Pronunciation Key

The symbol (ʹ), as in **grocer** (grōʹsə) and in **greengrocer** (grēnʹgrōˊsə), is used to mark primary stress; the syllable preceding it is pronounced with greater prominence than all other syllables in the word, compound word, or phrase. The symbol (ˊ), as in **greengrocer,** is used to mark secondary stress; the syllable preceding a secondary stress is pronounced with less prominence than the one marked (ʹ) but with more prominence than those syllables in polysyllabic words bearing no stress mark at all. Isolated monosyllables, such as **green** (grēn), are not marked for stress; they are to be read with primary stress.

ă cat, tack
ā age, say
ä ark, car

b back, cab
ch charm, march
d do, odd

ĕ led, dell
ē eat, tea
ĕə aired, dare

f file, life
g gas, sag
h hot, ahead

ĭ pit, tip
ī ice, sigh
ĭə fear, here

j germ, merge
k cap, pack
l law, all

m mate, tame
n no, own
ng song, hanger

ŏ sob, boss
ō oats, stow
ô ought, tore
oi toil, boy
o͝o look, put
o͞o fool
ou out, now
o͝oə poor, tour

p pitch, chip
r red, try
s sell, less
sh sham, mash
t ton, nut
th thick, kith
th̸ then, smooth

ŭ luck, cull
û curt, Turk

v vain, nave
w wine, twine
y yawn, yes
z zone, nose
zh leisure, invasion

ə occurs only in unstressed syllables and indicates the sound of
a *in* alone
e *in* system
i *in* terrible
o *in* gallop
u *in* circus

Foreign Sounds

ȧ as in French *ami*: a vowel intermediate in quality between (ă) of *cat* and (ŭ) of *cut*

ė as in French *été*: a vowel intermediate in quality between (ē) of *beat* and (ĕ) of *bet*

KH as in German *ach*; Scottish *loch*: a consonant made by raising the tongue almost to the position for (k), as in *keep, cool,* while breathing out forcibly and trying to pronounce (h)

N as in French *un bon vin blanc* (œN bȯN văN bläN): a vowel modifier, used to indicate nasalization of the preceding vowel

ȯ as in French *beau*: a vowel intermediate in quality between (ô) of *shore* and (o͞o) of *shoe*

œ as in French *peu, peur*; German *schön*: a vowel made with the lips rounded as for (ô) of *court* or (ŏ) of *cot* while trying to say (ĕ) of *set*

Y as in French *rue*; German *über*: a vowel made with the lips rounded as for (o͞o) of *food* while trying to say (ē) of *see*

Encyclopedic World Dictionary

First published in 1971 by
The Hamlyn Publishing Group Limited
London · New York · Sydney · Toronto
Astronaut House, Feltham, Middlesex, England

Reprinted 1976, 1979

ISBN 0 600 00007 9

Filmset in Great Britain by Keyspools Limited,
Golborne, Lancs.

Printed and bound in Great Britain
by Cox & Wyman Ltd
London, Fakenham and Reading

Encyclopedic World Dictionary

Editor
Patrick Hanks

Editorial Consultant
Simeon Potter

Hamlyn

London · New York · Sydney · Toronto

Special Consultants

THE ARTS
Art and Architecture
TREWIN COPPLESTONE, N.D.D., A.T.D., Lecturer, Extramural Department, University of London, Lecturer, Study Centre, Victoria and Albert Museum

MUSIC
GUY HALAHAN
G. S. HINDLEY, M.A.

BANKING AND FINANCE
W. G. HANKS, Cert.A.I.B.

DOMESTIC SCIENCE
CAROL M. DIXON, Home Economist
VIVIEN TILLEY, Home Economist

GEOGRAPHY
CHRISTINE WILLS, B.Sc.
MICHAEL FREEBERNE, M.A., Lecturer, School of Oriental and African Studies, University of London

LAW
HARVEY TEFF, M.A., of the Middle Temple, Barrister-at-Law, Lecturer in Law at City of Westminster College

LINGUISTICS
General Advisers
SIMEON POTTER, Ph.D., Professor Emeritus, Liverpool University
J. A. SHEARD, Ph.D., King's College, University of London

African Usage
MALCOLM GUTHRIE, B.Sc., Ph.D., A.R.S.M., Professor of Bantu Languages and Head of the Department of Africa, School of Oriental and African Studies, University of London
D. K. RYCROFT, School of Oriental and African Studies, University of London
RACILIA NELL, B.A., Dip.Lib., F.S.A.L.A.

Australian and New Zealand Usage
W. S. RAMSON, Ph.D., Senior Lecturer, Department of English, The Australian National University

Etymologies
KEMP MALONE, Professor Emeritus of English Literature, Johns Hopkins University, U.S.A.

Phonetics
GORDON F. ARNOLD, B.A., Reader in Phonetics, University College, London

Epigraphy
DAVID DIRINGER, M.A., D.LITT., Fellow, Royal Anthropological Society, Senior Member, University College, Cambridge, The Alphabet Museum, Cambridge and Tel Aviv, Guest Professor, Bar Ilan University, Israel.

Synonyms and Antonyms
MILES L. HANLEY, Professor of English, University of Wisconsin, U.S.A.
JOAN HUDDLESTON, M.A., Lecturer, College of Further Education, Bracknell, Berks.

MEDICINE
R. W. M. BALDWIN, M.B., B.S., M.R.C.S., L.R.C.P., D.Obst.R.C.O.G., Senior House Officer, Anaesthetics, Charing Cross Hospital, London
M. E. ROBERTS, M.B., B.S., M.R.C.S., L.R.C.P., House Physician, St Bartholomew's Hospital, London

MILITARY TERMS
BRIGADIER D. R. L. BRIGHT, O.B.E.
MAJOR G. DONOVAN BOYD, T.D.

NATURAL HISTORY
Botany and Flora
G. J. CUNNELL, B.Sc., Ph.D., Lecturer, Department of Botany, Westfield College, University of London

Zoology and Fauna
Michael Boorer, B.Sc., Education Officer, The Zoological Society of London
Ken Denham, formerly of the Zoological Society of London, former curator of the Oceanarium, Morecambe

NAUTICAL TERMS
Captain A. G. Course, A.M.Inst.T., member of the Honourable Company of Master Mariners

PHILOSOPHY AND LOGIC
E. G. Reeve, M.Sc., Ph.D.

PRINTING
Philip Cohen, Book Production Consultant,
British Standards Institution, London

RELIGION
R. C. N. Thomas, B.A.

SCIENCE
General Editor
Alan Isaacs, B.Sc., Ph.D., A.C.G.I., D.I.C.
Aeronautics and Astronautics
Maurice Allward, Deputy Manager, Technical Publications Department, Hawker Siddeley Aviation
Biochemistry
J. D. Killip, B.Sc., Ph.D., Editorial Assistant, *Biochemical Journal*
Automatic Data Processing and Electronics
Colin D. Bright, B.A., Centre for Computing and Automation, Imperial College of Science and Technology, University of London

SOCIOLOGY
Judith M. Fido, B.A.

SPORT
Graeme Kent

STATISTICS
Albert Dickson, Executive Editor, *The Journal of the Royal Statistical Society*

TECHNOLOGY
C. T. G. Boucher, M.Sc., Ph.D., A.R.I.B.A., A.M.I.Struct.E., Lecturer
University of Manchester
Institute of Science and Technology

Editorial Staff

Editor
Patrick Hanks

Deputy Editor
Janet Liebster

Associate Editors
John Bailie
Bridget Hadaway
Jocelyn Pearson

Assistant Editors
Peter Levy
Paul Procter
Kate Reddick
Adrian Shire
Linda Stanton
Della Summers
Adèle Wainwright
Kenneth Williamson

Contents

General Introduction

Patrick Hanks

The aim of the *Encyclopedic World Dictionary* is to provide the general reader with as much up-to-date information about words and facts as can be comprehended within a single manageable volume, in the most readily accessible presentation. In the past forty-odd years, since the last volume of the great *Oxford English Dictionary* (OED) was published, there has been a significant shift in the vocabulary and preoccupations of most educated English-speaking people. The EWD is the first general dictionary published in England to take account of this shift. Since the beginning of this century the emphasis of education has shifted from the classics to the sciences. At the same time the world has contracted from a great area on which human populations took weeks and months to make contact with each other, to what Marshall McLuhan has called an electronic village. Furthermore, in the last half century linguists have made considerable advances in the study of languages and psychologists have developed techniques of presenting information which have contributed to the principles on which modern dictionaries are based.

Of all these and many other developments, the editors, contributors, and staff of the EWD have taken note, and at the same time we have endeavoured to preserve all that is best in the great tradition of English lexicography from Johnson to C. T. Onions. Indeed, this work goes further, in being based on one of the finest American dictionaries, the *American College Dictionary* (ACD). We were fortunate in being able to secure the right to use the definitions and principles of this book, which has been widely praised for its balanced scholarship, its lucidity, and wide coverage of Modern English.

The EWD, then, is a full and detailed record of Modern English on modern linguistic principles. It will provide the user with all the information he is likely to need about the spelling, pronunciation, meaning, and etymology of the words selected, and that selection has been made from a wide-ranging collection of information of many different types, designed to meet all the various reference needs of the educated Modern English speaker, and edited on rigorously scholarly principles. There are seven broad classes of entry in this dictionary, all contained for ease of reference in a single alphabetical list.

Clearly, the editors' first concern has been to describe the vocabulary common to all or most brands of English in the fullest and clearest possible form. Clarence Barnhart said in his preface to the ACD: 'This dictionary records the usage of speakers and writers of our language; no dictionary founded on the methods of modern scholarship can prescribe as to usage; it can only inform on the basic facts of usage. A good dictionary is a guide to usage much as a good map tells you the nature of the terrain over which you may want to travel. It is not the function of the dictionary-maker to tell you how to speak, any more than it is the function of the map-maker to move rivers or rearrange mountains or fill in lakes. A dictionary should tell you what is commonly accepted usage and wherein different classes of speakers or regions differ in their use of language.' This is now an accepted principle of modern lexicography, underlying the EWD as much as it did the ACD.

Since this is primarily a descriptive dictionary, the order of definitions is determined by the principle of placing the most common present-day meaning or group of meanings first, regardless of which is the earliest recorded sense. This has been made possible by the labours of Drs Lorge and Thorndike, whose semantic word count of some twenty-five million running words of text has established in the first place the frequency of occurrence of all the words in a representative sample of modern English prose. They went further, and counted the frequency of occurrence of the different meanings of about four and a half million words in context. Without such a basis, no dictionary could claim to be a scholarly and accurate record of what English words actually mean in the twentieth century. Thanks to their work, it is possible to state with confidence that the first meaning or group of meanings in this dictionary represent the most common usage of each word, except in a few instances where the editors have decided that the meanings of the word would be more clearly organized in historical or some other order.

Secondly, it has been our aim to give extensive coverage to the fast-changing vocabulary of science and technology. The ACD itself retained 355 special consultants, and their definitions have been checked, labelled, supplemented, and where necessary altered. This work has been done with the assistance of British and Commonwealth experts, besides a number of scholars who have freely given advice and information on specific points. Particular mention should be made of the work of Dr Alan Isaacs in this field; thanks to his massive contribution, along with that of our other technical consultants, the EWD is not only a dictionary of the common vocabulary of English, but also contains in the same alphabetical list the most up-to-date science dictionary available on the British market. Special attention has been given to fields such as computers, space travel, astronomy, and medicine, in which very rapid progress in understanding or technique are matched by a huge increase in vocabulary, both in the coinage of new words such as *algol*, *blast-off*, and *quasar*, and the extension to new and specialized senses of existing words—see for example definition 5 of *code*, definition 6 of *facility*, or definition 3 of *levitation*. These words and the many thousands of others used in the sciences and technologies are now so firmly established as part of everyday life that any major dictionary has a duty to define them accurately and clearly. One of the major functions of the EWD is to assist the layman in this way, bearing in mind that even scientists become laymen outside their disciplines.

A third aspect of dictionary-publishing in the 1970s is the speed of communication across the world, which is having a profound effect on the development and position of English, perhaps more than on any other language. No modern dictionary can afford to ignore that Southern British English (SBE) is not the only standard language that goes under the name of English, and few professional linguists today would dare to prescribe it as the only 'correct' form. This point is discussed more fully in the prefaces by Professor Simeon Potter on page 11, and Mr G. F. Arnold on page 15. The difficulties of representing more than one kind of pronunciation in a one-volume general dictionary are obvious. No attempt has been made, for instance, to indicate, for a word which is common to all or most brands of standard English, South African or Australian pronunciations when they are different from that current in Southern British English. However, vocabulary is a different matter. In at least three categories—technical terms, social terms, and flora and fauna—words are used as standard English in one part of the world which are little or never used elsewhere. The American word *faucet* corresponds to what other English speakers call a *tap*; the South Africans may call a rascal a *skelm*; the *belah* does not grow outside Australia, nor the *biddy-biddy* outside New Zealand. When New Yorkers hear the word *standee* they may think first of people standing in the theatre, whereas Londoners would more probably think of a bus. Previous dictionaries have tended to ignore such variants and treat British—or American—standard as the only 'correct' form. We believe that a modern dictionary of standard English cannot afford such a provincial attitude. The great English-speaking communities throughout the world are in daily verbal contact by communication satellites, by films and television programmes produced in one country and enjoyed throughout the world. At the same time, physical separation has diminished so that Australia and Great Britain, on opposite sides of the world, are only a matter of hours apart. For these reasons educated speakers of English in one part of the world are almost certain to be baffled from time to time by the standard language of some other English-speaking community. Special consultants on the EWD have collected extensive lists of such words, and they are fully defined here. Wherever our research has indicated that a word or sense is restricted to a particular kind or geographical area of English, the definition has been labelled or worded to make this clear. This aspect of the dictionary alone would justify its title as a world dictionary of the major world language.

A fourth need of the dictionary-user which it has been our aim to meet is in defining words restricted to a particular register. The labels *Colloq.*, *Slang*, *Dial.*, and the occasional formula 'not generally regarded as correct usage' are used to give as accurate as possible a record of levels of usage. A wide range of slang and colloquialisms has been selected for definition, on the basis of their frequency of occurrence, especially their frequency in modern literature. A particular aspect is that the standard vocabulary is constantly refurbished from these registers. For example, few people nowadays would regard *spree* as anything but Standard English, but when the relevant section of the Oxford English Dictionary was issued in 1915 the word was labelled *Colloq.* *Burgle* is now acceptable Standard English, but OED's comment (1888) is 'Colloq. or Humorous—of very recent appearance', while *perm* appeared only in time for the Supplement (1933), in which it is labelled *Colloq.* Because of this tendency of non-standard words to be upgraded, matched by the downgrading of certain standards (which is generally accompanied by a semantic change—see, for example, *awful*), the EWD editors have been conservative in the use of labels. Words which show signs of becoming standard have been given special attention, and in disputed cases the label has been omitted.

Attention has also been given to another rich source, historically at any rate, of Standard English—the dialects. The old South-East Midland dialect of Middle English has become, with various modifications, a 'class dialect'—the class in question being the vast English middle class. It is the basis of all other standard forms of English. When spoken with a Southern British English pronunciation, it is, as Mr Arnold points out on page 17, the most widely comprehended form of English. It may even become in the future the basis of international communication. Meanwhile other native dialects have, especially during the twentieth century, been battered into submission by the massive attack of the standard dialect through increased literacy, the press, radio and television, the cinema, and indeed the whole fabric of a mechanized urban society. Without question the dialects are in decline. Already in 1870, Aldis Wright, making the earliest proposal for a systematic record of dialect words—a proposal which gave rise to Joseph Wright's massive *English Dialect Dictionary*, and indirectly to the dialect surveys carried out at Leeds and Edinburgh universities—prophesied, 'In a few years it will be too late. Railroads and certificated teachers are doing their work.' Although one of the more curious effects of television has been to bring various regional accents into vogue for a time, the vogue has rarely extended to the point of choosing dialect words. It is only in communities strongly wedded to a traditional way of life and to some extent isolated from the mainstream of urban culture—in fact, mainly agricultural communities—that it is still possible to distinguish some eighty variant terms for, for example, 'the weakest pig in the litter'. Such variants are not the concern of the general lexicographer. However, there are still a number of terms widely distributed in dialects other than South-East Midland, which survive, are used in literature, television, etc., as marks of a dialect-speaker, are of such historical importance, or are of such great frequency that they do command the attention of a dictionary of this kind. Words such as *butty*, *mardy*, *gradely* will be found fully defined in this dictionary.

In this connection a word should be said about the status of the speech of Edinburgh. Unlike any other standard of English, it has a history as long, intricate, and fascinating as that of London. And unlike any other British dialect except that of London, it has won acceptance as the language of educated speakers outside the geographical area of its origin. In addition, many social customs and institutions are of course distinctive of Scotland. For these reasons the labels *Scot.* and *Scot. and N Dial.* will be found quite frequently throughout these pages: our policy has been to give full coverage to the principal terms of the language and institutions of Scotland, as to other standard languages. The difference is that the history of Scots is so long and the variants from Southern British English so numerous that it would be quite impossible to include *all* Scottish variants. Accordingly our source material was divided into essential terms, which because of peculiarity to Scotland, frequency, or some other consideration, are included in our dictionary, and words which, being mere phonetic variants of SBE, or obsolescent, rare, or local, do not qualify for entry in a modern international dictionary of general English.

It is worth noting that many words which have dropped out of SBE survive in the dialects or in Scots. In some cases this has influenced the decision on entry. Even where a word does not survive in the dialects, it may qualify for entry in this dictionary. The reading of educated people is of course not confined to the publications of the twentieth century, and it is precisely the words which have become obsolete or archaic which are likely to lead the modern reader to refer to a dictionary. For this reason this dictionary contains all words which have been in normal literary use at any time in the Modern English period (since about 1475), and where appropriate the labels *Obs.* or *Archaic* have been used.

The fifth class of information contained in the dictionary marks a startling departure from the terms of reference of traditional English lexicography. Because we intend the EWD to be a comprehensive reference book, a selection of commonly required encyclopedic information about facts, people, places, and the like has been included—once again, for ease of reference in the one alphabetical list. Systematic checks on, for example, biography, geography, institutions, and world currencies were carried out, and the same standards of defining have been applied to proper names as to the common vocabulary. We have tried to give the most significant facts about each person or place having importance today. We have included, for example, major writers in the chief European languages, all the most significant English writers, the most prominent scientists, inventors, statesmen, and other leading people in recorded history. We have included cities and towns throughout the world with more than 100,000 inhabitants, all those in Europe, South Africa, and the Commonwealth with more than 50,000, all those in Great Britain and Australia with more than 20,000. The latest available population figures have been obtained from the most reliable sources, and in this connection a special word of acknowledgement is due to the librarians and press officers of almost every embassy and High Commission in London. In addition, we have given information about many hundreds of smaller towns of historical, geographical, or political importance, about regions, administrative divisions, and features of physical geography throughout the world, especially the English-speaking world. We have defined all the currency units in the world, giving the latest available exchange rate with the pound sterling. The list of these systematic surveys is too great to give in full, but the above examples will give an idea of the kind of information the reader can expect to be provided with.

The sixth and seventh classes of entry call for no special comment. Foreign words and phrases have been included if they are generally used in an English context, and current standard abbreviations are also listed, especially those new ones which are so prominent in contemporary science, such as DNA and NMR.

All the seven classes of entry in this dictionary are given, as has been said, in a single alphabetical list. Each word entry in the dictionary is given in its standard modern spelling. If widely accepted variants exist, these are shown, if necessary with a restrictive label, at the end of the definitions. If the variant is more than a column distant from the main entry, a headword and cross-reference are inserted at the appropriate alphabetical place. Choice of which form of a variant is to carry the definition is governed by usage, frequency, modernity, and consistency. The choice of one form to carry a definition does not necessarily imply proscription of the others.

Each entry word is accompanied by a guide to pronunciation. The principles of this guide and of English pronunciation are explained on page 15 by Mr Arnold.

The pronunciation guide is followed by a part-of-speech label, and if the entry word is used in more than one grammatical form, the appropriate part-of-speech label precedes each group of definitions for that part of speech. Inflected forms are shown for those words which form an inflection other than by the simple addition of a regular ending, as in the change of *-y* to *-ies*.

Definitions are numbered for ease of reference; the basic principle governing their order is explained earlier in this preface. Technical senses, colloquial senses, and obsolete or archaic senses are normally placed at the end of the appropriate semantic or grammatical group of definitions. Special phrases come last of all within each group, unless there is reason for grouping a phrase with a particular definition. Where phrasal verbs are listed, the distinction between transitive and intransitive is not maintained. However, this distinction is maintained if the definition is numbered.

The definitions are followed by an etymology wherever one can be usefully given. The etymologies are basically those of Professor Kemp Malone and his staff, the method of which is explained in his preface on page 21. Occasionally these have been altered in the light of more recent research, and here we have been specially fortunate in securing the help of Professor Malcolm Guthrie for the etymologies of words of African origin.

Definitions may also be accompanied by an illustration. Captions explaining the illustrations, as under *abacus*, are also designed to supplement the definitions. Actual sizes of animals are given, instead of ratios of reduction which the user must work out, and usually doesn't. There are over 300 spot maps throughout the dictionary, showing the location of places of historical importance, such as the centres of the *Hanseatic League*, or places which have come into prominence over the past decade, as the countries of Africa, or which are hard to find in current atlases, as areas of historical importance, for example *Austria-Hungary, 1871–1914*.

Finally, the user is provided with a number of synonym studies and lists. These are keyed to particular definitions, and it is important to realize that different words are not synonymous in their entirety, but only in certain relatively narrow areas of meaning. For example, *unqualified* and *utter* are synonyms of *absolute* in the meaning 'free from limitation or restriction'; *complete* and *perfect*, however, are synonyms of *absolute* in the meaning 'free from imperfection'. For other areas of meaning of *absolute*, other synonyms exist; it is all-important to settle first on the common or core meaning of the synonyms to be distinguished, discriminating carefully among them, and to give examples illustrating the use of the synonymous words. Clear examples are almost as important as the discriminations; great pains have been taken to provide illustrative examples for each synonym. The synonym studies have as far as possible been placed under the better-known word. For a further explanation of the principles of handling synonyms and antonyms see the preface by Professor Miles L. Hanley on page 25.

It would be impossible to thank adequately all those who have helped in the preparation of this dictionary. Besides those mentioned individually, a great number of scholars have contributed their special knowledge to the solution of particular problems, and many members of the editorial staff of The Hamlyn Group have from time to time acted as patient guineapigs in frequency checks and in supplying other information. It is our hope to have produced a work worthy of its predecessor, the *American College Dictionary*, and of modern linguistic scholarship—a work which will be of good service to its users.

The English-Speaking World

Simeon Potter

This dictionary is concerned with the whole world of English from Alaska to New Zealand. People who speak English can be divided into three groups: those who have inherited it as their birth tongue, those who have acquired it as a second language, and those who are compelled to use it for some special purpose whether as diplomats, businessmen, journalists, consultants, scientists, technologists, or students of literature. One person in seven of the world's total population now belongs to one of these three groups.

In Shakespeare's day English was spoken by only five and a half million people, who were mainly confined to the British Isles. Even there, however, to quote Richard Mulcaster, the famous High Master of St Paul's School, it was not everywhere spoken. 'The English tongue', he said, 'is of small reach, stretching no further than this island of ours, nay not there over all.' Mulcaster had in mind not only those varieties of Celtic spoken in the Scottish Highlands, Wales, Devonshire, and Cornwall, but also those dialects of Scandinavian spoken in north-west Scotland, the Hebrides, and the Western Isles.

Before Shakespeare's death in 1616 the expansion of English had begun. It began with the founding of the Old Dominion State of Virginia by Captain John Smith in 1608 and the landing of the Pilgrim Fathers on Plymouth Rock in 1620. It continued with the westward migrations to New England and Canada in the seventeenth century and to various parts of all four continents outside Europe in the eighteenth. The time of this maximum expansion was exceptionally opportune for two simple but very important reasons. First, English began to expand only when, in the forms of its words and in the structures of its sentences, it had already settled down and attained maturity as an efficient instrument of communication. Secondly, it began to expand some good time after the invention of printing, when craftsmanship and artistic skill in the manipulation of movable types had already reached a high level of expertise, so that literature of all kinds might be disseminated speedily and cheaply.

Today, as we survey this widely diffused English-speaking world, we find it fairly stable in the British Isles, North America, and Australasia. We find it very much on trial, and subjected to varying degrees of stresses and strains, throughout Africa. In the Indian subcontinent and in the coastal countries, archipelagos and islands of south-east Asia, its future is unpredictable.

The United Kingdom of Great Britain and Northern Ireland with its population of fifty-six millions still contains one fifth of the people who have English as their mother tongue, and yet it includes two diminishing Celtic communities—Scots Gaelic in the Scottish Highlands and the Western Isles, and Welsh in the Principality of Wales. The latter is still spoken by one million people, of whom one half reside in Glamorganshire alone and the other half in the western counties from Anglesey to Carmarthen. Moreover, in the independent Republic of Ireland, the government encourages the resuscitation of Irish as the national language on the basis of the dialect of Munster, however stubbornly the inhabitants of Dublin decline to use any other form of speech than a particularly clear and attractive variety of English. Only in the counties of Mayo and Galway, Kerry and Cork, do people continue to speak Irish in spontaneous conversation.

In England the drift of population to the south-eastern counties continues and the speech of educated Londoners is accepted as Received Standard. It is this type of pronunciation that is taught in the schools and universities of Europe. English is now taught as the first foreign language in France, Belgium, Luxembourg, the Netherlands, West Germany, Denmark, Iceland, Norway, Sweden, and Finland.

Although it is the largest and wealthiest of British dominions, Canada remains persistently bilingual. One third of its eighteen million citizens, living mostly in Quebec and in the neighbouring provinces of Ontario and New Brunswick, speak French—a French in some respects nearer that of Voltaire than that of modern Paris. These *habitants* are indeed forced by circumstances to speak and read English as their first collateral language—as are, indeed, the Eskimos who inhabit the shores of Labrador and the autochthonous Algonquians who still live around the Great Lakes. But throughout the Dominion a policy of full linguistic equality and 'the same rights everywhere' is operated. Since the most densely populated regions lie in the St Lawrence basin, most Canadians live within one hundred miles of the open United States boundary and the influence of the speech of their southern neighbours is therefore powerful and unremittent.

Most of the first colonists who settled in New England were British, but Dutchmen founded New Amsterdam and held it until 1664, when it was taken by the British and renamed New York after the King's brother, the Duke of York. Ninety per cent of the settlers on the Atlantic seaboard before the confirmation of the Federal Constitution in 1778 were British, and they settled east of the Appalachian Mountains, but after that date the numerous immigrants who arrived from Ireland and Germany moved farther west. The potato famine in 1845 caused one and a half million Irishmen to enter the New World, and the European revolution of 1848 impelled as many Germans to settle in Pennsylvania, Oregon, and the Middle West. After the American Civil War one million Scandinavians made their homes in Minnesota and the upper Mississippi basin. Millions more Czechs, Slovaks, Serbs, Croats, and Italians followed them before the end of that century, and in the twentieth century these were joined by countless millions from all over Western Europe fleeing from political tyranny. To these were added French from Canada, Spanish from Mexico, and Chinese and Japanese from across the Pacific. Meanwhile the number of Negroes had not diminished. Today the fifty states of the great Federal Republic remain inherently cosmopolitan, comprising an open society with full linguistic liberty. No fewer than twenty-three native languages are still in use, of which Spanish, German, Italian, French, Polish, Dutch, and Hungarian are the first seven. Most of these speakers, however, are driven by daily need to make themselves bilingual and in the second and third generations their descendants will speak and write English with varying degrees of literacy. The Golden State of California has now surpassed New York in number of inhabitants, but radio and television networks link east and west, and join both with Europe. Apart from divergences in spelling, there are no longer any perceptible differences in style between essays and reports by British and American humanists and scientists, but in the lower registers of colloquial speech and slang the variations are considerable. Neologisms of many kinds proliferate more copiously in the New World, although, in these days of near-instantaneous telecommunication, they pass round the world with such speed that their places of origin are not easy to locate. Some newly coined words and phrases recorded for the first time in this dictionary are commonly assumed to be American, but it would be difficult to prove them so. From functional shifts (as old as Shakespeare) of noun into verb and verb into noun many new uses have arisen. One can now *audition* a person for competence to participate in a dramatic or musical programme; *headline* an important item of news; *highlight* the outstanding features of a picture, document, or argument; *invoice* a customer or club member to pay a bill or a back subscription; *pinpoint* the precise cause of a disaster; *process* a new brand of food; *service* a machine, car, or plane; and *steamroller* one's opponents in dialogue or debate. A contestant who wins no prize is an *also-ran*; a highly profitable purchase is a good *buy*; all articles of food offered for human consumption are *eats*; any creature or object whose best days are past is a *has-been*; technical expertise is *know-how*; and an unavoidable necessity is a *must*. By back-formation, or derivation in reverse, arise new verbs like *automate*, *bulldoze*, *burgle*, *commute*, *donate*, *eavesdrop*, *escalate*, *frivol*, *intuit*, *laze*, *liaise*, *reminisce*, *sculpt*, and *televise*. By blending or telescoping arise such new portmanteau-substantives as *contrail* 'condensation trail' of jet aircraft, *duralumin* 'durable aluminium', *magnalium* 'alloy of magnesium and aluminium', *motorcade* 'motor-car cavalcade', *nucleonics* 'nuclear electronics', *quark* 'question mark' in cableese, *quasar* 'quasi-stellar' source of radio energy, and *racon* 'radar beacon'.

Crossing the Atlantic Ocean from the New to the Third World, we find that in the Republic of South Africa, as in Canada, our language is compelled to live side by side with another European tongue, namely Cape Dutch or Afrikaans. The latter is indeed so much a simplified form of the European Dutch brought to Africa in colonizing days that it must now be classed as a new language in its own right. On the other hand the variety of English spoken within the Republic, and outside it in Botswana, Rhodesia, Zambia, Tanzania, Uganda, and Kenya has diverged little from that of London. Speakers of English in the Republic, it is true, use Dutch-derived words when referring to features peculiar to the African landscape, such as *kloof* 'cleft, ravine', *kopje* 'hill', *krantz* 'crag', *veld* 'treeless plain', and *vlei* 'watery hollow', and they naturally adhere to native names when talking about indigenous flora and fauna unknown in Europe. Words made famous in history like *trek* and *commando* now belong to our general vocabulary. When the British in Cape Province talk of *staking a claim* they probably have the days of the great gold rush still in mind. They speak of *outspanning* rather than of unyoking or unharnessing at the end of a journey on horseback or in a horse-drawn vehicle, and they put their cattle into a *kraal* for the night. Many of these one and a half million careful speakers of English hold influential positions as business executives, bank managers, medical practitioners, and lawyers. They are careful speakers because they know their language to be on trial. They are, in fact, slightly outnumbered by Afrikaners, most of whom are nevertheless forced to acquire a workable knowledge of English, whether they like it or not.

The four West African territories—Gambia, Sierra Leone, Ghana, and Nigeria—gained independence during that one decade (1955–65) which saw the relinquishment of colonial rule by all the European powers except Portugal in Angola and Mozambique. Far from implying linguistic recession, however, political withdrawal may make an interstate language a greater necessity than ever before. Much depends upon degrees of literacy among the peoples concerned. Two native languages, Hausa and Swahili, are rapidly extending their domains. Hausa, the speech of central Sudan and northern Nigeria, has become a useful *lingua franca* over much of West Africa. Swahili, the language of Zanzibar and the adjacent mainland coast, serves the same function over much of East Africa. Both Hausa and Swahili now compete healthily and advantageously with English as media of interstate communication and commerce.

In Gibraltar, Malta, and Cyprus, English is widely spoken side by side with other languages: in Gibraltar with Spanish, in Malta with Italian and Maltese, and in Cyprus with Greek and Turkish. Here and in many countries bordering on the southern and and eastern shores of the Mediterranean Sea—Libya, Egypt, Israel, Lebanon, and Syria—and yet farther afield in Iraq, Iran, Afghanistan, Pakistan, India, and Burma, professional men and women need at least a reading knowledge of English for proficiency in their daily occupations.

In the Indian subcontinent English now shares the title of an official language with no fewer than eleven others. Everywhere language is a highly charged issue tied up with salaried posts and political power. The British Raj (1757–1947) lasted little more than half as long as the Imperium Romanum (A.D. 43–410) in Britain, but it left behind an acute language problem that defies immediate solution. Language has set going more riots, more fasts, and more trouble for the central government than any other issue in recent years. In insisting that the link language must be Hindi, and only Hindi, and not even Hindustani, the Hindus completely ignore the claims of the Dravidian south with its one hundred million people speaking Tamil, Telugu, Kanarese, or Malayalam. Moreover, Hindustani itself has two forms, Urdu and Literary Hindi. Urdu is written in modified Arabic characters and is used in everyday intercourse by the Muslims. Literary Hindi, the same tongue fundamentally, is written in the Devanagari script and draws heavily on ancient Sanskrit for its learned vocabulary. It is this literary Hindi, and not popular Hindustani, that ardent nationalists wish to make the one official language of the Republic of India. On August 15th, 1967, the twentieth anniversary of India's achievement of independence, the Prime Minister declared that this premature insistence on the primacy of Hindi could lead only to separatism and 'in the present-day world India cannot afford to live in isolation'. Therefore, Mrs Gandhi maintained, India had to cope with three languages—regional, national, and international. She insisted that English should remain the one international language indefinitely. The subsequent census of 1968 showed that English was still spreading. Unfortunately, however, there are now unwelcome indications that efficiency in its use is declining even among the educated elite. Too many educated Indians and Pakistanis are content to use babu English or 'clerk's language', disregarding distinctions between archaic, literary, common, colloquial, and slang registers of speech. Nevertheless there is some consolation to be found in the fact that growing numbers of scientists and technologists relying upon western periodicals for the latest information on research have been less affected by this decline than students of literature and the humanities.

Moving on now to Thailand, Malaya, and south-east Asia, we find that there too English (including pidgin English) remains an indispensable international language, but that it has acquired an attractive competitor in Malay, which now ranks ninth among the world's languages in number of speakers. Malay is an advanced language, uninflected and largely monosyllabic, which has its home on the north coast of Sumatra. It owes much to English and it is clearly destined to hold a position of importance in the commerce and administration of the Far East. Under the name *Bahasa Indonesia* it has been adopted as the one official medium for that extensive region. In their own books and journals the Malays long employed an adapted Arabic alphabet, but more recently they have gone over to Roman letters. Many Malay words have already found their way into English: *bamboo*, *bantam*, *cockatoo*, *caddy* (for tea), *gong*, *gutta-percha*, *launch* in the sense of 'pinnace' (from the Malay adjective *lanchar* 'speedy, swift') and *raffia*. Throughout Malaya, Sarawak, North Borneo, and the thousands of islands in the South Pacific Ocean, English is well established as a second language. Over one quarter of the Filipinos speak American

English fluently although their official language is Tagalog. The Philippines with their population of nearly thirty millions were granted complete independence on July 4th, 1946.

Finally, passing in our survey to Australia and New Zealand, we have to note that the former has no rival European language within its shores and that in a population of over ten millions the Aborigines number less than three hundred thousand. People live mostly in the coastal towns and cities of the south-east, ranging from Brisbane to Adelaide. For them the open country behind them is the *outback*. There they find animals and plants hitherto unknown: trees that shed bark instead of leaves, and cherries that carry their stones outside instead of within. *Brush*, *bush*, *creek*, *paddock*, and *scrub* have acquired wider senses in a different landscape, whereas *brook*, *dale*, *field*, *forest*, and *meadow* are seldom used. A creek that leads off from a river and re-enters it downstream is called an *anabranch*, whereas a creek coming to a dead end is a *billabong*. *Dinkum* means 'genuine'. Completely trustworthy information or news is *dinkum oil*. Australian speech has slower rhythms and flatter intonations than British English. The neutral vowel (as in the final syllable of *butter*) is of frequent occurrence. *Archers* and *arches* are pronounced alike. Contrariwise, *taxis* and *taxes* are distinguished in Australian, and so are *candid* and *candied*. Inevitably, in both vocabulary and pronunciation, Australian English is constantly and strongly subjected to influences from the United States.

Although New Zealand lies over one thousand miles away, the English there spoken is similar to that of Australia, but there are discernible variations between North and South Islands. Aboriginal Maoris are more numerous in North Island, where their euphonious language commands respect. It belongs to the Malayo–Polynesian family and it is therefore akin to Tahitian, Samoan, and Hawaian. Educated Maoris are bilingual. When they speak English they do so with exceptional precision and care.

As a global language English now stands first. Its only rivals as world languages are Spanish, French, and Portuguese. It might be maintained that Mandarin Chinese possesses a yet greater number of speakers and that Hindustani and Russian are more formidable contestants than French and Portuguese. But Chinese, Hindustani, and Russian are confined to single large areas: they are like solid blocks in the Eurasian heartland. They are also hampered by antiquated scripts: Chinese by its ancient pictographic characters (although Romanization, too long deferred, is making progress) and Russian by its modified Cyrillic alphabet. In this respect, indeed, Hindustani is doubly handicapped because, as we have just seen, it is divided within itself by two scripts, one for the Hindi of India and Hinduism, and another for the Urdu of Pakistan and Islam. It is an inestimable blessing that the four world languages use one and the same Roman script.

Thus it may be said that English has now reached a most interesting point in its history. Its inflections are stable. It has succeeded in shedding all superfluities, retaining only minimal inflections for nouns, pronouns, and verbs. Alone among European languages, it has dispensed with adjectival inflections, but the other two morphological processes of affixation and composition are more alive than ever and generate an unparalleled wealth of derivatives and compounds capable of expressing the finest shades of meaning. Prefixes and suffixes especially, whether Greek or Latin or native, are being fully employed to produce yet greater succinctness and precision. The gate has been kept wide open to foreign elements, adopted or adapted as required. English-speaking scientists, whatever their nationality, continue to go to Classical Greek for their technical terms. They have come to regard Greek as a kind of quarry whence they can draw verbal materials to make new words or to modify words already in use. For instance, by prefixing the adverb *tele-* 'distant' to the existing compound *photography* the scientist creates the unambiguous term *telephotography* to denote the photography of distant objects by means of a specially constructed lens. Again, by inserting the adjective *micro-* 'small' into this same compound he creates the term *photomicrography* to denote the photography of minute objects like viruses and bacteria. As fields of research are subdivided, so fresh word-blocks are mined from the Greek quarry to describe the new specialisms. As the older life sciences of *biology*, *botany*, and *zoology* are departmentalized, so arise new names like *bacteriology*, *biochemistry*, *endocrinology*, *genetics*, and *immunology*. Such appellations are accepted by the whole world of learning. Is it fanciful therefore to see in this growing scientific nomenclature of today an adumbration of the international language of tomorrow?

Today our world is divided not only by language but also by religions and ideologies, by different degrees of industrialization, and by uneven distribution of wealth. It is, nevertheless, a shrinking world in which there will soon be no isolation. Before the end of this century every community on earth will have found ways and means to communicate with the rest of the world.

Pronunciation

Gordon F. Arnold

It is a common experience for any one of us, when reading, to be confronted with a word which is completely new to us. Sometimes the context in which the word occurs allows us to make a reasonable guess at its meaning; sometimes the context does not help at all. Either way our reaction may then be to reach for the dictionary to discover the meaning or to check the validity of our guess. With the meaning revealed to us our initial need is satisfied. Consulting the dictionary may, however, have served to heighten, not diminish, our curiosity; and we may well feel the need to push our enquiry further and to ascertain when and how to use the word when talking. The definitions in a dictionary help us to decide when to say a word; they do not tell us how to say it. In addition to the many other kinds of information which we come to expect of it, a dictionary must therefore provide, if it is to satisfy fully, clear indications of the way its entries are to be pronounced.

But a dictionary does not automatically provide such indications. The spelling form of a word cannot give all the guidance necessary for its pronunciation. Whatever may at one time have been the relation between them and however faithfully the one may have reflected the other, in present-day English, spelling is a most unreliable guide to pronunciation. Many books have been written, and will no doubt continue to be written, purporting to give worthwhile rules of pronunciation based on conventional spelling; but, as even the most casual glance at their contents reveals, these rules are for the most part subject to so many exceptions that their value is minimal and their validity suspect. If, however, against the evidence, we still cling to the notion that we can make do with the conventional spelling as a guide to pronunciation, we ought perhaps to remind ourselves of the considerable amount of time and energy which, in their early years at home and at school, we devote to teaching children to read—teaching them, that is, to match up the pronunciational forms of words, which they already know, with the corresponding spelling forms which they have still to master. Their difficulties stem from the unphonetic nature of our spelling: each letter or sequence of letters does not consistently stand for one and only one sound. We are all aware that in some English words a letter may have no pronunciational value whatsoever, that *knight* and *night* sound the same and that *thumb* rhymes with *plum*. We are perhaps rather less aware that a letter or sequence of letters is often used to indicate a wide variety of sounds. The seven words *cough, thought, through, rough, though, bough,* and *thorough* all contain the same *ough* letter sequence; yet in no two of these words does this letter sequence indicate the same pronunciation. All of us can rhyme the first six of these words with *off*, *sort*, *blue*, *cuff*, *go*, and *now*, the pronunciations of which, we can readily agree, have very little in common; a moment's reflection and we can persuade ourselves, and rightly so, that the end of *thorough* sounds like the end of *opera* or of *terror*. Likewise we may not altogether appreciate that what is in fact one and the same sound can, in the pronunciation of a number of words, be represented by an equivalent number of different spellings. In this dictionary we have represented the second sound of *me*, for instance, by the symbol (ē). Besides the spelling in *e*, we can find at least eight other ways in which our conventional orthography attempts to indicate this sound: *ee* in *breeze*, *ea* in *grease*, *ie* in *frieze*, *ei* in *seize*, *i* in *police*, *ey* in *key*, *ay* in *quay*, *eo* in *people*. Not all sounds of English are represented by so many divergent spellings as the (ē) sound of *me*, and not many sequences of letters can be pronounced in as many different ways as *ough*; but these are clear examples of the widespread lack of consistent relationship between the way we spell our language and the way we pronounce it. Obviously then, if we wish to give any consistent indication of the pronunciation of the entries in this dictionary, we need to include a specially designed pronunciation guide. We must rewrite each and every entry word so that a given symbol, or sequence of symbols, stands for one and only one sound: *breeze*, *grease*, *frieze*, *seize*, *police*, *key*, *quay*, and *people*, for instance, since they each contain the second sound of *me*, must all include the symbol (ē) when they are rewritten. In this dictionary the rewritten form, indicating the pronunciation of an entry, is given immediately after the conventional spelling form, and the value to be ascribed to each symbol of the rewritten form is exemplified in the Pronunciation Key on the endpapers of the dictionary.

Before we consider how best to rewrite the entries in this dictionary in conformity with the principle of 'one sound, one symbol', we ought perhaps to ask why it is that the conventional spelling serves us so ill as a guide to pronunciation. The lack of consistent correspondence between our spelling and our pronunciation results from two conflicting tendencies—tendencies which are exhibited by all languages having written as well as spoken forms, but which are most readily discernible in the case of English. On the one hand we find a marked tendency towards conservatism in orthographic practice: the spelling of English words has remained virtually unchanged for two centuries, despite great efforts by zealous would-be reformers to persuade us to adopt spelling forms which would more reliably reflect the way we speak. Of course English spelling has not always exhibited its present-day rigidity. Up to the 15th century a word was apt to appear in a wide variety of spelling guises; and part of our difficulty in understanding texts preserved from Saxon times, for instance, stems from the freedom of orthographic practice which their scribes enjoyed. Each scribe, bound by no generally accepted rules, attempted to spell in conformity with his own pronunciation; and his pronunciation, never wholly consistent or unchanging, was likewise never identical with that of any of his fellow scribes. Even as late as Shakespeare's day English people still had considerable latitude in the spelling of their words. The major turning point, however, came in the 15th century with the invention of printing. From then on obvious practical advantages, for reader and printer alike, were to be derived from the establishment of a standard spelling form for each individual word; and by the 18th century, when books and printed matter of all kinds began to be widely disseminated, our spelling had achieved the standardization we know today.

On the other hand there is an equally marked tendency for the pronunciation of English, like that of every other language, to change and evolve. In the last thirty years, it is true, the advent of radio and television, the spread of universal education, and an ever-increasing consciousness of the printed word have, in this country, all been contributing to some slowing down of the pace of pronunciational change. Yet there seems no likelihood whatsoever that our pronunciation will ever achieve the rigidity now presented by our spelling. Greater ease of travel and of communications generally has laid our pronunciation open to powerful, modifying influences from the Antipodes, from South Africa and above all from North America, all areas in which English is spoken as a native language but which hitherto, for reasons of geography, have been linguistically remote from the British Isles. At the same time we must recognize one very important characteristic of the human speech-mechanism which actively works to prevent our pronunciation from ever achieving a state of complete uniformity. Human beings are not talking machines; our control over our speech organs has not and cannot have machine-like precision. Consequently we do not always succeed in pronouncing a word in exactly the same way on all occasions. At any one moment the variation in sound may be quite small and of a transient nature, passing unnoticed. Over long periods of time, however, and with large numbers of individual speakers involved, this variation may develop into an appreciable, rather more longstanding pronunciational change. Such a change may be discernible in the speech of all speakers of the language in question. It may equally be limited to the speech of certain groups of speakers, while the speech of other groups exhibits a different pronunciational change or no change at all. It is, therefore, not surprising that 20th-century pronunciation is very different from that which Chaucer or Shakespeare used; nor should we be surprised that, despite the general accessibility of all areas, numerous regional accents continue to flourish within the narrow confines of the British Isles. Small wonder, too, that this ever-present tendency for pronunciation to change makes it very unlikely that our spelling will ever be reformed sufficiently drastically to allow it to become a reliable guide to English pronunciation. Even if we were prepared to forgo the advantages which our conservatism in orthographic matters has afforded us, reform of spelling could never ensure that our spelling remained in step with our pronunciation unless such reform were a continuing process; and frequent changes in our spelling practice would create at least as many problems as they would solve.

Any thoroughgoing reform of English spelling would not only have to rewrite English words in accordance with the principle 'one sound, one symbol'; it would also have to take account of a problem with which our present standardized spelling does not attempt to cope. The spelling *import*, for instance, is used whether we intend noun or verb; and for once the spelling is consistent since, noun or verb, both words present the same sequence of sounds. Yet the two words are not pronounced in identical fashion. If we are to say them correctly, we need to know that for the noun we place the maximum prominence—

or primary stress, as we shall call it—on the first syllable, whereas for the verb the primary stress is reserved for the second syllable. While not many words in English are distinguished simply by the positioning of the primary stress, the words spelt *import* nonetheless hint at another major, characteristic feature of English pronunciation. In English the position of the primary stress in a word of two syllables or more is not predictable; unlike Polish words, for instance, which invariably have primary stress on their penultimate syllable, some words in English show primary stress on their first syllable—*gen'erally*, for instance; some on their second syllable—for example, *decep'tively*; some on their third syllable, and so on. Nor can we readily determine the position of the primary stress in one word by consideration of its incidence in related words: the primary stress falls on the first syllable of *pho'tograph*, but the related words *photog'raphy* and *photograph'ic* take this stress on their second and third syllables, respectively. A moment's repetition of *photograph*, *photography*, and *photographic* illustrates another important feature of English pronunciation: where the primary stress falls quite often has a marked effect on the sequence of sounds which constitutes the pronunciational form of a word. The letter *a*, for instance, in *photograph* is sounded like the *a* of *calm* or, less commonly, like the *a* of *cat*; in *photography* like the *a* of *alone*; in *photographic* like the *a* of *cat*, never like the *a* of *calm*. These differences of pronunciation, as well as those exhibited by the two letters *o* in the same three words, can all be related in some measure to the incidence of the primary stress. Unlike the conventional, standardized spelling, therefore, the rewritten form of each word in this dictionary must not only be set down in such a way that a particular symbol always stands for one and the same sound; the rewritten form must also include the clearest indication as to which of its syllables are stressed and which are not.

So far we have been concerned with the difficulties of showing pronunciation in a dictionary such as this, and with the shortcomings of our conventional orthography. We have now to decide what kind of pronunciation is to be shown. The weight of tradition and the numbers of speakers involved effectively limit our choice to one of the two major types, American English or British English. The pronunciation indicated here for all native English words is therefore a British English one. However, there still exists a wide variety of pronunciations to be encountered over the length and breadth of the British Isles; although many factors are now tending more and more to blur the differences between the regional accents of this country, nonetheless, simply by listening to the way they talk, most of us can readily distinguish a Scot from a Welshman, a Yorkshireman from a Cockney, a Liverpudlian from a Bristolian. So we must again make a choice. Now there are some among us who will argue for one kind of British English pronunciation rather than another on allegedly aesthetic grounds: such people will champion a Scots pronunciation as being distinguished and beautiful or a West-Country brogue as being warm and friendly, but they will castigate a Cockney or a Liverpudlian as a slovenly speaker with an ugly accent. Generally, however, it would seem that this verdict is socially, not aesthetically, motivated: it is the man, rather than his accent, that is being judged. Whatever our views on the social standing or aesthetic value of each of our regional accents, we must never lose sight of the fact that the prime function of speech is communication, communication between man and man; and our choice of the type of pronunciation to be represented in this dictionary should be determined in the light of this overriding need for intelligibility. We must choose that type of pronunciation which is most readily intelligible to the largest possible number of native English speakers. For this reason and this reason alone this dictionary shows what we may call Southern British English pronunciation. Though a Scottish pronunciation for instance has great social standing all over the British Isles and a Liverpool accent perhaps rather less, we cannot doubt that, except to Scots and Liverpudlians, both are less readily and less widely intelligible than Southern British English, the present-day intelligibility and acceptance of which, whether within this country or abroad, are in no small measure due to the far-reaching influence of the B.B.C., particularly of its radio programmes.

Despite its name, Southern British English pronunciation no longer has any marked regional associations—perhaps this may partially account for its general acceptance—and speakers whose pronunciation approximates to Southern British English are now to be found in all parts of the British Isles and throughout the English-speaking world. Originally, however, as the name suggests, Southern British English pronunciation predominated in the south of the country, especially in the south-east, in and around the capital; it was a pronunciation intimately associated with the capital, with the royal court, and with the public schools. It consequently acquired great prestige and, in the 19th century particularly, when social distinctions were much more rigidly maintained than they are today, it was widely regarded as socially preferable to most, if not all, other British English pronunciations—and this notwithstanding, or perhaps because of, the fact that the total number of Southern British English speakers constituted but a very small minority of the overall population of these islands. Nowadays, though still regarded by some as socially and therefore aesthetically superior, the tendency is for these overtones to become more and more muted and for Southern British English pronunciation to acquire the stature of an unofficial standard which even the most partisan supporters of any one regional accent can accept as neutral, common ground between themselves and those who champion some other rival regional pronunciation.

Each type of pronunciation of each language can be analysed into its own individual set of distinctive sounds—sounds which a speaker must distinguish with the utmost clarity if he is to convey his meaning unambiguously to a listener. A speaker with a Southern British English pronunciation must, for instance, maintain a consistent difference between the sounds represented by *p* and *b* in *pit* and *bit*, because if he did not a listener would, in some circumstances at least, be unsure which of the two words and its associated meanings were intended; similarly he must distinguish sharply between the *a* of *bass*, a fish, and the *a* of *bass*, a term in music, a distinction which our conventional spelling patently fails to make. In all a Southern British English speaker needs to have at his command a repertoire of 44 distinctive sounds. To rewrite the entries in this dictionary for pronunciation purposes we therefore need an identical number of symbols, 44, if we are always to indicate each distinctive sound by its own, individual symbol. As the Pronunciation Key in the front endpapers of this dictionary shows, the symbols chosen to represent the 44 distinctive sounds of a Southern British English pronunciation consist, with one exception, either of a single letter with or without a superimposed diacritic, or a close-knit sequence of two letters, all drawn from our alphabet. Thus *cot*, *caught*, and *coat*, the pronunciation of each of which, in spite of the spelling, comprises three distinctive sounds with the first and third of these common to all three words, are differentiated by their middle sounds, written in the pronunciation guide of this dictionary (ŏ), (ô), and (ō), respectively. On the other hand *Caesar* and *seizure*, each consisting of four distinctive sounds, differ in the third sound: that for *Caesar* is represented in the rewritten form by the single letter (z), while that for *seizure* is indicated by the close-knit letter sequence (zh).

We have already touched upon the need to indicate in the rewritten form of any polysyllabic word or phrase the syllable which bears the primary stress. Except in the case of isolated monosyllables—*case* (kās), *load* (lōd), for instance—which, though followed by no stress mark, should be read with primary stress, primary stress is shown in this dictionary by the stress mark **′** placed immediately after the syllable to which it is appropriate. All native English words and phrases have one and only one primary stress. In addition it sometimes happens that one or more of the remaining syllables of phrases and of longer words are stressed, but to a lesser degree than the syllable carrying the primary stress. Such syllables are said to bear secondary stress, which is indicated by the stress mark ′, again placed after the syllable to which it refers. Except for the isolated monosyllables mentioned above, syllables followed by neither **′** nor by ′ are unstressed. Since both types of stress mark, **′** and ′, are placed immediately after the syllable to which each is appropriate, they also effectively act as markers of the boundary between the stressed syllable and any syllable, stressed or unstressed, immediately following. When a syllable is unstressed and hence not followed by either **′** or ′, the boundary between that syllable and any succeeding syllable is shown by a space. Thus the boundaries of the five syllables of *elimination* are marked in the rewritten form (ĭ lĭm′ĭ nā**′**shən) by a space after the first and third (unstressed) syllables, by ′ (secondary stress) after the second, and by **′** (primary stress) after the fourth.

The rewritten form of *elimination* brings us to consider the symbol (ə) which, exceptionally, is not drawn directly from our alphabet. In a language such as English, with its characteristic system of degrees of stress, there is always a strong tendency for stressed syllables to be said with great clarity and for the unstressed syllables to be uttered progressively less and less clearly. The greatest effect of this tendency to slur over unstressed syllables has been exerted on their vowels; and such has been the weakening of these unstressed vowels during the gradual development of Southern British English pronunciation that it is now impossible to detect any qualitative difference between the vowels which we write with *a* in *alone*, *e* in *system*, *i* in *terrible*, *o* in *gallop*, and *u* in *circus*. Though purists, with their eyes fastened on the orthographic differences, will no doubt continue to complain about mumbled and mangled vowels, this levelling of vowels in the unstressed syllables of many English words is a characteristic feature of most types of English pronunciation throughout the English-speaking world; and since it is in accord with the pronunciation practice of the vast majority of native English speakers, it has now to be regarded as correct usage. Though the vowel (ə) can be found only in unstressed syllables, it is by no means the case that every unstressed syllable must contain the vowel (ə). On the contrary: there are very many instances of vowels other than (ə) occurring in such syllables, the vowel (ô) for instance in the second, unstressed syllable of *import* said as a noun. We cannot therefore with any certainty infer the presence of the vowel (ə) from the absence of stress on a syllable. Consequently, wherever this vowel does in fact occur, it has to be specifically marked with its own distinctive symbol.

While the frequent occurrence of the vowel (ə) is a feature common to most types of native English pronunciation, Southern British English presents another characteristic which sets it apart from most other pronunciation types. Unlike the great majority of American speakers and unlike some British speakers, Scots and West-Country people for instance, all of whom pronounce *r* wherever it is written, Southern British English speakers give a pronunciational value to this letter only when the next sound in a word is a vowel sound. Thus while *red* and *around* for example must be said with the consonant (r), the *r* has no pronunciational value in words such as *arms* and *fort* where *m* and *t* follow with consonantal value. The result is that the pronunciation of *arms* is now indistinguishable from that of *alms* and *fort* and *fought* are likewise homophonous. Words spelt with a final letter *r* also illustrate the rule that *r* is pronounced only before a following vowel sound. When such words are said in isolation—*far, water*, for instance—the *r*, as we would expect, has no value in the pronunciation. But when, in phrase-making or in word-compounding, a word spelt with a final letter *r* is immediately followed by a further word the pronunciation of which starts with a vowel sound, in the phrase *Far East* or the compound word *water-inch* for example, this *r* can be and very often is sounded. Thus the pronunciation guide in this dictionary rewrites *far* and *water*, as (fä) and (wô′tə) when isolated forms, but as (fär′) and (wô′tər) in *Far East* and *water-inch*. This present-day distribution of the sound (r) in Southern British English pronunciation is a relatively recent development; it seems likely that in the speech of London and the south-east the letter *r* was pronounced in some way or another in all positions in the word—before consonants and at the end of a word as well as before vowels—as late as the middle of the 18th century.

Another striking feature of Southern British English pronunciation is its wealth of vowel sounds, some twenty in all. Twelve of these, the vowels of *calm* and *put* for instance, have a steady, unchanging quality and are known as pure vowels or monophthongs. The remainder, usually called diphthongs, begin with one vowel quality and end with a different vowel quality: the diphthong represented by the *ow* of *now* for example starts with a vowel quality resembling that in the word *calm* and ends with a quality not unlike that in *put*. Southern British English pronunciation possesses eight diphthongs, rather more than most other types of native English pronunciation, American and Scottish for instance; and some languages, like French and Spanish, have none at all. Four of these Southern British English diphthongs, those in *bait, bite, boat*, and *bout*, by an evolutionary process known to scholars of English as the Great Vowel Shift, have developed from vowels which in pre-Shakespearian times are thought to have been monophthongs. The diphthongs in words such as *peer, pear*, and *poor*, on the other hand, have resulted from the combination of something like the former vowel quality in these words with the pronunciation of the final *r* weakened to (ə).

The vast majority of words, phrases, and proper names included in this dictionary are native English. For the most part these each have only one pronunciational form in Southern British English, and are consequently shown here with only one rewritten form. Many native English words do however have alternative pronunciations in Southern British English. *Aesthetic*, for example, can be said with an initial (ē) or an initial (ĕ). Similarly the vowel in the first (unstressed) syllable of *report* can be either (ĭ) or (ə); indeed, many a non-final syllable in a word which we have shown with (ĭ) can be heard with (ə) instead. However, in Southern British English *aesthetic* with (ē) is considerably more common than the form with (ĕ), which seems typically American; *report* is most often said with (ĭ), the form in (ə) perhaps being more consistent with an Australian or a South African pronunciation. For all words, having two or more attested pronunciations in Southern British English, one of which is however clearly dominant, only the dominant form is given in this dictionary.

Occasionally two or more differing pronunciations of a native English word seem equally common in Southern British English; in these circumstances both, or all, alternatives are given. Sometimes these alternative pronunciations of the same word differ in respect of one or more of their constituent distinctive sounds: *room* can be pronounced either (rŏŏm) or (rōōm). Sometimes they differ in that a distinctive sound of one form is omitted from the other form: *history* is heard both as (hĭs′tə rĭ) and as (hĭs′trĭ). The vowel (ə), as in this last example, is nowadays particularly susceptible to being omitted when it occurs non-finally in the fuller form. Its omission often has the effect of reducing the number of syllables in a word by one, as the rewritten forms of *history* show. We should therefore not be surprised if the number of syllables in a rewritten form of a word does not always coincide with the apparent number of syllables in its corresponding conventional orthographic form; such a discrepancy is yet another manifestation of the conflict we have already mentioned, between the conservatism of our orthographic practice and the continuing evolution of our pronunciation. Nor is it surprising that the vowel (ə) shows this tendency to disappear; it has after all developed in unstressed, weakly articulated syllables and, in the development of a language, complete elimination is often the fate of weakly pronounced sounds. In present-day Southern British English pronunciation the omission of an expected (ə) is much more widespread than the rewritten forms of the words in this dictionary might suggest. Many words which we have rewritten with a non-final (ə)—*police* (pə lēs′) and *southern* (sŭth′ən), for instance—are now heard without this (ə); but these shortened forms have not been included in this dictionary since, for the moment at any rate, they appear to be minority pronunciations. For the same reason a rewritten form omitting an expected (ə) has on occasions been given in preference to the fuller form when it has been judged to represent the pronunciation of a majority of Southern British English speakers; typical examples are: *papal*, *total*, *focal*, *tribal*, *bridal*, *frugal*, *bitten*, and *ridden*, rewritten (pā′pl), (tō′tl), (fō′kl), (trī′bl), (brī′dl), (fro͞o′gl), (bĭt′n), and (rĭd′n), in all of which the spelling suggests a vowel sound between the penultimate and final consonants of each word. In these last examples, unlike *history* above, the omission of the expected vowel in no way affects the number of their constituent syllables: with or without the vowel they are disyllabic. Whether or not the omission of a sound brings about a reduction in the number of syllables in a word is always made clear by the relevant rewritten form.

This dictionary also includes a certain number of foreign words, phrases, and proper names. Where it is well attested, as in the case of *Paris* for example, an anglicized pronunciation is recorded for such entries, the appropriate rewritten form being drawn up in accordance with the practice followed for native English words. For some of the foreign entries, however, no anglicized pronunciation is at all common; and while it is possible to anglicize the pronunciation of any foreign word, we have in this dictionary adhered to the principle of including only those anglicizations which appear to have achieved a certain degree of currency in Southern British English. Some foreign entries have consequently been rewritten to show only the appropriate foreign pronunciation. In rewriting such native pronunciations of foreign entries we have adhered to the same broad general principle which has guided us in our treatment of native English words. For each foreign language each of its distinctive sounds is always represented by one and only one symbol, either a single letter or a close-knit sequence of two letters, and for each foreign language only as many symbols are used as the language has distinctive sounds. The number of distinctive sounds varies from language to language. While Southern British English has 44, and hence needs the 44 symbols given in the Pronunciation Key, the relevant figures for Polish and Modern Greek, for instance, are respectively 37 and 23.

We only need to listen for a short time to a foreign language being spoken to realize that its sounds are rarely, if ever, identical with those of Southern British English. Quite often, however, the difference between a foreign sound and the most similar Southern British English sound is not so great as to make the use of a common symbol to indicate both grossly misleading. We are thus able to use (ô) both for the vowel in English *saw* and for the first vowel in Russian *Sochi*, for instance, even though the ear of a trained phonetician would not accept them as identical. In any case what matters most is that, for each language, we employ only as many symbols as are sufficient to maintain all the essential differentiations between the distinctive sounds of that language: the precise phonetic value to be attributed to any particular symbol has obviously to be learned for each individual language. Nonetheless it sometimes happens that one language presents one or more phonetic features quite unknown to another. As we have already said, Southern British English contains a wealth of diphthongs whereas French has none. It would therefore seem helpful, when rewriting French entries and entries from other languages possessing no diphthongs, to avoid using those symbols—(ā), (ō), (ī), (ĭə), and so on—which designate Southern British English diphthongs. To ensure a sufficiency of symbols for French and other similar languages, we have instead made use of a limited set of special symbols, namely the vowels (ȧ), (ė), (ȯ), (œ), and (Y), the vowel modifier (N), and the consonant (KH). The phonetic significance of these special symbols is illustrated in the Pronunciation Key, to be found in the endpapers of this dictionary.

Treatment of Etymologies

Kemp Malone

Scientific investigation into the origin and history of words has never been more active than it is at the present time. English etymologists in particular have been busy, and their researches have cleared up many points once enigmatic or wrongly set forth. The writers of the etymologies here presented have taken due account of the learned publications in this field, and in a number of cases have made contributions of their own. They have provided in this dictionary a presentation of etymologies which is up to date in form and substance. Outmoded and pre-scientific terms like *Teutonic* and *Zend* have been avoided, and the reader will find, instead, the terminology now usual in linguistic science. The terms used are duly defined in the dictionary proper.

The treatment of the etymological material is conservative. The use of hypothetical or reconstructed forms has, in general, been avoided, and where such forms appear, they are marked with an asterisk. The origin of many words is put down as 'uncertain' or 'unknown', and plausible but doubtful etymologies are given (if at all) with a question mark. Rival explanations have been carefully weighed and, if the balance seemed even, both alternatives have been included. In sum, the etymologies here set down present, in succinct form, the fruits of scholarly research, old and new, on the origins of English words.

Extreme brevity of presentation commonly marks the etymologies given in a dictionary of this scope. In this dictionary, too, limitations of space have made brevity needful, but the etymological treatment remains remarkably full, and is combined with an exactness of detail rarely found even in dictionaries many times the size. The method of presentation used is described in the paragraphs which follow.

METHOD OF PRESENTATION

The etymological part of a word entry is normally the final section of the entry proper; it is set off from the rest of the entry by square brackets.

The etymology begins with some indication of the age of the word in English. This item of information is not etymological, strictly speaking, and might have been given elsewhere in the entry, but it has proved convenient to include it in the etymological part. If the word was current in English in the Middle Ages (before A.D. 1500), it is marked ME (Middle English); if the word was current in the early Middle Ages (before A.D. 1100), it is marked OE (Old English). Thus, the etymological part of the entry **guilt** reads: [ME *gilt*, OE *gylt* offence]. If the modern written form (spelling) of the word was already in use in Middle English, it is not repeated after 'ME'. Thus, for **name** we have: [ME; OE *nama*, . . .]. Here the semicolon marks the fact that ME and Modern English agree in the spelling of the word. If the Old English spelling likewise agrees with the one now current, the entry word is not repeated at all in the etymology. Thus, for **god** we have: [ME and OE, . . .]. If the word does not occur in English before the sixteenth century, no indication of its date is set down; this want of indication serves to mark the work as post-medieval.

NATIVE WORDS

Next comes the etymology proper. The fundamental distinction here is that between native words and words of foreign origin. The etymology of a native word like *guilt* or *god* is comparatively simple: after giving the oldest recorded form (if it differs from the current form), one lists the cognates; that is, the words in kindred tongues that correspond both formally and semantically. The etymological part of the word entry **god** reads: [ME and OE, c. D *god*, G *Gott*, Icel. *godh*, Goth. *guth*]. This means that *god* occurs in Middle English and Old English, and that it is cognate with Dutch *god*, German *Gott*, Icelandic *godh*, and Gothic *guth*. Not all the cognates are listed, of course. Thus, the Danish cognate *gud* is here omitted, and in most cases only one or two cognates can be given, for want of space. The etymology of *guilt* (given above) includes no cognates for the simple reason that none exists; this word occurs in English only, the kindred languages having no words with which *guilt* can be etymologically connected.

Most native words lack the simplicity of *guilt* and *god*. Even so, however, their etymology can usually be presented in a line, or less. Only now and then is more space required, as it is with **godsend**: [earlier *God's send*, var. (under influence of SEND, v.) of *God's sond* or *sand*, OE *sond*, *sand* message, service]. Here a mere analysis into *god* and *send* would have been insufficient. In many composite words, however, such an analysis meets every etymological need. Often, indeed, the word explains itself, so to speak. Thus, the structure of the adjective *godly* is evident, and the reader in search of etymological explanations need only take the word apart and look up its elements *god* and *-ly* in the dictionary. For this reason the entry **godly,** and many like entries, have no etymological section.

FOREIGN WORDS

The etymology of words of foreign origin takes up more space, on the average, if only because the language of origin must be specified. Moreover, many such words got into English, not directly from the tongues to which they were native, but through other tongues, and the etymology usually gives the intermediate stages as well as the ultimate source, so far as these can be determined. The word **heroine** is one of the simpler examples: [t. L, t. Gk, der. *hḗrōs* hero]. This means that the English word was taken from Latin, and that the Latin word had been taken from Greek, in both cases without change in spelling; further, that the Greek word was derived from the corresponding masculine word. The etymology of **honorary,** too, is simple: [t. L: m. s. *honōrārius* relating to honour]. This means that *honorary* was taken (into English) from Latin: more precisely, that the English form of the word is a modification of the stem of the Latin form. The technical term *stem* (abbreviated s.) is defined in the entry **stem** of this dictionary, and is used accordingly in the etymologies. The stem of Latin *honōrārius* is *honōrāri-* (the *-us* is an inflectional ending that marks the form as nominative, singular, and masculine). The Latin word was not taken into English in its stem form, however, but in a modification (m.) of that form required by a rule of English spelling; the letter *i* is not permitted at the end of a word and in this position is regularly replaced by *y*. In accordance with this rule we write *honorarium* but *honorary*, and the English word form *honorary* is explained, in our etymology above, as m. s. (that is, a modification of the stem of) L *honōrārius*. The colon is used to divide the general statement of origin (namely, that the word was taken from Latin) from the explanation of the precise written form of the English word.

The colon is also used in etymologies like that of **biceps**: [t. L: two-headed]. Here the English word and its Latin etymon agree in written form but differ in meaning. In English the word is a noun, used to name a muscle with a double attachment; in Latin, it is an adjective with no particular reference to muscles, though applicable enough to a muscle thought of as two-headed. In such cases the meaning of the etymon is set after the colon. In cases like **inspector,** however, no gloss is needed, and the etymological part of the entry reads simply: [t. L]. This etymology might have been expanded by reference to the entries INSPECT and -OR, where further etymological information is given, but space is precious and the user of the dictionary must make for himself this analysis of **inspector.**

CROSS-REFERENCES

References to other entries are made by printing the entry word in small capitals. Thus, the etymology of **mischance** reads: [ME *meschance*, t. OF: m. *mescheance*. See MIS-[1], CHANCE]. Here, at the end of the etymology, the reader is referred to two other entries, MIS- and CHANCE, where he will find further etymological information. In this case the reference takes the form 'see MIS-, CHANCE'. But a mere gloss, if printed in small capitals, serves also, as an entry reference. There are two such references in the etymology of **interregnum**: [t. L, f. *inter-* INTER- + *regnum* REIGN]. This etymological statement means that *interregnum* was taken from Latin, and that the Latin word was formed from *inter-* and *regnum*, both the meaning and the etymology of which may be found by consulting the entries INTER- and REIGN in this dictionary. The repetition here may seem needless, but is actually needful, because one must distinguish between Latin and English, even though the word forms are the same. In the sequence '*inter-* INTER-' the first form is Latin; the second, its English gloss.

FORMATIONS

Many English words were not taken, as such, from a foreign tongue but were made by putting together words or word elements of foreign origin, and therefore have a distinctly foreign look. Thus, the learned term **homoeomorphism** looks like a Greek word because its parts are Greek in origin. Its etymology reads [f. m. s. Gk *homoiómorphos* of like form + -ISM]. This means that the word was formed from a modification of the stem of Greek *homoiómorphos* plus the English word element *-ism*, itself of Greek origin. In this dictionary such words are carefully distinguished from words actually taken from a foreign language. The reader will note that the etymology begins with the abbreviation f. (formed from), not with t. (taken from).

REPLACEMENT

Another important feature of the English vocabulary is brought out in the etymologies by the abbreviation r. (replacing). The etymology of **horizon** serves for illustration: [t. L, t. Gk: bounding circle, horizon, prop. ppr., bounding; r. ME *orizonte*, t. OF]. The modern form of the word, which agrees with the Latin and Greek etymon, replaced a medieval form taken from Old French. This change marks part of a process of Latinization which the English language underwent during the Renaissance, a process which has continued, in various ways, to the present day. One result of it has been to reduce the number of French words in English vocabulary, replacing them by corresponding Latin or Greek words. In this dictionary systematic account has been taken of such replacements.

DESCENT VS. ADOPTION

The etymology of words taken from French and the other Romance languages makes special problems of presentation because of the very fact that these words can usually be traced back to Latin, the language out of which all the Romance languages grew. The Romance vocabulary is made up, in part, of words Latin by descent, having been handed down from generation to generation while spoken Latin was becoming Romance. In this dictionary such words are said to go back to Latin (abbreviated g. L). In the same way a native English word might go back to Germanic, but since such words are rarely traced back, in the etymologies, to Germanic times (for want of records), this parallel is of little practical importance here. Most of the Romance words of Latin origin, however, like the corresponding words in English, German, and other European languages, were simply taken from Latin by learned men at various times and added to the vernacular vocabulary. Such words are of course marked t. L, not g. L, in the etymologies. The two etymologies which follow illustrate the difference between the two kinds of Romance words of Latin origin:

ire [ME, t. OF, t. L: m. *īra*]
isle [ME *isle*, *ile*, t. OF, g. L *insula*]

SCANDINAVIAN WORDS

The English vocabulary includes many words of Scandinavian origin, most of them taken into English in the 10th and 11th centuries, though rarely recorded until Middle English times and often without record even then. It is usually impossible to say which particular Scandinavian language they came from. In such cases the etymology specifies Scandinavian origin and gives a pertinent form from some Scandinavian tongue, usually Icelandic, the classical language of the North. We illustrate with **bulk**: [ME *bolke* heap, t. Scand.; cf. Icel. *būlki* heap, cargo]. A like difficulty arises with many Romance words of Germanic origin, and the etymology of these is given in a like form.

DERIVATIVES

The expression 'derived from' (abbreviated der.) is used in the etymologies in its strict or narrow sense only. Thus, it appears in the etymology of **jaundice**: [ME *jaunes*, *jaundis*, t. OF: m. *jaunisse*, der. *jaune* yellow, g. L *galbinus* greenish yellow]. Here we are told that Old French *jaunisse* was derived from *jaune*. The derivative was made by adding to the basic word *jaune*, the noun suffix *-isse* -ICE, but this is left unexplained in the etymology. The reader will not find 'der.' used loosely in an etymology, to signify mere origin or the like. Thus, the etymology just given does not say that the English word *jaundice* was derived from French, or from Old French.

COMBINING FORMS

Most English words are composite; that is, they were made by putting together other words or word elements. In composition a word may have a special form, different from the one it has when used alone. In the etymologies of this dictionary such a special form is called a combining form (abbreviated comb. form). A familiar example is *thir-*, the combining form of *three*, as in *thirteen* and *thirty*. The numeral *ten* has two combining forms: *-teen*, as in *thirteen* (3 plus 10), and *-ty*, as in *thirty* (3 times 10). Other native words have combining forms, of course, but by far the greatest number of such forms are of classical (Latin and Greek) origin. These classical combining forms have a special interest for the historical linguist. Thus, the initial combining forms usually end in a vowel, often identical with the stem vowel of prehistoric times. In the classical period the vowel with which most prehistoric stems ended had become, functionally, a part (or the whole) of the inflectional ending, and was no longer treated as belonging to the stem. In an uninflected combining form, however, the old stem vowel may be kept as such. It must be added that these forms, even in classical times, tended to end in *o*, irrespective of etymology, and this tendency is still more marked in modern formations. The vowel *i* was also favoured in this position. In this dictionary many combining forms have entries of their own, and the others used in English words are duly identified in the etymologies. The same holds for the prefixes, the suffixes, and even the inflectional endings of English.

BLENDS

Many English words, though a very small proportion of the whole, are compounds of a special kind, technically known as blends (abbreviated b.). They usually have the appearance of simple words because of the way in which they were put together. An example is the word *boost*, a blend of *boom* and *hoist*. Each of the sources of a blend contributes something to the final product, but the contribution may be small. If a whole word as such enters into a compound, that compound is not a blend. In origin, the blend is usually slangy and jocular, but blends often become serious and respectable members of linguistic society. In this dictionary a number of words are etymologized as blends.

TRANSLITERATIONS

The forms given in the etymologies reproduce the spelling of the originals, with certain conventional changes. Letters not in the modern English alphabet are not used, but ligatures like *æ* and marks like the tilde are kept. The letter yogh of Middle English is represented by *y* or *gh*, according to its phonetic value. Old and Middle English thorn and eth are replaced by *th*, but for phonetic reasons the treatment of the corresponding Icelandic letters is different, thorn being represented by *th*, eth by *dh*. Old English and Icelandic long vowels are marked with a macron, but Middle English long vowels are left unmarked. In general, long vowels are marked in ancient word forms. In marking Latin quantities, Lewis and Short's and Harper's dictionaries have been followed. Greek quantities conform to Liddell and Scott.

ABBREVIATIONS

In the course of the discussion above, some of the abbreviations used in the etymologies have been explained. Many other abbreviations are used, of course, but these are too familiar to need explanation. A key to all the abbreviations will be found on the inside of the front cover, and a shorter key, giving only the most frequent abbreviations, appears at the bottom of every left-hand page. By the use of abbreviation it has proved possible to present in limited space a substantial amount of etymological information with clarity and precision. It is hoped that the reader will find the presentation convenient and informative.

Synonyms and Antonyms

Miles L. Hanley

I. WHAT ARE SYNONYMS?

Early writers referred to synonyms as words of identical meaning. To be sure, there have been groups of words in English which, for a period of time, could be considered synonymous in this oldest and strictest sense. But, like other languages, English is subject to what is known as *semantic change*, affecting the meanings of words. Many words, while usually keeping earlier meanings, at least for a time, have developed new ones; together with figurative uses, specialized uses, and differences of various other kinds. English has also borrowed freely from the languages with which it has come in contact; and when words have been borrowed, the meaning of any corresponding English terms, or that of the borrowed terms, or both, has commonly been changed. For example, at the time when the word *animal*—already widely known as a Latin word—was adopted into English, there was the native word *deer*, which had the same meaning. But after *animal* had come in as the general term, the word *deer* developed the specialized meaning of 'a horned beast'. Between words originally identical in meaning, therefore, differences great and small have developed, in one of their senses or in several.

That a word may now be truly synonymous with another word or words in some meanings but not in others, needs little proof. *Steal, rob,* and *pilfer* are quite clearly synonymous in the sense of 'to take away that which belongs to another'. They are quite as clearly not synonymous in the sense of 'to move quietly or furtively', another of the meanings of *steal*. Thus, the student who wrote 'The sun came pilfering through the leaves' was making the mistake of considering these synonyms as identical in all their meanings.

Important as semantic change is, a discussion of it is not practicable here; obviously we must consider words according to their current meanings and uses. We can, however, take some account of it in our definition of synonyms: THOSE WORDS ARE SYNONYMS FOR ONE ANOTHER WHICH HAVE THE SAME, OR A VERY SIMILAR, GENERAL MEANING, THOUGH ONE OR MORE OF THEIR OTHER MEANINGS MAY DIFFER MORE OR LESS WIDELY.

II. WHY STUDY SYNONYMS?

'To consider synonymous words *identical* is fatal to accuracy; to forget that they are *similar*, to some extent *equivalent*, and sometimes *interchangeable* is destructive of freedom and variety.' This statement (*Standard Dictionary*, 1894), which remains one of the best on the subject, points to some of the principal values in studying synonyms.

If one becomes aware of distinctions commonly (sometimes even unconsciously) made between similar words, one has added to one's understanding of those words. If one's attention is also drawn to some of the *ways* of distinguishing between words, and to some of the *kinds of differences* between words in some ways similar, one then has the equipment for gaining an understanding of further words which may be encountered.

A person can be said truly to have enlarged his vocabulary only with those words which he can use with precision and with judgement. A corollary of the statements preceding is, then, that by studying synonyms a person may learn not to use undiscriminatingly words which he does not understand, lest, in his attempts to be elegant, he succeed only in being ridiculous.

Discriminated studies of synonyms, especially, therefore, can be of assistance if one has such purpose as: (1) gaining freedom and ease in speaking and writing, (2) gaining a sense of appropriateness which will encourage careful discrimination, and (3) acquiring accuracy and precision in the use of words.

III. PRINCIPLES OF SELECTION OF SYNONYMS

A partial treatment of all possible synonyms, or a full treatment of even a part of all possible synonyms, would require volumes devoted exclusively to the subject. A chosen vocabulary of synonyms must necessarily be limited according to some principle or principles of selection.

In this book, lists of synonymous words have been provided where it was thought that these would be useful in throwing further light on the meaning, or meanings, of entry words of high frequency. The lists are in addition to, and exclusive of, words given in definitions and in the studies. Such lists were to serve not only as 'finding lists', but to encourage further exploration into the meanings of the headword.

In the discriminated studies, however, the first consideration was frequency of use. In the past, just as the earliest English dictionaries were lists of 'hard words', words of a literary tinge or words considered particularly difficult were likely to be selected for such study. Or those might be chosen which would be used in 'elegant' conversation (Mrs Thrale, *British Synonymy*, 1794). But a modern reference book cannot anticipate the infinite variety of needs that individual readers may have; only a word list chosen on the basis of frequency has a chance of being frequently useful to many.

It is, moreover, the frequently used, long-established word which has developed the greatest variety of meanings. And it is here that the general reader needs help. For example, in what contexts is 'little' more appropriate than 'small'? When and why is 'small' to be preferred?

It is only fair to say, at this point, that there are still many unsolved problems in determining frequency. Studies such as those of Lorge and Thorndike have revealed many useful facts. But so far, the choice of material for the study of frequency has necessarily limited, and to a degree distorted, the findings. Most of the material studied has been either literary or at least written; no account has been taken of the differences between vocabularies in oral and written materials. Much of the material has not been concerned with current usage, and until recently there has been no separation according to levels of formality, informality, etc.; or of parts of speech (when a single form may be used as noun and verb or as noun and adjective), though one part of speech may account for all but a small percentage of the occurrences, leaving the other part of speech as a rare word; or of the different definitions of any word (some uses being out of fashion so that only one or two may account for all or most of a fairly high frequency).

An outstanding advantage of this dictionary is the extensive use that has been made of the semantic word count of Drs Irving Lorge and Edward L. Thorndike. In this, the classifications and subdivisions of the great Oxford English Dictionary have been used in showing the relative frequency of various uses of a word. With this help we have been able to build on the studies and analyses made by some of our most distinguished English scholars over a period of more than seventy years.

In so far as frequency has been established, we have used it as our first principle. Almost all the words selected for study are from Thorndike's first 10,000, and well up in frequency as indicated in *The Teacher's Word Book of 30,000 Words*, by Thorndike and Lorge.

Other principles were used to a lesser degree. Some of them follow:

1. We have chosen words with which general readers have difficulty; that is, some of the words often enquired about in newspaper columns, radio programmes, university classes, and the like.
2. We have attempted to state concisely the distinctions between some words confused with one another and mistakenly thought to be synonyms, in such a way that the preferred usages will be clear.
3. We have taken into account the kinds of difficulty which persons learning English have; such studies as *judicious, judicial* are intended to be useful to this group of readers.
4. We have included a few examples from literature, especially from those texts which are commonly set for study in schools and universities.
5. Some of the words traditionally included in any treatment of synonyms have, of course, been considered.
6. A few groups needed to illustrate important principles (see Section V) have been added.

IV. METHOD OF TREATMENT OF SYNONYMS

In the synonym studies, the words discriminated have been limited to groups which have a considerable area of meaning in common. In order that the core meaning might be clear and might be stated in each study, the number of words compared in a study has been kept small—usually three or four, though sometimes only two, and only in a few instances five or more.

A study has practically always been placed under the entry of highest frequency, unless for a special reason (as *ado*, important for occurrence in literature; or *await*, a contrast with the modern form) it has seemed desirable to call greater attention to a word now less frequently used.

To call attention to the fact that the same word may have a number of different meanings; that other words may be its synonyms in one sense but not in another; and that a frequently used sense of one word may be a synonym for a less frequent one of another word, we have keyed each study to a particular sense of a word. With the other definitions of each word easily available, the reader may compare the other senses of the words as he wishes, and discover whatever additional area of synonymy there is. In some cases, different definitions of the same word are closely related in meaning—so closely at times that a number had to be arbitrarily assigned to the study—but in other cases the differences are great (as for example, *brazen*, 'of brass', and *brazen*, 'bold'). The hope is to lead the reader to consider the *various* definitions of a word and not merely to take the first one or two, if it has several. To examine all the meanings is essential to finding one which fits a context; and the habit is essential in learning to use unfamiliar synonyms discriminatingly—or even to discover which of the meanings are synonymous (the No. 1 definition of one word may be synonymous with the No. 5 of another word, but not with the first four).

In each study we give first a statement of the idea that the words have in common, to show how they are alike. We then go on to show how they differ, by giving the distinctive characteristics of each word. Sometimes it is felt that little more than a comparison of definitions is necessary—a first step in any discrimination. But various methods have been used to illustrate a variety of differences (see Section V).

In most cases, examples in context have been given, not to limit use by a single idiomatic example, but to illustrate an accepted use. It would have been possible to use literary, especially poetic, quotations, for many of the examples; but it has seemed wiser not to do so, since the poet or literary artist frequently finds an original, striking, or suggestive use which, in itself properly memorable, would be useable only rarely in everyday life. Therefore, the examples are expressions that are, or could be, found in ordinary conversation or writing. In a few instances, it has been possible to use all of the discriminated words in a single context, to show how the use of each word produces some difference in the meaning.

V. POINTS ILLUSTRATED IN THE SYNONYM STUDIES

We have tried to illustrate various ways in which words may be discriminated, or ways in which 'words that mean the same thing' may differ to the degree that they must be discriminated. A common question is, 'What is the difference between this word and that one?' Some of the differences we have illustrated are the following:

1. Between general and specific.
2. Between shades of meaning.
3. In emphasis.
4. In implication.
5. In application.
6. In connotation.
7. In emotional effect.
8. In levels of usage.
9. Between literary and colloquial usage.
10. Effects of prefixes and suffixes.
11. In idiom.
12. In British and American usage.
13. Between borrowed and native words.
14. Between literal and figurative uses.
15. Between concrete and abstract uses.
16. Between technical (or occupational) uses and popular uses.
17. In aspect of action.
18. Between local or provincial usages and general usage.

VI. WHAT ARE ANTONYMS?

When, in 1867, C. J. Smith coined the term *antonym*, he meant it to be used in the sense of 'counter-term' (such as 'non-x' for 'x'), a name already well known. *Antonym*, however, has since his time been variously interpreted.

As with *synonym*, the strictest interpretation has turned out to be too strict. If the strictest sense, 'word of (completely) contradictory meaning,' were adopted, most English words would not have antonyms. This is true, in any case, of scientific words, most of which are monosemantic. But it is perfectly obvious that, for a very large percentage of the non-scientific words, there are other words which offer a sharp contrast to at least some of the aspects or meanings.

Even such an unpromising word as *man*, for example, may be contrasted with other words which most emphatically do not mean the same thing as *man*: *woman* (different sex); *boy* (different age); *officer* (different rank), etc. Naturally this process could not be carried to the extreme of saying that all words not *man* are its antonyms because they differ from it in some respect. As with synonyms, there must first be some basis of likeness in classification; that is, for *man* the antonyms must be those referring to human beings, or at least to something living; an antonym for *black* should be the name of a colour; for *anger* should be the name of an emotion, and the like. Perhaps, however, this likeness in classification may be taken for granted.

Since there are, as yet, many unsolved problems concerning antonyms, trying to give a definition is very difficult. A narrow definition is unsatisfactory; but a broad one must have limitations. A tentative statement might be made as follows: AN ANTONYM IS A WORD WHICH EXPRESSES THE OPPOSITE OR THE NEGATIVE OF ONE OR MORE OF THE MEANINGS OF ANOTHER WORD.

The number of antonyms which any word can have is not limited to one. Indeed, most words which would have antonyms at all would have several, and some words have great numbers. In this book we have not attempted to give as many antonyms as possible (either for any word or in total). As with synonyms, we have keyed antonyms to specific meanings of entry words, and have usually given only one antonym; but that one a word whose usual meaning is in sharp contrast to the sense of the entry word indicated.

Table of Common English Spellings

In the following table the spellings of each sound are related to the phonetic symbols of the Encyclopedic World Dictionary (EWD) and of the International Phonetic Association (IPA). The most frequent spelling or spellings of each sound are indicated in bold-face italics.

EWD Symbol	IPA Symbol	Spellings	Examples
ă	æ	***a***, ai	hat, plaid
ā	eɪ	***a***, ***ai***, ao, au, ay, ***ea***, eh, ei, ey	ape, rain, gaol, gauge, ray, steak, eh, veil, obey
ä	ɑ	***a***, ah, al, ***ar***, au, ear, er	father, ah, palm, part, laugh, heart, clerk
b	b	***b***, bb	bed, hobby
ch	tʃ	***ch***, tch, te, ti, tu	chief, catch, righteous, question, natural
d	d	***d***, dd, ed	do, ladder, pulled
ĕ	e	a, ai, ay, ***e***, ea, ei, eo, ie, u	any, said, says, ebb, leather, heifer, leopard, friend, bury
ĕə	ɛə	ae, ***air***, ao, ar, ***are***, ayer, ear, eir, ere	aeroplane, chair, aorist, scarce, dare, prayer, wear, their, there
ē	i	ae, ay, ***e***, ***ea***, ***ee***, ei, eo, ey, i, ie, oe	Caesar, quay, equal, team, see, deceive, people, key, machine, field, amoeba
f	f	***f***, ff, gh, ph	feed, muffin, tough, physics
g	g	***g***, gg, gh, gu, gue	give, egg, ghost, guard, demagogue
h	h	***h***, wh	hit, who
ĭ	ɪ	a, e, ***i***, ie, o, u, ui, y	village, England, if, sieve, women, busy, build, hymn
iə	ɪə	e, ea, ear, ***eer***, eir, eo, ere, eu, ia, ier, ir	period, idea, hear, peer, weir, theological, here, museum, Ian, pier, fakir
ī	aɪ	ai, ay, ei, eigh, ey, ***i***, ***ie***, igh, uy, ***y***, ye	aisle, aye, either, height, eye, ice, tie, nigh, buy, sky, dye
j	dʒ	ch, de, dge, di, du, g, gg, ***j***	Greenwich, grandeur, bridge, soldier, procedure, magic, suggest, jump
k	k	***c***, cc, cch, ch, che, ***ck***, cq, cque, cu, gh, ***k***, qu	car, account, bacchanal, character, ache, back, acquaint, sacque, biscuit, lough, kill, liquor
l	l	***l***, ll	live, call
m	m	chm, gm, ***m***, mb, mm, mn	drachm, paradigm, more, limb, hammer, autumn
n	n	gn, kn, mn, ***n***, nn, pn	gnat, knife, mnemonic, not, runner, pneumatic
ng	ŋ	n, ***ng***, ngue	pink, ring, tongue
ŏ	ɒ	a, ach, au, ***o***, ou, ow	wander, yacht, sausage, box, cough, knowledge
ō	əʊ	au, eau, eo, ew, ***o***, oa, oe, oh, oo, ou, ough, ow, owe	mauve, beau, yeoman, sew, note, road, toe, oh, brooch, soul, though, flow, owe
ô	ɔ	a, ar, ***au***, ***aw***, oa, ***oar***, oor, ***or***, ***ore***, ough, ***our***	tall, war, fault, raw, broad, board, floor, order, more, ought, court
o͝o	ʊ	o, ***oo***, or, oul, ***u***	wolf, look, worsted, should, put
o͝oə	ʊə	ewer, oor, our, ***ur***, ***ure***	sewer, poor, tour, curious, endure
o͞o	u	eu, ew, o, oe, oeu, ***oo***, ou, ough, u, ue, ui	feud, grew, move, shoe, manoeuvre, food, group, through, rude, flue, fruit
oi	ɔɪ	***oi***, oy	oil, toy
ou	aʊ	eo, ***ou***, ough, ***ow***	Macleod, out, bough, brow
p	p	***p***, pp	pen, stopper
r	r	***r***, rh, rr, wr	red, rhythm, carrot, write
s	s	c, ce, ps, ***s***, sc, sch, se, ss	city, mice, psalm, see, scene, schism, case, loss
sh	ʃ	ce, ch, che, chsi, ci, s, sch, sci, ***sh***, shi, si, ssi, ti	ocean, machine, douche, fuchsia, special, sugar, schedule, conscience, ship, cushion, mansion, mission, mention
t	t	ed, pt, ***t***, th, tt	talked, ptarmigan, toe, thyme, bottom
th	θ	th	thin
t͟h	ð	th, the	then, bathe
ŭ	ʌ	o, oe, oo, ou, ***u***	son, does, flood, couple, cup
û	ɜ	ear, ***er***, err, eur, ***ir***, or, our, ***ur***, urr, ***yr***	learn, term, err, connoisseur, thirst, worm, journey, hurt, purr, myrtle
v	v	f, ph, ***v***, vv	of, Stephen, visit, flivver
w	w	o, u, ***w***, wh	choir, quiet, well, white
y	j	i, j, ***y***	union, hallelujah, yet
z	z	***s***, ss, x, ***z***, zz	has, scissors, Xerxes, zone, dazzle
zh	ʒ	ge, s, ***si***, z	garage, measure, division, seizure
ə	ə	***a***, ***ar***, e, eo, ***er***, i, ia, ***o***, oar, oi, ***or***, ou, ough, our, re, u, ur, ure	alone, particular, Scotsmen, dungeon, mother, possible, parliament, gallop, cupboard, porpoise, doctor, famous, borough, colour, centre, circus, grandeur, figure

Explanatory Notes

Material in this dictionary has been arranged in the order considered to be the most convenient for the user. All items in the dictionary are in one alphabetical list: words of the common vocabulary, names of persons, geographical names, abbreviations, foreign words and phrases, etc.

Similarly, all information within a vocabulary entry has been arranged for the convenience of the user. In general, information about spelling and pronunciation comes first, meanings next, etymologies and synonyms last. The sequence of material in the entries is as follows:

I. the entry of words or word.
II. the pronunciation.
III. the parts of speech.
IV. the inflected forms.
V. the restrictive label.
VI. the definition or definitions, including subentries and idiomatic phrases.
VII. variant spellings.
VIII. etymology.
IX. run-on (or, undefined derivative) entries.
X. synonym lists and studies.
XI. antonym lists.

Abbreviations used in this dictionary have been limited as far as possible to familiar ones. All abbreviations used appear in their individual alphabetical places in the dictionary itself.

I. ENTRY WORD OR WORDS

(A) The entry word appears in large bold-face type at the left, slightly farther into the left margin than the usual line of the text. (Example: **guard**)

(B) Each foreign word and phrase is followed by a label indicating the language of the word or phrase. (Example: **anno Domini**)

(C) Separate entries are made for all words which, though spelt identically, are of completely unrelated derivation; in such cases, each entry word is followed by a small superscript number. (Example: **gum**^{1}, **gum**^{2}, and **gum**^{3})

II. PRONUNCIATION

(A) The pronunciation follows the entry word, within parentheses. (Example: **grow**)

(B) The first pronunciation shown is, as a rule, the form in widest general use.

(C) Pronunciations are not usually given for run-on entries providing the pronunciation is easily ascertainable from the combination of the main entry and the suffix. (Example: **guardedly**)

A full key to the pronunciation system appears inside the front cover of this dictionary. In addition, for ready reference, an abbreviated pronunciation key appears at the bottom of each right-hand page.

III. PARTS OF SPEECH

(A) The pronunciation is followed by an abbreviation in italics, indicating the part of speech of the entry word.

(B) If the entry word is used in more than one grammatical form, an italicized abbreviation indicating the part of speech precedes each set of definitions to which it refers.

IV. INFLECTED FORMS

(A) If an entry word has irregularly inflected forms (any form not formed by the simple addition of the suffix to the main entry), the summary of these forms is given immediately after the pronunciation.

(B) If a word has variant inflected forms, these variants are shown. (Example: **grovel**)

(C) Regularly inflected forms, not generally shown, include:

(1) Nouns forming a plural merely by the addition of *-s* or *-es*, such as *dog* (*dogs*) or *class* (*classes*);
(2) Verbs forming the past tense by adding *-ed*, such as *halt* (*halted*);
(3) Verbs forming the present tense by adding *-s* or *-es*, such as *talk* (*talks*) or *smash* (*smashes*);
(4) Verbs forming the present participle by adding *-ing*, such as *walk* (*walking*);
(5) Adjectives forming the comparative and superlative by adding *-er*, *-est*, such as *black* (*blacker*, *blackest*).

Regular forms are given when necessary, however, for clarity, or the avoidance of confusion.

(D) In the case of inflected forms of verbs, if two forms are shown, the first represents the past tense and the past participle, while the second represents the present participle.

(E) If three inflected forms of verbs are shown, the first represents the past tense, the second the past participle, and the third the present participle.

(F) If necessary, variants of inflected forms are labelled as to level of usage or dialect distribution.

V. RESTRICTIVE LABELS

(A) Entries that are limited in usage as to level, region, time, or subject, are marked with such labels as: *Colloq.*, *Slang*, *U.S.*, *Dial.*, *Obs.*, *Archaic*, *Electronics*, *Chem.*, etc.

(B) If the restrictive label applies to the entire entry, it appears before the first part-of-speech label. (Example: **grouch**)

(C) If the restrictive label applies to only one part of speech, it appears after that part-of-speech label but before the definition numbers.

(D) If the restrictive label applies to only one definition, it appears after the definition number but before the definition itself. (Example: **grub,** def. 3)

VI. DEFINITIONS

(A) Definitions are individually numbered; numbers appear in a single sequence without regard to part of speech. The central meaning of each part of speech is put first; usually this is also the commonest meaning. The usual order after the central meaning is: figurative or transferred meanings, specialized meanings, general meanings, obsolete, archaic, or rare meanings. This order, however, has been broken, for example where it is desirable to group related meanings together.

(B) In some cases in which two definitions are very closely related, usually within the same field of information, they are marked with bold-face letters of the alphabet under the same definition number.

(C) If a meaning occurs with both capitalized and lower-case forms, an indication of this is given at the beginning of the definition. (Example: **Guernsey,** def. 3)

(D) Special effort has been made to indicate unique grammatical context wherever possible. Thus, the customary prepositional forms following certain words are often shown. (Example: **gulp,** def. 2)

(E) Idiomatic phrases, prepositional verb phrases, etc., are usually listed in secondary bold face alphabetically under main entries. Such entries are usually placed under the difficult or key word. (Example: **ground**)

VII. VARIANT SPELLINGS

Definitions always appear under the commonest spelling of a word.

(A) Less common variants merely cross-refer to the more common ones.

(B) At the end of the definitions of the most common spellings, the variants are usually shown.

(C) Variants are often labelled as to usage, either within specific fields (as *Law*) or within specific levels, regions, or times (as *Colloq.*, *U.S.*, *Archaic*, etc.).

VIII. ETYMOLOGIES

Etymologies appear in square brackets after the definition or definitions of the entry.

A full key to the etymology appears inside the front of this dictionary, and a short abbreviated key appears at the bottom of every left-hand page.

IX. RUN-ON ENTRIES

Words which are simple derivatives of the main entry, and which present no meaning problem, are run on after the etymology, or (if there is no etymology) after the last definition in the entry. Such entries appear in secondary bold-face type, followed by an indication of their grammatical form.

X. SYNONYMS

(A) Studies discriminating between synonyms appear with numbers corresponding to the definitions involved. These studies have been placed under the commonest of the synonyms under discussion, and cross-references are placed under the other terms.

(B) At the end of certain entries, lists of synonyms appear, each list being preceded by a number indicating the particular definition to which that list applies. In these lists, semicolons have been used to set off clusters of words with slightly different facets of meaning within the same general definitions.

XI. ANTONYMS

Lists of antonyms are shown throughout the book, preceded by a number indicating the definition to which the antonym list refers.

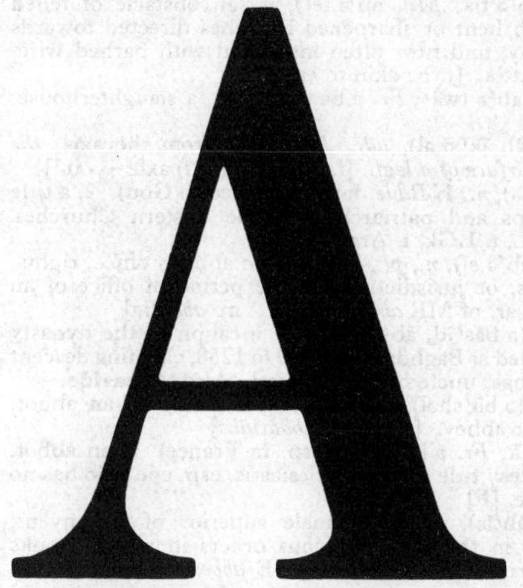

A Dictionary of the English Language

A, a (ā), *n., pl.* **A's, a's** or **As. 1.** the first letter of the English alphabet. **2.** the first in any series. **3.** the highest mark for school, college, or university work; alpha. **4.** *Music.* **a.** the sixth degree in the scale of C major, or the first in the relative minor scale (A minor). **b.** a written or printed note representing this tone. **c.** a string, key, or pipe tuned to this note. **d.** (in the fixed system of solmization) the sixth note of the scale, called **la. e.** the note to which concert performers tune their instruments; concert A. **5. from A to Z,** from beginning to end.

a[1] (ā; *unstressed* ə), *adj. or indef. article.* a word used esp. before nouns beginning with a consonant to mean: **1.** some (indefinite singular referring to one individual of a class): *a man, a house, a star.* **2.** another: *he is a Cicero in eloquence.* **3.** one: *two of a kind, a thousand.* **4.** any (a single): *not a one.* **5.** indefinite plural: *a few, a great many.* Also, *before a vowel,* **an.** [ME, phonetic var. of AN]

a[2] (ā; *unstressed* ə), *adj. or indef. article.* each; every: *three times a day.* [orig. *a,* prep., OE *an, on,* confused with the indefinite article. See A-[1]]

a[3] (ə), *prep. Colloq. or Dial.* of: *cloth a gold.* [OE *of* of]

a' (ä, ô), *adj. Scot.* all: *for a' that.* Also, **a.**

a-[1], a prefix, a reduced form of Old English prep. *on,* meaning 'on', 'in', 'into', 'to', 'towards', preserved before a noun in a prepositional phrase, forming a predicate adjective or an adverbial element, as in *afoot, abed, ashore, apart, aside,* and in archaic and dialectal use before a present participle in *-ing,* as in *to set the bells aringing.* [ME and late OE *a-,* var. of OE *an, on* at, on. See ON]

a-[2], a prefix, a reduced form of Old English *of,* as in *akin, afresh, anew.* [ME *a-,* OE *of* (prep.) off, of]

a-[3], an old point-action prefix, not referring to an act as a whole, but only to the beginning or end: *she awoke* (became awake), *they abided by these conclusions* (remained faithful to the end). [OE *ā-*; in some cases confused with OF *a-* (g. L *ad-* AD-) and erroneously refashioned after supposed L analogies, as in *a(l)lay*]

a-[4], var. of **ab-** before *m, p,* and *v,* as in *amove, aperient, avert.* [ME *a-,* t. F, g. L *ab-*; or t. L, reduced form of *ab-.* See AB-]

a-[5], var. of **ad-,** used: **1.** before *sc, sp, st,* as in *ascend.* **2.** in words of French derivation (often with the sense of increase, addition), as in *amass.* [ME *a-,* t. F, g. L *ad-,* or assimilated forms of *ad-,* such as *ab-, ac-, af-,* etc.; or t. L, reduced form of *ad-* AD-]

a-[6], var. of **an-**[1] before consonants, as in *achromatic.* [t. Gk, called alpha privative, before vowels *an-*; akin to L *in-* not, E UN-[1]]

A, 1. *Chem.* argon. **2.** *Physics.* **a.** Also, **Å.** angstrom unit. **b.** absolute temperature. **c.** ampere.

A (ā), *Cinema.* —*adj.* **1.** denoting a film which may be shown publicly to accompanied children as well as to adults. —*n.* **2.** such a film.

a., 1. about. **2.** acre; acres. **3.** adjective.

A-1 (ā′wŭn′), *adj.* **1.** *Naut.* registered as a first-class vessel in Lloyd's Register (or any other shipping register). **2.** *Colloq.* first-class; excellent. Also, **A-one.**

A.A., 1. Alcoholics Anonymous. **2.** anti-aircraft. **3.** Automobile Association.

A.A.A., Amateur Athletic Association.

Aachen (ä′kən; *Ger.* ȧ′KHən), *n.* a town in West Germany, in SW North Rhine-Westphalia. 177,900 (est. 1966). French, **Aix-la-Chapelle.**

Aalborg (*Dan.* ŏ′bôr), *n.* a seaport in N Denmark. 85,800 (est. 1960).

Aalto (*Fin.* äl′tô), *n.* **Alvar** (*Fin.* äl′vär), born 1898, Finnish architect and furniture designer.

A and M, 1. Agricultural and Mechanical. **2.** (of hymns) Ancient and Modern.

Aarau (*Ger.* ȧr′ou), *n.* a town in and capital of Aargau, in N Switzerland. 17,045 (1960).

aardvark (äd′väk), *n.* a large, nocturnal, burrowing mammal of Africa, subsisting largely on termites, and having a long, extensile tongue, claws, and conspicuously long ears. There is only one genus, *Orycteropus,* constituting a separate order, *Tubulidentata.* [t. Afrikaans, f. m. *aarde* earth + *vark* pig]

Aardvark, *Orycteropus afer* (Total length 5 to 6 ft, tail 2 to 2½ ft)

aardwolf (äd′wŏŏlf′), *n.* a striped, hyena-like African mammal, *Proteles cristatus,* which feeds on carrion and insects. [t. Afrikaans, f. m. *aarde* earth + *wolf* wolf]

Aargau (*Ger.* ȧr′gou), *n.* a canton in N Switzerland. 360,940 pop. (1960); 542 sq. mi. *Cap.:* Aarau. French, **Argovie.**

Aarhus (*Dan.* ôr′hōōs), *n.* a seaport in Denmark, in E Jutland. 119,568 (1960).

Aaron (ĕə′rən), *n.* the first high priest of the Hebrews and the brother of Moses. Exodus 4:14.

Aaronic (ĕə rŏn′ĭk), *adj.* **1.** pertaining to Aaron. **2.** pertaining or belonging to the Jewish priestly order. **3.** priestly; ecclesiastical. **4.** of the second or lesser order of priesthood among the Mormons. Also, (esp. def. 3) **Aaron′ical.**

Aaron's-beard (ēə′rənz bĭəd′), *n.* a creeping evergreen shrub, *Hypericum calycinum,* with large yellow flowers, a native of SE Europe frequently planted in shady places; rose of sharon.

Aaron's-rod (ĕə′rənz rŏd′), *n.* **1.** a widespread scrophulariaceous biennial plant, *Verbascum thapsus,* densely covered with woolly hairs and having erect spikes of yellow flowers. **2.** *Archit.* a decorative moulding of a tall straight stem with curling foliage.

Ab (ăb), *n.* (in the Jewish calendar) the eleventh month of the civil year and the fifth of the ecclesiastical year.

Ab, *Chem.* alabamine.

ab., about.

ab-, 1. Also, **abs-, a-**[4]. a prefix meaning 'off', 'away', 'from', as in *abduct, abjure.* **2.** *Physics.* a prefix attached to practical electrical units to denote the corresponding unit in the electromagnetic system. [t. L, repr. *ab,* prep., from, away; akin to Gk *apó,* Skt *ápa* from]

A.B., able-bodied (seaman).

A.B.A., Amateur Boxing Association.

aba (ăb′ə), *n.* a sleeveless outer garment, worn by Arabs. [t. Ar.: m. *'abā'a*]

Aba (ă bä′), *n.* a town in Nigeria, in the S Eastern Region. 58,000 (est. 1963).

abaca (ăb′ə kə), *n.* **1.** a Philippine plant, *Musa textilis.*

2. the fibre of this plant, Manila hemp, used in making rope. [t. Sp., t. Tagalog]

aback (ə băk′), *adv.* **1.** with the wind blowing against the forward side of a sail or sails, instead of the afterside. **2.** back against the mast, as sails, or with sails so placed. **3.** towards the back. **4. taken aback, a.** suddenly disconcerted. **b.** (of a ship) caught by the wind so as to press the sails back against the mast. **c.** (of sails) caught by a wind on the forward surface. [ME *abak*, OE *on*, prep., + *bæc* on or to the back]

abacus (ăb′ə kəs), *n.*, *pl.* **-ci** (-sī′). **1.** a contrivance for calculating, consisting of beads or balls strung on wires or rods set in a frame. **2.** *Archit.* a slab forming the top of the capital of a column. See diag. under **column.** [t. L, t. Gk: m. *ábax*]

A B

Chinese abacus: (Each vertical column = one integer; each bead in group A = 5 when lowered; each bead in group B = 1 when raised; value of this setting is 203,691,500)

Abadan (ăb′ə dän′), *n.* a city in SW Iran, on the Shatt-al-Arab: oil refineries. 230,000 (est. 1967).

Abaddon (ə băd′ən), *n.* **1.** the place of destruction; the depth of hell. **2.** Apollyon. Rev. 9:11. [t. Heb.: destruction]

abaft (ə băft′), *Naut.* —*prep.* **1.** in the rear of; behind. —*adv.* **2.** at or towards the stern; aft. [ME, f. A-¹ + *baft*, OE *bæftan*, *be æftan*. See BY, AFT]

abalone (ăb′ə lō′nĭ), *n.* a large snail of the genus *Haliotis* having a bowl-like shell bearing a row of respiratory holes; sea-ear. The flesh is used for food and the shell for ornament and mother-of-pearl objects. [t. Sp.]

abandon¹ (ə băn′dən), *v.t.* **1.** to leave completely and finally; forsake utterly; desert: *to abandon one's home.* **2.** to give up all concern in: *to abandon the cares of empire.* **3.** to give up (something begun) without finishing: *to abandon a cricket match because of rain.* **4.** to give up the control of: *to abandon a city to a conqueror.* **5.** to yield (oneself) unrestrainedly: *to abandon oneself to grief.* **6.** *Law.* to cast away or leave (one's property) with no intention of reclaiming it, thereby making the property available for appropriation by any person. **7.** *Law.* to relinquish (insured property) to the underwriter in case of partial loss, thus enabling the insured to claim a total loss. **8.** *Obs.* to banish. [ME *abandone(n)*, t. OF: m. *abandoner*, der. phrase *a bandon* under one's jurisdiction] —**aban′doner,** *n.* —**aban′donment,** *n.*

—**Syn. 2.** ABANDON, RELINQUISH, RENOUNCE mean to give up all concern in something. ABANDON means to give up (or discontinue any further interest in something, because of discouragement, weariness, distaste, etc.: *to abandon one's efforts.* RELINQUISH implies being (or feeling) compelled to give up something one would prefer to keep: *to relinquish a long-cherished desire.* RENOUNCE implies making (and perhaps formally stating) a voluntary decision to give something up: *to renounce worldly pleasures.* See also **desert².** **3.** give up, yield, surrender, resign, waive, abdicate. —**Ant. 3.** keep.

abandon² (ə băn′dən), *n.* a giving up to natural impulses; freedom from constraint or conventionality: *to do something with abandon.* [t. F]

abandoned (ə băn′dənd), *adj.* **1.** forsaken. **2.** unrestrained. **3.** shamelessly and recklessly wicked. —**Syn. 3.** See **immoral.**

abandonee (ə băn′dən ē′), *n.* *Law.* an insurer to whom a wreck has been abandoned. Cf. **abandon¹** (def. 7).

à bas (*Fr.* ȧ bä′), down with (the person or thing named)!

abase (ə bās′), *v.t.*, **abased, abasing. 1.** to reduce or lower, as in rank, office, estimation; humble; degrade. **2.** *Archaic.* to lower; bring down. [b. BASE² and ME *abesse(n)* (t. OF: m. *abaissier*, f. *a-* A-⁵ + *baissier* lower, ult. der. LL *bassus* low)] —**abase′ment,** *n.* —**abas′er,** *n.*

abash (ə băsh′), *v.t.* to destroy the self-possession of; make ashamed or embarrassed: *stand or feel abashed.* [ME *abashe(n)*, t. AF: m. *abaïss-*, var. of OF *esbaïss-*, s. *esbaïr* astonish] —**abash′ment,** *n.*

abate¹ (ə bāt′), *v.*, **abated, abating.** —*v.t.* **1.** to reduce in amount, intensity, etc.; lessen; diminish: *to abate a tax, one's enthusiasm, etc.* **2.** *Law.* to put an end to or suppress (a nuisance); suspend or extinguish (an action); annul (a writ). **3.** to deduct or subtract. **4.** to omit. —*v.i.* **5.** to decrease or become less in strength or violence: *the storm has abated.* **6.** *Obs. except Law.* to fail; become void. [ME *abate(n)*, t. OF: m. *abatre*, f. *a-* A-⁵ + *batre* beat] —**abat′able,** *adj.* —**abat′er;** *Law* **aba′tor,** *n.* —**Ant. 5.** increase, intensify.

abate² (ə bāt′), *v.i.* *Law, Obs.* to make an abatement (def. 4a). [t. OF: m. *enbatre* thrust in]

abatement (ə bāt′mənt), *n.* **1.** alleviation; mitigation. **2.** suppression or termination: *abatement of a nuisance.* **3.** decrease; reduction. **4.** *Law.* **a.** *Obs.* a wrongful entry on land made by a stranger, after the owner's death and before the owner's heir or devisee has obtained possession. **b.** a decrease in the legacies of a will when the assets of an estate are insufficient to pay all general legacies in full.

abatis (ăb′ə tĭs; *Mil.* ăb′ə tē′), *n.* an obstacle of felled trees with bent or sharpened branches directed towards the enemy, and now often interlaced with barbed wire. Also, **abattis.** [t. F; akin to ABATE]

abattoir (ăb′ə twä′; *Fr.* ȧ bȧ twȧr′), *n.* a slaughterhouse. [t. F]

abaxial (ăb ăk′sĭ əl), *adj.* *Bot.* away from the axis: *the abaxial surface of a leaf.* [f. AB- + L *axi(s)* axle + -AL¹]

Abba (ăb′ə), *n.* **1.** *Bible.* father (applied to God). **2.** a title of bishops and patriarchs in some Eastern Churches. [ME, t. L, t. LGk, t. Aram.]

abbacy (ăb′ə sĭ), *n.*, *pl.* **-cies. 1.** an abbot's office, rights, privileges, or jurisdiction. **2.** the period of office of an abbot. [var. of ME *abbatie*, t. LL: m. *abbātia*]

Abbasid (ə băs′ĭd, ăb′ə sĭd′), *n.* a caliph of the dynasty which ruled at Baghdad, A.D. 750 to 1258, claiming descent from Abbas, uncle of Mohammed. Also, **Abbaside.**

abbatial (ə bā′shəl), *adj.* of or pertaining to an abbot, abbess, or abbey. [t. LL: s. *abbātiālis*]

abbé (ăb′ā; *Fr.* ȧ bĕ′), *n.* (esp. in France) **1.** an abbot. **2.** a courtesy title for any ecclesiastic, esp. one who has no other title. [F]

abbess (ăb′ĭs), *n.* the female superior of a convent, regularly in the same religious orders in which monks are governed by an abbot. [ME *abbesse*, t. OF, g. LL *abbātissa*]

Abbevillian (ăb vĭl′ĭ ən, -yən), *adj.* of, pertaining to, or characteristic of a Palaeolithic culture in Europe, marked by the use of crude stone hand axes; Chellean. Also, **Abbevillean.** [named after *Abbeville*, town in France near which such objects were first found]

abbey (ăb′ĭ), *n.*, *pl.* **-beys. 1.** the religious body or establishment under an abbot or abbess; a monastery or convent. **2.** the monastic buildings. **3.** the church of an abbey. **4. the Abbey,** Westminster Abbey. **5.** a country residence that was formerly an abbatial house: *Newstead Abbey.* [ME *abbeye*, t. OF: m. *abaie*, g. LL *abbātia*]

Abbey Theatre, a theatre in Dublin associated with the Irish National Theatre Society (founded 1901) and the dramas of Synge, Yeats, and more recently Brendan Behan.

abbot (ăb′ət), *n.* the head or superior of a monastery. [ME, var. of ME and OE *abbod*, t. LL: m. s. *abbās*, t. LGk, t. Aram.: m. *abbā* father] —**ab′botship′, ab′botric,** *n.*

abbrev., abbreviation. Also, **abbr.**

abbreviate (ə brē′vĭ āt′), *v.t.*, **-ated, -ating,** to make brief; make shorter by contraction or omission: *to abbreviate 'foot' to 'ft'.* [t. L: m. s. *abbreviātus*, pp.] —**abbre′via′tor,** *n.* —**Syn.** See **shorten.**

abbreviation (ə brē′vĭ ā′shən), *n.* **1.** a shortened or contracted form of a word or phrase, used as a symbol for the whole. **2.** reduction in length; abridgement. **3.** *Music.* any of several signs or symbols used to abbreviate musical notation, as those indicating the repetition of a phrase or a note. [t. L: s. *abbreviātio*]

ABC (ā′bē′sē′), *n.* **1.** Also, *U.S.*, **ABCs.** the alphabet. **2.** a handbook (on any subject), often arranged alphabetically. **3.** the main or the basic facts, principles, etc. (of any subject).

Abd-el Krim (ăb′ dəl krĭm′), 1881–1963, Riff leader of a native revolt in Morocco, 1921–26.

abdicate (ăb′dĭ kāt′), *v.*, **-cated, -cating.** —*v.i.* **1.** to renounce a throne or some claim; relinquish a right, power, or trust. —*v.t.* **2.** to give up or renounce (office, duties, authority, etc.), esp. in a voluntary, public, or formal manner. [t. L: m. s. *abdicātus*, pp.] —**abdicable** (ăb′dĭ kə bl), *adj.* —**ab′dicative,** *adj.* —**ab′dica′tor, ab′dicant,** *n.*

abdication (ăb′dĭ kā′shən), *n.* the act of abdicating; renunciation, esp. of sovereign power.

abdomen (ăb′də mən, ăb dō′-), *n.* **1.** that part of the body of a mammal between the thorax and the pelvis; the visceral cavity containing most of the digestive organs; the belly. **2.** (in vertebrates below mammals) a region of the body corresponding to but not coincident with the human abdomen. **3.** *Entomol.* the posterior section of the body of an arthropod, behind the thorax or the cephalothorax. See diag. under **insect.** [t. L]

abdominal (ăb dŏm′ĭ nəl), *adj.* of, in, or on the abdomen: *abdominal muscles.* —**abdom′inally,** *adv.*

abdominous (ăb dŏm′ĭ nəs), *adj.* pot-bellied.

abduce (ăb dyōōs′), *v.t.* **-duced, -ducing.** abduct (def. 2). [t. L: m. s. *abdūcere*]

abducent (ăb dyōō′sənt), *adj.* *Physiol.* drawing away (applied to muscles, etc.).

abduct (ăb dŭkt′), *v.t.* **1.** to carry off surreptitiously or by force, esp. to kidnap. **2.** *Physiol.* to draw away from the original position (opposed to *adduct*). [t. L: s. *abductus*, pp.] —**abduc′tor,** *n.*

abduction[1] (ăb dŭk′shən), *n.* **1.** the act of fact of abducting. **2.** the state of being abducted. [t. F: f. s. L *abductus* + -*ion* -ION]

abduction[2] (ăb dŭk′shən), *n. Logic.* a syllogism whose major premise is certain but whose minor premise is probable. [t. NL: s. *abductio*: trans. of Gk *apagōgē*]

Abdul (ăb′dŏŏl), *n. Colloq.* (often derogatory) **1.** nickname for a Turk. **2.** (collectively) Turks.

Abdul-Hamid II (ăb′dŏŏl hă mēd′), 1842–1918, sultan of Turkey 1876–1909.

Abdul Rahman. See **Rahman, Tunku Abdul.**

abeam (ə bēm′), *adv. Naut.* at right angles to the keel of a ship; directly opposite the middle part of the ship.

abecedarian (ā′bē sē dĕə′rĭ ən), *n.* **1.** a pupil who is learning the letters of the alphabet. **2.** a beginner. —*adj.* **3.** alphabetical. **4.** primary; rudimentary. [f. s. ML *abecedārius* ABCD book + -AN]

abecedary (ā′bē sē′də rĭ), *n., pl.* **-ries.** abecedarian.

abed (ə bĕd′), *adv. Obs.* **1.** in bed. **2.** confined to bed.

Abednego (ə bĕd′nĭ gō′), *n.* See **Shadrach.**

Abel (ā′bl), *n. Bible.* the second son of Adam and Eve, slain by his brother, Cain. Gen. 4.

Abelard (ăb′ĭ läd′), *n.* **Peter,** 1079–1142, French scholastic philosopher, teacher, and theologian. His love affair with Héloise is one of the famous romances of history. Also, *French,* **Pierre Abélard** (*Fr.* pyĕr à bĕ lȧr′).

abele (ə bēl′, ā′bl), *n.* the white poplar tree, *Populus alba.* [t. D: m. *abeel,* t. OF: m. *abel,* g. LL *albellus,* dim. of L *albus* white]

abelmosk (ā′bl mŏsk′), *n.* a malvaceous plant, *Hibiscus abelmoschus,* of warm countries, cultivated for its musky seed, which is used in perfumery, etc. [t. NL: m. s. *Abelmoschus,* t. Ar.: m. *habb el mosk* grain of musk]

Abel Tasman National Park, a national park in New Zealand, in South Island, on Tasman Bay. 43,939 acres.

Abeokuta (ăb′ĭ ō kŏŏ′tə), *n.* a town in Nigeria, in W Western Region. 84,000 (est. 1963).

Aberavon (ăb′ə răv′ən), *n.* a town in Wales, in W Glamorganshire. 31,226 (1961).

Aberdare (ăb′ə dĕə′), *n.* a town in Wales, in N Glamorganshire. 39,155 (1961).

Aberdare Mountains, a mountain range in Kenya, N of Nairobi. Highest peak, 13,000 ft.

Aberdeen (ăb′ə dēn′), *n.* **1. George Hamilton Gordon, 4th Earl of,** 1784–1860, British statesman; prime minister 1852–55. **2.** a seaport in Scotland, the county town of Aberdeenshire. 185,034 (est. 1964). **3.** Aberdeenshire. —**Aberdonian** (ăb′ə dō′nyən), *adj., n.*

Aberdeen Angus (ăng′gəs), one of a breed of hornless beef cattle with smooth black hair, originally bred in Scotland.

Aberdeenshire (ăb′ə dēn′shĭə, -shə), *n.* a county in NE Scotland. 321,426 pop. (est. 1964); 1974 sq. mi. *Co. town:* Aberdeen. Also, **Aberdeen.** *Abbrev.:* A'deen.

Aberglaube (*Ger.* ȧ′bər glou bə), *n. German.* belief beyond what is justified by experience and knowledge.

Abernethy (ăb′ə nĕth′ĭ, -nē′thĭ), *n.* **John,** 1764–1831, English surgeon.

aberrant (ă bĕ′rənt), *adj.* **1.** straying from the right or usual course. **2.** deviating from the ordinary or normal type. [t. L: s. *aberrans,* ppr.] —**aber′rance, aber′rancy,** *n.*

aberration (ăb′ə rā′shən), *n.* **1.** the act of wandering from the usual way or normal course. **2.** deviation from truth or moral rectitude. **3.** lapse from a sound mental state. **4.** *Astron.* apparent displacement of a heavenly body, due to the joint effect of the motion of the rays of light proceeding from it and the motion of the earth. **5.** *Optics.* any disturbance of the rays of a pencil of light such that they can no longer be brought to a sharp focus or form a clear image. **6.** *Genetics.* deviation from type. [t. L: s. *aberrātio*] —**ab′erra′tional,** *adj.*

Abertillery (ăb′ə tĭ lĕə′rĭ), *n.* a town in Wales, in W Monmouthshire. 25,146 (1961).

Aberystwyth (ăb′ə rĭs′twĭth), *n.* a town in Wales, in Cardiganshire. 11,000 (est. 1964).

abet (ə bĕt′), *v.t.,* **abetted, abetting.** to encourage or countenance by aid or approval (used chiefly in a bad sense): *to abet evildoers, to abet a crime or offence.* [ME *abbette(n),* t. OF: m. *abeter,* f. *a-* A-[5] + *beter* (t. Scand.: cf. Icel. *beita* cause to bite. See BAIT)] —**abet′ment,** *n.*

abetter (ə bĕt′ə), *n.* one who abets. Also (esp. in legal use), **abettor.**

ab extra (ăb ĕk′strə), *Latin.* from the outside.

abeyance (ə bā′əns), *n.* **1.** temporary inactivity or suspension. **2.** *Law.* a state of waiting for the ascertainment of the person entitled to ownership: *an estate in abeyance.* [t. AF: m. *abeiance* expectation, der. OF *abeer* gape after, f. *a-* A-[5] + *beer, baer* gape, g. LL *badāre*]

abeyant (ə bā′ənt), *adj.* in abeyance.

Abhazia (ăb hä′zĭ ə), *n.* an autonomous republic in the SW Soviet Union, on the E coast of the Black Sea. 442,000 pop. (est. 1963); 3360 sq. mi. *Cap.:* Sukhumi. Also, **Abhasia, Abkhazia.**

abhor (əb hô′), *v.t.,* **-horred, -horring.** to regard with repugnance; loathe or abominate. [late ME, t. L: m. s. *abhorrēre*] —**abhor′rer,** *n.* —**Syn.** See **hate.**

abhorrence (əb hŏ′rəns), *n.* **1.** a feeling of extreme aversion. **2.** something detested.

abhorrent (əb hŏ′rənt), *adj.* **1.** feeling horror (fol. by *of*): *abhorrent of excess.* **2.** utterly opposed (fol. by *to*): *abhorrent to reason.* **3.** exciting horror; detestable. **4.** remote in character (fol. by *from*): *abhorrent from the principles of law.* —**abhor′rently,** *adv.*

Abib (ā′bĭb), *n.* Nisan.

abidance (ə bī′dns), *n.* **1.** the act of abiding. **2.** conformity (fol. by *by*): *abidance by rules.*

abide (ə bīd′), *v.,* **abode** or **abided, abiding.** —*v.i.* **1.** to remain; continue; stay: *abide with me.* **2.** to dwell; reside. **3.** to continue in a certain condition; remain steadfast or faithful. **4. abide by, a.** to stand by: *to abide by a friend.* **b.** to await or accept the consequences of: *to abide by the event.* —*v.t.* **5.** to wait for. **6.** to stand one's ground against; await or sustain defiantly. **7.** *Colloq.* to put up with; tolerate: *I can't abide such people.* **8.** to pay the price or penalty of; suffer for. [ME *abide(n),* OE *ābidan.* See A-[3]. In def. 8 confused with ABY] —**abid′er,** *n.*

abiding (ə bī′dĭng), *adj.* continuing; steadfast: *an abiding faith.* —**abid′ingly,** *adv.* —**abid′ingness,** *n.*

Abidjan (ăb′ĭ jän′; *Fr.* à bēd zhäN′), *n.* the capital of Ivory Coast, in the S part. 257,500 (est. 1964).

abietic acid (ăb′ĭ ĕt′ĭk), a yellow crystalline acid, $C_{19}H_{29}COOH$, derived from the resin of a species of pine, used in driers, varnishes, and soaps. [f. s. L *abiēs* fir + -IC + ACID]

abigail (ăb′ĭ gāl′), *n.* a lady's maid. [from *Abigail,* the 'waiting gentlewoman', in Beaumont and Fletcher's '*The Scornful Lady*'. See also I Sam. 25:23–42]

ability (ə bĭl′ĭ tĭ), *n., pl.* **-ties. 1.** power or capacity to do or act in any relation. **2.** competence in any occupation or field of action, from the possession of capacity, skill, means, or other qualification. **3.** (*pl.*) talents; mental gifts or endowments. [ME *(h)abilite,* t. F, t. L: m. s. *habilitas*; r. ME *ablete,* t. OF]

—**Syn. 1.** capability; proficiency, expertness, dexterity. **2.** ABILITY, FACULTY, TALENT denote mental qualifications or powers. ABILITY is a general word for mental power, native or acquired, enabling one to do things well: *a person of great ability, ability in mathematics.* FACULTY denotes a natural ability for a particular kind of action: *a faculty for saying what he means.* TALENT is often used to mean a native ability or aptitude in a special field: *a talent for music or art.*

Abingdon (ăb′ĭng dən), *n.* a town in England, in N Berkshire. 14,287 (1961).

ab initio (ăb′ĭ nĭsh′ĭ ō′), *Latin.* from the beginning.

ab intra (ăb ĭn′trə), *Latin.* from within; from inside.

abiogenesis (ā′bī ō jĕn′ĭ sĭs), *n. Biol.* **1.** the (hypothetical) production of living things from inanimate matter; spontaneous generation. **2.** the theory, belief, or doctrine that living things can be produced from inanimate matter. [f. A-[6] + BIO- + GENESIS] —**abiogenist** (ā′bī ŏj′ĭ nĭst).

abiogenetic (ā′bī ō jĭ nĕt′ĭk), *adj. Biol.* of or pertaining to abiogenesis. —**a′biogenet′ically,** *adv.*

abirritant (ăb ĭ′rĭ tənt), *Med.* —*n.* **1.** a soothing agent. —*adj.* **2.** reducing irritation.

abirritate (ăb ĭ′rĭ tāt′), *v.t.,* **-tated, -tating.** *Med.* to make less irritable. —**abir′rita′tion,** *n.*

abject (ăb′jĕkt), *adj.* **1.** utterly humiliating or disheartening: *abject poverty.* **2.** contemptible; despicable: *an abject liar.* **3.** humble; servile: *an abject apology.* **4.** *Obs.* cast aside. [ME, t. L: s. *abjectus,* pp., thrown away] —**abjec′tion,** *n.* —**abjectly** (ăb′jĕkt lĭ), *adv.* —**ab′jectness,** *n.*

abjuration (ăb′jŏŏ rā′shən), *n.* the act of abjuring; renunciation upon oath.

abjure (əb jŏŏə′), *v.t.,* **-jured, -juring. 1.** to renounce or repudiate; retract, esp. with solemnity: *to abjure one's errors.* **2.** to forswear: *to abjure allegiance.* [t. L: m. s. *abjūrare*] —**abjur′atory,** *adj.* —**abjur′er,** *n.*

Abkhazia (ăb kä′zĭ ə), *n.* Abhazia.

abl., ablative.

ablactate (ăb lăk′tāt), *v.t.,* **-tated, -tating.** to wean. [t. L: m. s. *ablactātus,* pp.] —**ab′lacta′tion,** *n.*

ablation (ăb lā′shən), *n.* **1.** *Med.* removal, esp. of organs, abnormal growths, or harmful substances, from the body by mechanical means, as by surgery. **2.** *Physics, Geol., etc.* erosion of a solid body by a fluid. [t. L: s. *ablātio* a carrying away]

ablative (ăb′lə tĭv), *Gram.* —*adj.* **1.** (in some inflected languages) denoting a case which has among its functions the indication of place from which, time when, place in which, manner, means, instrument, agent, etc. —*n.* **2.** the ablative case. **3.** a word in that case, as *Troiā* in Latin *Æneās Troiā vēnit*, 'Aeneas came from Troy'. [t. L: m. s. *ablātīvus* of removal; r. late ME *ablatif*, t. F]

ablative absolute, (in Latin grammar) a construction not dependent upon any other part of the sentence, consisting of a noun and a participle, noun and adjective, or two nouns, in which both members are in the ablative case, as Latin *viā factā*, 'the road having been made'.

ablator (ăb lā′tə), *n.* **1.** a disposable casing used to protect a spacecraft from excessive heating during re-entry into the earth's atmosphere. **2.** the material of such a casing.

ablaut (ăb′lout; *Ger.* äp′lout), *n. Gram.* **1.** regular change in the internal structure of roots, particularly in the vowel, showing alteration in function and meaning. **2.** such change in Indo-European languages, as in English *sing, sang, sung, song*; gradation. [t. G: f. *ab* off + *Laut* sound]

ablaze (ə blāz′), *adv.* **1.** on fire. —*adj.* **2.** gleaming as if on fire. **3.** excited; eagerly desirous. **4.** very angry.

able (ā′bl), *adj.*, **abler, ablest.** **1.** having sufficient power, strength, or qualifications; qualified: *a man able to perform military service.* **2.** having unusual intellectual qualifications: *an able minister,* **3.** showing talent or knowledge: *an able speech.* [ME, t. OF, g. L *habilis* easy to handle, fit]

—**Syn.** **1.** ABLE, CAPABLE, COMPETENT all mean possessing adequate power for doing something. ABLE implies power equal to effort required: *able to finish in time.* CAPABLE implies power to meet or fulfil ordinary, usual requirements: *a capable workman.* COMPETENT suggests power to meet demands in a completely satisfactory manner: *a competent nurse.* **2, 3.** talented, accomplished, gifted; skilled, clever.

-able, a suffix used to form adjectives, esp. from verbs, to denote ability, liability, tendency, worthiness, or likelihood, as in *teachable, perishable, obtainable,* but also attached to other parts of speech (esp. nouns) as in *objectionable, peaceable,* and even verb phrases, as in *get-at-able.* Many of these adjectives, such as *durable, tolerable,* have been borrowed directly from Latin or French, in which language they were already compounded. However, **-able** is attached freely (now usually with passive force) to stems of any origin. Also, **-ble, -ible.** [ME, t. OF, g. s. L *-ābilis*]

able-bodied (ā′bl bŏd′ĭd), *adj.* physically competent.

able-bodied seaman, an experienced seaman who has passed certain tests in the practice of seamanship.

ablegate (ăb′lĭ gāt′), *n.* a papal envoy to a newly appointed dignitary.

ablins (ā′blĭnz), *adv. Scot.* perhaps. Also, **aiblins.**

abloom (ə blo͞om′), *adv., adj.* in blossom.

abluent (ăb′lo͞o ənt), *adj.* **1.** cleansing. —*n.* **2.** a cleansing agent; a detergent. [t. L: m. s. *abluens*, ppr.]

ablution (ə blo͞o′shən), *n.* **1.** a cleansing with water or other liquid, as in ceremonial purification. **2.** the liquid used. **3.** (*pl.*) the act of washing oneself: *do one's ablutions.* [ME, t. L: s. *ablūtio*] —**ablu′tionary,** *adj.*

ably (ā′blĭ), *adv.* in an agile manner; competently.

Abnaki (ăb nä′kĭ), *n., pl.* **-kis,** (*esp. collectively*) **-ki.** **1.** a member of an American Indian people of Maine, New Brunswick, and Quebec. **2.** the language of the Abnaki, an Algonquian language.

abnegate (ăb′nĭ gāt′), *v.t.*, **-gated, -gating.** to refuse or deny to oneself; reject; renounce. [t. L: m. s. *abnegātus*, pp.] —**ab′nega′tion,** *n.* —**ab′nega′tor,** *n.*

abnormal (ăb nô′məl), *adj.* not conforming to rule; deviating from the type or standard. [f. s. L *abnormis* irregular + -AL[1]; r. *anormal*, t. F, t. ML: s. *anormalus* for L *anōmalus*, t. Gk: m. *anōmalos.* See ANOMALOUS] —**abnor′mally,** *adv.* —**Syn.** anomalous, aberrant, peculiar: exceptional, unusual; odd. See **irregular.**

abnormality (ăb′nô măl′ĭ tĭ), *n., pl.* **-ties.** **1.** an abnormal thing, happening, or feature. **2.** deviation from the standard, rule, or type; irregularity.

abnormal psychology, the study of mental phenomena, behaviour patterns, etc., of individuals who deviate widely from the average.

abnormity (ăb nô′mĭ tĭ), *n., pl.* **-ties.** **1.** abnormality; irregularity. **2.** malformation; monstrosity.

Abo (ăb′ō), *n. Austral. Colloq.* an Aborigine.

Åbo (*Sw.* ō′bo͞o), *n.* Swedish name of **Turku.**

aboard (ə bôd′), *adv.* **1.** on board; on or in a ship, train, bus, etc. **2.** alongside. —*prep.* **3.** on board of.

abode (ə bōd′), *n.* **1.** a dwelling place; a habitation. **2.** continuance in a place; sojourn; stay. —*v.* **3.** pt. and pp. of **abide.** [ME *abood*, OE *ābād*, pt. of *ābīdan* ABIDE]

aboil (ə boil′), *adj., adv.* **1.** on the boil; boiling. **2.** boiling with passion. [f. A-[1] + BOIL[1]]

abolish (ə bŏl′ĭsh), *v.t.* to do away with; put an end to; annul; destroy: *to abolish slavery.* [t. F: m. *aboliss-*, s. *abolir* make perish, g. s. L *abolescere* perish] —**abol′ishable,** *adj.* —**abol′isher,** *n.* —**abol′ishment,** *n.*

—**Syn.** suppress; annihilate; exterminate. ABOLISH, ERADICATE, STAMP OUT mean to do away completely with something. To ABOLISH is to cause to cease, often by a summary order: *to abolish a requirement.* STAMP OUT, stronger though less formal, implies forcibly making an end to something considered undesirable or harmful: *to stamp out the opium traffic.* ERADICATE (literally, to tear out by the roots), a formal word, suggests extirpation, leaving no vestige or trace: *to eradicate evil.*

abolition (ăb′ə lĭsh′ən), *n.* **1.** utter destruction; annulment; abrogation: *the abolition of laws, customs, debts, etc.* **2.** the legal extinction of Negro slavery. [t. L: s. *abolitio*] —**ab′oli′tionary,** *adj.* —**ab′oli′tionist.** *n.*

abolitionism (ăb′ə lĭsh′ə nĭz′əm), *n.* the principle or policy of abolition, esp. of Negro slavery.

abomasum (ăb′ə mā′səm), *n.* the fourth or true stomach of ruminants, lying next to the omasum. See diag. under **ruminant.** Also, **abomasus** (ăb′ə mā′səs). [t. NL, f. L *ab-* AB- + *omāsum* bullock's tripe]

A-bomb (ā′bŏm′), *n.* atomic bomb.

abominable (ə bŏm′ĭ nə bl), *adj.* **1.** detestable; loathsome. **2.** *Colloq.* shocking; unpleasant; bad. [ME, t. F, t. L: m. s. *abōminābilis*] —**abom′inableness,** *n.* —**abom′inably,** *adv.*

abominable snowman, a manlike creature supposed to inhabit the snows of Tibet; yeti.

abominate (ə bŏm′ĭ nāt′), *v.t.*, **-nated, -nating.** **1.** to regard with intense aversion; abhor. **2.** to dislike strongly. [t. L: m. s. *abōminātus*, pp., having deprecated as an ill omen] —**abom′ina′tor,** *n.* —**Syn.** **1.** See **hate.**

abomination (ə bŏm′ĭ nā′shən), *n.* **1.** an object greatly disliked or abhorred. **2.** intense aversion; detestation. **3.** a detestable action; a shameful vice.

aboriginal (ăb′ə rĭj′ĭ nəl), *adj.* **1.** pertaining to aborigines; primitive: *aboriginal customs.* **2.** original native; indigenous. —*n.* **3.** Aborigine. —**ab′orig′inal′ity,** *n.* —**ab′orig′inally,** *adv.*

ab origine (ăb′ō rĭj′ĭ nĭ), *Latin.* from the very first; from the source or origin.

aborigine (ăb′ə rĭj′ĭ nĭ), *n.* **1.** (*usually cap.*) one of a race of primitive people inhabiting Australia and the nearby islands. **2.** (*often cap.*) their language; native Australian. **3.** (*pl.*) the primitive inhabitants of a country; the people living in a country at the earliest period. **4.** (*pl.*) *Rare.* the original fauna or flora of a region. [t. L, der. *ab orīgine* from the beginning]

abort (ə bôt′), *v.i.* **1.** to miscarry before the foetus is viable. **2.** to develop incompletely, remaining in a rudimentary state or degenerating. **3.** to come to nothing; fail. **4.** *Slang.* to fail to complete a mission, or test of a mechanical device. —*v.t.* **5.** to cause to abort. [t. L: s. *abortus*, pp., having miscarried]

aborticide (ə bô′tĭ sīd′), *n.* **1.** destruction of a foetus in the uterus; foeticide. **2.** an abortifacient. [f. s. L *abortus* miscarriage + -(I)CIDE]

abortifacient (ə bô′tĭ fā′shənt), *adj.* **1.** causing abortion. —*n.* **2.** something used to produce abortion. [f. s. L *abortus* miscarriage + -(I)FACIENT]

abortion (ə bô′shən), *n.* **1.** the expulsion of a human foetus before it is viable (within the first 28 weeks of pregnancy). **2.** an immature and not viable birth product; miscarriage. **3.** *Biol.* the arrested development of an embryo or an organ at its (more or less) early stage. **4.** anything which fails in its progress before it is matured or perfected, as a design or project. [t. L: s. *abortio* miscarriage] —**abor′tional,** *adj.*

abortionist (ə bô′shə nĭst), *n.* one who produces or aims to produce a criminal abortion, esp. one who makes a practice of so doing.

abortive (ə bô′tĭv), *adj.* **1.** failing to succeed; miscarrying: *an abortive scheme.* **2.** born prematurely. **3.** imperfectly developed; rudimentary. **4.** *Med.* **a.** producing or intended to produce abortion; abortifacient. **b.** acting to halt progress of a disease. **5.** *Pathol.* (of the course of a disease) short and mild without the commonly pronounced clinical symptoms. —**abor′tively,** *adv.* —**abor′tiveness,** *n.*

Aboukir (ăb′o͞o kĭə′), *n.* a bay of the Mediterranean, on the N coast of Egypt: Battle of the Nile (defeat of French by British), 1798. Also, **Abukir.**

aboulia (ə bo͞o′lyə), *n. Psychol.* a form of mental derangement in which volition is impaired or lost. Also, **abulia.** [t. Gk: m. *aboulía* ill counsel] —**abou′lic,** *adj.*

abound (ə bound′), *v.i.* **1.** to be in great plenty; be very prevalent: *the discontent which abounds in the world.* **2.** to be rich (fol. by *in*): *some languages abound in figurative expressions.* **3.** to be filled; teem (fol. by *with*): *the ship abounds with rats.* [ME *aboundе(n)*, t. OF: m. *abunder*, g. L *abundāre*] —**abound′ing,** *adj.*

about (ə bout′), *prep.* **1.** of; concerning; in regard to: *to talk about secrets.* **2.** connected with: *instructions about the work.* **3.** somewhere near or in: *he is about the house.*

4. near; close to: *about my height*. 5. on every side of; around: *the railing about the tower*. 6. on or near (one's person): *they had lost all they had about them*. 7. on the point of (fol. by an infinitive): *about to leave*. 8. here and there in or on: *wander about the place*. 9. concerned with; engaged in doing. —*adv*. 10. near in time, number, degree, etc.; approximately: *about a hundred miles*. 11. *Colloq*. nearly; almost: *about ready*. 12. nearby: *he is somewhere about*. 13. on every side, in every direction: *look about*. 14. half round; in the reverse direction: *to spin about*. 15. *Naut*. on the opposite tack. 16. to and fro; here and there: *move furniture about*. 17. in rotation or succession; alternately: *turn about is fair play*. 18. on the move: *be up and about*. 19. *Archaic*. around. —*adj*. 20. **up and about,** astir; active (after sleep). [ME; OE *abūtan*, var. of *onbūtan*, *on būtan* on the outside (of)]

about-face (*n*. ə bout′fās′; *v*. ə bout′fās′), *n*., *v*., **-faced, -facing.** *Chiefly U.S.* about-turn.

about-ship (ə bout′shĭp′), *v.i.* *Naut*. to tack a ship.

about-sledge (ə bout′slĕj′), *n*. a large sledge-hammer used by blacksmiths in conjunction with a smaller hammer, alternate blows being given with each.

about turn, the military command to face to the rear in a prescribed manner while standing. Also, *Chiefly U.S.*, **about face.**

about-turn (ə bout′tûn′), *n*., *v*., **-turned, -turning.** —*n*. 1. a complete, sudden change in position, principle, attitude, etc.; volte-face. —*v.i.* 2. to turn in the opposite direction.

above (ə bŭv′), *adv*. 1. in or to a higher place; overhead: *the blue sky above*. 2. higher in rank or power: *appeal to the courts above*. 3. before in order, esp. in a book or writing: *from what has been said above*. 4. in heaven. —*prep*. 5. in or to a higher place than: *fly above the earth*. 6. more in quantity or number than: *the weight is above a ton*. 7. superior to, in rank or authority. 8. not capable of (an undesirable thought, action, etc.). 9. in preference to: *to favour one child above another*. 10. **above all,** principally; most important of all. 11. **above oneself, a.** over-excited; elated. **b.** conceited; smug; self-satisfied. —*adj*. 12. said, mentioned, or written above; foregoing: *the above explanation*. —*n*. 13. **the above,** that which was said, mentioned, or written previously. [ME; OE *abufan*, f. A-[1] + *bufan* above]

aboveboard (ə bŭv′bôd′), *adv*., *adj*. in open sight; without tricks, deceit, or disguise: *open and aboveboard actions*. Also (esp. in predicative use), **above board.**

above-ground (ə bŭv′ground′), *adv*., *adj*. alive, in the world; not buried. Also (esp. in predicative use), **above ground.**

ab ovo (ăb ō′vō), *Latin*. from the beginning. [L: from the egg]

Abp, Archbishop.

abracadabra (ăb′rə kə dăb′rə), *n*. 1. a mystical word used in incantations, or written in triangular form as a charm on an amulet. 2. any word charm or empty jingle of words. 3. gibberish; nonsense. [t. L]

abrachia (ā brăk′ĭ ə, ă brăk′-), *n*. *Anat*. a total absence of arms due to a developmental anomaly.

abradant (ə brā′dnt), *adj*., *n*. abrasive.

abrade (ə brād′), *v.t.*, *v.i.*, **abraded, abrading.** to wear off or down by friction; scrape off. [t. L: m. s. *abrādere* scrape off] —**abrad′er,** *n*.

Abraham (ā′brə hăm′, -həm), *n*. 1. *Bible*. the first of the great patriarchs, father of Isaac, and traditional founder of the Hebrew people. Gen. 11–25. 2. **Heights of,** a plateau in Canada near Quebec: battle 1759 in which the British under Wolfe defeated the French.

abranchiate (ā brăng′kĭ ĭt, -āt′), *adj*. *Zool*. without gills. Also, **abranchial** (ā brăng′kyəl). [f. A-[6] + s. Gk *bránchia* gills + -ATE[1]]

abrasion (ə brā′zhən), *n*. 1. the result of rubbing or abrading; an abraded spot or place. 2. the act or process of abrading. [t. L: s. *abrāsio* a scraping off]

abrasive (ə brā′sĭv, -zĭv), *n*. 1. any material or substance used for grinding, polishing, lapping, etc., as emery or sand. —*adj*. 2. tending to produce abrasion. 3. (of a personality) irritating; tending to annoy.

abreact (ăb′rĭ ăkt′), *v.t.* *Psychoanal*. to remove by abreaction.

abreaction (ăb′rĭ ăk′shən), *n*. *Psychoanal*. the release of mental tension due to an unpleasant experience, by reliving the experience in speech and action in the presence of a psychoanalyst. [f. AB- + REACTION. Cf. G *Abreagierung*]

abreast (ə brĕst′), *adv*., *adj*. 1. side by side. 2. alongside, in progress or attainment; equally advanced (fol. by *of* or *with*): *to keep abreast of the times in science*.

abridge (ə brĭj′), *v.t.*, **abridged, abridging.** 1. to shorten by condensation or omission, or both; rewrite or reconstruct on a smaller scale. 2. to lessen; diminish. 3. to deprive; cut off. [ME *abrege(n)*, t. OF: m. *abreger*, g. L *abbreviāre* shorten] —**abridge′able; abridg′able,** *adj*. —**abridged′,** *adj*. —**abridg′er,** *n*. —**Syn. 1.** cut down; epitomize; condense. See **shorten. 2.** contract. **3.** curtail. —**Ant. 1.** lengthen. **2.** expand.

abridgement (ə brĭj′mənt), *n*. 1. a condensation, as of a book; a reproduction of anything in reduced or condensed form. 2. the act of abridging. 3. the state of being abridged. Also, **abridgment.**

abroach (ə brōch′), *adv*. 1. broached. 2. **set abroach, a.** to cause (a cask, a barrel, etc.) to flow or to let out liquid. **b.** to give rise to; spread abroad.

abroad (ə brôd′), *adv*. 1. in or to a foreign country or countries: *to live abroad*. 2. out of doors: *the owl ventures abroad at night*. 3. astir; at large; in circulation: *rumours of disaster are abroad*. 4. broadly; widely. 5. wide of the truth. [ME *a brood*; f. A-[1] + BROAD. Cf. MnE *at large*]

abrogate (ăb′rə gāt′), *v.t.*, **-gated, -gating.** to abolish summarily; annul by an authoritative act; repeal: *to abrogate a law*. [t. L: m. s. *abrogātus*, pp.] —**abrogable** (ăb′rə gə bl), *adj*. —**ab′roga′tion,** *n*. —**ab′roga′tive,** *adj*. —**ab′roga′tor,** *n*.

abrupt (ə brŭpt′), *adj*. 1. terminating or changing suddenly: *an abrupt turn in a road*. 2. sudden; unceremonious: *an abrupt entrance*. 3. lacking in continuity; having sudden transitions from one subject to another: *an abrupt literary style*. 4. brusque; discourteous: *an abrupt manner*. 5. steep; precipitous: *an abrupt descent*. 6. *Bot*. truncated. [t. L: m. s. *abruptus*, pp., broken off] —**abrupt′ly,** *adv*. —**abrupt′ness,** *n*. —**Syn. 1.** See **sudden.**

abruption (ə brŭp′shən), *n*. a sudden breaking off.

Abruzzi (*It*. à broo͞t′tsē), *n*. **1. Duke of the** (*Prince Luigi Amedeo of Savoy-Aosta*), 1873–1933, Italian naval officer, mountaineer, and arctic explorer. **2. Abruzzi e Molise,** a region in S Italy. 1,584,777 pop. (1961); 5883 sq. mi. *Cap.*: Aquila.

abs-, var. of **ab-** before *c*, *q*, *t*, as in *abscond*, *absterge*.

Absalom (ăb′sə ləm), *n*. *Bible*. the third son of David, who rebelled against his father and was killed. II Sam. 13–19.

abscess (ăb′sĭs), *n*. a localized collection of pus in a cavity, caused by disintegration of body tissue, often accompanied by swelling and inflammation and usually caused by bacteria. [t. L: s. *abscessus* a going away] —**ab′scessed,** *adj*.

abscind (əb sĭnd′), *v.t.* to cut off; sever.

abscissa (ăb sĭs′ə), *n*., *pl*. **-scissas, -scissae** (-sĭs′ē). *Maths*. (in plane Cartesian coordinates) the *x*-coordinate of a point, i.e., its horizontal distance from the *y*-axis measured parallel to the *x*-axis. [t. L: short for *linea abscissa* line cut off]

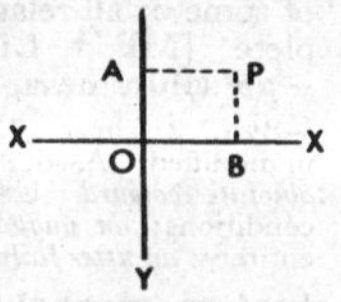

Y
A P
X O B X
Y

Abscissa: P, any point; AP or OB, abscissa of P; XX, axis of abscissa; YY, axis of the ordinate

abscission (ăb sĭzh′ən, -sĭsh′-), *n*. the act of cutting off; sudden termination. [t. L: s. *abscissio*]

abscond (əb skŏnd′), *v.i.* to depart in a sudden and secret manner, esp. to avoid legal process. [t. L: s. *abscondere* put away] —**abscond′er,** *n*.

abseil (*Ger*. ăp′sīl), *v.i.* *Mountaineering*. to lower oneself with a double rope down a rock face. [G: s. *abseilen*]

absence (ăb′səns), *n*. 1. a state of being away: *speak ill of no-one in his absence*. 2. a period of being away: *an absence of several weeks*. 3. lack; non-existence: *the absence of proof*. [ME, t. F, t. L: m. s. *absentia*]

absence of mind, absent-mindedness.

absent (*adj*. ăb′sənt; *v*. ăb sĕnt′), *adj*. 1. not in a certain place at a given time; away (opposed to *present*). 2. lacking: *revenge is absent from his mind*. 3. absentminded. —*v.t.* 4. to take or keep (oneself) away: *to absent oneself from home*. [ME, t. L: s. *absens*, ppr.] —**absentation** (ăb′sĕn tā′shən), *n*. —**absent′er,** *n*. —**ab′sentness,** *n*.

absentee (ăb′sən tē′), *n*. 1. one who is absent. 2. one who habitually lives away from his country, place of work, etc.

absenteeism (ăb′sən tē′ĭz′əm), *n*. 1. the practice of absenting oneself from duties, studies, employment, etc., often for inadequate reasons. 2. the practice of living away from one's estates, country, employment, source of income, etc.

absentee landlord, an owner, investor, or incumbent who lives in a place, region, or country other than that from which he draws his income.

absently (ăb′sənt lĭ), *adv*. inattentively.

absent-minded (ăb′sənt mīn′dĭd), *adj*. forgetful of one's immediate surroundings; preoccupied. —**ab′sent-mind′edly,** *adv*. —**ab′sent-mind′edness,** *n*.

—**Syn.** ABSENT-MINDED, ABSTRACTED, OBLIVIOUS all mean inattentive to immediate surroundings. ABSENT-MINDED suggests an unintentional wandering of the mind from the present: *an absent-minded professor.* ABSTRACTED implies that the mind has been drawn away from the immediate present by reflection upon some engrossing subject: *wearing an abstracted air.* OBLIVIOUS implies absorption in some thought which causes one to be completely forgetful of or unaware of one's surroundings: *oblivious of danger.*

absent without leave, away from military duties without permission, but without the intention of deserting. *Abbrev.:* A.W.O.L.

absinth (ăb′sĭnth), *n.* **1.** a strong, bitter, green-coloured, aromatic liqueur, 68° proof, made with wormwood, anise, and other herbs, having a pronounced liquorice flavour. **2.** wormwood (def. 2). **3.** *U.S.* sagebrush. Also, **absinthe.** [t. F, t. L: m. s. *absinthium,* t. Gk: m. *apsinthion* wormwood] —**absin′thial, absin′thian,** *adj.*

absinthism (ăb′sĭn thĭz′əm), *n.* a morbid condition due to excessive consumption of absinth. Cf. **alcoholism.**

absolute (ăb′sə lo͞ot′), *adj.* **1.** free from imperfection; complete; perfect: *absolute liberty.* **2.** not mixed; pure. **3.** free from restriction or limitation; unqualified: *absolute command.* **4.** arbitrary or despotic: *an absolute monarchy.* **5.** viewed independently; not comparative or relative: *absolute position.* **6.** positive: *absolute in opinion.* **7.** *Gram.* **a.** syntactically independent; not grammatically connected with any other element in the sentence, as *It being Sunday* in *It being Sunday, the family went to church.* **b.** (of a transitive verb) used with no object expressed, as *to give* in *the collectors for the charity asked him to give.* **c.** (of an adjective) having its noun understood, not expressed, as *poor* in *the poor are always with us.* **d.** characterizing the phonetic or phonemic form of a word or phrase occurring by itself, not influenced by surrounding forms (distinguished from *sandhi form*). Example: 'not' in 'is not' as opposed to 'isn't', or 'will' in 'they will' as opposed to 'they'll'. **8.** *Physics.* **a.** as nearly independent as possible of arbitrary standards or of properties of special substances or systems: *absolute zero of temperature.* **b.** pertaining to a system of units based on some primary units, esp. units of length, mass, and time: *c.g.s. units are absolute units.* **c.** pertaining to a measurement based on an absolute zero or unit: *absolute pressure.* **9.** *Law.* (of a court order, decree, etc.) unconditional; having full effect immediately (opposed to *nisi*). **10. the Absolute** (*sometimes l.c.*). *Metaphys.* **a.** that which is free from any restriction, or is unconditioned; the ultimate ground of all things. **b.** that which is independent of some or all relations. **c.** that which is perfect or complete. [ME, t. L: m. s. *absolūtus,* pp., loosened from] —**ab′solute′ness,** *n.*

—**Syn. 2.** sheer. **3.** ABSOLUTE, UNQUALIFIED, UTTER all mean unmodified. ABSOLUTE implies an unquestionable finality: *an absolute coward.* UNQUALIFIED means without reservations or conditions: *an unqualified success.* UTTER expresses totality or entirety: *an utter failure.*

absolute alcohol, ethyl alcohol containing not more than one per cent by weight of water.

absolute humidity, *Meteorol.* humidity (def. 2c).

absolutely (ăb′sə lo͞ot′lĭ; *emphatic* ăb′sə lo͞ot′lĭ), *adv.* **1.** completely; wholly. **2.** positively. **3.** *Colloq.* yes; certainly. **4.** (of transitive verbs) without an object.

absolute majority, the number by which votes cast for the leading candidate exceed those cast for all other candidates. Cf. **majority** (def. 3).

absolute music, music whose patterns in sound are not intended to illustrate, or describe (opposed to *programme music*).

absolute pitch, *Music.* **1.** the exact pitch of a note in terms of vibration per second. **2.** Also, **perfect pitch.** the ability to sing, or recognize the pitch of, a note by ear.

absolute temperature, *Physics.* temperature measured on the Kelvin scale.

absolute zero, *Physics, Chem.* the lowest possible temperature which the nature of matter admits, or that temperature at which the particles whose motion constitutes heat would be at rest, being defined as 273·16 degrees below the zero of the centigrade scale (or —459·69 degrees Fahrenheit). Cf. **absolute** (def. 8a).

absolution (ăb′sə lo͞o′shən), *n.* **1.** the act of absolving; release from consequences, obligations, or penalties. **2.** the state of being absolved. **3.** *Rom. Cath. Theol.* **a.** a remission of sin or of the punishment due to sin, which the priest, on the ground of authority received from Christ, makes in the sacrament of penance. **b.** the formula declaring such remission. **4.** *Prot. Theol.* a declaration or assurance of divine forgiveness to penitent believers, made after confession of sins. [t. L: s. *absolūtio* an acquittal; r. ME *absolucioun,* t. F]

absolutism (ăb′sə lo͞o tĭz′əm), *n.* **1.** the principle or the exercise of absolute power in government. **2.** *Philos.* the doctrine of an absolute or non-relative being. —**ab′solut′ist,** *n.* —**ab′solutis′tic,** *adj.*

absolutory (ăb sŏl′yo͞o tə rĭ, -trĭ), *adj.* giving absolution.

absolve (əb zŏlv′), *v.t.,* **-solved, -solving. 1.** to free from the consequences or penalties of actions (fol. by *from*): *to absolve one from moral blame.* **2.** to set free or release, as from some duty, obligation, or responsibility (fol. by *from*): *absolved from his oath.* **3.** to grant pardon for. **4.** *Eccles.* **a.** to grant or pronounce remission of sins to. **b.** to remit (sin). **c.** to declare (censure, as excommunication) removed. [t. L: m. s. *absolvere* loosen from] —**absolv′able,** *adj.* —**absolv′ent,** *adj., n.* —**absolv′er,** *n.*

—**Syn. 1.** ABSOLVE, ACQUIT, EXONERATE mean to free from blame. ABSOLVE is a general word for this idea. To ACQUIT is to release from a specific and usually formal accusation: *the court must acquit the accused if there is not enough evidence to prove guilt.* To EXONERATE is to consider a person clear of blame for an act (even when the act is admitted), or to justify him for having done it: *to exonerate one of a crime committed in self-defence.* **2.** liberate; exempt. —**Ant. 1.** blame.

absonant (ăb′sə nənt), *adj.* **1.** discordant (fol. by *from* or *to*). **2.** abhorrent; unnatural; incompatible (fol. by *from* or *to*). [f. AB- + s. L *sonans,* ppr., sounding]

absorb (əb sôb′, -zôb′), *v.t.* **1.** to swallow up the identity or individuality of: *the empire absorbed all the small states.* **2.** to engross wholly: *absorbed in a book.* **3.** to suck up or drink in (liquids): *a sponge absorbs water.* **4.** to assimilate (ideas, knowledge, etc.). **5.** to take up or receive in by chemical or molecular action: *carbonic acid is formed when water absorbs carbon dioxide.* **6.** to take in without echo or recoil: *to absorb sound.* **7.** *Obs.* to swallow up. [t. L: s. *absorbēre*] —**absorb′able,** *adj.* —**absorb′abil′ity,** *n.*

—**Syn. 1.** assimilate, consume, engulf.

absorbed (əb sôbd′, -zôbd′), *adj.* engrossed; preoccupied. —**absorbedly** (əb sô′bĭd lĭ, -zô′-), *adv.* —**absorb′edness,** *n.*

absorbefacient (əb sô′bĭ fā′shənt, -zô′-), *adj.* **1.** causing absorption. —*n.* **2.** a drug or other substance which causes absorption. [f. L *absorbē(re)* absorb + -FACIENT]

absorbent (əb sô′bənt, -zô′-), *adj.* **1.** capable of absorbing; performing the function of absorption. —*n.* **2.** a thing that absorbs. —**absorb′ency,** *n.*

absorbent cotton, *U.S.* cottonwool (def. 2).

absorber (əb sô′bə, -zô′-), *n.* **1.** one who or that which absorbs. **2.** *Nucleonics.* a material which will capture neutrons without generating others.

absorbing (əb sô′bĭng, -zô′-), *adj.* engrossing: *an absorbing pursuit.* —**absorb′ingly,** *adv.*

absorption (əb sôp′shən, -zôp′-), *n.* **1.** assimilation: *the absorption of small farms by a bigger one.* **2.** the sucking up or drawing in of a liquid by a porous substance. **3.** passage of substances to the blood, lymph, and cells, as from the alimentary canal (e.g., digested foods) or from the tissues. **4.** a taking in or reception by molecular or chemical action: *absorption of gases, light, etc.* **5.** preoccupation. [t. L: s. *absorptio*] —**absorp′tive,** *adj.* —**absorp′tiveness,** *n.*

absorption bands, *Optics.* the dark bands in a spectrum caused by the selective absorption of light of the medium traversed. Also, **absorption lines.**

absorption factor, *Optics.* a constant of any material giving its absorption power for light passing through it. Also, **absorption coefficient.**

absorption spectrum, *Optics.* a system of absorption bands, esp. such a system characteristic of a particular medium.

absorptivity (ăb′sôp tĭv′ĭ tĭ, -zôp-), *n.* *Physics.* the ratio between the radiation absorbed by a surface and the total energy striking the surface.

abstain (əb stān′), *v.i.* **1.** to refrain voluntarily, esp. from doing or enjoying something (fol. by *from*): *abstain from drinking intoxicants.* **2.** to refrain deliberately from casting one's vote. [ME *absteine(n),* t. F: m. *abstenir,* r. OF *astenir,* g. L *abstinēre*] —**abstain′er,** *n.* —**Syn.** forbear; desist, cease.

abstemious (əb stē′myəs), *adj.* **1.** sparing in diet; moderate in the use of food and drink; temperate. **2.** characterized by abstinence: *an abstemious life.* **3.** sparing: *an abstemious diet.* [t. L: m. *abstēmius*] —**abste′miously,** *adv.* —**abste′miousness,** *n.*

abstention (əb stĕn′shən), *n.* **1.** a holding off or refraining; abstinence from action. **2.** a deliberate withholding of one's vote. [f. s. L *abstentus,* pp., abstained + -ION] —**absten′tious,** *adj.*

absterge (əb stûj′), *v.t.,* **-sterged, -sterging. 1.** *Med.* to purge. **2.** to make clean by wiping. [t. L: m. s. *abstergēre* wipe off]

abstergent (əb stû′jənt), *adj.* **1.** cleansing; detergent. —*n.* **2.** a cleansing agent; a detergent, as soap.

abstersion (əb stû′shən), *n.* the act of absterging.

abstersive (əb stû′sĭv), *adj.* abstergent. —**abster′siveness,** *n.*

abstinence (ăb′stĭ nəns), *n.* **1.** forbearance from any indulgence of appetite, esp. from the drinking of alcohol: *total abstinence.* **2.** self-restraint; forbearance. **3.** *Eccles.* the refraining from certain kinds of food on certain days, as from meat on Fridays. Also, **ab′stinency.** [ME *abstynens,* t. L: m. s. *abstinentia*] —**ab′stinent,** *adj.* —**ab′stinently,** *adv.* —**Syn. 1.** abstemiousness; moderation, temperance.

abstract (*adj.* ăb′străkt; *n.* ăb′străkt; *v.* ăb străkt′ *for 10–13,* ăb′străkt *for 14*), *adj.* **1.** conceived apart from matter and from special cases: *an abstract number.* **2.** theoretical; not applied: *abstract science.* **3.** difficult to understand; abstruse: *abstract speculations.* **4.** of or pertaining to non-representational art; using only lines, colours, generalized or geometrical forms, etc. —*n.* **5.** a summary of a statement, document, speech, etc. **6.** that which concentrates in itself the essential qualities of anything more extensive or more general, or of several things; essence. **7.** an idea or term considered apart from some material basis or object. **8. the abstract,** the ideal. **9. in the abstract,** without reference to special circumstances or particular applications. —*v.t.* **10.** to draw or take away; remove. **11.** to withdraw or divert (the attention). **12.** *Colloq.* to steal. **13.** to consider as a general object apart from special circumstances: *to abstract the notions of time, of space, or of matter.* **14.** to summarize. [t. L: s. *abstractus,* pp., drawn away] —**abstract′er,** *n.* —**ab′stractly,** *adv.* —**ab′stractness,** *n.*

abstracted (ăb străk′tĭd), *adj.* **1.** lost in thought; preoccupied. **2.** withdrawn; removed. —**abstract′edly,** *adv.* —**abstract′edness,** *n.* —**Syn.** See **absent-minded.**

abstraction (ăb străk′shən), *n.* **1.** an abstract or general idea or term. **2.** an idea which cannot lead to any practical result; something visionary. **3.** the act of considering something as a general object apart from special circumstances. **4.** the act of taking away or separating; withdrawal: *the sensation of cold is due to the abstraction of heat from our bodies.* **5.** absent-mindedness; reverie. **6.** *Fine Arts.* **a.** a work of art **(pure abstraction)** using lines, shapes, and colours without reference to natural objects. **b.** a work of art **(near abstraction)** retaining representational characteristics but expressing them through geometrical or generalized forms. [t. L: s. *abstractio*]

abstractive (ăb străk′tĭv), *adj.* **1.** having the power of abstracting. **2.** pertaining to an epitome or summary.

abstract music, absolute music.

abstract noun, *Gram.* **1.** a noun having an abstract (as opposed to concrete) meaning, as *dread.* **2.** a noun made with an abstract suffix, as *witness.*

abstract of title, *Law.* an outline history of the title to a parcel of real property, showing the original grant, subsequent conveyances, mortgages, etc.

abstriction (ăb strĭk′shən), *n.* *Bot.* a method of spore formation in which successive portions of the sporophore are cut off through the growth of septa. [f. AB- + s. L *strictio* a drawing together]

abstruse (ăb stro͞os′), *adj.* **1.** difficult to understand; esoteric: *abstruse questions.* **2.** *Obs.* hidden. [t. L: m. s. *abstrūsus,* pp., concealed] —**abstruse′ly,** *adv.* —**abstruse′ness,** *n.*

absurd (əb sûd′), *adj.* **1.** contrary to reason or common sense; obviously false or foolish; logically contradictory; ridiculous: *an absurd statement.* **2.** comical; laughable. [t. L: s. *absurdus*] —**absurd′ly,** *adv.* —**absurd′ness,** *n.*

—**Syn.** ABSURD, RIDICULOUS, PREPOSTEROUS all mean inconsistent with reason or common sense. ABSURD means glaringly opposed to manifest truth or reason: *an absurd claim.* RIDICULOUS implies that something is fit only to be laughed at, perhaps contemptuously or derisively: *a ridiculous suggestion.* PREPOSTEROUS implies an amazing extreme of foolishness: *a preposterous proposal.*

absurdity (əb sû′dĭ tĭ), *n., pl.* **-ties. 1.** the state or quality of being absurd. **2.** something absurd.

Abu-Bekr (ə bo͞o′bĕk′ə), *n.* A.D. 573–634, first caliph of Mecca, A.D. 632–634; Mohammed's father-in-law and successor.

Abu Dhabi (ăb′o͞o dä′bĭ). See **Trucial States.**

Abukir (ăb′o͞o kĭə′), *n.* Aboukir.

abulia (ə byo͞o′lyə), *n.* aboulia.

abundance (ə bŭn′dəns), *n.* **1.** an overflowing quantity or supply: *an abundance of grain.* **2.** overflowing fullness: *abundance of the heart.* **3.** affluence; wealth. **4.** *Cards.* (in solo whist) a call of nine tricks. **5.** *Physics.* the ratio of the number of atoms of a certain isotope in a mixture of isotopes to the total number of atoms present, often expressed as a percentage. [ME, t. OF, g. L *abundantia*] —**Syn. 1.** copiousness, profusion. See **plenty.**

abundant (ə bŭn′dənt), *adj.* **1.** present in great quantity; fully sufficient: *an abundant supply.* **2.** possessing in great quantity; abounding (fol. by *in*): *a river abundant in salmon.* [ME, t. OF, g. s. L *abundans,* ppr.] —**abun′dantly,** *adv.* —**Syn. 1.** plentiful, copious, profuse, overflowing.

ab urbe condita (ăb û′bĭ kŏn′dĭ tə), *Latin.* from the founding of the city (Rome, ab. 753 B.C.). *Abbrev.:* A.U.C. The year 360 A.U.C. would be the 360th year after the founding of Rome.

abusage (ə byo͞o′sĭj), *n.* improper use of words; unidiomatic or ungrammatical language.

abuse (*v.* ə byo͞oz′; *n.* ə byo͞os′), *v.,* **abused, abusing,** *n.* —*v.t.* **1.** to use wrongly or improperly; misuse: *to abuse authority, to abuse a confidence.* **2.** to do wrong to; act injuriously towards: *to abuse one's wife.* **3.** to revile; malign. **4.** *Archaic.* to deceive. [ME *abuse(n),* t. F: m. *abuser,* ult. der. L *abūsus,* pp., having used up] —*n.* **5.** wrong or improper use; misuse: *the abuse of privileges.* **6.** insulting language. **7.** ill treatment of a person. **8.** a corrupt practice or custom; an offence: *the abuses of bad government.* **9.** *Archaic.* deception. [t. F: m. *abus,* t. L: s. *abūsus* a wasting, misuse] —**abus′er,** *n.*

—**Syn. 2.** ill use, maltreat. **3.** vilify, vituperate, berate, upbraid. **6.** ABUSE, CENSURE, INVECTIVE all mean strongly expressed disapproval. ABUSE implies an outburst of harsh and scathing words against another (often one who is defenceless): *abuse directed against an opponent.* CENSURE implies blame, adverse criticism, or hostile condemnation: *severe censure of acts showing bad judgement.* INVECTIVE applies to strong but formal denunciation in speech or print, often in the public interest: *invective against racketeering.*

Abu Simbel (ăb′o͞o sĭm′bl), a former village in Egypt, now covered by the Aswan Lake; site of two temples of Ramses II, figures from which were raised in 1966–67 above the level of the lake.

abusive (ə byo͞o′sĭv), *adj.* **1.** using harsh words or ill treatment: *an abusive author.* **2.** characterized by or containing abuse: *an abusive satire.* **3.** wrongly used; corrupt: *an abusive exercise of power.* [t. L: m. s. *abūsīvus*] —**abu′sively,** *adv.* —**abu′siveness,** *n.*

abut (ə bŭt′), *v.i.,* **abutted, abutting.** to be adjacent to (often fol. by *on, upon,* or *against*): *this piece of land abuts upon a street.* [ME *abutte(n),* t. OF: coalescence of *abouter* join end to end (der. *a-* A-[5] + *bout* end) and *abuter* make contact with one end (der. *a-* A-[5] + *but* end)] —**abut′tal,** *n.*

abutilon (ə byo͞o′tĭ lən), *n.* any plant of the malvaceous genus *Abutilon,* esp. the flowering mallow. [t. NL, t. Ar.: m. *aubūṭīlūn*]

abutment (ə bŭt′mənt), *n.* **1.** the state of being adjacent to something. **2.** that on which something abuts, as the part of a pier which receives the thrust of an arch; a part for sustaining or resisting pressure, as the part of a bridge pier exposed to the force of the current or of floating ice, or the structure supporting the shore ends of a bridge and restraining the embankment which supports the approaches. **3.** the place where projecting parts meet; junction.

Abutment: A, Arch abutment; B, Current abutment

abutter (ə bŭt′ə), *n.* *Chiefly U.S.* an owner of adjacent land.

abuzz (ə bŭz′), *adj., adv.* buzzing.

aby (ə bī′), *v.t.,* **abought, abying.** *Archaic.* to pay the penalty of. Also, **abye.** [ME *abye(n),* OE *ābyg-* s. *ābycgan,* f. *ā-* A-[3] + *bycgan* buy]

Abydos (ə bī′dŏs), *n.* **1.** an ancient ruined city in central Egypt; temples and tombs. **2.** an ancient town in NW Asia Minor, at the narrowest part of the Hellespont. See **Hero and Leander.**

abysm (ə bĭz′əm), *n.* *Poetic.* an abyss. [ME *abi(s)me,* t. OF, g. VL **abyssimus,* superl. of L *abyssus* ABYSS]

abysmal (ə bĭz′məl), *adj.* **1.** of or like an abyss. **2.** immeasurable: *abysmal ignorance.* **3.** immeasurably bad: *an abysmal performance.* —**abys′mally,** *adv.*

abyss (ə bĭs′), *n.* **1.** a bottomless gulf; any deep, immeasurable space. **2.** anything profound and unfathomable: *the abyss of time.* **3.** the bottomless pit; hell. [t. L: s. *abyssus,* t. Gk: m. *ábyssos* without bottom]

abyssal (ə bĭs′əl), *adj.* **1.** abysmal. **2.** of or pertaining to the lowest depths of the ocean.

Abyssinia (ăb′ĭ sĭn′yə), *n.* Ethiopia (def. 1). —**Ab′yssin′ian,** *adj., n.*

ac-, var. of **ad-** (by assimilation) before *c* and *qu,* as in *accede, acquire,* etc.

-ac, an adjective suffix meaning 'pertaining to', as in *elegiac, cardiac.* [repr. Gk adj. suffix *-akos,* whence L *-acus,* F *-aque*]

Ac, *Chem.* actinium.

AC, 1. Air Corps. **2.** aircraftman.

A/C., 1. account. **2.** account current.

a.c., *Elect.* alternating current. Also, **A.C.**

acacia (ə kā′shə), *n.* **1.** any tree or shrub of the mimosaceous genus *Acacia,* native in warm regions. **2.** one of several other plants, as the locust tree. **3.** gum arabic. [t. L, t. Gk: m. *akakía* a thorny Egyptian tree]

Academe (ăk'ə dēm'), *n. Poetic.* **1.** the Academy in Athens. **2.** (*l.c.*) any place of instruction.

academic (ăk'ə dĕm'ĭk), *adj.* Also, **ac'adem'ical. 1.** pertaining to an advanced institution of learning, as a college, university, or academy; relating to higher education. **2.** pertaining to those university subjects which are concerned with the refinement of the mind rather than the learning of skills (opposed to *technical*). **3.** theoretical; not practical. **4.** too much concerned with purely intellectual interests. **5.** conforming to set rules and traditions; conventional. —*n.* **6.** a member of a college or university. **7.** (*pl.*) discussions, arguments, etc., of purely theoretical interest. —**ac'adem'ically,** *adv.*

academicals (ăk'ə dĕm'ĭ klz), *n.pl.* academic dress.

academic dress, formal university dress, as cap and gown, and sometimes dark suit, etc.

academic freedom, freedom of a teacher to discuss social, economic, or political problems without interference from university or public officials.

academician (ə kăd'ə mĭsh'ən), *n.* a member of a society for promoting literature, art, or science.

academicism (ăk'ə dĕm'ĭ sĭz'əm), *n.* traditionalism or conventionalism in art, literature, etc.

academic year, that part of the calendar year during which the schools, universities, etc. are in session; starting in September or October.

Académie Française (*Fr.* à kà dē mē fräɴ sĕz'), French Academy.

academism (ə kăd'ə mĭz'əm), *n.* **1.** academicism. **2.** *Philos.* the doctrines of the school founded by Plato.

academy (ə kăd'ə mĭ), *n., pl.* **-mies. 1.** an association or institution for the promotion of literature, science, or art: *the Academy of Arts and Letters.* **2.** a school for instruction in a particular art or science: *a military academy.* **3.** (sometimes pejorative) a secondary school, esp. a private one. **4.** *Scot.* a grammar school. **5. the Academy, a.** the French Academy. **b.** (in England) the Royal Academy. **c.** the public grove in Athens, in which Plato taught. **d.** the Platonic school of philosophy. [t. L: m. s. *acadēmia*, t. Gk: m. *Akadḗmeia* (der. *Akádēmos*, an Attic hero)]

Acadia (ə kā'dyə), *n.* a former French colony in SE Canada: ceded to Great Britain 1713. French, **Acadie** (*Fr.* à kà dē').

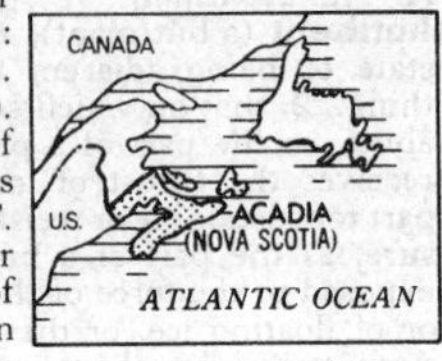

Acadia, *c.* 1605 1713

Acadian (ə kā'dyən), *adj.* **1.** of or pertaining to Acadia or its inhabitants. —*n.* **2.** Also, *U.S. Dial.*, **Cajun, Cajian.** a native or inhabitant of Acadia, or one of the descendants of these in Louisiana. **3.** *Geol.* of or pertaining to the major mountain-building episode which occurred in eastern North America in the late Devonian period.

acajou (ăk'ə zho͞o'), *n.* **1.** cashew. **2.** *French.* a kind of mahogany.

acaleph (ăk'ə lĕf'), *n.* one of the *Acalephae*, a group of coelenterate marine animals including the sea nettles and jellyfishes. Also, **acalephe** (ăk'ə lēf'). [t. NL: s. *Acalēpha*, t. Gk: m. *akalḗphē* nettle] —**acalephan** (ăk'ə lē'fən), *adj., n.*

acanthaceous (ăk'ən thā'shəs), *adj.* **1.** having prickly growths. **2.** belonging to the *Acanthaceae*, or acanthus family of plants.

acantho-, *Bot.* a word element meaning 'thorn', or 'thorny'. Also, before vowels, **acanth-.** [t. Gk: m. *akantho-*, comb. form of *ákantha* thorn]

acanthocephalan (ə kăn'thō sĕf'ə lən), *n.* any of the worms belonging to a phylum or class of internal parasitic worms, *Acanthocephala*, having a protrusile proboscis covered with recurved hooks and a hollow body without digestive tract, found in the intestine of vertebrates.

acanthodian (ăk'ăn thō'dyən), *n.* a spiny-finned shark-like fish of the late Silurian and Devonian periods.

acanthoid (ə kăn'thoid), *adj.* spiny; spinous.

acanthopterygian (ăk'ăn thŏp'tə rĭj'ĭ ən), *adj.* **1.** belonging or pertaining to the *Acanthopterygii*, the group of fishes with spiny fins, as the bass and perch. —*n.* **2.** an acanthopterygian fish. [f. ACANTHO- s. Gk *pterýgion* fin + -AN]

acanthous (ə kăn'thəs), *adj.* spinous.

Acanthus
A, Leaf of plant, *Acanthus mollis*; B, Architectural ornament, front and side view

acanthus (ə kăn'thəs), *n., pl.* **-thuses, -thi** (-thī). **1.** a plant of the genus *Acanthus*, of the Mediterranean regions, with large spiny or toothed leaves. **2.** an architectural ornament resembling the leaves of this plant, as in the Corinthian capital. Also, **acanth.** [t. L, t. Gk: m. *ákanthos* a thorny tree] —**acan'thine,** *adj.*

a cappella (ä'kə pĕl'ə; *It.* à käp pĕl'lä), *Music.* **1.** without instrumental accompaniment. **2.** in the style of church or chapel music. Also, **al'la cappel'la.** [It.]

a capriccio (ä'kə prĭch'ĭ ō'; *It.* à kä prēt'chō), *Music.* freely; at the whim of the performer (a musical direction). [It.: according to caprice]

Acapulco (ăk'ə po͝ol'kō), *n.* a seaport in SW Mexico. 48,846 (1965).

acariasis (ăk'ə rī'ə sĭs), *n.* **1.** infestation with acarids, esp. mites. **2.** a skin disease caused by such infestation. [f. m. Gk *ákar(i)* mite + -IASIS]

acarid (ăk'ə rĭd), *n.* any animal belonging to the *Acari* (or *Acarida*), an order of arachnids including the mites, ticks, etc. [f. m. Gk *ákar(i)* mite + -ID[2]]

acaridan (ə kĕə'rĭ dən), *adj.* **1.** belonging to the acarids. —*n.* **2.** an acarid.

acaroid (ăk'ə roid'), *adj.* resembling an acarid.

acaroid gum, a red resin which exudes from the trunk of the liliaceous Australian grass tree, *Xanthorrhoea hastilis*, and other species. Also, **acaroid resin.**

acarpellous (ā kä'pə ləs), *adj. Bot.* having no carpels. Also, *U.S.*, **acar'pelous.**

acarpous (ā kä'pəs), *adj. Bot.* not producing fruit; sterile; barren. [t. Gk: m. *ákarpos* without fruit]

acarus (ăk'ə rəs), *n., pl.* **-ri** (-rī'). an animal of the genus *Acarus*; a mite. [t. L, t. Gk; m. *ákari*]

acatalectic (ă kăt'ə lĕk'tĭk), *Pros.* —*adj.* **1.** not catalectic; complete. —*n.* **2.** a verse having the complete number of syllables in the last foot. See example under **catalectic.**

acaudal (ə kô'dl), *adj. Zool.* tailless. Also, **acaudate** (ə kô'dāt).

acaulescent (ăk'ô lĕs'ənt), *adj. Bot.* not caulescent; stemless; without visible stem. Also, **acauline** (ə kô'lĭn, -līn), **acaulose** (ə kô'lōs), **acaulous** (ə kô'ləs), —**ac'-aules'cence,** *n.*

acc., 1. accompaniment. **2.** accompanied (by). **3.** according (to). **4.** account. **5.** accusative.

Accad (ăk'ăd), *n.* Akkad.

accede (ăk sēd'), *v.i.,* **-ceded, -ceding. 1.** to give consent; agree; yield: *to accede to terms.* **2.** to attain, as an office or dignity; arrive at (fol. by *to*): *to accede to the throne.* **3.** *Internat. Law.* to become a party (*to*), as a nation signing a treaty. [t. L: m. s. *accēdere* go to] —**acced'ence,** *n.* —**acced'er,** *n.*

accel., accelerando.

accelerando (ăk sĕl'ə răn'dō; *It.* ät chĕ lĕ rän'dō), *adv., adj. Music.* gradually increasing in speed. [It.]

accelerant (ăk sĕl'ə rənt), *n. Chem.* accelerator.

accelerate (ăk sĕl'ə rāt'), *v.,* **-rated, -rating.** —*v.t.* **1.** to cause to move or advance faster: *accelerate growth.* **2.** to help to bring about more speedily than would otherwise have been the case: *to accelerate the fall of a government.* **3.** to increase or otherwise change the velocity of (a body) or the rate of (motion); cause to undergo acceleration. —*v.i.* **4.** to become faster; increase in speed. [t. L: m. s. *accelerātus*, pp.]

acceleration (ăk sĕl'ə rā'shən), *n.* **1.** the act of accelerating; increase of speed or velocity. **2.** a change in velocity.

accelerative (ăk sĕl'ə rə tĭv), *adj.* tending to accelerate; increasing the velocity (*of*). Also, **acceleratory** (ăk-sĕl'ə rə tə rĭ, -trĭ).

accelerator (ək sĕl'ə rā'tə), *n.* **1.** one that accelerates. **2.** *Motor Vehicles.* a device for opening and closing the throttle, esp. when operated by the foot. **3.** *Photog.* any substance, device, or the like, that shortens the time of exposure or development. **4.** *Chem.* **a.** any substance that increases the speed of a chemical change. **b.** any chemical which increases the rate of vulcanization of rubber. **5.** *Anat.* any muscle, nerve, or activating substance that quickens a movement. **6.** *Physics.* a device for producing high-energy particles, as a cyclotron. **7.** *Bldg Trades.* a pump for circulating water through a central-heating system.

accelerometer (ăk sĕl'ə rŏm'ĭ tə), *n.* an instrument for measuring acceleration, used in aircraft.

accent (*n.* ăk'sənt; *v.* ăk sĕnt'), *n.* **1.** the distinctive character of a vowel or syllable determined by its degree or pattern of stress or musical tone. **2.** any one of the degrees or patterns of stress used in a particular language as essential features of vowels, syllables, or words: *primary accent, falling accent, sentence accent.* **3.** a mark indicating stress, musical tone, or vowel quality. In English the accent mark (') is sometimes used to indicate a syllable which is stressed. French has three accent marks, the acute (´), the grave (`), and the circumflex (ˆ), which indicate vowel quality (or sometimes merely distinguish meaning, as *la* 'the' and *là* 'there').

b., blend of, blended; c., cognate with; d., dialect, dialectal; der., derived from; f., formed from; g., going back to; m., modification of; r., replacing; s., stem of; t., taken from; ?, perhaps. See full key on inside front cover.

4. *Pros.* **a.** regularly recurring stress. **b.** a mark indicating stress or some other distinction in pronunciation or value. **5.** any one of the musical tones or melodies used in a particular language as essential features of vowels or syllables. **6.** characteristic style of pronunciation: *foreign accent.* **7.** *Music.* **a.** stress or emphasis given to certain notes. **b.** a mark denoting this. **c.** stress or emphasis regularly recurring as a feature of rhythm. **8.** *Maths., etc.* a mark, or one of a number of marks, placed after a letter or figure: **a.** to distinguish similar quantities which differ in value, as in b', b'', b''', etc. (called *b prime, b second, b third,* etc., respectively). **b.** to indicate a particular unit or measure, as feet (') or inches (''): 5'3'', meaning *5 feet, 3 inches*; or as minutes (') or seconds ('') of time or a degree: 18'25'', meaning *18 minutes, 25 seconds.* **c.** to indicate the operation of differentiation in calculus. **9.** words or tones expressive of some emotion. **10.** (*pl.*) *Poetic.* words; language. **11.** distinctive character or tone. *—v.t.* **12.** to pronounce (a vowel, syllable, or word) with one of the distinctive accents of the language, esp. with a stress accent. **13.** to mark with a written accent or accents: *to accent a word to indicate its pronunciation.* **14.** *Chiefly U.S.* to emphasize; accentuate. [t. L: s. *accentus* tone]

accentor (ăk sĕn'tə), *n.* a large hedge-sparrow, *Prunella collaris,* with a black-spotted white throat, of European mountainous areas.

accentual (ăk sĕn'tyŏŏ əl), *adj.* **1.** pertaining to accent; rhythmical. **2.** *Pros.* of, pertaining to, or characterized by syllabic accent (distinguished from *quantitative*). **—accen'tually,** *adv.*

accentuate (ăk sĕn'tyŏŏ āt'), *v.t.,* **-ated, -ating. 1.** to emphasize. **2.** to mark or pronounce with an accent. [t. ML: m. s. *accentuātus,* pp.] **—accen'tua'tion,** *n.*

accept (ək sĕpt'), *v.t.* **1.** to take or receive (something offered); receive with approval or favour: *his proposal was accepted.* **2.** to admit and agree to; accede or assent to: *to accept a treaty, an excuse, etc.* **3.** to take with formal acknowledgement of responsibility or consequences: *to accept office.* **4.** to accommodate oneself to: *accept the situation.* **5.** to believe: *to accept a fact.* **6.** to receive as to meaning; understand. **7.** *Com.* to acknowledge, by signature, as calling for payment, and thus to agree to pay, as a draft. **8.** (in a deliberative body) to receive as an adequate performance of the duty with which an officer or a committee has been charged; receive for further action: *the report of the committee was accepted.* *—v.i.* **9.** *Archaic.* to accept an invitation, gift, position, etc. (sometimes fol by *of*). [ME *accept(en),* t. L: m. *acceptāre,* freq. of *accipere* take] **—accept'er;** *esp. Com.* **accep'tor,** *n.*

acceptable (ək sĕp'tə bl), *adj.* **1.** capable or worthy of being accepted. **2.** pleasing to the receiver; agreeable; welcome. **—accept'abil'ity, accept'ableness,** *n.* **—accept'ably,** *adv.*

acceptance (ək sĕp'təns), *n.* **1.** the act of taking or receiving something offered. **2.** favourable reception; favour. **3.** the act of assenting or believing: *acceptance of a theory.* **4.** the fact or state of being accepted or acceptable. **5.** *Com.* **a.** an engagement to pay an order, draft, or bill of exchange when it becomes due, as by the person on whom it is drawn. **b.** an order, draft, etc., which a person has accepted as calling for payment and has thus promised to pay: *a trade acceptance.*

acceptance house, *Banking.* a bank which specializes in handling bills of exchange for foreign trade.

acceptant (ək sĕp'tənt), *adj.* accepting; receptive.

acceptation (ăk'sĕp tā'shən), *n.* **1.** favourable regard. **2.** belief. **3.** usual or received meaning.

accepted (ək sĕp'tĭd), *adj.* customary; established; approved.

access (ăk'sĕs), *n.* **1.** the act or privilege of coming to; admittance; approach: *to gain access to a person.* **2.** way, means, or opportunity of approach. **3.** *Theol.* approach to God through Jesus Christ. Eph. 2:18. **4.** *Law.* **a.** the opportunity of marital intercourse between husband and wife. **b.** a parent's right to see a child. **5.** an attack, as of disease. **6.** a sudden outburst of passion. **7.** accession. [ME, t. L: s. *accessus* approach]

accessary (ək sĕs'ə rĭ), *n., pl.* **-ries,** *adj. Chiefly Law.* accessory. **—acces'sarily,** *adv.* **—acces'sariness,** *n.*

accessible (ək sĕs'ə bl), *adj.* **1.** easy of access; approachable. **2.** attainable: *accessible evidence.* **3.** open to the influence of (fol. by *to*): *accessible to bribery.* **—acces'sibil'ity,** *n.* **—acces'sibly,** *adv.*

accession (ək sĕsh'ən), *n.* **1.** the act of coming into the possession of a right, dignity, office, etc.: *accession to the throne.* **2.** an increase by something added: *an accession of territory.* **3.** something added. **4.** *Law.* addition to property by growth or improvement. **5.** consent: *accession to a demand.* **6.** *Internat. Law.* formal acceptance of a treaty, international convention, or other agreement between states. **7.** the act of coming near; approach. [t. L: s. *accessio* increase] **—acces'sional,** *adj.*

accessorial (ăk'sĕ sô'rĭ əl), *adj.* accessory.

accessory (ək sĕs'ə rĭ), *n., pl.* **-ries,** *adj.* *—n.* **1.** a subordinate part or object; something added or attached for convenience, attractiveness, etc., such as a spotlight, heater, driving mirror, etc., for a vehicle. **2.** (*pl.*) the additional parts of an outfit, as shoes, gloves, hat, handbag, etc. **3.** *Law.* one who, without being present at its commission, is guilty of aiding or abetting another who commits a felony: **an accessory before the fact** is not present when the act is done; **an accessory after the fact** knowingly conceals or assists another who has committed a felony. *—adj.* **4.** contributing to a general effect; subsidiary: *accessory sounds in music.* **5.** *Law.* giving aid as an accessory. **6.** *Geol.* denoting minerals present in relatively small amounts in a rock, and not mentioned in its definition, as zircon in granite. Also, **accessary.** [t. LL: m. s. *accessōrius*] **—acces'sorily,** *adv.* **—acces'soriness,** *n.* **—Syn. 1.** See **addition.**

access time, time taken to retrieve information from the memory of a digital computer.

acciaccatura (*It.* ät chäk kä tōō'rä), *n.* *Music.* **1.** a short appoggiatura. **2.** a short grace-note a semitone above or below, and struck just before (or sometimes simultaneously with) a principal note.

Written Played
A B A B

Acciaccatura (def. 2)
A, Grace-note; B, Principal note

accidence (ăk'sĭ dəns), *n.* **1.** the rudiments of any subject. **2.** *Gram.* **a.** that part of morphology dealing with inflection. **b.** an inflected form of a word. **c.** a property shown by such inflection. [var. of *accidents,* pl. of *accident* (def. 5), or t. L: m. s. *accidentia,* neut. pl. of *accidens,* ppr., striking, happening (as if fem. noun)]

accident (ăk'sĭ dənt), *n.* **1.** an undesirable or unfortunate happening; casualty; mishap. **2.** anything that happens unexpectedly, without design, or by chance. **3.** the operation of chance: *I was there by accident.* **4. a.** non-essential circumstance; occasional characteristic. **5.** *Gram.* an inflectional variation of a word, as *them* (an inflected form of *they*). **6.** *Geol.* an irregularity, generally on a small scale, on a surface, the explanation for which is not readily apparent. [ME, t. L: s. *accidens,* ppr., happening] **—Syn. 1.** mischance, misfortune, disaster, calamity, catastrophe.

accidental (ăk'sĭ dĕn'tl), *adj.* **1.** happening by chance or accident, or unexpectedly: *an accidental meeting.* **2.** non-essential; incidental; subsidiary: *accidental benefits.* **3.** *Music.* denoting or pertaining to sharps, flats, or naturals not in the key signature. *—n.* **4.** a non-essential or subsidiary circumstance or feature. **5.** *Music.* **a.** a sign placed before a note indicating a sharp, flat, or natural not in the key signature. **b.** the note so indicated. **6.** (*usually pl.*) *Fine Arts.* striking random effects of light in painting. **—ac'ciden'tally,** *adv.* **—ac'ciden'talness,** *n.*

—Syn. 1. ACCIDENTAL, CASUAL, FORTUITOUS all describe something outside the usual course of events. ACCIDENTAL implies occurring unexpectedly or by chance: *an accidental blow.* CASUAL describes a passing event of slight importance: *a casual reference.* FORTUITOUS is applied to events occurring without known cause: *a fortuitous shower of meteors.*

accident-prone (ăk'sĭ dənt prōn'), *adj.* abnormally susceptible to accidents.

accidie (ăk'sĭd ĭ), *n.* acedia.

accipiter (ăk sĭp'ĭ tə), *n., pl.* **-tres** (-trēz'). any bird of the subfamily *Accipitrinae* and genus *Accipiter,* which comprises short-winged, long-tailed hawks. [t. L]

accipitral (ăk sĭp'ĭ trəl), *adj.* accipitrine.

accipitrine (ăk sĭp'ĭ trīn', -trĭn), *adj.* **1.** belonging to the *Accipitrinae* (see **accipiter**). **2.** raptorial; like, or related to the birds of prey.

acclaim (ə klām'), *v.t.* **1.** to salute with words or sounds of joy or approval; applaud. **2.** to announce or proclaim by acclamation. *—v.i.* **3.** to make acclamation; applaud. *—n.* **4.** an oral vote, often unanimous, usually taken after the sense of a meeting is clear and unmistakeable. **5.** acclamation (defs. 1, 2). [t. L: m. s. *acclāmāre*] **—acclaim'er,** *n.*

acclamation (ăk'lə mā'shən), *n.* **1.** a shout or other demonstration of welcome, goodwill, or applause. **2.** the act of acclaiming. **3.** acclaim (def. 4). **—acclamatory** (ə klăm'ə tə rĭ, -trĭ), *adj.*

acclimate (ə klī'mĭt, ăk'lĭ māt'), *v.t., v.i.,* **-mated, -mating.** *U.S.* to acclimatize. **—acclimatable** (ə klī'mĭ tə bl), *adj.* **—acclimation** (ăk'lĭ mā'shən), *n.*

acclimatize (ə klī'mə tīz'), *v.t., v.i.,* **-tized, -tizing.** to habituate or become habituated to a new climate or environment. Also, **acclimatise.** [t. F: m. s. *acclimater*, der. *à* to + *climat* climate] —**accli′matiz′able,** *adj.* —**accli′matiza′tion,** *n.* —**accli′matiz′er,** *n.*

acclivity (ə klĭv′ĭ tĭ), *n., pl.* **-ties.** an upward slope, as of ground; an ascent. [t. L: m. s. *acclivitas* steepness]

accolade (ăk′ə lād′, ăk′ə lād′), *n.* **1.** a ceremony used in conferring knighthood, consisting at one time of an embrace, and afterwards of giving the candidate a light blow upon the shoulder with the flat of a sword. **2.** the blow itself. **3.** any award; honour. **4.** *Music.* a brace joining several staves. [t. F, t. It.: m. *accollata*, prop. fem. pp. of *accollare* embrace about the neck; r. ME *acolee*, t. OF]

accommodate (ə kŏm′ə dāt′), *v.*, **-dated, -dating.** —*v.t.* **1.** to do a kindness or a favour to; oblige: *to accommodate a friend.* **2.** to provide suitably; supply (fol. by *with*): *to accommodate a friend with money.* **3.** to provide with room and sometimes with food and entertainment. **4.** to make suitable or consistent; adapt: *to accommodate oneself to circumstances.* **5.** to bring into harmony; adjust; reconcile: *to accommodate differences.* **6.** to find or provide space for (something). —*v.i.* **7.** to become or be conformable; act conformably; agree. [t. L: m. s. *accommodātus*, pp., suited] —**accom′moda′tor,** *n.* —**Syn. 1.** serve, aid, assist. See **oblige. 6.** See **contain.**

accommodating (ə kŏm′ə dā′tĭng), *adj.* easy to deal with; obliging. —**accom′modat′ingly,** *adv.*

accommodation (ə kŏm′ə dā′shən), *n.* **1.** the act of accommodating. **2.** the state or process of being accommodated; adaptation. **3.** adjustment of differences; reconciliation. **4.** *Sociol.* a process of mutual adaptation between persons or social groups, usually through eliminating or lessening of factors of hostility. **5.** anything which supplies a want; a convenience. **6.** lodging, or food and lodging. **7.** a readiness to aid others; obligingness. **8.** a loan or pecuniary favour. **9.** *Physiol.* the automatic adjustment by which the eye adapts itself to distinct vision at different distances.

accommodation address, a private poste restante.

accommodation bill, a bill, draft, note, etc., drawn, accepted or endorsed by one person for another without consideration, to enable the second person to obtain credit or raise money. Also, *U.S.*, **accommodation draft, note, etc.**

accommodation ladder, a ladder or stairway hung from a ship's side to connect with boats below.

accommodative (ə kŏm′ə dā′tĭv), *adj.* tending to accommodate; adaptive. —**accom′moda′tiveness,** *n.*

accompaniment (ə kŭm′pə nĭ mənt, ə kŭmp′nĭ-), *n.* **1.** something incidental or added for ornament, symmetry, etc. **2.** *Music.* any subsidiary part or parts added to a solo or concerted composition to enhance the effect.

accompanist (ə kŭm′pə nĭst, ə kŭmp′nĭst), *n.* *Music.* one who plays an accompaniment. Also, *U.S.*, **accompanyist.**

accompany (ə kŭm′pə nĭ, ə kŭmp′nĭ), *v.t.*, **-nied, -nying. 1.** to go in company with; join in action: *to accompany a friend on a walk.* **2.** to be or exist in company with: *thunder accompanies lightning.* **3.** to put in company with; associate (fol. by *with*): *he accompanies his speech with gestures.* **4.** *Music.* to play or sing an accompaniment to. [ME *accompanye(n)*, t. F: m. *accompagner*, der. *à* to + *compagne* COMPANION] —**accom′panier,** *n.*

—**Syn. 1.** ACCOMPANY, ATTEND, CONVOY, ESCORT mean to go with someone (or something). To ACCOMPANY is to go as an associate on equal terms: *to accompany a friend on a shopping trip.* ATTEND implies going with usually to render service or perform duties: *to attend one's employer on a business trip.* To CONVOY is to accompany (especially ships) with an armed guard, for protection: *to convoy a fleet of merchant vessels.* To ESCORT is to accompany in order to protect, guard, honour, or show courtesy: *to escort a visiting dignitary.*

accomplice (ə kŏm′plĭs, -kŭm′-), *n.* an associate in a crime; partner in wrongdoing. [earlier *complice*, t. F, t. ML: m. s. *complex*, *complicis* close associate, confederate: the phrase *a complice* became *accomplice* by failure to recognize it as made up of two words]

accomplish (ə kŏm′plĭsh, -kŭm′-), *v.t.* **1.** to bring to pass; carry out; perform; finish: *to accomplish one's mission.* **2.** to complete (a distance or period of time). **3.** to make complete; equip perfectly. [ME *accomplice(n)*, t. OF: m. *acompliss-*, s. *acomplir*, g. LL *accomplēre*] —**accom′plishable,** *adj.* —**accom′plisher,** *n.* —**Syn. 1.** complete, fulfil; execute. See **do.**

accomplished (ə kŏm′plĭsht, -kŭm′-), *adj.* **1.** completed; effected: *an accomplished fact.* **2.** perfected; expert: *an accomplished scholar.* **3.** perfected in the graces and attainments of polite society.

accomplishment (ə kŏm′plĭsh mənt, -kŭm′-), *n.* **1.** the act of carrying into effect; fulfilment: *the accomplishment of our desires.* **2.** anything accomplished; achievement: *the accomplishments of scientists.* **3.** (*often pl.*) an acquired art or grace; polite attainment. —**Syn. 1.** completion.

accompt (ə kount′), *n., v.i., v.t.* *Archaic.* account.

accord (ə kôd′), *v.i.* **1.** to be in correspondence or harmony; agree. —*v.t.* **2.** to make to agree or correspond; adapt. **3.** to grant; concede: *to accord due praise.* **4.** *Archaic.* to settle; reconcile. —*n.* **5.** just correspondence of things; harmony of relation. **6.** a harmonious union of sounds. **7.** consent or concurrence of opinions or wills; agreement. **8.** an international agreement; settlement of questions outstanding between nations. **9. of one's own accord,** voluntarily. **10. with one accord,** with spontaneous agreement. [t. LL: s. *accordāre*; r. ME *acorde(n)*, t. OF: m. *acorder*] —**accord′able,** *adj.* —**accord′er,** *n.* —**Syn. 1.** See **agree.**

accordance (ə kô′dns), *n.* **1.** agreement; conformity. **2.** the act of according.

accordant (ə kô′dnt), *adj.* agreeing; conformable. —**accord′antly,** *adv.*

according (ə kô′dĭng), *adv.* **1. according to, a.** in accordance with: *according to his judgement.* **b.** proportionately. **c.** on the authority of; as stated by. **2. according as,** conformably or proportionately as. —*adj.* **3.** agreeing.

accordingly (ə kô′dĭng lĭ), *adv.* **1.** in accordance; correspondingly. **2.** in due course; therefore; so. —**Syn. 1, 2.** consequently, hence, thus. See **therefore.**

accordion (ə kô′dyən), *n.* **1.** a portable wind instrument with bellows and button-like keys sounded by means of metallic reeds. **2.** a piano accordion. —*adj.* **3.** having folds like the bellows of an accordion: *accordion pleats.* [f. ACCORD + -ION] —**accor′dionist.** *n.*

accost (ə kŏst′), *v.t.* **1.** to approach, esp. with a greeting or remark. **2.** to solicit as a prostitute. —*n.* **3.** greeting. [t. F: s. *accoster*, g. LL *accostāre* put side by side]

accouchement (ə ko͞osh′mənt; *Fr.* à ko͞osh mäɴ′), *n.* *French.* period of confinement in childbirth; labour.

accoucheur (ăk′o͞o shû′; *Fr.* à ko͞o shœr′), *n.* *French.* a man who acts as a midwife; an obstetrician.

accoucheuse (*Fr.* à ko͞o shœz′), *n.* *French.* a midwife.

account (ə kount′), *n.* **1.** a verbal or written recital of particular transactions and events; narrative: *an account of everything as it happened.* **2.** an explanatory statement of conduct, as to a superior. **3.** a statement of reasons, causes, etc., explaining some event. **4.** reason; consideration (prec. by *on*): *on all accounts.* **5.** consequence; importance: *things of no account.* **6.** estimation; judgement: *to take into account.* **7.** profit; advantage: *to turn anything to account.* **8. on account of, a.** because of; by reason of. **b.** for the sake of. **9.** a statement of pecuniary transactions. **10.** *Bookkeeping.* **a.** a formal record of the debits and credits relating to the person named (or caption placed) at the head of the ledger account. **b.** a balance of a specified period's receipts and expenditures. **11. for the account,** to be paid on the regular settlement day. **12. in account with,** having a credit arrangement with. **13. on** or **to account,** as an interim payment. **14. go to one's account,** go to the Last Judgement; die. **15. bring, call to account,** demand an explanation or justification of actions. [ME *acount(e)*, t. OF: m. *acont*, *acunt*, later *acompt*, f. *a* to + *cont*, g. LL *comptum*, L *computum* calculation] —*v.i.* **16.** to give an explanation (fol. by *for*): *to account for the accident.* **17.** to answer concerning one's conduct, duties, etc. (fol. by *for*): *to account for shortages.* **18.** to render an account, esp. of money. **19.** to cause death, capture, etc. (fol. by *for*). —*v.t.* **20.** to count; consider as: *I account myself well paid.* **21.** to assign or impute (fol. by *to*). [ME *acunte(n)*, t. OF: m. *acunter*, g. LL *accomptāre*] —**Syn. 1.** See **narrative.**

accountable (ə koun′tə bl), *adj.* **1.** liable to be called to account; responsible (*to* a person, *for* an act, etc.): *I am not accountable to any man for my deeds.* **2.** that can be explained. —**account′abil′ity, account′ableness,** *n.* —**account′ably,** *adv.*

accountancy (ə koun′tən sĭ), *n.* the art or practice of an accountant.

accountant (ə koun′tənt), *n.* a person whose profession is inspecting and auditing business accounts. —**account′antship′,** *n.*

account card, a small card which entitles the holder to have goods charged to an account, at a department store, etc.

accounting (ə koun′tĭng), *n.* the theory and system of setting up, maintaining, and auditing the books of a firm; the art of analysing the financial position and operating results of a business firm from a study of its sales, purchases, overheads, etc. (distinguished from *bookkeeping* in that a bookkeeper only makes the proper entries in books set up to the accountant's plan).

accouplement (ə kŭp′l mənt), *n.* *U.S.* **1.** the act of coupling. **2.** that which couples, esp. (in a building) a tie or brace. [t. F, der. *accoupler*, der. *à* to + *couple* COUPLE]

accoutre (ə ko͞o′tə), *v.t.* to equip or array, esp. with military accoutrements. Also, *U.S.*, **accouter.** [t. F: m. s. *accoutrer*]

accoutrements (ə ko͞o′trĭ mənts), *n.pl.* **1.** equipage; trappings. **2.** the equipment of a soldier except arms and clothing. Also, *U.S.*, **accouterments.**

Accra (ə krä′), *n.* a seaport in W Africa on Gulf of Guinea: the capital of Ghana. 337,770 (1960). Also, **Akkra.**

accredit (ə krĕd′ĭt), *v.t.* **1.** to ascribe or attribute to (fol. by *with*): *he was accredited with having said it.* **2.** to attribute; consider as belonging: *a discovery accredited to Edison.* **3.** to furnish (an officially recognized agent) with credentials: *to accredit an envoy.* **4.** to certify as meeting official requirements. **5.** to bring into credit; invest with credit or authority. **6.** to believe. [t. F: s. *accréditer*]

accrete (ə krēt′), *v.*, **-creted, -creting,** *adj.* —*v.i.* **1.** to grow together; adhere (fol. by *to*). —*v.t.* **2.** to add as by growth. —*adj.* **3.** *Bot.* grown together. [t. L: m. s. *accrētus*, pp., increased]

accretion (ə krē′shən), *n.* **1.** an increase by natural growth or by gradual external addition; growth in size or extent. **2.** the result of this process. **3.** an extraneous addition: *the last part of the legend is a later accretion.* **4.** the growing together of separate parts into a single whole. **5.** *Law.* increase of property by gradual additions caused by acts of nature, as of land by alluvion. **6.** *Pathol.* conglomeration; piling up of substances. [t. L: s. *accrētio*] —**accre′tive,** *adj.*

Accrington (ăk′rĭng tən), *n.* a town in England, in central Lancashire. 39,018 (1961).

accrual (ə kro͞o′əl), *n.* **1.** the act or process of accruing. **2.** something accrued; accretion.

accrue (ə kro͞o′), *v.i.*, **-crued, -cruing. 1.** to happen or result as a natural growth; arise in due course; come or fall as an addition or increment. **2.** *Law.* to become a present and enforceable right or demand. [der. *accrue*, obs. n., t. F, orig. fem. pp. of *accroître* increase, g. L *accrescere*] —**accrue′ment,** *n.*

accrued interest, the amount of interest accumulated at a given time but not yet paid (or received).

acct, account.

acculturation (ə kŭl′chə rā′shən), *n.* *Sociol.* the process and result of adopting the culture traits of another group.

accumbent (ə kŭm′bənt), *adj.* **1.** reclining: *accumbent posture.* **2.** *Bot.* lying against something. [t. L: m. s. *accumbens*, ppr.] —**accum′bency,** *n.*

accumulate (ə kyo͞o′myo͞o lāt′), *v.*, **-lated, -lating.** —*v.t.* **1.** to heap up; gather as into a mass; collect: *to accumulate wealth.* —*v.i.* **2.** to grow into a heap or mass; form an increasing quantity: *public evils accumulate.* [t. L: m. s. *accumulātus*, pp., heaped up]

accumulation (ə kyo͞o′myo͞o lā′shən), *n.* **1.** a collecting together. **2.** that which is accumulated. **3.** growth by continuous additions, as of interest to principal.

accumulative (ə kyo͞o′myo͞o lə tĭv), *adj.* tending to or arising from accumulation; cumulative. —**accu′mulatively,** *adv.* —**accu′mulativeness,** *n.*

accumulative sentence, *n.* *Law.* a sentence of imprisonment which is to be served after another sentence already imposed.

accumulator (ə kyo͞o′myo͞o lā′tə), *n.* **1.** one that accumulates. **2.** *Elect.* a secondary cell, or battery of secondary cells connected together in series or parallel, used for storing electrical energy; a storage battery. **3.** an electric device in arithmetic machines, as the main register of a digital computer, where the arithmetic operations are performed. **4.** *Horseracing.* a bet laid on four or more races from which the winnings and the original stake are carried forward to each race in turn. [t. L]

accuracy (ăk′yə rə sĭ), *n.* the condition or quality of being accurate; precision or exactness; correctness.

accurate (ăk′yə rĭt), *adj.* in exact conformity to truth, to a standard or rule, or to a model; free from error or defect: *an accurate typist.* [t. L: m. s. *accūrātus*, pp., exact, cared for] —**ac′curately,** *adv.* —**ac′curateness,** *n.* —**Syn.** See **correct.**

accursed (ə kû′sĭd, ə kûst′), *adj.* **1.** subject to a curse; ruined. **2.** worthy of curses; detestable. Also, **accurst.** —**accursedly** (ə kû′sĭd lĭ), *adv.* —**accurs′edness,** *n.*

accusation (ăk′yo͞o zā′shən), *n.* **1.** a charge of wrongdoing; imputation of guilt or blame. **2.** the specific offence charged: *the accusation is murder.* **3.** the act of accusing or charging. Also, **accusal** (ə kyo͞o′zəl). [t. L: s. *accūsātio*]

accusatival (ə kyo͞o′zə tī′vəl), *adj.* pertaining to the accusative case.

accusative (ə kyo͞o′zə tĭv), *adj.* **1.** (in Greek, Latin, and English grammar) denoting in Latin and Greek by means of its form, in English by means of its form or its position, a case which has as one of its chief functions the indication of the direct object of a finite verb, as in 'the boy loves *the girl*'. **2.** similar to such a case form in function or meaning. —*n.* **3.** the accusative case. **4. a.** word in that case: *Latin 'puellam' may be spoken of as an accusative.* **5.** a form or construction of similar meaning. [t. L: m. s. *accūsātīvus*, trans. of Gk (*ptôsis*) *aitiātikḗ* (case) pertaining to that which is caused] —**accu′satively,** *adv.*

accusatorial (ə kyo͞o′zə tô′rĭ əl), *adj.* pertaining to an accuser. —**accu′sato′rially,** *adv.*

accusatory (ə kyo͞o′zə tə rĭ, -trĭ), *adj.* containing an accusation; accusing: *he looked at the jury with an accusatory expression.*

accuse (ə kyo͞oz′), *v.t.*, **-cused, -cusing. 1.** to bring a charge against; charge with the fault or crime (*of*). **2.** to blame. [t. L: m. s. *accūsāre* accuse, blame; r. ME *acuse*, t. OF] —**accus′er,** *n.* —**accus′able,** *adj.* —**accus′ingly,** *adv.* —**Syn. 1.** arraign, indict; incriminate; impeach.

accused (ə kyo͞ozd′), *adj.* **1.** charged with a crime or the like. —*n.* **2.** the defendant or defendants in a criminal law case.

accustom (ə kŭs′təm), *v.t.* to familiarize by custom or use; habituate: *to accustom oneself to cold weather.* [late ME *acustume(n)*, t. OF: m. *acostumer*, der. *a* to + *costume* custom]

accustomed (ə kŭs′təmd), *adj.* **1.** customary; habitual: *in their accustomed manner.* **2.** in the habit of: *accustomed to doing good.* **3.** habituated; familiar with; used (*to*): *accustomed to good living.* —**accus′tomedness,** *n.*

ace (ās), *n.* **1.** a single spot or mark on a card or die. **2.** *Cards.* a playing card marked with a single spot, in most games counting as highest, lowest, or either, in its suit. **3.** *Dice.* a die or the face of a die marked with a single spot. **4.** (in tennis, badminton, etc.) **a.** a serve which the opponent fails to touch. **b.** the point thus scored. **5.** a very small quantity, amount, or degree; a particle: *within an ace of winning.* **6.** a highly skilled person; an adept: *an ace at tap-dancing.* **7.** a fighter pilot officially credited with shooting down five or more enemy aeroplanes. —*adj.* **8.** excellent; first in quality; outstanding. [ME *as*, t. OF, g. L, supposedly t. d. Gk, var. of Gk *heîs* one]

-acea, *Zool.* a suffix of (Latin) names of classes and orders of animals, as in *Crustacea.* [t. L, neut. pl. of *-āceus.* See -ACEOUS]

-aceae, *Bot.* a suffix of (Latin) names of families of plants, as in *Rosaceae.* [t. L, fem. pl. of *-āceus.* See -ACEOUS]

acedia (ə sē′dyə), *n.* sloth; spiritual apathy. Also, **accidie.** [t. ML, t. Gk: m. *akēdíā*]

Aceldama (ə sĕl′də mə, ə kĕl′də mə), *n.* **1.** the 'field of blood' near Jerusalem, purchased with the bribe Judas took for betraying Jesus. Matt. 27:8; Acts 1:19. **2.** any place of slaughter. [t. L, t. Gk: m. *Akeldamá*, t. Aram.: m. *hagal damā*]

acentric (ā sĕn′trĭk), *adj.* not centred; having no centre.

-aceous, a suffix of adjectives used in scientific terminology, as in *cretaceous, herbaceous*, and in adjectives derived from *-acea, -aceae.* [t. L: m. *-āceus* of the nature of]

acephalous (ə sĕf′ə ləs), *adj.* **1.** headless; lacking a distinct head. **2.** without a leader. [t. LL: m. *acephalus*, t. Gk: m. *aképhalos.* See A-[6], CEPHALOUS]

acerbate (*v.* ăs′ə bāt′; *adj.* ə sû′bĭt), *v.*, **-bated, -bating,** *adj.* —*v.t.* **1.** to make sour or bitter. **2.** to exasperate. —*adj.* **3.** embittered. [t. L: m. s. *acerbātus*, pp.]

acerbic (ə sû′bĭk), *adj.* sour; harsh, bitter. [f. L. s. *acerbus* + -IC]

acerbity (ə sû′bĭ tĭ), *n.*, *pl.* **-ties. 1.** sourness, with roughness or astringency of taste. **2.** harshness or severity, as of temper or expression. [t. F: m. *acerbité*, t. L: m. s. *acerbitas*]

acerose (ăs′ə rōs′), *adj.* *Bot.* needle-shaped, as the leaves of the pine. Also, **acerous** (ăs′ə rəs). [t. L: m. s. *acerōsus*, der. *acus* chaff, but confused with *acus* needle]

acervate (ə sû′vāt, -vĭt), *adj.* *Bot.* heaped; growing in heaps, or in closely compacted clusters. [t. L: m. s. *acervātus*, pp., heaped] —**acer′vately,** *adv.*

acescent (ə sĕs′ənt), *adj.* turning sour; slightly sour; acidulous. [t. L: m. s. *acescens*, ppr.] —**aces′cence, aces′cency,** *n.*

acet-, var. of **aceto-,** used before vowels, as in *acetaldehyde.*

acetabulum (ăs′ĭ tăb′yo͞o ləm), *n.*, *pl.* **-la** (-lə). *Anat.* the socket of the hipbone which receives the head of the thighbone. See diag. under **pelvis.** [t. L: vinegar cup, saucer] —**ac′etab′ular,** *adj.*

acetal (ăs′ĭ tl), *n.* **1.** a colourless, volatile fluid, $C_6H_{14}O_2$, used as a hypnotic or solvent. 2. (*pl.*) a class of compounds of aldehydes or ketones with alcohols.

acetaldehyde (ăs′ĭ tăl′dĭ hīd′), *n.* a volatile, colourless, aromatic liquid, CH_3CHO, used commercially in the silvering of mirrors and in organic synthesis.

acetamide (ăs′ĭ tăm′īd, ə sĕt′ĭ mīd′), *n.* *Chem.* the amide of acetic acid, a white crystalline solid, CH_3CONH_2, melting at 80°C. Also, **acetamid** (ăs′ĭ tăm′ĭd, ə sĕt′ĭ mĭd). [f. ACET(YL) + AMIDE]

acetanilide (ăs′ĭ tăn′ĭ līd′), *n.* an organic compound, C_8H_9ON, derived by the action of glacial acetic acid upon aniline, used as a remedy for fever, headache, rheumatism, etc., and in the lacquer industry; antifebrin. Also, **acetanilid** (ăs′ĭ tăn′ĭ lĭd). [f. ACET(YL) + ANIL(INE) + -IDE]

acetate (ăs′ĭ tāt′), *n.* *Chem.* a salt or ester of acetic acid. [f. ACET- + -ATE[1]] —**ac′eta′ted,** *adj.*

acetate rayon, a rayon made from the acetic ester of cellulose, differing from viscose rayon in having a greater strength when wet and in being more sensitive to high temperature.

acetic (ə sē′tĭk, ə sĕt′ĭk), *adj.* pertaining to, derived from, or producing vinegar or acetic acid.

acetic acid, a colourless liquid, CH_3COOH, the essential constituent of vinegar, used in the manufacture of acetate rayon and the production of numerous esters as solvents and flavouring agents.

acetic anhydride, a colourless, pungent fluid, $(CH_3.CO)_2O$, the anhydride of acetic acid, used as a reagent and in the production of plastics, film, and fabrics derived from cellulose.

acetify (ə sĕt′ĭ fī′), *v.t., v.i.,* **-fied, -fying.** to turn into vinegar; make or become acetous. [f. ACET- + -(I)FY] —**acet′ifica′tion,** *n.* —**acet′ifi′er,** *n.*

aceto-, a word element indicating the presence of acetic acid or the radical acetyl. Also, **acet-.** [comb. form repr. L *acētum* vinegar]

acetone (ăs′ĭ tōn′), *n.* a colourless, volatile, inflammable liquid, $(CH_3)_2CO$, formed in the distillation of acetates, etc., used as a solvent and in smokeless powders, varnishes, etc. [f. ACET- + -ONE]

acetone bodies, *Pathol.* acetone and related compounds found in blood, urine, etc., during ketosis; ketone bodies.

acetous (ăs′ĭ təs), *adj.* 1. containing or producing acetic acid. 2. sour; vinegary. Also, **acetose** (ăs′ĭ tōs′). [t. LL: m. s. *acētōsus*]

acetum (ə sē′təm), *n.* a preparation made with vinegar or dilute acetic acid as the solvent. [t. L: vinegar]

acetyl (ăs′ĭ tĭl), *n.* *Chem.* a radical, CH_3CO-, in acetic acid. [f. ACET- + -YL] —**ac′etyl′ic,** *adj.*

acetylate (ə sĕt′ĭ lāt′), *v.t.,* **-lated, -lating.** *Chem.* to combine (a compound) with one or more acetyl groups. —**acet′yla′tion,** *n.*

acetylcholine (ăs′ĭ tĭl kō′lēn, -ĭn), *n.* 1. an alkaline organic compound, $C_7H_{17}O_3N$, found in the animal body and in certain plants; it is released at parasympathetic nerve endings when they are stimulated, and is thought to be responsible for the transmission of nerve impulses across synapses. 2. this substance prepared from ergot, and used medicinally to decrease the blood pressure or to set up peristalsis.

acetylene (ə sĕt′ĭ lēn′), *n.* a colourless gas, C_2H_2, prepared by the action of water on calcium carbide, used in metal welding and cutting, as an illuminant, and in organic synthesis.

acetylene series, *Chem.* a series of unsaturated aliphatic hydrocarbons containing a triple bond and having the general formula C_nH_{2n-2}.

acetylsalicylic acid (ăs′ĭ tĭl săl′ĭ sĭl′ĭk, ə sē′tĭl-), aspirin.

acey-deucy (ā′sĭ dyōō′sĭ), *n.* a form of backgammon.

A.C.G.B., Arts Council of Great Britain.

Achaean (ə kē′ən), *adj.* 1. of Achaia or the Achaeans. 2. Greek. —*n.* 3. an inhabitant of Achaia. 4. a Greek. Also, **Achaian** (ə kī′ən). [f. s. L *Achaeus* (t. Gk: m. *Achaiós*) + -AN]

Achaean League, a political confederation of Achaean and other Greek cities, 281–146 B.C.

Achaia (ə kī′ə), *n.* an ancient country in S Greece, on the Gulf of Corinth. Also, **Achaea** (ə kē′ə). See map under **Attica.**

Achates (ə kā′tēz), *n.* 1. (in Virgil's *Aeneid*) the companion and friend of Aeneas. 2. a faithful comrade.

ache (āk), *v.,* **ached, aching,** *n.* —*v.i.* **1.** to suffer pain; have or be in continuous pain: *his whole body ached.* **2.** to be eager; yearn; long. —*n.* **3.** pain of some duration, in opposition to sudden twinges or spasmodic pain. **4.** a longing. [ME *aken,* v., *ache,* n.; OE *acan,* v., *æce,* n. The MnE word has the spelling of the ME noun with the pronunciation of the ME verb] —**ach′ingly,** *adv.* —**ach′age,** *n.* —**ach′y,** *adj.* —**Syn. 3.** See **pain.**

Achelous (ăk′ĭ lō′əs), *n.* *Gk Myth.* a river god, defeated by Hercules in a struggle over Deianira.

achene (ə kēn′), *n.* *Bot.* a small, dry, hard, one-seeded, indehiscent fruit. Also, **akene.** [t. NL: m. s. *achaenium,* f. Gk *a-* A-[6] + m. s. Gk *chainein* gape + *-ium* -IUM] —**achenial** (ə kē′nĭ əl), *adj.*

Achernar (ā′kə nä′), *n.* a first-magnitude star in the constellation Eridanus.

Acheron (ăk′ə rŏn′), *n.* **1.** *Class. Myth.* a river in Hades, over which Charon ferried the souls of the dead. **2.** the lower world; hell. —**Ach′eron′tic,** *adj.*

Acheulian (ə shōō′lĭ ən, -yən), *adj.* of, pertaining to, or characteristic of the lower Palaeolithic culture in Europe, marked by the use of finely made bifacial tools with multiple cutting edges. Also, **Acheulean.** [named after St *Acheul,* village in France where remains were first found]

à cheval (*Fr.* ȧ shə vȧl′), *French.* by horse; on horseback.

achieve (ə chēv′), *v.,* **achieved, achieving.** —*v.t.* **1.** to bring to a successful end; carry through; accomplish. **2.** to bring about, as by effort; gain or obtain: *to achieve victory.* —*v.i.* **3.** to accomplish some enterprise; bring about a result intended. [ME *acheve(n),* t. OF: m. *achever,* der. phrase (*venir*) *a chief* = LL *ad caput venire* come to a head] —**achiev′able,** *adj.* —**achiev′er,** *n.* —**Syn. 1.** consummate, complete; effect, execute. See **do. 2.** attain, realize, win.

achievement (ə chēv′mənt), *n.* **1.** something accomplished, esp. by valour, boldness, or superior ability; a great or heroic deed. **2.** the act of achieving; accomplishment: *the achievement of one's object.*

—**Syn. 1.** ACHIEVEMENT, EXPLOIT, FEAT are terms for a noteworthy act. ACHIEVEMENT connotes final accomplishment of something noteworthy, after much effort and often in spite of obstacles and discouragements: *a scientific achievement.* EXPLOIT connotes boldness, bravery, and usually ingenuity: *the famous exploit of an aviator.* FEAT connotes the performance of something difficult, generally demanding skill and strength: *a feat of horsemanship.*

achievement age, *Psychol.* the age at which, according to an accepted standard of capability, any young person should be able to carry out a selected task successfully.

achievement quotient, *Psychol.* educational age divided by actual age. Thus a child of 10 years whose educational achievement equals that of the average 12-year-old has an achievement quotient of 1·2 (commonly expressed as 120). *Abbrev.:* AQ Cf. **intelligence quotient.**

achievement test, *Psychol.* a test designed to measure the results of learning or teaching, as contrasted with tests of native ability or aptitude. Cf. **intelligence test.**

Achill (ăk′ĭl), *n.* an island off the coast of Ireland, in county Mayo. 56 sq. mi.

Achilles (ə kĭl′ēz), *n.* *Gk Legend.* the hero of Homer's *Iliad,* the greatest Greek warrior in the Trojan war, who came to be the ideal of Greek manhood. According to legend, he died when Paris wounded him in the heel, where he was vulnerable. —**Achillean** (ăk′ĭ lĭən′), *adj.*

Achilles heel, one's only vulnerable spot.

Achilles tendon, *Anat.* the tendon joining the calf muscles to the heelbone; the hamstring.

achlamydate (ā klăm′ĭ dāt′, -dĭt), *adj.* *Zool.* not chlamydate; having no mantle or pallium.

achlamydeous (ăk′lə mĭd′ĭ əs), *adj.* *Bot.* not chlamydeous; having no floral envelope. [f. A-[6] + s. Gk *chlamýs* cloak + -EOUS]

achondroplasia (ă kŏn′drō plā′zyə), *n.* *Med.* a form of dwarfism characterized by short limbs and a large head. [f. A-[6] + m. s. Gk *chóndros* cartilage + -PLASIA] —**achon′droplas′tic,** *adj.*

achromatic (ăk′rə măt′ĭk), *adj.* **1.** *Optics.* free from colour produced by the decomposition of light in chromatic aberration. **2.** *Biol.* **a.** containing or consisting of achromatin. **b.** resisting dyes. **3.** *Music.* without accidentals or changes in key. [f. s. Gk *achrṓmatos* colourless + -IC] —**ach′romat′ically,** *adv.*

achromatin (ə krō′mə tĭn), *n.* *Biol.* that portion of the nucleus of a cell which is less highly coloured by staining agents than the rest of the cell.

achromatism (ə krō′mə tĭz′əm), *n.* freedom from chromatic aberration. Also, **achromaticity** (ə krō′mə tĭs′ĭ tĭ).

achromatize (ə krō′mə tīz′), *v.t.,* **-tized, -tizing.** to make achromatic; deprive of colour. Also, **achromatise.**

achromatous (ə krō′mə təs), *adj.* without colour; of a lighter colour than normal. [t. Gk: m. *achrṓmatos*]

achromic (ə krō′mĭk), *adj.* colourless; without colouring matter. Also, **achro′mous.** [f. A-[6] + m. Gk *chrôma* colour + -IC]

acicula (ə sĭk′yōō lə), *n., pl.* **-lae** (-lē′). a needle-shaped part or process; a spine, bristle, or needle-like crystal. [t. L, dim. of *acus* needle]

acicular (ə sĭk′yo͝o lə), *adj.* needle-shaped. —**acic′ularly,** *adv.*

aciculate (ə sĭk′yo͝o lĭt, -lāt′), *adj.* **1.** having aciculae. **2.** marked as with needle scratches. **3.** needle-shaped; acicular. Also, **acic′ulat′ed.**

aciculum (ə sĭk′yo͝o ləm), *n., pl.* **-lums, -la** (-lə). **1.** an acicula. **2.** *Zool.* one of the slender sharp stylets embedded in the parapodia of some annelids, as the *Polychaeta.* [erroneous var. of ACICULA]

acid (ăs′ĭd), *n.* **1.** *Chem.* a compound (usually having a sour taste and capable of neutralizing alkalis and reddening blue litmus paper) containing hydrogen which can be replaced by a metal or an electropositive radical to form a salt. Acids are proton donors, and yield hydronium ions in water solution. **2.** a substance with a sour taste. —*adj.* **3.** *Chem.* **a.** belonging or pertaining to acids or the anhydrides of acids. **b.** having only a part of the hydrogen of an acid replaced by a metal or its equivalent: *an acid phosphate, etc.* **4.** tasting sharp or sour: acid fruits. **5.** sour; sharp; ill-tempered: *an acid remark, wit, etc.* **6.** *Geol.* (of igneous rocks) containing 66 per cent or more silica. [t. L: s. *acidus* sour]

—**Syn. 5.** ACID, ASTRINGENT are used figuratively of wit or humour. ACID suggests a sharp biting, or ill-natured quality: *an acid joke about an opponent.* ASTRINGENT connotes severity but usually also a bracing quality, as of something applied with curative intent: *much-needed astringent criticism.*

acid drop, a sharp-tasting boiled sweet of sugar and tartaric acid.

acid-fast (ăs′ĭd fāst′), *adj.* resistant to decolorating by acid after staining.

acid-forming (ăs′ĭd fô′mĭng), *adj.* **1.** yielding acid in chemical reaction; acidic. **2.** (of food) containing a large amount of acid ash after complete oxidation.

acidic (ə sĭd′ĭk), *adj.* **1.** *Geol.* containing a large amount of silica. **2.** acid-forming (def. 1).

acidify (ə sĭd′ĭ fī′), *v.t., v.i.,* **-fied, -fying.** to make or become acid; convert into an acid. [f. ACID + -(I)FY] —**acid′ifi′able,** *adj.* —**acid′ifica′tion,** *n.* —**acid′ifi′er,** *n.*

acidimeter (ăs′ĭ dĭm′ĭ tə), *n. Chem.* an instrument used to measure the amount of acid present in a solution.

acidimetry (ăs′ĭ dĭm′ĭ trĭ), *n. Chem.* the measurement of the amount of acid present in a solution. —**acidimetric** (ăs′ĭ dĭ mĕt′rĭk), *adj.* —**ac′idimet′rically,** *adv.*

acidity (ə sĭd′ĭ tĭ), *n., pl.* **-ties. 1.** the quality or extent of being acid. **2.** sourness; tartness. **3.** excessive acid quality, as of the gastric juice.

acidometer (ăs′ĭ dŏm′ĭ tə), *n.* a type of hydrometer, chiefly used for measuring the specific gravity of the electrolyte in an accumulator.

acidophil (ăs′ĭ də fĭl, ə sĭd′ə-), *n. Biol.* a cell or cell constituent with selective affinity for acid dyes.

acidophilus (ăs′ĭ dŏf′ĭ ləs), *n.* See **lactobacillus.**

acidophilus milk, a fermented milk which alters the bacterial content of the intestines. The fermenting bacteria are *Lactobacilli acidophili.*

acidosis (ăs′ĭ dō′sĭs), *n. Pathol.* poisoning by acids formed within the body under morbid conditions. [irreg. f. ACID + -OSIS] —**acidotic** (ăs′ĭ dŏt′ĭk), *adj.*

acid soil, a soil of acid reaction, or having predominance of hydrogen ions, tasting sour in solution.

acid test, a critical test; final analysis.

acidulate (ə sĭd′yo͝o lāt′), *v.t.,* **-lated, -lating. 1.** to make somewhat acid. **2.** to sour; embitter. —**acid′ula′tion,** *n.*

acidulous (ə sĭd′yo͝o ləs), *adj.* **1.** slightly sour. **2.** sharp; caustic. **3.** subacid. [t. L: m. *acidulus,* dim. of *acidus*]

aciduric (ăs′ĭ dyo͝oə′rĭk), *adj.* (of bacteria) capable of growth in an acid environment.

acid value, *Chem.* the number of milligrams of N/10 potassium hydroxide required to neutralize the free fatty acids in one gram of a fat, oil, or resin. Also, **acid number.**

acidy (ăs′ĭ dĭ), *adj.* of or resembling acid; sour: *an acidy taste.*

acierate (ăs′ĭ ə rāt′), *v.t.,* **-rated, -rating.** to convert (iron) into steel. [f. F *acier* steel + -ATE[1]] —**ac′iera′tion,** *n.*

aciform (ăs′ĭ fôm′), *adj.* needle-shaped; acicular. [f. s. L *acus* needle + -(I)FORM]

acinaciform (ăs′ĭ năs′ĭ.fôm′), *adj. Bot.* scimitar-shaped, as a leaf. [f. s. L *acinacēs* short sword (t. Gk: m. *akinákēs*) + -(I)FORM]

Acinaciform leaf

aciniform (ə sĭn′ĭ fôm′), *adj.* **1.** clustered like grapes. **2.** acinous. [f. s. L *acinus* grape + -(I)FORM]

acinous (ăs′ĭ nəs), *adj.* consisting of acini. Also, **acinose** (ăs′ĭ nōs′). [t. L: m. s. *acinōsus* like grapes]

acinus (ăs′ĭ nəs), *n., pl.* **-ni** (-nī′). **1.** *Bot.* one of the small drupelets or berries of an aggregate baccate fruit, as the blackberry, etc. **2.** a berry, as a grape, currant, etc. **3.** *Anat.* **a.** a minute rounded lobule. **b.** the smallest secreting portion of a gland. [t. L: berry, grape]

-acious, an adjective suffix made by adding **-ous** to nouns ending in **-acity** (the *-ty* being dropped), as *audacious.*

-acity, a suffix of nouns denoting quality and the like. [t. F: m. *-acité,* t. L: m. s. *-ācitas,* or directly t. L]

ack., acknowledgement.

ack-ack (ăk′ăk′), *n. Slang.* **1.** anti-aircraft fire. **2.** anti-aircraft arms. —*adj.* **3.** anti-aircraft. [used by radio operators for A.A. (anti-aircraft)]

ack-emma (ăk′ĕm′ə), *adv. Slang.* a.m. [used by radio operators]

acknowledge (ək nŏl′ĭj), *v.t.,* **-edged, -edging. 1.** to admit to be real or true; recognize the existence, truth, or fact of: *to acknowledge belief in God.* **2.** to express recognition or realization of: *to acknowledge an acquaintance by bowing.* **3.** to recognize the authority or claims of: *to acknowledge his right to vote.* **4.** to indicate appreciation or gratitude for. **5.** to admit or certify the receipt of: *to acknowledge a letter.* **6.** *Law.* to own as binding or of legal force: *to acknowledge a deed.* [b. obs. *acknow* (OE *oncnāwan* confess) and *knowledge,* v., admit] —**acknowl′edgeable,** *adj.* —**acknowl′edger,** *n.*

—**Syn. 1.** ACKNOWLEDGE, ADMIT, CONFESS agree in the idea of declaring something to be true. ACKNOWLEDGE implies making a statement reluctantly, often about something previously denied: *to acknowledge a fault.* ADMIT especially implies acknowledging something under pressure: *to admit a charge.* CONFESS usually means stating somewhat formally an admission of wrongdoing, crime, or shortcoming: *to confess guilt, to an inability to understand.* —**Ant. 1.** deny.

acknowledgement (ək nŏl′ĭj mənt), *n.* **1.** the act of acknowledging or admitting. **2.** a recognition of the existence or truth of anything: *the acknowledgement of a sovereign power.* **3.** an expression of appreciation. **4.** a thing done or given in appreciation or gratitude. **5.** *Law.* **a.** an admission of a debt or obligation, esp. a written admission that a debt is due. **b.** declaration by a testator before witnesses that he has signed a will. Also, **acknowledgment.**

aclinic (ə klĭn′ĭk), *adj.* free from inclination or dip of the magnetic needle. [f. m. s. Gk *aklinḗs* not bending + -IC]

aclinic line, *n.* an imaginary line around the earth near the equator where the magnetic needle remains horizontal.

acme (ăk′mĭ), *n.* the highest point; culmination. [t. Gk: m. *akmḗ*]

acmite (ăk′mīt), *n.* aegirite.

acne (ăk′nĭ), *n.* an inflammatory disease of the sebaceous glands, characterized by an eruption (often pustular) of the skin, esp. of the face. [orig. uncert.]

acnode (ăk′nōd), *n. Maths.* a node (def. 5) at which the tangents to two curves are imaginary and distinct. Cf. **crunode.** [f. s. L *acus* needle + NODE] —**acno′dal,** *adj.*

acock (ə kŏk′), *adv., adj.* in a cocked position.

acoelomate (ā sē′lə māt′), *adj. Zool.* having no coelom.

acol (ăk′l), *n.* a system of conventions in bridge, standard in British tournament play. [named after *Acol* Road in NW London, where the bridge club in which it was first played is situated]

acolyte (ăk′ə līt′), *n.* **1.** an altar attendant of minor rank; server. **2.** *Rom. Cath. Ch.* a member of the highest of the four minor orders, ranking next below a subdeacon. **3.** an attendant; an assistant. [ME *acolyt,* t. ML: m. s. *acolitus,* t. Gk: m. *akólouthos* follower]

Aconcagua (ăk′ŏng kä′gwə; *Sp.* ä kōn kä′gwä), *n.* a mountain in W Argentina, in the Andes: the highest peak in the Western Hemisphere. 22,834 ft.

aconite (ăk′ə nīt′), *n.* **1.** any plant of the ranunculaceous genus *Aconitum,* including plants with poisonous and medicinal properties, as monkshood or wolf's-bane. **2.** an extract or tincture made from the root of any of these plants. Also, **aconitum** (ăk′ə nī′təm). [t. L: m. s. *aconitum,* t. Gk: m. *akóniton*] —**aconitic** (ăk′ə nĭt′ĭk), *adj.*

acorn (ā′kôn), *n.* the fruit of the oak, a nut in a hardened scaly cup. [d. ME *acorne,* r. ME *akern,* OE *æcern,* c. Icel. *akarn*]

acotyledon (ə kŏt′ĭ lē′dn), *n. Bot.* a plant without cotyledons. [f. A-[6] COTYLEDON] —**acotyledonous** (ə-kŏt′ĭ lē′də nəs), *adj.*

acouchi (ə ko͞o′shĭ), *n.* any of the small rodents of the genus *Myoprocta,* of South America. Also, **acouchy.**

acoustic (ə ko͞os′tĭk), *adj.* **1.** Also, **acous′tical,** pertaining to the sense or organs of hearing, or to the science of sound. —*n.* **2.** a remedy for deafness or imperfect hearing. [t. F: m. *acoustique,* t. Gk: m. s. *akoustikós*] —**acous′tically,** *adv.*

acoustician (ăk′o͞o stĭsh′ən), *n.* an acoustic engineer.

acoustic mine, a mine designed to be exploded by

vibration, as by that from the propeller of a passing ship.

acoustics (ə ko͞os′tĭks), *n.* **1.** *Physics.* the science of sound. **2.** (*construed as pl.*) acoustic properties, as of an auditorium. [pl. of ACOUSTIC. See -ICS]

acoustic tile, *Bldg Trades.* a tile of some soft, sound-absorbent material, as cork, used for the interiors of recording studios, concert halls, etc.

à couvert (*Fr.* ȧ ko͞o vĕr′), *French.* under cover.

A.C.P., Association of Correctors of the Press.

acquaint (ə kwānt′), *v.t.* **1.** to make more or less familiar or conversant (fol. by *with*): *to acquaint him with our plan.* **2.** to furnish with knowledge; inform: *to acquaint a friend with one's efforts.* [ME *acointe(n)*, t. OF: m. *acointer*, g. LL *adcognitāre* make known]

acquaintance (ə kwān′təns), *n.* **1.** a person (or persons) known to one, esp. a person with whom one is not on terms of great intimacy. **2.** the state of being acquainted; personal knowledge. —**acquaint′anceship′,** *n.*

—**Syn. 1.** ACQUAINTANCE, ASSOCIATE, COMPANION, FRIEND refer to a person with whom one is in contact. An ACQUAINTANCE is someone recognized by sight or someone known, though not intimately: *a casual acquaintance.* An ASSOCIATE is a person who is often in one's company, usually because of some work, enterprise, or pursuit in common: *a business associate.* A COMPANION is a person who shares one's activities, fate, or condition: *a travelling companion, companion in despair.* A FRIEND is a person with whom one is on intimate terms and for whom one feels a warm affection: *a trusted friend.* **2.** association, familiarity, intimacy.

acquainted (ə kwān′tĭd), *adj.* having personal knowledge; informed (fol. by *with*): *acquainted with law.*

acquest (ă kwĕst′), *n.* an acquisition.

acquiesce (ăk′wĭ ĕs′), *v.i.*, **-esced, -escing.** to assent tacitly; comply quietly; agree; consent (often fol. by *in*): *to acquiesce in an opinion.* [t. L: m. s. *acquiescere*] —**ac′quiesc′ingly,** *adv.*

acquiescence (ăk′wĭ ĕs′əns), *n.* **1.** the act or condition of acquiescing or giving tacit assent; a silent submission, or submission with apparent consent. **2.** *Law.* such neglect to take legal proceedings in opposition to a matter as implies consent thereto.

acquiescent (ăk′wĭ ĕs′ənt), *adj.* disposed to acquiesce or yield; submissive. —**ac′quies′cently,** *adv.*

acquire (ə kwī′ə), *v.t.*, **-quired, -quiring. 1.** to come into possession of; get as one's own: *to acquire property, a title, etc.* **2.** to gain for oneself through one's actions or efforts: *to acquire learning, a reputation, etc.* **3.** *Colloq.* to steal. [t. L: m. s. *acquīrere*; r. ME *acquere(n)*, t. OF: m. *acquerre*] —**acquirable** (ə kwī′ə rə bəl), *adj.* —**acquir′er,** *n.* —**Syn. 1.** obtain, procure, secure; win, earn; attain. See **get.**

acquired characteristics, *Biol.* characteristics that are the results of environment, use, or disuse, rather than of heredity. Also, *U.S.*, **acquired characters.**

acquired taste, 1. an unusual liking acquired through experience. **2.** the thing so liked.

acquirement (ə kwī′ə mənt), *n.* **1.** the act of acquiring, esp. the gaining of knowledge or mental attributes. **2.** (*often pl.*) that which is acquired; attainment.

acquisition (ăk′wĭ zĭsh′ən), *n.* **1.** the act of acquiring or gaining possession: *the acquisition of property.* **2.** something acquired: *a valued acquisition.* [t. L: s. *acquīsītio*]

acquisitive (ə kwĭz′ĭ tĭv), *adj.* tending to make acquisitions; fond of acquiring possessions: *an acquisitive society.* —**acquis′itively,** *adv.* —**acquis′itiveness,** *n.*

acquit (ə kwĭt′), *v.t.*, **-quitted, -quitting. 1.** to relieve from a charge of fault or crime; pronounce not guilty (fol. by *of*). **2.** to release or discharge (a person) from an obligation. **3.** to settle (a debt, obligation, claim, etc.). **4. acquit oneself, a.** to behave; bear or conduct oneself: *he acquitted himself well in battle.* **b.** to clear oneself: *he acquitted himself of suspicion.* [ME *aquite(n)*, t. OF: m. *aquiter.* See AD-, QUIT] —**acquit′ter,** *n.* —**Syn. 1.** See **absolve.**

acquittal (ə kwĭt′l), *n.* **1.** the act of acquitting; discharge. **2.** the state of being acquitted; release. **3.** *Law.* judicial deliverance from a criminal charge on a verdict or finding of not guilty.

acquittance (ə kwĭt′ns), *n.* **1.** discharge of or from debt or obligation. **2.** a document certifying this; a receipt. **3.** acquittal.

acr-, var. of **acro-,** used before vowels.

acre (ā′kə), *n.* **1.** a common unit of land measure, now equal in English-speaking countries to 4840 sq. yds. **2.** (*pl.*) fields or land in general. **3.** (*pl.*) *Colloq.* large quantities. **4.** *Obs.* an open ploughed or sown field. [ME *aker*, OE *æcer*, c. G *Acker*]

Acre (ā′kə), *n.* a seaport in NW Israel: captured during the Third Crusade by Richard the Lion-Heart 1191. 57,500 (1963).

acreage (ā′kə rĭj), *n.* acres collectively; extent in acres.

acred (ā′kəd), *adj.* having acres; landed.

acre-foot (ā′kə fo͝ot′), *n.* a unit of volume of water in irrigation: the amount covering one acre to a depth of one foot (43,560 cubic feet).

acre-inch (ā′kər ĭnch′), *n.* one-twelfth of an acre-foot.

acrid (ăk′rĭd), *adj.* **1.** sharp or biting to the taste; bitterly pungent; irritating. **2.** violent; stinging: *acrid remarks.* [f. s. L *ācer* sharp + -ID[4]] —**acridity** (ə krĭd′ĭ tĭ), **ac′ridness,** *n.* —**ac′ridly,** *adv.*

acridine (ăk′rĭ dēn′, -dĭn), *n.* a crystalline substance, $C_{13}H_9N$, part of the anthracene fraction of coal tar. It occurs as needle-shaped crystals and is a source of synthetic dyes and drugs.

acriflavine (ăk′rĭ flā′vĭn, -vēn), *n.* a derivative of acridine, $C_{14}H_{14}N_3Cl$, used as an antiseptic; trypaflavine.

Acrilan (ăk′rĭ lăn′), *n.* *Trademark.* an acrylic fibre used in textiles, characterized chiefly by softness, strength, and crease-resistance.

acrimonious (ăk′rĭ mō′nyəs), *adj.* caustic; stinging; bitter; virulent: *an acrimonious answer.* —**ac′rimo′niously,** *adv.* —**ac′rimo′niousness,** *n.*

acrimony (ăk′rĭ mə nĭ), *n.*, *pl.* **-nies.** sharpness or severity of temper; bitterness of expression proceeding from anger or ill nature. [t. L: m. s. *ācrimōnia*]

acritical (ā krĭt′ĭ kl), *adj.* **1.** not critical. **2.** *Med.* (of a disease) not showing a crisis.

acro-, a word element meaning 'tip', 'top', 'apex', or 'edge', as in *acrogen.* Also, before vowels, **acr-.** [t. Gk: m. *akro-*, comb. form of *ákros* at the top or end]

acrobat (ăk′rə băt′), *n.* **1.** a skilled performer who can walk on a tightrope, perform on a trapeze, or do other similar feats. **2.** one who makes striking changes of opinion, as in politics, etc. [t. F: m. *acrobate*, t. Gk: m. s. *akróbatos* walking on tiptoe] —**ac′robat′ic,** *adj.* —**ac′robat′ically,** *adv.*

acrobatics (ăk′rə băt′ĭks), *n.pl.* **1.** the feats of an acrobat; gymnastics. **2.** skilled tricks like those of an acrobat. Also, **ac′robat′ism.**

acrocarpous (ăk′rə kä′pəs), *adj.* *Bot.* having the fruit at the end of the primary axis.

acrodont (ăk′rə dŏnt′), *adj.* *Anat.*, *Zool.* **1.** with rootless teeth fastened to the alveolar ridge of the jaws. **2.** with sharp tips on the crowns of the cheek teeth.

acrodrome (ăk′rə drōm′), *adj.* *Bot.* running to a point: said of a venation with the nerves terminating in, or curving inward to, the point of a leaf. Also, **acrodromous** (ə krŏd′rə məs).

acrogen (ăk′rə jən), *n.* *Bot.* a flowerless plant growing at the apex only, as ferns and mosses. —**acrogenic** (ăk′rə jĕn′ĭk), **acrogenous** (ə krŏj′ĭ nəs), *adj.* —**acrog′enously,** *adv.*

acrolein (ə krō′lĭ ĭn), *n.* *Chem.* a colourless, pungent liquid, acrylic aldehyde, C_3H_4O, obtained in the decomposition of glycerol. [f. ACR(ID) + L *olē(re)* smell + -IN[2]]

acrolith (ăk′rə lĭth), *n.* a sculptured figure having only the head and extremities made of marble or other stone. [t. L: s. *acrolithus*, t. Gk: m. *akrólithos*] —**ac′rolith′ic,** *adj.*

acromegalic (ăk′rō mĭ găl′ĭk), *adj.* **1.** pertaining to or suffering from acromegaly. —*n.* **2.** a person suffering from acromegaly.

acromegaly (ăk′rō mĕg′ə lĭ), *n.* *Pathol.* a chronic disease characterized by excessive growth of the head, feet, hands, and sometimes the chest extremities and other structures, due to overactivity of the pituitary gland. [t. F: m. *acromégalie.* See ACRO-, MEGALO-]

acromion (ə krō′mĭ ən), *n.*, *pl.* **-mia** (-mĭ ə). *Anat.* the outward end of the spine of the scapula or shoulder-blade. See diag. under **shoulder.** Also, **acromion process.** [t. NL, t. Gk: m. *akrṓmion*] —**acro′mial,** *adj.*

acronychal (ə krŏn′ĭ kl), *adj.* occurring at sunset, as the rising or setting of a star. Also, *U.S.*, **acronical.** [f. m. s. Gk *akrónychos* at nightfall + -AL[1]]

acronym (ăk′rə nĭm), *n.* a word formed from the initial letters of other words, as *NATO* (from *North Atlantic Treaty Organization*) or *radar* (from *radio detection and ranging*). [f. ACR(O)- + m. Gk *ónyma* name (Doric), modelled on HOMONYM]

acropetal (ə krŏp′ĭ tl), *adj.* *Bot.* (of an inflorescence) developing upwards, towards the apex.

acrophobia (ăk′rə fō′byə), *n.* *Psychol.* a pathological dread of high places.

acropolis (ə krŏp′ə lĭs), *n.* **1.** the citadel of an ancient Greek city. **2. the Acropolis,** the citadel of Athens. [t. L. Gk: m. *akrópolis* the upper city]

acrospire (ăk′rə spī′ə), *n.* *Bot.* the first sprout appearing in the germination of grain; the developed plumule of the seed. [f. ACRO- + SPIRE[1]]

across (ə krŏs′), *prep.* **1.** from side to side of: *a bridge across a river.* **2.** on the other side of: *across the sea.* **3.** so as to meet or fall in with: *we came across our friends.*

—*adv.* **4.** from one side to another: *I came across in a steamer.* **5.** on the other side: *we'll soon be across.* **6.** crosswise: *with arms across.* **7.** *Slang.* so as to pay or own up: *come across,* [f. A-[1] + CROSS]

acrostic (ə krŏs′tĭk), *n.* **1.** a series of lines or verses in which the first, last, or other particular letters form a word, phrase, the alphabet, etc. —*adj.* **2.** of or forming an acrostic. [t. L: m. s. *acrostichis,* t. Gk: m. *akrostichis.* See ACRO-, STICHIC] —**acros′tically,** *adv.*

acroter (ə krō′tə, ăk′rə tə), *n.* *Archit.* **1.** a plinth or pedestal placed at the apex or ends of a pediment to receive an ornament or statue. **2.** such a plinth and the object on it.

acrotism (ăk′rə tĭz′əm), *n.* *Pathol.* absence or weakness of the pulse. [f. A-[6] + m. s. Gk *krótos* a beat + -ISM] —**acrotic** (ə krŏt′ĭk), *adj.*

acryl (ăk′rĭl), *n.* *Chem.* the hypothetical radical of the allyl series, C_3H_3O. [f. ACR(OLEIN) + -YL] —**acrylic** (ə krĭl′ĭk), *adj.*

acrylic acid, *Chem.* one of a series of acids derived from the alkenes, with the general formula, $C_nH_{2n-2}O_2$.

acrylic ester, *Chem.* one of the series of esters derived from the acrylic acids.

acrylic resin, *Chem.* one of the group of thermoplastic resins formed by polymerizing the esters or amides of acrylic acid, used chiefly when transparency is desired. Perspex and Plexiglas are in this group.

A.C.T., Australian Capital Territory.

act (ăkt), *n.* **1.** anything done of performed; a doing; deed. **2.** the process of doing: *caught in the act.* **3.** a decree, edict, law, statute, judgement, resolve, or award: *an act of Parliament.* **4.** a deed of instrument recording a transaction. **5.** one of the main divisions of a play or opera. **6.** an individual performance forming part of a variety show, radio programme, etc. —*v.i.* **7.** to do something; exert energy or force; be employed or operative: *his mind acts sluggishly.* **8.** to be employed or operate in a particular way; perform specific duties or functions: *to act as chairman.* **9.** to produce effect; perform a function: *the medicine failed to act.* **10.** to behave: *to act well under pressure.* **11.** to pretend. **12.** to perform as an actor: *did she ever act on the stage?* **13.** to be capable of being acted on the stage: *his plays don't act well.* **14.** to serve or substitute (fol. by *for*). **15. act on** or **upon, a.** to act in accordance with; follow: *he acted upon my suggestion.* **b.** to affect: *alcohol acts on the brain.* **16. act up (to), a.** to come up to a standard set; fulfil. **b.** *Colloq.* to play up, take advantage of. —*v.t.* **17.** to represent (a fictitious or historical character) with one's person: *to act Macbeth.* **18.** to feign; counterfeit: *to act outraged virtue.* **19.** to behave as: *he acted the fool.* **20.** *Obs.* to actuate. [ME, t. L: s. *actum* a thing done, and s. *actus* a doing] —**Syn. 1.** feat, exploit; achievement; transaction. See **action.**

actable (ăk′tə bl), *adj.* **1.** capable of being acted (on the stage). **2.** capable of being carried out in practice. —**act′abil′ity,** *n.*

Actaeon (ăk tē′ən), *n.* *Class. Legend.* a hunter, who, having seen Artemis (Diana) bathing, was changed by her into a stag.

actg, acting.

ACTH, 1. a hormone produced by the pituitary gland which stimulates the activity of the cortical substance of the adrenal glands. **2.** this hormone extracted from the pituitary of pigs and used medicinally against rheumatic fever, rheumatoid arthritis, and various allergic disorders. [initials of *adreno-cortico-tropic hormone*]

actin (ăk′tĭn), *n.* *Biochem.* a globular or fibrous protein present in muscle plasma which, in connection with myosin, plays an important role in muscle contraction.

actinal (ăk′tĭ nəl), *adj.* *Zool.* having tentacles or rays. —**ac′tinally,** *adv.*

acting (ăk′tĭng), *adj.* **1.** serving temporarily; substitute: *acting governor.* **2.** that acts; functioning. **3.** provided with stage directions; designed to be used for performance: *an acting version of a play.*

actinia (ăk tĭn′ĭ ə), *n., pl.* **-tiniae** (-tĭn′ĭ ē′), a sea-anemone of the genus *Actinia.*

actinic (ăk tĭn′ĭk), *adj.* **1.** pertaining to actinism. **2.** (of radiation) chemically active. —**actin′ically,** *adv.*

actinic rays, light of shorter wavelengths (violet and ultraviolet) which produces photochemical effects.

actinide (ăk′tĭ nīd′), *n.* *Chem.* any of the series of elements with atomic numbers between 89 and 103; analogous to a lanthanide; actinon.

actiniform (ăk tĭn′ĭ fôm′), *adj.* *Zool.* having a radiate form.

actinism (ăk′tĭ nĭz′əm), *n.* the action or the property of radiant energy of producing chemical changes.

actinium (ăk tĭn′ĭ əm), *n.* *Chem.* a radioactive chemical element, an isotope of mesothorium, occurring in pitchblende, and resembling the rare earths in chemical behaviour and valency. *Symbol:* Ac; *at. no.:* 89; *at. wt of most stable isotope:* 227; *radioactive half-life:* 27·7 years. [f. ACTIN(O)- + -IUM]

actino-, 1. *Chem.* a word element used in compounds relating to actinism or actinic activity, as in *actinotherapy.* **2.** *Zool.* a word element used in compounds relating to radiate structures, as in *actinoid.* Also, **actin-.** [t. Gk: m. *aktīno-,* comb. form of *aktís* ray]

actinogram (ăk tĭn′ə grăm′), *n.* a record made by an actinograph.

actinograph (ăk tĭn′ə grăf′, -gräf′), *n.* a recording actinometer. —**actin′ograph′ic,** *adj.*

actinography (ăk′tĭ nŏg′rə fĭ), *n.* the recording of actinic power by an actinograph.

actinoid (ăk′tĭ noid′), *adj.* raylike; radiate.

actinolite (ăk tĭn′ə līt′), *n.* a variety of amphibole, occurring in greenish bladed crystals or in masses.

actinometer (ăk′tĭ nŏm′ĭ tə), *n.* an instrument for measuring the intensity of radiation, whether by the chemical effects or otherwise. —**ac′tinom′etry,** *n.* —**actinometric** (ăk′tĭ nō mĕt′rĭk), **ac′tinomet′rical,** *adj.*

actinomorphic (ăk′tĭ nō mô′fĭk), *adj.* **1.** having radial symmetry. **2.** *Bot.* (of certain flowers, as the buttercup) divisible vertically into similar halves by each of a number of planes. Also, **ac′tinomor′phous.**

actinomycete (ăk′tĭ nō mī sēt′), *n.* any member of the *Actinomycetes,* a group of micro-organisms commonly regarded as filamentous bacteria.

actinomycosis (ăk′tĭ nō mī kō′sĭs), *n.* *Vet. Sci., Med.* an infectious inflammatory disease of cattle and other animals and of man, due to certain parasites and causing lumpy, often suppurating tumours, esp. about the jaws. —**actinomycotic** (ăk′tĭ nō mī kŏt′ĭk), *adj.*

actinon (ăk′tĭ nŏn′), *n.* *Chem.* **1.** an inert gas, an isotope of radon, of mass number 219, produced by the disintegration of actinium. *Symbol:* An. **2.** actinide.

actinopod (ăk tĭn′ə pŏd′), *n.* any protozoan of the subclass *Actinopoda,* including the heliozoans and radiolarians, having stiff, rodlike, radiating pseudopodia.

actinozoan (ăk′tĭ nō zō′ən), *n., adj.* *Zool.* anthozoan.

action (ăk′shən), *n.* **1.** the process or state of acting or of being active: *the machine is not now in action.* **2.** something done; an act; deed. **3.** (*pl.*) habitual or usual acts; conduct. **4.** energetic activity. **5.** an exertion of power or force: *the action of wind upon a ship's sails.* **6.** *Physiol.* a change in organs, tissues, or cells leading to performance of a function, as in muscular contraction. **7.** way or manner of moving: *the action of a machine or of a horse.* **8.** the mechanism by which something is operated, as that of a breech-loading rifle or a piano. **9.** *Physics.* the product of work and time. **10.** a small battle. **11.** military and naval combat. **12.** the main subject or story, as distinguished from an incidental episode. **13.** *Drama.* **a.** one of the three unities. See **unity** (def. 10). **b.** an event or happening that is part of a dramatic plot: *the action of a scene, a bit of action.* **14.** the gestures or deportment of an actor or speaker. **15.** *Fine Arts.* the appearance of animation, movement, or passion given to figures by their attitude, position, or expression. **16.** *Law.* **a.** a proceeding instituted by one party against another. **b.** the right of bringing it. **c. take action,** to commence legal proceedings. —*v.t.* **17.** to take action concerning. [t. L: s. *actio;* r. ME *accion,* t. OF] —**ac′tionless,** *adj.*

—**Syn. 2.** ACTION, ACT both mean something done. ACTION applies esp. to the doing; ACT to the result of the doing. An ACTION usually lasts through some time and consists of more than one act: *to take action on a petition.* An ACT is single and of slight duration: *an act of kindness.* **10.** See **battle**[1].

actionable (ăk′shə nə bl), *adj.* **1.** furnishing ground for a law suit. **2.** liable to a law suit. —**ac′tionably,** *adv.*

action painting, a form of abstract painting which concentrates on the effects gained by random application of pigment, as by splashing, trickling, scratching, smearing, etc.

action stations, 1. a. *Mil.* stations to be taken up in readiness for or during battle. **b.** *Colloq.* positions taken up preparatory to action. **2. a.** *Mil.* the command to take up action stations. **b.** *Colloq.* a warning or command to get ready for action.

Actium (ăk′tĭ əm), *n.* a promonotory in NW ancient Greece: Antony and Cleopatra were defeated by Octavian and Agrippa in a naval battle near here, 31 B.C.

activate (ăk′tĭ vāt′), *v.t.,* **-vated, -vating. 1.** to make active. **2.** *Physics.* to render radioactive. **3.** to aerate (sewage) as a purification measure. **4.** *Chem.* **a.** to make more active: *to activate carbon, a catalyst, molecules.* **b.** to hasten (reactions) by various means, such as heating. **5.** *U.S. Mil.* to mobilize. —**ac′tiva′tion,** *n.*

activated sludge, aerated sewage sludge, added to raw sewage to hasten bacterial decomposition.

activator (ăk′tĭ vā′tə), *n.* a catalyst.

active (ăk′tĭv), *adj.* **1.** in a state of action; in actual progress or motion: *active hostilities.* **2.** constantly engaged in action; busy: *an active life.* **3.** having the power of quick motion; nimble: *an active animal.* **4.** moving in considerable volume; brisk; lively: *an active market.* **5.** causing change; capable of exerting influence: *active treason.* **6.** *Gram.* denoting a voice of verb inflection, in which the subject is represented as performing the action expressed by the verb (opposed to *passive*). For example: In English, *he writes the letter* (active); *the letter was written* (passive). **7.** requiring action; practical: *the intellectual and the active mental powers.* **8.** *Theol.* devoted to good works (opposed to *contemplative*). **9.** (of a volcano) in eruption. **10.** *Accounting.* profitable; busy: *active accounts* (ones having current transactions). **11.** interest-bearing: *active paper.* **12.** *Med.* acting quickly; producing immediate effects: *active remedies.* **—*n.* 13.** *Gram.* **a.** the active voice. **b.** a form of construction in that voice. **14.** (of a communications satellite) able to retransmit signals. [t. L: m. s. *actīvus*; r. ME *actif*, t. F] **—ac′tively,** *adv.* **—ac′tiveness,** *n.*

—Syn. 1. acting; working; operative. **2.** ACTIVE, ENERGETIC, STRENUOUS, VIGOROUS imply a liveliness and briskness in accomplishing something. ACTIVE suggests quickness and diligence as opposed to laziness or dilatory methods: *an active and useful person.* ENERGETIC suggests forceful and intense, sometimes nervous activity: *conducting an energetic campaign.* STRENUOUS implies eager and zealous activity with a sense of urgency: *making a strenuous effort.* VIGOROUS suggests strong, effective activity: *using vigorous measures to accomplish an end.* **3.** agile, sprightly.

active immunity, immunity achieved by the manufacture of antibodies within the organism.

active list, *Mil.* a list of officers on full pay available for or engaged in service.

active service, 1. the performance of military duty in the field in time of war. **2.** the state of being on full duty with full pay.

activist (ăk′tĭ vĭst), *n.* a zealous worker for a cause, esp. a communist worker who raises productivity by his efforts. **—ac′tivism,** *n.*

activity (ăk tĭv′ĭ tĭ), *n., pl.* **-ties. 1.** the state of action; doing. **2.** the quality of acting promptly; energy. **3.** a specific deed or action; sphere of action: *social activities.* **4.** an exercise of energy or force; an active movement or operation. **5.** liveliness; agility. **6.** *Physics.* the number of disintegrations taking place in a radioactive specimen in a given time.

act of faith, 1. an act which demonstrates or tests the strength of a person's convictions, as a personal sacrifice. **2.** *Colloq.* a risk or gamble, esp. one taken because of a hunch.

act of God, *Law.* a direct, sudden, and irresistible action of natural forces, such as could not humanly have been foreseen or prevented.

act of grace, an act of Parliament granting a general pardon.

act of indemnity, an act of Parliament passed to exempt persons from punishment for illegal actions undertaken in the public interest, as in wartime.

act of Parliament, a legislative decree passed by Parliament and bearing the Royal Assent.

act of war, an illegal act of aggression by a country against another with which it is nominally at peace.

actomyosin (ăk′tō mī′ə sĭn), *n.* *Biochem.* a complex of actin and myosin which is the major constituent of muscle. The shortening of actomyosin fibrils causes muscle contraction.

Acton (ăk′tən), *n.* **1. John Emerich Edward, 1st Baron,** 1834–1902, English historian. **2.** a district of the W outer London borough of Ealing.

actor (ăk′tə), *n.* **1.** one who represents fictitious or historical characters in a play, film, broadcast, etc. **2.** one who acts; doer. [t. L]

actress (ăk′trĭs), *n.* a female actor.

Acts of the Apostles, the fifth book in the New Testament. Also, **Acts.**

actual (ăk′cho͝o əl), *adj.* **1.** existing in act or fact; real. **2.** now existing; present: *the actual position of the moon.* **3.** *Obs.* exhibited in action. [t. LL: s. *actuālis* active, practical; r. ME *actuel*, t. OF] **—ac′tualness,** *n.* **—Syn. 1.** true, genuine. See **real**[1].

actual grace, *Rom. Cath. Ch.* supernatural help given by God to enlighten the mind and strengthen the will to do good and avoid evil.

actuality (ăk′cho͝o ăl′ĭ tĭ), *n., pl.* **-ties. 1.** actual existence; reality. **2.** (*pl.*) actual conditions or circumstances; facts: *he had to adjust to the actualities of life.*

actualize (ăk′cho͝o ə līz′), *v.t.,* **-lized, -lizing.** to make actual; realize in action or fact. Also, **actualise. —ac′tualiza′tion,** *n.*

actually (ăk′cho͝o ə lĭ), *adv.* as an actual or existing fact; really.

actual sin, *Theol.* the sin of an individual, as contrasted with original sin.

actuary (ăk′tyo͝o ə rĭ), *n., pl.* **-ries. 1.** *Insurance.* an officer who computes risks, rates, etc., according to probabilities indicated by recorded facts. **2.** (formerly) a registrar or clerk. [t. L: m. s. *actuārius*] **—actuarial** (ăk′tyo͝o-ĕə′rĭ əl), *adj.* **—ac′tuar′ially,** *adv.*

actuate (ăk′tyo͝o āt′), *v.t.,* **-ated, -ating. 1.** to incite to action: *actuated by selfish motives.* **2.** to put into action. [t. ML: m. s. *actuātus*, pp.] **—ac′tua′tion,** *n.* **—ac′tua′tor,** *n.*

acuate (ăk′yo͝o ĭt, -āt′), *adj.* sharpened; pointed. [t. ML: m. s. *acuātus*, pp.]

acuity (ə kyo͞o′ĭ tĭ), *n.* sharpness; acuteness: *acuity of vision.* [t. L: m. s. *acuitas*]

aculeate (ə kyo͞o′lĭ ĭt, -āt′), *adj.* **1.** *Biol.* having or denoting any sharp-pointed structure. **2.** having a slender ovipositor or sting, as the hymenopterous insects. **3.** pointed; stinging. Also, **acu′leat′ed.** [t. L: m. s. *aculeātus* prickly]

aculeus (ə kyo͞o′lĭ əs), *n.* **1.** *Bot.* a prickle or thorn, esp. one growing from the stem of a rose tree. **2.** *Zool.* an ovipositor or sting.

acumen (ə kyo͞o′mĕn, ăk′yo͝o mĕn′), *n.* quickness of perception; mental acuteness; keen insight. [t. L] **—acu′minous,** *adj.*

acuminate (*adj.* ə kyo͞o′mĭ nĭt, -nāt′; *v.* ə kyo͞o′mĭ nāt′), *adj., v.,* **-nated, -nating. —*adj.* 1.** *Bot., Zool., etc.* pointed; tapering to a point. **—*v.t.* 2.** to make sharp or keen. [t. L: m. s. *acūminātus*, pp.] **—acu′mina′tion,** *n.*

Acuminate leaf

acupuncture (*n.* ăk′yo͝o pŭngk′chə; *v.* ăk′yo͝o-pŭngk′chə), *n., v.,* **-tured, -turing. —*n.* 1.** a Chinese medical practice that attempts to cure disease by puncturing certain areas of the skin with needles. **2.** *Med.* the puncture of a tissue with a needle, as for drawing off fluids or relieving pain. **—*v.t.* 3.** to perform an acupunture on. [f. L *acu(s)* needle + PUNCTURE]

acushla (ə ko͞osh′lə), *adj., n.* *Irish.* darling. [t. Irish, from phr. *a cushla mo chroidhe* oh pulse of my heart]

acutance (ə kyo͞o′tns), *n.* a measure of the sharpness with which a film can reproduce the edge of an object.

acute (ə kyo͞ot′), *adj.* **1.** sharp at the end; ending in a point (opposed to *blunt* or *obtuse*). **2.** sharp in effect; intense; poignant: *acute sorrow.* **3.** severe; crucial: *an acute shortage.* **4.** brief and severe, as disease (opposed to *chronic*). **5.** sharp or penetrating in intellect, insight, or perception: *an acute observer.* **6.** having quick sensibility; susceptible to slight impressions: *acute eyesight.* **7.** high in pitch, as sound (opposed to *grave*). **8.** *Geom., etc.* (of an angle) less than 90°. See diag. under **angle. 9.** *Gram.* designating or having a particular accent (′) indicating: **a.** (orig.) a raised pitch (as in ancient Greek). **b.** (later) stress (as in the Spanish *adiós*), quality of sound (as in the French *résumé*), vowel length (as in Hungarian), etc. **—*n.* 10.** the acute accent. [t. L: m. s. *acūtus*, pp., sharpened] **—acute′ly,** *adv.* **—acute′ness,** *n.*

—Syn. 5. keen, astute, discerning, perspicacious; sharp-witted. ACTIVE, PENETRATING, SHREWD imply a keenness of understanding, perception, or insight. ACUTE suggests particularly a clearness of perception and a realization of related meanings: *an acute intellect.* PENETRATING adds the idea of depth of perception and a realization of implications: *a wise and penetrating judgement.* SHREWD adds the idea of knowing how to apply practically (or to one's own advantage) what one perceives and understands: *wary and shrewd.*

-acy, a suffix of nouns of quality, state, office, etc., many of which accompany adjectives in *-acious* or nouns or adjectives in *-ate*, as in *efficacy, fallacy,* etc., *advocacy, primacy,* etc., *accuracy, delicacy,* etc. [repr. L *-ācia, -ātia*, and Gk *-áteia*]

acyclic (ā sī′klĭk, ā sĭk′lĭk), *adj.* **1.** *Bot.* not occurring in cycles; not periodic. **2.** *Bot.* not arranged in whorls. **3.** *Chem.* aliphatic. [f. A-[6] + CYCLIC]

acyl group (ăs′ĭl), *Chem.* any organic acid radical.

ad[1] (ăd), *n.* *Colloq.* advertisement.

ad[2] (ăd), *n.* *Tennis.* advantage (def. 5).

ad-, a prefix of direction, tendency, and addition, attached chiefly to stems not found as words themselves, as in *advert, advent.* Also, **ac-, af-, ag-, al-, an-, ap-, ar-, as-, at-,** and **a-**[5]. [t. L, repr. *ad*, prep., to, towards, at, about]

-ad, 1. a suffix forming nouns denoting a collection of a certain number, as in *triad.* **2.** a suffix found in words and names proper to Greek myth, as in *dryad, Pleiad.* **3.** a literary suffix used in titles imitating *Iliad*, as in *Dunciad.* [repr. Gk *-áda*, acc. (nom. *-ás*)]

A.D., (L *anno Domini*) in the year of our Lord; since Christ was born. From 20 B.C. to A.D. 50 is 70 years.

adactylous (ā dăk′tĭ ləs), *adj. Zool.* without fingers or toes. [f. A-[6] + DACTYL + -OUS]

adage (ăd′ĭj), *n.* a proverb. [t. F, t. L; m. s. *adagium*]

adagio (ə dä′jĭ ō′; *It.* ä dä′jō), *adv., adj., n., pl.* **-gios.** *Music, etc.* —*adv.* **1.** in a leisurely manner; slowly. —*adj.* **2.** slow. —*n.* **3.** an adagio movement or piece. [It.]

Adam (ăd′əm), *n.* **1.** the name of the first man: progenitor of the human race. Genesis 2:7. **2. the old Adam,** the evil inherent in man. —**Adamic** (ă dam′ĭk), *adj.*

Adam (ăd′əm), *n.* **1. James,** 1730–94, and his brother, **Robert,** 1728–92, architects and furniture designers in the classical manner. —*adj.* **2.** (of furniture) pertaining to or in the style of these two brothers.

adamant (ăd′ə mənt), *n.* **1.** (in ancient times) some impenetrably hard substance, variously identified later as the diamond or lodestone. **2.** any impenetrably hard substance. —*adj.* **3.** hard as adamant; adamantine. **4.** hard-hearted. [t. L: s. *adamas,* t. Gk; r. ME *adamaunt* (t. OF), and OE *athamans* (repr. LL var. of *adamas*)]

adamantine (ăd′ə măn′tĭn), *adj.* **1.** impenetrable. **2.** like a diamond in lustre.

Adamite (ăd′ə mīt′), *n.* **1.** a descendant of Adam; a human being. **2.** a nudist. —**Adamitic** (ăd′ə mĭt′ĭk), *adj.*

Adams (ăd′əmz), *n.* **1. Charles Francis,** 1807–86, U.S. statesman: minister to Great Britain 1861–68 (son of John Quincy Adams). **2. John,** 1735–1826, second president of the U.S., 1797–1801; leader in the American War of Independence. **3. John Quincy** (kwĭn′sĭ), 1767–1848, sixth president of the U.S. 1825–29; secretary of state 1817–25 (son of John Adams). **4. Mount, a.** a mountain in the U.S., in SW Washington, in the Cascade Range. 12,307 ft. **b.** a mountain in the U.S., in N New Hampshire, in the White Mountains. 5,798 ft.

Adam's ale, *Colloq.* water.

Adam's apple, *n.* **1.** a projection of the thyroid cartilage at the front of the (male) throat. **2.** forbidden fruit.

adamsite (ăd′əm zīt′), *n.* a yellow irritant smoke, containing a form of arsenic that is poisonous, used as a harassing agent. *Symbol:* DM. [named after Major Roger *Adams,* U.S. soldier, born 1889, who invented it. See -ITE[1]]

Adam's-needle (ăd′əmz nē′dl), *n. U.S.* a species of yucca, *Yucca filamentosa,* much cultivated for ornament.

Adana (ăd′ə nə; *Turk.* ä′dä nä), *n.* a city in S Turkey. 231,548 (1960).

Adapazari (*Turk.* ä dä′pä zä rĭ), *n.* a town in NW Turkey. 79,420 (1960).

adapt (ə dăpt′), *v.t.* to make suitable to requirements; adjust or modify fittingly. [t. L: s. *adaptāre*] —**Syn.** fit, accommodate, suit, compose, reconcile. See **adjust.**

adaptable (ə dăp′tə bl), *adj.* **1.** capable of being adapted. **2.** able to adapt oneself easily to new conditions. —**adapt′-abil′ity, adapt′ableness,** *n.*

adaptation (ăd′ăp tā′shən), *n.* **1.** the act of adapting. **2.** the state of being adapted; adjustment. **3.** something produced by adapting. **4.** a literary work rewritten for presentation in a different medium: *an adaptation of a novel for the stage.* **5.** *Biol.* **a.** alteration in the structure or function of organisms which enables them to survive and multiply in a changed environment. **b.** a form or structure modified in response to a changed environment. **6.** *Physiol.* the response of sensory receptor organs, as those of vision, touch, temperature, olfaction, audition, and pain, to constantly applied stimuli from a changing environment. **7.** Also, **adaption** (ə dăp′shən). *Sociol.* a slow, usually unconscious modification of individual and social activity in adjustment to cultural surroundings. —**ad′apta′tional,** *adj.*

adaptive (ə dăp′tĭv), *adj.* serving to adapt; showing adaptation: *adaptive colouring of a chameleon.* —**adap′-tively,** *adv.* —**adap′tiveness,** *n.*

adaptor (ə dăp′tə), *n.* **1.** one that adapts. **2.** a device for fitting together parts having different sizes or designs. **3.** an accessory to convert a machine, tool, etc., to a new or modified use. **4.** *Elect.* an accessory plug for connecting a piece of apparatus fitted with one type of terminals to a supply point with a different type. Also, **adapter.**

Adar (ā′dä), *n.* (in the Jewish calendar) the sixth month of the civil year and the twelfth of the ecclesiastical year. [Heb.]

ad astra per aspera (ăd ăs′trə pər ăs′pə rə), *Latin.* to the stars through difficulties.

adaxial (ăd ăk′sĭ əl), *adj. Bot.* situated on the side towards the axis. [f. AD- + s. L *axi(s)* axle + -AL[1]]

A.D.C., aide-de-camp.

ad captandum (vulgus) (ăd′ kăp tăn′dəm vŏŏl′gəs), *Latin.* in order to please (the mob); emotional.

add (ăd), *v.t.* **1.** to unite or join so as to increase the number, quantity, size, or importance: *to add another stone to the pile.* **2.** to find the sum of (often fol. by *up*). **3.** to say or write further. **4.** to include (fol. by *in*). —*v.i.* **5.** to perform the arithmetical operation of addition. **6.** to be or serve as an addition (fol. by *to*): *to add to one's grief.* **7. add up, a.** to amount (*to*): *it adds up to murder.* **b.** to make the desired or expected total: *these figures don't add up.* **c.** *Colloq.* to make sense, be logically consistent: *the facts don't add up.* [ME *adde(n),* t. L: m. *addere*] —**add′ible, add′able,** *adj.* —**add′er,** *n.* —**Syn. 1.** append; attach.

Addams (ăd′əmz), *n.* **1. Jane,** 1860–1935, U.S. social worker and writer. **2. Charles (Samuel),** born 1912, U.S. macabre cartoonist.

addax (ăd′ăks), *n.* a large pale-coloured antelope, *Addax nasomaculatus,* of North Africa, with loosely spiral horns. [t. L; of ancient North African orig.]

Addax, *Addax nasomaculatus* (3 ft high at the shoulder, 6 ft long, horns 3 or 4 ft long)

added line, *U.S. Music.* a ledger line.

addend (ăd′ĕnd, ə dĕnd′), *n. Chiefly U.S.* summand.

addendum (ə dĕn′dəm), *n., pl.* **-da** (-də). **1.** a thing to be added; an addition. **2.** an appendix to a book. **3.** *Mach.* **a.** the distance between the tip of a tooth and the pitch circle or pitch line of a toothed wheel or rack. **b.** Also, **addendum circle,** an imaginary circle touching the ends of the teeth of a toothed wheel. [t. L, neut. ger. of *addere* add]

adder (ăd′ə), *n.* **1.** the common European viper, *Vipera berus,* a small venomous snake, widespread in northern Eurasia. **2.** any of various other snakes, venomous or harmless, resembling the viper. [var. of ME *nadder* (*a nadder* being taken as *an adder*), OE *nǣdre*]

adder's-meat (ăd′əz mēt′), *n.* the greater stitchwort, *Stellaria holostea.*

adder's-tongue (ăd′əz tŭng′), *n.* a fern of the genus *Ophioglossum,* with a spore-bearing spike.

adder's-wort (ăd′əz wûrt′), *n.* bistort (def. 1).

addict (*n.* ăd′ĭkt; *v.* ə dĭkt′), *n.* **1.** one who is addicted to a practice or habit: *a drug addict.* —*v.t.* **2.** to give (oneself) over, as to a habit or pursuit; apply or devote habitually (fol. by *to*): *addict oneself to science.* [t. L: s. *addictus,* pp., adjudged, devoted]

addicted (ə dĭk′tĭd), *adj.* devoted or given up (to a practice, habit, or substance) (fol. by *to*): *addicted to drugs.* —**addict′edness,** *n.*

addiction (ə dĭk′shən), *n.* the state of being addicted to some habit, practice, or substance, esp. to narcotics.

addictive (ə dĭk′tĭv), *adj.* **1.** (esp. of drugs) causing or tending to cause addiction. —*n.* **2.** an addictive agent.

adding machine, any of various, usually monetary, calculating machines.

Addis Ababa (ăd′ĭs ăb′ə bə), the capital of Ethiopia, in the central part. 450,000 (est. 1964).

Addison (ăd′ĭ sən), *n.* **Joseph,** 1672–1719, English essayist and poet. —**Addisonian** (ăd′ĭ sō′nyən), *adj.*

Addison's disease, *Pathol.* a disease characterized by asthenia, low blood-pressure, and a brownish coloration of the skin, due to progressive destruction of the suprarenal cortex. [named after T. *Addison,* 1793–1860, English physician, who first described it]

additament (ə dĭt′ə mənt), *n.* something added; an addition. [t. L: s. *additāmentum*]

addition (ə dĭsh′ən), *n.* **1.** the act or process of adding or uniting. **2.** the process of uniting two or more numbers into one sum, denoted by the symbol +. **3.** the result of adding; anything added. **4.** *Obs.* a particularizing designation added to a person's name. **5.** *U.S.* wings, rooms, etc., added to a building, or land added to property already owned. **6. in addition to,** besides; as well as. [t. L: s. *additio*; r. ME *addicioun,* t. F]

—**Syn. 3.** increase, enlargement; increment; accession, supplement; appendix. ADDITION, ACCESSORY, ADJUNCT, ATTACHMENT mean something joined on to or used with something else. ADDITION is the general word, carrying no implication of size, importance, or kind, but merely that of being joined to something previously existing: *an addition to an income, to a building, to one's cares.* An ACCESSORY is a subordinate addition to a more important thing, for the purpose of aiding, completing, ornamenting, etc.: *accessories to an outfit.* An ADJUNCT is a subordinate addition that aids or assists a main thing or person but is often separate: *a second machine as an adjunct to the first.* An ATTACHMENT is an accessory part which may be easily connected and removed: *a pleating attachment for a sewing-machine.*

additional (ə dĭsh′ə nəl), *adj.* added; supplementary: *additional information.* —**addi′tionally,** *adv.*

additive (ăd′ĭ tĭv), *adj.* **1.** to be added; of the nature of an addition; characterized by addition: *an additive process.*

—*n.* **2.** something added. [t. L: m. s. *additīvus*] —**ad′ditively,** *adv.*

addle (ăd′l), *v.*, **addled, addling,** *adj.* —*v.t., v.i.* **1.** to make or become muddled or confused. **2.** to make or become spoiled or rotten, as eggs. —*adj.* **3.** mentally confused; muddled, as in the combinations **ad′dle-brained′, ad′dle-head′ed, ad′dle-pat′ed. 4.** rotten: *addled eggs.* [OE *adela* liquid filth, c. MLG *adele* mud]

address (ə drĕs′), *n., v.,* **-dressed** or **-drest, -dressing.** —*n.* **1.** a formal speech or writing directed to a person or a group of persons: *an address on current problems.* **2.** a direction as to name and residence inscribed on a letter, etc. **3.** a place where a person lives or may be reached. **4.** *Computers.* a number or symbol which identifies a particular register in the memory of a digital computer. **5.** manner of speaking to persons; personal bearing in conversation. **6.** skilful management; adroitness: *to handle a matter with address.* **7.** (*usually pl.*) attentions paid by a lover; courtship. **8.** (*usually cap.*) *Parl. Proc.* the reply to the Queen's speech in parliament. **9.** *U.S.* a request to the executive by a legislature to remove a judge for unfitness. **10.** *Obs.* preparation. —*v.t.* **11.** to direct speech or writing to: *to address an assembly, how does one address the governor?* **12.** to direct to the ear or attention: *to address a warning to someone.* **13.** to apply in speech (used reflexively, fol. by *to*): *he addressed himself to the chairman.* **14.** to direct for delivery; put a direction on: *to address a letter.* **15.** to direct the energy or force of (used reflexively, fol. by *to*): *he addressed himself to the work in hand.* **16.** to pay court to; woo; court. **17.** *Golf.* to adjust and apply the club to (the ball) in preparing for a stroke. **18.** *Obs. except in Golf.* to give direction to; aim. **19.** *Obs.* to prepare. —*v.i.* **20.** *Obs.* to make an appeal. **21.** *Obs.* to make preparations. [ME *addresse(n)*, t. F: m. *adresser*, earlier *adrecier*, ult. der. L *ad* to + *dīrectus* straight] —**address′er, address′or,** *n.* —**Syn. 1.** discourse, lecture. See **speech. 6.** adroitness, dexterity; cleverness, ingenuity; tact.

addressee (ăd′rĕs ē′), *n.* one to whom anything is addressed.

addressograph (ə drĕs′ə grăf′, -gräf′), *n.* **1.** a machine that prints addresses upon envelopes, etc., from stencils. **2.** (*cap.*) a trademark for this machine.

adduce (ə dyōōs′), *v.t.,* **-duced, -ducing.** to bring forward in argument; cite as pertinent or conclusive: *to adduce reasons.* [t. L: m. s. *addūcere* lead to] —**adduc′ible,** *adj.* —**adduc′er,** *n.*

adducent (ə dyōō′sənt), *adj. Physiol.* drawing towards; adducting. [t. L: s. *addūcens*, ppr., leading to]

adduct (ə dŭkt′), *v.t. Physiol.* to draw towards the main axis (opposed to *abduct*). [t. L: s. *adductus*, pp., led to] —**adduc′tive,** *adj.* —**adduc′tor,** *n.*

adduction (ə dŭk′shən), *n.* **1.** *Physiol.* the action of the adductor or adducent muscles. **2.** the act of adducing.

-ade[1], **1.** a suffix found in nouns denoting action or process, product or result of action, person or persons acting, often irregularly attached, as in *blockade, escapade, masquerade.* **2.** a noun suffix indicating a drink made of a particular fruit, as in *orangeade.* [t. F, t. Pr.: m. *-ada*, g. L *-āta*; in some words -ADE is for Sp. and Pg. *-ado*, It. *-ato*, g. L *-ātus*]

-ade[2], a collective suffix, var. of **-ad** (def. 1), as in *decade.*

A'deen, Aberdeenshire.

Adelaide (ăd′ĭ lād′), *n.* a city in S Australia, the capital of the state of South Australia: university, founded 1874. pop. with suburbs 607,800 (est. 1965). See map under **Canberra.**

Adélie Land (ăd′ĭ lĭ; *Fr.* à dė lē′), a coastal region of Antarctica south of Australia: under French sovereignty. Also **Adélie Coast.**

ademption (ə dĕmp′shən), *n. Law.* the failure of a specific legacy because the subject matter no longer belongs to the testator's estate at his death. [t. L: s. *ademptio*]

Aden (ā′dn), *n.* **1.** a former British colony in S Arabia. 210,000 pop. (est. 1964); 75 sq. mi. **2.** the former capital of this colony; a seaport. **3. Gulf of,** an arm of the Arabian Sea between the E tip of Africa and the Arabian peninsula. See **South Yemen.**

adenalgia (ăd′ĭ năl′jə), *n. Pathol.* pain in a gland.

Adenauer (ăd′n ou′ə; *Ger.* à′də nou ə), *n.* **Konrad** (kŏn′răd; *Ger.* kôn′ràt), 1876–1967, chancellor of the German Federal Republic 1949–63.

adenine (ăd′ĭ nĭn, -nēn′, -nīn′), *n. Biochem.* a purine base, $C_5H_5N_5$, present in all living cells, mainly in combined form, as in nucleic acids.

adeno-, *Anat.* a word element meaning 'gland'. Also, before vowels, **aden-.** [t. Gk, comb. form of *adḗn*]

adenoid (ăd′ĭ noid′), *n.* **1.** (*usually pl.*) an enlarged mass of lymphoid tissue in the upper pharynx, common in children, often preventing nasal breathing. —*adj.* **2.** Also, **ad′enoi′dal.** pertaining to the lymphatic glands. [t. Gk: m. s. *adenoeidḗs* glandular]

adenoidectomy (ăd′ĭ noi dĕk′tə mĭ), *n., pl.* **-mies.** *Surg.* the operation of removing the adenoids.

adenoma (ăd′ĭ nō′mə), *n., pl.* **-mas, -mata** (-mə tə), *Pathol.* **1.** a tumour originating in a gland. **2.** a tumour of glandlike structure. —**adenomatous** (ăd′ĭ nŏm′ə təs, -nō′mə-), *adj.*

adenosine (ă dĕn′ə sēn′, ăd′ĭ nō′sēn), *n. Biochem.* a compound of adenine and ribose, present in all living cells, mainly in combined form, as in ribonucleic acids.

adenosine triphosphate, *Biochem.* the triphosphate of adenosine, present in all living cells, which represents a store of chemical energy that is immediately available to the cell for use in biosynthesis, etc. *Abbrev.*: ATP.

adenovirus (ăd′ĭ nō vī′ə rəs), *n.* a virus causing infection of the upper respiratory tract. [f. ADENO- + VIRUS]

adenylic acid (ăd′ĭ nĭl′ĭk), *Biochem.* the monophosphate of adenosine, present in all living cells, mainly in combined form, as in ribonucleic acids.

adept (ăd′ĕpt), *n.* **1.** one who has attained proficiency; one fully skilled in anything. —*adj.* **2.** highly skilled; proficient. [t. L: s. *adeptus*, pp., having attained] —**ad′eptly,** *adv.* —**ad′eptness,** *n.*

adequacy (ăd′ĭ kwə sĭ), *n.* the state or quality of being adequate; a sufficiency for a particular purpose.

adequate (ăd′ĭ kwĭt), *adj.* **1.** equal to the requirement or occasion; fully sufficient, suitable, or fit (often fol. by *to* or *for*). **2.** *Law.* reasonably sufficient for starting legal action: *adequate grounds.* [t. L: m. s. *adaequātus*, pp., equalized] —**ad′equately,** *adv.* —**ad′equateness,** *n.* —**Syn. 1.** satisfactory.

ad eundum (gradum) (ăd′ā ŏŏn′dŏŏm grä′dŏŏm), *Latin.* to the same (degree). A graduate from one university may be admitted without examination to an *ad eundum* degree in the same subject at another university.

à deux (*Fr.* à dœ′), *French.* of or for two; two at a time.

ad extremum (ăd′ĕks trē′məm), *Latin.* to the extreme; at last; finally.

ad fin., (L *ad finem*) to, towards, or at the end.

ad gloriam (ăd glô′rĭ ăm′), *Latin.* for glory.

adhere (əd hĭə′), *v.i.,* **-hered, -hering. 1.** to stick fast; cleave; cling (fol. by *to*). **2.** to be devoted; be attached as a follower or upholder (fol. by *to*): *to adhere to a party a leader, a church, a creed, etc..* **3.** to hold closely or firmly (fol. by *to*): *to adhere to a plan.* **4.** *Obs.* to be consistent. [t. L: m. s. *adhaerēre*] —**adher′er,** *n.* —**Syn. 1.** See **stick.**

adherence (əd hĭə′rəns), *n.* **1.** the quality of adhering; fidelity; steady attachment: *adherence to a party, rigid adherence to rules.* **2.** the act or state of adhering; adhesion.

adherent (əd hĭə′rənt), *n.* **1.** one who follows or upholds a leader, cause, etc.; supporter; follower (fol. by *of*). —*adj.* **2.** sticking; clinging; adhering. **3.** *Bot.* adnate. **4.** *Gram.* standing before and modifying a noun. —**adher′ently,** *adv.* —**Syn. 1.** See **follower.**

adhesion (əd hē′zhən), *n.* **1.** the act or state of adhering, or of being united: *the adhesion of parts united by growth.* **2.** steady attachment of the mind or feelings; adherence. **3.** *Physics.* the molecular force exerted across the surface of contact between unlike liquids and solids which resists their separation. **4.** *Pathol.* **a.** the abnormal union of adjacent tissues due to inflammation. **b.** the tissue involved. [t. L: m. s. *adhaesio*]

adhesive (əd hē′sĭv), *adj.* **1.** clinging; tenacious; sticking fast. —*n.* **2.** a substance for sticking things together. —**adhe′sively,** *adv.* —**adhe′siveness,** *n.*

adhesive tape, a plastic or fabric tape coated on one side with an adhesive, used for binding, etc.

adhibit (əd hĭb′ĭt), *v.t.* **1.** to take or let in; admit. **2.** to use or apply. **3.** *Rare.* to attach. [t. L: s. *adhibitus*, pp., applied] —**adhibition** (ăd′hĭ bĭsh′ən), *n.*

ad hoc (ăd hŏk′), *Latin.* for this (special purpose); with respect to this (subject or thing). An **ad hoc committee** is one set up to deal with one subject only (opposed to *omnibus*).

ad hominem (ăd hŏm′ĭ nĕm′), *Latin.* to the man; personal. An argument *ad hominem* appeals to a person's prejudices or special interests instead of to his intellect.

adiabatic (ăd′yə băt′ĭk, ā′dyə-), *adj. Physics., Chem.* without gain or loss of heat (distinguished from *isothermal*). [f. s. Gk *adiábatos* impassable + -IC] —**ad′iabat′ically,** *adv.*

adiaphorism (ăd′ĭ ăf′ə rĭz′əm), *n.* tolerance by the Church of actions not specifically prohibited by the Scriptures; indifferentism. [t. Gk: m. *adiáphoros*]

adiaphorous (ăd′ĭ ăf′ə rəs), *adj.* doing neither good nor harm, as a medicine.

adiathermancy (ăd′yə thû′mən sĭ), *n. Physics.* inability to transmit heat radiation. —**ad′iather′manous,** *adj.*

adieu (ə dyōō′; *Fr.* à dyœ′), *interj.*, *n.*, *pl.* **adieus, adieux** (ə dyōōz′; *Fr.* à dyœ′). —*interj.* **1.** goodbye; farewell. —*n.* **2.** the act of taking one's leave; a farewell. [ME, t. F, g. L *ad Deum* (I commend you) to God]

Adige (*It.* à′dē jè), *n.* a river in N Italy, flowing SE to the Adriatic. ab. 220 mi.

ad inf., ad infinitum.

ad infinitum (ăd′ ĭn fĭ nī′təm), *Latin.* to infinity; endlessly; without limit.

ad init., ad initium.

ad initium (ăd′ ĭ nĭsh′ĭ əm), *Latin.* at the beginning.

ad int., ad interim.

ad interim (ăd ĭn′tə rĭm), *Latin.* in the meantime.

adios (*Sp.* à dyós′), *interj.* *Spanish.* goodbye; farewell.

adipic acid (ə dĭp′ĭk), *Chem.* a white, crystalline solid, $(CH_2)_4(COOH)_2$, slightly soluble in water, used in the synthesis of nylon. [ADIP(OSE) + -IC]

adipocere (ăd′ĭ pō sĭə′), *n.* a waxy substance sometimes formed from dead animal bodies in moist burial places or under water. [f. *adipo-* (comb. form repr. L *adeps* fat) + m. L *cēra* wax] —**adipocerous** (ăd′ĭ pŏs′ə rəs), *adj.*

adipose (ăd′ĭ pōs′), *adj.* **1.** fatty; consisting of, resembling, or having relation to fat: *adipose tissue.* —*n.* **2.** animal fat stored in the fatty tissue of the body. [t. NL: m. s. *adipōsus* fatty, der. L *adeps* fat] —**ad′ipose′ness, adiposity** (ăd′ĭ pŏs′ĭ tĭ), *n.*

adipose fin, *Ichthyol.*, a finlike projection, fleshy and lacking rays, behind the dorsal fin.

Adirondack Mountains (ăd′ĭ rŏn′dăk), a mountain range in the U.S., in NE New York State: a part of the Appalachian system. Highest peak, Mt Marcy, 5344 ft. Also, **Adirondacks.**

adit (ăd′ĭt), *n.* **1.** an entrance or a passage. **2.** *Mining.* a nearly horizontal passage leading into a mine. **3.** access. [t. L: s. *aditus* approach]

adj., **1.** adjective. **2.** adjourned. **3.** adjunct. **4.** *Banking.* adjustment. **5.** adjutant.

adjacency (ə jā′sən sĭ), *n.*, *pl.* **-cries. 1.** the state of being adjacent. **2.** (*usually pl.*) that which is adjacent.

adjacent (ə jā′sənt), *adj.* lying near, close, or contiguous; adjoining; neighbouring: *a field adjacent to the main road.* [t. L: s. *adjacens*, ppr.] —**adja′cently,** *adv.* —**Syn.** abutting, bordering. See **adjoining.**

adjacent angles, *Geom.* two angles having the same vertex and having a common side between them.

adjective (ăj′ĭk tĭv), *n.* **1.** *Gram.* **a.** one of the major parts of speech of many languages, comprising words used to qualify or limit a noun. **b.** such a word, as *wise* in *a wise ruler*, or in *he is wise.* **c.** any word or phrase of similar function or meaning. —*adj.* **2.** *Gram.* pertaining to an adjective; functioning as an adjective; adjectival: *the adjective use of a noun.* **3.** not able to stand alone; dependent. **4.** *Law.* concerning methods of enforcement of legal rights, as pleading and practice (opposed to *substantive*). **5.** *Dyeing.* (of colours) requiring a mordant or the like to render them permanent (opposed to *substantive*). [t. L: m. s. *adjectīvus*] —**adjectival** (ăj′ĭk tī′vəl), *adj.* —**ad′jecti′vally, ad′jectively,** *adv.*

adjoin (ə join′), *v.t.* **1.** to be in connection or contact with; abut on: *his house adjoins the lake.* —*v.i.* **2.** to lie or be next, or in contact. [ME *ajoine(n)*, t. OF: m. *adjoindre*, g. L *adjungere* join to]

adjoining (ə joi′nĭng), *adj.* bordering; contiguous: *the adjoining room.*

—**Syn.** ADJOINING, ADJACENT, BORDERING all mean near or close to something. ADJACENT implies being nearby or next to: *adjacent angles.* ADJOINING implies touching, having a common point or line: *an adjoining yard.* BORDERING means having a common boundary with: *France is a country bordering on Spain.*

adjourn (ə jûn′), *v.t.* **1.** to suspend the meeting of, as a public or private body, to a future day or to another place: *adjourn the court.* **2.** to defer or postpone to a future meeting of the same body: *the court adjourned consideration of the question.* **3.** to put off; defer; postpone. —*v.i.* **4.** to postpone, suspend, or transfer proceedings. [ME *adjourne(n)*, t. OF: m. *ajorner*, from phr. *a jorn nome* until an appointed day]

adjournment (ə jûn′mənt), *n.* **1.** the act of adjourning. **2.** a state or period of being adjourned.

adjt, adjutant.

Adjt Gen., Adjutant General.

adjudge (ə jŭj′), *v.t.*, **-judged, -judging. 1.** to pronounce formally; decree: *the will was adjudged void.* **2.** to award judicially; assign: *the prize was adjudged to him.* **3.** to decide by a judicial opinion or sentence: *to adjudge a case.* **4.** to sentence or condemn: *he was adjudged to die.* **5.** to deem: *it was adjudged wise to avoid war.* [ME *ajuge(n)*, t. OF: m. *ajugier*, g. L *adjūdicāre*]

adjudicate (ə jōō′dĭ kāt′), *v.*, **-cated, -cating.** —*v.t.* **1.** to pronounce or decree by judicial sentence; settle judicially; pass judgement on; to determine (an issue or dispute) judicially. —*v.i.* **2.** to sit in judgement (fol. by *upon*). **3.** to act as a judge in an amateur competition of the arts. [t. L: m. s. *adjūdicātus*, pp.] —**adju′dica′tive,** *adj.* —**adju′dica′tor,** *n.*

adjudication (ə jōō′dĭ kā′shən), *n.* **1.** the act of adjudicating. **2.** *Law.* **a.** the act of a court in making an order, judgement, or decree. **b.** a judicial decision or sentence.

adjunct (ăj′ŭngkt), *n.* **1.** something added to another thing but not essentially a part of it. **2.** a person joined to another in some duty or service; an assistant. **3.** *Gram.* a qualifying form, word, phrase, etc., depending on some other form, word, phrase, etc. **4.** *Logic.* a non-essential attribute. —*adj.* **5.** joined to a thing or person, esp. subordinately; associated; auxiliary. [t. L: s. *adjunctus*, pp.] —**Syn. 1.** See **addition.**

adjunctive (ə jŭngk′tĭv), *adj.* forming an adjunct. —**adjunc′tively,** *adv.*

adjure (ə jōōə′), *v.t.*, **-jured, -juring. 1.** to charge, bind, or command, earnestly and solemnly, often under oath or the threat of a curse. **2.** to entreat or request earnestly. [ME *adjure(n)*, t. L: m. *adjūrāre*] —**adjuration** (ăj′ōōə-rā′shən), *n.* —**adjuratory** (ə jōōə′rə tə rĭ, -trĭ), *adj.* —**adjur′er, adju′ror,** *n.*

adjust (ə jŭst′), *v.t.* **1.** to fit, as one thing to another, make correspondent or conformable; adapt; accommodate: *to adjust things to a standard.* **2.** to put in working order; regulate; bring to a proper state or position: *to adjust an instrument.* **3.** to settle or bring to a satisfactory state, so that parties are agreed in the result: *to adjust differences.* **4.** *Insurance.* to fix (the sum to be paid on a claim); settle (a claim). **5.** to systematize. **6.** *Mil.* to correct the elevation and deflection of (a gun). —*v.i.* **7.** to adapt oneself; become adapted. [t. F (obs.): s. *adjuster*, t. ML: m. *adjūstāre*, erroneous Latinization of OF *ajouster*, g. LL *adjuxtāre*] —**adjust′able,** *adj.* —**adjust′ably,** *adv.* —**adjust′er, adjus′tor,** *n.*

—**Syn. 2.** ADJUST, ADAPT, ALTER in their literal meanings imply making necessary or desirable changes (as in position, shape, and the like). TO ADJUST is to move into the proper position for use: *to adjust the eyepiece of a telescope.* TO ADAPT is to make a change in character, to make something useful in a new way: *to adapt a paperclip to a hairpin.* TO ALTER is to change the appearance but not the use: *to alter the height of a table.* **3.** arrange, rectify; reconcile.

adjustable-pitch (ə jŭst′ĭ bl pĭch′), *adj.* *Aeron.* (of a propeller) having blades whose pitch can be changed while the propeller is stationary to suit various conditions of flight.

adjustment (ə jŭst′mənt), *n.* **1.** the act of adjusting; act of adapting to a given purpose. **2.** the state of being adjusted; orderly relation of parts or elements. **3.** a means of adjusting: *the adjustment of a microscope.* **4.** *Sociol.* a process of fitting individual or collective patterns of activity to other such patterns carried out with some awareness or purposefulness. **5.** *Insurance.* the act of ascertaining the amount of indemnity which the party insured is entitled to receive under the policy, and of settling the claim. **6.** a settlement of a disputed account or claim.

adjutant (ăj′ə tənt), *n.* **1.** *Mil.* a staff officer who assists the commanding officer. **2.** an assistant. **3.** the adjutant bird. [t. L: s. *adjūtans*, ppr., aiding] —**ad′jutancy,** *n.*

adjutant bird, a large stork, *Leptoptilus dubius*, of India. Also, **adjutant crane, adjutant stork.**

adjutant general, *pl.* **adjutants general.** *Mil.* **1.** (in the British Army). **a.** the head of a department of the general staff. **b.** an executive officer of a general. **2.** *U.S.* **a. the Adjutant General,** the chief administrative officer of the Army. **b.** a member of the Adjutant General's Department, from which adjutants for higher command are assigned. **3.** *U.S.* a high, often the highest, officer of the National Guard of a state or territory.

adjuvant (ăj′ə vənt), *adj.* **1.** serving to help or assist. —*n.* **2.** a person or thing aiding or helping. **3.** *Med.* whatever aids in removing or preventing a disease, esp. a substance added to a prescription to aid the operation of the main ingredient. [t. L: s. *adjuvans*, ppr.]

Adler (ăd′lə; *Ger.* àd′lər), *n.* **Alfred,** 1870–1937, Austrian psychiatrist and psychologist. —**Adlerian** (ăd lĭə′rĭ ən), *adj.*

ad lib., ad libitum.

ad-lib (ăd lĭb′), *v.i.*, *v.t.*, **-libbed, -libbing.** *Colloq.* to improvise, as notes, words, or business, during rehearsal or performance. [v. use of AD LIB.]

ad libitum (ăd lĭb′ĭ təm), *Latin.* at pleasure; to any extent; without restriction: used in music to indicate that the manner of performance of a passage is left to the discretion of the performer. *Abbrev.*: **ad lib.**

ad litteram (ăd lĭt′ə răm′), *Latin.* to the letter; exactly. One cites an author *verbatim* and *ad litteram.*

ad loc., (L *ad locum*) at or to the place.

Adm., 1. Admiral. 2. Admiralty.

ad majorem Dei gloriam (ăd′ mä jô′rĕm dā′ē glô′rĭ ăm′), *Latin.* for the greater glory of God (motto of the Jesuit order).

adman (ăd′măn′), *n.* one who takes part in advertising, esp. via the mass media. [short for *advertisement man*]

admass (ăd′măs′), *n.* the consumers who make up the audience of advertising via the mass media. [short for *advertisement mass*]

admeasure (ăd mĕzh′ə), *v.t.*, **-ured, -uring.** to measure off or out; apportion. [f. AD- + MEASURE; r. ME *amesure*, t. OF: m. *amesurer*, g. LL *admēnsūrāre*]

admeasurement (ăd mĕzh′ə mənt), *n.* **1.** the process of measuring. **2.** the number, dimensions, or measure of anything. **3.** apportionment.

Admetus (ăd mē′təs), *n. Gk Legend.* a Thessalian king, one of the Argonauts and husband of Alcestis.

adminicle (əd mĭn′ĭ kl), *n.* an aid; auxiliary. [t. L: m. s. *adminiculum* a prop] —**adminicular** (ăd′mĭ nĭk′yŏŏ lə), *adj.*

administer (əd mĭn′ĭs tə), *v.t.* **1.** to manage (affairs, a government, etc.); have charge of the execution of: *to administer laws.* **2.** to bring into use or operation; dispense: *to administer justice.* **3.** to make application of; give: *to administer medicine.* **4.** to tender or impose: *to administer an oath.* **5.** *Law.* to manage or dispose of, as the deceased's estate by an executor or administrator, or a trust estate by a trustee. —*v.i.* **6.** to contribute assistance; bring aid or supplies (fol. by *to*): *to administer to the needs of the poor.* **7.** to perform the duties of an administrator. [t. L: m. s. *administrāre*; r. ME *amynistre*, t. OF: m. *aministrer*] —**administrable** (əd mĭn′ĭs trə bl), *adj.* —**administrant** (əd mĭn′ĭs trənt), *adj.*, *n.* —**Syn.** **1.** conduct, control. See **rule.** **3.** apply.

administrate (əd mĭn′ĭs trāt′), *v.t.*, **-trated, -trating.** to administer.

administration (əd mĭn′ĭs trā′shən), *n.* **1.** the management or direction of any office or employment. **2.** the function of a political state in exercising its governmental duties. **3.** any body of men entrusted with administrative powers. **4.** the duty or duties of an administrator. **5.** *Chiefly U.S.* the political leaders of a country who wield power; the government. **6.** *Chiefly U.S.* the period of service of a government. **7.** *U.S.* those executive functions of government, both general and local, which are neither legislative nor judicial. **8.** *Law.* management of the estate of a deceased person by an executor or administrator, or of a trust estate by a trustee. **9.** the act of dispensing, esp. formally: *administration of the sacraments.* **10.** the act of tendering: *the administration of an oath.* **11.** the applying of a medicine, etc.

administrative (əd mĭn′ĭs trə tĭv), *adj.* pertaining to administration; executive: *administrative ability, problems, etc.* —**admin′istratively,** *adv.*

administrative law, law relating to the powers, duties, and organization of public administrative authorities.

administrator (əd mĭn′ĭs trā′tə), *n.* **1.** one who directs or manages affairs of any kind. **2.** a person with a talent for managing or organizing: *he is a born administrator.* **3.** *Law.* a person appointed by a court to take charge of the estate of a person who died without appointing an executor. [t. L]

administratix (əd mĭn′ĭs trā′trĭks), *n.*, *pl.* **-trices** (-trĭ sēz′). *Law.* a female administrator.

admirable (ăd′mə rə bl), *adj.* worthy of admiration; exciting approval, reverence, or affection; excellent. [t. L: m. s. *admīrābilis*] —**ad′mirableness,** *n.* —**ad′mirably,** *adv.* —**Syn.** estimable, praiseworthy.

admiral (ăd′mə rəl), *n.* **1.** the commander-in-chief of a navy (in Britain formerly the *Lord High Admiral*). **2.** a naval officer of the highest rank. **3.** a naval officer of high rank. The grades in the Royal Navy are: **admiral of the fleet, admiral, vice-admiral** and **rear-admiral.** **4.** the ship of an admiral; flagship. **5. a.** the master of a fishing fleet. **b.** the chief ship in it. **6.** any of various butterflies, as the **red admiral** (*Vanessa atalanta*). [var. of ME *amiral*, t. OF, t. Ar: m. *amīr al* (chief of) in various phrases, e.g. *amīr al bahr* commander of the sea; var. *admiral* arose by assoc. with L *admīrābilis* admirable, etc.] —**ad′miralship′,** *n.*

admiralty (ăd′mə rəl tĭ), *n.*, *pl.* **-ties,** *adj.* —*n.* **1.** the office or jurisdiction of an admiral. **2.** the officials or the department of state having charge of naval affairs (in Britain now the **Admiralty Board,** part of the Ministry of Defence). **3. the Admiralty,** the official building in London which formerly housed the admiralty (def. 2). —*adj.* **4.** pertaining to the sea: *admiralty law.*

Admiralty Islands, a group of islands in the SW Pacific, N of New Guinea: under Australian administration. 18,835 pop. (1962); ab. 800 sq. mi.

Admiralty Range, a mountain range in Antarctica, NW of the Ross Sea.

admiration (ăd′mə rā′shən), *n.* **1.** a feeling of wonder, pleasure, and approbation. **2.** the act of looking on or contemplating with pleasure: *admiration of a pretty girl.* **3.** an object of wonder or approbation: *she was the admiration of everyone.* **4.** *Archaic.* wonder. —**Syn.** **1.** approval; esteem; veneration.

admire (əd mī′ə), *v.*, **-mired, -miring.** —*v.t.* **1.** to regard with wonder, pleasure, and approbation. **2.** to regard with wonder or surprise (now usually ironical or sarcastic): *I admire your audacity.* —*v.i.* **3.** to feel or express admiration. **4.** *U.S. Dial.* to like or desire (to do something). [t. L: m. s. *admīrārī* wonder at] —**admir′ingly,** *adv.* —**Syn.** **1.** esteem; revere, venerate.

admirer (əd mī′ə rə), *n.* **1.** one who admires. **2.** a lover.

admissible (əd mĭs′ə bl), *adj.* **1.** that may be allowed or conceded; allowable. **2.** capable or worthy of being admitted. **3.** *Law.* allowable as evidence. —**admis′sibil′ity, admis′sibleness,** *n.* —**admis′sibly,** *adv.*

admission (əd mĭsh′ən), *n.* **1.** the act of allowing to enter; entrance afforded by permission, by provision or existence of means, or by the removal of obstacles: *the admission of aliens into a country.* **2.** power or permission to enter: *to grant a person admission.* **3.** the price paid for entrance, as to a theatre, etc. **4.** the act or condition of being received or accepted in a position or office; appointment: *admission to the practice of law.* **5.** confession of a charge, an error, or a crime; acknowledgement: *his admission of the theft solved the mystery.* **6.** an acknowledgement of the truth of something. **7.** a point or statement admitted; concession. [t. L: s. *admissio*] —**Syn.** **1.** See **entrance**[1].

admissive (əd mĭs′ĭv), *adj.* tending to admit.

admit (əd mĭt′), *v.*, **-mitted, -mitting.** —*v.t.* **1.** to allow to enter; grant or afford entrance to: *to admit a student to college.* **2.** to give right or means of entrance to. **3.** to permit; allow. **4.** to permit to exercise a certain function or privilege: *admitted to the bar.* **5.** to allow as valid: *to admit the force of an argument.* **6.** to have capacity for the admission of at one time: *this passage admits two abreast.* **7.** to acknowledge; confess: *he admitted his guilt.* **8.** to grant in argument; concede: *the fact is admitted.* —*v.i.* **9.** to leave room for (fol. by *of*): *this situation admits of no other solution.* **10.** to give access; grant entrance: *this key admits to the garden.* [t. L: m. s. *admittere*; r. late ME *amitte(n)*, t. F: m. *amettre*] —**admit′ter,** *n.* —**Syn.** **7.** own; avow. See **acknowledge.**

admittance (əd mĭt′ns), *n.* **1.** permission to enter; the power or right of entrance: *admittance into the church.* **2.** the act of admitting. **3.** actual entrance. **4.** *Elect.* the reciprocal of impedance. —**Syn.** **1.** See **entrance**[1].

admittedly (əd mĭt′ĭd lĭ), *adv.* by acknowledgement; confessedly: *he was admittedly the one who had lost the documents.*

admix (əd mĭks′), *v.t.*, *v.i.* to mingle with or add to something else. [back-formation from ME *admixt*, t. L: s. *admixtus*, pp., mingled with]

admixture (əd mĭks′chə), *n.* **1.** the act of mixing. **2.** the state of being mixed. **3.** anything added; any alien element or ingredient.

admonish (əd mŏn′ĭsh), *v.t.* **1.** to counsel against something; caution or advise. **2.** to notify of or reprove for a fault, esp. mildly: *to admonish someone as a brother.* **3.** to recall or incite to duty; remind: *to admonish someone about his obligations.* [back-formation from ADMONITION; r. ME *amonesten*, t. OF] —**admon′isher,** *n.* —**admon′ishingly,** *adv.* —**admon′ishment,** *n.* —**Syn.** **1.** See **warn.** **2.** rebuke, censure.

admonition (ăd′mə nĭsh′ən), *n.* the act of admonishing; counsel or advice; gentle reproof; caution. [t. L: s. *admonitio*; r. ME *amonicioun*, t. OF]

admonitor (əd mŏn′ĭ tə), *n.* an admonisher. [t. L]

admonitory (əd mŏn′ĭ tə rĭ, -trĭ), *adj.* tending or serving to admonish: *an admonitory gesture.*

adnate (ăd′nāt), *adj. Bot., Zool., etc.* grown fast to something; congenitally attached. [t. L: m. s. *adnātus* born to]

adnation (ăd nā′shən), *n.* adnate condition.

ad nauseam (ăd nô′zĭ ăm′, -sĭ-), *Latin.* to a sickening or disgusting extent.

adnoun (ăd′noun′), *n. Gram.* an adjective in its substantival use: *the useful.* The more common term is *adjective used as a noun.* [f. AD- + NOUN, modelled on ADVERB] —**adnominal** (əd nŏm′ĭ nəl), *adj.*

A, Adnate stipule

ado (ə dōō′), *n.* activity; bustle; fuss. [d. ME *ado*, *at do* to do]

—**Syn.** ADO, TO-DO, COMMOTION, STIR, TUMULT suggest a great deal of fuss and noise. ADO implies a confused bustle of activity,

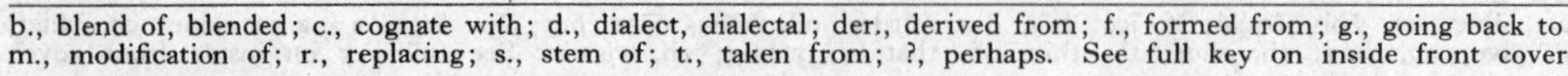

a considerable emotional upset, and a great deal of talking: *much ado about nothing.* TO-DO, now more commonly used, may mean merely excitement and noise, and may be pleasant or unpleasant: *a great to-do over a film star.* COMMOTION suggests a noisy confusion and babble: *commotion at the scene of an accident.* STIR suggests excitement and noise, with a hint of emotional cause: *the report was followed by a tremendous stir in the city.* TUMULT suggests disorder with noise and violence: *a tumult as the mob stormed the Bastille.*

adobe (ə dō′bĭ), *n.* **1.** the sun-dried brick in common use in countries having little rainfall. **2.** a yellow silt or clay, deposited by rivers, used to make bricks. **3.** a building constructed of adobe. **4.** a dark, heavy soil, containing clay. [t. Sp.]

adobe flat, a plain consisting of adobe deposited by short-lived rainfall or thaw streams, usually having a smooth or unmarked surface.

adolescence (ăd′ə lĕs′əns), *n.* **1.** the transition period between puberty and adult stages of development; youth. It extends from about 14 to 25 years of age in man, and from 12 to 21 in woman. **2.** the quality or state of being adolescent; youthfulness. Also, **ad′oles′cency.**

adolescent (ăd′ə lĕs′ənt), *adj.* **1.** growing to adulthood: youthful. **2.** having the characteristics of adolescence or of an adolescent. —*n.* **3.** an adolescent person. [t. L: s. *adolescens*, ppr.]

Adonai (ăd′ō nī′, -nā′ī), *n.* **1.** Also, **Adonoy** (ăd′ō noi′). *Hebrew.* a title of reverence for God. **2.** *Eccles.* the second person of the Trinity; Jesus Christ. [t. Hebrew: lit., my Lord; spoken in place of the ineffable name YAHWEH]

Adonic (ə dō′nĭk), *adj.* **1.** *Pros.* denoting a verse consisting of a dactyl (– ⏑ ⏑) followed by a spondee (– –) or trochee (– ⏑). **2.** of Adonis. —*n.* **3.** *Pros.* an Adonic verse or line. [t. ML: s. *adōnicus*]

Adonis (ə dō′nĭs), *n.* **1.** *Gk Myth.* a favourite of Aphrodite, killed by a wild boar, but permitted by Zeus to pass four months every year in the lower world with Persephone, four with Aphrodite, and four wherever else he chose. In another account he spent half the year on earth and thus symbolically represented the vegetation cycle. **2.** (*often l.c.*) a very handsome young man. **3.** (*l.c.*) a beau or dandy.

adonize (ăd′ō nīz′), *v.i.*, **-nized, -nizing.** *Colloq.* to adorn or dandify oneself. Also, **adonise.**

adopt (ə dŏpt′), *v.t.* **1.** to choose for or take to oneself; make one's own by selection or assent: *to adopt a name or idea.* **2.** to take as one's own child, specif. by a formal legal act. **3.** to vote to accept: *the House adopted the report.* **4.** to take or receive into any kind of new relationship: *to adopt a person as an heir.* **5.** to nominate (a candidate) for political office. [t. L: s. *adoptāre*] —**adopt′able,** *adj.* —**adopt′er,** *n.* —**adop′tion,** *n.*

adoptive (ə dŏp′tĭv), *adj.* **1.** related by adoption: *an adoptive father or son.* **2.** tending to adopt. —**adop′tively,** *adv.*

adorable (ə dô′rə bl), *adj.* **1.** worthy of being adored. **2.** *Colloq.* arousing strong liking. —**ador′ableness, ador′abil′ity,** *n.* —**ador′ably,** *adv.*

adoration (ăd′ô rā′shən), *n.* **1.** the act of paying honour as to a divine being; worship. **2.** reverent homage. **3.** fervent and devoted love.

adore (ə dô′), *v.*, **adored, adoring.** —*v.t.* **1.** to regard with the utmost esteem, love, and respect. **2.** to honour as divine; worship: *to be adored as gods.* **3.** *Colloq.* to like greatly. —*v.i.* **4.** to worship. [t. LL: m. s. *adorāre* worship, L address; r. ME *aoure(n)*, t. OF: m. *ao(u)rer*] —**ador′er,** *n.* —**ador′ing,** *adj.* —**ador′ingly,** *adv.* —**Syn. 1.** reverence, revere, venerate.

adorn (ə dôn′), *v.t.* **1.** to make pleasing or more attractive; embellish; add lustre to: *the piety which adorns his character.* **2.** to increase or lend beauty to, as by dress or ornaments; decorate: *garlands of flowers adorning her hair.* [t. L: s. *adornāre*; r. ME *aourne*, t. OF: m. *ao(u)rner*] —**adorn′er,** *n.* —**adorn′ingly,** *adv.* —**Syn. 2.** beautify; deck, bedeck.

adornment (ə dôn′mənt), *n.* **1.** ornament: *the adornments and furnishings of a room.* **2.** an adorning; ornamentation: *personal adornment.*

adown (ə doun′), *adv., prep. Poetic.* down.

A.D.P., automatic data processing.

ad patres (ăd pä′trēz), *Latin.* to (his) fathers; dead.

adpressed (ăd prĕst′), *adj.* pressed closely against or fitting closely to something. Also, **appressed.**

ad quem (ăd kwĕm′), *Latin.* at or to which; the goal.

Adrastus (ə drăs′təs), *n. Gk Legend.* a king of Argos and leader of the Seven against Thebes.

ad rem (ăd rĕm′), *Latin.* to the matter or thing. To reply *ad rem* is to keep to the subject being considered.

adrenal (ə drē′nəl), *Anat., Zool.* —*adj.* **1.** situated near or on the kidneys; suprarenal. **2.** of or produced by the adrenal glands. —*n.* **3.** one of the adrenal glands. [f. AD- + s. L *rēnēs* kidneys + -AL[1]]

adrenalectomy (ə drē′nə lĕk′tə mĭ), *n.*, *pl.* **-mies.** *Surg.* the removal of one or both adrenal glands.

adrenal glands, *Anat., Zool.* suprarenal glands.

adrenaline (ə drĕn′ə lĭn, -ə lēn′), *n.* **1.** a white or whitish crystalline compound, $C_9H_{13}NO_3$, a hormone produced by the adrenal medulla; epinephrine. **2.** this substance purified from the suprarenal secretion of animals and used as a drug to speed heart action, contract blood vessels, etc. Also, **adrenalin.**

adret (ăd′rĕt; *Fr.* à drė′), *n.* the side of a hill facing the equator and therefore receiving the maximum sunshine. [t. F: Swiss dial. for *à droite* on the right]

Adrian (ā′drĭ ən), *n.* **1.** name of six popes, esp. **Adrian I,** died A.D. 795, pope A.D. 772–795, and **Adrian IV** *c.* 1100–59, pope 1154–59, the only Englishman ever to become pope. **2.** Hadrian. **3. Edgar Douglas, 1st Baron,** born 1889, English physiologist.

Adrianople (ā′drĭ ə nō′pl), *n.* former name of **Edirne.**

Adriatic Sea (ā′drĭ ăt′ĭk), an arm of the Mediterranean between Italy and Yugoslavia. ab. 500 mi. long.

Adriatic Sea

adrift (ə drĭft′), *adv., adj.* **1.** not fastened by any kind of moorings; at the mercy of winds and currents. **2.** swayed by any chance impulse. **3.** *Colloq.* confused; wide of the mark. [f. A-[1] + DRIFT]

adroit (ə droit′), *adj.* expert in the use of the hand or mind; possessing readiness of resource; ingenious. [t. AF, der. phrase *à droit* rightly, *droit* g. L *dīrectus* straight] —**adroit′ly,** *adv.* —**adroit′ness,** *n.* —**Syn.** dexterous; skilful, clever; deft.

à droite (*Fr.* à drwàt′), *French.* to (or on) the right.

adscititious (ăd′sĭ tĭsh′əs), *adj.* added or derived from without; supplemental; additional. [f. s. L *adscītus*, pp., derived + -ITIOUS]

adscript (ăd′skrĭpt), *adj.* written after (distinguished from *subscript, superscript*). [t. L: s. *adscriptus*, pp.]

adscription (əd skrĭp′shən), *n.* ascription.

adsorb (əd sôb′), *v.t.* to gather (a gas, liquid, or dissolved substance) on a surface in a condensed layer, as when charcoal adsorbs gases. [f. AD- + s. L *sorbēre* suck in, modelled on ABSORB] —**adsorb′ent,** *adj., n.* —**adsorption** (əd sôp′shən), *n.* —**adsorp′tive,** *adj., n.*

adularia (ăd′yŏŏ lĕə′rĭ ə), *n. Mineral.* a transparent or translucent variety of orthoclase, often pearly or opalescent, as the moonstone. [named after the *Adula* mountain group in Switzerland. See -ARIA]

adulate (ăd′yŏŏ lāt′), *v.t.*, **-lated, -lating.** to show pretended or undiscriminating devotion to; flatter servilely. [t. L: m. s. *adūlātus*, pp.] —**ad′ula′tion,** *n.* —**ad′ula′ter,** *n.* —**adulatory** (ăd′ yŏŏ lā′tə rĭ), *adj.*

adult (ə dŭlt′, ăd′ŭlt), *adj.* **1.** having attained full size and strength; grown up; mature: *an adult person, animal, or plant.* **2.** pertaining to or designed for adults: *adult education.* —*n.* **3.** a person who is grown up or of age. **4.** a full-grown animal or plant. **5.** *Common Law.* a person who has attained 21, or in some circumstances 18, years of age. **6.** *Civil Law.* a male after attaining 14, or a female after attaining 12, years of age. [t. L: s. *adultus*, pp.] —**adult′hood,** *n.* —**adult′ness,** *n.*

adult education, the part-time education of adults, esp. by evening classes.

adulterant (ə dŭl′tə rənt), *n.* **1.** a substance used for adulterating. —*adj.* **2.** adulterating.

adulterate (*v.* ə dŭl′tə rāt′; *adj.* ə dŭl′tə rĭt, -tə rāt′), *v.*, **-rated, -rating,** *adj.* —*v.t.* **1.** to debase by adding inferior materials or elements; make impure by admixture; use cheaper, inferior, or less desirable goods in the production or marketing of (any professedly genuine article): *to adulterate food.* —*adj.* **2.** adulterated. **3.** adulterous. [t. L: m. s. *adulterātus*, pp., defiled] —**adul′tera′tor,** *n.*

adulteration (ə dŭl′tə rā′shən), *n.* **1.** the act or process of adulterating. **2.** the state of being adulterated. **3.** something adulterated.

adulterer (ə dŭl′tə rə), *n.* a person, esp. a man, guilty of adultery. —**adulteress** (ə dŭl′tə rĭs), *n.fem.*

adulterine (ə dŭl′tə rĭn, -tə rīn′), *adj.* **1.** characterized by adulteration; spurious. **2.** born of adultery. **3.** of or involving adultery. [t. L: m. s. *adulterīnus*]

adulterous (ə dŭl′tə rəs), *adj.* **1.** characterized by, pertaining to, or guilty of adultery. **2.** *Obs.* spurious.

adultery (ə dŭl′tə rĭ), *n.*, *pl.* **-teries.** voluntary sexual intercourse between a married person and any other than the lawful spouse. [t. L: m. s. *adulterium*; r. ME *avoutrie*, t. OF]

adumbral (ăd ŭm′brəl), *adj.* shadowy; shady.

adumbrate (ăd′ŭm brāt′), *v.t.*, **-brated, -brating. 1.** to give a faint shadow or resemblance of; outline or shadow forth. **2.** to foreshadow; prefigure. **3.** to darken or conceal partially; overshadow. [t. L: m. s. *adumbrātus*, pp., shadowed] —**ad′umbra′tion,** *n.*

adumbrative (ăd ŭm′brə tĭv), *adj.* shadowing forth; indicative. —**adum′bratively,** *adv.*

adunc (ə dŭngk′), *adj.* curved inwards; hooked. Also, **aduncous** (ə dŭng′kəs), **aduncate** (ăd′ŭng kāt′, ə dŭng′-kāt). [t. L: s. *aduncus* crooked] —**aduncity** (ə dŭn′ sĭ tĭ), *n.*

adust (ə dŭst′), *adj.* **1.** dried or darkened as by heat; burnt; scorched. **2.** atrabilious; sallow; gloomy. [t. L: s. *adūstus*, pp.]

ad utrumque paratus (ăd′o͞o tro͞om′kwā pə rä′to͞os), *Latin.* ready for either alternative.

Aduwa (ăd′o͞o wə), *n.* a town in N Ethiopia: the Ethiopians defeated the Italians here 1896. 6000 (est. 1964).

adv., 1. adverb. **2.** adverbial. **3.** adverbially. **4.** advocate.

ad val., ad valorem.

ad valorem (ăd′və lô′ rĕm), in proportion to the value. An *ad valorem* duty charged on goods entering a country is fixed at a percentage of the customs value as stated on the invoice. [t. L]

advance (əd väns′), *v.*, **-vanced, -vancing,** *n.*, *adj.* —*v.t.* **1.** to move or bring forwards in place: *the troops were advanced to the new position.* **2.** to bring to view or notice; propose: *to advance an argument.* **3.** to improve; further: *to advance one's interests.* **4.** to raise in rank; promote. **5.** to raise in rate: *to advance the price.* **6.** to bring forwards in time; accelerate: *to advance growth.* **7.** to supply beforehand; furnish on credit, or before goods are delivered or work is done. **8.** to supply or pay in expectation of reimbursement: *to advance money on loan.* **9.** *Archaic.* to raise, as a banner.
—*v.i.* **10.** to move or go forwards; proceed: *the troops advanced.* **11.** to improve or make progress; grow: *to advance in knowledge or rank.* **12.** to increase in quantity, value, price, etc.: *stocks advanced three points.*
—*n.* **13.** a moving forwards; progress in space: *advance to the sea.* **14.** advancement; promotion: *an advance in rank.* **15.** a step forwards; actual progress in any course of action: *the advance of knowledge.* **16.** (*usually pl.*) an effort to bring about acquaintance, accord, understanding, etc. **17.** addition to price; rise in price: *an advance in cottons.* **18.** *Com.* **a.** a giving beforehand; a furnishing of something before an equivalent is received. **b.** the money or goods thus furnished. **c.** a loan against securities, or in advance of payment due. **19.** *Mil.* (formerly) the order or a signal to advance. **20.** *U.S.* the leading body of an army. **21. in advance, a.** before; in front. **b.** beforehand; ahead of time: *he insisted on paying his rent in advance.*
—*adj.* **22.** made or given in advance: *an advance payment.* **23.** issued in advance: *an advance copy.* **24.** advanced; having progressed beyond others or beyond the average: *an advance student.* **25.** going before. [ME *avaunce(n)*, t. OF: m. *avancier*, g. LL *abanteāre*, der. *abante* (f. *ab* + *ante*) from before] —**advanc′er,** *n.*
—**Syn. 2.** adduce; propound, offer. **5.** increase. **6.** quicken, hasten, speed up. **10.** ADVANCE, MOVE ON, PROCEED all imply movement forwards. ADVANCE applies to forward movement, esp. towards an objective: *to advance to a platform.* PROCEED emphasizes movement as from one place to another, and often implies continuing after a halt: *to proceed on one's journey.* MOVE ON, a more informal expression, is similar in meaning to PROCEED; it does not, however, imply a definite goal: *the crowd was told to move on.* **11.** thrive, flourish; prosper. **12.** rise. **16.** overture; proposal.

advanced (əd vänst′), *adj.* **1.** placed in advance: *with foot advanced.* **2.** far on in progress; beyond the average: *an advanced class in French.* **3.** far on in time: *an advanced age.*

advance guard, a body of troops going before the main force to clear the way, guard against surprise, etc. Also, **advanced guard.**

Advanced Level, *Educ.* the second grade of the General Certificate of Education, for which public examinations are taken in Britain and elsewhere, at sixth-form level, qualifying students for entry into colleges, universities, etc. Also, **A Level.**

advanced student, *Educ.* one studying at a university, usually for a higher degree.

advancement (əd väns′mənt), *n.* **1.** the act of moving forwards. **2.** promotion in rank or standing; preferment: *his hopes of advancement failed.* **3.** *Law.* money or property given during his lifetime by a person subsequently dying intestate and deducted from the intestate share of the recipient.

advantage (əd vän′tĭj), *n.*, *v.*, **-taged, -taging.** —*n.* **1.** any state, circumstance, opportunity, or means specially favourable to success, interest, or any desired end: *the advantage of a good education.* **2.** benefit; gain; profit: *it is to his advantage.* **3.** superiority or ascendancy (often fol. by *over* or *of*): *to have the advantage of age.* **4.** a position of superiority (often fol. by *over* or *of*): *don't let him have the advantage of us.* **5.** *Tennis.* the first point scored after deuce, or the resulting state of the score; vantage. **6. take advantage of, a.** to make use of: *to take advantage of an opportunity.* **b.** to impose upon: *to take advantage of someone.* **7. to advantage,** with good effect; advantageously. —*v.t.* **8.** to be of service to; yield profit or gain to; benefit. [ME *avantage*, t. OF, der. *avant* before, forward, g. LL *abante.* See ADVANCE]
—**Syn. 2.** ADVANTAGE, BENEFIT, PROFIT all mean something that is of use or value. ADVANTAGE is anything that places one in an improved position, esp. in coping with competition or difficulties: *it is to one's advantage to have travelled widely.* BENEFIT is anything that promotes the welfare or improves the state of a person or group: *a benefit to society.* PROFIT is any valuable, useful, or helpful gain: *profit from trade or experience.*

advantageous (ăd′vən tā′jəs), *adj.* of advantage; furnishing convenience or opportunity; profitable; useful; beneficial: *an advantageous position.* —**ad′vanta′geously,** *adv.* —**ad′vanta′geousness,** *n.*

advection (əd vĕk′shən), *n.* **1.** the transfer of heat by horizontal movements of air; horizontal convection. **2.** the movement of air horizontally. [t. L: s. *advectio* a carrying]

advent (ăd′vənt), *n.* **1.** a coming into place, view, or being; arrival: *the advent of death.* **2.** (*often cap.*) the coming of Christ into the world. **3.** (*cap.*) a season (including four Sundays) preceding Christmas, commemorative of Christ's coming. **4. Second Advent,** the second coming of Christ to establish a personal reign upon the earth as its king. [ME, t. L: s. *adventus* arrival]

Adventist (ăd′vən tĭst), *n.* a member of any of certain Christian denominations which maintain that the second coming of Christ is near at hand; Second Adventist. —**Ad′ventism,** *n.*

adventitious (ăd′vĕn tĭsh′əs), *adj.* **1.** accidentally or casually acquired; added extrinsically; foreign. **2.** *Bot.*, *Zool.* appearing in an abnormal or unusual position or place, as a root. [t. L: m. *adventicius* coming from abroad] —**ad′venti′tiously,** *adv.* —**ad′venti′tiousness,** *n.*

adventive (əd vĕn′tĭv), *Bot.*, *Zool.* —*adj.* **1.** not native and usually not yet well established, as exotic plants or animals. —*n.* **2.** an adventive plant or animal.

Advent Sunday, the first Sunday in Advent, being the Sunday nearest to St Andrew's Day (Nov. 30th).

adventure (əd vĕn′chə), *n.*, *v.*, **-tured, -turing.** —*n.* **1.** an undertaking of uncertain outcome; a hazardous enterprise. **2.** an exciting experience. **3.** participation in exciting undertakings or enterprises: *the spirit of adventure.* **4.** a commercial or financial speculation of any kind; a venture. **5.** *Obs.* peril; danger. **6.** *Obs.* chance. —*v.t.* **7.** to risk or hazard. **8.** to take the chance of; dare. **9.** to venture to say or utter: *to adventure an opinion.* —*v.i.* **10.** to take the risk involved. **11.** to venture. [ME *aventure*, t. OF, g. L *adventūra*, future p., (sc. *rēs*) (a thing) about to happen]

adventurer (əd vĕn′chə rə), *n.* **1.** one who adventures. **2.** a seeker of fortune in daring enterprises; a soldier of fortune. **3.** one who undertakes any great commercial risk; a speculator. **4.** a seeker of fortune by underhand or equivocal means.

adventuresome (əd vĕn′chə səm), *adj.* bold; daring; adventurous.

adventuress (əd vĕn′chə rĭs), *n.* **1.** a female adventurer. **2.** a woman who schemes to win social position, money, etc., by equivocal methods.

adventurism (əd vĕn′chə rĭz′əm), *n.* defiance of accepted standards of behaviour.

adventurous (əd vĕn′chə rəs), *adj.* **1.** inclined or willing to engage in adventures. **2.** attended with risk; requiring courage. —**adven′turously,** *adv.* —**adven′turousness,** *n.*
—**Syn. 1.** daring, venturous, venturesome.

adverb (ăd′vûb′), *n.* **1.** one of the major parts of speech comprising words used to qualify or limit a verb, a verbal noun (also, in Latin, English, and some other languages, an adjective or another adverb), or an adverbial phrase or clause. An adverbial element expresses some relation of place, time, manner, attendant circumstance, degree, cause, inference, result, condition, exception, concession, purpose, or means. **2.** such a word, as *well* in English *she sings well.* **3.** any word or phrase of similar function or meaning. [earlier *adverbe*, t. L: m. s. *adverbium*] —**adverbial** (əd vû′byəl), *adj.* —**adver′bially,** *adv.* —**ad′verbless,** *adj.*

ad verbum (ăd vû′bəm), *Latin.* to the word; exact in wording according to an original.

adversaria (ăd′və sēə′rĭ ə), *n.pl.* notes or jottings, as in a commonplace book. [t. L]

adversary (ăd′və sə rĭ), *n., pl.* **-saries.** **1.** an unfriendly opponent. **2.** an opponent in a contest; a contestant. **3. the Adversary,** the Devil; Satan. [ME *adversarie*, t. L: m. *adversārius*]

—Syn. 1. ADVERSARY, ANTAGONIST mean a person, a group, or a personified force, contending against another. ADVERSARY suggests an enemy who fights determinedly, continuously, and relentlessly: *a formidable adversary.* ANTAGONIST suggests one who, in hostile spirit, opposes another, often in a particular contest or struggle: *a duel with an antagonist.* **—Ant. 1.** ally, supporter.

adversative (əd vû′sə tĭv), *adj.* **1.** expressing contrariety, opposition, or antithesis: *'but' is an adversative conjunction.* *—n.* **2.** an adversative word or proposition. [t. LL: m. s. *adversātīvus*] **—adver′satively,** *adv.*

adverse (ăd vûs′, ăd′vûs), *adj.* **1.** antagonistic in purpose or effect: *adverse criticism, adverse to slavery.* **2.** opposing one's interests or desire: *adverse fate, fortune, influences, or circumstances.* **3.** being or acting in a contrary direction; opposed or opposing: *adverse winds.* **4.** opposite; confronting: *the adverse page.* **5.** *Bot.* turned towards the axis, as a leaf. **6.** *Law.* **a.** opposed to the examining party in a law suit: *an adverse witness.* **b. adverse possession,** an occupation or possession of land by one who has no lawful title to it, which, if unopposed for a certain period, extinguishes the right and title of the true owner. [ME, t. L: m. *adversus*, pp., turned against, turned towards] **—adverse′ly,** *adv.* **—adverse′ness,** *n.* **—Syn. 1.** hostile, inimical. **2.** unfavourable; unlucky, disastrous. See **contrary.**

adversity (əd vû′sĭ tĭ), *n., pl.* **-ties.** **1.** adverse fortune or fate; a condition marked by misfortune, calamity, or distress: *his struggles with adversity.* **2.** an unfortunate event or circumstance: *the prosperities and adversities of this life.* [ME *adversite*, t. L: m. *adversitas* opposition] **—Syn. 2.** See **affliction.**

advert[1] (əd vût′), *v.i.* **1.** to make a remark or remarks (about or in relation to); refer (fol. by *to*): *he adverted briefly to the occurrences of the day.* **2.** to turn the attention (fol. by *to*). [t. L: s. *advertere* turn to; r. ME *averte(n)*, t. OF: m. *avertir*]

advert[2] (ăd′vût), *n. Colloq.* an advertisement. [shortened form of ADVERTISEMENT]

advertent (əd vû′tnt), *adj.* attentive; heedful. **—advert′ence, advert′ency,** *n.* **—advert′ently,** *adv.*

advertise (ăd′və tīz′), *v.,* **-tised, -tising.** *—v.t.* **1.** to give information to the public concerning; make public announcement of, by publication in periodicals, by printed posters, by broadcasting over the radio, television, etc.: *to advertise a reward.* **2.** to praise the good qualities of, in order to induce the public to buy or invest in. **3.** to offer (an article) for sale or (a vacancy) to applicants, etc., by placing an advertisement in a newspaper, magazine, etc.: *he advertised the post of private secretary.* **4.** *Archaic.* to give notice, advice, or information to; inform. **5.** *Obs.* to admonish; warn. *—v.i.* **6.** to ask (*for*) by placing an advertisement in a newspaper, magazine, etc.: *to advertise for a house to rent.* Also, *U.S.,* **advertize.** [ME *advertise(n)*, t. MF: m. *advertiss-*, s. *advertir*, t. L: m. *advertere*] **—ad′vertis′er,** *n.*

advertisement (əd vû′tĭz mənt), *n.* any device or public announcement, as a printed notice in a newspaper, a commercial film on television, a neon sign, etc., designed to attract public attention, bring in custom, etc. Also, *U.S.,* **advertizement.** [ME, t. MF: m. *advertissement*]

advertising (ăd′və tī′zĭng), *n.* **1.** the act or practice of bringing anything, as one's wants or one's business, into public notice, esp. by paid announcements in periodicals, on hoardings, etc., or on television: *to secure customers by advertising.* **2.** paid announcements; advertisements. **3.** the profession of designing and writing advertisements. Also, *U.S.,* **advertizing.**

advice (əd vīs′), *n.* **1.** an opinion recommended, or offered, as worthy to be followed: *I shall act on your advice.* **2.** a communication, esp. from a distance, containing information: *advice from abroad.* [late ME *advyse* (r. ME *avys*, t. OF: m. *avis* opinion), f. L: *ad-* AD- + s. *visum*, pp. neut., what seems best]

—Syn. 1. admonition. ADVICE, COUNSEL are suggestions given by a (presumably) wiser or more highly trained person to one considered in need of guidance. ADVICE is a practical recommendation as to action or conduct: *advice about purchasing land.* COUNSEL is weighty and serious advice, given after careful deliberation: *counsel about one's career.* **2.** information, news, tidings; report.

advisable (əd vī′zə bl), *adj.* **1.** proper to be advised or to be recommended. **2.** open to or desirous of advice. **—advis′abil′ity, advis′ableness,** *n.* **—advis′ably,** *adv.* **—Syn. 1.** expedient, politic, proper, prudent, sensible.

advise (əd vīz′), *v.,* **-vised, -vising.** *—v.t.* **1.** to give counsel to; offer an opinion to, as worthy or expedient to be followed: *I advise you to be cautious.* **2.** to recommend as wise, prudent, etc.: *he advised secrecy.* **3.** to give (a person, etc.) information or notice (fol. by *of*): *the merchants were advised of the risk.* *—v.i.* **4.** to offer counsel; give advice: *I shall act as you advise.* **5.** *Chiefly U.S.* to take counsel (fol. by *with*): *I shall advise with my friends.* [t. LL: m. s. *advīsāre*; r. ME *avise(n)*, t. OF] **—Syn. 1.** admonish, caution. See **warn. 3.** inform, notify, apprise.

advised (əd vīzd′), *adj.* **1.** considered: now chiefly in *ill-advised* or *well-advised.* **2.** informed: *kept thoroughly advised.* **—advisedness** (əd vī′zĭd nĭs), *n.*

advisedly (əd vī′zĭd lĭ), *adv.* after due consideration; deliberately.

advisement (əd vīz′mənt), *n. U.S.; Archaic in Britain.* careful deliberation; consultation: *the application was taken under advisement.*

adviser (əd vī′zə), *n.* **1.** one who gives advice. **2.** *Educ.* a peripatetic specialist who advises schools on the organization and teaching of a particular subject. **3.** *U.S.* a teacher who helps students choose their course of study, etc.

advisory (əd vī′zə rĭ), *adj.* of, or giving, advice; having power to advise: *an advisory council.*

advocaat (ăd′vō kä′, -kät′), *n.* **1.** a liqueur containing brandy, eggs and flavouring. **2.** *Archaic.* a similar drink used for medicinal purposes. [t. D, orig. *advocatenborrel* the drink of advocates]

advocacy (ăd′və kə sĭ), *n.* an act of pleading for, supporting, or recommending; active espousal.

advocate (*v.* ăd′və kāt′; *n.* ăd′və kĭt, -kāt′), *v.,* **-cated, -cating,** *n.* *—v.t.* **1.** to plead in favour of; support or urge by argument; recommend publicly: *he advocated isolationism.* *—n.* **2.** one who defends, vindicates, or espouses a cause by argument; an upholder; a defender (fol. by *of*): *an advocate of peace.* **3.** one who pleads for or in behalf of another; intercessor. **4.** *Chiefly Scot., sometimes English, and formerly U.S.* one who pleads the cause of another in a court of law; a barrister. **5. Lord Advocate,** the chief law officer in Scotland. [t. L: m. s. *advocātus* (prop. pp.) one summoned to help another (in legal case); r. ME *avocat*, t. OF] **—ad′voca′tor,** *n.*

advocation (ăd′və kā′shən), *n.* **1.** *Law.* the calling of an action before itself by a superior (papal or Scottish) court. **2.** *Obs.* advocacy. **3.** *Obs.* the act of summoning.

advocatory (əd vŏk′ə tə rĭ), *adj.* of an advocate or his functions.

advocatus diaboli (ăd′və kä′təs dī ăb′ə lī′), *Medieval Latin.* **1.** the devil's advocate. **2.** an adverse critic, esp. of what is deemed good; a detractor.

advowson (əd vou′zən), *n. Law.* the right of presentation to a benefice. [t. AF; r. ME *avoweson*, t. OF: m. *avoeson*, g. L *advocātio*]

advt, advertisement.

adynamia (ăd′ĭ nā′myə), *n. Pathol.* weakness; debility; asthenia. [t. Gk]

adynamic (ăd′ĭ năm′ĭk, ā′dī-), *adj. Pathol.* lacking strength; asthenic.

adytum (ăd′ĭ təm), *n., pl.* **-ta** (-tə). **1.** (in ancient worship) a sacred place which the public was not allowed to enter; an inner shrine. **2.** the most sacred or reserved part of any place of worship. [t. L, t. Gk: m. *ádyton* not to be entered]

adze (ădz), *n.* a heavy chisel-like steel tool fastened at right angles to a wooden handle, used to dress timber, etc. Also, *U.S.,* **adz.** [ME *adese*, OE *adesa*]

A B

Adze
A, Carpenter's adze;
B, Cooper's adze

ae (ā), *adj. Scot.* one.

æ, **1.** a digraph or ligature appearing in Latin and Latinized Greek words. In English words of Latin or Greek origin, *æ* is now usually reduced to *e*, except generally in proper names (*Caesar*), in words belonging to Roman or Greek antiquities (*aegis*), and in modern words of scientific or technical use (*aecium*). **2.** an early English ligature representing a vowel sound like the *a* in modern *bad.* The long *æ* continued in use until about 1250, but was finally replaced by *e*. The short *æ* was given up by 1150, being replaced usually by *a* but sometimes by *e*.

ae-. For words with initial **ae-,** see also **e-.**

A.E., pen-name of George William **Russell.** Also, **Æ.**

ae., (L *aetatis*) at the age of; aged.

A.E.A., Atomic Energy Authority.

Aeacus (ē′ə kəs), *n. Gk Myth.* a son of Zeus; grandfather of Achilles and a judge in the lower world. Cf. **Minos, Rhadamanthys.**

aecial stage (ē′shĭ əl), *Bot.* the part of the life cycle of the rust fungi in which aecia are formed.

aecidial stage (ē sĭd′ĭ əl), *Bot.* the part of the life cycle of the rust fungi in which aecidia are formed.

aecidium (ē sĭd′ĭ əm), *n.*, *pl.* **-cidia** (-sĭd′ĭ ə). *Bot.* an aecium in which the spores are always formed in chains and enclosed in a cup-shaped peridium. [NL: dim. of Gk *aikía* injury]

aeciospore (ē′sĭ ə spô′), *n. Bot.* a spore borne by an aecium.

aecium (ē′shĭ əm, ē′sĭ-), *n.*, *pl.* **-cia** (-shĭ ə, -sĭ ə). *Bot.* the sorus of rust fungi which arises from the haploid mycelium, commonly accompanied by spermogonia and bearing chainlike or stalked spores. [t. NL: f. m. s. Gk *aikía* an injurious effect + *-ium* -IUM] —**aecial** (ē′shĭ əl, -sĭ əl), *adj.*

aëdes (ā ē′dēz), *n.* **1.** the mosquito, *Aëdes aegypti*, which transmits yellow fever and dengue. **2.** any mosquito of the genus *Aëdes*. [t. NL, t. Gk: unpleasant]

aedicule (ē′dĭ kyōōl′), *n. Archit.* **1.** a small shrine, esp. one between two pillars. **2.** any small building. [t. L: m. s. *aedicula*, dim. of *aedes* temple]

aedile (ē′dīl), *n.* (in ancient Rome) one of a board of magistrates in charge of public buildings, streets, markets, games, etc. [t. L: m. s. *aedīlis*] —**ae′dileship′**, *n.*

Aeëtes (ē ē′tēz), *n. Gk Legend.* a king of Colchis, father of Medea, and custodian of the Golden Fleece.

Aegean (ē jē′ən), *adj.* denoting or pertaining to the civilization which preceded the historic Hellenic period and which flourished in various islands in, and lands adjacent to, the Aegean Sea, as Crete, Argolis, etc. [f. m. s. L *Aegaeus* (t. Gk: m. *Aigaîos*) + -AN]

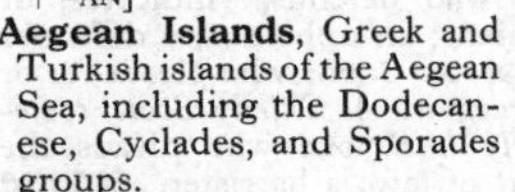

Aegean Sea

Aegean Islands, Greek and Turkish islands of the Aegean Sea, including the Dodecanese, Cyclades, and Sporades groups.

Aegean Sea, an arm of the Mediterranean between Greece and Asia Minor. ab. 350 mi. long; ab. 200 mi. wide.

aegerite (ā′jə rīt′, ē′jə-), *n.* a mineral consisting of a sodium and iron silicate, $Na_2O.Fe_2O_34SiO_2$; acmite. [f. AEGIR + -ITE[1]]

Aegeus (ē′jyōōs, ē′jĭ əs), *n. Gk Legend.* king of Athens and father of Theseus.

Aegina (ē jī′nə), *n.* **1. Gulf of,** a gulf in SE Greece. **2.** an island in this gulf. 10,052 pop. (1963); 32 sq. mi. **3.** a seaport on this island. 5820 (1963).

Aegir (ā′gĭə, ē′jĭə), *n. Scand. Myth.* the sea-god, the husband of Ran. [t. Icel.]

aegis (ē′jĭs), *n.* **1.** *Gk Myth.* **a.** the shield of Zeus. **b.** the shield lent by Zeus to other deities, esp. Athene. **2.** protection; sponsorship: *under the imperial aegis*. [t. L, t. Gk: m. *aigís*, lit., a goatskin]

Aegisthus (ē jĭs′thəs), *n. Gk Legend.* the cousin of Agamemnon. He seduced Clytemnestra in the absence of her husband, Agamemnon, and was later killed by her son, Orestes.

Aegospotami (ē′gŏs pŏt′ə mī′), *n.* a creek in ancient Thrace, flowing into the Hellespont: near its mouth the Athenian fleet was defeated by Lysander, 405 B.C. leading to the termination of the Peloponnesian War.

aegrotat (ē grō′tăt, ē′grō tăt′, ī′grō-), *n.* (in universities) **1.** an official certificate of illness allowing a candidate to pass an examination even though he failed to attend part of it. **2.** the degree thus taken. [t. L: he is ill]

Aegyptus (ē jĭp′təs), *n. Gk Legend.* a king of Egypt and twin brother of Danaüs.

Ælfric (ăl′frĭk), *n.* (‘*Ælfric Grammaticus*’), A.D. *c.* 955–*c.* 1020, English abbot and writer.

-aemia, *Med.* a suffix referring to the state of the blood, as in *toxaemia*. Also, **-emia, -haemia, -hemia.** [NL: also *-hemia, -haemia*, t. Gk: m. *-aimia* (as in *anaimia* want of blood), der. *haîma* blood]

Aeneas (ĭ nē′əs), *n. Class. Myth.* the son of Anchises and Aphrodite (Venus): a Trojan hero, who became the founder of Rome. See **Aeneid.** [t. L, t. Gk: m. *Aineías*]

Aeneid (ĭ nē′ĭd), *n.* a Latin epic poem by Virgil, reciting the adventures of Aeneas after the fall of Troy.

aeneous (ā ē′nĭ əs), *adj.* bronze-coloured. [t. L: m. *aēneus* brazen]

Aeolian (ē ō′lyən), *adj.* **1.** belonging to a branch of the Greek race named after Aeolus, the legendary founder; Aeolic. —*n.* **2.** a member of one of the three great divisions of the ancient Greek race, the two other divisions being the Dorian and the Ionian. **3.** Aeolic [f. m. s. Gk *Aioleús* Aeolus + -IAN]

Aeolian (ē ō′lyən), *adj.* **1.** pertaining to Aeolus, or to the winds in general. **2.** (*l.c.*) due to atmospheric action; wind blown. **3.** (*l.c.*) *Geol.* deposited or formed by wind, as loess or dunes. [f. m. s. Gk *Aíolos* Aeolus + -IAN]

aeolian harp, a box over which are stretched a number of strings of equal length, tuned in unison and sounded by the wind. Also, **aeolian lyre; wind harp.**

Aeolian mode, *Music.* a scale, represented by the white keys of a keyboard instrument, beginning on A.

Aeolic (ē ŏl′ĭk), *n.* **1.** the dialect of Greek spoken by the Aeolians. —*adj.* **2.** Aeolian.

aeolipile (ē ŏl′ĭ pīl′), *n.* an instrument consisting essentially of a round vessel rotated by the force of steam generated within, and escaping through, bent arms. Also, **aeolipyle.** [t. L: m. s. *aeolipila*, orig. *Aeolī pila* ball of Aeolus, or *Aeolī pylae* doorway of Aeolus]

Aeolis (ē′ə lĭs), *n.* an ancient coastal region and Greek colony in NW Asia Minor.

aeolotropic (ē′ə lō trŏp′ĭk), *adj. Physics.* not isotropic; anisotropic. [f. m. Gk *aiólo(s)* changeful + -TROPIC] —**aeolotropy** (ē′ə lŏt′rə pĭ), **aeolotropism** (ē′ə lŏt′rə pĭz′-əm), *n.*

Aeolus (ē′ə ləs), *n. Gk Myth.* the ruler of the winds.

aeon (ē′ən), *n.* **1.** an indefinitely long period of time; an age. **2.** (*cap.*) (in the Gnostic doctrine) one of a class of powers or beings conceived as emanating from the Supreme Being and performing various functions in the operations of the universe. **3.** *Geol.* the largest division of geological time, comprising two or more eras. Also, **eon.** [t. L, t. Gk: m. *aiṓn* lifetime, age]

aeonian (ē ō′nyən), *adj.* eternal. [f. m. s. Gk *aiṓnios* agelong + -AN]

aer-, var. of **aero-** before vowels.

aerate (ēə′rāt), *v.t.*, **-rated, -rating.** **1.** to charge or treat with air or a gas, esp. with carbon dioxide. **2.** to expose to the free action of the air: *to aerate milk in order to remove unpleasant smells.* **3.** *Physiol.* to expose (a medium or tissue) to air, as in the oxygenation of the blood in respiration. [f. AER- + -ATE[1]] —**aera′tion,** *n.*

aerator (ēə′rā′tə), *n.* **1.** an apparatus for aerating water or other fluids. **2.** a contrivance for fumigating wheat and other grain, to bleach it and destroy fungi and insects.

A.E.R.E., Atomic Energy Research Establishment.

aerial (ēə′rĭ əl), *n.* **1.** *Radio.* that part of a radio system designed to radiate or receive electromagnetic waves into or from free space; an antenna. —*adj.* **2.** of, in, or produced by the air: *aerial currents.* **3.** inhabiting or frequenting the air: *aerial creatures.* **4.** reaching far into the air; high; lofty: *aerial spires.* **5.** partaking of the nature of air; airy: *aerial beings.* **6.** unsubstantial; visionary: *aerial fancies.* **7.** having a light and graceful beauty; ethereal: *aerial music.* **8.** *Biol.* growing in the air, as the adventitious roots of some trees. See illus. under **banyan.** **9.** pertaining to or used for, against, or in aircraft. [f. s. L *āerius* airy (t. Gk: m. *āérios*) + -AL[1]] —**aer′ially,** *adv.*

aerialist (ēə′rĭ ə lĭst), *n. U.S.* a trapeze artist.

aeriality (ēə′rĭ ăl′ĭ tĭ), *n.* unsubstantiality.

aerial perspective, that branch of perspective which considers the variations of light, shade, and colour in objects delineated or photographed, according to their distances, the quality of light falling on them, and the medium through which they are seen.

aerial photograph, a photograph taken from the air. —**aerial photography.**

aerie (ēə′rĭ, ĭə′rĭ), *n.* eyrie. Also, **aery.** [t. ML: m. *aeria*, t. OF: m. *aire*, g. L *ārea* AREA or L *ātrium* ATRIUM]

aeriferous (ēə rĭf′ə rəs), *adj.* conveying air, as the bronchial tubes. [f. AER- + -(I)FEROUS]

aeriform (ēə′rĭ fôm′), *adj.* **1.** having the form or nature of air; gaseous. **2.** unsubstantial; unreal.

aero (ēə′rō), *adj.* **1.** of or for aircraft. **2.** of aeronautics.

aero-, a word element meaning: **1.** air; atmosphere. **2.** gas. **3.** aeroplane. [t. Gk, comb. form of *āḗr* air]

aerobatic (ēə′rō băt′ĭk), *adj.* of or pertaining to displays of manoeuvring and other stunts in an aircraft.

aerobatics (ēə′rō băt′ĭks), *n.pl.* **1.** stunts carried out by aircraft; aerial acrobatics. **2.** (*construed as sing.*) the skill of giving an aerobatic display.

aerobe (ēə′rōb), *n. Biol.* a bacterium or other micro-organism whose existence requires, or is not destroyed by, the presence of free oxygen (opposed to *anaerobe*). [t. NL: m. *aerobia*, f. Gk: *āero-* AERO- + m. *bíos* life]

aerobee (ēə′rə bē′), *n. Astronautics.* a type of research rocket capable of carrying scientific payloads to altitudes of between 75 and 350 miles.

aerobic (ēə rō′bĭk), *adj.* **1.** (of organisms or tissues) requiring, or not destroyed by, the presence of free oxygen. **2.** pertaining to or caused by the presence of oxygen: *aerobic respiration.* —**aero′bically,** *adv.*

aerobiont (ēə rō′bĭ ŏnt′), *n. Biol.* aerobe.

aerobiosis (ēə′rō bī ō′sĭs), *n.* existence in the presence

of free oxygen. —**aerobiotic** (ēə′rō bī ŏt′ĭk), *adj.*
aerobium (ĕə rō′bĭ əm), *n., pl.* **-bia** (-bĭ ə). *Biol.* aerobe.
aerodonetics (ēə′rō də nĕt′ĭks), *n.* the study of gliding or soaring flight; the science dealing with gliding craft. [f. s. Gk *āerodónētos* air tossed + -ICS]
aerodrome (ēə′rə drōm′), *n.* a landing field for aeroplanes, esp. private aeroplanes, having permanent buildings, equipment, hangars, etc. but usually smaller than an airport. Also, *U.S.*, **airdrome.**
aerodynamics (ēə′rō dī năm′ĭks), *n.* the science that treats of the motion of the air and other gases, or of their properties and mechanical effects when in motion. Cf. **aerostatics.** —**aer′odynam′ic,** *adj.* —**aer′odynam′icist,** *n.*
aerodyne (ēə′rō dīn′), *n.* any heavier-than-air craft.
aero-elastic (ēə′rō ĭ lăs′tĭk), *adj. Aeron.* (of an airframe) deformable by aerodynamic forces. —**aer′o-elastic′ity,** *n.* —**aer′o-elastic′ian,** *n.*
aeroembolism (ēə′rō ĕm′bə lĭz′əm), *n.* a morbid condition caused by substantial decrease in atmospheric pressure, as in high-altitude flying, and characterized by the formation of nitrogen bubbles in the blood, pains in the lungs, etc. Cf. **bends** and **caisson disease.**
aero-engine (ēə′rō ĕn′jĭn), *n. Aeron.* the source of power in an aircraft.
aerofoil (ēə′rō foil′), *n.* any surface, such as a wing, aileron, or stabilizer, designed to help in lifting or controlling an aircraft by making use of the current of air through which it moves.
aerogram (ēə′rə grăm′), *n.* **1.** a radio telegram. **2.** a message carried by an aircraft.
aerograph (ēə′rə grăf, -gräf′), *n.* a spray gun for paint, lacquer, etc.
aerography (ēə rŏg′rə fĭ), *n.* description of the air or atmosphere. —**aerog′rapher,** *n.* —**aerographic** (ēə′rəgrăf′ĭk), **aer′ograph′ical,** *adj.*
aerolite (ēə′rə līt′), *n.* a meteorite consisting mainly of stony matter. Also, **aerolith** (ēə′rə lĭth). —**aerolitic** (ēə′rə lĭt′ĭk), *adj.*
aerology (ēə rŏl′ə jĭ), *n.* the study of the properties of air and of the atmosphere. —**aerologic** (ēə′rə lŏj′ĭk), **aer′olog′ical,** *adj.* —**aerol′ogist,** *n.*
aeromarine (ēə′rō mə rēn′), *adj. Aeron.* denoting or pertaining to navigation of aircraft above the ocean.
aeromechanic (ēə′rō mĭ kăn′ĭk), *n.* **1.** an aviation mechanic. —*adj.* **2.** of or pertaining to aeromechanics.
aeromechanics (ēə′rō mĭ kăn′ĭks), *n.* the mechanics of air or gases. —**aer′omechan′ical,** *adj.*
aerometer (ēə rŏm′ĭ tə), *n.* an instrument for determining the weight, density, etc., of air or other gases.
aerometry (ēə rŏm′ĭ trĭ), *n.* pneumatics. —**aerometric** (ēə′rə mĕt′rĭk), *adj.*
aeron., aeronautics.
aeronaut (ēə′rə nôt′), *n.* **1.** the pilot of a balloon or other lighter-than-air craft. **2.** a traveller in an airship. [backformation from AERONAUTICS. Cf. F *aéronaute*]
aeronautic (ēə′rə nô′tĭk), *adj.* of aeronautics or aeronauts. Also, **aer′onau′tical.** [t. NL: s. *aeronautica,* neut. pl. adj., pertaining to sailing in the air] —**aer′onau′tically,** *adv.*
aeronautical engineer, one versed in the design and construction of aeroplanes, etc.
aeronautical engineering, the action, work, or profession of an aeronautical engineer.
aeronautics (ēə′rə nô′tĭks), *n.pl., construed as sing.* the science or art of flight. [pl. of AERONAUTIC. See -ICS]
aeropause (ēə′rə pôz′), *n.* a region of the upper atmosphere marking the boundary between the denser portion of the atmosphere and outer space.
aerophagia (ēə′rə fā′jə), *n. Psychiatry.* morbid swallowing of air due to neurotic gastric disturbances.
aerophobia (ēə′rə fō′byə), *n. Psychiatry.* morbid fear of draughts of air, gases, and airborne noxious influences.
aerophyte (ēə′rə fīt′), *n. Bot.* epiphyte.
aeroplane (ēə′rə plān′), *n.* an aircraft, heavier than air, kept aloft by the upward thrust exerted by the passing air on its fixed wings, and driven by propellers, jet propulsion, etc. Also, *Chiefly U.S.*, **airplane.**
aeroplane spin, *Wrestling.* a manoeuvre in which a wrestler hauls his opponent on to his shoulders and spins round to make him giddy.
aerosol (ēə′rə sŏl′), *n.* **1.** *Phys. Chem.* a system consisting of colloidal particles dispersed in a gas; a smoke or fog. **2.** an aerosol container. [f. AERO- + SOL[4]]
aerosol bomb, an aerosol container for spraying insecticides on a large scale, esp. agriculturally.
aerosol container, a small metal container for storing under pressure, and subsequently dispensing as a spray, such domestic products in the aerosol form as insecticides, waxes, lacquers, etc. Also, **aerosol pack.**
aerospace (ēə′rə spās′), *n.* **1.** the earth's envelope of air and the space beyond it, in which rockets and space vehicles fly. —*adj.* **2.** pertaining to aeronautics and astronautics considered together.
aerostat (ēə′rə stăt′), *n.* a balloon, airship, or any lighter-than-air craft. [f. AERO- + -STAT]
aerostatic (ēə′rə stăt′ĭk), *adj.* **1.** of aerostatics. **2.** of, or capable of supporting, aerostats. Also, **aer′ostat′ical.**
aerostatics (ēə′rə stăt′ĭks), *n.* **1.** the science of the equilibrium of air and other gases, and of the equilibrium of bodies sustained in them. **2.** the science of lighter-than-air craft.
aerostation (ēə′rə stā′shən), *n.* the operation of aerostats. [t. F, der. *aérostat* AEROSTAT]
aerotherapeutics (ēə′rō thĕ′rə pyōō′tĭks), *n.* that branch of therapeutics which deals with the curative use of air or of artificially prepared atmospheres. Also, **aerotherapy** (ēə′rō thĕ′rə pĭ).
Aertex (ēə′tĕks), *n. Trademark.* a cellular cotton fabric used for underwear, sports shirts, etc.
aeruginous (ĭə rōō′jĭ nəs), *adj.* bluish green; like verdigris. [t. L: m. s. *aerūginōsus*]
aery[1] (ēə′rĭ, ā′ə rĭ), *adj. Poetic.* ethereal; lofty. [t. L: m. s. *āerius* airy]
aery[2] (ēə′rĭ, ĭə′rĭ), *n., pl.* **aeries.** eyrie.
Aeschines (ĕs′kĭ nēz′), *n.* 389–314 B.C. Athenian orator: rival of Demosthenes.
Aeschylus (ēs′kĭ ləs), *n.* 525–456 B.C., Greek tragic poet and dramatist. —**Aeschylean** (ēs′kĭ lē′ən), *adj.*
Aesculapian (ēs′kyōō lā′pyən), *adj.* **1.** pertaining to Aesculapius. **2.** medical. —*n.* **3.** a physician.
Aesculapius (ēs′kyōō lā′pyəs), *n. Rom. Myth.* the god of medicine and healing.
Aesir (ā′sĭə, ē′-), *n.pl.* the gods of the Scandinavian mythology, dwelling in Asgard. [t. Icel., pl. of *āss* god]
Aesop (ē′sŏp), *n.* 620?–560? B.C., Greek writer of fables. —**Aesopian** (ē sŏp′yən), *adj.*
aesthesia (ēs thē′zyə), *n.* sensitivity; feeling; perceptibility. Also, *U.S.*, **esthesia.** [NL, t. Gk: m. *aisthēsia* perceptive state]
aesthesis (ēs thē′sĭs), *n.* aesthesia. Also, *U.S.*, **esthesis.** [t. Gk: m. *aísthēsis* a perceiving]
aesthete (ēs′thēt), *n.* **1.** one who cultivates the sense of the beautiful; one very sensitive to the beauties of art or nature. **2.** one who affects great love of art, music, poetry, etc., and indifference to practical matters. Also, *U.S.*, **esthete.** [t. Gk: m. s. *aisthētḗs* one who perceives]
aesthetic (ēs thĕt′ĭk, ĕs-), *adj.* **1.** pertaining to the sense of the beautiful or the science of aesthetics. **2.** having a sense of the beautiful; characterized by a love of beauty. Also, *U.S.*, **esthetic.** [t. Gk: m. s. *aisthētikós* perceptive]
aesthetical (ēs thĕt′ĭ kl, ĕs-), *adj.* of or relating to aesthetics. Also, *U.S.*, **esthetical.**
aesthetically (ēs thĕt′ĭ klĭ, ĕs-), *adv.* **1.** according to aesthetics or its principles. **2.** in an aesthetic manner. Also, *U.S.*, **esthetically.**
aesthetician (ēs′thĭ tĭsh′ən, ĕs′-), *n.* one versed in aesthetics. Also, *U.S.*, **esthetician.**
aestheticism (ēs thĕt′ĭ sĭz′əm, ĕs-), *n.* **1.** the acceptance of artistic beauty and taste as a fundamental standard, ethical and other standards being secondary. **2.** an exaggerated devotion to art, music, or poetry with indifference to practical matters. Also, *U.S.*, **estheticism.**
aesthetics (ēs thĕt′ĭks, ĕs-), *n.* **1.** *Philos.* the science which deduces from nature and taste the rules and principles of art; the theory of the fine arts; the science of the beautiful, or that branch of philosophy which deals with its principles or effects; the doctrines of taste. **2.** *Psychol.* the study of the mind and emotions in relation to the sense of beauty. Also, *U.S.*, **esthetics.** [pl. of AESTHETIC. See -ICS]
aestival (ēs tī′vəl), *adj.* pertaining or appropriate to summer. Also, *U.S.*, **estival.** [t. L: m. s. *aestīvālis*]
aestivate (ēs′tĭ vāt′), *v.i.*, **-vated, -vating. 1.** to spend the summer. **2.** *Zool.* to pass the summer in a torpid condition. Also, *U.S.*, **estivate.** —**aes′tiva′tor,** *n.*
aestivation (ēs′tĭ vā′shən), *n.* **1.** *Zool.* the act of aestivating. **2.** *Bot.* the arrangement of the parts of a flower in the bud. Also, *U.S.*, **estivation.**
aetatis suae (ē tä′tĭs sōō′ē), *Latin.* in a certain year of one's age.
aether (ē′thə), *n.* ether (defs 2, 3, 4). —**aethereal** (ē thĭə′rĭ əl), *adj.*
aetiology (ē′tĭ ŏl′ə jĭ), *n.* the study of the causes of anything, esp. of diseases. Also, *U.S.*, **etiology.** [t. L: m. s. *aetiologia,* t. Gk: m. *aitiología,* der. *aitía* cause. See -LOGY] —**aetiological** (ē′tĭ ə lŏj′ĭ kl), *adj.* —**ae′tiolog′ically,** *adv.* —**ae′tiol′ogist,** *n.*
Aetna (ĕt′nə), *n.* **Mount.** See **Etna, Mount.**
Aetolia (ē tō′lyə), *n.* an ancient district in W Greece.
A.E.U., Amalgamated Engineering Union.

af-, var. of **ad-** (by assimilation) before *f*, as in *affect.*
AF, Anglo-French. Also, **A.F.**
A.F., audio frequency. Also, **a.f.**
A.F.A., Amateur Football Alliance.
A.F.A.M., Ancient Free and Accepted Masons.
afar (ə fä′), *adv.* **1.** from a distance (usually prec. by *from*): *he came from afar.* **2.** far away; at or to a distance (usually fol. by *off*): *he saw the place afar off.* [ME *a fer.* See A-[1], FAR]
A.F.C., **1.** Air Force Cross. **2.** automatic flight control. **3.** automatic frequency control.
afeard (ə fĭəd′), *adj. Archaic or Dial.* afraid. Also, **afeared.** [ME *afered*, OE *āfǣred*]
afebrile (ă fē′brĭl, ā′-), *adj.* without fever; feverless. [f. A-[6] + FEBRILE]
affable (ăf′ə bl), *adj.* **1.** easy to talk to or to approach; polite; friendly: *an affable and courteous gentleman.* **2.** expressing affability; mild; benign: *an affable countenance.* [t. F, t. L: m. s. *affābilis* able to be spoken to] **—af′fabil′ity, af′fableness,** *n.* **—af′fably,** *adv.* **—Syn. 1.** courteous; urbane. See **civil.**
affair (ə fēə′), *n.* **1.** anything done or to be done; that which requires action or effort; business; concern: *an affair of great moment, the affairs of state.* **2.** (*pl.*) matters of interest or concern; particular doings or interests: *put your affairs in order.* **3.** an event or a performance; a particular action, operation, or proceeding: *when did this affair happen?* **4.** thing; matter (applied to anything made or existing, with a descriptive or qualifying term): *this machine is a complicated affair.* **5.** a private or personal concern; a special function, business, or duty: *attend to your own affairs.* **6.** a love affair. [t. F: m. *affaire*, g. *à faire* to do; r. ME *afere*, t. OF: m. *afaire*]
affaire de cœur (*Fr.* å fĕr də kœr′), *French.* an affair of the heart; a love affair.
affaire d'honneur (*Fr.* å fĕr dō nœr′), *French.* a duel.
affect[1] (*v.* ə fĕkt′; *n.* ăf′ĕkt), *v.t.* **1.** to act on; produce an effect or a change in: *cold affects the body.* **2.** to impress; move (in mind or feelings): *the poetry affected me deeply.* **3.** (of pain, disease, etc.) to attack or lay hold of. **—***n.* **4.** *Psychol.* feeling or emotion. **5.** *Obs.* affection; passion; sensation; inclination; inward disposition or feeling. [t. L: s. *affectus*, pp., influenced, attacked]
—Syn. 1. AFFECT, EFFECT agree in the idea of exerting influence. To AFFECT is to concern, be of interest or importance to; to produce an effect in or upon something: *to affect one's conduct or health.* To EFFECT is to accomplish or bring about something: *to effect a reconciliation.* **2.** touch; move, stir.
affect[2] (ə fĕkt′), *v.t.* **1.** to make a show of; put on a pretence of; pretend; feign: *to affect ignorance.* **2.** to make a show of liking or imitating: *to affect an Oxford accent.* **3.** to use or adopt by preference; choose; prefer: *the peculiar costume which he affected.* **4.** to assume the character or attitude of: *to affect the freethinker.* **5.** to tend towards habitually or naturally: *a substance which affects colloidal form.* **6.** (of animals and plants) to inhabit; frequent: *moss affects the northern slopes.* **7.** *Archaic.* to take pleasure in; fancy; like. **8.** *Archaic.* to aim at; aspire to. **—***v.i.* **9.** to profess; pretend: *he affected to be wearied.* [t. F: s. *affecter*, t. L: m. *affectāre*] **—affect′er,** *n.* **—Syn. 1.** See **pretend.**
affectation (ăf′ĕk tā′shən), *n.* **1.** a striving for the appearance of (a quality not really or fully possessed); pretence of the possession or character; effort for the reputation (fol. by *of*): *an affectation of wit, affectation of great wealth.* **2.** artificiality of manner or conduct; effort to attract notice by pretence, assumption, or any assumed peculiarity: *his affectations are insufferable.* **3.** *Obs.* strenuous pursuit or desire (fol. by *of*). [t. L: s. *affectātio* a pursuit after] **—Syn. 2.** airs, mannerisms.
affected[1] (ə fĕk′tĭd), *adj.* **1.** acted upon; influenced. **2.** influenced injuriously; impaired; attacked, as by climate or disease. **3.** moved; touched: *she was deeply affected.* [pp. of AFFECT[1]]
affected[2] (ə fĕk′tĭd), *adj.* **1.** assumed artificially: *affected airs, affected diction.* **2.** assuming or pretending to possess characteristics which are not natural: *an affected lady.* **3.** inclined or disposed: *well affected towards a project.* [pp. of AFFECT[2]] **—affect′edly.** *adv.* **—affect′edness** *n.* **—Syn. 1.** pretended, feigned.
affecting (ə fĕk′tĭng), *adj.* having power to excite or move the feelings; tending to move the affections. **—affect′ingly,** *adv.* **—Syn.** touching, pathetic.
affection[1] (ə fĕk′shən), *n.* **1.** a settled goodwill, love, or attachment: *the affection of a parent for his child.* **2.** the state of having one's feelings affected; emotion or feeling: *over and above our reason and affections.* **3.** *Pathol.* a disease, or the condition of being diseased; a morbid or abnormal state of body or mind: *a gouty affection.* **4.** the act of affecting; act of influencing or acting upon. **5.** the state of being affected. **6.** *Philos.* a contingent, alterable, and accidental state or quality of being. **7.** *Psychol.* the affective aspect of a mental process. **8.** *Archaic.* a bodily state due to any influence. **9.** *Obs.* bent or disposition of mind. [t. L: s. *affectio* influence (active), state of mind, favourable disposition (passive)] **—Syn. 1.** devotion, fondness. See **love. 3.** See **disease. —Ant. 1.** dislike.
affection[2] (ə fĕk′shən), *n. Obs.* affectation. [f. AFFECT[2], V. + -ION]
affectional (ə fĕk′shə nəl), *adj.* relating to or implying affection. [f. AFFECTION[1] + -AL[1]]
affectionate (ə fĕk′shə nĭt), *adj.* **1.** characterized by or manifesting affection; possessing or indicating love; tender: *an affectionate embrace.* **2.** having great love or affection; warmly attached: *your affectionate brother.* **3.** *Obs.* strongly disposed or inclined. **4.** *Obs.* biased; partisan. **—affec′tionately,** *adv.* **—affec′tionateness,** *n.* **—Syn. 1.** loving, fond. **2.** devoted.
affective (ə fĕk′tĭv), *adj.* **1.** pertaining to the affections; emotional. **2.** exciting emotion; affecting. **3.** *Psychol.* pertaining to feeling or emotion, esp. to pleasurable or unpleasurable aspects of mental process. **—affec′tively,** *adv.* **—affectivity** (ăf′ĕk tĭv′ĭ tĭ), *n.*
afferent (ăf′ə rənt), *adj. Physiol.* bringing to or leading towards a central organ or point (opposed to *efferent*): *afferent nerves or veins.* [t. L: s. *afferens*, ppr., bringing to]
affetuoso (ə fĕt′yōō ō′zō; *It.* äf fĕt twō′zō), *adv., adj. Music.* with feeling. [It.]
affiance (ə fī′əns), *v.*, **-anced, -ancing,** *n.* **—***v.t.* **1.** to bind by promise of marriage; betroth: *to affiance a daughter.* **—***n.* **2.** the pledging of faith; esp. a marriage contract. **3.** trust; confidence; reliance. [ME, t. OF: m. *afiance*, der. *afier*, g. LL *affīdāre* pledge]
affianced (ə fī′ənst), *adj.* betrothed.
affiant (ə fī′ənt), *n. U.S. Law.* one who makes an affidavit.
affiche (*Fr.* å fēsh′), *n. French.* a posted notice; poster.
affidavit (ăf′ĭ dā′vĭt), *n. Law.* a written declaration upon oath, esp. one made before an authorized official. [t. L: he has made oath]
affiliate (*v.* ə fĭl′ĭ āt′; *n.* ə fĭl′ĭ ĭt, -āt′), *v.*, **-ated, -ating,** *n.* **—***v.t.* **1.** to attach as a branch or part; unite; associate (fol. by *to* in Brit. usage, by *with* in U.S. usage): *affiliated to the church.* **2.** to bring into association or close connection: *the two banks were affiliated.* **3.** to connect in the way of descent or derivation (fol. by *upon*). **4.** *Law.* **a.** to fix the paternity of, as an illegitimate child. **b.** to refer to as being the child of or belonging to. **—***v.i.* **5.** to associate oneself; be intimately united in action or interest. **—***n.* **6.** one who or that which is affiliated; associate or auxiliary. [t. LL: m. s. *affiliātus*, pp., adopted as a son]
affiliation (ə fĭl′ĭ ā′shən), *n.* **1.** the act of affiliating. **2.** the state of being affiliated; association.
affiliation order, *Law.* an order made by a magistrate making the proven father of an illegitimate child pay maintenance for a specified period.
affined (ə fīnd′), *adj.* **1.** related; connected. **2.** *Obs.* bound. [f. s. F *affiné* related + -ED[2]]
affinitive (ə fĭn′ĭ tĭv), *adj.* characterized by affinity; closely related.
affinity (ə fĭn′ĭ tĭ), *n.*, *pl.* **-ties. 1.** a natural liking for, or attraction to, a person or thing. **2.** inherent likeness or agreement as between things; close resemblance or connection. **3.** relationship by marriage or by ties other than those of blood (distinguished from *consanguinity*). **4.** one for whom such a natural liking or attraction is felt. **5.** *Biol.* the phylogenetic relationship between two organisms or groups of organisms resulting in a resemblance in general plan or structure, or in the essential structural parts. **6.** *Chem.* that force by which the atoms of bodies of dissimilar nature unite in certain definite proportions to form a compound. [ME, t. F: m. *af(f)inité*, t. L: m. s. *affīnitas*]
affirm (ə fûm′), *v.t.* **1.** to. state or assert positively; maintain as true: *to affirm one's loyalty to one's country.* **2.** to establish, confirm, or ratify: *the appellate court affirmed the judgement of the lower court.* **3.** *Logic.* to state in the affirmative. **4.** *Law.* to declare solemnly without oath. **—***v.i.* **5.** to declare positively; assert solemnly. **6.** *Law.* to declare solemnly before a court or magistrate, but without oath (a practice allowed where the affirmant has scruples, usually religious, against taking an oath). [t. L: s. *affirmāre*; r. ME *aferme(n)*, t. OF: m. *afermer*] **—affirm′able,** *adj.* **—affirm′ably,** *adv.* **—affirm′er,** *n.* **—Syn. 1.** See **declare.**
affirmant (ə fû′mənt), *n.* one who affirms.
affirmation (ăf′û mā′shən), *n.* **1.** the assertion that something is, or is true. **2.** that which is affirmed; a proposition that is declared to be true. **3.** establishment of something of prior origin; confirmation; ratification.

4. *Law.* a solemn declaration accepted instead of a statement under oath. Also, **affirmance** (ə fûr′məns).

affirmative (ə fûr′mə tĭv), *adj.* **1.** giving affirmation or assent; confirmatory; not negative: *an affirmative answer.* **2.** *Logic.* denoting a proposition or judgement that asserts a relation between its terms, or asserts that the predicate applies to the subject. —*n.* **3.** that which affirms or asserts; a positive proposition: *two negatives make an affirmative.* **4.** an affirmative word or phrase, as *yes* or *I do.* **5. the affirmative,** the agreeing or concurring side. [t. LL: m. s. *affirmātivus*; r. ME *affirmatyff*, t. OF] —**affirm′atively,** *adj.*

affirmatory (ə fûr′mə tə rĭ, -trĭ), *adj.* affirmative.

affix (*v.* ə fĭks′; *n.* ăf′ĭks), *v.t.* **1.** to fix; fasten, join, or attach (fol. by *to*): *to affix stamps to a letter.* **2.** to impress (a seal or stamp). **3.** to attach (blame, reproach, ridicule, etc.). —*n.* **4.** that which is joined or attached. **5.** *Gram.* any meaningful element (prefix, infix, or suffix) added to a stem or base, as *-ed* added to *want* to form *wanted.* [t. ML: s. *affixāre*, freq. of L *affīgere* fasten to] —**affix′er,** *n.*

affixture (ə fĭks′chə), *n.* the act of affixing; attachment.

afflated (ə flā′tĭd), *adj.* inspired.

afflatus (ə flā′təs), *n.* **1.** inspiration; an impelling mental force acting from within. **2.** divine communication of knowledge. Also, **afflation.** [t. L: a blast]

afflict (ə flĭkt′), *v.t.* **1.** to distress with mental or bodily pain; trouble greatly or grievously: *to be afflicted with the gout.* **2.** *Obs.* to overthrow; rout. [t. L: s. *afflictus*, pp., thrown down] —**afflict′er,** *n.* —**Syn. 1.** vex, harass, torment, plague.

affliction (ə flĭk′shən), *n.* **1.** a state of pain, distress, or grief: *they sympathized with us in our affliction.* **2.** a cause of continual pain of body or mind, as sickness, loss, calamity, persecution, etc. [ME, t. L: s. *afflictio*]
—**Syn. 1.** AFFLICTION, ADVERSITY, MISFORTUNE, TRIAL refer to an event or circumstance which is hard to bear. A MISFORTUNE is any seriously adverse or unfavourable occurrence: *he had the misfortune to break his leg.* AFFLICTION suggests not only a misfortune but the emotional effect of this: *blindness is one kind of affliction.* ADVERSITY suggests one of a succession of mishaps and afflictions: *Job remained patient under all his adversities.* TRIAL emphasizes the testing of one's character in undergoing misfortunes, trouble, etc.: *his son's conduct was a great trial to him.*

afflictive (ə flĭk′tĭv), *adj.* characterized by or causing pain; distressing. —**afflic′tively,** *adv.*

affluence (ăf′lo͝o əns), *n.* **1.** abundance of material goods; wealth: *to live in great affluence.* **2.** an abundant supply, as of thoughts, words, etc.; a profusion. **3.** a flowing to or towards; afflux. [t. F, t. L: m. s. *affluentia*]

affluent (ăf′lo͝o ənt), *adj.* **1.** abounding in means; rich: *an affluent person.* **2.** abounding in anything; abundant. **3.** flowing freely: *an affluent fountain.* —*n.* **4.** a tributary stream. [ME, t. L: s. *affluens*, ppr., flowing to] —**af′fluently,** *adv.* —**Syn. 1.** See **rich.**

afflux (ăf′lŭks), *n.* **1.** that which flows to or towards a point: *an afflux of blood to the head.* **2.** the act of flowing to; a flow. [t. ML: s. *affluxus*, n., der. L *affluere* flow to]

afford (ə fôd′), *v.t.* **1.** to have the means (often prec. by *can* or *may* and fol. by an infinitive): *we can afford to sell cheap.* **2.** to be able to meet the expense of; spare the price of (often prec. by *can* or *may*): *he can't afford a car.* **3.** to be able to give or spare (often prec. by *can* or *may*): *I can't afford the loss of a day.* **4.** to supply; furnish: *the transaction afforded him a good profit.* **5.** to be capable of yielding or providing: *the records afford no explanation.* **6.** to give or confer upon: *to afford one great pleasure, etc.* [ME *aforthen*, OE *geforthian* further, accomplish] —**afford′able,** *adj.*

afforest (ə fŏ′rĭst), *v.t.* to convert (bare or cultivated land) into forest, originally for the purpose of providing hunting grounds. [t. ML: s. *afforestāre.* See AD-, FOREST] —**affor′esta′tion,** *n.*

affranchise (ə frăn′chīz), *v.t.*, **-chised, -chising.** to free from a state of dependence, servitude, or obligation. [t. F: m. (by assoc. with FRANCHISE, n.) *affranchiss-*, s. of *affranchir.* See AD-, FRANK[1]]

affray (ə frā′), *n.* **1.** a public fight; a noisy quarrel; a brawl. **2.** *Law.* the fighting of two or more persons in a public place. —*v.t.* **3.** *Archaic.* to frighten. [ME *a(f)fray-(en)*, t. AF, var. of *effrayer*, OF *effreer*, g. LL *exfridāre*, f. *ex-* EX-[1] + *-fridāre*, der. *fridus* peace (of Gmc orig.)]

affreightment (ə frāt′mənt), *n.* *Com.* a contract made by a shipowner to carry goods for payment. [f. obs. *affreight* (t. F: m. s. *affréter*, remodelled on FREIGHT) + -MENT]

affricate (ăf′rĭ kit), *n.* *Phonet.* a composite speech sound beginning with a stop and ending with a fricative, such as *ch* in *church* (which begins like *t* and ends like *sh*). Also, **affricative** (ə frĭk′ə tĭv). [t. L: m. s. *affricātus*, pp., rubbed on or against] —**af′frica′tion,** *n.*

affright (ə frīt′), *Archaic.* —*v.t.* **1.** to frighten. —*n.* **2.** sudden fear or terror; fright. **3.** a source of terror. **4.** the act of terrifying. [ME *afrighten*, OE *āfyrhtan*, f. *ā-* (intensive) + *fyrhten* frighten] —**affright′edly,** *adv.*

affront (ə frŭnt′), *n.* **1.** a personally offensive act or word; an intentional slight; an open manifestation of disrespect; an insult to the face: *an affront to the king.* **2.** an offence to one's dignity or self-respect. —*v.t.* **3.** to offend by an open manifestation of disrespect or insolence: *an affronting speech.* **4.** to put out of countenance; make ashamed or confused. **5.** to meet or encounter face to face; confront: *to affront death.* **6.** *Archaic.* to front; face. [ME *afront(en)*, t. OF: m. *afronter*, g. LL *affrontāre*] —**affront′er,** *n.* —**affront′ingly,** *adv.* —**Syn. 1.** impertinence, indignity.

affrontive (ə frŭn′tĭv), *adj.* *Archaic.* insulting.

affusion (ə fyo͞o′zhən), *n.* the pouring on of water or other liquid, esp. in baptism. [f. s. L *affūsus*, pp., poured + -ION]

Afgh., Afghanistan.

Afghan (ăf′găn), *n.* **1.** a native of Afghanistan. **2.** Pushtu (language). **3.** (*l.c.*) a kind of woollen blanket, knitted, crocheted, or woven, usually in a geometric pattern. **4.** Afghan hound. —*adj.* **5.** of Afghanistan or its people.

Afghan hound, a breed of greyhound with a very long silky coat.

Afghani (ăf găn′ĭ, -gä′nĭ), *n.* **1.** Afghan. **2.** the monetary unit of Afghanistan, equivalent to about £0·0093 sterling. **3.** an alloy coin of this value. —*adj.* **4.** Afghan.

Afghanistan (ăf găn′ĭ stăn′, -ĭ stän′), *n.* a kingdom in S Asia, NW of India, E of Iran, and S of the Soviet Union. ab. 13,800,000 pop. (est. 1965); 250,000 sq. mi. *Cap.*: Kabul.

Afghanistan

aficionado (ə fĭsh′yə nä′dō; *Sp.* ä fē thyō nä′dō), *n.* an ardent devotee. [Sp.]

afield (ə fēld′), *adv.* **1.** abroad; away from home. **2.** off the beaten path; far and wide: *to stray far afield in one's reading.* **3.** in or to the field or fields.

afire (ə fī′ə), *adv., adj.* on fire: *to set something afire.*

aflame (ə flām′), *adv., adj.* **1.** on fire; ablaze: *the house was all aflame.* **2.** inflamed; aroused; glowing: *aflame with curiosity.*

afloat (ə flōt′), *adv., adj.* **1.** borne on the water; in a floating condition: *the ship is afloat.* **2.** on board ship; at sea: *cargo afloat and ashore.* **3.** flooded: *the main deck was afloat.* **4.** moving without guide or control: *our affairs are all afloat.* **5.** passing from place to place; in circulation: *a rumour is afloat.*

aflutter (ə flŭt′ə), *adv., adj.* in a flutter.

A.F.M., Air Force Medal.

afocal (ā fō′kl), *adj.* having no finite focal point, as a telescope.

afoot (ə fo͝ot′), *adv., adj.* **1.** on foot; walking: *I came afoot.* **2.** astir; in progress: *there is mischief afoot.*

afore (ə fô′), *adv., prep., conj.* *Archaic or Dial.* before. [ME *aforne*, OE *on foran.* See A-[1], FORE[1]]

aforementioned (ə fô′mĕn′shənd), *adj.* mentioned earlier or previously.

aforesaid (ə fô′sĕd′), *adj.* said or mentioned previously.

aforethought (ə fô′thôt′), *adj.* **1.** thought of beforehand; premeditated: *malice aforethought.* —*n.* **2.** premeditation; forethought.

aforetime (ə fô′tīm′), *adj.* **1.** in time past; in a former time; previously. —*adj.* **2.** former; previous.

a fortiori (ā′fô tĭ ô′rĭ), *Latin.* for a still stronger reason; even more certain; all the more.

afoul (ə foul′), *adv., adj.* **1.** in a state of collision or entanglement: *a ship with its shrouds afoul.* **2. run afoul of,** to become entangled with: *run afoul of the law.*

Afr., **1.** Africa. **2.** African.

afraid (ə frād′), *adj.* **1.** feeling fear; filled with apprehension: *afraid to go.* **2.** reluctantly or regretfully of the opinion (sometimes fol. by *that*). [ME *afraied*, orig. pp. of AFFRAY]
—**Syn. 1.** scared, fearful. AFRAID, ALARMED, FRIGHTENED, TERRIFIED all indicate a state of fear. AFRAID implies inner apprehensive disquiet: *afraid of (or in) the dark.* ALARMED implies that the feelings are aroused through realization of some imminent or unexpected danger to oneself or others: *alarmed by (or about) someone's illness.* FRIGHTENED means shocked with sudden, but usually short-lived, fear, esp. that arising from apprehension of physical harm: *frightened by (or about) an accident.* TERRIFIED suggests the emotional reaction when one is struck with a violent, overwhelming fear: *terrified by an earthquake.*

afreet (ăf′rēt), *n.* *Arabian Myth.* a powerful evil demon or monster. Also, **afrit.** [t. Ar.: m. *'ifrīt*]

afresh (ə frĕsh′), *adv.* anew; again: *to start afresh.*

Afric (ăf′rĭk), *adj. Archaic.* African.

Africa (ăf′rĭ kə), *n.* the second largest continent, S of Europe and between the Atlantic and Indian Oceans. 258,000,000 pop. (est. 1964); ab. 11,700,000 sq. mi.; ab. 4970 mi. long; ab. 4700 mi. wide.

African (ăf′rĭ kən), *adj.* **1.** of or from Africa; belonging to the black race of Africa; Negro. *—n.* **2.** a native of Africa; a member of the black race of Africa; a Negro.

Africanism (ăf′rĭ kə nĭz′əm), *n.* **1.** an African characteristic. **2.** the study of Africa or Africans. **3.** the policy of asserting the unity and identity of interests of Africa as a whole.

Africanist (ăf′rĭ kə nĭst), *n.* one specially knowledgeable about or interested in Africa or Africans.

Africanize (ăf′rĭ kə nīz′), *v.*, **-nized, -nizing.** *—v.t.* **1.** to hand over the control or (something) to Africans; make African. *—v.i.* **2.** to assume or affect Africanisms. Also, **Africanise.** —**Af′ricaniza′tion,** *n.*

African lily, agapanthus.

African sleeping sickness, *Pathol.* a disease, generally fatal, common in parts of Africa, usually marked by fever, wasting, and progressive lethargy, and caused by a parasitic protozoan, *Trypanosoma gambiense.* It is carried by a tsetse fly, *Glossina palpalis.*

African violet, a plant, *Saintpaulia ionantha,* with violet, pink, or white flowers, popular in cultivation.

Afrikaans (ăf′rĭ käns′), *n.* a language of South Africa, developed out of the speech of 17th-century settlers from Holland and still very like Dutch; South African Dutch; Taal. [var. sp. of D *Afrikaansch*]

Afrikaner (ăf′rĭ kä′nə), *n.* an Afrikaans-speaking native of the Republic of South Africa born of white parents of Dutch, German, or Huguenot descent. Also, **Afrikander.** [t. Afrikaans: m. *Afrikaander,* b. *Afrikaans* and *Hollander*]

afrit (ăf′rēt), *n.* afreet.

Afro-, a combining form meaning 'African', 'Negro'. [t. L: m. s. *Afer* African]

Afro-American (ăf′rō ə mĕ′rĭ kən), *adj.* **1.** pertaining to Americans of African origin or descent. *—n.* **2.** an American Negro.

Afro-Asian (ăf′rō ā′shən), *adj.* **1.** consisting of or pertaining to Africa and Asia, or Africans and Asians, considered together. **2.** of Asian descent and African citizenship. **3.** of mixed African and Asian descent. *—n.* **4.** an Asian living in Africa. **5.** one of mixed African and Asian blood.

aft (äft), *adv., adj. Naut.* at, in, or towards the stern. [OE *æftan* from behind (f. *æft-* behind + *-an,* suffix marking motion from), c. Goth. *aftana*]

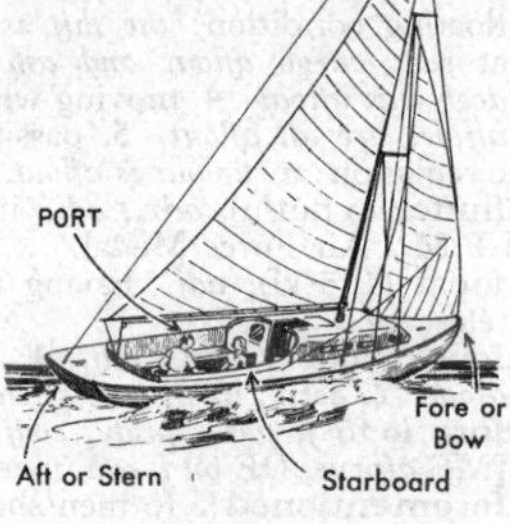

Aft

after (äf′tə), *prep.* **1.** behind in place; following behind: *men placed in a line one after another.* **2.** in pursuit of; in search of; with or in desire for: *run after him.* **3.** concerning: *to inquire after a person.* **4.** later in time than; in succession to; at the close of: *after supper, time after time I urged him to do it.* **5.** subsequent to and in consequence of: *after what has happened, I can never return.* **6.** below in rank or excellence; next to: *Milton is usually placed after Shakespeare among English poets.* **7.** in imitation of, or in imitation of the style of: *after Raphael, to make something after a model.* **8.** with with name of: *he was named after his uncle.* **9.** in proportion to; in accordance with: *after their intrinsic value.* **10.** according to the nature of; in agreement or unison with; in conformity to: *he swore after the manner of his faith.* *—adv.* **11.** behind; in the rear: *Jill came tumbling after.* **12.** later in time; afterwards: *happy ever after.* *—adj.* **13.** later in time; next; subsequent; succeeding: *in after years.* **14.** *Naut.* farther aft, or towards the stern of the ship: *the after sail.* *—conj.* **15.** subsequent to the time that: *after the boys left.* [ME, OE *æfter* (f. *æf-* away from + *-ter,* comp. suffix)] **—Syn. 1.** See **behind.**

afterbirth (äf′tə bûth′), *n.* the placenta and foetal membranes expelled from the uterus after parturition.

afterbrain (äf′tə brān′), *n.* metencephalon.

afterburner(äf′tə bû′nə), *n.* a device for reheating, as a ramjet coupled to the exhaust of a jet engine to provide added thrust.

afterburning (äf′tə bû′nĭng), *n.* **1.** *Astronautics.* the irregular burning of fuel left in the firing chamber of a rocket after main burning has ceased. **2.** combustion in an afterburner.

after-care (äf′tə kēə′), *n.* treatment, supervision, or assistance of convalescents, newly released mental patients, or discharged convicts.

afterdamp (äf′tə dămp′), *n.* an irrespirable mixture of gases, consisting chiefly of carbon dioxide and nitrogen, left in a mine after an explosion or fire; chokedamp.

afterdeck (äf′tə dĕk′), *n. Naut.* the weather deck abaft the midship house.

after-effect (äf′tə rĭ fĕkt′), *n.* **1.** a delayed effect; effect that follows later. **2.** *Med.* a result appearing after the first effect due to an agent, usually a drug, has gone.

afterglow (äf′tə glō′), *n.* **1.** the glow frequently seen in the sky after sunset. **2.** a second or secondary glow.

afterheat (äf′tə hēt′), *n. Physics.* the heat generated in a nuclear reactor after it has been shut down, due to the radioactive substances formed in the fuel elements.

after-image (äf′tər ĭm′ĭj), *n. Psychol.* a visual image or other sense impression that persists after the withdrawal of the exciting stimulus.

afterlife (äf′tə līf′), *n.* **1.** life after death. **2.** later life.

aftermath (äf′tə măth′), *n.* **1.** resultant conditions, esp. of a catastrophe: *the aftermath of the storm.* **2.** a second mowing or crop of grass from land in the same season. [f. AFTER + *math* a mowing (OE *mǣth*)]

aftermost (äf′tə mōst′, -məst), *adj.* **1.** *Naut.* farthest aft. **2.** hindmost. [ME *aftermest,* OE *æftemest* last; the *-r-* owing to assoc. with *after.* See AFT, -MOST]

afternoon (äf′tə no͞on′), *n.* **1.** the time from noon until evening. **2.** the latter part: *the afternoon of life.* *—adj.* **3.** pertaining to the latter part of the day.

after-pains (äf′tə pānz′), *n.pl.* pains, caused by contraction of the uterus, experienced after childbirth.

after peak, *Naut.* an enclosed space aft under decks, used as a store or for keeping drinking water.

afterpiece (äf′tə pēs′), *n.* a short dramatic piece performed after a play.

afters (äf′təz), *n.pl. Colloq.* dessert.

aftershaft (äf′tə shäft′), *n. Ornith.* **1.** a supplementary feather, usually small, arising from the underside of the base of the shafts of certain feathers in many birds. **2.** the shaft of such a feather.

aftertaste (äf′tə tāst′), *n.* **1.** a taste remaining after the substance causing it is no longer in the mouth. **2.** a slight lingering after-effect, often an unpleasant one.

afterthought (äf′tə thôt′), *n.* **1.** reflection after an act; some answer, expedient, or the like, that occurs to one's mind too late, or afterwards. **2.** a later or second thought. **3.** an action, remark, etc., prompted by an afterthought.

aftertime (äf′tə tīm′), *n.* future time.

afterwards (äf′tə wədz), *adv.* in later or subsequent time; subsequently. Also, **af′terward.** [OE *æfterweard(es),* var. of OE *æfteweard(es).* See AFT, -WARDS; for *-r-,* see AFTERMOST]

afterworld (äf′tə wûld′), *n.* the future world.

ag-, var. of **ad-** (by assimilation) before *g,* as in *agglutinate.*

AG, (G *Aktiengesellschaft*) joint-stock company.

Ag, *Chem.* (L *argentum*) silver.

A.G., **1.** Adjutant General. **2.** Attorney General.

aga (ä′gə), *n.* (in Turkey) **1.** a title of honour, usually implying respect for age. **2.** a general. Also, **agha.**

Agadir (ăg′ə dĭə′), *n.* a seaport in SW Morocco: international crisis 1911. 16,695 (1960).

again (ə gĕn′, ə gān′), *adv.* **1.** once more; in addition; another time; anew: *he did it all over again.* **2.** in an additional case or instance; moreover; besides; furthermore. **3.** on the other hand: *it might happen and again it might not.* **4.** back; in return; in reply: *to answer again.* **5.** in the opposite direction; to the same place or person: *to return again.* **6. again and again,** often; with frequent repetition. **7. as much again,** twice as much. [ME; OE *ongegn,* adv. and prep., opposite (to), towards, again, f. *on* in + *gegn* straight]

against (ə gĕnst′, ə gānst′), *prep.* **1.** in an opposite direction to, so as to meet; towards; upon: *to ride against the wind, the rain beats against the window.* **2.** in contact with, or in pressure upon: *to lean against a wall.* **3.** in opposition to; adverse or hostile to: *twenty votes against ten, against reason.* **4.** in resistance to or defence from: *protection against burglars.* **5.** in preparation for; in provision for: *money saved against a rainy day.* **6.** in contrast with; having as background: *the pictures stand out against the dark wall.* **7.** in exchange for; in return for; as a balance to: *draw against merchandise shipped.* **8.** instead of, as an alternative to, in contrast with, (sometimes prec. by *as*): *the advantages of flying against going by train.* **9.** *Obs.* directly opposite; facing; in front of (now *over against*). *—conj.* **10.** *Archaic or Dial.* by the time that. [f. AGAIN + -(*e*)*s,* adv. gen. suff. + *-t* added later; for this *-t* see WHILST, etc.]

Aga Khan (ä′gə kän′), *n.* **1.** the title of the leader of the Ismailian sect of Muslims in Pakistan and India. **2. Aga Khan III** (*Aga Sultan Sir Mohammed Shah*), 1872–1957, leader of the Ismailian sect 1855–1957. **3. Aga Khan IV** (*Shah Karim al-Husainy*), born 1936, grandson of Aga Khan III, leader of the Ismailian sect since 1957.

agama (ăg′ə mə, ə găm′ə), *n.* any lizard of the Old World family *Agamidae*, allied to the iguanas and including large and brilliantly coloured species. [t. Carib]

Agamemnon (ăg′ə mĕm′nŏn, -nən), *n. Gk Legend.* a king of Mycenae, son of Atreus and brother of Menelaus. He led the Greeks against Troy. Upon his return he was treacherously slain by his faithless wife, Clytemnestra.

agamic (ə găm′ĭk), *adj.* **1.** *Biol.* **a.** asexual. **b.** occurring without sexual union; germinating without impregnation; not gamic. **2.** *Obs. Bot.* cryptogamic. Also, **agamous** (ăg′ə məs). [f. s. Gk *ágamos* unwed + -IC] —**agam′ically,** *adv.*

agamogenesis (ăg′ə mō jĕn′ĭ sĭs), *n. Biol.* asexual reproduction by buds, offshoots, cell division, etc. [f. Gk *ágamo(s)* unmarried + GENESIS] —**agamogenetic** (ăg′ə-mō jĭ nĕt′ĭk), *adj.*

Agaña (ə gä′nyə), *n.* the capital of Guam. 1642 (1960).

agapanthus (ăg′ə păn′thəs), *n.* any of several African liliaceous plants constituting the genus *Agapanthus* with umbels of blue or white flowers; African lily. [f. Gk: s. *agápē* love + m. *ánthos* flower]

agape[1] (ə gāp′), *adv., adj.* wide open; with the mouth wide open; in an attitude of wonder or eagerness.

agape[2] (ăg′ə pĭ), *n.* an early Christian love-feast at which communion was held and gifts were collected for the poor, in commemoration of the Lord's Supper. [t. Gk]

agar (ā′gə), *n.* **1.** *Biol.* a culture medium with an agar-agar base: *a spore agar.* **2.** agar-agar.

agar-agar (ā′gər ā′gə), *n.* a gelatine-like product of certain seaweeds, used to solidify culture media and, esp. in the Orient, for soups, etc. [t. Malay]

agaric (ăg′ə rĭk, ə gă′rĭk), *n.* an agaricaceous fungus. [t. L: s. *agaricum*, t. Gk: m. *agarikón*; named after *Agaria*, a place in Sarmatia]

agaricaceous (ə gă′rĭ kā′shəs), *adj.* belonging to the *Agaricales* or *Agaricaceae*, a family of fungi including mushrooms having blade-shaped gills on the underside of the cap.

Agassiz (ăg′ə sĭ; *for 2 also, Fr.* à gà sē′), *n.* **1. Alexander,** 1835–1910, U.S. zoologist and geologist. **2.** his father, **(Jean) Louis (Rodolphe)** (*Fr.* zhäN lwē rŏ dŏlf′), 1807–73, Swiss zoologist and geologist in the U.S.

agate (ăg′ĭt), *n.* **1.** a variegated variety of quartz (chalcedony) showing coloured bands or other markings (clouded, mosslike, etc.). **2.** a child's playing marble made of this substance, or of glass in imitation of it. **3.** *U.S.* the printing type ($5\frac{1}{2}$ point) ruby (def. 5). [t. F: m. *agathe*, g. L *achātēs*, t. Gk] —**ag′ate-like′,** *adj.*

agateware (ăg′ĭt wēə′), *n.* pottery variegated to resemble agate.

Agathocles (ə găth′ə klēz′), *n.* 361–289 B.C., tyrant of Syracuse.

agatize (ăg′ə tīz′), *v.t.*, **-tized, -tizing.** to change into, or make like, agate. Also, **agatise.**

à gauche (*Fr.* à gōsh′), *French.* on or to the left-hand side.

agave (ə gā′vĭ), *n.* any plant of the American (chiefly Mexican) amaryllidaceous genus *Agave*, species of which yield useful fibres, are used in making a fermented beverage, a distilled spirit, or a soap substitute, or are cultivated for ornament, as the century plant. [t. NL, t. Gk: m. *Agauē*, proper n., fem. of *agauós* noble]

agaze (ə gāz′), *adj., adv.* gazing.

agcy, agency.

age (āj), *n., v.*, **aged, ageing** or **aging.** —*n.* **1.** the length of time during which a being or thing has existed; length of life or existence to the time spoken of or referred to: *his age is 20 years, a tree or building of unknown age.* **2.** the lifetime of an individual, or of the individuals of a class or species on an average: *the age of the horse is from 25 to 30 years.* **3.** a period of human life, usually marked by a certain stage of physical or mental development, esp. a degree of development, measured by years from birth, which involves legal responsibility and capacity: *the age of discretion, the age of consent.* **4. of age,** *Law.* **a.** being any of several ages, usually 21 or 18, at which certain legal rights, as voting or marriage, are acquired. **b.** being 21 years old, in possession of full legal rights and responsibilities. **5.** the particular period of life at which one becomes naturally or conventionally qualified or disqualified for anything: *under age or over age for conscription.* **6.** one of the periods or stages of human life: *a person of middle age,* **7.** old age: *his eyes were dim with age.* **8.** a particular period of history, as distinguished from others; a historical epoch: *the age of Pericles, the Stone Age, the Middle Ages.* **9.** the people who live at a particular period. **10.** a generation or a succession of generations: *ages yet unborn.* **11.** *Colloq.* a great length of time: *I haven't seen you for an age* or *for ages.* **12.** *Psychol.* the comparative mental, emotional, or other development of a person, expressed by equating performance in various tests to the average age at which the same result is attained. **13.** *Geol.* a long or short part of the world's history distinguished by special features: *the Ice Age.* **14.** any one of the stages in the history of mankind divided, according to Hesiod, into the golden, silver, bronze, heroic, and iron ages. The happiest and best was the first (or golden) age, and the worst the iron age. —*v.i.* **15.** to grow old; develop the characteristics of old age: *he is ageing rapidly.* —*v.t.* **16.** to make old; cause to grow old or to seem old; *fear aged him overnight.* **17.** to bring to maturity or to a state fit for use: *to age wine.* [ME, t. OF: m. *aage*, earlier *e(d)age*, ult. f. m. L *aetas* + suffix *-āticum* -AGE]

—**Syn. 8.** AGE, EPOCH, ERA, PERIOD all refer to an extent of time. AGE usually implies a considerable extent of time, esp. one associated with a dominant personality, influence, characteristic, or institution: *the age of chivalry.* EPOCH and ERA are often used interchangeably, but an ERA is properly an extent of time characterized by changed conditions and new undertakings: *an era of invention.* An EPOCH is properly the beginning of an era: *an epoch of armed aggression.* A PERIOD may be long or short, but usually has a marked condition or feature: *the glacial period, a period of expansion.*

-age, a noun suffix, common in words taken from French, as in *baggage, language, savage, voyage,* etc., now a common English formative, forming: **1.** collective nouns from names of things, as in *fruitage, leafage.* **2.** nouns denoting condition, rank, service, fee, etc., from personal terms, as in *bondage, parsonage.* **3.** nouns expressing various relations, from verbs, as in *breakage, cleavage, postage.* [t. OF, g. L *-āticum*, neut. adj. suffix]

aged (ā′jĭd *for 1, 2, 4, 5;* ājd *for 3*), *adj.* **1.** having lived or existed long: *an aged man or tree.* **2.** pertaining to or characteristic of old age: *aged wrinkles.* **3.** of the age of: *a man aged 40 years.* **4.** *Phys. Geog.* old; approaching the state of a peneplain. **5.** (of horses) over 6 (or sometimes 8) years old. —**a′gedly,** *adv.* —**a′gedness,** *n.* —**Syn. 1.** See **old.** —**Ant. 1.** young.

agee (ə jē′), *adv., adj. Scot. or Dial.* ajee.

age-group (āj′gro͞op′), *n.* a group of persons having similar ages, and sometimes other characteristics in common, as scholastic ability.

ageing (ā′jĭng), *adj.* **1.** growing old; elderly. **2.** causing someone or something to grow old. **3.** causing a person to appear old, or older: *an ageing hat.* —*n.* **4.** the process of growing old. **5.** the process of causing someone or something to grow old. **6. the ageing,** elderly people. Also, **aging.**

ageless (āj′lĭs), *adj.* never growing old.

age-long (āj′lŏng′), *adj.* lasting for an age.

agency (ā′jən sĭ), *n., pl.* **-cies. 1.** a commercial or other organization furnishing some form of service for the public: *an advertising agency.* **2.** the place of business of an agent. **3.** the office of agent; the business of an agent entrusted with the concerns of another. **4.** the state of being in action or of exerting power; action; operation: *the agency of Providence.* **5.** a mode of exerting power; a means of producing effects; instrumentality: *by the agency of friends.* **6.** an Indian agency.

agenda (ə jĕn′də), *n.pl., sing.* **-dum** (-dəm). **1.** things to be done. **2.** matters to be brought before a committee, council, board, etc., as things to be done. **3.** (construed as *sing.*) a programme or list of things to be done, discussed, etc. [t. L, neut. pl. of gerundive of *agere* do]

agene (ā′jēn), *n.* nitrogen trichloride, NCl_3, a heavy explosive liquid. It is used in minute quantities as a preservative in bread, and to whiten flour.

agenize (ā′jĭ nīz′), *v.t.*, **-nized, -nizing.** to treat with agene. Also, **agenise.**

agent (ā′jənt), *n.* **1.** a person acting on behalf of another: *my agent has power to sign my name.* **2.** one who or that which acts or has the power to act: *a moral agent.* **3.** a natural force or object producing or used for obtaining specific results; instrumentality: *many insects are agents of fertilization.* **4.** an active cause; an efficient cause. **5.** an official: *an agent of Lloyd's.* **6.** a representative of a business firm, esp. a commercial traveller; a canvasser; solicitor. **7.** *Chem.* a substance which causes a reaction. **8.** a campaign manager; an election agent. **9.** *U.S.* an Indian agent. —*adj.* **10.** acting (opposed to *patient* in the sense of sustaining action). [t. L: s. *agens*, ppr., driving, doing] —**Syn. 1.** representative, deputy.

agential (ā jĕn′shəl), *adj.* **1.** pertaining to an agent or to an agency. **2.** *Gram.* agentive.

agentival (ā′jən tī′vəl), *adj.* agentive.

agentive (ā′jən tĭv), *Gram.* —*adj.* **1.** pertaining to, or productive of, a form which indicates agent or agency. —*n.* **2.** an agentive element or formation, as English *-er* in *painter.*

agent provocateur (*Fr.* à zhäɴ prō vō kȧ tœr′), *pl.* **agents provocateurs** (à zhäɴ prō vō kȧ tœr′). *French.* a secret agent hired to incite suspected persons to some illegal action, outbreak, etc., that will make them liable to punishment.

age of consent, the age at which one, esp. a female, is considered by law to be able to give consent to marriage or sexual intercourse.

age of discretion, *Law.* the age at which a person becomes legally responsible for certain acts and competent to exercise certain powers.

Age of Reason, any period in history, esp. the eighteenth century in Europe, characterized by a critical approach to religious, social, and philosophical matters that seeks to repudiate beliefs or systems not based on or justifiable by reason.

age-old (āj′ōld′), *adj.* very old.

ageratum (ăj′ĭ rā′təm), *n.* **1.** any plant of the asteraceous genus *Ageratum,* as *A. houstonianum,* a garden annual with small, dense, blue or white flower heads. **2.** any of various other composite plants, bearing blue, or sometimes white, flowers. [t. L, t. Gk: m. *agēraton* kind of plant, prop. neut. adj., not growing old]

aggiornamento (*It.* ȧd jōr nȧ mėn′tō), *n., pl.* **-ti** (-tē). *Italian.* the act of bringing customs, etc., up to date.

agglomerate (*v.* ə glŏm′ə rāt′; *adj., n.* ə glŏm′ə rĭt, -ə rāt′), *v.,* **-rated, -rating,** *adj., n.* —*v.t., v.i.* **1.** to collect or gather into a mass. —*adj.* **2.** gathered together into a ball or mass. **3.** *Bot.* crowded into a dense cluster, but not cohering. —*n.* **4.** a mass of things clustered together. **5.** a rock formation composed of large angular volcanic fragments. [t. L: m. s. *agglomerātus,* pp., wound into a ball] —**agglom′erative,** *adj.*

agglomeration (ə glŏm′ə rā′shən), *n.* **1.** an indiscriminately formed mass. **2.** the act or process of agglomerating.

agglutinant (ə glōō′tĭ nənt), *adj.* **1.** uniting, as glue; causing adhesion. —*n.* **2.** an agglutinating agent.

agglutinate (*v.* ə glōō′tĭ nāt′; *adj.* ə glōō′tĭ nĭt, -nāt′), *v.,* **-nated, -nating,** *adj.* —*v.t., v.i.* **1.** to unite or cause to adhere, as with glue. **2.** *Gram.* to form by agglutination. —*adj.* **3.** united by or as by glue. **4.** *Gram.* agglutinative. [t. L: m. s. *agglūtinātus,* pp., pasted to]

agglutinating language, a language whose affixes are invariable and are juxtaposed instead of fused. Turkish and Hungarian are agglutinating languages. See **agglutination,** (def. 6).

agglutination (ə glōō′tĭ nā′shən), *n.* **1.** the act or process of uniting by glue or other tenacious substance. **2.** the state of being thus united; adhesion of parts. **3.** that which is united; a mass or group cemented together. **4.** *Chem.* the coalescing or clumping of small suspended particles into larger masses. **5.** *Immunol.* the clumping of bacteria, red blood corpuscles, or other cells, due to introduction of an antibody. **6.** *Gram.* a pattern or process of inflection and word formation in some languages, in which the constituent elements of words are relatively distinct and constant in form and meaning; esp. such a process involving the addition of several suffixes to a single root or stem. In Turkish *ev* means 'house', *ev-ler* means 'houses', *ev-den* means 'from a house', and *ev-ler-den* means 'from houses'.

agglutinative (ə glōō′tĭ nə tĭv), *adj.* **1.** tending or having power to agglutinate or unite: *an agglutinative substance.* **2.** *Gram.* (of a language or construction) characterized by agglutination.

agglutinin (ə glōō′tĭ nĭn), *n.* *Immunol.* an antibody which causes agglutination.

agglutinogen (ăg′lōō tĭn′ə jən), *n.* *Immunol.* an antigen present in a bacterial body which when injected into an animal causes the production of agglutinins.

aggrade (ə grād′), *v.t.,* **-graded, -grading.** *Phys. Geog.* to raise the grade or level of (a river valley, a stream bed, etc.), as by depositing detritus. [f. AG- + GRADE, v.] —**aggradation** (ăg′rə dā′shən), *n.*

aggrandize (ăg′rən dīz′, ə grăn′dīz), *v.t.,* **-dized, -dizing.** **1.** to widen in scope; increase in size or intensity; enlarge; extend. **2.** to make great or greater in power, wealth, rank, or honour. **3.** to make (something) appear greater. Also, **aggrandise.** [t. F: m. *agrandiss-,* s. *agrandir,* g. L *ad-* AD- + *grandire* make great] —**aggrandizement** (ə grăn′dĭz mənt), *n.* —**ag′grandiz′er,** *n.*

aggravate (ăg′rə vāt′), *v.t.,* **-vated, -vating.** **1.** to make worse or more severe; intensify, as anything evil, disorderly, or troublesome: *to aggravate guilt; grief aggravated her illness.* **2.** *Colloq.* to provoke; irritate; exasperate: *threats will only aggravate her.* [t. L: m. s. *aggravātus,* pp., added to the weight of] —**ag′gravat′ed,** *adj.* —**ag′gravat′ing,** *adj.* —**ag′gravat′ingly,** *adv.* —**ag′grava′tor,** *n.*

—**Syn. 1.** heighten. AGGRAVATE, INTENSIFY both mean to increase in degree. To AGGRAVATE is to make more serious or more grave: *to aggravate a danger, an offence, a wound.* To INTENSIFY is perceptibly to increase intensity, force, energy, vividness, etc.: *to intensify heat, colour, rage.*

aggravation (ăg′rə vā′shən), *n.* **1.** increase of the intensity or severity of anything; act of making worse: *an aggravation of pain.* **2.** *Colloq.* something that irritates or exasperates.

aggregate (*adj., n.* ăg′rĭ gĭt, -gāt′; *v.* ăg′rĭ gāt′), *adj., n., v.,* **-gated, -gating.** —*adj.* **1.** formed by the conjunction or collection of particulars into a whole mass or sum; total; combined: *the aggregate amount of indebtedness.* **2.** *Bot.* **a.** (of a flower) formed of florets collected in a dense cluster but not cohering as in composite plants. **b.** (of a fruit) composed of a cluster of carpels belonging to the same flower, as the raspberry. —*n.* **3.** a sum, or assemblage of particulars; a total or gross amount: *the aggregate of all past experience.* **4. in the aggregate,** taken together; considered as a whole; collectively. **5.** *Geol.* a mixture of different mineral substances separable by mechanical means, as granite. **6.** any hard material added to cement to make concrete. —*v.t.* **7.** to bring together; collect into one sum, mass, or body. **8.** to amount to (the number of): *the guns captured will aggregate five or six hundred.* —*v.i.* **9.** to combine and form a collection or mass. [t. L: m. s. *aggregātus,* pp., added to] —**ag′gregately,** *adv.* —**aggregative** (ăg′rĭ gā′tĭv), *adj.*

aggregation (ăg′rĭ gā′shən), *n.* **1.** a combined whole; an aggregate: *an aggregation of isolated settlements.* **2.** the act of collection into an unorganized whole. **3.** the state of being so collected. **4.** *Ecol.* a group of organisms of the same or different species living closely together but less integrated than a society.

aggress (ə grĕs′), *v.i.* **1.** to commit the first act of hostility or offence; attack first. **2.** to begin a quarrel.

aggression (ə grĕsh′ən), *n.* **1.** the action of a state in violating by force the rights of another state, particularly its territorial rights. **2.** any offensive action or procedure; an inroad or encroachment: *an aggression upon one's rights.* **3.** the practice of making assaults or attacks; offensive action in general. **4.** *Psychol.* the emotional drive to attack; an offensive mental attitude (rather than defensive). [t. L: s. *aggressio*]

aggressive (ə grĕs′ĭv), *adj.* **1.** characterized by aggression; tending to aggress; making the first attack: *an aggressive foreign policy.* **2.** *Chiefly U.S.* energetic; vigorous. —**aggres′sively,** *adv.* —**aggres′siveness,** *n.*

aggressor (ə grĕs′ə), *n.* a person who attacks first; one who begins hostilities; an assailant or invader. [t. L]

aggrieve (ə grēv′), *v.t.,* **-grieved, -grieving.** to oppress or wrong grievously; injure by injustice (used now chiefly in the passive). [ME *agreve(n),* t. OF: m. *agrever,* g. L *aggravāre* exasperate]

aggrieved (ə grēvd′), *adj.* **1.** injured; oppressed; wronged: *he felt himself aggrieved.* **2.** *Law.* deprived of legal rights or claims. **3.** *Colloq.* feeling that one has been wronged; hurt; resentful: *an aggrieved expression on someone's face.*

agha (ä′gə), *n.* aga.

aghast (ə gäst′), *adj.* struck with amazement; stupefied with fright or horror: *they stood aghast at this unforeseen disaster.* [ME *agast,* pp. of *agasten* terrify. Cf. OE *gǣstan* in same sense]

agila (ăg′ĭ lä′), *n.* eaglewood. [t. Pg. or Sp.]

agile (ăj′īl), *adj.* **1.** quick and light in movement: *a robust and agile frame.* **2.** active; lively: *an agile mind.* [t. L: m. s. *agilis*] —**ag′ilely,** *adv.* —**Syn. 1.** nimble, sprightly.

agility (ə jĭl′ĭ tĭ), *n.* the power of moving quickly and easily; nimbleness: *agility of the body or mind.* [late ME *agilite,* t. F, t. L: m. s. *agilitas*]

Agilon (ăj′ĭ lŏn′), *n.* *Trademark.* an elasticized nylon yarn used in the manufacture of hosiery and underwear.

Agincourt (ăj′ĭn kôt′), *n.* a village in N France, near Calais: site of a decisive victory of the English under Henry V over the French, 1415. French, **Azincourt** (*Fr.* à zăɴ kōōr′).

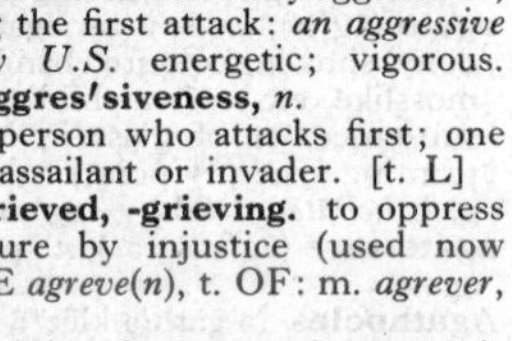

Agincourt

agio (ăj′ĭ ō′), *n., pl.* **-os.** **1.** a premium on money in exchange. **2.** an allowance for the difference in value of two currencies. **3.** an allowance given or taken on bills of exchange from other countries, to balance out exchange expenses. **4.** agiotage. [t. It.: m. *aggio* exchange, premium = *aggio*, g. L *habeo* I have]

agiotage (ăj′ə tĭj), *n.* **1.** the business of exchange. **2.** speculative dealing in securities. [t. F, der. It. *aggio* AGIO]

agist (ă jĭst′), *v.t.* **1.** to take in and feed or pasture (livestock) for payment. **2.** to lay a public burden, as a tax, on (land or its owner). [ME, t. OF: s. *agister*, f. *à* to + *giste* resting-place (ult. der. L *jacere* lie)] —**agis′tor,** *n.*

agistment (ă jĭst′mənt), *n.* **1.** the act of agisting. **2.** the price paid for pasturing livestock. **3.** a burden or tax.

agitate (ăj′ĭ tāt′), *v.*, **-tated, -tating.** —*v.t.* **1.** to move or force into violent irregular action; shake or move briskly: *the wind agitates the sea.* **2.** to move to and fro; impart regular motion to: *to agitate a fan, etc.* **3.** to disturb, or excite into tumult; perturb: *the mind of man is agitated by various emotions.* **4.** to call attention to by speech or writing; discuss; debate: *to agitate the question.* **5.** *Archaic.* to consider or revolve in the mind. —*v.i.* **6.** to arouse or attempt to arouse public feeling as in some political or social question: *to agitate for the repeal of a tax.* [t. L: m. s. *agitātus*, pp., aroused, excited] —**ag′itat′edly,** *adv.*

agitation (ăj′ĭ tā′shən), *n.* **1.** the act of agitating. **2.** a state of being agitated: *she walked away in great agitation.* **3.** persistent urging of a political or social question before the public. —**agitative** (ăj′ĭ tə tĭv), *adj.*

—**Syn.** 2. AGITATION, DISTURBANCE, EXCITEMENT, TURMOIL imply inner unrest and a nervous condition. AGITATION implies a shaken state of emotions, usually perceptible in the face or movements: *with evident agitation she opened the telegram.* DISTURBANCE implies an inner disquiet caused by worry, indecision, apprehension, and the like: *long-continued mental disturbance is a cause of illness.* EXCITEMENT implies a highly emotional state caused by either agreeable or distressing circumstances: *excitement over a proposed trip, unexpected good news, a fire.* TURMOIL suggests such a struggle or conflict of emotions that one is unable to think consecutively: *her thoughts were in a hopeless turmoil.*

agitato (ăj′ĭ tä′tō), *adj. Music.* agitated; restless or hurried in movement or style. [It.]

agitator (ăj′ĭ tā′tə), *n.* **1.** one who stirs up others, with the view of strengthening his own cause or that of his party, etc. **2.** a machine for agitating and mixing.

agitprop (ăj′ĭt prŏp′, ăj′ĭt prŏp′), *n.* **1.** agitation and propaganda esp. for the cause of communism. **2.** (*often cap.*) an agency or department, as of a government, that directs and coordinates agitation and propaganda. **3.** one who is trained or takes part in such activities. —*adj.* **4.** of or pertaining to agitprop. **5.** *Theat.* pertaining to a dramatic style or technique of social protest and Marxist attitudes. [t. Russ.: b. *agitatsiya* agitation + *propaganda* propaganda]

Aglaia (ə glī′ə), *n. Gk Myth.* one of the Graces.

agleam (ə glēm′), *adv., adj.* gleaming.

aglet (ăg′lĭt), *n.* **1.** a metal tag at the end of a lace. **2.** the points or ribbons generally used in the 16th and 17th centuries to fasten or tie dresses. **3.** aiguillette. Also, **aiglet.** [ME, t. F: m. *aiguillette* point, ult. der. L *acus* needle]

agley (ə glē′, ə glī′, ə glā′), *adv. Chiefly Scot. and N Dial.* off the right line; awry; wrong. [f. A-[1] + Scot. *gley* squint]

aglimmer (ə glĭm′ə), *adv., adj.* glimmering.

aglitter (ə glĭt′ə), *adv., adj.* glittering.

aglossa (ə glŏs′ə), *n.* any frog of the genus *Aglossa*, family *Pipidae*, of South America and Africa, which have no tongues; tongueless frog. [f. A-[6] + Gk *glôssa* tongue]

aglow (ə glō′), *adv., adj.* glowing.

agminate (ăg′mĭ nĭt, ăg′mĭ nāt′), *adj.* aggregated or clustered together. Also, **ag′minat′ed.** [f. s. L *agmen* troop + -ATE[1]]

agnail (ăg′nāl′), *n.* hangnail.

agnate (ăg′nāt), *n.* **1.** a kinsman whose connection is traceable exclusively through males. **2.** any male relation by the father's side. —*adj.* **3.** related or akin through males or on the father's side. **4.** allied or akin. [t. L: m. s. *agnātus*, pp., born to] —**agnatic** (ăg năt′ĭk), *adj.* —**agnation** (ăg nā′shən), *n.*

Agni (ŭg′nĭ), *n. Hindu Myth.* the god of fire, one of the three chief divinities of the Vedas. [t. Skt]

agnomen (ăg nō′mĕn), *n.*, *pl.* **-nomina** (-nŏm′ĭ nə). **1.** an additional (fourth) name given to a person by the ancient Romans in allusion to some achievement or other circumstance, as *Africanus* in *Publius Cornelius Scipio Africanus.* **2.** any nickname. [t. L: f. *ag-* AG- + *nōmen* name] —**agnominal** (ăg nŏm′ĭ nəl), *adj.*

agnostic (ăg nŏs′tĭk), *n.* **1.** one who holds that the ultimate cause (God) and the essential nature of things are unknown or unknowable or that human knowledge is limited to experience. —*adj.* **2.** pertaining to the agnostics or their doctrines. **3.** asserting the relativity and uncertainty of all knowledge. [f. A-[6] + s. Gk *gnōstikós* knowing. Coined by T. Huxley in 1869] —**agnos′tically,** *adv.* —**Syn. 1.** See **atheist.**

agnosticism (ăg nŏs′tĭ sĭz′əm), *n.* **1.** the doctrine maintained by agnostics. **2.** an intellectual attitude or doctrine which asserts the relativity and therefore the uncertainty of all knowledge.

Agnus Dei (ăg′nōōs dā′ē). **1.** *Eccles.* **a.** a figure of a lamb as emblematic of Christ. **b.** such a representation with the nimbus inscribed with the cross about its head, and supporting the banner of the cross. **2.** *Rom. Cath. Ch.* **a.** a wax medallion stamped with this figure and blessed by the pope, or a fragment of such a medallion. **b.** a triple chant, beginning 'Agnus Dei', preceding the communion in the mass. **c.** the music accompanying this prayer. **3.** *C. of E.* **a.** an invocation beginning 'O Lamb of God', said or sung in the communion service. **b.** a musical setting for this. [LL: Lamb of God. See John 1:29]

ago (ə gō′), *adv.* in past time; past: *some time ago, long ago.* [ME, var. of *agoon*, OE *āgān*, pp. of *āgān* go by, pass]

agog (ə gŏg′), *adj.* **1.** highly excited by eagerness or curiosity. —*adv.* **2.** in a state of eager desire; with excitement. [t. F: m. *en gogues* in a merry mood]

agogic (ə gŏj′ĭk), *adj. Music.* producing an effect similar to an accent by sustaining one of a pair of notes slightly beyond its written value.

-agogue, a word element meaning 'leading' or 'guiding', found in a few agent nouns (often with pejorative value), as in *demagogue, pedagogue.* [t. Gk: m. s. *agōgós* leading]

agon (ăg′ŏn, -ŏn), *n.*, *pl.* **agones** (ă gō′nēz). *Gk Antiq.* a contest for a prize, whether of athletes in the games or of poets, painters, and the like. [t. Gk]

agone (ə gŏn′), *adv., adj. Archaic.* ago.

agonic (ə gŏn′ĭk), *adj.* not forming an angle. [f. s. Gk *ágōnos* without angles + -IC]

agonic line, a line on the earth's surface connecting points at which the declination of the earth's magnetic field is zero.

agonist (ăg′ə nĭst), *n.* **1.** *Physiol.* an actively contracting muscle considered in relation to its opposing muscle (the antagonist). **2.** a competitor.

agonistic (ăg′ə nĭs′tĭk), *adj.* **1.** combative; striving to overcome in argument. **2.** aiming at effect; strained. **3.** pertaining to contests. Also, **ag′onis′tical.** [t. Gk: m. s. *agōnistikós*] —**ag′onis′tically,** *adv.* —**ag′onis′tics,** *n.*

agonize (ăg′ə nīz′), *v.*, **-nized, -nizing.** —*v.i.* **1.** to writhe with extreme pain; suffer violent anguish. **2.** to make great effort of any kind. —*v.t.* **3.** to distress with extreme pain; torture. Also, **agonise.** [t. ML: m. s. *agōnizāre*, t. Gk: m. *agōnízesthai* contend] —**ag′oniz′ingly,** *adv.*

agony (ăg′ə nĭ), *n.*, *pl.* **-nies.** **1.** extreme, and generally prolonged, pain; intense suffering. **2.** intense mental excitement of any kind. **3.** the struggle preceding natural death: *mortal agony.* **4. the agony,** Christ's suffering in the garden of Gethsemane. **5. put, pile, turn on the agony,** *Colloq.* to exaggerate a story, misfortunes, etc. for effect. **6.** *Rare.* a violent struggle. [ME *agonye*, t. LL: m. *agōnia*, t. Gk: contest, anguish] —**Syn. 1.** throe, paroxysm, pang; ache. See **pain. 2.** anguish, torment, torture.

agony column, *Colloq.* a newspaper column of advertisements, esp. those arising from personal distress; personal column.

agora[1] (ăg′ə rə), *n.*, *pl.* **-rae** (-rē′). (in ancient Greece) **1.** a popular political assembly. **2.** the place of such assembly, originally the market place. [t. Gk]

agora[2] (ăg′ə rä′), *n. pl.* **agorot** (ăg′ə rōt′), an Israeli currency unit, equal to the hundredth part of a pound. [t. Heb.]

agoraphobia (ăg′ə rə fō′byə), *n. Psychol.* a morbid fear of being in an open space. [f. AGORA + -PHOBIA]

agouti (ə gōō′tĭ), *n.*, *pl.* **-tis, -ties.** **1.** any of several short-haired, short-eared, rabbit-like rodents of the genus *Dasyprocta*, of South and Central America and the West Indies, destructive to sugar cane. **2.** an irregularly barred pattern of the fur of certain rodents. **3.** an animal having fur of this pattern. [t. F, t. Sp.: m. *aguti*, t. Tupi]

Agouti, *Dasyprocta aguti* (19 to 22 in. long)

agouty (ə gōō′tĭ), *n.*, *pl.* **-ties.** agouti.

Agra (ä′grə), *n.* a city in N India, in Uttar Pradesh; site of the Taj Mahal. 462,029 (1961).

agraffe (ə grăf′), *n.* **1.** a small cramp iron. **2.** a clasp for hooking together parts of clothing, etc. **3.** a device for checking vibration in a piano string. [t. F, var. of *agrafe* hook, f. *à* A-⁵ + *grafe* sharp-pointed tool (g. L *graphium*, t. Gk: m. *grapheîon* pencil); F meaning influenced by *agrappe* hook]

Agram (*Ger.* ä′gräm), *n.* German name of **Zagreb.**

agranulocytosis (ə grăn′yo͞o lō sī tō′sĭs), *n. Pathol.* a serious, often fatal, blood disease, marked by a great reduction of the leucocytes.

agraphia (ə grăf′yə), *n. Pathol.* a cerebral disorder marked by total or partial inability to write. [t. NL, f. Gk: *a-* A-⁶ + *-graphia* writing] —**agraph′ic,** *adj.*

agrarian (ə grêə′rĭ ən), *adj.* **1.** relating to land, land tenure, or the division of landed property: *agrarian laws.* **2.** pertaining to the advancement of agricultural groups: *an agrarian experiment.* **3.** rural; agricultural. **4.** growing in fields; wild: *an agrarian plant.* —*n.* **5.** one who favours the equal division of land. [f. s. L *agrārius* pertaining to land + -AN] —**agrar′ianism,** *n.*

agree (ə grē′), *v.*, **agreed, agreeing.** —*v.i.* **1.** to yield assent; consent (often fol. by *to*, esp. with reference to things and acts): *he agreed to accompany the ambassador, do you agree to the conditions?* **2.** to be of one mind; harmonize in opinion or feeling (often fol. by *with*, esp. with reference to persons): *I don't agree with you.* **3.** to live in concord or without contention; harmonize in action. **4.** to come to one opinion or mind; come to an arrangement or understanding; arrive at a settlement (sometimes fol. by *upon*). **5.** to be consistent; harmonize (fol. by *with*): *this story agrees with others.* **6.** to be applicable or appropriate; resemble; be similar (fol. by *with*): *the picture does not agree with the original.* **7.** to be accommodated or adapted; suit (fol. by *with*): *the same food does not agree with every person.* **8.** *Gram.* to correspond in inflectional form, as in number, case, gender, or person (fol. by *with*). —*v.t.* **9.** to concede; grant (fol. by noun clause): *I agree that he is the ablest of us.* **10.** to determine; settle (usually fol. by noun clause): *It was agreed that we should meet again.* [ME *agre(en)*, t. OF: m. *agréer*, der. phrase *a gré* at pleasure]

—**Syn. 5.** AGREE, ACCORD, CORRESPOND imply comparing persons or things and finding that they harmonize. AGREE implies having or arriving at a condition in which no essential difference of opinion or detail is evident: *all the reports agree.* ACCORD emphasizes agreeing exactly, both in fact and in point of view: *this report accords with the other.* CORRESPOND suggests having an obvious similarity, though not agreeing in every detail: *part of this report corresponds with the facts.*

agreeable (ə grĭə′bl), *adj.* **1.** to one's liking; pleasing: *agreeable manners.* **2.** willing or ready to agree or consent: *are you agreeable?* **3.** suitable; conformable (fol. by *to*). —**agree′abil′ity, agree′ableness,** *n.* —**agree′ably,** *adv.*

agreed (ə grēd′), *adj.* arranged by common consent: *they met at the agreed time.*

agreement (ə grē′mənt), *n.* **1.** the act of coming to a mutual arrangement. **2.** the arrangement itself. **3.** unanimity of opinion; harmony in feeling: *agreement among the members.* **4.** the state of being in accord; concord; harmony; conformity: *agreement between observation and theory.* **5.** *Gram.* correspondence in number, case, gender, person, or some other formal category between syntactically connected words, esp. between one or more subordinate words and the word or words upon which they depend. For example: in *the boy runs*, *boy* is a singular noun and *runs* is a distinctively singular form of the verb. **6.** collective agreement. **7.** *Law.* **a.** an expression of assent by two or more parties to the same object. **b.** the phraseology, written or oral, of an exchange of promises.

—**Syn. 2.** AGREEMENT, BARGAIN, COMPACT, CONTRACT all suggest a binding arrangement between two or more parties. AGREEMENT ranges in meaning from mutual understanding to binding obligation. BARGAIN applies particularly to agreements about buying and selling. COMPACT applies to treaties or alliances between nations or to formal personal pledges. CONTRACT is used especially in law and business for such agreements as are legally enforceable.

agréments (*Fr.* ä grĕ mäɴ′), *n.pl. French.* **1.** agreeable qualities or circumstances. **2.** *Music.* ornaments. Also, **agrémens.**

agrestic (ə grĕs′tĭk), *adj.* **1.** rural; rustic. **2.** unpolished. [f. s. L *agrestis* rural + -IC]

agric., 1. agricultural. **2.** agriculture. Also, **agr.**

Agricola (ə grĭk′ə lə), *n.* **Gnaeus Julius** (nē′əs jo͞o′lyəs), A.D. 37–93, Roman general: governor of Britain.

agriculture (ăg′rĭ kŭl′chə), *n.* the cultivation of land, as in the raising of crops; husbandry; tillage; farming (in a broad sense, including horticulture, forestry, stock-raising, etc.). [t. L: m. s. *agricultūra*, f. *agrī*, gen. of *ager* land + *cultūra* cultivation] —**ag′ricul′tural,** *adj.* —**ag′ricul′turally,** *adv.*

agriculturist (ăg′rĭ kŭl′chə rĭst), *n.* **1.** a farmer. **2.** an expert in agriculture. Also, **agriculturalist** (ăg′rĭ kŭl′chə rə lĭst).

Agrigento (*It.* ä grē jĕn′tō), *n.* a town in S Sicily. 51,387 (1966). Formerly, **Girgenti.**

agrimony (ăg′rĭ mə nĭ), *n.*, *pl.* **-nies. 1.** any plant of the rosaceous genus *Agrimonia*, esp. *A. eupatoria*, a perennial herb with pinnate leaves and small yellow flowers. **2.** any of certain other plants, as hemp agrimony or bur marigold. [t. L: m. s. *agrimōnia*, var. of *argemōnia* a plant, t. Gk: m. *argemṓnē*; r. ME *egrimoigne*, t. OF: m. *aigremoine*]

Agrippa (ə grĭp′ə), **Marcus Vipsanius** (mä′kəs vĭp sā′nĭ əs), 63–12 B.C. Roman statesman, general, engineer: victor over Antony and Cleopatra at Actium.

Agrippina II (ăg′rĭ pī′nə), A.D. 16?–59?, mother of the Roman emperor Nero.

agro-, a word element meaning 'soil', 'field', as in *agrology.* [t. Gk, comb. form of *agrós*]

agrobiology (ăg′rō bī ŏl′ə jĭ), *n.* the quantitative science of plant life and plant nutrition. —**agrobiologic** (ăg′rō-bī′ə lŏj′ĭk), **ag′robi′olog′ical,** *adj.* —**ag′robi′olog′ically,** *adv.* —**ag′robiol′ogist,** *n.*

agrology (ə grŏl′ə jĭ), *n.* the applied phases of soil science. See **pedology¹.** —**agrologic** (ăg′rə lŏj′ĭk), **ag′rolog′ical,** *adj.*

agron., agronomy.

agronomics (ăg′rə nŏm′ĭks), *n.* the art and science of managing land and crops.

agronomy (ə grŏn′ə mĭ), *n.* **1.** the applied phases of both soil science and the several plant sciences, often limited to applied plant sciences dealing with crops. **2.** agriculture. —**agronomic** (ăg′rə nŏm′ĭk), **ag′ronom′ical,** *adj.* **agron′omist,** *n.*

agrostology (ăg′rə stŏl′ə jĭ), *n.* the part of botany that treats of grasses. [f. s. Gk *ágrōstis* kind of grass + -(O)LOGY]

aground (ə ground′), *adv.*, *adj.* on the ground; stranded: *the ship ran aground.*

Agt, agent. Also, **agt.**

Aguascalientes (*Sp.* ä′gwäs kä lyĕn′tĕs), *n.* a town in central Mexico. 147,727 (est. 1965).

ague (ā′gyo͞o), *n.* **1.** *Pathol.* a malarial fever characterized by regularly returning paroxysms, marked by successive cold, hot, and sweating fits. **2.** a fit of shaking or shivering as if with cold; a chill. [ME, t. OF, t. Pr., t. L: m. s. *acūta (febris)* acute (fever)] —**a′gued,** *adj.* —**a′guish,** *adj.* —**a′guishly,** *adv.* —**a′gue-like′,** *adj.*

Aguinaldo (*Sp.* ä gē näl′dō), *n.* **General Emilio** (*Sp.* ĕ mē′lyō), 1869–1964, Filipino leader against Spain during the Spanish-American War and against the U.S. after the war.

Agulhas (ə gŭl′əs; *Port.* ä go͞o′lyäsh), *n.* **Cape,** the southernmost point of Africa.

ah (ä), *interj.* (an exclamation expressing pain, surprise, pity, complaint, dislike, joy, etc., according to the manner of utterance.) [ME]

A.H., (L *anno Hejirae*) in the year of or from the Hegira (A.D. 622) (in the Muslim system of dating).

a.h., *Elect.* ampere-hour.

aha (ä hä′), *interj.* (an exclamation expressing triumph, contempt, mockery, irony, surprise, etc., according to the manner of utterance.) [ME]

Ahab (ā′hăb), *n. Bible.* king of Israel of the ninth century B.C., husband of Jezebel. I Kings 16–22.

Ahasuerus (ə hăz′yo͞o ĭə′rəs), *n. Bible.* king of Persia (known by the Greeks as Xerxes), husband of Esther. Book of Esther; Ezra 4:6.

ahead (ə hĕd′), *adv.* **1.** in or to the front; in advance; before. **2.** forward; onward. **3. be ahead,** to be to the good; be winning: *I was well ahead in the deal.* **4. get ahead of,** to surpass. [f. A-¹ + HEAD]

ahem (ə hĕm′), *interj.* (an utterance designed to attract attention, express doubt, etc.)

Ahidjo (*Fr.* ä ĕd zhō′), *n.* **Ahmadou** (*Fr.* ä mä do͞o′), born 1924, president of Cameroun since 1960.

ahimsa (ä hĭm′sä), *n.* the Buddhist duty of harmlessness to living things. [t. Skt]

Ahmedabad (ä′mə də băd′), *n.* a city in W India, in Gujarat state. 1,206,001 (1961). Also, **Ahmadabad.**

Ahmednagar (ä′məd nŭg′ə), *n.* a city in W India, in Maharashtra state. 119,020 (1961). Also, **Ahmadnagar.**

ahoy (ə hoi′), *interj. Naut.* (a call used in hailing.) [f. *a*, interj. + HOY]

Ahriman (ä′rĭ mən), *n. Zoroastrianism.* the wicked Devil, supreme spirit of evil, antagonistic to Ormazd.

ahungered (ə hŭng′gəd), *adj. Archaic.* hungry.

Ahura Mazda (ä′ho͞o rə măz′də), Ormazd.

Ahvenanmaa (*Finn.* äh′vĕ näm mä), *n.* Finnish name of **Åland Islands.**

Ahwaz (ä wäz′), *n.* a town in SW Iran. 123,000 (est. 1968).

ai (ä′ĭ), *n., pl.* **ais** (ä′ĭz), a large three-toed sloth, *Bradypus tridactylus,* of Central and South America. [t. Tupi: m. (*h*)*aī*, imit. of its cry]

A.I., artificial insemination.

A.I.A., Associate of the Institute of Actuaries.

A.I.A.A., Architect Associate of the Incorporated Association of Architects and Surveyors.

A.I.A.C., Associate of the Institute of Company Accountants.

A.I.A.S., Surveyor Associate of the Incorporated Association of Architects and Surveyors.

aiblins (ā′blĭnz), *adv. Scot.* ablins.

Aichinger (*Ger.* īKH′ĭng ər), *n.* **Ilse** (*Ger.* ĭl′zə), born 1921, German writer.

aid (ād), *v.t.* **1.** to afford support or relief to; help. **2.** to promote the course of accomplishment of; facilitate. **3.** to give financial support to: *a state-aided school.* —*v.i.* **4.** to give help or assistance. —*n.* **5.** help; support; assistance. **6.** one who or that which aids or yields assistance; a helper; an auxiliary. **7. in aid of,** directed towards; intended to achieve. **8.** a payment made by feudal vassals to their lord on special occasions. **9.** *Eng. Hist.* any of a variety of revenues received by the king in the Middle Ages after 1066 from his feudal vassals and from others of his subjects. **10.** *U.S.* aide-de-camp. [ME *aide*(*n*), t. OF: m. *aidier*, g. L *adjūtāre*] —**aid′er,** *n.* —**aid′less,** *adj.* —**Syn. 1.** See **help. 5.** succour; relief; subsidy; subvention. —**Ant. 2.** hinder.

A.I.D., artificial insemination (by) donor.

Aidan (ā′dn), *n.* **Saint,** died A.D. 651, English monk at Iona; bishop of Northumbria *c.* A.D. 635–651.

aide (ād), *n.* an aide-de-camp. [t. F]

aide-de-camp (ād′də kŏng′), *n., pl.* **aides-de-camp.** a military or naval officer acting as a confidential assistant to a superior, esp. a general, governor, etc. [t. F: camp assistant]

aide-mémoire (*Fr.* ĕd mė mwär′), *n. French.* a reminder; a memorandum of discussion, agreement, or action.

Aidin (*Turk.* äy′dĭn), *n.* Aydin.

aiglet (ā′glĭt), *n.* aglet.

aigrette (ā′grĕt, ā grĕt′), *n.* **1.** an egret. **2.** a plume or tuft of feathers arranged as a head ornament, esp. the back plumes of various herons. **3.** a copy in jewellery of such a plume. **4.** the feathery pappus of the dandelion, thistle, and other plants. [t. F]

aiguille (ā gwēl′, ā′gwēl), *n.* **1.** a needle-like rock mass or mountain peak. **2.** a slender stone-boring tool. [t. F, in OF *aguille* needle, g. LL dim. of L *acus* needle]

aiguillette (ā′gwĭ lĕt′), *n.* an ornamental tagged cord or braid on a uniform; aglet. [t. F, dim. of *aiguille.* See AGLET]

A.I.H., artificial insemination (by) husband.

Aiken (ā′kĭn), *n.* **Conrad Potter,** born 1889, U.S. poet.

ail (āl), *v.t.* **1.** to affect with pain or uneasiness; trouble. —*v.i.* **2.** to feel pain; be ill (usually in a slight degree); be unwell. [ME *ailen*, OE *eglan*, c. Goth *agljan*]

ailanthus (ā lăn′thəs), *n.* a simaroubaceous tree, *Ailanthus altissima,* with pinnate leaves and greenish flowers, native in eastern Asia and planted in Europe and America as a shade tree; tree of heaven. [t. NL, t. Amboinan: m. *aylanto* tree of heaven] —**ailan′thic,** *adj.*

aileron (ā′lə rŏn′), *n. Aeron.* a hinged, movable flap of an aeroplane wing, usually part of the trailing edge, used primarily to maintain lateral balance or to bank, roll, etc. [t. F, dim. of *aile* wing. See AISLE]

ailing (ā′lĭng), *adj.* sickly. —**Syn.** See **sick.**

ailment (āl′mənt), *n.* a morbid affection of the body or mind; indisposition: *a slight ailment.*

A.I.Loco. E., Associate of the Institution of Locomotive Engineers.

aim (ām), *v.t.* **1.** to give a certain direction and elevation to (a gun or the like), for the purpose of causing the projectile, when the weapon is discharged, to hit the object. **2.** to direct or point (something) at something: *the satire was aimed at the Church.* —*v.i.* **3.** to level a gun; give direction to a blow, missile, etc. **4.** to strive; try (followed by *at* or *to*): *they aim at saving something every month.* **5.** to direct efforts towards an object: *to aim high, at the highest.* **6.** *Colloq.* to intend: *she aims to go tomorrow.* **7.** *Obs.* to estimate; guess. —*n.* **8.** the act of aiming or directing anything at or towards a particular point or object. **9.** the direction in which a missile is pointed; the line of sighting: *to take aim.* **10.** the point intended to be hit; thing or person aimed at. **11.** something intended or desired to be attained by one's efforts; purpose. **12.** *Obs.* conjecture; guess. [ME *ayme*(*n*), t. OF: m. (*a*)*esmer*, g. L (*ad*)*aestimāre* estimate] —**aim′er,** *n.*

—**Syn. 11.** AIM, END, OBJECT all imply something which is the goal of one's efforts. AIM implies that towards which one makes a direct line, refusing to be diverted from it: *a nobleness of aim, one's aim in life.* END emphasizes the goal as a cause of efforts: *the end for which one strives.* OBJECT emphasizes the goal as that towards which all efforts are directed: *the object of years of study.*

A.I.Mech.E., Associate of the Institution of Mechanical Engineers.

A.I.Min.E., Associate of the Institution of Mining Engineers.

aimless (ām′lĭs), *adj.* without aim; purposeless. —**aim′lessly,** *adv.* —**aim′lessness,** *n.*

ain (ān), *adj. Scot.* own.

Ain (*Fr.* ăN), *n.* a department in E France. 327,146 pop. (1962); 2249 sq. mi. *Cap.:* Bourg.

aîné (*Fr.* ĕ nė′), *adj. French.* of the greater age; elder; eldest. —**aînée,** *adj. fem.*

Ainsworth (ānz′wûth′), *n.* **W(illiam) Harrison,** 1805–82, English novelist.

ain't (ānt), (generally considered to be bad usage) **1.** a contraction of *am not,* extended in use as contraction of *are not* and *is not.* **2.** a contraction (with loss of *h*) of *have not* or *has not.*

Aintab (īn tăb′), *n.* Gaziantep.

Ainu (ī′nōō), *n.* **1.** a member of an aboriginal race of the northernmost islands of Japan, having Caucasian features, light skin, and hairy bodies. **2.** the language of the Ainus, of uncertain relationship.

air[1] (ĕə), *n.* **1.** a mixture of oxygen, nitrogen and other gases, which surrounds the earth and forms its atmosphere. **2.** a movement of the atmosphere; a light breeze. **3.** *Obs.* breath. **4.** circulation; publication; publicity: *to give air to one's ideas.* **5.** the general character or complexion of anything; appearance. **6.** the peculiar look, appearance, and bearing of a person. **7.** (*pl.*) affected manner; manifestation of pride or vanity; assumed haughtiness: *to put on airs.* **8.** *Music.* **a.** a tune; a melody. **b.** the soprano or treble part. **c.** an aria. **d.** an Elizabethan song. **9.** *Radio.* the atmosphere through which radio waves are sent. **10. clear the air,** to eliminate dissension, ambiguity, or tension from a discussion, situation, etc. **11. in the air, a.** without foundation or actuality; visionary or uncertain. **b.** in circulation. **c.** undecided or unsettled (often prec. by *up*). **12. into thin air,** completely or entirely out of sight or reach. **13. off the air,** no longer being broadcast; not on the air. **14. on the air,** in the act of broadcasting; being broadcast. **15. take the air,** to go out of doors; walk or ride a little distance. **16. walk** (or **tread**) **on air,** to feel very happy or elated. —*v.t.* **17.** to expose to the air; give access to the open air; ventilate. **18.** to expose to warm air; to dry with heated air: *to air sheets.* **19.** to expose ostentatiously; bring into public notice; display: *to air one's opinions or theories.* [ME *ayre, eir,* t. OF: m. *air,* g. L *āēr,* t. Gk: air, mist] —**air′like′,** *adj.*

air[2] (ĕə), *adv. Scot.* early. [see ERE]

Air (ä′ĭə; *Fr.* ȧ ēr′), *n.* a former native kingdom in Niger, in Africa, consisting of a plateau and oasis region in the Sahara. ab. 30,000 sq. mi. Also, **Asben.**

air alert, *U.S. Mil.* **1.** the act of flying while waiting for orders or for enemy aeroplanes to appear. **2.** the signal to take stations for such action.

air-base (ĕə′bās′), *n.* an operations centre for units of an airforce.

air-bed (ĕə′bĕd′), *n.* an inflatable mattress.

air-bell (ĕə′bĕl′), *n.* **1.** bubble of air. **2.** *Photog.* bubble of air which leaves marks on a photograph during processing.

air-bladder (ĕə′blăd′ə), *n.* **1.** a vesicle or sac containing air. **2.** *Ichthyol.* a symmetrical sac filled with air whose principal function is the regulation of the hydrostatic equilibrium of the body; a swim bladder.

airborne (ĕə′bôn′), *adj.* **1.** borne up, carried, or transported by air. **2.** in the air; (of aircraft) having taken off. **3.** *Mil.* trained for and allotted to air operations: *an airborne division.*

air-bound (ĕə′bound′), *adj.* stopped up by air.

air-brake (ĕə′brāk′), *n.* **1.** *Aeron.* a hinged flap or other extendable device for reducing the speed of an aircraft. **2.** a brake or system of brakes operated by compressed air.

airbrick (ĕə′brĭk′), *n.* a perforated block let into a wall for ventilation.

air-bridge (ĕə′brĭj′), *n.* a transport link by aeroplane between two places.

air-brush (ĕə′brŭsh′), *n.* an atomizer for spraying liquid paint upon a surface.

airbus (ĕə′bŭs′), *n.* a passenger aircraft operating over short routes.

air-cell (ĕə′sĕl′), *n.* a small cavity full of air in plant or animal tissue; air-sac; air-bladder.

air-chamber (ĕə′chām′bə), *n.* **1.** a chamber containing air, as in a pump or a lifeboat. **2.** a compartment of a hydraulic system containing air which by its elasticity equalizes the pressure and flow of liquid within the system.

air chief marshal, 1. an officer in the Royal Air Force or any of various other airforces equivalent in rank to a general in the army. 2. the rank.

air-cock (ĕə′kŏk′), *n.* an air-valve.

air commodore, 1. an officer in the Royal Air Force or any of various other airforces equivalent in rank to a commodore in the navy. 2. the rank.

air-condenser (ĕə′kən dĕn′sə), *n.* 1. *Radio.* a capacitor in which the dielectric is air. 2. a machine for condensing air.

air-condition (ĕə′kən dĭsh′ən), *v.t.* 1. to furnish with an air-conditioning system. 2. to treat (air) with such a system. —**air′-condi′tioned,** *adj.* —**air′-condi′tioner,** *n.*

air-conditioning (ĕə′kən dĭsh′ə nĭng), *n.* 1. a system of treating air in buildings to assure temperature, humidity, dustlessness, and movement at levels most conducive to personal comfort or manufacturing processes. —*adj.* 2. denoting or pertaining to such a system.

air-cool (ĕə′ko͞ol′), *v.t.* 1. *Mach.* to remove the heat of combustion, friction, etc., from, as by a stream of air flowing over a finned engine cylinder. 2. to air-condition. —**air′cooled′,** *adj.*

air-corridor (ĕə′kŏ′rĭ dô′), *n.* a route along which flying is permitted in a restricted area, as from Berlin to the West.

aircraft (ĕə′kräft′), *n., pl.* **-craft.** any machine supported for flight in the air by buoyancy (such as balloons and other lighter-than-air craft) or by dynamic action of air on its surfaces (such as aeroplanes, helicopters, gliders, and other heavier-than-air craft).

aircraft-carrier (ĕə′kräft kă′rĭ ə), *n.* a warship, of varying size, equipped with a deck for the taking off and landing of aircraft, and storage space for the aircraft.

aircraftman (ĕə′kräft′mən), *n., pl.* **-men.** one of the lowest rank in the Royal Air Force. Also, **aircraftsman.** —**air′craft′wom′an, air′crafts′wom′an,** *n. fem.*

aircrew (ĕə′kro͞o′), *n.* the crew of an aircraft.

air-curtain (ĕə′kû′tn), *n.* a stream of compressed air directed, usually downwards, across a doorway, to form a shield against draughts, etc.

air-cushion (ĕə′ko͝osh′ən), *n.* 1. an inflatable airtight cushion. 2. air-chamber (def. 2). 3. the cushion of air supporting a hovercraft. —*adj.* 4. denoting or pertaining to a hovercraft.

air-cylinder (ĕə′sĭl′ĭn də), *n.* a cylinder containing air, esp. (with a piston) as a device for checking the recoil of a gun.

air-drain (ĕə′drān′), *n.* a cavity in the external walls of a building to prevent damp from penetrating.

Airdrie (ĕə′drĭ), *n.* a burgh in Scotland, in NE Lanarkshire. 33,620 (1961).

airdrome (ĕə′drōm′), *n. U.S.* an aerodrome.

airdrop (ĕə′drŏp′), *n.* delivery of supplies, troops, etc., by parachute.

air-dry (ĕə′drī′), *v.,* **-dried, -drying.** *adj.* —*v.t.* 1. to remove moisture from by evaporation in free air. —*adj.* 2. dry beyond further evaporation.

air-duct (ĕə′dŭkt′), *n. Engineering.* 1. a channel or pipe carrying warmed air in a heating system. 2. a channel, tube, or pipe which forms part of a ventilation system.

Airedale (ĕə′dāl′), *n.* a large heavy kind of terrier with a rough brown or tan coat which is black or grizzled over the back. [from *Airedale* in Yorkshire]

Airedale (Ab. 2 ft high at the shoulder)

airer (ĕə′rə), *n.* a wooden frame or other device for airing clothes.

airfield (ĕə′fēld′), *n.* a level area, usually equipped with hard-surfaced runways, on which aeroplanes take off and land.

airflow (ĕə′flō′), *n.* air currents caused by a moving aircraft, car, etc.

airfoil (ĕə′foil′), *n. U.S.* aerofoil.

airforce (ĕə′fôs′), *n.* 1. the branch of the armed forces of any country concerned with military aircraft. —*adj.* 2. of or pertaining to an airforce.

Air Force, Royal Air Force.

airframe (ĕə′frām′), *n. Aeron.* the whole body of an aeroplane without its engines.

airfreight (ĕə′frāt′), *n.* 1. cargo transported by aircraft. 2. the charge made for this service.

air-gap (ĕə′găp′), *n. Elect.* 1. an air-insulated gap in a magnetic circuit. 2. a spark gap in air between two conducting electrodes.

Airgraph (ĕə′grăf′, -gräf′), *Trademark.* —*n.* 1. a letter photographed on film, sent by air, and then enlarged. —*v.t.* 2. to send by Airgraph.

airgun (ĕə′gŭn′), *n.* a gun operated by compressed air.

airhole (ĕə′hōl′), *n.* 1. an opening to admit or discharge air. 2. a natural opening in the frozen surface of a river or pond. 3. *Aeron.* air-pocket.

air-hostess (ĕə′hōs′tĭs), *n.* a stewardess on an airliner.

airily (ĕə′rĭ lĭ), *adv.* 1. in a gay manner; jauntily. 2. lightly; delicately. —**airiness** (ĕə′rĭ nĭs), *n.*

airing (ĕə′rĭng), *n.* 1. an exposure to the air, or to a fire, as for drying. 2. a walk, drive, or the like, in the open air.

air-intake (ĕər′ĭn′tāk), *n.* 1. an opening in an aircraft for introducing air, mainly for the engines. 2. the opening through which air enters a carburettor. 3. a quantity of air taken in.

air-jacket (ĕə′jăk′ĭt), *n.* 1. an envelope of enclosed air about part of a machine, as for checking the transmission of heat. 2. a lifebelt.

airlane (ĕə′lān′), *n.* a route regularly used by aeroplanes; airway.

airless (ĕə′lĭs), *adj.* 1. lacking air. 2. without fresh air; stuffy. 3. still.

air-letter (ĕə′lĕt′ə), *n.* a sheet of very lightweight paper, folded and sent as a letter by airmail.

airlift (ĕə′lĭft′), *n.* 1. a system of transport by aircraft, esp. that established in 1948 by the Western powers to supply Berlin during the Soviet blockade. 2. the act or process of transporting such a load. —*v.t.* 3. to transport by airlift.

airline (ĕə′līn′), *n.* 1. a system furnishing (usually) scheduled air transport between specified points. 2. the aeroplanes, airports, navigational aids, etc., of such a system. 3. a company that owns or operates such a system. 4. a scheduled route followed by such a system. 5. *U.S.* a beeline.

airliner (ĕə′lī′nə), *n.* a large passenger aircraft operated by an airline.

airlock (ĕə′lŏk′), *n.* 1. *Civ. Eng.* an airtight transition compartment at the entrance of a pressure chamber, as in a spacecraft or a submerged caisson. 2. *Engineering.* an obstruction to or stoppage of the flow of liquid in a pipe, caused by an air bubble.

airmail (ĕə′māl′), *n.* 1. the system of transmitting mail by aircraft. 2. mail transmitted by aircraft. —*adj.* 3. of or sent by airmail.

airman (ĕə′mən), *n., pl.* **-men.** an aviator, esp. a member of an airforce. —**air′manship′,** *n.*

air marshal, *n.* 1. an officer in the Royal Air Force or any of various other airforces, equivalent in rank to a lieutenant general in the army. 2. the rank.

air-mass (ĕə′măs′), *n. Meteorol.* a body of air which approximates horizontal uniformity in its properties.

air mattress, an air-bed.

air-minded (ĕə′mīn′dĭd), *adj.* 1. interested in aviation or in the aviation aspects of problems. 2. favouring increased use of aircraft. —**air′-mind′edness,** *n.*

airplane (ĕə′plān′), *n. Chiefly U.S.* aeroplane.

air plant, *Bot.* epiphyte.

air-pocket (ĕə′pŏk′ĭt), *n. Aeron.* 1. a downward current of air, usually causing a sudden loss of altitude. 2. any pocket of air, as in a mine, where gas or water is held back by the air-pressure in the pocket.

airport (ĕə′pôt′), *n.* a tract of land or water with facilities for aircraft landing, take-off, shelter, supply, and repair, often used regularly for receiving or discharging passengers and cargo.

air-pressure (ĕə′prĕsh′ə), *n.* 1. the pressure of the atmosphere. 2. the pressure exerted by the air, as inside a tyre.

airproof (ĕə′pro͞of′), *adj.* 1. impervious to air. —*v.t.* 2. to make impervious to air.

airpump (ĕə′pŭmp′), *n.* an apparatus for drawing in, compressing, and discharging air.

air-raid (ĕə′rād′), *n.* a raid or incursion by hostile aircraft, esp. for dropping bombs or other missiles. —**air′-raid′er,** *n.*

air-raid shelter, a security area or place used as a refuge during an air-raid.

air-raid warden, a person who has temporary police duties during an air-raid alert.

air-rifle (ĕə′rī′fəl), *n.* an airgun with rifled bore.

air-route (ĕə′ro͞ot′), *n.* an established flight path from one place to another, usually organized into stages with intermediate stopping points, etc.

air-sac (ĕə′săk′), *n.* 1. a sac containing air. 2. any of certain cavities in a bird's body connected with the lungs. 3. a saclike dilatation of an insect trachea.

airscrew (ĕə′skro͞o′), *n.* an aeroplane propeller.

airshaft (ĕə′shäft′), *n.* a ventilating shaft, esp. in a tunnel or mine.

airship (ĕə′shĭp′), *n.* a self-propelled, lighter-than-air craft with means of controlling the direction of flight, usually classed as rigid, semirigid, or non-rigid.

airsick (ĕə'sĭk'), *adj.* ill as the result of travelling in the air. —**air'sick'ness,** *n.*

air-slake (ĕə'slāk'), *v.t.*, **-slaked, -slaking.** to slake by moist air, as lime.

airsock (ĕə'sŏk'), *n.* windsock.

airspace (ĕə'spās'), *n.* the region of the atmosphere above the territory of a nation, etc.

airspeed (ĕə'spēd'), *n.* the forward speed of an aircraft relative to the air through which it moves.

air-spray (ĕə'sprā'), *adj.* pertaining to compressed-air spraying devices or to liquids used in them.

airstream (ĕə'strēm'), *n.* **1.** an airflow. **2.** a wind, esp. one at a high altitude.

airstrip (ĕə'strĭp'), *n.* *Aeron.* a runway, esp. a single runway forming a landing ground in a remote place.

air-switch (ĕə'swĭch'), *n.* *Elect.* a switch in which the interruption of the circuit occurs in air.

airt (ĕət; *Scot.* ėrt), *Scot.* —*n.* **1.** a direction. —*v.t.* **2.** to point out the way. Also, **airth** (ĕəth; *Scot.* ėrth). [t. Gaelic: m. *aird* height]

air-terminal (ĕə'tû'mĭ nəl), *n.* a place of assembly for air passengers, not necessarily at an airport, with administrative offices, etc.

airtight (ĕə'tīt'), *adj.* **1.** so tight or close as to be impermeable to air. **2.** having no weak points or openings of which an opponent may take advantage.

air-trap (ĕə'trăp'), *n.* a device which uses a water seal to prevent the escape of foul air from sinks, drains, etc.

air turbine. See **turbine** (def. 2).

air-valve (ĕə'vălv'), *n.* **1.** a device for controlling the flow of air through a pipe. **2.** a device for releasing air that has accumulated in a pipeline, as at the top of a hill.

air vesicle, *Bot.* a large air-filled pocket, present mainly in plants which float on water.

air vice-marshal (ĕə'vīs mä'shəl), **1.** an officer in the Royal Air Force or any of various other airforces, equivalent in rank to a major general in the army. **2.** the rank.

airwards (ĕə'wədz), *adv.* up in the air; towards the air. Also, **airward.**

airway (ĕə'wā'), *n.* **1.** an air-route fully equipped with emergency landing fields, beacon lights, radio beams, etc. **2.** any passage in a mine used for purposes of ventilation; an air course. **3.** *Med.* a tube used to achieve unobstructed respiration in general anaesthesia.

air-well (ĕə'wĕl'), *n.* airshaft.

airwoman (ĕə'wo͝om'ən), *n.*, *pl.* **-women.** a woman aviator.

airworthy (ĕə'wû'thĭ), *adj.* *Aeron.* meeting accepted standards for safe flight; equipped and maintained in condition to fly. —**air'wor'thiness,** *n.*

airy (ĕə'rĭ), *adj.* **airier, airiest. 1.** open to a free current of air; breezy: *airy rooms.* **2.** consisting of or having the character of air; immaterial: *airy phantoms.* **3.** light in appearance; thin: *airy lace.* **4.** light in manner; sprightly; gay; lively: *airy songs.* **5.** light in movement; graceful; delicate: *an airy tread.* **6.** light as air; unsubstantial; unreal; imaginary: *airy dreams.* **7.** visionary; speculative. **8.** performed in the air; aerial. **9.** lofty; high in the air. **10.** casual, off-hand; superficial, flippant.

airy-fairy (ĕə'rĭ fēə'rĭ), *adj.* *Colloq.* light and delicate; whimsical; fanciful.

Aisha (ä'ĭ shə), *n.* A.D. 613?–678, favourite wife of Mohammed and daughter of Abu-Bekr. Also, **Ayesha.**

aisle (īl), *n.* **1.** a passageway between seats in a church, hall, etc. **2.** *Archit.* **a.** a lateral division of a church or other building separated from the nave by piers or columns. See diag. under **basilica. b.** a similar division at the side of the choir or a transept. **c.** any of the lateral divisions of a church or hall, as the nave. [var. of *isle*, trans. of late ML *insula* aisle (in L island); r. ME *ele*, t. OF, g. L *āla* shoulder, wing; *ai-* of current sp. from F *aile*] —**aisled** (īld), *adj.*

Aisne (ān; *Fr.* ĕn), *n.* **1.** a river in N France, flowing into the river Oise; battles, 1914, 1917, 1918. See map under **Compiègne. 2.** a department in N France. 512,920 pop. (1962); 2868 sq. mi. *Cap.*: Laon.

ait (āt), *n.* a small island. Also, **eyot.** [ME *eyt*, OE *igeoth*, dim. of *ieg* island; history of forms not clear]

aitch (āch), *n.* the letter *H*, *h*.

aitchbone (āch'bōn'), *n.* **1.** the rump bone, as of beef. **2.** the cut of beef which includes this bone. [ME *nache-bone*; *a nache-bone* became *an aitch-bone* by false division into words; *nache*, t. OF, ult. der. L *natis* buttock]

Aitken (āt'kĭn), *n.* **William Maxwell.** See **Beaverbrook.**

Aix-en-Provence (*Fr.* ĕks äɴ prŏ väɴs'), *n.* a town in SE France, N of Marseilles. 67,943 (1962). Also, **Aix.**

Aix-la-Chapelle (āks'lä shă pĕl'; *Fr.* ĕks lȧ shȧ pĕl'), *n.* French name of **Aachen.**

Aizuwakamatsu (ī'zo͞o wä'kə măt'so͞o), *n.* a town in Japan, in N central Honshu island. 102,239 (1965).

Ajaccio (ə yăch'ĭ ō'; ə jăs'ĭ ō'; *Fr.* ȧ zhak syō'), *n.* a seaport in and the capital of Corsica: birthplace of Napoleon. with suburbs, 83,337 (1962).

ajar[1] (ə jä'), *adj.*, *adv.* neither quite open nor shut; partly opened: *leave the door ajar.* [ME *on char* on the turn; *char*, OE *cerr* turn. See A-[1], CHARWOMAN]

ajar[2] (ə jä'), *adv.*, *adj.* out of harmony; jarring: *ajar with the world.* [for *at jar* at discord. See JAR[2], n.]

Ajax (ā'jăks), *n.* *Gk Legend.* **1.** a mighty warrior of the Greeks in the siege of Troy. He killed himself in chagrin when Achilles' armour was awarded to Odysseus. **2. the lesser Ajax,** a Locrian king, a hero in the Trojan War, second in speed only to Achilles. [t. L, t. Gk: m. *Aíās*]

ajee (ə jē'), *adv.*, *adj.* *Scot. or Dial.* to one side; awry. Also, **agee.** [f. A-[1] + Scot. d. *jee* to move]

Ajman (ăj män'), *n.* See **Trucial States.**

Ajmer (ŭj mĭə'), *n.* a city in NW India in Rajasthan. 231,240 (1961). Formerly part of **Ajmer-Merwara** province within, though not part of, Rajputana.

Akashi (ä'kə shĭ), *n.* a seaport in Japan, in W Honshu island. 159,299 (1956).

Akbar (ăk'bä), *n.* 1542–1605, Mogul emperor of India 1556–1605.

akela (ä kā'lə), *n.* the adult in charge of a pack of cubs in the Scout movement. [named after *Akela*, leader of the wolf pack in the '*Jungle Book*' of Rudyard Kipling]

akene (ə kēn'), *n.* achene.

Akhnaton (ăk nä'tŏn), *n.* Amenhotep IV.

Akhmatora (*Russ.* ȧкн mȧ'tə rə), *n.* **Anna** (*Russ.* ȧn'nə), 1888–1966, Russian poet.

akimbo (ə kĭm'bō), *adv.* with hand on hip and elbow bent outwards: *to stand with arms akimbo.* [ME *in kene bowe*, appar., in keen bow, in a sharp bent; but cf. Icel. *kengboginn* bent double, crooked]

akin (ə kĭn'), *adj.* **1.** of kin; related by blood. **2.** allied by nature; partaking of the same properties. [f. A-[2] + KIN] —**Syn. 2.** cognate; similar, analogous.

Akita (ä'kĭ tä'), *n.* a seaport in N Japan, on Honshu island. 216,607 (1965).

Akkad (ăk'ăd), *n.* **1.** Also, **Accad.** one of the four cities of Nimrod's kingdom. Gen. 10:10. In the cuneiform inscriptions it evidently includes most of N Babylonia. —*adj.* **2.** Akkadian. See map under **Chaldea.**

Akkadian (ə kā'dyən), *n.* **1.** the eastern group of Semitic languages, all extinct, including Babylonian and Assyrian. **2.** any member of this group. **3.** one of the Akkadian people. —*adj.* **4.** of or belonging to Akkad. **5.** designating or pertaining to the primitive inhabitants of Babylonia or the non-Semitic language ascribed to them. **6.** designating or pertaining to the (later) Semitic language of Babylonia.

Akkerman (ăk'ə män'), *n.* former name of **Belgorod-Dnestrovski.**

Akkra (ə krä'), *n.* Accra.

Akola (ə kō'lə), *n.* a town in India, in E Bombay. 115,760 (1961).

Akron (ăk'rən), *n.* a city in the U.S., in NE Ohio. 290,351 (1960).

Aksum (äk'so͞om), *n.* the capital of an ancient Ethiopian kingdom. Also, **Axum.**

à l', *French.* form of à la used for either gender before a vowel or mute *h*.

al-, var. of **ad-** before *l*, as in *allure.*

-al[1], an adjective suffix meaning 'of or pertaining to', 'connected with', 'of the nature of', 'like', 'befitting', etc., occurring in numerous adjectives and in many nouns of adjectival origin, as *annual, choral, equal, regal.* [t. L: s. *-ālis* (neut. *-āle*) pertaining to; often r. ME *-el*, t. F]

-al[2], a suffix forming nouns of action from verbs, as in *refusal, denial, recital, trial.* [t. L: m. *-āle* (pl. *-ālia*), neut. of adj. suffix *-ālis*; often r. ME *-aille*, t. OF]

-al[3], *Chem.* a suffix indicating that a compound includes an alcohol or aldehyde group, as in *chloral.* [short for AL(COHOL) or AL(DEHYDE)]

AL, Anglo-Latin. Also **A.L.**

Al, *Chem.* aluminium.

ala (ā'lə), *n.*, *pl.* **alae** (ā'lē). **1.** a wing. **2.** a winglike part, process, or expansion, as of a bone, a shell, a seed, a stem, etc. **3.** one of the two side petals of a papilionaceous flower. [t. L: wing]

à la (ä'lä; *Fr.* ȧ lȧ), **1.** according to the: *à la carte, à la mode.* **2.** (short for *à la mode (de)*) after the manner or fashion of: *à la parisienne.* [t. F: at, to, in + the; fem. form used before a word beginning with a consonant]

Ala., Alabama.

Alabama (ăl'ə băm'ə), *n.* **1.** a state in the SE United States. 3,266,740 pop. (1960); 51,609 sq. mi. *Cap.*: Montgomery. *Abbrev.*: Ala. **2.** a river flowing from central Alabama SW to the Mobile river. 315 mi. —**Alabamian** (ăl'ə băm'yən), **Al'abam'an,** *adj. n.*

alabaster (ăl′ə băs′tə), *n.* **1.** a finely granular variety of gypsum, often white and translucent, used for ornamental objects or work, such as lamp bases, figurines, etc. **2.** a variety of calcite, often with a banded structure, used for similar purposes (**oriental alabaster**). **—***adj.* Also, **alabastrine** (ăl′ə băs′trĭn, -bäs′-). **3.** made of alabaster: *an alabaster column.* **4.** resembling alabaster; smooth and white as alabaster: *her alabaster throat.* [ME, t. L, t. Gk: m. *alábastros*, var. of *alábastos* an alabaster box]

à la bonne heure (*Fr.* à lȧ bō nœr′), *French.* **1.** at the right moment. **2.** just right; excellent; very well.

à la carte (ä′lä kät′; *Fr.* à lȧ kȧrt′), according to the menu; with a stated price for each dish: *dinner à la carte.* [t. F]

alack (ə lăk′), *interj. Archaic.* (an exclamation of sorrow, regret, or dismay.) Also, **alackaday** (ə lăk′ə dā′).

alacrity (ə lăk′rĭ tĭ), *n.* **1.** liveliness; briskness; sprightliness. **2.** cheerful readiness or willingness. [t. L: m. s. *alacritas*] **—alac′ritous,** *adj.*

Ala Dagh (*Turk.* ä′lä däKH′), **1.** a mountain range in S Turkey. Highest peak, ab. 11,000 ft. **2.** a mountain range in E Turkey. Highest peak, ab. 11,500 ft.

Aladdin (ə lăd′ĭn), *n.* (in *The Arabian Nights' Entertainments*) the son of a poor widow in China. He becomes the possessor of a magic lamp and ring, with which he commands two genii who gratify all his wishes.

Alagöz (*Turk.* ä lä gœz′), *n.* a volcanic mountain in the SE Soviet Union in the Armenian Republic. 13,435 ft.

Alai Mountains (ä′lī), a mountain range in the SW Soviet Union in Asia, in Kirghiz Republic: a part of the Tien Shan mountain system. Peaks, 16,000 to 19,500 ft.

alalia (ə lā′lyə), *n. Med.* loss of the power of speech. [t. Gk]

alameda (ăl′ə mā′də), *n. Chiefly South-Western U.S.* a public walk shaded with poplar or other trees. [t. Sp., der. *alamo* poplar]

Alamein (ăl′ə mān′), *n.* See **El Alamein.**

alamo (ăl′ə mō′), *n., pl.* **-mos.** *South-Western U.S.* a cottonwood. [t. Sp.: poplar]

Alamo (ăl′ə mō′), *n.* a mission building in San Antonio, Texas, which underwent a terrible siege by Mexicans in February, 1836, was taken on March 6th, and its entire garrison of American rebels killed.

alamode (ăl′ə mōd′), *n.* glossy silk for scarfs, etc.

à la mode (ä′lä mōd′; *Fr.* à lȧ mŏd′), **1.** in or according to the fashion. **2.** *Cookery.* (of beef) larded and braised or stewed with vegetables, herbs, etc., and served with a rich brown gravy. Also, **alamode.** [t. F]

à la mort (*Fr.* à lȧ mŏr′), *French.* **—***adj.* **1.** half dead. **2.** melancholy; dispirited. **—***adv.* **3.** mortally.

Alanbrooke (ăl′ən brŏŏk′), *n.* **Alan Francis Brooke, 1st Viscount,** 1883–1963, British field marshal.

Åland Islands (ä′lənd, ô′-; *Swed.* ō′lȧnd), a group of Finnish islands in the Baltic between Sweden and Finland. 22,144 pop. (1959); 572 sq. mi. Finnish, **Ahvenanmaa.**

alanine (ăl′ə nēn′, -nĭn′), *n. Biochem.* an amino acid, $CH_3CH(NH_2)COOH$, found in many proteins.

alar (ā′lə), *adj.* **1.** pertaining to or having wings; alary. **2.** winglike; wing-shaped. **3.** *Anat., Bot.* axillary. [t. L: s. *ālāris*, der. *āla* wing]

Alarcón y Mendoza (*Sp.* à lȧr kōn′ ē mĕn dō′thȧ), *n.* **Juan Ruiz de** (*Sp.* KHwȧn′ rwēth′ dė), *c.* 1580–1639, Spanish playwright, born in Mexico.

Alaric (ăl′ə rĭk), *n.* A.D. *c.*370–410, king of the Visigoths: captured Rome A.D. 410.

alarm (ə läm′), *n.* **1.** a sudden fear or painful suspense excited by an apprehension of danger; apprehension; fright. **2.** any sound, outcry, or information intended to give notice of approaching danger: *a false alarm.* **3.** a self-acting contrivance of any kind used to call attention, rouse from sleep, warn of danger, etc. **4.** a warning sound; signal for attention. **5.** a call to arms. **6.** *Fencing.* an appeal or a challenge made by a step or stamp on the ground with the advancing foot. **—***v.t.* **7.** to surprise with apprehension of danger; disturb with sudden fear. **8.** to give notice of danger to; rouse to vigilance and exertions for safety. [ME *alarme*, t. OF, t. It.: m. *allarme* tumult, fright, der. *all' arme* to arms] **—alarmed′,** *adj.* **—alarm′ingly,** *adv.* **—Syn. 1.** consternation; terror, panic. See **fear. 7.** See **afraid.**

alarm clock, a clock which can be set to sound a bell or the like at a particular time, used to rouse people from sleep.

alarmist (ə lä′mĭst), *n.* one given to raising alarms, esp. without sufficient reason, as by exaggerating dangers, prophesying calamities, etc. **—alarm′ism,** *n.*

alarum (ə lă′rəm, ə lĕə′-), *n.* **1.** *Archaic.* alarm. **2.** *Horol.* **a.** a device designed to ring a warning bell at a certain hour. **b.** the bell itself.

alary (ā′lə rĭ, ăl′ə-), *adj.* **1.** of or pertaining to wings. **2.** *Biol.* wing-shaped. [t. L: m. s. *ālārius*, der. *āla* wing]

alas (ə lăs′, ə läs′), *interj.* (an exclamation expressing sorrow, grief, pity, concern, or apprehension of evil.) [ME *allas*, t. OF: m. *a las, ha las*, f. *a, ha* ah + *las* miserable, g. L *lassus* weary]

Alas., Alaska.

Alaska (ə lăs′kə), *n.* **1.** a state of the United States, in NW North America. 226,167 (1960); 586,400 sq. mi. *Cap.:* Juneau. *Abbrev.:* Alas. **2.Gulf of,** a large gulf of the Pacific, on the S coast of Alaska. **3.** (*l.c.*) *Textiles.* a yarn made of cotton mixed with wool or mohair. **—Alas′kan,** *adj., n.*

Alaska Highway, a road extending from E British Columbia, Canada, to Fairbanks, Alaska: built as a U.S. military supply route, 1942. 1523 mi. Unofficially, **Alcan Highway.**

Alaska Peninsula, a long, narrow peninsula forming the SW extension of the mainland of Alaska. ab. 400 mi. long.

Alaska Range, a mountain range in S Alaska. Highest peak, Mt McKinley, 20,300 ft.

alastrim (ə lăs′trĭm), *n. Med.* a mild form of smallpox. [t. Pg.]

alate (ā′lāt), *adj.* **1.** winged. **2.** having membranous expansions like wings. Also, **a′lated.** [t. L: m. s. *ālātus* winged]

alb (ălb), *n. Eccles.* a white linen robe with close sleeves, worn by an officiating priest. [ME and OE *albe*, t. L: m. *alba* (*vestis*) white (garment)]

Alb

Alb., **1.** Also, **Alba.** Alberta (Canada). **2.** Albania.

Alba (ăl′bə), *n.* **Duke of.** See **Alva.**

Albacete (*Sp.* ȧl bȧ thė′tė), *n.* a town in SE Spain. 78,926 (1965).

albacore (ăl′bə kô′), *n., pl.* **-cores,** (*esp. collectively*) **-core. 1.** the long-finned tunny, *Germo alalunga*, common in all warm or temperate seas, and highly valued for canning. **2.** any of various fishes related to or resembling the tunny. [t. Pg.: m. *albacor*(*a*), t. Ar.: m. *al bakūra*]

Alba Longa (ăl′bə lŏng′gə), a city of ancient Latium, SE of Rome: fabled birthplace of Romulus and Remus.

Albania (ăl bā′nyə), *n.* **1.** a republic in S Europe, in the Balkan Peninsula between Yugoslavia and Greece. 1,665,000 pop. (1961); 10,632 sq. mi. *Cap.:* Tirana. See map under **Macedonia. 2.** *Obs. Rare.* Scotland.

Albanian (ăl bā′nyən), *adj.* **1.** pertaining to Albania (def. 1), its inhabitants, or their language. **—***n.* **2.** a native or inhabitant of Albania. **3.** the language of Albania (def. 1), an Indo-European language.

Albany (ôl′bə nĭ), *n.* **1.** a city in the U.S., the capital of New York State, in the E part, on the Hudson. 129,726 (1960). **2.** a river in central Canada, flowing from W Ontario E to James Bay, 610 mi. **3.** Also, **Alban.** *Poetic.* Britain, England, or (esp.) Scotland.

albata (ăl bā′tə), *n.* a variety of German silver. [t. NL, prop. fem. of L *albātus*, pp., made white]

albatross (ăl′bə trŏs′), *n.* any of various large web-footed seabirds related to the petrels, esp. of the genus *Diomedea*, of the Pacific and southern waters, noted for their powers of flight. [var. of *algatross*, t. Pg.: m. *alcatraz* seafowl, cormorant; change of *-g-* to *-b-*? by association with L *alba* white (the bird's colour)]

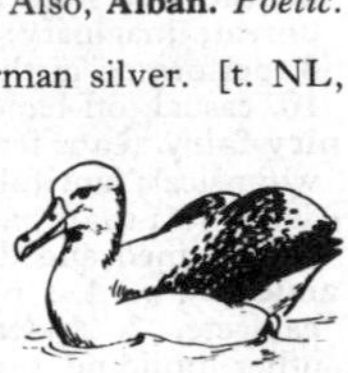

Wandering albatross, *Diomedea exulans* (3½ ft long, wingspan 11 ft)

Albay (ăl bī′), *n.* former name of **Legaspi.**

albedo (ăl bē′dō), *n.* **1.** *Astron.* the ratio of the light reflected by a planet or satellite to that received by it. **2.** *Physics.* the ratio of the neutrons reflected (in a neutron reflector) to those absorbed. [t. L: whiteness]

Albee (ăl′bē, ôl′bē), *n.* **Edward,** born 1928, U.S. dramatist.

albeit (ôl bē′ĭt), *conj.* although; notwithstanding that: *to choose a strategic albeit inglorious retreat.* [ME *al be it* although it be]

Albemarle Sound (ăl′bĭ mäl′), a sound on the Atlantic coast of the U.S., in NE North Carolina, ab. 60. mi. long.

Albéniz (*Sp.* ȧl bė′nēth), *n.* **Isaac** (*Sp.* ē sȧ ȧk′), 1860–1909, Spanish composer and pianist.

Alberich (*Ger.* ȧl′bə rĭKH), *n. Medieval Legend.* king of the dwarfs and chief of the Nibelungs.

albert (ăl′bət), *n.* **1.** Also, **Albert chain.** a kind of watch-chain. **2.** a standard size of notepaper, 6 × 3⅞ inches. [named after Prince *Albert*]

Albert (ăl′bət), *n.* **1. Prince** (*Francis Charles Augustus Albert Emanuel, Prince of Saxe-Coburg-Gotha*), 1819–61, German prince, husband of Queen Victoria; known as Prince Consort. **2. Lake.** Also, **Albert Nyanza.** a lake in central Africa between Uganda and the Congo: a source of the Nile. ab. 100 mi. long; ab. 2000 sq. mi.; altitude ab. 2200 ft.

Albert I, 1875–1934, king of the Belgians 1909–34.

Alberta (ăl bû′tə), *n.* a province in W Canada. 1,451,000 pop. (est. 1965); 255,285 sq. mi. *Cap.*: Edmonton.

Albert Edward, a mountain peak of the Owen Stanley range in SE New Guinea. 13,080 ft.

Alberti (*It.* ȧl bĕr′tē), *n.* **Leon Battista** (*It.* lė ȯn′ bȧt-tēs′tȧ), 1440–72, Italian architect, artist, musician, and poet.

Albert Medal, an award for bravery in saving life (orig. at sea).

Albert Nyanza (nyăn′zə). See **Albert, Lake.**

Albertus Magnus (ăl bû′təs măg′nəs) (*Albert von Böllstadt*), 1193?–1280, German scholastic philosopher; teacher of Thomas Aquinas; canonized in 1932.

albescent (ăl bĕs′ənt), *adj.* becoming white; whitish. [t. L: s. *albescens*, ppr.] **—albes′cence,** *n.*

Albi (*Fr.* ȧl bē′), *n.* a town in S France: centre of the Albigenses. 41,268 (1962).

Albigenses (ăl′bĭ jĕn′sēz), *n.pl.* the members of several Catharist or Manichean sects, or of a crusade against them, in the south of France in the 12th and 13th centuries. [ML, der. ALBI] **—Albigensian** (ăl′bĭ jĕn′sĭ ən, -shən), *adj.*, *n.*

albinism (ăl′bĭ nĭz′əm), *n.* the state or condition of being an albino. **—albinistic** (ăl′bĭ nĭs′tĭk), *adj.*

albino (ăl bē′nō), *n.*, *pl.* **-nos. 1.** a person with a pale, milky skin, light hair, and pink eyes, resulting from a congenital absence of pigmentation. **2.** an animal or plant with a marked deficiency in pigmentation. *—adj.* **3.** of or pertaining to albinos or albinism. [t. Pg., der. *albo*, g. L *albus* white]

Albion (ăl′byən), *n.* *Poetic.* Britain. [t. L, said to be der. *albus* white]

albite (ăl′bīt), *n.* a very common mineral of the plagioclase felspar group, sodium aluminium silicate, $NaAlSi_3O_8$, usually white, occurring in many igneous rocks. [f. s. L *albus* white + -ITE[1]]

Alboin (ăl′boin, -bō ĭn), *n.* died A.D. 573?, king of the Langobards from A.D. 561? until his death.

album (ăl′bəm), *n.* **1.** a book consisting of blank leaves for the insertion or preservation of photographs, stamps, autographs, etc. **2.** a book of selections, esp. of music. **3.** a folder containing two or more long-playing records. **4.** *U.S.* a visitors' book. [t. L: tablet, prop. neut. of *albus* white]

albumen (ăl′byōō mĭn), *n.* **1.** the white of an egg. **2.** *Bot.* the nutritive matter about the embryo in a seed. **3.** *Biochem.* albumin. [t. L (def. 1), der. *albus* white]

albumenize (ăl byōō′mĭ nīz′), *v.t.*, **-nized, -nizing.** to treat with an albuminous solution. Also, **albumenise.**

albumin (ăl′byōō mĭn), *n.* *Biochem.* any of a class of water-soluble proteins composed of nitrogen, carbon, hydrogen, oxygen and sulphur, occurring in animal and vegetable juices and tissues. [t. L: s. *albūmen* ALBUMEN]

albuminate (ăl byōō′mĭ nāt′), *n.* *Biochem.* a compound resulting from the action of an alkali or an acid upon albumin.

albuminoid (ăl byōō′mĭ noid′), *n.* *Biochem.* **1.** a scleroprotein; one of a class of simple proteins which are insoluble in all neutral solvents, as keratin, gelatine, collagen, etc. *—adj.* **2.** resembling albumen or albumin. [f. s. L *albūmen* white of egg + -OID] **—albu′minoi′dal,** *adj.*

albuminous (ăl byōō′mĭ nəs), *adj.* **1.** of albumin. **2.** containing albumin. **3.** resembling albumin.

albuminuria (ăl byōō′mĭ nyōōə′rĭ ə), *n.* *Pathol.* the presence of albumin in the urine. [f. ALBUMIN + -URIA] **—albu′minur′ic,** *adj.*

Albuquerque (ăl′bə kû′kĭ), *n.* a city in the U.S., in central New Mexico. 201,189 (1960).

alburnum (ăl bû′nəm), *n.* *Bot.* the softer part of the wood between the inner bark and the heartwood; sapwood. [t. L, der. *albus* white]

Albury (ôl′bə rĭ), *n.* a town in SE Australia, in New South Wales. 23,950 (est. 1964).

Alcaeus (ăl sē′əs), *n.* fl. *c.* 600 B.C., Greek lyric poet of Mytilene.

alcahest (ăl′kə hĕst′), *n.* alkahest.

Alcaic (ăl kā′ĭk), *adj.* **1.** pertaining to Alcaeus or to certain metres or a form of strophe or stanza used by, or named after, him. *—n.* **2.** (*pl.*) Alcaic verses or strophes.

alcaide (ăl kād′; *Sp.* ȧl kȧ′ē ᵺė), *n.* (in Spain, Portugal, South-Western U.S., etc.) **1.** a commander of a fortress. **2.** a jailer; the governor or keeper of a prison. Also, **alcayde.** [t. Sp., t. Ar.: m. *al qā'id* the commander]

alcalde (ăl kăl′dĭ; *Sp.* ȧl kȧl′dė), *n.* (in Spain and South-Western U.S.) a chief municipal officer with judicial powers. Also, *South-Western U.S.*, **alcade** (ăl kād′). [t. Sp., t. Ar.: m. *al qādī* the judge. See CADI]

Alcan Highway (ăl′kăn), unofficial name of **Alaska Highway.**

Alcatraz (ăl′kə trăz′), *n.* an island in W California in San Francisco Bay; site of a former U.S. prison.

Alcazar (ăl′kə zä′; *Sp.* ȧl kȧ′thȧr), *n.* **1.** the palace of the Moorish kings (later, of Spanish royalty) at Seville. **2.** (*l.c.*) a palace of the Spanish Moors. [t. Sp., t. Ar.: m. *al qaṣr* the castle (*qaṣr*, t. L: m. s. *castrum* fortress)]

Alcestis (ăl sĕs′tĭs), *n.* *Gk Legend.* the wife of the Thessalian king Admetus, whose life she saved by dying in his place. She was brought back from Hades by Hercules.

alchemist (ăl′kĭ mĭst), *n.* one who practises or is versed in alchemy. **—al′chemis′tic, al′chemis′tical,** *adj.*

alchemize (ăl′kĭ mīz′), *v.t.*, **-mized, -mizing.** to change by alchemy; transmute, as metals. Also, **alchemise.**

alchemy (ăl′kĭ mĭ), *n.* **1.** *Medieval Chem.* an art which sought in particular to transmute baser metals into gold, and to find a universal solvent and an elixir of life. **2.** any magical power or process of transmuting. [ME *alkamye*, t. OF: m. *alcamie*, t. ML: m. *alchimia*, t. Ar.: m. *al kīmīyā'* (*kīmīyā'* ?t. LGk: m. *chýma* molten metal)] **—alchemic** (ăl kĕm′ĭk), **alchem′ical,** *adj.* **—alchem′ically,** *adv.*

Alcibiades (ăl′sĭ bī′ə dēz′), *n.* 450?–404 B.C., Athenian politician and general.

Alcides (ăl sī′dēz), *n.* Hercules.

alcidine (ăl′sĭ dīn′, -dĭn), *adj.* *Ornith.* pertaining to or resembling the *Alcidae*, the auk family.

Alcinoüs (ăl sĭn′ō əs), *n.* *Homeric Legend.* a king of the Phaeacians, at whose court Odysseus related the story of his wanderings; the father of Nausicaä.

A.L.C.M., Associate of the London College of Music.

Alcman (ălk′mən), *n.* fl. 620 B.C., Greek lyric poet.

Alcmene (ălk mē′nĭ), *n.* *Gk Myth.* mother of Hercules by Zeus, who visited her in the guise of her husband.

Alcock (ôl′kŏk′), *n.* **Sir John William,** 1892–1919, English aviator; made the first flight across the Atlantic with A. W. Brown in 1919.

alcohol (ăl′kə hŏl′), *n.* **1.** a colourless, inflammable liquid (**ethyl alcohol,** C_2H_5OH), the intoxicating principle of fermented liquors, formed from certain sugars (esp. glucose) by fermentation, now usually prepared by treating grain with malt and adding yeast. **2.** any intoxicating liquor containing this spirit. **3.** *Chem.* any of a class of chemical compounds having the general formula ROH, where R represents an alkyl group; derived from the hydrocarbon by replacement of a hydrogen atom by the hydroxyl radical, OH. [t. ML: orig., fine powder; hence, essence or rectified spirits, t. Ar.: m. *al kuḥl* the powdered antimony, kohl]

alcoholic (ăl′kə hŏl′ĭk), *adj.* **1.** pertaining to or of the nature of alcohol. **2.** containing or using alcohol. **3.** caused by alcohol. **4.** suffering from alcoholism. **5.** preserved in alcohol. *—n.* **6.** a person suffering from alcoholism. **7.** one addicted to intoxicating drinks.

alcoholicity (ăl′kə hŏ lĭs′ĭ tĭ), *n.* alcoholic quality or strength.

alcoholism (ăl′kə hŏ lĭz′əm), *n.* a diseased condition due to the excessive use of alcoholic beverages.

alcoholize (ăl′kə hŏ līz′), *v.t.*, **-lized, -lizing. 1.** to treat with alcohol. **2.** to make alcoholic. Also, **alcoholise.**

alcoholometer (ăl′kə hŏ lŏm′ĭ tə), *n.* an instrument for finding the percentage of alcohol in a liquid. **—al′coholom′etry,** *n.*

Alcoran (ăl′kŏ rän′), *n.* the Koran. [ME *alkaron*, ult. t. Ar.: m. *al qor'ān*, lit., the reading]

Alcott (ôl′kət), *n.* **1. (Amos) Bronson,** 1799–1888, U.S. transcendentalist philosopher, writer, and reformer. **2.** his daughter, **Louisa May,** 1832–88, U.S. author.

alcove (ăl′kōv), *n.* **1.** a recess opening out of a room. **2.** a recess in a room for a bed, for books in a library, or for other similar furnishings. **3.** any recessed space, as in a garden. [t. F, t. Sp.: m. *alcoba*, t. Ar.: m. *al qubba* the vaulted space]

Alcuin (ăl′kwĭn), *n.* A.D. 735–804, English churchman and scholar; teacher and friend of Charlemagne.

alcyonarian (ăl′sĭ ə nēə′ rĭ ən), *n.* **1.** any anthozoan of the subclass *Alcyonaria*, having the body parts in groups of eight. *—adj.* **2.** belonging to the *Alcyonaria*.

Alcyone (ăl sī′ə nĭ), *n.* a star of the third magnitude in the constellation Taurus: the brightest star in the group known as the Pleiades. [t. L, t. Gk: m. *Alkyónē*]

Ald., Alderman. Also, **ald.**

Aldan (*Russ.* ȧl dȧn′), *n.* a river flowing from the Yablonoi Mountains in the SE Soviet Union in Asia NE to the river Lena. ab. 1300 mi.

Aldebaran (ăl dĕb′ə rən), *n.* one of the brightest stars in the sky, orange in colour, in the constellation Taurus. [t. Ar.: the follower (i.e. of the Pleiades)]

aldehyde (ăl′dĭ hīd′), *n.* one of a group of organic compounds with the general formula R–CHO, which yield acids when oxidized and alcohols when reduced. [short for NL *al*(*cohol*) *dehyd*(*rogenātum*) alcohol deprived of hydrogen] —**al′dehy′dic,** *adj.*

alder (ôl′də), *n.* **1.** any shrub or tree of the betulaceous genus *Alnus* growing in moist places in northern temperate or colder regions. **2.** any of various trees or shrubs resembling this genus. [ME; OE *alor, aler*]

alder buckthorn, a deciduous, rhamnaceous shrub or small tree of Europe and Asia, *Frangula alnus*, with small greenish flowers and black fleshy fruits.

alderfly (ôl′də flī′), *n., pl.* **-flies.** any of several dark neuropterous insects of the family *Sialidae*, much used as a fishing fly.

alderman (ôl′də mən), *n., pl.* **-men. 1.** (in Great Britain) one of the members, chosen by the elected councillors, in a borough or county council. **2.** *Hist.* ealdorman. **3.** a local government officer in any of various other countries, as the U.S., having powers varying according to locality. [ME; OE *aldormann, ealdormann*, f. *ealdor* chief, elder + *mann* man] —**aldermanity** (ôl′də măn′ĭ tĭ), **al′dermanship′,** *n.* —**al′derman′ic,** *adj.*

aldermanry (ôl′də mən rĭ), *n., pl.* **-ries.** a district of a borough represented by an alderman.

Aldermaston (ôl′də mäs′tən), *n.* a village in England, in Berkshire: atomic weapons research establishment.

aldern (ôl′dûn, -dən), *adj. Archaic.* made of alder wood.

Alderney (ôl′də nĭ), *n.* **1.** the northernmost of the Channel Islands in the English Channel, 17 mi. NE of Guernsey. 1449 pop. (1961); 3 sq. mi. **2.** one of a breed of cattle originally reared in the Channel Islands, as Jersey or Guernsey cattle.

Aldershot (ôl′də shŏt′), *n.* **1.** a town in England, in Hampshire, SW of London. 33,690 (1964). **2.** a large permanent military camp there.

Aldine (ôl′dīn), *adj.* **1.** of or from the press of Aldus Manutius and his family, of Venice (about 1490–1597), chiefly noted for compactly printed editions of the classics. —*n.* **2.** any Aldine or other early edition. **3.** any of certain styles of printing types.

Aldington (ôl′dĭng tən), *n.* **Richard,** 1892–1962, English poet and novelist.

Aldis lamp (ôl′dĭs), *Trademark.* a portable signalling lamp.

Aldm., alderman. Also, **ald.**

aldol (ăl′dŏl), *n. Chem.* a colourless fluid, $C_4H_8O_2$, from an acetaldehyde condensation, used medicinally as a sedative and hypnotic. [f. ALD(EHYDE) + (ALCOH)OL]

aldose (ăl′dōs), *n. Chem.* a monosaccharose sugar containing the aldehyde group.

Aldrin (ôl′drĭn), *n.* **Edwin** (‘*Buzz*’), born 1930, U.S. astronaut, with Neil Armstrong one of the first men to land on the moon.

Aldus Manutius (ôl′dəs mə nyo͞o′shəs). See **Manutius.**

ale (āl), *n.* **1.** any of various beers lighter and paler than stout, especially pale ale (or bitter) and mild ale. See **beer. 2.** beer. **3.** *Obs.* any unhopped beer. [ME; OE *ealu*, c. Icel. *öl*]

aleatory (ā′lyə tə rĭ), *adj.* **1.** *Law.* **a.** depending on a contingent event. **b. aleatory contract,** a wagering contract; a bet. **2.** *Sociol.* having or pertaining to accidental causes and hence not predictable; felt to be a matter of luck, and thus attributed to benevolent or malevolent forces. [t. L: m. s. *āleātōrius*, der. *āleātor* dice-player]

alecost (āl′kŏst′), *n.* costmary.

Alecto (ə lĕk′tō), *Gk Myth.* one of the Furies.

alee (ə lē′), *adv. Naut.* on or towards the leeside of a ship (opposed to *aweather*).

alegar (ăl′ĭ gə, ā′lĭ-), *n.* ale vinegar; sour ale.

alehouse (āl′hous′), *n.* a house where ale is retailed.

Alekhine (ăl′ĭk hĕn′, ăl′ĭ kĕn′), *n.* **Alexander** (*Aleksandr Alekhin*), 1892–1946, Russian World Champion chess-player, living in France.

Aleksandropol (*Russ.* ə lĭk sȧn drô′pəly), *n.* former name of **Leninakan.**

Aleksandrovsk (*Russ.* ə lĭk sȧn′drəfsk), *n.* former name of **Zaporozhe.**

Alemannic (ăl′ĭ măn′ĭk), *n.* **1.** the High German speech of Swabia, Württemberg, Switzerland, and Alsace. —*adj.* **2.** of or pertaining to the Alemanen, an early people of SW Germany, or their dialect. Also, **Alemanic.** [f. s. L *Aleman*(*n*)*ī* name of a Gmc tribe + -IC]

Alembert, d′ (*Fr.* dȧ läɴ bĕr′), **Jean le Rond** (*Fr.* zhäɴ lə rôɴ′), 1717?–83, French mathematician, philosopher, and writer: associate of Diderot.

alembic (ə lĕm′bĭk), *n.* **1.** a vessel with a beaked cap or head, formerly used in distilling; an ancient retort. **2.** anything that transforms, purifies, or refines. [ME *alambic*, t. ML: s. *alambicus*, t. Ar.: m. *al anbiq* the still (*anbīq* t. Gk: m. *ámbix* cup)] —**alem′bic′ated,** *adj.*

A, Alembic; B, Lamp; C, Receiver

Alençon (*Fr.* ȧ läɴ sôɴ′), *n.* a town in NW France, in Orne department. 27,024 (1963).

Alençon lace (ə lĕn′sən, -sŏn; *Fr.* ȧ läɴ sôɴ′), **1.** a delicate needlepoint lace made in Alençon. **2.** a machine reproduction of this lace, with a cordlike outline.

Aleppo (ə lĕp′ō), *n.* a city in NW Syria. 670,230 (est. 1964).

Aleppo gall, the gall of the oak tree, rich in tannin; nut-gall.

alerce (ə lûs′; *Sp.* ȧ lĕr′thĕ), *n.* the sandarac tree.

alert (ə lûrt′), *adj.* **1.** vigilantly attentive: *an alert mind.* **2.** moving with celerity; nimble. —*n.* **3.** an attitude of vigilance or caution: *on the alert.* **4.** an air-raid warning. **5.** the period during which an air-raid warning is in effect. —*v.t.* **6.** to prepare (troops, etc.) for action. **7.** to warn of an impending raid or attack. [t. F: m. *alerte*, t. It.: m. *all′ erta* on the lookout] —**alert′ed,** *adj.* —**alert′ly,** *adv.* —**alert′ness,** *n.*

—**Syn. 1.** ALERT, VIGILANT, WATCHFUL imply a wide-awake attitude, as of someone keenly aware of his surroundings. ALERT describes a ready and prompt attentiveness together with a quick intelligence: *the visitor to the city was alert and eager to see the points of interest.* VIGILANT suggests some immediate necessity for keen, active observation, and for continuing alertness: *knowing the danger, the scout was unceasingly vigilant.* WATCHFUL suggests carefulness and preparedness: *watchful waiting.* **2.** brisk, lively, quick, active.

-ales, *Bot.* a suffix of (Latin) names of orders. [t. L, pl. of *-ālis*, adj. suffix. See -AL[1]]

Alessandria (ăl′ĭ săn′drĭ ə), *n.* a town in NW Italy, in Piedmont. 98,069 (1966).

aleurone (ə lyo͝oə′rən, -rōn), *n.* minute albuminoid granules (protein) found in connection with starch and oily matter, in the endosperm of ripe seeds, and in a special layer of cells in grains of wheat, etc. [t. Gk: m. *áleuron* flour] —**aleuronic** (ăl′yo͝o rŏn′ĭk), *adj.*

Aleut (ăl′ĭ o͞ot′), *n.* **1.** a native of the Aleutian Islands. **2.** the language spoken by the Aleutian Indians.

Aleutian (ə lo͞o′shən), *adj.* **1.** of or pertaining to the Aleutian Islands. —*n.* **2.** Aleut (def. 1).

Aleutian Islands, an archipelago extending W from the Alaska Peninsula for ab. 1200 mi.: a part of Alaska. Also, **Aleutians.**

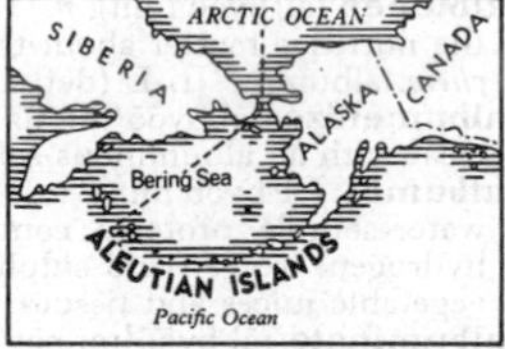

Aleutian Islands

A level, Advanced level.

alevin (ăl′ĭ vĭn), *n.* a young fish, esp. a salmon. [t. F]

alewife (āl′wīf′), *n., pl.* **-wives.** a woman who keeps an alehouse. [f. ALE + WIFE]

Alexander (ăl′ĭg zän′də), *n.* **Harold R. L. G., 1st Earl of Tunis,** 1891–1969, British field marshal: governor-general of Canada 1946–52; British minister of defence 1952–54.

Alexander I, 1. (Russ.: *Aleksandr Pavlovich*), 1777–1825, tsar of Russia 1801–25. **2.** (Serb.: *Aleksandar Obrenović*), 1876–1903, king of Serbia 1889–1903. **3.** (son of Peter I of Serbia), 1888–1934, king of Yugoslavia 1921–34.

Alexander I Island, an island off the coast of Antarctica, W of Graham Land.

Alexander II (Russ.: *Aleksandr Nikolaevich*), 1818–81, tsar of Russia 1855–81.

Alexander III (Russ.: *Aleksandr Aleksandrovich*), 1845–94, tsar of Russia 1881–94 (son of Alexander II).

Alexander VI (*Roderigo Lanzol y Borgia*), 1431?–1503, pope 1492–1503.

Alexander Archipelago, a group of coastal islands in SE Alaska.

Alexander Nevski (nĕv′skĭ, nĕf′-), 1220?–63, Russian prince, warrior, and statesman.

alexanders (ăl′ĭg zän′dəz), *n., pl.* **alexanders.** a biennial umbelliferous plant of southern Europe, *Smyrnium olusatrum*, with dense umbels of yellowish flowers and black fruits.

Alexander Severus (sĭ vĭə′rəs), A.D. 208?–235, Roman emperor, A.D. 222–235.

Alexander the Great, 356–323 B.C., king of Macedonia 336–323 B.C.; conqueror of Greek city-states and Persian Empire from Asia Minor and Egypt to India.

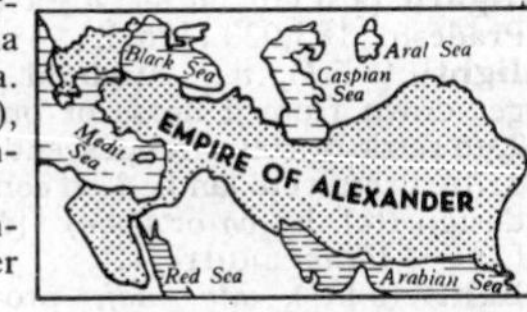

Empire of Alexander the Great

Alexandra (ăl′ĭg zăn′drə), *n.* 1844–1925, queen consort of Edward VII.

Alexandretta (ăl′ĭg zăn-drĕt′ə, -zän-), *n.* former name of **Iskenderun.**

Alexandria (ăl′ĭg zăn′drĭ ə, -zän′-), *n.* a port in N Egypt, on the Nile delta: founded by Alexander the Great, 332 B.C.; ancient seat of learning. 1,513,000 (1960). See map under **Suez.**

Alexandrian (ăl′ĭg zăn′drĭ ən, -zän′-), *adj.* **1.** of Alexandria. **2.** pertaining to the schools of philosophy, literature, and science in ancient Alexandria. **3.** erudite and critical rather than original or creative. **4.** of Alexander the Great. —*n.* **5.** a native or inhabitant of Alexandria.

Alexandrine (ăl′ĭg zăn′drĭn, -zän′-), *n.* **1.** *Pros.* **a.** a verse or line of poetry of six iambic feet. **b.** (in French poetry) a verse of alternate couplets of twelve and thirteen syllables. —*adj.* **2.** *Pros.* designating such a verse or line. **3.** of or pertaining to Alexandria. [t. F: m. *alexandrin,* from poems in this metre on *Alexander* the Great]

alexandrite (ăl′ĭg zăn′drīt, -zän′-), *n.* a variety of chrysoberyl, green by daylight and red-violet by artificial light, used as a gem. [f. ALEXANDER II of Russia + -ITE[1]]

Alexandroupolis (ăl′ĭg zän drōō′pə lĭs), *n.* a seaport in NE Greece, in Western Thrace. 18,712 (1961). Formerly, **Dede Agach.**

alexia (ə lĕk′sĭ ə), *n.* *Psychol.* a cerebral disorder marked by inability to read. [f. A-[6] + s. Gk *léxis* a speaking + -IA]

alexin (ə lĕk′sĭn), *n.* *Immunol.* **1.** any of certain substances in normal blood serum which destroy bacteria, etc. **2.** complement (def. 9). [f. s. Gk *aléxein* ward off + -IN[2]] —**alexinic** (ăl′ĕk sĭn′ĭk), *adj.*

alexipharmic (ə lĕk′sĭ fä′mĭk), *Med.* —*adj.* **1.** warding off poisoning or infection; antidotal; prophylactic. —*n.* **2.** an alexipharmic agent, esp. an internal antidote. [t. Gk: m. s. *alexiphármakon* a remedy against poison; final syll., prop. *-ac,* conformed to the suffix -IC]

Alexius I (ə lĕk′sĭ əs), (*Alexius Comnenus*), 1048–1118, emperor of the Byzantine Empire 1081–1118.

alfalfa (ăl făl′fə), *n.* a European fabaceous forage plant, *Medicago sativa,* with bluish purple flowers; lucerne. [t. Sp., t Ar.: m. *al faṣfaṣa* the best sort of fodder]

Alfieri (*It.* äl fyĕ′rē), *n.* **Count Vittorio** (*It.* vēt tô′ryô), 1749–1803, Italian dramatist and poet.

al fine (ăl fē′nĭ), *Music.* to the end (a direction, as after a *da capo* or *dal segno,* to continue to *fine,* the indicated end). [It.]

Alfol (ăl′fŏl), *n.* *Trademark.* an insulating material made of aluminium foil.

Alfonso XII (ăl fŏn′sō, -zō; *Sp.* äl fôn′sô), 1857–85, king of Spain 1874–85.

Alfonso XIII, 1886–1941, king of Spain from 1886 until deposed in 1930.

alforja (ăl fô′jə), *n.* *South-Western U.S.* **1.** a leather bag or saddlebag. **2.** a cheek pouch. [t. Sp., t. Ar.: m. *al khorj* the double saddlebag]

Alfred the Great (ăl′frĭd), A.D. 849–899, king of England, 871–899; defeated invading Danes and established the overlordship of the West Saxon royal house, built the first English fleet, encouraged education, and translated several Latin works into English, becoming the father of English prose literature.

alfresco (ăl frĕs′kō), *adj.* **1.** open-air: *an alfresco cafe.* —*adv.* **2.** in the open air; out-of-doors: *to dine alfresco.* [t. It. *al fresco* in the cool]

Alg., Algeria.

alg., algebra.

alga (ăl′gə), *n., pl.* **-gae** (-jē). any chlorophyll-containing plant belonging to the phylum *Thallophyta,* comprising the seaweeds and various freshwater forms and varying in form and size, from a single microscopic or sometimes large and branching cell, to forms with trunklike stems many feet in length. They constitute a subphylum, the *Algae.* [t. L: seaweed] —**al′gal,** *adj.*

algarroba (ăl′gə rō′bə), *n.* **1.** any of certain mesquites, esp. *Prosopis juliflora* and its botanical variety *glandulosa.* **2.** its beanlike pod. **3.** the carob (tree). **4.** its beanlike fruit. Also, **algaroba, algarrobo.** [t. Sp., t. Ar.: m. *al kharrūba.* See CAROB]

algebra (ăl′jĭ brə), *n.* **1.** the mathematical art of reasoning about (quantitative) relations by means of a systematized notation including letters and other symbols; the analysis of equations, combinatorial analysis, theory of fractions, etc. **2.** any special system of notation adapted to the study of a special system of relationships: *algebra of classes.* [t. ML, t. Ar.: m. *al jebr, al jabr* bone-setting, hence algebraic redintegration]

algebraic (ăl′jĭ brā′ĭk), *adj.* of or occurring in algebra. Also, **al′gebra′ical.** —**al′gebra′ically,** *adv.*

algebraist (ăl′jĭ brā′ĭst), *n.* an expert in algebra.

Algeciras (ăl′jĭ sĭə′rəs, *Sp.* äl KHē thē′räs), *n.* a seaport in S Spain, on the Strait of Gibraltar. 26,000 (est. 1963).

Algeria (ăl jĭə′rĭ ə), *n.* a republic in NW Africa: formerly comprising 13 departments of France; became independent, July 3rd, 1962. 10,786,000 pop. (1960); 113,833 sq. mi. *Cap.*: Algiers. —**Alge′rian, Algerine** (ăl′jə rēn′), *adj., n.*

-algia, a noun suffix meaning 'pain', as in *neuralgia.* [t. NL, t. Gk]

algid (ăl′jĭd), *adj.* cold or chilly, esp. applied to a cold fit at the onset of fever. [t. L: s. *algidus*] —**algid′ity,** *n.*

Algiers (ăl jĭəz′), *n.* **1.** a seaport in and the capital of Algeria, in the N part. 883,879 (1960). **2.** one of the former Barbary States in N Africa, notorious for its pirates; modern Algeria.

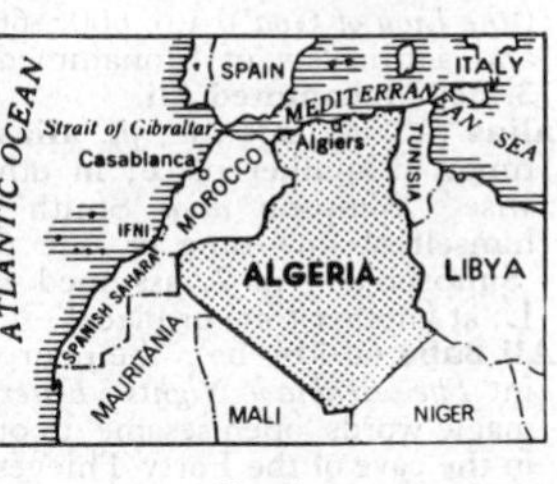

Algeria

algin (ăl′jĭn), *n.* *Chem.* any hydrophilic, colloidal substance found in or obtained from various kelps, esp. from *Macrocystis pyrifera.* [f. ALG(A) + -IN[2]]

alginate (ăl′jĭ nāt′), *n.* a gelatinous substance, the sodium salt of alginic acid, extracted from various kelps, used in the manufacture of ice-cream, in sizing cloth, in dyes, plastics, and explosives, and for various other industrial purposes. [f. ALGIN + -ATE[2]]

alginic acid (ăl jĭn′ĭk), *Chem.* insoluble acid, $(C_6H_8O_6)n$, found in certain seaweeds; used as a thickening agent in foods and for sizing paper.

algo-, a word element meaning 'pain', as in *algolagnia.* [comb. form repr. Gk *álgos*]

Algoa Bay (ăl gō′ə), an indentation of the Indian Ocean in South Africa, in Cape Province.

algoid (ăl′goid), *adj.* like algae. [f. ALG(A) + -OID]

Algol (ăl′gŏl), *n.* a star of the second magnitude in the constellation Perseus (def. 2). It is remarkable for its variability, which is due to periodic eclipse by a fainter stellar companion. [t. Ar.: the demon]

algol (ăl′gŏl), *n.* an internationally accepted autocode in which computer programmes are written, in algebraic notation following the rules of Boolean algebra. [f. ALGO(RITHMIC) + L(ANGUAGE)]

algolagnia (ăl′gə lăg′nĭ ə), *n.* *Psychol.* morbid enjoyment of sexually related pain, including both sadism and masochism. [f. ALGO- + m. Gk *lagneía* lust] —**al′golag′nic,** *adj.* —**al′golag′nist,** *n.*

algology (ăl gŏl′ə jĭ), *n.* the branch of botany that deals with algae. —**algological** (ăl′gə lŏj′ĭ kl), *adj.* —**algol′ogist,** *n.*

algometer (ăl gŏm′ĭ tə), *n.* a device for determining sensitiveness to pain due to pressure. —**algometric** (ăl′gə mĕt′rĭk), **al′gomet′rical,** *adj.* —**algom′etry,** *n.*

Algonquian (ăl gŏng′kĭ ən, -kwĭ ən), *n.* **1.** one of the principal linguistic stocks of North America, belonging to the Algonquian-Mosan phylum, and including languages spoken or formerly spoken from Labrador southwards and westwards through Canada and the northern U.S. to the Rocky Mountains, including Micmac, Ojibwa, Penobscot, Delaware, Cree, Fox, Blackfoot, Cheyenne, Arapaho, etc. **2.** an Algonquian tribe member. —*adj.* **3.** belonging to or constituting this stock.

Algonquian-Mosan (mō′sən), *n.* a great linguistic phylum of North America including Algonquian, Salishan, and Wakashan.

Algonquin (ăl gŏng′kĭn, -kwĭn), *n.* **1.** a member of a group of North American Indian tribes formerly along the Ottawa river and the northern tributaries of the St Lawrence. **2.** their language, of Algonquian stock. **3.** any Algonquian Indian. Also, **Algonkin.**

algophobia (ăl′gə fō′byə), *n.* *Psychol.* an abnormal dread of pain.

algor (ăl′gô), *n.* *Pathol.* coldness or chill, esp. at the onset of fever. [t. L: cold]

algorism (ăl′gə rĭz′əm), *n.* **1.** the Arabic system of arithmetical notation (with the figures 1, 2, 3, etc.). **2.** the art of computation with the Arabic figures, one to nine, plus the zero; arithmetic. **3.** algorithm. [ME *algorisme*, t. OF, t. ML: m. s. *algorismus*, t. Ar.: m. *al Khwārizmī* the native of *Khwārizm* Khiva (i.e. *Abū Ja'far Mohammed ibn Mūsā*, 9th-century Arab mathematician, author of a famous treatise on algebra translated into ML]

algorithm (ăl′gə rĭth′əm), *n. Maths.* any systematic procedure for solving a particular mathematical problem. Also, **algorism.** [var. of ALGORISM by assoc. with ARITHMETIC] —**al′gorith′mic,** *adj.*

alhaji (ăl hăj′ĭ), *n.* **1.** a Muslim who has made a pilgrimage to Mecca. **2.** (*cap.*) a title of respect accorded to one who has done this. [t. Ar.]

Alhambra (ăl hăm′brə), *n.* the palace of the Moorish kings at Granada, Spain, completed in the 14th century. [t. Sp., t. Ar.: m. *al hamā'* the red (referring to the colour of the soil)]

alhambresque (ăl′hăm brĕsk′), *adj.* resembling the fanciful style of ornamentation of the Spanish Alhambra.

Ali (ä′lĭ), *n.* **1. Ali ibn Abu Talib** (ä′lĭ ĭb ən ä′bo͞o tä lēb′) (‘*the Lion of God*’), A.D. 600?–661, Arabian caliph, cousin and son-in-law of Mohammed. **2.** See **Mehemet Ali. 3.** See **Mohammed Ali.**

alias (ā′lĭ əs), *adv.*, *n.*, *pl.* **aliases.** —*adv.* **1.** at another time; in another place; in other circumstances; otherwise. ‘Simpson *alias* Smith’ means a person calling himself at one time or one place ‘Smith’, at another ‘Simpson’. —*n.* **2.** assumed name; another name. [t. L: at another time or place]

Ali Baba (ăl′ĭ bä′bə), the poor woodcutter, hero of a tale in *The Arabian Nights' Entertainments*, who uses the magic words ‘open sesame’ to open the door to the wealth in the cave of the Forty Thieves.

alibi (ăl′ĭ bī′), *n.*, *pl.* **-bis. 1.** *Law.* a defence by an accused person that he was elsewhere at the time the offence with which he is charged was committed. **2.** the evidence that proves one was elsewhere. **3.** *Colloq.* an excuse. [t. L: elsewhere]

alible (ăl′ĭ bl), *adj.* nutritive. [t. L: m. s. *alibilis*] —**al′ibil′ity,** *n.*

Alicante (ăl′ĭ kăn′tĭ; *Sp.* ä lē kän′tē), *n.* a seaport in SE Spain, on the Mediterranean. 132,809 (1965).

Alice Springs (ăl′ĭs sprĭngz′), *n.* a town in the Northern Territory of Australia. 5124 (1961).

alicyclic (ăl′ĭ sī′klĭk, -sĭk′lĭk), *adj.* denoting organic compounds, essentially aliphatic in chemical behaviour, but differing structurally in that the essential carbon atoms are connected as in a ring instead of an open chain.

alidade (ăl′ĭ dād′), *n. Survey, Chiefly U.S.* **1.** a telescope equipped with vertical circle and stadia crosshairs and mounted on a flat base, used to make measurements from a plane-table. **2.** a similar instrument consisting of a brass rule with sighting holes at the ends. Also, **alidad** (ăl′ĭ dăd′). [ME, t. ML: m. s. *alhidada*, t. Ar.: m. *al 'idāda* the revolving radius of a graduated circle]

alien (ā′lyən, ā′lĭ ən), *n.* **1.** one born in or belonging to another country who has not acquired citizenship by naturalization and is not entitled to the privileges of a citizen. **2.** a foreigner. **3.** one who has been estranged or excluded; an outsider. —*adj.* **4.** residing under another government or in another country than that of one's birth, and not having rights of citizenship in such a place of residence. **5.** belonging or pertaining to aliens: *alien property.* **6.** foreign; strange; not belonging to one: *alien speech.* **7.** opposed; incompatible; repugnant (fol. by *to*): *ideas alien to our way of thinking.* [ME, t. L: s. *aliēnus* belonging to another] —**Syn. 2.** See **stranger.**

alienable (ā′lyə nə bl, ā′lĭ ə-), *adj. Law.* capable of being sold or transferred. —**a′lienabil′ity,** *n.*

alienage (ā′lyə nĭj, ā′lĭ ə-), *n.* the state of being an alien; the legal standing of an alien.

alienate (ā′lyə nāt′, ā′lĭ ə-), *v.t.*, **-nated, -nating. 1.** to make indifferent or averse; estrange. **2.** to turn away: *to alienate the affections.* **3.** *Law.* to transfer or convey, as title, property, or other right, to another: *to alienate lands.* [t. L: m. s. *aliēnātus*, pp., estranged] —**a′liena′tor,** *n.*

alienation (ā′lyə nā′shən, ā′lĭ ə-), *n.* **1.** a withdrawal or estrangement, as of feeling or the affections. **2.** *Law.* a transfer of the title to property by one person to another by conveyance or will (as distinguished from *inheritance*). **3.** *Psychol.* mental or psychiatric illness. [ME, t. L: s. *aliēnātio* a transferring, also insanity]

alienee (ā′lyə nē′, ā′lĭ ə-), *n. Law.* one to whom property is alienated.

alienism (ā′lyə nĭz′əm, ā′lĭ ə-), *n.* **1.** alienage. **2.** the study or treatment of mental diseases.

alienist (ā′lyə nĭst, ā′lĭ ə-), *n. Obs.* a psychiatrist or other specialist in mental diseases. [t. F: m. *aliéniste*, f. s. L *aliēnus* insane + *-iste* -IST]

alienor (ā′lyə nə, ā′lĭ ə-, ā′lyə nô′, ā′lĭ ə-), *n. Law.* one who transfers property.

aliform (ā′lĭ fôm′), *adj.* wing-shaped; winglike; alar. [f. s. L *āla* wing + -(I)FORM]

Aligarh (ä′lĭ gû′, ăl′ĭ-), *n.* a city in N India, in Uttar Pradesh. 185,020 (1961).

alight[1] (ə līt′), *v.i.*, **alighted** or **alit, alighting. 1.** to get down from a horse or out of a vehicle; dismount. **2.** to settle or stay after descending: *a bird alights on a tree.* **3.** (of aircraft) to land. **4.** to come accidentally, or without design (fol. by *on* or *upon*). [ME *alighte(n)*, OE *alīhten*, f. A-[1] + *līhtan* LIGHT[2], v.]

alight[2] (ə līt′), *adv.*, *adj.* provided with light; lighted up; burning. [ME; orig. pp. of *alight*, v., light up, but now regarded as f. A-[1] + LIGHT[1], n. Cf. AFIRE]

align (ə līn′), *v.t.* **1.** to adjust to a line; lay out or regulate by line; form in line. **2.** to bring into line. —*v.i.* **3.** to fall or come into line; be in line. **4.** to join with others in a cause. Also, **aline.** [t. F: s. *aligner*, f. *à* A-[5] + *ligner* (g. L *līneāre* line)] —**align′er,** *n.*

alignment (ə līn′mənt), *n.* **1.** an adjustment to a line; arrangement in a line. **2.** the line or lines formed. **3.** a taking of sides; joining a group, party or cause. **4.** the cause, group, or attitude so supported. **5.** a ground plan of a railway or road. **6.** *Archaeol.* a line or an arrangement of parallel or converging lines of upright stones (menhirs). Also, **alinement.**

alike (ə līk′), *adv.* **1.** in the same manner, form, or degree; in common; equally: *known to treat all customers alike.* —*adj.* **2.** having resemblance or similarity; having or exhibiting no marked or essential difference (used regularly of a plural substantive or idea, and only in the predicate): *he thinks all politicians are alike.* [ME, t. Scand.; cf. Icel. *ālīka* similar]

aliment (*n.* ăl′ĭ mənt; *v.* -mĕnt′), *n.* **1.** that which nourishes; nutriment; food. **2.** that which sustains; support. —*v.t.* **3.** to sustain; support. [t. L: s. *alimentum* food] —**al′imen′tal,** *adj.* —**al′imen′tally,** *adv.*

alimentary (ăl′ĭ mĕn′tə rĭ), *adj.* **1.** concerned with the function of nutrition. **2.** pertaining to food; nutritious. **3.** providing sustenance or maintenance. **4.** *Law.* protective: *an alimentary trust.*

alimentary canal, the digestive passage in any animal from mouth to anus. Also, **alimentary tract.**

alimentation (ăl′ĭ mĕn tā′shən), *n.* **1.** nourishment; nutrition. **2.** maintenance; support.

alimentative (ăl′ĭ mĕn′tə tĭv), *adj.* nutritive.

alimony (ăl′ĭ mə nĭ), *n.* **1.** *Law.* an allowance paid to a woman by her husband or former husband for her maintenance, granted by a court while action is pending. In the case of his insanity a husband may receive alimony. **2.** *U.S.* maintenance. [t. L: m. s. *alimōnia* sustenance]

aline (ə līn′), *v.t.*, *v.i.*, **alined, alining.** align. —**aline′ment,** *n.* —**alin′er,** *n.*

Ali Pasha (ä′lĭ pä′sha) (‘*the Lion of Janina*’), 1741–1822, Turkish governor of Albania and part of Greece.

aliped (ăl′ĭ pĕd′), *adj. Zool.* having the toes connected by a winglike membrane, as the bats. [t. L: s. *ālipēs* having winged feet]

aliphatic (ăl′ĭ făt′ĭk), *adj. Chem.* pertaining to or concerned with those organic compounds which are open chains, as the paraffins or olefins. [f. m. s. Gk *áleiphar* oil, fat + -IC]

aliquant (ăl′ĭ kwənt), *adj. Maths.* contained in a number or quantity, but not dividing it evenly: *5 is an aliquant part of 16.* [t. L: s. *aliquantus* some]

aliquot (ăl′ĭ kwŏt′), *adj. Maths.* forming an exact proper divisor: *5 is an aliquot part of 15.* [t. L: some, several]

aliquot scaling, *Music.* a method (used by some pianoforte makers) of producing a fuller tone in the upper strings of a piano by adding a set of sympathetic strings sounding an octave higher.

alit (ə lĭt′), *v.* pt. and pp. of **alight**[1].

aliunde (ā′lĭ ŭn′dĭ), *adv.*, *adj.* from another place: *evidence aliunde* (evidence outside the record). [L: from another place]

alive (ə līv′), *adj.* (*rarely used attributively*) **1.** in life or existence; living. **2.** (by way of emphasis) of all living: *the proudest man alive.* **3.** in a state of action; in force or operation; unextinguished: *keep a memory alive.* **4.** full of life; lively: *alive with excitement.* **5. alive to,** attentive to; awake or sensitive to. **6.** filled as with living things; swarming; thronged; teeming. **7.** (of electric circuits or equipment) functioning; connected to a power supply; live. [ME; OE *on līfe* in life] —**alive′ness,** *n.* —**Ant. 1.** dead. **4.** lifeless.

alizarin (ə lĭz′ə rĭn), *n.* one of the earliest known dyes, orig. obtained from madder but now made from anthraquinone. [t. F: m. *alizarine*, der. *alizari*, t. Ar.: m. *al 'uṣāra* the extract]

alk., alkali.

alkahest (ăl′kə hĕst′), *n.* the universal solvent sought by the alchemists. Also, **alcahest.** [t. NL, prob. coined by Paracelsus]

alkalescent (ăl′kə lĕs′ənt), *adj.* tending to become alkaline; slightly alkaline. —**al′kales′cence, al′kales′cency,** *n.*

alkali (ăl′kə lī′), *n., pl.* **-lis, -lies. 1.** *Chem.* **a.** any of various bases, the hydroxides of the alkali metals and of ammonium, which neutralize acids to form salts and turn red litmus paper blue. **b.** any of various other more or less active bases, as calcium hydroxide. **c.** *Obsolesc.* any of various other compounds, as the carbonates of sodium and potassium. **2.** *Agric.* a soluble mineral salt, or a mixture of soluble salts, occurring in soils, etc., usually to the damage of crops. [ME *alkaly*, t. MF: m. *alcali*, t. Ar.: m. *al qily*, later *al qalī* the saltwort ashes]

alkalify (ăl′kə lĭ fī′, ăl kăl′ĭ-), *v.*, **-fied, -fying.** —*v.t.* **1.** to alkalize. —*v.i.* **2.** to become alkaline. —**alkalifiable** (ăl′kə lĭ fī′ə bl, ăl kăl′ĭ-), *adj.*

alkali metal, *Chem.* a monovalent metal, one of the first group of the periodic system, including potassium, sodium, lithium, rubidium, caesium, and francium, whose hydroxides are alkalis.

alkalimeter (ăl′kə lĭm′ĭ tə), *n.* an instrument for determining the concentration of alkalis in solution. —**al′kalim′etry,** *n.*

alkaline (ăl′kə līn′), *adj.* of or like an alkali; having the properties of an alkali.

alkaline-earth metal, *Chem.* a bivalent metal, one of the second group of the periodic system, including calcium, strontium, barium, and radium. Sometimes beryllium and magnesium are also included.

alkaline earths, *Chem.* the oxides of barium, strontium, calcium, radium, and sometimes magnesium and beryllium.

alkalinity (ăl′kə lĭn′ĭ tĭ), *n.* **1.** alkaline condition; the quality which constitutes an alkali. **2.** the extent to which a solution is alkaline. See ***p*H.**

alkali soil, any of various soils in poorly drained or arid regions, containing a large amount of soluble mineral salts (chiefly of sodium) which in dry weather appear on the surface as a (usually white) crust or powder.

alkalize (ăl′kə līz′), *v.t.*, **-lized, -lizing.** to make alkaline; change into an alkali. Also, **alkalise.** [f. ALKAL(I) + -IZE] —**al′kaliza′tion,** *n.*

alkaloid (ăl′kə loid′), *n.* **1.** one of a class of basic nitrogenous organic compounds occurring in plants, such as nicotine, atropine, morphine, or quinine. —*adj.* **2.** Also, **al′kaloi′dal,** resembling an alkali; alkaline.

alkalosis (ăl′kə lō′sĭs), *n.* *Physiol.* excessively alkaline state of the body tissue and blood. [f. ALKAL(I) + -OSIS]

alkane (ăl′kān), *n.* *Chem.* any member of the methane series.

alkanet (ăl′kə nĕt′), *n.* **1.** a European boraginaceous plant, *Alkanna tinctoria*, whose root yields a red dye. **2.** the root. **3.** the dye; anchusin. **4.** any of several similar plants, as the bugloss (*Anchusa officinalis*) and the puccoon (*Lithospermum*). [ME, t. Sp.: m. *alcaneta*, dim. of *alcana* henna, t. Ar.: m. *al ḥennā'*]

alkene (ăl′kēn), *n.* *Chem.* any member of the ethylene series.

Alkmaar (*Du.* ŏlk′măr), *n.* a town in the Netherlands in central North Holland. 45,479 (1963).

Alkoran (ăl′kŏ rän′), *n.* the Koran.

alkyd resins (ăl′kĭd), *Plastics.* glyptal resins.

alkylation (ăl′kĭ lā′shən), *n.* *Chem.* the replacement of a hydrogen atom in a cyclic organic compound by an alkyl group.

alkyl group (ăl′kĭl), *Chem.* a univalent group or radical derived from an aliphatic hydrocarbon, by removal of a hydrogen atom, having the general formula C_nH_{2n+1}. Also, **alkyl radical.** [f. ALK(ALI) + -YL]

alkyl halide, *Chem.* an organic compound with the type formula RX, where R is a radical derived from a hydrocarbon of the methane series and X is a halogen, as methyl chloride, CH_3Cl.

alkyne (ăl′kīn), *n.* *Chem.* any member of the acetylene series. Also, **alkine.**

all (ôl), *adj.* **1.** the whole of (with reference to quantity, extent, duration, amount, or degree): *all Europe, all the year round.* **2.** the whole number of (with reference to individuals or particulars, taken collectively): *all men.* **3.** a plurality of; many (chiefly with kinds, sorts, manner). **4.** any; any whatever: *beyond all doubt.* **5.** the greatest possible: *with all speed.* —*pron.* **6.** the whole quantity or amount: *to eat all of something.* **7.** the whole number: *all of us.* **8.** everything: *is that all?* —*n.* **9.** a whole; a totality of things or qualities. **10.** one's whole interest, concern, or property: *to give, or lose one's all.* **11.** Some special noun phrases are:

above all, before everything else.

after all, 1. after everything has been considered; notwithstanding. **2.** in spite of all that was done, said, etc.: *he lost the fight after all.*

all in all, 1. (taking) everything together. **2.** one's sole and exclusive concern in life: *he is her all in all.*

and all, as well as everything else; moreover.

and all that, and so on; et cetera.

at all, 1. in any degree: *not bad at all.* **2.** for any reason: *I was surprised at his coming at all.* **3.** in any way: *no offence at all.*

for all that, notwithstanding; in spite of.

for good and all, forever; finally.

in all, all included: *a hundred people in all.*

once (and) for all, for the final time.

—*adv.* **12.** wholly; entirely; quite: *all alone.* **13.** only; exclusively: *he spent his income all on pleasure.* **14.** each; apiece: *the score was one all.* **15.** by so much; to that extent (fol. by *the* and a comparative adjective): *rain made conditions all the worse.* **16.** *Archaic and Poetic.* even; just. [ME; OE *all, eall*, c. G *all*]

all-, var. of **allo-** before vowels, as in *allonym.*

alla breve (ä′lä brā′vĭ; *It.* äl lȧ brĕv′ė), *Music.* **1.** an expression denoting a species of time in which every bar contains a breve, or four minims. **2.** a time value of four crotchets to a bar, but taken with the minim as the unit, i.e. twice as fast. [It.]

Allah (ăl′ə), *n.* the Muslim name of the Supreme Being. [t. Ar.: m. *Allāh*, contr. of *al ilāh* the God]

Allahabad (ăl′ə hə băd′, -bäd′), *n.* a city in India, the capital of Uttar Pradesh, in the SE part, at the confluence of Ganges and Jumna rivers. 411,955 (1961).

Allan-a-Dale (ăl′ən ə dāl′), *n.* (in English balladry) a youth, befriended by Robin Hood, who kept his sweetheart from wedding an aged knight and took her for his own bride.

allanite (ăl′ə nīt′), *n.* a mineral, a silicate of calcium, cerium, aluminium, and iron, chiefly occurring in brown to black masses or prismatic crystals; orthite. [named after Thomas *Allan*, 1777–1833, English mineralogist. See -ITE[1]]

allantoic (ăl′ən tō′ĭk), *adj.* *Zool.* pertaining to the allantois.

allantoid (ə lăn′toid), *adj.* **1.** *Zool.* allantoic. **2.** *Bot.* sausage-shaped. —*n.* **3.** the allantois. —**allantoidal** (ăl′ən toi′dl), *adj.*

allantois (ə lăn′tois, ăl′ən tois′), *n.* *Zool.* a foetal appendage of mammals, birds, and reptiles, typically developing as an extension of the urinary bladder. [t. NL, earlier *allantoides*, t. Gk: m. *allantoeidēs* sausage-shaped]

alla prima (ä′lä prē′mə), *Art.* (of a painting) completed by a single application of pigments, as distinguished from painting built up in stages by applying successive layers of pigments.

allargando (ä′lä găn′dō; *It.* äl lȧr gȧn′dȯ), *adj.* *Music.* progressively slower and often increasing in power. [It.]

allay (ə lā′), **-layed, -laying.** —*v.t.* **1.** to put at rest; quiet (tumult, fear, suspicion, etc.); appease (wrath). **2.** to mitigate; relieve or alleviate: *to allay pain.* —*v.i.* **3.** to abate. [ME *aleyen*, OE *ālecgan* put down, suppress, f. *ā*- A-[3] + *lecgan* lay; sp. *all*- by false identification of prefix *a*- with L *ad*-] —**allay′er,** *n.*

—**Syn. 1.** ALLAY, MODERATE, SOOTHE mean to reduce excitement or emotion. To ALLAY is to lay to rest or lull to a sense of security, possibly by making the emotion seem unjustified: *to allay suspicion, anxiety, fears.* To MODERATE is to tone down any excess and thus to restore calm: *to moderate the expression of one's grief.* To SOOTHE is to exert a pacifying or tranquillizing influence: *to soothe a terrified child.* **2.** lessen, diminish, reduce. —**Ant. 1.** excite.

All Black, a member of a New Zealand rugby team.

all-burnt (ôl′bûnt′), *n.* *Aeron.* the stage in the operation of a rocket motor when the supply of fuel has been exhausted and ceases to provide thrust; burnout.

all clear, a signal, etc., that an air-raid, or other cause for alarm or activity, is over.

allegation (ăl′ĭ gā′shən), *n.* **1.** a mere assertion made without proof. **2.** a statement offered as a plea, an excuse, or a justification. **3.** the act of alleging; affirmation. **4.** an assertion made by a party in a legal proceeding, which he undertakes to prove. [ME t. L: s. *allēgātio*]

allege (ə lĕj′), *v.t.*, **-leged, -leging. 1.** to assert without proof. **2.** to declare before a court, or elsewhere as if upon oath. **3.** to declare with positiveness; affirm; assert. **4.** to plead in support of; urge as a reason or excuse. **5.** *Archaic.* to cite or quote in confirmation. [ME *allegge(n)*, t. AF: m. *alegier* (g. L *ex*- EX[1]- + *lītigāre* sue), with sense of L *allēgāre* adduce] —**allege′able,** *adj.* —**alleg′er,** *n.*

allegedly (ə lĕj′ĭd lĭ), *adv.* according to allegation.

Allegheny (ăl′ĭ gā′nĭ), *n.* a river in the U.S., flowing from SW New York State through W Pennsylvania into the Ohio river at Pittsburgh. 325 mi.

Allegheny Mountains, a mountain range in the U.S., in Pennsylvania, Maryland, West Virginia, and Virginia: a part of the Appalachian system. Also, **Alleghenies.**

allegiance (ə lēʹjəns), *n.* **1.** the obligation of a subject or citizen to his sovereign or government; duty owed to a sovereign or state. **2.** observance of obligation; faithfulness to any person or thing. [ME *alegeaunce* (with *a-* of obscure orig.), t. OF: m. *ligeance.* See LIEGE] —**Syn. 1, 2.** See **loyalty.**

allegiant (ə lēʹjənt), *adj.* loyal.

allegorical (ălʹĭ gŏrʹĭ kl), *adj.* consisting of or pertaining to allegory; of the nature of or containing allegory; figurative: *an allegorical poem, meaning, etc.* Also, **alʹlegorʹic, —alʹlegorʹically,** *adv.*

allegorist (ălʹĭ gə rĭst), *n.* one who uses or writes allegory.

allegoristic (ălʹĭ gə rĭsʹtĭk), *adj.* relating in the form of allegory, interpreting with allegorical meaning.

allegorize (ălʹĭ gə rīzʹ), *v.*, **-rized, -rizing.** —*v.t.* **1.** to turn into allegory; narrate in allegory. **2.** to understand in an allegorical sense; interpret allegorically. —*v.i.* **3.** to use allegory. Also, **allegorise.** —**allegorization** (ălʹĭ gə rĭ zāʹshən), *n.* —**alʹlegorizʹer,** *n.*

allegory (ălʹĭ gə rĭ), *n., pl.* **-ries. 1.** figurative treatment of one subject under the guise of another; a presentation of an abstract or spiritual meaning under concrete or material forms. **2.** a symbolic narrative: *the political allegory of Piers Plowman.* **3.** *Obs.* an emblem. [ME *allegorie,* t. L: m. *allēgoria,* t. Gk]

allegretto (ălʹĭ grĕtʹō; *It.* äl lė grĕtʹtȯ), *adj., n., pl.* **-tos.** *Music.* —*adj.* **1.** more rapid than andante, but slower than allegro. —*n.* **2.** an allegretto movement, of a graceful character. [It., dim. of *allegro* ALLEGRO]

allegro (ə lāʹgrō, ə lĕgʹ-; *It.* äl lėʹgrȯ), *adj., n., pl.* **-gros.** *Music.* —*adj.* **1.** brisk; rapid. —*n.* **2.** an allegro movement. [It., g. L *alacer* brisk]

allele (ə lēlʹ), *n. Biol.* an allelomorph. [t. Gk: m. s. *allḗlōn* (gen.) reciprocally] —**allelic** (ə lēʹlĭk), *adj.*

allelomorph (ə lēʹlə môfʹ, ə lĕlʹə-), *n. Biol.* one of two or more alternative, hereditary units or genes at identical loci of homologous chromosomes, giving rise to contrasting Mendelian characters. [f. *allelo-* (comb. form of ALLELE) + -MORPH] —**alleʹlomorʹphic,** *adj.* —**alleʹlomorʹphism,** *n.*

alleluia (ălʹĭ lo͞oʹyə), *interj.* **1.** praise to the Lord; hallelujah. —*n.* **2.** a song of praise to God. [t. L, t. Gk: m. *allēloúia,* t. Heb.: m. *hallēlūyāh* praise ye Jehovah]

allemande (ălʹĭ măndʹ; *Fr.* äl mäNdʹ), *n.* **1.** either of two dances of German origin. **2.** a piece of music in moderate common measure, usually starting with a short up-beat: it often follows the prelude in the classical suite. **3.** a figure performed in a quadrille. [F: lit., German]

all-embracing (ôlʹĭm brāʹsĭng), *adj.* applying to the whole of a group; covering every eventuality.

Allen (ălʹĭn), *n.* **1. Grant,** 1848–99, British novelist and writer on science, born in Canada. **2. Sir Hugh Percy,** 1869–1946, English organist, conductor and teacher: director of the Royal College of Music. **3. Bog of,** a series of morasses in central Ireland, E of the river Shannon. ab. 240,000 acres. **4. Lough,** a lough in Antrim, in Ireland, on the river Shannon. ab. 7 mi. long and 3 mi. wide.

Allenby (ălʹən bĭ), *n.* **Edmund, 1st Viscount,** 1861–1936, British field marshal: commander of British forces in Palestine and Syria in World War I.

Allentown (ălʹĭn tounʹ), *n.* a city in E Pennsylvania. 108,347 (1960).

Alleppey (ŭlʹə pĭ), *n.* a seaport in India, in central W Kerala. 138,834 (1961).

allergen (ălʹə jĕnʹ), *n. Immunol.* any substance which might induce an allergy. [f. ALLER(GY) + -GEN]

allergenic (ălʹə jĕnʹĭk), *adj.* causing allergic sensitization.

allergic (ə lûʹjĭk), *adj.* **1.** of or pertaining to allergy. **2.** affected with allergy.

allergy (ălʹə jĭ), *n., pl.* **-gies. 1.** a state of physical hypersensitivity to certain things, as pollens, food, fruits, etc., which are normally harmless. Hay fever, asthma, and hives are common allergies. **2.** the symptoms produced by reaction to an allergen, as oedema and inflammation. **3.** altered or acquired susceptibility produced by a first inoculation or treatment as exhibited in reaction to a subsequent one of the same nature. See **anaphylaxis. 4.** *Colloq.* a dislike or antipathy: *an allergy to hard work.* [t. NL: m. s. *allergia,* f. Gk: s. *állos* other + *-ergia* work]

alleviate (ə lēʹvĭ ātʹ), *v.t.*, **-ated, -ating.** to make easier to be endured; lessen; mitigate: *to alleviate sorrow, pain, punishment, etc.* [t. LL: m. s. *alleviātus,* pp.] —**alleʹviaʹtor,** *n.*

alleviation (ə lēʹvĭ āʹshən), *n.* **1.** the act of alleviating. **2.** something that alleviates.

alleviative (ə lēʹvyə tĭv, ə lēʹvĭ āʹtĭv), *adj.* **1.** serving to alleviate. —*n.* **2.** something that alleviates. —**alleʹviant,** *n., adj.*

alleviatory (ə lēʹvĭ āʹtə rĭ, ə lēʹvyə tə rĭ), *adj.* alleviative.

alley[1] (ălʹĭ), *n., pl.* **alleys. 1.** a narrow enclosed lane. **2.** a narrow backstreet. **3.** a walk, enclosed with hedges or shrubbery, in a garden. **4.** a long narrow enclosure with a smooth wooden floor for bowling, etc. [ME *aley,* t. OF: m. *alee* a going, passage, der. *aler* go] —**Syn. 1.** See **street.**

alley[2] (ălʹĭ), *n., pl.* **alleys.** a choice large playing marble. [dim. abbrev. of ALABASTER]

alleyway (ălʹĭ wāʹ), *n.* **1.** a narrow passageway between buildings. **2.** an alley (def. 1).

all-fired (ôlʹfīʹəd), *adj. U.S. Slang.* **1.** infernal; cursed; blasted. **2.** utter.

all-fives (ôlʹfīvzʹ), *n.* a variety of the game of dominoes.

All Fools' Day, April Fools' Day.

all fours, 1. all four legs of an animal, or both arms and both legs of man (formerly *all four*): *to crawl on all fours.* **2. on all fours,** even (*with*); presenting exact comparison (*with*). **3.** Also, **all-fours.** a card game played by two or more persons, seven points constituting a game.

all-good (ôlʹgo͝odʹ), *n.* Good-King-Henry.

all hail, *Archaic.* a salutation of greeting or welcome.

Allhallowmass (ôlʹhălʹō măsʹ), *n.* the feast of Allhallows.

Allhallows (ôlʹhălʹōz), *n.* All Saints' Day.

Allhallowtide (ôlʹhălʹō tīdʹ), *n.* the time or season of Allhallows.

allheal (ôlʹhēlʹ), *n.* **1.** a panacea. **2.** valerian (def. 1).

alliaceous (ălʹĭ āʹshəs), *adj.* **1.** *Bot.* belonging to the genus *Allium,* which includes the garlic, onion, leek, etc. **2.** having the smell or taste of garlic, onion, etc.

alliance (ə līʹəns), *n.* **1.** the state of being allied or connected; relation between parties allied or connected. **2.** marriage, or the relation or union brought about between families through marriage. **3.** formal agreement by two or more nations to cooperate for specific purposes. **4.** any joining of efforts or interests by persons, families, states, or organizations: *an alliance between church and state.* **5.** the persons or parties allied. **6.** relationship in qualities; affinity: *the alliance between logic and metaphysics.* **7.** *Bot.* a subclass; a group of related families of plants. [ME *aliaunce,* t. OF: m. *aliance.* See ALLY]

—**Syn. 1.** association; coalition, combination; partnership. **3.** ALLIANCE, CONFEDERATION, LEAGUE, UNION all mean the joining of states for mutual benefit or to permit the joint exercise of functions. An ALLIANCE may apply to any connection entered into for mutual benefit. LEAGUE usually suggests closer combination or a more definite object or purpose. CONFEDERATION applies to a permanent combination for the exercise in common of certain governmental functions. UNION implies an alliance so close and permanent that the separate states or parties become essentially one.

allied (ə līdʹ, ălʹīd), *adj.* **1.** joined by treaty. **2.** related: *allied species.* **3.** (*cap.*) pertaining to the Allies.

Allier (*Fr.* ȧ lyėʹ), *n.* **1.** a river flowing from S France N to the river Loire. ab. 250 mi. **2.** a department in central France. 380,221 pop. (1962); 2850 mi. *Cap.:* Moulins.

allies (ălʹīz, ə līzʹ), *n.pl.* **1.** pl. of **ally. 2.** (*cap.*) (in World War I) the powers of the Triple Entente (Great Britain, France, Russia), with the nations allied with them (Belgium, Serbia, Japan, Italy, etc., not including the United States), or, in loose use, with all the nations (including the United States) allied or associated with them as opposed to the Central Powers. **3.** (*cap.*) (in World War II) the countries that fought against the Axis powers.

alligator (ălʹĭ gāʹtə), *n.* **1.** the broad-snouted representative of the crocodile group found in the south-eastern U.S. **2.** any crocodilian (usually but not always applied to broad-snouted species) in other parts of the world. **3.** *Metall.* a machine for bringing the balls of iron from a puddling furnace into compact form so that they can be handled. [t. Sp.: m. *el lagarto* the lizard, ult. g. L *lacertus* lizard]

alligator pear, avocado (def. 1).

all-important (ôlʹĭm pôʹtnt), *adj.* essential; important above all things.

all in, *Colloq.* exhausted.

all-in (ôlʹĭnʹ), *adj.* **1.** with extras included; inclusive: *at the all-in rate.* **2.** without restrictions: *all-in wrestling.*

alliterate (ə lĭtʹə rātʹ), *v.*, **-rated, -rating.** —*v.i.* **1.** to show alliteration (*with*): *the 'h' in 'harp' does not alliterate with the 'h' in 'honoured'.* **2.** to use alliteration: *Swinburne often alliterates.* —*v.t.* **3.** to compose or arrange with alliteration: *he alliterates the 'w's' in that line.*

alliteration (ə lĭtʹə rāʹshən), *n.* **1.** the commencement of two or more stressed syllables of a word group: **a.** with the same consonant sound or sound group (**consonantal alliteration**), as in *from stem to stern.* **b.** with a vowel sound which may differ from syllable to syllable (**vocalic alliteration**), as in *each to all.* **2.** the commencement of two or more words of a word group with the same letter, as in *apt alliteration's artful aid.* [f. AL- + s. L *lītera* letter + -ATION]

alliterative (ə lĭt′ə rə tĭv), *adj.* pertaining to or characterized by alliteration: *alliterative verse.* —**allit′eratively,** *adv.* —**allit′erativeness,** *n.*

allium (ăl′ĭ əm), *n. Bot.* a flower or plant of the liliaceous genus *Allium*, comprising bulbous plants with a peculiar pungent smell, including the onion, leek, shallot, garlic, and chive. [t. L: garlic]

all-night (ôl′nīt′), *adj.* **1.** in operation throughout the night; open all night. **2.** continuing all night.

allo-, a word element indicating difference, alternation, or divergence, as in *allonym, allomerism.* Also, **all-.** [t. Gk, comb. form of *állos* other]

Alloa (ăl′ə wə), *n.* a seaport in Scotland, the county town of Clackmannanshire, in the S part. 13,895 (1961).

allocate (ăl′ə kāt′), *v.t.*, **-cated, -cating. 1.** to set apart for a particular purpose; assign or allot: *to allocate shares.* **2.** to fix the place of; locate. [t. ML: m. s. *allocātus*, pp. of *allocāre*, f. L: *al-* AL- + *locāre* place] —**Syn. 1.** See **assign.**

allocation (ăl′ə kā′shən), *n.* **1.** the act of allocating; apportionment. **2.** the share or proportion allocated. **3.** *Accounting.* a system of dividing expenses and incomes among the various branches, etc., of a business.

allocution (ăl′ə kyōō′shən), *n.* an address, esp. a formal, authoritative one. [t. L: s. *allocūtio*]

allodial (ə lō′dyəl), *adj.* free from the tenurial rights of a feudal overlord. Also, **alodial.** [t. ML: s. *allōdiālis*]

allodium (ə lō′dyəm), *n., pl.* **-dia** (-dyə). land owned absolutely, not subject to any rent, service, or other tenurial right of an overlord. Also, **alodium.** [t. ML, t. OLG: m. *allōd* (f. *all* ALL + *ōd* property). See -IUM]

alloerotism (ăl′ō ĕ′rə tĭz′əm), *n. Psychoanal.* sexual love in relation to another person (opposed to *autoerotism*). Also, **alloeroticism** (ăl′ō ĭ rŏt′ĭ sĭz′əm).

allogamy (ə lŏg′ə mĭ), *n.* cross-fertilization. —**allog′amous,** *adj.*

allomerism (ə lŏm′ə rĭz′əm), *n.* variability in chemical constitution without change in crystalline form. [f. ALLO- + s. Gk *méros* part + -ISM] —**allom′erous,** *adj.*

allomorphism (ăl′ə mô′fĭz′əm), *n.* variability in crystalline form without change in chemical constitution: a form of allotropy. —**allomor′phous,** *adj.*

allonge (ə lŏnj′), *n. Com.* a slip of paper attached to a bill of exchange to take further endorsements. [F: lengthening]

allonym (ăl′ə nĭm), *n.* the name of someone else assumed by the author of a work. [f. ALL(O)- + m. Gk *ónyma* name]

allopath (ăl′ə păth′), *n.* one who practises or favours allopathy. Also, **allopathist** (ə lŏp′ə thĭst).

allopathy (ə lŏp′ə thĭ), *n.* the method of treating disease by the use of agents producing effects different from those of the disease treated (opposed to *homeopathy*). —**allopathic** (ăl′ə păth′ĭk), *adj.* —**al′lopath′ically,** *adv.*

allophane (ăl′ə fān′), *n.* a mineral, an amorphous hydrous silicate of aluminium, occurring in blue, green, or yellow masses, resinous to earthy. [t. Gk: m. s. *allophanḗs* appearing otherwise (with reference to its change of appearance under the blowpipe)]

allophone (ăl′ə fōn′), *n. Phonet.* one of several phones belonging to the same phoneme.

alloplasm (ăl′ə plăz′əm), *n. Biol.* that part of protoplasm which is differentiated to perform a special function, as that of the flagellum.

allopolyploid (ăl′ə pŏl′ĭ ploid′), *Biol.* —*adj.* **1.** having more than two haploid sets of chromosomes that are dissimilar and derived from different species. —*n.* **2.** an allopolyploid cell or organism. [ALLO- + POLYPLOID] —**allopolyploidy** (ăl′ə pŏl′ĭ ploi′dĭ), *n.*

allot (ə lŏt′), *v.t.*, **-lotted, -lotting. 1.** to divide or distribute as by lot; distribute or parcel out; apportion: *to allot shares.* **2.** to appropriate to a special purpose: *to allot money for a new park.* **3.** to assign as a portion (*to*); set apart; appoint. [t. MF: m. s. *aloter*, f. *a* to + *loter* divide by lot, der. *lot* lot, of Gmc orig.] —**allot′ter,** *n.* —**Syn. 1.** See **assign.**

allotment (ə lŏt′mənt), *n.* **1.** the act of allotting; distribution; apportionment. **2.** a portion, share, or thing allotted. **3.** a small plot of land let out by a public authority to individuals for gardening, esp. vegetable-growing.

allotrope (ăl′ə trōp′), *n.* one of two or more existing forms of a chemical element: *charcoal, graphite, and diamond are allotropes of carbon.*

allotropic (ăl′ə trŏp′ĭk), *adj.* pertaining to or characterized by allotropy. Also, **al′lotrop′ical.** —**al′lotrop′ically,** *adv.* —**allotropicity** (ăl′ə trə pĭs′ĭ tĭ), *n.*

allotropy (ə lŏt′rə pĭ), *n.* a property of certain chemical elements, as carbon, sulphur and phosphorus, of existing in two or more distinct forms in the solid, liquid, or gaseous state. Also **allot′ropism.** [t. Gk: m. s. *allotropía* variety. See ALLO-, -TROPY]

all' ottava (ăl′ə tä′və; *It.* àl lòt tà′và), *Music.* a direction (8va) placed above or below the stave, to indicate that the passage covered is to be played one octave higher or lower respectively. [It.]

allottee (ə lŏt′ē′), *n.* one to whom something is allotted.

all-out (ôl′out′), *adj.* using all one's resources; complete; total: *an all-out effort.*

all-over (ôl′ō′və), *adj.* extending or repeated all over, as a decorative pattern on embroidered or lace fabrics.

allow (ə lou′), *v.t.* **1.** to grant permission to or for; permit: *to allow a student to be absent, no smoking allowed.* **2.** to let have; grant or give as one's share or suited to one's needs; assign as one's right: *to allow a person £100 for expenses, to allow someone so much a year.* **3.** to permit involuntarily, by neglect or oversight: *to allow an error to occur.* **4.** to admit; acknowledge; concede: *to allow a claim.* **5.** to take into account; set apart; abate or deduct: *to allow an hour for changing trains.* **6.** *U.S. Dial.* to say or think. **7.** *Archaic.* to approve; sanction. —*v.i.* **8.** to permit; make possible: *to spend more than one's salary allows.* **9. allow for,** to make concession, allowance, or provision for: *to allow for breakage.* [ME *alowe(n)*, t. OF: m. OF *alouer* assign (g. LL *allocāre*)]

—**Syn. 1.** ALLOW, LET, PERMIT imply granting or conceding the right of someone to do something. ALLOW and PERMIT are often interchangeable, but PERMIT is the more positive. ALLOW implies complete absence of an attempt, or even an intent, to hinder. PERMIT suggests formal or implied assent or authorization. LET is the familiar, conversational term for both ALLOW and PERMIT. —**Ant. 1.** forbid.

allowable (ə lou′ə bl), *adj.* that may be allowed; legitimate; permissible. —**allow′ableness,** *n.* —**allow′ably,** *adv.*

allowance (ə lou′əns), *n., v.*, **-anced, -ancing.** —*n.* **1.** a definite amount or share allotted; a ration. **2.** a definite sum of money allotted or granted to meet expenses or requirements: *an allowance of pocket-money.* **3.** an addition on account of some extenuating or qualifying circumstance. **4.** a deduction: *allowance for breakages.* **5.** acceptance; admission: *the allowance of a claim.* **6.** sanction; tolerance. **7.** *Minting.* tolerance (def. 6). **8.** *Mach.* a prescribed variation in dimensions. Cf. **tolerance** (def. 5). —*v.t.* **9.** to put upon an allowance. **10.** to limit (supplies, etc.) to a fixed or regular amount.

allowedly (ə lou′ĭd lĭ), *adv.* admittedly; in a manner that is allowed.

alloy (*n.* ăl′oi, ə loi′; *v.* ə loi′), *n.* **1.** a substance composed of two or more metals (or, sometimes, a metal and a nonmetal) which have been intimately mixed by fusion, electrolytic deposition, or the like. **2.** a less costly metal mixed with a more valuable one. **3.** standard; quality; fineness. **4.** admixture, as of good with evil. **5.** a deleterious element. —*v.t.* **6.** to mix (metals) so as to form an alloy. **7.** to reduce a value by an admixture of a less costly metal. **8.** to debase, impair, or reduce by admixture. [t. F: m. *aloyer*, OF *aleier*, g. L *alligāre* combine]

all-powerful (ôl′pou′ə fəl), *adj.* having or exercising exclusive and unlimited authority; omnipotent.

all-purpose (ôl′pû′pəs), *adj.* for every purpose.

all right, 1. safe and sound: *are you all right?* **2.** yes; very well; okay. **3.** satisfactory; acceptable: *his work is all right, but I have seen better employees.* **4.** satisfactorily; acceptably; correctly: *he did the job all right.* **5.** without fail; certainly (often ironically): *all right! you'll be sorry.*

all-round (ôl′round′), *adj.* **1.** able to do many things. **2.** having general use; not too specialized. **3.** *U.S.* extending all about. Also, *U.S.*, **all′-around′.**

all-rounder (ôl′roun′də), *n.* **1.** one able to do many things with equal competence (opp. to *specialist*). **2.** *Sport.* **a.** one skilled in all aspects of a game, as a cricketer who bowls, bats, and fields equally well. **b.** one skilled in many sports.

All Saints' Day, a church festival celebrated on Nov. 1st, in honour of all the saints; Allhallows.

allseed (ôl′sēd′), *n.* any of various many-seeded plants, as a goosefoot, *Chenopodium polyspermum*, and the knotgrass, *Polygonum aviculare.*

All Souls' Day, a day of prayer for the souls of the dead, on Nov. 2nd.

allspice (ôl′spīs′), *n.* **1.** the berry of a tropical American myrtaceous tree, *Pimenta officinalis.* **2.** a mildly sharp and fragrant spice made from it; pimento.

all-star (ôl′stä′), *adj.* (of a theatre production or the like) having all or many of the parts played by stars.

all-time (ôl′tīm′), *adj.* (greatest) of all time to date; outstanding: *he's an all-time rogue.*

allude (ə lōōd′), *v.i.*, **-luded, -luding. 1.** to make an allusion: refer casually or indirectly (fol. by *to*): *he often alluded to his poverty.* **2.** to contain a casual or indirect reference (fol. by *to*): *the letter alludes to something now forgotten.* [t. L: m. s. *allūdere* play with]

allure (ə lyōōə′), *v.*, **-lured, -luring,** *n.* —*v.t.* **1.** to attract by the offer of some real or apparent good; tempt by something flattering or acceptable. **2.** to fascinate; charm. —*n.* **3.** fascination; charm. [ME *alure(n)*, t. OF: m. *alurer*, f. *a* to + *lurer* LURE] —**allur′er,** *n.*

allurement (ə lyōōə′mənt), *n.* **1.** fascination; charm. **2.** the means of alluring. **3.** the act or process of alluring.

alluring (ə lyōōə′rĭng), *adj.* **1.** tempting; enticing; seductive. **2.** fascinating; charming. —**allur′ingly,** *adv.* —**allur′ingness,** *n.*

allusion (ə lōō′zhən), *n.* **1.** a passing or casual reference; an incidental mention of something, either directly or by implication: *a classical allusion.* **2.** *Obs.* a metaphor. [t. L: s. *allūsio* playing with]

allusive (ə lōō′sĭv), *adj.* **1.** having reference to something not fully expressed; containing, full of, or characterized by allusions. **2.** *Obs.* metaphorical. —**allu′sively,** *adv.* —**allu′siveness,** *n.*

alluvial (ə lōō′vyəl), *adj.* **1.** of or pertaining to alluvium. —*n.* **2.** alluvial soil. **3.** *Austral.* gold-bearing alluvial soil. [f. s. L *alluvium* ALLUVIUM + -AL[1]]

alluvial fan, *Phys. Geog.* a fan-shaped alluvial deposit formed by a stream where its velocity is abruptly decreased, as at the mouth of a ravine or at the foot of a mountain. Also, **alluvial cone.**

alluvion (ə lōō′vyən), *n.* **1.** alluvium. **2.** *Law.* land gained gradually on a shore or a river bank through the recent action or recession of water, whether from natural or artificial causes. **3.** overflow; flood. [t. F, t. L: s. *alluvio* inundation]

alluvium (ə lōō′vyəm), *n.*, *pl.* **-via** (-vyə), **-viums. 1.** a deposit of sand, mud, etc., formed by flowing water. **2.** the sedimentary matter deposited thus within recent times, esp. in the valleys of large rivers. [t. L, neut. of *alluvius* alluvial, washed to]

all-weather (ôl′wĕth′ə), *adj.* of or for any or all types of weather.

ally (*v.* ə lī′; *n.* ăl′ī, ə lī′), *v.*, **-lied, lying,** *n.*, *pl.* **-lies.** —*v.t.* **1.** to unite by marriage, treaty, league, or confederacy; connect by formal agreement (fol. by *to* or *with*). **2.** to bind together; connect by some relation, as by resemblance or friendship; associate. —*v.i.* **3.** to enter into an alliance; join or unite. —*n.* **4.** one united or associated with another, esp. by treaty or league; an allied nation, sovereign, etc. **5.** one who helps another or cooperates with him; supporter; associate. [t. F: m. *allier*, g. L *alligāre* bind to; r. ME *alie(n)*, t. OF: m. *alier*]

allyl alcohol (ăl′ĭl), a colourless liquid, C_3H_5OH, whose vapour is very irritating to the eyes; propenol.

allyl group, *Chem.* a univalent aliphatic radical, C_3H_5, with a double bond. [f. L *all(ium)* garlic + -YL] —**allylic** (ə lĭl′ĭk), *adj.* Also, **allyl radical.**

allyl resin, *Chem.* any of a class of synthetic resins formed by the polymerization of compounds containing the allyl group.

allyl sulphide, *Chem.* a colourless or pale yellow liquid with antiseptic properties, $(C_3H_5)_2S$, found in garlic; oil of garlic.

Alma-Ata (ăl′mə ä′tə; *Russ.* àl mà′à tà′), *n.* a city in the S Soviet Union in Asia: the capital of Kazakhstan. 623,000 (est. 1965). Formerly, **Vyernyi.**

almacantar (ăl′mə kăn′tə), *n.* almucantar.

Almadén (*Sp.* àl mà dĕn′), *n.* a town in S Spain: mercury mines. 12,468 (1963).

Almagest (ăl′mə jĕst′), *n.* **1.** a treatise in Greek on astronomy by Ptolemy. **2.** (*l.c.*) any of various medieval works of a like kind, as on astrology or alchemy. [ME *almageste*, t. OF, ult. t. Ar.: m. *al majistī*, f. *al* the + m. Gk *megístē* (*sýntaxis*) greatest (composition)]

almah (ăl′mə), *n.* (in Egypt) a professional dancing or singing girl. Also, **alma, alme, almeh.** [t. Ar.: m. *'ālima* (fem.) learned]

alma mater (ăl′mə mä′tə, mā′tə), (*sometimes caps.*) one's school, college, or university. [t. L: foster mother]

almanac (ôl′mə năk′), *n.* a calendar of the days of the year, in weeks and months, indicating the time of various events or phenomena during the period, as anniversaries, sunrise and sunset, changes of the moon and tides, etc., or giving other pertinent information. Also, **almanack.** [ME *almenak*, t. ML: m. *almanac, almanach*, t. Sp., ? t. Ar.: m. * *al manākh*]

almandine (ăl′mən dēn′, -dīn′), *n.* a mineral, iron aluminium garnet, $Fe_3Al_2Si_3O_{12}$, used as a gem and abrasive. [f. ML *almand(īna)* (var. of *alabandīna*, der. L *Alabanda*, name of a city in Asia Minor) + -INE[2]]

al Mansur (ăl′măn sōōə′), (*Abu Djafar Abdallah*), A.D. 712?–775, Eastern caliph A.D. 754–775; founder of Baghdad.

Alma-Tadema (ăl′mə tăd′ĭ mə), *n.* **Sir Lawrence,** 1836–1912, British painter born in the Netherlands.

alme (ăl′mĭ), *n.* almah. Also, **almeh.**

Almelo (*Du.* ŏl′mə lò), *n.* a town in the Netherlands, in SE Overijssel province. 55,753 (1965).

Almería (ăl′mə rĭə′; *Sp.* àl mĕ rē′à), *n.* a seaport in S Spain, on the Mediterranean. 88,852 (1965).

almery (äm′rĭ), *n.* ambry.

almighty (ôl mī′tĭ), *adj.* **1.** possessing all power; omnipotent: *God Almighty.* **2.** having great might; overpowering: *the almighty power of the press.* **3.** *Colloq.* great; extreme: *he's in an almighty fix.* —*n.* **4. the Almighty,** God. [ME; OE *ælmihtig, ealmihtig* all mighty] —**almight′ily,** *adv.* —**almight′iness,** *n.*

almond (ä′mənd), *n.* **1.** the stone (nut) or kernel (sweet or bitter) of the fruit of the almond tree, *Amygdalus prunus*, which grows in warm temperate regions. **2.** the tree itself. **3.** a flavour or flavouring of or like almonds. **4.** a delicate pale tan colour. **5.** almond green. **6.** anything shaped like an almond. [ME *almonde*, t. OF: m. *almande, alemandle*, g. L *amygdala*, t. Gk: m. *amygdálē*] —**al′mond-like′,** *adj.*

almond-eyed (ä′mənd īd′), *adj.* having eyes with a long or narrow oval shape.

almond green, the pale clear green colour of the fruit of the almond.

almond oil, 1. a colourless, fatty oil expressed from almonds and used in cosmetics, as a lubricant, etc. **2.** Also, **bitter almond oil,** an oil extracted from bitter almonds whose chief constituent is benzaldehyde, used in medicine, for flavouring, etc. **3.** any of various nut oils similar to bitter almond oil. **4.** benzaldehyde.

almoner (ä′mə nə), *n.* **1.** a social worker with some medical training attached to a hospital. **2.** *Hist.* a dispenser of alms or charity, esp. for a religious house, a princely household, etc. [ME *aumoner*, t. OF, g. LL *eleēmosynārius* of alms, der. LL *eleēmosyna* ALMS]

almonry (ä′mən rĭ), *n.*, *pl.* **-ries.** *Hist.* the place where an almoner resides, or where alms are distributed.

almost (ôl′mōst′), *adv.* very nearly; all but. [ME; OE *eal māst*, var. of *æl mǣst* nearly]

—**Syn.** ALMOST, NEARLY, WELLNIGH all mean with a small degree of or short space of. ALMOST implies very little short of: *almost exhausted, almost home.* NEARLY implies a slightly greater distance or degree than ALMOST: *nearly well, nearly to the city.* WELLNIGH, a more literary word, implies a barely appreciable distance or extent: *wellnigh forgotten, wellnigh home.*

alms (ämz), *n. sing. or pl.* that which is given to the poor or needy; anything given as charity. [ME *almes*, OE *ælmysse*, t. LL: m. s. *eleēmosyna*, t. Gk: m. *eleēmosýnē* compassion, alms]

almsgiving (ämz′gĭv′ĭng), *n.* the act or practice of giving alms. —**alms′giv′er,** *n.*

almshouse (ämz′hous′), *n.* a house endowed to give free or cheap accommodation to the poor.

almsman (ämz′mən), *n.*, *pl.* **-men;** *fem.* **-woman,** *pl.* **-women.** *Hist.* one who lives on alms.

almucantar (ăl′myōō kăn′tə), *n.* *Astron.* **1.** a circle of altitude, parallel to the horizontal plane. **2.** an instrument for measuring altitudes and azimuths. Also, **almacantar.**

Alnico (ăl′nĭ kō′), *n.* *Trademark.* an alloy of iron, nickel, aluminium, and cobalt, used for permanent magnets.

alodium (ə lō′dyəm), *n.*, *pl.* **-dia** (-dyə). allodium. —**alo′dial,** *adj.*

aloe (ăl′ō), *n.*, *pl.* **-oes. 1.** any plant of the liliaceous genus *Aloe*, chiefly African, various species of which yield a drug (**aloes**) and a fibre. **2.** (*often pl. construed as sing.*) a bitter purgative drug, the inspissated juice of the leaves of several species of *Aloe.* **3.** American aloe; the century plant. **4.** (*pl. construed as sing.*) a fragrant resin of wood from the heart of an East Indian tree, the eaglewood. [ME (usually pl.) *aloen*, OE *aluwan*, t. L: m. *aloē*, t. Gk] —**aloetic** (ăl′ō ĕt′ĭk), *adj.*

aloft (ə lŏft′), *adv.*, *adj.* **1.** high up; in or into the air; above the ground. **2.** *Naut.* at or towards the masthead; in the upper rigging. [ME, t. Scand.; cf. Icel. *ā lopti* in the air]

alogical (ā lŏj′ĭ kl, ə-), *adj.* outside the domain or operation of logic. [f. A-[6] + LOGICAL] —**alog′ically,** *adv.*

aloin (ăl′ō ĭn), *n.* *Chem.* an intensely bitter, crystalline, purgative substance obtained from aloes.

alone (ə lōn′), *adj.* (*used in the pred. or following the noun*). **1.** apart from another or others: *to be alone.* **2.** to the exclusion of all others or all else: *man shall not live by bread alone.* **3. leave alone, a.** to allow (someone) to be by himself. **b.** *Colloq.* to refrain from bothering or interfering with. **4. let alone, a.** not to mention. **b.** to refrain from bothering or interfering with. 5. *Obs.* unique. —*adv.* 6. solitarily. 7. only; merely. [ME *al one* ALL (wholly) ONE] —**alone′ness,** *n.*

—**Syn.** 1. ALONE, LONE, LONELY, LONESOME all imply being without companionship or association. ALONE is colourless unless reinforced by *all*: it then suggests solitariness or desolation: *alone in the house, all alone on an island.* LONE is somewhat poetic or is intended humorously: *a lone sentinel, widow.* LONELY implies a sad or disquieting feeling of isolation. LONESOME connotes emotion, a longing for companionship.

along[1] (ə lŏng′), *prep.* 1. implying motion or direction through or by the length of; from one end to the other of: *to walk along a road.* 2. by the length of; parallel to or in a line with the length of: *a row of primroses along the hedge.* —*adv.* 3. in a line, or with a progressive motion; onwards. 4. by the length; lengthways. 5. in company; together (fol. by *with*): *I'll go along with you.* 6. as a companion; with one: *he took his sister along.* 7. **all along, a.** all the time. **b.** throughout; continuously. **c.** from end to end. **d.** at full length. 8. **be along,** *Colloq.* to come to a place: *he will soon be along.* 9. **get along,** *Colloq.* **a.** to be on amicable terms. **b.** to go; depart. [ME; OE *andlang*]

along[2] (ə lŏng′), *adv. Dial.* owing to; on account of (fol. by *of*). [ME; OE *gelang*]

alongshore (ə lŏng′shôr′), *adv.* by or along the shore or coast.

alongside (ə lŏng′sīd′), *adv.* 1. along or by the side; at or to the side of anything: *we brought the boat alongside.* —*prep.* 2. beside; by the side of.

Alonso (*Sp.* ȧ lōn′sō), *n.* **Dámaso** (*Sp.* dȧ′mȧ sō), born 1898, Spanish poet.

aloof (ə lo͞of′), *adv.* 1. at a distance, but within view; withdrawn: *to stand aloof.* —*adj.* 2. reserved; unsympathetic; disinterested. [f. A-[1] + *loof* LUFF, windward] —**aloof′ly,** *adv.* —**aloof′ness,** *n.* —**Ant.** 1. near.

alopecia (ăl′ə pē′shə), *n. Pathol.* 1. loss of hair; baldness. 2. **alopecia areata** (ĕə′rĭ ā′tə), a condition in which patches of hair fall out. [t. L, t. Gk: m. *alōpekía* mange of foxes]

aloud (ə loud′), *adv.* 1. with the natural tone of the voice as distinguished from in a whisper or silently: *to read aloud.* 2. with a loud voice; loudly: *to cry aloud.*

alow (ə lō′), *adv. Archaic or Naut.* low down; below.

alp (ălp), *n.* 1. a high mountain. 2. **the Alps.** See **Alps.** [t. L: s. *Alpēs*, pl., the Alps; ? from Celtic]

alpaca (ăl păk′ə), *n.* 1. a domesticated sheeplike South American ruminant of the genus *Lama* allied to the llama and the guanaco, having long, soft, silky hair or wool. 2. the hair. 3. a fabric made of it. 4. a glossy, wiry, commonly black woollen fabric with cotton warp. 5. a rayon and alpaca crepe, with a viscose and acetate rayon warp. [t. Sp., from *paco*, Peruv. animal name (to which the Ar. article, *al*, has been prefixed)]

Alpaca, *Lama pacos* (5 ft high)

alpenglow (ăl′pən glō′), *n.* a reddish glow often seen on the summits of mountains before sunrise and after sunset. [trans. of G *Alpenglühen*]

alpenhorn (ăl′pən hôn′), *n.* a long, powerful horn of wood or bark used in the Alps, as by cowherds. Also, **alphorn.** [t. G]

alpenstock (ăl′pən stŏk′), *n.* a strong staff pointed with iron, used by mountain climbers. [t. G]

Alpes-Maritimes (*Fr.* ȧlp mȧ rē tēm′), *n.* a department in SE France. 618,265 pop. (1962); 1527 sq. mi. *Cap.:* Nice.

alpestrine (ăl pĕs′trĭn), *adj.* 1. alpine. 2. *Bot.* subalpine (def. 2). [f. s. ML *alpestris* (der. L *Alpēs* Alps) + -INE[1]]

alpha (ăl′fə), *n.* 1. the first letter in the Greek alphabet (Α, α), corresponding to A. 2. the first; beginning. 3. the highest mark in an examination. 4. *Astron.* a star, usually the brightest of a constellation. 5. *Chem.* (of a compound) one of the possible positions of substituted atoms or groups.

alpha and omega, beginning and end. Rev. 1:8.

alphabet (ăl′fə bĕt′), *n.* 1. the letters of a language in their customary order. 2. any system of characters or signs for representing sounds or ideas. 3. first elements; simplest rudiments: *the alphabet of radio.* [t. L: s. *alphabētum*, t. Gk: m. *alphábētos*, f. *álpha* A + m. *bêta* B]

alphabetical (ăl′fə bĕt′ĭ kl), *adj.* 1. in the order of the alphabet: *alphabetical arrangement.* 2. pertaining to an alphabet; expressed by an alphabet: *alphabetical writing.* Also, **al′phabet′ic.** —**al′phabet′ically,** *adv.*

alphabetize (ăl′fə bə tīz), *v.t.*, **-tized, -tizing.** 1. to arrange in order of the alphabet: *to alphabetize a list of names.* 2. to express by an alphabet. Also, **alphabetise.** —**alphabetization** (ăl′fə bĕt′ī zā′shən), *n.* —**al′phabetiz′er,** *n.*

alpha-eucaine (ăl′fə yo͞o′kān), *n.* eucaine (def. 1).

alpha iron, a form of iron which, when pure, exists up to approximately 900 degrees centigrade; consisting of body-centred cubic crystals.

alphanumeric (ăl′fə nyo͞o mĕ′rĭk), *adj.* (of a set of characters) conveying information by using both letters and numbers. Also, **al′phanumer′ical.** [b. ALPHA(BET) + NUMERIC(AL) —**al′phanumer′ically,** *adv.*

alpha particle, *Physics.* a positively charged particle composed of two protons and two neutrons (and therefore equivalent to the nucleus of a helium atom) and spontaneously emitted by some radioactive material such as radium.

alpha ray, *Physics.* a stream of alpha particles.

Alpheus (ăl fē′əs), *n. Gk Myth.* a river god, son of Oceanus and Tethys, who fell in love with the nymph Arethusa and, when she became a spring to escape him, changed into a river and mingled with her.

alphorn (ălp′hôn′), *n.* alpenhorn.

alphosis (ăl fō′sĭs), *n. Pathol.* lack of pigment in the skin, as in albinism. [f. s. Gk *alphós* kind of leprosy + -OSIS]

alpine (ăl′pīn), *adj.* 1. of or pertaining to any lofty mountain. 2. very high; elevated. 3. (*cap.*) of or pertaining to the Alps. 4. *Bot.* growing on mountains, above the limit of tree growth. 5. (*cap.*) *Geol.* of or pertaining to the major mountain-building episode which occurred in Europe and N Africa in the Tertiary period. [t. L: m. s. *Alpīnus*, der. *Alpēs* the ALPS]

alpinism (ăl′pĭ nĭz′əm), *n.* mountain climbing, esp. in the Alps. —**al′pinist,** *n.*

Alps (ălps), *n.* a mountain system in S Europe, extending from France through Switzerland and Italy to Austria and Yugoslavia. Highest peak, Mont Blanc, 15,781 ft. [see ALP]

already (ôl rĕd′ĭ), *adv.* by this (or that) time; previously to or at some specified time. [ME *al redy* all ready. See ALL, READY]

alright (ôl′rīt′), *adv.* (not generally regarded as good usage) all right.

Alsace (ăl′săs; *Fr.* ȧl zȧs′), *n.* 1. an administrative region in NE France between the Vosges mountains and the Rhine. 1,318,070 pop. (1962); 3202 sq. mi. *Prefecture:* Strasbourg. 2. a former province in NE France.

Alsace-Lorraine (ăl′săs lō rān′; *Fr.* ȧl zȧs lō rĕn′), *n.* a region in NE France, including the former provinces of Alsace and Lorraine: a part of Germany 1871–1919 and 1940–44. 1,986,969 pop. (1954); 5607 sq. mi.

BELGIUM
PRUSSIA
LUXEMBOURG
PALATINATE
BADEN
ALSACE-LORRAINE
FRANCE
1871-1919
SWITZERLAND

Alsace-Lorraine

Alsatia (ăl sā′shə), *n.* 1. *Obs.* Alsace. 2. *Hist.* a cant term for Whitefriars, London, once a sanctuary for debtors and lawbreakers. [t. ML, Latinization of G *Elsass* ALSACE, lit., foreign settlement]

Alsatian (ăl sā′shən), *adj.* 1. of or pertaining to Alsace. 2. of or pertaining to Alsatia. —*n.* 3. a native or inhabitant of Alsace. 4. *Hist.* an inhabitant of Alsatia (Whitefriars); a criminal. 5. a highly intelligent wolf-like breed of dog much used by the police, or as a guide-dog, etc.

al Shaab (ăl shäb′). See **Medina al Shaab.**

alsike (ăl′sīk, -sĭk, ôl′-), *n.* a European clover, *Trifolium hybridum*, with whitish or pink flowers. Also, **alsike clover.** [named after *Alsike*, in Sweden]

alsinaceous (ăl′sĭ nā′shəs), *adj. Bot.* 1. caryophyllaceous. 2. relating to or resembling the chickweed. [f. Gk *alsin(ē)* + -ACEOUS]

Al Sirat (ăl′sĭ răt′), *Islam.* 1. the correct path of religion. 2. the bridge, fine as a razor's edge, over which all who enter paradise must pass. [t. Ar.: m. *al sirāt* the road, from L (*via*) *strāta* paved (road). Cf. STREET]

also (ôl′sō), *adv.* in addition; too; further. [ME; OE *alswā, ealswā* all (wholly or quite) so] —**Syn.** besides, moreover.

also-ran (ôl′sō răn′), *n.* 1. an unplaced horse in a race. 2. a nonentity.

alt (ălt), *Music.* —*adj.* 1. high. —*n.* 2. **in alt,** in the first octave above the treble stave. [t. It.: s. *alto* high]

alt-, var. of **alto-** before vowels.

alt., 1. alternate. 2. altitude. 3. alto.

Alta, Alberta (Canada).

Altaic (ăl tā′ĭk), *n.* 1. a family of languages consisting of the Turkic, Tungusic, and Mongolian branches or subfamilies. —*adj.* 2. belonging, or pertaining to these languages.

Altai Mountains (*Russ.* àl tày′), a mountain system in central Asia, mostly in the Mongolian People's Republic and the S Soviet Union in Asia. Highest peak, Belukha, 15,157 ft.

Altair (ăl tēə′), *n.* a star of the first magnitude in the constellation Aquila. [t. Ar.: m. *al ṭā'ir* the bird]

Altamira (ăl′tə mĭə′rə), *n.* a cave in N Spain, near Santander: Old Stone Age colour drawings of animals.

altar (ôl′tə), *n.* **1.** an elevated place or structure, on which sacrifices are offered or at which religious rites are performed. **2.** (in most Christian churches) the communion table. **3.** *Civ. Eng.* one of the steps in a dry-dock wall. **4.** (*cap.*) *Astron.* the southern constellation Ara. **5. lead to the altar,** to marry (a woman). [ME *alter*, OE *altar(e)*, t. LL. Cf. L *altāria*, pl., high altar]

altar boy, acolyte (def. 1).

altarpiece (ôl′tə pēs′), *n.* a work of art or decorative screen behind and above an altar; a reredos.

altazimuth (ăl tăz′ĭ məth), *n.* a mounting of telescopes or theodolites which provides two axes, one horizontal and one vertical, so that the instrument may be turned in the plane of the horizon and in any vertical plane. Altazimuths are used to determine altitudes and azimuths of heavenly bodies. [f. ALT(ITUDE) + AZIMUTH]

Altdorf (ălt′dôf; *Ger.* àlt′dôrf), *n.* a town in central Switzerland: the legendary home of William Tell. 7477 (1964).

alter (ôl′tə), *v.t.* **1.** to make different in some particular; modify. **2.** *U.S. and Austral. Colloq.* to castrate or spay. —*v.i.* **3.** to become different in some respect. [t. F: s. *altérer*, ult. der. L *alter* other] **—Syn. 1.** See **adjust** and **change.**

alter., alteration.

alterable (ôl′tə rə bl), *adj.* capable of being altered. —**al′terabil′ity, al′terableness,** *n.* —**al′terably,** *adv.*

alterant (ôl′tə rənt), *adj.* **1.** producing alteration. **2.** *Med.* gradually restoring healthy bodily functions. —*n.* **3.** something that causes alteration. **4.** *Med.* an alterant drug or medicine.

alteration (ôl′tə rā′shən), *n.* **1.** the act of altering. **2.** the condition of being altered. **3.** a change; modification.

alterative (ôl′tə rə tĭv), *adj.* **1.** tending to alter. **2.** *Med. Obs.* alterant. —*n.* **3.** *Med. Obs.* an alterant drug or medicine.

altercate (ôl′tə kāt′), *v.i.*, **-cated, -cating.** to argue with zeal, heat, or anger; wrangle. [t. L: m. s. *altercātus*, pp., having wrangled]

altercation (ôl′tə kā′shən), *n.* a heated or angry dispute; a noisy wrangle. —**al′terca′tive,** *adj.*

altered chord, *Music.* a chord in which at least one note has been changed from its normal pitch in the key.

alter ego (ăl′tər ē′gō, ĕg′ō), *Latin.* **1.** a second self. **2.** an inseparable friend. [L: lit., another I]

alter idem (ăl′tər ī′dĕm), *Latin.* another exactly similar.

alterity (ôl tĕ′rĭ tĭ, ăl-), *n.* otherness.

alternant (ôl tû′nənt), *Chiefly U.S. adj.* alternating. [t. L: s. *alternans*, ppr.]

alternate (*v.* ôl′tə nāt′; *adj.*, *n.* ôl tû′nĭt), *v.*, **-nated, -nating,** *adj.*, *n.* —*v.i.* **1.** to follow one another in time or place reciprocally (usually fol. by *with*): *day and night alternate with each other.* **2.** to change about by turns between points, states, actions, etc.: *he alternates between hope and despair.* **3.** *Elect.* to reverse direction or sign periodically. **4.** *Theat.* to understudy. —*v.t.* **5.** to perform by turns, or one after another. **6.** to interchange successively: *to alternate hot and cold compresses.* —*adj.* **7.** arranged or following each after the other, in succession: *alternate winter and summer.* **8.** every other one of a series: *read only the alternate lines.* **9.** reciprocal. **10.** *Bot.* **a.** (of leaves, etc.) placed singly at different heights on the axis, on each side alternately, or at definite angular distances from one another. **b.** opposite to the intervals between other organs: *petals alternate with sepals.* —*n.* **11.** *U.S.* a person authorized to take the place of and act for another in his absence; substitute. [t. L: m. s. *alternātus*] —**alter′nateness,** *n.*

Alternate leaves

alternate angles, *Geom.* two non-adjacent angles made by the crossing of two lines by a third line, both angles being either interior or exterior, and being on opposite sides of the third line.

alternately (ôl tû′nĭt lĭ), *adv.* **1.** in alternate order; by turns. **2.** in alternate position.

alternating current, *Elect.* a current that reverses direction in regular cycles. *Abbrev.*: a.c.

alternation (ôl′tə nā′shən), *n.* alternate succession; appearance, occurrence, or change by turns.

alternation of generations, *Biol.* an alternating in a line of reproduction, between generations unlike and generations like a given progenitor, esp. the alternation of asexual with sexual reproduction.

alternative (ôl tû′nə tĭv), *n.* **1.** a possibility of one out of two (or, less strictly, more) things: *the alternative of remaining neutral or attacking.* **2.** one of the things thus possible: *they chose the alternative of attacking.* **3.** a remaining course or choice: *we had no alternative but to move.* —*adj.* **4.** affording a choice between two things, or a possibility of one thing out of two. **5.** (of two things) mutually exclusive, so that if one is chosen the other must be rejected: *alternative results of this or that course.* **6.** *Logic.* (of a proposition) asserting two or more alternatives, at least one of which is true. [t. ML: m. s. *alternātīvus*] —**alter′natively,** *adv.* —**alter′nativeness,** *n.* **—Syn. 1.** option, selection. See **choice.**

alternator (ôl′tə nā′tə), *n.* *Elect.* a generator of alternating current.

althaea (ăl thē′ə), *n.* **1.** any plant of the genus *Althaea.* **2.** a malvaceous flowering garden shrub, *Hibiscus syriacus*; Aaron's-beard. **3.** (*cap.*) *Gk Legend.* the mother of Meleager. Also, **althea.** [t. L, t. Gk: m. *althaía* wild mallow]

Althing (ăl′thĭng), *n.* the Icelandic parliament, consisting of an upper and a lower house.

althorn (ălt′hôn′), *n.* a valved brass instrument, a horn, a fourth or fifth below the ordinary cornet; a tenor saxhorn. Also, **alto horn.**

although (ôl ŧħō′), *conj.* even though (practically equivalent to *though*, but often preferred to it in stating fact). Also, **altho′.** [ME, f. *al* even + THOUGH. See ALL, adv.] **—Syn.** though, not withstanding (that), even if.

alti-, var. of **alto-.**

altimeter (ăl tĭm′ĭ tə, ăl′tĭ mē′tə), *n.* **1.** a sensitive aneroid barometer calibrated and graduated to measure altitudes by the decrease of atmospheric pressure with height, used in aircraft for finding distance above sea-level, terrain, or some other reference point. **2.** any device used for the same purpose which operates by some other means, as by radio waves, etc. [f. ALTI + METER[1]] —**altim′etry,** *n.*

Althorn

altissimo (ăl tĭs′ĭ mō; *It.* àl tēs′sē mô), *Music.* —*adj.* **1.** very high. —*n.* **2. in altissimo,** in the second octave above the treble stave. [It.]

altitude (ăl′tĭ tyo͞od′), *n.* **1.** the height above sea-level of any point on the earth's surface or in the atmosphere. **2.** extent or distance upwards. **3. a.** *Astron.* the angular distance of a star, planet, etc., above the horizon. **b.** *Survey, etc.* the angle of elevation of any point above the horizon. **4.** *Geom.* **a.** the perpendicular distance from the base of a figure to its highest point. **b.** the line through the highest point of a figure perpendicular to the base. **5.** a high point or region: *mountain altitudes.* **6.** high or exalted position, rank, etc. [ME, t. L: m. *altitūdo* height] **—Syn. 2.** See **height. —Ant. 2.** depth.

altitudinal (ăl′tĭ tyo͞o′dĭ nəl), *adj.* relating to height.

alto (ăl′tō), *n.*, *pl.* **-tos,** *adj.* —*n. Music.* **1.** the lowest female voice; contralto. **2.** the highest male voice; countertenor. **3.** a singer with an alto voice. **4.** a musical part for an alto voice. **5.** the viola. **6.** an althorn. —*adj.* **7.** *Music.* of the alto; having the compass of the alto. **8.** high. [t. It., g. L *altus* high]

alto-, a word element meaning 'high', as in *altostratus.* Also, **alt-, alti-.** [comb. form repr. L *altus*]

alto clef, *Music.* a sign placing middle C on the third line of the stave. See illus. under **clef.**

altocumulus (ăl′tō kyo͞o′myo͝o ləs), *n.* *Meteorol.* a cloud type consisting of globular masses or patches, more or less in a layer, somewhat darker underneath and larger than cirrocumulus.

altogether (ôl′tə gĕŧħ′ə), *adv.* **1.** wholly; entirely; completely; quite: *altogether bad.* **2.** in all: *the debt amounted altogether to twenty pounds.* **3.** on the whole: *altogether, I'm glad it's over.* —*n.* **4.** a whole. **5. the altogether,** *Colloq.* the nude. [var. of ME *altogeder*, f. *al* ALL, adj. + *togeder* TOGETHER]

alto horn, althorn.

Altona (*Ger.* àl′tô nà), *n.* a metropolitan district of Hamburg, in N West Germany: formerly an independent city.

alto-rilievo (ăl′tō rĭ lē′vō), *n.*, *pl.* **-vos.** sculpture in high relief, in which the figures project from the background by at least half their depth (contrasted with *bas-relief*). Also, **alto-relievo.** [t. It.]

altostratus (ăl′tō strā′təs), *n.* *Meteorol.* a moderately high, veil-like or sheetlike cloud, without definite configurations, more or less grey or bluish.

altricial (ăl trĭsh′əl), *adj. Ornith.* confined to the nesting place for a period after hatching. [t. NL: s. *altriciālis*, der. L *altrix* nurse]

Altrincham (ôl′trĭng əm), *n.* a town in England, in NE Cheshire. 41,122 (1961).

altruism (ăl′trōō ĭz′əm), *n.* the principle or practice of seeking the welfare of others (opposed to *egoism*). [t. F: m. *altruisme*, der. It. *altrui* of or to others]

altruist (ăl′trōō ĭst), *n.* a person devoted to the welfare of others (opposed to *egoist*).

altruistic (ăl′trōō ĭs′tĭk), *adj.* regardful of others; having regard to the well-being or best interests of others (opposed to *egoistic*). **—al′truis′tically,** *adv.*

Al'Ubaid (ăl yōō′bī ĭd), *n.* **1.** an early phase of Mesopotamian culture. **—***adj.* **2.** pertaining to or characteristic of this culture. [named after *Al'Ubaid* in S Iraq, site of an ancient Sumerian city.]

alula (ăl′yōō lə), *n., pl.* **-lae** (-lē′). *Ornith.* the group of 3 to 6 small, rather stiff, feathers growing on the first digit, pollex, or thumb of a bird's wing. [t. NL, dim. of L *āla* wing] **—al′ular,** *adj.*

alum (ăl′əm), *n.* **1.** an astringent crystalline substance, a double sulphate of aluminium and potassium, $K_2SO_4 \cdot Al_2(SO_4)_3 \cdot 24H_2O$, used in medicine, dyeing, and many technical processes. **2.** one of a class of double sulphates analogous to the potassium alum, having the general formula $R_2SO_4 . X_2(SO_4)_3 . 24H_2O$, where R is a monovalent alkali metal or ammonium, and X one of a number of trivalent metals. **3.** *Obsolesc.* aluminium sulphate $Al_2(SO_4)_3$. [ME, t. OF, f. L *alūmen*]

alumina (ə lyōō′mĭ nə), *n.* **1.** *Mineral.* the oxide of aluminium, Al_2O_3, occurring widely in nature as corundum (in the ruby and sapphire, emery, etc.). **2.** *Obs.* aluminium. [t. NL, der. L *alūmen* alum]

aluminate (ə lyōō′mĭ nāt′), *n.* **1.** *Chem.* a salt of the acid form of aluminium hydroxide. **2.** *Mineral.* a metallic oxide combined with alumina.

aluminiferous (ə lyōō′mĭ nĭf′ə rəs), *adj.* containing or yielding aluminium.

aluminium (ăl′yōō mĭn′yəm), **1.** a silver-white metallic element, light in weight, ductile, malleable, and not readily oxidized or tarnished, occurring combined in nature in igneous rocks, shales, clays, and most soils. It is much used in alloys and for lightweight utensils, castings, aeroplane parts, etc. *Symbol:* Al; *at. wt:* 26·9815; *at. no.:* 13; *sp. gr.:* 2·70 at 20°C. **—***adj.* **2.** belonging to or containing aluminium. Also, *U.S.*, **aluminum.** [t. NL, der. L *alūmen* alum]

aluminium foil, a thin sheet of aluminium used for wrapping food, tobacco, and other domestic articles.

aluminize (ə lyōō′mĭ nīz′), *v.t.*, **-nized, -nizing.** to treat with aluminium. Also, **aluminise.**

aluminothermy (ə lyōō′mĭ nō thûr′mĭ), *n. Metall.* a process of producing high temperatures by causing finely divided aluminium to react with the oxygen from another metallic oxide. Also, **alu′minother′mics.** [f. *alumino-* (comb. form of ALUMINIUM) + -THERMY]

aluminous (ə lyōō′mĭ nəs), *adj.* of the nature of or containing alum or alumina. [t. L: m. s. *alūminōsus*]

aluminum (ə lyōō′mĭ nəm), *n. U.S.* aluminium.

alumna (ə lŭm′nə), *n., pl.* **-nae** (-nē). *Chiefly U.S.* fem. of **alumnus.**

alumnus (ə lŭm′nəs), *n., pl.* **-ni** (-nī). *Chiefly U.S.* a graduate or former student of a school, college, university, etc. [t. L: foster child, pupil]

alumroot (ăl′əm rōōt′), *n.* **1.** any of several plants of the saxifragaceous genus *Heuchera*, with astringent roots, esp. *H. sanguinea*. **2.** the root. Also, **al′umstone′.**

alunite (ăl′yōō nīt′), *n.* a mineral, a hydrous sulphate of potassium and aluminium, $KAl_3(SO_4)_2(OH)_6$, commonly occurring in fine-grained masses. [f. F *alun* alum + -ITE[1]]

Alva (ăl′və; *Sp.* äl′bä), *n.* **Fernando Álvarez de Toledo** (*Sp.* fĕr nän′dō äl′ba rĕth dĕ tō lĕ′dō), **Duke of,** 1508–82, Spanish general who ruthlessly suppressed a Protestant rebellion in the Netherlands in 1567. Also, **Alba.**

Alvarado (*Sp.* äl bä rä′dō), *n.* **1. Alonso de** (*Sp.* ä lōn′sō dĕ), died 1553?, Spanish soldier in conquests of Mexico and Peru. **2. Pedro de** (*Sp.* pĕ′drō dĕ), 1495?–1541, Spanish soldier: chief aide of Cortez in conquest of Mexico.

Álvarez Quintero (*Sp.* äl′bä rĕth kēn tĕ′rō), **Joaquín** (*Sp.* KHwä kēn′), 1873–1944, and his brother **Serafín** (*Sp.* sĕ rä fēn′), 1871–1938, Spanish dramatists.

Alvaro (*It.* äl vä′rō), *n.* **Corrado** (*It.* kōr rä′dō), born 1895, Italian writer.

alveolar (ăl vē′ə lə), *adj.* **1.** *Anat., Zool.* pertaining to an alveolus or to alveoli. **2.** *Phonet.* with the tongue touching or near the alveolar ridge.

alveolar arch, that part of the upper jawbone in which the teeth are set.

alveolar ridge, the ridgelike inward projection of the gums between the hard palate and the upper front teeth.

alveolar theory, the theory that protoplasm consists of viscid bubbles or chambers filled with more fluid substances.

alveolate (ăl vē′ə lĭt, -lāt′), *adj.* **1.** having alveoli; deeply pitted, as a honeycomb. **2.** inserted in an alveolus. Also, **alve′olat′ed. —alve′ola′tion,** *n.*

alveolus (ăl vē′ə ləs), *n., pl.* **-li** (-lī′), *Anat., Zool.* **1.** a little cavity, pit, or cell, as a cell of a honeycomb. **2.** an air-cell of the lungs, formed by the terminal dilation of tiny air passageways. **3.** one of the terminal secretory units of a racemose gland. **4.** the socket within the jawbone in which the root or roots of a tooth are set. **5.** (*pl.*) alveolar ridge. [t. L, dim. of *alveus* a hollow]

alvine (ăl′vĭn, -vīn), *adj. Med., Obs.* pertaining to the belly; intestinal. [t. L: m. s. *alvīnus*, der. *alvus* belly]

alway (ôl′wā′), *adv. Archaic.* always. [ME; OE *ealneweg*, orig. *ealne weg*. See ALL, WAY]

always (ôl′wāz′, -wĭz), *adv.* **1.** all the time; uninterruptedly. **2.** every time; on every occasion (opposed to *sometimes* or *occasionally*): *he always works on Saturday.* [ME, f. ALWAY + adv. gen. suffix *-(e)s*] **—Syn. 1.** perpetually, everlastingly, for ever, continually.

alyssum (ăl′ĭ səm), *n.* **1.** any of the herbs constituting the brassicaceous genus *Alyssum*, characterized by small yellow or white racemose flowers. **2.** sweet alyssum. [t. NL, t. Gk: m. *álysson* name of a plant, lit., curing (canine) madness]

am (ăm; *unstressed* əm, m), *v.* 1st pers. sing. pres. indic. of **be.** [OE *am*, *eam*, var. of *eom*, c. Icel. *em*, Goth. *im.* Cf. Irish *am*, Gk *eimí*]

a.m., **1.** (L *ante meridiem*) before noon. **2.** the period from 12 midnight to 12 noon.

AM, *Radio.* amplitude modulation.

A.M., **1.** *U.S.* (L *Artium Magister*) Master of Arts. **2.** Albert Medal.

Am., **1.** America. **2.** American.

amadavat (ăm′ə də văt′), *n.* a small finchlike Indian bird, *Estrilda amandava*, exported as a cagebird. Also, **avadavat.** [t. Gujarati: named after AHMEDABAD]

amadou (ăm′ə dōō′), *n.* a spongy substance prepared from fungi (*Polyporus* [*Fomes*] *fomentarius* and allied species) growing on trees, used as tinder and in surgery. [t. F]

Amagasaki (ăm′ə gə sä′kĭ), *n.* a town in S Japan, on W Honshu island, near Osaka. 500,990 (1965).

amah (ä′mə, ăm′ə), *n.* (used among Europeans in the Far East). **1.** a nurse, esp. a wet nurse. **2.** a maidservant. [Anglo-Indian, t. Pg.: m. *ama*]

amain (ə mān′), *adv. Archaic.* **1.** with full force; vigorously; violently. **2.** at full speed. **3.** suddenly; hastily. **4.** exceedingly; greatly. [f. A-[1] + MAIN[1]]

Amalfi (ə măl′fĭ; *It.* ä mäl′fē), *n.* a seaport in Italy, in Campania, SE of Naples: important commercial centre 9th–14th centuries. 12,365 (1966).

amalgam (ə măl′gəm), *n.* **1.** a mixture or combination. **2.** an alloy of mercury with another metal or metals. **3.** a rare mineral, an alloy of silver and mercury, occurring as silver-white crystals or grains. [ME, t. ML: s. *amalgama*, appar. m. L *malagma* poultice, t. Gk]

amalgamate (ə măl′gə māt′), *v.*, **-mated, -mating. —***v.t.* **1.** to mix so as to make a combination; blend; unite; combine: *to amalgamate two companies.* **2.** *Metall.* to mix or alloy (a metal) with mercury. **—***v.i.* **3.** to combine, unite, or coalesce. **4.** to blend with another metal, as mercury. **—amal′gamable,** *adj.* **—amal′gama′tive,** *adj.* **—amal′gama′tor,** *n.*

amalgamation (ə măl′gə mā′shən), *n.* **1.** the act of amalgamating. **2.** the resulting state. **3.** *Com.* a merger or two or more companies. **4.** *Ethnol.* the biological fusion of diverse racial stocks. **5.** *Metall.* the extraction of the precious metals from their ores by treatment with mercury.

Amalthaea (ăm′ăl thē′ə), *n. Gk Myth.* **1.** a nymph who nursed Zeus on goat's milk. **2.** the goat itself. Also, **Amalthea.**

amanita (ăm′ə nī′tə), *n. Bot.* any fungus of the agaricaceous genus *Amanita*, comprised chiefly of poisonous species. [t. NL, t. Gk: m. *amanîtai*, pl., kind of fungi]

amanuensis (ə măn′yōō ĕn′sĭs), *n., pl.* **-ses** (-sēz). a person employed to write or type what another dictates or to copy what has been written by another; secretary. [t. L: secretary, orig. adj., f. (*servus*) *ā manū* secretary + *-ensis* belonging to]

amaranth (ăm′ə rănth′), *n.* **1.** *Poetic.* a flower that never fades. **2.** any plant of the genus *Amaranthus*, which includes species cultivated for their showy flowers, as the love-lies-bleeding, or their coloured foliage (green, purple, etc.). 3. *U.S.* a purplish red azo dye used to colour foods. [var. (by assoc. with Gk *ánthos* flower) of *amarant*, t. L: s. *amarantus*, t. Gk: m. *amárantos* unfading]

amaranthaceous (ăm′ə răn thā′shəs), *adj. Bot.* belonging to the family *Amaranthaceae* (or *Amarantaceae*), comprising mostly herbaceous or shrubby plants, as the cockscomb, the amaranth, etc.

amaranthine (ăm′ə răn′thĭn), *adj.* **1.** of or like the amaranth. **2.** unfading; everlasting. **3.** purplish.

Amaravati (ăm′ə rä′və tĭ), *n.* Amraoti.

amarelle (ăm′ə rĕl′), *n. U.S.* morello cherry.

Amarillo (ăm′ə rĭl′ō), *n.* a town in the U.S., in NW Texas. 137,969 (1960).

amaryllidaceous (ăm′ə rĭl′ĭ dā′shəs), *adj. Bot.* belonging to the *Amaryllidaceae*, or amaryllis family of plants, which includes the amaryllis, narcissus, snowdrop, etc.

amaryllis (ăm′ə rĭl′ĭs), *n.* **1.** a bulbous plant, *Amaryllis belladonna*, the belladonna lily, with large, lily-like, normally rose-coloured flowers. **2.** any of several related plants once referred to the genus *Amaryllis*. **3.** (*cap.*) a shepherdess or country girl (in classical and later pastoral poetry). [t. L, t. Gk (def. 3)]

Amaryllis, *Amaryllis belladonna*

amasi (ə mä′sĭ), *n. S African.* maas.

amass (ə măs′), *v.t.* **1.** to gather for oneself; collect as one's own: *to amass a fortune.* **2.** to collect into a mass or pile; bring together. [t. F: s. *amasser*, der. *masse* mass, g. L *massa* lump (of dough, etc.)] —**amass′able,** *adj.* —**amass′er,** *n.* —**amass′ment,** *n.*

amateur (ăm′ə tû′, ăm′ə tyŏŏə′), *n.* **1.** one who cultivates any study or art or other activity for personal pleasure instead of professionally or for gain. **2.** an athlete who has never competed for money. **3.** a superficial or unskilful worker; dabbler. **4.** *Obs.* one who admires. [t. F, t. L: m. s. *amātor* lover] —**am′ateurship′,** *n.* —**Syn. 3.** dilettante, tiro, novice. —**Ant. 1–3.** professional.

amateurish (ăm′ə tû′rĭsh, -tyŏŏə′-), *adj.* characteristic of an amateur; having the faults or deficiencies of an amateur. —**am′ateur′ishly,** *adv.* —**am′ateur′ishness,** *n.*

amateurism (ăm′ə tə rĭz′əm, -tyŏŏə-), *n.* the practice or character of an amateur.

Amati (ə mä′tĭ; *It.* à mà′tē), *n.* **1.** a family of violinmakers of Cremona, Italy, who flourished in the 16th and 17th centuries. **2.** a violin made by a member of this family. **3. Nicolò** (*It.* nē kò lò′), 1596–1684, Italian violin-maker; teacher of Antonio Stradivari.

amative (ăm′ə tĭv), *adj.* disposed to loving; amorous. [f. s. L *amātus*, pp., loved + -IVE] —**am′atively,** *adv.* —**am′ativeness,** *n.*

amatol (ăm′ə tŏl′), *n.* an explosive mixture of ammonium nitrate and TNT.

amatory (ăm′ə tə rĭ), *adj.* pertaining to lovers or lovemaking; expressive of love: *amatory poems, an amatory look.* Also, **amatorial** (ăm′ə tô′rĭ əl). [t. L: m. s. *amātōrius*]

amatungulu (ăm′ə tŭng′gyŏŏ lōō′), *n. S African.* matungulu.

amaurosis (ăm′ô rō′sĭs), *n.* partial or total loss of sight without obvious disease of the optic nerve or retina. [NL, t. Gk, der. *amaurós* dim] —**amaurotic** (ăm′ô-rŏt′ĭk), *adj.*

amaze (ə māz′), *v.*, **amazed, amazing,** *n.* —*v.t.* **1.** to overwhelm with surprise; astonish greatly. **2.** *Obs.* to bewilder. —*n.* **3.** *Archaic.* amazement. [OE *āmasian.* Cf. MAZE] —**amazedly** (ə mā′zĭd lĭ), *adv.* —**amaz′edness,** *n.* —**Syn. 1.** astound, dumbfound. See **surprise.**

amazement (ə māz′mənt), *n.* **1.** overwhelming surprise or astonishment. **2.** *Obs.* stupefaction. **3.** *Obs.* perplexity. **4.** *Obs.* consternation.

amazing (ə mā′zĭng), *adj.* causing great surprise; wonderful. —**amaz′ingly,** *adv.*

Amazon (ăm′ə zən), *n.* **1.** a river in N South America, flowing from the Peruvian Andes E through N Brazil to the Atlantic: the largest river in the world. ab. 3600 mi. See map under **Guiana.** **2.** *Gk Legend.* one of a race of female warriors said to dwell near the Black Sea. **3.** one of a mythical tribe of female warriors in South America. **4.** (*often l.c.*) a tall, powerful, aggressive woman. [(def. 2) ME, t. L, t. Gk, ult. orig. uncert.; the name of the river refers to female warriors seen in its vicinity]

Amazon ant a species of red ant, *Polyergus rufescens*, that steals and enslaves the young of other species.

Amazonian (ăm′ə zō′nyən), *adj.* **1.** characteristic of an Amazon; warlike; masculine. **2.** pertaining to the river Amazon or the country adjacent to it.

amazon-stone (ăm′ə zən stōn′), *n. Mineral.* a green felspar, a variety of microcline, used as an ornamental material. Also, **amazonite** (ăm′ə zə nīt′). [f. AMAZON river + STONE]

ambages (ăm bā′jēz), *n.pl. Archaic.* winding or roundabout ways. [t. L: circuits]

ambagious (ăm bā′jəs), *adj.* roundabout. —**amba′giously,** *adv.* —**amba′giousness,** *n.*

Ambala (əm bä′lə), *n.* a town in N India, in E Punjab. 105,543 (1961).

ambary (ăm bä′rĭ), *n.* **1.** a plant of India, *Hibiscus cannabinus*, which yields a useful fibre. **2.** the fibre itself. Also, **ambari.** [t. Hind.]

ambassador (ăm băs′ə də), *n.* **1.** a diplomatic agent of the highest rank, sent by one sovereign or state to another either as resident representative (**ordinary** or **resident ambassador,** or (with full powers) **ambassador plenipotentiary**) or on temporary special service (**ambassador extraordinary** or *U.S.* **ambassador-at-large**). **2.** an authorized messenger or representative. [ME *ambassadour*, t. F: m. *ambassadeur*, t. It.: m. *ambasciatore*; prob. of Celtic orig.] —**ambassadorial** (ăm băs′ə dô′rĭ əl), *adj.* —**ambas′sadorship′,** *n.*

ambassadress (ăm băs′ə drĭs), *n.* **1.** a female ambassador. **2.** the wife of an ambassador.

Ambato (*Sp.* àm bà′tò), *n.* a town in central Ecuador, near Mt Chimborazo. 52,713 (est. 1962).

amber (ăm′bə), *n.* **1.** a pale yellow, sometimes reddish or brownish, fossil resin of vegetable origin, translucent, brittle, and capable of gaining a negative electrical charge by friction. **2.** the yellowish brown colour of resin. **3.** an amber light used as a warning in signalling. **4.** of amber. **5.** resembling amber. **6.** yellowish brown. [ME *ambra*, t. ML, t. Ar.: m. *'anbar* ambergris]

ambergris (ăm′bə grēs′, -grĭs), *n.* an opaque, ash-coloured substance, a morbid secretion of the sperm whale, fragrant when heated, usually found floating on the ocean or cast ashore, used chiefly in perfumery. [late ME *imbergres*, t. F: m. *ambre gris* grey amber]

amberoid (ăm′bə roid′), *n.* synthetic amber made by compressing pieces of various resins, esp. amber, at a high temperature. Also, **ambroid.**

ambi-, a word element meaning 'both', 'around', 'on both sides', as in *ambidextrous.* [comb. form repr. L *ambi-* around, or *ambo* both]

ambidexter (ăm′bĭ dĕk′stə), *n.* **1.** a person who uses both hands equally well. **2.** *Archaic.* a double-dealer, esp. a deceitful lawyer or juror. —*adj.* **3.** *Archaic.* ambidextrous. [t. ML, f. *ambi-* AMBI- + *dexter* right]

ambidexterity (ăm′bĭ dĕks tĕ′rĭ tĭ), *n.* **1.** ambidextrous facility. **2.** unusual cleverness. **3.** *Archaic.* duplicity.

ambidextrous (ăm′bĭ dĕks′trəs), *adj.* **1.** able to use both hands equally well. **2.** unusually skilful; facile. **3.** *Archaic.* double-dealing; deceitful. Also, **am′bidex′tral.** —**am′bidex′trously,** *adv.* —**am′bidex′trousness,** *n.*

ambience (ăm′bĭ əns), *n.* **1.** environment; surrounding atmosphere. **2.** the mood, character, quality, atmosphere, etc., as of a place or milieu. [t. F]

ambient (ăm′bĭ ənt), *adj.* **1.** completely surrounding: *ambient air.* **2.** circulating. [t. L: s. *ambiens*, ppr., going around]

ambiguity (ăm′bĭ gyōō′ĭ tĭ), *n., pl.* **-ties.** **1.** doubtfulness or uncertainty of meaning: *to speak without ambiguity.* **2.** an equivocal or ambiguous word or expression: *the law is free of ambiguities.* [ME *ambiguite*, t. L: m. s. *ambiguitas*] —**Ant. 1.** explicitness.

ambiguous (ăm bĭg′yŏŏ əs), *adj.* **1.** open to various interpretations; having a double meaning; equivocal: *an ambiguous answer.* **2.** of doubtful or uncertain nature; difficult to comprehend, distinguish, or classify: *a rock of ambiguous character.* **3.** lacking clearness or definiteness; obscure; indistinct. [t. L: m. *ambiguus* doubtful] —**ambig′uously,** *adv.* —**ambig′uousness,** *n.*

—**Syn. 1.** AMBIGUOUS, EQUIVOCAL describe that which is not clear in meaning. That which is AMBIGUOUS leaves the intended sense doubtful; it need not be purposely deceptive. That which is EQUIVOCAL is equally capable of two or more interpretations, and is usually intended to be so for the purpose of mystifying. **3.** puzzling, enigmatic.

ambit (ăm′bĭt), *n.* **1.** boundary; limits; sphere. **2.** scope; extent. **3.** circumference. [ME, t. L: s. *ambitus* compass]

ambitendency (ăm′bĭ tĕn′dən sĭ), *n. Psychol.* the coexistence of opposite tendencies.

ambition (ăm bĭsh′ən), *n.* **1.** an eager desire for distinction, preferment, power, or fame. **2.** the object desired or sought after: *the crown was his ambition.* **3.** desire for work or activity; energy. —*v.t.* **4.** *Obs.* to desire strongly; have as an ambition. [ME, t. L: s. *ambitio* striving for honours] —**ambi′tionless,** *adj.* —**Syn. 1.** aspiration.

ambitious (ăm bĭsh′əs), *adj.* **1.** having ambition; eagerly desirous of obtaining power, superiority, or distinction. **2.** showing ambition; aiming high: *an ambitious undertaking.* **3.** intended to be, or appearing to be, superior, distinctive, etc.: *an ambitious style.* **4.** strongly desirous; eager: *ambitious of power.* [ME, t. L: m. s. *ambitiōsus*] —**ambi′tiously,** *adv.* —**ambi′tiousness,** *n.*

—**Syn. 1.** AMBITIOUS, ASPIRING, ENTERPRISING describe one who wishes to rise above his present position or condition. The AMBITIOUS man wishes to attain wordly success, and puts forth effort towards this end: *ambitious for social position.* The ENTERPRISING man is characterized by energy and daring in undertaking projects. The ASPIRING man wishes to rise (mentally or spiritually) to a higher level or plane, or to attain some end that he feels to be above his ordinary expectations.

ambivalence (ăm bĭv′ə ləns), *n.* **1.** the coexistence in one person of opposite and conflicting feelings towards the same person or object. **2.** uncertainty or ambiguity, esp. due to inability to make up one's mind. —**ambiv′alent,** *adj.*

ambiversion (ăm′bĭ vû′shən), *n. Psychol.* a state or condition intermediate between extrovert and introvert personality types.

ambivert (ăm′bĭ vût′), *n. Psychol.* one who is intermediate between an introvert and an extrovert.

amble (ăm′bl), *v.*, **-bled, -bling,** *n.* —*v.i.* **1.** to move with the gait of a horse, when it lifts first the two legs on one side and then the two on the other. **2.** to go at an easy pace. —*n.* **3.** an ambling gait. **4.** an easy or gentle pace. [ME, t. OF: m. *ambler,* g. L *ambulāre* walk] —**am′bler,** *n.* —**am′bling,** *adv.*

amblygonite (ăm blĭg′ə nīt′), *n.* a rare mineral, a lithium aluminium fluophosphate, $Li(AlF)PO_4$. [t. G: m. *Amblygonit,* f. s. Gk *amblygōnios* obtuse-angled + *-it* -ITE[1]]

amblyopia (ăm′blĭ ō′pĭ ə), *n. Pathol.* dimness of sight, without apparent organic defect. [t. NL, t. Gk] —**amblyopic** (ăm′blĭ ŏp′ĭk), *adj.*

ambo (ăm′bō), *n., pl.* **-bos, -bones** (ăm bō′nēz). (in early Christian churches) one of the two raised desks from which gospels and epistles were read or chanted. [t. ML, t. Gk: m. *ámbōn*]

amboceptor (ăm′bō sĕp′tə), *n. Immunol.* a substance which develops during infection in the blood and which according to Ehrlich has affinities for both the bacterial cell or red blood cells and the complement. [f. L *ambo* both + -CEPTOR]

Amboina (ăm boi′nə), *n.* **1.** an island in Indonesia, in the Moluccas. 66,821 pop. (1963); 314 sq. mi. **2.** a seaport on this island. **3.** amboyna. —**Amboi′nan, Am′boinese′,** *n., adj.*

Amboise (*Fr.* äɴ bwȧz′), *n.* a historic town in central France, E of Tours: famous castle, long a royal residence. 4244 (1963).

amboyna (ăm boi′nə), *n.* the wood of an East Indian papilionaceous tree, *Pterocarpus indicus.* Also, **amboina.**

ambroid (ăm′broid), *n.* amberoid.

Ambrose (ăm′brōz), *n.* **Saint,** A.D. 340?–397, bishop of Milan. —**Ambrosian** (ăm brō′zyən), *adj.*

ambrosia (ăm brō′zyə), *n.* **1.** the food of the gods of classical mythology, imparting immortality. **2.** anything imparting the sense of divinity, as poetic inspiration, music, etc. **3.** something especially delicious to taste or smell. **4.** fungi cultivated for food by ambrosia beetles. **5.** bee-bread. **6.** any plant of the composite genus *Ambrosia,* comprising the American ragweeds. [t. L, t. Gk: food of the gods, der. *ámbrotos* immortal]

ambrosia beetle, a bark-beetle of the family *Scolytidae.*

ambrosiaceous (ăm brō′zĭ ā′shəs), *adj. Bot.* belonging to the *Ambrosiaceae,* or ragweed family of plants, which includes the ragweed, marsh elder, etc.

ambrosial (ăm brō′ zyəl), *adj.* **1.** exceptionally pleasing to taste or smell; especially delicious, fragrant, or sweet-smelling. **2.** worthy of the gods; divine. Also, **ambro′sian.** —**ambro′sially,** *adv.*

Ambrosian chant, a mode of singing or chanting introduced by St Ambrose in Milan.

ambry (ăm′brĭ), *n., pl.* **-bries. 1.** a cupboard; dresser. **2.** a storeroom; pantry. **3.** a recess for church vessels. Also, **aumbry, almery.** [ME *almarie,* ult. t. L: m. *armārium* closet]

ambs-ace (āmz′ās′, ămz′-), *n.* **1.** the double ace, the lowest throw at dice. **2.** bad luck; misfortune. **3.** the smallest amount or distance. Also, **ames-ace.** [ME *ambes as,* t. OF, g. L *ambās as* double ace]

ambulacral (ăm′byŏŏ lā′krəl), *adj. Zool.* denoting the radial areas of an echinoderm bearing the tubular protrusions by which the creature moves. [f. s. L *ambulācrum* walk, avenue + -AL[1]]

ambulance (ăm′byŏŏ ləns), *n.* a vehicle, boat, or aircraft equipped for carrying sick or wounded persons. [t. F, der. (*hôpital*) *ambulant* walking (hospital)]

ambulance-chaser (ăm′byŏŏ ləns chā′sə), *n. Chiefly U.S. Slang.* a disreputable solicitor who incites persons to sue for damages because of an accident.

ambulant (ăm′byŏŏ lənt), *adj.* **1.** moving from place to place; shifting. **2.** *Med.* ambulatory (def. 4). [t. L: s. *ambulans,* ppr., walking]

ambulate (ăm′byŏŏ lāt′), *v.i.*, **-lated, -lating.** to walk or move about, or from place to place. [t. L: m. s. *ambulātus,* pp., walked] —**am′bula′tion,** *n.*

ambulatory (ăm′byŏŏ lə tə rĭ, -trĭ), *adj., n., pl.* **-ries.** —*adj.* **1.** pertaining to or capable of walking. **2.** adapted for walking, as the limbs of many animals. **3.** moving about; not stationary. **4.** *Med.* not confined to bed: *ambulatory patient.* **5.** *Law.* not fixed; alterable or revocable: *ambulatory will.* —*n.* **6.** *Archit.* a place for walking: **a.** the side aisle surrounding the choir or chancel of a church. **b.** the arcaded walk around a cloister.

ambury (ăm′bə rĭ, -brĭ), *n.* anbury.

ambuscade (ăm′bəs kād′), *n., v.*, **-caded, -cading.** —*n.* **1.** an ambush. —*v.i.* **2.** to lie in ambush. —*v.t.* **3.** to attack from a concealed position. [t. F: m. *embuscade,* der. *embusquer,* b. It. *imboscata* and OF *embûcher.* See AMBUSH] —**am′buscad′er,** *U.S., n.*

ambuscado (ăm′bəs kā′dō), *n., pl.* **-dos.** *Obs.* ambuscade.

ambush (ăm′bŏŏsh′), *n.* Also, **am′bushment. 1.** the act of lying concealed so as to attack by surprise. **2.** the act of attacking unexpectedly from a concealed position. **3.** a secret or concealed position where men lie in wait to attack unawares. **4.** a person or body of men lying in wait. —*v.t.* **5.** to attack from ambush. [ME *enbusshe,* t. OF: m. *embusche,* ult. der. *bûche* bush, of Gmc orig.] —**am′bush′er,** *n.* —**am′bush-like′,** *adj.*

A.M.D.G., (L *ad majorem Dei gloriam*) to the greater glory of God.

ameba (ə mē′bə), *n., pl.* **-bas, -bae** (-bē), *U.S.* amoeba. —**ame′bic,** *adj.*

ameer (ə mĭə′), *n.* amir.

ameliorate (ə mē′lyə rāt′), *v.t., v.i.* **-rated, -rating.** to make or become better; improve; meliorate. [f. s. F *améliorer* + -ATE[1]; modelled on earlier MELIORATE] —**ame′liorable,** *adj.* —**ameliorant** (ə mē′lyə rənt), *n.* —**ame′liorative,** *adj.* —**ame′liora′tor,** *n.* —**Syn.** See **improve.**

amelioration (ə mē′lyə rā′shən), *n.* **1.** the act of ameliorating. **2.** the resulting state. **3.** something which is improved; an improvement.

amen (ā′mĕn′, ä′-), *interj.* **1.** it is so; so be it (used after a prayer, creed, or other formal statement). —*adv.* **2.** verily; truly. —*n.* **3.** an expression of concurrence or assent. **4.** the last word. —*v.t.* **5.** to say amen to. [OE, t. LL, t. Gk, t. Heb.: certainty, truth]

Amen (ä′mən), *n.* a minor Theban god with the head of a ram, symbolizing fertility and life, later identified by the Egyptians with the sun-god, Amen-Ra, their principal deity. Also, **Amon.** [t. Egypt., explained as 'the one who hides his name']

amenable (ə mē′nə bl), *adj.* **1.** disposed or ready to answer, yield, or submit; submissive; tractable. **2.** liable to be called to account; answerable; legally responsible. **3.** liable or exposed (to charge, claim, etc.): *amenable to criticism.* [f. s. F *amener* bring to (f. *à* to + *mener* bring, g. L *mināre* drive) + -ABLE] —**ame′nabil′ity, ame′nableness,** *n.* —**ame′nably,** *adv.*

amen corner, *U.S.* **1.** a place in a church, usually at one side of the pulpit, once occupied by those worshippers who led the responsive amens during the service. **2.** any special place in a church occupied by zealous worshippers.

amend (ə mĕnd′), *v.t.* **1.** to alter (a motion, bill, constitution, etc.) by due formal procedure. **2.** to change for the better; improve: *to amend one's ways.* **3.** to remove or correct faults in; rectify: *an amended spelling.* —*v.i.* **4.** to grow or become better by reforming oneself. [ME *amende(n),* t. OF: m. *amender,* g. L *ēmendāre* correct] —**amend′able,** *adj.* —**amend′er,** *n.*

amendatory (ə mĕn′də tə rĭ, -trĭ), *adj. U.S.* serving to amend; corrective.

amendment (ə mĕnd′mənt), *n.* **1.** the act of amending; correction; improvement. **2.** the alteration of a motion, bill, constitution, etc. **3.** a change so made, either by way of correction or addition.

amends (ə mĕndz′), *n. sing. or pl.* **1.** reparation or compensation for a loss, damage, or injury of any kind; recompense: *to make amends.* **2.** *Obs.* recovery of health. [ME *amendes,* t. OF, pl. of *amende* reparation]

Amenhotep III (ä′mĭn hō′tĕp, ăm′ĭn-), king of Egypt 1411? B.C.–1375 B.C. Also, **Amenophis III** (ăm′ĭ nō′fĭs).

Amenhotep IV, died *c.* 1357 B.C. king of Egypt *c.* 1375–*c.* 1357 B.C. the first ruler in history to declare his belief in one god. Also, **Akhnaton, Amenophis IV, Ikhnaton.**

amenity (ə mĕn′ĭ tĭ, -mē′nĭ-), *n., pl.* **-ties. 1.** (*pl.*) agreeable features, circumstances, ways, etc. **2.** (*pl.*) features,

facilities, or services of a house, estate, district, etc., which make for a comfortable and pleasant life. **3.** the quality of being pleasant or agreeable in situation, prospect, disposition, etc.; pleasantness: *the amenity of the climate.* [late ME, t. L: m. s. *amoenitas*]
amenorrhoea (ă mĕn′ə rĭə′, ā-), *n. Pathol.* absence of menstruation. Also, *Chiefly U.S.*, **amenorrhea.** [f. A-[6] + *meno-* (comb. form repr. Gk *men* month) + -(R)RHOEA]
Amen-Ra (ä′mən rä′), *n.* See **Amen** (god).
ament[1] (ə mĕnt′, ā′mənt), *n. Psychol.* a mentally deficient person; one suffering from amentia.
ament[2] (ăm′ənt, ā′mənt), *n. Bot.* amentum.
amentaceous (ăm′ĭn tā′shəs), *adj.* **1.** consisting of a catkin. **2.** bearing catkins.
amentia (ə mĕn′shə), *n. Psychol.* lack of intellectual development; mental deficiency. [t. L: lack of reason]
amentiferous (ăm′ĭn tĭf′ə rəs), *adj., Bot.* bearing amenta or catkins.
amentiform (ə mĕn′tĭ fôm′), *adj.* catkin-shaped.
amentum (ə mĕn′təm), *n., pl.* **-ta.** *Bot.* a spike of unisexual apetalous flowers with scaly bracts, usually deciduous; a catkin. Also, **ament.** [t. L: strap, thong]

Amenta
A, Staminate; B, Pistillate

Amer., **1.** America. **2.** American.
amerce (ə mûs′), *v.t.,* **amerced, amercing. 1.** to punish by an arbitrary or discretionary fine, i.e., one not fixed by statute. **2.** to punish by inflicting a discretionary penalty of any kind. [ME *amercy*, ult. der. OF phrase (*estre*) *a merci* (to be) at the mercy of] **—amerce′able,** *adj.* **—amerce′ment,** *n.* **—amerc′er,** *n.*
America (ə mĕ′rĭ kə), *n.* **1.** the United States of America. **2.** North America. **3.** South America. **4.** North, Central, and South America together with the offshore islands. [named after *Americus* Vespucius. See VESPUCCI]
American (ə mĕ′rĭ kən), *adj.* **1.** of or pertaining to the United States of America: *an American citizen.* **2.** of or pertaining to North or South America. **3.** *Ethnol.* denoting or pertaining to the so-called 'red' race, characterized by a reddish or brownish skin, dark eyes, black hair, and prominent cheekbones, and embracing the aborigines of North and South America (sometimes excluding the Eskimos), known as American Indians or Amerindians. **—*n.* 4.** a citizen of the United States of America. **5.** a native or an inhabitant of the western hemisphere. **6.** an aborigine of the western hemisphere. **7.** the English language as spoken in the United States.
Americana (ə mĕ′rĭ kä′nə), *n.pl.* books, papers, etc., relating to America, esp. to its history and geography. [t. NL. See -ANA]
American aloe, the century plant.
American cheese, *U.S.* a smooth white or yellow hard cheese with a slightly acid flavour, similar to Cheddar.
American cloth, a cloth glazed on one side, used for upholstery, etc. Also, **American leather, enamelled cloth.**
American eagle, the bald eagle, esp. as depicted on the coat of arms of the United States.
American football, a game similar to Rugby football, played by two teams of eleven players, each of which tries to score touchdowns by running or passing the ball to the opponent's goal line and field goals by kicking the ball over the cross bars of the opponent's goalpost.
American Indian, Amerindian.
Americanism (ə mĕ′rĭ kə nĭz′əm), *n* **1.** an English language usage peculiar to the people of the United States. **2.** a custom, trait, or thing peculiar to the United States of America or its citizens. **3.** devotion to or preference for the United States and its institutions.
Americanize (ə mĕ′rĭ kə nīz′), *v.t., v.i.,* **-nized, -nizing.** to make or become American in character; assimilate to the customs and institutions of the United States. Also, **Americanise. —Amer′icaniza′tion,** *n.*
American Legion, a society, organized in 1919, composed of former members of the U.S. armed forces who served in World Wars I and II and the Korean War.
American organ, *Music.* a keyboard instrument similar to the harmonium, but in which the air is sucked through the reeds.
American Revolution, *U.S.* the War of American Independence.
American Samoa, the islands of the Samoa group belonging to the U.S., including mainly Tutuila and the Manua islands. 20,051 pop. (1960); 76 sq. mi. *Cap.*: Pago Pago.
americium (ăm′ə rĭs′ĭ əm), *n.* a radioactive element, one of the products of the bombardment of uranium and plutonium by very energetic helium ions. *Symbol:* Am; *at. no.:* 95. [f. AMERIC(A) + -IUM]
Amerigo Vespucci (ə mĕ′rĭ gō vĕs po͞o′chĭ). See **Vespucci.**
Amerind (ăm′ə rĭnd), *n.* Amerindian (def. 1). **—Am′erin′dic,** *adj.*
Amerindian (ăm′ə rĭn′dĭ ən, -dyən), *n.* **1.** a member of the aboriginal race of America or of any of the aboriginal North and South American stocks, often excepting the Eskimos. **2.** any of the languages of the Amerindians. **—*adj.* 3.** denoting, belonging to, or pertaining to the race embracing the aborigines of America. **4.** of or pertaining to any of the Amerindian languages. [b. AMER(ICAN) + INDIAN]
Amersfoort (*Du.* ä′mərs fört), *n.* a town in the Netherlands, in E Utrecht province. 73,965 (1965).
ames-ace (āmz′ās′, ămz′-), *n.* ambs-ace.
amethyst (ăm′ĭ thĭst), *n.* **1.** *Mineral.* a coarsely crystallized purple or violet quartz used in jewellery. **2.** the violet sapphire (**oriental amethyst**). **3.** a purplish tint. [t. L: s. *amethystus*, t. Gk: m. *améthystos* lit., remedy for drunkenness: r. ME *ametiste*, t. OF] **—amethystine** (ăm′ĭ thĭs′tĭn), *adj.* **—am′ethyst-like′,** *adj.*
ametropia (ăm′ĭ trō′pyə), *n. Pathol.* an abnormal condition of the eye causing faulty refraction of light rays, as in astigmatism, myopia, etc. [t. NL, f. Gk: s. *ámetros* irregular + *-opia* -OPIA] **—ametropic** (ăm′ĭ trŏp′ĭk), *adj.*
Amhara (ăm hä′rə), *n.* **1.** a former kingdom in NW Ethiopia. *Cap.:* Gondar. **2.** an inhabitant of this kingdom. **—Amha′ran,** *n., adj.*
Amharic (ăm hă′rĭk), *n.* **1.** the language spoken by the Amharas: one of the semitic languages of Ethiopia. **—*adj.* 2.** of or pertaining to Amhara.
Amherst (ăm′əst, ăm′hûst), *n.* **Jeffrey, Baron,** 1717–97, British field marshal: took Canada from the French, 1758–60.
ami (*Fr.* à mē′), *n. French.* friend.
amiable (ā′myə bl), *adj.* **1.** having or showing agreeable personal qualities, as sweetness of temper, kindheartedness, etc. **2.** friendly; kindly: *an amiable mood.* **3.** *Obs.* lovable, lovely. [ME *amyable*, t. OF: m. *amiable*, g. L *amicābilis* friendly] **—a′miabil′ity, a′miableness,** *n.* **—a′miably,** *adv.* **—Syn. 1.** gracious.
amianthus (ăm′ĭ ăn′thəs), *n. Mineral.* a fine variety of asbestos, with delicate, flexible filaments. [var. (with *-th* from *polyanthus*) of *amiantus*, t. L, t. Gk: m. *amíantos* (*líthos*) undefiled (stone)]
amic (ăm′ĭk), *adj. Chem.* of an amide or amine.
amicable (ăm′ĭ kə bl), *adj.* characterized by or exhibiting friendliness; friendly; peaceable: *an amicable settlement.* [t. L: m. s. *amīcābilis*] **—am′icabil′ity, am′icableness,** *n.* **—am′icably,** *adv.*
amice[1] (ăm′ĭs), *n. Eccles.* an oblong piece of linen worn about the neck and shoulders under the alb, or, formerly, on the head. [ME *amyse*, t. OF: m. *amis*, g. L *amictus* cloak]
amice[2] (ăm′ĭs), *n.* a furred hood or hooded cape, with long ends hanging down in front, formerly worn by the clergy. [late ME *amisse*, t. F: m. *aumusse*, t. Pr.: m. *almussa*, f. Ar. *al* the + m. G *Mütze* cap]
A.M.I.C.E., Associate Member of the Institution of Civil Engineers.
A.M.I. Chem. E., Associate Member of the Institution of Chemical Engineers.
amicus curiae (ă mē′ko͞os kyo͞o′ə′rĭ ē′), *Law.* a person not a party to the litigation who volunteers or is invited by the court to give advice to the court upon some matter pending before it. [L: a friend of the court]
amid (ə mĭd′), *prep.* in the midst of or surrounded by; among; amidst. [ME *amidde*, OE *amiddan*, for *on middan* in the middle. See MID[1]] **—Syn.** See **among.**
amide (ăm′īd, -ĭd), *n. Chem.* **1.** a metallic derivative of ammonia in which the NH_2 grouping is retained, as *potassium amide*, KNH_2. **2.** an organic compound obtained by replacing the OH group in acids by the NH_2 radical. [f. AM(MONIA) + -IDE] **—amidic** (ə mĭd′ĭk), *adj.*
amidin (ăm′ĭ dĭn), *n.* the soluble matter of starch. [f. s. ML *amidum*, var. of L *amylum* (t. Gk: m. *ámylon* fine meal) + -IN[2]]
amidmost (ə mĭd′mōst′), *adv., prep.* in the very middle (of).
amido-, *Chem.* **1.** a prefix denoting the replacement of an OH group by the NH_2 radical. **2.** (sometimes) amino-. [comb. form of AMIDE] **—amido** (ə mē′dō, ăm′ĭ dō′), *adj.*
amidogen (ə mē′də jən, ə mĭd′ə-), *n. Chem.* the NH_2 radical. If attached to CO in a compound it is called an **amido group;** without CO, an **amino group.**
Amidol (ăm′ĭ dŏl′), *n. Trademark.* a colourless crystalline phenol derivative, $C_6H_8N_2O.2HCl$, used as a photographic developer.

---

b., blend of, blended; c., cognate with; d., dialect, dialectal; der., derived from; f., formed from; g., going back to; m., modification of; r., replacing; s., stem of; t., taken from; ?, perhaps. See full key on inside front cover.

amidships (ə mĭd′shĭps′), *adv. Naut.* **1.** in or towards the middle of a ship, or the part midway between stem and stern. **2.** lengthways. Also, **amid ship.**

amidst (ə mĭdst′), *prep.* amid. [ME *amiddes*, f. *amidde* amid + adv. gen. *-s;* for later *-t*, cf. AGAINST, etc.]

amie (*Fr.* à mē′), *n., pl.* **amies** (à mē′), *French.* fem. of **ami.**

A.M.I.E.E., Associate Member of the Institution of Electrical Engineers.

Amiens (ăm′yənz; *Fr.* à myăɴ′), *n.* a city in N France, on the river Somme: cathedral; battles, 1914, 1918, 1944. 105,433 (1962). See map under **Compiègne.**

amigo (ă mē′gō; *Sp.* à mē′gô), *n., pl.* **-gos** (-gōz; *Sp.* -gôs). *Spanish.* friend.

A.M.I. Loco. E., Associate Member of the Institute of Locomotive Engineers.

A.M.I.Mech.E., Associate Member of the Institution of Mechanical Engineers.

amine (ə mēn′, ăm′ĭn), *n. Chem.* any of a class of compounds prepared from ammonia by replacing one, two, or all hydrogen atoms with organic radicals. [f. AM(MONIA) + -INE[2]]

amino-, *Chem.* a prefix denoting an amino group [comb. form of AMINE]

amino acid (ăm′ĭ nō′, ə mē′nō), *Chem.* any of a group of organic compounds derived from the acids, RCOOH, by replacement of hydrogen in the (R) group by the (NH_2) radical. They are the basic constituents of proteins.

amino group, the universal basic radical, NH_2. Also, **amino radical.**

aminophylline (ə mē′nō fĭl′ēn), *n. Pharm.* a mixture of theophylline and ethylene diamine used as a vasodilator and antispasmodic.

amino resin, any of a class of thermosetting resins formed by the interaction of an amine with an aldehyde, used chiefly for coatings for paper and textiles.

A.M.Inst.T.E., Associate Member of the Institution of Transport Engineers.

amir (ə mĭə′), *n.* **1.** emir. **2.** (*cap.*) the former title of the ruler of Afghanistan. **3.** former title of certain Turkish officials. Also, **ameer.** [t. Ar.: m. *amīr* commander. See EMIR]

Amis (ā′mĭs), *n.* **Kingsley,** born 1922, English novelist.

amiss (ə mĭs′), *adv.* **1.** out of the proper course or order; in a faulty manner; wrongly: *to speak amiss.* **2. take amiss,** to be offended at; resent. **3. come amiss,** to be unwelcome; be received with ingratitude; be inopportune. —*adj.* **4.** (used only predicatively) wrong; faulty; out of order; improper (sometimes fol. by *with*): *there is something amiss with it.* [ME *amis*, f. A-[1] + *mis* wrong. See MISS[1]]

amitosis (ăm′ĭ tō′sĭs), *n. Biol.* the direct method of cell division characterized by simple cleavage of the nucleus, without the formation of chromosomes. [f. A-[6] + MITOSIS] —**amitotic** (ăm′ĭ tŏt′ĭk), *adj.*

amity (ăm′ĭ tĭ), *n., pl.* **-ties,** friendship; harmony; good understanding, esp. between nations. [ME *amytie*, t. F: m. *amité*, ult. der. L *amīcus* friend]

Amman (ə män′), *n.* the capital of Jordan, in the central part. 296,358 (1962). See map under **Jordan.**

ammeter (ăm′mē′tə, ăm′ĭ tə), *n. Elect.* an instrument for measuring the strength of electric currents in amperes. [f. AM(PERE) + -METER[1]]

ammiaceous (ăm′ĭ ā′shəs), *adj. Bot.* apiaceous.

ammine (ăm′ēn, ə mēn′), *n. Chem.* a compound containing one or more ammonia molecules in coordinate linkage. [f. AMM(ONIA) + -INE[2]]

ammo (ăm′ō), *n. Colloq.* ammunition.

ammocete (ăm′ə sēt′), *n.* the larval stage of a lamprey, used as bait. It resembles the theoretical ancestor of the vertebrates. Also, **ammocoete.** [t. NL: m. s. *ammocoetes* something bedded in sand, f. Gk: s. *ámmos* sand + m. *koítē* bed]

ammon (ăm′ən), *n.* the argali.

Ammon (ăm′ən), *n.* classical name of the Egyptian divinity Amen, whom the Greeks identified with Zeus, the Romans with Jupiter. [t. L, t. Gk, t. Egypt.: m. *Amen*]

Ammon (ăm′ən), *n.* a biblical semi-nomadic Semitic people living east of the Jordan.

ammonal (ăm′ə nəl), *n.* a high explosive, a mixture of ammonium nitrate and powdered aluminium. [short for *ammon(ium nitrate and) al(uminium)*]

ammonia (ə mō′nyə, ə mō′nĭ ə), *n.* **1.** a colourless, pungent, suffocating gas, NH_3, a compound of nitrogen and hydrogen, very soluble in water. **2.** Also, **ammonia water** or **aqueous ammonia.** this gas dissolved in water, the common commercial form. [t. NL; so called as being obtained from sal *ammoniac.* See AMMONIAC]

ammoniac (ə mō′nĭ ăk′), *n.* **1.** gum ammoniac. —*adj.* **2.** ammoniacal. [ME, t. L: s. *ammōniacum*, t. Gk: m. *ammōniakón*, applied to a salt and a gum said to come from near the shrine of AMMON[1] in Libya]

ammoniacal (ăm′ə nī′ə kl), *adj.* **1.** consisting of, containing, or using ammonia. **2.** like ammonia.

ammoniate (ə mō′nĭ āt′), *v.,* **-ated, -ating,** *n.* —*v.t.* **1.** to treat or cause to unite with ammonia. —*n.* **2.** a compound formed with ammonia.

ammonic (ə mŏn′ĭk, ə mō′nĭk), *adj.* of or pertaining to ammonia or ammonium.

ammonify (ə mŏn′ĭ fī′, ə mō′nĭ-), *v.t., v.i.* **-fied, -fying.** *Chiefly U.S.* **1.** to ammoniate. **2.** to ammonize. —**ammon′ifica′tion,** *n.*

ammonite (ăm′ə nīt′), *n.* one of the coiled, chambered fossil shells of the extinct cephalopod molluscs, suborder *Ammonoidea.* [t. NL: m. s. *Ammōnītes*, der. ML *cornū Ammōnis* horn of Ammon]

ammonium (ə mō′nĭ əm, -nyəm), *n. Chem.* a radical, NH_4, which plays the part of a metal in the compounds (**ammonium salts**) formed when ammonia reacts with acids. [f. AMMON(IA) + -IUM]

ammonium chloride, a white granular powder, NH_4Cl, used medicinally and industrially; sal ammoniac.

ammonium hydroxide, a basic compound, NH_4OH, made by dissolving ammonia in water, used extensively as a weak alkali.

ammonium nitrate, a white, soluble solid, the nitrate of ammonia, NH_4NO_3, used in explosives, freezing mixtures, and the preparation of nitrous oxide.

ammonization (ăm′ə nī zā′shən), *n.* the formation of ammonia or its compounds, as in soil, etc., by soil organisms. Also, **ammonisation.** [f. AMMON(IA) + -IZATION]

ammonize (ăm′ə nīz′), *v.,* **-nized, -nizing.** —*v.t.* **1.** to convert into ammonia or ammonium compounds. —*v.i.* **2.** to become ammonized; produce ammonization. Also, **ammonise.**

ammunition (ăm′yo͞o nĭsh′ən), *n.* **1.** all the material used in discharging all types of firearms or any weapon that throws projectiles; powder, shot, shrapnel, bullets, cartridges, and the means of igniting and exploding them, as primers and fuses. Chemicals, bombs, grenades, mines, pyrotechnics are also ammunition. **2.** any material or means used in combat. **3.** *Obs.* military supplies. —*adj.* **4.** supplied from army stores. —*v.t.* **5.** to supply with ammunition. [t. F (obs.): m. *amunition* for *munition*, *la munition* being understood as *l'amunition*]

amnesia (ăm nē′zyə), *n. Psychol.* loss of a large block of interrelated memories. [t. NL, t. Gk: forgetfulness] —**amnesiac** (ăm nē′zĭ ăk′), **amnesic** (ăm nē′sĭk, -zĭk), **amnestic** (ăm nĕs′tĭk), *adj.*

amnesty (ăm′nəs tĭ), *n., pl.* **-ties,** *v.,* **-tied, -tying.** —*n.* **1.** a general pardon for offences against a government. **2.** the granting of immunity for past offences against the laws of war. **3.** *Law.* a pardon granted by an act of Parliament originated by the Crown. **4.** *U.S. Law.* protection against punishment granted a witness in order to compel him to testify to incriminating facts. **5.** a forgetting or overlooking of any offence. —*v.t.* **6.** to grant amnesty to; pardon. [t. L: m. s. *amnēstia*, t. Gk: forgetfulness]

amnion (ăm′nĭ ən), *n., pl.* **-nia** (-nĭ ə). *Anat., Zool.* the innermost of the embryonic or foetal membranes of insects, reptiles, birds, and mammals; the sac containing the amniotic fluid and the embryo. [t. NL, t. Gk] —**amnionic** (ăm′nĭ ŏn′ĭk), *adj.*

amniotic (ăm′nĭ ŏt′ĭk), *adj. Anat., Zool.* of or pertaining to the amnion.

amniotic fluid, *Anat., Zool.* the watery fluid in the amniotic sac, in which the embryo is suspended.

amoeba (ə mē′bə), *n., pl.* **-bae** (-bē), **-bas.** *Zool.* **1.** a microscopic, one-celled animal consisting of a naked mass of protoplasm constantly changing in shape as it moves and engulfs food. **2.** a protozoan of the genus *Amoeba.* Also, *U.S.,* **ameba.** [t. NL, t. Gk: m. *amoibḗ* change] —**amoe′ba-like′,** *adj.*

amoebaean (ăm′ĭ bē′ən), *adj. Pros.* alternately responsive, as verses in dialogue. Also, **amoebean.**

amoebic (ə mē′bĭk), *adj.* **1.** of, pertaining to, or resembling an amoeba. **2.** characterized by, or due to the presence of, amoebae, as certain diseases. Also, *U.S.,* **amebic.**

amoebic dysentery, a variety of dysentery whose causative agent is a protozoan, *Endamoeba histolytica,* characterized esp. by intestinal ulceration.

amoeboid (ə mē′boid), *adj. Biol.* resembling or related to amoebae. Also, *U.S.,* **ameboid.** [f. AMOEB(A) + OID]

amok (ə mŭk′, ə mŏk′), *n.* **1.** a psychic disturbance characterized by depression followed by overwhelming desire to murder. —*adv.* **2. run amok.** See **amuck.** [t. Malay: m. *amoq*]

amole (ə mō′lā; *Sp.* à mô′lĕ), *n. South-Western U.S.* **1.** the roots of any of various plants, as Mexican species of agave, used as a substitute for soap. **2.** any such plant. [t. Mex. Sp., t. Nahuatl]

Amon (ä′mən), *n.* Amen (god).

among (ə mŭng′), *prep.* **1.** in or into the midst of; in association or connection with; surrounded by: *he fell among thieves.* **2.** to each of; by or for distribution to: *divide these among you.* **3.** in the number, class, or group of; of or out of: *that's among the things we must do.* **4.** with or by all or the whole of: *popular among the people.* **5.** by the joint or reciprocal action of: *settle it among yourselves.* **6.** each with the other; mutually: *to quarrel among themselves.* [OE *amang,* for *on (ge)mang* in the crowd, in the midst of]

—**Syn. 1.** AMONG, AMID, BETWEEN imply a position in the middle of. AMONG suggests a relationship with a group of objects considered collectively: *one idea among many.* AMID, a more literary word, implies being in the middle place or surrounded by something: *to stand amid ruins.* BETWEEN refers to two or more separate objects, each being individually related to the rest: *a war between three states.*

amongst (ə mŭngst′), *prep.* among. [ME *amonges,* f. AMONG + adv. gen. *-es;* for later *-t* after the gen. *-s,* cf. AGAINST, etc.]

amontillado (ə mŏn′tĭ lä′dō; *Sp.* ȧ mōn tē lyä′dō), *n.* a pale-coloured, medium dry, Spanish sherry. [t. Sp.]

amoral (ă mŏ′rəl, ā′-), *adj.* without moral quality; neither moral nor immoral. [f. A-[6] + MORAL] —**amorality** (ăm′ō-răl′ĭ tĭ, ā′mŏ-), *n.* —**amor′ally,** *adv.*

—**Syn.** AMORAL, IMMORAL and NON-MORAL are sometimes confused. AMORAL means having no moral standards, either good or bad, by which one may be judged. IMMORAL means not conforming to a given set of moral standards. NON-MORAL means not dealing or concerned with moral matters or standards at all.

amoretto (ăm′ə rĕt′ō; *It.* ȧ mō rĕt′tō), *n., pl.* **-retti** (rĕt′ĭ; *It.* -rĕt′tē), a little cupid. [t. It., dim. of *amore,* g. L *amor* love]

amorino (ăm′ō rē′nō), *n., pl.* **-ni** (-nē). amoretto.

amorist (ăm′ə rĭst), *n.* **1.** a lover; a gallant. **2.** one who writes about love. **3.** one who seeks sexual experiences. [f. L *amor* love + -IST] —**am′orism,** *n.*

amoroso (ăm′ə rō′sō; *It.* ȧ mō rō′sō), *adj., adv. Music.* tender; tenderly. [t. It.]

amorous (ăm′ə rəs), *adj.* **1.** inclined or disposed to love: *an amorous disposition.* **2.** in love; enamoured. **3.** showing love: *amorous sighs.* **4.** pertaining to love: *amorous poetry.* [ME, t. OF, g. L *amōrōsus,* der. *amor* love] —**am′orously,** *adv.* —**am′orousness,** *n.* —**Syn. 1.** loving; amatory. **3.** fond, tender.

amor patriae (ăm′ô păt′rĭ ē′), *Latin.* love of one's country; patriotism.

amorphism (ə mô′fĭz′əm), *n.* **1.** the state or quality of being amorphous. **2.** nihilism (def. 3).

amorphous (ə mô′fəs), *adj.* **1.** lacking definite form; having no specific shape. **2.** of no particular kind or character; indeterminate; formless; unorganized: *an amorphous style.* **3.** *Geol.* occurring in a mass, as without stratification or crystalline structure. **4.** *Chem.* non-crystalline. [t. Gk: m. *ámorphos*] —**amor′phously,** *adv.* —**amor′phousness,** *n.*

amortization (ə mô′tĭ zā′shən), *n.* **1.** the act of amortizing a debt. **2.** the money devoted to this purpose. Also, **amortisation, amortisement, amortizement** (ə mô′tĭz-mənt).

amortize (ə mô′tīz), *v.t.,* **-tized, -tizing. 1.** to liquidate or extinguish (an indebtedness or charge) usually by periodic payments (or by entries) made to a sinking fund, to a creditor, or to an account. **2.** *Old Eng. Law.* to convey to a corporation; alienate in mortmain. Also, **amortise.** [ME *amortise(n),* t. OF: m. *amortiss-,* s. *amortir* deaden, buy out, der. *mort* death. Cf. ML *admortizāre*] —**amor′tiz′able,** *adj.*

Amos (ā′mŏs), *n.* **1.** a Hebrew prophet of the eighth century B.C., author of the Old Testament book bearing his name. **2.** this book.

amount (ə mount′), *n.* **1.** quantity or extent: *the amount of resistance.* **2.** the full effect, value, or import. **3.** the sum total of two or more sums or quantities; the aggregate: *the amount of 7 and 9 is 16.* **4.** the sum of the principal and interest of a loan. —*v.i.* **5.** to reach, extend, or be equal in number, quantity, effect, etc. (fol. by *to*). [ME *amount(en),* t. OF: m. *amonter* mount up to, der. *amont* upward, orig. phrase *a mont* to the mountain]

amour (ə mo͝oə′), *n.* a love affair, esp. a clandestine one. [t. F, prob. t. Pr.: m. *amor,* g. L *amor* love]

amour-propre (*Fr.* ȧ mo͝or prŏ′pr), *n. French.* self-esteem; self-respect.

amove (ə mo͞ov′), *v.t. Law.* to remove; remove from office. [t. L: m. s. *āmovēre,* move away] —**amo′tion,** *n.*

Amoy (ə moi′), *n.* a seaport in Fukien province in SE China, on an island in Taiwan Strait. 308,000 (est. 1958).

amp., 1. amperage. **2.** ampere.

ampelopsis (ăm′pĭ lŏp′sĭs), *n.* any plant of the vitaceous genus *Ampelopsis,* comprising climbing woody vines or shrubs, esp. Virginia creeper. [t. NL, f. s. Gk *ámpelos* vine + *-opsis* -OPSIS]

amperage (ăm′pə rĭj), *n. Elect.* the strength of an electric current measured in amperes.

ampere (ăm′pēə), *n. Elect.* the basic SI unit of current, defined as the current which, if maintained in two parallel conductors of infinite length, of negligible cross-section, and separated by one metre in a vacuum, would produce a force of 2×10^{-7} newtons per metre. *Symbol:* A. Also, **ampère.**

Ampère (ăm′pēə; *Fr.* äɴ pĕr′), *n.* **André Marie** (*Fr.* äɴ drē mȧ rē′), 1775–1836, French physicist.

ampere-hour (ăm′pēər ou′ə), *n. Elect.* a unit equal to 3600 coulombs; the quantity of electricity transferred by a current of one ampere in one hour.

ampere-turn (ăm′pēə tûn′), *n. Elect.* **1.** one complete turn or convolution of a conducting coil, through which one ampere of current passes. **2.** the magnetomotive force produced by one ampere passing through one complete turn or convolution of a coil.

ampersand (ăm′pə sănd′), *n.* the name of the character &, meaning *and.* [contraction of *and per se–and,* & by itself (as a mere symbol given after the letters of the alphabet, and called *and*)]

amphetamine (ăm fĕt′ə mēn′, -mĭn), *n. Pharm.* a drug which, diluted with water, is used as a spray or inhaled to relieve nasal congestion and is taken internally to stimulate the central nervous system. See **purple hearts.**

amphi-, a word element meaning 'on both sides', 'on all sides', 'around', 'round about', as in *amphicoelous.* [t. Gk, repr. *amphí,* prep. and adv.]

amphiarthrosis (ăm′fĭ ä thrō′sĭs), *n., pl.* **-ses** (-sēz). *Anat.* a form of articulation which permits slight motion, as that between the bodies of the vertebrae. [f. AMPHI- + Gk *árthrōsis* articulation]

amphiaster (ăm′fĭ ăs′tə), *n. Biol.* the achromatic spindle with two asters that forms during mitosis.

amphibian (ăm fĭb′ĭ ən), *n.* **1.** any animal of the class *Amphibia,* that class of vertebrates that comprises the frogs, salamanders, and caecilians (with various extinct types), representing the essential basic characteristics of the ancestral stock of all land vertebrates. Typically they lay eggs that hatch in water and the young go through a fishlike, larval, or tadpole stage, later metamorphosing into lung-breathing quadrupeds. **2.** an amphibious plant. **3.** an aeroplane that can take off from and land on either land or water. **4.** an amphibious vehicle. —*adj.* **5.** belonging to the class *Amphibia.* **6.** capable of operating on land or water; amphibious. [f. s. NL *Amphibia* (neut. pl. of *amphibius,* t. Gk: m. *amphíbios* living a double life) + -AN]

amphibiotic (ăm′fĭ bī ŏt′ĭk), *adj. Zool.* living on land during an adult stage and in water during a larval stage. [f. AMPHI- + m. s. Gk *biōtikós* pertaining to life]

amphibious (ăm fĭb′ĭ əs), *adj.* **1.** living both on land and in water; belonging to both land and water. **2.** capable of operating on both land and water: *amphibious plane.* **3.** of a twofold nature. [t. Gk: m. *amphíbios* living a dual life] —**amphib′iously,** *adv.* —**amphib′iousness,** *n.*

amphibole (ăm′fĭ bōl′), *n. Mineral.* any of a complex group of hydrous silicate minerals, containing chiefly calcium, magnesium, sodium, iron, and aluminium, and including hornblende, tremolite, asbestos, etc., and occurring as important constituents of many rocks. [t. F, t. Gk: m. s. *amphíbolos* ambiguous]

amphibolic[1] (ăm′fĭ bŏl′ĭk), *adj.* of or pertaining to amphibole. [f. AMPHIBOL(E) + -IC]

amphibolic[2] (ăm′fĭ bŏl′ĭk), *adj.* equivocal; uncertain; changing; ambiguous. [f. AMPHIBOL(Y) + -IC]

amphibolite (ăm fĭb′ə līt′), *n. Geol.* a metamorphic rock composed basically of amphibole or hornblende. [f. AMPHIBOL(E) + -ITE[1]]

amphibology (ăm′fĭ bŏl′ə jĭ), *n., pl.* **-gies.** ambiguity of speech, esp. from uncertainty of the grammatical construction rather than of the meaning of the words, as in *The Duke yet lives that Henry shall depose.* [t. LL: m. s. *amphibologia,* r. L *amphibolia* (see AMPHIBOLY), which was remodelled after *tautologia* and the like] —**amphibological** (ăm fĭb′ə lŏj′ĭ kl), *adj.*

amphibolous (ăm fĭb′ə ləs), *adj. Logic.* ambiguous; equivocal; susceptible of two meanings. [t. L: m. *amphibolus,* t. Gk: m. *amphíbolos* thrown around]

amphiboly (ăm fĭb′ə lĭ), *n., pl.* **-lies.** amphibology. [t. L: m. s. *amphibolia* ambiguity, t. Gk]

amphibrach (ăm′fĭ brăk′), *n. Pros.* a trisyllabic foot in which the syllables come in the following order: short, long, short (quantitative metre), or unstressed, stressed, unstressed (accentual metre). Thus, *together* is an accentual amphibrach. [t. L: s. *amphibrachys,* t. Gk: short on both sides]

amphichroic (ăm′fĭ krō′ĭk), *adj. Chem.* giving either of two colours, one with acids and one with alkalis. Also, **amphichromatic** (ăm′fĭ krō măt′ĭk). [f. AMPHI- + s. Gk *chróa* colour + -IC]

amphicoelous (ăm′fĭ sē′ləs), *adj. Anat., Zool.* concave on both sides, as the bodies of the vertebrae of fishes. [t. Gk: m. *amphíkoilos* hollowed all round]

amphictyon (ăm fĭk′tĭ ən), *n.* a deputy to the council of an amphictyony. [t. Gk: m. s. *amphiktýones*, pl., dwellers around, neighbours]

amphictyonic (ăm fĭk′tĭ ŏn′ĭk), *adj.* of or pertaining to an amphictyon or an amphictyony.

amphictyony (ăm fĭk′tĭ ə nĭ), *n., pl.* **-nies.** a religious league of ancient Greek states participating in the cult of a common deity. [t. Gk: m. s. *amphiktyonía*]

amphidiploid (ăm′fĭ dĭp′loid), *n. Genetics.* a plant type possessing the sum of the chromosome numbers of two parental species, ordinarily arising from the doubling of the chromosomes of a hybrid of two species.

amphigory (ăm′fĭ gə rĭ), *n., pl.* **-ries.** a meaningless rigmarole, as of nonsense verses or the like; a nonsensical parody. —**amphigoric** (ăm′fĭ gŏ′rĭk), *adj.*

amphigouri (ăm′fĭ gōōə′rĭ), *n., pl.* **-ris.** amphigory. [t. F; orig. unknown]

amphimacer (ăm fĭm′ə sə), *n. Pros.* a trisyllabic foot in which the syllables come in the following order: long, short, long (quantitative metre), or stressed, unstressed, stressed (accentual metre). Thus, *anodyne* is an accentual amphimacer. [t. L: m. s. *amphimacrus*, t. Gk: m. *amphímakros* long on both sides]

amphimixis (ăm′fĭ mĭk′sĭs), *n.* **1.** *Biol.* the merging of the germ plasm of two organisms in sexual reproduction. **2.** *Embryol., Genetics.* the combining of paternal and maternal hereditary substances. [f. AMPHI- + Gk *míxis* a mingling]

Amphion (ăm fī′ən), *n. Gk Myth.* the son of Antiope by Zeus, twin brother of Zethus, and husband of Niobe, who with his brother fortified Thebes with a wall, charming the stones into place by his lyre.

amphioxus (ăm′fĭ ŏk′səs), *n. Zool.* a small fishlike animal, the lancelet, showing vertebrate characteristics but lacking a vertebral column, important in discussions of vertebrate ancestry. [t. NL, f. Gk: *amphi-* AMPHI- + m. *oxýs* sharp]

amphipod (ăm′fĭ pŏd′), *n.* **1.** any of a type of small crustaceans, *Amphipoda*, including beach fleas, etc. —*adj.* **2.** of or pertaining to the amphipods.

amphiprostyle (ăm fĭp′rə stīl′, ăm′fĭ prō′stīl), *adj. Archit.* having a prostyle porch in front and rear but no columns along the sides. [t. L: m. s. *amphiprostȳlos*, t. Gk]

amphisbaena (ăm′fĭs bē′nə), *n.* **1.** a burrowing, blind, and limbless snakelike lizard of the family *Amphisbaenidae*, with obtuse head and tail, moving forwards or backwards with equal ease. **2.** *Class. Myth.* a mythical venomous serpent having a head at each end and able to move in either direction. [t. L, t. Gk: m. *amphísbaina*] —**am′phisbae′nic,** *adj.*

amphitheatre (ăm′fĭ thĭə′tə), *n.* **1.** a level area of oval or circular shape surrounded by rising ground. **2.** any place for public contests or games; an arena. **3.** a building with tiers of seats around an arena or central area, as those used in ancient Rome for gladiatorial contests. **4.** a semicircular sloping gallery in a modern theatre. Also, *U.S.,* **amphitheater.** [t. L: m. s. *amphitheātrum*, t. Gk: m. *amphithéātron*] —**amphitheatric** (ăm′fĭ thĭ ăt′rĭk), **am′phitheat′rical,** *adj.* —**am′phitheat′rically,** *adv.*

amphithecium (ăm′fĭ thē′sĭ əm), *n., pl.* **-cia** (-sĭ ə). *Bot.* the layer or layers of cells in the capsule of a moss surrounding the spores. [t. NL, f. *amphi-* AMPHI- + *thēcium* (t. Gk: m. *thēkíon*, dim. of *thḗkē* case)]

amphitricha (ăm fĭt′rĭ kə), *n.pl.* bacteria having the organs of locomotion on both poles. [f. AMPHI- + m. *trich-* (s. Gk *thríx* hair)] —**amphit′richate, amphit′richous,** *adj.*

Amphitrite (ăm′fĭ trī′tĭ), *n. Gk Myth.* the goddess of the sea, daughter of Nereus and wife of Poseidon.

Amphitryon (ăm fĭt′rĭ ən), *n.* **1.** *Gk Legend.* the husband of Alcmene. **2.** a host; an entertainer.

amphiuma (ăm′fĭ yōō′mə), *n.* an aquatic, eel-like salamander of the genus *Amphiuma*, of south-eastern North America, having two pairs of very small feet. [t. NL]

amphora (ăm′fə rə), *n., pl.* **-rae** (-rē′). a two-handled, narrow-necked vessel, commonly big-bellied and narrowed at the base, used by the ancient Greeks and Romans for holding wine, oil, etc. [t. L, t. Gk: m. *amphoreús*, short for *amphiphoreús*] —**am′phoral,** *adj.*

Amphorae

amphoric (ăm fŏ′rĭk), *adj.* producing or like the sound made by blowing across the top of a bottle: *amphoric breathing.*

amphoteric (ăm′fə tĕ′rĭk), *adj. Chem.* functioning as an acid or as a base. [f. s. Gk *amphóteros* (comp. of *ámphō* both) + -IC]

ample (ăm′pl), *adj.,* **-pler, -plest. 1.** of great extent, size, or amount; large; spacious. **2.** in full or abundant measure; copious; liberal. **3.** fully sufficient for the purpose or for needs; enough and to spare. **4.** rather bulky or full in form or figure. [late ME, t. L: m. s. *amplus*] —**am′pleness,** *n.*

—**Syn. 2.** AMPLE, COPIOUS, LIBERAL describe an abundant supply of something. AMPLE describes a plentiful amount: *to give ample praise.* COPIOUS implies an apparently inexhaustible and lavish abundance: *a copious flow of tears.* LIBERAL implies a generous supply (more than AMPLE but less than COPIOUS) together with a free and unrestricted dispensing of it: *liberal amounts of food were distributed to the needy.* —**Ant. 2.** scanty, meagre.

amplexicaul (ăm plĕk′sĭ kôl′), *adj. Bot.* clasping the stem, as some leaves do at their base. [t. NL: s. *amplexicaulis*, f. L: m. s. *amplexus* embracing + *caulis* stem]

Amplexicaul leaves

ampliation (ăm′plĭ ā′shən), *n. Archaic.* enlargement; amplification. [t. L: s. *ampliātio*]

amplification (ăm′plĭ fĭ kā′shən), *n.* **1.** the act of amplifying. **2.** expansion of a statement, narrative, etc., as for rhetorical purposes. **3.** a statement, narrative, etc., so expanded. **4.** an addition made in expanding. **5.** *Elect.* increase in the strength of current, voltage, or power. [t. L: s. *amplificātio*] —**amplificatory** (ăm′plĭ fĭ kā′tə rĭ), *adj.*

amplifier (ăm′plĭ fī′ə), *n.* **1.** one who amplifies or enlarges. **2.** *Elect.* a device for increasing the amplitudes of electric waves or impulses by means of the control exercised by the input over the power supplied to the output from a local source of energy. Commonly it is a radio valve or transistor, or a device employing them. **3.** such a device used to magnify the sound produced by a radio, record-player, or any of certain musical instruments, as an electric guitar. **4.** *Photog.* an additional lens for expanding the field of vision.

amplify (ăm′plĭ fī′), *v.,* **-fied, -fying.** —*v.t.* **1.** to make larger or greater; enlarge; extend. **2.** to expand in stating or describing, as by details, illustrations, etc. **3.** *Elect.* to increase the amplitude of (impulses or waves). **4.** to make louder; magnify (the sound of). **5.** *U.S. Colloq.* to exaggerate. —*v.i.* **6.** to discourse at length; expatiate or dilate (usually fol. by *on*). [ME *amplify(en)*, t. F: m. *amplifier*, t. L: m. s. *amplificāre* enlarge. See -FY] —**Ant. 1.** contract. **2.** condense.

amplitude (ăm′plĭ tyōōd′), *n.* **1.** extension in space, esp. breadth or width; largeness; extent. **2.** large or full measure; abundance; copiousness. **3.** *Physics.* the distance or range from one extremity of an oscillation to the middle point or neutral value. **4.** *Elect.* the maximum strength of an alternating current during its cycle, as distinguished from the mean or effective strength. **5.** *Astron.* the arc of the horizon from the east or west point to a heavenly body at its rising or setting. [t. L: m. *amplitūdo*]

amplitude modulation, *Electronics.* a system of radio transmission in which the carrier wave is modulated by changing its amplitude (distinguished from *frequency modulation*). *Abbrev.*: AM.

amply (ăm′plĭ), *adv.* in an ample manner; sufficiently.

ampoule (ăm′pōōl), *n. Med.* a sealed glass bulb used to hold hypodermic solutions. [t. F, g. L *ampulla* bottle]

ampulla (ăm pōōl′ə), *n., pl.* **-pullae** (-pōōl′ē). **1.** *Anat.* a dilated portion of a canal or duct, esp. of the semicircular canals of the ear. **2.** *Eccles.* **a.** a vessel for the wine and water used at the altar. **b.** a vessel for holding consecrated oil. **3.** a two-handled bottle used by the ancient Romans for oil, etc. **4.** ampoule. [t. L] —**ampul′lary,** *adj.*

ampullaceal (ăm′pōō lā′shəl), *adj.* like an ampulla; bottle-shaped. Also, **am′pulla′ceous.**

amputate (ăm′pyōō tāt′), *v.t.,* **-tated, -tating. 1.** to cut off (a limb, arm, etc.) by a surgical operation. **2.** *Obs.* to prune, as branches of trees. [t. L: m. s. *amputātus*, pp.] —**am′puta′tion,** *n.* —**am′puta′tor,** *n.*

amputee (ăm′pyōō tē′), *n.* one who has lost an arm, hand, leg, etc., by amputation.

Amraoti (ăm′rä′ə tĭ, ŭm′-), *n.* a town in India, in NE Maharashtra. 137,875 (1961). Also, **Amaravati.**

Amravati (ăm rä′və tĭ), *n.* Amraoti.

amrita (ăm rē′tə), *n. Hindu Myth.* **1.** the ambrosial drink of immortality. **2.** the immortality conferred by it. Also, **amreeta.** [t. Skt: m. *amṛta* immortal; as n., the drink of immortality. Cf. Gk *ám(b)rotos* immortal]

Amritsar (ăm rĭt′sə), *n.* a city in NW India, in Punjab. 376,295 (1961).

Amstelveen (*Du.* ŏm stəl vĕn′), *n.* a town in the Netherlands, in S North Holland, S of Amsterdam. 56,761 (1966).

Amsterdam (ăm′stə dăm′; *Du.* ŏm stər dŏm′), *n.* a seaport in and the parliamentary capital of the Netherlands, in North Holland, on the IJssel Lake: ship canal. 866,290 (1965). See map under **The Hague.**

amt, amount.

amu (ăm′yōō), *n. Physics.* atomic mass unit.

amuck (ə mŭk′), *adv.* (*orig. adj.*) **1. run amuck, a.** to rush about in a murderous frenzy. **b.** to rush about wildly. —*n.* **2.** amok. [var. of AMOK]

Amu Darya (*Russ.* ȧ mōō′ dȧ ryȧ′), a river flowing from the Pamirs in central Asia NW to the Aral Sea. ab. 1400 mi. Also, **Oxus.**

amulet (ăm′yōō lĭt), *n.* an object superstitiously worn to ward off evil; a protecting charm. [t. L: s. *amulētum*]

Amundsen (ä′mōōnd sən), *n.* **Roald** (rō′äl), 1872–1928, Norwegian explorer: discovered the South Pole in December, 1911.

Amur (ə mōōə′), *n.* a river in E Asia, forming most of the boundary between N Manchuria and the SE Soviet Union, flowing into the Sea of Okhotsk. ab. 2700 mi.

amuse (ə myōōz′), *v.t.*, **amused, amusing. 1.** to hold the attention of agreeably; entertain; divert. **2.** to excite mirth in. **3.** to cause (time, leisure, etc.) to pass agreeably. **4.** *Archaic.* to keep in expectation by flattery, pretences, etc. **5.** *Obs.* to engross. **6.** *Obs.* to puzzle. [late ME, t. MF: m. s. *amuser* occupy with trifles, divert, f. *a* to + *muser* stare. See MUSE[1]] **—amus′able,** *adj.* **—amus′er,** *n.*

—Syn. 1. AMUSE, DIVERT, ENTERTAIN mean to occupy the attention with something pleasant. That which AMUSES dispels the tedium of idleness or pleases the fancy. DIVERT implies turning the attention from serious thoughts or pursuits to something light, amusing, or lively. That which ENTERTAINS usually does so because of a plan or programme which engages and holds the attention by being pleasing and sometimes instructive.

amused (ə myōōzd′), *adj.* **1.** filled with interest; pleasurably occupied. **2.** displaying amusement: *an amused expression.* **3.** aroused to mirth. **—amusedly** (ə myōō′zĭd lĭ), *adv.*

amusement (ə myōōz′mənt), *n.* **1.** the state of being amused; enjoyment. **2.** that which amuses; pastime; entertainment. **3.** a mechanical entertainment, as a roundabout at a fair. [t. F] **—Syn. 1.** recreation, frolic, pleasure, merriment. **2.** diversion, game.

amusement arcade, a covered way or shop having coin-operated mechanical games and gambling machines.

amusement park, a commercially run enclosed ground where amusements are permanently situated.

amusing (ə myōō′zĭng), *adj.* **1.** pleasantly entertaining or diverting. **2.** exciting moderate mirth; delighting the fancy. **—amus′ingly,** *adv.* **—amus′ingness,** *n.*

—Syn. 2. AMUSING, COMICAL, DROLL describe that which causes mirth. That which is AMUSING is quietly humorous or funny in a gentle, good-humoured way: *the baby's attempts to talk were amusing.* That which is COMICAL causes laughter by being incongruous, witty, or ludicrous: *his huge shoes made the clown look comical.* DROLL adds to COMICAL the idea of strange or peculiar, and sometimes that of sly, waggish, humour or clowning.

amusive (ə myōō′zĭv), *adj.* amusing or entertaining.

amydaloidal (ə mĭ′də loi′dl), *adj. Geol.* **1.** (of rocks) containing amygdales. —*n.* **2.** *Obs.* amydaloidal rock. Also, **amy′daloid′, amygdaloid.**

amygdala (ə mĭg′də lə), *n.*, *pl.* **-lae** (-lē′). **1.** *Anat.* **a.** an almond-shaped part. **b.** (*pl.*) the tonsils. **c.** a lobe of the cerebellum. **2.** *Obs.* an almond. [t. L, t. Gk: m. *amygdálē* almond. Cf. OE *amygdal*]

amygdalate (ə mĭg′də lĭt, -lāt′), *adj.* pertaining to, resembling, or made of almonds.

amygdale (ə mĭg′dāl), *n. Geol.* an almond-shaped cavity in an igneous rock, formed by the expansion of steam and later filled with minerals. Also, **amygdule.**

amygdalin (ə mĭg′də lĭn), *n.* a crystalline principle, $C_{20}H_{27}NO_{11} + 3H_2O$, existing in bitter almonds, and in the leaves, etc., of species of the genus *Prunus* and of some of its near allies.

amygdaline (ə mĭg′də lĭn, -līn′), *adj.* of or pertaining to the amygdalae.

amygdaloid (ə mĭg′də loid′), *n.*, *adj.* amydaloidal. Also, **amyg′daloi′dal.**

amygdule (ə mĭg′dyōōl), *n.* amygdale.

amyl (ăm′ĭl), *n. Chem.* a univalent radical C_5H_{11}, derived from pentane. Its compounds are found in fusel oil, fruit extracts, etc. [t. L: s. *amylum* starch (t. Gk: m. *ámylon*); the *-yl* was identified with -YL]

amylaceous (ăm′ĭ lā′shəs), *adj.* of the nature of starch; starchy. [f. AMYL(O)- + -ACEOUS]

amyl acetate, *Chem.* a colourless liquid, $CH_3COOC_5H_{11}$, with a smell of pear drops, used as a solvent, in perfumes, and as a flavouring.

amyl alcohol, *Chem.* a colourless liquid, $C_5H_{11}OH$, consisting of a mixture of two or more isomeric alcohols, derived from the pentanes and serving as a solvent and intermediate for organic syntheses.

amylase (ăm′ĭ lās′), *n. Biochem.* any of several starch-splitting enzymes, occurring in digestive juices, blood, and plants, which hydrolyse starches to simple sugars such as glucose and maltose.

amylene (ăm′ĭ lēn′), *n. Chem.* any of certain unsaturated isomeric hydrocarbons with the formula C_5H_{10}; pentene.

amylo-, a combining form of **amyl** and **amylum.** Also, **amyl-.**

amyloid (ăm′ĭ loid′), *n. Pathol.* a hard, homogeneous, glossy substance deposited in tissues in certain kinds of degeneration. **—am′yloi′dal,** *adj.*

amyloidosis (ăm′ĭ loi dō′sĭs), *n. Pathol.* a disease resulting from the deposit of amyloid in tissue or organs.

amylolysis (ăm′ĭ lŏl′ĭ sĭs), *n. Biochem.* the conversion of starch into sugar. [f. AMYLO- + -LYSIS] **—amylolytic** (ăm′ĭ lō lĭt′ĭk), *adj.*

amylopectin (ăm′ĭ lō pĕk′tĭn), *n. Chem.* the gel component of starch. It turns red in iodine.

amylopsin (ăm′ĭ lŏp′sĭn), *n. Biochem.* an enzyme of the pancreatic juice, capable of converting starch into sugar; pancreatic amylase. [b. AMYLO(LYSIS) and (PE)PSIN]

amylose (ăm′ĭ lōs′), *n. Chem.* the sol or soluble component of starch. It turns intense blue in iodine.

amylum (ăm′ĭ ləm), *n.* starch (def. 1). [t. L, t. Gk: m. *ámylon* fine meal, starch]

amytal (ăm′ĭ tăl′), *n. Pharm.* a colourless crystalline substance, $C_{11}H_{18}N_2O_3$, used esp. as a sedative.

AN, Anglo-Norman.

An, *Chem.* actinon.

an[1] (ăn; *unstressed* ən), *adj. or indefinite article.* the form of **a** before an initial vowel sound. See **a**[1]. [ME; OE *ān*. See ONE]

an[2] (ăn; *unstressed* ən), *conj.* **1.** *Dial. and Colloq.* and. **2.** *Archaic and Dial.* if. Also, **an′.** [var. of AND]

an-[1], a prefix meaning 'not', 'without', 'lacking', used before vowels and *h*, as in *anarchy.* Also, **a-**[6]. [t. Gk]

an-[2], var. of **ad-,** before *n*, as in *announce.*

an-[3], var. of **ana-,** used before vowels, as in *anaerobe.*

-an, a suffix meaning: **1.** 'belonging to', 'pertaining or relating to', 'adhering to', and commonly expressing connection with a place, person, reader, class, order, sect, system, doctrine, or the like, serving to form adjectives, many of which are also used as nouns, as *American, Christian, Elizabethan, republican,* and hence serving to form other nouns of the same type, as *historian, theologian.* **2.** *Zool.* 'relating to a certain class', as in *mammalian.* [t. L: s. *-ānus*; r. ME *-ain, -en*, t. OF]

an., (L *anno*) in the year.

ana[1] (ä′nə), *n.* **1.** a collection of miscellaneous information, esp. in the form of table talk, gossip, etc. **2.** the information so collected. [independent use of -ANA]

ana[2] (ăn′ə), *adv. Pharm.* in equal quantities; of each (used in medical prescriptions, with reference to ingredients, and often written āā). [ML, t. Gk. See ANA-]

ana-, a prefix meaning 'up', 'throughout', 'again', 'back', occurring originally in words from the Greek, but used also in modern words (English and other) formed on the Greek model, as in *anabatic.* [t. Gk, repr. *aná*, prep.]

-ana, a noun suffix denoting a collection of material pertaining to a given subject, as in *Shakespeariana, Americana.* [t. L, neut. pl. of *-ānus* -AN]

anabaena (ăn′ə bē′nə), *n.*, *pl.* **-nas.** *Bot.* any of the freshwater algae constituting the genus *Anabaena*, commonly occurring in masses, and often contaminating drinking water, giving it a fishy taste and smell. [t. NL, der. Gk *anabaínein* go up]

anabantid (ăn′ə băn′tĭd), *n.* **1.** any of several fishes of the family *Anabantidae*, comprising the labyrinth fishes. —*adj.* **2.** belonging to or pertaining to the *Anabantidae.* [t. NL: s. *Anabantidae* (f. ANABAS + -IDAE)]

Anabaptist (ăn′ə băp′tĭst), *n.* **1.** an adherent of a religious and social movement which arose in Europe shortly after 1520 and was distinguished by its insistence on its members being baptized again, its rejection of infant baptism, and by its attempts to establish a Christian communism. **2.** (*l.c.*) a member of a later sect or religious body holding the same doctrines. **3.** *Archaic.* Baptist (def. 1). **—an′abap′tism,** *n.*

anabaptize (ăn′ə băp′tīz, -băp tīz′), *v.t.* to baptize again. Also, **anabaptise.**

anabas (ăn′ə băs′), *n.* any fish of the genus *Anabas* of southern Asia, etc., as the climbing fish, *A. testudineus.* [t. NL, t. Gk, aorist participle of *anabaínein* go up]

anabasis (ə năb′ə sĭs), *n.*, *pl.* **-ses** (-sēz′), **1.** a march from the coast into the interior, as that of Cyrus the Younger against Artaxerxes II, described by Xenophon in his *Anabasis.* **2.** any military expedition. [t. Gk]

anabatic (ăn′ə băt′ĭk), *adj. Meteorol.* (of winds and air currents) moving upwards or up a slope. [t. Gk: m. s. *anabatikós* pertaining to climbing]

anabiosis (ăn′ə bī ō′sĭs), *n.* a bringing back or returning to consciousness; reanimation (after apparent death). [t. NL, t. Gk: revival] —**anabiotic** (ăn′ə bī ŏt′ĭk), *adj.*

anabolism (ə năb′ə lĭz′əm), *n. Biol.* constructive metabolism (opposed to *catabolism*). [f. s. Gk *anabolē* a throwing up + -ISM] —**anabolic** (ăn′ə bŏl′ĭk), *adj.*

anabranch (ăn′ə brănch′), *n. Phys. Geog.* a branch of a river which leaves the main stream and either enters it again, dries up, or sinks into the ground. [short for *anastomosing branch*]

anacardiaceous (ăn′ə kä′dĭ ā′shəs), *adj.* belonging to the *Anacardiaceae*, a family of trees and shrubs including the cashew, mango, pistachio, sumach, etc. [f. s. NL *Anacardiāceae* (f. *ana-* ANA- + s. Gk *kardía* heart + *-āceae* -ACEAE) + -OUS]

anachronism (ə năk′rə nĭz′əm), *n.* **1.** an error assigning a custom, event, person, or thing to an age other, esp. earlier, than the correct one. **2.** something placed or occurring out of its proper time. [t. Gk: s. *anachronismós*]

anachronistic (ə năk′rə nĭs′tĭk), *adj.* containing an anachronism. Also, **anach′ronis′tical.**

anachronous (ə năk′rə nəs), *adj.* anachronistic. —**anach′ronously,** *adv.*

anaclisis (ăn′ə klī′sĭs), *n. Psychoanal.* the choice of an object of libidinal attachment on the basis of a resemblance to early childhood protective and parental figures. [t. Gk: m. *anáklisis* a leaning back]

anaclitic (ăn′ə klĭt′ĭk), *adj. Psychoanal.* exhibiting or pertaining to anaclisis.

anacoluthia (ăn′ə kə lo͞o′thĭ ə), *n.* lack of grammatical sequence or coherence, esp. in the same sentence. [t. L, t. Gk: m. *anakolouthia*] —**an′acolu′thic,** *adj.*

anacoluthon (ăn′ə kə lo͞o′thŏn), *n., pl.* **-tha** (-thə). *Rhet.* a construction involving a break in grammatical sequence; a case of anacoluthia. [t. L, t. Gk: m. *anakólouthon*, neut. adj., inconsequent]

anaconda (ăn′ə kŏn′də), *n.* **1.** a large South American snake, *Eunectes murinus*, of the boa family. **2.** any boa constrictor. [orig. unknown: ? t. Sinhalese]

Anaconda (ăn′ə kŏn′də), *n.* a town in the U.S., in SW Montana: largest copper smelter in the world. 12,054 (1960).

Anacreon (ə năk′rĭ ən), *n. c.* 563–*c.* 478 B.C., Greek lyric poet known for his love poems and drinking songs.

Anacreontic (ə năk′rĭ ŏn′tĭk), *adj.* Also, **anacreontic. 1.** of or in the manner of Anacreon. **2.** convivial; amatory. —*n.* **3.** (*l.c.*) an Anacreontic poem.

anacrusis (ăn′ə kro͞o′sĭs), *n. Pros.* an unstressed syllable or syllable group which begins a line of verse but is not counted as part of the first foot, which properly begins with a stressed syllable. [t. L, t. Gk: m. *anákrousis*, der. *anakroúein* strike up]

anadem (ăn′ə dĕm′), *n. Poetic.* a garland or wreath for the head. [t. L: m. *anadēma*, t. Gk: fillet]

anadiplosis (ăn′ə dĭ plō′sĭs), *n. Rhet.* repetition in the first part of one clause of a prominent word in the latter part of the preceding clause. [t. Gk: repetition]

anadromous (ə năd′rə məs), *adj.* (of fishes) going from the sea up a river or into coastal waters to spawn (contrasted with *catadromous*). [t. Gk: m. *anádromos* running up]

anaemia (ə nē′mĭ ə), *n.* **1.** *Pathol.* a quantitative deficiency of the haemoglobin, often accompanied by a reduced number of red blood cells, and causing pallor, weakness, and breathlessness. **2.** bloodlessness; paleness. Also, *Chiefly U.S.*, **anemia.** [NL, t. Gk: m. *anaimía* want of blood]

anaemic (ə nē′mĭk), *adj.* **1.** suffering from anaemia. **2.** sickly, colourless; without body or vigour. Also, *Chiefly U.S.*, **anemic.**

anaerobe (ă nĕə′rōb), *n.* a bacterium or other microorganism which does not require free oxygen or is not destroyed by its absence (opposed to *aerobe*). [backformation from *anaerobia*, pl. of ANAEROBIUM]

anaerobic (ăn′ĕə rō′bĭk), *adj.* **1.** *Biol.*, *Physiol.* (of organisms or tissues) requiring the absence of free oxygen or not destroyed by its absence. **2.** pertaining to or caused by the absence of oxygen. **3.** affected by or involving the activities of anaerobes. —**an′aero′bically,** *adv.*

anaerobiont (ăn′ĕə rō′bĭ ənt), *n. Biol.* anaerobe.

anaerobiosis (ăn′ĕə rō bĭ ō sĭs), *n. Biol.* life in the absence of oxygen. —**anaerobiotic** (ăn′ĕə rō bĭ ŏt′ĭk), *adj.* —**an′aerobiot′ically,** *adv.*

anaerobium (ăn′ĕə rō′bĭ əm), *n., pl.* **-bia** (-bĭ ə). *Biol.* anaerobe. [NL, f. Gk: *an-* AN-[1] + *āero-* AERO- + m. *bíos* life]

anaesthesia (ăn′ĭs thē′zyə), *n.* **1.** *Med.* general or local insensibility, as to pain and other sensation, induced by certain drugs. **2.** *Pathol.* general loss of the senses of feeling, such as pain, heat, cold, touch, and other less common varieties of sensation. **3.** the science of anaesthetics. Also, *Chiefly U.S.*, **anesthesia.** [t. NL, t. Gk: m. *anaisthēsia* insensibility]

anaesthesin (ăn′ĭs thē′zĭn), *n. Chem.* benzocaine.

anaesthetic (ăn′ĭs thĕt′ĭk), *n.* **1.** a substance such as ether, chloroform, cocaine, etc., that produces anaesthesia. —*adj.* **2.** pertaining to or causing physical insensibility. **3.** insensitive. Also, *Chiefly U.S.*, **anesthetic.**

anaesthetist (ə nēs′thə tĭst), *n.* a person who administers anaesthetics, usually a specially trained doctor. Also, *Chiefly U.S.* **anesthetist.**

anaesthetize (ə nēs′thə tīz′), *v.t.*, **-tized, -tizing.** to render physically insensible, as by an anesthetic. Also, **anaesthetise, anesthetise**; *Chiefly U.S.*, **anesthetize.** —**anaes′thetiza′tion,** *n.*

anaglyph (ăn′ə glĭf), *n.* **1.** something executed in low relief, as a cameo or an embossed ornament. **2.** *Photog.* a picture composed of two images, one red and one green, which, when viewed through red and green spectacles, appears stereoscopic. [t. Gk: s. *anáglyphos* wrought in low relief] —**anaglyphic** (ăn′ə glĭf′ĭk), **anaglyptic** (ăn′ə glĭp′tĭk), *adj.*

anagoge (ăn′ə gōj′ĭ), *n.* **1.** the spiritual interpretation or application of words, as of Scriptures. **2.** *Theol.* the application of the types and allegories of the Old Testament to subjects of the New Testament. [t. LL, t. Gk: a bringing up, elevation] —**anagogic** (ăn′ə gŏj′ĭk), **an′agog′ical,** *adj.* —**an′agog′ically,** *adv.*

anagram (ăn′ə grăm), *n.* **1.** a transposition of the letters of a word or sentence to form a new word or sentence, as *Galenus* is an anagram of *angelus.* —*v.t.*, *v.i.* **2.** to anagrammatize. [t. NL: m. *anagramma*, backformation from Gk *anagrammatismós* transposition of letters] —**anagrammatic** (ăn′ə grə măt′ĭk), **an′agrammat′ical,** *adj.* —**an′agrammat′ically,** *adv.*

anagrammatize (ăn′ə grăm′ə tīz′), *v.*, **-tized, -tizing.** —*v.t.* **1.** to transpose into an anagram. —*v.i.* **2.** to make anagrams. Also, **anagrammatise.** —**an′agram′matism,** *n.* —**an′agram′matist,** *n.*

Anaheim (ăn′ə hīm′), *n.* a town in the U.S., in SW California, SE of Los Angeles. 104,184 (1960).

anal (ā′nəl), *adj.* of, pertaining to, or near the anus.

anal., **1.** analogous. **2.** analogy. **3.** analysis.

analcite (ă năl′sīt, ăn′əl sīt′), *n.* a white or slightly coloured zeolite mineral, generally found in crystalline form. Also, **analcime** (ă năl′sĭm, -sīm). [f. m. s. Gk *analkḗs* weak + -ITE[1]]

analects (ăn′ə lĕkts′), *n.pl.* selected passages from the writings of an author or of different authors. Also, **analecta** (ăn′ə lĕk′tə). [t. L: (m.) *analecta*, pl., t. Gk: m. *análekta* things gathered] —**an′alec′tic,** *adj.*

analeptic (ăn′ə lĕp′tĭk), *Med.* —*adj.* **1.** restoring; invigorating; giving strength after disease. **2.** awakening, esp. from drug stupor. —*n.* **3.** an analeptic remedy. [t. Gk: m. s. *analēptikós* restorative]

anal fin, (in fishes) the median ventral unpaired fin.

analgesia (ăn′əl jē′zyə, -syə), *n. Med.* absence of sense of pain. [t. NL, t. Gk]

analgesic (ăn′əl jē′zĭk, -sĭk), *Med.* —*n.* **1.** a remedy that relieves or removes pain. —*adj.* **2.** pertaining to or causing analgesia.

analogical (ăn′ə lŏj′ĭ kl), *adj.* based on, involving, or expressing an analogy. Also, **an′alog′ic.** —**an′alog′ically,** *adv.*

analogist (ə năl′ə jĭst), *n.* **1.** one who employs or argues from analogy. **2.** one who looks for analogies. —**anal′ogism,** *n.*

analogize (ə năl′ə jīz′), *v.*, **-gized, -gizing.** —*v.t.* **1.** to study or explain by analogy. —*v.i.* **2.** to make use of analogy in reasoning, argument, etc. **3.** to be analogous; exhibit analogy. Also, **analogise.**

analogous (ə năl′ə gəs), *adj.* **1.** having analogy; corresponding in some particular. **2.** *Biol.* corresponding in function, but not evolved from corresponding organs, as the wings of a bee and those of a hummingbird. [t. L: m. *analogus*, t. Gk: m. *análogos* proportionate] —**anal′ogously,** *adv.* —**anal′ogousness,** *n.*

analogue (ăn′ə lŏg′), *n.* **1.** something having analogy to something else. **2.** *Biol.* an organ or part analogous to another. [t. F, t. Gk: m. s. *análogon*]

analogue computer. See **computer.**

analogy (ə năl′ə jĭ), *n., pl.* **-gies. 1.** an agreement, likeness, or correspondence between the relations of things to one another; a partial similarity in particular circumstances on which a comparison may be based: *the analogy between the heart and a pump.* **2.** agreement; similarity. **3.** *Biol.* an analogous relationship. **4.** (in linguistic change) the tendency of inflections and formations to follow existing models and regular patterns: *'adnoun' is formed on the analogy of 'adverb'*. **5.** *Logic.* a form of reasoning in which similarities are inferred from a similarity of two or more things in certain particulars. [t. L: m. s. *analogia*, t. Gk: orig., equality of ratios, proportion]

analphabetic (ăn′ăl fə bĕt′ĭk), *adj.* **1.** not alphabetical. **2.** unable to read and write; illiterate.

analyse (ăn′ə līz′), *v.t.*, **-lysed, -lysing. 1.** to resolve into elements or constituent parts; determine the elements or essential features of: *to analyse an argument.* **2.** to examine critically, so as to bring out the essential elements or give the essence of: *to analyse a poem.* **3.** to subject to mathematical, chemical, grammatical, etc., analysis. **4.** psychoanalyse. Also, *U.S.*, **analyze.** [backformation from ANALYSIS] —**an′alys′able,** *adj.* —**an′alys′er,** *n.*

analysis (ə năl′ə sĭs), *n.*, *pl.* **-ses** (-sēz′). **1.** separation of a whole, whether a material substance or any matter of thought, into its constituent elements (opposed to *synthesis*). **2.** this process as a method of studying the nature of a thing or of determining its essential features: *the grammatical analysis of a sentence.* **3.** a brief presentation of essential features; an outline or summary, as of a book; a synopsis. **4.** *Maths.* **a.** an investigation based on the properties of numbers. **b.** the discussion of a problem by algebra as opposed to geometry. **5.** *Chem.* **a.** intentionally produced decomposition or separation of a substance into its ingredients or elements, to find their kind or quantity. **b.** the ascertainment of the kind or amount of one or more of the constituents of a substance, whether actually obtained in separate form or not. **6.** psychoanalysis. [t. ML, t. Gk: a breaking up]

analysis of variance, *Statistics.* a procedure for resolving the total variance of a set of variates into component variances, which are associated with various factors affecting the variates.

analyst (ăn′ə lĭst), *n.* **1.** one who analyses or who is skilled in analysis. **2.** a psychoanalyst.

analytic (ăn′ə lĭt′ĭk), *adj.* **1.** pertaining to or proceeding by analysis (opposed to *synthetic*). **2.** (of languages) characterized by the use of separate words (**free forms**) rather than of inflectional adjuncts (**bound forms**) to show syntactic relationships, as in English or Chinese (opposed to *synthetic*). **3.** *Logic.* (of a proposition) necessarily true because its denial involves a contradiction, as *all spinsters are unmarried.* Also, **an′alyt′ical.** [t. ML: s. *analyticus*, t. Gk: m. *analytikós*] —**an′alyt′ically,** *adv.*

analytical geometry, geometry treated by algebra, the position of any point being determined by numbers which are its coordinates with respect to a system of coordinates.

analytics (ăn′ə lĭt′ĭks), *n.* mathematical or algebraic analysis. [n. use of ANALYTIC. See -ICS]

Anam (ă năm′, ăn′ăm), *n.* Annam.

anamnesis (ăn′ăm nē′sĭs), *n.* **1.** the recalling of things past; recollection. **2.** *Med.* a case history. [t. NL, t. Gk: a recalling to mind]

anamorphoscope (ăn′ə mô′fə skōp′), *n.* *Photog.* **1.** a camera or viewing device designed to produce an anamorphic image, in the form of radial slits on a rotating disc. **2.** a curved mirror or other device for giving a correct image of a picture or the like distorted by anamorphosis.

anamorphosis (ăn′ə mô′fə sĭs), *n.*, *pl.* **-ses** (-sēz′). **1.** a distorted image, esp. a drawing, which appears in natural form under certain conditions, as when viewed at a raking angle or reflected from a curved mirror. **2.** the method of producing such images. [t. NL, t. Gk: a forming anew] —**an′amor′phic, an′amor′phous,** *adj.*

anandrous (ă năn′drəs), *adj.* *Bot.* having no stamens. [t. Gk: m. *ánandros* without a man]

Ananias (ăn′ə nī′əs), *n.* **1.** *Bible.* a man who was struck dead for lying. Acts 5:1–5. **2.** a liar.

ananthous (ă năn′thəs), *adj.* *Bot.* without flowers. [f. AN-[1] + s. Gk *ánthos* flower + -OUS]

anapaest (ăn′ə pĕst′, ăn′ə pēst′), *n.* *Pros.* a foot of three syllables, two short followed by one long (quantitative metre), or two unstressed followed by one stressed (accentual metre). Thus, *for the nonce* is an accentual anapaest. Also, **anapest.** [t. L: m. s. *anapaestus*, t. Gk: m. *anápaistos* struck back, reversed (as compared with a dactyl)] —**an′apaes′tic,** *adj.*, *n.*

anaphase (ăn′ə fāz′), *n.* *Biol.* the stage in mitotic cell division after cleavage of the chromosomes, in which the chromosomes move away from each other to opposite ends of the cell.

anaphora (ə năf′ə rə), *n.* *Rhet.* repetition of the same word or words at the beginning of two or more successive verses, clauses, or sentences. [t. L, t. Gk: a bringing up]

anaphrodisiac (ăn′ăf rə dĭz′ĭ ăk′), *Med.* —*adj.* **1.** capable of diminishing sexual desire. —*n.* **2.** an anaphrodisiac agent. [f. AN-[1] + APHRODISIAC]

anaphylaxis (ăn′ə fĭ lăk′sĭs), *n.* *Pathol.* increased susceptibility to a foreign protein resulting from previous exposure to it, as in serum treatment. [t. NL, f. Gk: *ana-* ANA- + *phýlaxis* a guarding] —**an′aphylac′tic,** *adj.*

anaplasmosis (ăn′ə plăz mō′sĭs), *n.* *Vet. Sci.* a disease of cattle caused by a blood-infecting protozoan parasite, transmitted by bloodsucking flies and ticks.

anaplastic (ăn′ə plăs′tĭk), *adj.* **1.** *Surg.* plastic (def. 6). **2.** *Pathol.* **a.** (of cells) having reverted to a more primitive form. **b.** (of tumours) having a high degree of malignancy.

anaplasty (ăn′ə plăs′tĭ), *n.* anaplastic surgery. [f. s. Gk *anáplastos* plastic + -Y[3]]

anaptotic (ăn′ăp tŏt′ĭk), *adj.* (of languages) tending to become uninflected, in accordance with a theory that languages evolve from uninflected to inflected and back. [f. AN-[3] + s. Gk *áptōtos* indeclinable + -IC]

anarch (ăn′äk), *n.* *Archaic.* an anarchist.

anarchic (ă nä′kĭk), *adj.* **1.** of, like, or tending to anarchy. **2.** advocating anarchy. **3.** lawless. Also, **anar′chical.** —**anar′chically,** *adv.*

anarchism (ăn′ə kĭz′əm), *n.* **1.** the doctrine (advocated under various forms) urging the abolition of government and governmental restraint as the indispensable condition of political and social liberty. **2.** the methods or practices of anarchists.

anarchist (ăn′ə kĭst), *n.* **1.** one who advocates anarchy as a political idea; a believer in an anarchic theory of society, esp. an adherent of the social theory of Proudhon, Bakunin, or Kropotkin. **2.** one who seeks to overturn by violence all constituted forms and institutions of society and government, with no purpose of establishing any other system of order in the place of that destroyed. **3.** any person who promotes disorder or excites revolt against an established rule, law, or custom. [f. s. Gk *ánarchos* without a ruler + -IST] —**anarchistic** (ăn′ə kĭs′tĭk), *adj.*

anarchize (ăn′ä kīz′), *v.t.* to make anarchic. Also **anarchise.**

anarchy (ăn′ə kĭ), *n.* **1.** a state of society without government or law. **2.** political and social disorder due to absence of governmental control. **3.** absence of government or governmental restraint. **4.** a theory which regards the union of order with the absence of all direct or coercive government as the political ideal. **5.** confusion in general; disorder. [t. Gk: m. s. *anarchía* lack of a ruler]

anarthrous (ă nä′thrəs), *adj.* **1.** *Zool.* without joints or articulated limbs. **2.** (esp. in Greek grammar) used without the article. [t. Gk: m. *ánarthros*]

anasarca (ăn′ə sä′kə), *n.* *Pathol.* a pronounced generalized dropsy. [? m. Gk phrase *anà sárka* up flesh] —**an′asar′cous,** *adj.*

anastigmatic (ăn′ə stĭg măt′ĭk, ă năs′tĭg-), *adj.* *Optics.* (of a lens) not astigmatic; forming point images of a point object located off the lens AXIS.

anastomose (ə năs′tə mōz′), *v.t.*, *v.i.*, **-mosed, -mosing.** *Physiol.* to communicate or connect by anastomosis.

anastomosis (ə năs′tə mō′sĭs), *n.*, *pl.* **-ses** (-sēz). **1.** *Physiol.* communication between blood vessels by means of collateral channels. **2.** *Biol.* connection between parts of any branching system. [t. NL, t. Gk: opening] —**anastomotic** (ə năs′tə mŏt′ĭk), *adj.*

anastrophe (ə năs′trə fĭ), *n.* *Rhet.* inversion of the usual order of words. [t. L, t. Gk: a turning back]

anat., **1.** anatomical. **2.** anatomy.

anatase (ăn′ə tās′), *n.* a black to brown mineral, titanium dioxide, TiO_2, occurring in octahedral crystals; octahedrite. [t. F, t. Gk: m. *anátasis* extension]

anathema (ə năth′ĭ mə), *n.*, *pl.* **-mas. 1.** a formal ecclesiastical curse involving excommunication. **2.** any imprecation of divine punishment. **3.** a curse; an execration. **4.** a person or thing accursed or consigned to damnation or destruction. **5.** a person or thing detested or loathed. [t. LL, t. Gk: something devoted (to evil)]

anathematize (ə năth′ĭ mə tīz′), *v.*, **-tized, -tizing.** —*v.t.* **1.** to pronounce an anathema against; denounce; curse. —*v.i.* **2.** to pronounce anathemas; curse. Also, **anathematise.** —**anath′ematiza′tion,** *n.* —**anath′emat′ic,** *adj.*

anatine (ăn′ə tīn′, -tĭn), *adj.* **1.** of or pertaining to the *Anatidae*, the duck family. **2.** resembling a duck; ducklike. [t. L: m. s. *anatīnus*]

Anatolia (ăn′ə tō′lyə), *n.* a vast plateau between the Black Sea and the Mediterranean: in ancient usage, synonymous with the peninsula of Asia Minor; in modern usage, applied to Turkey in Asia.

Anatolian (ăn′ə tō′lyən), *adj.* **1.** of Anatolia. **2.** of, or belonging to, a group or family of languages that includes cuneiform Hittite and its nearest congeners.

anatomical (ăn′ə tŏm′ĭ kl), *adj.* **1.** pertaining to anatomy. **2.** *Slang.* bawdy; sexual. Also, **an′atom′ic.** —**an′atom′ically,** *adv.*

anatomist (ə năt′ə mĭst), *n.* an expert in anatomy.

anatomize (ə năt′ə mīz′), *v.t.*, **-mized, -mizing. 1.** to dissect, as a plant or an animal, to show the position, structure, and relation of the parts; display the anatomy of. **2.** to analyse or examine very minutely. Also, **anatomise.** —**anat′omiza′tion,** *n.*

anatomy (ə năt′ə mĭ), *n., pl.* **-mies. 1.** the structure of an animal or plant, or of any of its parts. **2.** the science of the structure of animals and plants. **3.** dissection of animals or plants, or their parts, for study of structure, position, etc. **4.** an anatomical subject or model. **5.** a skeleton. **6.** any analysis or minute examination. **7.** *Colloq.* body; bodily form; figure. [t. LL: m. s. *anatomia*, t. Gk, var. of *anatomē* dissection; r. ME *anothomia*, t. ML]

anatropous (ə năt′rə pəs), *adj. Bot.* (of an ovule) inverted at an early stage of growth, so that the micropyle is turned towards the funicle, the chalaza being situated at the opposite end. [t. NL: m. *anatropus* inverted. See ANA-, -TROPOUS]

anatto (ə năt′ō), *n.* annatto.

Anaxagoras (ăn′ăk săg′ə rəs), *n.* 500?–428 B.C., Greek philosopher.

Anaximander (ə năk′sĭ măn′də), *n.* 611?–547? B.C., Greek philosopher.

Anaximenes (ăn′ăk sĭm′ĭ nēz′), *n.* 6th century B.C., Greek philosopher of Miletus.

anbury (ăn′bə rĭ, -brĭ), *n.* **1.** a soft, spongy tumour or wart of horses, oxen, etc. **2.** a disease of cruciferous plants, esp. the turnip, in which the roots become clubbed. Also, **ambury, anberry.** [orig. uncert.; ? der. OE *ang-* pain + BERRY. Cf. HANGNAIL]

anc., ancient.

-ance, a suffix of nouns denoting action, state, or quality, or something exemplifying one of these, often corresponding to adjectives in *-ant*, as *brilliance, distance*, or formed directly from verbs, as in *assistance, defiance.* Cf. **-ence.** [ME *-ance*, t. F, g. L *-antia, -entia*, orig. ppr. endings]

ancestor (ăn′sĭs tə), *n.* **1.** one from whom a person is descended, usually distantly; a forefather; a progenitor. **2.** *Biol.* the actual or hypothetical form or stock of an earlier and presumably lower type, from which any organized being is known or inferred to have developed. **3.** *Law.* one from whom an inheritance is derived (correlative of *heir*). [ME *ancestre*, t. OF, g. L *antecessor* predecessor] —**ancestress** (ăn′sĭs trĭs), *n. fem.*

ancestral (ăn sĕs′trəl), *adj.* pertaining to ancestors; descending or claimed from ancestors: *an ancestral home.* —**ances′trally,** *adv.* —**Syn.** hereditary, inherited.

ancestry (ăn′sĭs trĭ), *n., pl.* **-tries. 1.** ancestral descent. **2.** honourable descent. **3.** a series of ancestors.

Anchises (ăn kī′sēz), *n. Class. Legend.* a prince of Troy, father of Aeneas.

anchor (ăng′kə), *n.* **1.** a device for holding boats, vessels, floating bridges, etc., in place. **2.** any similar device for holding fast or checking motion. **3.** a metallic strap or belt built into masonry to hold facing or other materials. **4.** a means of stability: *hope is his anchor.* **5.** *Mil.* a key defensive position. **6.** *Colloq.* a home. **7. at anchor,** held still by an anchor; anchored. **8. cast anchor,** to put down or drop the anchor. **9. weigh anchor,** to take up the anchor. —*v.t.* **10.** to hold fast by an anchor. **11.** to fix or fasten; affix firmly. —*v.i.* **12.** to drop anchor. **13.** to lie or ride at anchor. **14.** to keep hold or be firmly fixed. **15.** *Colloq.* to take up residence (in a place); settle. [ME *anker, ancre*, OE *ancor*, t. L: s. *ancora*, t. Gk: m. *ankȳra*] —**an′chorless,** *adj.* —**an′chor-like′,** *adj.*

anchorage (ăng′kə rĭj), *n.* **1.** a place for anchoring. **2.** a charge for anchoring. **3.** the act of anchoring. **4.** the state of being anchored. **5.** that to which anything is fastened. **6.** a means of anchoring or making fast. **7.** a means of support or stability, esp. for the mind.

Anchorage (ăng′kə rĭj), *n.* a seaport in the U.S., in S Alaska: earthquake 1964. 44,237 (1960).

anchor buoy, *Naut.* a small buoy made fast to an anchor and floating above it, to indicate its position.

anchoress (ăng′kə rĭs), *n.* a female anchorite.

anchoret (ăng′kə rĭt, -rĕt′), *n.* anchorite. [t. LL: m. s. *anachōrēta* (t. Gk: m. *anachōrētēs* a recluse) by assoc. with obs. *anchor* hermit (OE *ancora*)] —**anchoretic** (ăng′kə rĕt′ĭk), *adj.*

anchor-ice (ăng′kə rīs′), *n.* ground ice.

anchorite (ăng′kə rīt′), *n.* one who has retired to a solitary place for a life of religious seclusion; a hermit; a recluse. [ME *ancorite*, t. ML: m. s. *anachōrita*, var. of LL *anachōrēta*] —**anchoritic** (ăng′kə rĭt′ĭk), *adj.*

anchor light, *Naut.* a light carried at the bow or stern of a ship at anchor, visible from any direction for at least two miles. Also, **riding light.**

anchovy (ăn′chə vĭ), *n., pl.* **-vies. 1.** a small herring-like marine fish, *Engraulis encrasicholus*, abundant in S Europe, much used pickled and in the form of a salt paste. **2.** any fish of the same family (*Engraulidae*). **3.** *U.S.* any smelt. [t. Sp. and Pg.: m. *anchova*, prob. t. d. It. (Genoese): m. *anciova*, g. LL *apiuva*, t. Gk: m. *aphýē*]

anchovy pear, 1. the fruit of a West Indian tree, *Grias cauliflora*, often pickled, and somewhat resembling the mango. **2.** the tree.

anchusa (ăng kyōō′sə), *n.* any plant of the boraginaceous genus *Anchusa*, rough hairy plants including the bugloss. [t. L, t. Gk: m. *ánchousa* alkanet]

anchusin (ăng kyōō′sĭn), *n.* alkanet (def. 3).

anchylose (ăng′kĭ lōz′), *v.t., v.i.*, **-losed, -losing.** ankylose. —**an′chylo′sis,** *n.* —**anchylotic** (ăng′kĭ lŏt′ĭk), *adj.*

anchylostomiasis (ăng′kĭ lŏs′tə mī′ə sĭs), *n.* ankylostomiasis.

ancienne noblesse (*Fr.* äɴ syĕn nŏ blĕs′), *French.* the ancient nobility, esp. of the ancien régime.

ancien régime (*Fr.* äɴ syăɴ rĕ zhĕm′), *French.* **1.** the political and social system of France before the Revolution of 1789. **2.** a former system of government.

ancient[1] (ān′shənt), *adj.* **1.** of or in time long past, esp. before the end of the Western Roman Empire, A.D. 476: *ancient history.* **2.** dating from a remote period; of great age. **3.** very old (applied to persons). **4.** *Archaic.* venerable. **5.** *Law.* having been in existence for a statutory period of time, often 20 years: *in ancient matters the normal requirements of proof are relaxed.* —*n.* **6.** a person who lived in ancient times, esp. one of the ancient Greeks, Romans, Hebrews, etc. **7.** (*usually pl.*) one of the classical writers of antiquity. **8.** an old man. [ME *auncien*, t. OF: m. *ancien*, g. LL *antiānus* former, old, der. L *ante* before] —**an′cientness,** *n.*

—**Syn. 2.** ANCIENT, ANTIQUATED, ANTIQUE, OLD-FASHIONED refer to something dating from the past. ANCIENT implies existence or first occurrence in the past: *an ancient custom.* ANTIQUATED connotes something too old or no longer useful: *an antiquated building.* ANTIQUE suggests a curious or pleasing quality in something old: *antique furniture.* OLD-FASHIONED may disparage something as being out of date or may approve something old as being superior: *an old-fashioned hat, old-fashioned courtesy.* —**Ant. 2.** new.

ancient[2] (ān′shənt), *n. Obs.* **1.** the bearer of a flag. **2.** a flag, banner, or standard; an ensign. [var. of ENSIGN]

Ancient Greek, Greek as spoken before *c.* 300 B.C. See **Greek** (def. 4).

ancient history, 1. history before the end of the Western Roman Empire in A.D. 476. **2.** *Colloq.* information or events of the recent past which are common knowledge or are no longer relevant.

ancient lights, *Law.* the legal right of a window to receive a certain amount of daylight, after it has done so for 27 years.

anciently (ān′shənt lĭ), *adv.* in ancient times; of old.

Ancient of Days, the eternal Supreme Being.

ancientry (ān′shən trĭ), *n. Archaic.* **1.** ancient character or style. **2.** ancient times. **3.** ancient lineage.

ancillary (ăn sĭl′ə rĭ), *adj.* accessory; auxiliary. [t. L: m. *ancillāris* pertaining to a handmaid]

ancipital (ăn sĭp′ĭ tl), *adj. Bot., Zool.* two-edged: *ancipital stems.* Also, **ancipitous** (ăn sĭp′ĭ təs). [f. s. L *anceps* two-headed + -AL[1]]

Ancohuma (ăng′kō ōō′mə), *n.* See **Sorata, Mount.**

ancon (ăng′kŏn), *n., pl.* **ancones** (ăng kō′nēz), **1.** *Archit.* any projection, as a console, supporting a cornice or the like. **2.** *Anat.* the elbow. [t. L, t. Gk: m. *ankṓn* a bend, the elbow] —**anconeal** (ăng kō′nĭ əl), *adj.*

Ancona (ăn kō′nə), *n.* a seaport in Italy, in the Marches on the Adriatic. 101,769 (1966).

-ancy, an equivalent of **-ance,** used chiefly in nouns denoting state or quality, as in *buoyancy.* [t. L: m. s. *-antia*]

ancylostomiasis (ăn′sĭ lŏs′tə mī′ə sĭs), *n.* ankylostomiasis.

and (ănd; *unstressed* ənd, ən), *conj.* **1.** with; along with; together with; besides; also; moreover (used to connect grammatically coordinate words, phrases, or clauses): *pens and pencils.* **2.** as well as: *nice and warm.* **3.** *Colloq.* to (used between verbs): *try and do it.* **4.** *Archaic.* also; then (used to introduce a sentence, implying continuation): *And he said unto Moses.* **5.** *Archaic or Dial.* if: *and you please.* —*n.* **6.** the ampersand sign. **7.** (*often pl.*) an additional consideration, detail, or the like. [OE; akin to G *und*]

and., andante.

Andalusia (ăn′də lo͞o′zyə), *n.* a region in S Spain, bordering on the Atlantic and the Mediterranean. 33,712 sq. mi. Spanish, **Andalucia** (*Sp.* än dä lo͞o thē′ä), —**An′dalu′sian,** *adj.*, *n.*

andalusite (ăn′də lo͞o′sīt), *n.* a mineral, aluminium silicate, Al_2SiO_5, found in schistose rocks. [named after ANDALUSIA. See -ITE[1]]

Andaman and Nicobar Islands (ăn′də mən; nĭk′ō bä′), two groups of islands in the Bay of Bengal, SW of Burma, a centrally administered territory of India. 63,548 pop. (1961); 3143 sq. mi. *Cap.*: Port Blair.

andamento (ăn′də mĕn′tō; *It.* än dä mĕn′tō), *n. Music.* an elaborate fugue subject, often in two sections. [t. It.]

andante (ăn dăn′tĭ; *It.* än dän′tė), *Music.* —*adj.*, *adv.* **1.** moderately slow and even. —*n.* **2.** an andante movement or piece. [It.: lit., walking]

andantino (ăn′dăn tē′nō; *It.* än dän tē′nō), *adj.*, *adv.*, *n.*, *pl.* **-nos.** *Music.* —*adj.*, *adv.* **1.** slightly faster than andante. —*n.* **2.** an andantino movement or piece. [It., dim. of *andante* ANDANTE]

Andean (ăn dē′ən, ăn′dĭ-), *adj.* of or like the Andes.

Anderlecht (*Flem.* ŏn′dər lĕKHt), *n.* a suburb of Brussels. 88,326 (est. 1952).

Andersen (ăn′də sən), *n.* **Hans Christian** (hänz′ krĭs′-chən), 1805–75, Danish author, esp. of fairytales.

Anderson (ăn′də sən), *n.* **1. Elizabeth Garrett,** 1836–1917, first British woman physician. **2. Marian,** born 1908, U.S. contralto.

Andes (ăn′dēz), *n.pl.* a lofty mountain system in South America, extending ab. 4500 mi. from N Colombia and Venezuela S to Cape Horn. Highest peak (of the Western Hemisphere), Aconcagua, 22,834 ft.

andesine (ăn′dĭ zēn′, -zĭn), *n.* a plagioclase mineral occurring as crystals in igneous rocks. [f. ANDES + -INE[2]]

andesite (ăn′dĭ zīt′), *n.* a volcanic rock composed essentially of plagioclase felspar, resembling trachyte in appearance. [f. ANDES + -ITE[1]]

Andhra Pradesh (ăn′drə prä dĕsh′), a state in SE India, formed in 1953 from parts of Madras and Hyderabad. 35,983,447 pop. (1961); 105,963 sq. mi. *Cap.*: Hyderabad.

andiron (ănd′ī′ən), *n.* one of a pair of metallic stands used to support wood in an open fire: a firedog. [ME *andyre*, t. OF: m. *andier*, ? t. Gallic: m. **andera* young cow (through use of cows' heads as decorations on andirons); *-iron* by assoc. with *iron*]

Andizhan (*Russ.* ən dĭ zhän′), *n.* a town in the SW Soviet Union in Asia, in Uzbekistan. 150,000 (est. 1963).

and/or, and *or* or: *history and/or art* (meaning 'history and art' or 'history or art').

Andorra (ăn dô′rə; *Sp.* än dô′rä), *n.* a small republic in the E Pyrenees between France and Spain, under the joint suzerainty of France and the Spanish Bishop of Urgel. 5000 pop. (est. 1964). 191 sq. mi. *Cap.*: Andorra. French, **Andorre** (*Fr.* äN-dŏr′).

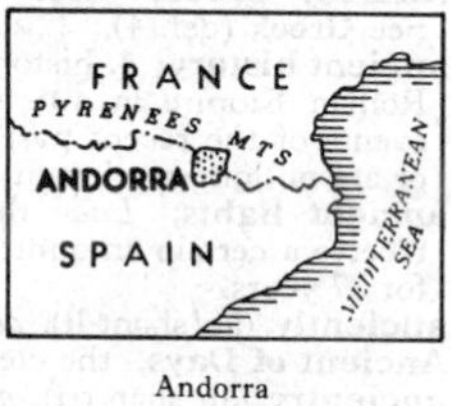

Andorra

Andover (ăn′dō′və), *n.* a town in England, in NW Hampshire. 16,985 (1961).

andr-, var. of **andro-,** used before vowels, as in *androecium.*

andradite (ăn′drə dīt′), *n.* a mineral, calcium-iron garnet, $Ca_3Fe_2Si_3O_{12}$, occurring in brown, green, or black crystals. [named after José Bonifacio d'*Andrada* e Silva, 1763–1838, Brazilian mineralogist; see -ITE[1]]

andrase (ăn′drās, -drāz), *n. Zool.* an androgenic enzyme or hormone.

Andrássy (ăn drăs′ĭ; *Hung.* ŏn′drä shē), *n.* **1. Count Julius,** 1823–90, Hungarian statesman. **2.** his son, **Count Julius** (*Gyula*), 1860–1929, Hungarian statesman.

Andrea del Sarto (ăn′drĭ ə dĕl sä′tō). See **Sarto.**

Andreanof Islands (ăn′drĭ ä′nŏf), a group of islands in the W part of the Aleutian Islands. 1432 sq. mi.

Andrew (ăn′dro͞o), *n. Bible.* one of the twelve apostles of Jesus. Mark 3:18; John 1:40–42.

Andrewes (ăn′dro͞oz), *n.* **Lancelot,** 1555–1626, English bishop and theologian.

Andreyev (*Russ.* än dryĕ′yŭf), *n.* **Leonid Nikolayevich** (*Russ.* lĭ ä nĕt′nĭ kä lä′yĭ vĭch), 1871–1919, Russian writer and dramatist.

Andria (*It.* än′dryä), *n.* a town in Italy, in N Apulia. 75,168 (1966).

Andrić (*Serb.* än′drēch), *n.* **Ivo** (*Serb.* ē′vô), born 1892, Yugoslav novelist.

andro-, *Biol.* a word element meaning 'man', 'male', as contrasted with 'female', as in *androsphinx.* Also, **andr-.** [t. Gk, comb. form of *anḗr* man, male]

Androcles (ăn′drə klēz′), *n. Rom. Legend.* a slave spared in the arena by a lion from whose foot he had years before extracted a thorn. Also, **Androclus** (ăn′drə kləs).

androclinium (ăn′drə klĭn′ĭ əm), *n. Bot.* clinandrium.

androecium (ăn drē′sĭ əm), *n.*, *pl.* **-cia** (-sĭ ə). *Bot.* the stamens of a flower collectively. [t. NL, f. Gk: *andr-* ANDR- + m. *oikíon* house] —**androe′cial,** *adj.*

androgen (ăn′drə jən), *n. Biochem.* any substance, natural or synthetic, which promotes masculine characteristics. —**androgenic** (ăn′drə jĕn′ĭk), *adj.*

androgynous (ăn drŏj′ĭ nəs), *adj.* **1.** *Bot.* having staminate and pistillate flowers in the same inflorescence. **2.** being both male and female; hermaphroditic. [t. L: m. *androgynus*, t. Gk: m. *andrógynos* hermaphrodite] —**androg′yny,** *n.*

Andromache (ăn drŏm′ə kĭ), *n. Gk Legend.* the wife of Hector and mother of Astyanax.

Andromeda (ăn drŏm′ĭ də), *n.* **1.** *Gk Myth.* the daughter of Cassiopeia and wife of Perseus, by whom she was rescued from a sea-monster. **2.** *Astron.* a northern constellation containing within its borders the external stellar system known as the Great Nebula in Andromeda.

androsphinx (ăn′drə sfĭngks′), *n.* a sphinx with the head of a man.

androsterone (ăn drŏs′tə rōn′), *n. Biochem.* an androgenic sex hormone, $C_{19}H_{30}O_2$, usually present in male urine.

-androus, a word element meaning 'male', as in *polyandrous.* [t. NL: m. *-andrus*, t. Gk: m. *-andros* of a man]

Andvari (ăn′dwä rĭ), *n. Scand. Myth.* a dwarf who owned a great treasure (the hoard of the Nibelungs). It was taken from him by Loki.

ane (ān), *adj.*, *n.*, *pron. Scot. and N Dial.* one.

-ane, **1.** a noun suffix used in chemical terms, esp. names of hydrocarbons of the methane or paraffin series, as *decane, pentane, propane.* **2.** an adjective suffix used when a similar form (with a different meaning) exists in **-an,** as *human, humane.* [t. L: m. *-ānus*, adj. suffix]

anear (ə nĭə′), *adv.*, *prep. Poetic.* near.

anecdotage[1] (ăn′ĭk dō′tĭj), *n.* anecdotes collectively. [f. ANECDOT(E) + -AGE]

anecdotage[2] (ăn′ĭk dō′tĭj), *n. Humorous.* a state of old age in which a person is given to excessive reminiscence. [b. ANECDOTE + DOTAGE]

anecdotal (ăn′ĭk dō′tl), *adj.* pertaining to, marked by, or consisting of anecdotes.

anecdote (ăn′ĭk dōt′), *n.* a short narrative of a particular incident or occurrence of an interesting nature. [t. ML: m. s. *anecdota*, t. Gk: m. *anékdota* things unpublished]

anecdotic (ăn′ĭk dŏt′ĭk), *adj.* **1.** anecdotal. **2.** given to relating anecdotes. Also, **an′ecdot′ical.**

anecdotist (ăn′ĭk dō′tĭst), *n.* a relater of anecdotes.

anechoic (ăn′ĭ kō′ĭk), *adj.* having a low degree of reverberation, esp. of a recording studio, etc.

anele (ə nēl′), *v.t.*, **aneled, aneling.** *Archaic.* to administer extreme unction to. [ME *anelien*, f. *an-* on + *elien* to oil, der. OE *ele* oil, t. L: m. *oleum*]

anemia (ə nē′mĭ ə), *n. Chiefly U.S.* anaemia. —**ane′mic,** *adj.*

anemo-, a word element meaning 'wind', as in *anemometer.* [t. Gk, comb. form of *ánemos* wind]

anemogram (ə nĕm′ə grăm′), *n.* an anemographic record.

anemograph (ə nĕm′ə grăf′, -gräf′), *n. Meteorol.* an instrument for measuring and recording the velocity, force, or direction of the wind. —**anemographic** (ə-nĕm′ə grăf′ĭk), *adj.* —**anemography** (ăn′ĭ mŏg′rə fĭ), *n.*

anemology (ăn′ĭ mŏl′ə jĭ), *n.* the science of winds.

anemometer (ăn′ĭ mŏm′ĭ tə), *n.* **1.** *Meteorol.* an instrument for indicating wind velocity. **2.** any instrument for measuring the rate of flow of a fluid. —**anemometric** (ăn′ĭ mō mĕt′rĭk), **an′emomet′rical,** *adj.* —**an′emom′etry,** *n.*

anemone (ə nĕm′ə nĭ), *n.* **1.** any plant of the ranunculaceous genus *Anemone*, esp. the **wood anemone** or windflower, *A. nemorosa*, a rhizomatous perennial producing abundant white flowers in early spring. **2.** sea-anemone. [t. L, t. Gk: windflower]

anemophilous (ăn′ĭ mŏf′ĭ ləs), *adj. Bot.* (of seed plants) fertilized by windborne pollen. [f. ANEMO- + -PHILOUS; lit., wind-loving] —**an′emoph′ily,** *n.*

anemoscope (ə nĕm′ə skōp′), n. *Meteorol.* any device showing the existence and direction of the wind.

anenst (ə nĕnst′), *prep. Archaic and Dial.* anent. [earlier *anent(i)st*, var. (with excrescent *-t*) of ME *anentes*, gen. of ANENT]

anent (ə nĕnt′), *prep.* **1.** *Archaic and Scot.* in regard to; concerning. **2.** *Archaic and Dial.* opposite to; over against; close to. [var. (with excrescent *-t*) of ME *anen*, OE *on emn, on efen* on even (ground), with, beside]

anergy (ăn′ə jĭ), *n.* **1.** *Pathol.* deficiency of energy.

2. *Med.* lack of immunity to an antigen. [t. NL: m. s. *anergia*, f. Gk: *an-* AN-[1] + *-ergia* work]

aneroid (ăn′ə roid′), *adj.* **1.** using no fluid. **—*n.* 2.** an aneroid barometer. [f. A-[6] + s. Gk *nērós* liquid + -OID]

aneroid barometer, an instrument for measuring atmospheric pressure and, indirectly, altitude, by registering the pressure exerted on the elastic top of a box or chamber exhausted of air.

anesthesia (ăn′ĭs thē′zyə), *n. Chiefly U.S.* anaesthesia. **—anesthetic** (ăn′ĭs thĕt′ĭk), *adj., n.* **—anesthetist** (ə-nēs′thə tĭst), *n.*

anesthesiology (ăn′ĭs thē′zĭ ŏl′ə jĭ), *n. U.S.* anaesthesia (def. 3). **—an′esthe′siol′ogist,** *n.*

anesthetize (ə nēs′thə tīz′), *v.t.,* **-tized, -tizing.** *Chiefly U.S.* anaesthetize. **—anes′thetiza′tion,** *n.*

anethole (ăn′ĭ thōl′), *n. Chem.* a compound, $C_{10}H_{12}O$, found in anise and fennel oils, and used in perfumes and as an antiseptic and carminative, etc. [f. s. Gk *ánēthon* anise (prop., dill) + -OLE]

Aneto (*Sp.* ä nĕ′tô), *n.* Spanish name of **Néthou, Pic de.**

aneuploid (ăn′yo͞o ploid′), *adj. Bot.* not having an integral multiple of the haploid set of chromosomes and therefore genetically unbalanced.

aneurin (ə nyo͝oə′rĭn), *n. Chem.* vitamin B_1. See **thiamine.**

aneurysm (ăn′yo͝oə rĭz′əm), *n. Pathol.* a permanent cardiac or arterial dilatation usually caused by weakening of the vessel wall by diseases such as syphilis or arteriosclerosis. Also, **aneurism.** [t. Gk: m. *aneúrysma* dilatation] **—an′eurys′mal, an′euris′mal,** *adj.*

anew (ə nyo͞o′), *adv.* **1.** over again; once more: *to write a story anew.* **2.** in a new form or manner. [ME *onew,* etc., OE *of-niowe,* r. OE *edniwe* once more]

anfractuosity (ăn′frăk tyo͞o ŏs′ĭ tĭ), *n., pl.* **-ties. 1.** the state or quality of being anfractuous. **2.** a channel, crevice, or passage full of windings and turnings.

anfractuous (ăn frăk′tyo͞o əs), *adj.* characterized by windings and turnings; sinuous; circuitous: *an anfractuous path.* Also, **anfractuose** (ăn frăk′tyo͞o ōs′). [t. L: m. s. *anfractuōsus* winding]

Angara (*Russ.* ən gä rä′), *n.* a river in the S Soviet Union in Asia, rising NE of Lake Baikal and flowing through it NW to the Yenisei river; called the Upper Tunguska in its lower course. ab. 1300 mi.

angary (ăng′gə rĭ), *n. Internat. Law.* the right of a belligerent state to seize and use the property of neutrals for purposes of warfare, subject to payment of full compensation. [t. L: m. s. *angaria* forced service (to a lord), t. Gk: m. *angareía* post service]

angel (ān′jəl), *n.* **1.** *Theol.* one of a class of spiritual beings, attendants of God (in medieval angelology divided, according to their rank, into nine orders, ranging from highest to lowest as follows: seraphim, cherubim, thrones, dominations or dominions, virtues, powers, principalities or princedoms, archangels, angels). **2.** a conventional representation of such a being, in human form, with wings. **3.** a messenger, esp. of God. **4.** a person, esp. a woman, who resembles an angel in beauty, kindliness, etc. **5.** an attendant or guardian spirit. **6.** *Colloq.* a financial backer of a play, campaign, actor, candidate, etc. **7.** an English gold coin, struck between 1470 and 1634, in value from 6*s.* 8*d.* to 10*s.*, bearing a figure of the archangel Michael overcoming the dragon. [ME and OE, var. of *engel,* pre-E **angil,* t. L: m. s. *angelus,* t. Gk: m. *ángelos,* orig., messenger] **—an′-gelhood′,** *n.*

angel cake, a delicate white cake made without fat.

angelfish (ān′jəl fĭsh′), *n., pl.* **-fishes,** (*esp. collectively*) **-fish. 1.** any shark of the genus *Squatina* of Atlantic and Pacific waters, with a depressed flat body and large, winglike pectoral fins. **2.** any of the South American freshwater ciclids of the genus *Pterophyllum,* commonly kept in aquariums. **3.** a butterfly fish, *Holacanthus nicobariensis,* of the Indian Ocean, having blue and black stripes. **4.** *U.S.* any of several brightly coloured marine fishes of the coasts of North America, as *Chaetodipterus faber* and *Angelichthys ciliaris.*

angelic (ăn jĕl′ĭk), *adj.* **1.** of or belonging to angels. **2.** like an angel; saintly. Also, **angel′ical. —angel′-ically,** *adv.*

angelica (ăn jĕl′ĭ kə), *n.* **1.** any plant of the genus *Angelica,* tall umbelliferous plants found in both hemispheres, esp. *A. orchangelica* (*Archangelica officinalis*), cultivated in Europe for its aromatic smell and medicinal root and for its stalks, which are preserved as a cake decoration, etc.; archangel. **2.** the preserved stalks. [t. ML: angelic (herb)]

Angelico (ăn jĕl′ĭ kō′), *n.* **Fra** (frä) (*Giovanni da Fiesolé*), 1387–1455, Italian painter.

Angell (ān′jəl), *n.* **Sir Norman** (*Ralph Norman Angell Lane*), 1874–1967, English writer.

angelo-, a combining form of **angel.**

angelolatry (ān′jĭ lŏl′ə trĭ), *n.* angel-worship.

angelology (ān′jĭ lŏl′ə jĭ), *n.* doctrine concerning angels.

angelshark (ān′jəl shäk′), *n.* angelfish (def. 1).

angels-on-horseback (ān′jəlz ŏn hôs′băk′), *n.* a rich savoury dish of oysters and bacon on toast.

angelus (ăn′jĭ ləs), *n. Rom. Cath. Ch.* **1.** (*often cap.*) a devotion in memory of the Annunciation. **2.** the bell (**angelus bell**) tolled in the morning, at noon, and in the evening, to indicate the time when the angelus is to be recited. [t. LL (the first word of the recitation). See ANGEL]

Angelus Silesius (*Ger.* ȧng′gė lo͞os zĭ lė′zĭ o͞os), *n.* (*Johannes Scheffler*), 1624–77, German poet.

angel-water (ān′jəl wô′tə), *n.* a scented water originally made with angelica but later with various other substances, as ambergris or rosewater.

anger (ăng′gə), *n.* **1.** a strongly felt displeasure aroused by real or supposed wrongs, often accompanied by an impulse to retaliate; wrath; ire. **2.** *Obs. or Dial.* pain or smart, as of a sore. **3.** *Obs.* grief; trouble. **—*v.t.* 4.** to excite to anger or wrath. **5.** *Obs. or Dial.* to cause to smart; inflame. [ME, t. Scand.; cf. Icel. *angr* grief, sorrow]

—Syn. 1. displeasure; resentment, exasperation. ANGER, FURY, INDIGNATION, RAGE imply deep and strong feelings aroused by injury, injustice, wrong, etc. ANGER is a sudden violent emotion often associated with revengeful feelings: *a burst of anger.* INDIGNATION, a more formal word, implies a deep and justified anger, often directed against something unworthy: *indignation at cruelty or against corruption.* RAGE is vehement anger: *rage at being frustrated.* FURY is rage so great that it resembles insanity: *the fury of a woman scorned.*

angerly (ăng′gə lĭ), *adv. Archaic.* angrily.

Angers (*Fr.* äN zhĕ′), *n.* a city in W France, capital of Maine-et-Loire department. 115,252 (1962).

Angevin (ăn′jĭ vĭn), *adj.* **1.** of or from Anjou. **2.** relating to the counts of Anjou or their descendants, esp. those who ruled in England, or to the period when they ruled. **—*n.* 3.** an inhabitant of Anjou. **4.** a member of an Angevin royal house, esp. that of the Plantagenets. [t. F]

angina (ăn jī′nə), *n. Pathol.* **1.** any inflammatory affection of the throat or fauces, as quinsy, croup, mumps, etc. **2.** angina pectoris. [t. L: quinsy, lit., strangling. Cf. Gk *anchónē*] **—angi′nal,** *adj.*

angina pectoris (pĕk′tə rĭs), *Pathol.* a syndrome characterized by paroxysmal, constricting pain below the sternum, most easily precipitated by exertion or excitement and caused by ischaemia of the heart muscle, usually due to a coronary artery disease, such as arteriosclerosis. [NL: angina of the chest]

angio-, a word element meaning 'vessel', or 'container', as in *angiology.* [t. NL, t. Gk: m. *angeio-,* comb. form of *angeîon* vessel]

angiology (ăn′jĭ ŏl′ə jĭ), *n.* the part of the science of anatomy that deals with blood vessels and lymphatics.

angioma (ăn′jĭ ō′mə), *n., pl.* **-mas, -mata** (-mə tə). a tumour consisting chiefly of dilated or newly formed blood or lymph vessels. [f. ANGI(O)- + -OMA] **—angiomatous** (ăn′jĭ ŏm′ə təs, -ō′mə-), *adj.*

angiosperm (ăn′jĭ ə spûm′), *n.* a plant having its seeds enclosed in an ovary (opposed to *gymnosperm*). **—an′-giosper′mous,** *adj.*

Angkor (ăng′kô), *n.* a ruined city in NW Cambodia: the site of **Angkor Wat** (wŏt), an ancient Khmer temple.

angle[1] (ăng′gl), *n., v.,* **-gled, -gling. —*n.* 1.** *Geom.* **a.** the space within two lines or three planes diverging from a common point, or within two planes diverging from a common line. **b.** the figure so formed. **c.** the amount of rotation needed to bring one line or plane into coincidence with another. **2.** an angular projection; a projecting corner: *the angles of a building.* **3.** an angular recess; a nook, corner. **4.** a point of view; standpoint: *a new angle on the problem.* **5.** an aspect, side; phase: *to consider all angles of the question.* **6.** *Engineering.* angle iron. **7. at an angle,** slanting; not perpendicular (to). **—*v.t.* 8.** to move, direct, bend or present at an angle or in an angular course. **9.** to put a slant or bias on (a question, statement, etc.). **10.** to put into a corner; corner. **—*v.i.* 11.** to move or bend in angles. [ME, t. F, g. L *angulus*]

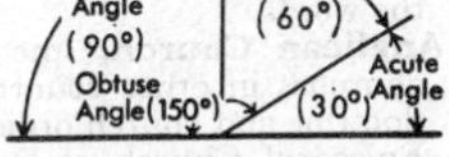

Right Angle (90°) · Acute Angle (60°) · Obtuse Angle (150°) · Acute Angle (30°)

Angles

angle[2] (ăng′gl), *v.,* **-gled, -gling,** *n.* **—*v.i.* 1.** to fish with hook and line. **2.** to try by artful means to get: *to angle for a compliment.* **—*n.* 3.** *Archaic.* a fishhook or fishing tackle. [OE *angel, angul;* akin to ANGLE[1]]

Angle (ăng′gl), *n.* one of a West Germanic people that migrated from Schleswig to Britain in the 5th century A.D. and founded the kingdoms of East Anglia, Mercia, and Northumbria. As early as the 6th century their name was extended to all the Germanic inhabitants of Britain. [OE *Angle*, orig. the inhabitants of *Angel*, a district of what is now Schleswig, said to be named from its hooklike shape]

angle bracket, an L-shaped metal bracket used to support a shelf, etc.

angled (ăng′gld), *adj.* having an angle or angles.

angle iron, 1. a bar of iron in the form of an angle. **2.** a rolled iron or steel bar with an L-shaped cross-section, used mainly in iron constructions. Also, **angle, angle section.**

angle of attack, *Chiefly U.S.* angle of incidence (def. 2).

angle of incidence, 1. the angle that a line, ray of light, etc., meeting a surface, makes with the perpendicular to that surface at the point of meeting. **2.** the acute angle between the chord line of an aircraft wing or other aerofoil and its direction of motion relative to the air. **3. rigging angle of incidence,** the fixed angle between the chord line of the wing or tail-plane and the axis of the fuselage.

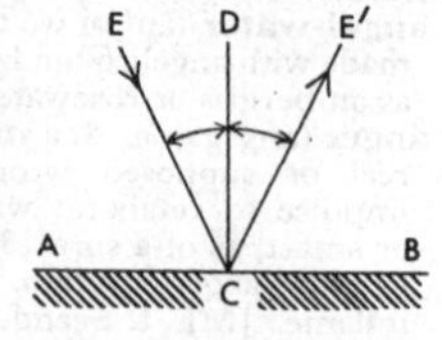

ECD, Angle of incidence on surface AB; CD, Perpendicular; E′CD, Angle of reflection

angle of reflection, the angle that a ray of light, or the like, reflected from a surface, makes with a perpendicular to that surface at the point of reflection.

angle of refraction, the angle that a refracted ray of light makes with the perpendicular to the interfacial surface at the point of refraction.

angler (ăng′glə), *n.* **1.** one who angles; one who fishes for pleasure. **2.** a fish, *Lophius piscatorius* of the coasts of Europe or *L. americanus* of America, which attracts small fish by the movement of a wormlike filament attached to its head just above the mouth; the devilfish. **3.** any of various related fishes, with a modified free dorsal spine above the mouth, constituting the order *Pediculati.*

Anglesey (ăng′gl sĭ), *n.* an island and county in NW Wales. 51,700 pop. (1961); 276 sq. mi. *Co. town:* Holyhead.

anglesite (ăng′gl sīt′), *n.* a mineral, lead sulphate, $PbSO_4$, found in massive forms or in colourless or variously tinted crystals: a common lead ore. [named after ANGLESEY. See -ITE[1]]

angleworm (ăng′gl wûm′), *n.* an earthworm used for bait in angling.

Anglia (ăng′glĭ ə), *n.* Latin name of **England.**

Anglian (ăng′glĭ ən), *adj.* **1.** of or relating to the Angles or to East Anglia. *—n.* **2.** an Angle. **3.** the northern and eastern group of Old English dialects.

Anglic (ăng′glĭk), *adj. Rare.* Anglian.

Anglican (ăng′glĭ kən), *adj.* **1.** of or pertaining to the Church of England. **2.** related in origin to and in communion with the Church of England, as various episcopal churches in other parts of the world. **3.** *Chiefly U.S.* English. *—n.* **4.** a member of the Church of England or of a church in communion with it. **5.** one who upholds the system or teachings of the Church of England. **6.** one who emphasizes the authority of that church; a High-Churchman. [t. ML: s. *Anglicānus*]

Anglican Chant, *Music.* the type of harmonized melody in common use for psalms in Church of England services, the rhythm being altered in each verse to accommodate the words.

Anglican Church, the Church of England and the churches in other countries in full accord with it as to doctrine and church order, as the Church of Ireland, the Episcopal Church of Scotland, the Church of Wales, the Protestant Episcopal Church in the U.S., etc.

Anglicanism (ăng′glĭ kə nĭz′əm), *n.* Anglican principles; the Anglican Church system.

Anglice (ăng′glĭ sĭ), *adv.* in English; as the English would say it; according to the English way, as *Córdoba, Anglice Cordova.* [t. ML, der. *Anglicus* English]

Anglicism (ăng′glĭ sĭz′əm), *n.* an English idiom.

Anglicist (ăng′glĭ sĭst), *n.* an authority on English language and literature. [f. s. L *Anglicus* English + -IST]

anglicize (ăng′glĭ sīz′), *v.t., v.i.,* **-cized, -cizing.** (*sometimes cap.*) to make or become English in form or character: *to anglicize the pronunciation of a Russian name.* Also, **anglicise.** —**an′gliciza′tion,** *n.*

Anglify (ăng′glĭ fī′), *v.t., v.i.,* **-fied, -fying.** to anglicize.

angling (ăng′glĭng), *n.* the act or art of fishing with a hook and line, usually attached to a rod.

Anglist (ăng′glĭst), *n.* an authority on England. [t. G]

Anglo-, a word element meaning 'pertaining to England or the English', as in *Anglo-American.* [comb. form repr. ML *Anglus* Englishman, *Anglī* (pl.) the English]

Anglo-American (ăng′glō ə mĕ′rĭ kən), *adj.* **1.** belonging or relating to, or connected with, England and America, esp. the United States, or with the people of both: *Anglo-American commerce.* **2.** pertaining to the English who have settled in America, esp. in the United States, or have become American citizens. *—n.* **3.** a native or descendant of a native of England who has settled in America, esp. in the United States, or has become an American citizen.

Anglo-Catholic (ăng′glō kăth′ə lĭk), *n.* **1.** one who emphasizes the Catholic character of the Anglican Church. **2.** an Anglican Catholic, as opposed to a Roman or Greek Catholic. *—adj.* **3.** of or pertaining to Anglo-Catholicism or Anglo-Catholics. —**Anglo-Catholicism** (ăng′glō kə-thŏl′ĭ sĭz′əm), *n.*

Anglo-French (ăng′glō frĕnch′), *adj.* **1.** English and French. **2.** pertaining to Anglo-French (def. 3). *—n.* **3.** that dialect of French current in England from the Norman Conquest to the end of the Middle Ages.

Anglo-Indian (ăng′glō ĭn′dyən), *n.* **1.** a person of mixed English and Indian parentage; a Eurasian. **2.** a person of British birth who has lived long in India. *—adj.* **3.** Eurasian. **4.** of, pertaining to, or relating to England and India as politically associated. **5.** of the English language as spoken in India.

Anglo-Irish (ăng′glō ī′rə rĭsh), *adj.* **1.** English and Irish. **2.** pertaining to the English who have settled in Ireland. *—n.* **3.** the people of English birth or descent living in Ireland.

Anglomania (ăng′glō mā′nyə), *n.* an excessive attachment to, respect for, or imitation of English institutions, manners, customs, etc. —**An′gloma′niac′,** *n.*

Anglo-Norman (ăng′glō nô′mən), *adj.* **1.** pertaining to that period, 1066–1154, when England was ruled by Normans. **2.** pertaining to the Normans who settled in England, or their descendants, or their dialect of French. *—n.* **3.** a Norman who settled in England after 1066, or one of his descendants. **4.** Anglo-French.

Anglophil (ăng′glō fĭl), *n.* one who is friendly to or admires England or English customs, institutions, etc. Also, **Anglophile** (ăng′glō fīl′).

Anglophobe (ăng′glō fōb′), *n.* one who hates or fears England or the English.

Anglophobia (ăng′glō fō′byə), *n.* an intense hatred or fear of England, or of whatever is English.

Anglo-Saxon (ăng′glō săk′sən), *n.* **1.** one who belongs to the English-speaking world, irrespective of historical periods, political boundaries, geographical areas, or racial origins (the only medieval sense). **2.** an Englishman of the period before the Norman conquest. **3.** a person of English stock and traditions; in the U.S., usually a person of colonial descent and/or British origin. **4.** Old English (def. 1). **5.** the English language. **6.** plain English. **7.** pre-English (def. 1). *—adj.* **8.** of, pertaining to, or characteristic of the Anglo-Saxons. **9.** pertaining to Anglo-Saxon. [t. ML: s. *Anglo-Saxonēs* the English people; r. OE *Angulseaxan*, t. ML: m. *Anglī Saxonēs*, Latinizations of the OE folk names *Angle* and *Seaxan*]

Angola (ăng gō′lə), *n.* an overseas territory of Portugal in SW Africa. 4,832,677 pop. (1960); 481,226 sq. mi. *Cap.:* Luanda. Also, **Portuguese West Africa.**

Angora (ăng gô′rə *for 1, 2, and 3*; ăng gô′rə, ăng′gə rə *for 4*), *n.* **1.** an Angora rabbit. **2.** an Angora cat. **3.** (*sometimes l.c.*) **a.** the hair of the Angora goat or rabbit. **b.** a yarn or fabric made from this. **4.** Ankara.

Angora cat, a long-haired variety of the domestic cat, orig. from Angora.

Angora goat, a variety of goat, orig. from Angora, reared for its long, silky hair which is called mohair.

Angora rabbit, a long-haired variety of domestic rabbit.

Angostura (*Sp.* än gôs tōō′rä), *n.* former name of **Ciudad Bolívar.**

angostura bark (ăng′gəs tyŏŏə′rə), *n.* the bitter aromatic bark of a South American rutaceous tree of the genus *Cusparia* (or *Galipea*), supposed to be valuable as a tonic. Also, **angostura.** [named after ANGOSTURA]

angostura bitters, 1. a bitter aromatic tonic prepared in Trinidad from barks, roots, herbs, etc., under a secret formula. **2.** (*caps.*) a trademark for this tonic.

Angoulême (*Fr.* äN gōō lĕm′), *n.* a town in France, capital of Charente department. 51,223 (1962).

Angra do Heroismo (*Port.* ən′grə dōō ē rōō ēzh′mōō), a seaport in the Azores, on Terceira island: former capital of the Azores. 96,174 (1960).

angry (ăng′grĭ), *adj.,* **-grier, -griest. 1.** feeling or showing anger or resentment (*with* or *at* a person, *at* or *about* a thing). **2.** characterized by anger; wrathful: *angry words.* **3.** *Med.* inflamed, as a sore; exhibiting inflammation.

4. *Colloq.* expressing the attitude of an angry young man. [ME; f. ANGER + -Y[1]] **—an′grily,** *adv.* **—an′griness,** *n.* **—Syn. 1.** irate, incensed, enraged.

angry young man, 1. a young man, esp. a writer, outspokenly disgusted with the existing social order. 2. (*also caps.*) one of a group of young English writers of the 1950s, esp. those thought to share attitudes expressed by the protagonist of John Osborne's play *Look Back in Anger.*

Angst (*Ger.* ȧngst). *n., pl.* **Ängste** (*Ger.* ĕng′stə), *German.* a feeling or outlook of dread, fear, etc.

angstrom unit (ăng′strŭm, -strəm), a unit of length for measuring very short wavelengths and distances between atoms in molecules, equal to 10^{-10} metres. Symbols: Å, A, Å.U. or A.U. Also, **angstrom, Ångström.** [named after A. J. *Ångström,* 1814–74, Swedish physicist]

anguilliform (ăng gwĭl′ĭ fôm′), *adj.* having the shape or form of an eel. [f. s. L *anguilla* eel + -(I)FORM]

anguine (ăng′gwĭn), *adj.* pertaining to or resembling a snake. [t. L: m. s. *anguīnus*]

anguish (ăng′gwĭsh), *n.* **1.** excruciating or agonizing pain of either body or mind; acute suffering or distress: *the anguish of grief.* **—***v.t., v.i.* **2.** to affect with or suffer anguish. [ME, t. OF: m. *anguisse, angoisse,* g. L *angustia* straitness, pl. straits, distress] **—Syn. 1.** agony, torment, torture. See **pain. —Ant. 1.** delight.

angular (ăng′gyŏŏ lə), *adj.* **1.** having an angle or angles. **2.** consisting of, situated at, or forming an angle. **3.** of, pertaining to, or measured by an angle. **4.** bony; gaunt. **5.** acting or moving awkwardly. **6.** stiff in manner; unbending. [t. L: s. *angulāris*] **—an′gulary,** *adv.* **—an′gularness,** *n.* **—Ant. 1.** round. **4.** rotund.

angular acceleration, *Maths.* rate of change of angular velocity.

angular diameter, *Astron.* the angle which the apparent diameter of a celestial body subtends at the observer's eye.

angular distance, *Astron.* the distance between two bodies in terms of the angle subtended by them at the point of observation.

angular frequency, the frequency of a periodic phenomenon expressed in radians per second, which is equal to 2π multiplied by the frequency in cycles per second.

angularity (ăng′gyŏŏ lă′rĭ tĭ), *n., pl.* **-ties. 1.** angular quality. **2.** (*pl.*) sharp corners; angular outlines.

angular leaf spot, a disease of plants, characterized by angular, watery spots on the leaves and fruit, caused by any of several bacteria, as *Pseudomanas lachrymans.*

angular momentum, *Physics.* the product of the angular velocity of a rotating body and its moment of inertia with respect to the same axis.

angular velocity, *Maths.* velocity measured in terms of a rate of motion through an angle about an axis.

angulated (ăng′gyŏŏ lā′tĭd), *adj.* of angular form; angled: *angulated stems.* Also, **angulate** (ăng′gyŏŏ lĭt, -lāt′). [t. L: m. s. *angulātus,* pp., made angular]

angulation (ăng′gyŏŏ lā′shən), *n.* angular formation.

Angus (ăng′gəs), *n.* a county in E Scotland. 280,156 pop. (est. 1964); 873 sq. mi. *Co. town:* Forfar.

angwantibo (ăng gwăn′tĭ bō′), *n.* a small golden-coloured primate of the loris family, *Arctocelus calabarensis,* of W Africa.

Anhalt (*Ger.* ȧn′hȧlt), *n.* a former state in central Germany.

anhinga (ăn hĭng′gə), *n.* snakebird.

Anhwei (ăn′wā′), *n.* a province in eastern China. 33,560,000 pop. (est. 1957); 56,371 sq. mi. *Cap.:* Hofei. Also, **Nganhwei.**

anhydride (ăn hī′drīd, -drĭd), *n. Chem.* **1.** a compound formed by abstraction of water, an oxide of a non-metal (**acid anhydride**) or a metal (**basic anhydride**) which forms an acid or a base, respectively, when united with water. **2.** a compound from which water has been abstracted. [f. s. Gk *ánydros* without water (with etymological *h* inserted) + -IDE]

anhydrite (ăn hī′drīt), *n.* a mineral anhydrous calcium sulphate, $CaSO_4$, usually in whitish or slightly coloured masses.

anhydrous (ăn hī′drəs), *adj. Chem.* indicating loss of all water, esp. water of crystallization. [t. Gk: m. *ánydros* without water (with *h* from *hydrous*)]

ani (ä′nĭ), *n., pl.* **anis.** either of two black cuckoo-like birds of the genus *Crotophaga,* inhabiting the warmer parts of America. [t. Sp. or Pg., t. Tupi]

anil (ăn′ĭl), *n.* **1.** a fabaceous shrub, *Indigofera suffruticosa,* one of the plants which yield indigo, native to the West Indies. **2.** indigo; deep blue. [t. F, t. Pg., t. Ar.: m. *al -nīl,* f. *al* the + *nīl* (t. Skt: m. *nīlī* indigo)]

anile (ăn′ĭl, ā′nīl), *adj.* of or like a weak old woman: *anile ideas.* [t. L: m. s. *anīlis,* der. *anus* old woman]

aniline (ăn′ĭ lĭn, -lēn′), *n.* **1.** an oily liquid, $C_6H_5NH_2$, obtained first from indigo but now prepared from benzene, and serving as the basis of many brilliant dyes, and in the manufacture of plastics, resins, etc. **—***adj.* **2.** pertaining to or derived from aniline: *aniline colours.* [f. ANIL + -INE[2]]

aniline dye, any organic dye made from a coal-tar base (because the earliest ones were made from aniline).

anility (ə nĭl′ĭ tĭ), *n., pl.* **-ties. 1.** an anile state. **2.** an anile notion or procedure.

anima (ăn′ĭ mə), *n.* **1.** soul; life. **2.** (in the psychology of C. G. Jung) **a.** the inner personality that is turned towards the unconscious of the individual (contrasted with *persona*). **b.** the feminine principle, esp. as present in men (contrasted with *animus*). [L: breath, soul]

animadversion (ăn′ĭ măd vû′shən), *n.* **1.** a remark, usually implying censure; a criticism or comment. **2.** the act or fact of criticizing. [t. L: s. *animadversio*]

animadvert (ăn′ĭ măd vût′), *v.i.* **1.** to comment critically; make remarks by way of criticism or censure (fol. by *on* or *upon*). **2.** *Obs.* to take cognizance or notice. **—***v.t.* **3.** to consider. **4.** to remark. [t. L: s. *animadvertere* regard, notice]

animal (ăn′ĭ məl), *n.* **1.** any living thing that is not a plant, generally capable of voluntary motion, sensation, etc. **2.** any animal other than man. **3.** an inhuman person; brutish or beastlike person. **—***adj.* **4.** of, pertaining to, or derived from animals: *animal life, animal fats.* **5.** pertaining to the physical or carnal nature of man, rather than his spiritual or intellectual nature: *animal needs.* [t. L: living being]

—Syn. 1, 3. ANIMAL, BEAST, BRUTE refer to sentient creatures as distinct from minerals and plants; fig., they usually connote qualities and characteristics below the human level. ANIMAL is the general word; fig., it applies merely to the body or animal-like characteristics: *an athlete is a magnificent animal.* BEAST refers to four-footed animals; fig., it suggests a base, sensual nature: *a glutton is a beast.* BRUTE implies absence of ability to reason; fig., it connotes savagery as well: *a drunken brute.*

animal black, any black pigment made from calcined bone or similar animal matter.

animalcule (ăn′ĭ măl′kyōōl), *n.* **1.** a minute or microscopic animal, nearly or quite invisible to the naked eye, as an infusorian or rotifer. **2.** *Rare.* a tiny animal, such as a mouse, fly, etc. [t. NL: m. s. *animalculum,* dim. of L *animal* animal] **—an′imal′cular,** *adj.*

animalculum (ăn′ĭ măl′kyŏŏ ləm), *n., pl.* **-la** (-lə). animalcule.

animal husbandry, the science of breeding, feeding, and care of animals, esp. on a farm.

animalism (ăn′ĭ mə lĭz′əm), *n.* **1.** an animal state; state of being actuated by sensual appetites, and not by intellectual or moral forces; sensuality. **2.** the doctrine that human beings are without a spiritual nature.

animalist (ăn′ĭ mə lĭst), *n.* **1.** one who believes in the doctrine of animalism. **2.** a painter, sculptor, writer, etc., who portrays animals. **—an′imalis′tic,** *adj.*

animality (ăn′ĭ măl′ĭ tĭ), *n.* **1.** the animal nature in man. **2.** animal life.

animalize (ăn′ĭ mə līz′), *v.t.,* **-lized, -lizing.** to excite the animal passions of; brutalize; sensualize. Also, **animalise. —an′imaliza′tion,** *n.*

animal kingdom, the animals of the world collectively (distinguished from *vegetable kingdom*).

animally (ăn′ĭ mə lĭ), *adv.* physically.

animal magnetism, 1. attractive power or charm exerted by one's physical or animal nature, esp. by physical beauty, strength, etc. **2.** *Obs.* **a.** hypnotism. **b.** hypnotic powers.

animal spirits, exuberance of health and life; animation and good humour; buoyancy.

animal starch, glycogen.

animate (*v.* ăn′ĭ māt′; *adj.* ăn′ĭ mĭt), *v.,* **-mated, -mating,** *adj.* **—***v.t.* **1.** to give life to; make alive. **2.** to make lively, vivacious, or vigorous. **3.** to encourage: *to animate weary troops.* **4.** to move to action; actuate: *animated by religious zeal.* **5.** to cause to appear or move as if alive, as in an animated cartoon. **—***adj.* **6.** alive; possessing life: *animate creatures.* **7.** lively. [t. L: m. s. *animātus*] **—an′imat′er, an′imat′or,** *n.* **—an′imat′ingly,** *adv.*

—Syn. 1. vivify, quicken, vitalize. **2.** ANIMATE, INVIGORATE, STIMULATE mean to enliven. To ANIMATE is to create a liveliness: *health and energy animated his movements.* To INVIGORATE means to give physical vigour, to refresh, to exhilarate: *mountain air invigorates.* To STIMULATE is to arouse a latent liveliness on a particular occasion: *alcohol stimulates.*

animated (ăn′ĭ mā′tĭd), *adj.* **1.** full of life, action, or spirit; lively; vigorous: *an animated debate.* **2.** moving or made to move as if alive. **—an′imat′edly,** *adv.*

animated cartoon, a film consisting of a series of drawings, each slightly different from the ones before and after it, run through a projector.

animation (ăn′ĭ mā′shən), *n.* **1.** animated quality; liveliness; vivacity; spirit; life. **2.** the act of animating; act of enlivening. **3.** the process of preparing animated cartoons. **—Syn. 1.** vigour, energy; enthusiasm, ardour.

animatism (ăn′ĭ mə tĭz′əm), *n.* the attribution of consciousness to inanimate objects.

animato (ăn′ĭ mä′tō), *adj.*, *adv.* *Music.* animated; animatedly (often taken as indicating a quickening of tempo).

animé (ăn′ĭ mā′, -mĭ), *n.* any of various resins or copals, esp. that from *Hymenaea courbaril*, a tree of tropical America, used in making varnish, scenting pastilles, etc. [t. Sp., prob. t. native dialect]

animism (ăn′ĭ mĭz′əm), *n.* **1.** the belief that all natural objects and the universe itself possess a soul. **2.** the belief that natural objects have souls which may exist apart from their material bodies. **3.** the doctrine that the soul is the principle of life and health. **4.** belief in spiritual beings or agencies. [f. s. L *anima* soul + -ISM] **—an′imist,** *n.*, *adj.* **—an′imis′tic,** *adj.*

animosity (ăn′ĭ mŏs′ĭ tĭ), *n.*, *pl.* **-ities.** a feeling of ill will or enmity animating the conduct, or tending to display itself in action (fol. by *between* or *towards*). [late ME *animosite*, t. L: m. s. *animōsitas* courage]

animus (ăn′ĭ məs), *n.* **1.** hostile spirit; animosity. **2.** purpose; intention; animating spirit. **3.** (in the psychology of C. G. Jung) the masculine principle, esp. as present in women (contrasted with *anima*).

anion (ăn′ī′ən), *n.* *Phys. Chem.* **1.** a negatively charged ion which is attracted to the anode in electrolysis. **2.** any negatively charged atom, radical, or molecule. [t. Gk: going up (ppr. neut.)]

anise (ăn′ĭs), *n.* **1.** a herbaceous plant, *Pimpinella anisum*, of Mediterranean regions, yielding aniseed. **2.** aniseed. [ME *anys*, t. OF: m. *anis*, t. L: s. *anīsum*, t. Gk: m. *ánīson* dill, anise]

aniseed (ăn′ĭ sēd′), *n.* the aromatic seed of the anise, used in medicine, in cookery, etc.

anisette (ăn′ĭ zĕt′, -sĕt′), *n.* a cordial or liqueur flavoured with aniseed. [t. F]

aniso-, a word element meaning 'unlike' or 'unequal'. [comb. form repr. Gk *ánisos* unequal, f. *an-* AN-[1] + *ísos* equal]

anisocarpic (ăn ī′sō kär′pĭk, ăn′ī-), *adj.* *Bot.* (of a flower) having fewer carpels than other floral parts.

anisodactylous (ăn ī′sō dăk′tĭ ləs, ăn′ī-), *adj.* **1.** *Zool.* unequal-toed; having the toes unlike. **2.** *Ornith.* having three toes pointing forwards and one backwards.

anisole (ăn′ĭ sōl′), *n.* a colourless fluid, C_7H_8O, used in the perfume industry and for killing lice. [f. s. L *anīsum* ANISE + -OLE]

anisomerous (ăn′ĭ sŏm′ə rəs), *adj.* *Bot.* unsymmetrical (applied to flowers which do not have the same number of parts in each circle). **—an′isom′ery,** *n.*

anisometric (ăn ī′sō mĕt′rĭk, ăn′ī-), *adj.* **1.** not isometric; of unequal measurement. **2.** (of crystals) having three dimensionally unequal axial directions.

anisometropia (ăn ī′sō mə trō′pyə, ăn′ī-), *n.* *Pathol.* inequality in the power of the two eyes to refract light. [t. NL: f. *aniso-* ANISO- + s. Gk *métron* measure + *-opia* -OPIA]

anisotropic (ăn ī′sō trŏp′ĭk, ăn′ī-), *adj.* **1.** *Physics.* of different properties in different directions. **2.** *Bot.* of different dimensions along the different axes. **—anisotropy** (ăn′ī sŏt′rə pĭ), *n.*

Anjou (*Fr.* äN zho͞o′), *n.* a region and former province in W France, in the Loire valley.

Ankara (ăng′kə rə), *n.* the capital of Turkey, in the central part. 650,067 (1960). Also, **Angora.**

Ankara

ankerite (ăng′kə rīt′), *n.* a mineral related to dolomite but containing iron in place of part of the magnesium. [named after Prof. M. J. *Anker*, died 1843, Austrian mineralogist; see -ITE[1]]

ankh (ăngk), *n.* *Egypt. Art.* a tau cross with a loop at the top, used as a symbol of generation or enduring life. [t. Egypt.: life, soul]

ankle (ăng′kl), *n.* **1.** the aggregate joint connecting the foot with the leg. **2.** the slender part of the leg above the foot. [ME *ankel*, t. Scand. (cf. Dan. *ankel*); r. OE *anclēow(e)*]

anklebone (ăng′kl bōn′), *n.* the astragalus.

ankled (ăng′kld), *adj.* having ankles.

ankle-deep (ăng′kl dēp′), *adj.*, *adv.* high or deep enough to cover the ankles.

Ankh

ankle-sock (ăng′kl sŏk′), *n.* a sock which reaches just above the ankle.

anklet (ăng′klĭt), *n.* an ornament for the ankle, corresponding to a bracelet for the wrist or forearm. **2.** *U.S.* an ankle-sock.

Ankrah (ăng′krə), *n.* **Joseph Arthur,** born 1915, Ghanaian army officer and politician, head of government 1966–69.

ankus (ăng′kəs), *n.* an elephant goad. [t. Hind.]

ankylose (ăng′kĭ lōz′), *v.t.*, *v.i.*, **-losed, -losing.** to grow together and consolidate, as two otherwise freely approximating similar or dissimilar hard tissues, like the bones of a joint or the root of a tooth and its surrounding bone. Also, **anchylose.**

ankylosis (ăng′kĭ lō′sĭs), *n.* **1.** *Pathol.* morbid adhesion of the bones of a joint. **2.** *Anat.* consolidation or union of two similar or dissimilar hard tissues previously freely approximating, as the bones of a joint, or the root of a tooth and its surrounding bone. Also, **anchylosis.** [t. NL, t. Gk: stiffening of the joints] **—ankylotic** (ăng′kĭ lŏt′ĭk), *adj.*

ankylostomiasis (ăng′kĭ lŏs′tə mī′ə sĭs), *n.* hookworm disease. Also, **anchylostomiasis, ancylostomiasis.** [f. m. NL *Ancylostom(a)* genus of hookworms (f. Gk: *ankýlo(s)* bent, hooked + *stóma* mouth) + -IASIS]

anlace (ăn′lĭs), *n.* a medieval dagger or short sword, worn in front of the person. [ME, t. OF: m. *ale(s)naz*, der. *alesne* awl, t. Gmc: m. *alisna*]

anlage (ăn′lä′gə), *n.*, *pl.* **-gen** (-gən). *Embryol.* **1.** primordium. **2.** blastema. [G: set-up, layout]

ann., **1.** annual. **2.** annals. **3.** (L *anni*) years. **4.** annuity.

anna (ăn′ə), *n.* **1.** a former unit of currency in India, the sixteenth part of a rupee. **2.** a former coin of this value. [t. Hind.: m. *ānā*]

Annaba (ăn′ə bə; *Fr.* à nà bà′), *n.* a seaport in NE Algeria, E of Algiers. 164,000 (est. 1964). Formerly, **Bône.** See **Hippo Regius.**

annabergite (ăn′ə bû′gīt), *n.* a mineral, hydrous nickel arsenate, $Ni_3As_2O_8.8H_2O$, occurring in apple-green crystalline masses; nickel bloom. [named after *Annaberg*, town in Saxony. See -ITE[1]]

annal (ăn′əl), *n.* a register or record of the events of a year. See **annals.**

annalist (ăn′ə lĭst), *n.* a chronicler of yearly events. **—an′nalis′tic,** *adj.* **—an′nalis′tically,** *adv.*

annals (ăn′əlz), *n.pl.* **1.** history or relation of events recorded year by year. **2.** historical records generally. **3.** a periodical publication containing formal reports of learned societies, etc. [t. L: m. *annālēs* (*librī* books) yearly records]

Annam (ă năm′, ăn′ăm), *n.* **1.** former name of Vietnam (until 1945). **2.** a region in central Vietnam, now divided between South and North Vietnam. Also, **Anam.**

Annamese (ăn′ə mēz′), *adj.*, *n.*, *pl.* **-mese.** *—adj.* **1.** of or pertaining to Annam, its people, or their language. *—n.* **2.** a native of Annam. **3.** (formerly) the Vietnamese language. **4.** the linguistic family to which this belongs, widespread in Tonkin and Annam, and of no certainly known relationships.

Annamite (ăn′ə mīt′), *n.*, *adj.* Annamese.

Annapolis (ə năp′ə lĭs), *n.* a seaport in the U.S., the capital of Maryland; naval academy. 23,385 (1960).

Annapolis Royal, a town in W Nova Scotia, on an arm of the Bay of Fundy: the first settlement in Canada (1605). Formerly, **Port Royal.**

Annapurna (ăn′ə po͝oə′nə), *n.* a mountain in the Himalayas, in Nepal. 26,503 ft.

annates (ăn′āts, -əts), *n.pl.* *Eccles.* (formerly) first fruits; the first year's revenue of a see or benefice, payable to the pope. Also, **annats** (ăn′ăts, -əts). [t. ML: m. *annāta* time, work, yield of a year, der. L *annus* year]

annatto (ə năt′ō), **1.** a small tree, *Bixa orellana*, of tropical America. **2.** a yellowish red dye obtained from the pulp enclosing its seeds, used for colouring fabrics, butter, varnish, etc. Also, **anatto, annatta, anatta, arnotto** [t. Carib]

Anne (ăn), *n.* **1. Queen,** 1665–1714, queen of England 1702–14. (daughter of James II of England). **2. Saint,** (popularly held to be) the mother of the Virgin Mary.

anneal (ə nēl′), *v.t.* **1.** to heat (glass, earthenware, metals, etc.) to remove or prevent internal stress. **2.** to free from internal stress by heating and gradually cooling. **3.** to toughen or temper: *to anneal the mind.* [ME *anele(n)*, OE *anǣlan*, f. *an* on + *ǣlan* burn]

Anne Boleyn (bo͝ol′ĭn, bo͞o lĭn′), See **Boleyn.**

Annecy (*Fr.* àn sē′), *n.* a town in France, the capital of Haute-Savoie. 45,715 (1962).

annelid (ăn′ə lĭd), *n.* *Zool.* a member of the *Annelida*, a phylum of worms comprising earthworms, leeches, various marine worms, etc., characterized by their ringed or segmented bodies. [t. F: m. *annélide*, f. m. s. L *ānellus* (dim. of *ānulus* ring) + *-ide* -ID[2]]

Anne of Austria, 1601–66, queen of Louis XIII of France: regent during minority of her son Louis XIV.

Anne of Bohemia, 1366–94, queen of Richard II of England.

Anne of Cleves (klēvz), 1515–57, the fourth wife of Henry VIII of England.

annex (*v.* ə nĕks′; *n.* ăn′ĕks), *v.t.* **1.** to attach, join, or add, esp. to something larger or more important; unite; append; subjoin. **2.** to take possession of, take to one's own use permanently. **3.** *Colloq.* to take without permission; appropriate. —*n.* **4.** something annexed or added, esp. a supplement to a document: *an annex to a treaty.* **5.** *Chiefly U.S.* annexe. [ME *a(n)nexe(n)*, t. ML: m. *annexāre*, ult. der. L *annexus*, pp. joined] —**annex′able,** *adj.*

annexation (ăn′ĭk sā′shən, -ĕk-), *n.* **1.** the act of annexing, esp. new territory. **2.** the fact of being annexed. **3.** something annexed. —**an′nexa′tionist,** *n.*

annexe (ăn′ĕks), *n.* **1.** a subsidiary building or an addition to a building. **2.** something annexed. Also, **annex.** [t.F]

annexment (ə nĕks′mənt), *n. Obs.* that which is annexed.

Annigoni (ăn′ĭ gō′nĭ; *It.* ä nē gô′nē), *n.* **Pietro** (*It.* pyĕ′trô), born 1910, Italian portrait painter.

annihilable (ə nī′ə lə bl), *adj.* susceptible of annihilation. —**anni′hilabil′ity,** *n.*

annihilate (ə nī′ə lāt′), *v.t.*, **-lated, -lating.** **1.** to reduce to nothing; destroy utterly: *the bombing annihilated the city.* **2.** to destroy the form or collective existence of: *to annihilate an army.* **3.** to cancel the effect of; annul: *to annihilate a law.* **4.** *Colloq.* to defeat utterly, as in argument, competition, or the like. [t. LL: m. s. *annihilātus*, pp.] —**annihilative** (ə nī′ə lə tĭv), *adj.* —**anni′hila′tor,** *n.*

annihilation (ə nī′ə lā′shən), *n.* **1.** the act of annihilating. **2.** extinction; destruction. —**anni′hila′tionist,** *n.*

annihilation radiation, *Physics.* the electromagnetic radiation resulting from the annihilation of matter when a particle and its corresponding anti-particle collide.

anniversary (ăn′ĭ vûr′sə rĭ), *n.*, *pl.* **-ries,** *adj.* —*n.* **1.** the yearly recurrence of the date of a past event. **2.** the celebration of such a date. —*adj.* **3.** returning or recurring each year. **4.** pertaining to an anniversary: *an anniversary gift.* [t. L: m. s. *anniversārius*]

anno aetatis suae (ăn′ō ē tä′tĭs sōō′ē), *Latin.* in the year of his age.

anno Domini (ăn′ō dŏm′ĭ nī′), *Latin.* in the year of our Lord. *Abbrev.:* A.D., as A.D. 597.

anno regni (ăn′ō rĕg′nī), *Latin.* in the year of the reign.

annotate (ăn′ō tāt′), *v.*, **-tated, -tating.** —*v.t.* **1.** to supply with notes; remark upon in notes: *to annotate the works of Bacon.* —*v.i.* **2.** to make annotations or notes. [t. L: m. s. *annotātus*, pp.] —**an′nota′tor,** *n.*

annotation (ăn′ō tā′shən), *n.* **1.** the act of annotating. **2.** a note commenting upon, explaining, or criticizing some passage of a book or other writing.

announce (ə nouns′), *v.t.*, **-nounced, -nouncing.** **1.** to make known publicly; give notice of. **2.** to state the approach or presence of: *to announce guests or dinner.* **3.** to make known to the mind or senses. [ME *announce(n)*, t. OF: m. *anoncier*, g. L *annuntiāre*]

—**Syn. 1.** ANNOUNCE, PROCLAIM, PUBLISH mean to communicate something in a formal or public way. To ANNOUNCE is to give out news, often of something expected in the future: *to announce a lecture series.* To PROCLAIM is to make a widespread and general announcement of something of public interest: *to proclaim a holiday.* To PUBLISH is to make public in an official way, now esp. by printing: *to publish a book.*

announcement (ə nouns′mənt), *n.* **1.** public or formal notice announcing something. **2.** the act of announcing.

announcer (ə noun′sə), *n.* one who announces, esp. on radio or television.

anno urbis conditae (an′ō ûr′bĭs kŏn′dĭ tē′), *Latin.* in the year after the founding of the city (of Rome, traditionally in 753 B.C.). *Abbrev.:* A.U.C.

annoy (ə noi′), *v.t.* **1.** to disturb (a person) in a way that displeases, troubles, or slightly irritates him. **2.** *Mil.* to molest; harm. —*v.i.* **3.** to be disagreeable or troublesome. —*n.* **4.** *Archaic or Poetic.* something annoying. [ME *anoye*, t. OF: m. *enui*, der. *en(n)uyer* displease, g. LL *inodiāre*, der. *in odiō* in hatred] —**annoy′er,** *n.* —**Syn. 1.** harass, pester. See **bother, worry.**

annoyance (ə noi′əns), *n.* **1.** that which annoys; a nuisance: *some visitors are an annoyance.* **2.** the act of annoying. **3.** the feeling of being annoyed. **4.** *Acoustics.* the (degree of) psychological distress caused by excessive noise.

annoying (ə noi′ĭng), *adj.* causing annoyance: *annoying habits.* —**annoy′ingly,** *adv.* —**annoy′ingness,** *n.*

annual (ăn′yŏŏ əl), *adj.* **1.** of, for, or pertaining to a year; yearly. **2.** occurring or returning once a year: *an annual celebration.* **3.** *Bot.* living only one growing season, as beans or maize. **4.** performed during a year: *the annual course of the sun.* —*n.* **5.** a plant living only one year or season. **6.** a literary production published annually. [t. LL: s. *annuālis*; r. ME *annuel*, t. OF] —**an′nually,** *adv.*

annual parallax. See **parallax** (def. 3).

annual ring, one of the yearly growth rings on a cross-section of a tree.

annuitant (ə nyōō′ĭ tənt), *n.* one who receives an annuity.

annuit coeptis (ăn′yŏŏ ĭt sĕp′tĭs), *Latin.* He (God) has favoured our undertakings (adapted from Virgil, *Aeneid*, IX, 625; motto on reverse of the great seal of the United States).

annuity (ə nyōō′ĭ tĭ), *n.*, *pl.* **-ties.** **1.** a specified income payable at stated intervals for a fixed or a contingent period, often for the recipient's life, in consideration of a stipulated premium paid either in prior instalment payments or in a single payment. **2.** the right to receive such an income, or the duty to make such a payment or payments. [ME *annuitee*, t. F: m. *annuité*, ult. der. L *annuus* yearly]

annul (ə nŭl′), *v.t.*, **annulled, annulling.** **1.** to make void or null; abolish (used esp. of laws or other established rules, usages, and the like): *to annul a marriage.* **2.** to reduce to nothing; obliterate. [ME *anulle(n)*, t. LL: m. *annullāre*] —**annul′lable,** *adj.*

annular (ăn′yŏŏ lə), *adj.* **1.** having the form of a ring. **2.** bearing a ring. —*n.* **3.** the ring finger. [t. L: s. *annulāris*] —**annularity** (ăn′yŏŏ lă′rĭ tĭ), *n.* —**an′nularly,** *adv.*

annular eclipse, *Astron.* an eclipse of the sun in which a portion of its surface is visible as a ring surrounding the dark moon (opposed to *total eclipse*).

annular ligament, *Anat.* the general ligamentous envelope which surrounds the wrist or ankle.

annulate (ăn′yŏŏ lĭt, -lāt′), *adj.* **1.** formed of ringlike segments, as an annelid worm. **2.** having rings or ringlike bands.

annulated (ăn′yŏŏ lā′tĭd), *adj.* **1.** *Archit.* (of a column) formed of several shafts banded together. **2.** annulate.

annulation (ăn′yŏŏ lā′shən), *n.* **1.** formation with or into rings. **2.** a ringlike formation or part.

annulet (ăn′yŏŏ lĭt), *n.* **1.** a little ring. **2.** *Archit.* an encircling band, moulding, or fillet, as on a Doric capital. **3.** *Her.* a small circle. [f. s. L *annulus* ring + -ET]

annulment (ə nŭl′mənt), *n.* **1.** an invalidation, as of a marriage. **2.** act of annulling.

annulose (ăn′yŏŏ lōs′), *adj.* furnished with rings; composed of rings: *annulose animals.* [t. NL: m. s. *annulōsus*, der. L *annulus* ring]

annulus (ăn′yŏŏ ləs), *n.*, *pl.* **-li** (-lī′), **-luses.** a ring; a ringlike part, band, or space. [t. L, var. of *ānulus* ring]

annunciate (ə nŭn′shĭ āt′, -sĭ-), *v.t.*, **-ated, -ating.** to announce. [ME *annunciat*, ppl. adj., announced, t. ML: s. *annunciātus*, r. L *annuntiātus*, pp.]

annunciation (ə nŭn′sĭ ā′shən), *n.* **1.** (*often cap.*) the announcement by the angel Gabriel to the Virgin Mary of the incarnation of Christ. **2.** (*cap.*) the festival (March 25th) instituted by the church in memory of this. **3.** *Rare.* the act of announcing; proclamation.

annunciator (ə nŭn′sĭ ā′tə), *n.* **1.** an announcer. **2.** an apparatus which indicates visually which of a number of electric circuits has caused a bell to ring. **3.** *Railways.* any apparatus which gives an audible signal of the passage of a train past a point.

Annunzio d′ (*It.* dän nōōn′tsyô), **Gabriele** (*It.* gä bryĕ′lĕ). See **d'Annunzio.**

annus mirabilis (ăn′ŏŏs mĭ răb′ĭ lĭs), *Latin.* year of wonders; wonderful year.

anoa (ə nō′ə), *n.* a dwarf buffalo, *Anoa depressicornis*, of Indonesia: the smallest wild representative of the cattle tribe.

anociassociation (ə nō′sĭ ə sō′sĭ ā′shən), *n. Surg.* a method for preventing shock and other harmful effects resulting from an operation, consisting principally in giving general and local anaesthesia and in avoiding all unnecessary trauma during the operation. Also, **anociation** (ə nō′sĭ ā′shən). [f. A-[6] + *noci-* (comb. form repr. L *nocēre* harm) + ASSOCIATION]

anodal (ă nō′dl), *adj.* anodic.

anode (ăn′ōd), *n.* **1.** the electrode which gives off positive ions, or towards which negative ions or electrons move or collect, in a voltaic cell, radio valve, or other device. **2.** the positive pole of a battery or other source of current. (opposed to *cathode*). **3.** the plate of a radio valve. [t. Gk: m. s. *ánodos* way up]

anodic (ă nŏd′ĭk), *adj.* pertaining to an anode or the phenomena in its vicinity. Also, **anodal.**

anodize (ăn′ə dīz′), *v.t.*, **-dized, -dizing.** *Chem.* to coat a metal, esp. magnesium or aluminium, with a protective film by chemical or electrolytic means. Also, **anodise.** [f. ANOD(E) + -IZE]

anodyne (ăn′ə dīn′), *n.* **1.** a medicine, esp. a drug, that relieves or removes pain. **2.** anything relieving distress.

—*adj.* **3.** relieving pain. **4.** soothing to the feelings. [t. L: m. s. *anōdynus*, t. Gk: m. *anṓdynos* freeing from pain]

anoestrus (ăn ēs′trəs), *n. Zool.* the resting period of the oestrous cycle, when the animal is not on heat. —**anoestrous,** *adj.*

anoint (ə noint′), *v.t.* **1.** to put oil on; apply an unguent or oily liquid to. **2.** to smear with any liquid. **3.** to consecrate by applying oil. [ME *anoynte(n)*, t. OF: m. *enoint*, pp. of *enoindre*, g. L *inunguere*] —**anoint′er,** *n.* —**anoint′ment,** *n.*

anole (ə nōl′), *n.* any of numerous American iguanid lizards of the genus *Anolis*, capable of changing the colour of the skin.

anolyte (ăn′ə līt′), *n.* that part of an electrolyte which surrounds the anode in electrolysis. [b. ANODE and ELECTROLYTE]

anomalism (ə nŏm′ə lĭz′əm), *n. Obs.* **1.** anomalous quality. **2.** an anomaly.

anomalistic (ə nŏm′ə lĭs′tĭk), *adj.* of or pertaining to an anomaly.

anomalistic month, *Astron.* the average interval between consecutive passages of the moon through the perigee.

anomalistic year, *Astron.* the average interval between consecutive passages of the earth through the perihelion.

anomalous (ə nŏm′ə ləs), *adj.* deviating from the common rule, type, or form; abnormal; irregular. [t. L: m. *anōmalus*, t. Gk: m. *anṓmalos* irregular] —**anom′alously,** *adv.* —**anom′alousness,** *n.*

anomaly (ə nŏm′ə lĭ), *n., pl.* **-lies. 1.** deviation from the common rule or analogy. **2.** something anomalous: *the anomalies of human nature.* **3.** *Astron.* **a.** an angular quantity used in defining the position of a point in an orbit. **b. true anomaly,** the angular distance of a planet from the perihelion of its orbit, as observed from the sun. **c. mean anomaly,** a quantity increasing uniformly with the time and equal to the true anomaly at perihelion and aphelion. [t. L: m. s. *anōmalia*, t. Gk]

anomie (ăn′ō mĭ), *n. Sociol.* a social vacuum marked by the absence of social norms or values, as in the case of an area of lodging houses for single people in a large city. [t. F, t. Gk: m. *anomía* lawlessness] —**anom′ic,** *adj.*

anon (ə nŏn′), *adv. Archaic.* **1.** in a short time; soon. **2.** at another time. **3.** at once; immediately. **4. ever and anon,** now and then. [ME; OE *on ān* into one, *on āne* in one, immediately]

anon., anonymous.

anonym (ăn′ə nĭm), *n.* **1.** an assumed or false name. **2.** an anonymous person or publication.

anonymous (ə nŏn′ĭ məs), *adj.* **1.** without any name acknowledged, as that of author, contributor, or the like: *an anonymous pamphlet.* **2.** of unknown name; whose name is withheld: *an anonymous author.* **3.** lacking individuality; without distinguishing features; without identity. [t. Gk: m. *anṓnymos*] —**anonymity** (ăn′ə nĭm′ĭ tĭ), **anon′ymousness,** *n.* —**anon′ymously,** *adv.*

anopheles (ə nŏf′ĭ lēz′), *n., pl.* **-les.** any mosquito of the genus *Anopheles*, which, when infested with the organisms causing malaria, may transmit the disease to human beings. [t. NL, t. Gk: useless, hurtful]

Anopheles, *Anopheles quadrimaculatus* (¼ in. long)

anorak (ăn′ə răk′), *n.* a strong waterproof jacket with a hood, originally for use in polar regions, now commonly used for any outdoor activity. [t. Eskimo: m. *anoraq*]

anorexia (ăn′ô rĕk′sĭ ə), *n. Med.* lack of appetite. Also **anorexy.** [f. AN-[1] + m. Gk *órexis* longing]

anorthic (ăn ô′thĭk), *adj. Crystall.* triclinic.

anorthite (ăn ô′thīt), *n.* a mineral of the plagioclase felspar group, calcium aluminium silicate, $CaAl_2Si_2O_8$, occurring in basic igneous rocks; indianite. [f. AN-[1] + s. Gk *orthós* straight + -ITE[1]] —**anorthitic** (ăn′ô thĭt′ĭk), *adj.*

anorthosite (ăn ô′thə sīt′), *n. Geol.* a granular igneous rock composed largely of labradorite or a more calcic felspar. [f. AN-[1] + Gk *orthós* straight + -ITE[1]. Cf. F *anorthose* a felspar]

anosmia (ăn ŏz′mĭ ə, ăn ŏs′-), *n. Pathol.* loss of the sense of smell. [t. NL, f. Gk: *an-* AN-[1] + s. *osmḗ* smell + *-ia* -IA] —**an′osmat′ic,** *adj.*

another (ə nŭth′ə), *adj.* **1.** a second; a further; an additional: *another piece of cake.* **2.** a different; a distinct; of a different kind: *at another time, another man.* —*pron.* **3.** one more; an additional one: *try another.* **4.** a different one; something different: *going from one house to another.* **5.** one just like. **6. one another,** one the other; each other: *love one another.* [ME; orig. *an other*]

Anouilh (*Fr.* à nōōy′), *n.* **Jean** (*Fr.* zhäN), born 1910, French playwright.

ans., answer.

ansate (ăn′sāt), *adj.* having a handle or handle-like part: *an ansate cross* (ankh). [t. L: m. s. *ansātus*]

Anschluss (ăn′shlōōs), *n. German.* union, esp. the political union of Austria with Germany in 1938.

Anselm (ăn′sĕlm), *n.* **Saint,** 1033–1109, archbishop of Canterbury, scholastic theologian and philosopher.

anserine (ăn′sə rīn′, -sə rĭn), *adj.* **1.** *Ornith.* of or pertaining to the subfamily *Anserinae*, the goose family. **2.** resembling a goose; gooselike. **3.** stupid; foolish; silly. [t. L: m. s. *anserīnus*]

Ansermet (*Fr.* äN sĕr mĕ′), *n.* **Ernest Alexandre** (*Fr.* ĕr nĕst ȧlĕk säN′dr), born 1883, Swiss orchestral conductor.

Anshan (ăn′shăn′), *n.* a town in NE China, in Liaoning province. 833,000 (est. 1958).

answer (än′sə), *n.* **1.** a spoken or written reply to a question, request, letter, etc. **2.** a reply or response in act: *the answer was a volley of fire.* **3.** a reply to a charge or an accusation. **4.** *Law.* a pleading of facts by a defendant in opposition to those stated in the plaintiff's declaration. **5.** a solution to a doubt or problem, esp. in mathematics. **6.** a piece of work (written or otherwise) performed as a demonstration of knowledge or ability in a test or examination. **7.** a re-echoing, imitation, or repetition of sounds. **8.** *Music.* the entrance of a fugue subject, usually on the dominant, after its first presentation in the main key. —*v.i.* **9.** to make answer; reply. **10.** to respond by a word or act: *to answer with a nod.* **11.** to respond (to a stimulus, direction, command, etc.); obey; acknowledge (fol. by *to*): *to answer to the whip, to one's name.* **12.** to be or declare oneself responsible or accountable (fol. by *for*): *I will answer for his safety.* **13.** to give assurance of; vouch (fol. by *for*): *he answered for the truth of the statement.* **14.** to act or suffer in consequence of (fol. by *for*): *to answer for one's sins.* **15.** to be satisfactory or serve (fol. by *for*): *to answer for a purpose.* **16.** to correspond; conform (fol. by *to*): *to answer to a description.* **17. answer back,** to make a rude or impertinent reply. —*v.t.* **18.** to make answer to; to reply or respond to: *to answer a person or a question.* **19.** to give as an answer. **20.** to make a defence against (a charge); meet or refute (an argument). **21.** to act in reply or response to: *to answer the bell, answer a summons.* **22.** to respond to (mechanical direction or steering): *the car answered the wheel.* **23.** to serve or suit: *this will answer the purpose.* **24.** to discharge (a responsibility, claim, debt, etc.). **25.** to conform or correspond to; be similar or equivalent to: *to answer a description.* **26.** to atone for; make amends for. [ME; OE *andswaru*, f. *and-* against + *swaru*, akin to *swerian* swear] —**an′swerer,** *n.* —**an′swerless,** *adj.*

—**Syn. 1.** ANSWER, REPLY, RESPONSE, RETORT all mean words used to meet a question, remark, charge, etc. An ANSWER is a return remark: *an answer giving the desired information.* REPLY is somewhat more formal than ANSWER: *a reply to a letter.* A RESPONSE often suggests an answer to an appeal, exhortation, etc., or an expected or fixed reply: *a response to enquiry, a response in a church service.* A RETORT implies a keen, prompt answer, esp. one that turns a remark upon the person who made it: *a sharp retort.*

answerable (än′sə rə bl), *adj.* **1.** accountable, responsible (*for* a person, act, etc.): *I am answerable for his safety.* **2.** liable to be called to account or asked to defend one's actions (*to* a person): *he is answerable to his employer.* **3.** capable of being answered. **4.** proportionate; correlative (fol. by *to*). **5.** corresponding; suitable (fol. by *to*). —**an′swerableness,** *n.* —**an′swerably,** *adv.*

ant (ănt), *n.* **1.** any of certain small hymenopterous insects constituting the family *Formicidae*, very widely distributed in thousands of species, all of which have some degree of social organization. **2.** a termite. **3. have ants in one's pants,** *Slang.* to be restless or impatient. [ME *amte*, OE *ǣmete*] —**ant′like′,** *adj.*

an't (änt *for 1*; änt *or* ănt *for 2*; ānt, änt *or* änt *for 3*), **1.** contraction of *are not.* **2.** contraction of *am not* (as an interrogative). **3.** *Obs. or Dial.* contraction of *is not, has not, have not, or am not* (as a statement).

ant-, var. of **anti-** esp. before a vowel or *h*, as in *antacid.*

-ant, 1. adjective suffix, orig. participial, as in *ascendant, pleasant.* **2.** noun suffix used in words of participial origin, denoting agency or instrumentality, as in *servant, irritant.* Cf. **-ent.** [t. F, g. L *-ant-*, nom. *-ans*, ppr. ending]

ant., antonym.

anta (ăn′tə), *n., pl.* **-tae** (-tē). *Archit.* a square pier or pilaster, formed by thickening a wall at its extremity, often having a base and a capital. [t. L (found only in pl.)]

Antabuse (ăn′tə byōōs′), *n. Trademark.* a drug, tetraethylthiuram disulphide, used in the treatment of alcoholism. It produces highly unpleasant symptoms when alcohol is taken following administration of the drug.

antacid (ănt ăs′ĭd), *adj.* **1.** neutralizing acids; counteracting acidity, as of the stomach. —*n.* **2.** an antacid agent or remedy. [f. ANT- + ACID]

Antaeus (ăn tē′əs), *n. Gk Myth.* an African giant who

was invincible when in contact with the earth, but was lifted into the air and crushed by Hercules. —**Antae′an,** *adj.*

antagonism (ăn tăg′ə nĭz′əm), *n.* **1.** the activity or the relation of contending parties or conflicting forces; active opposition. **2.** an opposing force, principle, or tendency. [t. Gk: m. s. *antagṓnisma*]

antagonist (ăn tăg′ə nĭst), *n.* **1.** one who is opposed to or strives with another in any kind of contest; opponent; adversary. **2.** *Physiol.* a muscle which acts in opposition to another (the agonist). [t. Gk: s. *antagōnistḗs*] —**Syn. 1.** See **adversary.**

antagonistic (ăn tăg′ə nĭs′tĭk), *adj.* acting in opposition; mutually opposing. —**antag′onis′tically,** *adv.*

antagonize (ăn tăg′ə nīz′), *v.,* **-nized, -nizing.** —*v.t.* **1.** to make hostile; make an antagonist of: *his speech antagonized half the voters.* **2.** *Physiol.* to counteract the action of; act in opposition to. **3.** *Now U.S.* to oppose. Also, **antagonise.**

Antakiya (ăn′tä kē′yə), *n.* Arabic name of **Antioch.**

antalkali (ănt ăl′kə lī′), *n., pl.* **-lis, -lies.** something that neutralizes alkalis or counteracts alkalinity. —**antalkaline** (ănt ăl′kə līn′, -lĭn), *adj., n.*

Antalya (*Turk.* än täl′ yä), *n.* a seaport in SW Turkey, on the Mediterranean. 50,908 (1960).

Antananarivo (ăn′tə năn′ə rē′vō), *n.* Tananarive.

antarctic (ănt äk′tĭk), *adj.* **1.** of, at, or near the South Pole. —*n.* **2. the Antarctic,** the Antarctic Ocean and Antarctica. [t. L: s. *antarcticus,* t. Gk: m. *antarktikós* opposite the north; r. ME *antartik,* t. OF: m. *antartique*]

Antarctica (ănt äk′tĭ kə), *n.* the continent around the South Pole, almost wholly covered by a vast continental icesheet, ab. 5,000,000 sq. mi. Also, **Antarctic Continent.** See map under **South Pole.**

Antarctic Circle, the northern boundary of the South Frigid Zone, 23° 28′ from the South Pole.

Antarctic Ocean, the ocean S of the Antarctic Circle.

Antarctic Zone, the South Frigid Zone, between the Antarctic Circle and the South Pole.

Antares (ăn tēə′rēz), *n.* a red giant star of the first magnitude in Scorpio. [t. Gk, f. *ant(i)* compared with + *Arēs* Mars; so called because its colour resembles that of the planet]

ant-bear (ănt′bēə′), *n.* **1.** a large terrestrial tropical American edentate, the great anteater, *Myrmecophaga jubata,* subsisting on termites, ants, and other insects, and having powerful front claws, a long, tapering snout and extensile tongue, and a shaggy grey coat marked with a conspicuous black band. **2.** the aardvark.

Ant-bear (def. 1), *Myrmecophaga jubata* (23 in. high, overall length 7 ft, tail 2½ ft)

ante (ăn′tĭ), *n., v.,* **-ted** or **-teed, -teing.** —*n.* **1.** *Poker.* a stake put into the pool by each player after seeing his hand but before drawing new cards, or, sometimes, before seeing his hand. —*v.i., v.t.* **2.** *Poker.* to put (one's stake) into the pool. **3.** *Slang.* to pay (one's share) (usually fol. by *up*). [Cf. L *ante* before]

ante-, a prefix meaning 'before in space or time', as in *antedate, antediluvian, anteroom, antecedent.* [t. L]

anteater (ănt′ē′tə), *n.* **1.** any of three related edentates of tropical America, feeding chiefly on termites: **a.** the ant-bear or **great anteater. b.** the tamandua or **lesser anteater. c. silky** or **two-toed anteater,** a yellowish, arboreal, prehensile-tailed species, *Cyclopes didactylus,* about the size of a rat. **2.** the aardvark. **3.** any of the pangolins or scaly anteaters of Africa and tropical Asia. **4.** any of the echidnas or spiny anteaters of Australia and New Guinea. **5. banded anteater,** an almost extinct insectivorous marsupial, *Myrmecobius fasciatus,* of South and West Australia.

antebellum (ăn′tĭ bĕl′o͝om), *adj.* before the war, esp. before the American Civil War. [L: *ante bellum*]

antecede (ăn′tĭ sēd′), *v.t.,* **-ceded, -ceding.** to go before, as in order; precede. [back-formation from ANTECEDENT]

antecedence (ăn′tĭ sē′dns), *n.* **1.** the act of going before; precedence. **2.** the quality or condition of being antecedent. **3.** *Astron.* (of a planet) apparent retrograde motion. Also, **antecedency** (ăn′tĭ sē′dn sĭ).

antecedent (ăn′tĭ sē′dnt), *adj.* **1.** going or being before; preceding; prior (often fol. by *to*): *an antecedent event.* —*n.* **2.** (*pl.*) **a.** ancestry. **b.** one's past history. **3.** a preceding circumstance, event, etc. **4.** *Gram.* the word or phrase, usually a noun or its equivalent, which is replaced by a pronoun or other substitute later (or rarely, earlier) in the sentence or in a subsequent sentence. In *Jack lost a hat and he can't find it, Jack* is the antecedent of *he,* and *hat* is the antecedent of *it.* **5.** *Maths.* the first term of a ratio; the first or third term of a proportion. **6.** *Logic.* the first member of a conditional or hypothetical proposition. [t. L: s. *antecēdens,* ppr.] —**an′teced′ently,** *adv.*

antecessor (ăn′tĭ sĕs′ə), *n. Rare.* one who goes before; a predecessor.

antechamber (ăn′tĭ chām′bə), *n.* a chamber or an apartment through which access is had to a principal apartment. [t. F: m. *antichambre,* t. It.: m. *anticamera,* f. *anti-* ANTE- + *camera* chamber (g. L *camera* vault)]

antechapel (ăn′tĭ chăp′l), *n.* (in a school or college) an outer part or lobby at the west end of the chapel.

antechoir (ăn′tĭ kwīə′), *n.* an enclosed space in front of the choir of a church.

antedate (*v.* ăn′tĭ dāt′, ăn′tĭ dāt′; *n.* ăn′tĭ dāt′), *v.,* **-dated, -dating,** *n.* —*v.t.* **1.** to be of older date than; precede in time: *the Peruvian empire antedates that of Mexico.* **2.** to affix a date earlier than the true one to (a document, etc.): *to antedate a cheque.* **3.** to assign to an earlier date: *to antedate a historical event.* **4.** to cause to return to an earlier time. **5.** to cause to happen sooner; accelerate. **6.** to take or have in advance; anticipate. —*n.* **7.** a prior date.

antediluvian (ăn′tĭ dĭ lo͞o′vyən), *adj.* **1.** belonging to the period before the Flood. Gen. 7, 8. **2.** antiquated; primitive: *antediluvian ideas.* —*n.* **3.** one who lived before the Flood. **4.** one who is very old or old-fashioned. [f. ANTE- + s. L *dīluvium* deluge + -AN]

antefix (ăn′tĭ fĭks′), *n., pl.* **-fixes, -fixa.** *Archit.* **1.** an upright ornament at the eaves of a tiled roof, to conceal the foot of a row of convex tiles which cover the joints of the flat tiles. **2.** an ornament above the top moulding of a cornice. [t. L: s. *antefixum,* prop. neut. of *antefixus* fixed before] —**an′tefix′al,** *adj.*

anteflexion (ăn′tĭ flĕk′shən), *n. Pathol.* a bending forwards, esp. of the body of the uterus.

antelope (ăn′tĭ lōp′), *n., pl.* **-lopes,** (*esp. collectively*) **-lope. 1.** a slenderly built, hollow-horned ruminant allied to cattle, sheep, and goats, found chiefly in Africa and Asia. **2.** leather made from its skin. **3.** *U.S.* pronghorn. [ME, t. OF: m. *antelop,* t. ML: m. s. *antalopus,* t. LGk: m. *anthólops*]

ante meridiem (ăn′tĭ mə rĭd′ĭ əm), *Latin.* **1.** before noon. **2.** the time between 12 midnight and 12 noon. *Abbrev.:* A.M. or a.m. —**an′temerid′ian,** *adj.*

ante-mortem (ăn′tĭ mô′təm), *adj. Latin.* before death: *an ante-mortem confession.*

antemundane (ăn′tĭ mŭn′dān), *adj.* before the creation of the world.

antenatal (ăn′tĭ nā′tl), *adj.* **1.** before birth; during pregnancy: *an antenatal clinic.* —*n.* **2.** an antenatal examination.

antenna (ăn tĕn′ə), *n., pl.* **-tennae** (-tĕn′ē) *for 1;* **-tennas** *for 2.* **1.** *Zool.* one of the jointed appendages occurring in pairs on the heads of insects, crustaceans, etc., often called feelers. See diag. under **insect. 2.** a radio aerial. [t. L: a sailyard] —**anten′nal, anten′nary,** *adj.*

antenniform (ăn tĕn′ĭ fôm′), *adj.* shaped like an antenna.

antennule (ăn tĕn′yo͞ol), *n.* a small antenna, specif. one of the anterior pair in crustaceans.

antependium (ăn′tĭ pĕn′dĭ əm), *n., pl.* **-dia** (-dĭ ə). the decoration of the front of an altar, as a covering of silk, or a painted panel. [t. ML. See ANTE, PEND, -IUM]

antepenult (ăn′tĭ pĭ nŭlt′), *n.* the last syllable but two in a word, as *-syl-* in *monosyllable.* [t. L: short for *antepaenultima* (*syllaba*)]

antepenultimate (ăn′tĭ pĭ nŭl′tĭ mĭt), *adj.* **1.** last but two. —*n.* **2.** the last but two; the third from the end.

anterior (ăn tĭə′rĭ ə), *adj.* **1.** placed before; situated more to the front (opposed to *posterior*). **2.** going before in time; preceding; earlier: *an anterior age.* [t. L: compar. adj. der. *ante* before] —**anteriority** (ăn tĭə′rĭ ŏ′rĭ tĭ), *n.* —**ante′riorly,** *adv.*

anteroom (ăn′tĭ ro͞om′, -ro͝om′), *n.* **1.** a smaller room through which access is had to a main room. **2.** a waiting room.

anteversion (ăn′tĭ vû′shən), *n. Pathol.* a tipping forward of the uterus with its fundus directed towards the pubis. [t. L: s. *anteversio* a putting before]

antevert (ăn′tĭ vût′), *v.t. Pathol.* to displace (the uterus) by tipping forward. [t. L: s. *antevertere* precede]

anthelion (ănt hē′lĭ ən, ăn thē′-), *n., pl.* **-lia** (-lĭ ə). (esp. in polar regions) a luminous ring seen round the shadow of the observer's head as thrown by the sun on a cloud, fogbank, or moist surface. [t. Gk, prop. neut. of *anthḗlios* opposite the sun]

anthelmintic (ăn′thĕl mĭn′tĭk), *Med.* —*adj.* **1.** destroying or expelling intestinal worms. —*n.* **2.** an anthelmintic remedy. [f. ANT- + m s. Gk *hélmins* worm + -IC]

anthem (ăn′thəm), *n.* **1.** a hymn, as of praise, devotion, or patriotism. **2.** a piece of sacred vocal music, usually with words taken from the Scriptures. **3.** a hymn sung in alternate parts. *—v.t.* **4.** to celebrate with an anthem. [ME *antem*, OE *antemn(e)*, *antefn(e)*, t. VL: m. *antefna*, g. LL *antifona*, var. of *antiphōna*, t. Gk. See ANTIPHON]

anthemion (ăn thē′myən), *n.*, *pl.* **-mia** (-myə). an ornament of floral forms in a flat radiating cluster, as in architectural decoration, vase painting, etc. [t. NL, t. Gk: flower]

anther (ăn′thə), *n. Bot.* the pollen-bearing part of a stamen. See diag. under **flower.** [t. NL: s. *anthēra*, t. Gk, fem. of *anthērós* flowery]

antheridium (ăn′thə rĭd′ĭ əm), *n.*, *pl.* **-ridia** (-rĭd′ĭ ə). *Bot.* a male sex organ containing motile male gametes. [t. NL, dim. of Gk *antherá* ANTHER]

antherozoid (ăn′thə rə zō′ĭd, ăn′thə rə zoid′), *n. Bot.* the motile male gamete produced in an antheridium.

anthesis (ăn thē′sĭs), *n. Bot.* the period or act of expansion in flowers, esp. the maturing of the stamens. [t. NL, t. Gk: full bloom]

anthill (ănt′hĭl′), *n.* a mound of earth, leaves, etc., formed by a colony of ants in constructing their habitation.

antho-, a word element meaning 'flower', as in *anthocyanin.* [t. Gk, comb. form of *ánthos*]

anthocyanin (ăn′thō sī′ə nĭn), *n.* any of a class of water-soluble pigments including most of those that give red and blue flowers these colours. Also, **anthocyan** (ăn′-thō sī′ən).

anthodium (ăn thō′dyəm), *n.*, *pl.* **-dia** (-dyə). *Bot.* a flower head or capitulum, esp. the head (or so-called compound flower) of a composite plant. [t. NL, f. s. Gk *anthṓdēs* flower-like + *-ium* -IUM]

anthologize (ăn thŏl′ə jīz′), *v.*, **-gized, -gizing.** *—v.i.* **1.** to make an anthology. *—v.t.* **2.** to include in an anthology. Also, **anthologise.**

anthology (ăn thŏl′ə jĭ), *n.*, *pl.* **-gies.** **1.** a collection of short, choice poems, especially epigrams, of varied authorship. **2.** any collection of literary pieces of varied authorship. [t. Gk: m. s. *anthología*, lit., a flower-gathering] **—anthological** (ăn′thə lŏj′ĭ kl), *adj.* **—anthol′ogist,** *n.*

Anthony (ăn′tə nĭ), *n.* **Saint,** A.D. 251?–356?, Egyptian hermit; founder of Christian monasticism. Also, **Antony.**

Anthony of Padua (ăn′tə nĭ), **Saint,** 1195–1231, Franciscan monk and preacher in Italy and France.

anthophore (ăn′thə fô′), *n. Bot.* a form of floral stipe, produced by the elongation of the internode between the calyx and the corolla, and bearing the corolla, stamens, and pistil. [t. Gk: m. s. *anthophóros* flower-bearing]

A

Section of flower of wild pink, *Silene caroliniana*, showing A, anthophore within the calyx

anthotaxy (ăn′thə tăk′sĭ), *n. Bot.* the arrangement of flowers on the axis of growth; inflorescence.

anthozoan (ăn′thə zō′ən), *n.* **1.** any animal of the *Anthozoa*, a class of the phylum *Coelenterata*, comprising sessile marine animals of the polyp type, single or colonial, having a columnar body with the interior partitioned by septa and an oral disc with one to many circles of tentacles. It includes anemones, corals, sea-pens, etc. *—adj.* **2.** belonging to this class.

anthracene (ăn′thrə sēn′), *n.* a hydrocarbon, $C_{14}H_{10}$, found in coal tar, important commercially as a source of alizarin. [f. m. s. Gk *ánthrax* coal + -ENE]

anthracite (ăn′thrə sīt′), *n.* a mineral coal containing little of the volatile hydrocarbons and burning almost without flame; hard coal. [t. L: m. s. *anthracītes*, t. Gk: m. *anthrakítēs* kind of precious stone (prop., coal-like)] **—anthracitic** (ăn′thrə sĭt′ĭk), *adj.*

anthracnose (ăn thrăk′nōs), *n.* a necrotic plant disease with restricted lesions, as of bean and cotton plants. [f. Gk: m. s. *ánthrax* carbuncle, coal + m. s. *nósos* disease]

anthracoid (ăn′thrə koid′), *adj.* resembling anthrax.

anthracosis (ăn′thrə kō′sĭs), *n.* a diseased condition of the lungs caused by inhalation of coaldust in mines.

anthraquinone (ăn′thrə kwĭ nōn′, -kwĭn′ōn), *n. Chem.* a yellow crystalline substance, $C_{14}H_8O_2$, obtained from anthracene or phthalic anhydride, used in the preparation of alizarin. [f. ANTHRA(CENE) + QUINONE]

anthrax (ăn′thrăks), *n.*, *pl.* **-thraces** (-thrə sēz′). **1.** a malignant infectious disease of cattle, sheep, and other animals and of man, caused by *Bacillus anthracis.* **2.** a malignant carbuncle which is the diagnostic lesion of anthrax disease in man. [t. L, t. Gk: carbuncle, coal] **—anthrac′ic,** *adj.*

anthrop., **1.** anthropological. **2.** anthropology.

anthropo-, a word element meaning 'man', 'human being', as in *anthropocentric.* Also, **anthrop-.** [t. Gk, comb. form of *ánthrōpos*]

anthropocentric (ăn′thrə pō sĕn′trĭk), *adj.* **1.** regarding man as the central fact of the universe. **2.** assuming man to be the final aim and end of the universe. **3.** viewing and interpreting everything in terms of human experience and values. **—anthropocentricism** (ăn′thrə pō sĕn′trĭ-sĭz′əm), *n.*

anthropogenesis (ăn′thrə pō jĕn′ĭ sĭs), *n.* the genesis or development of the human race, esp. as a subject of scientific study. Also, **anthropogeny** (ăn′thrə pŏj′ĭ nĭ). **—an′thropogen′ic,** *adj.*

anthropogeography (ăn′thrə pō jĭ ŏg′ rə fĭ), *n.* the study of the geographical distribution of human communities and the relationship between such communities and their natural environment.

anthropography (ăn′thrə pŏg′rə fĭ), *n.* the branch of anthropology that describes the varieties of mankind and their geographical distribution.

anthropoid (ăn′thrə poid′), *adj.* Also, **an′thropoid′al.** **1.** resembling man. *—n.* **2.** an anthropoid ape. [t. Gk: m. s. *anthrōpoeidḗs*]

anthropoid ape, any ape of the family *Pongida*, comprising the gorilla, chimpanzee, orang-utan, and gibbon, without cheek pouches or developed tail.

anthropol., anthropology.

anthropologist (ăn′thrə pŏl′ə jĭst), *n.* one who studies or is versed in anthropology.

anthropology (ăn′thrə pŏl′ə jĭ), *n.* **1.** the science that treats of the origin, development (physical, intellectual, moral, etc.), and varieties, and sometimes esp. the cultural development, customs, beliefs, etc., of mankind. **2.** the study of man's agreement with and divergence from other animals. **3.** the science of man and his works. **—anthropological** (ăn′thrə pə lŏj′ĭ kl), **an′thropolog′ic,** *adj.* **—an′thropolog′ically,** *adv.*

anthropometrics (ăn′thrə pə mĕt′rĭks), *n.* the science of anthropometry.

anthropometry (ăn′thrə pŏm′ĭ trĭ), *n.* the measurement of the size and proportions of the human body. **—anthropometric** (ăn′thrə pə mĕt′rĭk), **an′thropomet′rical,** *adj.*

anthropomorphic (ăn′thrə pə mô′fĭk), *adj.* ascribing human form or attributes to beings or things not human, esp. to a deity.

anthropomorphism (ăn′thrə pə mô′fĭz′əm), *n.* anthropomorphic conception or representation, as of a deity. **—an′thropomor′phist,** *n.*

anthropomorphize (ăn′thrə pə mô′fīz), *v.t.*, *v.i.* **-phized, -phizing.** to ascribe human form or attributes (to). Also, **anthropomorphise.**

anthropomorphosis (ăn′thrə pə mô′fə sĭs), *n.* transformation into human form.

anthropomorphous (ăn′thrə pə mô′fəs), *adj.* **1.** having or resembling the human form. **2.** anthropomorphic. [t. Gk: m. *anthrōpómorphos*]

anthroponomy (ăn′thrə pŏn′ə mĭ), *n.* the science that treats of the laws regulating the development of the human organism in relation to other organisms and to environment. Also, **anthroponomics** (ăn′thrə pə nŏm′ĭks). **—an′-thropono m′ical,** *adj.*

anthropopathy (ăn′thrə pŏp′ə thĭ), *n.* ascription of human passions or feelings to beings not human, esp. to God. Also, **an′thropop′athism.** [t. Gk: m. s. *anthrōpopátheia* humanity]

anthropophagi (ăn′thrə pŏf′ə gī′), *n.pl.*, *sing.* **-agus** (-ə gəs). man-eaters; cannibals. [t. L, pl. of *anthrōpophagus*, t. Gk: m. *anthrōpophágos*]

anthropophagite (ăn′thrə pŏf′ə gīt′), *n.* a man-eater; a cannibal.

anthropophagy (ăn′thrə pŏf′ə jĭ), *n.* the eating of human flesh; cannibalism. **—anthropophagic** (ăn′thrə pə făj′-ik), **an′thropophag′ical, anthropophagous** (ăn′thrə pŏf′ə gəs), *adj.*

anthroposophy (ăn′thrə pŏs′ə fĭ), *n.* **1.** wisdom arising from knowledge of the nature of man. **2.** the spiritualistic system of religion and philosophy taught by Rudolf Steiner. [f. ANTHROPO- + -SOPHY] **—an′thropos′ophist,** *n.*

anti (ăn′tĭ), *n.*, *pl.* **-tis.** **1.** one who is opposed to a particular practice, party, policy, action, etc. *—adj.* **2.** against; opposed to; antagonistic (to).

anti-, a prefix meaning 'against', 'opposed to', with the following particular meanings: **1.** opposed; in opposition: *anti-British, antislavery.* **2.** rival or spurious; pseudo-: *antibishop, anti-Messiah.* **3.** the opposite or reverse of: *antihero, anticlimax.* **4.** not; un-: *antilogical, antigrammatical.* **5.** placed opposite: *antipole, anti-chorus.* **6.** moving in a reverse or the opposite direction: *anticyclone.* **7.** *Med.* corrective; preventive; curative: *antifat, antipyretic; antistimulant.* Also, **ant-.** [t. Gk]

anti-aircraft (ăn′tĭ ĕə′kräft′), *adj.* designed for or used in defence against enemy aircraft.
antiar (ăn′tĭ ä′), *n.* **1.** the upas tree. **2.** an arrow poison prepared from its sap. [t. Javanese: m. *antjar*]
antibiosis (ăn′tĭ bī ō′sĭs), *n. Biol.* an association between organisms which is injurious to one of them. [f. ANTI- + Gk *bíōsis* act of living]
antibiotic (ăn′tĭ bī ŏt′ĭk), *Biochem.* —*n.* **1.** a chemical substance produced by micro-organisms which, in dilute solutions, may inhibit the growth of and even destroy bacteria and other micro-organisms. **2.** such a substance isolated and purified (examples: penicillin, streptomycin) and used in the treatment of infectious diseases of man, animals, and plants. —*adj.* **3.** of or involving antibiotics. **4.** *Obs.* inimical to life; destroying.
antibody (ăn′tĭ bŏd′ĭ), *n., pl.* **-bodies.** any of various substances existing in the blood or developed in immunization which counteract bacterial or viral poisons or destroy bacteria in the system.
antic (ăn′tĭk), *n., adj., v.,* **-ticked, -ticking.** —*n.* **1.** (*often pl.*) a grotesque, fantastic, or ludicrous gesture or posture; fantastic trick. **2.** *Archaic.* a grotesque pageant; ridiculous interlude. **3.** *Archaic.* an actor playing a grotesque or ludicrous part; buffoon; clown. **4.** *Obs.* a grotesque, caricatured, or distorted artistic representation, esp. in architecture, as a gargoyle. —*adj.* **5.** *Archaic* fantastic; odd; grotesque: *an antic disposition.* —*v.i.* **6.** *Obs.* to perform antics; to caper. [t. It.: m. *antico* old (but used as if It. *grottesco* grotesque), g. L *antīquus*]
anticatalyst (ăn′tĭ kăt′ə lĭst), *n. Chem.* a substance which prevents or slows a chemical reaction (opposed to *catalyst*).
anticathode (ăn′tĭ kăth′ōd), *n.* the plate, often of platinum, on which cathode rays impinge in an X-ray tube, thus producing X-rays.
antichlor (ăn′tĭ klô′), *n. Chem.* any of various substances, esp. sodium thiosulphate, used for removing excess chlorine from paper pulp, textiles, fibres, etc., after bleaching. [f. ANTI- + CHLOR(INE)] —**antichloristic** (ăn′tĭ klô rĭs′tĭk) *adj.*
anticholinergic (ăn′tĭ kŏl′ĭ nû′jĭk), *adj.* **1.** antagonistic to acetylcholine. —*n.* **2.** an anticholinergic substance.
Antichrist (ăn′tĭ krīst′), *n. Theol.* **1.** a particular personage or power (variously identified or explained) conceived as appearing in the world as a mighty antagonist of Christ. **2.** (*sometimes l.c.*) an opponent of Christ; a person or power antagonistic to Christ. [t. Gk: s. *antíchrīstos*; r. ME *antecrist*, t. OF] —**antichristian** (ăn′tĭ krĭs′chən), *adj., n.*
anticipant (ăn tĭs′ĭ pənt), *adj.* **1.** anticipative (fol. by *of*). —*n.* **2.** one who anticipates.
anticipate (ăn tĭs′ĭ pāt′), *v.,* **-pated, -pating.** —*v.t.* **1.** to realize beforehand; foretaste or foresee: *to anticipate pleasure.* **2.** to expect: *to anticipate an acquittal.* **3.** to perform (an action) before another has had time to act. **4.** to be before (another) in doing something; forestall: *anticipated by his predecessors.* **5.** to consider or mention before the proper time: *to anticipate more difficult questions.* **6.** *Finance.* **a.** to expend (funds) before they are legitimately available for use. **b.** to discharge (an obligation) before it is due. —*v.i.* **7.** to think, speak, act, etc., in advance or prematurely. [t. L: m. s. *anticipātus*, pp.] —**antic′ipa′tor,** *n.* —**antic′ipa′table,** *adj.* —**Syn. 1.** See **expect. 3.** preclude, obviate, prevent.
anticipation (ăn tĭs′ĭ pā′shən), *n.* **1.** the act of anticipating. **2.** realization in advance; foretaste; expectation; hope. **3.** previous notion; slight previous impression; intuition. **4.** *Law.* the act of expending funds before they are legally due. **5.** *Music.* a note introduced in advance of its harmony so that it sounds against the preceding chord.

A, Anticipation (def. 5)

anticipative (ăn tĭs′ĭ pā′tĭv, ăn tĭs′ĭ pə tĭv), *adj.* anticipating or tending to anticipate; containing anticipation: *an anticipative action or look.* —**antic′ipa′tively,** *adv.*
anticipatory (ăn tĭs′ĭ pā′tə rĭ, ăn tĭs′ĭ pə trĭ), *adj.* of, showing, or expressing anticipation. —**antic′ipa′torily,** *adv.*
anticlastic (ăn′tĭ klăs′tĭk), *adj. Maths.* (of a surface) having principal curvatures of opposite sign at a given point opposed to *synclastic.*
anticlerical (ăn′tĭ klĕr′ĭ kl), *adj.* opposed to the influence and activities of the clergy in public affairs. —**anti′cler′icalism,** *n.*
anticlimax (ăn′tĭ klī′măks), *n.* **1.** a noticeable or ludicrous descent in discourse from lofty ideas or expressions to what is much less impressive. **2.** an abrupt descent in dignity; an inglorious or disappointing conclusion. —**anticlimactic** (ăn′tĭ klī măk′tĭk), *adj.*
anticlinal (ăn′tĭ klī′nəl), *adj.* **1.** inclining in opposite directions from a central axis. **2.** *Geol.* **a.** inclining downwards on both sides from a median line or axis, as an upward fold of rock strata. **b.** pertaining to such a fold. [f. ANTI- + CLIN(O)- + -AL[1]]

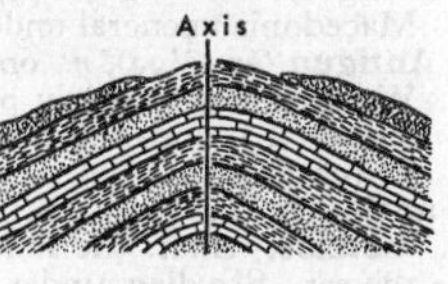

Cross-section of anticlinal fold

anticline (ăn′tĭ klīn′), *n. Geol.* an anticlinal rock structure.
anticlinorium (ăn′tĭ klī nô′rĭ əm), *n., pl.* **-oria** (-ô′rĭ ə). *Geol.* a compound anticline, consisting of a series of subordinate anticlines and synclines, the whole having the general contour of an arch.
anticlockwise (ăn′tĭ klŏk′wīz′), *adj., adv.* in a direction opposite to that of the rotation of the hands of a clock.
anticoagulant (ăn′tĭ kō ăg′yŏŏ lənt), *adj.* **1.** preventing or reducing coagulation, esp. of blood. —*n.* **2.** an anticoagulant agent.
Anticosti (ăn′tĭ kŏs′tĭ), *n.* an island in E Canada, in the estuary of the St Lawrence: a part of Quebec. ab. 130 mi. long; 3043 sq. mi.
anticyclone (ăn′tĭ sī′klōn), *n. Meteorol.* an extensive horizontal movement of the atmosphere spirally around and away from a gradually progressing central region of high barometric pressure, the spiral motion being clockwise in the Northern Hemisphere, anticlockwise in the Southern. —**anticyclonic** (ăn′tĭ sī klŏn′ĭk), *adj.*
antidazzle (ăn′tĭ dăz′əl), *adj. Motor Vehicles.* designed to reduce the dazzle or glare of headlights.
antidepressant (ăn′tĭ dĭ prĕs′ənt), *Med.* —*n.* **1.** any of a class of drugs used for raising the spirits in treating mental depression. —*adj.* **2.** of, pertaining to, or denoting, this class of drugs.
antidiphtheritic (ăn′tĭ dĭf′thə rĭt′ĭk), *Med.* —*adj.* **1.** curing or preventing diphtheria. —*n.* **2.** an antidiphtheritic remedy.
antidote (ăn′tĭ dōt′), *n.* **1.** a medicine or other remedy for counteracting the effects of poison, disease, etc. **2.** whatever prevents or counteracts injurious effects. [t. L: m. s. *antidotum*, t. Gk: m. *antídotos* (verbal adj.) given against] —**an′tidot′al,** *adj.*
antidromic (ăn′tĭ drŏm′ĭk), *adj.* **1.** *Physiol.* conducting nerve impulses in a direction opposite to the usual one. **2.** *Bot.* (of a species of plant) exhibiting both left- and right-hand twining. [ANTI- + s. Gk *drómos* a running + -IC]
Antietam (ăn tē′təm), *n.* a small river in the U.S., flowing from S Pennsylvania through NW Maryland into the Potomac: American Civil War battle 1862.
antifebrile (ăn′tĭ fē′brĭl), *Med.* —*adj.* **1.** efficacious against fever; febrifuge; antipyretic. —*n.* **2.** an antifebrile agent.
antifebrin (ăn′tĭ fē′brĭn), *n. Chem.* acetanilide.
Antifederalist (ăn′tĭ fĕd′ə rə lĭst, -fĕd′rə-), *n. U.S. Hist.* a member or supporter of the Antifederal Party. —**An′tifed′eralism,** *n.*
Antifederal Party (ăn′tĭ fĕd′ər əl, -fĕd′rəl), *U.S. Hist.* the party which, before 1789, opposed the adoption of the proposed Constitution and after that favoured its strict construction.
antifouling (ăn′tĭ fou′lĭng), *adj.* **1.** preventing growth of marine organisms on a ship's bottom. —*n.* **2.** an antifouling agent, usually in the form of a paint.
antifreeze (ăn′tĭ frēz′), *n.* a liquid used in the radiator of an internal-combustion engine to lower the freezing point of the cooling medium.
antifriction (ăn′tĭ frĭk′shən), *adj.* **1.** preventing or reducing friction; lubricating. —*n.* **2.** an antifriction agent.

---

an′ti-al′cohol′ic, *adj., n.*
an′ti-al′coholism, *n.*
an′tibacter′ial, *adj.*
an′ticen′sorship′, *n.*
an′ticlas′sical, *adj.*
an′ticlas′sically, *adv.*
an′ticlas′sicism, *n.*
an′ticlas′sicist, *n.*
an′ticom′munism, *n.*
an′ticom′munist, *n., adj.*
an′ticonserv′atism, *n.*
an′ticonserv′ative, *n., adj.*
an′ticonserv′atively, *adv.*
an′ti-Corn′-Law′, *adj.*
an′ticorro′sive, *adj.*
an′tidaz′zle, *adj.*
an′tidem′ocrat, *n.*
an′tidem′ocrat′ic, *adj.*
an′tidem′ocrat′ically, *adv.*
an′tidis′estab′lishmentar′ian, *n., adj.*
an′tidis′estab′lishmentar′ianism, *n.*
an′tidi′uret′ic, *adj., n.*
an′ti-en′zyme, *n.*
an′tifas′cism, *n.*
an′tifas′cist, *n., adj.*
an′tifem′inism, *n.*
an′tifem′inist, *n., adj.*

---

antigen (ăn′tĭ jən), *n.* any substance which when injected into animal tissues will stimulate the production of antibodies. [f. ANTI(BODY) + -GEN] —**antigenic** (ăn′tĭ jĕn′ĭk), *adj.*

Antigone (ăn tĭg′ə nĭ), *n. Gk Legend.* a daughter of Oedipus by his mother, Jocasta. For performing funeral rites (forbidden by edict of Creon, King of Thebes) over her brother Polynices, she was condemned to be buried alive, and hanged herself.

Antigonus (ăn tĭg′ə nəs), *n.* ('*Cyclops*'), 382?–301 B.C., Macedonian general under Alexander the Great.

Antigua (ăn tē′gə), *n.* one of the Leeward Islands, in the West Indies, formerly part of the British colony of the Leeward Islands. 65,100 pop. (1962); 108 sq. mi. *Cap.:* St John's.

antihelix (ăn′tĭ hē′lĭks), *n., pl.* **-helices** (-hē′lĭ sēz′), **-helixes.** *Anat.* the inner curved ridge of the pinna of the ear. See diag. under **ear.**

antihero (ăn′tĭ hĭə′rō), *n.* a hero or central character who does not possess the traditional heroic virtues or characteristics. —**antiheroic** (ăn′tĭ hĭ rō′ĭk), *adj.*

antihistamine (ăn′tĭ hĭs′tə mēn′, -mĭn), *n. Pharm.* any of certain medicines or drugs which neutralize or inhibit the effect of histamine in the body, used mainly in the treatment of allergic disorders. —**antihistamine, an′ti-his′tamin′ic,** *adj.*

antiketogenesis (ăn′tĭ kē′tō jĕn′ĭ sĭs), *n. Med.* prevention of the excessive formation of acetone bodies in the body, such as occurs in diabetes. [f. ANTI- + KETO(SIS) + -GENESIS] —**an′tike′togen′ic,** *adj.*

antiknock (ăn′tĭ nŏk′), *n.* a material, usually a lead compound, added to the fuel to eliminate or minimize detonation in an internal-combustion engine.

Anti-Lebanon (ăn′tĭ lĕb′ə nən), *n.* a mountain range in SW Syria, E of the Lebanon Mountains.

antilegomena (ăn′tĭ lĕ gŏm′ĭ nə), *n.pl.* a group of books now part of the New Testament which were not at first universally accepted, including the Apocalypse. [t. Gk: (neut. pl. ppr. pass.) things spoken against]

Antilles (ăn tĭl′ēz), *n.pl.* a chain of islands in the West Indies, divided into the **Greater Antilles** (Cuba, Hispaniola, Jamaica, and Puerto Rico), and the **Lesser Antilles** (a group of smaller islands to the SE). —**Antillean** (ăn′tĭ lē′ən, ăn tĭl′ĭ ən), *adj.*

antilog (ăn′tĭ lŏg′), *n.* antilogarithm.

antilogarithm (an′tĭ lŏg′ə rĭth′əm), *n. Maths.* the number corresponding to a logarithm.

antilogism (ăn tĭl′ə jĭz′əm), *n. Logic.* a group of three inconsistent propositions, two of which are premises of a syllogism that contradicts the third.

antilogy (ăn tĭl′ə jĭ), *n., pl.* **-gies.** a contradiction in terms or ideas. [t. Gk: m. s. *antilogía* contradiction] —**antilogous** (ən tĭl′ə gəs), *adj.*

antimacassar (ăn′tĭ mə kăs′ə), *n.* an ornamental covering for the backs and arms of chairs, sofas, etc., to keep them from being soiled by hair oil. [f. ANTI- + *Macassar*, hair oil obtained from MACASSAR]

antimalarial (ăn′tĭ mə lēə′rĭ əl), *Med.* —*adj.* **1.** preventive of or efficacious against malaria. —*n.* **2.** an antimalarial agent.

antimasque (ăn′tĭ măsk′), *n.* a comic or grotesque interlude between the acts of a masque. Also, **antimask.**

antimatter (ăn′tĭ măt′ə), *n. Physics, Chem.* the analogue of matter, possessing charges opposite to those of matter, as negatively charged nuclei (antiprotons) surrounded by positively charged electrons (positrons).

antimere (ăn′tĭ mĭə′), *n. Zool.* actinomere. —**antimeric** (ăn′tĭ mĕ′rĭk), *adj.* —**antimerism** (ăn tĭm′ə rĭz′əm), *n.*

antimissile (ăn′tĭ mĭs′īl), *adj.* **1.** designed or used in defence against guided missiles. —*n.* **2.** a ballistic device with a homing instrument, for defence.

antimonic (ăn′tĭ mŏn′ĭk), *adj.* of or containing antimony, esp. in the pentavalent state.

antimonite (ăn′tĭ mə nīt′), *n.* stibnite.

antimonous (ăn′tĭ mə nəs), *adj. Chem.* containing trivalent antimony. Also, **antimonious** (ăn′tĭ mō′nĭ əs).

antimonsoon (ăn′tĭ mŏn sōōn′), *n. Meteorol.* a current of air moving in a direction opposite to that of a given monsoon and lying above it.

antimony (ăn′tĭ mə nĭ), *n.* a brittle, lustrous, white metallic element occurring in nature free or combined, used chiefly in alloys and (in compounds) in medicine. *Symbol:* Sb; *at. no.:* 51; *at. wt:* 121·75. [late ME, t. ML: m. s. *antimōnium*] —**antimonial** (ăn′tĭ mō′nĭ əl), *adj., n.*

antimony glance, stibnite.

antimonyl (ăn′tĭ mə nĭl, ăn tĭm′ə-), *n. Chem.* a radical containing antimony and oxygen (SbO) which forms salts. [f. ANTIMON(Y) + -YL]

antineuralgic (ăn′tĭ nyōōə răl′jĭk), *Med.* —*adj.* **1.** preventing or relieving neuralgia or neuralgic pain. —*n.* **2.** an antineuralgic substance.

antineutrino (ăn′tĭ nyōō trē′nō), *n. Physics, Chem.* the antiparticle of a neutrino.

antineutron (ăn′tĭ nyōō′trŏn), *n. Physics, Chem.* an antiparticle which annihilates a neutron on collision.

anting (ăn′tĭng), *n.* the placing by certain birds of ants among their feathers, apparently to kill parasites.

antinode (ăn′tĭ nōd′), *n. Physics.* a point, line, or region in a vibrating medium at which the amplitude of variation of the disturbance is greatest, situated halfway between two adjacent nodes.

antinomian (ăn′tĭ nō′myən), *n.* one who maintains that Christians are freed from the moral law by the dispensation of grace set forth in the gospel. —**an′tino′mian,** *adj.* —**an′tino′mianism,** *n.*

antinomy (ăn tĭn′ə mĭ), *n., pl.* **-mies. 1.** opposition between laws and principles; contradiction in law. **2.** *Philos.* the mutual contradiction of two principles or correctly drawn inferences, each of which is supported by reason. [t. L: m. s. *antinomia*, t. Gk]

antinovel (ăn′tĭ nŏv′əl), *n.* a novel in which the traditional approach to such aspects as plot, form, character, etc., is deliberately rejected.

Antioch (ăn′tĭ ŏk′), *n.* a town in S Turkey: capital of the ancient kingdom of Syria 300–64 B.C. 30,000 (est. 1964). Arabic, **Antakiya.** —**Antiochian** (ăn′tĭ ō′kyən), *adj.*

Antioch

Antiochus III (ăn tī′ə kəs) ('*the Great*'), 241?–187 B.C., king of Syria 223–187 B.C.; fought against the Romans.

Antiochus IV (*Antiochus Epiphanes*), died 164? B.C., king of Syria 175–164? B.C.

Antiope (ăn tī′ə pē), *n. Gk Myth.* the mother of Amphion and Zethus.

anti-oxidant (ăn′tĭ ŏk′sĭ dənt), *n.* **1.** any substance which when added to rubber inhibits its deterioration. **2.** any substance inhibiting oxidation.

antiparallel (ăn′tĭ păr′rə lĕl′), *adj. Physics.* rotating in opposite directions.

antiparticle (ăn′tĭ pä′tĭ kl), *n. Physics.* the particle (sometimes hypothetical), with which annihilation of a given particle can take place.

antipasto (*It.* än tē päs′tō), *n. Italian.* an appetizer course of relishes, smoked meat, fish, etc.; hors d'œuvres.

Antipater (ăn tĭp′ə tə), *n.* 398?–319 B.C., general under Alexander the Great; regent of Macedonia.

antipathetic (ăn tĭp′ə thĕt′ĭk, ăn′tĭ pə-), *adj.* having a natural antipathy, contrariety, or constitutional aversion (often fol. by *to*): *he was antipathetic to any change.* Also, **antip′athet′ically,** *adv.*

antipathy (ăn tĭp′ə thĭ), *n., pl.* **-thies. 1.** a natural or settled dislike; repugnance; aversion. **2.** an instinctive contrariety or opposition in feeling. **3.** an object of natural aversion or settled dislike. [t. L: m. s. *antipathīa*, t. Gk: m. *antipátheia*, der. *antipathḗs* having opposite feelings] —**Syn. 1.** See **aversion.** —**Ant. 1.** attraction.

antiperiodic (ăn′tĭ pĭə′rĭ ŏd′ĭk), *adj.* **1.** efficacious against periodic diseases, as intermittent fever. —*n.* **2.** an antiperiodic agent.

antiperistalsis (ăn′tĭ pĕ′rĭ stăl′sĭs), *n. Physiol.* inverted peristaltic action of the intestines, by which their contents are carried upwards. —**an′tipe′ristal′tic,** *adj.*

antipersonnel (ăn′tĭ pû′sə nĕl′), *adj. Mil.* used against individuals rather than against mechanized vehicles, material, etc.: *antipersonnel bombs.*

antiperspirant (ăn′tĭ pûs′pə rənt), *n.* any preparation for retarding perspiration.

antiphlogistic (ăn′tĭ flə jĭs′tĭk), *adj. Med.* **1.** checking inflammation. —*n.* **2.** an antiphlogistic remedy.

antiphon (ăn′tĭ fən), *n.* **1.** a verse sung in response. **2.** *Eccles.* **a.** a psalm, hymn, or prayer sung in alternate parts. **b.** a verse or a series of verses sung as a prelude or

an′tigov′ernment, *adj.*
an′ti-ic′er, *n.*
an′ti-ic′ing, *adj.*
an′ti-im′migra′tion, *adj.*
an′ti-imper′ialism, *n.*
an′ti-imper′ialist, *adj., n.*
an′ti-in′tellec′tual, *adj., n.*
an′timagnet′ic, *adj.*
an′timalar′ial, *adj.*
an′timil′itarism, *n.*
an′timil′itarist, *n., adj.*
an′timil′itary, *adj.*
an′timonar′chic, *adj.*
an′timonar′chical, *adj.*
an′timonar′chically, *adv.*
an′timon′archism, *n.*
an′timon′archist, *n., adj.*
an′timon′archy, *n.*
an′tina′tional, *adj.*
an′tina′tionaliza′tion, *n.*
an′tipa′pal, *adj.*
an′tipar′liamen′tary, *adj.*

conclusion to some part of the service. [t. ML: s. *antiphōna*, t. Gk: (prop. neut. pl.) sounding in answer]

antiphonal (ăn tĭf′ə nəl), *adj.* **1.** pertaining to antiphons or antiphony; responsive. —*n.* **2.** an antiphonary. —**antiph′onally,** *adv.*

antiphonary (ăn tĭf′ə nə rĭ), *n.*, *pl.* **-naries.** a book of antiphons. Also, **antiphoner** (ăn tĭf′ə nə).

antiphony (ăn tĭf′ə nĭ), *n.*, *pl.* **-nies. 1.** alternate or responsive singing by a choir in two divisions. **2.** a psalm, etc., so sung; an antiphon. **3.** a responsive musical utterance. —**antiphonic** (ăn′tĭ fŏn′ĭk), *adj.*

antiphrasis (ăn tĭf′rə sĭs), *n.* *Rhet.* the use of words in a sense opposite to the proper meaning; irony. [t. L, t. Gk] —**antiphrastic** (ăn′tĭ frăs′tĭk), *adj.* —**an′tiphras′tically,** *adv.*

antipode (ăn′tĭ pōd′), *n.* *Chiefly U.S.* the direct or exact opposite.

antipodes (ăn tĭp′ə dēz′), *n.pl.* **1.** points diametrically opposite to each other on the earth or any globe. **2.** those who dwell there. **3.** the part or parts of the world diametrically opposite. **4.** (*sometimes construed as sing.*) the direct or exact opposite. [t. L, t. Gk: pl. of *antípous* with feet opposite] —**antipodean** (ăn tĭp′ə dē′ən), *adj.*, *n.*

Antipodes (ăn tĭp′ə dēz′), *n.pl.* a group of small uninhabited islands, ab. 460 mi. SE of and belonging to New Zealand. ab. 20 sq. mi.

antipope (ăn′tĭ pōp′), *n.* one who is elected pope in opposition to another held to be canonically chosen.

antiproton (ăn′tĭ prō′tŏn), *n.* *Physics, Chem.* a subatomic particle of unit negative charge with a mass equal to that of a proton. [f. ANTI- + PROTON]

antipyretic (ăn′tĭ pī rĕt′ĭk), *Med.* —*adj.* **1.** checking or preventing fever. —*n.* **2.** an antipyretic agent.

antipyrine (ăn′tĭ pī′rĭn, -rēn), *n.* *Pharm.* a white powder, $C_{11}H_{12}N_2O$, used as a sedative, antipyretic, antirheumatic, and antineuralgic.

antiq., antiquity.

antiquarian (ăn′tĭ kwâr′ĭ ən), *adj.* **1.** pertaining to the study of antiquities or to antiquaries. —*n.* **2.** antiquary. **3.** *Paper.* a standard size of drawing paper, 53 × 31 inches. —**an′tiquar′ianism,** *n.*

antiquary (ăn′tĭ kwə rĭ), *n.*, *pl.* **-quaries.** an expert on ancient things; a student or collector of antiquities. [t. L: m. s. *antīquārius* of antiquity]

antiquate (ăn′tĭ kwāt′), *v.t.*, **-quated, -quating. 1.** to make old and useless by substituting something newer and better. **2.** to make antique. [t. L: m. s. *antīquātus*, pp., made old] —**an′tiqua′tion,** *n.*

antiquated (ăn′tĭ kwā′tĭd), *adj.* **1.** grown old; obsolete or obsolescent. **2.** ill adapted to present use. **3.** aged. —**an′tiquat′edness,** *n.* —**Syn. 2.** See **ancient**[1].

antique (ăn tēk′). *adj.*, *n.*, *v.*, **-tiqued, -tiquing.** —*adj.* **1.** belonging to former times as contrasted with modern. **2.** dating from an early period: *antique furniture.* **3.** *Colloq.* old-fashioned; antiquated: *an antique garment.* **4.** *Archaic.* aged; ancient. —*n.* **5.** an object of art or a furniture piece of a former period. **6.** the antique (usually Greek or Roman) style, esp. in art. **7.** *Print.* a style of boldface type. —*v.t.* **8.** to make appear antique. [t. L: m. s. *antīquus* old] —**antique′ly,** *adv.* —**antique′ness,** *n.* —**Syn. 2.** See **ancient**[1].

antiquity (ăn tĭk′wĭ tĭ), *n.*, *pl.* **-ties. 1.** the quality of being ancient; great age: *a family of great antiquity.* **2.** ancient times; former ages: *the errors of dark antiquity.* **3.** the time before the Middle Ages. **4.** the ancients collectively; the people of ancient times. **5.** (*usually pl.*) something belonging to or remaining from ancient times.

antirachitic (ăn′tĭ rə kĭt′ĭk), *adj.* pertaining to the prevention or cure of rickets.

antiremonstrant (ăn′tĭ rĭ mŏn′strənt), *n.* **1.** one opposed to remonstrance or to those who remonstrate. **2.** (*cap.*) one of that party in the Dutch Calvinistic Church which opposed the Remonstrants or Arminians.

antirheumatic (ăn′tĭ ro͞o măt′ĭk), *Med.* —*adj.* **1.** preventing or relieving rheumatism or rheumatic pain. —*n.* **2.** antirheumatic substance.

antirrhinum (ăn′tĭ rī′nəm), *n.* any of the genus *Antirrhinum*, of scrophulariaceous herbs, natives of the Old World; snapdragon. [t. NL, t. Gk: m. *antírrhinon* calf's snout]

antiscorbutic (ăn′tĭ skô byo͞o′tĭk), *Med.* —*adj.* **1.** efficacious against scurvy. —*n.* **2.** an antiscorbutic agent.

anti-Semite (ăn′tĭ sĕm′īt, -sē′mīt), *n.* one hostile to the Jews. —**anti-Semitic** (ăn′tĭ sĭ mĭt′ĭk), *adj.* —**an′ti-Semit′ically,** *adv.* —**anti-Semitism** (ăn′tĭ sĕm′ĭ tĭz′əm), *n.*

antisepsis (ăn′tĭ sĕp′sĭs), *n.* destruction of the microorganisms that produce sepsis or septic disease.

antiseptic (ăn′tĭ sĕp′tĭk), adj. **1.** pertaining to or causing antisepsis. —*n.* **2.** an antiseptic agent. —**antiseptically** (ăn′tĭ sĕp′tĭ klĭ), *adv.*

antisepticize (ăn′tĭ sĕp′tĭ sīz′), *v.t.*, **-cized, -cizing.** to treat with antiseptics. Also, **antisepticise.**

antiserum (ăn′tĭ sĭə′rəm), *n.*, *pl.* **-serums, -sera** (-sĭə′rə). serum containing antibodies, as antitoxins or agglutinins, obtained by inoculation of animals and used for injection into the bloodstream of other animals to provide immunity to a specific disease.

antislavery (ăn′tĭ slā′və rĭ), *adj.* *Chiefly U.S. Hist.* opposed to slavery, esp. Negro slavery.

antisocial (ăn′tĭ sō′shəl), *adj.* **1.** unwilling or unable to associate normally with one's fellows. **2.** opposed, damaging, or motivated by antagonism to social order, or to the principles on which society is constituted. —**an′tiso′cially,** *adv.*

antispasmodic (ăn′tĭ spăz mŏd′ĭk), *adj.* **1.** checking spasms. —*n.* **2.** an antispasmodic agent.

Antisthenes (ăn tĭs′thĭ nēz′), *n.* 444?–365? B.C., Greek philosopher, founder of the Cynic philosophy.

antistrophe (ăn tĭs′trə fĭ), *n.* **1.** the part of an ancient Greek choral ode, answering to a previous strophe, sung by the chorus when returning from left to right. **2.** the second of two metrically corresponding systems in a poem. [t. L, t. Gk: a turning about] —**antistrophic** (ăn′tĭ strŏf′ĭk), *adj.*

antitank (ăn′tĭ tăngk′), *adj.* *Mil.* designed for use against tanks or other armoured vehicles: *antitank gun.*

antithesis (ăn tĭth′ĭ sĭs), *n.*, *pl.* **-ses** (-sēz′). **1.** opposition; contrast: *the antithesis of theory and fact.* **2.** the direct opposite (fol. by *of* or *to*). **3.** *Rhet.* **a.** the setting of one clause or other member of a sentence against another to which it is opposed. **b.** a clause or member thus set in opposition, [t. LL, t. Gk: opposition]

antithetic (ăn′tĭ thĕt′ĭk), *adj.* **1.** of the nature of or involving antithesis. **2.** directly opposed or contrasted. Also, **an′tithet′ical.** —**an′tithet′ically,** *adv.*

antitoxic (ăn′tĭ tŏk′sĭk), *adj.* **1.** counteracting toxic influences. **2.** of or serving as an antitoxin.

antitoxin (ăn′tĭ tŏk′sĭn), *n.* **1.** a substance formed in the body, which counteracts a specific toxin. **2.** the antibody formed in immunization with a given toxin, used in treating or immunizing against certain infectious diseases.

antitrade (ăn′tĭ trād′), *n.* **1.** any of the upper tropical winds moving counter to and above the trade winds, but descending beyond the trade wind limits, and becoming the westerly winds of middle latitudes. —*adj.* **2.** denoting such a wind.

antitragus (ăn tĭt′rə gəs), *n.*, *pl.* **-gi** (-jī′). *Anat.* a process of the external ear. See diag. under **ear.** [t. NL, t. Gk: m. *antítragos*]

antitrust laws (ăn′tĭ trŭst′), *U.S.* legislation for the protection of trade from monopolistic restraints.

antitype (ăn′tĭ tīp′), *n.* that which is foreshadowed by a type or symbol, as a New Testament event prefigured in the Old Testament. [t. Gk: m. s. *antítypos* corresponding as a stamp to the die] —**antitypic** (ăn′tĭ tĭp′ĭk), **an′tityp′ical,** *adj.*

antivenin (ăn′tĭ vĕn′ĭn), *n.* **1.** an antitoxin produced in the blood by repeated injections of venom, as of snakes. **2.** the antitoxic serum obtained from such blood.

antivivisectionist (ăn′tĭ vĭv′ĭ sĕk′shə nĭst), *n.* one who opposes the practice of vivisection. —**an′tiviv′isec′tion,** *adj.* —**an′tiviv′isec′tionism,** *n.*

antler (ănt′lə), *n.* one of the solid deciduous horns, usually branched, of an animal of the deer family. [ME *auntelere*, t. OF: m. *antoillier*, ult. der. L *ant(e)* before + *oculus* eye]

antlered (ănt′ləd), *adj.* **1.** having antlers. **2.** decorated with antlers.

ant-lion (ănt′lī′ən), *n.* a larval neuropterous insect of the family *Myrmeleontidae*, the larva of which digs a pit in sand, where it lies in wait for ants, etc.

Antler of a stag
A, Brow antler;
B, Bay antler;
C, Royal antler;
D, Crown antler

Antofagasta (ăn′tə fə găs′tə; *Sp.* än tō fä gäs′tä), *n.* a seaport in N Chile. 100,000 (est. 1968).

an′tipar′liamentar′ian, *n.*, *adj.*
an′tipar′liamentar′ianism, *n.*
an′tipat′riot′ic, *adj.*
an′tipoet′ic, *adj.*
an′tira′cial, *adj.*
an′tira′cially, *adv.*
an′tirad′ical, *n.*, *adj.*
an′tirad′icalism, *n.*
an′tireform′, *adj.*
an′tireform′ing, *adj.*
an′tireli′gious, *adj.*
an′tirevi′sionist, *adj.*, *n.*
an′tiroy′alism, *n.*
an′tiroy′alist, *n.*, *adj.*
an′tislav′ery, *adj.*, *n.*
an′tiso′cialist, *n.*, *adj.*
an′tiso′cialism, *n.*
an′tistat′ic, *adj.*
an′tithe′ism, *n.*
an′tithe′ist, *n.*
an′ti-un′ion, *adj.*
an′ti-un′ionist, *n.*

Antoinette (ăn′twə nĕt′; *Fr.* äɴ twȧ nĕt′), *n.* **Marie** (mä′rĭ; *Fr.* mȧ rē′). See **Marie Antoinette.**

Antoninus (ăn′tə nī′nəs), *n.* **Marcus Aurelius.** See **Aurelius.**

Antoninus Pius (pī′əs), A.D. 86–161, emperor of Rome A.D. 138–161.

Antonioni (ăn′tō nĭ ō′nĭ; *It.* ȧn tō nyō′nē), *n.* **Michelangelo,** born 1915, Italian film director.

Antonius (ăn tō′nyəs), *n.* See **Antony, Mark.**

antonomasia (ăn′tə nə mā′shə), *n. Rhet.* **1.** the identification of a person by an epithet or appellative not his name, as *his lordship.* **2.** the use of a personal name to denote a class of similar persons, as *a Shylock.* [t. L, t. Gk, der. *antonomázein* call instead]

Antony (ăn′tə nĭ), *n.* **1. Mark** (*Marcus Antonius*), 83?–30 B.C., Roman general: friend of Caesar; member of second triumvirate and rival of Octavian. **2. Saint.** See **Anthony.**

antonym (ăn′tə nĭm), *n.* a word opposed in meaning to another (opposed to *synonym*): *'good' is the antonym of 'bad'.* [f. ANT- + s. Gk *ónyma* name; modelled on SYNONYM]

antre (ăn′tə), *n. Chiefly Poetic.* a cavern; a cave. [t. F, t. L: m. s. *antrum*, t. Gk: m. *ántron*]

Antrim (ăn′trĭm), *n.* a county in NE Northern Ireland. 278,600 pop. (1962); 1098 sq. mi. *Co. town:* Belfast.

Antrim Hills, a range of low mountains in Co. Antrim, in Northern Ireland. Highest peak, Troskan, 1817 ft. Also, **Antrim Mountains.**

antrorse (ăn trôs′), *adj. Bot., Zool.* bent or directed forwards or upwards. [t. NL: m. s. *antrorsus*, f. L *antero-* front + *versus*, pp., turned] —**antrorse′ly,** *adv.*

antrum (ăn′trəm), *n., pl.* **-tra** (-trə). *Anat.* a cavity in a bone, esp. that in the maxilla. [t. L, t. Gk: m. *ántron*]

Antung (ăn′tŏŏng′), *n.* a seaport in NE China, at the mouth of the Yalu river. 370,000 (est. 1958).

Antwerp (ănt′wûp), *n.* **1.** a province in N Belgium. 1,468,450 pop. (est. 1963); 1104 sq. mi. **2.** a seaport in and the capital of this province. 251,419 (1962). French, **Anvers** (äɴ vĕr′). Flemish, **Antwerpen** (ŏnt′vĕr pə).

Anubis (ə nyōō′bĭs), *n. Egypt. Myth.* a son of Osiris identified by the Greeks with Hermes, and represented as having the head of a dog. [t. L, t. Gk: m. *Anoubis*, t. Egypt.: m. *Anup* jackal]

anural (ə nyŏŏə′rəl), *adj. Zool.* **1.** tailless. **2.** salientian. Also, **anur′an, anur′ous.** [f. AN-[1] + m. s. Gk *ourá* tail + -AL[1]]

anuria (ə nyŏŏə′rĭ ə), *n. Med.* the absence or suppression of urine.

anus (ā′nəs), *n. Anat.* the opening at the lower end of the alimentary canal, through which the solid refuse of digestion is excreted. [t. L]

anvil (ăn′vĭl), *n.* **1.** a heavy iron block with a smooth face, frequently of steel, on which metals, usually red- or white-hot, are hammered into desired shapes. **2.** anything on which blows are struck. **3.** the fixed jaw in certain measuring instruments. **4.** *Anat.* the incus. **5. on the anvil,** unformulated; under discussion. [ME *anvilt*, OE *anfilt(e)*, c. MD *anvilte*]

Anvil (def. 1)

anvilbird (ăn′vĭl bûd), *n.* tinkerbird.

anxiety (ăng zī′ə tĭ), *n., pl.* **-ties. 1.** distress or uneasiness of mind caused by apprehension of danger or misfortune. **2.** solicitous desire; eagerness. **3.** *Psychol.* a state of apprehension and psychic tension found in some forms of mental disorder. [t. L: m. s. *anxietas*] —**Syn. 1.** See **apprehension.**

anxious (ăngk′shəs, ăng′-), *adj.* **1.** full of anxiety or solicitude; greatly troubled or solicitous: *to be anxious about someone's safety.* **2.** earnestly desirous (fol. by infinitive or *for*): *anxious to please.* **3.** attended with or showing solicitude or uneasiness: *anxious forebodings.* **4.** causing anxiety or worry; difficult: *an anxious business, an anxious time.* [t. L: m. *anxius* troubled] —**anx′iously,** *adv.* —**anx′iousness,** *n.* —**Syn. 1.** concerned, worried, disturbed.

any (ĕn′ĭ), *adj.* **1.** one, a, an, or (with plural noun) some; whatever or whichever it may be: *if you have any witnesses, produce them.* **2.** in whatever quantity or number, great or small: *have you any butter?* **3.** every: *any schoolboy would know that.* **4.** (with a negative) none at all. **5. any one,** any single or individual (person or thing): *any one part of the town.* **6.** a great or unlimited (amount): *any number of things.* —*pron.* **7.** (*construed as sing.*) any person; anybody, or (*construed as pl.*) any persons: *he does better than any before him; unknown to any.* **8.** any single one or any ones; any thing or things; any quantity or number: *I haven't any.* —*adv.* **9.** in any degree; to any extent; at all: *Do you feel any better? Will this route take any longer?* [ME; OE *ǣnig*, der. *ān* one] —**Syn. 2.** See **some.**

anybody (ĕn′ĭ bŏd′ĭ, -bə dĭ), *pron., n., pl.* **-bodies. 1.** any person. **2.** a person of little importance.

anyhow (ĕn′ĭ hou′), *adv.* **1.** in any case; at all events. **2.** in a careless manner. **3.** in any way whatever.

anyone (ĕn′ĭ wŭn′, -wən), *pron.* **1.** any person; anybody. —*adj.* **2.** any one. See **any** (def. 5).

anything (ĕn′ĭ thĭng′), *pron.* **1.** any thing whatever; something, no matter what. —*n.* **2.** a thing of any kind. —*adv.* **3.** in any degree; to any extent. **4. like anything,** *Colloq.* greatly; with great energy or emotion.

any way, 1. in any way or manner. **2.** carelessly; haphazardly; anyhow.

anyway (ĕn′ĭ wā′), *adv.* in any case; anyhow.

anyways (ĕn′ĭ wāz′), *adv. U.S.* **1.** any way. **2.** anyway.

anywhere (ĕn′ĭ wĕə′), *adv.* in, at, or to any place.

anywise (ĕn′ĭ wīz′), *adv. U.S.* in any way or respect.

Anzac (ăn′zăk), *n.* **1.** a member of the Australian and New Zealand Army Corps during World War I. **2.** a soldier from Australia or New Zealand.

Anzac Day, April 25th, the anniversary of the Anzac landing on Gallipoli in 1915: a public holiday in Australia and New Zealand.

ANZUS (ăn′zəs), *n.* Australia, New Zealand, and the United States, esp. as associated in the mutual defence treaty (**ANZUS Pact** or **Treaty**) of 1952.

A.O.C.-in-C., Air Officer Commanding-in-Chief.

Aomori (ä′ō mô′rĭ), *n.* a seaport in N Japan, at the N end of Honshu island. 224,433 (1965).

A-one (ā′wŭn′), *adj.* A-1.

Aorangi (ā′ō răng′gĭ), *n.* See **Cook, Mount.**

aorist (ā′ə rĭst, ĕə′rĭst), *n. Gram.* **1.** a tense of the Greek verb expressing action (in the indicative, past action) without further limitation or implication. —*adj.* **2.** of or in the aorist. [t. Gk: s. *aóristos* indefinite]

aoristic (ā′ə rĭs′tĭk, ĕə rĭs′-), *adj.* **1.** *Gram.* pertaining to the aorist. **2.** indefinite; indeterminate.

aorta (ā ô′tə), *n., pl.* **-tas, -tae** (-tē). *Anat.* the main trunk of the arterial system, conveying blood from the left ventricle of the heart to all of the body except the lungs. See diag. under **heart.** [t. NL, t. Gk: m. *aortḗ*] —**aor′tic, aor′tal,** *adj.*

aoudad (ä′ŏŏ dăd′), *n.* a wild sheep of northern Africa, *Ammotragus lervia.* [t. F, t. Berber: m. *audad*]

ap-, var. of **ad-,** before *p* as in *appear.*

Ap., Apostle.

A.P., 1. Associated Press. **2.** Associated Presbyterian.

apace (ə pās′), *adv.* with speed; quickly; swiftly.

apache (ə păsh′, ə păsh′; *Fr.* ȧ pȧsh′), *n.* a Parisian gangster or tough. [t. F, special use of APACHE]

Apache (ə păch′ĭ), *n., pl.* **Apaches, Apache. 1.** one of a group of Indian tribes of Athabascan speech stock in the south-western U.S. **2.** any of several Athabascan languages of Arizona and the Rio Grande basin.

apagoge (ăp′ə gō′jĭ), *n. Logic.* the technique of indirectly proving something by showing that the alternative is false, impossible, or absurd. [t. Gk: a leading away] —**apagogic** (ăp′ə gŏj′ĭk), **ap′agog′ical,** *adj.* —**ap′agog′ically,** *adv.*

apanage (ăp′ə nĭj), *n.* appanage.

aparejo (*Sp.* ȧ pȧ rĕ′ĸнō), *n., pl.* **-jos** (*Sp.* -ĸнōs). *Spanish.* a Mexican pack-saddle formed of stuffed leather cushions.

Aparri (ȧ pä′rĭ), *n.* a seaport in the Philippines on N Luzon. 24,974 (1963).

apart (ə pät′), *adv.* **1.** in pieces, or to pieces: *to take a watch apart.* **2.** separately or aside in motion, place, or position. **3.** to or at one side, with respect to purpose or function: *to set something apart.* **4.** separately or individually in consideration. **5.** aside (used with a gerund or noun): *joking apart, what do you think?* **6. apart from,** aside from: *apart from other considerations.* —*adj.* **7.** separate; independent: *a class apart.* [ME, t. OF: m. *a part*, g. L *ad partem* to the side]

apartheid (ə pät′hīt, -hāt), *n.* (in South Africa) racial segregation. [t. Afrikaans, f. *apart* APART + *-heid* -HOOD]

apartment (ə pät′mənt), *n.* **1.** a single room in a building. **2.** (*pl.*) a suite of furnished rooms, among others in a building. **3.** *Chiefly U.S.* a flat. [t. F: m. *appartement*, t. It.: m. *appartemento*, der. *appartare* separate. See APART]

apartment house, *U.S.* a building divided into apartments (def. 3).

apatetic (ăp′ə tĕt′ĭk), *adj. Zool.* assuming colours and forms which effect deceptive camouflage. [t. Gk: m. s. *apatētikós* fallacious]

apathetic (ăp′ə thĕt′ĭk), *adj.* **1.** having or exhibiting little or no emotion. **2.** indifferent. Also, **ap′athet′ical.** —**ap′athet′ically,** *adv.*

apathy (ăp′ə thĭ), *n., pl.* **-thies. 1.** lack of feeling; absence or suppression of passion, emotion, or excitement. **2.** lack of interest in things which others find moving or exciting. [t. L: m. s. *apathīa*, t. Gk: m. *apátheia* insensibility] **—Ant. 1.** ardour.

apatite (ăp′ə tīt′), *n.* a common mineral, calcium fluorophosphate, $Ca_5FP_3O_{12}$, occurring crystallized and massive, and varying in colour, used in the manufacture of phosphate fertilizers. [f. s. Gk *apátē* deceit + -ITE[1]: so called because often mistaken for other minerals]

ape (āp), *n.*, *v.*, **aped, aping.** *—n.* **1.** a tailless monkey or a monkey with a very short tail. **2.** an anthropoid ape. **3.** an imitator; a mimic. **4.** any monkey. *—v.t.* **5.** to imitate servilely; mimic. [ME; OE *apa*; c. G *Affe*] **—ape′like′,** *adj.*

apeak (ə pēk′), *adv. Naut.* in a vertical position or direction, or nearly so.

Apeldoorn (ăp′l dôn′; *Du.* ȧ′pəl dórn), *n.* a town in the Netherlands, in central Gelderland. 112,235 (1965).

Apelles (ə pĕl′ēz), *n.* 360?–315? B.C., Greek painter.

Apennines (ăp′ĭ nīnz′), *n.pl.* a mountain range traversing Italy from NW to SW. Highest peak, Monte Corno, 9585 ft.

aperçu (*Fr.* ȧ pĕr sʏ′), *n.*, *pl.* **-çus** (*Fr.* -sʏ′) *French.* **1.** a hasty glance; a glimpse. **2.** an outline or summary. [F, prop. pp. of *apercevoir* perceive]

aperient (ə pĭə′rĭ ənt), *Med. —adj.* **1.** purgative; laxative. *—n.* **2.** a medicine or an article of diet that acts as a mild laxative. [t. L: s. *aperiens*, ppr., opening]

aperiodic (ā′pĭə rĭ ŏd′ĭk), *adj.* **1.** not periodic; irregular. **2.** *Physics.* deadbeat. [f. A-[6] + PERIODIC] **—aperiodicity** (ā′pĭə rĭ ə dĭs′ĭ tĭ), *n.*

apéritif (*Fr.* ȧ pė rē tēf′), *n. French.* an aperitive.

aperitive (ə pĕ′rĭ tĭv), *n.* a small alcoholic drink taken to whet the appetite before a meal. Also, **aperitif** (ə pĕ′rĭ tĭf). [t. F: m. APÉRITIF]

aperture (ăp′ə chə), *n.* **1.** a hole, slit, crack, gap, or other opening. **2.** *Optics.* an opening that limits the quantity of light that can enter an optical instrument. [t. L: m. s. *apertūra*]

aperture synthesis, *Astron.* the use of two small aerials in a radio telescope to synthesize a large aperture.

apery (ā′pə rĭ), *n.*, *pl.* **-eries. 1.** apish behaviour; mimicry. **2.** a silly trick. [f. AP(E) + -ERY]

apetalous (ā pĕt′ə ləs), *adj. Bot.* having no petals.

apex (ā′pĕks), *n.*, *pl.* **apexes, apices** (ā′pĭ sēz′). **1.** the tip, point, or vertex of anything; the summit. **2.** climax; acme. [t. L: point, summit]

aph-, var. of **ap-, apo-** used before an aspirate.

aph., aphetic.

aphaeresis (ə fĭə′rĭ sĭs), *n.* the omission of a letter, phoneme, or unstressed syllable at the beginning of a word, as in *squire* for *esquire* Also, *Chiefly U.S.*, **apheresis.** [t. L, t. Gk: m. *aphaíresis* removal] **—aphaeretic** (ăf′ĭ rĕt′ĭk), *adj.*

aphanite (ăf′ə nīt′), *n. Geol.* any fine-grained igneous rock having such compact texture that the constituent minerals cannot be detected with the naked eye. [f. s. Gk *aphanḗs* obscure + -ITE[1]] **—aphanitic** (ăf′ə nĭt′ĭk), *adj.*

aphasia (ə fā′zyə), *n. Pathol.* impairment or loss of the faculty of speech. [t. NL, t. Gk: speechlessness]

aphasiac (ə fā′zĭ ăk′), *n. Pathol.* one affected with aphasia.

aphasic (ə fā′zĭk, -sĭk), *Pathol. —adj.* **1.** pertaining to or affected with aphasia. *—n.* **2.** an aphasiac.

aphelion (ə fē′lĭ ən), *n.*, *pl.* **-lia** (-lĭ ə). *Astron.* the point of a planet's, comet's, or artificial satellite's orbit most distant from the sun (opposed to *perihelion*). [Hellenized form of NL *aphēlium*. See APH-, HELIO-]

Aphelion

apheresis (ə fĭə′rĭ sĭs), *n. Chiefly U.S.* aphaeresis.

aphesis (ăf′ĭ sĭs), *n.* (in historical linguistic process) the gradual disappearance of an unstressed initial vowel or syllable, as in *mend* from *amend.* [t. Gk: a letting go]

aphetic (ə fĕt′ĭk), *adj.* of, pertaining to, or due to aphesis.

aphid (ā′fĭd), *n.* any of the plant-sucking insects of the family *Aphididae*; greenfly; plant-louse. [t. NL: s. *aphis*] **—aphidian** (ə fĭd′ĭ ən), *adj.*, *n.*

aphis (ā′fĭs), *n.*, *pl.* **aphides** (ā′fĭ dēz′). an aphid.

Apple tree aphid, *Aphis mali* (⅛ in. long)

aphonia (ə fō′nyə), *n. Pathol.* loss of voice, due to an organic or functional disturbance of the vocal organs. [t. Gk: speechlessness]

aphonic (ə fŏn′ĭk), *adj.* **1.** *Phonet.* **a.** unvoiced; without sound. **b.** voiceless (def. 5). **2.** *Pathol.* affected with aphonia. *—n.* **3.** *Pathol.* one affected with aphonia.

aphorism (ăf′ə rĭz′əm), *n.* a terse saying embodying a general truth. [ML: s. *aphorismus*, t. Gk: m. *aphorismós* definition, a short pithy sentence] **—aph′oris′mic, aphorismatic** (ăf′ə rĭz măt′ĭk), *adj.*

aphorist (ăf′ə rĭst), *n.* a maker of aphorisms.

aphoristic (ăf′ə rĭs′tĭk), *adj.* **1.** of, like, or containing aphorisms: *his sermons were always richly aphoristic.* **2.** given to making or quoting aphorisms. **—aph′oris′tically,** *adv.*

aphorize (ăf′ə rīz′), *v.i.*, **-rized, -rizing.** to utter aphorisms; write or speak in aphorisms. Also, **aphorise.**

aphrodisiac (ăf′rə dĭz′ĭ ăk′), *Med. —adj.* **1.** arousing sexual desire. *—n.* **2.** a drug or food that arouses sexual desire. [t. Gk: m. s. *aphrodīsiakós* venereal]

Aphrodite (ăf′rə dī′tĭ), *n.* the Greek goddess of love and beauty, identified by the Romans with Venus.

aphyllous (ə fĭl′əs), *adj. Bot.* naturally leafless. [t. Gk: m. *áphyllos* leafless]

aphylly (ə fĭl′ĭ), *n. Bot.* leaflessness.

Apia (ă pĭə′, ăp′ĭ ə), *n.* a seaport in and the capital of Western Samoa, on Upolu island. 21,699 (1961).

apiaceous (ā′pĭ ā′shəs), *adj. Bot.* related to the umbelliferous genus *Apium*, including parsley, celery, etc. [f. s. L *apium* parsley + -ACEOUS]

apian (ā′pyən), *adj.* of or pertaining to bees. [t. L: s. *apiānus*]

apiarian (ā′pĭ ĕə′rĭ ən), *adj.* relating to the breeding and care of bees.

apiarist (ā′pyə rĭst), *n.* one who keeps an apiary; a beekeeper.

apiary (ā′pyə rĭ), *n.*, *pl.* **-ries.** a place in which bees are kept; a stand or shed containing a number of beehives. [t. L: m. s. *apiārium*]

apical (ăp′ĭ kl, ā′pĭ-), *adj.* of, at, or forming the apex. [f. s. L *apex* summit + -AL[1]] **—ap′ically,** *adv.*

apices (ā′pĭ sēz), *n.*, *pl.* of **apex.**

apiculate (ə pĭk′yŏŏ lĭt, -lāt′), *adj. Bot.* tipped with a short, abrupt point, as a leaf.

apiculture (ā′pĭ kŭl′chə), *n.* the rearing of bees. [f. L *api(s)* bee + CULTURE] **—a′picul′tural,** *adj.* **—a′picul′turist,** *n.*

apiece (ə pēs′), *adv.* for each piece, thing, or person; for each one; each: *an orange apiece, costing a shilling apiece.* [orig. two words, *a* to or for each + PIECE]

à pied (*Fr.* ȧ pyė′), *French.* afoot; walking; on foot.

Apis (ā′pĭs), *n.* the sacred bull of the ancient Egyptians, to which divine honours were paid. [t. L, t. Gk: m. *Apis*, t. Egyptian: m. *ḥapi*, prob. the running (bull)]

apish (ā′pĭsh), *adj.* **1.** having the qualities, appearance, or ways of an ape. **2.** slavishly imitative. **3.** foolishly affected. **—ap′ishly,** *adv.* **—ap′ishness,** *n.*

apivorous (ā pĭv′ə rəs), *adj. Zool.* feeding on bees, as certain birds. [f. L *api(s)* bee + -VOROUS]

Apl, April.

aplacental (ā′plə sĕn′tl, ăp′lə-), *adj. Zool.* not placental; having no placenta, as the lowest mammals.

aplanatic (ăp′lə năt′ĭk), *adj. Optics.* free from spherical aberration and coma. [f. m. s. Gk *aplánētos* not wandering + -IC] **—aplan′atism,** *n.*

aplastic anaemia (ā plăs′tĭk), *Pathol.* a severe anaemia due to destruction or depressed function of the bone marrow, with no regenerative hyperplasia.

aplite (ăp′līt), *n.* a fine-grained granite composed essentially of felspar and quartz. [f. m. s. Gk *haplóos* single, simple + -ITE[1]] **—aplitic** (ă plĭt′ĭk), *adj.*

aplomb (ə plŏm′; *Fr.* ȧ plôɴ′), *n.* **1.** imperturbable self-possession, poise, or assurance. **2.** a perpendicular position. [t. F: f. *à* according to + *plomb* plummet]

apnoea (ăp nĭə′), *n. Pathol.* **1.** suspension of respiration. **2.** asphyxia. Also, *U.S.*, **apnea.** [t. NL, t. Gk: m. *ápnoia* lack of wind] **—apnoeal′, apnoeic** (ăp nē′ĭk), *adj.*

Apo (ā′pō), *n.* a volcano in the Philippines on S Mindanao, near Davao: the highest peak in the Philippines. 9610 ft.

apo-, a prefix meaning 'from', 'away', 'off', 'asunder', as in *apomorphine, apophyllite.* Also, **ap-, aph-.** [t. Gk. Cf. AB-]

Apoc., **1.** Apocalypse. **2.** Apocrypha. **3.** Apocryphal.

apocalypse (ə pŏk′ə lĭps), *n.* **1.** (*cap.*) the Revelation of St John the Divine. **2.** any of a class of writings, Jewish and Christian, which appeared from about 200 B.C. to A.D. 350, assuming to make revelation of the ultimate divine purpose. **3.** revelation; discovery; disclosure. [ME *apocalipse*, t. L: m. s. *apocalypsis*, t. Gk: m. *apokálypsis*]

apocalyptic (ə pŏk′ə lĭp′tĭk), *adj.* **1.** of or like an apocalypse; affording a revelation. **2.** pertaining to the Apocalypse, or book of Revelation. Also, **apoc′alyp′tical. —apoc′alyp′tically,** *adv.*

apocarp (ăp′ə käp′), *n. Bot.* a gynoeceum with apocarpous carpels.

apocarpous (ăp′ə kä′pəs), *adj. Bot.* having the carpels separate. [f. APO- + m. s. Gk *karpós* fruit + -OUS]

apochromatic (ăp′ə krə măt′ĭk), *adj. Optics.* having a high degree of correction for chromatic and spherical aberration and for coma. [modelled on ACHROMATIC. See APO-]

Apocarpous flower

apocopate (ə pŏk′ə pāt′), *v.t.*, **-pated, -pating.** to shorten by apocope. —**apoc′opa′tion,** *n.*

apocope (ə pŏk′ə pĭ), *n.* the cutting off of the last sound of a word, as in *cinema* from *cinematograph.* [t. L, t. Gk: m. *apokopē* a cutting off]

apocrypha (ə pŏk′rĭ fə), *n.pl.* (*now construed as sing.*) **1.** (*cap.*) fourteen books, not considered canonical, included in the Septuagint and the Vulgate as an appendix to the Old Testament, but usually omitted from Protestant editions of the Bible. **2.** various religious writings of uncertain origin regarded by some as inspired, but rejected by most authorities. **3.** works of doubtful authorship or authenticity. [t. LL, neut. pl. of *apocryphus,* t. Gk: m. *apókryphos* hidden]

apocryphal (ə pŏk′rĭ fəl), *adj.* **1.** of doubtful authorship or authenticity. **2.** *Eccles.* **a.** (*cap.*) of or pertaining to the Apocrypha. **b.** of doubtful sanction; uncanonical. **3.** false; spurious. **4.** fabulous; fictitious; mythical. —**apoc′ryphally,** *adv.* —**apoc′ryphalness,** *n.*

apocynaceous (ə pŏs′ĭ nā′shəs), *adj. Bot.* belonging to the *Apocynaceae,* or dogbane family, which includes the dogbane, periwinkle, oleander, and various other plants, mostly tropical, some having medicinal and industrial uses. [f. s. NL *Apocynum* the dogbane genus (t. Gk: m. *apókynon* kind of plant) + -ACEOUS]

apodal (ăp′ə dl), *adj. Zool.* **1.** having no distinct feet or footlike members. **2.** belonging to the *Apoda* or *Apodes* (various groups of apodal animals). Also, **apod** (ăp′ŏd). [f. s. Gk *ápous* footless + -AL[1]]

apodictic (ăp′ə dĭk′tĭk), *adj.* **1.** incontestable because demonstrated or demonstrable. **2.** *Logic.* descriptive of a proposition (in Aristotelian logic) or a judgement (in Kantian), the truth of which it claims to be necessary. Also, **apodeictic** (ăp′ə dīk′tĭk), **ap′odic′tical.** [t. Gk: m. s. *apodeiktikós* demonstrative] —**ap′odic′tically,** *adv.*

apodosis (ə pŏd′ə sĭs), *n., pl.* **-ses** (-sēz′). (in a conditional sentence) the clause stating the consequence. [t. L, t. Gk: return, answering clause]

apogamy (ə pŏg′ə mĭ), *n. Bot.* the development of a sporophyte from a cell or cells of the gametophyte other than the egg. [f. APO- + -GAMY] —**apogamic** (ăp′ə găm′ĭk), **apog′amous,** *adj.*

apogee (ăp′ə jē′), *n.* **1.** *Astron.* the point in the orbit of a heavenly body most distant from the earth (opposed to *perigee*). **2.** the highest or most distant point; climax. [t. F: m. *apogée,* t. L: m. *apogēum,* t. Gk: m. *apógaion* (*diástēma*) (distance) from the earth] —**ap′oge′al, ap′oge′an,** *adj.*

Apogee

apogeotropism (ăp′ə jĭ ŏt′rə pĭz′əm), *n. Bot.* growth or tendency away from the earth; negative geotropism. —**apogeotropic** (ăp′ə jĭə trŏp′ĭk), *adj.*

Apollinaire (ə pŏl′ĭ nĕə′; *Fr.* ȧ pŏ lē nĕr′), *n.* **Guillaume** (*Fr.* gē yōm′) (*Wilhelm Apollinaris de Kostrowitzki*), 1880–1918, French poet, novelist, and prose-writer.

Apollo (ə pŏl′ō), *n., pl.* **-los. 1.** a Greek (and Roman) deity, the god of light, healing, music, poetry, prophecy, youthful manly beauty, etc. **2.** a very beautiful young man. [t. L, t. Gk: m. s. *Apóllōn*]

Apollo Belvedere, a marble statue of Apollo, found in 1485, and now in the Belvedere, Rome: probably a Roman copy of a Greek original.

apollonian (ăp′ə lō′nyən), *adj.* **1.** (*cap.*) pertaining to the cult of Apollo. **2.** serene; stately; poised; having the properties of classic beauty.

Apollyon (ə pŏl′yən), *n. Bible.* the destroyer; the angel of the bottomless pit. Rev. 9:11. [t. Gk: prop. adj., destroying]

apologetic (ə pŏl′ə jĕt′ĭk), *adj.* **1.** making apology or excuse for fault, failure, etc. **2.** defending by speech or writing. Also, **apol′oget′ical.** [t. LL: s. *apologēticus,* t. Gk: m. *apologētikós*] —**apol′oget′ically,** *adv.*

apologetics (ə pŏl′ə jĕt′ĭks), *n.* **1.** the science or technique of defensive argument. **2.** the branch of theology concerned with the defence of Christianity.

apologia (ăp′ə lō′jĭ ə), *n.* a formal defence or justification in speech or writing, as of a cause or doctrine. [t. L, t. Gk: a speech in defence]

apologist (ə pŏl′ə jĭst), *n.* **1.** one who makes an apology or defence in speech or writing. **2.** *Eccles.* **a.** a defender of Christianity. **b.** one of the authors of the early Christian apologies.

apologize (ə pŏl′ə jīz′), *v.i.*, **-gized, -gizing. 1.** to offer excuses or regrets for some fault, insult, failure, or injury. **2.** to make a formal defence in speech or writing. Also, **apologise.** —**apol′ogiz′er,** *n.*

apologue (ăp′ə lŏg′), *n.* **1.** a didactic narrative; a moral fable. **2.** an allegory. [t. F, t. L: m. s. *apologus,* t. Gk: m. *apólogos* a story, tale]

apology (ə pŏl′ə jĭ), *n., pl.* **-gies. 1.** an expression of regret offered for some fault, failure, insult, or injury. **2.** an apologia. **3.** a poor specimen or substitute; a makeshift: *a sad apology for a hat.* [see APOLOGIA] —**Syn. 1.** See **excuse. 2.** justification, vindication.

apolune (ăp′ə lo͞on′), *n.* the highest point in the orbit of a body which is circling the moon, with respect to the moon's centre. [f. APO- + *lune* (m. s. L *lūna* moon), modelled on APOGEE]

apomorphine (ăp′ə mô′fēn), *n. Pharm.* an artificial crystalline alkaloid prepared from morphine: used in the form of the hydrochloride as an emetic and expectorant. Also, **apomorphin** (ăp′ə mô′fĭn), **apomorphia** (ăp′ə-mô′fy ə).

aponeurosis (ăp′ə nyo͞oə rō′sĭs), *n., pl.* **-ses** (-sēz). *Anat.* a whitish fibrous membrane formed by the expansion of a tendon. [t. NL, t. Gk, der. *aponeuroûsthai* become a tendon] —**aponeurotic** (ăp′ə nyo͞oə rŏt′ĭk), *adj.*

apopemptic (ăp′ə pĕmp′tĭk), *adj.* pertaining to sending away; valedictory. [t. Gk: m. s. *apopemptikós*]

apophasis (ə pŏf′ə sĭs), *n. Rhet.* denial of an intention to speak of something which is at the same time hinted or insinuated. [t. L, t. Gk: denial]

apophthegm (ăp′ə thĕm′), *n.* a short, pithy, instructive saying; a terse remark or aphorism. Also, **apothegm.** [t. Gk: m. *apóphthegma*] —**apophthegmatic** (ăp′ə thĭg-măt′ĭk), **ap′ophthegmat′ical,** *adj.*

apophthegmatize (ăp′ə thĕg′mə tīz′), *v.i.*, **-tized, -tizing.** to speak in apophthegms. Also, **apophthegmatise.** —**ap′ophtheg′matist,** *n.*

apophyge (ə pŏf′ĭ jĭ), *n. Archit.* **1.** the small, hollow outward spread at the bottom of the shaft of a column by which it joins the base. See diag. under **column. 2.** a similar but slighter spread at the top of the shaft. [t. Gk: lit., an escape]

apophyllite (ə pŏf′ĭ līt′, ăp′ō fĭl′īt), *n.* a mineral, a hydrous potassium and calcium, occurring in white crystals. [f. APO- + s. Gk *phýllon* leaf + -ITE[1]; so named because of its tendency to exfoliate]

apophysis (ə pŏf′ĭ sĭs), *n., pl.* **-ses** (-sēz′). *Anat., Bot., etc.* an outgrowth; a process; a projection or protuberance. [t. NL, t. Gk: an offshoot]

apoplectic (ăp′ə plĕk′tĭk), *adj.* Also, **ap′oplec′tical. 1.** of or pertaining to apoplexy. **2.** having or inclined to apoplexy. **3.** *Colloq.* bad-tempered; choleric. —*n.* **4.** a person having or disposed to apoplexy. —**ap′oplec′tically,** *adv.*

apoplexy (ăp′ə plĕk′sĭ), *n. Pathol.* **1.** marked loss of bodily function due to cerebral haemorrhage. **2.** haemorrhage into the tissue of any organ, esp. the brain. [ME *apoplexie,* t. L: m. *apoplēxia,* t. Gk, der. *apoplēssein* disable by a stroke]

aport (ə pôt′), *adv. Naut.* on or towards the port side.

aposiopesis (ăp′ə sī′ō pē′sĭs), *n. Rhet.* a sudden breaking off in the middle of a sentence, as if from unwillingness to proceed. [t. L, t. Gk, der. *aposiōpân* be silent] —**aposiopetic** (ăp′ə sī′ō pĕt′ĭk), *adj.*

apostasy (ə pŏs′tə sĭ), *n., pl.* **-sies.** a total desertion of, or departure from, one's religion, principles, party, cause, etc. [ME *apostasie,* t. L: m. *apostasia,* t. Gk, var. of *apóstasis* defection, revolt]

apostate (ə pŏs′tāt, -tĭt), *n.* **1.** one who forsakes his church, cause, party, etc. —*adj.* **2.** guilty of apostasy.

apostatize (ə pŏs′tə tīz′), *v.i.*, **-tized, -tizing.** to commit apostasy. Also, **apostatise.**

a posteriori (ā′ pŏs tē′rĭ ô′rī), from effect to cause; based upon actual observation or upon experimental data (opposed to *a priori*): *an a posteriori argument.* [t. L: from the subsequent or latter]

apostil (ə pŏs′tĭl), *n.* a marginal annotation or note. Also, **apostille.** [t. F: (m.) *apostille,* der. *apostiller,* f. *à* to + *postille* marginal note, prob. t. ML: m. *postilla,* f. *post* after + *illa* those things]

apostle (ə pŏs′əl), *n.* **1.** one of the twelve disciples sent forth by Christ to preach the gospel. **2.** (among the Jews of the Christian epoch) a title borne by persons sent on foreign missions. **3.** *Mormon Ch.* one of a council of twelve officials presiding over the Church and administering its ordinances. **4.** a pioneer of any great moral reform. **5.** a vigorous and zealous upholder (of a principle, cause, etc.). [ME *apostel,* OE *apostol,* t. L: s. *apostolus,*

t. Gk: m. *apóstolos* one sent away. Cf. ME *apostle*, t. OF] —**apos′tleship′**, *n.*

Apostles' Creed, a creed of virtually universal acceptance in the Christian Church, dating back to about A.D. 500 and traditionally ascribed to Christ's apostles. It begins 'I believe in God the Father Almighty'.

apostle spoon, a small silver spoon with a figure of an apostle at the end of the handle; formerly a common christening present.

apostolate (ə pŏs′tə lĭt, -lāt′), *n.* **1.** the dignity or office of an apostle. **2.** *Rom. Cath. Ch.* the dignity or office of the pope, the holder of the Apostolic See.

apostolic (ăp′ə stŏl′ĭk), *adj.* **1.** pertaining to or characteristic of an apostle, esp. of the twelve apostles. **2.** derived from the apostles in regular sequence. **3.** of the pope; papal. Also, **ap′ostol′ical.** —**ap′ostol′ically,** *adv.* —**apostolicism** (ăp′ə stŏl′ĭ sĭz′əm), *n.* —**apostolicity** (ə-pŏs′tə lĭs′ĭ tĭ), *n.*

Apostolic Fathers, **1.** the fathers of the Church whose lives overlapped those of any of the apostles. **2.** works dating from the second century, reputed to have been written by them.

Apostolic See, **1.** the Church of Rome, traditionally founded by St Peter. **2.** (*l.c.*) any of the churches founded by apostles.

apostolic succession, *Eccles.* the descent of faith and order from Christ's apostles through the consecration of bishops.

apostrophe[1] (ə pŏs′trə fĭ), *n.* the sign (') used to indicate: **1.** the omission of one or more letters in a word, as in *o'er* for *over*, *halo'd* for *haloed*. **2.** the possessive case, as in *lion's*, *lions'*. **3.** certain plurals, as in *several M.D.'s*. [special use of APOSTROPHE[2], by confusion with F *apostrophe*, t. L: m. s. *apostrophus*, t. Gk: m. *apóstrophos* turned away, elided] —**apostrophic** (ăp′ə strŏf′ĭk), *adj.*

apostrophe[2] (ə pŏs′trə fĭ), *n.* a digression from a discourse, esp. in the form of a personal address to someone not present. [t. L, t. Gk: a turning away] —**apostrophic** (ăp′ə strŏf′ĭk), *adj.*

apostrophize (ə pŏs′trə fīz′), *v.*, **-phized, -phizing.** *Rhet.* —*v.t.* **1.** to address by apostrophe. —*v.i.* **2.** to utter an apostrophe. Also, **apostrophise.**

apothecaries' measure, a system of units used in compounding and dispensing liquid drugs. In Great Britain 20 minims (♏) = 1 fluid scruple (f℈); 3 fluid scruples = 1 fluid drachm (fʒ); 8 fluid drachms = 1 fluid ounce (f℥); 20 fluid ounces = 1 pint; 8 pints = 1 imperial gallon (277·274 cubic inches). In the United States 60 minims = 1 fluid dram; 8 fluid drams = 1 fluid ounce; 16 fluid ounces = 1 pint; 8 pints = 1 U.S. gallon (231 cubic inches).

apothecaries' weight, a system of weights used in compounding and dispensing drugs: 20 grains = 1 scruple (℈); 3 scruples = 1 drachm (ʒ); 8 drachms = 1 ounce (℥); 12 ounces = 1 pound. The grain, ounce, and pound are the same as in troy weight, the grain alone being the same as in avoirdupois weight.

apothecary (ə pŏth′ĭ kə rĭ), *n.*, *pl.* **-ries.** **1.** *Archaic.* a chemist; a pharmacist. **2.** *Law.* a chemist licensed to prescribe medicine by the Apothecaries' Society of London, or the Apothecaries' Hall of Ireland. [ME *apothecarie*, t. LL: m. *apothēcārius* shopkeeper, der. L *apothēca*, t. Gk: m. *apothḗkē* storehouse; r. ME *apotecarie*, t. OF: m. *apotecaire*. See -ARY[1]]

apothecium (ăp′ə thē′sĭ əm), *n.*, *pl.* **-cia** (-sĭ ə). *Bot.* the fruit of certain lichens, usually an open, saucer- or cup-shaped body, the inner surface of which is covered with a layer which bears asci. [t. NL, f. L: s. *apothēca* (t. Gk: m. *apothḗkē* storehouse) + dim. *-ium*] —**apothecial** (ăp′ə-thē′sĭ əl), *adj.*

apothegm (ăp′ə thĕm′), *n.* an apophthegm. —**apothegmatic** (ăp′ə thĭg măt′ĭk), **ap′othegmat′ical,** *adj.*

apothem (ăp′ə thĕm′), *n.* *Geom.* a perpendicular from the centre of a regular polygon to one of its sides. [f. APO- + m. Gk *théma*, der. *tithénai* set]

AB, Apothem

apotheosis (ə pŏth′ĭ ō′sĭs), *n.*, *pl.* **-ses** (-sēz). **1.** exaltation to the rank of a god. **2.** the glorification of any person. **3.** a deified or glorified ideal. [t. L, t. Gk: deification]

apotheosize (ə pŏth′ĭ ə sīz′), *v.t.*, **-sized, -sizing.** to deify. Also, **apotheosise.**

app., **1.** apparent. **2.** appendix. **3.** appointed.

appal (ə pôl′), *v.t.*, **-palled, -palling.** **1.** to overcome with fear; fill with consternation and horror. **2.** *Colloq.* to shock; dismay; displease. [ME *apalle(n)*, t. OF: m. *apallir* become or make pale] —**Syn.** **1.** See **frighten.**

Appalachian (ăp′ə lā′chĭ ən), *n.* *Geol.* the major mountain-building episode which occurred in eastern North America in the late Devonian and early Mississippian periods.

Appalachian Mountains, a mountain system of E North America, extending from Quebec province in Canada to N Alabama. Highest peak, Mt Mitchell, 6684 ft. Also, **Appalachians.**

Appalachian tea, **1.** the leaves of any of certain plants of the genus *Ilex* of the eastern U.S., as the shrub or small tree, *I. vomitoria*, sometimes used as a tea. **2.** a plant yielding such leaves. **3.** a shrub, *Viburnum cassinoides*, of the eastern U.S.

appall (ə pôl′), *v.t.* *U.S.* appal.

appalling (ə pô′lĭng), *adj.* **1.** causing dismay or horror: *an appalling accident.* **2.** *Colloq.* very bad; objectionable. **3.** *Colloq.* noticeable. —**appall′ingly,** *adv.*

appanage (ăp′ə nĭj), *n.* **1.** land or some other source of revenue assigned for the maintenance of a member of the family of a ruling house. **2.** whatever belongs or falls to one's rank or station in life. **3.** a natural or necessary accompaniment. Also, **apanage.** [t. F, der. OF *apaner*, t. ML: m. *appānāre* furnish with bread]

appar., **1.** apparent. **2.** apparently.

apparatus (ăp′ə rā′təs), *n.*, *pl.* **-tus, -tuses.** **1.** an assemblage of instruments, machinery, appliances, materials, etc., for a particular use. **2.** any complex appliance for a particular purpose. **3.** *Physiol.* a collection of organs, differing in structure, which all minister to the same function. **4.** an organization or subdivision of an organization, esp. that part concerned with general administration: *the apparatus of a political party.* [t. L: preparation]

apparel (ə păr′əl), *n.*, *v.*, **-relled, -relling,** or (*U.S.*) **-reled, -reling.** —*n.* **1.** a person's outer clothing; raiment. **2.** *Archaic.* aspect; guise. **3.** *Naut.* the furnishings or equipment of a ship, as sails, anchors, guns, etc. —*v.t.* **4.** *Archaic.* to dress or clothe; adorn; ornament. [ME *aparaile(n)* t. OF: m. *apareiller* clothe, ult. der. L *ad-* AD- + dim. of *par* equal] —**Syn.** **1.** clothes, dress, attire, garb.

apparent (ə păr′ənt), *adj.* **1.** capable of being clearly perceived or understood; plain or clear. **2.** seeming; ostensible: *the apparent motion of the sun.* **3.** observed without correction (as opposed to *mean* or *true*). **4.** exposed to the sight; open to view. **5.** absolutely entitled to an inherited throne, title, or other estate, by right of birth (opposed to *presumptive*): *the heir apparent.* [t. L: s. *appārens* appearing; r. ME *aparant*, t. OF] —**appar′ently,** *adv.* —**appar′entness,** *n.*

—**Syn.** **1.** APPARENT, EVIDENT, OBVIOUS, PATENT all refer to something easily perceived. APPARENT applies to that which can readily be seen or perceived: *an apparent effort.* EVIDENT applies to that which facts or circumstances make plain: *his innocence was evident.* OBVIOUS applies to that which is unquestionable, because completely manifest or noticeable: *an obvious change of method.* PATENT, a more formal word, applies to that which is open to view or understanding by all: *a patent error.*

apparition (ăp′ə rĭsh′ən), *n.* **1.** a ghostly appearance; a spectre or phantom. **2.** anything that appears, esp. something remarkable or phenomenal. **3.** the act of appearing [t. LL: s. *appāritio*, in L service] —**ap′pari′tional,** *adj.*

—**Syn.** **1.** APPARITION, PHANTASM, PHANTOM are terms for a supernatural appearance. An APPARITION of a person or thing is an immaterial appearance which seems real, and is generally sudden or startling in its manifestation: *an apparition of a headless horseman.* Both PHANTOM and PHANTASM denote an illusory appearance, as in a dream; the former is usually pleasant and the latter frightening: *a phantom of a garden, a monstrous phantasm.*

apparitor (ə păr′ĭ tə), *n.* **1.** a subordinate official of an ancient Roman magistrate. **2.** a subordinate official of an ecclesiastical court. **3.** a university beadle. [t. L: (public) servant]

appassionato (ə păs′yə nä′tō), *adj.* *Music.* impassioned; with passion or strong feeling. [It.]

appeal (ə pēl′), *n.* **1.** a call for aid, support, mercy, etc.; an earnest request or entreaty. **2.** application or reference to some person or authority for corroboration, vindication, decision, etc. **3.** *Sport.* a call from a player to the referee or umpire for his decision on a point of play. **4.** *Law.* **a.** an application or proceeding for review by a higher tribunal. **b.** *Obs.* a formal charge or accusation. **5.** power to attract or to move the feelings: *the game has lost its appeal; sex appeal.* **6.** *Obs.* a summons or challenge. —*v.i.* **7.** to call for aid, mercy, sympathy, or the like; make an earnest entreaty. **8.** *Law.* to apply to a higher tribunal for review of a case or particular issue. **9.** to resort for proof, decision, or settlement: *to appeal to force.* **10.** *Sport.* to appeal to the referee or umpire for his decision. **11.** to offer a peculiar attraction, interest, enjoyment, etc.: *this colour appeals to me.* —*v.t.* **12.** *Law.* **a.** to apply to a higher tribunal for review of (a case). **b.** *Obs.* to charge with a crime before a tribunal. [ME *apele(n)*, t. OF: m. *apeler*, g. L *appellāre* approach, address, summon] —**appeal′able,** *adj.* —**appeal′er,** *n.* —**appeal′ingly,** *adv.*

—**Syn. 1.** prayer, supplication. **7.** APPEAL, ENTREAT, PETITION, SUPPLICATE mean to ask for something wished for or needed. APPEAL and PETITION may concern groups and formal or public requests. ENTREAT and SUPPLICATE are usually more personal and emotional. To APPEAL is to ask earnestly for help or support, on grounds of reason, justice, common humanity, etc.: *to appeal for contributions to a cause.* To PETITION is to ask by written request, by prayer, or the like, that something be granted: *to petition for more playgrounds.* ENTREAT suggests pleading: *the child entreated his father not to punish him.* To SUPPLICATE is to beg humbly, usually from a superior, powerful, or stern (official) person: *to supplicate that the lives of prisoners be spared.*

appear (ə pĭə′), *v.i.* **1.** to come into sight; become visible: *a cloud appeared on the horizon.* **2.** to have an appearance; seem; look: *to appear wise.* **3.** to be obvious; be clear or made clear by evidence: *it appears to me that you are right.* **4.** to come or be placed before the public: *his biography appeared last year.* **5.** *Law.* to come formally before a tribunal, authority, etc., as defendant, plaintiff, or counsel. [ME *apere(n)*, t. OF: m. *aper-*, s. *apareir*, g. L *appārēre*] —**Syn. 2.** See **seem.**

appearance (ə pĭə′rəns), *n.* **1.** the act or fact of appearing, as to the eye, the mind, or the public. **2.** *Law.* **a.** the formal coming into court of a party to a suit. **b.** formal notice of intent to defend an action. **3.** outward look or aspect; mien: *a man of noble appearance.* **4.** outward show or seeming; semblance: *to avoid the appearance of coveting an honour.* **5.** (*pl.*) outward signs; indications; apparent conditions or circumstances: *don't judge by appearances.* **6. keep up appearances,** to maintain a (socially acceptable) outward show (often to conceal inner fault). **7. to all appearances,** apparently; so far as can be seen. **8.** an apparition. **9.** *Philos.* the sensory, or phenomenal, aspect of existence to an observer.

—**Syn. 3.** APPEARANCE, ASPECT, GUISE refer to the way in which something outwardly presents itself to view. APPEARANCE refers to the outward look: *the shabby appearance of his car.* ASPECT refers to the appearance at some particular time or in special circumstances; it often has emotional implications, either ascribed to the object itself or felt by the beholder: *in the dusk the forest had a terrifying aspect.* GUISE suggests a misleading appearance, assumed for an occasion or a purpose: *under the guise of friendship.*

appease (ə pēz′), *v.t.*, **-peased, -peasing. 1.** to bring to a state of peace, quiet, ease, or content: *to appease an angry king.* **2.** to satisfy: *to appease one's hunger.* **3.** to accede to the belligerent demands of (a country, government, etc.) by a sacrifice of justice. [ME *apese(n)*, t. OF: m. *apaisier*, der. *a* to + *pais* (g. L *pax*) peace] —**appeas′able,** *adj.* —**appease′ment,** *n.* —**appeas′er,** *n.*

—**Syn. 1.** pacify, calm, placate. **2.** allay, assuage. **3.** APPEASE, CONCILIATE, PROPITIATE imply trying to preserve or obtain peace. To APPEASE is to make anxious overtures and often undue concessions to satify the demands of someone with a greed for power, territory, etc.: *Chamberlain tried to appease Hitler at Munich.* To CONCILIATE is to win an enemy or opponent over by displaying a willingness to be just and fair: *when mutual grievances are recognized, conciliation is possible.* To PROPITIATE is to admit a fault, and, by trying to make amends, to allay hostile feeling: *to propitiate an offended neighbour.* —**Ant. 1.** enrage. **2.** sharpen. **3.** defy.

appel (ə pĕl′), *n. Fencing.* **1.** a tap or stamp of the foot, formerly serving as a warning of one's intent to attack. **2.** a smart stroke with the blade used for the purpose of procuring an opening. [t. F]

appellant (ə pĕl′ənt), *n.* **1.** one who appeals. **2.** *Law.* one who appeals to a higher tribunal. —*adj.* **3.** appellate. [t. L: s. *appellans*, ppr., appealing]

appellate (ə pĕl′ĭt), *adj. Law.* **1.** pertaining to appeals. **2.** having power to review and decide appeals. [t. L: m. s. *appellātus*, pp., appealed]

appellation (ăp′ĭ lā′shən), *n.* **1.** a name, title, or designation. **2.** the act of naming. [t. L: s. *appellātio* name]

appellative (ə pĕl′ə tĭv), *n.* **1.** a common noun as opposed to a proper name. **2.** a descriptive name; a designation, as *Odd* in *Odd John.* —*adj.* **3.** pertaining to a common noun. **4.** designative; descriptive. —**appel′latively,** *adv.*

appellee (ăp′ĕ lē′, ə pĕl′ē′), *n. Law.* **1.** *U.S.* the respondent in an appellate proceeding. **2.** *Hist.* one challenged or accused. [t. F: m. *appelé*, pp. of *appeler* APPEAL]

appellor (ə pĕl′ə), *n. Law, Hist.* one who challenges, esp. to trial by combat.

append (ə pĕnd′), *v.t.* **1.** to add, as an accessory; subjoin; annex. **2.** to attach as a pendant. [t. L: s. *appendere* hang (something) on]

appendage (ə pĕn′dĭj), *n.* **1.** a subordinate attached part of anything. **2.** *Biol.* any member of the body diverging from the axial trunk. **3.** *Bot.* any subsidiary part superadded to another part.

appendant (ə pĕn′dənt), *adj.* **1.** hanging to; annexed; attached. **2.** associated as an accompaniment or consequence: *the salary appendant to a position.* **3.** *Law.* pertaining to a legal appendant. —*n.* **4.** a person or thing attached or added. **5.** *Law.* an interest (usually in land) connected with or dependent on some other interest. Also, **append′ent.** —**append′ance, append′ence,** *n.*

appendicectomy (ə pĕn′dĭ sĕk′tə mĭ), *n., pl.* **-mies.** *Surg.* excision of the vermiform appendix. [f. s. L *appendix* APPENDIX + -ECTOMY] Also, *U.S.*, **appendectomy** (ăp′ĕn dĕk′tə mĭ).

appendicitis (ə pĕn′dĭ sī′tĭs), *n. Pathol.* inflammation of the vermiform appendix. [t. NL, f. s. L *appendix* APPENDIX + *-ītis* -ITIS]

appendicle (ə pĕn′dĭ kl), *n.* a small appendage. [t. L: m. s. *appendicula*, dim. of *appendix* APPENDIX] —**appendicular** (ăp′ĕn dĭk′yŏŏ lə), **appendiculate** (ăp′ĕn dĭk′yŏŏ lĭt, -lāt′), *adj.*

appendix (ə pĕn′dĭks), *n., pl.* **-dixes, -dices** (-dĭ sēz′). **1.** matter which supplements the main text of a book, generally explanatory, statistical, or bibliographic material. **2.** *Anat.* **a.** a process or projection. **b.** the vermiform appendix. [t. L: appendage, addition]

—**Syn. 1.** APPENDIX, SUPPLEMENT both mean material added after the end of a book. An APPENDIX gives useful additional information, without which, however, the rest of the book is complete: *in the appendix are forty detailed charts.* A SUPPLEMENT, bound in the book or published separately, is given for comparison, as an enhancement, to provide corrections, to present later information, and the like: *a yearly supplement is issued.*

Appenzell (*Ger.* à pən tsĕl′, à′pən tsĕl), *n.* a canton in NE Switzerland. 61,863 pop. (1960); 161 sq. mi.

apperceive (ăp′ə sēv′), *v.t.*, **-ceived, -ceiving.** *Psychol.* **1.** to be conscious of perceiving; comprehend. **2.** to comprehend by assimilating (a new idea) with the mass of concepts, etc., already in the mind. [der. APPERCEPTION, modelled on *perceive, perception*]

apperception (ăp′ə sĕp′shən), *n. Psychol.* **1.** conscious perception. **2.** the act of apperceiving. [t. F] —**ap′percep′tive,** *adj.*

appertain (ăp′ə tān′), *v.i.* to belong as a part, member, possession, attribute, etc.; pertain (fol. by *to*). [ME *aperteine(n)*, t. OF: m. *apertenir*, g. LL *appertinēre*]

appetence (ăp′ĭ təns), *n.* **1.** strong natural craving; appetite; intense desire. **2.** instinctive inclination or natural tendency. **3.** material or chemical attraction or affinity. [t. L: m. s. *appetentia* seeking after] —**ap′petent,** *adj.*

appetency (ăp′ĭ tən sĭ), *n., pl.* **-cies.** appetence.

appetite (ăp′ĭ tīt′), *n.* **1.** a desire for food or drink: *to work up an appetite.* **2.** a desire to supply any bodily want or craving: *the natural appetites.* **3.** an innate or acquired demand or propensity to satisfy a want: *an appetite for reading.* [ME *appetit*, t. OF, t. L: s. *appetītus* onset, desire for] —**Syn. 1–3.** longing, hunger.

appetitive (ə pĕt′ĭ tĭv, ăp′ĭ tī′tĭv), *adj.* pertaining to appetite.

appetizer (ăp′ĭ tī′zə), *n.* a food or drink that stimulates the desire for food. Also, **appetiser.**

appetizing (ăp′ĭ tī′zĭng), *adj.* exciting or appealing to the appetite. Also, **appetising.** —**ap′petiz′ingly,** *adv.*

Appian Way (ăp′ĭ ən), an ancient Roman road extending from Rome to Brundisium (now Brindisi): begun 312 B.C. by Appius Claudius Caecus. ab. 350 mi.

applaud (ə plôd′), *v.i.* **1.** to express approval by clapping the hands, shouting, etc. **2.** to give praise; express approval. —*v.t.* **3.** to praise or show approval of by clapping the hands, shouting, etc.: *to applaud an actor.* **4.** to praise in any way; commend; approve: *to applaud one's conduct.* [t. L: s. *applaudere*] —**applaud′er,** *n.*

applause (ə plôz′), *n.* **1.** hand-clapping, shouting, or other demonstration of approval. **2.** any expression of approbation or approval. [t. L: m. s. *applausus*, pp.] —**applausive** (ə plô′zĭv), *adj.* —**Syn. 2.** acclamation.

apple (ăp′l), *n.* **1.** the edible fruit, usually round and red, of a rosaceous tree, *Malus pumila* (*Pyrus malus*). **2.** the tree, cultivated in most temperate regions. **3.** the fruit of any of certain other species of tree of the same genus. **4.** any of these trees. **5.** any of various other fruits, or fruitlike products or plants, usually specially designated, as the custard-apple, love apple (tomato), oak-apple. **6.** the forbidden fruit of the tree in the Garden of Eden; temptation. [ME; OE *æppel*, c. G *Apfel*]

applecart (ăp′l kät′), *n.* **1.** a cart or market barrow for apples. **2. upset the applecart,** to disrupt plans.

apple green, a clear, light green.

applejack (ăp′l jăk′), *n.* a brandy distilled from fermented (i.e. rough) cider. See **cider.**

apple of discord, *Gk Myth.* the golden apple inscribed 'For the fairest', thrown by the goddess of discord among the Greek gods and awarded by Paris to Aphrodite. His award led to the destruction of Troy.

apple of the eye, 1. the pupil of the eye. 2. something very precious or dear.
apple-pie (ăp′l pī′), *n.* 1. a pie made with apples. 2. **apple-pie order,** perfect order. 3. **apple-pie bed,** a bed with the sheet doubled back, or in any way made uncomfortable as a joke.
apple sauce, 1. apples stewed to soft pulp. 2. *U.S. Slang.* nonsense; rubbish.
Appleton (ăp′l tən), *n.* **Sir Edward Victor,** 1892–1965, English scientist.
Appleton layers, the upper layers of the ionosphere, beyond the Heaviside layer, important in the reflection of radio waves. [named after Sir Edward APPLETON]
appliable (ə plī′ə bl), *adj. Rare.* applicable.
appliance (ə plī′əns), *n.* 1. an instrument, apparatus, or device for a particular use. 2. a fire-engine. 3. the act of applying; application. 4. *Obs.* compliance. [f. m. APPLY + -ANCE]
applicable (ăp′lĭ kə bl, ə plĭk′ə-), *adj.* capable of being applied; fit; suitable; relevant. **—ap′plicabil′ity, ap′plicableness,** *n.* **—ap′plicably,** *adv.*
applicant (ăp′lĭ kənt), *n.* one who applies; a candidate: *an applicant for a position.* [t. L: s. *applicans,* ppr.]
application (ăp′lĭ kā′shən), *n.* 1. the act of putting to a special use or purpose: *the application of common sense to a problem.* 2. the quality of being useable for a particular purpose or in a special way; relevance: *this has no application to the case.* 3. use (of a word, phrase, etc.) with assignation of a particular meaning or reference. 4. the lesson, point, or bearing (of a fable). 5. the act of applying: *the application of salve to a wound.* 6. the thing or remedy applied. 7. the act of requesting. 8. a written or spoken request or appeal. 9. close attention; persistent effort: *application to one's studies.* [t. L: s. *applicātio* a joining to] **—Syn.** 8. solicitation, petition. 9. See **effort.**
applicative (ăp′lĭ kə tĭv), *adj.* applying or capable of being applied; applicatory; practical.
applicator (ăp′lĭ kā′tə), *n.* any device used for applying, as a rodlike instrument for applying medication.
applicatory (ăp′lĭ kā′tə rĭ), *adj.* fitted for application or use; practical.
applied (ə plīd′), *adj.* 1. put to practical use, as a science when its laws are concrete phenomena (distinguished from *abstract, theoretical,* or *pure* science). 2. laid flat against.
appliqué (ă plē′kā; *Fr.* à plē kė′), *adj., n., v.,* **-quéd, -quéing.** *—adj.* 1. formed with ornamentation of one material sewn or otherwise applied to another. *—n.* 2. the ornamentation used to make an appliqué material. 3. work so formed. *—v.t.* 4. to apply or form as in appliqué work. [t. F, pp. of *appliquer* put on]
apply (ə plī′), *v.,* **-plied, -plying.** *—v.t.* 1. to lay on; bring into physical proximity or contact: *to apply a match to powder.* 2. to bring to bear; put into practical operation, as a principle, law, rule, etc. 3. to put to use; employ: *they know how to apply their labour.* 4. to devote to some specific purpose: *to apply a sum of money to pay a debt.* 5. to use (a word or statement) with reference to some person or thing as applicable or pertinent: *to apply the testimony to the case.* 6. to give with earnestness or assiduity; employ with attention; set: *to apply one's mind to one's lessons.* 7. to appliqué. *—v.i.* 8. to have a bearing or reference; be pertinent: *the argument applies to the case.* 9. to make application or request; ask: *to apply for a job.* [ME *aplie(n),* t. OF: m. *aplier,* g. L *applicāre* attach] **—appli′er,** *n.* **—Syn.** 4. appropriate, allot, assign. 9. petition.
appoggiatura (ə pŏj′ə-to͞o′rə; *It.* à pòd jà to͞o′-rà), *n. Music.* a note of embellishment (short or long) preceding another note and taking a portion of its time. [It., der. *appoggiare,* prop., lean]

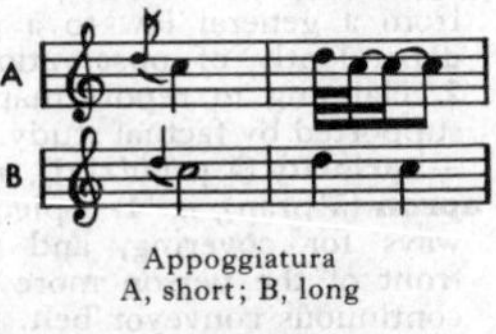

Appoggiatura
A, short; B, long

appoint (ə point′), *v.t.* 1. to nominate or assign to a position, or to perform a function; set apart; designate: *to appoint a new secretary.* 2. to constitute, ordain, or fix by decree, order, or decision; decree: *laws appointed by God.* 3. to determine by authority or agreement; fix; settle: *a time appointed for the meeting.* 4. *Law.* to designate (a person) to take the benefit of an estate created by a deed or will. 5. to provide with what is requisite; equip. 6. *Obs.* to point at by way of censure. *—v.i.* 7. *Obs.* to ordain; resolve; determine. [ME *apoint(en),* t. OF: m. *apointer,* der. *a-* A-⁵ + *pointer* POINT] **—appoint′er,** *n.* **—Syn.** 2. prescribe, establish. 5. supply. See **furnish.**
appointee (ə poin′tē′, ăp′oin tē′), *n.* 1. a person appointed. 2. a beneficiary under a legal appointment.
appointive (ə poin′tĭv), *adj. Chiefly U.S.* pertaining to or dependent on appointment: *an appointive office.*
appointment (ə point′mənt), *n.* 1. the act of appointing, designating, or placing in office: *to fill a vacancy by appointment.* 2. an office held by a person appointed. 3. the act of fixing by mutual agreement; engagement: *an appointment to meet at six o'clock.* 4. (*usually pl.*) equipment, as for a ship, hotel, etc. 5. decree; ordinance.

—Syn. 2. APPOINTMENT, OFFICE, POST, STATION all mean a place of duty or employment. APPOINTMENT refers to a position for which special qualifications are required. OFFICE often suggests a position of trust or authority. POST is a general term and may be used of any position, esp. a military one. STATION is a formal word usually restricted to military or other high public positions; it emphasizes the location or social sphere of the occupation. See **position.**

appointor (ə poin′tə, ə poin′tô′), *n. Law.* one who exercises a power of appointment of property.
Appomattox (ăp′ə măt′əks), *n.* a town in the U.S., in central Virginia: Lee surrendered to Grant here, April 9th, 1865.
apportion (ə pô′shən), *v.t.* to divide and assign in just proportion or according to some rule; distribute or allocate proportionally: *to apportion expenses.* [t. F: m. s. *apportionner,* f. *à* to + *portionner* PORTION, v.]
apportionment (ə pô′shən mənt), *n.* 1. the act of apportioning. 2. *U.S.* the distribution of representation in the federal House of Representatives among the several states (or, in state legislatures, among the counties or other local areas).
appose (ə pōz′), *v.t.,* **-posed, -posing.** 1. to put or apply (one thing) to or near to another. 2. to place next, as one thing to another; place side by side, as two things. [t. F: m. s. *apposer,* f. *à* AD- + *poser* POSE², assoc. with derivatives of L *apponere.* See APPOSITE]
apposite (ăp′ə zĭt), *adj.* suitable; well-adapted; pertinent: *an apposite answer.* [t. L: m. s. *appositus,* pp., put to] **—ap′positely,** *adj.* **—ap′positeness,** *n.*
apposition (ăp′ə zĭsh′ən), *n.* 1. the act of adding to or together; a placing together; juxtaposition. 2. *Gram.* a syntactic relation between expressions, usually consecutive; which have the same function and the same relation to other elements in the sentence, the second expression identifying or supplementing the first. For example: *Adam, the first man,* has *the first man* in apposition to *Adam.* **—ap′posi′tional,** *adj.* **—ap′posi′tionally,** *adv.*
appositive (ə pŏz′ĭ tĭv), *Gram. —adj.* 1. placed in apposition. *—n.* 2. a word or phrase placed in apposition. **—appos′itively,** *adv.*
appraisal (ə prā′zəl), *n.* 1. the act of assessing the worth, quality, or condition of anything. 2. an assessment or statement of worth, quality, or condition. 3. the act of placing an estimated value on an asset or assets. 4. valuation; an estimate of value, as for sale.
appraise (ə prāz′), *v.t.,* **-praised, -praising.** 1. to estimate generally, as to quality, size, weight, etc. 2. to value in current money; estimate the value of. Also, **apprize.** [b. APPRIZE and PRAISE] **—apprais′able,** *adj.* **—apprais′er,** *n.* **—apprais′ingly,** *adv.*
appraisement (ə prāz′mənt), *n.* appraisal (defs 3 and 4).
appreciable (ə prē′shĭ ə bl, -shə bl), *adj.* 1. capable of being perceived or estimated; noticeable. 2. fairly large. **—appre′ciably,** *adv.*
appreciate (ə prē′shĭ āt′), *v.,* **-ated, -ating.** *—v.t.* 1. to place a sufficiently high estimate on: *his great ability was not appreciated.* 2. to be fully conscious of; be aware of; detect: *to appreciate the dangers of a situation.* 3. to be sensible of the good qualities (of a person, thing, or action); to be pleased or grateful with. 4. to raise in value. *—v.i.* 5. to increase in value. [t. L: m. s. *appretiātus,* pp., appraised] **—appre′cia′tor,** *n.*

—Syn. 1. APPRECIATE, ESTEEM, PRIZE, VALUE imply holding something in high regard. To APPRECIATE is to exercise wise judgement, delicate perception, and keen insight in realizing the worth of something. To ESTEEM is to feel respect combined with a warm, kindly feeling. To VALUE is to attach importance to a thing because of its worth (material or otherwise). To PRIZE is to value highly and cherish.

appreciation (ə prē′shĭ ā′shən), *n.* 1. the act of estimating the qualities of things and giving them their due value. 2. clear perception or recognition, esp. of aesthetic quality. 3. sensibility to good qualities or good actions; pleasure; gratitude. 4. increase in value, as of property. 5. a critical essay, esp. a favourable one.
appreciative (ə prē′shĭ ə tĭv, -shə tĭv), *adj.* capable of appreciating; feeling or manifesting appreciation. **—appre′ciatively,** *adv.* **—appre′ciativeness,** *n.*
appreciatory (ə prē′shə tə rĭ, -trĭ), *adj.* appreciative. **—appre′ciatorily,** *adv.*
apprehend (ăp′rĭ hĕnd′), *v.t.* 1. to take into custody;

arrest by legal warrant or authority. **2.** to grasp the meaning of; understand; conceive. **3.** to entertain suspicion or fear of; anticipate: *I apprehend no violence.* —*v.i.* **4.** to understand. **5.** to be apprehensive; fear. [t. L: s. *apprehendere* seize] —**ap'prehend'er,** *n.*

apprehensible (ăp'rĭ hĕn'sə bl), *adj.* capable of being understood. —**ap'prehen'sibil'ity,** *n.*

apprehension (ăp'rĭ hĕn'shən), *n.* **1.** anticipation of adversity; dread or fear of coming evil. **2.** the faculty of apprehending; understanding. **3.** a view, opinion, or idea on any subject. **4.** the act of arresting; seizure. [t. L: s. *apprehensio*]

—**Syn. 1.** APPREHENSION, ANXIETY, MISGIVING imply an unsettled and uneasy state of mind. APPREHENSION is an active state of fear, usually of some danger or misfortune: *apprehension before opening a telegram.* ANXIETY is a somewhat prolonged state of apprehensive worry: *anxiety because of a reduced income.* MISGIVING implies a dubious uncertainty or suspicion, as well as uneasiness: *to have misgivings about the investment.*

apprehensive (ăp'rĭ hĕn'sĭv), *adj.* **1.** uneasy or fearful about something that may happen: *apprehensive of* (or *for*) *one's safety.* **2.** quick to learn or understand. **3.** perceptive (fol. by *of*). —**ap'prehen'sively,** *adv.* —**ap'prehen'siveness,** *n.*

apprentice (ə prĕn'tĭs), *n.*, *v.*, **-ticed, -ticing.** —*n.* **1.** one who works for another with obligations to learn a trade. **2.** a learner; a novice. —*v.t.* **3.** to bind to or put under the care of an employer for instruction in a trade. [ME *aprentys*, t. OF: m. *aprentis*, der. *a(p)prendre* teach, learn, APPREHEND] —**appren'ticeship',** *n.*

appressed (ə prĕst'), *adj.* adpressed.

apprise (ə prīz'), *v.t.*, **-prised, -prising.** to give notice to; inform; advise (often fol. by *of*). Also, **apprize.** [t. F: m. *a(p)pris*, pp. of *a(p)prendre* learn, teach. See APPRENTICE]

apprize (ə prīz'), *v.t.*, **-prized, -prizing.** *Now Rare.* appraise. Also, **apprise.** [ME *aprise(n)*, t. OF: m. *apriser*, der. phrase *à pris* for sale] —**appriz'er,** *n.*

appro (ăp'rō), *n. Colloq.* **1.** approval. **2.** approbation.

approach (ə prōch'), *v.t.* **1.** to come nearer or near to: *to approach the city.* **2.** to come near to in quality, character, time, or condition: *approaching Homer as a poet.* **3.** to bring near to something. **4.** to make advances or a proposal to: *to approach the minister with a suggestion.* **5.** to begin work on; set about: *to approach a problem.* —*v.i.* **6.** to come nearer; draw near: *the storm approaches.* **7.** to come near in character, time, amount, etc.; approximate. —*n.* **8.** the act of drawing near: *the approach of a horseman.* **9.** nearness or close approximation: *a fair approach to accuracy.* **10.** any means of access; the area through which one approaches: *the approaches to a city.* **11.** the method used or steps taken in setting about a task, problem, etc. **12.** (*sing. or pl.*) advances made to a person. **13.** (*pl.*) *Mil.* works for protecting forces in an advance against a fortified position. **14.** *Golf.* a stroke after teeing off, by which a player endeavours to get his ball on the putting green. [ME *aproche(n)*, t. OF: m. *aprochier*, g. LL *appropiāre*]

approachable (ə prō'chə bl), *adj.* **1.** capable of being approached; accessible. **2.** (of a person) easy to approach. —**approach'abil'ity, approach'ableness,** *n.*

approach beacon, a localizer beacon.

approbate (ăp'rə bāt'), *v.t.*, **-bated, -bating. 1.** *Scot. Law.* to accept as valid. **2. approbate and reprobate,** *Law.* to accept those parts of a legal instrument which are favourable to one while repudiating the unfavourable parts. **3.** *Chiefly U.S.* to approve officially. [t. L: m. s. *approbātus*, pp., favoured]

approbation (ăp'rə bā'shən), *n.* **1.** approval; commendation. **2.** sanction. **3.** *Obs.* conclusive proof.

approbatory (ăp'rə bā'tə rĭ), *adj.* approving; expressing approbation. Also, **approbative** (ăp'rə bā'tĭv).

appropriable (ə prō'prĭ ə bl), *adj.* capable of being appropriated.

appropriate (*adj.* ə prō'prĭ ĭt; *v.* ə prō'prĭ āt'), *adj.*, *v.*, **-ated, -ating.** —*adj.* **1.** suitable or fitting for a particular purpose, person, occasion, etc.: *an appropriate example.* **2.** belonging or peculiar to one: *each played his appropriate part.* —*v.t.* **3.** to set apart for some specific purpose or use: *the legislature appropriated funds for the university.* **4.** to take to or for oneself; take possession of. **5.** to filch; annex; steal. [t. L: m. s. *appropriātus*, pp., made one's own] —**appro'priately,** *adv.* —**appro'priateness,** *n.* —**appro'priative,** *adj.* —**appro'pria'tor,** *n.* —**Syn. 1.** befitting, apt, meet, felicitous.

appropriation (ə prō'prĭ ā'shən), *n.* **1.** anything appropriated for a special purpose, as money. **2.** the act of appropriating. **3.** an act of a legislature authorizing money to be paid from the treasury for a special use.

approval (ə prōō'vəl), *n.* **1.** the act of approving; approbation. **2.** sanction; official permission. **3. on approval,** for examination, without obligation to buy.

approve[1] (ə prōōv'), *v.*, **-proved, -proving.** —*v.t.* **1.** to pronounce or consider good; speak or think favourable of: *to approve the policies of the government.* **2.** to confirm or sanction officially; ratify. **3.** *Obs.* to demonstrate in practice; show. **4.** *Obs.* to make good; attest. **5.** *Obs.* to prove by trial. **6.** *Obs.* to convict. —*v.i.* **7.** to speak or think favourably (usually fol. by *of*): *to approve of him.* [ME *aprove(n)*, t. OF: m. *aprover*, g. L *approbāre*] —**approv'able,** *adj.* —**approv'er,** *n.* —**approv'ingly,** *adv.*

—**Syn. 1.** APPROVE, COMMEND, PRAISE mean to have, and usually to express, a favourable opinion. TO APPROVE is to have a very good opinion, expressed or not, of someone or something: *he approved the new plan.* TO COMMEND is to speak or write approvingly, often formally and publicly, to congratulate or honour for something done: *to commend a fireman for a heroic feat.* TO PRAISE is to speak or write, often in glowing and emotional terms, to or about one or more persons: *to praise the Boy Scouts.* **2.** authorize, endorse.

approve[2] (ə prōōv'), *v.t.*, **-proved, -proving.** *Law.* to improve; increase the value of; turn to one's own profit. [t. ONF: m. *approer* profit]

approved school, (in Britain) a school for education and therapeutic treatment of delinquent children, committed to it on the instructions of a magistrate.

approvement (ə prōōv'mənt), *n. Law.* enclosure of part of a stretch of common land.

approver (ə prōō'və), *n.* **1.** *Law.* an accomplice in a crime who turns queen's evidence. **2.** an informer.

approx., approximately.

approximal (ə prŏk'sĭ məl), *adj. Anat.* near or adjacent, as surfaces of teeth.

approximate (*adj.* ə prŏk'sĭ mĭt; *v.* ə prŏk'sĭ māt'), *adj.*, *v.*, **-mated, -mating.** —*adj.* **1.** nearly exact, equal, or perfect. **2.** inaccurate; rough. **3.** near; close together. **4.** very similar. —*v.t.* **5.** to come near to; approach closely to: *to approximate a solution to a problem.* **6.** to bring near. —*v.i.* **7.** to come near in position, character, amount, etc. [t. L: m. s. *approximātus*, pp.] —**approx'imately,** *adv.*

approximation (ə prŏk'sĭ mā'shən), *n.* **1.** a drawing, moving, or advancing near in space, position, degree, or relation. **2.** a result which is not exact, but is sufficiently so for a given purpose.

appurtenance (ə pû'tĭ nəns), *n.* **1.** something accessory to another and more important thing; an adjunct. **2.** *Law.* a right, privilege, or improvement belonging to and passing with a principal property. **3.** (*pl.*) apparatus; mechanism. [ME *appurtena(u)nce*, t. AF: m. *apurtenance*, ult. der. L *appertinēre* belong to]

appurtenant (ə pû'tĭ nənt), *adj.* **1.** appertaining or belonging; pertaining. —*n.* **2.** an appurtenance.

Apr., April.

après moi le déluge (*Fr.* à prĕ mwå' lə dĕ lyzh'), *French.* after me the deluge (attributed to Louis XV).

apricot (ā'prĭ kŏt'), *n.* **1.** the downy yellow fruit, somewhat resembling a small peach, of the tree *Prunus armeniaca.* **2.** the tree. **3.** a pinkish yellow or yellowish pink. [var. of *apricock*, appar. b. L *praecoqua* apricots (neut. pl. of *praecoquus* early ripe) and F *abricot* apricot, t. Pg.: m. *albricoque*, t. Sp.: m. *albar(i)coque*, t. Ar.: m. *al barqūq*, t. LGk: m. *praikókion*, t. L (as above)]

April (ā'prəl), *n.* the fourth month of the year, containing 30 days. [t. L: s. *Aprīlis*]

April fool, 1. a victim on April Fools' Day. **2.** a joke played on April Fools' Day.

April Fools' Day, April 1; All Fools' Day; the day observed by playing jokes on unsuspecting people.

a priori (ā' prī ô'rī, ä' prĭ ô'rĭ). **1.** from cause to effect; from a general law to a particular instance; valid independently of observation (opposed to *a posteriori*). **2.** claiming to report matters of fact but actually not supported by factual study. [t. L: from something prior] —**apriority** (ā'prī ŏ'rĭ tĭ), *n.*

apron (ā'prən), *n.* **1.** a piece of clothing made in various ways for covering, and usually also protecting, the front of the person more or less completely. **2.** a flat continuous conveyor belt. **3.** *Mach.* that part of a lathe carriage containing the clutches and gears that transmit feeder or lead screw motion to the carriage. **4.** *Civ. Eng.* **a.** any device for protecting a surface of earth such as a river bank, from the action of moving water. **b.** a platform to receive the water falling over a dam. **5.** a panel or board below a window, projecting slightly into a room. **6.** a paved or hard-packed area abutting on airfield buildings and hangars. **7.** the part of the stage in front of the proscenium arch. **8.** *Geol.* a deposit of gravel and sand extending forward from a moraine. —*v.t.* **9.** to put an apron on; furnish with an apron. [ME *napron* (*a napron* being later taken as *an apron*), t. OF: m. *naperon*, dim. of *nape*, g. L *nappa* napkin, cloth] —**a'pron-like',** *adj.*

apron-strings (ā′prən strĭngz′), *n.pl.* **1.** the ties of an apron. **2. tied to the apron-strings,** emotionally dependent on or bound to a person, as a child is to its mother.

apropos (ăp′rə pō′), *adv.* **1.** to the purpose; opportunely. **2.** with reference or regard; in respect (fol. by *of*): *apropos of nothing.* **3.** by the way. —*adj.* **4.** opportune; pertinent: *apropos remarks.* [t. F: m. *à propos*]

apse (ăps), *n.* **1.** *Archit.* a vaulted semicircular or polygonal recess in a building, esp. at the end of the choir of a church. See diag. under **basilica. 2.** *Astron.* **a.** an apsis. **b. apse line,** line of apsides. [t. L: m. s. *apsis,* t. Gk: m. *(h)apsís,* loop, circle, bow, arch, apse] —**apsidal** (ăp′sĭ dl), *adj.*

apsis (ăp′sĭs), *n., pl.* **apsides** (ăp sī′dēz, ăp′sĭ dēz′). **1.** *Astron.* **a.** either of two points in an eccentric orbit, the one (**higher apsis**) farthest from the centre of attraction, and the one (**lower apsis**) nearest to it. **b. line of apsides,** the line coinciding with the major axis of an orbit. **2.** *Archit.* an apse. [t. L. See APSE]

apt (ăpt), *adj.* **1.** inclined; disposed; prone: *too apt to slander others.* **2.** unusually intelligent; quick to learn: *an apt pupil.* **3.** suited to the purpose or occasion: *an apt metaphor.* **4.** *Archaic.* prepared; ready; willing. [ME, t. L: s. *aptus* fastened, joined, fitted] —**apt′ly,** *adv.* —**apt′ness,** *n.*

—**Syn. 2.** clever, bright. **3.** APT, PERTINENT, RELEVANT all refer to something suitable or fitting. APT means to the point and particularly appropriate: *an apt comment.* PERTINENT means pertaining to the matter in hand: *a pertinent remark.* RELEVANT means directly related to and important to the subject: *a relevant opinion.*

apteral (ăp′tə rəl), *adj.* *Archit.* without columns or a porch along the sides.

apterous (ăp′tə rəs), *adj.* **1.** *Zool.* wingless, as some insects. **2.** *Bot.* without membranous expansions, as a stem. [t. Gk: m. *ápteros* without wings]

apterygial (ăp′tə rĭj′ĭ əl), *adj.* *Zool.* without wings, fins, or limbs, as snakes and eels. [f. A-[6] + s. Gk *pterýgion* little wing + -AL[1]]

apteryx (ăp′tə rĭks), *n., pl.* **-teryxes** (-tə rĭk′sĭz), any of several flightless ratite birds of New Zealand, constituting the genus *Apteryx,* allied to the extinct moa; kiwi. [t. NL, f. Gk: *a-* A-[6] + *ptéryx* wing]

Apteryx, *Apteryx australis* (27 in. long)

aptitude (ăp′tĭ tyo͞od′), *n.* **1.** a natural tendency or acquired inclination; both capacity and propensity for a certain course. **2.** readiness in learning; intelligence; talent. **3.** the state or quality of being apt; special fitness. [t. ML: m. *aptitūdo,* der. L *aptus* fit]

aptitude test, a test for special fitness; a test given to find out what sort of work a person has the ability to learn, such as clerical work, mechanical work, etc.

Apuleius (ăp′yo͝o lē′əs), *n.* **Lucius** (lo͞o′syəs), born A.D. 125?, Roman philosopher and satirist.

Apulia (ə pyo͞o′lyə), *n.* a region in SE Italy. 3,409,687 pop. (1961); 7442 sq. mi. *Cap.:* Bari. Italian, **Puglia.**

Apure (ă po͞oə′rĭ; *Sp.* à po͞o′rĕ), *n.* a river flowing from W Venezuela E to the Orinoco. ab. 300 mi.

Apurímac (ăp′o͞o rē′măk; *Sp.* à po͞o rē′mák′), *n.* a river flowing from S Peru NW to the Ucayali river. ab. 500 mi.

apyretic (ăp′ī rĕt′ĭk), *adj.* *Pathol.* free from fever. [f. s. Gk *apýretos* without fever + -IC]

AQ, achievement quotient.

Aq., (L *aqua*) water. Also, **aq.**

Aqaba (ăk′ə bə), *n.* a seaport in SW Jordan at the N end of the **Gulf of Aqaba,** an arm of the Red Sea. 9228 (1961).

aqua (ăk′wə), *n., pl.* **aquae** (ăk′wē). *Chiefly Pharm.* water; a liquid; a solution. [t. L: water]

aqua ammoniae (ə mō′nĭ ē′), ammonia (def. 2). Also, **aqua ammonia.** [NL]

aqua fortis (fô′tĭs), concentrated nitric acid. [NL: strong water]

aqualung (ăk′wə lŭng′), *n.* a cylinder of compressed air, usually strapped on to the back, with a tube leading to a special mouthpiece or watertight mask, which enables a swimmer to move about freely at a considerable depth for an extended length of time.

aquamarine (ăk′wə mə rēn′), *n.* **1.** a transparent light-blue or greenish blue variety of beryl, used as a gem. **2.** light blue-green or greenish blue. [t. L: m. *aqua marina* sea water; r. *aigue marine,* t. F]

aquanaut (ăk′wə nôt′), *n.* a skin-diver.

aquanautics (ăk′wə nô′tĭks), *n.pl.* (*construed as sing.*) the practice of skin-diving. —**aqu′anau′tic,** *adj.*

aquaplane (ăk′wə plān′), *n., v.,* **-planed, -planing.** —*n.* **1.** a single broad water-ski. —*v.i.* **2.** to ride an aquaplane. **3.** (of a motor vehicle, etc.) to ride up at high speed on water on the road surface so that the wheels lose contact with the surface. [f. L *aqua* water + -PLANE[2]; modelled on AEROPLANE]

aqua regia (rē′jĭ ə), a mixture of one part of nitric acid and three parts of hydrochloric acid. [t. NL: royal water (with allusion to its power to dissolve gold)]

aquarelle (ăk′wə rĕl′), *n.* a painting in transparent watercolours. [t. F, t. It.: m. *acquarello,* dim. of *acqua* water] —**aq′uarel′list,** *n.*

aquarist (ăk′wə rĭst), *n.* **1.** a curator of an aquarium. **2.** a student of marine life.

aquarium (ə kwĕə′rĭ əm), *n., pl.* **aquariums, aquaria** (ə kwĕə′rĭ ə). a pond, tank, or establishment in which living aquatic animals or plants are kept, as for exhibition. [t. L, prop. neut. of *aquārius* pertaining to water]

Aquarius (ə kwĕə′rĭ əs), *n., gen.* **Aquarii** (ə kwĕə′rĭ ī′). **1.** *Astron.* a zodiacal constellation; the Water-bearer. **2.** the eleventh sign of the zodiac. See diag. under **zodiac.** [t. L: water-bearer, prop. adj., pertaining to water]

aquatic (ə kwăt′ĭk, ə kwŏt′-), *adj.* **1.** of or pertaining to water. **2.** living or growing in water. **3.** practised on or in water: *aquatic sports.* [t. L: s. *aquāticus* watery]

aquatics (ə kwăt′ĭks, ə kwŏt′-), *n.pl.* (*construed as sing.*) sports practised on or in water.

aquatint (ăk′wə tĭnt′), *n.* **1.** a process imitating the broad flat tints of ink or wash drawings by etching a microscopic crackle on the copperplate intended for printing. **2.** an etching made by this process. —*v.t., v.i.* **3.** to etch in aquatint. [t. F: m. *aquatinte,* t. It.: m. *acqua tinta,* g. L *aqua tincta* tinted water]

aqua vitae (vī′tē), **1.** alcohol. **2.** spirituous drink, as brandy or whisky. [t. ML: water of life]

aqueduct (ăk′wĭ dŭkt′), *n.* **1.** *Civ. Eng.* **a.** a conduit or artificial channel for conducting water from a distance, the water usually flowing by gravity. **b.** a structure which carries a conduit or canal across a valley or over a river. **2.** *Anat.* a canal or passage through which liquids pass. [t. L: m. *aquae ductus* conveyance of water]

aqueous (ā′kwĭ əs, ăk′wĭ-), *adj.* **1.** of, like, or containing water; watery. **2.** (of rocks) formed of matter deposited in or by water.

aqueous ammonia, ammonia (def. 2).

aqueous humour, *Anat.* the limpid watery fluid which fills the space between the cornea and the crystalline lens in the eye.

aquiculture (ā′kwĭ kŭl′chə, ăk′wĭ-), *n.* cultivation of the resources of the sea or of inland waters, as opposed to their exploitation. [f. *aqui-* (comb. form repr. L *aqua* water) + CULTURE]

aquifer (ăk′wĭ fə), *n.* a layer of rock which holds water and allows water to percolate through it. Also, **aquafer.**

Aquila (ăk′wĭ lə, ə kwĭl′ə), *n., gen.* **-lae** (-lē′). *Astron.* a northern constellation, the Eagle, lying south of Cygnus, and containing the bright star Altair. [t. L: eagle]

Aquila (*It.* à′kwē là), *n.* a town in central Italy. 60,000 (est. 1968).

aquilegia (ăk′wĭ lē′jĭ ə), *n.* *Bot.* any columbine. [t. ML, var. of *aquilēja* columbine]

Aquileia (ăk′wĭ lē′ə), *n.* an ancient city at the N end of the Adriatic: important Roman centre.

aquiline (ăk′wĭ līn′), *adj.* **1.** of or like the eagle. **2.** (of the nose) curved like an eagle's beak; hooked. [t. L: m. s. *aquilīnus*]

Aquinas (ə kwī′nəs), *n.* **Thomas** (‘*the Angelic Doctor*’), 1225?–1274, Italian scholastic philosopher and one of the great theologians of the Roman Catholic Church.

Aquitaine (ăk′wĭ tān′; *Fr.* à kē tĕn′), *n.* **1.** an administrative region in SW France. 2,312,464 pop. (1962); 16,374 sq. mi. *Prefecture:* Bordeaux. **2.** an ancient Roman province in Gaul, and later a medieval duchy. Latin, **Aquitania** (ăk′wĭ tā′nyə).

Duchy of Aquitaine, 1360

a quo (ä kwō′), *Latin.* from which; a point of departure (for something, an idea, etc.).

ar-, var. of **ad-** (by assimilation) before *r,* as in *arrear.*

-ar[1], **1.** an adjective suffix meaning ‘of or pertaining to’, ‘of the nature of’, ‘like’, as in *linear, regular.* **2.** a suffix forming adjectives not directly related to nouns, as *similar, singular.* [t. L: s. *-āris;* r. ME *-er,* t. AF]

-ar[2], a noun suffix, as in *vicar, scholar, collar.* [repr. L *-ārius, -āris,* etc.]

-ar[3], a noun suffix denoting an agent (replacing regular **-er**[1]), as in *beggar, liar.* [special use of -AR[2]]

Ar, *Chem.* (an alternative symbol for) argon.

Ar., 1. Arabic. **2.** Aramaic. **3.** argumentum.

A.R.A., Associate of the Royal Academy.

Ara (ä′rə), *n., gen.* **Arae** (ä′rē). *Astron.* the Altar, a southern constellation near Scorpio.

Arab (ăr′əb), *n.* **1.** a member of the Arabic race (now widely spread in Asia and Africa, and formerly in southern Europe). **2.** a native of Arabia; an Arabian. **3.** a horse of a graceful, intelligent breed, native to Arabia and adjacent countries. **4.** a street Arab. —*adj.* **5.** belonging or pertaining to Arabs. **6.** inhabited by Arabs. [back-formation from ARABY] —**Syn. 5.** See **Arabic.**

Arab., 1. Arabia. 2. Arabic.

arabesque (ăr′ə bĕsk′), *n.* **1.** a kind of ornament in which flowers, foliage, fruits, vases, animals, and figures (in strict Muslim use, no animate objects) are represented in a fancifully combined pattern. **2.** a pose in ballet in which one leg is stretched horizontally behind and the body lowered forward from the hips. **3.** *Music.* a short composition with florid decoration. —*adj.* **4.** in the Arabian style, esp. of ornamentation. [t. F: Arabian, t. It.: m. *arabesco*, der. *Arabo* Arab]

Arabia (ə rā′byə), *n.* a peninsula in SW Asia, including Saudi Arabia, Yemen, Muscat and Oman, South Yemen, and other political divisions: divided in ancient time into **Arabia Deserta** (dĭ zû′tə), the N part, **Arabia Felix** (fē′lĭks), the S part (sometimes restricted to Yemen) and **Arabia Petraea** (pĕ trē′ə), the NW part. 10,000,000 pop. (est. 1964); ab. 1,000,000 sq. mi.

Arabian (ə rā′byən), *adj.* **1.** pertaining or belonging to the Arabs. **2.** in Arabia. —*n.* **3.** a native or inhabitant of Arabia. **4.** an Arab (def. 1). —**Syn. 1.** See **Arabic.**

Arabian camel. See **camel** (def. 1a).

Arabian Desert, a large desert in Egypt between the Nile valley and the Red Sea.

Arabian Nights' Entertainments, The, a collection of Eastern folk tales derived in part from Indian and Persian sources and dating from the 10th century A.D. Also, **The Thousand and One Nights.**

Arabian Sea, the NW part of the Indian Ocean, between India and Arabia.

Arabic (ăr′ə bĭk), *adj.* **1.** of or pertaining to Arabia or the Arabs. **2.** pertaining to or derived from the languages or culture of Arabia or the Arabs. **3.** (*l.c.*) designating certain species of acacia growing in Arabia and other eastern countries. —*n.* **4.** any of the languages that developed out of the language of the Arabians of the time of Mohammed, now spoken in North Africa, Egypt, Arabia, Jordan, Syria, and Iraq. **5.** the standard literary and classical language as established by the Koran. [t. L: s. *Arabicus*]

Arabic numerals, the characters 0, 1, 2, 3, 4, 5, 6, 7, 8, 9, introduced into general Western use since the 12th century. Also, **Arabic figures.**

arabinose (ə răb′ĭ nōs′, ăr′ə bĭ-), *n.* the pentose sugar, $C_5H_{10}O_5$, derived from plant gums or made synthetically from glucose. [f. ARAB(IC) + -IN² + -OSE²]

arabis (ăr′ə bĭs), *n.* any plant of the cruciferous genus *Arabis*; rock-cress. [t. LL]

Arabist (ăr′ə bĭst), *n.* an authority on Arabia and the Arabs or on the Arabic language and literature.

arable (ăr′ə bl), *adj.* **1.** capable, without much modification, of producing crops by means of tillage. —*n.* **2.** arable land. [t. L: m. s. *arābilis* that can be ploughed; r. *earable* (f. *ear*, v., plough + -ABLE)] —**ar′abil′ity,** *n.*

Arab League, a limited confederation formed in 1945 by Arab Palestine and Trans-Jordan (now Jordan), Egypt, Iraq, Lebanon, Saudi Arabia, and Yemen; subsequently joined by Algeria, Kuwait, Libya, Morocco, Sudan, and Tunisia.

Arab Palestine. See **Palestine** (def. 2).

Araby (ăr′ə bĭ), *n. Poetic.* Arabia. [ME *Arabye*, t. F]

araceous (ə rā′shəs), *adj. Bot.* belonging to the *Araceae*, or arum family of plants, which includes the arums, cuckoopint, taro, etc. [f. AR(UM) + -ACEOUS]

Arachne (ə răk′nĭ), *n. Gk Myth.* a Lydian maiden who challenged Athene to a contest in weaving, and was turned into a spider. [t. L, t. Gk: lit., spider]

arachnid (ə răk′nĭd), *n.* any arthropod of the class *Arachnida*, which includes the spiders, scorpions, mites, etc. [t. NL: s. *Arachnida*, f. s. Gk *aráchnē* spider, spider's web + *-ida* -ID²] —**arachnidan** (ə răk′nĭ dən), *adj., n.*

arachnoid (ə răk′noid), *adj.* **1.** resembling a spider's web. **2.** of or belonging to the arachnids. **3.** *Anat.* pertaining to the serous membrane (between the dura mater and the pia mater) enveloping the brain and spinal cord. **4.** *Bot.* formed of or covered with long, delicate hairs or fibres. —*n.* **5.** an arachnid. **6.** the arachnoid membrane. [t. Gk: m. s. *arachnoeidḗs* like a cobweb]

A.R.A.D., Associate of the Royal Academy of Dancing.

Arad (ăr′ăd; *Rum.* ä räd′), *n.* a city in W Rumania, on the Mures river. 113,730 (1961).

Arafura Sea (ä′rə fo͝o′rə), a sea between N Australia and SW New Guinea.

Aragon (*Fr.* à rà gôɴ′), *n.* **Louis** (*Fr.* lwē), born 1897, French writer and poet.

Aragon (ăr′ə gən; *Sp.* ä rä gôn′), *n.* a region in NE Spain: formerly a kingdom; later a province. 18,181 sq. mi.

Kingdom of Aragon, 1492

aragonite (ə răg′ə nīt′), *n.* a mineral, calcium carbonate, $CaCO_3$, chemically identical with calcite but differing in crystallization, and in having a higher specific gravity, less marked cleavage, etc. [f. ARAGON + -ITE¹]

Araguaya (*Port.* ä rä gwä′yä), *n.* a river in central Brazil, flowing N to the river Tocantins. ab. 1000 mi.

Arak (ä räk′), *n.* a town in E central Iran. 66,838 (est. 1964).

aralia (ə rā′lyə), *n.* any plant of the *Aralia* genus, a group of decorative ivies much grown for indoor ornament.

araliaceous (ə rā′lĭ ā′shəs), *adj. Bot.* belonging to the *Araliaceae*, the ivy family, including the aralias, ginseng, etc.

Aral Sea (ăr′əl), an inland sea in the SW Soviet Union in Asia, E of the Caspian Sea. 26,166 sq. mi. Also, **Lake Aral.**

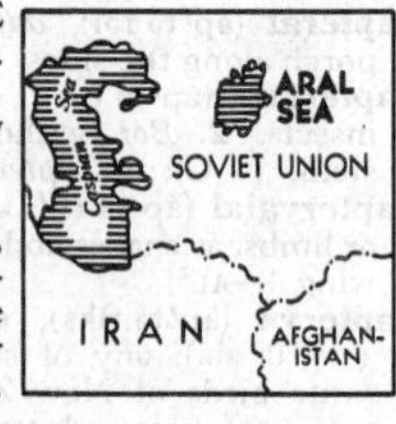

Aral Sea

Aram (ĕə′răm, ĕə′rəm), *n.* Hebrew name of ancient Syria.

Aram., Aramaic.

Aramaean (ăr′ə mē′ən), *n.* Also, **Aramean. 1.** a Semite of the division associated with Aram. **2.** the Aramaic language. —*adj.* **3.** of or pertaining to Aram or Aramaic. [f. s. L *Aramaeus* (t. Gk: m. *Aramaîos*) pertaining to Aram or Syria + -AN]

Aramaic (ăr′ə mā′ĭk), *n.* **1.** any of a group of Semitic languages which became the speech of Syria, Palestine, and Mesopotamia after circa 300 B.C., including Syriac and the language of Christ. —*adj.* **2.** pertaining to Aram, or to the languages spoken there.

Aran Islands (ăr′ən), a group of three islands of Co. Galway, off the W coast of Ireland. 2588 pop. (1953); 18 sq. mi.

Arapaho (ə răp′ə hō′), *n., pl.* **-ho. 1.** (*pl.*) a tribe of North American Indians, of Algonquian speech stock, once dwelling in the Colorado plains, and now in Oklahoma and Wyoming. **2.** a member of this tribe. **3.** their language. Also, **Arapahoe.**

arapaima (ăr′ə pī′mə), *n.* a large freshwater fish, *Arapaima gigas*, of Brazil and Guiana, said to attain a length of 15 feet and a weight of 400 pounds. [t. Pg., t. Tupi]

Ararat (ăr′ə răt′), *n.* a volcanic mountain with two peaks, in E Turkey, near the boundary with Iran and the Soviet Union: mentioned in Gen. 8:4. 16,696 ft.

Mount Ararat

Aras (ä räs′), *n.* a river flowing from E Turkey along a portion of the border between NW Iran and the SW Soviet Union into the river Kura. Ancient, **Araxes** (ə răk′sēz).

Araucania (ăr′rô kā′nyə), *n.* a region in central Chile.

Araucanian (ăr′rô kā′nyən), *n.* **1.** one of a tribe of South American Indians in central Chile. **2.** a linguistic stock of Chile and northern Argentina.

araucaria (ăr′rô kĕə′rĭ ə), *n.* any tree of the pinaceous genus *Araucaria* of South America, Australia, and Polynesia, esp. the monkey-puzzle tree. [t. NL: f. *Arauco*, province of S Chile + *-āria* -ARIA]

Arawak (ăr′ə wăk′), *n.* one of a numerous and widely scattered Amerindian language stock of northern and north-eastern South America and the West Indies. —**A′rawak′an,** *adj.*

arbalest (är′bə lĭst), *n.* a powerful medieval crossbow. Also, **arbalist.** [OE *arblast*, t. OF: m. *arbaleste* kind of catapult, g. L *arcuballista*. See ARC, BALLISTA] —**ar′balester,** *n.*

Arbela (ä bē′lə), *n.* an ancient city of Assyria, E of

Nineveh: Alexander defeated Darius near here 331 B.C.

arbiter (ä′bĭ tə), *n.* **1.** a person empowered to decide points at issue. **2.** one who has the sole or absolute power of judging or determining. [t. L: witness, judge]

arbitrable (ä′bĭ trə bl), *adj.* capable of arbitration; subject to the decision of an arbiter or arbitrator.

arbitrage (ä′bĭ trĭj, ä′bĭ träzh′ *for 1*; ä′bĭ trĭj *for 2*), *n.* **1.** *Finance.* the simultaneous purchase and sale of the same securities, commodities, or moneys in different markets to profit from unequal prices. **2.** *Rare.* arbitration. [t. F, der. *arbitrer* arbitrate] —**ar′bitrager,** *n.*

arbitral (ä′bĭ trəl), *adj. Scot. Law.* pertaining to an arbiter or to arbitration. [t. LL: s. *arbitrālis*, der. L *arbiter* judge]

arbitrament (ä bĭt′rə mənt), *n.* **1.** arbitration. **2.** the decision or sentence pronounced by an arbiter. **3.** the power of absolute and final decision. [t. ML: s. *arbitrāmentum*; r. ME *arbitrement*, t. OF]

arbitrary (ä′bĭ trə rĭ), *adj., n., pl.* **-ries.** —*adj.* **1.** subject to individual will or judgement; discretionary. **2.** not attributable to any rule or law; accidental. **3.** capricious; uncertain; unreasonable: *an arbitrary interpretation.* **4.** uncontrolled by law; using or abusing unlimited power; despotic; tyrannical: *an arbitrary government.* —*n.* **5.** *Print.* a special sort. [t. L: m. s. *arbitrārius* of arbitration, uncertain] —**ar′bitrarily,** *adv.* —**ar′bitrariness,** *n.*

arbitrate (ä′bĭ trāt′), *v.,* **-trated, -trating.** —*v.t.* **1.** to decide as arbiter or arbitrator; determine. **2.** to submit to arbitration; settle by arbitration: *to arbitrate a dispute.* —*v.i.* **3.** to act as arbiter; decide between opposing parties or sides. **4.** to submit a matter to arbitration. [t. L: m. s. *arbitrātus*, pp.] —**ar′bitra′tive,** *adj.*

arbitration (ä′bĭ trā′shən), *n.* **1.** *Law.* the hearing and determining of a dispute between parties by a person or persons chosen or agreed to by them. **2.** *Internat. Law.* the application of judicial methods to the settlement of international disputes. —**ar′bitra′tional,** *adj.*

arbitrator (ä′bĭ trā′tə), *n.* a person chosen to decide a dispute, esp. one empowered to examine the facts and to decide an issue. Also, *Obs.,* **arbitrer** (ä′bĭ trə).

arbitratrix (ä′bĭ trā′trĭks), *n.* a female arbitrator.

arbitress (ä′bĭ trĭs), *n.* a female arbiter.

Arblay, d′ (dä′blā; *Fr.* dȧr blĕ′), *n.* **Madame** (*Frances* or *Fanny Burney*), 1752–1840, English novelist.

arbor[1] (ä′bə), *n. U.S.* arbour.

arbor[2] (ä′bə), *n.* **1.** *Mach.* **a.** a beam, shaft, axis, or spindle. **b.** a bar or shaft used to support either the work or the cutting tools during a machining process. **2.** *Foundry.* a reinforcing member of a core or mould. [Latinized var. of earlier *arber*, t. F: m. *arbre*]

arbor[3] (ä′bô), *n., pl.* **arbores** (ä′bə rēz′). a tree (used chiefly in botanical names). [t. L]

arboreal (ä bô′rĭ əl), *adj.* **1.** pertaining to trees; treelike. **2.** living in or among trees. **3.** *Zool.* adapted for living and moving about in trees, as the limbs and skeleton of opossums, squirrels, monkeys, and apes.

arboreous (ä bô′rĭ əs), *adj.* **1.** abounding in trees; wooded. **2.** arboreal. **3.** arborescent. [t. L: m. *arboreus* pertaining to trees]

arborescent (ä′bə rĕs′ənt), *adj.* treelike in size and form. [t. L: s. *arborescens*, ppr., becoming a tree] —**ar′bores′cence,** *n.*

arboretum (ä′bə rē′təm), *n., pl.* **-ta** (-tə). a plot of land where different trees or shrubs are grown for study or popular interest. [t. L: a plantation of trees]

arboriculture (ä′bə rĭ kŭl′chə), *n.* the cultivation of trees and shrubs. [f. *arbori-* (comb. form repr. L *arbor* tree) + CULTURE]

arborist (ä′bə rĭst), *n.* a specialist in the care and cultivation of trees.

arborization (ä′bə rĭ zā′shən), *n.* a treelike appearance, as in certain minerals or fossils. Also, **arborisation.**

arborous (ä′bə rəs), *adj.* of or pertaining to trees.

arbor vitae (ä′bô vī′tē). **1.** an evergreen tree of the coniferous genus *Thuja*, esp. *T. occidentalis*, planted for hedges, etc. See **red cedar** (def. 1). **2.** *Anat.* a treelike appearance in a vertical section of the cerebellum, due to the arrangement of the white and grey nerve tissues. Also, **ar′borvi′tae.** [t. L: tree of life]

arbour (ä′bə), *n.* **1.** a bower formed by trees, shrubs, or vines, often on a trellis. **2.** *Obs.* a grass plot; lawn; garden; orchard. Also, *U.S.,* **arbor.** [ME (*h*)*erber*, t. AF, var. of OF (*h*)*erbier*, g. L *herbārium*, der. *herba* plant; influenced by L *arbor* tree]

Arbroath (ä brōth′), *n.* a royal burgh in Scotland, in SE Angus. 19,533 (1961).

Arbuthnot (ä bŭth′nət), *n.* **John,** 1667–1735, English satirist and physician: friend of Swift and Pope.

arbutus (ä byōō′təs), *n.* **1.** any of the evergreen shrubs or trees of the ericaceous genus *Arbutus*, esp. *A. unedo*, of southern Europe, with scarlet berries, cultivated for ornament and food. **2.** a creeping ericaceous plant, *Epigaea repens*, of the U.S., with fragrant white and pink flowers (**trailing arbutus**). [t. L: strawberry tree]

arc (äk), *n., v.,* **arced** (äkt), **arcing** (ä′kĭng) or **arcked, arcking.** —*n.* **1.** *Geom.* any part of a circle or other curved line. **2.** *Elect.* the luminous bridge formed by the passage of a current across a gap between two conductors or terminals, due to the incandescence of the conducting vapours. **3.** *Astron.* the part of a circle representing the apparent course of a heavenly body. **4.** anything bow-shaped. —*v.i.* **5.** to form an electric arc. [ME *ark*, t. L: m. s. *arcus* bow]

Arcs of circles

Arc, d′ (*Fr.* dȧrk), *n.* **Jeanne** (*Fr.* zhȧn). See **Joan of Arc.**

A.R.C.A., Associate of the Royal College of Art.

arcade (ä kād′), *n., v.,* **-caded, -cading.** —*n.* **1.** *Archit.* **a.** a series of arches supported on piers or columns. **b.** an arched, roofed-in gallery. **2.** an arched or covered passageway with shops on either side. **3.** a pedestrian way with a colonnade on one side and shops on the other. —*v.t.* **4.** to provide with or form as an arcade or arcades. [t. F, t. It.: m. *arcata* arch, der. *arco* bow, arch, g. L *arcus*]

Arcadia (ä kā′dyə), *n.* a mountainous district in ancient Greece, proverbial for the contented pastoral simplicity of its people. [t. L, t. Gk: m. *Arkadía*]

Arcadian (ä kā′dyən), *adj.* **1.** of Arcadia. **2.** pastoral; rustic; simple; innocent. —*n.* **3.** a native of Arcadia.

Arcady (ä′kə dĭ), *n. Poetic.* Arcadia.

arcane (ä kān′), *adj.* mysterious; secret; obscure: *poor writing can make even the most familiar things seem arcane.* [t. L: m. s. *arcānus*, der. *arcēre* shut up, keep]

arcanum (ä kā′nəm), *n., pl.* **-na** (-nə). **1.** (*often pl.*) a secret; a mystery. **2.** a supposed great secret of nature which the alchemists sought to discover. **3.** a secret and powerful remedy. [t. L, neut. of *arcānus* secret, hidden]

arc-boutant (*Fr.* ȧrk bōō täɴ′), *n., pl.* **arcs-boutants** (*Fr.* ȧrk bōō täɴ′). *French.* a flying buttress.

arch[1] (äch), *n.* **1.** a curved structure resting on supports at both extremities, used to sustain weight, to bridge or roof an open space, etc. **2.** an archway. **3.** something bowed or curved; any bowlike part: *the arch of the foot.* **4.** any curvature in the form of an arch: *the arch of the heavens.* **5.** one of the principal ridge-shapes of a fingerprint, forming a set of simple curves (distinguished from *loop* and *whorl*). —*v.t.* **6.** to cover with a vault, or span with an arch. **7.** to throw or make into the shape of an arch or vault; curve: *a horse arches its neck.* —*v.i.* **8.** to form an arch. [ME, t. OF: m. *arche*, a fem. var. of *arc* (g. L *arcus* bow), due to confusion with *arche* ark (g. L *arca* coffer)]

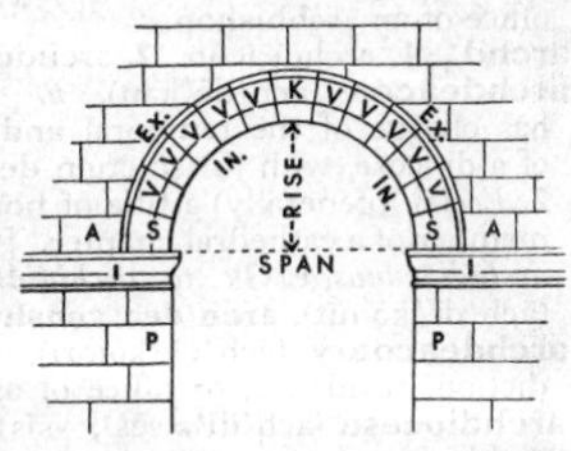

Arch
A, Abutment; S, Springer; V, Voussoir; In., Intrados; Ex., Extrados; K, Keystone; I, Impost; P, Pier

arch[2] (äch), *adj.* **1.** chief; most important; principal: *the arch rebel.* **2.** cunning; sly; roguish: *an arch smile.* —*n.* **3.** *Obs.* a chief. [separate use of ARCH-] —**arch′ly,** *adv.* —**arch′ness,** *n.*

arch-, a prefix meaning 'first', 'chief', as in *archbishop, arch-priest.* [ME *arch-*, OE *arce-*, *erce-*, t. L: m. *arch-*, *arche-*, *archi-*, t. Gk, comb. forms of *archós* chief]

-arch, a suffix meaning 'chief', as in *monarch.* [see ARCH-]

Arch., archbishop.

arch., **1.** archaic. **2.** archaism. **3.** archery. **4.** archipelago. **5.** architect. **6.** architectural. **7.** architecture.

Archaean (ä kē′ən), *Geol.* —*n.* **1.** (formerly) the Pre-Cambrian era or series of rocks. **2.** (formerly) the early Pre-Cambrian era or series of predominantly igneous and metamorphic rocks formed then. —*adj.* **3.** pertaining to a division of early Pre-Cambrian rocks. Also, **Archean.** [f. ARCHAE(O)- + -AN]

archaeo-, a word element meaning 'primeval', 'primitive', 'ancient', as in *archaeology, archaeopteryx.* Also, (*esp. before a vowel*) **archae-**; **archeo-.** [t. Gk: m. *archaio-* comb. form of *archaîos*]

archaeol., **1.** archaeological. **2.** archaeology.

archaeological (ä′kĭ ə lŏj′ĭ kl), *adj.* of or pertaining to archaeology. Also, **archeological, ar′chaeolog′ic.** —**ar′chaeolog′ically,** *adv.*

archaeology (ä′kĭ ŏl′ə jĭ), *n.* **1.** the scientific study of any culture, esp. a prehistoric one, by excavation and description of its remains. **2.** *Now Rare.* ancient history; the study of antiquity. Also, **archeology.** [t. Gk: m. s. *archaiologia* antiquarian lore] —**ar′chaeol′ogist,** *n.*

archaeopteryx (ä′kĭ ŏp′tə rĭks), *n.* a fossil bird, the oldest known avian type, with teeth and a long, feathered, vertebrate tail, found in the later Jurassic. [t. NL, f. *archaeo-* ARCHAEO- + Gk *ptéryx* wing, bird]

Archaeozoic (ä′kĭ ə zō′ĭk), *adj.* **1.** pertaining to the most ancient period of the earth's history, during which the earliest forms of life presumably appeared. —*n.* **2.** the Archaeozoic era. **3.** *Geol.* the series of rocks preceding the Proterozoic. Also, **Archeozoic.** [f. ARCHAEO- + s. Gk *zōē* life + -IC]

archaic (ä kā′ĭk), *adj.* **1.** marked by the characteristics of an earlier period; old-fashioned. **2.** no longer used in ordinary speech or writing; borrowed from older usage (distinguished from *obsolete*). [t. Gk: m. s. *archaïkós* antique] —**archa′ically,** *adv.*

archaism (ä′kĭ ĭz′əm, -kā-), *n.* **1.** something archaic, as a word or expression. **2.** the use of what is archaic, as in literature. **3.** archaic quality or style. [t. Gk: s. *archaïsmós*] —**ar′chaist,** *n.* —**ar′chais′tic,** *adj.*

archaize (ä′kĭ īz′, -kā-), *v.*, **-ized, -izing.** —*v.t.* **1.** to give an archaic appearance or quality to. —*v.i.* **2.** to use archaisms. Also, **archaise.** —**ar′chaiz′er,** *n.*

archangel (äk′ān′jəl), *n.* **1.** a chief or principal angel; one of a particular order of angels. **2.** *Bot.* angelica (def. 1). **3.** deadnettle. **4.** a breed of pigeon. [ME, t. L: s. *archangelus,* t. Gk: m. *archángelos* chief angel] —**archangelic** (äk′ăn jĕl′ĭk), *adj.*

Archangel (äk′ān′jəl), *n.* a seaport in the NW Soviet Union in Europe, on the **Gulf of Archangel** (Dvina Bay), an arm of the White Sea. 303,000 (est. 1965). Russian, **Arkhangelsk.**

archbishop (äch′bĭsh′əp), *n.* a bishop of the highest rank. [OE *arcebiscop* (r. *hēahbiscop* high bishop), repr. L *archiepiscopus,* t. Gk: m. *archiepískopos.* See ARCH-, BISHOP]

archbishopric (äch′bĭsh′əp rĭk), *n.* the see, diocese, or office of an archbishop.

archd., **1.** archdeacon. **2.** archduke.

archdeacon (äch′dē′kən), *n.* **1.** an ecclesiastic who has charge of the temporal and external administration of a diocese, with jurisdiction delegated from the bishop. **2.** *Eccles.* (generally) a title of honour conferred only on a member of a cathedral chapter. [OE *arcediacon,* t. L: m. s. *archidiāconus,* t. Gk: m. *archidiákonos*] —**archdeaconate** (äch′dē′kə nĭt), **arch′dea′conship′,** *n.*

archdeaconry (äch′dē′kən rĭ), *n.*, *pl.* **-ries.** the jurisdiction, residence, or office of an archdeacon.

archdiocese (äch′dī′ə sēs′, -sĭs), *n.* the diocese of an archbishop.

archducal (äch′dyōō′kl), *adj.* pertaining to an archduke or an archduchy.

archduchess (äch′dŭch′ĭs), *n.* **1.** the wife of an archduke. **2.** a princess of the Austrian imperial family.

archduchy (äch′dŭch′ĭ), *n.*, *pl.* **-ies.** the territory of an archduke or an archduchess.

archduke (äch′dyōōk′), *n.* a title of the sovereign princes of the former ruling house of Austria. —**arch′duke′dom,** *n.*

arche-[1], var. of **archi-,** as in *archegonium.*

arche-[2], var. of **archae-.**

Archean (ä kē′ən), *n., adj.* *Geol.* Archaean.

arched (ächt), *adj.* **1.** made, covered, or spanned with an arch. **2.** having the form of an arch.

arched dam, a dam having in plan the shape of an arch, in order to resist the pressure of impounded water.

archegonium (ä′kĭ gō′nyəm), *n.*, *pl.* **-nia** (-nyə). *Bot.* the female reproductive organ in ferns, mosses, etc. [t. NL, f. s. Gk *archégonos* first of a race + *-ium* -IUM] —**ar′chego′nial, archegoniate** (ä′kĭ gō′nĭ ĭt, -āt′), *adj.*

archenemy (äch′ĕn′ĭ mĭ), *n.*, *pl.* **-mies.** **1.** a chief enemy. **2.** Satan; the Devil.

archenteron (ä kĕn′tə rŏn′), *n.* *Embryol.* the primitive enteron or digestive cavity of a gastrula. [f. ARCH- + Gk *énteron* intestine] —**archenteric** (ä′kĕn tĕ′rĭk), *adj.*

archeo-, var. of **archaeo-.** Also, (before a vowel) **arche-.**

archeology (ä′kĭ ŏl′ə jĭ), *n.* archaeology. —**archeological** (ä′kĭ ə lŏj′ĭ kl), **ar′cheolog′ic,** *adj.* —**ar′cheolog′ically,** *adv.* —**ar′cheol′ogist,** *n.*

Archeozoic (ä′kĭ ə zō′ĭk), *adj., n.* Archaeozoic.

archer (ä′chə), *n.* **1.** one who shoots with a bow and arrow; a bowman. **2.** (*cap.*) *Astron.* **a.** the zodiacal constellation Sagittarius. **b.** the sign named from it. [ME, t. AF, var. of OF *archier,* g. L *arcārius,* der. *arcus* bow]

Archer (ä′chə), *n.* **William,** 1856–1924, Scottish translator, esp. of Ibsen, and dramatist.

archerfish (ä′chə fĭsh′), *n.* **1.** a small, black and white, tropical fish, *Toxotes jaculator,* which catches insects by stunning them with drops of water ejected from its mouth. **2.** any of various similar fish.

archery (ä′chə rĭ), *n.* **1.** the practice, art, or skill of an archer. **2.** archers collectively. **3.** an archer's bows, arrows, and other weapons.

archespore (ä′kĭ spô′), *n.* *Bot.* the primitive cell, or group of cells, which give rise to the cells from which spores are derived. Also, **archesporium** (ä′kĭ spô′rĭ əm). —**ar′chespo′rial,** *adj.*

archetype (ä′kĭ tīp′), *n.* a model or first form; the original pattern or model after which a thing is made. [t. L: m. s. *archetypum,* t. Gk: m. *archétypon,* neut. of *archétypos* first-moulded, original] —**archetypal** (ä′kĭ-tī′pl), **archetypical** (ä′kĭ tĭp′ĭ kl), *adj.*

archfiend (äch′fēnd′), *n.* **1.** a chief fiend. **2.** Satan.

archi-, a prefix: **1.** var. of **arch-.** **2.** *Biol.* 'original' or 'primitive', as in *archicarp.* [t. L, t. Gk. See ARCH-]

archicarp (ä′kĭ käp′), *n.* *Bot.* the female sex organ in various ascomycetous fungi, commonly a multicellular coiled hypha differentiated into a terminal trichogyne and the ascogonium.

archidiaconal (ä′kĭ dī ăk′ə nəl), *adj.* of or pertaining to an archdeacon or his office. —**archidiaconate** (ä′kĭ dī-ăk′ə nĭt), *n.*

archiepiscopal (ä′kĭ ĭ pĭs′kə pl), *adj.* of or pertaining to an archbishop or his office. —**archiepiscopate** (ä′kĭ ĭ pĭs′kə pĭt, -pāt′), **archiepiscopacy** (ä′kĭ ĭ pĭs′-kə pə sĭ), *n.*

archil (ä′chĭl), *n.* orchil.

archimandrite (ä′kĭ măn′drīt), *n.* *Gk Ch.* **1.** the head of a monastery; an abbot. **2.** a superior abbot, having charge of several monastries. **3.** a title given to distinguished celibate priests. [t. ML: m. *archimandrita,* t. LGk: m. s. *archimandrī́tēs*]

Archimedes (ä′kĭ mē′dēz), *n.* 287?–212 B.C., a Greek mathematician, physicist, and inventor: discovered principles of specific gravity and of the lever. —**Archimedean** (ä′kĭ mē′dĭ ən, -mĭ dē′ən), *adj.*

Archimedes' principle, the principle that the apparent loss in weight of a body totally or partially immersed in a liquid is equal to the weight of the liquid displaced.

Archimedes' screw, a device consisting essentially of a spiral passage within an inclined cylinder for raising water to a height when rotated.

arching (ä′chĭng), *n.* arched work or formation.

archipelago (ä′kĭ pĕl′ĭ gō′), *n.*, *pl.* **-gos, -goes.** **1.** any large body of water with many islands. **2.** the island groups in such a body of water. **3. the Archipelago,** the Aegean Sea, with its many islands. [t. It.: m. *arcipelago,* lit., chief sea, f. *arci-* ARCHI- + m. Gk *pélagos* sea] —**archipelagic** (ä′kĭ pĭ lăj′ĭk), *adj.*

archiplasm (ä′kĭ plăz′əm), *n.* archoplasm.

archit., architecture.

architect (ä′kĭ tĕkt′), *n.* **1.** one whose profession it is to design buildings and superintend their construction. **2.** the deviser, maker, or creator of anything. [t. L: s. *architectus,* t. Gk: m. *architéktōn* chief builder]

architectonic (ä′kĭ tĕk tŏn′ĭk), *adj.* **1.** pertaining to architecture. **2.** pertaining to construction or design of any kind. **3.** resembling architecture in manner or technique of structure. **4.** (of a science or structure) giving the principle of organization of a system. [t. L: s. *architectonicus,* t. Gk: m. *architektonikós*] —**ar′chitecton′ical,** *adj.* —**ar′chitecton′ically,** *adv.*

architectonics (ä′kĭ tĕk tŏn′ĭks), *n.* **1.** the science of architecture. **2.** the (science of the) systematic arrangement of knowledge.

architectural (ä′kĭ tĕk′chə rəl), *adj.* **1.** of or pertaining to architecture. **2.** conforming to the basic principles of architecture. **3.** having the qualities of architecture. —**ar′chitec′turally,** *adv.*

architecture (ä′kĭ tĕk′chə), *n.* **1.** the art or science of building, including plan, design, construction, and decorative treatment. **2.** the style of building. **3.** the action or process of building; construction. **4.** a building. **5.** buildings collectively. [t. L: m. s. *architectūra*]

architrave (ä′kĭ trāv′), *n.* *Archit.* **1.** the lowest division of an entablature, resting immediately on the columns. See diag. under **column.** **2.** a band of mouldings or other ornamentation about a rectangular door or other opening or a panel. **3.** a decorative band about openings or panels of any shape. [t. It.: f. *archi-* ARCHI- + *trave* (g. L *trabs* beam)]

archival (ä kī′vəl), *adj.* pertaining to archives or valuable records; contained in such archives or records.

archives (ä′kīvz), *n.pl.* **1.** a place where public records or other historical documents are kept. **2.** documents or records relating to the activities, rights, claims, treaties,

constitutions, etc., of a family, corporation, community, or nation. [t. F, t. L: m. *archīvum*, t. Gk: m. *archeîon* public building, pl., records]
archivist (ä′kĭ vĭst), *n.* a custodian of archives.
archivolt (ä′kĭ vōlt′), *n.* *Archit.* a band of mouldings or other ornamentation about an arched opening. [t. It.: s. *archivolto*, f. *archi-* ARCH + *volto* turned]
archlet (äch′lĭt), *n.* a small arch.
archlute (äch′lo͞ot′), *n.* the theorbo.
archon (ä′kŏn), *n.* **1.** a higher magistrate in ancient Athens. **2.** any ruler. [t. Gk: m. *árchōn* ruler, prop. ppr. of *árchein* be first, rule] —**ar′chonship′,** *n.*
archoplasm (ä′kə plăz′əm), *n.* **1.** protoplasm. **2.** *Cytology.* (in cell division) the substance surrounding the centrosome. Also, **archiplasm.**
archpriest (äch′prēst′), *n.* **1.** a priest holding first rank, as among the members of a cathedral chapter or among the clergy of a district outside the episcopal city. **2.** *Rom. Cath. Ch.* a priest acting as superior of the Roman Catholic secular clergy in England, first appointed in 1598 and superseded by a vicar apostolic in 1623. —**arch′priest′hood,** *n.*
archway (äch′wā′), *n.* *Archit.* **1.** an entrance or passage under an arch. **2.** a covering or enclosing arch.
archwise (äch′wīz′), *adv.* in the shape of an arch.
-archy, a word element meaning 'rule', 'government', as in *monarchy*. [t. Gk: m. *-archía*]
arc light, 1. Also, **arc lamp.** a lamp in which the light source of high intensity is an electric arc, usually between carbon rods. **2.** the light produced.
A.R.C.M., Associate of the Royal College of Music.
arco (ä′kō), *Music.* —*adj.* **1.** played with the bow, as the violin. —*n.* **2.** a passage so played. [t. It.: bow]
A.R.C.O., Associate of the Royal College of Organists.
arcograph (ä′kə grăf′, -gräf′), *n.* *Geom., etc.* an instrument once used for drawing arcs, having a flexible arc-shaped part adjusted by an extensible straight bar connecting its sides; cyclograph.
A.R.C.S., Associate of the Royal College of Science.
arc sine, tangent, etc., *Trig.* the angle, measured in radians, whose sine, tangent, etc., is a given number.
arctic (äk′tĭk), *adj.* **1.** of, at, or near the North Pole; frigid. **2.** extremely cold. **3.** *Astron.* of, near, or lying under the Great and the Little Bear. —*n.* **4.** the arctic regions. [t. L: s. *arcticus*, t. Gk: m. *arktikós* of the Bear (constellation), northern; r. ME *artik*, t. OF: m. *artique*]
Arctic Circle, the southern boundary of the North Frigid Zone, 23° 28′ from the North Pole.
Arctic Ocean, an ocean N of North America, Asia, and the Arctic Circle. ab. 5,400,000 sq. mi.
Arctic Zone, the section of the earth's surface lying between the Arctic Circle and the North Pole.
Arcturus (äk tyo͝oə′rəs), *n.* *Astron.* a bright star of the first magnitude in the constellation Boötes. [t. L, t. Gk: m. *Arktoûros*, lit., guard of the Bear, f. *árktos* a bear, the Great Bear + *oûros* guardian]
arcuate (ä′kyo͞o ĭt, -āt′), *adj.* curved like a bow. Also, **ar′cuat′ed.** [t. L: m. s. *arcuātus*, pp.] —**ar′cua′tion,** *n.*
-ard, a noun suffix, orig. intensive but now often depreciative or without special force, as in *coward, drunkard, wizard.* Also, **-art.** [t. OF: *-ard, -art*, t. G: m. *-hart, -hard* hardy, c. HARD]
ardeb (ä′dĕb), *n.* a unit of capacity used for dry measure in Egypt and neighbouring countries, officially equivalent in Egypt to 5·44 bushels, but varying in different places. [t. Ar.: m. *ardabb*, t. Gk: m. *artábē*, t. OPers.: m. *artaba*]
Ardèche (*Fr.* àr dĕsh′), *n.* a department in SE France. 249,077 pop. (1962); 2145 sq. mi. *Cap.:* Privas.
Arden (ä′dn), *n.* **Forest of,** a forest district in N Warwickshire, formerly occupying a large area in central and E England: scene of Shakespeare's *As You Like It.*
ardency (ä′dn sĭ), *n.* warmth of feeling; ardour.
Ardennes (ä dĕn′; *Fr.* àr dĕn′), *n.* **1.** a department in NE France. 300,247 pop. (1962); 2029 sq. mi. *Cap.:* Charleville-Mézières. **2. Forest of,** a wooded plateau along the river Meuse, in NE France, SE Belgium, and Luxembourg: German counteroffensive in World War II.
ardent (ä′dnt), *adj.* **1.** glowing with feeling, earnestness, or zeal; passionate; fervent: *ardent vows, an ardent patriot.* **2.** glowing; flashing. **3.** burning, fiery, or hot. [t. L: s. *ardens*, ppr., burning; r. ME *ardaunt*, t. OF: m. *ardant*] —**ar′dently,** *adv.* —**Syn. 1.** fervid, eager, enthusiastic; vehement.
ardent spirits, strong alcoholic drinks made by distillation, as brandy, whisky, or gin.
ardour (ä′də), *n.* **1.** warmth of feeling; fervour; eagerness; zeal. **2.** burning heat. Also, *U.S.,* **ardor.** [ME, t. OF, g. L] —**Syn. 1.** fervency, passion, zeal.
arduous (ä′dyo͞o əs), *adj.* **1.** requiring great exertion; laborious; difficult: *an arduous enterprise.* **2.** energetic; strenuous: *making an arduous effort.* **3.** hard to climb; steep: *an arduous path.* **4.** hard to endure; severe; full of hardships: *an arduous winter.* [t. L: m. *arduus*] —**ar′duously,** *adv.* —**ar′duousness,** *n.* —**Syn. 1.** toilsome, onerous, wearisome, exhausting.
are[1] (ä; *unstressed* ə), *v.* pres. indic. pl. of the verb **be.** [d. OE (Northumbrian) *aron*]
are[2] (ä), *n.* a metric surface measure equal to 100 square metres, or 119·6 square yards; a hundredth of a hectare. [t. F, t. L: m. s. *ārea* AREA]
area (ēə′rĭ ə), *n., pl.* **areas,** (*in Biol., often*) **areae** (ēə′rĭ ē′). **1.** any particular extent of surface; region; tract: *the settled area.* **2.** extent, range, or scope: *the whole area of science.* **3.** a piece of unoccupied ground; an open space. **4.** a sunken space leading to a cellar or basement entrance, or in front of basement or cellar windows. **5.** *Maths.* amount of surface (plane or curved); two-dimensional extent. **6.** *Anat., Physiol.* a zone of the cerebral cortex with a specific function. [t. L: piece of level ground, open space] —**a′real,** *adj.*
area rule, *Aeron.* a method of design for obtaining minimum drag from the overall configuration of an aircraft.
areaway (ēə′rĭ ə wā′), *n.* *U.S.* **1.** area (def. 4). **2.** a passageway.
areca (ă′rĭ kə, ə rē′-), *n.* **1.** any palm of the genus *Areca*, of tropical Asia and the Malay Archipelago, esp. *A. catechu*, the betel palm, which bears a nut (the **areca nut**). **2.** the nut itself. **3.** any of various palms formerly referred to the genus *Areca.* Also, **areca palm** for defs 1, 3. [t. Pg., t. Malayalam: m. *ādekka*, ult. t. Tamil]
Arecibo (*Sp.* à rė sē′bō), *n.* a town in NW Puerto Rico. 69,879 (1960).
Aref (ă rĕf′), *n.* **Abdul Rahman Mohammed** (ăb′do͝ol rä′mən mə hăm′ĭd), born 1916, president of Iraq 1966–68.
arena (ə rē′nə), *n.* **1.** the oval space in a Roman amphitheatre for combats or other performances. **2.** an enclosure for sports contests, shows, etc. **3.** a field of conflict or endeavour: *the arena of politics.* [t. L: sand, sandy place]
arenaceous (ă′rĭ nā′shəs), *adj.* **1.** sandlike; sandy. **2.** *Geol.* of or pertaining to sedimentary rock composed of sand particles and others down to 0·002 mm. in diameter. [t. L: m. *arēnāceus* sandy]
arenicolous (ă′rĭ nĭk′ə ləs), *adj.* inhabiting sand. [f. s. L *arēna* sand + -(I)COLOUS]
aren't (änt), **1.** contraction of *are not.* **2.** contraction of *am not* (as an interrogative). **3.** *Illiterate or Dial.* contraction of *am not* (as a statement).
areocentric (ēə′rĭ ō sĕn′trĭk), *adj.* *Astron.* having the planet Mars as centre. [f. *areo-* (comb. form of ARES) + CENTRIC]
areola (ə rīə′lə), *n., pl.* **-lae** (-lē), *Biol.* **1.** a ring of colour, as around a pustule or the human nipple. **2.** a small interstice, as between the fibres of connective tissue. [t. L, dim. of *ārea* AREA] —**are′olar,** *adj.* —**areolate** (ə rīə′lĭt, -lāt), *adj.* —**areolation** (ə rīə′lā′shən), *n.*
areole (ēə′rĭ ōl′), *n.* *Biol.* an areola. [t. F, t. L: m. *areola*, dim. of *area* open space]
Areopagite (ă′rĭ ŏp′ə jīt′, -gīt′), *n.* *Gk Hist.* a member of the council of the Areopagus. —**Areopagitic** (ă′rĭ ŏp′ə-jĭt′ĭk), *adj.*
Areopagus (ă′rĭ ŏp′ə gəs), *n.* **1.** a hill in Athens, to the west of the Acropolis. **2.** *Gk Hist.* the council which met on this hill, originally having wide public functions but later a purely judicial body. **3.** any high tribunal. [t. L, t. Gk: m. *Areiópagos* hill of Ares. Cf. Acts, 17, 19, 22]
Arequipa (ă′rĭ kē′pə; *Sp.* à rė kē′pà), *n.* a city in S Peru. 156,657 (1961).
Ares (ēə′rēz), *n.* the Greek god of war, identified by the Romans with Mars. [t. L, t. Gk]
arête (ə rāt′), *n.* *Phys. Geog.* a sharp ridge of a mountain; the divide between two glaciated valleys. [t. F, g. L *arista* awn, spine]
Arethusa (ă′rĭ thyo͞o′zə), *n.* *Gk Myth.* a nymph changed into a spring on the island of Ortygia (near Syracuse, Sicily) to save her from the pursuing river god, Alpheus.
Aretino (ă′rĭ tē′nō; *It.* à rė tē′nō), *n.* **Pietro** (*It.* pyĕ′trō), 1492–1556, Italian satirist and dramatist.
Arezzo (ə rĕt′sō; *It.* à rĕt′tsō), *n.* a town in Italy in Tuscany. 82,247 (1966).
Arg., Argentina.
arg., argentum.
argal[1] (ä′gl), *n.* argol.
argal[2] (ä′gl), *n.* argali.
argali (ä′gə lĭ), *n., pl.* **-li.** a wild sheep of Asia, *Ovis ammon*, with long, thick, spirally curved horns; the ammon. Also **argal.** [t. Mongolian]

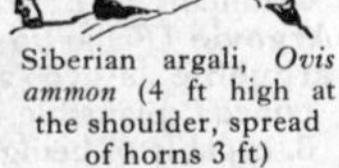
Siberian argali, *Ovis ammon* (4 ft high at the shoulder, spread of horns 3 ft)

argent (ä′jənt), *n.* **1.** *Archaic.* silver. **2.** *Her.* the silver or silvery white used in armorial bearings. **3.** *Obs.* money. —*adj.* **4.** like silver; silvery white. [t. F, g. L *argentum* silver]

argental (ä jĕn′tl), *adj.* of, pertaining to, containing, or resembling silver.

argenteous (ä jĕn′tĭ əs), *adj.* *Rare.* silvery. [t. L: m. *argenteus*]

Argenteuil (*Fr.* ȧr zhäɴ tœy′), *n.* a town in N France, in Seine-et-Oise department, on the Seine. 82,458 (1962).

argentic (ä jĕn′tĭk), *adj.* *Chem.* of or containing silver, with a valency greater than the corresponding argentous compound.

argentiferous (ä′jən tĭf′ə rəs), *adj.* silver-bearing. [f. s. L *argentum* silver + -(I)FEROUS]

Argentina (ä′jən tē′nə; *Sp.* ȧr кнĕn tē′nȧ), *n.* a republic in S South America. 20,959,100 pop. (1960); 1,084,120 sq. mi. *Cap.:* Buenos Aires.

argentine (ä′jən tīn′), *adj.* **1.** pertaining to or resembling silver. —*n.* **2.** a silvery substance obtained from fish scales, used in making imitation pearls. [f. s. L *argentum* silver + -INE[1]]

Argentine (ä′jən tēn′, -tīn′), *n.* **1.** a native or inhabitant of Argentina. **2.** **the Argentine,** Argentina. —*adj.* **3.** of or pertaining to Argentina. Also, **Argentinean** (ä′jən-tĭn′ĭ ən).

argentite (ä′jən tīt′), *n.* silver sulphide, Ag_2S, a dark lead-grey sectile mineral, crystalline or massive: an important ore of silver; silver glance. [f. s. L *argentum* silver + -ITE[1]]

argentous (ä jĕn′təs), *adj.* *Chem.* containing monovalent silver, as *argentous chloride*, AgCl.

argentum (ä jĕn′təm), *n.* *Chem.* silver. [t. L]

argie-bargie (ä′jĭ bä′jĭ), *v.i.*, *n.* argy-bargy.

argil (ä′jĭl), *n.* clay, esp. potter's clay. [var. of *argil(l)e*, t. L: m. *argilla*, t. Gk: white clay]

argillaceous (ä′jĭ lā′shəs), *adj.* **1.** of the nature of or resembling clay; clayey. **2.** *Geol.* of or pertaining to sedimentary rock composed of particles less than 0·002 mm. in diameter.

argilliferous (ä′jĭ lĭf′ə rəs), *adj.* containing clayey matter.

argillite (ä′jĭ līt′), *n.* any compact sedimentary rock composed mainly of clay minerals. [f. s. L *argilla* white clay + -ITE[1]]

arginine (ä′jĭ nīn′), *n.* one of the essential amino acids, $C_6H_{14}O_2N_4$, which make up plant and animal proteins.

arginine phosphate, *Biochem.* the phosphate of arginine, present as the phosphagen in tissues of most invertebrates.

Argive (ä′jīv, -gīv), *adj.* **1.** of or pertaining to Argos. **2.** Greek. —*n.* **3.** a native of Argos. **4.** any Greek.

argle-bargle (ä′gl bä′gl), *v.i.*, *n.* argy-bargy.

Argo (ä′gō), *n.* **1.** *Astron.* a very large southern constellation, now divided into four, lying largely south of Canis Major. **2.** *Gk Legend.* the ship in which Jason sailed in quest of the Golden Fleece.

argol (ä′gŏl), *n.* crude tartar. Also, **argal.** [ME *argoile*, t. AF: m. *argoil*]

Argolis (ä′gə lĭs), *n.* **1.** an ancient district in SE Greece. **2.** **Gulf of,** a gulf of the Aegean, in SE Greece.

argon (ä′gŏn), *n.* a colourless, odourless, chemically inactive, monatomic, gaseous element. *Symbol:* Ar; *at. no.:* 18; *at. wt:* 39·948. [t. NL, t. Gk, prop. neut. of *argós* idle]

Argonaut (ä′gə nôt′), *n.* **1.** *Gk Legend.* a member of the band that sailed to Colchis with Jason in the ship Argo in search of the Golden Fleece. **2.** (*l.c.*) the paper nautilus. [t. L: s. *Argonauta*, t. Gk: m. *Argonaútēs* (f. *Argó* Argo + *naútēs* sailor)] —**Ar′go-nau′tic,** *adj.*

Argonne Forest (ä′gŏn; *Fr.* ȧr gŏn′), a wooded region in NE France: battles, 1918, 1944.

Argonne Forest

Argos (ä′gŏs), *n.* an ancient city in SE Greece, the centre of Argolis: a powerful rival of Sparta, Athens, and Corinth.

argosy (ä′gə sĭ), *n.*, *pl.* **-sies.** **1.** a large merchant ship, esp. one with a rich cargo. **2.** a fleet of such ships. [t. It.: m. *Ragusea* a vessel of RAGUSA]

argot (ä′gō), *n.* the peculiar language or jargon of any class or group; cant; originally, that of thieves and vagabonds, devised for purposes of disguise and concealment. [t. F; orig. unknown] —**argotic** (ä gŏt′ĭk), *adj.*

Argovie (*Fr.* ȧr gô vē′), *n.* French name of **Aargau.**

arguable (ä′gyōō ə bl), *adj.* **1.** capable of being maintained; plausible. **2.** open to dispute or argument. **3.** capable of being argued. —**ar′guably,** *adv.*

argue (ä′gyōō), *v.*, **-gued, -guing.** —*v.i.* **1.** to present reasons for or against a thing: *to argue for or against a proposed law.* **2.** to contend in argument; dispute: *to argue with someone about something.* —*v.t.* **3.** to state the reasons for or against: *counsel argued the cause.* **4.** to maintain in reasoning: *to argue that something must be so.* **5.** to argue in favour of; support by argument: *his letter argues restraint.* **6.** to persuade, drive, etc., by reasoning: *to argue one out of a plan.* **7.** to show; prove or imply: *his clothes argue poverty.* [ME *argue(n)*, t. OF: m. *arguer*, g. L *argūtāre*, freq. of *arguere* show] —**ar′guer,** *n.*

—**Syn.** **1.** ARGUE, DEBATE, DISCUSS imply using reasons or proofs to support or refute an assertion, proposition, or principle. ARGUE implies reasoning or trying to understand; it does not necessarily imply opposition: *to argue with oneself.* To DISCUSS is to present varied opinions and views: *to discuss ways and means.* To DEBATE is to interchange formal (usually opposing) arguments, esp. on public questions: *to debate a proposed amendment.*

argufy (ä′gyōō fī′), *v.t.*, *v.i.*, **-fied, -fying.** *Illit.* or *Dial.* to argue or wrangle. [f. ARGU(E) + -FY]

argument (ä′gyōō mənt), *n.* **1.** an argumentation; debate. **2.** a matter of contention. **3.** a process of reasoning; series of reasons. **4.** a statement or fact tending to improve a point. **5.** an address or composition intended to convince others of the truth of something. **6.** an abstract or summary of the chief points in a book or sections of a book. **7.** the theme or thesis of a literary composition. **8.** *Maths.* (of a function) an independent variable. **9.** *Obs.* evidence or proof. [ME, t. L: s. *argūmentum* proof]

—**Syn.** **1.** ARGUMENT, CONTROVERSY, DISPUTE imply the expression of opinions for and against some idea. An ARGUMENT usually arises from a disagreement between two persons, each of whom advances facts supporting his own point of view. A CONTROVERSY or a DISPUTE may involve two or more persons. A DISPUTE is an oral contention, usually brief, and often of a heated, angry, or undignified character: *a violent dispute over a purchase.* A CONTROVERSY is an oral or written expression of contrary opinions, and may be dignified and of some duration: *a political controversy.*

argumentation (ä′gyōō mĕn tā′shən), *n.* **1.** debate; discussion; reasoning. **2.** the setting forth of reasons together with the conclusion drawn from them; formal or logical reasoning. **3.** the premises and conclusion so set forth.

argumentative (ä′gyōō mĕn′tə tĭv), *adj.* **1.** given to argument; disputatious. **2.** controversial. —**ar′gumen′tatively,** *adv.* —**ar′gumen′tativeness,** *n.*

argumentum (ä′gyōō mĕn′tōōm), *n.* *Latin.* argument, as **argumentum ad hominem,** argument designed to appeal to the prejudices of an audience or attack the character of an opponent; or **argumentum ad rem,** argument confined strictly to relevant issues.

Argus (ä′gəs), *n.* **1.** *Gk Legend.* a giant with a hundred eyes, set to guard the heifer Io. His eyes were transferred, after his death, to the peacock's tail. **2.** any observant or vigilant person. **3.** (*l.c.*) any pheasant of the Malayan genera *Argusianus* and *Rheinardia*, marked with eyelike spots.

Argus-eyed (ä′gəs īd′), *adj.* keen-eyed; vigilant.

argy-bargy (ä′jĭ bä′jĭ), *n.*, *v.*, **-bargied, -bargying.** *Colloq.* —*n.* **1.** argumentative talk; wrangling; disputation. —*v.i.* **2.** to wrangle; argue tediously; bandy words. Also, **argie-bargie, argle-bargle.**

Argyle (ä gīl′), *n.* **1.** (*also l.c.*) a diamond-shaped pattern of two or more colours, used in knitting socks, sweaters, etc. —*adj.* **2.** (*also l.c.*) having such a pattern. [var. of ARGYLL; arbitrary designation]

Argyll (ä gīl′), *n.* a county in W Scotland. 59,345 pop. (1961); 3110 sq. mi. *Co. town:* Lochgilphead. Also, **Argyllshire** (ä gīl′shĭə, -shə).

argyrol (ä′jĭ rōl′, ä jī′ə rəl), *n.* *Pharm.* **1.** a compound of silver and a protein, applied to mucous membranes as a mild antiseptic. **2.** (*cap.*) a trademark for this substance. [f. s. Gk *árgyros* silver + *-ol* (unexplained)]

arhat (ä′hət), *n.* a Buddhist who has attained nirvana.

arhythmia (ə rĭth′mĭ ə), *n.* *Pathol.* arrhythmia.

aria (ä′rĭ ə), *n.* **1.** an air or melody. **2.** an elaborate melody for a single voice, with accompaniment, in an opera, oratorio, etc., esp. one consisting of a principal and a subordinate section, and a repetition of the first with or without alterations. [t. It., g. L *āer* air]

-aria, *Bot.*, *Zool.* a suffix used in names of genera and groups. [t. L, neut. pl. n. and adj. termination]

Ariadne (ăr′ĭ ăd′nĭ), *n.* *Gk Legend.* a daughter of Minos and Pasiphaë. She gave Theseus the thread whereby he escaped from the Labyrinth.

Arian (ĕə′rĭ ən), *adj.* **1.** pertaining to Arius. —*n.* **2.** an adherent of the Arian doctrine. See **Arius.** [t. L: s. *Ariānus*, der. *Arius*] —**Ar′ianism,** *n.*

Arian (ĕə′rĭ ən), *adj.*, *n.* Aryan.

-arian, a compound suffix of adjectives and nouns, often referring to pursuits, doctrines, etc., or to age, as in *antiquarian, humanitarian, octogenarian.* [f. -ARY[1] + -AN]

A.R.I.B.A., Associate of the Royal Institute of British Architects.

Arica (ə rē′kə; *Sp.* ä rē′kä), *n.* **1.** a seaport in N Chile. 46,542 (1960). **2.** See **Tacna-Arica.**

arid (ăr′ĭd), *adj.* **1.** dry; without moisture; parched with heat. **2.** uninteresting; dull; unrewarding. **3.** barren; unproductive; lacking spiritual or creative life. [t. L: s. *āridus* dry] —**aridity** (ə rĭd′ĭ tĭ), **ar′idness,** *n.* —**ar′idly,** *adv.* —**Syn. 1.** See **dry.** —**Ant. 1.** humid.

Ariège (*Fr.* ä ryĕzh′), *n.* a department in S France. 137,192 pop. (1962); 1893 sq. mi. *Cap.:* Foix.

ariel (ĕə′rĭ əl), *n.* an Arabian gazelle, *Gazella arabica.* Also, **ariel gazelle.** [t. Ar.: m. *aryal* stag or ibex]

Ariel (ĕə′rĭ əl), *n.* **1.** (in Shakespeare's *Tempest*) a spirit of the air having magical powers. **2.** *Astron.* one of the five satellites of Uranus. [t. LL, t. Gk, t. Heb.: m. *arī'ēl*]

Aries (ĕə′rēz), *n., gen.* **Arietis** (ə rī′ə tĭs). **1.** the Ram, a zodiacal constellation between Pisces and Taurus. **2.** the first sign of the zodiac (♈), which the sun enters about March 21. See **zodiac.** [t. L: a ram]

arietta (ăr′ĭ ĕt′ə; *It.* ä rē ĕt′tä), *n. Music.* a short aria. Also, **ariette** (ăr′ĭ ĕt′). [It., dim. of *aria.* See ARIA]

aright (ə rīt′), *adv.* rightly; correctly; properly.

aril (ăr′ĭl), *n. Bot.* an accessory covering or appendage of certain seeds, esp. one arising from the placenta, funicle or hilum. [t. NL: m. s. *arillus,* der. ML *arillī* dried grapes, t. Sp.: m. *arillos*]

arillate (ăr′ĭ lāt′), *adj. Bot.* having an aril.

arillode (ăr′ĭ lōd′), *n. Bot.* a false aril; an aril which originates from the micropyle instead of at or below the hilum, as in the nutmeg. [see ARIL, -ODE[1]]

Arimathaea (ăr′ĭ mə thĭə′), *n.* a town in ancient Palestine. Matt. 27:57. Also, **Arimathea.**

ariose (ăr′ĭ ōs′, ăr′ĭ ōs′), *adj. Rare.* characterized by melody; songlike. [Anglicization of ARIOSO]

arioso (ä′rĭ ō′zō, ăr′ĭ-), *adj., adv. Music.* in the manner of an air or melody. [It., der. *aria* ARIA]

Ariosto (ăr′ĭ ŏs′tō; *It.* ä ryŏs′tō), *n.* **Ludovico** (*It.* lōō dō vē′kō), 1474–1533, Italian poet, author of *Orlando Furioso.*

-arious, an adjective suffix meaning 'connected with', 'having to do with', as in *gregarious.* [t. L: m. *-ārius*]

arise (ə rīz′), *v.i.,* **arose, arisen, arising. 1.** to come into being or action; originate; appear: *new questions arise.* **2.** to result or proceed (fol. by *from*). **3.** to move upwards. **4.** *Literary or Formal.* to rise; get up from sitting, lying, or kneeling. [ME *arise(n),* OE *ārīsan,* f. *ā-* up + *rīsan* rise]

arista (ə rĭs′tə), *n., pl.* **-tae** (-tē). **1.** *Bot.* a bristle-like appendage of grain, etc.; an awn. **2.** *Entomol.* a prominent bristle on the antenna of some dipterous insects. [t. L. See ARÊTE]

aristate (ə rĭs′tāt), *adj.* **1.** *Bot.* having aristae; awned. **2.** *Zool.* tipped with a thin spine. [t. LL: m. s. *aristātus,* der. L. *arista* awn]

Aristides (ăr′ĭs tī′dēz), *n.* ('*the Just*'), 530?–468? B.C., Athenian statesman and general.

Aristippus (ăr′ĭs tĭp′əs), *n.* 435?–356? B.C., Greek philosopher who founded a school at Cyrene.

aristo-, a word element meaning 'best', 'superior', as in *aristocratic.* [t. Gk, comb. form of *áristos* best]

aristocracy (ăr′ĭ stŏk′rə sĭ), *n., pl.* **-cies. 1.** a government or a state characterized by the rule of a nobility, elite, or privileged upper class. **2.** a body of persons holding exceptional prescriptive rank or privileges; a class of hereditary nobility. **3.** government by the best men in the state. **4.** a governing body composed of the best men in the state. **5.** any class ranking as socially or otherwise superior. [t. L: m. s. *aristocratia,* t. Gk: m. *aristokratía* rule of the best. See ARISTO-, -CRACY]

aristocrat (ăr′ĭs tə krăt′), *n.* **1.** one who has the tastes, manners, etc., of the members of a superior group or class. **2.** (one of) the best of its kind. **3.** a member of an aristocracy. **4.** an advocate of an aristocratic form of government. —**a′ristoc′ratism,** *n.*

aristocratic (ăr′ĭs tə krăt′ĭk), *adj.* **1.** befitting an aristocrat; stylish, grand, or exclusive. **2.** like an aristocrat. **3.** belonging to or favouring the aristocracy. **4.** of or pertaining to government by an aristocracy. Also, **a′ristocrat′ical.** —**a′ristocrat′ically,** *adv.*

aristolochiaceous (ə rĭs′tə lō′kĭ ā′shəs), *adj. Bot.* belonging to the *Aristolochiaceae,* a family of plants including birthwort, Dutchman's-pipe, etc. [f. s. L *Aristolochia* birthwort genus (t. Gk: m. *aristolócheia*) + -ACEOUS]

Aristophanes (ăr′ĭ stŏf′ə nēz′), *n.* 448?–385? B.C., Athenian poet and writer of comedy.

Aristotelian (ăr′ĭs tō tē′lyən, -tē′lĭ ən), *adj.* **1.** of or pertaining to Aristotle or to his doctrines. —*n.* **2.** a follower of Aristotle. **3.** one who thinks in particulars and scientific deductions as distinct from the metaphysical speculation of Platonism. Also, **Aristotelean.** —**Ar′istote′lianism,** *n.*

Aristotelian logic, 1. the logic of Aristotle, esp. in the modified form taught in the Middle Ages. **2.** formal logic, dealing with the logical form, rather than the content, of propositions, and based on the four propositional forms; all S is P; no S is P; some S is P; some S is not P.

Aristotle (ăr′ĭ stŏt′l), *n.* 384–322 B.C., Greek philosopher: pupil of Plato; tutor of Alexander the Great.

arith., 1. arithmetic. **2.** arithmetical.

arithmetic (*n.* ə rĭth′mə tĭk; *adj.* ăr′ĭth mĕt′ĭk), *n.* **1.** the art or skill of computation with figures (the most elementary branch of mathematics). **2.** Also, **theoretical arithmetic.** the theory of numbers; the study of the divisibility of whole numbers, the remainders after division, etc. **3.** a book on this subject. —*adj.* **4.** of or pertaining to arithmetic. [t. L: s. *arithmētica,* t. Gk: m. *arithmētiké,* prop. fem. of *arithmētikós* of or for reckoning; r. ME *arsmetik,* t. OF: m. *arismetique*]

arithmetical (ăr′ĭth mĕt′ĭ kl), *adj.* of or pertaining to arithmetic. —**ar′ithmet′ically,** *adv.*

arithmetical progression, a sequence in which each term is obtained by the addition of a constant number to the preceding term. For example: 1, 4, 7, 10, 13, and 6, 1, −4, −9, −14. Also, **arithmetic series.**

arithmetician (ə rĭth′mə tĭsh′ən, ăr′ĭth-), *n.* an expert in arithmetic.

arithmetic mean, *Maths.* the mean obtained by adding several quantities together and dividing the sum by the number of quantities. For example: the arithmetic mean of 1, 5, 2, 8 is 4.

Arius (ĕə′rĭ əs), *n.* died A.D. 336, Christian priest at Alexandria, who held that Christ the Son was not consubstantial with God the Father.

a rivederci (*It.* ä rē vĕ dĕr′chē), *Italian.* See **arrivederci.**

Ariz., Arizona.

Arizona (ăr′ĭ zō′nə), *n.* a state in the SW United States. 1,302,161 pop. (1960); 113,909 sq. mi. *Cap.:* Phoenix. *Abbrev.:* Ariz.

Arjuna (ä′jōō nə), *n. Hindu Myth.* the chief hero of the Bhagavad-gita.

ark (äk), *n.* **1.** the vessel built by Noah for safety during the Flood. Gen. 6–9. **2.** any similar large floating vessel. **3.** Also, **ark of the covenant.** a chest or box of great sanctity representing the presence of the Deity, borne by the Israelites in their desert wandering (Num. 10:35), the most sacred object of the tabernacle and of the temple in Jerusalem, where it was kept in the holy of holies. **4.** *Now Dial.* a chest; box. **5. out of the ark,** *Colloq.* very old. [ME; OE *arc, earc,* t. L: m. s. *arca* a chest, coffer]

Ark., Arkansas.

Arkansas (ä′kən sô′; *also for 2* ä kăn′zəs), *n.* **1.** a state in the S central United States. 1,786,272 pop. (1960); 53,103 sq. mi. *Cap.:* Little Rock. *Abbrev.:* Ark. **2.** a river flowing from the Rocky Mountains in central Colorado into the Mississippi in SE Arkansas. 1450 mi.

Arkhangelsk (*Russ.* är KHän′gĭlysk), *n.* Russian name of **Archangel.**

arkose (ä′kōs), *n. Geol.* a coarse, hard sandstone composed of quartz and at least 10 per cent felspar.

Arkwright (äk′rīt), *n.* **Sir Richard,** 1732–92, English inventor of the spinning jenny.

Arlberg (äl′bûg; *Ger.* ärl′bĕrk), *n.* **1.** a mountain pass in W Austria. ab. 5900 ft high. **2.** a tunnel beneath this.

Arles (älz; *Fr.* ärl), *n.* a town in SE France, in Bouches-du-Rhône, on the river Rhône: Roman ruins. 42,353 (1966).

Arlington (ä′lĭng tən), *n.* a county in the U.S., in NE Virginia: site of a U.S. national cemetery.

arm[1] (äm), *n.* **1.** the upper limb of the human body from the shoulder to the hand. **2.** this limb, exclusive of the hand. **3.** the forelimb of any vertebrate. **4.** some part of an organism like or likened to an arm. **5.** any armlike part, as of a lever or of the yard (**yardarm**) of a ship. **6.** a covering for the arm, as the sleeve of a garment. **7.** a branch or subdivision of an organization. **8.** a projecting support for the forearm at the side of a chair, sofa, etc. **9.** an inlet, creek, or cove: *an arm of the sea.* **10.** power; might; strength; authority: *the arm of the law.* **11. arm in arm,** with arms linked; close together. **12. at arm's length,** at a distance, yet almost within reach. **13. in arms,** carried in the arms, as a child; unready; not yet independent or fully developed. **14. with open arms,** cordially. —*v.t.* **15.** to escort arm in arm. [OE *arm, earm,* c. G *Arm,* L *armus* shoulder, Gk *harmós* joint] —**arm′less,** *adj.* —**arm′like′,** *adj.*

arm[2] (äm), *n.* **1.** (*usually pl.*) an offensive or defensive implement for use in war; a weapon. **2.** *Mil.* a fighting branch of the military service, as the infantry, cavalry, field artillery, air corps, etc. —*v.i.* **3.** to enter into a state of hostility or of readiness for war. —*v.t.* **4.** to equip with arms. **5.** to cover or provide with whatever will add strength, force, or security. **6.** to fit or prepare (a thing) for any specific purpose or effective use. [ME *arme(n)*, t. F: m. *armer*, g. L *armāre*]

Armada (ä mä′də), *n.* **1.** Also, the **Spanish** or **Invincible Armada.** a fleet sent by Spain against England in 1588, but shattered and dispersed by storms. **2.** (*l.c.*) any fleet of warships. [t. Sp., g. L *armāta* armed forces (prop. pp. neut. pl. of *armāre* ARM², V.). See ARMY]

armadillo (ä′mə-dĭl′ō), *n.*, *pl.* **-los.** any of a great variety of burrowing mammals, having a jointed, protective covering of bony plates. They constitute a suborder, *Cingulata*, of the edentates, distributed in many species throughout South America and north as far as Texas, and widely used for food. They are omnivorous and mostly nocturnal. The **Texas armadillo,** *Dasypus novemcinctus*, is unique for always producing quadruplets of one sex. [t. Sp., dim. of *armado* armed, g. L *armātus*, pp.]

Armadillo, *Dasypus novemcinctus* (2½ ft long)

Armageddon (ä′mə gĕd′n), *n.* **1.** *Bible.* the place where the final battle will be fought between the forces of good and evil (probably named in reference to Megiddo). Rev. 16:16. **2.** any great crucial armed conflict.

Armagh (ä mä′), *n.* **1.** a county in Northern Ireland. 118,600 pop. (est. 1963); 489 sq. mi. **2.** its county town. 9000 (est. 1963).

armament (ä′mə mənt), *n.* **1.** the weapons with which a military unit, esp. an aeroplane, vehicle, or warship, is equipped. **2.** a land, sea, or air force equipped for war. **3.** the process of equipping or arming for war. [t. L: s. *armāmenta*, pl., implements, equipment, ship's tackle]

armature (ä′mə chə), *n.* **1.** armour. **2.** *Biol.* the protective covering of an animal or plant, or any part serving for defence or offence. **3.** *Elect.* **a.** the iron or steel applied across the poles of a permanent magnet to close it, or to the poles of an electromagnet to communicate mechanical force. See illus. under **electromagnet. b.** the part of an electrical machine which includes the main current-carrying winding (distinguished from the *field*). **c.** a pivoted part of an electrical device, as a buzzer or relay, activated by a magnetic field. **4.** *Sculpture.* a framework built as a support for clay figures during construction. [t. L: m. s. *armātūra* armour]

armband (äm′bănd′), *n.* a band of material worn round the sleeve to indicate authority, allegiance, etc., or, if black, mourning.

armchair (äm′chēə′), *n.* **1.** a chair with arms to support the forearms or elbows. —*adj.* **2.** stay-at-home; amateur: *an armchair critic.* **3.** seen or enjoyed at home: *the armchair theatre.*

armed (ämd), *adj.* **1.** bearing arms. **2.** supported or maintained by arms: *armed peace.* **3.** provided with a defence; ready.

armed bullhead, the pogge.

armed forces, all of the principal naval or military forces, including the army, navy, marines, airforce, etc. Also, **armed services.**

Armenia (ä mē′nĭ ə, -mē′nyə), *n.* **1.** an ancient country in W Asia: now a region in the SW Soviet Union, E Turkey, and NW Iran. **2.** Official name, **Armenian Soviet Socialist Republic.** a constituent republic of the Soviet Union, in S Caucasia. 2,007,000 pop. (1963); ab. 11,500 sq. mi. *Cap.*: Erivan.

Armenian Soviet Socialist Republic

Armenian (ä mē′nĭ ən, -mē′nyən), *adj.* **1.** pertaining to Armenia or to its inhabitants. —*n.* **2.** a native of Armenia. **3.** the language of the Armenians, an Indo-European language.

Armentières (ä′mən tĭəz′; *Fr.* är mäN tyĕr′), *n.* a town in extreme N France, in Nord department: battles, 1914, 1918. 18,691 (1963).

armet (ä′mĕt), *n.* *Armour.* a helmet with movable front plates to cover the face. [t. F, dim. of *arme* ARM²]

armful (äm′fo͝ol′), *n.*, *pl.* **-fuls.** as much as the arm, or both arms, can hold.

armhole (äm′hōl′), *n.* a hole in a garment for the arm.

armiger (ä′mĭ jə), *n.* **1.** one entitled to armorial bearings. **2.** an armour-bearer to a knight; a squire. [t. ML: squire, L armour-bearer]

armillary (ä′mĭ lə rĭ, ä mĭl′ə rĭ), *adj.* consisting of hoops or rings. [f. s. L *armilla* armlet, ring + -ARY¹]

armillary sphere, *Astron.* an arrangement of rings, all circles of a single sphere, showing the relative positions of the principal circles of the celestial sphere.

arming (ä′mĭng), *n.* *Naut.* a piece of tallow placed in a cavity at the lower end of a sounding lead to bring up a sample of the sand, mud, etc., of the sea bottom.

Arminian (ä mĭn′ĭ ən), *adj.* **1.** of or pertaining to Jacobus Arminius or his doctrines. —*n.* **2.** an adherent of the Arminian doctrines. —**Armin′ianism,** *n.*

Arminius (ä mĭn′ĭ əs), *n.* **1.** (*Hermann*), 17? B.C.–A.D. 21, Germanic hero: defeated Roman army, A.D. 9. **2. Jacobus** (jə kō′bəs) (*Jacob Harmensen*), 1560–1609, Dutch Protestant theologian who modified certain Calvinistic doctrines, esp. that of predestination.

armipotent (ä mĭp′ə tənt), *adj.* mighty in arms or war. [ME, t. L: s. *armipotens* powerful in arms]

armistice (ä′mĭ stĭs), *n.* a temporary suspension of hostilities by agreement of the parties, as to discuss peace; a truce. [t. NL: m. s. *armistitium*, f. L: *armi-* (comb. form of *arma* arms) + *-stitium* (der. *sistere* stop)]

Armistice Day, November 11th, the anniversary of the cessation of hostilities of World War I in 1918; kept on Remembrance Sunday since 1946.

armlet (äm′lĭt), *n.* **1.** an ornamental band worn on the arm. **2.** a little arm: *an armlet of the sea.*

armoire (ä mwä′; *Fr.* är mwär′), *n.* a large wardrobe or movable cupboard, with doors and shelves. [t. F. See AMBRY]

armor (ä′mə), *n.*, *v.t.* *U.S.* armour.

armorial (ä mô′rĭ əl), *adj.* **1.** belonging to heraldry or to heraldic bearing. —*n.* **2.** a book containing heraldic bearings and devices.

armorial bearings, a coat of arms.

Armorica (ä mŏ′rĭ kə), *n.* an ancient region in NW France, corresponding generally to Brittany.

Armorican (ä mŏ′rĭ kən), *adj.* **1.** pertaining to Armorica or an Armorican. **2.** *Geol.* of or pertaining to the major mountain-building episode which occurred in Europe in the Upper Carboniferous and Permian periods; Hercynian. —*n.* **3.** a native of Armorica. **4.** the Breton language. Also, **Armo′ric** for defs 1, 3, and 4.

armorist (ä′mə rĭst), *n.* one skilled in heraldry or the blazoning of arms.

armory (ä′mə rĭ), *n.*, *pl.* **-ries.** **1.** *Heraldry.* the art of blazoning arms. **2.** *Archaic.* heraldic bearings or arms. **3.** *Chiefly U.S.* an armourer's shop; an arsenal. **4.** *U.S.* armoury. [var. spelling of ARMOURY]

armour (ä′mə), *n.* **1.** defensive equipment; any covering worn as a protection against offensive weapons. **2.** a metallic sheathing or protective covering, esp. metal plates used on warships, armoured vehicles, aeroplanes, and fortifications. **3.** any protective covering, as the scales of a fish. **4.** that which serves as a protection or safeguard. **5.** the outer wrapping of metal, usually fine, braided steel wires, on a cable, primarily for the purpose of mechanical protection. —*v.t.* **6.** to cover with armour or armour plate. Also, *U.S.*, **armor.** [ME *armure*, t. OF: m. *armeüre*, g. L *armātūra*]

Suit of armour
A, Pauldron; B, Breastplate; C, Tasset; D, Cuisse; E, Kneepiece; F, Greave; G, Solleret; H, Helmet; I, Gorget; J, Brassard; K, Elbowpiece; L, Gauntlet

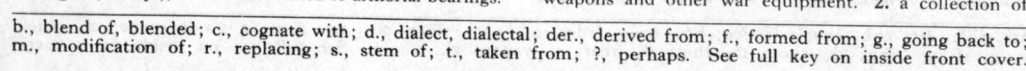

armour-bearer (ä′mə bēə′rə), *n.* a retainer bearing the armour or arms of a warrior. Also, *U.S.*, **armor-bearer.**

armoured (ä′məd), *adj.* **1.** protected by armour or armour-plate. **2.** consisting of troops using armoured vehicles: *an armoured division.* Also, *U.S.*, **armored.**

armoured car, a military vehicle with wheels, light armour, and, usually, machine-guns. Also, *U.S.*, **armored car.**

armourer (ä′mə rə), *n.* **1.** a maker or repairer of armour. **2.** a manufacturer of arms. **3.** an official, soldier, or sailor in charge of the upkeep of small arms in a regiment or on a naval vessel. Also, *U.S.*, **armorer.**

armour-plate (ä′mə plāt′), *n.* a plate or plating of specially hardened steel used to cover warships, tanks, aircraft, fortifications, etc., to protect them from enemy fire. Also, *U.S.*, **armor plate**; **ar′mour-plat′ing.** —**ar′mour-plat′ed,** *adj.*

armoury (ä′mə rĭ), *n.*, *pl.* **-ries.** **1.** a storage place for weapons and other war equipment. **2.** a collection of arms or armour. 3. armour collectively. 4. armory. Also, *U.S.*, **armory.** [ME *armurie.* See ARMOUR, -Y[3]]

armpit (ämʹpĭtʹ), *n. Anat.* the hollow under the arm at the shoulder; the axilla.

armrest (ämʹrĕstʹ), *n.* a rest or support, as on a chair, for the arm.

arms (ämz), *n.pl.* 1. arm[2] (def. 1). 2. *Mil.* small arms. 3. heraldic bearings. 4. (**up**) **in arms, a.** armed and prepared to resist. **b.** angry; in rebellion (against something); violently resentful. 5. **under arms,** armed. 6. **bear arms,** to serve as a soldier. 7. **take arms,** to resort to fighting; fight. [ME *armes,* t. OF, g. L *arma*]

arms race, competition between nations in building up military resources.

Armstrong (ämʹstrŏngʹ), *n.* 1. **Louis** (*'Satchmo'*), born 1900, U.S. jazz trumpeter and composer. 2. **Neil,** born 1930, U.S. astronaut, first man to walk on the moon.

army (äʹmĭ), *n., pl.* **-mies.** 1. (*cap. or l.c.*) the military forces of a nation, exclusive of the naval and, in some countries, the airforces. 2. (in large military land forces) the second largest unit, consisting of two or more corps. 3. a large body of men trained and armed for war. 4. any body of persons organized for any cause: *the Salvation Army.* 5. a host; a great multitude. [ME *armee,* t. OF, g. L *armāta* armed forces]

army ant, any ant of the tropical and subtropical genus *Dorylinae,* that travel in vast swarms.

army list, a list of all commissioned officers.

army of occupation, an army established in conquered territory to maintain order and to ensure the carrying out of peace or armistice terms.

army worm, 1. a kind of caterpillar, the larva of a noctuid moth, *Leucania unipuncta,* which often travels in hosts over a region, destroying grass, grain, etc. 2. some similarly destructive larva.

Arne (än), *n.* **Thomas Augustine,** 1710–78, English composer.

Arnhem (änʹəm), *n.* a city in the Netherlands, in S Gelderland, on the Rhine: battle 1944. 130,399 (1965).

Arnhem Land, 1. (formerly) the whole of the peninsula N of the Victoria and Roper rivers, in Northern Territory, Australia. 2. an Aboriginal reserve in the NE of this area.

arnica (äʹnĭ kə), *n.* 1. any plant of the asteraceous genus *Arnica,* esp. *A. montana.* 2. a tincture of the flowers of such a plant, applied medicinally to sprains and bruises.

Arnim (*Ger.* ärʹnĭm), *n.* **Achim von** (*Ger.* äʹKHĭm fōn), 1781–1831, German poet and author.

Arno (äʹnō), *n.* a river flowing from the Apennines in central Italy W through Florence to the Ligurian Sea. ab. 140 mi.

Arnold (äʹnəld), *n.* 1. **Sir Edwin,** 1832–1904, English poet and journalist. 2. **Matthew,** 1822–88, English essayist, poet, and literary critic. 3. **Thomas,** 1795–1842, English clergyman: headmaster of Rugby (father of Matthew).

Arnold von Winkelried (*Ger.* ärʹnōlt fōn vĭngʹkəl rēt), died 1386?, Swiss hero in the battle of Sempach (1386), fought against the Austrians.

arnotto (ä nŏtʹō), *n.* annatto.

aroid (ăʹroid, ĕəʹ-), *Bot.* —*adj.* 1. araceous. —*n.* 2. any araceous plant. [f. AR(UM) + -OID]

aroideous (ə roiʹdĭ əs), *adj.* araceous.

aroint thee (ə rointʹ), *Archaic.* avaunt! begone!

aroma (ə rōʹmə), *n.* 1. a smell arising from spices, plants, etc., esp. an agreeable smell; fragrance. 2. (of wines and spirits) the smell or bouquet. 3. a characteristic, subtle quality. [t. L, t. Gk: spice, sweet herb] —**Syn.** 1. See **perfume.**

aromatic (ăʹrə mătʹĭk), *adj.* 1. having an aroma; fragrant; sweet-scented; spicy. 2. *Chem.* of or pertaining to aromatic compounds. —*n.* 3. a plant, drug, or medicine yielding a fragrant smell, as certain spices, oils, etc. —**arʹomatʹically,** *adv.* —**aromaticity** (ăʹrə mə tĭsʹĭ tĭ), *n.*

aromatic compound, *Chem.* any of a class of organic compounds including benzene, naphthalene, anthracene, and their derivatives, which contain an unsaturated ring of carbon atoms. Many have an agreeable smell.

aromatization (ə rōʹmə tī zāʹshən), *n. Chem.* the catalytic conversion of aliphatic hydrocarbons to aromatic hydrocarbons. Also, **aromatisation.**

aromatize (ə rōʹmə tīzʹ), *v.t.*, **-tized, -tizing.** to make aromatic or fragrant. Also, **aromatise.**

arose (ə rōzʹ), *v.* pt. of **arise.**

around (ə roundʹ), *adv.* 1. in a circle or sphere; round about; on every side. 2. here and there; about: *to travel around.* 3. *Colloq.* somewhere about or near: *to hang around for a person.* —*prep.* 4. about; on all sides; encircling; encompassing: *a halo around his head.* 5. *Colloq.* here and there in: *to roam around the country.* 6. *Colloq.* somewhere in or near: *to stay around the house.* 7. *Colloq.* approximately; near in time, amount, etc.: *around ten o'clock, around a million.* [f. A-[1] + ROUND]

arouse (ə rouzʹ), *v.*, **aroused, arousing.** —*v.t.* 1. to excite into action; stir or put in motion; call into being: *aroused to action, arousing suspicion.* 2. to wake from sleep. —*v.i.* 3. to become aroused. [der. ROUSE[1], modelled on ARISE] —**arousal** (ə rouʹzəl), *n.* —**arousʹer,** *n.* —**Syn.** 1. animate, inspirit; incite; stimulate.

A.R.P., air-raid precautions.

Arp (*Fr.* ärp), *n.* **Jean** (*Fr.* zhäN) or **Hans** (*Fr.* äns), born 1888, French sculptor.

arpeggio (ä pĕjʹĭ ōʹ), *n., pl.* **-os.** *Music.* 1. the sounding of the notes of a chord separately and in succession instead of simultaneously. 2. (esp. on keyboard instruments and the harp) the breaking or spreading of a chord so that the notes are sounded in very rapid succession and finally all sound together. 3. a chord sounded in either of these ways. [t. It., der. *arpeggiare* play on the harp]

Written Played

Arpeggio

arpent (äʹpənt; *Fr.* är päNʹ), *n.* an old French unit of area equal to about one acre. It is still used in the province of Quebec and in parts of Louisiana.

arquebus (äʹkwĭ bəs), *n.* a light hand gun with matchlock or wheel-lock mechanism, formerly in use. Also, **harquebus.** [t. F: m. *arquebuse,* t. It. (obs.): m. *arcobuso,* t. D: m. *haakbus*]

arr., 1. arranged. 2. arrival. 3. arrive; arrived.

A.R.R. (L *anno regni Regis* or *Reginae*), in the year of the King's (or Queen's) reign.

arrack (ăʹrək), *n.* any of various spirits distilled in the East Indies and elsewhere in the East from toddy (def. 2), molasses, or other materials. [ult. t. Ar.: m. *'araq* (fermented) juice]

arraign (ə rānʹ), *v.t.* 1. *Law.* to call or bring before a court to answer to a charge or accusation. 2. to accuse or charge in general. —*n.* 3. *Obs. or Law.* arraignment. [ME *araine(n),* t. AF: m. *arainer,* ult. g. ML* *arratiōnāre* call to account] —**arraignʹer,** *n.*

arraignment (ə rānʹmənt), *n.* 1. *Law.* the act of arraigning. 2. a calling in question for faults; accusation.

Arran (ăʹrən), *n.* an island in SW Scotland, in the Firth of Clyde. 4506 pop. (1963); 166 sq. mi.

arrange (ə rānjʹ), *v.*, **-ranged, -ranging.** —*v.t.* 1. to place in proper, desired, or convenient order; adjust properly: *to arrange books on a shelf.* 2. to come to an agreement or understanding regarding: *to arrange a bargain.* 3. to prepare or plan: *to arrange the details of a meeting.* 4. *Music.* to adapt (a composition) for a particular mode of rendering by voices or instruments. —*v.i.* 5. to make a settlement; come to an agreement. 6. to make preparations. [ME *arayngе(n),* t. OF: m. s. *arangier,* f. *a-* A-[5] + *rangier* RANGE, v.] —**arrangʹer,** *n.* —**Syn.** 1. array; group, sort. 2. settle, determine.

arrangement (ə rānjʹmənt), *n.* 1. the act of arranging. 2. the state of being arranged. 3. the manner in which things are arranged. 4. a final settlement; adjustment by agreement. 5. (*usually pl.*) preparatory measure; previous plan; preparation. 6. something arranged in a particular way: *a floral arrangement.* 7. *Music.* **a.** the adaptation of a composition to voices or instruments, or to a new purpose. **b.** a piece so adapted. [t. F]

arrant (ăʹrənt), *adj.* 1. downright; thorough: *an arrant fool.* 2. notorious. 3. *Obs.* wandering. [var. of ERRANT] —**arʹrantly,** *adv.*

arras (ăʹrəs), *n.* 1. rich tapestry. 2. a tapestry weave. 3. a wall hanging. [named after ARRAS]

Arras (ăʹrəs; *Fr.* à răsʹ), *n.* a town in N France, in Pas de Calais department: battles in World War I. 36,400 (1963).

array (ə rāʹ), *v.t.* 1. to place in proper or desired order, as troops for battle. 2. to clothe with garments, esp. of an ornamental kind; deck. —*n.* 3. order, as of troops drawn up for battle. 4. an impressive group of things on exhibition, as a window display. 5. regular order or arrangement. 6. attire; dress. [ME, t. AF: m. *arai,* var. of OF *arei,* f. *a* to + *rei* order, of Gmc origin] —**Syn.** 1. arrange, range, marshal.

arrayal (ə rāʹəl), *n.* 1. the act of arraying; muster; array. 2. whatever is arrayed.

arrear (ə rĭəʹ), *n.* 1. (*usually pl.*) the state of being behind or behindhand. 2. (*usually pl.*) that which is behind in payment; a debt which remains unpaid, though due. 3. **in arrear** or **in arrears,** behind in payments. 4. *Archaic.* the rear. [ME *arere,* t. OF, g. L *ad-* AD- + *retrō* backwards]

arrearage (ə rĭəʹrĭj), *n.* 1. the state or condition of being behind in payments due or in arrears. 2. arrears; amount or amounts overdue. 3. a thing or part kept in reserve. [ME *arerage,* t. OF. See ARREAR, -AGE]

arrest (ə rĕstʹ), *v.t.* 1. to seize (a person) by legal authority or warrant. **2.** to capture; seize. **3.** to catch and fix: *to arrest the attention.* **4.** to bring to a standstill; stop; check: *to arrest the current of a river.* **5.** *Med.* to stop the active growth of: *arrested cancer.* —*n.* **6.** taking a person into custody in connection with a legal proceeding. **7.** any seizure or taking by force. **8.** the act of stopping. **9.** the state of being stopped. **10.** *Mach.* any device for arresting motion in a mechanism. [ME *arest(e)*, t. OF: (m.) *areste* stoppage, der. *arester*, g. LL *adrestāre* (f. L: *ad-* AD- + *restāre* stop)] —**arrest′er,** *n.* —**Syn. 4.** See **stop. 6.** apprehension, imprisonment. **8.** stoppage, halt.

arrestee (ə rĕs′tē′), *n. Scot. Law.* one who is under an arrestment (def. 2).

arresting (ə rĕs′tĭng), *adj.* catching the attention; striking: *an arresting painting.*

arrestment (ə rĕst′mənt), *n.* **1.** *Law.* the state of being under arrest; detention. **2.** *Scot. Law.* the prevention of a debtor (the arrestee) from paying a creditor, until a claim upon that creditor by another person (the arrester) has been met.

Arrhenius (*Swed.* ä rē′nē o͞os), *n.* **Svante August** (*Swed.* svän′tə ou′go͝ost), 1859–1927, Swedish scientist.

arrhythmia (ə rĭth′mĭ ə), *n. Pathol.* any disturbance in the rhythm of the heartbeat. [t. Gk: want of rhythm] —**arrhythmic** (ə rĭth′mĭk), *adj.*

arride (ə rīd′), *v.t.*, **-rided, -riding.** *Obs.* to be agreeable or pleasing to. [t. L: m. s. *arrīdēre* smile at]

arrière-ban (ă′rĭ ĕə băn′; *Fr.* ä ryĕr bäN′), *n.* **1.** a group of vassals who owed military service, esp. to French kings. **2.** the message calling on this group for duty. [t. F, f. Gmc: *hari, heri* army + *ban* proclamation]

arrière-pensée (*Fr.* ä ryĕr päN sĕ′), *n. French.* a mental reservation; hidden motive.

arris (ă′rĭs), *n. Archit.* **1.** a sharp ridge, as between adjoining channels of a Doric column. **2.** the line, edge, or hip in which the two straight or curved surfaces of a body, forming an exterior angle, meet. [t. F: m. *areste*, g. L *arista* ear of grain, bone of a fish]

arrival (ə rī′vəl), *n.* **1.** the act of arriving: *the time of arrival.* **2.** the reaching or attainment of any object or condition: *arrival at a decision.* **3.** the person or thing that arrives, or has arrived. —**Syn. 1.** advent, coming.

arrive (ə rīv′), *v.*, **-rived, -riving.** —*v.i.* **1.** to come to a certain point in the course of travel; reach one's destination. **2.** to reach in any course or process; attain (fol. by *at*): *to arrive at a conclusion.* **3.** to come: *the time has arrived.* **4.** to happen; occur. **5.** to attain a position of success in the world. **6.** *Obs.* to come to shore. —*v.t.* **7.** *Obs.* to reach; come to. **8.** *Obs.* to happen to. [ME *a(r)rive(n)*, t. OF: m. *a(r)river*, g. LL *arrīpāre* come to shore]

—**Syn. 1.** ARRIVE, COME both mean to reach a stopping place. ARRIVE directs the attention to the final point of an activity or state: *the train arrived at noon.* COME rarely refers to the actual moment of arrival but refers instead to the progress towards it. —**Ant. 1.** depart.

arrivederci (*It.* ä rē vĕ dĕr′chē), *Italian.* until we see each other again; goodbye for the present.

arriviste (*Fr.* ä rē vēst′), *n. French.* an ambitious person; social climber or careerist.

arroba (ə rō′bə), *n.* **1.** a Spanish and Portuguese unit of weight of varying value, in Mexico, etc., equal to 25·37 pounds avoirdupois, and in Brazil to 32·98 pounds avoirdupois. **2.** a unit of liquid measure of varying value, used in Spain, etc., and commonly equal (when used for wine) to 3·5 imperial gallons or (when used for oil) to 2·75 imperial gallons. [t. Sp., t. Ar.: m. *al -rub'* the quarter]

arrogance (ă′rə gəns), *n.* the quality of being arrogant; offensive exhibition of assumed or real superiority; overbearing pride. Also, **ar′rogancy.** [ME, t. F, t. L: m. s. *arrogantia*] —**Syn.** haughtiness, insolence, disdain.

arrogant (ă′rə gənt), *adj.* **1.** making unwarrantable claims or pretensions to superior importance or rights; overbearingly assuming; insolently proud. **2.** characterized by or proceeding from arrogance: *arrogant claims.* [ME, t. L: s. *arrogans*, ppr., assuming] —**ar′rogantly,** *adv.* —**Syn. 1.** presumptuous, haughty, imperious, supercilious. See **proud.** —**Ant. 1.** meek. **2.** modest.

arrogate (ă′rə gāt′), *v.t.*, **-gated, -gating. 1.** to claim unwarrantably or presumptuously; assume or appropriate to oneself without right. **2.** to attribute or assign to another without just reason. [t. L: m. s. *arrogātus*, pp., assumed, asked of] —**ar′roga′tion,** *n.*

arrondissement (*Fr.* ä rôN dēs mäN′), *n.*, *pl.* **-ments** (-mäN′). *French.* **1.** the largest administrative division of a French department. Each arrondissement is divided into cantons. **2.** a borough of Paris.

arrow (ă′rō), *n.* **1.** a slender, straight, generally pointed, missile weapon made to be shot from a bow. The shaft is nearly always made of light wood, fitted with feathers at the nock end to help guide it. **2.** anything resembling an arrow in form. **3.** a figure of an arrow used to indicate direction. **4.** (*pl.*) *Colloq.* the game of darts. **5.** (*cap.*) *Astron.* Sagitta. **6.** See **broad arrow.** [ME and OE *arwe*, c. Icel. *ör*] —**ar′rowless,** *adj.* —**ar′row-like′,** *adj.* —**ar′row-shaped′,** *adj.*

arrow-grass (ă′rō grăs′), *n.* any one of the grasslike marsh plants of the genus *Triglochin*; the burst seed capsule resembles an arrowhead.

arrowhead (ă′rō hĕd′), *n.* **1.** the head of an arrow, usually wedge-shaped or barbed. **2.** any plant of the genus *Sagittaria*, usually aquatic, species of which have arrow-shaped leaves. **3.** anything shaped like an arrowhead; a wedge-shaped design or ornament.

arrow-poison frog (ăr′ō poi′zən), dendrobates.

arrowroot (ă′rə ro͞ot′), *n.* **1.** a tropical American plant, *Maranta arundinacea*, or related species, whose rhizomes yield a nutritious starch. **2.** the starch itself. **3.** a similar starch from other plants, used in puddings, biscuits, etc.

arrowshot (ă′rō shŏt′), the range of an arrow.

arrowwood (ă′rō wo͝od′), *n. U.S.* any of several shrubs and small trees, as the wahoo and certain viburnums, with tough, straight shoots, once used for arrows.

arrowworm (ă′rō wûm′), *n.* a small transparent pelagic animal of elongate form with fins, comprising the class or phylum *Chaetognatha.*

arrowy (ă′rō ĭ), *adj.* **1.** like an arrow in shape, speed, effect, etc.; swift or piercing. **2.** consisting of arrows.

arse (äs), *Taboo.* —*n.* **1.** rump; bottom; buttocks; posterior. **2.** *Slang.* a person, esp. a foolish one. —*v.i.* **3. arse about,** *Slang.* to fool around. [ME; OE *ears*]

arsenal (ä′sə nəl), *n.* **1.** a repository or magazine of arms and military stores of all kinds for land or naval service. **2.** a building having that incidental purpose but used mainly for the training of troops. **3.** a public establishment where military equipment or munitions are manufactured. [t. It.: m. *arsenale* dock (Venetian d. *arzanà*), t. Ar.: m. *dar ṣinā'a* workshop]

arsenate (ä′sĭ nāt′, -nĭt), *n. Chem.* salt of arsenic acid.

arsenic (*n.* äs′nĭk; *adj.* ä sĕn′ĭk), *Chem.* —*n.* **1.** a greyish white element having a metallic lustre, volatilizing when heated, and forming poisonous compounds. *Symbol:* As; *at. wt:* 74·9216; *at. no.:* 33. **2.** arsenic trioxide or white arsenic, As_2O_3, which is used in medicine and the arts, and in poison for vermin. **3.** a mineral, the native element, occurring in white or grey masses. —*adj.* **4.** of or containing arsenic, esp. in the pentavalent state. [ME *arsenik*, t. L: m. s. *arsenicum*, t. Gk: m. *arsenikón* orpiment]

arsenic acid, *Chem.* a water-soluble crystalline compound, H_3AsO_4, used in the manufacture of arsenates.

arsenical (ä sĕn′ĭ kl), *adj.* **1.** containing or relating to arsenic. —*n.* **2.** (*pl.*) a group of insecticides, drugs, etc., containing arsenic.

arsenide (ä′sĭ nīd′), *n. Chem.* a compound containing two elements, of which arsenic is the negative one, as **silver arsenide,** Ag_3As.

arsenite (ä′sĭ nīt′), *n. Chem.* **1.** a salt of any of the hypothetical arsenous acids. **2.** arsenic (def. 2).

arseniuret (ä sē′nyo͞o rĭt, -sĕn′yo͞o-), *n. Chem.* arsenide. [f. ARSENI(C) + URET]

arseniuretted (ä sē′nyo͞o rĕt′ĭd, -sĕn′yo͞o-), *adj. Chem.* combined with arsenic so as to form an arsenide. Also, *U.S.*, **arseniureted.**

arsenopyrite (ä′sĭ nō pī′ə rīt′, ä sĕn′ə-), *n.* a common mineral, iron arsenic sulphide, FeAsS, occurring in silver-white to steel-grey crystals or masses, an ore of arsenic. [f. *arseno-* (comb. form of ARSENIC) + PYRITE]

arsenous (ä′sĭ nəs), *adj. Chem.* containing trivalent arsenic, as *arsenous chloride*, $AsCl_3$.

arsine (ä′sēn), *n. Chem.* **1.** arseniuretted hydrogen, AsH_3, a colourless, inflammable, highly poisonous gas, with a fetid garlic-like smell, used in chemical warfare. **2.** any derivative of this compound, in which one or more hydrogen atoms are replaced by organic radicals. [f. ARS(ENIC) + -INE[2]]

arsis (ä′sĭs), *n.*, *pl.* **-ses** (-sēz). **1.** *Pros.* **a.** (originally) the unaccented syllable of a foot in verse. **b.** (in later use) the unstressed part of a rhythmical unit (opposed to *thesis*). **2.** *Music.* the anacrusis, or upbeat (opposed to *thesis*). [t. L, t. Gk: a raising (appar. of hand or voice)]

arson (ä′sən), *n. Law.* the malicious burning of a house or outbuilding belonging to another, or (as fixed by statute) the burning of any building (including one's own). [t. AF, g. LL *arsio* a burning]

arsphenamine (äs′fĕn ə mēn′, -fĕn ăm′ĭn), *n. Pharm.* a yellow crystalline powder subject to rapid oxidization, $C_{12}H_{12}N_2O_2As_2 . 2HCl + 2H_2O$, used to treat diseases caused by spirochete organisms, esp. syphilis and trench mouth; first known as '606'. [f. ARS(ENIC) + PHEN(YL) + AMINE]

ars poetica (äz′ pō ĕt′ĭ kə), *Latin.* the art of poetry or poetics.

art[1] (ät), *n.* **1.** the production or expression of what is beautiful (esp. visually), appealing, or of more than ordinary significance. **2.** *Journalism.* any illustration in a newspaper or magazine. **3.** a department of skilled performance: *industrial art.* **4.** (*pl.*) a branch of learning or university study. **5.** (*pl.*) liberal arts. **6.** skilled workmanship, execution, or agency (often opposed to *nature*). **7.** a skill or knack; a method of doing a thing, esp. if it is difficult. **8.** craft; cunning: *glib and oily art.* **9.** studied action; artificiality in behaviour. **10.** (*usually pl.*) an artifice or artful device: *the arts and wiles of politics.* **11.** *Archaic.* learning or science. **12. art and part,** wholly involved; wholeheartedly. [ME, t. OF, g. s. L *ars* skill, art]

art[2] (ät), *v. Archaic.* 2nd pers. sing. pres. indic. of **be.** [ME; OE *eart*]

-art, var. of **-ard,** as in *braggart.*

art., 1. article. 2. artificial.

artal (ä′täl), *n.* pl. of **rotl.**

Artaxerxes I (ä′tə zûk′sēz), **1.** son of Xerxes, king of Persia 464–425 B.C. **2.** died A.D. 242, king of Persia A.D. 212?–242; founder of the dynasty and empire of the Sassanidae.

Artaxerxes II (ä′tə zûk′sēz), died 359? B.C., king of Persia 404?–359 B.C.

Artaxerxes III (ä′tə zûk′sēz), died 338 B.C., king of Persia 359–338 B.C.

artefact (ä′tĭ făkt′), *n.* **1.** any object made by man with a view to subsequent use. **2.** *Biol.* a substance, structure, or the like, not naturally present in tissue but formed by reagents, death, etc. Also, **artifact.** [f. L: *arti-* (comb. form of *ars* art) + s. *factus,* pp., made]

artel (ä tĕl′), *n.* (in the Soviet Union) a peasants' or workers' cooperative enterprise. [t. Russ.]

Artemis (ä′tĭ mĭs), *n. Gk Myth.* a goddess, sister of Apollo, represented as a virgin huntress and associated with the moon: identified with Diana. [t. L, t. Gk]

artemisia (ä′tĭ mĭz′ĭ ə, -mĭs′ĭ ə), *n.* any of a very large genus of composite plants, *Artemisia,* abundant in dry regions, and mostly of the northern hemisphere, including wormwood, mugwort, the North American sagebrush, etc. [t. L, t. Gk]

arterial (ä tĭə′rĭ əl), *adj.* **1.** *Physiol.* pertaining to the blood in the arteries which has been charged with oxygen during its passage through the lungs, and, in the higher animals, is usually bright red. **2.** *Anat.* of, pertaining to, or resembling the arteries. **3.** having a main channel and many branches: *arterial drainage.* **4.** carrying the main flow of traffic between large towns: *an arterial road.* —*n.* **5.** an arterial road.

arterialize (ä tĭə′rĭ ə līz′), *v.t.,* **-lized, -lizing.** to make arterial. Also, **arterialise.** —**arte′rializa′tion,** *n.*

arteriole (ä tĭə′rĭ ōl′), *n.* a small artery. [t. NL: m. s. *arteriola,* dim. of *artēria* artery]

arteriosclerosis (ä tĭə′rĭ ō sklĭə rō′sĭs), *n. Pathol.* an arterial disease occurring esp. in the elderly, characterized by inelasticity and thickening of the vessel walls, with lessened blood flow. [t. NL, f. Gk: *artērio-* (comb. form of *artēría* artery) + m. *sklḗrōsis* hardening] —**arteriosclerotic** (ä tĭə′rĭ ō sklĭə rŏt′ĭk), *adj.*

arteritis (ä′tə rī′tĭs), *n. Med.* inflammation of an artery. [f. s. L *artēria* artery + -ITIS]

artery (ä′tə rĭ), *n., pl.* **-teries. 1.** *Anat.* a blood vessel which conveys blood from the heart to any part of the body. **2.** a main channel in any ramifying system of communications or transport, as in drainage or roads. [ME *arterie,* t. L: m. *arteria,* t. Gk]

artesian well (ä tē′zyən), a well whose shaft penetrates through an impervious layer into a water-bearing stratum from which the water rises by hydrostatic pressure. [t. F: m. *artésien* pertaining to ARTOIS, where such wells are bored]

Cross-section of an artesian well
A, Impermeable strata;
B, Permeable strata;
C, Artesian boring and well

Arteveld (ä′tə vĕlt′), *n.* **1. Jacob van** (yăk′ŏb văn), 1290?–1345, statesman of Flanders. **2.** his son, **Philip van** (fĭl′ĭp văn), 1340?–82, popular leader of Flanders. Also, **Artevelde** (ä′tə vĕl′də).

artful (ät′fəl), *adj.* **1.** crafty; cunning; tricky: *artful schemes.* **2.** skilful in adapting means to ends; ingenious.

arthralgia (ä thrăl′jə), *n. Pathol.* pain in a joint. —**arthral′gic,** *adj.*

arthritic (ä thrĭt′ĭk), *adj.* **1.** suffering or tending to suffer from arthritis. **2.** of or of the nature of arthritis. —*n.* **3.** an arthritic person.

arthritis (ä thrī′tĭs), *n. Pathol.* inflammation of a joint, as in gout or rheumatism. [t. L, t. Gk: joint disease]

arthro-, *Anat.* a word element meaning 'joint', as in *arthropod.* Also, **arthr-.** [t. Gk, comb. form of *árthron*]

arthromere (ä′thrə mĭə′), *n. Zool.* one of the segments or parts into which the body of articulated animals is divided.

arthropod (ä′thrə pŏd′), *n.* **1.** any of the *Arthropoda,* the phylum of segmented invertebrates, having jointed legs, as the insects, arachnids, crustaceans, and myriapods. —*adj.* **2.** Also, **arthropodal** (ä′thrə pō′dl, ä thrŏp′ə dl), **arthropodous** (ä thrŏp′ə dəs). belonging to or pertaining to the *Arthropoda.*

arthrospore (ä′thrə spô′), *n.* **1.** *Bacteriol.* an isolated vegetative cell which has passed into a resting state, occurring in bacteria, and not regarded as a true spore. **2.** *Bot.* one of a number of spores of various low fungi and algae, united in the form of a string of beads, formed by fission.

Arthur (ä′thə), *n.* **1.** legendary king in ancient Britain: leader of Knights of the Round Table. **2. Chester Alan,** 1830–86, 21st president of the U.S., 1881–85.

Arthurian (ä thyŏŏə′rĭ ən), *adj.* of or pertaining to Arthur, who, with his knights, forms the subject of a great body of medieval romantic literature.

artichoke (ä′tĭ chōk′), *n.* **1.** a herbaceous, thistle-like plant, *Cynara scolymus,* with an edible flower head. **2.** the edible portion, used as a table vegetable. **3.** Jerusalem artichoke. [t. d. It.: m. *articiocco,* t. Pr.: m. *arquichaut,* t. Ar.: m. *al kharshūf*]

Artichoke, *Cynara scolymus*

article (ä′tĭ kl), *n., v.,* **-cled, -cling.** —*n.* **1.** a literary composition on a specific topic, forming an independent part of a book or literary publication, esp. of a newspaper, magazine, review, or other periodical. **2.** an individual piece or thing of a class; an item or particular: *an article of food or dress.* **3.** a thing, indefinitely: *what is that article?* **4.** (in some languages) any word, as the English words *a* or *an* (**indefinite article**) and *the* (**definite article**), whose main function is to precede nouns of a certain class (**common nouns**), esp. when these are not preceded by other limiting modifiers. **5.** a clause, item, point, or particular in a contract, treaty, or other formal agreement; a condition or stipulation in a contract or bargain. **6.** a separate clause or provision of a statute. **7.** (*pl.*) a document drawn up in articles; an agreement or code. **8.** a matter or subject. **9.** *Archaic.* juncture or moment. —*v.t.* **10.** to set forth in articles; charge or accuse specifically. **11.** to bind by articles of covenant or stipulation: *to article an apprentice.* **12.** to bind by articles of agreement. —*v.i.* **13.** *U.S.* to make specific changes. [ME, t. F, t. L: m. *articulus,* dim. of *artus* joint]

articles of association, the regulations and constitution of a registered company in Great Britain and elsewhere, or the document containing them.

Articles of Confederation, *U.S. Hist.* the first constitution of the thirteen American colonies, adopted in 1781 by the Continental Congress and lasting till 1788.

articles of faith, (a statement of) the essential points of faith held by a particular Church. See **Thirty-nine Articles.**

articles of war, *Hist.* the disciplinary code by which the British army and navy were bound before the 19th century.

articular (ä tĭk′yŏŏ lə), *adj.* of or pertaining to the joints. [t. L: s. *articulāris*]

articulate (*adj., n.* ä tĭk′yŏŏ lĭt; *v.* ä tĭk′yŏŏ lāt′), *adj., v.,* **-lated, -lating,** *n.* —*adj.* **1.** clear; distinct. **2.** uttered clearly in distinct syllables. **3.** capable of speech; not speechless. **4.** Also, **articulated.** having joints or articulations; composed of segments. —*v.t.* **5.** to utter articulately. **6.** *Phonet.* to make the movements and adjustments of the speech organs necessary to utter (a speech sound). **7.** to unite by a joint or joints. —*v.i.* **8.** to utter distinct syllables or words: *to articulate distinctly.* **9.** *Phonet.* to articulate a speech sound. **10.** to form a joint. —*n.* **11.** *Rare.* a segmented invertebrate. [t. L: m. s. *articulātus,* pp.] —**artic′ulately,** *adv.* —**artic′ulateness,** *n.* —**artic′ulator,** *n.*

articulated lorry, a lorry having a detachable tractor able to move at an angle to the body, designed for easier manoeuvre when turning. Also, **articulated truck.**

articulation (ä tĭk′yŏŏ lā′shən), *n.* **1.** *Phonet.* **a.** the act or process of articulating speech. **b.** the adjustments and movements of speech organs involved in pronouncing a particular sound, taken as a whole. **c.** any of these adjustments and movements. **d.** any speech sound, esp. a consonant. **2.** clarity of diction; distinctness. **3.** the act of jointing. **4.** a jointed state or formation; a joint. **5.** *Bot.* **a.** a joint or place between two parts where separation may take place spontaneously, as at the point of attachment of a leaf. **b.** a node in a stem, or the space between two nodes. **6.** *Anat., Zool.* a joint, as the joining or juncture of bones or of the movable segments of an arthropod. **7.** *Art.* the way in which the elements of an architectural design are interrelated through different degrees of emphasis.

artifact (ä′tĭ făkt′), *n.* artefact.

artifice (ä′tĭ fĭs), *n.* **1.** a crafty device or expedient; a clever trick or stratagem. **2.** craft; trickery. **3.** skilful or apt contrivance. **4.** *Obs.* workmanship. [t. F, t. L: m. s. *artificium*] **—Syn. 1.** ruse, subterfuge, wile. **2.** guile, deception, deceit. See **cunning.**

artificer (ä tĭf′ĭ sə), *n.* **1.** a skilful or artistic worker; craftsman. **2.** one who is skilful in devising ways of making things; an inventor. **3.** *Mil.* a soldier or sailor mechanic who does repairs, maintains machinery, etc.

artificial (ä′tĭ fĭsh′əl), *adj.* **1.** made by human skill and labour (opposed to *natural*). **2.** made in imitation of or as a substitute; not genuine. **3.** feigned; fictitious; assumed. **4.** full of affectation; affected. **5.** *Biol.* based on arbitrary rather than organic criteria. **6.** *Obs.* artful; crafty. [ME t. L: s. *artificiālis*] **—ar′tifi′cially,** *adv.* **—ar′tifi′cialness,** *n.*

artificial horizon, 1. a level reflector, as a surface of mercury, used in determining the altitudes of stars, etc. **2.** the bubble in a sextant or octant for aerial use.

artificial insemination, a method of inducing pregnancy by artificial introduction of viable sperm into the canal of the cervix: widely practised on cattle and horses for the purpose of selective breeding.

artificiality (ä′tĭ fĭsh′ĭ ăl′ĭ tĭ), *n., pl.* **-ties. 1.** artificial quality. **2.** an artificial thing or trait.

artificial radioactivity, *Physics.* induced radioactivity.

artificial respiration, a method for restarting the breathing of a person who has been half-drowned or otherwise asphyxiated, as by alternately pressing on and releasing the rib cage, or by the kiss of life.

artificial selection. See **selection** (def. 6).

artificial silk, rayon or any other similar synthetic material.

artillery (ä tĭl′ə rĭ), *n.* **1.** mounted guns, movable or stationary, light or heavy, as distinguished from small arms. **2.** the troops, or the branch of an army, concerned with the service of such guns. **3.** the science which treats of the use of such guns. [ME *artilrie*, t. OF: m. *artillerie* implements of war]

artilleryman (ä tĭl′ə rĭ mən), *n., pl.* **-men.** one who serves a piece of artillery, or is in a regiment of artillery. Also, **artil′lerist.**

artiodactyl (ä′tĭ ō dăk′tĭl), *adj.* **1.** *Zool.* having an even number of toes or digits on each foot. **—***n.* **2.** any animal of the mammalian order *Artiodactylia*, which comprises the even-toed quadrupeds, as the swine, the hippopotamuses and the ruminants: cattle, sheep, goats, deer, camels, etc., sometimes classified as a suborder of ungulates. [f. Gk: *ártio(s)* even + m. s. *dáktylos* finger or toe] **—ar′tiodac′tylous,** *adj.*

artisan (ä′tĭ zən, ä′tĭ zăn′), *n.* **1.** one skilled in an industrial or applied art; a craftsman. **2.** a member of the urban working classes. **3.** any of certain ratings in the Royal Navy. **4.** *Obs.* an artist. [t. F, t. It.: m. *artigiano*, der. *arte* guild] **—Syn. 1.** See **artist.**

artist (ä′tĭst), *n.* **1.** a person who practises one of the fine arts, esp. a painter or a sculptor. **2.** a member of one of the histrionic professions, as an actor or singer. **3.** one who exhibits art in his work, or makes an art of his employment. **4.** *Obs.* an artisan. [t. F: m. *artiste*, t. It.: m. *artista*, g. LL. See ART[1], -IST]

—Syn. 1. ARTIST, ARTISAN are persons having superior skill or ability, or capable of a superior kind of workmanship. An ARTIST is a person engaged in some type of fine art. An ARTISAN is engaged in a commerical or manual enterprise.

artiste (ä tēst′; *Fr.* är tēst′), *n. French.* an artist, esp. an actor, singer, dancer, or other public performer.

artistic (ä tĭs′tĭk), *adj.* **1.** conformable to the standards of art; aesthetically excellent or admirable. **2.** of, like, or befitting an artist. **3.** stormy, emotional, and capricious, as temperament or behaviour popularly ascribed to artists. Also, **artis′tical. —artis′tically,** *adv.*

artistry (ä′tĭs trĭ), *n., pl.* **-tries. 1.** artistic workmanship, effect, or quality. **2.** artistic pursuits.

artless (ät′lĭs), *adj.* **1.** free from deceit, cunning, or craftiness; ingenuous: *an artless mind.* **2.** natural; simple: *artless beauty.* **3.** lacking art, knowledge, or skill. **—art′lessly,** *adv.* **—art′lessness,** *n.*

Art Nouveau (ä′noo͞ vō′; *Fr.* är noo͞ vō′), *Fine Arts.* an international decorative style, based on organic and growth forms in nature, widely common between 1890 and 1914. **—Art′-Nouveau′,** *adj.* [t. F: lit., new art; named after a shop in Paris]

Artois (*Fr.* är twä′), *n.* a former province in N France: artesian wells. See map under **Agincourt.**

Arts Council of Great Britain, a semiofficial cultural organization which promotes and subsidizes the arts all over Britain, and seeks to maintain cultural standards esp. in music, drama, and poetry.

art silk, artificial silk.

artwork (ät′wûk′), *n. Print.* any piece of specially designed material from which a printer's plate or block, etc., is composed.

arty (ä′tĭ), *adj.*, **-tier, -tiest.** *Colloq.* ostentatious in display of artistic interest. **—art′iness,** *n.*

arty-crafty (ä′tĭ kräf′tĭ), *adj.* affectedly artistic; artistic but useless, pretentious, or trivial.

Aruba (ə roo͞′bə; *Du.* ō rʏ′bä), *n.* an island in the Netherlands Antilles, off the NW coast of Venezuela. 59,315 pop. (1963); 69 sq. mi.

Aru Islands (ä′roo͞), an island group in Indonesia, SW of New Guinea. 3306 sq. mi.

arum (ĕə′rəm), *n.* **1.** any plant of the genus *Arum*, having an inflorescence consisting of a spadix enclosed in a large spathe, as the cuckoopint. **2.** any of various allied plants in cultivation, as the calla lily. [t. L, t. Gk: m. *áron* the wake-robin] **—ar′um-like′,** *adj.*

Arundel (ă′rən dl), *n.* a town in SE England, in Sussex: castle. 2650 (est. 1962).

arundinaceous (ə rŭn′dĭ nā′shəs), *adj. Bot.* pertaining to or like a reed or cane; reedlike; reedy. [t. L: m. *arundināceus*, der. *(h)arundo* reed]

Arup (*Dan.* ō′rôb), *n.* **Ove Nyquist** (*Dan.* ō′və nʏ′kvēst), born 1895, British engineer born in Denmark.

A.R.V., American Revised Version (of the Bible).

arvo (ä′vō), *n. Austral. and N.Z. Slang.* afternoon.

-ary[1], **1.** an adjective suffix meaning 'pertaining to', attached chiefly to nouns (*honorary*) and to stems appearing in other words (*voluntary*). **2.** a suffix forming nouns from other nouns or adjectives indicating location or repository (*dictionary, granary, apiary*), officers (*functionary, secretary*), or other relations (*adversary*). **3.** a suffix forming collective numeral nouns, esp. in time units (*centenary*). [t. L: m. *-ārius*, neut. *-ārium*]

-ary[2], var. of **-ar**[1], as in *exemplary, military.*

Aryan (ĕə′rĭ ən), *n.* **1.** *Ethnol.* a member or descendant of the prehistoric people who spoke Indo-European. **2.** (in Nazi doctrine) a non-Jewish Caucasian, esp. one of Nordic physical type. **3. a.** Indo-European. **b.** the hypothetical parent language of Indo-European. **—***adj.* **4.** of or pertaining to an Aryan or the Aryans. **5.** Indo-European. Also, **Arian.** [f. Skt *Arya*, name by which the Sanskrit-speaking immigrants into India called themselves + -AN]

Aryanize (ĕə′rĭ ə nīz′), *v.t.*, **-nized, -nizing.** (in Nazi doctrine) to remove all non-Aryan persons from (office, business, etc.). Also, **Aryanise.**

aryl (ă′rĭl), *adj. Chem.* of or pertaining to any of the organic radicals obtained from the aromatic hydrocarbons by removing a hydrogen atom, as phenyl (C_6H_5) from benzene (C_6H_6). [f. AR(OMATIC) + -YL]

arylamine (ă′rĭ lə mēn′, -lăm′ĭn), *n. Chem.* any of a group of amines in which one or more of the hydrogen atoms of ammonia are replaced with aromatic radicals.

arytenoid (ă′rĭ tē′noid), *Anat.* **—***adj.* Also, **arytenoidal** (ă′rĭ tĭ noi′dl). **1.** ladle- or cup-shaped (applied to two small cartilages at the top of the larynx, and to some of the muscles connected with them). **—***n.* **2.** an arytenoid cartilage. Also, **arytaenoid.** [t. Gk: m. s. *arytainoeidēs* ladle-shaped]

as[1] (ăz; *unstressed* əz), *adv.* **1.** to such a degree or extent: *as good as gold.* **2. as well as,** as much or as truly as; just as; equally as; as also; in addition to: *goodness as well as beauty.* **3. as well, a.** equally; also; too: *beautiful, and good as well.* **b.** as well as not; equally well; better; advisable: *it is as well to avoid trouble.* **—***conj.* **4.** the consequent in the correlations *as* (or *so*) . . . *as, same . . . as*, etc., denoting degree, extent, manner, etc. (*as good as gold, in the same way as before*), or in the correlations *so as, such as*, denoting purpose or result (fol. by infinitive): *to listen so as to hear.* **5.** (without antecedent) in the degree, manner, etc., of or that: *quick as thought, speak as he does.* **6.** according to what, or the manner in which, or the extent to which: *as I hear, we help as we are able.* **7.** though: *bad as it is, it could be worse.* **8.** as if; as though: *he spoke quietly,* *as to himself.* **9.** when or while. **10.** since; because. **11.** for instance. **12. as for, as to,** with regard or respect to; for the matter of. **13. as if, as though,** as it would be if. **14. as it were,** in some sort; so to speak. **15. as yet, a.** up to now; even yet. **b.** for the moment; in the near future; just yet. *—rel.pron.* **16.** that; who; which (esp. after *such* and *the same*). **17.** (of) which fact, contingency, etc. (referring to a statement): *I may fail you, as you realize.* *—prep.* **18.** in the role, function, status, or manner of: *to appear as Othello, serve as a warning.* [ME *as, als, alse, also,* OE *alswā, ealswā* all so, quite so, quite as, as. Cf. ALSO] **—Syn. 10.** See **because.**

as² (ăs), *n., pl.* **asses** (ăs′ĭz). **1.** a copper coin, the unit of the early monetary system of Rome, first nominally of the weight of a pound (12 ounces). About 80 B.C., having fallen to half an ounce, it ceased to be issued. **2.** a unit of weight: 12 ounces; the pound, equal to 327·4 grammes, or 5053 grains. [t. L]

ås (*Sw.* ōs), *n., pl.* **åsar** (*Sw.* ōs′ăr), *Geol.* an esker. [Sw.]

as-, var. of **ad-** before *s,* as in *assert.*

As, *Chem.* arsenic.

AS, Anglo-Saxon. Also, **A.-S., A.S.**

A.S.A., Amateur Swimming Association.

A.S.A.A., Associate of the Society of Incorporated Accountants and Auditors.

asafoetida (ăs′ə fēt′ĭ də), *n.* a gum resin having an obnoxious, alliaceous smell, obtained from the roots of several species of the umbelliferous genus *Ferula* and used in medicine. Also, **asafetida, assafoetida, assafetida.** [t. ML: f. *asa* (t. Pers.: m. *azā* mastic) + L *foetida* fetid]

Asahikawa (ä sä′hĭ kə wə), *n.* a town in Japan, on central Hokkaido island. 245,246 (1965).

Asansol (ăs′ăn sōl′), *n.* a town in India, in W Bengal. 103,405 (1961).

asarabacca (ăs′ə rə băk′ə), *n.* an aristolochiaceous perennial evergreen, *Asarum europaeum,* of the woodlands of Europe and W Asia. [f. L: m. *asarum* this plant + *bacca* berry]

Asben (ăs bĕn′), *n.* Air (Niger).

asbestos (ăs bĕs′təs, ăz-), *n.* **1.** *Mineral.* **a.** a fibrous amphibole, used for making incombustible or fireproof articles. **b.** the mineral chrysotile, similarly used. **2.** a fire-resistant fabric woven from asbestos fibres. *—adj.* **3.** Also, **asbestine** (ăs bĕs′tĭn, ăz-). made of or pertaining to this fabric. [t. L, t. Gk: unquenchable; r. ME *asbeston,* t. OF]

ascarid (ăs′kə rĭd), *n. Zool.* any of the *Ascaridae,* a family of nematode worms including the roundworm and pinworm. [t. NL: s. *ascaridae,* t. Gk: m. *askarídes* (pl.) threadworms]

ascend (ə sĕnd′), *v.i.* **1.** to climb or go upwards; mount; rise. **2.** to rise to a higher point or degree; proceed from an inferior to a superior degree or level. **3.** to go towards the source or beginning; go back in time. **4.** *Music.* to rise in pitch; pass from any tone to a higher one. *—v.t.* **5.** to go or move upwards upon or along; climb; mount: *to ascend a hill or ladder.* [ME *ascende(n),* t.L: m. *ascendere* climb up] **—ascend′ible, ascend′able,** *adj.* **—Syn. 1.** soar. **2.** tower. **5.** see **climb.**

ascendancy (ə sĕn′dən sĭ), *n.* the state of being in the ascendant; governing or controlling influence; domination. Also, **ascendency, ascend′ance, ascend′ence.**

ascendant (ə sĕn′dənt), *n.* **1.** a position of dominance or controlling influence; superiority; predominance: *in the ascendant.* **2.** an ancestor (opposed to *descendant*). **3.** *Astrol.* **a.** the point of the ecliptic or the sign of the zodiac rising above the horizon at the time of a birth, etc. **b.** the horoscope. *—adj.* **4.** superior; predominant. **5.** *Bot.* directed or curved upwards. **6.** rising. Also, **ascendent.**

ascender (ə sĕn′də), *n.* **1.** one who or that which ascends. **2.** *Print.* the part of such letters as *b, h, d,* and *f* that rises above the body of most lower-case letters.

ascending (ə sĕn′dĭng), *adj.* **1.** rising. **2.** *Bot.* growing or directed upwards, esp. obliquely or in a curve from the base.

ascension (ə sĕn′shən), *n.* **1.** the act of ascending; ascent. **2.** (*often cap.*) *Eccles.* the bodily passing of Christ from earth to heaven. Acts 1:9. **3.** (*cap.*) Ascension Day. [ME, t. L: s. *ascensio*]

Ascension (ə sĕn′shən), *n.* a British island in the S Atlantic. 478 pop. (1963); 34 sq. mi.

Ascension Day, the fortieth day after Easter, commemorating the ascension of Christ; Holy Thursday.

Ascensiontide (ə sĕn′shən tīd′), *n.* the period between Ascension Day and Whitsunday.

ascensive (ə sĕn′sĭv) *adj.* ascending; rising.

ascent (ə sĕnt′), *n.* **1.** the act of ascending; upward movement; rise. **2.** a rising from a lower to a higher state, degree, or grade; advancement. **3.** the act of climbing or travelling up. **4.** the way or means of ascending; upward slope. **5.** a procedure towards a source or beginning. **6.** gradient. [der. ASCEND modelled on DESCENT]

ascertain (ăs′ə tān′), *v.t.* **1.** to find out by trial, examination, or experiment, so as to know as certain; determine. **2.** *Archaic.* to make certain, clear, or definitely known. [ME *ascertain,* t. OF: s. *ascertener* make certain, der. *a-* A-⁵ + *certain* CERTAIN] **—as′certain′able,** *adj.* **—as′certain′ableness,** *n.* **—as′certain′ably,** *adv.* **—as′certain′ment,** *n.* **—Syn. 1.** See **learn.**

ascetic (ə sĕt′ĭk), *n.* **1.** a person who leads an abstemious life. **2.** one who practises religious austerities. **3.** (in the early Christian Church) a monk; hermit. *—adj.* **4.** pertaining to asceticism or ascetics. **5.** rigorously abstinent; austere. **6.** unduly strict in religious exercises or mortifications. [t. Gk: m. s. *askētikós* pertaining to a monk or hermit, der. *askētḗs* monk, hermit (orig. athlete)]

ascetical (ə sĕt′ĭ kl), *adj.* pertaining to ascetic discipline or practice. **—ascet′ically,** *adv.*

asceticism (ə sĕt′ĭ sĭz′əm), *n.* **1.** the life or practice of an ascetic; the principles and historic course of the ascetics. **2.** *Theol.* the theory or systemic exposition of the means (whether negative, as self-denial and abstinence, or positive, as the exercise of natural and Christian virtues) by which a complete conformity with the divine will may be attained. **3.** rigorous self-discipline.

Aschaffenberg (*Ger.* ä shä′fən bĕrk), *n.* a town in West Germany, in NW Bavaria. 55,800 (est. 1966).

Ascham (ăs′kəm), *n.* **Roger,** 1515–68, English scholar and writer: tutor of Queen Elizabeth.

asci (ăs′ī), *n.* pl. of **ascus.**

ascidian (ə sĭd′ĭ ən), *Zool.* *—n.* **1.** a tunicate or sea-squirt. *—adj.* **2.** of or belonging to the *Ascidia* or *Tunicata.* [f. ASCIDI(UM) + -AN]

ascidium (ə sĭd′ĭ əm), *n., pl.* **-cidia** (-sĭd′ĭ ə). *Bot.* a baglike or pitcher-shaped part. See illus. under **pitcher-plant.** [t. NL, t. Gk: m. *askídion,* dim. of *askós* bag]

ascites (ə sī′tēz), *n. Pathol.* an abnormal collection of fluid in the peritoneal cavity. [t. L, t. Gk: m. *askítēs* (sc. *nósos* disease) a kind of dropsy, der. *askós* bag, belly] **—ascitic** (ə sĭt′ĭk), *adj.*

asclepiadaceous (ăs klē′pĭ ə dā′shəs), *adj. Bot.* belonging to the *Asclepiadaceae,* or milkweed family of plants. [f. s. NL *Asclēpias* the milkweed genus (t. Gk: m. *asklēpiás* kind of plant, named after *Asklēpiós* Asclepius) + -ACEOUS]

Asclepiadean (ăs klē′pĭ ə dē′ən), *Class. Pros.* *—adj.* **1.** denoting or pertaining to a kind of verse consisting of a spondee, two (or three) choriambi, and an iamb. *—n.* **2.** an Asclepiadean verse. [so called after the Greek poet *Asclepiades*]

Asclepius (ăs klē′pĭ əs), *n. Gk Myth.* the god of medicine and a son of Apollo. Aesculapius is his Roman counterpart.

asco-, a word element meaning 'bag'. [t. Gk: m. *asko-,* comb. form of *askós*]

ascocarp (ăs′kə kärp′), *n. Bot.* (in ascomycetous fungi) the fructification bearing the asci, a general term embracing apothecium, perithecium, etc.

ascogonium (ăs′kə gō′nyəm), *n., pl.* **-nia** (-nyə). *Bot.* (in certain ascomycetous fungi) **1.** the female sexual organ; the archicarp. **2.** the portion of the archicarp which receives the antheridial nuclei and puts out the hyphae bearing the asci. **—as′cogo′nial,** *adj.*

Ascoli Piceno (*It.* äs′kō lē pē chĕ′nō), a town in Italy, in the Marches. 54,017 (1966).

ascomycete (ăs′kə mī sēt′), *n. Bot.* a fungus of the class *Ascomycetes,* including the yeasts, mildews, truffles, etc., characterized by bearing the sexual spores in a sac.

ascomycetous (ăs′kə mī sē′təs), *adj. Bot.* belonging or pertaining to the *Ascomycetes.*

ascorbic acid (ə skô′bĭk), *Biochem.* the antiscorbutic vitamin, or vitamin C, $C_6H_8O_6$ found in citrus fruits, tomatoes, paprika, and green vegetables, and also made industrially.

ascospore (ăs′kə spô′), *n. Bot.* a spore formed in an ascus. **—ascosporous** (ăs kŏs′pə rəs, ăs′kə spô′rəs), **ascosporic** (ăs′kə spô′rĭk), *adj.*

Ascot (ăs′kət), *n.* **1.** a town in England, in Berkshire. **2.** a racecourse near this town. *—adj.* **3.** denoting or pertaining to the race meetings held at Ascot.

ascribe (ə skrīb′), *v.t.,* **ascribed, ascribing. 1.** to attribute impute, or refer, as to a cause or source; assign: *the alphabet is usually ascribed to the Phoenicians.* **2.** to consider or allege to belong. [t. L: m. s. *ascribere* add to a writing; r. ME *ascrive(n),* t. OF: m. *ascriv-,* s. *ascrire*] **—ascrib′able,** *adj.* **—Syn. 1.** See **attribute.**

ascription (ə skrĭp′shən), *n.* **1.** the act of ascribing. **2.** a statement ascribing something, specif., praise to the Deity. Also, **adscription.**

ascus (ăs′kəs), *n.*, *pl.* **asci** (ăs′ī). *Bot.* the sac in ascomycetes in which the sexual spores are formed. [t. NL, t. Gk: m. *askós* bag, wineskin, bladder]

asdic (ăz′dĭk), *n.* a device to determine the presence and location of objects under water by measuring the direction and return time of a sound echo. [acronym from *Allied Submarine Detection Investigation Committee*]

-ase, *Chem.* a noun suffix used in names of enzymes, as in *lactase, pectase.* [der. (DIAST)ASE]

A.S.E., Amalgamated Society of Engineers.

asepsis (ə sĕp′sĭs, ā-), *n.* **1.** absence of the micro-organisms that produce sepsis or septic disease. **2.** *Med.* methods or treatment, as by surgical operation, characterized by the use of instruments, dressings, etc., that are free from such micro-organisms. [f. A-[6] + SEPSIS]

aseptic (ə sĕp′tĭk, ā-), *adj.* free from the living germs of disease, fermentation, or putrefaction. **—asep′tically,** *adv.*

asexual (ā sĕk′syo͞o əl, ā-), *adj.* *Biol.* **1.** not sexual. **2.** having no sex or no sexual organs. **3.** independent of sexual processes. **—asexuality** (ā sĕk′syo͞o ăl′ĭ tĭ), *n.* **—asex′ually,** *adv.*

Asgard (ăs′gäd), *n.* *Scand. Myth.* the heavenly abode of the gods, connected with the earth by a rainbow bridge (Bifrost). Also, **Asgarth** (ăs′gäth), **Asgardhr** (ăs′gä′thə). [t. Icel.: m. s. *āsgardhr*, f. *āss* god + *gardhr* YARD]

Asgeirsson (*Icel.* åws′gyĕyr sŏn), *n.* **Asgeir** (*Icel.* åws′-gyĕyr), born 1894, president of Iceland 1952–68.

ash[1] (ăsh), *n.* **1.** (*usually pl., used as sing. chiefly in scientific and commercial language*) the powdery residue of matter that remains after burning: *hot ashes: soda ash.* **2.** *Geol.* finely pulverized lava thrown out by a volcano in eruption. See **ashes.** [ME; OE *asce, æsce*]

ash[2] (ăsh), *n.* **1.** any tree of the oleaceous genus *Fraxinus*, esp. *F. excelsior* of Europe and Asia or *F. americana* of North America (**white ash**). **2.** the wood, tough, straight-grained, and elastic, and valued as timber. **3.** (in the Southern Hemisphere) any of several trees resembling the ash. [ME *asch*, OE *æsc*, c. G *Esche*]

ash[3] (ăsh), *n.* the name of the old English letter *æ.* See **æ** (def. 2).

ashamed (ə shāmd′), *adj.* **1.** feeling shame; abashed by guilt. **2.** unwilling or restrained through fear of shame: *ashamed to speak.* **3.** loath to acknowledge (fol. by *of*): *ashamed of her husband.* **—ashamedly** (ə shā′mĭd lĭ), *adv.* **—asham′edness,** *n.*

—Syn. 1. ASHAMED, HUMILIATED, MORTIFIED refer to a condition of discomfort and embarrassment. ASHAMED describes a feeling of guilt combined with regret: *ashamed of a fault.* HUMILIATED describes a feeling of being humbled or disgraced: *humiliated by public ridicule.* MORTIFIED describes a feeling of deep chagrin embarrassment, and confusion: *mortified by her clumsiness.* **—Ant. 1.** proud.

Ashanti (ə shăn′tĭ), *n.* **1.** an area in W Africa, now part of Ghana; a former native kingdom and a former British colony. 1,108,548 pop. (1963); 24,379 sq. mi. *Cap.:* Kumasi. **2.** a native or an inhabitant of Ashanti.

ash bin, a bin or metal receptacle for ashes. Also, **ash bucket.**

Ashburton (ăsh′bû′tn), *n.* **1. Alexander Baring, 1st Baron,** 1774–1848, British statesman. **2.** a river in Australia flowing W through Western Australia to the Indian Ocean. Course ab. 400 mi.

ash can, *U.S.* **1.** a dustbin. **2.** an ash bin.

Ashcroft (ăsh′krŏft′), *n.* **Dame Peggy,** born 1907, English actress.

Ashdod (ăsh′dŏd), *n.* a port in W Israel, S of Jaffa. 27,000 (est. 1967).

ashen[1] (ăsh′ən), *adj.* **1.** ash-coloured; grey. **2.** consisting of ashes. [f. ASH[1] + -EN[2]]

ashen[2] (ăsh′ən), *adj.* **1.** pertaining to the ash tree or its timber. **2.** made of wood from the ash tree. [f. ASH[2] + -EN[2]]

ashes (ăsh′ĭz), *n. pl.* **1.** ruins, as from destruction by burning: *the ashes of an ancient empire.* **2.** the remains of the human body after cremation. **3.** a dead body or corpse; mortal remains. **4. the Ashes,** the trophy, a wooden urn containing a cremated cricket stump, played for by England and Australia in test cricket. See also **ash**[1].

Ashford (ăsh′fəd), *n.* a town in England, in Kent. 27,996 (1961).

ash-grey (ăsh′ grā′), *n.*, *adj.* pale grey of ashes. Also, **ash colour;** *U.S.*, **ash-gray.**

Ashikaga (ā shē′kə gə, -kəng ə), *n.* a town in Japan, in E central Honshu island. 150,259 (1965).

Ashkenazim (ăsh′kə nä′zĭm), *n. pl.* German, Polish, and Russian Jews (as distinguished from the *Sephardim* or Spanish-Portuguese Jews). [Heb., pl. of *Ashk'naz*, a descendant of Japheth (Gen. 10:3); also, in medieval use, Germany] **—Ash′kena′zic,** *adj.*

Ashkenazy (*Russ.* əsh kĭ nä′zĭ), *n.* **Vladimir** (*Russ.* vlä dĕ′mĭr), born 1937, Soviet pianist.

Ashkhabad (ăsh′kə băd′), *n.* a city in the Soviet Union, the capital of Turkmenistan, in the S central part. 226,000 (est. 1965). Formerly, **Poltoratsk.**

ashlar (ăsh′lə), *n.* *Bldg Trades.* **1.** a squared block of building stone, finished or rough. **2.** such stones collectively. **3.** masonry made of them. **4.** one of the pieces of timber used in ashlaring; a stud. Also, **ashler.** [ME *asheler*, t. OF: m. *aisselier*, ult. der. L *axis* board]

ashlaring (ăsh′lə rĭng), *n.* *Bldg Trades.* pieces of timber fixed between the rafters and floor joists of an attic to form a partition wall cutting off the angle where the joists and rafters meet. Also, **ashlar pieces, ashlering.**

ashlering (ăsh′lə rĭng), *n.* *Bldg Trades.* **1.** ashlar (def. 3). **2.** ashlaring.

Ashmole (ăsh′mōl′), *n.* **Elias** (ĭ lī′əs), 1617–92, English antiquary.

ashore (ə shô′), *adv.*, *adj.* *Naut.* **1.** to shore; on or to the land. **2.** on land (opposed to *aboard* or *afloat*).

Ashton (ăsh′tən), *n.* **Sir Frederick William,** born 1906, English dancer and choreographer.

Ashton-under-Lyne (ăsh′tən ŭn′də līn′), *n.* a town in England, in SE Lancashire, near Manchester. 49,810 (est. 1962).

Ashtoreth (ăsh′tə rĕth′), *n.* an ancient Semitic goddess. See **Astarte.** [t. Heb.]

ashtray (ăsh′trā′), *n.* a small tray, saucer, or bowl for tobacco ash.

Ashur (ăsh′o͝oə), *n.* Assur.

Ashurbanipal (ăsh′o͝oə bä′nĭ păl′), *n.* died 626? B.C., king of Assyria 668?–626? B.C.

Ash Wednesday, the first day of Lent.

ashy (ăsh′ĭ), *adj.*, **ashier, ashiest. 1.** ash-coloured; pale. **2.** of ashes. **3.** sprinkled or covered with ashes.

Asia (ā′shə), *n.* the largest continent, bounded by Europe and the Pacific, Arctic, and Indian oceans. 1,600,000,000 pop. (est. 1961); ab. 16,000,000 sq. mi.

Asia Minor, a peninsula in W Asia between the Black and the Mediterranean seas, including most of Asiatic Turkey. See **Anatolia.**

Asian (ā′shən), *adj.* **1.** of or belonging to, or characteristic of Asia or its inhabitants. **—***n.* **2.** a native of Asia. **—Asianic** (ā′shĭ ăn′ĭk), *adj.*

Asian flu, *Pathol.* a form of influenza caused by a virus believed to have been carried from Asia. Also, **Asian influenza;** *Chiefly U.S.*, **Asiatic flu, Asiatic influenza.**

Asiatic (ā′shĭ ăt′ĭk), *adj.*, *n.* Asian.

Asiatic cholera, *Pathol.* an infectious epidemic disease, originally from Asia, which is often fatal. See **cholera** (def. lb).

aside (ə sīd′), *adv.* **1.** on or to one side; to or at a short distance; apart; away from some position or direction: *to turn inside.* **2.** away from one's thoughts or consideration: *to put one's cares aside.* **—***n.* **3.** *Theat.* a part of an actor's lines not supposed to be heard by others on the stage and intended only for the audience. **4.** words spoken in an undertone, so as not to be heard by some of the people present.

asinine (ăs′ĭ nīn′), *adj.* stupid; obstinate. [t. L: m. s. *asininus*, der. *asinus* ass] **—as′inine′ly,** *adv.* **—asininity** (ăs′ĭ nĭn′ĭ tĭ), *n.*

Asir (ă sĭə′), *n.* a district in SW Saudi Arabia.

-asis, a word element forming names of diseases. [t. L, t. Gk]

ask (äsk), *v.t.* **1.** to put a question to: *ask him.* **2.** to seek to be informed about: *to ask the way;* (or, with a double object) *to ask him the way.* **3.** to seek by words to obtain; request: *to ask advice or a favour.* **4.** to solicit from; request of (with a personal object, and with or without *for* before the thing desired): *I ask you a great favour, ask him for advice.* **5.** to demand; expect: *to ask a price for something.* **6.** to call for; require: *the job asks time.* **7.** to invite: *to ask guests.* **8.** to publish (banns); publish the banns of (persons). **—***v.i.* **9.** to make inquiry; inquire: *she asked after or about him.* **10.** to request or petition (fol. by *for*): *ask for bread.* **11. ask for it,** *Colloq.* to behave so as to invite trouble. [ME *asken*, OE *āscian*, also *ācsian*, c. OHG *eiscōn*] **—ask′er,** *n.* **—Syn. 9.** See **inquire.**

askance (ə skăns′), *adv.* **1.** with suspicion, mistrust, or disapproval: *he looked askance at my offer.* **2.** with a side glance; sideways. Also, **askant** (ə skănt′). [orig. uncert.]

Aske (ăsk), *n.* **Robert,** died 1537, English attorney who led the Pilgrimage of Grace, and was hanged.

askew (ə skyo͞o′), *adv.* **1.** to one side; out of line; obliquely; awry. **—***adj.* **2.** oblique. [f. A-[1] + SKEW]

asking price, the price demanded by a seller, usually considered as subject to bargaining or discount.

Askja (äsk′yə), *n.* a volcano in Iceland. 3376 ft.

aslant (ə slănt′), *adv.* **1.** at a slant; slantingly; obliquely.

—*adj.* 2. slanting; oblique. —*prep.* 3. slantingly across; athwart. [ME *on slont*, *on slent* on slope. Cf. Sw. *slänt* slope]

asleep (ə slēp′), *adv.* 1. in or into a state of sleep. —*adj.* 2. sleeping. 3. dormant; inactive. 4. (of the foot, hand, leg, etc.) numb. 5. dead.

A.S.L.E.F., Associated Society of Locomotive Engineers and Firemen.

A.S.L.I.B., Association of Special Libraries and Information Bureaux. Also, **Aslib** (ăz′lĭb).

aslope (ə slōp′), *adv.* 1. at a slope. —*adj.* 2. sloping.

Asmara (ăs mä′rə), *n.* a city in Ethiopia, in Eritrea. 120,000 pop. (est. 1964); altitude ab. 7700 ft.

Asmodeus (ăs mō′dyəs, ăs′mō dīəs′), *n.* (in Jewish demonology) an evil spirit. [t. L: m. *Asmodaeus*, t. Gk: m. *Asmodaîos*, t. Heb.: m. *Ashmadai*]

Asnières (*Fr.* ȧ nyĕr′), *n.* a suburb of Paris. 82,201 (1962).

asocial (ā sō′shəl), *adj.* 1. *Psychol., Sociol., etc.* avoiding or withdrawn from the environment; not social. 2. inconsiderate of others; selfish; not scrupulous.

Asoka (ə sō′kə), *n.* died 226? B.C., Buddhist king in India 264?–226? B.C.

Asosan (ăs′ō săn′), *n.* a volcano in SW Japan, on Kyushu island. 5225 ft high; crater, 12 mi. across.

asp[1] (ăsp). *n.* 1. any of several poisonous snakes, esp. the Egyptian cobra, *Naja naja*, said to have caused Cleopatra's death, and much used by snake-charmers. 2. the common European viper or adder. 3. *Archaeol.* the uraeus. [t. L: m. *aspis*, t. Gk]

asp[2] (ăsp) *n., adj. Poetic or Obs.* aspen. [OE *æspe* (see ASPEN)]

asparagine (ə spăr′ə jēn′, -jĭn), *n.* an amino acid, NH_2-$COCH_2CH(NH_2)COOH$, occurring in proteins.

asparagus (ə spăr′ə gəs), *n.* 1. any plant of the liliaceous genus *Asparagus*, esp. *A. officinalis*, cultivated for its edible shoots. 2. the shoots, used a a table vegetable. [t. L, t. Gk: m. *aspáragos*]

aspartic acid (ăs pä′tĭk), *Biochem.* an amino acid, $HOOCCH_2CH(NH_2)COOH$, occurring in proteins.

Aspasia (ăs pā′shə, -zhə), *n.* fl. *c.* 445 B.C., Athenian courtesan, mistress of Pericles.

aspect (ăs′pĕkt), *n.* 1. appearance to the eye or mind; look: *the physical aspect of the country.* 2. countenance; facial expression. 3. a way in which a thing may be viewed or regarded: *both aspects of a question.* 4. view commanded; exposure: *the house has a southern aspect.* 5. the side or surface facing a given direction: *the dorsal aspect of a fish.* 6. *Gram.* a. (in some languages) a category of verb inflection denoting various relations of the action or state of the verb to the passage of time, as duration, repetition, or completion. Examples: *he ate* (completed action); *he was eating* (incompleted action); *he ate and ate* (durative action). b. (in other languages) one of several contrasting constructions with similar meanings: *the durative aspect.* c. a set of such categories or constructions in a particular language. d. the meaning of, or typical of, such a category or construction. e. such categories or constructions, or their meanings collectively. 7. *Astrol.* the relative position of planets as determining their influence. 8. *Archaic.* a look; glance. [ME, t. L: s. *aspectus*, der. *aspicere* look at] —**Syn.** 1. See **appearance.** 4. prospect, outlook.

aspect ratio, *Aeron.* the ratio of the span of an aerofoil to its mean chord.

aspectual (ăs pĕk′tyo͝o əl), *adj. Gram.* 1. of, pertaining to, or producing a particular aspect or aspects. 2. used as or like a form inflected for a particular aspect.

aspen (ăs′pən), *n.* 1. any of various species of poplar, as *Populus tremula* of Europe, and *P. tremuloides* (**quaking aspen**) or *P. alba* (**white aspen**) in America, with leaves that tremble in the slightest breeze. —*adj.* 2. of or pertaining to the aspen. 3. trembling or quivering, like the leaves of the aspen. [ME *aspen*, adj., f. *asp* white poplar (OE *æspe*) + -EN[2]]

asper (ăs′pə), *n.* a former Egyptian and Turkish silver coin, equal to $^1/_{120}$ of a piastre. [t. F: m. *aspre* (or t. It.: m. *aspero*), t. MGk: m. *áspron* white (coin)]

Asperges (ăs pû′jēz), *n. Eccles.* 1. the rite of sprinkling the altar, clergy, and people with holy water before High Mass on Sundays. 2. the anthem beginning 'Asperges', sung while the priest performs this rite. [L: thou shalt sprinkle]

aspergillosis (ăs pû′jĭ lō′sĭs), *n., pl.* **-ses** (-sēz). *Vet. Sci.* disease in an animal caused by aspergilli.

aspergillum (ăs′pə jĭl′əm), *n., pl.* **-gilla** (-jĭl′ə), **-gillums.** *Eccles.* a brush or instrument for sprinkling holy water; aspersorium. [f. L: s. *aspergere* sprinkle + *-illum*, dim. suffix]

aspergillus (ăs′pə jĭl′əs), *n., pl.* **-gilli** (-jĭl′ī). *Bot.* any fungus of the genus *Aspergillus*, family *Aspergillaceae*, whose sporophores are distinguished by a bristly, knoblike top. [See ASPERGILLUM]

asperity (ăs pĕr′ĭ tĭ), *n., pl.* **-ties.** 1. roughness or sharpness of temper; severity; acrimony. 2. hardship; difficulty; rigour. 3. roughness of surface; unevenness. 4. something rough or harsh. [t. L: m. s. *asperitas* roughness; r. ME *asprete*, t. OF]

asperse (ə spûs′), *v.t.*, **aspersed, aspersing.** 1. to assail with damaging charges or insinuations; cast reproach upon; slander. 2. to sprinkle; bespatter. [t. L: m. s. *aspersus*, pp., sprinkled] —**aspers′er,** *n.*

aspersion (ə spû′shən), *n.* 1. a damaging imputation; a derogatory criticism: *to cast aspersions on one's character.* 2. the act of aspersing: *to baptize by aspersion.* 3. a shower or spray.

aspersorium (ăs′pə sô′rĭ əm), *n., pl.* **-soria** (-sô′rĭ ə), **-soriums.** *Eccles.* 1. a vessel for holding holy water. See illus. under **stoup.** 2. aspergillum. [t. ML. See ASPERSE, -ORIUM]

asphalt (ăs′fălt), *n.* 1. any of various dark-coloured, solid bituminous substances, composed mostly of mixtures of hydrocarbons, occurring native in various parts of the earth. 2. a similar artificial substance, the by-product of petroleum-cracking operations. 3. a mixture of such a substance with crushed rock, etc., used for roads, etc. —*v.t.* 4. to cover or pave with asphalt. [t. LL: s. *asphaltum*, t. Gk: m. *ásphalton*] —**asphal′tic,** *adj.* —**as′phalt-like′,** *adj.*

asphaltum (ăs făl′təm), *n.* asphalt.

asphodel (ăs′fə dĕl′), *n.* 1. any of various liliaceous plants of the genera *Asphodelus* and *Asphodeline*, natives of southern Europe, with white, pink, or yellow flowers; in Greek mythology, the flower of the dead. 2. any of various other plants, as the daffodil. [t. L: s. *asphodelus*, t. Gk: m. *asphódelos*]

asphyxia (ăs fĭk′sĭ ə), *n. Pathol.* the extreme condition caused by lack of oxygen and excess of carbon dioxide in the blood, caused by sufficient interference with respiration, as in choking. [t. Gk: stopping of the pulse]

asphyxiant (ăs fĭk′sĭ ənt), *adj.* 1. asphyxiating or tending to asphyxiate. —*n.* 2. an asphyxiating agent or substance. 3. an asphyxiating condition.

asphyxiate (ăs fĭk′sĭ āt′), *v.*, **-ated, -ating.** —*v.t.* 1. to produce asphyxia in. —*v.i.* 2. to become asphyxiated. —**asphyx′ia′tion,** *n.* —**asphyx′ia′tor,** *n.*

aspic[1] (ăs′pĭk), *n.* an appetizing, preservative jelly used as a garnish or as a base for meat, vegetables, etc. [t. F; orig. uncert.]

aspic[2] (ăs′pĭk), *n. Poetic.* an asp[1]. [t. F, g. L *aspis*]

aspic[3] (ăs′pĭk), *n.* the great lavender, *Lavandula latifolia*, yielding an oil used in perfumery. [t. F, t. ML: m. (*lavendula*) *spica* (lavender) spike]

aspidistra (ăs′pĭ dĭs′trə), *n.* a smooth, stemless Asian herb, *Aspidistra elatior*, family *Liliaceae*, bearing large evergreen leaves often striped with white, once widely grown as a house plant: often seen as a symbol of genteel respectability. [t. NL, der. Gk *aspis* shield]

aspirant (ə spī′ə rənt, ăs′pĭ rənt), *n.* 1. a person who aspires; one who seeks advancement, honours, a high position, etc. —*adj.* 2. *Rare.* aspiring.

aspirate (*v.* ăs′pĭ rāt′; *n., adj.* ăs′pĭ rĭt), *v.* **-rated, -rating,** *n., adj.* —*v.t.* 1. *Phonet.* a. to release (a stop) in such a way that the breath escapes with audible friction, as in *title* where the first *t* is aspirated, the second is not. b. to begin (a word or syllable) with an *h* sound, as in *when* (pronounced *hwen*), *howl*, opposed to *wen*, *owl.* 2. *Med.* to remove (fluids) from body cavities by use of an aspirator. 3. to draw or remove by suction. —*n.* 4. *Phonet.* a puff of unvoiced air before or after another sound, represented in many languages by *h*, and in Greek by the sign of rough breathing (ʽ). —*adj.* 5. *Phonet.* aspirated. [t. L: m. s. *aspīrātus*, pp., breathed on]

aspiration (ăs′pĭ rā′shən), *n.* 1. the act of aspiring; lofty or ambitious desire. 2. an act of aspirating; a breath. 3. *Phonet.* a. the fricative unstopping or release of a stop consonant, as in *too*, where the breath escapes with audible friction as the *t* is brought to an end by the withdrawal of the tongue from contact with the gums. b. the use of an aspirate in pronunciation. 4. *Med.* the act of removing a fluid, as pus or serum, from a cavity of the body, by a hollow needle or trocar connected with a suction syringe.

aspirator (ăs′pĭ rā′tə), *n.* 1. an apparatus or device employing suction. 2. a jet pump used in laboratories to produce a partial vacuum. 3. *Med.* an instrument for removing fluids from the body by suction.

aspiratory (ə spī′ə rə tə rĭ, -trĭ), *adj.* pertaining to or suited for aspiration.

aspire (ə spī′ə), *v.i.*, **-spired, -spiring.** 1. to long, aim, or seek ambitiously; be eagerly desirous, esp. for something great or lofty (fol. by *to, after*, or an infinitive): *to aspire after immortality, to aspire to be a leader among men.* **2.** *Archaic or Poetic.* to rise up; soar; mount; tower. [ME *aspyre*, t. L: m. s. *aspīrāre* breathe on] **—aspir'er,** *n.* **—aspir'ing,** *adj.* **—Syn. 1.** See **ambitious.**

aspirin (ăs'prĭn), *n. Pharm.* a white crystalline derivative of salicylic acid, $C_9H_8O_4$, used to relieve the pain of headache, rheumatism, gout, neuralgia, etc; acetylsalicylic acid. [t. G (orig. trademark): f. *A(cetyl)* ACETYL + *Spir(säure)* salicylic (acid) (see SPIRAEA) + -in -IN[2]]

Asplund (*Sw.* äs'plo͞ond), *n.* **Gunnar** (*Sw.* go͞on'är), 1885–1940, Swedish architect.

asprawl (ə sprôl'), *adv., adj.* sprawling; in a sprawl.

asquint (ə skwĭnt'), *adv., adj.* with an oblique glance. [f. A-[1] + *squint* (of obscure orig.; cf. D *schuinte* slope)]

Asquith (ăs'kwĭth), *n.* **Herbert Henry** (*1st Earl of Oxford and Asquith*), 1852–1928, British statesman: prime minister 1908–16.

ass (ăs), *n.* **1.** a long-eared, usually ash-coloured mammal, *Equus asinus*, related to the horse, serving as a slow, patient, sure-footed beast of burden; the donkey. **2.** any allied wild species, as the **Mongolian wild ass,** *E. hemionus.* See illus. under **onager. 3.** a fool; a blockhead. **4.** *Taboo.* arse. [ME; OE *assa*, t. OWelsh: m. *asyn* ass, t. L: m. s. *asinus*]

Ass, *Equus asinus* (Ab. 3 ft high at the shoulder)

assafetida (ăs'ə fĕt'ĭ də), *n.* asafoetida. Also, **assafoetida.**

assagai (ăs'ə gī'), *n., pl.* **-gais,** *v.t.,* **-gaied, -gaiing.** assegai.

assai (ă sī'; *It.* äs sāy'), *adv. Music.* very: *allegro assai* (very quick). [It.]

assail (ə sāl'). *v.t.* **1.** to set upon with violence; assault. **2.** to set upon vigorously with arguments, entreaties, abuse, etc. **3.** to undertake with the purpose of mastering. [ME *asaile(n)*, t. OF: m. *asalir*, g. VL *adsalīre*, f. L: *ad-* AD- + *salīre* leap] **—assail'able,** *adj.* **—assail'er,** *n.* **—assail'ment,** *n.* **—Syn. 1.** See **attack.**

assailant (ə sā'lənt), *n.* **1.** one who assails. **—***adj.* **2.** assailing; attacking.

Assam (ăs'ăm, ă săm'), *n.* a state in NE India. 11,872,722 pop. (1961); 85,012 sq. mi. *Cap.*: Shillong. **—Assamese** (ăs'ə mēz'), *adj., n.*

assassin (ə săs'ĭn), *n.* **1.** one who undertakes to murder, esp. from fanaticism or for a reward. **2.** (*cap.*) one of an order of Muslim fanatics, active in Persia and Syria from about 1090 to 1272, whose chief object was to assassinate Crusaders. [t. F, t. ML: s. *assassīnus*, t. Ar.: m. *hashshāshin*, pl., hashish eaters]

assassinate (ə săs'ĭ nāt'), *v.t.,* **-nated, -nating. 1.** to kill by sudden or secret, premeditated assault, esp. for political or religious motives. **2.** to blight or destroy treacherously: *to assassinate a person's character.* [t. ML: m. s. *assassinātus*, pp.] **—assas'sina'tion,** *n.* **—assas'sina'tor,** *n.* **—Syn. 1.** murder.

assassin bug, any insect of the heteropterous family *Reduviidae.* Most are predacious and some are blood-sucking parasites of warm-blooded animals.

assault (ə sôlt'), *n.* **1.** the act of assailing; an attack; onslaught. **2.** *Mil.* the stage of close combat in an attack. **3.** *Law.* an unlawful physical attack upon another; an attempt or offer to do violence to another, with or without a battery, as by holding a stone or club in a threatening manner. **4.** indecent assault. **—***v.t.* **5.** to make an assault upon; attack; assail. **6.** to rape or attempt to rape. [ME *assaut*, t. OF, der. *asalir* ASSAIL] **—assault'er,** *n.* **—Syn. 1.** onset, charge. **5.** See **attack.**

assault and battery, *Law.* an assault with an actual touching or other violence upon another.

assay (*v.* ə sā'; *n.* ə sā', ăs'ā), *v.t.* **1.** to examine by trial; put to test or trial: *to assay one's strength.* **2.** *Metall.* to analyse (an ore, alloy, etc.) in order to determine the quantity of gold, silver, or other metal in it. **3.** *Pharm., etc.* to subject (a drug, etc.) to an analysis for the determination of its potency. **4.** to try in combat. **5.** to attempt; endeavour; essay. **6.** to judge the quality of; evaluate. **—***v.i.* **7.** to make an attempt; endeavour; try. **8.** *U.S.* to contain, as shown by analysis, a certain proportion of (usually precious) metal. **—***n.* **9.** *Metall.* determination of the amount of metal, esp. gold or silver, in an ore, alloy, etc. **10.** *Pharm., etc.* determination of the strength, purity, etc., of a pharmaceutical substance or ingredient. **11.** a substance undergoing analysis or trial. **12.** a listing of the findings in assaying a substance. **13.** examination; trial; attempt; essay. [ME, t. OF, g. LL *exagium* a weighing. Cf. ESSAY, n.] **—assay'er,** *n.* **—assay'able,** *adj.*

assegai (ăs'ĭ gī'), *n., pl.* **-gais,** *v.,* **-gaied, -gaing,** or **-gaiing.** **—***n.* **1.** the slender throwing spear of the Bantu peoples of southern Africa. **2.** a South African cornaceous tree, *Curtisia faginea*, from whose wood such spears are made. **—***v.t.* **3.** to pierce with an assegai. Also, **assagai.** [t. Sp.: m. *azagaya*, t. Ar.: f. *al* the + (Berber) *zaghāyah* spear]

assemblage (ə sĕm'blĭj), *n.* **1.** a number of persons or things assembled; an assembly. **2.** the act of assembling. **3.** the state of being assembled. [t. F]

assemble (ə sĕm'bl), *v.,* **-bled, -bling. —***v.t.* **1.** to bring together; gather into one place, company, body or whole. **2.** to put or fit (parts) together; put together the parts of (a mechanism, etc.). **—***v.i.* **3.** to come together; gather; meet. [ME *as(s)emble(n)*, t. OF: m. *as(s)embler*, g. LL* *assimulāre* compare, imitate] **—assem'bler,** *n.* **—Syn. 1.** See **gather. 2.** See **manufacture. 3.** congregate.

assemblé (*Fr.* ä säɴ blĕ'), *n. French.* (in ballet) a leap with one leg extended, followed by a landing with the feet crossed.

assembly (ə sĕm'blĭ), *n., pl.* **-blies. 1.** a company of persons gathered together, usually for the same purpose, whether religious, political, educational, or social. **2.** (*cap.*) *Govt.* a legislative body, sometimes esp. a lower house of a legislature. **3.** (*cap.*) *French Hist.* National Assembly. **4.** the act of assembling. **5.** the state of being assembled. **6.** *Mil.* a signal, as by drum or bugle, for troops to fall into ranks or otherwise assemble. **7.** the putting together of complex machinery, as aeroplanes, from interchangeable parts of standard dimensions. **8.** such parts, before or after assembling. [ME *as(s)emblee*, t. OF] **—Syn. 1.** assemblage, gathering. See **convention.**

assembly line, an arrangement of machines, tools, and workers in which each worker performs a special operation on an incomplete unit, which usually passes down a line of workers until it is finished.

assemblyman (ə sĕm'blĭ mən), *n., pl.* **-men.** *U.S.* a member of a legislative assembly, esp. of a lower house.

assembly room, 1. a room for public balls or other entertainment. **2.** (*pl.*) a number of such rooms in a building designed for public functions.

Assen (*Du.* ŏs'ə), *n.* a town in the Netherlands, in Drenthe province. 35,080 (1967).

assent (ə sĕnt'), *v.i.* **1.** to agree by expressing acquiescence or admitting truth; express agreement or concurrence (often fol. by *to*): *to assent to a statement.* **—***n.* **2.** agreement, as to a proposal; acquiescence; concurrence. **3.** Also, **Royal assent.** the formal act of recognition by the sovereign which transforms a parliamentary bill into an act of Parliament. [ME *as(s)ente(n)*, t. OF: m. *as(s)enter*, g. L *assentārī*, freq. of *assentīrī*] **—assen'ter,** *n.* **—Syn. 1.** acquiesce, accede, concur. See **consent.**

assentation (ăs'ĕn tā'shən), *n.* the practice of assenting, esp. obsequiously.

assentor (ə sĕn'tə), *n. Govt.* one of the eight voters who endorse the nomination, by a proposer and seconder, of a candidate for election to Parliament, as required by law.

assert (ə sûť), *v.t.* **1.** to state as true; affirm; declare: *to assert that one is innocent.* **2.** to maintain or defend (claims, rights, etc.). **3.** to put (oneself) forward boldly and insistently. [t. L: s. *assertus*, pp., joined to] **—assert'er, asser'tor,** *n.* **—Syn. 1.** See **declare. —Ant. 1.** deny.

assertion (ə sû'shən), *n.* **1.** a positive statement; an unsupported declaration. **2.** the act of asserting. **—Syn. 1.** allegation.

assertive (ə sû'tĭv), *adj.* given to asserting; positive; dogmatic. **—asser'tively,** *adv.* **—asser'tiveness,** *n.*

assertoric (ăs'û tŏ'rĭk), *adj. Logic.* (in Kantian logic) descriptive of a proposition or judgement which claims to be true, but is not necessarily true.

assertory (ə sû'tə rĭ), *adj.* affirming; assertive.

asses' bridge, *Geom.* pons asinorum (Euclid, I 5).

assess (ə sĕs'), *v.t.* **1.** to estimate officially the value of (property, income, etc.) as a basis for taxation (fol. by *at*): *the property was assessed at two million pounds.* **2.** to fix or determine the amount of (damages, a tax, a fine, etc.). **3.** to impose a tax or other charge on. [ME *assesse(n)*, t. OF: m. *assesser*, g. LL *assessāre* fix a tax, freq. of L *assidēre* sit at] **—assess'able,** *adj.*

assessment (ə sĕs'mənt), *n.* **1.** the act of assessing. **2.** an amount assessed as payable; an official valuation of taxable property, etc., or the value assigned.

assessor (ə sĕs'ə), *n.* **1.** one who makes assessments, as of damage for insurance purposes. **2.** *U.S.* an inspector of taxes. **3.** an advisory associate or assistant. **4.** one who advises a court on questions which involve technical or scientific knowledge. **5.** one who shares another's position, rank, or dignity. [t. L: assistant judge, ML assessor of taxes; r. ME *assessour*, t. OF] **—assessorial** (ăs'ĕ sô'rĭ əl), *adj.*

asset (ăs′ĕt), *n.* **1.** a useful thing or quality: *neatness is an asset.* **2.** a single item of property.

assets (ăs′ĕts), *n.pl.* **1.** *Com.* resources of a person or business consisting of such items as real property, machinery, inventories, notes, securities, cash, etc. **2.** property or effects (opposed to *liabilities*). **3.** *Accounting.* the detailed listing of property owned by a firm and money owing to it. **4.** *Law.* **a.** property in the hands of an executor or administrator sufficient to pay the debts or legacies of the testator or intestate. **b.** any property available for paying debts, etc. [ME, t. AF: m. OF *asetz*, adv., enough, taken as pl. noun, g. L *ad-* AD- + *satis* enough]

asseverate (ə sĕv′ə rāt′), *v.t.*, **-rated, -rating.** to declare earnestly or solemnly; affirm positively. [t. L: m. s. *asseverātus*, pp.]

asseveration (ə sĕv′ə rā′shən), *n.* **1.** the act of asseverating. **2.** an emphatic assertion.

Asshur (ăsh′ŏŏə), *n.* Assur.

assibilate (ə sĭb′ĭ lāt′), *v.*, **-lated, -lating.** *Phonet.* —*v.t.* **1.** to change into or pronounce with the accompaniment of a sibilant sound or sounds. —*v.i.* **2.** to change by assibilation. **3.** to become a sibilant or a sound containing a sibilant. —**assibilation** (ə sĭb′ĭ lā′shən), *n.*

assiduity (ăs′ĭ dyōō′ĭ tĭ), *n.*, *pl.* **-ties. 1.** constant or close application; diligence. **2.** (*pl.*) devoted or solicitous attentions.

assiduous (ə sĭd′yōō əs), *adj.* **1.** constant; unremitting: *assiduous reading.* **2.** constant in application; attentive; devoted. [t. L: m. *assiduus* sitting down to] —**assid′uously,** *adv.* —**assid′uousness,** *n.*

assign (ə sīn′), *v.t.* **1.** to make over or give, as in distribution; allot: *assign rooms at a hotel.* **2.** to appoint, as to a post or duty: *assign to stand guard.* **3.** to designate; specify: *to assign a day.* **4.** to ascribe; attribute; refer: *to assign a reason.* **5.** *Law.* to transfer: *to assign a contract.* **6.** *Mil.* to place permanently on duty with a unit or under a commander. —*v.i.* **7.** *Law.* to transfer property, esp. in trust for the benefit of creditors. —*n.* **8.** (*usually pl.*) *Law.* a person to whom the property or interest of another is or may be transferred: *my heirs and assigns.* [ME *assigne(n)*, t. OF: m. *as(s)igner*, g. L *assignāre*] —**assign′er;** *Chiefly Law,* **assignor** (ăs′ĭ nô′), *n.*

—**Syn. 1.** ASSIGN, ALLOCATE, ALLOT mean to apportion or measure out. To ASSIGN is to distribute available things, designating them to be given to or reserved for specific persons or purposes: *to assign duties.* To ALLOCATE is to earmark or set aside parts of things available or expected in the future, each for a specific purpose: *to allocate income to various types of expenses.* To ALLOT implies making restrictions as to amount, size, purpose, etc., and then apportioning or assigning: *to allot spaces for parking.*

assignable (ə sī′nə bl), *adj.* **1.** capable of being specified. **2.** capable of being attributed. **3.** *Law.* capable of being assigned. —**assign′abil′ity,** *n.* —**assign′ably,** *adv.*

assignat (ăs′ĭg năt′, ăs′ĭ nyä′; *Fr.* ȧ sēn yȧ′), *n.* *French Hist.* one of the notes (paper currency) issued from 1789–96 by the revolutionary government on the security of confiscated lands. [t. F, t. L: s. *assignātus*, pp. See ASSIGN, V.]

assignation (ăs′ĭg nā′shən), *n.* **1.** an appointment for a meeting, now esp. an illicit love-meeting. **2.** the act of assigning; assignment.

assignee (ăs′ĭ nē′), *n.* *Law.* one to whom some right or interest is transferred, either for his own enjoyment or in trust.

assignment (ə sīn′mənt), *n.* **1.** something assigned, as a particular task or duty. **2.** the act of assigning. **3.** *Law.* **a.** the transference of a right, interest, or title, or the instrument of transfer. **b.** a transference of property to assignees for the benefit of creditors. **4.** *Austral.* a system under which convicts were assigned as servants.

assimilable (ə sĭm′ĭ lə bl), *adj.* capable of being assimilated. —**assim′ilabil′ity,** *n.*

assimilate (ə sĭm′ĭ lāt′), *v.*, **-lated, -lating.** —*v.t.* **1.** to take in and incorporate as one's own; absorb (fol. by *to* or *with*). **2.** *Physiol.* to convert (food, etc.) into a substance suitable for absorption into the system. **3.** to make like; cause to resemble (fol. by *to* or *with*). **4.** to compare; liken (fol. by *to* or *with*). **5.** *Phonet.* to articulate more like another sound in the same utterance, as *ant* for earlier *amt.* —*v.i.* **6.** to be or become absorbed. **7.** *Physiol.* (of food, etc.) to be converted into the substance of the body; be absorbed into the system. **8.** to become or be like; resemble (fol. by *to* or *with*). [t. L: m. s. *assimilātus*, pp., likened]

assimilation (ə sĭm′ĭ lā′shən), *n.* **1.** the act or process of assimilating. **2.** the state or condition of being assimilated. **3.** *Physiol.* the conversion of absorbed food into the substance of the body. **4.** *Bot.* the total process of plant nutrition, including absorption of external foods and photosynthesis. **5.** *Zool.* the resemblance of an animal to its surroundings, in both shape and colour. **6.** *Sociol.* the merging of cultural traits from previously distinct cultural groups, not involving biological amalgamation. **7.** *Phonet.* the changing of a sound to one more like, or the same as, another sound near it.

assimilative (ə sĭm′ĭ lə tĭv), *adj.* characterized by assimilation; assimilating. Also, **assimilatory** (ə sĭm′ĭ lə tə rĭ, -trĭ).

Assiniboin (ə sĭn′ĭ boin′), *n.* a Siouan language.

Assiniboine (ə sĭn′ĭ boin′), *n.* a river in S Canada, flowing from SE Saskatchewan into the Red River in S Manitoba. ab. 450 mi.

Assisi (ə sē′zĭ), *n.* a town in central Italy, in Umbria, SE of Perugia: birthplace of St Francis. 27,000 (est. 1964).

assist (ə sĭst′), *v.t.* **1.** to give support, help, or aid to in some undertaking or effort, or in time of distress. **2.** to be associated with as an assistant. —*v.i.* **3.** to give aid or help. **4.** *Obs.* to be present, as at a meeting, ceremony, etc. —*n.* **5.** *Ice Hockey.* a play which helps a team-mate to score, officially scored and credited as such. [t. F: s. *assister*, t. L: m. *assistere* stand by] —**assist′er;** *Law,* **assis′tor,** *n.* —**Syn. 1.** sustain, befriend; back. See **help.** —**Ant. 1.** block, frustrate.

assistance (ə sĭs′təns), *n.* **1.** the act of assisting; help; aid. **2.** *Colloq.* national assistance. [t. F; r. ME *assystence*, t. ML: m. s. *assistentia*]

assistant (ə sĭs′tənt), *n.* **1.** one who assists a superior in some office or work; helper. —*adj.* **2.** assisting; helpful. **3.** associated with a superior in some office or work: *assistant manager.* —**Syn. 1.** aide, adjutant.

assistant chief constable, 1. a police officer ranking below chief constable. **2.** the rank.

Assiut (ă syōōt′), *n.* Asyut.

assize (ə sīz′), *n.* **1.** (*usually pl.*) (in England and Wales) a trial session, civil or criminal, held periodically in specific locations by a judge (usually of the High Court) on circuit through the English counties. **2.** judgement: *the last or great assize.* **3.** *Scot. Law.* **a.** a trial by jury. **b.** a jury. **4.** *U.S.* a sitting of a legislative or administrative agency. **5.** *U.S.* an edict, ordinance, or enactment made at such a sitting, or issued by such an agency. [ME, t. OF: m. *as(s)ise* session, der. *aseeir*, g. L *assidere* sit by]

assn, association. Also, **Assn.**

assoc., **1.** associate. **2.** associated. **3.** association.

associable (ə sō′shĭ ə bl, -shə bl), *adj.* capable of being associated. [t. F] —**asso′ciabil′ity,** *n.*

associate (*v.* ə sō′shĭ āt′; *n.*, *adj.* ə sō′shĭ ĭt, -āt′), *v.*, **-ated, -ating,** *n.*, *adj.* —*v.t.* **1.** to connect by some relation, as in thought. **2.** to join as a companion, partner, or rally. **3.** to unite; combine: *coal associated with shale.* —*v.i.* **4.** to enter into a league or union; unite. **5.** to keep company, as a friend or intimate: *to associate only with wealthy people.* —*n.* **6.** a partner in interest, as in business or in an enterprise or action. **7.** a companion or comrade: *my most intimate associates.* **8.** a confederate; an accomplice; an ally. **9.** anything usually accompanying or associated with another; an accompaniment or concomitant. **10.** one who is admitted to a subordinate degree of membership in an association or institution: *an associate of the Royal Academy.* —*adj.* **11.** associated, esp. as a companion or colleague: *an associate partner.* **12.** having subordinate membership; without full rights and privileges. **13.** allied; concomitant. [orig. adj., ME *associat*, t. L: s. *associātus*, pp., joined to] —**Syn. 6.** See **acquaintance.**

Associated Press, a business organization of newspapers throughout the U.S. together with correspondents abroad for the reporting and distribution of news. *Abbrev.*: A.P.

association (ə sō′sĭ ā′shən, -shĭ-), *n.* **1.** an organization of people with a common purpose and having a formal structure. **2.** the act of associating. **3.** the state of being associated. **4.** companionship or intimacy. **5.** connection or combination. **6.** the connection of ideas in thought, or an idea connected with or suggested by a subject of thought. **7.** *Ecol.* a group of plants of one or more species living together under uniform environmental conditions and having a uniform and distinctive aspect. **8.** association football. —**asso′cia′tional,** *adj.* —**Syn. 1.** alliance, union. **4.** fellowship.

association football, a form of football in which the use of the hands and arms is prohibited except to the goalkeeper: it is played with a spherical ball and a team of eleven players; soccer.

association of ideas, *Psychol.* the tendency of a sensation, perception, thought, etc., to recall others previously coexisting in consciousness with it or with states similar to it.

associative (ə sō′shyə tĭv), *adj.* **1.** pertaining to or resulting from association. **2.** tending to associate or unite. —**asso′ciatively,** *adv.*

assoil (ə soil′), *v.t. Archaic.* **1.** to absolve; acquit; pardon. **2.** to atone for. [ME, t. OF, pres. indic. of *a(s)soldre,* g. L *absolvere* loosen]

assonance (ăs′ə nəns), *n.* **1.** resemblance of sounds. **2.** a substitute for rhyme, in which the same vowel sounds, though with different consonants, are used in the terminal words of lines, as *penitent* and *reticence.* **3.** alliteration; use of the same consonant sounds and different vowels, as *cheery* and *chary.* **4.** partial agreement. [t. F, der. *assonant,* t. L: s. *assonans,* ppr., sounding to] —**as′sonant,** *adj., n.* —**assonantal** (ăs′ə năn′tl), *adj.*

assonate (ăs′ə nāt′), *v.i.,* **-nated, -nating. 1.** to have corresponding vowel sounds. **2.** to use assonance.

assort (ə sôrt′), *v.t.* **1.** to distribute according to sort or kind; classify. **2.** to furnish with a suitable assortment or variety of goods; make up of articles likely to suit a demand. **3.** to group or classify (*with*). —*v.i.* **4.** to agree in sort or kind; be matched or suited. **5.** *Archaic.* to associate; consort. [late ME, t. MF: s. *assorter* distribute, join, der. *a-* A-[5] + *sorte* kind, b. with *sort* lot, fate]

assorted (ə sôr′tĭd), *adj.* **1.** consisting of selected kinds; arranged in sorts or varieties. **2.** consisting of various kinds; miscellaneous. **3.** matched; suited.

assortment (ə sôrt′mənt), *n.* **1.** the act of assorting; distribution; classification. **2.** an assorted collection.

ASSR, Autonomous Soviet Socialist Republic. Also, **A.S.S.R.**

asst, assistant.

assuage (ə swāj′), *v.t.,* **-suaged, -suaging. 1.** to make milder or less severe; mitigate; ease: *to assuage grief or wrath.* **2.** to appease; satisfy: *to assuage appetite, thirst, craving, etc.* **3.** to mollify; pacify. [ME *assuage(n),* t. OF: m. *a(s)suagier,* ult. f. L: *ad-* AD- + deriv. of *suāvis* sweet] —**assuage′ment,** *n.* —**assuag′er,** *n.*

Assuan (ăs wăn′), *n.* Aswan. Also, **Assouan.**

assuasive (ə swā′sĭv), *adj.* soothing; alleviative.

assume (ə syōōm′), *v.t.,* **-sumed, -suming. 1.** to take for granted or without proof; suppose as a fact: *assume a principle in reasoning.* **2.** to take upon oneself; undertake: *to assume office, an obligation,* etc. **3.** to take on or put on oneself: *to assume new habits of life.* **4.** to pretend to have or be; feign: *to assume a false humility.* **5.** to appropriate or arrogate: *to assume a right to oneself.* **6.** *Archaic.* to take into relation or association; adopt. —*v.i.* **7.** to be arrogant; make presumptuous claims. [late ME: t. L: m. s. *assūmere* take up] —**assum′able,** *adj.* —**assum′er,** *n.* —**Syn. 1.** presuppose. **4.** See **pretend.**

assumed (ə syōōmd′), *adj.* **1.** pretended. **2.** taken for granted. **3.** usurped. —**assumedly** (ə syōō′mĭd lĭ), *adv.*

assuming (ə syōō′mĭng), *adj.* arrogant; presuming. —**assum′ingly,** *adv.*

assumpsit (ə sŭmp′sĭt), *n. Law.* **1.** *Hist.* a legal action for breach of a simple contract (a promise not under seal): abolished 1875. **2.** an actionable promise. [t. L: he undertook]

assumption (ə sŭmp′shən), *n.* **1.** the act of taking for granted or supposing. **2.** something taken for granted; a supposition. **3.** the act of taking to or upon oneself. **4.** arrogance; presumption. **5.** *Eccles.* **a.** (*often cap.*) the bodily taking up into heaven of the Virgin Mary after her death. **b.** (*cap.*) a feast commemorating it, celebrated on August 15th. **6.** *Logic.* the minor premise of a syllogism. —**Syn. 2.** conjecture, hypothesis, theory, postulate. **4.** effrontery, forwardness.

assumptive (ə sŭmp′tĭv), *adj.* **1.** taken for granted. **2.** characterized by assumption. **3.** presumptuous.

Assur (ăs′ə), *n.* the supreme national god of Assyria. Also, **Ashur, Asshur, Asur.**

assurance (ə shōōə′rəns, ə shô′-), *n.* **1.** a positive declaration intended to give confidence. **2.** pledge; guarantee; surety. **3.** full confidence or trust; freedom from doubt; certainty. **4.** freedom from timidity; self-reliance; courage. **5.** presumptuous boldness; impudence. **6.** insurance (now usually restricted to life insurance). **7.** *Law.* the transference and securing of the title to property. —**Syn. 3.** See **trust. 4, 5.** See **confidence.**

assure (ə shōōə′, ə shô′), *v.t.,* **-sured, -suring. 1.** to declare earnestly to; inform or tell positively. **2.** to make (one) sure or certain; convince, as by a promise or declaration. **3.** to make (a future event) sure; ensure: *this assures the success of our work.* **4.** to secure or confirm; render safe or stable: *to assure a person's position.* **5.** to give confidence to; encourage. **6.** to insure, esp. against death. **7.** *Law.* to transfer or convey (property). [ME *assure(n),* t. OF: m. *aseürer,* g. LL *assēcūrāre*] —**assurer;** *Law,* **assur′or,** *n.*

assured (ə shōōəd′, ə shôd′), *adj.* **1.** made sure; sure; certain. **2.** bold; confident. **3.** boldly presumptuous. —*n.* **4.** *Insurance.* **a.** the beneficiary under a policy. **b.** the person whose life or property is covered by a policy. —**assuredly** (ə shōōə′rĭd lĭ, ə shô′-), *adv.* —**assur′edness,** *n.*

assurgent (ə sûr′jənt), *adj.* **1.** *Bot.* curving upwards, as leaves; ascending. **2.** *Her.* shown rising out of the sea. [t. L: s. *assurgens,* ppr., rising up] —**assur′gency,** *n.*

Assyria (ə sĭr′ĭ ə), *n.* an ancient empire in SW Asia: greatest extent ab. 750–612 B.C. *Cap.:* Nineveh.

Assyrian Empire, 7th century B.C.

Assyrian (ə sĭr′ĭ ən), *adj.* **1.** pertaining to Assyria, the Assyrians, or their language. —*n.* **2.** a native or an inhabitant of Assyria. **3.** a Semitic language of the Akkadian group, spoken in northern Mesopotamia.

Assyriology (ə sĭr′ĭ ŏl′ə jĭ), *n.* the science of Assyrian antiquities. —**Assyr′iol′ogist,** *n.*

Astarte (ăs tär′tĭ), *n.* an ancient Semitic deity, goddess of fertility and reproduction worshipped by the Phoenicians, corresponding to the Hebrew Ashtoreth and the Babylonian and Assyrian Ishtar, and regarded as a moon goddess by the Greeks and Romans. [t. L, t. Gk, t. Phoenician: m. *Ashtareth*]

astatic (ə stăt′ĭk, ā-), *adj.* **1.** unstable; unsteady. **2.** *Physics.* having no tendency to take a definite position. [f. s. Gk *ástatos* unstable + -IC] —**astat′ically,** *adv.* —**astaticism** (ə stăt′ĭ sĭz′əm, ā-), *n.*

astatic galvanometer, *Physics.* a moving-magnet galvanometer in which the magnets are so arranged that the earth's magnetic field (or any other uniform field) exerts no controlling torque on the moving system.

astatine (ăs′tə tēn′, -tĭn), *n. Chem.* a rare element of the halogen family. *Symbol:* At; *at. no.:* 85. [f. Gk *ástatos* unstable + -INE[2]]

aster (ăs′tə), *n.* **1.** *Bot.* any plant of the large composite genus *Aster,* having rays varying from white or pink to blue around a yellow disc. **2.** a plant of some allied genus, as *Callistephus chinensis* (**China aster**). **3.** *Biol.* either of two star-shaped structures formed in a cell during mitosis. [t. L, t. Gk: star]

-aster[1], a suffix used to form nouns denoting something that imperfectly resembles or merely apes the true thing, or an inferior or petty instance of something, as *criticaster, poetaster, oleaster.* [t. L]

-aster[2], *Chiefly Biol.* a suffix meaning 'star'. [repr. Gk *astḗr*]

asteraceous (ăs′tə rā′shəs), *adj. Bot.* belonging to the *Asteraceae* or *Carduaceae,* the aster family of plants, usually included in the *Compositae.*

asteria (ăs tĭə′rĭ ə), *n. Min.* a precious stone which shows asterism when cabochon-cut, as the star-sapphire.

asteriated (ăs tĭə′rĭ ā′tĭd), *adj. Crystall.* exhibiting asterism. [f. s. Gk *astérios* starry + -AT(E)[1] + -ED[2]]

asterisk (ăs′tə rĭsk), *n.* **1.** the figure of a star (*), used in writing and printing as a reference mark or to indicate omission, doubtful matter, etc. **2.** something in the shape of a star or asterisk. [t. LL: m. s. *asteriscus,* t. Gk: m. *asterískos,* dim. of *astḗr* star]

asterism (ăs′tə rĭz′əm), *n.* **1.** *Astron.* **a.** a group of stars. **b.** a constellation. **2.** *Crystall.* a property of some crystallized minerals of showing a starlike luminous figure in transmitted light or, in a cabochon-cut stone, by reflected light. **3.** three asterisks (⁂ or ⁎⁎⁎) placed before a passage to direct attention to it. [t. Gk: s. *asterismós,* der. *asterízein* mark with stars]

astern (ə stûrn′), *adv., adj. Naut.* **1.** to the rear (of); behind; in a backward direction. **2.** in the rear; in a position behind.

asternal (ă stûr′nəl), *adj. Anat., Zool.* not reaching to or connected with the sternum. [f. A-[6] + STERNAL]

asteroid (ăs′tə roid′), *n.* **1.** *Zool.* any of the *Asteroidea,* a class of echinoderms characterized by a starlike body with radiating arms or rays, as the starfishes. **2.** *Astron.* one of several hundred planetoids with orbits lying mostly between those of Mars and Jupiter. —*adj.* **3.** starlike. **4.** *Zool.* belonging to or pertaining to the asteroids (def. 1). [t. Gk: m. s. *asteroeidḗs* starlike]

asteroidean (ăs′tə roi′dĭ ən), *n. adj., Zool.* asteroid (defs. 1 and 4).

asthenia (ăs thē′nyə), *n. Pathol.* lack or loss of strength; debility. [NL, t. Gk: m. *asthéneia*]

asthenic (ăs thĕn′ĭk), *adj.* **1.** of or pertaining to asthenia. **2.** weak; lacking strength. **3.** *Anat.* of a physical type characterized by a small trunk, slight muscular development, and long limbs (associated by Kretschmer with schizophrenic mental traits). —*n.* **4.** an asthenic person or type.

asthenosphere (əs thē′nə sfĭə′, -thĕn′-), *n.* the zone of

rock below the lithosphere or earth's crust; it is in a relatively plastic condition.
asthma (ăs′mə), *n.* a paroxysmal disorder of respiration, with laboured breathing, a feeling of constriction in the chest, and coughing. [t. Gk: panting; r. ME *asma*, t. ML]
asthmatic (ăs măt′ĭk), *adj.* **1.** suffering from asthma. **2.** pertaining to asthma. —*n.* **3.** one suffering from asthma. —**asthmat′ically,** *adv.*
Asti (ăs′tĭ; *It.* äs′tē), *n.* a town in NW Italy, in Piedmont. 69,182 (1966).
astigmatic (ăs′tĭg măt′ĭk), *adj.* pertaining to, exhibiting, or correcting astigmatism.
astigmatism (ə stĭg′mə tĭz′əm), *n.* a defect of the eye or of a lens whereby rays of light from an external point converge unequally in different meridians, thus causing imperfect vision or images. [f. A-[6] + s. Gk *stigma* point + -ISM]
astilbe (ə stĭl′bĭ), *n.* any plant of the saxifragaceous genus *Astilbe*, grown for the clusters of small, showy flowers.
astir (ə stû′), *adj.*, *adv.* **1.** in a stir; in motion or activity. **2.** up and about; out of bed.
Astolat (ăs′tō lăt′), *n.* a place in the Arthurian romances, possibly in Surrey.
astomatous (ă stŏm′ə təs, ă stō′mə-), *adj. Zool., Bot.* having no mouth, stoma, or stomata. [f. A-[6] + s. Gk *stóma* mouth + -OUS]
Aston (ăs′tn), *n.* **Francis William,** 1877–1945 English physicist.
astonied (ə stŏn′ĭd), *adj. Archaic.* dazed; bewildered.
astonish (ə stŏn′ĭsh), *v.t.* to strike with sudden and overpowering wonder; surprise greatly; amaze. [earlier *astony*, ? OE *āstunian*, intensive of *stunian* resound. Cf. ASTOUND, STUN] —**aston′isher,** *n.* —**Syn.** astound, startle, shock. See **surprise.**
astonishing (ə stŏn′ĭ shĭng), *adj.* causing astonishment; amazing. —**aston′ishingly,** *adv.*
astonishment (ə stŏn′ĭsh mənt), *n.* **1.** overpowering wonder or surprise; amazement. **2.** an object or cause of amazement.
Astor (ăs′tə), *n.* **1. John Jacob,** 1763–1848, U.S. capitalist and fur merchant, born in Germany. **2. John Jacob, 1st Baron of Hever,** born 1886, English newspaper proprietor. **3. Nancy, Viscountess,** 1879–1964, first woman to take a seat in the British House of Commons. **4. William Waldorf, 1st Viscount of Hever Castle,** 1848–1919, British newspaper proprietor and U.S. diplomat, born in the U.S. **5.** his son, **Waldorf, 2nd Viscount,** 1879–1952, British politician and newspaper proprietor.
astound (ə stound′), *v.t.* **1.** to overwhelm with amazement; astonish greatly. —*adj.* **2.** *Archaic.* astonished. [pp. of obs. *astone, astun.* See ASTONISH, STUN] —**astound′ingly,** *adv.* —**Syn. 1.** See **surprise.**
astr., **1.** astronomer. **2.** astronomical. **3.** astronomy.
astraddle (ə străd′l), *adv.*, *adj.* with one leg on each side; in a straddling position; astride.
Astraea (ăs trē′ə), *n. Gk Myth.* the goddess of justice, daughter of Zeus and Themis, the last of the immortals to leave mankind.
astragal (ăs′trə gl), *n.* **1.** *Archit.* **a.** a small convex moulding cut into the form of a string of beads. **b.** a plain convex moulding. See diag. under **column. 2.** any similar moulding, as in carpentry or metalwork. **3.** (*pl.*) dice. [t. L: s. *astragalus.* See ASTRAGALUS]
astragalus (ăs trăg′ə ləs), *n.*, *pl.* **-li** (-lī′). *Anat.* the uppermost bone of the tarsus; anklebone; talus; tibiale. [t. L, t. Gk: m. *astrágalos*] —**astrag′alar,** *adj.*
astrakhan (ăs′trə kăn′), *n.* **1.** a kind of fur of young lambs, with lustrous closely curled wool, from Astrakhan. **2.** Also, **astrakhan cloth.** a fabric with curled pile resembling it.
Astrakhan (ăs′trə kăn′; *Russ.* äs′trə KHəny), *n.* a city at the mouth of the Volga, in the SE Soviet Union in Europe. 342,000 (est. 1965).
astral (ăs′trəl), *adj.* **1.** pertaining to or proceeding from the stars; consisting of or resembling stars; starry; stellar. **2.** *Biol.* relating to or resembling an aster: star-shaped. **3.** *Theosophy.* pertaining to a supersensible substance supposed to pervade all space and form the substance of a second body belonging to each individual. [t. L: s. *astrālis*, der. *astrum* star, t. Gk: m. *ástron*]
astray (ə strā′), *adv.*, *adj.* out of the right way or away from the right; straying; wandering.
astrict (ə strĭkt′), *v.t.* **1.** to bind fast; confine; constrain or restrict. **2.** to bind morally or legally. [t. L: s. *astrictus*, pp., drawn close] —**astric′tion,** *n.*
astride (ə strīd′), *adv.*, *adj.* **1.** in the posture of striding or straddling. —*prep.* **2.** with a leg on each side of.
astringe (ə strĭnj′), *v.t.*, **astringed, astringing.** to compress; bind together; constrict. [t. L: m. s. *astringere*]
astringent (ə strĭn′jənt), *adj.* **1.** *Med.* contracting; constrictive; styptic. **2.** stern or severe; austere. —*n.* **3.** *Med.* a substance which contracts the tissues or canals of the body, thereby diminishing discharges, as of blood. [t. L: s. *astringens*, ppr.] —**astrin′gency,** *n.* —**astrin′gently,** *adv.* —**Syn. 2.** See **acid.**
astro-, a word element meaning 'star', as in *astrology*. [t. Gk, comb. form of *ástron*]
astrobee (ăs′trə bē′), *n. Aerospace.* a research rocket capable of carrying scientific payloads to altitudes of between 200 and 1800 miles. [f. ASTRO- + BEE[1]]
astrobiology (ăs′trō bī ŏl′ə jĭ), *n.* the study of the possibility that life exists outside the earth's immediate environment.
astrobotany (ăs′trō bŏt′ə nĭ), *n.* the study of the possibility that plant life exists outside the earth's immediate environment.
astrocompass (ăs′trō kŭm′pəs), *n.* a compass for indicating direction relative to the stars.
astrodome (ăs′trə dōm′), *n. Aeron.* a transparent dome on the top of the fuselage of an aeroplane, for astronomical observation. [f. ASTRO- + DOME]
astrogeology (ăs′trō jĭ ŏl′ə jĭ), *n.* the study of the geological structure of planets other than the earth, and of other bodies in the solar system.
astrol., **1.** astrologer. **2.** astrological. **3.** astrology.
astrolabe (ăs′trə lāb′), *n.* an astronomical instrument for taking the altitude of the sun or stars and for the solution of other problems in astronomy and navigation. [t. ML: m. s. *astrolabium*, t. Gk: m. *astrolábon* (*órganon*) armillary sphere; r. ME *astrelabe*, t. OF]
astrology (ə strŏl′ə jĭ), *n.* **1.** a study which assumes, and professes to interpret, the influence of the heavenly bodies on human affairs. **2.** (formerly) practical astronomy, the earliest form of the science. [ME, t. L: m. s. *astrologia*, t. Gk. See ASTRO-, -LOGY] —**astrol′oger,** *n.* —**astrological** (ăs′trə lŏj′ĭ kl), **as′trolog′ic,** *adj.* —**as′trolog′ically,** *adv.*
astrometry (ə strŏm′ĭ trĭ), *n.* measurement of the positions, motions, and distances of the celestial bodies.
astron., **1.** astronomer. **2.** astronomical. **3.** astronomy.
astronaut (ăs′trə nôt′), *n.* a traveller outside the atmosphere of the earth. [back-formation from ASTRONAUTICS]
astronautic (ăs′trə nô′tĭk), *adj.* of astronautics or astronauts. Also, **as′tronau′tical.** [f. ASTRO- + NAUTIC(AL)] —**as′tronau′tically,** *adv.*
astronautics (ăs′trə nô′tĭks), *n.* the science or art of flight outside the atmosphere of the earth. [pl. of ASTRONAUTIC. See -ICS]
astronavigation (ăs′trō năv ĭg ā′shən), *n.* navigation by observation of the stars.
astronomer (ə strŏn′ə mə), *n.* an expert in astronomy; a scientific observer of the celestial bodies.
astronomical (ăs′trə nŏm′ĭ kl), *adj.* **1.** of, pertaining to, or connected with astronomy. **2.** very large, like the numbers used in astronomical calculations. Also, **as′tronom′ic.** —**as′tronom′ically,** *adv.*
astronomical clock, an electrically controlled pendulum clock which reads sidereal time.
astronomical unit, the mean distance between the centre of the earth and the centre of the sun, about 92·9 million miles, used as a unit of distance within the solar system. *Abbrev.*: AU. Also, **astronomic unit.**
astronomical year. See **year** (def. 5).
astronomy (ə strŏn′ə mĭ), *n.* the science of the celestial bodies, their motions, positions, distances, magnitudes, etc. [ME *astronomie*, t. L: m. *astronomia*, t. Gk. See ASTRO-, -NOMY]
astrophotography (ăs′trō fə tŏg′rə fĭ), *n.* the photography of stars and other celestial objects.
astrophysics (ăs′trō fĭz′ĭks), *n.* astronomical physics, treating of the physical properties and phenomena of the celestial bodies. —**as′trophys′ical,** *adj.* —**astrophysicist** (ăs′trō fĭz′ĭ sĭst), *n.*
astrosphere (ăs′trə sfĭə′), *n. Biol.* **1.** the central portion of an aster, in which the centrosome lies. **2.** the whole aster exclusive of the centrosome; attraction sphere.
astucious (ăs tyōō′shəs), *adj. Rare.* astute. [t. F: m. *astucieux*]
Asturias (ăs tōō′rĭ ăs′; *Sp.* äs tōōr′yäs), *n.* a former kingdom and province in NW Spain.
astute (ə styōōt′), *adj.* of keen penetration or discernment; sagacious; shrewd; cunning. [t. L: m. s. *astūtus*, der. *astus* adroitness, cunning] —**astute′ly,** *adv.* —**astute′ness,** *n.* —**Syn.** artful, crafty, wily, sly.
Astyanax (ăs tī′ə năks′), *n. Gk Legend.* the young son of Hector and Andromache, thrown from the walls of Troy by the victorious Greeks.
astylar (ă stī′lə, ā-), *adj. Archit.* without columns. [f. s. Gk *ástylos* without columns + -AR[1]]
Asunción (ə sōōn′sĭ ōn′; *Sp.* ä sōōn thyōn′), *n.* the capital

of Paraguay, in the S part, on the Paraguay river. 305,160 (1962).

asunder (ə sŭn′də), *adv.*, *adj.* **1.** into separate parts; in or into pieces: *to tear asunder.* **2.** apart or widely separated: *as wide asunder as the poles.* [ME *asunder*, *o(n)sunder*, OE *on sundran* apart. See A-[1], SUNDER]

Asur (äs′ə), *n.* Assur.

Aswan (äs wän′), *n.* **1.** a town in SE Egypt, on the Nile. 48,000 (est. 1960). **2.** a large dam across the Nile nearby. 6400 ft long. Also, **Assuan, Assouan.**

asyllabic (ās′ĭ lăb′ĭk, ā′sĭ-), *adj.* not syllabic.

asylum (ə sī′ləm), *n.* **1.** an institution for the maintenance and care of the insane, the blind, orphans or the like. **2.** an inviolable refuge, as formerly for criminals and debtors; a sanctuary. **3.** *Internat. Law.* a temporary refuge granted political offenders, esp. in a foreign legation. **4.** any secure retreat. [t. L, t. Gk: m. *ásylon*, neut. of *ásylos* inviolable] **—Syn. 1.** See **hospital.**

asymmetric (ăs′ĭ mĕt′rĭk, ā′sĭ-), *adj.* **1.** not symmetrical; without symmetry. **2.** *Logic.* denoting relations which, if they hold between one term and a second, do not hold between the second and the first: *the relation 'being an ancestor of' is asymmetric.* Also, **a′symmet′rical. —a′symmet′rically,** *adv.*

asymmetry (ā sĭm′ĭ trĭ), *n.* lack of symmetry or proportion. [t. Gk: m. s. *asymmetría*]

asymptote (ăs′ĭm tōt′), *n. Maths.* a straight line that is the limit of a tangent to a curve as the point of contact moves off to infinity. [t. Gk: m. s. *asýmptōtos* not close] **—asymptotic** (ăs′ĭm tŏt′ĭk), **as′ymptot′ical,** *adj.* **—as′ymptot′ically,** *adv.*

A B

A B

AB, Asymptote

asynchronism (ā sĭng′krə nĭz′əm, ā sĭn′-), *n.* want of synchronism, or coincidence in time. **—asyn′chronous,** *adj.*

asyndeton (ă sĭn′dĭ tən), *n. Rhet.* the omission of conjunctions. [t. L, t. Gk, neut. of *asýndetos* unjoined] **—asyndetic** (ăs′ĭn dĕt′ĭk), *adj.* **—as′yndet′ically,** *adv.*

Asyut (ä syo͞ot′), *n.* a city in N central Egypt, on the Nile. 122,000 (1960).

At, astatine.

at (ăt; *unstressed* ət), *prep.* a particle specifying a point occupied, attained, sought, or otherwise concerned, as in place, time, order, experience, etc., and hence used in many idiomatic phrases expressing circumstantial or relative position, degree or rate, action, manner: *to stand at the door, to aim at a mark, at home, at hand, at noon, at zero, at work, at ease, at length, at a risk, at cost, at one's best.* [ME; OE *æt*; c. Icel. *at*, L *ad* AD-]

at-, var. of **ad-** before *t*, as in *attend.*

at., atomic.

a.t., ampere turn. Also, **A.T.**

atabal (ăt′ə băl′), *n.* a kind of drum used by the Moors. Also, **attabal.** [t. Sp., t. Ar.: m. *aṭ tabl* the drum]

atabrine (ăt′ə brĭn, -brēn′), *n. Pharm.* an antimalarial substance, $C_{23}H_{30}N_3OCl$, a hydrochloride of mepacrine, with properties similar to plasmochin. Also, **atabrin.**

Atacama (ăt′ə kä′mə; *Sp.* ä tä kä′mä), *n.* an extensive desert along the W coast of S America, including much of Chile and parts of the Argentine and Bolivia: nitrates, silver, and copper mining.

atactic (ə tăk′tĭk), *adj.* pertaining to or afflicted with ataxia. Also, **atax′ic.**

Atahualpa (ät′ə wäl′pə), *n.* died 1533, last Inca king of Peru.

ataghan (ăt′ə găn′), *n.* yataghan.

Atalanta (ăt′ə lăn′tə), *n. Gk Myth.* a virgin huntress who helped to kill the Calydonian boar (see **Meleager**). All suitors whom she could outrun were put to death, but she was vanquished by one who dropped three golden apples given him by Aphrodite, which Atalanta stopped to pick up.

ataman (ăt′ə mən), *n., pl.* **-mans.** a chief of Cossacks, elected by the whole group, serving as a chairman in peace, a leader in war; a hetman. [t. Russ.]

ataraxia (ăt′ə răk′sĭ ə), *n.* a state of tranquillity, free from emotional disturbance and anxiety. Also, **ataraxy** (ăt′ə răk′sĭ). [NL, t. Gk: impassiveness] **—at′arac′tic** (-răk′tĭk), **at′arax′ic,** *adj., n.*

Atatürk (ăt′ə tûk′; *Turk.* ä tä tyrk′), *n.* **Kemal** (*Turk.* kĕ mäl′), 1880–1938, founder of the Turkish republic, president of Turkey 1923–38.

atavic (ə tăv′ĭk), *adj.* **1.** of or pertaining to remote ancestors. **2.** atavistic.

atavism (ăt′ə vĭz′əm), *n.* **1.** *Biol.* the reappearance in an individual of characteristics of some more or less remote ancestor that have been absent in intervening generations. **2.** reversion to an earlier type. [f. s. L *atavus* ancestor + -ISM] **—at′avist,** *n.* **—at′avis′tic,** *adj.*

ataxia (ə tăk′sĭ ə), *n. Pathol.* **1.** loss of coordination of the muscles, esp. of the extremities. **2.** locomotor ataxia. [t. NL, t. Gk: disorder] **—atax′ic, atac′tic,** *adj.*

Atbara (ăt′bə rə, ăt bä′rə), *n.* a river flowing from NW Ethiopia NW to the Nile in the Sudan, ab. 500 mi.

A.T.C., **1.** Air Training Corps. **2.** Air Traffic Control.

ate (ĕt), *v.* pt. of **eat.**

Ate (ā′tĭ, ä′tĭ), *n. Gk Myth.* a goddess personifying the fatal blindness or recklessness which produces crime, and the divine punishment which follows it. [t. Gk]

-ate[1], a suffix forming: **1.** adjectives equivalent to **-ed** (in participial and other adjectives), as in *accumulate, separate.* **2.** nouns denoting esp. persons charged with some duty or function, or invested with some dignity, right, or special character, as in *advocate, candidate, curate, legate, prelate.* **3.** nouns denoting some product or result of action, as in *mandate* (lit., a thing commanded). **4.** verbs, orig. taken from Latin past participles but now formed from any Latin or other stem, as in *actuate, agitate, calibrate.* [t. L: m. *-ātus, -āta, -ātum*]

-ate[2], *Chem.* a suffix forming nouns denoting a salt formed by action of an acid on a base, esp. where the name of the acid ends in *-ic*, as in *acetate.* [t. L: m. *-ātum* neut. of *-ātus* -ATE[1]]

-ate[3], a suffix forming nouns denoting condition, estate, office, officials, or an official, etc., as in *consulate, senate.* [t. L: m. *-ātus*, suffix making nouns of 4th declension]

Atebrin (ăt′ə brĭn, -brēn′), *n. Pharm., Trademark.* atabrine.

atelier (ăt′ə lyā′; *Fr.* ȧ tə lyĕ′), *n.* the workshop or studio of an artist. [t. F: workplace, orig. pile of chips, der. OF *astele* chip, g. LL *astella*, r. L *astula*]

a tempo (ä tĕm′pō), *Music.* resuming the speed which obtained preceding *rit.* or *accel.* [It.]

Aten (ä′tən), *n.* a sun-god introduced into Egyptian religion by Amenhotep IV as the only god. Also, **Aton.**

Athabascan (ăth′ə băs′kən), *n.* an American Indian linguistic stock of the Na-Dene phylum, including languages of NW Canada and Alaska (e.g., Ojibwa), of the Pacific coast, esp. Oregon and California (e.g., Hupa), and of Arizona and the Rio Grande basin (notably Navaho and Apache). Also, **Athapascan.**

Athabaska (ăth′ə băs′kə), *n.* **1. Lake,** a lake in W Canada, in NW Saskatchewan and NE Alberta, ab. 200 mi. long; ab. 3000 sq. mi. **2.** a river flowing from W Alberta NE to Lake Athabaska. 765 mi.

athanasia (ăth′ə nā′syə), *n.* deathlessness; immortality. Also, **athanasy** (ə thăn′ə sĭ). [t. Gk]

Athanasian (ăth′ə nā′shən), *adj.* **1.** of or pertaining to Athanasius. **—*n.* 2.** *Theol.* a follower of Athanasius or a believer in his creed.

Athanasian Creed, *Theol.* a (probably) post-Augustinian creed of the Christian faith, of unknown authorship, formerly ascribed to Athanasius.

Athanasius (ăth′ə nā′shəs), *n.* **Saint,** A.D. 296?–373, bishop of Alexandria: opponent of Arianism.

Athapascan (ăth′ə păs′kən), *n.* Athabascan.

Atharva-Veda (ə tä′və vā′də), *n.* See **Veda.**

atheism (ā′thĭ ĭz′əm) *n.* **1.** the doctrine that there is no God. **2.** disbelief in the existence of a God (or gods). **3.** godlessness. [f. s. Gk *átheos* without a god + -ISM]

atheist (ā′thĭ ĭst), *n.* one who denies or disbelieves the existence of God or gods.

—Syn. ATHEIST, AGNOSTIC, INFIDEL, SCEPTIC refer to persons not inclined towards religious belief. An ATHEIST is one who denies the existence of a Deity or divine beings. An AGNOSTIC is one who believes it impossible to know anything about God or about the creation of the universe. INFIDEL means an unbeliever, especially a non-believer in Islam or Christianity. A SCEPTIC doubts and is critical of all accepted doctrines and creeds.

atheistic (ā′thĭ ĭs′tĭk), *adj.* pertaining to or characteristic of atheists; involving, containing, or tending to atheism. Also, **a′theis′tical. —a′theis′tically,** *adv.*

atheling (ăth′ĭ lĭng), *n. Early English Hist.* a man of royal blood; a prince. [ME; OE *ætheling*, f. *æthelu* noble family + *-ing*, suffix of appurtenance]

Athelstan (ăth′əl stən), *n.* A.D. 895?–940, king of England A.D. 925–940.

Athena (ə thē′nə), *n.* the Greek goddess of wisdom, arts, industries, and prudent warfare, identified by the Romans with Minerva. Also, **Athene** (ə thē′nĭ). [t. Gk: m. *Athḗnē*]

athenaeum (ăth′ĭ nē′əm), *n.* **1.** an institution for the promotion of literary or scientific learning. **2.** a library or reading room. **3.** (*cap.*) a sanctuary of Athena at Athens, built by the Roman emperor Hadrian, and frequented by poets and men of learning. Also, **atheneum.** [t. L, t. Gk: m. *Athḗnaion* temple of Athena]

Athenagoras (ăth′ĭn ăg′ə rəs), *n.* 2nd century B.C., Greek Christian apologist.

Athenian (ə thē′nyən), *adj.* **1.** pertaining to Athens. —*n.* **2.** a native or citizen of Athens.

Athens (ăth′ĭnz), *n.* the capital of Greece, in the SE part. 1,852,709 (1961). Greek, **Athenai** (*Gk* ä thē′nĕ). See map under **Marathon.**

athermancy (ă thû′mən sĭ), *n. Physics.* the power of stopping radiant heat.

athermanous (ă thû′mə nəs), *adj. Physics.* impermeable to or able to stop radiant heat. [f. A-[6] + s. Gk *thermaínein* heat + -OUS]

atheroma (ăth′ə rō′mə), *n. Pathol.* atherosclerosis. [t. Gk] —**ath′ero′matous,** *adj.*

atherosclerosis (ăth′ə rō sklĭə rō′sĭs), *n. Pathol.* a form of arteriosclerosis in which fatty substances deposit in and beneath the intima of the arteries. [NL, f. m. Gk *athḗr* chaff + SCLEROSIS]

athirst (ə thûst′), *adj.* **1.** having a keen desire; eager (often fol. by *for*). **2.** *Archaic.* thirsty.

athlete (ăth′lēt), *n.* **1.** anyone trained to exercises of physical agility and strength. **2.** one trained for track and field events only. [t. L: m. s. *āthlēta*, t. Gk: m. *āthlētḗs* contestant in games]

athlete's foot, a contagious disease, a ringworm of the feet, caused by a fungus that thrives on moist surfaces.

athletic (ăth lĕt′ĭk), *adj.* **1.** physically active and strong. **2.** of, like, or befitting an athlete. **3.** of a physical type characterized by long limbs, large chest, and well-developed muscles. **4.** of or pertaining to athletics. —**athlet′ically,** *adv.* —**athleticism** (ăth lĕt′ĭ sĭz′əm), *n.*

athletics (ăth lĕt′ĭks), *n.* **1.** (*usually construed as pl.*) athletic sports, as running, rowing, boxing, etc. **2.** (*usually construed as sing.*) track and field events only. **3.** (*usually construed as sing.*) the practice of athletic exercises; the principles of athletic training.

athodyd (ăth′ō dĭd′), *n. Aeron.* a ramjet. [from *a*(*ero*)-*th*(*erm*)*ody*(*namic*) *d*(*uct*)]

at-home (ət hōm′), *n.* **1.** a reception in one's home. **2.** a day when a factory, school, or other institution is open to inspection by members of the public.

Athos (ăth′ŏs, ā′thŏs; *Gk* ä′thôs), *n.* **Mount, 1.** the easternmost of three prongs of the peninsula of Chalcidice, in NE Greece: site of an independent republic of 20 monasteries. 3086 pop. (1951); 131 sq. mi.; about 35 mi. long. **2.** a headland there. 6350 ft.

athwart (ə thwôt′), *adv.* **1.** from side to side (often in an oblique direction): transversely. **2.** perversely; awry; wrongly. **3.** *Naut.* at right angles to a ship's keel. —*prep.* **4.** from side to side of; across. **5.** in opposition to; contrary to. **6.** *Naut.* across the line or course of. [f. A-[1] + THWART, adv.]

atilt (ə tĭlt′), *adj., adv.* **1.** at a tilt or inclination; tilted. **2.** in a tilting encounter.

-ation, a suffix forming nouns denoting action or process, state or condition, a product or result, or something producing a result, often accompanying verbs or adjectives of Latin origin ending in *-ate*, as in *agitation, decoration, elation, migration, separation*, but also formed in English from any stem, as in *botheration, flirtation, starvation.* See **-ion, -tion.** [t. L: s. *-ātio* = -ATE[1] + -ION; identical with G *-ation*, F *-ation*, etc., all from L]

-ative, an adjective suffix expressing tendency, disposition, function, bearing, connection, etc., as in *affirmative, demonstrative, talkative.* See **-ive.** [t. L: m. s. *-ātivus* = -ATE[1] + -IVE; repr. also F *-atif* (masc.), *-ative* (fem.)]

Atkins (ăt′kĭnz), *n.* **Tommy.** See **Tommy Atkins.**

Atlanta (ət lăn′tə), *n.* a city in the U.S., the capital of Georgia, in the N part. 487,455 (1960).

Atlantean (ăt′lăn tē′ən), *adj.* **1.** pertaining to the demigod Atlas. **2.** having the strength of Atlas. **3.** pertaining to Atlantis. [f. s. L. *Atlantēus* pertaining to Atlas + -AN. See ATLAS]

atlantes (ət lăn′tēz), *n. pl., sing.* **atlas.** *Archit.* figures of men used as supporting or decorative columns. [t. L, t. Gk. See ATLAS (def. 4)]

Atlantic (ət lăn′tĭk), *n.* **1.** the Atlantic Ocean. —*adj.* **2.** of or pertaining to the Atlantic Ocean. **3.** pertaining to the demigod Atlas. [t. L: s. *Atlanticus*, t. Gk: m. *Atlantikós* pertaining to Atlas]

Atlantic Charter, the joint declaration of Roosevelt and Churchill (August 14, 1941) resulting from a meeting at sea, and setting forth a programme of postwar peace aims.

Atlantic City, a town in the U.S., in SE New Jersey: coastal resort. 59,544 (1960).

Atlantic Ocean, an ocean bordered by North and South America in the Western Hemisphere, and Europe and Africa in the Eastern Hemisphere: divided by the equator into the **North Atlantic** and the **South Atlantic.** ab. 31,530,000 sq. mi.; with connecting seas, ab. 41,000,000 sq. mi.; greatest known depth, 30,246 ft.

Atlantic Pact, the treaty (1949) which established the North Atlantic Treaty Organization.

Atlantis (ət lăn′tĭs), *n.* a mythical island in the Atlantic Ocean, first mentioned by Plato, supposedly west of Gibraltar, said to have finally sunk into the sea.

atlas (ăt′ləs), *n.* **1.** a bound collection of maps. **2.** a volume of plates or tables illustrating any subject. **3.** *Anat.* the first cervical vertebra, which supports the head. **4.** (*cap.*) a demigod in classical mythology, condemned to support the sky on his shoulders, and identified with the Atlas Mountains. **5.** (*cap.*) one who supports a heavy burden; a mainstay. **6.** sing. of **atlantes. 7.** a size of paper, 26 × 34 inches. [t. L, t. Gk: defs 1–3, 5–7 are special uses of 4]

Atlas Mountains, a mountain range in NW Africa, extending for ab. 1500 mi. through Morocco, Algeria, and Tunisia. Highest peak, Mt Tizi, 14,764 ft.

Atli (ăt′lĭ), *n. Scand. Legend.* the king of the Huns who married Gudrun, widow of Sigurd, for her inheritance, slew her brothers, and was killed by her in turn. [Icel. var. of ATTILA]

atman (ăt′mən), *n. Hinduism.* **1.** the breath. **2.** the principle of life. **3.** the individual soul. **4.** (*cap.*) the World Soul, from which all individual souls derive, and to which they return as the supreme goal of existence. **5.** (*cap.*) Brahma, the Supreme Being. [Skt]

atmolysis (ăt mŏl′ĭ sĭs), *n. Chem.* the separation of a mixture of gases through the walls of a porous vessel due to the different diffusion rates of the constituent molecules.

atmosphere (ăt′mə sfĭə′), *n.* **1.** the gaseous fluid surrounding the earth; the air. **2.** this medium at a given place. **3.** *Astron.* the gaseous envelope surrounding any of the heavenly bodies. **4.** *Chem.* any gaseous envelope or medium. **5.** a conventional unit of pressure, the normal pressure of the air at sea-level, about 14·72 pounds per square inch. **6.** environing or pervading influence: *an atmosphere of freedom.* **7.** the quality in a work of art which produces a predominant mood or impression. [t. NL: m. s. *atmosphaera*, f. Gk: *atmó*(*s*) vapour + m. *sphaîra* SPHERE]

atmospheric (ăt′məs fĕ′rĭk), *adj.* Also, **at′mospher′ical. 1.** pertaining to, existing in, or consisting of the atmosphere: *atmospheric vapours.* **2.** caused, produced, or operated on by the atmosphere: *atmospheric pressure.* —*n.* **3.** (*pl.*) *Radio.* extraneous noises, crackling, etc., caused by stray electrical currents from storms or other atmospheric disturbance being picked up by the receiver; static. —**at′mospher′ically,** *adv.*

at. no., atomic number.

atoll (ăt′ŏl, ə tŏl′), *n.* a ringlike coral island enclosing a lagoon. [t. Maldive: m. *atol*]

atom (ăt′əm), *n.* **1.** *Physics, Chem.* the smallest unitary constituent of a chemical element, composed of a more or less complex aggregate of protons, neutrons, and electrons, whose number and arrangement determine the element. **2.** (esp. formerly) a hypothetical particle of matter so minute as to admit of no division. **3.** anything extremely small; a minute quantity. [t. L: s. *atomus*, t. Gk: m. *átomos* indivisible] —**Syn. 3.** iota.

atomic (ə tŏm′ĭk), *adj.* **1.** pertaining to atoms. **2.** propelled or driven by atomic energy. **3.** using or having developed atomic weapons. **4.** *Chem.* existing as free uncombined atoms. **5.** extremely minute. Also, **atom′ical.** —**atom′ically,** *adv.*

atomic age, the period in history initiated by the first use of the atomic bomb and characterized by atomic energy as a military, political, and industrial factor.

atomic bomb, 1. a bomb whose potency is derived from nuclear fission of atoms of fissionable material, with consequent conversion of part of their mass into energy. **2.** a bomb whose explosive force comes from a chain reaction based on nuclear fission in U-235 or in plutonium. It was first used militarily on Hiroshima, Japan (August 6th, 1945). The explosion of such a bomb is extremely violent and is attended by great heat, a brilliant light, and strong gamma-ray radiation. Also, **atom bomb, A-bomb.**

atomic clock, a highly accurate clock in which an electric oscillator, as a crystal, is regulated by the vibration of an atomic system.

atomic energy, energy obtained from changes within the atomic nucleus, chiefly from nuclear fission.

Atomic Energy Authority, the body responsible for the development and control of atomic energy in Britain. The corresponding body in the U.S. is the **Atomic Energy Commission.**

atomic heat, *Chem.* the product of the specific heat and the atomic weight of an element; approximately equal to 6 calories per gram per degree for solid elements at normal temperatures.

atomicity (ăt′ə mĭs′ĭ tĭ), *n. Chem.* **1.** the number of atoms in the molecule of a gas. **2.** *Obs.* valency.

atomic mass unit, *Physics.* a unit for expressing the mass of an individual isotope, based on the isotope of carbon, $^{12}_{6}$C. It is approximately equal to $1{\cdot}7 \times 10^{-24}$ grams.

atomic number, *Chem., Physics.* the number of protons in the nucleus of an atom of a given element. *Abbrev.:* at. no.

atomic philosophy, atomism (def. 2).

atomic pile, pile[1] (def. 7).

atomic power, **1.** energy released in nuclear reactions. **2.** a world power having developed its own atomic weapons.

atomics (ə tŏm′ĭks), *n. U.S. Colloq.* the branch of nuclear physics dealing with atomic energy, nuclear fission, etc.

atomic structure, *Physics.* the theoretically derived concept of an atom composed of a positively charged nucleus surrounded and electrically neutralized by negatively charged electrons, revolving in orbits at varying distances from the nucleus, the constitution of the nucleus and the arrangement of the electrons differing with the different chemical elements.

atomic theory, **1.** *Physics, Chem.* the modern theory of the atom as having a complex internal structure and electrical properties. **2.** *Physics.* the mathematical and geometrical description of the motions of the electrons in the atom about the nucleus. **3.** *Philos.* atomism (def. 2). Also, **atomic hypothesis.**

atomic warfare, warfare in which atomic weapons are used.

atomic weapon, any weapon (esp. a bomb, shell, or missile) in which the destructive power is derived from atomic energy.

atomic weight, *Chem.* the average weight of the atoms of a given specimen of an element, measured in atomic mass units. *Abbrev.:* at. wt, a.w.

atomism (ăt′ə mĭz′əm), *n.* **1.** atomic theory. **2.** *Philos.* the theory that minute discrete, finite, unchangeable, and indivisible elements are the ultimate constituents of all matter; and that all observable change is attributable to change in the relation of such elements to one another. —**at′omist,** *n.* —**at′omis′tic,** *adj.*

atomize (ăt′ə mīz′), *v.t.,* **-mized, -mizing.** **1.** to reduce to atoms. **2.** to reduce to fine particles or spray. Also, **atomise.** —**at′omiza′tion,** *n.*

atomizer (ăt′ə mī′zə), *n.* an apparatus for reducing liquids to a fine spray, as for medicinal application. Also, **atomiser.**

atom-smasher (ăt′əm smăsh′ə), *n. Colloq.* any device for disintegrating or splitting atoms, as an accelerator.

atomy[1] (ăt′ə mĭ), *n., pl.* **-mies.** *Archaic.* **1.** an atom; a mote. **2.** a pygmy. [t. L: m. *atomī* atoms]

atomy[2] (ăt′ə mĭ), *n., pl.* **-mies.** *Obs.* a skeleton. [der. ANATOMY, taken as *an atomy*]

Aton (ä′tən), *n.* Aten.

atonal (ă tō′nəl), *adj. Music.* having no key. [f. A-[6] + TONAL] —**aton′alism,** *n.* —**aton′alis′tic,** *adj.* —**aton′ally,** *adv.*

atonality (ăt′ō năl′ĭ tĭ), *n. Music.* **1.** the absence of key or tonal centre. **2.** an atonal principle or style of composition.

atone (ə tōn′), *v.,* **atoned, atoning.** —*v.i.* **1.** to make amends or reparation, as for an offence or a crime, or for an offender (fol. by *for*). **2.** to make up, as for errors or deficiencies (fol. by *for*). **3.** *Obs.* to agree. —*v.t.* **4.** to make amends for; expiate. **5.** *Rare.* to harmonize; make harmonious. **6.** *Obs.* to bring into unity. [back-formation from ATONEMENT] —**aton′er,** *n.* —**aton′able,** *adj.*

atonement (ə tōn′mənt), *n.* **1.** satisfaction or reparation for a wrong or injury; amends. **2.** *Theol.* the reconciliation of God and man by means of the life, sufferings, and death of Christ. **3.** *Obs.* reconciliation; agreement. [f. phrase *at one* in accord + -MENT]

atonic (ă tŏn′ĭk), *adj.* **1.** *Phonet.* **a.** unaccented. **b.** *Obs.* voiceless (def. 5). **2.** *Pathol.* characterized by atony. —*n.* **3.** *Gram.* an unaccented word, syllable, or sound.

atony (ăt′ə nĭ), *n. Pathol.* lack of tone or energy; muscular weakness, esp. in a contractile organ. [t. ML: m. s. *atonia,* t. Gk: languor]

atop (ə tŏp′), *adv.* **1.** on or at the top. —*prep.* **2.** on the top of: *atop the house.*

ATP, *Biochem.* adenosine triphosphate.

atrabilious (ăt′rə bĭl′yəs), *adj.* melancholic or hypochondriac; splenetic. Also, **at′rabil′iar.** [f. L *ātra bīli(s)* black bile + -OUS] —**at′rabil′iousness,** *n.*

atremble (ə trĕm′bl), *adv.* in a trembling state.

Atreus (ā′trĭ o͞os′, ā′trĭ əs), *n. Gk Legend.* a king of Mycenae, and a son of Pelops. His evil deeds and those of his house gave many themes to the Greek dramatists.

atrip (ə trĭp′), *adj. Naut.* (of an anchor) raised just enough to clear the bottom.

atrium (ā′trĭ əm, ä′trĭ əm), *n., pl.* **atria** (ā′trĭ ə, ä′trĭ ə), **1.** *Archit.* **a.** the central main room of an ancient Roman private house. **b.** a courtyard, mostly surrounded by colonnades, in front of an early Christian or medieval church. **2.** *Zool.* an internal cavity or space; applied variously to different cavities in different organisms, but esp., in the developing vertebrate heart, to the space which later forms the auricles. [(def. 1) t. L; (def. 2) t. NL, special use of L *atrium*]

atrocious (ə trō′shəs), *adj.* **1.** extremely or shockingly wicked or cruel; heinous. **2.** shockingly bad or lacking in taste; execrable. **3.** *Colloq.* very bad. [f. ATROCI(TY) + -OUS] —**atro′ciously,** *adv.* —**atro′ciousness,** *n.*

atrocity (ə trŏs′ĭ tĭ), *n., pl.* **-ties.** **1.** the quality of being atrocious. **2.** an atrocious deed or thing. [t. L: m. s. *atrōcitas*]

atrophied (ăt′rə fĭd), *adj.* exhibiting or affected with atrophy; wasted.

atrophy (ăt′rə fĭ), *n., v.,* **-phied, -phying.** —*n.* **1.** *Pathol.* wasting away of the body or of an organ or part, as from defective nutrition or other cause. **2.** degeneration; reduction in size and functional power through lack of use. —*v.t., v.i.* **3.** to affect with or undergo atrophy. [earlier *atrophie,* t. L: m. *atrophia,* t. Gk: lack of nourishment] —**atrophic** (ə trŏf′ĭk), *adj.*

atropine (ăt′rə pēn′, -pĭn), *n.* a poisonous crystalline alkaloid, $C_{17}H_{23}NO_3$, obtained from belladonna (deadly nightshade) and other solanaceous plants, which prevents the response of various body structures to certain types of nerve stimulation. Also, **atropin** (ăt′rə pĭn). [f. s. NL *Atropa,* the belladonna genus (t. Gk: m. *átropos.* See ATROPOS) + -INE[2]]

atropism (ăt′rə pĭz′əm), *n. Pathol.* the morbid state induced by atropine.

Atropos (ăt′rə pŏs′), *n. Gk Myth.* one of the Fates. She cut off the thread of life. [t. Gk: lit., inflexible]

Ats, atmospheres (def. 5).

A.T.S., Auxiliary Territorial Service (organized in 1941 for women serving in the British Army; became part of the Army in 1949 as W.R.A.C.). Also, **ATS** (ăts).

att., attorney.

attabal (ăt′ə băl′), *n.* atabal.

attacca (*It.* ät täk′kä), *v.i.* (*usually imperative*). *Music.* to begin (the next movement) without a pause. [t. It.: impv. of *attaccare* ATTACK]

attach (ə tăch′), *v.t.* **1.** to fasten to; affix; join; connect: *to attach a cable.* **2.** to join in action or function. **3.** to place on duty with or in assistance to an organization or working unit temporarily, esp. a military unit. **4.** to connect as an adjunct; associate: *a curse is attached to this treasure.* **5.** to assign or attribute: *to attach significance to a gesture.* **6.** to bind by ties of affection or regard. **7.** *Law.* to arrest (a person) or distrain (property) in payment of a debt by legal authority. **8.** *Obs.* to lay hold of; seize. —*v.i.* **9.** to adhere; pertain; belong (fol. by *to* or *upon*): *no blame attaches to him.* [ME *attache(n),* t. OF: m. *atachier,* f. *a-* AD- + word akin to TACK[1]] —**attach′able,** *adj.* —**Syn. 1.** subjoin.

attaché (ə tăsh′ā; *Fr.* ȧ tȧ shĕ′), *n.* one attached to an official staff, esp. that of an embassy or legation. [F, prop. pp. of *attacher* ATTACH]

attaché case, a small rectangular leather case for documents, etc.

attachment (ə tăch′mənt), *n.* **1.** the act of attaching. **2.** the state of being attached. **3.** affection that binds one to another person or to a thing; regard. **4.** that which attaches; a fastening or tie: *the attachments of a pair of skis or of a harness.* **5.** an adjunct or supplementary device: *attachments to a reaping machine.* **6.** *Law.* **a.** arrest of a person, for contempt of court, by legal authority. **b.** the process of ordering someone (the garnishee) who owes money to a judgement debtor, to pay this money to the judgement creditor, in settlement of the judgement debt. —**Syn. 3.** love, devotedness, devotion. **4.** junction, connection. **5.** See **addition.**

attack (ə tăk′), *v.t.* **1.** to set upon with force or weapons; begin hostilities against: *attack the enemy.* **2.** to direct unfavourable criticism, argument, etc., against; blame or abuse violently. **3.** to set about (a task) or go to work on (a thing) vigorously. **4.** (of disease, destructive agencies, etc.) to begin to affect. —*v.i.* **5.** to make an attack; begin hostilities. —*n.* **6.** the act of attacking; onslaught; assault. **7.** criticism; abuse; calumny. **8.** an offensive military operation with the aim of overcoming the enemy and destroying his armed forces and will to resist. **9.** *Pathol.* seizure by disease. **10.** the initial (offensive) movement in a contest; onset. **11.** the act or manner of beginning anything; start; approach. **12.** vigour, precision, and flair in approach to or execution of anything, esp. in the performance of a musical work. **13.** *Hockey.* the forward line. [t. F: m. *attaquer*, t. It.: m. *attaccare* attack, ATTACH] —**attack′er,** *n.*

—**Syn. 1.** ATTACK, ASSAIL, ASSAULT, MOLEST all mean to set upon someone forcibly, with hostile or inimical intent. ATTACK is the most general word and applies to a beginning of hostilities, esp. those definitely planned: *to attack from ambush.* ASSAIL implies vehement, sudden, and sometimes repeated attack: *to assail with weapons, with gossip.* ASSAULT almost always implies bodily violence: *to assault with intent to kill.* TO MOLEST is to interfere with, to threaten, or to assault: *he was safe, and where no one could molest him.* **2.** criticize, censure, impugn. —**Ant. 1.** defend.

attain (ə tān′). *v.t.* **1.** to reach, achieve, or accomplish by continued effort: *to attain one's ends.* **2.** to come to or arrive at in due course: *to attain the opposite shore.* —*v.i.* **3. attain to,** to arrive at; succeed in reaching or obtaining. [ME *attaine(n)*, t. OF: m. *ataindre*, g. L *attingere* touch upon] —**Syn. 1.** secure. See **gain¹**.

attainable (ə tā′nə bl), *adj.* capable of being attained. —**attain′abil′ity, attain′ableness,** *n.*

attainder (ə tān′də), *n.* **1.** *Hist.* the legal consequence of judgement of death or outlawry for treason or felony, involving the loss of all civil rights; abolished 1870. **2.** *Obs.* dishonour. [ME, t. OF: m. *ataindre* ATTAIN; later assoc. with F *taindre* stain, g. L *tingere.* See ATTAINT]

attainment (ə tān′mənt), *n.* **1.** the act of attaining. **2.** something attained; a personal acquirement.

attainment test, *Educ.* a test designed to measure the level of knowledge attained by an individual, as opposed to native ability or intelligence; achievement test.

attaint (ə tānt′), *v.t.* **1.** *Law, Hist.* to condemn by a sentence or a bill or act of attainder. **2.** to disgrace. **3.** *Archaic.* to accuse. **4.** *Obs.* to prove the guilt of. —*n.* **5.** attainder. **6.** *Obs.* a stain, disgrace; taint. **7.** *Obs.* a touch or hit, esp. in tilting. [ME *ataynte(n)*, t. OF: m. *ataint*, pp. of *ataindre* ATTAIN; in part confused with TAINT]

attainture (ə tān′chə), *n.* **1.** attainder. **2.** imputation.

attar (ăt′ə), *n.* a perfume or essential oil obtained from flowers or petals, esp. of damask roses. [t. Pers.: m. *'atar*, t. Ar.: m. *'itr*]

attemper (ə tĕm′pə), *v.t.* **1.** to qualify, modify, or moderate by mixing or blending (with something different or opposite). **2.** to regulate or modify the temperature of. **3.** to soothe; mollify; mitigate. **4.** to accommodate; adapt (fol. by *to*). [t. L: s. *attemperāre* fit; r. ME *atempre(n)*, t. OF: m. *atemprer*]

attempt (ə tĕmpt′), *v.t.* **1.** to make an effort at; try; undertake; seek: *to attempt a conversation, to attempt to study.* **2.** to attack; make an effort against: *to attempt a person's life.* **3.** *Archaic.* to tempt. —*n.* **4.** effort put forth to accomplish something; a trial or essay. **5.** an attack or assault: *an attempt upon one's life.* [t. L: s. *attemptāre* try] —**attempt′abil′ity,** *n.* —**attempt′able,** *adj.* —**attempt′er,** *n.* —**Syn. 1.** See **try. 4.** undertaking, endeavour.

attend (ə tĕnd′), *v.t.* **1.** to be present at: *to attend school or a meeting.* **2.** to go with as a concomitant or result; accompany: *a cold attended with fever.* **3.** to minister to; devote one's services to. **4.** to wait upon or accompany as a servant. **5.** to take charge of; tend. **6.** *Obs.* to wait for; expect. —*v.i.* **7.** to give attention; pay regard or heed. **8.** to apply oneself: *to attend to one's work.* **9.** to take care or charge of: *to attend to a task.* **10.** to be consequent (*on*) **11.** to wait (*on*) with service. **12.** *Obs.* to wait. [ME *atende(n)*, t. OF: m. *atendre*, g. L *attendere* stretch towards] —**Syn. 4.** See **accompany.**

attendance (ə tĕn′dəns), *n.* **1.** the act of attending. **2.** the (number of) persons present. **3.** the number of times (out of a maximum) that a person is present. **4.** *Obs.* attendants collectively.

attendant (ə tĕn′dənt), *n.* **1.** one who attends another, as for service or company. **2.** one employed to take care or charge of someone or something, esp. when this involves directing or assisting the public: *a cloakroom attendant.* **3.** one who is present, as at a meeting. **4.** that which goes along with or follows as a natural consequence. —*adj.* **5.** being present or in attendance; accompanying. **6.** concomitant; consequent: *attendant evils.* —**Syn. 1.** escort; retainer, servant.

attention (ə tĕn′shən), *n.* **1.** the act or faculty of attending. **2.** *Psychol.* concentration of the mind upon an object; maximal integration of the higher mental processes. **3.** observant care; consideration; notice: *your letter will receive early attention.* **4.** civility or courtesy: *attention to a stranger.* **5.** (*pl.*) acts of courtesy indicating regard, as in courtship. **6.** *Mil.* **a.** a command to take an erect position, with eyes to the front, arms hanging to the sides, heels together, and toes turned outwards at an angle of 45 degrees. **b.** the state of so standing: *at attention.* [ME *attencioun*, t. L: m. s. *attentio*] —**Syn. 4.** homage, deference; respect.

attentive (ə tĕn′tĭv), *adj.* **1.** characterized by or giving attention; observant. **2.** assiduous in service or courtesy; polite; courteous. —**atten′tively,** *adv.* —**atten′tiveness,** *n.* —**Syn. 1.** regardful, mindful.

attenuant (ə tĕn′yo͞o ənt), *adj.* diluting, as a liquid. [t. L: s. *attenuans*, ppr.]

attenuate (*v.* ə tĕn′yo͞o āt′; *adj.* ə tĕn′yo͞o ĭt, -āt′), *v.,* **-ated, -ating,** *adj.* —*v.t.* **1.** to make thin; make slender or fine; rarify. **2.** to weaken or reduce in force, intensity, effect, quantity, or value. —*v.i.* **3.** to become thin or fine. **4.** to grow less; weaken. —*adj.* **5.** attenuated; thin. **6.** *Bot.* tapering gradually to a narrow extremity. [t. L: m. s. *attenuātus*, pp., made thin]

attenuation (ə tĕn′yo͞o ā′shən), *n.* **1.** the act of attenuating. **2.** the resulting state. **3.** *Physics.* the loss of power suffered by radiation when it passes through matter.

attenuator (ə tĕn′yo͞o ā′tə), *n.* **1.** one who or that which attenuates. **2.** *Electronics.* an electronic network that reduces the amplitude of a signal without distortion.

attest (ə tĕst′), *v.t.* **1.** to bear witness to; certify; declare to be correct, true, or genuine; declare the truth of, in words or writing; esp., affirm in an official capacity: *to attest the truth of a statement.* **2.** to give proof or evidence of; manifest: *his works attest his industry.* —*v.i.* **3.** to certify to the genuineness of a document by signing as witness. —*n.* **4.** *Archaic.* witness; testimony; attestation. [t. L: s. *attestāi* bear witness] —**attest′or, attes′ter,** *n.*

attestation (ăt′ĕs tā′shən), *n.* **1.** the act of attesting. **2.** an attesting declaration; testimony; evidence.

Att. Gen., Attorney General.

attic (ăt′ĭk), *n.* **1.** that part of a building, esp. a house, directly under a roof; a garret. **2.** a room or rooms in that part. **3.** a low storey or decorative wall above an entablature or the main cornice of a building. [t. F: m. *attique*, t. L: m. s. *Atticus* Attic (orig., as applied to a square column in building)]

Attic (ăt′ĭk), *adj.* **1.** pertaining to Attica. **2.** (*often l.c.*) displaying simple elegance, incisive intelligence, and delicate wit. —*n.* **3.** a native or an inhabitant of Attica; an Athenian. **4.** the Ionic dialect of ancient Athens which became the standard of Greek literature (from the 5th century B.C.). [t. L: s. *Atticus*, t. Gk: m. *Attikós*]

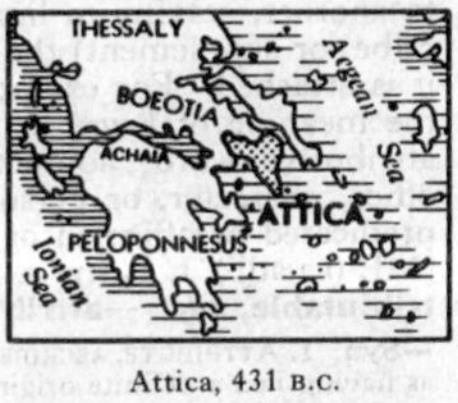

Attica (ăt′ĭ kə), *n.* the region around Athens, in SE Greece.

Attica, 431 B.C.

Attic faith, inviolable faith.

Atticism (ăt′ĭ sĭz′əm), *n.* **1.** peculiarity of style or idiom belonging to Attic Greek. **2.** Attic elegance of diction. **3.** concise and elegant expression. Also, **at′ticism.**

Atticize (ăt′ĭ sīz′), *v.,* **-cized, -cizing.** —*v.i.* **1.** to affect Attic style, usages, etc.: intermingle with Attic elements. **2.** to favour or side with the Athenians. —*v.t.* **3.** to make conformable to Attic usage. Also, **Atticise, atticise, atticize.** [t. Gk: m. s. *Attikízein* (def. 2)]

Attic salt, dry, delicate wit. Also, **Attic wit.**

Attila (ăt′ĭ lə), *n.* (*'Scourge of God'*), died A.D. 453, king of the Huns who invaded Europe; defeated at Châlons, A.D. 451, by the Romans and Visigoths.

attire (ə tī′ə), *v.,* **-tired, -tiring,** *n.* —*v.t.* **1.** to dress, array, or adorn, esp. for special occasions, ceremonials, etc. —*n.* **2.** clothes or apparel, esp. rich or splendid garments. **3.** the horns of a deer. [ME *atire(n)*, t. OF: m. *atirer* put in order, der. *a-* AD- + *tire* row]

atirement (ə tī′ə mənt), *n.* *Obs.* dress; attire

attitude (ăt′ĭ tyo͞od′), *n.* **1.** position, disposition, or manner with regard to a person or thing: *a menacing attitude.* **2.** position of the body appropriate to an action, emotion, etc. **3.** *Aeron.* the inclination of the three principal axes of an aircraft relative to the wind, to the ground, etc. **4.** a pose in ballet in which the dancer stands on one leg, the other bent behind. [t. F, t. It.: m. *attitudine* aptness, t. ML: m. s. *aptitūdo* APTITUDE] —**at′titu′dinal,** *adj.* —**Syn. 2.** See **position.**

attitudinarian (ăt′ĭ tyo͞o′dĭ nĕə′rĭ ən), *n.* one who studies attitudes.

attitudinize (ăt′ĭ tyo͞o′dĭ nīz′), *v.i.,* **-nized, -nizing.** to assume affected attitudes; pose for effect. Also, **attitudinise.** —**at′titu′diniz′er,** *n.*

Attlee (ăt′lĭ), *n.* **Clement Richard, 1st Earl,** 1833–1967, British statesman; prime minister 1945–51.

attorn (ə tûn′), *Law.* —*v.i.* **1.** to acknowledge the relation of tenant to a new landlord. —*v.t.* **2.** to turn over to another; transfer. [t. ML: s. *attornāre*, t. OF: m. *at-*

orner transfer, f. *a-* AD- + *torner* turn] —**attorn′ment,** *n.*

attorney (ə tûr′nĭ), *n., pl.* **-neys. 1.** one duly appointed or empowered by another to transact any business for him (**attorney in fact**). **2. power of attorney.** Also, **letter of attorney, warrant of attorney.** a formal document by which one person authorizes another to act for him. **3.** *Now Chiefly U.S.* lawyer. [ME *atorne*, t. OF, pp. of *atorner* assign]

attorney at law, *Law, Now Chiefly U.S.* a solicitor; an officer of the court authorized to appear before it as representative of a party to a legal controversy.

attorney general, *pl.* **attorneys general, attorney generals,** the chief law officer of a state or nation and head of its legal department.

attract (ə trăkt′), *v.t.* **1.** to act upon by a physical force causing or tending to cause approach or union (opposed to *repel*). **2.** to draw by other than physical influence; invite or allure; win: *to attract attention or admirers.* —*v.i.* **3.** to possess or exert the power of attraction. [t. L: s. *attractus*, pp., drawn to] —**attract′able,** *adj.* **attrac′tor, attract′er,** *n.*

attraction (ə trăk′shən), *n.* **1.** the act, power, or property of attracting. **2.** allurement; enticement. **3.** that which allures or entices; a charm. **4.** *Physics.* a force which draws two or more bodies together, or causes them to orbit about a common centre. **5.** an entertainment offered to the public. **6.** *Gram.* the tendency (uncommon in English) for a word to be altered from its correct case, number, or gender to agree with a word near to it, as in *the wages of sin is death*, where *is* agrees with *death* instead of *wages*.

attraction sphere, *Biol.* astrosphere.

attractive (ə trăk′tĭv), *adj.* **1.** appealing to one's liking or admiration; engaging; alluring; pleasing. **2.** having the quality of attracting. —**attrac′tively,** *adv.* —**attrac′tiveness,** *n.*

attrahent (ăt′rə hənt, ə trā′ənt), *adj.* drawing; attracting. [t. L: s. *attrahens*, ppr., drawing to]

attrib., 1. attribute. **2.** attributive. **3.** attributively.

attribute (*v.* ə trĭb′yo͞ot; *n.* ăt′rĭ byo͞ot′), *v.,* **-uted, -uting,** *n.* —*v.t.* **1.** to consider as belonging; regard as owing, as an effect to a cause (often fol. by *to*). —*n.* **2.** something attributed as belonging; a quality, character, characteristic, or property: *wisdom is one of his attributes.* **3.** *Gram.* **a.** a word or phrase grammatically subordinate to another, serving to limit (identify, particularize, describe, or supplement) the meaning of the form to which it is attached. For example: in *the red house, red* limits the meaning of *house*; it is an attribute of *house*. **b.** an attributive word; adjunct. **4.** *Fine Arts.* a symbol of office, character, or personality. **5.** *Logic.* that which is predicated or affirmed of a subject. **6.** *Obs.* reputation. [ME (as adj.), t. L: m. s. *attribūtus*, pp., assigned] —**attrib′utable,** *adj.* —**attrib′uter, attrib′utor,** *n.*

—**Syn. 1.** ATTRIBUTE, ASCRIBE, IMPUTE imply regarding something as having had a definite origin. ATTRIBUTE and ASCRIBE are often used interchangeably, to imply something's having originated with a definite person or from a definite cause. ASCRIBE is, however, neutral as to implications; whereas, possibly because of an association with *tribute*, ATTRIBUTE is coming to have a complimentary connotation: *to ascribe one's health to outdoor life, an accident to carelessness; to attribute one's success to a friend's encouragement.* IMPUTE has gained uncomplimentary connotations, and usually means to accuse or blame someone or something as a cause or origin: *to impute dishonesty to him.* **2.** See **quality.**

attribution (ăt′rĭ byo͞o′shən), *n.* **1.** the act of attributing; ascription. **2.** that which is ascribed; an attribute. **3.** authority or function assigned.

attributive (ə trĭb′yo͝o tĭv), *adj.* **1.** pertaining to or having the character of attribution or an attribute. **2.** *Gram.* expressing an attribute; in English, applied esp. to adjectives and adverbs preceding the words which they modify (distinguished from *predicate* and *appositive*), as *first* in *the first day*. —*n.* **3.** a word expressing an attribute; attributive word, phrase, or clause. —**attrib′utively,** *adv.* —**attrib′utiveness,** *n.*

attrite (ə trīt′), *adj. Obs.* worn by rubbing or attrition. Also, **attrit′ed.** [t. L: m. s. *attrītus*, pp.]

attrition (ə trĭsh′ən), *n.* **1.** a rubbing against; friction. **2.** a wearing down or away by friction; abrasion. **3.** *Theol.* imperfect sorrow for one's sins. [t. L: s. *attrītio*]

attune (ə tyo͞on′), *v.t.,* **-tuned, -tuning.** to adjust to tune or harmony; bring into accord. [f. AT- + TUNE]

atty, attorney.

atwain (ə twān′), *adv. Archaic.* in twain; in two; asunder. Also, **atwo** (ə to͞o′). [ME; f. A-[1] + TWAIN]

atween (ə twēn′), *prep., adv. Archaic.* between.

at. wt, atomic weight.

atypical (ā tĭp′ĭ kl), *adj.* not typical; not conforming to the type; irregular; abnormal. Also, **atyp′ic.** [f. A-[6] + TYPICAL] —**atyp′ically,** *adv.*

au (*Fr.* ō), *French.* to the; at the; with the. See **à la.**

AU, 1. astronomical unit. **2.** angstrom unit. Also, **a.u., A.U., Au, A.u.**

Au, *Chem.* (L *aurum*) gold.

aubade (*Fr.* ō băd′), *n. French.* a piece sung or played outdoors at dawn, usually as a compliment to someone.

Aube (*Fr.* ōb), *n.* a department in NE France. 255,099 pop. (1962); 2327 sq. mi. *Cap.*: Troyes.

Auber (*Fr.* ō bĕr′), *n.* **Daniel François Esprit** (*Fr.* dȧ nyĕl fräɴ swȧ zĕs prē′), 1782–1871, French composer.

auberge (ō bĕəzh′; *Fr.* ō bĕrzh′), *n. French.* an inn; tavern.

aubergine (ō′bə zhēn′; *Fr.* ō bĕr zhēn′), *n.* **1.** a plant, *Solanum melongena*, cultivated for its edible, more or less egg-shaped fruit, dark purple (or sometimes white or yellow) in colour; eggplant. **2.** the fruit, used as a table vegetable. **3.** the colour, a deep reddish purple. —*adj.* **4.** aubergine in colour. [t. F]

Aubervilliers (*Fr.* ō bĕr vē lyē′), *n.* a suburb of Paris in N France. 70,836 (1962).

aubrietia (ô brē′shə), *n.* any of the trailing, purple-flowered plants of the cruciferous genus *Aubrietia*, much grown in rock gardens.

auburn (ô′bən), *n.* **1.** a reddish brown or golden brown colour. —*adj.* **2.** having auburn colour: *auburn hair.* [ME *auburne*, t. OF: m. *auborne*, g. L *alburnus* whitish, der. *albus* white]

Aubusson rug (*Fr.* ō bʏ sôɴ′), a fine French rug, handmade, with a flat tapestry weave.

A.U.C. 1. ab urbe condita. **2.** anno urbis conditae.

Auchinleck (ô′kĭn lĕk′), *n.* **Sir Claude John Eyre,** born 1884, British field marshal.

Auckland (ôk′lənd), *n.* the principal seaport of New Zealand, on N North Island. 588,400 (est. 1969).

au contraire (*Fr.* ō kôɴ trĕr′), *French.* **1.** on the contrary. **2.** on the opposite or adverse side.

au courant (*Fr.* ō ko͞o räɴ′), *French.* up to date.

auction (ôk′shən), *n.* **1.** a public sale at which property or goods are sold to the highest bidder. **2.** *Cards.* **a.** auction bridge. **b.** (in bridge or certain other games) the competitive bidding to fix a contract that a player or players undertake to fulfil. —*v.t.* **3.** to sell by auction (sometimes fol. by *off*): *he auctioned off his furniture.* [t. L: s. *auctio* an increasing]

auction bridge, a variety of bridge in which all tricks won, whether bid or not, score towards game. Cf. **contract.**

auctioneer (ôk′shə nĭə′), *n.* **1.** one who conducts sales by auction. —*v.t.* **2.** to auction.

auctorial (ôk tô′rĭ əl), *adj.* of or pertaining to an author; authorial. [f. L *auctor* originator + -IAL]

audacious (ô dā′shəs), *adj.* **1.** bold or daring; spirited; adventurous: *audacious warrior.* **2.** reckless or bold in wrongdoing; impudent and presumptuous. [f. AUDACI(TY) + -OUS] —**auda′ciously,** *adv.* —**auda′ciousness,** *n.* —**Syn. 2.** unabashed, shameless.

audacity (ô dăs′ĭ tĭ), *n.* **1.** boldness or daring, esp. reckless boldness. **2.** effrontery or insolence. [f. s. L *audācia* daring + -TY[2]]

Aude (*Fr.* ōd), *n.* a department in S France. 269,782 pop. (1962); 2449 sq. mi. *Cap.*: Carcassonne.

Auden (ô′dn), *n.* **Wystan Hugh** (wĭs′tən), born 1907, English poet.

audible (ô′dĭ bl), *adj.* capable of being heard; actually heard; loud enough to be heard. [t. ML: m. s. *audibilis*, der. L *audire* hear] —**au′dibil′ity, au′dibleness,** *n.* —**au′dibly,** *adv.*

audience (ô′dyəns), *n.* **1.** an assembly of hearers or spectators: *the audience at a film.* **2.** the persons reached by a book, radio broadcast, etc.; public. **3.** liberty or opportunity of being heard or of speaking with or before a person or group. **4.** *Govt.* admission of a diplomatic representative to a sovereign or high officer of government; formal interview. **5.** the act of hearing or attending to words or sounds. [ME, t. OF, g. L *audientia* attention, hearing]

audient (ô′dyənt), *adj.* **1.** hearing; listening. —*n.* **2.** a listener. [t. L: s. *audiens*, ppr.]

audile (ô′dĭl), *n.* **1.** *Psychol.* one in whose mind auditory images are especially distinct. —*adj.* **2.** of or pertaining to hearing.

audio (ô′dĭ ō′), *adj. Electronics.* designating electronic apparatus using audio frequencies: *audio amplifier.*

audio-, a word element meaning 'hear', 'of or for hearing', as in *audiometer*. [comb. form repr. L *audire* hear]

audio frequency, *Physics, Electronics.* any frequency at which a sound wave is audible to the human ear, in the range 15 cycles per second to 20,000 cycles per second.

audiometer (ô′dĭ ŏm′ĭ tə), *n. Med.* an instrument for gauging and recording the power of hearing. —**audiometric** (ô′dĭ ō mĕt′rĭk), *adj.*

audiovisual (ô′dĭ ō vĭz′yo͞o əl), *adj.* involving or directed simultaneously at the faculties of seeing and hearing: *an audiovisual aid to teaching.*

audiphone (ô′dĭ fōn′), *n. Med.* a kind of diaphragm held against the upper teeth to assist hearing by transmitting sound vibrations to the auditory nerve.

audit (ô′dĭt), *n.* **1.** an official examination and verification of accounts and records, esp. of financial accounts. **2.** an account or a statement of account. **3.** a calling to account. **4.** *Archaic.* a judicial hearing. **5.** *Rare.* audience. —*v.t.* **6.** to make audit of; examine (accounts, etc.) officially. **7.** *U.S.* to attend (lectures, classes, etc.) as an auditor. —*v.i.* **8.** to examine and verify an account or accounts by reference to vouchers. [late ME *audite*, t. L: m. s. *audītus* a hearing]

audition (ô dĭsh′ən), *n.* **1.** the act, sense, or power of hearing. **2.** a hearing given to a musician, speaker, etc., to test voice qualities, performance, etc. **3.** *Rare.* what is heard. —*v.t., v.i.* **4.** to give an audition (to). [t. L: s. *audītio* a hearing]

auditive (ô′dĭ tĭv), *adj.* auditory.

auditor (ô′dĭ tə), *n.* **1.** a hearer; listener. **2.** a person appointed and authorized to examine accounts and accounting records, compare the charges with the vouchers, verify balance sheet and income items, and state the result. **3.** *U.S.* a university student who is registered as taking a given course but not for credit and without obligation to do the work of the course. —**auditress** (ô′dĭ trĭs), *n. fem.*

auditorium (ô′dĭ tô′rĭ əm), *n., pl.* **-toriums, -toria** (-tô′rĭ ə). the space for the audience in a concert hall, theatre, school, or other building. [t. L]

auditory (ô′dĭ tə rĭ, -trĭ), *adj., n., pl.* **-ries.** —*adj.* **1.** *Anat., Physiol.* pertaining to hearing, to the sense of hearing, or to the organs of hearing: *the auditory nerve.* —*n.* **2.** an assembly of hearers; an audience. **3.** an auditorium. [t. L: m. s. *audītōrius* (-*ōrium*, neut.)]

Audubon (ô′də bŏn′), *n.* **John James,** 1785?–1851, U.S. naturalist, who painted and wrote about the birds of North America.

au fait (ō fā′, *Fr.* ō fĕ′), *French.* having experience or practical knowledge of a thing; expert; versed.

Aufklärung (*Ger.* ouf klĕ′ro͝ong), *n. German.* **1.** enlightenment. **2.** *Europ. Hist.* enlightenment (def. 3). [G: lit., clearing up]

au fond (*Fr.* ō fôɴ), *French.* at bottom or to the bottom; thoroughly; in reality; fundamentally.

auf Wiedersehen (*Ger.* ouf vē′dər zā ən), *German.* until we meet again; goodbye for the present.

Aug., August.

aug., augmentative.

Augean stables (ô jē′ən), *Gk Legend.* the stables in which a king (**Augeas**) kept 3000 oxen and which had not been cleaned for thirty years. Hercules accomplished the task in a single day by turning the river Alpheus through the stable.

auger (ô′gə), *n.* **1.** a carpenter's tool larger than a gimlet, with a spiral groove for boring holes in wood. **2.** a large tool for boring holes deep in the ground. [ME, var. of *nauger* (*a nauger* being taken as *an auger*), OE *nafogār*]

Augers (def. 1)

aught[1] (ôt), *n.* **1.** anything whatever; any part: *for aught I know.* —*adv.* **2.** *Archaic* or *Dial.* in any degree; at all; in any respect. Also, **ought.** [ME *aught, ought,* OE *āwiht, ōwiht* at all, anything, f. *ā, ō* ever + *wiht* thing]

aught[2] (ôt), *n. Obs.* nought; zero (0). [appar. alt. of NAUGHT; *a naught* being taken as *an aught*]

Augier (*Fr.* ō zhyē′), *n.* **Guillaume Victor Émile** (*Fr.* gē yōm vēk tôr ē mēl′), 1820–89, French dramatist.

augite (ô′jīt), *n.* a mineral, a silicate, chiefly of calcium, magnesium, iron, and aluminium, a dark green to black variety of pyroxene, characteristic of basic eruptive rocks like basalt. [t. L: m. *augītēs* precious stone, t. Gk] —**augitic** (ô jĭt′ĭk), *adj.*

augment (*v.* ôg mĕnt′; *n.* ôg′mənt), *v.t.* **1.** to make larger; enlarge in size or extent; increase. **2.** *Gram.* to add an augment to. —*v.i.* **3.** to become larger. —*n.* **4.** *Gram.* (in Greek, Sanskrit, etc.) a prefixed vowel or a lengthened initial vowel, which characterizes certain forms in the inflection of verbs. [ME *augment(en),* t. L: m. *augmentāre* increase] —**augment′able,** *adj.* —**augment′er,** *n.* —**Syn. 1.** See **increase.**

augmentation (ôg′mĕn tā′shən), *n.* **1.** the act of augmenting. **2.** an augmented state. **3.** that by which anything is augmented. **4.** *Music.* modification of a theme by increasing the time value of all its notes (opposed to *diminution*).

augmentative (ôg mĕn′tə tĭv), *adj.* **1.** serving to augment. **2.** *Gram.* pertaining to or productive of a form denoting increased size or intensity. In Spanish, *-ón* added to a word indicates increased size (*silla*, 'chair'; *sillón*, 'armchair'); hence it is an augmentative suffix. —*n.* **3.** *Gram.* an augmentative element or formation.

augmented (ôg mĕn′tĭd), *adj. Music.* (of an interval) greater by a semitone than the corresponding perfect or major interval.

augmentor (ôg mĕnt′ə), *n.* **1.** *Zool.* any nerve that increases the activity rate of an organ as a gland or muscle. **2.** *Zool.* (in vertebrates) the nerve which increases the heartbeat rate. **3.** *Aerospace.* a device, as an afterburner, which achieves additional thrust from a jet or rocket engine.

Augrabies Falls (ô grä′bĭ, ô KHrä′bĭ), a cascade on the Orange river in S Africa. 480 ft.

au gratin (ō grăt′ĭn; *Fr.* ō grȧ tăɴ′), *French.* cooked or baked covered with browned crumbs or cheese, or with both.

Augsburg (ougz′bûg; *Ger.* ouks′bo͝ork), *n.* a city in S West Germany, in W Bavaria. 212,200 (est. 1966).

augur (ô′gə), *n.* **1.** one of a body of ancient Roman officials charged with observing and interpreting omens, for guidance in public affairs. **2.** any soothsayer; prophet. —*v.t.* **3.** to divine or predict, as from omens; prognosticate. **4.** to afford an omen of. —*v.i.* **5.** to conjecture from signs or omens; presage. **6.** to be a sign; bode (*well* or *ill*). [t. L] —**augural** (ô′gyo͞o rəl), *adj.* —**au′gurship′,** *n.*

augury (ô′gyo͞o rĭ), *n., pl.* **-ries. 1.** the art or practice of an augur; divination. **2.** a rite or observation of an augur. **3.** an omen, token, or indication. [ME, t. L: m. s. *augurium*]

august (ô gŭst′), *adj.* **1.** inspiring reverence or admiration; of supreme dignity or grandeur; majestic: *an august spectacle.* **2.** venerable: *your august father.* [t. L: s. *augustus*] —**august′ly,** *adv.* —**august′ness,** *n.*

August (ô′gəst), *n.* the eighth month of the year, containing 31 days. [named after AUGUSTUS]

Augusta (ô gŭs′tə), *n.* a city in the U.S., the capital of Maine, in the SW part. 21,680 (1960).

Augustan (ô gŭs′tən), *adj.* **1.** pertaining to Augustus Caesar, the first Roman emperor, or to his reign (the **Augustan Age**), which marked the golden age of Latin literature. **2.** pertaining to the Augustan Age in Roman literature or to the highest point in the literature of any country. **3.** having some of the characteristics of Augustan literature, as classicism, correctness, brilliance, nobility. —*n.* **4.** an author in an Augustan age.

Augustine (ô gŭs′tĭn), *n.* **1. Saint** (*Austin*), A.D. 354–430, leader of the early Christian Church: author of *City of God* and *Confessions*; bishop of Hippo Regius in N Africa. **2. Saint,** died A.D. 604, Roman monk: headed group of missionaries that landed in England A.D. 597 and began the conversion of the English to Christianity; first archbishop of Canterbury. **3.** an Augustinian.

Augustinian (ô′gəs tĭn′ĭ ən), *adj.* **1.** pertaining to St Augustine (A.D. 354–430), to his doctrines, or to any religious order following his rule. —*n.* **2.** a member of any of several religious orders deriving their name and rule from St Augustine, esp. a member of the order of mendicant friars (**Hermits of St Augustine** or **Austin Friars**). **3.** one who adopts the views or doctrines of St Augustine. —**Au′gustin′ianism, Augustinism** (ô-gŭs′tĭ nĭz′əm), *n.*

Augustus (ô gŭs′təs), *n.* (*Gaius Julius Caesar Octavianus, Augustus Caesar*), 63 B.C. – A.D. 14, first Roman emperor, 27 B.C. to A.D. 14: reformer, patron of arts and literature; heir and successor to Julius Caesar. Before 27 B.C., called **Octavian.**

au jus (*Fr.* ō zhʏ′), *French.* (meat) served in its own gravy.

auk (ôk), *n.* **1.** any of certain short-winged, three-toed diving birds of the family *Alcidae* of northern seas, esp. certain species of this family, as the **razor-billed auk,** *Alca torda,* and the extinct, flightless **great auk,** *Pinguinis impennis.* **2. little auk,** a small, short-billed black and white bird, *Plautus alle,* of Greenland, Novaya Zemlya, etc. [t. Scand.: cf. Dan. *alke*]

Razor-billed auk, *Alca torda* (17 in. long)

auklet (ôk′lĭt), *n.* any of various small members of the auk family found in north Pacific waters, as the **crested auklet,** *Aethia cristatella,* and its allies.

au lait (ō lā′; *Fr.* ō lĕ′), *French.* prepared or served with milk.

auld (ôld), *adj. Scot.* old.

auld lang syne (ôld′ lăng sīn′), *Scot.* **1.** old times, esp. times fondly remembered. **2.** old or long friendship.

aulic (ô′lĭk), *adj.* pertaining to a royal court. [t. L: s. *aulicus*, t. Gk: m. *aulikós* of the court]
Aulic Council, a personal council of the Holy Roman Emperor exercising chiefly judicial powers.
aulos (ô′ləs), *n., pl.* **-loi** (-loi). an ancient Greek double-reed wind instrument.
aumbry (ôm′brĭ), *n.* ambry.
au naturel (*Fr.* ō nȧ tʏ rĕl′), *French.* **1.** in the natural state; naked. **2.** cooked plainly. **3.** uncooked.
aunt (änt), *n.* **1.** the sister of one's father or mother. **2.** the wife of one's uncle. **3.** a term of address used by children to a female friend of the family.
Aunt Sally, 1. a figure, typically of a woman smoking a pipe, at which objects are thrown at a fair. **2.** a person who is the butt of jibes, insults, etc.
aunty (än′tĭ), *n.* a familiar or diminutive form of **aunt.** Also, **auntie.**
au pair (ō pēə′; *Fr.* ō pĕr′), *French.* **1.** by exchange; used **a.** of a system whereby young people living in different countries stay in each other's homes to learn the language. **b.** of young girls, esp. foreigners, who do domestic work for a small payment and their keep. **2.** a girl or, occasionally, a boy, who does this.
aura (ô′rə), *n., pl.* **auras, aurae** (ô′rē). **1.** a distinctive air, atmosphere, character, etc.: *an aura of culture.* **2.** a subtle emanation proceeding from a body and surrounding it as an atmosphere. **3.** *Elect.* the motion of the air at an electrified point. **4.** *Pathol.* a sensation, as of a current of cold air, or other sensory experience, preceding an attack of epilepsy, hysteria, etc. [t. L, t. Gk: breath of air]
aural[1] (ô′rəl), *adj.* of or pertaining to an aura. [f. AUR(A) + -AL[1]]
aural[2] (ô′rəl), *adj.* of, or perceived by, the organs of hearing. [f. s. L *auris* ear + -AL[1]] **—au′rally,** *adv.*
Aurangzeb (ô′rəng zĕb′), *n.* 1618–1707, Mogul emperor of Hindustan 1658–1707. Also, **Aurungzeb, Aurengzebe** (ô′rəng zēb′).
aureate (ô′rĭ ĭt, -āt′), *adj.* **1.** golden. **2.** brilliant; splendid. [ME *aureat,* t. L: s. *aureātus* adorned with gold]
Aurelian (ô rē′lĭ ən, -rēl′yən), *n.* (*Lucius Domitius Aurelianus*), A.D. 212?–275, Roman emperor A.D. 270–275.
Aurelius (ô rē′lĭ əs, ô rē′lyəs), *n.* **Marcus** (mä′kəs) (*Marcus Aurelius Antoninus*), A.D. 121–180, emperor of Rome A.D. 161–180: Stoic philosopher and writer. **—Aure′lian,** *adj.*
aureole (ô′rĭ ōl′), *n.* **1.** a radiance surrounding the head or the whole figure in the representation of a sacred personage. **2.** any encircling ring of light or colour; a halo. **3.** *Astron.* corona (defs 1, 2). Also, **aureola** (ô rē′ə lə). [t. L: m. *aureola,* fem. of *aureolus* golden]
aureomycin (ô′rĭ ō mī′sĭn), *n. Med.* **1.** an antibiotic effective against diseases caused by bacteria and also by certain viruses and Rickettsia, such as typhus. **2.** (*cap.*) a trademark for this substance.
au revoir (ō′rə vwä′; *Fr.* ō rə vwȧr′), *French.* until we see each other again; goodbye for the present.
auric (ô′rĭk), *adj. Chem.* of or containing gold, esp. in the trivalent state. [f. s. L *aurum* gold + -IC]
auricle (ô′rĭ kl), *n.* **1.** *Anat.* **a.** the projecting outer portion of the ear; the pinna. **b.** one of two chambers of the heart through which blood from the veins passes into the ventricles. See diag. under **heart. 2.** *Bot., Zool.* a part like or likened to an ear. [t. L: m. s. *auricula,* dim. of *auris* ear] **—au′ricled,** *adj.*
auricula (ə rĭk′yo͝o lə), *n., pl.* **-lae** (-lē′). any of a wide variety of cultivated primulaceous plants derived from *Primula auricula,* native in the Alps.
auricular (ô rĭk′yo͝o lə), *adj.* **1.** of or pertaining to the organs of hearing. **2.** perceived by or addressed to the ear: *auricular confession.* **3.** dependent on hearing; aural. **4.** shaped like an ear; auriculate. **5.** *Anat.* pertaining to an auricle of the heart. **6.** *Ornith.* denoting certain feathers, usually of peculiar structure, which overlie and defend the outer opening of a bird's ear. **—***n.* **7.** (*usually pl.*) *Ornith.* an auricular feather.
auriculate (ô rĭk′yo͝o lĭt, -lāt′), *adj.* **1.** having auricles, or earlike parts. **2.** shaped like an ear. Also, **auric′ula′ted.**
auriferous (ô rĭf′ə rəs), *adj.* yielding or containing gold. [f. L *aurifer* gold-bearing + -OUS]
Auriga (ô rī′gə), *n.* a northern constellation containing Capella. [t. L: charioteer]
Aurignacian (ô′rĭg nā′shən), *adj.* of or belonging to a sequence of related Upper Palaeolithic cultures. [named after *Aurignac,* a village in S France where remains were first found]
Aurillac (*Fr.* ō rē yȧk′), *n.* a town in central France, the capital of Cantal department. 27,000 (est. 1962).
Auriol (*Fr.* ō ryōl′), *n.* **Vincent** (*Fr.* văɴ säɴ′), 1884–1966, president of France 1947–54.
aurist (ô′rĭst), *n.* a physician expert in treating diseases of the ear; an otologist. [f. s. L *auris* ear + -IST]
aurochs (ô′rŏks), *n., pl.* **-rochs.** a European wild ox, *Bos primigenius,* now extinct; the urus. [t. G, var. of *Auerochs,* MHG *ūr-ochse,* f. *ūr* (c. OE *ūr* wild ox) + *Ochse* ox]

Aurochs, *Bos primigenius* (Ab. 6 ft high at the shoulder)

Aurora (ô rô′rə), *n.* **1.** *Class. Myth.* dawn, often personified by the Romans and others, as a goddess (Eos). **2.** (*l.c.*) the rise or dawn of something. **3.** (*l.c.*) *Meteorol.* an electrical atmospheric phenomenon, consisting of streamers, bands, curtains, arcs, etc., of light, ordinarily confined to high altitudes; the polar lights (aurora borealis or aurora australis). [t. L]
aurora australis (ŏ strā′lĭs), *Meteorol.* the aurora of the Southern Hemisphere, a phenomenon similar to the aurora borealis. [NL]
aurora borealis (bô′rĭ ā′lĭs), *Meteorol.* the aurora of the Northern Hemisphere, a luminous meteoric phenomenon appearing at night. [NL]
auroral (ô rô′rəl), *adj.* **1.** of or like the dawn. **2.** pertaining to a polar aurora. **—auro′rally,** *adv.*
aurorean (ô rô′rĭ ən), *adj. Poetic.* belonging to the dawn; auroral.
aurous (ô′rəs), *adj.* **1.** *Chem.* containing monovalent gold. **2.** of or containing gold. [f. AUR(UM) + -OUS]
aurum (ô′rəm), *n. Chem.* gold. *Symbol:* Au.
Auschwitz (oush′vĭts; *Ger.* oush′vĭts), *n.* a town in SW Poland. 14,400 (est. 1957). Site of Nazi concentration camp during World War II. Polish, **Oświęcim.**
auscultate (ô′skəl tāt′), *v.t., v.i.,* **-tated, -tating.** *Med.* to examine by auscultation. **—auscultative** (ô′skəl-tā′tĭv, ô skŭl′tə-). **—aus′culta′tor,** *n.*
auscultation (ô′skəl tā′shən), *n.* **1.** *Med.* the act of listening, either directly or through a stethoscope or other instrument, to sounds within the body, as a method of diagnosis, etc. **2.** the act of listening. [t. L: s. *auscultātio* a listening]
Ausgleich (*Ger.* ous′glīKH), *n., pl.* **-gleiche** (*Ger.* -glī KHə). *German.* **1.** an arrangement or compromise between parties. **2.** the agreement made between Austria and Hungary in 1867, regulating the relations between the countries and setting up the Dual Monarchy.
Ausonius (ô sō′nĭ əs), *n.* **Decimus Magnus** (dĕs′ĭ məs măg′nəs), *c.* A.D. 310–395, Roman poet.
auspex (ô′spĕks), *n., pl.* **auspices** (ô′spĭ sēz′). an augur (def. 1). [t. L]
auspicate (ô′spĭ kāt′), *v.,* **-cated, -cating.** *Obs. or Rare.* **—***v.t.* **1.** to initiate with ceremonies calculated to ensure good luck; inaugurate. **—***v.i.* **2.** to augur. [t. L: m. s. *auspicātus,* pp.]
auspice (ô′spĭs), *n., pl.* **auspices** (ô′spĭ sĭz). **1.** (*usually pl.*) favouring influence; patronage: *under the auspices of the Home Office.* **2.** a propitious circumstance. **3.** a divination or prognostication, originally from birds. [t. F, t. L: m. s. *auspicium*]
auspicial (ô spĭsh′əl), *adj.* **1.** of or pertaining to auspices: *auspicial rites.* **2.** *Rare.* auspicious.
auspicious (ô spĭsh′əs), *adj.* **1.** of good omen; betokening success; favourable; an auspicious moment. **2.** favoured by fortune; prosperous; fortunate. [f. s. L *auspicium* divination + -OUS] **—auspi′ciously,** *adv.* **—auspi′ciousness,** *n.*
Aussie (ŏz′ĭ), *n. Colloq.* **1.** an Australian. **2.** Australia.
Austen (ô′stĭn, ŏs′tĭn), *n.* **Jane,** 1775–1817, English novelist.
austenite (ô′stə nīt′), *n. Metall.* the solid solution of carbon and/or alloying elements in gamma iron.
Auster (ô′stə), *n. Poetic.* the south wind personified. [t. L]
austere (ô stĭə′), *adj.* **1.** harsh in manner; stern in appearance; forbidding. **2.** severe in disciplining or restraining oneself; morally strict. **3.** grave; sober; serious. **4.** severely simple; without ornament: *austere writing.* **5.** rough to the taste; sour or harsh in flavour. [ME, t. L: m. s. *austērus,* t. Gk: m. *austērós*] **—austere′ly,** *adv.* **—austere′ness,** *n.*
austerity (ŏ stĕ′rĭ tĭ), *n., pl.* **-ties. 1.** austere quality; severity of manner, life, etc.; lack of luxury or ornament. **2.** (*usually pl.*) a severe or ascetic practice. **—***adj.* **3.** evincing austerity; adopted for the sake of, or because of, austerity. **—Syn. 2.** See **hardship.**
Austerlitz (ô′stə lĭts; *Ger.* ous′tər lĭts), *n.* a town in central Czechoslovakia, in Moravia: Napoleon defeated the combined Russian and Austrian armies here 1805.

Austin (ô′stĭn, ŏs′tĭn), *n.* **1. Alfred,** 1835–1913, English poet **2. John,** 1790–1859, English writer on law. **3.** Augustine (def. 1). **4.** a city in the U.S., the capital of Texas, in the central part, on the Colorado river. 186,545 (1960).

Austin friar. See **Augustinian** (def. 2).

austral (ô′strəl), *adj.* **1.** southern. **2.** (*cap.*) Australian. [t. L: s. *austrālis* (def. 2)]

Austral., **1.** Australasia. **2.** Australia.

Australasia (ŏs′trə lā′zhə, -shə), *n.* Australia, New Zealand, and neighbouring islands of the S Pacific Ocean. —**Aus′trala′sian,** *adj., n.*

Australia (ŏ strā′lyə), *n.* **1.** the continent SE of Asia. 2,948,366 sq. mi. **2. Commonwealth of,** a member of the Commonwealth of Nations, consisting of the federated states and territories of Australia and Tasmania. 11,135,539 pop. (est. 1964); 2,974,581 sq. mi. *Cap.:* Canberra.

Australian (ŏ strā′lyən), *adj.* **1.** of or pertaining to Australia. —*n.* **2.** a native or inhabitant of Australia. **3.** an Australian aborigine. **4.** any of the languages of the Australian aborigines. **5.** the English language as spoken in Australia.

Australian Alps, a mountain range in SE Australia. Highest peak, Mt Kosciusko, 7316 ft.

Australian ballot, *Govt.* a ballot which ensures secrecy in voting, originally used in South Australia.

Australian Capital Territory, a federal territory in SE Australia, within New South Wales: Canberra, the capital, is situated here. 80,413 pop. (est. 1964); 939 sq. mi. Formerly, **Federal Capital Territory.**

Australianism (ŏ strā′lyə nĭz′əm), *n.* an English usage originating in or peculiar to Australia.

Australian Rules, a game of football played in the southern and western states of Australia.

australopithecine (ŏs′trə lō pĭth′ĭ sēn′), *n.* **1.** a primate of the extinct genus *Australopithecus,* of the Pleistocene epoch, found first in southern Africa, having jaws resembling those of man and a skull resembling that of the apes. —*adj.* **2.** belonging or pertaining to the genus *Australopithecus.* [f. *australopithec(us)* (NL, f. *australo-,* comb. form of *australis* southern + *pithecus,* t. Gk: m. *píthēkos* ape) + -INE[1]]

Australorp (ŏs′trəlôrp′), *n.* *Austral.* an Australian breed of Orpington fowl.

Austrasia (ŏ strā′zhə, -shə), *n.* the E part of the kingdom of the Franks comprising parts of what is now NE France, W Germany, and Belgium. *Cap.:* Metz. —**Austra′sian,** *adj., n.*

Austrasia, 5th century A.D.

Austria (ŏs′trĭ ə), *n.* a country in central Europe. 7,073,807 pop. (1961); 32,381 sq. mi. *Cap.:* Vienna. German, **Österreich.** —**Aus′trian,** *adj., n.*

Austria-Hungary (ŏs′trĭ ə hŭng′ gə rĭ), *n.* a former monarchy in central Europe, including the empire of Austria, kingdom of Hungary and various crownlands: dissolved 1918. —**Austro-Hungarian** (ŏs′trō hŭng gēə′rĭ ən), *adj.*

Austria–Hungary, 1871–1914

Austro-, a word element, meaning 'Austria', 'Austrian'.

Austronesia (ŏs′trō nē′zhə, -shə), *n.* islands of the central and south Pacific. [f. *austro-* (repr. AUSTER) + s. Gk *nêsos* island + -IA]

Austronesian (ŏs′trō nē′zhən, -shən), *adj.* **1.** of or pertaining to Austronesia. —*n.* **2.** a family of languages spoken in the Pacific, consisting of four divisions, Indonesian, Melanesian, Micronesian, and Polynesian; Malayo-Polynesian.

aut-, var. of **auto-**[1] before most vowels, as in *autacoid.*

autacoid (ô′tə koid′), *n.* *Physiol.* a substance secreted by one organ into the bloodstream or lymph, and controlling organic processes elsewhere in the body; a hormone. [f. AUT- + m. s. Gk *ákos* remedy + -OID]

autarchy (ô′tä′kĭ), *n., pl.* **-chies. 1.** absolute sovereignty. **2.** self-government. **3.** autarky. [t. Gk: m. s. *autarchía* self-rule] —**autar′chic,** *adj.*

autarky (ô′tä kĭ), *n., pl.* **-kies. 1.** the condition of self-sufficiency, esp. economic, as applied to a state. **2.** a national policy of economic independence. Also, **autarchy.** [t. Gk: m. s. *autárkeia*] —**autar′kical,** *adj.* —**au′tarkist,** *n., adj.*

autecism (ô tē′sĭz əm), *n.* *U.S.* autoecism.

autecology (ô′tĭ kŏl′ə jĭ), *n.* that branch of ecology which deals with the individual organism and its environment. Cf. **synecology.**

auth., **1.** author. **2.** authorized.

authentic (ô thĕn′tĭk), *adj.* **1.** entitled to acceptance or belief; reliable; trustworthy: *an authentic story.* **2.** of the authorship or origin reputed; of genuine origin: *authentic documents.* **3.** *Law.* executed with all due formalities: *an authentic deed.* **4.** *Music.* (of a church mode) having a range extending from the final to the octave above. Cf. **plagal. 5.** *Obs.* authoritative. Also, **authen′tical.** [t. LL: s. *authenticus,* t. Gk: m. *authentikós* warranted] —**authen′tically,** *adv.*

authenticate (ô thĕn′tĭ kāt′), *v.t.,* **-cated, -cating. 1.** to make authoritative or valid. **2.** to establish as genuine. —**authenticable** (ô thĕn′tĭ kə bl), *adj.* —**authen′tica′tion,** *n.* —**authen′tica′tor,** *n.*

authenticity (ô′thĕn tĭs′ĭ tĭ), *n.* the quality of being authentic; reliability; genuineness.

author (ô′thə), *n.* **1.** a person who writes a novel, poem, essay, etc.; the composer of a literary work, as distinguished from a compiler, translator, editor, or copyist. **2.** the originator, beginner, or creator of anything. **3.** the literary production(s) of a writer: *to find a passage in an author.* [ME *autor,* t. OF, t. L: m. *auctor* originator] —**authoress** (ô′thə rĭs), *n. fem.* —**authorial** (ô thô′rĭ əl), *adj.* —**au′thorless,** *adj.*

authoritarian (ô thŏ′rĭ tēə′rĭ ən), *adj.* **1.** favouring the principle of subjection to authority as opposed to that of individual freedom. —*n.* **2.** one who favours authoritarian principles. [f. AUTHORIT(Y) + -ARIAN] —**author′itar′ianism,** *n.*

authoritative (ô thŏ′rĭ tə tĭv), *adj.* **1.** having due authority; having the sanction or weight of authority: *an authoritative opinion.* **2.** having an air of authority; positive; peremptory; dictatorial. —**author′itatively,** *adv.* —**author′itativeness,** *n.* —**Syn. 1.** conclusive, unquestioned. **2.** impressive, dogmatic.

authority (ô thŏ′rĭ tĭ), *n., pl.* **-ties. 1.** the right to determine, adjudicate, or otherwise settle issues or disputes; the right to control, command, or determine. **2.** a person or body with such rights. **3.** an accepted source of information, advice, etc. **4.** a standard author or his writing; an expert on a subject. **5.** a statute, court rule, or judicial decision which establishes a rule or principle of law; a ruling. **6.** title to respect or acceptance; commanding influence. **7.** a warrant for action; justification. **8.** testimony; witness. [ME *auctorite,* t. L: m. s. *auctōritas*] —**Syn. 1.** AUTHORITY, CONTROL, INFLUENCE denote a power or right to direct the actions or thoughts of others. AUTHORITY is a power or right, usually because of rank or office, to issue commands and to punish for violations: *to have authority over subordinates.* CONTROL is either authority or influence applied to the complete and successful direction or manipulation of persons or things: *to be in control of a project.* INFLUENCE is a personal and unofficial power derived from deference of others to one's character, ability, or station; it may be exerted unconsciously or may operate through persuasion: *to have influence over one's friends.*

authorization (ô′thə rī zā′shən), *n.* the act of authorizing; permission from or establishment by an authority. Also, **authorisation.**

authorize (ô′thə rīz′), *v.t.,* **-rized, -rizing. 1.** to give authority or legal power to; empower (to do something). **2.** to give authority for; formally sanction (an act or proceeding). **3.** to establish by authority or usage: *authorized by custom.* **4.** to afford a ground for; warrant; justify. Also, **authorise.** —**au′thoriz′er,** *n.*

authorized (ô′thə rīzd′), *adj.* **1.** authoritative; endowed with authority. **2.** legally or duly sanctioned.

Authorized Version, an English revision of the Bible prepared under James I and published in 1611.

authorling (ô′thə lĭng), *n.* an insignificant author. [f. AUTHOR + -LING[1]]

authorship (ô′thə shĭp′), *n.* **1.** the occupation or career of writing books, articles, etc. **2.** origin as to author, composer, or compiler: *the authorship of a book.*

Auth. Ver., Authorized Version (of the Bible).

autism (ô′tĭz′əm), *n.* *Psychol.* **1.** fantasy; introverted thought; daydreaming; marked subjectivity of interpretation. **2.** such a state, with introversive behaviour, noted in several psychopathological conditions. [f. AUT- + -ISM] —**autistic** (ô tĭs′tĭk), *adj.*

auto (ô′tō), *n., pl.* **-tos.** *Chiefly U.S.* automobile. [shortened form]

auto-[1], a word element meaning 'self', 'same', as in *autograph.* Also, **aut-.** [t. Gk, comb. form of *autós*]

auto-[2], a combining form of **automobile.**
auto., automobile.
Autobahn (ô′tə bän′; *Ger.* ou′tō bän), *n.*, *pl.* **-bahnen** (*Ger.* -bä nən). (in Germany) a motorway.
autobiographical (ô′tə bī′ə grăf′ĭ kl), *adj.* dealing with one's life history. Also, **au′tobi′ograph′ic.** —**au′tobi′ograph′ically,** *adv.*
autobiography (ô′tə bī ŏg′rə fĭ), *n.*, *pl.* **-phies.** an account of a person's life written by himself. —**au′tobiog′rapher,** *n.*
autocade (ô′tō kād′), *n.* *U.S.* motorcade.
autocephalous (ô′tō sĕf′ə ləs), *adj.* **1.** not under the jurisdiction of another. **2.** *Eastern Ch.* (of a church) appointing its own bishop, though still in communion with the ecumenical patriarch. [t. MGk: m. *autoképhalos* having its own head. See AUTO-[1], -CEPHALOUS] —**au′toceph′aly,** *n.*
autochthon (ô tŏk′thən), *n.*, *pl.* **-thons, -thones** (-thə nēz′). **1.** an aboriginal inhabitant. **2.** *Ecol.* one of the indigenous animals or plants of a region. [t. Gk: lit., sprung from the land itself]
autochthonous (ô tŏk′thə nəs), *adj.* pertaining to autochthons; aboriginal; indigenous. Also, **autoch′thonal, autochthonic** (ô′tŏk thŏn′ĭk). —**autoch′thonism, autoch′thony,** *n.*
autoclave (ô′tə klāv′), *n.* **1.** a heavy vessel in which chemical reactions take place under high pressure. **2.** a pressure cooker. **3.** *Med.* a strong closed vessel in which steam under pressure effects sterilization. [t. F: self-regulation, f. *auto-* AUTO-[1] + m. s. L *clāvis* key]
autocode (ô′tō kōd′), *n.* any of several language systems in which computer programs are written, as algol.
autocracy (ô tŏk′rə sĭ), *n.*, *pl.* **-cies. 1.** uncontrolled or unlimited authority over others, invested in a single person; the government or power of an absolute monarch. **2.** independent or self-derived power. [t. Gk: m. s. *autokráteia* absolute power]
autocrat (ô′tə krăt′), *n.* **1.** an absolute ruler; a monarch who holds and exercises the powers of government as by inherent right, not subject to restrictions. **2.** a person invested with, or claiming to exercise, absolute authority. [t. Gk: m. s. *autokratḗs* ruling by oneself]
autocratic (ô′tə krăt′ĭk), *adj.* pertaining to or of the nature of autocracy; absolute; holding independent and unlimited powers of government. Also, **au′tocrat′ical.** —**au′tocrat′ically,** *adv.*
auto-da-fé (ô′tō dä fā′), *n.*, *pl.* **autos-da-fé.** the public declaration of the judgement passed on persons tried in the courts of the Spanish Inquisition, followed by execution of the sentences imposed, including burning (by civil authorities) of heretics at the stake. Also, *Spanish,* **auto de fé** (*Sp.* ou′tō dĕ fĕ′). [t. Pg.: act of (the) faith]
autodidact (ô′tō dī dăkt′), *n.* a person who is self-taught. [f. AUTO-[1] + m. s. Gk *didaktós* taught] —**au′todidac′tic,** *adj.*
autodigestion (ô′tō dĭ jĕs′chən), *n.* autolysis. —**au′todiges′tive,** *adj.*
autoecism (ô tē′sĭz′əm), *n.* *Bot.* the development of the entire life cycle of a parasitic fungus on a single host or group of hosts. Also, *U.S.*, **autecism.** [f. AUT- + m. s. Gk *oikos* house + -ISM] —**autoecious** (ô tē′shəs), *adj.*
autoerotic (ô′tō ĭ rŏt′ĭk), *adj.* *Psychoanal.* producing sexual emotion without association with another person.
autoerotism (ô′tō ĕ′rə tĭz′əm), *n.* *Psychoanal.* the arousal and satisfaction of sexual emotion within or by oneself, usually by masturbation. Also, **autoeroticism** (ô′tō-ĭ rŏt′ĭ sĭz′əm).
autogamy (ô tŏg′ə mĭ), *n.* *Bot.* fecundation of the ovules of a flower by its own pollen; self-fertilization (opposed to *allogamy*). —**autog′amous,** *adj.*
autogenesis (ô′tō jĕn′ĭ sĭs), *n.* *Biol.* abiogenesis. Also, **autogeny** (ô tŏj′ĭ nĭ).
autogenetic (ô′tō jĭ nĕt′ĭk), *adj.* **1.** self-generated. **2.** *Biol.* of autogenesis. —**au′togenet′ically,** *adv.*
autogenous (ô tŏj′ĭ nəs), *adj.* **1.** self-produced; self-generated. **2.** *Physiol.* pertaining to substances generated in the body. [f. s. Gk *autogenḗs* self-produced + -OUS] —**autog′enously,** *adv.*
autogiro (ô′tō jī′ə rō′), *n.* autogyro.
autograft (ô′tə gräft′), *n.* *Med.* a graft transferred from one part of a patient's body to another.
autograph (ô′tə grăf′, -gräf′), *n.* **1.** a person's own signature. **2.** a person's own handwriting. **3.** a manuscript in the author's handwriting. —*adj.* **4.** written by a person's own hand: *an autograph letter.* **5.** containing autographs: *an autograph album.* —*v.t.* **6.** to write one's name on or in: *to autograph a book.* **7.** to write with one's own hand. [t. L: s. *autographum,* t. Gk: m. *autógraphon.* See AUTO-[1], -GRAPH] —**autographic** (ô′tə-grăf′ĭk), **au′tograph′ical,** *adj.* —**au′tograph′ically,** *adv.*
autography (ô tŏg′rə fĭ), *n.* **1.** autograph writing. **2.** exact reproduction of the outline of a drawing or writing; production of a facsimile.
autogyro (ô′tō jī′ə rō′), *n.* an aircraft with horizontally rotating blades turned in flight by air forces resulting from its forward motion. [t. Sp. See AUTO-[1], GYRO-]
autoharp (ô′tō häp′), *n.* a zither played with the fingers or a plectrum, which is capable of playing chords by arrangements of dampers and is easily learned.
autohypnosis (ô′tō hĭp nō′sĭs), *n.* self-induced hypnosis or hypnotic state. —**autohypnotic** (ô′tō hĭp nŏt′ĭk), *adj.*
autoicous (ô toi′kəs), *adj.* *Bot.* having antheridia and archegonia on the same plant: synoicous, paroicous, or otherwise. [f. AUT- + m. s. Gk *oikos* house + -OUS]
auto-ignition (ô′tō ĭg nĭsh′ən), *n.* **1.** the ignition of the fuel and air mixture in an internal-combustion engine due to the heat of the combustion chamber or to compression. **2.** spontaneous combustion.
auto-immunization (ô′tō ĭm′yŏŏ nī zā′shən), *n.* *Med.* the sensitization of a person to a substance elaborated in his own body. Also, **auto-immunisation.**
auto-infection (ô′tō ĭn fĕk′shən), *n.* *Pathol.* infection from within the body.
auto-inoculation (ô′tō ĭ nŏk′yŏŏ lā′shən), *n.* inoculation of a healthy part with an infective agent from a diseased part of the same body.
auto-intoxication (ô′tō ĭn tŏk′sĭ kā′shən), *n.* *Pathol.* poisoning with toxic substances formed within the body, as during intestinal digestion.
autokinetic (ô′tō kĭ nĕt′ĭk, -kī-), *adj.* self-moving; automatic. [f. s. Gk *autokínētos* self-moved + -IC]
Autolycus (ô tŏl′ĭ kəs), *n.* a light-hearted thief, trickster, or plagiarist; an opportunist (from the character in Shakespeare's *Winter's Tale*).
autolysin (ô′tə lī′sĭn, ô tŏl′ĭ-), *n.* an autolytic agent.
autolysis (ô tŏl′ĭ sĭs), *n.* *Biochem.* the breakdown of plant or animal tissue by the action of enzymes contained in the tissue affected; self-digestion. [f. AUTO-[1] + -LYSIS] —**autolytic** (ô′tə lĭt′ĭk), *adj.*
automat (ô′tə măt′), *n.* an automatic apparatus for serving articles, esp. food, to customers upon the dropping of the proper coins or tokens into a slot. [t. Gk: s. *autómaton.* See AUTOMATON]
automata (ô tŏm′ə tə), *n.* pl. of **automaton.**
automate (ô′tə māt′), *v.t.*, **-mated, -mating. 1.** to apply the principles of automation to (a mechanical process). **2.** to operate or control by automation. [back-formation from AUTOMATION]
automatic (ô′tə măt′ĭk), *adj.* **1.** having the power of self-motion; self-moving or self-acting; mechanical. **2.** *Physiol.* occurring independently of volition, as certain muscular actions. **3.** (of a firearm, pistol, etc.) utilizing the recoil, or part of the force of the explosive, to eject the spent cartridge shell, introduce a new cartridge, cock the arm, and fire it repeatedly. **4.** done unconsciously or from force of habit; mechanical (opposed to *voluntary*). —*n.* **5.** a machine which operates automatically. **6.** automatic rifle. **7.** automatic pistol. [f. s. Gk *autómatos* self-acting + -IC] —**au′tomat′ically,** *adv.*

—**Syn. 2.** AUTOMATIC, INVOLUNTARY both mean not under the control of the will. That which is AUTOMATIC, however, is an invariable reaction to a fixed type of stimulus: *the patella reflex is automatic.* That which is INVOLUNTARY is an unexpected response which varies according to the occasion, circumstances, mood, etc.: *an involuntary cry of pain.*

automatic computer, a digital computer.
automatic control, the control of a system by a mechanism which is capable of acting to compensate for disturbances in the system without human intervention.
automatic data processing, the use of computers and other information-handling machines to store, organize, and perform calculations on large quantities of numerical data with the minimum of human intervention. *Abbrev.:* A.D.P.
automatic dialling code, *Teleph.* the series of numbers and letters used in subscriber trunk dialling.
automatic pilot, *Aeron.* an automatic steering device in an aircraft.
automatic pistol, a pistol that has a mechanism that throws out the empty cartridge case, puts in a new one, and prepares the pistol to be fired again.
automatic rifle, a type of rifle which can be fired by single shots or several shots in succession automatically.
automatic transmission, transmission on a motor vehicle in which gear-changing is operated mechanically in accordance with car or engine speed, rather than manually by the driver.
automation (ô′tə mā′shən), *n.* **1.** the science of applying automatic control to industrial processes; the replacement of manpower by sophisticated machinery. **2.** the process or

act of automating a mechanical process. **3.** the degree to which a mechanical process is automatically controlled. [b. AUTOM(ATIC) + (OPER)ATION]

automatism (ô tŏm′ə tĭz′əm), *n.* **1.** action or condition of being automatic; mechanical or involuntary action. **2.** *Philos.* the doctrine that all activities of animals, including men, are controlled only by physiological causes, consciousness being considered a non-causal by-product; epiphenomenonalism. **3.** *Physiol.* the involuntary functioning of an organic process, esp. muscular, without neural stimulation. **4.** *Psychol.* an act performed by an individual without his awareness or will, as sleepwalking. **5.** *Surrealism.* relaxing or evading of conscious thought to bring unconscious and repressed ideas and feelings to artistic expression. —**autom′atist,** *n.*

automaton (ô tŏm′ə tən), *n., pl.* **-tons, -ta** (-tə). **1.** a mechanical figure or contrivance constructed to act as if spontaneously through concealed motive power. **2.** a person who acts in a monotonous routine manner, without active intelligence. **3.** something capable of acting spontaneously or without external impulse. [t. Gk, prop. neut. of *autómatos* self-acting]

automobile (ô′tə mə bēl′), *n.* **1.** *Chiefly U.S.* a motor car (or other self-propelled road transport vehicle). —*adj.* **2.** automotive. [t. F. See AUTO-[1], MOBILE] —**automobilist** (ô′tə mō′bĭ lĭst), *n.*

automotive (ô′tə mō′tĭv), *adj.* **1.** propelled by a self-contained power plant. **2.** *U.S.* of or pertaining to motor vehicles.

autonomic (ô′tə nŏm′ĭk), *adj.* **1.** autonomous. **2.** *Physiol.* pertaining to or designating a system of nerves and ganglia (the **autonomic, involuntary,** or **vegetative nervous system**) leading from the spinal cord and brain to glands, blood vessels, the viscera, and the heart and smooth muscles, constituting their efferent innervation and controlling their involuntary functions (opposed to *cerebrospinal*). **3.** *Bot.* produced by internal forces or causes; spontaneous. **4.** of or pertaining to autonomics. —**au′tonom′ically,** *adv.*

autonomics (ô′tə nŏm′ĭks), *n. construed as sing.* the science, study, or pratice of developing a number of self-governing systems, as within a large business organization.

autonomous (ô tŏn′ə məs), *adj.* **1.** *Govt.* **a.** self-governing; independent; subject to its own laws only. **b.** pertaining to an autonomy. **2.** independent; self-contained; self-sufficient; self-governing. **3.** *Philos.* containing its own guiding principles. **4.** *Biol.* existing as an independent organism and not as a mere form or state of development of an organism. **5.** *Bot.* spontaneous. [t. Gk: m. *autónomos*] —**auton′omously,** *adv.*

autonomy (ô tŏn′ə mĭ), *n., pl.* **-mies. 1.** *Govt.* **a.** the condition of being autonomous; self-government, or the right of self-government. **b.** a self-governing community. **2.** independence; self-sufficiency; self-regulation. **3.** *Philos.* the doctrine that the individual human will contains its own principles and laws. [t. Gk: m. s. *autonomía*] —**auton′omist,** *n.*

autonym (ô′tə nĭm), *n.* a work published under the author's own name. [f. AUT- + m. s. Gk *ónyma* name]

autoplasty (ô′tə plăs′tĭ), *n. Surg.* the repair of defects with the tissue from another part of the patient. Also, **autoplastic transplantation.** [f. s. Gk *autóplastos* self-formed + -Y[3]]

autopsy (ô′tŏp′sĭ, ô′təp-), *n., pl.* **-sies. 1.** inspection and dissection of a body after death, as for determination of the cause of death; a post-mortem examination. **2.** personal observation. [t. Gk: m. s. *autopsía* seeing with one's own eyes]

autoradiograph (ô′tō rā′dĭ ō grăf′, -grăf′), *n.* an image obtained on a photographic plate by placing on it a specimen containing a radioactive isotope. The result shows the distribution of the radioactive element in the specimen. —**autoradiography** (ô′tō rā′dĭ ŏg′rə fĭ), *n.*

autosome (ô′tə sōm′), *n. Genetics.* any chromosome other than the sex chromosome in species having both types of chromosomes.

autosuggestion (ô′tō sə jĕs′chən), *n. Psychol.* suggestion arising from within a person (as opposed to one from an outside source, esp. another person).

autotomy (ô tŏt′ə mĭ), *n. Zool.* self-crippling by casting off damaged or trapped appendages such as tails by lizards, legs by spiders and crabs, etc.

autotoxaemia (ô′tō tŏk sē′mĭ ə), *n.* auto-intoxication. Also, **au′totoxe′mia.**

autotoxin (ô′tə tŏk′sĭn), *n. Pathol.* a toxin or poisonous principle formed within the body and acting against it. —**au′totox′ic,** *adj.*

autotrophic (ô′tə trŏf′ĭk), *adj. Bot.* (of plants) building their own nutritive substances, esp. by photosynthesis or chemosynthesis.

autotruck (ô′tō trŭk′), *n. U.S.* a lorry.

autotype (ô′tə tīp′), *n.* **1.** facsimile. **2.** a photographic process for producing permanent prints in a carbon pigment. **3.** a picture so produced. —*v.t.* **4.** to produce by an autotypic process. —**autotypic** (ô′tə tĭp′ĭk), *adj.* —**autotypy** (ô′tə tī′pĭ), *n.*

autoxidation (ô tŏk′sĭ dā′shən), *n. Chem.* **1.** the oxidation of a compound by its exposure to air. **2.** an oxidation reaction in which another substance must be included for the reaction to be completed.

autumn (ô′təm), *n.* **1.** the third season of the year, between summer and winter. **2.** a period of maturity passing into decline. [t. L: s. *autumnus*; r. ME *autompne,* t. OF]

autumnal (ô tŭm′nəl), *adj.* **1.** belonging to or suggestive of autumn; produced or gathered in autumn. **2.** past maturity or middle life. —**autum′nally,** *adv.*

autumnal equinox. See **equinox** (def. 1). Also, **autumnal point.**

autumn crocus, any of several liliaceous plants of the genus *Colchicum*, producing their flowers in autumn, esp. *C. autuminale.* Also, **meadow saffron.**

autunite (ô′tə nīt′), *n.* a yellow mineral, a hydrous calcium uranium phosphate, $CaU_2P_2O_{12}.8H_2O$, occurring in crystals as nearly square tablets: a minor ore of uranium. [named after *Autun*, a town in eastern France. See -ITE[1]]

Auvergne (ō vĕən′, ō vûn′; *Fr.* ō vĕrny′), *n.* **1.** an administrative region in central France. 1,273,162 pop. (1962); 10,107 sq. mi. *Prefecture:* Clermont-Ferrand. **2.** a former province in central France.

aux (*Fr.* ō), *French.* to the; at the; with the. See **à la.**

aux., auxiliary. Also, **auxil.**

auxanometer (ôk′sə nŏm′ĭ tə), *n. Bot.* an instrument which measures the growth of plants. [f. *auxano-* (m. s. Gk *auxánein* increase) + -METER[1]]

Aux Cayes (ō kā′; *Fr.* ō kȧy′), former name of **Les Cayes.**

auxiliary (ôg zĭl′yə rĭ), *adj., n., pl.* **-ries.** —*adj.* **1.** giving support; helping; aiding; assisting. **2.** subsidiary; additional: *auxiliary troops.* **3.** used as a reserve: *an auxiliary engine.* —*n.* **4.** person or thing that gives aid of any kind; helper. **5.** auxiliary verb. **6.** (*pl.*) foreign troops in the service of a nation at war. **7.** a sailing vessel carrying auxiliary power. [t. L: m. s. *auxiliārius*, der. *auxilium* aid] —**Syn. 2.** subordinate, ancillary. **4.** ally.

auxiliary note, *Music.* a melody note not part of the harmony, to which a part moves by one step up or down in between two harmony notes.

auxiliary verb, a verb customarily preceding certain forms of other verbs, used to express distinctions of time, aspect, mood, etc., as *do, am,* etc., in I *do* think; I *am* going; we *have* spoken; *may* we go?; *can* they see?; we *shall* walk.

auxin (ôk′sĭn), *n. Bot., Chem.* a class of substances which in minute amounts regulate or modify the growth of plants, esp. root formation, bud growth, fruit and leaf drop, etc. [? var. of *auxein*, f. Gk *aúxē* increase + -IN[2]]

auxochrome (ôk′sə krōm′), *n. Chem.* any group of atoms which make a chromogen acidic or basic, giving it the ability to adhere to wool and silk. [f. *auxo-* (repr. Gk *auxánein* increase) + CHROME]

aux Sources (ō sŏŏəs′), **Mount,** a peak in S Africa, on the borders of the Orange Free State, Natal, and Lesotho. 10,822 ft.

av., **1.** average. **2.** avoirdupois.

A/V, ad valorem. Also, **a.v.**

A.V., Authorized Version (of the Bible).

avadavat (ăv′ə də văt′), *n.* amadavat.

avail (ə vāl′), *v.i.* **1.** to have force or efficacy; be of use; serve. **2.** to be of value of profit. —*v.t.* **3.** to be of use or value to; profit; advantage. **4. avail oneself of,** to give oneself the advantage of; make use of. —*n.* **5.** efficacy for a purpose; advantage to an object or end: *of little or no avail.* **6.** (*pl.*) *Now Chiefly U.S.* profits or proceeds. [ME, f. OF: *a-* A-[5] + *vail*, 1st person sing. pres. indic. of *valoir*, g. L *valēre* be strong, have effect] —**avail′ingly,** *adv.*

availability (ə vā′lə bĭl′ĭ tĭ), *n., pl.* **-ties. 1.** the state of being available: *the availability of a candidate.* **2.** that which or one who is available.

available (ə vā′lə bl), *adj.* **1.** suitable or ready for use; at hand; of use or service: *available resources.* **2.** having sufficient power or efficacy; valid. **3.** *Archaic.* profitable; advantageous. —**avail′ableness,** *n.* —**avail′ably,** *adv.* —**Syn. 1.** accessible, usable.

avalanche (ăv′ə länch′), *n., v.,* **-lanched, -lanching.** —*n.* **1.** a large mass of snow, ice, etc., detached from a mountain slope and sliding or falling suddenly downwards. **2.** anything like an avalanche in suddenness and destructiveness: *an avalanche of misfortunes.* **3.** *Physics.*

a shower of particles resulting from the collision of a high energy particle, such as a cosmic ray, with any other form of matter. —*v.i.* **4.** to come down in, or like, an avalanche. [t. F: b. d. *avaler* go down (der. L *ad-* AD- + *vallis* valley) and d. F (Swiss) *lavenche* of pre-Latin orig.]

Avalon (ăv′ə lŏn′), *n. Celtic Legend.* an island represented as an earthly paradise in the western seas, to which King Arthur and other heroes were carried at death. Also, **Avallon.** [t. ML: (m.) s. (*insula* island) *Avallōnis* (Geoffrey of Monmouth)]

avant-garde (ăv′ŏng gäd′; *Fr.* ȧ väɴ gȧrd′), *n.* **1.** the vanguard; the leaders in progress in any field, esp. the arts; the new ideas or thinkers. —*adj.* **2.** of or pertaining to the avant-garde. **3.** modern; experimental; (affectedly) ultra-modern. [t. F: vanguard]

avanturine (ə văn′tyo͞o rĭn), *n., adj.* aventurine.

Avar (ä′vä), *n.* one of a people, probably of Asiatic origin, who invaded Europe in the 6th century A.D. See map under **Byzantine Empire.**

avarice (ăv′ə rĭs), *n.* insatiable greed for riches; inordinate, miserly desire to gain and hoard wealth. [ME, t. OF, t. L: m. s. *avāritia* greed] —**Syn.** cupidity.

avaricious (ăv′ə rĭsh′əs), *adj.* characterized by avarice; greedy; covetous. —**av′ari′ciously,** *adv.* —**av′ari′ciousness,** *n.*

avast (ə väst′), *interj. Naut.* stop! hold! cease! stay! [prob. t. D: m. *houd vast* hold fast]

avatar (ăv′ə tä′), *n.* **1.** *Hindu Myth.* the descent of a deity to the earth in an incarnate form or some manifest shape; the incarnation of a god. **2.** a supreme manifestation; embodiment. [t. Skt: m. *avatāra* descent]

avaunt (ə vônt′), *adv. Archaic.* away! go! [ME, t. F: m. *avant* forward, g. L *abante* from before]

avdp., avoirdupois.

ave (ä′vĭ), *interj.* **1.** hail! welcome! —*n.* **2.** the salutation 'ave'. **3.** (*cap.*) Ave Maria. **4.** (*cap.*) the time for the recitation of the Angelus, so called because the Ave Maria is thrice repeated in it. [t. L, impv. of *avēre* be or fare well]

Ave., avenue. Also, **ave.**

Avebury (āv′bə rĭ), *n.* **1. Baron.** See **Lubbock, Sir John. 2.** a village in Wiltshire, near Stonehenge: site of a large system of prehistoric megaliths.

avec plaisir (*Fr.* ȧ vĕk plĕ zēr′), *French.* with pleasure.

Avellaneda (*Sp.* ȧ vė lyȧ nė′dȧ), *n.* a town in E Argentina, near Buenos Aires. 100,000 (est. 1964).

Ave Maria (ä′vĭ mə rĭə′), **1.** the 'Hail, Mary', a prayer in the Roman Catholic Church, based on the salutation of the angel Gabriel to the Virgin Mary and the words of Elizabeth to her. Luke 1:28, 42. **2.** the hour for saying the prayer. **3.** a recitation of this prayer. **4.** the bead or beads on a rosary used to count off each prayer as spoken. **5.** any of the numerous musical settings of the Ave Maria, for choirs, orchestra, etc. Also, **Ave Mary** (ä′vĭ mĕə′rĭ). [L: hail, Mary]

avenaceous (ăv′ĭ nā′shəs), *adj. Bot.* of or like oats; of the oat kind. [t. L: m. *avēnāceus,* der. *avēna* oats]

avenge (ə vĕnj′), *v.,* **avenged, avenging.** —*v.t.* **1.** to take vengeance or exact satisfaction for: *to avenge a death.* **2.** to take vengeance on behalf of: *avenge your brother.* —*v.i.* **3.** to take vengeance. [ME *avenge(n),* t. OF: m. *avengier,* f. *a-* A-[5] + *vengier* revenge, g. L *vindicāre* punish] —**aveng′er,** *n.* —**avenge′ment,** *n.*

—**Syn. 1, 2.** AVENGE, REVENGE both mean to inflict pain or harm in return for pain or harm inflicted on oneself or those persons or causes to which one feels loyalty. The two words were formerly interchangeable, but have been differentiated until they now convey widely diverse ideas. AVENGE is now restricted to inflicting punishment as an act of retributive justice or as a vindication of the right: *to avenge a murder by bringing the criminal to trial.* REVENGE implies inflicting pain or harm to retaliate for real or fancied wrongs; a reflexive pronoun is now usually used with this verb: *Iago wished to revenge himself upon Othello.*

avens (ăv′ĭnz), *n.* **1.** any of the perennial rosaceous herbs constituting the genus *Geum,* as the **water avens,** *G. rivale,* and **wood avens** (herb bennet). **2.** mountain avens. [ME, t. OF: m. *avence,* t. ML: m. s. *avencia* kind of clover]

Aventine (ăv′ĭn tīn′, -tĭn), *n.* one of the Seven Hills of Rome. [t. L: m. s. *Aventīnus*]

aventurine (ə vĕn′tyo͞o rĭn), *n.* **1.** an opaque, brown glass containing fine, gold-coloured particles. **2.** any of several varieties of minerals, esp. quartz or felspar, spangled with bright particles of mica, haematite, or other minerals. —*adj.* **3.** spangled; glittering. Also, **avanturine.** [t. F, t. It.: m. *avventurina,* der. *aventura* chance (the mineral being rare and found only by chance)]

avenue (ăv′ĭ nyo͞o′), *n.* **1.** the main way of approach, lined with trees, through grounds to a country house or monumental building. **2.** any double row of trees, whether lining a road or not. **3.** a wide street (sometimes lined with trees). **4.** a way or opening for entrance into a place: *the avenue to India.* **5.** means of access or attainment: *avenue of escape, avenues of success.* [t. F, orig. pp. fem. of *avenir,* g. L *advenīre* come to] —**Syn. 3.** See **street.**

aver (ə vû′), *v.t.,* **averred, averring. 1.** to affirm with confidence; declare in a positive or peremptory manner. **2.** *Law.* to allege as a fact. [ME *aver(en),* t. OF: s. *averer,* ult. der. L *ad-* AD- + *vērus* true]

average (ăv′ə rĭj, ăv′rĭj), *n., adj., v.,* **-raged, -raging.** —*n.* **1.** an arithmetical mean. **2.** *Maths.* a quantity intermediate to a set of quantities. **3.** the ordinary, normal, or typical amount, rate, quality, kind, etc.; the common run. **4.** *Com.* **a.** a small charge paid by the master on account of the ship and cargo, such as pilotage, towage, etc. **b.** an expense, partial loss, or damage to ship or cargo. **c.** the incidence of such an expense or loss on the owners or their insurers. **d.** an equitable apportionment among all the interested parties of such an expense or loss. —*adj.* **5.** of or pertaining to an average; estimated by average; forming an average. **6.** intermediate, medial, or typical in amount, rate, quality, etc. —*v.t.* **7.** to find an average value for; reduce to a mean. **8.** to result in, as an arithmetical mean; amount to, as a mean quantity: *wheat averages 56 pounds to a bushel.* —*v.i.* **9.** to have or show an average: *to average as expected.* **10. average down,** to purchase more of a security or commodity at a lower price to reduce the average cost of one's holdings. **11. average up,** to purchase more of a security or commodity at a higher price to take advantage of a contemplated further rise in prices. [cf. F *avarie* customs duty, etc. c. It. *avaria,* t. Ar.: m. *'awārīya* damages. See -AGE] —**av′eragely,** *adv.*

averment (ə vû′mənt), *n.* **1.** the act of averring. **2.** a positive statement. **3.** *Law.* an allegation.

Avernus (ə vû′nəs), *n.* **1.** a lake near Naples, Italy, looked upon by the ancients as an entrance to hell, from whose waters vile-smelling vapours arose, supposedly killing birds over it. **2.** hell. [t. L] —**Aver′nal,** *adj.*

Averroës (ə vĕ′rō ēz′), *n.* 1126?–1198, Arab philosopher in Spain: influence on Christian and Jewish thought. Arabic, **ibn-Rushd.** Also, **Averrhoës.**

Averroism (ăv′ə rō′ĭz′əm), *n.* the philosophy of Averroës, consisting chiefly of a pantheistic interpretation of the doctrines of Aristotle. Also, **Averrhoism.** —**Av′erro′ist,** *n.* —**Av′errois′tic,** *adj.*

averse (ə vûs′), *adj.* **1.** disinclined, reluctant, or opposed: *averse to* (formerly *from*) *flattery.* **2.** *Bot.* turned away from the central axis (opposed to *adverse*). [t. L: m. s. *āversus,* pp., turned away] —**averse′ly,** *adv.* —**averse′ness,** *n.* —**Syn. 1.** unwilling, loath. See **reluctant.**

aversion (ə vû′shən), *n.* **1.** an averted state of the mind or feelings; repugnance, antipathy, or rooted dislike (usually fol. by *to*). **2.** a cause of dislike; an object of repugnance. **3.** *Obs.* a turning away.

—**Syn. 1.** distaste, abhorrence. AVERSION, ANTIPATHY, LOATHING connote strong dislike or detestation. AVERSION is an unreasoning desire to avoid that which displeases, annoys, or offends: *an aversion to* (or *towards*) *cats.* ANTIPATHY is a distaste, dislike, or disgust towards something: *an antipathy towards* (or *for*) *braggarts.* LOATHING connotes a combination of hatred and disgust, or detestation: *a loathing for* (or *towards*) *venison, a criminal.*

avert (ə vût′), *v.t.* **1.** to turn away or aside: *to avert one's eyes.* **2.** to ward off; prevent: *to avert evil.* [ME, t. OF: s. *avertir,* g. L *āvertere* turn away] —**avert′er,** *n., adj.* —**avertedly** (ə vû′tĭd lĭ), *adv.*

avertin (ə vû′tĭn), *n.* **1.** tribromoethanol. **2.** (*cap.*) a trademark for it.

Aves (ā′vēz), *n.pl. Zool.* the class of vertebrates comprising the birds, distinguished from all other animals by their feathers, and from their closest relatives, the *Reptilia,* by their warm-bloodedness, the hard shell of their eggs, and significant anatomical features. [t. L, pl. of *avis* bird]

Avesta (ə vĕs′tə), *n.* the Books of Wisdom, or sacred scriptures, of Zoroastrianism.

Avestan (ə vĕs′tən), *n.* **1.** the language of the Avesta, closely related to Old Persian. —*adj.* **2.** of or pertaining to the Avesta or its language. [f. AVESTA + -AN]

Aveyron (*Fr.* ȧ vĕ rôɴ′), *n.* a department in S France. 290,442 pop. (1962); 3387 sq. mi. *Cap.:* Rodez.

avi-, a word element meaning 'bird'. [t. L, comb. form of *avis* bird]

avian (ā′vyən), *adj. Zool.* of or pertaining to birds.

aviary (ā′vyə rĭ), *n., pl.* **-ries.** a large cage or enclosure in which birds are kept. [t. L: m. s. *aviārium,* der. *avis* bird]

aviate (ā′vĭ āt′), *v.i.,* **-ated, -ating.** to fly in an aircraft. [back-formation from AVIATION]

aviation (ā′vĭ ā′shən), *n.* **1.** the act, art, or science of flying by mechanical means, esp. with heavier-than-air craft. 2. the aircraft (with equipment) of an air force. [t. F. See AVI-, -ATION]

aviator (ā′vĭ ā′tə), *n.* a pilot of an aeroplane or other heavier-than-air craft. —**aviatrix** (ā′vĭ ā′trĭks), **aviatress** (ā′vĭ ā′trĭs), *n. fem.*

Avicenna (ăv′ĭ sĕn′ə), *n.* A.D. 980–1037, Arab physician and philosopher. Arabic, **ibn-Sina.**

aviculture (ā′vĭ kŭl′chə), *n.* the rearing or keeping of birds. —**a′vicul′turist,** *n.*

avid (ăv′ĭd), *adj.* **1.** keenly desirous; eager; greedy (often fol. by *of* or *for*): *avid of pleasure or power.* **2.** keen: *avid hunger.* [t. L: s. *avidus* eager] —**av′idly,** *adv.*

avidin (ăv′ĭ dĭn, ə vĭd′ĭn), *n. Biochem.* a substance found in the white of egg which combines with biotin causing a biotin deficiency in the diet of the consumer.

avidity (ə vĭd′ĭ tĭ), *n.* eagerness; greediness.

avifauna (ā′vĭ fô′nə), *n.* the birds of a given region; avian fauna. —**a′vifau′nal,** *adj.*

Avignon (*Fr.* à vē nyôɴ′), *n.* a town in SE France, on the river Rhône: papal residence 1309–77. 75,181 (1962).

avion (*Fr.* à vyôɴ′), *n. French.* aeroplane.

avionics (ā′vĭ ŏn′ĭks), *n. Aeron.* the study and use of electronic equipment for aircraft. [f. AVI(ATION) + (ELECTR)ONICS]

avirulent (ă vĭ′ro͞o lənt), *adj.* (of organisms) having no virulence, as a result of age, heat, etc.

aviso (ə vī′zō), *n., pl.* **-sos. 1.** dispatch. **2.** a boat used esp. for carrying dispatches. [t. Sp.]

avitaminosis (ā vĭt′ə mĭ nō′sĭs, ăv′ĭ tăm′ĭ-), *n. Pathol.* a disease caused by a lack of vitamins. [f. A-[6] + VITAMIN + -OSIS]

Avlona (ăv lō′nə), *n.* Valona.

A.V.M., air vice-marshal.

avocado (ăv′ə kä′dō), *n., pl.* **-dos. 1.** a tropical American fruit, green to black in colour and commonly pear-shaped, borne by the lauraceous tree, *Persea americana*, and its variety *drymifolia*, eaten raw, esp. as a salad fruit; alligator pear. **2.** the tree. Also, **avocado pear.** [t. d. Sp. (lit., lawyer) alter. of *oguacate*, t. Nahuatl: m. *ahuacatl* lit., testicle]

Avocado, *Persea americana*

avocation (ăv′ə kā′shən), *n.* **1.** minor or occasional occupations; hobbies. **2.** (*also pl.*) one's regular occupation, calling, or vocation. **3.** diversion or distraction. [t. L: s. *āvocātio* a calling off]

avocatory (ə vŏk′ə tə rĭ, -trĭ), *adj.* calling away, off, or back.

avocet (ăv′ə sĕt′), *n.* any of several long-legged, web-footed shorebirds constituting the *Recurvirostra*, having a long, slender beak curving upwards towards the end. Also, **avoset.** [t. F: m. *avocette*, t. It.: m. *avocetta*]

Avogadro (*It.* à vò gà′drò), *n.* **Count Amadeo** (*It.* à mà dĕ′ò), 1776–1856, Italian physicist and chemist.

Avogadro's hypothesis, *Chem.* the hypothesis which states that equal volumes of gases under the same conditions of temperature and pressure contain equal numbers of molecules. Cf. **Avogadro's number.**

Avogadro's number, *Chem.* the number of molecules in a gram-molecule or atoms in a gram-atom; $6{\cdot}02257 \times 10^{23}$. Also, **Avogadro's constant.**

avoid (ə void′), *v.t.* **1.** to keep away from; keep clear of; shun; evade: *to avoid a person or a danger.* **2.** *Law.* to make void or of no effect; invalidate. **3.** *Obs.* to empty; eject or expel. —*v.i.* **4.** *Obs.* to go away; leave. [ME *avoide(n)*, t. AF: m. *avoider*, var. of OF *esvuidier* empty out; f. *es-* EX-[1] + *vuidier* (g. L *viduāre*) empty. See VOID, *adj.*] —**avoid′able,** *adj.* —**avoid′ably,** *adv.* —**avoid′er,** *n.*

—**Syn. 1.** AVOID, ESCAPE mean to come through peril, actual or potential, without suffering serious consequences. To AVOID is to succeed in keeping away from something harmful or undesirable: *to avoid meeting an enemy.* ESCAPE suggests encountering peril but coming through it safely: *to escape drowning.*

avoidance (ə voi′dns), *n.* **1.** the act of keeping away from: *avoidance of scandal.* **2.** *Law.* a making void. **3.** tax avoidance.

avoir., avoirdupois.

avoirdupois (ăv′ə də poiz′, ăv′wä dyo͞o pwä′), *n.* **1.** avoirdupois weight. **2.** *U.S. Colloq.* weight; heaviness. [ME *avoir de pois*, t. OF: goods sold by weight, lit., to have weight]

avoirdupois weight, the system of weights in British and U.S. use for goods other than gems, precious metals, and drugs: $27^{11}/_{32}$ grains = 1 dram; 16 drams = 1 ounce; 16 ounces = 1 pound; 112 pounds (Brit.) or 100 pounds (U.S.) = 1 hundredweight; 20 hundredweight = 1 ton. The pound contains 7000 grains.

Avon (ā′vən), *n.* **1. Earl of.** See **Eden, (Robert) Anthony. 2.** a river in central England, flowing SE past Stratford to the Severn. 80 mi. **3.** a river in S England, flowing W to the mouth of the Severn. 75 mi. **4.** a river in S England, flowing S to the English Channel. ab. 60 mi.

avoset (ăv′ə sĕt′), *n.* avocet.

à votre santé (*Fr.* à vŏ trə säɴ tĕ′), *French.* to your health.

avouch (ə vouch′), *v.t. Archaic.* **1.** to make frank affirmation of; declare or assert with positiveness. **2.** to assume responsibility for; guarantee. **3.** to admit; confess. [ME *avouche(n)*, t. OF: m. *avochier*, t. L: m. *advocāre* summon] —**avouch′ment,** *n.*

avow (ə vou′), *v.t.* **1.** to admit or acknowledge frankly or openly; own; confess. **2.** to state; assert; affirm; declare. [ME *avowe(n)*, t. OF: m. *avoer*, g. L *advocāre* summon] —**avow′able,** *adj.* —**avow′er,** *n.*

avowal (ə vou′əl), *n.* **1.** frank acknowledgement or admission. **2.** open declaration; assertion; affirmation.

avowed (ə voud′), *adj.* acknowledged; declared: *an avowed enemy.* —**avowedly** (ə vou′ĭd lĭ), *adv.* —**avow′edness,** *n.*

avulsed (ə vŭl′sĭd), *adj. Surg.* (of a wound) having the tissue torn away.

avulsion (ə vŭl′shən), *n.* **1.** a tearing away. **2.** *Law.* the sudden removal of soil by change in a river's course or by a flood, from the land of one owner to that of another. **3.** a part torn off. [t. L: s. *āvulsio*]

avuncular (ə vŭng′kyo͞o lə), *adj.* of or pertaining to an uncle; like an uncle; *avuncular affection.* [f. s. L *avunculus* uncle (dim. of *avus* grandfather) + -AR[1]]

a.w., atomic weight.

awa (ə wô′, ə wä′), *adv. Scot.* away.

await (ə wāt′), *v.t.* **1.** to wait for; look for or expect. **2.** to be in store for; be ready for. **3.** *Obs.* to lie in wait for. —*v.i.* **4.** *Chiefly U.S.* to wait, as in expectation. [ME *awaite(n)*, t. ONF: m. *awaitier*, f. *a-* A-[5] + *waitier* watch. See WAIT] —**Syn. 1.** See **expect.**

awake (ə wāk′), *v.,* **awoke** or **awaked, awaking,** *adj.* —*v.t., v.i.* **1.** to wake; wake up. **2.** to come or bring to a realization of the truth; to rouse to action, attention, etc.: *he awoke to the realities of life.* —*adj.* **3.** waking not sleeping. **4.** vigilant; alert: *awake to a danger.* [ME; OE weak v. *awacian* and (for pret. and pp.) OE strong v. *onwæcnan*, later *awæcnan* (pret. *onwōc*, *awōc*, pp. *onwacen*, *awacen*)]

awaken (ə wā′kən), *v.t., v.i.* to waken. [ME *awak(e)ne(n)*, OE *onwæcnian*, later *awæcnian*] —**awak′ener,** *n.*

awakening (ə wā′kə nĭng), *adj.* **1.** rousing; reanimating; alarming. —*n.* **2.** the act of awaking from sleep. **3.** an arousal or revival of interest or attention; a waking up, as from indifference, ignorance, etc.

award (ə wôd′), *v.t.* **1.** to adjudge to be due or merited; assign or bestow: *to award prizes.* **2.** to bestow by judicial decree; assign or appoint by deliberate judgement, as in arbitration. —*n.* **3.** something awarded, as a payment or medal. **4.** *Law.* **a.** the decision of arbitrators on points submitted to them. **b.** a decision after consideration; a judicial sentence. [ME *awarde(n)* t. AF: m. *awarder*, var. of *esguarder* observe, decide, f. L: *ex-* EX-[1] + *guardāre* watch, guard, of Gmc orig.] —**award′able,** *adj.* —**award′er,** *n.*

aware (ə wĕə′), *adj.* cognizant or conscious (*of*); informed: *aware of the danger.* [ME; OE *gewær* watchful. See WARE[2], WARY] —**aware′ness,** *n.* —**Syn.** See **conscious.**

awash (ə wŏsh′), *adv., adj.* **1.** *Naut.* just level with the surface of the water, so that the waves break over. **2.** covered with water. **3.** washing about; tossed about by the waves.

away (ə wā′), *adv.* **1.** from this or that place; off: *to go away.* **2.** apart; at a distance: *to stand away from the wall.* **3.** aside: *turn your eyes away.* **4.** out of possession, notice, use, or existence: *to give money away.* **5.** continuously; on: *to blaze away.* **6.** without hesitation: *fire away.* **7.** immediately; forthwith: *right away.* **8. away with,** take away: *away with this man.* **9. do** or **make away with,** to put out of existence; get rid of; kill. —*adj.* **10.** absent: *away from home.* **11.** distant: *six miles away.* **12.** *Colloq.* on the move; having started; in full flight. **13.** *Sport.* **a.** (played) on the opponents' ground. **b.** *Racing.* of or pertaining to the outward or first half of the race. —*interj.* **14.** go away! depart! [ME; OE *aweg*, earlier *on weg* on way]

awe (ô), *n., v.,* **awed, awing.** —*n.* **1.** respectful or reverential fear, inspired by what is grand or sublime: *in awe of God.* **2.** *Archaic.* power to inspire fear or reverence. **3.** *Obs.* fear or dread. —*v.t.* **4.** to inspire with awe. **5.** to influence or restrain by awe. [ME, t. Scand.; cf. Icel. *agi* fear]

aweather (ə wĕth′ə), *adv., adj. Naut.* on or to the weather side of a vessel; in the direction of the wind (opposed to *alee*).

aweigh (ə wā′), *adj.* *Naut.* (of an anchor) raised just enough to be clear of the bottom.

awe-inspiring (ô′ĭn spī′ə rĭng), *adj.* **1.** filling one with awe. **2.** worthy of awe; magnificent. **3.** *Colloq.* amazing; exciting; worthy of amazement, excitement, or admiration: *not an awe-inspiring performance.*

aweless (ô′lĭs), *adj.* without awe; fearless; not to be awed. Also, *U.S.*, **awless.**

awesome (ô′səm), *adj.* **1.** inspiring awe. **2.** characterized by awe. —**awe′somely,** *adv.* —**awe′someness,** *n.*

awe-struck (ô′strŭk′), *adj.* filled with awe. Also, **awe-stricken** (ô′strĭk′ən).

awful (ô′fəl), *adj.* **1.** *Colloq.* extremely bad; unpleasant; ugly. **2.** *Colloq.* very; very great. **3.** inspiring fear; dreadful; terrible. **4.** full of awe; reverential. **5.** inspiring reverential awe; solemnly impressive. [ME; f. AWE + -FUL, r. OE *egeful* dreadful] —**aw′fully,** *adv.* —**aw′fulness,** *n.*

awhile (ə wīl′), *adv.* for a short time or period.

awkward (ô′kwəd), *adj.* **1.** lacking dexterity or skill; clumsy; bungling. **2.** ungraceful; ungainly; uncouth: *awkward gestures.* **3.** ill-adapted for use or handling; unhandy: *an awkward method.* **4.** requiring caution; somewhat hazardous: *there's an awkward step there.* **5.** difficult to handle; dangerous: *an awkward customer.* **6.** embarrassing or trying: *an awkward predicament.* **7.** deliberately obstructive, difficult, or perverse. **8.** *Obs.* oblique; backward; inverted. [f. *auk* backhanded (t. Scand.; cf. Icel. *öfugr* turned the wrong way) + -WARD] —**awk′wardly,** *adv.* —**awk′wardness,** *n.* —**Syn. 1.** unskilful, unhandy, inexpert; inept.

awl (ôl), *n.* *Carp., etc.* a pointed instrument for piercing small holes in leather, wood, etc. [ME *al*, OE *æl*, c. G *Ahle*]

Awls
A, Bradawl;
B, Sewing awl

awless (ô′lĭs), *adj.* *U.S.* aweless.

awlwort (ôl′wût′), *n.* a small stemless, aquatic cruciferous plant, *Subularia aquatica*, with slender, sharp-pointed leaves.

awn (ôn), *n.* *Bot.* **1.** a bristle-like appendage of a plant, esp. on the glumes of grasses. **2.** such appendages collectively, as those forming the beard of wheat, barley, etc. **3.** any similar bristle. [ME, t. Scand.; cf. Sw. *agn*, Icel. *ögn* husk] —**awned,** *adj.* —**awn′less,** *adj.*

awning (ô′nĭng), *n.* **1.** a rooflike shelter of canvas, etc., before a window or door, over a deck, etc., as for protection from the sun. **2.** a shelter. [orig. unknown]

awoke (ə wōk′), *v.* pt. and (*Rare or Dial.*) pp. of **awake.**

A.W.O.L. (*pronounced as initials or, in Mil. Slang.* ā′wŏl), *Mil.* absent without leave.

awry (ə rī′), *adv., adj.* **1.** with a turn or twist to one side; askew: *to glance or look awry.* **2.** away from reason or the truth. **3.** amiss; wrong: *our plans went awry.* [ME *on wry.* See A-[1], WRY]

ax., axiom.

axe (ăks), *n., pl.* **axes,** *v.,* **axed, axing.** —*n.* **1.** an instrument with a bladed head on a handle or helve, used for hewing, cleaving, chopping, etc. **2. have an axe to grind,** to have a private purpose or selfish end to attain. **3. the axe,** *Colloq.* **a.** a drastic cutting down (of expenses). **b.** dismissal from a job, position, or the like: the sack. —*v.t.* **4.** to shape or trim with an axe. **5.** *Colloq.* to cut down; reduce (expenditure, prices, etc.) sharply. Also, *Chiefly U.S.*, **ax.** [ME; OE *æx*, akin to G *Axt*, L *ascia*, Gk *axínē*] —**axe′like′,** *adj.*

axeman (ăks′mən), *n., pl.* **-men** (-mən). **1.** one who wields an axe. **2.** *Colloq.* a personnel officer or the like, one of whose duties is to dismiss staff. Also, *Chiefly U.S.*, **axman.**

axes[1] (ăk′sēz), *n.* pl. of **axis.**

axes[2] (ăk′sĭz), *n.* pl. of **axe.**

axial (ăk′sĭ əl), *adj.* **1.** of, pertaining to, or forming an axis. **2.** situated in an axis or on the axis. Also, **axile** (ăk′sĭl, -sīl).

axially (ăk′sĭ ə lĭ), *adv.* in the line of the axis.

axil (ăk′sĭl), *n.* *Bot.* the angle between the upper side of a leaf or stem and the supporting stem or branch. [t. L: m. s. *axilla* armpit]

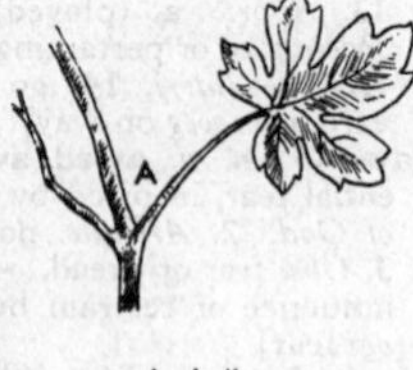

A, Axil

axilla (ăk sĭl′ə), *n., pl.* **axillae** (ăk sĭl′ē). **1.** *Anat.* the armpit. **2.** *Ornith.* the corresponding region on a bird. **3.** *Bot.* an axil. [t. L]

axillary (ăk sĭl′ə rĭ), *adj., n., pl.* **-aries.** —*adj.* **1.** pertaining to the axilla. **2.** *Bot.* pertaining to or growing from the axil (of plants). —*n.* **3.** *Ornith.* (*usually pl.*) a feather growing from the axilla (def. 2). Also, **axil′lar.**

axiology (ăk′sĭ ŏl′ə jĭ), *n.* *Philos.* the science of values in general, including ethics, aesthetics, religion, etc. [f. Gk *áxio(s)* worthy + -LOGY] —**axiological** (ăk′sĭ ə lŏj′ĭ kl), *adj.*

axiom (ăk′sĭ əm), *n.* **1.** a recognized truth. **2.** an established and universally accepted principle or rule. **3.** *Logic, Maths., etc.* a proposition which is assumed without proof for the sake of studying the consequences that follow from it. [t. L: m. *axiōma*, t. Gk: a requisite]

axiomatic (ăk′sĭ ə măt′ĭk), *adj.* **1.** pertaining to or of the nature of an axiom; self-evident. **2.** aphoristic. Also, **ax′iomat′ical.** —**ax′iomat′ically,** *adv.*

axis[1] (ăk′sĭs), *n., pl.* **axes** (ăk′sēz). **1.** the line about which a rotating body, such as the earth, turns. **2.** the central line of any symmetrical, or nearly symmetrical, body: *the axis of a cylinder, of the eye, etc.* **3.** a fixed line adopted for reference, as in plotting a curve on a graph, in crystallography, etc. **4.** *Anat.* **a.** a central or principal structure, about which something turns or is arranged: *the skeletal axis.* **b.** the second cervical vertebra. **5.** *Bot.* the longitudinal support on which organs or parts are arranged; the stem, root; the central line of any body. **6.** *Aeron.* any one of three lines defining the lines of an aeroplane, one being generally determined by the direction of forward motion and the other two at right angles to it. **7.** *Fine Arts.* one or more theoretical central lines around which an artistic form is organized or composed. **8.** an alliance of two or more nations to coordinate their foreign and military policies, and to draw in with them a group of dependent or supporting powers. **9. the Axis,** the alliance of Germany, Italy, and Japan prior to and during World War II, beginning with the Rome–Berlin Axis (1936). [t. L: axle, axis, board. Cf. AXLE]

axis[2] (ăk′sĭs), *n.* any of several species of East Asiatic deer, as *Axis axis* and related forms, with white spots. Also, **axis deer.** [t. L]

axis of symmetry, *Maths.* a straight line for which every point on a given curve has corresponding to it another point such that the line connecting the two points is bisected by the given line.

axle (ăk′səl), *n.* **1.** *Mach.* the pin, bar, shaft, or the like, on which or with which a wheel or pair of wheels rotate. **2.** either end (spindle) of an axletree or the like. **3.** the whole (fixed) axletree, or a similar bar connecting and turning with two opposite wheels of a vehicle. [OE *eaxl(e)* shoulder, crossbeam (in *eaxle-gespann* crossbeam attachment place). Cf. Icel. *öxl* shoulder, axle]

axletree (ăk′səl trē′), *n.* a bar fixed crosswise under a vehicle, with a rounded spindle at each end upon which a wheel rotates. [ME, f. AXLE + TREE]

axman (ăks′mən), *n.; pl.* **-men** (-mən). *Chiefly U.S.* axeman.

Axminster carpet (ăks′mĭn′stə), a kind of carpet having a stiff jute back and a cut pile of wool. [named after *Axminster*, a town in Devonshire]

axolotl (ăk′sə lŏt′l, ăk′sə lŏt′l), *n.* **1.** any of several Mexican salamanders that breed in the larval stage, in Mexico prized as food. **2.** the larva of any salamander (esp. of the genus *Ambystoma*) that matures sexually in the larval stage. [t. Nahuatl]

Axolotl, *Ambystoma mexicanus* (6 to 12 in. long)

axon (ăk′sŏn), *n.* *Anat.* the appendage of the neuron which transmits impulses away from the cell. Also, **axone** (ăk′sōn). See diag. under **nerve cell.** [t. Gk: axis]

axonometric (ăk′sə nə mĕt′rĭk), *adj.* (of a projection, drawing, etc.) having all lines in a representation of a three-dimensional object drawn to scale, resulting in the optical distortion of diagonals and curves.

Axum (äk′so͞om), *n.* Aksum.

ay[1] (ī), *adv., n., pl.* **ayes.** —*adv.* **1.** yes. —*n.* **2.** an affirmative vote or voter, esp. in the House of Commons. Also, **aye.** [earlier *I*, ? var. of ME *yie*, OE *gī* YEA (with loss of *y* as in IF)]

ay[2] (ā), *interj.* *Archaic or Dial.* ah! oh! [ME *ey*, m. phrase *ay me*, t. F: m. *ahi, aï.* Cf. It. *ahime*, Sp. *ay de mi*]

ay[3] (ā), *adv., n.* aye[1].

Ayacucho (ä′yə ko͞o′chō; *Sp.* ä yä ko͞o′chô), *n.* a town in SW Peru: victory of Bolívar near here ended Spain's domination in the New World, 1824. 22,000 (1961).

ayah (ī′ə), *n.* (in India) a native maid or nurse. [t. Hind.: m. *āya*, t. Pg.: m. *aia*, fem. of *aio* tutor]

Aydin (*Turk.* äy′dĭn), *n.* a town in W Turkey, SE of Izmir: ancient ruins. Also, **Aidin.**

aye[1] (ā), *adv. Poetic or Dial.* ever; always. Also, **ay.** [ME *ei*, *ai*, t. Scand.: cf. Icel. *ei*, c. OE *ā* ever]

aye[2] (ī *or* ā), *adv.* ay[1].

aye-aye (ī′ī′), *n.* a nocturnal lemur, *Daubentonia madagascariensis*, of Madagascar, about the size of a cat and with rodent-like front teeth. [t. F, t. Malagasy: m. *aiay*; prob. imit. of its cry]

Aye-aye, *Daubentonia madagascariensis* (Total length, 3 ft, 8 in. high)

Ayer (ĕə), *n.* **A(lfred) J(ules),** born 1910, English philosopher and teacher.

Ayers Rock (ĕəz), the largest monolith in the world, in Northern Territory, Australia; 1100 ft high; 5½ mi. round at the base.

Ayesha (ä′ĭ shə), *n.* Aisha.

Aylesbury (ālz′bə rĭ, -brĭ), *n.* **1.** a town in England, in Buckinghamshire. 34,680 (1964). **2.** Also, **Aylesbury duck.** one of a breed of white, domestic ducks.

Aymara (ī′mə rä′; *Sp.* ȧy mȧ rȧ′), *n.* an important Indian nationality and speech group in Bolivia and Peru, still existing around Lake Titicaca. **—Aymaran** (ī′mə răn′), *adj.*

Aymé (*Fr.* ĕ mē′), *n.* **Marcel** (*Fr.* mȧr sĕl′), born 1902, French novelist.

Ayr (ĕə), *n.* **1.** a seaport in Scotland, the county town of Ayrshire. 45,697 (est. 1964). **2.** Ayrshire.

Ayr., Ayrshire.

ayre (ĕə), *n. Archaic.* air (def. 8).

Ayrshire (ĕə′shĭə, -shə), *n.* **1.** Also, **Ayr.** a county in SW Scotland. 347,389 pop. (1961); 1132 sq. mi. *Co. town:* Ayr. **2.** one of a hardy breed of dairy cattle, well-muscled, of medium size, brown and white in colour, originating in the county of Ayr.

Ayub Khan (ī yo͞ob′ kän′, ī′yo͞ob), **Mohammed** (mō hăm′ĭd), born 1908, Pakistani field marshal and statesman: president of Pakistan 1958–69.

Ayuthia (ä yo͞o′thĭ ə), *n.* a city in central Thailand, on the Menam: former capital of the country. 15,821 (1963). Also, **Ayudhya** (ä yo͞o′dyə), **Ayutthaya** (ä yo͞o′tə yə).

az-, var. of **azo-** used before vowels, as in *azole*.

azalea (ə zā′lyə), *n.* any plant of a particular group (*Azalea*) of the ericaceous genus *Rhododendron*, comprising species with handsome, variously coloured flowers, some of which are familiar in cultivation. *Azalea* was once a botanical genus but is now a nursery or horticultural classification. [t. NL, t. Gk: (fem. adj.) dry; so named as growing in dry soil]

azan (ä zän′), *n.* (in Muslim countries) the call to prayer, proclaimed by the crier (muezzin) from the minaret of a mosque five times daily. [t. Ar.: m. *adhān* invitation. See MUEZZIN]

Azaña y Díez (*Sp.* ȧ thȧ′nyȧ ē dē′ĕth), **Manuel** (*Sp.* mȧn wĕl′), 1880–1940, Spanish statesman: prime minister 1931–33, 1936; president 1936–39.

Azazel (ə zā′zəl, ăz′ə zĕl′), *n.* **1.** the leader of the rebellious sons of God who entered into sexual relations with the daughters of men. Gen. 6:1–4. **2.** (in Arabic writers) one of the jinn imprisoned by the angels for their transgressions.

azedarach (ə zĕd′ə răk′), *n.* the chinaberry. [t. F: m. *azédarac*, ult. der. Pers. *āzād dirakht* noble tree]

azeotrope (ə zē′ə trōp′), *n. Phys. Chem.* any solution having constant minimum and maximum boiling points. [f. A-[6] + *zeo-* (comb. form repr. Gk *zeîn* boil) + -TROPE]

Azerbaijan (äz′ə bī-jän′), *n.* **1.** Official name, **Azerbaijan Soviet Socialist Republic.** one of the constituent republics of the Soviet Union, in Caucasia. 4,200,000 pop. (est. 1963); ab. 33,000 sq. mi. *Cap.:* Baku. **2.** a province in NW Iran. 3,500,000 pop. (est. 1964); ab. 35,000 sq. mi. *Cap.:* Tabriz. Also, **Azerbaidzhan.**

Azerbaijan Soviet Socialist Republic

Azerbaijani (äz′ə bī jä′nĭ), *n., pl.* **-nis,** (*esp. collectively*) **-ni. 1.** a native or inhabitant of Azerbaijan. **2.** a member of a Turkic-speaking people of Azerbaijan both in the Soviet Union and in NW Iran. **3.** the Turkic language of the Azerbaijani. **—***adj.* **4.** of or pertaining to the Azerbaijani people or language. Also, **Azerbaijanian** (äz′ə-bī jä′nyən).

azide (ā′zīd), *n. Chem.* a salt, or other derivative, of hydrazoic acid, many of which are explosive.

Azikiwe (ă zē′kĭ wā′, -kwā, äz′ĭ kē′wā), *n.* **Nnamdi** (ən-năm′dĭ), born 1904, president of the Federal Republic of Nigeria 1963–66.

azimuth (ăz′ĭ məth), *n.* **1.** *Astron., Navig.* the arc of the horizon from the celestial meridian to the foot of the great circle passing through the zenith, the nadir, and the point of the celestial sphere in question (in astronomy commonly reckoned from the south point of the horizon towards the west point: in navigation reckoned from the north point of the horizon towards the east point). **2.** *Survey., Gunnery, etc.* an angle measured clockwise from the south or north. [ME *azimut*, t. OF, t. Ar.: m. *assumūt*, f. *as* (= *al*) the + *sumūt*, pl. of *samt* way] **—azimuthal** (ăz′ĭ mŭth′əl), *adj.* **—az′imuth′ally,** *adv.*

azimuthal projection, *Cartog.* a map projection based on the concept of projecting the earth's surface on to a tangent plane surface; zenithal projection.

azine (ăz′ēn, -ĭn), *n. Chem.* any of a group of organic compounds having six atoms, one or more of them nitrogen, arranged in a ring, the number of nitrogen atoms being indicated by a prefix, as in *diazine, triazine, tetrazine.* Also, **azin** (ăz′ĭn). [f. AZ- + -INE[2]]

azo-, *Chem.* a word element meaning nitrogen. [t. Gk: s. *ázōos* lifeless] **—azo** (ăz′ō), *adj.*

azobenzene (ăz′ō bĕn′zēn, -bĕn zēn′), *n. Chem.* an orange-red crystalline substance, $C_6H_5N = NC_6H_5$, obtained from nitrobenzene in an alkaline solution.

azo dye, *Chem.* any of a large group of synthetic colouring substances which contain the **azo group,** —N=N—.

azoic (ə zō′ĭk), *adj. Geol.* pertaining to geologic time before life appeared. [f. s. Gk *ázōos* lifeless + -IC]

azole (ăz′ōl, ə zōl′), *n. Chem.* any of a group of organic compounds having five atoms, one or more of them nitrogen, arranged in a ring. The number of nitrogen atoms is indicated by a prefix, as in *diazole.* [f. AZ- + -OLE]

azonal soil (ā zō′nəl), *n. Geol.* one of a group of immature soils on which climate and vegetation have had little influence.

azonic (ā zŏn′ĭk), *adj.* not confined to any particular zone or region; not local.

Azores (ə zôz′), *n.* a group of islands in the N Atlantic, W of and belonging to Portugal. 350,000 pop. (1964); 890 sq. mi.

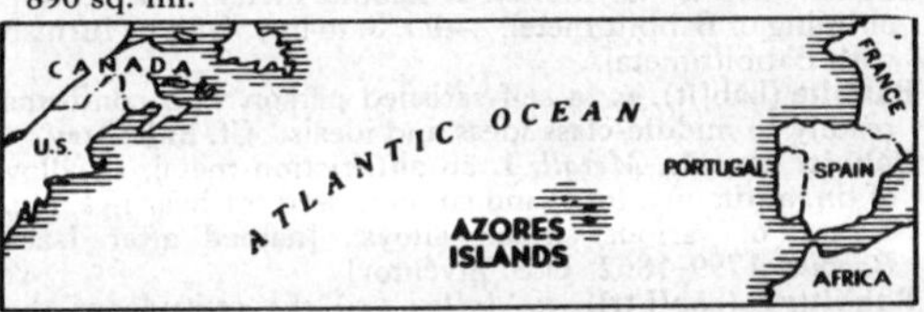

Azores Islands

Azorín (*Sp.* ȧ thō rēn′), *n.* (*José Martinez Ruiz*), 1874–1967, Spanish novelist, dramatist, and critic.

azote (ăz′ōt, ə zōt′), *n. Obs.* nitrogen. [t. F, t. Gk: m. s. *ázōtos*, prop., ungirt (mistakenly thought to mean lifeless, the gas being unfit to support life in respiration)] **—azoted** (ăz′ō tĭd, ə zō′tĭd), *adj.*

azoth (ăz′ŏth), *n. Alchemy.* **1.** mercury, as the assumed first principle of all metals. **2.** the universal remedy of Paracelsus. [t. F, var. of *azoch*, t. Ar.: m. *az zāwūq* the mercury]

azotic (ə zŏt′ĭk), *adj.* of or pertaining to azote; nitric.

azotize (ăz′ə tīz′), *v.t.,* **-tized, -tizing.** to nitrogenize. Also, **azotise.**

Azov (ä′zŏv; *Russ.* ȧ zôf′), *n.* **Sea of,** a sea NE of the Black Sea and connected with it by Kerch Strait. ab. 14,500 sq. mi. Also, **Azof.** See map under **Black Sea.**

Azrael (ăz′rāl, ăz′rĭ əl), *n.* (in Jewish and Muslim angelology) the angel who separates the soul from the body at the moment of death.

Aztec (ăz′tĕk), *n.* **1.** a member of an Indian people dominant in Central Mexico at the time of the Spanish invasion (1519). **2.** a Uto-Aztecan language of the Nahuatl subgroup, still extensively spoken in Mexico; Nahuatl. **—Az′tecan,** *adj.*

azure (ăzh′ə, ăz′yo͞oə), *adj.* **1.** of a sky blue colour. **—***n.* **2.** the blue of an unclouded sky. **3.** a blue pigment, now esp. cobalt blue. **4.** the sky. [ME, t. OF: m. *azur*, t. Ar.: m. *lāzward*, t. Pers.: m. *lajward* lapis lazuli]. **—az′ury,** *adj.*

azurite (ăzh′o͝o rīt′), *n.* **1.** a blue mineral, a hydrous copper carbonate $[Cu_3(CO_3)_2(OH)_2]$, an ore of copper; chessylite. **2.** a gem of moderate value, ground from this mineral.

azygous (ăz′ĭ gəs), *adj. Zool., Bot.* not being one of a pair; single. [t. Gk: m. *ázygos*]

B

B, b (bē), *n., pl.* **B's** or **Bs, b's** or **bs. 1.** the second letter of the English alphabet. **2.** the second in any series: *schedule B.* **3.** the second highest mark for school, college, or university work; beta. **4.** *Music.* **a.** the seventh degree in the scale of C major or the second degree in the relative minor scale (A minor). **b.** a written or printed note representing this tone. **c.** a key, string, or pipe tuned to this note. **d.** (in solmization) the seventh note of the scale of C, called **te.**

B, *Chem.* boron.

B., 1. bay. **2.** Bible. **3.** British. **4.** Brotherhood.

b., 1. born. **2.** bass. **3.** basso. **4.** blend of; blended. **5.** book. **6.** *Cricket.* bowled. **7.** breadth. **8.** brother. **9.** (euphemistic for) any obscene or taboo word beginning with b.

Ba, *Chem.* barium.

B.A., 1. (L *Baccalaureus Artium*) Bachelor of Arts. **2.** British America. **3.** British Association.

baa (bä), *v.,* **baaed, baaing,** *n.* —*v.i.* **1.** to cry as a sheep; bleat. —*n.* **2.** the bleating of a sheep. [imit.]

baal (bäl), *adv., interj. Austral.* no; not. [t. native Australian]

Baal (bā′əl, bāl), *n., pl.* **Baalim** (bā′ə lĭm). **1.** any of numerous local deities among the ancient Semitic peoples, typifying the productive forces of nature and worshipped with much sensuality. **2.** a solar deity, the chief god of the Phoenicians. **3.** any false god. [t. Heb.: m. *ba'al* lord] —**Ba′alism,** *n.* —**Ba′alist, Baalite** (bā′ə līt′), *n.*

Baalbek (bäl′bĕk), *n.* a ruined city in E Lebanon: Temple of the Sun. Ancient Greek, **Heliopolis.**

baardman (bät′măn′), *n.* a small pink-billed weaverbird, *Spropiper squamifrons,* of dry areas in southern Africa. [t. Afrikaans]

baas (bäs), *n. S African.* sir; master; boss. [t. Afrikaans. See BOSS]

baba (bä′bä; *Fr.* bȧ bȧ′), *n.* a yeast-raised cake of brioche dough, flavoured with rum, etc., and baked.

babbitt (băb′ĭt), *n. Metall.* **1.** Babbitt metal. **2.** a bearing or lining of Babbitt metal. —*v.t.* **3.** to line, face, or furnish with Babbitt metal.

Babbitt (băb′ĭt), *n.* a self-satisfied person who conforms readily to middle-class ideas and ideals. Cf. **Babbittry.**

Babbitt metal, *Metall.* **1.** an antifriction metal, an alloy of tin, antimony, lead, and copper, used for bearings, etc. **2.** any of various similar alloys. [named after Isaac *Babbitt,* 1799–1862, U.S. inventor]

Babbittry (băb′ĭ trĭ), *n.* (*often l.c.*) the attitude of the self-satisfied middle class, having social conformity and business success as its ideals, as typified by the title character of Sinclair Lewis's novel *Babbitt* (1922).

babble (băb′l), *v.,* **-led, -ling,** *n.* —*v.i.* **1.** to utter words imperfectly or indistinctly. **2.** to talk idly, irrationally, or foolishly; chatter. **3.** to make a continuous murmuring sound: *a babbling stream.* —*v.t.* **4.** to utter incoherently or foolishly. **5.** to reveal foolishly or thoughtlessly: *to babble a secret.* —*n.* **6.** inarticulate speech. **7.** senseless or foolish prattle. **8.** a murmuring sound. [ME *babele(n)*; of imit. orig. Cf. Icel. *babla*] —**bab′blement,** *n.* —**bab′bly,** *adj.*

babbler (băb′lə), *n.* **1.** one who or that which babbles. **2.** any of the tropical and subtropical African birds of the family *Timaliidae.*

babe (bāb), *n.* **1.** baby. **2.** an innocent or inexperienced person. **3.** *U.S. Slang.* girl. [ME]

Babel (bā′bl), *n.* **1.** *Bible.* an ancient city (Babylon) where the building of a tower intended to reach heaven was begun and a confounding of the language of the people took place. Gen 11:4–9. **2.** (*usually l.c.*) a confused mixture of sounds. **3.** (*usually l.c.*) a scene of noise and confusion. [t. Heb.: m. *Bābel* Babylon]

Bab el Mandeb (băb′ ĕl măn′dĕb), a strait between E Africa and SW Arabia, connecting the Red Sea and the Gulf of Aden. 20 mi. wide.

Baber (bä′bə), *n.* (*Zahir ed-Din Mohammed*), 1483–1530, founder of Mogul Empire. Also **Babar.**

babies'-breath (bā′bĭz brĕth′), *n.* **1.** a tall herb, *Gypsophila paniculata,* of the pink family, bearing numerous small, fragrant, white or pink flowers. **2.** any of certain other plants, as the grape hyacinth, *Muscari.* Also, **baby's-breath.**

babiroussa (băb′ĭ roō′sə), *n.* an East Indian swine, *Babirussa babyrussa.* The male has peculiar curved tusks growing upwards, one pair from each jaw. Also, **babirussa, babirusa.** [t. Malay: m. *bābi rūsa* hog-deer]

Babiroussa, *Babirussa babyrussa* (2 ft or more high at the shoulder)

Babism (bä′bĭz′əm), *n.* the doctrine of a pantheistic Persian sect, founded about 1844, inculcating a high morality, recognizing the equality of the sexes, and forbidding polygamy. —**Bab′ist,** *n., adj.*

baboon (bə boōn′), *n.* any of various large, terrestrial monkeys, with a doglike muzzle, large cheek pouches, and a short tail, which constitute the genus *Papio* of Africa and Arabia. [ME *babewyne,* t. OF: m. *babouin* stupid person] —**baboon′ish,** *adj.*

baboonery (bə boō′ nə rĭ), *n.* baboonish behaviour.

babu (bä′boō), *n.* **1.** (formerly) a title in Bengal corresponding to English *Mr.* **2.** a Hindu gentleman. **3.** an Indian clerk who writes English. **4.** any Indian having a smattering of English culture, esp. with ludicrous results. Also, **baboo.** [t. Hind.] —**ba′buism,** *n.*

babu English, English as used by babus, full of long and learned words, frequently misapplied, esp. with a ludicrous effect.

babul (bä boōl′, bä′boōl), *n.* **1.** any of several trees of the mimosaceous genus *Acacia,* which yield a gum, esp. *A. arabica* of India. **2.** the gum, pods, or bark of such a tree. [t. Hind.]

babushka (bə boōsh′kə), *n.* a woman's scarf, often triangular, used as a hood with the ends tied under the chin. [t. Russ.: lit., grandmother]

Babushkin (*Russ.* bȧ′boōsh kĭn), *n.* a town in the central Soviet Union in Europe, a suburb of Moscow. 112,000 (est. 1959).

baby (bā′bĭ), *n., pl.* **-bies,** *adj., v.,* **-bied, -bying.** —*n.* **1.** an infant; young child of either sex. **2.** a young animal. **3.** the youngest member of a family, group, etc. **4.** a childish person (usually derogatory). **5.** *S African, Austral., etc.* a machine for sorting diamondiferous gravel. **6.** *Slang.* an invention or creation of which one is particularly proud. **7.** *U.S. Slang.* girl. **8. hold the baby,** *Colloq.* to carry the responsibility for something in the default of others. —*adj.* **9.** of, like, or suitable for a baby; *baby carriage.* **10.** infantile; babyish: *a baby face.* **11.** small; comparatively little: *a baby grand (piano).* —*v.t.* **12.** to treat like a young child; pamper. [ME *babi, babee,* dim. of BABE] —**ba′byhood′,** *n.* —**ba′byish,** *adj.* —**ba′byishly,** *adv.* —**ba′byishness,** *n.* —**ba′by-like′,** *adj.*

Babylon (băb′ĭ lən), *n.* **1.** an ancient city of SW Asia, on the river Euphrates, noted for its magnificence and culture: the capital of Babylonia and later of the Chaldean Empire. **2. Hanging Gardens of,** its gardens, probably built in the form of a tower or pyramid. One of the Seven Wonders of the World. **3.** any great, rich, and luxurious or wicked city. [t. L, t. Gk, t. Akkadian: m. *Bāb Ilu* the gate of the god *Il*]

Babylon

Babylonia (băb′ĭ lō′nyə), *n.* an ancient empire in SW Asia, in the lower Euphrates valley: period of greatness, 2800–1750 B.C.

Babylonian (băb′ĭ lō′nyən), *adj.* **1.** pertaining to Babylon or Babylonia. **2.** sinful. —*n.* **3.** an inhabitant of ancient Babylonia. **4.** a language of Babylonia, esp. the Semitic language of the Akkadian group.

baby-sit (bā′bĭ sĭt′), *v.i.,* **-sat, -sitting.** to take charge of a child while the parents are out. —**ba′by-sit′ter,** *n.*

baccalaureate (băk′ə lô′rĭ ĭt), *n.* **1.** the bachelor's degree. **2.** (in France) the first grade of university examination, taken by high-school pupils. **3.** *U.S.* a religious service usually associated with commencement ceremonies. [t. ML: m. s. *baccalaureātus,* der. *baccalaureus* (as if f. L *bacca* berry + *laureus* of laurel), var. of *baccalārius* BACHELOR] —**bac′calau′rean,** *adj.*

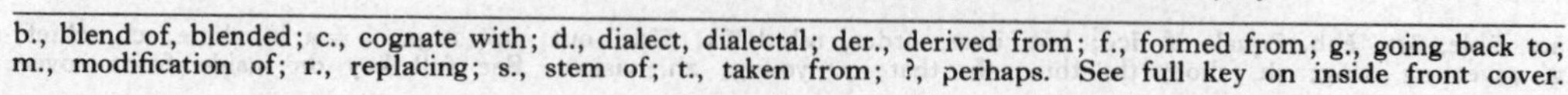

baccarat (băk′ə rä′, băk′ə rä′; *Fr.* bȧ kȧ rȧ′), *n.* a gambling game at cards played by a banker and two or more punters. Also, **baccara.** [t. F; orig. unknown]

baccate (băk′āt), *adj. Bot.* **1.** berry-like. **2.** bearing berries. [t. L: m. s. *baccātus* berried]

Bacchae (băk′ē), *n.pl. Class. Myth.* **1.** the female attendants of Bacchus. **2.** the priestesses of Bacchus. **3.** the women who took part in the Bacchanalia.

bacchanal (băk′ə nəl), *n.* **1.** a follower of Bacchus. **2.** a drunken reveller. **3.** an occasion of drunken revelry; an orgy. *—adj.* **4.** pertaining to Bacchus; bacchanalian. [t. L: s. *bacchānālis*]

Bacchanalia (băk′ə nā′lyə), *n.pl.* **1.** a Roman festival in honour of Bacchus. **2.** (*l.c.*) drunken orgies. [L, neut. pl. of *bacchānālis* BACCHANAL, adj.] **—bac′chana′lian,** *adj.* **—bac′chana′lianism,** *n.*

bacchant (băk′ənt), *n., pl.* **bacchants, bacchantes** (bə-kăn′tiz). **1.** a priest, priestess, or votary of Bacchus; a bacchanal. **2.** a drunken reveller. [t. L: s. *bacchans*, ppr., celebrating the festival of Bacchus] **—bacchantic** (bə-kăn′tĭk), *adj.*

bacchante (bə kăn′tĭ), *n.* a female bacchant. [t. F, t. L: m. s. *bacchans* BACCHANT]

Bacchic (băk′ĭk), *adj.* **1.** relating to or in honour of Bacchus; connected with bacchanalian rites or revelries. **2.** (*l.c.*) jovial; riotously or jovially intoxicated; drunken.

bacchius (bă kī′əs), *n., pl.* **-chii.** *Pros.* a foot of three syllables, the first short (or unaccented) and the other two long (or stressed).

Bacchus (băk′əs), *n. Rom. Myth.* the god of wine. See **Dionysus.** [t. L, t. Gk: m. *Bákchos*]

bacci-, *Bot.* a word element meaning 'berry', as in *bacciform.* [t. L, comb. form of *bacca*]

bacciferous (băk sĭf′ə rəs), *adj. Bot.* bearing or producing berries. [f. L *baccifer* + -OUS]

bacciform (băk′sĭ fôm′), *adj. Bot.* berry-shaped.

baccivorous (băk sĭv′ə rəs), *adj.* feeding on berries.

baccy (băk′ĭ), *n. Colloq.* tobacco. Also, **bacco.** [abbrev. of TOBACCO]

bach (băch), *n.* **1.** *Colloq.* a bachelor. **2.** *Chiefly N.Z.* a holiday house; beach hut. *—v.i.* **3.** *Slang.* to keep house alone. [short for BACHELOR]

Bach (bäKH; *Ger.* bȧKH), *n.* **1. Johann Sebastian** (*Ger.* yō′hȧn zė bȧs′tĭ ȧn), 1685–1750, German organist and composer. **2.** his sons: **Johann Christian** (*Ger.* yō′hȧn krĭs′tĭ ȧn), 1735–82; **Karl Philipp Emanuel** (*Ger.* kȧrl fē′lĭp ė mȧn′o͞o ĕl), 1714–88; **Wilhelm Friedmann** (*Ger.* vĭl′hĕlm frēt′mȧn), 1710–84, German musicians and composers.

bach., bachelor.

bachelor (băch′ə lə, băch′lə), *n.* **1.** an unmarried man of any age. **2.** a person who has taken the first or lowest degree at a university: *bachelor of arts.* **3.** a young knight who followed the banner of another. **4.** a young male fur seal kept from the breeding grounds by the older males. [ME *bacheler*, t. OF, t. ML: m. s. *baccalāris, baccalārius*, appar. orig. small dairy farmer, ? akin to L *baculum* staff] **—bachelordom** (băch′ə lə dəm, băch′lə-), *n.* **—bach′elorhood′,** *n.* **—bach′elorism,** *n.* **—bach′elorship′,** *n.*

bachelor-at-arms (băch′ə lər ət ämz′, băch′lər-), *n., pl.* **bachelors-at-arms.** bachelor (def. 3).

bachelor-girl (băch′ə lə gûl′), *n.* a young unmarried woman, esp. one living away from home.

bachelor's-button (băch′ə ləz bŭt′n, băch′ləz-), *n.* any of various plants with round flower heads, esp. the cornflower, or double-flowered varieties of ranunculus.

Bachman (*Ger.* bȧKH′mȧn), *n.* **Ingeborg** (*Ger.* ĭng′ə bŏrk), born 1926, Austrian poetess.

Bach trumpet, clarion.

bacillary (bə sĭl′ə rĭ), *adj.* **1.** Also, **bacilliform** (bə-sĭl′ĭ fôm′), of or like a bacillus; rod-shaped. **2.** *Bacteriol.* characterized by bacilli. Also, **bacillar** (bə sĭl′ə). [f. s. L *bacillus* little rod + -ARY[2]]

bacillus (bə sĭl′əs), *n., pl.* **-cilli** (-sĭl′ī). *Bacteriol.* **1.** any of the group of rod-shaped bacteria which produce spores in the presence of free oxygen. See illus. under **bacteria. 2.** (formerly) any of the rod-shaped or cylindrical bacteria. [t. LL, dim. of *baculus* rod]

bacitracin (băs′ĭ trā′sĭn), *n. Med.* an antibiotic effective against diseases caused by certain bacteria, viruses, and Rickettsia. [f. BACI(LLUS) + (Margaret) *Trac(y)* name of American patient in whose tissues such bacteria were first identified + -IN[2]]

back[1] (băk), *n.* **1.** the hinder part of the human body, extending from the neck to the end of the spine. **2.** the part of the body of animals corresponding to the human back. **3.** the rear portion of any part or organ of the body: *the back of the head.* **4.** the whole body, with reference to clothing: *the clothes on his back.* **5.** the part opposite to or farthest from the face or front; the hinder side; the rear part: *the back of a hall.* **6.** the part covering the back, as of clothing. **7.** the spine: *to break one's back.* **8.** any rear part of an object serving to support, protect, etc.: *the back of a book.* **9.** *Naut.* the keel and keelson of a vessel. **10.** the strength to carry a burden or responsibility. **11.** *Football, etc.* **a.** one of the defending players behind the forwards. **b.** the position occupied by such a player. **12.** *Mining.* (of a level or layer) the side nearest the surface of the ground, including the earth between that level and the next. **13.** Some special noun phrases are:

behind one's back, in secret; deceitfully; in one's absence.

break the back of, 1. to deal with or accomplish the most difficult or arduous part of (a task, etc.). **2.** to overburden or overwhelm.

get off one's back, *Colloq.* to cease to criticize or interfere with someone.

on the back of, close behind; immediately following in space or time.

put one's back into, to do (something) with all one's energy and strength.

put one's back up, to arouse one's resentment.

see the back of, 1. to be rid of, as a person. **2.** to finish with; complete.

turn one's back on, to disregard, neglect, or ignore.

—v.t. **14.** to support, as with authority, influence, or money (often fol. by *up*). **15.** to cause to move backwards; reverse the action of: *to back a car.* **16.** to bet in favour of: *to back a horse in the race.* **17.** to get upon the back of; mount. **18.** to furnish with a back: *to back a book.* **19.** to lie at the back of; form a back or background for: *a beach backed by hills.* **20.** to write on the back of; endorse.

—v.i. **21.** to go backwards (often fol by *up*). **22.** *Naut.* (of wind) to change direction anticlockwise.

—v. **23.** Some special verb phrases are:

back and fill, 1. *Naut.* to trim the sails so that the wind strikes them first on the forward and then on the after side (done against the wind in a narrow channel to manoeuvre a ship from bank to bank without making headway but floating with the current). **2.** *Colloq.* to vacillate.

back down, 1. to retreat from or abandon an argument, opinion, claim, etc. **2.** *Rowing.* to row a boat backwards.

back out or **out of, 1.** to withdraw from or abandon (an engagement, promise, etc.). **2.** to go or cause to move out backwards.

back up, 1. to give support to; encourage. **2.** to go or cause to move backwards. **3.** *Mountaineering.* to climb a chimney or cleft by pressing the feet on one side and the back on the other.

back water, *Naut.* to reverse the direction of a vessel.

—adj. **24.** lying or being behind: *a back door.* **25.** away from the front position or rank; remote: *back country.* **26.** belonging to the past: *back files.* **27.** overdue: *back pay.* **28.** coming or going back; backward: *back current.* **29.** *Phonet.* pronounced with the tongue drawn back in the mouth as, in most varieties of English, the vowels of *bought, boat,* and *boot.* **30. (in) back of,** *U.S. Colloq.* behind. [ME *bak*, OE *bæc*, c. Icel. *bak*] **—back′er,** *n.* **—back′less,** *adj.*

—Syn. 24. BACK, HIND, POSTERIOR, REAR refer to something situated behind something else. BACK means the opposite of front: *back window.* HIND, and the more formal word POSTERIOR, suggest the rearmost of two or more, often similar, objects: *hind legs, posterior lobe.* REAR is used of buildings, conveyances, etc., and in military language it is the opposite of fore: *rear end of a train.*

back[2] (băk), *adv.* **1.** at, to, or towards the rear; backwards: *to step back.* **2.** towards the past: *to look back on one's youth.* **3.** towards the original starting point, place, or condition: *to go back to the old home.* **4.** returned home; in the original starting point, place, or condition again: *back where he started from.* **5.** in reply; in return: *to pay back a loan.* **6.** in reversal of the usual course: *to take back a gift.* **7. back and forth,** from side to side, to and fro. [aphetic var. of ABACK]

back[3] (băk), *n.* a tub or vat. [t. D: m. *bak*, t. F: m. *bac* tub, trough, ferryboat]

backache (băk′āk′), *n.* an ache in one's back.

backbencher (băk′bĕn′chə), *n.* **1.** a member of the British House of Commons who does not hold a ministerial position and who therefore sits on a bench behind the front bench. **2.** any person holding a similar position in any other assembly. **—back′bench′,** *adj.*

backbite (băk′bīt′), *v.*, **-bit, -bitten** or (*Colloq.*) **-bit, -biting.** *—v.t.* **1.** to attack the character or reputation of secretly. *—v.i.* **2.** to speak evil of the absent. **—back′bit′er,** *n.* **—back′bit′ing,** *n.*

backblocks (băk′blŏks′), *n., pl. Austral. and N.Z.* remote, sparsely inhabited inland country. **—back′block′,** *adj.* **—back′block′er,** *n.*

backboard (băk′bôd′), *n.* **1.** a board placed at or forming the back of anything. 2. *Med.* a board worn to support or straighten the back.

backboiler (băk′boi′lə), *n.* a domestic boiler heated through a vent at the back of the hearth of an open fire, stove, etc.

back bond, *Law.* a bond of indemnity given to a surety.

backbone (băk′bōn′), *n.* **1.** *Anat.* the spinal or vertebral column; the spine. **2.** something resembling a backbone in appearance, position, or function. **3.** strength of character; resolution. **4. to the backbone,** through and through. —**back′boned′,** *adj.* —**back′bone′less,** *adj.*

backbreaking (băk′brā′kĭng), *adj.* physically exhausting.

backchat (băk′chăt′), *n.* impertinent talk; answering back.

backcloth (băk′klŏth′), *n.* *Theat.* the painted curtain or hanging at the back of a set; backdrop.

backcomb (băk′kōm′), *v.t.* to ruffle (a woman's hair) by combing it towards the roots in order to make a bouffant hairstyle.

back country, *Chiefly Austral.* sparsely populated rural areas.

backcross (băk′krŏs′), *Genetics.* —*v.t.* **1.** to cross a hybrid (of the first generation) with either of its parents. —*n.* **2.** an instance of such crossing.

backdate (băk′dāt′), *v.t.* to date before the true time; apply retrospectively: *the pay rise was backdated.*

backdoor (băk′dô′), *n.* **1.** a door at the rear of a building. **2.** any secret approach; a hidden, obscure, or dishonourable means of entry. —*adj.* **3.** secret; clandestine.

back-draught (băk′dräft′), *n.* a backward current.

backdrop (băk′drŏp′), *n.* *Theat.* backcloth.

backed (băkt), *adj.* **1.** having a back: *a high-backed chair.* **2.** having backing: *a government-backed measure.*

back end, **1.** the rear end. **2.** the end part of a season, esp. the late autumn.

backfall (băk′fôl′), *n.* **1.** that which falls back. **2.** *Wrestling.* a fall in which a wrestler is thrown upon his back.

backfire (băk′fī′ə), *v.,* **-fired, -firing,** *n.* —*v.i.* **1.** (of an internal-combustion engine) to have a premature explosion in the cylinder or in the admission or exhaust passages. **2.** *Chiefly U.S.* to check a forest or prairie fire by burning off an area in advance of it. **3.** to bring results opposite to those planned: *the plot backfired.* —*n.* **4.** (in an internal-combustion engine) premature ignition of fuel, resulting in loss of power and loud explosive sound in the manifold. **5.** an explosion coming out of the breech of a firearm. **6.** *Chiefly U.S.* a fire deliberately started in front of a forest or prairie fire in order to check it.

back-formation (băk′fô mā′shən), *n.* *Gram.* **1.** the formation of a word from one that is wrongly (or humorously) taken to be its derivative, as *typewrite* from typewriter, *donate* from donation. **2.** a word so formed.

backgammon (băk′găm′ən, băk′găm′ən), *n.* **1.** a game played by two persons on a board having two tables or parts, with pieces or men moved in accordance with throws of dice. **2.** a victory at this game, esp. one resulting in a tripled score. —*v.t.* **3.** to defeat at backgammon, esp. to win a triple score over. [f. BACK[1], adj. + GAMMON[1]; game so called because the pieces often go back and re-enter]

background (băk′ground′), *n.* **1.** the ground or parts situated in the rear. **2.** the surface or ground against which the parts of a picture are relieved, or the portions of a picture represented as more distant (opposed to *foreground*). **3.** the social, historical, and other antecedents which explain an event or condition: *the background of the war.* **4.** a person's origin, education, etc., in relation to present character, status, etc. **5. in the background,** out of sight or notice; in obscurity. **6.** *Physics.* the counting rate of a Geiger counter or other counter tube due to radioactive sources other than the one being measured. —*adj.* **7.** of or pertaining to the background; in the background.

backhand (băk′hănd′), *n.* **1.** the hand turned backwards in making a stroke, as in tennis. **2.** a stroke, as in tennis, by a right-handed player from the left of the body (or the reverse for a left-handed player). **3.** writing which slopes backwards or to the left. —*adj.* **4.** backhanded. —**Ant. 1.** forehand.

backhanded (băk′hăn′dĭd), *adj.* **1.** performed with the hand turned backwards, crosswise, or in any oblique direction, or with the back of the hand in the direction of the stroke. **2.** sloping to the left: *backhanded writing.* **3.** oblique or opposite in meaning; indirect: *a backhanded compliment.* **4.** (of a rope) twisted in the opposite way from the usual or right-handed method. —**back′hand′edly,** *adv.* —**back′hand′edness,** *n.*

backhander (băk′hăn′də), *n.* **1.** a backhanded blow or stroke. **2.** an insincere or indirect remark. **3.** *Colloq.* a bribe.

Backhaus (băk′hous′; *Ger.* bȧk′hous), *n.* **Wilhelm** (*Ger.* vĭl′hĕlm), 1884–1969, German pianist.

backhouse (băk′hous′), *n.* *Chiefly U.S.* **1.** an outbuilding. **2.** a privy.

backing (băk′ĭng), *n.* **1.** aid or support of any kind. **2.** supporters or backers collectively. **3.** that which forms the back or is placed at or attached to the back of anything to support or strengthen it.

backing store, *Computers.* an auxiliary memory store attached to a digital computer.

backlash (băk′lăsh′), *n.* **1.** *Mach.* the jarring reaction, or the play, between loosely fitting or worn parts of a machine or mechanical device. **2.** *Angling.* a tangled line on a reel, caused by a faulty cast. **3.** any sudden, violent, or unexpected reaction.

backlog (băk′lŏg′), *n.* **1.** an accumulation (of business resources, stock, etc.) acting as a reserve. **2.** an accumulation (of work, correspondence, etc.) awaiting attention. **3.** *Chiefly U.S.* a log at the back of a fire.

backmost (băk′mōst′), *adj.* farthest to the back.

back number, **1.** an out-of-date issue of a serial publication. **2.** anything out of date.

back of beyond, a remote, inaccessible place.

back of Bourke (bûk), *Austral. Colloq.* back of beyond; the most remote country imaginable.

back-pedal (băk′pĕd′l), *v.i.,* **-alled, -alling,** or (*U.S.*) **-aled, -aling.** **1.** to press the pedals of a bicycle backwards, as in slowing down. **2.** *Colloq.* to make an effort to slow down, or reverse one's course, as to avoid danger. **3.** *Boxing.* to retreat still facing one's opponent.

backroom (băk′ro͝om′, -ro͞om′), *adj.* doing or pertaining to important work behind the scenes: *backroom boys.*

Backs (băks), *n.pl.* the borders of the river Cam at the back of the colleges in Cambridge, famous for their beauty.

back-saw (băk′sô′), *n.* a saw with a thickened ridge on the back for stiffness.

back seat, **1.** a seat at the back. **2. take a back seat,** to retire into obscurity, or into an insignificant or subordinate position.

back-seat driver, *Colloq.* **1.** a passenger in a car who offers unnecessary advice to the driver, as though trying to drive the car himself. **2.** one who interferes with advice or orders in matters which are not his responsibility.

backset (băk′sĕt′), *n.* **1.** a setback; a reverse. **2.** an eddy or counter-current.

backsheesh (băk′shēsh), *n., v.t., v.i.* baksheesh. Also, **backshish.**

backside (băk′sīd′), *n.* **1.** the back part. **2.** the rump.

backsight (băk′sīt′), *n.* *Survey.* **1.** a sight on a previously occupied instrument station. **2.** (in levelling) the reading on a rod that is held on a point of known elevation, used in computing the height of the instrument.

back slang, a form of slang in which words are pronounced as though spelt backwards.

backslide (băk′slīd′), *v.i.,* **-slid, -slidden** or **-slid, -sliding.** to relapse into error or sin. —**back′slid′er,** *n.*

backspin (băk′spĭn′), *n.* reverse spinning of a ball causing it to bounce backwards, as in tennis.

backspring (băk′sprĭng′), *n.* *Naut.* a rope leading from a point forward on a ship to a point aft on the quay, or vice versa, to prevent the moored ship surging ahead or astern.

backstage (băk′stāj′), *adv.* **1.** out of the view of the audience in a theatre; in the wings or dressing rooms, or behind the curtain on the stage. **2.** towards the rear of the stage; upstage. **3.** *Colloq.* behind the scenes; in private. —*adj.* **4.** situated, occurring, etc., backstage.

backstairs (băk′stēəz′), *n.* **1.** a secondary staircase, originally for servants. —*adj.* **2.** Also, **back′stair′.** indirect; underhand.

backstay (băk′stā′), *n.* **1.** *Mach.* a supporting or checking piece in a mechanism. **2.** *Naut.* a stay or supporting rope leading from a masthead backwards to the ship's side or stern.

backstitch (băk′stĭch′), *n.* **1.** stitching or a stitch in which the thread doubles back each time on the preceding stitch. —*v.t., v.i.* **2.** to sew by backstitch.

backstop (băk′stŏp′), *n.* **1.** *Rowing.* a wooden block at the bow end of the seat slide, to prevent the seat running off the runners. **2.** *U.S. Sport.* a long stop; a person, screen, or the like, to prevent a ball going too far.

back straight, *Athletics.* the straight part of a circuit track on the opposite side to the home straight.

back-strapped (băk′străpt′), *adj.* **1.** *Naut.* (of a vessel) held powerless by wind or tide in a dangerous or difficult position. **2.** (of a person) in a difficult situation; powerless.

backstreet (băk′strēt′), *n.* **1.** a small, unimportant street in a town. —*adj.* **2.** illegal, illicit, or improper: *backstreet abortions.*

backstroke (băk′strōk′), *n.* **1.** a backhanded stroke.

2. a blow or stroke in return; recoil. **3.** *Swimming.* a stroke made while on one's back.

backsword (băk′sôd′), *n.* **1.** a sword with only one sharp edge; a broadsword. **2.** a cudgel with a basket hilt, used like a foil in fencing.

backswordsman (băk′sôdz′mən), *n., pl.* **-men.** one who uses a backsword. Also, **back′sword′man.**

back talk, backchat.

back-to-back (băk′tə băk′), *adj.* (of houses) built so as to abut at the rear, characteristic of 19th-century housing in poor industrial districts.

backtrack (băk′trăk′), *v.i.* **1.** to return over the same course or route. **2.** to withdraw from an undertaking, position, etc.; pursue a reverse policy.

backward (băk′wəd), *adj.* **1.** directed towards the back or past. **2.** reversed; returning: *a backward movement or journey.* **3.** behind in time or progress; late; slow: *a backward child or country.* **4.** reluctant; hesitating; bashful. *—adv.* **5.** *Now Chiefly U.S.* backwards. [ME *bakward,* f. *bak* BACK[1] + -WARD] **—back′wardly,** *adv.* **—back′wardness,** *n.* **—Syn. 4.** disinclined; timid; retiring.

backwardation (băk′wə dā′shən), *n. Stock Exchange.* the percentage paid by a seller of stock in consideration of the postponement of delivery until the next account day (opposed to *contango*).

backwards (băk′wədz), *adv.* **1.** towards the back or rear. **2.** with the back foremost. **3.** in the reverse of the usual or right way; retrogressively: *to read or spell backwards.* **4.** towards the past. **5.** in time past. **6. backwards and forwards,** to and fro. **7. bend, lean,** or **fall over backwards,** *Colloq.* to go to great trouble, even to the point of personal inconvenience. Also, *Now Chiefly U.S.,* **backward.** [ME *bakweardes.* See BACKWARD, -WARDS]

backwash (băk′wŏsh′), *n.* **1.** *Naut.* the water thrown back by oars, paddlewheels, or the like. **2.** a condition lasting after the event which caused it. *—v.t.* **3.** to remove the oil from (combed wool).

backwater (băk′wô′tə), *n.* **1.** water held or forced back, as by a dam, flood, tide, etc. **2.** a pool or stretch of stagnant water connected to a river. **3.** a place or state of stagnant backwardness. **4.** backwash. *—v.i.* **5.** to move a boat backwards by paddling with the oars.

backwoods (băk′wo͝odz′), *n.pl.* **1.** *Chiefly U.S.* wooded or partially uncleared and unsettled districts. **2.** any unfamiliar or unfrequented area: *the backwoods of English literature.* *—adj.* Also, **back′wood′. 3.** of or pertaining to the backwoods. **4.** unsophisticated; uncouth.

backwoodsman (băk′wo͝odz′mən), *n., pl.* **-men. 1.** one living in the backwoods. **2.** *Colloq.* a hereditary peer who seldom attends the House of Lords. **3.** *U.S. Colloq.* an uncouth person.

backyard (băk′yäd′), *n.* a yard behind a house.

Bacolod (bə kōl′əd), *n.* a town in the Philippines, in NE Negros. 119,315 (1960).

bacon (bā′kən), *n.* **1.** meat from the back and sides of the pig, salted and dried or smoked. **2. save one's bacon,** *Colloq.* to save one from a dangerous or awkward situation. [ME, t. OF, t. Gmc; cf. OHG *bahho,* MHG *bache* buttock, ham]

Bacon (bā′kən), *n.* **1. Francis** (*Baron Verulam, Viscount St Albans*), 1561–1626, English essayist, philosopher, and statesman. **2. Francis,** born 1910, English painter born in Ireland. **3. Roger** (*Friar Bacon, 'the Admirable Doctor'*), 1214?–94?, English philosopher and scientist.

bacon-and-eggs (bā′kən ənd ĕgz′), *n.* bird's-foot trefoil.

Baconian (bā kō′nyən), *adj.* **1.** of or pertaining to Francis Bacon or his doctrines. *—n.* **2.** an adherent of Baconian philosophy.

bacteraemia (băk′tə rē′mĭ ə), *n. Pathol.* the presence (for transient periods) of bacteria in the blood. Also, *U.S.,* **bacteremia.**

bacteri-, a word element meaning 'bacteria' or 'bacterial'. Also, **bacter-, bacterio-, bactero-.** [comb. form of BACTERIUM]

bacteria (băk tĭə′rĭ ə), *n., pl. of* **bacterium.** the morphologically simplest group of non-green vegetable organisms, various species of which are concerned in fermentation and putrefaction, the production of disease, the fixing of atmospheric nitrogen, etc.; a schizomycete. [t. NL. See BACTERIUM] **—bacte′rial,** *adj.* **—bacte′rially,** *adv.*

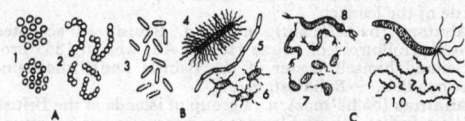

Bacteria (greatly magnified)
A, Cocci (spherical): 1. *Staphylococcus aureus*; 2. *Streptococcus pyogenes*. B, Bacilli (rod): 3. *Clostridium cadaveris*; 4. *Proteus vulgaris*; 5. *Bacillus subtilis*; 6. *Bacillus typhosus*. C, Spirilla (spiral): 7. *Vibrio comma*; 8. *Spirillum undula*; 9. *Theospirillum*; 10. *Spirochaeta*.

bactericide (băk tĭə′rĭ sīd′), *n.* an agent capable of destroying bacteria. **—bacte′ricid′al,** *adj.*

bacterin (băk′tə rĭn), *n. Med.* a vaccine prepared from bacteria. [f. BACTER(I-) + -IN[2]]

bacteriochlorophyll (băk tĭə′rĭ ō klŏ′rə fĭl), *n. Bacteriol.* a green substance similar to chlorophyll, found in certain bacteria.

bacteriol., bacteriology.

bacteriology (băk tĭə′rĭ ŏl′ə jĭ), *n.* the science that deals with bacteria. **—bacteriological** (băk tĭə′rĭ ə lŏj′ĭ kl), *adj.* **—bacte′riolog′ically,** *adv.* **—bacte′riol′ogist,** *n.*

bacteriolysis (băk tĭə′rĭ ŏl′ĭ sĭs), *n.* disintegration or dissolution of bacteria. **—bacteriolytic** (băk tĭə′rĭ ə lĭt′ĭk), *n., adj.*

bacteriophage (băk tĭə′rĭ ə fāj′), *n. Bacteriol.* a virus that specifically attacks bacteria.

bacteriostasis (băk tĭə′rĭ ō stā′sĭs), *n. Bacteriol.* the inhibition of the multiplication of bacteria without actually destroying them. **—bacteriostatic** (băk tĭə′rĭ ō stăt′ĭk), *adj.*

bacteriotoxic (băk tĭə′rĭ ō tŏk′sĭk), *adj. Bacteriol.* **1.** harmful to bacteria. **2.** caused by toxins or poisons of bacterial origin.

bacterium (băk tĭə′rĭ əm), *n. Bacteriol.* **1.** sing. of **bacteria. 2.** a group of non-spore-forming, non-motile, rod-shaped bacteria (as distinct from the bacillus and clostridium groups). [t. NL, t. Gk: m. *baktḗrion,* dim. of *báktron* stick]

bactero-, var. of **bacteri-.**

bacteroid (băk′tə roid′), *Bacteriol.* *—n.* **1.** one of the minute rodlike or branched organisms (regarded as forms of bacteria) in the root nodules of nitrogen-fixing plants, as the legumes. *—adj.* **2.** resembling a bacterium.

Bactria (băk′trĭ ə), *n.* an ancient country in W Asia between the Oxus river and the Hindu Kush mountains. **—Bac′trian,** *adj., n.*

Bactrian camel, the two-humped camel, *Camelus bactrianus.*

Bactrian camel, *Camelus bactrianus* (Ab. 9 ft long, ab. 7½ ft high at the humps)

baculiform (bə kyo͞o′lĭ fôm′, băk′yo͞o-), *adj. Biol.* rod-shaped. [f. s. L *baculum* rod + -(I)FORM]

baculine (băk′yo͞o lĭn, -līn′), *adj.* pertaining to the cane or to its use in punishing. [f. s. L *baculum* rod + -INE[1]]

Bacup (bā′kəp), *n.* a town in England, in SE Lancashire. 17,308 (1961).

bad[1] (băd), *adj.,* **worse, worst,** *n., adv.* *—adj.* **1.** not good: *bad conduct, a bad life.* **2.** defective; worthless: *a bad coin, a bad debt.* **3.** unsatisfactory; poor; below standard; inadequate: *bad heating, a bad businessman.* **4.** incorrect; faulty: *a bad shot.* **5.** unskilful; incompetent (fol. by *at*): *bad at tennis.* **6.** not valid; not sound: *a bad claim.* **7.** having an injurious or unfavourable tendency or effect: *bad air, bad for him.* **8.** in ill health; sick: *to feel bad.* **9.** regretful; contrite; sorry; upset: *to feel bad about an error.* **10.** unfavourable; unfortunate: *bad news.* **11.** offensive; disagreeable; painful: *a bad temper.* **12.** severe: *a bad sprain.* **13.** rotten; decayed. **14. go bad,** decay; rot. *—n.* **15.** that which is bad. **16.** a bad condition, character, or quality. **17. go to the bad,** become morally ruined, wicked, or corrupt. **18. to the bad,** in deficit; out of pocket: *two hundred pounds to the bad.* *—adv.* **19.** badly. [ME *badde;* ? back-formation from OE *bǣddel* effeminate person] **—bad′ness,** *n.*

—Syn. 1. depraved, corrupt, base, sinful, criminal, villainous, atrocious. BAD, EVIL, ILL, WICKED are closest in meaning, in reference to that which is lacking in moral qualities or is actually vicious and reprehensible. BAD is the broadest and simplest term: *a bad man, bad habits.* EVIL applies to that which violates or leads to the violation of moral law: *evil practices.* ILL now appears mainly in certain fixed expressions, with a milder implication than that in EVIL: *ill will, ill-natured.* WICKED implies wilful and determined doing of what is very wrong: *a wicked plan.* **3.** inferior, poor, deficient. **7.** disadvantageous. **10.** adverse.

bad[2] (băd), *v.* pt. of **bid.**

Badajoz (băd′ə hŏz′; *Sp.* bä dä KHōth′), *n.* a town in SW Spain. 102,499 (1965).

Badalona (*Sp.* bä dä lō′nä), *n.* a seaport in NE Spain. 120,014 (1965).

bad blood, hate; long-standing enmity; dislike.

baddish (băd′ĭsh), *adj.* fairly bad.

bade (băd), *v.* pt. of **bid.**

Baden (bä′dn; *Ger.* bä′dən), *n.* **1.** a former state in SW

West Germany, now Baden-Württemberg. **2.** Also, **Ba'den-Ba'den.** a town in West Germany, in Baden-Württemberg. 40,200 (est. 1963).

Baden-Powell (bā'dn pō'ĭl), *n.* **Robert Stephenson Smyth, 1st Baron,** 1857–1941, British general: founded the Boy Scouts in 1908.

Baden-Württemberg (*Ger.* bä'dən vʏr'təm bĕrk), *n.* a Land in SW West Germany; formerly Baden. 8,534,100 pop. (est. 1966); 13,803 sq. mi. *Cap.*: Stuttgart.

Bader (bä'də), *n.* **Douglas R. S.,** born 1910, British fighter pilot who fought in World War II after losing both legs.

bad form, a breach of good manners.

badge (băj), *n.* **1.** a mark, token, or device worn as a sign of allegiance, membership, authority, achievement, etc. **2.** any emblem, token, or distinctive mark. [ME *bage, bagge*; orig. unknown]

badger (băj'ə), *n.* **1.** any of the various burrowing carnivorous mammals of the *Mustelidae*, as *Meles meles*, a European species about two feet long, and *Taxidea taxus*, a similar American species. **2.** the fur of this mammal. **3.** a wombat. **4.** a bandicoot (def. 2). **5.** a hyrax. **6.** a ratel. **7.** a brush, esp. a paint-brush, of badger's hair. —*v.t.* **8.** to harass; torment. [earlier *bageard*, ? f. BADGE (with allusion to white mark on head) + -ARD]

Badger, *Meles meles* (Ab. 2 ft long)

Bad Godesberg (*Ger.* bȧd'gō'dəs bĕrk), a town in West Germany, in North Rhine-Westphalia, near Bonn. 70,700 (est. 1966).

badinage (băd'ĭ näzh'), *n.* light, playful banter or raillery. [t. F, der. *badiner* jest, der. *badin* fool, t. Pr., der. *badar* gape, g. LL *badāre*]

badlands (băd'lăndz'), *n.pl. U.S.* a barren area in which soft rock strata are eroded into varied, fantastic forms.

Bad Lands, a barren, badly eroded region in the U.S., in SW South Dakota and NW Nebraska.

badly (băd'lĭ), *adv.* **1.** in a bad manner; ill. **2.** very much: *to need or want badly.*

badminton (băd'mĭn tən), *n.* a game, similar to lawn tennis, but played with a high net and shuttlecock. [named after *Badminton*, village in Gloucestershire]

Badoglio (*It.* bȧ dōl'lyō), *n.* **Pietro** (*It.* pyĕ'trō), 1871–1956, Italian general.

bad shot, 1. a badly aimed shot. **2.** a wrong guess. **3.** an unsuccessful attempt. **4.** a poor marksman.

bad-tempered (băd'tĕm'pəd), *adj.* cross; cantankerous.

Baeda (bē'də), *n.* Bede.

Baedeker (bā'dĭ kə), *n.* any of the series of guidebooks for travellers issued by the German publisher Karl Baedeker, 1801–59, and his successors.

Baekeland (bāk'lănd'; *Flem.* bȧ'kə lŏnt), *n.* **Leo Hendrik** (lē'ō hĕn'drĭk; *Flem.* lĕ'ō), 1863–1944, U.S. chemist born in Belgium. Cf. **Bakelite.**

baff (băf), *Golf.* —*v.i.* **1.** to strike the ground with the club in making a stroke. —*n.* **2.** a baffing stroke, unduly lofting the ball. [? imit.]

Baffin (băf'ĭn), *n.* **William,** 1584–1622, English navigator who explored arctic North America.

Baffin Bay, a part of the Arctic Ocean between Greenland and the Canadian arctic islands.

Baffin Island, a large Canadian island between Greenland and Hudson Bay. ab. 1000 mi. long.

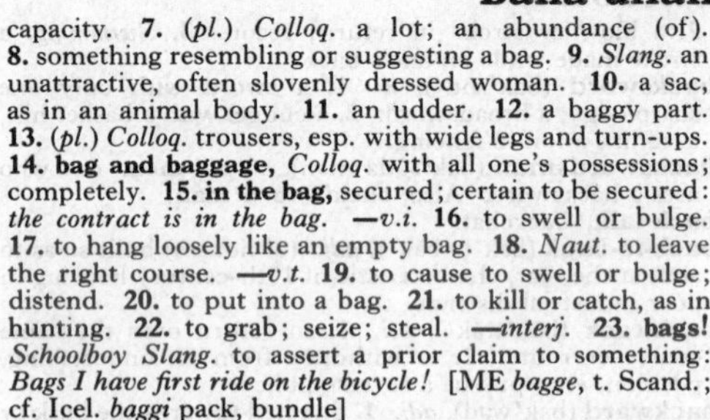

Baffin Bay

baffle (băf'əl), *v.*, **-fled, -fling,** *n.* —*v.t.* **1.** to thwart or frustrate disconcertingly; balk; confuse. **2.** to puzzle or mystify. **3.** *Naut.* (of the wind, current, etc.) to force (a ship, etc.) to take a variable course by being greatly changeable. **4.** *Obs.* to hoodwink; cheat. —*v.i.* **5.** to struggle ineffectually, as a ship in a gale. —*n.* **6.** an artificial obstruction for checking or deflecting the flow of gases (as in a boiler), sounds (as in a radio), etc. **7.** *Obs.* a balk or check; perplexity. [orig. uncert.] —**baf'flement,** *n.* —**baf'fler,** *n.* —**baf'fling,** *adj.* —**baf'flingly,** *adv.*

baffy (băf'ĭ), *n.*, *pl.* **baffies.** *Golf.* a short wooden club with a deeply pitched face, for lofting the ball.

bag (băg), *n.*, *v.*, **bagged, bagging,** *interj.* —*n.* **1.** a receptacle of leather, cloth, paper, etc. **2.** a suitcase or other portable receptacle for carrying articles as in travelling. **3.** a handbag. **4.** the contents of a bag. **5.** *Hunting.* a sportsman's take of game, etc. **6.** any of various measures of capacity. **7.** (*pl.*) *Colloq.* a lot; an abundance (of). **8.** something resembling or suggesting a bag. **9.** *Slang.* an unattractive, often slovenly dressed woman. **10.** a sac, as in an animal body. **11.** an udder. **12.** a baggy part. **13.** (*pl.*) *Colloq.* trousers, esp. with wide legs and turn-ups. **14. bag and baggage,** *Colloq.* with all one's possessions; completely. **15. in the bag,** secured; certain to be secured: *the contract is in the bag.* —*v.i.* **16.** to swell or bulge. **17.** to hang loosely like an empty bag. **18.** *Naut.* to leave the right course. —*v.t.* **19.** to cause to swell or bulge; distend. **20.** to put into a bag. **21.** to kill or catch, as in hunting. **22.** to grab; seize; steal. —*interj.* **23. bags!** *Schoolboy Slang.* to assert a prior claim to something: *Bags I have first ride on the bicycle!* [ME *bagge*, t. Scand.; cf. Icel. *baggi* pack, bundle]

—**Syn. 1.** BAG, SACK, are often used interchangeably. A BAG, though it may be of any size, is usually small, and made of such materials as paper, leather, etc. A SACK is usually large, oblong, and made of coarse material.

bagasse (bə găs'), *n.* crushed sugar cane or beet refuse from sugar-making. [t. F, t. Pr.: m. *bagasso*]

bagatelle (băg'ə tĕl'), *n.* **1.** something of little value; a trifle. **2.** a game played on a board having at one end holes into which balls are to be struck with a cue. **3.** pinball. **4.** a short and light musical composition, usually for the piano. [t. F, t. It.: m. *bagattella*, dim. of *baga, baca* berry]

Bagehot (băj'ət), *n.* **Walter,** 1826–77, English economist and literary critic.

bagel (bā'gl), *n.* a small ring-shaped, hard roll. Also, **beygel.** [t. Yiddish: m. *beygel*]

bagful (băg'fo͝ol'), *n.* as much as a bag will hold.

baggage (băg'ĭj), *n.* **1.** luggage, esp. in bulk, as for a major expedition. **2.** the portable equipment of an army. **3.** *U.S.* any luggage. **4.** *Colloq.* an ugly or difficult old woman. **5.** *Colloq.* a pert or impudent young woman. **6.** *Colloq.* an immoral woman; a prostitute.

bagging (băg'ĭng), *n.* woven material, as of hemp or jute, for bags.

baggy (băg'ĭ), *adj.*, **-gier, -giest.** baglike; hanging loosely. —**bag'gily,** *adv.* —**bag'giness,** *n.*

Baghdad (băg dăd'), *n.* the capital of Iraq, in the central part, on the Tigris river. 862,076; with suburbs, 1,313,012 (1965). Also, **Bagdad.**

bagman (băg'mən), *n.*, *pl.* **-men.** *Obs.* a travelling pedlar.

bagnio (bä'nyō), *n.*, *pl.* **bagnios. 1.** a prison for slaves, as in the Orient. **2.** a brothel. **3.** a bath or bathing house. [t. It.: m. *bagno*, g. L *balneum* bath]

bagpipe (băg'pīp'), *n.* (*often pl.*) a reed instrument consisting of a melody pipe and one or more accompanying drone pipes protruding from a windbag into which the air is blown by the mouth or a bellows. —**bag'piper,** *n.*

Bagpipes

Bagrit (băg'rĭt), *n.* **Sir Leon,** born 1902, English scientist and businessman.

Bagshot (băg'shŏt'), *n.* a town in England, in W Surrey. 16,744 (1961).

baguette (bă gĕt'), *n.* **1.** a gem cut in a long, rectangular shape. **2.** this shape. **3.** *Archit.* a small, convex, semicircular moulding. Also, **baguet.** [t. F: wand, rod, t. It.: m. *bacchetta*, dim. of *bacchio*, g. L *baculum*]

Baguio (băg'ĭ ō'; *Sp.* bȧ'gyō), *n.* **1.** a town in the Philippines, on Luzon: summer capital. 4961 ft high. 36,531 (est. 1960). **2.** a tropical cyclone in the Philippines.

bagworm (băg'wûm'), *n.* the caterpillar of any moth of the *Psychidae*. It constructs a bag of silk, leaves, etc., in which it lives.

bah (bä), *interj.* (an exclamation of contempt.)

bahadur (bə hä'də), *n.* a title of respect commonly affixed to the names of officers and public figures in India.

Bahai (bə hä'ĭ), *n.*, *pl.* **-hais,** *adj.* —*n.* **1.** an adherent of Bahaism. —*adj.* **2.** of or pertaining to Bahaism or a Bahai. [t. Pers.: m. *Baha'* (*ullah*) splendour (of God), title of the leader]

Bahaism (bə hä'ĭz'əm), *n.* *Relig.* Babism as accepted by the followers of Mirza Husain Ali, who in 1863 proclaimed himself leader of the Babists under the name Baha'ullah. —**Baha'ist,** *n.*, *adj.*

Bahamas (bə hä'məz), *n.* a group of islands in the British West Indies, SE of Florida: an internally self-governing colony since 1964. 138,749 pop. (est. 1964); 4404 sq. mi. *Cap.*: Nassau. Also, **Bahama Islands.** See map under **Haiti.**

Baha'ullah (bä'hä o͞ol'ə), *n.* (*Husain Ali*), 1817–92, Persian religious leader, founder of the Bahai faith.

Bahawalpur (bə hä′wəl po͝oə′, bä′wəl-), *n.* **1.** a division of West Pakistan, formerly a state. 3,205,000 pop. (1961); 32,443 sq. mi. **2.** a city, formerly capital of the state. 84,377 (1961).

Bahia (bə hē′ə; *Port.* bȧ ē′ȧ), *n.* São Salvador.

Bahía Blanca (bə hē′ə blăng′kə; *Sp.* bȧ ē′ȧ blän′kȧ), a seaport in E Argentina. 135,800 (est. 1960).

Bahrain (bä rān′), *n.* a British protectorate consisting of a group of islands in the W Persian Gulf. 143,213 pop. (1959); 232 sq. mi. *Cap.*: Manama. Also, **Bahrein.**

baht (bät), *n., pl.* **bahts, baht. 1.** the monetary unit of Thailand, equal to 100 satang, and equivalent to about £0·02 sterling. **2.** a banknote or cupronickel coin of this value. [t. Thai]

Baiae (bī′ē), *n.* an ancient resort in SW Italy: villas of Julius Caesar, Nero, and Pompey.

Baikal (bī kăl′; *Russ.* bȧy-kȧl′), *n.* **Lake,** a lake in the S Soviet Union in Asia: the deepest lake in the world. ab. 13,000 sq. mi.; ab. 5000 ft deep.

Lake Baikal

bail[1] (bāl), *Law.* —*n.* **1.** property given as surety that a person released from custody will return at an appointed time. **2.** the person or persons giving it. **3.** the position or the privilege of being bailed. **4.** release from prison on bond. **5.** the court granting such a release. —*v.t.* **6.** to grant or to obtain the liberty of (a person under arrest) on security given for his appearance when required, as in court for trial. **7.** to deliver possession of (goods, etc.) for storage, hire, or other special purpose, without transfer of ownership. **8. bail up,** to hold up and rob. [ME *bayle,* t. OF: m. *bail* control, *baillier* deliver, g. L *bājulāre* carry]

bail[2] (bāl), *n.* **1.** the semicircular handle of a kettle or pail. **2.** a hooplike support, as for a wagon cover. [ME *beyl,* prob. t. Scand.; cf. Icel. *beyglast* become bent]

bail[3] (bāl), *v.t., v.i., n.* bale[3].

bail[4] (bāl), *n.* **1.** *Cricket.* either of the two small bars or sticks laid across the tops of the stumps which form the wicket. **2.** a bar for separating horses in a stable. **3.** *Austral. and N.Z.* a framework for securing a cow's head during milking. **4.** (*pl.*) *Obs.* the wall of an outer court of a feudal castle. —*v.t.* **5. bail up,** *Austral.* to secure the head of (a cow) in a bail. [ME *baile,* t. OF: barrier; of obscure origin]

bailable (bā′lə bl), *adj. Law.* **1.** capable of being set free on bail. **2.** admitting of bail: *a bailable offence.*

bailee (bā′lē′), *n. Law.* one to whom goods are delivered in bailment.

bailer (bā′lə), *n.* **1.** baler. See **bale**[3]. **2.** *Cricket.* a ball which strikes or removes the bails without disturbing the stumps.

bailey (bā′lĭ), *n., pl.* **-leys.** *Archaic.* the wall of defence about the outer court of a feudal castle, or the outer court itself (still used in some proper names, as in the *Old Bailey,* London). [ME *baily;* var. of BAIL[4]]

Bailey bridge, a bridge of prefabricated steel units for spanning rivers, first used in World War II. [named after Sir Donald *Bailey,* born 1910, the inventor]

bailie (bā′lĭ), *n.* (in Scotland) a municipal officer or magistrate, corresponding to an English alderman. [ME *bailli,* t. OF, var. of *baillif* BAILIFF]

bailiff (bā′lĭf), *n.* **1.** an officer employed by a sheriff to serve writs, execute processes, make arrests, collect fines, summon juries, etc. **2.** (formerly) a person charged with local administration of justice. **3.** an overseer of a landed estate. [ME *baillif,* t. OF, der. *baillir* govern. See BAIL[4]]

bailiwick (bā′lĭ wĭk), *n.* **1.** the district within which a bailiff or sheriff has jurisdiction. **2.** a person's area of skill, work, etc. [f. BAILIE + *wick* office (ME *wike,* OE *wice*)]

bailment (bāl′mənt), *n. Law.* **1.** the act of bailing a prisoner or accused person. **2.** the act of bailing goods, etc.

bailor (bā′lə, bā′lô′), *n. Law.* one who delivers goods, etc., in bailment.

bailsman (bālz′mən), *n., pl.* **-men.** *Law.* one who gives bail or security.

bain-marie (*Fr.* băɴ mȧ rē′), *n., pl.* **bains-marie** (băɴ-mȧ rē′), a vessel containing hot water, in which another vessel is placed to heat its contents. [F: bath of Miriam (sister of Moses), in the Middle Ages considered an alchemist]

Bairam (bī răm′, bī′răm), *n.* either of two Muslim festivals, **lesser Bairam** immediately after Ramadan, and **greater Bairam** 70 days after it. [t. Turk.: m. *bai ram*]

Baird (bĕəd), *n.* **John Logie** (lō′gĭ), 1888–1946, Scottish inventor: demonstrated the first television transmission in 1926.

Baird Mountains (bĕəd), a mountain range in NW Alaska, forming the W end of the Brooks Range.

bairn (bĕən), *n. Scot. and N Dial.* a child; a son or daughter. [Scot. var. of obs. E *barn(e)* childe, OE *bearn*]

Bairnsfather (bĕənz′fä′thə), *n.* **Bruce,** 1889–1959, British cartoonist.

bait (bāt), *n.* **1.** food or some substitute, used as a lure in angling, trapping, etc. **2.** an allurement; enticement. **3.** a halt for refreshment or rest during a journey. **4.** *Colloq.* a rage; temper. —*v.t.* **5.** to prepare (a hook or trap) with bait. **6.** to lure as with bait; captivate. **7.** to set dogs upon (an animal) for sport. **8.** to worry; torment. **9.** to give food and drink to (horses, etc.) esp. during a journey. —*v.i.* **10.** to stop for food or refreshment during a journey. **11.** to take food; feed. [ME, t. Scand.; cf. Icel. *beita*] —**bait′er,** *n.*

baize (bāz), *n., v.,* **baized, baizing.** —*n.* **1.** a soft, usually green, woollen fabric resembling felt, used chiefly for the tops of billiard tables. **2.** a table cover of this fabric, esp. on a billiard table. —*v.t.* **3.** to cover or line with baize. [earlier *bays,* t. F: m. *baies,* pl., der. *bai* bay-coloured, g. L *badius*]

Baja California (*Sp.* bȧ′KHȧ kȧ lē fôr′nyȧ), Spanish name of **Lower California.**

bake (bāk), *v.,* **baked, baking,** *n.* —*v.t.* **1.** to cook by dry heat in an oven, under coals, or on heated metals or stones. **2.** to harden by heat. —*v.i.* **3.** to bake bread, etc. **4.** to become baked. **5.** *Colloq.* to become very hot, esp. by sunbathing. —*n.* **6.** *U.S.* a social occasion at which baked food is served. **7.** *Scot.* a kind of biscuit. [ME *bake(n),* OE *bacan,* c. G *backen*]

bakehouse (bāk′hous′), *n.* a bakery.

Bakelite (bā′kə līt′), *n.* a trademark for a thermosetting plastic derived by heating phenol or cresol with formaldehyde and ammonia under pressure, used for making radio cabinets, telephone receivers, electric insulators, and moulded plastic ware. [named after L. H. BAEKELAND]

baker (bā′kə), *n.* one who bakes; one who makes and sells bread, cake, etc.

Baker (bā′kə), *n.* **Mount,** a mountain in the U.S., in NW Washington, in the Cascade Range. 10,750 ft.

baker's dozen, thirteen, reckoned as a dozen.

bakery (bā′kə rĭ), *n., pl.* **-ries. 1.** a building or room to bake in; bakehouse. **2.** a baker's shop.

Bakewell tart (bāk′wəl), an open tart with a pastry base and a cakelike filling. [named after *Bakewell,* a town in Derbyshire]

baking (bā′kĭng), *n.* **1.** the act of one who or that which bakes. **2.** the quantity baked at one time; a batch. —*adj.* **3.** *Colloq.* very hot; sweltering.

baking powder, any of various powders used as a substitute for yeast in baking, composed of sodium bicarbonate mixed with an acid substance capable of setting carbon dioxide free when the mixture is moistened.

baking soda, sodium bicarbonate, $NaHCO_3$.

baklava (bä′klə vä′), *n.* a Near-Eastern pastry of very thin dough, nuts, and honey. [t. Turk.]

baksheesh (băk′shēsh), (used in India, Turkey, etc.) —*n.* **1.** a tip, present, or gratuity. —*v.t., v.i.* **2.** to give a tip (to). Also, **bakshish, backsheesh, backshish.** [t. Pers.: m. *bakhshīsh,* der. *bakhshīdan* give]

Bakst (*Russ.* bȧkst), *n.* **Leon Nikolaevich** (*Russ.* lĭ ôn′ nĭ kȧ lȧ′yĭ vĭch), 1866–1924, Russian painter and designer.

Baku (bä ko͞o′; *Russ.* bȧ ko͞o′), *n.* a seaport in the S Soviet Union in Europe, on the Caspian Sea: capital of Azerbaijan. 1,147,000 with suburbs (est. 1965).

Bakunin (*Russ.* bȧ ko͞o′nĭn), *n.* **Mikhail Aleksandrovich** (*Russ.* mĭ KHȧ ēl′ ə lĭk sȧn′drə vĭch), 1814–76, Russian anarchist and writer.

bal., balance.

B.A.L., British anti-lewisite; dimercaprol.

Balaam (bā′lăm), *n.* **1.** a Mesopotamian diviner who, when commanded to curse the Israelites, blessed them and uttered favourable prophecies, after having been rebuked by the ass he rode. Num. 22–23. **2.** a person likened to Balaam; a prophet who changes his mind, esp. from wrong to right. **3.** *Journalism.* journalistic material kept in reserve for filling up a newspaper. —**Ba′laamite′,** *n.* —**Balaamitical** (bā′lə mĭt′ĭ kl), *adj.*

balaclava helmet, a warm woollen hood which covers the ears, orig. worn by soldiers in the Crimea. Also, **balaclava.**

Balaklava (băl′ə klä′və; *Russ.* bə lȧk lȧ′və), *n.* a seaport in the SW Soviet Union in Europe, on the Black Sea: scene of the charge of the Light Brigade in the Crimean War, 1854. Also, **Balaclava.**

balalaika (băl′ə lī′kə), *n.* a Russian musical instrument with a triangular body and a guitar-like neck. [t. Russ.]

Balalaika

Bala Lake, the largest natural lake in Wales, in Merionethshire. 1·8 sq. mi. Welsh, **Llyn Tegid.**

balance (băl′əns), *n.*, *v.*, **-anced, -ancing.** —*n.* **1.** an instrument for weighing, typically a bar poised or swaying on a central support according to the weights borne in scales (pans) suspended at the ends. **2.** power to decide as by a balance; authoritative control. **3.** a state of equilibrium or equipoise; equal distribution of weight, amount, etc. **4.** mental steadiness; habit of calm behaviour, judgement, etc. **5.** harmonious arrangement or adjustment, esp. in the arts of design. **6.** something used to produce equilibrium; a counterpoise. **7.** the act of balancing; comparison as to weight, amount, importance, etc.; estimate. **8.** *Colloq.* the remainder or rest. **9.** *Com.* **a.** equality between the totals of the two sides of an account. **b.** the difference between the debit total and the credit total of an account. **c.** unpaid difference represented by the excess of debits over credits. **10.** an adjustment of accounts. **11.** *Horol.* a wheel which oscillates against the tension of a hairspring for regulating the beats of a watch or clock. **12.** (*cap.*) *Astron.*, *Astrol.* the zodiacal constellation or sign Libra. **13.** *Dancing.* a balancing movement. —*v.t.* **14.** to weigh in a balance. **15.** to estimate the relative weight or importance of; compare: *balance probabilities.* **16.** to serve as a counterpoise to; counterbalance; offset. **17.** to bring to or hold in equilibrium; poise: *to balance a book on one's head.* **18.** to arrange, adjust, or proportion the parts of symmetrically. **19.** to be equal or proportionate to. **20.** *Com.* **a.** to add up the two sides of (an account) and determine the difference. **b.** to make the necessary entries in (an account) so that the sums of the two sides will be equal. **c.** to settle by paying what remains due on an account; equalize or adjust. **21.** *Dancing.* to move in rhythm to and from: *to balance one's partner.* —*v.i.* **22.** to have an equality or equivalence in weight, parts, etc.; be in equilibrium: *the account doesn't balance; do these scales balance?* **23.** *Com.* to reckon or adjust accounts. **24.** to waver, hesitate. **25.** *Dancing.* to move forwards and backwards, or in opposite directions; set. [ME, t. OF, g. LL *bilanx* having two scales] —**bal′anceable,** *adj.* —**Syn. 4.** poise, composure. **8.** See **remainder.**

balance bar, any projecting bar which offsets the weight of a hinged gate, as the beam projecting from a lock gate.

balance of payments, the difference between a nation's total payments to foreign countries (debits) and its total receipts from foreign sources (credits).

balance of power, a distribution and an opposition of forces among nations such that no single nation will be strong enough to dominate all the others.

balance of trade, the difference between the value of the exports and imports of a country, said to be favourable or unfavourable as exports are greater or less than imports.

balancer (băl′ən sə), *n.* **1.** one who or that which balances. **2.** *Entomol.* haltere. **3.** an acrobat.

balance sheet, *Com.* **1.** a tabular statement of both sides of a set of accounts, in which the debit and credit balances add up as equal. **2.** a statement of the financial position of a business on a specified date.

balance spring, a hairspring.

balance wheel, *Horol.* balance (def. 11).

balanitis (băl′ə nī′tĭs), *n.* *Med.* inflammation of the glans penis.

Balarama (bŭl′ə rä′mə), *n.* *Hindu Myth.* the elder brother of Krishna and an incarnation of Vishnu.

balas (băl′əs, bā′ləs), *n.* *Mineral.* a rose red variety of spinel. Also, **balas ruby.** [ME, t. OF: m. *balais*, t. Ar.: m. *balakhsh* kind of ruby, t. Pers.: m. *Badakhshān*, a province where found]

balata (băl′ə tə), *n.* **1.** the dried juice or gum (**balata gum**) obtained from the bully tree, *Manilkara bidentata*, used as a substitute for gutta-percha and in making chewing gum. **2.** the bully tree. [t. Amer. Sp.]

Balaton (băl′ə tən; *Hung.* bŏl′ŏ tŏn), *n.* a lake in W Hungary; the largest lake in central and western Europe. 266 sq. mi.; ab. 50 mi. long. German, **Plattensee.**

Balbo (băl′bō: *It.* bäl′bô), *n.* **Italo** (*It.* ē′tä lô), 1896–1940, Italian aviator, general, and statesman.

Balboa (băl bō′ə; *Sp.* bäl bô′ä), *n.* **1. Vasco Núñez de** (*Sp.* bäs′kô nōō′nyĕth dĕ), 1475?–1517, Spanish adventurer and explorer: discovered the Pacific Ocean in 1513. **2.** a seaport in the Canal Zone at the Pacific terminus of the Panama Canal. 4162 (1960). **3.** (*l.c.*) the monetary unit of Panama, equal to 100 cents, and valued at one U.S. dollar. **4.** (*l.c.*) a silver coin of this value.

balbriggan (băl brĭg′ən), *n.* a kind of unbleached cotton, originally made at Balbriggan, in Ireland, used esp. in hosiery and underwear.

balcony (băl′kə nĭ), *n.*, *pl.* **-nies. 1.** a balustraded or raised and railed platform projecting from the wall of a building. **2.** (in some cinemas, theatres, etc.) the highest gallery. [t. It.: m. *balcone*, der. *balco* scaffold, t. OHG. See BALK] —**bal′conied,** *adj.*

bald (bôld), *adj.* **1.** lacking hair on some part of the scalp: *a bald head or person.* **2.** destitute of some natural growth or covering: *a bald mountain.* **3.** bare; plain; unadorned: *a bald prose style.* **4.** open; undisguised: *a bald lie.* **5.** *Zool.* having white on the head: *bald eagle.* [ME *balled*, f. obs. *ball* white spot (cf. Welsh *bali* whiteness) + -ED[3]] —**bald′ing, bald′ish,** *adj.* —**bald′ly,** *adv.* —**bald′ness,** *n.*

baldachin (bôl′də kĭn), *n.* **1.** *Archit.* a fixed canopy, of metal, wood, or stone, above the isolated high altar of a church or above a tomb. **2.** a portable canopy carried in religious processions. Also, **baldaquin.** [t. F: m. *baldaquin*, t. It.: m. *baldacchino*, orig., silk from Baghdad, der. *Baldacco* Baghdad]

bald eagle, a large eagle, *Haliaetus leucocephalus*, of the U.S. and Canada, having a fully feathered head and, when adult, a white head and tail.

Bald eagle, *Haliaetus leucocephalus* (Ab. 3 ft high, wingspan 7 ft)

Balder (bôl′də), *n.* *Scand. Myth.* son of Odin, and one of the chief deities, god of the summer sun, and called 'the Good'. Also, **Baldr** (bäl′də).

balderdash (bôl′də dăsh′), *n.* **1.** idle, ill-informed talk; rubbish. **2.** a senseless jumble of words; nonsense. **3.** *Obs.* a mixture of spirits.

baldhead (bôld′hĕd′), *n.* one who has a bald head. —**bald′-head′ed,** *adj.*

baldmoney (bôld′mŭn′ĭ), *n.* spignel.

baldpate (bôld′pāt′), *n.* one who has a bald head. —**bald′-pat′ed,** *adj.*

baldric (bôl′drĭk), *n.* a belt, sometimes richly ornamented, worn diagonally from shoulder to hip, supporting a sword, horn, etc. [ME *bawdrik*, orig. and history obscure; akin to MHG *balderich* girdle; r. ME *baudry*, t. OF, t. MHG (as above)]

Baldwin (bôld′wĭn), *n.* **1. James,** born 1924, U.S. writer. **2. Stanley** (*Earl Baldwin of Bewdley*), 1867–1947, British statesman: prime minister 1923–24, 1924–29, 1935–37.

Baldwin I, 1058–1118, crusader and first king of Jerusalem, 1100–1118.

bale[1] (bāl), *n.*, *v.*, **baled, baling.** —*n.* **1.** a large bundle or package prepared for storage or transportation, esp. one closely compressed and secured by cords, wires, hoops, or the like, sometimes with a wrapping: *a bale of hay.* —*v.t.* **2.** to make into bales. [ME, t. Flem., t. OF: m. *balle*, t. Gmc (cf. OHG: m. *balla* BALL[1])] —**bal′er,** *n.*

bale[2] (bāl), *n.* *Archaic.* **1.** evil; harm; misfortune. **2.** woe; misery; sorrow. [ME; OE *balu*, *bealo*]

bale[3] (bāl), *v.*, **baled, baling,** *n.* —*v.t.* **1.** to dip out of or remove from a boat, as with a bucket or a can: *to bale water out of a boat.* **2.** to clear of water by dipping (usually fol by *out*): *to bale out a boat.* —*v.i.* **3.** to bale water. **4.** to make a parachute jump from a plane (fol. by *out*). **5.** *Colloq.* to abandon a dangerous position or course (fol. by *out*). —*n.* **6.** a bucket or other vessel for baling. Also, **bail.** [ME *bayle*, t, OF: m. *baille* bucket, g. VL *bājula* vessel] —**bal′er,** *n.*

Bâle (*Fr.* bàl), *n.* French name of **Basle.**

Balearic Islands (băl′ĭ ă′rĭk), a group of islands in the W Mediterranean: a province of Spain. 442,000 pop. (est. 1963); 1936 sq. mi. *Cap.*: Palma. Spanish, **Baleares** (*Sp.* bä lĕ ä′rĕs).

baleen (bə lēn′), *n.* *Zool.* whalebone (def. 1). [ME *balene*, t. OF: m. *baleine*, g. L *balaena* whale]

balefire (bāl′fī′ə), *n.* **1.** a large fire in the open air, bonfire. **2.** *Archaic.* a beacon or signal fire. **3.** *Archaic.* the fire of a funeral pyre. [ME *balefyre*, OE *bǣlfȳr*]

baleful (bāl′fəl), *adj.* **1.** full of menacing or malign influences; pernicious. **2.** *Archaic.* wretched; sorrowful. [ME; OE *bealofull*] —**bale′fully,** *adv.* —**bale′fulness,** *n.*

Balewa (bə lā′wə), *n.* **Alhaji Sir Abubakar Tafawa.** See **Tafawa Balewa.**

Balfour (băl′fô, -fə, -fōōə), *n.* **Arthur James** (*1st Earl of Balfour*), 1848–1930, British statesman and writer: prime minister 1902–05.

Balfour Declaration, a statement (Nov. 2nd, 1917) that the British government 'view with favour the establishment in Palestine of a National Home for the Jewish people', but that 'nothing shall be done which may prejudice the civil and religious rights of existing non-Jewish communities in Palestine'.

Bali (bä′lĭ), *n.* an island in Indonesia, E of Java. 1,775,000 pop. (est. 1961); 2147 sq. mi. *Cap.*: Singaraja.

Bali

Balikesir (*Turk.* bä lĭk′ĕ sĕr), *n.* a town in NW Turkey. 61,145 (1960).

Balinese (bä′lĭ nēz′), *adj., n., pl.* **-nese.** —*adj.* **1.** of or pertaining to Bali, its people, or their language. —*n.* **2.** a native or inhabitant of Bali. **3.** the language of Bali, an Indonesian language.

Baliol (bā′lyəl, bā′lĭ əl), *n.* **John de,** 1249–1315, king of Scotland 1292–96.

balk (bôk), *v.i.* **1.** to stop, as at an obstacle: *he balked at making the speech.* **2.** (of horses) to stop short and stubbornly refuse to go on. —*v.t.* **3.** to place a balk in the way of; hinder; thwart: *balked in one's hopes.* **4.** to let slip; fail to use: *to balk an opportunity.* —*n.* **5.** a check or hindrance; a defeat or disappointment. **6.** a miss, slip, or failure: *to make a balk.* **7.** a strip of land left unploughed. **8.** a crossbeam in the roof of a house which unites and supports the rafters. **9.** a squared timber. **10.** a rope connecting a line of fishing nets. **11.** *Billiards, Chiefly U.S.* baulk. Also, **baulk.** [ME; OE *balca* ridge, c. OHG *balco* beam] —**balk′er,** *n.*

Balkan (bôl′kən), *adj.* **1.** pertaining to the Balkan States or their inhabitants. **2.** pertaining to the Balkan Peninsula. **3.** pertaining to the Balkan Mountains. —*n.* **4. the Balkans,** the Balkan States or the Balkan Peninsula.

Balkanize (bôl′kə nīz′), *v.t.*, **-nized, -nizing.** to divide into small states hostile to one another. Also, **Balkanise.** —**Bal′kaniza′tion,** *n.*

Balkan Mountains, a mountain range extending from W Bulgaria to the Black Sea. Highest peak, ab. 7800 ft.

Balkan Peninsula, a peninsula in S Europe, bordered by the Adriatic, Ionian, Aegean, and Black seas.

Balkan States, the countries in the Balkan Peninsula: Yugoslavia, Rumania, Bulgaria, Albania, Greece, and the European part of Turkey.

Balkhash (băl kăsh′), *n.* a salt lake in the SW Soviet Union in Asia, in Kazakhstan. 7115 sq. mi.

balky (bô′kĭ), *adj.*, **balkier, balkiest.** *U.S.* given to balking: *a balky horse.*

ball[1] (bôl), *n.* **1.** a spherical or approximately spherical body; a sphere. **2.** a round or roundish body, of different materials and sizes, hollow or solid, for use in various games, as cricket, football, tennis, or golf. **3.** a game played with a ball. **4.** a throw, play, action, movement, etc., of a ball: *a low or high ball, a flighted ball.* **5.** *Mil.* **a.** a solid projectile, usually spherical, for a cannon, rifle, pistol, etc. (distinguished from a *shell*). **b.** projectiles, esp. bullets, collectively. **6.** any part of a thing, esp. of the human body, that is rounded or protuberant: *the ball of the thumb.* **7.** (*pl.*) *Taboo Slang.* **a.** testicles. **b.** balderdash; rubbish; nonsense. **8.** *Astron.* a planetary or celestial body, esp. the earth. **9. have the ball at one's feet,** be on the road to success. **10. keep the ball rolling,** *Colloq.* to keep something going; to keep up the rate of progress or activity. **11. on the ball,** *Slang.* in touch with a situation, reality, etc.; alert; sharp. **12. play ball,** *U.S. Colloq.* to work together (with); cooperate. **13. start the ball rolling,** to start an operation; set an activity in motion. —*v.t.* **14.** to make into a ball or balls. **15.** to clog or entangle. **16.** *Taboo Slang.* to bring to a state of hopeless confusion or difficulty (fol. by *up*). —*v.i.* **17.** to form or gather into a ball. [ME *bal*, t. Scand.; cf. Icel. *böllr*]

—**Syn. 1.** BALL, GLOBE, SPHERE, ORB agree in referring to a round or rounded object. BALL may be applied to any round or roundish object or part: *a rubber ball.* GLOBE and SPHERE denote something thought of as either exactly or approximately round: *in the form of a globe, a perfect sphere.* ORB is now found only in elevated or scientific use; it is applied esp. to the eye and to the heavenly bodies: *the orb of the full moon.*

ball[2] (bôl), *n.* a social assembly for dancing. [t. F: m. *bal*, der. OF *baler* dance, g. LL *ballāre*]

Ball (bôl), *n.* **John,** died 1381, English priest: one of the leaders of Wat Tyler's peasants' revolt in 1381.

ballad (băl′əd), *n.* **1.** a simple, often crude, narrative poem, of popular origin, composed in short stanzas, esp. one of romantic character and adapted for singing. **2.** any poem written in similar style. **3.** any light, simple song, esp. one of sentimental or romantic character, having two or more stanzas, all sung to the same melody. **4.** the musical setting for a ballad. [ME *balade*, t. OF, t. Pr.: m. *balada* dance, der. *balar* dance, g. LL *ballāre*]

ballade (bə läd′; *Fr.* bȧ lȧd′), *n.* **1.** a poem consisting commonly of three stanzas having an identical rhyme scheme, followed by an envoy. The same last line is used for each of the stanzas and the envoy. **2.** *Music.* a composition in free style and romantic mood, often for solo piano or for orchestra. [t. F. See BALLAD]

ballad-monger (băl′əd mŭng′gə), *n.* **1.** a seller of ballads. **2.** a bad poet.

ballad opera, a light opera, often humorous or satirical, in which the tunes are taken from popular songs, and the dialogue is spoken.

balladry (băl′ə drĭ), *n.* ballad poetry.

ballad stanza, the metrical form for ballad verse, ordinarily consisting of four lines.

ballan (băl′ən), *n.* a species of wrasse, *Labrus maculatus.* [t. Irish]

ball and chain, 1. a heavy iron ball fastened by a chain to a prisoner's leg. **2.** any restraint.

ball-and-socket joint (bôl′ən sŏk′ĭt), a joint formed by a ball or knob in a socket, admitting a degree of rotary movement in every direction.

Ballarat (băl′ə răt′, băl′ə răt′), *n.* a town in SE Australia, in Victoria. 57,290 (est. 1964).

ballast (băl′əst), *n.* **1.** any heavy material carried by a ship or boat for ensuring proper stability, so as to avoid capsizing and to secure the greatest effectiveness of the propelling power. **2.** something heavy, as bags of sand, placed in the car of a balloon for control of altitude or, less frequently, of attitude. **3.** anything that gives mental, moral, or political stability or steadiness. **4.** gravel, broken stone, slag, etc., placed between and under railway sleepers to give stability, provide drainage, and distribute the load. **5.** a mixture of small stones and sand, used as a building material. —*v.t.* **6.** to furnish with ballast: *to ballast a ship.* **7.** to give steadiness to; keep steady. [t. MLG: f. *bal* bad + *last* load; but cf. ODan. *barlast* (f. *bar* BARE[1], mere + *last* load)]

ball-bearing (bôl′bēə′rĭng), *n. Mach.* **1.** a bearing in which the shaft or journal turns upon a number of steel balls running in an annular track. **2.** any of the steel balls so used.

ball boy, *Tennis.* a person employed to retrieve balls and return them to the server.

ballcock (bôl′kŏk′), *n.* a device for regulating the supply of water in a tank, cistern, or the like, consisting essentially of a valve connected with a hollow floating ball which by its rise or fall shuts or opens the valve.

ballerina (băl′ə rē′nə; *It.* bäl lė rē′nȧ), *n., pl.* **-nas,** (*It.*) **-ne** (-nė). **1.** the principal female dancer in a ballet company. **2.** any female ballet-dancer. [t. It.]

ballet (băl′ā; *Fr.* bȧ lĕ′), *n.* **1.** a spectacular entertainment, often designed to tell a story, and rendered by a company of professional dancers. **2.** the style of dancing employed in such a performance, using intricate steps and expressive gestures. **3.** the music for a ballet. **4.** the choreography of a ballet. **5.** a dance interlude in an operatic or dramatic performance. **6.** a company of dancers. [t. F, t. It.: m. *balletto*, dim. of *ballo* BALL[2]]

ballet-dancer (băl′ĭ dän′sə), *n.* a male or female dancer trained in ballet techniques.

balletomane (băl′ĭ tə mān′), *n.* a ballet enthusiast.

balletomania (băl′ĭ tə mā′nyə), *n.* great or excessive enthusiasm for ballet.

ballflower (bôl′flou′ə), *n. Archit.* a medieval ornament resembling a ball placed in a circular flower, the three (or four) petals of which form a cup around it.

ball-frame (bôl′frām′), *n.* an abacus.

ballista (bə lĭs′tə), *n., pl.* **-tae** (-tē). an ancient military engine for throwing stones or other missiles. [t. L, der. Gk *bállein* throw]

Ballista

ballistic (bə lĭs′tĭk), *adj.* **1.** relating to projectiles. **2.** relating to an instrument, as a ballistic galvanometer, for measuring the effect of a transient source of energy or an impact.

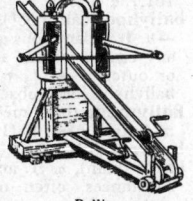

ballistic galvanometer, a galvanometer for measuring surges of electric current.

ballistic missile, a missile, such as a rocket, which is propelled and guided only in the initial phase of its flight, but reaches its target by a ballistic descent.

ballistic pendulum, a heavy block of wood suspended on strings so that it can swing in one plane only, used for measuring the momentum of bullets, etc.

ballistics (bə lĭs′tĭks), *n.* the science or study of the motion of projectiles, such as bullets, shells, bombs, rockets, etc., proceeding under no power and acted upon only by gravitational forces and the resistance of the

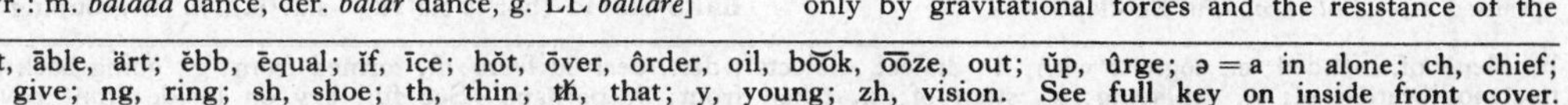

medium through which they pass. **Interior ballistics** is the study of the motion of projectiles within the bore of a gun or of rocket missiles under the influence of burning fuel; **exterior ballistics** is the study of the motion of projectiles after they leave the muzzle of a gun or of rocket missiles when influenced only by the atmosphere or space and gravity. —**ballistician** (băl′ĭs tĭsh′ən), *n.*

ballonet (băl′ə nĕt′), *n.* an air or gasbag compartment in a balloon, etc., used to control buoyancy and maintain shape. [t. F: m. *ballonnet*, dim. of *ballon* balloon]

balloon (bə lo͞on′), *n.* **1.** a bag made of some material impermeable to gas and filled with some gas lighter than ordinary air, designed to rise and float in the atmosphere, and in the large forms having a car or compartment attached for passengers. **2.** an inflatable rubber bag, usually brightly coloured, used as a children's toy. **3.** *Chem.* a round-bottomed flask. **4.** (in drawings, etc.) a balloon-shaped figure enclosing words represented as issuing from the mouth of the speaker. **5.** a kick or stroke which sends a ball high into the air. —*v.i.* **6.** to go up or ride in a balloon. **7.** to swell or puff out like a balloon. —*v.t.* **8.** to fill with air; inflate or distend (something) like a balloon. **9.** to send (a ball) high into the air. —*adj.* **10.** puffed out like a balloon: *balloon sleeves.* [t. It.: m. *ballone*, aug. of *balla* ball] —**balloon′ist,** *n.*

balloon barrage, a barrage of anchored balloons intended to destroy or deter low-flying hostile aircraft.

balloon glass, a pear-shaped glass, narrowing at the top to intensify the aroma of the brandy, for which it is principally used.

balloon jib, *Naut.* a large triangular sail of light canvas used by yachts in light winds, instead of the jib.

balloon tyre, a large pneumatic tyre in which the pressure is low to prevent the shock of uneven surfaces.

balloon vine, a sapindaceous tropical climbing plant, *Cardiospermum halicacabum*, with big bladder-like pods; heartseed.

ballot (băl′ət), *n.*, *v.*, **-loted, -loting.** —*n.* **1.** a ticket, paper, etc., used in voting. **2.** the whole number of votes cast or recorded: *there was a large ballot.* **3.** the method of secret voting by means of printed or written ballots, or by means of voting machines. **4.** voting in general, or a round of voting. **5.** (formerly) a little ball used in voting. —*v.i.* **6.** to vote by ballot. **7.** to draw lots: *to ballot for places.* [t. It.: m. *ballotta* bullet, lot, dim. of *balla* ball] —**bal′lotter,** *n.*

ballot-box (băl′ət bŏks′), *n.* a box to receive ballots.

ballot-paper (băl′ət pā′pə), *n.* a slip of paper bearing a ballot vote.

ballottement (bə lŏt′mənt), *n.* *Med.* **1.** an unreliable method of diagnosing pregnancy by the rebound of a foetal part displaced from its position by a sudden push with the examining finger. **2.** a similar method employed in testing for a floating kidney, movable abdominal tumours, etc. [t. F: a tossing, der. *ballotter* toss as a ball]

ballpoint pen (bôl′point′), a fountain pen in which the point is a fine ball-bearing, depositing an extremely thin film of ink. It will write for a longer period with a single reservoir of ink than a conventional pen.

ballroom (bôl′ro͝om′, -ro͞om′), *n.* a large room in a private residence, hotel, etc., in which dances are held.

balls-up (bôlz′ŭp′), *n.* *Taboo Slang.* **1.** confusion arising from a mistake; a mess. **2.** the mistake itself. Also, *U.S.*, **ball-up.**

bally (băl′ĭ), *Slang.* —*adj.* **1.** confounded (used humorously or for emphasis). —*adv.* **2.** very. [? orig. euph. for BLOODY]

Bally (băl′ĭ), *n.* a town in India, in E West Bengal. 101,159 (1961).

ballyhoo (băl′ĭ ho͞o′), *n.*, *pl.* **-hoos,** *v.*, **-hooed, -hooing.** —*n.* **1.** a clamorous attempt to win customers or advance any cause; blatant advertising or publicity. **2.** clamour or outcry. —*v.t.*, *v.i.* **3.** *U.S.* to advertise or push by ballyhoo. [orig. obscure]

Ballymena (băl′ĭ mē′nə), *n.* a town in Northern Ireland, in Antrim. 14,740 (1961).

ballyrag (băl′ĭ răg′), *v.t.* bullyrag.

balm (bäm), *n.* **1.** any of various oily, fragrant, resinous substances, often of medicinal value, exuding from certain plants, esp. tropical trees of the burseraceous genus *Commiphora.* **2.** a plant or tree yielding such a substance. **3.** any aromatic or fragrant ointment. **4.** aromatic fragrance; sweet smell. **5.** any of various aromatic menthaceous plants, esp. of the genus *Melissa*, as *M. officinalis*, a lemon-scented perennial herb. **6.** anything which heals, soothes, or mitigates pain. [ME *basme*, t. OF, g. L *balsamum* BALSAM]

balmacaan (băl′mə kăn′), *n.* a man's short, full-skirted overcoat of rough woollen cloth, with raglan shoulders. [named after *Balmacaan*, in Scotland]

Balmain (băl mān′), *n.* a town in Australia, in New South Wales, a suburb of Sydney. 28,268 (1947).

balm of Gilead, **1.** any of several species of the genus *Commiphora* (esp. *C. opobalsamum* and *C. meccanensis*), which yield a fragrant oleoresin. **2.** the resin itself. **3.** a hybrid female poplar, *Populus gileadensis.*

Balmoral (băl mŏ′rəl), *n.*, **1.** a castle in Scotland, near Braemar: a royal residence. **2.** a coloured woollen petticoat formerly worn under a looped-up skirt. **3.** (*also l.c.*) a kind of laced shoe. **4.** a kind of brimless Scottish cap with a flat top projecting all round the head.

Balmung (băl′mo͝ong), *n.* (in the *Nibelungenlied*) the sword of Siegfried.

balmy (bä′mĭ), *adj.*, **balmier, balmiest.** **1.** mild and refreshing; soft; soothing: *balmy weather.* **2.** having the qualities of balm; aromatic; fragrant: *balmy leaves.* **3.** producing balm. **4.** *Slang.* barmy. —**balm′ily,** *adv.* —**balm′iness,** *n.* —**Syn. 1.** fair, gentle, temperate, clement.

balneal (băl′nĭ əl), *adj.* of or pertaining to baths or bathing. [f. s. L *balneum* bath + -AL[1]]

balneology (băl′nĭ ŏl′ə jĭ), *n.* *Med.* the science of using baths and bathing in therapeutics. [f. s. L *balneum* bath + -(O)LOGY]

baloney (bə lō′nĭ), *n.* *Slang.* nonsense; insincere or idle talk; eyewash; waffle. Also, **boloney.**

balsa (bôl′sə), *n.* **1.** a bombacaceous tree, *Ochroma lagopus*, of tropical America, with an exceedingly light wood used for life-preservers, rafts, etc. **2.** a raft made of balsa wood. **3.** any raft. [t. Sp.]

balsam (bôl′səm), *n.* **1.** any of various fragrant exudations from certain trees, esp. of the burseraceous genus *Commiphora* (see **balm** def. 1), as the balm of Gilead (**balsam of Mecca**). **2.** a similar product (**balsam of Peru** and **balsam of Tolu**) yielded by the leguminous trees, *Myroxylon pereirae* and *M. balsamum* of Central and South America. **3.** oleoresin (def. 1). **4.** any of certain transparent turpentines, as Canada balsam. **5.** a plant or tree yielding a balsam. **6.** the balsam fir. **7.** any of various plants of the balsaminaceous genus *Impatiens*, as *I. balsamina*, a common garden annual. **8.** any aromatic ointment, whether for ceremonial or medicinal use. **9.** any healing or soothing agent or agency. [OE, t. L: s. *balsamum*, t. Gk: m. *bálsamon*] —**balsamaceous** (bôl′sə mā′shəs), *adj.*

balsam fir, **1.** a North American species of fir, *Abies balsamea*, which yields Canada balsam. **2.** the wood of this tree. **3.** any of certain other firs.

balsamic (bôl săm′ĭk, bŏl-), *adj.* of, like, or containing balsam. —**balsam′ically,** *adv.*

balsamiferous (bôl′sə mĭf′ə rəs, bŏl′-), *adj.* yielding balsam. [f. BALSAM + -(I)FEROUS]

balsaminaceous (bôl′sə mĭ nā′shəs, bŏl′sə-), *adj.* *Bot.* belonging to the *Balsaminaceae*, a family of plants with odd-shaped flowers, including many tropical species and also the balsams of the genus *Impatiens.* [f. s. Gk *balsamínē* balsam plant + -ACEOUS]

balsam poplar, a poplar, *Populus tacamahaca*, with broad heart-shaped leaves, cultivated as a shade tree.

balsam spruce, either of two North American conifers of the genus *Picea*, *P. pungens* (the **blue spruce**) and *P. engelmanni.*

Balt., Baltic.

Baltic (bôl′tĭk), *adj.* **1.** of, near, or on the Baltic Sea. **2.** of or pertaining to the Baltic States. —*n.* **3. the Baltic,** the Baltic Sea, Baltic States, and surrounding area. **4.** a group of Indo-European languages, including Lettish, Lithuanian, and the extinct Old Prussian. [t. ML: s. *Balticum*, ? der. L *balteus* belt]

Baltic Sea

Baltic Sea, a sea in N Europe, bounded by Sweden, Finland, the Soviet Union, Poland, Germany and Denmark. ab. 160,000 sq. mi.

Baltic States, the formerly independent republics of Estonia, Latvia, and Lithuania, sometimes including Finland.

Baltimore (bôl′tĭ mô′), *n.* **1.** a seaport in the U.S., in N Maryland, on an estuary near Chesapeake Bay. 939,024 (1960). **2. Lord.** See **Calvert, Sir George.**

Baltimore oriole, an American oriole, *Icterus galbula*; the firebird. [so named because the black and orange of the male were the colours of Lord Baltimore's livery]

Balto-Slavic (bôl′tō slä′vĭk, -slăv′ĭk), *n.* a grouping of

Indo-European languages comprising the Baltic and Slavic groups.

Baluchi (bə lo͞o′chĭ), *n.*, *pl.* **Baluchi, Baluchis. 1.** a member of a Muslim people living in Baluchistan. **2.** the Iranian language of this people.

Baluchistan (bə lo͞o′chĭ stän′, -stăn′), *n.* **1.** an arid mountainous region in S Asia, in SE Iran and NW West Pakistan, bordering on the Arabian Sea. **2.** a former territory of W British India, now incorporated into West Pakistan.

baluster (băl′ə stə), *n. Archit.* one of a series of short pillar-like supports (usually of stone) for a coping or railing, as of a parapet. [t. F: m. *balustre*, t. It.: m. *balaust(r)o*, t. L: m. *balaustium*, t. Gk: m. *balaústion* pomegranate flower]

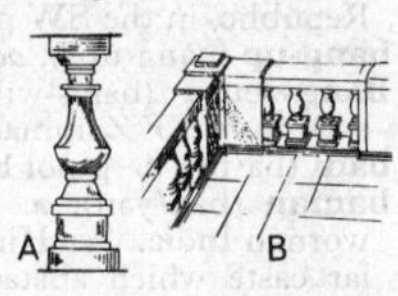

A, Baluster; B, Balustrade

balustrade (băl′ə strād′), *n. Archit.* a coping or railing with the row of balusters supporting it, as in parapet.

Balzac (băl′zăk; *Fr.* bȧl zak′), *n.* **Honoré de** (*Fr.* ŏ nō rĕ′ də), 1799–1850, French novelist.

Bamako (*Fr.* bȧ mȧ kō′), *n.* the capital of Mali, in the SW part. 120,000 (est. 1963).

Bamberg (băm′bûg; *Ger.* bȧm′bĕrk), *n.* a town in West Germany, in N Bavaria. 72,200 (est. 1966).

bambino (băm bē′nō; *It.* bȧm bē′nō), *n.*, *pl.* **-ni** (-nē). **1.** a child or baby. **2.** an image of the infant Jesus. [t. It., dim of *bambo* simple]

bamboo (băm bo͞o′), *n.*, *pl.* **-boos. 1.** any of the woody or treelike tropical and semitropical grasses of the genus *Bambusa* (or *Bambos*) and allied genera. **2.** the hollow woody stem of such a plant, used for building purposes and for making furniture, poles, etc. [earlier *bambus*, t. D: m. *bamboes*, ult. t. Malay: m. *mambu*]

bamboo curtain, the state of censorship between Communist countries of Asia, esp. China, and the rest of the world.

bamboozle (băm bo͞o′zəl), *v.*, **-zled, -zling.** *—v.t.* **1.** to deceive by trickery; impose upon. **2.** to perplex; mystify. *—v.i.* **3.** *Chiefly U.S.* to practise imposition or trickery. [? of cant orig.] **—bamboo′zlement,** *n.* **—bamboo′zler,** *n.*

bamboo-fish (băm bo͞o′fĭsh′), *n.* a striped fish, *Sarpa salpa*, of African waters, belonging to the bream family.

ban[1] (băn), *v.*, **banned, banning,** *n.* *—v.t.* **1.** to prohibit; interdict: *to ban a meeting or book.* **2.** *Archaic.* to pronounce an ecclesiastical curse upon. **3.** *Archaic.* to curse; execrate. *—n.* **4.** an authoritative interdiction. **5.** informal denunciation or prohibition, as by public opinion. **6.** *Law.* a sentence of outlawry. **7.** *Eccles.* a formal ecclesiastical denunciation; excommunication. **8.** a malediction; curse. [ME, t. Scand.; cf. Icel. *banna* forbid, curse, c. OE *bannan* summon] **—Syn. 1.** forbid. **4.** prohibition, proscription, taboo.

ban[2] (băn), *n.* **1.** a public proclamation or edict. **2.** (*pl.*) banns. **3.** (in feudal times) the summons of the sovereign's vassals for military service, or the whole body liable to the summons. [OE *gebann*]

ban[3] (băn), *n. Hist.* **1.** the governor of Croatia and Slavonia. **2.** one of the wardens of the southern marches of Hungary. [t. Hung., t. Pers.: lord]

ban[4] (bän), *n.*, *pl.* **bani** (bä′nĭ). a Rumanian coin worth one-hundredth part of a leu. [Rum.]

banal (bə näl′), *adj.* hackneyed; trite. [t. F, der. OF *ban*, t. Gmc: proclamation, c. BAN[2]] **—banality** (bə năl′ĭ tĭ), *n.* **—banal′ly,** *adv.* **—Syn.** See **commonplace.**

banana (bə nä′nə), *n.* **1.** a plant of the tropical genus *Musa*, of which various species are cultivated for their nutritious fruit. **2.** the fruit, esp. that of *M. sapientum*, with yellow or red rind. [t. Pg., Sp., from native name]

banana oil, *Chem.* amyl acetate, $CH_3CO_2C_5H_{11}$, a sweet-smelling, colourless, liquid ester, used as a solvent and in artificial fruit flavours.

banana republic, any small tropical country, esp. of South or Central America, considered as backward, politically unstable, etc., and dependent on the trade of rich foreign nations.

Banbury (băn′bə rĭ), *n.* a town in England, in Oxfordshire, esp. important in 16th and 17th centuries. 21,410 (est. 1962).

banbury cake, a kind of mince pie.

banbury tale, an untrue tale.

band[1] (bănd), *n.* **1.** a company of persons (rarely animals) joined or acting together; a company, party, or troop. **2.** a company of musicians playing instruments usually for marching or open-air performance, namely, brass, woodwind, and percussion. **3.** an orchestra playing popular music, esp. for dancing. **4.** a division of a nomadic tribe; a group of individuals who move and camp together. *—v.t.* **5.** to unite in a troop, company, or confederacy. *—v.i.* **6.** to unite; confederate (usually fol. by *together*). [t. F: m. *bande*, ult. from Gmc, but sense devel. purely Rom.] **—Syn. 1.** See **company.**

band[2] (bănd), *n.* **1.** a thin, flat strip of some material for binding, confining, trimming, or some other purpose: hatband, rubber band. **2.** a fillet, belt, or strap. **3.** a stripe, as of colour or decorative work. **4.** the form of falling or flat collar commonly worn by men and women in the 17th century in western Europe. **5.** (*pl.*) a linen or cambric collar with two pendent strips in front, sometimes worn by clergymen (Geneva bands); also in legal and university dress. **6.** *Radio.* a range of frequencies lying between any two well-defined limits. *—v.t.* **7.** to mark with bands; stripe. [ME *bande*, t. F, ult. c. BAND[3]]

band[3] (bănd), *n.* **1.** (*usually pl.*) anything which binds the person or the limbs; a shackle, manacle, or fetter. **2.** an obligation; bond: *the nuptial bands.* [ME, t. Scand.; cf. Icel. *band*]

Banda (băn′də), *n.* **Dr Hastings Kamuzu** (kă mo͞o′zo͞o), born 1906, prime minister of Malawi from 1963; president from 1966.

bandage (băn′dĭj), *n.*, *v.*, **-daged, -daging.** *—n.* **1.** a strip of cloth or other material used to bind up a wound, hold a dressing in place, etc. **2.** anything used as a band or ligature. *—v.t.* **3.** to bind or cover with a bandage. [t. F, der. *bande* band] **—band′ager,** *n.*

bandanna (băn dä′nə, -dăn′ə), *n.* **1.** a large coloured handkerchief with spots or figures, usually white on a red or blue background. **2.** any large handkerchief. Also, **bandan′a.** [appar. der. Hind. *bandhnu*, mode of dyeing in which the cloth is tied so as to prevent parts from receiving the dye]

Bandar (băn′dä, -də), *n.* See **Masulipatam.**

Bandaranaike (băn′də rə nī′ĭ kə), *n.* **1. Mrs Sirimavo** (sĭ′rĭ mä′vō), born 1916, wife of **Solomon**: prime minister of Ceylon 1960–65 and since 1970. **2. Solomon,** 1899–1959, Ceylonese statesman: prime minister 1956–59.

Bandar Maharani (băn′də mä′hə rä′nĭ), a seaport in Malaysia, in SW Johore, on the Strait of Malacca.

Banda Sea (băn′də), a sea between Celebes and New Guinea, S of the Moluccas and N of Timor.

b. & b., **1.** bed and breakfast. **2.** bread and butter.

bandbox (bănd′bŏks′), *n.* a light box of pasteboard, thin wood, etc., for holding a hat, collars, etc.

bandbrake (bănd′brāk′), *n.* a braking device consisting of a band which tightens round a wheel or drum.

bandeau (băn′dō), *n.*, *pl.* **-deaux** (-dōz). a band worn about or on the head; a headband; a fillet. [t. F, dim. of *bande* BAND[2]]

banded (băn′dĭd), *adj.* **1.** striped. **2.** fastened (as with a band).

banderol (băn′də rōl′), *n.* **1.** a small flag or streamer borne on a lance, at a masthead, etc. **2.** a narrow scroll, esp. one bearing an inscription. **3.** a sculptured band adapted to receive an inscription. Also, **banderole, bannerol.** [t. F, t. It.: m. *banderola* small banner, der. *bandiera* banner]

bandicoot (băn′dĭ ko͞ot′), *n.* **1.** any of the very large East Indian rats constituting the genus *Nesokia*, as *N. bandicota*; Malabar rat; pig-rat. **2.** any of various long-clawed, insectivorous marsupials of the family *Peramelidae* of Australia, etc. [t. Telugu: m. *pandikokku* pig-rat]

Bandicoot, *Macrotis lagotis* (Total length 2 ft, tail 8 in.)

bandit (băn′dĭt), *n.*, *pl.* **-dits, banditti** (băn dĭt′ĭ). **1.** a robber, esp. one who robs by violence. **2.** an outlaw. [t. It.: m. *bandito*, prop. pp. of *bandire* proscribe]

banditry (băn′dĭ trĭ), *n.* **1.** the work or practice of bandits. **2.** bandits collectively; banditti.

bandmaster (bănd′mäs′tə), *n.* the conductor of a band.

bandog (băn′dŏg′), *n.* **1.** any dog kept chained. **2.** a mastiff or bloodhound. [ME *band-dogge*; f. BAND[3] + DOG]

bandolier (băn′də lĭə′), *n.* a broad belt worn over the shoulder by soldiers, and having a number of small loops or pockets, each containing a cartridge or cartridges. Also, **bandoleer.** [t. F: m. *bandoulière*, t. Sp.: m. *bandolera*, der. *banda* band, sash, t. It., of Gmc orig.]

bandoline (băn′də lēn′), *n.* a mucilaginous preparation used for keeping the hair smooth or in curls, waves, etc. [t. F, b. *bandeau* band + L *linere* smear]

bandore (băn dô′, băn′dô), *n.* an old musical stringed instrument resembling the lute or the guitar. Also, **pandora, pandore.** [t. Sp.: m. *bandurria*, var. of *pandora*, t. LL: m. *pandūra*, t. Gk: m. *pandoûra* musical instrument with three strings]

bandsaw (bănd′sô′), *n. Mach.* a saw consisting of an endless toothed steel band passing over two wheels.

bandsman (băndz′mən), *n.*, *pl.* **-men.** a musician who plays in a band.

band spectrum, *Physics.* an emission or absorption spectrum consisting of a number of bands of lines, as produced by molecules.

bandstand (bănd′stănd′), *n.* a platform, often roofed, for outdoor band performances.

Bandung (băn′dŏŏng), *n.* a city in Indonesia, in W Java; Afro-Asian conference, 1955. 972,566 (1961).

band wagon, 1. *U.S.* a wagon carrying a band for music, as at the head of a procession or parade. **2.** the successful or winning side or cause. **3. climb** or **jump on the band wagon,** *Colloq.* to join the winning side; take advantage of a popular movement or fashion; follow the crowd.

bandy (băn′dĭ), *v.*, **-died, -dying,** *adj.*, *n.*, *pl.* **-dies.** —*v.t.* **1.** to pass from one to another, or back and forth; give and take: *to bandy blows or words.* **2.** to throw or strike to and fro, or from side to side, as a ball in tennis. —*adj.* **3.** (of legs) having a bend or crook outward. **4.** bandy-legged. —*n. Obs.* **5.** an old form of tennis. **6.** bandy-ball. **7.** an early kind of hockey stick. [orig. obscure. Cf. F *bander* bandy, *se bander* band together, ? der. *bande* side]

bandy-ball (băn′dĭ bôl′), *n. Obs.* an early form of hockey.

bandy-bandy (băn′dĭ băn′dĭ), *n.* a poisonous Australian ringed snake, *Furina annulata.*

bandy-legged (băn′dĭ lĕg′ĭd, -lĕgd′), *adj.* having crooked legs; bowlegged.

bane (bān), *n.* **1.** that which causes death or destroys life. **2.** *Archaic.* a deadly poison. **3.** a thing that ruins or spoils. **4.** *Archaic.* ruin; destruction; death. [ME; OE *bana* slayer]

baneberry (bān′bə rĭ, -brĭ), *n.*, *pl.* **-ries. 1.** any plant of the ranunculaceous genus *Actaea,* comprising herbs which bear nauseous poisonous berries, esp. *A. spicata,* herb Christopher. **2.** the berry.

baneful (bān′fəl), *adj.* destructive; pernicious; poisonous: *a baneful superstition, baneful herbs.* —**bane′fully,** *adv.* —**bane′fulness,** *n.*

Banff (bămf), *n.* **1.** a burgh in Scotland, the county town of Banffshire. 3233 (est. 1962). **2.** Banffshire. **3.** a resort in **Banff National Park,** a scenic park (2585 sq. mi.) in the Rocky Mountains in SW Alberta, Canada. 2337 (1951).

Banffs., Banffshire.

Banffshire (bămf′shĭə, -shə), *n.* a county in NE Scotland. 46,400 pop. (est. 1964); 630 sq. mi. *Co. town:* Banff. *Abbrev.:* Banffs.

bang[1] (băng), *n.* **1.** a loud, sudden explosive noise, as the discharge of a gun. **2.** a resounding stroke or blow. **3.** *Colloq.* a sudden, impetuous movement: *he started off with a bang.* **4.** a knock; a bump. **5.** *U.S. Colloq.* energy; spirit. **6.** *U.S. Slang.* thrill; excitement. —*v.t.* **7.** to strike or beat resoundingly; slam: *to bang a door.* **8.** to knock or bump: *he banged his head.* **9.** to place or move with a bang: *to bang a plate down.* —*v.i.* **10.** to strike violently or noisily: *to bang on the door.* **11.** to make a loud noise as of violent blows: *the guns banged away.* **12.** to slam; to slam repeatedly: *the door banged.* **13. bang a market,** *Com.* to sell stock recklessly in the open market, thereby lowering prices. —*adv.* **14.** with a bang; suddenly and loudly; abruptly. [cf. Icel. *banga* to hammer, *bang* hammering, bungling]

bang[2] (băng), *n.* **1.** a fringe of banged hair. —*v.t.* **2.** to cut (the hair) so as to form a fringe over the forehead. **3.** to dock (the tail of a horse, etc.). [short for BANGTAIL]

bang[3] (băng), *n.* bhang.

Bangalore (băng′gə lô′), *n.* a city in S India, the capital of Mysore state, in the SE part. 905,134 (1961).

bangalow (băng′ə lō′), *n.* a palm, *Archontophoenix cunninghamii,* found in E Australia. [t. native Australian]

banger (băng′ə), *n. Colloq.* **1.** a sausage. **2.** a firework that makes a bang. **3.** a dilapidated vehicle.

Bangka (băng′kə; *Du.* bȧng′kȧ), *n.* an island in Indonesia, E of Sumatra: tin mines. 250,452 pop. (est. 1961); 4611 sq. mi. *Cap.:* Muntok. Also, **Banka.**

Bangkok (băng′kŏk, băng kŏk′), *n.* **1.** the capital of Thailand, on the Menam river: the principal port of Thailand. With suburbs, 1,669,246 (1964). **2.** (*l.c.*) a kind of straw from Thailand. **3.** (*l.c.*) a hat woven of this straw.

bangle (băng′gl), *n.* **1.** a bracelet in the form of a ring, without a clasp. **2.** an ornamental anklet. [t. Hind.: m. *bangrī* bracelet of glass]

bang-on (băng′ŏn′), *adj.*, *adv. Colloq.* **1.** right on the mark; dead-centre. **2.** first-rate. Also (esp. in predicative use), **bang on.**

Bangor (băng′gô, -gə), *n.* **1.** a town in Wales, in Caernarvonshire, on the Menai Strait. 13,993 (1961). **2.** a town in Northern Ireland, in County Down. 23,865 (1961).

Bang's disease (băngz), *Vet. Sci.* an infectious disease of cattle caused by a bacterium, *Brucella abortus,* which infects the genital organs and frequently causes abortions. It also causes undulant fever or brucellosis in man.

bangtail (băng′tāl′), *n.* **1.** a docked tail. **2.** an animal with a docked tail, esp. a horse. **3. bangtail muster,** *Austral. Colloq.* a round-up of cattle for counting. [f. *bang* (nasal var. of *bag* cut) + TAIL[1]] —**bang′-tailed′,** *adj.*

Bangui (*Fr.* bäɴ gē′), *n.* the capital of the Central African Republic, in the SW part. 82,500 (est. 1964).

bang-up (băng′ŭp′), *adj. U.S. Slang.* first-rate; bang-on.

Bangweulu (băng′wĭ ōō′lōō), *n.* a shallow lake and swamp in NE Zambia. ab. 50 mi. long.

bani (bä′nĭ), *n.* pl. of **ban**[4].

banian (băn′yən), *n.* **1.** a loose shirt, jacket, or gown worn in India. **2.** a Hindu trader or merchant of a particular caste which abstains from eating flesh. **3.** banyan. [t. Pg., prob. t. Ar.: m. *banyān,* t. Gujarati: m. *vāniyo* merchant, t. Skt: m. *vanij*]

banish (băn′ĭsh), *v.t.* **1.** to condemn to exile; expel from or relegate to a country or place by authoritative decree. **2.** to compel to depart; send, drive, or put away: *to banish sorrow.* [ME *banysshe(n),* t. OF: m. *baniss-,* s. *banir,* g. LL *bannīre* ban; of Gmc orig. and akin to BAN[1], v.] —**ban′isher,** *n.* —**ban′ishment,** *n.* —**Syn. 1.** exile, expatriate, outlaw.

banister (băn′ĭs tə), *n.* **1.** one of the supports of a stair rail, either plain or resembling a pillar. **2.** (*pl.*) a stair rail and its supports. Also, **bannister.** [var. of BALUSTER]

Banjermasin (băn′jə mä′sĭn), *n.* a seaport in Indonesia, on the S coast of Borneo. 214,096 (1961).

banjo (băn′jō), *n.*, *pl.* **-jos. 1.** a musical instrument of the guitar family, having a circular body covered in front with tightly stretched parchment, and played with the fingers or a plectrum. **2.** *Austral. Slang.* a frying pan. [var. of BANDORE] —**ban′joist,** *n.*

Banjo

banjolele (băn′jə lā′lĭ), *n.* a small banjo with gut strings. [b. BANJO and (UKU)LELE]

bank[1] (băngk), *n.* **1.** a long pile or heap: *a bank of earth, snow, or clouds.* **2.** a slope or acclivity. **3.** *Phys. Geog.* the slope immediately bordering a stream course along which the water normally runs. **4.** *Oceanog.* a broad submarine elevation in the continental shelf lying some distance off the coast, over which the water is relatively shallow. **5.** *Coal Mining.* the surface around the mouth of a shaft. **6.** *Aeron.* the lateral inclination of an aeroplane, esp. during a curve. —*v.t.* **7.** to border with or like a bank; embank. **8.** to form into a bank or heap (fol. by *up*): *to bank up the snow.* **9.** *Aeron.* to tip or incline (an aeroplane) laterally. **10.** to cover up (a fire) with ashes or fuel and close the dampers, to make it burn long and slowly. —*v.i.* **11.** to rise in or form banks, as clouds or snow. **12.** *Aeron.* to tip or incline an aeroplane laterally. [ME *banke,* prob. t. Scand.] —**Syn. 1.** embankment, mound, ridge. **3.** See **shore**[1].

bank[2] (băngk), *n.* **1.** an institution for receiving and lending money (in some cases, issuing notes or holding current accounts that serve as money) or transacting other financial business. **2.** the office or quarters of such an institution. **3.** (in games) **a.** the stock or fund of pieces from which the players draw. **b.** the fund of the manager or the dealer. **4.** any storage place. **5.** any store or reserve: *a blood bank.* **6.** *Obs.* a sum of money, esp. as a fund for use in business. **7.** *Obs.* a moneychanger's table, counter, or shop. —*v.i.* **8.** to exercise the functions of a bank or banker. **9.** to keep money in, or have an account with, a bank. **10.** (in games) to hold the bank. **11.** *Colloq.* to rely or count (fol. by *on* or *upon*). —*v.t.* **12.** to deposit in a bank. [ME *banke,* t. F: m. *banque,* t. It.: m. *banca,* orig. bench, table; of Gmc orig. See BANK[1], BENCH]

bank[3] (băngk), *n.* **1.** an arrangement of objects in line. **2.** *Music.* a row of keys in an organ. **3.** a bench for rowers in a galley. **4.** a row or tier of oars. **5.** the rowers on one bench or to one oar. —*v.t.* **6.** to arrange in a bank. [ME *banck,* t. OF: m. *banc* bench, t. LL: s. *bancus;* from the Gmc source of BENCH]

Banka (băng′kə), *n.* Bangka.

bankable (băng′kə bl), *adj.* receivable by a bank.

bank acceptance, a draft endorsed or otherwise formally acknowledged by a bank on which it is drawn.

bank account, 1. an account with a bank. **2.** balance standing to the credit of a depositor at a bank.

bankbill (băngk′bĭl′), *n.* bank-draft.

bankbook (băngk′bŏŏk′), *n.* a book held by a depositor in which a bank enters a record of his account; a bank passbook or a series of bank statements.

bank charge, a small charge for bank services debited to a customer's account.

bank clerk, one employed in a bank to receive or pay out money over the counter. Also, *U.S.*, **teller.**

bank-draft (băngk′dräft′), *n.* a draft drawn by one bank on another, payable on demand or at a specified future date. Also, **bankbill.**

banker[1] (băng′kə), *n.* **1.** one who manages a bank or is in the banking business. **2.** one who holds or supplies money for another. **3.** (in games) the keeper or holder of the bank. **4.** a gambling card game. [f. BANK[2] + -ER[1]]

banker[2] (băng′kə), *n.* **1.** a vessel employed in the cod fishery on the banks off Newfoundland. **2.** *Austral.* a river running bank high: *to run a banker.* [f. BANK[1] + -ER[2]]

banker[3] (băng′kə), *n. Bldg Trades.* the bench or table upon which bricklayers and stonemasons prepare and shape their material. [f. BANK[3] + -ER[2]. Cf. It. *banco*]

banker's card, a small card issued on request by certain banks to credit-worthy customers, undertaking that the holder's cheques up to a specified amount will be honoured.

banker's draft, bank-draft.

banker's order, a customer's written order to a bank to make a payment or a series of payments on his behalf.

bank holiday, **1.** a weekday on which banks are closed by law; legal holiday. **2.** a secular day on which banks are closed and the law therefore exempts the parties to negotiable paper from their obligations.

banking[1] (băng′kĭng), *n.* **1.** the business of a bank or banker. *—adj.* **2.** pertaining to a bank or banking.

banking[2] (băng′kĭng), *n.* superelevation.

banknote (băngk′nōt′), *n.* **1.** a promissory note, payable on demand, issued by a bank and intended to circulate as money. *—adj.* **2.** pertaining to a bank or banking.

Bank of England, the central bank of the United Kingdom, under the control of a governor and a board of directors, which fixes the bank rate, regulates loans by private banks, and houses the government's capital reserves.

bank passbook, a bankbook for a deposit account.

bank rate, **1.** the rate of discount fixed by a bank or banks. **2.** the rate at which the central bank of a country is prepared to discount bills, as the Bank of England.

bankrupt (băng′krŭpt, -krəpt), *n.* **1.** *Law.* a person who upon his own petition or that of his creditors is adjudged insolvent by a court, and whose property is administered for and divided among his creditors, under a bankruptcy law. **2.** any insolvent debtor; one unable to satisfy any just claims made upon him. *—adj.* **3.** *Law.* subject to, or under, legal process because of insolvency; insolvent. **4.** at the end of one's resources; lacking (fol. by *in*): *to be bankrupt in thanks.* **5.** pertaining to bankrupts. *—v.t.* **6.** to make bankrupt. [t. F: m. (after L *ruptus* broken) *banqueroute*, t. It.: m. *bancarotta* bankruptcy, f. *banca* bank + *rotta*, pp. fem. of *rompere* break, g. L *rumpere*]

bankrupt certificate, a certificate issued by a court, authorizing the appointment of an administrator to a bankrupt estate.

bankruptcy (băng′krəp sĭ), *n., pl.* **-cies.** **1.** the state of being or becoming bankrupt. **2.** utter ruin; failure of a source: *the bankruptcy of a writer's imagination.*

Banks (băngks), *n.* **Sir Joseph,** 1743–1820, English naturalist.

banksia (băngk′sĭ ə), *n.* any plant of the Australian genus *Banksia* comprising shrubs and trees with leathery leaves and dense cylindrical heads of flowers. [t. NL, named after Sir Joseph BANKS]

Bankside (băngk′sīd′), *n.* a former theatrical district in London, along the south bank of the Thames, the site of Shakespeare's Globe Theatre.

Banks Peninsula, a promontory on the E coast of South Island, New Zealand. ab. 33 mi. long and 15 mi. wide.

bank statement, a printed sheet bearing a complete record of a current account, sent periodically to a customer.

bank transfer, a credit transfer.

banner (băn′ə), *n.* **1.** the flag of a country, army, troop, etc. **2.** an ensign or the like bearing some device or motto, as one borne in processions. **3.** a piece of cloth, attached by one side to a pole or staff, formerly used as the standard of a sovereign, lord, or knight. **4.** anything displayed as a profession of principles: *the banner of freedom.* **5.** *Her.* a square flag bearing heraldic devices. **6.** *Journalism.* the headline which extends across the width of the newspaper, usually at the top of the first page. *—adj.* **7.** leading; foremost: *a banner year for crops.* [ME *banere*, t. OF, der. LL *bandum* standard; of Gmc orig. (cf. Goth. *bandwo* sign)] **—ban′nered,** *adj.*

banneret (băn′ə rĭt, -ə rĕt′), *n.* **1.** *Hist.* a knight who could bring a company of followers into the field under his own banner. **2.** a rank of knighthood; knight banneret. **3.** a bannerette. [ME *baneret*, t. OF, der. *baniere* BANNER]

bannerette (băn′ə rĕt′), *n.* a small banner. Also, **banneret.** [t. OF, dim. of *baniere* BANNER]

bannerol (băn′ə rōl′), *n.* banderol.

bannister (băn′ĭs tə), *n.* banister.

bannock (băn′ək), *n. Scot. and N Dial.* a flat cake made of oatmeal, barley meal, etc., commonly baked on a griddle. [OE *bannuc* bit, small piece, t. OBrit. Cf. OCornish *banna* drop]

Bannockburn (băn′ək bûn′), *n.* a village in central Scotland, in Stirlingshire: site of the victory of the Scots (1314) under Robert the Bruce over the English, which assured the independence of Scotland.

banns (bănz), *n.pl. Eccles.* notice of an intended marriage, given three times in the parish church of each of the betrothed. Also, **bans.** [var. of *bans*, pl. of BAN[2], n.]

banquet (băng′kwĭt), *n., v.,* **-queted, -queting.** *—n.* **1.** a feast. **2.** a ceremonious public dinner. *—v.t., v.i.* **3.** to entertain (another) or regale (oneself) at a banquet. [t. F, t. It.: m. *banchetto*, dim. of *banco* bench] **—ban′queter,** *n.* **—Syn. 1.** See **feast.**

banquette (băng kĕt′), *n.* **1.** *Fort.* a platform or step along the inside of a parapet or trench, for soldiers to stand on when firing. **2.** *Archaic.* a bench for passengers on top of a stagecoach. **3.** *Southern U.S.* pavement.

banshee (băn′shē, băn shē′), *n. Irish and Scot.* a supernatural being supposed to give warning by its wails of an approaching death in the family. Also, **ban′shie.** [t. Irish: m. *bean sidhe* woman of the fairies]

bant (bănt), *v.i.* to reduce weight by banting. [back-formation from BANTING]

bantam (băn′təm), *n.* **1.** (*often cap.*) a domestic fowl of any of certain varieties or breeds characterized by very small size. **2.** a small person, esp. a quarrelsome one. *—adj.* **3.** diminutive, tiny; small but spirited.

Bantam (băn′təm; *Du.* bŏn′tŏm), *n.* a village in W Java: first Dutch settlement in the East Indies.

bantamweight (băn′təm wāt′), *n.* a boxer of very light weight (not more than 8 st. 6 lbs in professional boxing, or 8 st. 7 lbs in amateur boxing).

banteng (băn′tĕng), *n.* a wild ox, *Bos banteng*, of SE Asia, sometimes domesticated. [t. Malay]

banter (băn′tə), *n.* **1.** playfully teasing language; good-humoured raillery. *—v.t.* **2.** to address with banter; chaff. *—v.i.* **3.** to use banter. [orig. unknown] **—ban′terer,** *n.* **—ban′teringly,** *adv.* **—Syn. 1.** badinage, joking, jesting. **2.** tease.

banting (băn′tĭng), *n.* a method of reducing one's weight, based upon a high protein and low fat and carbohydrate diet. [named after William *Banting*, 1797–1878, English dietitian] **—ban′tingism,** *n.*

Banting (băn′tĭng), *n.* **Sir Frederick Grant,** 1891–1941, Canadian physician: discoverer of insulin treatment of diabetes.

bantling (bănt′lĭng), *n. Archaic.* a young child; brat. [t. G: m. *Bänkling* bastard. See BENCH, -LING[1]]

Bantu (băn′to͞o, băn to͞o′), *n., pl.* **-tu, -tus,** *adj.* *—n.* **1.** a principal linguistic family of Africa, its languages being prevalent from the Equator to South Africa, including Swahili, Tswana, Zulu, Ganda, and Kongo. **2.** (*pl.*) a large family of Negro tribes inhabiting central and southern Africa. **3.** a member of any of these tribes. *—adj.* **4.** of or pertaining to the Bantu tribes or languages.

Bantustan (băn′to͞o stän′), *n.* (in the Republic of South Africa) an area set up for Africans as a self-contained and theoretically self-governing settlement. [f. BANTU + *-stan* as in PAKISTAN]

Banville (*Fr.* bäɴ vēl′), *n.* **Théodore Faullain de** (*Fr.* tē ō dôr fō lăɴ′ də), 1823–91, French poet and dramatist.

banyan (băn′yən), *n.* an East Indian fig tree, *Ficus benghalensis*, whose branches send out adventitious roots to the ground, sometimes causing the tree to spread over a wide area. Also, **banian.** [orig. a particular tree under which BANIAN traders had built a pagoda]

Banyan, *Ficus benghalensis* (70 to 100 ft high)

banzai (băn′zī′), *interj.* **1.** (a Japanese complimentary salutation or patriotic shout, as in honour of the emperor, meaning): **a.** long life. **b.** forward; attack. *—adj.* **2.** reckless; suicidal. [t. Jap.: ten thousand years]

baobab (bā′ō băb′), *n.* a large exceedingly thick-trunked bombacaceous tree of the genus *Adansonia*, esp. *A. digitata*, native to tropical Africa, bearing a gourdlike fruit; the monkey-bread tree. [t. native African]

B.A.O.R., British Army of the Rhine.

bap (băp), *n.* a roll or small loaf of bread, usually elliptical, with a thin, soft crust. [orig. unknown]

Bapt., 1. Baptist. 2. (*l.c.*) baptized. Also, **Bap.**

baptism (băp′tĭz′əm), *n.* **1.** *Eccles.* a ceremonial immersion in water, or application of water, as an initiatory rite or sacrament of the Christian church. **2.** any similar ceremony or action of initiation, dedication, etc. —**baptismal** (băp tĭz′məl), *adj.* —**baptis′mally,** *adv.*

baptism of fire, **1.** the first battle a soldier experiences. **2.** any severe ordeal; crucial test.

Baptist (băp′tĭst), *n.* **1.** *Relig.* a member of a Christian denomination which maintains that baptism (usually implying immersion) should follow only upon a personal profession of Christian faith. **2.** one who baptizes. **3. the Baptist,** John, the forerunner of Christ.

baptistery (băp′tĭs tə rĭ, -tĭs trĭ), *n., pl.* **-ries.** **1.** a building, or a part of a church, in which baptism is administered. **2.** (in Baptist Churches) a tank containing water for baptism by immersion. Also, **baptistry.** [t. L: m. s. *baptistērium*, t. Gk: m. *baptistḗrion*]

baptize (băp tīz′), *v.,* **-tized, -tizing.** —*v.t.* **1.** to immerse in water, or sprinkle or pour water on, in the Christian rite of baptism. **2.** to cleanse spiritually; initiate or dedicate by purifying. **3.** to christen. —*v.i.* **4.** to administer baptism. Also, **baptise.** [ME *baptise(n)*, t. OF: m. *baptiser*, t. LL: m. *baptizāre*, t. Gk: m. *baptízein* immerse] —**baptiz′er,** *n.*

bar[1] (bä), *n., v.,* **barred, barring,** *prep.* —*n.* **1.** a relatively long and evenly shaped piece of some solid substance, esp. one of wood or metal used as a guard or obstruction, or for some mechanical purpose: *the bars of a fence or gate.* **2.** crowbar. **3.** an oblong piece of any solid material: *a bar of soap or toffee.* **4.** the amount of material in a bar. **5.** *Com.* an ingot, lump, or wedge of gold or silver. **6.** a band or stripe: *a bar of light.* **7.** *Oceanog.* a long ridge of sand or gravel in coastal waters, near or slightly above the surface, and extending across the mouth of a bay or parallel to the shore. **8.** anything which obstructs, hinders, or impedes; an obstacle; a barrier: *a bar to vice.* **9.** *Music.* **a.** the unit of music between two bar lines; the distance between two vertical lines. **b.** *U.S.* bar line. **c.** See **double bar.** **10.** a counter or a room where alcoholic drinks, etc., are served to customers. **11.** any counter or place specializing in the sale of one particular commodity: *stocking bar.* **12.** practising barristers collectively. **13.** *Chiefly U.S.* the legal profession, esp. that in a given community. **14.** a railing in a courtroom separating the general public from the part of the room occupied by the judges, jury, barristers, solicitors, and other members of the legal profession. **15.** the place in court where prisoners stand or sit: *a prisoner at the bar.* **16.** (in a house of parliament) a bar or line opposite the Speaker's chair, marking the boundary of the house. **17.** *Law.* **a.** an objection which nullifies an action or claim. **b.** a stoppage or defeat of an alleged right of action. **18.** any tribunal: *the bar of public opinion.* **19.** *Physics.* a unit of pressure equal to 1,000,000 dynes per square centimetre. **20.** (in lace) bride[2] (def. 1). **21.** *Her.* a band, properly horizontal, crossing the field. **22.** a strip of silver or some other metal added to a medal below the clasp as a further distinction: *D.S.O. and bar.* —*v.t.* **23.** to provide or fasten with a bar or bars: *to bar the door.* **24.** to shut in or out by or as by bars. **25.** to block (a way, etc.) as with a barrier; prevent or hinder, as access. **26.** to exclude; except. **27.** to forbid; preclude: *no holds barred.* **28.** to mark with bars, stripes, or bands. —*prep.* **29.** except; omitting; but: *bar none.* [ME *barre*, t. OF, g. LL *barra*, of disputed origin]
—**Syn.** 8. BAR, BARRIER, BARRICADE mean something put in the way of advance. BAR has the general meaning of hindrance or obstruction: *a bar across the doorway.* BARRIER suggests an impediment to progress, literal or figurative, or a defensive obstruction against attack: *a river barrier.* A BARRICADE is esp. a pile of articles hastily gathered or a rude earthwork for protection in street fighting: *a barricade of wooden boxes.*

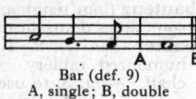

A B
Bar (def. 9)
A, single; B, double

bar[2] (bä), *n. U.S.* a mosquito net. [t. Creole F (Louisiana d.): m. *bère*; orig. unknown]

bar., **1.** barometer. **2.** barrel. **3.** barrister.

Barabbas (bə răb′əs), *n. Bible.* a condemned robber or insurrectionist whose release was demanded of Pilate by the mob when they had an opportunity to free Jesus. Mark 15:6–11; John 18:40.

Baracaldo (*Sp.* bä rä käl′dô), *n.* a town in N Spain. 99,130 (1965).

Baranagar (bə răn′ə gə), *n.* a town in India, in E West Bengal. 107,837 (1961).

barb[1] (bäb), *n.* **1.** a point or pointed part projecting backwards from a main point, as of a fishhook, an arrowhead, or a fence wire. **2.** a sharp or unkind implication in a remark; cutting comment. **3.** *Bot., Zool.* a beardlike growth or part. **4.** *Ornith.* one of the processes attached to the rachis of a feather. **5.** a breed of domestic pigeons similar to the carriers or homers, having a short, broad bill. **6.** any of a large number of small, Old World cyprinoid fishes of the genera *Barbus* or *Puntius* widely cultivated for home aquariums. **7.** (*usually pl.*) *Vet. Sci.* a small protuberance under the tongue in horses and cattle, esp. when inflamed and swollen. **8.** a linen covering for the throat and breast, formerly worn by women mourners, and now by nuns. **9.** *Obs.* a beard. —*v.t.* **10.** to furnish with a barb or barbs: *to barb a hook.* [ME *barbe*, t. OF, g. L *barba* beard] —**barbed,** *adj.*

barb[2] (bäb), *n.* a horse of a breed brought from Barbary to Spain by the Moors. [t. F: m. *barbe*]

Barbados (bä bā′dōz), *n.* an island in the West Indies, in the E Lesser Antilles: an independent state and a member of the Commonwealth of Nations. 245,275 pop. (est. 1966); 166 sq. mi. *Cap.*: Bridgetown.

barbarian (bä bēə′rĭ ən), *n.* **1.** a man in a rude, savage state; an uncivilized person. **2.** an uncultured person; a philistine. **3.** a foreigner (orig. a non-Greek). —*adj.* **4.** uncivilized. **5.** foreign. [t. F: m. *barbarien*, der. L *barbaria* barbarous country] —**barbar′ianism,** *n.*
—**Syn.** 4. rude, savage, primitive, wild. BARBARIAN, BARBARIC, BARBAROUS pertain to uncivilized people. BARBARIAN is the general word for anything uncivilized: *a barbarian tribe.* BARBARIC has both unfavourable and mildly favourable connotations, implying crudeness of taste or practice, or conveying an idea of rude magnificence and splendour: *barbaric noise.* BARBAROUS emphasizes the inhumanity and cruelty of barbarian life: *barbarous customs.*

barbaric (bä băr′ĭk), *adj.* **1.** uncivilized: *barbaric invaders.* **2.** of, like, or befitting barbarians: *a barbaric empire.* **3.** crudely rich or splendid: *barbaric decorations.* [ME *barbarik*, t. L: m. s. *barbaricus*, t. Gk: m. *barbarikós* foreign, barbaric] —**barbar′ically,** *adv.* —**Syn. 1.** See **barbarian.**

barbarism (bä′bə rĭz′əm), *n.* **1.** barbarous or uncivilized condition. **2.** something belonging or proper to a barbarous condition; a barbarous act. **3.** the use in a language of forms or constructions felt by some to be undesirably alien to the established mode or custom of the language. **4.** such a form or construction, as *complected, all the farther.*

barbarity (bä băr′rĭ tĭ), *n., pl.* **-ties.** **1.** brutal or inhuman conduct; cruelty. **2.** an act of cruelty or inhumanity. **3.** crudity of style, taste, etc.

barbarize (bä′bə rīz′), *v.i., v.t.,* **-rized, -rizing.** to make or become barbarous. Also, **barbarise.** —**bar′bariza′tion,** *n.*

Barbarossa (bä′bə rŏs′ə), *n.* surname of Emperor Frederick I of Germany, meaning 'red beard'.

barbarous (bä′bə rəs), *adj.* **1.** uncivilized: *barbarous countries.* **2.** excessively harsh: *barbarous treatment.* **3.** harsh-sounding: *wild and barbarous music.* **4.** not conforming or conformed to classical standards or accepted usage, as language. **5.** foreign (orig. non-Greek). [t. L: m. *barbarus*, t. Gk: m. *bárbaros*, orig., babbling] —**bar′barously,** *adv.* —**bar′barousness,** *n.* —**Syn. 1.** See **barbarian. 2.** cruel, ferocious, inhuman, brutal.

Barbary (bä′bə rĭ), *n.* a region in N Africa, extending from W of Egypt to the Atlantic, and including the former Barbary States.

Barbary ape, an ape, *Macaca sylvana*, of northern Africa and Gibraltar.

Barbary Coast, the Mediterranean coastline of the former Barbary States: once infested with pirates who harassed Mediterranean trade.

Barbary Coast

Barbary States, Morocco, Algiers, Tunis, and Tripoli.

barbate (bä′bāt), *adj.* *Zool., Bot.* bearded; tufted or furnished with hairs. [t. L: m. s. *barbātus* bearded]

barbecue (bä′bĭ kyoo͞′), *n., v.,* **-cued, -cuing.** —*n.* **1.** a large social entertainment, usually in the open air, at which animals are roasted whole. **2.** a dressed ox or other animal roasted whole. **3.** a framework on which animals are roasted whole or in large pieces. **4.** pieces of meat roasted over an open fire, esp. when basted in a highly seasoned sauce. —*v.t.* **5.** to roast whole or in large pieces before an open fire, on a spit or gridiron. **6.** to cook (slices of meat or fish) in a highly seasoned sauce. [t. Sp.: m. *barbacoa*, t. Haitian: m. *barboka*]

barbed wire, steel wire to which barbs are attached at short intervals, used largely for fencing in livestock, protecting a defensive military position, etc.

barbel (bä′bl), *n.* **1.** a slender cylindrical tactile process appended to the mouth of certain fishes. **2.** any of various cyprinoid fishes of the genus *Barbus*, esp. *B. barbus*, of Europe. [ME *barbelle*, t. OF: m. *barbel*, *g.* LL *barbellus*, dim. of *barbus*]

barbell (bä′bĕl′), *n.* an apparatus in weight-lifting consisting of a steel bar, about 7 ft long, to the ends of which disc-shaped weights are attached.

barbellate (bä′bĭ lāt′, bä bĕl′ĭt, -āt), *adj. Bot., Zool.* having short, stiff hairs. [f. s. NL *barbella* (dim. of L *barbula* little beard) + -ATE¹]

barber (bä′bə), *n.* **1.** one whose occupation it is to shave or trim the beard and to cut and dress the hair of customers. —*v.t.* **2.** to trim or dress the beard and hair of. [ME *barbour*, t. AF, ult. der. L *barba* beard]

Barber (bä′bə), *n.* **Samuel,** born 1910, American composer.

barberry (bä′bə rĭ), *n., pl.* **-ries. 1.** a shrub of the genus *Berberis*, esp. *B. vulgaris*. **2.** its red, elongated, acid fruit. [ME *barbere*, t. ML: m. s. *barbaris, berberis*]

barber's pole, a pole painted in red and white spirals, often with a brass bowl attached, displayed outside many barbers' shops as a sign of their trade.

barbet (bä′bĭt), *n.* **1.** a dog with long curly hair; poodle. **2.** any of numerous tropical non-passerine birds of the family *Capitonidae*, most of which are brightly coloured and large-headed, and have bristles at the base of the bill. [t. F, masc. dim. of *barbe* beard]

barbette (bä bĕt′), *n.* **1.** a platform or mound of earth within a fortification, from which guns may be fired over the parapet instead of through embrasures. **2.** *Naval.* an armoured cylinder to protect a turret on a warship. [t. F, fem. dim. of *barbe* beard]

barbican (bä′bĭ kən), *n.* **1.** an outwork of a castle or fortified place. **2.** an outpost of any nature, as a bridge tower, or a defence outside of the moat protecting the approach to the drawbridge. [ME, t. OF: m. *barcane*, t. ML: m. *barbicana*; ult. orig. obscure, ? t. Ar.Pers.: m. *bāb khāne* gatehouse, or Pers. *bālā khāne* high house]

barbicel (bä′bĭ sĕl′), *n. Ornith.* one of the minute processes fringing the barbules of certain feathers. [t. NL: m. s. *barbicella*, dim. of L *barba* beard]

bar billiards, a game resembling billiards, played on a small table with certain obstacles against a time limit, after the expiry of which a bar drops, preventing the return of balls for play.

Barbirolli (bä′bĭ rŏl′ĭ), *n.* **Sir John,** 1899–1970, British conductor.

barbital (bä′bĭ tăl′), *n. U.S.* barbitone.

barbital sodium, *Pharm.* a sleeping powder, $C_8H_{11}N_2O_3Na$, the sodium salt of barbitone.

barbitone (bä′bĭ tōn′), *n. Pharm.* a drug, diethylbarbituric acid, sold as sleeping pills; Veronal. [f. BARBIT(URIC) + -ONE]

barbiturate (bä bĭt′yŏŏ rĭt, -rāt′), *n. Chem.* a derivative of barbituric acid, esp. a sedative drug.

barbituric acid (bä′bĭ tyŏŏ′rĭk), *Chem.* an acid, $C_4H_4N_2O_3$, a crystalline powder from which several hypnotic and sedative drugs are derived; malonyl urea. [*barbituric*, f. s. Gk *bárbiton* lyre + URIC]

Barbizon School (bä′bĭ zŏn′; *Fr.* bȧr bē zôɴ′), a group of French landscape painters of the late 19th century, including Théodore Rousseau and Daubigny, who worked chiefly at Barbizon, a village in N France.

Barbuda (bä bo͞o′də), *n.* a British colony in the Leeward Islands, in the West Indies: a dependency of Antigua. 979 pop. (1964); 62 sq. mi.

barbule (bä′byo͞ol), *n.* **1.** a little barb. **2.** one of the small processes fringing the barbs of a feather. [t. L: m. s. *barbula*, dim. of *barba* beard]

Barbusse (*Fr.* bȧr bʏs′), *n.* **Henri** (*Fr.* äɴ rē′), 1873?–1935, French journalist and author.

Barca (bä′kə), *n.* **1.** a politically influential family of ancient Carthage. Hamilcar, Hasdrubal, and Hannibal belonged to it. **2.** Cyrenaica.

barcarole (bä′kə rōl′), *n.* **1.** a boating song of the Venetian gondoliers. **2.** a piece of music composed in the style of such songs. Also, **barcarolle.** [t. F: m. *barcarolle*, t. It.: m. *barcar(u)ola* boatman's song, der. *barcar(u)olo* a boatman, der. *barca* BARQUE]

Barcelona (bä′sĭ lō′nə; *Sp.* bȧr thĕ lô′nä), *n.* a seaport in NE Spain, on the Mediterranean. 1,696,008 (1965). See map under **Barbary Coast.**

barchan (bä kän′), *n. Geog.* a crescent-shaped sand-dune with the horns pointing downwind, found especially in the deserts of Turkestan. Also, **barkhan.** [t. Turk.: sandhill]

Barclay de Tolly (bä′klĭ də tŏl′ĭ), **Prince Mikhail** (mē′kĭ ĭl), 1716–1818, Russian field marshal: commander-in-chief against Napoleon in 1812.

Barcoo (bä′ko͞o), *n.* a river of Australia flowing SW through Queensland, joining with the Thomson river to form Cooper Creek. 330 mi.

bard¹ (bäd), *n.* **1.** one of an ancient Celtic order of poets. **2.** a strolling minstrel. **3.** *Archaic.* a poet. **4. the Bard,** Shakespeare. [ME, t. Celtic (cf. Irish *bard*, Welsh *bardd*), whence also L *bardus*, Gk *bárdos*] —**bard′ic,** *adj.*

bard² (bäd), *Obs.* —*n.* **1.** any of the various pieces of defensive armour for a horse. —*v.t.* **2.** to caparison with bards. Also, **barde.** [t. F, t. Ar.: m. *hardha'ah* pack-saddle]

bardolatry (bäd ŏl′ə trĭ), *n. Colloq.* excessive adulation of Shakespeare. [f. BARD¹ (def. 4) + -OLATRY]

bardy (bä′dĭ), *n. Austral.* an edible grub eaten by Australian Aborigines. [t. native Australian]

bare¹ (bĕə), *adj.* **barer, barest,** *v.*, **bared, baring.** —*adj.* **1.** without covering or clothing; naked or nude: *bare knees.* **2.** with the head uncovered. **3.** without the usual furnishings, contents, etc.: *bare walls.* **4.** open to view; unconcealed; undisguised. **5.** unadorned; bald; plain: *the bare facts.* **6.** napless or threadbare. **7.** scarcely or just sufficient: *bare necessities.* —*v.t.* **8.** to make bare. [ME; OE *bær*, c. G *bar*] —**bare′ness,** *n.* —**barish** (bĕə′rĭsh), *adj.* —**Syn. 7.** See **mere**¹. **8.** uncover; strip.

bare² (bĕə), *v. Archaic.* pt. of bear.

bareback (bĕə′băk′), *adv., adj.* with the back (of a horse, etc.) bare; without saddle. —**bare′backed′,** *adj.*

barefaced (bĕə′fāst′), *adj.* **1.** with the face uncovered. **2.** undisguised; boldly open. **3.** shameless; impudent; audacious: *a barefaced lie.* —**barefacedly** (bĕə′fāst′lĭ) *adv.* —**bare′faced′ness,** *n.*

barefoot (bĕə′fo͝ot′), *adj., adv.* with the feet bare.

barefooted (bĕə′fo͝ot′ĭd), *adj.* having the feet bare.

barehanded (bĕə′hăn′dĭd), *adj.* **1.** with hands uncovered. **2.** with empty hands; without means.

bareheaded (bĕə′hĕd′ĭd), *adj., adv.* with the head uncovered.

Bareilly (bə rā′lĭ), *n.* a city in India, in W central Uttar Pradesh. 254,409 (1961).

barelegged (bĕə′lĕg′ĭd, -lĕgd′), *adj.* with bare legs.

barely (bĕə′lĭ), *adv.* **1.** only; just; no more than: *she is barely sixteen.* **2.** *Colloq.* not quite; nearly. **3.** without disguise or concealment; openly: *a question barely put.* **4.** nakedly. **5.** *Archaic.* merely; only. —**Syn. 1.** See **hardly.**

Barenboim (bă′rən boim′), *n.* **Daniel** (dăn′yəl), born 1942, Israeli pianist and conductor, born in the Argentine.

Barents Sea (bă′rənts), a part of the Arctic Ocean between NE Europe and the islands of Spitsbergen, Franz Josef Land, and Novaya Zemlya. [named after Willem *Barents*, died 1597, Dutch navigator and explorer]

baresark (bĕə′säk), *n.* **1.** *Scand. Legend.* a berserker. —*adv.* **2.** without armour. [translation var. of *berserk* taken as *bare* + *serk* sark, shirt]

bargain (bä′gĭn), *n.* **1.** an agreement between parties settling what each shall give and take, or perform and receive, in a transaction. **2.** such an agreement as affecting one of the parties: *a losing bargain.* **3.** *Stock Exchange.* an agreement to sell or to purchase; a sale or purchase. **4.** that which is acquired by bargaining. **5.** an advantageous purchase. **6. into the bargain,** over and above what is stipulated; moreover; besides. **7. strike a bargain,** to make a bargain; come to terms. —*v.i.* **8.** to discuss the terms of a bargain; haggle over terms. **9.** to come to an agreement; make a bargain. **10. bargain for,** to be prepared for; expect: *he got more than he bargained for.* **11. bargain on,** to count on; rely on. —*v.t.* **12.** to arrange by bargain; stipulate. [ME, t. OF: m. *bargaigne*] —**bar′gainer,** *n.* —**Syn. 1.** See **agreement. 8.** See **trade.**

barge (bäj), *n., v.*, **barged, barging.** —*n.* **1.** a vessel, usually unpowered, used for transporting freight; a lighter. **2.** a vessel of state used in pageants. **3.** a ship's boat used in visits of courtesy. **4.** *Naval.* a boat reserved for a flag officer. —*v.t.* **5.** to carry or transport by barge. —*v.i.* **6.** to move in the slow, heavy manner of a barge. **7.** *Colloq.* to bump; collide. **8. barge in,** *Colloq.* to force one's presence rudely or clumsily. [ME, t. OF, g. der. of L *bāris*, t. Gk: (Egyptian) boat, barge]

bargeboard (bäj′bôd′), *n.* an overhanging board along the projecting sloping edge of a gable roof.

barge couple, one of the pair of rafters in a gable carrying the overhanging portion of the roof.

barge course, the part of a gable roof that projects beyond the end wall.

bargee (bä jē′), *n.* **1.** one of the crew of a barge. **2.** one who has charge of a barge. Also, *Chiefly U.S.*, **bargeman** (bäj′mən).

barge pole, 1. a pole used to propel a barge. **2. not to touch with a barge pole,** to have nothing to do with; not to go near.

Bari (bä′rĭ), *n.* a seaport in SE Italy, in Apulia, on the Adriatic. 339,185 (1966). Italian, **Bari delle Puglie** (*It.* bä′rē dĕl lĕ po͞o′lyĕ).

baric[1] (bĕə′rĭk, bă′rĭk), *adj. Chem.* of or containing barium. [f. BAR(IUM) + -IC]

baric[2] (bă′rĭk), *adj.* of or pertaining to weight, esp. that of the atmosphere. [f. s. Gk *báros* weight + -IC]

barilla (bə rĭl′ə), *n.* **1.** either of two European saltworts, *Salsola kali* and esp. *S. soda,* whose ashes yield an impure carbonate of soda. **2.** the alkali obtained from the ashes of these and certain other maritime plants. [t. Sp.: m. *barrilla*]

Baring (bĕə′rĭng), *n.* **Alexander.** See **Ashburton.**

barit., *Music.* baritone.

barite (bĕə′rīt), *n.* barytes.

baritone (bă′rĭ tōn′), *Music.* —*n.* **1.** a male voice or voice part intermediate between tenor and bass. **2.** a singer with such a voice. **3.** a large, valved brass instrument, slightly smaller in bore than a euphonium, used chiefly in military bands. **4.** barytone. —*adj.* **5.** of or pertaining to the baritone; having the compass of the baritone. Also, **barytone.** [t. Gk: m. s. *barýtonos* deep sounding]

barium (bĕə′rĭ əm), *n. Chem.* a whitish, malleable, active, divalent, metallic element occurring in combination chiefly as barytes or as witherite. *Symbol:* Ba; *at. wt:* 137·34; *at. no.:* 56; *sp. gr.:* 3·5 at 20°C. [t. NL; f. BAR(YTES) + -IUM]

bark[1] (bäk), *n.* **1.** the abrupt, explosive cry of a dog. **2.** a similar sound made by another animal or by a person. **3.** *Colloq.* a cough. —*v.i.* **4.** to utter an abrupt, explosive cry or a series of such cries, as a dog. **5.** to make a similar sound: *the big guns barked.* **6.** to speak or cry out sharply or gruffly. **7.** *Slang.* to advertise a cheap show at its entrance. **8.** *Colloq.* to cough. **9. bark up the wrong tree,** to mistake one's object; assail or pursue the wrong person or purpose. —*v.t.* **10.** to utter or give forth with a bark; to bark out an order. [ME *berke(n)*, OE *beorcan*]

bark[2] (bäk), *n.* **1.** *Bot.* the external covering of the woody stems, branches, and roots of plants, as distinct and separable from the wood itself. **2.** *Tanning.* a mixture of oak and hemlock barks. —*v.t.* **3.** to strip off the bark of; peel. **4.** to remove a circle of bark from. **5.** to cover or enclose with bark. **6.** to treat with a bark infusion; tan. **7.** to rub off the skin of: *to bark one's shins.* [ME, t. Scand.; cf. Dan. *bark*] —**bark′er,** *n.*

bark[3] (bäk), *n.* barque.

bark beetle, any beetle of the family *Scolytidae,* the adults and larvae of which do great damage to living trees, esp to conifers.

bark-bound (bäk′bound′), *adj.* (of a tree) having the internal tissues compressed and damaged due to failure of the bark to split.

barkeeper (bä′kē′pə), *n. U.S.* **1.** the owner or manager of a bar. **2.** a barman. Also, *U.S.,* **barkeep.**

barkentine (bä′kən tēn′), *n.* barquentine.

barker (bä′kə), *n.* **1.** an animal or person that barks. **2.** *Colloq.* one who stands before a shop, nightclub, etc., calling passers-by to enter. [f. BARK[1] + -ER[1]]

barkhan (bä kän′), *n.* barchan.

Barking (bä′kĭng), *n.* an E outer borough of London. 178,900 (1965).

Barkly Tableland, a plateau on the border of Northern Territory and Queensland, Australia. Average height, 900 ft. ab. 50,000 sq. mi.

barky (bä′kĭ), *adj.,* **barkier, barkiest.** consisting of or containing bark; covered with or resembling bark.

Barletta (*It.* bȧr lĕt′tȧ), *n.* a seaport in SE Italy, in Apulia, on the Adriatic. 13,178 (1966).

barley (bä′lĭ), *n.* a widely distributed cereal plant of the genus *Hordeum,* whose awned flowers grow in tightly bunched spikes, with three small additional spikes at each node. It is used as food, and in the making of beer, ale, and whisky. [ME *barly,* OE *bærlic*; cf. BARN[1]]

barleycorn (bä′lĭ kôn′), *n.* **1.** barley, or a grain of barley. **2.** a measure equal to one third of an inch.

barley sugar, sugar boiled, formerly in a decoction of barley, until it has become brittle and transparent.

barley wine, a strong ale.

bar line, *Music.* the vertical line dividing two bars.

barm (bäm), *n.* yeast formed on malt liquors while fermenting. [ME *berme,* OE *beorma,* c. G *Bärme*]

barmaid (bä′mād′), *n.* a woman or girl who serves drinks in a bar.

barman (bä′mən), *n., pl.* **-men.** a man who mixes and serves drinks in a bar; bartender.

Barmecide (bä′mĭ sīd′), *n.* a member of a noble Persian family of Baghdad who, according to a tale in *The Arabian Nights' Entertainments,* gave a beggar a pretended feast with empty dishes.

Barmen (bä′mən; *Ger.* bȧr′mən), *n.* See **Wuppertal.**

bar mizvah (bä mĭts′və), *Judaism.* **1.** a boy of thirteen, the age at which he acquires religious obligations. **2.** the ceremony and feast marking this. Also, **bar mitzvah.** [t. Heb.]

barmy (bä′mĭ), *adj.,* **barmier, barmiest. 1.** containing or resembling barm; frothy. **2.** *Slang.* silly; stupid; mad.

barn[1] (bän) **1.** a building for storing hay, grain, etc., and often for stabling livestock. —*v.t.* **2.** to store in a barn. [ME *bern,* OE *berern,* f. *bere* barley + *ærn* place, house]

barn[2] (bän), *n. Physics.* a unit used in measuring cross-sectional areas of atomic nuclei, equal to 10^{-24} sq. cm. [special use of BARN[1]]

Barnabas (bä′nə bəs), *n.* the surname of the Cyprian Levite Joseph, an apostle and companion of Paul. Acts 4:36, 37.

barnacle[1] (bä′nə kl), *n.* **1.** any of certain crustaceans of the group *Cirripedia,* as the **goose barnacles,** stalked species which cling to ship bottoms and floating timber, and the **rock barnacles,** species which attach themselves to marine rocks. **2.** a thing or person that clings tenaciously. **3.** the barnacle goose. [late ME *bernacle,* of obscure orig. (cf. ML *bernacula,* F *bernicle, barnacle*); r. ME *bernekke, bernake* (cf. ML *bernaca,* OF *bernaque*)] —**bar′nacled,** *adj.*

Goose barnacle, *Lepas fasicularis*

barnacle[2] (bä′nə kl), *n.* **1.** (*usually pl.*) an instrument with two hinged branches for pinching the nose of an unruly horse. **2.** (*pl.*) *Colloq.* spectacles. [ME *bernacle,* t. OF: m. *bernac*]

barnacle goose, a wild goose of N Europe, allied to the brent, and often confused with it. Also, **bernicle goose.**

Barnardo (bä nä′dō, bə-), *n.* **Dr Thomas,** 1845–1905, a philanthropist who founded homes for destitute children in England.

Barnaul (*Russ.* bər nȧ o͞ol′), *n.* a city in the S Soviet Union in Asia, on the Ob river. 382,000 (est. 1965).

barn-dance (bän′däns′), *n.* a country dance similar to a schottische.

Barnes (bänz), *n.* a district of the SW outer London borough of Richmond upon Thames.

Barnet (bä′nĭt), *n.* a NW outer borough of London. 316,400 (1965).

Barneveldt (*Du.* bŏr′nə vĕlt), *n.* **Jan van Olden** (*Du.* yŏn vŏn ôl′dən), 1547–1619, Dutch statesman and patriot.

barney (bä′nĭ), *n. Slang.* **1.** humbug; cheating. **2.** an unfair contest or prizefight. **3.** a spree; a shindy.

barn owl, a widely distributed owl, *Tyto alba,* commonly frequenting barns, where it destroys mice.

Barnsley (bänz′lĭ), *n.* a town in central England, in the West Riding of Yorkshire, N of Sheffield. 74,650 (1961).

Barnstaple (bän′stə pl), *n.* a seaport in England, in N Devon. 15,944 (1961).

barnstorm (bän′stôm′), *v.i. Chiefly U.S. Colloq.* **1.** to travel around acting in plays in small country towns where there are no theatres. **2.** to act badly; overact; rant. **3.** to conduct a campaign or speaking tour in rural areas. **4.** to attack something violently. [back-formation from *barnstormer,* lit., one who storms the barn] —**barn′storm′er,** *n.* —**barn′storm′ing,** *n., adj.*

barn swallow. See **swallow**[2] (def. 1).

Barnum (bä′nəm), *n.* **Phineas Taylor** (fĭn′ĭ əs), 1810–91, U.S. showman; established circus 1871.

barnyard (bän′yäd′), *n.* **1.** a yard next to a barn. —*adj.* **2.** found in a barnyard. **3.** appropriate to a barnyard: *barnyard behaviour.*

baro-, a word element meaning 'weight', 'pressure', as in *barogram.* [comb. form repr. Gk *báros* weight]

Barocchio (*It.* bȧ rŏk′kyō), *n.* See **Vignola.**

Baroda (bə rō′də), *n.* **1.** a former native state in W India, now part of Bombay state. **2.** a city in India, in W Madhya Pradesh, N of Bombay, formerly capital of Baroda state. 295,144 (1961).

barogram (bă′rə grăm′), *n. Meteorol.* a record traced by a barograph or similar instrument.

barograph (bă′rə grăf′, -gräf′), *n. Meteorol.* an automatic recording barometer. —**barographic** (bă′rə grăf′ĭk), *adj.*

Baroja (*Sp.* bȧ rô′KHȧ), *n.* **Pio** (*Sp.* pē′ô), 1872–1956, Spanish novelist.

barometer (bə rŏm′ĭ tə), *n.* **1.** an instrument for measuring atmospheric pressure, thus determining height, weather changes, etc. **2.** anything that indicates changes: *the barometer of public opinion.* —**barometric** (bă′rə mĕt′rĭk), **bar′omet′rical,** *adj.* —**bar′omet′rically,** *adv.* —**barom′etry,** *n.*

baron (bă′rən), *n.* **1.** a member of the lowest rank of the peerage. **2.** *Hist.* **a.** a feudal tenant-in-chief holding the

---

b., blend of, blended; c., cognate with; d., dialect, dialectal; der., derived from; f., formed from; g., going back to; m., modification of; r., replacing; s., stem of; t., taken from; ?, perhaps. See full key on inside front cover.

lands directly from a king. **b.** any great lord. **3.** *Obs.* a former title of judges of the Court of Exchequer. **4.** *Orig. U.S.* a powerful industrialist or financier: *a press baron.* **5.** baron of beef. [ME, t. OF, g. L *bāro* hulking fellow]

baronage (bă′rə nĭj), *n.* **1.** the whole body of barons. **2.** barony.

baroness (bă′rə nĭs), *n.* **1.** the wife of a baron. **2.** a lady holding a baronial title in her own right.

baronet (bă′rə nĭt, -rə nĕt′), *n.* a member of a British hereditary order of honour, ranking below the barons and made up of commoners, designated by *Sir* before the name, and *Baronet*, usually abbreviated *Bart.*, after: *Sir John Smith, Bart.*

baronetage (bă′rə nĭ tĭj), *n.* **1.** the order of baronets; baronets collectively. **2.** baronetcy.

baronetcy (bă′rə nĭt sĭ, bă′rə nĕt′sĭ), *n.*, *pl.* **-cies.** the rank or patent of a baronet.

barong (bă rŏng′), *n.* a large, broad-bladed knife or cleaver used by the Moros. [native name]

baronial (bə rō′nyəl), *adj.* **1.** pertaining to a baron, a barony, or to the order of barons. **2.** befitting a baron.

baron of beef, a joint of beef consisting of the two sirloins joined at the backbone.

barony (bă′rə nĭ), *n.*, *pl.* **-nies.** **1.** the rank or dignity of a baron. **2.** the domain of a baron. [ME *baronie*, t. OF, der. *baron* BARON]

baroque (bə rōk′, bə rŏk′), *n.* **1.** *Art.* **a.** a style developed in Italy in the 16th century, characterized by asymmetry, bold and contorted forms and exaggeration of ornamental and pictorial effects. **b.** work of this style and period. **2.** *Music.* the ornate style of composition characteristic of the 17th and early 18th centuries. **3.** anything extravagantly ornamented. *—adj.* **4.** pertaining to the baroque. **5.** extravagantly ornamented. [t. F, t. Pg.: m. *barroco* irregular]

baroscope (bă′rə skōp′), *n.* an instrument showing roughly the variations in atmospheric pressure. —**baroscopic** (bă′rə skŏp′ĭk), *adj.*

barostat (bă′rō stăt′), *n.* a device for maintaining a constant pressure, esp. in aircraft, to compensate for variation of atmospheric pressure with altitude.

barotrauma (bă′rō trô′mə), *n. Med.* injury to the eardrum or Eustachian tube caused by difference between atmospheric and intratympanic pressure.

barouche (bə ro͞osh′), *n.* a four-wheeled carriage with a seat outside for the driver, and seats inside for two couples facing each other, and with a folding hood over the back seat. [t. d. G: m. *Barutsche*, t. It.: m. *biroccio*, g. L *birolus* two-wheeled]

Barouche

barque (bäk), *n.* **1.** *Naut.* a sailing vessel having three or more masts, square-rigged on all but the aftermost mast, which is fore-and-aft rigged. **2.** *Poetic.* any boat or sailing vessel. Also, **bark.** [ME; ult. der. LL *barca*]

barquentine (bä′kən tēn′), *n. Naut.* a sailing vessel having three or more masts, square-rigged on the foremast and fore-and-aft rigged on the other masts. Also, **barquantine, barkentine.** [f. BARQUE + (BRIGA)NTINE]

Barquisimeto (*Sp.* bär kē sē mĕ′tō), *n.* a town in W Venezuela. 199,691 (1961).

Barra (bă′rə), *n.* an island of the Outer Hebrides. 1467 pop. (1961); 35 sq. mi.

barrack[1] (bă′rək), *n.* (*usually pl.*) **1.** a building or range of buildings for lodging soldiers, esp. in garrison. **2.** any large, plain building in which many people are lodged. *—v.t., v.i.* **3.** to lodge in barracks. [t. F: m. *baraque*, t. It.: m. *baracca*; orig. uncert.]

barrack[2] (bă′rək), *v.i.* **1.** to shout boisterously against a player, team, or the like; jeer. **2. barrack for,** to support; shout encouragement and approval. *—v.t.* **3.** to shout for or against. [? back-formation from *barracking* banter, var. of *barrakin, barrikin* gibberish (Cockney slang)]

barracuda (bă′rə kyo͞o′də), *n.*, *pl.* **-da, -das.** any of several species of elongate, predaceous, tropical and subtropical marine fishes of the genus *Sphyraena*, some of which are extensively used for food. [t. Sp., t. W. Ind.]

barrage (bă′räzh), *n.*, *v.*, **-raged, -raging.** *—n.* **1.** *Mil.* a barrier of artillery fire used to prevent the enemy from advancing, to enable troops behind it to operate with a minimum of casualties, or to cut off the enemy's retreat in one or more directions. **2.** any similar defensive device, as a balloon barrage. **3.** any overwhelming quantity: *a barrage of questions.* **4.** *Civ. Eng.* an artificial obstruction in a watercourse to increase the depth of the water, facilitate irrigation, etc. **5.** *Fencing.* a tie in a bout. *—v.t.* **6.** to cut off by or subject to a barrage. [t. F, der. *barrer*, v. Cf. F phrase *tir de barrage* barrage fire]

barrage balloon, a balloon used in a balloon barrage.

barramunda (bă′rə mŭn′də), *n.*, *pl.* **-da, -das.** a lungfish, *Neoceratodus forsteri*, of the rivers of Australia. Also, **barramundi** (bă′rə mŭn′dĭ). [t. native Australian]

barranca (bə răng′kə; *Sp.* bär rän′kä), *n. U.S.* a steep-walled ravine or gorge. [t. Sp.]

Barranquilla (*Sp.* bär rän kē′lyä), *n.* a port in N Colombia, on the Magdalena river. 498,301 (1964).

barrator (bă′rə tə), *n. Law.* one who commits barratry. Also, **barrater.** [ME *baratour*, t. OF: m. *barateor* fraudulent dealer, der. *barater* exchange, cheat]

barratry (bă′rə trĭ), *n. Law.* **1.** fraud by a master or crew at the expense of the owners of the ship or its cargo. **2.** the offence of frequently exciting and stirring up suits and quarrels. **3.** the purchase or sale of ecclesiastical preferments or of offices of state. [ME *barratrie*, t. OF: m. *baraterie.* See BARRATOR] —**bar′ratrous,** *adj.* —**bar′ratrously,** *adv.*

Barrault (*Fr.* bä rō′), *n.* **Jean-Louis** (*Fr.* zhäɴ lwē′), born 1910, French actor and director.

barred (bäd), *adj.* **1.** provided with one or more bars: *a barred gate.* **2.** striped; streaked: *barred fabrics.*

barrel (bă′rəl), *n.*, *v.*, **-relled, -relling,** or (*U.S.*) **-reled, -reling.** *—n.* **1.** a wooden cylindrical vessel, with slightly bulging sides made of staves hooped together and with flat, parallel ends. **2.** the quantity which such a vessel of some standard size can hold (as not less than 36 imperial gallons of beer or other liquids). **3.** any vessel, case, or part similar in form. **4.** *Ordn.* the tube of a gun. **5.** *Mach.* the chamber of a pump, in which the piston works. **6.** *Horol.* the cylindrical case in a watch or clock within which the mainspring is coiled. **7.** *Ornith.* the hard, horny, hollow part of the stem at the base of a feather; the calamus or quill. **8.** *Naut.* the main portion of a capstan, about which the rope winds, between the drumhead at the top and the pawl rim at the bottom. See illus. under **capstan.** *—v.t.* **9.** to put or pack in a barrel or barrels. [ME *barel*, t. OF: m. *baril*, prob. der. *barre* bar, stave]

barrelful (bă′rəl fo͝ol′), *n.*, *pl.* **-fuls.** as much as a barrel will hold.

barrel-house (bă′rəl hous′), *adj. Jazz, Orig. U.S.* in a rough and crude style, as in low-class nightclubs where (usually) only blues are played and sung. [orig. a cheap drinking establishment with a row of barrels in evidence]

barrel organ, a musical instrument in which air from a bellows is admitted to a set of pipes by means of pins inserted into a revolving barrel; hand organ.

barrel vault, *Archit.* a simple hemicylindrical vault. See illus. under **vault**[1].

barren (bă′rən), *adj.* **1.** incapable of producing, or not producing, offspring; sterile: *a barren woman.* **2.** unproductive; unfruitful: *barren land.* **3.** destitute of interest or attraction. **4.** mentally unproductive; dull; stupid. **5.** not producing results; fruitless: *a barren pen.* *—n.* **6.** (*usually pl.*) *U.S.* level or slightly rolling land, usually with a sandy soil and few trees, relatively infertile. [ME *barein*, t. OF: m. *baraine*, of pre-L orig.] —**bar′renly,** *adv.* —**bar′renness,** *n.*

Barren Grounds, a region of windswept, almost uninhabited tundras in N Canada, esp. around Hudson Bay. Also, **Barren Lands.**

barren strawberry, a rosaceous herb, *Potentilla sterilis*, of Europe.

barrenwort (băr′ən wût′), *n.* a rhizomatous berberidaceous herb, *Epimedium alpinus*, a native of S Europe, commonly cultivated.

Barrès (*Fr.* bä rĕs′), *n.* **Maurice** (*Fr.* mō rēs′), 1862–1923, French novelist, writer on politics, and politician.

barret (bă′rĭt), *n.* a kind of small cap, esp. a biretta. [t. F: m. *barrette* cap, t. It.: m. *berretta.* See BIRETTA]

barrette (bă rĕt′), *n.* a clasp for holding a woman's hair. [t. F, dim. of *barre* bar]

Barrhead (bä′hĕd′), *n.* a burgh in Scotland, in Renfrewshire, near Glasgow. 14,422 (1961).

barricade (bă′rĭ kād′, bă′rĭ kād′), *n.*, *v.*, **-caded, -cading.** *—n.* **1.** a defensive barrier hastily constructed, as in a street, to stop an enemy. **2.** any barrier or obstruction to passage: *a barricade of rubbish.* *—v.t.* **3.** to obstruct or block with a barricade. **4.** to shut in and defend with or as with a barricade. [t. F, prob. t. Pr.: m. *barricada* a barricade, orig. made of casks filled with earth, der. *barrica* cask] —**bar′ricad′er,** *n.* **—Syn. 1.** See **bar**[1].

Barrie (bă′rĭ), *n.* **Sir James Matthew,** 1860–1937, Scottish novelist, short-story writer, and playwright.

barrier (bă′rĭ ə), *n.* **1.** anything built or serving to bar passage, as a stockade or fortress, or a railing. **2.** any natural bar or obstacle: *a mountain barrier.* **3.** anything that restrains or obstructs progress, access, etc.: *a trade barrier.* **4.** a limit or boundary of any kind: *the barriers of caste.* **5.** (*often cap.*) *Phys. Geog.* the portion of the polar icecap of Antarctica extending miles out beyond land, and resting in places on the ocean bottom. **6.** *Oceanog.* a bar formed offshore by the action of waves and currents, separated from the mainland by lagoons or marshes. **7.** *Horseracing.* the starting gate. **8.** (*pl.*) the palisades or railing surrounding the ground where tourneys and jousts were carried on. [ME *barrere,* t. AF, der. *barre* bar] —**Syn. 1.** See bar[1].

barrier reef, *Oceanog.* a long narrow ridge of coral close to or above the surface of the sea off the coast of a continent or island: *the Great Barrier Reef.*

barring (bä′rĭng), *prep.* excepting; except for: *barring accidents, I'll be there.*

barrio (*Sp.* bȧr′ryȯ), *n., pl.* **-rios.** (in Spain and countries colonized by Spain) one of the divisions into which a town or city, together with the contiguous rural territory is divided. [t. Sp.]

barrister (bă′rĭs tə), *n.* a lawyer admitted to plead at the bar in any court. [f. *barri-* (comb. form of BAR[1]) + -STER]

Barros (*Port.* bȧr′ro͞osh), *n.* **João de** (*Port.* zhwəʊɴ′ də) (*'the Portuguese Livy'*), 1496–1570, Portuguese historian.

barrow[1] (bă′rō), *n.* **1.** a two-wheeled handcart, esp. one used by a costermonger. **2.** a wheelbarrow. **3.** *Obs.* a flat frame for carrying a load. [ME *barewe,* OE *bearwe;* prob. akin to OE *beran* BEAR[1], v.]

barrow[2] (bă′rō), *n.* **1.** an ancient or prehistoric burial mound; a tumulus. **2.** a hill (now chiefly in placenames). [ME *berwe,* OE *beorg* hill, mound, c. G *Berg* hill, mountain]

barrow[3] (bă′rō), *n.* a castrated male swine. [ME *barow,* OE *bearg*]

Barrow (bă′rō), *n.* **1.** Also, **Barrow-in-Furness** (bă′rō ĭn-fû′nĭs). a seaport in NW England, in Lancashire. 64,624 (1961). **2.** a river of SE Ireland flowing S to Waterford. 119 mi. **3. Point,** the N tip of Alaska.

barrow boy, a costermonger.

Barry (bă′rĭ; *Fr.* bȧ rē′), *n.* **Madame Du.** See **Du Barry.**

Barry (bă′rĭ), *n.* **1. Sir Charles,** 1795–1860, English architect. **2.** a town in Wales, in Glamorganshire. 42,084 (1961).

Barrymore (bă′rĭ mô′), *n.* U.S. family of actors: **Maurice** (*Herbert Blythe*), 1847–1905, father of **Ethel,** 1879–1959, **John,** 1882–1942, and **Lionel,** 1878–1954.

Barry Mountains, a mountain range in E Victoria, Australia. Highest point, Mt Hotham, 6101 ft.

bar sinister, 1. *Her.* (erroneously) a baton or a bend sinister. See illus. under **bend sinister. 2.** the implication or proof of bastard birth.

Bart., Baronet.

bartender (bä′tĕn′də), *n. Chiefly U.S.* a barman.

barter (bä′tə), *v.i.* **1.** to trade by exchange of commodities rather than by the use of money. —*v.t.* **2.** to exchange in trade as one commodity for another; trade. **3.** to bargain away unwisely or dishonourably (fol. by *away*). —*n.* **4.** the act of bartering. **5.** the thing bartered. [ME *bartre,* freq. of obs. *barrat,* v., t. OF: m. *barater* exchange, cheat. Cf. BARRATOR] —**bar′terer,** *n.* —**Syn. 1, 2.** See **trade.**

Barth (*Ger.* bȧrt), *n.* **Karl,** 1886–1968, Swiss Protestant theologian.

Bartholdi (bä thŏl′dĭ; *Fr.* bȧr tŏl dē′), *n.* **Frédéric Auguste** (*Fr.* frė dė rēk ō gʏst′), 1834–1904, French sculptor who executed the Statue of Liberty.

Bartholomew (bä thŏl′ə myo͞o′), *n. Bible.* one of the twelve apostles. Mark 3:18.

bartizan (bä′tĭ zən, bä′tĭ zăn′), *n. Archit.* a small overhanging turret on a wall or tower. [alter. of BRATTISHING] —**bartizaned** (bä′tĭ zənd, bä′tĭ zănd′), *adj.*

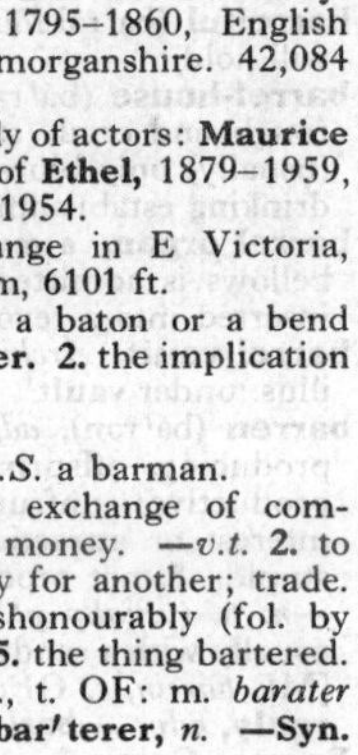

Bartizan

Bartle Frere (bä′tl frĭə′), a mountain peak in E Queensland, Australia. 5287 ft.

Bartlett (bät′lĭt), *n. Hort.* a large, yellow, juicy variety of pear. Also, **Bartlett pear.**

Bartók (bä′tŏk), *n.* **Béla** (bā′lə, bĕl′ə), 1881–1945, Hungarian composer.

Bartolommeo (*It.* bȧr tȯ lȯ mĕ′ȯ), **Fra** (*It.* frȧ) (*Baccio della Porta*), 1475–1517, Italian painter.

Baruch (bä′rŏŏk, bĕə′-), *n. Bible.* the amanuensis and friend of Jeremiah and nominal author of the Book of Baruch in the Apocrypha. Jer. 32:13.

Baruch (bə ro͞ok′), *n.* **Bernard Mannes** (măn′əs), 1870–1965, U.S. statesman and financier.

Barwon (bä′wən), *n.* a river, forming part of the Darling river, flowing SW through New South Wales, Australia.

barye (bă′rĭ), *n. Physics.* a unit of pressure equal to one dyne per sq. cm.

baryon (bă′rĭ ən), *n. Physics.* one of the group of elementary particles consisting of nucleons and hyperons.

baryta (bə rī′tə), *n. Chem.* **1.** barium oxide, BaO. **2.** barium (in phrases): *carbonate of baryta.* [see BARYTES] —**barytic** (bə rĭt′ĭk), *adj.*

barytes (bə rī′tēz), *n.* a common mineral, barium sulphate, $BaSO_4$, occurring in tabular crystals: the principal ore of barium; heavy spar. Also, **barite.** [t. Gk: weight]

barytone[1] (bă′rĭ tōn′), *Music.* —*n.* **1.** Also, **baryton.** a form of bass viol having sympathetic strings. **2.** a baritone. —*adj.* **3.** baritone.

barytone[2] (bă′rĭ tōn′), *adj.* **1.** (in Greek) pronounced with the (theoretical) grave accent on the last syllable. —*n.* **2.** a barytone word. [t. Gk: m. s. *barýtonos* with grave accent]

basal (bā′səl), *adj.* **1.** of, at, or forming the base. **2.** fundamental: *basal characteristics.* **3.** *Physiol.* **a.** indicating a standard low level of activity of an organism as present during total rest. **b.** of an amount required to maintain this level. —**bas′ally,** *adv.*

basal metabolic rate, *Physiol.* the rate of oxygen intake and heat discharge in an organism in a basal state.

basal metabolism, *Physiol.* the energy turnover of the body at a standard low level of activity.

basalt (băs′ôlt, bā′sôlt), *n.* the dark, dense igneous rock of a lava flow or minor intrusion, composed essentially of plagioclase and pyroxene, and often displaying a columnar structure. [t. L: s. *basaltes* a dark, hard marble of Ethiopia] —**basaltic** (bə sôl′tĭk), *adj.*

basaltware (băs′ôlt wĕə′, bā′sôlt-), *n.* unglazed stoneware developed by Josiah Wedgwood, usually black, with a dull gloss.

bascule (băs′kyo͞ol), *n. Civ. Eng.* a device operating like a balance or seesaw, esp. an arrangement of a movable bridge (**bascule bridge**) by which the rising floor or section is counterbalanced by a weight. [t. F: a seesaw, r. *bacule,* appar. f. *ba(ttre)* strike and *cul* the posterior]

base[1] (bās), *n., adj., v.,* **based, basing.** —*n.* **1.** the bottom of anything, considered as its support; that on which a thing stands or rests. **2.** a fundamental principle or groundwork; foundation; basis. **3.** *Archit.* **a.** that part of a column on which the shaft rests. See diag. under **column. b.** the lowest member of a wall, monument, or the like. **c.** the lower elements of a complete structure. **4.** *Bot., Zool.* **a.** the part of an organ nearest its point of attachment. **b.** the point of attachment. **5.** the principal element or ingredient of anything, considered as its fundamental part. **6.** that from which a commencement, as of action or reckoning, is made. **7.** *Baseball, etc.* one of the four fixed stations to which players run. **8.** a starting point for competitors in a race or the like. **9.** the goal in hockey and in certain other games. **10.** *Mil.* **a.** a fortified or more or less protected area or place from which the operations of an army or an airforce proceed. **b.** a supply installation for a large military force. **11.** *Geom.* the line or surface forming that part of a figure on which it is supposed to stand. **12.** *Maths.* the number which serves as a starting point for a logarithmic or other numerical system. **13.** baseline. **14.** *Electronics.* the part of a transistor which controls the current flow. **15.** *Chem.* **a.** a compound which reacts with an acid to form a salt, as ammonia, calcium hydroxide, certain nitrogen-containing organic compounds (as the amines and alkaloids), etc. **b.** the hydroxide of a metal or of an electropositive element or radical. **c.** a radical or molecule which takes up or accepts protons. **16.** *Gram.* the form to which affixes are added in the construction of a complex word, sometimes equivalent to *root* or *stem.* For example: *want* is the base in *unwanted.* **17.** *Her.* the lower part of a shield. —*adj.* **18.** serving as a base. —*v.t.* **19.** to make or form a base or foundation for. **20.** to establish, as a fact or conclusion (fol. by *on* or *upon*). **21.** to place or establish on a base or basis; ground; found; establish. [ME, t. OF, t. L: m. s. *basis,* t. Gk: a stepping, a step, pedestal, base]

—**Syn. 1.** BASE, BASIS, FOUNDATION refer to anything upon which a structure is built and upon which it rests. BASE usually refers to a literal supporting structure: *the base of a statue.* BASIS more often refers to a figurative support: *the basis of a report.* FOUNDATION implies a solid, secure understructure: *the foundation of a skyscraper or a rumour.*

base[2] (bās), *adj.,* **baser, basest,** *n.* —*adj.* **1.** morally low; without dignity of sentiment; mean-spirited; selfish; cowardly. **2.** characteristic of an inferior person or thing. **3.** of little value: *the base metals.* **4.** debased or counterfeit: *base coin.* **5.** of illegitimate birth. **6.** *Old Eng. Law.* **a.** not held or holding by honourable tenure. **b. base estate,** an estate held by services not honourable, or by villeinage. **c. base tenant,** the tenant of such an estate. **7.** not classical or refined: *base language.* **8.** *Obs.* deep or grave in sound; bass: *the base tones of a piano.* **9.** *Archaic.* of humble origin or station. **10.** *Archaic.* of small height. **11.** *Archaic.* low in place, position, or degree. **—n. 12.** *Music. Obs.* bass[1]. [ME, t. OF: m. *bas*, g. LL *bassus* low] **—base′ly,** *adv.* **—base′ness,** *n.* **—Syn. 1.** despicable, contemptible. See **mean**[2]. **2.** servile, ignoble.

baseball (bās′bôl′), *n.* **1.** a game of ball played by two sides of nine players each, on a diamond enclosed by lines connecting four bases, a complete circuit of which must be made by a player after batting, in order to score a run. **2.** the ball used in playing this game.

baseboard (bās′bôd′), *n.* **1.** a board forming the base of anything. **2.** *U.S.* a skirting board.

baseborn (bās′bôn′), *adj.* **1.** of humble birth. **2.** born out of wedlock. **3.** base-natured; mean.

baseburner (bās′bû′nə), *n.* *U.S.* a stove or furnace with a self-acting fuel hopper over the fire chamber.

Basel (*Ger.* bä′zəl), *n.* Basle.

baseless (bās′lĭs), *adj.* having no base; without foundation; groundless: *a baseless claim.*

base level, *Phys. Geog.* the lowest level to which running water can theoretically erode the land.

baseline (bās′līn′), *n.* **1.** *Survey.* an accurately measured line forming one side of a triangle or system of triangles from which all other sides are computed. **2.** *Tennis.* a line at the end of the court. **3.** *Baseball.* a line joining bases. **4.** a line at the base of anything.

basement (bās′mənt), *n.* **1.** a storey of a building partly or wholly underground. **2.** the portion of a structure which supports those portions which come above it. **3.** the substructure of a columnar or arched construction.

basenji (bə sĕn′jĭ), *n.* a small smooth-haired dog of an African breed, having a chestnut or black coat, characterized by its inability to bark. [t. Lingala (a Bantu language of the Congo): from the bush, t. Swahili: m. *washenzi* savage, worthless]

bases[1] (bā′sēz), *n.* pl. of **basis.**

bases[2] (bā′sĭz), *n.* pl. of **base**[1].

bash (băsh), *Dial. or Slang.* **—v.t. 1.** to strike with a crushing or smashing blow. **—n. 2.** a crushing blow. **3. have a bash,** make an attempt. [b. BAT[1] and MASH]

Bashan (bā′shăn), *n.* a fertile region E of the Jordan in ancient Palestine: famous for its cattle and sheep. See map under **Tyre.**

bashaw (bə shô′), *n.* **1.** pasha. **2.** *Colloq.* an important personage; a bigwig. [t. Turk.: m. *bāsha*, var. of *pāsha* PASHA]

bashful (băsh′fəl), *adj.* **1.** uncomfortably diffident or shy; timid and easily embarrassed. **2.** indicative of, accompanied with, or proceeding from bashfulness. [f. obs. *bash*, v. (aphetic var. of ABASH) + -FUL] **—bash′fully,** *adv.* **—bash′fulness,** *n.* **—Syn. 1.** See **shy**[1].

bashibazouk (băsh′ĭ bə zo͝ok′), *n.* *Hist.* one of a class of irregular mounted troops in the Turkish military service. [t. Turk.: m. *bashi-bozuq* irregular soldier, lit., wrong-headed]

Bashkir (băsh kĭə′), *n.* an autonomous republic in the E Soviet Union in Europe. 3,603,000 pop. (est. 1963); ab. 54,200 sq. mi. *Cap.:* Ufa. Official name, **Bashkir Autonomous Soviet Socialist Republic.**

basic (bā′sĭk), *adj.* **1.** of, pertaining to, or forming a base; fundamental: *a basic principle, ingredient, etc.* **2.** *Chem.* **a.** pertaining to, of the nature of, or containing a base. **b.** not having all of the hydroxyls of the base replaced by the acid radical, or having the metal or its equivalent united partly to the acid radical and partly to oxygen. **c.** alkaline. **3.** *Metall.* denoting, pertaining to, or made by a steelmaking process in which the furnace is lined with a basic or non-siliceous material, principally burnt magnesite and a small amount of ground basic slag, to aid in sintering. **4.** *Geol.* (of rocks) having relatively little silica. **5.** *Mil.* **a.** primary: *basic training.* **b.** *U.S.* receiving basic training: *a basic airman.* **—n. 6.** *U.S. Mil.* a soldier or airman receiving basic training.

basically (bā′sĭ klĭ), *adv.* fundamentally.

Basic English, a simplified English with a restricted vocabulary, intended as an international auxiliary language and for use in teaching English.

basicity (bā sĭs′ĭ tĭ), *n.* *Chem.* **1.** the state of being a base. **2.** the power of an acid to react with bases, dependent on the number of replaceable hydrogen atoms of the acid.

basic slag, the slag in a basic lined furnace used to remove impurities from metal, as in steelmaking, and as a fertilizer.

basidiomycete (bă sĭd′ĭ ō mī sēt′), *n.* *Bot.* a basidiomycetous organism. [t. NL: m. *Basidiomycētes.* See BASIDIUM, MYCETES]

basidiomycetous (bă sĭd′ĭ ō mī sē′təs), *adj.* *Bot.* belonging or pertaining to the *Basidiomycetes*, a large group of fungi which bear the spores on a basidium, including the smuts, rusts, mushrooms, puffballs, etc.

basidiospore (bă sĭd′ĭ ō spô′), *n.* *Bot.* a spore that is produced by a basidium.

basidium (bă sĭd′ĭ əm), *n.*, *pl.* **-sidia** (-sĭd′ĭ ə). *Bot.* a special form of sporophore, characteristic of basidiomycetous fungi, on which the sexual spores are borne, usually at the tips of slender projections. [f. BAS(IS) + -IDIUM] **—basid′ial,** *adj.*

Basidia

basil (băz′əl), *n.* a plant of the mint family *Labiatae*, genus *Ocimum*, as **sweet basil,** *O. basilicum.* [ME *basile*, t. OF, t. L: short for *basilicum*, t. Gk: m. *basilikón* (neut.), lit., royal]

Basil (băz′əl), *n.* **Saint** (‘*the Great*’), A.D. 329?–379, bishop of Caesarea, in Asia Minor. Also, **Basilius.**

Basilan (bă sē′lăn), *n.* a town in the Philippines, on **Basilan Island.** 155,712 (1960).

Basildon (băz′ĭl dən), *n.* a new town in England, in SE Essex. 53,752 (1961).

basilar (băs′ĭ lə), *adj.* **1.** pertaining to or situated at the base, esp. the base of the skull. **2.** basal. Also, **basilary** (băs′ĭ lə rĭ).

basilic (bə zĭl′ĭk), *adj.* **1.** kingly; royal. **2.** of a basilica. Also, **basilican** (bə zĭl′ĭ kən), **basilical.** [t. F, m. *basilique*, t. L: m. s. *basilicus*, t. Gk: m. *basilikós* kingly]

basilica (bə zĭl′ĭ kə), *n.* **1.** (*cap.*) (in ancient Rome) a large oblong building near the Forum, used as a hall of justice and public meeting place. **2.** *Archit.* an oblong building, esp. a church with a nave higher than its aisles. **3.** one of the seven main churches of Rome or another Roman Catholic church accorded the same religious privileges. [t. L, t. Gk: m. *basilikḗ*, fem. of *basilikós* royal]

Christian basilica (def. 2) A, Apse; B, Secondary apse; C, High altar; D, Transept; E, Nave; F, Aisle

Basilicata (bă sĭl′ĭ kä′tə; *It.* bä zē lĕ-kä′tä), *n.* a region in S Italy. 748,085 pop. (1963); 3856 sq. mi. *Cap.:* Potenza. Ancient, **Lucania.**

basilic vein, *Anat.* a large vein on the inner side of the arm.

basilisk (băs′ĭ lĭsk, băz′-), *n.* **1.** *Class. Legend.* a mythical creature (serpent, lizard, or dragon) said by the ancients to kill by its breath or look. **2.** a tropical American lizard of the genus *Basiliscus*, of the family *Iguanidae*, with a crest on the back of the head and along the back and tail. **3.** a kind of ancient brass cannon. [t. L: m. s. *basiliscus*, t. Gk: m. *basilískos*, prop. dim. of *basileús* king]

Hooded basilisk, *Basiliscus mitratu* (2½ to 3 ft long)

Basilius (bə sĭl′ĭ əs, -zĭl′-), *n.* Basil.

basil-thyme (băz′əl tīm′), *n.* a labiate annual herb, *Acinos arvensis*, of Europe and Asia.

basin (bā′sən), *n.* **1.** a circular container of greater width than depth, contracting towards the bottom, used chiefly to hold water or other liquid, esp. for washing. **2.** a small circular container of approximately equal width and depth, used chiefly for mixing, cooking, etc. **3.** any container of similar shape. **4.** the quantity held by such a container. **5.** a natural or artificial hollow place containing water, esp. one in which ships are docked. **6.** *Geol.* an area in which the strata dip from the margins towards a common centre. **7.** *Phys. Geog.* **a.** a hollow or depression in the earth's surface, wholly or partly surrounded by higher land: *ocean basin, lake basin, river basin.* **b.** the tract of country drained by a river and its tributaries. [ME, t. OF: m. *bacin*, g. LL *bachīnus*, der. *bacca* water vessel] **—ba′sined,** *adj.* **—ba′sin-like′,** *adj.*

basinet (băs′ĭ nĭt, -nĕt′), *n.* *Armour.* a steel globe-shaped cap. [ME, t. OF: m. *bacinet*, dim. of *bacin* BASIN]

basinful (bā′sən fo͝ol′), *n.* **1.** as much as a basin contains. **2.** *Colloq.* a sufficiency or superabundance of trouble, distress, etc.

Basingstoke (bā′zĭng stōk′), *n.* a town in England, in N Hampshire. 25,980 (1961).

basipetal (bā sĭp′ĭ tl), *adj. Bot.* (of a plant structure) developing towards the base during growth.
basiphil (bā′sĭ fĭl), *Biol.* —*adj.* **1.** having an affinity for basic dyes. —*n.* **2.** a cell or cells exhibiting such an affinity. [f. BASI(C) + -PHIL]
basis (bā′sĭs), *n., pl.* **-ses** (-sēz). **1.** the bottom or base of anything, or that on which it stands or rests. **2.** a groundwork or fundamental principle. **3.** the principal constituent; a fundamental ingredient. [t. L, t. Gk. See BASE[1]] —**Syn. 1, 2.** See **base**[1].
bask (bäsk), *v.i.* **1.** to lie in or be exposed to a pleasant warmth: *to bask in the sunshine.* **2.** to enjoy a pleasant situation: *he basked in royal favour.* —*v.t.* **3.** *Archaic.* to expose to warmth or heat, etc. [ME *baske(n)*, t. Scand.: cf. Icel. *badhask*, refl. of *badha* bathe]
Baskerville (băs′kə vĭl), *n.* a style of type. [named after John *Baskerville*, 1706–75, English typographer]
basket (bäs′kĭt), *n.* **1.** a receptacle made of twigs, rushes, thin strips of wood, or other flexible material, woven together. **2.** a container made of pieces of thin veneer, used for packing berries, vegetables, etc. **3.** the contents of a basket. **4.** anything like a basket in shape or use. **5.** *Basketball.* **a.** a short open net suspended before the backboard through which the ball must pass to score points. **b.** a score, counting one point on a free throw and two for a field goal. [ME; orig. unknown] —**bas′-ketful′**, *adj.* —**bas′ketless,** *adj.* —**bas′ket-like′,** *adj.*
basketball (bäs′kĭt bôl′), *n.* **1.** an American game similar to netball played, usually indoors, by two teams of five men (or six women) each. Points are scored by throwing the ball through the baskets placed at either end of the oblong court. **2.** the round leather ball used in this game.
basket chair, a chair made of basketwork.
basket hilt, a basket-like hilt of a sword, etc., serving to cover and protect the hand. —**bas′ket-hilt′ed,** *adj.*
basketry (bäs′kĭ trĭ), *n.* **1.** basketwork; baskets. **2.** the art or process of making baskets.
basket weave, a plain weave with two or more yarns woven together, resembling that of a basket.
basketwork (bäs′kĭt wûk′), *n.* work of the basket kind or weave; wickerwork; interwoven work.
basking shark (bäs′kĭng), a very large shark, *Cetorhinus maximus*, which frequently comes to the surface to bask in the sun.
Basle (bäl), *n.* **1.** a canton in NW Switzerland. 148,282 pop. (1960); 165 sq. mi. **2.** a city in NE Switzerland on the Rhine, on the borders of France and West Germany; formerly part of Basle canton, now itself an independent canton. 212,700 (1964). French, **Bâle;** German, **Basel.**
basophile (bā′sə fĭl′), *n.* basiphil.
Basque (băsk), *n.* **1.** one of a people of unknown origin inhabiting the western Pyrenees regions in France and Spain. **2.** their language, historically connected only with Iberian. **3.** (*l.c.*) a woman's bodice extending over the hips. **4.** (*l.c.*) a short skirt or piece hanging from the waistline of a woman's (formerly a man's) garment. —*adj.* **5.** of or pertaining to the Basques or their language. [t. F, g. L *Vasco* inhabitant of *Vasconia* Gascony]
Basque Provinces, a region in N Spain, bordering on the Bay of Biscay, populated mostly by Basques.
Basra (băz′rə), *n.* a river port in SE Iraq, N of the Persian Gulf. 673,623 (1965). Also, **Busra, Busrah.**
bas-relief (bä′rĭ lēf′, băs′-; bä′rĭ lēf′, băs′-), *n.* sculpture in low relief, in which the figures project only slightly from the background. [t. F, t. It.: m. *basso-rilievo* low relief]
Bas-Rhin (*Fr.* bȧ răN′), *n.* a department of E France. 770,150 pop. (1962); 1848 sq. mi. *Cap.:* Strasbourg.
bass[1] (bās), *Music.* —*adj.* **1.** low in pitch; of the lowest pitch or range: *a bass voice, part, singer, or instrument.* **2.** of or pertaining to the lowest part in harmonized music. —*n.* **3.** the bass part. **4.** a bass voice, singer, or instrument. [var. of BASE[2] (see def. 12)]
bass[2] (băs), *n., pl.* **basses,** (*esp. collectively*) **bass. 1.** any of the spiny-finned sea-fish of the family *Serranidae*, esp. *Labrax lupus.* **2.** any of several similar fishes of other families. [var. of d. E *barse*, OE *bærs*]
bass[3] (băs), *n.* **1.** *Bot.* bast. **2.** the basswood or linden. [alter. of BAST]
Bassano (bə sä′nō; *It.* bȧs sȧ′nȯ), *n.* **Jacopo da Ponte,** (*It.* yȧ′kȯ pȯ dȧ pȯn′tė), 1510–92, Italian painter of the Venetian school. [named after *Bassano*, in N Italy, his native town]
bass clef (bās), *Music.* the symbol placed on the fourth line of a stave to indicate that the notes are pitched below middle C; F clef. See illus. under **clef.**
bass drum (bās), *Music.* a musical instrument, the largest of the drum family, having a cylindrical body and two membranes.
Basse-Normandie (*Fr.* bȧs nŏr mäN dē′), *n.* an administrative region of N France. 1,188,113 pop. (1962); 6865 sq. mi. *Prefecture:* Caen.
Basses-Alpes (*Fr.* bȧs ȧlp′), *n.* a department of SE France. 91,843 pop. (1962); 2698 sq. mi. *Cap.:* Digne.
Basses-Pyrénées (*Fr.* bȧs pē rė nė′), *n.* a department of SW France. 466,038 pop. (1962); 2978 sq. mi. *Cap.:* Pau.
basset[1] (băs′ĭt), *n.* a long-bodied, short-legged dog resembling a dachshund but larger and heavier. Also, **basset hound.** [t. F, orig. dim. of *bas* low]

Basset (11 to 15 in. high at the shoulder)

basset[2] (băs′ĭt), *n., v.,* **-seted, -seting.** *Geol., Mining.* —*n.* **1.** an outcrop, as of the edges of strata. —*v.i.* **2.** to crop out. [? t. F: something low. See BASSET[1]]
Basseterre (bäs tĕə′), *n.* a seaport in the West Indies: the capital of St Kitts. 15,897 (1960).
Basse-Terre (băs tĕə′; *Fr.* bȧs tĕr′), *n.* a seaport in and the capital of Guadeloupe, in the French West Indies. 13,978 (1963).
basset horn, *Music.* an alto clarinet with a soft tone. [t. G: m. *Bassett-horn*, f. *Bassett* voice (or instrument) pitched between tenor and bass (t. It.: m. *bassetto*, dim. of *basso* low) + *Horn*, pun on name of inventor]
bass horn (bās), *Music.* **1.** a tuba. **2.** *Obsolesc.* a wind instrument related to the serpent.
bassinet (băs′ĭ nĕt′, băs′ĭ nĕt′), *n.* **1.** a basket with a hood over one end, for use as a baby's cradle; Moses basket. **2.** a form of perambulator. [t. F, dim. of *bassin* BASIN]
basso (băs′ō; *It.* bȧs′sȯ), *n., pl.* **-sos, -si** (-sē). *Music.* one who sings bass; a bass. [t. It., g. LL *bassus* low]
bassoon (bə so͞on′), *n. Music.* **1.** a woodwind instrument of the oboe class in baritone range, having a doubled wooden tube or body and a long, curved metallic crook to receive the reed. **2.** a reed stop on the organ whose tone resembles that of the orchestral bassoon. [t. F: m. *basson*, t. It.: m. *bassone*, aug. of *basso* low] —**bassoon′ist,** *n.*

Bassoon

basso profundo (prə fŭn′dō; *It.* prŏ-fo͞on′dȯ), *Music.* the lowest bass singer. [t. It.: deep bass]
basso-rilievo (băs′ō rĭ lē′vō), *n., pl.* **-vos.** bas-relief. Also, **basso-relievo.**
Bass Strait (băs), a strait between Australia and Tasmania. 80–150 mi. wide.
bass viol (bās), *Music.* viola da gamba (def. 1).
basswood (băs′wo͝od′), *n.* **1.** a North American linden, esp. *Tilia americana.* **2.** its wood, much used for furniture.
bast (băst), *n.* **1.** *Bot.* phloem. **2.** the inner bark of the lime and other trees, used in making matting, etc. [ME; OE *bæst*, c. G *Bast*]
bastard (băs′təd, bäs′-), *n.* **1.** an illegitimate child. **2.** something irregular, inferior, spurious, or unusual. **3.** *Colloq.* an unpleasant or despicable person. **4.** *Colloq.* any person (without pejorative sense). —*adj.* **5.** illegitimate in birth. **6.** spurious; not genuine; false. **7.** of abnormal or irregular shape or size; of unusual make or proportions. **8.** having the appearance of; resembling in some degree. [ME, t. OF: prob. f. *bast* packsaddle + *-ard* -ARD, through meaning of mule; for semantic development, cf. MULATTO]
bastard balm, a strong-smelling labiate herb, *Melittis melissophylum*, of the woods of S and central Europe.
bastardize (băs′tə dīz′, bäs′-), *v.t.,* **-dized, -dizing. 1.** to declare or prove to be a bastard. **2.** to debase. Also, **bastardise.** —**bas′tardiza′tion,** *n.*
bastard kudu, the South African antelope, *Tragelaphus angasi*; inyala.
bastardly (băs′təd lĭ, bäs′-), *adj. Obs.* **1.** bastard; baseborn. **2.** spurious; counterfeit.
bastard wing, *Ornith.* alula.
bastardy (băs′tə dĭ, bäs′-), *n., pl.* **-dies. 1.** condition of a bastard; illegitimacy. **2.** *Obs.* the act of begetting a bastard.
baste[1] (bāst), *v.t.,* **basted, basting.** to sew slightly; sew with temporary stitches, as a garment in the first stages of making; tack. [ME, t. OF: m. *bastir*, t. OG; cf. OHG *bestan* sew with bast, der. *bast* BAST]
baste[2] (bāst), *v.t.,* **basted, basting.** to moisten (meat, etc.) while cooking, with dripping, butter, etc. [? t. F: cf. OF *basser* soak, moisten]
baste[3] (bāst), *v.t.,* **basted, basting. 1.** to beat with a stick thrash; cudgel. **2.** to denounce or scold vigorously. [t. Scand.; cf. Icel. *beysta* beat, thresh]

b., blend of, blended; c., cognate with; d., dialect, dialectal; der., derived from; f., formed from; g., going back to; m., modification of; r., replacing; s., stem of; t., taken from; ?, perhaps. See full key on inside front cover.

Bastia (*Fr.* bȧs tyȧ′), *n.* a seaport on the NE coast of Corsica; the former capital of Corsica. 50,881 (1962).

bastille (băs tēl′; *Fr.* bȧs tēy′), *n.* **1. the Bastille,** a famous fortress in Paris, used as a prison, built in the 14th century and destroyed July 14th, 1789. **2.** any prison, esp. one conducted in a tyrannical way. **3.** a tower, as of a castle; a small fortress. Also, **bastile.** [ME, t. F, der. *bastir* build]

Bastille Day, July 14th, a national holiday of the French republic, commemorating the fall of the Bastille.

bastinado (băs′tĭ nā′dō), *n., pl.* **-does,** *v.,* **-doed, -doing.** —*n.* **1.** a blow or a beating with a stick, etc. **2.** an oriental mode of punishment consisting of blows with a stick on the soles of the feet, or on the buttocks. **3.** a stick or cudgel. —*v.t.* **4.** to beat with a stick, etc., esp. on the soles of the feet or on the buttocks. Also, *Archaic,* **bastinade** (băs′tĭ nād′). [t. Sp.: m. *bastonada,* der. *baston* stick]

basting (bās′tĭng), *n.* **1.** sewing with slight or temporary stitches. **2.** (*pl.*) the stitches taken, or the threads used. [f. BASTE[1] + -ING[1]]

bastion (băs′tĭ ən), *n.* **1.** *Fort.* projecting portion of a rampart or fortification, forming an irregular pentagon attached at the base to the main work. **2.** a fortified place. **3.** any person or object which affords support or defence. [t. F, t. It.: m. *bastione,* der. *bastire* build] —**bas′tioned,** *adj.*

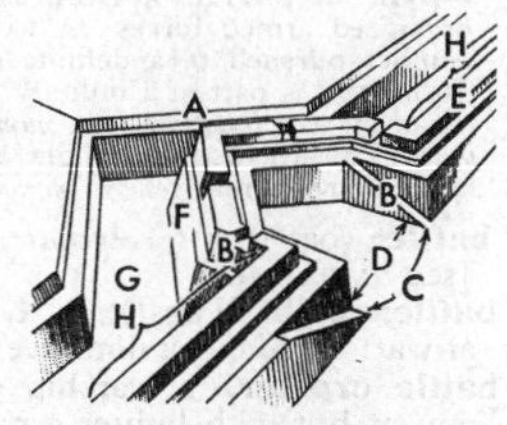

Bastion: A, Salient angle; B, Flank; C, Ramp; D, Gorge; E. Parapet; F, Face; G, Moat; H, Curtain

Basutoland (bəsōō′tōlănd′), *n.* former name of **Lesotho.**

bat[1] (băt), *n., v.,* **batted, batting.** —*n.* **1.** *Sports.* **a.** the club used in certain games, as cricket and baseball, to strike the ball. **b.** a racket, esp. one used in table tennis. **c.** the right or turn to bat. **2.** batsman: *he is a good bat.* **3.** a heavy stick, club, or cudgel. **4.** *Colloq.* a blow as with a bat. **5.** any fragment of brick or hardened clay. **6.** *Dial. or Colloq.* rate of motion, or speed. **7.** *Slang.* a spree; binge: *to go on a bat.* **8.** batt. **9. carry one's bat, a.** *Cricket.* to remain at the wicket as a batsman throughout an innings. **b.** *Colloq.* to accomplish any difficult, lengthy, or dangerous task. **10. off one's own bat,** independently; without prompting or assistance. —*v.t.* **11.** to strike or hit with or as with a bat or club. —*v.i.* **12.** *Cricket, etc.* **a.** to strike at the ball with the bat. **b.** to take one's turn as a batsman. **13.** *Slang.* to rush. [ME *batte,* OE *batt* cudgel]

bat[2] (băt), *n.* **1.** any of the nocturnal or crepuscular flying mammals constituting the order *Chiroptera,* characterized by modified forelimbs which serve as wings and are covered with a membranous skin extending to the hind limbs. **2. bats in the belfry,** mad notions. [var. of ME *bakke,* t. Scand.; cf. Dan. *-bakke*] —**bat′like′,** *adj.*

Silver-haired bat, *Lasionycteris noctivagans* (4 in. long)

bat[3] (băt), *v.t.,* **batted, batting.** *Colloq.* to wink. [var. of *bate* flutter, t. OF: m. *batre,* g. LL *batere* beat]

Bataán (bə tăn′, bə tän′), *n.* a peninsula in the Philippines, in W Luzon.

Bataán

Batangas (bə tăng′găs), *n.* a seaport in the Philippines, in SW Luzon. 736,000 (1962).

batata (bə tä′tə), *n.* the sweet potato. [t. Sp., t. Haitian; c. POTATO]

Batavia (bə tä′vyə), *n.* a former Dutch name of **Djakarta.**

batch (băch), *n.* **1.** the quantity of bread made at one baking. **2.** a quantity or number coming at one time or taken together: *a batch of prisoners.* **3.** the quantity of material prepared or required for one operation. [ME *batche,* OE *gebæc* baking, der. *bacan* bake]

batch costing, *Com.* a form of job costing in which a convenient unit or quantity of production is treated as a batch or job.

bate (bāt), *v.t.,* **bated, bating. 1.** to moderate or restrain (the breath): *to wait with bated breath.* **2.** to lessen; abate. [aphetic var. of ABATE]

bateau (*Fr.* bȧ tō′), *n., pl.* **-teaux** (*Fr.* -tō′). **1.** a light boat, esp. one having a flat bottom and tapering ends. **2.** a pontoon of a floating bridge. [t. F, in OF *batel.* Cf. ML *batellus,* dim. of *bat(t)us* boat, prob. t. OE: m. *bāt*]

bateleur eagle (băt′ə lû′), a large African eagle, *Terathopius ecaudatus,* with white underwings. [*bateleur* t. F, lit., puppeteer]

batfish (băt′fĭsh′), *n.* any of the flat-bodied marine fishes of the family *Ogcocephalidae,* as *Ogcocephalus vespertilio,* common along the southern Atlantic coast of the U.S. [f. BAT[2] + FISH, n.]

batfowl (băt′foul′), *v.i.* to catch birds at night by dazzling them with a light, then taking them in a net. [prob. f. BAT[1] + FOWL, v.] —**bat′fowl′er,** *n.*

bath[1] (bäth), *n.* **1.** a washing of the body in, or an exposure of it to the action of, water or other liquid, or vapour, etc., as for cleansing, refreshment, medical treatment, etc. **2.** water or other agent used for this purpose. **3.** a vessel for containing this, as a bathtub. **4.** a room equipped for bathing; bathroom. **5.** a building containing apartments for bathing, or fitted up for bathing. **6.** (*often pl.*) a swimming pool. **7.** (*often pl.*) one of the elaborate bathing establishments of the ancients. **8.** (*usually pl.*) a town or place resorted to for medical treatment by bathing, etc. **9.** a preparation, as an acid solution, in which something is immersed. **10.** the vessel containing such a preparation. **11.** a device for heating or cooling apparatus by means of a surrounding medium such as sand, water, or oil. **12.** the state of being covered by a liquid. —*v.t.* **13.** to put or wash in a bath. [ME; OE *bæth,* c. G *Bad*] —**bath′less,** *adj.*

bath[2] (băth), *n.* either of two Hebrew units of liquid measure, about 8·33 and 8·95 imperial gallons respectively. [t. Heb.]

Bath (bäth), *n.* a city in England, in Somerset: mineral springs; Roman remains. 80,856 (1962).

Bath (bäth), *n.* **Order of the,** an order of knighthood founded in 1725.

bath brick, a compacted mass of fine siliceous sand, used for scouring metal. [named after *Bath,* England]

bath bun, a sweet, spiced bun with dried fruit in it.

bathchair (bäth′chēə′), *n.* a type of invalid's wheel chair.

bathe (bāth), *v.,* **bathed, bathing,** *n.* —*v.t.* **1.** to immerse in water or other liquid for cleansing, refreshment, etc. **2.** to wet; wash. **3.** to moisten or suffuse with any liquid. **4.** to apply water or other liquid to, with a sponge, cloth, etc. **5.** to cover or surround with anything like water. —*v.i.* **6.** to take a bath. **7.** to swim for pleasure. **8.** to be covered or surrounded as if with water. —*n.* **9.** the act of bathing, as in the sea. [ME *bathien,* OE *bathian,* der. *bæth* bath] —**bath′er,** *n.*

Bathgate (bäth′gāt′), *n.* a burgh in Scotland, in West Lothian. 12,686 (1961).

bathhouse (bäth′hous′), *n.* a house or building for bathing or containing dressing-rooms for bathers.

bathing suit, a swimming costume, usually for a woman. Also, **bathing dress, bathing costume.**

bathing trunks, a man's swimming costume.

batho-, a word element meaning 'deep', as in *batholith.* [comb. form repr. Gk *báthos* depth]

batholith (băth′ə lĭth′), *n.* *Geol.* a large body of igneous rock, bounded by irregular, cross-cutting surfaces or fault planes, and believed to have crystallized at a considerable depth below the earth's surface. Also, **batholite** băth′ə līt′), **bathylith.** —**bath′olith′ic, batholitic** (băth′ə lĭt′ĭk), *adj.*

bathometer (bə thŏm′ĭ tə), *n.* *Oceanog.* a device for ascertaining the depth of water. Also, **bathymeter.** —**bathometric** (băth′ə mĕt′rĭk), *adj.* —**bathom′etry,** *n.*

bathos (bā′thŏs), *n.* **1.** a ludicrous descent from the elevated to the commonplace; anticlimax. **2.** triteness or triviality in style. **3.** insincere pathos; sentimentality. [t. Gk: depth] —**bathetic** (bə thĕt′ĭk), *adj.*

bathrobe (bäth′rōb′), *n.* a loose garment, often long, for wear in going to and from a bath.

bathroom (bäth′rŏŏm′, -rōōm′), *n.* a room fitted with a bath.

baths (bäthz), *n.pl.* **1.** pl. of **bath. 2.** (*sometimes construed as sing.*) **a.** a building containing public washing facilities. **b.** a public swimming pool.

Bathsheba (băth shē′bə, băth′shĭ-), *n.* *Bible.* wife of Uriah the Hittite, loved by David; later, David's wife and mother of Solomon. II Sam. 11, 12.

bath stone, a building stone quarried near Bath.

bathtub (bäth′tŭb′), *n.* a tub to bathe in, esp. one forming a permanent fixture in a bathroom.

Bathurst (băth′əst), *n.* **1.** a seaport in and the capital of Gambia. With suburbs, 40,017 (1963). **2.** a town in SE Australia, in New South Wales. 17,330 (est. 1964).

bathylith (băth′ĭ lĭth′), *n.* batholith.

bathymeter (bə thĭm′ĭ tə), *n.* bathometer. —**bathymetric** (băth′ĭ mĕt′rĭk), *adj.*—**bathym′etry,** *n.*

bathysphere (băth′ĭ sfĭə′), *n. Oceanog.* a spherical diving apparatus from which to study deep-sea life. Also, **bathyscape** (băth′ĭ skāp′), **bathyscaphe** (băth′ĭ skāf′), **bathyscope** (băth′ĭ skōp′). [f. Gk *bathý(s)* deep + -SPHERE]

batik (băt′ĭk), *n.* **1.** a method of printing cloth using a wax deposit to achieve the desired pattern. **2.** the fabric so decorated. Also, **battik.** [t. Malay (Javanese)]

Batista y Zaldívar (*Sp.* bä tēs′tä ē thäl dē′bär), **Fulgencio** (*Sp.* fo͞ol KHĕn′thyō), born 1901, Cuban military leader: president of Cuba 1940–44, 1952–59.

batiste (bă tēst′), *n.* a fine, delicate cotton fabric of plain weave. [t. F: m. *Baptiste,* name of the alleged first maker]

Batley (băt′lĭ), *n.* a town in England, in the West Riding of Yorkshire. 39,639 (1961).

batman (băt′mən), *n., pl.* **-men.** a British army officer's assigned soldier-servant.

baton (băt′ŏn; *Fr.* bä tôN′), *n.* **1.** a staff, club, or truncheon, esp. as a mark of office or authority. **2.** *Music.* the wand used by a conductor. **3.** *Her.* a sinister ordinary cut off at each end, borne in England as a mark of bastardy. **4.** *Athletics.* (in relay racing) a metal or wooden tube, handed on by one relay runner to the next. [t. F, r. obs. *baston,* t. OF, der. LL *bastum*; orig. uncert.]

Baton Rouge (băt′n ro͞ozh′), a town in the U.S., the capital of Louisiana, in the SE part: a port on the Mississippi. 152,419 (1960).

batrachian (bə trā′kyən), *Zool. —adj.* **1.** of or pertaining to the *Batrachia,* a term formerly applied to the *Amphibia,* though sometimes restricted to the salientians. *—n.* **2.** an amphibian, esp. a salientian. [f. s. Gk *bátrachos* frog + -IAN]

bats (băts), *adj. Colloq.* mad. See **bat**² (def. 2).

bats-in-the-belfry (băts′ĭn thə bĕl′frĭ), *n.* a hairy perennial campanulaceous herb with blue flowers, *Campanula trachelium,* of Europe and W Asia.

batsman (băts′mən), *n., pl.* **-men.** *Cricket, etc.* one who wields a bat or whose turn it is to bat.

batt (băt), *n.* a sheet of matted cottonwool. Also, **bat.**

batt., 1. battalion. **2.** battery.

battalion (bə tăl′yən), *n.* **1.** *Mil.* a ground-force unit composed of three or more companies or similar units. **2.** an army in battle array. **3.** (*often pl.*) a large number; force. [t. F: m. *bataillon,* t. It.: m. *battaglione*]

Battambang (băt′əm băng′), *n.* a town in W Cambodia. 40,000 (est. 1962).

battels (băt′lz), *n.pl.* (at Oxford University) accounts for provisions and stores supplied by colleges to their members.

batten¹ (băt′n), *v.i.* **1.** to thrive as by feeding; grow fat. **2.** to feed gluttonously; live in luxury at the expense of others. *—v.t.* **3.** to cause to thrive as by feeding; fatten. [t. Scand.; cf. Icel. *batna* improve, der. *bati* change for the better. Cf. OE *bet* better]

batten² (băt′n), *n.* **1.** a light strip of wood usually having an oblong cross-section and used to fasten main members of a structure together. **2.** *Naut.* **a.** a thin strip of wood inserted in a sail to keep it flat. **b.** a strip of wood, as one used to secure the edges of a tarpaulin over a hatchway. *—v.t.* **3.** to furnish with battens. **4.** *Naut.* to fasten (as hatches) with battens and tarpaulins (usually fol. by *down*). [var. of BATON]

Battenburg cake (băt′n bûg′), an oblong sponge cake divided sectionally into four squares in two colours, with jam between the squares and a marzipan outer covering.

batter¹ (băt′ə), *v.t.* **1.** to beat persistently or hard; pound. **2.** to damage by beating or hard usage. *—v.i.* **3.** to deal heavy, repeated blows; pound. *—n.* **4.** *Print.* **a.** a damaged spot on the face of type or a plate. **b.** the resulting defect in print. [ME *batere(n)*; freq. of BAT¹]

batter² (băt′ə), *n.* a mixture of flour, milk or water, eggs, etc., beaten together for use in cookery. [late ME *bater, n.* use of batter¹, but cf. OF *bature* beating]

batter³ (băt′ə), *n.* **1.** one who or that which bats. **2.** *Baseball.* the batsman.

batter⁴ (băt′ə), *Archit. —v.i.* **1.** (of walls, etc.) to slope backwards from the base. *—n.* **2.** the receding slope, usually decreasing in thickness. [orig. uncert.]

battering ram, an ancient military engine with a heavy horizontal beam for battering down walls, etc.

Battersea (băt′ə sĭ), *n.* a district in the SW London borough of Wandsworth.

battery (băt′ə rĭ), *n., pl.* **-ries. 1.** *Elect.* a galvanic cell or group of cells which produce electrical energy by chemical means. **2.** a set or series of similar machines, parts, or the like, as a group of boilers. **3.** a large number of cages in which chickens, etc., are reared for intensive productivity. **4.** *Mil.* **a.** a parapet or fortification equipped with artillery. **b.** two or more pieces of artillery used for combined action. **c.** a tactical unit of artillery, usually consisting of four guns together with the artillerymen, equipment, etc. **d.** the personnel or complement of officers and men attached to it. **e. in battery,** (of an artillery piece) in firing position, having recuperated from recoil. **5.** *Naval.* a group of guns on, or the whole armament of, a vessel of war. **6.** *Music.* the percussion section of an orchestra collectively. **7.** the act of beating or battering. **8.** *Law.* an unlawful attack upon another by beating or wounding, or by touching in an offensive manner. **9.** the instrument used in battering. [t. F: m. *batterie,* der. *battre* beat]

battik (băt′ĭk), *n.* batik.

batting (băt′ĭng), *n.* **1.** the act or manner of using a bat in a game of ball. **2.** cotton or wool in batts or sheets, used as filling for quilts or bed covers.

battle¹ (băt′l), *n., v.,* **battled, battling.** *—n.* **1.** a hostile encounter or engagement between opposing forces. **2.** participation in such hostile engagements: *wounds received in battle.* **3.** a fight between two persons or animals. **4.** *Archaic.* a battalion. *—v.i.* **5.** to engage in battle. **6.** to struggle; strive: *to battle for freedom. —v.t.* **7.** to fight. [ME *batayle,* t. OF: m. *bataille,* g. LL *battālia,* der. L *battuere* beat] **—bat′tler,** *n.*

—Syn. 1. BATTLE, ACTION, SKIRMISH mean a conflict between organized armed forces. A BATTLE is a prolonged and general conflict pursued to a definite decision: *the Battle of Waterloo.* An ACTION is part of a military operation, offensive or defensive: *the army was involved in a number of brilliant actions during the battle.* A SKIRMISH is a slight engagement, often preparatory to larger movements: *several minor skirmishes.* **2.** warfare, combat.

battle² (băt′l), *v.t. Archaic.* to furnish with battlements. [see BATTLEMENT]

battleaxe (băt′l ăks′), *n.* **1.** an axe for use as a weapon of war. **2.** *Slang.* a domineering older woman.

battle cruiser, a warship of maximum speed and fire power, but with lighter armour than a battleship.

battle cry, 1. a cry or shout of troops in battle. **2.** the phrase or slogan in any contest or campaign.

battledore (băt′l dô′), *n., v.,* **-dored, -doring.** *—n.* **1.** an instrument shaped like a tennis racket, but smaller, used in striking a shuttlecock in play. **2.** Also, **battledore and shuttlecock.** the game played with this racket and a shuttlecock. **3.** a wooden instrument used to strike clothes to wash them. *—v.t., v.i.* **4.** to toss to and fro. [ME *batyldore,* ? f. *bater* BATTER¹ + *dore* beetle, with dissimilation]

battledress (băt′l drĕs′), *n.* a simple, tough uniform without ornamental features, as worn by soldiers in battle.

battle fatigue, *Psychol.* a type of neurosis occurring among soldiers engaged in active warfare, and often making continued service in danger zones impossible; combat fatigue.

battlefield (băt′l fēld′), *n.* the field or ground on which a battle is fought. Also, **battleground** (băt′l ground′).

battlement (băt′l mənt), *n.* (*often pl.*) *Archit.* an indented parapet, having a series of openings, orig. for shooting through; a crenellated upper wall. [ME *batelment,* ? ult. der. OF *bastiller* fortify] **—battlemented** (băt′l mən-tĭd), *adj.*

A A B C D D

Battlement
A, Merlon; B, Crenel; C, Loophole; D, Machicolation

battleplane (băt′l plān′), *n. U.S.* a military aeroplane.

battle royal, 1. a fight in which more than two combatants are engaged. **2.** a hard fight or a heated argument; a fight to the finish.

battle-scarred (băt′l skäd′), *adj.* bearing scars or damages received in battle.

battleship (băt′l shĭp′), *n.* one of a class of warships which are the most heavily armoured and equipped with the most powerful batteries.

battue (bă to͞o′, -tyo͞o′; *Fr.* bä tʏ′), *n.* **1.** *Hunting.* **a.** the beating or driving of game from cover, to be killed by sportsmen. **b.** a hunt of this kind. **2.** indiscriminate slaughter of defenceless or unresisting crowds. [t. F, prop. fem. pp. of *battre* beat]

batty (băt′ĭ), *adj.,* **-ier, -iest. 1.** *Slang.* crazy; silly. **2.** of or like a bat. [f. BAT² (def. 2.) + -Y¹]

Batum (bä to͞om′), *n.* a seaport in the SW Soviet Union in Europe, on the SE coast of the Black Sea. 96,000 (est. 1965).

bauble (bô′bl), *n.* **1.** a cheap piece of ornament; trinket; gewgaw. **2.** a jester's staff. [ME *babel,* t. OF: toy, prob. der. *bel,* g. L *bellus* pretty]

Baucis and Philemon (bô′sĭs; fĭ lē′mŏn), a poor and aged Phrygian couple who offered hospitality to Zeus and Hermes in disguise, and as a reward were saved from a flood and granted long life and simultaneous death, whereupon they were turned into two trees.

Baudelaire (*Fr.* bōd lĕr′), *n.* **Pierre Charles** (*Fr.* pyĕr shärl′), 1821–67, French poet and critic.

Baudouin I (*Fr.* bô dwăN′), born 1930, king of the Belgians since 1951.

baudrons (bô′drənz), *n. Scot.* **1.** a cat. **2.** a hare.

Bauhaus (*Ger.* bou′hous), *n. German.* a school established in Weimar in 1918 by Walter Gropius to create a functional experimental architecture, utilizing all the resources of art, science, and technology.

bauhinia (bō hĭn′ĭ ə, bō-), *n.* any evergreen leguminous tropical shrub of the genus *Bauhinia*, now widely cultivated.

baulk (bôk), *n.* **1.** *Billiards.* **a.** any of the eight panels or compartments lying between the cushions of the table and the baulk lines. **b. in baulk,** inside any of these spaces. **2.** a balk. —*v.i., v.t.* **3.** to balk.

baulk line, *Billiards.* **1.** a straight line drawn across the table, behind which the cue balls are placed in beginning the game; string line. **2.** any of four lines, each near to and parallel with one side of the cushion, which divide the table into a large central panel or compartment and eight smaller compartments (**baulks**) lying between this. **3.** baulk.

Bautzen (*Ger.* bout′sən), *n.* a town in E East Germany, on the river Spree: site of Napoleon's victory over the Prussians and Russians, 1813. 42,008 (1955).

bauxite (bôk′sīt), *n.* a rock, consisting chiefly of aluminium oxide or hydroxide with various impurities: the principal ore of aluminium. [f. Les *Baux*, in southern France + -ITE[1]]

bauxite cement, a quick-setting cement consisting principally of calcium aluminate, made from bauxite and lime.

Bavaria (bə vĕə′rĭ ə), *n.* a Land in S West Germany; formerly a kingdom. 10,216,800 pop. (est. 1966); 27,239 sq. mi. *Cap.*: Munich. German, **Bayern.**

Bavaria

Bavarian (bə vĕə′rĭ ən), *adj.* **1.** of or pertaining to Bavaria, its inhabitants, or their dialect. —*n.* **2.** a native or an inhabitant of Bavaria. **3.** the High German speech of most of Bavaria and Austria, and of the Sudeten Germans.

bawbee (bô bē′), *n. Scot.* **1.** an old Scottish bullion coin, originally worth about three halfpence of English coin, later sixpence. **2.** *Colloq.* a halfpenny. [named after a Scottish mint master, the laird of Sille*bawby*]

bawcock (bô′kŏk′), *n. Archaic. or Dial.* (used familiarly) a fine fellow. [t. F: m. *beau coq* fine cock]

bawd (bôd), *n.* **1.** a procuress. **2.** *Hist.* a procurer. [ME *bawde*, ? t. F: m. *baud* gay, t. W Gmc; cf. OE *bald* bold]

bawdy (bô′dĭ), *adj.* **-dier, -diest,** *n.* —*adj.* **1.** obscene; indecent. —*n.* **2.** bawdry. —**bawd′ily,** *adv.* —**bawd′iness,** *n.*

bawdy house, a brothel.

bawdry (bô′drĭ), *n.* **1.** promiscuous sexual behaviour. **2.** procuring. **3.** indecent or lewd talk.

bawl (bôl), *v.t.* **1.** to utter or proclaim by outcry; shout out. **2.** to cry for sale, as a hawker. **3.** *Orig. U.S.* to scold (fol. by *out*). —*v.i.* **4.** to cry or wail lustily. —*n.* **5.** a loud shout; an outcry. [ME *bawl(en)*, prob. t. ML: m. *baulāre* bark as a dog; but cf. Icel. *baula* low as a cow] —**bawl′er,** *n.*

Baxter (băk′stə), *n.* **Richard,** 1615–91, English Puritan preacher, scholar, and writer.

bay[1] (bā), *n. Phys. Geog.* **1.** a recess or inlet in the shore of a sea or lake between two capes or headlands, not as large as a gulf but larger than a cove. **2.** a recess of land, partly surrounded by hills or woods. **3.** *U.S.* an arm of a prairie, extending into woods, and partly surrounded by them. [ME *baye*, t. OF: m. *baie*, g. LL *baia*, of doubtful orig.]

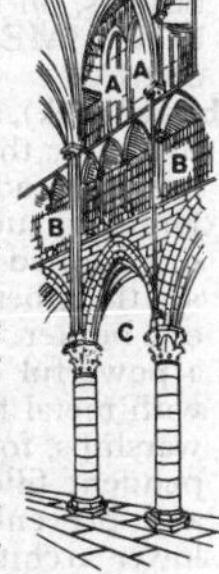

Architectural bays
A, Window bay; B, Triforium; C, Arch of aisle

bay[2] (bā), *n.* **1.** *Archit.* **a.** the part of a window included between two mullions. **b.** a recessed space projecting outwards from the line of a wall, as to contain a window. **c.** a bay window. **d.** a space or division of a wall, building, etc., between two vertical architectural features or members. **2.** *Aeron.* **a.** any portion of an aeroplane set apart by two successive bulkheads or other bracing members. **b.** a compartment in an aircraft: *a bomb bay, an engine bay.* **3.** a compartment, as in a barn for storing hay. **4.** a recess or area set back from the general flow of traffic: *parking bay.* **5.** *Naut.* the forward part of a ship between decks on either side, formerly often used as a hospital. [ME, t. OF: m. *baee* an opening, ult. der. LL *batāre* gape]

bay[3] (bā), *n.* **1.** a deep, prolonged bark, as of a hound or hounds in hunting. **2.** a stand made by a hunted animal to face or repel pursuers, or of a person forced to face a foe or difficulty: *to stand at bay, be brought to bay.* **3.** the position of the pursuers or foe thus kept off. —*v.i.* **4.** to bark, esp. with a deep prolonged sound, as a hound in hunting. —*v.t.* **5.** to beset with deep prolonged barking. **6.** to express by barking. **7.** to bring to or hold at bay. [ME *baye(n)*, aphetic var. of *abay*, t. OF: m. *abaier*]

bay[4] (bā), *n.* **1.** the European laurel, *Laurus nobilis*; sweet bay. **2.** a West Indian tree, *Pimenta acris*, whose leaves are used in making bay rum. **3.** any of various laurel-like trees. **4.** any of several magnolias. **5.** an honorary garland or crown bestowed for victory or excellence. **6.** (*pl.*) fame; renown. [ME, t. OF: m. *baie*, g. L *bāca, bacca* berry]

bay[5] (bā), *n.* **1.** reddish brown. **2.** a bay horse or animal. —*adj.* **3.** (of horses, etc.) of the colour bay. [ME, t. OF: m. *bai*, g. L *badius*]

Bayamón (*Sp.* bä yä mōn′), *n.* a town in NE Puerto Rico. 72,134 (1960).

Bayard (*Fr.* bȧ yȧr′), *n.* **1. Pierre Terrail, Seigneur de** (pyĕr tĕ rȧy′ sĕn yœr′ də), *c.* 1473–1524, the heroic French knight 'without fear and without reproach'. **2.** any man of heroic courage and unstained honour.

Bayard (bā′əd), *n.* **1.** a magical legendary horse in medieval chivalric romances. **2.** a mock-heroic name for any horse. **3.** (*l.c.*) *Archaic.* a bay horse. [ME, t. OF: f. *bai* BAY + *-ard* -ARD]

bayberry (bā′bə rĭ), *n.*, *pl.* **-ries. 1.** any of certain North American shrubs or trees of the genus *Myrica*, as *M. cerifera* (wax-myrtle). **2.** the berry of such a plant. **3.** a West Indian tree, *Pimenta acris*, whose leaves are used in making bay rum. [f. BAY[4] + BERRY]

Bayern (*Ger.* bī′ərn), *n.* German name of **Bavaria.**

Bayeux tapestry (bī yû′; *Fr.* bȧ yœ′), a strip of linen 231 feet long and 20 inches wide, preserved in Bayeux, a town in NW France. Its coloured embroidery depicts events leading to the Norman conquest of England, and it probably dates from the 12th century.

Bayle (*Fr.* bĕl), *n.* **Pierre** (*Fr.* pyĕr), 1647–1706, French philosopher and critic.

Baylis (bā′lĭs), *n.* **Lilian M.,** 1874–1937, theatrical manager of the Old Vic and Sadlers Wells.

bayonet (bā′ə nĭt), *n.*, *v.*, **-neted, -neting.** —*n.* **1.** a stabbing or slashing instrument of steel, made to be attached to or at the muzzle of a rifle. —*v.t.* **2.** to kill or wound with the bayonet. [t. F: m. *baïonette*, der. BAYONNE, in France, where such weapons were first manufactured]

bayonet cap, *Elect.* the type of head of an electric lamp or appliance which is held in place by two opposite pins and a spring on the terminal plates.

bayonet holder, *Elect.* a socket designed to receive a bayonet cap.

Bayonne (*Fr.* bȧ yŏn′), *n.* a seaport in SW France, in Basses-Pyrénées department. 32,600 (est. 1962).

bayou (bī′yōō), *n.*, *pl.* **-yous.** *Southern U.S.* an arm or outlet of a lake, river, etc. [t. Louisiana F, t. Choctaw (Muskhogean): m. *bayuk* small stream]

Bayreuth (bī′roit; *Ger.* bī rŏYt′), *n.* a town in West Germany, in N Bavaria: music festivals founded by Richard Wagner. 63,100 (est. 1966).

bay rum, a fragrant liquid used as a cosmetic, etc., esp. after shaving, prepared by distilling the leaves of the bayberry, *Pimenta acris*, with rum, or by mixing oil from them with alcohol, water, and other oils.

bay salt, a coarse-grained salt obtained by the evaporation of sea water.

bay tree, the European laurel, *Laurus nobilis.*

bay window, a window forming an extension in a room and projecting outwards from the wall of the building, esp. one rising from the ground or basement.

bazaar (bə zä′), *n.* **1.** a marketplace or quarter containing shops, particularly in the Orient. **2.** any place where miscellaneous goods are sold. **3.** a sale of miscellaneous articles, as for some charitable purpose. [t. F: m. *bazar*, t. Ar., t. Pers.]

Bazaine (*Fr.* bȧ zĕn′), *n.* **François Achille** (*Fr.* fräN swȧzȧ shēl′), 1811–88, French general and marshal.

Bazin (*Fr.* bȧ zăN′), *n.* **René François Nicolas Marie** (*Fr.* rə nė fräN swȧ nē kō lȧ mȧ rē′), 1853–1932, French novelist.

bazooka (bə zōō′kə), *n. Mil.* a cylindrical rocket-launcher, an individual infantry weapon that fires a rocket capable of penetrating several inches of armour-plate, used to destroy tanks and other armoured military vehicles. [fanciful coinage, orig. applied to an invented musical instrument]

B.B.C., British Broadcasting Corporation.

bbl., *pl.* **bbls.** barrel.

B.C., 1. Battery Commander. **2.** before Christ: *from 20* B.C. *to* A.D. *50 is 70 years.* **3.** Board of Control. **4.** British Columbia.

b.c., bayonet cap.

B.C.E., Bachelor of Civil Engineering.

B.Ch., (L *Baccalaureus Chirurgiae*) Bachelor of Surgery.

BCG, (F *Bacille Calmette Guérin*) a strain of attenuated bovine tubercle bacilli, used in immunization against tuberculosis.

B.C.L., Bachelor of Civil Law.

B. Com., Bachelor of Commerce.

bd, *pl.* **bds. 1.** board. **2.** bond. **3.** bound.

b/d, brought down.

B.D., Bachelor of Divinity.

B.D.A., British Dental Association.

bdellium (dĕl′ĭ əm, -yəm), *n.* **1.** a fragrant gum resin obtained from certain burseraceous plants, as *Commiphora.* **2.** a plant yielding it. **3.** a substance mentioned in the Bible (Gen. 2:12 and Num. 11:7), variously interpreted to mean gum resin, carbuncle, crystal, or pearl. [t. L (Vulgate) (Gen. 2:12 and Num. 11:7), t. Gk: m. *bdéllion,* translating Heb. *b'dōlakh*; r. ME *bdelyum* (Wyclif)]

bd ft, 1. board feet. **2.** board foot.

bdl., *pl.* **bdls.** bundle.

B.D.S., Bachelor of Dental Surgery.

be (bē; *unstressed* bĭ), *v., pres. indic. sing.* 1 **am**; 2 **are** or (*Archaic*) **art**; 3 **is**; *pl.* **are**; *pt. indic.* 1 **was**; 2 **were** or (*Archaic*) **wast** or **wert**; 3 **was**; *pl.* **were**; *pres. subj.* **be**; *pt. subj.* 1 **were**; 2 **were** or (*Archaic*) **wert**; 3 **were**; *pl.* **were**; *pp.* **been**; *ppr.* **being.** —*substantive.* **1.** to exist; have reality; live; take place; occur; remain as before: *he is no more, it was not to be, think what might have been, the wedding was last week.* —*copula.* **2.** (a link connecting a subject with predicate or qualifying words in assertive, interrogative, and imperative sentences, or serving to form infinitive and participial phrases): *you are late, he is much to blame, is he here? try to be just, the art of being agreeable.* —*auxiliary.* **3.** (used with the present participle of a principal verb to form the progressive tense (*I am waiting*), or with a past participle in passive forms, regularly of transitive verbs (*the date was fixed, it must be done*) and formerly, as still to some extent, of intransitives (*I am done, he is come*)). [ME *been,* OE *beon,* g. IE base *bheu-* become; now used to make inf., pres. and past participles, and pres. subj.; for pres. ind., see AM, IS, ARE (g. IE base *es-* exist); for pret., see WAS, WERE (g. IE base *wes-* remain)]

be-, a prefix of W Germanic origin, meaning 'about', 'around', 'all over', and hence having an intensive and often disparaging force, much used as an English formative of verbs (and their derivatives), as in *besiege, becloud, bedaub, beplaster, bepraise,* and often serving to form transitive verbs from intransitives or from nouns or adjectives, as in *begrudge, belabour, befriend, belittle.* [OE, unstressed form of *bī* by]

Be, *Chem.* beryllium.

B.E., 1. Bachelor of Engineering. **2.** bill of exchange.

B/E, bill of exchange. Also, **b.e.**

B.E.A., British European Airways.

beach (bēch), *n.* **1.** the sand or loose water-worn pebbles of the seashore. **2.** that part of the shore of the sea, or of a large river or lake, washed by the tide or waves. —*v.t., v.i.* **3.** *Naut.* to run or haul up (a ship or boat) on the beach. [? der. OE *bece* brook with sense devel. 'pebbly course of stream', hence 'shingle'] —**beach′less,** *adj.* —**Syn. 2.** coast, seashore, strand. See **shore**[1].

beachcomber (bēch′kō′mə), *n.* **1.** one who lives by gathering articles along the beaches, as from wreckage; a vagrant of the beach or coast, esp. a white man in South Pacific regions. **2.** a long wave rolling in from the ocean.

beach flea, any of various small hopping amphipods (family *Orchestidae*) found on beaches; a sandhopper.

Beach flea, *Orchestia agilis* (enlarged)

beachhead (bēch′hĕd′), *n.* the area of lodgement which is the first objective of a military force landing on an enemy shore.

beach hut, a cabin or cubicle on a seafront for changing into and from swimming costumes, or for living in.

beaching (bē′chĭng), *n.* gravel providing an artificial beach, as for a reservoir.

beach-la-mar (bēch′lə mä′), *n.* former name of **Neo-Melanesian.** [corruption of F BÊCHE-DE-MER lit., sea spade, m. Pg. *bicho do mar* trepang, so called because this pidgin was originally used in the trepang trade]

beachy (bē′chĭ), *adj. Obs.* covered with pebbles or sand.

Beachy Head, a headland of E Sussex, on the English Channel. 575 ft.

beacon (bē′kən), *n.* **1.** a guiding or warning signal, such as a fire, esp. one on a pole, tower, hill, etc. **2.** a tower or hill used for such purposes. **3.** a lighthouse, signal buoy, etc., on a coast or over dangerous spots at sea to warn and guide vessels. **4.** a radio beacon. **5.** any person, thing, or act that warns or guides. **6.** Belisha beacon. —*v.t.* **7.** to serve as a beacon to; guide. **8.** to furnish or mark with beacons. —*v.i.* **9.** to serve or shine as a beacon. [ME *beken,* OE *bēac(e)n*] —**bea′conless,** *adj.*

Beaconsfield (bē′kənz fēld′), *n.* See **Disraeli.**

bead (bēd), *n.* **1.** a small ball of glass, pearl, wood, etc., with a hole through it, strung with others like it, and used as an ornament or in a rosary. **2.** (*pl.*) a necklace. **3.** (*pl.*) a rosary. **4. say, tell,** or **count one's beads,** to say prayers and count them off by means of the beads on the rosary. **5.** any small globular or cylindrical body. **6.** a bubble rising through effervescent liquid. **7.** a mass of such bubbles on the surface of a liquid. **8.** a drop of liquid: *beads of sweat, etc.* **9.** the front sight of a gun. **10.** *U.S.* aim. **11.** *Archit., etc.* **a.** a narrow convex moulding, usually more or less semicircular in section. **b.** any of various pieces similar in some sections to this type of moulding. **12.** *Chem.* a globule of borax or some other flux, supported on a platinum wire, in which a small amount of some substance is heated in a flame as a test for its constituents, etc. **13.** *Metall.* the rounded mass of refined metal obtained by cupellation. —*v.t.* **14.** to ornament with beads. —*v.i.* **15.** to form beads; form in beads or drops. [ME *bede* prayer, rosary bead, aphetic var. of *ibed,* OE *gebed* prayer] —**bead′ed,** *adj.* —**bead′like′,** *adj.*

beadhouse (bēd′hous′), *n.* an almshouse whose beneficiaries were required to pray for the founder. Also, **bedehouse.**

beading (bē′dĭng), *n.* **1.** material composed of or adorned with beads. **2.** narrow lacelike trimming. **3.** narrow openwork trimming through which ribbon may be run. **4.** a narrow ornamental strip of wood used on walls, furniture, etc. **5.** bead (def. 11).

beadle (bē′dl), *n.* **1.** Also, *esp. Oxford and Cambridge,* **bedel, bedell.** an official in British universities who, bearing a mace, supervises and leads processions. **2.** *Eccles.* a parish officer having various subordinate duties. [south-eastern ME *bedel,* OE *bydel* apparitor, herald]

beadledom (bē′dl dəm), *n.* a stupid show or exercise of authority, as by subordinate officials.

beadroll (bēd′rōl′), *n.* **1.** *Rom. Cath. Ch.* a list of persons to be prayed for. **2.** any list or catalogue.

bead-ruby (bēd′ro͞o′bĭ), *n., pl.* **-bies.** the false lily of the valley, *Maianthemum canadense,* a low herb, with small white flowers and red bead-shaped berries.

beadsman (bēdz′mən), *n., pl.* **-men. 1.** one who prays for another, as a duty, and esp. when paid for it. **2.** an inmate of a poorhouse. Also, **bedesman.** —**beadswoman** (bēdz′wo͝om′ən), *n., fem.*

beadwork (bēd′wûk′), *n.* **1.** ornamental work made of or with beads. **2.** beading.

beady (bē′dĭ), *adj.,* **beadier, beadiest. 1.** beadlike; small, globular, and glittering: *beady eyes.* **2.** covered with or full of beads.

beagle (bē′gl), *n., v.,* **-gled, -gling.** —*n.* **1.** one of a breed of small hounds with short legs and drooping ears, used esp. in hunting. **2.** a spy; manhunter. —*v.i.* **3.** to hunt with beagles, on foot not on horseback. [ME *begle*; orig. uncert.]

Beagle (15 in. high at the shoulder)

beak[1] (bēk), *n.* **1.** the horny bill of a bird; the neb. **2.** a similar horny head part in certain animals such as the turtle, duck-billed platypus, etc. **3.** *Slang.* a person's nose. **4.** anything beaklike or ending in a point, as the lip of a pitcher or a beaker. **5.** *Bot.* a narrowed or prolonged tip. **6.** *Naut.* a powerful construction of metal, or of timber sheathed with metal forming a part of the bow of many older-type warships, for ramming an enemy's ship. **7.** *Archit.* a little pendent fillet, with a channel behind it forming a drip and preventing water from trickling down the faces of lower architectural members. [ME *beke,* t. OF: m. *bec,* g. L *beccus,* of Celtic orig.] —**beaked** (bēkt), *adj.* —**beak′less,** *adj.* —**beak′like′,** *adj.* —**beak′y,** *adj.*

beak[2] (bēk), *n. Colloq.* **1.** magistrate; judge. **2.** *Slang.* schoolmaster. [orig. unknown]

beaker (bē′kə), *n.* **1.** a large drinking vessel with a wide mouth. **2.** contents of a beaker. **3.** a flat-bottomed cylin-

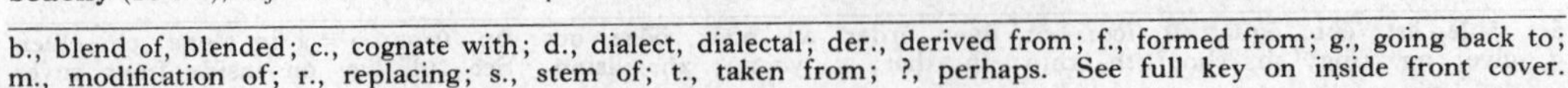

drical vessel, usually with a pouring lip. [var. (influenced by BEAK[1]) of d. E *bicker*, ME *biker*, t. Scand.; cf. Icel. *bikarr* (? ult. t. L: m. *bicārium*)]

Beaker (def. 3)

Beaker Folk, *Anthropol.* the round-headed, square-jawed inhabitants of parts of Britain in the early Bronze Age who made bell-shaped metal beakers, found in typical round barrows.

be-all and end-all, the final and exclusive aim; the ultimate conclusion.

beam (bēm), *n.* **1.** a thick, long piece of timber, shaped for use. **2.** a similar piece of metal, stone, etc. **3.** *Bldg Trades.* one of the main horizontal supporting members in a building or the like, as for supporting a roof or floor. **4.** *Shipbuilding.* one of the strong transverse pieces of timber or metal stretching across a ship to support the deck, hold the sides in place, etc. **5.** *Naut.* **a.** the side of a vessel, or the direction at right angles to the keel, with reference to the wind, sea, etc. **b.** the greatest breadth of a ship. **6.** the widest part. **7.** *Mach.* **a.** an oscillating lever of a steam engine, transferring the motion from piston rod to crankshaft. **b.** a roller or cylinder in a loom, on which the warp is wound before weaving. **c.** a similar cylinder on which cloth is wound as it is woven. **8.** the transverse bar of a balance from the ends of which the scales or pans are suspended. **9.** a ray, or bundle of parallel rays, of light or other radiation. **10.** the angle at which a microphone or loudspeaker functions best. **11.** the cone-shaped range of effective use of a microphone or loudspeaker. **12.** a gleam; suggestion: *a beam of hope.* **13.** *Radio, Aeron.* a signal transmitted along a narrow course, used to guide pilots through darkness, bad weather, etc. **14. on the beam, a.** on the course indicated by a radio beam. **b.** *Naut.* at right angles with the keel. **c.** *Slang.* just right; exact; correct; in touch with the situation. **15. fly** or **ride the beam,** *Radio, Aeron.* to be guided by a beam. **16. off the beam, a.** not on the course indicated by a radio beam. **b.** *Slang.* wrong; incorrect; out of touch with the situation. —*v.t.* **17.** to emit in or as in beams or rays. **18.** *Radio.* to transmit (a signal) on a narrow beam. —*v.i.* **19.** to emit beams, as of light. **20.** to look or smile radiantly. [ME *beem*, OE *bēam* tree, piece of wood, ray of light, c. G *Baum* tree] —**beamed,** *adj.* —**beam′less,** *adj.* —**beam′like′,** *adj.* —**Syn.** 19. See **shine.**

beam-ends (bēm′ĕndz′), *n.pl.* **1.** *Naut.* the ends of a ship's beams. **2. on her beam-ends,** *Naut.* so far inclined on one side that the deck beams are practically vertical. **3. on one's beam-ends,** *Colloq.* in acute distress, poverty, or the like.

beamer (bē′mə), *n.* *Cricket, Colloq.* a ball aimed high by the bowler, often to the height of the batsman's head.

beam hole, *Physics.* a hole in the shielding of a nuclear reactor through which a beam of radiation, esp. of neutrons, can be made to escape for experimental use.

beaming (bē′mĭng), *adj.* radiant; bright; cheerful. —**beam′ingly,** *adv.*

beam-riding (bēm′rī′dĭng), *n.* *Radio, Aeron.* the guidance of missiles along the axis of a beam. —**beam′-ri′der,** *n.*

beam tube, *Radio.* a valve in which the stream of electrons flowing to the plate is focused by the action of a set of auxiliary, charged elements.

beamy (bē′mĭ), *adj.,* **beamier, beamiest. 1.** *Colloq.* emitting beams, as of light; radiant. **2.** broad in the beam, as a ship. **3.** *Zool.* having antlers, as a stag.

bean (bēn), *n.* **1.** the edible nutritious seed of various species of leguminous plants, esp. of the genus *Phaseolus.* **2.** a plant producing such seeds, used either fresh or dried. **3.** any of various other beanlike seeds or plants, as the coffee bean. **4.** *Colloq.* a coin; anything of the least value: *I haven't a bean.* **5.** *Slang.* head. **6. full of beans,** energetic; vivacious. **7. spill the beans,** *Colloq.* to divulge information, often unintentionally. [ME *bene*, OE *bēan*, c. G *Bohne*] —**bean′like′,** *adj.*

beanbag (bēn′băg′), *n.* a small cloth bag filled with beans, used as a toy.

bean caper, a small tree, *Zygophyllum fabago*, of the eastern Mediterranean regions, whose flower buds are used as a substitute for capers.

beanfeast (bēn′fēst′), *n.* *Colloq.* a festivity; celebration.

Beannabeola (byŭn′ə byō′lə), *n.* **Twelve Bens** or **Pins of,** a group of low mountains in the Republic of Ireland, in NW Co. Galway. Highest peak, Benbarn, 2395 ft.

beano (bē′nō), *n.* *Slang.* beanfeast.

beanpole (bēn′pōl′), *n.* **1.** a tall pole for a bean plant to climb on. **2.** *Slang.* a tall, lanky person.

beansprout (bēn′sprout′), *n.* the sprout of newly germinated millet, eaten as a vegetable. Also, **bean′shoot′.**

beanstalk (bēn′stôk′), *n.* the stem of a bean plant.

bean tree, any of several trees bearing pods resembling those of a bean, as the catalpa and the carob tree.

bear[1] (bĕə), *v.,* **bore** or (*Archaic*) **bare, borne** or **born, bearing** (bĕə′rĭng). —*v.t.* **1.** to hold up; support: *to bear the weight of the roof.* **2.** to carry: *to bear gifts.* **3.** to conduct; guide; take: *they bore him to his quarters.* **4.** to press or push against: *the crowd was borne back by the police.* **5.** to render; afford; give: *to bear witness.* **6.** to transmit or spread (gossip, tales, etc.). **7.** to sustain without yielding or suffering injury (usually negative unless qualified): *I can't bear your scolding.* **8.** to undergo; suffer: *to bear pain.* **9.** to accept or have as an obligation: *to bear responsibility, cost, blame, etc.* **10.** to hold up under; be capable of: *his claim doesn't bear close examination.* **11.** to be fit for or worthy of: *the story doesn't bear repeating.* **12.** to have and be entitled to: *to bear title.* **13.** to possess as a quality, characteristic, etc.; have in or on: *bear traces, an inscription, etc.* **14.** to stand in (a relation or ratio); *the relation that price bears to profit.* **15.** to carry in the mind: *to bear love, a grudge, etc.* **16.** to exhibit; show. **17.** to have and use; exercise: *to bear sway.* **18.** to manage (oneself, one's body, head, etc.): *to bear oneself erectly.* **19.** to conduct (oneself). **20.** to give birth to: *to bear quintuplets.* **21.** to produce by natural growth: *plants bear leaves.* **22. bear a hand,** to give assistance. **23. bear out,** to confirm; prove right: *the facts bear me out.* —*v.i.* **24.** to hold, or remain firm, as under pressure (often fol. by *up*). **25.** to be patient (fol. by *with*). **26.** to press (fol. by *on, against, down,* etc.). **27.** to have an effect, reference, or bearing (fol. by *on*): *time bears heavily on him.* **28.** to tend in course or direction; move; go: *the ship bears due west.* **29.** to be located or situated: *the headland bears due west from us.* **30.** to bring forth young, fruit, etc. **31. bear down,** *Med.* (of a woman in labour) to make a voluntary muscular expulsive effort. **32. bring to bear,** to bring into effective operation; bring about. [ME *bere(n)*, OE *beran*; akin to G *gebären* bring forth, L *ferre* bear, Gk *phérein*, Skt *bhar-*] —**bear′able,** *adj.* —**bear′ableness,** *n.* —**bear′ably,** *adv.*

—**Syn. 4.** thrust, drive, force. **7.** tolerate, brook, abide. **8.** BEAR, STAND, ENDURE refer to supporting the burden of something distressing, irksome, or painful. BEAR is the general word and STAND its colloquial equivalent, but with an implication of stout spirit: *to bear a disappointment well, to stand a loss.* ENDURE implies continued resistance and patience in bearing through a long time: *to endure torture.*

bear[2] (bĕə), *n., adj., v.,* **beared, bearing.** —*n.* **1.** any of the plantigrade, carnivorous or omnivorous mammals of the family *Ursidae*, having massive bodies, coarse, heavy fur, relatively short limbs, and almost rudimentary tails. **2.** any of various animals resembling the bear, as the ant-bear. **3.** a gruff, clumsy, or rude person. **4.** (in general business) one who believes that conditions are or will be unfavourable. **5.** *Stock Exchange.* one who sells (often what he does not possess) with the expectation of buying in at a lower price and making a profit of the difference (opposed to a *bull*). **6.** (*cap.*) *Astron.* either of two constellations in the Northern Hemisphere, the **Great Bear** (Ursa Major) and the **Little Bear** (Ursa Minor). —*adj.* **7.** *Stock Exchange.* of, having to do with, or caused by declining prices in stocks, etc.: *a bear market.* —*v.t., v.i.* **8.** *Stock Exchange, etc.* to attempt to lower the price of (stocks); operate in (stocks) for a decline in price. [ME *bere*, OE *bera*, c. G *Bär*]

Black bear, *Ursus americanus* (5 ft long)

bear-baiting (bĕə′bā′tĭng), *n.* the entertainment of setting dogs to fight a captive bear.

bearberry (bĕə′bə rĭ), *n., pl.* **-ries. 1.** a trailing, evergreen, ericaceous shrub, *Arctostaphylos uva-ursi*, bearing small, bright red berries and tonic, astringent leaves. **2.** a related species, *A. alpina*, bearing black berries (**alpine bearberry** or **black bearberry**).

beard (bĭəd), *n.* **1.** the growth of hair on the face of an adult man, sometimes exclusive of the moustache. **2.** *Zool.* a tuft, growth, or part resembling or suggesting a human beard, as the tuft of long hairs on the lower jaw of a goat, or a cluster of fine, hairlike feathers at the base of the beak of certain birds. **3.** *Bot.* a tuft or growth of awns or the like, as in wheat, barley, etc. **4.** a barb or catch on an arrow, fishhook, knitting needle, crochet hook, etc. **5.** *Print.* the part of a type which connects the face with the shoulder of the body; the neck. See diag. under **type.** —*v.t.* **6.** to seize, or pull the beard of. **7.** to oppose boldly; defy. **8.** to supply with a beard. [ME *berd*, OE *beard*, c. G *Bart*] —**beard′ed,** *adj.* —**beard′less,** *adj.* —**beard′lessness,** *n.* —**beard′like′,** *adj.*

bearded tit, the reedling. Also, **bearded titmouse.**

bearded vulture, the lammergeyer.
beard grass, a grass, *Polypogon monspeliensis*, of marshy areas near the sea.
Beardsley (bĭədz′lĭ), *n.* **Aubrey Vincent** (ô′brĭ), 1872–98, English artist and illustrator.
beard-tongue (bĭəd′tŭng′), *n.* any plant of the scrophulariaceous genus *Penstemon.*
bearer (bĕə′rə), *n.* **1.** a person or thing that carries, upholds, or brings. **2.** (in India and Africa, formerly) a native servant of a European. **3.** one who presents an order for money or goods. **4.** a tree or plant that yields fruit or flowers. **5.** the holder of rank or office. **6.** pallbearer.
bear garden, 1. (formerly) a place for keeping or exhibiting bears, as for bear-baiting. **2.** any place of tumult.
bear hug, *Wrestling.* a hold in which the wrestler squeezes his opponent around the body as hard as possible.
bearing (bĕə′rĭng), *n.* **1.** the manner in which a person bears or carries himself, including posture, gestures, etc.: *a man of dignified bearing.* **2.** the act, capability, or period of producing or bringing forth: *a tree past bearing.* **3.** that which is produced; a crop. **4.** the act of enduring or capacity to endure. **5.** reference or relation (fol. by *on*): *some bearing on the problem.* **6.** *Archit.* **a.** a supporting part, as in a structure. **b.** the contact area between a load-carrying member and its support. **7.** *Mach.* a part in which a journal, pivot, or the like, turns or moves. **8.** (*often pl.*) direction or relative position: *the pilot lost his bearings.* **9.** *Geog.* a horizontal angle measured from 0 to 90° fixing the direction of a line with respect to either the north or south direction. **True bearings** are referred to the true north direction, **magnetic bearings** to magnetic north (or south). **10.** *Her.* any single device on a coat of arms; a charge. **—Syn. 1.** See **manner.**
bearing rein, a short rein attached to the saddle of a harness to prevent a horse from lowering its head.
bearish (bĕə′rĭsh), *adj.* **1.** like a bear; rough; burly; morose; rude. **2.** *Stock Exchange, etc.* unfavourable and tending to cause a decline in price. **—bear′ishly,** *adv.* **—bear′ishness,** *n.*
Bear River, a river in the U.S., in Utah, Wyoming, and Idaho, flowing into Great Salt Lake. ab. 450 mi.
bear's-breech (bĕəz′brēch′), *n.* a perennial acanthaceous herb, *Acanthus mollis*, with whitish flowers, of S Europe. Also, **bear's-breeches** (bĕəz′brĭch′ĭz).
Bearsden (bĕəz dĕn′), *n.* a burgh in Scotland, in Dunbarton. 17,022 (1961).
bear's-foot (bĕəz′fo͝ot′), *n.* any of various species of hellebore, esp. *Helleborus foetidus* and *H. viridis.*
bearskin (bĕə′skĭn′), *n.* **1.** the skin or pelt of a bear. **2.** a tall black fur cap worn esp. by soldiers. **3.** a coarse, shaggy woollen cloth for overcoats.
beast (bēst), *n.* **1.** any animal except man, but esp. a large four-footed one. **2.** the animal nature common to man and non-humans. **3.** a coarse, filthy, or otherwise beastlike human. **4.** (*cap.*) *Bible.* Antichrist. Rev. 13:18. [ME *beste*, t. OF, g. LL *besta*, var. of L *bestia*] **—beast′-like′,** *adj.* **—Syn. 1.** See **animal.**
beastly (bēst′lĭ), *adj.*, **-lier, -liest. 1.** of or like a beast; bestial. **2.** *Slang.* nasty; disagreeable. **—beast′liness,** *n.*
beast of burden, an animal used for carrying loads.
beat (bēt), *v.*, **beat, beaten** or **beat, beating,** *n.*, *adj.* *—v.t.* **1.** to strike repeatedly and, usually, violently. **2.** to thrash, cane, or flog, as a punishment. **3.** to whisk; stir, as in order to thicken or aerate: *to beat cream, beat egg-white.* **4.** to dash against: *rain beating the trees.* **5.** to assault; cause damage to (usually fol. by *up*). **6.** to flutter or flap: *a bird beating its wings.* **7.** to sound as on a drum. **8.** to hammer (metal) thin; flatten (usually fol. by *out*). **9.** to forge or make by repeated blows (usually fol. by *out*). **10.** to produce or elucidate (an idea, attitude, etc.) (usually fol. by *out*). **11.** to make (a path) by repeated treading. **12.** *Music.* to mark (time) by strokes, as with the hand or a metronome. **13.** *Hunting.* to scour (forest, grass, bush, etc.) in order to rouse game. **14.** to overcome in a contest; defeat. **15.** to break or destroy (a habit or the like). **16.** to be superior to. **17.** to frustrate or baffle; be too difficult for: *it beats me how he survived the avalanche.* **18.** to take measure to counteract or offset: *leaving early to beat the rush hour.* **19.** *U.S. Slang.* to swindle or cheat: *to beat someone out of five hundred dollars.*
—v.i. **20.** to strike repeated blows; pound. **21.** to throb or pulsate. **22.** to dash (*against, on*, etc.). **23.** to resound under blows, as a drum. **24.** to play, as on a drum. **25.** to scour cover in order to rouse game. **26.** to permit or admit of beating: *this cream won't beat.* **27.** *Physics.* to make a beat or beats. **28.** *Naut.* to make progress to windward by sailing full and by, first on one tack and then on the other.
—v. **29.** Some special verb phrases are:
beat about the bush, to approach a matter in a roundabout way; avoid coming to the point.
beat a retreat, to withdraw hurriedly.
beat back, to force back; compel to withdraw.
beat down, 1. to subdue; subject: overcome. **2.** to suppress or override (opposition, etc.). **3.** *Colloq.* to secure a lower price from by haggling.
beat it, *Slang.* to go away; depart.
beat off, to repulse; thrust aside.
beat the bounds, 1. to define the boundaries (of a parish) by striking the ground with rods, or some other method. **2.** to delimit or define the scope, as of a topic, argument, or the like.
beat up, to assault or damage.
—n. **30.** a stroke or blow. **31.** the sound made by it. **32.** a throb or pulsation. **33.** *Horol.* the stroke made by the action of the escapement of a watch or clock. **34.** a beaten path or habitual round, as of a policeman. **35.** *Music.* **a.** the audible, visual, or mental marking of the metrical divisions of music. **b.** a stroke of the hand, baton, etc., marking time division or accent for music during performance. **36.** *Pros.* the accent stress, or ictus, in a foot or rhythmical unit of poetry. **37.** *Physics.* a periodic pulsation caused by simultaneous occurrence of two waves, currents, or sounds of slightly different frequency. **38.** *Hunting.* **a.** the act of scouring for game. **b.** a shoot in which game is raised by beating. **39.** *Slang.* a beatnik. **40.** *Slang.* a deadbeat; loafer; sponger. *—adj.* **41.** *Colloq.* exhausted; worn out. **42.** *Colloq.* defeated. **43.** of or pertaining to the beat generation or their culture. **44.** abhorring traditional conventions of dress, behaviour, etc.; cool. [ME *bete(n)*, OE *bēatan*, c. Icel. *bauta*]
—Syn. 1. BEAT, HIT, POUND, STRIKE, THRASH refer to the giving of a blow or blows. BEAT implies the giving of repeated blows: *to beat a rug.* To HIT is usually to give a single blow, definitely directed: *to hit a ball.* To POUND is to give heavy and repeated blows, often with the fist: *to pound a nail, the table.* To STRIKE is to give one or more forceful blows suddenly or swiftly: *to strike a gong.* To THRASH implies inflicting repeated blows as punishment, to show superior strength, and the like: *to thrash a child.* **21.** See **pulsate.**
beaten (bē′tn), *adj.* **1.** having undergone blows; hammered. **2.** much trodden; commonly used: *the beaten track.* **3.** defeated. **4.** exhausted.
beater (bē′tə), *n.* **1.** a person or thing that beats. **2.** an implement or device for beating something: *an egg-beater.* **3.** *Hunting.* one who rouses or beats up game.
beat generation, members of the generation that came of age after World War II, who reject traditional standards of behaviour, dress, etc., and adopt an attitude of mystical detachment and relaxation.
beat group, a group of performers, usually youthful, of beat music.
beatific (bē′ə tĭf′ĭk), *adj.* **1.** rendering blessed. **2.** blissful: *a beatific vision or smile.* [t. LL: s. *beātificus*] **—be′atif′-ically,** *adv.*
beatification (bĭ ăt′ĭ fĭ kā′shən), *n.* **1.** the act of beatifying. **2.** the state of being beatified. **3.** *Rom. Cath. Ch.* the official act of the pope whereby a deceased person is declared to be enjoying the happiness of heaven, and therefore a proper subject of religious honour and public cult in certain places.
beatify (bĭ ăt′ĭ fī′), *v.t.*, **-fied, -fying. 1.** to make blissfully happy. **2.** *Rom. Cath. Ch.* to declare (a deceased person) to be among the blessed, and thus entitled to specific religious honour. [t. F: m. s. *béatifier*, t. L: m. *beātificāre* make happy]
beating (bē′tĭng), *n.* **1.** the act of a person or thing that beats. **2.** the same act administered as punishment; whipping. **3.** a defeat. **4.** a pulsation or throb.
beatitude (bĭ ăt′ĭ tyo͞od′), *n.* **1.** supreme blessedness; exalted happiness. **2.** (*often cap.*) *Theol.* any one of the declarations of blessedness pronounced by Christ in the Sermon on the Mount, as 'Blessed are the poor', etc. Matt. 5:3–11. [t. L: m. *beātitūdo*]
Beatles (bē′tlz), *n.pl.*, **The,** an English beat group: **George Harrison,** born 1943, **John Lennon,** born 1940, **Paul McCartney,** born 1942, and **Ringo Starr** (*Richard Starkey*), born 1940.
beat music, pop music with a strong, insistent, syncopated beat, using electronically amplified instruments.
beatnik (bēt′nĭk), *n.* *Colloq.* **1.** a member of the beat generation; a beat. **2.** one who avoids traditional conventions of behaviour, dress, etc.
Beatrice (bĭə′trĭs; *It.* bĕ ä trĕ′chĕ), *n.* (in Dante's *Vita Nuova* and *Commedia Divina*) a symbolic figure developed from the lady of Dante's love on earth.
Beatty (bē′tĭ), *n.* **David** (*1st Earl of the North Sea and of Brooksby*), 1871–1936, British admiral.
beau (bō), *n.*, *pl.* **beaus, beaux** (bōz). **1.** a lover; swain. **2.** a lady's escort. **3.** a dandy; fop. [ME, t. OF, n. use of *beau* (earlier *bel*) handsome, g. L *bellus.* See BELLE] **—beau′ish,** *adj.*

Beau Brummell (brŭm′əl), **1.** (*George Bryan Brummell*) 1778–1840, a man who set the fashion in men's clothes in England. **2.** a fop; dandy.

Beaufort scale (bō′fət), *Meteorol.* a numerical scale for indicating the force or velocity of the wind, ranging from 0 for calm to 12 for hurricane, or velocities above 75 miles per hour. [named after Sir Francis *Beaufort*, 1774–1857, British admiral who devised it]

beau geste (*Fr.* bō zhĕst′), *pl.* **beaux gestes** (*Fr.* bō zhĕst′). *French.* a fine gesture, often only for effect.

Beauharnais (*Fr.* bō ăr nĕ′), *n.* **1. Eugénie Hortense de,** (*Fr.* œ zhē nē ŏr täNs′ də), 1783–1837, queen of Holland: wife of Louis Bonaparte. **2. Joséphine de** (*Fr.* zhō zē fēn′ də), 1763–1814, first wife of Napoleon: empress of France 1804–09.

beau ideal (ī dē′əl, ī dēl′), **1.** a conception of perfect beauty. **2.** a model of excellence. [t. F]

Beaujolais (bō′zhə lā′; *Fr.* bō zhŏ lĕ′), *n.* **1.** a region in SE France. **2.** the wine from that region.

Beaumarchais (*Fr.* bō măr shĕ′), *n.* **Pierre Augustin Caron de** (*Fr.* pyĕr ō gʏ stăN kă rōN′ də), 1732–99, French dramatist.

beau monde (bō′mŏnd′; *Fr.* bō mōNd′), *French.* the fashionable world.

Beaumont (bō′mŏnt), *n.* **1.** a town in the U.S., in SE Texas. 119,175 (1960). **2. Francis,** 1584–1616, English dramatist: collaborated with John Fletcher.

Beaune (bōn; *Fr.* bōn), *n.* **1.** town in E France, in Côte d'Or department. 14,695 (1963). **2.** the wine grown nearby.

beauteous (byōō′tyəs), *adj. Chiefly Poetic.* beautiful. **—beau′teously,** *adv.* **—beau′teousness,** *n.*

beautician (byōō tĭsh′ən), *n.* a person who operates or works in a beauty parlour. [f. BEAUT(Y) + *-ician* of PHYS(ICIAN)]

beautiful (byōō′tĭ fəl), *adj.* having beauty; delighting the eye; admirable to the taste or the mind. **—beau′tifully,** *adv.*

—Syn. BEAUTIFUL, HANDSOME, LOVELY, PRETTY refer to a pleasing appearance. That is BEAUTIFUL which has perfection of form, colour, etc., or noble and spiritual qualities: *a beautiful landscape, girl* (not *man*). HANDSOME often implies stateliness or pleasing proportion and symmetry: *a handsome man.* That which is LOVELY is beautiful but in a warm and endearing way: *a lovely smile.* PRETTY implies a moderate but noticeable beauty, esp. in that which is small or of minor importance: *a pretty child.* **—Ant.** ugly.

beautify (byōō′tĭ fī′), *v.t., v.i.*, **-fied, -fying.** to make or become beautiful. [f. BEAUTY + -FY] **—beautification** (byōō′tĭ fĭ kā′shən), *n.* **—beau′tifi′er,** *n.*

beauty (byōō′tĭ), *n., pl.* **-ties. 1.** that quality of any object or sense or thought whereby it excites an admiring pleasure; qualification of a high order for delighting the eye or the aesthetic sense. **2.** something beautiful, esp. a woman. **3.** a grace, charm, or pleasing excellence. **4.** *Colloq.* an excellent example of its kind. **5.** *Colloq.* a particular advantage: *one of the beauties of this job is that I have so much spare time.* [ME *beute*, t. OF: m. *beaute*, der. *beau.* See BEAU] **—Syn. 1.** loveliness, pulchritude.

Beauty of Bath, a cultivated variety of apple, yellow with red mottling, having an astringent flavour.

beauty parlour, *Chiefly U.S.* an establishment for the hairdressing, manicuring, etc., of women. Also, *U.S.*, **beauty parlor, beauty shop.**

beauty spot, 1. a patch worn on the face or elsewhere to set off the fairness of the skin. **2.** a mole or other trifling mark on the skin. **3.** a place of scenic beauty. **4.** any spot, place, or feature of especial beauty.

Beauvais (*Fr.* bō vĕ′), *n.* a town in NW France, in Oise department. 36,533 (1962).

Beauvoir (*Fr.* bō vwăr′), *n.* **Simone de** (*Fr.* sē mŏn′ də), born 1908, French novelist and essayist.

beaux (bōz), *n.* a pl. of **beau.**

beaux-arts (*Fr.* bōz ăr′), *n.pl. French.* the fine arts, as painting, sculpture, etc.

beaux-esprits (*Fr.* bōz ĕs prē′), *n. French.* pl. of **bel-esprit.**

beaver[1] (bē′və), *n.* **1.** an amphibious rodent of the genus *Castor*, valued for its fur and formerly for castor, and noted for its ingenuity in damming streams with trees, branches, stones, mud, etc. **2.** its fur. **3.** a flat, round hat made of beaver fur or a similar fabric. **4.** a man's high silk hat. **5.** a heavy woollen cloth. [ME *bever*, OE *beofor*, akin to G *Biber*] **—bea′ver-like′,** *adj.*

Beaver, *Castor canadensis* (3½ ft long, including tail)

beaver[2] (bē′və), *n.* **1.** a piece of armour protecting the lower part of the face. **2.** a visor (def. 1). **3.** a full style of beard. [late ME *baviere*, t. MF: orig., bib, der. *bave* saliva]

beaverboard (bē′və bôd′), *n.* **1.** a light, stiff sheeting made of wood fibre and used in building, esp. for partitions, temporary structures, etc. **2.** (*cap.*) a trademark for this substance.

Beaverbrook (bē′və brŏŏk′), *n.* **William Maxwell Aitken** (āt′kĭn), **1st Baron,** 1879–1964, British newspaper proprietor, born in Canada.

B, Beaver[2] (def. 1)

bebeerine (bə bĭə′rēn, -rĭn), *n. Pharm.* an alkaloid resembling quinine, obtained from the bark of the greenheart and other plants.

bebeeru (bə bĭə′rōō), *n.* greenheart (def. 1). [native name in Guyana]

Bebel (*Ger.* bē′bəl), *n.* **Ferdinand August** (*Ger.* fĕr′dĭ nänt ou′gŏŏst), 1840–1913, German socialist and writer.

Bebington (bĕb′ĭng tən), *n.* a town in England, in Cheshire. 52,814 (1961).

beblubbered (bĭ blŭb′əd), *adj.* disfigured by weeping.

bebop (bē′bŏp′), *n. Jazz.* a style of composition and performance characterized by dissonant harmony, complex rhythmic devices, and experimental, often bizarre, instrumental effects. Also, **bop, rebop.** [fanciful coinage] **—be′bop′per,** *n.*

becalm (bĭ käm′), *v.t.* **1.** (*usually in pp.*) to halt (a ship, etc.) through lack of wind. **2.** to calm.

became (bĭ kām′), *v.* pt. of **become.**

because (bĭ kŏz′, bĭ kəz′), *conj.* **1.** for the reason that; due to the fact that: *the game was abandoned because it rained.* **—***adv.* **2.** by reason; on account (fol. by *of*): *the game was abandoned because of rain.* [ME *bi cause* by cause]

—Syn. 1. BECAUSE, AS, SINCE, FOR, INASMUCH AS agree in implying a reason for an occurrence or action. BECAUSE introduces a direct reason: *I was sleeping because I was tired.* AS and SINCE are casual and merely imply circumstances attendant on the main statement: *as* (or *since*) *I was tired, I was sleeping.* The reason, proof, or justification introduced by FOR is like an afterthought or a parenthetical statement: *I was sleeping, for I was tired.* INASMUCH AS implies concession; the main statement is true in view of the circumstances introduced by this conjunction: *inasmuch as I was tired, it seemed best to sleep.*

beccafico (bĕk′ə fē′kō), *n., pl.* **-cos.** any of several small European birds, esp. the garden warbler, *Sylvia hortensis*, esteemed as a delicacy in Italy. [t. It.: f. *becca*(*re*) peck + *fico* fig]

béchamel sauce (*Fr.* bē shă mĕl′), a white sauce flavoured with carrots, onions, seasoning, etc. [t. F, named after the inventor, Louis de *Béchamel*, steward of Louis XIV]

bechance (bĭ chäns′), *v.*, **-chanced, -chancing,** *adv.* **—***v.i., v.t.* **1.** to befall. **—***adv.* **2.** by chance.

Béchar. See **Colomb-Béchar.**

becharm (bĭ chäm′), *v.t.* to charm; captivate.

bêche-de-mer (*Fr.* bĕsh də mĕr′), *n.* **1.** an edible sea-cucumber. **2.** Neo-Melanesian. [See BEACH-LA-MAR]

Bechuana (bĕch′ŏŏ ä′nə), *n., pl.* **-na, -nas.** Tswana.

Bechuanaland (bĕch′ŏŏ ä′nə lănd′), *n.* former name of **Botswana.**

beck[1] (bĕk), *n.* **1.** a beckoning gesture. **2.** *Scot.* a bow or curtsy of greeting. **3. at one's beck and call,** ready to obey one immediately; subject to one's slightest wish. **—***v.t., v.i.* **4.** to beckon. [short for BECKON]

beck[2] (bĕk), *n. Dial.* a brook. [ME, t. Scand.; cf. Icel. *bekkr*, akin to OE *bece*]

Beckenham (bĕk′ə nəm), *n.* a district of the SE outer London borough of Bromley.

becket (bĕk′ĭt), *n. Naut.* **1.** any of various contrivances for holding spars, etc., in position, as a short rope with a knot at one end which can be secured in a loop at the other end. **2.** a loop or ring of rope forming a handle, or the like. [orig. unknown]

Becket (bĕk′ĭt), *n.* **Saint Thomas** (à), 1118?–70, archbishop of Canterbury: murdered because of his opposition to Henry II's policies towards the Church.

becket bend, *Naut.* sheet bend.

Beckett (bĕk′ĭt), *n.* **Samuel,** born 1906, Irish author and playwright, writing in French and English.

Beckford (bĕk′fəd), *n.* **William,** 1759–1844, English writer.

Beckmann (bĕk′mən; *Ger.* bĕk′măn), *n.* **Max,** 1884–1950, German expressionist painter.

Bechmann thermometer, a type of differential thermometer, used for measuring small changes in temperature.

beckon (bĕk′ən), *v.t., v.i.* **1.** to signal, summon, or direct by a gesture of the head or hand. **2.** to lure; entice. **—***n.* **3.** a beckoning. [ME *beknen*, OE *bēcnan*, der. *bēacen* sign. Cf. BEACON] **—beck′oner,** *n.*

becloud (bĭ kloud′), *v.t.* **1.** to darken or obscure with clouds. **2.** to make confused: *becloud the argument.*

become (bĭ kŭm′), *v.*, **became, become, becoming.** —*v.i.* **1.** to come into being; come or grow to be (as stated): *he became tired.* **2.** to be the fate (of): *what will become of him?* —*v.t.* **3.** to befit; suit: *that dress becomes you.* [ME *becume(n)*, OE *becuman* come about, happen]

becoming (bĭ kŭm′ĭng), *adj.* **1.** attractive: *a becoming dress.* **2.** suitable; proper: *a becoming sentiment.* —*n.* **3.** any process of change. **4.** *Aristotelian Metaphys.* any change involving realization of potentialities, as a movement from the lower level of potentiality to the higher level of actuality. —**becom′ingly,** *adv.* —**becom′ingness,** *n.* —**Syn. 2.** fitting, meet, appropriate.

Becquerel (*Fr.* bĕ krĕl′), *n.* **1. Alexandre Edmond** (*Fr.* ȧ lĕg zäɴ drĕd mōɴ′), 1820–91, French physicist (son of Antoine César and father of Antoine Henri). **2. Antoine César** (*Fr.* äɴ twȧn sė zȧr′), 1788–1878, French physicist. **3. Antoine Henri** (*Fr.* äɴ twȧn äɴ rē′), 1852–1908, French physicist.

Becquerel rays, *Obsolesc.* rays emitted by radioactive substances. [named after A. H. BECQUEREL]

bed (bĕd), *n., v.*, **bedded, bedding.** —*n.* **1.** a piece of furniture upon which or within which a person sleeps. **2.** the mattress and bedclothes together with the bedstead. **3.** the bedstead alone. **4.** the use of a bed for the night; lodging. **5.** matrimonial rights and duties; the union of man and woman, especially as father and mother. **6.** *Colloq.* sexual intercourse. **7.** any resting place. **8.** something resembling a bed in form or position. **9.** a piece of ground (in a garden) in which plants are grown. **10.** the ground under a body of water. **11.** a piece or part forming a foundation or base. **12.** a rock layer or stratum. **13.** a foundation surface of earth or rock supporting a track or pavement: *a road bed.* **14.** the undersurface of a brick, shingle, slate, or tile in position. **15.** either of the horizontal surfaces of a stone in position. **16.** *Print.* the flat surface in a printing press on which the forme of type is laid. **17.** *Zool.* flesh enveloping the base of a claw. **18. put to bed, a.** to help (someone) to go to bed. **b.** *Printing.* to lock up (formes) in a press before printing. **c.** *Colloq.* to prepare (an edition of a newspaper, etc.) for press, by working on it up to the time of going to press. —*v.t.* **19.** to provide with a bed. **20.** to put to bed. **21.** to make a bed for (a horse, cattle, etc.) (fol. by *down*). **22.** *Hort.* to plant in or as in a bed. **23.** to lay flat, or in a bed or layer. **24.** to embed, as in a substance. **25.** to go to bed with, usually for the purpose of sexual intercourse. —*v.i.* **26.** to go to bed. **27.** *Geol.* to form a compact layer or stratum. [ME; OE *bedd*, c. D *bed*, G *Bett*] —**bed′like′,** *adj.*

bed and breakfast, (in a hotel or the like) the provision of sleeping accommodation and breakfast. *Abbrev.:* b. & b.

bedaub (bĭ dôb′), *v.t.* **1.** to daub all over; besmear; soil. **2.** to ornament gaudily or excessively.

bedazzle (bĭ dăz′əl), *v.t.*, **-zled, -zling.** to blind or confuse by dazzling.

bedbug (bĕd′bŭg′), *n.* a small flat, wingless, hemipterous, bloodsucking insect, *Cimex lectularius*, that infests houses and esp. beds; cimex.

Bedbug, *Cimex lectularius* (⅛ in. long)

bedchamber (bĕd′chām′bə), *n.* *Archaic.* bedroom.

bedclothes (bĕd′klōz′, -klōthz′), *n.pl.* coverings for a bed; sheets, blankets, etc.

bedder (bĕd′ə), *n.* *Colloq.* (at Cambridge University) a bedmaker.

bedding (bĕd′ĭng), *n.* **1.** blankets, sheets, for a bed; bedclothes. **2.** litter; straw, etc., as a bed for animals. **3.** *Bldg Trades.* foundation or bottom layer of any kind. **4.** *Geol.* arrangement of rocks in strata.

Beddington (bĕd′ĭng tən), *n.* a district of the S outer London borough of Sutton.

Beddoes (bĕd′ōz), *n.* **Thomas Lovell** (lŭv′əl), 1803–49, English dramatist and poet.

Bede (bēd), *n.* **Saint** (*'the Venerable Bede'*), A.D. 673?–735, English monk, historian, and theologian: wrote earliest history of England. Also, **Baeda.**

bedeck (bĭ dĕk′), *v.t.* to deck out; showily adorn.

bedeguar (bĕd′ĭ gə), *n.* a mossy growth on the stems of roses, caused by gall. [t. F: *bédeguar*, der. Pers. *bādāwar* brought by the wind]

bedehouse (bēd′hous′), *n.* beadhouse.

bedel (bē′dl), *n.* *Archaic, but still used at Oxford and Cambridge.* beadle. Also, **bedell.**

bedesman (bēdz′mən), *n., pl.* **-men.** beadsman. —**bedeswoman** (bēdz′wo͝om′ən), *n. fem.*

bedevil (bĭ dĕv′əl), *v.t.*, **-illed, -illing,** or (*U.S.*) **-iled, -iling. 1.** to treat diabolically; torment maliciously. **2.** to possess as with a devil; bewitch. **3.** to confound; muddle; spoil. —**bedev′ilment,** *n.*

bedew (bĭ dyo͞o′), *v.t.* to wet with or as with dew.

bedfast (bĕd′făst′), *adj.* confined to bed.

bedfellow (bĕd′fĕl′ō), *n.* **1.** a sharer of one's bed. **2.** close companion: *politics makes strange bedfellows.*

Bedford (bĕd′fəd), *n.* **1. John Plantagenet, Duke of,** 1389–1435, English regent of France. **2.** a town in England, the county town of Bedfordshire. 64,740 (est. 1962). **3.** Bedfordshire.

Bedford cord, a fabric, esp. wool, distinctively woven with a lengthwise or diagonal corded effect.

Bedfordshire (bĕd′fəd shĭə′, -shə), *n.* a county in central England. 380,804 pop. (1961); 473 sq. mi. *Co. town:* Bedford. *Abbrev.:* Beds. Also, **Bedford.**

bedight (bĭ dīt′), *v.t.*, **-dight, -dight** or **-dighted, -dighting.** *Archaic.* to deck out; array.

bedim (bĭ dĭm′), *v.t.*, **-dimmed, -dimming.** to make dim. —**Ant.** illuminate, illumine.

Bedivere (bĕd′ĭ vĭə′), *n.* **Sir,** *Arthurian Legend.* the knight who brought the dying King Arthur to the barge in which the three queens bore him to the Isle of Avalon.

bedizen (bĭ dī′zən, -dĭz′ən), *v.t.* to dress or adorn gaudily. [f. BE- + DIZEN] —**bedi′zenment,** *n.*

bedlam (bĕd′ləm), *n.* **1.** a scene of wild uproar and confusion. **2.** (*cap.*) the former Royal Bethlehem Hospital, a lunatic asylum in SE London. **3.** any lunatic asylum; a madhouse. [ME *bedlem*, alter. of *Bethlehem*]

bedlamite (bĕd′lə mīt′), *n.* a lunatic.

bed linen, sheets and pillowcases.

Bedlington (bĕd′lĭng tən), *n.* **1.** a town in England, in E Northumberland. 29,373 (1961). **2.** a light, neat kind of terrier with a thick, woolly coat which may be white, blue, sandy, or liver-coloured.

Bedloe Island (bĕd′lō), former name (until 1958) of **Liberty Island.**

bedmaker (bĕd′mā′kə), *n.* **1.** one who makes beds. **2.** (at Cambridge University) a college servant, among whose duties is the making of beds.

bed moulding, *Archit.* **1.** the moulding, or series of mouldings, between the corona and the frieze of an entablature. **2.** any moulding under a projection.

Bedouin (bĕd′o͝o ĭn), *n.* **1.** an Arab of the desert, in Asia or Africa; nomadic Arab. **2.** a nomad; wanderer. [t. F, t. Ar.: m. *badawiyīn*, pl. of *badawī* desert dweller]

bedpan (bĕd′păn′), *n.* **1.** a shallow toilet pan for use by persons confined to bed. **2.** a warming pan.

bedplate (bĕd′plāt′), *n.* a plate, platform, or frame supporting the lighter parts of a machine.

bedpost (bĕd′pōst′), *n.* one of the upright supports of a bedstead.

bedraggle (bĭ drăg′l), *v.t.*, **-gled, -gling.** to make limp and soiled as with wet or dirt.

bedrail (bĕd′rāl′), *n.* a board connecting the headboard and footboard along the side of a bed.

bedrid (bĕd′rĭd′), *adj.* **1.** bedridden. **2.** worn out. [ME *bedrede*, OE *bedreda, -rida* lit., bed-rider]

bedridden (bĕd′rĭd′n), *adj.* confined to bed. [var. (by confusion with pp.) of BEDRID]

bedrock (bĕd′rŏk′), *n.* **1.** *Geol.* unbroken solid rock, overlaid in most places by soil or rock fragments. **2.** bottom layer; lowest stratum. **3.** any firm foundation.

bedroom (bĕd′ro͞om′, -ro͝om′), *n.* a sleeping room.

Beds., Bedfordshire.

bedside (bĕd′sīd′), *n.* **1.** the side of a bed, esp. as the place of one in attendance on the sick. —*adj.* **2.** attending a sick person: *a good bedside manner.* **3.** at or for a bedside: *a bedside table.*

bed-sitter (bĕd′sĭt′ə), *n.* *Colloq.* bed-sitting room.

bed-sitting room, a single-room dwelling place with both a bed and daytime living facilities.

bedsore (bĕd′sô′), *n.* a sore due to prolonged confinement in bed, as in a long illness.

bedspread (bĕd′sprĕd′), *n.* an outer covering, usually decorative, for a bed.

bedspring (bĕd′sprĭng′), *n.* one of a set of springs for the support of a mattress.

bedstead (bĕd′stĕd′, -stĭd), *n.* the framework of a bed supporting the springs and a mattress.

bedstraw (bĕd′ strô′), *n.* a rubiaceous plant, *Galium verum* (**our Lady's bedstraw**), or some allied species: formerly used as straw for beds.

bedtime (bĕd′tīm′), *n.* time to go to bed.

bedward (bĕd′wəd), *adv.* to bed. Also, **bed′wards.**

Bedwelty (bĕd′wəl tĭ), *n.* a town in England, in W Monmouthshire. 27,336 (1961).

Bedworth (bĕd′wəth), *n.* a town in England, in N Warwickshire. 32,501 (1961).

bee[1] (bē), *n.* **1.** any of various hymenopterous insects of the super-family *Apoidea*, which includes many social and solitary bees of several families, as the bumblebees, honeybees, etc. **2.** the common honeybee, *Apis mellifera.*

3. **bee in one's bonnet,** a. an obsession. b. a slightly crazy idea, attitude, fad, etc. 4. *Chiefly U.S.* a local gathering for work, entertainment, contests, etc.: *spelling bee.* [ME; OE *bēo*, c. D *bij*, Icel. *bȳ*] —**bee'like',** *adj.*

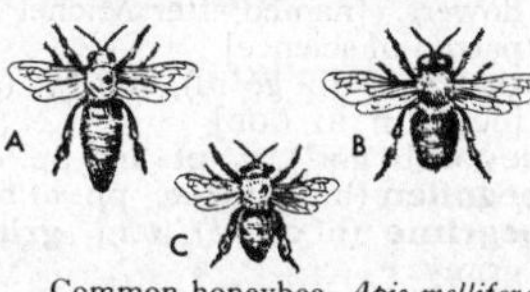

Common honeybee, *Apis mellifera* A, Queen; B, Drone; C, Worker

bee[2] (bē), *n. Naut.* a piece of hard wood, bolted to the side of the bowsprit, through which to reeve stays. [ME *beh* ring, OE *bēag, bēah* ring]

bee-beetle (bē'bē'tl), *n.* a European beetle, *Trichodes apiarius*, which sometimes infests beehives.

bee-bread (bē'brĕd'), *n.* a protein food mixture, containing pollen, manufactured and stored up by bees for their young; ambrosia.

beech (bēch), *n.* 1. any tree of the genus *Fagus*, of temperate regions, having a smooth grey bark, and bearing small edible triangular nuts. 2. the wood of such a tree. [ME *beche*, OE *bēce*] —**beech'en,** *adj.*

Beecham (bē'chəm), *n.* **Sir Thomas,** 1879–1961, English orchestral conductor.

Beeching (bē'chĭng), *n.* **Richard, Baron,** born 1913, British industrialist; chairman of the British Railways Board 1963–65.

beech mast, the edible nuts of the beech, esp. when lying on the ground.

beechnut (bēch'nŭt'), *n.* the small, triangular, edible nut of the beech.

bee-eater (bē'ē'tə), *n.* any of the family *Meropidae*, comprising European insectivorous birds with long, slender bills and brilliant plumage.

beef (bēf), *n., pl.* **beeves** (bēvz) for 1; **beefs** for 5; *v.* —*n.* 1. a bull, cow, or steer of the genus *Bos*, esp. if intended for meat. 2. the flesh of such an animal, used for food. 3. *Colloq.* brawn; muscular strength. 4. *Colloq.* weight, as of human flesh. 5. *Chiefly U.S. Slang.* a complaint. —*v.i.* 6. *Chiefly U.S. Slang.* to complain; grumble. [ME, t. OF: m. *boef*, g. L *bōs* ox] —**beef'less,** *adj.*

beef cattle, cattle raised for beef.

beefeater (bēf'ē'tə), *n.* 1. one who eats beef. 2. a yeoman of the guard or a warder of the Tower of London. 3. *U.S. Slang.* an Englishman.

bee-fly (bē'flī'), *n.* any fly of the dipterous family *Bombyliidae*, members of which more or less resemble bees.

beefsteak (bēf'stāk'), *n.* a prime slice of beef for grilling or frying, as fillet, rump, sirloin, etc.

beef tea, an extract of beef made by heating chopped beef in water and straining it.

beef-witted (bēf'wĭt'ĭd), *adj.* thick-witted; stupid.

beefwood (bēf'wŏŏd'), *n.* any of several trees of the genus *Casuarina*, of Australia and the East Indies.

beefy (bē'fĭ), *adj.,* **beefier, beefiest.** fleshy; brawny; solid; heavy. —**beef'iness,** *n.*

beehive (bē'hīv'), *n.* 1. a hive or receptacle, traditionally dome-shaped, serving as a habitation for bees. 2. a crowded, busy place. 3. a hat, house, or other object shaped like a traditional beehive. —*adj.* 4. dome-shaped, like a traditional beehive.

beehive house, a prehistoric circular building, found throughout Europe, usually of stone and having a dome-shaped covering.

beekeeper (bē'kē'pə), *n.* one who keeps bees. Also, **beemaster** (bē'mäs'tə).

bee-killer (bē'kĭl'ə), *n.* a robber fly (family *Asilidae*).

beeline (bē'līn'), *n.* a direct line, like the course of bees returning to a hive: *the hungry children made a beeline for the food.*

Beelzebub (bĭ ĕl'zĭ bŭb'), *n.* 1. *Bible.* 'the prince of the devils' (Matt. 12:24); the devil. 2. a devil. 3. (in Milton's *Paradise Lost*) one of the fallen angels, second only to Satan himself. [ult. t. Heb.: m. *Ba'al-zebub* Philistine god, II Kings 1:2 (? meaning 'lord of flies')]

bee-moth (bē'mŏth'), *n.* a brown moth, *Galleria mellonella*, whose larvae feed on beeswax. Also, **wax-moth.**

been (bĕn), *v.* pp. of **be.**

bee orchid, a European orchidaceous, perennial herb, *Ophrys apifera*, bearing a flower said to resemble a bumblebee.

bee plant, any plant much used by bees for food materials.

beer (bĭə), *n.* 1. an alcoholic beverage made by brewing and fermentation from cereals, usually malted barley and flavoured with hops, etc., to give a bitter taste. 2. any of various beverages, whether alcoholic or not, made from roots, molasses, or sugar, yeast, etc.: *root beer, ginger beer.* [ME *bere*, OE *bēor*, c. G *Bier*]

beer and skittles, drinks and pleasure; any pleasurable activity.

Beerbohm (bĭə'bōm), *n.* **Sir Max,** 1872–1956, English author and caricaturist.

beer money, *Colloq.* 1. a gratuity. 2. any money set aside for spending on pleasure, especially by a husband.

Beersheba (bĭə shē'bə), *n.* a town in S Israel, near the southern extremity of biblical Palestine. 62,000 (est. 1964). See **Dan**[1] (def. 3).

beery (bĭə'rĭ), *adj.,* **beerier, beeriest.** 1. of, like, or abounding in beer. 2. affected by or suggestive of beer. —**beer'iness,** *n.*

beestings (bēs'tĭngz), *n.pl.* colostrum, the first milk of a mammal, esp. a cow, after giving birth. Also, **biestings.** [OE var. of *bȳsting*, der. *bēost* beestings, c. G *Biest*]

Beeston (bē'stən), *n.* a town in England, in Nottinghamshire. (with Stapleford) 55,995 (1961).

beeswax (bēz'wăks'), *n.* 1. the wax secreted by bees, of which they construct their honeycomb; wax (def. 1). —*v.t.* 2. to rub, polish, or treat with beeswax.

beeswing (bēz'wĭng'), *n.* a thin film formed on port and some other wines after long keeping. —**beeswinged** (bēz'wĭngd'), *adj.*

beet (bēt), *n.* 1. any of various biennial plants of the chenopodiaceous genus *Beta*, whose varieties include the **red beet,** which has a fleshy edible root, and the **sugar beet,** which yields sugar. 2. the root of such a plant. 3. the leaves served as a salad or cooked vegetable. [OE *bēte*, t. L: m. *bēta*] —**beet'like',** *adj.*

beetfly (bēt'flī'), *n.* a dipterous insect, *Pegomya nyoscyami*, var. *betae-curt*; a very common pest of beet and other root crops. Also, **mangold fly.**

Beethoven (bā'tō vən; *Ger.* bĕt'hō fən), *n.* **Ludwig van** (*Ger.* lōōt'vĭкн fän), 1770–1827, German composer.

beetle[1] (bē'tl), *n., v.,* **-tled, -tling.** —*n.* 1. any insect of the order *Coleoptera*, characterized by having forewings modified as hard, horny structures, useless in flight. 2. any of various insects resembling beetles, as the common cockroach. —*v.i.* 3. *Slang.* to move swiftly, especially in an aeroplane (often fol. by *off* or *along*). [ME *bētylle, bityl*, OE *bitula* lit., biter]

Beetle, *Calosoma sycophanta* (Ab. 1 in. long)

beetle[2] (bē'tl), *n., v.,* **-tled, -tling.** —*n.* 1. a heavy hammering or ramming instrument, usually of wood, used to drive wedges, force down paving stones, consolidate earth, etc. 2. any of various wooden instruments for beating linen, mashing potatoes, etc. —*v.t.* 3. to use a beetle on; drive, ram, beat, or crush with a beetle. 4. to finish (cloth) by means of a beetling machine. [ME and d. OE *bētel*, r. OE *bietl*, der. *bēatan* beat]

beetle[3] (bē'tl), *adj., v.,* **-tled, -tling.** —*adj.* 1. projecting, overhanging: *beetle brows.* —*v.i.* 2. to project; jut out; overhang. [back-formation from BEETLE-BROWED] —**bee'tling,** *adj.*

beetle-browed (bē'tl broud'), *adj.* 1. having heavy projecting eyebrows. 2. scowling; sullen. [ME *bitelbrowed*, f. *bitel* biting + BROW + -ED[3]. See BEETLE[1]]

beetlehead (bē'tl hĕd'), *n.* a stupid person; blockhead. [see BEETLE[2]] —**bee'tlehead'ed,** *adj.*

Beeton (bē'tn), *n.* **Isabella Mary,** 1836–65, English cookery writer.

beetroot (bēt'rōōt'), *n.* the edible root of the red beet.

beet sugar, sugar from the roots of the sugar beet.

beeves (bēvz), *n.* pl. of **beef** (def. 1).

bef., before.

B.E.F., British Expeditionary Force.

befall (bĭ fôl'), *v.,* **-fell, -fallen, -falling.** —*v.i.* 1. to happen or occur. 2. *Archaic.* to come (*to*) as by right. —*v.t.* 3. to happen to. [ME *befallen*, OE *befeallan*]

befit (bĭ fĭt'), *v.t.,* **-fitted, -fitting.** to be fitting or appropriate for; be suited to: *his clothes befit the occasion.*

befitting (bĭ fĭt'ĭng), *adj.* fitting; proper. —**befit'tingly,** *adv.* —**Syn.** appropriate, suitable, seemly.

befog (bĭ fŏg'), *v.t.,* **-fogged, -fogging.** to involve in fog or obscurity; confuse.

befool (bĭ fōōl'), *v.t.* 1. to fool; deceive; dupe. 2. to treat as a fool.

before (bĭ fô'), *adv.* 1. in front; in advance; ahead. 2. in time preceding; previously. 3. earlier or sooner: *begin at noon, not before.* —*prep.* 4. in front of; ahead of; in advance of: *before the house.* 5. previously to; earlier than: *before the war.* 6. ahead of; in the future of; awaiting: *the golden age is before us.* 7. in preference to; rather than: *they would die before yielding.* 8. in precedence of, as in order or rank: *we put freedom before fame.* 9. in the presence or sight of: *before an audience.* 10. under the jurisdiction or consideration of: *before a magistrate.* 11. **before the wind,** *Naut.* blown along by the wind. —*conj.* 12. previously to the time when: *before we go.*

13. sooner than; rather than: *I will die before I submit.* [ME *before(n)*, OE *beforan*, f. *be* by + *foran* before] —**Ant.** 1. behind. 2. afterwards. 3. later.

beforehand (bĭ fôʹhănd′), *adv., adj.* in anticipation; in advance; ahead of time.

beforetime (bĭ fôʹtīm′), *adv. Archaic.* formerly.

befoul (bĭ foulʹ), *v.t.* to make foul; defile; sully.

befriend (bĭ frĕndʹ), *v.t.* to act as a friend to; aid.

befuddle (bĭ fŭdʹl), *v.t.*, **-dled, -dling.** 1. to make stupidly drunk. 2. to confuse, as with glib argument.

beg (bĕg), *v.*, **begged, begging.** —*v.t.* 1. to ask for in charity; ask as alms. 2. to ask for, or of, with humility or earnestness, or as a favour: *to beg forgiveness, to beg him to forgive me.* 3. to assume or demand permission (to say or do something): *beg to differ, beg to point out an error.* 4. to take for granted without justification. 5. **beg the question, a.** to assume the very point raised in a question. **b.** to evade the point at issue. —*v.i.* 6. to ask alms or charity; live by asking alms. 7. to ask humbly or earnestly: *begging for help.* 8. **go begging,** to be unwanted; be unclaimed. [ME *beggen*, OE *bedecian*]
—**Syn.** 2. entreat, pray, crave, implore, beseech, petition. BEG and REQUEST are used in certain conventional formulas, in the sense of *ask.* BEG, once a part of many formal expressions used in letter-writing, debate, etc., is now used chiefly in courteous formulas like *I beg your pardon, the Committee begs to report,* etc. REQUEST, more impersonal and now more formal, is used in giving courteous orders (*you are requested to report*) and in commercial formulas like *to request payment.*

began (bĭ gănʹ), *v.* pt. of **begin.**

begat (bĭ gătʹ), *v. Archaic.* pt. of **beget.**

beget (bĭ gĕtʹ), *v.t.*, **begot, begotten** or **begot, begetting.** 1. to procreate or generate (used chiefly of the male parent). 2. to cause; produce as an effect. [ME *begete(n)*, f. BE- + GET; r. OE *begitan*] —**begetʹter,** *n.*

beggar (bĕgʹə), *n.* 1. one who begs alms, or lives by begging. 2. a penniless person. 3. (in playful use) a wretch or rogue: *a dear little beggar.* —*v.t.* 4. to reduce to beggary; impoverish. 5. to exhaust the resources of: *to beggar description.* [ME *begger*, f. BEG + -ER[1]. See -AR[3]] —**beggardom** (bĕgʹə dəm), **begʹgarhood′,** *n.* —**begʹgarman′,** *n.*

beggarly (bĕgʹə lĭ), *adj.* like or befitting a beggar; wretchedly poor; mean. —**begʹgarliness,** *n.*

beggar-my-neighbour (bĕgʹə mĭ nāʹbə), *n.* a common card game for two players. Also, **beggar-your-neighbour.**

beggar's-lice (bĕgʹəz līs′), *n.* 1. (*construed as pl.*) seeds or fruits which stick to clothing. 2. (*sing. or pl.*) any plant producing them. Also, **begʹgar-lice′.**

beggar's-tick (bĕgʹəz tĭk′), *n.* 1. one of the prickly awns of *Bidens frondosa* or similar plants. 2. (*pl.*) the plant itself.

beggar-tick (bĕgʹə tĭk′), *n.* 1. beggar's-tick. 2. beggar's-lice.

beggary (bĕgʹə rĭ), *n.* 1. the condition of utter poverty. 2. beggars collectively.

Beghard (bĕgʹəd, bĭ gädʹ), *n.* a member of one of certain former religious communities of men which arose in Flanders in the 13th century, living after the manner of the Beguines. Also, **Beguin.** [t. ML: s. *Beghardus*]

begin (bĭ gĭnʹ), *v.*, **began, begun, beginning.** —*v.i.* 1. to enter upon an action; take the first step; commence; start. 2. to come into existence; arise; originate. 3. **to begin with, a.** in the first place; firstly. **b.** as a start. —*v.t.* 4. to take the first step in; set about; start; commence. 5. to originate; be the originator of. [ME *beginne(n)*, OE *beginnan*] —**beginʹner,** *n.*
—**Syn.** 4. BEGIN, COMMENCE, INITIATE, START (when followed by noun or gerund) refer to setting into motion or progress something which continues for some time. BEGIN is the common term: *to begin knitting a sweater.* COMMENCE is a more formal word, often suggesting a more prolonged or elaborate beginning: *to commence proceedings in court.* INITIATE implies a careful and often ingenious first act in a new field: *to initiate a new procedure.* START means to make a first, often sudden, move or to set out on a course of action: *to start a race, start paving a street.* 5. institute, inaugurate, initiate. —**Ant.** 1. end.

beginning (bĭ gĭnʹĭng), *n.* 1. the act or fact of entering upon an action or state. 2. the point of time or space at which anything begins: *the beginning of the Christian era.* 3. the first part or initial stage of anything: *the beginnings of science.* 4. origin; source; first cause: *humility is the beginning of wisdom.* —**Syn.** 1. initiation, inauguration, inception. 2. start. —**Ant.** 1. ending. 2. end.

begird (bĭ gûdʹ), *v.t.*, **-girt** or **-girded, -girding.** to gird about; encompass; surround. [ME *begirden*, OE *begyrdan.* See BE-, GIRD[1]]

begone (bĭ gŏnʹ), *v.i.* to go away, depart (usually as an imperative).

begonia (bĭ gōʹnyə), *n.* any plant of the tropical genus *Begonia*, including species much cultivated for their handsome, succulent, often varicoloured leaves and waxy flowers. [named after Michel *Bégon*, 1638–1710, French patron of science]

begorrah (bĭ gŏʹrə), *interj.* (an oath). Also, **begorra.** [euph. m. BY GOD]

begot (bĭ gŏtʹ), *v.* pt. and pp. of **beget.**

begotten (bĭ gŏtʹn), *v.* pp. of **beget.**

begrime (bĭ grīmʹ), *v.t.*, **-grimed, -griming.** to make grimy.

begrudge (bĭ grŭjʹ), *v.t.*, **-grudged, -grudging.** 1. to be discontented at seeing (a person) have (something): *to begrudge a man his good fortune.* 2. to be reluctant to give, grant, or allow: *to begrudge him the money he earned.* —**Syn.** 1. See **envy.**

beguile (bĭ gīlʹ), *v.t.*, **-guiled, -guiling.** 1. to influence by guile; mislead; delude. 2. to take away from by artful tactics (fol. by *of*). 3. to charm or divert. 4. to while away (time) pleasantly. —**beguileʹment,** *n.* —**beguilʹer,** *n.* —**Syn.** 1. deceive, cheat.

Beguin (bĕgʹĭn; *Fr.* bĕ găɴʹ), *n.* a Beghard.

beguine (bĭ gēnʹ), *n.* 1. a South American dance in bolero rhythm. 2. a modern social dance based on the beguine. 3. music for either of these dances. [t. Creole F: fem. form of *béguin* flirtation]

Beguine (bĕgʹēn; *Fr.* bĕ gēnʹ), *n.* a member of one of certain communities of Roman Catholic women who devote themselves to a religious life but retain private property and may leave at any time. The first of these communities was founded at Liège in the 12th century. [ME *begyne*, t. OF: m. *béguine*, der. Lambert le *Bègue* (i.e., Stammerer), founder of the order]

begum (bēʹgəm), *n.* (in India) 1. a Muslim woman ruler. 2. a high-ranking Muslim lady, often a widow. [t. Hind.: m. *begam*]

begun (bĭ gŭnʹ), *v.* pp. of **begin.**

behalf (bĭ häfʹ), *n.* 1. side, interest, or aid (prec. by *on*): *on behalf of his country.* 2. *U.S.* favour or interest (prec. by *in*). [ME *behalve* beside, in OE a phrase, *be healfe* (*him*) by (his) side; later used as n. by confusion with ME *on his halve* on his side. See HALF]

Behan (bēʹən), *n.* **Brendan (Francis),** 1923–64, Irish dramatist.

behave (bĭ hāvʹ), *v.*, **-haved, -having.** —*v.i.* 1. to conduct oneself or itself; act: *the ship behaves well.* 2. to act in a socially acceptable manner: *did the child behave?* —*v.t.* 3. **behave oneself, a.** to conduct oneself in a specified way. **b.** to conduct oneself properly. [late ME, appar. f. BE- + HAVE hold oneself a certain way]

behaviour (bĭ hāʹvyə), *n.* 1. manner of behaving or acting. 2. *Psychol.* the actions or activities of the individual as matters of psychological study. 3. the action of any material: *the behaviour of tin under heat.* Also, *U.S.*, **behavior.** —**behavʹioural;** *U.S.* **behavioral,** *adj.*
—**Syn.** 1. demeanour, manners. BEHAVIOUR, CONDUCT, DEPORTMENT refer to one's mode of acting. BEHAVIOUR refers to one's actions before or towards others, esp. on a particular occasion: *his behaviour at the party was childish.* CONDUCT refers to actions viewed collectively, esp. as measured by an ideal standard of behaviour: *conduct is judged according to principles of ethics.* DEPORTMENT is behaviour as related to a code or to an arbitrary standard: *deportment is guided by rules of etiquette.*

behaviourism (bĭ hāvʹyə rĭz′əm), *n. Psychol.* a theory or method that regards objective and accessible facts of behaviour or activity of man and animals as the only proper subject for psychological study. Also, *U.S.*, **behaviorism.** —**behavʹiourist;** *U.S.* **behaviorist,** *n., adj.*

behaviour pattern, *Sociol.* a recurrent way of acting by an individual or group towards a given object or in a given situation.

behead (bĭ hĕdʹ), *v.t.* to cut off the head of; kill or execute by decapitation.

beheld (bĭ hĕldʹ), *v.* pt. and pp. of **behold.**

behemoth (bĭ hēʹmŏth), *n.* 1. *Bible.* an animal, perhaps the hippopotamus, mentioned in Job 40:15. 2. *Colloq.* a huge and powerful man, beast, etc. [t. Heb.: m. *behēmōth*, pl. (intensive form) of *behēmah* beast]

behest (bĭ hĕstʹ), *n.* bidding or injunction; mandate or command. [ME; OE *behǣs* promise]

behind (bĭ hīndʹ), *prep.* 1. at the back of; at the rear of: *behind the house.* 2. after; later than: *behind schedule.* 3. less advanced than; inferior to: *behind his class in mathematics.* 4. on the farther side of; beyond: *behind the mountain.* 5. supporting; promoting: *a millionaire is behind the play.* 6. hidden or unrevealed by: *malice lay behind her smile.* —*adv.* 7. at or towards the back; in the rear. 8. in a place, state, or stage already passed: *he left his wallet behind.* 9. remaining; in reserve: *greater support is behind.* 10. in arrears; behindhand: *behind with the rent.* 11. slow, as a watch or clock. —*n.* 12. the hindquarters of a man or animal. [ME *behinden*, OE *behindan.* See BE-, HIND[1]]

—**Syn.** 1, 2. BEHIND, AFTER both refer to a position following something else. BEHIND applies primarily to position in space, and suggests that one person or thing is at the back of another: it may also refer to (a fixed) time: *he stood behind the chair, the train is behind schedule.* AFTER applies primarily to time; when it denotes position in space, it is not used with precision, and refers usually to bodies in motion: *rest after a hard day's work; they entered the room, one after another.*

behindhand (bĭ hīnd′hănd′), *adv., adj.* **1.** late. **2.** behind in progress; backward. **3.** in debt.

Behistun (*Pers.* bā hĕs to͞on′), *n.* a ruined town in W Iran: site of a cliff containing an account carved in Persian, Elamite, and Babylonian cuneiform, which provided the key to cuneiform. Also, **Bisutun.**

behold (bĭ hōld′), *v.*, **-held, -holding,** *interj.* —*v.t.* **1.** to observe; look at; see. —*interj.* **2.** look! see! [ME *beholde(n)*, OE *behaldan* keep] —**behold′er,** *n.*

beholden (bĭ hōl′dən), *adj.* under an obligation; indebted.

behoof (bĭ ho͞of′), *n.* use; advantage; benefit. [ME *behove*, OE *behōf* profit, need, c. G *Behuf*]

behove (bĭ hōv′), *v.*, **-hoved, -hoving.** —*v.t.* **1.** to be needful or proper for or incumbent on (now only in impersonal use): *it behoves me to see him.* —*v.i.* **2.** *Archaic.* to be needful, proper, or due (in impersonal use). Also, *Chiefly U.S.*, **behoove** (bĭ ho͞ov′). [ME *behove(n)*, OE OE *behōfian* need. See BEHOOF]

Behrens (*Ger.* bē′rəns), *n.* **Peter,** 1868–1940, German expressionist architect.

Behring (*Ger.* bē′rĭng), *n.* **1. Emil von** (*Ger.* ĕ′mēl fŏn), 1854–1917, German physician and bacteriologist. **2. Vitus** (*Dan.* vē′to͞os). See **Bering, Vitus.**

beige (bāzh), *n., adj.* very light brown, as of undyed wool; light grey with brownish tinge. [t. F]

Beilan Pass (bā lăn′), a mountain pass NW of Aleppo: the ancient gateway from Asia Minor to Syria.

being (bē′ĭng), *n.* **1.** existence, as opposed to non-existence. **2.** conscious existence; life: *the aim of our being.* **3.** mortal existence; lifetime. **4.** substance or nature: *of such a being as to arouse fear.* **5.** something that exists: *inanimate beings.* **6.** a living thing. **7.** a human being; person. **8.** (*cap.*) God. **9.** *Philos.* **a.** that which has actuality either materially or in idea. **b.** absolute existence in a complete or perfect state, lacking no essential characteristic; essence.

Beira (bī′ə rə; *Port.* bəy′rə), *n.* a seaport in Mozambique. 58,235 (1960).

Beirut (bā′ro͞ot, bā ro͞ot′), *n.* a seaport in and the capital of Lebanon. 500,000 (est. 1963). Also, **Beyrouth.**

Bejaia (*Fr.* bĕ zhȧ yȧ′), *n.* a seaport in NE Algeria. 63,000 (est. 1960). French, **Bougie.**

bejewel (bĭ jo͞o′əl), *v.t.*, **-elled, -elling** or (*U.S.*) **-eled, -eling.** to adorn with or as with jewels.

Békéscsaba (*Hung.* bē′kēsh chŏ bŏ), *n.* a town in SE Hungary. 51,000 (est. 1962).

bel (bĕl), *n. Physics.* the unit which measures power ratios equal to the logarithm to the base 10 of the ratio of any two powers. [named after A. G. BELL]

Bel (bāl), *n.* a deity of the Babylonians and Assyrians, god of the earth. [t. L: s. *Bēlus*, t. Gk: m. *Bêlos* BAAL]

belabour (bĭ lā′bə), *v.t.* **1.** to beat vigorously; ply with heavy blows. **2.** to assail persistently, as with ridicule. **3.** *Obs.* to labour at. Also, *U.S.*, **belabor.**

belah (bĭ lä′, bē′lä), *n.* an Australian tree, *Casuarina glauca.* [t. native Australian]

belated (bĭ lā′tĭd), *adj.* coming or being late or too late. —**belat′edly,** *adv.* —**belat′edness,** *n.*

Belaúnde (*Sp.* bĕ lȧ o͞on′dĕ), *n.* **Fernando** (*Sp.* fĕr nȧn′dŏ) (*Fernando Belaúnde Terry*), born 1913, president of Peru 1963–68.

belay (bĭ lā′), *v.t., v.i.*, **-layed, -laying,** *n.* —*v.t.* **1.** *Naut.* to fasten (a rope) by winding around a pin or short rod inserted in a holder so that both ends of the rod are clear. **2.** *Mountaineering.* to secure (a rope or person) by a turn of rope round a rock or piton. —*v.i.* **3.** to stop (used chiefly in the imperative). **4.** to make a rope fast. —*n.* **5.** *Mountaineering.* a knot or turn of rope round a rock or piton by which a climbing-rope is held secure. [ME *belegge(n)*, OE *belecgan* cover. See BE-, LAY[1]]

belaying pin, *Naut.* a pin for use in securing the ends of ropes.

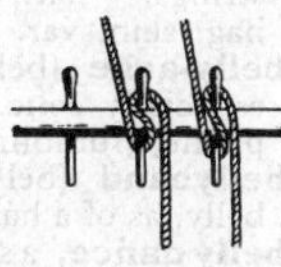
Belaying pins, with ropes belayed on them

bel canto (bĕl kăn′tō), *Music.* a smooth, cantabile style of singing. [It.]

belch (bĕlch), *v.i.* **1.** to eject wind spasmodically and noisily from the stomach through the mouth; eructate. **2.** to emit contents violently, as a gun, geyser, or volcano. **3.** to issue spasmodically; gush forth. —*v.t.* **4.** to eject spasmodically or violently; give forth. —*n.* **5.** a belching; eructation. **6.** a burst of flame, smoke, gas, etc. [ME *belche(n)*. Cf. OE *belcettan*] —**belch′er,** *n.*

belcher (bĕl′chə), *n.* a dark blue kerchief with blue-centred white spots. [named after Jim *Belcher*, 1783–1854, a boxer]

beldam (bĕl′dəm), *n. Archaic.* **1.** an old woman, esp. an ugly one; hag. **2.** grandmother. Also, **beldame** (bĕl′dəm). [ME: grandmother, f. *bel-* (t. OF: *bel, belle* fair) used like GRAND (def. 12) + *dam* DAME]

beleaguer (bĭ lē′gə), *v.t.* **1.** to surround with an army. **2.** to surround: *beleaguered with annoyances.* [t. D: m. s. *belegeren*, der. *be-* about + *leger* camp] —**belea′guered,** *adj.* —**belea′guerer,** *n.*

Belém (*Port.* bə ləyɴ′), *n.* a seaport in N Brazil, on the Pará river. 402,170 (1960). Also, **Pará.**

belemnite (bĕl′əm nīt′), *n. Palaeontol.* a conical fossil, several inches long, consisting of the internal calcareous rod of an extinct animal allied to the cuttlefish; a thunder-stone. [f. s. Gk *bélemnon* dart + -ITE[1]]

bel-esprit (*Fr.* bĕl ĕs prē′), *n., pl.* **beaux-esprits** (bō-zĕs prē′). *French.* a person of great wit or intellect.

Belfast (bĕl′făst; bĕl făst′), *n.* a seaport in and the capital of Northern Ireland, the county town of Antrim, also in Co. Down: the Queen's University (founded 1908).

Belfort (*Fr.* bĕl fŏr′), *n.* **1.** a territory in E France. 109,371 pop. (1962); 235 sq. mi. **2.** a fortress town in and the capital of this territory, strategically situated on a pass between the Vosges and Jura mountains: siege 1870–71; battle 1944. 48,070 (1962).

belfry (bĕl′frĭ), *n., pl.* **-fries.** **1.** a belltower, either attached to a church or other building or standing apart. **2.** that part of a steeple or other structure in which a bell is hung. **3.** a frame of timberwork which may sustain a bell. **4.** *Hist.* **a.** a watchtower. **b.** a movable tower for attacking fortifications. **5.** *Colloq.* the head or mind. [ME *belfray*, dissimilated var. of *berfrey*, t. OF: m. *berfrei*, t. Gmc; cf. MHG *bercfrit* defence shelter]

Belg., **1.** Belgian. **2.** Belgium.

Belgaum (bĕl′goum), *n.* a town in India, in NW Mysore. 127,885 (1961).

Belgian (bĕl′jən), *n.* **1.** a native or an inhabitant of Belgium. —*adj.* **2.** of or pertaining to Belgium.

Belgian Congo, a former Belgian colony in central Africa: now an independent republic. See **Congo** (def. 1).

Belgian endive, chicory.

Belgian hare, one of a breed of domestic rabbits notable for large size.

Belgic (bĕl′jĭk), *adj.* **1.** of the Belgae, an ancient people of N Gaul. **2.** Belgian. [t. L: s. *Belgicus*, der. *Belgae*]

Belgium (bĕl′jəm), *n.* a kingdom in W Europe, on the North Sea, N of France. 9,251,414 pop. (1962); 11,779 sq. mi. *Cap.:* Brussels. Flemish, **België** (*Flem.* bĕl′-KHē ə). French, **Belgique** (*Fr.* bĕl zhĕk′).

Belgorod-Dnestrovski (*Russ.* byĕl′gə rət dnyĭs trôf′ skĭ), *n.* a seaport in the SW Soviet Union in Europe, on the Black Sea at the mouth of the Dniester river. 39,000 (est. 1966). Formerly, **Akkerman.**

Belgrade (bĕl grād′), *n.* the capital of Yugoslavia, in the E part, on the Danube. 598,346 (1961). Serbian, **Beograd.**

Belgravia (bĕl grā′vyə), *n.* a fashionable district in London, adjoining Hyde Park.

Belgravian (bĕl grā′vyən), *adj.* **1.** of Belgravia. **2.** aristocratic; fashionable.

Belial (bē′lĭ əl, bē′lyəl), *n.* **1.** *Theol.* the spirit of evil personified; the devil; Satan. **2.** (in Milton's *Paradise Lost*) one of the fallen angels. **3.** (in the Bible and rabbinical commentary) worthlessness, wickedness, or destruction. [t. Heb.: m. *belī-ya'al* worthlessness]

belie (bĭ lī′), *v.t.*, **-lied, -lying.** **1.** to misrepresent: *his face belied his thoughts.* **2.** to show to be false: *his trembling belied his calm words.* **3.** to prove false to; fail to justify: *to belie one's faith.* **4.** to lie about; slander. [ME *belye(n)*, OE *belēogan*, f. *be-* BE- + *lēogan* LIE[1]] —**beli′er,** *n.*

belief (bĭ lēf′), *n.* **1.** that which is believed; an accepted opinion. **2.** conviction of the truth or reality of a thing, based upon grounds insufficient to afford positive knowledge: *statements unworthy of belief.* **3.** confidence; faith; trust: *a child's belief in his parents.* **4.** a religious tenet or tenets: *the Christian belief.* [ME *bilēve* (with *-ē-* from v.), r. early ME *bilēafe*, r. OE *gelēafa*, c. G *Glaube*]

—**Syn.** 2. BELIEF, CERTAINTY, CONVICTION refer to acceptance of, or confidence in, an alleged fact or body of facts as true or right without positive knowledge or proof. BELIEF is such acceptance in general: *belief in astrology.* CERTAINTY indicates unquestioning belief and positiveness in one's own mind that something is true: *I know this for a certainty.* CONVICTION is settled, profound, or earnest belief that something is right: *a conviction that a decision is just.*

believe (bĭ lēv′), *v.*, **-lieved, -lieving.** —*v.i.* **1.** to have confidence (*in*); trust; rely through faith (*on*). **2.** to be persuaded of the truth of anything; accept a doctrine, principle, system, etc. (fol. by *in*): *to believe in public schools.* —*v.t.* **3.** to have belief in; credit; accept as true: *to believe a person or a story.* **4.** to think: *I believe he has left the city.* [ME *bileve(n)*, f. *bi-* + *lēven*, d. OE *lēfan*; r. OE *(ge)līefan*, c. G *glauben*] —**believ′able,** *adj.* —**believ′er,** *n.* —**believ′ingly,** *adv.*

belike (bĭ līk′), *adv. Archaic or Dial.* very likely; perhaps; probably. [f. BE- + LIKE[1]]

Belisarius (bĕl′ĭ sĕə′rĭ əs), *n.* A.D. 505?–565, general of the Eastern Roman Empire.

Belisha beacon (bə lē′shə), a yellow globe, usually mounted on a black-and-white ringed post, and containing an intermittently flashing light, to mark a pedestrian crossing. [named after Leslie Hore-*Belisha*, 1893–1957, British politician: minister of transport 1934–37]

Belitong (bĭ lē′tŏng), *n.* Billiton.

belittle (bĭ lĭt′l), *v.t.*, **-tled, -tling.** to make little or less important; depreciate; disparage.

belive (bĭ līv′), *adv. Scot. or Archaic.* before long; soon.

Belize (bĕ lēz′), *n.* a seaport in and the capital of British Honduras. 32,690 (1960).

bell[1] (bĕl), *n.* **1.** a sounding instrument, usually of metal, cup-shaped with a flaring mouth, rung by the strokes of a clapper, tongue, or hammer suspended within it. **2.** any instrument emitting a ringing signal, esp. an electrical device in which an electromagnet causes a hammer to strike repeatedly a hollow metal hemisphere, producing a continuous ringing sound, as a doorbell. **3.** the stroke, sound, or signal emitted by such an instrument. **4.** *Naut.* the half-hourly subdivisions of a watch of four hours, each being marked by single or double strokes of a bell. **5.** any object in the shape of a traditional bell (def. 1). **6.** the end of a musical wind instrument, or any tube when its edge has been turned out and enlarged. **7.** *Zool.* umbrella (def. 2). —*v.t.* **8.** to put a bell on. **9. to bell the cat,** to undertake a dangerous enterprise for the common good. **10.** to cause to swell into a bell shape. —*v.i.* **11.** to take or have the form of a bell. [ME and OE *belle.* See BELL[2], BELLOW] —**bell′-like′,** *adj.*

bell[2] (bĕl), *v.i., v.t.* **1.** to bellow like a deer in the rutting season. **2.** *Obs.* to bellow; roar. —*n.* **3.** the cry of a rutting deer. [ME *belle(n)*, OE *bellan* roar, c. G *bellen* bark]

Bell (bĕl), *n.* **Alexander Graham,** 1847–1922, U.S. scientist, born in Scotland: invented the telephone.

belladonna (bĕl′ə dŏn′ə), *n.* **1.** a poisonous solanaceous plant, *Atropa belladonna*; deadly nightshade. **2.** either of two drugs, atropine and hyoscyamine, obtained from this plant. [t. It.: lit., fair lady]

belladonna lily, the amaryllis (def. 1).

Bellamy (bĕl′ə mĭ), *n.* **Edward,** 1850–98, U.S. author.

Bellay (*Fr.* bĕ lĕ′), *n.* **Joachim du.** See **Du Bellay, Joachim.**

bellbine (bĕl′bīn′), *n.* a convolvulaceous climbing perennial herb, *Calystegia cepium*, with large white funnel-shaped flowers.

bellbird (bĕl′bûd′), *n.* any of various birds of the Southern Hemisphere whose notes resemble the sound of a bell, as the honey-eater.

bell, book, and candle, *Colloq.* the trappings of a religious service, esp. as formerly used in excommunication.

bell-bottomed (bĕl′bŏt′əmd), *adj.* widening into a bell-shape at the lower end.

bellboy (bĕl′boi′), *n. Chiefly U.S.* a pageboy.

bell buoy, *Naut.* a buoy containing a bell which is rung by the action of the waves.

bellcote (bĕl′kōt′), *n.* a framework in a roof from which bells are hung.

belle (bĕl), *n.* a woman or girl admired for her beauty; a reigning beauty. [t. F, fem. of *beau* BEAU]

belleek (bə lēk′), *n.* a fragile, ornamental porcelain with a bright lustre. Also, **Belleek ware.** [named after *Belleek*, in Northern Ireland]

Belle Isle, Strait of, the strait between Labrador and Newfoundland. 10–15 mi. wide.

Bellerophon (bə lĕ′rə fən), *n. Gk Legend.* a hero of Corinth who, on the winged horse Pegasus, slew the monster Chimera.

belles-lettres (bĕl lĕt′r), *n.pl.* the finer or more elegant forms of literature; literature regarded as a fine art. [F] —**belletrist** (bĕl lĕt′rĭst), *n.* —**belletristic** (bĕl′lĕ trĭs′tĭk), *adj.* —**Syn.** See **literature.**

bellflower (bĕl′flou′ə), *n.* a campanula.

bell-foundry (bĕl′foun′drĭ), *n.* a place where bells are made. —**bell′-found′er,** *n.*

bell glass, bell jar.

bell heather, a perennial ericaceous shrub, *Erica cinerea*, of W Europe.

bellhop (bĕl′hŏp′), *n. U.S.* pageboy.

bellicose (bĕl′ĭ kōs′), *adj.* inclined to war; warlike; pugnacious. [t. L: m. s. *bellicōsus*, der. *bellum* war] —**bel′licose′ly,** *adv.* —**bellicosity** (bĕl′ĭ kŏs′ĭ tĭ), *n.*

belligerence (bĭ lĭj′ə rəns), *n.* **1.** warlike nature. **2.** the state or act of carrying on war; warfare. **3.** the state of being actually at war. Also, **belligerency.**

belligerent (bĭ lĭj′ə rənt), *adj.* **1.** warlike; given to waging war. **2.** of warlike character: *a belligerent tone.* **3.** waging war; engaged in war: *the belligerent powers.* **4.** pertaining to war, or to those engaged in war: *belligerent rights, etc.* —*n.* **5.** a state or nation at war, or a member of the military forces of such a state. [t. L: m. s. *belligerans*, ppr.] —**bellig′erently,** *adv.*

Bellini (*It.* bĕl lē′nē), *n.* **1. Gentile** (*It.* jĕn tē′lė), 1427?–1507, Venetian painter (son of Jacopo). **2. Giovanni** (*It.* jō vän′nē), 1430?–1516, Venetian painter (son of Jacopo). **3. Jacopo** (*It.* yä′kō pō), 1400?–70, Venetian painter. **4. Vincenzo** (*It.* vēn chĕn′tsō), 1801?–35, Italian composer of opera.

bell jar, a bell-shaped glass vessel or cover, as for protecting delicate instruments, bric-a-brac, etc., or for holding gases in chemical operations. Also, **bell glass.**

bellman (bĕl′mən), *n., pl.* **-men.** *Archaic.* a man who carries or rings a bell, esp. a town crier or watchman.

bell metal, a hard alloy of copper and tin of low damping capacity, used for bells.

bell-mouthed (bĕl′mouthd′, -moutht′), *adj.* having a flaring mouth like that of a bell.

Belloc (bĕl′ək, -ŏk), *n.* **Hilaire** (hĭ lĕə′), 1870–1953, British essayist, poet, and satirist, born in France.

Bello Horizonte (*Port.* bĕ′lō rē zōn′tē), Belo Horizonte.

Bellona (bĕ lō′nə), *n. Rom. Myth.* goddess of war (sister or wife of Mars). [t. L]

bellow (bĕl′ō), *v.i.* **1.** to make a hollow, loud, animal cry, as a bull or cow. **2.** to roar; bawl: *bellowing with rage.* —*v.t.* **3.** to utter in a loud deep voice: *to bellow forth an answer.* —*n.* **4.** the act or sound of bellowing. [ME *belwe(n)*, appar. b. OE *bellan* BELL[2] and *bylgan* bellow] —**bel′lower,** *n.* —**Syn. 2.** See **cry.**

Bellow (bĕl′ō), *n.* **Saul,** born 1915, U.S. novelist and playwright, born in Canada.

bellows (bĕl′ōz), *n. sing. and pl.* **1.** an instrument or machine for producing a strong current of air, as for a draught for a fire or sounding an organ or other musical instrument, consisting essentially of an air-chamber which can be expanded to draw in air through a valve and contracted to expel the air through a tube or tubes. **2.** anything resembling or suggesting a bellows, as the collapsible part of a camera or enlarger. **3.** *N Dial. and Colloq.* the lungs. [ME *belwes*, pl., OE *belg* short for *blǣst-belg* blast-bag. See BELLY]

bellpull (bĕl′pŏŏl′), *n.* a rope or handle for sounding a bell.

bellpush (bĕl′pŏŏsh′), *n.* a button for operating an electric bell.

bellringer (bĕl′rĭng′ə), *n.* **1.** one who rings church bells. **2.** a performer playing musical handbells. —**bell′-ring′ing,** *n.*

bell tent, a tent shaped like a traditional bell.

belltower (bĕl′tou′ə), *n.* a campanile.

bellwether (bĕl′wĕth′ər), *n.* **1.** a wether or other male sheep which leads the flock, usually bearing a bell. **2.** a person whom others follow blindly.

bellwort (bĕl′wût′), *n.* **1.** any campanulaceous plant. **2.** *U.S.* a plant of the liliaceous genus *Uvularia*, bearing a delicate, slenderly bell-shaped, yellow flower.

belly (bĕl′ĭ), *n., pl.* **-ies,** *v.,* **-ied, -ying.** —*n.* **1.** the front or underpart of a vertebrate body from the breastbone to the pelvis, containing the abdominal viscera; the abdomen. **2.** the stomach with its adjuncts. **3.** appetite for food; gluttony. **4.** the womb. **5.** the inside or interior of anything: *the belly of a ship.* **6.** a protuberant or bulging surface of anything: *the belly of a flask.* **7.** *Anat.* the fleshy part of a muscle. **8.** the front, inner, or under-surface or part (opposed to *back*). **9.** *Music.* the front surface of a violin or similar instrument, bearing the strings. —*v.t., v.i.* **10.** to swell out. [ME *bely*, OE *belig* bag, skin, var. of *belg* (whence *bellow(s)*)]

belly-ache (bĕl′ĭ āk′), *n.* **1.** a pain in the stomach, especially colic. **2.** *Slang.* Also, **belly-aching.** a complaint; grumbling. —*v.i.* **3.** *Slang.* to complain or grumble.

bellyband (bĕl′ĭ bănd′), *n.* a band worn about the belly, as of a harnessed horse.

belly dance, a solo dance of oriental origin performed by a woman by movements of the abdominal muscles.

belly-flop (bĕl′ĭ flŏp′), *n., v.,* **-flopped, -flopping.** —*n.* **1.** a bad dive in which one falls on to the surface of the water. —*v.i.* **2.** to dive in such a way.

bellyful (bĕl′ĭ fŏŏl′), *n. Slang.* **1.** repletion. **2.** pregnancy.

belly laugh, a deep, loud, and uninhibited laugh.

Belo Horizonte (*Port.* bĕ′lò rē zòn′tē), a city in SE Brazil. 693,328 (1962). Also, **Bello Horizonte.**

belong (bĭ lŏng′), *v.i.* **1.** to have one's rightful place; to bear relation as a member, adherent, inhabitant, etc. (fol. by *to*): *he belongs to Glasgow.* **2. belong to, a.** to be the property of: *the book belongs to him.* **b.** to be an appurtenance, adjunct, or part of: *that cover belongs to this jar.* **c.** to be a property, function, or concern of: *attributes which belong to nature.* **3.** to have the proper social qualifications: *he doesn't belong.* **4.** to be proper or due. [ME *belonge(n)*, f. BE- + *longen* belong, adj., aphetic var. of d. *along*, OE *gelang* belonging to]

belonging (bĭ lŏng′ĭng), *n.* **1.** something that belongs. **2.** (*pl.*) possessions; goods; personal effects.

beloved (bĭ lŭv′ĭd, -lŭvd′), *adj.* **1.** greatly loved; dear to the heart. —*n.* **2.** one who is greatly loved.

Belovo (*Russ.* byĕ′lə və), *n.* a town in the N Soviet Union in Asia. 107,000 (est. 1959).

below (bĭ lō′), *adv.* **1.** in or to a lower place; lower down; beneath. **2.** on or to a lower floor; downstairs. **3.** on earth. **4.** in hell or the infernal regions. **5.** at a later point on a page or in writing: *see the statistics below.* **6.** in a lower rank or grade: *he was demoted to the class below.* —*prep.* **7.** lower down than: *below the knee.* **8.** lower in rank, degree, amount, rate, etc., than: *below cost.* **9.** too low or base to be worthy of. **10.** downstream of: *below the bridge.* [ME *bilooghe* by low. See BE-, LOW[1]]

—**Syn.** 7. BELOW, UNDER, BENEATH indicate position in some way lower than something else. BELOW implies being in a lower plane: *below the horizon, the waterline.* UNDER implies being lower in a perpendicular line: *the plaything is under a chair.* BENEATH has a meaning between BELOW and UNDER and usually denotes being under so as to be covered, overhung, or overtopped: *the pool beneath the falls.*

Bel Paese (*It.* bĕl′pä ĕ′zĕ), *Trademark.* a mild Italian table cheese.

Belper (bĕl′pə), *n.* a town in England, in S central Derbyshire. 15,563 (1961).

Belsen (bĕl′sən; *Ger.* bĕl′zən), *n.* a village in NW West Germany; the site of a Nazi concentration camp during World War II. Also, **Bergen-Belsen.**

Belshazzar (bĕl shăz′ə), *n.* son of Nebuchadnezzar, and king of Babylonia. Dan. 5. [t. Heb.]

belt (bĕlt), *n.* **1.** a band of flexible material for encircling the waist. **2.** *Sport.* such a band as a token of honour or achievement. **3.** any encircling or transverse band, strip, or strips. **4.** a large strip of land having distinctive properties or characteristics: *the cotton belt.* **5.** *Mach.* **a.** a flexible band or cord connecting and passing about each of two or more wheels, pulleys or the like, to transmit or change the direction of motion. See illus. under **shafting. b.** conveyor belt. **6.** *Naval.* a series of armour-plates around a ship. **7.** *Mil.* **a.** a cloth strip with loops, or a series of metal links with grips, for holding cartridges which are fed into an automatic gun. **b.** a band of leather or webbing, worn round the waist and used as a support for weapons, ammunition, etc. **8.** *Boxing.* an imaginary line round the body at the level of the navel below which the boxer must not strike. **9. below the belt,** against the rules; unfairly. —*v.t.* **10.** to gird or furnish with a belt. **11.** to surround or mark as if with a belt. **12.** to fasten on (a sword, etc.) by means of a belt. **13.** to beat with a belt, strap, etc. **14.** *Colloq.* to give a thwack or blow to. —*v.i.* **15. belt up,** *Slang.* be quiet; shut up. [ME and OE, prob. ult. t. L: m. s. *balteus*] —**belt′less,** *adj.*

—**Syn.** 4. BELT and ZONE both mean a region with special characteristics. BELT still retains its original sense of a strip or band, and is a less formal term: *the green belt.* ZONE can refer to a region of any shape and tends to be used in political and technical language: *the danger zone, the Torrid Zone.*

Beltane (bĕl′tān, -tən), *n.* an ancient Celtic festival observed on May Day in Scotland and Ireland. [ME (Scot.), t. Gaelic: m. *bealltainn*; of obscure orig.]

belting (bĕl′tĭng), *n.* **1.** material for belts. **2.** belts collectively. **3.** a belt. **4.** *Colloq.* a thrashing or beating.

beluga (bĭ lo͞o′gə), *n.* **1.** the white whale, a cetacean, *Delphinapterus leucas*, chiefly arctic, having a rounded head, and white in colour. **2.** a white sturgeon, *Acipenser huso*, of the Caspian and the Black Sea, yielding caviar and isinglass. [t. Russ.: m. *bielukha*, der. *bielo-* white]

belvedere (bĕl′vĭ dĭə′; *It.* bĕl vĕ dĕ′rĕ), *n.* **1.** an upper storey or any structure or building designed to afford a fine view. **2.** (*cap.*) the Vatican art gallery in Rome. [t. It.: beautiful view]

B.E.M., British Empire Medal.

bema (bē′mə), *n.*, *pl.* **-mata** (-mə tə). **1.** a rostrum from which ancient Greek orators made speeches. **2.** *Gk Orth. Ch.* the enclosed space surrounding the altar; the sanctuary or chancel. [t. Gk: step, platform]

bemaul (bĭ môl′), *v.t.* to maul severely.

bemean (bĭ mēn′), *v.t.* to make mean; debase (oneself).

bemire (bĭ mī′ə), *v.t.*, **-mired, -miring. 1.** to soil with mire. **2.** to sink in mire.

bemoan (bĭ mōn′), *v.t.* **1.** to moan over; bewail; lament. **2.** to express pity for. —*v.i.* **3.** to lament; mourn. [f. BE- + MOAN; r. ME *bemene(n)*, OE *bemǣnan*]

bemused (bĭ myo͞ozd′), *adj.* **1.** confused; muddled; stupefied. **2.** lost in thought; preoccupied.

ben[1] (bĕn), *n.* *Scot.* the inner room (parlour) of a two-roomed cottage, the other room being the but. [ME, var. of *binne*, OE *binnan* within, c. G *binnen*]

ben[2] (bĕn), *n.* **1.** a tree, *Moringa oleifera*, of Arabia, India, and elsewhere, bearing a winged seed (nut) which yields an oil (**oil of ben**), used in extracting flower perfumes, lubricating delicate machinery, etc. **2.** the seed of such a tree. [t. Ar.: m. *bān*]

ben[3] (bĕn), *n.* *Scot.* a mountain peak. [t. Gael.: m. *beann*]

benadryl (bĕn′ə drĭl), *n.* *Pharm.* **1.** a synthetic drug, diphenhydramine hydrochloride, used esp. to relieve hay fever and hives. **2.** (*cap.*) a trademark for this drug.

bename (bĭ nām′), *v.t.*, **-named; -named, -nempt,** or **-nempted; -naming.** *Archaic.* to name; denominate.

Benares (bĭ nä′rĭz), *n.* former name of **Varanasi.**

Benbecula (bĕn bĕk′yo͝o lə), *n.* an island of the Outer Hebrides. 1390 pop. (1961).

Ben Bella (bĕn bĕl′ə), **Ahmed,** born 1919, Algerian statesman: premier 1962–65; president 1963–65.

Benbow (bĕn′bō), *n.* **John,** 1653–1702, English admiral.

bench (bĕnch), *n.* **1.** a long seat with or without a back to accommodate several people. **2.** a seat in the Houses of Parliament. **3.** the seat on which judges sit in court. **4.** the position or office of a judge: *appointed to the bench.* **5.** the body of persons sitting as judges. **6.** the bishops of the Church of England. **7.** a seat occupied by a person in his or her official capacity. **8.** the persons themselves. **9.** the strong work-table of a carpenter or other mechanic. **10.** a platform on which animals are placed for exhibition, esp. at a dog show. **11.** a dog show. **12.** berm (def. **1**). **13.** *Mining.* a step or working elevation in a mine. **14.** *Phys. Geog.* a flat, terrace-like tract of land on a valley slope above the stream bed, or along a coast above the level of sea or lake. —*v.t.* **15.** to furnish with benches. **16.** to seat on a bench. **17.** to place in exhibition: *to bench a dog.* [ME; OE *benc.* See BANK[2], BANK[3]] —**bench′less,** *adj.*

bencher (bĕn′chə), *n.* **1.** a senior member of an Inn of Court. **2. frontbencher,** a minister of the Crown or an Opposition spokesman. **3. backbencher,** an M.P. not holding ministerial office and not appointed Opposition spokesman.

benchmark (bĕnch′mäk′), *n.* *Survey.* a point of known elevation, usually a mark cut into some durable material, as stone or a concrete post with a bronze plate, to serve as a reference point in running a line of levels for the determination of elevations.

bench warrant, *Law.* a warrant issued or ordered by a judge or court for the apprehension of an offender.

bend[1] (bĕnd), *v.*, **bent** or (*Archaic*) **bended, bending,** *n.* —*v.t.* **1.** to bring (a bow, etc.) into a state of tension by curving it. **2.** to force into a different or particular, esp. curved, shape, as by pressure. **3.** to cause to submit: *to bend someone to one's will.* **4.** to turn in a particular direction. **5.** to incline mentally (fol. by *to* or *towards*). **6.** *Naut.* to fasten. **7.** *Archaic.* to strain or brace tensely (fol. by *up*). —*v.i.* **8.** to become curved, crooked, or bent. **9.** to assume a bent posture; stoop. **10.** to bow in submission or reverence; yield; submit. **11.** to turn or incline in a particular direction; be directed. **12.** to direct one's energies. **13. bend over backwards,** to exert oneself to the utmost; make a strenuous effort. —*n.* **14.** the act of bending. **15.** the state of being bent. **16.** a bent thing or part; curve; crook. **17.** *Naut.* a knot by which a rope is fastened to another rope or to something else. **18. round the bend,** *Colloq.* mad. **19. the bends,** *Colloq.* **a.** caisson disease. **b.** aeroembolism. [ME *bende(n)*, OE *bendan* bind, bend (a bow)] —**bend′able,** *adj.*
—**Syn.** 2. curve, crook, flex. 9. bow, stoop.

bend[2] (bĕnd), *n.* *Her.* a diagonal band extending from the dexter chief to the sinister base. [OE *bend* band; in ME identified with OF *bende* band]

bender (bĕn′də), *n.* **1.** one who or that which bends. **2.** *Slang.* a drinking spree.

Bendigo (bĕn′dĭ gō′), *n.* a town in SE Australia, in Victoria: gold mining. 42,940 (est. 1964).

bend sinister, *Her.* a diagonal band extending from the sinister chief to the dexter base (a supposed mark of bastardy).

Bend sinister

bene-, a word element meaning 'well', as in *benediction.* [t. L, comb. form of *bene*, adv.]

beneath (bĭ nēth′), *adv.* **1.** below; in a lower place, position, state, etc. **2.** underneath: *the heaven above and the earth beneath.* —*prep.* **3.** below; under: *beneath the same roof.* **4.** farther down than; underneath; lower in place than. **5.** lower down on a slope than: *beneath the crest of a hill.* **6.** inferior in position, power, etc., to: *a captain is beneath a major.* **7.** unworthy of; below the level or dignity of: *beneath contempt.* [ME *benethe*, OE *beneothan*, f. *be* by + *neothan* below] —**Syn. 3.** See **below.** —**Ant. 1.** above.

Benedicite (bĕn′ĭ dĭ′sĭ tĭ), *n.* **1.** *Eccles.* the canticle beginning in Latin 'Benedicite, omnia opera Domini', and in English 'O all ye works of the Lord'. **2.** a musical setting for it. **3.** (*l.c.*) an invocation for a blessing. —*interj.* **4.** (*l.c.*) bless you! [t. L, 2nd pers. pl. impv. of *benedicere* bless]

Benedick (bĕn′ĭ dĭk), *n.* **1.** (in Shakespeare's *Much Ado About Nothing*) the confident bachelor who courts and finally marries Beatrice. **2.** (*l.c.*) Also, **benedict.** a newly married man, esp. one who has been long a bachelor.

Benedict (bĕn′ĭ dikt), *n.* the name adopted by 15 popes, esp.: **1. XIV,** 1675–1758, Italian ecclesiastic: pope 1704–58: patron of art, archaeology, and learning. **2. XV,** 1854–1922, Italian ecclesiastic: pope 1914–22.

Benedict (bĕn′ĭ dĭkt), *n.* **Saint,** A.D. 480?–543?, Italian monk: founded Benedictine order.

Benedictine (bĕn′ĭ dĭk′tĭn, -tīn *for 1*; bĕn′ĭ dĭk′tēn *for 2*), *n.* **1.** *Eccles.* a member of an order of monks founded at Monte Cassino, between Rome and Naples, by St Benedict about A.D. 530, or of various congregations of nuns following his rule. The rules of the order (**Benedictine rule**) enjoined silence and useful employment when not in divine service. **2.** (*usually l.c.*) a French liqueur orig. made by Benedictine monks. —*adj.* **3.** pertaining to St Benedict or to an order following his rule. [t. F: m. *bénédictin*]

benediction (bĕn′ĭ dĭk′shən), *n. Eccles.* **1.** the act of uttering a blessing. **2.** the form of blessing pronounced by an officiating minister, as at the close of divine service, etc. **3.** a ceremony by which things are set aside for sacred uses, as a church, vestments, bells, etc. **4.** the advantage conferred by blessing; a mercy or benefit. [ME, t. L: s. *benedictio*] —**ben′edic′tional,** *adj.* —**benedictory** (bĕn′ĭ dĭk′tə rĭ), *adj.*

Benedict's test, *Med.* a chemical test for detecting the presence of reducing sugars in urine. [named after Stanley R. *Benedict*, 1884–1936, U.S. biochemist]

Benedictus (bĕn′ĭ dĭk′təs), *n. Eccles.* **1.** the short canticle or hymn beginning in Latin 'Benedictus qui venit in nomine Domini', and in English 'Blessed is He that cometh in the name of the Lord'. **2.** the canticle or hymn beginning in Latin 'Benedictus Dominus Deus Israel', and in English 'Blessed be the Lord God of Israel'. **3.** a musical setting of either of these canticles. [t. L: pp., blessed]

benefaction (bĕn′ĭ făk′shən), *n.* **1.** the act of conferring a benefit; doing good. **2.** the benefit conferred; charitable donation. [t. LL: s. *benefactio*]

benefactor (bĕn′ĭ făk′tə, bĕn′ĭ făk′-), *n.* **1.** one who confers a benefit; kindly helper. **2.** one who makes a bequest or endowment. [t. L] —**benefactress** (bĕn′ĭ făk′trĭs, bĕn′ĭ făk′-), *n. fem.*

benefic (bĭ nĕf′ĭk), *adj. Archaic.* beneficent.

benefice (bĕn′ĭ fĭs), *n., v.,* **-ficed, -ficing.** —*n.* **1.** an ecclesiastical living. **2.** the revenue itself. —*v.t.* **3.** to invest with a benefice or ecclesiastical living. [ME, t. OF, t. L: m. s. *beneficium* benefit, favour]

beneficence (bĭ nĕf′ĭ səns), *n.* **1.** the doing of good; active goodness or kindness; charity. **2.** beneficent act or gift; benefaction. [t. L: m. s. *beneficentia*]

beneficent (bĭ nĕf′ĭ sənt), *adj.* doing good or causing good to be done; conferring benefits; kindly in action or purpose. —**benef′icently,** *adv.*

beneficial (bĕn′ĭ fĭsh′əl), *adj.* **1.** conferring benefit; advantageous; helpful. **2.** *Law.* **a.** helpful in the meeting of needs: *a beneficial association.* **b.** involving the personal enjoyment of proceeds: *a beneficial owner.* —**ben′efi′cially,** *adv.* —**Syn. 1.** salutary, wholesome, serviceable. —**Ant. 1.** harmful.

beneficiary (bĕn′ĭ fĭsh′ə rĭ), *n., pl.* **-aries. 1.** one who receives benefits, profits, or advantages. **2.** *Law.* a person designated as the recipient of funds or other property under a trust, insurance policy, etc. **3.** *Eccles.* the holder of a benefice.

benefit (bĕn′ĭ fĭt), *n., v.,* **-fited, -fiting.** —*n.* **1.** an act of kindness. **2.** anything that is for the good of a person or thing. **3.** a theatrical performance or other public entertainment to raise money for a worthy purpose. **4.** a payment or other assistance given by an insurance company, mutual benefit society, or public agency. —*v.t.* **5.** to do good to; be of service to. —*v.t.* **6.** to gain advantage; make improvement. [partial Latinization of ME *benfet*, t. AF, g. L *benefactum*, f. *bene-* BENE- + *factum* thing done. See and cf. FACT] —**Syn. 1.** favour, service. **2.** See **advantage.**

benefit of clergy, 1. *Colloq.* church rites, as marriage. **2.** an early right of church authorities to try, in an ecclesiastical court, any clergyman accused of serious crime (abolished in England in 1827 and in the U.S. in 1790).

benefit society, *U.S. Insurance.* a form of friendly society. Also, **benefit association.**

Benelux (bĕn′ĭ lŭks′), *n.* **1.** a customs union (since Jan. 1st, 1948) of Belgium, the Netherlands, and Luxembourg, now part of the Common Market. **2.** these countries collectively.

benempt (bĭ nĕmpt′), *v. Archaic.* a pp. of **bename.**

Benenden (bĕn′ən dən), *n.* a village in England, in central Kent; girls' school, formed 1924.

Beneš (*Cz.* bĕn′ĕsh), *n.* **Eduard** (*Cz.* ĕ′do͞o ärt), 1884–1948, Czechoslovakian patriot and statesman: president of Czechoslovakia, 1935–38 and 1945–48.

Benét (bĭ nā′), *n.* **Stephen Vincent,** 1898–1943, U.S. poet.

Benevento (bĕn′ĭ vĕn′tō; *It.* bĕ nĕ vĕn′ tō), *n.* a city in S Italy: site of the Arch of Trajan. 58,351 (1966).

benevolence (bĭ nĕv′ə ləns), *n.* **1.** desire to do good for others; goodwill; charitableness. **2.** an act of kindness; charitable gift. **3.** *Eng. Hist.* a forced contribution to the sovereign. —**Ant. 1.** malevolence.

benevolent (bĭ nĕv′ə lənt), *adj.* **1.** desiring to do good for others. **2.** intended for benefits rather than profit: *a benevolent institution.* [t. L: s. *benevolens* well-wishing; r. ME *benyvolent*, t. OF: m. *benivolent*] —**benev′olently,** *adv.*

benevolent society, form of friendly society. Also, **benevolent association.**

Benfleet (bĕn′flēt′), *n.* a town in England, in Essex. 32,395 (1961).

Bengal (bĕn gôl′, bĕng-), *n.* **1.** a former province in NE India: now divided into **East Bengal** (in Pakistan) and **West Bengal** (in India). **2. Bay of,** a part of the Indian Ocean between India and Burma.

Bengalese (bĕn′gə lēz′, bĕng′-), *adj., n., pl.* **-lese.** —*adj.* **1.** of or pertaining to Bengal. —*n.* **2.** a native or inhabitant of Bengal.

Bengali (bĕn gô′lĭ, bĕng-), *n.* **1.** a native or an inhabitant of Bengal. **2.** the language of Bengal, an Indic language. —*adj.* **3.** of or pertaining to Bengal, its inhabitants, or their language; Bengalese.

bengaline (bĕng′gə lēn′, bĕng′gə lēn′), *n.* a corded fabric resembling poplin but with heavier cords. It may be silk or rayon with worsted cord. [t. F]

Bengal light, a vivid, sustained, blue light used in signalling, fireworks, etc. Also, **Bengal match.**

Benghazi (bĕn gä′zĭ), *n.* a seaport in N Libya. 70,000 (est. 1965).

Benguela (*Port.* bĕng gwĕl′ə), *n.* a town in Angola, in the W part. 52,300 (est. 1960).

Ben-Gurion (bĕn′go͝o′rĭ ən), *n.* **David,** born 1886, Israeli statesman: prime minister of Israel 1949–53, 1955–63.

Beni (*Sp.* bĕ′nē), *n.* a river flowing from W Bolivia NE to the Madeira river. ab. 600 mi.

benighted (bĭ nī′tĭd), *adj.* **1.** intellectually or morally ignorant; unenlightened. **2.** overtaken by darkness or night. [pp. of *benight*, v., der. BE- + NIGHT]

benign (bĭ nīn′), *adj.* **1.** of a kind disposition; kind. **2.** showing or caused by gentleness or kindness: *a benign smile.* **3.** favourable; propitious: *benign planets.* **4.** (of weather) salubrious. **5.** *Pathol.* not malignant: *a benign tumour.* [ME *benigne*, t. OF, t. L: m. s. *benignus* kind] —**benign′ly,** adv. —**Ant. 2.** sinister. **3.** malign.

benignant (bĭ nĭg′nənt), *adj.* **1.** kind, esp. to inferiors; gracious. **2.** exerting a good influence; beneficial. **3.** *Pathol.* benign. [b. BEN(IGN) and (MAL)IGNANT] —**benignancy** (bĭ nĭg′nən sĭ), *n.* —**benig′nantly,** *adv.*

benignity (bĭ nĭg′nĭ tĭ), *n., pl.* **-ties. 1.** the quality of being benign; propitiousness; kindness. **2.** a good deed.

Beni Hasan (bĕn′ĭ hŭs′än), a village in central Egypt, on the Nile, N of Asyut: ancient cliff tombs.

Benin (bĕ nēn′, bĕ nĭn′), *n.* **1.** a former kingdom in W Africa: now a district in Western Nigeria. 8482 sq. mi. **2.** a town in Benin district. 54,000 (est. 1964). **3.** a river in S Nigeria flowing into the **Bight of Benin,** a wide bay in the Gulf of Guinea.

benison (bĕn′ĭ zən, -sən), *n. Archaic.* benediction. [ME *benisoun*, t. OF: m. *beneison*, g. s. L *benedictio*]

Beni Suef (bĕn′ĭ so͞o ĕf′), a town in N Egypt, on the Nile. 79,000 (est. 1960).

benjamin (bĕn′jə mĭn), *n.* benzoin (def. 1). [var. (by assimilation to *Benjamin*) of *benjoin* BENZOIN]

Benjamin (bĕn′jə mĭn), *n.* **1.** *Bible.* **a.** the youngest and favourite son of Jacob by Rachel, and brother of Joseph. **b.** a tribe of Israel said to have Benjamin as its ancestor. **2. Arthur,** 1893–1960, Australian composer and pianist.

Ben Lomond (bĕn lō′mənd), a mountain in W Scotland, E of Loch Lomond. 3192 ft.

benne (bĕn′ĭ), *n.* the sesame, *Sesamum indicum*, from the seeds of which a fixed oil (**oil of benne** or **benne oil**) is expressed. [t. Malay]

bennet (bĕn′ĭt), *n.* herb bennet.

Bennett (bĕn′ĭt), *n.* **1. (Enoch) Arnold,** 1867–1931, English novelist. **2. Richard Bedford, 1st Viscount,** 1870–1947, Canadian statesman. **3. Richard Rodney,** born 1936, English composer. **4. William Sterndale,** 1816–75, English musician and composer.

Ben Nevis (bĕn nĕv′ĭs), a peak in W Scotland in Inverness-shire, near Fort William: the highest point in the British Isles. 4406 ft.

Bennington (bĕn′ĭng tən), *n.* a women's college in the U.S., at Bennington, Vermont, founded in 1932.

Benoni (bĭ nō′nĭ), *n.* a town in the Republic of South Africa, near Johannesburg: gold mines. 140,790 (1960).

bent[1] (bĕnt), *adj.* **1.** curved; crooked: *a bent stick, bow, etc.* **2.** determined; set; resolved (fol. by *on*). **3.** *Slang.* stolen: *to sell bent goods.* **4.** *Slang.* thievish; having little or no regard for the law. **5.** *Slang.* homosexual; queer. **—*n.*** **6.** bent state or form. **7.** direction taken (usually figurative); inclination; leaning; bias: *a bent for painting.* **8.** capacity of endurance. **9.** *Civ. Eng.* a transverse frame of a bridge or a building, designed to support either vertical or horizontal loads. [pp. of BEND[1]] **—Syn.** **7.** tendency, propensity, proclivity, predilection.

bent[2] (bĕnt), *n.* **1.** bent grass. **2.** a stalk of such grass. **3.** (formerly) any stiff grass or sedge. **4.** *Scot. and N Dial.* a grassy tract, a moor, or a hillside. [ME; OE *beonet*, c. G *Binse* rush]

bent grass, any of the species of the gramineous genus *Agrostis*, esp. *A. tenuis.*

Bentham (bĕn′thəm), *n.* **Jeremy** (jĕ′ rə mĭ), 1748–1832, English jurist and utilitarian philosopher.

Benthamism (bĕn′thə mĭz′əm), *n.* the variety of utilitarianism put forth by Jeremy Bentham, characterized esp. by moral and ethical evaluation of actions in terms of their power to produce pleasure (the only good) or pain (the only evil). **—Benthamite** (bĕn′thə mīt′), *n., adj.*

benthos (bĕn′thŏs), *n. Ecol.* the animals and plants that are fixed to or crawl upon the sea bottom. Also, **benthon.** [t. Gk: depth (of the sea)] **—benthic,** *adj.*

Bentinck (bĕn′tĭngk), *n.* **1. William Henry Cavendish, Duke of Portland,** 1738–1809, British statesman, prime minister 1787; 1807–09. **2.** his son, **Lord William Cavendish,** 1774–1839, British governor-general of India 1828–35.

Bentley (bĕnt′lĭ), *n.* **Richard,** 1662–1742, British scholar and critic.

bentwood (bĕnt′wŏŏd′), *n.* **1.** wood steamed and bent for use in furniture. **—*adj.*** **2.** of or denoting such furniture.

Benue (bĕn′ōō ĭ), *n.* a river in W Africa, flowing from Cameroun W to the river Niger in Nigeria. ab. 800 mi. See map under **Nigeria.**

benumb (bĭ nŭm′), *v.t.* **1.** to make numb; deprive of sensation: *benumbed by cold.* **2.** to render inactive; stupefy. [ME *benome(n)*, OE *benumen*, pp. of *beniman* deprive]

benz-, var. of **benzo-,** chiefly used before vowels.

benzaldehyde (bĕn zăl′dĭ hīd′), *n. Chem.* an aldehyde, C_6H_5CHO, obtained from natural oil of bitter almonds or other oils, or produced artificially, used in dyes, as a flavouring agent, etc.

benzamine (bĕn′zə mēn′), *n.* eucaine (def. 2); beta-eucaine.

Benzedrine (bĕn′zĭ drēn′, -drĭn), *n.* **1.** *Trademark.* amphetamine. **2.** (*l.c.*) *Colloq.* amphetamine, or any stimulant drug.

benzene (ben′zēn, bĕn zēn′), *n. Chem.* a colourless, volatile, inflammable, liquid, aromatic hydrocarbon, C_6H_6, obtained chiefly from coal tar, and used as a solvent for resins, fats, etc., and in the manufacture of dyes, etc.

benzene ring, *Chem.* the graphic representation of the structure of benzene as a hexagon with a carbon atom at each of its points. Each carbon atom is united with an atom of hydrogen, one or more of which may be replaced to form benzene derivatives. Also, **benzene nucleus.**

benzidine (bĕn′zĭ dēn′, -dĭn), *n. Chem.* a basic compound, $NH_2C_6H_4C_6H_4NH_2$, occurring as greyish scales or a crystalline powder, used in the manufacture of certain dyes, as Congo red. [f. BENZ- + -ID[3] + -INE[2]]

benzine (bĕn′zēn, bĕn zēn′), *n.* a colourless, volatile, inflammable liquid, a mixture of various hydrocarbons, obtained in the distillation of petroleum, and used in cleaning, dyeing, etc.

benzo-, *Chem.* a combining form meaning 'pertaining to or derived from benzene' or designating the presence of benzoic acid. Also, **benz-.**

benzoate (bĕn′zō āt′, -ĭt), *n. Chem.* a salt or ester of benzoic acid.

benzocaine (bĕn′zō kān′), *n. Chem.* a water-insoluble crystalline ester, $NH_2C_6H_4COOC_2H_5$ (ethyl p-aminobenzoate), used as a local anaesthetic. Also, **anaesthesin.**

benzoic acid (bĕn zō′ĭk), *Chem., Pharm., etc.* a white, crystalline acid, C_6H_5COOH, obtained from benzoin and other balsams or from toluene, used in medicine, aniline dye manufacture, as a food preservative, etc.

benzoin (bĕn′zoin, -zō ĭn, bĕn zō′ĭn), *n.* **1.** a balsamic resin obtained from species of *Styrax*, esp. *S. benzoin*, a tree of Java, Sumatra, etc., and used in perfumery, medicine, etc. **2.** any plant of the lauraceous genus *Lindera* (also known as *Benzoin*) which includes the spicebush and other aromatic plants. [earlier *benjoin*, t. F, through Sp. or Pg., t. Ar.: m. *lubān jāwi* incense of Java ((*lu-* appar. taken as 'the')]

benzol (bĕn′zŏl), *n.* crude industrial benzene. Also, **benzole.**

benzophenone (bĕn′zō fĭ nōn′), *n. Chem.* a water-insoluble crystalline ketone, $C_6H_5COC_6H_5$, used in organic synthesis. [f. BENZO- + PHEN- + -ONE]

benzoquinone (bĕn′ zō kwĭ nōn′), *n. Chem.* quinone (def. 1).

benzoyl (bĕn′zō ĭl), *n. Chem.* a univalent radical, C_6H_5CO, present in benzoic acid and allied compounds.

benzpyrene (bĕnz pī′ə rēn′,-pī′rēn) *n. Chem.* a yellow crystalline polycyclic hydrocarbon, $C_{20}H_{12}$, occurring in minute quantities in coal tar. It is carcinogenic, and thought to be one of the most harmful constituents of tobacco smoke.

Ben-Zvi (bĕn′zvē′), *n.* **Izhak** (ī′zək), 1884–1963, Israeli statesman: president 1952–63.

benzyl (bĕn′zĭl), *n. Chem.* a univalent organic radical, $C_6H_5CH_2$, from toluene.

Beograd (*Serb.* bĕ ô′ grăd), *n.* Serbian name of **Belgrade.**

Beowulf (bā′ə wŏŏlf′), *n.* **1.** an Old English alliterative epic poem of the early 8th century. **2.** its hero.

Beppu (bĕp′ōō), *n.* a town in Japan, in NE Kyushu. 118,938 (1965).

bequeath (bĭ kwēth′, -kwēth′), *v.t.* **1.** *Law.* to dispose by last will of (personal property, esp. money). **2.** to hand down; pass on. **3.** *Obs.* to commit; entrust. [ME *bequethe(n)*, OE *becwethan*, f. BE- + *cwethan* say] **—bequeathal** (bĭ kwē′thəl), *n.*

bequest (bĭ kwĕst′), *n.* **1.** *Law.* a disposition in a will concerning personal property, esp. money. **2.** a legacy. [ME *biqueste*, OE *gequis*, c. Goth. *gakwiss* consent]

Ber., Berwickshire.

Béranger (*Fr.* bĕ räɴ zhĕ′), *n.* **Pierre Jean de** (*Fr.* pyĕr zhäɴ′ də), 1780–1857, French poet.

Berar (bĕ rä′), *n.* a former division of the Central Provinces in central India; now part of Madhya Pradesh.

berate (bĭ rāt′), *v.t.*, **-rated, -rating.** to scold.

Berber (bû′bə), *n.* **1.** a member of a group of North African tribes living in Barbary and the Sahara. **2.** the Hamitic languages of the Berbers, spoken from Tunisia, west to the Atlantic and in the Sahara, including Kabyle, Tuareg, and other languages. **—*adj.*** **3.** of or pertaining to the Berbers or their language.

Berbera (bû′bə rə), *n.* a seaport in the Somali Republic, on the Gulf of Aden; formerly capital of British Somaliland. 20,000 (est. 1965).

berberidaceous (bû′bə rĭ dā′shəs), *adj.* belonging to the *Berberidaceae*, a family of plants including the barberry, May apple, etc.

berberine (bû′bə rēn′). *n. Chem.* a widely distributed alkaloid, $C_{20}H_{19}NO_5$, found in the barberry and a considerable number of plants whose extracts have a yellow colour and a bitter taste.

berceuse (*Fr.* bĕr sœz′), *n., pl.* **-ceuses** (*Fr.* -sœz′). *Music.* a cradlesong; lullaby. [F]

Berchtesgaden (*Ger.* bĕrKH təs gä′dən), *n.* a town in West Germany, in S Bavaria: site of the fortified mountain chalet of Adolf Hitler. 5752 (1958).

Berdichev (*Russ.* bĭr dĕ′chĭf), *n.* a town in the SW Soviet Union, in the Ukranian Republic. 66,306 (1963).

Berdyaev (*Russ.* bĭr dyä′ yĭf), *n.* **Nikolas** (*Nikolai Aleksandrovich*), 1874–1948, Russian idealistic philosopher.

bereave (bĭ rēv′), *v.t.*, **-reaved** or **-reft, -reaving.** **1.** to deprive (*of*) ruthlessly, esp. of hope, joy, etc.: *bereft of all their lands.* **2.** to make desolate through loss (*of*), esp. by death: *bereaved of their mother.* **3.** *Obs.* to take away by violence. [ME *bereve(n)*, OE *berēafian*, f. BE + *rēafian* rob] **—bereave′ment,** *n.*

Berenice's Hair (bĕ′ rĭ nī′sēz), *Astron.* the constellation Coma Berenices.

Berenson (bĕ′rən sən), *n.* **Bernard,** 1865–1959, U.S. art critic and writer, born in Lithuania.

beret (bĕ′rā; *Fr.* bė rė′), *n.* a soft, round, peakless cap that fits closely. [t. F, t. Béarn dialect: m. *berreto,* g. Gallo-Rom. *birretum* cap, der. LL *birrum* cloak]

Berezina (*Russ.* bĭ rĭ zĭ nä′), *n.* a river in the W Soviet Union, flowing SE to the river Dnieper: crossed with heavy losses by Napoleon's army during the retreat of 1812. ab. 350 mi.

Berezniki (*Russ.* bĭ rĭz nĭ kē′), *n.* a town in the NE Soviet Union in Europe. 106,000 (est. 1959).

berg[1] (bûg), *n.* iceberg. [short for ICEBERG]

berg[2] (bûg), *n.* (in South Africa) a mountain. [t. Afrikaans]

Berg (*Ger.* bĕrk), *n.* **Alban** (*Ger.* äl′bän), 1885–1935, Austrian composer.

Bergamo (bû′gə mō′; *It.* bĕr′gä mō), *n.* a city in N Italy, in Lombardy. 122,187 (1966).

bergamot (bû′gə mŏt′), *n.* **1.** a small tree of the citrus family, *Citrus bergamia,* the rind of whose fruit yields a fragrant essential oil (**essence of bergamot**). **2.** the oil or essence itself. **3.** any of various plants of the mint family, as *Mentha citrata,* yielding an oil resembling essence of bergamot. **4.** *Hort.* one of a group of globular oblate, evenly and regularly shaped pears. [t. F: m. *bergamote,* t. It.: m. *bergamotta,* appar. t. Turk: m. *begarmūdi* prince's pear]

Bergen (bû′gən; *Norw.* bĕr′gən). *n.* a seaport in SW Norway, on the Atlantic. 117,290 (1965).

Bergen-Belsen (*Ger.* bĕr′gən bĕl′zən), *n.* Belsen.

Bergerac (*Fr.* bĕr zhə räk′), *n.* **(Savinien) Cyrano de** (*Fr.* sȧ vē nyăɴ sē rä nō′ də), 1619–55, French soldier, duellist, and romantic writer: hero of play by Rostand.

Bergman (bûg′mən; *Sw.* bĕry′män), *n.* **Ingmar** (ĭng′-mä; *Sw.* ĕng′mär), born 1918, Swedish film director.

bergpruim (bĕək′proim), *n.* a tree or shrub, *Pappea capensis,* of southern Africa, the fruit of which is used for making vinegar. [t. Afrikaans: f. *berg* mountain + *pruim* plum]

Bergson (bûg′sən; *Fr.* bĕrg sōɴ′), *n.* **Henri** (*Fr.* äɴ rē′), 1859–1941, French philosopher and writer. —**Bergsonian** (bûg sō′nyən), *adj., n.*

Bergsonism (bûg′sə nĭz′əm), *n.* *Philos.* Henri Bergson's doctrine of creative evolution, emphasizing duration as the central fact of experience and an *élan vital* (vital drive) as an original life-force essentially governing all organic processes.

bergwind (bûg′wĭnd′), *n.* (in South Africa) a hot, dry, oppressive wind blowing down from the plateau towards the coast.

berhyme (bĭ rīm′), *v.t.,* **-rhymed, -rhyming.** to celebrate in verse. Also, **berime.**

Beria (*Russ.* byĕ′rĭ yə), *n.* **Lavrenti Pavlovich** (*Russ.* läv ryĕn′tĭy päv′lə vĭch), 1899–1953, Soviet leader; executed for treason.

beribboned (bĭ rĭb′ənd), *adj.* adorned with ribbons.

beri-beri (bĕ′rĭ bĕ′rĭ), *n.* *Pathol.* a disease of the peripheral nerves caused by deficiency in vitamin B_1 and marked by pain in and paralysis of the extremities, and severe emaciation or swelling of the body. [t. Sinhalese, redupl. of *beri* weakness]

Bering (bĕ′rĭng, bĕə′-; *Dan.* bė′rĭng), *n.* **Vitus** (*Dan.* vē′-tōōs), 1680–1741, Danish navigator and explorer of the N Pacific for Russia. Also, **Behring.**

Bering Sea (bĕ′rĭng, bĕə′-), a part of the N Pacific N of the Aleutian Islands. ab. 878,000 sq. mi. See map under **Kamchatka.**

Bering Strait, the strait between Alaska and the Soviet Union in Asia, connecting the Bering Sea and the Arctic Ocean. 36 mi. wide.

berk (bûk), *n.* *Slang.* a fool.

Berkeleian (bä klē′ən), *adj.* **1.** pertaining or relating to George Berkeley, or his philosophy. —*n.* **2.** one who holds George Berkeley's system of idealism; one who denies the existence of a material world. —**Berkele′-ianism,** *n.*

Berkeley (bäk′lĭ), *n.* **1. George,** 1685–1753, Irish bishop and philosopher. **2. Lennox (Randal Francis),** born 1903, English composer.

Berkeley (bûk′lĭ), *n.* a town in the U.S., in W California, on San Francisco Bay: University of California, founded 1868. 111,268 (1960).

berkelium (bə kē′lĭ əm), *n.* *Chem.* a synthetic, radioactive, metallic element. *Symbol*: Bk; *at. no.*: 97. [f. BERKEL(EY), Calif., where first identified + -IUM]

Berkhampstead (bû′kəm stĭd), *n.* a town in England in W Hertfordshire. 13,051 (1961). Also, **Berkhamsted.**

Berks., Berkshire.

Berkshire (bäk′shĭə, -shə), *n.* **1.** a county in S England. 503,357 pop. (1961); 725 sq. mi. *Co. town*: Reading. **2.** one of a breed of black pigs originating in Berkshire, characterized by white markings on feet, face, and tail.

Berlage (*Du.* bĕr′lä ᴋʜə), *n.* **Hendrikus Petrus,** 1856–1934, Dutch architect.

berlin (bə lĭn′, bû′lĭn), *n.* **1.** large four-wheeled closed carriage hung between two perches, having two interior seats. **2.** berline. **3.** Berlin wool. [named after BERLIN]

Berlin

Berlin (bû lĭn′; *also Ger.* bĕr lēn′ *for 2*), *n.* **1. Irving,** born 1888, U.S. songwriter. **2.** a city in central East Germany, the former capital of Prussia and of Germany: divided since 1945 into American, British, and French sectors (later **western sector**) and a **Soviet sector.** See **East Berlin, West Berlin.** See map under **Nuremburg.**

berline (bû lĭn′; *Fr.* bĕr lĕn′), *n.* a saloon car with a movable glass partition behind the driver's seat.

Berlin wool, a soft woollen yarn for tapestry work, etc.

Berlioz (bĕə′lĭ ōz′; *Fr.* bĕr lyōz′), *n.* **Louis Hector** (*Fr.* lwē ĕk tŏr′), 1803–69, French composer.

berm (bûm), *n.* **1.** Also, **berme.** *Fort.* a narrow terrace between the rampart and moat. **2.** the ledge or shoulder alongside a road. [t. F: (m.) *berme,* t. MD]

Bermejo (*Sp.* bĕr mĕ′ᴋʜō), *n.* a river in N Argentina, flowing SE to the Paraguay river. ab. 1000 mi.

Bermondsey (bû′mənd zĭ), *n.* a district of the S inner London borough of Southwark.

Bermuda (bə myōō′də), *n.* a group of islands in the Atlantic, 580 miles E of North Carolina: a British colony; resort. 45,921 pop. (est. 1962); 19 sq. mi. *Cap.*: Hamilton. Also, **Bermudas.** —**Bermudan** (bə myōō′-dən), *adj., n.*

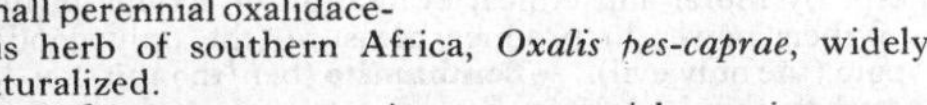

Bermuda

Bermuda buttercup, a small perennial oxalidaceous herb of southern Africa, *Oxalis pes-caprae,* widely naturalized.

Bermuda grass, a gramineous perennial creeping grass, *Cynodon dactylon,* of temperate regions.

Bermuda onion, *Hort.* any of several mild flat varieties of onion grown in Bermuda and on a large scale in Texas and, to some extent, in other parts of the U.S.

Bermuda shorts, shorts reaching to the knee, worn by men and women for informal dress, esp. in the U.S.

Bernadette (bû′nə dĕt′), *n.* **Saint** (*Marie Bernarde Soubirous*), 1844–1879, French visionary at Lourdes.

Bernadotte (bû′nə dŏt′; *Fr.* bĕr nä dŏt′), *n.* **Jean Baptiste Jules** (*Fr.* zhäɴ bä tēst zhʏl′), 1764–1844, French marshal under Napoleon: king of Sweden and Norway, 1818–44, as Charles XIV.

Bernanos (*Fr.* bĕr nä nōs′), *n.* **Georges** (*Fr.* zhōrzh), 1888–1948, French novelist and polemicist.

Bernard (bû′nəd, bə näd′). **1. Saint** (*Bernard of Menthon*), A.D. 923–1008, French monk. **2. Saint** (*Bernard of Cluny*), fl. 1140, French monk. **3. Saint** (*Bernard of Clairvaux, 'the Mellifluous Doctor'*), 1090?–1153, French monk, preacher, and mystical writer.

Bernardine (bû′nə dĭn, -dēn′), *adj.* **1.** of or pertaining to St Bernard of Clairvaux. **2.** of or pertaining to the Cistercians. —*n.* **3.** a Cistercian.

Berne (bûn; *Fr.* bĕrn), *n.* **1.** the capital of Switzerland, in the W part. 166,900 pop. (1962). **2.** a canton in W Switzerland. 889,523 pop. (1960); 2658 sq. mi. *Cap.*: Berne. Also, **Bern.** —**Bernese** (bû nēz′), *n., adj.*

Berne convention, an international convention, 1886, to protect literary and artistic copyright.

Bernese Alps, a range of the Alps in SW Switzerland. Highest peak, 14,026 ft. Also, **Bernese Oberland** (ō′bə lănd′; *Ger.* ō′bər länt).

Bernhardi (*Ger.* bĕrn här′ dē), *n.* **Friedrich (A. J.) von** (*Ger.* frē′drĭᴋʜ fōn), 1849–1930, German general.

Bernhardt (bûn′hät; *Fr.* bĕr när′), *n.* **Sarah** (*Rosine Bernard*), 1845–1923, French actress.

bernicle goose (bû′nĭ kl), barnacle goose.

Bernina (*It.* bĕr nē′nä), *n.* a mountain peak (13,295 ft) in SE Switzerland, in the Rhaetian Alps, traversed by **Bernina Pass** (7640 ft high), leading to N Italy.

Bernini (bû nē′nĭ, bĕə-; *It.* bĕr nē′nē), *n.* **Gianlorenzo** (*It.* jän lō rĕn′tsō) 1598–1680, Italian sculptor and architect.

Bernouilli (*Fr.* bĕr nōō yē′; *Ger.* bĕr nōō′lĭ), *n.* **1. Daniel,** 1700–82, son of Jean, Swiss scientist in hydrodynamics.

2. **Jacques,** 1654–1705, Swiss mathematician. 3. **Jean,** 1667–1748, brother of Jacques, Swiss mathematician: discovered the exponential calculus.

Bernstein (bûn′stīn), *n.* **Leonard,** born 1918, U.S. conductor and composer.

berretta (bĭ rĕt′ə), *n. Eccles.* biretta.

berried (bĕ′rĭd), *adj.* 1. covered with berries. 2. of or like a berry; baccate. 3. (of lobsters, etc.) having eggs.

Berruguete (*Sp.* bėr ro͞o gė′tė), *n.* **Pedro,** fl. 1483–1503, Spanish painter.

berry (bĕ′rĭ), *n., pl.* **-ries,** *v.,* **-ried, -rying.** —*n.* 1. any small, (usually) stoneless and juicy fruit, irrespective of botanical structure, as the gooseberry, strawberry, holly berry, rose hip, etc. 2. a dry seed or kernel, as of wheat. 3. a knob on a swan's bill. 4. *Bot.* a simple fruit having a pulpy pericarp in which the seeds are embedded, as the grape, gooseberry, currant, tomato, etc. 5. one of the eggs of the lobster. —*v.i.* 6. to bear or produce berries. 7. to gather berries. [ME and OE *berie,* c. G *Beere*] —**ber′ryless,** *adj.* —**ber′ry-like′,** *adj.*

Berry (bĕ′rĭ; *Fr.* bĕ rē′), *n.* a former province in central France. Also, **Berri.**

bersagliere (bĕə′sä lyĕə′rĭ; *It.* bėr säl lyĕ′rė), *n., pl.* **-ri** (-rĭ; *It.* -rē). one of a class of riflemen or marksmen in the Italian army.

berserk (bû sûk′), *adj.* 1. violently and destructively frenzied. —*n.* 2. berserker.

berserker (bû sû′kə), *n. Scand. Legend.* one of the ancient Norse warriors of great strength and courage, reputed to have fought with frenzied fury in battle; baresark. [t. Icel.: m. *berserkr* wild warrior; orig. uncert.]

berth (bûth), *n.* 1. a shelflike space, bunk, or whole room allotted to a traveller on a vessel or a train as a sleeping space. 2. *Naut.* **a.** room for a vessel to moor at a dock or ride at anchor. **b.** a space allowed for safety or convenience between a vessel and other vessels, rocks, etc. 3. any place allotted to a person. 4. *Colloq.* job; position. 5. **give a wide berth to,** to avoid; keep away from. —*v.t.* 6. *Naut.* to assign or allot anchoring ground to; give space to lie in, as a ship in a dock. —*v.i.* 7. *Naut.* to come to a dock, anchorage, or mooring. [prob. der. BEAR[1]]

bertha (bû′thə), *n.* a kind of collar or trimming, as of lace, worn about the shoulders by women, as on a low-necked dress. [t. F: m. *berthe,* der. *Berthe* Bertha, Charlemagne's mother, noted for her modesty]

Bertha (bû′thə), *n.* Big Bertha.

Bertillon system (bû′tĭ lŏn′; *Fr.* bĕr tē yôN′), a system of identifying persons, esp. criminals, by a record of individual physical measurements and peculiarities. [named after the inventor, Alphonse *Bertillon,* 1853–1914, French anthropologist]

Berwickshire (bĕ′rĭk shĭə′, -shə), *n.* a county in SE Scotland. 22,044 pop. (est. 1964); 457 sq. mi. *Co. town*: Duns. Also, **Berwick** (bĕ′rĭk).

Berwick-upon-Tweed (bĕ′rĭk ə pŏn twēd′), *n.* a town in England, in N Northumberland. 12,166 (1965).

beryl (bĕ′rĭl), *n.* 1. a mineral, beryllium aluminium silicate, $Be_3Al_2Si_6O_{18}$, usually green (but also blue, rose, white, and golden) and both opaque and transparent, the latter variety including the gems emerald and aquamarine: the principal ore of beryllium. 2. pale bluish green; sea-green. [ME, t. L: m. s. *bēryllus,* t. Gk: m. *bēryllos*] —**beryline** (bĕ′rĭ lĭn, -līn′), *adj.*

beryllium (bĕ rĭl′yəm), *n. Chem.* a steel grey, divalent, hard, light, metallic element, the salts of which are said to have a sweetish taste (hence it is called glucinum by the French). Its chief use is in copper alloys not subject to fatigue, used for springs and contacts. *Symbol*: Be; *at. wt*: 9·0122; *at. no.*: 4; *sp. gr.*: 1·8 at 20°C. [f. BERYL + -IUM]

Berzelius (bə zē′lĭ əs; *Swed.* bĕr sė′lē o͝os), *n.* **Jöns Jakob** (*Swed.* yœns yä′kōb), **Baron,** 1779–1848, Swedish chemist.

Bes (bĕs), *n. Egypt. Relig.* a beneficent god of pleasure.

Besançon (*Fr.* bə zäN sôN′), *n.* a city in E France, on the river Doubs, capital of Doubs department: Roman ruins. 95,642 (1962).

Besant (bĕz′ənt *for 1*; bə zănt′ *for 2*), *n.* 1. **Annie (Wood),** 1847–1933, British social and political reformer and theosophist. 2. **Sir Walter,** 1836–1901, English novelist.

beseech (bĭ sēch′), *v.t.,* **-sought** or **-seeched, -seeching.** 1. to implore urgently. 2. to beg eagerly for; solicit. [ME *biseche(n),* f. BE- + *sechen,* OE *sēcan* seek] —**beseech′er,** *n.* —**beseech′ing,** *adj.* —**beseech′ingly,** *adv.* —**beseech′ingness,** *n.* —**Syn.** 1. entreat, pray.

beseem (bĭ sēm′), *v.t.* 1. to be fit for or worthy of. —*v.i.* 2. to be seemly or fitting.

beset (bĭ sĕt′), *v.t.,* **-set, -setting.** 1. to attack on all sides; assail; harass: *beset by enemies, difficulties, etc.* 2. to surround; hem in. [ME *besette(n),* OE *besettan,* f. BE- + *settan* SET] —**beset′ment,** *n.*

besetting (bĭ sĕt′ĭng), *adj.* constantly attacking, tempting, etc.: *our besetting sins.*

beshrew (bĭ shro͞o′), *v.t. Archaic.* to curse; invoke evil upon. [ME *beshrewen,* f. BE- + SHREW[1]]

beside (bĭ sīd′), *prep.* 1. by or at the side of; near: *sit down beside me.* 2. compared with. 3. *Rare.* over and above; in addition to; besides. 4. apart from; not connected with: *beside the point or question.* 5. **beside oneself,** out of one's senses through strong emotion. —*adv.* 6. in addition; besides. [ME; OE *be sīdan* by side]

—**Syn.** 1. BESIDE, BESIDES may both be used as prepositions, though with different meanings. BESIDE is almost exclusively used as a preposition meaning 'by the side of': *beside the house, the stream.* BESIDES is used as a preposition meaning 'in addition to' or 'over and above': *besides these honours he received a pension.*

besides (bĭ sīdz′), *adv.* 1. moreover. 2. in addition. 3. otherwise; else. —*prep.* 4. over and above; in addition to. 5. other than; except. [f. BESIDE + adv. *-s*]

—**Syn.** 1. BESIDES, MOREOVER both indicate something additional to what has already been stated. BESIDES often suggests that the addition is in the nature of an afterthought: *the bill cannot be paid as yet; besides the work is not completed.* MOREOVER is more formal and implies that the addition is something particular, emphatic, or important: *I did not like the house; moreover, it was too high-priced.* 4. See **beside.**

besiege (bĭ sēj′), *v.t.,* **-sieged, -sieging.** 1. to lay siege to. 2. to crowd round. 3. to assail or ply, as with requests, etc. —**besiege′ment,** *n.* —**besieg′er,** *n.*

besmear (bĭ smĭə′), *v.t.* 1. to smear over. 2. to sully; soil. [ME *bismeren,* OE *besmerian.* See BE-, SMEAR]

besmirch (bĭ smûch′), *v.t.* 1. to soil; stain, as with soot. 2. to detract from the honour of: *to besmirch one's name.*

besom (bē′zəm), *n.* 1. brush or twigs bound together as a broom. 2. a broom of any kind. [ME *besum* broom, rod, OE *besema,* c. G *Besen*]

besot (bĭ sŏt′), *v.t.,* **-sotted, -sotting.** 1. to infatuate. 2. to make stupid or foolish. 3. to stupefy with drink.

besought (bĭ sôt′), *v.* pt. and pp. of **beseech.**

bespake (bĭ spāk′), *v. Archaic.* pt. of **bespeak.**

bespangle (bĭ spăng′gl), *v.t.,* **-gled, -gling.** to adorn with, or as with, spangles.

bespatter (bĭ spăt′ə), *v.t.* 1. to soil by spattering; sprinkle with mud, dirty water, etc. 2. to slander.

bespeak (bĭ spēk′), *v.,* **-spoke** or (*Archaic*) **-spake, -spoken** or **-spoke, -speaking,** *n.* —*v.t.* 1. to ask for in advance; stipulate: *to bespeak a calm hearing or the reader's patience.* 2. to reserve beforehand; engage in advance; make arrangements for: *to bespeak a seat in a theatre.* 3. *Poetic.* to speak to; address. 4. to show; indicate: *this bespeaks a kindly heart.* —*n.* 5. *Obs.* an actor's benefit performance. [ME *bespeken,* OE *besprecan* speak against, speak of, f. *be-* BE- + *sprecan* (for loss of *-r-* see SPEAK)]

bespectacled (bĭ spĕk′tə kld), *adj.* wearing spectacles.

bespoke (bĭ spōk′), *adj.* 1. made to order: *bespoke goods.* 2. working to order: *a bespoke tailor.*

bespread (bĭ sprĕd′), *v.t.,* **-spread, -spreading.** to spread over; cover with.

besprent (bĭ sprĕnt′), *adj. Poetic.* besprinkled; bestrewed. [pp. of *bespreng* (obs.), OE *besprengan*]

besprinkle (bĭ sprĭng′kl), *v.t.,* **-kled, -kling.** to sprinkle over with something; bespatter.

Bessarabia (bĕs′ə rā′byə), *n.* a territory in the SW Soviet Union: formerly a province of Rumania. 17,151 sq. mi. —**Bes′sara′bian,** *adj., n.*

Bessarabia

Bessemer (bĕs′ĭ mə), *n.* **Sir Henry,** 1813–98, English engineer: inventor of Bessemer process.

Bessemer converter, *Metall.* a huge pear-shaped metal container used in the Bessemer process.

Bessemer process, *Metall.* a process of producing steel, in which impurities are removed by forcing a blast of air through molten iron.

best (bĕst), *adj.* (*superlative of* **good**). 1. of the highest quality, excellence, or standing: *the best judgement.* 2. most advantageous, suitable, or desirable: *the best way.* 3. largest; most: *the best part of a day.* —*adv.* (*superlative of* **well**). 4. most excellently or suitably; with most advantage or success. 5. in or to the highest degree; most fully. 6. **had best,** would be wiser, safer, etc., to. —*n.* 7. the best thing, state, or part. 8. one's finest clothing. 9. utmost or best quality: *at one's best.* 10. **at best, a.** in the best circumstances. **b.** in the most favourable view. 11. **for the best, a.** having an unexpectedly good result. **b.** with good intentions or motives. 12. **get** or **have the best of,** to defeat. 13. **make**

the best of, to manage as well as one can (in unfavourable or adverse circumstances). —*v.t.* **14.** to defeat; beat. **15.** to outdo; surpass. [ME *beste,* OE *betst,* c. Goth. *batist-*]

best boat, *Rowing.* a shell (def. 13).

bestead (bĭ stĕd′), *v.,* **-steaded, -steaded** or **-stead, -steading,** *adj.* —*v.t.* **1.** to help; assist; serve; avail. —*adj.* **2.** *Archaic.* placed; situated. [ME, f. BE- + *stead,* v., help, be of use to, der. *stead,* n., profit, support]

bestial (bĕs′tyəl), *adj.* **1.** of or belonging to a beast. **2.** brutal; inhuman; irrational. **3.** depravedly sensual; carnal. [ME, t. L: s. *bestiālis*] —**bes′tially,** *adv.*

bestiality (bĕs′tĭ ăl′ĭ tĭ), *n.* **1.** bestial character or conduct; beastliness. **2.** excessive appetites or indulgence. **3.** unnatural sexual relations with an animal; sodomy.

bestialize (bĕs′tyə līz′), *v.t.,* **-lized, -lizing.** to make bestial. Also, **bestialise.**

bestiary (bĕs′tyə rĭ), *n., pl.* **-ries.** a type of book very popular in the Middle Ages, consisting of a collection of moralized fables about natural history objects, mostly animals, modelled on one attributed to an Alexandrian Greek of the 4th century after Christ. [t. ML: m. s. *bestiārium,* prop. neut. of L *bestiārius* pertaining to beasts]

bestir (bĭ stû′), *v.t.* (generally reflexive), **-stirred, -stirring.** to stir up; rouse to action. [ME *bestyrie(n),* OE *bestyrian* heap up]

best man, the chief attendant of the bridegroom at a wedding.

bestow (bĭ stō′), *v.t.* **1.** to present as a gift; give; confer. **2.** to dispose of; apply to some use. **3.** *Colloq.* to provide quarters for. **4.** to put; stow; deposit; store. —**bestow′al, bestow′ment,** *n.*

bestraddle (bĭ străd′l), *v.t.,* **-dled, -dling.** to bestride.

bestrew (bĭ stro͞o′), *v.t.,* **-strewed, -strewn** or **-strewed, -strewing.** **1.** to strew or cover (a surface). **2.** to strew or scatter about. **3.** to lie scattered over. [ME *bistrewe(n),* OE *bestrēowian*]

bestride (bĭ strīd′), *v.t.,* **-strode** or **-strid, -stridden** or **-strid, -striding.** **1.** to get or be astride of; spread the legs on both sides of. **2.** to step over or across. [ME *bestride(n),* OE *bestrīdan,* f. BE- + *strīdan* stride]

best-seller (bĕst′sĕl′ə), *n.* **1.** a book that has a very large sale during a given period. **2.** the author of such a book.

bestud (bĭ stŭd′), *v.t.,* **-studded, -studding.** to set with studs distributed over a surface; dot.

bet (bĕt), *v.,* **bet** or **betted, betting,** *n.* —*v.t.* **1.** to pledge as a forfeit to another who makes a similar pledge in return, in support of an opinion; stake; wager. —*v.i.* **2.** to lay a wager. **3.** to make a practice of betting. **4. you bet,** *Slang.* you may be sure; certainly. —*n.* **5.** a pledge of something to be forfeited, in case one is wrong, to another who has the opposite opinion. **6.** that which is pledged. **7.** chance of success. **8.** a thing, person, or eventuality on which to gamble or stake one's hopes: *he's a bad bet.* [orig. uncert.] —**bet′ter, bet′tor,** *n.*

bet., between.

beta (bē′tə), *n.* the second letter of the Greek alphabet (Β, β), often used to designate the second in a series, esp. in scientific classification, as: **a.** *Astron.* (of a constellation) the second brightest star: *Rigel is* β *(or Beta) Orionis.* **b.** *Chem.* (of a compound) one of the possible positions of substituted atoms or groups. **c.** (in examinations, etc.) the second highest mark or grade.

beta decay, *Physics.* a radioactive disintegration in which an electron or a positron is emitted.

beta-eucaine (bē′tə yo͞o′kān), *n.* eucaine (def. 2). Also, **betacaine** (bē′tə kān′).

betaine (bē′tə ēn′, -ĭn; bĭ tā′ēn, -ĭn), *n. Chem.* a nonpoisonous crystalline substance, $C_5H_{11}O_2N(H_2O)$, a sweetish-tasting alkaloid, found in sugar beets, cottonseed, the sprouts of wheat and barley; related chemically to glycine. [f. L *bēta* beet + -INE[2]]

betake (bĭ tāk′), *v.t.* (generally reflexive), **-took, -taken, -taking.** **1.** to go: *she betook herself to the market.* **2.** to resort to; undertake: *he betook himself to flight.*

beta-naphthol (bē′tə năf′thŏl), *n. Chem.* a crystalline antiseptic, $C_{10}H_7OH$.

beta particle, *Physics.* an electron or positron emitted during a beta decay.

beta ray, *Physics.* a stream of beta particles.

beta transformation, beta decay.

betatron (bē′tə trŏn′), *n. Physics.* a device based on the principle of the transformer, which accelerates electrons to high energy by a magnetic field varying with time.

betel (bē′tl), *n.* an East Indian pepper plant, *Piper betle.* Cf. **betel nut.** [t. Pg.: m. *betele,* earlier *vitele,* t. Malay: m. *vettila,* Tamil *vettilei*]

Betelgeuse (bē′tl jûz′, bē′tl jûz′), *n. Astron.* a giant reddish star of the first magnitude in the constellation Orion. Also, **Be′telgeux′.** [t. F, ? t. Ar.: m. *bit-al-jāuza* the giant's shoulder]

betel nut, the areca nut, chewed extensively with lime by Indians, Pakistanis, and others.

betel palm, a tall, graceful, Asiatic palm, *Areca catechu,* that bears the areca nut or betel nut, so named from its association in native usage with the betel plant.

bête noire (bĕt′nwä′; *Fr.* bĕt nwȧr′), *French.* something that one especially dislikes or dreads, either a person, task, or object; bugbear. [F: black beast]

Bethany (bĕth′ə nĭ), *n.* a village in Israeli-occupied Jordan near Jerusalem, at the foot of the Mount of Olives.

bethel (bĕth′əl), *n.* **1.** a hallowed spot. Gen. 28:19. **2.** a dissenters' chapel or meeting house. **3.** *Chiefly U.S.* a church or chapel for seamen, often afloat in a harbour. [t. Heb.: m. *bēth-ēl* house of God]

Bethel (bĕth′əl), *n.* an ancient town in NW Jordan, near Jerusalem.

Bethesda (bĕ thĕz′də), *n.* **1.** *Bible,* a pool in Jerusalem, having healing powers. John 5:2-4. **2.** a chapel.

bethink (bĭ thĭngk′), *v.,* **-thought, -thinking.** *Archaic.* —*v.t.* (generally reflexive) **1.** to remember; recall. **2.** to think; consider. **3.** to determine; resolve. **4.** to bear in mind; remember. —*v.i.* **5.** to consider; meditate. [ME *bethenken,* OE *bethencan,* f. BE- + *thencan* consider]

Bethlehem (bĕth′lĭ hĕm′, -lĭ əm), *n.* a town in Israeli-occupied Jordan, near Jerusalem; birthplace of Jesus and of David. 15,000 (est. 1965).

Bethlehem

Bethmann-Hollweg (*Ger.* bĕt′män hôl′ vĕk), *n* **Theobald von** (*Ger.* tė′ō bȧlt fōn), 1856–1921, German statesman: chancellor 1909–17.

Bethnal Green (bĕth′nəl), a district of the E inner London borough of Tower Hamlets.

bethought (bĭ thôt′), *v.* pt. and pp. of **bethink.**

Bethsaida (bĕth sā′də), *n.* an ancient town in N Israel, near the N shore of the Sea of Galilee.

betide (bĭ tīd′), *v.,* **-tided, -tiding.** *Archaic.* —*v.t.* **1.** to happen; befall; come to: *woe betide the villain!* —*v.i.* **2.** to come to pass. [ME *betide(n),* f. BE- + *tiden,* OE *tīdan* betide]

betimes (bĭ tīmz′), *adv.* **1.** before it is too late; early. **2.** soon. [ME *betymes,* f. *betime* by time + adv. *-s*]

bêtise (*Fr.* bĕ tēz′), *n.* **1.** stupidity. **2.** a stupid or foolish act or remark. **3.** an absurdity; trifle. [F, der. *bête* beast]

Betjeman (bĕch′ə mən), *n.* **John,** born 1906, English poet and writer.

betoken (bĭ tō′kən), *v.t.* **1.** to give evidence of; indicate. **2.** to be or give a token of; portend.

béton (bĕt′ən; *Fr.* bė tôɴ′), *n.* a kind of concrete composed of a mixture of cement, sand, and gravel.

betony (bĕt′ə nĭ), *n.* **1.** a plant, *Stachys* (formerly *Betonica*) *officinalis,* of the mint family, formerly used in medicine and dyeing. **2.** any of various similar plants. [t. LL: m. *betoni(ca)*; r. ME *beteine,* t. OF; r. OE *betonice,* t. LL (as above)]

betook (bĭ to͝ok′), *v.* pt. of **betake.**

betray (bĭ trā′), *v.t.* **1.** to deliver or expose to an enemy by treachery or disloyalty. **2.** to be unfaithful in keeping or upholding: *to betray a trust.* **3.** to be disloyal to; disappoint the hopes or expectations of. **4.** to reveal or disclose in violation of confidence: *to betray a secret.* **5.** to reveal unconsciously (something one would preferably conceal). **6.** to show; exhibit. **7. betray oneself,** to reveal one's real character, plans, etc. **8.** to deceive; mislead. **9.** to seduce and desert. [ME *bitraien,* f. *bi-* BE- + *traien,* t. OF: m. *traïr,* ult. g. L *trādere* give over] —**betray′al,** *n.* —**betray′er,** *n.*

betroth (bĭ trōth′, -trōth′), *v.t.* **1.** to promise to marry. **2.** to arrange for the marriage of; affiance. [ME *betrouthen,* var. of *betreuthien,* der. BE- + *treuthe,* OE *trēowth* pledge. See TROTH, TRUTH]

betrothal (bĭ trō′thəl), *n.* the act or ceremony of betrothing; engagement. Also, **betroth′ment.**

betrothed (bĭ trōthd′, -trōtht′), *adj.* **1.** engaged to be married. —*n.* **2.** an engaged person.

better (bĕt′ə), *adj.* (*comparative of* **good**). **1.** of superior quality or excellence: *a better position.* **2.** of superior value, use, fitness, desirability, acceptableness, etc.: *a better time for action.* **3.** larger; greater: *the better part of a lifetime.* **4.** improved in health; healthier. **5.** completely recovered in health; well. —*adv.* (*comparative of* **well**). **6.** in a more excellent way or manner: *to behave better.* **7.** in a superior degree: *to know a man better.* **8.** more: *better than a mile to town.* **9. had better,** would be wiser, safer, etc., to. **10. better off,** in better circumstances.

11. **think better of,** a. to reconsider and decide more wisely. b. to think more favourably of. —*v.t.* 12. to make better; improve; increase the good qualities of. 13. **better oneself,** to improve one's social standing, education, etc. 14. to improve upon; surpass; exceed; *they bettered working conditions.* —*v.i.* 15. *Colloq. or Dial.* to become better. —*n.* 16. that which has superior excellence, etc.: *the better of two choices.* 17. (*usually pl.*) one's superior in wisdom, wealth, etc. 18. superiority: *to get the better of someone.* [ME *bettre*, OE *betera*, c. Goth. *batiza*] —**Syn.** 12. See **improve.**

better half, *Colloq.* one's wife.

betterment (bĕt′ə mənt), *n.* 1. improvement. 2. (*usually pl.*) *Law.* an improvement of real property, other than mere repairs.

Betterton (bĕt′ə tən), *n.* **Thomas,** 1635?–1710, English actor.

Betti (*It.* bĕt′tē), *n.* **Ugo** (*It.* ōō′gō), 1892–1953, Italian poet and dramatist.

betting shop, a licensed bookmaking establishment that takes off-course bets on horseraces, etc.

bettong (bĕt′ŏng), *n.* *Austral.* a kangaroo rat of the genus *Bettongia.* [t. native Australian]

betulaceous (bĕt′yōō lā′shəs), *adj.* *Bot.* belonging to the *Betulaceae*, a family of trees and shrubs including the birch, alder, etc. [f. s. L *betula* birch + -ACEOUS]

between (bĭ twēn′), *prep.* 1. in the space separating (two or more points, objects, etc.). 2. intermediate to, in time, quantity, or degree; *between 12 and 1 o'clock, between pink and red.* 3. connecting: *a link between parts.* 4. involving; concerning; of: *war between nations, choice between things.* 5. by joint action or possession of: *to own land between them.* 6. distinguishing one thing from another: *he can't tell the difference between butter and margarine.* 7. **between you and me** or **between ourselves,** in confidence. 8. **go between,** to act as a mediator. —*adv.* 9. in the intervening space or time; in an intermediate position or relation: *visits far between.* [ME *betwene*, OE *betwēonan, betwēonum*, f. *be* by + *-twēonan, twēonum*, der. *twā* two] —**Syn.** 1. See **among.**

betweenwhiles (bĭ twēn′wīlz′), *adv.* in the meantime; in between other activities. Also, **between-time.**

betwixt (bĭ twĭkst′), *prep., adv.* 1. *Archaic.* between. 2. **betwixt and between,** neither the one nor the other; in a middle position. [ME *betwix*, OE *betweox*; for final *-t* cf. *against*, etc.]

beukenhout (byōō′kən hout′, -hōt′), *n.* a timber tree, *Faurea mcnaughtonii*, of southern Africa. [t. Afrikaans: f. *beuk(en)* beech + *hout* timber]

Beulah (byōō′lə), *n.* *Bible.* the land of Israel. Isa. 62:4. [t. Heb.: m. *bĕʿūlāh* married]

Beuthen (*Ger.* boy′tən), *n.* German name of **Bytom.**

BeV, *U.S.* billion electron-volts; GeV.

Bevan (bĕv′ən), *n.* **Aneurin** (ə nī′ə rĭn), 1897–1960, British politician.

bevatron (bĕv′ə trŏn′), *n.* *Physics.* a synchroton type of particle accelerator, capable of accelerating electrons to very high energies.

bevel (bĕv′əl), *n., v.,* **-elled, -elling** or (*U.S.*) **-eled, -eling,** *adj.* —*n.* 1. the inclination that one line or surface makes with another when not at right angles. 2. an adjustable instrument used by woodworkers for laying out angles or adjusting the surface of wood to a particular inclination. —*v.t., v.i.* 3. to cut or slant at a bevel. —*adj.* 4. oblique; sloping; slanted. [orig. obscure] —**bev′eller,** *n.*

Bevel (def. 2)

bevel gear, *Mach.* a gear in which the axis or shaft of the driver forms an angle with the axis or shaft of the wheel driven. See illus. under **gear.**

bevel square, bevel (def. 2).

beverage (bĕv′ə rĭj, bĕv′rĭj), *n.* a drink of any kind: *intoxicating beverages.* [ME, t. OF: m. *bevrage*, der. *bevre*, g. L *bibere* drink]

Beveridge (bĕv′ə rĭj, bĕv′rĭj), *n.* **Sir William Henry, 1st Baron,** 1879–1963, British economist.

Beverley (bĕv′ə lĭ), *n.* a town in England, in the E Riding of Yorkshire. 16,031 (1961).

Beverly Hills, a town in SW California, near Los Angeles. 30,817 (1960).

Bevin (bĕv′ĭn), *n.* **Ernest,** 1881–1951, British trade unionist and statesman: foreign minister 1945–51.

bevy (bĕv′ĭ), *n., pl.* **bevies.** 1. a flock of birds, esp. larks or quails. 2. a group, esp. of girls or women. [ME *bevey*; orig. uncert.]

bewail (bĭ wāl′), *v.t.* 1. to express deep sorrow for; lament. —*v.i.* 2. to express grief.

beware (bĭ wâ′), *v.* (now only used as imperative or infinitive). —*v.i.* 1. to be wary, cautious, or careful (fol. by *of* or a clause). —*v.t.* 2. *Archaic.* be wary of.

Bewick (byōō′ĭk), *n.* **Thomas,** 1753–1828, English wood-engraver and illustrator.

bewigged (bĭ wĭgd′), *adj.* wearing a wig.

bewilder (bĭ wĭl′də), *v.t.* to confuse or puzzle completely; perplex. [f. BE- + WILDER] —**bewil′dered,** *adj.* —**bewil′deredly,** *adv.* —**bewil′dering,** *adj.* —**bewil′deringly,** *adv.* —**Syn.** mystify, nonplus, confound, daze. See **puzzle.**

bewilderment (bĭ wĭl′də mənt), *n.* bewildered state.

bewitch (bĭ wĭch′), *v.t.* 1. to affect by witchcraft or magic; throw a spell over. 2. to enchant. —**bewitch′er,** *n.* —**bewitch′ery,** *n.* —**bewitch′ing,** *adj.* —**bewitch′ingly,** *adv.* —**bewitch′ment,** *n.* —**Syn.** 2. fascinate, captivate.

bewray (bĭ rā′), *v.t.* *Obs.* 1. to reveal. 2. to betray. [ME *bewreien*, f. BE- + *wreien*, OE *wrēgan* accuse]

Bexhill (bĕks′hĭl′), *n.* a town in England, in East Sussex. 28,941 (1961).

Bexley (bĕks′lĭ), *n.* a SE outer borough of London. 212,900 (1965).

bey (bā), *n., pl.* **beys.** 1. (formerly) the governor of a minor Turkish province. 2. a Turkish title of respect. 3. (formerly) the title of the native ruler of Tunis. [t. Turk.: m. *beg*]

beygel (bā′gl), *n.* bagel.

Beyle (*Fr.* bĕl), *n.* **Marie Henri** (*Fr.* mȧ rē äN rē′), real name of **Stendhal.**

Beyoglu (*Turk.* bĕy′ō lōō), *n.* a modern part of Istanbul, in Turkey in Europe, on the Golden Horn. 253,588 (1950). Formerly, **Pera.**

beyond (bĭ yŏnd′), *prep.* 1. on or to the farther side of: *beyond the house.* 2. farther on than; more distant than: *beyond the horizon.* 3. later than: *they stayed beyond the time limit.* 4. outside the understanding, limits, or reach of; past: *beyond human comprehension.* 5. superior to; surpassing; above: *wise beyond all others.* 6. more than; in excess of; over and above. —*adv.* 7. farther on or away; *as far as the house and beyond.* —*n.* 8. the life after the present one. [ME *beyonde*, OE *begeondan*, f. *be* by + *geondan* beyond]

Beyrouth (bā rōōt′), *n.* Beirut.

bezant (bĕz′ənt, bĭ zănt′), *n.* 1. the solidus, a gold coin of the Byzantine emperors, widely circulated in Europe during the Middle Ages. 2. *Archit.* an ornament in the form of a flat disc. 3. *Her.* a small gold circle. [ME, t. OF: m. *besant*, g. L *Byzantius* Byzantine]

bezel (bĕz′əl), *n.* 1. a sloping face or edge of a chisel or other cutting tool. 2. the upper oblique faces of a brilliant-cut gem. 3. the grooved ring or rim holding a gem or watch crystal in its setting. [prob. t. F, der. *biais* slant. See BIAS]

Béziers (*Fr.* bē zyē′), *n.* a town in S France, in Hérault department. 75,541 (1962).

bezique (bĭ zēk′), *n.* a card game for two or more players, played with 64 cards. [t. F: m. *bésigue*]

bezoar (bē′zô), *n.* 1. a calculus or concretion found in the stomach or intestines of certain animals, esp. ruminants, formerly reputed to be efficacious against poison. 2. *Obs.* a counterpoison or antidote. [t. Ar.: m. *bāzahr*, t. Pers.: m. *pādzahr* counterpoison]

bezonian (bĭ zō′nĭ ən), *n.* *Archaic.* an indigent rascal; scoundrel. [der. obs. *besonio*, t. It.: m. *bisogno* need, needy fellow]

Bezwada (bāz′wä′də), *n.* Vijayawada.

b.f., 1. *Colloq.* bloody fool. 2. Also, **bf.** *Printing.* boldface.

b/f, *Com.* brought forward.

Bhagalpur (bä′gl pōōə′), *n.* a town in India, in E Bihar. 143,850 (1961).

Bhagavad-gita (bŭg′ə vəd gē′tə), *n.* *Hinduism.* a famous episode of eighteen chapters in the Mahabharata, wherein the divine incarnation Krishna expounds the duties of the caste system together with devotion to the Deity. [t. Skt: the Song of the Blessed One]

bhang (băng), *n.* 1. the Indian hemp plant. 2. a preparation of its leaves and tops used in India as an intoxicant and narcotic. Also, **bang.** [t. Hind.: m. *bhāng*, g. Skt *bhangā* hemp]

bharal (bä′rəl), *n.* a wild goat, *Pseudois nayaur*, of the Himalayas.

Bhatpara (bät pä′rə), *n.* a town in India, in W West Bengal, near Calcutta. 147,630. (1961).

Bhaunagar (bou nŭg′ə), *n.* a seaport in S Gujarat, W India. 171,039 (1962). Also, **Bhavnagar** (bŭv nŭg′ə).

Bhave (bä′vä), *n.* **Vinoba** (vĭ nō′bə), born 1895, Indian land reformer.

bheesti (bēs′tĭ), *n.* (in India) a water-carrier. Also, **bheesty, bheestie, bhistee.** [t. Hind.: m. *bhistī*, t. Pers.: m. *bihishti* water-carrier, deriv. (presumably jocular) of *bihisht* paradise]

Bhoodan (bo͞o dän′), *n.* (in India) a socio-agricultural reform movement, in which landowners give land to the community, founded by Vinoba Bhave in 1951.

Bhopal (bō päl′), *n.* **1.** a former state in the central part of India, now part of Madhya Pradesh. **2.** the capital of Madhya Pradesh, in the W central part. 185,374 (1962).

b.h.p., brake horsepower.

Bhumibol Adulyadej (bo͞o′mĭ pōn ə do͞o′lyə dĕt′), born 1927, king of Thailand since 1946.

Bhutan (bo͞o tän′), *n.* a kingdom in the Himalayas NE of India: partly controlled by India. 850,000 pop. (est. 1964); ab. 18,000 sq. mi. *Cap.:* Thimphu. See map under **Everest.**

Bi, *Chem.* bismuth.

bi-, a prefix meaning 'twice, doubly, two', as in *bicarbonate, bilateral, binocular, biweekly.* Also, **bin-.** [t. L, comb, form of *bis* twice, doubly]

Biafra (bĭ ăf′rə), *n.* **1.** the Eastern Region of Nigeria, having a predominantly Ibo population; independent May 1967–January 1970, war with the rest of Nigeria 1967–70. **2. Bight of,** a wide bay in the E part of the Gulf of Guinea, off the W coast of Africa.

Białystok (*Pol.* byȧ wĭ′stŏk), *n.* a city in E Poland. 134,000 (1964). Russian, **Byelostok.**

biangular (bī ăng′gyo͝o lə), *adj.* having two angles or corners.

biannual (bī ăn′yo͝o əl), *adj.* occurring twice a year. —**bian′nually,** *adv.*

biannulate (bī ăn′yo͝o lĭt, -lāt′), *adj. Zool.* having two rings or ringlike bands, as of colour.

Biarritz (bĭə′rĭts, bĭə rĭts′; *Fr.* byȧ rēts′), *n.* a town in SW France, on the Bay of Biscay: resort. 22,000 (est. 1964).

bias (bī′əs) *n., adj., adv., v.,* **biased, biasing.** —*n.* **1.** an oblique or diagonal line of direction, esp. across a woven fabric: *to cut cloth on the bias.* **2.** a particular tendency or inclination, esp. one which prevents unprejudiced consideration of a question. **3.** *Bowling.* **a.** a bulge or a greater weight on one side of the bowl, causing it to swerve. **b.** the swerved course of a bowl, due to shape or weighting. **4.** *Radio.* the direct voltage placed on the grid of an electronic valve. —*adj.* **5.** cut, set, folded, etc., diagonally. —*adv.* **6.** slantingly; obliquely. —*v.t.* **7.** to influence, usually unfairly; prejudice; warp. [t. F: m. *biais* slant, prob. g. L *biaxius* having two axes]

—**Syn. 2.** BIAS, PREJUDICE mean a strong inclination of the mind or a preconceived opinion about something or someone. A BIAS may be favourable or unfavourable: *bias in favour of or against an idea.* PREJUDICE implies a preformed judgement even more unreasoning that BIAS, and usually implies an unfavourable opinion: *prejudice against a race.* —**Ant. 2.** impartiality. **5.** straight.

biathlon (bī ăth′lŏn), *n. Sport.* a cross-country ski contest combined with rifle marksmanship. [f. BI- + Gk *âthlon* contest]

biauricular (bī′ô rĭk′yo͝o lə), *adj. Anat.* **1.** having two auricles. **2.** pertaining to the two ears.

biauriculate (bī′ô rĭk′yo͝o lĭt, -lāt′), *adj. Biol.* having two auricles or earlike parts.

biaxial (bī ăk′sĭ əl), *adj.* **1.** having two axes. **2.** (of a crystal) having two directions in which no double refraction occurs. —**biax′ially,** *adv.*

bib (bĭb), *n., v.,* **bibbed, bibbing.** —*n.* **1.** an article of clothing worn under the chin by a child, esp. while eating, to protect the dress. **2.** the upper part of an apron. **3.** an edible fish, *Gadus luscus,* of the NE Atlantic; pout. —*v.t.* **4.** *Obs.* to tipple. [ME *bibben*; orig. uncert., ? t. L: m. *bibere* drink] —**bib′like′,** *adj.*

Bib., **1.** Bible. **2.** biblical.

bib and tucker, *Colloq.* clothes, esp. one's best: *for the party she put on her best bib and tucker.*

bibasic (bī bā′sĭk), *adj. Chem.* dibasic.

bibber (bĭb′ə), *n.* a steady drinker; tippler.

bibcock (bĭb′kŏk′), *n. Plumbing.* a tap having a nozzle bent downwards.

bibelot (bĭb′lō; *Fr.* bē blō′), *n.* small object of curiosity, beauty, or rarity. [t. F]

bi-bivalent (bī′bī vā′lənt, bī bĭv′ə-), *adj. Chem.* denoting an electrolytic compound which splits into two ions, each with a valency of two.

bibl., **1.** biblical. **2.** bibliographical.

Bible (bī′bl), *n.* **1.** the collection of sacred writings of the Christian religion, comprising the Old and the New Testament. **2.** the Old Testament only. **3.** (*often l.c.*) the sacred writings of any religion. **4.** (*l.c.*) any book accepted as authoritative. [ME *bibul,* t. ML: m. s. *biblia,* t. Gk: pl. of *biblíon,* dim. of *bíblos* book]

Bible Belt, an area of the Southern U.S. noted for its fundamentalist religious beliefs.

biblical (bĭb′lĭ kl), *adj.* **1.** of or in the Bible. **2.** in accord with the Bible. —**bib′lically,** *adv.*

Biblical Aramaic. See **Chaldean.**

Biblical Latin, the form of Latin used in the translation of the Bible, which became current in Western Europe at the beginning of the Middle Ages.

biblicist (bĭb′lĭ sĭst), *n.* **1.** an adherent of the letter of the Bible; a fundamentalist. **2.** (*l.c.*) a biblical scholar. —**bib′licism,** *n.*

biblio-, a word element meaning: **1.** book, as in *bibliophil.* **2.** Bible, as in *bibliolatry.* [t. Gk, comb. form of *biblíon* book]

bibliofilm (bĭb′lĭ ō fĭlm′), *n.* a microfilm used esp. in libraries for reproducing the pages of valuable or much-used books.

bibliog., **1.** bibliographer. **2.** bibliography.

bibliographer (bĭb′lĭ ŏg′rə fə), *n.* one occupied with or expert in bibliography. Also, **bibliograph** (bĭb′lĭ ō grăf′, -gräf′). [f. s. Gk *bibliográphos* book-writer + -ER[1]]

bibliography (bĭb′lĭ ŏg′rə fĭ), *n., pl.* **-phies. 1.** a complete or selective list of literature on a particular subject. **2.** a list of works by a given author. **3.** a list of source materials used or consulted in the preparation of a work. **4.** the systematic description, history, classification, etc., of books and other written or printed works. —**bibliographic** (bĭb′lĭ ō grăf′ĭk), **bib′liograph′ical,** *adj.*

bibliolatry (bĭb′lĭ ŏl′ə trĭ), *n.* excessive reverence for the Bible. —**bib′liol′ater,** *n.* —**bib′liol′atrous,** *adj.*

bibliomancy (bĭb′lĭ ō măn′sĭ), *n.* divination by means of a book, as the Bible, opened at random at some verse taken as significant.

bibliomania (bĭb′lĭ ō mā′nyə), *n.* an enthusiasm for collecting books. —**bibliomaniac** (bĭb′lĭ ō mā′nĭ ăk′), *adj., n.* —**bibliomaniacal** (bĭb′lĭ ō mə nī′ə kl), *adj.*

bibliopegy (bĭb′lĭ ŏp′ĭ jĭ), *n.* the art of binding books. [f. BIBLIO- + m. s. Gk *-pēgía,* der. *pēgnýnai* fasten]

bibliophil (bĭb′lĭ ō fĭl), *n.* a lover of books. Also, **bibliophile** (bĭb′lĭ ō fīl′), **bibliophilist** (bĭb′lĭ ŏf′ĭ lĭst). [t. F. See BIBLIO-, -PHIL] —**bib′lioph′ilism,** *n.* —**bib′lioph′ilis′tic,** *adj.*

bibliopole (bĭb′lĭ ō pōl′), *n.* a bookseller, esp. a dealer in books unique for their rarity, artistic format, etc. Also, **bibliopolist** (bĭb′lĭ ŏp′ə lĭst). [t. L: m. *bibliopōla,* t. Gk: m. *bibliopṓlēs*] —**bibliopolic** (bĭb′lĭ ō pŏl′ĭk), **bib′liopol′ical,** *adj.* —**bibliopolism** (bĭb′lĭ ŏp′ə lĭz′əm), **bib′liop′oly,** *n.*

Biblist (bĭb′lĭst, bī′blĭst), *n.* **1.** one who regards the Bible as the only rule of faith. **2.** a biblicist.

bibulous (bĭb′yo͝o ləs), *adj.* **1.** in the habit of alcoholic drinking. **2.** absorbent; spongy. [t. L: m. *bibulus* freely drinking] —**bib′ulously,** *adv.* —**bib′ulousness,** *n.*

bicameral (bī kăm′ə rəl), *adj. Govt.* having two branches, chambers, or houses, as a legislative body.

bicarb., sodium bicarbonate.

bicarbonate (bī kä′bə nĭt, -nāt′), *n. Chem.* a salt of carbonic acid, containing the HCO_3 radical; an acid carbonate, as *sodium bicarbonate,* $NaHCO_3$.

bicarbonate of soda, sodium bicarbonate.

bice (bīs), *n.* blue or green pigment as of carbonates of copper. [ME *bis,* t. OF: dark-coloured, brownish grey]

bicentenary (bī′sĕn tē′nə rĭ), *adj., n., pl.* **-naries.** —*adj.* **1.** of or pertaining to a 200th anniversary. —*n.* **2.** a 200th anniversary. **3.** its celebration.

bicentennial (bī′sĕn tĕn′yəl), *adj.* **1.** consisting of or lasting 200 years: *a bicentennial period.* **2.** recurring every 200 years. —*n.* **3.** *U.S.* a bicentenary.

bicephalous (bī sĕf′ə ləs), *adj. Bot., Zool.* having two heads. [f. BI- + m. s. Gk *kephalḗ* head + -OUS]

biceps (bī′sĕps), *n. Anat., Zool.* a muscle having two heads of origin, esp. in Anat.: **a. biceps brachii,** the muscle on the front of the upper arm, which bends the forearm. **b. biceps femoris,** the hamstring muscle on the back of the thigh. [t. L: two-headed]

bichloride (bī klô′rīd), *n. Chem.* **1.** a compound in which two atoms of chlorine are combined with another element or radical. **2.** mercuric chloride.

bichloride of mercury, *Chem.* corrosive sublimate.

bichromate (bī krō′māt, -mĭt), *n. Chem.* **1.** dichromate. **2.** chromate of potassium, $K_2Cr_2O_7$.

bicipital (bī sĭp′ĭ tl), *adj.* **1.** having two heads. **2.** *Anat.* pertaining to the biceps. [f. s. L *biceps* two-headed + -AL[1]]

bicker (bĭk′ə), *v.i.* **1.** to engage in petulant argument; wrangle. **2.** to run rapidly; move quickly; rush; hurry. **3.** to quiver; flicker; glitter. —*n.* **4.** an angry dispute; squabble. [ME *biker(en).* Cf. MLG *bicken* prick, thrust] —**bick′erer,** *n.*

bicollateral (bī′kŏ lăt′ə rəl), *adj. Bot.* (of a bundle) having the xylem lined with phloem on both its inner and outer faces.

bicolour (bī′kŭl′ə), *adj.* of two colours: *a bicolour flower.* Also, **bi′col′oured;** *U.S.,* **bicolor, bicolored.**

biconcave (bī kŏn′kāv, bī′kŏn kāv′), *adj.* concave on both sides, as a lens. See illus. under **lens.**

biconjugate (bī kŏn′jŏŏ gĭt, -gāt′), *adj. Bot.* (of leaves) having two pairs of leaflets or pinnae. [f. BI- + CONJUGATE]

biconvex (bī kŏn′vĕks, bī′kŏn vĕks′), *adj.* convex on both sides, as a lens. See illus. under **lens.**

bicorn (bī′kôrn′), *adj. Bot., Zool.* having two horns or hornlike parts. Also, **bicornuate** (bī kôr′nyŏŏ ĭt, -āt′). [t. L: s. *bicornis* two-horned]

bicorporal (bī kôr′pə rəl), *adj.* having two bodies. Also, **bicorporeal** (bī′kôr pôr′rĭ əl).

bicron (bī′krŏn, bĭk′rŏn), *n. U.S. Physics.* one U.S. billionth (0·000,000,001) of a metre.

bicuspid (bī kŭs′pĭd), *adj.* Also, **bicuspidate** (bī kŭs′pĭ dāt′). **1.** having two cusps or points, as certain teeth. —*n.* **2.** *Anat.* one of eight such teeth in man, four on each jaw between the cuspid and the first molar teeth. [f. BI- + s. L *cuspis* point]

bicycle (bī′sĭ kl), *n., v.,* **-cled, -cling.** —*n.* **1.** a vehicle with two wheels, one in front of the other, and having a saddle-like seat for the rider. It is steered by handlebars and driven by pedals or a motor. —*v.t.* **2.** to ride a bicycle. [t. F: f. *bi-* BI- + m. s. Gk *kýklos* circle, wheel] —**bi′cyclist,** *n.*

bicyclic (bī sī′klĭk, -sĭk′lĭk), *adj.* **1.** consisting of or having two circles. **2.** *Bot.* in two whorls, as the stamens of a flower. Also, **bicy′clical.**

bid (bĭd), *v.* **bade** or **bad** (for 1, 2) or **bid** (for 3–8), **bidden** or **bid, bidding,** *n.* —*v.t.* **1.** to command; order; direct: *bid them depart.* **2.** to say as a greeting or benediction: *to bid farewell.* **3.** *Com.* to offer, as a price at an auction or as terms in a competition to secure a contract. **4.** *Com.* **a.** to overbid all offers for (property) at an auction in order to retain ownership (fol. by *in*). **b.** to increase (the market price) by increasing bids (fol. by *up*). **5.** *Cards.* to enter a bid of a given quantity or suit; call: *to bid two no-trumps.* —*v.i.* **6.** to make an offer to purchase at a price. **7. bid fair,** to seem likely. —*n.* **8.** the act of one who bids. **9.** an offer, as at an auction. **10.** the price of terms offered. **11.** *Cards.* **a.** the number of points or tricks a player offers to make. **b.** the turn of a person to bid. **12.** an attempt to attain some goal or purpose: *a bid for power.* [ME *bidde(n),* OE *(ge)bidden* beg, ask, pray; sense devel. influenced by ME *bede(n),* OE *bēodan* offer, proclaim, command] —**bid′der,** *n.* —**Syn. 1.** charge.

bidarka (bī där′kə), *n.* the sealskin boat of the Alaskan Eskimo. Also, **bidarkee** (bī där′kē). [t. Russ., dim. of *baidara* coracle]

biddable (bĭd′ə bl), *adj.* **1.** willing to do what is asked; obedient; docile. **2.** *Cards.* adequate to bid upon: *a biddable hand at bridge.*

bidden (bĭd′n), *v.* pp. of **bid.**

bidding (bĭd′ĭng), *n.* **1.** invitation; command; order. **2.** a bid. **3.** bids collectively.

Biddle (bĭd′l), *n.* **John,** 1615–62, English theologian: founder of Unitarianism in England.

Biddulph (bĭd′ŭlf), *n.* a town in England, in N Staffordshire. 14,060 (1961).

biddy (bĭd′ĭ), *n., pl.* **-dies. 1.** *Dial.* chicken. **2.** *Slang.* old woman. [orig. uncert.]

biddy-biddy (bĭd′ĭ bĭd′ĭ), *n.* a low-growing plant of New Zealand, *Acaena viridior,* with a clinging bur. Also, **bidi-bidi.** [t. Maori: m. *piri-piri*]

bide (bīd), *v.,* **bided** (for 1) or **bode** (for 2), **biding.** —*v.t.* **1. bide one's time,** to wait for a favourable opportunity. **2.** *Archaic.* to endure; bear. —*v.i.* **3.** *Archaic.* to dwell; abide; wait; remain; continue. [ME *biden,* OE *bīdan*]

Bideford (bĭd′ĭ fəd), *n.* a town in England, in N Devonshire. 10,498 (1961).

bidet (bē′dā; *Fr.* bē dĕ′), *n.* a small low bath, straddled by the user, for washing the genitals. [F]

Biedermeier (bē′də mī′ə), *adj.* **1.** pertaining to a conventional style of interior decoration, furniture, etc., common among the middle classes in German-speaking countries during the 19th century. **2.** conventional in outlook. [named after Gottlieb *Biedermeier,* fictitious philistine contributor to 19th-century German literary periodicals]

Biel (*Ger.* bēl), *n.* a town in Switzerland, in N Berne canton. 66,600 (1964).

bield (bēld), *n. Scot. and N Dial.* shelter.

Bielefeld (*Ger.* bē′lə fĕlt), *n.* a city in West Germany, in NE North Rhine-Westphalia. 170,600 (1966).

Biella (*It.* byĕl′lä), *n.* a town in Italy, in NW Piedmont. 52,468 (1966).

bien entendu (*Fr.* byăN näN täN dʏ′), *French.* naturally; of course.

Bienne (*Fr.* byĕn), *n.* **Lake of,** a lake in NW Switzerland: traces of prehistoric lake dwellings. 16 sq. mi. German, **Bielersee** (*Ger.* bē′lər zē).

biennial (bī ĕn′ĭ əl), *adj.* **1.** happening every two years: *biennial games.* **2.** *Bot.* completing its normal term of life in two years, flowering and fruiting the second year, as beet, winter wheat. —*n.* **3.** any event occurring once in two years. **4.** *Bot.* a biennial plant. [f. s. L *biennium* two-year period + -AL[1]] —**bien′nially,** *adv.*

bienvenu (*Fr.* byăN və nʏ′), *adj. French.* welcome. —**bienvenue′,** *adj., fem.*

Bienville (*Fr.* byăN vēl′), *n.* **Jean Baptiste Le Moyne, Sieur de** (*Fr.* zhäN bȧ tēst lə mwȧn′, syœr′ də), 1680–1768, French governor of Louisiana: founder of New Orleans.

bier (bĭə), *n.* a frame or stand on which a corpse, or the coffin containing it, is laid before burial. [ME *bere,* OE *bēr, bǣr,* c. G *Bahre*]

biestings (bēs′tĭngz), *n. pl.* beestings.

B.I.F., British Industries Fair.

bifacial (bī fā′shəl), *adj.* **1.** having two faces or fronts. **2.** having the opposite surfaces alike. **3.** *Bot.* having the opposite surfaces unlike, as a leaf.

bifarious (bī fĕə′rĭ əs), *adj. Bot.* in two vertical rows. [t. L: m. *bifārius* twofold] —**bifar′iously,** *adv.*

biff (bĭf), *Colloq.* —*n.* **1.** a blow; punch. —*v.t.* **2.** to punch.

biffin (bĭf′ĭn), *n.* a red variety of winter cooking apple. [var. of *beefing,* f. BEEF (from the colour) + -ING[1]]

bifid (bī′fĭd), *adj.* cleft into two parts or lobes. [t. L: s. *bifidus*] —**bifid′ity,** *n.* —**bi′fidly,** *adv.*

bifilar (bī fī′lə), *adj.* furnished or fitted with two filaments or threads. —**bifi′larly,** *adv.*

biflagellate (bī flăj′ĭ lāt′, -lĭt), *adj. Zool.* having two whiplike appendages or flagella.

biflex (bī′flĕks), *adj.* bent at two places.

bifocal (bī fō′kl), *adj.* **1.** *Chiefly Optics.* having two foci. **2.** (of spectacle lenses) having two portions, one for near and one for far vision. —*n.* **3.** (*pl.*) spectacles with bifocal lenses.

bifoliate (bī fō′lĭ ĭt, -āt′), *adj.* having two leaves or leaflets.

biform (bī′fôm′), *adj.* having or combining two forms, as a centaur, mermaid, etc. Also, **bi′formed.** [t. L: s. *biformis*]

Bifrost (bĭv′rŏst), *n. Scand. Myth.* the rainbow bridge of the gods from heaven to earth. [t. Icel.: m. *Bifröst*]

bifurcate (bī′fû kāt′; *adj. also* -kĭt), *v.,* **-cated, -cating,** *adj.* —*v.t., v.i.* **1.** to divide or fork into two branches. —*adj.* **2.** divided into two branches. [t. ML: m. s. *bifurcātus,* der. L *bi-* BI- + *furca* fork] —**bi′furca′tion,** *n.*

big (bĭg), *adj.,* **bigger, biggest,** *adv.* —*adj.* **1.** large in size, height, width, amount, etc. **2.** pregnant: *big with child.* **3.** filled; teeming: *eyes big with tears.* **4.** loud: *a big voice.* **5.** large in compass or conception; magnanimous; generous; liberal: *a big heart, big gesture.* **6.** important in influence, standing, wealth, etc.: *big business, a big financier.* **7.** haughty; pompous; boastful: *big words, a big talker.* **8.** *Obs.* very strong; powerful. —*adv.* **9.** *Colloq.* boastfully: *to talk big.* **10.** *Colloq.* on a grand scale; liberally: *to think big.* [ME; orig. uncert.] —**big′gish,** *adj.* —**big′ness,** *n.* —**Syn. 1.** large, huge, immense; bulky, massive; capacious, voluminous; extensive. See **great. 6.** consequential. **7.** inflated, arrogant. —**Ant. 1.** little, small.

bigamist (bĭg′ə mĭst), *n.* a person guilty of bigamy.

bigamous (bĭg′ə məs), *adj.* **1.** having two wives or husbands at the same time; guilty of bigamy. **2.** involving bigamy. [t. ML: m. *bigamus,* f. *bi-* BI- + *-gamus* (t. Gk: m. *-gamos* married)] —**big′amously,** *adv.*

bigamy (bĭg′ə mĭ), *n. Law.* the crime of marrying while one has a wife or husband still living, from whom no valid divorce has been effected. [ME *bigamie,* t. OF, der. *bigame* BIGAMOUS]

bigarreau (bĭg′ə rō′, bĭg′ə rō′), *n. Hort.* a kind of large, sweet, heart-shaped cherry with firm flesh. [t. F]

big bang theory, *Astron.* the cosmological theory that the universe originated with an explosion of a single superdense agglomeration of matter. The observed expansion of the universe is explained as the fragments from this explosion continuing to fly apart. Cf. **steady state theory.**

Big Ben, 1. the bell in the clock tower of the Houses of Parliament in London. **2.** the clock. **3.** the tower. [named after Sir *Ben(jamin Hall),* First Commissioner of Works at the time of building]

Big Bertha, *Colloq.* a German gun or cannon, esp. one of large size, as used during World War I.

Big Brother, a dictator, esp. one who tries to control people's private lives and thoughts. [from a character in Orwell's novel '*1984*']

big business, powerful financial or business resources, esp. considered collectively.

Big Dipper, 1. *Astron., Chiefly U.S.* the Plough. See **Ursa Major. 2.** (*l.c.*) See **roller-coaster.**

big end, *Motor Vehicles.* the larger end of the connecting rod in a reciprocating engine, which bears on the crankshaft. [short for *big end bearing*]

Big Five, **1.** the United States, Great Britain, France, Italy, and Japan, in World War I and at the Paris Peace Conference, 1919. **2.** the United States, Great Britain, the Soviet Union, Nationalist China, and France, in the United Nations.

Big Four, the United States, Great Britain, the Soviet Union, and France in the United Nations.

big game, **1.** large animals, esp. when hunted for sport. **2.** an important prize or objective.

biggin (bĭg′ĭn), *n.*, **1.** a cap, esp. a child's. **2.** *Dial.* a nightcap. [t. F: m. *béguin* cap worn by Beguines]

bigging (bĭg′ĭng), *n.* *Scot. and N Dial.* a building; home. [der. *big* build (ME *biggen*, t. Scand.)]

bighead (bĭg′hĕd′), *n.* **1.** *Vet. Sci.* an inflammatory swelling of the tissues of the head of sheep. **2.** *Colloq.* a conceited person. —**big′-head′ed,** *adj.*

big-hearted (bĭg′hä′tĭd), *adj.* generous; kind.

bighorn (bĭg′hôn′), *n.*, *pl.* **-horn, -horns.** a wild sheep of the U.S., *Ovis canadensis*, of the Rocky Mountains, with large, curving horns.

Bighorn, *Ovis canadensis* ($3\frac{1}{2}$ ft high at the shoulder, 5 ft 10 in. long)

Big Horn, a river in the U.S. flowing from central Wyoming to the Yellowstone river in S Montana. 336 mi.

Big Horn Mountains, a mountain range in the U.S. in N Wyoming, in the Rocky Mountains. Highest peak, Cloud Peak, 13,165 ft. Also, **Big Horns.**

bight (bīt), *n.* **1.** the part of a rope between the ends. **2.** the loop or bent part of a rope, as distinguished from the ends. **3.** a bend or curve in the shore of a sea or a river. **4.** a body of water bounded by such a bend; a bay. —*v.t.* **5.** to fasten with a bight of rope. [ME *byght*, OE *byht* a bend]

big noise, *Slang.* an important person; bigwig.

bignonia (bĭg nō′nyə), *n.* any plant of the genus *Bignonia*, which comprises climbing shrubs, American and mostly tropical, much cultivated for their showy trumpet-shaped flowers. [t. NL; named after the Abbé *Bignon*, librarian to Louis XV]

bignoniaceous (bĭg nō′nĭ ā′shəs), *adj.* *Bot.* belonging or pertaining to the *Bignoniaceae*, a family of plants including the trumpet flower, catalpa, etc.

bigot (bĭg′ət), *n.* a person who is intolerantly convinced of the rightness of a particular creed, opinion, practice, etc. [t. F; orig. uncert.]

bigoted (bĭg′ə tĭd), *adj.* of or denoting a bigot or his actions. —**big′otedly,** *adv.*

bigotry (bĭg′ə trĭ), *n.*, *pl.* **-ries.** **1.** intolerant attachment to a particular creed, opinion, practice, etc. **2.** the actions or beliefs of a bigot.

big shot, *Slang.* big noise; bigwig.

big-time (bĭg′tīm′), *Slang.* —*adj.* **1.** at the top level in any business or pursuit: *big-time boys.* —*n.* **2.** the top level, esp. in business.

big toe, (in man) the hallux.

big top, **1.** the main tent in a circus. **2.** the circus.

big tree, an extremely large coniferous tree of California, *Sequoiadendron giganteum* (formerly *Sequoia gigantea*). Cf. **sequoia.**

bigwig (bĭg′wĭg′), *n.* *Colloq.* a very important person.

Bihar (bĭ hä′), *n.* **1.** a state in NE India. 46,455,610 pop. (1961); 67,164 sq. mi. *Cap.:* Patna. **2.** a town in this state. 78,581 (1961).

bihourly (bī ou′ə lĭ), *adj.* occurring every two hours.

Biisk (*Russ.* bēysk), *n.* a town in the SW Soviet Union in Asia. 146,000 (est. 1959). Also, **Biysk.**

bijou (bē′zhōō), *n.*, *pl.* **-joux** (-zhōōz). **1.** a jewel. **2.** something small and choice. —*adj.* **3.** small and choice: *bijou cottage.* [t. F]

bijouterie (bĭ zhōō′tə rĭ), *n.* jewellery. [t. F]

bijugate (bī′jŏŏ gāt′, bī jōō′gāt), *adj.* *Bot.* (of leaves) having two pairs of leaflets or pinnae. Also, **bijugous** (bī′jŏŏ gəs). [f. BI- + JUGATE]

Bikaner (*Hind.* bē kä nėr′), *n.* **1.** a former native state in NW India, in Rajputana, now in Rajasthan. **2.** a city in Rajasthan, former capital of the native state. 150,634 (1961).

bike (bīk), *n.*, *v.*, **biked, biking.** *Colloq.* bicycle. [alter. of BICYCLE]

bikini (bĭ kē′nĭ), *n.* a very brief two-piece bathing suit.

Bikini (bĭ kē′nĭ), *n.* an atoll in the N Pacific, in the Marshall Islands: atomic bomb tests, 1946. 3 sq. mi.

bilabial (bī lā′byəl), *Phonet.* —*adj.* **1.** pronounced with the two lips brought close together or touching. In the English bilabial consonants *p*, *b*, and *m*, the lips touch; in the bilabial *w*, they do not. —*n.* **2.** a bilabial speech sound.

bilabiate (bī lā′bĭ āt′, -ĭt), *adj.* *Bot.* two-lipped, as a corolla.

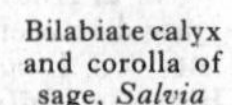

Bilabiate calyx and corolla of sage, *Salvia*

bilander (bĭl′ən də), *n.* *Naut.* a small merchant vessel with two masts, used on canals and along the coast in Holland, etc. [t. D: m. *bijlander*, f. *bij* by + *land* land + *-er* -ER[1]]

bilateral (bī lăt′ə rəl), *adj.* **1.** pertaining to, involving, or affecting two sides or parties. **2.** *Law, etc.* (of a contract) binding the parties to reciprocal obligations. **3.** *Bot., Zool.* pertaining to both sides: *bilateral symmetry.* **4.** disposed on opposite sides of an axis; two-sided. **5.** *Educ.* (of a British school) providing two of the three main types of secondary education (modern, technical, or grammar). —**bilat′eralism, bilat′eralness,** *n.* —**bilat′erally,** *adv.*

Bilbao (bĭl bä′ō; *Sp.* bĕl bä′ó), *n.* a seaport in N Spain, near the Bay of Biscay. 350,884 (1965).

bilberry (bĭl′bə rĭ, -brĭ), *n.*, *pl.* **-ries.** a deciduous ericaceous shrub, *Vaccinium myrtillus*, of the Old World, bearing black edible fruits; blaeberry; whortleberry. [f. *bil* (t. Scand.; cf. Dan. *bølle* bilberry) + BERRY]

bilbo[1] (bĭl′bō), *n.*, *pl.* **-boes.** (*usually pl.*) a long iron bar or bolt with sliding shackles and a lock, formerly used to confine the feet of prisoners. [orig. uncert.]

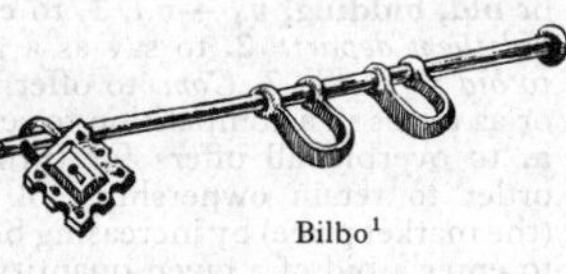

Bilbo[1]

bilbo[2] (bĭl′bō), *n.*, *pl.* **-boes.** *Archaic.* a sword. [short for *Bilbo sword* sword of Bilbao (Spain)]

bilby (bĭl′bĭ), *n.* a nocturnal rat-kangaroo of Australia, *Thalacomys lagotis.* [t. native Australian]

bile (bīl), *n.* **1.** *Physiol.* a bitter yellow or greenish liquid secreted by the liver and aiding in digestion, principally by emulsifying fats. **2.** ill nature; peevishness. [t. F, t. L: m. *bīlis*]

bilection (bī lĕk′shən), *n.* *Archit.* bolection.

bile pigments, *Physiol.* decomposition products of haemoglobin present in bile.

bile salts, *Physiol.* substance (sodium taurocholate and sodium glycocholate) present in bile which aid emulsification of fats in the intestine.

bilestone (bĭl′stōn′), *n.* *Pathol.* a gallstone.

bilge (bĭlj), *n.*, *v.*, **bilged, bilging.** —*n.* **1.** *Naut.* **a.** either of the rounded underportions at either side of a ship's hull. **b.** the lowest portion of a ship's interior. **c.** Also, **bilge water.** foul water that collects in a ship's bilge. **2.** *Slang.* eyewash; rubbish. **3.** the wider part or belly of a cask. —*v.i.* **4.** *Naut.* to spring a leak in the bilge. **5.** to bulge or swell out. —*v.t.* **6.** *Naut.* to break in the bilge of. [orig. unknown]

bilge keel, *Naut.* either of two keel-like projections extending lengthwise along a ship's bilge, one on each side, to retard rolling. Also, **bilge piece.**

bilgy (bĭl′jĭ), *adj.* *Naut.* smelling like bilge water.

bilharzia (bĭl hä′zĭ ə), *n.* **1.** any parasite blood fluke of the family *Schistosomidae*; a schistosome. **2.** bilharziasis. [named after Theodor *Bilharz*, 1829–94, German physician]

bilharziasis (bĭl′hä zī′ə sĭs), *n.* *Med., Vet. Sci.* a chronic disease of man and other animals caused by the presence of the bilharzia worm in the blood; common in tropical and subtropical climates. Also, **bilharziosis** (bĭl hä′-zĭ ō′sĭs).

biliary (bĭl′yə rĭ), *adj.* **1.** *Physiol.* **a.** of bile. **b.** conveying bile: *a biliary duct.* See diag. under **stomach.** **2.** *Pathol.* bilious: *biliary colic.* [t. NL: m. *bīliāris*, der. L *bīlis* bile]

bilinear (bī lĭn′ĭ ə), *adj.* *Maths.* of, pertaining to, or having reference to two lines: *bilinear coordinates.*

bilingual (bī lĭng′gwəl), *adj.* **1.** able to speak one's native language and another with approximately equal facility. **2.** expressed or contained in two different languages. —*n.* **3.** a bilingual person. [f. s. L *bilinguis* speaking two languages + -AL[1]] —**bilin′gually,** *adv.*

bilingualism (bī lĭng′gwə lĭz′əm), *n.* **1.** habitual use of two languages. **2.** ability in being bilingual.

bilious (bĭl′yəs), *adj.* **1.** *Physiol., Pathol.* pertaining to bile or to an excess secretion of bile. **2.** *Pathol.* suffering from, caused by, or attended by trouble with the bile or liver. **3.** peevish; testy; cross. **4.** sickly; nauseating: *a bilious colour.* [t. L: m. s. *bīliōsus* full of bile] **bil′iously,** *adv.* —**bil′iousness,** *n.*

bilirubin (bĭl′ĭ rōō′bĭn), *n.* *Physiol.* the major bile pigment, orange in colour.

-bility, a suffix forming nouns from adjectives in *-ble*, as in *nobility*. [ME *-bilite*, t. F, t. L: m. s. *-bilitas*]

biliverdin (bĭl′ĭ vû′dĭn), *n. Physiol.* a bile pigment, green in colour.

bilk (bĭlk), *v.t.* **1.** to evade payment of (a debt). **2.** to defraud; cheat. **3.** to frustrate. **4.** to escape from; elude. —*n.* **5.** a trick; a fraud. **6.** a cheater; a swindler. [orig. unknown] —**bilk′er,** *n.*

bill[1] (bĭl), *n.* **1.** an account of money owed for goods or services supplied. **2.** a slip or ticket showing the amount owed for goods consumed or purchased, esp. in a restaurant. **3.** *Govt.* a form or draft of a proposed statute presented to a legislature, but not yet enacted or passed and made law. **4.** a written or printed public notice or advertisement: *stick no bills.* **5.** any written paper containing a statement of particulars: *a bill of charges or expenditures.* **6.** a bill of exchange. **7.** *U.S.* a piece of paper money; note. **8.** *Law.* a bill of indictment. **9.** a printed theatre programme or the like. **10.** programme; entertainment: *there is a good bill at the theatre.* **11.** *Obs.* an acknowledgement of debt; a promissory note. —*v.t.* **12.** to announce by bill or public notice: *a new actor was billed for this week.* **13.** to schedule as part of a programme. [ME *bille*, t. Anglo-L: m. *billa*, var. of ML *bulla* seal (see BULL[3])] —**Syn. 4.** poster, notice, advertisement.

bill[2] (bĭl), *n.* **1.** that part of the jaws of a bird covered with a horny sheath; a beak. **2.** *Geog.* a beaklike promontory or headland. —*v.i.* **3.** to join bills or beaks, as doves. **4.** *Colloq.* to kiss. **5. bill and coo, a.** (of doves etc.) to join beaks and make soft murmuring sounds. **b.** *Colloq.* to kiss and talk fondly. [ME; OE *bile* beak]

bill[3] (bĭl), *n.* **1.** a medieval shafted weapon with a broad hook-shaped blade and a spike at the back. **2.** a billhook. **3.** *Naut.* the point or extremity of the fluke of an anchor. [OE *bill* sword, c. G *Bille* pickaxe]

bill[4] (bĭl), *n.* the cry of the bittern. [cf. OE *bylgan* bellow, c. Icel. *bylga* roar]

billabong (bĭl′ə bŏng′), *n. Austral.* **1.** a branch of a river flowing away from the main stream, in some cases returning to it lower down. **2.** a stagnant backwater. **3.** a channel or watercourse that dries up outside the rainy season. [t. native Australian]

billboard[1] (bĭl′bôd′), *n. Chiefly U.S.* a board on which notices or advertisements are posted; a hoarding. [f. BILL[1] (def. 4.) + BOARD]

billboard[2] (bĭl′bôd′), *n. Naut.* a projection placed abaft the cathead, for the bill or fluke of an anchor to rest on. [f. BILL[3] (def. 3) + BOARD]

billet[1] (bĭl′ĭt), *n., v.,* **-eted, -eting.** —*n.* **1.** lodging for a soldier, esp. lodging in private or non-military public buildings. **2.** *Mil.* an official order, written or verbal, directing the person to whom it is addressed to provide such lodging. **3.** a place assigned, as a berth or the like to a member of a ship's crew. **4.** job; appointment. **5.** a small paper or note in writing. —*v.t.* **6.** *Mil.* to direct (a soldier) by ticket, note, or verbal order, where to lodge. **7.** to provide lodging for; quarter. [ME *billette*, t. OF, b. *bille* a writing and *bullette* certificate, der. *bulle* BULL]

billet[2] (bĭl′ĭt), *n.* **1.** a small thick stick of wood, esp. one cut for fuel. **2.** *Metall.* a bar or slab of iron or steel, esp. when obtained from an ingot by forging, etc. **3.** *Archit.* one of a series of short rods forming part of a moulding. **4.** a short strap used for connecting various straps and portions of a harness. **5.** a pocket or loop into which the end of a strap is inserted after passing through a buckle. [ME *billette*, t. OF: m. *billete*, dim. of *bille* log]

Architectural billets

billet-doux (bĭl′ĭ do͞o′; *Fr.* bē yė do͞o′), *n., pl.* **billets-doux** (bĭl′ĭ do͞oz′; *Fr.* bē yė do͞o′). a love-letter. [t. F: lit., sweet note]

billfish (bĭl′fĭsh′), *n., pl.* **-fishes,** (*esp. collectively*) **-fish.** *Chiefly U.S.* any of various fish with a long bill or snout, as the gar, needlefish, or marlin.

billfold (bĭl′fōld′), *n. U.S.* a wallet or pocket-book.

billhead (bĭl′hĕd′), *n.* **1.** a printed heading on paper for making out bills. **2.** a sheet of paper with such a heading. **3.** a printed form for itemized statements.

billhook (bĭl′ho͝ok′), *n.* an instrument with a curved, hooked blade for pruning, etc. Also, **bill.**

billiard (bĭl′yəd), *adj.* of or used in billiards.

billiards (bĭl′yədz), *n.* a game played by two or more persons on a rectangular table enclosed by an elastic ledger or cushion, with balls (**billiard balls**) of ivory or other hard material, driven by means of cues. [t. F: m. *billard*, der. *bille* log. Cf. BILLET[2]] —**bil′liardist,** *n.*

Billhook

billing (bĭl′ĭng), *n.* the relative position in which a performer or act is listed on handbills, posters, etc.

Billingham (bĭl′ĭng əm), *n.* a town in England, in SE Durham. 32,130 (1960).

Billings (bĭl′ĭngz), *n.* **Josh** (*H. W. Shaw*), 1818–85, U.S. humorist.

billingsgate (bĭl′ĭngz gāt′), *n.* coarse language or abuse. [orig., the kind of language heard at BILLINGSGATE]

Billingsgate (bĭl′ĭngz gāt′), *n.* a fish market in central London.

billion (bĭl′yən), *n.* **1.** (in Great Britain, Germany, etc.) a million millions. **2.** (in the U.S., France, etc.) a thousand millions. [t. F: f. *bi-* + (*mi*)*llion*, i.e., the second power of one million (def. 1 agrees with earlier, def. 2 with later, F usage)] —**bil′lionth,** *adj., n.*

billionaire (bĭl′yə nĕə′), *n.* the owner of a billion pounds, dollars, francs, etc.

Billiton (bĭl′lĭ tŏn′, bĭ lē′tŏn), *n.* an island in Indonesia, SW of Borneo. 1866 sq. mi. Also, **Belitong.**

bill of attainder, formerly, a legal act depriving a person of his property if found guilty of treason or a felony.

bill of exchange, a written authorization or order to pay a specified sum of money to a specified person.

bill of fare, a list of foods that are served; menu.

bill of health, a certificate as to the health of a ship's company at the time of her clearing any port.

bill of indictment, a written accusation of crime delivered to a court (formerly to a grand jury), which becomes an indictment if endorsed by the court.

bill of lading, a written receipt given by a carrier for goods accepted for transporting.

bill of quantities, *Bldg Trades.* a document giving all particulars of materials and labour necessary for the erection of a building.

bill of rights, 1. a formal statement of the fundamental rights of the people of a nation. **2.** (*caps.*) an English statute of 1689 confirming, with minor changes, the Declaration of Rights, declaring the rights and liberties of the subjects and settling the succession in William III and Mary II. **3.** (*caps.*) such a statement incorporated in the Constitution of the United States as Amendments 1–10, and in all state constitutions.

bill of sale, a document transferring title in personal property from one person to another, either temporarily as security against a loan or debt (**conditional bill of sale**), or permanently (**absolute bill of sale**).

billon (bĭl′ən), *n.* **1.** an alloy used in coinage, consisting of gold or silver with a preponderating admixture of some base metal. **2.** an alloy of silver with copper or the like, used for coins of small denomination. **3.** any coin struck from such an alloy. [t. F, der. *bille* log]

billow (bĭl′ō), *n.* **1.** a great wave or surge of the sea. **2.** any surging mass: *billows of smoke.* —*v.i.* **3.** to rise or roll in or like billows; surge. [t. Scand.; cf. Icel. *bylgja*]

Billows, Bay of, a plain on the face of the moon.

billowy (bĭl′ō ĭ), *adj.,* **-lowier, -lowiest.** full of billows; surging: *billowy flames.* —**bil′lowiness,** *n.*

billposter (bĭl′pōs′tə), *n.* one who posts bills and advertisements. Also, **billsticker** (bĭl′stĭk′ə).

billy[1] (bĭl′ĭ), *n., pl.* **-ies. 1.** a small cudgel. **2. like billy-o,** *Colloq.* with great vigour or force: *raining like billy-o.* [special use of *Billy*, pet var. of *William*, man's name]

billy[2] (bĭl′ĭ), *n.* (esp. in Australia) a tin kettle or pot, used by bushmen or campers to boil tea, etc. Also, **billycan** (bĭl′ĭ kăn′). [? t. native Australian: m. *billa* water]

billycock (bĭl′ĭ kŏk′), *n. Colloq.* **1.** a round, low-crowned, soft felt hat. **2.** a bowler hat. [var. of *bully-cocked* (*hat*), i.e. hat cocked in the style of a bully]

billy-goat (bĭl′ĭ gōt′), *n.* a male goat.

bilobed (bī′lōbd′), *adj.* having or divided into two lobes. Also, **bilobated.**

bilocular (bī lŏk′yo͞o lə), *adj.* divided into two compartments, or containing two cells internally. Also, **biloculate** (bī lŏk′yo͞o lĭt, -lāt′).

Bilston (bĭl′stən), *n.* a town in England, in S Staffordshire. 33,067 (1961).

biltong (bĭl′tŏng′), *n.* (in South Africa) strips of lean meat dried in the open air. [t. Afrikaans]

bimanous (bĭm′ə nəs, bī mā′-), *adj. Zool.* two-handed. [f. s. NL *bimana* (*animālia*) two-handed (animals) + -OUS]

bimanual (bī măn′yo͞o əl), *adj.* involving the use of both hands. —**biman′ually,** *adv.*

bimbil (bĭm′bĭl), *n.* the eucalyptus, *Eucalyptus populifolia*, of Australia. [t. native Australian]

bimensal (bī mĕn′səl), *adj.* occurring once in two months; bimonthly.

bimestrial (bī mĕs′trĭ əl), *adj.* **1.** occurring every two months; bimonthly. **2.** lasting two months. [f. s. L *bimestri*(*s*) of two months' duration + -AL[1]]

bimetallic (bī′mĭ tăl′ĭk), *adj.* **1.** of two metals. **2.** pertaining to bimetalism. [t. F: m. *bimétallique*]

bimetallism (bī mĕt′ə lĭz′əm), *n.* **1.** the use of two metals, ordinarily gold and silver, at a fixed relative value, as the monetary standard. **2.** the doctrine or policies supporting such a standard. —**bimet′allist,** *n.*

bimonthly (bī mŭnth′lĭ), *adj., n., pl.* **-lies,** *adv.* —*adj.* **1.** occurring every two months. **2.** occurring twice a month; semi-monthly. —*n.* **3.** a bimonthly publication. —*adv.* **4.** every two months. **5.** twice a month; semi-monthly.

bin (bĭn), *n., v.,* **binned, binning.** —*n.* **1.** a box or enclosed place used for storing grain, coal, refuse, and the like. —*v.t.* **2.** to store in a bin. [ME *binne,* OE *binn(e)* crib]

bin-, a form of **bi-,** sometimes used before a vowel, as in *binaural.* [prop. t. L: m. *bīnī* two apiece]

binary (bī′nə rĭ), *adj., n., pl.* **-ries.** —*adj.* **1.** consisting of, indicating, or involving two. **2.** using, involving, or expressed in the binary number system. —*n.* **3.** a whole composed of two. **4.** *Astron.* a binary star. **5.** the binary number system. [t. L: m. s. *bīnārius* consisting of two things]

binary arithmetic, arithmetic using the binary number system.

binary code, any means of representing information by a sequence of the digits 1 and 0.

binary compound, *Chem.* a compound containing only two elements or radicals.

binary digit, a single digit in a binary number.

binary form, *Music.* a form founded on two themes, or on two balancing or answering sections or phrases.

binary notation, the binary number system.

binary number, a number expressed in the binary number system.

binary number system, a number system which uses only the digits 1 and 0, based on the rules $1 + 0 = 1$, $1 + 1 = 10$. Also, **binary system.**

binary scale, binary number system.

binary star, *Astron.* a system of two stars which revolve round their common centre of gravity.

binate (bī′nāt), *adj. Bot.* double; produced or borne in pairs. [t. NL: m. s. *bīnātus,* der. L *bīnī* two at a time] —**bi′nately,** *adv.*

binaural (bĭn ô′rəl), *adj.* **1.** of, with, or for both ears: *binaural hearing, a binaural stethoscope.* **2.** having two ears.

binaural broadcasting, a system of radio broadcasting in which a microphone in one part of a studio broadcasts via FM and one in another part via AM. FM and AM receivers similarly placed provide a stereophonic effect.

bind (bīnd), *v.,* **bound, binding,** *n.* —*v.t.* **1.** to make fast with a band or bond. **2.** to encircle with a band or ligature: *bind up one's hair.* **3.** to swathe or bandage (often fol. by *up*). **4.** to fasten around; fix in place by girding. **5.** to cause to cohere or harden. **6.** to unite by any legal or moral tie: *bound by duty, debt, etc.* **7.** to hold to a particular state, place, employment, etc. **8.** to place under obligation or compulsion (usually passive): *all are bound to obey the laws.* **9.** *Law.* to put under legal obligation (fol. by *over*): *to bind a man over to keep the peace.* **10.** to make compulsory or obligatory: *to bind an order with a deposit.* **11.** to indenture as an apprentice (often fol. by *out*). **12.** *Pathol.* to hinder or restrain (the bowels) from their natural operations; constipate. **13.** to fasten or secure within a cover, as a book. **14.** to cover the edge of, as for protection or ornament. —*v.i.* **15.** to become compact or solid; cohere. **16.** to be obligatory: *an obligation that binds.* **17.** to tie up anything, esp. sheaves of grain. —*n.* **18.** something that binds. **19.** *Colloq.* a nuisance; bore. **20.** a bine. **21.** *Mining.* hardened clay between layers of coal. **22.** *Music.* a tie. **23.** *Fencing.* a thrust which forces the opponent's sword diagonally across the target. [ME *binden,* OE *bindan,* c. G *binden*] —**Syn. 1.** gird, fasten, attach, tie. —**Ant. 1.** free.

binder (bīn′də), *n.* **1.** a person or thing that binds. **2.** a detachable cover for loose papers. **3.** one who binds books; a bookbinder. **4.** *Agric.* **a.** an attachment to a harvester or reaper for binding the cut grain. **b.** a machine that both cuts and binds grain. **5.** *Law.* an informal contract, in force while a more formal document is being drawn up. **6.** a tie beam, esp. in a floor. **7.** *Metall.* a substance used: **a.** to hold crushed ore dust together before and during sintering or refining. **b.** to hold metallic powders (mixed sometimes with non-metals) together after compacting and before sintering in powder metallurgy. **8.** *Bldg Trades.* a material, as cement, used to join masonry.

bindery (bīn′də rĭ), *n.* an establishment for binding books.

binding (bīn′dĭng), *n.* **1.** the act of fastening or uniting. **2.** anything that binds. **3.** the covering within which the leaves of a book are bound. **4.** a strip that protects or adorns the edge of cloth, etc. —*adj.* **5.** having power to bind or oblige; obligatory: *a binding engagement.* —**bind′ingly,** *adv.* —**bind′ingness,** *n.*

binding energy, *Physics.* the energy required to split an atomic nucleus into its constituent nucleons.

Bin Dinh (bĭn′dĭn′), a town in South Vietnam. ab. 147,000 (est. 1968).

bindweed (bīnd′wēd′), *n.* any of various twining or vinelike plants, esp. certain species of *Convolvulus.*

bine (bīn), *n.* **1.** a twining plant stem, as of the hop. **2.** any bindweed. **3.** woodbine (defs 1, 2). [var. of BIND]

Binet (bē′nā; *Fr.* bē nĕ′), *n.* **Alfred** (*Fr.* àl frĕd′), 1857–1911, French psychologist: deviser of Binet test.

Binet test (bē′nā; *Fr.* bē nĕ′), *Psychol.* a test for determining the relative development of the intelligence of children and others, consisting of a series of questions and tasks graded with reference to the ability of the normal child to deal with them at successive age levels. Also, **Binet-Simon test** (-sī′mən; *Fr.* -sē mōɴ′).

binge (bĭnj), *n. Slang.* a spree; a period of excessive indulgence, as in eating or drinking. [Lincolnshire d.: *binge* (v.) to soak]

Bingen (*Ger.* bĭng′ən), *n.* a town in W West Germany, on the Rhine: whirlpool; tourist centre. 15,373 (est. 1963).

bingey (bĭn′jĭ), *n. Austral. and N.Z. Colloq.* the stomach; belly. Also, **bingy.** [t. native Australian]

binghi (bĭng′ī), *n. Austral. Slang.* an Aborigine. [t. native Australian]

Bingley (bĭng′lĭ), *n.* a town in England, in the central West Riding of Yorkshire. 22,308 (1961).

bingo (bĭng′gō), *n.* **1.** a widely popular game of chance in which numbers are selected at random and contestants cover corresponding numbers on individual cards. —*interj.* **2.** (an exclamation expressing triumph at a discovery or achievement.)

binnacle (bĭn′ə kl), *n. Naut.* a special stand of non-magnetic material built in the hull of a ship for housing the compass and fitted with lights by which the compass can be read at night. [earlier *bittacle,* t. Pg.: m. *bitacola,* or t. Sp.: m. *bitácula,* ult. t. L: m. *habitāculum* dwelling place]

binocle (bĭn′ŏk′l), *n.* a pair of binoculars. [t. F, t. NL: m. s. *bīnoclus,* f. L: *bīn(ī)* two at a time + m. *oculus* eye]

binocular (bĭ nŏk′yŏŏ lə, bī-), *adj.* **1.** involving (the use of) two eyes: *binocular vision.* —*n.* **2.** (*pl.*) a double telescope used by both eyes at once; field-glasses. —**binocularity** (bĭ nŏk′yŏŏ lăr′ĭ tĭ), *n.* —**binoc′ularly,** *adv.*

binomial (bī nō′myəl), *n.* **1.** *Alg.* an expression which is a sum or difference of two terms, as $3x + 2y$ and $x^2 - 4x$. **2.** *Zool., Bot.* binominal. —*adj.* **3.** *Alg.* consisting of or pertaining to two terms or a binomial. **4.** *Zool., Bot.* binominal. [f. s. LL *binōmius* having two names + -AL[1]] —**bino′mially,** *adv.*

binomial distribution, *Statistics.* a distribution giving the probability of obtaining a specified number of successes in a set of trials where each trial can end in either a success or a failure.

binomial theorem, *Alg.* a formula giving the power of any binomial without multiplying out all the terms.

binominal (bī nŏm′ĭ nəl), *n. Zool., Bot.* **1.** a name consisting of two terms, denoting respectively genus and species, as *Felis leo,* the lion. —*adj.* **2.** consisting of or characterized by binominals. Also, **binomial.** [f. BI- + NOMINAL]

bint (bĭnt), *n. Slang.* a girl. [t. Ar.]

binturong (bĭn′tyŏŏ rŏng′, bĭn tyŏŏə′rŏng), *n.* a large, arboreal SE Asian civet, *Arctictis binturong.*

binucleate (bī nyŏŏ′klĭ āt′, -ĭt), *adj.* having two nuclei, as some cells. Also, **binu′clear, binu′cleat′ed.**

Binyon (bĭn′yən), *n.* **Lawrence,** 1869–1943, English poet, translator, and art historian.

bio-, a word element meaning 'life', 'living things', as in *biology.* [t. Gk, comb. form of *bios* life]

bioastronautics (bī′ō ăs′trə nô′tĭks), *n.* (*construed as sing.*) the science dealing with the effects of space travel on animals and plants.

Bío-Bío (*Sp.* bē′ō bē′ō), *n.* a river in central Chile flowing from the Andes NW to the Pacific at Concepción. ab. 250 mi.

biocellate (bī ŏs′ĭ lāt′, -lĭt, bī′ō sĕl′ĭt), *adj. Zool., Bot.* marked with two ocelli or eyelike parts.

biochemistry (bī′ō kĕm′ĭs trĭ), *n.* the chemistry of living matter. *Abbrev.*: biochem. —**biochemical** (bī′ō kĕm′ĭ kl), **bi′ochem′ic,** *adj.* —**bi′ochem′ically,** *adv.* —**bi′ochem′ist,** *n.*

bioclimatology (bī′ō klī′mə tŏl′ə jĭ), *n.* the study of the effect of climate on the life and health of animals, esp. humans.

biodynamics (bī′ō dī năm′ĭks, -dĭ-), *n.* the branch of biology that treats of energy, or of the activity of living organisms (opposed to *biostatics*). **—bi′odynam′ic, bi′odynam′ical,** *adj.*

biog., 1. biographical. 2. biography.

biogenesis (bī′ō jĕn′ĭ sĭs), *n. Biol.* the doctrine that living organisms come from other living organisms only. Also, **biogeny** (bī ŏj′ĭ nĭ). **—biogenetic** (bī′ō jĭ nĕt′ĭk), *adj.* **—bi′ogenet′ically,** *adv.*

biogeography (bī′ō jĭ ŏg′rə fĭ), *n. Ecol.* the study of the geographical distribution of living things.

biographer (bī ŏg′rə fə), *n.* a writer of biography.

biographical (bī′ə grăf′ĭ kl), *adj.* **1.** of or pertaining to a person's life. **2.** pertaining to biography. Also, **bi′ograph′ic. —bi′ograph′ically,** *adv.*

biography (bī ŏg′rə fĭ), *n., pl.* **-phies. 1.** a written account of a person's life. **2.** such writings collectively. **3.** the study of the lives of individuals. **4.** the art of writing a biography. [t. Gk: m. s. *biographia*]

biol., 1. biological. 2. biology.

biological (bī′ə lŏj′ĭ kl), *adj.* Also, **bi′olog′ic. 1.** pertaining to biology. **2.** of or pertaining to the products and operations of applied biology: *a biological preparation or test.* **—***n.* **3.** *Biol., Pharm.* any biochemical product, esp. serums, vaccines, etc., produced from micro-organisms. **—bi′olog′ically,** *adv.*

biological control, a method of controlling pests by introducing one of their natural enemies.

biological shield, a thick wall surrounding a nuclear reactor, to protect workers from radiation.

biological warfare, warfare which makes use of biologically produced poisons that affect man, domestic animals, or food crops, esp. bacteria or viruses. Also, **B.W.**

biology (bī ŏl′ə jĭ), *n.* the science of life or living matter in all its forms and phenomena, esp. with reference to origin, growth, reproduction, structure, etc. **—biol′ogist,** *n.*

bioluminescence (bī′ō lo͞o′mĭ nĕs′əns), *n.* the production of light by living organisms. **—bi′olu′mines′cent,** *adj.*

biolysis (bī ŏl′ĭ sĭs), *n. Biol.* dissolution of a living being; death; the destruction of the phenomena of life, esp. the chemical decomposition of organic matter. **—biolytic** (bī′ō lĭt′ĭk), *adj.*

biometrics (bī′ō mĕt′rĭks), *n.* **1.** *Biol.* the application of mathematical-statistical theory to biology. **2.** biometry. **—bi′omet′ric, bi′omet′rical,** *adj.* **—bi′omet′rically,** *adv.*

biometry (bī ŏm′ĭ trĭ), *n.* the calculation of the probable duration of human life.

Bion (bī′ŏn), *n.* fl. *c.* 100 B.C. Greek pastoral poet.

bionomics (bī′ō nŏm′ĭks), *n.* ecology (def. 1). [f. BIO- + *-nomics,* as in ECONOMICS] **—bi′onom′ic, bi′onom′ical,** *adj.* **—bi′onom′ically,** *adv.* **—bionomist** (bī ŏn′əmĭst), *n.*

biophysics (bī′ō fĭz′ĭks), *n.* that branch of biology which deals with biological structures and processes in terms of physics. **—bi′ophys′ical,** *adj.*

biopsy (bī′ŏp′sĭ), *n. Med.* the excision and diagnostic study of a piece of tissue from a living body.

bioscope (bī′ə skōp′), *n.* **1.** *Now Chiefly S African.* cinema. **2.** an early form of film projector (about 1900). **3.** *Obs.* a film, esp. a newsreel.

bioscopy (bī ŏs′kə pĭ), *n. Med.* examination of the body to discover whether or not it is alive.

-biosis, a word element meaning 'way of life', as in *symbiosis.* [comb. form repr. Gk *biōsis*]

biosphere (bī′ə sfĭə′), *n.* the part of the earth where living organisms are to be found.

biostatics (bī′ō stăt′ĭks), *n.* the branch of biology that treats of the structure of organisms in relation to their functions (opposed to *biodynamics*). **—bi′ostat′ic, bi′ostat′ical,** *adj.*

biosynthesis (bī′ō sĭn′thĭ sĭs), *n. Biochem.* the synthesis of complex substances from simpler compounds by living organisms.

biota (bī ō′tə), *n. Ecol.* the animal and plant life of a region or period. [t. NL, t. Gk: m. *biotē* life]

biotic (bī ŏt′ĭk), *adj.* pertaining to life. Also, **biot′ical.**

biotin (bī′ə tĭn), *n. Biochem.* a crystalline acid, $C_{10}H_{16}N_2O_3S$, one of the vitamin B complex factors; vitamin H. It will prevent the death of animals which have been fed large quantities of raw white of eggs.

biotite (bī′ə tīt′), *n.* a very common mineral of the mica group, occurring in dark brown or green or black sheets and scales, an important constituent of igneous rocks. [named after J. B. *Biot,* 1774–1862, French physicist. See -ITE[1]] **—biotitic** (bī′ə tĭt′ĭk), *adj.*

biotype (bī′ə tīp′), *n. Biol.* a group of organisms with the same hereditary characteristics; genotype. **—biotypic** (bī′ə tĭp′ĭk), *adj.*

biparietal (bī′pə rī′ĭ tl), *adj. Anat.* pertaining to both parietal bones.

biparous (bĭp′ə rəs), *adj.* **1.** *Zool.* bringing forth offspring in pairs. **2.** *Bot.* bearing two branches or axes.

bipartisan (bī′pä tĭ zăn′), *adj.* representing, supported, or characterized by two parties, esp. political parties. **—bi′partisan′ship,** *n.*

bipartite (bī pä′tīt), *adj.* **1.** *Law.* **a.** being in two corresponding parts: *a bipartite contract.* **b.** affecting two parties; bilateral. **2.** *Bot.* divided into two parts nearly to the base, as a leaf. [t. L: m. s. *bipartītus,* pp., divided into two parts] **—bipar′titely,** *adv.* **—bipartition** (bī′pä tĭsh′ən), *n.*

biped (bī′pĕd), *Zool.* **—***n.* **1.** a two-footed animal. **—***adj.* **2.** having two feet. [t. L: s. *bipēs* two-footed]

bipedal (bī′pĕd′l), *adj.* biped.

bipetalous (bī pĕt′ə ləs), *adj. Bot.* having two petals.

biphenyl (bī fēn′əl, -fē′nəl), *n. Chem.* a colourless crystalline compound, $C_6H_5C_6H_5$, composed of two phenyl groups. The benzidine dyes are derivatives of biphenyl.

bipinnate (bī pĭn′āt, bī pĭn′ĭt), *adj. Bot.* pinnate, as a leaf, with the divisions also pinnate.

biplane (bī′plān′), *n.* an aeroplane or glider with two pairs of wings, one above and usually slightly forward of the other.

bipod (bī′pŏd), *n.* a two-legged support, as for a machine-gun. [f. BI- + -POD. Cf. TRIPOD]

Bipinnate leaf

bipolar (bī pō′lə), *adj.* **1.** having two poles. **2.** pertaining to or found at both poles. **—bipolarity** (bī′pō lăr′ĭ tĭ), *n.*

bipropellant (bī′prə pĕl′ənt), *n. Astronautics.* a liquid rocket propellant in the form of two substances, a fuel and an oxidant.

biquadrate (bī kwŏd′rāt, -rĭt), *n. Maths.* the fourth power.

biquadratic (bī′kwŏd răt′ĭk), *adj. Maths.* involving the fourth, but no higher, power of the unknown or variable.

biradial symmetry (bī rā′dyəl), *Biol.* symmetry manifested both bilaterally and radially in the same creature, as in ctenophores.

birch (bûch), *n.* **1.** any tree or shrub of the genus *Betula,* comprising species with a smooth, laminated outer bark and close-grained wood. **2.** the wood itself. **3.** a birch rod, or a bundle of birch twigs, used as a whip. **—***adj.* **4.** of or pertaining to birch. **5.** consisting or made of birch. **—***v.t.* **6.** to beat or punish with a birch. [ME *birche,* OE *bierce,* c. G *Birke*]

Birch (bûch), *n.* See **John Birch Society.**

birchen (bû′chən), *adj. Archaic.* birch.

Birchite (bû′chīt), *n.* a member or follower of the John Birch Society and its principles. Also, **Bircher. —Bir′chism,** *n.*

bird[1] (bûd), *n.* **1.** any of the *Aves,* a class of warm-blooded vertebrates having a body more or less completely covered with feathers, and the forelimbs so modified as to form wings by means of which most species fly. **2.** *Sport.* **a.** a game bird. **b.** a clay pigeon. **3.** *Slang.* a person, esp. one having some peculiarity. **4.** *Slang.* a sound of derision, esp. hissing: *to get the bird.* **5.** *Archaic.* the young of any fowl. **—***v.i.* **6.** to catch or shoot birds. [ME *byrd, bryd,* OE *brid(d)* young bird, chick] **—bird′less,** *adj.* **—bird′like′,** *adj.*

bird[2] (bûd), *n. Colloq.* a girl; a girlfriend. [alter. of BURD]

birdbath (bûd′bäth′), *n.* a small bath, usually of stone, placed in a garden for wild birds.

birdcage (bûd′kāj′), *n.* a wicker or wire cage for tame birds.

bird call, 1. a sound made by a bird. **2.** a sound imitating that of a bird. **3.** a device used to imitate the sound of a bird.

bird-cherry (bûd′chĕ′rĭ), *n.* **1.** an Old World wild cherry, *Prunus padus.* **2.** its fruit.

bird dog, *U.S.* a gun dog.

bird-fancier (bûd′făn′sĭ ə, -făn′syə), *n.* one who rears or sells birds.

bird-foot (bûd′fo͝ot′), *n.* bird's-foot.

birdie (bû′dĭ), *n.* **1.** bird; small bird. **2.** *Golf.* a score of one stroke under par on a hole.

birdlime (bûd′līm′), *n., v.,* **-limed, -liming. —***n.* **1.** a sticky material, prepared from holly, mistletoe or other plants and smeared on twigs to catch small birds which light on it. **—***v.t.* **2.** to smear or catch with or as with birdlime.

birdman (bûd′măn′, -mən), *n., pl.* **-men** (-mĕn′, -mən). **1.** fowler. **2.** ornithologist. **3.** *Colloq.* aviator.

bird of paradise, any bird of the family *Paradiseidae,* of New Guinea, etc., noted for magnificent plumage, as *Paradisea apoda.*

bird of passage, 1. a bird that migrates seasonally. **2.** a restless person; one who does not stay in one place for long.

bird of peace, dove.

bird of prey, *Ornith.* any of numerous predatory, flesh-eating birds such as the eagles, hawks, kites, vultures, owls, etc., most of which have strong beaks and claws for catching, killing and tearing to pieces the animals on which they feed.

bird pepper, a variety of extremely strong pepper, *Capsicum frutescens,* with small, elongated berries.

birdseed (bûd′sēd′), *n.* small seed, esp. that of a grass, *Phalaris canariensis,* used as food for birds.

bird's-eye (bûdz′ī′), *adj.* **1.** seen from above: *a bird's-eye view of a city.* **2.** general; not detailed: *a bird's-eye view of history.* **3.** having spots or markings resembling birds' eyes: *bird's-eye maple.* **—***n.* **4.** any of various plants with small, round, bright-coloured flowers, as a primrose, *Primula farinosa,* the germander speedwell, *Veronica chamaedrys,* or a variety of tobacco. **5.** a type of weave with small, eyelike figures. **6.** a fabric, either cotton or linen, of such a weave, used esp. for towelling.

bird's-foot (bûdz′fo͝ot′), *n.* any of the slender leguminous herbs of the genus *Ornithopus,* esp. *O. perpusillus,* in which the pods on each stalk are spread out and resemble the claws of a bird's foot.

bird's-foot trefoil, **1.** a fabaceous plant, *Lotus corniculatus,* the legumes of which spread like a crow's foot. **2.** any similar plant of the same genus.

bird's-foot violet, a violet, *Viola pedata,* cultivated for its large light-blue or whitish flowers with yellow eyes.

bird's-nest (bûdz′nĕst′), *v.i.* to search for bird's nests, often in order to steal the eggs.

bird's-nest orchid, a perennial orchid, *Neottia nidus-avis,* with a mass of thick, fleshy roots, growing in dense woods usually of beech.

bird's-nest soup, a Chinese soup prepared from the gelatinous nests of any of several species of Indo-Australian swift of the *Collocalia* family.

birds of a feather, people of similar worth or character (often derogatory).

birdsong (bûd′sŏng′), *n.* the song of a bird.

bird-spider (bûd′spī′də), *n.* any of several large bird-eating spiders found in Brazil, of the family *Aviculariidae.*

bird-table (bûd′tā′bl), *n.* a table in a garden on which scraps, etc., are put for wild birds, esp. in winter.

birdwoman (bûd′wo͝om′ən), *n., pl.* **-women.** *Colloq.* a female aviator.

Birdwood (bûd′wo͝od′), *n.* **William Riddell, 1st Baron,** 1865–1951, British soldier and educationist.

birefringence (bī′rĭf rĭn′jəns), *n. Mineral.* double refraction of light, as exhibited by crystalline minerals esp. calcite. [BI- + REFRINGENCE] **—bi′refrin′gent,** *adj.*

bireme (bī′rēm), *n.* a galley having two banks or tiers of oars. [t. L: m.s. *birēmis,* lit., two-oared]

biretta (bĭ rĕt′ə), *n.* a stiff, square cap with three (or four) upright projecting pieces extending from the centre of the top to the edge, worn by Roman Catholic ecclesiastics. Also, **berretta.** [t. It.: m. *berretta,* der. L *birrus* cap]

Biretta

Birkenhead (bûr′kən hĕd′, bû′kən hĕd′), *n.* **1. Frederick Edwin Smith, 1st Earl of,** 1872–1930, British lawyer, statesman, and writer. **2.** a port in England, in NW Cheshire, on the Mersey opposite Liverpool. 143,680 (1965).

Birkett (bû′kĭt), *n.* **William Norman, 1st Baron,** 1883–1962, English lawyer and politician.

birl (bûl), *v.t., v.i. U.S.* **1.** *Lumbering.* to cause (a floating log) to rotate rapidly by treading upon it. **2.** to cause (a coin, etc.) to spin.

Birmingham (bû′mĭng əm *for 1*; -hăm′ *for 2*), *n.* **1.** a city in central England, in NW Warwickshire: industrial centre: university (founded 1960). 1,115,630 (1961). **2.** a town in the U.S., in central Alabama. 340,887 (1960).

Biro (bī′ə rō), *n. Trademark.* a type of ballpoint pen.

birth (bûth), *n.* **1.** the fact of being born: *the day of his birth.* **2.** the act of bearing or bringing forth; parturition. **3.** lineage; extraction; descent: *of Grecian birth.* **4.** high or noble lineage. **5.** supposedly natural heritage: *a musician by birth.* **6.** that which is born. **7.** any coming into existence; origin: *the birth of Protestanism.* [ME *byrth(e),* t. Scand.; cf. Icel. *byrdh*] **—Syn. 3.** parentage, race, family.

birth certificate, a certificate issued by a registrar upon the birth of each person, recording sex and parentage.

birth control, the regulation of birth through the deliberate control or prevention of conception.

birthday (bûth′dā′), *n.* **1.** (of persons) the day of one's birth. **2.** (of things) origin or beginning. **3.** the anniversary of one's birth or the origin of something. **—***adj.* **4.** given on, held on, or connected with a birthday.

birthday honours, (in Britain) honours conferred on the official birthday of the ruling monarch.

birthday suit, *Colloq.* the naked skin; state of nakedness.

birthmark (bûth′mäk′), *n.* a congenital mark on the body.

birthnight (bûth′nīt′), *n.* the night of one's birth.

birthplace (bûth′plās′), *n.* place of birth or origin.

birthrate (bûth′rāt′), *n.* the proportion of the number of births in a place in a given time to the total population.

birthright (bûth′rīt′), *n.* any right or privilege to which a person is entitled by birth.

birthroot (bûth′ro͞ot′), *n.* **1.** a species of trillium, *Trillium erectum,* the roots of which are used in medicine. **2.** any of certain other species of trillium.

birthwort (bûth′wût′), *n.* **1.** a plant, *Aristolochia clematitis,* a native of Europe, said to ease childbirth. **2.** any of certain other species of the genus *Aristolochia.* **3.** birthroot.

bis (bĭs), *adv.* **1.** twice. **2.** a second time: used (esp. in music) to direct a repetition. [t. L. See BI-]

bis., bissextile.

Bisayan (bĭ sī′ən), *n.* Visayan.

Bisayas (*Sp.* bē sȧ′yȧs), *n.* Spanish name of the **Visayan Islands.**

Biscay (bĭs′kā, -kĭ), *n.* **Bay of,** a large bay of the Atlantic between W France and N Spain.

biscuit (bĭs′kĭt), *n.* **1.** a small, dry cake made from stiff sweet dough, chopped, rolled, or sliced, and then baked. **2.** *U.S.* a bap. **3.** a pale brown colour. **4.** pottery after the first baking and before glazing. **—***adj.* **5.** pale brown. [ME *besquite,* t. OF: m. *bescuit,* f. *bes* (g. L *bis*) twice + *cuit,* pp. of *cuire* cook (g. L *coquere*)] **—bis′cuit-like′, bis′cuity,** *adj.*

bise (bēz), *n.* a dry, cold north or north-east wind in south-eastern France, Switzerland, and adjoining regions. [t. F, t. Gmc; cf. OHG *bisa*]

bisect (bī sĕkt′), *v.t.* **1.** to cut or divide into two parts. **2.** *Geom.* to cut or divide into two equal parts. **—***v.i.* **3.** to split into two, as a road; fork. **—bisec′tion,** *n.* **—bisec′tional,** *adj.* **—bisec′tionally,** *adv.*

bisector (bī sĕk′tə), *n. Geom.* a line or plane bisecting an angle or line segment.

biserrate (bī sĕ′rāt, -rĭt), *adj. Bot.* double serrate; notched like a saw, with the teeth also notched.

bisexual (bī sĕk′syo͞o əl), *adj. Biol.* **1.** of both sexes. **2.** combining male and female organs in one individual; hermaphroditic. **—***n.* **3.** *Biol.* one who has the reproductive organs of both sexes. **4.** a person sexually attracted to either sex. **—bisex′ualism,** *n.* **—bisex′ually,** *adv.*

bishop (bĭsh′əp), *n.* **1.** a clergyman consecrated for the spiritual direction of a diocese, being in the Greek, Roman Catholic, Anglican, and other churches a member of the highest order in the ministry. **2.** a spiritual overseer in the early Christian Church, either of a local church or of a number of churches. **3.** *Chess.* a piece which moves obliquely on squares of the same colour. **4.** a hot drink made of port wine, oranges, cloves, etc. [ME; OE *bisc(e)op,* t. VL: (m.) s. *(e)biscopus,* var. of L *episcopus,* t. Gk: m. *episkopos* overseer] **—bish′opless,** *adj.*

bishopbird (bĭsh′əp bûd′), *n.* any of various brightly coloured African birds of the weaver family, as the **red bishopbird,** *Pyromelana orix.*

Bishop Aukland, a town in England, in county Durham. 35,276 (1961).

bishopric (bĭsh′əp rĭk), *n.* the see, diocese, or office of a bishop. [ME *bisshoprike,* OE *bisceoprīce,* f. *bisceop* bishop + *rice* dominion]

bishop's-cap (bĭsh′əps kăp′), *n.* mitrewort.

Bishop's Stortford (stô′fəd), a town in England, in E Hertfordshire. 18,342 (1961).

bishop's-weed (bĭsh′əps wēd′), *n.* an umbelliferous perennial herb with long rhizomes, *Aegopodium podagraria,* a native of Europe and temperate Asia, but widely naturalized elsewhere and frequently becoming a persistent weed; herb Gerard; goutweed; ground elder.

bisk (bĭsk), *n.* bisque[1].

Biskra (bĭs′krä), *n.* a town and oasis in NE Algeria, in the Sahara. 55,400 (est. 1966).

Bismarck (bĭz′mäk; *Ger.* bĭs′märk), *n.* **1. Otto von** (*Ger.* ŏt′ō fōn) (*Prince Otto Eduard Leopold von Bismarck Schönhausen*), 1815–98, German statesman: first chancellor of the modern German Empire, 1871–90. **2.** a city in the U.S., the capital of North Dakota, in the central part. 27,670 (1960).

Bismarck Archipelago, a group of islands in the SW Pacific NE of New Guinea, including the Admiralty Islands, New Britain, New Ireland, and adjacent islands: under Australian administration. ab. 23,000 sq. mi.

bismillah (bĭz mĭl′ə, bĭs-), *interj.* in the name of Allah. [Ar.]

bismuth (bĭz′məth), *n. Chem.* a brittle, metallic element, having compounds used in medicine. *Symbol*: Bi; *at. no.*: 83; *at. wt*: 208·98; *sp. gr.*: 9·8 at 20° C. [t. G, var. of *Wismut*; orig. uncert.] —**bis′muthal,** *adj.*

bismuthic (bĭz myōō′thĭk, -mŭth′ĭk), *adj. Chem.* of or containing bismuth, esp. in the pentavalent state.

bismuthinite (bĭz mŭth′ĭ nīt′), *n.* a mineral, bismuth sulphide, Bi_2S_3, occurring in lead-coloured masses; an ore of bismuth.

bismuthous (bĭz′mə thəs), *adj. Chem.* containing trivalent bismuth.

bison (bī′sən), *n., pl.* **-son.** *Zool.* **1.** a large North American bovine ruminant, *Bison bison* (**American bison,** or buffalo), with high, well-haired shoulders. **2.** the aurochs. [t. L, t. Gmc; cf. G *Wisent*]

American bison, *Bison bison* (10 to 12 ft long, ab. 6 ft high at the shoulder)

bisque[1] (bĭsk), *n.* **1.** any smooth, creamy soup. **2.** a thick soup made of shellfish or game stewed long and slowly. Also, **bisk.** [t. F]

bisque[2] (bĭsk), *n.* a point, extra turn, or the like, allowed to a player as odds in tennis and other games. [t. F; orig. unknown]

bisque[3] (bĭsk), *n.* **1.** pottery which has been baked but not glazed; biscuit. **2.** a variety of white unglazed porcelain. [short for BISCUIT]

Bissao (*Port.* bē sȧw′), *n.* a seaport in and capital of Portuguese Guinea. 24,936 (1960). Also, **Bissau.**

bissextile (bĭ sĕks′tĭl), *adj.* **1.** containing or denoting the extra day of leap year. —*n.* **2.** a leap year. [t. LL: m. s. *bissextilis* (*annus*) leap year]

bistort (bĭs′tôt), *n.* **1.** a European perennial herb, *Polygonum bistorta*, with a twisted root, which is sometimes used as an astringent; snakeweed; adder's-wort. **2.** a plant of other allied species, as **Virginia bistort,** *P. virginianum*, and **Alpine bistort,** *P. viviparum*. [f. L: *bis* twice + s. *torta*, pp. fem., twisted]

bistoury (bĭs′tōō rĭ), *n., pl.* **-ries.** a small, narrow surgical knife. [t. F: m. *bistouri*]

bistre (bĭs′tə), *n.* **1.** a brown pigment extracted from the soot of wood, much used in pen and wash drawings. **2.** a dark brown colour. Also, *U.S.*, **bister.** [t. F: m. *bistre*; orig. unknown, ? akin to F *bis* dark grey]

bistro (bēs′trō; *Fr.* bēs trō′), *n. Colloq.* a small, modern restaurant or cafe. [t. F]

bisulphate (bī sŭl′fāt), *n. Chem.* a salt of sulphuric acid, containing the radical HSO_4.

bisulphide (bī sŭl′fīd), *n. Chem.* disulphide.

bisulphite (bī sŭl′fīt), *n. Chem.* a salt of sulphurous acid, containing the radical HSO_3.

Bisutun (bē′sōō tōōn′), *n.* Behistun.

bisymmetrical (bī′sĭ mĕt′rĭ kl), *adj. Bot.* having two planes of symmetry at right angles to each other. Also, **bi′symmet′ric.** —**bi′symmet′rically,** *adv.* —**bisymmetry** (bī sĭm′ĭ trĭ), *n.*

bit[1] (bĭt), *n., v.,* **bitted, bitting.** —*n.* **1.** the metallic mouthpiece of a bridle, with the adjacent parts to which the reins are fastened. See illus. under **harness. 2.** anything that curbs or restrains. **3.** *Mach.* the cutting or penetrating part of various tools: **a.** the cutting portion of an axe or hatchet or the removable cutter in the plane, brace, etc. **b.** the movable boring or drilling part (in many forms) used in a carpenter's brace, a drilling machine, or the like. **4.** the part of a key which enters the lock and acts on the bolt and tumblers. **5. take the bit between one's teeth, a.** to throw off control; rush headlong. **b.** to take the plunge, rejecting all restraint; throw one's energies into something. —*v.t.* **6.** to put up a bit in the mouth of. **7.** to curb; restrain. **8.** to grind a bit on. [ME *byt*, OE *bite* action of biting] —**bit′less,** *adj.*

Spiral bits (def. 3b)

bit[2] (bĭt), *n.* **1.** a small piece or quantity of anything: *a bit of string, a bit of one's mind.* **2.** a short time: *wait a bit.* **3.** a coin worth more than one unit of currency: *threepenny bit, two shilling bit.* **4.** the smallest amount; jot; whit. **5.** share or part of a duty, task, etc.: *do one's bit.* **6.** *U.S. Colloq.* twelve and a half cents. **7. bit by bit,** slowly; gradually; in stages. **8. a bit of,** rather: *a bit of a nuisance.* **9. not a bit of it,** not at all; by no means. [ME *bite*, OE *bita* bit, morsel] —**Syn. 1.** particle, speck, grain, mite; scrap, fragment.

bit[3] (bĭt), *n.* a single, basic unit of information, used in connection with computers and communication theory. [short for B(INARY DIG)IT]

bitartrate (bī tä′trāt), *n. Chem.* a tartrate in which only one of the acid hydrogens of tartaric acid is replaced by a metal or a positive radical; an acid tartrate.

bitch (bĭch), *n.* **1.** a female dog. **2.** a female of canines generally. **3.** *Slang.* a woman, esp. a disagreeable or malicious one. **4.** *Slang.* a complaint. —*v.i.* **5.** *Slang.* to complain. —*v.t.* **6.** *Slang.* to spoil; bungle. [ME *biche*, OE *bicce*, c. Icel *bikkja*]

bite (bīt), *v.,* **bit, bitten** or **bit, biting,** *n.* —*v.t.* **1.** to cut into or wound, or cut (*off, out,* etc.) with the teeth. **2.** to grip with the teeth. **3.** to cut or pierce. **4.** to sting, as an insect. **5.** to cause to smart or sting. **6.** to eat into or corrode, as an acid does. **7.** *Slang.* to trouble; worry; disturb: *what's biting him?* **8.** *Etching.* to use acid for eating into such parts of a copper or other surface as are left bare of a protective coating. **9.** to make a great impression on: *bitten by the love of music.* **10.** to close the teeth tightly on. **11.** to take firm hold or act effectively on. **12.** to cheat; deceive. —*v.i.* **13.** to press the teeth (*into, on,* etc.); snap. **14.** *Angling.* (of fish) to take the bait. **15.** to accept a deceptive offer or suggestion. **16.** to act effectively; grip; hold. —*n.* **17.** the act of biting. **18.** a wound made by biting. **19.** a cutting, stinging, or nipping effect. **20.** pungency; sharpness. **21.** a small piece bitten off. **22.** food: *not a bite to eat.* **23.** a small meal. **24.** *Mach.* **a.** the catch or hold that one object or one part of a mechanical apparatus has on another. **b.** a surface brought into contact to obtain a hold or grip, as in a lathe, chuck, or similar device. **25.** (in a file) the roughness or power of abrasion. [ME *biten*, OE *bītan*, c. G *beissen*] —**bit′er,** *n.*

Bithynia (bĭ thĭn′ĭ ə), *n.* an ancient country in NW Asia Minor.

biting (bī′tĭng), *adj.* **1.** nipping; keen: *biting cold.* **2.** cutting; sarcastic: *a biting remark.* —**bit′ingly,** *adv.*

Bitolj (*Serb.* bē′tôly), *n.* a town in S Yugoslavia. 49,001 (1961). Turkish, **Monastir.**

bitonality (bī′tō năl′ĭ tĭ), *n. Music.* the use in composition, etc., of two keys simultaneously.

bit part, *Theat.* a small or unimportant role.

bitstock (bĭt′stŏk′), *n. Mach.* a brace.

bitt (bĭt), *Naut.* —*n.* **1.** a strong post of wood or iron projecting (usually in pairs) above the deck of a ship, and used for securing cables, lines for towing, etc. —*v.t.* **2.** to put (a cable, etc.) round the bitts. [var. of BIT[1]]

bitten (bĭt′n), *v.* pp. of **bite.**

bitter (bĭt′ə), *adj.* **1.** having a harsh, disagreeable taste, like that of quinine. **2.** hard to admit or receive: *a bitter lesson.* **3.** hard to bear; grievous; distressful: *a bitter sorrow.* **4.** causing pain; piercing; stinging: *bitter cold.* **5.** characterized by intense animosity: *bitter hatred.* **6.** harsh; sarcastic; cutting: *bitter words.* —*n.* **7.** that which is bitter; bitterness. **8.** a kind of light draught beer. —*v.t.* **9.** to make bitter. [OE *biter*; akin to BITE] —**bit′terish,** *adj.* —**bit′terly,** *adv.* —**bit′terness,** *n.* —**Syn. 6.** acrimonious, caustic. —**Ant. 1.** sweet. **2.** pleasant.

bittercress (bĭt′ə krĕs′), *n.* any herb of the cruciferous genus *Cardamine*, as the **hairy bittercress,** *C. hirsuta.*

bitter end, 1. *Naut.* the extreme tail-end of a cable or rope. The bitter end of an anchor cable is secured to the ship inside the chain locker. **2. to the bitter end,** to the very end (usually of something difficult or unpleasant): *they fought to the bitter end.* [*bitter* (f. BITT + -ER [1]) + END[1]]

Bitter Lakes, two lakes that form part of the Suez Canal, in NE Egypt.

bittern[1] (bĭt′ən), *n.* any of several herons, as the **common bittern,** *Botaurus stellaris*, of Europe, and *Botaurus lentiginosus* of North America. [ME *bitter, botor*, t. OF: m. *butor*; orig. uncert. Cf. L *būtio* bittern]

bittern[2] (bĭt′ən), *n.* a bitter, oily liquid remaining as a by-product of salt-making after the salt has crystallized out of sea water or brine, used as a source of bromine, etc. [d. var. of *bittering*, f. BITTER + -ING[1]]

Bittern, *Botaurus stellaris* (Ab. 28 in. long)

Bitterroot Range, a range of the Rocky Mountains, on the boundary between Idaho and Montana. Highest peak, ab. 10,000 ft. Also, **Bitter Root Range.**

bitters (bĭt′əz), *n.pl.* **1.** a spirituous or other drink in which bitter herbs or roots are steeped. **2.** *Pharm.* **a.** a liquid, usually alcoholic, impregnated with a bitter medicine, as gentian, quassia, etc., used as a stomachic, tonic, or the like. **b.** bitter medicinal substances in general, as quinine, gentian, etc.

bittersweet (*n.* bĭt′ə swēt′; *adj.* bĭt′ə swēt′), *n.* **1.** the woody nightshade, *Solanum dulcamara*, a climbing or trailing solanaceous plant with scarlet berries. **2.** any climbing plant of the genus *Celastrus*, with orange capsules opening to expose red-coated seeds, esp. *Celastrus scandens*. *—adj.* **3.** both bitter and sweet to the taste. **4.** both pleasant and painful.

bitterwood (bĭt′ə wo͝od′), *n.* **1.** any tree of the tropical simaroubaceous genus *Picrasma*. **2.** the bitter wood of this tree, from which a substitute for quassia is prepared.

bitty (bĭt′ĭ), *adj.* **1.** scrappy; disjointed; not unified. **2.** (of a liquid) containing bits of skin, sediment, etc.: *bitty milk, bitty paint.*

bitumen (bĭt′yo͝o mĭn), *n.* **1.** any of various natural substances, as asphalt, maltha, gilsonite, etc., consisting mainly of hydrocarbons. **2.** a brown tar or asphalt-like substance used in painting. [t. L] —**bituminoid** (bĭ tyo͝o′mĭ noid′), *adj.*

bituminize (bĭ tyo͝o′mĭ nīz′), *v.t.*, **-nized, -nizing.** to convert into or treat with bitumen. Also, **bituminise.** —**bitu′miniza′tion,** *n.*

bituminous (bĭ tyo͝o′mĭ nəs), *adj.* of, like, or containing bitumen: *bituminous shale.*

bituminous coal, soft coal; a mineral coal which contains volatile hydrocarbons and tarry matter, and burns with a yellow, smoky flame.

bivalent (bī vā′lənt, bĭv′ə-), *adj.* **1.** *Chem.* **a.** having a valency of 2. **b.** having two valencies, as mercury, with valencies 1 and 2. **2.** *Biol.* pertaining to composites of two similar or identical chromosomes, or chromosome sets. *—n.* **3.** *Biol.* a bivalent pair or set of chromosomes. —**bivalence** (bī vā′ləns, bĭv′ə ləns), **biva′lency,** *n.*

bivalve (bī′vălv′), *n. Zool.* **1.** a mollusc having two shells hinged together, as the oyster, clam, mussel; a lamellibranch. *—adj.* **2.** *Bot.* having two valves, as a seed case. **3.** *Zool.* having two shells, usually united by a hinge. —**bivalvular** (bī văl′vyo͝o lə), *adj.*

bivouac (bĭv′o͞o ăk′, bĭv′wăk), *n., v.*, **-acked, -acking.** *—n.* **1.** a temporary camp, esp. a military one, made out in the open with little or no equipment. *—v.i.* **2.** to sleep out; make a bivouac. [t. F, prob. t. d. G: m. *Biwache*. Cf. G *Beiwacht* patrol]

biweekly (bī wēk′lĭ), *adj., n., pl.* **-lies,** *adv.* *—adj.* **1.** occurring every two weeks. **2.** occurring twice a week; semiweekly. *—n.* **3.** a periodical issued every other week. *—adv.* **4.** every two weeks. **5.** twice a week.

biyearly (bī yiə′lĭ), *adj., adv.* **1.** biennial. **2.** twice yearly.

Biysk, Biisk.

bizarre (bĭ zä′), *adj.* singular in appearance, style, or general character; whimsically strange; odd. [t. F: odd, t. Sp.: m. *bizarro* brave, ? t. Basque: m. *bizar* beard] —**bizarre′ly,** *adv.* —**bizarre′ness,** *n.*

Bizerte (bĭ zû′tə; *Fr.* bē zĕrt′), *n.* a seaport in N Tunisia. 46,681 (1959). Also, **Bizerta** (bĭ zû′tə). Ancient, **Hippo Zarytus.**

Bizet (bē′zā; *Fr.* bē zĕ′), *n.* **Georges** (*Fr.* zhôrzh) (*Alexandre César Léopold Bizet*), 1838–75, French composer.

Bjoerling (*Swed.* byœr′lĕng), *n.* **Jussi** (*Swed.* yo͞o′sē), 1911–60, Swedish operatic tenor.

Björnson (*Norw.* byœrn′sŏn), *n.* **Björnstjerne** (*Norw.* byœrn′styĕr nə), 1832–1910, Norwegian poet, novelist, and dramatist.

bk, **1.** bank. **2.** book.

bkg, banking.

bl., **1.** bale; bales. **2.** barrel; barrels.

B.L., Bachelor of Law.

b.l., **1.** *Com.* bill of lading. **2.** *Ordn.* breech-loading.

blaasop (blä′sŏp), *n.* a poisonous fish of the genus *Tetrodon*, of South African waters of the Indian Ocean, having the habit of inflating itself when brought to the surface; a puffer. [t. Afrikaans: f. *blaas* bladder + *op* UP]

blab (blăb), *v.*, **blabbed, blabbing,** *n.* *—v.t.* **1.** to reveal indiscreetly and thoughtlessly. *—v.i.* **2.** to talk or chatter indiscreetly and thoughtlessly. **3.** to let out a secret; tell tales; talk. *—n.* **4.** idle, indiscreet chattering. **5.** a person who blabs. [orig. uncert.; cf. Icel. *blabbra*, OHG *blabbizōn*]

blabber (blăb′ə), *n.* **1.** one who blabs. *—v.t., v.i.* **2.** to blab.

blabbermouth (blăb′ə mouth′), *n., pl.* **-mouths** (-mouthz′). *Colloq.* one who talks too much or who talks indiscreetly.

black (blăk), *adj.* **1.** without brightness or colour; absorbing all or nearly all the rays emitted by a light source. **2.** wearing black or dark clothing, armour, etc.: *the black prince.* **3.** *Anthropol.* **a.** pertaining or belonging to an ethnic group characterized by dark skin pigmentation. **b.** pertaining specifically to the 'black races' of Africa, Oceania, and Australia: the Negroes, Negritos, Papuans, Melanesians, and Australian Aborigines. **4.** soiled or stained with dirt. **5.** characterized by absence of light; involved or enveloped in darkness: *a black night.* **6.** gloomy; dismal: *a black outlook.* **7.** boding ill; sullen; forbidding: *black words, black looks.* **8.** without any moral light or goodness; evil; wicked. **9.** caused or marked by ruin or desolation. **10.** indicating censure, disgrace, or liability to punishment: *a black mark on one's record.* **11.** illicit. **12.** prohibited or banned by a trade union. **13.** (of coffee) without milk or cream. *—n.* **14.** a colour without hue at one extreme end of the scale of greys, opposite to white. A black surface absorbs light of all hues equally. **15.** (*sometimes cap.*) a member of a dark-skinned people; a Negro. **16.** a black speck, flake, or spot, as of soot. **17.** black clothing, esp. as a sign of mourning: *to be in black.* **18.** *Chess, Draughts.* the dark-coloured men or pieces. **19.** black pigment: *lampblack.* **20. in the black,** financially solvent. *—v.t.* **21.** to make black; put black on. **22.** to clean and polish (shoes) with blacking. **23.** (of a trade union) to ban or prevent normal industrial working in (a factory, industry, or the like). **24. black out, a.** to obscure by concealing all light in defence against air-raids. **b.** to jam (a radio). **c.** to suppress (news). *—v.i.* **25.** to become black; take on a black colour. **26.** to lose consciousness (fol. by *out*). [ME *blak*, OE *blæc*, c. OHG *blah-*, *blach-*] —**black′ish,** *adj.* —**black′ishly,** *adv.* —**black′ness,** *n.* —**Syn. 1.** sable, ebon; swart, swarthy; dark, dusky; sooty, inky. —**Ant. 1.** colourful. **4.** clean. **6.** hopeful.

blackamoor (blăk′ə mo͝oə′, -mô′), *n. Archaic.* **1.** a Negro. **2.** any dark-skinned person. [var. of *black Moor*]

black-and-blue (blăk′ən blo͞o′), *adj.* discoloured, as by bruising. Also (esp. in predicative use), **black and blue.**

Black and Tan, a member of an armed force of about 6000 men sent by the British government to Ireland in June 1920, to suppress revolutionary activity; so called from the colour of their uniforms.

black and white, **1.** print or writing. **2.** a drawing or picture done in black and white only.

black art, witchcraft; magic.

blackball (blăk′bôl′), *v.t.* **1.** to ostracize. **2.** to vote against. **3.** to reject (a candidate) by placing a black ball in the ballot box. *—n.* **4.** an adverse vote. **5.** a black ball placed in a ballot box signifying a negative vote. —**black′-ball′er,** *n.*

black bass, an American freshwater fish of the genus *Micropterus.*

black bear, a species of American bear, *Euarctos americanus*, with a pale face and dense black fur.

Blackbeard (blăk′bĭəd′), *n.* See **Teach, Edward.**

black beetle, a cockroach.

black belt, *Judo.* **1.** a belt worn by an experienced contestant ranking up to eighth Dan. **2.** a contestant entitled to wear this.

blackberry (blăk′bə rĭ, -brĭ), *n., pl.* **-ries. 1.** the fruit, black or very dark purple when ripe, of certain species of the genus *Rubus.* **2.** the plant bearing this fruit; the bramble. *—v.i.* **3. go blackberrying,** to go out to pick blackberries. [ME *blakeberie*, OE *blace berian* (pl.)] —**black′berry-like′,** *adj.*

black bindweed, **1.** a slender twining plant, *Polygonum convolvulus*, found widely as a weed. **2.** black bryony.

blackbird (blăk′bûd′), *n.* **1.** a European songbird of the thrush family, *Turdus merula.* **2.** any of various unrelated birds having black plumage in the male. **3.** *U.S.* any of various American birds of the family *Icteridae.* **4.** *Chiefly Austral.* (formerly) a Kanaka kidnapped and transported as a slave labourer.

blackbirding (blăk′bû′dĭng), *n. Chiefly Austral.* (formerly) trade in kidnapped Kanaka slaves. —**black′-bird′er,** *n.*

blackboard (blăk′bôd′), *n.* a smooth dark board, used in schools, etc., for writing or drawing on with chalk.

black body, *Physics.* a body which emits a continuous spectrum of light radiation, the spectral distribution of which depends only on its temperature.

black-body radiator (blăk′bŏd′ĭ), *Physics.* a full radiator.

black book, **1.** a book of names of people liable to censure or punishment. **2. to be in one's black books,** to be in disfavour.

black box, **1.** *Aerospace.* a unit, not necessarily coloured black, which contains and protects electronic equipment, esp. equipment which automatically records information about an aircraft's flight, which may be inspected after a crash. **2.** *Journalism Slang.* any device, invention, etc., the workings of which are mysterious or kept secret.

black bread, pumpernickel.

black-browed (blăk′broud′), *adj.* **1.** having black eyebrows. **2.** having a sullen, brooding, or angry appearance.

black bryony, a twining Old World perennial vine of the genus *Dioscorea* with red berries, *Tamus communis.*

black buck, a common Indian antelope, *Antilope cervicapra*, of medium size and blackish brown colour.

Blackburn (blăk′bûn), *n.* a town in NW England, in Lancashire. 106,242 (1961).

blackbutt (blăk′bŭt′), *n.* any of several eucalyptus trees of Australia.

Black Canyon, a canyon in the U.S. of the Colorado river between Arizona and Nevada: site of Boulder Dam.

black cap, (formerly in Britain) the cap put on by a judge before pronouncing a death sentence.

blackcap (blăk′kăp′), *n.* **1.** a black-headed warbler, *Sylvia atricapilla.* **2.** any of several other birds having the top of the head black, as certain warblers. **3.** *U.S.* a popular name of the plant and fruit of the black raspberry, *Rubus occidentalis.*

black cock, the male of the European black grouse, *Lyrurus tetrix.*

black comedy, a comedy expressing an underlying pessimism or bitterness, or one dealing with a tragic or gruesome subject.

black cotton soil, regur.

Black Country, a district in England, in the Midlands around Birmingham, thought of as begrimed by numerous factories, etc.

blackcurrant (blăk′kŭ′rənt), *n.* **1.** the small, black edible fruit of the shrub *Ribes nigrum.* **2.** the shrub itself.

blackdamp (blăk′dămp′), *n. Mining.* air in which the oxygen has been replaced by carbon dioxide.

Black Death, bubonic plague, which spread over Europe in the 14th century.

black diamond, **1.** a carbonado (def. 2). **2.** (*pl.*) coal.

black disease, *Vet. Sci.* an acute, often fatal disease of sheep caused by general intoxication from *Clostridium novyi,* an anaerobic organism which multiplies in the liver in areas damaged by the common liver fluke.

black earth, **1.** any of various dark-coloured, fertile, calcareous soils, very good for cereal production, esp. that which covers a large area of southern Russia; chernozem. **2.** regur.

blacken (blăk′ən), *v.,* **-ened, -ening.** *—v.t.* **1.** to make black; darken. **2.** to speak evil of; defame. *—v.i.* **3.** to grow or become black. **—black′ener,** *n.*

Blackett (blăk′ĭt), *n.* **Patrick Maynard Stuart,** born 1897, English physicist.

black eye, bruising round the eye, resulting from a blow, etc.

blackface (blăk′fās′), *n.* **1.** *Theat.* **a.** an entertainer who blacks his face, hands, etc., to mimic a Negro. **b.** the make-up for such an entertainer. **2.** *Print.* bold-face type.

blackfellow (blăk′fĕl′o), *n.* an Aborigine of Australia.

blackfish (blăk′fĭsh′), *n., pl.,* **-fishes,** (*esp. collectively*) **-fish.** **1.** the black whale. **2.** a salmon just after it has spawned. **3.** any of various dark-coloured fishes, as the black ruff or the sea-bass, the South African edible fish *Centrolophus niger,* or the American tautog.

black flag, the pirate flag, usually of black cloth with the white skull and crossbones on it.

black fly, any of the minute, black-bodied gnats of the dipterous family *Simuliidae*; the larvae are aquatic.

Blackfoot (blăk′fo͝ot′), *n., pl.* **-feet** (-fēt′), **-foot.** **1.** a member of a North American tribe of Indians (the Blackfeet) of Algonquian stock. **2.** an Algonquian language of Saskatchewan, Alberta, and Montana. *—adj.* **3.** of or pertaining to the Blackfeet.

Black Forest, a forest-covered mountainous region in SW West Germany. Highest peak, Feldberg, ab. 4700 ft. German, **Schwarzwald.**

Black Forest

Black Friar, **1.** a Dominican friar (from the distinctive black mantle). **2.** a Benedictine monk.

Blackfriars (blăk′frī′əz, -frī′əz), *n.* a district of central London.

black frost, a hard frost with no rime or snow.

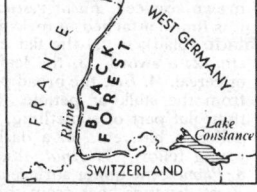

black grouse, a large grouse, *Lyrurus tetrix,* found in the northern parts of Europe and western Asia. The male is black, the female mottled grey and brown.

blackguard (blăg′äd), *n.* **1.** a coarse, despicable person; a scoundrel. *—v.t.* **2.** to revile in scurrilous language. *—v.i.* **3.** to behave like a blackguard. [f. BLACK + GUARD] **—black′guardism,** *n.*

blackguardly (blăg′äd lĭ), *adj.* **1.** of, like, or befitting a blackguard. *—adv.* **2.** in the manner of a blackguard.

black gum, a tree of the family *Nyssaceae,* as *Nyssa sylvatica.* See **tupelo.**

Black Hand, **1.** an anarchistic society in Spain, suppressed in 1883. **2.** a criminal secret society in the U.S., esp. of Italians organized for blackmail and deeds of violence about the last decade of the 19th century. **3.** any similar group. [trans. of Sp. *mano negra*]

blackhead (blăk′hĕd′), *n.* **1.** a small black-tipped, fatty mass in a follicle of the face. **2.** any of several birds having a black head, as the scaup duck. **3.** *Vet. Sci.* a malignant, infectious, protozoan disease of turkeys, chickens, and many wild birds, attacking esp. the intestines and liver.

blackheart (blăk′hät′), *n.* **1.** a plant disease, as of potatoes and various trees, in which internal plant tissues blacken. **2.** a kind of cherry bearing a large, sweet, somewhat heart-shaped fruit with a nearly black skin.

black-hearted (blăk′hä′tĭd), *adj.* evil.

Black Hills, a group of mountains in the U.S., in W South Dakota and NE Wyoming. Highest peak, Kearney Peak, 7242 ft.

Black Hole, **1.** a small prison cell in Fort William, Calcutta, into which, in 1756, 146 Europeans were thrust for a night, only 23 of whom were alive in the morning. **2.** (*l.c.*) *Colloq.* any small, overcrowded room. **3.** (*l.c.*) a military cell or lock-up. Also, **Black Hole of Calcutta.**

black horehound, a fetid European weed, *Ballota nigra,* with purple flowers, prevalent in waste land.

blacking (blăk′ĭng), *n.* any preparation for producing a black coating or finish, as on shoes, stoves, etc.

blackjack (blăk′jăk′), *n.* **1.** *Hist.* a large drinking cup or jug for beer, ale, etc., orig. one made of leather coated externally with tar. **2.** the black flag of a pirate. **3.** *U.S.* a short club, usually leather-covered, consisting of a heavy head on an elastic shaft. **4.** *Mineral.* a dark, iron-rich variety of sphalerite; blende. **5.** caramel, burnt sugar, treacle, black toffee, liquorice, or any other dark sweet substance. **6.** *Cards.* **a.** pontoon². **b.** the ace of spades. **c.** a variety of pontoon in which any player may become dealer. *—v.t. U.S.* **7.** to strike or beat with a blackjack. **8.** to compel by threat.

Leather blackjacks

black knot, a fungus plant disease appearing as black knotlike masses on the branches, esp. on plums and cherries.

black lead, graphite; plumbago.

black-lead (blăk′lĕd′), *v.t.* to blacken or polish with black lead.

blackleg (blăk′lĕg′), *n., v.,* **-legged, -legging.** *—n.* **1.** one who continues to work during a strike, takes a striker's place, refuses to join a union, etc. **2.** a swindler, esp. in racing or gambling. **3.** *Vet. Sci.* an infectious, generally fatal disease of cattle and sheep characterized by painful, gaseous swellings in the muscles, usually of the upper parts of the legs. **4.** a plant disease, as of cabbage and potato, in which the lower stems turn black and decay. *—v.t., v.i.* **5.** to refuse to join (one's fellow workers) in a strike.

black-letter (blăk′lĕt′ə), *Print.* *—n.* **1.** a heavy-faced type in gothic style like that in early English printed books. *—adj.* **2.** of, pertaining to, set in, or resembling black-letter.

black-letter day, an unlucky day.

black list, a list of persons under suspicion, disfavour, censure, etc., or a list of fraudulent or unreliable customers or firms.

black-list (blăk′lĭst′), *v.t.* to put on a black list.

blackly (blăk′lĭ), *adv.* darkly; gloomily; wickedly.

black magic, magic used for evil purposes.

blackmail (blăk′māl′), *n.* **1.** *Law.* **a.** any payment extorted by intimidation, as by threats of injurious revelations or accusations. **b.** the extortion of such payment. **2.** a tribute formerly exacted in the north of England and in Scotland by freebooting chiefs for protection from pillage. *—v.t.* **3.** to extort blackmail from. [f. BLACK + *mail* coin, rent (ME *maille,* t. OF)] **—black′-mail′er,** *n.*

Black Maria (mə rī′ə), *Colloq.* a closed vehicle used for conveying prisoners to and from jail.

black mark, a mark of failure or censure.

black market, an illegal market violating price controls, rationing, etc.

black marketeer, a dealer on a black market.

black mass, a travesty of the mass, as performed by devil-worshippers.

black measles, *Pathol.* a severe form of measles characterized by a haemorrhagic rash.

black medick. See **medick.**

Blackmore (blăk′mô′), *n.* **Richard Doddridge** (dŏd′rĭj), 1825–1900, English novelist.

Black Mountains, a mountain range in the U.S., in W North Carolina: a part of the Appalachian system. Highest peak, Mt Mitchell, 6684 ft.
Black Muslim, a member of a Negro organization in the U.S., advocating modified teachings of Islam and racial segregation.
black nightshade, a common weed, *Solanum nigrum*, with white flowers and black berries.
blackout (blăk′out′), *n.* **1.** the extinguishing of all visible lights in a city, etc., as a wartime protection. **2.** the extinguishing or failure of light as in a power failure. **3.** *Theat.* the extinguishing of all stage lights. **4.** temporary loss of consciousness or vision, esp. in aviation due to high acceleration. **5.** loss of memory. **6.** fade-out of radio signals.
black pepper, a hot, sharp condiment prepared from the dried berries of a tropical vine, *Piper nigrum*.
black plate, sheet steel or iron which has not been coated with a covering of tin.
blackpoll (blăk′pōl′), *n.* a North American warbler, *Dendroica striata*, the adult male of which has the top of the head black.
Blackpool (blăk′po͞ol′), *n.* a seaport in NW England, in Lancashire: resort. 153,185 (1961).
Black Power, a Negro movement originating in the U.S. advocating the advancement of Negroes through violent and/or political means.
Black Prince, the, 1330–76, Edward Prince of Wales (the son of Edward III).
black pudding, a dark sausage made of blood, suet, and other ingredients.
black rhinoceros, a two-horned rhinoceros, *Rhinoceros bicornis*, of Africa, characterized by a pointed upper lip.
Black Rod, an usher (**gentleman usher of the black rod**) of the King's chamber, the Order of the Garter, and the House of Lords (so called from the rod he carries).
black rot, *Bot.* any of various diseases of vegetables caused by bacteria, esp. *Pseudomonas campestris*, or fungi, producing black discoloration and decay.
black rust, *Bot.* an obligate fungal parasite of cereals, *Puccinia graminis*, which follows part of its life cycle in the common barberry.
black saltwort, the sea-milkwort.
Black Sea, a sea S of E Europe, bounded by the Soviet Union, Turkey, Rumania, and Bulgaria. ab. 168,000 sq. mi.; greatest depth, ab. 7200 ft. Also, **Euxine Sea.** Ancient, **Pontus Euxinus.**

Black Sea

black sheep, a person regarded as worthless despite good background.
Blackshirt (blăk′shûrt′), *n.* *Europ. Hist.* a member of a fascist organization in Europe, such as the Italian fascist militia or the British Union of Fascists.
blacksmith (blăk′smĭth′), *n.* **1.** a person who makes horseshoes and shoes horses. **2.** an artisan who works in iron. [f. BLACK (in ref. to iron or black metal) + SMITH[1]. Cf. WHITESMITH]
blacksnake (blăk′snāk′), *n.* **1.** a deadly venomous snake, *Pseudechis porphyriacus*, of Australia, allied to the cobra. **2.** a non-venomous snake, *Coluber constrictor*, of the U.S., attaining a length of 5 to 6 ft, and notably agile and strong. **3.** *U.S.* a heavy, tapering, flexible whip of braided cowhide or the like. Also, **black snake.**
black spot, a place on a road where accidents frequently occur.
black spruce, **1.** a conifer of North America, *Picea mariana*, noted for its extremely dark green needles. **2.** an easily worked light wood from this tree.
Blackstone (blăk′stōn, -stən), *n.* **Sir William,** 1723–80, English judge and writer on law.
black tea, a tea which has been allowed to wither and ferment in the air for some time, before being subjected to a heating process.
blackthorn (blăk′thôn′), *n.* **1.** a much-branched, thorny shrub, *Prunus spinosa*, bearing white flowers and small plumlike fruits; sloe. **2.** its wood.
black tie, **1.** a black bow tie for men, worn with a formal style of evening dress. **2.** a formal style of evening dress for men, of which the characteristic garments are a black bow tie and a dinner jacket (distinguished from *white tie*).
blacktop (blăk′tŏp′), *Chiefly U.S.* —*n.* **1.** a bituminous substance, as asphalt, used for surfacing roads, specif. as a top dressing for concrete roads. **2.** a road surfaced with blacktop. —*adj.* **3.** of or surfaced with blacktop.
blacktracker (blăk′trăk′ə), *n.* *Austral.* an Aborigine tracker employed by the police.
black twitch, an annual gramineous grass, *Alopecurus myosuroides*, common as a weed in SE England.
black velvet, a drink of champagne mixed with stout.
Black Volta. See **Volta** (def. 2).
black vomit, *Pathol.* **1.** a dark-coloured substance, consisting chiefly of altered blood, vomited in some cases of yellow fever, usually presaging a fatal issue of the disease. **2.** the act of throwing up this matter. **3.** the disease itself.
Blackwall hitch (blăk′wôl′), a hitch made with a rope over a hook so that it holds fast when pulled but is loose otherwise. See illus. under **knot.**
Blackwall Tunnel, a road tunnel under the Thames in E London connecting Poplar with Greenwich.
black walnut, **1.** a tree, *Juglans nigra*, of North America, which yields a valuable timber. **2.** the nut thereof. **3.** the wood of this tree.
Blackwater (blăk′wô′tə), *n.* a river in the S Republic of Ireland, flowing SE to the Atlantic. 100 mi.
blackwater fever, *Pathol.* a severe form of malaria found chiefly in the tropics but occasionally in the southern U.S.
black whale, a dolphin-like cetacean of the genus *Globicephalus*; a blackfish.
black widow, a poisonous female spider, *Latrodectus mactans*, that eats its mate, common in the U.S.
Blackwood (blăk′wo͝od′), *n.* **1. Algernon,** 1869–1951, English writer. **2. William,** 1776–1834, Scottish publisher. **3.** a river in SW Australia flowing into the Indian Ocean. ab. 190 mi.
bladder (blăd′ə), *n.* **1.** *Anat., Zool.* **a.** a distensible pelvic sac with membranous and muscular walls, for storage and expulsion of urine by the kidneys. **b.** any similar sac or receptacle. **2.** *Bot.* a sac or the like containing air, as in certain seaweeds. **3.** any inflatable or distensible bag, as the inner bag of a football, or the bellows of bagpipes. **4.** anything inflated, empty, or unsound. [ME; OE *blǣdre* bladder, blister, akin to BLOW[2], v., BLAST] —**blad′derless,** *adj.* —**blad′der-like′,** *adj.* —**blad′dery,** *adj.*
bladder campion, a plant, *Silene latifolia* (*Silene inflata*), so called from its inflated calyx.
bladder fern, any fern of the rhizomatous genus *Cystopteris*, esp. the **brittle bladder fern,** *C. fragilis*.
bladdernose (blăd′ə nōz′), *n.* a large seal, *Cystophora cristata*, of the northern Atlantic, the male of which has a large, distensible, hoodlike sac upon the head; the hooded seal.
bladdernut (blăd′ə nŭt′), *n.* **1.** the bladder-like fruit capsule of any shrub or small tree of the genus *Staphylea*, as *S. pinnata* of southern Europe. **2.** the shrub itself.
bladder-seed (blăd′ə sēd′), *n.* an umbelliferous Old World herb, *Physospermum cornubiense*, with inflated fruits.
bladder senna, a leguminous shrub, *Solutea arborescens*, of the Mediterranean region, with inflated membranous pods.
bladder worm, *Zool.* the bladder-like encysted larva of a tapeworm; a cysticercus, coenurus, or hyatid.
bladderwort (blăd′ə wût′), *n.* any of various herbs of the large genus *Utricularia*, including aquatic, terrestrial, and epiphytic forms throughout the world.
bladderwrack (blăd′ə răk′), *n.* a common branched brown seaweed, *Fucus vesciculosus*, bearing air-bladders; it is found attached to rocks in the intertidal zone.
blade (blād), *n.* **1.** the flat cutting part of sword, knife, etc. **2.** a sword. **3.** the leaf of a plant, esp. of a grass or cereal. **4.** *Bot.* the broad part of a leaf, as distinguished from the stalk or petiole. See illus. under **leaf. 5.** a thin, flat part of something, as of a bone, an oar, a propeller, a bat, etc. **6.** a dashing, swaggering, or rakish young fellow. **7.** *Anat.* the scapula or shoulder-blade. **8.** *Phonet.* the upper surface and edges of the tongue for a short distance back from the tip. [ME; OE *blæd*, c. G *Blatt*] —**blad′ed,** *adj.* —**blade′less,** *adj.* —**blade′-like′,** *adj.*
blaeberry (blā′bə rĭ), *n., pl.* **-ries,** bilberry. [ME *blaberie*; f. OE *blæ-* blue (c. ON *blār*) + BERRY]
Blagoyevgrad (*Russ.* blə gə yĭv grăt′), *n.* a town in the SE Soviet Union in Asia. 104,000 (est. 1963). Formerly, **Blagoveshchensk** (*Russ.* blə gă vyĕsh′chĭnsk).
blah (blä), *n. Colloq.* high-sounding empty talk; eloquent rubbish.
blain (blān), *n. Pathol.* an inflammatory swelling or sore. [ME *bleine*, OE *blegen*]
Blake (blāk), *n.* **1. Robert,** 1599–1657, English admiral. **2. William,** 1757–1827, English poet and artist.
blamable (blā′mə bl), *adj.* deserving blame; censurable. Also, **blameable.** —**blam′ableness,** *n.* —**blam′ably,** *adv.*

blame (blām), *v.*, **blamed, blaming,** *n.* —*v.t.* **1.** to lay the responsibility of (a fault, error, etc.) on a person: *I blame the accident on him.* **2.** to find fault with; censure: *I blame you for that.* **3.** *U.S. Slang and Dial.* to blast (as a humorous imperative or optative): *blame my hide if I go.* **4. to blame,** responsible for a fault or error; blamable; culpable: *he is to blame.* —*n.* **5.** imputation of fault; censure. **6.** responsibility for a fault, error, etc. [ME *blamen*, t. OF: m. *blasmer*, g. LL *blasphēmāre* BLASPHEME] —**Syn. 1, 2.** reproach, reprove, reprehend. BLAME, CENSURE, CONDEMN imply finding fault with someone (or something). TO BLAME is to hold accountable for some error, mistake, omission, neglect, or the like: *who is to blame for the disaster?* The verb CENSURE differs from the noun in connoting scolding or rebuking even more than adverse criticism: *to censure one for extravagance.* TO CONDEMN is to express an adverse (esp. legal) judgement, without recourse: *to condemn a man to death.* **5.** reprehension, condemnation, stricture. **6.** guilt, culpability, fault. —**Ant. 2.** praise.

blamed (blāmd), *U.S. Slang and Dial.* —*adj.* **1.** confounded. —*adv.* **2.** confoundedly; excessively.

blameful (blām′fəl), *adj.* deserving blame. —**blame′fully,** *adv.* —**blame′fulness,** *n.*

blameless (blām′lĭs), *adj.* free from blame; guiltless. —**blame′lessly,** *adv.* —**blame′lessness,** *n.* —**Syn.** irreproachable. See **innocent.** —**Ant.** guilty.

Blanc (*Fr.* bläɴ), *n.* **1. Jean Joseph Charles Louis** (*Fr.* zhäɴ zhô zĕf shärl lwē′), 1811–82, French socialist and historian. **2. Mont** (*Fr.* môɴ), a mountain on the French-Italian border: the highest peak of the Alps. 15,781 ft.

blanc fixe (blŏng′fĭks′; *Fr.* bläɴ fēks′), *n. Chem.* artificial barium sulphate, used in paints as an extender. [t. F: lit., fixed white]

blanch (blänch), *v.t.* **1.** to whiten by removing colour. **2.** *Hort.* to whiten or prevent from becoming green by excluding the light (a process applied to the stems or leaves of plants, such as celery, lettuce, etc.). **3.** to remove the skin from (nuts, fruits, etc.) by immersion in boiling water, then in cold. **4.** to separate (the grains or strands of rice, macaroni, etc.) by immersing in boiling water, then in cold. **5.** to scald (meat, etc.). **6.** *Metall.* to give a white lustre to (metals), as by means of acids. **7.** to make pale, as with sickness or fear. —*v.i.* **8.** to become white; turn pale. [ME *blaunche(n)*, t. OF: m. *blanchir*, der. *blanc* white. See BLANK] —**blanch′er,** *n.* —**Syn. 1.** See **whiten.**

blancmange (blə mŏnzh′), *n.* a jelly-like preparation of milk thickened with cornflour, gelatine, or the like, and flavoured. [ME *blancmanger*, t. OF: lit., white food]

bland (blănd), *adj.* **1.** (of a person's manner) suave; (deliberately) agreeable or pleasant but often without real feelings. **2.** soothing or balmy, as air. **3.** mild, as food or medicines: *a bland diet.* **4.** non-stimulating, as medicines. [t. L: s. *blandus*] —**bland′ly,** *adv.* —**bland′ness,** *n.* —**Syn. 1.** suave, urbane. **3.** soft, mild.

blandish (blăn′dĭsh), *v.t.* to treat flatteringly; coax; cajole. [ME *blaundysh(en)*, t. OF: m. *blandiss-*, s. *blandir*, g. L *blandīre* flatter] —**blan′disher,** *n.*

blandishment (blăn′dĭsh mənt), *n.* (*often pl.*) flattering action or speech.

blank (blăngk), *adj.* **1.** (of paper, etc.) free from marks; not written or printed on. **2.** not filled in: *a blank cheque.* **3.** unrelieved or unbroken by ornament or opening: *a blank wall.* **4.** lacking some usual or completing feature; empty. **5.** void of interest, results, etc. **6.** showing no attention, interest, or emotion: *a blank face.* **7.** disconcerted; nonplussed: *a blank look.* **8.** complete, utter, or unmitigated: *blank stupidity.* **9.** white or pale. **10.** *Colloq.* (euphemistic for any vulgar or taboo epithet). —*n.* **11.** a place where something is lacking: *a blank in one's memory.* **12.** a void; emptiness. **13.** a space left (to be filled in) in written or printed matter. **14.** a printed form containing such spaces. **15.** a dash put in place of an omitted letter or word, esp. profanity or obscenity. **16.** *Mach.* a piece of metal prepared to be stamped or cut into a finished object, such as a coin or key. **17.** *Archery.* the white mark in the centre of a butt or target at which an arrow is aimed. **18.** a blank cartridge. **19.** a domino unmarked on one or both of its halves. **20.** a lottery ticket which does not win. **21. draw (a) blank,** get no results; fail. **22. in blank,** (of a document) with spaces left to be filled in. —*v.t.* **23.** to make blank or void: *to blank out an entry.* **24.** *Mach.* to stamp or punch out of flat stock as with a die. [ME, t. OF: m. *blanc* white, t. Gmc; cf. G *blank* bright, shining] —**blank′ness,** *n.* —**Syn. 1–4.** See **empty.**

Blank (blăngk), *n.* **Joost de** (yōs′ də), 1908–68, British ecclesiastic born in Holland; Anglican Archbishop of Cape Town 1957–63.

blank cartridge, *Ordn.* a cartridge containing powder only, without a bullet.

blank cheque, 1. a cheque bearing a signature but no stated amount. **2.** a free hand; carte blanche.

blank endorsement, *Com.* an endorsement on a cheque or note naming no payee, and payable to bearer.

blanket (blăng′kĭt), *n.* **1.** a large rectangular piece of soft, loosely woven fabric, usually wool, used esp. as a bed covering. **2.** a covering for a horse, etc. **3.** *U.S. and Can.* the chief garment worn by some Indians. **4.** any heavy concealing layer or covering: *a blanket of clouds.* —*v.t.* **5.** to cover with or as with a blanket. **6.** to obscure by increasing prominence of the background (often fol. by *out*). **7.** to toss in a blanket, as for punishment. **8.** *Naut.* to take the wind out of the sails of (a vessel) by passing to windward of it. —*adj.* **9.** covering or intended to cover a group or class of things, conditions, etc.: *a blanket indictment.* [ME, t. OF: m. *blancquete*, dim. of *blanc* white] —**blan′ketless,** *adj.*

blanketing (blăng′kĭ tĭng), *n.* **1.** *Radio.* the effect of a signal from a powerful transmitter which interferes with or prevents the reception of other signals. **2.** cloth for making blankets. **3.** a tossing in a blanket.

blanket stitch, the loop stitch used to bind the edges of blankets, etc.

blankly (blăngk′lĭ), *adv.* **1.** without expression or understanding. **2.** flatly; directly; point-blank.

blank verse, 1. unrhymed verse. **2.** the unrhymed iambic pentameter verse most frequently used in English dramatic, epic, and reflective poems.

Blantyre (blăn tī′ə), *n.* a town in S Malawi. 120,000 (est. 1966).

blare (blĕə), *v.*, **blared, blaring,** *n.* —*v.i.* **1.** to emit a loud raucous sound. —*v.t.* **2.** to sound loudly; proclaim noisily. —*n.* **3.** a loud raucous noise. **4.** glaring intensity of colour. [ME *blaren*, t. MD]

blarney (blä′nĭ), *n.*, *v.*, **-neyed, -neying.** —*n.* **1.** flattering or wheedling talk; cajolery. —*v.t.*, *v.i.* **2.** to ply or beguile with blarney; use blarney; wheedle. [see BLARNEY STONE]

Blarney stone, a stone in Blarney Castle near Cork, Ireland, said to confer skill in flattery to anyone who kisses it.

Blasco Ibáñez (*Sp.* blās′kô ē bä′nyĕth), **Vicente** (*Sp.* bē thĕn′tĕ), 1867–1928, Spanish novelist.

blasé (blä zā′, blä′zā; *Fr.* blä zĕ′), *adj.* indifferent to and bored by pleasures of life. [t. F, pp. of *blaser* exhaust, satiate, ? t. D: m. *blasen* blow]

blaspheme (blăs fēm′), *v.*, **-phemed, -pheming.** —*v.t.* **1.** to speak impiously or irreverently of (God or sacred things). **2.** to speak evil of; abuse. —*v.i.* **3.** to utter impious words. [t. LL: m. s. *blasphēmāre*, t. Gk: m. *blasphēmeîn* speak ill; r. ME *blasfeme(n)*, t. OF: m. *blasfemer*] —**blasphem′er,** *n.* —**Syn. 1.** See **curse.**

blasphemous (blăs′fĭ məs), *adj.* uttering, containing, or exhibiting blasphemy. —**blas′phemously,** *adv.* —**blas′phemousness,** *n.*

blasphemy (blăs′fĭ mĭ), *n.*, *pl.* **-mies. 1.** impious utterance or action concerning God or sacred things. **2.** *Judaism.* **a.** (in Talmudic law) cursing and reviling the 'ineffable name' of the Lord. **b.** (in later Hebrew history) the violation of religious law by pronouncing one of the four-letter symbols for God rather than using one of the substitute words. **3.** *Theol.* the crime of assuming to oneself the rights or qualities of God. **4.** irreverent behaviour towards anything held sacred. [t. LL: m. s. *blasphēmia*, t. Gk: slander; r. ME *blasfemie*, t. OF] —**Syn. 1.** profanity, cursing, swearing.

blast (bläst), *n.* **1.** a sudden blowing or gust of wind. **2.** the blowing of a trumpet, whistle, etc. **3.** the sound produced by this. **4.** a forcible stream of air from the mouth, from bellows, or the like. **5.** *Metall.* air under pressure directed into a blast furnace, cupola, etc., to support combustion. **6.** a jet of exhaust steam directed into a chimney to augment the draught, as in a locomotive. **7.** a draught thus increased. **8.** *Mining, Civ. Eng., etc.* the charge of dynamite or other explosive used at one firing in blasting operations. **9.** the act of exploding; explosion. **10.** the forcible movement of air, or the shock wave, caused by an explosion. **11.** any pernicious or destructive influence, esp. on animals or plants; a blight. **12. full blast,** *Colloq.* very actively; very successfully. —*v.t.* **13.** to blow (a trumpet, etc.). **14.** to cause to shrivel or wither; blight. **15.** to affect with any pernicious influence; ruin; destroy: *to blast one's hopes.* **16.** to tear (rock, etc.) to pieces with an explosive. —*v.i.* **17.** to wither; be blighted. —*interj.* **18.** (an exclamation of anger or irritation). [ME; OE *blǣst*] —**blas′ter,** *n.* —**Syn. 1.** See **wind**[1].

-blast, *Biol.* a combining form meaning 'embryo', 'sprout', 'germ', as in *ectoblast.* [t. Gk: s. *blastós*]

blasted (bläs′tĭd), *adj.* **1.** withered; shrivelled; blighted. **2.** (used euphemistically) damned.

blastema (blăs tē′mə), *n.*, *pl.* **-mata** (-mə tə). *Embryol.*

an aggregation of embryonic cells, capable of differentiation into primordia and organs. [t. NL, t. Gk: sprout] —**blastemic** (blăs tēm′ĭk, -tē′mĭk), *adj.*

blast furnace, *Metall.* a vertical, steel cylindrical furnace using a forced blast to produce molten iron which may be converted into steel or formed into pig-iron.

blasto-, *Biol.* a word element meaning 'embryo' or 'germ', as in *blastocyst.* Also, before vowels, **blast-.** [t. Gk, comb. form of *blastós*]

blastocoel (blăs′tō sēl′), *n. Embryol.* the cavity of a a blastula, arising in the course of cleavage. Also, **blastocoele.**

blastocyst (blăs′tō sĭst′), *n. Embryol.* **1.** the germinal vesicle. **2.** the vesicular stage in early mammalian development, following cleavage.

blastoderm (blăs′tō dûm′), *n. Embryol.* **1.** the primitive membrane or layer of cells which results from the segmentation of the ovum. **2.** the membrane forming the wall of the blastula, and in most vertebrates enclosing a cavity or a yolk mass. —**blas′toder′mic,** *adj.*

blastodisc (blăs′tō dĭsk′), *n. Embryol.* the small disc of protoplasm, containing the egg nucleus, which appears on the surface of the yolk mass in very heavily yolked eggs, as of birds and reptiles.

blast-off (bläst′ŏf′), *n. Aerospace.* lift-off.

blastogenesis (blăs′tō jĕn′ĭ sĭs), *n. Biol.* **1.** reproduction by gemmation or budding. **2.** the theory of the transmission of hereditary characters by germ plasm.

blastomere (blăs′tō mĭə′), *n. Embryol.* any cell produced during the early stages of cleavage. —**blastomeric** (blăs′tō mĕ′rĭk), *adj.*

blastopore (blăs′tō pô′), *n. Embryol.* the orifice of an archenteron. —**blastoporic** (blăs′tō pŏ′rĭk), *adj.*

blastosphere (blăs′tō sfĭə′), *n. Embryol.* **1.** a blastula. **2.** a blastocyst (def. 2).

blastula (blăs′tyŏŏ lə), *n., pl.* **-lae** (-lē′). *Embryol.* an early developmental stage of a metazoan, consisting in typical cases of a hollow sphere formed by a single layer of cells. [t. NL, dim. of Gk *blastós* sprout, germ] —**blas′tular,** *adj.*

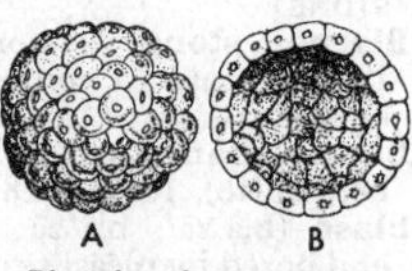

Blastula, after numerous cleavages: A, Exterior view; B, Cross-section

blatant (blā′tnt), *adj.* **1.** (of actions, etc.) flagrantly obvious or undisguised: *a blatant error, a blatant lie.* **2.** (of persons) offensively conspicuous in or unconcerned by (bad) behaviour; brazen; barefaced. **3.** *Obs.* bleating: *blatant herds.* [coined by Spenser. Cf. L *blatire* babble] —**bla′tancy,** *n.* —**bla′tantly,** *adv.*

blather (blăth′ə), *n.* **1.** foolish talk. —*v.i., v.t.* **2.** to talk or utter foolishly. Also, **blether.** [ME, t. Scand.; cf. Icel. *bladhra* talk nonsense]

blatherskite (blăth′ə skīt′), *n.* one given to voluble, empty talk. Also, **blatherskate, bletherskate.** [f. BLATHER + *skite* SKATE[3]]

blaubok (blou′bŏk′), *n., pl.* **-bok, -boks.** a bluish antelope of southern Africa, *Hippotragus leucophaeus*, extinct since 1800, with backward-curving horns. [t. Afrikaans: m. *blauwbok* blue buck]

Blaue Reiter (*Ger.* blou′ə rī tər), **der** (*Ger.* dĕr), a group of artists formed in Munich in 1911, including Kandinsky, Marc, and Klee. [G: lit., the blue rider]

Blavatsky (blə văt′skĭ), *n.* **Madame** (*Elena Petrovna Blavatskaya, nee Hahn*), 1831–91, Russian theosophist.

Blaydon (blā′dn), *n.* a town in England, in N Durham, near Newcastle-upon-Tyne. 30,615 (1961).

blaze[1] (blāz), *n., v.,* **blazed, blazing.** —*n.* **1.** a bright flame or fire. **2.** a bright, hot gleam or glow: *the blaze of day.* **3.** a sparkling brightness: *a blaze of jewels.* **4.** a sudden, intense outburst, as of fire, passion, fury. **5.** (*pl.*) *Slang.* hell. —*v.i.* **6.** to burn brightly. **7.** to shine like flame. **8.** (of guns) to fire continuously. **9.** *Poetic.* to be meritoriously conspicuous. —*v.t.* **10.** to exhibit vividly. [ME and OE *blase* torch, flame] —**Syn. 1.** See **flame.**

blaze[2] (blāz), *n., v.,* **blazed, blazing.** —*n.* **1.** a spot or mark made on a tree, as by removing a piece of the bark, to indicate a boundary or a path in a forest. **2.** a white spot on the face of a horse, cow, etc. —*v.t.* **3.** to mark with blazes. **4. blaze a trail, a.** to mark out a trail with blazes. **b.** to break new ground; pioneer. [t. LG: m. *bläse* white mark on head of horse or steer, c. Icel. *blesa*]

blaze[3] (blāz), *v.t.,* **blazed, blazing. 1.** to make known; proclaim; publish. **2.** *Obs.* to blow, as from a trumpet. [ME *blase(n)*, t. MD, c. Icel. *blāsa* blow]

blazer (blā′zə), *n.* **1.** one who or that which blazes. **2.** *Colloq.* anything intensely bright or hot. **3.** a lightweight summer jacket, often brightly coloured, as worn by sportsmen. **4.** a jacket, usually bearing some badge or crest, as worn by schoolchildren.

blazing (blā′zĭng), *adj.* **1.** burning fiercely. **2.** very hot; scorching. **3.** bright; dazzling. **4.** violently angry. **5.** noticeable as an outstanding example of its kind: *a blazing indiscretion.*

blazon (blā′zən), *v.t.* **1.** to set forth conspicuously or publicly; display; proclaim. **2.** to describe in heraldic terminology. **3.** to depict (heraldic arms, etc.) in proper form and colour. —*n.* **4.** a heraldic shield; armorial bearings. **5.** the heraldic description or armorial bearings. [ME *blason*, t. OF: shield, later armorial bearings] —**bla′zoner,** *n.*

blazonry (blā′zən rĭ), *n.* **1.** *Her.* **a.** armorial bearings. **b.** a description of heraldic devices. **2.** brilliant decoration or display.

bldg, building.

-ble, var. of **-able,** as in *noble*; occurring first in words of Latin origin which came into English through French, later in words taken directly from Latin. Also, after consonant stems, **-ible.** [t. OF, g. L *-bilis*, suffix forming verbal adjectives]

bleach (blēch), *v.t., v.i.* **1..** to make or become white, pale, or colourless. —*n.* **2.** a bleaching agent. **3.** degree of paleness achieved in bleaching. **4.** the act of bleaching. [ME *blechen*, OE *blǣcean*] —**bleach′er,** *n.* —**Syn. 1.** See **whiten.**

bleacher (blē′chə), *n.* **1.** one who or that which bleaches. **2.** a vessel used in bleaching. **3.** (*usually pl.*) *U.S.* an uncovered seat or stand for spectators at games.

bleachery (blē′chə rĭ), *n., pl.* **-ries.** *Obs.* a place or establishment where bleaching is carried on.

bleaching powder, a powder used for bleaching, esp. chloride of lime.

bleak[1] (blēk), *adj.* **1.** bare, desolate, and windswept: *a bleak plain.* **2.** cold and piercing: *a bleak wind.* **3.** dreary: *a bleak prospect.* [ME *bleke* pale, b. *bleche* (OE *blǣc*) and *blake* (OE *blāc*), c. G *bleich*] —**bleak′ly,** *adv.* —**bleak′ness,** *n.*

bleak[2] (blēk), *n.* a small freshwater European fish, *Alburnus lucidus*, with small, shiny scales. [t. Scand. (cf. Icel. *bleikja*); r. OE *blǣge*, d. *blay.*]

blear (blĭə), *v.t.* **1.** to make (the eyes or sight) dim, as with tears or inflammation. —*adj.* **2.** bleary. **3.** a blur; a bleared state. [ME *blere(n)* (orig. adj.); orig. uncert]

blear-eyed (blĭər′īd′), *adj.* **1.** having bleared eyes. **2.** dull of perception. Also, **blear′y-eyed′.**

bleary (blĭə′rĭ), *adj.,* **blearier, bleariest. 1.** (of the eyes) dim from a watery discharge, or from tiredness. **2.** blear-eyed. **3.** misty; dim; indistinct. [f. BLEAR + -Y[1]] —**blear′ily,** *adv.* —**blear′iness,** *n.*

bleat (blēt), *v.i.* **1.** to cry as a sheep, goat, or calf. **2.** to speak with a bleating sound. **3.** to complain; moan. —*v.t.* **4.** to give forth with a bleat. —*n.* **5.** the cry of a sheep, goat, or calf. **6.** any similar sound. **7.** a feeble protest or complaint. [ME *blete(n)*, OE *blǣtan*] —**bleat′er,** *n.* —**bleat′ingly,** *adv.*

bleb (blĕb), *n. Rare.* **1.** a blister or pustule. **2.** a bubble. —**bleb′by,** *adj.*

bleed (blēd), *v.,* **bled** (blĕd), **bleeding,** *n.* —*v.i.* **1.** to lose blood, from the body or internally from the vascular system. **2.** to be severely wounded or die, as in battle: *bled for the cause.* **3.** to cause blood to flow, esp. surgically. **4.** (of blood, etc.) to flow out. **5.** to exude sap, juice, etc. **6.** (of colour in dyeing) to run. **7.** to feel pity, sorrow, or anguish: *a nation bleeds for its dead heroes.* **8.** *Slang.* to pay money as when overcharged or threatened with extortion. **9.** *Print.* to run off the edges of a printed page, either by design or through mutilation caused by too close trimming. —*v.t.* **10.** to cause to lose blood, esp. surgically. **11.** to lose or emit (blood or sap). **12.** to drain, draw sap, liquid, etc., from. **13.** *Colloq.* to obtain, as in excessive amount, or extort money from. **14.** *Print.* **a.** to permit (printed illustrations or ornamentation) to run off the page or sheet. **b.** to trim the margin of (a book or sheet) so closely as to mutilate the text or illustration. —*n.* **15.** *Print.* a sheet or page margin trimmed in this way. **16.** a part thus trimmed off. [ME *blede(n)*, OE *blēdan*, der. *blōd* blood]

bleeder (blē′də), *n.* **1.** a person predisposed to bleeding; haemophiliac. **2.** *Slang.* **a.** (a term of abuse.) **b.** person; fellow. **3.** *Slang.* an extortioner.

bleeding (blē′dĭng), *n., adj.* —*n.* **1.** loss of blood. **2.** letting of blood. **3.** exuding of sap from a cut. —*adj.* **4.** emanating pity. —*adj., adv.* **5.** *Slang.* bloody.

bleeding-heart (blē′dĭng hät′), *n.* any of various plants of the genus *Dicentra*, esp. *D. spectabilis*, a common garden plant with racemes of red, heart-shaped flowers.

bleep (blēp), *v.i.* **1.** to emit a high-pitched broken sound, or a radio signal. —*n.* **2.** a single short high-pitched sound. [imit.]

blemish (blĕm′ĭsh), *v.t.* **1.** to destroy the perfection of.

—*n.* **2.** a defect; a disfigurement; stain. [ME *blemissh(en)*, t. OF: m. *blemiss-*, s. *ble(s)mir* make livid] —**blem′isher,** *n.* —**Syn. 1.** injure, mar, damage, impair, deface. **2.** See **defect.**

blench[1] (blĕnch), *v.i.* to shrink; flinch; quail. [ME *blenchen*, OE *blencan* deceive] —**blench′er,** *n.*

blench[2] (blĕnch), *v.i.*, *v.t.* to make or become pale or white; blanch. [var. of BLANCH]

blend (blĕnd), *v.*, **blended** or **blent, blending,** *n.* —*v.t.* **1.** to mix smoothly and inseparably together. **2.** to mix (various sorts or grades) in order to obtain a particular kind or quality. **3.** to prepare by such mixture. —*v.i.* **4.** to mix or intermingle smoothly and inseparably. **5.** to have no perceptible separation: *sea and sky seemed to blend.* —*n.* **6.** the act or manner of blending: *tea of our own blend.* **7.** a mixture or kind produced by blending. **8.** *Linguistics.* a word made by putting together parts of other words, as *dandle*, a blend of *dance* and *handle*. [ME *blenden*, OE *blendan*, *blandan*, c. Icel. *blanda*] —**Syn. 1.** mingle, combine, coalesce. See **mix.**

blende (blĕnd), *n.* **1.** sphalerite; zinc sulphide. **2.** any of certain other sulphides. [t. G, der. *blenden* blind, deceive]

blended (blĕn′dĭd), *adj.* (of a whisky) consisting of either two or more whiskies, or of whiskies and neutral spirits.

Blenheim (blĕn′ĭm), *n.* village in S West Germany, on the Danube: victory of the Duke of Marlborough over the French, 1704. German, **Blindheim.**

Blenheim Palace, a mansion in Oxfordshire built for the Duke of Marlborough after his victory at Blenheim.

Blenheim spaniel, one of a breed of small spaniels with short heads and very long ears, kept as pets. [from BLENHEIM PALACE]

blennioid (blĕn′ĭ oid′), *adj.* *Ichthyol.* **1.** resembling a blenny. **2.** pertaining to the blennies.

blennorrhagia (blĕn′ə rā′jĭ ə), *n.* *Pathol.* blennorrhoea (def. 2). [t. Gk: m. *blénnos* slime + -RHAGIA]

blennorrhoea (blĕn′ə rĭə′), *n.* *Pathol.* **1.** a discharge of mucus. **2.** a discharge of mucus from the genital organs, due to gonorrhoea. **3. acute blennorrhoea,** purulent conjunctivitis caused by gonorrhoea. Also, *Chiefly U.S.*, **blennorrhea.** [f. Gk: m. *blénnos* slime + m. *rhoía* -(R)RHOEA modelled on GONORRHOEA]

blenny (blĕn′ĭ), *n.*, *pl.* **-ies.** any of various fishes of the genus *Blennius* and allied genera, with an elongated tapering body and small pelvic fins inserted farther forward than the pectoral fins. [t. L: m. s. *blennius*, t. Gk: m. *blénnos* blenny, orig. slime]

blent (blĕnt), *v.* pt. and pp. of **blend.**

blephar-, a word element meaning 'eyelid', as in *blepharitis.* Also, **blepharo-.** [comb. form. repr. Gk *blépharon* eyelid]

blepharitis (blĕf′ə rī′tĭs), *n.* *Pathol.* inflammation of the eyelids. [f. BLEPHAR- + -ITIS]

Blériot (blĕ′rĭ ō′; *Fr.* blė ryō′), *n.* **Louis** (*Fr.* lwē), 1872–1936, French aeroplane inventor and aviator.

blesbok (blĕs′bŏk′), *n.* a large antelope of southern Africa, *Damaliscus albifrons*, having a blaze on the face. Also, **blesbuck** (blĕs′bŭk′), [t. Afrikaans: blaze buck]

blesmol (blĕs′mŏl, -mōl), *n.* any of several greyish southern African burrowing rodents of the family *Bathyergidae*, harmful to crops. [t. Afrikaans: blaze mole]

bless (blĕs), *v.t.*, **blessed** or **blest, blessing. 1.** to consecrate by a religious rite; make or pronounce holy. **2.** to request of God the bestowal of divine favour on. **3.** to bestow good of any kind upon: *a nation blessed with peace.* **4.** to feel thankful or grateful for (something) or grateful to (someone). **5.** to extol as holy; glorify. **6.** to protect or guard from evil. **7.** *Eccles.* to make the sign of the cross over. [ME *blessen*, OE *blētsian*, *blēdsian* consecrate, orig. with blood, der. *blōd* blood]

blessed (blĕs′ĭd, blĕst), *adj.* **1.** consecrated; sacred; holy. **2.** divinely or supremely favoured; fortunate; happy. **3.** beatified. **4.** bringing happiness; pleasurable. **5.** (in euphemistic use) damned. **6.** (used for emphasis): *every blessed penny.* —*n.* **7.** those who are blessed. —**bless′edly,** *adv.* —**bless′edness,** *n.*

Blessed Sacrament. See **sacrament** (def. 3).

Blessed Trinity, Trinity (def. 1).

Blessed Virgin, the Virgin Mary.

blessing (blĕs′ĭng), *n.* **1.** the act or words of one who blesses. **2.** a special favour, mercy, or benefit. **3.** a favour or gift bestowed by God, thereby bringing happiness. **4.** the invoking of God's favour upon a person. **5.** praise; devotion; worship. **6.** (in euphemistic use) a cursing.

blest (blĕst), *v.* **1.** pt. and pp. of **bless.** —*adj.* **2.** blessed.

Bletchley (blĕch′lĭ), *n.* a town in England, in NE Buckinghamshire. 17,093 (1961).

blether (blĕth′ə), *v.i.*, *v.t.*, *n.* blather.

bletherskate (blĕth′ə skāt′), *n.* blatherskite. Also, **bletherskite.**

blew (blōō), *v.* pt. of **blow.**

blewits (blōō′ĭts), *n.* a common edible mushroom, *Tricholoma personatum*, with a pale brown cap and mauve stalk; bluelegs.

Blida (blē′də), *n.* a town in N Algeria. 93,000 (est. 1960).

Bligh (blī), *n.* **William,** *c.* 1753–1817, English naval officer and admiral: commander in 1789 of H.M.S. *Bounty.*

blight (blīt), *n.* **1.** a widespread and destructive plant disease, such as **chestnut blight, potato late blight,** and **apple fire blight. 2.** any cause of destruction, ruin, or frustration. —*v.t.* **3.** to cause to wither or decay; blast. **4.** to destroy; ruin; frustrate. —*v.i.* **5.** to suffer blight. [orig. unknown]

blightbird (blīt′bûd′), *n.* a small New Zealand bird, *Zosterops caerulescens.*

blighter (blī′tə), *n.* *Slang.* **1.** a person; fellow. **2.** a despicable person; cad.

Blighty (blī′tĭ), *n.* *Mil. Slang.* **1.** England; one's home country. **2.** (chiefly in World War I) a wound serious enough to get one sent back to England. Also, **blighty.** [t. Hind.: m. *bilāyatī* foreign, European, c. VILAYET]

blimey (blī′mĭ), *interj.* *Slang.* (an exclamation expressing surprise or amazement.) Also, **blimy.** [See GORBLIMEY]

blimp[1] (blĭmp), *n.* **1.** (formerly) a small, non-rigid airship or dirigible, used chiefly for observation. **2.** *Colloq.* any dirigible. [orig. uncert.]

blimp[2] (blĭmp), *n.* an elderly person, usually military, with reactionary views. [from Colonel *Blimp*, cartoon character created by David Low]

blind (blīnd), *adj.* **1.** lacking the sense of sight. **2.** unwilling, or unable to try, to understand: *blind to all arguments.* **3.** not controlled by reason: *blind tenacity.* **4.** not possessing or proceeding from intelligence. **5.** lacking all awareness: *a blind stupor.* **6.** drunk. **7.** hard to see or understand: *blind reasoning.* **8.** hidden from view: *a blind corner.* **9.** having no outlets. **10.** closed at one end: *a blind street.* **11.** done without seeing: *blind flying.* **12.** made without knowledge in advance: *a blind date.* **13.** of or pertaining to blind persons. —*v.t.* **14.** to make blind, as by injuring, dazzling, or bandaging the eyes. **15.** to make obscure or dark. **16.** to deprive of discernment or judgement. **17.** to outshine; eclipse. —*n.* **18.** something that obstructs vision or keeps out light. **19.** a shade for a window, as a strip of cloth on a roller, or a venetian blind. **20.** a blinker for a horse. See illus. under **harness. 21.** *Chiefly U.S.* a lightly built structure of brush or other growths, esp. one in which hunters conceal themselves; a hide. **22.** a cover for masking action or purpose; decoy. **23.** *Slang.* a bout of excessive drinking; drinking spree. **24. the blind,** sightless people. —*adv.* **25.** without being able to see one's way: *to fly blind.* **26.** without assessment or prior consideration: *to enter into a deal blind.* [OE, c. G *blind*] —**blind′ing,** *adj.* —**blind′ingly,** *adv.* —**blind′ly,** *adv.* —**blind′ness,** *n.*

—**Syn. 1.** BLIND, STONE-BLIND, PURBLIND mean lacking in vision. BLIND means unable to see with the physical eyes. STONE-BLIND emphasizes complete blindness. PURBLIND refers to weakened vision, literally or figuratively. **3.** irrational, uncritical. **19.** See **curtain. 21.** hiding place, ambush.

blindage (blīn′dĭj), *n.* *Mil.* a screen or other structure as for protecting men in a trench. [t. F, der. *blinder* to armour, t. G: m. *blinden* blind]

blind alley, **1.** a road, street, etc., closed at one end. **2.** a position or situation offering no hope of progress or improvement.

blind copy, a copy of a letter, etc., sent to someone other than the person addressed, no mention of this being made on the addressee's copy.

blinder (blīn′də), *n.* **1.** a person or thing that blinds. **2.** *U.S.* a blinker for a horse. **3.** a blind (def. 23); spree.

blindfish (blīnd′fĭsh′), *n.* any of various small fishes, as of the genus *Amblyopsis*, having rudimentary functionless eyes; found in subterranean streams.

blindfold (blīnd′fōld′), *v.t.* **1.** to prevent sight by covering (the eyes); cover the eyes of. **2.** to impair the clear thinking of. —*n.* **3.** a bandage over the eyes. —*adj.* **4.** with eyes covered: *a blindfold test.* **5.** rash; unthinking. [f. BLIND + FOLD[1] wrap up, r. *blindfell*, lit., a blind-fall. Cf. OE *(ge)blindfellian* make blind]

Blindheim (*Ger.* blĭnt′hīm), *n.* German name of **Blenheim.**

blind man's buff (blīnd′ mănz bŭf′), a game in which a blindfolded player tries to catch and identify one of the others. [see BUFF[2]]

blind spot, **1.** *Anat.* a small area on the retina, insensitive to light, at which the optic nerve leaves the eye. See diag. under **eye. 2.** a matter about which one is ignorant or unintelligent, despite knowledge of related things. **3.** *Radio.* an area in which signals are weak and their reception poor.

blind staggers, *Vet. Sci.* stagger (def. 12).
blindstorey (blīnd′stô′rĭ), *n., pl.* **-ries.** *Archit.* triforium.
blindworm (blīnd′wûm′), *n.* slow-worm.
blink (blĭngk), *v.i.* **1.** to wink, esp. rapidly and repeatedly. **2.** to look with winking or half-shut eyes. **3.** to cast a glance; take a peep. **4.** to look evasively or with indifference; ignore (often fol. by *at*). **5.** to shine unsteadily or dimly; twinkle. *—v.t.* **6.** to cause to blink. **7.** to shut the eyes to; evade, shirk. *—n.* **8.** a blinking. **9.** a glance or glimpse. **10.** a gleam; glimmer. **11.** *Meteorol.* iceblink. **12. on the blink,** *Slang.* not working properly. [ME *blinken*, var. of *blenken* blench. Cf. G *blinken*] **—Syn. 1.** See **wink.**
blinker (blĭng′kə), *n.* **1.** a device for flashing light signals. **2.** either of two flaps on a bridle, to prevent a horse from seeing sideways or backwards.
blinking (blĭng′kĭng), *adj. Slang.* confounded; blasted. **—blink′ingly,** *adv.*
blinks (blĭngks), *n.* a small portulacaceous herb, *Montia fontana.*
blip (blĭp), *n.* a spot of light on a radar screen indicating the position of an aeroplane, submarine, or other object.
bliss (blĭs), *n.* **1.** lightness of heart; blitheness; gladness. **2.** supreme happiness or delight. **3.** *Theol.* the joy of heaven. **4.** a cause of great joy or happiness. [ME *blisse*, OE *bliss*, *blīths*, der. *blīthe* BLITHE] **—Syn. 2.** See **happiness. —Ant. 2.** despair.
Bliss (blĭs), *n.* **Sir Arthur,** born 1891, English composer.
blissful (blĭs′fəl), *adj.* full of, abounding in, enjoying, or conferring bliss; supremely joyful. **—bliss′fully,** *adv.* **—bliss′fulness,** *n.*
blister (blĭs′tə), *n.* **1.** a thin vesicle on the skin, containing watery matter or serum, as from a burn or other injury. **2.** any similar swelling, as an air bubble in a casting or a paint blister. **3.** (formerly) a transparent bulge on the fuselage of an aeroplane, usually for mounting a gun. **4.** a blister plaster. **5.** *Colloq.* an unpleasant person. *—v.t.* **6.** to raise a blister or blisters on. **7.** to apply a blister plaster to. **8.** to subject to burning scorn, sarcasm, or criticism. *—v.i.* **9.** to rise in blisters; become blistered. [ME *blister*, *blester*, ? t. OF: m. *blestre* clod, lump (prob. of Gmc orig.)] **—blis′tery,** *adj.*
blister beetle, any of various beetles of the family *Meloidae*, many of which produce a secretion capable of blistering the skin, as the Spanish fly. Also, **blister fly.**
blister gas, *Chem. Warfare.* a poison gas that burns or blisters the tissues of the body.
blister plaster, *Med.* a plaster (often bearing blister beetles) applied to the skin to raise blisters.
blister rust, *Bot.* a disease, esp. of white pine trees, manifested by cankers and in the spring by blisters, raised by fungi of the genus *Cronartium.*
B. Lit., Bachelor of Literature.
blithe (blīth), *adj.* joyous, merry, or gay in disposition; glad; cheerful. [ME; OE *blīthe* kind, pleasant, joyous] **—blithe′ly,** *adv.* **—Syn.** mirthful, sprightly, light-hearted, buoyant. **—Ant.** solemn.
blithering (blĭth′ə rĭng), *adj.* **1.** nonsensical; jabbering. **2.** blinking.
blithesome (blīth′səm), *adj.* lighthearted; merry; cheerful: *a blithesome nature.* **—blithe′somely,** *adv.* **—blithe′someness,** *n.*
B. Litt., Bachelor of Letters.
blitz (blĭts), *n.* **1.** *Mil.* war waged by surprise, swiftly and violently, as by the use of aircraft. **2. the Blitz,** the night air-raids by German bombers in World War II on London and elsewhere, esp. in the period 1940–41. **3.** any swift, vigorous attack. *—v.t.* **4.** to attack with a blitz. Also, **blitzkrieg** (blĭts′krēg′). [t. G: lightning (war)]
blizzard (blĭz′əd), *n.* **1.** a violent windstorm with dry, driving snow and intense cold. **2.** a widespread and heavy snowstorm. [var. of d. *blizzer* blaze, flash, blinding flash of lightning; sense widened from lightning to storm. Cf. OE *blysa*, *blyse* torch, and *blysian* burn]
B. LL., Bachelor of Laws.
bloat (blōt), *v.t.* **1.** to make distended, as with air, water, etc.; cause to swell. **2.** to puff up; make vain or conceited. **3.** to cure (fishes) as bloaters. *—v.i.* **4.** to become swollen; be puffed out or dilated. *—n.* **5.** *Vet. Sci.* Also, **bloating.** (in cattle, sheep, and horses) a distension of the rumen or paunch or of the large colon by gases of fermentation, caused by ravenous eating of green forage, esp. legumes. [der. *bloat*, adj., ME *blout* puffy, t. Scand.; cf. Icel. *blautr* soft]
bloater (blō′tə), *n.* **1.** a herring cured by being salted and briefly smoked and dried. **2.** a mackerel similarly cured.
blob (blŏb), *n.* **1.** a small globe of liquid; a bubble. **2.** a small lump, drop, splotch, or daub. **3.** *Colloq.* (in cricket) nought; no runs: *out for a blob.* [? imit.]
bloc (blŏk), *n.* **1.** a group of states or territories united by some common factor. **2.** *Europ. Politics.* a coalition of factions or parties for a particular measure or purpose. **3.** *U.S. Politics.* a group of legislators, usually of both parties, who vote together for some particular interest: *the farm bloc in Congress.* [t. F. See BLOCK]
Bloch (blôk; *Ger.* blôKH), *n.* **Ernest,** 1880–1959, U.S. composer born in Switzerland.
block (blŏk), *n.* **1.** a solid mass of wood, stone, etc., usually with one or more plane or approximately plane faces. **2.** a child's building brick. **3.** a mould or piece on which something is shaped or kept in shape, as a hat block. **4.** a piece of wood prepared for cutting, or as cut, for wood engraving. **5.** *Print.* a letterpress printing plate, mounted on a base to make it type-high. **6.** a (wooden) bench or board for chopping or cutting on. **7.** the support on which a person about to be beheaded lays his head. **8.** a platform from which an auctioneer sells. **9.** *Mech.* **a.** a device consisting of one or more grooved pulleys mounted in a casing or shell, to which a hook or the like is attached, used for transmitting power, changing the direction of motion, etc. **b.** the casing or shell holding the pulley. **10.** an obstacle or hindrance. **11.** a blocking or obstructing, or blocked or obstructed state or condition. **12.** *Pathol.* an obstruction, as of a nerve. **13.** a dull, stolid, or insensitive person. **14.** *Slang.* the head. **15.** *Sport.* a hindering of an opponent's actions. **16.** *Cricket.* a mark made by the batsman on the crease when taking guard. **17.** a quantity, portion, or section taken as a unit or dealt with at one time: *block of tickets.* **18.** a row of contiguous buildings, or one large building, divided into separate houses, flats, shops, etc. **19.** *U.S.* **a.** a portion of a city, town, etc., enclosed by (usually four) neighbouring and intersecting streets. **b.** the length of one side of this; distance between one intersection and the next. **20.** a block section. **21.** a large number of shares taken together, as on the stock exchange. **22.** a writing or sketching pad. **23.** *Philately.* a group of four or more unseparated stamps, not in a strip. **24.** *Athletics.* a starting block. **25.** a blocked shoe. *—v.t.* **26.** to fit with blocks; mount on a block. **27.** to shape or prepare on or with a block. **28.** to cut into blocks. **29.** to sketch or outline roughly or in a general plan, without details (often fol. by *out*). **30.** to obstruct (a space, progress); check, hinder or prevent (a person) by placing obstacles in the way; stop up. **31.** to restrict the use of (a currency, etc.). **32.** *Pathol., Physiol.* to stop the passage of impulses in (a nerve, etc.). *—v.i.* **33.** to act so as to obstruct an opponent (as in football, boxing, etc.). **34.** *Cricket.* to stop the ball with the bat. [ME *blok*, appar. t. OF: m. *bloc* block, mass, t. Gmc (cf. G *Block*)] **—block′er,** *n.*

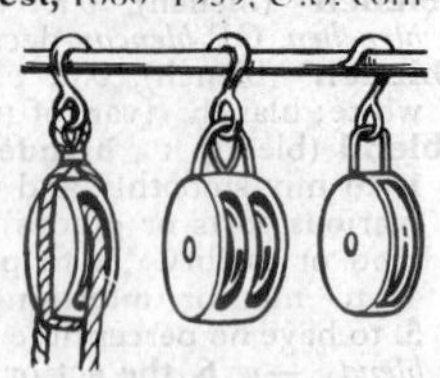

Single and double blocks (def. 9)

blockade (blŏ kād′), *n., v.,* **-kaded, -kading.** *—n.* **1.** *Naval, Mil.* the shutting up of a place, esp. a port, harbour, or part of a coast by hostile ships or troops to prevent entrance or exit. **2.** any obstruction of passage or progress. *—v.t.* **3.** to subject to a blockade. **—blockad′er,** *n.*
blockage (blŏk′ĭj), *n.* an obstruction.
block and tackle, the pulley blocks and ropes used for hoisting.
blockbuster (blŏk′bŭs′tə), *n.* **1.** an aerial bomb containing high explosives and weighing from 4 to 8 tons, used as a large-scale demolition bomb. **2.** *Colloq.* anything violent or violently unexpected.
block diagram, *Electronics, Engineering.* a diagram which shows the interconnections between the parts of a system.
blocked shoe, a dance shoe with a stiffened toe, worn by a ballerina to enable her to dance on the tip of her toes. Also, **point shoe.**
block grant, a fixed general grant to cover all subsidized activities of an organization.
blockhead (blŏk′hĕd′), *n.* a stupid fellow; a dolt.
blockhouse (blŏk′hous′), *n.* **1.** *Mil.* a fortified structure with ports or loopholes for gunfire, used against bombs, artillery, and small-arms fire. **2.** (formerly) a building, usually of hewn timber and with a projecting upper storey, having loopholes for musketry. **3.** a house built on squared logs.
blockish (blŏk′ĭsh), *adj.* like a block; dull; stupid. **—block′ishly,** *adv.* **—block′ishness,** *n.*
block lava, *Geol.* lava flows composed of rough angular blocks.
block letter, **1.** Also, **block capital.** a plain typelike capital letter. **2.** *Print.* a typeface or letter designed without serifs.
block plane, a small plane used for cutting across the grain of the wood.

block print, *Fine Arts.* a design printed by means of blocks of wood or metal.
block release, *Educ.* (in Britain) day release of a group of workers.
block section, one of the short sections into which a railway is divided for signalling purposes.
block signal, a fixed railway signal governing the movements of trains entering and using a block section.
block system, a system of controlling train movements by allowing only one train at a time into a block section.
block tin, pure tin.
block type, block letter (def. 2).
Bloemfontein (blo͞om′fŏn tān′), *n.* a city in the central part of the Republic of South Africa: capital of Orange Free State. 145,273 (1960).
Blois (*Fr.* blwȧ), *n.* a town in central France, in Loire-et-Cher department, on the river Loire; historic castle. 36,426 (1961).
Blok (*Russ.* blŏk), *n.* **Aleksandr Aleksandrovich** (*Russ.* ə lĭk sän′dr ə lĭk sän′drə vĭch), 1880–1921, Russian poet.
bloke (blōk), *n. Colloq.* man; fellow; guy. [t. Shelta]
blond (blŏnd), *adj.* **1.** light-coloured. **2.** (of a person) having light-coloured hair and skin. *—n.* **3.** a blond person. **4.** lace or net of silk, orig. unbleached, manufactured in France, now, esp. black silk lace. [t. F, t. ML: s. *blondus* yellow. Cf. OE *blondenfeax* grey-haired] **—blonde,** *adj., n., fem.* **—blond′ness,** *n.*
blood (blŭd), *n.* **1.** the fluid that circulates in the arteries and veins or principal vascular system of animals, in man being of a red colour and consisting of a pale yellow plasma containing semisolid corpuscles. **2.** body fluids spilling or spilled out; gore. **3.** the vital principle; life. **4.** bloodshed; slaughter; murder. **5.** the juice or sap of plants. **6.** temper or state of mind: *a person of hot blood.* **7.** man's fleshly nature: *the frailty of men's blood.* **8.** a man of fire or spirit. **9.** a rake. **10.** physical and cultural extraction. **11.** royal extraction. **12.** descent from a common ancestor: *related by blood.* **13.** *Stock Breeding.* recorded and respected ancestry; pure-bred breeding. **14.** *Slang.* a lurid piece of fiction; thriller; sex novel. **15. in cold blood,** calmly, coolly, and deliberately. **16. one's blood is up,** one's anger or belligerence is aroused. *—v.t.* **17.** to cause to bleed. **18.** *Slang.* to extort money from; bleed. **19.** *Hunting.* **a.** to give (hounds, etc.) a first taste or sight of blood. **b.** to smear with blood, as after a hunt. **20.** to initiate. [ME; OE *blōd*, c. G *Blut*] **—blood′like′,** *adj.*
blood and thunder, violence; sensationalism; bombast.
blood-and-thunder (blŭd′ən thŭn′də), *adj.* (of films, plays, etc.) characterized by violence and bombast.
blood bank, a place where blood is stored.
bloodbath (blŭd′bäth′), *n.* **1.** a massacre. **2.** a bath in blood.
blood blister, a blister containing a bloody fluid.
blood brother, one who has sworn lifelong brotherhood to, and mingled his blood with, another.
blood count, the count of the number of red or white blood cells in a specific volume of blood.
bloodcurdling (blŭd′kûd′lĭng), *adj.* frightening; terrifyingly horrible.
blood donor, one who gives blood for a blood bank or transfusion.
blooded (blŭd′ĭd), *adj.* **1.** having blood: *warm-blooded animals.* **2.** (of horses, etc.) derived from ancestors of good blood; having a good pedigree. **3.** having been through battle: *blooded troops.* **4.** initiated.
blood feud, a vendetta.
blood group, one of several classifications into which the blood may be grouped according to its agglutinogens. Also, **blood type.**
blood guilt, guilt of murder or bloodshed. **—blood′-guilt′y,** *adj.* **—blood′-guilt′iness,** *n.*
blood heat, the normal temperature (about 98 4°F or 37°C) of human blood.
bloodhound (blŭd′hound′), *n.* **1.** one of a breed of large, powerful dogs with a very acute sense of smell, used for tracking game, human fugitives, etc. **2.** *Colloq.* a detective; sleuth.

Bloodhound (25 to 27 in. high at the shoulder)

bloodless (blŭd′lĭs), *adj.* **1.** without blood; pale. **2.** free from bloodshed: *a bloodless victory.* **3.** spiritless; without energy. **4.** cold-hearted: *bloodless charity.* **—blood′lessly,** *adv.* **—blood′lessness,** *n.*
Bloodless Revolution, The, the Glorious Revolution of 1688.
blood-letting (blŭd′lĕt′ĭng), *n.* the act of letting blood by opening a vein.
bloodmobile (blŭd′mə bēl′), *n. U.S.* a vehicle containing medical equipment for receiving blood donations.
blood money, 1. a fee paid to a hired murderer. **2.** compensation paid to the survivors of a slain man.
blood orange, a variety of orange with blood-red flesh and skin when ripe.
blood plasma, the liquid part of human blood, often stored in hospitals, etc., for transfusions.
blood-poisoning (blŭd′poiz′nĭng), *n. Pathol.* a morbid condition of the blood due to the presence of toxic matter or micro-organisms; toxaemia; septicaemia; pyaemia.
blood pressure, *Physiol.* the pressure of the blood against the inner walls of the blood vessels, varying in different parts of the body, during different phases of contraction of the heart, and under different conditions of health, exertion, etc.
blood pudding, black pudding.
blood rain, rain coloured red by small particles of dust, as in the desert.
blood-red (blŭd′rĕd′), *adj.* **1.** of the deep red colour of blood. **2.** red with blood.
blood relation, one related by birth. Also, **blood relative.**
bloodroot (blŭd′ro͞ot′), *n.* **1.** the tormentil. **2.** a North American papaveraceous plant, *Sanguinaria canadensis,* with red root and root sap.
blood serum, serum (def. 1).
bloodshed (blŭd′shĕd′), *n.* destruction of life; slaughter.
bloodshot (blŭd′shŏt′), *adj.* (of the eyes) red from dilated blood vessels. [var. of *blood-shotten,* f. BLOOD + *shot(ten),* pp. of SHOOT]
blood sports, sports involving bloodshed, as hunting.
bloodstain (blŭd′stān′), *n.* a spot or trace of blood.
bloodstained (blŭd′stānd′), *adj.* **1.** stained with blood. **2.** guilty of bloodshed.
bloodstock (blŭd′stŏk′), *n.* thoroughbred stock, esp. stud horses.
bloodstone (blŭd′stōn′), *n. Jewellery.* a greenish variety of chalcedony with small bloodlike spots of red jasper scattered through it; heliotrope.
bloodstream (blŭd′strēm′), *n.* the blood flowing through a circulatory system.
bloodsucker (blŭd′sŭk′ə), *n.* **1.** any animal that sucks blood, esp. a leech. **2.** *Colloq.* an extortioner. **3.** *Colloq.* a sponger (def. 2).
blood test, a test of a sample of blood to determine blood type, presence of infection, parentage, etc.
bloodthirsty (blŭd′thûs′tĭ), *adj.* eager to shed blood; murderous. **—blood′thirst′ily,** *adv.* **—blood′thirst′iness,** *n.*
blood transfusion, the injection of blood from one person or animal into the bloodstream of another.
blood vessel, any of the vessels (arteries, veins, capillaries) through which the blood circulates.
bloodworm (blŭd′wûm′), *n.* a red aquatic larva or small dipteran of the genus *Chironomus.*
bloody (blŭd′ĭ), *adj.,* **bloodier, bloodiest,** *v.,* **bloodied, bloodying,** *adv.* *—adj.* **1.** stained with blood. **2.** attended with bloodshed: *a bloody battle.* **3.** inclined to bloodshed. **4.** of, of the nature of, or pertaining to blood; containing or composed of blood. **5.** *Colloq.* damned. **6.** *Colloq.* **a.** (of people) difficult; obstinate; cruel. **b.** (of events) cruel; unjust; unbearable. *—v.t.* **7.** to stain with blood. *—adv.* **8.** *Colloq.* very. [ME *blody,* OE *blōdig*] **—blood′ily,** *adv.* **—blood′iness,** *n.* **—Syn. 3.** bloodthirsty, murderous.
bloody mary, a cocktail consisting chiefly of tomato juice and vodka. Also, **bloody Mary.**
bloody-minded (blŭd′ĭ mīn′dĭd), *adj. Colloq.* **1.** obstructive; unhelpful; difficult. **2.** deliberately cruel or unpleasant. **—blood′y-mind′edness,** *n.*
bloom[1] (blo͞om), *n.* **1.** the flower of a plant. **2.** flowers collectively. **3.** the state of having the buds opened. **4.** a flourishing, healthy condition: *the bloom of youth.* **5.** prime; state of full development; perfection. **6.** a glow or flush on the cheek indicative of youth and health. **7.** *Bot.* a whitish powdery deposit or coating, as on the surface of certain fruits and leaves. **8.** any similar surface coating or appearance. **9.** any of certain minerals occurring as a pulverulent encrustation. *—v.i.* **10.** to produce or yield blossoms. **11.** to flourish. **12.** to be in a state of healthy beauty and vigour. **13.** to glow with a warm colour. [ME *blom(e),* t. Scand.; cf. Icel. *blōm* flower, *blōmi* prosperity] **—bloom′less,** *adj.* **—Syn. 4.** freshness, glow, flush.
bloom[2] (blo͞om), *n.* a semi-finished steel ingot rolled to reduced size. [OE *blōma* lump of metal]
bloomer[1] (blo͞o′mə), *n.* **1.** a plant which blooms. **2.** *Colloq.* an embarrassingly foolish mistake; laughable blunder. [f. BLOOM[1] + -ER[1]]
bloomer[2] (blo͞o′mə), *n.* **1.** (*pl.*) loose trousers gathered at the knee, formerly much worn by women as part of gymnasium, riding, or other like dress. **2.** (*pl.*) a woman's

undergarment so designed. **3.** a costume for women, advocated about 1850 by Mrs Amelia Bloomer of New York, consisting of a short skirt and loose trousers buttoned around the ankle. [named after Mrs *Bloomer*. See def. 3]

bloomer[3] (blo͞o′mə), *n.* an oblong loaf of white bread.

blooming (blo͞o′mĭng), *adj.* **1.** in bloom; blossoming; in flower. **2.** glowing as with youthful freshness and vigour. **3.** flourishing; prospering. **4.** *Slang.* (as a euphemism) damned. —**bloom′ingly,** *adv.*

Bloomsbury (blo͞omz′bə rĭ, -brĭ), *n.* a district in central London, noted as a centre for writers and publishers.

Bloomsbury Group, a group of literary and artistic friends, meeting in Bloomsbury ab. 1906–30, including E. M. Forster, Virginia Woolf, and Lytton Strachey.

bloomy (blo͞o′mĭ), *adj.* **1.** covered with blossoms; in full flower. **2.** having a bloom (def. 7), as fruit.

blossom (blŏs′əm), *n. Bot.* **1.** the flower of a plant, esp. of one producing an edible fruit. **2.** the flowers of a fruit tree, collectively: *apple blossom.* **3.** the state of flowering: *the apple tree is in blossom.* —*v.i.* **4.** *Bot.* to produce or yield blossoms. **5.** to flourish; develop (often fol. by *out*). [ME *blosme, blossem,* OE *blōs(t)m(a)* flower] —**blos′somless,** *adj.* —**blos′somy,** *adj.*

blot[1] (blŏt), *n., v.,* **blotted, blotting.** —*n.* **1.** a spot or stain, esp. of ink on paper. **2.** a blemish or reproach on character or reputation. **3.** an erasure or obliteration, as in a writing. —*v.t.* **4.** to spot, stain, or bespatter. **5.** to darken; make dim; obscure or eclipse. **6.** to make indistinguishable (fol. by *out*): *blot out a memory.* **7.** to dry with absorbent paper or the like. **8.** to destroy; wipe out completely (fol. by *out*). **9.** to paint coarsely; daub. —*v.i.* **10.** (of ink, etc.) to spread in a stain. **11.** to become blotted or stained: *this paper blots easily.* [ME; orig. uncert.] —**blot′less,** *adj.* —**Syn. 1.** blotch.

blot[2] (blŏt), *n.* **1.** *Backgammon.* an exposed piece liable to be taken or forfeited. **2.** an exposed or weak point, as in an argument or course of action. [t. D or LG: *bloot* bare, c. G *bloss*]

blotch (blŏch), *n.* **1.** a large irregular spot or blot. —*v.t.* **2.** to mark with blotches; blot, spot, or blur. [b. BLOT[1] and BOTCH[1]] —**blotch′y,** *adj.*

blotter (blŏt′ə), *n.* **1.** anything used to absorb excess ink. **2.** a piece, book, or pad of blotting paper.

blotting paper, a soft, absorbent, unsized paper, used esp. for drying ink.

blotto (blŏt′ō), *adj. Slang.* unconscious, esp. under the influence of drink.

blouse (blouz), *n.* **1.** a light, loosely fitting bodice or shirt worn by a woman, esp. one that is gathered or held in at the waist. **2.** a jockey's silk jacket. **3.** a loose upper garment, reaching about to the knees, worn esp. by peasants; a smock frock. **4.** a waist-length, single-breasted jacket forming part of army battledress. [t. F, ? t. Pr.: m. (*lano*) *blouso* short (wool)] —**blouse′like′,** *adj.*

bloused (blouzd), *adj.* (of women's clothes) having fullness above the waistline or belt, esp. at the back; blouse-like. [f. BLOUS(E) + -ED[3]]

blow[1] (blō), *n.* **1.** a sudden stroke with hand, fist, or weapon. **2.** a sudden shock, or a calamity or reverse. **3.** a sudden attack or drastic action. **4. at one blow,** with a single act. **5. come to blows,** to start to fight. [northern ME *blaw*; orig. uncert.]

—**Syn. 1.** buffet, thump, thwack, rap, slap, cuff, box. BLOW, STROKE both refer to a sudden and forceful impact, but differ both literally and figuratively, in that the first emphasizes the violence of the impact: *a blow from a hammer, a blow to one's hopes.* STROKE indicates precision and finality, often together with the idea of unexpectedness: *the stroke of a piston, a forehand stroke, a stroke of lightning.*

blow[2] (blō), *v.,* **blew, blown, blowing,** *n.* —*v.i.* **1.** (of the wind or air) to be in motion. **2.** to move along, carried by or as by the wind: *the dust was blowing.* **3.** to produce or emit a current of air, as with the mouth, a bellows, etc.: *blow on your hands.* **4.** *Music.* (of horn, trumpet, etc.) to give out sound. **5.** to make a blowing sound; whistle. **6.** to breathe hard or quickly; pant. **7.** *Colloq.* to boast; brag. **8.** *Slang.* to depart. **9.** *Zool.* (of a whale) to spout. **10.** (of a fuse, light bulb, radio valve, tyre, etc.) to burn out or perish; become unusable (often fol. by *out*). **11.** to be extinguished, as by the wind (fol. by *out*). **12. blow in,** *Colloq.* to make an unexpected visit; drop in; call. **13. blow over, a.** to cease; subside. **b.** to be forgotten. **14. blow up, a.** to come into being: *a storm blew up.* **b.** to explode: *the ship blew up.* **c.** *Colloq.* to lose one's temper. **d.** *Colloq.* to scold; abuse. —*v.t.* **15.** to drive by means of a current of air. **16.** to spread by report. **17.** to divulge (a secret). **18.** to drive a current of air upon. **19.** to extinguish (a flame, etc.) with a puff of air (fol. by *out*). **20.** to clear or empty by forcing air through. **21.** to shape (glass, etc.) with a current of air. **22.** to cause to sound, esp. by a current of air. **23.** to cause to explode (fol. by *up, to bits,* etc.). **24.** to inflate (fol. by *up*). **25.** *Photog.* to reproduce by enlargement (fol. by *up*). **26.** to expel noisily (fol. by *off*). **27.** to put (a horse) out of breath by fatigue. **28.** (pp. **blowed**) *Slang.* (used euphemistically) to damn. **29.** *Colloq.* to squander; spend quickly. —*n.* **30.** a blast of air or wind. **31.** the act of producing a blast of air, as in playing a wind instrument. **32.** *Colloq.* a walk in the fresh air; airing. **33.** *Colloq.* boasting or bragging. **34.** *Metall.* **a.** the blast of air used in making steel in a converter. **b.** the time during which, or that part of a process in which, it is used. [ME *blowe(n),* OE *blāwan*]

blow[3] (blō), *v.,* **blew, blown, blowing,** *n.* —*v.i., v.t.* **1.** to blossom; bloom; flower. —*n.* **2.** a yield or display of blossoms. **3.** the state of blossoming. [ME *blowen,* OE *blōwan*]

Blow (blō), *n.* **John,** 1649–1708, English composer and organist.

blower (blō′ə), *n.* **1.** a person or thing that blows. **2.** a machine for forcing air through a furnace, building, mine, etc. **3.** a whale. **4.** *Slang.* a telephone or speaking tube.

blowfish (blō′fĭsh′), *n.* puffer (def. 2).

blowfly (blō′flī′), *n., pl.* **-flies. 1.** any of various true flies, *Diptera,* which deposit their eggs or larvae on carcasses or meat, or in sores, wounds, etc. **2.** the bluebottle (def. 1).

blowgun (blō′gŭn′), *n.* a blowpipe (def. 1).

blowhole (blō′hōl′), *n.* **1.** an air or gas vent. **2.** either of two nostrils or spiracles, or a single one, at the top of the head in whales and other cetaceans, through which they breathe. **3.** a hole in the ice to which whales or seals come to breathe. **4.** *Metall.* a defect in a casting caused by trapped steam or gas.

blowing (blō′ĭng), *n.* **1.** the sound of any vapour or gas issuing from a vent under pressure. **2.** *Metall.* a disturbance caused by gas or steam blowing through molten metal.

blowlamp (blō′lămp′), *n.* a small portable apparatus which gives a hot flame by forcing paraffin under pressure through a small nozzle and burning it in air; used in plumbing, etc.

blown[1] (blōn), *adj.* **1.** inflated; distended. **2.** out of breath; fatigued; exhausted. **3.** flyblown. **4.** formed by blowing: *blown glass.* [see BLOW[2]]

blown[2] (blōn), *adj. Hort.* fully expanded or opened, as a flower. [see BLOW[3]]

blown oil, vegetable oil which has been thickened by having air blown through it at an elevated temperature.

blow-out (blō′out′), *n.* **1.** a rupture of a motor-car tyre. **2.** the blowing of a fuse. **3.** a sudden or violent escape of air, steam, or the like. **4.** *Colloq.* a big meal or lavish entertainment; spree.

blowpipe (blō′pīp′), *n.* **1.** a pipe or tube through which missiles are blown by the breath. **2.** a tube through which a stream of air or gas is forced into a flame to concentrate and increase its heating action. **3.** *Glass-blowing.* a long iron pipe used to gather and blow the viscous glass. **4.** *Med.* an instrument used to observe or clean a cavity.

blowtorch (blō′tôch′), *n. U.S.* a blowlamp.

blow-up (blō′ŭp′), *n.* **1.** an explosion or other drastic trouble. **2.** a violent outburst of temper or scolding. **3.** *Photog.* an enlargement.

blowy (blō′ĭ), *adj.* windy.

blowzy (blou′zĭ), *adj.,* **blowzier, blowziest. 1.** dishevelled; unkempt: *blowzy hair.* **2.** red-faced. Also, **blowzed** (blouzd). [der. *blowze* wench, of unknown origin]

blub (blŭb), *v.i.* **blubbed, blubbing.** *Colloq.* to weep; cry noisily. [short for BLUBBER]

blubber (blŭb′ə), *n.* **1.** *Zool.* the fat found between the skin and muscle of whales and other cetaceans, from which oil is made. **2.** the act of blubbering. —*v.i.* **3.** to weep, usually noisily and with contorted face. —*v.t.* **4.** to say while weeping. **5.** to disfigure with weeping. —*adj.* **6.** swollen. [ME *bluber,* n., *blubren,* v.; appar. imit. Cf. G *blubbern* bubble] —**blub′berer,** *n.* —**blub′beringly,** *adv.*

blubbery (blŭb′ə rĭ), *adj.* **1.** abounding in or resembling blubber. **2.** (of a cetacean) fat. **3.** blubbered; disfigured; swollen.

blucher (blo͞o′kə, -chə), *n.* **1.** a kind of strong leather half-boot. **2.** a shoe with the vamp continued up beneath the top, which laps over it from the sides. [named after Field Marshal von BLÜCHER]

Blücher (blo͞o′kə, -chə; *Ger.* blʏ′KHər), *n.* **Gebhart Leberecht von** (*Ger.* gĕp′härt lĕ′bə rĕKHT fōn), 1742–1819, Prussian field marshal.

bludge (blŭj), *v.,* **bludged, bludging.** *Austral. Colloq.* —*v.i.* **1.** to evade responsibilities. **2.** to impose on others. [short for BLUDGEON] —**bludg′er,** *n.*

bludgeon (blŭj′ən), *n.* **1.** a short, heavy club with one end loaded, or thicker and heavier than the other. —*v.t.*

2. to strike or fell with a bludgeon. 3. to force (someone) into something; bully. [orig. unknown] —**bludg′eoner,** *n.*

blue (blo͞o), *n., adj.,* **bluer, bluest,** *v.,* **blued, blueing** or **bluing.** —*n.* **1.** the pure hue of clear sky; deep azure (between green and violet in the spectrum). **2. the blue, a.** the sky. **b.** the sea. **c.** the unknown; the dim distance; nowhere: *out of the blue.* **3.** a substance, as indigo, used to whiten clothes in laundering them. **4.** a blue thing. **5.** a person who wears blue, or is a member of a group characterized by a blue symbol. **6. a.** a sportsman who represents or has represented his university in a contest with another, esp. Oxford (**dark blue**) and Cambridge (**light blue**). **b.** the honour awarded for this. **c.** the colours awarded for this. **7.** *Colloq.* a Tory. **8.** blue clothes. **9.** a bluestocking. **10.** (*pl.*) See **blues. 11.** *Austral. Slang.* a fight; dispute. —*adj.* **12.** of the colour blue. **13.** tinged with blue. **14.** (of the skin) discoloured by cold, contusion, fear, rage, or vascular collapse. **15.** Tory. **16.** right-wing. **17.** depressed in spirits. **18.** dismal: *a blue day.* **19.** *Slang.* drunk. **20.** obscene, or pertaining to obscenity. **21.** thick; teeming; crammed (fol. by *with*). **22. once in a blue moon,** rarely and exceptionally. —*v.t.* **23.** to make blue; dye a blue colour. **24.** to treat (laundry) with blue. **25.** *Slang.* to spend wastefully; squander. [ME *blew,* t. OF: m. *bleu,* t. Gmc (cf. G *blau*)] —**blue′ly,** *adv.* —**blue′ness,** *n.* —**Syn. 17.** despondent, dejected.

blue baby, an infant with congenital cyanosis.

Bluebeard (blo͞o′bĭəd′), *n.* **1.** (in folklore) a nickname of the chevalier Raoul, whose seventh wife found in a forbidden room the bodies of the other six. **2.** any man alleged to have murdered a number of his wives or other women.

bluebell (blo͞o′bĕl′), *n.* **1.** a liliaceous Old World plant, *Scilla nonscripta,* with drooping blue flowers. **2.** any of various other plants with blue bell-shaped flowers, as the harebell (**bluebell of Scotland**).

blueberry (blo͞o′bə rĭ, -brĭ), *n., pl.* **-ries. 1.** the edible berry, usually bluish, of any of various shrubs of the ericaceous genus *Vaccinium.* **2.** any of these shrubs.

bluebird (blo͞o′bûd′), *n.* **1.** any bird of the genus *Sialia,* comprising small North American passerine songbirds whose prevailing colour is blue; esp. the well-known eastern bluebird, *S. sialis,* which appears early in the spring. **2.** any of various other birds of which the predominant colour is blue.

blue-black (blo͞o′blăk′), *n., adj.* black tinged with blue, or with a blue sheen.

blue blood, aristocratic blood; the imagined hereditary exclusiveness of aristocrats. —**blue′-blood′ed,** *adj.*

blue-bonnet (blo͞o′bŏn′ĭt), *n.* **1.** a broad, flat bonnet of blue wool, formerly much worn in Scotland. **2.** a Scottish soldier who wore such a bonnet. **3.** any Scot. Also, **bluecap.**

bluebook (blo͞o′bo͝ok′), *n.* **1.** a British parliamentary or other official publication, bound in a blue cover. **2.** *U.S. Colloq.* a directory of socially prominent persons.

bluebottle (blo͞o′bŏt′l), *n.* **1.** any of several large, metallic blue and green flies of the dipterous family *Calliphoridae*; the larvae of some are parasites of domestic animals. **2.** the cornflower. **3.** any of various other plants with blue flowers, esp. of the genera *Campanula* and *Scilla.* **4.** *Slang.* a policeman. **5.** (in Australia) the Portuguese man-of-war.

blue butcher, the early purple orchid, *Orchis mascula.*

bluecap (blo͞o′kăp′), *n.* **1.** a year-old salmon, with blue markings on its head. **2.** the blue titmouse. **3.** a bluebonnet.

blue cheese, cheese marked with a blue mould; introduced by passing copper wires through the cheese during processing. Also, **blue vein.**

blue chip, 1. a blue-coloured poker chip, usually of high value. **2.** a reliable industrial share. **3.** a valuable asset.

blue-chip (blo͞o′chĭp′), *adj.* **1.** pertaining to or constituting a blue chip. **2.** having an outstanding quality among items in a particular group.

Bluecoat School, Christ's Hospital.

blue devils, 1. low spirits. **2.** delirium tremens.

Blue Ensign, the flag of H.M. Naval Reserve, blue with a Union Jack in the top left-hand corner.

blue-eyed (blo͞o′īd′), *adj.* **1.** having blue eyes. **2.** *Colloq.* darling; favourite.

blue-eyed grass (blo͞o′īd′), any of numerous plants of the iridaceous genus *Sisyrinchium,* having grasslike leaves and small, usually blue, flowers.

blue-eyed mary, a boraginaceous perennial, *Omphalodes verna,* of W Europe, with bright blue flowers.

Bluefields (blo͞o′fēldz′), *n.* a seaport in E Nicaragua. 17,649 (1963).

bluefish (blo͞o′fĭsh′), *n., pl.* **-fishes,** (*esp. collectively*) **-fish. 1.** a predacious marine food fish, *Pomatomus saltatrix,* bluish or greenish in colour, of the Atlantic coast of the Americas. **2.** any of many diverse kinds of fishes, usually of a bluish colour.

blue fox, 1. a variety of the small arctic fox, *Alopex lagopus,* having a year-round bluish pelt. **2.** any fox of this species while having a bluish fur in the summer season. **3.** the blue fur. **4.** any white fox fur dyed blue.

blue funk, *Slang.* a state of extreme fear.

bluegill (blo͞o′gĭl′), *n.* a freshwater sunfish, *Lepomis macrochirus,* of the Mississippi and its tributaries, much used for food and important among the smaller game fishes.

bluegrass (blo͞o′gräs′), *n.* **1.** any of various grasses of the genus *Poa,* as the **Kentucky bluegrass,** *P. pratensis,* etc. **2. the Bluegrass,** the Bluegrass Region.

Bluegrass Region, a region in the U.S., in central Kentucky, famous for its luxuriant crops of bluegrass.

blue-green (blo͞o′grēn′), *n., adj.* (of) a colour about midway between blue and green in the spectrum.

blue-green algae, *Bot.* unicellular or filamentous, asexual algae belonging to the class *Myxophyceae* (*Cyanophyceae*), usually bluish green as the result of blue pigments added to their chlorophyll.

blue-grey (blo͞o′grā′), *n., adj.* (of) a colour between blue and grey.

blue ground, *Mineral.* a blue-grey decomposed agglomerate which contains diamonds, found chiefly in Brazil and southern Africa.

blue gum, eucalyptus.

blueing (blo͞o′ĭng), *n.* **1.** the process of colouring or tingeing something blue. **2.** the production of a film of blue oxide on polished steel. **3.** treatment of clothes with blue to increase their whiteness. Also, **bluing.**

blueish (blo͞o′ĭsh), *adj.* bluish.

bluejacket (blo͞o′jăk′ĭt), *n.* **1.** a rating in the Royal Navy. **2.** any sailor.

bluejay (blo͞o′jā′), *n.* a well-known crested jay, *Cyanocitta cristata,* of the eastern U.S. and Canada.

bluelegs (blo͞o′lĕgz′), *n.* (*construed as sing. or pl.*) blewits.

Blue Mountains, 1. a dissected plateau in New South Wales, Australia; average height 3000 ft. **2.** a low range of mountains in the U.S., in NE Oregon and SE Washington.

Blue Nile. See **Nile, Blue.**

blue-pencil (blo͞o′pĕn′səl), *v.t.,* **-cilled, -cilling,** or (*U.S.*) **-ciled, -ciling.** to alter, abridge, or cancel with, or as with, a pencil that makes a blue mark, as in editing a manuscript, or in censoring.

blue peter, *Naut.* a blue flag with a white square in the centre, hoisted as a signal for immediate sailing, to recall boats, etc. [f. BLUE + *peter,* orig. REPEATER]

Blue peter

blue pointer, a large shark, *Isuropsis mako,* of the coasts of southern Australia and New Zealand.

blueprint (blo͞o′prĭnt′), *n.* **1.** a process of photographic printing, based on ferric salts, in which the prints are white on a blue ground; cyanotype: used chiefly in making copies of tracings. **2.** a copy made using this process. **3.** a detailed outline or plan. —*v.t.* **4.** to make a blueprint of.

blue racer, a variety of blacksnake, occurring in the central U.S.

blue riband, 1. a distinction awarded for the fastest crossing of the Atlantic by a liner. **2.** any high distinction.

blue ribbon, 1. blue riband. **2.** a blue ribbon worn as a badge of honour, esp. by members of the Order of the Garter.

Blue Ridge, a mountain range in the U.S., extending SW from N Virginia to N Georgia: a part of the Appalachians.

blue ruin, *Colloq.* gin[1].

blues (blo͞oz), *n.pl.* **1.** despondency; melancholy. **2.** *Jazz.* a type of song, of American Negro origin, predominantly melancholy in character and usually performed in slow tempo. [short for BLUE DEVILS]

blue shark, a shark, *Carcharias glaucus,* found in British waters.

blue sow-thistle, a tall composite herb, *Cicerbita alpina,* of the mountains of Europe.

Blue Stack Mountains, a range of low mountains in the Republic of Ireland in Co. Donegal. Highest point, Lavagh More, 2211 ft.

bluestocking (blo͞o′stŏk′ĭng), *n.* **1.** a woman who devotes herself to literary or intellectual pursuits (often to the detriment of femininity). **2.** a member of a mid-18th century London literary circle. —*adj.* **3.** of or pertaining to literary or intellectual women. [so called because

members of this group (def. 2) wore blue woollen instead of formal black silk stockings]
bluestone (blo͞o′stōn′), *n.* **1.** blue vitriol. **2.** a bluish argillaceous sandstone used for building purposes, flagging, etc.
blue streak, *Colloq.* something moving very fast.
bluetit (blo͞o′tĭt′), *n.* a species of titmouse with a blue patch on the head and blue wingtips.
bluetongue (blo͞o′tŭng′), *n.* a common lizard of Australia, *Tiliqua scincoides scincoides,* having a cobalt-coloured tongue.
blue vitriol, sulphate of copper, $CuSO_4 . 5H_2O$, a compound occurring in large, transparent, deep blue triclinic crystals, used in calico printing, medicine, etc. Also, **bluestone.**
blueweed (blo͞o′wēd′), *n. U.S.* viper's bugloss.
blue whale, the sulphur-bottom.
blue-winged teal (blo͞o′wĭngd′), a small pond and river duck, *Anas discors,* of North America, with greyish blue patches on the wings.
bluey (blo͞o′ĭ), *adj.* **1.** somewhat blue; bluish. **—*n.*** **2.** *Austral.* a swag.
bluff[1] (blŭf), *adj.* **1.** somewhat abrupt and unconventional in manner; hearty; frank. **2.** presenting a bold and nearly perpendicular front, as a coastline. **3.** *Naut.* (of a ship) presenting a broad, flattened front. **—*n.*** **4.** a cliff, headland, or hill with a broad, steep face. [prob. t. LG: m. *blaf* flat] **—bluff′ly,** *adv.* **—bluff′ness,** *n.* **—Syn. 1.** See **blunt. 2.** steep, precipitous.
bluff[2] (blŭf), *v.t.* **1.** to mislead by presenting a bold front. **2.** to gain by bluffing: *he bluffed his way.* **3.** *Poker.* to deceive by a show of confidence in the strength of one's cards. **—*v.i.*** **4.** to mislead someone by presenting a bold front. **—*n.*** **5.** an act of bluffing. 6. one who bluffs; a bluffer. [orig. uncert.] **—bluff′er,** *n.*
bluing (blo͞o′ĭng), *n.* **1.** *Chiefly U.S.* blue (def. 3). **2.** blueing.
bluish (blo͞o′ĭsh), *adj.* somewhat blue. Also, **blueish. —blu′ishness,** *n.*
Blum (*Fr.* blo͞om), *n.* **Léon** (*Fr.* lĕ ôɴ′), 1872–1950, French statesman.
blunder (blŭn′də), *n.* **1.** a gross or stupid mistake. **—*v.i.*** **2.** to move or act blindly, stupidly, or without direction or steady guidance. **3.** to make a gross or stupid mistake, esp. through mental confusion. **—*v.t.*** **4.** to bungle; botch. **5.** to utter thoughtlessly; blurt out. [ME *blondren,* t. Scand.; cf. OSw. *blundra*] **—blun′derer,** *n.* **—blun′deringly,** *adv.* **—Syn. 1.** error. See **mistake.**
blunderbuss (blŭn′də bŭs′), *n.* **1.** a short musket of wide bore with expanded muzzle to scatter shot, bullets, or slugs at close range. **2.** a stupid blundering person. [alter. of D *donderbus,* f. *donder* thunder + *buss* gun, orig. box]
blunge (blŭnj), *v.t.,* **blunged, blunging.** to mix (clay or the like) with water, forming a liquid suspension. [b. BLEND and PLUNGE]
blunger (blŭn′jə), *n.* a large vessel containing rotating arms for mechanical mixing.
blunt (blŭnt), *adj.* **1.** having an obtuse, thick, or dull edge or tip; rounded; not sharp. **2.** abrupt in address or manner; forthright; plain-spoken. **3.** slow in perception or understanding; dull. **—*v.t.*** **4.** to make blunt. **5.** to weaken or impair the force, keenness, or susceptibility of. [ME; orig. unknown] **—blunt′ly,** *adv.* **—blunt′ness,** *n.* **—Syn.** 1. See **dull.** 2. BLUNT, BLUFF, BRUSQUE, CURT characterize manners and speech. BLUNT suggests lack of polish and of regard for the feelings of others: *blunt and tactless.* BLUFF implies an unintentional roughness together with so much good-natured heartiness that others rarely take offence: *a bluff sea-captain.* BRUSQUE connotes sharpness and abruptness of speech or manner: *a brusque denial.* CURT applies esp. to disconcertingly or discourteously concise language: *a curt reply.*
blur (blû), *v.,* **blurred, blurring,** *n.* **—*v.t.*** **1.** to obscure or sully as by smearing with ink, etc. **2.** to obscure by making confused in form or outline; make indistinct. **3.** to dim the perception or susceptibility of; make dull or insensible. **—*v.i.*** **4.** to become indistinct: *the vision blurred.* **5.** to make blurs. **—*n.*** **6.** a smudge or smear which obscures. **7.** a blurred condition; indistinctness. [? akin to BLEAR] **—blur′ry,** *adj.*
blurb (blûb), *n.* an announcement or advertisement, usually an effusively laudatory one, esp. on the jacket flap of a book. [coined by Gelett Burgess]
blurt (blût), *v.t.* **1.** to utter suddenly or inadvertently; divulge unadvisedly (usually fol. by *out*). **—*n.*** **2.** an abrupt utterance. [? imit.]
blush (blŭsh), *v.i.* **1.** to redden as from embarrassment, shame, or modesty. **2.** to feel shame (*at, for,* etc.). **3.** (of the sky, flowers, etc.) to become rosy. **—*v.t.*** **4.** to make red; flush. **5.** to make known by a blush. **—*n.*** **6.** a reddening, as of the face. **7.** a rosy or pinkish tinge. **8. at the first blush,** at first sight. **—*adj.*** **9.** pale pink. [ME *blusche(n),* OE *blyscan* redden] **—blush′er,** *n.* **—blush′ful,** *adj.* **—blush′less,** *adj.* **—blush′ingly,** *adv.*
bluster (blŭs′tə), *v.i.* **1.** to roar and be tumultuous, as wind. **2.** to be loud, noisy, or swaggering; utter loud, empty menaces or protests. **—*v.t.*** **3.** to force or accomplish by blustering. **—*n.*** **4.** boisterous noise and violence. **5.** noisy, empty menaces or protests; inflated talk. [cf. Icel. *blāstr* blowing] **—blus′terer,** *n.* **—blus′teringly,** *adv.* **—blus′tery, blus′terous,** *adj.*
Blyth (blīth), *n.* a seaport in England, in S Northumberland. 35,921 (1961).
Blyton (blī′tn), *n.* **Enid (Mary),** 1896–1968, English author, esp. of children's stories.
B.M., British Museum.
B.M.A., British Medical Association.
B.M.E., Bachelor of Mining Engineering.
B.Met., Bachelor of Metallurgy.
B. Mus., 1. Bachelor of Music. **2.** British Museum.
bn, battalion.
B'nai B'rith (bə nā′ bə rēth′, brĭth′), a fraternal organization of Jewish men. [t. Heb.: m. *bĕnē bĕrīth* sons of the covenant]
Bnei Brak (bə nā′brăk′), a town in W Israel, near Tel Aviv. 57,000 (est. 1964).
BO, *Colloq.* body odour, esp. due to excessive perspiration.
b/o, *Com.* buyer's option.
bo (bō), *interj.* (an exclamation used to surprise or startle, esp. children.) Also, **boh.**
Bo (bō), *n.* a town in S central Sierra Leone: administrative headquarters. 88,000 (est. 1961).
boa (bō′ə), *n., pl.* **boas. 1.** any of various non-venomous snakes of the family *Boidae,* notable for their vestiges of hind limbs, as the boa constrictor of the American tropics. **2.** a long, snake-shaped wrap of silk, feather, or other material, worn about the neck by women. [t. L]
Boabdil (bō′ăb dĭl; *Sp.* bō āb dēl′), *n.* (*abu-Abdallah,* '*El Chicho*') died 1492?, last Moorish king of Granada, 1482–92.
B.O.A.C., British Overseas Airways Corporation.
boa constrictor, 1. a boa, *Constrictor constrictor,* of Central and South America, noted for its size and crushing power. **2.** any large python or other snake of the boa family.
Boadicea (bō′ə dĭ sĭə′), *n.* died A.D. 62, queen of the Iceni who led an unsuccessful revolt against the Roman government of Britain. Also, **Boudicca.**
Boanerges (bō′ə nû′jēz), *n.* **1.** (*construed as pl.*) *Bible.* surname given by Christ to James and John, explained as meaning 'sons of thunder'. Mark, 3:17. **2.** (*construed as sing.*) a vociferous preacher or orator. [t. LL, t. Gk, t. Aram.: surname equiv. to Heb. *bĕnē regesh* 'sons of thunder']
boar (bô), *n.* **1.** an uncastrated male pig. **2.** a wild boar. [ME *boor,* OE *bār*]
board (bôd), *n.* **1.** a piece of timber sawn thin, and of considerable length and breadth compared with the thickness. **2.** (*pl.*) *Theat.* the stage. **3.** *Austral., N.Z.* **a.** the floor of a woolshed. **b.** the number of shearers employed in a woolshed. **4.** a flat slab of wood for some specific purpose: *an ironing-board.* **5.** a sheet of wood, paper, etc., with or without markings, for some special use: *a chessboard.* **6.** a blackboard. **7.** stiff cardboard covered with paper, cloth, or the like, to form the binding for a book. **8.** a table, esp. to serve food on. **9.** daily meals, esp. as provided for pay. **10.** an official body of persons who direct or supervise some activity: *a board of directors, board of trade.* **11.** the border or edge of anything, as in *seaboard.* **12.** *Naut.* **a.** the side of a ship. **b.** one leg, or tack, of the course of a ship beating to windward. **13. by the board,** over the ship's side. **14. go by the board,** to be discarded, neglected, or destroyed. **15. on board,** on or in a ship, aeroplane, or vehicle. **—*v.t.*** **16.** to cover or close with boards. **17.** to furnish with food, or with food and lodging, esp. for pay. **18.** to arrange for the furnishing of meals and lodging to (sometimes fol. by *out*). **19.** to go on board of or enter (a ship, train, etc.). **20.** to come up alongside of (a ship), as to attack or to go on board. **21.** to approach; accost. **—*v.i.*** **22.** to take one's meals, or be supplied with food and lodging at a fixed price. **23. board out,** to take meals and lodging away from home. [OE *bord* board, table, shield]
boarder (bô′də), *n.* **1.** one who is supplied with meals and lodging. **2.** a pupil at a boarding school. **3.** a person chosen to board an enemy ship.
board foot, a unit of measure equal to the cubic contents of a piece of timber one foot square and one inch thick, used in measuring logs and timber.
boarding (bô′dĭng), *n.* **1.** wooden boards collectively. **2.** a structure of boards, as in a fence or a floor.

boarding house, a place, usually a home, at which board is furnished, often with lodging.

boarding school, a school at which board and lodging are furnished for the pupils.

board measure, *Bldg Trades.* a system of cubic measure in which the unit is the board foot.

Board of Trade, (in Britain) the ministry that supervises and encourages commerce and industry.

Board of Trade unit, a kilowatt-hour. *Abbrev.:* B.T.U.

board rule, a measuring device having scales for finding the cubic contents of a board without calculation.

board school, *Educ. Hist.* (in Britain) an elementary school, providing free compulsory education under the Education Act, 1872.

boarfish (bôr′fĭsh′), *n.* any of various fishes of different genera which have a projecting snout, esp. a small spiny-rayed European fish, *Capros aper.*

boarhound (bôr′hound′), *n.* any of various large dogs used orig. for hunting wild boars, esp. a dog of a German breed (**German boarhound**) or a Great Dane.

boarish (bôr′rĭsh), *adj.* swinish; sensual; cruel.

boast[1] (bōst), *v.i.* **1.** to speak exaggeratedly and objectionably, esp. about oneself. **2.** to speak with pride (fol. by *of*). —*v.t.* **3.** to speak of with excessive pride, vanity, or exultation. **4.** to be proud in the possession of: *the town boasts a new school.* —*n.* **5.** a thing boasted of. **6.** exaggerated or objectionable speech; bragging. [ME *bosten*; orig. unknown] —**boast′er,** *n.* —**boast′ingly,** *adv.*

—**Syn. 1, 2.** BOAST, BRAG imply vocal self-praise or claims to superiority over others. BOAST usually refers to a particular ability, possession, etc., which may be one of such kind as to justify a good deal of pride: *he boasts of his ability as a singer.* BRAG, a more colloquial term, usually suggests a more ostentatious and exaggerated boasting but less well-founded: *he loudly brags of his marksmanship.*

boast[2] (bōst), *v.t.* to dress or shape (stone, etc.) roughly. [orig. uncert.]

boaster (bōs′tə), *n.* a steel chisel with a two-inch cutting edge for boasting.

boastful (bōst′fəl), *adj.* given to or characterized by boasting. —**boast′fully,** *adv.* —**boast′fulness,** *n.*

boat (bōt), *n.* **1.** a vessel for transport by water, constructed to provide buoyancy by excluding water and shaped to give stability and permit propulsion. **2.** a small ship, generally for specialized use. **3.** a small vessel carried for use by a large one. **4.** *Colloq.* a ship. **5.** an open dish resembling a boat: *a gravy boat.* **6. in the same boat,** faced with the same, esp. unfortunate, circumstances. **7. burn one's boats,** to commit oneself; make an irrevocable decision. —*v.i.* **8.** to go in a boat. —*v.t.* **9.** to transport in a boat. [ME *boot*, OE *bāt*, c. Icel. *beit*]

boatbill (bōt′bĭl′), *n.* a bird of the genus *Cochlearius*, of the heron family, containing the single species *C. cochlearius*, of tropical America.

boat-deck (bōt′dĕk′), *n.* the top deck of a ship where the small boats are carried.

boater (bō′tə), *n.* **1.** one who is boating. **2.** a straw hat with a flat hard brim.

boatful (bōt′fo͝ol′), *n.* as much as a boat will hold.

boathook (bōt′ho͝ok′), *n.* a metal hook fixed to a pole, for pulling or pushing a boat.

boathouse (bōt′hous′), *n.* a house or shed for sheltering boats.

boating (bō′tĭng), *n.* the use of boats, esp. for pleasure.

boatload (bōt′lōd′), *n.* **1.** the cargo that a vessel carries. **2.** the cargo that a vessel is capable of carrying.

boatman (bōt′mən), *n., pl.* **-men.** a person skilled in the use of small craft. —**boat′manship′,** *n.*

boat race, 1. a race between rowing boats. **2. the Boat Race,** a rowing race between Oxford and Cambridge Universities held annually on the Thames between Putney and Mortlake.

boatswain (bō′sən; *rarely* bōt′swān′), *n.* a warrant officer on a warship, or a petty officer on a merchant vessel, in charge of rigging, anchors, cables, etc. Also, **bo's'n, bosun.** [OE *bātswegen* boatman]

boatswain's chair, *Naut.* a cradle (def. 5). Also, **bosun's chair.**

boat-train (bōt′trān′), *n.* a train making connection with a ship.

Boaz (bō′ăz), *n. Bible.* husband of Ruth. Ruth 2–4.

bob[1] (bŏb), *n., v.,* **bobbed, bobbing.** —*n.* **1.** a short jerky motion: *a bob of the head.* **2.** a quick curtsy. —*v.t.* **3.** to move quickly down and up: *to bob the head.* **4.** to indicate with such a motion: *to bob a greeting.* —*v.i.* **5.** to make a jerky motion with head or body. **6.** to curtsy. **7.** to move up and down with a bounding motion, as a boat. **8.** to rise to the surface or into view suddenly or jerkily (fol. by *up*). **9.** to move about with jerky motions. [ME; orig. uncert.]

bob[2] (bŏb), *n., v.,* **bobbed, bobbing.** —*n.* **1.** a style of short haircut for women and children. **2.** a horse's tail cut short. **3.** a small dangling or terminal object, as the weight on a pendulum or a plumbline. **4.** *Poetry.* **a.** a short line either at the end of a stanza or followed by a wheel (see **bob and wheel**). **b.** a short-lined refrain or burden. **5.** *Angling.* **a.** a knot of worms, rags, etc., on a string. **b.** a float for a fishing line. **6.** *Colloq.* a bunch; a cluster. **7.** a bobsleigh or one of its runners. —*v.t.* **8.** to cut short; dock. —*v.i.* **9.** *Angling.* to fish with a bob. [ME *bobbe* bunch, cluster, knob; orig. obscure]

bob[3] (bŏb), *n., v.,* **bobbed, bobbing.** —*n.* **1.** a tap; light blow. —*v.t.* **2.** to tap; strike lightly. [ME *bobben*; ? imit.]

bob[4] (bŏb), *n. Colloq.* a shilling. [orig. uncert.]

bob[5] (bŏb), *n. Bellringing.* a name given to a set of changes rung on six (**bob minor**), eight (**bob major**), ten (**bob royal**), or twelve (**bob maximus**) bells.

Bobadilla (*Sp.* bō bä thē′lyä), *n.* **Francisco de** (*Sp.* frän thēs′kō dē), died 1502, Spanish colonial governor in the West Indies: sent Columbus back to Spain in chains.

bob and wheel, *Poetry.* a short line (the bob) followed by a group of longer lines (the wheel) usually at the end of a stanza.

bobber (bŏb′ə), *n.* **1.** one who or that which bobs. **2.** a fishing bob.

bobbery (bŏb′ərĭ), *n., pl.* **-ries.** *Colloq.* a disturbance. [? Anglo-Ind., t. Hindi: m. *bāp re* O father!]

bobbin (bŏb′in), *n.* a reel, cylinder, or spool upon which yarn or thread is wound, as used in spinning, machine sewing, etc. [t. F: m. *bobine*, der. *bobiner* to wind up]

bobbinet (bŏb′ĭ nĕt′), *n.* lacelike fabric of hexagonal mesh, made on a lace machine. [var. of *bobbin-net*, f. BOBBIN NET[1]]

bobbin lace, lace made by hand with bobbins of thread, the threads being twisted round pins stuck into a pattern place on a pillow.

bobble (bŏb′l), *n.* **1.** a small pendant ball, usually of wool, for trimming scarves or other garments. **2.** any small ball which dangles or bobs.

bobby (bŏb′ĭ), *n., pl.* **-ies.** *Colloq.* a policeman. [special use of *Bobby*, for Sir *Robert* Peel]

bobby pin, *U.S.* a hairgrip.

bobbysocks (bŏb′ĭ sŏks′), *n.pl. Chiefly U.S. Colloq.* ankle-socks, esp. as worn by young girls.

bobbysoxer (bŏb′ĭ sŏk′sə), *n. Chiefly U.S. Colloq.* an adolescent or teenage girl.

bobcat (bŏb′kăt′), *n.* an American wildcat, esp. the species *Lynx rufus*, which is widespread in the U.S.

Bobo-Dioulasso (*Fr.* bō bō dyo͞o lä sō′), *n.* a town in W Upper Volta. 51,500 (est. 1963).

bobolink (bŏb′ə lĭngk′), *n.* a common North American passerine songbird, *Dolichonyx oryzivorus*, which winters in South America. [short for *Bob o' Lincoln*, supposed to be the bird's call]

Bobolink, *Dolichonyx oryzivorus* (7 to 7½ in. long)

bobotie (bō′bə tĭ, bə bō′tĭ), *n. S African.* a dish of minced meat seasoned with curry and spices, and served with a cream sauce. [t. Afrikaans, ? t. Malay: m. *burbur* potage or pulp]

bobsled (bŏb′slĕd′), *n., v.,* **-sledded, -sledding.** bobsleigh.

bobsleigh (bŏb′slā′), *n.* **1.** a racing sledge carrying two or more people, having two sets of runners, one at the back and one at the front. **2.** (formerly) a sleigh formed of two short sledges coupled one behind the other. **3.** either of these two short sledges. —*v.i.* **4.** to ride on a bobsleigh. [f. BOB[2] + SLEIGH]

bobstay (bŏb′stā′), *n. Naut.* a rope, chain, or rod from the outer end of the bowsprit to the cutwater, holding the bowsprit in. See illus. under **bowsprit.**

bobtail (bŏb′tāl′), *n.* **1.** a short or docked tail. **2.** a bobtailed animal. —*adj.* **3.** bobtailed; cut short. —*v.t.* **4.** to cut short the tail of; dock.

bobwig (bŏb′wĭg′), *n.* a short curled wig.

Boccaccio (bō kä′chĭ ō′; *It.* bōk kät′chō), *n.* **Giovanni** (*It.* jō vän′nē), 1313–75, Italian writer and poet.

Boccherini (bŏk′ə rē′nĭ; *It.* bōk kē rē′nē), *n.* **Luigi** (*It.* lwē′jē), 1743–1805, Italian cellist and composer.

Boccioni (bŏch′ĭ ō′nĭ; *It.* bōt chō′nē), *n.* **Umberto** (*It.* o͞om bĕr′tō), 1882–1916, Italian futurist painter.

boche (bŏsh), *n. Slang.* (offensively) a German. Also, **Boche.** [t. F, ? alter. of F *caboche* head, pate, noddle, der. d. stem *cab-*, g. L *caput* head]

Bochum (*Ger.* bō′KHo͞om), *n.* a town in West Germany, in W North Rhine-Westphalia, in the Ruhr. 355,500 (est. 1966).

bock beer (bŏk), a strong, dark German beer. Also,

bock. [t. G: m. *Bockbier*, for *Eimbocker Bier* beer of Eimbock, or Einbeck, in Lower Saxony]

bocking (bŏk′ĭng), *n. Textiles.* a coarse woollen fabric, resembling baize, formerly used as a floor-covering. [named after *Bocking*, a village in Essex]

bod (bŏd), *n. Slang.* a person: *an odd bod.* [short for BODY]

bode[1] (bōd), *v.*, **boded, boding.** —*v.t.* **1.** to be an omen of; portend. **2.** *Archaic.* to announce beforehand; predict. —*v.i.* **3.** to portend. [ME *boden*, OE *bodian* announce, foretell, der. *boda* messenger] —**bode′ment,** *n.*

bode[2] (bōd), *v.* pt. and pp. of **bide** (def. 2).

bodega (bō dē′gə), *n.* a wineshop. [Sp., g. L *apothēca*, t. Gk: m. *apothḗkē* storehouse]

Bodensee (*Ger.* bō′dən zė), *n.* German name of **Lake Constance.** Also, **Boden See.**

bodhisattva (bō′dĭ săt′və, bŏd′ĭ-, -wə), *n. Buddhism.* an enlightened being who delays entry into nirvana in order to help others to attain enlightenment. [t. Skt: enlightened being]

bodice (bŏd′ĭs), *n.* **1.** the fitted upper part of or body of a woman's dress. **2.** an undergarment covering the upper part of the body, usually of a warm material, worn by very young girls. **3.** a woman's laced outer garment covering the waist and bust, common in peasant dress. **4.** *Obs.* stays or a corset. [var. of *bodies*, pl. of BODY]

Peasant bodice

bodiless (bŏd′ĭ lĭs), *adj.* having no body or material form; incorporeal.

bodily (bŏd′ĭ lĭ), *adj.* **1.** of or pertaining to the body. **2.** corporeal or material, in contrast with spiritual or mental. —*adv.* **3.** as a whole; without taking apart. —**Syn. 2.** See **physical.**

boding (bō′dĭng), *n.* **1.** a foreboding; omen. —*adj.* **2.** foreboding; ominous. —**bod′ingly,** *adv.*

bodkin (bŏd′kĭn), *n.* **1.** a small pointed instrument for making holes in cloth, etc. **2.** a blunt needle-like instrument for drawing tape, cord, etc., through a loop, hem, or the like. **3.** a long pin-shaped instrument used by women to fasten up the hair. **4.** *Obs.* a small dagger; a stiletto. [ME *boydekin* dagger; orig. unknown]

Bodleian (bŏd lē′ən, bŏd′lĭ-), *n.* the chief library of Oxford University, re-established by Sir Thomas Bodley, 1545–1613, English diplomat and scholar.

Bodoni (bə dō′nĭ *for 2; It.* bō dō′nē *for 1*), *n.* **1. Giambattista** (*It.* jäm bät tēs′tä), 1740–1813, Italian printer. **2.** *Print.* a style of type originally designed by Giambattista Bodoni.

body (bŏd′ĭ), *n., pl.* **bodies,** *v.,* **bodied, bodying,** *adj.* —*n.* **1.** the physical structure of an animal (and sometimes, in *Biol.*, of a plant) living or dead. **2.** a corpse; carcass. **3.** the trunk or main mass of a thing. **4.** *Zool.* the physical structure of an animal minus limbs and head. **5.** *Archit.* the central structure of a building, esp. the nave of a church; the major mass of a building. **6.** a vehicle minus wheels and other appendages. **7.** *Naut.* the hull of a ship. **8.** *Aeron.* the fuselage of an aeroplane. **9.** *Print.* the shank of a type, supporting the face. **10.** *Geom.* a figure having the three dimensions, length, breadth, and thickness; a solid. **11.** *Physics.* anything having inertia; a mass. **12.** any of the larger visible spherical objects in space, as a sun, moon, or planet: *heavenly bodies.* **13.** the major portion of an army, population, etc. **14.** the central part of a speech or document, minus introduction, conclusion, indexes, etc. **15.** *Colloq. and Dial.* a person. **16.** *Law.* the physical person of an individual. **17.** a collective group, or an artificial person: *body politic, body corporate.* **18.** a number of things or people taken together. **19.** consistency or density; substance; strength as opposed to thinness: *wine of a good body.* **20.** matter or physical substance (as opposed to spirit or soul). **21.** that part of a dress which covers the trunk, or the trunk above the waist. —*v.t.* **22.** to invest with or as with a body. **23.** to represent in bodily form (usually fol. by *forth*). —*adj.* **24.** *Print.* (of printed matter) used mainly for the text, generally less than 14 point (as distinguished from *display matter*). [ME; OE *bodig*, c. MHG *potih*] —**bod′ied,** *adj.*

—**Syn. 1, 2.** BODY, CARCASS, CORPSE agree in referring to a physical organism. BODY refers to the material organism of an individual man or animal, either living or dead: *the muscles in a horse's body, the body of a victim (man or animal).* CARCASS refers only to the dead body of an animal, unless applied humorously or contemptuously to the human body: *a sheep's carcass, save your carcass.* CORPSE refers only to the dead body of a man: *preparing a corpse for burial.*

body blow, 1. *Boxing.* a blow to an opponent's body between the breastbone and the waistline. **2.** a serious (but not decisive) setback or defect.

body cavity, *Zool., Anat., etc.* the general or common cavity of the body, as distinguished from special cavities or those of particular organs.

body-centred (bŏd′ĭ sĕn′təd), *adj. Crystall.* (of a crystal structure) having atomic or ionic centres at the midpoint of each cubic cell, as at the corners. Cf. **face-centred.**

bodycheck (bŏd′ĭ chĕk′), *n.* **1.** *Lacrosse.* the act of placing oneself between an opponent and his objective. **2.** *Wrestling.* the act of striking or stopping a moving opponent with the whole body. —*v.i.* **3.** to perform a bodycheck. —*v.t.* **4.** to obstruct.

body corporate, *Law.* a person, association, or group of persons legally incorporated; a corporation.

bodyguard (bŏd′ĭ gäd′), *n.* **1.** a personal or private guard, as for a high official. **2.** a retinue; escort.

bodyline (bŏd′ĭ līn′), *adj. Cricket.* (of bowling) fast and aimed at the batsman's body.

body politic, a people as forming a political body under an organized government.

body scissors, *Wrestling.* a hold in which a wrestler falls to the canvas and holds both legs around his opponent's body and squeezes.

body-servant (bŏd′ĭ sû′vənt), *n.* a valet.

body-snatching (bŏd′ĭ snăch′ĭng), *n.* the act of robbing a grave to obtain a body for dissection. —**bod′y-snatch′er,** *n.*

bodystocking (bŏd′ĭ stŏk′ĭng), *n.* a one-piece undergarment for women completely covering the torso.

bodywork (bŏd′ĭ wûk′), *n.* the outer shell of the body of a vehicle, or its construction.

Boehm (bûm; *Ger.* bœm), *n.* **Theobald** (thĭə′bôld; *Ger.* tē′ō bält), ? 1793–1881, German flautist and musician: invented the Boehm system.

Boehm system, *Music.* a system of fingering now widely used for the flute and occasionally the oboe, and later adapted to the clarinet. [invented by Theobald BOEHM]

Boeotia (bĭ ō′shyə), *n.* a district and republic in ancient Greece, NW of Athens. *Cap.:* Thebes.

Boeotian (bĭ ō′shyən), *adj.* **1.** of or pertaining to Boeotia or the Boeotians. **2.** dull; stupid. —*n.* **3.** a native or inhabitant of Boeotia. **4.** a dull, stupid person.

Boer (bō′ə, bô; *Afrik.* bo͝or), *n.* **1.** a South African of Dutch extraction. —*adj.* **2.** of or pertaining to the Boers. [t. D: peasant, countryman. See BOOR]

boerboon (bo͝oə′bo͞on′), *n.* a large shrub, *Schotia speciosa,* of southern Africa, the bark of which is used medicinally and in tanning. [t. Afrikaans: Boer bean]

Boer War, 1. a war in which Great Britain fought against the Transvaal and Orange Free State, 1899–1902. **2.** a war between Great Britain and the Transvaal, 1880–81.

Boethius (bō ē′thyəs), *n.* **Anicius Manlius Severinus** (ə nĭsh′ĭ əs măn′lĭ əs sĕv′ə rī′nəs), A.D. 475?–525?, Roman philosopher and statesman. Also, **Boece** (bō ēs′), **Boetius** (bō ē′shəs).

boffin (bŏf′ĭn), *n. Slang.* a scientist, esp. one engaged in military research.

Bofors gun (bō′fəz), an automatic anti-aircraft gun. [named after *Bofors*, town in S Sweden, where it was first made]

B. of T., Board of Trade.

bog (bŏg), *n., v.,* **bogged, bogging.** —*n.* **1.** wet, spongy ground, with soil composed mainly of decayed vegetable matter. **2.** an area or stretch of such ground. **3.** *Slang.* a lavatory or latrine. —*v.t., v.i.* **4.** to sink in or as in a bog. [t. Irish or Gaelic: soft] —**bog′gish,** *adj.* —**bog′gy,** *adj.* —**bog′giness,** *n.*

bog asphodel, either of two liliaceous plants, *Nathecium ossifragum* of Europe, and *N. americanum* of the U.S., growing in boggy places.

bog bean, buck bean.

bogey (bō′gĭ), *n., pl.* **-geys. 1.** *Golf.* **a.** par (def. 4). **b.** one stroke above par on a hole. **2.** a bogy. [var. of BOGY]

boggle[1] (bŏg′l), *v.,* **-gled, -gling,** *n.* —*v.i.* **1.** to take alarm; start with fright. **2.** to hesitate, as if afraid to proceed; waver; shrink. **3.** to dissemble; equivocate. **4.** to be awkward; bungle. —*n.* **5.** the act of shying or taking alarm. **6.** *Colloq.* bungle; botch. [? special use of BOGGLE[2]] —**bog′gler,** *n.*

boggle[2] (bŏg′l), *n.* bogle.

bogie[1] (bō′gĭ), *n.* **1.** a low truck or trolley. **2.** one of a pair of pivoted trucks supporting a railway locomotive, carriage, tram, etc. **3.** bogy. [? var. of BOGY]

bogie[2] (bō′gĭ), *n. Austral. Slang.* **1.** a swim or bath. **2.** a swimming hole. [t. native Australian]

bogle (bō′gl, bŏg′l), *n.* a bogy; a spectre. Also, **boggle.** [der. obs. *bog*, var. of BUG bugbear]

bog moss, sphagnum.

bog myrtle, an aromatic marsh shrub, *Myrica gale*; sweet gale.

Bognor Regis (bŏg′nə rē′jĭs), a seaside resort in England, in West Sussex. 28,064 (1961).

bog oak, oak (or other wood) preserved in peat bogs.

Bogong (bō′gŏng), *n.* **Mount,** a peak in SE Victoria, Australia. 6516 ft.

bogong (bō′gŏng), *n.* bugong.

Bogor (bō′gô), *n.* a city in Indonesia, in W Java. 154,092 (1961).

bog orchid, an orchid, *Hammarbya paludosa,* with greenish yellow flowers.

Bogotá (bŏg′ə tä′; *Sp.* bô gô tä′), *n.* the capital of Colombia, in the central part. 1,697,311 (1964).

bog rush, a cyperaceous tufted perennial, *Schoenus nigricans,* growing in temperate regions near the sea.

bog spavin, *Vet. Sci.* a swelling on the hock joint of a horse. See **spavin.**

bogtrotter (bŏg′trŏt′ə), *n.* **1.** one who lives among bogs. **2.** *Colloq.* (in contemptuous use) a rural Irishman.

bogus (bō′gəs), *adj.* counterfeit; spurious; sham. [orig. uncert.]

bogy (bō′gĭ), *n., pl.* **-gies. 1.** a hobgoblin; evil spirit. **2.** anything that haunts and annoys one. **3.** *Mil. Slang.* an unidentified aircraft. Also, **bogey, bogie.** [der. obs. *bog.* See BOGLE]

Bohemia (bō hē′myə), *n.* **1.** Czech, **Čechy.** a region in W Czechoslovakia. 20,101 sq. mi. **2.** a district inhabited by Bohemians (def. 3). **3.** the social circles in which a Bohemian atmosphere is prevalent.

Bohemia

Bohemian (bō hē′myən), *n.* **1.** a native or inhabitant of Bohemia. **2.** the Czech language. **3.** (*often l.c.*) a person with artistic or intellectual tendencies who lives and acts with disregard for conventional rules of behaviour. **4.** a Gipsy. *—adj.* **5.** pertaining to Bohemia, its people, or their language. **6.** pertaining to or characteristic of Bohemians (def. 3). **—Bohe′mianism,** *n.*

Bohemian Forest, a low forest-covered mountain range on the boundary between SW Czechoslovakia and SE West Germany. Highest peak, Arber, 4780 ft. German, **Böhmerwald** (*Ger.* bœ′mər vält). See map under **Moravian Gate.**

Bohol (bō hôl′), *n.* one of the Philippine islands, in the central part. 750,000 pop. (est. 1968); 1492 sq. mi.

Bohr (bô), *n.* **Niels** (nēls), 1885–1962, Danish physicist.

Bohr theory, *Physics.* a theory of atomic structure in which the electrons are described as revolving in individual orbits about a central nucleus. [named after Niels BOHR]

bohunk (bō′hŭngk′), *n. U.S. Slang.* (in contemptuous use) an unskilled or semiskilled foreign-born labourer, specif., a Bohemian, Magyar, Slovak, or Croatian. Cf. **hunky**[2].

Boiardo (*It.* bô yär′dô), *n.* **Matteo Maria** (*It.* mät tĕ′ô mä rē′ä), 1434–94, Italian poet.

boil[1] (boil), *v.i.* **1.** to change from liquid to gaseous state, producing bubbles of gas that rise to the surface of the liquid, agitating it as they rise. **2.** to be in a similarly agitated state: *the sea was boiling.* **3.** to be agitated by angry feeling. **4.** to contain, or be contained in, a liquid that boils: *the pot is boiling, the meat is boiling.* **5.** *Colloq.* to feel very hot. **6. boil over, a.** to overflow while boiling. **b.** to be unable to suppress excitement, anger, etc. *—v.t.* **7.** to cause to boil. **8.** to cook by boiling. **9.** to separate (sugar, salt, etc.) from something containing it by heat. **10. boil down, a.** to reduce by boiling. **b.** to shorten; abridge. *—n.* **11.** the act of boiling. **12.** the state or condition of boiling. **13.** the agitated flow of silt, etc., into an excavation due to the pressure of water in the surrounding earth. [ME *boile(n),* t. OF: m. *boillir,* g. L *bullīre*]

—Syn. 3. BOIL, SEETHE, SIMMER are used figuratively to refer to agitated states of emotion. To BOIL suggests the state of being very hot with anger or rage: *rage made his blood boil.* To SEETHE is to be deeply stirred, violently agitated, or greatly excited: *a mind seethes with conflicting ideas.* To SIMMER means to be on the point of bursting out or boiling over: *to simmer with curiosity.*

boil[2] (boil), *n. Pathol.* a painful, suppurating, inflammatory sore forming a central core, caused by microbic infection, *Staphylococcus aureus*; a furuncle. [ME *bule,* OE *bȳl,* c. G *Beule*]

Boileau-Despréaux (*Fr.* bwȧ lō dĕ prĕ ō′), *n.* **Nicolas** (*Fr.* nē kô lä′), 1636–1711, French critic and poet.

boiled shirt, *Colloq.* a white or dress shirt.

boiler (boi′lə), *n.* **1.** a closed vessel together with its furnace, in which steam or other vapour is generated for heating or for driving engines. **2.** a stove or kitchen fire for heating water, or the stove and water tank. **3.** a tank for storing hot water. **4.** a vessel for boiling or heating, esp. a copper one. **5.** a chicken which should be cooked by boiling. **6.** one who boils.

boilersuit (boi′lə syōōt′), *n.* a one-piece suit of some cheap tough material for rough work.

boiling point, 1. the temperature at which the vapour pressure of a liquid is equal to the pressure of the atmosphere on the liquid, equal for water to 212°F or 100°C at sea-level. **2.** the peak of excitement or emotion.

boiling-water reactor, *Physics.* a type of nuclear reactor in which water is used both as coolant and moderator.

Boise (boi′zĭ, -sĭ), *n.* a town in the U.S., the capital of Idaho, in the SW part. 51,977 (1963).

Bois-le-Duc (*Fr.* bwȧ lə dʏk′), *n.* French name of **'s Hertogenbosch.**

boisterous (boi′stə rəs), *adj.* **1.** rough and noisy; clamorous; unrestrained. **2.** (of waves, weather, wind, etc.) rough and stormy. **3.** *Obs.* rough and massive. [ME *boistrous,* earlier *boistous*; orig. unknown] **—bois′terously,** *adv.* **—bois′terousness,** *n.* **—Syn. 1.** uproarious, obstreperous, roistering. **—Ant. 1.** sedate.

Boito (boi′tō; *It.* bŏy′tô), *n.* **Arrigo** (*It.* är rē′gô), 1842–1918, Italian poet and composer esp. of opera.

Bojardo (*It.* bô yär′dô), *n.* Boiardo.

Bojer (*Norw.* bō′yər), *n.* **Johan** (*Norw.* yô hän′), 1872–1959, Norwegian novelist and playwright.

bok-bok (bŏk′bŏk′), *n. S African.* a form of chain leapfrog played by two teams. [t. Afrikaans: lit., goat-goat or buck-buck]

Bokhara (bō kä′rə), *n.* Bukhara.

bokmakierie (bŏk′mə kĭə′rĭ), *n.* **1.** a large grey-green and yellow shrike, *Telophorus zeylonus,* family *Laniidae,* of southern Africa. **2.** the kokkewiet. [t. Afrikaans]

Bokmål (*Norw.* bōōk′môl), *n.* Riksmal; Dano-Norwegian. [Norw.: book-speech]

boko (bō′kō), *n. Slang.* the nose.

Boksburg (bŏks′bûg), *n.* a town in the Republic of South Africa, in S Transvaal. 71,029 (1960).

Bol., Bolivia.

bola (bō′lə), *n.* a weapon used by the Indians and Gauchos of southern South America, consisting of two or more heavy balls secured to the ends of one or more strong cords, which entangle the victim at which it is thrown. Also, **bolas** (bō′ləs). [t. Sp.: a ball, g. L *bulla* bubble, round object]

Bolan Pass (bō län′), a pass in NE Baluchistan. ab. 54 mi. long.

bolar (bō′lə), *adj.* of or pertaining to bole or clay.

bold (bōld), *adj.* **1.** not hesitating in the face of actual or possible danger or rebuff. **2.** not hesitating to breach the rules of propriety; forward. **3.** calling for daring, unhesitating action. **4.** overstepping usual bounds or conventions. **5.** conspicuous to the eye: *bold handwriting.* **6.** steep; abrupt: *a bold promontory.* **7.** *Print.* (of type, etc.) with heavy lines; in bold face. **8.** *Obs.* trusting; assured. **9. make bold to,** to venture to. [ME; OE *b(e)ald,* c. G *bald*] **—bold′ly,** *adv.* **—bold′ness,** *n.*

—Syn. 1. fearless, courageous, brave, intrepid, daring. **2.** BOLD, BRAZEN, FORWARD, PRESUMPTUOUS may refer to manners in a derogatory sense. BOLD suggests impudence, shamelessness, and immodesty (esp. in women): *a bold stare.* BRAZEN suggests the same, together with a defiant manner: *a brazen hussy.* FORWARD implies making oneself unduly prominent or bringing oneself to notice with too much assurance. PRESUMPTUOUS implies overconfidence, effrontery, taking too much for granted. **—Ant. 2.** modest.

bold face, *Print.* type that has thick, heavy lines, used for emphasis, etc. **—bold-face** (bōld′fās′), *adj.*

bold-faced (bōld′fāst′), *adj.* **1.** impudent; brazen. **2.** *Print.* (of type) having thick lines.

Boldon (bōl′dən), *n.* a town in England, in NE Durham. 25,218 (1961).

bole[1] (bōl), *n. Bot.* the stem or trunk of a tree. [ME, t. Scand.; cf. Icel. *bolr*]

bole[2] (bōl), *n.* **1.** any one of a class of soft, brittle, unctuous clays, varying in colour and affording pigments. **2.** a reddish pigment of this class used as a foundation for gilt work or gold leaf. [t. LL: m. s. *bōlus,* t. Gk: m. *bôlos* clod, lump]

bolection (bō lĕk′shən), *n. Archit.* a moulding which projects beyond the surface of the work it decorates. Also, **bilection.** [orig. uncert.]

bolero (bə lĕə′rō *for 1 and 2*; bŏl′ə rō *for 3*; *Sp.* bô lĕ′rô), *n., pl.* **-ros. 1.** a lively Spanish dance in three-four time. **2.** the music for it. **3.** a short jacket ending above or at the waistline. [t. Sp.]

boletus (bō lē′təs), *n.* any species of the genus *Boletus,* a group of umbrella-shaped mushrooms in which the stratum of tubes on the underside of the cap is easily separable. [t. L, t. Gk: m. *bōlítēs* kind of mushroom]

Boleyn (bōōl′ĭn, bōō lĭn′), *n.* **Anne,** 1507–36, second wife of Henry VIII of England; mother of Queen Elizabeth I.

bolide (bō′lĭd, -lĭd), *n. Astron.* a large, brilliant meteor, esp. one that explodes; a fireball. [t. F, t. L: m. s. *bolis* large meteor, t. Gk: missile]

Bolingbroke (bŏl′ĭng brōōk′; *older* bōōl′-), *n.* **Henry**

St John (sĭn′jən), **1st Viscount,** 1678–1751, British statesman and writer.

bolivar (bŏl′ĭ vä′; *Sp.* bò lē′bär), *n., pl.* **bolivars;** *Sp.* **bolívares** (*Sp.* bò lē′bärės). **1.** the monetary unit of Venezuela, equal to about £0·092 sterling. **2.** a silver coin of this value. *Abbrev.:* B. [named after Simón BOLÍVAR]

Bolívar (bō lē′vä; *Sp.* bò lē′ bär), *n.* **Simón** (sī′mən; *Sp.* sē mòn′), 1783–1830, Venezuelan statesman: leader of revolt of South American colonies from Spanish rule.

Bolivia (bə lĭv′ĭ ə; *Sp.* bò lē′byä), *n.* a republic in W South America. 3,509,000 pop. (est. 1962); 404,388 sq. mi. *Capitals:* La Paz and Sucre. —**Boliv′ian,** *adj., n.*

boliviano (bŏl′ĭ vyä′nō), *n., pl.* **-nos** (-nōz). until 1963 the monetary unit of Bolivia; equal to 0·001 of a **peso boliviano.** [t. Bolivian Sp.]

boll[1] (bōl), *n.* a rounded seed vessel or pod of a plant, as of flax or cotton. [var. of BOWL[1]]

boll[2] (bōl), *n. Scot. and N Dial.* **1.** a measure of capacity for grain, equal to 6 (Scotland) or 2 to 6 (England) imperial bushels. **2.** a measure of weight for flour, equal to 140 lbs. [t. Scand.; cf. Icel. *bolli,* c. OE *bolla* bowl]

Böll (*Ger.* bœl), *n.* **Heinrich** (*Ger.* hīn′rĭKH), born 1917, German author.

bollard (bŏl′əd), *n.* **1.** a strong post on a kerb or traffic island used as a protection or to prevent vehicles from mounting pavements. **2.** *Naut.* a vertical post on which hawsers are made fast. **3.** *Mountaineering.* a pillar of snow or ice, used as an anchor. [? f. BOLE[1] + -ARD]

bollocks (bŏl′əks), *n.pl. Taboo Slang.* balls. See **ball**[1] (def. 7).

boll weevil (bōl), a beetle of the southern U.S., *Anthonomus grandis,* that attacks the bolls of cotton.

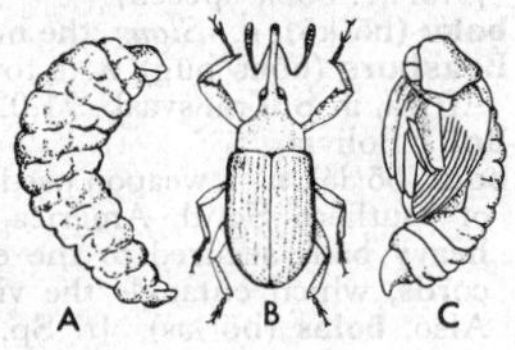

Cotton boll weevil, *Anthonomus grandis*
A, Larva; B, Adult; C, Pupa

bollworm (bōl′wûm′), *n.* any of various moth larvae which attack cotton bolls, as the **pink bollworm,** the larva of the moth *Platyeara gossypiella,* of the U.S., or the larva of *Earias insulana* or *Earias fabia* of Egypt and India.

Bologna (bə lōn′yə, -lŏn′-; *It.* bò lòn′nyä), *n.* **1. Giovanni da** (*It.* jò vän′nē), 1529–1608, Italian sculptor. **2.** a city in N Italy, in Emilia. 480,697 (1966). —**Bolognese** (bŏl′ə nēz′), *adj., n., sing. and pl.*

bologna sausage, a large-sized variety of sausage containing a mixture of meats. Also, **bologna** (bə lō′nə, -lōn′yə,-lō′nĭ).

bolograph (bō′lə grăf′, -gräf′), *n. Physics.* a record made by a bolometer. [f. s. Gk *bolḗ* ray + -(O)GRAPH] —**bolographic** (bō′lə grăf′ĭk), *adj.*

bolometer (bō lŏm′ĭ tə), *n. Physics.* an electrical resistance element for measuring minute amounts of radiant energy. [f. s. Gk *bolḗ* ray + -(O)METER[1]] —**bolometric** (bō′lə mĕt′rĭk), *adj.*

boloney (bə lō′nĭ), *n.* **1.** *U.S. Colloq.* bologna sausage. **2.** baloney.

Bolshevik (bŏl′shĭ vĭk), *n., pl.* **Bolsheviks; Bolsheviki** (-vē′kĭ). **1.** (in Russia) **a.** (1903–17) a member of the more radical majority of the Social Democratic Party, advocating abrupt and forceful seizure of power by the proletariat. **b.** (since 1918) a member of the Soviet Communist Party. **2.** (in any country) a member of a Communist Party. **3.** (in derisive use) any radical or progressive. Also, **bolshevik.** [t. Russ., der. *bolshe* greater, more, with allusion to the majority (Russ. *bolshinstvo*) of the party at the 1903 party congress]

bolshevism (bŏl′shĭ vĭz′əm), *n.* **1.** the doctrines, methods, or procedure of the Bolsheviks. **2.** the principles or practices of ultraradical socialists or political ultraradicals generally.

bolshevist (bŏl′shĭ vĭst), *n.* **1.** a follower or advocate of the doctrines or methods of the Bolsheviks. **2.** (*sometimes l.c.*) an ultraradical socialist; any political ultraradical. —*adj.* **3.** bolshevistic.

bolshevistic (bŏl′shĭ vĭs′tĭk), *adj.* pertaining to or characteristic or suggestive of bolshevists or bolshevism.

bolshevize (bŏl′shĭ vīz′), *v.,* **-vized, -vizing.** —*v.t.* **1.** to bring under the influence or domination of bolshevists; render Bolshevik or bolshevistic. —*v.i.* **2.** to become Bolshevik or bolshevistic; act like a Bolshevik. Also, **bolshevise.** —**bol′sheviza′tion,** *n.*

bolshie (bŏl′shĭ), *Colloq.* —*n.* **1.** (*sometimes cap.*) Bolshevik. —*adj.* **2.** bolshevistic. **3.** obstinate; difficult; tiresome. Also, **bolshy.**

bolson (bōl sōn′), *n. Phys. Geog.* a broad and nearly flat mountain-rimmed desert basin with interior drainage. [t. Sp.: large purse. See BURSE]

bolster (bōl′stə), *n.* **1.** a long ornamental pillow for a bed, sofa, etc. **2.** something resembling this in form or use. **3.** a pillow, cushion, or pad. **4.** a support, as one for a bridge truss. —*v.t.* **5.** to support with or as with a pillow. **6.** to prop, support, or uphold (something weak, unworthy, etc.) (often fol. by *up*). [ME *bolstre,* OE *bolster,* c. G *Bolster*] —**bol′sterer,** *n.*

bolt[1] (bōlt), *n.* **1.** a movable bar which when slid into a socket fastens a door, gate, etc. **2.** the part of a lock which is protruded from and drawn back into the case, as by the action of the key. **3.** a strong metal pin, often with a head at one end and with a screw thread at the other to receive a nut. See illus. under **nut. 4. a.** a woven length of cloth. **b.** a roll of wallpaper. **5.** the uncut edge of a sheet folded to make a book. **6.** a sudden swift motion or escape. **7.** any sudden dash, run, flight, etc. **8.** a jet of any liquid, esp. molten glass. **9.** an arrow, esp. one for a crossbow. **10.** a rod or bar which closes the breech of a rifle. **11.** a shaft of lightning; a thunderbolt. **12. bolt from the blue,** a sudden and entirely unexpected occurrence. **13. have shot one's bolt,** to have reached the limit of one's endurance or effort. —*v.t.* **14.** to fasten with or as with bolts. **15.** to shoot; discharge (a missile). **16.** to blurt; utter hastily. **17.** to swallow (one's food) hurriedly or without chewing. **18.** to make (cloth, wallpaper, etc.) into bolts. —*v.i.* **19.** to run away in alarm and uncontrollably, esp. of horses and rabbits. **20.** *U.S.* to desert a political party, etc. —*adv.* **21.** suddenly; with sudden meeting or collision. **22. bolt upright,** stiffly upright. [ME and OE, c. G *Bolzen*] —**bolt′er,** *n.* —**bolt′less,** *adj.* —**bolt′like′,** *adj.*

bolt[2] (bōlt), *v.t. Archaic.* **1.** to sift through a cloth or sieve. **2.** to examine or search into, as if by sifting. Also, **boult.** [ME *bult(en),* t. OF: m. *bulter* sift, t. MD: m. *buitelen*] —**bolt′er,** *n.*

bolthead (bōlt′hĕd′), *n.* **1.** the head of a bolt. **2.** *Chem.* (formerly) a matrass.

bolthole (bōlt′hōl′), *n.* any refuge; place or means of escape.

Bolton (bōl′tən), *n.* a town in NW England, in Lancashire. 160,887 (1961).

boltonia (bōl tō′nyə), *n.* a tall asteraceous perennial, genus *Boltonia,* of the U.S., sometimes cultivated. [t. NL; after James *Bolton,* died 1795, English botanist]

boltrope (bōlt′rōp′), *n.* **1.** *Naut.* a rope or the cordage sewn on the edges of a sail or the like to strengthen it. **2.** a superior grade of rope.

Boltzmann (*Ger.* bōlts′män), *n.* **Ludwig** (*Ger.* lōōt′vĭKH), 1844–1906, Austrian physicist.

bolus (bō′ləs), *n. Med.* **1.** a round mass of medicine, larger than an ordinary pill, forming a dose. **2.** a lump of masticated food which enters the oesophagus at one swallow. [t. LL, t. Gk: m. *bôlos* lump]

Bolzano (*It.* bòl tsä′nò), *n.* a town in Italy, in Trentino-Alto Adige. 99,843 (1966). German, **Bozen.**

bomb (bŏm), *n.* **1.** a hollow projectile filled with an explosive charge. **2.** any similar missile or explosive device. **3.** *Geol.* a rough spherical or ellipsoidal mass of lava ejected from a volcano. —*v.t.* **4.** to hurl bombs at; drop bombs upon, as from an aeroplane; bombard. —*v.i.* **5.** to hurl or drop bombs. **6.** to explode a bomb or bombs. [t. F: m. *bombe,* t. It.: m. *bomba,* g. L *bombus* a booming sound, t. Gk: m. *bómbos*]

bombacaceous (bŏm′bə kā′shəs), *adj. Bot.* belonging to the *Bombacaceae,* a family of woody plants including the silk-cotton trees and the baobab. [f. s. LL *bombax* (for L *bombyx,* t. Gk: silkworm, silk) + -ACEOUS]

bombard (*v.* bŏm bäd′; *n.* bŏm′bäd), —*v.t.* **1.** to attack or batter with artillery. **2.** to attack with bombs. **3.** *Physics.* to direct a constant stream of high-speed particles towards. **4.** to assail vigorously: *bombard someone with questions.* —*n.* **5.** the earliest kind of cannon, orig. throwing stone balls. [ME *bombarde,* t. OF: cannon, der. L *bombus* loud noise. See BOMB] —**bombard′ment,** *n.*

bombardier (bŏm′bə dĭə′), *n.* **1.** *Mil.* the lowest rank of NCO in the Royal Artillery. **2.** *Mil.* the member of a bomber crew who operates the bomb release mechanism. **3.** *Hist.* artilleryman. [t. F]

bombardon (bŏm′bə dən, bŏm bä′dn), *n. Music.* **1.** a bass reedstop of the organ. **2.** a large, deep-toned, valved brass instrument not unlike a tuba. [t. It.: m. *bombardone;* akin to BOMBARD]

bombasine (bŏm′bə zēn′, bŏm′bə zēn′), *n.* a fine-twilled fabric with a silk warp and worsted weft, formerly much used (in black) for mourning. Also, **bombazine.** [t. F: m. *bombasin,* t. LL: s. *bombasinum,* der. *bombax.* See BOMBAST]

bombast (bŏm′băst), *n.* **1.** high-sounding and often insincere words; verbiage. **2.** *Obs.* cotton or other material used to stuff garments; padding. —*adj.* **3.** *Obs.* bombastic.

[earlier *bombace*, t. F, g. LL *bombax* cotton, for L *bombyx* silkworm, silk, t. Gk]

bombastic (bŏm băs′tĭk), *adj.* (of speech, etc.) high-sounding; high-flown; inflated; turgid. Also, **bombas′tical.** —**bombas′tically,** *adv.*

Bombay (bŏm bā′), *n.* **1.** a former state in W India: previously a province of British India; enlarged in 1956 and in 1960 divided into two new states, Gujarat and Maharashtra. **2.** the capital of Maharashtra state: a port on the Arabian Sea. 4,152,056 (1962). See map under **Delhi.**

Bombay duck, a dried fish (the bummalo), eaten as a savoury with curries.

bomb bay, *Aeron., Mil.* the compartment of an aeroplane in which bombs are carried.

bombe (*Fr.* bôɴb), *n.* *French.* **1.** a sweet consisting of sponge, meringue, and cream, etc., with ice-cream. **2.** the circular mould or dish for containing such a sweet.

bomber (bŏm′ə), *n.* *Mil.* an aeroplane employed to carry and drop bombs.

bombload (bŏm′lōd′), *n.* the load of bombs carried by an aeroplane.

bombora (bŏm bô′rə), *n.* *Austral.* **1.** a submerged reef of rocks. **2.** a dangerous current over a reef. [t. native Australian]

bombproof (bŏm′pro͞of′), *adj.* strong enough to resist the impact and explosive force of bombs or shells.

bomb rack, a device for carrying bombs in an aircraft.

bombshell (bŏm′shĕl′), *n.* **1.** a bomb. **2.** a sudden or devastating action or effect: *his resignation was a bombshell.*

bombsight (bŏm′sīt′), *n.* *Mil.* an aiming instrument used to tell when to drop a bomb from an aircraft so that it will hit a specified target.

bombsite (bŏm′sīt′), *n.* the remains of a building which has been destroyed by a bomb.

bombycid (bŏm′bĭ sĭd), *n.* any of the *Bombycidae*, the family of moths that includes the silkworm moths. [f. s. L *bombyx* silkworm (t. Gk) + -ID[2]]

Bon (bŏn), *n.* **Cape,** a cape on the NE coast of Tunisia: surrender of the German Afrika Korps, May 12th, 1943.

bona fide (bō′nə fī′dĭ), in good faith; without fraud. [t. L] —**bona-fide,** *adj.*

Bonaire (bŏn′ĕə′; *Du.* bô nĕr′), *n.* an island in the Netherlands Antilles. 5661 pop. (1955); 95 sq. mi.

bon ami (*Fr.* bôɴ nȧ mē′), *French.* **1.** a good friend. **2.** a lover.

bonanza (bō năn′zə), *n.* **1.** a mine of wealth; good luck. **2.** *U.S.* a rich mass of ore, as found in mining. [t. Sp.: fair weather, prosperity, der. L *bonus* good]

Bonaparte (bō′nə pät′; *Fr.* bŏ nȧ pȧrt′), *n.* **1. Jérôme** (jə rōm′; *Fr.* zhĕ rôm′), 1784–1860, king of Westphalia (brother of Napoleon I). **2. Joseph** (jō′zĭf; *Fr.* zhô zĕf′), 1768–1844, king of Naples and Spain (brother of Napoleon I). **3. Louis** (*Fr.* lwē; *Du.* lo͞o ē′), 1778–1846, king of Holland (brother of Napoleon I). **4. Louis Napoléon** (lo͞o′ĭ nə pō′lyən), Napoleon III. **5. Lucien** (lo͞o′syən; *Fr.* ly syăɴ′), 1775–1840, Prince of Cannino (brother of Napoleon I). **6. Napoléon** (nə pō′lyən; *Fr.* nȧ pô lĕ ôɴ′), See **Napoleon I, Napoleon II.** Also, *Italian,* **Buonaparte.**

Bonapartism (bō′nə pä′tĭz əm), *n.* adherence to the Bonapartes or their policies. —**Bo′napart′ist,** *n., adj.*

bon appétit (*Fr.* bôɴ nȧ pĕ tē′), *French.* (I wish you) a hearty appetite.

Bonaventure (bŏn′ə vĕn′chə), *n.* **Saint** ('*the Seraphic Doctor*'), 1221–74, Italian scholastic theologian. Also, *Italian,* **Bonaventura** (*It.* bô nȧ vĕn to͞o′rȧ).

bonbon (bŏn′bŏn′; *Fr.* bôɴ bôɴ′), *n.* **1.** a fondant, fruit, or nut centre dipped in fondant or chocolate. **2.** a piece of confectionery. [t. F, der. *bon* good]

bonbonnière (*Fr.* bôɴ bŏ nyĕr′), *n.* *French.* a box of chocolates.

bond (bŏnd), *n.* **1.** something that binds, fastens, confines, or holds together. **2.** a cord; rope; band; ligament. **3.** something that unites individual people into a group. **4.** something that constrains a person to a certain line of behaviour. **5.** a bondsman or security. **6.** a sealed instrument under which a person or corporation guarantees to pay a stated sum of money on or before a specified day. **7.** any written obligation under seal. **8.** *Law.* **a.** a written acknowledgement of a debt. **b.** such an acknowledgement dependent upon the condition that one party shall do or refrain from doing a certain action. **9.** the state of dutiable goods on which the duties are unpaid (esp. in phrase *in bond*). **10.** *Finance.* a certificate of ownership of a specified portion of a debt due by government or other corporation to individual holders, and usually bearing a fixed rate of interest. **11.** *Insurance.* **a.** a surety agreement. **b.** the money deposited, or the promissory arrangement entered into, under any such agreement. **12.** a substance that causes particles to adhere; a binder. **13.** *Chem.* any valency linkage between atoms in a compound, esp. a unit of combining equivalent to that of one hydrogen atom. **14.** bond paper. **15.** *Bldg Trades.* the connection of the stones or bricks in a wall, etc., made by overlapping them in order to bind the whole into a compact mass. —*v.t.* **16.** to put (goods, an employee, official, etc.) in or under bond. **17.** *Finance.* to place a bonded debt on; mortgage. **18.** *Bldg Trades.* to cause (bricks or other building materials) to hold together firmly by laying them in some overlapping pattern. —*v.i.* **19.** to hold together from being bonded, as bricks in a wall. [ME, var. of BAND[3]] —**bond′er,** *n.*

—**Syn. 3.** BOND, LINK, TIE agree in referring to a force or influence which unites people. BOND and TIE are sometimes used interchangeably. BOND, however, usually emphasizes the strong and enduring quality of affection; whereas TIE may refer more especially to duty, obligation, or responsibility. A LINK is a definite connection, though a slighter one; it may indicate affection or merely some traceable influence or desultory communication: *a close link between friends.*

bondage (bŏn′dĭj), *n.* **1.** slavery or involuntary servitude; serfdom. **2.** the state of being bound by or subjected to external control. **3.** *Early Eng. Law.* tenure of land by villeinage. —**Syn. 1.** See **slavery.**

bonded (bŏn′dĭd), *adj.* **1.** secured by or consisting of bonds: *bonded debt.* **2.** placed in bond: *bonded goods.*

bonded carman, a carrier licensed to carry goods which are still in bond.

bonded warehouse, a warehouse for holding goods in bond. See **bond** (def. 9).

bond energy, *Chem.* the energy required to separate two atoms joined by a bond.

bondholder (bŏnd′hōl′də), *n.* a holder of bonds issued by a government or corporation. —**bond′hold′ing,** *adj., n.*

bond length, *Chem.* the distance between nuclei of atoms joined by a bond.

bondmaid (bŏnd′mād′), *n.* **1.** a female slave. **2.** a female bound to service without wages.

bondman (bŏnd′mən), *n., pl.* **-men. 1.** a male slave. **2.** a man bound to service without wages. **3.** *Early Eng. Law.* a villein or other unfree tenant. Also, **bondsman.**

bond paper, a superior variety of white paper.

bondservant (bŏnd′sû′vənt), *n.* one who serves in bondage; a slave.

bondsman (bŏndz′mən), *n., pl.* **-men. 1.** *Law.* one who is bound or who by bond becomes surety for another. **2.** bondman.

Bond Street, a street in the West End of London, noted for fashion shops.

bondwoman (bŏnd′wo͝om′ən), *n., pl.* **-women.** a female slave. Also, **bondswoman** (bŏndz′wo͝om′ən).

bone (bōn), *n., v.,* **boned, boning.** —*n.* **1.** *Anat., Zool.* **a.** any of the separate pieces of which the skeleton of a vertebrate is composed. **b.** the hard tissue which composes the skeleton. **2.** a bone or piece of a bone with the meat adhering to it, as an article of food. **3.** (*pl.*) the skeleton. **4.** (*pl.*) a body. **5.** any of various similar substances, such as ivory, whalebone, etc. **6.** something made of bone, or of a substance resembling bone. **7.** a strip of whalebone used to stiffen corsets, etc. **8.** (*pl.*) dice. **9.** (*pl.*) *Theat.* **a.** noisemakers of bone or wood used by a minstrel endman. **b.** an endman in a minstrel troupe. **10.** (*pl.*) *Colloq.* a surgeon. **11.** (in certain phrases) a point of dispute: *I have a bone to pick with you, he made no bones about it.* **12. feel in one's bones,** to feel intuitively. —*v.t.* **13.** to take out the bones of: *to bone a turkey.* **14.** to put whalebone into (clothing). **15.** *Agric.* to put ground bone into, as fertilizer. **16.** *Slang.* to steal. **17.** *Austral. Colloq.* to bring or wish bad luck on, orig. by sorcery with bones. —*v.i.* **18.** *U.S. Slang.* to study hard and fast; cram (often fol. by *up*). [ME *boon,* OE *bān,* c. G *Bein* leg] —**boned,** *adj.* —**bone′less,** *adj.* —**bone′like′,** *adj.*

Bône (*Fr.* bôn), *n.* former name of **Annaba.** Also, **Bona** (bō′nə).

bone ash, the remains of bones calcined in the air. Also, **bone earth.**

bone bed, *Geol.* a layer of rock containing bone remains.

boneblack (bōn′blăk′), *n.* a black carbonaceous substance obtained by calcining bones in closed vessels.

bone china, a kind of china in which bone ash is used.

bone-dry (bōn′drī′), *adj.* *Colloq.* dry as a bone; very dry.

bone earth, bone ash.

bonehead (bōn′hĕd′), *n.* *Colloq.* a stupid, obstinate person; a blockhead. —**bone′head′ed,** *adj.*

bone-idle (bōn′ī′dl). *adj.* *Colloq.* extremely lazy.

bonemeal (bōn′mēl′), *n.* bones ground to a coarse powder, used as a fertilizer or animal feed.

bone oil, a fetid, tarry liquid obtained in the dry distillation of bone.

bonesetter (bŏn′sĕt′ə), *n.* a medical practitioner who treats broken bones and similar disorders without the formal qualifications of a surgeon; an osteopath.

boneshaker (bōn′shā′kə), *n.* **1.** an early type of bicycle with solid tyres and no springs. **2.** *Colloq.* any ancient and rickety bicycle or other vehicle.

bonfire (bŏn′ fī′ə), *n.* **1.** a large fire in an open place, for entertainment, celebration, or as a signal. **2.** any fire built in the open. [earlier *bonefire*; heaps of wood and bones were burned at certain old festivals]

bongo[1] (bŏng′gō), *n., pl.* **-gos.** a large forest-dwelling antelope, *Taurotragus eurycerus*, of tropical Africa, of a chestnut colour striped with white, with spiralling horns.

bongo[2] (bŏng′gō), *n., pl.* **-gos, -goes.** one of a pair of small drums, played by beating with the fingers. [t. Amer. Sp.]

Bongo (bŏn′gō; *Fr.* bôɴ gô′), *n.* **Albert Bernard** (*Fr.* ȧl bĕr bĕr nȧr′), born 1935, president of Gabon since 1967.

Bonheur (*Fr.* bŏ nœr′), *n.* **Rosa** (*Fr.* rô zȧ′) (*Marie Rosalie Bonheur*), 1822–99, French painter of animals.

bonhomie (bŏn′ə mĭ; *Fr.* bŏ nŏ mē′), *n.* frank and simple good-heartedness; a good-natured manner. Also, **bonhommie.** [t. F, der. *bonhomme* good man]

Boniface (bŏn′ĭ fās′), *n.* **1.** name given to nine popes, esp. **Boniface VIII** (*Benedetto Gaetani*), *c.* 1235–1303, Italian ecclesiastic: pope 1294–1303. **2. Saint** (*Wynfrith*), A.D. 680?–755?, English monk who became a missionary in Germany.

Bonington (bŏn′ĭng tən), *n.* **Richard Parkes,** 1801–28, English landscape painter.

bonito (bə nē′tō), *n., pl.* **-tos, -toes. 1.** any of the mackerel-like fishes of the genus *Sarda*, as *S. sarda* of the Atlantic. **2.** any of several related species, as the **oceanic bonito** or skipjack, *Katsuwonus pelamis*. [t. Sp.]

bonjour (*Fr.* bôɴ zhōōr′), *n., interj. French.* good day; hello.

bonkers (bŏng′kəz), *adj. Slang.* crazy.

bon mot (*Fr.* bôɴ mô′), *pl.* **bons mots** (*Fr.* bôɴ mô′), a particularly appropriate word or expression; a clever saying; witticism. [F: lit., good word]

Bonn (bŏn; *Ger.* bŏn), *n.* a city in West Germany, in S North Rhine-Westphalia, on the Rhine: capital of Federal Republic of Germany; Beethoven's birthplace: university, founded 1818. 140,500 (est. 1966).

Bonnard (*Fr.* bŏ nȧr′), *n.* **Pierre** (*Fr.* pyĕr), 1867–1947, French impressionist painter.

bonne (*Fr.* bŏn), *n. French.* **1.** a maidservant. **2.** a child's nurse. [F, fem. of *bon* good. See BOON[2]]

bonne amie (*Fr.* bŏn ȧ mē′), *French.* fem. of **bon ami.**

bonne bouche (*Fr.* bŏn bōōsh′), *pl.* **bonnes bouches** (bŏn bōōsh′). *French.* a titbit.

bonne foi (*Fr.* bŏn fwȧ′), *French.* good faith; sincerity.

bonnet (bŏn′ĭt), *n.* **1.** a woman's or child's outdoor head covering, commonly fitting down over the hair, and often tied under the chin. **2.** *Chiefly Scot.* a man's or boy's cap. **3.** any of various hoods, covers, or protective devices. **4.** a cowl for a chimney to stabilize the draught. **5.** the cover of a motor car or other engine. **6.** *Naut.* an additional piece of canvas laced to the foot (formerly the top) of a jib or other sail. *—v.t.* **7.** to put a bonnet on. [ME *bonet*, t. OF: cap (orig. its material); ? of Gmc orig.] **—bon′net-like′,** *adj.*

bonnet rouge (*Fr.* bŏ nĕ rōōzh′), *pl.* **bonnets rouges** (*Fr.* bŏ nĕ rōōzh′). *French.* **1.** a red liberty cap, worn by extremists at the time of the French Revolution. **2.** an extremist or radical. [F: red cap]

bonny (bŏn′ĭ), *adj.,* **-ier, -iest. 1.** radiant with health; handsome; pretty. **2.** *Scot. and N Dial.* fine (often used ironically). Also, **bonnie.** [ME *bonie.* See BOON[2]] **—bon′nily,** *adv.* **—bon′niness,** *n.*

bonnyclabber (bŏn′ĭ klăb′ə), *n.* sour, thick milk. [t. Irish: m. *bainne clabair*, lit., milk of the clabber (i.e. ? the churn-dasher)]

bonsoir (*Fr.* bôɴ swȧr′), *n., interj. French.* good evening; good night.

bonspiel (bŏn′spēl, -spəl), *n. Scot.* a curling match between two clubs, parishes, etc. [orig. obscure]

bontebok (bŏn′tĭ bŏk′), *n.* a large, red, antelope of southern Africa, *Damaliscus pygargus*, with a blaze on the face, now almost extinct. [t. Afrikaans: pied buck]

bon ton (*Fr.* bôɴ tôɴ′), good or elegant form or style; good breeding; fashionable society. [F: good tone]

bonus (bō′nəs), *n.* **1.** something given or paid over and above what is due. **2.** a sum of money paid to a shareholder, partner, employee, or agent of a company, a returned soldier, etc., over and above his regular dividend or pay. **3.** something free added in a corporate sale of securities. **4.** *Insurance.* **a.** dividend. **b.** a percentage of the net profits of a company added to a policy when it matures. **5.** a premium paid for a loan, contract, etc. **6.** *Colloq.* a bribe. **7.** any unsolicited or unexpected gift. [t. L: (adj.) good]

bon vivant (*Fr.* bôɴ vē väɴ′), *pl.* **bons vivants** (*Fr.* bôɴ vē väɴ′). *French.* **1.** a person who lives luxuriously, self-indulgently, etc. **2.** a jovial companion.

bon viveur (*Fr.* bôɴ vē vœr′), *French.* a bon vivant.

bonne viveuse (*Fr.* bŏn vē vœz′), *French.* fem. of **bon viveur.**

bon voyage (*Fr.* bôɴ vwȧ yȧzh′), *French.* pleasant trip.

bony (bō′nĭ), *adj.,* **bonier, boniest. 1.** of or like bone. **2.** full of bones. **3.** having prominent bones; big-boned. **—bon′iness,** *n.*

bonze (bŏnz), *n.* a Buddhist monk, esp. of Japan or China. [t. F, t. Pg.: m. *bonzo*, t. Jap.: m. *bonzô*, t. Chinese: m. *fan sung* ordinary (member) of the assembly]

bonzer (bŏn′zə), *adj. Austral. Colloq.* excellent.

boo (bōō), *interj., n., pl.* **boos,** *v.,* **booed, booing.** *—interj.* **1.** (an exclamation used to express contempt, disapprobation, etc., or to frighten.) *—n.* **2.** this exclamation. *—v.i.* **3.** to cry 'boo'. *—v.t.* **4.** to cry 'boo' at; show disapproval of by booing.

booay (bōō′ī), *n. N.Z. Colloq.* a remote country district. Also, **booai.** [t. Maori: m. *puhoi*]

boob (bōōb), *n. Slang.* **1.** a fool; a dunce. **2.** a foolish mistake. *—v.i.* **3.** to blunder; make a mistake. [see BOOBY]

boobialla (bōō′bĭ ä′lə), *n.* a tree, *Acacia longifolia*, of Australia; grown elsewhere as a greenhouse shrub. [t. native Australian]

boobook (bōō′bŏŏk), *n.* a small owl, *Ninox boobook*, widespread in Australia. [t. native Australian]

booby (bōō′bĭ), *n., pl.* **-bies. 1.** a stupid person; a dunce. **2.** the worst student, player, etc., of a group. **3.** Also, **booby gannet.** any of various gannets, as the **white-bellied booby** (*Sula leucogaster*) of the Bahamas, etc. [prob. t. Sp.: m. *bobo* fool, also the bird booby, g. L *balbus* stammering] **—boo′byish,** *adj.*

booby hatch, 1. *Naut.* a wooden hood over a hatch. **2.** *U.S. Colloq.* lunatic asylum. **3.** *U.S. Slang.* jail.

booby prize, a prize given in consolation or good-natured ridicule to the worst player in a game or contest.

booby trap, 1. an object so placed as to fall on or trip up an unsuspecting person. **2.** *Mil.* a hidden or disguised bomb or mine so placed that it will be set off by an unsuspecting person.

boodle (bōō′dl), *n., v.,* **-dled, -dling.** *U.S. Slang. —n.* **1.** (often in contemptuous use) the lot, pack, or crowd: *the whole boodle.* **2.** a bribe or other illicit gain in politics. *—v.i.* **3.** to obtain money dishonestly, as by corrupt bargains. [t. D: m. *boedel, boel* stock, lot] **—boo′dler,** *n.*

boogie-woogie (bōō′gĭ wōō′gĭ), *n. Jazz.* a form of instrumental blues using melodic variations over a constantly repeated bass figure.

boohoo (bōō′hōō′), *v.,* **-hooed, -hooing,** *n., pl.* **-hoos.** *—v.i.* **1.** to weep noisily; blubber. *—n.* **2.** the sound of noisy weeping. [imit.]

book (bŏŏk), *n.* **1.** a written or printed work of some length, as a treatise or other literary composition, esp. on consecutive sheets fastened or bound together. **2.** a number of sheets of writing paper bound together and used for making entries, as of commercial transactions. **3.** a division of a literary work, esp. one of the larger divisions. **4. the Book,** the Bible. **5.** *Music.* the text of an opera, operetta, etc. **6.** a record of bets, as on a horse-race. **7.** *Cards.* the number of tricks or cards which must be taken before any trick counts in the score: in bridge six tricks. **8.** a set of tickets, cheques, stamps, etc., bound together like a book. **9.** a pile or package of leaves, as of tobacco. **10.** anything that serves for the recording of facts or events: *the book of Nature.* **11. bring to book,** to bring to account. **12. by (the) book, a.** formally. **b.** authoritatively; correctly. **13. a. in one's good books,** in favour. **b. in one's bad books,** out of favour. **14. on the books,** entered on the list of members. **15. take a leaf out of one's book,** to emulate. **16. throw the book at,** to bring all possible charges against (an offender); sentence (an offender) to the maximum penalties; punish severely. **17. without book, a.** by memory. **b.** without authority. *—v.t.* **18.** to enter in a book or list; record; register. **19.** to engage (a place, passage, etc.) beforehand. **20.** to put (somebody, something) down for a place, passage, etc. **21.** to engage (a person or company) for a performance or performances. **22.** to record the name of, with a view to possible prosecution for a minor offence: *the police booked him for speeding.* *—v.i.* **23.** to register one's name. **24.** to engage a place, services, etc. [ME; OE *bōc*, c. G *Buch*] **—book′less,** *adj.*

bookbinder (bŏŏk′bīn′də), *n.* one whose business or work is the binding of books. **—book′bind′ing,** *n.*

bookcase (bŏŏk′kās′), *n.* a set of shelves for books.

book club, 1. a club which lends or sells (usually at a discount) books to its members. 2. a club organized for the discussion and reviewing of books.

book debt, an amount showing in a trader's accounts as due to him.

book end, a support placed at the end of a row of books to hold them upright.

bookie (bŏŏk′ĭ), *n. Colloq.* bookmaker (def. 2).

booking (bŏŏk′ĭng), *n.* **1.** advance engagement of a place or passage. **2.** an engagement to perform.

booking clerk, an official who sells tickets, as for a railway journey.

booking office, a place where tickets are sold, as at a railway station.

bookish (bŏŏk′ĭsh), *adj.* **1.** given to reading or study. **2.** more acquainted with books than with real life. **3.** of or pertaining to books; literary. **4.** stilted; pedantic. —**book′ishly,** *adv.* —**book′ishness,** *n.*

bookkeeping (bŏŏk′kē′pĭng), *n.* the work or skill of keeping account books or systematic records of money transactions. —**book′kee′per,** *n.*

book-learning (bŏŏk′lû′nĭng), *n.* knowledge gained by reading books, as distinguished from that obtained through observation and experience. Also, **book knowledge, booklore** (bŏŏk′lô′). —**book-learned** (bŏŏk′lû′nĭd), *adj.*

booklet (bŏŏk′lĭt), *n.* a little book, esp. one with paper covers; pamphlet.

booklouse (bŏŏk′lous′), *n., pl.* **-lice** (-līs′). any insect of the order *Corrodentia,* which damages books by eating away the glue, and is injurious to other products in houses, granaries, etc.

bookmaker (bŏŏk′mā′kə), *n.* **1.** a maker of books. **2.** a professional betting man, who accepts the bets of others, as on horses in racing. —**book′mak′ing,** *n.*

bookman (bŏŏk′mən), *n., pl.* **-men. 1.** a studious or learned man; a scholar. **2.** *Colloq.* a person whose occupation is selling or publishing books.

bookmark (bŏŏk′mäk′), *n.* **1.** a ribbon or the like placed between the pages of a book to mark a place. **2.** a bookplate. Also, **book′mark′er.**

Book of Common Prayer, the service book of the Church of England, essentially adopted but changed in details by other churches of the Anglican communion.

Book of Mormon. See **Mormon** (def. 2).

book of prime entry, *Com.* a book of account in which transactions are initially recorded before being transferred to the ledger, as a cashbook or daybook. Also, **book of original entry, book of originating entry;** *U.S.,* **book of account.**

bookplate (bŏŏk′plāt′), *n.* a label, bearing the owner's name, a design, etc., for pasting in a book.

book post, an arrangement for the conveyance of books at cheaper rates than other parcels.

bookrack (bŏŏk′răk′), *n.* **1.** a rack for supporting an open book. **2.** a rack for holding books.

book scorpion, any of the minute arachnids, superficially resembling a tailless scorpion, which constitute the order *Chelonethi* (*Pseudoscorpionida*), as *Chelifer cancroides,* found in old books, etc.

bookseller (bŏŏk′sĕl′ə), *n.* a person whose occupation or business is selling books.

bookshelf (bŏŏk′shĕlf′), *n.* a shelf for holding books.

bookshop (bŏŏk′shŏp′), *n.* a shop where books are sold.

bookstall (bŏŏk′stôl′), *n.* **1.** a stall, especially at a station or airport, where newspapers, magazines, and books are sold. **2.** a stall at which books (usually secondhand) are sold.

bookstand (bŏŏk′stănd′), *n.* **1.** bookrack. **2.** bookstall.

book-token (bŏŏk′tō′kən), *n.* a gift token for books to a stated value.

book trade, publishers, printers and booksellers together; all those engaged in the manufacture and selling of books.

bookworm (bŏŏk′wûm′), *n.* **1.** any of various insects that feed on books. **2.** a person closely addicted to reading or study.

Boolean algebra (bōō′lĭ ən), a mathematical means of representing statements in logic. [named after George *Boole,* 1815–65, English mathematician]

boom[1] (bōōm), *v.i.* **1.** to make a deep, prolonged, resonant sound; make a rumbling, humming, or droning noise. **2.** to move with a resounding rush or great impetus. **3.** to progress or flourish vigorously, as a business, a city, etc. —*v.t.* **4.** to give forth with a booming sound (usually fol. by *out*): *the clock boomed out twelve.* **5.** to push (a cause, a new product, etc.) vigorously. —*n.* **6.** a deep, hollow, continued sound. **7.** a roaring, rumbling, or reverberation, as of waves or distant guns. **8.** the cry of the bittern. **9.** a buzzing, humming, or droning, as of a bee or beetle. **10.** a rapid increase in prices, business activity, etc. **11. a.** a rise in popularity, as of a political candidate. **b.** efforts to bring this about. —*adj.* **12.** caused by a boom: *boom prices.* [imit. Cf. ZOOM] —**Ant. 10.** depression, slump.

boom[2] (bōōm), *n.* **1.** *Naut.* a long pole or spar used to extend the foot of certain sails. **2.** a chain or cable or a series of connected floating timbers, etc., serving to obstruct navigation, to confine floating timber, etc. **3.** the area thus shut off. **4.** *Mach.* a spar or beam projecting from the mast of a derrick, supporting or guiding the weights to be lifted. **5.** (in a television or film studio) a movable arm supporting a microphone or floodlight above the actors, or an aerial camera. [t. D: tree, beam. See BEAM]

B, Boom; G, Gaff

boom[3] (bōōm), *n. S African Colloq.* marijuana. [orig. uncert. ? t. Afrikaans: tree]

boomer (bōō′mə), *n. Austral. Colloq.* a large male kangaroo.

boomerang (bōō′mə răng′), *n.* **1.** a bent or curved piece of hard wood used as a missile by the native Australians, one form of which can be so thrown as to return to the thrower. **2.** a scheme, plan, argument, etc., which recoils upon the user. —*v.i.* **3.** (of a scheme, etc.) to cause unexpected harm to the originator. [t. native Australian]

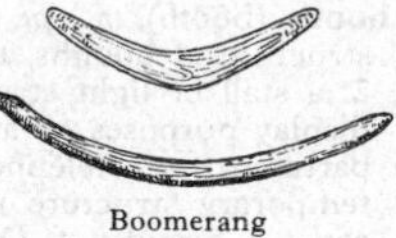
Boomerang

boomslang (bōōm′slăng′), *n.* a poisonous tree snake, *Dispholidus typus,* of southern Africa. [t. Afrikaans: tree snake]

boomtown (bōōm′toun′), *n. Chiefly U.S.* a town that has grown rapidly or is enjoying a spell of prosperity.

boomvaring (bōōm fā′rĭng), *n. S African.* tree fern. [t. Afrikaans]

boon[1] (bōōn), *n.* **1.** a benefit enjoyed; a thing to be thankful for; a blessing. **2.** *Archaic.* that which is asked; a favour sought. [ME, t. Scand.; cf. Icel. *bōn* request, petition]

boon[2] (bōōn), *adj.* jolly; jovial; convivial: *boon companion.* [ME, t. OF: m. *bon,* g. L *bonus* good]

boondocks (bōōn′dŏks′), *n. Chiefly U.S. Slang.* **1.** an uninhabited and densely overgrown area, as a swamp, forest, etc. **2.** a remote suburb or rural area: *the firm moved to the boondocks.*

boondoggle (bōōn′dŏg′l), *n., v.,* **-doggled, -doggling.** *U.S.* —*n.* **1.** a belt, knife sheath, axe handle, or other product of simple manual skill. **2.** *Slang.* work of little or no practical value. —*v.i.* **3.** *Slang.* to do work of little or no practical value. —**boon′dog′gler,** *n.* —**boon′dog′gling,** *n.*

Boone (bōōn), **Daniel,** 1735–1820, American pioneer, esp. in Kentucky.

boor (bōōə), *n.* **1.** a rude or unmannerly person. **2.** a peasant; a rustic. **3.** an illiterate or clownish peasant. **4.** a Dutch or German peasant. **5.** any foreign peasant. **6.** (*cap.*) Boer. [t. D: m. *boer* peasant, or t. LG: m. *būr* peasant]

boorish (bōōə′rĭsh), *adj.* of or like a boor; rustic; rude. —**boor′ishly,** *adv.* —**boor′ishness,** *n.*

boost (bōōst), *v.t.* **1.** to lift or raise by pushing from behind or below. **2.** to advance or aid by speaking well of. **3.** to increase; push up: *to boost prices.* **4.** *Aeron., Motor Vehicles.* to supercharge. —*n.* **5.** an upward shove or push. **6.** an aid that helps one to rise in the world. **7.** *Aeron., Motor Vehicles.* the difference between the induction pressure in a supercharged internal-combustion engine and the atmospheric pressure. [b. BOOM and HOIST]

booster (bōō′stə), *n.* **1.** one who or that which boosts. **2.** *Elect.* a device connected in series with a current for increasing or decreasing the nominal circuit voltage. **3.** *Aeron., Motor Vehicles.* a supercharger in an internal-combustion engine. **4.** *Astronautics.* **a.** a rocket engine used as the main supply of thrust in a missile flight. **b.** the stage of a missile containing this engine, usually detached at all-burnt. **5.** *Pharm.* a substance, usually injected, for prolonging a person's immunity to a specific infection.

boot[1] (bōōt), *n.* **1.** a heavy shoe, esp. one reaching above the ankle. **2.** a covering, usually of leather, rubber, or a similar synthetic material, for the foot and leg, reaching up to and sometimes beyond the knee. **3.** *Hist.* an instrument of torture for the leg. **4.** a protective covering for the foot and part of the leg of a horse. **5.** a receptacle or place for baggage usually at the rear of a vehicle. **6.** a kick. **7.** *Slang.* a dismissal; discharge. **8. boot's on the other foot,** the true position is the reverse. **9. heart in one's**

boots, extreme despondency; loss of morale. **10. lick the boots of,** to be subservient to; flatter. *—v.t.* **11.** to put boots on. **12.** *Hist.* to torture with the boot. **13.** *Slang.* to kick; drive by kicking. **14.** *Slang.* to dismiss; discharge. [ME *bote,* t. OF; of Gmc orig. See SABOT]

boot[2] (bo͞ot), *n.* **1. to boot,** into the bargain; in addition. **2.** *Archaic or Dial.* something given into the bargain. **3.** *Obs.* advantage. **4.** *Obs.* remedy. *—v.i.* **5.** *Obs. or Poetic.* to be of profit, advantage, or avail: *it boots not to complain.* [ME *bote,* OE *bōt* advantage]

boot[3] (bo͞ot), *n. Archaic.* booty; spoil; plunder. [special use of BOOT[2] by assoc. with BOOTY]

bootblack (bo͞ot′blăk′), *n.* a person whose occupation it is to shine shoes, boots, etc.

booted (bo͞o′tĭd), *adj.* **1.** equipped with boots. **2.** *Ornith.* (of the tarsus of certain birds) covered with a continuous horny, bootlike sheath.

bootee (bo͞o tē′; *or esp. for 1* bo͞o′tē), *n.* **1.** a baby's knitted shoe. **2.** a kind of half-boot for women.

Boötes (bō ō′tēz), *n.* a northern constellation containing the first magnitude star Arcturus; the Herdsman. [t. L, t. Gk: ox-driver]

booth (bo͞oth), *n., pl.* **booths** (bo͞othz). **1.** a temporary structure of boughs, canvas, boards, etc., as for shelter. **2.** a stall or light structure for the sale of goods or for display purposes, as at a market or fair. **3.** a small compartment for a telephone, film projector, etc. **4.** a small temporary structure used by voters at elections. [ME *bōthe,* t. Scand.; cf. Dan. *bod*]

Booth (bo͞oth), *n.* **1. Edwin Thomas,** 1833–93, U.S. actor. **2.** his brother, **John Wilkes,** 1838–65, U.S. actor: assassin of Abraham Lincoln. **3. Junius Brutus,** 1796–1852, British actor in England and America (father of Edwin and John). **4. William,** 1829–1912, English preacher: founder of the Salvation Army.

Boothia (bo͞o′thĭ ə), *n.* **1.** an arctic peninsula in N Canada: northernmost part of the mainland of North America: former location of the north magnetic pole. **2. Gulf of,** a gulf between this peninsula and Baffin Island.

bootjack (bo͞ot′jăk′), *n.* a device used to hold a boot while the foot is drawn out of it.

bootlace (bo͞ot′lās′), *n.* **1.** a string or lace for fastening a boot. **2.** a shoelace.

Bootle (bo͞o′tl), *n.* a seaport in NW England, on the Mersey estuary near Liverpool. 82,829 (1961).

bootleg (bo͞ot′lĕg′), *n., v.,* **-legged, -legging,** *adj. Chiefly U.S. —n.* **1.** alcoholic drink secretly and unlawfully made, sold, or transported. **2.** that part of a boot which covers the leg. *—v.t.* **3.** to deal in (spirits or other goods) illicitly. *—v.i.* **4.** to carry goods, as spirits, about secretly for illicit sale. *—adj.* **5.** made, sold, or transported unlawfully. **6.** unlawful; clandestine. **7.** of or pertaining to bootlegging. [def. 2 orig. meaning; others arose from the practice of concealing illegal spirits in the bootleg] **—boot′leg′ger,** *n.*

bootless (bo͞ot′lĭs), *adj.* without advantage; unavailing; useless. [OE *bōtlēas* unpardonable, f. *bōt* BOOT[2] + *-lēas* -LESS] **—boot′lessly,** *adv.* **—boot′lessness,** *n.*

bootlicker (bo͞ot′lĭk′ə), *n. Slang.* one who curries favour; a flatterer.

boots (bo͞ots), *n., pl.* **boots.** a servant, as at a hotel, who cleans shoes, carries luggage, etc.

boots and saddles, *U.S.* a cavalry bugle call for mounted formation.

boot tree, *U.S.* a shoetree.

booty (bo͞o′tĭ), *n., pl.* **-ties. 1.** spoil taken from an enemy in war; plunder; pillage. **2.** that which is seized by violence and robbery. **3.** a prize or gain, without reference to use of force. [late ME *boyte;* cf. G *Beute*]

booze (bo͞oz), *n., v.,* **boozed, boozing.** *Colloq. —n.* **1.** alcoholic drink. **2.** a drinking bout; spree. *—v.i., v.t.* **3.** to drink immoderately. [ME *bouse,* t. MD: m. *būsen*] **—booz′er,** *n.*

boozy (bo͞o′zĭ), *adj.* **boozier, booziest.** *Colloq.* **1.** drunken. **2.** addicted to alcohol. **—booz′iness,** *n.*

bop (bŏp), *n.* bebop.

bor., 1. borough. **2.** boron.

bora[1] (bô′rə), *n. Meteorol.* a violent, dry, cold wind on the coasts of the Adriatic, blowing from the north or north-east. [t. d. It., g. L *boreas* north wind]

bora[2] (bô′rə), *n. Austral.* an Aborigine initiation rite. [t. native Australian]

boracic (bə răs′ĭk), *adj. Chem.* boric.

boracite (bô′rə sīt′), *n.* a mineral, a borate and chloride of magnesium, $Mg_6Cl_2B_{14}O_{26}$, occurring in white or colourless crystals or fine-grained masses, strongly pyro-electric. [f. *borac-,* s. ML *borax* BORAX + -ITE[1]]

borage (bŏ′rĭj, bŭ′rĭj), *n.* **1.** a plant, *Borago officinalis,* native of southern Europe, with hairy leaves and stems, used in salads and medicinally. **2.** any of various allied or similar plants. [ME, t. AF: m. *burage,* var. of OF *bourrace,* der. *bourrer* stuff, ult. der. ML *burra* wool]

boraginaceous (bə răj′ĭ nā′shəs), *adj.* belonging to the *Boraginaceae,* or borage family of plants, including borage, bugloss, heliotrope, forget-me-not, etc.

borak (bô′răk), *n. Austral. Colloq.* ridicule: *to poke borak at someone.* [t. native Australian]

borane (bô′rān), *n. Chem.* a hydride of boron, used industrially as a high-energy fuel.

Borås (*Sw.* bo͞o rós′), *n.* a town in SW Sweden. 68,948 (1964).

borate (*n.* bô′rāt, -rĭt; *v.* bô′rāt), *n., v.,* **-rated, -rating.** *Chem. —n.* **1.** a salt of orthoboric acid. **2.** (loosely) a salt of any boric acid. *—v.t.* **3.** to treat with borate, boric acid, or borax.

borax (bô′răks), *n.* a white, crystalline sodium borate, $Na_2B_4O_7 . 10\,H_2O$, occurring naturally or prepared artificially and used as a flux, cleansing agent, in the manufacture of glass, etc. [t. ML, t. Ar.: m. *būraq,* t. Pers.: m. *bōrah* (OPers. *bōrak*); r. ME *boras,* t. OF]

borazon (bô′rə zŏn′, -zən), *n. Chem.* a very hard substance compounded industrially of boron and nitrogen.

Borchert (*Ger.* bŏr′ KHərt), *n.* **Wolfgang** (*Ger.* vŏlf′găng), 1921–47, German novelist and essayist.

Bordeaux (bô dō′; *Fr.* bŏr dó′), *n.* **1.** a seaport in SW France, in Gironde department, on the river Garonne. 249,688 (1962). **2.** wine produced in the region surrounding Bordeaux. Red Bordeaux wines are called *clarets.* White Bordeaux wines include *sauternes* (sweet) and *graves* (dry). **3.** Bordeaux mixture.

Bordeaux mixture, *Hort.* a fungicide consisting of a mixture of copper sulphate, lime, and water.

bordelaise (bô′də lāz′; *Fr.* bŏr də lĕz′), *n. Cookery.* a brown sauce flavoured with red wine.

bordello (bô dĕl′ō), *n.* a brothel. [t. It.]

border (bô′də), *n.* **1.** a side, edge, or margin. **2.** the line that separates one country, state, or province from another; frontier line. **3.** the district or region that lies along the boundary line of a country. **4. the Border,** the region along the boundary between England and Scotland. **5.** *U.S. Hist.* a newly settled, pioneer area of North America. **6.** brink; verge. **7.** an ornamental strip or design around the edge of a printed page, a drawing, etc. **8.** a piece of ornamental trimming around the edge of a garment, cap, etc. **9.** *Hort.* a narrow strip of ground in a garden, enclosing a portion of it. *—v.t.* **10.** to make a border about; adorn with a border. **11.** to form a border or boundary to. **12.** to lie on the border of; adjoin. *—v.i.* **13. border on** or **upon, a.** to touch or abut at the border. **b.** to approach closely in character; verge. [ME *bordure,* t. OF, der. *bord* side, edge; of Gmc orig. See BOARD] **—bor′dered,** *adj.* **—bor′derless,** *adj.* **—Syn. 1.** See **edge. 12.** See **adjoining.**

borderer (bô′də rə), *n.* one who dwells on or near the border of a country, region, etc., esp. that between England and Scotland.

borderland (bô′də lănd′), *n.* **1.** land forming a border or frontier. **2.** an uncertain intermediate district, space, or condition.

borderline (bô′də līn′), *adj.* **1.** on or near a border or boundary. **2.** uncertain; indeterminate. **3.** (in examinations, etc.) qualifying or failing to qualify by a narrow margin. **4.** *Educ. Psychol.* between backward and subnormal. **5.** verging on insanity.

Border States, 1. *U.S. Hist.* the slave states inclined to compromise instead of seceding: Delaware, Maryland, Virginia, Kentucky, Missouri; sometimes extended to include North Carolina, Tennessee, and Arkansas. **2.** *U.S.* the states touching the Canadian border. **3.** (prior to 1940) certain of the countries of central and northern Europe, bordering on the Soviet Union and formerly belonging to the Russian Empire: Finland, Poland, Estonia, Latvia, and Lithuania.

bordure (bô′dyo͞oə), *n. Her.* the outer fifth of the shield. [ME, t. OF. See BORDER]

bore[1] (bô), *v.,* **bored, boring,** *n. —v.t.* **1.** to pierce (a solid substance) or make (a round hole, etc.) with an auger, drill, or other rotated instrument. **2.** to force by persistent forward thrusting. **3.** *Horseracing.* to push aside persistently; crowd out. *—v.i.* **4.** to make a hole, as with an auger or drill. **5.** to admit of being pierced with an auger or the like, as a substance. *—n.* **6.** a hole made by boring, or as if by boring. **7.** the inside diameter of a hollow cylindrical object or device, such as a bush or bearing, or the barrel of a gun. [ME *boren,* OE *borian,* c. G *bohren;* akin to L *forāre* pierce] **—Syn. 1.** perforate.

bore[2] (bô), *v.,* **bored, boring,** *n. —v.t.* **1.** to weary by tedious repetition, dullness, unwelcome attentions, etc. *—n.* **2.** a dull, tiresome, or uncongenial person. **3.** a cause of ennui or annoyance. [orig. unknown]

bore[3] (bô), *n.* an abrupt rise of the tide which breaks in an estuary, rushing violently up the channel. [ME, t. Scand.; cf. Icel. *bāra* wave]
bore[4] (bô), *v.* pt. of **bear**[1].
boreal (bôʹrĭ əl), *adj.* **1.** pertaining to the north wind. **2.** northern. **3.** pertaining to Boreas. [t. L: s. *boreālis*, der. *Boreas* north wind]
Boreas (bôʹrĭ ăsʹ), *n.* the north wind, as personified or deified by the Greeks.
boredom (bôʹdəm), *n.* the state or an instance of being bored; tedium; ennui.
boree (bôʹrē, bô rēʹ), *n.* a weeping tree, *Acacia pendula*, common in Australia; myall. [t. native Australian]
borehole (bôʹhōlʹ), *n.* a hole bored into the surface of the earth, as for extracting oil.
borer (bôʹrə), *n.* **1.** one who or that which bores or pierces. **2.** *Mach.* a tool used for boring; an auger. **3.** *Entomol.* any insect that burrows in trees, fruits, etc., esp. any beetle of certain groups. **4.** *Zool.* any of various molluscs, etc., that bore into wood, etc. **5.** a marsipobranch fish, as a hagfish, that bores into other fish to feed on their flesh.
Borgerhout (*Flem.* bôr KHər hôwtʹ), *n.* a town in N Belgium, near Antwerp. 51,115 (1962).
Borghese (*It.* bòr gèʹzè), *n.* a noble Italian family, orig. from the republic of Siena, important in Italian society and politics from the 16th to the early 19th century.
Borgia (bôʹjyə; *It.* bŏrʹjä), *n.* **1. Cesare** (*It.* chèʹzä rè), 1476–1507, Italian cardinal, military leader, and politician. **2. Lucrezia** (*It.* lōō krĕtʹtsyä), 1480–1519, sister and the political tool of Cesare; patroness of culture; Duchess of Ferrara. **3. Rodrigo Lanzol** (*It.* rŏ drēʹgò län zòlʹ), 1431–1503, Italian cardinal: became Pope Alexander VI (father of Cesare and Lucrezia Borgia).
Borglum (bôʹgləm), *n.* **(John) Gutzon** (gŭtʹsən), 1867–1941, U.S. sculptor and painter.
Borg Olivier (bôj/ŏl ĭ vĭəʹ), **George** (jôj), born 1911, prime minister of Malta since 1962.
boric (bôʹrĭk), *adj.* *Chem.* of or containing boron. Also, **boracic.**
boric acid, *Chem.* any of a group of acids derived from boron trioxide with varying amounts of water, esp. orthoboric acid, $B_2O_3.3H_2O$ (or H_3BO_3) but also metaboric acid, $B_2O_3.H_2O$ (or HBO_2), pyroboric acid, $2B_2O_3.3H_2O$ (or $H_6B_4O_9$), or tetraboric acid, $2B_2O_3.H_2O$ (or $H_2B_4O_7$).
boride (bôʹrīd), *n.* *Chem.* any hard, heat-resistant compound, usually containing two elements only, of which boron is the more electropositive.
boring (bôʹring), *n.* *Mach.* **1.** the act or process of piercing or perforating. **2.** the hole so made. **3.** (*pl.*) the chips, fragments, or dust produced in boring.
born (bôn), *adj.* **1.** brought forth by birth. **2.** possessing from birth the quality or character stated: *a born fool.* —*v.* **3.** a pp. of **bear,** now normally replaced in all senses by **borne.** [prop. pp. of BEAR[1]; ME and OE *boren*]
Born (bôn), *n.* **Max,** 1882–1970, British physicist, born in Germany.
borne (bôn), *v.* pp. of **bear.**
Borneo (bôʹnĭ ōʹ), *n.* an island in the Malay Archipelago, including Brunei, the Malaysian states of Sabah and Sarawak, and Indonesian Borneo (Kalimantan). ab. 290,000 sq. mi.

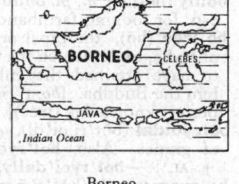

Borneo

borneol (bôʹnĭ ŏlʹ), *n.* *Chem.*, *Bot.* terpene alcohol, $C_{10}H_{17}$-OH, closely resembling common camphor, found in concrete masses in the trunk of *Dryobalanops aromatica*, a large tree of Borneo, Sumatra, etc. [f. BORNEO + -OL[1]]
Bornholm (bônʹhōm), *n.* a Danish island in the Baltic, S of Sweden. 48,823 (1964).
bornite (bôʹnīt), *n.* a common mineral, copper iron sulphide, Cu_5FeS_4, occurring in masses of brownish colour on fresh surfaces: an important ore of copper. [after I. von *Born*, 1742–91, Austrian mineralogist. See -ITE[1]]
Bornu (bô nōōʹ), *n.* a former sultanate in W Africa, S and W of Lake Chad: now largely a province in Nigeria. ab. 5,000,000 pop.; ab. 50,000 sq. mi.
Borodin (bŏʹrə dĭn; *Russ.* bə rä dēnʹ), *n.* **Aleksandr Porfirevich** (*Russ.* ə lĭk sänʹdr pər fĭr yèʹvĭch), 1834–87, Russian composer.
Borodino (bŏʹrə dēʹnō; *Russ.* bə rə dĭ nôʹ), *n.* a village in the W Soviet Union, 70 mi. W of Moscow: Napoleon's victory here made possible the capture of Moscow, 1812.
boron (bôʹrŏn), *n.* *Chem.* a non-metallic element present in borax, etc., and obtained in either an amorphous or a crystalline form when reduced from its compound. *Symbol*: B; *at. wt*: 10·811; *at. no.*: 5. [b. BORAX and CARBON]
boronia (bô rōʹnĭ ə, -nyə), *n.* any one of a number of common Australian shrubs of the genus *Boronia.*
boron trioxide, *Chem.* a colourless crystalline solid, B_2O_3, which forms boric acid on hydration. Also, **boron oxide.**
borosilicate (bôʹrō sĭlʹĭ kĭt, -kətʹ), *n.* *Chem.* a salt of boric and silicic acids.
borosilicic acids (bôʹrō sī lĭsʹĭk), *Chem.* hypothetical acids yielding borosilicate.
borough (bŭʹrə), *n.* **1.** an urban community incorporated by royal charter. **2.** an urban electoral constituency, usually subdivided. **3.** (formerly) a fortified town, or a town possessing municipal organization. **4.** *U.S.* **a.** one of the five administrative divisions of New York City. **b.** (in certain states) a municipality smaller than a city. [ME *burgh* town, OE *burg* stronghold, c. G *Burg*]
borough-English (bŭʹrə ĭngʹglĭsh), *n.* *Law* a customary system of inheritance in parts of England which gave the entire estate to the youngest son.
Borromini (bŏʹrō mēʹnĭ; *It.* bòr rò mēʹnē), *n.* **Francesco,** 1599–1667, Italian architect.
borrow (bŏʹrō), *v.t.* **1.** to take or obtain (a thing) on the promise to return it or its equivalent; obtain the temporary use of. **2.** to get from another or from a foreign source; appropriate or adopt: *borrowed words.* **3.** *Arith.* (in subtraction) to take from one denomination to add to the next lower. —*v.i.* **4.** to borrow something. [ME *borowe(n)*, OE *borgian*, der. *borg* a pledge] —**borʹrower,** *n.*
Borrow (bŏʹrō), *n.* **George,** 1803–81, English traveller, writer, and student of languages, esp. Romany.
Bors (bôs), *n.* **Sir,** *Arthurian Legend.* **1.** Also, **Sir Bors de Ganis.** a knight of the Round Table, nephew of Lancelot. **2.** a natural son of King Arthur.
borsh (bôsh), *n.* a Russian stock soup containing beets, served hot or chilled. Also, **borsch, borscht** (bôsht), **borshch** (bôshch). [t. Russ.: m. *borshch*]
borstal (bôsʹtl), *n.* **1.** a reformatory for young offenders between the ages of 16 and 21. —*adj.* **2.** coming from or having to do with a borstal. [named after *Borstal*, village in Kent, where the first such reformatory is situated]
bort (bôt), *n.* flawed, low quality diamonds, and diamond fragments, valuable only for crushing to diamond dust. [cf. OF *bort* bastard] —**bortʹy,** *adj.*
borzoi (bôʹzoi), *n.*, *pl.* **-zois.** a large swift dog with a soft coat and long, pointed nose, orig. bred in Russia; Russian wolfhound. [t. Russ: lit., swift]

Borzoi (29 in. high at the shoulder)

boscage (bŏsʹkĭj), *n.* a mass of growing trees or shrubs; woods, groves, or thickets. Also, **boskage.** [ME. t. OF, der. *bosc*, t. Gmc. See BOSKY]
Bosch (bŏsh), *n.* **Hieronymus** (hĭə rŏnʹĭ məs), 1450?–1516, Dutch painter.
boschbok (bŏshʹbŏkʹ), *n.* bushbuck. [t. Afrikaans]
boschvark (bŏshʹväkʹ), *n.* bushpig. [t. Afrikaans: woodpig]
Bose (bōs), *n.* **1. Sir Jagadis Chandra** (jə gə dēsʹ chŭnʹdrə), 1858–1937, Indian physicist and plant physiologist. **2. Satyendra Nath** (să tyĕnʹdrə nätʹ), born 1894, Indian physicist.
Bose-Einstein statistics, *Physics.* a system of statistical mechanics applicable to elementary particles which do not obey the exclusion principle. [named after S. N. BOSE and A. EINSTEIN]
bosh[1] (bŏsh), *n.* *Colloq.* complete nonsense; absurd or foolish talk or opinions. [t. Turk.: empty, vain]
bosh[2] (bŏsh), *n.* the lower portion of a blast furnace, extending from the widest part to the hearth. [cf. G *Böschung* slope]
bosket (bŏsʹkĭt), *n.* a grove; a thicket. Also, **bosquet.** [t. F: m. *bosquet*, t. It.: m. *boschetto*, dim. of *bosco* wood. See BUSH[1]]
bosky (bŏsʹkĭ), *adj.* **1.** woody; covered with bushes. **2.** shady. [f. ME *bosk* (var. of *busk*, var. of BUSH[1]) + -Y[1]]
bo'sʹn (bōʹsən), *n.* *Naut.* boatswain.
Bosnia (bŏzʹnĭ ə), *n.* a former Turkish province in S Europe: part of Austria 1878–1918; now part of Yugoslavia. See map under **Austria-Hungary.** —**Bosʹnian,** *adj.*, *n.*
Bosnia and Herzegovina (hĕəʹtsĭ gō vēʹnə), a constituent republic of Yugoslavia, in the W part. 3,277,948 pop. (1961); 19,909 sq. mi. *Cap.*: Sarajevo.
bosom (bŏŏzʹəm), *n.* **1.** the breast of a human being, esp. a woman. **2.** that part of a garment which covers the breast. **3.** the breast, conceived of as the seat of

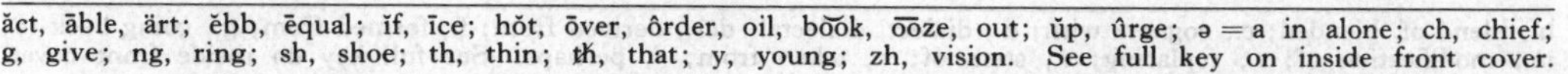

thought or emotion. **4.** the enclosure formed by the breast and the arms; affectionate embrace. **5.** something likened to the human bosom: *the bosom of the earth.* —*adj.* **6.** of or pertaining to the bosom. **7.** intimate or confidential: *a bosom friend.* —*v.t.* **8.** to take to the bosom; embrace; cherish. **9.** to hide from view; conceal. [ME; OE *bōsm*, c. G *Busen*]

bosomy (bo͝oz′ə mĭ), *adj.* (of a woman) having large or prominent breasts.

boson (bō′sŏn), *n. Physics.* any of a group of elementary particles which have integral spin and obey Bose-Einstein statistics. [named after S. N. BOSE. See (I)ON]

Bosporus (bŏs′pə rəs), *n.* a strait connecting the Black Sea and the Sea of Marmara. 18 mi. long.

bosquet (bŏs′kĭt), *n.* bosket.

boss[1] (bŏs), *n. Colloq.* **1.** one who employs or superintends workmen; a foreman or manager. **2.** anyone who asserts mastery, esp. one who controls a political or other body. —*v.t.* **3.** to be master of or over; manage; direct; control. —*v.i.* **4.** to be boss. **5.** to be domineering. —*adj.* **6.** chief; master. [t. D: m. *baas* master. See BAAS]

boss[2] (bŏs), *n.* **1.** *Bot., Zool.* a protuberance or roundish excrescence on the body or on some organ of an animal or plant. **2.** *Geol.* a knoblike mass of rock, esp. such an outcrop of eruptive rock. **3.** an ornamental protuberance of metal, ivory, etc. **4.** *Archit.* a knoblike projection of ornamental character, as at the intersection of ribs or groins. **5.** *Mach.* the enlarged part of a shaft. —*v.t.* **6.** to ornament with bosses. **7.** to emboss[1]. [ME *bos*, t. OF: m. *boce.* See BOTCH[2]]

bossa nova (bŏs′ə nō′və), **1.** jazz-influenced music of Brazilian origin, rhythmically related to the samba. **2.** a dance performed to this music.

bossboy (bŏs′boi′), *n. S African.* the African supervisor of an African labour force.

boss cockie, *Austral. Slang.* **1.** a farmer who employs labour. **2.** a boss.

bosset (bŏs′ĭt), *n.* the rudimentary stub of a horn or antler on a young deer. [f. BOSS[2] + -ET]

boss-eyed (bŏs′īd′), *adj.* **1.** having a squint. **2.** *Colloq.* lacking in perception; based on false perception: *a boss-eyed attempt.*

boss-shot (bŏs′shŏt′), *n.* a wild error or blunder.

Bossuet (*Fr.* bô swĕ′), *n.* **Jacques Bénigne** (*Fr.* zhàk bė nĕny′), 1627–1704, French bishop and writer.

bossy[1] (bŏs′ĭ), *adj.*, **bossier, bossiest.** *Colloq.* given to acting like a boss; domineering. [f. BOSS[1] + -Y[1]]

bossy[2] (bŏs′ĭ), *adj.* studded with ornamental bosses; projecting as decorative work. [f. BOSS[2] + -Y[1]]

Boston (bŏs′tən), *n.* **1.** a city in the U.S., the capital of Massachusetts, in the E part: the largest city and seaport in New England. 697,197 (1960). **2.** a town in England, in Holland, Lincolnshire. 24,915 (1961). **3.** (*l.c.*) a game of cards, played by four persons with two packs of cards. **4.** (*l.c.*) a social dance, a modification of the waltz. —**Bostonian** (bŏs tō′nyən), *adj., n.*

Boston Massacre, *U.S. Hist.* a riot on March 5th 1770, arising from the resentment of Boston citizens against British troops quartered in the city.

Boston Tea Party, *U.S. Hist.* a raid on British ships in Boston Harbour on December 16th, 1773, in which colonists of Boston, disguised as Indians, threw tea into the harbour as a protest against British taxes on tea.

Boston terrier, any of a breed of small, smooth-coated dogs with short hair and brindle or dark brown coat with white markings, originated in the U.S. by crossing the English bulldog and the bull-terrier. Also, **Boston bull.**

Boston terrier (12 to 16 in. high)

bosun (bō′sən), *n.* boatswain.

bosun's chair, boatswain's chair.

Boswell (bŏz′wel, -wəl), *n.* **1. James,** 1740–95, Scottish author: biographer of Samuel Johnson. **2.** any devoted biographer. —**Boswellian** (bŏz wĕl′ĭ-ən), *adj.*

Bosworth Field (bŏz′wûth, -wəth), the site of a battlefield near Leicester, where Richard III was defeated and slain by the future Henry VII (the first Tudor ruler of England) in 1485.

bot (bŏt), *n.* an insect larva infesting the skin, sinuses, nose, eye, stomach, or other parts of animals or man. Also, **bott.** See **botfly.** [orig. uncert.]

bot., 1. botanical. **2.** botanist. **3.** botany.

B.O.T., Board of Trade.

botanical (bə tăn′ĭ kl), *adj.* Also, **botan′ic. 1.** pertaining to plants: *botanical survey, botanical drugs.* —*n.* **2.** *Pharm.* a drug made from part of a plant, as from roots, leaves, bark, etc. [f. ML *botanicus* (t. Gk: m. *botanikós*) + -AL[1]] —**botan′ically,** *adv.*

botanist (bŏt′ə nĭst), *n.* one who is skilled in botany.

botanize (bŏt′ə nīz′), *v.*, **-nized, -nizing.** —*v.i.* **1.** to study plants botanically. **2.** to collect plants for botanical study. —*v.t.* **3.** to explore botanically. Also, **botanise.** —**bot′aniz′er,** *n.*

botany (bŏt′ə nĭ), *n., pl.* **-nies. 1.** the science of plants; the branch of biology that deals with plant life. **2.** the plant life of a region: *the botany of Cuba.* **3.** the biology of a plant or plant group: *the botany of deciduous trees.* [f. *botan(ic)* (see BOTANICAL) + -Y[3]]

Botany Bay, 1. a bay on the SE coast of Australia, near Sydney: former British penal colony. **2.** any place of detention or punishment.

Botany wool, a fine wool obtained from merino sheep. Also, **Botany.**

botch[1] (bŏch), *v.t.* **1.** to spoil by poor work; bungle. **2.** to do or say in a bungling manner. **3.** to mend or patch in a clumsy manner (often fol. by *up*). —*n.* **4.** a clumsy or poor piece of work; a bungle: *his carpentry was a complete botch.* **5.** a clumsily added part or patch. [ME *bocchen*; orig. uncert.] —**botch′er,** *n.* —**botch′ery,** *n.*

botch[2] (bŏch), *n. Archaic or Dial.* a swelling on the skin; a boil; an eruptive disease. [ME *boche*, t. ONF, var. of *boce* ulcer]

botchy (bŏch′ĭ), *adj.*, **botchier, botchiest.** poorly made or done; bungled.

botfly (bŏt′flī′), *n., pl.* **-flies.** any of a number of dipterous insects of the families *Oestridae* and *Gastrophilidae*, the larvae of which are parasitic in the skin or other parts of animals or man. [see BOT]

both (bōth), *adj., pron.* **1.** the one and the other; the two together: *give both dates, both had been there.* —*conj., adv.* **2.** alike; equally: *both men and women, he is both ready and willing.* [ME *bothe, bathe*, t. Scand.; cf. Icel. *bādhir*, c. G *beide*]

Botha (bō′tə), *n.* **Louis** (lo͞o′ĭ), 1863–1919, South African general and statesman.

bother (bŏth′ə), *v.t.* **1.** to give trouble to; annoy; pester; worry. **2.** to bewilder; confuse. —*v.i.* **3.** to trouble oneself. **4.** to cause annoyance or trouble. —*n.* **5.** something bothersome. **6.** an annoying disturbance. **7.** worried or perplexed state. **8.** someone who bothers. —*interj.* **9.** (a mild exclamation.) [orig. unknown]

—**Syn. 1.** BOTHER, ANNOY, PLAGUE imply persistent interference with one's comfort or peace of mind. BOTHER suggests causing trouble or weariness or repeatedly interrupting in the midst of pressing duties. To ANNOY is to vex or irritate by bothering. PLAGUE is a strong word, connoting unremitting annoyance and harassment.

botheration (bŏth′ə rā′shən), *interj.* (a mild exclamation indicating vexation or annoyance.)

bothersome (bŏth′ə səm), *adj.* troublesome.

Bothnia (bŏth′nĭ ə), *n.* **Gulf of,** an arm of the Baltic, extending N between Sweden and Finland. ab. 400 mi. long. See map under **Baltic.**

Bothwell (bŏth′wĕl, -wəl, bŏth′-), *n.* **James Hepburn, Earl of,** 1536?–78, third husband of Mary, Queen of Scots.

bothy (bŏth′ĭ), *n., pl.* **bothies.** *Scot.* a hut or small cottage, esp. for lodging farmhands or workmen. [? der. BOOTH]

bo tree (bō), the pipal or sacred fig tree, *Ficus religiosa*, of India, under which the founder of Buddhism is reputed to have attained the enlightenment which constituted him the Buddha. [*bo*, t. Sinhalese, t. Pali: m. *bodhi-(taru)* perfect knowledge (tree)]

botryoidal (bŏt′rĭ oi′dl), *adj.* having the form of a bunch of grapes. Also, **bot′ryoid′.** [f. m. s. Gk *botryoeidḗs* + -AL[1]] —**bot′ryoi′dally,** *adv.*

botryomycosis (bŏt′rĭ ō mī kō′sĭs), *n.* a disease of horses, usually following castration, in which there is tumefaction of the stump of the spermatic cord.

botryose (bŏt′rĭ ōs′), *adj.* **1.** botryoidal. **2.** racemose.

bots (bŏts), *n.* (*construed as pl.*) a disease caused by the attachment of the larvae of botflies to the stomach of a horse.

Botsares (bŏt′sə rēs′), *n.* **Markos** (mä′kŏs). See **Bozzaris, Marco.**

Botswana (bŏt swä′nə), *n.* a republic in southern Africa, formerly a British protectorate: a member of the Commonwealth of Nations. 548,000 pop. (est. 1965); ab. 275,000 sq. mi. *Cap.:* Gaberones. Formerly, **Bechuanaland.** See map under **Cape of Good Hope.**

bott (bŏt), *n.* bot.

botte (*Fr.* bŏt), *n. Fencing.* a thrust or hit. [t. F]

Botticelli (bŏt′ĭ chĕl′ĭ; *It.* bôt tē chĕl′lē), *n.* **Sandro** (săn′drō; *It.* sàn′dro) (*Alessandro di Mariano dei Filipepi*), 1447–1510, Italian painter.

bottle[1] (bŏt′l), *n., v.*, **-tled, -tling.** —*n.* **1.** a portable vessel with a neck or mouth, now commonly made of glass, used for holding liquids. **2.** the contents of a bottle; as much as a bottle contains: *a bottle of wine.* **3.** a bottle with a rubber nipple from which a baby sucks milk, etc. **4. the bottle, a.** intoxicating drink. **b.** bottled milk for babies (opposed to *the breast*): *raised on the bottle.* —*v.t.* **5.** to put into or seal in a bottle; to preserve (fruit or vegetables) in bottles. **6. bottle up,** to shut in or restrain closely: *to bottle up one's feelings.* [ME *botel,* t. OF: m. *botele,* g. LL *butticula,* dim. of *buttis* BUTT⁴] —**bot′tle-like′,** *adj.* —**bot′tler,** *n.*

bottle² (bŏt′l), *n. Dial.* a bundle, esp. of hay. [ME *botel,* t. OF, dim. of *botte* bundle]

bottle-brush (bŏt′l brŭsh′), *n.* **1.** a brush for cleaning bottles. **2.** any tree of the genus *Calistemon,* having large red flowers, found in Australia. **3.** any similar tree.

bottle-feed (bŏt′l fēd′), *v.t., v.i.,* **-fed, -feeding.** to feed (a baby) with prepared milk from a bottle (opposed to *breastfeed*).

bottle-glass (bŏt′l gläs′), *n.* a kind of thick, dark green glass used for making bottles.

bottle green, deep green.

bottle-holder (bŏt′l hōl′də), *n. Colloq.* **1.** a boxer's or wrestler's second. **2.** any supporter or assistant.

bottleneck (bŏt′l nĕk′), *n.* **1.** a narrow entrance or passage-way. **2.** a place, or stage in a process, where progress is retarded. **3. a.** a narrow part of a road between two wide stretches. **b.** a congested junction, road, town, etc., fed by several roads, where traffic is likely to be held up.

bottle nose, a swollen red or purple pimply nose, popularly believed to be caused by alcoholic drink. —**bottle-nosed** (bŏt′l nōzd′), *adj.*

bottlenose (bŏt′l nōz′), *n.* any of various cetaceans, as *Hyperoodon ampullatus.*

bottle-o (bŏt′l ō′), *n. Austral. Colloq.* a collector of empty bottles.

bottle party, a party to which each guest brings a bottle of some alcoholic drink.

bottle-store (bŏt′l stô′), *n. S African.* an off-licence.

bottle tree, any of several trees, species of the genus *Sterculia* (*Firmiana*), native to warmer regions, as *S. rupestris* (**narrow-leaved bottle tree**) and *S. trichosiphon* (**broad-leaved bottle tree**)

bottle-washer (bŏt′l wŏsh′ə), *n.* **1.** one whose occupation is washing bottles. **2.** *Colloq.* a factotum.

bottling (bŏt′lĭng), *n.* the act, process, or business of preserving fruit, etc., in bottles or jars.

bottom (bŏt′əm), *n.* **1.** the lowest or deepest part of anything, as distinguished from the top: *the bottom of a hill, of a page, etc.* **2.** the place of least honour, dignity, or achievement: *the bottom of the class, of the table, etc.* **3.** the lowest gear of a motor; first gear. **4.** the underside: *the bottom of a flatiron.* **5.** the ground under any body of water: *the bottom of the sea.* **6.** *Phys. Geog.* low-lying alluvial land adjacent to a river. **7.** *Naut.* **a.** the part of a ship below the wales. **b.** a ship. **8.** the seat of a chair. **9.** the buttocks. **10.** the fundamental part; basic aspect: *from the bottom of my heart.* **11.** the inmost part or inner end of a recess, bay, lane, etc. **12. at bottom,** in reality; fundamentally. —*v.t.* **13.** to furnish with a bottom. **14.** to base or found (fol. by *on* or *upon*). **15.** to get to the bottom of; fathom. —*v.i.* **16.** to be based; rest. **17.** to strike against the bottom or end; reach the bottom. —*adj.* **18.** lowest; undermost. **19.** fundamental: *the bottom cause.* [ME; OE *botm,* c. G *Boden*] —**Syn. 1.** base, foot.

bottom drawer, a repository of articles hoarded by a young woman against marriage. Also, *U.S.,* **hope chest.**

bottomless (bŏt′əm lĭs), *adj.* **1.** without a bottom. **2.** immeasurably deep. **3. the bottomless pit,** hell.

bottommost (bŏt′əm mōst′), *adj.* lowest; at the very bottom.

bottomry (bŏt′əm rĭ), *n., pl.* **-ries.** *Marine Law.* a contract, of the nature of a mortgage, by which the owner of a ship borrows money to make a voyage, pledging the ship as security. [modelled on D *bodemerij*]

Bottrop (*Ger.* bŏt′rŏp), *n.* a town in West Germany, in W central North Rhine-Westphalia, near Essen. 112,300 (est. 1966).

botulin (bŏt′yo͝o lĭn), *n.* the toxin causing botulism.

botulinus (bŏt′yo͝o lī′nəs), *n.* the bacterium *Clostridium botulinum,* which forms botulin.

botulism (bŏt′yo͝o lĭz′əm), *n.* a disease of the nervous system caused by botulin developed in spoiled sausage, preserved and other foods eaten by animals and man. [f. s. L *botulus* sausage + -ISM]

B.o.T. unit, Board of Trade unit.

Bouaké (*Fr.* bwȧ kĕ′), *n.* a town in S central Ivory Coast. 80,000 (est. 1964).

Boucher (*Fr.* bo͞o shĕ′), *n.* **François** (*Fr.* fräɴ swȧ′), 1703–70, French painter.

Bouches-du-Rhône (*Fr.* bo͞osh dʏ rōn′), *n.* a department in SE France. 1,248,355 pop. (1962); 2026 sq. mi. *Cap.:* Marseilles.

Boucicault (bo͞o′sĭ kō′), *n.* **Dion** (dī′ŏn, -ən), 1822–90, Irish dramatist and actor.

bouclé (bo͞o′klā; *Fr.* bo͞o klĕ′), *n.* yarn with loops, which produces a woven or knitted fabric with rough appearance. [t. F]

Boudicca (bō dĭk′ə), *n.* Boadicea.

Boudin (*Fr.* bo͞o dăɴ′), *n.* **Eugène** (*Fr.* œ zhĕn′), 1824–98, French painter.

boudoir (bo͞o′dwä, -dwô), *n.* a lady's bedroom or private room. [t. F, der. *bouder* pout, sulk]

bouffant (bo͞o′fŏng; *Fr.* bo͞o fäɴ′), *adj. French.* puffed out; full, as sleeves, hairstyle, or draperies. —**bouffante** (bo͞o′fŏnt; *Fr.* bo͞o fäɴt′), *adj. fem.*

bougainvillaea (bo͞o′gən vĭl′ĭ ə), *n.* any plant of the nyctaginaceous South American genus *Bougainvillaea,* comprising shrubs with small flowers, species of which are cultivated for ornament.

Bougainville (bo͞o′gən vĭl′; *Fr.* bo͞o găɴ vēl′), *n.* **1. Louis Antoine de** (*Fr.* lwē äɴ twȧn′ də) 1729–1811, French navigator. **2.** the largest of the Solomon Islands, in the S Pacific. 64,080 pop. (1964); 4080 sq. mi.

bough (bou), *n.* **1.** a branch of a tree, esp. one of the larger of the main branches. **2.** *Archaic.* the gallows. [ME; OE *bōg, bōh* shoulder, bough, c. D *boeg,* LG *bug,* Icel. *bōgr* shoulder, bow of a ship] —**bough′less,** *adj.* —**Syn. 1.** See **branch.**

bought (bôt), *v.* pt. and pp. of **buy.**

bougie (bo͞o′zhē; *Fr.* bo͞o zhē′), *n.* **1.** *Med.* **a.** a slender flexible instrument for introduction into passages of the body for dilating or opening, etc. **b.** a suppository. **2.** a wax candle. [t. F, name of BOUGIE, Algerian town, centre of wax trade]

Bougie (*Fr.* bo͞o zhē′). See **Bejaia.**

Bouguereau (*Fr.* bo͞o grō′), *n.* **Adolphe William** (*Fr.* ȧ dŏlf wēl yȧm′), 1825–1905, French painter.

bouillabaisse (bo͞o′yə bĕs′; *Fr.* bo͞o yȧ bĕs′), *n.* a kind of stew made of fish and vegetables. [t. F, t. Pr.: m. *bouiabaisso,* f. *boui* boil + *abaisso* (go) down]

bouillon (bo͞o′yŏng; *Fr.* bo͞o yôɴ′), *n.* a clear, thin soup made by boiling meat, etc. [t. F, der. *bouillir* boil]

Boulanger (*Fr.* bo͞o läɴ zhĕ′), *n.* **1. Georges Ernest Jean Marie** (*Fr.* zhŏrzh ĕr nĕst zhäɴ mȧ rē′), 1837–91, French general and politician. **2. Nadia (Juliette)** (*Fr.* nȧ dyȧ zhʏ lyĕt′), born 1887, French conductor and music teacher.

boulder (bōl′də), *n.* a detached and rounded or worn rock, esp. a large one. [short for *boulder stone,* ME *bulder-,* t. Scand.; cf. d. Sw. *bulldersten* big stone (in a stream)]

Boulder Canyon, the canyon of the Colorado river above Boulder Dam, between Arizona and Nevada.

boulder clay, *Geol.* a layer of clay containing boulders and stones, deposited by ancient glaciers.

Boulder Dam, a large dam in the U.S., on the Colorado river, in SE Nevada and NW Arizona: the highest dam in the world. 727 ft high; 1180 ft long. Official name, **Hoover Dam.**

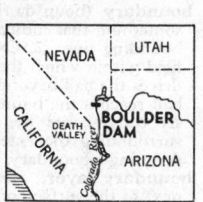

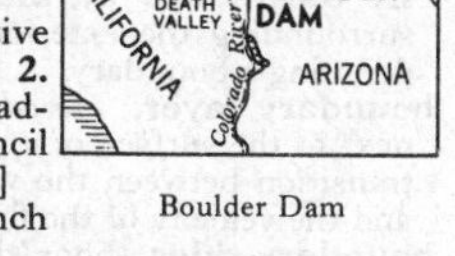

Boulder Dam

Boule (bo͞o′lĭ), *n.* **1.** the legislative assembly of modern Greece. **2.** (*sometimes l.c.*) a legislative, advisory, or administrative council in ancient Greek states. [t. Gk]

boules (*Fr.* bo͞ol), *n.pl.* a French game resembling bowls.

boulevard (bo͞ol′vä, -väd), *n.* a broad avenue of a city, often having trees and used as a promenade. [t. F, t. MLG: m. *boleverk.* See BULWARK] —**Syn.** See **street.**

boulevardier (bo͞ol vä′dĭ ā′; *Fr.* bo͞ol vȧr dyĕ′), *n.* one who frequents boulevards; a pleasure seeker.

bouleversement (*Fr.* bo͞ol vĕrs mäɴ′), *n. French.* an overturning; upsetting; confusion; turmoil.

Boulogne (bo͞o loin′; *Fr.* bo͞o lŏny′), *n.* a seaport in N France, in Pas de Calais department. 50,036 (1962). Also, **Boulogne-sur-Mer** (*Fr.* bo͞o lŏny sʏr mĕr′).

Boulogne, Bois de (*Fr.* bo͞o lŏny′, bwȧ də), a park in W Paris.

Boulogne Billancourt (*Fr.* bo͞o lŏny bē yäɴ ko͞or′), a suburb SW of Paris in N France. 107,074 (1962). Also, **Boulogne-sur-Seine** (*Fr.* bo͞o lŏny sʏr sĕn′).

Boult (bōlt), *n.* **Sir Adrian (Cedric),** born 1889, English conductor.

boulter (bōl′tə), *n.* a long, stout fishing line with several hooks attached.

Boulton (bōl′tən), *n.* **Matthew,** 1728–1809, English engineer, partner of James Watt.

Boumédienne (bōō mā′dĭ ĕn′; *Fr.* bōō mė dyĕn′), **Houari** (hou′ərĭ), born 1927, prime minister of Algeria since 1965.

bounce (bouns), *v.*, **bounded, bouncing,** *n.*, *adv.* —*v.i.* **1.** to move with a bound, and rebound, as a ball: *a ball bounces back from the wall.* **2.** to burst egregiously (*into* or *out of*): *to bounce into and out of a room.* **3.** to boast; show off. **4.** *Colloq.* (of cheques) to be dishonoured; to be returned unpaid. —*v.t.* **5.** to cause to bound or rebound: *to bounce a ball, to bounce a child up and down.* **6.** *Slang.* to eject or discharge summarily. **7.** to persuade (someone) by bluff. —*n.* **8.** a rebound or bound: *catch the ball on the first bounce.* **9.** a sudden spring or leap. **10.** impudence; bluster; swagger. **11.** ability to bounce; resilience. **12.** *U.S. Slang.* expulsion; discharge; dismissal. —*adv.* **13.** with a bounce; suddenly. [ME *bunsen* thump, t. LG, der. *bums*! thump! Cf. D *bonzen* thwack, etc.]

bouncer (boun′sə), *n.* **1.** one who or that which bounces. **2.** *Slang.* one employed in a place of public resort to eject disorderly persons. **3.** something large of its kind. **4.** an impudent, brash person. **5.** *Cricket.* a bumper. **6.** *Slang.* a gross untruth; a lie. **7.** *Slang.* a dishonoured cheque.

bouncing (boun′sĭng), *adj.* **1.** stout, strong, or vigorous: *a bouncing baby.* **2.** exaggerated; big; hearty; noisy: *a bouncing lie.*

bouncing Bett (bĕt), the common soapwort. Also, **bouncing Bess** (bĕs), **bouncing Bet.**

bound[1] (bound), *adj.* **1.** tied; in bonds: *a bound prisoner.* **2.** made fast as by a band or bond: *bound by one's word.* **3.** secured within a cover, as a book. **4.** under obligation, legally or morally: *in duty bound to help.* **5.** destined or sure: *it is bound to happen.* **6.** determined or resolved: *he is bound to go.* **7.** *Pathol.* constipated; costive. **8. bound up in** or **with, a.** inseparably connected with. **b.** having the affections centred in: *his life is bound up in his children.* [pp. of BIND]

bound[2] (bound), *v.i.* **1.** to move by leaps; leap; jump; spring. **2.** to rebound, as a ball. —*v.t.* **3.** to cause to bound. —*n.* **4.** a leap onwards or upwards; a jump. **5.** a rebound. [t. F: m. s. *bondir* leap, orig., resound, ? g. L *bombitāre* hum] —**Syn. 1.** See **skip**[1].

bound[3] (bound), *n.* **1.** (*usually pl.*) a limiting line, or boundary: *the bounds of space and time.* **2.** that which limits, confines, or restrains. **3.** (*pl.*) territory on or near a boundary. **4.** (*pl.*) an area included within boundary lines: *within the bounds of his estate, within the bounds of reason.* **5. out of bounds,** forbidden of access to certain persons or to the general public. —*v.t.* **6.** to limit as by bounds. **7.** to form the boundary or limit of. **8.** to name the boundaries of. —*v.i.* **9.** to have boundaries (*on*); abut. [ME *bounde, boune,* t. OF: m. *bodne,* g. LL *butina*] —**Syn. 1.** border, frontier. **6.** demarcate, circumscribe.

bound[4] (bound), *adj.* **1.** going or intending to go; on the way (*to*); destined (*for*): *the train is bound for Edinburgh.* **2.** *Archaic.* prepared; ready. [ME *boun,* t. Scand.; cf. Icel. *būinn,* pp. of *būa* get ready]

boundary (boun′də rĭ, -drĭ), *n.*, *pl.* **-ries,** *adj.* —*n.* **1.** something that indicates bounds or limits; a limiting or bounding line. **2.** *Cricket.* **a.** the marked limits of the field within which the game is played. **b.** a stroke which drives the ball beyond those limits. **c.** the four, or, if the ball reaches the boundary without touching the ground, six runs scored by such a stroke. —*adj.* **3.** *Physics.* surrounding the exterior of a solid or liquid body. **4.** denoting a boundary.

boundary layer, *Aerodynamics.* the thin layer of fluid next to the surface of a moving body in which there is a transition between the velocity of the body on one side, and the velocity of the fluid on the other.

boundary-rider (boun′də rĭ rī′də, -drĭ-), *n.* *Austral.* a station hand who keeps fences in good repair and prevents stock from straying.

bounden (boun′dən), *adj.* morally obligatory (only in phrase *bounden duty*). [var. of BOUND[1]; orig. pp. of BIND]

bounder (boun′də), *n.* *Colloq.* an obtrusive, ill-bred person; a vulgar upstart.

bound form, a linguistic form which never occurs by itself but always as part of some larger construction, as *-ed* in *seated.*

boundless (bound′lĭs), *adj.* without bounds; unlimited: *his boundless energy amazed them.* —**bound′lessly,** *adv.* —**bound′lessness,** *n.*

bounteous (boun′tĭ əs), *adj.* **1.** giving or disposed to give freely; generously liberal. **2.** freely bestowed; plentiful; abundant. [f. *bounte* (earlier var. of BOUNTY) + -OUS; r. ME *bontyvous,* der. OF *bontif* benevolent] —**boun′teously,** *adv.* —**boun′teousness,** *n.*

bountiful (boun′tĭ fəl), *adj.* **1.** liberal in bestowing gifts, favours, or bounties; munificent; generous. **2.** abundant; ample: *a bountiful supply.* —**boun′tifully,** *adv.* —**boun′tifulness,** *n.*

bounty (boun′tĭ) *n.*, *pl.* **-ties. 1.** generosity in giving. **2.** whatever is given bounteously; a benevolent, generous gift. **3.** a premium or reward, esp. one offered by a government. [ME *bounte,* t. OF: m. *bonte(t),* g. L *bonitas* goodness] —**Syn. 1.** munificence, liberality, charity.

Bounty (boun′tĭ), *n.* a ship commanded by William Bligh, whose crew mutinied near Tahiti in 1789.

bouquet (bō kā′, bōō-, *for 1;* bōō kā′ *for 2; Fr.* bōō kĕ′), *n.* **1.** a bunch of flowers; a nosegay. **2.** the characteristic aroma of wines, liqueurs, etc. [t. F: bunch, clump of trees, d. var. of OF *bosquet* little wood, dim. of *bosc* wood. See BUSH[1]]

bouquet garni (bōō′kā gä nē′; *Fr.* bōō kĕ gȧr nē′), *French.* a bunch of herbs used to give flavour to soups, stews, and sauces.

Bourbon (bŏŏə′bən, *Fr.* bōōr bôɴ′ *for 1–3;* bû′bən *for 4.*) *n.* **1.** a member of the last house of the royal family of France, or of any of its branches, as the former royal family of Spain. **2. Charles** (*Fr.* shȧrl), 1490–1527, French general. **3.** *Chiefly U.S.* (in derogatory use) an extreme reactionary, or one devoted to ideas suited only to past conditions. **4.** (*l.c.*) *U.S.* Also, **bourbon whiskey.** a kind of whisky distilled from a mash containing 51 per cent or more maize; orig. the maize whisky produced in Bourbon County, Kentucky.

Bourbonism (bŏŏə′bə nĭz′əm), *n.* **1.** adherence to the system of government and the ideas for which the Bourbons stood. **2.** *U.S.* extreme conservatism, as in politics. —**Bour′bonist,** *n.*

bourdon (bŏŏə′dn, bô′dn), *n.* *Music.* **1.** the drone of a bagpipe, or of a monotonous and repetitious ground melody. **2.** a low-pitched tone; a bass. **3.** an organ stop producing such a tone. [t. F]

bourg (bŏŏəg; *Fr.* bōōr), *n.* **1.** a town. **2.** a French market town. [t. F, g. LL *burgus,* t. Gmc. See BOROUGH]

Bourg (*Fr.* bōōrk), *n.* a town in E France, capital of Ain department. 2518 (1962).

bourgeois[1] (bŏŏə′zhwä; *Fr.* bōōr zhwȧ′), *n.*, *pl.* **-geois,** *adj.* —*n.* **1.** a member of the middle class. **2.** a shopkeeper or other trader. **3.** one whose outlook is said to be determined by a concern for property values; a capitalist as opposed to a member of the wage-earning class. —*adj.* **4.** belonging to or consisting of the middle class. **5.** lacking in refinement or elegance; conventional. **6.** dominated or characterized by a concern for property values or by materialistic pursuits. [t. F; c. BURGESS] —**bourgeoise** (bŏŏə′zhwäz; *Fr.* bōōr zhwȧz′), *n.*, *adj. fem.*

bourgeois[2] (bû jois′), *n.* a printing type (9 point) of a size between brevier and long primer. [? proper name]

bourgeoisie (bŏŏə′ zhwä zē′; *Fr.* bōōr zhwȧ zē′), *n.* **1.** the bourgeois class. **2.** (in Marxist ideology) the class opposed to the proletariat or wage-earning class. [t. F]

bourgeon (bû′jən), *n.*, *v.* burgeon.

Bourges (*Fr.* bōōrzh), *n.* a city in central France, in Cher department. 63,479 (1962).

Bourget (*Fr.* bōōr zhĕ′), *n.* **Paul** (*Fr.* pŏl), 1852–1935, French novelist and critic.

Bourgogne (*Fr.* bōōr gōny′), *n.* French name of **Burgundy.**

Bourguiba (bŏŏə gē′bə; *Fr.* bōōr gē bȧ′), *n.* **Habib** (hä-bēb′), born 1903, leader of the Tunisian independence movement: president of Tunisia since 1957.

bourn[1] (bôn), *n.* a small, intermittent stream in limestone or chalk country. [var. of BURN[2]]

bourn[2] (bôn), *n.* **1.** a bound; limit. **2.** destination; goal. **3.** realm; domain. Also, **bourne.** [t. F: m. *borne*]

Bournemouth (bôn′məth), *n.* a town in England, in SW Hampshire: seaside resort. 153,965 (1961).

bournonite (bô′nə nīt′), *n.* *Chem.* a mineral sulphide of lead, copper, and antimony; occurring in wheel-shaped twins; wheel ore.

bourrée (bōō′rā; *Fr.* bōō rė′), *n.* **1.** an old French and Spanish dance, resembling a gavotte. **2.** the music for it.

Bourse (bŏŏəs; *Fr.* bōōrs), *n.* a stock exchange, esp. that of Paris. [t. F: orig., purse, g. LL *bursa,* t. Gk: m. *býrsa* hide]

bouse[1] (bouz), *v.t.*, **boused, bousing.** *Naut.* to haul with tackle. Also, **bowse.** [orig. unknown]

bouse[2] (bōōz), *n.*, *v.*, **boused, bousing.** booze.

boustrophedon (bōō′strə fē′dn, bou′-), *n.* an ancient method of writing in which the lines run alternately from right to left and from left to right. [t. Gk: adv., with turning like that of oxen in ploughing]

bousy (bōō′zĭ), *adj.* boozy.

bout (bout), *n.* **1.** a contest; a trial of strength. **2.** a turn at work or any action. **3.** period; spell: *a bout of illness.* [var. of obs. *bought* bend, turn, der. BOW[1]]

boutique (bōō′tēk; *Fr.* bōō tēk′), *n.* a small shop selling fashionable or luxury articles esp. for women. [t. F]

bouttonniere (bōō′tŏ nĭ ĕə′), *n.* a buttonhole bouquet or flower. [t. F: buttonhole]

bovid (bō′vĭd), *adj. Zool.* of or pertaining to the *Bovidae*, or ox family, comprising the hollow-horned ruminants, as oxen, sheep, and goats.

bovine (bō′vīn), *adj.* **1.** of the ox family (*Bovidae*). **2.** oxlike. **3.** stolid; dull. —*n.* **4.** a bovine animal. [t. LL: m. s. *bovinus*, der. L *bōs* ox]

bow[1] (bou), *v.i.* **1.** to bend or curve downwards; stoop: *the pines bowed low.* **2.** to yield; submit: *to bow to the inevitable.* **3.** to bend the body or head in worship, reverence, respect, or submission. **4.** to incline the head or body, or both, in salutation etc. **5. bow and scrape,** to be servile. —*v.t.* **6.** to bend or incline in worship, submission, respect, civility, or agreement: *to bow one's head.* **7.** to cause to submit; subdue; crush. **8.** to cause to stoop: *age had bowed his head.* **9.** to express by a bow, or by bowing: *to bow one's thanks.* **10.** to usher (*in, out,* etc.) with a bow. **11.** *Archaic and Dial.* to cause to bend; make curved or crooked. —*n.* **12.** an inclination of the head or body in salutation, assent, thanks, reverence, respect, or submission. [ME *bowe(n)*, OE *būgan*, c. G *biegen* bend] —**bowed** (boud), *adj.*

bow[2] (bō), *n.* **1.** a strip of flexible wood or other material bent by a string stretched between its ends, used for shooting arrows. **2.** a bend or curve. **3.** something curved or arc-shaped. **4.** a looped knot, as of ribbon, composed of one or two loops and two ends. See illus. under **knot.** **5.** *Music.* **a.** an implement, orig. curved but now almost always straight, with horsehairs stretched upon it, for playing any member of the violin family of instruments. **b.** a single stroke of such an implement. **6.** the arched front part of a saddle. **7.** a U-shaped piece under an animal's neck to hold a yoke. **8.** a rainbow. **9.** Also, **bow collector.** *Railways, etc.* a triangular-shaped current collector used on some electric railways, tramways, etc. See **trolley** (def. 4). —*adj.* **10.** curved; bent like a bow: *bow legs.* —*v.t., v.i.* **11.** to bend into the form of a bow; curve. **12.** *Music.* **a.** to perform by means of a bow upon a stringed instrument. **b.** to make a single downward or upward stroke of the bow. [ME *bowe*, OE *boga*, c. G *Bogen*] —**bow′less,** *adj.* —**bow′like′,** *adj.*

bow[3] (bou), *n.* **1.** (*sometimes pl.*) the front or forward part or end of a ship, boat, airship, etc. See illus. under **aft.** **2.** the foremost oar used in rowing a boat. **3.** the person who pulls that oar; the bow oar; bowman. **4. on the port** (or **starboard**) **bow,** within 45° to port (or starboard) of the direction in which the stem of the ship is pointing. [t. LG: m. *boog*, or D: m. *boeg*. Cf. Dan. *bov*, c. BOUGH]

bow compass (bō), *Geom.* any of various compasses, as one having the legs joined by a bow-shaped piece.

bowdlerize (boud′lə rīz′), *v.t.*, **-rized, -rizing.** to expurgate prudishly. Also, **bowdlerise.** [from Thomas *Bowdler*, who in 1818 published an expurgated edition of Shakespeare] —**bowd′lerism, n.** —**bowd′leriza′tion,** *n.* —**bowd′leriz′er,** *n.*

bowel (bou′əl), *n., v.*, **-elled, -elling,** or (*U.S.*) **-eled, -eling.** —*n.* **1.** *Anat.* **a.** an intestine. **b.** (*usually pl.*) the parts of the alimentary canal below the stomach; the intestines or entrails. **2.** the inward or interior parts. **3.** (*pl.*) *Archaic.* feelings of pity or compassion. —*v.t.* **4.** to disembowel. [ME *bouel*, t. OF: m. *boel*, g. L *botellus*, dim. of *botulus* sausage]

bower[1] (bou′ə), *n.* **1.** a leafy shelter or recess; an arbour. **2.** *Archaic.* a rustic dwelling; a cottage. **3.** *Poetic.* a chamber; a boudoir. —*v.t.* **4.** to enclose in or as in a bower; embower. [ME *bour*, OE *būr* a dwelling, cottage, akin to *būan* dwell] —**bow′erlike′,** *adj.*

bower[2] (bou′ə), *n.* an anchor carried at a ship's bow. Also, **bower anchor.** [f. BOW[3] + -ER[2]]

bower[3] (bou′ə), *n.* (in euchre and other card games) the knave of trumps (**right bower**) or the other knave of the same colour (**left bower**); the highest cards in the game, unless the joker (often called the **best bower**) is used. [t. G: m. *Bauer* peasant, jack (in cards)]

bower[4] (bou′ə), *n.* one who or that which bows or bends. [f. BOW[1] + -ER[1]]

bower[5] (bō′ə), *n. Music.* a player with the bow on a violin or other stringed instruments. [f. BOW[2] + -ER[1]]

bowerbird (bou′ə bûd′), *n.* any of various Australian and Papuan oscine birds, related to birds of paradise, as *Ptilonorhynchus violaceus*, which build bowerlike structures, used, not as nests, but as places of resort to attract the females.

bowery[1] (bou′ə rī), *adj.* bowerlike; containing bowers; shady: *a bowery maze.*

bowery[2] (bou′ə rī), *n., pl.* **-eries.** **1.** *U.S.* (among the Dutch settlers of New York) a farm or country seat. **2. the Bowery,** a long, wide street in New York City, notorious for its saloons, squalid hotels, etc. [t. D: m. *bouwerij* (def. 1), der. *bouwer* farmer]

bowfin (bō′fĭn′), *n.* a North American freshwater ganoid fish, *Amia calva.*

bow hand (bō), **1.** *Archery.* the hand that holds the bow, usually the left hand. **2.** *Music.* the hand that draws the bow, usually the right hand.

bowhead (bō′hĕd′), *n.* a whale, *Balaena mysticetus*, of arctic seas.

bowie knife (bō′ĭ), a heavy sheath-knife having a long, single-edged blade. [named after James *Bowie*, 1796–1836, American pioneer]

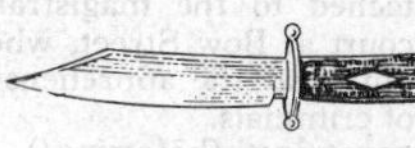
Bowie knife

bowing (bō′ĭng), *n. Music.* the style in which the bow is used in playing a particular passage.

bowl[1] (bōl), *n.* **1.** a rather deep, round dish or basin, used chiefly for holding liquids, food, etc. **2.** the contents of a bowl. **3.** a rounded, hollow part: *the bowl of a pipe.* **4.** a large drinking cup; a goblet. **5.** festive drinking; conviviality. **6.** any bowl-shaped depression or formation. **7.** an edifice with a bowl-like interior, as for athletic contests, etc. [ME *bolle*, OE *bolla*, c. Icel. *bolli.* See BOLL[1]] —**bowl′-like′,** *adj.*

bowl[2] (bōl), *n.* **1.** one of the biased or weighted balls used in the game of bowls. **2.** one of the balls, having little or no bias, used in playing ninepins or tenpin bowling. **3.** a cast or delivery of the ball in bowling. **4.** *Mach.* a rotating cylindrical part in a machine, as one to reduce friction. —*v.i.* **5.** to play with bowls, or at bowling. **6.** to roll a bowl, as in the game of bowls. **7.** to move along smoothly and rapidly. **8.** *Cricket.* to deliver the ball with a straight arm in such a way that it bounces once before reaching the batsman. —*v.t.* **9.** to roll or trundle, as a ball, hoop, etc. **10.** to knock or strike, as by the ball in bowling (fol. by *over* or *down*). **11.** to disconcert; upset (fol. by *over*). **12.** to carry or convey as in a wheeled vehicle. **13.** *Cricket.* to eliminate (a batsman) by delivering a ball which breaks the batsman's wicket. [ME *boule*, t. OF: ball, g. L *bulla* bubble]

bowleg (bō′lĕg′), *n. Pathol.* **1.** outward curvature of the legs causing a separation of the knees when the ankles are close or in contact. **2.** a leg so curved. —**bow-legged** (bō′lĕg′ĭd, bō′lĕgd′), *adj.*

bowler[1] (bō′lə), *n.* a hard felt hat with a rounded crown and narrow brim. [f. BOWL[1] + -ER[2]]

bowler[2] (bō′lə), *n.* one who bowls (a ball). [f. BOWL[2] + -ER[1]]

bowler hat, a bowler[1]. —**bowler-hatted** (bō′lə hăt′ĭd), *adj.*

bowline (bō′lĭn), *n.* **1.** Also, **bowline knot.** a knot which forms a non-slipping loop. **2.** *Naut.* **a.** a rope leading forward and fastened to the leech of a square sail, used to steady the weather leech of the sail and keep it forward. **b. on a bowline,** sailing close to the wind.

Bowline (def. 1)

bowling (bō′lĭng), *n.* **1.** the act of playing with or at bowls. **2.** the game of bowls. **3.** *Cricket.* the act of delivering the ball to the batsman. **4.** tenpin bowling.

bowling alley, **1.** a long enclosure for playing bowls, etc. **2.** a covered place with a long, narrow, planked enclosure, for tenpin bowling.

bowling crease. See **crease** (def. 3a).

bowling green, a level plot of turf for bowling.

bowls (bōlz), *n.* **1.** a game, common in Great Britain, the Commonwealth, and parts of the U.S. and Canada, in which the players roll biased or weighted balls along the sward in an effort to bring them as near as possible to a stationary ball called the *jack.* **2.** skittles, ninepins, or tenpin bowling.

bowman[1] (bō′mən), *n., pl.* **-men.** **1.** an archer. **2.** (in medieval warfare) a soldier armed with a bow. [f. BOW[2] + MAN]

bowman[2] (bou′mən), *n., pl.* **-men.** bow[3] (def. 3). [f. BOW[3] + MAN]

bow oar (bou), bow[3] (def. 3).

bow pen (bō), *Geom.* a bow compass with a pen at the end of one leg.

bowsaw (bō′sô′), *n.* a saw with a thin blade held taut in a bowlike frame, used especially for cutting curves. See illus. under **saw.**

bowse (bouz), *v.t.*, **bowsed, bowsing.** bouse[1].

bowser (bou′zə), *n.* **1.** a vehicle supplying aviation spirit to aircraft. **2.** *Austral. and N.Z. Colloq.* a petrol pump. [orig. trademark, from personal name]

bowser bag, *U.S.* a bag provided by a restaurant or the like, for carrying home scraps, as for a dog. [*bowser* ? der BOW-WOW]

bowshot (bō′shŏt′), *n.* the distance a bow sends an arrow.

bowsprit (bō′sprĭt′), *n. Naut.* a large spar projecting forward from the stem of a ship or other vessel. [ME *bousprete*, f. *bou* bow of a ship + *spret* (OE *sprēot* pole)]

Bow Street (bō), a street in London, in which there is a metropolitan magistrates' court.

Bow Street runner, *Hist.* (1749–1829) an officer attached to the magistrates' court at Bow Street, whose duty was the apprehension of criminals.

A, Bowsprit; B, Jib boom; C, Bobstay

bowstring (bō′strĭng′), *n.*, *v.*, **-stringed** or **-strung, -stringing.** —*n.* **1.** the string of a bow. **2.** a string used, as by the Turks, for execution by strangling. —*v.t.* **3.** to strangle with a bowstring or any string or band.

bowstring hemp, any of various fibrous plants of the genus *Sansevieria* of Asia and Africa.

bow tie (bō), a small, bow-shaped tie.

bow window (bō), **1.** a rounded bay window. **2.** *Colloq.* a protuberant or pregnant belly.

bow-wow (bou′wou′), *n.* **1.** the bark of a dog. **2.** an imitation of this. **3.** (in childish use) a dog.

bowyangs (bō′yăngz), *n.* *Austral. Colloq.* a string tied round the trouser leg to prevent the turnup from dragging. [orig. uncertain]

bowyer (bō′yə), *n.* a maker or seller of bows.

box[1] (bŏks), *n.* **1.** a case or receptacle, usually rectangular, of wood, metal, cardboard, etc., with a lid or removable cover. **2.** the quantity contained in a box. **3.** a packet or case containing presents. **4.** the present or gift itself, esp. as given to tradesmen at Christmas; Christmas box. **5.** a collection of money for a charitable purpose, etc. **6.** a compartment or place shut or railed off for the accommodation of a small number of people in a public place, esp. in theatres, opera houses, ballrooms, etc. **7.** (in a court of law) a stand or pew reserved for witnesses, the accused or the jury. **8.** a small shelter: *a watchman's box.* **9.** a small house, as for use while following some sport: *a shooting box.* **10.** the driver's seat on a horse-drawn carriage. **11.** a loosebox. **12.** part of a page of a periodical set off by lines, border, or white space. **13.** *Mach.* an enclosing, protecting, or hollow part; a casing; a chamber; a bush; a socket. **14.** *Sport.* a shaped device of some light, tough material worn inside a supporter for protection. **15.** *Baseball.* the space where the batter stands (or, less often, the pitcher or coaches). **16.** *Agric.* a bowl or pit cut in the side of a tree for collecting sap. —*v.t.* **17.** to put into a box. **18.** to enclose or confine as in a box (often fol. by *up*). **19.** to furnish with a box. **20.** to form into a box or the shape of a box. **21.** *Naut.* to boxhaul (often fol. by *off*). **22.** to make a hole or cut in (a tree) for the sap to collect. **23. box up,** to bring about a state of confusion as a result of mismanagement. **24. box the compass,** *Naut.* to name the compass points in order. [special use of BOX[3]] —**box′ful′,** *n.* —**box′ like′,** *adj.*

box[2] (bŏks), *n.* **1.** a blow as with the hand or fist. —*v.t.* **2.** to strike with the hand or fist, esp. on the ear. **3.** to fight in a boxing match. —*v.i.* **4.** to fight with the fists; spar. [ME; orig. unknown]

box[3] (bŏks), *n.* **1.** an evergreen shrub or small tree of the genus *Buxus*, esp. *B. sempervivens*, much used for ornamental borders, hedges, etc., and yielding a hard, durable wood. **2.** the wood itself. See **boxwood. 3.** any of various other shrubs or trees, esp. species of eucalyptus. [ME and OE, t. L: m. s. *buxus*, t. Gk: m. *pýxos*]

box bed, 1. a bed completely enclosed so as to resemble a box. **2.** a bed that folds up in the form of a box.

boxberry (bŏks′bə rĭ, -brĭ), *n.*, *pl.* **-ries.** the checkerberry.

boxboard (bŏks′bôd′), *n.* a thin, tough board made from wood and wastepaper pulp.

box calf, a chrome-tanned calfskin with square markings produced by graining.

box camera, a boxlike camera, without bellows.

boxcar (bŏks′kä′), *n.* *U.S. Railways.* a large, enclosed and covered freight van.

boxcloth (bŏks′klŏth′), *n.* a heavy cloth, usually light brown, used in making warm coats.

box coat, 1. an outer coat with a straight, unfitted back. **2.** (formerly) a heavy overcoat worn by coachmen.

box elder, a fast-growing North American maple, *Acer negundo*, cultivated for shade.

boxer (bŏk′sə), *n.* **1.** one who boxes; a pugilist. **2.** a smooth-coated, brown dog of medium size, related to the bulldog and terrier.

Boxer (bŏk′sə), *n.* a member of a Chinese secret society, which practised ritualistically the traditional Chinese posture boxing, supposed to make them immune to bullets and swords. In 1900 they attacked foreigners and Chinese Christians and besieged the legations at Peking until an international expeditionary force raised the siege.

boxfish (bŏks′fĭsh′), *n.* trunkfish (defs 2 and 3).

box-frame (bŏks′frām′), *n.* *Bldg Trades.* a rigid frame, usually of steel, used as a basis for certain structures.

boxhaul (bŏks′hôl′), *v.t.* *Naut.* to veer (a ship) round on her heel by bracing the head yards aback, etc.

boxing[1] (bŏk′sĭng), *n.* **1.** the material used to make boxes or casings. **2.** a boxlike enclosure. **3.** the act of putting into or furnishing with a box. [f. BOX[1] + -ING[1]]

boxing[2] (bŏk′sĭng), *n.* the act or art of fighting with the fists, with or without boxing gloves. [f. BOX[2] + -ING[1]]

Boxing Day, the first weekday after Christmas, when Christmas gifts are traditionally given to employees, tradesmen, etc.

boxing glove, a padded glove worn in boxing.

boxing match, an organized fight following strict rules, between two pugilists.

box iron, a smoothing iron which is heated by placing a hot iron in its boxlike holder.

box junction, 1. *Elect.* a box of some non-magnetic material as cast-iron, containing a cable joint or joints. **2.** a road junction marked with crossed yellow lines on the road surface, which traffic may not enter unless an exit is clear.

box kite, a kite consisting of a light, box-shaped frame, covered except on the ends and a space along the middle.

box number, a number given in a newspaper advertisement as an address to which replies may be directed, care of the newspaper office.

box office, 1. the office in which tickets are sold at a theatre or other place of public entertainment. **2.** receipts from a play or other entertainment. **3.** the ability of an entertainment or performer to draw an audience: *this show will be good box office.*

box pleat, a double pleat, with the material folded under at each side.

boxroom (bŏks′ ro͝om′, -ro͞om′), *n.* a storage room for pieces of furniture, etc.

box seat, a seat in a theatre box, etc.

box spanner, a hollow tube shaped at one or both ends to fit a nut, and turned by a bar inserted through the diameter.

boxthorn (bŏks′thôn′), *n.* matrimony vine.

boxwood (bŏks′wo͝od′), *n.* **1.** the hard, fine-grained, compact wood of the box: much used for wood engravers' blocks, musical and mathematical instruments, etc. **2.** the tree or shrub itself. Cf. **box**[3].

boy (boi), *n.* **1.** a male child, from birth to full growth, but esp. to the beginning of youth. **2.** a young man who lacks maturity, vigour, judgement, etc. **3.** a grown man. **4.** a boyfriend. **5.** a young servant; a page. **6.** (in India, Africa, China, Japan, etc.) a native male servant, working as a butler, waiter, houseboy, etc. —*interj.* **7.** (an exclamation of surprise, delight, etc.) [ME; orig. uncert.]

boyar (bō yä′, boi′ə), *n.* **1.** *Russian Hist.* a member of the old nobility of Russia, before Peter the Great made rank depend on state service. **2.** (formerly) one of a privileged class in Rumania. Also, **boyard** (bō yäd′, boi′əd). [t. Russ.: m. *boyarin* lord]

boycott (boi′kŏt), *v.t.* **1.** to combine in abstaining from, or preventing dealings with, as a means of intimidation or coercion: *to boycott a person, foreign goods, etc.* **2.** to abstain from buying or using: *to boycott a commercial product.* —*n.* **3.** the practice of boycotting. **4.** an instance of boycotting. [from Captain *Boycott*, the first victim (1880), agent of an Irish landlord]

Boyd Orr (boid′ô′), **John, Baron,** born 1880, Scottish biologist.

boyfriend (boi′frĕnd′), *n.* **1.** a man by whom a girl or woman is courted. **2.** any young male friend.

boyhood (boi′ho͝od′), *n.* the state or period of being a boy.

boyish (boi′ĭsh), *adj.* of, like, or befitting a boy; high-spirited. —**boy′ishly,** *adv.* —**boy′ishness,** *n.*

boyla (boi′lə), *n.* *Austral.* an Aboriginal sorcerer. [t. native Australian]

Boyle (boil), *n.* **Robert,** 1627–91, English chemist and physicist.

Boyle's law, *Physics.* the principle that at a constant temperature the volume occupied by a given quantity of an ideal gas is inversely proportional to the pressure upon the gas. [named after Robert BOYLE]

Boyne (boin), *n.* a river in the E Republic of Ireland, near which William III defeated James II (1690). 70 mi.

Boys' Brigade, an organization founded in 1883 to promote obedience, reverence and self-respect among boys.

boy scout, 1. a member of an organization of boys (the **Boy Scouts),** founded in England in 1908 by Lt Gen.

Sir Robert S. S. Baden-Powell, to develop in its members manly character, self-reliance, and usefulness to others. **2.** a member of any similar society elsewhere.
boysenberry (boiʹzən bə rĭ, -brĭ), *n., pl.* **-ries.** a blackberry-like fruit with a flavour similar to that of raspberries, developed by crossing various species of *Rubus*. [named after R. *Boysen*, 20th-cent. U.S. botanist]
Bozcaada (*Turk*. bôzʹchȧ ȧ dȧʹ), *n.* Tenedos.
Bozen (*Ger.* bōʹtsən), *n.* German name of **Bolzano.**
Bozzaris (bō zăʹrĭs, -zäʹ-), *n.* **Marco** (mäʹkō), 1788?–1823, Greek patriot.
bp., **1.** bishop. **2.** baptized. **3.** birthplace.
b.p., **1.** Also, **B/P.** *Com.* bills payable. **2.** *Physics, Chem.* boiling point.
B.P., **1.** British Pharmacopoeia. **2.** blood pressure.
B.Pharm., Bachelor of Pharmacy.
B. Phil., Bachelor of Philosophy. Also, **B.Ph.**
Br, *Chem.* bromine.
Br., **1.** Britain. **2.** British.
br., **1.** branch. **2.** brig. **3.** bronze. **4.** brother.
b.r., *Com.* bills receivable. Also, **B/R, b.rec.**
B.R., British Railways (British Rail).
bra (brä), *n. Colloq.* a brassiere.
braaivleis (brīʹflās), *n. S African.* a barbecue. [t. Afrikaans: roast meat]
Brabant (brə băntʹ; *Du.* bräʹbônt; *Fr.* brȧ bäNʹ), *n.* **1.** a former duchy in W Europe: now divided into two provinces, one in Belgium (Brabant) and one in the Netherlands (North Brabant). See map under **Agincourt.** **2.** a province in central Belgium. 2,052,913 pop. (est. 1963); 1268 sq. mi. *Cap.:* Brussels. **3.** a province in the S Netherlands. 2,085,294 pop. (1965); 1894 sq. mi. *Cap.:* 's Hertogenbosch.
braccate (brăkʹāt), *adj. Ornith.* having legs covered by feathers. [t. L: m. s. *brac(c)atus* having breeches]
brace (brās), *n., v.,* **braced, bracing.** **—***n.* **1.** something that holds parts together or in place, as a clasp or clamp. **2.** anything that imparts rigidity or steadiness. **3.** *Mach.* a device for holding and turning tools for boring or drilling. See illus. under **brace and bit.** **4.** *Bldg Trades.* a piece of timber, metal, etc., used to support or position another piece or portion of a framework. **5.** *Naut.* (on a square-rigged ship) a rope by which a yard is swung about and secured horizontally. **6.** *Music.* leather loops sliding upon the tightening cords of a drum to change their tension and therewith the pitch. **7.** (*often pl.*) *Dentistry.* a round or flat metal wire placed against surfaces of the teeth, and used to straighten irregularly arranged teeth. **8.** *Med.* an appliance for supporting a weak joint or joints. **9.** (*pl.*) straps or bands worn over the shoulders for holding up the trousers. **10.** a pair; a couple. **11.** one of two characters { or } for connecting written or printed lines. **12.** *Music.* connected staves. **13.** a defence or protection for the arm, specif. one used in archery.
—v.t. **14.** to furnish, fasten, or strengthen with or as with a brace. **15.** to fix firmly; make steady. **16.** to make tight; increase the tension of. **17.** to act as a stimulant to. **18.** *Naut.* to swing or turn round (the yards of a ship) by means of the braces. *—v.i.* **19. brace up,** *Colloq.* to rouse one's strength or vigour. [ME *brase(n)*, t. OF: m. *bracier* embrace, der. *brace* the two arms (cf. def. 10), g. L *brāchia*] **—Syn. 10.** See **pair.**
brace and bit, a boring tool consisting of a bit and a handle for rotating it.

Brace and bit

bracelet (brāsʹlĭt), *n.* **1.** an ornamental band or circlet for the wrist or arm. **2.** *Slang.* a handcuff. [ME, t. OF, dim. of *bracel*, ult. der. L *brāc(c)hium* arm]
bracer[1] (brāʹsə), *n.* **1.** one who or that which braces, binds, or makes firm. **2.** *Colloq.* a stimulating drink; tonic. [f. BRACE + -ER[1]]
bracer[2] (brāʹsə), *n. Archery.* a guard for the left wrist and lower arm worn as a protection against the friction or the catching of the bowstring. [ME *braser*, t. OF: m. *brasseüre*, der. *bras* arm, g. L *brāchium*]
brach (brăch), *n. Obs.* a bitch of the hound kind. Also, **brachet** (brăchʹĭt). [ME *braches*, pl., t. OF, pl. of *brachet*, dim. of *brac*, t. OHG: m. *bracco* a hound hunting by scent]
brachial (brāʹkyəl, brăkʹyəl), *adj. Zool.* **1.** belonging to the arm, foreleg, wing, pectoral fin, or other forelimb of a vertebrate. **2.** belonging to the upper part of such member, from the shoulder to the elbow. **3.** armlike, as an appendage. [t. L: s. *brāchiālis*]
brachialgia (brāʹkĭ ălʹ jə, brăkʹĭ-), *n. Pathol.* pain in the nerves of the upper arm.
brachiate (brāʹkĭ ĭt, -ātʹ, brăkʹĭ-), *adj. Bot.* having widely spreading branches in alternate pairs.
brachio-, a word element meaning 'arm', as in *brachiopod.* Also (before a vowel), **brachi-.** [t. NL, comb. form repr. L *brāchium*, or its source, Gk *brachīōn*]
brachiopod (brāʹkĭ ə pŏdʹ, brăkʹĭ-), *n. Zool.* any of the *Brachiopoda*, a largely extinct phylum of mollusc-like animals, the lamp-shells, having dorsal and ventral shells.
brachiosaur (brăkʹĭ ō sôʹ), *n.* one of the *Brachiosaurus*, a genus of large dinosaurs of the Upper Jurassic period.
brachium (brāʹkĭ əm, brăkʹĭ-), *n., pl.* **brachia** (brāʹkĭ ə, brăkʹĭ ə). *Anat., Zool.* **1.** the arm as a whole. **2.** the upper arm, from the shoulder to the elbow. **3.** the part of any limb, as in the wing of a bird, corresponding to the upper arm. **4.** an armlike part or process. [t. L: arm]
brachy-, a word element meaning 'short', as in *brachycephalic.* [t. Gk, comb. form of *brachýs*]
brachycephalic (brăkʹĭ sĭ fălʹĭk), *adj. Anat.* short-headed (opposed to *dolichocephalic*); having a breadth of head at least four-fifths the length from front to back. Also, **brachycephalous** (brăkʹĭ sĕfʹə ləs). **—brachʹycephʹaly,** *n.*
brachylogy (brə kĭlʹə jĭ), *n., pl.* **-gies.** brevity of diction; a concise or abridged form of expression. [t. Gk: m. s. *brachylogía.* See BRACHY-, -LOGY]
brachypterous (brə kĭpʹtə rəs), *adj. Ornith.* short-winged. [f. BRACHY- + -PTEROUS]
brachyuran (brăkʹĭ yo͞oʹrən), *adj.* **1.** belonging or pertaining to the *Brachyura*, a group of stalk-eyed decapod crustaceans with short tails, the common crabs. **—***n.* **2.** a brachyuran crustacean.
brachyurous (brăkʹĭ yo͞oʹrəs), *adj. Zool.* short-tailed, as the crabs (opposed to *macrurous*).
bracing (brāʹsĭng), *adj.* **1.** strengthening; invigorating. **—***n.* **2.** a brace. **3.** braces collectively. **—bracʹingly,** *adv.*
bracken (brăkʹən), *n.* **1.** a large, coarse fern or brake, esp. *Pteridium aquilinum.* **2.** a clump of ferns. [ME *braken*, t. Scand.; cf. Sw. *bräken* fern]
bracket (brăkʹĭt), *n.* **1.** a wooden, metal, etc., support of triangular outline placed under a shelf or the like. **2.** a shelf or shelves supported by a bracket. **3.** *Archit.* an ornamental projection from the face of a wall, intended to support a statue, pier, etc.; a corbel. See illus. under **corbel.** **4.** a projecting fixture for gas or electricity. **5.** one of two marks, [or], used in writing or printing to enclose parenthetical matter, interpolations, etc. **6.** *Maths.* **a.** (*pl.*) parentheses of various forms indicating that the enclosed quantity is to be treated as a unit. **b.** (loosely) vinculum (def. 2). **7.** a grouping of persons, esp. as based on the amount of their taxable income: *low income bracket.* **8.** *Gunnery.* range or elevation producing both shorts and overs on a target. **—***v.t.* **9.** to furnish with or support by a bracket or brackets. **10.** to place within brackets; couple with a brace. **11.** to associate or mention together, implying equality of some kind. **12.** *Gunnery.* to place (shots) both over and short of a target. [earlier *bragget*, t. F: m. *braguette*, t. Pr., or Sp., dim. of *bragga*, g. L *brācae*, pl., breeches, of Celtic orig.]
bracketing (brăkʹĭ tĭng), *n. Archit.* the series of wooden supports, often of fanciful jigsaw form, nailed to the ceiling, joists, and battening to support cornices.
brackish (brăkʹĭsh), *adj.* **1.** slightly salt; having a salty or briny flavour. **2.** distasteful. [f. *brack* brackish (t. D: m. *brak*) + -ISH[1]] **—brackʹishness,** *n.*
Bracknell (brăkʹnəl), *n.* a new town in England, in E Berkshire. 25,448 (1965).
bract (brăkt), *n. Bot.* a specialized leaf or leaflike part, usually situated at the base of a flower or inflorescence. [t. L: m. s. *bractea* thin plate of metal] **—bracteal** (brăkʹtĭ əl), *adj.* **—bractʹless,** *adj.*
bracteate (brăkʹtĭ ĭt, -ātʹ), *n.* **1.** *Archeol.* a thin ornamental plate of gold or silver. **—***adj.* **2.** *Bot.* having bracts.
bracteolate (brăkʹtĭ ə lĭt, -lātʹ), *adj. Bot.* having bracteoles.
bracteole (brăkʹtĭ ōlʹ), *n. Bot.* a small or secondary bract, as on a pedicel. Also, **bractlet** (brăktʹlĭt).

A, Bract of marigold

brad (brăd), *n.* **1.** a small wire nail with a head projecting on only one side, or not projecting at all. **—***v.t.* **2.** to turn down (the end of a nail which projects a short way through the work). [ME *brad*, var. of *brod*, t. Scand.; cf. Icel. *broddr* spike]
bradawl (brădʹôlʹ), *n. Carp.* an awl for making small holes in wood for brads, etc. See illus. under **awl.**
Bradford (brădʹfəd), *n.* a city in England, in the West Riding of Yorkshire. 295,768 (1962).
Bradlaugh (brădʹlô), *n.* **Charles,** 1833–91, English social reformer.
Bradley (brădʹlĭ), *n.* **1. James,** 1693–1762, English astronomer. **2. Omar Nelson,** born 1893, U.S. general.
Bradman (brădʹmən), *n.* **Sir Donald (George),** born 1908, Australian cricketer.

Bradshaw (brăd′shô), *n.* a British railway timetable, issued annually 1839–1961. [named after George *Bradshaw,* the publisher]

bradycardia (brăd′ĭ kä′dĭ ə), *n. Med.* abnormal slowness of the pulse, usually below 60 beats per minute. [f. Gk, comb. form of *bradýs* slow + m. *kardía* heart]

brae (brā), *n. Scot. and N Dial.* a slope; a declivity; a hillside. [ME *bra*, t. Scand.; cf. Icel. *brā* eyelash, c. OE *brēaw* eyebrow, eyelid; G *Braue* eyebrow]

Braemar (brā mä′), *n.* a village in Scotland, in Aberdeenshire: annual Highland games. with Crathie 1018 (1961).

brag (brăg), *v.*, **bragged, bragging,** *n., adj.* —*v.i.* **1.** to use boastful language; boast. —*n.* **2.** a boast or vaunt; bragging. **3.** a thing to boast of. **4.** a boaster. **5.** a card game similar to poker. [t. Scand.; cf. Icel. *bragga sig* take heart, *braggasi* thrive] —**brag′ger,** *n.* —**Syn. 1.** See **boast**[1].

Bragg (brăg), *n.* **1. Sir William Henry,** 1862–1942, English physicist. **2.** his son, **Sir William Lawrence,** born 1890, British physicist, born in Australia.

braggadocio (brăg′ə dō′chĭ ō′), *n., pl.* **-os. 1.** empty boasting; brag. **2.** a boasting person; a braggart. [from *Braggadochio,* name of a boastful character in Spenser's '*Faerie Queen*']

braggart (brăg′ət), *n.* **1.** one given to bragging. —*adj.* **2.** bragging; boastful. [f. BRAG + *-art*, m. -ARD; cf. F (obs.) *bragard* boastful] —**brag′gartism,** *n.*

Bragi (brä′gĭ), *n. Scand. Myth.* son of Odin, and god of poetry; Odin's principal skald in Valhalla. His wife is Ithunn. Also, **Brage** (brä′gə).

Brahe (brä; *Dan.* brȧ′ə), *n.* **Tycho** (*Dan.* tʏ′gō), 1546–1601, Danish astronomer.

brahma (brä′mə), *n.* a breed of large domestic fowls, of Asiatic origin, with feathered legs and small wings and tail. [named after and short for BRAHMAPUTRA]

Brahma (brä′mə), *n.* **1.** (in philosophic Hinduism) the impersonal Supreme Being, the primal Source and the ultimate Goal of all being; Atman, the World Soul. **2.** (in later Hinduism) a trinity of the personal Creator together with Vishnu the Preserver and Siva the Destroyer. [t. Skt: m. *bráhma*, neut., worship, prayer, the impersonal divinity (see def. 1); m. *brahmá* masc., worshipper, priest, the divinity as personified (see def. 2)]

brahman (brä′mən), *n. U.S.* brahmin, esp. a variety bred in the southern U.S.

Brahman (brä′mən), *n., pl.* **-mans.** a member of the highest, or priestly, caste among the Hindus. Also, **Brahmin.** [t. Skt: m. *brāhmana*] —**Brahmanic** (brä-măn′ĭk), **Brahman′ical,** *adj.*

Brahmanism (brä′mə nĭz′əm), *n.* the religious and social system of the Brahmans and orthodox Hindus, characterized by the caste system and diversified pantheism. —**Brah′manist,** *n.*

Brahmaputra (brä′mə pōō′trə), *n.* a river flowing from SW Tibet through NE India, joining the Ganges in E Pakistan to flow into the Bay of Bengal. ab. 1800 mi. See map under **Lhasa.**

brahmin (brä′mĭn), *n.* an animal of a breed of cattle of the species *Bos indicus,* originating in India.

Brahmin (brä′mĭn), *n., pl.* **Brahmin. 1.** Brahman. **2.** (*often l.c.*) a person of great culture and intellect. **3.** (*often l.c.*) a snobbish or aloof intellectual.

Brahms (brämz; *Ger.* brȧms), *n.* **Johannes** (*Ger.* yō hȧn′əs), 1833–97, German composer.

braid (brād), *v.t.* **1.** to weave together strips or strands of; plait. **2.** to form by such weaving. **3.** to bind or confine (the hair) with a band, ribbon, etc. **4.** to trim (garments) with braid. —*n.* **5.** a braided length, or plait, of hair, etc. **6.** a narrow band or tape, formed by plaiting or weaving together several strands of silk, cotton, wool, or other material, often with gold or silver wire, used as trimming for garments, etc. **7.** a band, ribbon, etc., for binding or confining the hair. [ME *braide(n)*, OE *bregdan* move quickly, move to and fro, weave, c. Icel. *bregdha*] —**braid′er,** *n.*

braiding (brā′dĭng), *n.* **1.** braids collectively. **2.** braided work.

brail (brāl), *n.* **1.** *Naut.* one of certain ropes made fast to the after leech of a sail, to assist in taking in the sail. —*v.t.* **2.** to gather or haul in (a sail) by means of brails (usually fol. by *up*). [ME *brayle*, t. OF: m. *braiel* cincture, g. L *brācāle* belt, der. *brācae* breeches]

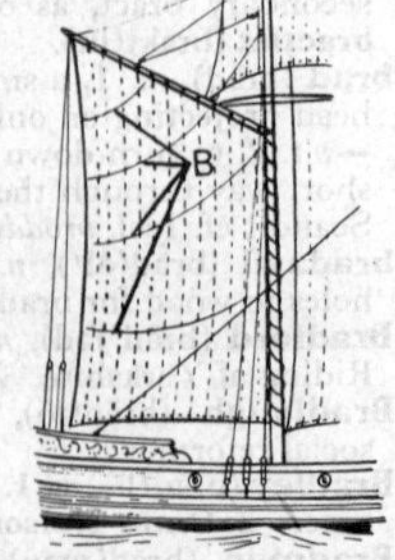

B, Brail

Brăila (*Rum.* brə ē′lȧ), *n.* a town in E Rumania: a port on the Danube. 116,364 (1961).

Braille (brāl), *n.* (*sometimes l.c.*) a system of writing or printing for the blind, in which combinations of tangible points are used to represent letters, etc. [after Louis *Braille,* 1809–52, the inventor]

brain (brān), *n.* **1.** (*sometimes pl.*) the soft convoluted mass of greyish and whitish nerve substance which fills the cranium of man and other vertebrates. **2.** *Zool.* (in many invertebrates) a part of the nervous system more or less corresponding to the brain of vertebrates. **3.** (*usually pl.*) understanding; intellectual power; intelligence. **4.** *Colloq.* a highly intelligent or well-informed person. **5. have something on the brain,** to have an obsession; to be preoccupied with. **6. pick someone's brains,** to use another person's work or ideas to one's own advantage. —*v.t.* **7.** to dash out the brains of. [ME; OE *bregen*, c. MLG *bregen*] —**Syn. 3.** See **mind.**

brain cell, *Anat.* a neurone in the brain.

brainchild (brān′chīld′), *n., pl.* **-children.** a product of one's creative work or thought.

brain drain, *Colloq.* the steady flow of young British scientists, etc., emigrating to work in the U.S.

brainfag (brān′făg′) *n.* mental exhaustion.

brain fever, *Pathol.* cerebrospinal meningitis.

brainless (brān′lĭs), *adj.* mentally weak; witless; stupid. —**brain′lessness,** *n.*

brainpan (brān′păn′), *n.* the skull or cranium.

brainsick (brān′sĭk′), *adj. Chiefly U.S.* crazy; mad. —**brain′sick′ly,** *adv.* —**brain′sick′ness,** *n.*

brainstorm (brān′stôm′), *n.* **1.** a sudden, violent attack of mental disturbance. **2.** *Colloq.* a sudden inspiration, idea, etc.

brainstorming (brān′stô′mĭng), *n. U.S.* a technique in which a group meets in order to stimulate creative thinking, develop new ideas, etc.

brains trust, 1. a group of informed persons who discuss topics for public entertainment. **2.** *U.S.* Also, **brain trust.** a group of experts who give counsel, help shape policy, etc.

brainwash (brān′wŏsh′), *v.t.* to indoctrinate by brainwashing. [back-formation from *brainwashing*] —**brain′-wash′er,** *n.*

brainwashing (brān′wŏsh′ĭng), *n.* systematic indoctrination that changes or undermines one's political convictions.

brainwave (brān′wāv′), *n.* **1.** *Colloq.* a sudden idea or inspiration. **2.** (*pl.*) *Med.* electroencephalogram.

brainy (brā′nĭ), *adj.*, **brainier, brainiest.** having brains; intelligent; clever. —**brain′iness,** *n.*

braise (brāz), *v.t.*, **braised, braising.** to cook (meat or vegetables) by sautéing in fat and then cooking slowly in very little moisture. [t. F: m. *braiser*, der. *braise* hot charcoal, live coals; of Gmc orig.]

brak (brăk), *n. S African.* a mongrel dog. [t. Afrikaans, t. D: beagle, c. BRACH]

brake[1] (brāk), *n., v.*, **braked, braking.** — *n.* **1.** any mechanical device for arresting the motion of a wheel, a motor, or a vehicle, chiefly by means of friction or pressure. **2.** (*pl.*) the drums, shoes, tubes, levers, etc., making up the brake system. **3.** a tool or machine for breaking up flax or hemp, to separate the fibre. **4.** a heavy kind of harrow. **5.** Also, **break.** shooting brake. **6.** a brake van. **7.** *Obs.* an old instrument of torture. —*v.t.* **8.** to slow or stop the motion of (a wheel, motor vehicle, etc.) as by a brake. **9.** to furnish with brakes. **10.** to process (flax or hemp) by crushing it in a brake. —*v.i.* **11.** to use or apply a brake. **12.** to run a hoisting machine. **13.** to slow down. [ME, t. MLG and/or MD; akin to BREAK] —**brake′-less,** *adj.*

brake[2] (brāk), *n.* a place overgrown with bushes, shrubs, brambles, or cane; a thicket. [cf. MLG *brake*]

brake[3] (brāk), *n.* any large or coarse fern, esp. *Pteridium aquilina* or some allied species. [ME, var. of BRACKEN]

brake[4] (brāk), *v. Obs. or Archaic.* pt. of **break.**

brakeage (brā′kĭj), *n.* **1.** the action of a brake or set of brakes, as in stopping a vehicle. **2.** brakes collectively.

brake band, a part of brake mechanism consisting of a flexible band which grips a drum when tightened.

brake block, (on railway vehicles, bicycles, etc.) the brake shoe.

brake drum, the steel or cast-iron part attached to the wheel hub or transmission shaft to which a brake lining is applied.

brake horsepower, the useful horsepower developed by an engine or motor as measured by the resistance offered by a brake. *Abbrev.:* b.h.p.

brakelight (brāk′līt′), *n. Motor Vehicles.* a tail-light linked to the brakes so that it shows when they are applied. Also, **stoplight.**

brake lining, a material, usually asbestos combined with other materials, used as the friction-producing element of a brake; brake shoe.

brake parachute, a parachute attached to the tail of an

aeroplane which may be opened to assist as a brake when landing.

brake shoe, the part of a brake which presses against the brake drum or wheel to slow it.

brakesman (brāks′mən), *n., pl.* **-men.** **1.** *Mining.* a winch operator at a pithead. **2.** *Railways, Chiefly U.S.* Also, **brakeman.** (on transcontinental trains) an official whose duties are similar to those of a guard on British trains.

brake van, *Railways.* the coach on a train from which a braking system may be applied; the guard's van.

Brakpan (brăk′păn′), *n.* a town in the Republic of South Africa, in S Transvaal. 77,777 (1960).

Bramante (*It.* brä män′tė), *n.* **Donato** (*It.* dō nä′tō), 1444?–1514, Italian architect and painter.

bramble (brăm′bl), *n., v.,* **-bled, -bling.** —*n.* **1.** the common blackberry, *R. fruticosus.* **2.** any plant of the rosaceous genus *Rubus.* **3.** any rough prickly shrub, as the dogrose. —*v.i.* **4.** to gather blackberries. [OE *bræmbel, brembel,* var. of *brǣmel, brēmel,* der. *brōm* broom] —**bram′bly,** *adj.*

brambling (brăm′blĭng), *n.* an Old World finch, *Fringilla montifringilla,* closely related to the chaffinch. [earlier *bramling,* f. d. m. BROOM + -LING[1]]

Bramley's seedling (brăm′lĭz), a vigorous variety of cooking apple having firm, juicy flesh. Also, **Bramley.**

bran (brăn), *n.* **1.** the ground husk of wheat or other grain, separated from flour or meal by bolting. **2.** by-products or grain processing used as feed. [ME, t. OF]

Bran (brăn), *n.* a Brython deity, and early mythical king of Britain.

branch (bränch), *n.* **1.** *Bot.* a division or subdivision of the stem or axis of a tree, shrub, or other plant (the ultimate or smaller ramifications being called branchlets, twigs, or shoots). **2.** a limb, offshoot, or ramification: *the branches of a deer's horns.* **3.** any member or part of a body or system; a section or subdivision: *the various branches of learning.* **4.** a local operating division of a company, chain-store, library, or the like. **5.** a line of family descent, in distinction from some other line or lines from the same stock. **6.** (in the classification of languages) a subdivision of a family; a group. **7.** *Geog.* **a.** a tributary stream. **b.** any stream that is not a large river or a creek. —*v.i.* **8.** to put forth branches; spread in branches. **9.** to divide into separate parts or subdivisions; diverge. **10.** **branch out,** to expand in a new direction. —*v.t.* **11.** to divide as into branches. **12.** to adorn with needlework; decorate with embroidery, as in textile fabrics. [ME, t. OF: m. *branche,* g. LL *branca* paw, claw] —**branch′less,** *adj.* —**branch′like′,** *adj.* —**branch′y,** *adj.*

—**Syn.** **1.** BRANCH, BOUGH, LIMB refer to divisions of a tree. BRANCH is general, meaning either a large or a small division. BOUGH refers only to the larger branches: *a bough loaded with apples.* A LIMB is a large primary division of a tree trunk or of a bough: *to climb out on a limb.*

branchia (brăng′kĭ ə), *n.pl.* *Ichthyol.* branchiae. [t. L (sing.), t. Gk: m. *bránchia* (neut. pl.) gills] —**bran′chial,** *adj.*

branchiae (brăng′kĭ ē′), *n.pl.* *Ichthyol.* the respiratory organs or gills of fishes, etc.

branchiate (brăng′kĭ ĭt, -āt′), *adj.* *Ichthyol.* having branchiae.

branchiopod (brăng′kĭ ə pŏd′), *n.* *Zool.* any of the *Branchiopoda,* a group of crustaceans having branchiae or gills on the feet. [f. s. Gk *bránchia* gills + -(O)POD]

branch line, a minor railway line, often connected to the main line at one end only.

Brancusi (brăng ko͞o′zĭ; *Rum.* brəng ko͞oshy′), **Constantin,** 1876–1957, French sculptor born in Rumania.

brand (brănd), *n.* **1.** a trademark or trade name to identify a product, as that of a distributor, or a manufacturer or other producer. **2.** kind, grade, or make, as indicated by a brand, stamp, trademark, or the like. **3.** a mark made by burning or otherwise, to indicate kind, grade, make, ownership, etc. **4.** a mark formerly put upon criminals with a hot iron. **5.** any mark of infamy; a stigma. **6.** an iron for branding. **7.** a burning or partly burnt piece of wood. **8.** *Archaic or Poetic.* a torch. **9.** *Archaic or Poetic.* a sword. —*v.t.* **10.** to mark with a brand. **11.** to mark with infamy; stigmatize. [ME and OE; akin to BURN[1]] —**brand′er,** *n.*

Brandeis (brăn′dīs), *n.* a private university in the U.S., at Waltham, Massachusetts, founded 1947.

Brandenburg (brăn′dən bûg′; *Ger.* brän′dən bo͝ork), *n.* **1.** a former province in East Germany. **2.** a town in central East Germany, the former capital of this province. 89,243 (1963).

Brandenburg Gate, a triumphal arch in Berlin standing on the border between East and West Berlin. German, **Brandenburger Tor** (*Ger.* brän′dən bo͝or gər tōr).

Brandes (*Dan.* brän′dəs), *n.* **George Morris Cohen** (*Dan.* gė′ŏrg mŏ′rēs kō′ən), 1842–1927, Danish critic and scholar.

brandied (brăn′dĭd), *adj.* flavoured with brandy.

brandish (brăn′dĭsh), *v.t.* **1.** to shake or wave, as a weapon; flourish. —*n.* **2.** a wave or flourish, as of a weapon. [ME *braundish(en),* t. OF: m. *brandiss-,* s. *brandir,* der. *brand* sword; of Gmc orig. See BRAND] —**bran′disher,** *n.*

brandling (brănd′lĭng), *n.* a small, reddish brown earthworm, *Helodrilus foetidus,* with yellow markings, found chiefly in manure heaps, used as a bait in fishing. [f. BRAND + -LING[1]]

brand-new (brănd′nyo͞o′, brăn′nyo͞o′), *adj.* completely new. [f. BRAND + NEW]

Brandon (brăn′dən), *n.* a town in England, in central Durham. 19,531 (1961).

brandreth (brănd′rĭth), *n.* a rail or frame of wood or metal.

Brandt (*Ger.* bränt), *n.* **Willi** (*Ger.* vĭl′ē), born 1913, German statesman: chancellor of West Germany since 1969.

brandy (brăn′dĭ), *n., pl.* **-dies,** *v.,* **-died, -dying.** —*n.* **1.** the spirit distilled from the fermented juice of grapes or, sometimes, of apples, peaches, plums, etc. —*v.t.* **2.** to mix, flavour, or preserve with brandy. [short for *brandywine,* t. D: m. *brandewijn* burnt (i.e. distilled) wine]

brandyball (brăn′dĭ bôl′), *n.* a small, round, brandy-coloured sweet.

brandy-bottle (brăn′dĭ bŏt′l), *n.* the yellow waterlily.

brandysnap (brăn′dĭ snăp′), *n.* a thin, sticky ginger biscuit flavoured with brandy.

Brangwyn (brăng′wĭn), *n.* **Sir Frank,** 1867–1956, British painter.

branks (brăngks), *n.pl.* a bridle formerly used to punish a scold. [orig. uncert]

branny (brăn′ĭ), *adj.* of, containing, or like bran.

brant (brănt), *n.* *Now Chiefly U.S.* brent.

Brantford (brănt′fəd), *n.* a town in SE Canada, in Ontario, near Hamilton. 56,741 (1961).

Braque (bräk, brăk), *n.* **Georges** (*Fr.* zhŏrzh), 1881–1963, French painter.

brash (brăsh), *adj.* **1.** impertinent; impudent; forward. **2.** headlong; hasty; rash. —*n.* **3.** loose fragments of rock. **4.** any fragmented rubbish, as hedge-clippings. **5.** *Naut.* small fragments of crushed ice collected by winds or currents near the shore. **6.** an acidulous eructation from the stomach. **7.** *Dial.* an attack of illness. **8.** *Dial.* a shower of rain. [orig. obscure]

brashy (brăsh′ĭ), *adj.* **1.** loosely fragmented; rubbishy. **2.** brittle; liable to break into fragments.

brasier (brā′zyə), *n.* brazier.

Brasil (*Port.* brä zēl′; *Sp.* brä sēl′), *n.* Portuguese and Spanish name of **Brazil.**

Brasilia (brə zĭl′yə), *n.* a city in and the capital of Brazil, on the central plateau. 141,742 (1960).

brasilin (brăz′ĭ lĭn), *n.* *Chem.* brazilin.

Braşov (*Rum.* brä shôv′), *n.* a city in central Rumania. 137,231 (1964). Formerly (1950–60), **Stalin.** German, **Kronstadt.** Hungarian, **Brassó.**

brass (bräs), *n.* **1.** a durable, malleable, and ductile yellow alloy, consisting essentially of copper and zinc. **2.** a utensil, ornament, or other article made of brass. **3.** *Mach.* a bearing, bush, or the like. **4.** a collective term for musical instruments of the trumpet and horn families (**brass instruments**), usually made of brass and having a funnel-shaped mouthpiece without a reed. **5.** a memorial tablet incised with an effigy, coat of arms or the like. **6.** metallic yellow; lemon, amber, or reddish yellow. **7.** *Slang.* **a.** high-ranking military officers. **b.** any important officials. **8.** *Colloq.* excessive assurance; impudence; effrontery. **9.** *Slang.* money. —*adj.* **10.** of brass. **11.** using musical instruments of the horn and trumpet family. [ME *bras,* OE *bræs*] —**brass′like′,** *adj.*

brassage (brä′sĭj), *n.* a charge to cover costs of coining money. [t. F, der. *brasser* stir (welded metal), ult. der. L *brace* white corn, of Celtic orig.]

brassard (brăs′äd), *n.* **1.** a badge worn round the upper arm. **2.** *Armour.* Also, **brassart** (brăs′ət). a piece of armour for the arm. See illus. under **armour.** [t. F, der. *bras* arm]

brass band, a band made up chiefly or exclusively of instruments of the horn and trumpet families.

brasserie (brăs′ə rĭ), *n.* an establishment where drinks, especially beer, and food are served to the public. [t. F: brewery]

brassey (brăs′ĭ, brä′sĭ), *n.* brassy[2]

brass hat, *Slang.* a high-ranking army, navy, or airforce officer.

brassicaceous (brăs′ĭ kā′shəs), *adj.* *Bot.* belonging to the family *Brassicaceae* (often called *Cruciferae*) of herbaceous plants, including the common cabbage, watercress, etc. [f. s. L *brassica* cabbage + -ACEOUS]

brassie (bräs′ĭ, brä′sĭ), *n.* brassy².

brassiere (bräs′ĭ ə′, bräz′-), *n.* a woman's undergarment which supports the breasts. [t. F: little camisole, der. *bras* arm]

Brassó (*Hung.* brŏsh′shō), *n.* Hungarian name of **Braşov.**

brass tacks, *Colloq.* basic facts; realities.

brassware (bräs′wēə′), *n.* articles of brass.

brass wind, *Music.* brass (def. 4).

brassy¹ (brä′sĭ), *adj.*, **brassier, brassiest. 1.** made of or covered with brass. **2.** resembling brass. **3.** harsh and metallic: *brassy tones.* **4.** *Colloq.* brazen. [f. BRASS + -Y¹] **—brass′ily,** *adv.* **—brass′iness,** *n.*

brassy² (bräs′ĭ, brä′sĭ), *n.*, *pl.* **-ies.** *Golf.* a club (No. 2 wood) with a long shaft and a wooden head. Also, **brassey, brassie.**

brat (brăt), *n.* a child (used usually in contempt or irritation). [cf. d. *brat* rag, trash, OE *bratt* cloak]

Bratislava (brăt′ĭ slä′və), *n.* a city in S Czechoslovakia, on the Danube: a former capital of Hungary. 266,000 (est. 1965). German, **Pressburg.** Hungarian, **Pozsony.**

brattice (brăt′ĭs), *n.*, *v.*, **-ticed, -ticing.** **—***n.* **1.** a partition or lining, as of planks or cloth, forming an air passage in a mine. **—***v.t.* **2.** to provide with a brattice; line with planks or cloth. [ME *bretage*, t. OF: m. *bretesche* parapet, ? t. OE: m. *brittisc* British, i.e., foreign or Celtic (fortification)]

brattishing (brăt′ĭ shĭng), *n.* *Archit.* ornamental work along the cornice or coping of a building. Also, **bratticing.** [alter. of BRATTICE + -ING¹]

brattle (brăt′l), *n.*, *v.*, **-tled, -tling.** **—***n.* **1.** a clattering noise. **—***v.i.* **2.** to scamper noisily.

Braun (*Ger.* broun), *n.* **Wernher von** (*Ger.* vĕr′nər fōn), born 1912, German missile designer in the U.S.

braunite (brou′nīt), *n.* a mineral, manganese oxide and silicate, Mn_7SiO_{12}, an ore of manganese. [named after A.E. *Braun*, 1809–56, German archaeologist]

Braunschweig (*Ger.* broun′shvīk), *n.* German name of **Brunswick.**

bravado (brə vä′dō), *n.*, *pl.* **-does, -dos.** boasting; swaggering pretence. [t. Sp.: m. *bravada.* See BRAVE] **—Syn.** See **courage.**

brave (brāv), *adj.*, **braver, bravest,** *n.*, *v.*, **braved, braving.** **—***adj.* **1.** possessing or exhibiting courage or courageous endurance. **2.** making a fine appearance. **3.** *Archaic.* excellent; fine; admirable. **—***n.* **4. the brave,** brave people collectively. **5.** a North American Indian or other savage warrior. **6.** *Obs.* a bully. **7.** *Archaic.* a boast; a challenge; a defiance. **—***v.t.* **8.** to meet or face courageously: *to brave misfortunes.* **9.** to defy; challenge; dare. **10.** *Obs.* to make splendid. **11. brave it out,** to ignore or defy suspicion, blame or impudent gossip. **—***v.i.* **12.** *Obs.* to boast; brag. [t. F, t. It.: m. *bravo* brave, bold, fine, t. Sp.: vicious (first applied to bulls)] **—brave′ly,** *adv.* **—brave′ness,** *n.*

—Syn. 1. BRAVE, COURAGEOUS, FEARLESS, GALLANT refer to confident bearing in the face of difficulties or dangers. BRAVE is the most comprehensive; it is especially used of that confident fortitude or daring that actively faces and endures anything threatening. COURAGEOUS implies a higher or nobler kind of bravery, esp. as resulting from an inborn quality of mind or spirit which faces or endures perils or difficulties without fear and even with enthusiasm. FEARLESS implies unflinching spirit and coolness in the face of danger. GALLANT implies chivalrous, impetuous, dashing, or showy bravery.

bravery (brā′və rĭ), *n.*, *pl.* **-ries. 1.** brave spirit or conduct; courage; valour. **2.** *Archaic.* showiness; splendour; magnificence. **—Syn. 1.** intrepidity, fearlessness, boldness, daring, prowess, heroism, pluck. See **courage.**

bravo¹ (brä vō′), *interj.*, *n.*, *pl.* **-vos.** **—***interj.* **1.** well done! good! **—***n.* **2.** a shout of 'bravo!' [t. It., prop. adj. See BRAVE]

bravo² (brä′vō), *n.*, *pl.* **-voes, -vos.** a daring bandit or assassin or murderer. [t. It. See BRAVE]

bravura (brə vŏŏə′rə, -vyŏŏ′rə; *It.* brȧ vōō′rȧ), *n.* **1.** *Music.* a florid passage or piece, requiring great skill and spirit in the performer. **2.** a display of daring; brilliant performance. **—***adj.* **3.** *Music.* spirited; florid; brilliant. [t. It.: bravery, spirit]

braw (brô, brä), *adj.* *Scot. and N Dial.* fine or fine-looking; excellent. [var. of BRAVE]

brawl¹ (brôl), *n.* **1.** a noisy quarrel; a squabble. **2.** a bubbling or roaring noise; a clamour. **—***v.i.* **3.** to quarrel angrily, noisily; wrangle. **4.** to make a bubbling or roaring noise, as water flowing over a rocky bed. [ME *brall(en)*, der. *brawl* brawler, var. of *broll* brat, contr. of *brothel* good-for-nothing, der. OE *brēothan* go to ruin] **—brawl′er,** *n.* **—Syn. 1.** See **disorder.**

brawl² (brôl), *n.* an old folk dance of French origin. [orig. unknown]

brawn (brôn), *n.* **1.** well-developed muscles. **2.** muscular strength. **3.** meat, esp. pork, boiled, pickled, and pressed into a mould. [ME *brawne*, t. OF: m. *braon*, t. Gmc; cf. G *braten* roast]

brawny (brô′nĭ), *adj.*, **brawnier, brawniest.** muscular; strong. **—brawn′iness,** *n.*

braxy (brăk′sĭ), *Vet. Sci.* **—***n.* **1.** an acute bacterial disease of sheep involving inflammation of the bowels, usually fatal. **—***adj.* **2.** affected with braxy. [prob. n. use of adj., OE *brǣcsēoc* ill with falling sickness, f. *brǣc* rheum + *sēoc* sick]

bray¹ (brā), *n.* **1.** a harsh, breathy cry, as of the donkey. **2.** any similar loud, harsh sound. **3.** a harsh, noisy human utterance, as a protest or laugh. **—***v.i.* **4.** to utter a loud, harsh cry as the donkey. **5.** to make a loud, harsh, disagreeable sound, as a trumpet. **6.** to utter a harsh, noisy sound, as a protest or laugh. **—***v.t.* **7.** to utter with a loud, harsh sound, like the donkey. [ME *braye(n)*, t. OF: m. *braire*] **—bray′er,** *n.*

bray² (brā), *v.t.* to pound or crush fine, as in a mortar. [ME *braye(n)*, t. OF: m. *breier*]

brayer (brā′ə), *n.* **1.** an instrument for crushing; a pestle. **2.** *Print.* a small roller for inking type or plates by hand (usually for making a proof). [f. BRAY² + -ER¹]

Braz., 1. Brazil. 2. Brazilian.

braza (brä′zə; *Sp.* brä′thä), *n.* a unit of length in Spanish-speaking countries, representing the reach of outspread arms, officially 5·48 ft in Spain, and 5·68 ft in Argentina. [t. Sp., der. *brazo* arm, g. L *brāchium*]

braze¹ (brāz), *v.t.*, **brazed, brazing. 1.** to make of brass. **2.** to cover or ornament with brass, or as if with brass. **3.** to make brasslike. [OE *brǣsian*, der. *brǣs* brass]

braze² (brāz), *v.t.*, **brazed, brazing.** *Metall.* to unite (pieces of brass, steel, etc.) by intensely heating the parts to be joined and applying any one of a number of high melting solders which range in melting point from alloys rich in silver to pure copper. [? t. F: m. *braser*, der. *braise* live coals. See BRAISE]

brazen (brā′zən), *adj.* **1.** made of brass. **2.** like brass, as in sound, colour, strength, etc. **3.** shameless or impudent: *brazen effrontery.* **—***v.t.* **4.** to face with boldness and effrontery (fol. by *out*). **5.** to make brazen or bold. [ME *brasen*, OE *brǣsen*, der. *brǣs* brass] **—bra′zenly,** *adv.* **—bra′zenness,** *n.* **—Syn. 3.** See **bold.**

brazen-faced (brā′zən fāst′), *adj.* openly shameless; impudent.

brazier¹ (brā′zyə), *n.* a person who works in brass. Also, **brasier.** [ME *brasiere*; f. BRAZE¹, v. + -IER]

brazier² (brā′zyə), *n.* a metal receptacle for holding burning charcoal or other fuel, as for heating a room. Also, **brasier.** [t. F: m. *brasier*, der. *braise* live coals. See BRAISE, -ER²]

brazil (brə zĭl′), *n.* **1.** a wood from various tropical American trees of the genus *Caesalpinia* (esp. *C. echinata*) and allied genera, yielding red and purple dyes. **2.** the red dye extracted from it. **3.** (orig.) a hard East Indian wood yielding a red colour, from the tree *Caesalpinia sappan.* **4.** a brazil nut. [ME *brasile*, t. Sp. or Pg.: m. *brasil*, t. OF: m. *brésil* reddish-tinted wood, der. *brèze*, *braise* glowing coals; Brazil was named after the tree]

Brazil (brə zĭl′), *n.* a republic in South America. 70,967,185 pop. (1960); 3,286,170 sq. mi. *Cap.:* Brasilia. Official name, **United States of Brazil.** Portuguese and Spanish, **Brasil.** **—Brazilian** (brə zĭl′yən), *adj.*, *n.*

brazilin (brăz′ĭ lĭn), *n.* *Chem.* a yellow substance, $C_{16}H_{14}O_5$, from brazil, used as a dye and indicator. Also, **brasilin.**

brazil nut, the triangular edible seed (nut) of the tree *Bertholletia excelsa* and related species, of Brazil and elsewhere.

brazilwood (brə zĭl′wŏŏd′), *n.* brazil.

Brazos (brä′zōs; *locally* brăz′əs, brā′zəs), *n.* a river in the southern U.S., flowing from N Texas SE to the Gulf of Mexico. 870 mi.

Brazzaville (*Fr.* brȧ zȧ vēl′), *n.* the capital of the Republic of Congo and former capital of French Equatorial Africa: a port on the river Congo. 135,632 (1962). See map under **Congo.**

B.R.C.S., British Red Cross Society.

breach (brēch), *n.* **1.** the act or result of breaking; a break or rupture. **2.** a gap made in a wall, dyke, fortification, etc; rift; fissure. **3.** an infraction or violation, as of law, trust, faith, promise, etc. **4.** a severance of friendly relations. **5.** the springing of a whale from the water. **6.** *Obs.* a wound. **—***v.t.* **7.** to make a breach or opening in. [ME *breche*, t. OF, t. Gmc (cf. OHG *brecha*); r. ME *bruche*, OE *bryce*, akin to BREAK]

breach of contract, *Law.* the breaking, by action or omission, of an obligation imposed by a contract.

breach of privilege, *Law.* an abuse of any of the privileges accorded to members of parliament and peers; contempt of the High Court of Parliament.

breach of promise, *Law.* a violation of one's promise to marry.

breach of the peace, *Law.* a violation of the public peace, by a riot, disturbance, etc.

breach of trust, 1. *Law.* a violation of duty by a trustee. 2. *Colloq.* a violation of duty by any fiduciary.

bread (brĕd), *n.* 1. a food made of flour or meal, milk or water, etc., made into a dough or batter, with or without yeast or the like, and baked. 2. food or sustenance; livelihood: *to earn one's bread.* 3. *Eccles.* the wafer or bread used in the Eucharist. 4. **break bread, a.** to partake of or share food. **b.** *Eccles.* to administer or join in Communion. —*v.t.* 5. *Cookery.* to cover or dress with breadcrumbs or meal. [ME *breed,* OE *brēad,* c. G *Brot*] —**bread′less,** *adj.*

bread and butter, 1. bread spread with butter. 2. *Colloq.* means of living; livelihood.

bread-and-butter (brĕd′n bŭt′ə), *adj.* 1. seeking the means of living; mercenary. 2. *Colloq.* belonging to or in the stage of adolescence. 3. *Colloq.* matter-of-fact. 4. expressing thanks for hospitality, as a letter.

breadbasket (brĕd′bäs′kĭt), *n.* 1. a basket for containing bread. 2. *Colloq.* the stomach.

breadbin (brĕd′bĭn′), *n.* a bin for containing bread.

breadboard (brĕd′bôd′), *n.* a wooden board on which bread is sliced.

breadcrumb (brĕd′krŭm′), *n., v.,* **-crumbed** (-krŭmd′), **-crumbing.** —*n.* 1. (*usually pl.*) a small fragment of bread. 2. the soft, spongy inner part of a loaf. —*v.t.* 3. to dress (food) with breadcrumbs.

breadfruit (brĕd′froot′), *n.* 1. a large, round, starchy fruit yielded by a moraceous tree, *Artocarpus communis* (*A. altilis*), of the Pacific islands, etc., much used, baked or roasted, for food. 2. the tree bearing this fruit.

breadknife (brĕd′nīf′), *n.* a knife, usually with a serrated edge, for cutting bread.

breadline (brĕd′līn′), *n.* 1. a line of needy persons assembled to receive food given as charity. 2. **on the breadline,** living at subsistence level, sustained by public assistance or charity.

breadmould (brĕd′mōld′), *n.* a black fungus, *Rhizopus nigricans,* often seen on bread.

breadroot (brĕd′root′), *n.* the edible farinaceous root of *Psoralea esculenta,* a fabaceous plant of central North America.

bread sauce, a sauce made of milk infused with onion, bay leaf and pepper, and strained over breadcrumbs.

breadth (brĕdth, brĕtth), *n.* 1. *Maths.* the measure of the second principal diameter of a surface or solid, the first being length, and the third (in the case of a solid) thickness; width. 2. an extent or piece of something as measured by its width, or of definite or full width: *a breadth of cloth.* 3. freedom from narrowness or restraint; liberality: *breadth of understanding.* 4. size in general; extent. 5. *Art.* broad or general effect due to subordination of details or non-essentials. [f. earlier *breade* (OE *brǣdu*) + -TH[1]; modelled on LENGTH]

breadthways (brĕdth′wāz′, brĕtth′-), *adv.* in the direction of the breadth. Also, *esp. U.S.,* **breadthwise** (brĕdth′-wīz′, brĕtth′-).

bread tree, chinaberry.

breadwinner (brĕd′wĭn′ə), *n.* one who earns a livelihood for himself and those dependent upon him.

break (brāk), *v.,* **broke** or (*Archaic*) **brake; broken,** or (*Archaic*) **broke; breaking,** *n.* —*v.t.* 1. to divide into parts violently; reduce to pieces or fragments. 2. to violate: *to break a law or promise.* 3. to dissolve or annul (often fol. by *off*). 4. to fracture a bone of. 5. to lacerate; wound: *to break the skin.* 6. to discontinue abruptly; interrupt; suspend: *to break the silence.* 7. to destroy the regularity of. 8. to put an end to; overcome. 9. to interrupt the uniformity or sameness of: *to break the monotony.* 10. to destroy the unity, continuity, or arrangement of. 11. to exchange for a smaller amount or smaller units. 12. to make one's way through; penetrate. 13. *Law.* to open or force one's way into (a dwelling, store, etc.). 14. to make one's way out of: *to break jail.* 15. to surpass; outdo: *to break a record.* 16. to disclose or divulge, with caution or delicacy. 17. to disable or destroy by or as by shattering or crushing. 18. to ruin financially, or make bankrupt. 19. to reduce in rank. 20. to impair or weaken in strength, spirit, force, or effect. 21. to train to obedience; tame (often fol. by *in*). 22. to train away from a habit or practice (fol. by *of*). 23. *Elect.* to render (a circuit) incomplete; stop the flow of (a current). 24. *Music.* to arpeggiate. 25. *Cricket.* to strike so as to dislodge the bails from (a wicket). 26. to void or expel: *to break wind.* —*v.i.* 27. to become broken; separate into parts or fragments, esp. suddenly and violently. 28. to become suddenly discontinuous or interrupted; leave off abruptly (fol. by *off,* etc.). 29. to become detached (fol. by *off, from,* etc.). 30. to make a pause (often fol. by *off*). 31. to dissolve and separate (fol. by *up*). 32. to sever relations (fol. by *with*). 33. (of a ball) to change direction on bouncing. 34. (of a wave) to topple forward after developing a crest through the opposing pull of an undertow in shallow water. 35. to free oneself or escape suddenly, as from restraint (often fol. by *away*). 36. to force a way (fol. by *in, through, out,* etc.). 37. to burst (fol. by *in, forth, from,* etc.). 38. to come suddenly, as into notice. 39. to change state or activity (fol. by *into*). 40. to dawn, as the day. 41. (of a fish) to come to the surface. 42. to give way or fail as under strain (often fol. by *down*). 43. (of the heart) to be crushed or overwhelmed, esp. by grief. 44. (of stock-exchange prices) to drop quickly and considerably. 45. (of the voice) to vary between two registers, esp. in emotion or during adolescence. 46. *Music.* to change or go from one register to another, as a musical instrument. 47. *Linguistics.* to undergo breaking. 48. *Billiards.* to make a break (def. 69). 49. *Boxing.* to discontinue a clinch. 50. *Rugby.* to disband, as a scrummage. —*v.* 51. Some special verb phrases are:

break away, 1. (in racing) to start prematurely. 2. (of footballers) to elude (with the ball) defending players. 3. to secede.

break camp, to pack up tents and equipment and resume a march.

break down, 1. to take down or destroy by breaking. 2. to overcome. 3. to analyse. 4. to collapse. 5. to cease to function.

break even, to reach a point at which the total income is equal to the total investment.

break in, 1. to interrupt. 2. to adapt to one's convenience by use. 3. to enter (a house or the like) forcibly, as a burglar.

break off, 1. to sever by breaking. 2. to put a sudden stop to; discontinue. 3. to cease suddenly.

break out, 1. to issue forth; arise. 2. *Pathol.* (of certain diseases) to appear in eruptions. 3. to have a sudden appearance of various eruptions on the skin.

break step, *Mil.* to cease marching in cadence.

break up, 1. to separate; disband (esp. a school at end of term). 2. to put an end to; discontinue. 3. to cut up (fowl, etc.).

—*n.* 52. a forcible disruption or separation of parts; a breaking; a fracture, rupture, or shattering. 53. an opening made by breaking; a gap. 54. a rush away from a place; an attempt to escape: *a break for freedom.* 55. an interruption of continuity; suspension; stoppage. 56. an abrupt or marked change, as in sound or direction. 57. *Colloq.* an opportunity; chance. 58. *Chiefly U.S. Colloq.* a social error or slip; an unfortunate remark. 59. a small amount; portion. 60. a brief rest, as from work, esp. a midmorning pause, usually of fifteen minutes, between school classes. 61. *Pros.* a pause or caesura. 62. *Jazz.* a solo passage, usually of about two bars, during which the band accompaniment breaks off, or rests. 63. *Music.* the point in the scale where the quality of voice of one register changes to that of another, as from chest to head. 64. *Stock Exchange.* a sudden drop in prices. 65. *Elect.* an opening or discontinuity in a circuit. 66. *Print.* a wordbreak. 67. **a.** a series of successful shots, strokes, or the like, in a game. **b.** *Billiards.* the score made in such a series. 68. any continuous run, esp. of good fortune. 69. *Billiards.* **a.** the shot that breaks or scatters the balls at the beginning of the game. **b.** the right to the first shot. 70. a premature start in racing. 71. *Cricket, etc.* change in direction of a ball when it bounces, usually caused by a spinning motion imparted by the bowler. 72. *Tenpin Bowling.* a failure to knock down all ten pins after bowling twice. 73. shooting brake. [ME *breke(n),* OE *brecan,* c. G *brechen,* Goth. *brikan*] —**break′able,** *adj.*

—**Syn.** 1. BREAK, CRUSH, SHATTER, SMASH mean to reduce to parts, violently or by force. BREAK means to divide by means of a blow, a collision, a pull, or the like: *to break a chair, a leg, a strap.* To CRUSH is to subject to (usually heavy or violent) pressure so as to press out of shape or reduce to shapelessness or to small particles: *to crush a beetle.* To SHATTER is to break in a way that causes the pieces to fly in many directions: *to shatter an electric light bulb.* To SMASH is to break noisily and suddenly into many pieces: *to smash a tumbler.* 2. transgress, disobey, contravene.

breakage (brā′kĭj), *n.* 1. an act of breaking; a break. 2. the amount or quantity of things broken. 3. an allowance or compensation for loss or damage of articles broken in transit or in use.

breakaway (brā′kə wā′), *n.* 1. *Chiefly U.S.* a premature start (in racing); break. 2. *Football.* elusion by an attacking player with the ball of the defending players. 3. secession. —*adj.* 4. having seceded or having secession as an objective.

breakbone fever (brāk′bōn′), *Pathol.* dengue.

brewis (brōō′ĭs), *n. Now Dial.* **1.** broth. **2.** bread soaked in broth, gravy, etc. [ME *browes*, t. OF: m. *broez*, ult. t. OHG: m. *brod* BROTH]

brewster (brōō′stə), *n. Archaic and Dial.* one who brews; a brewer. [ME, f. BREW + -STER]

Brewster (brōō′stə), *n.* **1. Sir David,** 1781–1868, Scottish physicist. **2. William,** 1560?–1644, English colonist: leader of the Pilgrims at Plymouth.

brewster sessions, a meeting, now annual, of licensing justices in Great Britain.

Brezhnev (brĕzh′nĕv; *Russ.* bryĕzh′nĭf), *n.* **Leonid Ilyich** (*Russ.* lĭ ä nĕt′ ēl′yĭch), Soviet politician: first secretary of the Soviet Communist Party since 1964.

Briand (*Fr.* brē äN′), *n.* **Aristide** (*Fr.* ȧ rēs tēd′), 1862–1932, French statesman: prime minister of France 11 times.

briar (brī′ə), *n.* **1.** the white heath, *Erica arborea*, of France and Corsica, whose woody root is used for making tobacco pipes. **2.** a pipe made of this or similar wood. Also, **brier.** [t. F: m. *bruyère* heath, g. a LL deriv. of Gallic *brūcus* heather] —**bri′ary,** *adj.*

Briareus (brī ĕə′rĭ əs), *n. Gk Myth.* a hundred-armed, fifty-headed giant who helped Zeus against the Titans. —**Briar′ean,** *adj.*

briar-root (brī′ə rōōt′), *n.* **1.** the rootwood of the briar. **2.** certain other woods from which tobacco pipes are made. **3.** a pipe made of briar-root. Also, **brier-root.**

briarwood (brī′ə wŏŏd′), *n.* briar-root. Also, **brierwood.**

bribe (brīb), *n., v.,* **bribed, bribing.** —*n.* **1.** any valuable consideration given or promised for corrupt behaviour in the performance of official or public duty. **2.** anything given or serving to persuade or induce. **3.** *Textiles.* a length of damaged woollen fabric removed from a piece of cloth. —*v.t.* **4.** to give or promise a bribe to. **5.** to influence or corrupt by a bribe. —*v.i.* **6.** to give bribes; practise bribery. [ME; cf. OF *bribe* piece of bread given to a beggar, *briber* beg, c. Sp. *bribar*] —**brib′able,** *adj.* —**brib′abil′ity,** *n.* —**brib′er,** *n.*

bribery (brī′bə rĭ), *n., pl.* **-ries.** the act or practice of giving or accepting bribes.

bric-a-brac (brĭk′ə brăk′), *n.* miscellaneous ornamental articles of antiquarian, decorative, or other interest. Also, **bric-à-brac.** [t. F]

brick (brĭk), *n.* **1.** a block of clay, usually rectangular, hardened by drying in the sun or burning in a kiln, and used for building, paving, etc. **2.** such blocks collectively. **3.** the material. **4.** any similar block, esp. a small one of painted wood, used as a child's toy. **5.** *Colloq.* a good fellow. **6.** *Colloq.* a social blunder or solecism: *to drop a brick.* —*v.t.* **7.** to lay, line, wall, build, or enclose with brick (often fol. by *up*). [ME *brik*, t. MD: m. *bricke*, akin to BREAK] —**brick′like′,** *adj.*

brickbat (brĭk′băt′), *n.* **1.** a piece of broken brick, esp. one used as a missile. **2.** any rocklike missile. **3.** *Colloq.* an unkind remark; caustic criticism.

brickfield (brĭk′fēld′), *n.* a place where bricks are made.

brickfielder (brĭk′fēl′də), *n.* a dry, dusty wind blowing from the north in Victoria, Australia.

brick-kiln (brĭk′kĭln′), *n.* a kiln or furnace in which bricks are baked or burned.

bricklaying (brĭk′lā′ĭng), *n.* the art or occupation of laying bricks in construction. —**brick′lay′er,** *n.*

brick red, yellowish or brownish red.

brickwork (brĭk′wûk′), *n.* brick construction (as contrasted with that of other materials).

bricky (brĭk′ĭ), *adj.* consisting or made of bricks.

brickyard (brĭk′yäd′), *n.* a brickfield.

bricole (brĭ kōl′, brĭk′l), *n.* **1.** *Billiards.* a shot in which the cue ball strikes the cushion first. **2.** *Real Tennis.* a stroke rebounding from the side wall of the court. **3.** an indirect action or unexpected stroke. [t. F, t. Pr.: m. *bricola* catapult]

bridal (brī′dl), *adj.* **1.** of or pertaining to a bride or a wedding. —*n.* **2.** a wedding. **3.** *Archaic.* a wedding feast. [ME *bridale*, OE *brȳdealo* bride ale, f. *brȳd* bride + *ealo* ale, feast, assoc. with adj. suffix -AL[1]]

bridal wreath, any of several shrubs of the rosaceous genus *Spiraea*, bearing sprays of small white flowers, esp. *S. prunifolia.*

bride[1] (brīd), *n.* a woman newly married, or about to be married. [ME; OE *brȳd*, c. G *Braut*]

bride[2] (brīd), *n.* **1.** (in needlework, lacemaking, etc.) a bar, link, or tie between patterns. **2.** an ornamental bonnet string. [t. F: bridle, string, tie, t. Gmc. See BRIDLE]

Bride (brīd), *n.* **Saint.** See **Brigid, Saint.**

bridegroom (brīd′grōōm′, -grŏŏm′), *n.* a man newly married, or about to be married. [var. of ME *bridegome*, OE *brȳdguma*, f. *brȳd* bride + *guma* man (c. L *homo*)]

bridesmaid (brīdz′mād′), *n.* a young unmarried woman who attends the bride at a wedding.

bridewell (brīd′wĕl, -wəl), *n.* **1.** a house of correction for the confinement of vagrants and disorderly persons. **2.** *Obs. Colloq.* any prison or house of correction. [from a former prison in London at *St Bride's Well*]

bridge[1] (brĭj), *n., v.,* **bridged, bridging.** —*n.* **1.** a structure spanning a river, chasm, road, or the like, and affording passage. **2.** *Naut.* a raised platform from side to side of a ship above the rail, for the officer in charge. **3.** *Anat.* the ridge or upper line of the nose. **4.** *Dentistry.* an artificial replacement of a missing tooth or teeth, supported by natural teeth adjacent to the space. A bridge may be fixed or removable. **5.** *Music.* a thin support across which the strings of a stringed instrument are stretched above the sounding-board. **6.** (on spectacles) the part which joins the two lenses and rests on the bridge or sides of the nose. **7.** *Elect.* an instrument for measuring electrical impedance. **8.** *U.S. Railways.* a signal gantry. **9.** *Metall.* a ridge or wall-like projection of firebrick or the like, at either end of the hearth in a metallurgical furnace. **10.** *Billiards.* a notched piece of wood with a long handle, used to support a cue when the distance is otherwise too great to reach; rest. —*v.t.* **11.** to make a bridge over; span. **12.** to make (a way) by a bridge. [ME *brigge*, OE *brycg*, c. G *Brücke*] —**bridge′able,** *adj.* —**bridge′less,** *adj.*

bridge[2] (brĭj), *n. Cards.* a game for four players, derived from whist, in which one partnership plays to fulfil a certain declaration against opponents acting as defenders. See **contract** (def. 6) and **auction bridge.** [orig. uncert.]

bridgeboard (brĭj′bôd′), *n. U.S.* notchboard.

bridgehead (brĭj′hĕd′), *n.* **1.** a position held on the enemy side of a river or defile, to cover the crossing of friendly troops. **2.** any fortified position established in enemy territory, as by parachute troops. **3.** a defensive work covering or protecting the end of a bridge towards the enemy.

bridgehouse (brĭj′hous′), *n.* a house built at one end of a bridge, as for the purpose of defending it, collecting tolls, etc.

Bridgend (brĭj′ĕnd′), *n.* a town in S Wales, in Glamorganshire. 15,156 (1961).

Bridge of Sighs, a bridge in Venice through which prisoners are said to have been led for trial in the ducal palace.

Bridgeport (brĭj′pôt′), *n.* a city in the U.S., a seaport in SW Connecticut, on Long Island Sound. 156,748 (1960).

Bridges (brĭj′ĭz), *n.* **Robert,** 1844–1930, English poet.

Bridget (brĭj′ĭt), *n.* **Saint.** See **Brigid, Saint.**

Bridgetown (brĭj′toun′), *n.* a seaport in and the capital of Barbados. 94,000 (est. 1966).

Bridgewater Canal (brĭj′wô′tə), a canal between Worsley and Manchester, 42 miles long, the first major British artificial inland waterway. [named after Francis Egerton, 1763–1803, 3rd Duke of *Bridgewater*]

bridgework (brĭj′wûk′), *n.* **1.** *Dentistry.* **a.** dental bridges collectively. **b.** any of several different types of dental bridges. **2.** the building of bridges.

bridging (brĭj′ĭng), *n. Bldg Trades.* a piece or an arrangement of pieces fixed between floor or roof joists to keep them in place.

Bridgwater (brĭj′wô′tə), *n.* a town in England, in central Somerset. 25,582 (1961).

Bridie (brī′dĭ), *n.* **James** (*Osborne Henry Mavor*), 1888–1951, Scottish physician and dramatist.

bridle (brī′dl), *n., v.,* **-dled, -dling.** —*n.* **1.** the part of the harness of a horse, etc., about the head, consisting usually of headstall, bit, and reins, and used to restrain and guide the animal. **2.** anything that restrains or curbs. **3.** *Mach.* a link, flange, or other attachment for limiting the movement of any part of a machine. **4.** *Naut.* a short chain or rope span, both ends of which are made fast. **5.** a bridling, or drawing up of the head, as in disdain. —*v.t.* **6.** to put a bridle on. **7.** to control as with a bridle; restrain; curb. —*v.i.* **8.** to draw up the head and draw in the chin, as in disdain or resentment; to be resentful or annoyed (often fol. by *at*). [ME; OE *brīdel*, earlier *brigdils*] —**bri′dler,** *n.*

bridlepath (brī′dl päth′), *n.* a path suitable for use by horseback riders.

Bridlington (brĭd′lĭng tən), *n.* a town in England in the E East Riding of Yorkshire: seaside resort. 26,023 (1961).

bridoon (brĭ dōōn′), *n.* a light snaffle or bit without crossbars, and on a rein, used in certain military bridles in addition to the principal bit and its rein. [t. F: m. *bridon*, der. *bride* bridle]

Brie (brē), *n.* a kind of salted, white, soft cheese, ripened through bacterial action, waxy to semiliquid, as made in Brie, a district in northern France.

brief (brēf), *adj.* **1.** of little duration. **2.** using few words; concise; succinct. **3.** abrupt or curt. —*n.* **4.** a short and concise writing or statement. **5.** an outline, the form of which is determined by set rules, of all the possible arguments and information on one side of a controversy: *a debater's brief.* **6.** *Law.* a writ summoning one to answer to any action. **7.** *Law.* a memorandum of points of fact or of law, etc., for use in conducting a case. **8.** a briefing. **9.** *Rom. Cath. Ch.* a papal letter less formal than a bull, sealed with the pope's signet ring or stamped with the device borne on this ring. **10.** *Obs.* a letter. **11. in brief,** in few words; in short. —*v.t.* **12.** to instruct by a brief or briefing. **13.** *Law.* to retain as advocate in a suit. [t. F, g. L *brevis*] —**brief′ly,** *adv.* —**brief′ness,** *n.* —**Syn. 1.** short-lived, fleeting, transitory, ephemeral. See **short. 2.** terse, compact. **4.** See **summary.**

briefcase (brēf′kās′), *n.* a flat, rectangular leather case used for carrying documents, books, manuscripts, etc. Also, **dispatch case.**

briefing (brē′fĭng), *n.* a short, accurate summary of the details of a plan or operation as one given to a military unit, crew of an aeroplane, etc., before it undertakes the operation.

briefs (brēfs), *n.* legless underpants.

brier[1] (brī′ə), *n.* **1.** a prickly plant or shrub, esp. the sweetbrier, or a greenbrier. **2.** a tangled mass of prickly plants. **3.** a thorny stem or twig. Also, **briar.** [ME *brere,* OE *brēr*] —**bri′ery,** *adj.*

brier[2] (brī′ə), *n.* briar.

Brierley Hill (brī′ə lĭ hĭl′), a town in England, in S Staffordshire. 56,377 (1961).

brier-root (brī′ə ro͞ot′), *n.* briar-root.

brierwood (brī′ə wo͝od′), *n.* briarwood.

Brieux (*Fr.* brē œ′), *n.* **Eugène** (*Fr.* œ zhĕn′), 1858–1932, French dramatist.

brig[1] (brĭg), *n.* *Naut.* **1.** a two-masted vessel square-rigged on both masts. **2.** *U.S.* the compartment of a ship where prisoners are confined. [shortened form of BRIGANTINE]

brig[2] (brĭg), *n., v.* *Scot. and N Dial.* bridge.

Brig., *Mil.* **1.** Brigade. **2.** Brigadier.

brigade (brĭ gād′), *n., v.,* **-gaded, -gading.** —*n.* **1.** a unit consisting of several regiments, squadrons, groups, or battalions. **2.** a large body of troops. **3.** a body of individuals organized for a special purpose: *a fire brigade.* —*v.t.* **4.** to form into a brigade. **5.** to group together. [t. F, t. It.: m. *brigata* troop, der. *brigare* strive, contend]

brigade major, the adjutant or chief staff officer of a brigade.

brigadier (brĭg′ə dĭə′), *n.* *Mil.* **1.** a rank between colonel and major general in the British Army. **2.** an equivalent rank in any other army. **3.** an officer of either of these ranks. **4.** *U.S. Army Colloq.* a brigadier general. **5.** (formerly) a non-commissioned rank in the Napoleonic armies. [t. F, der. *brigade* BRIGADE. See -IER]

brigadier general, *pl.* **brigadier generals. 1.** (formerly) a brigadier in the British Army. **2.** *U.S. Army.* **a.** an officer between colonel and major general. **b.** this rank.

brigalow (brĭg′ə lō′), *n.* any of various acacias of Australia and New Zealand. [t. native Australian]

brigand (brĭg′ənd), *n.* a bandit; one of a gang of robbers in mountain or forest regions. [ME *brigant,* t. OF, t. It.: m. *brigante,* der. *brigare.* See BRIGADE] —**brig′andish,** *adj.*

brigandage (brĭg′ən dĭj), *n.* the practice of being a brigand; plundering. Also, **brig′andry.**

brigandine (brĭg′ən dēn′, -dīn′), *n.* *Armour.* a flexible body armour of overlapping steel plates riveted to the exterior covering of linen, velvet, leather, etc. [late ME *brigandyne,* t. OF: m. *brigandine*]

brigantine (brĭg′ən tēn′, -tīn′), *n.* *Naut.* a two-masted vessel in which the foremast is square-rigged and the mainmast bears a fore-and-aft mainsail and square topsails. [t. F: m. *brigantin,* t. It.: m. *brigantino,* der. *brigante* BRIGAND]

Brighouse (brĭg′hous′), *n.* a town in England, in the W West Riding of Yorkshire. 30,804 (1961).

bright (brīt), *adj.* **1.** radiating or reflecting light; luminous; shining. **2.** filled with light. **3.** vivid or brilliant, as colour. **4.** clear or translucent, as liquids. **5.** radiant or splendid. **6.** illustrious or glorious, as a period. **7.** quick-witted or intelligent. **8.** clever or witty, as a remark. **9.** animated; lively; cheerful, as a person. **10.** characterized by happiness or gladness. **11.** favourable or auspicious: *bright prospects.* —*n.* **12.** *Archaic.* brightness; splendour. —*adv.* **13.** in a bright manner; brightly. [ME; OE *bryht, beorht,* c. OHG *beraht,* Icel. *bjartr,* Goth. *bairhts*] —**bright′ly,** *adv.*

—**Syn. 1.** refulgent, effulgent, lustrous, lucent, beaming, lambent. BRIGHT, BRILLIANT, RADIANT, SHINING refer to that which gives forth, is filled with, or reflects light. BRIGHT suggests the general idea: *bright flare, stars, mirror.* BRILLIANT implies a strong, unusual, or sparkling brightness, often changeful or varied and too strong to be agreeable: *brilliant sunlight.* RADIANT implies the pouring forth of steady rays of light, esp. such as is agreeable to the eyes: *a radiant face.* SHINING implies giving forth or reflecting a strong or sparkling light: *shining eyes.* —**Ant. 1.** dull, dim.

Bright (brīt), *n.* **John,** 1811–89, British orator and statesman.

brighten (brī′tn), *v.i., v.t.* to become or make bright or brighter. —**bright′ener,** *n.*

brightness (brīt′nĭs), *n.* **1.** bright quality. **2.** luminosity apart from hue; value. Pure white is of maximum brightness and pure black is of zero brightness.

Brighton (brī′tn), *n.* **1.** a town in SE England, in W East Sussex, on the English Channel: seaside resort: University of Sussex, founded 1961. 162,757 (1961). **2.** a town in Australia, in Victoria, near Melbourne. 41,302 (1961).

Bright's disease, *Pathol.* a disease of the kidneys characterized by albuminuria and heightened blood pressure. [named after Richard *Bright,* 1789–1858, English physician, who described it]

Brigid (brĭj′ĭd, brē′ĭd), *n.* **Saint,** A.D. 453–523, Irish abbess: a patron saint of Ireland. Also, **Bride, Bridget, Brigit** (brĭj′ĭt, brē′ĭt).

brill (brĭl), *n., pl.* **brill** or **brills,** a European flatfish, *Scophthalmus rhombus,* closely allied to the turbot.

brillante (*It.* brēl län′tē), *Music. adj.* **1.** lively, brilliant. —*adv.* **2.** in a lively or brilliant manner.

brilliance (brĭl′yəns), *n.* **1.** great brightness; splendour; lustre. **2.** remarkable excellence or distinction; conspicuous mental ability. **3.** brightness (def. 2). **4.** *Music.* **a.** (of tone) abundance in high harmonies. **b.** (of style in playing) vivacity; liveliness. Also, **bril′liancy.** —**Syn. 1.** radiance, effulgence.

brilliant (brĭl′yənt), *adj.* **1.** shining brightly; sparkling; glittering; lustrous. **2.** distinguished; illustrious: *a brilliant achievement.* **3.** having or showing great intelligence or mental ability. **4.** *Music.* **a.** (of tone) characterized by the presence of a number of high harmonies. **b.** Also, *Italian,* **brillante.** (of style in playing) lively; vivacious. —*n.* **5.** a diamond (or other gem) of a particular cut, typically round in outline and shaped like two pyramids united at their bases, the top one cut off near the base and the bottom one close to the apex, with many facets on the slopes. **6.** this form. **7.** a printing type (about 3 point). [t. F: m. *brillant,* ppr. of *briller,* corresponding to It. *brillare* shine, sparkle, ? g. LL *brillāre,* der. L *bēryllus* BERYL] —**bril′liantly,** *adv.* —**bril′liantness,** *n.* —**Syn. 1.** See **bright.**

brilliantine (brĭl′yən tēn′), *n.* **1.** a toilet preparation for the hair; hairdressing. **2.** *U.S.* a dress fabric resembling alpaca. [t. F]

brim (brĭm), *n., v.,* **brimmed, brimming.** —*n.* **1.** the upper edge of anything hollow; rim: *the brim of a cup.* **2.** a projecting edge: *the brim of a hat.* **3.** *Archaic.* edge or margin. —*v.i.* **4.** to be full to the brim; to be full to overflowing: *a brimming glass.* —*v.t.* **5.** to fill to the brim. [ME *brimme* shore, OE *brim* sea. Cf. Icel. *brim* surf] —**Syn. 1.** See **rim.**

brimful (brĭm′fo͝ol′), *adj.* full to the brim; completely full. Also, **brimfull.**

brimmer (brĭm′ə), *n.* a cup or bowl full to the brim.

brimstone (brĭm′stən), *n.* **1.** sulphur. **2.** a virago. **3.** a common yellow butterfly, *Gonepteryx rhamni,* of the family *Pieridae.* [ME *brinston,* etc., f. *brinn(en)* burn + *ston* stone] —**brim′stony,** *adj.*

Brindisi (brĭn′dĭ zĭ), *n.* a seaport in SE Italy, in Apulia: an important Roman city and naval base. 78,307 (1966). Ancient, **Brundisium.**

brindle (brĭn′dl), *n.* **1.** a brindled colouring. **2.** a brindled animal. [back-formation from BRINDLED]

brindled (brĭn′dld), *adj.* grey or tawny with darker streaks or spots. Also, **brinded** (brĭn′dĭd). [cf. Icel. *bröndōttr;* ? akin to BRAND]

Brindley (brĭnd′lĭ), *n.* **James,** 1716–72, English canal engineer.

brine (brīn), *n., v.,* **brined, brining.** —*n.* **1.** water saturated or strongly impregnated with salt. **2.** water strongly salted for pickling. **3.** the sea or ocean. **4.** the water of the sea. —*v.t.* **5.** to treat with or steep in brine. [ME; OE *brȳne,* c. D *brijn*] —**brin′ish,** *adj.*

Brinell machine (brĭ nĕl′), *Metall.* an instrument for calculating the hardness (**Brinell hardness**) of metal, esp. heat-treated steels, by forcing a hard steel or tungsten carbide ball of standard dimensions into the material being tested, under a fixed pressure. [named after J. A. *Brinell,* 1849–1925, Swedish engineer]

Brinell number, *Metall.* a numerical expression of Brinell hardness, found by determining the diameter of a dent made by the Brinell machine.

bring (brĭng), *v.t.*, **brought, bringing. 1.** to cause to come with oneself; take along to the place or person sought; conduct or convey. **2.** to cause to come, as to a recipient or possessor, to the mind or knowledge, into a particular position or state, to a particular opinion or decision, or into existence, view, action, or effect. **3.** to lead or induce: *he couldn't bring himself to do it.* **4.** *Law.* to put forward before a tribunal; declare in or as if in court. **5.** *Taboo.* to cause to have an orgasm. —*v.* **6.** Some special verb phrases are:
bring about, 1. to cause; accomplish. **2.** *Naut.* to turn (a ship) on to the opposite tack.
bring back, to recall to the mind; remind one of.
bring down, 1. to shoot down (a plane). **2.** to reduce (a price); lower in price. **3.** to humble or subdue.
bring forth, 1. to produce. **2.** to give rise to; cause.
bring forward, 1. to produce to view. **2.** to adduce. **3.** *Com.* to transfer (a figure) to the top of the next column.
bring in, 1. to introduce. **2.** to pronounce (a verdict). **3.** to produce; yield (an income, cash, etc.).
bring off, 1. to bring to a successful conclusion; achieve. **2.** to bring away (from a ship, etc.). **3.** *Taboo.* to induce an orgasm in.
bring on, 1. to induce; cause. **2.** to cause to advance. **3.** *Taboo.* to excite sexually, so as to induce orgasm.
bring out, 1. to expose; show; reveal. **2.** to encourage (a timid or diffident person). **3.** to publish. **4.** to formally introduce (a girl) into society. **5.** to induce (workers, etc.) to leave work and go on strike.
bring over, to convince; convert.
bring round, 1. to convince of an opinion. **2.** to restore to consciousness, as after a faint.
bring to, 1. to bring back to consciousness. **2.** *Naut.* to head a ship close to or into the wind and kill her headway by manipulating helm and sails.
bring under, to subdue.
bring up, 1. to care for during childhood; rear. **2.** to introduce to notice or consideration. **3.** to cause to advance, as troops. **4.** to vomit. **5.** *Naut.* to stop (a ship); make fast to a buoy or quay, etc.
[ME *bringen*, OE *bringan*, c. G *bringen*] —**bring′er,** *n.*
—**Syn. 1.** transport. BRING, FETCH imply conveying or conducting to or towards the place where the speaker is. To BRING is simply so to convey or conduct: *bring it to me, I'm permitted to bring my dog here with me.* (It is the opposite of TAKE, which means to convey or conduct away from the place where the speaker is: *bring it back here, take it back there.*) FETCH usually means to go, get, and bring back: *fetch it tomorrow.* —**Ant. 1.** take.

bringing-up (brĭng′ĭng ŭp′), *n.* upbringing.

brinjal (brĭn′jəl), *n.* an aubergine. [t. Skt]

brink (brĭngk), *n.* **1.** the edge or margin of a steep place or of land bordering water. **2.** any extreme edge; verge. [ME, t. Scand.; cf. Dan. *brink*]

brinkmanship (brĭngk′mən shĭp′), *n.* *Colloq.* the practice of courting disaster, esp. nuclear war, to gain one's ends.

briny (brī′nī), *adj.*, **brinier, briniest. 1.** of or like brine; salty. —*n.* **2.** *Colloq.* the sea. —**brin′iness,** *n.*

Bri-Nylon (brī′nī′lŏn), *n.* *Trademark.* nylon manufactured in Britain.

brio (brē′ō), *n.* liveliness; spirit; vivacity. [t. It.]

brioche (brē′ōsh, -ŏsh; *Fr.* brē ōsh′), *n.* a kind of light, sweet bun or roll, raised with eggs and yeast. [t. F, der. *brier*, d. form of *broyer* knead]

briolette (brē′ō lĕt′; *Fr.* brē ō-), *n.* a pear-shaped gem having its entire surface cut with triangular facets. [t. F]

briquette (brĭ kĕt′), *n.* a moulded block of compacted coal dust for fuel. Also, **briquet.** [t. F]

brisance (brē′zəns; *Fr.* brē zäɴs′), *n.* the shattering power of high explosives. [t. F]

Brisbane (brĭz′bān, -bən), *n.* **1.** a seaport in E Australia: capital of Queensland. 663,500 (1964). **2.** a river in Australia, flowing E through Brisbane to the Pacific. 214 mi.

Briseis (brī sē′ĭs), *n.* (in the *Iliad*) a beautiful maiden allotted as booty to Achilles: the cause of his quarrel with Agamemnon.

brise-soleil (brēz′sŏ lā′; *Fr.* brēz sŏ lĕy′), *n.* *Archit.* a structure, usually of horizontal or vertical strips of concrete, etc., used in hot climates to shade a window from the sun; a sunbreak. [t. F: *brise* (verbal n. of *briser* to break) + *soleil* sun]

brisk (brĭsk), *adj.* **1.** quick and active; lively: *a brisk breeze, a brisk walk.* **2.** sharp and stimulating: *brisk weather.* **3.** (of alcoholic drinks) effervescing vigorously: *brisk cider.* —*v.t., v.i.* **4.** to make or become brisk; liven (*up*). [? akin to BRUSQUE] —**brisk′ish,** *adj.* —**brisk′ly,** *adv.* —**brisk′ness,** *n.* —**Syn 1.** spry, energetic. —**Ant. 1.** languid.

brisket (brĭs′kĭt), *n.* the breast of an animal, or the part of the breast lying next to the ribs. [ME *brusket*, appar. t. OF: m. *bruschet*, t. Gmc; cf. LG *bröske*, Icel. *brjōsk* cartilage]

brisling (brĭs′lĭng), *n.* the sprat.

bristle (brĭs′əl), *n., v.*, **-tled, -tling.** —*n.* **1.** one of the short, stiff, coarse hairs of certain animals, esp. swine, used extensively in making brushes, etc. **2.** any short, stiff hair or hairlike appendage (often used facetiously of human hair). —*v.i.* **3.** to stand or rise stiffly, like bristles. **4.** to erect the bristles, as an irritated animal: *the dog bristled.* **5.** to be thickly set with something suggestive of bristles: *the plain bristled with bayonets, the enterprise bristled with difficulties.* **6.** to be visibly roused to anger, hostility, or resistance. —*v.t.* **7.** to erect like bristles. **8.** to furnish with a bristle or bristles. **9.** to make bristly. [ME *bristel*, f. *brist* (OE *byrst*) + *-el*, dim. suffix] —**bris′tly,** *adj.*

bristlegrass (brĭs′əl gräs′), *n.* any grass of the widespread genus *Setaria.*

bristletail (brĭs′əl tāl′), *n.* any of various wingless insects of the order *Thysanura*, having long bristle-like caudal appendages.

Bristol (brĭs′tl), *n.* a seaport in SW England, in S Gloucestershire, on the river Avon near its confluence with the Severn estuary: university founded in 1909. 437,048 (1961).

Bristol board, a fine, smooth kind of pasteboard, sometimes glazed.

Bristol Channel, an arm of the Atlantic between Wales and SW England. ab. 85 mi. long and from 5 to 43 mi. wide.

Bristol diamond, *Min.* a lustrous rock-crystal from the limestone near Bristol.

Bristol fashion, all in order; shipshape; with perfect efficiency and neatness.

brit (brĭt), *n.* the young of herring and sprat. [t. Cornish; akin to Welsh *brith* speckled]

Brit., 1. Britain. **2.** British.

Britain (brĭt′n), *n.* **1.** Great Britain. **2.** Britannia (def. 1a). **3. Battle of,** the series of heavy bombing attacks on Britain by the German air force in August–October 1940, repulsed by a small force of Royal Air Force fighters. [ME *Bretayne*, t. OF: m. *Bretaigne*, t. L: m. *Britannia.* See BRITISH]

Britannia (brĭ tăn′yə), *n.* **1.** Roman name for: **a.** the largest island of the British Isles. **b.** the Roman province in that island. **2.** the British Empire. **3.** Great Britain. **4.** *Chiefly Poetic.* England, Scotland, and Ireland. **5.** the feminine personification of Great Britain or the British Empire. **6.** Britannia metal. [t. L]

Britannia metal, a white alloy of tin, copper, and antimony, usually with small amounts of zinc, etc., used for tableware.

Britannic (brĭ tăn′ĭk), *adj.* **1.** British: *Her Britannic Majesty.* **2.** Brythonic. [t. L: s. *Britannicus*]

Briticism (brĭt′ĭ sĭz′əm), *n.* *Chiefly U.S.* an English usage peculiar to British people. The use of *lift* (cf. U.S. *elevator*) is a typical Briticism.

Briticize (brĭt′ĭ sīz′), *v.t.*, **-cized, -cizing.** *Chiefly U.S.* to assimilate to British culture or usage. Also, **Briticise.**

British (brĭt′ĭsh), *adj.* **1.** of or pertaining to Great Britain, the Commonwealth of Nations, the former British Empire, or their inhabitants. **2.** of or pertaining to the ancient Britons. —*n.* **3.** the British people, taken collectively. **4.** the language of the ancient Britons and the languages which have developed from it, namely Welsh, Cornish (no longer spoken), and Breton. **5.** *Chiefly U.S.* the standard English language as spoken in southern England. [ME *Brytysshe*, OE *Bryttisc*, der. *Bryttas*, *Brettas* Britons, from Celtic]

British Antarctic Territory, a colony created in 1962 from certain of the Falkland Islands Dependencies and comprising the south Shetland Islands, the south Orkney Islands and Graham Land.

British anti-lewisite, dimercaprol.

British Association for the Advancement of Science, a society founded in 1831 to give impulse and direction to scientific research and to promote the interchange of scientific ideas.

British Columbia, a province in W Canada, on the Pacific coast. 1,789,000 pop. (est. 1965); 366,255 sq. mi. *Cap.:* Victoria.

British Commonwealth of Nations. See **Commonwealth of Nations.**

British Council, an autonomous organization, financed by the British Government, to promote British culture, esp. in foreign countries.

British Empire, 1. (formerly) the dominions, colonies, protectorates, dependencies, trusteeships, etc., collectively, under the control of the British Crown. **2. Order of the,** a military and civil order of knighthood.

Britisher (brĭt′ĭ shə), *n. Now Rare.* a native or inhabitant of Britain.

British Guiana, former name of **Guyana.**

British Honduras, a former British crown colony in N Central America, self-governing internally since 1964. 90,019 pop. (1960); 8867 sq. mi. *Cap.:* Belize.

British India, that part of India (17 provinces) which until 1947 was subject to British law; now divided between India and Pakistan.

British Indian Ocean Territory, a British colony in the Indian Ocean, 1200 mi. NE of Mauritius, comprising some islands of the Seychelles and the Chagos Archipelago: created 1965 to provide U.K. and U.S. defence facilities. 1384 pop. (est. 1965); ab. 120 sq. mi.

British Isles, a group of islands in W Europe, comprising Great Britain, Ireland, the Isle of Man, and adjacent islands. 55,656,364 pop. (1963); 120,592 sq. mi.

British Legion, an organization formed in 1921 to assist former members of the armed services.

British Museum, a museum in London containing art collections, antiquities, etc., and housing the national library.

British North America, 1. Canada. **2.** *Hist.* the British colonies of Canada and the east coast of America.

British Somaliland, a former British protectorate in E Africa, on the Gulf of Aden: now part of the Somali Republic.

British Standards Institution, an association founded in 1901 to prepare uniform standards for use in industry, communications, etc.

British Standard Time, the standard time of the British Isles, one hour ahead of Greenwich Mean Time: the same as Central European Time. *Abbrev.:* B.S.T.

British Summer Time, a time formerly adopted in the summer, one hour ahead of Greenwich Mean Time: standard in the British Isles 1916–67.

British thermal unit, the amount of heat required to raise the temperature of 1 lb. of water by 1° Fahrenheit. *Abbrev.:* B.T.U., B.th.u.

Briton (brĭt′n), *n.* **1.** a native or inhabitant of Great Britain, or (sometimes) of the Commonwealth. **2.** one of the Celtic people who in early times occupied the southern part of the island of Britain. [t. ML: s. *Brito*; r. ME *Breton*, t. OF, g. L *Bretto*]

britska (brĭts′kə), *n.* britzka.

Brittany (brĭt′ə nĭ), *n.* **1.** an administrative region of NW France forming a peninsula between the English Channel and the Bay of Biscay. 2,395,582 pop. (1962); 10,940 sq. mi. *Prefecture:* Rennes. **2.** a former duchy and province. French, **Bretagne.**

Britten (brĭt′n), *n.* **Benjamin,** born 1913, English composer, pianist, and conductor.

brittle (brĭt′l), *adj.* **1.** breaking readily with a comparatively smooth fracture, as glass. —*n.* **2.** a sweet made with treacle and nuts: *peanut brittle.* [ME *britel*, der. OE *brēotan* break] —**brit′tleness,** *n.* —**Syn. 1.** fragile. See **frail**[1].

brittle-star (brĭt′l stä′), *n.* a starfish of the class *Ophiuroidea*, having slender arms sharply marked off from the central disc.

britzka (brĭts′kə), *n.* an open carriage with a calash top. Also, **britska, britzska.** [t. Pol.: m. *bryczka*, dim. of *bryka* wagon]

Brno (bû′nō), *n.* a city in central Czechoslovakia: the capital of Moravia. 314,379 (1961). German, **Brunn.**

bro., pl. **bros.** brother. Also, **Bro.**

broach (brōch), *n.* **1.** *Mach.* an elongated and tapered tool with serrations which enlarges a given hole as the tool is pulled through the hole, which may be round, square, etc. See illus. under **reamer. 2.** (in a lock) the pin about which the barrel of the key fits. **3.** *Archit.* the projecting corner of the tower of a broach spire. **4.** a spit for roasting meat. **5.** a gimlet for tapping casks. **6.** a brooch. —*v.t.* **7.** to enlarge and finish with a broach. **8.** to tap or pierce. **9.** to draw as by tapping: *to broach liquor.* **10.** to mention or suggest for the first time: *to broach a subject.* —*v.i.* **11.** *Naut.* (of a ship) to veer to windward, esp. so as to be broadside to the wind (fol. by *to*). [ME *broche*, t. OF, g. L *brocc(h)us* projecting] —**broach′er,** *n.*

broach spire, *Archit.* an octagonal spire rising from a square tower.

broad[1] (brôd), *adj.* **1.** of great breadth: *a broad river or street.* **2.** of great extent; large: *the broad expanse of ocean.* **3.** widely diffused; open; full: *broad daylight.* **4.** not limited or narrow; liberal: *broad experience.* **5.** of extensive range or scope: *broad sympathies.* **6.** main or general: *the broad outlines of a subject.* **7.** plain or clear: *a broad hint.* **8.** bold; plain-spoken. **9.** indelicate; indecent: *a broad joke.* **10.** (of conversation) rough; coarse; countrified. **11.** unconfined; free; unrestrained: *broad mirth.* **12.** (of pronunciation) strongly dialectal: *broad Scots.* **13. broad a,** the *a* (ä) sound in *father*, esp. in a word which has this vowel in standard British usage, but in standard American usage is customarily pronounced with the *a* (a) of *glad*, as in *half* or *can't* or *laughable.* —*adv.* **14.** fully: *broad awake.* —*n.* **15.** the broad part of anything. **16.** *Slang, Chiefly U.S.* a woman, esp. a prostitute. [ME *brood*, OE *brād*, c. G *breit*] —**broad′ish,** *adj.* —**broad′ly,** *adv.* —**Syn. 1.** See **wide. 2.** extensive, ample, vast. —**Ant. 1.** narrow.

broad[2] (brôd), *n.* a shallow lake, esp. one in East Anglia.

broad arrow, 1. a mark of the shape of a broad arrowhead, placed upon British governmental stores, and formerly on prison clothing. **2.** *Archery.* an arrow having an expanded head.

broadaxe (brôd′ăks′), *n.* **1.** an axe for hewing timber. **2.** a battleaxe. Also, *U.S.*, **broadax.**

broad bean, an erect annual leguminous herb, *Vicia faba*, often cultivated for its large edible seeds.

broadbill (brôd′bĭl′), *n.* **1.** any of various birds with a broad bill, as the scaup duck, shoveler, and spoonbill. **2.** a swordfish.

broadbrim (brôd′brĭm′), *n.* **1.** a hat with a broad brim, as that worn by Quakers. **2.** (*cap.*) *U.S. Colloq.* a Friend or Quaker.

broadcast (brôd′käst′), *v.*, **-cast** or **-casted, -casting,** *n. adj., adv.* —*v.t.* **1.** to send (messages, speeches, music, etc.) by radio. **2.** to cast or scatter abroad over an area, as seed in sowing. **3.** to spread or disseminate widely: *to broadcast gossip.* —*v.i.* **4.** to send radio messages, speeches, etc. **5.** to scatter or disseminate something widely. —*n.* **6.** that which is broadcast. **7.** *Radio.* **a.** the broadcasting of radio messages, speeches, etc. **b.** a radio programme. **c.** a single period of broadcasting. **8.** a method of sowing by scattering seed. —*adj.* **9.** sent out by broadcasting, as radio messages, speeches, music, etc. **10.** of or pertaining to broadcasting. **11.** cast abroad or all over an area, as seed sown thus. **12.** widely spread or disseminated: *broadcast discontent.* —*adv.* **13.** so as to reach an indefinite number of radio receiving stations or instruments in various directions. **14.** so as to be cast abroad over an area: *seed sown broadcast.* —**broad′cast′er,** *n.*

Broad Church, *Eccles.* those members of the Anglican communion who favour a liberal interpretation of doctrine and ritual, and such conditions of membership as will promote wide Christian inclusiveness. —**Broad′-Church′,** *adj.* —**Broad′-Church′man,** *n.*

broadcloth (brôd′klŏth′), *n.* **1. cotton broadcloth,** cotton shirting or dress material, usually mercerized, resembling fine poplin. **2. rayon broadcloth,** spun rayon fabric similar to cotton broadcloth. **3. woollen broadcloth,** woollen dress goods with nap laid parallel with selvage.

broaden (brô′dn), *v.i., v.t.* to become or make broad; widen.

broad gauge. See **gauge** (def. 14). Also, **broad gage.** —**broad′-gauged′, broad′-gaged′,** *adj.*

broad jump, *U.S.* long jump.

broadleaf (brôd′lēf′), *n.* **1.** any of several cigar tobaccos which have broad leaves. —*adj.* **2.** having broad leaves.

broadloom carpet (brôd′lo͞om′), any kind of carpet, from 54 inches to 18 feet wide, woven on a broad loom to avoid the need for seams.

broad-minded (brôd′ mīn′dĭd), *adj.* free from prejudice or bigotry; liberal; tolerant. —**broad′-mind′edly,** *adv.* —**broad′-mind′edness,** *n.*

Broadmoor (brôd′mô′), *n.* a prison in Berkshire, England, for mentally ill criminals.

broad seal, the official seal of a country or state.

broadsheet (brôd′shēt′), *n.* **1.** a sheet of paper, esp. of large size, printed on one side only, as for distribution or posting. **2.** a ballad, song, tract, etc., printed or originally printed on a broadsheet. —*adj.* **3.** (of a ballad) printed or originally printed on a broadsheet.

broadside (brôd′sīd′), *n.* **1.** *Naut.* the whole side of a ship above the waterline, from the bow to the quarter. **2.** *Naval.* **a.** all the guns that can be fired to one side of a ship. **b.** a simultaneous discharge of all the guns on one side of a vessel of war. **3.** any comprehensive attack, as of criticism. **4.** a broadsheet (def. 1). **5.** any broad surface or side, as of a house. —*adv.* **6.** broadways.

Broadstairs (brôd′stĕəz′), *n.* a town in England, in E Kent, on the Strait of Dover: seaside resort. 16,979 (1961).

broadsword (brôd′sôd′), *n.* a straight, broad, flat sword, usually with a basket hilt.

broadway (brôd′wā′), *n.* **1.** a broad street (often the name given to the main street or centre of a town). **2.** (*cap.*) a street in New York City, famous for its theatres.

broadways (brôd′wāz′), *adv.* breadthways; along or

across the breadth: laterally (often fol. by *on*). Also, *esp. U.S.*, **broadwise** (brôd′wīz′).

Brobdingnag (brŏb′dĭng năg′), *n.* the region in Swift's *Gulliver's Travels* where everything was of enormous size. —**Brob′dingnag′ian,** *adj.*, *n.*

brocade (brə kād′), *n.*, *v.*, **-caded, -cading.** —*n.* **1.** fabric woven with an elaborate design from any yarn. The right side has a raised effect. —*v.t.* **2.** to weave with a design or figure. [t. Sp.: m. *brocado*, c. It. *broccato*, der. *broccare* interweave with gold or silver, der. L *brocc(h)us*. See BROACH] —**brocad′ed,** *adj.*

brocatelle (brŏk′ə tĕl′), *n.* **1.** a kind of brocade, in which the design is in high relief. **2.** an ornamental marble with variegated colouring, esp. from Italy and Spain. Also, *U.S.*, **brocatel.** [t. F, t. It.: m. *broccatello*]

broccoli (brŏk′ə lĭ), *n.* **1.** a plant of the mustard family, *Brassica oleracea* var. *botrytis*, resembling the cauliflower. **2.** a form of this plant which does not produce a head, the green saps and the stalk of which are a common vegetable. Also, **broccoli sprouts.** [t. It., pl. of *broccolo* sprout, der. L *brocchus* projecting]

broché (brō′shā; *Fr.* brŏ shĕ′), *adj.* woven with a pattern; brocaded. [t. F, pp. of *brocher* BROCADE, v.]

brochette (brŏ shĕt′), *n.* **1.** a skewer, for use in cookery. **2. en brochette** (ŏn; *Fr.* äN), on a small spit. [t. F, dim. of *broché* spit. See BROACH]

brochure (brō′shyŏŏə; *Fr.* brŏ shʏr′), *n.* a pamphlet. [t. F, der. *brocher* stitch]

brock (brŏk), *n.* a badger. [OE *brocc*, t. Gaelic *broc*]

Brocken (*Ger.* brŏk′ən), *n.* a mountain in E West Germany and W East Germany: the highest peak in the Harz Mountains; prominent in German folklore. 3745 ft.

brocket (brŏk′ĭt), *n.* **1.** the male red deer in the second year, with the first growth of straight horns. **2.** a small swamp deer, genus *Mazama*, of tropical America.

brogan (brō′gən), *n.* a coarse, stout shoe. [t. Irish]

Broglie (*Fr.* brŏy), *n.* **1. Achille Charles Léonce Victor de** (*Fr.* à shēl shárl lĕ ōNs vĕk tŏr′ də), 1785–1870, French statesman. **2. Louis Victor de** (*Fr.* lwē vĕk tŏr′ də), born 1892, French physicist.

brogue[1] (brōg), *n.* a broad soft accent, esp. Irish, in the pronunciation of English. [appar. special use of BROGUE[2]]

brogue[2] (brōg), *n.* a strongly made, comfortable type of ordinary shoe, often with decorative perforations on the vamp and upper. [t. Irish, Gaelic: m. *brōg* shoe]

broider (broi′də), *v.t.* *Archaic.* to embroider. [ME *broudre(n)*, t. OF: m. *bro(u)der*, *brosder*, of Gmc orig.] —**broi′dery,** *n.*

broil[1] (broil), *v.t.* **1.** to cook by direct heat, as on a gridiron or in an oven broiler; grill. **2.** to scorch; make very hot. —*v.i.* **3.** to be subjected to great heat. **4.** to burn with impatience, etc. —*n.* **5.** a broiling. **6.** something broiled. [ME *brule(n)*, ? t. OF: m. *bruiller* burn, g. LL verb, prob. b. Gmc *brand* a burning and L *ustulāre* burn a little (der. *ūrere* burn)]

broil[2] (broil), *n.* **1.** an angry quarrel or struggle; a disturbance; a tumult. —*v.i.* **2.** to quarrel; brawl. [ME, t. OF: m. *brouiller* disorder, prob. der. *bro(u)* broth, t. OHG: m. *brod.* Cf. BREWIS]

broiler (broi′lə), *n.* **1.** any device for broiling meats or fish; a grate or pan for broiling. **2.** a young chicken suitable for broiling.

brokage (brō′kĭj), *n.* brokerage.

broke (brōk), *v.* **1.** pt. of **break. 2.** *Archaic or Colloq.* pp. of **break.** —*adj.* **3.** *Colloq.* out of money; bankrupt.

broken (brō′kən), *v.* **1.** pp. of **break.** —*adj.* **2.** reduced to fragments. **3.** ruptured; torn; fractured. **4.** fragmentary or incomplete: *a broken set.* **5.** infringed or violated. **6.** interrupted or disconnected: *broken sleep.* **7.** uneven; (of ground) rough; (of water) choppy; (of weather) patchy, unsettled. **8.** weakened in strength, spirit, etc. **9.** reduced to submission; tamed: *the horse was not yet broken to the saddle.* **10.** imperfectly spoken, as language. **11.** ruined; bankrupt. **12.** *Phonet.* (of a vowel) diphthongized. —**bro′kenly,** *adv.* —**bro′kenness,** *n.*

broken-down (brō′kən doun′), *adj.* shattered or collapsed; having given way.

broken-hearted (brō′kən hä′tĭd), *adj.* crushed by grief.

Broken Hill, 1. a town in SE Australia, in New South Wales: the centre of a rich mining district. 29,810 (1964). **2.** a town in Zambia: zinc, vanadium, and lead mining. 30,000 (est. 1966).

broken white, an off-white colour in which the whiteness has been slightly yellowed or browned.

broken wind, *Vet. Sci.* heaves. —**bro′ken-wind′ed,** *adj.*

broker (brō′kə), *n.* **1.** an agent who buys or sells for a principal on a commission basis without having title to the property. **2.** a middleman or agent. [ME *brocor*, t. AF: m. *brocour*, orig., broacher (of casks), tapster (hence retailer); akin to BROACH]

brokerage (brō′kə rĭj), *n.* **1.** the business of a broker. **2.** the commission of a broker.

brolga (brŏl′gə), *n.* a crane, *Grus rubicunda*, common in Australia; native companion. [t. native Australian]

brolly (brŏl′ĭ), *n.* **1.** *Colloq.* an umbrella. **2.** *Mil. Slang.* a parachute.

bromal (brō′məl), *n.* *Chem.*, *Pharm.* a colourless, oily liquid, CBr_3CHO, used in medicine as an anodyne and hypnotic. [f. BROM(INE) + AL(COHOL)]

bromate (brō′māt), *n.*, *v.*, **-mated, -mating.** —*n.* **1.** *Chem.* a salt of bromic acid. —*v.t.* **2.** to combine with bromine.

Bromberg (brŏm′bûg; *Ger.* brŏm′bĕrk), *n.* German name of **Bydgoszcz.**

brome grass (brōm), any grass of the genus *Bromus*, widely distributed in about 40 species, esp. *B. inermis*, a perennial used for hay and pasture. Also, **brome.** [*brome*, t. L: m. s. *bromus*, t. Gk: m. *brómos* kind of oats]

bromeliaceous (brō mē′lĭ ā′shəs), *adj.* *Bot.* belonging to the *Bromeliaceae*, a large family of herbaceous plants, mostly of the tropical Americas, and including the pineapple and many ornamentals. [f. s. NL *Bromelia* (named after Olaf *Bromel*, 1639–1705, Swedish botanist) + -ACEOUS]

bromic (brō′mĭk), *adj.* *Chem.* containing pentavalent bromine (Br^{+5}).

bromic acid, *Chem.* an acid, $HBrO_3$, containing bromine and oxygen, used as an oxidizing agent.

bromide (brō′mīd), *n.* **1.** *Chem.* a compound usually containing two elements only, one of which is bromine. **2.** silver bromide, esp. in photography. **3.** *Slang.* a person who is platitudinous and boring. **4.** *Slang.* a tiresome platitude. [defs 3 and 4 from the use of certain bromides as sedatives]

brominate (brō′mĭ nāt′), *v.t.*, **-nated, -nating.** *Chem.* to treat or combine with bromine. —**bro′mina′tion,** *n.*

bromine (brō′mēn, -mĭn), *n.* *Chem.* an element, a dark-reddish fuming liquid, resembling chlorine and iodine in chemical properties. *Symbol:* Br; *at. wt:* 79·909; *at. no.:* 35; *sp. gr.* (*liquid*): 3·119 at 20°C. [f. s. Gk *brômos* stench + -INE[2]]

bromism (brō′mĭz′əm), *n.* *Pathol.* poisoning by bromides, characterized by psychosis, skin rashes, muscle tremors, etc.

Bromley (brŏm′lĭ), *n.* a SE outer borough of London. 294,300 (1965).

Bromsgrove (brŏmz′grōv′), *n.* a town in England, in NE Worcestershire. 34,474 (1961).

bronchi (brŏng′kī), *n.* *Anat.* pl. of **bronchus.**

bronchia (brŏng′kĭ ə), *n.pl.* *Anat.* the ramifications of the bronchi or tubes. [t. LL, t. Gk, der. *brónchos* windpipe]

bronchial (brŏng′kyəl), *adj.* *Anat.* pertaining to the bronchia or bronchi.

bronchial tubes, *Anat.* the bronchi, or the bronchi and their ramifications. See diag. under **lung.**

bronchiole (brŏng′kĭ ōl′), *n.* *Anat.* one of the small subdivisions of a bronchus. [t. NL: m. s. *bronchiolum*, f. s. *bronchi(a)* BRONCHIA + *-olum* dim. suffix]

bronchitis (brŏng kī′tĭs), *n.* *Pathol.* inflammation of the membrane lining of the bronchial tubes. [NL; f. BRONCH(O)- + -ITIS] —**bronchitic** (brŏng kĭt′ĭk), *adj.*

broncho (brŏng′kō), *n.*, *pl.* **-chos.** broncho.

broncho-, a word element meaning 'bronchial'. Also, **bronch-.** [t. Gk, comb. form of *brónchos* windpipe]

bronchopneumonia (brŏng′kō nyŏŏ mō′nyə), *n.* *Pathol.* inflammation of the bronchia and lungs; a form of pneumonia.

bronchoscope (brŏng′kə skōp′), *n.* *Med.* a tubular instrument for examining bronchi and for the removal of foreign bodies therefrom.

bronchus (brŏng′kəs), *n.*, *pl.* **-chi** (-kī). *Anat.* either of the two main branches of the trachea. See diag. under **lung.** [t. NL, t. Gk: m. *brónchos* windpipe]

bronco (brŏng′kō), *n.*, *pl.* **-cos.** a pony or mustang of the western U.S., esp. one that is not broken, or is only imperfectly broken in. Also, **broncho.** [t. Sp.: rough, rude]

bronco-buster (brŏng′kō bŭs′tə), *n.* *Western U.S.* one who breaks in broncos. Also, **broncobuster.**

Brontë (brŏn′tĭ), *n.* **1. Anne** (*Acton Bell*), 1820–49, English novelist. **2.** her sister, **Charlotte** (*Currer Bell*), 1816–1855, English novelist. **3.** her sister, **Emily Jane** (*Ellis Bell*), 1818–48, English novelist.

brontosaurus (brŏn′tə sô′rəs), *n.* a large amphibious herbivorous dinosaur of the

Brontosaurus, *Apatasaurus excelsus* (66 ft long, 12 ft high)

American Jurassic, 60 feet or more in length. [f. *bronto-*, comb. form of Gk *brontḗ* thunder + -SAURUS]

Bronx (brŏngks), *n.* **The,** a N borough of New York City. 1,424,815 pop. (1960); 43·4 sq. mi.

bronze (brŏnz), *n., v.,* **bronzed, bronzing.** —*n.* **1.** *Metall.* **a.** a durable brown alloy, consisting essentially of copper and tin. **b.** any of various other copper base alloys, such as **aluminium bronze, manganese bronze, silicon bronze,** etc. The term implies a product superior in some way to brass. **2.** a metallic brownish colour. **3.** a work of art, as a statue, statuette, bust, or medal, composed of bronze, whether cast or wrought. —*adj.* **4.** of the colour of bronze. —*v.t.* **5.** to give the appearance or colour of bronze to. **6.** to make brown, as by exposure to the sun. —*v.i.* **7.** to turn a bronze colour; become sunburnt. [t. F, t. It.: m. *bronzo*] —**bronz′y,** *adj.*

Bronze Age, 1. *Archaeol.* the age in the history of mankind (between the Stone and Iron Ages) marked by the use of bronze implements. **2.** (*l.c.*) *Gk Myth.* the third period of the history of man, marked by war and violence, following the golden and silver ages.

bronzewing (brŏnz′wĭng′), *n.* any of several pigeons of Australia, as *Phaps chalcoptera.*

Bronzino (*It.* brôn dzē′nô), *n.* **Angelo,** 1503–72, Italian mannerist painter.

brooch (brōch), *n.* a clasp or ornament for the dress, having a pin at the back for passing through the clothing and a catch for securing the pin. [var. of BROACH, n.]

brood (brōōd), *n.* **1.** a number of young creatures produced or hatched at one time; a family of offspring or young. **2.** breed or kind. —*v.t.* **3.** to sit as a bird over (eggs or young); incubate. **4.** to dwell persistently or moodily in thought on; ponder. —*v.i.* **5.** to sit as a bird over eggs to be hatched. **6.** to rest fixedly. **7.** to meditate with morbid persistence. —*adj.* **8.** kept for breeding purposes: *a brood mare.* [ME; OE *brōd,* c. G *Brut.* Cf. BREED]

—**Syn. 1.** BROOD, LITTER refer to young creatures. BROOD is esp. applied to the young of fowls and birds hatched from eggs at one time and raised under their mother's care: *a brood of young turkeys.* LITTER is applied to a group of young animals brought forth at a birth: *a litter of kittens or pups.*

brooder (brōō′də), *n.* **1.** a device or structure for the artificial rearing of young chickens or other birds. **2.** one who or that which broods.

broody (brōō′dĭ), *adj.,* **broodier, broodiest. 1.** moody. **2.** inclined to brood or sit on eggs: *a broody hen.*

brook[1] (brŏŏk), *n.* a small, natural stream of fresh water, flowing through a glen or through woods, meadows, etc. [ME; OE *brōc* stream, c. G *Bruch* marsh] —**Syn.** rivulet, run, burn, branch.

brook[2] (brŏŏk), *v.t.* to bear; suffer; tolerate (usually in a negative sentence). [ME *brouke(n),* OE *brūcan,* c. G *brauchen* use; akin to L *fruī* enjoy]

Brooke (brŏŏk), *n.* **1. Alan Francis.** see **Alanbrooke. 2. Basil Stanlake.** see **Brookeborough. 3. Sir James,** 1803–68, British soldier and adventurer: raja of Sarawak. **4. Rupert,** 1887–1915, English poet.

Brookeborough (brŏŏk′bə rə, -brə), *n.* **Basil Stanlake Brooke, 1st Viscount,** born 1888, Northern Irish statesman: prime minister 1943–63.

Brook Farm, the scene of a famous, but unsuccessful, communistic experiment in the U.S. at West Roxbury, Massachusetts, 1841–47, participated in by George Ripley, C. A. Dana, Nathaniel Hawthorne, and others.

brooklet (brŏŏk′lĭt), *n.* a little brook.

brooklime (brŏŏk′līm′), *n.* a kind of speedwell, *Veronica beccabunga,* common in wet places.

Brooklyn (brŏŏk′lĭn), *n.* a borough of New York City, on W Long Island. 2,627,319 pop. (1960); 76·4 sq. mi.

Brooks Range, a mountain range in the U.S., in N Alaska, forming a watershed between the Yukon river and the Arctic Ocean. Highest peak, ab. 10,000 ft.

brookweed (brŏŏk′wēd′), *n.* either of two primulaceous plants, the water-pimpernel, *Samolus valerandi,* of Europe, and *S. floribundus,* of North America, both bearing small white flowers.

broom (brōōm, brŏŏm), *n.* **1.** a sweeping implement consisting of a flat brush of bristles, nylon, etc., on a long handle. **2.** a sweeping implement consisting of a bunch of twigs or plant stems on a handle; besom. **3.** any of the shrubby fabaceous plants of the genus *Cytisus,* esp. *C. scoparius,* common in western Europe, which grows on uncultivated ground and has long, slender branches bearing yellow flowers. **4.** any of several shrubs of the papilionaceous genus *Crenista,* as the **madeira broom,** *C. virgata.* —*v.t.* **5.** to sweep. [ME *brōme,* OE *brōm,* c. OHG *brāmo.* Cf. BRAMBLE] —**broom′y,** *adj.*

broomcorn (brōōm′kôn′, brŏŏm′-), *n.* a variety of sorghum with long, stiff panicles, used in brooms.

broomrape (brōōm′rāp′, brŏŏm′-), *n.* any of various parasitic plants, esp. of the genus *Orobanche,* living on the roots of broom and other plants.

broomstick (brōōm′stĭk′, brŏŏm′-), *n.* the long stick forming the handle of a broom.

bros., brothers. Also, **Bros.**

brose (brōz), *n. Scot.* a dish made by stirring boiling liquid into oatmeal or other meal. [Scot. var. of BREWIS]

Brosse (*Fr.* brôs), *n.* **Salmon de** (*Fr.* sȧl môɴ′ də), 1571–1626, French architect.

broth (brŏth), *n.* **1.** thin soup of concentrated meat or fish stock. **2.** water in which meat or fish has been boiled, sometimes with vegetables or barley. [ME and OE, c. OHG *brod.* Cf. BREW, BREWIS]

brothel (brŏth′əl), *n.* a house of prostitution. [ME; orig. worthless person, later whore, der. OE *brothen* ruined, degenerate, pp. of *brēothan* decay; in mod. use, short for *brothel-house* whorehouse]

brother (brŭth′ə), *n., pl.* **brothers, brethren,** *v.* —*n.* **1.** a male child of the same parents (**full brother** or **brother-german**). **2.** a male child of only one of one's parents (**half-brother**). **3.** a male member of the same kinship group, nationality, profession, etc.; an associate; a fellow countryman, fellow man, etc. **4.** *Eccles.* **a.** a male lay member of a religious organization which has a priesthood. **b.** a man who devotes himself to the duties of a religious order without taking holy orders, or while preparing for holy orders. **5.** (*pl.*) all members of a particular race, or of the human race in general. —*v.t.* **6.** to treat or address as a brother. [ME; OE *brōthor,* c. G *Bruder*]

—**Syn. 1.** BROTHERS, BRETHREN are plurals of *brother.* BROTHERS are kinsmen, sons of the same parents: *my mother lives with my brothers.* BRETHREN, now archaic in the foregoing sense, is used of male members of a congregation or of a fraternal organization: *the brethren will meet at the church.*

brotherhood (brŭth′ə hŏŏd′), *n.* **1.** condition or quality of being a brother or brothers. **2.** quality of being brotherly. **3.** a fraternal or trade organization. **4.** all those engaged in a particular trade or profession.

brother-in-law (brŭth′ər ĭn lô′), *n., pl.* **brothers-in-law. 1.** one's husband's or wife's brother. **2.** one's sister's husband. **3.** the husband of one's wife's or husband's sister.

Brother Jonathan (jŏn′ə thən), *U.S. Colloq.* **1.** the government of the United States of America. **2.** a typical American.

brotherly (brŭth′ə lĭ), *adj.* **1.** of, like, or befitting a brother; fraternal. —*adv.* **2.** as a brother, fraternally. —**broth′erliness,** *n.*

brougham (brōō′əm, brōōm), *n.* **1.** a four-wheeled, box-like, closed carriage for two or four persons, with the driver's perch outside. **2.** an early type of motor car, often battery driven. [named after Lord *Brougham,* 1778–1868, British statesman]

brought (brôt), *v.* pt. and pp. of **bring.**

brow (brou), *n.* **1.** the ridge over the eye. **2.** the hair growing on that ridge; eyebrow. **3.** (*sing. or pl.*) the forehead: *to knit one's brows.* **4.** the countenance. **5.** the edge of a steep place. **6.** *Mining.* the top of the shaft; pithead. **7.** *Naut.* a narrow gangway. [ME *browe,* OE *brū*]

browbeat (brou′bēt′), *v.t.,* **-beat, -beaten, -beating.** to intimidate by overbearing looks or words; bully.

brown (broun), *n.* **1.** a dark shade with yellowish or reddish hue. —*adj.* **2.** of the colour brown. **3.** having skin of that colour. **4.** sunburned or tanned. —*v.t., v.i.* **5.** to make or become brown. [ME; OE *brūn,* c. G *braun*] —**brown′ish,** *adj.* —**brown′ness,** *n.*

Brown (broun), *n.* **1. Sir Arthur Whitten,** 1886–1948. See **Alcock. 2. Ford Madox,** 1821–93, English historical painter. **3. John** ('*of Osawatomie*'), 1800–59, U.S. abolitionist who incited the slaves to a rebellion but was captured at Harpers Ferry, tried, and hanged. **4. Lancelot** ('*Capability Brown*'), 1716–83, English landscape gardener. **5. Robert,** 1773–1858, Scottish botanist. **6.** a university in the U.S. at Providence, Rhode Island, founded in 1764.

brown ale, a sweet dark ale, heavily malted.

brown algae, *Bot.* algae belonging to the class *Phaeophyceae,* usually brown as a result of brown pigments added to their chlorophyll.

brown bear, 1. a variety of the black bear of Europe and America, *Ursus arctos,* inhabiting northern regions. **2.** a variety of the common black bear, *Ursus americanus,* having a brownish coat.

brown bread, any bread made of flour darker in colour than the bolted wheat flour.

brown coal, lignite.

Browne (broun), *n.* **1. Charles Farrar** (făr′ə). See **Ward, Artemus. 2. Hablot Knight.** See **Phiz. 3. Sir Thomas,** 1605–82, English physician and author.

browned off, *Colloq.* bored; discontented; fed up. Also (esp. in attributive positions), **browned-off** (bround′ ŏf′).

brown forest soil, *Geog.* a soil rich in humus derived from leaves, characteristic of temperate areas where the natural vegetation is or was deciduous forest. Also, **brown earth.**

Brownhills (broun′hĭlz′), *n.* a town in England, in S Staffordshire. 26,392 (1961).

Brownian movement (brou′nĭ ən), *Physics.* a rapid oscillatory motion often observed in very minute particles suspended in water or other liquid. Also, **Brownian motion.** [first noticed (in 1827) by Robert BROWN]

brownie (brou′nĭ), *n.* **1.** (in folklore) a little brown goblin, esp. one who helps secretly in household work. **2.** (*cap.*) a trademark for a type of inexpensive camera. **3.** (*cap.*) a member of the junior division (ages 8–11) of the Girl Guides or an associate organization in any of several other countries. **—Syn. 1.** See **fairy.**

browning (brou′nĭng), *n.* **1.** the process of turning something brown. **2.** a substance or preparation used to turn something brown, esp. gravy.

Browning (brou′nĭng), *n.* **1. Elizabeth Barrett** (băr′rĭt), 1806–61, English poetess. **2.** her husband, **Robert,** 1812–89, English poet. **3.** *Trademark.* a type of pistol.

brown owl, 1. the tawny owl. **2.** the woman in charge of a group of Brownies (def. 3).

brown paper, a type of strong, coarse, brown-coloured paper, used mainly for wrapping.

brown rice, rice from which the bran layers and germs have not been removed by polishing.

brown rot, *Plant Pathol.* a disease, as of apples, peaches, plums, etc., caused by fungi of the genus *Sclerotinia.*

Brownshirt (broun′shûrt′), *n.* **1.** a member of Hitler's storm-troopers. **2.** (loosely) any Nazi.

brownstone (broun′stōn′), *n.* *U.S.* **1.** a reddish brown sandstone, extensively used by the prosperous classes as a building material. *—adj.* **2.** belonging or pertaining to the well-to-do class.

brown study, deep, serious absorption in thought.

brown sugar, unrefined or partially refined sugar.

brown trout, the common river-trout of northern Europe, *Salmo trutta fario.*

browse (brouz), *v.*, **browsed, browsing,** *n.* *—v.t.* **1.** (of cattle, deer, etc.) to nibble at; eat from. **2.** (of cattle, deer, etc.) to feed on; pasture on; graze. *—v.i.* **3.** (of cattle, etc.) to graze. **4.** to glance at random through a book or books. *—n.* **5.** tender shoots or twigs of shrubs and trees as food for cattle, deer, etc. [appar. t. MF: m. *broust* young sprout, t. Gmc; cf. OS *brustian* to sprout] **—brows′er,** *n.*

B.R.S., British Road Services.

Bruce (bro͞os), *n.* **1. Robert the** (*Robert I, Robert Bruce*), 1274–1329, king of Scotland 1306–29: preserved the independence of Scotland by victory over the English at Bannockburn in 1314. **2. Stanley Melbourne, Viscount,** 1883–1967, Australian statesman, prime minister of Australia 1923–29. **3. Mount,** a peak in Western Australia, 4027 ft.

brucellosis (bro͞o′sĭ lō′sĭs), *n.* *Vet. Sci., Pathol.* infection with bacteria of the *Brucella* group, frequently causing abortions in animals and undulant fever in man. [t. NL: f. s. *Brucella* genus name (f. Sir David *Bruce*, 1855–1931, Australian physician + *-ella* dim. suffix) + *-osis* -OSIS]

brucine (bro͞o′sēn, -sĭn), *n.* *Pharm., Chem.* a bitter, poisonous alkaloid, $C_{23}H_{26}N_2O_4$, obtained from the nux vomica tree, *Strychnos nux vomica*, and from other species of the same genus, resembling strychnine in action but less powerful. [f. James *Bruce*, 1730–94, Scottish explorer of Africa + -INE[2]]

Brücke (*Ger.* brʏ′kə), *n.* **die** (*Ger.* dē), a group of expressionist painters and illustrators formed in Dresden in 1905. [G: lit. the bridge]

Bruckner (bro͝ok′nə; *Ger.* bro͝ok′nər), *n.* **Anton** (ăn′tŏn; *Ger.* ȧn′tôn), 1824–96, Austrian composer and organist.

Brueghel (broi′gl; *Flem.* brœ′KHəl), *n.* a Flemish family of genre and landscape painters: **Pieter,** 1525?–69, and his sons **Pieter,** 1564–1637, and **Jan,** 1568–1625. Also, **Brue′gel, Breu′ghel.**

Bruges (bro͞ozh; *Fr.* brʏzh), *n.* a city in NW Belgium: connected by canal with its seaport, Zeebrugge. 52,463 (1962). Flemish, **Brugge** (broʏe′KHə).

bruin (bro͞o′ĭn), *n.* a bear. [t. MD: lit., brown, the name of the bear in *Reynard the Fox*]

bruise (bro͞oz), *v.*, **bruised, bruising,** *n.* *—v.t.* **1.** to injure by striking or pressing, without breaking the skin or drawing blood. **2.** to injure or hurt superficially: *to bruise a person's feelings.* **3.** to crush (drugs or food) by beating or pounding. *—v.i.* **4.** to develop a discoloured spot on the skin as the result of a blow, fall, etc. **5.** to be injured superficially: *his feelings bruise easily.* *—n.* **6.** an injury due to bruising; a contusion. [ME *bruse(n)*, *brise(n)*, coalescence of OE *brȳsan* crush, bruise and OF *br(u)isier* break, ult. der. Gallic *bris-*, *brus-* beat]

bruiser (bro͞o′zə), *n.* **1.** a boxer. **2.** *Colloq.* a tough fellow; bully.

bruit (bro͞ot), *v.t.* **1.** to noise abroad; rumour (mainly in the passive): *the report was bruited about.* *—n.* **2.** *Archaic.* rumour. **3.** *Archaic.* a din. [ME, t. OF, der. *bruire* make a noise]

brum (brŭm), *n., adj.* *Dial., Slang.* (*sometimes cap.*) Brummagem.

Brumaire (*Fr.* brʏ mĕr′), *n.* the second month, October 22nd to November 20th, in the calendar adopted (1793) by the first French republic. [t. F, der. *brume* BRUME]

brumal (bro͞o′məl), *adj.* wintry. [t. L: s. *brūmālis*]

brumby (brŭm′bĭ), *n.* *Austral., N.Z.* a wild horse, esp. one descended from runaway stock. [? t. native Australian]

brume (bro͞om), *n.* mist; fog. [t. F: fog, t. Pr.: m. *bruma*, g. L *brūma* winter, winter solstice, lit., shortest day]

brumous (bro͞o′məs), *adj.*

Brummagem (brŭm′ə jəm), *n.* **1.** *Dial.* or *Colloq.* Birmingham. **2.** (*l.c.*) a showy but inferior and worthless thing. *—adj.* **3.** (*l.c.*) showy but inferior and worthless. **4.** *Dial. or Colloq.* pertaining to or inhabiting Birmingham.

Brummell (brŭm′əl), *n.* See **Beau Brummell.**

brummy (brŭm′ĭ), *n.* *Dial., Slang.* (*sometimes cap.*) **1.** an inhabitant of Birmingham. *—adj.* **2.** born and bred in Birmingham.

brunch (brŭnch), *n.* a midmorning meal that serves as both breakfast and lunch. [b. BREAKFAST and LUNCH]

Brundisium (bro͞on dĭz′ĭ əm), *n.* ancient name of **Brindisi.**

Brunei (bro͞o nī′, bro͞o′nī), *n.* **1.** a sultanate under British protection in NW Borneo. 98,438 pop. (est. 1963); ab. 2220 sq. mi. **2.** the capital of this sultanate: a seaport. 47,317 (est. 1964).

Brunel (bro͞o nĕl′), *n.* **Isambard Kingdom,** 1806–59, English civil engineer.

Brunelleschi (*It.* bro͞o nĕl lĕs′kē), *n.* **Filippo** (*It.* fē lĕp′pô), 1377?–1446, Florentine architect.

brunet (bro͞o nĕt′), *adj.* **1.** brunette. *—n.* **2.** *Obs.* a man or boy with dark hair, skin, and eyes. [t. F, dim. of *brun*, fem. *brune* brown; of Gmc orig. Cf. BROWN]

brunette (bro͞o nĕt′), *adj.* **1.** (of skin, eyes, or hair) dark; brown. **2.** (of a person) having dark or brown hair, eyes, or skin. *—n.* **3.** a woman or girl with dark hair, skin, and eyes.

Brunhild (bro͞on′hĭld; *Ger.* bro͞on′hĭlt), *n.* **1.** (in the *Nibelungenlied*) a legendary queen of Iceland, wife of King Gunther, for whom she is won by Siegfried. **2.** (in the corresponding Scandinavian legend) a Valkyrie, won by Sigurd for Gunnar. Also, **Brynhild.** [t. G. Cf. Icel. *Brynhildr*]

Brünn (*Ger.* brʏn), *n.* German name of **Brno.**

Brünnhilde (*Ger.* brʏn′hĭl′də), *n.* the heroine of Wagner's *Ring of the Nibelungs.* Cf. **Siegfried.**

Bruno (bro͞o′nō; *It.* bro͞o′nô), *n.* **1. Giordano** (*It.* jôr dä′nô), 1548?–1600, Italian philosopher. **2. Saint,** *c.* 1030–1101, German monk, born at Cologne: founder of Carthusian order.

Brunswick (brŭnz′wĭk), *n.* **1.** a former state in central Germany. 1418 sq. mi. Now part of Lower Saxony. **2.** a city in West Germany, in E Lower Saxony, the former capital of this state; a member of the Hanseatic League. 233,000 (est. 1966). German, **Braunschweig.** See map under **Hanseatic League.**

Brunswick black, a dark, glossy opaque varnish consisting of gilsonite or petroleum pitch dissolved in white spirit or aromatic hydrocarbons.

Brunswick blue, white paint stained blue with ferrocyanide.

Brunswick green, cupric oxychloride, a green pigment.

brunt (brŭnt), *n.* **1.** the shock or force of an attack, etc.; the main stress, force, or violence: *to bear the brunt of their criticism.* **2.** *Archaic.* a violent attack.

Brusa (*Turk.* bro͞o′sä), *n.* Bursa.

brush[1] (brŭsh), *n.* **1.** an instrument consisting of bristles, hair, or the like, set in or attached to a handle, used for painting, cleaning, polishing, rubbing, etc. **2.** an act of brushing; an application of a brush. **3.** the bushy tail of an animal, esp. of a fox. **4.** the art or skill of a painter of pictures. **5.** a painter. **6.** a slight skimming touch or contact. **7.** a brief hostile encounter; argument; skirmish. **8.** *Elect.* **a.** a conductor serving to maintain electric contact between stationary and moving parts of a machine or other apparatus. **b.** corona (def. 7). *—v.t.* **9.** to sweep, rub, clean, polish, etc., with a brush. **10.** to touch lightly in passing; pass lightly over. **11.** to remove by brushing or by lightly passing over (usually fol. by *aside*). **12. brush up, a.** to polish up; smarten. **b.** to revise and renew or improve one's skill in. *—v.i.* **13.** to move or skim with a slight contact. [ME *brusshe*, t. OF: m. *broisse*, t. Gmc; cf. MHG *büriste* brush] —**brush′y,** *adj.* —**Syn. 7.** See **struggle.**

brush[2] (brŭsh), *n.* **1.** a dense growth of bushes, shrubs, etc.; scrub; a thicket. **2.** backwoods; a sparsely settled region covered with scrub. [ME *brusche*, t. OF: m. *broce.* See BRUSH[1]] —**brush′y,** *adj.*

brush discharge, *Elect.* corona (def. 7).

brush-off (brŭsh′ŏf′), *n. Slang.* an abrupt or final dismissal or refusal.

brushstroke (brŭsh′strōk′), *n.* the stroke of a brush, as in painting.

brush turkey, *Austral.* a mound-building bird, *Alecturus lathami.*

brushwood (brŭsh′wo͝od′), *n.* **1.** branches of trees cut or broken off. **2.** densely growing small trees and shrubs. [f. BRUSH[2] + WOOD[1]]

brushwork (brŭsh′wûk′), *n.* **1.** the skill, style, or manner in which a painter uses his brush. **2.** painting or other work done with a brush.

brusque (bro͞osk, bro͝osk; *Fr.* brʏsk), *adj.* abrupt in manner; blunt; rough: *a brusque welcome.* [t. F, t. It.: m. *brusco* rude, sharp, g. L *bruscum*, b. L *ruscum* butcher's-broom and *brūcum* broom] —**brusque′ly,** *adv.* —**brusque′ness,** *n.* —**Syn.** See **blunt.**

brusquerie (*Fr.* brʏs kə rē′), *n.* brusqueness. [F]

Brussels (brŭs′əlz), *n.* the capital of Belgium, in the central part. 1,029,693 (1962). French, **Bruxelles.** Flemish, **Brussel** (*Flem.* brʏ′səl).

Brussels carpet, a kind of worsted carpet woven on a Jacquard loom, in which uncut loops form a heavy pile.

Brussels lace, handmade lace from Brussels.

Brussels sprout, (*sometimes l.c.*) **1.** a plant, *Brassica oleracea*, var. *gemmifera*, having small edible heads or sprouts along the stalk, which resemble miniature cabbage heads. **2.** one of the heads or sprouts themselves. Also, **Brussel sprout.**

Brussels sprout

brut (*Fr.* brʏt), *adj.* (of wines, usually champagne) very dry. [t. F: raw]

brutal (bro͞o′tl), *adj.* **1.** savage; cruel; inhuman. **2.** crude; coarse; harsh. **3.** irrational; unreasoning. **4.** of or pertaining to lower animals. —**bru′tally,** *adv.* —**Syn. 1.** See **cruel.**

brutalism (bro͞o′tə lĭz′əm), *n.* a modern architectural style expressing structure and using materials with machine-like directness.

brutality (bro͞o tăl′ĭ tĭ), *n., pl.* **-ties. 1.** quality of being brutal. **2.** a brutal act.

brutalize (bro͞o′tə līz′), *v.t., v.i.,* **-lized, -lizing.** to make or become brutal. Also, **brutalise.** —**bru′taliza′tion,** *n.*

brute (bro͞ot), *n.* **1.** a non-human animal; beast. **2.** a brutal person. **3.** *Colloq.* a selfish or unsympathetic person. **4.** the animal qualities, desires, etc., of man. —*adj.* **5.** wanting reason; animal; not human. **6.** not characterized by intelligence; irrational. **7.** characteristic of animals; of brutal character or quality. **8.** savage; cruel. **9.** sensual; carnal. [t. F: m. *brut*, t. L: s. *brūtus* dull] —**Syn. 1.** See **animal.**

brutify (bro͞o′tĭ fī′), *v.t., v.i.,* **-fied, -fying.** to brutalize.

brutish (bro͞o′tĭsh), *adj.* **1.** brutal. **2.** gross; carnal; bestial. **3.** uncivilized; like an animal. —**brut′ishly,** *adv.* —**brut′ishness,** *n.*

Brutus (bro͞o′təs), *n.* **Marcus Junius** (mä′kəs jo͞o′nyəs), 85?–42 B.C., Roman provincial administrator; one of the assassins of Julius Caesar.

Bruxelles (*Fr.* brʏ sĕl′; *local* brʏk sĕl′), *n.* French name of **Brussels.**

Bryansk (brĭ ănsk′; *Russ.* bryănsk), *n.* a city in the W Soviet Union in Europe. 267,000 (est. 1965).

Bryce (brīs), *n.* **James, Viscount,** 1838–1922, British historical and political writer, and diplomat.

Brynhild (brĭn′hĭld; *Icelandic* brʏn′-), *n.* Brunhild.

Bryn Mawr (brĭn′môr′), *n.* a women's college in the U.S., in Pennsylvania, founded in 1885.

bryology (brī ŏl′ə jĭ), *n.* the part of botany that treats of bryophytes. [f. Gk *brýo(n)* moss + -LOGY] —**bryological** (brī′ə lŏj′ĭ kl), *adj.* —**bryol′ogist,** *n.*

bryony (brī′ə nĭ), *n., pl.* **-nies. 1.** any plant of the Old World cucurbitaceous genus *Bryonia*, comprising vines or climbers with acrid juice and emetic and purgative properties as white bryony, *Bryonia dioica.* **2.** black bryony. [t. L: m. s. *bryōnia*, t. Gk]

bryophyte (brī′ə fīt′), *n. Bot.* any of the *Bryophyta*, a primary division or group of plants comprising the true mosses and liverworts. [t. NL: m. *Bryophyta*, pl., f. Gk *brýo(n)* moss + *-phyta* (see -PHYTE)] —**bryophytic** (brī′ə fĭt′ĭk), *adj.*

bryozoan (brī′ə zō′ən), *Zool.* —*adj.* **1.** of or pertaining to the *Bryozoa*, a phylum of marine and freshwater animals, of sessile habits, forming branching, encrusting, or gelatinous colonies of many small polyps, each having a circular or horseshoe-shaped ridge bearing ciliated tentacles. Branching marine types are termed sea-moss and are used as ornaments. —*n.* **2.** any of the *Bryozoa.* Also, **polyzoan.** [f. Gk *brýo(n)* moss + -ZO(A) + -AN]

Brython (brĭth′ən), *n.* **1.** a Celt in Britain using the Brythonic form of the Celtic language, which was confined mainly to the western part of southern Britain after the English conquest. **2.** a Briton. [t. Welsh]

Brythonic (brĭ thŏn′ĭk), *adj.* **1.** pertaining to the Celtic dialects used in north-western and south-western England, Wales and Brittany. —*n.* **2.** the British subgroup of Celtic (distinguished from *Goidelic*).

Brześć nad Bugiem (*Pol.* bzhĕshch′ nȧd bo͞o′gyĕm), *n.* Polish name of **Brest Litovsk.**

B.S., **1.** Bachelor of Science. **2.** Bachelor of Surgery.

b.s., *Com.* **1.** balance sheet. **2.** bill of sale.

B.S.A., Birmingham Small Arms (company).

B.Sc., (L *Baccalaureus Scientiae*) Bachelor of Science.

B.S.I., British Standards Institution.

B.S.S., British Standards Specification.

B.S.T., **1.** British Standard Time. **2.** (formerly) British Summer Time.

Bt, Baronet.

B.T.C., (formerly) British Transport Commission.

B.Th., (L *Baccalaureus Theologia*) Bachelor of Theology.

B.T.U., **1.** Board of Trade unit. **2.** Also, **B.th.u.** British thermal unit.

bu., bushel; bushels.

bub (bŭb), *n. Taboo Slang.* one of the breasts of a woman.

bubal (byo͞o′bl), *n.* a large antelope, one of the hartebeests, *Alcelaphus boselaphus*, of northern Africa. Also, **bubalis** (byo͞o′bə lĭs). [t. L: s. *būbalus* an oxlike antelope, t. Gk: m. *boúbalos*]

bubaline (byo͞o′bə līn′, -lĭn), *adj.* **1.** (of antelopes) resembling or like the bubal, as the hartebeests, blesbok, etc. **2.** pertaining to or resembling the true buffaloes.

bubble (bŭb′l), *n., v.,* **-bled, -bling.** —*n.* **1.** a small globule of gas in or rising through a liquid. **2.** a small globule of gas in a thin liquid envelope. **3.** a globule of air or gas, or a globular vacuum, in a solid substance. **4.** anything that lacks firmness, substance, or permanence; a delusion; a worthless, deceptive matter. **5.** an inflated speculation, esp. if fraudulent. **6.** the act or sound of bubbling. —*v.i.* **7.** to send up bubbles; effervesce. **8.** to flow or run with a gurgling noise; gurgle. —*v.t.* **9.** to cause to bubble; make (bubbles) in. **10.** *Archaic.* to cheat; deceive; swindle. [ME *bobel*, c. D *bobbelen*, Sw. *bubla.* Cf. BURBLE]

bubble-and-squeak (bŭb′l ən skwēk′), *n.* **1.** left-over potato and cabbage fried together. **2.** left-over meat and vegetables fried together.

bubble car, a small motor car with a bubble-shaped body.

bubble chamber, *Physics.* an apparatus for determining the movements of charged particles by producing visible tracks of bubbles in their paths as they traverse a transparent medium.

bubblegum (bŭb′l gŭm′), *n.* a type of chewing gum which can be blown into bubbles.

bubbly (bŭb′lĭ), *adj.* **1.** containing bubbles; bubbling. **2.** of or like bubbles. —*n.* **3.** *Slang.* champagne.

Buber (bo͞o′bə), *n.* **Martin,** 1878–1965, Jewish theologian and philosopher, born in Austria.

bubo (byo͞o′bō), *n., pl.* **-boes.** *Pathol.* an inflammatory swelling of a lymphatic gland, esp. in the groin or armpit. [t. LL, t. Gk: m. *boubṓn*, lit., groin]

bubonic (byo͞o bŏn′ĭk), *adj. Pathol.* **1.** of or pertaining to a bubo. **2.** accompanied by or affected with buboes.

bubonic plague, *Pathol.* a contagious epidemic disease in which the victims suffer chills, fevers, and buboes, and are prostrate, and which often has rat-fleas as its carrier.

bubonocele (byo͞o bŏn′ə sēl′), *n. Pathol.* an inguinal hernia, esp. one in which the protrusion of the intestine is limited to the region of the groin.

Bucaramanga (*Sp.* bo͞o kȧ rȧ mȧn′gȧ), *n.* a town in N Colombia. 229,748 (1964).

buccal (bŭk′l), *adj. Anat.* **1.** of or pertaining to the cheek. **2.** pertaining to the sides of the mouth or to the mouth; oral. **3.** pertaining to the mouth as a whole. [f. s. L *bucca* cheek, mouth + -AL[1]]

buccaneer (bŭk′ə nĭə′), *n.* **1.** a pirate. **2.** one of the piratical adventurers who raided Spanish colonies and shipping in America. —*v.i.* **3.** to act like, or lead the life of, a buccaneer. [t. F: m. *boucanier*, der. *boucan* frame for curing meat, t. Tupi: alter. of *mukém*] —**buc′caneer′ing,** *n., adj.*

buccinator (bŭk′sĭ nā′tə), *n. Anat.* a thin, flat muscle lining the cheek, assisting in mastication, blowing wind instruments, etc. [t. L: trumpeter, der. *buccināre* blow a trumpet] —**buc′cina′tory,** *adj.*

bucentaur (byo͞o sĕn′tô), *n.* the state barge of Venice, from which the doge and other officials on Ascension Day performed the ceremonial marriage of the state with the Adriatic, by dropping a ring into the sea. [t. It.: m. *bucentoro*, orig. uncert.; said to be f. Gk: m. *boûs* ox + m. s. *kéntauros* centaur (said to be from the figurehead of such a barge, representing a mythical beast, half bull, half man)]

Bucephalus (byo͞o sĕf′ə ləs), *n.* the warhorse of Alexander the Great.

Buchan (bŭk′ən), *n.* **John** (*Baron Tweedsmuir*), 1875–1940, Scottish novelist and historian: governor-general of Canada, 1935–40.

Buchanan (byo͞o kăn′ən), *n.* **1. Sir Colin,** born 1907, English town-planner. **2. James,** 1791–1868, 15th president of the U.S., 1857–61.

Bucharest (byo͞o′kə rĕst′, bo͞o′-), *n.* the capital of Rumania, in the S part. 1,239,458 (est. 1964). Rumanian, **Bucureşti.** See map under **Bessarabia.**

Buchenwald (bo͞o′kən väld′; *Ger.* bo͞o′KHən vält), *n.* a former Nazi concentration camp in central Germany, near Weimar, infamous for atrocities perpetrated there.

Buchmanism (bŭk′mə nĭz′əm), *n.* the Moral Rearmament movement. [named after Frank *Buchman*, 1878–1961, who founded it] —**Buchmanite** (bŭk′mə nīt′), *n.*

Büchner (*Ger.* bʏKH′nər), *n.* **Georg** (*Ger.* gė′ŏrk), 1813–37, German poet and dramatist.

buchu (bo͞o′ko͞o), *n.* **1.** any of several rutaceous shrubs of southern Africa, as *Barosma crenulata* and *B. betulina*, having small pale pink flowers and aromatic leaves; used medicinally and in flavouring brandy. **2.** the dried leaves of such a shrub. [t. Hottentot]

buck[1] (bŭk), *n.* **1.** the male of the deer, antelope, rabbit, or hare. **2.** the male fallow deer. **3.** the male of certain animals. **4.** a fop; dandy. **5.** *U.S. Colloq.* (used disparagingly) a male Indian or Negro. **6.** *U.S. Slang.* a dollar. [ME *bukke*, coalescence of OE *bucca* he-goat and *bucc* male deer, c. G *Bock*]

buck[2] (bŭk), *v.i.* **1.** (of a saddle or pack animal) to leap with arched back and come down with head low and forelegs stiff, in order to dislodge rider or pack. **2.** *U.S. Colloq.* to resist obstinately; object strongly: *to buck at improvements.* **3.** *Colloq.* to hurry (fol. by *up*). **4.** *Colloq.* to become more cheerful, vigorous, etc. (fol. by *up*). **5.** to boast. —*v.t.* **6.** to throw or attempt to throw (a rider) by bucking. **7.** *U.S. Colloq.* to resist obstinately; object strongly to. **8.** *Colloq.* to force or urge (someone) to hurry (fol. by *up*). **9.** *Colloq.* to make more cheerful, vigorous, etc. (fol. by *up*). —*n.* **10.** an act of bucking. [special use of BUCK[1]]

buck[3] (bŭk), *n. Gymnastics.* a horse (def. 6). [t. D: m. *zaagbok*]

buck[4] (bŭk), *n.* **1.** *Poker.* any object in the pot which reminds the winner that he has some privilege or duty when his turn to deal next comes. **2. pass the buck,** *Colloq.* to shift the responsibility or blame to another person. [orig. uncert.]

Buck (bŭk), *n.* **Pearl S(ydenstricker)** (sī′dn strĭk′ə), born 1892, U.S. novelist.

buckaroo (bŭk′ə ro͞o′, bŭk′ə ro͞o′), *n., pl.* **-roos.** *Western U.S.* a cowboy. Also, **buckayro** (bə kē͡ə′rō).

buck bean, a plant, *Menyanthes trifoliata*, with white or pink flowers, growing in bogs; bog bean.

buckboard (bŭk′bôd′), *n. U.S.* a light four-wheeled carriage in which a long elastic board or lattice frame is used in place of body and springs.

Buckboard

buckeen (bŭ kēn′), *n.* (in Ireland) a young man of the middle class or lower aristocracy who copies the habits of wealthier people.

bucker (bŭk′ə), *n.* a horse that bucks.

bucket (bŭk′ĭt), *n., v.,* **-eted, -eting.** —*n.* **1.** a vessel, usually round with flat bottom and a semicircular handle, for carrying water, sand, etc. **2.** anything resembling or suggesting this. **3.** one of the scoops attached to or forming the endless chain in certain types of conveyers or elevators. **4.** a cupped vane of a waterwheel, turbine, etc. **5.** a bucketful. **6. kick the bucket,** *Slang.* to die. —*v.t.* **7.** to lift, carry, or handle in a bucket (often fol. by *up* or *out*). **8.** to shake or toss jerkily (fol. by *about*). **9.** to handle (orders, etc.) as in a bucket shop. —*v.i.* **10.** *Colloq.* to move or drive fast (often fol. by *along*). **11.** to be shaken or tossed jerkily (fol. by *about*). [ME *bocket*, appar. t. OF: m. *buket* pail, tub, prob. der. some cognate of OE *būc* pitcher] —**bucketful** (bŭk′ĭt fo͝ol′), *n.*

bucket seat, a seat for one person in cars, aeroplanes, etc., usually curved laterally to hold the passenger in place.

bucket shop, *Finance.* a broker's establishment which is not part of, or subject to the rules of, any recognized stock exchange, and which speculates against its customers' purchases and sales by failing to execute some, so that customers' gains are the establishment's loss and vice versa. [orig. (U.S.) a place where liquor was obtained and carried away in buckets brought by the customers]

buckeye (bŭk′ī′), *n.* any of various trees or shrubs of the U.S., genus *Aesculus*, allied to the true horse chestnut, as *A. glabra* (**Ohio buckeye**), a large tree with an ill-smelling bark. [f. BUCK[1] stag + EYE, in allusion to the appearance of the seed]

Buckhaven (bŭk′hā′vən), *n.* a burgh in Scotland, in SE Fife. with Methil 21,104 (1961).

buckhorn (bŭk′hôn′), *n.* the hard material of which a buck's horn consists, used to manufacture knife handles, etc. Also, **buck's-horn.**

buckhound (bŭk′hound′), *n.* a hound for hunting bucks, etc., similar to the staghound, but smaller.

Buckingham (bŭk′ĭng əm), *n.* **1. George Villiers** (vĭl′əz, -yəz), **1st Duke of,** 1592–1628, English courtier, politician, and military leader: lord high admiral, 1617. **2.** his son, **George Villiers, 2nd Duke of,** 1628–87, English courtier and writer. **3.** Buckinghamshire.

Buckingham Palace, the London residence of the British sovereign, at the west end of St James's Park.

Buckinghamshire (bŭk′ĭng əm shĭə′, -shə), *n.* a county in S England. 486,183 pop. (1961); 749 sq. mi. *Co. town:* Aylesbury. Also, **Buckingham.** *Abbrev.:* Bucks.

buckish (bŭk′ĭsh), *adj.* **1.** (of a horse) inclined to buck. **2.** *Slang* (of a person) in fine form; fit and lively. **3.** foppish; dapper. —**buck′ishly,** *adv.* —**buck′ishness,** *n.*

buckjump (bŭk′jŭmp′), *v.i. Chiefly Austral.* (of a horse) to buck. [f. BUCK[2] + JUMP]

buckjumper (bŭk′jŭm′pə), *n. Chiefly Austral.* **1.** a horse which bucks. **2.** a rider of such a horse.

buckle (bŭk′l), *n., v.,* **-led, -ling.** —*n.* **1.** a clasp consisting of a rectangular or curved rim with one or more movable tongues, used for fastening together two loose ends, as of a belt or strap. **2.** any similar contrivance used for such a purpose. **3.** an ornament of metal, beads, etc., of similar appearance. **4.** a bend, bulge, or kink, as in a saw blade. —*v.t.* **5.** to fasten with a buckle or buckles. **6.** to bend and shrivel, by applying heat or pressure; warp; curl. **7.** to prepare (oneself) for action; apply (oneself) vigorously to something. —*v.i.* **8.** to set to work with vigour (fol. by *down to* or (absolutely) *to*). **9.** to bend, warp, or give way suddenly, as with heat or pressure. **10.** to grapple; contend. [ME *bocle*, t. F: m. *boucle* buckle, boss of a shield, g. L *buccula*, dim. of *bucca* cheek, mouth]

Buckle (bŭk′l), *n.* **Henry Thomas,** 1821–62, English historian.

buckler (bŭk′lə), *n.* **1.** a round shield, with grip for holding, and sometimes with straps through which the arm is passed. **2.** any means of defence; a protection. [ME *bokeler*, t. OF: m. *boucler* shield, orig., one with a boss, der. *boucle* boss. See BUCKLE, n.]

buckler-fern (bŭk′lə fûn′), *n.* any of several species of ferns of the genus *Dryopteris*, as *D. dilatata*, the **broad buckler-fern.**

Buckley's chance (bŭk′lĭz), *Austral., N.Z. Colloq.* a very slim chance; forlorn hope. [prob. after William *Buckley*, died 1856, Australian convict]

buckra (bŭk′rə), *n.* a white man (used among the Negroes of the African coast, the West Indies, and the southern U.S.). [? t. West African (Calabar): m. *mbākara* demon, powerful being, white man]

buck rarebit, a dish consisting of Welsh rarebit topped by a poached egg. Also, **buck rabbit.**

buckram (bŭk′rəm), *n., v.,* **-ramed, -raming.** —*n.* **1.** stiff cotton fabric for interlining, binding books, etc. **2.** stiffness of manner; extreme preciseness or formality. —*v.t.* **3.** to strengthen with buckram. **4.** to give (a person, etc.) a false appearance of importance or strength. [ME *bokeram.* Cf. OF *boquerant*, It. *bucherame*, ? ult. der. BUKHARA, where the cloth was exported]

Bucks., Buckinghamshire.

bucksaw (bŭk′sô′), *n.* a saw consisting of a blade set across an upright frame or bow, one bar of which is extended to form a handle, used with both hands in cutting wood.

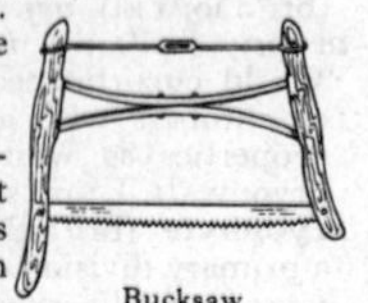
Bucksaw

b., blend of, blended; c., cognate with; d., dialect, dialectal; der., derived from; f., formed from; g., going back to; m., modification of; r., replacing; s., stem of; t., taken from; ?, perhaps. See full key on inside front cover.

buckshee (bŭk′shē′), *adj.* *Slang.* free of charge. [var. of BAKSHEESH]

buck's-horn (bŭks′hôrn′), *n.* buckhorn.

buck's-horn plantain, a small biennial herbaceous plant, *Plantago coronopus,* found in sandy coastal districts.

buckshot (bŭk′shŏt′), *n.* a large size of lead shot used on big game.

buckskin (bŭk′skĭn′), *n.* **1.** the skin of a buck or deer. **2.** a strong, soft, yellowish or greyish leather, orig. prepared from deerskin, now usually from sheepskin. **3.** (*pl.*) *U.S.* breeches made of buckskin.

buckthorn (bŭk′thôrn′), *n.* **1.** any of several trees or shrubs (sometimes thorny) belonging to the genus *Rhamnus,* as *R. cathartica,* a shrub whose berries were formerly much used in medicine as a purgative, and *R. frangula,* yielding the **buckthorn bark** used in medicine. **2.** a tree or shrub of the sapotaceous genus *Bumelia,* esp. *B. lycioides,* a tree common in the southern U.S.

bucktooth (bŭk′to͞oth′), *n., pl.* **-teeth** (-tēth′). a projecting tooth.

buckwheat (bŭk′wēt′), *n.* **1.** a herbaceous plant, *Fagopyrum sagittatum,* cultivated for its triangular seeds, which are used as a food for animals, and in the U.S. made into a flour for cakes, etc. **2.** the seeds of the buckwheat. **3.** buckwheat flour. [f. *buck* (OE *bōc* beech) + WHEAT. Cf. D *boekweit,* G *Buckweizen* buckwheat, lit., beech wheat; so called from its beechnut-shaped seed]

bucolic (byo͞o kŏl′ĭk), *adj.* Also, **bucol′ical. 1.** of or pertaining to shepherds; pastoral. **2.** rustic; rural; agricultural: *bucolic isolation* —*n.* **3.** a farmer; a shepherd; a rustic. **4.** a pastoral poem. [t. L: s. *būcolicus,* t. Gk: m. *boukolikós* rustic] —**bucol′ically,** *adv.*

Bucovina (bo͞o′kə vē′nə; *Rum.* bo͞o kȯ vē′nȧ), *n.* Bukovina.

Bucureşti (*Rum.* bo͞o ko͞o rĕshty′), *n.* Rumanian name of **Bucharest.**

bud[1] (bŭd), *n., v.,* **budded, budding.** —*n.* **1.** *Bot.* **a.** a small axillary or terminal protuberance on a plant, containing rudimentary foliage (**leaf bud**), the rudimentary inflorescence (**flower bud**), or both (**mixed bud**). **b.** an undeveloped or rudimentary stem or branch of a plant. **2.** *Zool.* (in certain animals of low organization) a prominence which develops into a new individual, sometimes permanently attached to the parent and sometimes becoming detached; a gemma. **3.** *Anat.* any small rounded part, as a tactile bud or a gustatory bud. **4.** an immature or undeveloped person or thing. **5. nip in the bud,** to stop (something) before it really gets started. —*v.i.* **6.** to put forth or produce buds, as a plant. **7.** to begin to grow and develop. **8.** to be in an early stage of development. —*v.t.* **9.** to cause to bud. **10.** *Hort.* to graft by inserting a single bud into the stock. [ME *budde*; orig. uncert.]

Leaf buds of the elm (def. 1a)

bud[2] (bŭd), *n.* *U.S. Colloq.* **1.** brother. **2.** man or boy (as a term of address). [alter. of BROTHER]

Budapest (byo͞o′də pĕst′; *Hung.* bo͞o′dŏ pĕsht), *n.* the capital of Hungary, on the Danube: formed by the union of the cities of Buda and Pest (1872). 1,875,000 (1960).

Buddha (bo͝od′ə), *n.* 'The Enlightened One', a title applied esp. to the great religious teacher, variously known as Siddhartha and Gautama (or Gotama), or Sakyamuni, who flourished in India about the 6th century B.C., regarded by his followers as the latest of a series of teachers (Buddhas) possessing perfect enlightenment and wisdom. [t. Skt: wise, enlightened]

Buddhism (bo͝od′ĭz′əm), *n.* the cult, founded by Buddha, which teaches that life is intrinsically full of suffering and that the supreme felicity (Nirvana) is to be striven for by psychological and ethical self-culture. —**Bud′dhist,** *n., adj.* —**Buddhis′tic,** *adj.*

buddle (bŭd′l), *n., v.,* **-dled, -dling,** *Mining.* —*n.* **1.** an inclined trough used for washing ore. —*v.t.* **2.** to wash (ore) with a buddle. [orig. unknown]

buddleia (bŭd′lĭ ə), *n.* any shrub of the genus *Buddleia,* mainly tropical ornamental perennials of the family *Loganiaceae,* having a two-celled, many-seeded fruit. [NL; after Adam *Buddle,* died 1715, English botanist]

buddy (bŭd′ĭ), *n., pl.* **-dies.** *U.S. Colloq.* a comrade or mate. [see BUD[2]]

Budeonny (bo͞o dĕn′ĭ; *Russ.* bo͞o dyôn′nĭy), *n.* **Semeon Mikhailovich** (*Russ.* sĭ myôn mĭ KHȧy′lə vĭch), born 1883, Russian general in 1917 Revolution and World War II.

budge (bŭj), *v.,* **budged, budging.** —*v.i.* **1.** to move slightly; give way (usually with negative). —*v.t.* **2.** to cause to budge (usually with negative). [t. F: m. s. *bouger,* ult. der. L *bullire* BOIL[1]]

Budge (bŭj), *n.* **Sir Ernest Alfred Wallis,** 1857–1934, English archaeologist and Egyptologist.

budgeree (bŭj′ə rē′, bŭj′ə rē′), *adj.* *Austral. Slang.* good, fine. [t. native Australian]

budgerigar (bŭj′ə rĭ gä′), *n.* a small parakeet of Australia, *Melopsittacus undulatus.* [t. native Australian]

budget (bŭj′ĭt), *n., v.,* **-eted, -eting.** —*n.* **1.** an estimate, often itemized, of expected income and expenditure, or operating results, for a given period in the future. **2.** specifically, the economic proposals made annually by the British Chancellor of the Exchequer in the House of Commons. **3.** a plan of operations based on such an estimate. **4.** an itemized allotment of funds for a given period. **5.** a stock; a collection. **6.** *Obs.* a small bag; a pouch. —*v.t.* **7.** to plan allotment of (funds, time, etc.). **8.** to deal with (specific funds) in a budget. [late ME *bougette,* t. F, dim. of *bouge* bag, g. L *bulga*] —**budgetary** (bŭj′ĭ tə rĭ, -trĭ), *adj.*

budget account, an account with a department store, etc., enabling a customer to obtain goods of a specified value, and pay for them over a maximum of eight months.

budgie (bŭj′ĭ), *n.* *Colloq.* budgerigar.

Budweis (*Ger.* bo͞ot′vīs), *n.* German name of **České Budějovice.**

Buenos Aires (bwā′nəs ī′rĭz; *Sp.* bwĕ′nȯs ȧy′rĕs), a seaport in and the capital of Argentina, in the E part, on the river Plate. 2,966,816 (1960).

buff[1] (bŭf), *n.* **1.** a kind of thick leather, orig. and properly made of buffalo skin but later also of other skins, light yellow with napped surface, used for making belts, pouches, etc. **2.** a thick coat of buff leather, worn esp. by soldiers. **3.** yellowish brown; medium or light tan. **4.** a buffwheel. **5.** *Colloq.* the bare skin. —*adj.* **6.** made of buff (leather). **7.** having the colour of buff. —*v.t.* **8.** to polish (metal) or to give a grainless finish of high lustre to (plated surfaces). **9.** to dye or stain in a buff colour. [appar. for earlier *buffle,* t. F: buffalo, t. It.: m. *bufalo.* See BUFFALO]

buff[2] (bŭf), *v.t.* **1.** to reduce or deaden the force of, as a buffer. —*n.* **2.** a blow; a slap; a buffet: *blindman's buff.* [late ME *buffe,* ? t. OF; or back-formation from BUFFET[1]. But cf. LG *buff* blow]

buffalo (bŭf′ə lō′), *n., pl.* **-loes, -los,** (*esp. collectively*) **-lo.** any of several mammals of the ox kind, as **1.** *Bos bubalus* or *Bubalus buffelus,* an Old World species, orig. from India, valued as a draught animal. **2.** *Bos caffer* or *Bubalus caffer* (**Cape buffalo**), a species of southern Africa. **3.** *Bison bison* (the **American buffalo** or bison). [t. It.: m. *bufalo,* g. d. L *būfalus,* var. of *būbalus* BUBAL]

Buffalo (bŭf′ə lō′), *n.* **1.** a city in the U.S., in W New York State; a port on Lake Erie. 532,759 (1960). **2.** a river in the Republic of South Africa flowing S through Natal to the Tugela river. ab. 200 mi.

Buffalo Bill. See **Cody, William Frederick.**

buffalo grass, 1. a short grass, *Buchloë dactyloides,* very prevalent on the dry plains of the Midwestern U.S. **2.** any of many species of short grasses.

Buffalo Indian, Plains Indian.

buffer[1] (bŭf′ə), *n.* **1.** an apparatus, such as one of the two at each end of a railway carriage, for absorbing the concussion between a moving body and something against which it strikes. **2.** anything serving to neutralize the shock of opposing forces. **3.** *Electronics.* a circuit which links two electronic systems which cannot be joined directly together. —*v.t.* **4.** *Chem.* to oppose a change of composition, especially of acidity or alkalinity. [f. BUFF[2], v. + -ER[1]]

buffer[2] (bŭf′ə), *n.* **1.** a device for polishing; buffwheel or buffstick. **2.** one who uses such a device. [f. BUFF[1] + -ER[1]]

buffer[3] (bŭf′ə), *n.* a foolish man, especially one elderly and pompous. [ME, ? alter. of BUFFOON]

buffer solution, *Chem.* a solution whose acidity or alkalinity remains almost unchanged by dilution or by the addition of acid or alkali.

buffer state, a smaller state lying between potentially hostile larger states.

buffet[1] (bŭf′ĭt), *n., v.,* **-feted, -feting.** —*n.* **1.** a blow, as with the hand or fist. —*v.t.* **2.** to strike, as with the hand or fist. **3.** to contend against; battle. —*v.i.* **4.** to struggle with blows of hand or fist. **5.** to force one's way by a fight, struggle, etc. [ME, t. OF, dim. of *buffe* a blow] —**buf′feter,** *n.*

buffet[2] (bo͝of′ā *for 1, 2, 3, and 5*; bŭf′ĭt or bo͝of′ā *for 4*; *Fr.* bʏ fĕ′), *n.* **1.** a counter, bar, or the like, for lunch or refreshments. **2.** a restaurant containing such a counter or bar. **3.** a meal so served. **4.** a sideboard or cabinet for holding china, plate, etc. —*adj.* **5.** (of a meal) spread on tables or buffets from which the guests serve themselves. [t. F: orig., chair, table]

Buffet (*Fr.* bʏ fĕ′), *n.* **Bernard** (*Fr.* bĕr nȧr′), born 1928, French painter.

buffeting (bŭf′ĭ tĭng), *n.* **1.** a pushing or jostling, as by wind. **2.** a series of physical or mental blows. **3.** *Aeron.*

the vibration of all or part of an aircraft, induced by its own aerodynamic wake.

buffing wheel (bŭf′ĭng), buffwheel.

bufflehead (bŭf′əl hĕd′), *n.* **1.** a small North American duck, *Glaucionetta albeola*, the male of which has fluffy head plumage; butterball. **2.** a foolish, ignorant fellow. [f. *buffle* buffalo + HEAD]

buffo (bōōf′ō; *It.* bōōf′fô), *n.*, *pl.* **-fi** (-fē). *Music.* (in opera) a comedy part, usually bass. [t. It.: ridiculous, der. *buffare* blow with puffed cheeks]

Buffon (*Fr.* bʏ fôɴ′), *n.* **Georges Louis Leclerc** (*Fr.* zhôrzh lwē lə klĕr′), **Comte de** (kôɴt də), 1707–88, French naturalist.

buffoon (bə fōōn′), *n.* **1.** one who amuses others by tricks, odd gestures and postures, jokes, etc. **2.** one given to coarse or undignified joking. [t. F: m. *bouffon*, t. It.: m. *buffone* jester, der. *buffa* a jest] **—buffoonery** (bə fōō′nə rĭ), *n.* **—buffoon′ish,** *adj.*

buffstick (bŭf′stĭk′), *n.* a small stick covered with leather or the like, used in polishing.

buffwheel (bŭf′wēl′), *n.* a wheel for polishing metal, etc., usually covered with leather bearing a polishing powder.

bufo (bōō′fō), *n.* any member of the *Bufonidae* family of toads. Also, **bufo frog.**

bug (bŭg), *n.*, *v.t.*, **bugged, bugging.** *—n.* **1.** *Chiefly U.S.* loosely, any insect, esp. one of the suborder *Heteroptera* (order *Hemiptera*), characterized by having the forewings thickened at base and membranous at tip, and the hindwings membranous. Sucking mouth parts enable the majority to suck plant juices and others to feed on animals, including man. **2.** the bedbug. **3.** *Colloq.* a malady, esp. a virus infection. **4.** (*often pl.*) *Colloq.* defect or difficulty: *eliminating the bugs in television.* **5.** *Colloq.* an idea or belief with which one is obsessed. **6.** a bogy; hobgoblin. **7.** *Slang.* a microphone hidden in a room to tap conversation. *—v.t.* **8.** *Slang.* to install a bug in (a room, etc.). **9.** *Slang.* to cause inconvenience or distress to (a person). **10.** to put a sudden end to (a plan, etc.). [ME *bugge.* Cf. Welsh *bug* bogy, ghost]

Bug (*Pol. and Russ.* bōōk), *n.* **1.** a river forming part of the boundary between E Poland and the W Soviet Union, flowing NW to the Vistula. 450 mi. **2.** a river in the SW Soviet Union, flowing SE to the estuary of the Dnieper. 470 mi.

bugaboo (bŭg′ə bōō′), *n.*, *pl.* **-boos.** some imaginary thing that causes fear or worry; a bugbear; a bogy. [f. BUG bogy + BOO (def. 1); for the *-a-*, cf. BLACKAMOOR]

Buganda (bōō găn′də), *n.* a province of Uganda, in the SE part.

bugbane (bŭg′bān′), *n.* *Chiefly U.S.* any of various tall erect herbs of the ranunculaceous genus *Cimicifuga*, as *C. americana* of the eastern U.S., bearing clusters of white flowers supposed to repel insects.

bugbear (bŭg′bĕə′), *n.* **1.** any source, real or imaginary, of needless fright or fear. **2.** *Obs.* a goblin that eats up naughty children. [f. BUG (def. 6) + BEAR[2]]

bugger (bŭg′ə), *n.* **1.** one who practises bestiality or sodomy. **2.** *Taboo Slang.* a foul, contemptible person. **3.** *Taboo Slang.* (not always pejorative) person; child. *—v.t.* **4.** to practise bestiality or sodomy on. **5.** *Taboo Slang.* to cause damage, frustration, or inconvenience to. *—v.i.* **6. bugger off,** *Taboo Slang.* (abusively) to remove oneself; depart. *—interj.* **7.** *Taboo.* (a strong exclamation of annoyance, disgust, etc.) [t. F: m. *bougre*, t. ML: m. s. *Bulgarus* a Bulgarian, a heretic; certain Bulgarian heretics being charged with this activity] **—bug′gery,** *n.*

buggy[1] (bŭg′ĭ), *n.*, *pl.* **-gies.** **1.** a two-wheeled horse-drawn carriage with or without a hood. **2.** *U.S.* a light four-wheeled carriage with a single seat and a transverse spring. **3.** *Colloq.* a motor car. [orig. uncert.]

buggy[2] (bŭg′ĭ), *adj.*, **-gier, -giest.** infested with bugs. [f. BUG + -Y[1]]

bug-hunter (bŭg′hŭn′tə), *n.* *Colloq.* a collecting entomologist.

bugle[1] (byōō′gl), *n.*, *v.*, **-gled, -gling.** *—n.* **1.** a cornet-like military wind instrument, usually metal, used for sounding signals and sometimes furnished with keys or valves. *—v.i.* **2.** to sound a bugle. [ME, t. OF, f. L *būculus*, dim. of *bōs* ox] **—bu′gler,** *n.*

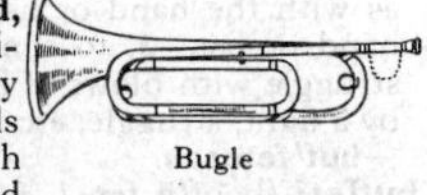
Bugle

bugle[2] (byōō′gl), *n.* any plant of the menthaceous genus *Ajuga*, esp. *A. reptans*, a low, blue-flowered herb. [t. F, g. LL *bugula* kind of plant]

bugle[3] (byōō′gl), *n.* a tubular glass bead, usually black, used for ornamenting dresses. [orig. uncert.]

bugloss (byōō′glŏs), *n.* any of various boraginaceous plants, as *Anchusa officinalis*, a European medicinal herb with rough leaves, and *Lycopsis arvensis*, a bristly, blue-flowered herb. [t. F: m. *buglosse*, t. L: m. *būglossa*, t. Gk: m. *boúglōssos* ox-tongue]

bugong (byōō′gŏng), *n.* an Australian noctuid moth, *Agrotis infusa.* Also, **bogong.** [t. native Australian]

buhl (bōōl), *n.* elaborate inlaid work of woods, metals, tortoiseshell, ivory, etc. Also, **buhlwork** (bōōl′wûk′). [appar. Germanized sp. of F *boulle* or *boule*, named after A. C. *Boulle* or *Boule*, 1642–1732, French cabinet-maker]

buhrstone (bû′stōn′), *n.* burstone.

build (bĭld), *v.*, **built** or (*Archaic*) **builded, building,** *n.* *—v.t.* **1.** to construct (something relatively complex) by assembling and combining parts: *build a house or an empire.* **2.** to establish, increase, and strengthen (often fol. by *up*): *build up a business.* **3.** to base; form; construct: *to build one's hopes on promises.* **4.** to fill in with houses (usually fol. by *up*). **5.** *Games.* **a.** to make (words) from letters. **b.** to add (cards) to each other according to number, suit, etc. **6.** to claim public attention for (a person or product) by means of an advertising campaign (fol. by *up*). *—v.i.* **7.** to engage in the art or business of building. **8.** to form or construct a plan, system of thought, etc. (fol. by *on* or *upon*). *—n.* **9.** manner or form of construction: *a person's build.* [ME *bilden, bulde(n)*, OE *byldan*, der. *bold* dwelling, house]

builder (bĭl′də), *n.* **1.** a person who builds. **2.** a person who contracts for the construction of buildings and supervises the workmen who build them.

building (bĭl′dĭng), *n.* **1.** anything built or constructed. **2.** the act, business, or art of constructing houses, etc. **—Syn.** **1.** BUILDING, EDIFICE, STRUCTURE refer to something built. BUILDING and STRUCTURE may apply to either a finished or an unfinished product of construction, and carry no implications as to size or condition. EDIFICE is not only a more formal word but narrower in application, referring to a completed structure, and usually a large and imposing one. BUILDING generally connotes a useful purpose (houses, schools, business offices, etc.); STRUCTURE suggests the planning and constructive process.

building line, a boundary set on either side of a street by a planning authority, beyond which buildings may not project.

building society, a business organization that advances money to enable people to buy or build a house.

build-up (bĭld′ŭp′), *n.* **1.** any progressive increase. **2.** *Mil.* a concentration of troops, etc., for an offensive. **3.** a publicity campaign on behalf of a person or a product.

built (bĭlt), *v.* pt. and pp. of **build.**

built-in (bĭlt′ĭn′), *adj.* built so as to be an integral, permanent part of a larger unit, as a bookcase.

built-up area (bĭlt′ŭp′), an area of dense habitation, within which speed-limits apply to traffic.

Buitenzorg (*Du.* bœy′tən zôrкн), *n.* the former Dutch name of **Bogor.**

B.U.J., (L *Baccalaureus utriusque juris*) Bachelor of Canon and Civil Law.

Bujumbura (bōō′jəm bōōə′rə), *n.* a town in and the capital of Burundi. 70,000 (est. 1966).

Bukhara (*Russ.* bōō кнä′rə), *n.* **1.** a former state in W Asia: now a region in the Uzbek Republic of the Soviet Union. **2.** the chief city of this region. 50,400 (est. 1964). Also, **Bokhara.**

Bukharin (*Russ.* bōō кнä′rĭn), *n.* **Nikolai Ivanovich** (*Russ.* nĭ kä lăy′ ĭ vän′ə vĭch), 1888–1938, Soviet editor, writer, and communist leader.

Bukovina (bōō′kə vē′nə; *Rum.* bōō kô vē′nä), *n.* **1.** a former province in N Rumania. 1912 sq. mi. **2. Northern,** a region in the SW Soviet Union, in the Ukrainian Republic: formerly a part of Rumania. Also, **Bucovina.**

Bulawayo (bōōl′ə wä′ō), *n.* a city in SW Rhodesia: mining centre. 214,400 (est. 1964).

bulb (bŭlb), *n.* **1.** *Bot.* **a.** a bud, having fleshy leaves and usually subterranean, in which the stem is reduced to a flat disc, rooting from the underside, as in the onion, lily, etc. **b.** a plant growing from a bulb. **2.** any round, enlarged part, esp. one at the end of a long, slender body: *the bulb of a thermometer.* **3.** *Elect.* **a.** the glass housing, in which partial vacuum has been established, which contains the filament of an incandescent electric lamp. **b.** an incandescent electric lamp. **4.** a valve (def. 7). **5.** *Anat.* **a. bulb of the spinal cord** or **brain,** the medulla oblongata. **b. bulb of the urethra,** the rounded mass of erectile tissue that surrounds the urethra at the posterior end of the penis, just in front of the anus. [t. L: s. *bulbus*, t. Gk: m. *bolbós*] **—bulbar** (bŭl′bə), *adj.* **—bulb′like′,** *adj.*

bulbiferous (bŭl bĭf′ə rəs), *adj.* producing bulbs.

bulbil (bŭl′bĭl), *n.* *Bot.* **1.** a little bulb. **2.** a small aerial bulb growing in the axils of leaves, as in the tiger lily, or replacing flower buds, as in the common onion. [t. NL: m. s. *bulbillus*, dim. of L *bulbus* BULB]

bulbous (bŭl′bəs), *adj.* **1.** bulb-shaped; bulging. **2.** having, or growing from, bulbs. Also, **bulbaceous** (bŭl bā′shəs).

bulbul (bōōl′bōōl), *n.* any bird of the tropical oriental

family *Pycnonotidae*, much referred to in Persian poetry, and noted as songsters. [t. Pers.]
Bulg., 1. Bulgaria. 2. Bulgarian.
Bulganin (bo͝ol gä′nĭn; *Russ.* bo͝ol gä′nĭn), *n.* **Nikolai Aleksandrovich** (*Russ.* nĭ kä lāy′ə lĭk sän′drə vĭch), born 1895, Soviet statesman: prime minister 1955–58.
Bulgar (bŭl′gä, bo͝ol′gä), *n.* Bulgarian.
Bulgaria (bŭl gĕə′rĭ ə, bo͝ol-), *n.* a republic in SE Europe. 8,226,564 pop. (1965); 42,818 sq. mi. *Cap.*: Sofia.
Bulgarian (bŭl gĕə′rĭ ən, bo͝ol-), *n.* **1.** a native or inhabitant of Bulgaria. **2.** a Slavic language, the language of Bulgaria. —*adj.* **3.** of or pertaining to Bulgaria, its people, or their language.
bulge (bŭlj), *n.*, *v.*, **bulged, bulging.** —*n.* **1.** a rounded projecting or protruding part; protuberance; hump. **2.** *Obs. Naut.* the bilge, or bottom of a ship's hull. —*v.i.* **3.** to swell out; be protuberant. —*v.t.* **4.** to make protuberant. [ME, t. OF: m. *boulge*, g. L *bulga* bag, of Celtic orig.] —**bulg′y,** *adj.*
Bulge (bŭlj), *n.* **Battle of the,** the final German counter-offensive of World War II, begun Dec. 16th, 1944, and thrusting deep into Allied territory in N and E Belgium: repulsed, Jan., 1945.
bulger (bŭl′jə), *n.* *Golf.* a club with a convex face.
bulimia (byo͞o lĭm′ĭ ə), *n.* *Pathol.* morbidly voracious appetite; a disease marked by constant hunger. Also, **bulimy** (byo͞o′lĭ mĭ). [t. NL, t. Gk: m. *boulīmía* great hunger] —**bulim′ic,** *adj.*
bulk (bŭlk), *n.* **1.** magnitude in three dimensions: *a ship of great bulk.* **2.** the greater part; the main mass or body: *the bulk of a debt.* **3.** goods or cargo not in packages, boxes, bags, etc. **4. in bulk, a.** unpackaged. **b.** in large quantities. **5.** *Rare.* the body of any large living creature. —*v.i.* **6.** to be of bulk, size, weight, or importance. [ME *bolke* heap, t. Scand.; cf. Icel. *búlki* heap, cargo] —**Syn. 1.** See **size.**
bulkhead (bŭlk′hĕd′), *n.* **1.** *Naut.* one of the upright partitions dividing a ship into compartments. **2.** a partition built to withstand pressure, as between the airlock and the cabin of a submarine or spacecraft. **3.** *Civ. Eng.* a partition built in a subterranean passage to prevent the passage of air, water, or mud. **4.** *Bldg Trades.* **a.** a horizontal or inclined outside door over a stairway leading to a cellar. **b.** a boxlike structure on a roof, etc., covering the head of a staircase or other opening.
bulky (bŭl′kĭ), *adj.*, **bulkier, bulkiest.** of great and cumbersome bulk or size. —**bulk′ily,** *adv.* —**bulk′iness,** *n.* —**Syn.** massive, ponderous, unwieldy.
bull[1] (bo͝ol), *n.* **1.** the male of a bovine animal, esp. of the genus *Bos*, with sexual organs intact and capable of reproduction. **2.** the male of certain other animals: *a bull elephant.* **3.** a violent or powerful, bull-like person. **4.** (in general business) one who believes that conditions are or will be favourable. **5.** *Stock Exchange.* one who buys in the hope of selling later at a profit due to a rise in prices (opposed to *bear*). **6.** (*cap.*) *Astron.* **a.** the zodiacal constellation Taurus. **b.** the sign named after it. **7.** *Mil. Slang.* the polishing and cleaning of equipment. **8.** *Slang.* nonsense. **9.** *Slang.* boastful talk. —*adj.* **10.** male. **11.** bull-like; large. **12.** (in the stock exchange, etc.) pertaining to the bulls; marked by a rise in price. —*v.t.* **13.** *Taboo Slang.* to have intercourse with (a woman). **14.** (in the stock exchange, etc.) to endeavour to raise the price of (stocks, etc.). **15.** to operate in, for a rise in price. [ME *bule*, OE *bula*; also ME *bulle*, OE *bull-* in *bulluc* bull calf. Cf. Icel. *boli*]
bull[2] (bo͝ol), *n.* a ludicrously inconsistent statement; an unintentional pun. Also, **Irish bull.** [ME, t. F: m. *boule* deceit, ? t. L: m. *bulla* bubble, knob]
bull[3] (bo͝ol), *n.* **1.** a bulla or seal. **2.** *Rom. Cath. Ch.* a formal papal document having a bulla attached. [ME *bulle*, t. L: m. *bulla*, ML seal, document, L bubble, knob]
bull[4] (bo͝ol), *n.* **1.** a bull's-eye (def. 1). **2.** a bull's-eye (def. 2). **3.** the score-value of a bull's-eye: *he scored a bull.*
Bull (bo͝ol), *n.* **1. John,** 1563–1628, English composer and organist. **2. John.** See **John Bull.**
bulla (bo͝ol′ə, bŭl′ə), *n.*, *pl.* **bullae** (bo͝ol′ē, bŭl′ē). **1.** a seal attached to an official document, as a papal bull. **2.** *Pathol.* **a.** a large vesicle. **b.** a blister-like or bubble-like part of a bone. [t. ML. See BULL[3]]
bullace (bo͝ol′ĭs), *n.* **1.** a rosaceous shrub or small tree, *Prunus domestica* subspecies *insititia*. **2.** the drupaceous fruit of this plant. [ME *bolace*, t. OF: m. *beloce*]
bullate (bo͝ol′āt, -ĭt, bŭl′-), *adj.* **1.** *Bot., Zool.* having the surface covered with irregular and slight elevations, giving a blistered appearance. **2.** *Anat.* inflated; vaulted. [t. L: m. s. *bullātus* having bubbles]
bullbat (bo͝ol′băt′), *n.* the nighthawk (def. 2).
bulldog (bo͝ol′dŏg′), *n.* **1.** a large-headed, short-haired, heavily built variety of dog, of comparatively small size but very muscular and courageous. **2.** a short-barrelled revolver of large calibre. **3.** the servant or assistant who accompanies the proctor at Oxford and Cambridge Universities when on duty. —*adj.* **4.** like or characteristic of a bulldog: *bulldog tenacity.*

English bulldog (13 in. or more high at the shoulder)

bulldog ant, a primitive ant, *Myrmecia gulosa*, of Australia, having a powerful sting.
bulldog clip, a type of spring-operated clip, originally having teeth-like serrations to hold papers, etc.
bulldoze (bo͝ol′dōz′), *v.t.*, **-dozed, -dozing.** **1.** *Slang.* to coerce or intimidate by violence or threats. **2.** to use a bulldozer on. [f. BULL[1] + *doze* (southern U.S. d. var. of DOSE), i.e., give a dose fit for a bull]
bulldozer (bo͝ol′dō′zə), *n.* **1.** a powerful caterpillar tractor having a vertical blade at the front end for moving earth, tree stumps, rocks, etc. **2.** *Slang.* a person who intimidates.
Buller (bo͝ol′ə), *n.* **1. Sir Redvers Henry** (rĕd′vəz), 1839–1908, British general in the Boer War. **2.** a river in NW South Island, New Zealand, flowing W to the Tasman Sea. 110 mi.
bullet (bo͝ol′ĭt), *n.* **1.** a small metal projectile, part of a cartridge, for firing from small arms. See diag. under **cartridge.** **2.** a small ball. [t. F: m. *boulet(te)*, dim. of *boule* ball]
bullet-head (bo͝ol′ĭt hĕd′), *n.* **1.** a round head. **2.** a person having such a head. **3.** an obstinate or stupid person. —**bul′let-head′ed,** *adj.*
bulletin (bo͝ol′ĭ tĭn), *n.* **1.** a brief account or statement, as of news or events, issued for the information of the public. **2.** a periodical publication, as of a learned society. —*v.t.* **3.** to make known by a bulletin. [t. F, t. It.: m. *bullettino*, dim. of *bulletta*, dim. of *bulla* edict. See BULL[3], BULLA]
bulletproof (bo͝ol′ĭt pro͞of′), *adj.* capable of resisting the impact of a bullet.
bullfight (bo͝ol′fīt′), *n.* a combat between men and a bull or bulls in an enclosed arena. —**bull′fight′er,** *n.* —**bull′fight′ing,** *n.*
bullfinch[1] (bo͝ol′fĭnch′), *n.* **1.** a rosy-breasted European fringilline bird, *Pyrrhula pyrrhula*, with a short, stout bill, valued as a cagebird. **2.** any of various allied or similar birds. [f. BULL[1] + FINCH]
bullfinch[2] (bo͝ol′fĭnch′), *n.* a hedge high enough to impede mounted hunters. [orig. uncert.]
bullfrog (bo͝ol′frŏg′), *n.* a large frog, as the American *Rana catesbeiana*, which has an exceptionally deep bass voice.
bullhead (bo͝ol′hĕd′), *n.* **1.** a small freshwater fish, *Cottus gobio*, having a number of strong spines, but devoid of scales. **2.** an obstinate or stupid person.
bull-headed (bo͝ol′hĕd′ĭd), *adj.* obstinate; blunderingly stubborn; stupid. —**bull′-head′edness,** *n.*
bullion (bo͝ol′yən), *n.* **1.** gold or silver in the mass. **2.** gold or silver in the form of bars or ingots. **3.** a cordlike trimming made of twisted gold or silver wire, or a trimming of cord covered with gold or silver thread (**bullion fringe**), used to ornament uniforms, etc. [ME *bullioun*, t. AF: m. *bullion* mint, der. *bouillir* boil, g. L *bullīre*; in part confused with OF *billon* debased metal]
bullish (bo͝ol′ĭsh), *adj.* **1.** like a bull. **2.** obstinate or stupid. **3.** (in the stock exchange, etc.) tending to cause a rise in price. **4.** optimistic.
bull-mastiff (bo͝ol′măs′tĭf), *n.* one of a breed of dogs produced by crossing the mastiff with the bulldog.
bull-necked (bo͝ol′nĕkt′), *adj.* thick-necked.
bull nose, **1.** *Vet. Sci.* a disease of swine caused by bacterial infection of the tissues of the snout causing gross malformation of the part and frequently serious blocking of the nasal passages. **2.** a brick having one corner rounded off.
bullock (bo͝ol′ək), *n.* a castrated male of a bovine animal, not having been used for reproduction; ox; steer. [ME *bullok*, OE *bulluc*. See BULL[1], -OCK]
bullocky (bo͝ol′ə kĭ), *n.* *Austral., N.Z.* the driver of a bullock team.
bullpen (bo͝ol′pĕn′), *n.* **1.** a pen for a bull or bulls. **2.** *U.S. Colloq.* a place for the temporary confinement of prisoners or suspects.
bullring (bo͝ol′rĭng′), *n.* an arena for a bullfight.
bullroarer (bo͝ol′rô′rə), *n.* a long, thin, narrow piece of wood attached to a string, by which it is whirled in the air, making a roaring sound: used for religious rites by certain primitive tribes, as Australian aborigines, American Indians, etc., and as a children's toy; thunder stick.

Bull Run, a small river in the U.S., in NE Virginia: two important battles of the American Civil War were fought near here, both resulting in defeat for the Union forces, 1861, 1862.

bull's-eye (bŏŏlz′ī′), *n.* **1.** the central spot, usually black, of a target. **2.** a shot that strikes the bull's-eye. **3.** a small circular opening or window. **4.** a thick disc or lenslike piece of glass inserted in a deck or the like to admit light. **5.** the central boss in a sheet of blown glass. **6.** *Naut.* an oval or circular wooden block having a groove around it and a hole in the centre through which to reeve a rope. **7.** a big, round, hard sweet, often of peppermint.

bullshit (bŏŏl′shĭt′), *n.* *Taboo.* **1.** the excrement of bulls. **2.** *Slang.* meaningless humbug. **3.** *Mil. Slang.* bull (def. 7).

bull's wool, *Austral., N.Z., Slang.* nonsense; humbug.

bull-terrier (bŏŏl′tĕr′rĭ ə), *n.* one of a breed of dogs produced by crossing the bulldog and the terrier.

Bull-terrier, white variety (18 in. high at the shoulder)

bull-trout (bŏŏl′trout′), *n.* **1.** the sea-trout. **2.** any large trout. **3.** the salmon.

bully[1] (bŏŏl′ĭ), *n., pl.* **-lies,** *v.,* **-lied, -lying,** *adj., interj.* —*n.* **1.** a blustering, quarrelsome, overbearing person who browbeats smaller or weaker people. **2.** *Archaic.* a man hired to do violence. **3.** *Obs.* a pimp; procurer. **4.** *Obs.* good friend; good fellow. **5.** *Obs.* sweetheart; darling. —*v.t.* **6.** to act the bully towards. —*v.i.* **7.** to be loudly arrogant and overbearing. —*adj.* **8.** *Colloq.* fine; excellent; very good. **9.** dashing; jovial; high-spirited. —*interj.* **10.** *Colloq.* good! well done! [t. D: m. *boele* lover]

bully[2] (bŏŏl′ĭ), *n.* bully beef. [? t. F: m. *bouilli* boiled beef, prop. pp. of *bouillir* boil]

bully[3] (bŏŏl′ĭ), *n.* *Hockey.* **1.** the procedure by which play is started or restarted. Two opposing players with the ball between them strike the ground and the opponent's stick alternately three times, and then try to strike the ball first. —*v.i.* **2.** Also, **bully off.** to start play in this way.

bully beef, *Colloq.* corned beef.

bullyrag (bŏŏl′ĭ răg′), *v.t.,* **-ragged, -ragging.** to bully; badger; abuse; tease. Also, **ballyrag.**

bully tree, any of various sapotaceous trees of tropical America, as *Manilkara bidentata* of Guiana, which yields the gum balata. [*bully,* said to be m. BALATA]

Bülow (*Ger.* bʏ′lō), *n.* **1. Prince Bernhard von** (*Ger.* bĕrn′hȧrt fōn), 1849–1929, chancellor of Germany, 1900–09. **2. Friedrich Wilhelm, Baron von,** 1755–1816, Prussian general. **3. Hans Guido von** (*Ger.* hȧns gē′dō fōn), 1830–94, German pianist and conductor.

bulrush (bŏŏl′rŭsh′), *n.* **1.** (in biblical use) the papyrus, *Cyperus papyrus.* **2.** any of various large rushes or rushlike plants of the genus *Scirpus,* as *S. lacustris,* a tall perennial from which mats, bottoms of chairs, etc., are made. [f. *bull* large (cf. BULL-TROUT) + RUSH[2]]

bulwark (bŏŏl′wək), *n.* **1.** *Fort.* a defensive mound of earth or other material situated round a place; a rampart. **2.** any protection against annoyance or injury from outside. **3.** (*usually pl.*) *Naut.* a solid part of a ship's side extending like a fence above the level of the deck. —*v.t.* **4.** to fortify with a bulwark or rampart; secure by a fortification; protect. [ME *bulwerk.* Cf. G *Bollwerk,* appar. orig. bole (tree trunk) work. Cf. BOULEVARD]

Bulwer (bŏŏl′wə), *n.* **William Henry Lytton Earle** (lĭt′n) (*Baron Dalling and Bulwer*), 1801–72, British diplomat and author, known as Sir Henry Bulwer.

Bulwer-Lytton (bŏŏl′wə lĭt′n), *n.* See **Lytton.**

bum (bŭm), *n., v.,* **bummed, bumming.** —*n.* **1.** *Taboo.* the rump; buttocks. **2.** a shiftless or dissolute person. **3.** a habitual loafer and tramp. **4.** *Slang.* a drunken orgy; a debauch. —*v.t.* **5.** *Slang.* to get for nothing; borrow without expectation of returning. —*v.i.* **6.** *Slang.* to sponge on others for a living; lead an idle or dissolute life. —*adj.* **7.** *Slang.* of poor, wretched, or miserable quality; bad. [akin to BUMP] —**bum′mer,** *n.*

bumbailiff (bŭm′bā′lĭf), *n.* *Archaic.* (contemptuous) a bailiff or underbailiff employed in serving writs, making arrests, etc.

bumblebee (bŭm′bl bē′), *n.* any of various large, hairy social bees of the family *Bombidae.* Also, **humblebee.** [f. *bumble* buzz + BEE[1]]

Bumblebee (worker), *Bombus terrestris* (Length ⅞ in.)

bumbledom (bŭm′bl dəm), *n.* a petty officiousness in a minor office. [after *Bumble* in Dickens's '*Oliver Twist*']

bumboat (bŭm′bōt′), *n.* *Naut.* a boat used in peddling provisions and small wares among vessels lying in port or offshore. —**bumboatman** (bŭm′bōt′mən), *n.*

bumf (bŭmpf, bŭmf), *n.* bumph.

bumkin (bŭm′kĭn), *n.* *Naut.* a bumpkin[2].

bummalo (bŭm′ə lō′), *n.* Bombay duck. [t. Marathi: m. *bombīla*]

bummaree (bŭm′ə rē′), *n.* **1.** a dealer at a fish market, esp. Billingsgate. **2.** a porter at Smithfield meat market. [orig. obscure]

bump (bŭmp), *v.t.* **1.** to come more or less heavily in contact with; strike; collide with. **2.** to cause to strike or collide: *to bump one's head against the wall.* **3.** *Colloq.* to increase (in extent, etc.) (fol. by *up*). **4.** *Chiefly School Slang.* to toss, as in a sheet or holding by the arms and legs, usually to celebrate the birthday of the person bumped. **5.** *Rowing.* to beat in a race by making a successful bump on. **6.** *Cricket.* to bowl (the ball) in such a way that it bounces high on pitching. **7. bump off,** *Colloq.* to kill. —*v.i.* **8.** to come in contact with; collide (often fol. by *against, into*). **9.** to jolt in the course of movement (often fol. by *about*). **10.** *Rowing.* to make a successful bump. **11.** *Cricket.* (of the ball) to bounce high on pitching when bowled. —*n.* **12.** the act of bumping; a blow. **13.** a dull thud; the noise of collision. **14.** the shock of a blow or collision. **15.** a swelling or contusion from a blow. **16.** a small area raised above the level of the surrounding surface, as on the skull or on a road. **17.** *Aeron.* a rapidly rising current of air which gives an aeroplane a dangerous jolt or upward thrust. **18.** *Rowing.* the contact between the bows of the pursuing boat and the stern or any other part of the pursued, by which the pursuer is deemed successful in the race and starts the next day's racing ahead of the bumped boat. [imit.]

bump ball, *Cricket.* a ball which strikes the ground immediately after being struck by the batsman, and which therefore does not put him out if it is caught.

bumper (bŭm′pə), *n.* **1.** a person or thing that bumps. **2.** a horizontal bar affixed to the front or rear of a vehicle to give some protection in collisions. **3.** a cup or glass filled to the brim, esp. when drunk as a toast. **4.** *Colloq.* something unusually large or full. —*adj.* **5.** unusually abundant: *bumper crops.* **6.** *Cricket.* a ball which is so bowled that it bounces high when it pitches; bouncer. —*v.t.* **7.** to fill to the brim. **8.** to drink a bumper as a toast to. —*v.i.* **9.** to drink toasts.

bumph (bŭmpf, bŭmf), *n.* **1.** written information, esp. when presented in wordy officialese. **2.** *Slang.* toilet paper. Also, **bumf.** [var. of BUMF, short for *bum fodder*]

bumping race, *Rowing.* a race in which the object is to catch up and bump the boat in front.

bumpkin[1] (bŭmp′kĭn), *n.* an awkward, clumsy yokel. [t. MD: m. *bommekyn* little barrel]

bumpkin[2] (bŭmp′kĭn), *n.* *Naut.* a beam or spar projecting outwards from the bow, side, or stern of a ship to extend a sail, secure blocks, or the like. Also, **bumkin.** [t. MD: m. *boomken* little tree]

bumptious (bŭmp′shəs), *adj.* offensively self-assertive: *he's a bumptious young upstart.* [f. BUMP + *-tious,* modelled on FRACTIOUS, etc.] —**bump′tiously,** *adv.* —**bump′tiousness,** *n.*

bumpy (bŭm′pĭ), *adj.,* **bumpier, bumpiest. 1.** of uneven surface: *a bumpy road.* **2.** full of jolts: *a bumpy ride.* **3.** giving rise to jolts: *bumpy air.* —**bump′ily,** *adv.* —**bump′iness,** *n.*

bun (bŭn), *n.* **1.** a kind of bread roll, usually slightly sweetened and round-shaped, and sometimes containing spice, dried currants, citron, etc. **2.** hair arranged at the back of the head in a bun shape. [ME *bunne*; orig. uncert.]

buna (bōō′nə, byōō′-), *n.* *Chem.* **1.** any synthetic rubber made by copolymerizing butadiene with other material. **2.** (orig.) a synthetic rubber made by polymerizing butadiene by means of styrene. [f. BU(TADIENE) + NA (the symbol for sodium)]

bunce (bŭns), *n.* *Slang.* **1.** profit, esp. unexpected. **2.** a share or commission. [orig. obscure]

bunch (bŭnch), *n.* **1.** a connected group; cluster: *a bunch of bananas.* **2.** a group of things; lot; *a bunch of papers.* **3.** *Colloq.* a group of human beings: *a fine bunch of boys.* **4.** a knob; lump; protuberance. —*v.t.* **5.** to group together; make a bunch of. —*v.i.* **6.** to gather into a cluster or protuberance; gather together. [ME *bunche*; orig. uncert.] —**Syn. 1, 2.** See **bundle.**

buncher resonator. See **klystron.**

bunch of fives, *Slang.* the fist.

bunchy (bŭn′chĭ), *adj.,* **bunchier, bunchiest. 1.** having bunches. **2.** bulging or protuberant.

bunco (bŭng′kō), *n., pl.,* **-cos,** *v.,* **-coed, -coing.** bunko.

buncombe (bŭng′kəm), *n.* *U.S.* bunkum.

bund (bŭnd), *n.* (in India, China, Japan, etc.) an embankment; an embanked quay. [t. Hind.: m. *band*]
Bund (bo͝ond; *Ger.* bo͝ont), *n.*, *pl.* **Bünde** (*Ger.* bʏn′də). **1.** a short form of 'German-American Volksbund', a former Nazi-inspired and directed organization in the U.S. **2.** an alliance or league. [t. G]
Bundaberg (bŭn′də bûg′), *n.* a town in Australia, in E Queensland. 23,750 (est. 1964).
Bundelkhand (bŭn′dl kŭnd′, -KHŭnd′), *n.* (formerly) a group of native states in central India: now a part of Madhya Pradesh.
Bundesrat (*Ger.* bo͝on′dəs råt), *n.* **1.** (formerly) a federal legislative council of representatives from the 26 states of the German Empire. Now upper house of the Federal German Parliament. **2.** the federal council of Switzerland. Also, **Bundesrath** (*Ger.* bo͝on′dəs råt). [G]
Bundestag (bo͝on′dəz täg′; *Ger.* bo͝on′dəs tåk), *n.* the lower house of the Federal German Parliament.
bundle (bŭn′dl), *n.*, *v.*, **-dled, -dling.** —*n.* **1.** a group loosely held together: *a bundle of hay.* **2.** something wrapped for carrying; package. **3.** a number of things considered together. **4.** *Biol.* an aggregation of strands of specialized conductive and mechanical tissue. **5.** *Textiles.* a measure of cloth, equal to 60,000 yards of linen yarn, or 20 hanks of cotton cloth. —*v.t.* **6.** to tie or wrap in a bundle. **7.** to dress snugly (fol. by *up*). **8.** to send away hurriedly or unceremoniously (fol. by *off, out,* etc.). —*v.i.* **9.** to leave hurriedly or unceremoniously (fol. by *off, out,* etc.). **10.** to dress warmly (fol. by *up*). **11.** to sleep or lie in the same bed without undressing, esp. of sweethearts, as formerly in Wales and New England. [ME *bundel*, t. MD, c. G *Bündel*; akin to OE *byndele* binding together] —**bun′dler,** *n.*

—**Syn.** **1.** BUNDLE, BUNCH refer to a number of things or an amount of something fastened or bound together. BUNDLE implies a loose or haphazard binding or grouping together: *a bundle of old clothes.* A BUNCH consists of a number of objects, usually of the same kind, esp. a number of straight objects held together at one point: *a bunch of roses or of keys.*

bundu (bo͝on′do͞o), *n.* *Rhodesian and S African.* wild country; bush or veld. [t. Shona: m. *bundo* grazing grass]
bung (bŭng), *n.* **1.** a stopper, as for the hole of a cask or for laboratory glassware. **2.** a bunghole. —*v.t.* **3.** to close with or as a bung (often fol. by *up*). **4.** to beat; bruise; maul (often fol. by *up*). **5.** *Slang.* to toss to another person; throw. [ME *bunge*, t. MD: m. *bonghe*]
bungaloid (bŭng′ə loid′), *adj.* pertaining to or characterized by bungalows. [f. BUNGAL(OW) + -OID modelled on FUNGOID]
bungalow (bŭng′gə lō′), *n.* **1.** a cottage, usually of only one storey, esp. for country or seaside residence. **2.** (in India) a house, usually surrounded by a veranda. [t. Hind.: m. *banglā*, lit., of Bengal]
bunghole (bŭng′hōl′), *n.* a hole or orifice in a cask through which it is filled.
bungle (bŭng′gl), *v.*, **-gled, -gling,** *n.* —*v.i.* **1.** to do something awkwardly and clumsily. —*v.t.* **2.** to do clumsily and awkwardly; botch. —*n.* **3.** a bungling performance. **4.** a bungled job. [? imit.] —**bun′gler,** *n.* —**bun′glingly,** *adv.*
Bunin (*Russ.* bo͞o′nĭn), *n.* **Ivan Alekseevich** (*Russ.* ĭ vän′ ə lĭk syĕ′yĭ vĭch), 1870–1953, Soviet poet and novelist.
bunion (bŭn′yən), *n.* *Pathol.* a swelling on the foot caused by the inflammation of a synovial bursa, esp. of the great toe. [orig. obscure]
bunk[1] (bŭngk), *n.* **1.** a built-in platform bed, as on a ship. **2.** *Colloq.* any bed. —*v.i.* **3.** *Colloq.* to occupy a bunk; sleep, esp. in rough quarters. [orig. unknown]
bunk[2] (bŭngk), *n.* *Slang.* humbug; nonsense. [short for BUNKUM]
bunk[3] (bŭngk), *n.* **to do a bunk,** to run away; take flight.
bunker[1] (bŭng′kə), *n.* **1.** a chest or box; a large bin or receptacle: *a coal bunker.* **2.** *Golf.* an obstacle, usually a small ridge, generally preceded by a sand-trap. —*v.t.* **3.** *Golf.* **a.** to drive (a ball) into a bunker. **b.** to impede or trap (as a sand trap). [orig. uncert.]
bunker[2] (bŭng′kə), *n.* a bombproof underground shelter. [t. G]
Bunker Hill, a hill in Charlestown, Massachusetts: the first major battle of the American War of Independence was fought on adjoining Breed's Hill, June 17, 1775.
bunkering (bŭng′kə rĭng), *n.* refuelling, as of vessels or vehicles, esp. with heavy fuels.
bunkhouse (bŭngk′hous′), *n.* a rough building used for sleeping quarters.
bunko (bŭng′kō), *n.*, *pl.* **-kos,** *v.*, **-koed, -koing.** *U.S. Colloq.* —*n.* **1.** a swindle or confidence trick, esp. at cards. —*v.t.* **2.** to swindle or trick. [short for BUNKUM]
bunko steerer, *U.S. Colloq.* a swindler.
bunkum (bŭng′kəm), *n.* **1.** insincere talk; claptrap; humbug. **2.** *Chiefly U.S.* insincere speechmaking intended merely to please political constituents. Also, *U.S.*, **buncombe.** [alter. of *Buncombe*, a county in the U.S., in North Carolina, from its Congressional representative's phrase, 'talking for Buncombe']
bunny (bŭn′ĭ), *n.*, *pl.* **-nies.** *Colloq.* **1.** a rabbit. **2.** *U.S.* a squirrel.
Bunsen (bŭn′sən; *Ger.* bo͝on′zən), *n.* **Robert Wilhelm** (*Ger.* rō′bĕrt vĭl′hĕlm), 1811–99, German chemist.
Bunsen burner, a type of gas burner with which a very hot, practically non-luminous flame is obtained by allowing air to enter at the base and mix with the gas. [named after R. W. BUNSEN]
bunt[1] (bŭnt), *v.i.* **1.** (of a goat or calf) to push with the horns or head. —*v.t.* **2.** to push (something) with the horns or head. —*n.* **3.** a push with the head or horns; butt. [nasalized var. of BUTT[2]]
bunt[2] (bŭnt), *n.* **1.** *Naut.* the middle part of a square sail. **2.** the bagging part of a fishing net or the like. [orig. unknown]
bunt[3] (bŭnt), *n.* a disease of wheat in which the kernels are replaced by black fungus spores. [orig. unknown]
bunting[1] (bŭn′tĭng), *n.* **1.** a coarse open fabric of worsted or cotton used for flags, signals, etc. **2.** flags, esp. a vessel's flags, collectively. [cf. G *bunt* particoloured]
bunting[2] (bŭn′tĭng), *n.* any of numerous small fringilline birds of the genera *Emberiza, Passerina,* and *Plectrophenax* as, respectively, the **reed bunting** (*E. shoeniclus*) of Europe, the **indigo bunting** (*P. cyanea*) of the U.S. and Canada, and the **snow bunting** (*P. nivalis*) of arctic regions. [ME *bountyng*; orig. uncert.]
buntline (bŭnt′lĭn, -līn′), *n.* *Naut.* one of the ropes attached to the foot of a square sail to haul it up to the yard for furling. [f. BUNT[2] + LINE[1]]
Buñuel (*Sp.* bo͞on̄y wĕl′), *n.* **Luis** (*Sp.* lwēs), born 1900, Spanish film director, associated with early surrealism.
bunya-bunya (bŭn′yə bŭn′yə), *n.* a tall, dome-shaped coniferous tree of Australia, *Araucaria bidwilli,* bearing edible seeds. [t. native Australian]
Bunyan (bŭn′yən), *n.* **John,** 1628–88, English preacher.
bunyip (bŭn′yĭp), *n.* *Austral.* an imaginary creature of Aborigine legend. [t. native Australian]
Buonaparte (*It.* bwō nä pär′tĕ), *n.* Italian spelling of **Bonaparte.**
Buonarroti (*It.* bwō när rōt′ē), *n.* See **Michelangelo.**
buoy (boi), *n.* *Naut.* **1.** a distinctively marked and shaped anchored float, sometimes carrying a light, whistle, or bell, marking a channel or obstruction. **2.** a lifebuoy. —*v.t.* **3.** to support by or as by a buoy; keep afloat in a fluid. **4.** *Naut.* to furnish or mark with a buoy or buoys: *to buoy or buoy off a channel.* **5.** to bear up or sustain, as hope or courage does. —*v.i.* **6.** to float; rise by reason of lightness. [ME *boye*, t. MD: m. *boeie* buoy, ult. t. L: m. *boia* fetter]

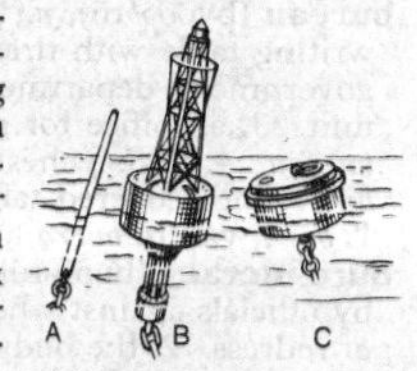

Buoys (def. 1)
A, Spar buoy;
B, Light buoy;
C, Mooring buoy

buoyage (boi′ĭj), *n.* *Naut.* **1.** a system of buoys. **2.** buoys collectively. **3.** the providing of buoys.
buoyancy (boi′ən sĭ), *n.* **1.** the power to float or rise in a fluid; relative lightness. **2.** the power of supporting a body so that it floats; upward pressure exerted by the fluid in which a body is immersed. **3.** elasticity of spirit; cheerfulness.
buoyant (boi′ənt), *adj.* **1.** tending to float or rise in a fluid. **2.** capable of keeping a body afloat, as a liquid. **3.** not easily depressed; cheerful. **4.** cheering or invigorating. —**buoy′antly,** *adv.*
B.U.P., British United Press.
buprestid (byo͞o prĕs′tĭd), *n.* any beetle of the family *Buprestidae,* comprising the metallic wood-borers, noted for their brilliant coloration. [f. s. L *būprestis*, t. Gk: m. *boúprēstis*, lit., ox-burner + -ID[2]]
bur[1] (bû), *n.*, *v.*, **burred, burring.** —*n.* **1.** *Bot.* the rough, prickly case around the seeds of certain plants, as of the chestnut and burdock. **2.** any bur-bearing plant. **3.** something or someone that adheres like a bur. **4.** any of various knots, knobs, lumps, or excrescences. **5.** burr[1] (defs 1, 2, 3). —*v.t.* **6.** burr[1]. [ME *burre*, t. Scand.; cf. Dan. *borre*]
bur[2] (bû), *n.*, *v.*, **burred, burring.** burr[2].
buran (bo͞o rän′), *n.* a violent storm of wind on the steppes of Russia and Siberia, esp. one accompanied by driving snow and intense cold. [t. Turk.]
Burbage (bû′bĭj), *n.* **Richard,** 1567?–1619, English actor: associate of Shakespeare.
Burberry (bû′bə rĭ), *n.* *Trademark.* a waterproof gaberdine raincoat.

burble (bû′bl), *v.*, **-bled, -bling,** *n.* —*v.t.* **1.** to make a bubbling sound; bubble. **2.** to speak with a burble. —*n.* **3.** a bubbling or gentle gush. **4.** a bubbling flow of speech. **5.** *Aeron.* the breakdown of smooth airflow around a wing at a high angle of incidence. [prob. imit.]
burbot (bû′bət), *n.*, *pl.* **-bots,** (*esp. collectively*) **-bot.** a freshwater fish of the cod family, *Lota lota,* of Europe, Asia, and North America, with an elongated body and a barbel on the lower jaw. [ME *borbot,* t. F: m. *borbote* (appar. der. L *barba* beard, b. with *borbe* slime)]
burd (bûd), *n.* *Scot., Poetic.* a lady; a maiden. See **bird**[2]. [ME *burde* lady; OE *byrde* well-born, akin to BIRTH]
Burdekin (bû′də kĭn), *n.* a river in Australia, in E Queensland, flowing into the Pacific Ocean. 425 mi.
burden[1] (bû′dn), *n.* **1.** that which is carried; a load. **2.** that which is borne with difficulty: *burden of responsibilities.* **3.** *Com.* the duty to discharge an obligation or responsibility: *the burden of a contract.* **4.** *Costing.* that part of the cost of manufacture which is not directly productive; oncost. **5.** *Naut.* **a.** the weight of a ship's cargo. **b.** the carrying capacity of a ship: *a ship of a hundred tons burden.* —*v.t.* **6.** to load heavily. **7.** to load oppressively; oppress. Also, *Archaic,* **burthen.** [var. of BURTHEN OE *byrthen*; akin to BEAR[1]] —**Syn. 1.** See **load.**
burden[2] (bû′dn), *n.* **1.** something often repeated or much dwelt upon; the principal idea. **2.** *Music.* **a.** the refrain or recurring chorus of a song. **b.** bourdon. [ME *burdoun,* t. OF: m. *bourdon* a humming, the drone of a bagpipe, der. L *burda* pipe; later assoc. with BURDEN[1]]
burden of proof, *Chiefly Law.* **1.** the obligation, in English criminal law incumbent in the first place upon the prosecution, to offer evidence which the court or jury could reasonably believe, in support of a contention, failing which the party will lose its case. **2.** the obligation to establish an alleged fact by convincing the tribunal of its probable truth (**the burden of persuasion**).
burdensome (bû′dn səm), *adj.* oppressively heavy. Also, *Archaic,* **burthensome.** —**bur′densomely,** *adv.* —**bur′densomeness,** *n.*
burdock (bû′dŏk′), *n.* a plant of the composite genus *Arctium,* esp. *A. lappa,* a coarse, broad-leaved weed with prickly heads or burs which stick to the clothing. [f. BUR + DOCK[1]]
Burdwan (bo͝oə′dwän), *n.* a town in India, in West Bengal. 108,224 (1961).
bureau (byo͝oə′rō), *n.*, *pl.* **-eaus, -eaux** (-ōz). **1.** a desk or writing table with drawers for papers. **2.** a division of a government department or independent administrative unit. **3.** an office for giving out information, etc.: *travel bureau.* **4.** *U.S.* a chest of drawers. [t. F: desk, office, OF *burel* cloth-covered table, kind of woollen cloth, ult. der. L *būra,* var. of *burra* long-haired woollen cloth]
bureaucracy (byo͝o rŏk′rə sĭ), *n.*, *pl.* **-cies. 1.** government by officials against whom there is inadequate public right of redress. **2.** the body of officials administering bureaus. **3.** excessive multiplication of, and concentration of power in, administrative bureaus; a system characterized by power without responsibility. **4.** excessive governmental red tape and routine. [t. F: m. *bureaucratie.* See BUREAU, -CRACY]
bureaucrat (byo͝oə′rə krăt′), *n.* **1.** an official of a bureaucracy. **2.** an official who works by fixed routine without exercising intelligent judgement. —**bu′reaucrat′ic,** *adj.* —**bu′reaucrat′ically,** *adv.*
burette (byo͝o rĕt′), *n.* *Chem.* a graduated glass tube, commonly having a stopcock at the bottom, used for accurately measuring, or measuring out, small quantities of liquid. [t. F: cruet, dim. of *buire* vessel for wine, etc. Cf. BUCKET]
burg (bûg), *n.* **1.** *Hist.* a fortified town. **2.** *U.S. Colloq.* a city or town. [var. of BURGH]
burgage (bû′gĭj), *n.* *Hist. Law.* **1.** (in England) a tenure whereby burgesses or townsmen held their lands or tenements of the king or other lord, usually for a fixed money rent: abolished in 1922. **2.** (in Scotland) that tenure by which the property in royal burghs is held under the crown, proprietors being liable to the (nominal) service of watching and warding. [t. ML: m. *burgāgium,* der. *burgus,* Latinized form of BURG(H), BOROUGH]
Burgas (*Bulg.* bo͞or gäs′), *n.* a seaport in E Bulgaria, on the **Gulf of Burgas** (inlet of Black Sea). 76,100 (1959).
burgee (bû′jē), *n.* *Naut.* a swallow-tailed flag or pennant, in the merchant service generally bearing the ship's name. [orig. uncert.; ? der. *burge* burgeon]
Burgenland (*Ger.* bo͞or′gən länt), *n.* a province in E Austria. 271,001 pop. (1961); 1526 sq. mi. *Cap.:* Eisenstadt.
burgeon (bû′jən), *v.i.* **1.** to begin to grow, as a bud; to put forth buds, shoots, as a plant (often fol. by *out, forth*). —*v.t.* **2.** to put forth as buds. —*n.* **3.** a bud; a sprout. Also, **bourgeon.** [ME *burjon,* t. OF, ? t. Gmc]
Bürger (*Ger.* bʏr′gər), *n.* **Gottfried August** (*Ger.* gŏt′frēt ou′go͞ost), 1747–94, German poet.
burgess (bû′jĭs), *n.* **1.** an inhabitant, esp. a citizen or freeman, of an English borough. **2.** *Hist.* a representative of a borough, corporate town, or university in Parliament. **3.** *U.S. Hist.* a representative in the popular branch of the colonial legislature of Virginia or Maryland. [ME *burgeis,* t. OF, g. LL *burgēnsis* a citizen. Cf. BOURGEOIS]
Burgess (bû′jĭs), *n.* (**Frank**) **Gelett** (jĭ lĕt′), 1866–1951, U.S. illustrator and humorist.
burgh (bû′rə), *n.* a borough (applied to chartered towns in Scotland). [var. of BOROUGH] —**burgh′al** (bû′gl), *adj.*
burgher (bû′gə), *n.* an inhabitant of a borough; a citizen.
Burghley (bû′lĭ), *n.* **William Cecil,** 1520–98, English statesman: adviser to Elizabeth I. Also, **Burleigh.**
burglar (bû′glə), *n.* one who commits burglary. [cf. Anglo-L *burglātor,* var. of *burgātor,* Latinization of AF *burgur* burglar, der. *burgier* pillage]
burglar alarm, an electric device which sounds a loud alarm if a building is forcibly entered.
burglarious (bû glĕə′rĭ əs), *adj.* pertaining to or involving burglary. —**burglar′iously,** *adv.*
burglarize (bû′glə rīz′), *v.t., v.i.,* **-rized, -rizing.** *U.S.* to burgle.
burglary (bû′glə rĭ), *n.*, *pl.* **-ries.** *Criminal Law.* the felony of breaking into and entering the house of another at night with intent to commit a felony therein.
burgle (bû′gl), *v.t., v.i.,* **-gled, -gling.** to commit burglary (in). [back-formation from BURGLAR]
burgomaster (bû′gə mäs′tə), *n.* the chief magistrate of a municipal town in Holland, Flanders, Germany, or Austria. [t. D: m. *burgemeester,* lit., town master]
burgonet (bû′gə nĕt′), *n.* *Armour.* an open helmet usually with pivoted peak and hinged cheek-pieces. [t. F: m. *bourguignotte,* der. *Bourgogne* Burgundy]
burgoo (bû′go͞o, bû go͞o′), *n.*, *pl.* **-goos. 1.** a thick oatmeal gruel, esp. as eaten by seamen. **2.** *U.S. Dial.* a kind of thick, highly seasoned soup. **3.** *U.S. Dial.* a picnic at which such soup is served. [orig. uncert.]
Burgos (*Sp.* bo͞or′gŏs), *n.* a city in N Spain: famous cathedral. 88,825 (1965).
Burgoyne (bû goin′, bû′goin), *n.* **John,** 1722–92, British general in the War of American Independence.
burgrave (bû′grāv), *n.* *German Hist.* **1.** the appointed head of a fortress. **2.** hereditary governor of a castle or town. [t. G: m. *Burggraf,* f. *Burg* castle + *Graf* count]
Burgundian (bə gŭn′dyən), *adj.* **1.** of or pertaining to Burgundy or its people. —*n.* **2.** a native or an inhabitant of Burgundy.
Burgundy (bû′gən dĭ), *n.*, *pl.* **-dies. 1.** an administrative region in SE France. 1,439,388 pop. (1962); 12,263 sq. mi. *Prefecture:* Dijon. **2.** a former kingdom, duchy, and province. **3.** (*often l.c.*) wine, of many varieties, red and white, mostly still, full, and dry, produced in the Burgundy region. **4.** (*often l.c.*) some similar wine made elsewhere. **5.** (*l.c.*) dull reddish blue (colour). French (*for defs 1, 2*), **Bourgogne.**
burial (bĕ′rĭ əl), *n.* the act of burying. [f. BURY + -AL[2] (cf. *funeral*); r. ME *buriel,* OE *byrgels* burying place, g. pre-E **burgh-* + *-ils* (var. of *-isl*) suffix; for dropping of *-s* (mistaken for plural sign), cf. RIDDLE, CHERRY]
burial ground, a tract of land for burial of the dead.
burial mound, a barrow[2].
burial society, an insurance society providing for funeral expenses.
burier (bĕ′rĭ ə), *n.* one who or that which buries.
burin (byo͝oə′rĭn), *n.* **1.** a tempered steel rod, with a lozenge-shaped point and a rounded handle, used for engraving furrows in metal. **2.** a similar tool used by marble-workers. **3.** an engraver's individual style. [t. F, prob. of Gmc orig.; cf. OHG *bora* gimlet. See BORE[1]] —**bur′inist,** *n.*
burke (bûk), *v.t.*, **burked, burking. 1.** to murder, as by suffocation, so as to leave no or few marks of violence. **2.** to get rid of by some indirect manoeuvre. **3.** to silence or suppress. [from W. *Burke,* hanged at Edinburgh in 1829 for murders of this kind]
Burke (bûk), *n.* **Edmund,** 1729–97, British statesman, orator, and writer.
burl (bûl), *n.* **1.** a small knot or lump in wool, thread, or cloth. **2.** a dome-shaped growth on the trunk of a tree; a wartlike structure sometimes two feet across and a foot or more in height, sliced to make a veneer known as **burlwood veneer.** —*v.t.* **3.** to remove burls from (cloth) in finishing. [ME *burle,* t. OF: m. *bourle,* ult. der. LL *burra* flock of wool] —**burled,** *adj.*
burlap (bû′lăp′), *n.* *U.S.* hessian; gunny.
Burleigh (bû′lĭ), *n.* Burghley.
burlesque (bû lĕsk′), *n., adj., v.,* **-lesqued, -lesquing.** —*n.*

1. an artistic composition, esp. literary or dramatic, which, for the sake of laughter, vulgarizes lofty material or treats ordinary material with mock dignity. **2.** any ludicrous take-off or debasing caricature. **3.** *U.S.* a theatrical or cabaret entertainment featuring coarse, crude, often vulgar comedy and dancing. *—adj.* **4.** involving ludicrous or debasing treatment of a serious subject. **5.** of or pertaining to risqué burlesque. *—v.t.* **6.** to make ridiculous by mocking representation. *—v.i.* **7.** to use caricature. [t. F, t. It.: m. *burlesco*, der. *burla* jest, mockery] **—burles′quer,** *n.*

—Syn. 2. BURLESQUE, CARICATURE, PARODY, TRAVESTY agree in indicating a ludicrous imitation. BURLESQUE is especially applied to theatrical entertainment and to action, and emphasizes the intention to cause laughter by ridicule. CARICATURE is especially applied to imitation of figure or feature, and emphasizes the exaggeration of reality. PARODY applies to imitation of style and manners, esp. verbal, and emphasizes the satirical intent. TRAVESTY is a general term, and emphasizes the inadequacy and gross inferiority of the imitation.

Burlington (bû′lĭng tən), *n.* **Richard Boyle, 3rd Earl of,** 1694–1753, English Palladian architect and patron of architects.

burly (bû′lĭ), *adj.*, **-lier, -liest. 1.** great in bodily size; stout; sturdy. **2.** bluff; brusque. [ME *borli, burlich, burli*; orig. uncert.] **—bur′lily,** *adv.* **—bur′liness,** *n.*

Burma (bû′mə), *n.* an independent republic in SE Asia, until 1948 a British dependency: historically subdivided into **Lower Burma** (coastal region W of Thailand), **Upper Burma** (inland districts), and the Shan States. 23,750,000 pop. (est. 1963); 261,789 sq. mi. *Cap.:* Rangoon.

Burman (bû′mən), *adj., n.* Burmese.

bur marigold, any of various herbs of the composite genus *Bidens*, esp. those with conspicuous yellow flowers.

Burma Road, a mountainous road extending from Lashio in Burma through China to Kunming, terminating at Chungking: used in World War II for supplying Allied forces in China.

Burmese (bû mēz′), *n., pl.* **-mese,** *adj.* *—n.* **1.** a native or inhabitant of Burma. **2.** the principal language of Burma, a Sino-Tibetan language. *—adj.* **3.** of or pertaining to Burma, its people, or their language.

burn[1] (bûn), *v.*, **burnt** or **burned, burning,** *n.* *—v.i.* **1.** to be on fire: *the fuel burns.* **2.** (of a furnace, etc.) to contain fire. **3.** to feel heat or a physiologically identical sensation: *his face burned in the wind.* **4.** to give light: *the lights in the house burn all night.* **5.** to glow like fire. **6.** (in games) to be extremely close to finding a concealed object or guessing an answer. **7.** to feel strong passion: *he was burning with anger.* **8.** *Chem.* to undergo combustion; oxidize. **9.** to become discoloured, tanned, or charred through heat. **10.** *U.S. Slang.* to be electrocuted in an electric chair. **11. burn out,** to die out for want of fuel. *—v.t.* **12.** to consume, partly or wholly, with fire. **13.** to put to death by burning: *they were burnt at the stake.* **14.** to cause to feel the sensation of heat. **15.** to injure, discolour, char, or treat with heat. **16.** to produce with fire: *to burn charcoal.* **17.** *Chem.* to cause to undergo combustion; oxidize. **18.** to calcine (earth, etc.) so as to obtain a pigment: *burnt sienna, burnt umber.* **19.** to pass through or over quickly and easily (fol. by *up*): *to burn up the miles in a car.* **20. burn one's fingers,** to suffer through rash interference or imprudence. **21. burn the water,** to spear salmon by torchlight. *—n.* **22.** a burned place. **23.** *Pathol.* an injury produced by heat or by abnormal cold, chemicals, poison gas, electricity, or lightning. A **first-degree burn** is characterized by reddening; a **second-degree burn** by blistering; a **third-degree burn** by charring. **24.** the operation of burning or baking, as in brickmaking. **25.** *Colloq.* a cigarette. [coalescence in later ME of OE *beornan*, v.i. (c. Goth. *brinnan*) and OE *bærnan*, v.t. (c. Goth. *brannjan*) with (weak) inflection of *bærnan* and phonetic form of *beornan*]

—Syn. 12. BURN, SCORCH, SEAR, SINGE refer to the effect of fire or heat. To BURN is to consume, wholly or in part, by contact with fire of excessive heat: *to burn leaves.* SCORCH implies superficial or slight burning on the surface, resulting in a change of colour or in injury to the texture because of shrivelling or curling: *to scorch a dress while ironing.* SEAR refers to the withering, drying, or hardening (esp. of living tissue) caused by heat or a hot object, and often implies acute pain. SINGE applies esp. to a superficial burning that takes off ends of projections: *to singe hair.*

burn[2] (bûn), *n.* *Scot. and N Dial.* a brook or rivulet. [ME *burne, bourne*, OE *burna, burne*, akin to G *Born, Brunnen* spring]

Burne-Jones (bûn′jōnz′), *n.* **Sir Edward,** 1833–1898, English painter and designer.

burner (bû′nə), *n.* **1.** one who or that which burns. **2.** that part of a gas fitting, lamp, etc., from which flame issues or in which it is produced.

burnet (bû′nĭt), *n.* **1.** a plant of the rosaceous genus *Sanguisorba*, esp. *S. minor*, an erect herb whose leaves are used for salad. **2.** one of several similar or related plants. **3.** a burnet moth. [ME, t. OF: m. *brunette*, dim. of *brun* brown]

burnet moth, 1. any moth of the genus *Zygaena*, with bright red hind wings, and spots of the same colour in the dark green forewing. **2.** any of several other moths having a dark green colouring, as *Anthrocera filipendula.*

burnet rose, a short, erect, very prickly rosaceous shrub with creamy-white flowers, *Rosa pimpinellifolia*, widespread in Europe and temperate Asia. Also, **Scotch rose.**

burnet saxifrage, an umbelliferous plant, *Pimpinella saxifraga*, with foliage resembling that of the burnet.

Burney (bû′nĭ), *n.* **Frances** (or **Fanny**) (*Madame d'Arblay*), 1752–1840, English novelist and diarist.

Burnham (bû′nəm), *n.* **(Linden) Forbes (Sampson),** born 1923, prime minister of Guyana since 1966.

Burnham scale (bû′nəm), the scale by which the salaries of teachers in English state schools are determined. [named after H. L. W. Lawson, 1st Viscount *Burnham*, English politician]

burning (bû′nĭng), *adj.* **1.** intense; serious; much-discussed: *a burning question.* *—n.* **2.** the final heat treatment used to develop hardness and other properties in ceramic products. **—burn′ingly,** *adv.*

burning bush, 1. any of various plants, esp. those of the genus *Fraxinella*, which yield a volatile and inflammable oil. **2.** the bush which burned but was not consumed, out of which God addressed Moses (Ex. 3:2–4); the symbol of the Church of Scotland.

burning-glass (bû′nĭng gläs′), *n.* a convex lens used to produce heat or ignite substances by focusing the sun's rays.

burnish (bû′nĭsh), *v.t.* **1.** to polish (a surface) by friction. **2.** to make smooth and bright. *—n.* **3.** gloss; brightness; lustre. [ME *burnissh(en)*, t. OF: m. *burniss-*, s. *burnir* make brown, polish, der. *brun* brown, t. Gmc; see BROWN]

burnisher (bû′nĭ shə), *n.* a tool, usually with a smooth, slightly convex head, used for polishing, as in dentistry, etc.

Burnley (bûn′lĭ), *n.* a town in NW England, in Lancashire. 79,250 (1964).

burnous (bû nōōs′, -nōōz′), *n.* a hooded mantle or cloak, such as that worn by Arabs, etc. Also, **burnouse** (bû nōōz′). [t. F: (m.) *burnous*, t. Ar.: m. *burnus*]

burnout (bûn′out′), *n.* *U.S.* all-burnt.

Burns (bûnz), *n.* **Robert,** 1759–96, Scottish poet.

burnsides (bûn′sīdz′), *n.pl.* *U.S.* a style of beard consisting of side-whiskers and a moustache, the chin being clean-shaven. [named after A. E. *Burnside*, 1824–81, general in the American Civil War]

burnt (bûnt), *v.* a pt. and pp. of **burn.**

Burnous

burnt offering, 1. an offering burnt upon an altar in sacrifice to a deity. **2.** *Colloq.* overcooked food.

burn-up (bûn′ûp′), *n.* *Colloq.* an unregulated trial of speed, esp. on a motorcycle.

burp (bûp), *n.* *Colloq.* **1.** a belch (def. 5). *—v.i.* **2.** to belch (def. 1). *—v.t.* **3.** cause (a baby) to belch, esp. to relieve flatulence after feeding. [imit.]

bur-parsley (bû′pä′slĭ), *n.* any annual umbelliferous herb of the genus *Caucalis*, bearing spring fruits.

burr[1] (bû), *n.* **1.** any of various tools and appliances for cutting or drilling. **2.** a rough protuberance, ridge, or area left on metal after cutting, drilling, or ploughing with an engraver's tool, etc. **3.** a rough or irregular protuberance on any object, as on a tree. **4.** bur[1]. *—v.t.* **5.** to form a rough point or edge on. [var. of BUR]

burr[2] (bû), *n.* **1.** a washer placed at the head of a rivet. **2.** the blank punched out of a piece of sheet metal. [ME *burwhe* circle, t. Scand.; cf. Icel. *borg* wall]

burr[3] (bû), *n.* **1.** a guttural pronunciation of the letter *r* (as in certain Northern English dialects). **2.** any rough or dialectal pronunciation. **3.** a whirring noise or sound. *—v.i.* **4.** to speak with a burr. **5.** to speak roughly, indistinctly, or inarticulately. **6.** to make a whirring noise or sound. *—v.t.* **7.** to pronounce with a burr. [appar. imit.; ? assoc. with idea of roughness in BUR]

burr[4] (bû), *n.* **1.** burstone. **2.** a mass of harder siliceous rock in soft rock. [orig. uncert.; ? akin to BUR]

burrawang (bŭ′rə wăng′), *n.* any Australian plant of the genus *Macrozamia*, having an edible nut. [t. native Australian]

bur-reed (bû′rēd′), *n.* any plant of the genus *Sparganium*, whose species have ribbon-like leaves and burlike heads of fruit.

burro (bŏŏ′rō), *n.*, *pl.* **-ros.** **1.** a pack donkey. **2.** any donkey. [t. Sp., der. *burrico* small horse, g. L *burricus*]

burrow (bŭ′rō), *n.* **1.** a hole in the ground made by a rabbit, fox, or similar small animal, for refuge and habitation. **2.** a similar place of retreat, shelter, or refuge. *—v.i.* **3.** to make a hole or passage (*in, into,* or *under* something). **4.** to lodge in a burrow. **5.** to hide. *—v.t.* **6.** to put a burrow or burrows into (a hill, etc.). **7.** to hide (oneself), as in a burrow. [ME *borow.* Cf. OE *beorg* burial place, *gebeorg* refuge, *burgen* grave] **—bur′rower,** *n.*

burrowing owl, a long-legged, terrestrial owl, *Speotyto cunicularia,* of North and South America, which digs its nesting burrow in open prairie land; ground owl.

burrstone (bû′stōn′), *n.* burstone.

burry (bû′rĭ), *adj.* full of burs; burlike; prickly.

bursa (bû′sə), *n.*, *pl.* **-sae** (-sē), **-sas.** *Anat., Zool.* a pouch, sac, or vesicle, esp. a sac containing synovia, to facilitate motion, as between a tendon and a bone. [t. ML: bag, purse, t. Gk: m. *býrsa* hide] **—bur′sal,** *adj.*

Bursa (*Turk.* bŏŏr′sâ), *n.* a city in NW Turkey: one-time capital of the Ottoman Empire. 153,866 (1960). Also, **Brusa.**

bursar (bû′sə), *n.* **1.** a treasurer or business officer, esp. of a college. **2.** (in Scotland) a student holding a bursary. [t. ML: m. *bursārius,* der. *bursa* purse] **—bur′sarship′,** *n.*

bursarial (bû sĕə′rĭ əl), *adj.* of, pertaining to, or paid to or by a bursar, or a bursary.

bursary (bû′sə rĭ), *n.*, *pl.* **-ries.** **1.** the treasury of a monastery or other institution. **2.** (in Scotland) a scholarship granted by a college. [t. ML: m. s. *bursāria*]

Burschenschaft (*Ger.* bŏŏr′shən shâft), *n.*, *pl.* **-schaften** (-shâf tən). *German.* any of certain associations of students at German universities, formed to promote patriotism, Christian conduct, and liberal ideas, but now purely social fraternities. [G, der. *Bursch* student]

burse (bûs), *n.* **1.** a pouch or case for some special purpose. **2.** (in Scotland) **a.** a fund to provide allowances for students. **b.** an allowance so provided. **3.** *Eccles.* a case or receptacle for the corporal. [t. F: m. *bourse* wallet, g. L *bursa,* t. Gk: m. *býrsa* hide]

burseraceous (bû′sə rā′shəs), *adj. Bot.* belonging to the family *Burseraceae,* of shrubs or trees of warm, often arid, countries, with compound leaves. [f. NL *Bursera* type genus (named after J. *Burser,* 1593–1649, German botanist) + -ACEOUS]

bursiform (bû′sĭ fôm′), *adj. Anat., Zool.* pouch-shaped; saccate. [f. s. ML *bursa* bag, purse + -(I)FORM]

bursitis (bû sī′tĭs), *n. Pathol.* inflammation of a bursa. [t. NL. See BURSA, -ITIS]

burst (bûst), *v.*, **burst, bursting,** *n.* *—v.i.* **1.** to fly apart or break open with sudden violence; explode. **2.** to issue forth suddenly and forcibly from or as from confinement. **3.** to break or give way from violent pain or emotion: *to burst into speech or tears.* **4.** to be extremely full, as if ready to break open. **5.** to become visible, audible, evident, etc., suddenly and clearly. *—v.t.* **6.** to cause to burst; break suddenly and violently. **7.** to cause or suffer the rupture of. *—n.* **8.** the act of bursting. **9.** a sudden display of activity or energy: *a burst of applause or speed.* **10.** a sudden expression or manifestation of emotion, etc. **11.** a sudden and violent issuing forth. **12.** *Mil.* **a.** the explosion of a projectile, esp. in a specified place: *an air burst.* **b.** a series of shots fired by one pressure on the trigger of an automatic weapon. **13.** the result of bursting: *a burst in the dyke.* **14.** a sudden opening to sight or view. [ME *berst(en), burst(en),* etc., OE *berstan;* form *burst* orig. past only; c. G *bersten,* Icel. *bresta*] **—burst′er,** *n.*

burstone (bû′stōn′), *n.* **1.** *Geol.* any of various siliceous rocks used for millstones. **2.** a millstone of such material. Also, **buhr, buhrstone, burrstone.** [f. BUR(R)[3] + STONE]

burthen (bû′thən), *n.*, *v.t. Archaic.* burden[1]. **—bur′thensome,** *adj.*

burton (bû′tn), *n. Naut.* **1.** any of various kinds of tackle used for setting up rigging, raising sails, etc. **2.** any of various small tackles, esp. one having a two-sheave and a one-sheave block. **3. go for a burton,** to be killed or destroyed; to disappear. [? var. of BRETON]

Burton (bû′tn), *n.* **1. Sir Richard Francis,** 1821–90, English traveller and writer. **2. Robert,** 1577–1640, English clergyman, scholar, and writer.

Burton-on-Trent (bû′tn ŏn trĕnt′), *n.* a town in England, in E Staffordshire: brewing. 50,766 (1961).

Burundi (bə rŏŏn′dĭ), *n.* a kingdom in central Africa, E of the Republic of Congo: formerly comprising the southern part of the Belgian trust territory of Ruanda-Urundi; became independent on July 1st, 1962. 2,213,480 pop. (1962); 10,747 sq. mi. *Cap.:* Usumbura. See map under **Rwanda.**

burweed (bû′wēd′), *n.* any of various plants having a burlike fruit, as the cocklebur, burdock, etc.

bury (bĕ′rĭ), *v.t.*, **buried, burying.** **1.** to put in the ground and cover with earth. **2.** to put (a corpse) in the ground or a vault, or into the sea, often with ceremony. **3.** to cause to sink in: *to bury a dagger in one's heart.* **4.** to cover in order to conceal from sight. **5.** to occupy (oneself) completely: *he buried himself in his work.* **6.** to put out of one's mind: *to bury an injury.* **7. to bury the hatchet,** to be reconciled after hostilities. [ME *berien, buryen,* OE *byrgan,* akin to OE *beorg* burial place] **—bur′ier,** *n.* **—Syn. 2.** inter, entomb, inhume.

Bury (bĕ′rĭ), *n.* a town in England, in SE Lancashire. 62,080 (est. 1964).

burying beetle, any beetle of the genus *Necrophorus,* esp. *N. vestigator,* that buries small creatures as food for its larvae.

Bury St Edmunds (bĕ′rĭ sənt ĕd′məndz), a town in England, in West Suffolk: famous medieval shrine. 21,680 (est. 1962).

bus (bŭs), *n.*, *pl.* **buses** or **busses,** *v.*, **bussed, bussing** or **bused, busing.** *—n.* **1.** a vehicle with a long body equipped with seats or benches for passengers, usually operating as part of a scheduled service; an omnibus. **2.** *Colloq.* a motor car or aeroplane. **3. miss the bus,** to miss an opportunity; be too late. *—v.i.* **4.** to travel by bus. [short for OMNIBUS]

bus., **1.** business. **2.** bushel; bushels.

busbar (bŭs′bä′), *n. Elect.* a metal bar which supplies power to several electrical units.

bus boy, *U.S.* a waiter's helper in a restaurant or other public dining room, for the more menial tasks.

busby (bŭz′bĭ), *n.*, *pl.* **-bies.** **1.** a tall fur hat with a bag hanging from the top over the right side, worn by hussars, etc., in the British Army. **2.** bearskin (def. 2). [? akin to obs. *buzz wig*]

Busby

bush[1] (bŏŏsh), *n.* **1.** a woody plant, esp. a low one, with many branches which usually arise from or near the ground. **2.** *Bot.* a small cluster of shrubs appearing as a single plant. **3.** something resembling or suggesting this, as a thick, shaggy head of hair. **4.** a fox's tail. **5.** *Geog.* a stretch of land covered with bushy vegetation or trees. **6.** *Chiefly Austral., N.Z.* the countryside in general, as opposed to the towns. **7.** *Hist.* a bunch of ivy, etc., hung as a sign before a tavern or vintner's shop. **8. beat about the bush,** to fail to come to the point; prevaricate. *—v.i.* **9.** to be or become bushy; branch or spread as or like a bush. *—v.t.* **10.** to cover with bushes; protect with bushes set round about; support with bushes. [ME; unexplained var. of *busk,* t. Scand.; cf. Dan. *busk*]

bush[2] (bŏŏsh), *Mach.* *—n.* **1.** a lining of metal or the like let into an orifice to guard against wearing by friction, erosion, etc. **2.** a metal lining, usually detachable, used as a bearing. *—v.t.* **3.** to furnish with a bush; line with metal. [t. MD: m. *busse,* n.]

bush., bushel; bushels.

bushbaby (bŏŏsh′bā′bĭ), *n.* any of the small lemurs of the loris family, of the genus *Galago,* esp. *G. grassicaudatus,* of E Africa, with nocturnal habits.

bushbuck (bŏŏsh′bŭk′), *n.* a small African antelope, *Tragelaphus scriptus,* frequenting forests and bushy regions. Also, **boschbok.**

bushed (bŏŏsht), *adj. Austral.* lost in the bush.

bushel (bŏŏsh′əl), *n.* **1.** a unit of dry measure containing 4 pecks, equivalent in Great Britain to 2219·36 cubic inches (**imperial bushel**) and in the U.S. (and formerly in England) to 2150·42 cubic inches (**Winchester bushel**). **2.** a container of this capacity. **3.** a unit of weight equal to the weight of a bushel of a given commodity. **4. hide one's light under a bushel,** to conceal one's abilities or good qualities. [ME *boyschel,* t. OF: m. *boissiel,* dim. of *boisse,* ult. der. Gallic word meaning hollow of the hand]

bush fire, a fire in forest or scrub country.

bush hammer, a hammer studded with pyramidal points or the like for dressing stone.

bush harrow, a harrow consisting of a heavy frame to which bushes or branches are attached, used for clearing land and sweeping earth over grass seed.

bushido (bŏŏ′shĭ dō′), *n.* **1.** a code of behaviour attributed to the warriors of feudal Japan, actually a growth of the end of the feudal period, tinged with Confucian influences. **2.** (in modern usage) fanatical disregard of life in the service of the Japanese emperor. [Jap.: lit. the way of the warrior]

bushiness (bŏŏsh′ĭ nĭs), *n.* bushy state or form.

bushing (bŏŏsh′ĭng), *n. Elect.* a lining for a hole, in-

tended to insulate and/or protect from abrasion conductors which pass through it. [f. BUSH² + -ING¹]
Bushire (byōō shīr′ə), *n.* a seaport in SW Iran, on the Persian Gulf. 25,000 (est. 1964).
bush-lawyer (bŏŏsh′lô′yə), *n.* **1.** a New Zealand bramble, *Rubus australis.* **2.** *Austral., N.Z.* one who pretends to a knowledge of the law.
bushman (bŏŏsh′mən), *n., pl.* **-men. 1.** *Austral.* a pioneer; dweller in the bush. **2.** (*cap.*) a member of a South African racially distinct people. **3.** (*cap.*) the language of the bushmen.
bushmaster (bŏŏsh′mäs′tə), *n.* a large venomous snake, *Lachesis mutus,* of tropical America.
Bushongo (bōō shŏng′gō), *n.pl.* (esp. collectively). **1.** a member of a Bantu people of the central Congo. **2.** their language. —*adj.* **3.** of or pertaining to this people, their language, or their culture.
bushpig (bŏŏsh′pĭg′), *n.* a wild pig, *Potamochaerus porcus,* of S and E Africa, with white face markings; boschvark.
bushranger (bŏŏsh′rān′jə), *n.* *Austral.* a bandit or criminal who hides in the bush and leads a predatory life.
bush tea, 1. a leguminous shrub of the genus *Cyclopia* of southern Africa, the twigs and leaves of which are used dried to make a herb tea. **2.** the beverage.
bush telegraph, 1. a system of communication over wide distances among primitive peoples, by drumbeats or other means. **2.** *Austral., N.Z.* a bushranger's confederate who supplies information about police movements, etc. **3.** *Colloq.* a channel along which rumours spread.
bushtit (bŏŏsh′tĭt′), *n.* any of several small chickadee-like birds of the North American genus *Psaltiparus,* known for their pendent nests.
bushveld (bŏŏsh′vĕlt′-fĕlt′), *n.* veld in southern Africa, characterized by scrub and thornbush vegetation.
bush-walk (bŏŏsh′wôk′), *v.i. Austral.* to hike or tramp for pleasure. —**bush′-wal′ker,** *n.*
bushwhack (bŏŏsh′wăk′), *U.S.* —*v.i.* **1.** to live as a bushwhacker. **2.** to fight as a guerrilla. —*v.t.* **3.** to ambush. [back-formation from BUSHWHACKER]
bushwhacker (bŏŏsh′wăk′ə), *n.* **1.** *U.S.* one accustomed to range in the woods; one who dwells in a remote, wooded area. **2.** *U.S. Hist.* a Confederate guerrilla. **3.** any guerrilla. [f. BUSH¹ + WHACKER]
bushwhacking (bŏŏsh′wăk′ĭng), *n.* *U.S.* **1.** travel through bushy country, on foot or in a boat. **2.** guerrilla tactics.
bushy (bŏŏsh′ĭ), *adj.,* **bushier, bushiest. 1.** resembling a bush. **2.** full of or overgrown with bushes.
busily (bĭz′ĭ lĭ), *adv.* **1.** in a busy manner; actively. **2.** with an unnecessary flurry of activity; officiously.
business (bĭz′nĭs), *n.* **1.** one's occupation, profession, or trade. **2.** *Econ.* the purchase and sale of goods in an attempt to make a profit. **3.** *Com.* a person, partnership, or corporation engaged in this; an established or going enterprise or concern. **4.** volume of trade; patronage. **5.** one's place of work. **6.** that with which one is principally and seriously concerned. **7.** that with which one is rightfully concerned. **8.** affair; matter. **9.** *Theat.* any movement or gesture by an actor used for dramatic expression (generally not applied to actions like exits, etc.). **10.** *Colloq.* defecation. **11.** *Slang.* prostitution. **12. mean business,** to be in earnest. [ME *busines,* OE (North) *bisignes.* See BUSY, -NESS] —**Syn. 1.** See **occupation.**
businesslike (bĭz′nĭs līk′), *adj.* conforming to the methods of business or trade; methodical; systematic.
businessman (bĭz′nĭs măn′), *n., pl.* **-men** (-mĕn′). a man who engages in business or commerce. —**businesswoman** (bĭz′nĭs wŏŏm′ən), *n. fem.*
busk¹ (bŭsk), *n.* **1.** a strip of wood, steel, whalebone, or other stiffening material placed in the front of a corset to keep it in shape. **2.** *Dial.* the whole corset. [t. F: m. *busc,* t. It.: m. *busco* stick]
busk² (bŭsk), *v.i.* **1.** to perform as a busker. **2.** *Jazz.* to improvise freely within the framework of a given tune.
busker (bŭs′kə), *n.* a street entertainer who performs for queues outside theatres, etc., and begs money from them.
buskin (bŭs′kĭn), *n.* **1.** a half-boot, or outer covering for the foot and leg reaching to the calf or higher. **2.** the high shoe or cothurnus of ancient Greek and Roman tragic actors. **3.** tragedy; tragic drama. [orig. uncert. Cf. F (obs.) *brousequin,* D *broosken,* Sp. *borcegui,* It. *borzacchino*]

Buskins (def. 1)

buskined (bŭs′kĭnd), *adj.* **1.** wearing buskins. **2.** pertaining to tragedy.
busman (bŭs′mən), *n., pl.* **-men** (-mən). the driver or conductor of a bus.
busman's holiday, a holiday on which one does one's regular work or some similar activity.
Busoni (byōō sō′nĭ; *It.* bōō zô′nē), *n.* **Ferruccio Benvenuto** (*It.* fĕr rōōt′chô bĕn vĕ nōō′tô), 1866–1924, Italian composer.
Busra (bŭs′rə), *n.* Basra. Also, **Busrah.**
buss (bŭs), *n., v.t., v.i. Dial.* kiss. [cf. d. G *Buss*]
bus-shelter (bŭs′shĕl′tə), *n.* a rain-shelter beside a bus-stop.
bus-stop (bŭs′stŏp′), *n.* a place at the roadside, usually marked by a standard sign, where buses stop for people to board and alight.
bust¹ (bŭst), *n.* **1.** the head and shoulders of a person done in sculpture, either in the round or in relief. **2.** the chest or breast; the bosom. [t. F: m. *buste,* t. It.: m. *busto,* g. L *bustum* bust, funeral monument, funeral]
bust² (bŭst) *Colloq.* or *Slang.* —*v.i.* **1.** to burst. **2.** to go bankrupt (often fol. by *up*). **3.** to part finally; quarrel and part (fol. by *up*). —*v.t.* **4.** to burst. **5.** to bankrupt; ruin (often fol. by *up*). **6.** to interrupt violently a political meeting or other gathering. (fol. by *up*). **7.** *U.S. Slang.* to reduce in rank or grade; demote (often fol. by *down*). **8.** *U.S.* to subdue; break the spirits of (a bronco, etc.). —*n.* **9.** *U.S.* a complete failure; bankruptcy. **10.** a drunken party; brawl. —*adj.* **11.** broken. **12.** bankrupt. [d. or colloq. var. of BURST]
Bustamante (bŭs′tə măn′tĭ), *n.* **Sir Alexander,** born 1884, prime minister of Jamaica 1962– 67.
bustard (bŭs′təd), *n.* any of several large birds of the family *Otidiae* allied to both the cranes and the plovers, inhabiting open country of Europe and Africa. [ME, t. OF, b. *bistarde* (t. It.: m. *bistarda*) and *oustarde,* both g. L *avis tarda* slow bird]
buster (bŭs′tə), *n.* **1.** a person or thing that busts. **2.** *Chiefly U.S. Colloq.* a small boy. **3.** *Colloq.* (a term of address to a man or boy.) **4.** *Slang.* something very big or unusual for its kind. **5.** *U.S. Slang* a roisterer. **6.** *U.S. Slang.* a frolic; a spree. **7.** *Austral.* a violent, cold, southerly wind.
bustle¹ (bŭs′əl), *v.,* **-tled, -tling,** *n.* —*v.i.* **1.** to move or act with a great show of energy (often fol. by *about*). —*v.t.* **2.** to cause to bustle. —*n.* **3.** activity with great show of energy; stir, commotion. [? var. of obs. *buskle*] —**bus′tlingly,** *adv.*
bustle² (bŭs′əl), *n.* (formerly) a pad, cushion, or wire framework worn by women on the back part of the body below the waist, to expand and support the skirt. [? der. BUSTLE¹]
Busto Arsizio (*It.* bōō′stô är sēt′tsyô), a town in Italy, in Lombardy. 71,986 (1966).
bust-up (bŭst′ŭp′), *n.* *Colloq.* **1.** a disruption; disturbance or commotion, as one which brings a meeting to a sudden end. **2.** a final parting, often with ill-feeling. **3.** a financial or commercial failure.
busy (bĭz′ĭ), *adj.,* **busier, busiest,** *v.,* **busied, busying.** —*adj.* **1.** actively and attentively engaged: *busy with his work.* **2.** not at leisure; otherwise engaged. **3.** full of or characterized by activity. **4.** officious; meddlesome; prying. [ME *busi, bisi,* OE *bysig,* c. D *bezig,* LG *besig*] —*v.t.* **5.** to keep occupied; make or keep busy: *to busy oneself keeping the lawn in order.* [ME *bisien,* OE *bysgian,* der. *bysig* BUSY, adj.] —**bus′yness,** *n.*
—**Syn. 1.** BUSY, DILIGENT, INDUSTRIOUS imply active or earnest effort to accomplish something, or a habitual attitude of such earnestness. BUSY means actively employed, temporarily or habitually: *a busy official.* DILIGENT suggests earnest and constant effort or application, and usually connotes fondness for, or enjoyment of, what one is doing: *a diligent student.* INDUSTRIOUS often implies a habitual characteristic of steady and zealous application, often with a definite goal: *an industrious clerk working for promotion.*
busybody (bĭz′ĭ bŏd′ĭ), *n., pl.* **-bodies.** a person who pries into and meddles in the affairs of others.
but¹ (bŭt; *unstressed* bət), *conj.* **1.** on the contrary; yet: *they all went, but I didn't.* **2.** except, rather than, or save: *anywhere but here.* **3.** except that (followed by a clause, often with *that* expressed): *nothing would do but, or but that, I should come in.* **4.** without the circumstance that, or that not: *it never rains but it pours.* **5.** otherwise than: *I can do nothing but go.* **6.** that (esp. after *doubt, deny,* etc., with a negative): *I don't doubt but he will do it.* **7.** that not (after a negative or question); *the children never played but that a quarrel followed.* **8.** who or which not: *no leader worthy of the name ever existed but was an optimist* (who was not an optimist). **9. but for,** except for; had it not been for; were it not for. —*prep.* **10.** with the exception of; except; save: *no one replied but me.* —*adv.* **11.** only; just: *there is but one God.* **12. all but,** almost: *all but dead.* —*n.* **13.** a restriction or objection: *no buts about it.* [ME; OE *b(e)ūta(n)* on the outside, without, f. *be-* by + *ūt* out + *-an* adv. suffix]
—**Syn. 1.** BUT, HOWEVER, NEVERTHELESS, STILL, YET are words implying opposition (with a possible concession). BUT marks an opposition or contrast, though in a casual way: *we are going,*

but we shall return. HOWEVER indicates a less marked opposition, but displays a second consideration to be compared with the first: *we are going; however (notice this also) we shall return.* NEVERTHELESS implies a concession, something which should not be forgotten in making a summing up: *we are going; nevertheless (do not forget that) we shall return.* STILL implies that in spite of a preceding concession, something must be considered as possible or even inevitable: *we have to go on foot; still (it is probable and possible that) we'll get there.* YET implies that in spite of a preceding concession, there is still a chance for a different outcome: *we are going; yet (in spite of all, some day) we shall return.* 2. See **except**[1].

but[2] (bŭt), *n. Scot.* the outer room of a house consisting of two rooms; the kitchen, the other room being the ben. [n. use of BUT[1], adv. (etymological sense)]

butadiene (byo͞o′tə dī′ēn, -dī ēn′), *n. Chem.* an inflammable, colourless, hydrocarbon gas, C_4H_6, used in making synthetic rubber. [f. BUTA(NE) + DI-[1] + -ENE]

Butagas (byo͞o′tə găs′), *n. Trademark.* butane as sold under pressure in cylinders.

butane (byo͞o′tān, byo͞o tān′), *n. Chem.* a saturated aliphatic hydrocarbon, C_4H_{10}, existing in two isomeric forms and used as a fuel and a chemical intermediate. [f. BUT(YL) + -ANE]

butanol (byo͞o′tə nŏl′), *n. Chem.* butyl alcohol, usually the *n*-isomer.

butanone (byo͞o′tə nōn′), *n. Chem.* an inflammable ketone, C_4H_8O, used as a solvent and in making plastics.

butch (bo͝och), *n. Slang.* 1. a lesbian, homosexual, or woman exhibiting extravagantly masculine characteristics. 2. a man, esp. one of notable physical strength. —*adj.* 3. of a man or woman, exhibiting masculine characteristics. [? der. BUTCHER]

butcher (bo͝och′ə), *n.* 1. a retail dealer in meat. 2. one who slaughters certain domesticated animals, or dresses their flesh, for food or for market. 3. a person guilty of cruel or indiscriminate slaughter. —*v.t.* 4. to kill or slaughter for food or for market. 5. to murder indiscriminately or brutally. 6. to bungle; botch: *to butcher a job.* [ME *bocher,* t. OF, der. *boc* he-goat, t. Gmc. See BUCK[1]] —**Syn. 5.** See **slaughter.**

butcher-bird (bo͝och′ə bûd′), *n.* any of various shrikes of the genus *Lanius,* which impale their prey upon thorns.

butcherly (bo͝och′ə lĭ), *adj.* like a butcher; cruel.

butcher's-broom (bo͝och′əz bro͞om′, -bro͝om′), *n.* a shrubby, liliaceous evergreen, *Ruscus aculeatus,* of England, used for making brooms.

butchery (bo͝och′ə rĭ), *n., pl.* **-eries.** 1. the trade or business of a butcher. 2. brutal slaughter of human beings; carnage. 3. a slaughterhouse.

Bute (byo͞ot), *n.* 1. Also, **Buteshire** (byo͞ot′shĭə, -shə). a county in SW Scotland, composed of islands. 15,129 pop. (1961); 218 sq. mi. *Co. town:* Rothesay. 2. an island in the Firth of Clyde: a part of this county. 13,602 pop. (est. 1964); 50 sq. mi. **3. John Stuart, 3rd Earl of,** 1713–92, British statesman: prime minister 1761–63.

butene (byo͞o′tēn), *n. Chem.* butylene.

butler (bŭt′lə), *n.* 1. the head male servant of a household. 2. the male servant having charge of the wines, plate, etc. [ME *buteler,* t. AF: m. *butuiller,* der. *bouteille* bottle] —**but′lership′,** *n.*

Butler (bŭt′lə), *n.* **1. Joseph,** 1692–1752, English bishop, theologian, and author. **2. Samuel,** 1612–80, English poet and satirist. **3. Samuel,** 1835–1902, English novelist.

butler's pantry, a room between a kitchen and a dining room arranged for the storage of china and silverware and containing a sink.

butlery (bŭt′lə rĭ), *n., pl.* **-leries.** a butler's room or pantry; a buttery. [f. BUTLER + -Y[3]; r. ME *boteleryе,* t. OF: m. *bouteillerie* storeroom for wine]

butt[1] (bŭt), *n.* 1. the end or extremity of anything, esp. the thicker, larger, or blunt end, as of a rifle, fishing rod, whip handle, arrow, log, etc. 2. an end which is not used up: *a cigarette butt.* 3. buttock. [ME *bott* buttock; appar. short for BUTTOCK]

butt[2] (bŭt), *n.* 1. a person or thing that is an object of wit, ridicule, sarcasm, etc., or contempt. 2. (in rifle practice) **a.** a wall of earth behind the targets of a target range, which prevents bullets from scattering over a wide area. **b.** (*pl.*) a wall in front of the targets of a target range, behind which men can safely lower, score, and raise targets during firing. 3. the target for archery practice. 4. (*pl.*) a range for rifle or archery practice. 5. a low wall or bank from behind which sportsmen shoot game birds. 6. a hinge for a door or the like, secured to the butting surfaces or ends instead of the adjacent sides. 7. *Obs.* a goal; limit. —*v.i.* 8. to have an end or projection (*on*); be adjacent (*to*). —*v.t.* 9. to join an end of (something); join the ends of (two things) together. [late ME, t. OF: m. *bout* end, extremity, of Gmc orig.]

butt[3] (bŭt), *v.t.* 1. to strike with the head or horns. —*v.i.* 2. to strike something or at something with the head or horns. 3. to project. 4. *Colloq.* to interrupt; interfere; intrude (fol. by *in*). —*n.* 5. a push with head or horns. [ME *butt(en),* t. OF: m. *bouter* strike, thrust, abut, touch, der. *bout* end, of Gmc orig.]

butt[4] (bŭt), *n.* 1. a large cask for wine, beer, or ale. 2. any cask or barrel. 3. a unit of capacity, equal to two hogsheads. [late ME; cf. OF *botte, bote,* c. It. *botte,* g. LL *butta, buttis* vessel, cask]

Butt (bŭt), *n.* **Dame Clara,** 1873–1936, English opera singer.

butte (byo͞ot), *n. Western U.S. and Canada.* an isolated hill or mountain rising abruptly above the surrounding land. [t. F: hill, prop., mound for target]

butter (bŭt′ə), *n.* 1. the fatty portion of milk, separating as a soft whitish or yellowish solid when milk or cream is agitated or churned. 2. this substance, processed for cooking and table use. 3. any of various other spreads of similar consistence: *butter icing, peanut butter.* 4. any of various substances of butter-like consistency, as various metallic chlorides, and certain vegetable oils solid at ordinary temperatures. —*v.t.* 5. to put butter on or in. 6. *Colloq.* to flatter grossly (often fol. by *up*). [ME; OE *butere,* t. L: m. s. *būtyrum,* t. Gk: m. *boútyron*] —**but′ter-like′,** *adj.*

butter-and-eggs (bŭt′ər ən ĕgz′), *n.* any of certain plants whose flowers are of two shades of yellow, as the toadflax.

butterball (bŭt′ə bôl′), *n.* 1. the bufflehead. 2. *Colloq.* a fat, round person.

butterbean (bŭt′ə bēn′), *n.* a variety of small-seeded lima beans, *Phaseolus lunatus,* grown in the southern U.S.

butterbur (bŭt′ə bû′), *n.* a perennial herb composite, *Petasites vulgaris,* bearing large woolly leaves said to have been used to wrap butter.

buttercup (bŭt′ə kŭp′), *n.* a plant of the genus *Ranunculus,* esp. *R. acris* or *R. bulbosus,* with yellow cup-shaped flowers.

butterdish (bŭt′ə dĭsh′), *n.* a small container in which butter is placed on the table.

butterfat (bŭt′ə făt′), *n.* butter; milk fat; a mixture of glycerides, mainly butyrin, olein, and palmitin.

Butterfield (bŭt′ə fēld′), *n.* **William,** 1814–1900, English architect.

butter-fingers (bŭt′ə fĭng′gəz), *n.* a person who fails to catch or drops things easily.

butterfish (bŭt′ə fĭsh′), *n., pl.* **-fishes,** (*esp. collectively*) **-fish.** 1. an elongated blenny, *Pholis gunnellus,* of the coastal waters of the North Atlantic. 2. a small, flattened, marine food fish, *Poronotus triacanthus,* of the Atlantic coast of the U.S., having very small scales and smooth skin.

butterfly (bŭt′ə flī′), *n., pl.* **-flies.** 1. any of a group of lepidopterous insects characterized by clubbed antennae, large, broad wings, often conspicuously coloured and marked, and diurnal habits. 2. a person who flits gaily but aimlessly from one thing to another. 3. *Swimming.* a stroke made in the prone position in which both arms are lifted simultaneously out of the water and flung forwards. [OE *buttorflēoge,* f. *buttor-* (comb. form of *butere*) + *flēoge* fly, c. G *Butterfliege*; ? orig. used of a butter-coloured (yellow) species]

butterfly fish, any of the tropical marine fishes of the family *Chaetodontidae,* as *Chaetodon copistratus,* which are suggestive in shape or colouring of the butterfly.

butterfly nut, a metal nut turned by projecting finger grips, resembling the wings of a butterfly; wing nut.

butterfly table, a small, occasional table with drop leaves having butterfly-shaped supports.

butterfly weed, 1. either of two closely related North American milkweeds, *Asclepias tuberosa* and *A. decumbens,* bearing orange-coloured flowers. 2. an erect North American herb, *Gaura coccinea,* related to the evening primrose, with wandlike spikes of red flowers.

butterine (bŭt′ə rēn′, -ə rĭn), *n.* an artificial butter partly made from milk; oleomargarine.

butterknife (bŭt′ə nīf′), *n.* a blunt-edged, flat-bladed utensil for cutting and serving butter at table.

buttermilk (bŭt′ə mĭlk′), *n.* the more or less acidulous liquid remaining after the butter has been separated from milk or cream.

butternut (bŭt′ə nŭt′), *n.* 1. the edible oily nut of an American tree, *Juglans cinerea,* of the walnut family. 2. the tree itself. 3. the souari nut. 4. dark brown.

butterscotch (bŭt′ə skŏch′), *n.* 1. a kind of toffee made with butter. 2. a flavour produced in puddings, icing, ice-cream, etc., by a combination of brown sugar, vanilla extract, and butter, with other ingredients.

butterwort (bŭt′ə wût′), *n.* any plant of the genus *Pinguicula,* small herbs whose leaves secrete a viscid substance in which small insects are caught.

buttery[1] (bŭt′ə rĭ), *adj.* 1. like, containing, or spread with, butter. 2. *Colloq.* grossly flattering. [f. BUTTER + -Y[1]]

buttery[2] (bŭt′ə rĭ), *n., pl.* **-ries.** **1.** a room in which the wines, liquors, and provisions of a household are kept; a pantry. **2.** a room, as esp. in colleges at Oxford and Cambridge Universities, from which certain articles of food and drink are supplied to the students. [ME *boterie*, t. OF, der. *bot(t)e* cask]

butt joint, *Bldg Trades.* a joint formed by two pieces of wood or metal united end to end without overlapping.

buttock (bŭt′ək), *n.* **1.** *Anat.* **a.** either of the two protuberances which form the rump. **b.** (*pl.*) the rump. **2.** (*sing or pl.*) *Naut.* the convex aftermost portion of a ship's body above the waterline. **3.** *Wrestling.* any of various moves which involve the use of the buttocks as a fulcrum to throw the opponent. *—v.t.* **4.** *Wrestling.* to throw, using the buttocks as a fulcrum. [ME *buttok*, OE *buttuc*]

button (bŭt′n), *n.* **1.** a disc or knob on a piece of cloth which, when passed through a slit or loop either in the same piece or another, serves as a fastening. **2.** anything resembling a button. **3.** an object of little value: *not worth a button.* **4.** *Bot.* a bud or other protuberant part of a plant. **5.** a young or undeveloped mushroom. **6.** a disc pressed to close an electric circuit, as in ringing a bell; push-button. **7.** (*pl.*) *Colloq.* a page or bellboy. **8.** *Metall.* a globule or mass of metal lying at the bottom of a crucible after fusion. **9.** *Fencing.* the protective knob fixed to the point of a foil. *—v.t.* **10.** to fasten with a button or buttons. **11.** *Colloq.* to bring (a business transaction, etc.) to a successful conclusion (fol. by *up*). **12.** to provide with a button or buttons. **13.** *Fencing.* to touch with the button of the foil. **14.** *Rowing.* a leather projection round the loom of an oar to prevent it slipping through the rowlock. *—v.i.* **15.** to be capable of being buttoned. [ME *boton*, t. OF, der. *bouter* thrust. See BUTT[2]] **—but′toner,** *n.* **—but′ton-like′,** *adj.*

buttonball (bŭt′n bôl′), *n.* the buttonwood (def. 1).

buttonbush (bŭt′n bo͝osh′), *n.* a name given to *Cephalanthus occidentalis*, a North American shrub, on account of its globular flower heads.

buttonhole (bŭt′n hōl′), *n., v.,* **-holed, -holing.** *—n.* **1.** the hole, slit, or loop through which a button is passed. **2.** a small flower or nosegay worn in the buttonhole in the lapel of a jacket. *—v.t.* **3.** to sew with buttonhole stitch. **4.** to make buttonholes in. **5.** to seize by or as by the buttonhole in the lapel of the jacket and detain in conversation. **—but′tonhol′er,** *n.*

buttonhole stitch, *Sewing.* a looped stitch used to strengthen the edge of material, as in a buttonhole.

buttonhook (bŭt′n ho͝ok′), *n.* a small metal or other stiff hook used for buttoning shoes, gloves, etc.

buttonmould (bŭt′n mōld′), *n.* a disc of bone, wood, or metal, to be covered with fabric to form a button.

button quail, any bird of the family *Turnicidae*, superficially resembling the true quails but more closely related to the pigeons, esp. *Turnix sylvatica* of Spain, Africa, and southern Asia.

button tree, **1.** a tropical tree or shrub, *Conocarpus erecta*, with heavy, hard, compact wood and button-like fruits. **2.** the buttonwood.

buttonwood (bŭt′n wo͝od′), *n.* **1.** a tall, North American plane tree, *Platanus occidentalis*, yielding a useful timber (so called from its small pendulous fruit). **2.** the button tree.

buttony (bŭt′ə nĭ), *adj.* **1.** like a button. **2.** having many buttons.

buttress (bŭt′rĭs), *n.* **1.** *Archit.* a structure built against a wall or building for the purpose of giving it stability. **2.** any prop or support. **3.** a thing shaped like a buttress, as a rock-wall projecting from a mountainside. *—v.t.* **4.** *Archit.* to support by a buttress. **5.** to prop up; support. [ME *boterace*, t. OF: m. *bouterez*, pl., der. *bouter* thrust, abut]

A, Buttress; B, Flying buttress

butt weld, *Bldg Trades.* a weld formed by joining the flattened ends of two pieces of iron at a white heat.

butty[1] (bŭt′ĭ; *Dial.* bo͝ot′ĭ), *n. Dial.* a workmate, esp. in a colliery.

butty[2] (bŭt′ĭ; *Dial.* bo͝ot′ĭ), *n. Dial.* **1.** a slice of bread spread with butter. **2.** a sandwich.

butyl (byo͞o′tĭl), *n. Chem.* a univalent radical, C_4H_9, from butane. [f. BUT(YRIC) + -YL]

butyl alcohols, *Chem.* a group of three isomeric alcohols of the formula C_4H_9OH.

butylene (byo͞o′tĭ lēn′), *n. Chem.* any of three isomeric gaseous hydrocarbons of the formula C_4H_8, belonging to the ethylene series. [f. BUTYL + -ENE]

butyl rubber, *Chem.* **1.** a synthetic rubber, prepared by polymerization of butylene containing a little butadiene, used for inner tubes of motor-car tyres because of its airtight qual ties. **2.** (*cap.*) a trademark for this substance.

butyraceous (byo͞o′tĭ rā′shəs), *adj.* of the nature of, resembling, or containing butter. [f. s. L *būtyrum* butter + -ACEOUS]

butyrate (byo͞o′tĭ rāt′), *n. Chem.* a salt or ester of butyric acid.

butyric (byo͞o tĭ′rĭk), *adj. Chem.* pertaining to or derived from butyric acid. [f. s. L *būtyrum* butter + -IC]

butyric acid, *Chem.* either of two isomeric acids C_3H_7-COOH, esp. the one, a rancid liquid, present in spoiled butter, etc., as an ester and sometimes free.

butyrin (byo͞o′tĭ rĭn), *n. Chem.* a colourless liquid fat or ester present in butter, and formed from glycerine and butyric acid. [f. s. L *būtyrum* butter + -IN[2]]

buxom (bŭk′səm), *adj.* **1.** (of a woman) full-bosomed, plump, and attractive because of radiant health. **2.** (usually of a woman) healthy, attractive, cheerful, and lively. [ME; early ME *buhsum* pliant, der. OE *būgan* bend, bow. See -SOME[1]] **—bux′omly,** *adv.* **—bux′omness,** *n.*

Buxtehude (*Ger.* bo͝ok stə ho͞o′də), *n.* **Dietrich,** 1637–1707, Danish organist and composer in Germany.

Buxton (bŭk′stən), *n.* a town in England, in Derbyshire. 19,155 (1961).

buy (bī), *v.,* **bought, buying,** *n.* *—v.t.* **1.** to acquire the possession of, or the right to, by paying an equivalent, esp. in money. **2.** to acquire by giving any kind of recompense: *to buy favour with flattery.* **3.** to hire; bribe. **4.** *Chiefly Theol.* to redeem; ransom. **5.** to get rid of (a claim, opposition, etc.) by payment; purchase the non-intervention of; bribe (fol. by *off*). **6.** to secure all of (an owner's or partner's) share or interest in an enterprise (fol. by *out*). **7.** to buy as much as one can of (fol. by *up*). **8.** to recover for the owner at an auction (fol. by *in*). *—v.i.* **9.** to be or become a purchaser. **10. buy it,** *Colloq.* to die: *he bought it at Ypres.* *—n.* **11.** *Colloq.* a bargain: *a good buy.* [ME *b(u)yen* etc., OE *byg-*, s. *bycgan*, c. OS *buggian*, Goth. *bugjan*] **—buy′able,** *adj.*

—**Syn. 1.** BUY, PURCHASE imply obtaining or acquiring property or goods for a price. BUY is the common and informal word, applying to any such transaction: *to buy a house, vegetables at the market.* PURCHASE is more formal and may connote buying on a larger scale: *to purchase a year's supplies.* —**Ant. 1.** sell.

buyer (bī′ə), *n.* **1.** one who buys; a purchaser. **2.** a purchasing agent, as for a chain-store.

Buys Ballot's Law (bīs′bə lōts′, bois′-), the principle that in the N Hemisphere atmospheric pressure is higher on the left when facing into the wind; in the S Hemisphere it is higher on the right. [named after C. H. D. *Buys Ballot*, 1817–1890, Danish meteorologist]

buzz (bŭz), *n.* **1.** a low, vibrating, humming sound, as of bees. **2.** a rumour or report. **3.** *Colloq.* a telephone call. *—v.i.* **4.** to make a low, vibrating, humming sound. **5.** to speak or whisper with such a sound. **6.** to move busily from place to place (usually fol. by *about*). **7.** *Colloq.* to go; leave (usually fol. by *off* or *along*). *—v.t.* **8.** to make a buzzing sound with: *the fly buzzed its wings.* **9.** to spread (a rumour) secretively. **10.** to communicate with buzzes, as in signalling. **11.** *Colloq.* to make a telephone call to. **12.** *Colloq.* to throw; hurl. **13.** *Aeron. Colloq.* **a.** to fly an aeroplane very low over: *to buzz a field.* **b.** to signal or greet (someone) by flying an aeroplane low and slowing the motor spasmodically. **14.** *Colloq.* to drain (a bottle) to the last drop. [imit.]

buzzard (bŭz′əd), *n.* **1.** any of various more or less heavily built hawks of the genus *Buteo* and allied genera, as *B. vulgaris*, a rather sluggish European species. **2.** any of various carrion-eating birds, as the **honey buzzard,** *Pernis apivorus*, and the turkey buzzard or turkey vulture, *Cathartes aura.* **3.** a foolish person. **4.** a foolish or unsuccessful act, procedure, or the like. [ME *busard*, t. OF, der. *buse* buzzard, g. L *būteo* kind of hawk]

Turkey buzzard, *Cathartes aura* (Ab. 2½ ft long)

buzzbomb (bŭz′bŏm′), *n. Mil.* a type of self-steering aerial bomb, launched from large land-based rocket platforms, and used by the Germans in World War II over England.

buzzer (bŭz′ə), *n.* **1.** one who or that which buzzes. **2.** a signalling apparatus similar to an electric bell, but producing sound by the vibration of an armature.

buzz-saw (bŭz′sô′), *n.* a small circular saw, so named because of the noise it makes.

buzzwig (bŭz′wĭg′), *n.* **1.** a large, bushy wig. **2.** a person wearing such a wig. **3.** a person of consequence; bigwig.

B.V., **1.** (L *Beata Virgo*) Blessed Virgin. **2.** (L *bene vale*) farewell.

B.V.M., (L *Beata Virgo Maria*) Blessed Virgin Mary.

bvt, **1.** brevet. **2.** brevetted.

bwana (bwä′nə), *n.* sir; master. [t. Swahili]

B.W.R., boiling-water reactor.

by (bī), *prep.* **1.** near to: *a house by the river.* **2.** using as a route: *he came by the main road.* **3.** through or on as a means of conveyance: *he journeyed by water.* **4.** to and past a point near: *he went by the church.* **5.** within the compass or period of: *by day, by night.* **6.** not later than: *by two o'clock.* **7.** to the extent of: *longer by an inch.* **8.** through evidence or authority of: *by his own account.* **9.** with the participation of: *regretted by all.* **10.** in conformity with: *by any standards this is a good book.* **11.** before; in the presence of: *to swear by all that is sacred.* **12.** through the agency or efficacy of: *founded by Napoleon, done by force.* **13.** after; in serial order: *piece by piece.* **14.** combined with in multiplication or relative dimension: *five feet by six feet.* **15.** involving as unit of measure: *beef by the pound.* *—adv.* **16.** near to something: *it's close by.* **17.** to and past a point near something: *the car drove by.* **18.** aside: *put it by for the moment.* **19.** over; past: *in times gone by.* **20. by and by,** at some time in the future; before long; presently. **21. by and large,** in general; on the whole. *—adj.* **22.** situated to one side. **23.** secondary, incidental. *—n.* **24.** bye. [ME; OE *bī*, stressed form answering to unstressed *be-*, c. G *bei* by, near]

—Syn. 12. BY, THROUGH, WITH indicate agency or means of getting something done or accomplished. BY is regularly used to denote the agent (person or force) in passive constructions: *it is done by many, destroyed by fire.* It also indicates means: *send it by airmail.* WITH denotes the instrument (usually consciously) employed by an agent: *he cut it with the scissors.* THROUGH designates particularly immediate agency or instrumentality or reason or motive: *to yield through fear, wounded through carelessness.*

by-, a prefix meaning: **1.** secondary; incidental, as in *by-product.* **2.** out of the way; removed, as in *byway.* **3.** near, as in *bystander.* Also, **bye-**.

Bydgoszcz (*Pol.* bĭd′gôshch), *n.* a town in NW Poland. 250,000 (est. 1964). German, **Bromberg.**

bye (bī), *n.* Also, **by. 1.** *Sport.* the state of having no competitor in a contest where several competitors are engaged in pairs, conferring the right to compete in the next round in an eliminatory competition. **2.** *Golf.* the holes of a stipulated course still unplayed after the match is decided. **3.** *Cricket.* a run made on a ball not struck by the batsman. **4.** something subsidiary, secondary, or out of the way. **5. by the bye.** Also, **by the by,** incidentally; by the way. *—adj.* **6.** by. [var. spelling of BY prep., in noun use]

bye-, var. of **by-**.

bye-bye (bī′bī′ *for 1*; bī′bī′ *for 2*), *interj., n., pl.* **bye-byes.** *Childish or Colloq.* *—interj.* **1.** goodbye. *—n.* **2.** (*pl.*) sleep: *go to bye-byes.*

by-election (bī′ĭ lĕk′shən), *n.* a parliamentary election held between general elections, to fill a vacancy. Also, **bye-election.**

Byelorussian Soviet Socialist Republic (byĕl′ō rŭsh′-ən), White Russian Soviet Socialist Republic.

Byelostok (*Russ.* byĭ lä stôk′), *n.* Russian name of **Białystok.**

bygone (bī′gŏn′), *adj.* **1.** past; gone by; out of date: *bygone days.* *—n.* **2.** that which is past.

bylaw (bī′lô′), *n.* **1.** an ordinance of a local authority having legal effect only within the boundaries of that authority's jurisdiction. **2.** a subsidiary law. **3.** a standing rule, as of a company or society, not in its constitution. Also, **bye-law.** [f. BY- + LAW; r. ME *bilawe*, f. *by* town (t. Scand.; cf. Dan. *by*) + *lawe* law]

by-line (bī′līn′), *n.* **1.** *Journalism.* a line under the heading of a newspaper or magazine article giving the writer's name. **2.** Also, **goal line.** *Soccer.* a white line marking the limits of the playing area of a soccer pitch.

byname (bī′nām′), *n.* **1.** a secondary name; cognomen; surname. **2.** a nickname.

Byng (bĭng), *n.* **1. John,** 1704–57, English admiral; executed 'for neglect of duty.' **2. Julian Hedworth George** (*Viscount Byng of Vimy*), 1862–1935, British general: governor-general of Canada 1921–26.

bypass (bī′päs′), *n.* **1.** a road enabling motorists to avoid towns and other heavy traffic points or any obstruction to easy travel on a main road. **2.** a secondary pipe or other channel connected with a main passage as for conducting a liquid or gas around a fixture, pipe or appliance. **3.** *Elect.* a shunt (def. 8) *—v.t.* **4.** to avoid (obstructions, etc.) by following a bypass. **5.** to cause (fluid, traffic, etc.) to follow such a channel. **6.** to go over the head of (one's immediate supervisor, etc.).

bypath (bī′päth′), *n.* a private path; an indirect course or means; byway.

byplay (bī′plā′), *n.* action or speech carried on aside while the main action proceeds, esp. on the stage.

by-product (bī′prŏd′ŭkt), *n.* a secondary or incidental product, as in a process of manufacture.

Byrd (bûd), *n.* **1. Richard Evelyn,** 1888–1957, rear admiral in U.S. Navy: polar explorer. **2. William,** 1543–1623, English composer and organist.

byre (bī′ə), *n.* a cowhouse or shed. [OE *bȳre*, der. OE *būr* hut. Cf. BOWER[1]]

byrlaw (bīə′lô′), *n.* *Hist., Chiefly Scot.* the local custom of a district by which rustic disputes were settled by common consent without litigation. **—byr′law′man,** *n.*

byrnie (bû′nĭ), *n.* a shirt of mail; a hauberk. [var. of ME *brynie*, t. Scand.; cf. Icel. *brynja*, c. OE *byrne* coat of mail]

byroad (bī′rōd′), *n.* a side road.

Byron (bī′ə rən), *n.* **1. George Gordon, Lord** (*6th Baron Byron*), 1788–1824, English poet. **2. Cape,** a promontory on the coast of New South Wales forming the most easterly point of mainland Australia.

Byronic (bī rŏn′ĭk), *adj.* **1.** of or pertaining to Lord Byron. **2.** possessing the characteristics of Byron or his poetry, esp. melancholy, melodramatic energy, etc. **—Byron′ically,** *adv.* **—By′ronism,** *n.*

byssus (bĭs′əs), *n., pl.* **byssuses, byssi** (bĭs′ī), **1.** *Zool.* a collection of silky filaments by which certain molluscs attach themselves to rocks. **2.** (among the ancients) **a.** (orig.) a fine yellowish flax, or the linen made from it, as the Egyptian mummy-cloth. **b.** (later) cotton or silk. [t. L, t. Gk: m. *býssos*, of oriental orig.] **—byssaceous** (bĭ sā′shəs), *adj.*

bystander (bī′stăn′də), *n.* a person present but not involved; a chance looker-on.

bystreet (bī′strēt′), *n.* a separate, private, or obscure street; a side street; a byway.

Bytom (*Pol.* bĭ′tŏm), *n.* a town in S Poland: formerly in Germany. 192,000 (est. 1964). German, **Beuthen.**

byway (bī′wā′), *n.* **1.** a secluded, private, or obscure road. **2.** a subsidiary or obscure field of research, endeavour, etc.

bywoner (bī′vō′nə), *n.* a poor white squatter on a farm in southern Africa, who pays the owner of the farm through his labour or a proportion of his crops. [t. Afrikaans: one who lives near]

byword (bī′wûd′), *n.* **1.** the name of a quality or concept which characterizes some person or group; the epitome (of): *his name is a byword for courage.* **2.** a word or phrase used proverbially; a common saying; a proverb. **3.** an object of general reproach, derision, scorn. etc. **4.** an epithet, often of scorn. [OE *bīword*]

by-work (bī′wûk′), *n.* work done in addition to one's regular work, as in intervals of leisure.

by-your-leave (bī′yô lēv′), *n.* a request for permission, or an apology.

Byz., Byzantine.

Byzantine (bĭ zăn′tīn, bī-), *adj.* **1.** of or pertaining to Byzantium. **2.** of or pertaining to the Byzantine Empire. **3.** of, pertaining to, or resembling Byzantine architecture. *—n.* **4.** a native or inhabitant of Byzantium. [t. L: m. s. *Bȳzantinus*]

Byzantine architecture, a style of architecture developed in Byzantium and its provinces during the 5th and 6th centuries A.D., characterized by centralized plans, vaulting, and rich use of light, shade, colourful mosaics, paintings, and decoration.

Byzantine Church, Orthodox Church.

Byzantine Empire, the Eastern Roman Empire after the fall of the Western Empire in A.D. 476, having Constantinople as its capital.

Byzantine Empire

Byzantium (bĭ zăn′tĭ əm, bī-), *n.* an ancient Greek city on the Bosporus, commanding the entrance to the Black Sea: Constantine I built the city of Constantinople on this site, A.D. 330.

bz., benzene.

C

C, c (sē), *n., pl.* **C's** or **Cs, c's** or **cs. 1.** a consonant, the third letter of the English alphabet. **2.** *Music.* **a.** the first or keynote of the C major scale, the third degree of the relative minor scale (A minor). **b.** a written or printed note representing this tone. **c.** a key, string, or pipe tuned to this note. **d.** (in solmization) the first note of the scale of C, called **do. e.** middle C.

C, 1. *Elect.* capacitance. **2.** *Chem.* carbon. **3.** (L *centum*) 100. See **Roman numerals. 4.** centigrade. **5.** century: *C19*. **6.** *Music.* (as a time signature) common time. **7.** coulomb. **8.** *U.S. Slang.* a hundred-dollar bill.

C., 1. Cape. **2.** Catholic. **3.** Celsius (= centigrade). **4.** Celtic. **5.** centigrade. **6.** Conservative.

c., 1. *Elect.* capacity. **2.** cash. **3.** *Cricket.* caught. **4.** cent; cents. **5.** centigrade. **6.** centime. **7.** centimetre. **8.** century. **9.** chapter. **10.** Also, **c** (L *circa, circiter, circum*) about. **11.** cognate with. **12.** copyright. **13.** cubic. **14.** *Physics.* the velocity of light in a vacuum.

Ca, *Chem.* calcium.

ca, (L *circa*) about: *ca* A.D. 476.

ca' (kä, kô), *v.t., v.i. Scot.* to call, esp. in the (obs.) sense 'to drive'. [var. of CALL]

ca., centiare.

C.A., 1. capital account. **2.** Central America. **3.** chartered accountant. **4.** chief accountant. **5.** Consumers' Association.

Caaba (kä′bə), *n.* Kaaba.

cab¹ (kăb), *n.* **1.** taxicab. **2.** any of various one-horse vehicles for public hire, as the hansom or the brougham. **3.** the covered part of a locomotive or lorry, where the driver sits. [short for CABRIOLET]

cab² (kăb), *n.* a Hebrew measure equal to about three pints. Also, **kab.** [t. Heb.: m. *qab* vessel]

C.A.B., Citizens' Advice Bureau.

cabal (kə băl′), *n., v.,* **-balled, -balling.** **—***n.* **1.** the secret schemes of a small group of plotters; an intrigue. **2.** a small group of secret plotters. **3.** (*often cap.*) *Eng. Hist.* a group of five ministers of Charles II in 1672. **—***v.i.* **4.** to form a cabal; intrigue; conspire; plot. [var. of *cabbal*, t. ML: s. *cabbāla.* See CABBALA. Def. 3 from the names of the ministers: *C*(*lifford*), *A*(*rlington*), B(UCKINGHAM), *A*(*shley*), *L*(*auderdale*)]

cabala (kə bä′lə), *n.* cabbala. **—cabal′ism,** *n.* **—cabal′ist,** *n.*

caballero (kăb′ə lyĕə′rō; *Sp.* kä bä lyĕ′rô), *n., pl.* **-ros.** a Spanish gentleman. [t. Sp., g. L *caballārius* horseman. See CAVALIER]

cabana (kə bä′nə), *n. Chiefly U.S.* **1.** a cabin; cottage; hut. **2.** a bathhouse near the water's edge. Also, *Spanish,* **cabaña** (*Sp.* kä bä′nyä). [t. Sp.]

cabane (kə băn′), *n. Mountaineering.* a hut at a high altitude, used for overnight stays.

cabaret (kăb′ə rā′), *n.* **1.** a form of musical, variety, or other entertainment at a restaurant, nightclub, etc., often late into the night; a floor show. **2.** a club, etc., that provides such entertainment. [t. F: cellar, ult. orig. uncert.]

cabbage¹ (kăb′ĭj), *n., v.,* **-baged, -baging.** **—***n.* **1.** any of various cultivated varieties of the cruciferous plant *Brassica oleracea*, var. *capitata*, with short stem and leaves formed into a compact, edible head. **2.** any of various plants resembling a cabbage. **3.** the head of the ordinary cabbage. **—***v.i.* **4.** to form a head like a cabbage. [ME *caboche*, t. F, prob. t. Pr.: m. *caboso*, der. *cap* head, g. L *caput*]

cabbage² (kăb′ĭj), *n., v.,* **-baged, -baging.** **—***n.* **1.** something stolen, esp. pieces of cloth by a tailor when making garments. **—***v.t., v.i.* **2.** to steal; pilfer. [orig. uncert.]

cabbage butterfly, a large, white butterfly of the Old World, *Pieris brassicae*, the larvae of which feed on cabbage. Also, **cabbage white.**

cabbage fly, a small dipterous fly, *Erioischia brassicae*, the grubs of which feed on the roots of cabbage.

cabbage moth, a noctuid moth, *Mamestra brassicae*, the caterpillars of which infest cabbage.

cabbage palm, any of several palm trees with large terminal leaf buds which are eaten like cabbage, as *Oreodoxa* (*Roystonea*) *oleracea* of the West Indies. Also, **cabbage tree.**

cabbage tree, 1. cabbage palm. **2.** a palmaceous tree, *Livistona australis*, of Australia. **3.** *Austral.* a wide-brimmed hat made from the leaves of this tree.

cabbage white, cabbage butterfly.

cabbage worm, the larva of the cabbage butterfly.

cabbala (kə bä′lə), *n.* **1.** (among certain Jewish rabbis and medieval Christians) a system of esoteric theosophy, based on a mystical interpretation of the Scriptures. **2.** any occult or secret doctrine or science. Also, **cabala, kabala, kabbala.** [t. ML, t. Heb.: m. *qabbālāh* tradition] **—cabbal′ism,** *n.* **—cabbal′ist,** *n.*

cabbalistic (kăb′ə lĭs′tĭk), *adj.* **1.** pertaining to the cabbala. **2.** mystic; occult. Also, **cab′balis′tical.**

cabby (kăb′ĭ), *n., pl.* **-ies.** *Colloq.* a cab driver.

caber (kā′bə), *n. Scot.* a pole or beam, esp. one thrown as a trial of strength in the Highland game of **tossing the caber.** [t. Gaelic: m. *cabar* pole]

cabin (kăb′ĭn), *n.* **1.** a small house; hut, esp. a temporary structure as on a building site. **2.** an apartment or room in a ship, as for passengers. **3.** (in a passenger ship) a room used for the accommodation of higher-fare passengers or officers. **4.** (in a warship) the apartment used by the commanding officer or flag officer. **5.** *Aeron.* the enclosed place in an aircraft for the pilot, passengers, or cargo. **—***v.i.* **6.** to live in a cabin. **—***v.t.* **7.** to confine; enclose tightly; cramp. [ME *cabane*, t. F, t. Pr.: m. *cabana*, g. LL *capanna*, of uncert. orig.] **—Syn. 1.** cot, shanty, shack.

cabin boy, a boy employed to wait on the officers and passengers of a ship.

cabin class, a class of accommodation on a passenger ship superior to tourist class but inferior to first class.

cabin cruiser, a motor boat with a cabin and berths.

Cabinda (*Port.* kə bēn′də), *n.* a Portuguese enclave in the Republic of Congo, administered as part of Angola. 50,233 pop. (est. 1950); 2807 sq. mi.

cabinet (kăb′ĭ nĭt), *n.* **1.** (*also cap.*) a council advising a sovereign or chief executive; the group of ministers responsible for the government of a nation. See **shadow cabinet. 2.** a piece of furniture with shelves, drawers, etc., for holding or displaying valuable objects, dishes, etc. **3.** a piece of furniture holding a record-player, radio, television, or the like. **4.** a case with compartments for precious objects, etc. **5.** a private room. **6.** *Archaic.* a small room. **7.** *Obs.* a small cabin. **8.** a standard size for a sheet of paper (6 inches by 4 inches) or for a photographic print ($6\frac{1}{2}$ inches by $4\frac{1}{4}$ inches). **—***adj.* **9.** pertaining to a political cabinet: *a cabinet meeting.* **10.** pertaining to a private room. **11.** private; confidential; secret. **12.** of suitable value, beauty, or size for a private room, small case, etc.: *a cabinet edition of Milton.* **13.** (of a projection, drawing, etc.) having all vertical and horizontal lines in a representation of a three-dimensional object drawn to exact scale, with oblique lines reduced to about half scale so as to offset the appearance of distortion. [t. F, t. It.: m. *gabinetto*, ? der. *gabbia* cage, g. L *cavea*; in some senses, dim. of CABIN]

cabinet-maker (kăb′ĭ nĭt mā′kə), *n.* a workman who uses tools, woodworking machines, and wood to build items for storage and household equipment.

cabinet minister, a minister who is a member of the cabinet.

cabinet pudding, a steamed pudding made of bread, milk, eggs, dried fruit, and sugar.

cabinetwork (kăb′ĭ nĭt wûk′), *n.* **1.** the making of fine furniture, etc. **2.** the product made.

cable (kā′bl), *n., v.,* **-bled, -bling.** **—***n.* **1.** a thick, strong rope, often one of several wires twisted together. **2.** *Naut.* **a.** the rope or chain used to hold a vessel at anchor. **b.** cable's length. **3.** *Elect.* a stranded conductor, or a combination of conductors insulated from one another. **4.** a telegram sent abroad, esp. by submarine cable. **—***v.t.* **5.** to send (a message) by submarine cable. **6.** to send a cable to. **7.** to fasten with a cable. **8.** to furnish with a cable or cables. **—***v.i.* **9.** to send a message by submarine cable. [ME *cable, cabel*, c. D, MLG, MHG, G *Kabel*, all t. Rom.; cf. F *cable* (t. Pr.), Sp. *cable*, all g. LL *capulum* halter]

cable car, 1. a cable-hauled tramcar. **2.** a car on a cable-way.

cablegram (kā′bl grăm′), *n.* cable (def. 4).

cable-laid (kā′bl lād′), *adj.* (of a rope) made by laying three plain-laid ropes together with a left-handed twist.

cable lift, a ski-lift.

cable moulding, *Archit.* a style of moulding carved to resemble thick rope.

cable railway, 1. a funicular railway. **2.** a railway on which the cars are hauled by a moving cable.

cablese (kā′bl ēz′), *n.* the language used in cables, characterized by shortened forms, abbreviated syntax, blends, etc.

cable's length, *Naut.* a unit of length (608 ft in the British Navy; 720 ft in the U.S. Navy).

cable stitch, *Knitting.* a pattern whereby one set of stitches is crossed over another so that a ropelike effect is produced.

cablet (kā′blĭt), *n.* a small cable, esp. a cable-laid rope under 10 inches in circumference. [f. CABLE + -ET]

cable tram, cable car.

cable tramway, a tramway on which the cars are pulled by a moving cable under the roadway.

cableway (kā′bl wā′), *n.* a construction for transporting goods or passengers in which the car hangs from a cable and is pulled by another, between two terminal towers; a teleferic.

cabling (kā′blĭng), *n.* **1.** *Engineering.* a collection of electrical and wire-rope cables. **2.** *Textiles.* two tightly twisted yarns which are subsequently twisted loosely together. **3.** cable moulding.

cabob (kə bŏb′), *n.* kebab.

cabochon (kăb′ə shŏn′; *Fr.* kȧ bô shôɴ′), *n.* a precious stone of convex hemispherical form, which has been polished but not cut into facets. [t. F, der. *caboche* head]

caboodle (kə bo͞o′dl), *n. Colloq.* the (whole) lot, pack, or crowd. [unexplained var. of BOODLE (def. 1)]

caboose (kə bo͞os′), *n.* **1.** a kitchen on the deck of a ship; galley. **2.** *U.S.* a wagon (usually the last) on a goods train, used by the crew; guard's van. [t. LG: m. *kabūse*]

Cabot (kăb′ət), *n.* **1. John,** *c.* 1450–98?, Italian navigator who explored for England; discovered North America in 1497. **2.** his son, **Sebastian,** 1474?–1557, English navigator and explorer.

cab rank, a place in the street reserved for taxicabs to stand awaiting passengers.

cabriole (kăb′rĭ ōl′), *n.* **1.** *Furnit.* a leg, curved and tapering, often ending in the form of an animal's paw, used esp. by Chippendale. **2.** *Ballet.* a leap in which one leg is raised in the air and the other is brought up to beat against it. [t. F. See CAPRIOLE]

A B

Cabrioles
A, 17th century; B, 18th century

cabriolet (kăb′rĭ ō lā′), *n. Obs.* **1.** a type of motor car resembling a coupé, with a folding top; a convertible coupé. **2.** a light, hooded one-horse carriage with two seats. [t. F, der. *cabriole* a leap. See CAPRIOLE]

Cabriolet, 19th century

cac-, var. of **caco-.**

C.A.C., Central Advisory Committee.

ca'canny (kä kăn′ĭ, kô-), *Orig. Scot. Slang.* —*n.* **1.** a go-slow. —*v.i.* **2.** to go slow. [lit., drive gently. See CA' (CALL), V., CANNY]

cacao (kə kā′ō, -kä′ō), *n., pl.* **-caos. 1.** a small evergreen sterculiaceous tree, *Theobroma cacao,* a native of tropical America, cultivated for its seeds, the source of cocoa, chocolate, etc. **2.** the fruit and seeds of this tree. [t. Sp., t. Nahuatl: m. *caca-uatl*]

cacao bean, cocoa bean.

cacao butter, cocoa butter.

cachalot (kăsh′ə lŏt′), *n.* the sperm whale. [t. F, t. Pg.: m. *cachoiote,* ult. der. L *caccabus* pot]

cache (kăsh), *n., v.,* **cached, caching.** —*n.* **1.** a hiding place, esp. one in the ground, for provisions, treasure, etc. **2.** the store of provisions, etc., so hidden. **3.** a store of food collected by some animals for the winter. —*v.t.* **4.** to put in a cache; conceal; hide. [t. F, der. *cacher* hide]

cachet (kă shā′, kăsh′ā; *Fr.* kȧ shĕ′), *n.* **1.** a seal as on a letter. **2.** a distinguishing mark or characteristic. **3.** kudos; prestige. **4.** *Pharm.* a hollow wafer for enclosing an ill-tasting medicine. **5.** *Philately.* a slogan, design, etc., stamped or printed on mail. [t. F, der. *cacher* hide]

cachexia (kə kĕk′sĭ ə), *n. Pathol.* general ill health, with emaciation, due to a chronic disease, as cancer. Also, **cachexy** (kə kĕk′sĭ). [t. NL, t. Gk: bad condition] —**cachectic** (kə kĕk′tĭk), *adj.*

cachinnate (kăk′ĭ nāt′), *v.i.,* **-nated, -nating.** to laugh loudly or immoderately. [t. L: m. s. *cachinnātus,* pp.] —**cach′inna′tion,** *n.*

cachou (kăsh′o͞o, kă sho͞o′), *n.* **1.** catechu. **2.** a pill or pastille for sweetening the breath. [t. F, t. Pg.: m. *cachu,* t. Malay: m. *kāchu* CATECHU]

cachucha (kə cho͞o′chə), *n. Spanish.* **1.** a lively dance. **2.** the music for it.

cacique (kə sēk′), *n.* **1.** a chief of an Indian clan or tribe in Mexico and the West Indies. **2.** a local political boss (in Spain and Spanish America). **3.** any of a genus of American oscinine passerine birds of the family *Icteridae,* including numerous species from Mexico and Central and South America, typical forms having a large bill somewhat swollen at the base. [t. Sp., t. Arawak]

cack-handed (kăk′hăn′dĭd), *adj. Colloq.* **1.** clumsy with the hands; maladroit. **2.** left-handed. [orig. uncert.]

cackle (kăk′l), *v.,* **-led, -ling,** *n.* —*v.i.* **1.** to utter a shrill, broken sound or cry, as a hen after laying an egg. **2.** to laugh brokenly. **3.** to chatter noisily. —*v.t.* **4.** to utter with cackles; express by cackling. —*n.* **5.** the act or sound of cackling. **6.** idle talk. [ME *cakelen*; imit. Cf. D *kakelen,* LG *kâkeln,* Swed. *kackla*] —**cack′ler,** *n.*

caco-, a word element meaning 'bad', 'deformed', or 'unpleasant', often used in forming medical terms. Also, **cac-.** [t. Gk: m. *kako-,* comb. form of *kakós* bad]

cacodemon (kăk′ə dē′mən), *n.* an evil spirit; a devil. Also, **cacodaemon.** [t. Gk: m. *kakodaímōn*]

cacodyl (kăk′ə dĭl), *n. Chem.* **1.** any compound containing the $(CH_3)_2As$ radical. **2.** a poisonous, ill-smelling liquid, $As_2(CH_3)_4$. [f. m. s. Gk *kakṓdēs* ill-smelling + -YL] —**cac′odyl′ic,** *adj.*

cacoethes (kăk′ō ē′thēz), *n.* an irresistible urge; mania. [t. L, t. Gk: m. *kakóēthes* bad habit (prop. neut. of *kakoēthēs* malignant)]

cacogenics (kăk′ō jĕn′ĭks), *n. Sociol.* dysgenics. [f. CACO- + (EU)GENICS] —**cac′ogen′ic,** *adj.*

cacography (kă kŏg′rə fĭ), *n.* **1.** bad handwriting (opposed to *calligraphy*). **2.** incorrect spelling (opposed to *orthography*). —**cacog′rapher,** *n.* —**cacographic** (kăk′ə grăf′ĭk), **cac′ograph′ical,** *adj.*

cacomistle (kăk′ə mĭs′əl), *n.* a carnivorous animal, *Bassariscus astutus,* of Mexico and the south-western U.S., related to the raccoon but smaller, with a sharper snout and longer tail. Also, **cacomixle** (kăk′ə mĭs′əl, -mĭk′səl). [t. Sp.: m. *cacomixtle,* t. Nahuatl: m. *tlacomiztli,* f. *tlaco* middle-sized + *miztli* lion]

Cacomistle, *Bassariscus astutus* (Total length 32 in., tail 17 in.)

cacoon (kə ko͞on′), *n.* the shiny flattened seeds of the tropical fabaceous climber *Entada scandens.*

cacophonous (kă kŏf′ə nəs), *adj.* having a harsh sound; discordant.

cacophony (kă kŏf′ə nĭ), *n., pl.* **-nies. 1.** the quality of having a harsh sound; dissonance. **2.** *Music.* frequent use of discords of a harshness and relationship difficult to understand. [t. NL: m. s. *cacophonia,* t. Gk: m. *kakophōnía*]

cactaceous (kăk tā′shəs), *adj. Bot.* belonging to the *Cactaceae,* or cactus family.

cactus (kăk′təs), *n., pl.* **-ti** (-tī), **-tuses.** any of various fleshy-stemmed plants of the family *Cactaceae,* usually leafless and spiny, often producing showy flowers, chiefly natives of the hot, dry regions of America. [t. L, t. Gk: m. *káktos* kind of prickly plant]

cacuminal (kă kyo͞o′mĭ nəl), *Phonet.* —*adj.* **1.** pronounced with the tip of the tongue curled back so as to touch the roof of the mouth above the gums; cerebral. —*n.* **2.** a cacuminal consonant. [f. s. L *cacūmen* top + -AL[1]]

cad (kăd), *n.* **1.** *Slang.* a contemptible, ill-bred person; one who does not behave like a gentleman. **2.** *Oxford Univ. Slang.* a townsman; an inhabitant of the town (as opposed to a member of the university). [short for CADDIE (def. 2)]

cadastral map (kə dăs′trəl), *Survey.* a map showing boundaries and ownership of land.

cadastral survey, *Survey.* a survey relating to boundaries and subdivision of land.

cadastre (kə dăs′tə), *n.* an official register of property, with details of boundaries, ownership, etc. [t. F, t. It.: m. *catastro,* var. of *catastico,* t. LGk: m. *katástichon* register, der. phrase *katà stíchon* line by line]

cadaver (kə dăv′ə, -dā′və), *n.* a dead body, esp. of a human being; a corpse. [t. L] —**cadaveric** (kə dăv′ə rĭk), *adj.*

cadaverine (kə dăv′ə rēn′), *n. Biochem.* a colourless ptomaine, $NH_2(CH_2)_5NH_2$, produced by protein hydrolysis and by the putrefaction of animal tissues.

cadaverous (kə dăv′ə rəs), *adj.* **1.** of or like a corpse. **2.** pale, wan; ghastly. **3.** haggard and thin. —**cadav′erously,** *adv.* —**cadav′erousness,** *n.*

caddie (kăd′ĭ), *n., v.,* **-died, -dying.** —*n.* **1.** *Golf.* an attendant, hired to carry the player's clubs, find the ball, etc. **2.** a person who runs errands, does odd jobs, etc. —*v.i.*

3. to work as a caddie. Also, **caddy.** [t. F: m. *cadet* CADET]

caddis (kăd′ĭs), *n.* a kind of coarse woollen yarn or braid.

caddis fly (kăd′ĭs), any of various adult insects of the order *Trichoptera*, characterized by four membranous, more or less hairy wings. Also, **cad′dice fly.** [orig. uncert.]

caddish (kăd′ĭsh), *adj.* ill-bred; ungentlemanly: *caddish behaviour.* —**cad′dishly,** *adv.* —**cad′dishness,** *n.*

caddis worm, the larva of the caddis fly, used as fish bait. Also, **caddis, caddice** (kăd′ĭs).

A B C

Caddis fly and larvae A, Caddis fly; B, Larva in case formed of small stones; C, Larva in case formed of grass roots

Caddoan (kăd′ō ən), *n.* a family of North American Indian languages spoken in the upper Missouri valley in N Dakota, in the Platte valley in Nebraska (Pawnee), and in SW Arkansas and neighbouring parts of Oklahoma, Texas, and Louisiana.

caddy[1] (kăd′ĭ), *n., pl.* **-ies.** a small box, tin, or chest, esp. one for holding tea. [var. of CATTY[2]]

caddy[2] (kăd′ĭ), *n., pl.* **-dies,** *v.i.,* **-died, -dying.** caddie.

cade[1] (kād), *n.* a species of juniper, *Juniperus oxycedrus*, of the Mediterranean area, whose wood on destructive distillation yields an oily liquid **(oil of cade)** used in treating skin affections. [t. F, t. Pr.]

cade[2] (kād), *adj.* (of the young of animals) left by the mother and raised by hand: *a cade lamb.* [orig. uncert.]

Cade (kād), *n.* **Jack,** died 1450, English rebel, leader of the insurrection of 1450.

cadelle (kə dĕl′), *n.* a small blackish beetle, *Tenebrioides mauritanicus*, all stages of which are commonly destructive to cereals. [t. F, t. Pr.: m. *cadello*, g. L *catellus*, fem. *catella* little animal]

cadence (kā′dns), *n.* **1.** rhythmic flow, as of verses; rhythm. **2.** the beat of any rhythmical movement. **3.** a fall in pitch of the voice, as in speaking. **4.** the general modulation of the voice. **5.** *Music.* a sequence of notes or chords which indicates the momentary or complete end of a composition, section, phrase, etc. **6.** *Mil.* the rate of stepping in marching: *a cadence of 120 steps per minute.* Also, **ca′dency.** [ME, t. F, t. It.: m. *cadenza*, g. LL *cadentia*, der. s. L *cadens*, ppr., falling] —**ca′denced,** *adj.*

cadent (kā′dnt), *adj.* **1.** having cadence. **2.** *Archaic.* falling. [t. L: s. *cadens*, ppr., falling]

cadenza (kə dĕn′zə), *n. Music.* an elaborate flourish or showy passage introduced for a singer near the end of an aria or for the soloist in a movement of a concerto. [t. It. See CADENCE]

cadet (kə dĕt′), *n.* **1.** a youth undergoing training to qualify as an officer in the armed services or the police. **2.** (in France before 1789) a gentleman, usually a younger son, who entered the army to prepare for a subsequent commission. **3.** a younger son or brother. **4.** the youngest son. —*adj.* **5.** pertaining to or traced through a younger son: *the cadet branch of a family.* [t. F, t. Gascon: m. *capdet* chief, ult. der. L *caput* head] —**cadet′ship, cadetcy** (kə dĕt′sĭ), *n.*

cadge (kăj), *v.,* **cadged, cadging.** —*v.t.* **1.** to obtain by imposing on another's generosity or friendship. **2.** to borrow without intent to repay. **3.** to beg or obtain by begging. —*v.i.* **4.** to obtain things from others with no intention of repayment. **5.** to beg. [orig. unknown] —**cadg′er,** *n.*

cadgy (kăj′ĭ), *adj. Scot.* **1.** cheerful. **2.** wanton.

cadi (kä′dĭ, kā′-), *n., pl.* **-dis.** a judge in a Muslim community, whose decisions are based on Islamic religious law. Also, **kadi.** [t. Ar.: m. *qādī* judge]

Cadiz (kə dĭz′), *n.* a seaport in SW Spain, on the **Gulf of Cadiz,** a bay of the Atlantic. 128,460 (1965). See map under **Trafalgar.** Also, **Cádiz** (*Sp.* kä′dēth).

cadmium (kăd′mĭ əm), *n. Chem.* a white, ductile divalent metallic element like tin in appearance: used in plating and in making certain alloys. As it is a good absorber of neutrons it is also used in the control rods of nuclear reactors. *Symbol:* Cd; *at. wt:* 112·410; *at. no.:* 48; *sp. gr.:* 8·6 at 20°C. [t. NL, der. L *cadmia*, t. Gk: m. *kadmeía* (*gê*) Cadmean (earth), i.e. calamine (with which cadmium is usually associated)] —**cad′mic,** *adj.*

cadmium cell, *Physics.* Weston cell.

cadmium orange, a yellow colour approaching orange.

cadmium yellow, a bright, or lemon, yellow colour.

Cadmus (kăd′məs), *n. Gk Legend.* a Phoenician prince who planted the teeth of a dragon he had slain, from which many warriors suddenly sprang up who fought each other until only five survived. These five, led by Cadmus, founded Thebes. He is said by several accounts to have brought an alphabet from Phoenicia (or Egypt) to Greece. —**Cad′mean,** *adj.*

Cadorna (*It.* kȧ dôr′nȧ), *n.* **Count Luigi** (*It.* lwē′jē), 1850–1928, Italian general: chief of staff 1914–17.

cadre (kä′də), *n.* **1.** *Mil.* the key group of officers and other ranks necessary to establish and train a new military unit. **2.** a framework. [t. F: frame, t. It.: m. *quadro*, g. L *quadrum* a square]

caduceus (kə dyōō′syəs), *n., pl.* **-cei** (-sĭ ī′). **1.** the staff carried by Hermes, or Mercury, as herald or messenger of the gods. **2.** a similar staff used as an emblem of the medical profession and as the insignia of the Medical Corps of the armed services. [t. L, t. d. Gk: m. *kārýkeion* herald's staff] —**cadu′cean,** *adj.*

Caduceus
Collar badge of an Air Force Medical Officer

caducity (kə dyōō′sĭ tĭ), *n.* **1.** the infirmity of old age; senility. **2.** frailty; transitoriness. [t. F: m. *caducité.* See CADUCOUS]

caducous (kə dyōō′kəs), *adj.* **1.** *Bot.* **a.** tending to fall. **b.** deciduous; dropping off very early, as leaves. **2.** *Zool.* subject to shedding. **3.** transitory. [t. L: m. *cadūcus* falling]

Cadwallader (kăd wŏl′ə də), *n.* Welsh prince, died 1172.

caecilian (sē sĭl′yən), *n.* any of the limbless and elongate burrowing amphibians of the order *Apoda.* [f. s. L *caecilia* lizard + -AN]

caeco-, a word element meaning 'the caecum'. Also, before vowels, **caec-**.

caecum (sē′kəm), *n., pl.* **-ca** (-kə). *Anat., Zool.* a cul-de-sac, esp. the one at the beginning of the human large intestine, bearing the vermiform appendix. See diag. under **intestine.** [t. L, neut. of *caecus* blind] —**cae′cal,** *adj.*

Cædmon (kăd′mən), *n.* fl. A.D. 670, Anglo-Saxon religious poet.

Caelian (sē′lĭ ən), *n.* the south-eastern hill of the Seven Hills of ancient Rome.

Caen (kŏng; *Fr.* kän), *n.* a seaport in N France, in Calvados department, near the English Channel. 117,372 (1962).

caeno-, var. of **caino-**.

caeoma (sē ō′mə), *n. Bot.* (in fungi) an aecium in which the spores are formed in chains and not enclosed in a peridium. [f. m. s. Gk *kaíein* smelt + -OMA]

Caerleon (kä lē′ən), *n.* a village in Monmouthshire: site of an ancient Roman fortress; supposed seat of King Arthur's court. 4711 (est. 1964).

Caern., Caernarvonshire.

Caernarvon (kä nä′vən), *n.* **1.** a town in Wales, the county town of Caernarvonshire. 8998 (1961). **2.** Caernarvonshire.

Caernarvonshire (kä nä′vən shiə′, -shə), *n.* a county in NW Wales. 121,194 pop. (1961); 569 sq. mi. *Co. town:* Caernarvon. *Abbrev.:* Caern. Also, **Caernar′von, Carnar′von.**

Caerphilly (kĕə fĭl′ĭ, kä-), *n.* a creamy white, quick-maturing cheese with a mild, delicate flavour.

caerulean (sĭ′rōō′lyən), *adj., n.* cerulean.

caesalpiniaceous (sĕz′ăl′pĭ nĭ ā′shəs, sĕs′-), *adj. Bot.* belonging to the *Caesalpiniaceae*, a family of leguminous plants including the brazil, royal poinciana, and numerous tropical genera. [f. s. NL *Caesalpinia*, the typical genus (named after Andrea *Caesalpino*, 1519–1603, Italian botanist) + -ACEOUS]

Caesar (sē′zə), *n.* **1. Gaius Julius** (gā′əs jōō′lyəs), 102 or 100–44 B.C., Roman general, statesman, and historian: conqueror of Gaul, Britain, etc. **2.** a title of the Roman emperors from Augustus to Hadrian, and later of the heir presumptive. **3.** any emperor. **4.** a tyrant; dictator. [cf. KAISER, TSAR]

Caesarea (sē′zə rĭə′), *n.* **1.** an ancient seaport in NW Israel: the Roman capital of Palestine. **2.** ancient name of **Kayseri.**

Caesarean (sĭ zĕə′rĭ ən), *n.* **1.** a Caesarean section. —*adj.* **2.** pertaining to Caesar or the Caesars: *a Caesarean conquest.* Also, **Caesarian, Cesarean, Cesarian.**

Caesarean section, *Surg.* the operation by which a foetus is taken from the womb by cutting through the walls of the abdomen and womb (supposedly performed at the birth of Caesar).

Caesarism (sē′zə rĭz′əm), *n.* absolute government; imperialism. —**Cae′sarist,** *n.*

caesium (sē′zyəm), *n. Chem.* a rare, extremely active, soft, monovalent metallic element showing blue lines in the spectrum. *Symbol:* Cs; *at. wt:* 132·91; *at. no.:* 55; *sp. gr.* 1·9 at 20°C; melts at 28·5°C. The radioactive isotope, **caesium-137,** is obtained from nuclear reactors and is used in radiotherapy and for sterilizing foodstuffs. Also, **cesium.** [NL, special use of *caesium* (neut.) bluish grey]

caesium clock, a very accurate type of clock based on the frequency of a particular line in the spectrum of caesium.

caespitose (sĕs′pĭ tōs′), *adj. Bot.* matted together; growing in dense tufts. Also, *U.S.,* **cespitose.** [f. m. s. L *caespes* turf + -OSE[1]] **—caes′pitose′ly,** *adv.*

caesura (sĭ zyo͝o′rə), *n., pl.* **-ras, -rae** (-rē). **1.** *Eng. Pros.* a break, esp. a sense pause, usually near the middle of a verse, and marked in scansion by a double vertical line, as in *know then thyself* ‖ *presume not God to scan.* **2.** *Gk and Latin Pros.* a division made by the ending of a word within a foot (or sometimes at the end of a foot), esp. in certain recognized places near the middle of a verse. Also, **cesura.** [t. L: a cutting] **—caesu′ral,** *adj.*

cafe (kăf′ā, kăf′ĭ; *def. 3 sometimes* kăf, kāf; *Fr.* kȧ fĕ′), *n.* **1.** a room or building where coffee and light refreshments are served. **2.** (in continental Europe and other countries) a similar room or building where alcoholic and other refreshments are served. **3.** a restaurant, usually low-priced. Also, **café.** [t. F. See COFFEE]

café au lait (kăf′ĭ ō lā′; *Fr.* kȧ fĕ ȯ lĕ′), *French.* **1.** hot coffee with scalded milk. **2.** a light brown colour.

cafeteria (kăf′ĭ tĭə′rĭ ə), *n.* a self-service restaurant. [t. Amer. Sp.: coffee shop]

caff (kăf), *n. Slang.* a cafe.

caffeine (kăf′ēn, kăf′ĭ ēn′), *n.* a bitter crystalline alkaloid, $C_8H_{10}N_4O_2$, obtained from coffee, tea, etc., used in medicine as a stimulant, diuretic, etc. [t. F: m. *caféine,* der. *café* coffee. See -INE[2] (def. 3)]

caftan (kăf′tăn), *n.* **1.** a long garment having long sleeves and tied at the waist by a girdle, worn under a coat in the Near East. **2.** a loose dress, either short or floor length, with long, bell-shaped sleeves, worn by women in imitation of this garment. Also, **kaftan.** [t. Turk., Pers.: m. *qaftān*] **—caf′taned,** *adj.*

cage (kāj), *n., v.,* **caged, caging.** **—***n.* **1.** a box-shaped receptacle or enclosure for confining birds or other animals, made with openwork of wires, bars, etc. **2.** anything that confines or imprisons; prison. **3.** something like a cage in structure or purpose. **4.** the enclosed platform of a lift, esp. one in a coal mine. **5.** any skeleton framework. **6.** *U.S. Ordn.* a steel framework upon which guns are supported. **7.** *Hockey.* the structure forming the goal. **—***v.t.* **8.** to put or confine in or as in a cage. [ME, t. OF, g. L *cavea* enclosure]

cagebird (kāj′bûd′), *n.* a bird kept in a cage.

cageling (kāj′lĭng), *n.* a cagebird.

cagey (kā′jĭ), *adj.,* **cagier, cagiest.** *Colloq.* cautious; secretive. Also, **cag′y.** **—cag′ily,** *adv.* **—cag′iness,** *n.*

Cagliari (kăl yä′rĭ; *It.* kȧl′lyȧ rē), *n.* **1. Paolo** (*It.* pȧ′ȯ lȯ). See **Veronese. 2.** a seaport in and the capital of Sardinia, in the S part. 209,878 (1966). See map under **Sardinia.**

Cagliostro (kăl yŏs′trō; *It.* kȧl lyŏs′trȯ), *n.* **Count Alessandro di** (*It.* ȧ lĕs sȧn′drȯ dē) (*Giuseppe Balsamo*), 1743–95, unscrupulous Italian adventurer and supposed magician.

Caguas (*Sp.* kȧ′gwȧs), *n.* a town in Puerto Rico. 65,098 (1960).

cahier (*Fr.* kȧ yĕ′), *n.* **1.** a number of sheets of paper or leaves of a book placed together, as for binding. **2.** a report of the proceedings of any body. [t. F, g. LL word meaning fourth, group of four sheets. See QUIRE[1]]

cahoot (kə ho͞ot′), *n. Slang.* **1. in cahoot** or **cahoots,** in partnership; in league. **2.** *U.S.* **go cahoots,** to become partners. [? t. F: m. *cahute* hut, cabin]

Caiaphas (kī′ə făs′), *n.* a high priest of the Jews from some time before A.D. 37: presided at the Council of Sadducees which condemned Jesus to death.

Caicos Islands (kī′kŏs). See **Turks and Caicos Islands.**

caiman (kā′mən), *n.* cayman.

Cain (kān), *n.* **1.** the first son of Adam and Eve, who murdered his brother Abel. Gen. 4. **2.** a murderer.

caino-, a word element meaning 'new', 'recent', as in *Cainozoic.* Also, **ceno-, caeno-.** [See -CENE]

cainogenesis (kī′nō jĕn′ĭ sĭs), *n. Biol.* development of an individual which does not repeat the phylogeny of its race, stock, or group (opposed to *palingenesis*). Also, **kainogenesis;** *Chiefly U.S.,* **cenogenesis.** [f. CAINO- + GENESIS] **—cainogenetic** (kī′nō jĭ nĕt′ĭk), *adj.*

Cainozoic (kī′nō zō′ĭk, kā′-), *Geol.* **—***adj.* **1.** pertaining to the geological era of rocks of most recent age, extending to the present. **—***n.* **2.** the era or rocks representing the most recent major division of earth history. Also, **Cenozoic, Kainozoic.** [f. CAINO- + ZO(O)- + -IC]

caique (kĭ ēk′), *n.* a long, narrow skiff or rowing boat used on the Bosporus. [t. F, t. It.: m. *caicco,* t. Turk.: m. *kayik*]

ça ira (*Fr.* sȧ ē rȧ′), *French.* it will go on (refrain of a song of the French Revolution).

caird (kĕəd), *n. Scot.* a travelling tinker; a tramp or vagrant. [t. Gaelic: m. *ceard* tinker]

cairn (kĕən), *n.* a heap of stones set up as a landmark, monument, tombstone, etc. [Scot., t. Gaelic: m. *carn* pile of stones] **—cairned** (kĕənd), *adj.*

cairngorm (kĕən′gôm′), *n.* a yellow or brown ornamental quartz. [so called from the CAIRNGORMS]

Cairngorms (kĕən′gômz′), *n.pl.* a range of mountains in E central Scotland; continuation of the Grampians. Highest peak, Ben Macdhui, 4296 ft.

Cairns (kĕənz), *n.* a town in NE Australia, in Queensland. 26,200 (est. 1964).

cairn terrier, a short-legged, long-bodied terrier with silver grey wiry hair.

Cairo (kī′ə rō′), *n.* the capital of Egypt, in the N part, on the E bank of the Nile. 3,346,000 (1960). See map under **Suez.**

caisson (kə so͞on′, kā′sən), *n.* **1.** a structure in which men can work on river beds, etc., consisting essentially of an airtight box or chamber with an open bottom, the water being kept out by the high air pressure maintained within. **2.** a boatlike structure used as a gate for a dock or the like. **3.** pontoon[1] (def. 3). **4.** a wooden chest containing bombs or explosives, used as a mine; an ammunition chest. **5.** an ammunition wagon. **6.** *Bldg Trades.* a deeply recessed panel in a ceiling, archway, or the like. [t. F: b. *caisse* chest and earlier *casson* (t. It.: m. *cassone,* aug. of *cassa,* g. L *capsa* box). See CASE[2]]

caisson disease, *Pathol.* a disorder caused by a too rapid decrease in atmospheric pressure, found in divers and pilots of unpressurized aircraft; characterized by pains in limbs and joints, and the adoption of a bent posture; bends.

Caith., Caithness.

Caithness (kāth′nĕs, kāth nĕs′), *n.* a county in NE Scotland. 27,345 pop. (1961); 686 sq. mi. *Co. town:* Wick. *Abbrev.:* Caith.

caitiff (kā′tĭf), *Archaic and Poetic.* **—***n.* **1.** a base, despicable person. **—***adj.* **2.** base; despicable. [ME *caitif,* t. ONF, g. LL **cactīvus,* assimilatory var. of L *captīvus* (see CAPTIVE)]

Caius (kēz), *n.* **John,** 1510–73, English physician and scholar.

cajole (kə jōl′), *v.t., v.i.,* **-joled, -joling.** to persuade by flattery or promises; wheedle; coax. [t. F: m. s. *cajoler,* ? b. *caresser* caress and *enjôler* capture] **—cajole′ment,** *n.* **—cajol′er,** *n.*

cajolery (kə jō′lə rĭ), *n., pl.* **-ries.** persuasion by flattery or promises; wheedling; coaxing.

Cajun (kā′jən), *n.* (in Louisiana) a descendant of the exiles from Acadia; Acadian. Also, **Cajian.** [var. of ACADIAN. Cf. *Injun* for *Indian*]

cajuput (kăj′ə pŭt′), *n.* **1.** a small myrtaceous tree or shrub of the Moluccas and neighbouring islands, *Melaleuca cajuputi* or *minor,* a variety of *M. leucadendron.* **2.** a green oil having a distinctive smell, distilled from the leaves of this tree, used as a stimulant, antispasmodic, and diaphoretic. **3.** a lauraceous tree, *Umbellularia californica,* whose aromatic leaves are used medicinally. Also, **caj′eput.** [t. D: m. *kajoepoetih,* t. Malay, f. *kāyu* wood + *pūtih* white]

cake (kāk), *n., v.,* **caked, caking.** **—***n.* **1.** a sweet baked food in loaf or layer form, made with or without shortening, usually with flour, sugar, eggs, flavouring, usually with baking powder or soda, and a liquid. **2.** a flat, thin mass of bread, esp. unleavened bread. **3.** a shaped or moulded mass of other food. **4.** a shaped or compressed mass: *a cake of soap, ice, etc.* **5. piece of cake,** *Slang.* something easily accomplished or obtained. **6. take the cake, a.** to win the prize. **b.** to surpass all others; excel. **—***v.t.* **7.** to form into a cake or compact mass. **—***v.i.* **8.** to become formed into a cake or compact mass: *mud caked on his shoes.* [ME, t. Scand.; cf. Icel. *kaka;* akin to D *koek,* G *Kuchen*]

cakes and ale, the good things and pleasures of life.

cakewalk (kāk′wôk′), *n.* **1.** a promenade or march, of American Negro origin, in which the couples with the most intricate or eccentric steps receive cakes as prizes. **2.** a dance based on this promenade. **3.** music for this dance. **—***v.i.* **4.** to walk or dance in or as in a cakewalk. **—cake′walk′er,** *n.*

Cal., 1. California. 2. *Physics.* large calorie.

cal., 1. *Music.* calando. 2. calibre. 3. *Physics.* small calorie.

Calabar (kăl′ə bä′, kăl′ə bä′), *n.* **1.** a river and estuary in SE Nigeria. **2.** a seaport near the mouth of this river. 50,000 (est. 1967).

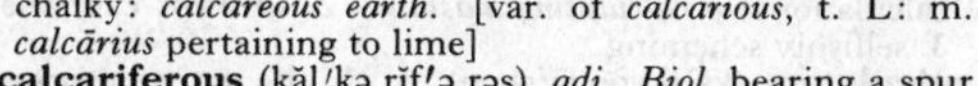

Calabar bean, the violently poisonous seed of a fabaceous African climbing plant, *Physostigma venenosum*, the active principle of which is physostigmine.

calabash (kăl′ə băsh′), *n.* **1.** any of various gourds, esp. the fruit of the bottle gourd, *Lagenaria siceraria.* **2.** any of the plants bearing them. **3.** the fruit of a bignoniaceous tree, *Crescentia cujete*, of tropical America. **4.** Also, **calabash tree.** the tree itself. **5.** the dried hollow shell of the calabash (either def. 1 or 3) used as a vessel or otherwise. **6.** a bottle, kettle, tobacco-pipe bowl, etc., made from it. **7.** a gourd used as a rattle, drum, etc., esp. by American Indians. [t. F: m. *calebasse*, t. Sp.: m. *calabaza* gourd, ? t. Pers.: m. *kharbuz* melon]

calabash nutmeg, *n.* **1.** the fruit of a tropical shrub, *Monodora myristica*, containing many aromatic oily seeds with the flavour of nutmegs. **2.** the shrub itself.

calaboose (kăl′ə bo͞os′, kăl′ə bo͞os′), *n. U.S. Colloq.* prison cell; jail. [t. Creole F, t. Sp.: m. *calabozo* dungeon, orig. uncert.]

Calabria (kə lā′brĭ ə; *It.* kȧ lȧ′brē ȧ), *n.* **1.** a region in SW Italy. 2,045,215 pop. (1961); 5828 sq. mi. *Cap.:* Reggio di Calabria. **2.** an ancient district at the SE extremity of Italy.

caladium (kə lā′dyəm), *n.* a plant of the araceous genus *Caladium*, mostly herbs of the American tropics, cultivated for their variegated, colourful leaves. [NL, t. Malay: m. *kaladi*]

Calais (kăl′ā, kăl′ĭ; *Fr.* kȧ lĕ′), *n.* a seaport in N France, in Pas de Calais department, on the Strait of Dover: the nearest French port to England. 74,605 (1962). See map under **Dunkirk.**

calamanco (kăl′ə măng′kō), *n., pl.* **-cos.** a glossy woollen fabric checked or brocaded in the warp so that the pattern shows on one side only, much used in the 18th century. [orig. uncert.; ? t. ML: m. *calamancus* kind of cap]

calamander (kăl′ə măn′də), *n.* the hard wood of a tree, *Diospyros quaesita*, of Ceylon and India, used for cabinetwork. [metathetic var. of COROMANDEL]

calamine (kăl′ə mīn′), *n.* **1.** Also, **calamine lotion.** a liquid soothing to the skin, prepared from zinc oxide with $\frac{1}{2}$ per cent ferric oxide. **2.** smithsonite (def. 1). **3.** *U.S.* hemimorphite. [t. F, t. ML: m. *calamīna*, appar. alter. of L *cadmia.* See CADMIUM]

calamint (kăl′ə mĭnt′), *n.* any plant of the labiate genus *Satureja*, esp. *S. calaminthe* and *S. nepeta.* [t. L: m. s. *calaminthē*, t. Gk: m. *kalamínthē*; r. ME *calament*, t. F, t. ML: s. *calamentum*]

calamite (kăl′ə mīt′), *n.* any of a group of extinct spore-bearing trees which flourished in the Carboniferous period. [t. NL: m. *Calamītes*, t. Gk: m. *kalamítēs* reedlike]

calamitous (kə lăm′ĭ təs), *adj.* causing or involving calamity; disastrous: *a calamitous defeat.* [t. L: m. s. *calamitōsus*] **—calam′itously,** *adv.* **—calam′itousness,** *n.*

calamity (kə lăm′ĭ tĭ), *n., pl.* **-ties. 1.** grievous affliction; adversity; misery. **2.** a great misfortune; a disaster. [late ME *calamyte*, t. L: m. s. *calamitas*] **—Syn. 2.** reverse, blow, catastrophe, cataclysm. See **disaster.**

calamus (kăl′ə məs), *n., pl.* **-mi** (-mī′), **1.** the sweet flag, *Acorus calamus.* **2.** its aromatic root. **3.** any palm of the genus *Calamus*, yielding rattan, canes, etc. **4.** the hollow base of a feather; a quill. [t. L, t. Gk: m. *kálamos* reed]

calando (kə lăn′dō; *It.* kȧ lăn′dô), *adj., n., pl.* **-dos** (-dōz; *It.* -dôs). *Music.* *—adj.* **1.** gradually diminishing in loudness and tempo. *—n.* **2.** a calando passage. [It.]

calash (kə lăsh′), *n.* **1.** a light, low-wheeled carriage, either with or without a folding top. **2.** the folding top (**calash top**) of such a vehicle. **3.** a kind of hood formerly worn by women. [t. F: m. *calèche*, t. G: m. *Kalesche*, t. Slavic; cf. Czech *kolésa*]

Calash

calcaneum (kăl kā′nyəm), *n., pl.* **-nea** (-nyə). calcaneus.

calcaneus (kăl kā′nyəs), *n., pl.* **-nei** (-nĭ ī′). **1.** *Anat.* (in man) the largest tarsal bone, forming the prominence of the heel. **2.** *Zool.* the corresponding bone in other vertebrates. Also, **calcaneum.** [t. L: heel]

calcar (kăl′kä), *n., pl.* **calcaria** (kăl kēə′rĭ ə). *Biol.* a spur, or spurlike process. [t. L: a spur]

calcarate (kăl′kə rāt′), *adj. Biol.* furnished with a calcar or calcaria; spurred. Also, **cal′carat′ed.**

Calcarate foot of pheasant

calcareous (kăl kēə′rĭ əs), *adj.* of, coated with, containing, or like calcium carbonate; chalky: *calcareous earth.* [var. of *calcarious*, t. L: m. *calcārius* pertaining to lime]

calcariferous (kăl′kə rĭf′ə rəs), *adj. Biol.* bearing a spur or spurs. [f. CALCAR + -(I)FEROUS]

calceiform (kăl′sĭ ĭ fôm′, kăl sē′-), *adj. Bot.* calceolate. [f. s. L *calceus* a shoe + -(I)FORM]

calceolaria (kăl′sĭ ə lēə′rĭ ə), *n.* any plant of the genus *Calceolaria*, often cultivated for its slipper-like flowers. [NL, f. s. L *calceolus* slipper (dim. of *calceus* shoe) + *-āria* -ARIA]

calceolate (kăl′sĭ ə lāt′), *adj. Bot.* having the form of a shoe or slipper, as the labellum of certain orchids.

calces (kăl′sēz), *n.* pl. of **calx.**

Calchas (kăl′kăs), *n. Gk Legend.* a priest of Apollo who aided the Greeks in the Trojan war.

calcic (kăl′sĭk), *adj.* pertaining to or containing lime or calcium. [f. s. L *calx* lime + -IC]

calciferol (kăl sĭf′ə rŏl′), *n. Biochem.* vitamin D_2; a fat-soluble, crystalline alcohol, $C_{28}H_{43}OH$, found in milk and fish-liver oils and produced by the activation of ergosterol by ultraviolet irradiation.

calciferous (kăl sĭf′ə rəs), *adj.* **1.** *Chem.* forming salts of calcium, esp. calcium carbonate. **2.** containing calcium carbonate. [f. s. L *calx* lime + -(I)FEROUS]

calcific (kăl sĭf′ĭk), *adj. Zool., Anat.* making or converting into salt of lime or chalk.

calcification (kăl′sĭ fĭ kā′shən), *n.* **1.** a changing into lime. **2.** *Physiol.* the deposition of lime or insoluble salts of calcium, as in a tissue. **3.** *Anat., Geol.* a calcified formation. **4.** a soil process in which the surface soil is supplied with calcium in such a way that the soil colloids are always close to saturation.

calcify (kăl′sĭ fī′), *v.t., v.i.,* **-fied, -fying.** *Physiol.* to make or become calcareous or bony; harden by the deposit of calcium salts. [f. s. L *calx* lime + -(I)FY]

calcimine (kăl′sĭ mīn′, -mĭn), *n., v.,* **-mined, -mining.** *—n.* **1.** a white or tinted wash for walls, ceilings, etc. *—v.t.* **2.** to wash or cover with calcimine. Also, **kalsomine.** [m. KALSOMINE by assoc. with CALCIUM]

calcine (kăl′sīn, -sĭn), *v.,* **-cined, -cining,** *n.* *—v.t., v.i.* **1.** to convert or be converted into calx by heat. **2.** to burn to a friable substance; roast. **3.** to oxidize by heating. **4.** to frit. *—n.* **5.** ore after it has been oxidized. [t. F: m. s. *calciner*, ult. der. L *calx* lime] **—calcination** (kăl′sĭ nā′shən), *n.* **—calcinatory** (kăl sĭn′ə tə rĭ, kăl′sĭn-, -trĭ), *adj., n.*

calcite (kăl′sīt), *n.* one of the commonest minerals, calcium carbonate, $CaCO_3$, occurring in a great variety of crystalline forms; calcspar. Limestone, marble, and chalk consist largely of calcite. [f. s. L *calx* lime + -ITE[1]]

calcium (kăl′sĭ əm), *n. Chem.* a silver-white divalent metal, occurring combined in limestone, chalk, gypsum, etc. *Symbol:* Ca; *at. wt:* 40·08; *at. no.:* 20; *sp. gr.:* 1·55 at 20°C. [t. NL, f. s. L *calx* lime + -IUM]

calcium carbide, *Chem.* a crystalline compound of calcium and carbon, CaC_2, which reacts with water to form acetylene.

calcium carbonate, *Chem.* a crystalline compound, $CaCO_3$, occurring in nature as calcite, etc.

calcium chloride, *Chem.* a white, deliquescent powder, $CaCl_2$, used as a drying agent, preservative, etc.

calcium hydroxide, *Chem.* slaked lime, $Ca(OH)_2$.

calcium light, a brilliant white light produced by heating lime to incandescence in an oxyhydrogen or other hot flame.

calcium phosphate, *Chem.* any of several phosphates of calcium occurring naturally in some rocks and in animal bones, and used in medicine, industry, etc.

calcium proprionate, *Chem.* a white, water-soluble powder, $Ca(CH_3CH_2COO)_2$, used in battery products to inhibit the growth of fungi.

calc-sinter (kălk′sĭn′tə), *n. Mineral.* travertine. [t. G: m. *Kalksinter* lime slag]

calcspar (kălk′spä′), *n.* calcite.

calc-tufa (kălk′to͞o′fə), *n. Geol.* calcareous tufa. See **tufa.** Also, **calc-tuff** (kălk′tŭf′).

calculable (kăl′kyo͝o lə bl), *adj.* **1.** that can be calculated. **2.** that can be counted on; reliable; dependable.

calculate (kăl′kyo͝o lāt′), *v.,* **-lated, -lating.** *—v.t.* **1.** to ascertain by mathematical methods; compute: *to calculate the velocity of light.* **2.** to make suitable, adapt, or fit for a purpose: *calculated to inspire confidence.* **3.** to do deliberately or cold-bloodedly: *a calculated insult.* **4.** to estimate the possibility of failure before undertaking (a course of action): *a calculated risk.* **5.** *U.S. Colloq. or Dial.* **a.** to think; suppose. **b.** to intend; plan. *—v.i.* **6.** to make a computation; form an estimate. **7.** to count or rely (fol. by *on* or *upon*). [t. L: m. s. *calculātus*, pp., counted. See CALCULUS] **—Syn. 1.** count, figure, cast, estimate, weigh.

calculating (kăl′kyo͝o lā′tĭng), *adj.* **1.** that performs calculations: *a calculating machine.* **2.** shrewd; cautious. **3.** selfishly scheming.

calculation (kăl′kyo͞o lā′shən), *n.* **1.** the act or process of calculating; computation. **2.** result or product of calculating. **3.** an estimate based on the various facts in a case; a forecast. **4.** forethought; prior or careful planning. —**calculative** (kăl′kyo͞o lə tĭv), *adj.* —**Syn. 4.** circumspection, caution, wariness. See **prudence.**

calculator (kăl′kyo͞o lā′tə), *n.* **1.** one who calculates or computes. **2.** a machine that performs mathematical operations mechanically, electro-mechanically or electronically. **3.** a set of tables that facilitates calculation. [t. L]

calculous (kăl′kyo͞o ləs), *adj. Pathol.* characterized by the presence of calculus or stone.

calculus (kăl′kyo͞o ləs), *n., pl.* **-luses** (*def. 1*), **-li** (-lī′) (*def. 2*). **1.** *Maths.* a method of calculation, esp. a highly systematic method of treating problems by a special system of algebraic notation. See **differential, infinitesimal,** and **integral calculus. 2.** *Pathol.* a stone or concretion found in the gall bladder, kidneys, or other parts of the body. [t. L: stone used in counting, dim. of *calx* small stone, lime]

Calcutta (kăl kŭt′ə), *n.* a seaport in NE India, in W Bengal, on the river Hooghly: capital of British India, 1772–1912. 2,927,289 (1961). See map under **Delhi.**

caldarium (kăl dēə′rĭ əm), *n., pl.* **-daria** (-dēə′rĭ ə). (in Roman baths) a room with hot water. [t. L]

Caldecott Award (kôl′dĭ kət), an annual award for an outstanding illustrated book for children, awarded at the same time as the Newbery Award. [named after Randolph *Caldecott*, 1846–86, English illustrator]

caldera (kăl dēə′rə), *n.* a large crater formed by the explosion or subsidence of the cone of a volcano. [t. Sp.: lit., cauldron]

Calderón de la Barca (kăl′də rŏn dĕl′ə bä′kə; *Sp.* käl dĕ rōn′ dĕ lä bär′kä), **Pedro** (*Sp.* pĕ′drō), 1600–81, Spanish dramatist and poet.

caldron (kôl′drən), *n.* cauldron.

Caldwell (kôld′wĕl, -wəl), *n.* **Erskine** (û′skĭn), born 1903, U.S. author.

Caleb (kā′lĕb), *n.* a Hebrew leader, sent as a spy into the land of Canaan. Num. 13:6, etc.

Caledon (kăl′ĭ dən), *n.* a river in S Africa flowing SW along the border of Lesotho and Orange Free State into the Orange River. 220 mi.

Caledonia (kăl′ĭ dō′nyə), *n. Chiefly Poetic.* Scotland.

Caledonian (kăl′ĭ dō′nyən), *adj.* **1.** *Chiefly Poetic.* Scottish. **2.** *Geol.* of or pertaining to the major mountain-building episode, which occurred in Europe, reaching its height at the end of the Silurian period. —*n.* **3.** a Scotsman.

Caledonian Canal, a ship canal traversing N Scotland, from the Atlantic NE to the North Sea. 60½ mi.

calefacient (kăl′ĭ fā′shənt), *n.* **1.** *Med.* a substance which produces a sensation of heat when applied to the body, as mustard. —*adj.* **2.** heating; warming. [t. L: s. *calefaciens*, ppr., making hot]

calefaction (kăl′ĭ făk′shən), *n.* **1.** the act of heating. **2.** a heated state. [t. L: s. *calefactio*] —**cal′efac′tive,** *adj.*

calefactory (kăl′ĭ făk′tə rĭ), *adj., n., pl.* **-ries.** —*adj.* **1.** serving to heat. —*n.* **2.** a heated sitting room in a monastery. [t. L: m. s. *calefactōrius* having heating power]

calendar (kăl′ĭn də), *n.* **1.** any of various systems of reckoning time, esp. with reference to the beginning, length, and divisions of the year: *the Gregorian calendar.* **2.** a tabular arrangement of the days of each month and week in a year. **3.** a list, index, or register, esp. one arranged chronologically, as a list of the cases to be tried in a court. **4.** *Obs.* a guide or example. —*v.t.* **5.** to enter in a calendar; register. [t. L: m. s. *calendārium* account book, der. *calendae* calends; r. ME *calender*, t. AF]

calendar day, the period from one midnight to the following one.

calendar month. See **month** (def. 2).

calendar week, the period from midnight on one Sunday to midnight on the following Sunday.

calendar year. See **year** (def. 1).

calender (kăl′ĭn də), *n.* **1.** a machine in which cloth, paper, or the like is smoothed, glazed, etc., by pressing between revolving cylinders. —*v.t.* **2.** to press in a calender. [t. F: m. *calandre*, prob. t. Pr.: m. *calandra*, ult. g. L *cylindrus* CYLINDER] —**cal′enderer,** *n.*

Calender (kăl′ĭn də), *n.* (*often l.c.*) (in Muslim countries) one of an order of mendicant dervishes founded in the 14th century. [t. Pers.: m. *qalandar*]

calends (kăl′ĭndz), *n.pl.* (in the Roman calendar) the first day of the month. Also, **kalends.** [ME *kalendes* (rarely sing.), OE *cālend* (beginning of) a month, t. L: s. *calendae* (usually *kalendae*)]

calendula (kə lĕn′dyo͞o lə), *n.* **1.** any plant of the asteraceous genus *Calendula*, esp. *C. officinalis*, a common marigold. **2.** the dried florets of this plant, used in medicine as a vulnerary, etc. [NL, dim. of L *calendae* CALENDS; so called as flowering almost every month of the year]

calenture (kăl′ən tyo͞oə′), *n.* a violent fever with delirium, affecting persons in the tropics. [t. F, t. Sp.: m. *calentura* heat, der. L *calēre* be hot]

calescent (kə lĕs′ənt), *adj.* growing warm; increasing in heat. [t. L: s. *calescens*, ppr., growing hot] —**cales′cence,** *n.*

calf[1] (käf), *n., pl.* **calves. 1.** the young of the cow or of other bovine mammals (in cattle usually under one year of age). **2.** the young of certain other animals, as the elephant, seal, and whale. **3.** calfskin leather. **4.** *Colloq.* an awkward, silly boy or man. **5.** a mass of ice detached from a glacier, iceberg, or floe. **6. kill the fatted calf,** to prepare an elaborate welcome. [ME and d. OE, r. OE *cealf*, c. G *Kalb*] —**calf′-like′,** *adj.*

calf[2] (käf), *n., pl.* **calves.** the fleshy part of the back of the human leg below the knee. [ME, t. Scand.; cf. Icel. *kālfi*]

calf love, temporary infatuation of a young boy or girl for a person of the opposite sex.

calfskin (käf′skĭn′), *n.* **1.** the skin or hide of a calf. **2.** leather made from it. —*adj.* **3.** of, or made of, calfskin.

calf's-snout (käfs′snout′), *n.* an Old World scrophulariaceous annual plant, *Antirrhinum orontium.* Also, **weasel's-snout.**

Calgary (kăl′gə rĭ), *n.* a city in SW Canada, in Alberta. 311,116 (1965).

Cali (*Sp.* kä′lē), *n.* a city in SW Colombia. 637,929 (1964).

Caliban (kăl′ĭ băn′), *n.* **1.** the ugly, beastlike slave of Prospero in Shakespeare's *The Tempest.* **2.** a man who has a degraded, bestial nature.

calibrate (kăl′ĭ brāt′), *v.t.,* **-brated, -brating. 1.** to determine the calibre of. **2.** to determine, check, or rectify the graduation or accuracy of (any instrument, machine, or gun). —**cal′ibra′tor,** *n.*

calibration (kăl′ĭ brā′shən), *n.* **1.** the act or process of calibrating. **2.** *Ordn.* the assessment of a gun for accuracy.

calibre (kăl′ĭ bə), *n.* **1.** the diameter of something of circular section, as a bullet, or esp. that of the inside of a tube, as the bore of a gun. **2.** *Ordn.* the diameter of the bore of a gun taken as a unit in stating its length: *a fifty-calibre 14-inch gun.* **3.** *Horol.* the arrangement of the components of a watch or clock. **4.** degree of capacity or ability; personal character. **5.** degree of merit, or importance; quality. Also, *U.S.,* **caliber.** [t. F, t. It.: m. *calibro*, t. Ar.: m. *qālib* mould]

calices (kăl′ĭ sēz′), *n.* pl. of **calix.**

caliche (kă lē′chĭ), *n. Geol.* **1.** a surface deposit consisting of sand or clay impregnated with crystalline salts, such as sodium nitrate or sodium chloride. **2.** a horizon of calcium or mixed carbonates in soils of semi-arid regions. [Sp., der. *cal* lime, g. L *calx*]

calicle (kăl′ĭ kl), *n.* a cuplike depression or formation, as in corals. [t. L: m. s. *caliculus*, dim. of *calix* cup]

calico (kăl′ĭ kō′), *n., pl.* **-coes, -cos,** *adj.* —*n.* **1.** white cotton cloth. **2.** *U.S.* a printed cotton cloth, superior to percale. **3.** (orig.) cotton cloth imported from India. —*adj.* **4.** made of calico. **5.** *Chiefly U.S.* resembling printed calico; spotted; piebald. [named after CALICUT]

Calicut (kăl′ĭ kət), *n.* former name of **Kozhikode.**

calif (kā′lĭf, kăl′ĭf), *n.* caliph.

Calif., official abbreviation for California.

califate (kăl′ĭ fāt′, -fĭt), *n.* caliphate.

California (kăl′ĭ fô′nyə, -fô′nĭ ə), *n.* **1.** a state in the W United States, on the Pacific coast. 15,717,204 pop. (1960); 158,693 sq. mi. *Cap.:* Sacramento. *Abbrev.:* Calif. **2. Gulf of,** an arm of the Pacific, extending NW between the W coast of Mexico and the peninsula of Lower California. ab. 750 mi. long. —**Cal′ifor′nian,** *adj., n.*

Californian poppy, a papaveraceous pale green herb with showy yellow flowers, *Eschscholtzia californica.*

californium (kăl′ĭ fô′nyəm), *n. Chem.* a synthetic, radioactive, metallic element. *Symbol:* Cf; *at. no.:* 98. [f. (University of) CALIFORN(IA), where first identified, + -IUM]

caliginous (kə lĭj′ĭ nəs), *adj. Rare.* misty; dim; dark. [t. L: m. s. *cālīginōsus* misty] —**caliginosity** (kə lĭj′ĭ nŏs′ĭ tĭ), *n.*

Caligula (kə lĭg′yo͞o lə), *n.* **Gaius Caesar** (gā′əs sē′zə), A.D. 12–41, Roman emperor A.D. 37–41.

calipash (kăl′ĭ păsh′), *n.* that part of a turtle next to the upper shield, a greenish gelatinous substance. Also, **callipash.** [orig. uncert.]

calipee (kăl′ĭ pē′), *n.* that part of a turtle next to the lower shield, consisting of a yellowish gelatinous substance. [cf. CALIPASH]

caliper (kăl′ĭ pə), *n.*, *v.t. Chiefly U.S.* calliper.

caliph (kā′lĭf, kăl′ĭf), *n.* successor (usually of Mohammed): a title for the head of a Muslim state. Also, **calif, kaliph, khalif, khalifa.** [ME *califfe*, t. OF: m. *calife*, t. ML: m. *calīpha*, t. Ar.: m. *khalīfa* successor, vicar]

caliphate (kăl′ĭ fāt′, -fĭt), *n.* the rank, jurisdiction or government of a caliph. Also, **califate.**

calisaya (kăl′ĭ sā′ə), *n.* the medicinal bark of the tree *Cinchona calisaya.* [t. S Amer. Sp., prob. t. Quechua]

calisthenics (kăl′ĭs thĕn′ĭks), *n.* callisthenics. **—cal′isthen′ic,** *adj.*

calix (kā′lĭks, kăl′ĭks), *n.*, *pl.* **calices** (kăl′ĭ sēz′). *Rom. Cath. Ch.* a chalice (def. 1). [t. L: cup]

calk[1] (kôk), *v.t.* caulk. **—calk′er,** *n.*

calk[2] (kôk), *n.* **1.** Also, **calkin.** a projection on a horseshoe to prevent slipping. See illus. under **horseshoe. 2.** *Chiefly U.S.* a similar device on the heel or sole of a shoe. **—***v.t.* **3.** to provide with calks. **4.** to injure with a calk. [ult. t. L: m. s. *calx* heel, or m. *calcar* spur]

calk[3] (kôk), *v.t.* to transfer (an outline or design) from a sheet backed with an unstable colouring material on to another sheet placed underneath by exerting pressure along the design with a blunt point. Also, **calque.** [t. L: m. s. *calcāre* to tread, der. *calx* heel. See CALK[2]]

call (kôl), *v.t.* **1.** to cry out in a loud voice. **2.** (of a bird or other animal) to utter (its characteristic cry). **3.** to announce; proclaim: *call a halt.* **4.** to read over (a roll or list) in a loud voice. **5.** to attract the attention of by loudly uttering something. **6.** to attract (someone's attention) to something: *he called the policeman's attention to the disturbance. She tried not to call attention to herself.* **7.** to rouse from sleep as by a call: *call me at 8 o'clock.* **8.** to command or request to come; summon: *the boy was called by his mother, call a cab, call a witness.* **9.** to summon to an office, duty, etc.: *call someone to the ministry.* **10.** to summon (a member of an Inn of Court) to the degree of barrister-at-law: *to call to the bar.* **11.** to convoke or convene, as a meeting or assembly: *call a committee meeting.* **12.** to bring under consideration or discussion: *call a case.* **13.** to telephone to (sometimes fol. by *up*). **14.** to attract or lure (wild birds, etc.) by a particular cry or sound. **15.** *U.S.* to demand payment or fulfilment of (a loan, etc.). **16.** *U.S.* to demand (bonds, etc.) for payment. **17.** to give a name to; name: *his parents named him James but the boys call him Jim.* **18.** to designate as something specified: *he called me a liar.* **19.** to reckon; consider; estimate: *to call a thing a success, I call that mean.* **20.** *Cricket.* **a.** to announce the end of (an over). **b.** to announce that (a bowler) has bowled a no-ball. **21.** *Billiards.* to request (the player) to state his intended shot. **22.** *Poker.* to require (a player) to show his hand, after equalling his bet. **23.** *Cards.* to bid.
—*v.i.* **24.** to speak loudly, as to attract attention; shout; cry: *who calls so loudly?* **25.** (of a bird or animal) to utter its characteristic cry. **26.** to make a short visit; stop at a place on some errand or business: *to call at a house or place for a person or thing, or upon a person.* **27.** to telephone a person. **28.** *Poker.* to demand a showing of hands.
—*v.* **29.** Some special verb phrases are:

call back, 1. to recall; summon or bring back. **2.** to revoke; retract: *call back one's words.*

call down, 1. to invoke from above; cause to descend. **2.** *U.S.* to reprimand; scold.

call for, 1. to go and get. **2.** to require; demand; need: *the occasion calls for a cool head.*

call forth, to bring or summon into action.

call in, 1. to collect: *call in debts.* **2.** to withdraw from circulation: *call in gold, notes.* **3.** to invite; summon to or as to one's assistance.

call into being, to create.

call into play, to activate.

call in(to) question, to throw doubt upon.

call it a day, to bring an activity to a close whether temporarily or permanently.

call off, 1. to order to desist. **2.** to cancel or postpone. **3.** to terminate an activity.

call on, 1. to appeal to: *call on a person for a song.* **2.** to make a short visit to: *to call on friends.*

call out, 1. to utter in a loud voice. **2.** to summon into service: *call out the militia.* **3.** to bring into play; elicit. **4.** *Obs.* to challenge to a duel.

call up, 1. to bring into action, discussion, etc. **2.** to require payment of. **3.** to summon for military service. **4.** to recollect: *call up my sorrows afresh.*
—*n.* **30.** a cry or shout. **31.** the cry of a bird or other animal. **32.** an instrument for imitating this cry and attracting or luring the animal. **33.** a summons or signal sounded by a bugle, bell, etc. **34.** a note blown on a horn to encourage hounds. **35.** a short visit: *to make a call on someone.* **36.** a conversation, connection, or request for a connection by telephone. **37.** a summons; invitation; bidding. **38.** *Theat.* a notice of rehearsal posted by the stage manager. **39.** a sense of divine appointment to a vocation or service. **40.** a request or invitation to take up a post, as a priest, or a professor in a university, etc. **41.** the summons (to the bar) to a member of an Inn of Court to receive the degree of barrister-at-law. **42.** a need or occasion: *he had no call to say such things.* **43.** a demand or claim: *to make a call on a person's time.* **44.** a rollcall. **45.** *Poker.* a demand for the showing of hands. **46.** a contract which permits its purchaser to buy a certain amount of stock, etc., at a specified price for a limited period of time. **47.** *Cards.* a bid. **48.** a demand for payment of an obligation, esp. where payment is at the option of the creditor. **49.** *Stock Exchange.* the option of claiming stock at or before a given date. **50. call for margin,** *Stock Exchange.* a demand for payment upon the balance owed a stockbroker because of the shrinking value of the security. **51. on call, a.** *Com.* payable or subject to return without advance notice. **b.** (of doctors, etc.) available for duty at short notice. **—***adj.* **52.** *Com.* repayable on demand: *call money, a call loan.* [ME *calle(n)* (cf. OE *calla* herald), r. OE *ceallian*, c. Icel. *kalla*]

—Syn. 1. CALL, INVITE, SUMMON imply requesting the presence or attendance of someone at a particular place. CALL is the general word: *to call a meeting.* To INVITE is to ask someone courteously to come as a guest, a participant, etc., leaving him free to refuse: *to invite guests to a concert, invite them to contribute to a fund.* SUMMON implies sending for someone, using authority or formality in requesting his presence, and (theoretically) not leaving him free to refuse: *to summon a witness.*

calla (kăl′ə), *n.* **1.** a plant of the genus *Zantedeschia* (or *Richardia*), native in Africa, esp. *Z. aethiopicum* (**calla lily**), which has a large white spathe enclosing a yellow spadix, and is familiar in cultivation. **2.** an araceous plant, *Calla palustris*, of cold marshes of Europe and North America, with heart-shaped leaves. [t. NL, ? special use of L *calla* plant name]

callable (kô′lə bl), *adj.* **1.** that may be called. **2.** subject to redemption upon notice, as a bond. **3.** subject to payment on demand, as money loaned.

callant (kä′lənt), *n. Scot. and N Dial.* a lad; a boy. Also, **callan** (kä′lən). [t. D or LG: m. *kalant*, t. F: m. *chaland* customer]

Callao (*Sp.* kä lyä′ō), *n.* a seaport in W Peru, near Lima. 161,286 (1961).

Callas (kăl′əs), *n.* **Maria** (mə rē′), born 1923, Greek operatic soprano, born in the U.S.

callbox (kôl′bŏks′), *n.* a public telephone kiosk.

callboy (kôl′boi′), *n.* **1.** a boy who summons actors just before they go on the stage. **2.** a pageboy.

caller[1] (kô′lə), *n.* **1.** one that calls. **2.** one who makes a short visit. [f. CALL + -ER[1]] **—Syn. 2.** See **visitor.**

caller[2] (kăl′ə, kä′lə), *adj. Scot. and N Dial.* **1.** fresh, as fish, vegetables, etc. **2.** fresh and cool. [? d. var. of *calver* fresh]

callgirl (kôl′gûl′), *n.* a prostitute who makes herself available for appointments by telephone.

calli-, a word element meaning 'beauty'. [t. Gk: m. *kalli-*, comb. form of *kállos*]

Callicrates (kə lĭk′rə tēz′), *n.* fl. 447–442 B.C., Athenian architect: part-designer of the Parthenon.

calligraphy (kə lĭg′rə fĭ), *n.* **1.** beautiful handwriting. **2.** handwriting; penmanship. [t. Gk: m. s. *kalligraphia*] **—callig′rapher, callig′raphist,** *n.* **—calligraphic** (kăl′ĭ grăf′ĭk), *adj.*

calling (kô′lĭng), *n.* **1.** the act of one that calls. **2.** a vocation, profession, or trade. **3.** a summons. **4.** an invitation. **5.** a convocation. **6.** *Cards.* a bidding.

calling card, a visiting card.

calliope (kə lī′ə pĭ), *n.* **1.** a harsh musical instrument consisting of a set of steam whistles, played from a keyboard. **2.** (*cap.*) *Gk Myth.* the Muse of heroic poetry. [t. L, t. Gk: m. *kalliópē*, lit. beautiful-voiced]

calliopsis (kăl′ĭ ŏp′sĭs), *n.* a coreopsis.

callipash (kăl′ĭ păsh′), *n.* calipash.

calliper (kăl′ĭ pə), *n.* **1.** (*usually pl.*) a tool in its simplest form having two legs and resembling a draughtsman's compass, used for obtaining inside and outside measurements, esp. across curved surfaces. **2.** Also, **calliper brake.** a brake on bicycles, etc., consisting of two brake blocks drawn towards each other through a central pivot and grip the rim of the wheel. **—***v.t.* **3.** to measure with callipers. Also, *Chiefly U.S.*, **caliper.** [var. of CALIBRE]

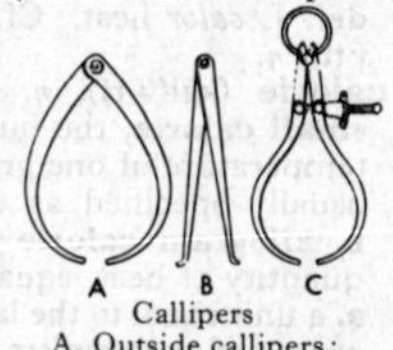

Callipers
A, Outside callipers; B, Inside callipers; C, Spring adjusting callipers

calliper rule, a calliper with one jaw fixed to, or integral with, a graduated straight bar on which the other jaw slides.

callipygian (kăl′ĭ pĭj′ĭ ən), *adj.* having well-shaped buttocks. Also, **callipygous** (kăl′ĭ pī′gəs). [t. Gk: m. s. *kallipýgos*]

callisthenics (kăl′ĭs thĕn′ĭks), *n.* **1.** (*construed as sing.*) the practice or art of callisthenic exercises; exercising the muscles for the purpose of gaining health, strength, and grace of form and movement; eurhythmics. **2.** (*construed as pl.*) light gymnastic exercises designed to develop grace as well as organic vigour and health. Also, **calisthenics.** [f. CALLI- + s. Gk *sthénos* strength + -ICS] —**cal′listhen′ic,** *adj.*

Callisto (kə lĭs′tō), *n. Gk Myth.* a nymph attendant on Artemis, punished for an amour with Zeus by being changed into a bear and slain by Artemis.

callosity (kă lŏs′ĭ tĭ), *n., pl.* **-ties. 1.** a callous condition. **2.** *Bot.* a hardened or thickened part of a plant. **3.** callus (def. 1a).

Callot (*Fr.* kȧ lō′), *n.* **Jacques** (*Fr.* zhȧk), 1592–1635, French etcher, engraver, and illustrator.

callous (kăl′əs), *adj.* **1.** hardened. **2.** hardened in mind, feelings, etc. **3.** having a callus; indurated, as parts of the skin exposed to friction. [t. L: m. s. *callōsus* hard-skinned] —**cal′lously,** *adv.* —**cal′lousness,** *n.* —**Syn. 1.** See **hard.**

call-over (kôl′ō′və), *n.* a rollcall.

callow (kăl′ō), *adj.* **1.** immature or inexperienced: *a callow youth.* **2.** (of a young bird) featherless; unfledged. [ME and OE *calu, calw-,* c. G *kahl*] —**cal′lowness,** *n.*

call sign, 1. a preliminary morse signal, as by a ship, to attract attention. **2.** the preliminary call of a radio station or transmitter which serves to identify it.

call-up (kôl′ŭp′), *n.* a summons to military service.

callus (kăl′əs), *n., pl.* **-luses,** *v.* —*n.* **1.** *Pathol., Physiol.* **a.** a hardened or thickened part of the skin; a callosity. **b.** a new growth of osseous matter at the ends of a fractured bone, serving to unite them. **2.** *Bot.* **a.** the tissue which forms over the wounds of plants, protecting the inner tissues and causing healing. **b.** a deposit on the perforated area of a sieve tube. —*v.i.* **3.** to make a callus. [t. L: hardened skin]

calm (käm), *adj.* **1.** without rough motion; still: *a calm sea.* **2.** not windy; of Beaufort scale force nil. **3.** free from excitement or passion; tranquil: *a calm face, voice, manner, etc.* —*n.* **4.** freedom from motion or disturbance; stillness. **5.** absence of wind. **6.** freedom from agitation, excitement, or passion; tranquillity; serenity. —*v.t.* **7.** to make calm: *calm fears, calm an excited dog, etc.* —*v.i.* **8.** to become calm (usually fol. by *down*). [ME *calme,* t. OF, t. It.: m. *calma* (as if orig., heat of the day, hence, time for resting, quiet), g. LL b. Gk *kaûma* burning heat and L *calēre* be hot] —**calm′ly,** *adv.* —**calm′ness,** *n.*

—**Syn. 1.** quiet, motionless. **3.** placid, peaceful, serene, self-possessed. CALM, COLLECTED, COMPOSED, COOL imply the absence of agitation. CALM implies an unruffled state, esp. under disturbing conditions: *calm in a crisis.* COLLECTED implies complete command of oneself, usually in spite of powerful stresses, and as the result of an effort: *he remained collected in spite of the excitement.* One who is COMPOSED has or has gained dignified self-possession: *pale but composed.* COOL implies the apparent absence of strong feeling or excitement, esp. in circumstances of danger or strain: *a mountaineer must have a cool head.* **7.** still, quiet, tranquillize. —**Ant. 3.** agitated, excited.

calmative (kăl′mə tĭv, kä′mə-), *adj., n. Med.* sedative.

calomel (kăl′ə mĕl′, -məl), *n. Pharm.* mercurous chloride, Hg_2Cl_2, a white, tasteless solid, used in medicine as a mercurial, a purgative, etc. [t. F, short for *calomélas,* f. Gk: m. s. *kalós* beautiful + *mélās* black]

calorescence (kăl′ə rĕs′əns), *n. Physics.* the absorption of radiation of one wavelength by a body and the subsequent emission of radiation of a different wavelength, especially of a shorter wavelength.

Calor gas (kăl′ə), *Trademark.* commercial butane.

caloric (kə lŏ′rĭk), *n.* **1.** heat. **2.** *Old Physics.* a hypothetical imponderable fluid whose presence in matter determined its thermal state. —*adj.* **3.** pertaining or relating to heat. **4.** (of engines) driven by heated air. [t. F: m. *calorique,* der. L *calor* heat. Cf. CALORIE] —**caloricity** (kăl′ə rĭs′ĭ tĭ), *n.*

calorie (kăl′ə rĭ), *n.* **1.** *Physics.* **a. gram calorie** or **small calorie,** the quantity of heat required to raise the temperature of one gram of water one degree centigrade, usually specified as determined at, or close to, 16°C. **b. kilogram calorie** or **large calorie,** (*usually cap.*) a quantity of heat, equal to 1000 gram calories. **2.** *Physiol.* **a.** a unit equal to the large calorie, used to express the heat output of an organism and the fuel or energy value of food. **b.** a quantity of food capable of producing such a unit of energy. Also, **calory.** [t. F, der. L *calor* heat]

calorific (kăl′ə rĭf′ĭk), *adj.* pertaining to conversion into heat. [t. L: s. *calōrificus* heat-producing]

calorific value, the amount of heat produced by the complete combustion of a given quantity of a substance, esp. a fuel.

calorimeter (kăl′ə rĭm′ĭ tə), *n. Physics, etc.* an apparatus for measuring quantities of heat. [f. L *calor* heat + -(I)METER[1]]

calorimetry (kăl′ə rĭm′ĭ trĭ), *n. Physics.* the measurement of heat. —**calorimetric** (kăl′ə rĭ mĕt′rĭk, kə lŏ′rĭ-), **cal′orimet′rical,** *adj.* —**cal′orimet′rically,** *adv.*

calory (kăl′ə rĭ), *n., pl.* **-ries.** calorie.

calotte (kə lŏt′), *n.* **1.** a plain skullcap, as that worn by Catholic ecclesiastics. **2.** *Archit.* a small dome in a low ceiling. [t. F, dim. of *cale* cap. Cf. CAUL]

caloyer (kăl′oi′ə, kă loi′ə), *n.* a monk of the Greek Orthodox Church. [t. F, t. It.: m. *caloiero,* t. LGk: m. *kalógēros* venerable, monk]

calpac (kăl′păk), *n.* kalpak.

calque (kôk), *v.t.,* **calqued, calquing.** calk[3]. [t. F]

Caltanissetta (*It.* käl tä nēs sĕt′tä), *n.* a town in central Sicily. 65,161 (1966).

caltrop (kăl′trəp), *n.* **1.** *Bot.* **a.** any of various plants having spiny heads or fruit, esp. of the genera *Tribulus* and *Kallstroemia.* **b.** the star thistle. **c.** an Old World plant, *Tribulus terrestris.* **d.** the water-chestnut. **2.** *Mil.* an iron ball with four projecting spikes so disposed that when the ball is on the ground one of them always points upwards, used to obstruct the passage of cavalry, etc. Also, **caltrap.** [ME *calketrappe,* OE *col(te)træppe, calcatrippe* spiny plant, appar. f. m. s. L *calx* heel + m. ML *trappa* trap]

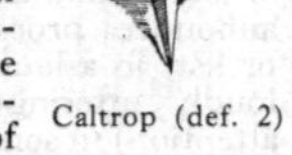
Caltrop (def. 2)

calumba (kəlŭm′bə), *n.* the root of an East African plant, *Jateorhiza columba,* used as a tonic.

calumet (kăl′yōō mĕt′), *n.* a long, ornamented tobacco pipe used by North American Indians on ceremonial occasions, esp. in token of peace. [t. d. F, g. dim. of L *calamus* reed]

calumniate (kə lŭm′nĭ āt′), *v.t.,* **-ated, -ating.** to make false and malicious statements about; slander. [t. L: m. s. *calumniātus,* pp.] —**calum′nia′tor,** *n.*

calumniation (kə lŭm′nĭ ā′shən), *n.* **1.** the act of calumniating; slander. **2.** a calumny.

calumnious (kə lŭm′nĭ əs), *adj.* of, involving, or using calumny; slanderous; defamatory. Also, **calumniatory** (kə lŭm′nyə tə rĭ, -trĭ). —**calum′niously,** *adv.*

calumny (kăl′əm nĭ), *n., pl.* **-nies. 1.** a false and malicious statement designed to injure someone's reputation. **2.** slander. [t. L: m. s. *calumnia*]

Calvados (kăl′və dŏs′; *Fr.* kȧl vȧ dōs′), *n.* **1.** a department in NW France. 480,686 pop. (1962); 2198 sq. mi. *Cap.:* Caen. **2.** (*sometimes l.c.*) a liqueur made from apple juice in Normandy; apple brandy.

calvaria (kăl vĕə′rĭ ə), *n.* the dome of the skull. [t. L. See CALVARY]

Calvary (kăl′və rĭ), *n., pl.* **-ries** (*def. 2*). **1.** Golgotha, the place where Jesus was crucified. Luke 23:33. **2.** (*l.c.*) a sculptured representation of the Crucifixion, usually erected in the open air. [t. L: m. s. *calvāria* skull, used to render the Aramaic name. See GOLGOTHA]

calve (käv), *v.,* **calved, calving.** —*v.i.* **1.** to give birth to a calf. **2.** (of a glacier, iceberg, etc.) to give off a detached piece. —*v.t.* **3.** to give birth to (a calf). **4.** to give off (a detached piece). [ME *calve(n),* der. *calf* calf; r. OE *cealfian,* der. *cealf* calf]

Calvé (*Fr.* kȧl vē′), *n.* **Emma** (*Fr.* ĕ mȧ′) (*Emma de Roquer Gaspari*), 1863?–1942, French operatic soprano.

Calvert (kăl′vət), *n.* **Sir George** (*1st Baron Baltimore*), *c.* 1580–1632, English statesman: founder of the colony of Maryland.

calves (kävz), *n.* pl. of **calf.**

Calvin (kăl′vĭn), *n.* **John,** 1509–64, religious reformer and theologian, born in France: leader of the Protestant Reformation in Geneva, Switzerland.

Calvinism (kăl′vĭ nĭz′əm), *n.* **1.** *Theol.* **a.** the doctrines and church practices taught by John Calvin, who emphasized the sovereignty of God, predestination, the authority of Scriptures, presbyterian polity, and strict church discipline. **b.** the doctrines of later theologians who accepted Calvin's teachings with various modifications. **2.** adherence to these doctrines. —**Cal′vinist,** *n., adj.* —**Cal′vinis′tic, Cal′vinis′tical,** *adj.*

calvities (kăl vĭsh′ĭ ēz′), *n. Chiefly Med.* baldness. [t. L]

Calwell (kôl′wĕl′), *n.* **Arthur,** born 1897, Australian politician.

calx (kălks), *n., pl.* **calces** (kăl′sēz), **calxes. 1.** the oxide or ashy substance which remains after metals, minerals, etc., have been thoroughly roasted or burnt. **2.** lime. [t. L: small stone, lime]

calyces (kăl′ĭ sēz′, kā′lĭ-), *n.* a pl. of **calyx.**

calycine (kăl′ĭ sĭn′), *adj.* pertaining to or resembling a calyx. Also, **calycinal** (kə lĭs′ĭ nəl).

calycle (kăl′ĭ kl), *n. Bot.* a set of bracts resembling an outer calyx. [t. L: m. s. *calyculus*, dim. of *calyx* calyx]

Calydon (kăl′ĭ dən), *n.* an ancient city in W Greece, in Aetolia. —**Calydonian** (kăl′ĭ dō′nyən), *adj.*

Calydonian hunt, *Gk Legend.* the pursuit, by Meleager and a band of heroes, of a savage boar (**Calydonian boar**) sent by Artemis to ravage Calydon.

calypso (kə lĭp′sō), *n., pl.* **-sos. 1.** a song, based on a musical pattern of West Indian origin, with topical, usually improvised, lyrics. **2.** a terrestrial orchid of the genus *Calypso* (*Cytherea*), widespread in the Northern Hemisphere, having a single variegated purple, yellow, and white flower. **3.** (*cap.*) *Gk Legend.* a sea-nymph who for seven years detained Odysseus on the island of Ogygia. —*adj.* **4.** pertaining to a calypso (def. 1).

calyptra (kə lĭp′trə), *n. Bot.* **1.** the hood which covers the lid of the capsule in mosses. **2.** a hoodlike part connected with the organs of fructification in flowering plants. **3.** a root cap. [t. NL, t. Gk: m. *kalýptra* veil] —**calyp′trate,** *adj.*

calyptrogen (kə lĭp′trə jən), *n. Bot.* the histogen layer which develops into the root cap.

calyx (kā′lĭks, kăl′ĭks), *n., pl.* **calyces** (kăl′ĭ sēz′, kā′lĭ-), **calyxes. 1.** *Bot.* the outermost group of floral parts, usually green; the sepals. **2.** *Anat., Zool.* a cuplike part. [t. L, t. Gk: m. *kályx* covering, husk, calyx]

A B

Calyces
A, Gamosepalous calyx; B, Bilabiate calyx

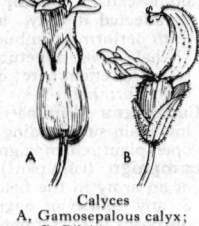

cam (kăm), *n. Mach.* a device for converting regular rotary motion into irregular rotary or reciprocating motion, etc., commonly consisting of an oval-, needle-, or heart-shaped, or other specially shaped flat piece, an eccentric wheel or the like, fastened on and revolving with a shaft, and engaging with other mechanism. [t. D or LG: m. *kam*, *kamm* cog. See COMB]

A B C

Cams
A, Elliptical cam; B, Cam wheel; C, Heart cam

Cam (kăm), *n.* a river in E England flowing NE by Cambridge into the Ouse; Granta. 40 mi.

Camagüey (*Sp.* kȧ mȧ gwĕy′), *n.* a city in central Cuba. 191,379 (1960).

camaraderie (kăm′ə rä′də rĭ), *n.* comradeship; close friendship. [t. F]

camarilla (kăm′ə rĭl′ə; *Sp.* kȧ mȧ rē′lyȧ), *n.* a group of private advisers; a cabal; a clique. [t. Sp., dim. of *cámara* CHAMBER]

camass (kăm′ăs), *n.* any of various plants of the lily family (genus *Camassia*), esp. *C. quamash*, a species in western North America, with sweet, edible bulbs. Also, **camas.** [t. N Amer. Ind., from Chinook jargon, der. *chamas* sweet (Nootka)]

camber (kăm′bə), *v.t., v.i.* **1.** to arch slightly; bend or curve upwards in the middle. —*n.* **2.** a slight arching or convexity above, as of a ship's deck or a road surface. **3.** a slightly arching piece of timber. **4.** *Aeron.* the rise of the curve of an aerofoil, usually expressed as the ratio of the rise to the length of the chord of the aerofoil. **5.** *Naut.* **a.** a small dock. **b.** a slipway for hauling ships on land. [t. d. F: m. *cambre*, adj., bent, g. L *camur*]

Camberwell (kăm′bə wĕl′, -wəl), *n.* a district of the S Inner London borough of Southwark.

Camberwell beauty, an Old World butterfly, *Nymphalis antiopa*, with velvety black wings tipped with yellow or white bands.

cambist (kăm′bĭst), *n.* **1.** a dealer in bills of exchange. **2.** an expert in the science of monetary exchange. **3.** a manual giving the moneys, weights, and measures of different countries, with their equivalents. [t. F: m. *cambiste*, t. It.: m. *cambista*, der. *cambiare* CHANGE]

cambium (kăm′bĭ əm), *n. Bot.* a cylindrical layer of meristematic cells which give rise to secondary tissues towards the inside and outside, thus causing increase in girth of a stem or root. [t. LL: exchange]

Cambodia (kăm bō′dyə), *n.* a kingdom in SE Asia, formerly a part of French Indochina. 5,748,842 pop. (1962); 69,866 sq. mi. *Cap.:* Pnom-Penh. French, **Cambodge** (*Fr.* käɴ bȯzh′). See map under **Indochina.** —**Cambod′ian,** *n., adj.*

cambogia (kăm bō′jĭ ə), *n. Pharm.* gamboge (def. 1).

Cambon (*Fr.* käɴ bôɴ′), *n.* **1. Jules Martin** (*Fr.* zhYl mȧr tăɴ′), 1845–1935, French diplomat and administrator. **2. Pierre Paul** (*Fr.* pyĕr pōl′), 1843–1924, French diplomat.

Camborne (kăm′bôn), *n.* a town in England, in Cornwall. (with Redruth) 36,090 (1961).

Cambrai (*Fr.* käɴ brĕ′), *n.* a city in N France, in Nord department: battles, 1917, 1918. 30,000 (est. 1964).

cambrel (kăm′brəl), *n.* a bent rod or stick on which butchers hang the carcasses of animals. [var. of GAMBREL]

Cambria (kăm′brĭ ə), *n.* medieval Latin name of Wales. [Latinization of Welsh *Cymry*]

Cambrian (kăm′brĭ ən), *adj.* **1.** *Geol.* pertaining to the oldest geological period or a system of rocks characterized by the presence of numerous well-preserved fossils. **2.** pertaining to Cambria (Wales). —*n.* **3.** *Geol.* the period or system comprising the first main division of the Palaeozoic era or rocks. **4.** a Welshman.

Cambrian Mountains, a range of low mountains extending through Wales from Carmarthenshire to Denbigh. Highest point, Aran Fawddwy, 2940 ft.

cambric (kām′brĭk), *n.* a cotton or linen fabric of fine close weave, usually white. [t. Flem.: m. *Kameryk* CAMBRAI]

Cambridge (kām′brĭj′), *n.* **1.** a city in E England. 95,358 (1961). **2.** the university situated there, founded 1209. **3.** a city in E Massachusetts, near Boston. 107,716 (1960). **4.** Cambridgeshire.

Cambridgeshire (kām′brĭj shĭə′, -shə), *n.* a county in E England. 189,913 pop. (1961); 492 sq. mi. *Co. town:* Cambridge. *Abbrev.:* Cambs. Also, **Cambridge.**

Cambs., Cambridgeshire.

Cambyses (kăm bī′sēz), *n.* died 522 B.C., son of Cyrus the Great and king of Persia 529–522 B.C.

Camden (kăm′dən), *n.* **1. William,** 1551–1623, English scholar, antiquary and historian. **2.** a NW inner borough of London. 246,000 (1964). **3.** a city in the U.S., in SW New Jersey: a port on the Delaware. 117,159 (1960).

came[1] (kām), *v.* pt. of **come.**

came[2] (kām), *n.* a slender grooved bar of lead for holding together the pieces of glass in windows of latticework or stained glass. [appar. var. of *calm* mould for casting metallic objects]

camel (kăm′əl), *n.* **1.** either of two large Old World ruminant quadrupeds of the genus *Camelus*, used as beasts of burden: **a.** the **Arabian camel,** or dromedary, with one hump (*C. dromedarius*). **b.** the **Bactrian camel,** with two humps (*C. bactrianus*). **2.** a brown colour somewhat lighter than fawn. **3.** *Civ. Eng., Naut.* a pontoon[1] (def. 2). [ME and OE, t. L: s. *camēlus*, t. Gk: m. *kámēlos*; of Semitic orig.] —**cam′elish, camel′-like′,** *adj.*

cameleer (kăm′ĭ lĭə′), *n.* **1.** a camel driver. **2.** a soldier on a camel.

camelhair (kăm′əl hĕə′), *n.* **1.** the hair of the camel, used for cloth, painters' brushes, certain oriental rugs, etc. **2.** cloth made of this hair, or of a substitute, usually tan in colour. —*adj.* **3.** made of camel's hair. **4.** (of a painter's brush) made from the tail hairs of squirrels.

camellia (kə mē′lyə), *n.* a plant, *Camellia* (or *Thea*) *japonica*, native in Asia, with glossy evergreen leaves and white, pink, red, or variegated waxy roselike flowers, familiar in cultivation. [named after G. J. *Kamel*, 1661–1706, Moravian Jesuit missionary]

Camelopard (kə mĕl′ə päd′, kăm′ĭ lə päd′), *n.* **1.** Also, **Camelopardalis** (kə mĕl′ə pä′də lĭs). *Astron.* a northern constellation. **2.** (*l.c.*) *Obs.* a giraffe. [t. LL: s. *camēlopardus*, L *camēlopardālis*, t. Gk: m. *kamēlopárdalis* giraffe]

Camelot (kăm′ĭ lŏt′), *n.* the legendary site of King Arthur's palace and court, thought to be near Exeter.

camel's-thorn (kăm′əlz thôn′), *n.* a thorny shrub, *Alhagi maurorum*, and a member of the family *Leguminosa*, found in the Mediterranean region and western Asia. Also, **camel-thorn** (kăm′əl thôn′).

Camembert (kăm′əm bĕə′; *Fr.* kȧ mäɴ bĕr′), *n.* a rich, cream-coloured variety of soft cheese.

Camenae (kə mē′nē), *n.pl.* (in early Roman religion) prophetic nymphs of the springs and fountains, later identified with the Greek Muses.

cameo (kăm′ĭ ō′), *n., pl.* **-os. 1.** an engraving in relief upon a gem, stone, etc., with differently coloured layers of the stone often utilized to produce a background of one hue and a design of another. **2.** a gem, stone, etc., so engraved. **3.** a short piece of ornate, highly polished writing. [t. It.: m. *cammeo*; prob. of oriental orig.]

cameo part, *Theat.* a minor role with attractive acting possibilities.

cameo ware, pottery with figures moulded in relief on a different-coloured background.

camera (kăm′ə rə, kăm′rə), *n.*, *pl.* **-eras** *for 1–2*, **-erae** (-ə rē′) *for 3.* **1.** a photographic apparatus in which sensitive plates or film are exposed, the image being formed by means of a lens. **2.** (in a television transmitting apparatus) the device in which the picture to be televised is formed before it is changed into electrical impulses. **3.** a judge's private room. **4. in camera, a.** *Law.* in the privacy of a judge's chambers. **b.** privately. [t. L: arch, vault, ML chamber, treasury. Cf. CHAMBER]

cameral (kăm′ə rəl), *adj.* pertaining to a camera (esp. defs. 3, 4).

camera lucida (lo͞o′sĭ də), *Optics.* an optical instrument by which the image of an external object is projected on a sheet of paper, etc., upon which it may be traced. [t. LL: light chamber]

cameraman (kăm′ə rə măn′, kăm′rə-), *n.*, *pl.* **-men.** a man who operates a camera, esp. a cinema or television camera.

camera obscura (ŏb skyo͝oə′rə), **1.** a darkened boxlike device in which images of external objects, received through an aperture, as with a convex lens, are exhibited in their natural colours on a surface arranged to receive them: used for sketching, exhibition purposes, etc. **2.** camera (def. 1). [t. LL: dark chamber]

Cameron (kăm′ə rən, kăm′rən), *n.* **Sir David Young,** 1865–1945, Scottish painter and etcher.

Cameroon (kăm′ə ro͞on′, kăm′ə ro͞on′), *n.* **1.** an active volcano on the N part of the coast of Cameroun: the highest peak on the W coast of Africa. 13,370 ft. **2.** Cameroun.

Cameroons (kăm′ə ro͞onz′), *n.* **1.** German, **Kamerun.** a region in W Africa: a former German protectorate; divided into two mandates of Cameroons (to Great Britain) and Cameroun (to France), 1919. **2.** former name, **British Cameroons.** the NW part of this region, comprising the **Northern Cameroons** (now part of Nigeria) and the **Southern Cameroons** (now part of Cameroun).

Cameroun (*Fr.* kȧm ro͞on′), *n.* an independent republic in W Africa, comprising the former French trusteeship of Cameroun and the former British trusteeship of Southern Cameroons. ab. 4,700,000 pop. (est. 1961); 183,350 sq. mi. *Cap.:* Yaoundé. Also, **Cameroon.** See map under **Nigeria.**

camion (kăm′yən; *Fr.* kȧ myôɴ′), *n.* a strongly built lorry or cart for carrying heavy loads. [t. F; orig. uncert.]

Camisard (kăm′ĭ zäd′; *Fr.* kȧ mĭ zär′), *n.* any of the French Protestants in the Cévennes region who in the early 18th century carried on an organized resistance to the revocation of the Edict of Nantes.

camisole (kăm′ĭ sōl′), *n.* **1.** an ornamental underbodice, worn under a thin outer bodice. **2.** a woman's dressing jacket. **3.** a sleeved jacket or jersey once worn by men. **4.** a type of straitjacket. [t. F, t. Sp.: m. *camisola*, dim. of *camisa* shirt]

camlet (kăm′lĭt), *n.* **1.** a durable waterproof cloth used for cloaks, etc. **2.** apparel made of this material. **3.** formerly, a rich fabric, apparently orig. made of camel's or goat's hair. [var. of *camelot*, t. F; r. late ME *chamelot*, t. OF, prob. t. Ar.: m. *khamla*, der. *khaml* nap]

Cammaerts (kăm′ĕəts), *n.* **Émile** (ĕ mēl′), 1878–1953, Belgian poet.

Camoëns (kăm′ō ĕns′), *n.* **Luis Vaz de** (*Port.* lwĕsh vȧsh də), 1524?–80, Portuguese poet. Portuguese, **Camões** (*Port.* kȧ môyɴsh′).

camomile (kăm′ə mīl′), *n.* **1.** any plant of the asteraceous genus *Anthemis*, esp. *A. nobilis* (the common camomile of Europe and of gardens elsewhere), a herb with strongly scented foliage and flowers which are used medicinally. **2.** any of various allied plants, as *Matricaria chamomilla* (**German** or **wild camomile**). Also, **chamomile.** [ME *camemille*, t. L: m. *chamomilla*, var. of *chamaemēlon*, t. Gk: m. *chamaímēlon* earth apple]

Camorra (kə mŏr′rə; *It.* kȧ mŏr′rȧ), *n.* **1.** a Neapolitan secret society, first publicly known about 1820, which developed into a powerful political organization and has been associated with blackmail, robbery, etc. **2.** (*l.c.*) some similar society or group. [t. It., t. Sp.: dispute, quarrel] —**Camor′rism,** *n.* —**Camor′rist,** *n.*

camouflage (kăm′o͝o fläzh′), *n.*, *v.*, **-flaged, -flaging.** —*n.* **1.** *Mil.* act, art, means, or result of disguising things to deceive the enemy, as by painting or screening objects so that they are lost to view in the background, or by making up objects which, from a distance, have the appearance of fortifications, guns, roads, etc. **2.** the means by which any object or creature renders itself indistinguishable from its background, as by assuming the colour, shape, or texture of objects in that background. **3.** disguise; deception; false pretence. —*v.t.* **4.** to disguise, hide, or deceive by means of camouflage: *camouflaged ships.* [t. F, der. *camoufler* disguise]

camouflet (kăm′o͝o flā′), *n.* *Mil.* a crater produced in a roadway or elsewhere by the placing and detonation of an explosive charge. [t. F]

camoufleur (kăm′o͝o flû′; *Fr.* kȧ mo͞o flœr′), *n.* *Mil.* one who conceals military objects by camouflage. [t. F]

camp[1] (kămp), *n.* **1.** a group of tents, caravans, or other temporary shelters in one place. **2.** the persons sojourning in such shelters. **3.** the place where the shelters are situated; a camping site. **4.** a site where soldiers are housed, in structures originally intended to be temporary. **5.** army life. **6.** a group of people favouring the same ideals, doctrines, etc.: *the socialist camp.* **7.** any position in which ideals, doctrines, etc., are strongly entrenched. —*v.i.* **8.** to establish or pitch a camp. **9.** to live temporarily in a tent (often fol. by *out*). —*v.t.* **10.** to put or station (troops, etc.) in a camp; shelter. [t. F, t. It.: m. *campo* field, g. L *campus*] —**camp′er,** *n.* —**camp′ing,** *n.*

camp[2] (kămp), *adj.* **1.** exaggerated and often amusing or effeminate in style. **2.** effeminate; given to acting and speaking with exaggerated mannerisms. **3.** homosexual. —*n.* **4.** an exaggerated, often amusing or effeminate style, mannerism, or the like. **5.** a person or his work displaying this quality. —*v.i.* **6.** to act in a camp manner. **7.** to be a homosexual. **8. camp it up, a.** to make an ostentatious or affected display. **b.** to flaunt homosexuality. —*v.t.* **9.** to perform or imbue (something) with a camp quality. [? dial. *camp* impetuous, uncouth person, hence objectionable, effeminate; in some senses, prob. special use of CAMP[1] brothel]

Campagna (kăm pä′nyə; *It.* kȧm pȧn′nyȧ), *n.* **1.** a low plain surrounding the city of Rome. **2.** (*l.c.*) any flat open plain; champaign. [t. It., g. L *campānia* level plain]

campaign (kăm pān′), *n.* **1.** the military operations of an army in the field during one season or enterprise. **2.** any course of aggressive activities for some special purpose: *a sales campaign.* **3.** the competition by rival political candidates and organizations for public office. —*v.i.* **4.** to serve in, or go on, a campaign. [t. F: m. *campagne*, ult. der. L *campus* plain] —**campaign′er,** *n.*

Campania (kăm pā′nyə; *It.* kȧm pȧn′nyȧ), *n.* a region in SW Italy. 4,756,094 pop. (1961); 5214 sq. mi. *Cap.:* Naples.

campanile (kăm′pə nē′lĭ; *It.* kȧm pȧ nē′lė), *n.*, *pl.* **-niles, -nili** (*It.* -nē′lē). a bell tower (often a detached structure). [t. It., der. *campana* bell, g. L]

campanology (kăm′pə nŏl′ə jĭ), *n.* **1.** the study of bells. **2.** the principles of bellringing, bell-founding, etc. [t. NL: m. s. *campanologia*, f. s. LL *campāna* bell + -(*o*)*logia* -(O)LOGY] —**cam′panol′ogist, cam′panol′oger,** *n.*

campanula (kəm păn′yo͝o lə), *n.* any plant of the genus *Campanula*, as the harebell or the Canterbury bell; a bellflower. [t. NL, dim. of LL *campāna* bell]

campanulaceous (kəm păn′yo͝o lā′shəs), *adj.* *Bot.* belonging to the *Campanulaceae*, or campanula family of plants.

campanulate (kəm păn′yo͝o lĭt, -lāt′), *adj.* bell-shaped, as a corolla.

camp bed, a light folding bed, usually of canvas stretched over a collapsible metal frame.

Campbell (kăm′bl), *n.* **1. Colin** (kŏl′ĭn) (*Baron Clyde*), 1792–1863, Scottish general. **2. Donald,** 1921–67, English speed record-holder. **3.** his father, **Sir Malcolm,** 1885–1948, English racing driver and speed record-holder. **4. Mrs Patrick** (*Beatrice Stella*), 1865–1940, English actress. **5. Thomas,** 1777–1844, Scottish poet and editor.

Campbell-Bannerman (kăm′bl băn′ə mən), *n.* **Sir Henry,** 1836–1908, British statesman: prime minister 1905–08.

Campbellite (kăm′bə līt′), *n.* a member of the body of Christians known as the Disciples of Christ. [f. *Campbell* + -ITE[1]; named after the Rev. Alexander *Campbell*, 1788–1866, U.S. religious leader born in Ireland, founder of the movement]

Campbelltown (kăm′bl toun′), *n.* a town in Australia, in E Tasmania. 24,400 (est. 1964).

camp chair, a light folding chair.

camp fire, 1. a fire in a camp for warmth or cooking. **2.** *Chiefly U.S.* a reunion of soldiers, scouts, etc.

camp follower, 1. a person who follows an army moving from camp to camp, without official connection, as a washerwoman, prostitute, etc. **2.** any unofficial or insignificant hanger-on, as of a political movement, a well-known personality, etc.

camphane (kăm′fān, kăm fān′), *n.* *Chem.* a white crystalline saturated hydrocarbon, $C_{10}H_{18}$, from which the camphor group is derived.

camphene (kăm′fēn, kăm fēn′), *n.* *Chem.* a white, feathery, unsaturated hydrocarbon, $C_{10}H_{16}$, present in certain essential oils.

camphol (kăm′fəl, -fōl), *n. Chem.* borneol.

camphor (kăm′fə), *n.* **1.** a whitish, translucent, crystalline, pleasant-smelling terpene ketone, $C_{10}H_{16}O$, obtained chiefly from the camphor tree and used in medicine, the manufacture of celluloid, etc. **2.** any of various similar substances. [t. ML: s. *camphora*, t. Ar.: m. *kāfūr*, t. Malay: m. *kāpūr*; r. ME *caumfre*, t. AF] —**camphoric** (kăm fō′rĭk), *adj.*

camphorate (kăm′fə rāt′), *v.t.*, **-rated, -rating.** to impregnate with camphor.

camphor ball, a mothball, usually consisting of naphthalene, and sometimes of camphor, etc.

camphor ice, *Med.* a preparation made chiefly of camphor, white wax, spermaceti, and castor oil, used esp. for skin infections.

camphor tree, **1.** a lauraceous tree, *Cinnamomum camphora,* of Japan, Taiwan, China, etc., yielding camphor. **2.** any of various similar trees, as *Dryobalanops aromatica* of Borneo, etc., which yields borneol.

Campinas (kəm pē′nəs; *Port.* kəm pē′nȧs), *n.* a town in S Brazil. 179,797 (1960).

camping site, a place where tents, caravans, etc., are or may be erected and parked as for holiday occupation.

campion (kăm′pyən), *n.* any of certain plants of the pink family, genera *Silene* or *Lychnis*, as the **rose campion,** *L. coronaria.* [prob. ult. der. L *campus* field]

Campion (kăm′pyən), *n.* **1. Edmund,** 1540–81, English Jesuit martyr. **2. Thomas,** 1567–1620, English musician and poet.

camp meeting, a religious gathering, usually lasting for some days, held in a tent or in the open air.

campo (kăm′pō), *n., pl.* **-pos.** (in South America) an extensive, nearly level, grassy plain. [t. Pg., Sp., g. L *campus* field, plain]

Campo Formio (kăm′pō fô′mĭ ō′), a village in NE Italy, in Friuli-Venezia Giulia: treaty between France and Austria, 1797. Modern, **Campoformido** (kăm′pō fô′mĭ dō′).

Campos (*Port.* kəm′pōōs), *n.* a city in E Brazil near Rio de Janeiro. 277,459 (est. 1957).

camp stool, a light folding seat.

campus (kăm′pəs), *n. U.S.* **1.** the grounds of a university or other institute of higher education. **2.** such a university, etc. [t. L: field]

Camrose (kăm′rōz′), *n.* **William Ewart Berry, 1st Viscount,** 1879–1954, British newspaper proprietor.

camshaft (kăm′shäft′), *n. Mach.* a shaft with cams.

Camus (*Fr.* kȧ mʏ′), *n.* **Albert** (*Fr.* ȧl bĕr′), 1913–60, French novelist.

camwheel (kăm′wēl′), *n.* a cam.

camwood (kăm′wood′), *n.* the hard red wood of the W African tree *Baphia nitida*, formerly used for making dye, etc. [orig. uncert.]

can[1] (kăn; *unstressed* kən), *v., pres. sing.* 1 **can**; 2 **can** or (*Archaic*) **canst**; 3 **can**; *pt.* **could.** —*aux.* **1.** to know how to; be able to; have the ability, power, right, qualifications, or means to: *you can lift the box.* **2.** *Colloq.* may; have permission: *Can I speak to you a moment?* —*v.t., v.i.* **3.** *Obs.* to know. [ME and OE *cann, can,* 1st and 3rd pers. sing. pres. ind. (pret. *cūthe*) of *cunnan,* c. G *können.* Cf. KEN and KNOW]

—**Syn.** **1.** CAN denotes power or ability to do something: *the child can talk.* MAY refers to probability, possibility, or permission: *our son may* (possibility or probability) *play football on Saturday if the doctor says he may* (permission). The two words are often confused in asking or granting permission; MAY is the politer usage. CANNOT may also be used to express either extreme negation of ability or negation of probability: *I cannot work such long hours, I cannot* (possibly) *be mistaken.* **2.** CAN BUT, CANNOT BUT are formal expressions suggesting that there is no possible alternative to doing a certain thing. CAN BUT is equivalent to informal CAN ONLY: *we can but do our best* (1. and *must* make the attempt; or 2. and no more than that should be expected of us). CANNOT BUT (do) is equivalent to informal CAN'T HELP (doing): *we cannot but protest against injustice* (we are under moral obligation to do so). CANNOT HELP BUT is common in familiar use, but is not otherwise considered good usage.

can[2] (kăn), *n., v.,* **canned, canning.** —*n.* **1.** a container, sometimes sealed, usually for a liquid and made of sheet iron coated with tin or other metal. **2.** the contents of a can. **3.** *Chiefly U.S.* a tin (def. 4). **4.** a drinking vessel. **5.** *Chiefly U.S.* a dustbin; wastebin. **6.** *Slang.* the blame for something: *to carry the can.* **7.** *U.S. Slang.* dismissal. **8.** *U.S. Slang.* the lavatory or bathroom. **9.** *U.S. Slang.* jail. **10.** *U.S. Slang.* the buttocks. **11.** *Naval Slang.* a depth charge. **12. in the can, a.** (of a film) ready for distribution; filmed, developed, and edited. **b.** completed; made final. —*v.t.* **13.** to put in a container, usually sealed for preservation. **14.** *U.S. Slang.* to dismiss; fire. **15. can it,** *Slang.* to shut up; be or become silent. [ME and OE *canne,* c. G *Kanne* can, pot, mug]

Can., **1.** Canada. **2.** Canadian.

can., **1.** canto. **2.** canton. **3.** cantoris.

Cana (kā′nə), *n.* an ancient town in N Israel, in Galilee: the scene of Jesus Christ's first miracle. John 2:1, 11.

Canaan (kā′nən), *n.* **1.** the ancient region, included in modern Palestine (now Israel and Jordan), lying between the Jordan, the Dead Sea, and the Mediterranean: the land promised by God to Abraham. Gen. 12. **2.** Palestine. **3.** any land of promise. **4.** *Bible.* the descendant of Ham, the son of Noah. Gen. 10. [t. Heb.: m. *kana'an*]

Canaan

Canaanite (kā′nə nīt′), *n.* **1.** a member of the Semitic people inhabiting Palestine at the time of the Hebrew conquest. **2.** a group of Semitic languages, including Hebrew and Phoenician, spoken chiefly in ancient Palestine and Syria. —**Ca′naanit′ish, Canaanitic** (kā′nə nĭt′ĭk), *adj.*

Canada (kăn′ə də), *n.* a country of North America and a member of the Commonwealth of Nations. 18,896,000 pop. (est. 1961); 3,690,410 sq. mi. *Cap.*: Ottawa.

Canada balsam, a transparent turpentine obtained from the balsam fir, *Abies balsamea*, used for mounting objects for the microscope.

Canada goose, the common wild goose, *Branta canadensis*, of North America.

Canada lily, a lily, *Lilium canadense*, with several nodding flowers and recurved sepals, common in Canada and the NE U.S.

Canadian (kə nā′dyən), *adj.* **1.** of Canada or its people. —*n.* **2.** a native or inhabitant of Canada.

Canadian pondweed, a submerged aquatic herb, *Elodea canadensis*, family *Hydrocharitaceae*, native of North America but naturalized and widespread in Europe.

Canadian River, a river flowing from the Rocky Mountains E to the Arkansas river in E Oklahoma. 906 mi.

canaille (*Fr.* kȧ nȧy′), *n.* riffraff; the rabble. [t. F, t. It.: m. *canaglia*, der. *cane* dog, g. L *canis*]

canal (kə năl′), *n., v.,* **-nalled, -nalling.** —*n.* **1.** an artificial waterway for navigation, drainage, irrigation, etc. **2.** a long, narrow arm of the sea penetrating far inland. **3.** a tubular passage or cavity for food, air, etc., esp. in an animal or plant; a duct. **4.** *Astron.* one of the long, narrow, dark lines on the surface of the planet Mars. **5.** *Obs.* a channel or watercourse. —*v.t.* **6.** to make a canal through. **7.** to furnish with canals. [late ME, t. L: s. *canālis* pipe, groove, channel]

canal boat, a craft built to fit canal locks.

Canaletto (kăn′ə lĕt′ō; *It.* kȧ nȧ lĕt′tȯ), *n.* **Antonio** (*It.* ȧn tȯ′nyȯ), 1697–1768, Italian painter.

canaliculus (kăn′ə lĭk′yŏŏ ləs), *n., pl.* **-li** (-lī′). *Anat., Zool.* a small canal or tubular passage, as in bone. [t. L, dim. of *canālis* channel. See CANAL] —**can′alic′ular, canaliculate** (kăn′ə lĭk′yŏŏ lĭt, -yŏŏ lāt′), **can′alic′ulat′ed,** *adj.*

canalize (kăn′ə līz′), *v.t.,* **-lized, -lizing.** **1.** to make a canal or canals through. **2.** to convert into a canal. **3.** to divert into certain channels; give a certain direction to or provide a certain outlet for. Also, **canalise.** —**canalization** (kăn′ə lī zā′shən), *n.*

canal rays, *Physics.* the rays (consisting of positively charged ions) which pass through a hole in the cathode, in a direction away from the anode, when an electric discharge takes place in a vacuum tube.

Canal Zone, a strip of territory 10 mi. wide across the Isthmus of Panama, on both sides of the Panama Canal, excl. cities of Panama and Colón: perpetually leased to and governed by U.S. 48,700 pop. (1963); 553 sq. mi.

canapé (kăn′ə pĭ, -pā′; *Fr.* kȧ nȧ pĕ′), *n.* **1.** a thin piece of bread, toast, etc., spread or topped with cheese, caviar, anchovies, or other appetizing foods. **2.** any of various types of 18th-century French sofas. [t. F. See CANOPY]

Canara (kə nä′rə), *n.* Kanara.

canard (kă näd′; *Fr.* kȧ nȧr′), *n.* **1.** a false story, report, or rumour; a hoax. **2.** *Aeron.* a very early kind of aeroplane, having a pusher engine with the rudder and elevator assembly in front of the wings. [t. F: lit., duck]

Canarese (kăn′ə rēz′), *n., adj.* Kanarese.

canary (kə nēə′rĭ), *n., pl.* **-ries.** **1.** Also, **canary bird.** a well-known cagebird, a kind of finch, *Serinus canarius*, native of the Canary Islands, and orig. of a brownish or greenish colour, but through modification in the domesticated state now usually a bright, clear yellow. **2.** Also, **canary yellow,** a bright, clear yellow colour. **3.** a sweet white wine of the Canary Islands, resembling sherry. **4.** *Obs.* a lively French and English dance, similar to the jig. —*adj.* **5.** canary-coloured; bright yellow. [named after the islands]

canary creeper, a climbing plant, *Tropaeolum aduncum*, having yellow flowers.

canary grass, any of various grasses of the genus *Phalaris*, as *P. canariensis*, native in the Canary Islands, which yields a seed used as food for cagebirds, or *P. arundinacea* (**reed canary grass**), a species widely used throughout the Northern Hemisphere as fodder.

Canary Islands, a group of mountainous islands in the Atlantic, near the NW coast of Africa, forming two provinces of Spain. 944,448 pop. (1960); 2894 sq. mi. Also, **Canaries.** [t. F: m. *Canarie* (the principal island), t. Sp.: m. *Canaria*, in L *canāria insula* isle of dogs]

canary pudding, a steamed sponge pudding made by placing canned or dried fruit, jam, etc., in the bottom of the basin before adding the pudding mixture.

canary seed, birdseed.

canasta (kə năs′tə), *n.* a card game of the rummy family in which the main object is to meld sets of seven or more cards. [t. Sp.: ? *canasta* kind of basket. Cf. CANISTER]

Canaveral (kə năv′ə rəl), *n.* **Cape,** former name of **Cape Kennedy.**

Canberra (kăn′bə rə, kăn′brə), *n.* the capital of Australia, in the SE part, in the Australian Capital Territory: Australian national university, founded 1946. 77,644 (est. 1964).

Canberra

cancan (kăn′kăn′; *Fr.* käɴ käɴ′), *n.* a form of quadrille marked by extravagant leaping and kicking, which came into vogue about 1830 in Paris. [t. F]

cancel (kăn′səl), *v.*, **-celled, -celling** or (*U.S.*) **-celed, -celing,** *n.* —*v.t.* **1.** to cross out (writing, etc.) by drawing a line or lines over. **2.** to make void; annul. **3.** to mark or perforate (a postage stamp, bus ticket, etc.) to render it invalid for re-use. **4.** to neutralize; counterbalance; compensate for. **5.** *Maths.* to eliminate by striking out (a factor common to both terms of a fraction, equivalent quantities on opposite sides of an equation, etc.). **6.** *Print.* to omit. —*n.* **7.** the act of cancelling. **8.** *Print.* omission. **9.** *Print., Bookbinding.* an omitted part, or the replacement for it. **10.** a piston for shutting off a group of stops on an organ. [late ME, t. L: m. s. *cancellāre* to make like a lattice, to strike out a writing] —**can′celler.** *n.*

—**Syn. 1, 3.** CANCEL, DELETE, ERASE, OBLITERATE indicate that something is no longer to be considered usable or in force. To CANCEL is to cross something out by stamping a mark over it, drawing lines through it, and the like: *to cancel a stamp, a word.* To DELETE is to omit something from written matter or from matter to be printed, often in accordance with a printer's symbol indicating this to be done: *to delete part of a line.* To ERASE is to remove by scraping or rubbing: *to erase something written in pencil.* To OBLITERATE is to blot out entirely, so as to remove all sign or trace of: *to obliterate a record, an inscription.* **2.** countermand, revoke, rescind.

cancellate (kăn′sĭ lāt′), *adj.* *Anat.* of spongy or porous structure, as bone. Also, **can′cellous.** [t. L: m. s. *cancellātus*, pp., latticed. See CANCEL]

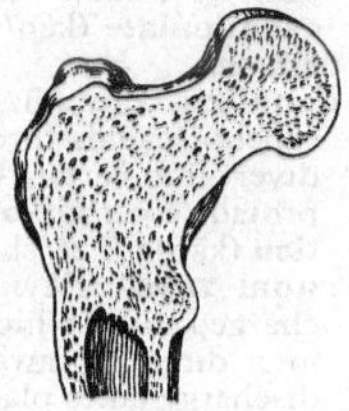

Cancellate bone structure

cancellation (kăn′sĭ lā′shən), *n.* **1.** the act of cancelling. **2.** the marks or perforations made in cancelling. **3.** something cancelled.

cancer (kăn′sə), *n.* **1.** *Pathol.* a malignant and invasive growth or tumour, esp. one originating in epithelium, tending to recur after excision and to metastasize to other sites. **2.** any evil condition or thing that spreads destructively. **3.** (*cap.*) *Astron.* a constellation and sign of the zodiac, represented by a crab. See illus. under **zodiac.** [t. L: crab, tumour] —**can′cerous,** *adj.*

Cancer (kăn′sə), *n.* **Tropic of.** See **tropic** (defs. 1a, 2a).

cancerophobia (kăn′sə rə fō′byə), *n.* a morbid fear of cancer.

cancroid (kăng′kroid), *adj.* **1.** *Pathol.* resembling a cancer, as certain tumours. **2.** *Zool.* resembling a crab. —*n.* **3.** *Pathol.* a form of cancer of the skin.

candela (kăn dē′lə, -dā′lə), *n.* the basic SI unit of luminous intensity: the brightness of a black body at the temperature of the solidification of platinum (2046°K) equals 60 candela per square cm. *Symbol:* cd [t. L: candle]

candelabra (kăn′dĭ lä′brə), *n.* **1.** a pl. of **candelabrum. 2.** (*pl. but taken as sing. with pl.* **-bras**). candelabrum.

candelabrum (kăn′dĭ lä′brəm), *n., pl.* **-bra** (-brə). an ornamental branched candlestick. [t. L, der. *candēla* candle]

candent (kăn′dənt), *adj.* glowing with heat; at a white heat. [t. L: s. *candens*, ppr., shining]

candescent (kăn dĕs′ənt), *adj.* glowing; incandescent. [t. L: s. *candescens*, ppr., beginning to glow] —**candes′cence,** *n.* —**candes′cently,** *adv.*

c. and f., cost and freight.

Candia (kăn′dĭ ə), *n.* **1.** Greek, **Herakleion.** a seaport in N Crete. 63,458 (1961). **2.** Crete.

candid (kăn′dĭd), *adj.* **1.** frank; outspoken; open and sincere: *candid account.* **2.** honest; impartial: *candid mind.* **3.** white. **4.** clear; pure. —*n.* **5.** a photograph having an unposed or informal subject. [t. L: s. *candidus* white, sincere] —**can′didly,** *adv.* —**can′didness,** *n.* —**Syn. 1.** See **frank.**

candidate (kăn′dĭ dāt′, -dĭt), *n.* **1.** one who seeks an office, an honour, etc. **2.** one who is selected by others as a contestant for an office, etc. **3.** one who seeks an academic qualification or the like, usually by examination. **4.** *Colloq.* a suitable subject: *that idea is a candidate for the wastepaper basket.* [t. L: m. s. *candidātus* clad in white, as a Roman candidate for office] —**candidacy** (kăn′ dĭ də sĭ), **candidature** (kăn′dĭ də chə), **can′didateship′,** *n.*

candid camera, a small handy camera, esp. one having a fast lens for unposed or informal pictures, often taken without the subject's knowledge.

candied (kăn′dĭd), *adj.* **1.** impregnated or encrusted with or as with sugar. **2.** crystallized, as sugar. **3.** honeyed or sweet; flattering.

Candiot (kăn′dĭ ŏt′), *adj.* **1.** Cretan. —*n.* **2.** a native or inhabitant of Crete. Also, **Candiote** (kăn′dĭ ōt′).

candle (kăn′dl), *n., v.,* **-dled, -dling.** —*n.* **1.** a long, usually slender, piece of tallow, wax, etc., with an embedded wick, burnt to give light. **2.** something like this in appearance or use. **3.** *Photom.* **a.** the luminous intensity of a standard candle. **b. standard candle,** a candle of specified size, composition, character of wick, and rate of burning, whose flame is taken as a unit of luminous intensity. **c. international candle,** a unit of luminous intensity established by international agreement, based on the standard candle but defined in terms of specially constructed electric lamps, now replaced by the **candela. 4. burn the candle at both ends,** to lead a too strenuous existence; attempt to do too much, as by making an excessive demand on one's available energy, rising early and retiring late, etc. **5. can't hold a candle to,** *Colloq.* to be totally inferior to. **6. not worth the candle,** not worth the effort or expense. —*v.i.* **7.** to examine (esp. eggs for freshness) by holding between the eye and a light. [OE *candel*, t. L: s. *candēla*]

candleberry (kăn′dl bə rĭ), *n., pl.* **-ries. 1.** the wax-myrtle (genus *Myrica*). **2.** its berry. **3.** the candlenut.

candlefish (kăn′dl fĭsh′), *n.* a small edible fish, *Thaleichthys pacificus*, of the north-western coast of America, of the smelt family, with flesh so oily that when the fish is dried it may be used as a candle.

candlelight (kăn′dl līt′), *n.* **1.** the light of a candle. **2.** artificial light. **3.** twilight; dusk.

Candlemas (kăn′dl məs), *n.* an ecclesiastical festival, Feb. 2nd, in honour of the presentation of the infant Jesus in the Temple and the purification of the Virgin Mary. Candles are blessed on this day. [ME *candelmasse*, OE *candelmæsse.* See CANDLE, -MAS]

candlenut (kăn′dl nŭt′), *n.* **1.** the oily fruit or nut of a euphorbiaceous tree, *Aleurites moluccana*, of the South Sea Islands, etc., the kernels of which, when strung together, are used as candles by the natives. **2.** the tree itself.

candlepin (kăn′dl pĭn′), *n.* **1.** a slender, candle-shaped pin used in ninepin or tenpin bowling. **2.** (*pl.*) a game using such pins.

candlepower (kăn′dl pou′ə), *n.* *Photom.* **1.** the illuminating capacity or luminous intensity of a candela or a standard candle. **2.** luminous intensity (of a light) or illuminating capacity (of a lamp or other device), measured in candelas or candles.

candlestick (kăn′dl stĭk′), *n.* a holder for a candle.

candletree (kăn′dl trē′), *n.* **1.** the candleberry (def. 1). **2.** the candlenut (def. 2).

candlewick (kăn′dl wĭk′), *n.* **1.** the wick of a candle. —*adj.* **2.** (of a fabric) usually unbleached cotton, into which small, short bunches of wicking have been hooked to form a design, used for bedspreads, etc.

candlewood (kăn′dl wŏŏd′), *n.* **1.** any resinous wood used for torches or as a substitute for candles. **2.** any of various trees or shrubs yielding such wood.

candour (kăn′də), *n.* **1.** frankness, as of speech; sincerity; honesty. **2.** freedom from bias; fairness; impartiality. **3.** *Obs.* kindliness. **4.** *Obs.* purity. Also, *U.S.*, **candor.** [t. L: radiance, purity, candour]

candy (kăn′dĭ), *n., pl.* **-dies,** *v.,* **-died, -dying.** —*n.* **1.** a sweet made of sugar crystallized by boiling. **2.** *U.S.* any of a variety of confections made with sugar, syrup, etc., combined with other ingredients. **3.** *U.S.* a single piece of such a confection. *—v.t.* **4.** to cook in heavy syrup until transparent, as fruit, fruit peel, or ginger. **5.** *U.S.* to cook in sugar or syrup, as yams. **6.** to reduce (sugar, etc.) to a crystalline form, usually by boiling down. **7.** to cover with sugar-like crystals, as of ice. **8.** to make sweet, palatable, or agreeable. *—v.i.* **9.** to become covered with sugar. **10.** to crystallize. [short for *sugar candy*, t. F: m. *sucre candi* candied sugar (*candi* der. Ar. *qand* sugar, t. Pers., appar. c. Skt *khanda* piece)]

candy floss, a fluffy, sweet confection whipped from white or coloured spun sugar.

candytuft (kăn′dĭ tŭft′), *n.* a plant of the brassicaceous genus *Iberis*, esp. *I. umbellata*, a cultivated annual with tufted flowers, orig. from Candia (Crete), and *I. amara*. [f. *Candy* (for CANDIA) + TUFT]

cane (kān), *n.*, *v.*, **caned, caning.** *—n.* **1.** a long, hollow or pithy, jointed woody stem, as that of bamboo, rattan, sugar cane, certain palms, etc. **2.** a plant having such a stem. **3.** such stems as a material. **4.** any of various tall, woody, bamboo-like grasses. **5.** the stem of the raspberry or blackberry. **6.** sugar cane. **7.** the stem of a bamboo, etc., used as a rod for flogging. **8.** a walking stick. **9.** a slender piece of sealing wax, etc. *—v.t.* **10.** to beat with a cane. **11.** to furnish or make with cane: *to cane chairs.* [ME, t. OF, t. Pr. or It., g. L *canna*, t. Gk: m. *kánna* reed. Cf. Heb. *qāneh*] *—***can′er,** *n.*

Canea (kă nĭə′), *n.* a seaport in and the capital of Crete. 38,467 (1961). Greek, **Khania.**

canebrake (kān′brāk′), *n.* *U.S.* a thicket of canes.

cane chair, a chair made of interwoven rattan cane.

canella (kə nĕl′ə), *n.* the cinnamon-like bark of a West Indian tree, *Canella winterana*, used as a condiment and in medicine. [t. ML: cinnamon, dim. of L *canna* CANE]

canephor (kăn′ĭ fô′), *n.* **1.** (in ancient Greece) one of the youths or maidens who bore upon their heads baskets containing the materials for sacrifice in certain religious festivals. **2.** *Archit.* a caryatid having a basket-like cushion upon the head. Also, **canephora** (kə nĕf′ə rə), *pl.* **-rae** (-rē′). [t. L, t. Gk: m. *kanēphóros* basket-bearer]

cane rat, a large nocturnal rodent, *Thryonomys swinderenianus*, of Africa, resembling a rat.

cane sugar, sugar obtained from sugar cane, $C_{12}H_{22}O_{11}$, identical with that obtained from the sugar beet; sucrose; saccharose.

canfield (kăn′fēld′), *n.* *Cards.* a game of patience often adapted for gambling purposes.

cangue (kăng), *n.* (in China, formerly) a kind of portable pillory worn about the neck by criminals. [t. F, prob. t. Pg.: m. *canga* yoke, t. Annamite: m. *gong*]

Canicula (kə nĭk′yŏŏ lə), *n.* *Astron.* Sirius; the Dog Star. [t. L: dim. of *canis* dog]

canicular (kə nĭk′yŏŏ lə), *adj.* *Astron., etc.* pertaining to the Dog Star or its rising.

canine (kā′nīn, kăn′īn), *adj.* **1.** of or like a dog; pertaining to or characteristic of dogs. **2.** *Anat., Zool.* of or pertaining to the four pointed teeth, esp. prominent in dogs, situated one on each side of each jaw, next to the incisors. *—n.* **3.** *Zool.* any animal of the dog family, the *Canidae*, including the wolves, jackals, hyenas, coyotes, and foxes. **4.** a dog. **5.** a canine tooth. [t. L: m. s. *caninus* pertaining to a dog]

canis (kā′nĭs), *n.* *Zool.* the canine genus that includes the domestic dog, *Canis familiaris*, the wild dogs, the wolves, and the jackals, all having 42 teeth. [t. L: dog]

Canis Major (kā′nĭs mā′jə), *gen.* **Canis Majoris** (mə jô′rĭs). *Astron.* the Great Dog, a southern constellation containing Sirius, the Dog Star, the brightest of the stars. [t. L: greater dog]

Canis Minor (kā′nĭs mī′nə), *gen.* **Canis Minoris** (mī nô′rĭs). *Astron.* the Little, or Lesser, Dog, a small ancient constellation following Orion and south of Gemini. It contains the star Procyon. [t. L: lesser dog]

canister (kăn′ĭs tə), *n.* **1.** a small box, usually of metal, for holding tea, coffee, etc. **2.** case shot (**canister shot**). [t. L: m. s. *canistrum*, t. Gk: m. *kánastron* wicker basket]

canker (kăng′kə), *n.* **1.** *Pathol.* a gangrenous or ulcerous sore, esp. in the mouth. **2.** *Vet. Sci.* a disease affecting horses' feet, usually the soles, characterized by a foul-smelling exudate. **3.** *Vet. Sci.* eczema in dogs' ears. **4.** *Vet. Sci.* an abscess or ulcer in birds. **5.** *Plant Pathol.* a stem disease in which a dead area is surrounded by living tissues. **6.** anything that corrodes, corrupts, destroys, or irritates. **7.** *Obs. or Dial.* dogrose. *—v.t.* **8.** to infect with canker. **9.** to corrupt; destroy slowly. *—v.i.* **10.** to become infected with or as with canker. [ME; OE *cancer*, t. L: m. *cancr-*, s. *cancer* gangrene]

cankerous (kăng′kə rəs), *adj.* **1.** of the nature of or resembling canker. **2.** causing canker.

cankerworm (kăng′kə wûm′), *n.* a striped green caterpillar injurious to fruit trees and other plants. It is the larva of any of several geometrid moths.

canna (kăn′ə), *n.* any plant of the tropical genus *Canna* (family *Cannaceae*), various species of which are cultivated for their large handsome leaves and showy flowers. [t. L: reed. See CANE]

cannabin (kăn′ə bĭn), *n.* a poisonous resin extracted from Indian hemp. [f. CANNAB(IS) + -IN[2]]

cannabis (kăn′ə bĭs), *n.* hashish; the dried pistillate parts of Indian hemp. [t. L: hemp]

Cannada (kăn′ə də), *n.* Kannada.

Cannae (kăn′ē), *n.* an ancient town in SE Italy: Romans defeated by Hannibal, 216 B.C.

canned (kănd), *adj.* *Orig. U.S.* **1.** preserved in a can, tin, or jar. **2.** *Slang.* recorded: *canned music.* **3.** *Slang.* prepared in advance. **4.** *Slang.* drunk.

cannel (kăn′əl), *n.* a compact coal burning readily and brightly. Also, **cannel coal.** [appar. for *candle coal*]

canneloni (kăn′ĭ lō′nĭ), *n.pl.* tubular or rolled pieces of pasta usually filled with a mixture of meat or cheese. [t. It.]

canner (kăn′ə), *n.* one who cans meat, fruit, etc., for preservation.

cannery (kăn′ə rĭ), *n.*, *pl.* **-ries.** a place where meat, fish, fruit, etc., are canned.

Cannes (kăn, kănz; *Fr.* kȧn), *n.* a seaport in SE France, in Alpes-Maritimes department, on the Mediterranean: coastal resort. 74,697 (1962).

cannibal (kăn′ĭ bl), *n.* **1.** a human being, esp. a savage, that eats human flesh. **2.** any animal that eats its own kind. *—adj.* **3.** pertaining to or characteristic of cannibals. **4.** given to cannibalism. [t. Sp.: m. *Canibal*, for *Caribal*, der. *Caribe* Carib]

cannibalism (kăn′ĭ bə lĭz′əm), *n.* **1.** the practice of eating one's own kind. **2.** savage cruelty; barbarism. *—***can′nibalis′tic,** *adj.* *—***can′nibalis′tically,** *adv.*

cannibalize (kăn′ĭ bə līz′), *v.t.*, **-lized, -lizing.** to repair (damaged motor vehicles, etc.) by the use of parts of other assembled vehicles, etc., instead of using spare parts. Also, **cannibalise.** *—***can′nibaliza′tion,** *n.*

cannikin (kăn′ĭ kĭn), *n.* a little can; a cup. [t. MFlem. or D: m. *cannekin* little can]

canning (kăn′ĭng), *n.* the act, process, or business of preserving meat, fruits, etc., in sealed cans or tins.

Canning (kăn′ĭng), *n.* **1. Charles John** (*Earl Canning*), 1812–62, governor-general and 1st viceroy of India. **2.** his father, **George,** 1770–1827, British statesman: prime minister 1827.

cannon (kăn′ən), *n.*, *pl.* **-nons,** (*esp. collectively*) **-non,** *v.* *—n.* **1.** a large ancient gun for firing heavy projectiles, mounted on a carriage. **2.** a powerful automatic gun for firing explosive shells, mounted on an aircraft. **3.** *Mach.* a hollow cylinder fitted over a shaft and capable of revolving independently. **4.** a smooth round bit. **5.** Also, **cannon bit, canon bit.** the part of a bit that is in the horse's mouth. **6.** the metal loop of a bell by which it is hung. **7.** *Zool.* **a.** the cannon bone. **b.** the part of the leg in which it is situated; instep. See illus. under **horse.** **8.** *Armour.* a cylindrical or semicylindrical plate covering the forearm or upper arm; rerebrace or vambrace. **9.** *Billiards.* a shot in which the ball struck with the cue is made to hit two balls in succession. **10.** any strike and rebound, as a ball striking a wall and glancing off. *—v.i.* **11.** to discharge cannon. **12.** to make a cannon in billiards. **13.** to come into collision with; crash into (fol. by *into*). [t. F: m. *canon*, t. It.: m. *cannone*, aug. of *canna* tube, g. L *canna*. See CANE]

cannonade (kăn′ə nād′), *n.*, *v.*, **-naded, -nading.** *—n.* **1.** a continued discharge of guns of any sort, esp. during an attack. *—v.t.*, *v.i.* **2.** to attack with or discharge cannon. [t. F: m. *canonnade*]

cannonball (kăn′ən bôl′), *n.* (formerly) a missile, usually round and made of iron or steel, designed to be fired from a cannon.

cannon bit, cannon (def. 5).

cannon bone, *Zool.* the greatly developed middle metacarpal or metatarsal bone of hoofed quadrupeds, extending from wrist or ankle to the first joint of the digit. See illus. under **horse.** [f. CANNON (as being tube-shaped) + BONE]

cannon fodder, soldiers (as the material used up in war).

cannonry (kăn′ən rĭ), *n.*, *pl.* **-ries.** **1.** a discharge of artillery. **2.** artillery (def. 1).

cannon shot, 1. a ball or shot for a cannon. **2.** the shooting of a cannon. **3.** the range of a cannon.

cannot (kăn′ŏt, kă nŏt′, kăn′ət), *v.* a form of **can not.** *—***Syn.** See **can**[1].

cannula (kăn′yŏŏ lə), *n.* *Surg.* a metal tube for insertion into the body, used to keep a passage open, to draw off fluid, or to introduce medication. [t. L, dim. of *canna.* See CANE]

cannular (kăn′yo͝o lə), *adj.* tubular. Also, **cannulate** (kăn′yo͝o lāt′, -lĭt).

canny (kăn′ĭ), *adj.*, **-nier, -niest,** *adv. Scot.* —*adj.* **1.** careful; cautious; wary. **2.** knowing; sagacious; shrewd; astute. **3.** frugal; thrifty. **4.** (chiefly with a negative) safe to deal or meddle with. **5.** pretty; attractive. **6.** *Archaic.* having supernatural powers. —*adv.* **7.**. in a canny manner. [appar. der. CAN[1]] —**can′nily,** *adv.* —**can′niness,** *n.*

canoe (kə no͞o′), *n.*, *v.*, **-noed, -noeing.** —*n.* **1.** any light and narrow boat, often canvas-covered, that is propelled by paddles in place of oars. **2.** any native boat of very light construction, as the Algonquian birchbark canoe. **3. paddle one's own canoe,** to be independent; manage on one's own. —*v.i.* **4.** to paddle a canoe. **5.** to go in a canoe. —*v.t.* **6.** to transport by canoe. [earlier *canow,* var. of *canoa,* t. Sp., t. Carib: m. *kanoa*] —**canoe′ing,** *n.* —**canoe′ist,** *n.*

canoewood (kə no͞o′ wo͝od′), *n.* the tulip tree.

canon[1] (kăn′ən), *n.* **1.** an ecclesiastical rule or law enacted by a council or other competent authority, and (in the Rom. Cath. Ch.) approved by the pope. **2.** the body of ecclesiastical law. **3.** any rule or law. **4.** a fundamental principle. **5.** a standard; criterion. **6.** the books of the Bible recognized by the Christian Church as genuine and inspired. **7.** any officially recognized set of sacred books. **8.** the body of works of a writer generally accepted as genuine. **9.** a catalogue or list, as of the saints acknowledged by the Church. **10.** *Liturgy.* that part of the mass between the Sanctus and the communion. **11.** *Music.* a kind of composition in which the same melody is played or sung through by two or more voice parts at the same or at a different pitch overlapping each other. **12.** a large size of printing type (48 point). [ME and OE, t. L: rule, canon, t. Gk: m. *kanṓn* straight rod, rule, standard] —**Syn. 4.** See **principle.**

canon[2] (kăn′ən), *n.* **1.** one of a body of dignitaries or prebendaries attached to a cathedral or a collegiate church; a member of the chapter of a cathedral or a collegiate church. **2.** *Rom. Cath. Ch.* one of the members (**canons regular**) of certain religious orders. [ME *canoun,* t. ONF: m. *canon,* t. ML. See CANNON]

cañón (kăn′yən; *Sp.* kä nyōn′), *n.* canyon.

canon bit, cannon (def. 5).

canoness (kăn′ə nĭs), *n.* one of a community of women living under a rule, but not under a vow.

canonical (kə nŏn′ĭ kl), *adj.* **1.** pertaining to, established by, or conforming to a canon or canons. **2.** included in the canon of the Bible. **3.** authorized; recognized; accepted: *canonical criticism.* —*n.* **4.** (*pl.*) the dress prescribed by canon for the clergy when officiating. [t. ML: s. *canonicālis,* der. L *canonicus,* t. Gk: m. *kanonikós.* See CANON[1]] —**canon′ically,** *adv.*

canonical hour, 1. *Eccles.* any of certain periods of the day set apart for prayer and devotion, namely, matins (with lauds), prime, tierce, sext, nones, vespers, and complin. **2.** any hour between 8 a.m. and 6 p.m., during which marriage may be legally performed in parish churches.

canonicate (kə nŏn′ĭ kāt′, -kĭt), *n.* the office or dignity of a canon; a canonry.

canonicity (kăn′ə nĭs′ĭ tĭ), *n.* canonical character.

canonist (kăn′ə nĭst), *n.* one versed in canon law.

canonize (kăn′ə nīz′), *v.t.*, **-nized, -nizing. 1.** *Eccles.* to place in the canon of saints. **2.** to glorify. **3.** to make canonical: *canonized books.* Also, **canonise.** —**can′oniza′tion,** *n.*

canon law, the body of ecclesiastical law.

canonry (kăn′ən rĭ), *n.*, *pl.* **-ries. 1.** the office or benefice of a canon. **2.** the body or group of canons.

canonship (kăn′ən shĭp′), *n.* the position or office of canon; canonry.

canoodle (kə no͞o′dl), *v.*, **-dled, -dling.** *Slang.* —*v.i.* **1.** to indulge in fondling and petting. —*v.t.* **2.** to fondle and pet.

can-opener (kăn′ōp′nə), *n.* a tin-opener.

Canopic (kə nō′pĭk), *adj.* **1.** *Archaeol.* of or from Canopus, as a kind of human-headed vase used to hold the entrails of embalmed bodies. **2.** denoting a vase used elsewhere to hold the ashes of the dead. [t. L: s. *Canōpicus,* der. *Canōpus* CANOPUS (def. 2)]

Canopus (kə nō′pəs), *n.* **1.** *Astron.* a star of the first magnitude in the constellation Carina: the second in order of brightness of the stars; Alpha Carinae. **2.** an ancient city on the seacoast of Lower Egypt, 15 mi. east of Alexandria.

canopy (kăn′ə pĭ), *n.*, *pl.* **-pies,** *v.*, **-pied, -pying.** —*n.* **1.** a covering suspended or supported over a throne, bed, etc., or held over a person, sacred object, etc. **2.** an overhanging protection or shelter. **3.** *Archit.* an ornamental roof-like projection or covering. **4.** the sky. **5.** the transparent, opening cover to the cockpit of some aircraft. **6.** fabric body of a parachute. —*v.t.* **7.** to cover with or as with a canopy: *clouds canopy the sky.* [ME *canape,* t. ML: s. *canapēum,* alter. of L *cōnōpēum* net curtains, t. Gk: m. *kōnōpeîon* mosquito net]

canorous (kə nô′rəs), *adj.* melodious; musical. [t. L: m. *canōrus*] —**cano′rously,** *adv.* —**cano′rousness,** *n.*

Canossa (kə nŏs′ə; *It.* kä nôs′sä), *n.* a ruined castle in N Italy: scene of the penance of the Holy Roman Emperor Henry IV before Pope Gregory VII in 1077.

Canova (*It.* kä nôv′ä), *n.* **Antonio** (*It.* än tô′nyô), 1757–1822, Italian sculptor.

Canrobert (*Fr.* käɴ rō bĕr′), *n.* **François Certain** (*Fr.* fräɴ swä sĕr tăɴ′), 1809–95, marshal of France.

Canso (kăn′sō), *n.* **Cape,** the NE extremity of the mainland of Nova Scotia.

canst (kănst), *v. Archaic or Poetic.* 2nd pers. sing. pres. of **can.**

cant[1] (kănt), *n.* **1.** insincere statements, esp. conventional pretence of enthusiasm for high ideals; insincere expressions of goodness or piety. **2.** the special secret language or jargon spoken by thieves, gipsies, etc.; argot. **3.** the words, phrases, etc., peculiar to a particular class, party, profession, etc. **4.** whining or singsong speech, esp. of beggars. —*v.i.* **5.** to make religious remarks insincerely or hypocritically; pretend goodness or piety. **6.** to speak in the whining or singsong tone of a beggar; beg. **7.** to use the secret language of thieves, gipsies, etc. [cf. OE *cantere* singer, t. L: m. *cantor*] —**can′ter,** *n.*

cant[2] (kănt), *n.* **1.** a salient angle. **2.** a sudden movement that tilts or overturns a thing. **3.** a slanting or tilted position. **4.** superelevation. **5.** an oblique line or surface, as one formed by cutting off the corner of a square or cube. **6.** an oblique or slanting face of anything. **7.** a sudden pitch or toss. —*v.t.* **8.** *Mech.* to bevel. **9.** to put in an oblique position; tilt; tip. **10.** to throw with a sudden jerk. —*v.i.* **11.** to take or have an inclined position; tilt; turn. —*adj.* **12.** tilted; at an angle. **13.** having flat surfaces and no curves: *a cant moulding.* [t. MD, or MLG: m. *kant,* both prob. t. ONF: m. *cant,* g. L *canthus* corner, side]

cant[3] (känt), *adj. Dial.* hearty; merry. [t. LG]

can't (känt), contraction of *cannot.*

Cant., 1. Canterbury. 2. Canticles.

Cantab., (ML *Cantabrigiensis*) of Cambridge.

cantabile (kän tä′bĭ lĭ), *Music.* —*adj.* **1.** with a singing tone; flowing in style. —*n.* **2.** a cantabile style, passage, or piece. [It., t. LL: m. s. *cantābilis* that may be sung]

Cantabrigian (kăn′tə brĭj′ĭ ən), *adj.* **1.** of Cambridge or Cambridge University. —*n.* **2.** a native or inhabitant of Cambridge. **3.** a student or graduate of Cambridge University. [f. s. *Cantabrigia* Latin form of the name Cambridge + -AN]

Cantal (*Fr.* käɴ tál′), *n.* a department in central France. 172,977 pop. (1962); 2231 sq. mi. *Cap.:* Aurillac.

cantaloup (kăn′tə lo͞op′), *n.* a variety of melon, *Cucumis melo,* var. *cantalupensis,* with hard, scaly, or warty rinds, esp. a small, ribbed, delicately flavoured muskmelon. Also, **cantaloupe.** [t. F: m. *cantaloup,* t. It.: m. *Cantalupo,* a former estate of the pope near Rome, where it was first grown in Europe]

cantankerous (kăn tăng′kə rəs), *adj.* ill-natured; quarrelsome; perverse or contrary, as in disposition: *a cantankerous old maid.* [? der. ME *contek* contention] —**cantan′kerously,** *adv.* —**cantan′kerousness,** *n.*

cantata (kăn tä′tə), *n. Music.* **1.** a choral composition, either sacred and resembling a short oratorio, or secular, as a lyric drama set to music but not to be acted. **2.** (orig.) a metrical narrative set to recitative, or alternate recitative and air, usually for a single voice, accompanied by one or more instruments. [t. It., der. *cantare* sing, g. L]

cantatrice (*It.* kän tä trē′chė; *Fr.* käɴ tä trēs′), *n.*, *pl. It.* **-trici** (-trē′chē), *Fr.* **-trices** (-trēs′). a female singer. [F and It., t. L: m. s. *cantātrix*]

cant dog, a wooden lever with a movable iron hook near the lower end, used for grasping and canting or turning over logs, etc. Also, **cant hook.**

Cant dog

canteen (kăn tēn′), *n.* **1.** a restaurant attached to a factory, office, etc., open only to employees. **2.** a place where refreshment and entertainment are provided for military personnel. **3.** the eating and drinking utensils of a soldier. **4.** a box containing a set of plate or cutlery. **5.** the cutlery itself. **6.** a small container used by soldiers and others for carrying water or other liquids. [t. F: m. *cantine,* t. It.: m. *cantina* cellar, wine cellar, der. *canto* side, g. L *canthus*]

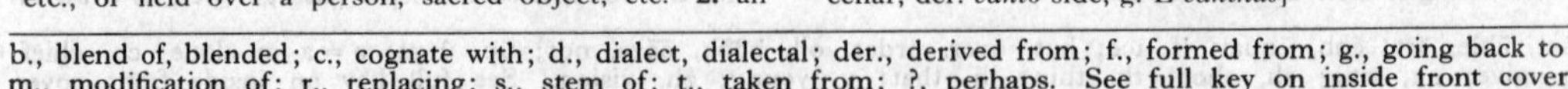

canter (kăn′tə), *n.* **1.** an easy gallop. —*v.i., v.t.* **2.** to go or ride at a canter. [short for *Canterbury gallop* (as of pilgrims to Canterbury)]

Canterbury (kăn′tə bə rĭ, -brĭ), *n.* a city in SE England, in Kent: famous cathedral; medieval pilgrimages to the tomb of Saint Thomas à Becket; its archbishop is primate of all England. 32,010 (est. 1964).

Canterbury bell, a plant, *Campanula medium*, having bell-shaped flowers of various colours ranging from violet-blue, to pink, to white.

Canterbury Bight, a wide bay on the E coast of South Island, New Zealand. ab. 128 mi. wide.

Canterbury Plains, an area of rich farmland along the E coast of South Island, New Zealand. ab. 4000 sq. mi.

cantharides (kăn thă′rĭ dēz′), *n.pl., sing.* **cantharis** (kăn′-thə rĭs). **1.** a preparation of powdered blister beetles, esp. the Spanish fly, *Lytta vesicatoria*, used medicinally as a skin irritant, diuretic, and aphrodisiac. **2.** (*sing.*) the beetle itself. [t. L, t. Gk: pl., blister flies]

cant hook, cant dog.

canthus (kăn′thəs), *n., pl.* **-thi** (-thī). *Anat.* the angle or corner on each side of the eye, formed by the junction of the upper and lower lids. [t. NL, t. Gk: m. *kanthós* corner of the eye]

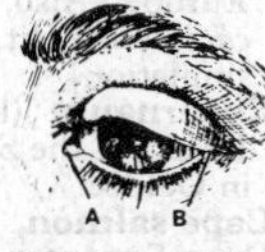

A, Inner canthus; B, Outer canthus

canticle (kăn′tĭ kl), *n.* **1.** one of the non-metrical hymns or chants, chiefly from the Bible, used in church services. **2.** a little song; a song. **3.** (*cap., pl.*) a book of the Old Testament, also known as the *Song of Solomon*. [ME, t. L: m. s. *canticulum*, dim. of *canticum* song]

cantilever (kăn′tĭ lē′və), *n.* **1.** *Mach.* a free part of any horizontal member projecting beyond a support. **2.** *Civ. Eng.* either of two bracket-like arms projecting towards each other from opposite banks or piers, serving to form the span of a bridge (**cantilever bridge**) when united. **3.** *Aeron.* a form of wing construction in which no external bracing is employed (**cantilever wing**). **4.** *Archit.* an extended bracket for supporting a balcony, cornice, or the like. [orig. uncert.]

cantle (kăn′tl), *n.* **1.** the hind part of a saddle, usually curved upwards. See illus. under **saddle. 2.** a corner; piece; portion. [ME *cantel*, t. ONF, dim. of *cant* corner, CANT[2]]

canto (kăn′tō), *n., pl.* **-tos. 1.** one of the main or larger divisions of a long poem, as in Dante's *Inferno*. **2.** *Music.* **a.** a song or melody. **b.** the part in a polyphonic composition which carries the melody, usually the soprano. [t. It., g. L *cantus* song]

canto fermo (kăn′tō fû′mō), cantus firmus.

canton (kăn′tŏn, kăn tŏn′ *for 1, 2 and 4*; kăn′tən *for 3*; kăn tŏn′ *for 5 and 6*; kən to͞on′ *for 7*), *n.* **1.** a small territorial district, esp. one of the states of the Swiss confederation. **2.** a subdivision of a French arrondissement. **3.** *Her.* a square division in the upper dexter corner of an escutcheon, etc. **4.** a division, part, or portion of anything. —*v.t.* **5.** to divide into parts or portions. **6.** to divide into cantons or territorial districts. **7.** to allot quarters to (soldiers, etc.). [t. F: corner, ult. der. L *canthus* corner, CANT[2]] —**cantonal** (kăn′tə nəl), *adj.*

Canton (kăn tŏn′), *n.* **1.** a seaport in SE China: the capital of Kwangtung province. 1,867,000 (est. 1958). See map under **Yangtze. 2.** a town in the U.S.A., in Ohio. 113,631 (1960).

Canton crepe (kăn′tən), a thin, light silk or rayon crepe with a finely wrinkled surface, heavier in texture than crepe de chine. [named after CANTON, China]

Cantonese (kăn′tə nēz′), *n., pl.* **-nese,** *adj.* —*n.* **1.** a Chinese language of southern China. **2.** a native or inhabitant of Canton. —*adj.* **3.** pertaining to Canton, its inhabitants, or their language.

Canton flannel (kăn′tən), a cotton twill fabric, napped on one side.

cantonment (kən to͞on′mənt), *n.* **1.** a camp (usually of large size) where men are trained for military service. **2.** military quarters. **3.** the quarters, esp. winter quarters, of an army in the field. [t. F: m. *cantonnement*]

Canton River (kăn tŏn′), Chu-Kiang.

cantor (kăn′tô), *n. Eccles.* **1.** an officer whose duty is to lead the singing in a cathedral or in a collegiate or parish church; a precentor. **2.** the Jewish religious official singing the liturgy. [t. L: singer]

cantoris (kăn tô′rĭs), *n.* the part of a cathedral choir on the north or precentor's side.

cantrip (kăn′trĭp), *n. Chiefly Scot.* **1.** a charm; a spell. **2.** a trick. [orig. unknown]

Cantuar (kăn′tyo͝o ä′), (ML *Cantuarensis*) of Canterbury, esp. the archbishopric.

cantus (kăn′təs), *n., pl.* **-tus. 1.** a song; melody. **2.** an ecclesiastical style of music. [t. L. See CHANT]

cantus firmus (kăn′təs fû′məs), **1.** *Eccles.* the ancient traditional vocal music of the Christian Church, having its form settled and its use prescribed by ecclesiastical authority. **2.** *Music.* a fixed melody to which other melodic parts are added. Also, **canto fermo.** [ML]

canty (kăn′tĭ, kän′-), *adj. Scot. and N Dial.* **1.** cheerful. **2.** lively; brisk. [t. LG: m. *kantig* cheerful]

Canuck (kə nŭk′), *n. Colloq. or Slang.* a Canadian, esp. a French Canadian.

Canute (kə nyo͞ot′), *n.* A.D. 994?–1035, Danish king of England 1017–35; of Denmark 1018–35; and of Norway 1028–35. Also, **Cnut, Knut.**

canvas (kăn′vəs), *n.* **1.** a closely woven, heavy cloth of hemp, flax, or cotton, used for tents, sails, etc. **2.** a piece of this material on which an oil painting is made. **3.** an oil painting on canvas. **4.** a tent, or tents collectively: *campers living under canvas.* **5.** sailcloth. **6.** sails collectively: *a ship under full canvas.* **7.** *Rowing.* the (orig. canvas-covered) narrowing part of a racing eight between the bow oarsman and the actual bow of the boat, or between the cox and the stern. **8.** *Rowing.* the corresponding part of any other racing boat. **9.** *Rowing.* this part considered as a unit of length: *to win by a canvas.* **10.** any fabric, of linen, cotton, etc., of a coarse loose weave, used as a foundation for embroidery stitches, for interlining, etc. [ME *canevas*, t. ONF, ult. der. L *cannabis* hemp]

canvasback (kăn′vəs băk′), *n.* a North American wild duck, *Aythya valisineria*, with a whitish back, prized for the delicacy of its flesh.

canvass (kăn′vəs), *v.t.* **1.** to solicit votes, subscriptions, opinions, etc., from (a district, group of people, etc.). **2.** to engage in a political campaign. **3.** to examine carefully; investigate by inquiry; discuss; debate. **4.** *Obs.* to criticize severely. —*v.i.* **5.** to solicit votes, opinions, etc. **6.** *U.S.* to review election returns. **7.** to engage in discussion or debate. —*n.* **8.** examination; close inspection; scrutiny. **9.** a soliciting of votes, orders, etc. **10.** *Chiefly U.S.* a campaign for election to government office. [var. of CANVAS n.; orig. meaning to toss (someone) in a canvas sheet (cf. def. 4)] —**can′vasser,** *n.*

canyon (kăn′yən), *n.* a deep valley with steep sides, often with a stream flowing through it. Also, **cañón.** [t. Sp.: m. *cañón* tube, der. *caña*, g. L *canna* reed]

canzone (kăn tsō′nĭ), *n., pl.* **-zoni** (-tsō′nĭ). **1.** a variety of lyric poetry in the Italian style, of Provençal origin, which closely resembles the madrigal. **2.** any ballad or song. [It., g. L *cantio* song]

canzonet (kăn′zə nĕt′), *n.* a short song, esp. a light and gay one.

caoutchouc (kou′cho͝ok), *n.* **1.** the gummy coagulated juice of certain tropical plants; indiarubber. **2.** pure rubber. [t. F, t. Sp.: m. *cauchú*, of S Amer. orig.]

cap (kăp), *n., v.,* **capped, capping.** —*n.* **1.** a covering for the head, esp. one fitting closely and made of softer material than a hat, and having little or no brim, but often having a peak, as worn by schoolboys. **2.** the flat, peaked headdress worn by soldiers and others. **3.** a special headdress denoting rank, occupation, etc.: *a cardinal's cap, nurse's cap.* **4.** a mortarboard. **5. a.** a headdress denoting that the wearer has been selected for a special team, as one representing his country, in certain sports, as cricket, football, etc. **b.** membership of such as team. **6.** a close-fitting waterproof headdress worn when swimming, etc. **7.** a covering of lace, etc., for a woman's head, usually worn indoors. **8.** the detachable protective top of a fountain pen, jar, etc. **9.** anything resembling or suggestive of a covering for the head in shape, use, or position. **10.** the acme. **11.** *Bot.* the pileus of a mushroom. **12.** a percussion cap. **13.** a noisemaking device for toy pistols, made of a small quantity of explosive wrapped in paper or other thin material. **14.** pessary (def. 3). **15. set one's cap at,** to ogle or try to capture the admiration and attention (of a man). —*v.t.* **16.** to provide or cover with or as with a cap. **17.** to select as a member of a representative team in football, cricket, etc. **18.** (in Scotland) to confer a degree on. **19.** to complete. **20.** to surpass; follow up with something as good or better. [ME *cappe*, OE *cæpe*, t. LL: m. *cappa*, *cāpa* cap, hooded cloak, cape, appar. der. *caput* head]

cap., **1.** capital. **2.** capitalize. **3.** capitalized. **4.** (*pl.* **caps**) capital letter. **5.** (L *capitulum, caput*) chapter.

capability (kā′pə bĭl′ĭ tĭ), *n., pl.* **-ties. 1.** quality of being capable; capacity; ability. **2.** quality of admitting of certain treatment. **3.** (*usually pl.*) a quality, ability, etc., that can be developed or used.

capable (kā′pə bl), *adj.* **1.** having much intelligence or ability; competent; efficient; able: *a capable instructor.* **2. capable of, a.** having the ability, strength, etc., to;

qualified or fitted for: *a man capable of judging art.* **b.** susceptible to; open to the influence or effect of: *a situation capable of improvement.* **c.** predisposed to; inclined to: *capable of murder.* [t. LL: m. *capābilis*] —**ca′pableness,** *n.* —**ca′pably,** *adv.* —**Syn. 1.** See **able.**

capacious (kə pā′shəs), *adj.* capable of holding much. [f. CAPACI(TY) + -OUS] —**capa′ciously,** *adv.* —**capa′ciousness,** *n.* —**Syn.** spacious, roomy.

capacitance (kə păs′ĭ təns), *n. Elect.* **1. a.** the property of a system which enables it to store electrical charge. **b.** the extent of this, usually measured in farads; electrical capacity. **2.** the ratio of a change in quantity of electricity (in a conductor) to the corresponding change in potential; electrical capacity. **3.** a capacitor. [f. CAPACIT(Y) + -ANCE]

capacitate (kə păs′ĭ tāt′), *v.t.*, **-tated, -tating. 1.** to make capable; enable. **2.** to furnish with legal powers. —**capac′ita′tion,** *n.*

capacitive (kə păs′ĭ tĭv), *adj. Elect.* pertaining to capacitance or capacity.

capacitor (kə păs′ĭ tə), *n. Elect.* a device for accumulating and holding an electric charge, consisting of two conducting surfaces separated by a non-conductor or dielectric; a condenser.

capacity (kə păs′ĭ tĭ), *n.*, *pl.* **-ties. 1.** the power of receiving or containing. **2.** cubic contents; volume. **3.** power of receiving impressions, knowledge, etc.; mental ability: *the capacity of a scholar.* **4.** power, ability, or possibility of doing something (fol. by *of, for,* or infinitive): *capacity for self-protection.* **5.** quality of being susceptible to certain treatment. **6.** position; function; relation: *in the capacity of legal adviser.* **7.** legal qualification or legal rights. **8.** *Elect.* **a.** capacitance. **b.** a measure of output performance. [late ME *capacyte*, t. L: m. s. *capācitas*] —**Syn. 4.** competence.

cap and bells, 1. the traditional dress of a jester. **2.** clownish behaviour.

cap and gown, academic dress.

Capaneus (kăp′ə nyōōs′, kə pā′nĭ əs), *n. Gk Legend.* one of the Seven against Thebes who was destroyed by Zeus with a thunderbolt for blasphemy. See **Seven against Thebes.**

cap-a-pie (kăp′ə pē′), *adv.* from head to foot. Also, **cap-à-pie.** [t. F (obs.)]

caparison (kə păr′ĭ sən), *n.* **1.** a covering, usually ornamental, laid over the saddle or harness of a horse, etc. **2.** dress; equipment; outfit. —*v.t.* **3.** to cover with a caparison. **4.** to dress finely; deck. [t. MF: m. *caparasson*, t. Sp.: m. *caparazón*, t. Pr.: m. *caparaso*, der. *capa* CAPE[1]]

cape[1] (kāp), *n.* a sleeveless garment fastened round the neck and falling loosely over the shoulders, worn separately or attached to a coat, etc. [t. F, t. Sp.: m. *capa*, g. LL *cāpa.* See CAP]

cape[2] (kāp), *n.* **1.** a piece of land jutting into the sea or some other body of water. **2. the Cape,** the Cape of Good Hope. [ME, t. F: m. *cap*, t. Pr., g. L *caput* head]

Cape (kāp), *adj. Geol.* **1.** pertaining to a mid-Palaeozoic period or system in S Africa, roughly equivalent to the Upper Silurian to Lower Carboniferous. —*n.* **2.** a period or system following the Nama and preceding the Karoo in S Africa.

Cape ash, the essenhout, *Ekebergia capensis.*

Cape Breton (brĭt′n, brĕt′n), an island forming the NE part of Nova Scotia. 163,000 pop. (est. 1964); 3970 sq. mi.

Cape buffalo, See **buffalo** (def. 1).

Cape Coast, a seaport in SW Ghana. 41,143 (1960).

Cape cobra, a large, common poisonous snake of southern Africa, *Naja nivea*, yellow or brown in colour; geelslang.

Cape Cod, a sandy peninsula in SE Massachusetts between **Cape Cod Bay** and the Atlantic Ocean.

Cape Colony, Cape Province.

Cape Coloured. See **coloured** (def. 7).

Cape Dutch. Afrikaans.

Cape Folded System, a series of fold mountain ranges in South Africa, in W and SW Cape Province, including the Zwartberg, Cedarberg, and Langeberg.

Cape gooseberry, 1. a tropical solanaceous herb, *Physalis peruviana*, cultivated for its yellow edible berry, native of S America, and naturalized in S Africa. **2.** its fruit.

Cape Horn (hôn), *n.* a headland on a small island at the S extremity of South America.

Cape ivy, a climbing plant, *Senecio macroglossus*, of southern Africa, having ivy-shaped leaves.

Capek (*Cz.* chä′pĕk), *n.* **Karel** (*Cz.* kä′rĕl), 1890–1938, Czech dramatist, novelist, and producer.

capelin (kăp′ĭ lĭn), *n.* either of two small fishes of the smelt family, of the North American coasts of the Atlantic (*Mallotus villosus*) and Pacific (*M. catervarius*). [t. F: m. *caplan, capelan*, prob. t. Pr. See CHAPLAIN]

Capella (kə pĕl′ə), *n. Astron.* a bright star of the first magnitude in the constellation Auriga. [t. L: lit., she-goat]

Cape of Good Hope, 1. a cape near the S extremity of Africa. **2.** Cape Province.

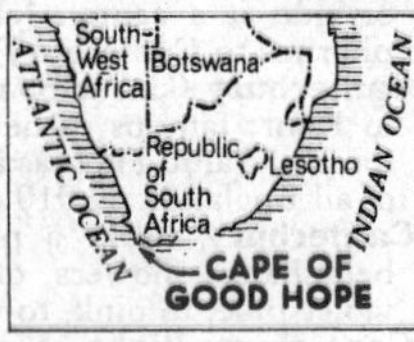

Cape of Good Hope

Cape pondweed, a perennial aquatic herb with floating leaves, *Aponogeton distachyos*, a native of southern Africa often planted and naturalized elsewhere.

Cape Province, a province in the Republic of South Africa. 5,362,853 pop. (1960); 277,169 sq. mi. *Cap.:* Cape Town.

caper[1] (kā′pə), *v.i.* **1.** to leap or skip about in a sprightly manner; prance. —*n.* **2.** a playful leap or skip. **3.** a prank; capricious action; harebrained escapade. [fig. use of L *caper* he-goat] —**ca′perer,** *n.*

caper[2] (kā′pə), *n.* **1.** a shrub, *Capparis spinosa*, of Mediterranean regions. **2.** its flower bud, which is pickled and used for garnish or seasoning. [ME *caperis*, t. L: m. *capparis*, t. Gk: m. *kápparis*]

capercailzie (kăp′ə kāl′yĭ, -kāl′zĭ), *n.* the woodgrouse, *Tetrao urogallus*, a very large gallinaceous bird of northern Europe. Also, **capercaillie** (kăp′ə kāl′yĭ). [t. Gaelic: m. *capullcoille*, lit., horse of the wood, with *r* for *l* by dissimilation]

Capernaum (kə pû′nyəm), *n.* an ancient town in N Israel, on the Sea of Galilee: the centre of Jesus's ministry in Galilee.

Cape salmon, geelbek (def. 2).

Cape Sparrow, mossie.

Capet (kā′pĭt, kăp′ĭt; *Fr.* kȧ pĕ′), *n.* **Hugh** or *Fr.* **Hugues** (Yg), A.D. 938?–996, king of France 987–996.

Cape teak, a large African tree, *Pterocarpus angolensis*, with durable wood resembling teak.

Capetian (kă pē′shən), *adj.* **1.** pertaining or relating to the French dynasty (987–1328) founded by Hugh Capet. —*n.* **2.** a member of this dynasty.

Cape Town, a seaport in the Republic of South Africa, near the Cape of Good Hope: seat of the legislature. With suburbs, 807,211 (1960). See map under **South Africa.**

Cape Verde Islands (vûd), a group of islands in the Atlantic, W of Senegal, an overseas territory of Portugal. 199,661 pop. (1961); 1557 sq. mi. *Cap.:* Praia. See map under **Dakar.**

Cape wren-warbler (rĕn′wô′blə), a small, brown warbler-like bird with speckled breast, *Prinia maculosa*, family *Muscicapidae*, of southern Africa. Also, *S African*, **tinktinkie.**

Cape York Peninsula, a large peninsula in NE Australia between the Gulf of Carpentaria and the Coral Sea.

capful (kăp′fo͝ol′), *n.*, *pl.* **-fuls.** as much as a cap will hold.

Cap Haïtien (*Fr.* kȧp ȧ ē syăN′), a seaport in N Haiti. 30,000 (est. 1965).

capias (kā′pĭ ăs′), *n. Law.* a writ commanding an officer to take a specified person into custody. [t. L: take thou]

capillaceous (kăp′ĭ lā′shəs), *adj.* hairlike; capillary. [t. L: m. *capillāceus* hairy]

capillarity (kăp′ĭ lăr′ĭ tĭ), *n.* **1.** the state of being capillary. **2.** *Physics.* capillary action.

capillary (kə pĭl′ə rĭ), *adj.*, *n.*, *pl.* **-laries.** —*adj.* **1.** pertaining to or occurring in or as in a tube of fine bore. **2.** *Physics.* **a.** pertaining to the property of surface tension. **b. capillary action,** the elevation or depression of the surface of liquids in fine tubes, etc., due to surface tension and the forces of cohesion and adhesion. **c. capillary attraction** or **repulsion,** the apparent attraction or repulsion between a liquid and a tube, etc., observed in such phenomena. **3.** *Bot.* resembling hair in the manner of growth or in shape. **4.** *Anat.* pertaining to a capillary or capillaries. —*n.* **5.** *Anat.* one of the minute blood vessels between the terminations of the arteries and the beginnings of the veins. **6.** Also, **capillary tube.** a tube with a small bore. [t. L: m. *capillāris* pertaining to the hair]

cap in hand, humbly, submissively; as a suppliant.

capita (kăp′ĭ tə), *n.* pl. of **caput.**

capital[1] (kăp′ĭ tl), *n.* **1.** the city or town which is the official seat of government in a country, state, etc. **2.** a capital letter. **3.** the wealth, whether in money or property, owned or employed in business by an individual, firm, etc. **4.** an accumulated stock of such wealth. **5.** any form of wealth employed or capable of being employed in the production of more wealth. **6.** *Accounting.* the ownership interest in a business. **7.** any source of profit, advantage, power, etc. **8.** capitalists as a group or class. **9.** resources. —*adj.* **10.** pertaining to capital: *capital stock.* **11.** principal; highly important. **12.** chief, esp. as being the official seat of government of a country, state, etc. **13.** excellent or first-rate. **14.** (of letters) of the large size used at the

beginning of a sentence or as the first letter of a proper name. **15.** involving the loss of the head or life, usually as punishment; punishable by death. **16.** fatal; serious: *a capital error.* **17.** of the largest, most heavily armed, etc., type: *a capital ship.* [ME, t. L: s. *capitālis* pertaining to the head or to life, chief (ML *capitāle*, n., wealth)]
—**Syn. 11.** The adjectives CAPITAL, CHIEF, MAJOR, PRINCIPAL apply to a main or leading representative of a kind. CAPITAL may mean larger or more prominent, or it may suggest pre-eminence: *capital letter, city.* CHIEF means leading, highest in office or power: *the chief clerk.* MAJOR may refer to greatness of importance, number, or quantity: *a major operation, the major part of a population.* PRINCIPAL refers to most distinguished, influential, or foremost: *principal export.* —**Ant. 11.** minor, lesser.

capital² (kăp′ĭ tl), *n. Archit.* the head, or uppermost part, of a column, pillar, etc. [ME *capital(e)*, t. L: m. s. *capitellum*, dim. of *caput* head; influenced by CAPITAL¹, adj.]

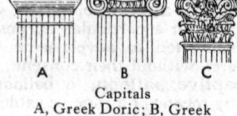

A B C
Capitals
A, Greek Doric; B, Greek Ionic; C, Greek Corinthian

capital account, 1. a business account stating the owner's or shareholder's interest in the assets. **2.** (*pl.*) *Accounting.* accounts showing the net worth, as in a business enterprise, as assets minus liabilities.

capital assets, fixed assets.

capital distribution, *Accounting.* the issue of bonus shares to shareholders in a company.

capital expenditure, *Accounting.* an addition to the value of a fixed asset, as by the purchase of a new building.

capital gains, profits from the sale of capital assets, such as bonds, real property, etc.

capital gains tax, a tax levied on capital gains.

capital goods, *Econ.* goods used in the production of other goods.

capitalism (kăp′ĭ tə lĭz′əm, kə pĭt′ə-), *n.* **1.** a system under which the means of production, distribution, and exchange are in large measure privately owned and directed. **2.** the concentration of capital in the hands of a few, or the resulting power or influence. **3.** a system favouring such concentration of wealth.

capital issue, capital distribution.

capitalist (kăp′ĭ tə lĭst, kə pĭt′ə-), *n.* **1.** one who has capital, esp. extensive capital employed in business enterprises. —*adj.* **2.** pertaining to capital or capitalists; founded on or believing in capitalism. —**cap′italis′tic,** *adj.* —**cap′italis′tically,** *adv.*

capitalization (kăp′ĭ tə lī zā′shən, kə pĭt′ə-), *n.* **1.** the act of capitalizing. **2.** the authorized and paid up shares or stock of a company. **3.** *Accounting.* **a.** the total investment of the owner or owners in a business enterprise. **b.** the total corporate liability. **c.** the total arrived at after addition of liabilities. **4.** conversion into stocks or bonds. **5.** the act of computing the present value of future periodical payments. Also, **capitalisation.**

capitalize (kăp′ĭ tə līz′, kə pĭt′ə līz′), *v.t.*, **-lized, -lizing.** **1.** to write or print in capital letters, or with an initial capital. **2.** to authorize a certain amount of stocks and bonds in the corporate charter: *to capitalize a company.* **3.** to convert (floating debt) into stock or shares. **4.** *Accounting.* to set up (expenditures) as business assets in the books of account instead of treating as expense. **5.** to supply with capital. **6.** to estimate the value of (a stock or an enterprise). **7.** to take advantage of; turn to one's advantage (often fol. by *on*): *capitalize on one's opportunities.* Also, **capitalise.**

capital levy, a tax based on total assets.

capitally (kăp′ĭ tə lĭ), *adv.* **1.** in a capital manner; excellently; very well. **2.** by capital punishment.

capital ship, one of a class of the largest warships; a battleship, battle cruiser, or aircraft-carrier.

capital stock, 1. the total shares issued by a company. **2.** the book value of all the shares of a company, including unissued shares and those not completely paid in.

capital sum, *Insurance.* the sum stated to be payable on the happening of some event against which insurance has been effected.

capital surplus, the surplus of a business, exclusive of its earned surplus.

capitate¹ (kăp′ĭ tāt′), *adj. Bot.* having a globular head; collected in a head. [t. L: m. s. *capitātus* having a head]

capitate² (kăp′ĭ tāt′), *n. Anat.* a small bone forming part of the carpus of the hand. [t. NL: m. s. *capitātum*, adj., in *os capitātum* capitate bone]

capitation (kăp′ĭ tā′shən), *n.* **1.** a numbering or assessing by the head. **2.** a poll tax. **3.** a fee or payment of a uniform amount for each person. [t. LL: s. *capitātio* poll tax]

Capitol (kăp′ĭ tl), *n.* **1.** the building at Washington, D.C., used by the Congress of the U.S. for its sessions. **2.** the ancient temple of Jupiter at Rome, on the Capitoline. **3.** the Capitoline. [ME *capitole*, t. L: m. s. *Capitōlium* (cf. defs 2, 3), der. *caput* head]

Capitoline (kə pĭt′ə līn′), *adj.* **1.** of or pertaining to the Capitol at Rome, the hill on which it stood, or the god Jupiter (who was worshipped there). —*n.* **2.** one of the Seven Hills of ancient Rome.

capitular (kə pĭt′yŏŏ lə), *n.* **1.** a member of an ecclesiastical chapter. **2.** (*pl.*) the laws or statutes of a chapter or of an ecclesiastical council. —*adj.* **3.** *Bot.* capitate. **4.** pertaining to an ecclesiastical or other chapter: *a capitular cathedral.* [t. ML: s. *capitulāris*, der. L *capitulum* CAPITULUM]

capitulary (kə pĭt′yŏŏ lə rĭ), *adj.*, *n.*, *pl.* **-ries.** —*adj.* **1.** pertaining to a chapter, esp. an ecclesiastical one. —*n.* **2.** a member of a chapter, esp. an ecclesiastical one. **3.** (*pl.*) the ordinances or laws of a Frankish sovereign.

capitulate (kə pĭt′yŏŏ lāt′), *v.i.*, **-lated, -lating.** to surrender unconditionally or on stipulated terms. [t. ML: m. s. *capitulātus*, pp. of *capitulāre* arrange in chapters, der. L *capitulum* CAPITULUM]

capitulation (kə pĭt′yŏŏ lā′shən), *n.* **1.** a surrender unconditionally or upon certain terms. **2.** the instrument containing a surrender. **3.** a statement of the heads of a subject; a summary or enumeration. **4.** (*pl.*) any of the treaties of the sultans of Turkey which granted to foreigners residing there rights of personalty of law, extraterritoriality, etc. **5.** a treaty by which Christian states obtained the right to establish courts for their nationals in non-Christian states.

capitulum (kə pĭt′yŏŏ ləm), *n.*, *pl.* **-la** (-lə). **1.** *Bot.* a close head of sessile flowers; a flower head. See illus. under **inflorescence.** **2.** *Anat.* the head of a bone. [t. L: small head, capital of column, chapter, dim. of *caput* head]

Cap'n (kăp′ən), *n.* Captain.

capon (kā′pən), *n.* a cock castrated to improve the flesh for use as food. [OE *capun*, t. L: m. s. *cāpo*]

Capone (kə pōn′), *n.* **Al,** 1899–1947, U.S. gangster.

caporal (kăp′ə räl′), *n.* a kind of tobacco. [t. F, t. It.: m. *caporale* superior. See CORPORAL]

Caporetto (kăp′ə rĕt′ō; *It.* kȧ pō rĕt′tō), *n.* a village in Yugoslavia, formerly in NE Italy: scene of a disastrous Italian defeat by the Austrians and Germans, 1917.

capote (kə pōt′; *Fr.* kȧ pōt′), *n.* **1.** a long cloak with a hood. **2.** a close, caplike bonnet worn by women and children. [t. F, dim. of *cape* hood]

Capote (kə pōt′), *n.* **Truman,** born 1924, U.S. writer.

Cappadocia (kăp′ə dō′syə), *n.* an ancient country in E Asia Minor: later a Roman province.

capparidaceous (kăp′ə rĭ dā′shəs), *adj. Bot.* belonging to the *Capparidaceae*, or caper family. [f. *capparid* (f. s. L *capparis* + -ID²) the caper plant + -ACEOUS]

capped hock, *Vet. Sci.* any swelling, inflammatory or otherwise, on the point of the hock of horses.

cappuccino (kăp′ŏŏ chē′nō), *adj.*, *n. Italian.* white (coffee).

capreolate (kăp′rĭ ə lāt′, kə prē′-), *adj.* **1.** *Bot.* having tendrils. **2.** *Anat.* resembling tendrils. [f. s. L *capreolus* tendril + -ATE¹]

Capri (kăp′rē; *It.* kȧ′prē), *n.* a rocky island off the Bay of Naples, in W Italy: famous for its scenery and grottoes. 10,600 pop. (est. 1964); 5½ sq. mi. See map under **Salerno.**

capriccio (kə prĭch′ĭ ō′; *It.* kȧ prēt′chō), *n.*, *pl.* **-cios,** *It.* **-ci** (*It.* -chē). **1.** a caper; a prank. **2.** a caprice. **3.** *Music.* a composition in a free, irregular style. [t. It., der. *capro* goat, g. L *caper*]

capriccioso (kə prĭch′ĭ ō′zō; *It.* kȧ prēt chō′sō), *adj. Music.* capricious; fantastic in style.

caprice (kə prēs′), *n.* **1.** a sudden change of mind without apparent or adequate motive; whim. **2.** a tendency to change one's mind without apparent or adequate motive; whimsicality; capriciousness. **3.** *Music.* capriccio (def. 3). [t. F, t. It.: *capriccio* CAPRICCIO]

capricious (kə prĭsh′əs), *adj.* **1.** subject to, led by, or indicative of caprice or whim. **2.** *Obs.* fanciful or witty. —**capri′ciously,** *adv.* —**capri′ciousness,** *n.*

Capricorn (kăp′rĭ kôn′), *n.* **1.** *Astron.* a zodiacal constellation between Sagittarius and Aquarius. **2.** Also, **Capricornus** (kăp′rĭ kô′nəs). the tenth sign of the zodiac. See diag. under **zodiac.** **3. Tropic of.** See **tropic** (1a, 2a). [t. L: s. *Capricornus*, lit., goat-horned]

caprifoliaceous (kăp′rĭ fō′lĭ ā′shəs), *adj. Bot.* belonging to the *Caprifoliaceae*, a family of plants including the honeysuckle, elder, viburnum, snowberry, etc. [f. s. ML *caprifolium* honeysuckle + -ACEOUS]

capriole (kăp′rĭ ōl′), *n.* **1.** a caper or leap. **2.** an upward spring made by a horse with all four feet and without advancing. —*v.i.* **3.** to execute a capriole. [t. F, t. It.: m. *capriola* caper, der. *capro* goat, g. L *caper*]

Caprivi Strip (kə prē′vĭ), a long, narrow strip of land in N South-West Africa bordered by Angola and Zambia. 300 mi. long. [named after Leo, Count von *Caprivi*, 1831–99, German soldier and statesman]

caproic acid (kə prō′ĭk). an organic acid, $CH_3(CH_2)_4$-COOH, found in fatty animal tissue and in coconut oil, used to make artificial flavouring agents. [f. *capro-* (comb. form repr. L *caper* goat) + -IC; so called from its smell]

caps, capital letters.

capsaicin (kăp sā′ĭ sĭn), *n. Chem.* a bitter irritant principle from paprika; colourless crystalline amide, $C_{18}H_{27}NO_3$, related to guaiacol. [f. L *capsa* box + -IC + -IN[2]]

capsicum (kăp′sĭ kəm), *n.* **1.** any plant of the solanaceous genus *Capsicum*, as *C. frutescens*, the common pepper of the garden, in many varieties, with mild to hot, pungent seeds enclosed in a podded or bell-shaped pericarp which also ranges from mild to extremely hot. **2.** the fruit of these plants, or some preparation of it, used as a condiment and once widely used internally and externally as a local irritant. [t. NL: f. s. L *capsa* box + *-icum*, neut. of *-icus* -IC]

capsize (kăp sīz′), *v.*, **-sized, -sizing.** —*v.i.* **1.** to overturn: *the boat capsized.* —*v.t.* **2.** to upset: *they capsized the boat.* [orig. unknown] —**Syn.** See **upset.**

capstan (kăp′stən), *n.* a device resembling a windlass but with a vertical axis, commonly turned by a bar or lever, and winding a cable, for raising weights (as an anchor) or drawing things closer (as a ship to its jetty). [ME, t. Pr.: m. *cabestan*, earlier *cabestran*, der. *cabestre*, g. L *capistrum* halter]

Capstan
A, Capstan head; B, Barrel; C, Toothed rim and pawls; D, Capstan bar

capstan bar, one of the levers, generally of wood, by which a capstan is turned.

capstan lathe, a lathe having the cutting tools mounted on a capstan-like holder.

capstone (kăp′stōn′), *n.* a coping.

capsular (kăp′syŏŏ lə), *adj.* of, in, or resembling a capsule.

capsulate (kăp′syŏŏ lāt′, -lĭt), *adj.* enclosed in or formed into a capsule. Also, **cap′sulat′ed.**

capsule (kăp′syŏŏl), **1.** a gelatinous case enclosing a dose of medicine. **2.** *Bot.* **a.** a dry dehiscent fruit, composed of two or more carpels. **b.** the spore case of various cryptogamic plants. **3.** *Anat.*, *Zool.* **a.** a membranous sac or integument. **b.** either of two strata of white matter in the cerebrum. **4.** the compartment of a spacecraft containing the crew or instruments. **5.** that part of a spacecraft or aircraft which is detachable. **6.** a small case, envelope, or covering. **7.** a thin metal covering for the mouth of a corked bottle. **8.** anything short or condensed, as a story or news item. [earlier *capsul*, t. L: s. *capsula*, dim. of *capsa* box]

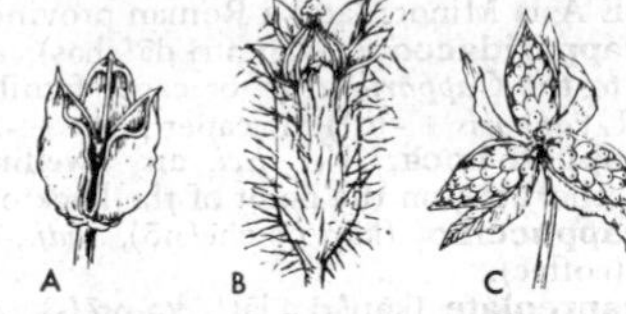

Capsules (def. 2a) after dehiscence
A, Asphodel; B, Prickly poppy; C, Violet

Capt., Captain.

captain (kăp′tĭn), *n.* **1.** one who is at the head of or in authority over others; a chief; leader. **2.** an officer in the British army, ranking above a lieutenant and below a major. **3.** an officer of corresponding rank in any other army. **4.** any military leader. **5.** the commander or master of a merchant ship or other vessel. **6.** an officer in the navy ranking above a commander and below a rear admiral, usually in command of a warship. **7.** the officer responsible for an aircraft while it is in flight, usually the senior pilot. **8.** the rank of a captain (defs 2, 3, or 6). **9.** the leader of a team, club, or side in any sport or game. **10.** the head boy of a school or division of a school. —*v.t.* **11.** to lead or command as a captain. [ME *capitain*, t. OF, t. LL: m. s. *capitāneus* chief, der. L *caput* head] —**cap′taincy,** *n.* —**cap′tainship′,** *n.*

Captain Cooker, *N.Z.* **1.** a wild boar. **2.** any pig, particularly a poor, mangy specimen.

caption (kăp′shən), *n.* **1.** a heading or title, as of a chapter, article, or page. **2.** *Print.* a legend for a picture or illustration. **3.** *Films.* the title of a scene, the text of a speech, etc., shown on the screen. **4.** *Law.* that part of a legal document which states on what authority it is made. —*v.t.* **5.** to provide with a caption. [t. L: s. *captio*]

captious (kăp′shəs), *adj.* **1.** apt to notice and make much of trivial faults or defects; fault-finding; difficult to please. **2.** proceeding from a fault-finding or cavilling disposition: *captious remarks.* **3.** apt or designed to ensnare or perplex, esp. in argument: *captious questions.* [t. L: m. s. *captiōsus* sophistical] —**cap′tiously,** *adv.* —**cap′tiousness,** *n.*

captivate (kăp′tĭ vāt′), *v.t.*, **-vated, -vating.** to enthral by beauty or excellence; enchant; charm. [t. LL: m. s. *captivātus*, pp., taken captive] —**cap′tiva′tion,** *n.* —**cap′tiva′tor,** *n.* —**Syn. 1.** See **charm.**

captive (kăp′tĭv), *n.* **1.** a prisoner. **2.** one who is enslaved by love, beauty, etc. —*adj.* **3.** made or held prisoner, esp. in war. **4.** kept in confinement or restraint. **5.** enslaved by love, beauty, etc.; captivated. **6.** of or pertaining to a captive. [t. L: m. s. *captivus*]

captive audience, people who have entered into a situation for a particular purpose, as at a restaurant, and are subjected to advertisements, propaganda, solicitations, etc., without their consent.

captive balloon, a balloon held in a particular place by means of a rope or cable, as for observation purposes.

captivity (kăp tĭv′ĭ tĭ), *n.*, *pl.* **-ties.** the state or period of being captive. —**Syn.** bondage, servitude, slavery.

captor (kăp′tə), *n.* a person who captures.

capture (kăp′chə), *v.*, **-tured, -turing,** *n.* —*v.t.* **1.** to take by force or stratagem; take prisoner; seize: *the chief was captured.* —*n.* **2.** the act of taking by force or stratagem. **3.** the thing or person captured. **4.** *Physics.* the process by which an atomic or nuclear system acquires an additional particle. **5.** *Geog.* the process by which one river acquires the tributaries of another, usually smaller and slower river. [t. F, t. L: m. *captūra*] —**cap′turer,** *n.* —**Syn. 1.** catch, arrest, snare, grab, nab. **2.** seizure, arrest.

Capua (kăp′yŏŏ ə; *It.* kä′pwä), *n.* a town in SW Italy, in Campania, near Naples. 10,220 (est. 1964).

capuche (kə pōōsh′), *n.* a hood or cowl; esp. the long, pointed cowl of the Capuchins. [t. F, t. It.: m. *cappuccio*]

capuchin (kăp′yŏŏ chĭn, -shĭn), *n.* **1.** a prehensile-tailed monkey of Central and South America, *Cebus capucinus*, whose head hair presents a cowl-like appearance. **2.** any monkey of the genus *Cebus.* **3.** a hooded cloak for women. **4.** (*cap.*) *Rom. Cath. Ch.* one of an order of Franciscan friars, a reformed branch of the Observants, wearing a long cowl. [t. F, t. It.: m. *cappuccino*, der. *cappuccio* hood]

Capuchin monkey, *Cebus capucinus* (Total length 3 ft, tail 15 in.)

caput (kā′pət, kăp′ət), *n.*, *pl.* **capita** (kăp′ĭ tə). *Anat.* any head or headlike expansion on a structure, as on a bone. [L: the head]

capybara (kăp′ĭ bä′rə), *n.* the largest living rodent, *Hydrochoerus hydrochaeris*, 3 or 4 feet long, living along the banks of South American rivers, sand-coloured and virtually tailless. [t. Pg.: m. *capibara*, t. Tupi: m. *kapigwara* grass-eater]

Capybara, *Hydrochoerus hydrochaeris* (3 to 4 ft long, ab. 2 ft high)

car (kä), *n.* **1.** a motor car. **2.** *Poetic.* a chariot, as of war or triumph. **3.** a vehicle of various kinds running on rails, as a restaurant car, tramcar, etc. **4.** *Chiefly U.S.* a railway carriage or wagon. **5.** the part of a balloon, lift, etc., in which the passengers, etc., are carried. [ME *carre*, t. ONF, g. LL *carrus*, of Celtic orig.]

carabin (kă′rə bĭn), *n.* **1.** carbine. **2.** *Hist.* a mounted soldier armed with a carbine. Also, **carabine** (kă′rə bīn′). [t. F: alter. of ONF *escarrabin* corpse-bearer, ult. der. L *scarabaeus* SCARAB]

carabineer (kă′rə bĭ nĭə′), *n.* (formerly) a soldier armed with a carbine. Also, **car′bineer′, car′abinier′.**

caracal (kă′rə kăl′), *n.* a large cat, *Felis caracal*, of Africa and parts of Asia, having reddish brown fur and tufted ears. [t. F or Sp., t. Turk., equiv. to *kara* black + *kulak* ear]

Caracalla (kă′rə kăl′ə), *n.* (*Marcus Aurelius Antonius Bassianus*), A.D. 188–217, Roman emperor A.D. 211–217.

caracara (kä′rə kä′rə), *n.* any of certain vulture-like birds of the subfamily *Polyborinae* of the warmer parts of America, as **Audubon's caracara** (*Polyborus cheriway*). [t. Sp., Pg., t. Tupi; imit. of its cry]

Caracas (kə răk′əs; *Sp.* kä rä′käs), *n.* the capital of Venezuela, in the N part; with suburbs, 1,336,119 (1961).

caracol (kă′rə kŏl), *n.*, *v.i.*, **-colled, -colling.** caracole.

caracole (kă′rə kōl′), *n.*, *v.*, **-coled, -coling.** —*n.* **1.** a half-turn executed by a horseman in riding. —*v.i.* **2.** to execute caracoles; wheel. [t. F, t. Sp.: m. *caracol* snail, wheeling movement]

Caractacus (kə răk′tə kəs), *n.* fl. A.D. *c.* 50, chieftain who opposed the Romans in Britain. Also, **Caradoc** (kə răd′ək).

caracul (kă′rə kŭl′), *n.* **1.** the skin of the very young of certain Asiatic or Russian sheep, karakul, dressed as a fur, resembling astrakhan, but with flatter, looser curl. **2.** karakul (sheep). Also, **karakul.** [named after *Kara Kul* (Turk.: Black Lake), in Uzbekistan, where the breed comes from]

carafe (kə răf′, -räf′), *n.* a glass bottle for water, wine, etc. [t. F, t. It.: m. *caraffa*, prob. t. Sp.: m. *garrafa*, t. Ar.: m. *gharrâf* drinking vessel]

caramba (kə răm′bə), *n.* carambola.

carambola (kă′rəm bō′lə), *n.* **1.** an oxalideaceous tree, *Averrhoa caramboia*, of SE Asia. **2.** the yellow, smooth-skinned, edible fruit of this tree. [t. Pg., t. Marathi: m. *karambal*]

caramel (kă′rə məl, -mĕl′), *n.* **1.** burnt sugar, used for colouring and flavouring food, etc. **2.** a kind of sweet, commonly in small blocks, made from sugar, butter, milk, etc. [t. F, t Sp.: s. *caramelo*]

caramelize (kă′rə mə līz′), *v.t.*, *v.i.*, **-lized, -lizing.** to convert or be converted into caramel. Also, **caramelise.**

carangoid (kə răng′goid), *adj.* **1.** belonging to or resembling the *Carangidae*, a family of spiny-rayed fishes including the cavally, pompano, pilot-fish, etc. —*n.* **2.** a carangoid fish. [f. s. NL *Caranx*, the typical genus (cf. Sp. *carangue* a West Indian flatfish) + -OID]

carapa (kă′rə pə, -pä′), *n.* any tree of the tropical meliaceous genus *Carapa.* [t. NL, t. Carib.: oil]

carapace (kă′rə pās′), *n.* a shield, test, or shell covering some or all of the dorsal part of an animal. [t. F, t. Sp.: m. *carapacho*]

carat (kă′rət), *n.* **1.** a unit of weight in gem stones, 200 mg. (about 3 grains of troy or avoirdupois weight). **2.** a twenty-fourth part (used in expressing the fineness of gold, pure gold being 24 carats fine). Also, **karat.** [t. F, t. It.: m. *carato*, t. Ar.: m. *qīraṭ* light weight, t. Gk: m. *kerátion* carob bean, carat, dim. of *kéras* horn]

Caravaggio (*It.* kä rä väd′jō), *n.* **Michelangelo Merisi** (*It.* mē kē län′jē lō mē′rē zē), 1573–1610, Italian painter.

caravan (kă′rə văn′), *n.* **1.** a vehicle in which people may live, whether temporarily or permanently, usually having two wheels and designed to be drawn by a motor car. **2.** such a vehicle having four cartwheels and horse-drawn, traditionally inhabited by gipsies and circus folk, etc. **3.** any large covered vehicle, for passengers or goods. **4.** a group of merchants or others travelling together, as for safety, esp. over deserts, etc., in Asia or Africa. —*v.i.* **5.** to live, as for a holiday, in a caravan. [t. F: m. *caravane*, t. Pers.: m. *kārwān*]

caravanserai (kă′rə văn′sə rī′, -rā′), *n.*, *pl.* **-ries.** **1.** (in the Near East) a kind of inn for the accommodation of caravans. **2.** any large inn or hotel. Also, **caravansary** (kă′rə văn′sə rĭ). [ult. t. Pers.: m. *kārwānsarāī*, f. *kārwān* caravan + *sarāī* inn]

caravel (kă′rə vĕl′), *n.* a kind of small three-masted ship formerly used esp. by the Spaniards and Portuguese. Also, **carvel.** [t. F: m. *caravelle*, t. It.: m. *caravella.* Cf. LL *carabus*, Gk *kárabos* kind of light ship]

caraway (kă′rə wā′), *n.* **1.** an umbelliferous condimental herb, *Carum carvi*, bearing aromatic seedlike fruit (**caraway seeds**) used in cookery and medicine. **2.** the fruit or seeds. [late ME, t. ML: m. *carui*, t. Ar.: m. *karawyā.* Cf. L *careum*, Gk *káron*]

carb-, var. of **carbo-** before vowels, as in *carbazole.*

carbamic acid (kä băm′ĭk), a hypothetical compound, NH_2COOH, known only in the form of its salts and esters. [f. CARB- + AM(IDE) + -IC]

carbamide (kä′bə mīd′), *n.* *Chem.* urea.

carbazole (kä′bə zōl′), *n.* a weakly acidic, crystalline compound, $C_{12}H_9N$, found with anthracene in coal tar. Many dyes are derived from it. [f. CARB- + AZ- + -OLE]

carbide (kä′bīd), *n.* *Chem.* **1.** a compound of carbon with a more electropositive element or radical. **2.** calcium carbide. [f. CARB- + -IDE]

carbine (kä′bīn), *n.* a short rifle (or, formerly, musket) carried by fighting soldiers and non-commissioned officers who are not equipped with rifles. Also, **carabin, carabine.** [t. F: m. *carabine*, orig. a small arquebus, der. *carabin* CARABIN]

carbineer (kä′bĭ nĭə′), *n.* carabineer.

carbinol (kä′bĭ nŏl′), *n.* *Chem.* **1.** methyl alcohol. **2.** an alcohol derived from it. [f. m. CARBON + -OL[1]]

carbo-, a word element meaning 'carbon', as in *carborundum.* Also, **carb-.** [comb. form of CARBON]

carbocyclic compounds (kä′bō sī′klĭk, -sĭk′lĭk), *Chem.* a group of organic compounds in which all the atoms composing the ring are carbon atoms, as naphthalene.

carboholic (kä′bō hŏl′ĭk), *n.* a person addicted to the consumption of carbohydrates. [b. CARBO(HYDRATE) + (ALCO)HOLIC]

carbohydrase (kä′bō hī′drāz), *n.* *Biochem.* any enzyme that acts upon carbohydrates.

carbohydrate (kä′bō hī′drāt), *n.* *Chem.* any of a class of organic compounds which are polyhydroxy aldehydes or polyhydroxy ketones, or change to such substances on simple chemical transformations, such as hydrolysis, oxidation, or reduction. Including sugars, starch, and cellulose, they form the supporting tissues of plants and are important food for animals.

carbolated (kä′bə lā′tĭd), *adj.* *Chem.* containing carbolic acid.

carbolic acid (kä bŏl′ĭk), *Chem.* phenol (def. 1). [f. CARB- + -OL[2] + -IC]

carbon (kä′bən), *n.* **1.** *Chem.* a widely distributed element which forms organic compounds in combination with hydrogen, oxygen, etc., and which occurs in a pure state as charcoal. *Symbol:* C; *at. wt:* 12·011; *at. no.:* 6; *sp. gr.:* (of diamond) 3·51 at 20°C; (of graphite) 2·26 at 20°C. **2.** *Elect.* **a.** the carbon rod through which current is conducted between the electrode-holder and the arc in carbon arc lighting or welding. **b.** the rod or plate, composed in part of carbon, used in batteries. **3.** a sheet of carbon paper. **4.** a carbon copy. **5.** the isotope carbon 14; radiocarbon. [t. F: m. *carbone*, t. L: m. s. *carbo* coal, charcoal]

carbonaceous (kä′bə nā′shəs), *adj.* *Chem.* of, like, or containing carbon.

carbonado (kä′bə nā′dō), *n.*, *pl.* **-does, -dos,** *v.*, **-does, -doing.** —*n.* **1.** a piece of meat, fish, etc., scored and broiled. **2.** an opaque, dark-coloured, massive form of diamond, found chiefly in Brazil, and used for drills; black diamond. —*v.t.* **3.** to score and broil. **4.** to slash; hack. [t. Sp.: m. *carbonada*, der. *carbón*, g. L *carbo* coal]

Carbonari (kä′bə nä′rĭ), *n.pl.*, *sing.* **-ro** (-rō). the members of a 19th-century secret political society, of revolutionary aims, in Italy, France, and Spain. [It., pl. of *carbonaro* charcoal-burner] —**Car′bona′rism,** *n.*

carbonate (*n.* kä′bə nāt′, -nĭt; *v.* kä′bə nāt′), *n.*, *v.*, **-nated, -nating.** —*n.* **1.** *Chem.* a salt of carbonic acid, as *calcium carbonate*, $CaCO_3$. —*v.t.* **2.** to form into a carbonate. **3.** to charge or impregnate with carbon dioxide. [t. NL: m. *carbonātum* (something) carbonated]

carbonation (kä′bə nā′shən), *n.* **1.** saturation with carbon dioxide, as in making soda-water. **2.** reaction with carbon dioxide to remove lime, as in sugar refining. **3.** carbonization. —**car′bona′tor,** *n.*

carbon black, the finely divided carbon produced by burning hydrocarbons, used in manufacturing ink, rubber products, etc.

carbon copy, a duplicate copy made by using carbon paper.

carbon cycle, **1.** *Biol.* the circulation on earth of carbon atoms, from the atmosphere through plants and animals back into the atmosphere. **2.** *Astrophysics.* a cycle of nuclear transformations, with the release of atomic energy, in the interiors of the stars, by means of which hydrogen is gradually converted into helium.

carbon dating, radiocarbon dating.

carbon dioxide, *Chem.* a colourless, odourless, incombustible gas, CO_2, used extensively in industry as dry ice, and in fizzy drinks, fire-extinguishers, etc. It is present in the atmosphere and formed during respiration.

carbon dioxide snow, *Chem.* carbon dioxide, CO_2, solidified under great pressure; dry ice. It is used as a refrigerant because it passes directly from a solid to a gas, absorbing a great amount of heat.

carbon disulphide, *Chem.* a colourless inflammable liquid, CS_2, used as a solvent in the rubber and plastic industries.

carbonic (kä bŏn′ĭk), *adj.* *Chem.* containing tetravalent carbon, as carbonic acid, H_2CO_3.

carbonic acid, *Chem.* the acid, H_2CO_3, formed when carbon dioxide dissolves in water, known in the form of its salts and esters, the carbonates.

carbonic acid gas, *Chem.* carbon dioxide.

Carboniferous (kä′bə nĭf′ə rəs), *Geol.* —*adj.* **1.** pertaining to a geological period or a system of rocks preceding the Permian, and following the Devonian; divided into **Upper Carboniferous, Lower Carboniferous,** and sometimes **Middle Carboniferous.** **2.** (*l.c.*) producing coal. —*n.* **3.** a late Palaeozoic period or system next following the Devonian. [f. CARBON + -(I)FEROUS]

carbonization (kä′bə nī zā′shən), *n.* **1.** *Chem.* formation of carbon from organic matter. **2.** coal distillation, as in coke ovens. Also, **carbonisation.**

carbonize (kä′bə nīz′), *v.t.*, **-nized, -nizing.** **1.** to char, forming carbon. **2.** to coat or enrich with carbon. Also, **carbonise.**

carbon monoxide, a colourless, odourless, poisonous gas, CO, burning with a pale blue flame, formed when carbon burns with an insufficient supply of air.

carbon paper, **1.** paper faced with a preparation of carbon or other material, used between two sheets of plain paper in order to reproduce upon the lower sheet that which is written or typed on the upper. **2.** a paper for making photographs by the carbon process.

carbon process, a method of making photographic prints by the use of a pigment, such as carbon, contained in sensitized gelatine.

carbon silicide, silicon carbide.

carbon tetrachloride, *Chem.* a non-inflammable, colourless liquid, CCl_4, used in medicine, and as a fire-extinguisher, cleaning fluid, solvent, etc.

carbonyl (kä′bə nīl), *n.* *Chem.* **1.** the divalent radical =CO occurring in acids, ketones, aldehydes, and their derivatives. **2.** a compound containing metal combined with carbon monoxide, as *nickel carbonyl*, $Ni(CO)_4$. [f. CARBON + -YL] —**car′bonyl′ic,** *adj.*

carborundum (kä′bə rŭn′dəm), *n.* **1.** *Chem.* silicon carbide, SiC, an important abrasive produced in the electric furnace. **2.** (*cap.*) a trademark for this substance. [f. CARBO- + (CO)RUNDUM]

carboxyl group (kä bŏk′sīl), *Chem.* a univalent radical, —COOH, present in and characteristic of the formulae of all organic acids. Also, **carboxyl radical.** [f. CARB- + OX(YGEN) + -YL]

carboy (kä′boi), *n.* a large glass bottle, esp. one protected by basketwork or a wooden box, as for containing acids. [t. Pers.: m. *qarābah* large flagon]

carbuncle (kä′bŭng′kl), *n.* **1.** a painful circumscribed inflammation of the subcutaneous tissue, resulting in suppuration and sloughing, and having a tendency to spread (somewhat like a boil, but more serious in its effects). **2.** a garnet cut in a convex rounded form without facets. **3.** (formerly) a rounded red gem, as a ruby or garnet. **4.** deep red. **5.** brownish red. [ME, t. ONF, g. L *carbunculus*, dim. of *carbo* (live) coal] —**car′bun′cled,** *adj.* —**carbuncular** (kä bŭng′kyŏŏ lə), *adj.*

carburant (kä′byŏŏ rənt), *n.* the fuel used in carburation.

carburation (kä′byŏŏ rā′shən), *n.* the process of mixing air and fuel in the proper proportions for combustion before feeding it into an internal-combustion engine. Also, **carburetion.**

carburet (kä′byŏŏ ret′), *v.t.*, **-retted, -retting** or (*U.S.*) **-reted, -reting.** to combine or mix with carbon or hydrocarbons. [f. CARB- + -URET]

carburettor (kä′byŏŏ rĕt′ə, kä′byŏŏ rĕt′ə), *n.* **1.** a device in an internal-combustion engine for mixing a volatile fuel with the correct proportion of air in order to form an explosive gas. **2.** an apparatus for adding hydrocarbons to non-luminous or poor gases, for the purpose of producing an illuminating or explosive gas. Also, **carburetter;** *U.S.*, **carburetor.**

carburize (kä′byŏŏ rīz′), *v.t.*, **-rized, -rizing.** **1.** to cause to unite with carbon. **2.** *Metall.* to introduce carbon into the surface of steel by heating it while it is in contact with a suitable source of carbon, as a form of case-hardening. **3.** to carburet. Also, **carburise.** —**car′buriza′tion,** *n.* —**car′buriz′er,** *n.*

carbylamine (kä′bĭ lə mēn′, -ăm′in), *n.* *Chem.* an organic compound containing the group –NC.

carcajou (kä′kə jōō′, -zhōō′), *n.* the American glutton, *Gulo gulo*; wolverine. [t. Canadian F, t. Amer. Ind. (Algonquian); cf. Montagnais *karkaju*, Ojibwa *gwingwaage*, Cree *kikkwahakes*]

carcanet (kä′kə nĕt′, -nĭt), *n.* **1.** *Archaic.* an ornamental collar or necklace. **2.** *Obs. or Hist.* an ornamental band for the head. [f. F *carcan* (of Gmc orig.) + -ET]

carcass (kä′kəs), *n.* **1.** the dead body of an animal or (now only in contempt) of a human being. **2.** (now chiefly in contempt or humour) a living body. **3.** the body of a slaughtered animal after removal of the offal, etc. **4.** anything from which life and power are gone. **5.** an unfinished framework or skeleton, as of a house or ship. Also, **car′case.** [t. F: m. *carcasse*, t. It.: m. *carcassa*; r. ME *carkeis*, t. AF] —**Syn.** **1.** See **body.**

Carcassonne (*Fr.* kȧr kȧ sŏn′), *n.* a town in S France, in Aude department. 38,100 (est. 1964).

carcinogen (kä sĭn′ə jən), *n.* *Pathol.* any substance which tends to produce a cancer in a body. —**carcinogenic** (kä′sĭ nō jĕn′ĭk), *adj.*

carcinogenesis (kä′sĭ nō jĕn′ĭ sĭs), *n.* *Pathol.* the inception or production and growth of cancer.

carcinoma (kä′sĭ nō′mə), *n.*, *pl.* **-mata** (-mə tə), **-mas.** *Pathol.* a malignant and invasive epithelial tumour that spreads by metastasis and often recurs after excision; a cancer. [t. L, t. Gk: m. *karkínōma* a cancer]

carcinomatosis (kä′sĭ nō mə tō′sĭs), *n.* *Pathol.* a condition marked by the production of an overwhelming number of carcinomata throughout the body. —**carcinomatous** (kä′sĭ nŏm′ə təs, -nō′mə-), *adj.*

card[1] (käd), *n.* **1.** a piece of stiff paper or thin pasteboard, usually rectangular, for various uses: *a visiting card, a union card* (showing membership of a trade union). **2.** a postcard. **3.** a piece of cardboard with more or less elaborate ornamentation, bearing complimentary greeting: *a Christmas card.* **4.** one of a set of small pieces of cardboard with spots or figures, used in playing various games, in prognostication, etc. **5.** (*pl.*) a game or games played with such a set. **6.** *Colloq.* a resource, plan, idea, approach to a problem or proposition, etc.: *that's his best card, to have a card up one's sleeve.* **7.** a programme of the events, as at horseraces. **8.** the circular piece of paper or other material on which the 32 points indicating direction are marked in a compass. **9.** *Textiles.* a perforated strip of cardboard, etc., used to control the pattern in weaving. **10.** *Colloq.* a person of some indicated characteristic: *a queer card.* **11.** *Colloq.* a likeable, amusing, or facetious person. **12.** (*pl.*) a person's national insurance and other papers held by his employer and handed over on termination of employment. **13. house of cards, a.** a structure, as made by children, of cards placed vertically and horizontally on top of each other. **b.** any flimsy structure of hopes or plans without foundation. [ME, t. F: m. *carte*, t. L: m. *charta* (see CHART)]

card[2] (käd), *n.* **1.** an implement used in disentangling and combing out fibres of wool, flax, etc., preparatory to spinning. **2.** a similar implement for raising the nap on cloth. —*v.t.* **3.** to dress (wool, etc.) with a card. [late ME *carde*, t. OF, ult. t. LL: m. *cardus*, L *carduus* thistle] —**card′er,** *n.*

Card., **1.** Cardiganshire. **2.** Cardinal.

cardamom (kä′də məm), *n.* **1.** the aromatic seed capsule of various zingiberaceous plants of the genera *Amomum* and *Elettaria*, native in tropical Asia, used as a spice or condiment and in medicine. **2.** any of the plants. Also, **cardamon** (kä′də mən), **cardamum.** [t. L: s. *cardamōmum*, t. Gk: m. *kardámōmon*]

cardan (kä′dn), *adj.* *Mach.* capable of transmitting rotary movement from a different angle than that of the final drive, as the wheels of a vehicle: *cardan joint, cardan shaft.* [named after G. *Cardano*, 1501–76, Italian mathematician]

cardboard (käd′bôd′), *n.* **1.** a thin, stiff pasteboard. —*adj.* **2.** made of cardboard. **3.** resembling cardboard in appearance, texture, etc. **4.** existing or performing a function in appearance only; insubstantial: *a cardboard prime minister, a cardboard empire.*

cardcase (käd′kās′), *n.* a small pocket case for visiting cards, etc.

card catalogue, a definite arrangement of cards of uniform size (**catalogue cards**) in drawers, each card usually identifying a single publication in a library.

cardi-, var. of **cardio-** before vowels, as in *cardialgia.*

cardiac (kä′dĭ ăk′), *adj.* **1.** pertaining to the heart. **2.** pertaining to the oesophageal portion of the stomach. [t. L: s. *cardiacus* of the heart, t. Gk: m. *kardiakós*]

cardiac glycoside, *Pharm.* one of a group of drugs used to stimulate the heart in cases of heart failure, obtained from a number of plants, as the foxglove, squill, or yellow oleander. Also, **cardiac glucoside.**

cardialgia (kä′dĭ ăl′jĭ ə), *n.* *Pathol.* pain in the region of the heart; heartburn (def. 1). [f. CARDI- + -ALGIA]

Cardiff (kä′dĭf), *n.* a seaport in and capital of Wales: county town of Glamorganshire. 256,270 (1961). See map under **Wales.**

cardigan (kä′dĭ gən), *n.* a close-fitting knitted woollen jacket. Also, **cardigan jacket, cardigan sweater.** [named after the 7th Earl of *Cardigan*, 1797–1868]

Cardigan (kä′dĭ gən), *n.* **1.** a town in Wales, the county town of Cardiganshire. 3789 (1961). **2.** Cardiganshire. **3.** a variety of the Welsh corgi breed of dogs. See **Welsh corgi.**

Cardigan Bay, a coastal indentation between Pembrokeshire and Caernarvonshire, on the W coast of Wales.

Cardiganshire (kä′dĭ gən shĭə′, -shə), *n.* a county in W Wales. 53,564 pop. (1961); 692 sq. mi. *Co. town:* Cardigan. *Abbrev.:* Card. Also, **Cardigan.**

cardinal (kä′dĭ nəl), *adj.* **1.** of prime importance; chief; principal; fundamental: *of cardinal significance.* **2.** deep rich red. —*n.* **3.** one of the seventy members of the Sacred College of the Roman Catholic Church, ranking next to the pope. **4.** Also, **cardinal bird, cardinal grosbeak.** a crested North American finch, *Richmondina cardinalis*, notable for its song. The male is brilliant red, the female brown. **5.** any of various similar birds. **6.** a deep rich red colour. **7.** a cardinal number. [ME, t. L: s. *cardinālis* pertaining to a hinge, chief] —**car′dinally,** *adv.* —**car′dinalship′,** *n.*

cardinalate (kä′dĭ nə lāt′), *n. Rom. Cath. Ch.* **1.** the body of cardinals. **2.** the office, rank, dignity, or incumbency of a cardinal.

cardinal flower, any of several species of the North American genus of plants *Lobelia,* as *L. cardinalis* or *L. fulgens,* having red, pink, or white flowers.

cardinal number, any of the numbers *one, two, three,* etc. (in distinction from *first, second, third,* etc. which are *ordinal numbers*). Also, **cardinal numeral.**

cardinal points, 1. the four chief directions of the compass; the north, south, east, and west points. **2.** *Optics.* (of a lens) the two principal foci, the two nodal points, and the two principal points.

cardinal sins. See **deadly sins.**

cardinal virtues, 1. the most important elements of good character. **2.** *Ancient Philos.* justice, prudence, temperance, and fortitude.

card index, 1. a case or file containing uniform cards arranged in a definite order, each bearing an item of information. **2.** the cards. **3.** the information.

carding (kä′dĭng), *n.* the process of preparing fibres as wool, cotton, etc., for spinning.

cardio-, a word element meaning 'heart'. Also, **cardi-.** [t. Gk: m. *kardio-,* comb. form of *kardía*]

cardiogram (kä′dĭ ō grăm′), *n.* an electrocardiogram.

cardiograph (kä′dĭ ō grăf′, -gräf′), *n.* an electrocardiograph. [f. CARDIO- + GRAPH] —**cardiographic** (kä′dĭ ō grăf′ĭk), *adj.* —**cardiography** (kä′dĭ ŏg′rə fĭ), *n.*

cardioid (kä′dĭ oid′), *n. Maths.* a somewhat heart-shaped curve, being the path of a point on a circle which rolls externally, without slipping on another equal circle. [t. Gk: m. s. *kardioeidḗs* heart-shaped. See CARDIO-, -OID]

Cardioid

cardiology (kä′dĭ ŏl′ə jĭ), *n.* the study of the heart and its functions. —**car′diol′ogist,** *n.*

carditis (kä dī′tĭs), *n. Pathol.* inflammation of the pericardium, myocardium, or endocardium, separately or in combination. [f. CARD(IO)- + -ITIS]

cardoon (kä do͞on′), *n.* a perennial edible plant, *Cynara cardunculus,* native in Mediterranean regions, related to the artichoke. [t. F: m. *cardon,* t. Pr., der. L *carduus* thistle]

cardpunch (käd′pŭnch′), *n. Computers.* a machine for preparing punched cards. Also, *U.S.,* **key punch.**

card-reader (käd′rē′də), *n. Computers.* a machine which senses the holes in a punched card and transmits the information obtained to other equipment.

cardsharp (käd′shäp′), *n.* a person, esp. a professional gambler, who cheats at card games. Also, **card′sharp′er.** —**card′sharp′ing,** *n.*

carduaceous (kä′dyo͞o ā′shəs), *adj. Bot.* belonging to the subfamily *Carduaceae,* regarded as part of the *Compositae* by most botanists, and including goldenrods, asters, fleabanes, and many other genera throughout the world. [f. s. NL *Carduāceae* (der. L *carduus* thistle) + -OUS]

Carducci (*It.* kär do͞ot′chē), *n.* **Giosuè** (*It.* jô swĕ′), 1835–1907, Italian poet.

card-vote (käd′vōt′), *n.* (at trade-union conferences, etc.) a vote in which each delegate carries a number of votes according to the number of card-carrying members he represents.

care (kẽə), *n., v.,* **cared, caring.** —*n.* **1.** worry; anxiety; concern: *care had aged him.* **2.** a cause of worry, anxiety, distress, etc.: *to be free from care.* **3.** serious attention; solicitude; heed; caution: *devote great care to work.* **4.** protection; charge: *under the care of a doctor.* **5.** an object of concern or attention. **6. care of.** Also, **c/o.** at the address of. —*v.i.* **7.** to be troubled; to be affected emotionally. **8.** to be concerned or solicitous; have thought or regard. **9.** to have a liking or taste (fol. by *for*; usually with a negative): *I don't care for cabbage.* **10.** to have a fondness or affection (fol. by *for*): *he cares greatly for her.* **11.** to look after; make provision (fol. by *for*): *the welfare state must care for the needy.* **12.** to be inclined: *I don't care to do it today.* [ME; OE *caru* (*cearu*), c. Goth. *kara*]

—**Syn.** 1. See **concern.** 3. To take CARE, PAINS, TROUBLE (to do something) implies watchful, conscientious effort to do something exactly right. To take CARE implies the performance of one particular detail: *she took care to feed the dog before going out.* To take PAINS suggests a sustained carefulness, an effort to see that nothing is overlooked but that every small detail receives attention: *to take pains with fine embroidery.* To take TROUBLE implies an effort which requires a considerable amount of activity and exertion: *to take the trouble to make suitable arrangements.*

careen (kə rēn′), *v.t.* **1.** to cause (a ship) to heel over or lie wholly or partly on its side, as for repairing or the like. **2.** to clean or repair (a ship in such a position). —*v.i.* **3.** to lean, sway, or tip to one side, as a ship. **4.** to careen a ship. —*n.* **5.** a careening. **6.** the position of a careened ship. [t. F: m. *carine,* t. L: m. *carīna* keel] —**careen′age,** *n.* —**careen′er,** *n.*

career (kə rĭə′), *n.* **1.** general course of action or progress of a person through life, as in some profession, in some moral or intellectual action, etc. **2.** an occupation, profession, etc., followed as one's lifework: *a career in law.* **3.** speed; full speed. **4.** *Obs.* a charge at full speed. —*v.i.* **5.** to run or move rapidly along. [t. F: m. *carrière,* t. It.: m. *carriera,* der. *carro,* g. L *carrus.* See CAR]

careerist (kə rĭə′rĭst), *n.* one intent on self-advancement.

carefree (kẽə′frē′), *adj.* without anxiety or worry.

careful (kẽə′fəl), *adj.* **1.** cautious in one's actions. **2.** taking pains in one's work; exact; thorough. **3.** (of things) done or performed with accuracy or caution. **4.** solicitously mindful (fol. by *of, about, in*). **5.** *Colloq.* mean; parsimonious. **6.** *Archaic.* troubled. **7.** *Archaic.* attended with anxiety. —**care′fully,** *adv.* —**care′fulness,** *n.*

—**Syn.** 1. watchful, guarded, chary, circumspect. CAREFUL, CAUTIOUS, DISCREET, WARY imply a watchful guarding against something. CAREFUL implies guarding against mistakes, by paying strict and close attention to details, and often, trying to use good judgement: *he was careful to distinguish between them.* CAUTIOUS implies a fear of some unfavourable situation, and investigation before coming to conclusions: *cautious about investments.* DISCREET implies being prudent in speech and action, and being trustworthy as a confidant: *discreet in manner, in keeping secrets.* WARY implies a vigilant lookout for a danger suspected or feared: *wary of polite strangers.* 2. painstaking, meticulous. 4. solicitous, attentive, heedful, regardful.

careless (kẽə′lĭs), *adj.* **1.** not paying enough attention to what one does. **2.** not exact or thorough: *careless work.* **3.** done or said heedlessly or negligently; unconsidered: *a careless remark.* **4.** not caring or troubling; having no care or concern; unconcerned (fol. by *of, about, in*): *careless of his health, about his person, in speech.* **5.** *Archaic.* free from anxiety. —**care′lessly,** *adv.* —**care′lessness,** *n.* —**Syn. 1.** incautious, unwary, indiscreet, reckless. **2.** inaccurate, negligent.

caress (kə rĕs′), *n.* **1.** an act or gesture expressing affection, as an embrace, pat, kiss, etc. —*v.t.* **2.** to touch or pat gently to show affection. **3.** to touch, etc., as if in affection. [t. F: m. *caresse,* t. It.: m. *carezza,* der. L *cārus* dear] —**caress′er,** *n.* —**caress′ingly,** *adv.*

caret (kă′rət), *n.* a mark (‸) made in written or printed matter to show the place where something is to be inserted. [t. L: there is lacking]

caretaker (kẽə′tā′kə), *n.* **1.** a person who takes care of a thing or place, esp. one whose job is to maintain and protect a building or group of buildings. —*adj.* **2.** holding office temporarily until a new appointment, election, etc., can be made, as an administration.

Carew (kə ro͞o′), *n.* **Thomas,** *c.* 1595–*c.* 1645, English poet.

careworn (kẽə′wôn′), *adj.* showing signs of care; tired and troubled with worries: *a careworn mother.*

car ferry, a ferry for transporting motor vehicles over a river, channel, etc.

cargo (kä′gō), *n., pl.* **-goes. 1.** the lading or freight of a ship. **2.** load. [t. Sp., der. *cargar* load]

Caria (kẽə′rĭ ə), *n.* an ancient district of SW Asia Minor.

Carib (kă′rĭb), *n.* **1.** a member of an Indian people of NE South America, formerly dominant through the Lesser Antilles. **2.** an extensive linguistic stock of the West Indies and of NE South America. [t. Sp.: m. *Caribe.* See CANNIBAL] —**Car′iban,** *adj.*

Caribbean Sea

Caribbean (kă′rĭ bē′ən), *adj.* **1.** pertaining to the Caribs, the Lesser Antilles, or the Caribbean Sea. —*n.* **2.** a Carib. **3.** Also, **Caribbean Sea.** a sea between Central America, the West Indies, and South America. ab. 750,000 sq. mi.; greatest known depth, 22,788 ft. **4.** the islands collectively of the Caribbean Sea.

caribou (kă′rĭ bo͞o′), *n., pl.* **-bou.** any of several North American species or varieties of reindeer, esp. *Rangifer caribou* and *R. tarandus.* [t. Canadian F, t. Algonquian (Micmac): m. *xalibu* pawer, scratcher]

Caribou, *Rangifer caribou* (Total length 6 ft, ab. 4 ft high at the shoulder)

caricature (kă′rĭ kə tyo͞oə′), *n., v.,* **-tured, -turing.** —*n.* **1.** a picture, description, etc., ludicrously exaggerating the peculiarities or defects of persons or things. **2.** the art or process of making such pictures, etc. **3.** any imitation or copy so inferior as to be ludicrous. —*v.t.* **4.** to make a caricature of; represent in caricature. [t. F, t. It.: m. *caricatura*, der. *caricare* (over)load, exaggerate. See CHARGE, v.] —**car′icatur′ist,** *n.* —**Syn. 3.** See **burlesque.**

caries (kēə′rĭ ēz′), *n.* decay, as of bone or teeth, or of plant tissue. [t. L]

carillon (kə rĭl′yən), *n.*, *v.*, **-lonned, -lonning.** —*n.* **1.** a set of stationary bells hung in a tower and sounded by manual or pedal action, or by machinery. **2.** a melody played on such bells. **3.** an organ stop which imitates the peal of bells. **4.** a set of horizontal metal plates, struck by hammers, used in the modern orchestra. —*v.i.* **5.** to play a carillon. [t. F: chime of (orig. four) bells, alter. of OF *carignon*, ult. der. L *quattuor* four]

carillonist (kə rĭl′yə nĭst), *n.* carillonneur.

carillonneur (kə rĭl′yə nû′; *Fr.* kȧ rē yŏ nœr′), *n.* one who plays a carillon. [F]

carina (kə rī′nə), *n.*, *pl.* **-nae** (-nē). *Bot.*, *Zool.* a keel-like part or ridge. See illus. under **papilionaceous.** [t. L: keel] —**cari′nal,** *adj.*

Carina (kə rī′nə), *n.*, *gen.* **-nae** (-nē). *Astron.* a southern constellation, containing the bright star, Canopus: one of the subordinate constellations into which Argo is divided.

carinate (kăr′ĭ nāt′), *adj.* *Bot.*, *Zool.* formed with a carina; keel-like. Also, **car′inat′ed.** [t. L: m. s. *carīnātus*, pp., keel-shaped]

Carinthia (kə rĭn′thĭ ə), *n.* a province in S Austria. 495,226 pop. (1961); 3681 sq. mi. *Cap.*: Klagenfurt. German, **Kärnten.**

Carioca (kăr′ĭ ō′kə; *Port.* kȧ ryŏk′ȧ), *n.* a native of Rio de Janeiro.

cariole (kăr′ĭ ōl′), *n.* **1.** a small, open, two-wheeled vehicle. **2.** a covered cart. Also, **carriole.** [t. F: m. *carriole*, t. It.: m. *carriuola*, ult. der. L *carrus*. Cf. CARRYALL]

carious (kēə′rĭ əs), *adj.* having caries, as teeth; decayed. [t. L: m. s. *cariōsus*] —**cariosity** (kēə′rĭ ŏs′ĭ tĭ), **car′iousness,** *n.*

carking (kä′kĭng), *adj.* *Archaic.* anxious; burdensome. [ME, ppr. of *cark(en)*, t. ONF: m. *carkier*, t. LL: m. *carcāre* burden, CHARGE]

carl (käl), *n.* **1.** *Archaic.* a churl. **2.** *Archaic.* a farmer. **3.** *Obs.* a bondman. Also, **carle.** [ME and OE, t. Scand.; cf. Icel. *karl* man, c. *Charles* proper name. Cf. CHURL]

Carletonville (käl′tən vĭl), *n.* a town in the Republic of South Africa, in S Transvaal. 56,246 (1960).

carline[1] (kä′lĭn), *n.* a biennial Old World composite plant, *Carlina vulgaris*. Also, **carline thistle.** [t. ML: m. *carlina*, ? fem. m. *Carolus* Charles, ult. orig. uncert.]

carline[2] (kä′lĭn), *n.* *Chiefly Scot.* **1.** an old woman. **2.** a hag; witch. [northern ME *kerling*, t. Scand.; cf. Icel. *kerling* old woman. See CARL]

carling (kä′lĭng), *n.* one of the fore-and-aft timbers in a ship which form part of the deck framework. [var. of CARLINE [2]]

Carlisle (kä līl′), *n.* a town in NW England, in Cumberland. 71,112 (1961). See map under **Hadrian's Wall.**

Carlist (kä′lĭst), *n.* **1.** a supporter of the claims of Don Carlos of Spain, or of his successors, to the Spanish throne. **2.** a partisan of Charles X of France, and of the elder branch of the Bourbons. —**Car′lism,** *n.*

Carlos (kä′lŏs; *Sp.* kȧr′lŏs), *n.* **Don** (dŏn; *Sp.* dŏn) (*Count of Molina*), 1788–1855, Spanish prince and pretender (second son of Charles IV, King of Spain).

Carlota (*Sp.* kȧr lŏ′tȧ), 1840–1927, wife of Maximilian, Archduke of Austria: Empress of Mexico 1864–67.

Carlovingian (kä′lō vĭn′jĭ ən), *adj.* Carolingian.

Carlow (kä′lō), *n.* **1.** a county in SE Ireland, in Leinster. 33,342 pop. (1961); 346 sq. mi. **2.** its county town. 7708 (1961).

Carlsbad (kälz′băd; *Ger.* kȧrls′bȧt), *n.* a town in W Czechoslovakia: mineral springs; Carlsbad decrees, 1819. 45,000 (1965). German, **Karlsbad.** Czech, **Karlovy Vary.**

Carlyle (kä līl′), *n.* **Thomas,** 1795–1881, Scottish essayist and historian.

Carm., Carmarthenshire.

carmagnole (kä′mən yōl′; *Fr.* kȧr mȧ nyŏl′), *n.* a dance and song popular during the French Revolution. [t. F, ? from *Carmagnola*, town in NW Italy]

carman (kä′mən), *n.*, *pl.* **-men.** a carrier or member of a firm of carriers.

Carmania (kä mā′nyə), *n.* a province of the ancient Persian Empire, on the Gulf of Oman.

Carmarthen (kä mä′t͟hən), *n.* **1.** a town in Wales, the county town of Carmarthenshire. 13,247 (1961). **2.** Carmarthenshire.

Carmarthenshire (kä mä′t͟hən shĭə′, -shə), *n.* a county in S Wales. 167,736 pop. (1961); 919 sq. mi. *Co. town:* Carmarthen. *Abbrev.:* Carm. Also, **Carmarthen.**

Carmel (kä′məl), *n.* **Mount,** a ridge in NW Israel, near the Mediterranean coast. ab. 14 mi. long; highest point, ab. 1800 ft.

Carmelite (kä′mə līt′), *n.* **1.** a mendicant friar belonging to a religious order founded at Mount Carmel in the 12th century; a White Friar. **2.** a nun belonging to this order. [t. LL: m. *Carmēlītēs*, t. Gk: m. *Karmēlítēs* inhabitant of Mt Carmel]

Carmichael (kä mī′kl), *n.* **Stokely** (stōk′lĭ), born 1941, U.S. Negro leader, born in Trinidad.

carminative (kä′mĭ nə tĭv), *n.* **1.** a drug causing expulsion of gas from the stomach or bowel. —*adj.* **2.** expelling gas from the body; relieving flatulence. [f. s. L *carminātus*, pp., carded + -IVE]

carmine (kä′mīn), *n.* **1.** a crimson or purplish red colour. **2.** a crimson pigment obtained from cochineal. —*adj.* **3.** crimson or purplish red. [t. ML: m. s. *carmīnus*, contr. of *carmesīnus*, der. Sp. *carmesí* CRIMSON]

carnage (kä′nĭj), *n.* **1.** the slaughter of a great number, as in battle; butchery; massacre. **2.** *Archaic.* dead bodies, as of men slain in battle. [t. F, t. It.: m. *carnaggio*, der. *carne* meat, g. s. L *caro* flesh]

carnal (kä′nəl), *adj.* **1.** not spiritual; merely human; temporal; worldly. **2.** pertaining to the flesh or the body, its passions and appetites; sensual. **3.** sexual. [ME, t. L: s. *carnālis*, der. L *caro* flesh] —**carnality** (kä năl′ĭ tĭ), *n.* —**car′nally,** *adv.* —**Syn. 2.** fleshly, bodily, animal. **3.** lustful, impure, gross, worldly.

carnallite (kä′nə līt′), *n.* a mineral, a hydrous potassium magnesium chloride, $KMgCl_3.6H_2O$: a valuable source of potassium. [named after R. von *Carnall*, 1804–74, Prussian mining official. See -ITE[1]]

Carnarvon (kä nä′vən), *n.* Caernarvon.

carnassial (kä năs′ĭ əl), *Zool.* —*adj.* **1.** (of teeth) adapted for shearing flesh, as certain of the upper and lower cheek teeth of cats, dogs, etc. —*n.* **2.** a carnassial tooth, esp. the last upper premolar or the first lower molar tooth of certain carnivores. [f. m. F *carnassier* flesh-eating (t. Pr.: m. *carnasier*, der. L *caro* flesh) + -AL[1]]

Carnatic (kä năt′ĭk), *n.* a historically important region on the SE coast of India: now in Madras state.

carnation (kä nā′shən), *n.* **1.** any of numerous cultivated varieties of clove pink, *Dianthus caryophyllus*, with fragrant flowers of various colours. **2.** pink; light red. **3.** the colours of flesh as represented in painting. —*adj.* **4.** coloured a light red. [t. L: s. *carnātio* fleshiness, NL representation of flesh in painting]

carnauba (kä nou′bə), *n.* **1.** the Brazilian wax-palm, *Copernicia cerifera*. **2.** a yellowish or greenish wax derived from the young leaves of this tree, used as a polish. [t. Brazilian Pg.]

Carnegie (kä nā′gĭ, -nĕg′ĭ), *n.* **Andrew,** 1835–1919, U.S. steel manufacturer and philanthropist, born in Scotland.

carnelian (kä nē′lyən), *n.* cornelian. [alter. (due to assoc. with L *caro* flesh) of CORNELIAN]

carnet (kä′nā; *Fr.* kȧr nĕ′), *n.* a customs licence for the temporary importation of a motor vehicle.

carnival (kä′nĭ vəl), *n.* **1.** revelry and merrymaking, usually riotous and noisy, and accompanied by processions, etc. **2.** a festive procession. **3.** a fair or amusement show, esp. one erected temporarily for a period of organized merrymaking. **4.** a period set aside for riotous merrymaking, esp. the season immediately preceding Lent. [t. It.: m. *carnevale*, alter. of *carnesciale*, der. *carnescialare*, *carnelasciare* leave off (eating) meat]

carnivore (kä′nĭ vô′), *n.* **1.** *Zool.* one of the *Carnivora*, the order of mammals, chiefly flesh-eating, that includes the cats, dogs, bears, seals, etc. **2.** *Bot.* a flesh-eating plant. [see CARNIVOROUS]

carnivorous (kä nĭv′ə rəs), *adj.* flesh-eating. [t. L: m. *carnivorus*] —**carniv′orously,** *adv.* —**carniv′orousness,** *n.*

Carnot (*Fr.* kȧr nō′), *n.* **1. Lazare Nicolas Marguerite** (*Fr.* lȧ zȧr nē kŏ lȧ mȧr gə rĕt′), 1753–1823, French general and statesman. **2.** his son, **Nicolas Léonard Sadi** (*Fr.* nē kŏ lȧ lė ŏ nȧr sȧ dē′), 1796–1832, French physicist.

Carnot cycle (kä′nō), a cycle of engine operations giving the maximum thermal efficiency obtainable by an engine working between any two temperatures. [named after N. L. S. CARNOT]

carnotite (kä′nə tīt′), *n.* a mineral, a yellow, earthy, hydrous potassium uranium vanadate: an ore of uranium. [named after A. *Carnot*, died 1920, French inspector general of mines. See -ITE[1]]

Carnot principle, *Physics.* the law which states that the efficiency of any reversible heat engine depends only on the range of temperature through which it works, and not on any of the properties of the materials used. [named after N. L. S. CARNOT]

Carnsore Point (kän′sô), the SE tip of Ireland, in Co. Wexford.

carob (kă′rəb), *n.* **1.** the fruit of a caesalpiniaceous tree, *Ceratonia siliqua*, of the Mediterranean regions, a long, dry pod containing hard seeds in a sweet pulp, used for feeding animals and sometimes eaten by man. **2.** the tree. [t. F: m. *carobe*, t. Ar.: m. *kharrūba*]

caroche (kə rōsh′), *n.* an old form of stately coach or carriage. [t. F (obs.): m. *carroche*, t. It.: m. *carroccio*, aug. of *carro* chariot, g. L *carrus*; akin to CAR]

carol (kă′rəl), *n.*, *v.*, **-rolled, -rolling** or (*U.S.*) **-roled, -roling. 1.** a song, esp. of joy. **2.** a Christmas song or hymn. **3.** *Obs.* a kind of circular dance. —*v.i.* **4.** to sing, esp. in a lively, joyous manner; warble. —*v.t.* **5.** to sing joyously. **6.** to praise or celebrate in song. [ME, t. OF: m. *carole*; prob. from Celtic root *cor-* circle, b. with L *choraula* minstrel, chorus leader, t. Gk: m. *choraúlēs*] —**car′oller,** *n.*

Carolean (kă′rə lē′ən), *adj.* Caroline.

Carolina (kă′rə lī′nə), *n.* **1.** a former English colony on the Atlantic coast of North America: officially divided into North Carolina and South Carolina, 1729. **2. the Carolinas,** North Carolina and South Carolina.

Carolina rice, a short-grained, unpolished rice used for sweet dishes and puddings.

Caroline (kă′rə līn′), *adj.* **1.** of or pertaining to the time of Charles I or Charles II: *Caroline drama.* **2.** of or pertaining to any other Charles, Charlemagne, etc.

Caroline Islands, a group of over 500 islands in the Pacific, E of the Philippine Islands: formerly a Japanese mandate; now under U.S. administration. 59,735 pop. (1964); 525 sq. mi.

Caroline Islands

Carolingian (kă′rə lĭn′jĭ ən), *adj.* belonging to the Frankish dynasty which reigned in France from A.D. 751 until A.D. 987 and in Germany until A.D. 911. Also, **Carlovingian.** [f. s. ML *Carolingī* (Latinized pl. of OG *Karling* descendant of *Karl*) + -IAN] —**Car′olin′gian,** *n.*

Carolinian (kă′rə lĭn′ĭ ən), *adj.* **1.** of or pertaining to North and South Carolina or to either one of them. **2.** Carolingian. **3.** Caroline. —*n.* **4.** a native or inhabitant of North or South Carolina.

carolus (kă′rə ləs), *n.*, *pl.* **-luses, -li** (-lī′). any of various coins issued under monarchs named Charles, esp. an English gold coin struck in the reign of Charles I, orig. worth 20 and later 23 shillings. [t. ML: Charles]

carom (kă′rəm), *n.* **1.** cannon (def. 9 and 10). —*v.i.* **2.** cannon (def. 12 and 13). Also, **carrom.** [earlier *carambole*, t. F, t. Sp.: m. *carambola*; special use of *carambola* CARAMBOLA (the fruit)]

Caro's acid (kä′rō, kă′rō), *Chem.* persulphuric acid (def. 1). [named after N. *Caro*, 1871–1935, German chemist]

carotene (kă′rə tēn′), *n.* *Chem.* any of three isomeric red hydrocarbons, $C_{40}H_{56}$, found in many plants, esp. carrots, and transformed to vitamin A in the liver. Also, **carotin** (kă′rə tĭn). [f. s. L *carota* CARROT + -ENE]

carotenoid (kə rŏt′ĭ noid′), *Chem.* —*n.* **1.** any of a group of red and yellow pigments, chemically similar to carotene, contained in animal fat and some plants. —*adj.* **2.** similar to carotene. **3.** pertaining to carotenoids. Also, **carotinoid.** [f. CAROTENE + -OID]

carotid (kə rŏt′ĭd), *Anat.* —*n.* **1.** either of the two great arteries, one on each side of the neck, which carry blood to the head. —*adj.* **2.** pertaining to the carotids. [t. Gk: s. *karōtídes*, pl., der. *káros* stupor (thought to be caused by compression of these arteries)] —**carot′idal,** *adj.*

carousal (kə rou′zəl), *n.* a noisy or drunken feast or other social gathering; jovial revelry. [f. CAROUSE, v. + -AL[2]]

carouse (kə rouz′), *n.*, *v.*, **-roused, -rousing.** —*n.* **1.** a noisy or drunken feast; jovial revelry. —*v.i.* **2.** to engage in a carouse; drink deeply. [n. and v. uses of obs. adv., t. G: m. *gar aus* (drink a cup) wholly out]

carousel (kă′rōō zĕl′, -sĕl′), *n.* carrousel.

carp[1] (käp), *v.i.* to find fault; cavil; complain unreasonably: *to carp at minor errors.* [ME *carpe(n)*, t. Scand.; cf. Icel *karpa* wrangle, dispute] —**carp′er,** *n.* —**carp′ingly,** *adv.*

carp[2] (käp), *n.*, *pl.* **carp. 1.** a large, coarse freshwater food fish, *Cyprinus carpio* (family *Cyprinidae*), commonly bred in ponds. **2.** any of various other fishes of the same family. [ME *carpe*, t. OF, t. Pr.: m. *carpa*, g. LL *carpa*; of Gmc orig.]

-carp, a noun termination meaning 'fruit', used in botanical terms, as *endocarp.* [comb. form repr. Gk *karpós*]

carp., carpentry.

carpal (kä′pl), *Anat.* —*adj.* **1.** pertaining to the carpus: *the carpal joint.* —*n.* **2.** a carpale. [t. NL: s. *carpālis*, der. L *carpus* wrist]

carpale (kä pā′lĭ), *n.*, *pl.* **-lia** (-lĭ ə). *Anat.* any of the bones of the wrist. Also, **carpal.** [t. NL, neut. of *carpālis* CARPAL]

car park, a place, usually in the open air, where cars may be parked.

Carpathian Mountains (kä pā′thyən), a mountain system in central Europe, extending to ab. 800 mi. from N Czechoslovakia to central Rumania. Highest peak, Gerlachovka, 8737 ft. Also, **Carpathians.** See map under **Walachia.**

Carpatho-Ukraine (kä pā′thō yōō krān′), *n.* a region in the SW Soviet Union, in the Ukrainian Republic: ceded by Czechoslovakia, 1945. 4871 sq. mi. Formerly, **Ruthenia** or **Carpathian Ruthenia.**

carpe diem (kä′pĭ dē′ĕm), *Latin.* enjoy the present day (trusting as little as possible to the future).

carpel (kä′pl), *n.* *Bot.* a simple pistil, or a single member of a compound pistil: regarded as a modified leaf. [t. NL: m. s. *carpellum.* der. Gk *karpós* fruit]

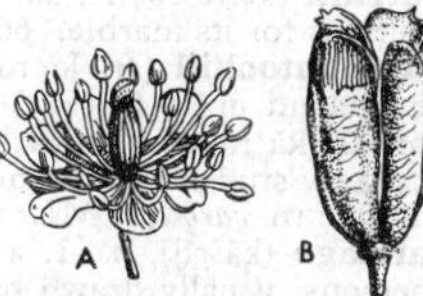

Carpels
A, Flower with simple pistils; B, Tricarpellary fruit

carpellary (kä′pĭ lə rĭ), *adj.* *Bot.* forming part of or arising from a carpel.

carpellate (kä′pĭ lāt′), *adj.* *Bot.* (of a flower) having carpels (opposed to *staminate*).

Carpentaria (kä′pən tĕə′rĭ ə), *n.* **Gulf of,** a large gulf on the N coast of Australia. ab. 420 mi. wide; ab. 480 mi. long.

carpenter (kä′pĭn tə), *n.* **1.** a workman who erects and fixes the wooden parts, etc., in the building of houses and other structures. **2.** *U.S.* a joiner. —*v.i.* **3.** to do carpenter's work. —*v.t.* **4.** to make by carpentry. [ME, t. ONF: m. *carpentier*, g. LL *carpentārius* wagon-maker, der. L *carpentum* wagon] —**car′pentry,** *n.*

carpenter bee, any of various solitary bees of the family *Xylocopidae* that make their nests in wood, boring tunnels in which to deposit their eggs.

carpet (kä′pĭt), *n.* **1.** a heavy fabric, commonly of wool, for covering floors. **2.** a covering of this material. **3.** any covering like a carpet: *they walked on the grassy carpet.* **4. on the carpet, a.** under consideration or discussion. **b.** before an authority for a reprimand. —*v.t.* **5.** to cover or furnish with, or as with, a carpet. **6.** *Colloq.* to reprimand. [ME *carpete*, t. ML: m. *carpeta*, ult. der. L *carpere* card (wool)]

carpetbag (kä′pĭt băg′), *n.* a bag for travelling, esp. one made of carpeting.

carpetbagger (kä′pĭt băg′ə), *n.* **1.** a person who takes up residence in a place, with no more property than he brings in a carpetbag, to seek special advantages for himself. **2.** (in U.S. history) (contemptuously) a Northerner who went to the South after the Civil War to seek political or other advantages made possible by the disorganized condition of political affairs.

carpet bedding, *Hort.* a system of planting flowers so that they produce a carpet-like pattern.

carpet beetle, a small beetle, *Anthrenus scrophulariae*, whose larvae are destructive to carpets and other woollen fabrics.

carpeting (kä′pĭ tĭng), *n.* **1.** material for carpets. **2.** carpets in general.

carpet slipper, one of a pair of soft slippers, usually with woollen uppers.

carpet snake, a large non-venomous snake of Australia, *Morelia variegata.*

carpet-sweeper (kä′pĭt swē′pə), *n.* a device for sweeping carpets, with a revolving brush, etc.

carpi (kä′pī), *n.* pl. of **carpus.**

-carpic, a word element related to **-carp,** as in *endocarpic.* [f. -CARP + -IC]

carpo-, a word element meaning 'fruit' as in *carpology.* [t. Gk: m. *karpo-*, comb. form of *karpós*]

carpogonium (kä′pə gō′nyəm), *n.*, *pl.* **-nia** (-nyə). *Bot.* the one-celled female sex organ of the red algae (*Rhodophyceae*) which, when fertilized, gives rise to the carpospores. [NL; see CARPO-, -GONIUM] —**car′pogo′nial,** *adj.*

carpology (kä pŏl′ə jĭ), *n.* the branch of botany that relates to fruits. —**carpological** (kä′pə lŏj′ĭ kl), *adj.* —**carpol′ogist,** *n.*

carpophagous (kä pŏf′ə gəs), *adj.* fruit-eating.

carpophore (kä′pə fô′), *n.* *Bot.* **1.** a slender pro-

A, Carpophore; B, Carpels

ăct, āble, ärt; ĕbb, ēqual; ĭf, īce; hŏt, ōver, ôrder, oil, bŏŏk, ōōze, out; ŭp, ûrge; ə = a in alone; ch, chief; g, give; ng, ring; sh, shoe; th, thin; ŧh, that; y, young; zh, vision. See full key on inside front cover.

longation of the floral axis, bearing the carpels of some compound fruits, as in the geranium and in many umbelliferous plants. **2.** the fruit body of the higher fungi.

carport (kä′pôt′), *n.* a roofed wall-less shed projecting from the side of a building, used as a shelter for a motor vehicle.

carpospore (kä′pə spô′), *n. Bot.* a non-motile spore of the red algae.

-carpous, a combining form related to **-carp,** as in *apocarpous.* [f. - CARP + - OUS]

carpus (kä′pəs), *n., pl.* **-pi** (-pī). *Anat.* the wrist, or the eight bones comprising it: the scaphoid, lunate, triquetral, pisiform, trapezoid, capitate, and hamate bones.

carrack (kă′rək), *n. Archaic.* a galleon. [ME *caracke,* t. OF: m. *carraque,* t. Sp., Pg.: m. *carraca,* t. Ar.: m. *qarāqīr,* pl. of *qurqūr* merchant vessel; or m. *harraqa* boat]

carrageen (kă′rə gēn′, kă′rə gēn′), *n.* Irish moss (def. 1). Also, **carragheen.** [named after *Carragheen,* in S Ireland]

Carrara (kə rä′rə; *It.* kär rä′ra), *n.* a town in NW Italy: famous for its marble. 66,743 (1966).

Carrauntoohill (*Ir.* kə rôn′tōō′əl), *n.* the highest peak in Ireland, in Co. Kerry. 3414 ft. Also, **Carrantuohill.**

carrel (kă′rəl), *n.* (in a library) a small area or cubicle used by students and others for individual study; a stall. [t. OF: m. *carole,* t. ML: m. *carola*]

carriage (kă′rij), *n.* **1.** a wheeled vehicle for conveying persons, usually drawn by horses, esp. one designed for comfort and elegance. **2.** *Railways.* a passenger-carrying vehicle unit. **3.** a wheeled support, as for a cannon. **4.** a part, as of a machine, designed for carrying something. **5.** manner of carrying the head and body; bearing: *the carriage of a soldier.* **6.** the act of transporting; conveyance: *the expenses of carriage.* **7.** the price or cost of conveyance. [ME *cariage,* t. ONF, der. *carier.* See CARRY] **—Syn. 5.** deportment.

carriageway (kă′rij wā′), *n.* that part of a road which carries vehicles.

carrick bend (kă′rik), *Naut.* a kind of knot for joining cables or hawsers. See illus. under **knot.** [*carrick* ? var. of CARRACK]

carrick bitt, *Naut.* one of the bitts which support the windlass.

carrier (kă′rĭ ə), *n.* **1.** a person or thing that carries. **2.** a person, company, etc., that undertakes to convey goods or persons for hire. **3.** *Mach.* a mechanism by which something is carried or moved. **4.** *Med.* an individual harbouring specific organisms, who, though often immune to the agent harboured, may transmit the disease to others. **5.** *Chem.* a catalytic agent which brings about a transfer of an element or group of atoms from one compound to another. **6.** *Radio.* **a.** Also, **carrier wave.** a wave whose amplitude, frequency, or phase is varied or modulated in order to transmit a signal. **b.** the mobile electrons or holes which carry the current in a semiconductor. **7.** *Physics, Biol.* an element which is added to radioactive isotopes of the same, or an analogous, element in order to provide sufficient material for a full-scale chemical or biological process to be followed. **8.** an aircraft-carrier. **9.** a carrier pigeon.

carrier bag, a bag made of strong paper, with string or paper handles.

carrier pigeon, 1. a pigeon trained to fly home from great distances and thus transport written messages; a homing pigeon. **2.** one of a breed of domestic pigeons characterized by a huge wattle at the base of the beak.

carriole (kă′rĭ ōl′), *n.* cariole.

carrion (kă′rĭ ən), *n.* **1.** dead and putrefying flesh. **2.** rottenness; anything vile. *—adj.* **3.** feeding on carrion. **4.** of or like carrion. [ME *carion, caroine,* t. ONF, var. of central OF *charoigne,* ult. der. L *caro* flesh]

carrion crow, 1. any of various crows, as the common European crow, *Corvus corone.* **2.** a black vulture, *Coragypo atratus,* of the southern U.S., etc.

carrion flower, any plant with fetid-smelling flowers which attract carrion flies, esp. members of the genera *Amorphophallus* and *Stapelia.*

Carroll (kă′rəl), *n.* **Lewis** (*Charles Lutwidge Dodgson*), 1832–98, English writer and mathematician.

carrom (kă′rəm), *n., v.i.,* carom.

carromata (kă′rə mä′tə), *n.* (in the Philippines) a light, two-wheeled covered vehicle, usually drawn by one horse. [t. Sp.: m. *carromato,* der. *carro* cart, g. L *carrus*]

carronade (kă′rə nād′), *n.* a short piece of muzzle-loading ordnance, formerly in use, esp. in ships. [der. *Carron* (Scotland), site of a cannon foundry]

carron oil (kă′rən), *Pharm.* a liniment containing lime-water and oil, formerly used for burns.

carrot (kă′rət), *n.* **1.** a plant of the umbelliferous genus *Daucus,* esp. *D. carota,* in its wild form a widespread, familiar weed, and in cultivation valued for its reddish edible root. **2.** the root. [t. F: m. *carotte,* t. L: m. s. *carōta,* t. Gk: m. *karōtón*]

carroty (kă′rə tĭ), *adj.* **1.** like a carrot root in colour; yellowish red. **2.** having red hair.

carrousel (kă′rōō zĕl′, -sĕl′), *n.* **1.** a merry-go-round (def. 1). **2.** a tournament in which horsemen executed various manoeuvres in formation. Also, **carousel.** [t. F, t. It.: m. *carosello,* der. *carro,* g. L *carrus* cart]

carry (kă′rĭ), *v.,* **-ried, -rying,** *n. pl.* **-ries.** *—v.t.* **1.** to convey from one place to another in a vehicle, ship, pocket, hand, etc. **2.** to transmit or transfer in any manner; take or bring: *the wind carries sounds, he carries his audience with him.* **3.** to bear the weight, burden, etc., of; sustain. **4.** to take a (leading or guiding part) in acting or singing; bear or sustain (a part or melody). **5.** to hold (the body, head, etc.) in a certain manner. **6.** to behave or comport (oneself). **7.** to take, esp. by force; capture; win. **8.** to secure the election of (a candidate) or the adoption of (a motion or bill). **9.** to print or publish in a newspaper or magazine. **10.** to extend or continue in a given direction or to a certain point: *to carry the war into enemy territory.* **11.** to lead or impel; conduct. **12.** to have as an attribute, property, consequence, etc.: *his opinion carries great weight.* **13** to support or give validity to (a related claim, etc.): *one decision carries another.* **14.** *Maths.* to transfer (a number) from one column to the next, as from units to tens, tens to hundreds, etc. **15.** *Com.* **a.** to keep on hand or in stock. **b.** to keep on one's account books, etc. **16.** to bear as a crop. **17.** to be pregnant with: *she is carrying her fifth child.* **18.** to support (cattle): *our grain supply will carry the cattle through the winter.* **19.** *Golf.* to advance beyond or go by (an object or expanse) with one stroke. **20.** *Hunting.* to retain and pursue (a scent). **21.** *Ice Hockey.* to move (the puck) along the ice; dribble. *—v.i.* **22.** to act as a bearer or conductor. **23.** to have or exert propelling force: *the rifle carries almost a mile.* **24.** to be transmitted, propelled, or sustained: *my voice carries farther than his.* **25.** to bear the head in a particular manner, as a horse.

—v. **26.** Some special verb phrases are:

carry away, to influence greatly or beyond reason.

carry forward, 1. to make progress with. **2.** *Bookkeeping.* to transfer (an amount, etc.) to the next column, page, etc.

carry off, 1. to win (the prize, honour, etc.). **2.** to face consequences boldly: *he carried it off well.* **3.** to cause the death of.

carry on, 1. to manage; conduct. **2.** to behave in an excited, foolish, or improper manner; flirt. **3.** to have a love affair (*with*). **4.** to continue; keep up without stopping.

carry out, to accomplish or complete (a plan, scheme, etc.): *to carry out the details of his plan.*

carry over, 1. to postpone; hold off until later. **2.** *Stock Exchange.* to defer completion of (a contract) so that it falls under a different account.

carry through, 1. to accomplish; complete. **2.** to support or help (in a difficult situation, etc.).

—n. **27.** range, as of a gun. **28.** *Golf.* the distance traversed by a ball before it alights. **29.** land separating navigable waters, over which a canoe or boat must be carried; a portage. **30.** a carrying. [ME *carie(n),* t. ONF: m. *carier,* g. LL *carricāre* convey by wagon, der. L *carrus.* See CAR]

—Syn. 1. CARRY, CONVEY, TRANSPORT, TRANSMIT, imply taking or sending something from one place to another. CARRY means to take by means of the hands, of a vehicle, etc.: *to carry a book.* CONVEY is a more formal word, suggesting a means of taking, but not any particular method of taking; it is also used figuratively: *to convey wheat to market, a message of sympathy.* TRANSPORT means to carry or convey goods, now usually by vehicle or vessel: *to transport milk to customers.* TRANSMIT implies chiefly sending or transferring messages, hereditary tendencies, etc.: *to transmit a telegram.*

carryall (kă′rĭ ôl′), *n. U.S.* **1.** a one-horse family carriage. **2.** a closed motor car having two passenger benches. **3.** a holdall. [f. CARRY + ALL; r. CARIOLE by pop. etym.]

carrycot (kă′rĭ kŏt′), *n.* the portable body of a light pram or cot, usually of canvas, with handles, sometimes considered together with its four-wheeled frame.

carry-on (kă′rĭ ŏn′), *n. Colloq.* foolish or unconventional behaviour or events. Also, **car′ryings-on′.**

carry-over (kă′rĭ ō′və), *n.* **1.** the part left over to a later period, account, etc. **2.** *Bookkeeping.* the total of one page on an account carried forward to the next. **3.** *Stock Exchange.* the practice of deferring completion of a contract from one account to another.

Carshalton (kə shôl′tən), *n.* a district of the S outer London borough of Sutton.

carsick (kä′sĭk′), *adj.* nauseated by the motion of a motor vehicle.

Carson (kä′sən), *n.* **1. Christopher** (‘*Kit*’), 1809–68, U.S. frontiersman and scout. **2. Sir Edward Henry** (*Baron Carson*), 1854–1935, British public official, born in Ireland.

Carson City, a city in the U.S., the capital of Nevada, in the W part. 5163 (1960).

cart (kät), *n.* **1.** a heavy vehicle, usually with solid tyres and made chiefly of wood, without springs, for the conveyance of heavy goods. **2.** a light two-wheeled vehicle with springs, used for business or pleasure. **3.** any small vehicle moved by hand. **4. in the cart,** *Slang.* in an awkward or unpleasant predicament. **5. put the cart before the horse, a.** to reverse the natural order. **b.** to confuse cause and effect. *—v.t.* **6.** to convey in or as in a cart. [metathetic var. of OE *cræt,* c. Icel *kartr*] **—cart′er,** *n.*

cartage (kä′tĭj), *n.* the act or cost of carting.

Cartagena (kä′tə jē′nə; *Sp.* kȧr tȧ KHĕ′nȧ), *n.* **1.** a seaport in SE Spain. 131,101 (1965). **2.** a seaport in N Colombia. 242,085 (1964).

carte[1] (kät; *Fr.* kȧrt), *n. Fencing.* quarte. [t. F: m. *quarte,* t. It.: m. *quarta* fourth]

carte[2] (kät; *Fr.* kȧrt), *n.* **1.** menu. Cf. **à la carte. 2.** *Now Rare or Obs.* a playing card. **3.** *Obs.* a map or chart. [t. F. See CARD[1]]

Carte (kät), *n.* **Richard D'Oyly** (doi′lĭ), 1844–1901, English theatrical producer, chiefly associated with Gilbert and Sullivan.

carte blanche (kät′blänch′; *Fr.* kȧrt bläNsh′), *pl.* **cartes blanches** (käts′blänch′; *Fr.* kȧrt bläNsh′). *French.* **1.** a signed paper left blank for the person to whom it is given to fill in his own conditions. **2.** unconditional authority; full power.

cartel (kä tel′), *n.* **1.** an international syndicate, combine, or trust generally formed to regulate prices and output in some field of business. **2.** a written agreement between belligerents, esp. for the exchange of prisoners. **3.** (*often cap.*) (in French or Belgian politics) a group acting as a unit towards a common goal. **4.** *Hist.* a challenge to single combat. [t. F, t. It.: m. *cartello,* dim. of *carta,* g. L *charta* paper. See CHART]

cartelize (kä′tə līz′), *v.i., v.t.,* **-lized, -lizing.** to organize into a cartel (def. 1). Also, **cartelise.** **—car′teliza′tion,** *n.*

Carter (kä′tə), *n.* **Howard,** 1873–1939, English Egyptologist.

Carteret (kä′tə rĭt), *n.* **John** (*Earl Granville*), 1690–1763, English statesman.

Cartesian (kä tē′zyən), *adj.* **1.** pertaining to Descartes, to his mathematical methods, or to his dualistic philosophy which began with the famous phrase *Cogito, ergo sum* (I think, therefore I am), saw physical nature mechanically, and in science emphasized rationalism and logic. *—n.* **2.** a believer in the philosophy of Descartes. [t. NL: s. *Cartesiānus,* der. *Cartesius,* Latinized form of the name of René DESCARTES] **—Carte′sianism,** *n.*

Cartesian coordinates, *Maths.* the coordinates of a point in a plane (or in a space) defined by the perpendicular distances of the point from two (or three) intersecting axes which are at right angles to each other.

Carthage (kä′thĭj), *n.* an ancient city-state in N Africa, near modern Tunis: destroyed by the Romans, 146 B.C. —**Carthaginian** (kä′thə jĭn′-yən), *adj., n.*

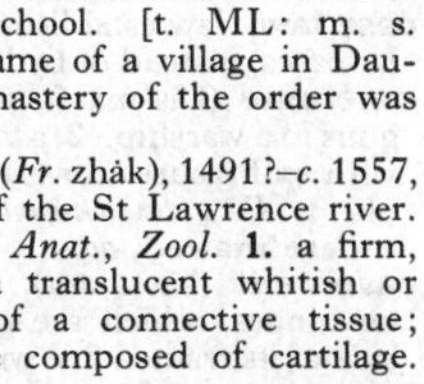

Carthage

carthorse (kät′hôs′), *n.* a large, extremely powerful kind of horse, used for heavy work.

Carthusian (kä thyōō′zyən), *n.* **1.** *Rom. Cath. Ch.* a member of an austere monastic order founded by St Bruno in 1086 near Grenoble, France. **2.** a pupil or former pupil of Charterhouse School. *—adj.* **3.** belonging to the Carthusian order. **4.** of or pertaining to Charterhouse School. [t. ML: m. s. *Cartusiānus,* der. *Chatrousse,* name of a village in Dauphiné near which the first monastery of the order was built]

Cartier (*Fr.* kȧr tyė′), *n.* **Jacques** (*Fr.* zhȧk), 1491?–*c.* 1557, French navigator: discoverer of the St Lawrence river.

cartilage (kä′tĭ lĭj, kät′lĭj), *n. Anat., Zool.* **1.** a firm, elastic, flexible substance of a translucent whitish or yellowish colour, consisting of a connective tissue; gristle. **2.** a part or structure composed of cartilage. [t. F, t. L: m. *cartilāgo* gristle]

cartilage bone, a bone that is developed from cartilage (distinguished from *membrane bone*).

cartilaginous (kä′tĭ lăj′ĭ nəs), *adj.* **1.** of or resembling cartilage. **2.** *Zool.* having the skeleton composed mostly of cartilage, as sharks and rays.

cartload (kät′lōd′), *n.* **1.** the amount a cart can hold. **2.** *Bldg Trades.* any amount between ¼ and ½ a cubic yard.

cartog., cartography.

cartogram (kä′tə grăm′), *n.* a diagrammatic presentation in highly abstracted or simplified form, commonly of statistical data, on a map base or distorted map base. [t. F: m. *cartogramme.* See CARD[1], -GRAM]

cartography (kä tŏg′rə fĭ), *n.* the production of maps, including construction of projections, design, compilation, drafting, and reproduction. Also, **chartography.** [f. *carto-* (comb. form of ML *carta* chart, map) + -GRAPHY] **—cartog′rapher,** *n.* **—cartographic** (kä′-tə grăf′ĭk), **car′tograph′ical,** *adj.* **—car′tograph′ically,** *adv.*

cartomancy (kä′tə măn′sĭ), *n.* divination by cards, whether a standard pack or a special one such as the tarot pack.

carton (kä′tn), *n.* **1.** a cardboard box. **2.** *Archery.* the white disc at the centre of a target. **3.** *Archery.* a shot which strikes the carton. [t. F. See CARTOON]

cartoon (kä tōōn′), *n.* **1.** a sketch or drawing as in a newspaper or periodical, symbolizing or caricaturing some subject or person of current interest, in an exaggerated way. **2.** *Art.* a drawing, of the same size as a proposed decoration or pattern in fresco, mosaic, tapestry, etc., for which it serves as a model to be transferred or copied. **3.** a comic strip. **4.** an animated cartoon. *—v.t.* **5.** to represent by a cartoon. [t. F: m. *carton,* t. It.: m. *cartone* pasteboard, cartoon, aug. of *carta,* g. L *charta* paper. See CHART] **—cartoon′ist,** *n.*

cartouche (kä tōōsh′), *n.* **1.** *Archit.* a French Renaissance motif, usually an oval tablet with ornamental scrollwork. **2.** an oval or oblong figure, as on ancient Egyptian monuments, enclosing characters which express royal names. **3.** the case containing the inflammable materials in certain fireworks. **4.** cartridge (def. 1). **5.** a box for cartridges. Also, **cartouch.** [t. F, t. It.: m. *cartoccio,* aug. of *carta,* g. L *charta* paper. See CHART]

cartridge (kä′trĭj), *n.* **1.** Also, **cartridge case.** a cylindrical case of pasteboard, metal, or the like, for holding a complete charge of powder, and often also the bullet or the shot, for a rifle, machine-gun, or other small arm. **2.** the case, charge, and bullet or shot; a round (def. 31). **3.** a case containing any explosive charge, as for blasting. **4.** anything resembling a cartridge, as the disposable container of ink for some types of fountain pen. **5.** a pick-up (def. 8). [m. CARTOUCHE]

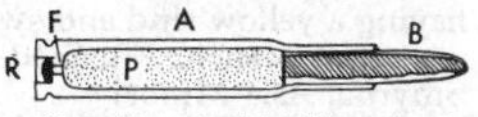

Cartridge: A, Metallic case of copper or brass; B, Bullet; R, Primer; F, Fulminate; P, Powder

cartridge belt, a belt (def. 7b) for ammunition with loops for cartridges or pockets for clips of cartridges.

cartridge clip, a metal frame or container holding cartridges for a magazine rifle or automatic pistol; clip.

cartridge paper, an uncoated type of drawing or printing paper, normally made from a bleached sulphate woodpulp, often with a percentage addition of esparto grass.

cartulary (kä′tyŏŏ lə rĭ), *n., pl.* **-ries.** a register of charters, title deeds, etc. Also, **chartulary.** [t. ML: m. s. *c(h)artulārium,* der. L *c(h)artula.* See CHARTER]

cartwheel (kät′wēl′), *n.* **1.** the wheel of a cart, usually large, wooden, with spokes and metal tyres. **2.** a somersault performed sideways, with legs and arms outstretched.

cartwright (kät′rīt′), *n.* a maker of carts, etc.

Cartwright (kät′rīt′), *n.* **Edmund,** 1743–1823, English clergyman: inventor of the power-driven loom.

caruncle (kă′rəng kl, kə rŭng′-), *n.* **1.** *Bot.* a protuberance at or surrounding the hilum of a seed. **2.** *Zool.* a fleshy excrescence, as on the head of a bird; a fowl's comb. [t. L: m. s. *caruncula,* dim. of *caro* flesh] **—caruncular** (kə rŭng′kyŏŏ lə), **carun′culous,** *adj.*

carunculate (kə rŭng′kyŏŏ lĭt, -lāt′), *adj.* having a caruncle or caruncles. Also, **carun′culat′ed.**

Caruso (kə rōō′sō; *It.* kȧ rōō′sȯ), *n.* **Enrico** (*It.* ėn rē′ko), 1873–1921, Italian operatic tenor.

carve (käv), *v.,* **carved, carving.** *—v.t.* **1.** to fashion by cutting: *to carve a block of stone into a statue.* **2.** to produce by cutting: *to carve a design in wood.* **3.** to cut into slices or pieces, as meat. **4.** to make or establish for oneself by one's own efforts (often fol. by *out*). **5.** *Slang.* to slash (a person) with a knife or razor (fol. by *up*). **6.** *Slang.* to cause (the driver of another vehicle) to swerve or slow suddenly to avoid collision (fol. by *up*). *—v.i.* **7.** to decorate by cutting figures, designs, etc. **8.** to cut meat. [ME *kerve(n),* OE *ceorfan* cut, c. G *Kerben* notch; akin to Gk *gráphein* mark, write] **—carv′er,** *n.*

carvel (kä′vəl), *n.* caravel.

carvel-built (kä′vəl bĭlt′), *adj.* (of a ship) built with the planks flush, not overlapping. Cf. **clinker-built.**

carven (kä′vən), *adj. Poetic.* carved.

Carver (kä′və), *n.* **1. George Washington,** *c.* 1864–1943, U.S. botanist and chemist. **2. John,** 1757?–1621, Pilgrim leader: first governor of Plymouth Colony.

carve-up (käv′ŭp′), *n. Slang.* **1.** a fight, esp. with knives or razors. **2.** any dispute, esp. one among drivers in traffic.

carving (kä′vĭng), *n.* **1.** the act of fashioning or producing by cutting. **2.** carved work; a carved design.

carving-knife (kä′vĭng nīf′), *n.* a large sharp knife for carving meat, etc.

Cary (kêə′rĭ), *n.* **1. Henry Francis,** 1772–1844, English writer and translator. **2. (Arthur) Joyce (Lunel),** 1888–1957, English novelist.

caryatid (kă′rĭ ăt′ĭd), *n., pl.* **-ids, -ides** (-ĭ dēz′). *Archit.* a figure of a woman used as a supporting column. [t. L: s. *Caryātides*, pl., t. Gk: m. *Karyátides*, lit., women of Caryae] —**car′yat′idal,** *adj.*

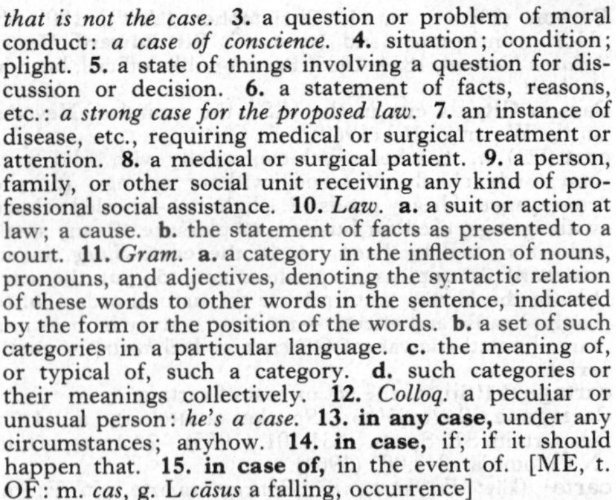

Caryatids

caryophyllaceous (kă′rĭ ō fĭ lā′shəs), *adj. Bot.* **1.** belonging to the *Caryophyllaceae* (sometimes called *Silenaceae*) or pink family of plants. **2.** resembling the pink. [f. m. s. Gk *karyóphyllon* clove tree + -ACEOUS]

caryopsis (kă′rĭ ŏp′sĭs), *n., pl.* **-opses** (-ŏp′sēz), **-opsides** (-ŏp′sĭ dēz′). *Bot.* a small, one-celled, one-seeded, dry, indehiscent fruit with the pericarp adherent to the seedcoat, as in wheat. [f. m. s. Gk *káryon* nut + -OPSIS]

casaba (kə sä′bə), *n.* a kind of winter muskmelon, having a yellow rind and sweet, juicy flesh. Also, **casaba melon, cassaba.** [named after *Kassaba*, town near Smyrna, Asia Minor]

Casablanca (kăs′ə blăng′kə), *n.* a seaport in NW Morocco. 1,085,000 (est. 1965).

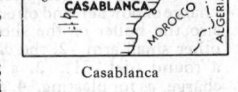

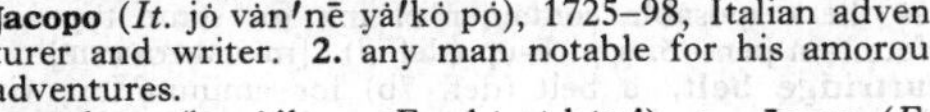

Casablanca

Casals (kă sălz′, *Sp.* kȧ säls′), *n.* **Pablo** (*Sp.* pȧ′blō), born 1876, Spanish cellist.

Casanova (kăz′ə nō′və, kăs′-; *It.* kȧ sȧ nô′vȧ), *n.* **1. Giovanni Jacopo** (*It.* jō vȧn′nē yȧ′kō pō), 1725–98, Italian adventurer and writer. **2.** any man notable for his amorous adventures.

Casaubon (kə sô′bən; *Fr.* kȧ zō bôN′), *n.* **Isaac** (*Fr.* ē zȧk′), 1559–1614, French classical scholar.

casbah (kăz′bä), *n.* kasbah.

cascade (kăs kād′), *n., v.,* **-caded, -cading.** —*n.* **1.** a waterfall over steep rocks, or a series of small waterfalls. **2.** an arrangement of lace, etc., in folds falling one over another in a zigzag fashion. **3.** a type of firework resembling a waterfall in effect. **4.** *Chem.* **a.** a series of vessels, from each of which a liquid successively overflows to the next, thus presenting a large absorbing surface, as to a gas. **b.** any process involving a number of repeated stages, each stage effecting an increase in the concentration of the desired end product. **5.** *Elect.* an arrangement of component devices, each of which feeds into the next in succession. —*v.i.* **6.** to fall in or like a cascade. [t. F, t. It.: m. *cascata*, der. *cascare*, der. L *cadere* fall]

Cascade Range, a mountain range on the Pacific coast of North America, extending from N California to British Columbia. Highest peak, Mt Rainier, 14,408 ft.

cascade shower, *Physics.* a fast-moving number of electrons, positrons, or photons which appear almost simultaneously from one high-energy particle as a result of pair production or radioactive collisions; soft shower.

Cascadian (kăs kā′dĭ ən, -dyən), *adj. Geol.* of or pertaining to the mountain-building episode in North America which reached its height at the end of the Tertiary period.

cascara (kăs kä′rə), *n.* a species of buckthorn, *Rhamnus purshiana*, of the Pacific coast of the U.S., yielding cascara sagrada. Also, **cascara buckthorn.** [t. Sp.: bark, der. *casca* bark, skin]

cascara sagrada (sə grä′də), the bark of the cascara, used as a cathartic or laxative. [t. Sp.: sacred bark]

cascarilla (kăs′kə rĭl′ə), *n.* **1.** Also, **cascarilla bark.** the bitter aromatic bark of any West Indian euphorbiaceous shrub of the genus *Croton*, as *C. elutaria*; used as a tonic. **2.** the shrub itself. [t. Sp., dim. of *cáscara* bark]

case[1] (kās), *n.* **1.** an instance of the occurrence, existence, etc., of something. **2.** the actual state of things: *that is not the case.* **3.** a question or problem of moral conduct: *a case of conscience.* **4.** situation; condition; plight. **5.** a state of things involving a question for discussion or decision. **6.** a statement of facts, reasons, etc.: *a strong case for the proposed law.* **7.** an instance of disease, etc., requiring medical or surgical treatment or attention. **8.** a medical or surgical patient. **9.** a person, family, or other social unit receiving any kind of professional social assistance. **10.** *Law.* **a.** a suit or action at law; a cause. **b.** the statement of facts as presented to a court. **11.** *Gram.* **a.** a category in the inflection of nouns, pronouns, and adjectives, denoting the syntactic relation of these words to other words in the sentence, indicated by the form or the position of the words. **b.** a set of such categories in a particular language. **c.** the meaning of, or typical of, such a category. **d.** such categories or their meanings collectively. **12.** *Colloq.* a peculiar or unusual person: *he's a case.* **13. in any case,** under any circumstances; anyhow. **14. in case,** if; if it should happen that. **15. in case of,** in the event of. [ME, t. OF: m. *cas*, g. L *cāsus* a falling, occurrence]

—**Syn. 1.** CASE, INSTANCE, EXAMPLE, ILLUSTRATION suggest the existence or occurrence of a particular thing representative of its type. CASE and INSTANCE are closely allied in meaning, as are EXAMPLE and ILLUSTRATION. CASE is a general word, meaning a fact, occurrence, or situation typical of a class: *a case of assault and battery.* An INSTANCE is a concrete factual case which is adduced to explain a general idea: *an instance of a brawl in which an assault occurred.* An EXAMPLE is one typical case, from many similar ones, used to make clear or explain the workings of a principle (what may be expected of any others of the group): *this boy is an example of the effect of strict discipline.* An ILLUSTRATION exemplifies a theory or principle similarly, except that the choice may be purely hypothetical: *the work of police dogs is an illustration of what is thought to be intelligence in animals.*

case[2] (kās), *n., v.,* **cased, casing.** —*n.* **1.** a thing for containing or enclosing something; a receptacle. **2.** a sheath or outer covering: *a knife case.* **3.** a box with its contents. **4.** the amount contained in a box or other container. **5.** a cased frame. **6.** *Metall.* the case-hardened surface of a piece of steel. **7.** *Bookbinding.* a completed book cover ready to be fitted to form the binding of a book. **8.** *Print.* a tray, of wood or metal, divided into compartments for holding types for the use of a compositor and usually arranged in a set of two, the **upper case** for capitals, etc., and the **lower case** for small letters, etc. —*v.t.* **9.** to put or enclose in a case; cover with a case. **10.** *Slang.* to examine or survey (a house, bank, etc.) in planning a crime. [ME *casse*, t. ONF, g. L *capsa* box, receptacle]

caseate (kā′sĭ āt′), *v.i.,* **-ated, -ating.** *Pathol.* to undergo caseous degeneration; become like cheese in consistency and appearance. [f. s. L *cāseus* cheese + -ATE[1]]

caseation (kā′sĭ ā′shən), *n. Pathol.* transformation into a soft cheeselike mass, as of tissue in tuberculosis.

casebook (kās′bo͝ok′), *n.* a book in which record is kept by doctors, social workers, etc., of their cases.

casebound (kās′bound′), *n., adj.* (of books) hardback.

cased frame, a framework, as of a door or window.

case-harden (kās′hä′dn), *v.t.* **1.** *Metall.* to make the outside surface of (alloys having an iron base) hard, leaving the interior tough and ductile by carburizing, cyanide hardening, or nitriding and suitable heat treatment. **2.** to harden in spirit so as to render insensible to external impressions or influences (as a judge).

case history, all the relevant information or material gathered about an individual, family, group, etc., for use by a caseworker, doctor, student, or the like, used esp. in social work, sociology, psychiatry, and medicine.

casein (kā′sĭ ĭn, -sēn), *n. Biochem.* a protein precipitated from milk, as by rennet, and forming the basis of cheese and certain plastics. [f. s. L *cāseus* cheese + -IN[2]]

caseinogen (kā′sĭ ĭn′ə jən, -sē′nə-), *n. Biochem.* the principal protein of milk, which in the presence of rennet is converted into casein.

case-knife (kās′nīf′), *n.* **1.** a knife carried or kept in a case. **2.** a table knife.

case law, law established by judicial decisions in particular cases, instead of by legislation.

casemate (kās′māt′), *n.* **1.** an armoured enclosure for guns in a warship. **2.** a vault or chamber, esp. in a rampart, with embrasures for artillery. [t. F, t. It.: m. *casamatta*, ult. t. Gk: m. *chásmata* opening (as military term)] —**case′mat′ed,** *adj.*

casement (kās′mənt), *n.* **1.** a window sash opening on hinges, which are generally attached to the upright side of its frame. **2.** a window with such sashes. **3.** *Poetic.* any window. **4.** a casing or covering. [f. CASE[2] + -MENT] —**case′mented,** *adj.*

Casement (kās′mənt), *n.* **(Sir) Roger (David),** 1864–1916, Irish patriot: hanged by the British for treason.

caseous (kā′sĭ əs), *adj.* of or like cheese. [f. s. L *cāseus* cheese + -OUS]

case record, a paper or papers containing a case history. Also, **case paper.**

casern (kə zûn′), *n.* (formerly) a lodging for soldiers in a garrison town; a barrack. Also, **caserne.** [t. F: m. *caserne,* orig., small room for soldiers, t. Pr.: m. *cazerna,* g. LL var. of *quaterna* group of four]

Caserta (*It.* kä zĕr′tä), *n.* a town in Italy, in Campania. 56,371 (1966).

case shot, a collection of small projectiles in a case, to be fired from a cannon.

casework (kās′wûk′), *n.* practical professional activity in the social services. —**case′work′er,** *n.*

caseworm (kās′wûm′), *n.* a caddis worm or other caterpillar that constructs a case around its body.

cash[1] (kăsh), *n.* **1.** money, esp. money on hand, as opposed to a money equivalent (as a cheque). **2.** money paid at the time of making a purchase, or sometimes an equivalent (as a cheque), as opposed to credit. —*v.t.* **3.** to give or obtain cash for (a cheque, etc.). **4. cash in one's chips, a.** (in poker, etc.) to hand in one's counters, etc., and get cash for them. **b.** *Colloq.* to die. —*v.i.* **5. cash in, a.** to obtain an advantage. **b.** *U.S. Colloq.* to die. **6. cash in on,** *Colloq.* **a.** to gain a return from. **b.** to turn to one's advantage. **7. cash up,** (of shopkeepers, etc.) to add up the takings. [t. F: m. *caisse,* t. Pr.: m. *caissa,* g. L *capsa* box]

cash[2] (kăsh), *n., pl.* **cash.** any of several low-denomination coins of China, India, and East Indies, esp. a Chinese copper coin. [t. Pg.: m. *caixa,* t. Tamil: m. *kāsu*]

cash account, 1. current account. **2.** *Bookkeeping.* a record kept of cash transactions.

cashbook (kăsh′bo͝ok′), *n.* a book in which to record money received and paid out.

cash desk, a desk in a shop, restaurant, or the like, where money is received from customers, in a till or drawer.

cash discount, 1. a term of sale by which the seller deducts a percentage from the bill if the purchaser pays within a stipulated period. **2.** the amount deducted.

cashew (kăsh′o͞o, kă sho͞o′), *n.* **1.** an anacardiaceous tree, *Anacardium occidentale,* native in tropical America, whose bark yields a medicinal gum. **2.** its fruit, a small, edible, kidney-shaped nut (**cashew nut**). [t. F: alter. of *acajou,* t. Brazilian Pg.: m. *acajú,* t. Tupi]

cashier[1] (kă shĭə′), *n.* one who has charge of cash or money, esp. one who superintends monetary transactions, as in a bank; bank clerk. [t. F: m. *caissier,* der. *caisse* cash box. See CASH[1]]

cashier[2] (kă shĭə′), *v.t.* **1.** to dismiss from a position of command or trust, esp. with disgrace. **2.** to discard; reject. [t. D: m. *kasseren,* t. F: m. *casser* break, discharge, annul, g. L *quassāre* shake, break, and LL *cassāre* annul]

cashmere (kăsh′mĭə), *n.* **1.** the fine downy wool at the roots of the hair of Kashmir goats of India. **2.** a shawl made of this hair. **3.** a wool fabric of twill weave.

Cashmere (kăsh mĭə′), *n.* Kashmir.

cash register, a till with a mechanism for indicating amounts of sales, etc.

casing (kā′sĭng), *n.* **1.** a case or covering. **2.** material for a case or covering. **3.** the framework around a door, window or staircase, etc. **4.** the outermost covering of a motor-vehicle tyre. **5.** any frame or framework. **6.** an iron pipe or tubing, esp. as used in oil and gas wells.

casino (kə sē′nō), *n., pl.* **-nos. 1.** a building or large room for meetings, amusements, gambling, etc. **2.** cassino. **3.** a small lodge or pavilion. [t. It., dim. of *casa* house, g. L *casa* cottage]

cask (käsk), *n.* **1.** a barrel-like container made of staves, and of varying size, for holding liquids, etc., often one larger and stronger than an ordinary barrel. **2.** the quantity such a container holds. [t. F: m. *casque,* t. Sp.: m. *casco* skull, helmet, cask (for wine, etc.), der. *cascar* break, g. LL *quassicāre,* der. *quassāre* break, shake]

casket (käs′kĭt), *n.* **1.** a small chest or box, as for jewels. **2.** *Chiefly U.S.* a coffin. —*v.t.* **3.** *Obs.* to put or enclose in a casket. [orig. uncert.]

Caslon (kăz′lən), *n.* **1. William,** 1692–1766, English type-founder. **2.** *Print.* an old-style type modelled on the types designed by William Caslon.

Casparian strip (kăs pēə′rĭ ən), *Bot.* an impervious thickened strip in the radial walls of some endodermal cells.

Caspian Sea (kăs′pĭ ən), a salt lake between SE Europe and Asia: the largest inland body of water in the world. ab. 169,000 sq. mi.; 85 ft below sea-level.

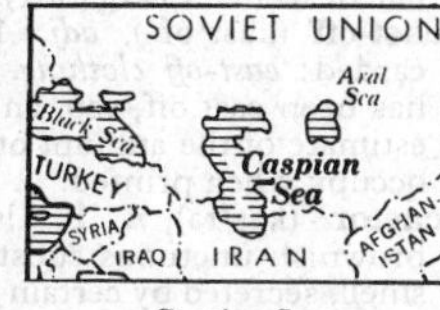

Caspian Sea

casque (käsk), *n. Chiefly Poetic.* a helmet (def. 1, esp. 1b). [t. F, t. Sp.: m. *casco* helmet. See CASK] —**casqued** (käskt), *adj.*

cassaba (kə sä′bə), *n.* casaba.

Cassandra (kə săn′drə), *n.* **1.** *Class. Legend.* a prophetess, daughter of Priam and Hecuba of ancient Troy, who was fated never to be believed. **2.** any woman who warns in vain of coming evil.

cassareep (kăs′ə rēp′), *n.* the inspissated juice of the root of the bitter cassava, used chiefly in West Indian cookery. [ult. t. Carib]

cassation (kă sā′shən), *n.* annulment; cancellation; reversal. [t. LL: s. *cassātio,* der. *cassāre* annul]

cassava (kə sä′və), *n.* **1.** any of several tropical euphorbiaceous plants of the genus *Manihot,* as *M. utilissima* (**bitter cassava**) and *M. dulci* (**sweet cassava**), cultivated for their tuberous roots, which yield important food products. **2.** a nutritious starch from the roots, the source of tapioca. [earlier *casavi,* t. Sp.: m. *cazabe,* t. Haitian (Taino): m. *cacábi, cazábbi*]

Cassegrainian telescope (kăs′ĭ grā′nyən), a reflecting telescope in which the primary mirror is perforated so that the light may pass through it to the eyepiece or photographic plate. Also, **Cassegrain telescope** (kăs′ĭ grān′). [named after N. *Cassegrain,* 17th-century French scientist; see -IAN]

Cassel (kăs′əl; *Ger.* käs′əl), *n.* Kassel.

casserole (kăs′ə rōl′), *n., v.,* **-roled, -roling.** —*n.* **1.** a baking dish of glass, pottery, etc., usually with a cover. **2.** any food, usually a mixture, baked in such a dish. **3.** a small dish with a handle, used in chemical laboratories. **4. en casserole** (*Fr.* äɴ käs rōl′), *French.* served or cooked in a casserole. —*v.t.* **5.** to bake in a casserole. [t. F, ult. der. *casse* pan, g. L *cattia,* t. Gk: m. *kyáthion* little cup, dim. of *kyáthos*]

cassette (kă sĕt′), *n.* **1.** *Photog.* the film-holder in certain types of camera; magazine (def. 7). **2.** (in a tape-recorder) a spool-holder resembling this. [t. F: fem. dim. of *casse* CASE[2]]

cassia (kăs′ĭ ə), *n.* **1.** a variety of cinnamon from the tree *Cinnamomum cassia,* of southern China (**cassia bark**). **2.** the tree itself. **3.** any of the caesalpiniaceous herbs, shrubs, and trees constituting the genus *Cassia,* as *C. fistula,* an ornamental tropical tree with long pods (**cassia pods**) whose pulp (**cassia pulp**) is a mild laxative, and *C. acutifolia* and *C. angustifolia,* which yield senna. **4.** cassia pods. **5.** cassia pulp. [OE, t. L, t. Gk: m. *kasía,* t. Heb.: m. *qətsīʿāh*]

cassimere (kăs′ĭ mĭə′), *n.* a plain or twilled woollen cloth. [var. of CASHMERE]

cassino (kə sē′nō), *n.* a game in which faced cards on the table are taken with eligible cards in the hand. Also, **casino.** [var. of CASINO]

Cassino (kə sē′nō; *It.* käs sē′nō), *n.* a town in central Italy, ab. 45 mi. NW of Naples: site of **Monte Cassino,** a famous Benedictine monastery; scene of bitter fighting between the Allied and Axis armies, Jan.–May, 1944. 21,105 (1961).

Cassiopeia (kăs′ĭ ə pē′ə), *n.* **1.** a northern circumpolar constellation east of Cepheus, on the opposite side of the Pole Star from Ursa Major. **2.** *Gk Myth.* the wife of Cepheus and mother of Andromeda.

Cassiopeia's Chair, the most conspicuous group of stars in the constellation Cassiopeia, supposed to resemble a chair in outline.

cassiopeium (kăs′ĭ ō′pĭ əm, -pyəm), *n. Chem.* lutetium.

cassiterite (kə sĭt′ə rīt′), *n.* a common mineral, tin dioxide, SnO_2: the principal ore of tin. [f. m. s. Gk *kassíteros* tin + -ITE[1]]

Cassius Longinus (kăs′yəs lŏn jī′nəs), **Gaius** (gā′əs), died 42 B.C., Roman politician and general, who led a conspiracy against Julius Caesar.

cassock (kăs′ək), *n.* **1.** a long, close-fitting garment worn by ecclesiastics and others engaged in church functions. **2.** a shorter, light, double-breasted coat or jacket, usually of black silk, worn under the Geneva gown. [t. F: m. *casaque,* t. It.: m. *casacca,* root *cas-* (cf. F *chasuble*), ? identical with L *casa* house, hut]

cassowary (kăs′ə wĕə′rĭ), *n., pl.* **-ries.** any of several large, three-toed, flightless, ratite birds constituting the genus *Casuarius,* of Australasian regions, superficially resembling the ostrich but smaller. [t. Malay: m. *kasuāri*]

Cassowary, *Casuarius casuarius* (Length 5 ft)

cast (käst), *v.,* **cast, casting,** *n.* —*v.t.* **1.** to throw; fling; hurl (often fol. by *away, off, out,* etc.). **2.** to throw off or away. **3.** to direct (the eye, a glance, etc.). **4.** to cause (light, etc.) to fall upon something or in a certain direction. **5.** to throw out (a fishing line, anchor, etc.). **6.** to throw down; throw (an animal) on its back or side. **7.** to part with; lose. **8.** to shed or drop (hair, fruit, etc), esp. prematurely. **9.** to bring forth (young), esp. abortively. **10.** to send off (a swarm), as bees do. **11.** *Obs.* to throw or set aside; discard or reject; dismiss or disband. **12.** to throw forth, as from within; emit or eject; vomit. **13.** to throw up (earth, etc.), as with a shovel. **14.** to put or place, esp. hastily or forcibly. **15.** to deposit (a vote, etc.). **16.** *Theat.* to allow parts, or parts of (a play) to actors; select (actors) for a play. **17.** *Metall.* to form (molten metal, etc.) into a particular shape by pouring into a mould; to produce (an object or article) by such a process. **18.** to compute or calculate; add, as a column of figures. **19.** to compute or calculate astrologically, as a horoscope; forecast. **20.** to ponder or consider; contrive, devise, or plan. **21.** to turn or twist; warp. **22.** *Naut.* to bring (a boat) round. **23.** *Naut.* to let go or let loose, as a vessel from a mooring (fol. by *loose, off,* etc.). *—v.i.* **24.** to throw a fishing line or the like. **25.** to calculate or add. **26.** *Obs.* to conjecture; forecast. **27.** to consider; plan or scheme (often fol. by *about*). **28.** to search this way and that, as for the scent in hunting (often fol. by *about*). **29.** to warp, as timber. **30.** *Naut.* to turn, esp. to get the boat's head away from the wind; tack. *—v.* **31.** Some special verb phrases are:

cast about, (fol. by *for* or an infinitive). **1.** to search mentally, as for an excuse. **2.** to scheme.

cast away, 1. to reject. **2.** to shipwreck.

cast back, 1. to refer to something past. **2.** to show resemblance to a remote ancestor.

cast down, to depress; discourage.

cast off, 1. to discard or reject. **2.** to let go. **3.** *Print.* to estimate the amount of space necessary for a piece of copy when printed. **4.** *Knitting.* to make the final row of stitches.

cast on, *Knitting.* to make the initial row of stitches.

cast up, 1. to compute; calculate. **2.** to eject; vomit. **3.** to turn up.

—n. **32.** the act of casting or throwing. **33.** that which is cast. **34.** the distance to which a thing may be cast or thrown. **35.** *Games.* **a.** a throw of dice. **b.** the number rolled. **36.** *Angling.* **a.** the act of throwing the line or net on the water. **b.** a line so thrown. **c.** the leader, with flies attached. **37.** *Hunting.* a dispersal of the hounds in all directions to recapture a scent. **38.** a secondary swarm of bees, etc. **39.** a stroke of fortune; fortune or lot. **40.** the form in which something is made or written; arrangement. **41.** *Theat.* the actors to whom the parts in a play are assigned. **42.** *Metall.* **a.** the act of casting or founding. **b.** the quantity of metal cast at one time. **43.** something shaped in a mould while in a fluid or plastic state; a casting. **44.** any impression or mould made from a thing. **45.** *Med.* rigid surgical dressing usually made of plaster-of-Paris bandage. **46.** a reproduction or copy, as a plaster model, made in a mould. **47.** outward form; appearance. **48.** sort; kind; style. **49.** tendency; inclination. **50.** a permanent twist or turn, esp. a squint: *to have a cast in one's eye.* **51.** a warp. **52.** a slight tinge of some colour; hue; shade. **53.** a dash or trace; a small amount. **54.** computation; calculation; addition. **55.** a conjecture; forecast. **56.** *Zool.* one of the wormlike coils of sand passed by the lugworm or other worms. **57.** *Geol.* a fossil showing surface features only of an organism. **58.** *Ornith.* a mass of feathers, fur, bones, or other indigestible matters ejected from the stomach by a hawk or other bird. **59.** *Pathol.* effused plastic matter produced in the hollow parts of various diseased organs. **60.** *Naut.* a sounding. *—adj.* **61.** discarded; lost: *the cast shoe of a horse.* **62.** moulded; having a certain shape. **63.** *Theat.* (of a production) having all actors selected. [ME *casten*, t. Scand.; cf. Icel. *kasta* throw] **—Syn. 1.** See **throw.** See **turn.**

Castalia (kăs tā′lyə), *n.* **1.** a spring on Mount Parnassus in Greece, sacred to Apollo and the Muses and regarded as a source of inspiration. **2.** any source of inspiration. —**Casta′lian,** *adj.*

castanet (kăs′tə nĕt′), *n.* a pair or one of a pair, of shells of ivory or hard wood held in the palm of the hand and struck together as an accompaniment to music and dancing, [t. Sp.: m. *castañeta*, dim. of *castaña*, g. L *castanea* chestnut]

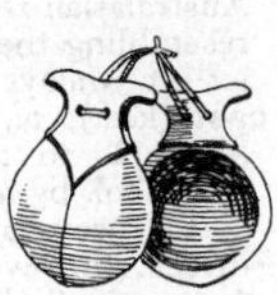

Castanets

castaway (käst′ə wā′), *n.* **1.** a shipwrecked person. **2.** an outcast. *—adj.* **3.** cast adrift.

caste (käst), *n.* **1.** *Sociol.* an endogamous and hereditary social group limited to persons in a given occupation or trade, having mores distinguishing it from other such groups. **2.** *Hinduism.* **a.** one of the artificial divisions or social classes into which the Hindus are rigidly separated and of which the privileges or disabilities are transmitted by inheritance. **b.** the system or basis of this division. **3.** any rigid system of social distinctions. **4.** the position or rank conferred by the Hindu social system or any similar system: *to lose caste.* [t. Sp., Pg.: m. *casta* breed, race, t. L: m. *castus* pure, CHASTE]

Castellammare di Stabia (*It.* käs tĕl lä mä′rĕ dē stä′byä), a seaport in Italy, in Campania, on the Bay of Naples. 68,746 (1966).

castellan (kăs′tĭ lən), *n.* the governor of a castle. [t. L: s. *castellānus* (der. *castellum*; see CASTLE); r. ME *castelain*, t. ONF]

castellany (kăs′tĭ lā′nĭ), *n., pl.* **-nies. 1.** the office of a castellan. **2.** the land belonging to a castle.

castellated (kăs′tĭ lā′tĭd), *adj.* **1.** *Archit.* built like a castle, esp. with turrets and battlements. **2.** having very many castles. —**cas′tella′tion,** *n.*

castellated nut, a nut having radial slits for the acceptance of a cotter pin; used as a locknut with a bolt having a corresponding hole.

Castellón (*Sp.* käs tĕ lyōn′), *n.* a seaport in E Spain. 70,417 (1965).

caster (käs′tə), *n.* **1.** one who or that which casts. **2.** castor[2].

castigate (kăs′tĭ gāt′), *v.t.,* **-gated, -gating.** to punish in order to correct; criticize severely. [t. L: m. s. *castīgātus*, pp.] —**cas′tiga′tion,** *n.* —**cas′tiga′tor,** *n.*

Castiglione (*It.* käs tēl lyō′nĕ), *n.* **Baldassare** (*It.* bäl däs-sä′rĕ), 1478–1529, Italian diplomat and author.

Castile (kăs tēl′), *n.* **1.** Spanish, **Castilla** (*Sp.* käs tē′lyä). a former kingdom comprising most of Spain. **2.** Also, **Castile soap.** a variety of hard soap made from olive oil and soda.

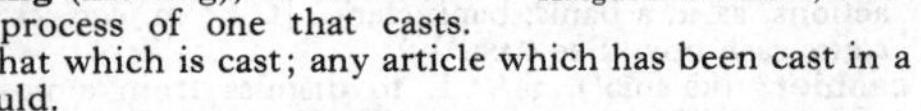

Kingdom of Castile, 1492

Castilian (kăs tĭl′yən), *n.* **1.** the accepted standard form of the Spanish language as spoken in Spain. **2.** the dialect of Castile. **3.** a native or inhabitant of Castile. *—adj.* **4.** of or pertaining to Castile.

casting (käs′tĭng), *n.* **1.** the act or process of one that casts. **2.** that which is cast; any article which has been cast in a mould.

casting vote, the deciding vote of the presiding officer when votes are equally divided.

cast iron, an alloy of iron, carbon, and other elements, cast as a soft and strong, or as a hard and brittle iron, depending on the mixture and methods of moulding.

cast-iron (käst′ī′ən), *adj.* **1.** made of cast iron. **2.** strong; hardy. **3.** inflexible; rigid; unyielding. **4.** incontrovertible: *a cast-iron alibi.*

castle (kä′səl), *n., v.,* **-tled, -tling.** *—n.* **1.** a fortified residence, as of a prince or noble in feudal times. **2.** the chief and strongest part of the fortifications of a medieval town. **3.** a strongly fortified, permanently garrisoned stronghold. **4.** a large and stately residence, esp. one which imitates the forms of a medieval castle. **5.** *Chess.* the rook. *—v.t.* **6.** to place or enclose in or as in a castle. **7.** *Chess.* to move (the king) in castling. *—v.i.* **8.** *Chess.* **a.** to move the king sideways two squares and bring the castle to the first square the king has passed over. **b.** (of the king) to be moved in this manner. [ME *castel*, t. ONF, g. L *castellum* fortress, dim. of *castrum* fortified place; r. OE *castel* village, t. L (Vulgate): m. s. *castellum*] —**cas′tled,** *adj.* **—Syn. 4.** palace, mansion.

Castleford (kä′səl fəd), *n.* a town in England, in the S West Riding of Yorkshire. 40,350 (1961).

castle in the air, a visionary project; a daydream. Also, **castle in Spain.**

Castlereagh (kä′səl rā′), *n.* **1. Robert Stewart, Viscount** (*2nd Marquess of Londonderry*), 1769–1822, British statesman. **2.** a river in Australia flowing E, S, then NW through New South Wales to join the Macquarie near its confluence with the Darling. 390 mi.

Castletown (kä′səl tən), *n.* a town on the S coast of the Isle of Man. 1549 (1961).

cast-off (käst′ŏf′), *adj.* **1.** thrown away; rejected; discarded: *cast-off clothing.* *—n.* **2.** a person or thing that has been cast off, esp. an article of clothing. **3.** *Print.* an estimate of the amount of space that a length of copy will occupy when printed.

castor[1] (käs′tə), *n.* **1.** Also, **castoreum** (käs tô′rĭ əm). a brownish unctuous substance with a strong, penetrating smell, secreted by certain glands in the groin of the beaver, used in medicine and perfumery. **2.** a beaver (hat).

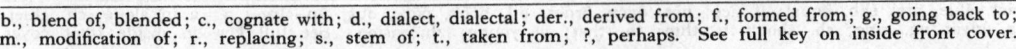

3. some similar hat. 4. a beaver. [t. L, t. Gk: m. *kástōr* beaver]

castor[2] (käs′tə), *n.* 1. a small wheel on a swivel, set under a piece of furniture, etc., to facilitate moving it. 2. a bottle or cruet with a perforated top, for holding a condiment. 3. a stand containing a set of such bottles. Also, **caster.** [var. of CASTER]

Castor (käs′tə), *n. Astron.* the more northerly of the two bright stars in Gemini; Alpha Geminorum.

Castor and Pollux, *Gk Myth.* twin sons of Leda and brothers of Helen (called the Dioscuri or sons of Zeus), famous for protection of sailors, and for brotherly affection. Pollux, who was immortal, spent alternate days with the gods and with his mortal brother in Hades.

castor bean, *U.S.* castor seed.

castor oil, a viscid oil obtained from castor seeds, used as a cathartic, lubricant, etc.

castor-oil plant (käs′tər oil′), a tall euphorbiaceous plant, *Ricinus communis*, native to India but widely naturalized, yielding castor seeds.

castor seed, the seed of the castor-oil plant.

castor sugar, finely ground white sugar.

castrametation (kăs′trə mĭ tā′shən), *n.* the laying out of camps. [t. F, f. L: *castra* camp + s. *mētātio* measurement]

castrate (kăs trāt′), *v.t.*, **-trated, -trating.** 1. to deprive of the testicles; emasculate. 2. to deprive of the ovaries. 3. to mutilate (a book, etc.) by removing parts; expurgate. [t. L: m. s. *castrātus*, pp.] —**castra′tion,** *n.*

castrato (kăs trä′tō), *n., pl.* **-ti** (-tē), **-tos.** 1. a male singer castrated in boyhood to preserve his voice in the upper registers. 2. the voice of or part sung by such a singer.

Castries (kăs trēs′), *n.* a seaport in the Windward Islands, the capital of St Lucia. 40,000 (1965).

Castro (kăs′trō; *Sp.* kȧs′trȯ), **Fidel** (fĭ dĕl′; *Sp.* fē dĕl′), born 1927, premier of Cuba since 1959.

Castrop-Rauxel (*Ger.* kȧs′trŏp rouk′səl), *n.* a town in West Germany, in central North Rhine-Westphalia. 86,200 (est. 1966). Also, **Kastrop-Rauxel.**

cast steel, *Metall.* steel rendered homogeneous by being melted in crucibles or pots.

casual (kăzh′yo͞o əl), *adj.* 1. happening by chance: *a casual meeting.* 2. unpremeditated; offhand; without any definite intention: *a casual remark, etc.* 3. careless; tending to leave things to chance; negligent; unconcerned: *a casual air.* 4. irregular; occasional: *a casual observer.* 5. informal: *casual clothes.* 6. accidental: *a casual fire.* 7. employed only irregularly. 8. *Obs.* pertaining to persons receiving charity from a district in which they do not permanently live. 9. *Obs.* uncertain. —*n.* 10. a worker employed only irregularly. 11. *Obs.* one who receives occasional relief at a workhouse, etc. 12. (*pl.*) relaxed, informal clothes, shoes, etc. [t. LL: s. *cāsuālis* by chance; r. ME *casuel*, t. OF] —**cas′ually,** *adv.* —**cas′ualness,** *n.* —**Syn.** 1. fortuitous, unforeseen. See **accidental.** —**Ant.** 1. planned. 2. deliberate.

casualty (kăzh′yo͞o əl tĭ), *n., pl.* **-ties.** 1. an unfortunate accident, esp. one involving bodily injury or death; a mishap. 2. *Mil.* **a.** a soldier who is missing in action, or who has been killed, wounded, or captured as a result of enemy action. **b.** (*pl.*) loss in numerical strength through any cause, as death, wounds, sickness, capture, or desertion. 3. one who is injured or killed in an accident. 4. any person injured accidentally.

casuarina (kăs′yo͞o ə rī′nə), *n.* any of the genus *Casuarina* of Australian and East Indian trees with jointed leafless branches; beefwood.

casuist (kăz′yo͞o ĭst), *n.* 1. one who studies and resolves cases of conscience or conduct. 2. an oversubtle or disingenuous reasoner upon such matters. [t. F: m. *casuiste*, der. L *cāsus* CASE[1]]

casuistic (kăz′yo͞o ĭs′tĭk), *adj.* 1. pertaining to casuists or casuistry. 2. oversubtle; intellectually dishonest; sophistical: *casuistic distinctions.* Also, **cas′uis′tical.** —**cas′uis′tically,** *adv.*

casuistry (kăz′yo͞o ĭs trĭ), *n., pl.* **-tries.** the application, or, from an outside point of view, misapplication, of general ethical principles to particular cases of conscience or conduct.

casus belli (kä′so͝os bĕl′ē), *Latin.* 1. an event or political occurrence which brings about a declaration of war. 2. any event which sparks off a quarrel.

cat (kăt), *n., v.,* **catted, catting.** —*n.* 1. a domesticated carnivore, *Felis domestica* (or *F. catus*), widely distributed in a number of breeds. 2. any digitate carnivore of the family *Felidae*, as the lion, tiger, leopard, jaguar, etc., of the genus *Felis*, and the short-tailed species that constitute the genus *Lynx*, and esp. any of the smaller species of either genus. 3. a spiteful and gossipy woman. 4. cat-o'-nine-tails. 5. *Games.* **a.** the tapering piece of wood used in the game of tipcat. **b.** the game itself. **c.** the bat used in this game. 6. a boy's game of ball. 7. a catboat. 8. a catfish. 9. *Naut.* a tackle used in hoisting an anchor to the cathead. 10. *Slang.* a person, esp. a young jazz musician or devotee of jazz. **11. let the cat out of the bag,** to disclose information, usually unintentionally. **12. rain cats and dogs,** to rain heavily. —*v.t.* 13. to flog with a cat-o'-nine-tails. 14. to hoist (an anchor) to the cathead. [ME; OE *catt, catte,* c. G *Katze*, F *chat*; ult. orig. unknown] —**cat′like′,** *adj.*

CAT (kăt), *n.* College of Advanced Technology.

cat., 1. catalogue. 2. catamaran. 3. catechism.

cata-, a prefix meaning 'down', 'against', 'back', occurring orig. in words from the Greek, but used also in modern words (English and other) formed after the Greek type, as in *catabolism, catalogue, catalysis, catastrophe.* Also (before a vowel), **cat-;** (before an aspirate), **cath-.** Also, **kata-.** [t. Gk: m. *kata-*, also (before a vowel) *kat-*, (before an aspirate) *kath-*, repr. *katá*, prep., down, through, against, according to]

catabolism (kə tăb′ə lĭz′əm), *n. Physiol., Biol.* a breaking down process; destructive metabolism (opposed to *anabolism*). Also, **katabolism.** [f. m. s. Gk *katabolḗ* a throwing down + -ISM] —**catabolic** (kăt′ə bŏl′ĭk), *adj.* —**cat′abol′ically,** *adv.*

catabolite (kə tăb′ə līt′), *n. Physiol., Biol.* a product of catabolic action.

catacaustic (kăt′ə kôs′tĭk, -kŏs′-), *adj. Maths, Optics.* denoting a caustic surface or curve formed by a reflection of light. See **diacaustic.**

catachresis (kăt′ə krē′sĭs), *n., pl.* **-ses** (-sēz). 1. misuse or strained use of words. 2. *Philol.* the employment of a word under a false form through misapprehension in regard to its origin: *causeway* and *crawfish* or *crayfish* have their forms by catachresis. [t. L, t. Gk: m. *katáchrēsis* misuse] —**catachrestic** (kăt′ə krĕs′tĭk), **cat′achres′tical,** *adj.* —**cat′achres′tically,** *adv.*

cataclinal (kăt′ə klī′nəl), *adj. Geog.* descending with the dip, as a valley. [f. CATA- + CLIN- + -AL[1]]

cataclysm (kăt′ə klĭz′əm), *n.* 1. any violent upheaval, esp. one of a social or political nature. 2. *Geog.* a sudden and violent physical action producing changes in the earth's surface. 3. an extensive flood. [t. L: s. *cataclysmos*, t. Gk: m. *kataklysmós* deluge]

cataclysmic (kăt′ə klĭz′mĭk), *adj.* 1. of, pertaining to or resulting from a cataclysm. 2. of the nature of, or having the effect of, a cataclysm: *cataclysmic changes.* Also, **cat′aclys′mal.**

catacomb (kăt′ə kōm′, -ko͞om′), *n.* 1. (*usually pl.*) an underground cemetery, esp. one consisting of tunnels and rooms with recesses dug out for coffins and tombs. 2. any series of underground tunnels and caves. [ME *catacombe*, OE *catacumbe*, t. LL: m. *catacumbas*]

catadromous (kə tăd′rə məs), *adj.* (of fishes) going down a river to the sea to spawn.

catafalque (kăt′ə fălk′), *n.* a raised structure on which the body of a deceased personage lies or is carried in state. [t. F, t. It.: m. *catafalco*, g. LL word f. *cata-* CATA- + s. *fala* tower + *-icum* -IC; akin to SCAFFOLD]

Catalan (kăt′ə lăn′, -lən), *adj.* 1. pertaining to Catalonia, its inhabitants, or their language. —*n.* 2. a native or inhabitant of Catalonia. 3. a Romance language spoken in Catalonia, closely related to Provençal. [t. Sp.]

catalase (kăt′ə lās′), *n. Chem.* an oxidizing enzyme which decomposes peroxides into water and oxygen. [f. CATAL(YSIS) + -ASE]

catalectic (kăt′ə lĕk′tĭk), *adj.* (of a line of poetry) lacking part of the last foot. Thus the italicized second line is catalectic:

> One more unfortunate,
> *Weary of breath.*

[t. LL: s. *catalēcticus*, t. Gk: m. *katalēktikós* incomplete]

catalepsy (kăt′ə lĕp′sĭ), *n. Pathol., Psychol.* a morbid bodily condition marked by suspension of sensation, muscular rigidity, fixity of posture, and often by loss of contact with environment. [t. LL: m. *catalēpsis*, t. Gk: m. *katálēpsis* seizure] —**cat′alep′tic,** *adj., n.*

catalo (kăt′ə lō′), *n., pl.* **-loes, -los.** a hybrid resulting from crossing the American bison (buffalo) with cattle of the domestic breeds. Also, **cattalo.** [b. CAT(TLE) and (BUFF)ALO]

catalogue (kăt′ə lŏg′), *n., v.,* **-logued, -loguing.** —*n.* 1. a list, usually in alphabetical order, with brief notes on the names, articles, etc., listed. 2. a record of the books and other resources of a library or a collection, indicated on cards, or, occasionally, in book form. 3. any list or register. —*v.t.* 4. to make a catalogue of; enter in a catalogue. 5. to describe the bibliographical and technical features of (a publication and the subject matter it treats). Also, *U.S.*, **catalog.** [t. F, t. LL: m. s. *catalogus*, t. Gk: m.

katálogos a list] —**cat′alogu′er, cat′alogu′ist,** *n.* —**Syn. 1.** See **list**[1].

Catalonia (kăt′ə lō′nyə), *n.* a region in NE Spain, formerly a province. Regional centre: Barcelona. Spanish, **Cataluña** (*Sp.* kä tä lo͞o′nyä).

catalpa (kə tăl′pə), *n.* any tree of the bignoniaceous genus *Catalpa*, of America and Asia, as *C. speciosa*, of the U.S., having large cordate leaves and bell-shaped white flowers. [t. NL, t. N Amer. Ind. (Creek): m. *kutuhlpa* winged head]

catalyse (kăt′ə līz′), *v.t.*, **-lysed, -lysing.** *Chem.* to act upon by catalysis. Also, *U.S.*, **catalyze.** —**cat′alys′er,** *n.*

catalysis (kə tăl′ĭ sĭs), *n.*, *pl.* **-ses** (-sēz′). *Chem.* the causing or accelerating of a chemical change by the addition of a substance (**catalyst**) which is not permanently affected by the reaction. [t. NL, t. Gk: m. *katálysis* dissolution] —**catalytic** (kăt′ə lĭt′ĭk), *adj.*, *n.* —**cat′alyt′ically,** *adv.*

catalyst (kăt′ə lĭst), *n.* *Chem.* a substance that causes catalysis.

catalytic cracking, *Chem.* the cracking of mineral oils of high boiling point by use of a catalyst.

catamaran (kăt′ə mə răn′), *n.* **1.** *Naut.* **a.** a float or raft, usually of several logs or pieces of wood lashed together. **b.** any craft with twin parallel hulls. **2.** *Colloq.* a quarrelsome person, esp. a woman. [t. Tamil: m. *katta-maram* tied tree or wood]

catamenia (kăt′ə mē′nyə), *n.pl.* *Physiol.* menses. [t. NL, t. Gk: m. *kataménia*, neut. pl. of *katamḗnios* monthly] —**cat′ame′nial,** *adj.*

catamite (kăt′ə mīt′), *n.* a boy or youth kept for or participating in homosexual activities. [t. L: m. s. *catamītus*; alter. of *Ganymedes* GANYMEDE]

catamount (kăt′ə mount′), *n.* catamountain.

catamountain (kăt′ə moun′tĭn), *n.* any wild animal of the cat family, as the European wildcat, or the leopard or panther. Also, **cat-o'-mountain.**

cat-and-dog (kăt′n dŏg′), *adj.* characterized by constant hostility and frequent quarrels: *they lead a cat-and-dog life together.*

Catania (kə tä′nyə), *n.* a seaport in E Sicily. 400,376 (1966).

Catanzaro (*It.* kä tän tsä′rô), *n.* a town in S Italy, in Calabria. 79,337 (1966).

cataphoresis (kăt′ə fə rē′sĭs), *n.* **1.** *Med.* the causing of medicinal substances to pass through or into living tissues in the direction of flow of a positive electric current. **2.** *Phys. Chem.* electrophoresis. [t. NL, f. Gk: m. *kata-* CATA- + *phórēsis* a carrying] —**cataphoretic** (kăt′ə fə rĕt′ĭk), *adj.*

cataphyll (kăt′ə fĭl), *n.* *Bot.* a simplified leaf form, as a bud scale or a scale on a cotyledon or rhizome.

cataplexy (kăt′ə plĕk′sĭ), *n.* *Zool.* a state of complete motionlessness; shamming death. [t. G: m. *Kataplexie*, t. Gk: m. s. *katáplēxis* amazement]

catapult (kăt′ə pŭlt′), *n.* **1.** a Y-shaped stick with an elastic strip between the prongs for propelling stones, etc. **2.** an ancient military engine for throwing darts, stones, etc. **3.** a device for launching an aeroplane from the deck of a ship, esp. a ship not equipped with a flight deck. —*v.t.* **4.** to hurl as from a catapult. **5.** to hit (an object) by means of a catapult. [t. L: s. *catapulta*, t. Gk: m. *katapéltēs*]

Catapult (def. 2)

cataract (kăt′ə răkt′), *n.* **1.** a descent of water over a steep surface; a waterfall, esp. one of considerable size. **2.** any furious rush or downpour of water; deluge. **3.** an abnormality of the eye, characterized by opacity of the lens. [ME *cataracte*, t. L: m. *cataracta* waterfall, t. Gk: m. *kataráktēs* down rushing]

catarrh (kə tä′), *n.* inflammation of a mucous membrane, esp. of the respiratory tract, accompanied by excessive secretions. [t. L: m. *catarrhus*, t. Gk: m. *katárrhous* running down] —**catarrh′al,** *adj.*

catarrhine (kăt′ə rīn′), *adj.* *Zool., Anthropol.* having a narrow ridge between the nostrils; belonging to one of the two divisions of primates (opposed to *platyrrhine*). [f. Gk: m. *kata-* CATA- + m. s. *rhī́s* nose]

catastasis (kə tăs′tə sĭs), *n.*, *pl.* **-ses** (-sēz′). the part of a drama, preceding the catastrophe, in which the action is at its height. [t. NL, t. Gk: m. *katástasis* appointment, settlement, condition]

catastrophe (kə tăs′trə fĭ), *n.* **1.** a sudden and widespread disaster. **2.** a final event or conclusion, usually an unfortunate one; a disastrous end. **3.** (in a drama) the point at which the circumstances overcome the central motive, introducing the close or conclusion; the denouement. **4.** a sudden violent disturbance, esp. of the earth's surface; a cataclysm. [t. Gk: m. *katastrophḗ* overturning] —**catastrophic** (kăt′ə strŏf′ĭk), *adj.* —**Syn. 2.** See **disaster.**

Catastrophe (kə tăs′trə fĭ), *n.* **Cape,** a headland on the coast of South Australia, forming the tip of the Eyre Peninsula.

catastrophism (kə tăs′trə fĭz′əm), *n.* *Geol.* the doctrine that certain vast geological changes in the earth's history were caused by catastrophes rather than gradual evolutionary processes. —**catas′trophist,** *n.*

catatonia (kăt′ə tō′nyə), *n.* *Psychol.* a syndrome seen most frequently in schizophrenia, with muscular rigidity and mental stupor, sometimes alternating with great excitement and confusion. [f. CATA- + Gk *-tonía*, der. *tónos* tension] —**catatonic** (kăt′ə tŏn′ĭk), *adj.*, *n.*

Catawba (kə tô′bə), *n.* a Siouan language of Virginia and the Carolinas.

catbird (kăt′bûd′), *n.* **1.** a slate-coloured North American songbird, *Dumetella carolinensis*, allied to the mockingbird, having a call resembling the mewing of a cat. **2.** any of several common birds of Australia which produce catlike cries.

catboat (kăt′bōt′), *n.* a boat with one mast, which is set well forward, and a single sail extended by gaff and boom.

cat-burglar (kăt′bû′glə), *n.* a burglar who enters by climbing.

catcall (kăt′kôl′), *n.* **1.** a cry like that of a cat, or an instrument for producing a similar sound, used to express disapproval, at a theatre, meeting, etc. —*v.i.* **2.** to sound catcalls. —*v.t.* **3.** to express disapproval of by catcalls.

catch (kăch), *v.*, **caught, catching,** *n.*, *adj.* —*v.t.* **1.** to capture, esp. after pursuit; take captive. **2.** to ensnare, entrap, or deceive. **3.** to be in time to reach (a train, boat, etc.). **4.** to come upon suddenly; surprise or detect, as in some action: *I caught him doing it.* **5.** to strike; hit: *the blow caught him on the head.* **6.** to intercept and seize (a ball, etc.). **7.** *Cricket.* to dismiss (a batsman) by intercepting and holding the ball after it has been struck by the bat and before it touches the ground. **8.** to check (one's breath, etc.). **9.** to get, receive, incur, or contract (often used figuratively): *to catch a cold, I caught the spirit of the occasion.* **10.** to lay hold of; grasp, seize, or snatch; grip or entangle: *a nail caught his sleeve.* **11.** to allow to be caught; be entangled with: *to catch one's finger in a door, catch one's coat on a nail.* **12.** to fasten with or as with a catch. **13.** to get by attraction or impression: *to catch the eye, the attention, etc.* **14.** to captivate; charm. **15.** to understand by the senses or intellect: *to catch a speaker's word.* —*v.i.* **16.** to become fastened or entangled: *the kite caught in the trees.* **17.** to take hold: *the door lock catches.* **18.** to become lit, take fire, ignite: *the wood caught instantly.* **19.** to spread or be communicated, as a disease. —*v.* **20.** Some special verb phrases are:

catch at, 1. to grasp or snatch. **2.** to be glad to get: *he caught at the chance.*

catch it, *Colloq.* to get a scolding or a beating.

catch on, *Colloq.* **1.** to become popular. **2.** to grasp mentally; understand.

catch out, to trap somebody, as into revealing a secret or displaying ignorance.

catch up, 1. to seize quickly: *he caught up the child in his arms.* **2.** to become embroiled or entangled in: *they were caught up in the crowd.* **3.** Also, **catch up with** or **catch up to.** to follow and reach, become level with, or overtake: *he caught her up by running; he caught up with the rest of the class by hard work.*

—*n.* **21.** the act of catching. **22.** anything that catches, esp. a device for checking motion. **23.** that which is caught, as a quantity of fish. **24.** anything worth getting. **25.** *Colloq.* a person of either sex regarded as a desirable matrimonial prospect. **26.** a fragment: *catches of a song.* **27.** *Music.* a round, esp. one in which the words are so arranged as to produce ludicrous effects. **28.** *Cricket.* **a.** the catching and holding of the ball after it has been struck and before it touches the ground. **b.** the wicket so gained. —*adj.* **29.** catchy (def. 2). [ME *cache(n)*, *cacche(n)*, t. ONF: m. *cachier*, g. LL *captiāre*, der. L *capere* take]

—**Syn. 10.** CATCH, CLUTCH, GRASP, SEIZE imply taking hold suddenly of something. To CATCH may be to reach after and get: *he caught my hand.* To CLUTCH is to take firm hold of (often out of fear or nervousness), and retain: *the child clutched his mother's hand.* To GRASP also suggests both getting and keeping hold of, with connotation of eagerness and alertness, rather than fear (lit. or fig.): *to grasp one's hand in welcome, to grasp an idea.* To SEIZE implies the use of force or energy in taking hold of suddenly (lit. or fig.): *to seize a criminal, seize an opportunity.*

catch-as-catch-can (kăch′əz kăch′kăn′), *n.* a style of wrestling in which any hold is allowed.

catch-basin (kăch′bā′sən), *n.* a receptacle at an opening into a sewer to retain matter that would not pass readily through the sewer. Also, **catchpit.**
catch-crop (kăch′krŏp′), *n.* a quick-growing crop grown between the rows of another crop, and harvested first.
catcher (kăch′ə), *n.* **1.** one who or that which catches. **2.** *Baseball.* the player who stands behind the bat or home base to catch the pitched ball.
catcher resonator. See **klystron.**
catchfly (kăch′flī′), *n.* any of various plants, esp. of the genus *Silene*, having a viscid secretion on stem and calyx in which small insects are sometimes caught.
catching (kăch′ĭng), *adj.* **1.** infectious. **2.** attractive; fascinating; captivating; alluring.
catchment area (kăch′mənt), **1.** Also, **catchment basin.** *Geog.* a drainage area, esp. of a reservoir or river. **2.** *Sociol.* the area from which persons may come to a central institution, as a school or hospital.
catchpenny (kăch′pĕn′ĭ), *adj., n., pl.* **-ies.** —*adj.* **1.** made to sell readily at a low price, regardless of value or use. —*n.* **2.** anything of little value or use, made merely for quick sale.
catchphrase (kăch′frāz′), *n.* a phrase caught up and repeated, often meaninglessly, during a vogue.
catchpit (kăch′pĭt′), *n.* a catch-basin.
catchpoints (kăch′points′), *n.pl. Railways.* a break in the rails on an up-gradient designed to catch and derail or divert any trucks accidentally descending against the flow of traffic.
catchpole (kăch′pōl′), *n. Archaic or Hist.* a petty officer of justice, esp. one who makes arrests for debt. Also, **catch′poll′.** [ME *cachepol*, OE *kæcepol*, t. ML: m. s. *cacepollus* chase-fowl. See CATCH, PULLET]
catchup (kăch′əp, kĕch′-), *n. Chiefly U.S.* ketchup. Also, **catsup.**
catchweight (kăch′wāt′), *n. Sport.* the chance or optional weight of a contestant, as contrasted with a weight fixed by agreement, etc.
catchword (kăch′wûd′), *n.* **1.** a word or phrase caught up and repeated for effect, as by a political party. **2.** a word printed at the top of a page in a dictionary or other reference book to indicate the first or last article on that page. **3.** a device, used esp. in old books, to assist the reader by inserting at the foot of the page the first word of the following page. **4.** an actor's cue.
catchy (kăch′ĭ), *adj.*, **catchier, catchiest. 1.** pleasing and easily remembered: *a catchy tune.* **2.** tricky; deceptive: *a catchy question.* **3.** occurring in snatches; fitful: *a catchy wind.*
cat-cracker (kăt′krăk′ə), *n. Colloq.* a plant in which oil is cracked catalytically.
cat-cracking (kăt′krăk′ĭng), *n. Colloq.* catalytic cracking.
cate (kāt), *n.* (*usually pl.*) *Archaic.* a choice food; a delicacy; a dainty. [aphetic var. of ME *acate*, t. ONF: m. *acat*, der. *acater* buy, g. LL *accaptāre* acquire]
catechesis (kăt′ĭ kē′sĭs), *n., pl.* **-ses** (-sēz). oral religious instruction, formerly esp. before baptism or confirmation. [t. L, t. Gk: m. *katēchesis* oral instruction]
catechetical (kăt′ĭ kĕt′ĭ kl), *adj.* pertaining to teaching by question and answer. Also, **cat′echet′ic.**
catechism (kăt′ĭ kĭz′əm), *n.* **1.** *Eccles.* **a.** an elementary book containing a summary of the principles of the Christian religion, esp. as maintained by a particular church, in the form of questions and answers. **b.** the contents of such a book. **2.** a similar book of instruction in other subjects. **3.** a series of formal questions designed to bring out a person's views. **4.** *Obs.* catechetical instruction. [t. LL: s. *catēchismus*, der. Gk *katēchízein.* See CATECHIZE]
catechist (kăt′ĭ kĭst), *n.* **1.** one who catechizes. **2.** *Eccles.* one appointed to instruct catechumens in the principles of religion as a preparation for baptism. —**cat′echis′tic, cat′echis′tical,** *adj.*
catechize (kăt′ĭ kīz′), *v.t.*, **-chized, -chizing. 1.** to instruct orally by means of questions and answers, esp. in Christian doctrine. **2.** to question with reference to belief. **3.** to question closely or excessively. Also, **catechise.** [t. LL: m. s. *catēchizāre*, t. Gk: m. *katēchízein*, teach orally] —**cat′echiza′tion,** *n.* —**cat′echiz′er,** *n.*
catechol (kăt′ĭ chŏl′, -kŏl′), *n. Chem., etc.* a white crystalline benzene derivative, $C_6H_4(OH)_2$, used in photography; pyrocatechol; pyrocatechin. [f. CATECH(U) + -OL[2]]
catechu (kăt′ĭ choo′), *n.* any of several astringent substances obtained from various tropical plants, esp. from the wood of two East Indian species of acacia, *Acacia catechu*, used in medicine, dyeing, tanning, etc. Also, **cutch.** [t. NL, t. Malay: m. (unexplained) *kachu*] —**cat′echu′ic,** *adj.*
catechumen (kăt′ĭ kyoo′mĕn), *n.* **1.** *Eccles.* one under instruction in the rudiments of Christianity, as in the early Church; a neophyte. **2.** a person being taught the elementary facts, principles, etc., of any subject. [t. LL: s. *catēchūmenus*, t. Gk: m. *katēchoúmenos*, ppr. pass. of *katēcheîn.* See CATECHIZE] —**cat′echu′menal,** *adj.*
categorical (kăt′ĭ gŏ′rĭ kl), *adj.* **1.** not involving a condition, qualification, etc.; explicit; direct: *a categorical answer.* **2.** *Logic.* (of a proposition) analysable into a subject and an attribute related by a copula, as in *all men are mortal.* **3.** of, pertaining to, or in a category. —**cat′egor′ically,** *adv.* —**cat′egor′icalness,** *n.*
categorical imperative, 1. *Ethics.* the rule of Immanuel Kant that one must do only what he can will that all others should do under similar circumstances. **2.** the unconditional command of conscience.
categorize (kăt′ĭ gə rīz′), *v.t.*, **-rized, -rizing.** to class in a category. Also, **categorise.** —**cat′egorist,** *n.*
category (kăt′ĭ gə rĭ), *n., pl.* **-ries. 1.** a classificatory division in any field of knowledge, as a phylum or any of its subdivisions in biology. **2.** any general or comprehensive division; a class. **3.** *Logic, Metaphys.* **a.** a basic mode or phase of existence, as space, quantity, quality. **b.** a basic form or organizing principle of reason, as the principle of causality. [t. L: m. s. *catēgoria*, t. Gk: m. *katēgoría* assertion]
catena (kə tē′nə), *n., pl.* **-nae** (-nē). a chain or connected series, esp. of extracts from the writings of the fathers of the Church. [t. L: chain]
catenary (kə tē′nə rĭ), *n., pl.* **-ries,** *adj.* —*n.* **1.** the curve assumed approximately by a heavy uniform cord or chain hanging freely from two points not in the same vertical line. **2.** a system of overhead conductor-wires on an electric railway in which the running wire is suspended from a slack wire strung between supports on either side of the line. —*adj.* **3.** Also, **catenarian** (kăt′ĭ nĕə′rĭ ən). pertaining to a catenary. [t. L: m. s. *catēnārius* relating to a chain]
catenate (kăt′ĭ nāt′), *v.*, **-nated, -nating,** *adj. Biol.* —*v.t.* **1.** to link together; form into a connected series. —*adj.* **2.** catenulate. [t. L: m. s. *catēnātus* chained] —**cat′ena′tion,** *n.*
catenulate (kə tĕn′yoo lāt′, -lĭt), *adj. Biol.* formed of a row or chain of cells or spores.
cater (kā′tə), *v.i.* to provide food and service, means of amusement, or the like (fol. by *for*). [v. use of obs. *cater*, ME *catour*, aphetic var. of *acatour* buyer of provisions, t. OF: m. *acateor* buyer. See CATE]
cateran (kăt′ə rən), *n. Hist.* a freebooter or marauder of the Scottish Highlands. [t. ML: s. *caterānus*, Latinization of ME (Scot.) *catherein*, etc., t. Gaelic: m. *ceathairne* peasantry. See KERN[1]]
cater-cornered (kăt′ə kô′nəd), *adj.* **1.** diagonal. —*adv.* **2.** diagonally. [f. *cater*, adv., diagonally (t. F: m. *quatre* four) + *cornered*]
cater-cousin (kā′tə kŭz′ən), *n. Archaic.* **1.** one related by or as by cousinship. **2.** an intimate friend.
caterer (kā′tə rə), *n.* a purveyor of food or provisions, as for entertainments, etc.; one who caters. —**cateress** (kā′tə rĭs), *n. fem.*
caterpillar (kăt′ə pĭl′ə), *n.* **1.** the wormlike larva of a butterfly or a moth. **2.** Also, **caterpillar tractor.** a tractor having the driving wheels moving inside endless tracks on either side, thus being capable of hauling heavy loads over rough or soft ground. **3.** the endless tracks themselves. **4.** any device, as a tank or steam-shovel, moving on endless belt (caterpillar) treads; a track-laying vehicle. **5.** *Obs.* one who preys on others; extortioner. [late ME *catyrpel(er)*, of uncert. orig. Cf. OF *chatepelose*, lit., hairy cat]
caterwaul (kăt′ə wôl′), *v.i.* **1.** to cry as cats on heat. **2.** to utter a similar sound; howl or screech. **3.** to quarrel like cats. —*n.* Also, **cat′erwaul′ing. 4.** the cry of a cat on heat. **5.** any similar sound. [ME *caterw(r)awen*, f. *cater* (cf. G *Kater* tomcat) + *wrawen* howl]
catfall (kăt′fôl′), *n. Naut.* the rope or tackle for hoisting an anchor to the cathead.
catfish (kăt′fĭsh′), *n., pl.* **-fishes,** (*esp. collectively*) **-fish. 1.** any of numerous fishes having some fancied resemblance to a cat, such as one of the fishes characterized by long barbels, of the North American freshwater family *Ameiuridae*, many of which are used for food. **2.** any fish of the order *Nematognathi*, as a bullhead.
catgut (kăt′gŭt′), *n.* **1.** the intestines of sheep or other animals, dried and twisted, used in surgery as ligatures, as strings for musical instruments, etc. **2.** *Colloq.* a violin. **3.** *Colloq.* stringed instruments collectively.
cath-, var. of **cata-** before an aspirate, as in *cathode.*
Cath., Catholic.
Catharist (kăth′ə rĭst), *n.* **1.** a member of one of several Provençal sects of the 12th and 13th centuries, who

believed in purification by mortification and spiritual baptism. —*adj.* **2.** of or pertaining to this sect or its tenets. [t. ML: s. *Catharista*, der. Gk *katharízein* purify]

catharsis (kə thä′sĭs), *n.* **1.** *Aesthetics.* the effect of art in purifying the emotions (applied by Aristotle to the relief or purgation of the emotions of the audience or performers effected through pity and terror by tragedy and certain kinds of music). **2.** *Psychol.* an effective discharge with symptomatic relief but not necessarily a cure of the underlying pathology. **3.** *Psychiatry.* psychotherapy which encourages and permits discharge of pent-up and socially unacceptable effects. **4.** *Med.* purgation. [t. NL, t. Gk: m. *kátharsis* a cleansing]

cathartic (kə thä′tĭk), *adj.* **1.** Also, **cathar′tical.** evacuating the bowels; purgative. —*n.* **2.** a purgative. [t. L: s. *catharticus*, t. Gk: m. *kathartikós* fit for cleansing, purgative]

Cathay (kă thā′), *n.* *Archaic or Poetic.* China. [t. ML: s. *Cat(h)aya*; cf. Russ. *Kitai*, said to be of Tatar orig.]

cathead (kăt′hĕd′), *n.* *Naut.* a projecting timber or beam near the bow, to which the anchor is hoisted.

cathedra (kə thē′drə), *n., pl.* **-drae** (-drē). **1.** the seat or throne of a bishop in the principal church of his diocese. **2.** an official chair, as of a professor in a university. See **ex cathedra.** [t. L, t. Gk: m. *kathédra* chair]

cathedral (kə thē′drəl), *n.* **1.** the principal church of a diocese, containing the bishop's throne. —*adj.* **2.** pertaining to or containing a bishop's throne. **3.** pertaining to or emanating from a chair of office or authority.

Catherine (kăth′rĭn, -ə rĭn), *n.* **Saint,** died A.D. 307, Christian martyr of Alexandria who was tortured on a spiked wheel and beheaded.

Catherine I, *c.* 1683–1727, consort of Peter the Great, and empress of Russia 1725–27.

Catherine II (*'the Great'*), 1729–96, consort of Tsar Peter III, and empress of Russia 1762–96.

Catherine of Aragon, 1485–1536, first wife of Henry VIII of England and mother of Mary I of England.

Catherine of Siena, Saint, 1347–80, Italian ascetic and mystic (Dominican tertiary).

catherine-wheel (kăth′rĭn wēl′), *n.* **1.** a firework which rotates as it burns. **2.** *Archit.* a rose window.

catheter (kăth′ĭ tə), *n.* *Med.* a flexible or rigid hollow tube employed to drain fluids from body cavities or to distend body passages, esp. one for passing into the bladder through the urethra to draw off urine. [t. LL, t. Gk: m. *kathetḗr*, der. *kathiénai* let down]

catheterize (kăth′ĭ tə rīz′), *v.t.,* **-rized, -rizing.** to introduce a catheter into. Also, **catheterise.**

cathetometer (kăth′ĭ tŏm′ĭ tə), *n.* *Physics.* a small telescope so mounted on a graduated vertical pillar that it can move up and down it; used to measure small vertical lengths at a distance of a few feet.

cathexis (kə thĕk′sĭs), *n.* *Psychol.* **1.** the investment of emotional significance in an activity, object, or idea. **2.** the charge of mental energy so invested. [t. Gk: m. *káthexis* holding, retention; rendering G *Besetzung* (Freud)]

cathode (kăth′ōd), *n.* **1.** (in a voltaic cell, radio valve, X-ray tube, or other device) the electrode which emits electrons or gives off negative ions and towards which positive ions move or collect. **2.** the negative pole of a battery or other source of electric current (opposed to *anode*). Also, **kathode.** [t. Gk: m. s. *káthodos* way down] —**cathodic** (kə thŏd′ĭk), *adj.*

cathode ray, a stream of electrons generated at the cathode during an electric discharge in a valve.

cathode-ray oscilloscope, *Physics.* an instrument which displays the shape of a voltage or current wave on a cathode-ray tube. Also, **cathode-ray oscillograph.**

cathode-ray tube, *Electronics.* a vacuum tube that generates a focused beam of electrons which can be deflected by electric and/or magnetic fields. The terminus of the beam is visible as a spot or line of luminescence caused by its impinging on a sensitized screen at one end of the tube. Cathode-ray tubes are used to study the shapes of electric waves, to reproduce pictures in television receivers, as an indicator in radar sets, etc.

catholic (kăth′ə lĭk, kăth′lĭk), *adj.* **1.** pertaining to the whole Christian body or Church. **2.** universal in extent; involving all; of interest to all. **3.** having sympathies with all; broad-minded; liberal: *to be catholic in one's tastes, interests, etc.* [t. L: s. *catholicus*, t. Gk: m. *katholikós* (def. 2)] —**catholically** (kə thŏl′ĭk lĭ), *adv.*

Catholic (kăth′ə lĭk, kăth′lĭk), *adj.* **1.** *Theol.* **a.** (among Roman Catholics) claiming to possess exclusively the notes or characteristics of the one, only, true, and universal Church—unity, visibility, indefectibility, apostolic succession, universality, and sanctity (used in this sense, with these qualifications, only by the Church of Rome, as applicable only to itself and its adherents, and to their faith and organization; often qualified, especially by those not acknowledging these claims, by prefixing the word *Roman*). **b.** (among Anglicans) denoting or pertaining to the conception of the Church as the body representing the ancient undivided Christian witness, comprising all the orthodox churches which have kept the apostolic succession of bishops, and including the Anglican Church, the Roman Catholic Church, the Eastern Orthodox Church, Church of Sweden, the Old Catholic Church (in the Netherlands and elsewhere), etc. **2.** pertaining to the Western Church. —*n.* **3.** a member of a Catholic Church, esp. of the Church of Rome.

Catholic Church, *Rom. Cath. Ch.* a visible society of baptized, professing the same faith under the authority of the invisible head (Christ) and the authority of the visible head (the pope and the bishops in communion with him).

Catholicism (kə thŏl′ĭ sĭz′əm), *n.* **1.** the faith, system, and practice of the Catholic Church, esp. the Roman Catholic Church. **2.** (*l.c.*) catholicity (def. 1).

catholicity (kăth′ə lĭs′ĭ tĭ), *n.* **1.** the quality of being catholic; universality; broad-mindedness. **2.** (*cap.*) the Roman Catholic Church, or its doctrines and usages.

catholicize (kə thŏl′ĭ sīz′), *v.t., v.i.,* **-cized, -cizing.** to make or become catholic or (*cap.*) Catholic. Also, **catholicise.**

catholicon (kə thŏl′ĭ kən), *n.* a universal remedy; a panacea. [t. Gk: m. *katholikón*]

Catiline (kăt′ĭ līn′), *n.* **1.** (*Lucius Sergius Catilina*), 108?–62 B.C., Roman politician and conspirator. **2.** any base political conspirator.

cation (kăt′ī′ən), *n.* *Phys. Chem.* **1.** a positively charged ion which is attracted to the cathode in electrolysis. **2.** any positively charged ion, radical, or molecule. Also, **kation.** [t. Gk: m. *katión*, ppr. neut., going down]

catkin (kăt′kĭn), *n.* *Bot.* an amentum, as of the willow or birch. [t. D: m. *katteken* little cat]

Catkins of birch
A, Male;
B, Female

catling (kăt′lĭng), *n.* *Now Rare.* **1.** a little cat; a kitten. **2.** catgut; a catgut string. **3.** a surgical knife. [f. CAT + -LING[1]]

catmint (kăt′mĭnt′), *n.* a plant, *Nepeta cataria*, of the mint family, with strongly scented leaves, of which cats are fond. Also, **catnip.** [f. CAT + MINT]

catnap (kăt′năp′), *n.* **1.** a short, light nap or doze. —*v.i.* **2.** to take a short, light nap; doze.

catnip (kăt′nĭp), *n.* catmint. [f. CAT + *nip*, var. of *nep* catnip, var. of *nept*, t. ML: s. *nepta*, L *nepeta*]

Cato (kā′tō), *n.* **1.** **Marcus Porcius** (mä′kəs pô′shĭ əs) (*'the Elder'* or *'the Censor'*), 234–149 B.C. Roman statesman, soldier, and writer. **2.** his great-grandson, **Marcus Porcius** (*'the Younger'*), 95–46 B.C., Roman statesman, soldier, and Stoic philosopher.

cat-o'-mountain (kăt′ə moun′tĭn), *n.* catamountain.

cat-o'-nine-tails (kăt′ə nīn′tālz′), *n., pl.* **-tails.** a whip, usually having nine knotted lines or cords fastened to a handle, used to flog offenders.

catoptrics (kə tŏp′trĭks), *n.* that branch of optics dealing with the formation of images by mirrors. [t. Gk: m. s. *katoptrikós* of or in a mirror. See -ICS] —**catop′tric, catop′trical,** *adj.*

cat-rigged (kăt′rĭgd′), *adj.* rigged like a catboat.

cat's cradle, **1.** a child's game in which two players alternately stretch a looped string over their fingers in such a way as to produce different designs; sometimes also played by one person alone. **2.** the pattern of string produced in such a game.

cat's-ear (kăts′ĭə′), *n.* any of several species of herb of the composite genus *Hypochoeris*, as *H. radicata.*

cat's-eye (kăts′ī′), *n.* **1.** any of certain gems exhibiting a chatoyant lustre, but esp. a variety of chrysoberyl (the **oriental** or **precious cat's-eye**). **2.** one of a pair of small reflectors set in rubber and steel holders, marking the centre or side of a road.

cat's-foot (kăts′fo͝ot′), *n.* a perennial composite herb, *Antennaria dioica.*

Catskill Mountains (kăts′kĭl), a range of low mountains in the U.S., in E New York State. Highest peak, Slide Mountain, 4204 ft. Also, **Catskills.**

cat's-paw (kăts′pô′), *n.* **1.** a person used by another to serve his purpose; a tool. **2.** *Naut.* a kind of hitch in the bight of a rope, made to hook a tackle on. **3.** *Naut.* a light breeze which ruffles the surface of the water over a comparatively small area. Also, **catspaw.**

cat's-tail (kăts′tāl′), *n.* **1.** a tall reedlike marsh plant,

Typha latifolia, with flowers in long, dense cylindrical spikes; reed mace. **2.** any of several other plants of the same genus. **3.** *Bot.* an amentum or catkin.
catstick (kăt′stĭk′), *n.* a stick used in certain games.
catsup (kăt′səp), *n.* ketchup.
cat's whisker, 1. *Radio, Obs.* the wire forming one contact of the crystal in a crystal detector. **2.** (*pl.*) *Slang.* an excellent proposal, person, etc.
cattalo (kăt′ə lō′), *n., pl.* **-loes, -los.** catalo.
Cattegat (kăt′ĭ găt′), *n.* Kattegat.
cattish (kăt′ĭsh), *adj.* **1.** catlike; feline. **2.** spiteful. **—cat′tishly,** *adv.* **—cat′tishness,** *n.*
cattle (kăt′l), *n.* **1.** ruminants of the bovine kind, of any age, breed, or sex. **2.** such animals together with horses and other domesticated animals. **3.** insects, vermin, or other animals considered contemptuously or in a mass. **4.** human beings considered contemptuously or in a mass. [ME *catel*, t. ONF, g. L *capitāle* wealth, stock. See CAPITAL[1], n.]
cattlegrid (kăt′l grĭd′), *n.* a pit covered by a grid set in a roadway, designed to prevent the passage of animals, at the same time allowing the passage of wheeled traffic.
cattleman (kăt′l mən), *n., pl.* **-men. 1.** a person employed in tending or rearing cattle. **2.** *U.S.* one who rears cattle on a large scale; the owner of a cattle ranch.
catty[1] (kăt′ĭ), *adj.*, **-ier, -iest. 1.** catlike. **2.** quietly or slyly malicious; spiteful: *a catty gossip.* [f. CAT + -Y[1]] **—cat′tily,** *adv.* **—cat′tiness,** *n.*
catty[2] (kăt′ĭ), *n., pl.* **-ies.** (in China and elsewhere in the East) a weight equal to about $1\frac{1}{3}$ lbs avoirdupois. [t. Malay: m. *katī*]
Catullus (kə tŭl′əs), *n.* **Gaius Valerius** (gā′əs və lĭə′rĭ əs), 84?–54? B.C., Roman lyric poet.
catwalk (kăt′wôk′), *n.* any narrow walking space, as on a bridge, or in an aircraft.
cat whisker, cat's whisker.
Caucasia (kô kā′zyə), *n.* a region in the Soviet Union between the Black Sea and the Caspian: divided by the Caucasus mountains into Ciscaucasia (in Europe) and Transcaucasia (in Asia). Also, **Caucasus.**
Caucasian (kô kā′zyən), *adj.* Also, **Caucasic** (kô kā′zĭk), **Caucasoid** (kô′kə zoid′). **1.** pertaining to the so-called 'white race', embracing the chief peoples of Europe, south-western Asia, and northern Africa, so named because the native peoples of the Caucasus were considered typical. **2.** of or pertaining to the Caucasus mountain range. **—*n.* 3.** a member of the Caucasian race. **4.** a native of the Caucasus.
Caucasus (kô′kə səs), *n.* **1.** a mountain range in the S European Soviet Union. Highest peak, Mt Elbrus (highest in Europe), 18,481 ft. **2.** Caucasia.
caucus (kô′kəs), *n.* **1.** a local committee of a political party exercising a certain control over its affairs or actions. **2.** *U.S.* a meeting of the local members of a political party to nominate candidates, elect delegates to a convention, etc., or of the members of a legislative body who belong to the same party to determine upon action in that body. **—*v.i.* 3.** to hold or meet in a caucus. [orig. unknown; ? alter. of *caulkers'* (*meeting*), from the fact that such meetings were orig. held where ship business was carried on, or ? of Amer. Ind. orig.]
caudad (kô′dăd), *adv.* *Anat., Zool.* towards the tail or posterior end of the body (opposed to *cephalad*). [f. L: s. *cauda* tail + *ad* to]
caudal (kô′dl), *adj.* *Zool.* **1.** of, at, or near the tail. **2.** tail-like: *caudal appendages.* See diag. under **spinal column.** [t. NL: s. *caudālis*, der. L *cauda* tail] **—cau′dally,** *adv.*
caudate (kô′dāt), *adj.* *Zool.* having a tail or tail-like appendage. Also, **cau′da′ted.** [t. NL: m. s. *caudātus*, der. L *cauda* tail]
caudex (kô′dĕks), *n., pl.* **-dices** (-dĭ sēz′), **-dexes.** *Bot.* **1.** the axis of a plant, including both stem and root. **2.** the woody or thickened persistent base of a herbaceous perennial. [t. L: tree trunk. See CODEX]
caudillo (kô dē′lyō; *Sp.* kåw dē′lyȯ), *n., pl.* **-los** (-lyōz; *Sp.* -lyȯs). (in some Spanish-speaking countries) the head of the state; leader.
Caudine Forks (kô′dīn), two narrow mountain passes in S Italy, near Benevento: site of a Roman defeat by the Samnites, 321 B.C.
caudle (kô′dl), *n.* *Obs.* a warm drink for the sick, as of wine or ale mixed with eggs, bread, sugar, spices, etc. [ME *caudel*, t. ONF, dim. of *caud*, g. L *calidus* warm]
caught (kôt), *v.* pt. and pp. of **catch.**
caul (kôl), *n.* **1.** a part of the amnion sometimes covering the head of a child at birth, superstitiously supposed to bring good luck and to be an infallible preservative against drowning. **2.** a thin membrane covering the lower intestines of various animals, formerly used to make sausage skins. **3.** *Carp.* a sheet of thin plywood or aluminium used to protect veneers in passing. [ME *calle*, t. F: m. *cale* kind of cap]
cauld (kôld, käld, kȯd), *adj., n.* *Scot.* cold.
cauldron (kôl′drən), *n.* a large kettle or boiler. Also, **caldron.** [ME *cauderon*, t. ONF: m. *caudron*, g. deriv. of L *caldāria*, der. *cal(i)dus* hot]
caulescent (kô lĕs′ənt), *adj.* *Bot.* having an obvious stem rising above the ground. [f. s. L *caulis* stalk + -ESCENT]
caulicle (kô′lĭ kl), *n.* *Bot.* a small or rudimentary stem. [t. L: m. s. *cauliculus*, dim. of *caulis* stalk]
cauliflower (kŏl′ĭ flou′ə), *n.* **1.** a cultivated cruciferous plant, *Brassica oleracea* var. *botrytis*, whose inflorescence forms a compact, fleshy head. **2.** the head, used as a vegetable. [half adoption, half trans. of NL *cauliflōra*, lit., cabbage-flower]
cauliflower ear, an ear that has been deformed permanently, esp. by blows in boxing.
cauline (kô′lĭn, -līn), *adj.* *Bot.* of or pertaining to a stem, esp. pertaining to or arising from the upper part of a stem. [f. s. L *caulis* stalk + -INE[1]]
caulis (kô′lĭs), *n., pl.* **-les** (-lēz). *Bot.* the main stalk or stem of a plant, esp. of a herbaceous plant. [t. L]
caulk (kôk), *v.t.* **1.** to fill or close (a seam, joint, etc.), as in a boat. **2.** to make (a vessel) watertight by filling the seams between its planks with oakum or other materials driven snug. **3.** to drive the edges of (plating) together to prevent leakage. **4.** to fill or close seams or crevices of (a tank, window, etc.) in order to make watertight, airtight, etc. Also, **calk.** [ME *caulke(n)*, t. ONF: m. *cauquer*, g. L *calcāre* tread, press]
caulker (kô′kə), *n.* **1.** one who caulks. **2.** a caulking tool or device. Also, **calker.** [f. CAULK + -ER[1]]
causal (kô′zəl), *adj.* **1.** of, constituting, or implying a cause. **2.** *Gram.* expressing a cause, as a conjunction. **—caus′ally,** *adv.*
causalgia (kô zăl′jĭ ə), *n.* a neuralgia distinguished by a burning pain along certain nerves, usually of the upper extremities. [f. m. s. Gk *kaûsis* burning heat + -ALGIA]
causality (kô zăl′ĭ tĭ), *n., pl.* **-ties. 1.** the relation of cause and effect. **2.** causal quality or agency.
causa sine qua non (kou′zə sī′nĭ kwā nŏn′), *Latin.* a requisite or indispensable condition.
causation (kô zā′shən), *n.* **1.** the action of causing or producing. **2.** the relation of cause to effect. **3.** anything that produces an effect; a cause.
causative (kô′zə tĭv), *n.* **1.** *Gram.* a word (usually a verb) denoting causation, as *made* in *he made me eat the apple.* **—*adj.* 2.** *Gram.* **a.** pertaining to an affix or other form by which causatives are derived from an underlying word. For example: Gothic *-jan* is a causative affix in *fulljan* (cause to be full, fill). **b.** pertaining to a word or words so derived, esp. one formed from an underlying word that lacks this meaning: *'to fell' is the causative of 'to fall'.* **3.** acting as a cause; productive (fol. by *of*). **—caus′atively,** *adv.* **—caus′ativeness,** *n.*
cause (kôz), *n., v.,* **caused, causing. —*n.* 1.** that which produces an effect; the thing, person, etc., from which something results. **2.** the ground of any action or result; reason; motive. **3.** good or sufficient reason: *to complain without cause.* **4.** *Law.* **a.** a ground of legal action; the matter over which a person goes to law. **b.** a case for judicial decision. **5.** any subject of discussion or debate. **6.** that side of a question which a person or party supports; the aim, purpose, etc. of a group. **7.** *Philos.* the end or purpose for which a thing is done or produced (now only in *final causes*). **—*v.t.* 8.** to be the cause of; bring about. [ME, t. L: m. *causa*] **—caus′able,** *adj.* **—cause′less,** *adj.* **—caus′er,** *n.*
—Syn. 1. CAUSE, OCCASION refer to the starting of effects into motion. A CAUSE is an agency, perhaps acting over a long period, or a long-standing situation, which produces an effect: *the cause of the quarrel between the two men was jealousy.* An OCCASION is an event which provides an opportunity for the effect to become evident, or perhaps promotes its becoming evident: *the occasion of the quarrel was a blow struck by John.* **3.** See **reason. 8.** effect, make, create, produce.
cause célèbre (*Fr.* kȯz sĕ lĕ′br), *French.* a celebrated legal case.
causerie (kō′zə rĭ; *Fr.* kȯz rē′), *n.* **1.** a talk or chat. **2.** a short, informal essay, article, etc. [t. F, der. *causer* talk, t. L: m. *causāri* plead]
causeway (kôz′wā′), *n.* **1.** a raised road or path, as across low or wet ground. **2.** a cobbled or paved way. **—*v.t.* 3.** to pave, as a road or street, with cobbles or pebbles. **4.** to provide with a causeway. [var. of *causey way.* See CAUSEY]
causey (kô′zĭ), *n., pl.* **-seys.** causeway. [ME *cauce*, t. ONF: m. *caucie*, earlier *cauciee* (cf. F *chaussée*), g. LL *calciāta* paved road]
causse (kōs; *Fr.* kȯs), *n.* *Geog.* a limestone plateau. [t. F]
caustic (kôs′tĭk, kŏs′-), *adj.* **1.** capable of burning, corrod-

ing, or destroying living tissue: *caustic soda.* **2.** severely critical or sarcastic: *a caustic remark.* **3.** *Maths, Optics.* **a.** denoting a surface to which all the light rays emanating from a single point and reflected by a curved surface (as a concave mirror) are tangent. **b.** denoting a curve formed by a plane section of such a surface. **c.** denoting an analogous surface or curve resulting from refraction. —*n.* **4.** a caustic substance: *lunar caustic.* **5.** *Maths, Optics.* a caustic surface or curve. [t. L: s. *causticus*, t. Gk: m. *kaustikós* capable of burning] —**caus'tically,** *adv.* —**causticity** (kôs tĭs'ĭ tĭ, kŏs-), *n.*

caustic potash, potassium hydroxide, KOH, used in the manufacture of soap, and glass.

caustic soda, sodium hydroxide, NaOH, used in metallurgy and photography.

cauter (kô'tə), *n.* a cautery.

cauterize (kô'tə rīz'), *v.t.*, **-rized, -rizing.** to burn with a hot iron, or with fire or a caustic, esp. for curative purposes; treat with a cautery. Also, **cauterise.** —**cau'teriza'tion,** *n.*

cautery (kô'tə rĭ), *n.*, *pl.* **-ries. 1.** an escharotic substance or a hot iron used to destroy tissue. **2.** the process of destroying tissue with a cautery. [t. L: m. s. *cautērium*, t. Gk: m. *kautḗrion*, dim. of *kautḗr* branding iron]

caution (kô'shən), *n.* **1.** prudence in regard to danger or evil; carefulness; wariness: *proceed with caution.* **2.** a warning. **3.** *Law.* a warning to a person that his words may be used in evidence. **4.** *Mil.* (in drill) a preliminary utterance by an instructor, etc., before a word of command; a precautionary word of command. **5.** *Colloq.* a person or thing that is unusual, odd, amazing, etc. —*v.t.* **6.** to give warning to; advise or urge to take heed. **7.** *Law.* to warn (a person) that his words may be used in evidence. [t. L: s. *cautio*; r. ME *caucion* security, t. OF] —**Syn. 1.** circumspectness, heed, care. **2.** admonition, advice. **6.** See **warn.** —**Ant. 1.** recklessness.

cautionary (kô'shə nə rĭ), *adj.* of the nature of or containing a warning: *cautionary advice.*

caution money, money paid in advance (e.g. by a student) as a security against future debts, for good conduct, etc.

cautious (kô'shəs), *adj.* having or showing caution or prudence to avoid danger or evil; very careful. —**cau'tiously,** *adv.* —**cau'tiousness,** *n.* —**Syn.** prudent, discreet, guarded, wary, circumspect. See **careful.** —**Ant.** rash, heedless.

Cauvery (kô'və rĭ), *n.* a river in S India, flowing from the Western Ghats SE to the Bay of Bengal: sacred to the Hindus. 475 mi. Also, **Kaveri.**

cav., cavalry.

Cavafy (kə vä'fĭ), *n.* **Constantine,** 1868–1933, Greek poet in Egypt. Greek, **Kavaphis.**

cavalcade (kăv'əl kād'), *n.*, *v.*, **-caded, -cading.** —*n.* **1.** a procession of persons on horseback or in horse-drawn carriages. **2.** any procession. —*v.i.* **3.** to ride in procession. [t. F, t. It.: m. *cavalcata*, der. *cavalcare*, g. LL *caballicāre* ride on horseback]

cavalier (kăv'ə lĭə'), *n.* **1.** a horseman, esp. a mounted soldier; a knight. **2.** one having the spirit or bearing of a knight; a courtly gentleman; a gallant. **3.** a man escorting a woman or acting as her partner in dancing. **4.** (*cap.*) an adherent of Charles I of England in his contest with Parliament. —*adj.* **5.** haughty, disdainful, or supercilious. **6.** offhand or unceremonious. **7.** (*cap.*) of or pertaining to the Cavaliers. —*v.i.* **8.** to play the cavalier. **9.** to be haughty or domineering. [t. F, t. It.: m. *cavalliere*, der. *cavallo* horse, g. L *caballus*]

cavalierly (kăv'ə lĭə'lĭ), *adv.* **1.** in a cavalier manner. —*adj.* **2.** characteristic of a cavalier; arrogant.

Cavalier poets, a group of English poets (Herrick, Carew, Lovelace, Suckling, etc.), mainly at the court of Charles I, who produced a body of graceful lyrical poetry.

cavalla (kə văl'ə), *n.*, *pl.* **-la, -las.** cavally.

cavally (kə văl'ĭ), *n.*, *pl.* **-lies. 1.** any of various carangoid fishes of the genus *Caranx*, esp. *C. hippos*, a food fish of both coasts of tropical America. **2.** the cero. [t. Pg.: m. *cavalla*, or t. Sp.: m. *caballa* horse-mackerel, g. L *caballa* mare]

cavalry (kăv'əl rĭ), *n.*, *pl.* **-ries. 1.** *Mil.* a unit, or units collectively, of an army, which in the past were mounted on horseback, and are now equipped with armoured vehicles in either an armoured or a reconnaissance role. **2.** horsemen, horses, etc., collectively. **3.** *Obs.* horsemanship, esp. of a knight. [t. F: m. *cavalerie*, t. It.: m. *cavalleria* knighthood, der. *cavalliere.* See CAVALIER] —**cavalryman** (kăv'əl rĭ mən), *n.*

Cavan (kăv'ən), *n.* **1.** a county in S Northern Ireland, in Ulster. 56,594 pop. (1961); 729 sq. mi. **2.** its county town. 3208 (1961).

cavatina (kăv'ə tē'nə; *It.* kä vä tē'nä), *n.*, *pl.* **-ne** (-nĭ; *It.* -nè). *Music.* a simple song or melody, properly one without a second part and a repeat; an air. [t. It.]

cave[1] (kāv), *n.*, *v.*, **caved, caving.** —*n.* **1.** a hollow in the earth, esp. one opening more or less horizontally into a hill, mountain, etc. **2.** *Eng. Hist.* a secession, or a group of seceders, from a political party on some special question. —*v.t.* **3.** to hollow out. **4.** to cause to fall (fol. by *in*). —*v.i.* **5.** to fall or sink, as ground (fol. by *in*). **6.** *Colloq.* to give, yield, or submit (fol. by *in*). [ME, t. OF, t. L: m. *cava* hollow (places), neut. pl.]

cave[2] (kā'vĭ), *Schoolboy Slang.* —*v.i.*, *imperative.* **1.** beware. —*n.* **2.** lookout: *to keep cave.* [t. L]

caveat (kā'vĭ ăt'), *n.* **1.** *Law.* a legal notice to a court or public officer to suspend a certain proceeding until the notifier is given a hearing: *a caveat filed against the probate of a will.* **2.** any warning or caution. [t. L: let him beware]

caveat emptor (kā'vĭ ăt ĕmp'tô), *Latin.* let the buyer beware (since he buys without recourse).

caveator (kā'vĭ ā'tə), *n.* one who enters a caveat.

cave-dweller (kāv'dwĕl'ə), *n.* a caveman.

cave-in (kāv'ĭn'), *n.* a collapse, as of a mine, etc.

Cavell (kăv'əl), *n.* **Edith Louisa,** 1865–1915, English nurse, executed by the Germans in World War I.

caveman (kāv'măn'), *n.* **1.** a cave-dweller; a man of the Palaeolithic era. **2.** *Colloq.* a man who behaves in a rough, primitive manner, esp. towards women.

cavendish (kăv'ən dĭsh), *n.* tobacco softened, sweetened, and pressed into cakes. [named after the maker]

Cavendish (kăv'ən dĭsh), *n.* **Henry,** 1731–1810, English physicist and chemist.

cavern (kăv'ən), *n.* a cave, esp. a large cave. [ME *caverne*, t. F, t. L: m. *caverna* cave]

cavernous (kăv'ə nəs), *adj.* **1.** containing caverns. **2.** deep-set: *cavernous eyes.* **3.** hollow and deep-sounding: *a cavernous voice.* **4.** full of small cavities; porous. **5.** of a cavern: *cavernous darkness.* —**cav'ernously,** *adj.*

cavesson (kə vĕs'ən, kăv'ĭ sən), *n.* the noseband of a bridle or a halter. [t. It.: m. *cavezzone*]

cavetto (kə vĕt'ō; *It.* kä vĕt'tó), *n.*, *pl.* **-ti** (-tĭ; *It.* -tē), **-tos.** *Archit.* a concave moulding, as in a cornice, with the curve usually a quarter circle. See diag. under **column.** [t. It., dim. of *cavo*, g. L *cavum* hollow (place)]

caviar (kăv'ĭ ä', kăv'ĭ ä'), *n.* **1.** the roe of sturgeon and other large fish, pressed and salted, considered a great delicacy. **2. caviar to the general,** something beyond appeal to the popular taste. Also, **caviare.** [t. F, t. It.: m. *caviaro*, t. Turk.: m. *khāviār*; r. *cavialy*, t. It.: m. *caviale*, var. of *caviaro*; ult. orig. unknown]

cavicorn (kăv'ĭ kôn'), *adj.* *Zool.* hollow-horned, as the ruminants with true horns, as distinguished from bony antlers. [f. L: *cavi-* (comb. form of *cavus* hollow) + s. *-cornis* horned]

cavil (kăv'ĭl), *v.*, **-illed, -illing** or (*U.S.*) **-iled, -iling,** *n.* —*v.i.* **1.** to raise irritating and trivial objections; find fault unnecessarily. —*n.* **2.** a trivial and annoying objection. **3.** the raising of such objections. [t. F: m. s. *caviller*, t. L: m. *cavillāri*, der. *cavilla* a jeering] —**cav'iller;** *U.S.*, **caviler,** *n.*

cavitation (kăv'ĭ tā'shən), *n.* *Engineering.* rapid formation and collapse of vapour pockets in a flowing liquid in regions of very low pressure, a frequent cause of serious structural damage to propellers, pumps, etc.

cavity (kăv'ĭ tĭ), *n.*, *pl.* **-ties. 1.** any hollow place; a hollow: *a cavity in the earth.* **2.** *Anat.* a hollow space within the body, an organ, a bone, etc. **3.** *Dentistry.* the loss of tooth structure, most commonly produced by caries. A cavity may be artificially made to support dental restorations. [t. F: m. *cavité*, t. LL: m. s. *cavitas* hollowness] —**Syn. 1.** See **hole.**

cavity block, *Bldg Trades.* a block used for cavity walls.

cavity wall, *Bldg Trades.* a type of double wall designed to retain heat in a building, and prevent the penetration of moisture, having a gap, usually of 2 inches, between its leaves.

cavort (kə vôt'), *v.i.* *Colloq.* to prance or caper about. [orig. unknown]

Cavour (kə vŏŏə'; *It.* kä vōōr'), *n.* **Camillo Benso di** (*It.* kä mĕl'lŏ bĕn'sŏ dē), 1810–61, Italian statesman who was a leader in the unification of Italy.

cavy (kā'vĭ), *n.*, *pl.* **-vies.** any of various short-tailed South American rodents, esp. those of the genus *Cavia* (including the domesticated guineapig) or the family *Caviidae.* [t. NL: m. s. *Cavia*, t. Galibi: m. *cabiai*]

caw (kô), *n.* **1.** the cry of the crow, raven, etc. —*v.i.* **2.** to utter this cry or a similar sound. [imit.]

Cawnpore (kôn'pô'), *n.* Kanpur. Also, **Cawnpur** (kôn'-pŏŏə').

Caxton (kăk'stən), *n.* **1. William,** 1422?–91, first English printer: translator and author. **2.** *Bibliog.* any book printed by Caxton, all of which are in black-letter. 3. *Print.* a kind of type imitating Caxton's black-letter.

cay (kā, kē), *n.* a small island; key. [t. Sp.: s. *cayo;* akin to QUAY]

cayenne (kā ĕn′), *n.* a hot, biting condiment composed of the ground pods and seeds of any of several varieties of *Capsicum;* red pepper. Also, **cayenne pepper.** [named after *Cayenne,* in French Guiana]

Cayenne (kā ĕn′), *n.* a seaport in and the capital of French Guiana. 18,635 (1961).

cayman (kā′mən), *n., pl.* **-mans.** any of several tropical American crocodilians having overlapping scutes, constituting the genus *Caiman* and related types. Also, **caiman.** [t. Sp., Pg.: m. *caiman,* t. Carib]

Cayman Islands (kī män′), three islands NW of Jamaica, in the West Indies; British dependencies. 8803 pop. (1960); 104 sq. mi.

Cayuga (kā yōō′gə, kī-), *n., pl.* **-ga, -gas.** a member of a tribe of North American Indians, the smallest tribe of the Iroquois confederacy. [t. Mohawk: m. *kweñiógwen* the place where locusts were taken out]

cayuse (kī yōōs′), *n. Western U.S.* an Indian pony. [named after the *Cayuse* Indians, now living in Oregon]

Cb, *Chem.* columbium.

C.B., Companion of the (Order of the) Bath.

c.b., confined to barracks.

C.B.E., Commander of the (Order of the) British Empire.

C.B.I., Confederation of British Industry.

cc., 1. cubic capacity. 2. cubic centimetre or centimetres. 3. carbon copy. Also, **c.c.**

C.C., 1. county council. 2. county court. 3. cricket club.

C clef, *Music.* a sign indicating the position of middle C on the stave.

Cd, *Chem.* cadmium.

cd, 1. cord; cords. 2. *Physics.* candela.

C.D., 1. Civil Defence (Corps). 2. corps diplomatique.

c/d, 1. carried down. 2. Also, **C/D.** cash against documents.

Cdr, commander.

Ce, *Chem.* cerium.

C.E., 1. chief engineer. 2. civil engineer(ing).

Ceará (*Port.* syä rä′), *n.* Fortaleza.

cease (sēs), *v.,* **ceased, ceasing,** *n.* —*v.i.* **1.** to stop (moving, speaking, etc.): *she ceased to cry.* **2.** to come to an end. **3.** *Obs.* to die. —*v.t.* **4.** to put a stop or end to; discontinue: *to cease work.* —*n.* **5.** *Obs.* cessation. **6. without cease,** endlessly. [ME *cess(en),* t. OF: m. *cesser,* g. L *cessāre,* freq. of *cēdere* go, yield] —**Syn. 1.** See **stop.** —**Ant. 1.** begin.

cease-fire (sēs′fī′ə), *n.* a truce.

ceaseless (sēs′lĭs), *adj.* without stop or pause; unending; incessant. —**cease′lessly,** *adv.*

Ceaucescu (*Rum.* chăw shĕs′kōō), *n.* **Nicolae** (*Rum.* nē′kô lăy), born 1918, Rumanian statesman, leader of Rumania since 1967.

Cebú (sĭ bōō′), *n.* **1.** one of the Philippine Islands, in the central part of the group. 1,183,000 pop. (est. 1963); 1703 sq mi. **2.** a seaport on this island. 251,146 (1960).

Čechy (*Cz.* chĕ′KHē), *n.* Czech name of **Bohemia.**

Cecil (sĕs′əl), *n.* **William.** See **Burghley.**

Cecilia (sĭ sēl′yə), *n.* **Saint,** died A.D. 230?, Roman martyr: patron saint of music.

cecity (sē′sĭ tĭ), *n. Archaic.* mental blindness. [t. L: m. s. *caecitas* blindness]

Cecrops (sē′krŏps), *n. Gk Legend.* the founder and first king of Attica: represented as half dragon.

cedar (sē′də), *n.* **1.** any of the Old World coniferous trees constituting the genus *Cedrus,* as *C. libani* (**cedar of Lebanon**), a stately tree native in Asia Minor, etc. **2.** any of various junipers, as *Juniperus virginiana* (**red cedar**), an American tree with a fragrant reddish wood used for making lead pencils, etc. **3.** any of various other coniferous trees, as *Chamaecyparis thyoides,* a species of the swamps of the eastern U.S., *Thuja occidentalis,* the arbor vitae (both called **white cedar**), and *Libocedrus decurrens,* the **incense cedar** of California. **4.** any of various non-pinaceous tropical trees, as *Cedrela odorata* (**Spanish cedar**), a timber tree whose wood is used for cigar boxes. **5.** the wood of any of these trees. [ME *cedir,* etc., OE *ceder,* t. L: m. s. *cedrus,* t. Gk: m. *kédros;* r. ME *cedre,* t. OF]

Cedarberg (sē′də bûg′), *n.* a mountain range in the Republic of South Africa, in SW Cape Province. Highest peak, 6339 ft.

cedarn (sē′dən), *adj. Poetic.* **1.** of cedar trees. **2.** made of cedar wood.

cede (sēd), *v.t.,* **ceded, ceding.** to yield or formally resign and surrender to another; make over, as by treaty: *to cede territory.* [t. L: m. s. *cēdere* go, withdraw, yield, grant] —**Syn.** grant, transfer. —**Ant.** retain.

cedi (sā′dĭ), *n., pl.* **cedi. 1.** the monetary unit of Ghana, equivalent to about £0·408 sterling. **2.** a note of this value.

cedilla (sĭ dĭl′ə), *n.* a mark placed under *c* before *a, o,* or *u,* as in *façade,* to show that it has the sound of *s.* [t. Sp.: *cedilla,* now *zedilla,* the mark (orig. a *z* written after *c*), g. dim. of L *zēta,* t. Gk: name of letter *z*]

cedula (sĕd′yōō lə; *Sp.* thĕ′dōō lä), *n.* **1.** (in Spanish-speaking countries) any of various orders, certificates, or the like. **2.** any of certain securities issued by South and Central American governments. **3.** (in the Philippine Islands) **a.** a personal registration tax certificate. **b.** the tax itself. [t. Sp. See SCHEDULE]

cee-spring (sē′sprĭng′), *n.* a spring, shaped like the letter C, which supports the body of a vehicle. Also, **C-spring.**

ceil (sēl), *v.t.* to overlay (the interior upper surface of a building or room) with wood, plaster, etc.; to provide with a ceiling. [late ME. Cf. F *ciel* sky, heaven, canopy, g. L *caelum* sky, heaven]

ceiling (sē′lĭng), *n.* **1.** the overhead interior lining of a room; the surface of a room opposite the floor. **2.** top limit: *price ceilings on rent.* **3.** *Naut.* the flooring, usually wooden, covering the double bottom tanks, at the bottom of a ship's hold. **4.** *Aeron.* **a.** the maximum altitude to which a particular aircraft can rise under specified conditions. **b.** the maximum altitude from which the earth can be seen on a particular day, usually equal to the distance between the earth and the base of the lowest cloudbank. **5.** *Obs.* the act of one who ceils. —*adj.* **6.** *Colloq.* maximum. [der. CEIL]

ceilometer (sē lŏm′ĭ tə), *n. Meteorol.* a device for measuring and recording the height of clouds, based on the reflection of a beam of light from a cloud base. [f. CEIL(ING) + -(O)METER[1]]

celadon (sĕl′ə dŏn′), *n.* **1.** a pale green colour. —*adj.* **2.** pale green. [t. F]

celandine (sĕl′ən dīn′), *n.* **1.** a papaveraceous plant, *Chelidonium majus* (**greater celandine**), with yellow flowers. **2.** a ranunculaceous plant, *Ranunculus ficaria* (**lesser celandine**), with yellow flowers. [ME *celidoine,* t. OF, g. L *chelidonia,* t. Gk: m. *chelidónion,* der. *chelidṓn* swallow]

celanese (sĕl′ə nēz′), *n.* **1.** an acetate rayon yarn or fabric. **2.** (*cap.*) a trademark for this yarn or fabric.

-cele[1], a word element meaning 'tumour', as in *varicocele.* [comb. form repr. Gk *kḗlē*]

-cele[2], var. of **-coele.**

Celebes (sĕl′ĭ bēz′, sĕ lē′bĭz), *n.* an island in Indonesia, separated from the Philippine Islands by the **Celebes Sea.** With adjacent islands, 7,000,000 pop. (est. 1961); 72,986 sq. mi. Also, Indonesian, **Sulawesi.**

Celebes

celebrant (sĕl′ĭ brənt), *n.* **1.** the officiating priest in the celebration of the Eucharist. **2.** a participant in a public religious rite. **3.** a participant in any celebration.

celebrate (sĕl′ĭ brāt′), *v.,* **-brated, -brating.** —*v.t.* **1.** to observe (a day) or commemorate (an event) with ceremonies or festivities. **2.** to make known publicly; proclaim. **3.** to sound the praises of; extol. **4.** to perform with appropriate rites and ceremonies; solemnize. —*v.i.* **5.** to observe a day or commemorate an event with ceremonies or festivities. **6.** to perform a religious ceremony, esp. mass. **7.** *Colloq.* to engage in a festive activity; have a party. [t. L: m. s. *celebrātus,* pp.] —**cel′ebra′tor,** *n.* —**Syn. 3.** laud, glorify, honour.

celebrated (sĕl′ĭ brā′tĭd), *adj.* famous; renowned; well-known. —**Syn.** See **famous.**

celebration (sĕl′ĭ brā′shən), *n.* **1.** the act of celebrating. **2.** that which is done to celebrate anything.

celebrity (sĭ lĕb′rĭ tĭ), *n., pl.* **-ties. 1.** a famous or well-known person. **2.** fame; renown.

celeriac (sĭ lĕ′rĭ ăk′), *n.* a variety of celery having a large bulbous root which is cooked as a vegetable.

celerity (sĭ lĕ′rĭ tĭ), *n.* swiftness; speed. [ME *celerite,* t. L: m. s. *celeritas*]

celery (sĕl′ə rĭ), *n.* a plant, *Apium graveolens,* of the parsley family, whose blanched leafstalks are used raw for salad, and cooked as a vegetable. [t. F: m. *céleri,* t. d. It.: m. *sellari* (pl.), g. LL *selinon,* t. Gk: parsley]

celesta (sĭ lĕs′tə), *n.* a musical instrument consisting essentially of steel plates struck by hammers, and having a keyboard. Also, **celeste** (sĭ lĕst′). [t. F: m. *céleste,* lit., heavenly]

celestial (sĭ lĕs′tyəl), *adj.* **1.** pertaining to the spiritual or invisible heaven; heavenly; divine: *celestial bliss.* **2.** pertaining to the sky or visible heaven. —*n.* **3.** an inhabitant of heaven. [ME, t. OF, f. *celesti-* (m. s. L *caelestis* heavenly) + *-al* -AL[1]] —**celes′tially,** *adv.*

Celestial City, the goal of the journey in Bunyan's *Pilgrim's Progress*; the heavenly Jerusalem. Rev. 21.

Celestial Empire, the former Chinese Empire.

celestial equator, *Astron., Navig.* a great circle of the celestial sphere, the plane of which is perpendicular to the axis of the earth.

celestial globe, *Astron.* a model of the celestial sphere, on which the relative positions of the stars may be indicated without distortion.

celestial latitude. See **latitude** (def. 3).

celestial longitude. See **longitude** (def. 2a).

celestial pole. See **pole**[2] (def. 2).

celestial sphere, *Astron.* the imaginary spherical shell formed by the sky, usually represented as an infinite sphere of which the observer's position is the centre.

Celestine V (sĕl′ĭ stīn′, sĭ lĕs′tĭn, -tīn), **Saint,** *c.* 1215–96, Italian hermit: pope in 1294.

celestite (sĕl′ĭ stīt′), *n. Chem.* a white to delicate blue mineral, strontium sulphate, $SrSO_4$, occurring in tabular crystals: the principal ore of strontium. Also, **celestine** (sĕl′ĭs tĭn, -ĭ stīn′). [f. m. s. L *caelestis* heavenly (in allusion to the delicate blue of some specimens) + -ITE[1]]

celiac (sē′lĭ ăk′), *adj. Anat.* coeliac.

celibacy (sĕl′ĭ bə sĭ), *n., pl.* **-cies.** **1.** the unmarried state. **2.** (of priests, etc.) abstention by vow from marriage.

celibate (sĕl′ĭ bĭt), *n.* **1.** one who remains unmarried, esp. for religious reasons. —*adj.* **2.** unmarried. [t. L: m. s. *caelibātus*, der. *caelebs* unmarried]

cell (sĕl), *n.* **1.** a small room in a convent, prison, etc. **2.** any small compartment, bounded area, receptacle, case, etc. **3.** a small group acting as a unit within a larger organization. **4.** *Biol.* **a.** a plant or animal structure, usually microscopic, containing nuclear and cytoplasmic material, enclosed by a semipermeable membrane (animal) or cell wall (plant); the structural unit of plant and animal life. **b.** a minute cavity or interstice, as in animal or plant tissue. **5.** *Entomol.* one of the areas into which an insect's wing is divided by the veins. **6.** *Bot.* the pollen sac of an anther. **7.** *Elect.* a device which generates electricity and which forms the whole, or a part of, a voltaic battery, consisting in one of its simplest forms of two plates, each of a different metal, placed in a jar containing a dilute acid or other electrolyte (**voltaic cell**). **8.** *Phys. Chem.* a device for producing electrolysis, consisting essentially of the electrolyte, its container, and the electrodes (**electrolytic cell**). **9.** *Aeron.* **a.** the part of the wing structure of a biplane on either side of the fuselage. **b.** the gas-container of a balloon. **10.** *Archit.* one of the compartments of a groin or rib vault; web. **11.** *Eccles.* a monastery or nunnery, usually small, dependent on a larger religious house. [ME *celle*, OE *cell*, t. L: s. *cella* room]

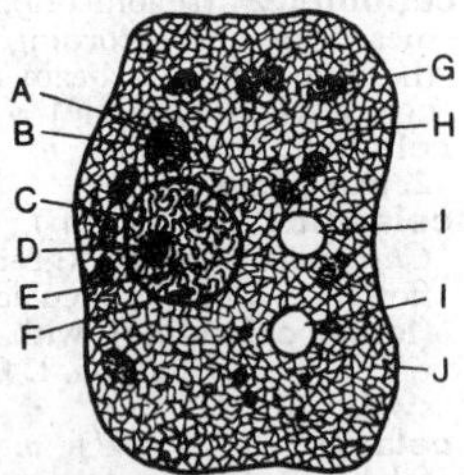

Diagram of an organic cell (def. 4a): A, Centrosphere; B, Centrosome; C, Nucleus; D, Nucleolus; E, Chromatin network; F, Karyosome; G, Plastid; H, Cytoplasm; I, Vacuole; J, Cell wall

cella (sĕl′ə), *n., pl.* **cellae** (sĕl′ē). *Archit.* (in ancient Greek or Roman temples) an enclosed inner room, the sanctuary containing the statue of the divinity. [t. L]

cellar (sĕl′ə), *n.* **1.** a room or set of rooms for the storage of foodstuffs, etc., now always either wholly or partly underground, and usually beneath a building. **2.** an underground room or store; basement. **3.** a wine cellar. **4.** a supply or stock of wines. **5.** a salt-cellar. —*v.t.* **6.** to place or store in a cellar. [t. L: m. s. *cellārium* pantry; r. ME *celer*, t. AF, var. of OF *celier*, g. L *cellārium*]

cellarage (sĕl′ə rĭj), *n.* **1.** cellar space. **2.** charges for storing in a cellar.

cellarer (sĕl′ə rə), *n.* the steward of a monastery.

cellaret (sĕl′ə rĕt′), *n.* a cabinet for wine bottles, etc.

cellarman (sĕl′ə măn′), *n.* a man in charge of a cellar, esp. that of a large public house.

cell-division (sĕl′dĭ vĭzh′ən), *n. Biol.* the division of a cell in reproduction or growth.

Celle (*Ger.* tsĕl′ə), *n.* a town in E central Lower Saxony. 58,300 (est. 1966).

Cellini (chĕ lē′nĭ; *It.* chĕl lē′nē), *n.* **Benvenuto** (*It.* bėn vė nōō′tò), 1500–71, Italian sculptor, artist in metal, and autobiographer.

cellist (chĕl′ĭst), *n.* a player on the cello. Also, **'cellist, violoncellist.**

cello (chĕl′ō), *n., pl.* **-los, -li.** the baritone of the violin family, which is rested vertically on the floor between the player's knees. Also, **'cello, violoncello.** [short form of VIOLONCELLO]

Cello

cellophane (sĕl′ə fān′), *n.* **1.** a transparent, paper-like product of viscose, impervious to moisture, germs, etc., used to wrap sweets, tobacco, etc. **2.** (*cap.*) a trademark for this product. [f. CELL(ULOSE) + -(O)-PHANE]

cell-sap (sĕl′săp′), *n.* the aqueous solution filling the vacuole of a plant cell.

cellular (sĕl′yŏŏ lə), *adj.* **1.** pertaining to or characterized by cellules or cells, esp. minute compartments or cavities. **2.** *Textiles.* loosely woven, with open airholes. [t. NL: s. *cellulāris*, der. L *cellula* little room]

cellule (sĕl′yōōl), *n.* a little cell. [t. L: m. *cellula*]

cellulitis (sĕl′yŏŏ lī′tĭs), *n. Pathol.* inflammation of cellular tissue. [t. NL, f. s. L *cellula* little cell + *-itis* -ITIS]

celluloid (sĕl′yŏŏ loid′), *n.* a substance consisting essentially of soluble guncotton and camphor, usually highly inflammable, variously used as a substitute for ivory, vulcanite, etc. [f. CELLUL(OSE) + -OID]

cellulose (sĕl′yŏŏ lōs′), *n.* **1.** *Chem.* an inert substance, a carbohydrate, the chief constituent of the cell walls of plants, and forming an essential part of wood, cotton, hemp, paper, etc. —*v.t.* **2.** to apply a cellulose lacquer to (a motor car, etc.). [f. s. L *cellula* little cell + -OSE[2]]

cellulose acetate, *Chem.* an acetic ester of cellulose used to make textiles, artificial leathers, yarns, etc.

cellulose lacquer, a quick-drying lacquer consisting of cellulose nitrate or of cellulose acetate, with suitable pigments and plasticizers dissolved in a volatile solvent.

cellulose nitrate, *Chem.* a nitric ester of cellulose used in the manufacture of lacquers and explosives.

cellulous (sĕl′yŏŏ ləs), *adj.* full or consisting of cells.

cell wall, *Biol.* the definite boundary or wall which is usually part of the structure of a biological cell, esp. a plant cell. See **cell** (def. 4a).

celom (sē′ləm), *n. Zool.* coelom.

Cels, Celsius.

Celsius thermometer (sĕl′syəs), **1.** centigrade thermometer. **2.** Also, **Celsius scale.** a centigrade scale or thermometer, from which the modern thermometer was developed (1743) by inverting the freezing point (orig. 100°) and boiling point (orig. 0°) of water. [named after A. *Celsius*, 1701–44, Swedish astronomer]

celt (sĕlt), *n. Archaeol.* an axe of stone or metal without perforation or groove for hafting. [t. LL: s. *celtis* chisel]

Celt (sĕlt, kĕlt), *n.* a member of an Indo-European people now represented chiefly by the Irish, Gaels, Welsh, and Bretons. Also, **Kelt.** [t. L: s. *Celtae*, pl., t. Gk: m. *Keltoí*]

Celt., Celtic.

Celtic (sĕl′tĭk, kĕl′tĭk), *n.* **1.** a group of Indo-European languages including Irish, Scottish, Gaelic, Welsh, Breton, etc., surviving now in Ireland, the Scottish Highlands, Wales, and Brittany. —*adj.* **2.** of the Celts or their language. Also, **Keltic.** —**Celticism** (sĕl′tĭ sĭz′əm, kĕl′-), *n.*

Celtic cross, a cross resembling a Latin cross, but having a circle around the upper members centred on their point of intersection. See illus. under **cross.**

Celto-, a word element meaning 'Celtic'.

cembalo (chĕm′bə lō′), *n. Music.* **1.** a dulcimer (def. 1). **2.** a harpsichord. [t. It.] —**cem′balist,** *n.*

cement (sĭ mĕnt′), *n.* **1.** any of various substances which are soft when first prepared but later become hard or stonelike, used for joining stones, making floors, etc. **2.** a material of this kind (the ordinary variety, often called **Portland cement**) commonly made by burning a mixture of clay and limestone, used for making concrete for foundations or the like, covering floors, etc. **3.** *Geol.* the compact groundmass surrounding and binding together the fragments of clastic rocks. **4.** anything that binds or unites. **5.** *Dentistry.* an adhesive plastic substance used to fill teeth or to pack fillings or inlays into teeth. **6.** *Dentistry.* cementum. **7.** *Metall.* the powder utilized during cementation. **8.** *Colloq.* concrete. —*v.t.* **9.** to unite by, or as by, cement: *a friendship cemented by time.* **10.** to coat or cover with cement. —*v.i.* **11.** to become cemented; join together or unite; cohere. [t. L: m. s. *caementum* rough stone; r. ME *siment*, t. OF] —**cement′er,** *n.*

cementation (sē′mĕn tā′shən), *n.* **1.** the act, process, or result of cementing. **2.** *Metall.* the heating of two substances in contact in order to effect some change in one of them; esp., the formation of steel by heating iron in powdered charcoal.

cementite (sĭ mĕn′tīt), *n.* *Metall.* a carbide of iron, Fe_3C, used in steel to add strength and hardness.

cement-mixer (sĭ mĕnt′mĭk′sə), *n.* a machine which prepares concrete from cement, sand, ballast, and water by mixing them in a revolving drum.

cementum (sĭ mĕn′təm), *n.* *Dentistry.* a hard tissue which forms the outer surfaces of the root of a tooth. See diag. under **tooth.**

cemetery (sĕm′ĭ trĭ), *n.*, *pl.* **-teries.** a burial ground, esp. one not attached to a church; graveyard. [late ME *cymytery*, t. LL: m. s. *coemētērium*, t. Gk: m. *koimētḗrion*]

-cene, a word element meaning 'recent', 'new', as in *Pleistocene.* [comb. form repr. Gk *kainós*]

cenesthesia (sē′nĭs thē′zyə), *n.* coenaesthesia. Also **cenesthesis** (sē′nĭs thē′sĭs).

Cenis (*Fr.* sə nē′), *n.* **Mont** (*Fr.* mōɴ). **1.** a pass in the Alps between France and Italy. 6835 ft high. **2.** a railway tunnel to the W of this pass. ab. 8 mi. long.

ceno-[1], var. of **caino-.**

ceno-[2], var. of **coeno-.** Also, before vowels, **cen-.**

cenobite (sē′nō bīt′), *n.* *Chiefly U.S.* coenobite. **—cenobitic** (sē′nō bĭt′ĭk), **ce′nobit′ical,** *adj.* **—cenobitism** (sē′nō bī′tĭz əm), *n.*

cenogenesis (sē′nō jĕn′ĭ sĭs), *n.*, *Biol.*, *Chiefly U.S.* cainogenesis. **—cenogenetic** (sē′nō jĭ nĕt′ĭk), *adj.*

cenotaph (sĕn′ə tăf′, -täf′), *n.* a sepulchral monument erected in memory of a deceased person whose body is elsewhere. [t. L: m. s. *cenotaphium*, t. Gk: m. *kenotáphion* an empty tomb] **—cen′otaph′ic,** *adj.*

Cenozoic (sē′nō zō′ĭk), *adj.*, *n.* *Chiefly U.S.* Cainozoic.

cense (sĕns), *v.t.*, **censed, censing.** to burn incense near or in front of; perfume with incense. [aphetic var. of INCENSE[1]]

censer (sĕn′sə), *n.* a container in which incense is burned. [ME *censere*, t. OF: m. *encensier.* See INCENSE[1]]

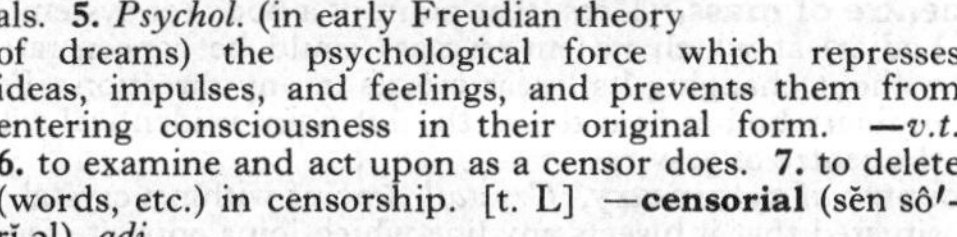
Censer

censor (sĕn′sə), *n.* **1.** an official who examines books, plays, news reports, films, radio programmes, etc., for the purpose of suppressing parts deemed objectionable on moral, political, military, or other grounds. **2.** any person who supervises the manners or morality of others. **3.** an adverse critic; a faultfinder. **4.** a member of the board of two officials of republican Rome who kept the register or census of the citizens, let public contracts, and supervised manners and morals. **5.** *Psychol.* (in early Freudian theory of dreams) the psychological force which represses ideas, impulses, and feelings, and prevents them from entering consciousness in their original form. **—*v.t.*** **6.** to examine and act upon as a censor does. **7.** to delete (words, etc.) in censorship. [t. L] **—censorial** (sĕn sô′rĭ əl), *adj.*

censorious (sĕn sô′rĭ əs), *adj.* severely critical; faultfinding; carping. **—censo′riously,** *adv.* **—censo′riousness,** *n.*

censorship (sĕn′sə shĭp′), *n.* **1.** the act of censoring. **2.** the office or power of a censor. **3.** the time during which a censor holds office. **4.** *Psychol.* censor (def. 5).

censurable (sĕn′shə rə bl), *adj.* deserving censure. **—cen′surableness, cen′surabil′ity,** *n.* **—cen′surably,** *adv.*

censure (sĕn′shə), *n.*, *v.*, **-sured, -suring.** **—*n.*** **1.** an expression of disapproval; adverse or hostile criticism; blaming. **—*v.t.*** **2.** to criticize adversely; disapprove; find fault with; condemn. **—*v.i.*** **3.** to give censure, adverse criticism, or blame. [ME, t. L: m. *censūra* censorship, judgement. Cf. CENSOR] **—cen′surer,** *n.* **—Syn. 1.** condemnation, reproof. See **abuse. 3.** reprove, rebuke, reprimand. See **blame. —Ant.** praise.

census (sĕn′səs), *n.* **1.** an official enumeration of inhabitants, with details as to age, sex, pursuits, etc. **2.** (in ancient Rome) the registration of citizens and their property, for purposes of taxation. [t. L] **—cen′sual,** *adj.*

cent (sĕnt), *n.* **1.** the hundredth part of the U.S. dollar. **2.** a bronze coin of this value. **3.** the hundredth part of monetary units elsewhere. [t. L: short for *centēsimus* hundredth]

cent-, var. of **centi-,** as in *centare.*

cent., 1. centigrade. **2.** central. **3.** centum (in *per cent*). **4.** century.

cental (sĕn′tl), *n.* *Rare.* a weight equal to 100 lbs avoirdupois. [f. s. L *centum* hundred + -AL[1]]

centare (sĕn′tĕə; *Fr.* säɴ tår′), *n.* centiare.

centaur (sĕn′tô), *n.* **1.** *Gk Legend.* one of a race of monsters having the head, trunk, and arms of a man, and the body and legs of a horse. **2.** (*cap.*) *Astron.* Centaurus. [ME, t. L: s. *centaurus*, t. Gk: m. *kéntauros*]

Centaurus (sĕn tô′rəs), *n.*, *gen.* **Centauri** (sĕn tô′rī). *Astron.* a southern constellation containing the first magnitude stars Alpha Centauri (the star nearest to the solar system) and Beta Centauri. [see CENTAUR]

centaury (sĕn′tô′rĭ), *n.*, *pl.* **-ries.** any of the Old World gentianaceous herbs belonging to the genus *Centaurium*, as the common centaury, *C. erythraea*, and *Centaurium umbellatum* (*Erythraea centaurium*), with medicinal properties. [ME *centaurie*, t. ML: m. *centauria*, r. L *centaurēum*, t. Gk: m. *kentaúreion*, der. *kéntauros* centaur (here the centaur Chiron, reputed discoverer of the plant's medicinal virtues)]

centavo (sĕn tä′vō; *Sp.* thĕn tä′bō), *n.*, *pl.* **-vos** (-vōs; *Sp.* -bōs). a small coin or minor monetary unit equal to the hundredth part of a particular monetary unit, esp. **a.** one hundredth of a peso, as in Mexico, the Philippine Islands, Cuba, etc. **b.** one hundredth of an escudo, in Portugal. [t. Sp. See CENT]

centenarian (sĕn′tĭ nĕə′rĭ ən), *adj.* **1.** pertaining to or having lived 100 years. **—*n.*** **2.** one who has reached the age of a hundred.

centenary (sĕn tē′nə rĭ), *adj.*, *n.*, *pl.* **-ries. —*adj.*** **1.** of or pertaining to a 100th anniversary. **—*n.*** **2.** a 100th anniversary. **3.** its celebration. **4.** a period of 100 years; a century. [t. L: m. s. *centēnārius* of or containing 100]

centennial (sĕn tĕn′yəl), *adj.* **1.** consisting of, or marking the completion of, 100 years. **2.** lasting 100 years. **3.** recurring every 100 years. **4.** 100 years old. **—*n.*** **5.** *U.S.* a centenary. [f. s. L *centennium* 100 years + -AL[1]; modelled on BIENNIAL] **—centen′nially,** *adv.*

center (sĕn′tə), *n.*, *v.* *U.S.* centre.

centering (sĕn′tə rĭng), *n.* a temporary framing, for supporting permanent framework during construction. Also, **centring.**

centesimal (sĕn tĕs′ĭ məl), *adj.* hundredth; pertaining to division into hundredths. [f. s. L *centēsimus* hundredth + -AL[1]] **—centes′imally,** *adv.*

centesimo (sĕn tĕs′ĭ mō′; *It.* chĕn tĕz′ē mō; *Sp.* thĕn-tĕs′ē mō), *n.*, *pl.* *It.* **-mi** (-mē), *Sp.* **-mos** (-mōs). **1.** an Italian copper coin and monetary unit, the hundredth part of a lira. **2.** the hundredth part of a peso in Uruguay and of a balboa in Panama. [t. It., g. L *centēsimus* hundredth]

centi-, a word element meaning 'hundred', applied in the metric system to the division of the unit by 100, as in *centigram.* Also, **cent-.** [t. L, comb. form of *centum*]

centiare (sĕn′tĭ ĕə′; *Fr.* säɴ tyår′), *n.* a square metre. Also, **centare.** [t. F. See CENTI-, ARE[2]]

centigrade (sĕn′tĭ grād′), *adj.* **1.** divided into 100 degrees, as a scale. **2.** pertaining to the centigrade thermometer. [t. F. See CENTI-, -GRADE]

centigrade thermometer, a thermometer based on a scale of equal degrees between zero (fixed at the melting point of ice) and 100° (fixed at the boiling point of water) at a pressure of 760 mm. of mercury; Celsius thermometer. See illus. under **thermometer.**

centigram (sĕn′tĭ grăm′), *n.* 1/100 of a gram, equivalent to 0·1543 grain. Also, **centigramme.** [t. F: m. *centigramme.* See CENTI-, -GRAM[2]]

centilitre (sĕn′tĭ lē′tə), *n.* one hundredth of a litre, equivalent to 0·6102 cubic inches, or 0·352 fluid ounces. Also, *U.S.*, **centiliter.** [t. F. See CENTI-, LITRE]

centillion (sĕn tĭl′ĭ ən, -yən), *n.* **1.** (in Britain and Germany) a cardinal number represented by 1 followed by 600 noughts; the hundredth power of a million. **2.** (in the U.S. and France) a cardinal number represented by 1 followed by 303 noughts.

centime (sŏn′tēm; *Fr.* säɴ tēm′), *n.* the hundredth part of a franc. [t. F: f. *cent* hundred + suffix *-ime*]

centimetre (sĕn′tĭ mē′tə), *n.* one hundredth of a metre, equivalent to 0·3937 in. Also, *esp. U.S.*, **centimeter.** [t. F: m. *centimètre.* See CENTI-, -METRE]

centimetre-gram-second (sĕn′tĭ mē tə grăm′sĕk′ənd), *adj.* of or pertaining to a system of units employed in science, based on the centimetre, gram, and second as the primary units of length, mass, and time. Also, **centimetre-gramme-second**; *U.S.*, **centimeter-gram-second.** *Abbrev.:* c.g.s.

céntimo (sĕn′tĭ mō′; *Sp.* thĕn′tē mō), *n.*, *pl.* **-mos** (-mōz′; *Sp.* -mōs), the hundredth part of a bolivar, colón, or peseta. [t. Sp., t. F: m. *centime*]

centipede (sĕn′tĭ pēd′), *n.* any member of the class *Chilopoda*, active, predacious, and mostly nocturnal arthropods having an elongated flattened body of numerous segments each with a single pair of legs, the first pair of which is modified into poison fangs. Few are dangerous to man. [t. L: m. s. *centipeda* hundred-footed insect]

centner (sĕnt′nə), *n.* **1.** (in several European countries) a unit of weight of 50 kilograms, equivalent to 110·23 lbs avoirdupois. **2.** *Rare.* a unit of 100 kilograms. [t.

Flem.: m. *centener*, t. L: m. s. *centēnārius* of a hundred]

cento (sĕn′tō), *n.*, *pl.* **-tos.** **1.** a poem composed wholly of quotations from other authors. **2.** *Archaic.* a patchwork. [t. L]

CENTO (sĕn′tō), *n.* an organization for economic and military cooperation, established in 1959, and comprising Great Britain, Iran, Pakistan, and Turkey. [*Cen*(*tral*) *T*(*reaty*) *O*(*rganization*)]

centr-, var. of **centro-** before vowels.

centra (sĕn′trə), *n.* pl. of **centrum.**

central (sĕn′trəl), *adj.* **1.** of or forming the centre. **2.** in, at, or near the centre. **3.** constituting that from which other related things proceed or upon which they depend. **4.** principal; chief; dominant: *the central idea, the central character in a novel.* **5.** *Anat., Physiol.* **a.** pertaining to the brain and spinal cord of the nervous system (as distinguished from *peripheral*). **b.** of or relating to the centrum or body of a vertebra. **6.** *Phonet.* pronounced with the tongue in a neutral position, as for example, the final vowel in *sofa* or *idea.* **—***n.* **7.** *U.S.* the office of a telephone system, in which connections are made between different lines. [t. L: s. *centrālis.* See CENTRE] **—cen′trally,** *adv.*

Central African Federation, Federation of Rhodesia and Nyasaland.

Central African Republic, an independent member of the French Community in central Africa. 1,256,000 pop. (1964); 238,000 sq. mi. *Cap.:* Bangui. Formerly, **Ubangi-Shari.**

Central America, continental North America S of Mexico, comprising the six republics of Guatemala, Honduras, El Salvador, Nicaragua, Costa Rica, Panama, and the colony British Honduras. 12,120,000 pop (est. 1961); 227,933 sq. mi. —**Central American.**

central bank, a bank which acts as banker to the government of a country and to other banks; it holds liquid funds and reserves, issues currency, and regulates the supply of credit.

Central Bay, a dark plain, *Sinus Medii*, in the centre of the face of the moon.

central cylinder, *Bot.* stele (def. 4).

Central European Time, the standard time adopted in all western European countries, the same as British Standard Time. *Abbrev.:* C.E.T.

central heating, a method of heating a building from a central system by circulating hot water, steam or air through pipes.

Centralia (sĕn trā′lyə), *n.* *Austral. Colloq.* the inland region of continental Australia.

Central India, a former group of states in central India, which constituted the **Central India Agency.**

Central Intelligence Agency, the U.S. federal government agency that coordinates intelligence, espionage, etc.

centralism (sĕn′trə lĭz′əm), *n.* **1.** centralization, or a centralizing system. **2.** the principle of centralization, esp. in government. **—cen′tralist,** *n., adj.*

centrality (sĕn trăl′ĭ tĭ), *n.* central position or state.

centralization (sĕn′trə lī zā′shən), *n.* **1.** the act of centralizing. **2.** the fact of being centralized. **3.** the concentration of administrative power in a central government. **4.** *Sociol.* a process whereby social groups and institutions become increasingly dependent on a central group or institution. Also, **centralisation.**

centralize (sĕn′trə līz′), *v.t.*, **-lized, -lizing.** **1.** to draw to or towards a centre. **2.** to bring under one control, esp. in government. **—***v.i.* **3.** to come together at a centre. Also, **centralise.** —**cen′traliz′er,** *n.*

central nervous system, the brain and spinal cord considered together. See **central** (def. 5).

Central Powers, (in World War I) Germany and Austria-Hungary, often with their allies Turkey and Bulgaria, as opposed to the Allies.

Central Provinces and Berar (bĕ rä′), a former province in central India, now a part of Madhya Pradesh.

Central Time, one of the four standard time zones in the U.S., lying on the 90th meridian, six hours behind **Greenwich Mean Time** and one hour behind **Eastern Time.**

centre (sĕn′tə), *n.*, *v.* **-tred, -tring.** **1.** *Geom.* the middle point, as the point within a circle or sphere equidistant from all points of the circumference or surface, or the point within a regular polygon equidistant from the vertexes. **2.** a point, pivot, axis, etc., round which anything rotates or revolves. **3.** a principal point, place, or object: *a shipping centre.* **4.** a person, thing, group, etc., occupying the middle position, esp. troops. **5.** (*usually cap.*) (in continental Europe) **a.** that part of a legislative assembly which sits in the centre of the chamber, a position customarily assigned to representatives holding views intermediate between those of the conservatives or right and the progressives or left. **b.** a party holding such views. **6.** *Football, Basketball, etc.* the middle player in the attacking or forward line; centre-forward. **7.** *Physiol.* a cluster of nerve cells governing a specific organic process: *the vasomotor centre.* **8.** *Mach.* **a.** a pointed rod mounted in the headstock spindle (**live centre**) or the tailstock spindle (**dead centre**) of a lathe, upon which the work to be turned is placed. **b.** one of two similar points on some other machine, as a planing machine, enabling an object to be turned on its axis. **c.** a tapered indentation in a piece to be turned on a lathe into which the centre is fitted. **—***v.t.* **9.** to place in or on a centre. **10.** to collect at a centre. **11.** to determine or mark the centre of. **12.** to adjust, shape, or modify (an object, part, etc.) so that its axis or the like is in a central or normal position. **13.** *Soccer, Hockey, etc.* to pass (the ball) from the wing to the midfield. **—***v.i.* **14.** to be at or come to a centre. **15.** *Soccer, Hockey, etc,* to centre the ball. Also, *U.S.*, **center.** [ME *centre*, t. OF, t. L: m. *centrum*, t. Gk: m. *kéntron* sharp point, centre] **—Syn. 1.** See **middle.**

Centre (*Fr.* säɴ′tr), *n.* an administrative region in central France. 1,858,297 pop. (1962); 15,266 sq. mi. *Prefecture:* Orléans.

centre-bit (sĕn′tə bĭt′), *n.* a carpenter's bit with a sharp, projecting centre point, used for boring holes.

centreboard (sĕn′tə bôd′), *n.* a movable fin keel in a boat, esp. a sailing dinghy, that can be drawn up in shoal water into a housing or well. Also, **centreplate.**

centre-forward (sĕn′tə fô′wəd), *n.* *Soccer, Hockey, etc.* the middle player in the forward line.

centre-half (sĕn′tə häf′), *n.* *Soccer, Hockey, etc.* the middle player in the half-back line.

centre of attraction, 1. the point towards which bodies tend by force of gravity or some other force. **2.** a person, place, etc., of greater interest than the surrounding people or places.

centre of buoyancy, the point in a floating body through which the buoyancy forces act; this is the same as the centre of gravity of the displaced fluid.

centre of curvature, 1. *Maths.* the point of intersection of any two normals to a curve. **2.** *Optics.* (of a lens or mirror) the centre of the sphere of which the surface of the lens or mirror forms a part.

centre of gravity, *Mech.* that point of a body (or system of bodies) from which it could be suspended or on which it could be supported and be in equilibrium in any position in a uniform gravitational field.

centre of inertia, centre of mass.

centre of mass, *Mech.* that point of a body (or system of bodies) at which its entire mass could be concentrated without changing its linear inertia in any direction. For ordinary bodies near the earth, this point is identical with the centre of gravity.

centre of symmetry, *Crystall.* a point within a crystal so situated that it bisects any line which joins opposite faces or edges of the crystal.

centrepiece (sĕn′tə pēs′), *n.* an ornamental object used in a central position, esp. on the centre of a dining table.

centreplate (sĕn′tə plāt′), *n.* centreboard.

centre-punch (sĕn′tə pŭnch′), *n.* **1.** a tool used to mark the centre of holes to be drilled, consisting of a punch with a conical point. **—***v.t.* **2.** to mark with this tool.

centre-three-quarter (sĕn′tə thrē kwô′tə), *n.* *Rugby Football.* one of two middle players in the three-quarter line.

centrewheel (sĕn′tə wēl′), *n.* the wheel which drives the minute and hour hands of a clock or watch.

centri-, var. of **centro-,** as in *centrifugal.*

centric (sĕn′trĭk), *adj.* pertaining to or situated at the centre; central. Also, **cen′trical.** **—cen′trically,** *adv.* **—centricity** (sĕn trĭs′ ĭ tĭ), *n.*

centrifugal (sĕn trĭf′yŏŏ gl, sĕn′trĭ fyōō′gl), *adj.* **1.** moving or directed outwards from the centre. **2.** pertaining to or operated by centrifugal force: *a centrifugal pump.* **3.** *Physiol.* efferent. **—***n.* **4.** a solid or perforated cylinder rotated rapidly to separate solids from liquid. [f. s. NL *centrifugus* centre-fleeing + -AL[1]] **—centrif′ugally,** *adv.* **—Ant. 1.** centripetal.

centrifugal force, the force exerted outwards by a body moving in a curved path; the reaction of centripetal force. Also, **centrifugal action.**

centrifugalize (sĕn′trĭ fyōō′gə līz′), *v.t.* centrifuge (def. 2). Also, **centrifugalise.**

centrifuge (sĕn′trĭ fyōōj′), *n.*, *v.*, **-fuged, -fuging.** **—***n.* **1.** a machine consisting of a rotating container, in which substances of different densities, as cream and milk, may be separated by centrifugal force or in which animals, humans, and instruments are subjected to prolonged accelerations. **—***v.t.* **2.** to subject to the action of a centrifuge. [t. F: centrifugal] **—centrifugation** (sĕn′trĭ fyōō gā′shən), *n.*

centring (sĕn′trĭng), *n.* centering.
centripetal (sĕn trĭp′ĭ tl, sĕn′trĭ pē′tl), *adj.* **1.** proceeding or directed towards the centre. **2.** operating by centripetal force. **3.** *Physiol.* afferent. [f. s. NL *centripetus* centre-seeking + -AL[1]] —**centrip′etally,** *adv.*
centripetal force, a force acting on a body, which is directed towards the centre of a circle or curve, which causes it to move in the circle or curve. Also, **centripetal action.**
centrist (sĕn′trĭst), *n.* (in continental Europe) a member of a political party of the Centre. See **centre** (def. 5a). [t. F: m. *centriste*, der. *centre* centre]
centro-, a word element meaning 'centre'. Also, **centr-, centri-.** [comb. form repr. L *centrum* and Gk *kéntron*]
centrobaric (sĕn′trō băr′ĭk), *adj.* pertaining to the centre of gravity. [f. CENTRO- + s. Gk *báros* weight + -IC]
centroclinal (sĕn′trō klī′nəl), *adj.* *Geol.* sloping down towards a central point from all directions.
centroid (sĕn′troid), *n.* *Mech.* the point in an area common to all lines whose moment of area is zero.
centrosome (sĕn′trə sōm′), *n.* *Biol.* a minute protoplasmic body regarded by some as the active centre of cell division in mitosis. See diag. under **cell.** [f. CENTRO- + -SOME[3]] —**centrosomic** (sĕn′trə sŏm′ĭk), *adj.*
centrosphere (sĕn′trə sfĭə′), *n.* **1.** *Biol.* the protoplasm around a centrosome; the central portion of an aster, containing the centrosome. See diag. under **cell. 2.** *Geol.* the central or interior portion of the earth.
centrum (sĕn′trəm), *n., pl.* **-trums, -tra** (-trə). **1.** a centre. **2.** *Zool.* the body of a vertebra. [t. L. See CENTRE]
centuple (sĕn′tyŏŏ pl), *adj., v.,* **-pled, -pling.** —*adj.* **1.** a hundred times as great; hundredfold. —*v.t.* **2.** to increase a hundred times. [t. F, t. LL: m. s. *centuplus* hundredfold]
centuplicate (*v.* sĕn tyōō′plĭ kāt′; *adj., n.* sĕn tyōō′plĭ kĭt, -kāt′), *v.,* **-cated, -cating,** *adj., n.* —*v.t.* **1.** to increase a hundred times; centuple. —*adj.* **2.** hundredfold. —*n.* **3.** a number or quantity increased a hundredfold. —**centu′plica′tion,** *n.*
centurial (sĕn tyŏŏə′rĭ əl), *adj.* pertaining to a century. [t. L: s. *centuriālis*]
centurion (sĕn tyŏŏə′rĭ ən), *n.* (in the Roman Army) the commander of a century. [ME, t. L: s. *centurio*, der. *centuria.* See CENTURY]
century (sĕn′chə rĭ), *n., pl.* **-ries. 1.** a period of one hundred years. **2.** one of the successive periods of 100 years reckoned forwards or backwards from a recognized chronological epoch, esp. from the assumed date of the birth of Jesus. **3.** any group or collection of 100, as 100 runs in cricket. **4.** (in the Roman Army) a company, consisting of approximately one hundred men. **5.** one of the voting divisions of the Roman people, each division having one vote. **6.** (*cap.*) *Print.* a style of type. [t. L: m. s. *centuria* a division of a hundred things]
century plant, a Mexican species of agave, *Agave americana*, cultivated for ornament: popularly supposed not to blossom until a century old.
ceorl (chēəl), *n.* *Early Eng. Hist.* a freeman of the lowest rank, neither a noble nor a slave. [OE. See CHURL] —**ceorl′ish,** *adj.*
cephal-, var. of **cephalo-,** before vowels, as in *cephalad.*
cephalad (sĕf′ə lăd′), *adv.* *Anat., Zool.* towards the head (opposed to *caudad*). [f. CEPHAL- + L *ad* to]
cephalic (sĭ făl′ĭk), *adj.* **1.** of or pertaining to the head. **2.** situated or directed towards the head. **3.** of the nature of a head. [t. L: s. *cephalicus*, t. Gk: m. *kephalikós* of the head]
-cephalic, a word element meaning 'head', as in *brachycephalic* (related to **cephalo-**).
cephalic index, *Anat., Anthropol.* the ratio of the greatest breadth of head to its greatest length from front to back, multiplied by 100.
cephalin (sĕf′ə lĭn, kĕf′-), *n.* *Biochem.* any of a group of closely related phosphatides occurring mainly in the brain. Also, **kephalin.**
cephalization (sĕf′ə lī zā′shən), *n.* *Zool.* a tendency in the development of animals to localization of important organs or parts in or near the head. Also, **cephalisation.**
cephalo-, a word element denoting the 'head', as in *cephalopod.* Also, **cephal-.** [t. Gk: m. *kephalo-*, comb. form of *kephalḗ*]
cephalochordate (sĕf′ə lō kô′dāt), *adj.* **1.** denoting or pertaining to the *Cephalochordata.* —*n.* **2.** a member of the *Cephalochordata*, a chordate subphylum including the lancelets, having fishlike characters but lacking a vertebral column. [f. CEPHALO- + CHORD + -ATE[1]]
cephalom., cephalometry.
cephalometer (sĕf′ə lŏm′ĭ tə), *n.* an instrument for measuring the head or skull; a craniometer.
cephalometry (sĕf′ə lŏm′ĭ trĭ), *n.* the science of the measurement of heads. [f. CEPHALO- + -METRY]
Cephalonia (sĕf′ə lō′nyə), *n.* the largest of the Ionian Islands, off the W coast of Greece. 46,302 pop. (1961); 287 sq. mi. Greek, **Kephallenia.**
cephalopod (sĕf′ə lə pŏd′), *n.* a member of the class *Cephalopoda*, the most highly organized class of molluscs, including the cuttlefish, squid, octopus, etc., the members of which have tentacles attached to the head. —**cephalopodan** (sĕf′ə lŏp′ə dən), *adj., n.* [f. CEPHALO- + -POD]
cephalothorax (sĕf′ə lō thô′răks), *n.* *Zool.* the anterior part of the body in certain arachnids and crustaceans, consisting of the coalesced head and thorax.
cephalous (sĕf′ə ləs), *adj.* having a head. [f. CEPHAL- + -OUS]
-cephalous, a word element related to **cephalo-.** [f. CEPHAL- + -OUS]
Cepheid variable (sē′fĭ ĭd), *Astron.* a variable star in which changes in brightness are due to bodily pulsations.
Cepheus (sē′fyōōs), *n.* **1.** *Astron.* a northern circumpolar constellation between Cassiopeia and Draco. **2.** *Gk Legend.* the Ethiopian king who was the husband of Cassiopeia and the father of Andromeda.
-ceptor, a word element meaning 'taker', 'receiver', as in *preceptor.* [t. L]
cer-, var. of **cero-,** used before vowels, as in *ceraceous.*
ceraceous (sĭ rā′shəs), *adj.* waxlike; waxy.
Ceram (sĭ răm′; *Port.* sĕ răN′; *Du.* sĕ′rŏm), *n.* an island of the Moluccas in Indonesia, W of New Guinea. 300,000 pop. (est. 1961); 7191 sq. mi.
ceramal (sə rām′əl), *n.* cermet. [f. CERAM(IC) + AL(LOY)]
ceramet (sĕ′rə mĕt′), *n.* cermet.
ceramic (sĭ răm′ĭk), *adj.* pertaining to products made from clay and similar materials, such as pottery, brick, etc., or to their manufacture: *ceramic art.* Also, **keramic.** [t. Gk: m. s. *keramikós* of or for potters' clay, pottery]
ceramics (sĭ răm′ĭks), *n.* **1.** (*construed as sing.*) the art and technology of making clay products and similar ware. **2.** (*construed as pl.*) articles of earthenware, porcelain, etc. Also, **keramics.** [pl. of CERAMIC. See -ICS] —**ceramist** (sĕ′rə mĭst), **ceram′icist,** *n.*
cerargyrite (sĭ rä′jĭ rīt′), *n.* a mineral, silver chloride: an important silver ore in some places; chlorargyrite; horn silver. [f. m. Gk *kér(as)* horn + s. Gk *árgyros* silver + -ITE[1]]
cerate (sĭə′rĭt, -rāt), *n.* *Pharm.* an unctuous (often medicated) preparation for external application, consisting of lard or oil mixed with wax, or the like, esp. one which has a firmer consistency than a typical ointment and does not melt when in contact with the skin. [t. L: m. s. *cērātum*, neut. pp., covered with wax]
ceratin (sĕ′rə tĭn, kĕ′-), *n.* *Zool.* keratin. [f. CERAT(O)- + -IN[2]]
cerato-, a word element meaning: **1.** *Zool.* horn, horny, or hornlike. **2.** *Anat.* the cornea. Also (before a vowel), **cerat-.** [t. Gk: m. *kerāto-*, comb. form of *kéras* horn]
ceratodus (sĭ răt′ə dəs, sĕ′rə tō′dəs), *n.* a fish of the extinct lungfish genus *Ceratodus*, or of the closely related existent genus *Neoceratodus*, as *N. forsteri*, the barramunda of Australia, so called from the hornlike ridges of the teeth. [NL, f. *cerat-* CERAT(O)- + m. Gk *odoús* tooth]
ceratoid (sĕ′rə toid′), *adj.* hornlike; horny. [t. Gk: m. s. *kerātoeidés* hornlike]
Cerberus (sû′bə rəs), *n.* **1.** *Class. Myth.* a dog, usually represented as having three heads, which guarded the entrance of the infernal regions. **2.** a watchful and formidable or surly keeper or guard. —**Cerberian** (sû bĭə′rĭ ən), *adj.*
cercaria (sû kĕə′rĭ ə), *n., pl.* **-cariae** (-kĕə′rĭ ē′). *Zool.* a larval stage of flukes, *Trematoda*, characterized by a body usually bearing a tail-like appendage, but sometimes enclosed in the tail. [NL, f. *cerc-* (comb. form repr. Gk *kérkos* tail) + *-āria* -ARIA] —**cercar′ial,** *adj.* —**cercar′ian,** *adj., n.*
cercus (sû′kəs), *n., pl.* **-ci** (sē). *Zool.* one of a pair of tail-like appendages in some insects and other arthropods, serving as tactile organs. [t. NL, t. Gk: m. *kérkos* tail] —**cercal** (sû′kl), *adj.*
cere[1] (sĭə), *n.* *Ornith.* a membrane of waxy appearance at the base of the upper mandible of certain birds, esp. birds of prey and parrots, in which the nostrils open. [late ME *sere*, t. ML: m. *cēra*, in L wax, c. Gk *kērós*]
cere[2] (sĭə), *v.t.,* **cered, cering. 1.** *Poetic.* to wrap in or as in a cerecloth, esp. a corpse. **2.** *Obs.* to wax. [ME, t. L: m. s. *cērāre*, to wax]
cereal (sĭə′rĭ əl), *n.* **1.** any gramineous plant yielding an edible farinaceous grain, as wheat, rye, oats, rice, maize, etc. **2.** the grain itself. **3.** some edible preparation of it, esp. a breakfast food made from some grain. —*adj.* **4.** of or pertaining to grain or the plants producing it. [t. L: s. *Cereālis* pertaining to Ceres]
cerebellum (sĕ′rĭ bĕl′əm), *n., pl.* **-bella** (-bĕl′ə). *Anat.,*

Zool. a large expansion of the hindbrain, concerned with the coordination of voluntary movements, posture, and equilibration. In man it lies at the back of and below the cerebrum and consists of two lateral lobes and a central lobe. [t. L, dim. of *cerebrum* brain] **—cer′ebel′lar,** *adj.*

cerebral (sĕ′rĭ brəl), *adj.* **1.** *Anat.*, *Zool.* of or pertaining to the cerebrum or the brain. **2.** thoughtful; intellectual. **3.** *Phonetics.* cacuminal. **—***n.* **4.** *Phonetics.* a cerebral consonant. [t. NL: s. *cerebrālis,* der. L *cerebrum* brain]

cerebral palsy, a form of paralysis caused by injury to the brain, most marked in certain motor areas. It is characterized by involuntary motions and difficulty in control of the voluntary muscles; sufferers are called spastics.

cerebrate (sĕ′rĭ brāt′), *v.i.*, **-brated, -brating.** **1.** *Rare.* to use the cerebrum or brain; experience brain action. **2.** *Colloq.* to think.

cerebration (sĕ′rĭ brā′shən), *n.* **1.** the action of the cerebrum or brain. **2.** thinking; thought.

cerebric (sĕ′rĭ brĭk), *adj.* pertaining to or derived from the brain.

cerebro-, a word element meaning 'cerebrum'. Also (before a vowel), **cerebr-.**

cerebroside (sĕ′rĭ brō′sīd), *n.* *Biochem.* any of a group of closely related lipids occurring in the brain.

cerebrospinal (sĕ′rĭ brō spī′nəl), *adj.* *Anat.*, *Physiol.* **1.** pertaining to or affecting both the brain and the spinal cord. **2.** pertaining to the central nervous system (distinguished from *autonomic*).

cerebrospinal meningitis, *Pathol.* an acute inflammation of the meninges of the brain and spinal cord caused by a specific organism, and accompanied by fever and occasionally red spots on the skin; brain fever. Also, **cerebrospinal fever.**

cerebrum (sĕ′rĭ brəm), *n., pl.* **-bra** (-brə). *Anat.*, *Zool.* **1.** the anterior and upper part of the brain, consisting of two hemispheres, partially separated by a deep fissure but connected by a broad band of fibres, and concerned with voluntary and conscious processes. **2.** these two hemispheres together with other adjacent parts; the prosencephalon, diencephalon, and mesencephalon together. [t. L: brain]

cerecloth (sĭə′klŏth′), *n.* **1.** a waxed cloth, used esp. for wrapping the dead. **2.** a piece of such cloth. [earlier *cered cloth.* See CERE[2], v.]

cerement (sĭə′mənt), *n.* (*usually pl.*) **1.** cerecloth. **2.** any grave-clothes. [f. CERE[2] + -MENT. Cf. F *cirement*]

ceremonial (sĕ′rĭ mō′nyəl), *adj.* **1.** pertaining to, used for, marked by, or of the nature of ceremonies or ceremony; ritual; formal. **—***n.* **2.** a system of ceremonies, rites, or formalities prescribed for or observed on any particular occasion; a rite or ceremony. **3.** *Rom. Cath. Ch.* **a.** the order for rites and ceremonies. **b.** a book containing it. **4.** formality, esp. of etiquette; the observance of ceremony. **—cer′emo′nialism,** *n.* **—cer′emo′nialist,** *n.* **—cer′emo′nially,** *adv.*

ceremonious (sĕ′rĭ mō′nyəs), *adj.* **1.** carefully observant of ceremony; formally or elaborately polite. **2.** pertaining to, marked by, or consisting of ceremony; formal. **—cer′emo′niously,** *adv.* **—cer′emo′niousness,** *n.*

ceremony (sĕ′rĭ mə nĭ), *n., pl.* **-monies.** **1.** the formalities observed on some solemn or important public or state occasion. **2.** a formal religious or sacred observance; a solemn rite. **3.** any formal act or observance, esp. a meaningless one. **4.** a gesture or act of politeness or civility. **5.** formal observances or gestures collectively; ceremonial observances. **6.** strict adherence to conventional forms; formality: *to leave a room without ceremony.* **7. stand on ceremony,** to be excessively formal or polite. [t. ML: m. s. *cēremōnia,* L *caerimōnia* sacred rite; r. ME *serimonie,* t. OF]

—**Syn.** **1, 2.** CEREMONY, RITE, RITUAL refer to set observances and acts traditional in religious services or on public occasions. CEREMONY applies to more or less formal dignified acts on religious or public occasions: *a marriage ceremony.* A RITE is an established, prescribed, or customary form of religious or other solemn practice: *the rite of baptism.* RITUAL refers to the form of conducting worship or to a code of ceremonies in general: *Masonic rituals.*

Cerenkov radiation (chĭ rĕng′kŏf; *Russ.* chĭ ryĕn′kəf), *Physics.* visible radiation emitted by charged particles when they travel through a transparent medium at a velocity greater than the velocity of light in that medium. Also, **Cherenkov radiation.** [named after P. A. *Cherenkov,* born 1904, Soviet physicist]

cereous (sĭə′rĭ əs), *adj.* waxlike; waxy. [t. L: m. *cereus*]

Ceres (sĭə′rēz), *n.* an ancient Italian goddess of tillage and corn, under whose name the Romans adopted the worship of the Greek goddess Demeter. [t. L]

ceresin (sĕ′rĭ sĭn), *n.* a hard and brittle paraffin wax used as a substitute for beeswax in paints and polishes.

cereus (sĭə′rĭ əs), *n.* any plant of the cactaceous genus *Cereus,* of tropical America, as *C. jamacaru,* of northern Brazil, which grows to about 40 feet. [t. L: wax candle]

ceria (sĭə′rĭ ə), *n.* *Chem.* cerium oxide, CeO_2, used in small amounts in gas mantles.

Cerigo (*It.* chĕ rē′gō), *n.* Italian name of **Cythera.**

cerik (sĭə′rĭk), *adj.* *Chem.* containing cerium, esp. in the tetravalent state.

cerise (sə rēz′, -rēs′), *n., adj.* mauve-tinged cherry red.

cerium (sĭə′rĭ əm), *n.* *Chem.* a steel grey, ductile metallic element of the rare-earth group found only in combination. *Symbol:* Ce; *at. wt:* 140·12; *at. no.:* 58. [t. NL, named after the asteroid *Ceres*]

cerium metals, *Chem.* See **rare-earth elements.**

cermet (sû′mĭt), *n.* *Metall.* a substance consisting of a sintered metal compacted with a ceramic material in order to modify the conductivity or heat resistance of the pure metal. Also, **ceramet, ceramal.** [CER(AMIC) + MET(AL)]

Cernăuţi (*Rum.* chĕr nə o͞otsy′), *n.* Rumanian name of **Chernovtsy.**

Černík (*Cz.* chĕr′nyēk), *n.* **Oldřich** (*Cz.* ŏl′drzhĕKH), born 1921, Czechoslovak statesman, prime minister 1968–70.

cernuous (sû′nyo͝o əs), *adj.* *Bot.* drooping or bowing down, as a flower. [t. L: m. *cernuus* stooping]

cero (sĭə′rō, sĭ′rō), *n., pl.* **-ros.** **1.** a large tropical Atlantic mackerel-like fish, *Scomberomorus regalis,* important for food and game. **2.** any related species. [t. Sp.: m. *sierra* saw, sawfish]

cero-, a word element meaning 'wax', as in *cerotype.* Also, **cer-.** [t. Gk: m. *kēro-,* comb. form of *kērós*]

cerograph (sĭə′rō grăf′, -gräf′), *n.* an engraving on wax. [CERO- + -GRAPH] **—cerographic** (sĭə′rō grăf′ĭk), **ce′rograph′ical,** *adj.* **—cerographist** (sĭə rŏg′rə fĭst), *n.*

cerography (sĭə rŏg′rə fĭ), *n.* the art of engraving on wax.

ceroplastic (sĭə′rō plăs′tĭk), *adj.* **1.** pertaining to modelling in wax. **2.** modelled in wax.

ceroplastics (sĭə′rō plăs′tĭks), *n.* **1.** the art of modelling in wax. **2.** waxworks.

cerotic acid (sĭ rŏt′ĭk), *Chem.* the monobasic fatty acid, $C_{26}H_{53}COOH$, of beeswax. [f. m. s. Gk *kērōtón* waxed + -IC]

cerotype (sĭə′rə tīp′), *n.* a process of engraving in which the design or the like is cut on a wax-coated metal plate, from which a printing surface is subsequently produced by stereotyping or by electrotyping.

cerous (sĭə′rəs), *adj.* *Chem.* containing trivalent cerium. [f. CER(IUM) + -OUS]

Cerro de Pasco (*Sp.* thĕr′rō dĕ päs′kō), a town in central Peru: famous silver mining district. 24,533 (est. 1954); 14,280 ft high.

cert (sût), *n.* *Colloq.* a certainty.

cert., **1.** certificate. **2.** certified. **3.** certify.

certain (sû′tn), *adj.* **1.** having no doubt; confident; assured (often fol. by *of* before a noun, gerund, or pronoun): *I am certain of being able to finish it by tomorrow.* **2.** sure; inevitable; bound to come (fol. by an infinitive): *it is certain to happen.* **3.** established as true or sure; unquestionable; indisputable: *it is certain that he tried.* **4.** fixed; agreed upon: *on a certain day.* **5.** definite or particular, but not named or specified: *certain persons.* **6.** that may be depended on; trustworthy; unfailing; reliable: *his aim was certain.* **7.** some though not much: *a certain reluctance.* **8.** *Obs.* steadfast. **—***n.* **9. for certain,** without any doubt; surely. [ME, t. OF, der. L *certus* fixed, certain, orig. pp.] **—Syn.** **1.** positive; convinced, satisfied. **2.** See **sure.** **3.** incontrovertible, irrefutable, incontestable. **4.** prescribed, specified.

certainly (sû′tn lĭ), *adv.* **1.** with certainty; without doubt; assuredly. **—***interj.* **2.** yes! of course!

certainty (sû′tn tĭ), *n., pl.* **-ties.** **1.** the state of being certain. **2.** something certain; an assured fact. **3.** *Colloq.* something regarded as certain to happen, to achieve a desired result as winning a race, etc.: *that horse is an absolute certainty.* **4. for a certainty,** without any doubt; surely.

certes (sû′tĭz), *adv.* *Archaic.* certainly; verily. [ME, t. OF, g. LL *certas,* adv., der. L *certus* CERTAIN]

certifiable (sû′tĭ fī′ə bl), *adj.* **1.** capable of being certified. **2.** committable to a mental institution. **—cer′tifi′ably,** *adv.*

certificate (*n.* sə tĭf′ĭ kĭt; *v.* sə tĭf′ĭ kāt′), *n., v.*, **-cated, -cating.** **—***n.* **1.** a writing on paper certifying to the truth of something or to status, qualifications, privileges, etc. **2.** a document issued to a person passing a particular examination, as the General Certificate of Education. **3.** *Law.* a statement, written and signed, which is by law made evidence of the truth of the facts stated, for all or for certain purposes. **4.** a share certificate. **5.** a trading certificate. **6.** a land certificate. **7.** the certificate held by the master of a ship. **8.** a bankrupt certificate. —*v.t.* **9.** to attest by a certificate. **10.** to furnish with or authorize by a certificate. [late ME, t. ML: m. s. *certificātum*, neut. pp. of *certificāre*. See CERTIFY]

certificate of deposit, a negotiable bearer security issued by an accepting house or an overseas or foreign bank for large sums of money, as for dealings between banks, finance houses, local authorities, etc. On the London money market they are normally issued in multiples of £10,000.

certificate of incorporation, a statement filed with the registrar of companies showing that a company is duly incorporated.

certificate of indebtedness, a short-term, negotiable, interest-bearing note representing indebtedness.

certificate of origin, a shipping document having consular certification that names a boat's origin and type of goods aboard, often required before importation.

certification (sû′tĭ fĭ kā′shən), *n.* **1.** the act of certifying. **2.** the state of being certified. **3.** a certified statement. **4.** the writing on the face of a cheque by which it is certified. **5.** *Law.* a certificate attesting the truth of some statement or event.

certified (sû′tĭ fīd′), *adj.* **1.** having, or proved by, a certificate. **2.** guaranteed; reliably endorsed. **3.** committed to a mental institution.

certified cheque, a cheque bearing a guarantee of payment by the bank on which it is drawn.

certify (sû′tĭ fī′), *v.t.*, **-fied, -fying. 1.** to guarantee as certain; give reliable information of. **2.** to testify to or vouch for in writing. **3.** to declare insane. **4.** to assure or inform with certainty. **5.** to guarantee; endorse reliably. **6.** *Chiefly U.S.* (of a bank, or one of its officials) to state in writing upon (a cheque) that the bank on which it is drawn has funds of the drawer sufficient to meet it. —*v.i.* **7.** to give assurance; testify (fol. by *to*); vouch (fol. by *for*). [ME *certifie(n)*, t. F: m. *certifier*, t. ML: m. *certificāre*] —**cer′tifi′er,** *n.*

certiorari (sû′tĭ ô rĕə′rī), *n. Law.* a writ issued from a superior court removing a case from a lower court or calling up the record of a proceeding in a lower court for review. [t. L: to be informed (lit., made more certain)]

certitude (sû′tĭ tyōōd′), *n.* sense of absolute conviction; certainty. [late ME, t. LL: m. *certitūdo*]

cerulean (sĭ rōō′lyən), *adj.*, *n.* sky blue; azure. Also, **caerulean.** [f. m. s. L *caeruleus* dark blue + -AN]

cerumen (sĭ rōō′mĕn), *n. Anat.* a yellowish waxlike secretion from certain glands in the external auditory canal, acting as a lubricant and arresting the entrance of dust, insects, etc.; earwax. [t. NL, der. L *cēra* wax]

ceruse (sə′rōōs), *n.* white lead; a mixture or compound of hydrate and carbonate of lead, much used in painting. [ME, t. OF, t. L: m. *cērussa*]

cerussite (siə′rə sīt′), *n. Chem.* a mineral, lead carbonate, $PbCO_3$, in white crystals or massive: an important ore of lead. [f. s. L *cērussa* white lead + -ITE[1]]

Cervantes Saavedra (sə văn′tēz; *Sp.* thĕr vän′tĕs sä ä vĕ′drä), **Miguel de** (*Sp.* mē gĕl′ dĕ), 1547–1616, Spanish novelist.

cervic-, a combining form of **cervical.** Also, **cervico-.**

cervical (sû′vĭ kl), *adj. Anat.* pertaining to the cervix or neck. See diag. under **spinal column.** [f. s. L *cervix* neck + -AL[1]]

cervicitis (sû′vĭ sī′təs), *n. Med.* inflammation of the cervix (of the uterus).

cervico-, var. of **cervic-** used before consonants.

Cervin (*Fr.* sĕr văɴ′), *n.* **Mont** (*Fr.* môɴ), French name of the **Matterhorn.**

cervine (sû′vīn), *adj.* **1.** deerlike. **2.** of deer or the deer family, the *Cervidae.* **3.** of a deep tawny colour. [t. L: m. s. *cervīnus* pertaining to deer]

cervix (sû′vĭks), *n.*, *pl.* **cervixes, cervices** (sə vī′sēz). *Anat.* **1.** the neck. **2.** the neck of the uterus, which dilates just before parturition. **3.** any necklike part. [t. L]

Cesarean (sĭ zĕə′rĭ ən), *adj.*, *n.* Caesarean. Also, **Cesarian.**

Cesena (*It.* chĕ zĕ′nä), *n.* a town in NE Italy, in Emilia. 83,688 (1966).

cesium (sē′zĭ əm), *n. Chem.* caesium.

Ceské Budějovice (*Cz.* chĕs′kĕ bōō′dyĕ yŏ vē tsĕ), a town in SW Czechoslovakia, on the river Vltava. 69,000 (est. 1965). German, **Budweis.**

cespitose (sĕs′pĭ tōs′), *adj. U.S.* caespitose.

cess[1] (sĕs), *n.* **1.** any of various special taxes, levies, or assessments, as (in Scotland) a land tax, or (in India) an import and sales tax. **2.** (in Ireland before 1919) the imposition of British soldiers upon the Irish people. —*v.t.* **3.** to assess for taxation. **4.** (in Ireland before 1919) to impose (soldiers) upon the populace for their keep. [aphetic var. of obs. n. use of ASSESS, v.]

cess[2] (sĕs), *n. Irish.* luck: *bad cess to you!* [? aphetic var. of SUCCESS]

cess[3] (sĕs), *n.* **1.** a cesspit or cesspool. **2.** a box at the end of a roof gutter above a drainpipe. **3.** a drain at the foot of a bank, as in a railway cutting. [t. It.: s. *cesso* privy, ? m. L *secessum* a place apart, neut. pp. of *secēdere* to go apart]

cessation (sĕ sā′shən), *n.* a ceasing; discontinuance; pause: *a cessation of hostilities.* [t. L: s. *cessātio*]

cesser (sĕs′ə), *n. Law.* the coming to an end, of, or as of the period of duration of a mortgage.

cession (sĕsh′ən), *n.* **1.** the act of ceding, as by treaty. **2.** something, as territory, ceded. **3.** the voluntary surrender by a debtor of his effects to his creditors. [t. L: s. *cessio*]

cessionary (sĕsh′ə nə rĭ), *n.*, *pl.* **-ries. 1.** a transferee. **2.** assignee. **3.** grantee.

cesspit (sĕs′pĭt′), *n.* a pit containing a cesspool.

cesspool (sĕs′pōōl′), *n.* **1.** a cistern, well, or pit for retaining the sediment of a drain or for receiving the filth of a water closet, etc. **2.** any filthy receptacle or place: *a cesspool of iniquity.*

c'est-à-dire (*Fr.* sĕ tȧ dēr′), *French.* that is to say.

c'est la guerre (*Fr.* sĕ lȧ gĕr′), *French.* that's war.

c'est la vie (*Fr.* sĕ lȧ vē′), *French.* that's life.

cestode (sĕs′tōd), *n.* a tapeworm, a member of the *Cestoda*, a class of internally parasitic platyhelminths or flatworms, characterized by the long tapelike body divided into joints. Also, **cestoidean** (sĕs toi′dĭ ən). [t. NL: m. *cestōdēs.* See CESTUS, -ODE[1]]

cestoid (sĕs′toid), *adj. Zool.* (of worms) ribbon-like.

cestus[1] (sĕs′təs), *n.* **1.** a belt or girdle. **2.** *Class. Myth.* the girdle of Aphrodite or Venus, which was said to be decorated with everything that could awaken love. [t. L, t. Gk: m. *kestós* girdle, lit., stitched]

cestus[2] (sĕs′təs), *Rom. Antiq.* a hand-covering made of leather strips often loaded with metal, worn by boxers. [t. L: m. *caestus*, prob. var. sp. of *cestus* CESTUS[1]]

cesura (sĭ zyōōə′rə), *n.* caesura. —**cesu′ral,** *adj.*

cet-, a word element meaning 'whale'. [comb. form repr. L *cētus* and Gk *kêtos* whale]

C.E.T., Central European Time.

cetacean (sĭ tā′shən), *adj.* **1.** belonging to the *Cetacea*, an order of aquatic, chiefly marine, mammals, including the whales, dolphins, porpoises, etc. —*n.* **2.** a cetacean mammal. [f. s. NL *Cetācea*, pl. (see CET-, -ACEA) + -AN] —**ceta′ceous,** *adj.*

cetane (sē′tān), *n. Chem.* a colourless, liquid, paraffin hydrocarbon, $C_{16}H_{34}$, found in petroleum; hexadecane.

cetane number, *Chem., etc.* a measure of the ignition quality of diesel-engine fuels. The fuel is compared with mixtures of the alpha form of methylnaphthalene (value = 0) and cetane (value = 100). Also, **cetane rating.**

Cetatea Albă (*Rum.* chĕ tȧ′tyȧ äl′bə), Rumanian name of **Akkerman.**

cetera desunt (kĕt′ə rə dē′sōōnt), *Latin.* the remaining (parts) are missing.

ceteris paribus (kĕt′ə rĭs pä′rĭ bōōs), *Latin.* the others (other things) being equal. *Abbrev.:* cet. par.

cetin (sē′tĭn), *n. Chem.* $C_{32}H_{64}O_2$, the chief constituent of spermaceti.

Cetinje (*Serb.* tsĕ′tē nyĕ), *n.* a town in SW Yugoslavia: former capital of Montenegro. 16,300 (est. 1964).

cet. par., ceteris paribus.

Cetus (sē′təs), *n., gen.* **Ceti** (sē′tī). *Astron.* a constellation, supposed to resemble a whale in outline, lying across the equator and containing an important variable star. [t. L, t. Gk. See CET-]

Cetywayo (sĕt′ĭ wä′ō), *n.* 1836–84, king of the Zulus. Also, **Cetewayo.**

Ceuta (syōō′tə; *Sp.* thĕw′tä), *n.* a Spanish seaport in Morocco, on the Strait of Gibraltar. 76,098 (1966).

Cévennes (*Fr.* sĕ vĕn′), *n.* a mountain range in S France. Highest peak, Mt Mézenc, 5753 ft.

Ceylon (sĭ lŏn′), *n.* an island in the Indian Ocean, S of India: member of the Commonwealth of Nations. 10,644,809 pop. (1963); 25,232 sq. mi. *Cap.:* Colombo. —**Ceylonese** (sē′lə nēz′), *adj., n.*

Ceylon

Ceylon moss, a red seaweed, *Gracilaria lichenoides*, of the East Indies: one of the algae from which agar-agar is obtained.

Cézanne (sā zăn′; *Fr.* sĕ zȧn′), *n.* **Paul** (*Fr.* pōl), 1839–1906, French painter.

cf., (L *confer*) compare.

c/f, carry forward; carried forward.

c.f.i., cost, freight, and insurance.

cg., centigram; centigrams.

C.G., 1. captain general. **2.** coastguard. **3.** Coldstream Guards. **4.** consul general.

c.g., centre of gravity.
C.G.M., Conspicuous Gallantry Medal.
C.G.S., Chief of General Staff.
c.g.s., *Physics.* centimetre-gram-second (system). Also, **cgs.**
ch., 1. chain (def. 9). 2. chapter. 3. *Chess.* check. 4. church.
C.H., Companion of Honour.
c.h., central heating.
chabazite (kăbʹə zītʹ), *n.* a zeolite mineral, essentially a hydrated sodium calcium aluminium silicate, occurring commonly in red to colourless crystals that are nearly cubes. [earlier *chabazie,* t. F, misspelling of Gk *chalázie* (voc.), der. *chálaza* hailstone. See -ITE[1]]
Chablis (shăbʹlĭ; *Fr.* shȧ blēʹ), *n.* a very dry white table wine from the Burgundy wine region in France. [named after *Chablis,* town in N central France]
chabouk (chäʹbo͝ok), *n.* a horsewhip used in eastern countries for inflicting corporal punishment. Also, **chabuk.** [t. Pers. and Hind.: m. *chābuk*]
cha-cha-cha (chäʹchä chäʹ), *n.* a dance of Latin American origin, similar to the mambo. Also, **cha-cha** (chäʹchä).
chacma (chăkʹmə), *n.* a large baboon, *Papio comatus,* of southern Africa, about the size of a mastiff. [t. Hottentot]
Chaco (chăkʹō; *Sp.* chäʹkō), *n.* 1. a part of the Gran Chaco region in central South America, formerly in dispute between Bolivia and Paraguay: boundary fixed by arbitration, 1938. ab. 100,000 sq. mi. 2. See **Gran Chaco.**
chaconne (shə kŏnʹ), *n.* 1. an ancient dance, probably of Spanish origin. 2. music for it. [t. F, t. Sp.: m. *chacona,* t. Basque: m. *chacun* pretty]

Chacma, *Papio comatus* (Total length 4½ ft, tail 21 in.)

chacun à son goût (*Fr.* shȧ kœɴ nȧ sôɴ go͞oʹ), *French.* everyone to his own taste.
Chad (chăd), *n.* 1. **Lake,** a lake in N Africa at the junction of Chad, Niger, and Nigeria. 10,000 to 20,000 sq. mi. (seasonal variation). See map under **Nigeria.** 2. Official name, **Republic of Chad.** an independent member of the French community E of this lake; formerly part of French Equatorial Africa. 2,730,000 pop. (est. 1959); 501,000 sq. mi. *Cap.:* Fort Lamy.
Chadwick (chădʹwĭk), *n.* **Sir James,** born 1891, English physicist.
Chaeronea (kĕʹrə nēʹə), *n.* an ancient city in E Greece, in Boeotia: victory of Philip of Macedon over the Athenians, 338 B.C.
chaeta (kēʹtə), *n., pl.* **-tae** (-tē). *Zool.* a bristle or seta, esp. of a chaetopod. [NL, t. Gk: m. *chaítē* hair]
chaeto-, a word element meaning 'hair', as in *chaetopod.* Also, before vowels, **chaet-.** [comb. form repr. Gk *chaítē*]
chaetophorous (kĭ tŏfʹə rəs), *adj. Zool.* bearing bristles; setigerous or setiferous.
chaetopod (kēʹtə pŏdʹ), *n. Zool.* any of the *Chaetopoda,* a class or group of annelids having the body made up of more or less similar segments provided with muscular processes bearing setae.
chafe (chāf), *v.,* **chafed, chafing,** *n.* —*v.t.* 1. to warm by rubbing. 2. to wear or abrade by rubbing. 3. to make sore by rubbing. 4. to irritate; annoy. 5. *Obs.* to heat; make warm. —*v.i.* 6. to rub; press with friction. 7. to become worn or sore by rubbing. 8. to be irritated or annoyed. 9. to become impatient; fret. —*n.* 10. irritation; annoyance. 11. heat, wear or soreness caused by rubbing. [ME *chaufe(n),* t. OF: m. *chaufer,* g. LL contr. of L *calefacere* make hot]
chafer (chāʹfə), *n.* any scarabaeid beetle. [ME *cheaffer, chaver,* OE *ceafor.* Cf. G *Käfer*]
chaff[1] (chăf), *n.* 1. the husks of grains and grasses separated from the seed. 2. straw cut small for fodder. 3. worthless matter; refuse; rubbish. [ME *chaf,* OE *ceaf,* c. D *kaf*] —**chaffʹlikeʹ,** *adj.* —**chaffʹy,** *adj.*
chaff[2] (chăf), *v.t., v.i.* 1. to ridicule or tease good-naturedly; banter. —*n.* 2. good-natured ridicule or teasing; raillery. [? special use of CHAFF[1]] —**chaffʹer,** *n.*
chaffer (chăfʹə), *n.* 1. bargaining; haggling. —*v.i.* 2. to bargain; haggle. 3. to bandy (words). —*v.t.* 4. *Obs.* trade or deal in; barter. 5. to bandy (words). [ME *chaffare,* earlier *chapfare* trading journey, f. OE *cēap* trade + *faru* a going] —**chafʹferer,** *n.*
chaffinch (chăfʹĭnch), *n.* a common European finch, *Fringilla coelebs,* with a pleasant short song, often kept as a cagebird. [OE *ceaffinc.* See CHAFF[1], FINCH]
chaffweed (chäfʹwēdʹ), *n.* a small annual primulaceous herb, *Anagallis minima,* having minute white or pink flowers.
chafing dish, a hotplate.
Chagall (*Fr.* shȧ gälʹ), *n.* **Marc,** born 1887, Russian painter in France and the U.S.
Chagres (*Sp.* chäʹgrĕs), *n.* a river in Panama, flowing through Gatún Lake to the Caribbean.
chagrin (shăgʹrĭn), *n.* 1. a feeling of vexation and disappointment or humiliation. —*v.t.* 2. to vex by disappointment or humiliation. [t. F. See SHAGREEN]
chain (chān), *n.* 1. a connected series of metal or other links for connecting, drawing, confining, restraining, etc., or for ornament. 2. something that binds or restrains. 3. (*pl.*) bonds or fetters. 4. (*pl.*) bondage. 5. a series of things connected or following in succession. 6. a range of mountains. 7. a number of similar establishments, as banks, theatres, hotels, etc., under one ownership and management. 8. *Chem.* a linkage of atoms of the same element, as carbon to carbon. 9. *Survey.* a. a measuring instrument consisting of 100 wire rods or links, each 7·92 inches long (**surveyor's** or **Gunter's chain**), or one foot long (**engineer's chain**). b. the length of a surveyor's chain (66 feet) or engineer's chain (100 feet). 10. *Aeron.* a number of radio stations cooperating for the purpose of providing a navigational system. —*v.t.* 11. to fasten or secure with a chain. 12. to fetter; confine: *chained to his desk.* 13. *Survey.* to measure (a distance on the ground) with a chain or tape. [ME *chayne,* t. OF: m. *chaeine,* g. L *catēna*] —**chainʹless,** *adj.*
chainage (chāʹnĭj), *n. Survey.* a length as measured by a surveyor's chain or tape.
chain-belt (chānʹbĕltʹ), *n.* chain-drive.
chain-bridge (chānʹbrĭjʹ), *n.* a suspension bridge.
chain-drive (chānʹdrīvʹ), *n.* 1. transmission of power by means of an endless chain moving between sprocket-wheels. 2. the endless chain itself.
chain-driven (chānʹdrĭvʹən), *adj.* driven by chain-drive.
chain-gang (chānʹgăngʹ), *n. Chiefly U.S.* a group of convicts chained together, usually while at work outside.
chain-gear (chānʹgĭəʹ), *n.* a gear in which motion is transmitted between sprockets, etc., by chain-drive.
chain-grate (chānʹgrātʹ), *n.* a form of mechanical boiler stoker in which the grate consists of an endless chain; as the chain slowly rotates fresh fuel is fed into the boiler.
chain-harrow (chānʹhăʹrō), *n.* a harrow composed of a number of chains attached to a bar dragged behind a tractor.
chain letter, a letter sent to a number of people, each of whom makes and sends copies to a number of other people who do likewise, the object being to spread a message or to raise money.
chain lightning, forked lightning.
chain mail, mail[2] (def. 1).
chainman (chānʹmən), *n., pl.* **-men.** a man who holds the chain in making surveying measurements; a surveyor's assistant.
chain-measure (chānʹmĕzhʹə), *n.* chain (def. 9).
chain-moulding (chānʹmōlʹdĭng), *n. Archit.* moulding in the pattern of a chain.
chainplate (chānʹplātʹ), *n. Naut.* one of a group of horizontal iron plates on the sides of a sailing ship, to which the lower rigging was secured.
chainpump (chānʹpŭmpʹ), *n.* a mechanism for raising water, etc., in buckets or the like attached to an endless moving chain.
chain-reacting (chānʹrĭ ăkʹtĭng), *adj. Physics.* (of a substance) undergoing or capable of undergoing a chain-reaction.
chain-reaction (chānʹrĭ ăkʹshən), *n.* 1. *Physics.* a nuclear reaction which produces enough neutrons to sustain itself. 2. *Chem.* a reaction which results in a product necessary for the continuance of the reaction. 3. *Colloq.* a series of reactions provoked by one event: *a pay-increase for railwaymen would provoke a chain-reaction of wage claims.*
chainsaw (chānʹsôʹ), *n.* 1. a power-driven crosscut saw with teeth mounted on an endless chain. 2. a similar saw used for cutting building stone.
chain-shot (chānʹshŏtʹ), *n. Ordn.* (formerly) a shot consisting of two balls or half balls connected by a short chain.
chain-smoke (chānʹsmōkʹ), *v.i., v.t.,* **-smoked, -smoking.** to smoke continually, as by lighting one cigarette from the preceding one. —**chainʹ-smokʹer,** *n.*
chain-stitch (chānʹstĭchʹ), *n.* 1. a kind of ornamental stitching in which each stitch forms a loop through the forward end of which the next stitch is taken. —*v.t., v.i.* 2. to sew with a chain-stitch.
chain-store (chānʹstôʹ), *n.* one of a group of retail stores under the same ownership and management and stocked from a common supply point or points.
chainwork (chānʹwûkʹ), *n.* decorative work esp. when looped or woven together as in the links of a chain.

chair (chĕə), *n.* **1.** a seat with a back and legs or other support, often with arms, usually for one person. **2.** anything resembling a chair in appearance or use. **3.** a seat of office or authority. **4.** the position of a judge, chairman, presiding officer, etc. **5.** the person occupying the seat or office, esp. the chairman of a meeting. **6.** the position of (chief) professor in a university faculty. **7.** electric chair. **8.** sedan chair. **9.** *Railways.* a metal block to support and secure a rail. **10. take the chair, a.** to assume the chairmanship of a meeting; begin or open a meeting. **b.** to preside at a meeting. —*v.t.* **11.** to place or seat in a chair. **12.** the install in office or authority. **13.** to conduct as chairman; preside over. **14.** to place in a chair and carry aloft, esp. in triumph. [ME *chaiere*, t. OF, g. L *cathedra* seat, t. Gk: m. *kathédra*]

chairborne (chĕə′bôn′), *adj. Colloq.* having a desk or office job (opposed to a more active one). [b. CHAIR and (AIR)BORNE]

chair lift, a series of chairs suspended from an endless cable driven by a motor, for conveying skiers up to the side of a slope.

chairman (chĕə′mən), *n., pl.* **-men. 1.** the presiding officer of a meeting, committee, board, etc. **2.** someone employed to carry or wheel a person in a chair. —**chair′manship′,** *n.*

chair rail, a moulding on an interior made to protect it from damage by the backs of chairs.

chairwoman (chĕə′wŏŏm′ən), *n., pl.* **-women.** a female chairman (def. 1).

chaise (shāz), *n.* **1.** a light, open carriage, usually with a hood, esp. a one-horse, two-wheeled carriage for two persons. **2.** a postchaise. [t. F: chair, chaise, var. of *chaire.* See CHAIR]

Chaise (def. 1)

chaise longue (shāz′lŏng′; *Fr.* shĕz lôNG′), a kind of couch or reclining chair with seat prolonged to form a full-length leg rest. [t. F: long chair]

chalaza (kə lā′zə), *n., pl.* **-zae** (-zē), **-zas. 1.** *Zool.* one of the two albuminous twisted cords which fasten an egg yolk to the shell membrane. **2.** *Bot.* the point of an ovule or seed where the integuments are united to the nucellus. See diag. under **orthotropous.** [t. NL, t. Gk: hail, lump] —**chala′zal,** *adj.*

chalcanthite (kăl kăn′thīt), *n.* blue vitriol.

Chalcedon (kăl′sĭ dŏn′, kăl′sĭ dən), *n.* an ancient city in NW Asia Minor, on the Bosphorus, opposite Byzantium.

chalcedony (kăl sĕd′ə nĭ), *n., pl.* **-nies.** a microcrystalline translucent variety of quartz, often milky or greyish. [ME, t. L (Vulgate): m. s. *chalcēdonius*, t. Gk: m. *chalkēdṓn* in Rev. 21:19] —**chalcedonic** (kăl′sĭ dŏn′ĭk), *adj.*

chalcid fly (kăl′sĭd), any of the *Chalcididae*, a family of small hymenopterous insects, often of bright metallic colours, whose larvae are mostly parasitic on various stages of other insects. Also, **chalcid.** [*chalcid*, f. s. Gk *chalkós* copper (with allusion to the metallic coloration) + -ID²]

Chalcidice (kăl sĭd′ĭ sĭ), *n.* a peninsula in NE Greece. Greek, **Khalkidike.**

chalco-, a word element meaning 'copper' or 'brass'. Also, before vowels, **chalc-.** [t. Gk: m. *chalko-*, comb. form of *chalkós*]

chalcocite (kăl′kə sīt′), *n.* a common mineral, cuprous sulphide, Cu_2S, an important ore of copper.

chalcography (kăl kŏg′rə fĭ), *n.* the art of engraving on copper or brass. —**chalcog′rapher,** *n.* —**chalcographic** (kăl′kə grăf′ĭk), **chal′cograph′ical,** *adj.*

chalcopyrite (kăl′kə pī′rīt, -pī′ə rīt′), *n.* a very common mineral, copper iron sulphide, $CuFeS_2$, occurring in brass-yellow crystals or masses: the most important ore of copper; copper pyrites.

Chaldaic (kăl dā′ĭk), *n., adj.* Chaldean (defs. 3, 4, and 5).

Chaldea (kăl dē′ə), *n.* ancient region in S Babylonia.

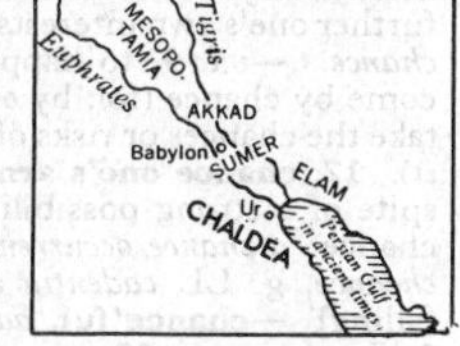

Chaldea

Chaldean (kăl dē′ən), *n.* **1.** one of an ancient Semitic people that formed the dominant element in Babylonia. **2.** an astrologer, soothsayer, or enchanter. Dan. 1:4; 2:2. **3.** biblical Aramaic. —*adj.* **4.** of or belonging to ancient Chaldea. **5.** pertaining to astrology, occult learning, etc. Also, **Chaldee** (kăl dē′). [f. m. s. L *Chaldaeus* (t. Gk: m. *Chaldaîos*) + -AN]

chaldron (chôl′drən), *n.* an old dry measure for coal, coke, lime, etc., equal to 32 or 36 or more bushels in different commodities and localities. [t. F: m. *chauldron* kettle; var. of CALDRON]

chalet (shăl′ā; *Fr.* shȧ lĕ′), *n.* **1.** a herdsman's hut in the Swiss mountains. **2.** a kind of cottage, low and with wide eaves, common in alpine regions. **3.** any cottage or villa built in this style. **4.** a small hut for holiday use, as at the seaside or in a holiday camp. [t. F (Swiss)]

Chaliapin (shăl′ĭ ä′pĭn; *Russ.* shȧ lyȧ′pĭn), *n.* **Feodor Ivanovich** (*Russ.* fyô′dər ĭ vä′nə vĭch), 1873–1938, Russian operatic bass singer.

chalice (chăl′ĭs), *n.* **1.** *Eccles.* **a.** a cup for the wine of the eucharist or mass. **b.** the wine contained in it. **2.** *Poet.* a drinking cup. **3.** a cuplike blossom. [ME, t. OF, g. L *calix* cup; r. ME *caliz, calc,* OE *calic,* t. L: m. *calix*] —**chaliced** (chăl′ĭst), *adj.*

chalk (chôk), *n.* **1.** *Geol.* **a.** a soft, white, pure limestone consisting of calcareous fossil skeletal fragments of microscopic algae. **b.** (*cap.*) that of the Upper Cretaceous system of England. **2.** a prepared piece of chalk or chalk-like substance, esp. calcium sulphate, for marking. **3.** a mark made with chalk. **4.** a score, or record of credit given, as at a tavern, etc. **5.** *Colloq.* a point in a person's favour. **6.** *Colloq.* (in phrases opposed to *cheese*) any thinly disguised substitute. **7. by a long chalk,** by far; by a considerable extent or degree. —*v.t.* **8.** to mark or write with chalk. **9.** to rub over or whiten with chalk. **10.** to treat or mix with chalk. **11.** to make pale; blanch. **12. chalk out,** to outline (a plan, etc.). **13. chalk up, a.** to score or earn: *they chalked up 360 runs in the first innings.* **b.** to ascribe to: *it may be chalked up to experience.* —*v.i.* **14.** to score, as in darts. [ME *chalke*, OE *cealc*, t. L: m. s. *calx* lime] —**chalk′like′,** *adj.* —**chalk′y,** *adj.* —**chalk′iness,** *n.*

chalkpit (chôk′pĭt′), *n.* a quarry for chalk.

challenge (chăl′ĭnj), *n., v.,* **-lenged, -lenging.** —*n.* **1.** a call to engage in a contest of skill, strength, etc. **2.** a call to fight, as a duel, etc. **3.** something that makes demands upon one's abilities, endurance, etc.: *this job is a challenge.* **4.** a demand to explain. **5.** *Mil.* the demand of a sentry for identification or the password. **6.** *Law.* a formal objection to the qualifications of a juror or to the legality of an entire jury. **7.** *U.S.* the assertion that a vote is invalid or that a voter is not legally qualified. —*v.t.* **8.** to summon to a contest of skill, strength, etc. **9.** to demand as of right; lay claim to; have a claim to. **10.** to make demands, esp. stimulating demands, upon: *this job will challenge your abilities.* **11.** to take exception to; call in question: *to challenge the wisdom of a procedure.* **12.** *Mil.* to halt and demand identification or password from. **13.** *Law.* to take formal exception to (a juror or jury). **14.** *U.S.* to assert that (a vote) is invalid or (a voter) is not qualified to vote. —*v.i.* **15.** to make or issue a challenge. **16.** *Hunting.* (of hounds) to cry or give tongue on picking up the scent. [ME *chalange*, t. OF: m. *chalenge*, g. L *calumnia* CALUMNY] —**chal′lengeable,** *adj.*

challenger (chăl′ĭn jə), *n.* **1.** one who or that which challenges. **2.** *Sport.* a contestant or member of a team that claims a championship or similar honour from the opponent.

challenging (chăl′ĭn jĭng), *adj.* **1.** stimulating; thought-provoking: *a challenging idea.* **2.** demanding; difficult but interesting: *a challenging job.* **3.** intriguing; enigmatic: *a challenging smile.*

challis (shăl′ĭ, shăl′ĭs), *n.* a printed fabric of plain weave in wool, cotton, or rayon. [orig. uncert.]

chalone (kăl′ōn), *n. Physiol.* an endocrine secretion which reduces physiological activity. [t. Gk: m. *chaloûn*, ppr., slackening]

Châlons (*Fr.* shȧ lôN′), *n.* **1.** Also, **Châlons-sur-Marne** (*Fr.* shȧ lôN sʏr märn′). a town in NE France: defeat of Attila, A.D. 451. 36,834 (1954). **2.** Also, **Châlons-sur-Saône** (*Fr.* shȧ lôN sʏr sōn′). a town in E France. 37,399 (1954).

chalumeau (shăl′yŏŏ mō′; *Fr.* shȧ lʏ mō′), *n. Music.* **1.** early reed pipe instruments collectively. **2.** the low register of the clarinet. [t. F, in OF *chalemel* a musical instrument, g. L *calamellus*, dim. of *calamus* reed]

chalybeate (kə lĭb′ĭ ĭt), *adj.* **1.** containing or impregnated with salts of iron, as a mineral spring, medicine, etc. —*n.* **2.** a chalybeate water, medicine, or the like. [appar. t. NL: m. s. *chalybēātus*, der. L *chalybēius* of steel, der. *chalybs*, t. Gk: m. *chálykps* iron]

chalybite (kăl′ĭ bīt′), *n.* siderite. [f. s. Gk *chálykps* iron + -ITE¹]

cham (kăm), *n. Archaic.* khan¹.

chamber (chām′bə), *n.* **1.** a room or apartment, usually a private room, and esp. a bedroom. **2.** a room in a palace or official residence. **3.** the meeting hall of a legislative or other assembly. **4.** (*pl.*) a place where a judge hears matters not requiring action in court. **5.** (*pl.*) quarters of barristers and others, esp. in the Inns of Court. **6.** *Obs.* the place where the moneys due to a government, etc., are received and kept; a treasury or chamberlain's office. **7.** a legislative, judicial, or other like body: *the upper or the lower chamber of a legislature.* **8.** a compartment or enclosed space; a cavity: *a chamber of the heart.* **9.** the space between the upper and lower gates of a lock on a navigable waterway. **10.** a receptacle for one or more cartridges in a firearm, or for a shell in a gun or other cannon. **11.** that part of the barrel of a gun which receives the charge. **12.** a chamber-pot. *—v.t.* **13.** to put or enclose in, or as in, a chamber. **14.** to provide with a chamber. [ME, t. OF: m. *chambre,* g. L *camera*] **—cham′bered,** *adj.*

chamber concert, a concert of chamber music.

chamberlain (chām′bə lĭn), *n.* **1.** an official charged with the management of a sovereign's or nobleman's living quarters. **2.** an official who receives rents and revenues, as of a municipal corporation; a treasurer. **3.** the high steward or factor of a nobleman. **4.** a high official of a royal court. [ME *chamberleyn,* t. OF: m. *chamberlenc,* t. OG; cf. OHG *chamarlinc*]

Chamberlain (chām′bə lĭn), *n.* **1. (Arthur) Neville** (nĕv′ĭl), 1869–1940, British prime minister 1937–40. **2. Joseph,** 1836–1914, British statesman (father of Sir Austen and Neville Chamberlain). **3. Sir (Joseph) Austen,** 1863–1937, British statesman.

chambermaid (chām′bə mād′), *n.* a female servant who takes care of bedrooms.

chamber music, music suited for performance in a room or a small concert hall, esp. for two or more (but usually less than ten) solo instruments.

chamber of commerce, an association, primarily of businessmen, to protect and promote the business activities of a city, etc.

chamber of horrors, 1. a place, as at a waxworks, where gruesome or horrible objects are exhibited. **2.** the objects collectively. **3.** any collection of things or ideas that might inspire horror.

chamber-pot (chām′bə pŏt′), *n.* a vessel for urine, used chiefly in bedrooms.

Chambers (chām′bəz), *n.* **Sir William,** 1723–96, British architect.

Chambéry (*Fr.* shäɴ bė rē′), *n.* a town in SE France, in Savoie department. 47,447 (1962).

chambray (shăm′brā), *n.* a fine variety of gingham, commonly plain, but with the warp and weft of different colours. [var. of CAMBRIC]

chameleon (kə mē′lyən), *n.* **1.** any of a group of lizards, *Chamaeleontidae,* esp. of the genus *Chamaeleon,* characterized by the greatly developed power of changing the colour of the skin, very slow locomotion, and a projectile tongue. **2.** an inconstant person. [ME *camelion,* t. L: m. *chamaeleon,* t. Gk: m. *chamailéōn,* lit., ground lion] **—chameleonic** (kə mē′lĭ ŏn′ĭk), *adj.* **—chame′leon-like′,** *adj.*

African chameleon, *Chamaeleon chamaeleon* (3 in. long)

chamfer (chăm′fə), *n.* **1.** an oblique surface cut on the edge or corner of a solid, usually a board, made by removing the arris and usually sloping at 45°. *—v.t.* **2.** to cut so as to form a chamfer. **3.** to cut channels or flutes in (a column). **4.** (fol. by *up*) to improve the appearance of; smarten. [appar. t. F: m. *chamfrain,* der. *chanfraindre,* f. *chant* side + *fraindre* (g. L *frangere* break)]

chamfrain (chăm′frĭn), *n.* armour made for a horse's head. Also, **chamfron** (chăm′frən), **chanfron.** [t. OF: m. *chanfrain*; orig. uncert.]

chamois (shăm′wä *for 1*; shăm′ĭ *for 2*; *Fr.* shȧ mwȧ′), *n., pl.* **-ois. 1.** an agile goatlike antelope, *Rupicapra rupicapra,* of high mountains of Europe and south-western Russia. **2.** Also, **cham′my.** a soft, pliable leather made from various skins dressed with oil (esp. fish oil), orig. prepared from the skin of the chamois; shammy. [t. F, g. LL *camox*]

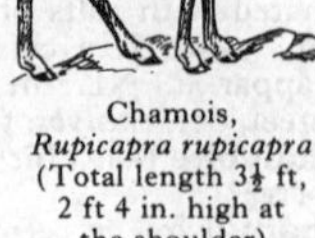

Chamois, *Rupicapra rupicapra* (Total length 3½ ft, 2 ft 4 in. high at the shoulder)

chamomile (kăm′ə mīl′), *n.* camomile.

Chamonix (shăm′ə nĭ; *Fr.* shȧ mō nē′), *n.* a mountain valley in E France, N of Mont Blanc: winter resort.

Chamorro (*Sp.* chȧ môr′rō), *n.* an inhabitant of Guam, the Marianas, etc.

champ¹ (chămp), *v.t.* **1.** to bite upon, esp. impatiently: *horses champing the bit.* **2.** to crush with the teeth and chew vigorously or noisily; munch. **3.** *Scot.* to mash; crush. *—v.i.* **4.** to make vigorous chewing or biting movements with the jaws and teeth. *—n.* **5.** the act of champing. [? nasalized var. (cf. BUNT) of *chop* bite at, der. *chap, chop* jaw]

champ² (chămp), *n. Slang.* a champion.

champagne (shăm pān′), *n.* **1.** a sparkling white wine produced in the wine region of Champagne, France, or elsewhere. **2.** the non-sparkling (still) dry white table wine produced in the region of Champagne. **3.** a very pale yellow or cream colour. *—adj.* **4.** having the colour of champagne.

Champagne (shăm pān′; *Fr.* shäɴ pȧny′), *n.* **1.** an administrative region in E France. 905,740 pop. (1962); 7911 sq. mi. *Prefecture:* Châlons-sur-Marne. **2.** a former province covering approximately the same area.

champaign (shăm pān′), *n.* **1.** level, open country; plain. *—adj.* **2.** level and open. [ME *champaigne,* t. OF, g. L *campānia.* See CAMPAIGN]

champak (chăm′păk, chŭm′pŭk), *n.* an East Indian tree, *Michelia champaca,* of the magnolia family, with fragrant golden flowers and a handsome wood used for making images, furniture, etc. Also, **champac.** [t. Hind.]

champerty (chăm′pə tĭ), *n. Law.* an illegal sharing in the proceeds of litigation by one who promotes it. [ME *champartie,* t. OF: m. *champart* share of the produce of land, g. L *campī pars* part of the field] **—cham′pertous,** *adj.*

champignon (chăm pĭn′yən; *Fr.* shäɴ pē nyôɴ′), *n.* a mushroom (defs. 2, 3). [t. F, ult. der. L *campānia* flat land, der. *campus* field]

Champigny-sur-Marne (*Fr.* shäɴ pē nyē sʏr märn′), *n.* a town in N France, in Seine department. 57,876 (1962).

champion (chăm′pyən), *n.* **1.** one who holds first place in any sport, etc., having defeated all opponents. **2.** anything that takes first place in competition. **3.** one who fights for or defends any person or cause: *a champion of the oppressed.* **4.** a fighter or warrior. *—v.t.* **5.** to act as champion of; defend; support. **6.** *Obs.* to defy. *—adj.* **7.** first among all contestants or competitors. **8.** *Dial.* first-rate. *—adv.* **9.** *Dial.* in a first-rate manner. [ME, t. OF, g. LL *campio,* der. L *campus* field (of battle)] **—championess** (chăm′pyə nĭs), *n. fem.* **—cham′pionless,** *adj.* **—Syn. 3.** defender, protector, vindicator. **5.** maintain, fight for, advocate.

championship (chăm′pyən shĭp′), *n.* **1.** the position of being a champion. **2.** the honour of being a champion in competition. **3.** a contest held to decide who shall be champion. **4.** advocacy or defence.

Champlain (shăm plān′; *also for 1, Fr.* shäɴ plăɴ′), *n.* **1. Samuel de** (*Fr.* sȧ mʏ ĕl′ də), 1567–1635, French explorer who founded Quebec: the first French governor of Canada. **2. Lake,** a lake in the U.S., between New York State and Vermont. 125 mi. long; ab. 600 sq. mi.

champlevé (shămp′lə vē′), *adj., n., pl.* **-vés** (-vēz′). *—adj.* **1.** of or pertaining to an enamel piece or enamelling technique in which enamel is fused on to the incised or hollowed areas of a metal base. *—n.* **2.** a champlevé enamel piece. **3.** the champlevé method. [t. F, lit. lifted field (i.e. the hollowed areas of the metal base)]

Champollion (*Fr.* shäɴ pō lyôɴ′), *n.* **Jean François** (*Fr.* zhäɴ fräɴ swȧ′), 1790–1832, French Egyptologist.

Champs Élysées (*Fr.* shäɴ zė lē zė′), a famous boulevard in Paris: cafes, shops, and theatres; a tourist centre. [F: lit. Elysian Fields]

chance (chäns), *n., v.,* **chanced, chancing,** *adj.* *—n.* **1.** the absence of any known reason why an event should turn out one way rather than another, spoken of as if it were a real agency: *chance governs all.* **2.** fortune; fate; luck. **3.** a possibility or probability of anything happening: *the chances are two to one against us.* **4.** an opportunity: *now is your chance.* **5.** a risk or hazard: *take a chance.* **6.** *Archaic.* an unfortunate event; a mishap. **7. by chance,** accidentally. **8. the main chance,** the opportunity to further one's own interests: *he had a constant eye to the main chance.* *—v.i.* **9.** to happen or occur by chance. **10.** to come by chance (fol. by *on* or *upon*). *—v.t.* **11.** *Colloq.* to take the chances or risks of; risk (usually fol by impersonal *it*). **12. chance one's arm,** to make an attempt, often in spite of a strong possibility of failure. *—adj.* **13.** due to chance: *a chance occurrence.* [ME *chea(u)nce,* t. OF: m. *cheance,* g. LL *cadentia* a falling out, der. *cadens* ppr., falling] **—chance′ful,** *adj.* **—chance′less,** *adj.* **—Syn. 9.** See **happen. 13.** casual, accidental, fortuitous.

chancel (chän′səl), *n.* the space about the altar of a church, usually enclosed, for the clergy, choir, etc. [ME, t. OF, g. LL *cancellus,* L *cancellī* bars, lattice (which enclosed the chancel)]

chancellery (chän′sə lə rĭ, -slə rĭ), *n., pl.* **-ries. 1.** the position of a chancellor. **2.** the office or department of a chancellor. **3.** the office attached to an embassy, etc. **4.** the building or room occupied by a chancellor's department. Also, **chancellory.** [ME *chancelerie*, t. OF, der. *chancelier* CHANCELLOR]

chancellor (chän′sə lə, -slə), *n.* **1.** the title of various important judges and other high officials. **2.** (*sometimes cap.*) the chief minister of state in any of various German-speaking countries, as present-day West Germany. **3.** a secretary, as of a king, nobleman, or embassy. **4.** the titular, honorary head of a university. **5.** *U.S.* the chief administrator in certain American universities. **6.** *U.S. and Obs.* a chancery judge. [ME *chanceler*, t. AF, var. of OF *chancelier*, g. L *cancellārius*, orig. officer stationed at a tribunal. See CHANCEL] —**chan′cellorship′,** *n.*

Chancellor (chän′sə lə), *n.* **Richard,** died 1556, English navigator.

Chancellor of the Duchy of Lancaster, (in Britain) a minister of the crown nominally appointed to administer crown lands in Lancashire, but in practice primarily concerned with special parliamentary duties determined by the prime minister.

Chancellor of the Exchequer, the minister in charge of finance in the British government.

chance-medley (chäns′mĕd′lĭ), *n. Law.* a sudden quarrel with violence, in the course of which one party kills or wounds another in self-defence or in the heat of passion. [t. AF: m. *chance medlée* mixed chance]

chancery (chän′sə rĭ), *n., pl.* **-ceries. 1.** the office or department of a chancellor. **2.** *Obs.* a chancellery. **3. a.** a court of record; an office of public records. **b.** (in Scotland) the record office in the General Register House in Edinburgh. **4.** (*cap.*) the Lord Chancellor's court, now a division of the High Court of Justice. **5.** *Law.* Also, **court of chancery.** a court having jurisdiction in equity. **6. in chancery, a.** *Law.* in litigation in a court of chancery. **b.** *Wrestling, Boxing.* (of a contestant's head) held under his opponent's arm. **c.** in a helpless or embarrassing position. [ME, var. of CHANCELLERY]

chancre (shăng′kə), *n. Pathol.* the initial lesion of syphilis, commonly a more or less distinct ulcer or sore with a hard base. [t. F, g. L *cancer* crab, cancer] —**chanc′rous,** *adj.*

chancroid (shăng′kroid), *Pathol.* —*n.* **1.** a soft, non-syphilitic venereal sore. **2.** the causative organism, *Haemophilus ducreyi.* —*adj.* **3.** of, pertaining to, or resembling a chancroid or chancre.

chancy (chän′sĭ), *adj.,* **chancier, chanciest.** *Colloq. or Dial.* uncertain; risky. Also, **chancey** (chän′sĭ). —**chan′-ciness,** *n.*

chandelier (shăn′dĭ lĭə′), *n.* a branched support for a number of lights, esp. one suspended from a ceiling. [t. F: f. *chandel* candle + suffix *-ier*]

chandelle (shăn dĕl′; *Fr.* shäɴ-), *n. Aeron.* an abrupt climbing turn approximating to a stall, in which momentum is used to obtain a higher rate of climb. [t. F]

Chandernagor (chŭn′də nə gô′), *n.* a town in NE India, in E West Bengal, near Calcutta: a port on the river Hooghly. Formerly a French dependency. 67,100 (1961). Also, **Chandarnagar** (chŭn′də nŭg′ə).

Chandigarh (chŭn′dĭ gä′), *n.* the capital of the state of Punjab, NW India. Established 1953. 89,300 (1961).

chandler (chän′dlə), *n.* **1.** a dealer or trader: *a ship's chandler.* **2.** one who makes or sells candles. **3.** *Obs.* a retailer of groceries, etc. [ME *cha(u)ndeler*, t. AF, var. of OF *chandelier* candle-seller, der. OF *chandelle* CANDLE]

chandlery (chän′dlə rĭ), *n., pl.* **-ries. 1.** a storeroom for candles. **2.** the warehouse, wares, or business of a chandler.

Chandragupta (chŭn′drə go͝op′tə), *n.* fl. *c.* 300 B.C., king of northern India *c.* 315–*c.* 296 or *c.* 291 B.C. Greek, **Sandrocottus.**

Chanel (*Fr.* shȧ nĕl′), *n.* **Gabrielle** (*Fr.* gȧb rē ĕl′) ('*Coco*'), born 1882, French fashion designer.

chanfron (chăn′frən), *n.* chamfrain.

Changchun (chăng′cho͞on′), *n.* a city in NE China: the capital of Kirin province. 975,000 (est. 1964). Also, **Hsinking.**

change (chānj), *v.,* **changed, changing,** *n.* —*v.t.* **1.** to make different; alter in condition, appearance, etc.; turn (often fol. by *into*): *change one's habits.* **2.** to substitute another or others for; exchange for something else: *to change one's job.* **3.** to give or get smaller money in exchange for: *to change a pound note.* **4.** to give or get different currency in exchange for: *to change pounds into francs.* **5.** to give and take reciprocally; interchange: *to change places with someone.* **6.** to remove and replace the coverings of: *to change a baby.* **7.** to select a higher or lower (gear of a motor vehicle). **8. change front,** *Mil.* to shift a military force in another direction. **9. change hands,** to pass from one hand or possessor to another. **10. change one's mind,** to alter one's intentions or opinion. **11. change one's tune,** to assume a different, usually humbler, attitude. —*v.i.* **12.** to become different; alter (sometimes fol. by *to* or *into*). **13.** to make a change or an exchange. **14.** to change trains or other conveyances. **15.** to change one's clothes. **16.** to change gear (fol. by *up* or *down*). —*n.* **17.** variation; alteration; modification; deviation; transformation. **18.** the substitution of one thing for another. **19.** variety or novelty. **20.** the passing from one place, state, form, or phase to another: *change of the moon.* **21.** the supplanting of one thing by another. **22.** that which is or may be substituted for another. **23.** a fresh set of clothing. **24.** information of advantage: *get no change out of someone.* **25.** a balance of money that is returned when the sum tendered is larger than the sum due. **26.** coins of low denomination. **27.** (*often cap.*) *Com.* a place where merchants meet for business transactions; an exchange. **28.** any of the various sequences in which a peal of bells may be rung. **29.** *Obs.* changefulness; caprice. **30. ring the changes,** to execute a number of manoeuvres or variations. [ME *change(n)*, t. OF: m. *changier*, g. LL *cambiāre*, L *cambīre*] —**chang′er,** *n.*

—**Syn. 1.** transmute, transform. CHANGE, ALTER both mean to make a difference in the state or condition of a thing or to substitute another state or condition. To CHANGE is to make a material difference so that the thing is distinctly other than it was: *to change one's opinion, one's shoes.* To ALTER is to make some partial change, as in appearance, but usually to preserve the identity: *to alter a dress* (*to change a dress* would mean to put on a different one).

changeable (chān′jə bl), *adj.* **1.** liable to change or to be changed; variable. **2.** *Archaic.* of changing colour or appearance: *changeable silk.* —**change′abil′ity, change′-ableness,** *n.* —**change′ably,** *adv.*

changeful (chānj′fəl), *adj.* changing; variable; inconstant. —**change′fully,** *adv.* —**change′fulness,** *n.*

changeless (chānj′lĭs), *adj.* unchanging. —**change′-lessly,** *adv.* —**change′lessness,** *n.*

changeling (chānj′lĭng), *n.* **1.** a child supposedly substituted secretly for another, esp. by fairies. **2.** *Archaic.* an inconstant person. **3.** *Archaic.* an idiot.

change of life, menopause.

change of venue, *Law.* the removal of trial to another jurisdiction.

changeover (chānj′ō′və), *n.* **1.** the transition from one system of working to another. **2.** a reversal of opinion, situation, etc. **3.** *Sport.* the movement of one team to positions at the other end of the field, as at half-time.

change-ringing (chānj′rĭng′ĭng), *n.* **1.** the act of ringing the changes on a peal of bells. **2.** variations on a subject.

Changsha (chăng′shä′), *n.* a city in SE China: the capital of Hunan province. 709,000 (est. 1950).

channel[1] (chăn′əl), *n., v.,* **-nelled, -nelling** or (*U.S.*) **-neled, -neling.** —*n.* **1.** the bed of a stream or waterway. **2.** the deeper part of a waterway. **3.** a wide strait, as between a continent and an island. **4.** *Naut.* a navigable route between two bodies of water. **5.** (*cap.*) the English Channel. **6.** a means of access. **7.** a course into which something may be directed. **8.** a route through which anything passes or progresses: *channels of communication.* **9.** a frequency band wide enough for one-way communication, the exact width of a channel depending upon the type of transmission involved (as telegraph, telephone, radio, television, etc.). **10.** a tubular passage for liquids or fluids. **11.** a groove or furrow. —*v.t.* **12.** to convey through a channel. **13.** to direct towards or into some particular course: *to channel one's interests.* **14.** to excavate as a channel. **15.** to form a channel in; groove. [ME *chanel*, t. OF, g. L *canālis* CANAL]

channel[2] (chăn′əl), *n.* one of the horizontal planks or ledges attached outside a ship to give more spread to the lower shrouds. [var. of *chain-wale* (see WALE[1])]

channel iron, a rolled iron, steel or aluminium bar whose section is shaped like three sides of a rectangle.

Channel Islands, a British group of islands in the English Channel, near the coast of France, consisting of Alderney, Guernsey, Jersey, Sark, and smaller islands. 152,529 pop. (1961); 75 sq. mi.

Channel tunnel, a projected tunnel linking France and England under the English Channel, started 1882.

chanson (shăn′sən; *Fr.* shäɴ sôɴ′), *n. French.* a song. [t. F, g. L *cantio*]

chanson de geste (*Fr.* shäɴ sôɴ də zhĕst′), *French.* one of a class of old French epic poems.

chant (chänt), *n.* **1.** a song; singing. **2.** a short, simple melody, specif. one characterized by single notes to which an indefinite number of syllables are intoned, used in singing the psalms, canticles, etc., in the church service. **3.** a psalm, canticle, or the like, chanted or for chanting. **4.** the singing or intoning of all or portions of the spoken parts of a church service. **5.** any monotonous song. **6.** a monotonous intonation of the voice in speaking.

—*v.t.* **7.** to sing. **8.** to celebrate in song. **9.** to sing to a chant, or in the manner of a chant, esp. in the church service. —*v.i.* **10.** to sing. **11.** to sing a chant. [ME *chaunte(n)*, t. OF: m. *chanter*, g. L *cantāre*, freq. of *canere* sing]

chantage (chän′tĭj; *Fr.* shäɴ tȧzh′), *n. French.* blackmail. [cf. F *faire chanter* to make (one) sing, to extort something]

chanter (chän′tə), *n.* **1.** one who chants; a singer. **2.** a chorister; a precentor. **3.** the chief singer or priest of a chantry. **4.** the pipe of a bagpipe, provided with finger holes for playing the melody.

chanterelle (chăn′tə rĕl′), *n.* the yellowish fungus, *Cantharellus cibarius*, a popular edible species in Europe. [t. F, t. NL: m. *cantharella*, dim. of L *cantharus* drinking vessel, t. Gk: m. *kántharos*]

chanteuse (*Fr.* shäɴ tœz′), *n. French.* a woman singer.

chantey (shăn′tĭ, chăn′-), *n.*, *pl.* **-teys.** *U.S.* shanty[2].

chanticleer (chăn′tĭ klĭə′), *n.* a name for the cock, orig. in the medieval epic *Reynard the Fox.* [ME *chauntecler*, t. OF: m. *Chantecler*, lit., clear singer, f. *chante* (impv. of *chanter* sing) + *cler* clear]

Chantilly (shăn tĭl′ĭ; *Fr.* shäɴ tē yē′), *n.* a town in N France, N of Paris: noted for its lace. 8324 (1962).

chantress (chän′trĭs), *n.* a female chanter or singer. [ME *chaunteresse*, t. OF: m. *chanteresse*]

Chantrey (chän′trĭ), *n.* **Sir Francis,** 1781–1851, English sculptor.

chantry (chän′trĭ), *n.*, *pl.* **-tries.** *Eccles.* **1.** an endowment for the singing or saying of mass for the souls of the founders or of persons named by them. **2.** a chapel or the like so endowed. **3.** the priests of a chantry endowment. [ME *chanterie*, t. F: singing]

chanty (shăn′tĭ, chăn′tĭ), *n.*, *pl.* **-ties.** shanty[2].

Chanukah (hä′no͝o kä′), *n.* Hanukkah.

Chao Phraya (chou′ prə yä′), Menam.

chaos (kā′ŏs), *n.* **1.** utter confusion or disorder, wholly without organization or order. **2.** (*usually cap.*) the infinity of space or formless matter supposed to have preceded the existence of the ordered universe. **3.** *Obs.* a chasm or abyss. [t. L, t. Gk]

chaotic (kā ŏt′ĭk), *adj.* in utter confusion or disorder. —**chaot′ically,** *adv.* —**Ant.** orderly, systematic.

chap[1] (chăp), *v.*, **chapped, chapping,** *n.* —*v.t.* **1.** (of cold or exposure) to crack, roughen, and redden (the skin). **2.** to cause (the earth, wood, etc.) to split, crack, open in clefts. —*v.i.* **3.** to become chapped. —*n.* **4.** a fissure or crack, esp. in the skin. **5.** *Scot.* a blow; a knock. [ME *chapp(en)*; orig. uncert.]

chap[2] (chăp), *n.* **1.** *Colloq.* a fellow; man or boy. **2.** *Obs. or Dial.* a customer. [short for CHAPMAN]

chap[3] (chŏp, chăp), *n.* chop[3]. [? special use of CHAP[1]]

chap., **1.** chaplain. **2.** chapter. Also, **Chap.**

chaparajos (*Sp.* chȧ pȧ rȧ′ᴋʜȯs), *n.pl.* chaps. Also, **chaparejos.**

chaparral (chăp′ə răl′), *n.* *South-Western U.S.* **1.** a close growth of low evergreen oaks. **2.** any dense thicket. [t. Sp., der. *chaparro* evergreen oak, ? t. Basque]

chaparral cock, a terrestrial cuckoo of the SW United States, *Geococcyx californianus*; the roadrunner.

chapatti (chə păt′ĭ, -pŭt′ĭ), *n.* a type of Indian flat dough cake. Also, **chapati.** [t. Hind.]

chapbook (chăp′bo͝ok′), *n.* one of a type of small books or pamphlets of popular tales, ballads, etc., such as were formerly hawked about by chapmen.

chape (chāp), *n.* the metal mounting or trimming of a scabbard, esp. at the point. [ME, t. F. See CAP]

chapeau (shăp′ō; *Fr.* shȧ pō′), *n.*, *pl.* **-peaux, -peaus** (-pōz; *Fr.* -pō′). a hat. [t. F, g. L *capellus*, dim. of *capa*, *cappa.* See CAP]

chapeau bras (shăp′ō brä′; *Fr.* shȧ pō brȧ′), *French.* a small three-cornered hat, formerly in use in the 18th century, which could be folded flat and carried under the arm. [F, f. *chapeau* hat + *bras* arm]

chapel (chăp′l), *n.* **1.** a private or subordinate place of prayer or worship; an oratory. **2.** a separately dedicated part of a church, or a small independent churchlike edifice, devoted to special services. **3.** a room or building for worship in a college or school, country house or royal court, etc. **4.** a place of worship of a religious body outside the established Church. **5.** a separate place of public worship dependent on the church of a parish. **6.** a religious service in a chapel. **7.** a choir or orchestra of a chapel, court, etc. **8.** a printing office. **9. a.** the body of members of a trade union in a printing or publishing house. **b.** a meeting of this body. [ME *chapele*, t. OF, g. LL *cappella* sanctuary for relics (such as the cape of St Martin), dim. of *capa*, *cappa.* See CAP]

chaperon (shăp′ə rōn′), *n.* **1.** an older person, usually a matron, who, for propriety, attends a young unmarried woman in public or accompanies a party of young unmarried men and women. —*v.t.* **2.** to attend or accompany as chaperon. Also, **chaperone.** [t. F: hood, der. *chape* CAPE[1]] —**chaperonage** (shăp′ə rə nĭj), *n.*

chapfallen (chăp′fô′lən), *adj.* dispirited; chagrined; dejected. Also, **chopfallen.**

chapiter (chăp′ĭ tə), *n. Archit.* a capital[2]. [t. F. See CHAPTER]

chaplain (chăp′lĭn), *n.* **1.** an ecclesiastic attached to the chapel of a royal court, or, formerly, a noble family, college, school, etc., or to a military unit. **2.** one who says the prayer, invocation, etc., for an organization or at an assembly or gathering. [ME *chapelayn*, t. OF: m. *chapelain*, g. LL *capellānus*, der. *capella* CHAPEL; r. OE *capellān*, t. LL (as above)] —**chap′laincy, chap′lainry, chap′lainship′,** *n.*

chaplet (chăp′lĭt), *n.* **1.** a wreath or garland for the head. **2.** a string of beads. **3.** *Rom. Cath. Ch.* **a.** a string of beads for counting prayers, one third the length of a rosary. **b.** the prayers so counted thereon. **4.** *Archit.* a small moulding carved in the shape of beads or the like. **5.** *Foundry.* a metal piece supporting the core in casting a cylindrical pipe. [ME *chapelet*, t. OF, dim. of *chapel* headdress. See CHAPEAU] —**chap′leted,** *adj.*

Chaplin (chăp′lĭn), *n.* **Charles Spencer** (‘*Charlie*’), born 1889, U.S. comedian, film actor, and film director, born in England. —**Chaplinesque** (chăp′lĭn ĕsk′), *adj.*

chapman (chăp′mən), *n.*, *pl.* **-men.** **1.** a hawker or pedlar. **2.** *Archaic.* a merchant. [ME; OE *cēapman*, f. *cēap* trade + *man* man]

Chapman (chăp′mən), *n.* **George,** 1559?–1634, English poet, dramatist, and translator.

chappie (chăp′ĭ), *n. Colloq.* chap[2] (def. 1).

chaps (chăps, shăps), *n.pl. Western U.S.* strong leather riding breeches or overalls, having no seat, worn esp. by cowboys. Also, **chaparajos, chaparejos.** [short for *chaparajos*, Mex. Sp. var. of *chaparreras* der. *chaparro* bramble bush]

chapter (chăp′tə), *n.* **1.** a main division, usually numbered, of a book, treatise, or the like. **2.** a branch, usually localized, of a society or fraternity. **3.** *Eccles.* **a.** an assembly of the monks in a monastery, or of those in a province, or of the entire order. **b.** a general assembly of the canons of a church. **c.** a meeting of the elected representatives of the provinces or houses of a religious community. **d.** the body of such canons or representatives collectively. **4.** a division of the acts of Parliament passed in a session. **5.** *Horol.* any one of the Roman figures used on clocks and watches to mark the time of day. **6.** *Liturgy.* a short scriptural quotation read at various parts of the office, as after the last psalm in the service of lauds, prime, tierce, etc. **7. chapter and verse,** an exact reference. **8. chapter of accidents,** a series of closely following misfortunes. —*v.t.* **9.** to divide into or arrange in chapters. [ME *chapitre*, t. OF, var. of *chapitle*, g. L *capitulum* small head, capital of column, chapter, dim. of *caput* head]

chapterhouse (chăp′tə hous′), **1.** *Eccles.* a building attached to a cathedral or monastery in which the chapter meets. **2.** the building of a chapter of a society, etc.

chaqueta (*Sp.* chȧ kĕ′tȧ), *n. Spanish.* a heavy jacket, esp. a leather one worn by cowboys. [Sp., t. F: m. *jaquette* jacket, der. *jaque* short garment, of obscure orig.]

char[1] (chä), *v.*, **charred, charring,** *n.* —*v.t.* **1.** to burn or reduce to charcoal. **2.** to burn slightly; scorch. —*v.i.* **3.** to become charred. —*n.* **4.** a charred substance. **5.** charcoal. [? short for CHARCOAL] —**char′ry,** *adj.*

char[2] (chä), *n.*, *pl.* **chars,** (*esp. collectively*) **char.** any trout of the genus *Salvelinus*, a land-locked relative of the salmon and trout; found in deep, cold lakes. Also, **charr.** [cf. Gaelic *ceara* red]

char[3] (chä), *n.*, *v.*, **charred, charring.** *Colloq.* —*n.* **1.** a charwoman. —*v.i.* **2.** to do housework by the hour or day for money. [ME *cherre*, OE *cerr*, *cyrr* turn, time, occasion, affair]

char[4] (chä), *n. Slang.* tea. [t. Hind.: m. *chā* TEA]

charabanc (shă′rə băng′; *Fr.* shȧ rȧ bäɴ′), *n.*, *pl.* **-bancs** (-băngz′; *Fr.* -bäɴ′). a motor coach, esp. an open one formerly much used in sightseeing. Also, **char-à-banc.** [t. F: m. *char à bancs* car with benches]

characin (kă′rə sĭn), *n.* a fish of the family *Characinidae*, native to Africa and South America. [t. NL: s. *Characinus* typical genus, der. Gk *chárax* a sea-fish] —**characinoid** (kə răs′ĭ noid′), *adj.*

character (kă′rĭk tə), *n.* **1.** the aggregate of qualities that distinguishes one person or thing from others. **2.** *Chiefly U.S.* one such quality; a characteristic. **3.** moral constitution, as of a person or people. **4.** good moral constitution or status. **5.** reputation. **6.** *Obs.* good repute. **7.** an account of the qualities or peculiarities of a person or thing. **8.** a formal statement from an employer concerning the qualities and habits of a former servant or employee. **9.** status or capacity. **10.** a person: *a strange character.* **11.** *Colloq.* an odd person. **12.** a person represented in a drama, story, etc. **13.** *Theat.* a part or role. **14.** *Genetics.* any trait, function, structure, or substance of an organism resulting from the development of a gene interacting with the environment and the remainder of the gene complex; a hereditary characteristic. **15.** a significant visual mark or symbol. **16.** a symbol as used in a writing system, as a letter of the alphabet. **17.** the symbols of a writing system collectively. **18.** a style of writing or printing. **19.** *Obs.* a cipher or cipher message. **20. in character,** consistent with what is known of previous character, behaviour, etc. **21. out of character,** inconsistent with what is known of previous character, behaviour, etc. *—v.t.* **22.** to portray; describe. **23.** *Archaic.* to engrave or inscribe. [t. L, t. Gk: m. *charaktēr* instrument for marking, mark; r. ME *caractere*, t. F] —**char′acterless,** *adj.*

—**Syn. 1.** CHARACTER, INDIVIDUALITY, PERSONALITY refer to the sum of the characteristics possessed by a person. CHARACTER refers esp. to moral qualities, ethical standards, principles, and the like: *a man of sterling character.* INDIVIDUALITY refers to the distinctive qualities which make one recognizable as a person differentiated from others: *a man of strong individuality.* PERSONALITY refers particularly to the combination of outer and inner characteristics that determine the impression which one makes upon others: *a man of vivid or pleasing personality.* **5.** See **reputation.**

character actor, an actor who portrays striking or eccentric characters.

characteristic (kă′rĭk tə rĭs′tĭk), *adj.* **1.** pertaining to, constituting, or indicating the character or peculiar quality; typical; distinctive. *—n.* **2.** a distinguishing feature or quality. **3.** *Maths.* the integral part of a logarithm. **—Syn. 2.** attribute, property, trait, peculiarity. See **feature.**

characteristically (kă′rĭk tə rĭs′ tĭ klĭ), *adv.* in a characteristic manner; typically.

characteristic velocity, *Astronautics.* the speed a rocket would attain with the complete consumption of its propellants if unaffected by external forces.

characterization (kă′rĭk tə rī zā′shən), *n.* **1.** portrayal; description. **2.** the act of characterizing. **3.** the creation of fictitious characters. Also, **characterisation.**

characterize (kă′rĭk tə rīz′), *v.t.*, **-rized, -rizing. 1.** to mark or distinguish as a characteristic; be a characteristic of. **2.** to describe the characteristic or peculiar quality of. **3.** to give character to. Also, **characterise.** —**char′acteriz′er,** *n.*

charactery (kă′rĭk tə rĭ, -trĭ), *n., pl.* **-ries. 1.** the use of characters or symbols for the expression of meaning. **2.** characters or symbols collectively.

charade (shə räd′), *n.* **1.** a parlour game in which a player or players act out in pantomime a word or phrase which the others try to guess. **2.** a ridiculous or pointless act or series of acts. [t. F, t. Pr.: m. *charrado* entertainment, der. *charra* chat]

charcoal (chä′kōl′), *n.* **1.** the carbonaceous material obtained by the imperfect combustion of wood or other organic substances. **2.** a drawing pencil of charcoal. **3.** a drawing made with charcoal. *—v.t.* **4.** to blacken, write or draw with charcoal. [ME *charcole*; orig. uncert.]

charcoal-burner (chä′kōl bû′nə), *n.* **1.** a person who makes charcoal, esp. (formerly) for a livelihood. **2.** a stove, etc., burning charcoal.

Charcot (*Fr.* shàr kō′), *n.* **Jean Martin** (*Fr.* zhäɴ màr tăɴ′), 1825–93, French specialist in nervous diseases.

chard (chäd), *n.* **1.** the blanched summer shoots of the globe artichoke, *Cynara scolymus.* **2.** the spring flowering shoots of salsify, *Tragopogon porrifolius.* **3.** a form of the common beet, *Beta vulgaris* var. *cicla*, with thick leafstalks (**Swiss chard**). [t. F: m. *charde*, g. L *carduus* thistle, artichoke]

Chardin (*Fr.* shàr dăɴ′), *n.* **Jean Baptiste Siméon** (*Fr.* zhäɴ bȧ tēst sē mė ôɴ′), 1699–1779, French still-life and genre painter.

Charente (*Fr.* shȧ räɴt′), *n.* a department in W France. 327,658 pop. (1962); 2306 sq. mi. *Cap.:* Angoulême.

Charente-Maritime (*Fr.* shȧ räɴt mȧ rē tēm′), *n.* a department in W France. 470,897 pop. (1962); 2792 sq. mi. *Cap.:* La Rochelle.

charge (chäj), *v.*, **charged, charging,** *n. —v.t.* **1.** to put a load or burden on or in. **2.** to fill or furnish (a thing) with the quantity, as of powder or fuel, that it is fitted to receive. **3.** to supply with a quantity of electricity or electrical energy: *to charge a battery.* **4.** to fill (air, water, etc.) with other matter in a state of diffusion or solution. **5.** to load or burden (the mind, heart, etc.). **6.** to lay a command or injunction upon. **7.** to instruct authoritatively, as a judge does a jury. **8.** to impute as a fault: *charge him with carelessness.* **9.** to lay blame upon: blame; accuse (usually fol. by *with*): *to charge someone with negligence.* **10.** to hold liable for payment; enter a debit against. **11.** to list or record as a debt or obligation; enter as a debit. **12.** to impose or ask as a price. **13.** to attack by rushing violently against. **14.** *Her.* to place a bearing on (a shield, etc.). *—v.i.* **15.** to make an onset; rush, as to an attack. *—n.* **16.** a load or burden. **17.** the quantity of anything which an apparatus is fitted to hold, or holds, at one time. **18.** *Elect.* an electric charge. **19.** a quantity of explosive to be set off at one time. **20.** a duty or responsibility laid upon or entrusted to one. **21.** care, custody, or superintendence: *to have charge of a thing.* **22.** anything or anybody committed to one's care or management. **23.** *Eccles.* a parish or congregation committed to the spiritual care of a minister or priest. **24.** a command or injunction; exhortation. **25.** *Law.* an address by a judge to a jury at the close of a trial, instructing them as to the legal points, the weight of evidence, etc., affecting their verdict in the case. **26.** an accusation or imputation of guilt: *he was arrested on a charge of murder.* **27.** expense or cost: *improvements made at a tenant's own charge.* **28.** a sum or price charged: *a charge of 5 shillings for admission.* **29.** a pecuniary burden, encumbrance, tax, or lien; cost; expense; liability to pay. **30.** an entry in an account of something due. **31.** an impetuous onset or attack, as of soldiers. **32.** a signal by bugle, drum, etc., for a military charge. **33.** the quantity of energy stored in a capacitor or electrical storage battery. **34.** *Her.* bearing (def. 10). **35.** *Slang.* a thrill; a kick. **36. in charge,** in command; having supervisory powers. **37. in charge of, a.** having the care or supervision of: *in charge of the class.* **b.** *U.S.* under the care or supervision of: *in charge of the teacher.* [ME *charge(n)*, t. OF: m. *charg(i)er*, g. LL *carricāre* load. See CAR] **—Syn. 6.** enjoin, exhort. **9.** indict, arraign. **26.** accusation, allegation. **28.** See **price. 31.** onslaught, assault. **—Ant. 9.** acquit, absolve.

chargeable (chä′jə bl), *adj.* **1.** that may or should be charged. **2.** liable to be accused or held responsible; indictable. **3.** liable to become a charge on the public.

chargé d'affaires (shä′zhā dă fĕə′; *Fr.* shȧr zhė dȧ fĕr′), *pl.* **chargés d'affaires. 1.** (in full: **chargé d'affaires ad interim**) an official placed in charge of diplomatic business during the temporary absence of the ambassador or minister. **2.** an envoy to a state to which a diplomat of higher grade is not sent. Also, **chargé.** [t. F: lit., entrusted with affairs]

charge hand, the next grade of workman below a foreman or ganger.

charger[1] (chä′jə), *n.* **1.** one who or that which charges. **2.** a horse intended, or suitable, to be ridden in battle. **3.** *Elect.* an apparatus which charges storage batteries. [f. CHARGE, V. + -ER[1]]

charger[2] (chä′jə), *n.* **1.** a platter. **2.** a large, shallow dish for liquids. [ME *chargeour*; akin to CHARGE]

charge sheet, a list of people awaiting a hearing in a magistrates' court, together with their charges.

charily (chĕə′rĭ lĭ), *adv.* **1.** carefully; warily. **2.** sparingly. **—Ant. 1.** boldly. **2.** liberally.

chariness (chĕə′rĭ nĭs), *n.* **1.** chary quality; caution; sparingness. **2.** *Obs.* scrupulous integrity.

Charing Cross (chă′rĭng), a district in central London.

chariot (chă′rĭ ət), *n.* **1.** a two-wheeled vehicle used by the ancients in war, racing, processions, etc. **2.** (in the 18th century) a light four-wheeled pleasure carriage. **3.** any more or less stately carriage. *—v.t.* **4.** to convey in a chariot. *—v.i.* **5.** to drive a chariot; ride in a chariot. [ME, t. OF, aug. of *char.* See CAR]

charioteer (chă′rĭ ə tĭə′), *n.* **1.** a chariot driver. **2.** (*cap.*) *Astron.* the northern constellation Auriga.

charisma (kə rĭz′mə), *n., pl.* **-mata** (-mə tə). **1.** *Theol.* a divinely conferred gift or power. **2.** those special spiritual powers or personal qualities that give an individual influence or authority over large numbers of people. Also, **charism** (kă′rĭz′əm). [t. Gk: *chárisma* gift] —**charismatic** (kă′rĭz măt′ĭk), *adj.*

charitable (chă′rĭ tə bl), *adj.* **1.** generous in gifts to relieve the needs of others. **2.** kindly or lenient in judging others. **3.** pertaining to or concerned with charity: *a charitable institution.* [ME, t. OF, der. *charite* CHARITY] —**char′itableness,** *n.* —**char′itably,** *adv.* **—Syn. 1.** beneficent, liberal, bountiful. **2.** broadminded. **—Ant. 1.** selfish. **2.** severe, intolerant.

Charites (kə rī′tēz), *n.pl. Gk Myth.* the three Graces, daughters of Zeus.

charity (chă′rĭ tĭ), *n., pl.* **-ties. 1.** almsgiving; the private or public relief of unfortunate or needy persons; benevolence. **2.** something given to a person or persons in need; alms. **3.** a charitable act or work. **4.** a charitable fund, foundation, or institution. **5.** benevolent feeling, esp. towards those in need. **6.** Christian love. I Cor. 13. [ME *charite*, t. OF, g. s. L *cāritas* dearness]

charity school, a day school for poor children in the 18th and 19th centuries; usually run by the Church of England.

charivari (shä′rĭ vä′rĭ), *n., pl.* **-ris.** a mock serenade of discordant noises made with pans, horns, etc., after a wedding. [t. F]

chark (chäk), *Dial.* —*n.* **1.** charcoal (def. 1). —*v.t.* **2.** to char; convert into coke. [back-formation from CHARCOAL]

charka (chä′kə), *n.* (in India and the East Indies) a cotton gin or spinning wheel. Also, **charkha.** [t. Hind.]

charlady (chä′lā′dĭ), *n., pl.* **-dies.** a charwoman.

charlatan (shä′lə tən), *n.* one who pretends to more knowledge or skill than he possesses; a quack. [t. F, t. It.: m. *ciarlatano* der. *ciarlare* chatter] —**charlatanic** (shä′-lə tăn′ĭk), *adj.*

charlatanism (shä′lə tə nĭz′əm), *n.* the practices of a charlatan. Also, **charlatanry** (shä′lə tən rĭ).

Empire of Charlemagne, 814 A.D.

Charlemagne (shä′lə mān′; *Fr.* shȧr lə mȧny′), *n.* (‘*Charles the Great*’), A.D. 742–814, king of the Franks A.D. 768–814: as Charles I, emperor of the Holy Roman Empire A.D. 800–814.

Charleroi (*Fr.* shȧr lə rwȧ′), *n.* a town in S Belgium. 25,662 (est. 1963). Also, **Charleroy.**

Charles (chälz), *n.* (*Prince of Wales*), born 1948, son of Queen Elizabeth II, heir apparent to the throne of Great Britain and Northern Ireland.

Charles I (chälz; *Fr.* shȧrl), **1.** Charlemagne. **2.** (‘*the Bald*’), A.D. 823–877, king of France A.D. 840–877: as Charles II, emperor of the Holy Roman Empire A.D. 875–877. **3.** 1600–49, king of England and Ireland from 1625 until executed in 1649 (son of James I). **4.** 1500–58, king of Spain 1516–56: as Charles V, emperor of the Holy Roman Empire 1519–56. **5.** 1887–1922, emperor of Austria 1916–18; as Charles IV, king of Hungary 1916–18.

Charles II, 1. See **Charles I** (def. 2). **2.** 1630–85, king of England and Ireland 1660–85 (son of Charles I).

Charles IV, 1. (‘*Charles the Fair*’), 1294–1328, king of France 1322–28. **2.** See **Charles I** (def. 5).

Charles V, 1. (‘*Charles the Wise*’), 1337–80, king of France 1364–80. **2.** See **Charles I** (def. 4).

Charles VI (‘*the Mad*’ or ‘*the Well-Beloved*’), 1368–1422, king of France 1380–1422.

Charles VII (‘*Charles the Victorious*’), 1403–61, king of France 1422–61 (son of Charles VI of France).

Charles IX, 1550–74, king of France 1560–74.

Charles X, 1757–1836, king of France 1824–30.

Charles XII, 1682–1718, king of Sweden 1697–1718.

Charles XIV, John, 1763–1844, king of Sweden and Norway 1818–44. See **Bernadotte.**

Charles Edward Stuart (‘*the Young Pretender*’ or ‘*Bonnie Prince Charlie*’), 1720–88, grandson of James II of Great Britain and Ireland.

Charles Louis (*Karl Ludwig Johann*), 1771–1847, archduke of Austria.

Charles Martel (mär tĕl′; *Fr.* mȧr-), A.D. 690?–741, ruler of the Franks, A.D. 714–41: grandfather of Charlemagne; checked Moorish invasion, A.D. 732.

Charles's law, *Physics.* the law which states that, for an ideal gas at constant pressure, a rise in temperature of 1°C will cause the gas to expand by $\frac{1}{273}$ of its volume. [named after J. A. C. *Charles*, 1746–1823, French physicist]

Charles's Wain (chäl′zĭz wān′), *Astron.* the Plough. [OE *Carles wægn* Carl's wagon (Carl = Charlemagne)]

Charles the Great, Charlemagne.

Charleston (chäl′stən), *n.* **1.** (*l.c.*) a kind of foxtrot, of Southern Negro origin, popular in the 1920s. **2.** a city in the U.S., the capital of West Virginia, in the W part. 104,800 (est. 1964). **3.** a seaport in the U.S., in SE South Carolina. 81,400 (est. 1964).

Charlestown (chälz′toun′), *n.* a former town in the U.S., in E Massachusetts: since 1874 a part of Boston: battle of Bunker Hill, June 17th, 1775.

Charleville-Mézières (*Fr.* shȧr lə vēl mė zyĕr′), *n.* a town in NE France, the capital of Ardennes department. 50,229 (1962).

charley horse, *U.S. Colloq.* stiffness in the leg; a sprain.

charlie (chä′lĭ), *n. Colloq.* a fool; a silly person. Also, **charley.**

charlock (chä′lŏk), *n.* the wild mustard, *Sinapis arvensis*, often troublesome as a weed in cornfields. [ME *carlok*, OE *cerlic*]

charlotte (shä′lət), *n.* a hot sweet dish commonly made by lining a fireproof dish with bread and filling with layers of fruit, bread, brown sugar, and shredded suet. [t. F, orig., woman's name]

Charlotte (shä′lət), *n.* a city in the U.S., in S North Carolina. 201,564 (1960).

Charlotte Amalie (shä′lət ə mä′lĭ ə), a seaport in and the capital of the Virgin Islands (U.S.), on St Thomas. 18,318 (1960). Formerly, **St Thomas.**

Charlottenburg (shä lŏt′ən bûg′; *Ger.* shȧr lŏt′ən-bo͝ork), *n.* a part of West Berlin.

charlotte russe (shä′lət ro͞os′), a mould of sponge fingers filled with a cream mousse mixture. [t. F: Russian charlotte]

Charlottetown (shä′lət toun′), *n.* a seaport in Canada, the capital of Prince Edward Island. 18,318 (1960).

charm[1] (chäm), *n.* **1.** an irresistible power to please and attract; fascination. **2.** some quality or feature exerting a fascinating influence: *feminine charms.* **3.** something which possesses this power. **4.** a trinket to be worn on a chain, bracelet, etc. **5.** something worn for its supposed magical effect; an amulet. **6.** any action supposed to have magical power. **7.** the chanting or recitation of a magic verse or formula. **8.** a verse or formula credited with magical power. **9. like a charm,** successfully; perfectly. —*v.t.* **10.** to attract powerfully by beauty, etc.; please greatly. **11.** to act upon with or as with a charm; enchant. **12.** to endow with or protect by supernatural powers. **13.** to calm, soothe, etc. —*v.i.* **14.** to be fascinating or pleasing. **15.** to use charms. **16.** to act as a charm. [ME *charme*, t. OF, g. L *carmen* song, incantation] —**charm′er,** *n.* —**Syn. 1.** attractiveness, allure. **11.** fascinate, captivate, entrance; enrapture, transport, ravish, delight; allure.

charm[2] (chäm), *n. Obs. or Dial.* blended singing of birds, children, etc. [ME *cherm(e)*, OE *cerm*, *ceorm*, var. of *cierm* outcry. Cf. CHIRM]

Charmeuse (*Fr.* shȧr mœz′), *n. Trademark.* a soft, dress fabric with a satin finish. [t. F: lit., charmer (fem.)]

charming (chä′mĭng), *adj.* **1.** pleasing; delightful. **2.** exercising magic power. —**charm′ingly,** *adv.*

charnel (chä′nəl), *n.* a repository for dead bodies. [ME, t. OF, g. LL *carnāle*, prop. neut. adj. See CARNAL]

charnel-house (chä′nəl hous′), *n.* a house or place in which the bodies or bones of the dead are deposited.

Charolais (shă′rə lā′; *Fr.* shȧ rō lĕ′), *n.* one of a breed of cattle, usually off-white or creamy white. Also, **Charollais.**

Charon (kēə′rən), *n.* **1.** *Class. Myth.* the ferryman who conveyed souls of the dead across the Styx. **2.** (in humorous use) any ferryman.

Charpentier (*Fr.* shȧr päɴ tyė′), *n.* **Gustave** (*Fr.* gʏs-tȧv′), 1860–1956, French composer.

charpoy (chä′poi), *n.* the common light bedstead of India. [t. Hind.: m. *chārpāī*, lit., four-footed, t. Pers.: m. *chahār-pāī*]

charqui (chä′kĭ), *n.* meat cut into strips and dried; jerked meat, esp. beef. [t. Sp., t. Quechua (Peruvian): m. *echarqui*]

charr (chä), *n., pl.* **charrs,** (*esp. collectively*) **charr.** char[2].

chart (chät), *n.* **1.** a sheet exhibiting information in tabulated or methodical form. **2.** a graphic representation, as by curves, of a dependent variable such as temperature, price, etc. **3.** a map, esp. a hydrographic or marine map. **4.** an outline map showing special conditions or facts: *a weather chart.* **5.** (*usually pl.*) a weekly list of the best-selling pop records. —*v.t.* **6.** to make a chart of. **7.** to plan: *to chart a course of action.* [t. F: m. *charte*, g. L *c(h)arta* paper, t. Gk: m. *chártēs* leaf of paper] —**chart′less,** *adj.* —**Syn. 3.** See **map.**

chartbound (chät′bound′), *adj. Colloq.* (of a pop-music record) likely to achieve a place in the charts of best-selling records each week.

charter (chä′tə), *n.* **1.** a written instrument or contract, esp. relating to land transfers. **2. a.** a written document, granted by a sovereign or legislature giving privileges, rights, the benefit of a new invention, a peerage, etc. **b.** a written grant by a sovereign power creating or incorporating a borough, university, company or a corporation, as the royal charters granted to British colonies in America. **3.** Also, **charter party.** a contract by which part or all of a ship is leased for a voyage or a stated time, and safe delivery of the cargo is agreed. **4.** special privilege or immunity. **5.** *U.S.* the articles or certificate of incorporation taken in connection with the law under which a corporation is organized. —*v.t.* **6.** to establish by charter. **7.** to lease or hire by charter party. **8.** to hire a vehicle, etc. —*adj.* **9.** done or held in accordance with a charter. **10.** founded, granted, or protected by a charter. **11.** hired for a particular purpose or journey: *a charter flight.* [ME *chartre*, t. OF, g. L *chartula*, dim. of *charta*]

Charterhouse (chä′tə hous′), *n.* **1.** a Carthusian monastery. **2.** an English boys' public school (founded 1611), now at Godalming, Surrey.
charter member, one of the original members.
charthouse (chät′hous′), *n.* chartroom.
Chartism (chä′tĭz′əm), *n.* the principles or movement of a party of political reformers, chiefly workingmen, active in England from 1838 to 1848 (so called from the **People's Charter,** the document which contained their principles and demands). [f. s. L *charta* charter + -ISM; pronunciation influenced by *charter*] —**Chart′ist,** *n., adj.*
chartography (kä tŏg′rə fĭ), *n.* cartography.
Chartres (shä′tr; *Fr.* shȧr′tr), *n.* a city in N France: famous cathedral. 33,992 (1962).
chartreuse (shä trûz′; *Fr.* shȧr trœz′), *n.* **1.** one of two aromatic liqueurs made by the Carthusian monks, at Grenoble, France, and (1901–46) in Tarragona, Spain. **2.** (*cap.*) a trademark for these liqueurs. **3.** a clear, light green with a yellowish tinge. **4.** a Carthusian monastery. —*adj.* **5.** of the colour chartreuse. [t. F]
chartroom (chät′ro͞om′, -ro͝om′), *n.* the room in a ship where charts are kept. Also, **charthouse.**
chartulary (chä′tyo͞o lə rĭ), *n., pl.* **-ries.** cartulary.
charwoman (chä′wo͝om′ən), *n., pl.* **-women.** a woman hired to do odd jobs of household work, or to do such work by the hour or day. [f. CHAR[3] + WOMAN]
chary (chēə′rĭ), *adj.,* **charier, chariest. 1.** careful; wary. **2.** shy. **3.** fastidious; choosy. **4.** sparing (often fol. by *of*): *chary of his praise.* [ME *chari,* OE *cearig* sorrowful, der. *caru* CARE] —**Ant. 1.** trustful. **2.** confident. **3.** uncritical. **4.** lavish.
Charybdis (kə rĭb′dĭs), *n. Gk Legend.* See **Scylla.** —**Caryb′dian,** *adj.*
chase[1] (chās), *v.,* **chased, chasing,** *n.* —*v.t.* **1.** to pursue in order to seize, overtake, etc. **2.** to pursue with intent to capture or kill, as game; hunt. **3.** to drive by pursuing. **4.** to put to flight. —*v.i.* **5.** to follow in pursuit: *to chase after someone.* **6.** *Colloq.* to run or hasten. —*n.* **7.** the act of chasing; pursuit. **8.** an object of pursuit; a thing chased. **9.** the occupation or sport of hunting. **10.** an unenclosed tract of privately owned land reserved for animals to be hunted. **11.** the right of keeping game or of hunting on the land of others. **12.** a steeplechase. **13.** *Tennis.* the second bounce of a ball that the opponent has failed or declined to return. [ME *chace(n),* t. OF: m. *chacier,* g. L *captiāre* seize. See CATCH]
chase[2] (chās), *n., v.,* **chased, chasing.** —*n.* **1.** a rectangular iron frame in which composed type, etc., is secured or locked, for printing or plate-making. **2.** a groove, furrow, or trench; a lengthened hollow. **3.** *Ordn.* **a.** the part of a gun in front of the trunnions. **b.** the part containing the bore. —*v.t.* **4.** to groove or indent, so as to make into a screw. **5.** to cut in making a screw thread. [t. F: m. *châsse,* g. L *capsa* box]
chase[3] (chās), *v.t.,* **chased, chasing.** to ornament (metal) by engraving or embossing. [aphetic var. of ENCHASE]
chaser[1] (chā′sə), *n.* **1.** one who or that which chases or pursues. **2.** *Colloq.* a drink of water, beer, or other mild beverage taken after a drink of spirits. **3.** Also, **chase-gun.** a gun on a vessel esp. for use when in chase or being chased. **4.** a hunter. **5.** a second-rate film. **6.** a clerk employed on a building site. [f. CHASE[1] + -ER[1]]
chaser[2] (chā′sə), *n.* a multiple-toothed tool used in cutting screw threads. [f. CHASE[2] + -ER[1]]
chaser[3] (chā′sə), *n.* a person who engraves metal. [f. CHASE[3] + -ER[1]]
chasm (kăz′əm), *n.* **1.** a yawning fissure or deep cleft in the earth's surface; a gorge. **2.** a breach or wide fissure in a wall or other structure. **3.** a marked interruption of continuity; gap. **4.** a sundering breach in relations: *the chasm of death.* **5.** a wide difference of feeling, interest, etc., between persons, groups, nations. [t. L: m. *chasma,* t. Gk] —**chasmal** (kăz′məl), *adj.*
chassé (shăs′ā), *n., v.,* **chasséd, chasséing.** *Dancing.* —*n.* **1.** a kind of gliding step in which one foot is kept in advance of the other. —*v.i.* **2.** to execute a chassé. [t. F: lit., chased]
chassepot (*Fr.* shȧs pō′), *n.* a breech-loading rifle, closed with a sliding bolt, introduced into the French army after the war between Austria and Prussia in 1866. [named after A. A. *Chassepot,* 1833–1905, the (French) inventor]
chasseur (shă sû′; *Fr.* shȧ sœr′), *n.* **1.** (in the French army) one of a body of troops (cavalry or infantry) equipped and trained for rapid movement. **2.** a uniformed footman or attendant; a liveried servant. **3.** a huntsman. [t. F: lit., chaser]
chassis (shăs′ĭ), *n., pl.* **chassis** (shăs′ĭz). **1.** the frame, wheels, and machinery of a motor vehicle, on which the body is supported. **2.** *Ordn.* the frame or rails on which a gun carriage moves backwards and forwards. **3.** the main landing gear of an aircraft; that portion of the landing gear that supports an aircraft. **4.** *Radio.* the foundation on which the sections of a television or radio set are mounted. [t. F: frame; akin to CHASE[2]]
chaste (chāst), *adj.* **1.** not having had sexual intercourse; virgin, esp. when considered as being virtuous. **2.** free from obscenity; decent. **3.** undefiled or stainless. **4.** pure in style; subdued; simple. **5.** *Obs.* unmarried. [ME, t. OF, g. L *castus* pure] —**chaste′ly,** *adv.* —**chaste′ness,** *n.* —**Ant. 1.** immoral. **2.** coarse. **3.** debased. **4.** ornate.
chasten (chā′sən), *v.t.* **1.** to inflict suffering upon for purposes of moral improvement; chastise. **2.** to restrain; subdue. **3.** to make chaste in style. [f. obs. *chaste,* v., chasten (t. OF: m. *chastier,* g. L *castigāre*) + -EN[1]] —**chas′tener,** *n.*
chastise (chăs tīz′), *v.t.,* **-tised, -tising. 1.** to inflict corporal punishment upon. **2.** *Archaic.* to restrain; chasten. **3.** *Archaic.* to refine; purify. [ME; f. obs. *chaste* CHASTEN + -ISE[2]] —**chastisement** (chăs′tĭz mənt), *n.* —**chastis′er,** *n.*
chastity (chăs′tĭ tĭ), *n.* the quality of being chaste. [ME *chastete,* t. OF, f. *chaste* CHASTE + *-te* -TY[2]]
chastity belt, a belt, from which is supported a padlocked device to prevent a woman having sexual intercourse, much used in the Middle Ages.
chasuble (chăz′yo͞o bl), *n. Eccles.* a sleeveless outer vestment worn by the celebrant at mass. [t. F (r. ME *chesible,* t. OF), g. LL *casubula,* for L *casula* cloak, dim. of *casa* house]

Chasuble

chat (chăt), *v.,* **chatted, chatting,** *n.* —*v.i.* **1.** to converse in a familiar or informal manner. —*v.t.* **2.** *Slang.* to talk persuasively to or flirt with (fol. by *up*): *to chat up a girl.* —*n.* **3.** informal conversation. **4.** any of several birds of the subfamily *Turdinae*; esp. the stonechat and whinchat, of the genus *Saxicola*; known for their harsh chattering cries. **5.** *U.S.* any of several passerine birds; a warbler. **6.** *Austral.* any bird of the genus *Ephthianura*; a wren. [short for CHATTER]
chateau (shăt′ō), *n., pl.* **-teaus, -teaux** (-tōz). **1.** a French castle. **2.** a stately residence in imitation of a French castle. **3.** a country estate, esp. a fine French one. Also, **château** (*Fr.* shȧ tō′). [t. F, g. L *castellum*]
Chateaubriand (*Fr.* shȧ tō brē äɴ′), *n.* **François René** (*Fr.* fräɴ swȧ rə nĕ′), **Vicomte de,** 1768–1848, French author and statesman.
chateaubriant (shăt′ō brē′ŏn; *Fr.* shȧ tō brē äɴ′), *n.* a fillet of beef cut thickly and grilled. Also, **chateaubriand.**
Château d'Yquem (*Fr.* shȧ tō dē kĕm′), a sweet white wine of France from the Sauternes district.
Châteauroux (*Fr.* shȧ tō ro͞o′), *n.* a town in central France, the capital of Indre department. 125,821 (1961).
Château-Thierry (shăt′ō tē′ə rĭ; *Fr.* shȧ tō tyĕ rē′), *n.* a town in N France, on the river Marne. 10,619 (1962).
chateau wine, the wine produced from grapes grown at a given vineyard or chateau in the Bordeaux wine region of France.
chatelaine (shăt′ə lān′), *n.* **1.** the mistress of a castle. **2.** the mistress of an elegant or fashionable household. **3.** a device for suspending keys, trinkets, etc., worn at the waist by women. Also, **châtelaine** (*Fr.* shȧt lĕn′). [t. F. See CASTELLAN]
Chatham (chăt′əm), *n.* **1. 1st Earl of.** See **Pitt, William. 2.** a seaport in England, in N Kent: naval dockyard. 49,520 (est. 1962).
Chatham Islands, an island group in the S Pacific, ab. 500 mi. E of and belonging to New Zealand. 487 pop. (1961); 372 sq. mi.
chatoyant (shə toi′ənt), *adj.* **1.** changing in lustre or colour. **2.** *Jewellery.* reflecting a single streak of light when cut in a cabochon. [t. F, ppr. of *chatoyer* change lustre like a cat's eye, der. *chat* cat]
Chattanooga (chăt′ə no͞o′gə), *n.* a city in the U.S., in SE Tennessee, on the Tennessee river. 130,009 (1960).
chattel (chăt′l), *n.* **1.** a moveable article of property. **2.** *Law.* **a. chattel personal,** articles of property both moveable and intangible, including debts, patents, copyrights, etc. **b. chattel real,** a leasehold interest in land. **3.** a slave. [ME *chatel,* t. OF. See CATTLE] —**Syn. 1.** See **property.**
chattel mortgage, *U.S.* a mortgage on household, moveable, or other personal property.
chatter (chăt′ə), *v.i.* **1.** to utter a succession of quick, inarticulate, speechlike sounds: *a chattering monkey.* **2.** to talk rapidly and to little purpose; jabber. **3.** to make a rapid clicking noise by striking together, as the teeth

from cold. **4.** *Mach.* to vibrate in cutting, so as to form a series of nicks or notches. —*v.t.* **5.** to utter rapidly or idly. **6.** to cause to chatter. —*n.* **7.** idle or foolish talk. **8.** the act or sound of chattering. [ME; imit.]

chatterbox (chăt′ə bŏks′), *n.* a very talkative person.

chatterer (chăt′ə rə), *n.* **1.** one who chatters. **2.** *U.S.* any bird of the genus *Bombycilla*; the waxwing; the three species of which are all found in the N hemisphere. **3.** *U.S.* any member of the tropical American bird family *Cotingidae*, fruit-eating birds of diverse coloration.

chatter marks, *Chiefly U.S.* **1.** marks left by a tool that has been chattering. **2.** stria (def. 2).

Chatterton (chăt′ə tən), *n.* **Thomas,** 1752–70, English poet.

chatty (chăt′ĭ), *adj.*, **-tier, -tiest.** given to or full of chat or familiar talk; conversational: *a chatty letter or person.* —**chat′tily,** *adv.* —**chat′tiness,** *n.*

Chaucer (chô′sə), *n.* **Geoffrey** (jĕf′rĭ), 1340?–1400, English poet.

Chaucerian (chô sĭə′rĭ ən), *adj.* **1.** of, pertaining to, or characteristic of Chaucer's writings. —*n.* **2.** a scholar devoted to the study of Chaucer. **3.** an imitator or follower of Chaucer: *the Scottish Chaucerians.*

chaudfroid (*Fr.* shō frwȧ′), *n.* a savoury or sweet white sauce, containing aspic, and used to coat cold meat, fish, fruit, etc. [t. F: lit., hot-cold]

chauffer (chô′fə), *n.* **1.** a metal basket for holding fire. **2.** a small, portable stove. [t. F: m. *chauffoir* heater]

chauffeur (shō′fə, shō fû′), *n.* a person, esp. male, employed to drive a private motor car. [t. F: stoker, der. *chauffer* heat. See CHAFE]

chauffeuse (shō fûz′; *Fr.* shō fœz′), *n.* a female chauffeur.

chaulmoogra (chôl mōō′grə), *n.* an East Indian tree of the genus *Taraktogenos* (or *Hydnocarpus*), the seeds of which yield a fixed oil used in the treatment of leprosy and skin diseases. [t. Bengali]

chausses (shōs), *n.pl. Hist.* medieval armour of mail for the legs and feet. [t. F, der. L *calceus* shoe]

chaussure (*Fr.* shō sʏr′), *n. French.* a foot covering. [F, der. *chausser* to shoe, g. L *calceāre*]

Chautauqua (shə tô′kwə), *n.* **1.** a village in SW New York State. **2.** a summer educational school, held there. **3.** (*often l.c.*) a system of home study originating in Chautauqua. **4.** (*often l.c.*) any similar assembly, esp. religious or educational. —*adj.* **5.** pertaining to an institution, or a system of popular education, employing summer schools assembling annually at Chautauqua, N.Y., with courses of home reading and study. **6.** (*often l.c.*) pertaining to a chautauqua: *a chautauqua programme.*

chauvinism (shō′vĭ nĭz′əm), *n.* blind enthusiasm for military glory; zealous and belligerent patriotism or devotion to any cause. [t. F: m. *chauvinisme*; from Nicolas *Chauvin*, an old soldier and overenthusiastic admirer of Napoleon I] —**chau′vinist,** *n., adj.* —**chau′vinis′tic,** *adj.* —**chau′vinis′tically,** *adv.*

Chavannes (*Fr.* shȧ vȧn′), *n.* **Puvis de** (*Fr.* pʏ vē′ də). See **Puvis de Chavannes.**

chaw (chô), *v.t., v.i., n. Dial.* chew.

chazzan (кнə zän′, кнä′zən), *n.* a Jewish cantor.

Ch.B., (L *Chirurgiae Baccalaureus*) Bachelor of Surgery.

Ch.E., Chemical Engineer.

Cheam (chēm), *n.* a district of the S outer London borough of Sutton.

cheap (chēp), *adj.* **1.** of a relatively low price; at a bargain. **2.** costing little labour or trouble. **3.** charging low prices: *a very cheap store.* **4.** of poor quality: *that material is cheap and nasty.* **5.** of little account; of small value; mean: *cheap conduct.* **6.** *Colloq.* embarrassed; sheepish: *feeling cheap about his mistake.* **7.** obtainable at a low rate of interest: *when money is cheap.* **8.** *U.S.* of decreased value or purchasing power, as currency depreciated due to inflation. —*adv.* **9.** at a low price; at small cost. —*n.* **10. on the cheap,** *Colloq.* at a low price. [ME *cheep* (in phrases as *greet cheep* cheap, lit., great bargain), OE *cēap*, c. G *Kauf* bargain] —**cheap′ly,** *adv.* —**cheap′ness,** *n.*

—**Syn. 1.** CHEAP, INEXPENSIVE agree in their suggestion of low cost. CHEAP now often suggests shoddiness, inferiority, showy imitation, complete unworthiness, and the like: *a cheap kind of fur.* INEXPENSIVE emphasizes lowness of price and suggests that the value is fully equal to the cost: *an inexpensive dress.* —**Ant. 1.** expensive, dear.

cheapen (chē′pən), *v.t.* **1.** to make cheap or cheaper. **2.** to belittle; bring into contempt. **3.** *Archaic.* to bargain for. —*v.i.* **4.** to become cheap or cheaper. —**cheap′ener,** *n.*

cheapjack (chēp′jăk′), *n.* **1.** a travelling hawker, selling cheap goods. —*adj.* **2.** shoddy; of poor quality.

Cheapside (chēp′sīd′), *n.* a central east-and-west thoroughfare of the City of London.

cheat (chēt), *n.* **1.** a fraud; swindle; deception. **2.** a person who cheats or defrauds. **3.** *Law.* the fraudulent obtaining of another's property by a false pretence or trick. **4.** an imposter. **5.** *U.S.* rye-brome. **6.** a card game, the object of which is to cheat without detection. —*v.t.* **7.** to defraud; swindle. **8.** to deceive; impose upon. **9.** to beguile; elude. —*v.i.* **10.** to practise fraud. [ME *chet(e)*, aphetic form of *achet*, var. of ESCHEAT] —**cheat′able,** *adj.* —**cheat′er,** *n.* —**cheat′ingly,** *adv.*

—**Syn. 1.** imposture, artifice, trick, hoax. **2.** swindler, trickster, sharper. **7.** CHEAT, DECEIVE, TRICK, VICTIMIZE refer to the use of fraud or artifice deliberately to hoodwink someone or to obtain an unfair advantage over him. CHEAT implies conducting matters fraudulently esp. for profit to oneself: *cheat him at cards.* DECEIVE suggests deliberately misleading or deluding, to produce misunderstanding or to prevent someone from knowing the truth: *to deceive one's parents.* TO TRICK is to deceive by a stratagem, often of a petty, crafty, or dishonourable kind: *to trick someone into signing a note.* TO VICTIMIZE is to make a victim of, to cause to suffer; the emotional connotation makes the cheating, deception, or trickery seem particularly dastardly: *to victimize a blind man.*

check (chĕk), *v.t.* **1.** to stop or arrest the motion of suddenly or forcibly. **2.** to restrain; hold in restraint or control. **3.** to investigate or verify as to correctness. **4.** *U.S.* to tick (often fol. by *off*). **5.** *U.S.* to leave in temporary custody: *check in your coat and hat.* **6.** *U.S.* to accept for temporary custody: *small parcels checked here.* **7.** *U.S.* to send luggage, etc., through to a final destination, but allowing the accompanying passenger to break the journey: *we checked two trunks through to New York.* **8.** *U.S.* to accept for conveyance, and to convey to a final destination: *check this trunk to New York.* **9.** to mark in a pattern of checks or squares: *a checked dress.* **10.** *U.S. Agric.* to mark the ground in order to plant in checkrows. **11.** *Chess.* to place (an opponent's king) under direct attack. **12.** *Naut.* to ease off; slacken: *to check a brace.* —*v.i.* **13.** to prove to be right; to correspond accurately: *the reprint checks with the original item for item.* **14.** to make an inquiry or investigation for verification, etc. (usually fol. by *up* or *on*): *I'll check up on the matter.* **15.** to make a stop; pause. **16.** *U.S.* to crack or split, usually in small cracks. **17.** *Hunting.* (of dogs) to stop on losing the scent or to verify it. **18.** *Falconry.* (of a hawk) to forsake the proper prey and follow baser game (fol. by *at*). **19.** to register one's arrival, as at a hotel, at work, etc. (fol. by *in*). **20.** to leave, as work or one's quarters at a hotel, etc. (fol. by *out*). —*n.* **21.** a person or thing that checks or restrains. **22.** a sudden arrest or stoppage; repulse; rebuff. **23.** control with a view to ascertaining performance or preventing error. **24.** *Angling.* a rachet device in a reel which controls the free running of the line. **25.** a controlled and carefully observed operation or test procedure to determine actual and potential performance. **26.** a means or standard to insure against error, fraud, etc. **27.** *U.S.* a tick. **28.** *U.S.* a cheque. **29.** *U.S.* bill[1] (def. 2). **30.** *U.S.* a ticket (def. 1). **31.** *Music.* the mechanism that holds a piano hammer after striking. **32.** a pattern formed of squares, as on a draughtboard. **33.** a fabric having a check pattern. **34.** *Chess.* the exposure of the king to direct attack. **35.** *U.S.* a counter used in card games; the chip in poker. **36.** *U.S.* a small crack. **37.** *Masonry.* a rabbet-shaped cutting on the edge of a stone, by which it is fitted to another stone. **38. in check, a.** under restraint. **b.** *Chess.* (of a player) having a king which is exposed to direct attack, or (of the king) being exposed to direct attack. —*adj.* **39.** serving to check, control, verify, etc. **40.** ornamented with a checked pattern; chequered. —*interj.* **41.** *Chess.* (an optional call to inform one's opponent that his king is exposed to direct attack.) [ME *chek*, t. OF: m. *eschec*, b. OF *eschac* check (ult. t. Pers.; see CHECKMATE) and OF *eschiec* booty (t. Gmc; cf. OHG *scāh*)] —**check′able,** *adj.* —**check′er,** *n.*

—**Syn. 1.** See **stop. 2.** CHECK, CURB, REPRESS, RESTRAIN refer to putting a control on movement, progress, action, etc. CHECK implies arresting suddenly, halting or causing to halt: *to check a movement towards reform.* CURB implies the use of a means such as a chain, strap, frame, wall, etc., to guide or control or to force to stay within definite limits: *to curb a horse.* REPRESS, formerly meaning to suppress, now implies preventing the action or development which might naturally be expected: *to repress evidences of excitement.* RESTRAIN implies the use of force to put under control, or chiefly, to hold back: *to restrain a person from violent acts.* **21.** obstacle, obstruction, hindrance, restriction, restraint, curb.

checkbook (chĕk′bŏŏk′), *n. U.S.* a chequebook.

checked (chĕkt), *adj.* **1.** having a pattern of squares; chequered. **2.** *Phonet.* situated in a closed syllable.

checker (chĕk′ə), *n.* **1.** *U.S.* a draughtsman. **2.** a chequered pattern. —*v.t., v.i.* **3.** *U.S.* chequer.

checkerberry (chĕk′ə bə rĭ, -brĭ), *n., pl.* **-ries. 1.** the red fruit of wintergreen, *Gaultheria procumbens.* **2.** the plant itself. Also, **boxberry, partridgeberry.**

checkerboard (chĕk′ə bôd′), *n. U.S.* a draughtboard; a chessboard.

checkered (chĕk′əd), *adj. U.S.* chequered.
checkers (chĕk′əz), *n. U.S.* draughts.
check-in (chĕk′ĭn′), *n. Chiefly U.S.* **1.** the act of registering one's arrival, as at work, at a hotel, etc. **2.** the place where arrival is registered.
checking account, *U.S.* a current account.
check list, *U.S.* items listed together for convenience of comparison or other checking purposes.
checkmate (chĕk′māt′), *n., v.,* **-mated, -mating,** *interj.* —*n.* **1.** *Chess.* **a.** the act of putting the opponent's king into an inextricable check, thus bringing the game to a close. **b.** the position of the pieces when a king is checkmated. **2.** defeat; overthrow. —*v.t.* **3.** *Chess.* to put (an opponent's king) into inextricable check. **4.** to check completely; defeat. —*interj.* **5.** *Chess.* (the announcing by a player that he has put his opponent's king into inextricable check.) [ME *chek mat,* ult. t. Ar.: m. *shāh māt* the king is dead]
checkout (chĕk′out′), *n.* the cash desk in a supermarket.
checkpoint (chĕk′point′), *n. Chiefly U.S.* a place where traffic is halted for inspection.
checkrail (chĕk′rāl′), *n. Railways.* an extra rail placed alongside the inner rail on curves, points, etc., to prevent derailment; guardrail.
check rein, 1. a short rein joining the bit of one of a span of horses to the driving rein of the other. **2.** a bearing rein.
checkroom (chĕk′ro͝om′, -ro͞om′), *n. U.S.* **1.** a left-luggage office. **2.** a cloakroom.
checkrow (chĕk′rō′), *U.S. Agric.* —*n.* **1.** one of a number of rows of trees or plants, esp. maize, in which the distance between adjacent trees or plants is equal to that between adjacent rows. —*v.t.* **2.** to plant in checkrows.
checkup (chĕk′ŭp′), *n.* **1.** an examination or close scrutiny for purposes of verification as to accuracy, comparison, etc. **2.** a comprehensive physical examination. **3.** an overhaul.
check valve, a valve which ensures one-way flow in a pipe.
Cheddar (chĕd′ə), *n.* a smooth white or yellow hard cheese with a slightly acid flavour. Cf. *U.S.* **American cheese.**
Cheddar Gorge, a gorge in the Mendip Hills, 400 ft deep, with large natural caves.
cheddite (chĕd′īt, shĕd′īt), *n.* an explosive used for blasting made up of a chlorate or perchlorate mixture with a fatty substance, such as castor oil. [t. F: f. *Chedde* place name (of Savoy) + *-ite* -ITE[1]]
cheek (chēk), *n.* **1.** either side of the face below eye level. **2.** the side wall of the mouth between the upper and lower jaws. **3.** something resembling the human cheek in form or position, as either of two parts forming corresponding sides of a thing. **4.** a buttock. **5.** one side of the head of a hammer. **6.** *Mach.* either of the sides of a pulley or block. **7.** *Print.* one of the sides of a block (def. 5). **8.** *Colloq.* impudence or effrontery. **9. cheek by jowl,** close together; adjacent. **10. turn the other cheek,** to accept provocation pacifistically. Matthew 5:39. **11. with one's tongue in one's cheek,** mockingly; insincerely. —*v.t.* **12.** *Colloq.* to address saucily; to be impudent. [ME *cheke,* OE *cēace,* c. D *kaak*]
cheekbone (chēk′bōn′), *n.* the bone or bony prominence below the outer angle of the eye.
cheek by jowl, side by side; in close intimacy.
cheek pouch, a bag in the cheek of certain animals, as squirrels, for carrying food.
cheektooth (chēk′to͞oth′), *n., pl.* **-teeth.** a molar or grinder.
cheeky (chē′kĭ), *adj.,* **cheekier, cheekiest.** *Colloq.* impudent; insolent: *a cheeky fellow, cheeky behaviour.* —**cheek′ily,** *adv.* —**cheek′iness,** *n.*
cheep (chēp), *v.i.* **1.** to chirp; peep. —*v.t.* **2.** to express by cheeps. —*n.* **3.** a chirp. [imit.]
cheeper (chē′pə), *n.* a young bird, esp. a game bird.
cheer (chĭə), *n.* **1.** a shout of encouragement, approval, congratulation, etc. **2.** that which gives joy or gladness; encouragement; comfort. **3.** state of feeling or spirits: *what cheer?* **4.** gladness, gaiety, or animation: *to make cheer.* **5.** food; provisions. **6. three cheers,** three shouts of hurrah, given as a token of approval for someone. **7.** *Archaic.* expression of countenance. —*v.t.* **8.** to salute with shouts of approval, congratulation, etc. **9.** to inspire with cheer; gladden (often fol. by *up*). **10.** to encourage or incite. —*v.i.* **11.** to utter cheers of approval, etc. **12.** to become cheerful (often fol. by *up*). **13.** *Obs.* to be in a particular state of spirits. —*interj.* **14.** (*pl.*) *Colloq.* to your health. [ME *chere,* t. OF: face, g. LL *cara*] —**cheer′er,** *n.* —**cheer′ingly,** *adv.*
—**Syn. 9.** CHEER, GLADDEN, ENLIVEN mean to make happy or lively. To CHEER is to comfort, to restore hope and cheerfulness to (now often CHEER UP, when thoroughness, a definite time, or a particular point in the action is referred to). (Cf. *eat up, drink up, hurry up*): *to cheer a sick person; soon cheered him up.* To GLADDEN does not imply a state of sadness to begin with, but suggests bringing pleasure or happiness to someone: *to gladden someone's heart with good news.* ENLIVEN suggests bringing vivacity and liveliness: *to enliven a dull evening, a party.* **10.** exhilarate, animate. **11.** shout, applaud, acclaim. —**Ant. 9.** depress. **10.** discourage.
cheerful (chĭə′fəl), *adj.* **1.** full of cheer; in good spirits: *a cheerful person.* **2.** promoting cheer; pleasant; bright: *cheerful surroundings.* **3.** arising from good spirits or cheerfulness: *cheerful song.* **4.** hearty or ungrudging: *cheerful giving.* —**cheer′fully,** *adv.* —**cheer′fulness,** *n.* —**Syn. 1.** cheery, gay, blithe.
cheerio (chĭə′rĭ ō′), *interj., n., pl.* **-os.** *Colloq.* **1.** goodbye. —*interj.* **2.** to your health.
cheerleader (chĭə′lē′də), *n. Chiefly U.S.* a person who leads cheering, esp. at sports matches.
cheerless (chĭə′lĭs), *adj.* without cheer; joyless; gloomy. —**cheer′lessly,** *adv.* —**cheer′lessness,** *n.*
cheerly (chĭə′lĭ), *adv.* cheerfully.
cheery (chĭə′rĭ), *adj.,* **-rier, -riest. 1.** in good spirits; blithe; gay. **2.** too obviously cheerful; over-hearty. **3.** promoting cheer; enlivening. —**cheer′ily,** *adv.* —**cheer′iness,** *n.*
cheese[1] (chēz), *n.* **1.** the curd of milk separated from the whey and prepared in many ways as a food. **2.** a cake or definite mass of this substance. **3.** something of similar shape or consistency, as a mass of pomace in cider-making. **4.** a conserve of fruit of the consistency of cream cheese. **5.** *Colloq.* (in phrases, opposed to *chalk*) the genuine article, not a substitute. **6.** *Obs.* a low curtsy. [ME *chese,* OE *cēse,* c. G *Käse,* ult. t. L: m. *cāseus*]
cheese[2] (chēz), *n. Slang.* the correct or proper thing. [prob. t. Pers., Hind.: m. *chīz* thing]
cheesecake (chēz′kāk′), *n.* **1.** a kind of cake or open pie filled with a custard-like preparation containing cheese. **2.** *Slang.* photographs of pretty girls in newspapers, magazines, etc., posed to display their bodies, and emphasizing their sex appeal. **3.** (usually derogatory) sex appeal.
cheesecloth (chēz′klŏth′), *n.* a coarse cotton fabric of open texture, orig. used in cheese-making, now also for costumes, etc.
cheese-cutter (chēz′kŭt′ə), *n.* **1.** that which cuts cheese, specif. a board and attached wire, the wire being drawn downwards through the cheese. **2.** a nautical peaked cap worn without a badge. **3.** *Naut.* a type of keel, fitted in a boat; lowered through the bottom when in use.
cheesed-off (chēzd′ŏf′), *adj. Slang.* bored; fed up. Also (esp. in predicative use), **cheesed off.**
cheese mite, a small arachnid, *Tyroglyphus longior,* that breeds in cheese and infests bran, flour, and hay.
cheeseparing (chēz′pĕə′rĭng), *adj.* **1.** meanly economical; parsimonious. —*n.* **2.** something of little or no value. **3.** niggardly economy. **4.** the remaining rind after the cheese has been pared off.
cheese straw, a long, thin cheese-flavoured biscuit.
cheesy (chē′zĭ), *adj.,* **-sier, -siest. 1.** like cheese: *cheesy taste or consistency.* **2.** *Slang.* smelly. **3.** *U.S. Slang.* of poor quality. —**chees′iness,** *n.*
cheetah (chē′tə), *n.* an animal of the cat family, *Acinonyx jubatus,* of south-western Asia and Africa, resembling the leopard but having certain doglike characteristics, often trained for hunting deer, etc.; fastest four-legged animal. Also, **chetah.** [t. Hind.: m. *chītā*]

Cheetah, *Acinonyx jubatus* (Total length ab. 7 ft, tail $2\frac{1}{2}$ ft, $2\frac{1}{2}$ ft high at the shoulder)

chef (shĕf), *n.* a cook, esp. a head cook. [t. F. See CHIEF]
chef-d'oeuvre (*Fr.* shĕ dœ′vr), *n., pl.* **chefs-d'oeuvre** (*Fr.* shĕ dœ′vr). *French.* a masterpiece, esp. of an author, painter, etc.
cheiro-, var. of **chiro-.**
Cheju (chĕ′jo͞o′), *n.* an island S of, and belonging to, South Korea; 718 sq. mi. Also, **Quelpart**; Japanese, **Saishuto**; Korean, **Saishu.**
Cheka (*Russ.* chĕ′kə), *n.* (formerly) the special commission in the Soviet Union for protection against counter-revolution; the secret police. The name was later changed to the G.P.U. [t. Russ.: f. *che* + *ka,* names of the initials of the *chrezvychainaya komissiya* extraordinary commission]
Chekhov (chĕk′ŏf; *Russ.* chĕ′KHəf), *n.* **Anton Pavlovich** (*Russ.* ȧn tôN′ pȧv′lə vĭch), 1860–1904, Russian short-story writer and dramatist. Also, **Tchekhoff.** —**Chekhovian** (chĕ kō′vyən), *adj.*
Chekiang (chĕ′kyăng′), *n.* a province in E China. 25,280,000 pop. (est. 1957). *Cap.:* Hangchow.

chela[1] (kē′lə), *n.*, *pl.* **-lae** (-lē). the nipper-like organ or claw terminating certain limbs of some arthropods. [t. NL, t. Gk: m. *chēlḗ* claw]

Chela of lobster

chela[2] (chā′lə), *n.* (in India) a disciple of a religious teacher. [t. Hind.: slave, disciple]
chelate (kē′lāt), *n.* **1.** *Chem.* a molecular structure in which a central polyvalent metal ion is combined into a ring of organic compounds or radicals. —*adj.* **2.** *Zool.* having a chela.
chelating agent, *Chem.* an organic chemical which is capable of removing unwanted metal ions by chelation.
chelation (kĭ lā′shən), *n.* *Chem.* the formation of a chelate.
cheli-, a word element meaning 'claws', as in *cheliferous.* [t. Gk: combining form of *chēlḗ* CHELA[1]]
chelicera (kĭ lĭs′ə rə), *n.*, *pl.* **-rae** (-rē′). one of the pre-oral appendages found in some spiders.
Chelidon (kĕl′ĭ dŏn′), *n.* *Class. Myth.* a maiden who was raped, enslaved, and then changed into a swallow.
cheliferous (kĭ lĭf′ə rəs), *adj.* bearing chelae.
cheliform (kē′lĭ fôm′), *adj.* nipper-like.
Chellean (shĕl′ĭ ən), *adj.* Abbevillian. [named after *Chelles*, Seine-et-Marne, France]
Chelmsford (chĕlms′fəd), *n.* a town in SE England, the county town of Essex. 49,908 (1961).
cheloid (kē′loid), *n.* *Pathol.* keloid.
chelonian (kĭ lō′nyən), *adj.* **1.** of or belonging to the *Chelonia*, an order or group of reptiles comprising the tortoises and turtles. —*n.* **2.** a tortoise or a turtle. [f. s. NL *Chelōnia*, pl. (cf. Gk *chelṓnē* tortoise) + -AN]
Chelsea (chĕl′sĭ), *n.* a district of the W inner London borough of Kensington and Chelsea; formerly an artists' and writers' district.
Chelsea bun, a round coiled yeast bun, containing currants, and decorated with sugar.
Chelsea pensioner, a pensioner at the Royal Hospital, Chelsea.
Cheltenham (chĕlt′nəm), *n.* **1.** a town in W England, in Gloucestershire. 74,910 (1964). **2.** *Print.* a style of type.
Chelyabinsk (*Russ.* chĭ lyä′bĭnsk), *n.* a city in the W Soviet Union in Asia, in the Ural area. 805,000 (est. 1965).
Chelyuskin (*Russ.* chĭ lyo͞os′kĭn), *n.* **Cape,** a cape in the N Soviet Union in Asia: northernmost point of Asia.
chem-, a word element representing chemic or chemical used before vowels. Also (esp. before a consonant), **chemo-.**
chem., **1.** chemical. **2.** chemist. **3.** chemistry.
chemic (kĕm′ĭk), *adj.* *Archaic.* **1.** alchemic. **2.** chemical. [short for ALCHEMIC]
chemical (kĕm′ĭ kl), *adj.* **1.** of or concerned with the science or the operations or processes of chemistry. —*n.* **2.** a substance produced by or used in a chemical process. —**chem′ically,** *adv.*
chemical affinity, **1.** chemical attraction; the force binding atoms together. **2.** the free energy change during a chemical reaction.
chemical engineer, one who practises chemical engineering.
chemical engineering, the science or profession concerned with the design, manufacture, and operation of plant or machinery used in industrial chemical processes.
chemical kinetics, the study of the rate at which chemical reactions proceed.
chemical reaction, a process involving two or more substances in which their molecular constitution is altered.
chemical warfare, warfare with asphyxiating, poisonous, and corrosive gases, oil flames, etc.
chemiluminescence (kĕm′ĭ lo͞o′mĭ nĕs′əns), *n.* (in chemical reactions) the production of light at low temperatures.
chemin de fer (*Fr.* shə măɴ də fĕr′), *French.* **1.** a railway. **2.** a variation of baccarat.
chemise (shə mēz′), *n.* **1.** a woman's loose-fitting shirt-like undergarment. **2.** (in women's fashions) a dress, suit, etc., designed to fit loosely at the waist and more tightly at the hips. **3.** a revetment for an earth embankment. [t. F, g. LL *camisia* shirt (prob. t. Celtic); r. ME *kemes*, OE *cemes*, t. LL: m. *camisia*]
chemisette (shĕm′ĭ zĕt′), *n.* a woman's garment of linen, lace, etc., worn with a low-cut or open bodice to cover the neck and breast. [t. F, dim. of *chemise*]
chemism (kĕm′ĭz′əm), *n.* chemical action.
chemisorb (kĕm′ĭ sôb′), *v.t.* to adsorb by chemisorption.
chemisorption (kĕm′ĭ sôp′shən), *n.* *Chem.* irreversible adsorption involving chemical forces.
chemist (kĕm′ĭst), *n.* **1.** one versed in chemistry or professionally engaged in chemical investigations. **2.** a retailer of medicinal drugs and toilet preparations. **3.** *Obs.* alchemist. [var. of ALCHEMIST]
chemistry (kĕm′ĭs trĭ), *n.*, *pl.* **-tries.** **1.** the science concerned with the composition of substances, the various elementary forms of matter, and the interactions between them. **2.** chemical properties, reactions, etc.: *the chemistry of carbon.* [f. CHEMIST + -RY]
chemmy (shĕm′ĭ), *n.* *Colloq.* chemin de fer (def. 2).
Chemnitz (*Ger.* kĕm′nĭts), *n.* former name of **Karl-Marx-Stadt.**
chemo-, var. of **chem-** used esp. before a consonant.
chemosphere (kĕm′ə sfĭə′), *n.* mesosphere (def. 2).
chemosynthesis (kĕm′ō sĭn′thĭ sĭs), *n.* *Bot.* production by plants of nutritive substances from carbon dioxide and water with energy derived from other chemical reactions. —**chemosynthetic** (kĕm′ō sĭn thĕt′ĭk), *adj.* —**chem′osynthet′ically,** *adv.*
chemotaxis (kĕm′ō tăk′sĭs), *n.* *Biol.* the property in a cell or organism, exhibiting attraction or repulsion to chemical substances. —**chem′otac′tic,** *adj.*
chemotherapeutics (kĕm′ō thĕ′rə pyo͞o′tĭks), *n.* *Med.* chemotherapy. —**chem′other′apeu′tic,** *adj.*
chemotherapy (kĕm′ō thĕ′rə pĭ), *n.* *Med.* treatment of disease by means of chemicals which have a specific toxic effect upon the disease-producing microorganisms. —**chem′other′apist,** *n.*
chemotropism (kĭ mŏt′rə pĭz′əm), *n.* *Bot.*, *Zool.* the property in plants and other organisms of turning or bending (towards or away), as by unequal growth, in response to the presence of chemical substances. —**chemotropic** (kĕm′ō trŏp′ĭk), *adj.* —**chem′otrop′ically,** *adv.*
Chemulpo (chĕm′o͝ol pō′), *n.* Inchon.
chemurgy (kĕm′û jĭ), *n.* a division of applied chemistry concerned with the industrial use of organic substances, esp. farm products. —**chemur′gic, chemur′gical,** *adj.*
Chenab (chĭ năb′), *n.* a river through S Kashmir and SW through Pakistan to the Sutlej in W Punjab. ab. 675 mi.
Chengchow (chĕng′chou′), *n.* a city in China; capital of Honan province. 785,000 (est. 1958).
Chengtu (chĕng′to͞o′), *n.* a walled city in central China, the capital of Szechwan province. 1,135,000 (est. 1958).
Chénier (*Fr.* shė nyė′), **André Marie de** (*Fr.* äɴ drė mȧ rē′ də), 1762–94, French poet.
chenille (shə nēl′), *n.* **1.** a velvety cord of silk or worsted, used in embroidery, fringe, etc. **2.** fabric made with a fringed silken thread used as the weft in combination with wool or cotton. [t. F: caterpillar, g. L *canicula* little dog]
chenopod (kē′nə pŏd′, kĕn′ə-), *n.* any plant of the genus *Chenopodium* or the family *Chenopodiaceae.* [f. *cheno-* (comb. form repr. Gk *chḗn* goose) + -POD]
chenopodiaceous (kē′nə pō′dĭ ā′shəs, kĕn′ə-), *adj.* *Bot.* belonging to the *Chenopodiaceae*, or goosefoot family of plants, which includes the beet and mangel-wurzel, spinach, and orach. [f. s. NL *Chenopodium* (see CHENOPOD) + -ACEOUS]
Cheops (kē′ŏps), *n.* fl. *c.* 2700 B.C., king of Egypt, of the 4th dynasty: builder of great pyramid at El Giza. Also, **Khufu.**
Chepstow (chĕp′stō), *n.* a town in England, in Monmouthshire. 6041 (1961).
cheque (chĕk), *n.* *Banking.* a written order, usually on a standard printed form directing a bank to pay a specified sum of money to, or to the order of, some particular person or the bearer, either *crossed* (payable only through a bank account), or *uncrossed* (payable on demand). Also, *U.S.*, **check.** [altered spelling of CHECK]
chequebook (chĕk′bo͝ok′), *n.* a book of printed forms for drawing cheques or orders on a bank. Also, *U.S.*, **checkbook.**
cheque card, a card issued by a bank to a customer allowing him to draw cash from any branch of that bank or from certain other banks.
chequer (chĕk′ə), *n.* **1.** a pattern of squares. **2.** (*pl.*) a draughtboard (esp. as an inn sign). **3.** a marble or similar token used in Chinese chequers. —*v.t.* **4.** to diversify in colour, variegate. **5.** to diversify in character; subject to alterations. Also, *U.S.*, **checker.** [ME *cheker*, t. AF: m. *escheker* chessboard, der. *eschec* CHECK]
chequerboard (chĕk′ə bôd′), *n.* a draughtboard. Also, *U.S.*, **checkerboard.**
chequered (chĕk′əd), *n.* **1.** marked by wide or frequent alteration; diversified: *a chequered career.* **2.** marked in squares. **3.** diversified in colour. Also, *U.S.*, **checkered.**
chequers (chĕk′əz), *n.* draughts.
Chequers (chĕk′əz), *n.* the British prime minister's official country house, situated near Aylesbury in Buckinghamshire.

Cher (*Fr.* shĕr), *n.* **1.** a department in central France. 293,514 pop. (1962); 2820 sq. mi. *Cap.:* Bourges. **2.** a river in central France, flowing NW to the river Loire. ab. 220 mi.

Cherbourg (shēə′bo͝oəg; *Fr.* shėr bo͞or′), *n.* a fortified seaport in NW France: taken by Allied forces, June 1944. 40,018 (1962). See map under **Normandy.**

cherchez la femme (*Fr.* shĕr shė lȧ fȧm′), *French.* search for the woman (as the cause of trouble).

Cherenkov radiation, Cerenkov radiation.

chérie (*Fr.* shė rē′), *n. French.* darling.

cherish (chĕr′ĭsh), *v.t.* **1.** to hold or treat as dear. **2.** to care for tenderly; nurture. **3.** to cling fondly to (ideas, etc.): *cherishing no resentment.* [ME *cherische(n)*, t. F: m. *chériss-*, s. *chérir*, der. *cher* dear, g. L *cārus*] —**che′risher, che′rishment,** *n.* —**che′rishingly,** *adv.*

—**Syn. 1.** CHERISH, FOSTER, HARBOUR imply giving affection, care, or shelter to something. CHERISH suggests regarding or treating something as valuable or as an object of affection or as valuable: *to cherish a memory or a friendship.* FOSTER implies sustaining and nourishing something with care, esp. in order to promote, increase, or strengthen it: *to foster a hope, enmity, crime.* HARBOUR suggests giving shelter to or entertaining something undesirable, esp. evil thoughts or intentions: *to harbour malice or a grudge.* —**Ant. 2.** neglect. **3.** relinquish.

Chernovtsy (*Russ.* chĭr nȧf tsĭ′), *n.* a town in the SW Soviet Union: formerly in Rumania. 145,000 (est. 1959). Rumanian, **Cernăuţi.** German, **Czernowitz.**

chernozem (chû′nō zĕm′), *n.* black earth.

Cherokee (chĕr′rə kē′, chĕ′rə kē′), *n., pl.* **-kee, -kees. 1.** a member of an important tribe of North American Indians of Iroquoian family whose present centre is Oklahoma. **2.** an Iroquoian language.

cheroot (shə ro͞ot′), *n.* a cigar having open, unpointed ends. [t. F: m. *chéroute*, t. Tamil: m. *shuruttu* a roll]

cherry (chĕ′rĭ), *n., pl.* **-ries,** *adj.* —*n.* **1.** the fruit of any of various trees of the genus *Prunus*, consisting of a pulpy, globular drupe enclosing a one-seeded smooth stone. **2.** the tree itself. **3.** its wood. **4.** any of various fruits or plants resembling the cherry. **5.** a bright red. —*adj.* **6.** bright red. **7.** made of the wood of the cherry tree. [ME *chery*, *chiri*, back-formation from OE *ciris* (the *-s* being taken for plural sign), t. VL: m. **ceresia*, der. L *cerasus* cherry tree, t. Gk: m. *kerasós.* Cf. F *cerise*, ONF *cherise*, etc., g. VL (as above)]

cherry bean, an annual herbaceous plant from Asia, *Virgna sinensis*; grown for green-manuring and cattle feed.

cherry laurel, an evergreen ornamental shrub, *Prunus laurocerasus.*

cherry-pie (chĕ′rĭ pī′), *n.* **1.** a pie made with cherries. **2.** the common heliotrope, *Heliotropium peruvianum.*

cherry-plum (chĕ′rĭ plŭm′), *n.* **1.** the red or yellow edible fruit of *Prunus cerasifera.* **2.** the tree itself.

cherry-stone (chĕ′rĭ stōn′), *n.* **1.** the endocarp of the cherry. **2.** *U.S.* a medium-sized clam.

chersonese (kû′sə nēs′), *n.* **1.** a peninsula. **2. the Chersonese,** Gallipoli Peninsula. [t. L: m. s. *chersonēsus*, t. Gk: m. *chersónēsos*]

chert (chût), *n.* a compact rock consisting essentially of cryptocrystalline quartz. [orig. d.; ult. orig. unknown] —**chert′y,** *adj.*

cherub (chĕ′rəb), *n., pl.* **cherubs** *for 3, 4;* **cherubim** (chĕ′rə bĭm, -ro͞o bĭm) *for 1, 2.* **1.** *Bible.* a kind of celestial being. Gen. 3:24; Ezek. 1 and 10. **2.** *Theol.* a member of the second order of angels, distinguished by knowledge, often represented as a beautiful winged child or as a winged head of a child. **3.** a beautiful or innocent person, esp. a child. **4.** a person with a chubby, innocent face. [ME and OE *cherubin*, pl., ult. t. Heb.: m. *kerūb* sing., *karūbīm*, pl.] —**cherubic** (chə ro͞o′bĭk), *adj.* —**cheru′bically,** *adv.*

Cherubini (*It.* kė ro͞o bē′nē), *n.* **Maria Luigi Carlo Zenobio Salvatore** (*It.* mȧ rē′ȧ lwē′jē kȧr′lō dzė nō′byō sȧl vȧ tō′rė), 1760–1842, Italian composer in France.

chervil (chû′vĭl), *n.* **1.** a herbaceous plant, *Anthriscus cerefolium*, of the parsley family, with aromatic leaves used to flavour soups, salads, etc. **2.** any of various plants of the same genus or allied genera. [ME *chervelle*, OE *cerfille*, t. L: m. s. *caerephylla*, pl. of *caerephyllum*, t. Gk: m. *chairéphyllon*]

Cherwell (chä′wəl), *n.* **Viscount.** See **Lindemann.**

Chesapeake Bay (chĕs′pēk′, chĕs′ə pēk′), a large inlet of the Atlantic, in Maryland and Virginia. ab. 200 mi. long; 4–40 mi. wide.

Cheshire (chĕsh′ə), *n.* **1.** a county in W England. 1,367,860 pop. (1961); 1015 sq. mi. *Co. town:* Chester. **2.** an orange or yellow, soft crumbly cheese, with a tangy flavour.

Cheshire cat, a constantly grinning cat, in *Alice in Wonderland*, named from the old simile 'to grin like a Cheshire cat'.

Cheshvan (KHĕsh′văn, hĕsh′-), *n.* Heshvan. Also, **Chesvan.**

chess[1] (chĕs), *n.* a game played by two persons, each with sixteen pieces, on a chequered board. [ME, t. OF: aphetic m. *esches*, *eschecs*, pl. See CHECK]

chess[2] (chĕs), *n., pl.* **chess, chesses.** one of the planks forming the roadway of a pontoon bridge. [orig. uncert.]

chess[3] (chĕs), *n. U.S.* rye-brome. [orig. uncert.]

chessboard (chĕs′bôd′), *n.* the board, identical with a draughtboard, used for playing chess.

chessman (chĕs′măn′, -mən), *n., pl.* **-men** (-mĕn′, -mən), one of the pieces used in the game of chess. [earlier *chessemeyne*, lit., chess-company]

chessylite (chĕs′ĭ līt′), *n.* azurite.

chest (chĕst), *n.* **1.** the trunk of the body from the neck to the belly; the thorax. **2.** a box, usually a large, strong one, for the safekeeping of valuables. **3.** the place where the funds of a public institution, etc., are kept. **4.** a box in which certain goods, as tea, are packed for transit. **5.** the quantity contained in such a box. **6. get (something) off one's chest,** to bring into the open (a pressing worry). [ME; OE *cest*, *cist*, t. L: s. *cista*, t. Gk: m. *kístē* box]

Chester (chĕs′tə), *n.* a walled city in W England, the county town of Cheshire. 59,288 (1961).

Chesterfield (chĕs′tə fēld′), *n.* **1. Philip Dormer Stanhope** (dô′mə stăn′əp), **4th Earl of,** 1694–1773, English statesman and author. **2.** a town in England, in E Derbyshire. 67,858 (1961). **3.** (*l.c.*) a sofa or divan with padded back and arms.

Chesterfieldian (chĕs′tə fēl′dyən), *adj.* like the Earl of Chesterfield; lordly; elegant; cold; suave.

Chesterton (chĕs′tə tən), *n.* **G(ilbert) K(eith),** 1874–1936, English essayist, critic, and novelist.

chestnut (chĕs′nŭt′), *n.* **1.** the edible nut of trees of the genus *Castanea*, of the beech family. **2.** any of the trees, as *C. sativa* (**Spanish chestnut**), *C. dentata* (**American chestnut**), or *C. crenata* (**Japanese chestnut**). **3.** the wood **4.** any of various fruits or trees resembling the chestnut, esp. the horse chestnut. **5.** reddish brown. **6.** a horse. **7.** *Colloq.* an old or stale joke, anecdote, etc. **8.** the callosity of the inner side of a horse's leg. See illus. under **horse.** —*adj.* **9.** reddish brown. **10.** (esp. of horses) sorrel. [f. obs. *chesten* chestnut (ME; OE *cisten-*, var. of **cesten*, g. WGmc **kastinia*, t. L: m. *castanea*, t. Gk: m. *kastanéa*) + NUT; r. ME *chasteine*, t. OF]

chestnut soil, *Geol.* a crumbly, dark brown soil overlaying a lighter calcareous layer, found in the drier steppes south of the black earth.

chest of drawers, a piece of furniture consisting of a set of drawers fitted into a frame, used for clothing, etc.

chest of viols, *Music.* a set of viols, for playing in consort.

chest-on-chest (chĕst′ŏn chĕst′), *n. U.S.* a tallboy.

chesty (chĕs′tĭ), *adj.*, **-tier, -tiest. 1.** *Colloq.* inclined to, or symptomatic of a chest disease. **2.** *Slang.* proud; conceited.

chetah (chē′tə), *n.* cheetah.

cheval-de-frise (shə văl′də frēz′), *n., pl.* **chevaux-de-frise** (shə vō′də frēz′). (*usually pl.*) *Mil.* an obstacle of projecting spikes or barbed wire used to close a gap to the enemy. [t. F: lit., horse of Friesland]

cheval glass (shə văl′), a full-length mirror mounted so as to swing in a frame. [*cheval*, t. F: support, horse]

chevalier (shĕv′ə lĭə′), *n.* **1.** a member of certain orders of honour or merit: *a chevalier of the Legion of Honour.* **2.** a knight. **3.** *French Hist.* **a.** the lowest title of rank in the old nobility. **b.** a cadet of the old nobility. **4.** a chivalrous man. **5.** an adventurer: *a chevalier of industry.* [ME *chevalere*, t. OF: m. *chevalier*, der. *cheval* horse, g. L *caballus.* See CAVALIER]

Chevalier (shə văl′ĭ ā′; *Fr.* shə vȧ lyė′), *n.* **Maurice** (mŏ′rĭs; *Fr.* mŏ rēs′), born 1888, French actor and singer.

Cheviot (chĕv′ĭ ət, chē′vĭ-), *n.* **1.** a breed of sheep valued for their thick wool (named after the Cheviots). **2.** (*l.c.*) a worsted fabric in a coarse twill weave used for coats, suits, etc.

Cheviots (chĕv′ĭ əts, chē′v-), *n.pl.* a range of hills on the boundary between England and Scotland; part of the range forms the Border National Park. Highest point, the Cheviot, 2681 ft. Also, **Cheviot Hills.**

chevron (shĕv′rən), *n.* **1.** a badge consisting of stripes meeting at an angle, worn on the sleeve (by non-commissioned officers, policemen, etc.) as an indication of rank, of service, etc. **2.** *Her.* the lower half of a bend and a bend sinister meeting at the centre of the shield, like an inverted V.

Chevrons
A, Army sergeant; B, Army corporal; C, Air Force sergeant (Aircrew); D, Air Force corporal

3. a similar decoration, as in an architectural moulding; a dancette. [t. F: rafter, chevron, der. F *chèvre* goat, g. L *caper*]

chevrotain (shĕv′rə tān′, -tĭn), *n.* any of the very small deerlike ruminants, family *Tragulidae*, of the genera *Tragulus* of Asia, and *Hyemoschus* of Africa. [t. F, dim. of OF *chevrot* kid, dim. of *chèvre* she-goat]

chevy (chĕv′ĭ), *v.*, **chevied, chevying,** *n.* —*v.t.* **1.** to chase; run after. **2.** to harrass; worry; nag. —*v.i.* **3.** to scamper; race. —*n.* **4.** a hunting cry. **5.** a hunt; chase. Also, **chevvy, chivvy.** [? short for CHEVY CHASE]

Chevy Chase. See **Otterburn.**

chew (cho͞o), *v.t.* **1.** to crush or grind with the teeth; masticate. **2.** to damage or destroy by or as if by chewing (fol. by *up*): *this machine has chewed up the carpet.* **3.** to meditate on; consider deliberately (fol. by *over*). —*v.i.* **4.** to perform the act of crushing or grinding with the teeth. **5.** to meditate. —*n.* **6.** the act of chewing. **7.** that which is chewed; a portion, as of tobacco, for chewing. [ME *chewen*, OE *cēowan*, akin to G *kauen*] —**chew′er,** *n.*

chewing gum (cho͞o′ĭng), a preparation for chewing, usually made of sweetened and flavoured chicle.

Chewings' fescue (cho͞o′ĭngz fĕs′kyo͞o), a valuable fodder grass, a form of red fescue, *Festuca rubra*, sub-species *commutata*, native of New Zealand. [named after Charles *Chewings*, died 1937, Australian botanist]

chewy (cho͞o′ĭ), *adj.* suitable for, and providing pleasure in, chewing, due to being tough or sticky.

Cheyenne (shī ăn′), *n., pl.* **-enne, -ennes. 1.** a member of a Plains tribe of Algonquian linguistic stock; now divided between Montana (**Northern Cheyenne**) and Oklahoma (**Southern Cheyenne**). **2.** a city in the U.S., the capital of Wyoming, in the SE part. 43,505 (1960). [t. Dakota Sioux: m. *shahi′yena, shai-ena*, or t. Teton Sioux: m. *shai-ela* people of alien speech, der. *sha′ia* speak a strange tongue]

chez (*Fr.* shė), *prep. French.* **1.** at the home of. **2.** in the works of: *chez Shakespeare.*

chg., *pl.* **chgs** charge.

chi (kī), *n.* the twenty-second letter (Χ, χ, = English ch or kh) of the Greek alphabet.

chiack (chī′ăk), *v.t. Austral. Slang.* to jeer; taunt; deride.

Chian (kī′ən), *adj.* **1.** of or pertaining to Chios. —*n.* **2.** a native or inhabitant of Chios. **3.** a rich, red wine from Chios, celebrated in classical times.

Chiang Kai-shek (chăng′kī shĕk′), born 1886, president of China, 1943–49; of Nationalist China since 1950.

Chiangmai (chăng′mī′), *n.* a town in NW Thailand. 65,736 (1964). Also, **Chiengmai** (chĕng′mī′).

Chianti (kĭ ăn′tĭ; *It.* kyȧn′tē), *n.* a medium to dry, red or white, full-bodied table wine, usually bottled in a colourful straw-covered bottle. [named after *Chianti* Mountains in Tuscany]

chiaroscuro (kĭ ä′rə sko͞o′rō), *n., pl.* **-ros. 1.** the treatment or general distribution of light and shade in a picture. **2.** pictorial art employing only light and shade. **3.** a sketch in light and shade. [t. It.: m. *chiaro-oscuro* bright-dark] —**chia′roscu′rist,** *n.* —**chia′roscu′rism,** *n.*

chiasm (kī′ăz′əm), *n. Anat.* a crossing or decussation, esp. that of the optic nerves at the base of the brain.

chiasma (kī ăz′mə), *n., pl.* **-mata** (-mə tə). *Biol.* a crossing point in conjugating chromosomes. [t. NL, t. Gk: arrangement in the form of the Greek letter *chi* (X)] —**chias′mal, chias′mic,** *adj.*

chiasmus (kī ăz′məs), *n. Rhet.* the reversal of the order in which two grammatical elements occur in a pair of parallel phrases: *I cannot dig, to beg I am ashamed* is an example of chiasmus. [t. NL, t. Gk: m. *chiasmós.* See CHIASMA] —**chiastic** (kī ăs′tĭk), *adj.*

chiastolite (kī ăs′tə līt′), *n. Mining.* a variety of andalusite, a section of which often exhibits the form of a cross.

Chiba (chē′bä′), *n.* a town in central Japan, on E central Honshu island, near Tokyo. 332,188 (1965).

Chibcha (chĭb′chə), *n.* **1.** (*pl.*) an extinct tribe of civilized South American Indians, formerly living in a high plateau of Bogotá, Colombia. **2.** a member of this tribe.

Chibchan (chĭb′chən), *n.* a South American Indian speech family including the Chibcha and other tribes of Colombia.

chibouk (chĭ bo͝ok′), *n.* a Turkish tobacco pipe with a long, stiff stem (sometimes 4 or 5 feet long). Also, **chibouque, chibuk.** [t. Turk.: m. *chibūq*]

chic (shēk, shĭk), *adj.* **1.** cleverly attractive in style; stylish. —*n.* **2.** style; cleverly attractive style, esp. in dress. [t. F, ? der. *chicane* CHICANE]

Chicago (shĭ kä′gō), *n.* a city in the U.S., in NE Illinois: a port on Lake Michigan; the second largest city in the U.S. 3,550,404 (1960). —**Chica′goan,** *n.*

chicane (shĭ kān′), *n., v.,* **-caned, -caning.** —*n.* **1.** chicanery. **2.** *Bridge.* a hand without trumps. **3.** *Motor Racing.* an artificial bend or series of bends, inserted in a straight stretch of a racetrack, in order to make the course more difficult. —*v.i.* **4.** to use chicanery. —*v.t.* **5.** to trick by chicanery. **6.** to quibble over; cavil at. [t. F, der. *chicaner* quibble, ?t. MLG: m. *schikken* arrange] —**chican′er,** *n.*

chicanery (shĭ kā′nə rĭ), *n., pl.* **-ries. 1.** legal trickery, quibbling, or sophistry. **2.** a quibble or subterfuge.

chicha (chē′chə), *n.* a beer of South and Central America, made from fermented maize. [t. Amer. Sp., t. Haitian native name]

Chichen Itzá (*Sp.* chē chĕn′ ēt thȧ′), the ruins of an ancient Mayan city, in SE Mexico.

Chichester (chĭch′ĭs tə), *n.* a city in England, the county town of West Sussex, in the W part. 20,124 (1961).

Chichester-Clark (chĭch′ĭs tə kläk′), *n.* **Major James (Dawson),** born 1923, prime minister of Northern Ireland since 1969.

chichi (shē′shē), *adj.* pretentiously elegant or stylish.

Chichihaerh (chē′chē hä′), *n.* a city in Heilungkiang province, in NE China. 704,000 (est. 1958).

chick (chĭk), *n.* **1.** a young chicken or other bird. **2.** a child. **3.** *Slang.* a young girl.

chickadee (chĭk′ə dē′), *n.* any of several North American birds of the family *Paridae.* [imit. of cry]

chickaree (chĭk′ə rē′), *n.* the red squirrel, *Sciurus hudsonius*, of North America. [imit. of cry]

Chickasaw (chĭk′ə sô′), *n., pl.* **-saw, -saws.** a member of a warlike Muskhogean tribe of North American Indians now in Oklahoma.

chicken (chĭk′ĭn), *n.* **1.** the young of the domestic fowl (or of certain other birds). **2.** a domestic fowl of any age, or its flesh. **3.** any of certain other birds as **Mother Carey's chicken** (the stormy petrel) or the **prairie chicken** (the prairie hen). **4.** *Colloq.* a young person, esp. a young girl. **5.** *Slang.* a coward. **6. count one's chickens before they are hatched,** *Colloq.* to act on an expectation which has not yet been fulfilled. —*adj.* **7.** *Slang.* cowardly. [ME *chiken*, OE *cicen, ciken.* Cf. D *kieken*]

chicken breast, *U.S. Pathol.* pigeon breast.

chickenfeed (chĭk′ĭn fēd′), *n.* **1.** poultry food. **2.** *Slang.* a meagre or insignificant sum of money. **3.** *Slang.* anything or anybody insignificant. **4.** *U.S. Slang.* small change; coins collectively of low denomination.

chicken-hearted (chĭk′ĭn hä′tĭd), *adj.* timid; cowardly.

chickenpox (chĭk′ĭn pŏks′), *n.* a mild, contagious eruptive disease, commonly of children, caused by a virus; varicella.

chickpea (chĭk′pē′), *n.* **1.** a leguminous plant, *Cicer arietinum*, bearing edible pealike seeds, much used for food in S Europe, Asia, and Africa. **2.** its seed. [earlier *chich* (*pease*), t. F: m. (*pois*) *chiche*, g. L *cicer* vetch]

chickweed (chĭk′wēd′), *n.* **1.** any of various plants of the caryophyllaceous genus *Stellaria*, esp. the widespread weed *S. media.* **2.** any of various allied plants.

chicle (chĭk′l), *n.* a gumlike substance obtained from certain tropical American trees, as the sapodilla, used in the manufacture of chewing gum, etc. Also, **chicle gum.** [t. Amer. Sp., t. Nahuatl: m. *chictli*]

chicory (chĭk′ə rĭ), *n., pl.* **-ries. 1.** a perennial herb, *Cichorium intylus*, with blue flowers, native of Europe and W Asia; the blanched shoots are used in salads, and the roasted, powdered roots added to coffee. **2.** *U.S.* endive or Belgian endive. [t. F: m. *chicorée*, t. L: m. s. *cichorēum*, t. Gk: m. *kichóreion*]

chide (chīd), *v.,* **chided** or **chid; chided, chid** or **chidden; chiding.** —*v.i.* **1.** to scold; find fault. —*v.t.* **2.** to dive, impel, etc., by chiding. **3.** to express disapproval of. [ME *chiden*, OE *cīdan*] —**chid′er,** *n.* —**chid′ingly,** *adv.* —**Syn. 3.** reprove, rebuke, censure.

chief (chēf), *n.* **1.** the head or leader of a body of men; the person highest in authority. **2.** the head or ruler of a clan, tribe, or military or youth organization, etc. **3.** *Chiefly U.S.* (*usually cap.*) a title of some advisers to the chief of staff who do not, in most instances, command the troop units of their arms or services. **4.** *Slang.* boss. **5.** *Her.* the upper third of an escutcheon. **6. in chief, a.** *Her.* borne in the upper part of the shield. **b.** especially, most of all. **c.** (of a command) held directly from the sovereign, or legislative power. —*adj.* **7.** highest in rank or authority. **8.** most important: *his chief merit, the chief difficulty.* **9.** standing at the head. —*adv.* **10.** *Archaic.* chiefly; principally. [ME, t. OF, g. L *caput* head] —**Syn. 8.** foremost, essential, leading, principal. See **capital**[1]. —**Ant. 7.** subordinate.

chief constable, 1. a police officer who is the head of a county or other police force, responsible ultimately to the Home Secretary. **2.** the rank.

chief inspector, 1. a police officer ranking above inspector and below superintendent. **2.** the rank.

chief justice, 1. (in various Commonwealth countries) the presiding judge of a supreme court of justice. 2. *U.S.* a. the presiding judge of a court having several members. b. the presiding judge of the U.S. Supreme Court (in full, **Chief Justice of the United States**). 3. (*caps.*) *Colloq.* Lord Chief Justice.

chiefly (chēf′lĭ), *adv.* 1. principally; above all. 2. mainly; mostly. **—Syn. 1, 2.** See **especially.**

chief of staff, 1. *Mil.* the principal staff officer, usually of the rank of major general, of a higher military formation, as a corps, who on behalf of his commander controls the staff in his headquarters. 2. any similar officer in any other army. 3. *U.S.* the senior officer of the army, navy, or air-force.

chief superintendent, 1. a police officer ranking above superintendent and below assistant chief constable or, in the London metropolitan police, below deputy commander. 2. the rank.

chieftain (chēf′tən, -tĭn), *n.* 1. a leader of a group, band, etc. 2. the chief of a clan or a tribe. [ME *chieftayne*, var. of *chevetaine*, t. OF, g. LL *capitānus*. See CAPTAIN] **—chief′taincy, chief′tainship′,** *n.*

chield (chēld), *n. Scot.* a young man; a fellow. Also, **chiel** (chēl). [var. of CHILD]

Chieti (*It.* kyĕ′tē), *n.* 1. a province in S Italy. 373,632 (1961). 2. the capital of this province. 51,265 (1966).

chiffchaff (chĭf′chăf′), *n.* a common, plain-coloured European warbler, *Phylloscopus collybita.* [imit.]

chiffon (shĭ fŏn′, shĭf′ŏn), *n.* 1. sheer fabric of silk, nylon, or rayon in plain weave. 2. any bit of feminine finery, as of ribbon or lace. [t. F, der. *chiffe* rag]

chiffonier (shĭf′ə nĭə′), *n.* 1. a high chest of drawers. 2. a low cupboard with shelves for books. Also, **chiffonnier.** [t. F: m. *chiffonnier*, der. *chiffon* rag]

chiffonière (chĭf′ə nĭə′), *n. French.* a small table with a single drawer.

Chigasaki (chē′gə sä′kĭ), *n.* a town in Japan, in SE central Honshu island. 100,081 (1965).

chigger (chĭg′ə), *n.* 1. the parasitic larva of certain kinds of mites, which causes severe itching when attached to the skin; the young of the harvest mite; redwing. 2. chigoe. [alter. of CHIGOE]

chignon (shē′nyŏn; *Fr.* shē nyôɴ′), *n.* a large rolled arrangement of the hair, worn at the back of the head by women. [t. F, ult. der. L *catēna* chain]

chigoe (chĭg′ō), *n.* a flea, *Tunga penetrans*, of the West Indies, South America, Africa, etc., the female of which buries itself in the skin of men and animals; chigger; jigger. [t. Carib. Cf. F *chique*]

Chigwell (chĭg′wəl), *n.* a district and former borough of NE London.

chihuahua (chĭ wä′wə), *n.* one of the smallest breeds of dog, originating in Mexico.

Chihuahua (*Sp.* chē wȧ′wȧ), *n.* a town in N Mexico. 198,461 (est. 1965).

chil-, var. of **chilo-,** used before vowels.

chilblain (chĭl′blān′), *n.* (*usually pl.*) *Pathol.* an inflammation on the hands and feet caused by exposure to cold and moisture. [f. CHIL(L) + BLAIN] **—chil′blained′,** *adj.*

child (chīld), *n., pl.* **children.** 1. a baby or infant. 2. a boy or girl. 3. *Law.* a person under the age of fourteen. 4. a childish person. 5. a son or daughter. 6. any descendant. 7. any person or thing regarded as the product or result of particular agencies, influences, etc.: *children of light.* 8. a disciple or follower. 9. *Dial.* a female infant. 10. *Archaic.* childe. 11. **with child,** pregnant. [ME *child*, pl. *childre(n)*, OE *cild*, pl. *cild(ru)*] **—child′less,** *adj.* **—child′lessness,** *n.*

child-bearing (chīld′bēə′rĭng), *n.* producing or bringing forth children.

childbed (chīld′bĕd′), *n.* the condition of a woman giving birth to a child; parturition.

childbed fever, puerperal fever.

childbirth (chīld′bûth′), *n.* parturition.

childe (chīld), *n. Archaic.* a youth of noble birth. Also, **child.** [var. spelling of CHILD]

Childermas (chĭl′də măs′), *n. Obs.* Holy Innocents' Day.

child guidance, *Sociol.* the readjustment, with psychiatric help, of difficult, retarded, etc., children.

childhood (chīld′hŏŏd), *n.* 1. the state of time of being a child. 2. **second childhood,** dotage; childishness in extreme old age.

childish (chīl′dĭsh), *adj.* 1. of, like, or befitting a child. 2. puerile; weak; silly. [ME *childisch*, OE *cildisc*] **—child′ishly,** *adv.* **—child′ishness,** *n.*

—Syn. 1, 2. CHILDISH, INFANTILE, CHILDLIKE refer to characteristics or qualities of childhood. The ending *-ish* has unfavourable connotations; CHILDISH therefore refers to characteristics which are undesirable and unpleasant: *childish selfishness, outbursts of temper.* INFANTILE, originally a general word, now often carries an even stronger idea of disapproval or scorn than does CHILDISH: *infantile reasoning, behaviour.* The ending *-like* has pleasing connotations; CHILDLIKE therefore refers to the characteristics which are desirable and admirable: *childlike innocence, trust.*

child labour, the employment in full-time occupations of children below the minimum age of fifteen. In most countries, the minimum age is the school-leaving age.

childlike (chīld′līk′), *adj.* like or befitting a child, as in innocence, frankness, etc. **—child′like′ness,** *n.* **—Syn.** See **childish.**

childly (chīld′lĭ), *adj. Rare.* childlike; childish.

children (chĭl′drən), *n.* pl. of **child.**

Children of Israel, the Hebrews; Jews.

child's play, something very easy or simple.

Chile (chĭl′ĭ; *Sp.* chē′lĕ), *n.* a republic in SW South America, on the Pacific coast. 7,339,546 pop. (1960); 286,396 sq. mi. *Cap.:* Santiago. **—Chil′ean,** *adj., n.*

Chile pine, the monkey-puzzle tree.

Chile saltpetre, sodium nitrate, $NaNO_3$, a crystalline compound used as a fertilizer. Also, **Chile saltpeter** or **chile nitre.**

chili[1] (chĭl′ĭ), *n., pl.* **-ies.** chilli.

chili[2] (chĭl′ĭ), *n., pl.* **-ies.** the hot, dry sirocco wind of N Africa. [ult. t. Berber]

chiliad (kĭl′ĭ ăd′), *n.* 1. a thousand. 2. a thousand years. [t. Gk: s. *chiliás*, der. *chī́lioi* thousand]

chiliarch (kĭl′ĭ äk′), *n. Gk and Roman Hist.* the commander of a thousand men. [t. Gk: s. *chiliárchēs*]

chiliasm (kĭl′ĭ ăz′əm), *n. Theol.* 1. the doctrine of the expected reign of Christ on earth for a thousand years. 2. the reign. [t. Gk: s. *chīliasmós*, der. *chīliás.* See CHILIAD] **—chiliast** (kĭl′ĭ ăst′), *n.* **—chil′ias′tic,** *adj.*

chill (chĭl), *n.* 1. coldness, esp. a moderate but penetrating coldness. 2. a sensation of cold, usually with shivering. 3. a cold stage, as a first symptom of illness. 4. a depressing influence or sensation. 5. a metal mould for making chilled castings. 6. a coldness of manner, lack of friendliness. **—***adj.* 7. cold; tending to cause shivering. 8. shivering with cold. 9. depressing or discouraging. 10. not warm or hearty: *a chill reception.* **—***v.i.* 11. to become cold. 12. to be seized with a chill. 13. *Metall.* to become hard, esp. on the surface, by sudden cooling, as a metal mould. **—***v.t.* 14. to affect with cold; make chilly. 15. to make cool or freeze: *to chill wines.* 16. to depress; discourage: *chill his hopes.* 17. *Metall.* to harden (cast-iron or steel) on the surface by casting in a metal mould. [ME *chile*, OE *ciele*, *cile* coolness; akin to COOL, COLD] **—chill′er,** *n.* **—chill′ingly,** *adv.* **—chill′ness,** *n.* **—Syn. 6.** See **cold.**

chilli (chĭl′ĭ), *n., pl.* **-ies.** the pod of species of capsicum, esp. *Capsicum frutescens.* Also, **chil′e, chil′i, chilli pepper.** [t. Amer. Sp.: m. *chile*, t. Nahuatl: m. *chili*]

chilli con carne (chĭl′ĭ kŏn kä′nĭ; *Sp.* chē′lē kȯn kȧr′nĕ), a popular Mexican dish made from meat and finely chopped red pepper, served with beans. Also, **chili con carne.** [t. Sp.: chilli with meat]

chilli sauce, a highly flavoured sauce made of tomatoes cooked with chilli, spices, and other seasonings.

Chillon (shĭ lŏn′; *Fr.* shē yôɴ′), *n.* an ancient castle in W Switzerland, at the E end of Lake Geneva.

chilly (chĭl′ĭ), *adj.*, **-ier, -iest,** *adv.* **—***adj.* 1. producing a sensation of cold; causing shivering. 2. feeling cold; sensitive to cold. 3. without warmth of feeling: *a chilly reception.* **—***adv.* 4. in a chill manner. **—chil′lily,** *adv.* **—chil′liness,** *n.* **—Syn. 1.** See **cold.**

chilo-, a word element meaning 'lip', 'labial'. [t. Gk: m. *cheilo-*, comb. form of *cheîlos* lip]

chiloplasty (kī′lə plăs′tĭ), *n.* plastic surgery of the lip.

chilopod (kī′lə pŏd′), *n.* a centipede.

Chiltern Hundreds (chĭl′tən), (in England) an office, technically one of profit under the crown, for which members of Parliament apply, by a legal fiction, in order to resign.

Chilterns (chĭl′tənz), *n.pl.* a range of chalk hills in England, extending from the Thames through Oxfordshire, Buckinghamshire, and Hertford. Highest point, 828 ft. Also, **Chiltern Hills.**

chimaera (kī mĭə′rə, kĭ-), *n.* 1. any of the fishes of the family *Chimaeridae.* The male has a spiny clasping organ over the mouth. 2. any similar fish of the group *Holocephali*, which includes this family. 3. chimera. [t. L. See CHIMERA]

chimar (chĭm′ə), *n.* chimer[2].

chimb (chĭm), *n.* chime[2].

Chimborazo (chĭm′bə rä′zō; *Sp.* chēm bȯ rȧ′thȯ), *n.* a volcanic mountain in central Equador, in the Andes. 20,702 ft.

chime[1] (chīm), *n., v.,* **chimed, chiming.** **—***n.* 1. an arrangement for striking a bell or bells so as to produce a musical sound: *a door chime, the chimes of Big Ben.* **2.** a set of vertical metal tubes struck with a hammer, as used in the modern orchestra. **3.** carillon (defs. 1, 3). **4.** (*often pl.*) carillon (def. 2). **5.** harmonious sound in general; music; melody. **6.** harmonious relation; accord. **7.** the rhythm of music, or the beat of verses of poetry. *—v.i.* **8.** to sound harmoniously or in chimes, as a set of bells. **9.** to produce a musical sound by striking a bell, etc.; ring chimes. **10.** to harmonize; agree. **11. chime in, a.** to break suddenly into a conversation, esp. to express agreement. **b.** to join in harmoniously (in music). *—v.t.* **12.** to give forth (music, etc.), as a bell or bells. **13.** to strike (a bell, etc.) so as to produce musical sound. **14.** to put, bring, indicate, etc., by chiming. **15.** to utter or repeat in cadence or singsong. [ME *chimbe*, appar. back-formation from OE *cimbal*, t. L: m. s. *cymbalum* cymbal]

chime[2] (chīm), *n.* the edge or brim of a cask or the like, formed by the ends of the staves beyond the head or bottom. Also, **chimb, chine.** [ME *chimb(e)*, OE *cimb* (in compounds and derivatives), c. G *Kimme* edge]

chimer[1] (chī′mə), *n.* one who or that which chimes.

chimer[2] (chĭm′ə), shĭm′-), *n.* a loose upper robe, esp. of a bishop, to which the lawn sleeves are usually attached. Also, **chimar, chimere** (chĭ mĭə′, shĭ-). [ME *chemer*, ? t. Anglo-L: m. s. *chimēra.* See SIMAR]

chimera (kī mĭə′rə, kĭ-), *n., pl.* **-ras. 1.** (*often cap.*) a mythological fire-breathing monster, commonly represented with a lion's head, a goat's body, and a serpent's tail. **2.** a grotesque monster, as in decorative art. **3.** a horrible or unreal creature of the imagination; a vain or idle fancy. **4.** *Genetics.* an organism composed of two or more genetically distinct tissues, as **a.** an organism which is partly male and partly female. **b.** an artificially produced creature having tissues of several species. Also, **chimaera.** [t. L: m. *chimaera*, t. Gk: m. *chímaira* lit., she-goat; r. ME *chimere*, t. F]

chimerical (kī mĕ′rĭ kl, kĭ-), *adj.* **1.** unreal; imaginary; visionary. **2.** wildly fanciful. Also, **chimer′ic. —chimer′ically,** *adv.*

Chimkent (*Russ.* chĭm kyĕnt′), *n.* a city in the S central Soviet Union in Asia. 200,000 (est. 1965).

chimney (chĭm′nĭ), *n., pl.* **-neys. 1.** a structure, usually vertical, containing a passage or flue by which the smoke, gases, etc., of a fire or furnace are carried off and by means of which a draught is created. **2.** that part of such a structure which rises above a roof. **3.** the smokestack or funnel of a locomotive, steamship, etc. **4.** a tube, commonly of glass, surrounding the flame of a lamp to promote combustion and keep the flame steady. **5.** anything resembling a chimney, such as the vent of a volcano. **6.** *Mountaineering.* a narrow cleft or opening in a rock face. **7.** *Now Dial.* fireplace. [ME *chiminee*, t. OF, g. LL *camīnāta*, der. L *camīnus* furnace, t. Gk: m. *kámīnos*] **—chim′neyless,** *adj.*

chimneybreast (chĭm′nĭ brĕst′), *n.* the projecting wall in a room which contains the fireplace and flues.

chimney corner, 1. the corner or side of a fireplace. **2.** a place near the fire. **3.** fireside.

chimneypiece (chĭm′nĭ pēs′), *n.* **1.** mantelpiece. **2.** *Obs.* a decoration over a fireplace.

chimneypot (chĭm′nĭ pŏt′), *n.* **1.** a cylindrical or other pipe, as of earthenware or sheet metal, fitted on the top of a chimney to increase draught, and carry off smoke. **2.** *Colloq.* a top-hat.

chimneystack (chĭm′nĭ stăk′), *n.* a group of flues, bricked together.

chimney swallow, 1. the common swallow, *Hirundo rustica*, which sometimes nests in barns or chimneys. **2.** the chimney swift, *Chaetura pelagica*, which often builds its nest in a disused chimney.

chimneysweep (chĭm′nĭ swē-p′), *n.* one whose business it is to clean out chimneys. Also, **chim′neysweep′er.**

chimney swift, chimney swallow (def. 2).

chimp (chĭmp), *n. Colloq.* a chimpanzee.

chimpanzee (chĭm′păn zē′), *n.* a highly intelligent anthropoid ape, *Pan troglodytes*, of equatorial Africa, smaller, with larger ears, and more arboreal than the gorilla. [t. a Bantu language in Angola, W. Africa; cf. Kongo *kimphenzi* chimpanzee, gorilla]

Chimpanzee, *Pan troglodytes* (4 ft long)

chin (chĭn), *n., v.,* **chinned, chinning.** *—n.* **1.** the lower extremity of the face, below the mouth. **2.** the point of the lower jaw. **3. keep one's chin up,** to remain cheerful, esp. under stress. **4. take it on the chin,** to take suffering or punishment stalwartly. *—v.t.* **5.** to bring one's chin up to (a horizontal bar, from which one is hanging), by bending the elbows; bring (oneself) to this position. *—v.i.* **6.** to chin oneself. **7.** *Colloq.* to talk. [ME; OE *cin*, c. G *Kinn*]

Chin., Chinese.

china[1] (chī′nə), *n.* **1.** a vitreous, translucent earthenware, orig. produced in China. **2.** any porcelain ware. **3.** plates, cups, etc., collectively. **4.** figurines of porcelain, esp. a collection. *—adj.* **5.** made of china.

china[2] (chī′nə), *n. Slang.* mate; friend. [rhyming slang, short for *china plate* mate]

China (chī′nə), *n.* **1.** a country in E Asia; under a communist government since 1949. Official name: **People's Republic of China.** Divided administratively into 22 provinces, 5 autonomous regions, and 2 cities directly under the central government. 656,630,000 pop (est. 1957), 770,000,000 (est. 1966); ab. 3,600,000 sq. mi. *Cap.:* Peking. **2. Republic of,** official name of **Nationalist China.**

China aster, any variety of a species of aster-like plant, *Callistephus chinensis.*

china bark (kī′nə, kē′nə, chī′nə), cinchona (def. 2).

chinaberry (chī′nə bə rĭ, -brĭ), *n., pl.* **-ries.** a tree, *Melia azedarach*, native to Asia but widely planted elsewhere for its ornamental yellow fruits. Also, **china tree.**

china clay, a natural form of hydrated aluminium silicate, used for making porcelain; kaolin; porcelain clay.

Chinaman (chī′nə mən), *n., pl.* **-men. 1.** a native or inhabitant of China; a Chinese. **2.** *Cricket.* an off break bowled by a left-handed bowler to a right-handed batsman.

China rose, 1. a rosaceous plant, *Rosa chinensis*, or *R. indica*, with red or white flowers. **2.** a dwarf rosaceous plant, *Rosa semperflorens*, with crimson flowers.

China Sea, a W part of the Pacific, divided by Taiwan Strait into the South and East China seas.

China stone, partly decomposed granite, used in porcelain manufacture.

Chinatown (chī′nə toun′), *n. Chiefly U.S.* the Chinese quarter of a city.

chinaware (chī′nə wēə′), *n.* dishes, etc., of china.

China wood-oil, tung oil.

chincapin (chĭng′kə pĭn), *n.* chinquapin.

chinch bug, a small American hemipterous insect of the genus *Blissus*, destructive to wheat, etc., esp. *B. leucopterus.* [*chinch* t. Sp.: m. *cinche*, g. L *cimex* bedbug]

chincherinchee (chĭn′chə rĭn chē′, -rĭn′chĭ), *n.* a bulbous liliaceous plant of southern Africa, *Ornithogalum lacteum* and *O. thyrsoides*, with showy, long-lasting flowers.

chinchilla (chĭn chĭl′ə), *n.* **1.** a small South American rodent of the genus *Chinchilla*, whose valuable skin is dressed as a fur. **2.** the fur itself. **3.** a thick, napped, woollen fabric for coats, esp. children's coats. **4.** one of a variety of any of certain animals, as a cat or rabbit, with long, soft, grey fur. [t. Sp., dim. of *chinche* bug]

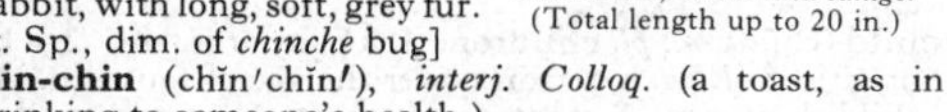

Chinchilla, *Chinchilla laniger* (Total length up to 20 in.)

chin-chin (chĭn′chĭn′), *interj. Colloq.* (a toast, as in drinking to someone's health.)

chin cough, *Obs.* whooping cough.

Chinchoy (chĭn′choi′), *n.* a city in Liaoning province, in NE China. 400,000 (est. 1958).

Chindit (chĭn′dĭt), *n.* a member of the British commando forces in Burma, 1943–44.

Chindwin (chĭn′dwĭn), *n.* a river in Burma, flowing S to the Irrawaddy. ab. 550 mi. long.

chine[1] (chīn), *n. Geog.* a ravine formed in rock by the action of running water. [ME, n. use of *chine*, v., crack, OE *cīnan*, akin to OE *cinu*, *cine* chink, fissure]

chine[2] (chīn), *n., v.,* **chined, chining.** *—n.* **1.** the backbone or spine. **2.** the whole or a piece of the backbone of an animal with adjoining parts, cut for cooking. **3.** a ridge or crest, as of land. *—v.t.* **4.** to cut along or across the backbone. [ME *chyne*, t. OF: m. *eschine*, t. Gmc. See SHIN]

chine[3] (chīn), *n.* chime[2].

chiné (shē′nā), *Textiles.* *—n.* **1.** material that is mottled, with the pattern printed on the warp. *—adj.* **2.** mottled, with the pattern printed on the warp.

Chinese (chī nēz′), *n., pl.* **-nese,** *adj.* *—n.* **1.** the standard language of China, based on the speech of Peking; Mandarin. **2.** a group of languages of the Sino-Tibetan family including standard Chinese and most of the other languages of China. **3.** any of the Chinese languages, which vary among themselves to the point of mutual unintelligibility. **4.** a native of or a descendant of a native of China. —*adj.* **5.** of China, its inhabitants, or their language. **6.** of or pertaining to the written characters of the Chinese language.

Chinese chequers, a game played by two or more persons with pegs or marbles, on a board with hollows or holes.

Chinese drive, *Cricket.* any unorthodox stroke.

Chinese hibiscus, a malvaceous shrub, *Hibiscus rosa-sinensis*, with showy flowers, single or double; greenhouse-cultivated.

Chinese lantern, **1.** a collapsible lantern of thin, coloured paper, often used for decorative lighting. **2.** a Japanese solanaceous herb, *Physalis franchetii*, often cultivated for its attractive orange-red inflated calyx.

Chinese puzzle, **1.** a very complicated puzzle; esp. a series of boxes in boxes. **2.** anything very complicated.

Chinese red, **1.** scarlet; orange-red; red chrome. **2.** a pigment consisting of basic lead chromate. Also, **chrome red.**

Chinese Wall. See **Great Wall of China.**

Chinese white, a pigment consisting of zinc oxide ground in water or oil.

Ch'ing (chĭng), *n.* the last imperial dynasty in China, 1644–1911, founded by the Manchus.

Chingford (chĭngʹfəd), *n.* a district in the NE outer London borough of Waltham Forest.

Chinghai (chĭngʹhīʹ), *n.* a province in W China. 2,050,000 (est. 1957). *Cap.*: Sining. Also, **Tsinghai.**

Chingola (chĭng gōʹlə), *n.* a town in central Zambia. 56,000 (est. 1963).

Chingtechen (chĭngʹtā chĕnʹ), *n.* Kingtehchen.

chink[1] (chĭngk), *n.* **1.** a crack, cleft, or fissure. **2.** a narrow opening. —*v.t.* **3.** *U.S.* to fill up chinks in. [appar. f. OE *cinu, cine* crack, fissure + *-k*, suffix. See -OCK]

chink[2] (chĭngk), *v.t., v.i.* **1.** to make, or cause to make, a short, sharp, ringing sound, as of coins or glasses striking together. —*n.* **2.** a chinking sound. [imit.]

Chink (chĭngk), *n. Slang.* (offensively) a Chinese.

chinkapin (chĭngʹkə pĭn), *n.* chinquapin.

chinless (chĭnʹlĭs), *adj.* **1.** with a receding chin; lacking a firm chin. **2.** lacking courage or firmness of purpose; vacillating; of weak character. **3. chinless wonder,** *Slang.* a foolish man, usually of good family.

chino (chēʹnō), *n. U.S.* a tough, twilled cotton cloth used for uniforms, sports clothes, etc.

Chino-, a combining form meaning 'Chinese'.

Chinoiserie (shēʹnwä zə rēʹ, shĭ nwäʹzə rĭ), *n.* a style of European art, current esp. in the 18th century, based on imitations of motifs in Chinese art.

Chinook (chĭ no͝okʹ, -no͝okʹ), *n., pl.* **-nook, -nooks. 1. Lower Chinook** and **Upper Chinook,** (*pl.*) North American Indian tribes of the Columbia river. **2.** a member of these tribes. **3.** a North American Indian linguistic family comprising two languages, **Lower Chinook** and **Upper Chinook,** and assigned by some linguists to the Penutian linguistic family. **4.** (*l.c.*) a warm, dry wind which blows at intervals down the eastern slopes of the Rocky Mountains. **5.** (*l.c.*) a warm, moist south-west wind on the coast of Washington and Oregon (**wet chinook**). [m. *Tsinúk* (Chehalis name)]

Chinookan (chĭ no͞oʹkən, -no͝okʹən), *n.* Chinook (def. 3).

Chinook jargon, a lingua franca composed of words from Chinook and other Indian languages and from English and French. It was formerly widely used among traders and Indians in the Columbia river country.

chinquapin (chĭngʹkə pĭn), *n.* **1.** the dwarf chestnut, *Castanea pumila*, a shrub or small tree of the U.S., bearing a small, edible nut, solitary in the bur. **2.** a fagaceous tree of the Pacific coast, *Castanopsis chrysophylla*. **3.** the nut of either of these trees. Also, **chincapin, chinkapin.** [t. N Amer. Ind. (Algonquian); cf. Delaware *činkwa* large, *min* fruit, seed]

chinrest (chĭnʹrĕstʹ), *n.* a device attached to a viola or a violin for controlling its position under the chin.

chinse (chĭns), *v.t.*, **chinsed, chinsing.** *Naut.* to caulk, esp. temporarily. [alter. of d. *chinch*, var. of CHINK[1]]

chinstrap (chĭnʹstrăpʹ), *n.* a strap under a chin for holding on a helmet.

chintz (chĭnts), *n., pl.* **chintzes. 1.** a printed cotton fabric, glazed or unglazed, used esp. for draperies. **2.** (orig.) painted or stained calico from India. [var. of *chints*, pl. of *chint*, t. Hind.: m. *chīnt*] —**chintzʹy,** *adj.*

chinwag (chĭnʹwăgʹ), *n. Slang.* a chat; a conversation.

chionodoxa (kīʹnə dŏkʹsə, chīʹnə-), *n.* any member of the small genus *Chionodoxa*, of liliaceous plants with blue flowers; native of Crete and Asia Minor.

Chios (kīʹŏs), *n.* **1.** a Greek island in the Aegean, near the W coast of Turkey. 62,233 pop. (1961); 322 sq. mi. **2.** the capital of this island: a seaport. 24,053 (1961). Greek, **Khios** (KHēʹôs).

chip[1] (chĭp), *n., v.*, **chipped, chipping.** —*n.* **1.** a small piece, as of wood, separated by chopping, cutting, or breaking. **2.** a very thin slice or piece of food, etc.: *chocolate chips.* **3.** a deep-fried finger of potato. **4.** a mark made by chipping. **5.** *Games.* a counter, as of ivory or bone, used in certain card games, etc. **6.** *Colloq.* a small (cut) piece of diamond, etc. **7.** *U.S.* anything trivial or worthless, or dried up or without flavour. **8.** *U.S.* a piece of dried dung. **9.** wood, straw, etc., in thin strips for weaving into hats, baskets, etc. **10.** *Golf.* chip shot. **11. chip off the old block,** *Colloq.* a person inheriting marked family characteristics. **12. chip on the shoulder,** *Colloq.* a grudge. —*v.t.* **13.** to hew or cut with an axe, chisel, etc. **14.** to cut or break off (bits or fragments). **15.** to disfigure by breaking off fragments. **16.** to shape or produce by cutting away pieces. **17.** *Colloq.* to contribute, as to a fund (often fol. by *in*). **18.** *Games.* to bet by means of chips, as in poker. —*v.i.* **19. a.** to cut potatoes into chips (def. 3). **b.** to cook chips. **20.** to break off in small pieces; to become chipped. **21.** *Colloq.* to taunt, chaff or poke fun at. **22.** *Golf.* to make a chip shot. **23. chip in, a.** to contribute money, help, etc. **b.** to interrupt. [ME *chippen*, OE *cippian*. Cf. MLG, MD *kippen* chip eggs, hatch]

chip[2] (chĭp), *n. Wrestling.* a tricky or special method by which an opponent can be thrown. [der. *chip*, v., trip. Cf. Icel. *kippa* scratch, pull]

chip basket, **1.** a basket of thin interwoven strips of wood used for packing fruit, etc. **2.** a wire basket in which chips are placed when frying.

chipboard (chĭpʹbôdʹ), *n.* **1.** a resin-bonded artificial wood made from waste wood, sawdust, etc., used in sheets for light structural work. **2.** a board, usually made of waste-paper, used in box-making, etc.

chip log. See **log** (def. 3b).

chipmunk (chĭpʹmŭngk), *n.* any of various small striped terrestrial squirrels of the N American genus *Tamias*, and the Asiatic and American genus *Eutamias*, esp. *T. striatus* of eastern North America. [t. N Amer. Ind. (Ojibwa): m. *ačitamo* squirrel]

Chipmunk, *Tamias striatus* (Total length 9 to 10 in.)

Chippendale (chĭpʹən dālʹ), *n.* **1. Thomas,** 1718?–79, English cabinet-maker and furniture designer. —*adj.* **2.** of, or in the style of, Thomas Chippendale.

Chippenham (chĭpʹə nəm), *n.* a town in England, in W Wiltshire. 17,543 (1961).

chipper[1] (chĭpʹə), *adj. Colloq.* lively; cheerful. [cf. Northern E *kipper* frisky]

chipper[2] (chĭpʹə), *n.* one who or that which chips or cuts. [f. CHIP[1] + -ER]

Chippewa (chĭpʹĭ wäʹ, -wə), *n.* **1.** an Ojibwa Indian. **2.** the Ojibwa language.

chipping (chĭpʹĭng), *n.* a fragment of stone, as used in surfacing roads.

chipping sparrow, any of several small North American sparrows of the genus *Spizella*, as *S. passerina*, commonly found about houses.

chip shot, *Golf.* a short shot using a wrist motion, made in approaching the green.

Chirico (*It.* kēʹrē kō), *n.* **Giorgio de** (*It.* jôrʹjō dĕ), born 1888, Greek-born metaphysical painter working mainly in Italy.

chirk (chûk), *v.i.* **1.** *Scot.* to make a strident grating sound. **2.** *U.S. Colloq.* to cheer (fol. by *up*). —*v.t.* **3.** *U.S. Colloq.* to cause to be cheered (fol. by *up*). —*adj.* **4.** *U.S. Colloq.* cheerful. [ME *chirken*, OE *circian* roar]

chirm (chûm), *v.i.* **1.** to chirp, as a bird; sing; warble. —*n.* **2.** the chirping of birds, etc.; charm. [ME; OE *cierm*]

chiro-, a word element meaning 'hand', as in *chiropractic.* [t. Gk: m. *cheiro-*, comb. form of *cheír*]

chirognomy (kī rŏgʹnə mĭ), *n.* the art of estimating a person's character by the appearance of the hand; palmistry.

chirography (kī rŏgʹrə fĭ), *n.* handwriting. —**chirogʹrapher,** *n.* —**chirographic** (kīʹrə grăfʹĭk), **chiʹrographʹical,** *adj.*

chiromancy (kīʹrə mănʹsĭ), *n.* the art of telling a person's fortune and character by the hand. —**chiʹromanʹcer,** *n.*

Chiron (kīʹrən), *n. Gk Myth.* a wise and beneficent centaur, teacher of Achilles, Asclepius, and others.

chironomid (kī rŏnʹə mĭd), *n.* one of a genus of midges, *Chironomus*, with aquatic larvae.

chiropody (kĭ rŏpʹə dĭ), *n.* the treatment of minor foot ailments, such as corns, bunions, etc. [f. CHIRO- + m. s. Gk *-podia*, der. *poús* foot] —**chiropʹodist,** *n.*

chiropractic (kī′rə prăk′tĭk), *n.* **1.** a therapeutic system based upon the premise that disease is caused by interference with nerve function, the method being to restore normal condition by adjusting the segments of the spinal column. **2.** a chiropractor. [f. CHIRO- + m. s. Gk *praktikós* practical]

chiropractor (kī′rə prăk′tə), *n.* one who practises chiropractic.

chiropter (kī rŏp′tə), *n.* any of the *Chiroptera*, the order of mammals that comprises the bats. [t. NL: s. *chiroptera*, pl., f. *chiro-* CHIRO- + Gk *pterá* wings]

chiropteran (kī rŏp′tə rən), *n.* **1.** chiropter. —*adj.* **2.** of or pertaining to a chiropter.

chirp (chûp), *v.i.* **1.** to make a short, sharp sound, as small birds and certain insects. **2.** to make any similar sound. —*v.t.* **3.** to sound or utter in a chirping manner. —*n.* **4.** a chirping sound. [? var. of CHIRK] —**chirp′er,** *n.*

chirpy (chû′pĭ), *adj. Colloq.* cheerful; lively; gay. —**chirp′ily,** *adv.*

chirr (chû), *v.i.* **1.** to make a shrill trilling sound, as a grasshopper. **2.** to make a similar sound. —*n.* **3.** the sound of chirring. Also, **chirre, churr.** [appar. back-formation from CHIRRUP]

chirrup (chĭr′əp), *v.*, **-ruped, -ruping,** *n.* —*v.i.* **1.** to chirp. **2.** to make a chirping sound, as to a cagebird or a horse. —*v.t.* **3.** to utter with chirps. —*n.* **4.** the act or sound of chirruping. [var. of CHIRP] —**chir′ruper,** *n.*

chirrupy (chĭr′ə pĭ), *adj.* chirpy.

chirurgeon (kī rû′jən), *n. Archaic.* a surgeon. [b. L *chirūrgus* surgeon (t. Gk: m. *cheirourgós*) and SURGEON; r. ME *cirurgien*, t. OF]

chirurgery (kī rû′jə rĭ), *n. Archaic.* surgery. —**chirur′gic, chirur′gical,** *adj.*

chisel (chĭz′əl), *n.*, *v.*, **-elled, -elling** or (*U.S.*) **-eled, -eling.** —*n.* **1.** a tool, as of steel, with a cutting edge at the extremity, usually transverse to the axis, for cutting or shaping wood, stone, etc. —*v.t.* **2.** to cut, shape, etc., with a chisel. **3.** *Slang.* **a.** to cheat; swindle. **b.** to get by cheating or trickery. —*v.i.* **4.** to work with a chisel. **5.** *Slang.* to use trickery; cheat. [ME, t. ONF, ult. der. L *caesus*, pp., cut] —**chis′eller;** *U.S.* **chis′eler,** *n.*

chiselled (chĭz′əld), *adj.* **1.** cut, shaped, etc., with a chisel. **2.** clear-cut. Also, *U.S.*, **chiseled.**

Chishima (chē′shē mä′), *n.* Japanese name of the **Kurile Islands.**

Chişinău (*Rum.* kē shē nəw′), *n.* Rumanian name of **Kishinev.**

Chislehurst (chĭz′əl hûst′), *n.* a district of SE London, now part of the outer London boroughs of Bexley and Bromley.

chi-square test (kī′skwĕə′), *Statistics.* a test devised for testing the mathematical goodness of fit of a frequency curve to an observed frequency distribution.

Chiswick (chĭz′ĭk), *n.* a district of the W outer London borough of Hounslow, on the Thames.

chit[1] (chĭt), *n.* **1.** a voucher of money owed for food, drink, etc. **2.** a note; a short memorandum. [short for CHITTY, t. Hind.: m. *chitthī*]

chit[2] (chĭt), *n.* a young person, esp. a pert girl. [? akin to KITTEN; assoc. with obs. *chit* sprout]

Chita (*Russ.* chĭ tá′), *n.* a city in the SE Soviet Union in Asia, E of Lake Baikal. 189,000 (est. 1963).

chitarra (kĭ tä′rə, chĭ tä′rə), *n.* an Italian guitar with wire strings.

chitarrone (kĭt′ä rō′nĭ, chĭt′ä-), *n.* a large double-necked theorbo or lute with wire strings.

chitchat (chĭt′chăt′), *n.* **1.** light conversation; small-talk. **2.** gossip. [varied redupl. of CHAT]

chitin (kī′tĭn), *n.* a characteristic horny organic component of the cuticula of arthropods. [t. F: m. *chitine*, der. Gk *chitṓn* tunic] —**chi′tinous,** *adj.*

chiton (kī′tən, -tŏn), *n.* **1.** *Gk Antiq.* a garment for both sexes, usually worn next to the skin. **2.** any of a group of sluggish, limpet-like molluscs which adhere to rocks. [t. Gk]

Chittagong (chĭt′ə gŏng′), *n.* a seaport in East Pakistan, near the Bay of Bengal. 364,205 (1961).

chitterling (chĭt′ə lĭng), *n.* **1.** (*usually pl.*) a part of the small intestine of pigs, etc., esp. as cooked for food. **2.** *Obs.* a frill or ruff. [cf. G *Kutteln* entrails]

chitty (chĭt′ĭ), *n.* chit[1].

chivalric (shĭv′əl rĭk), *adj.* **1.** pertaining to chivalry. **2.** chivalrous.

chivalrous (shĭv′əl rəs), *adj.* **1.** having the high qualities characteristic of chivalry, such as courage, courtesy, generosity, loyalty, etc. **2.** chivalric. **3.** having good and polished manners, and a consideration of others. [ME, t. OF: m. *chevalerous*, der. *chevalier* CHEVALIER] —**chiv′alrously,** *adv.* —**chiv′alrousness,** *n.*

chivalry (shĭv′əl rĭ), *n.* **1.** the ideal qualifications of a knight, such as courtesy, generosity, valour, dexterity in arms, etc. **2.** the rules and customs of medieval knighthood. **3.** the medieval system or institution of knighthood. **4.** a group of knights. **5.** gallant warriors or gentlemen. **6.** good manners; consideration of others. **7.** *Obs.* the position or rank of a knight. [ME, t. OF: m. *chevalerie*, der. *chevalier* CHEVALIER]

chive (chīv), *n.* a small bulbous plant, *Allium schoenoprasum*, related to the leek and onion, with long, slender leaves which are used as a seasoning in cookery. Also, **chive garlic.** [ME, t. ONF, g. L *caepa* onion]

chivvy (chĭv′ĭ), *v.*, **-vied, -vying,** *n.*, *pl.* **-vies.** chevy.

chizz (chĭz), *n. Slang.* a swindle; an unfair or unlucky event.

Ch.J., Chief Justice.

Chkalov (*Russ.* chká′ləf), *n.* former name (1938–57) of **Orenburg.**

chlamydate (klăm′ĭ dāt′, -dĭt), *adj. Zool.* having a mantle or pallium, as a mollusc. [f. s. Gk *chlamýs* mantle + -ATE[1]]

chlamydeous (klə mĭd′ĭ əs), *adj. Bot.* pertaining to or having a floral envelope. [f. s. NL *chlamydeae*, pl., (der. Gk *chlamýs* mantle) + -OUS]

chlamys (klā′mĭs, klăm′ĭs), *n.*, *pl.* **chlamydes** (klăm′ĭ dēz′). *Gk Antiq.* a short mantle or cloak worn by men. [t. L, t. Gk]

chloanthite (klō ăn′thīt), *n.* a mineral arsenide of nickel which is used as an ore of nickel; white nickel. Also, **cloanthite.** [f. s. Gk *chloanthḗs* pale (f. s. *chlóē* green vegetation + *-anthēs* flower) + -ITE[1]]

chloasma (klō ăz′mə), *n. Med.* hyperpigmentation of the facial skin in women, caused by increased deposits of melanin as a result of endocrine factors. [t. Gk: greenness]

Chlodwig (*Ger.* klōt′vĭKH), *n.* German name of **Clovis I.**

Chloe (klō′ĭ), *n.* (in pastoral and other literature) a name for a maiden, esp. one beloved. Also, **Chloë.**

chlor-[1], a word element meaning 'green', as in *chlorine*. Also, **chloro-**[1]. [t. Gk, comb. form of *chlōrós*]

chlor-[2], a combining form denoting 'chlorine', as in *chloral*. Also, **chloro-**[2].

chloracetic acid (klô′rə sē′tĭk), *Chem.* chloroacetic acid.

chloral (klô′rəl), *n. Chem.*, *Pharm.* **1.** a colourless, mobile liquid, CCl_3CHO, first prepared from chlorine and alcohol and used as a hypnotic. **2.** a white, crystalline substance, $CCl_3CH(OH)_2$ (**chloral hydrate**), formed by combining liquid chloral with water, and used as a hypnotic. [f. CHLOR-[2] + AL(COHOL)]

chloramine (klô′rə mēn′), *n. Chem.* **1.** one of a group of compounds obtained by the action of hypochlorite solutions on compounds containing NH or NH_2 groups; used as an antiseptic. **2.** an unstable, colourless liquid, NH_2Cl, with a pungent smell, derived from ammonia.

chloramphenicol (klô′răm fĕn′ĭ kŏl′), *n. Med.* chloromycetin.

chloranthy (klō răn′thĭ, klô′rən thĭ), *n. Bot.* an abnormal condition of a flower where all parts change into leafy structures.

chlorargyrite (klō rä′jĭ rīt′), *n.* cerargyrite.

chlorate (klô′rāt, -rĭt), *n. Chem.* a salt of chloric acid.

chlorella (klō rĕl′ə, klə-), *n.* a genus of microscopic unicellular green algae.

chlorenchyma (klə rĕng′kĭ mə), *n. Bot.* parenchyma tissue containing chlorophyll.

chloric (klô′rĭk), *adj. Chem.* of or containing chlorine in the pentavalent state. [f. CHLOR-[2] + -IC]

chloric acid, *Chem.* an acid, $HClO_3$, which exists only in solution and as salts.

chloride (klô′rīd), *n.* **1.** a compound usually of two elements only, one of which is chlorine. **2.** a salt of hydrochloric acid.

chloride of lime, *Chem., etc.* a white powder used in bleaching and disinfecting, made by treating slaked lime with chlorine, and regarded (when dry) as calcium oxychloride, $CaOCl_2$.

chlorinate (klô′rĭ nāt′), *v.t.*, **-nated, -nating.** **1.** *Chem.* to combine or treat with chlorine. **2.** to disinfect (water) by means of chlorine. **3.** *Metall.* to treat (a gold ore) with chlorine gas in order to remove the gold as a soluble chloride. —**chlo′rina′tion,** *n.* —**chlo′rina′tor,** *n.*

chlorine (klô′rēn), *n. Chem.* a greenish yellow gaseous element (occurring combined in common salt, etc.), incombustible, and highly irritating to the organs of respiration. It is used as a powerful bleaching agent and in various industrial processes. *Symbol:* Cl; *at. wt:* 35·453; *at. no.:* 17. Also, **chlorin** (klô′rĭn). [f. CHLOR-[1] + -INE[2]]

chlorite[1] (klô′rīt), *n.* a group of minerals, hydrous silicates of aluminium, ferrous iron, and magnesium, occurring in green platelike crystals or scales. [t. Gk: m. s. *chlōrîtis* kind of green stone]

chlorite[2] (klôʹrīt), *n.* *Chem.* a salt of chlorous acid, as **potassium chlorite,** $KClO$. [f. CHLOR-[2] + -ITE[1]]

chloro-[1], var. of **chlor-**[1], used before consonants, as in *chlorophyll.*

chloro-[2], var. of **chlor-**[2], used before consonants, as in *chloroform.*

chloroacetic acid (klôʹrō ə sēʹtĭk), *Chem.* any of three acetic acids: *monochloroacetic acid,* $CH_2Cl.COOH$, which forms rhombic crystals; *dichloroacetic acid,* $CHCl_2.COOH$, which is a colourless liquid; and *trichloroacetic acid,* $CCl_3.COOH$, which forms deliquescent rhombic crystals. All forms are used as wart-removers and in the manufacture of dyes. Also, **chloracetic acid.**

chloroform (klŏʹrə fôm′), *n.* *Chem., Pharm., etc.* a colourless volatile liquid, $CHCl_3$, used as an anaesthetic and solvent. —*v.t.* **2.** to administer chloroform to. **3.** to put chloroform on (a cloth, etc.). [f. CHLORO-[2] + FORM(YL)]

chlorohydrin (klô′rō hīʹdrĭn), *n.* *Chem.* any of a class of organic compounds containing a chlorine atom and a hydroxyl group, usually on adjacent carbon atoms.

chloromethane (klô′rō mēʹthān), *n.* *Chem.* a colourless gas, CH_3Cl, used as a refrigerant and in organic synthesis; methyl chloride.

chloromycetin (klô′rō mī sēʹtĭn), *n.* *Med.* **1.** an antibiotic, esp. effective against diseases caused by bacteria and certain viruses and Rickettsia, as undulant fever, typhoid fever, and typhus; chloramphenicol. **2.** (*cap.*) a trademark for this substance.

chlorophyll (klŏʹrə fĭl), *n.* *Bot., Biochem.* the green colouring substances of leaves and plants, having two forms: bluish black **chlorophyll a,** $C_{55}H_{72}MgN_4O_5$, and yellowish green **chlorophyll b,** $C_{55}H_{70}MgN_4O_6$. It is associated with the production of carbohydrates by photosynthesis in plants and is used as a dye for cosmetics and oils. Also, *U.S.*, **chlorophyl.** [f. CHLORO-[1] + -PHYLL]

chlorophyllous (klô′rō fĭlʹəs), *adj.* of or containing chlorophyll. Also, **chlorophyllose** (klô′rō fĭlʹōs).

chloropicrin (klô′rō pĭkʹrĭn, -pīʹkrĭn), *n.* *Chem., etc.* a colourless liquid, CCl_3NO_2, used as an insecticide and as a chemical agent in warfare; nitrochloroform; trichloronitromethane. Also, **chlorpicrin.** [f. CHLORO-[1] + PICR(IC) + -IN[2]]

chloroplast (klôʹrō plăst′), *n.* *Bot.* a plastid containing chlorophyll. [f. CHLORO-[1] + -PLAST]

chloroprene (klôʹrō prēn′), *n.* *Chem.* a colourless fluid, CH_2–CClCH–CH_2, produced from acetylene and hydrogen chloride, which polymerizes readily to neoprene.

chloroquine (klôʹrō kwēn′), *n.* *Pharm.* a synthetic antimalarial drug, $C_{18}H_{26}ClN_3$.

chlorosis (klô rōʹsĭs), *n.* **1.** abnormal yellow colour of a plant, as from lack of iron in the soil. **2.** a benign type of iron-deficiency anaemia in adolescent girls, marked by a pale yellow-green complexion. [t. NL; see CHLOR-[1], -OSIS]

chlorous (klôʹrəs), *adj.* *Chem.* containing trivalent chlorine, as **chlorous acid,** $HClO_2$, which occurs only in solution or as its salts, the chlorites. [f. CHLOR-[2] + -OUS]

chloropromazine (klô prōʹmə zēn′), *n.* *Pharm.* a drug which depresses the central nervous system and which is also antispasmodic, antihistaminic, and anticholinergic.

Ch.M., Master of Surgery.

chm., chairman. Also, **chmn, chn.**

choc (chŏk), *n.* *Colloq.* chocolate.

choc-ice (chŏkʹīs′), *n.* an ice-cream coated with chocolate.

chock (chŏk), *n.* **1.** a block or wedge of wood, etc., for filling in a space, esp. for preventing movement, as of a wheel or a cask. **2.** *Naut.* **a.** a metal or wooden fitting through which a mooring line, anchor cable, towline, or similar rope passes, usually on or in the rail. **b.** a shaped standard on which a boat, barrel, or other object rests. —*v.t.* **3.** to furnish with or secure by a chock or chocks. **4.** *Naut.* to place (a boat) upon chocks. —*adv.* **5.** as close or tight as possible; quite: *chock against the edge.* [prob. t. ONF: m. *choque* log or block of wood. Cf. It. *ciocco* burning log]

chock-a-block (chŏk′ə blŏkʹ), *adv.* **1.** *Naut.* with the blocks drawn close together, as when a tackle is hauled to the utmost. **2.** in a jammed or crowded condition.

chock-full (chŏk′fŏŏlʹ), *adj.* full to the utmost; crammed. Also, **chuck-full, choke-full.**

chock-stone (chŏkʹstōn′), *n.* *Mountaineering.* a stone jammed in a crack or cleft, intentionally or naturally, providing an anchor.

chocolate (chŏkʹə lĭt, chŏkʹlĭt), *n.* **1.** a preparation of the seeds of cacao, roasted, husked, and ground (without removing any of the fat), often sweetened and flavoured, as with vanilla. **2.** a beverage or confection made from this. **3.** dark brown. —*adj.* **4.** made or flavoured with chocolate. **5.** having the colour of chocolate. [t. Sp., t. Nahuatl: m. *chocolatl* bitter water]

Choctaw (chŏkʹtô), *n., pl.* **-taw, -taws. 1.** (*pl.*) a large Muskhogean tribe of North American Indians, formerly living chiefly in southern Mississippi, now in Oklahoma. **2.** a member of this tribe. **3.** their language.

Chofu (chō′fōōʹ), *n.* a town in Japan, in SE central Honshu island. 118,004 (1965).

choice (chois), *n., adj.*, **choicer, choicest.** —*n.* **1.** the act of choosing; selection. **2.** power of choosing; option. **3.** the person or thing chosen: *this book is my choice.* **4.** an abundance and variety from which to choose: *a wide choice of candidates.* **5.** that which is preferred or preferable to others; the best part of anything. **6.** an alternative. **7.** a well-chosen supply. —*adj.* **8.** worthy of being chosen; excellent; superior. **9.** carefully selected: *delivered in choice words.* [ME *chois,* t. OF, der. *choisir* choose, of Gmc orig. and akin to CHOOSE] —**choiceʹly,** *adv.* —**choiceʹness,** *n.*

—**Syn. 2.** CHOICE, ALTERNATIVE, OPTION, PREFERENCE all suggest the power of choosing between (two) things. CHOICE implies the opportunity to choose: *a choice of evils.* ALTERNATIVE suggests that one has a choice between only two possibilities. It is often used with a negative to mean that there is no second possibility: *to have no alternative.* OPTION emphasizes free right or privilege of choosing: *to exercise one's option.* PREFERENCE applies to a choice based on liking or partiality: *to state a preference.* **8.** See **fine**[1].

choir (kwīʹə), **1.** a company of singers, esp. an organized group employed in church service. **2.** any company or band, or a division of one: *string choir.* **3.** *Archit.* **a.** that part of a church used by the singers. **b.** (in a medieval cruciform church) the body of the church which extends from the crossing to the east, or altar, end. **c.** (in cathedrals, etc.) the area between the nave and the main altar. **4.** *Theol.* any of the nine orders of the celestial hierarchy. —*v.i., v.t.* **5.** *Poetic.* to sing in chorus. [ME *quer,* t. OF: m. *cuer,* g. L *chorus.* See CHORUS]

choirboy (kwīʹə boi′), *n.* a boy who sings in a choir.

choir loft, a gallery in which the choir is stationed.

choirmaster (kwīʹə mäs′tə), *n.* the leader or director of a choir.

choir organ, 1. a small organ for accompanying a choir. **2.** a division of an organ controlled by a separate manual.

choir school, a school for choirboys attached to a cathedral, etc.

choir screen, a screen separating the choir (def. 3b) from the nave of a church.

Choiseul (shwä zûlʹ; *Fr.* shwȧ zœlʹ), *n.* one of the British Solomon Islands, E of New Guinea. 4500 (est. 1951); 1500 sq. mi.

choke (chōk), *v.,* **choked, choking,** *n.* —*v.t.* **1.** to stop the breath of, by squeezing or obstructing the windpipe; strangle; stifle; suffocate. **2.** to stop, as the breath or utterance, by or as by strangling or stifling. **3.** to check or stop the growth, progress, or action of: *to choke off discussion.* **4.** to stop by filling; obstruct; clog; congest. **5.** to suppress, as a feeling or emotion. **6.** to fill chock-full. **7.** (in internal-combustion engines) to enrich the fuel mixture by diminishing the air supply to the carburettor, as when starting a motor. —*v.i.* **8.** to suffer strangling or suffocation. **9.** to be obstructed or clogged. **10.** to be temporarily overcome, as with emotion. —*n.* **11.** the act or sound of choking. **12.** (in internal-combustion engines) the mechanism by which the air supply to a carburettor is diminished or stopped. **13.** *Mach.* any such mechanism which, by blocking a passage, regulates the flow of air, etc. **14.** *Elect.* a choking coil. **15.** a narrowed part, as in a chokebore. **16.** the filamentous, inedible centre of the head of an artichoke. [ME *choke(n), cheke(n),* aphetic variants of ME *achoke(n), acheke(n),* OE *acēocian*]

chokeberry (chōkʹbə rĭ, -brĭ), *n., pl.* **-ries. 1.** the berry-like fruit of shrubs of the North American rosaceous genus *Aronia,* esp. *A. arbutifolia.* **2.** the plant bearing it.

chokebore (chōkʹbô′), *n.* **1.** (in a shotgun) a bore which narrows towards the muzzle to prevent shot from scattering too widely. **2.** a shotgun with such a bore.

chokecherry (chōkʹchĕ′rĭ), *n., pl.* **-ries. 1.** any of several species of cherry, esp. *Prunus virginiana* of North America, which bears an astringent fruit. **2.** the fruit.

chokedamp (chōkʹdămp′), *n.* *Mining.* mine atmosphere so low in oxygen and high in carbon dioxide as to cause choking; blackdamp.

choke-full (chōk′fŏŏlʹ), *adj.* chock-full.

choker (chōʹkə), *n.* **1.** one who or that which chokes. **2.** *Colloq.* a necklace worn tightly round the neck. **3.** *Colloq.* a neckcloth or a high collar.

choking (chōʹkĭng), *adj.* **1.** so full of emotion one almost chokes: *to speak in a choking voice.* **2.** that causes the sensation of being choked. —**chokʹingly,** *adv.*

choking coil, *Elect.* a coil of large inductance which

allows steady currents to pass freely but chokes off or greatly weakens all rapid fluctuations, esp. such a coil as is used in electronic apparatus.

choky (chō′kĭ), *n.*, *adj.*, **-kier, -kiest.** —*n.* **1.** *Slang.* prison. —*adj.* **2.** tending to choke or suffocate one. **3.** feeling choked or suffocated. Also, **chokey.**

chol-, a word element meaning 'gall' or 'bile'. Also, **chole-, cholo-.** [t. Gk, comb. form of *cholḗ* bile]

cholecystectomy (kŏl′ĭ sĭs tĕk′tə mĭ), *n.*, *pl.* **-mies.** *Surg.* removal of the gall bladder.

cholecystostomy (kŏl′ĭ sĭs tŏs′tə mĭ), *n.*, *pl.* **-mies.** *Surg.* a draining of the gall bladder with the organ left in place, usually done to remove stones.

choler (kŏl′ə), *n.* **1.** irascibility; anger; wrath; irritability. **2.** *Old Physiol.* bile (that one of the four humours supposed when predominant to cause irascibility and anger). **3.** *Obs.* biliousness. [t. LL: s. *cholera* bile, t. Gk: name of the disease; r. ME *colere*, t. OF]

cholera (kŏl′ə rə), *n.* **1.** *Pathol.* **a.** an acute, infectious disease, due to a specific micro-organism, endemic in India, etc., and epidemic generally, marked by profuse diarrhoea, vomiting, cramp, etc., and often fatal. **b.** an acute disorder of the digestive tract, marked by diarrhoea, vomiting, cramp, etc. (**sporadic cholera, bilious cholera,** or **cholera morbus**). **2.** *Vet. Sci.* any disease characterized by violent diarrhoea. See **swine fever** and **fowl cholera.** [t. L, t. Gk] —**choleraic** (kŏl′ə rā′ĭk), *adj.*

cholera infantum (ĭn făn′təm), *Pathol.* sporadic cholera in infants. [L: cholera of infants]

cholera morbus (môr′bəs), *Pathol.* sporadic cholera. Also, **cholera nostras** (nŏs′trăs). [L: cholera disease]

choleric (kŏl′ə rĭk), *adj.* **1.** irascible; angry. **2.** *Obs.* bilious. **3.** *Obs.* causing biliousness.

cholesterol (kə lĕs′tə rōl′), *n.* *Biochem.* a fatlike substance, $C_{27}H_{45}OH$, found in bile and gallstones, and in the blood and brain, the yolk of eggs, etc. Also, **cholesterin** (kə lĕs′tə rĭn). [f. CHOL(E)- + Gk *ster(eós)* solid + -OL²]

cholic acid (kō′lĭk, kŏl′ĭk), *Biochem.* a white crystalline hydroxy acid, $C_{23}H_{39}O_3.COOH$, derived from bile acids and related to the sex hormones and cholesterol. [*cholic* t. Gk: m. s. *cholikós* of bile]

choline (kō′lēn, kŏl′ēn, -ĭn), *n.* *Biochem.* a viscous organic base, $C_5H_{15}NO_2$, found in combined form in lecithin, acetylcholine, etc., which prevents the accumulation of fat in the liver and is often included in the vitamin B complex.

cholo-, var. of **chol-** before consonants.

Cholon (*Fr.* shō lôɴ′; *Annam.* chə lŭn′), *n.* a former town in South Vietnam, part of the Saigon-Cholon urban area. 481,000 (est. 1953).

Cholula (*Sp.* chō lo͞o′lä), *n.* a town in S central Mexico, near Puebla: ancient Aztec ruins. 12,833 (1960).

chondriosome (kŏn′drĭ ə sōm′), *n.* *Biol.* mitochondria. [f. Gk *chondrío(n)*, dim of *chóndros* cartilage + -SOME³]

chondroma (kŏn drō′mə), *n.*, *pl.* **-mas, -mata** (-mə tə). *Pathol.* a cartilaginous tumour or growth. [f. s. Gk *chóndros* cartilage + -OMA]

Chongjin (chŭng′jĭn′), *n.* Chungjin.

Chonju (chŭn′jo͞o′), *n.* a town in S South Korea. 212,326 (1964).

chook (cho͝ok), *n.* *Austral., N.Z. Colloq.* a fowl. [imit.]

choose (cho͞oz), *v.*, **chose, chosen** or (*Obs.*) **chose, choosing.** —*v.t.* **1.** to select from a number, or in preference to another or other things or persons. **2.** to prefer and decide (to do something): *he chose to stand for election.* **3.** to want; desire. —*v.i.* **4.** to make a choice. **5. cannot choose but,** cannot do otherwise than: *he cannot choose but hear.* [ME *chose(n)*, OE *ceōsan*; var. of ME *chēse(n)*, OE *cēosan*, c. G *kiesen*, Goth. *kiusan*; akin to L *gustāre* taste] —**choos′er,** *n.*

—**Syn. 1.** CHOOSE, SELECT, PICK, ELECT, PREFER indicate a decision that one or more possibilities are to be regarded more highly than others. CHOOSE suggests a decision on one of a number of possibilities because of its apparent superiority: *to choose a course of action.* SELECT suggests a choice made for fitness: *to select the proper golf club.* PICK, an informal word, suggests a selection on personal grounds: *to pick a winner.* The formal word ELECT suggests a kind of official action: *to elect a chairman.* PREFER, also formal, emphasizes the desire or liking for one thing more than for another or others: *to prefer coffee to tea.* —**Ant. 1.** reject.

choosy (cho͞o′zĭ), *adj.* *Colloq.* hard to please, particular, fastidious, esp. in making a choice: *choosy about food.* Also, **choos′ey.**

chop¹ (chŏp), *v.*, **chopped, chopping,** *n.* —*v.t.* **1.** to cut with a quick, heavy blow or series of blows, using an axe, etc. **2.** to make by so cutting. **3.** to cut in pieces. **4.** *Tennis, Cricket, etc.* to hit (a ball) with a chop stroke. **5.** *Colloq.* to dismiss; give the sack to; fire. —*v.i.* **6.** to make a quick, heavy stroke or a series of strokes, as with an axe. **7.** to go, come, or move suddenly or violently. —*n.* **8.** the act of chopping. **9.** a cutting blow. **10.** *Boxing.* a short, downward cutting blow. **11.** a chop stroke. **12.** a piece chopped off. **13.** a slice of mutton, lamb, veal, pork, etc., usually one containing a rib. **14.** a short, irregular, broken motion of waves. **15.** *Colloq.* one's deathblow: *he got the chop.* **16.** *Colloq.* the sack; dismissal. **17.** *Obs.* a chap; crack; cleft. [var. of CHAP¹] —**Syn. 1.** See **cut.**

chop² (chŏp), *v.*, **chopped, chopping.** —*v.i.* **1.** to turn, shift, or change suddenly, as the wind. **2.** *Obs.* to barter. **3.** *Obs.* to bandy words; argue. —*v.t.* **4.** *Dial.* to barter; exchange. **5. chop logic,** to reason or dispute argumentatively; argue. [var. of obs. *chap* barter, ME *chapien*, OE *cēapian*. Cf. CHEAP]

chop³ (chŏp), *n.* **1.** (*usually pl.*) a jaw. **2.** (*pl.*) the oral cavity. Also, **chap.** [? special use of CHOP¹]

chop⁴ (chŏp), *n.* **1.** (in India, China, etc.) **a.** an official stamp or seal, or a permit or clearance. **b.** a design, corresponding to a brand or trademark, stamped on goods to indicate their special identity. **2.** *Anglo-Indian Colloq.* quality. [t. Hind.: m. *chhāp* impression, stamp]

chop chop! (chŏp′chŏp′), bring it quickly. [Pidgin English *chop* quick]

chopfallen (chŏp′fô′lən), *adj.* chapfallen.

chophouse¹ (chŏp′hous′), *n.* an eating house making a speciality of chops, steaks, grills, and the like. [f. CHOP¹ + HOUSE]

chophouse² (chŏp′hous′), *n.* (in China, formerly) a customs house. [f. CHOP⁴ + HOUSE]

chopin (chŏp′ĭn), *n.* a kind of shoe with a very thick sole of cork or the like, sometimes suggesting a short stilt, formerly worn esp. by women. Also, **chopine** (chŏ pēn′, chŏp′ĭn). [t. Sp., der. *chapa* bit of leather, t. F: m. *chape* CHAPE]

Chopin (shŏp′ăng; *Fr.* shŏ păɴ′), *n.* **Frédéric François** (*Fr.* frĕ dĕ rēk′ fräɴ swȧ′), 1810–49, Polish-French pianist and composer.

chopper (chŏp′ə), *n.* **1.** one who or that which chops. **2.** a short axe with a large blade used for cutting up meat, etc.; a butcher's cleaver. **3.** *Colloq.* a helicopter.

chopping (chŏp′ĭng), *adj.* choppy (def. 1).

choppy (chŏp′ĭ), *adj.*, **-pier, -piest. 1.** (of the sea, etc.) forming short, irregular, broken waves. **2.** (of the wind) shifting or changing suddenly or irregularly; variable. [f. CHOP² + -Y¹]

chopstick (chŏp′stĭk′), *n.* one of a pair of thin sticks, as of wood or ivory, used by Chinese, etc., to raise food to the mouth. [f. Pidgin English *chop* quick + STICK¹]

chop stroke, *Tennis, Cricket, etc.* a downward stroke made with the racket or bat at an angle.

chop suey (chŏp′so͞o′ĭ), *Orig. U.S.* a mixed dish served in Chinese restaurants, consisting of small pieces of meat, chicken, etc., cooked together with onions, beansprouts, green peppers, mushrooms, or other vegetables and seasoning, in a gravy, eaten commonly with soya sauce and rice. Also, **chop sooy.** [t. Chinese: mixed bits]

choragus (kô rā′gəs), *n.*, *pl.* **-gi** (-jī). **1.** the leader and sponsor of an ancient Greek chorus. **2.** any conductor of an entertainment or festival. [t. L, t. Gk: m. *chorāgós*, *chorēgós* leader of the chorus] —**choragic** (kô răj′ĭk, -rā′jĭk), *adj.*

choral (*adj.* kô′rəl; *n.* kŏ räl′), *adj.* **1.** of a chorus or a choir. **2.** sung by or adapted for a chorus or a choir. —*n.* **3.** a chorale. [t. ML: s. *chorālis*, der. L *chorus.* See CHORUS] —**cho′rally,** *adv.*

chorale (kŏ räl′), *n.* **1.** a simple hymnlike tune in slow tempo usually sung by choir and congregation together. **2.** *U.S.* a choir or choral group.

chorargyrite (kô rä′jĭ rīt′), *n.* cerargyrite.

chord¹ (kôd), *n.* **1.** a string of a musical instrument. **2.** a feeling or emotion. **3.** *Geom.* that part of a straight line between two of its intersections with a curve. **4.** *Civ. Eng.* one of the main members which lie along the top or bottom edge of a truss framework. **5.** *Aeron.* a straight line joining the centres of curvature of the leading and trailing edges of an aerofoil section. **6.** *Anat.* a cord (def. 4). [t. L: s. *chorda* cord, string, t. Gk: m. *chordḗ* gut, string of a musical instrument. Cf. CORD] —**chord′al,** *adj.*

C A B

Geometrical chords: AB, AC chords, subtending arcs ACB, AC

chord² (kôd), *n.* *Music.* a combination of three or more notes in harmonic relation, sounded simultaneously. [var. spelling (influenced by CHORD¹) of *cord*, aphetic var. of ACCORD, n.]

chordate (kô′dāt), *Zool.* —*adj.* **1.** belonging or pertaining to the *Chordata*, the phylum that includes the

b., blend of, blended; c., cognate with; d., dialect, dialectal; der., derived from; f., formed from; g., going back to; m., modification of; r., replacing; s., stem of; t., taken from; ?, perhaps. See full key on inside front cover.

true vertebrates and those animals (*protochordates*) that have a notochord, such as the lancelets and the tunicates. —*n.* **2.** a chordate animal. [t. NL: m. s. *chordātus* having a chord. See CHORD[1]]

chording (kô′dĭng), *n. Music.* **1.** the distribution of notes within a chord. **2.** the intonation of a chord by instrumentalists or vocalists.

chore (chô), *n.* **1.** a small or odd job; a piece of minor domestic work. **2.** (*pl.*) routine work around a house or farm. **3.** a hard or unpleasant task. [ME *churre*, OE *cyrr*, var. of *cierr, cerr.* See CHAR[3]]

chorea (kŏ rĭə′), *n.* **1.** *Pathol.* an acute disease, esp. common among children, characterized by irregular, involuntary, and uncontrollable movements in the face or extremities; St Vitus's dance. **2.** *Vet. Sci.* a disease of the nervous system characterized by degenerations which cause irregular, jerky, involuntary muscular movements. It is frequent in dogs, usually as an after-effect of canine distemper. [t. NL, t. Gk: m. *choreía* dance]

choreographer (kŏ′rĭ ŏg′rə fə), *n.* a person who creates ballet and other dance compositions.

choreography (kŏ′rĭ ŏg′rə fĭ), *n.* **1.** the art of composing ballets, etc., and arranging separate dances. **2.** the art of representing the various movements in dancing by a system of notation. **3.** the art of dancing. Also, **choregraphy** (kŏ rĕg′rə fĭ). [f. *choreo-* (comb. form repr. Gk *choreía* dance) + -GRAPHY] —**choreographic** (kŏ′rĭ ə-grăf′ĭk), *adj.*

choriamb (kŏ′rĭ ămb′), *n. Pros.* a foot of four syllables, two short between two long.

choriambus (kŏ′rĭ ăm′bəs), *n., pl.* **-bi** (-bī), **-buses.** choriamb. [t. L, t. Gk: m. *choríambos*]

choric (kŏ′rĭk), *adj.* of or for a chorus.

chorioid (kô′rĭ oid′), *adj., n. Anat.* choroid.

chorion (kô′rĭ ən), *n. Embryol.* the outermost of the extra embryonic membranes of land vertebrates, contributing to the placenta in the placental mammals and next to the shell (or the shell membrane) in egg-laying types. [t. NL, t. Gk] —**chorionic** (kô′rĭ ŏn′ĭk), *adj.*

chorisis (kô′rĭ sĭs, kə rī′sĭs), *n. Bot.* an increase in the number of parts of a flower due to the branching of its primary members. [t. Gk: separation]

chorister (kŏ′rĭs tə), *n.* **1.** a singer in a choir. **2.** a male singer in a church choir; a choirboy. [f. s. ML *chorista* chorister + -ER[1]; r. ME *queristre*, t. AF, der. *quer* CHOIR]

Chorley (chô′lĭ), *n.* a town in England, in N Lancashire. 31,315 (1961).

chorography (kô rŏg′rə fĭ), *n. Geog.* the systematic description and analysis of regions or of a region. [t. L: m. s. *chōrographia*, t. Gk] —**chorog′rapher,** *n.* —**choro-graphic** (kŏ′rə grăf′ĭk), **cho′rograph′ical,** *adj.* —**cho′-rograph′ically,** *adv.*

choroid (kô′roid), *Anat.* —*adj.* **1.** like the chorion; membranous (applied esp. to a delicate, highly vascular membrane or coat of the eyeball between the sclerotic coat and the retina). —*n.* **2.** the choroid coat of the eye. Also, **chorioid.** See diag. under **eye.** [t. Gk: m. s. *choroeidēs*, prop. *chorioeidēs* like a membrane]

chorology (kŏ rŏl′ə jĭ), *n. Geog.* the systematic description and analysis of geographical distribution in regions. [f. *choro-* (comb. form of Gk *chôros* place) + -(O)LOGY] —**chorol′ogist,** *n.* —**chorological** (kŏ′rə lŏj′-ĭ kl), *adj.*

chortle (chô′tl), *v.,* **-tled, -tling,** *n.* —*v.t., v.i.* **1.** to chuckle or utter with glee. —*n.* **2.** a gleeful chuckle. [b. CHUCKLE and SNORT; coined by Lewis Carroll in '*Through the Looking-Glass*' (1871)] —**chor′tler,** *n.*

chorus (kô′rəs), *n., pl.* **-ruses,** *v.,* **-rused, -rusing.** —*n.* **1.** *Music.* **a.** a group of persons singing in concert. **b.** (in an opera, oratorio, etc.) such a company singing in connection with soloists or individual singers. **c.** a piece of music for singing in concert. **d.** a part of a song in which others join the principal singer or singers. **e.** any recurring refrain. **2.** simultaneous utterance in singing, speaking, etc. **3.** the sounds uttered. **4.** (in musical shows) **a.** the company of dancers and singers. **b.** the singing or song of such a company. **5.** (in ancient Greek use) **a.** a dance performed by a company of persons and accompanied with song or narration, orig. as a religious rite. **b.** a company of singers, dancers, or narrators supplementing the performance of the main actors. **6.** (in later use) **a.** a company of persons, or a single person, having a similar function in a play, esp. in the Elizabethan drama. **b.** a part of a drama rendered by such a company or person. —*v.t., v.i.* **7.** to sing or speak in chorus. [t. L, t. Gk: m. *chorós* dance, band of dancers, chorus]

chorus girl, *Theat.* a female member of the chorus (of a musical comedy or the like). —**chorus boy.**

Chorzów (*Pol.* KHŏ′zhōōf), *n.* a city in S Poland. 153,000 (est. 1964). Formerly, **Królewska Huta.** German, **Königshütte.**

chose[1] (chōz), *v.* pt. and obs. pp. of **choose.**

chose[2] (shōz), *n. Law.* a thing; an article of personal property. [t. F: thing, g. L *causa* CAUSE]

chose in action, *Law.* **1.** an intangible form of property as a debt, patent, share, etc., recoverable by an action. **2.** a right which can be protected only by legal action.

chosen (chō′zən), *v.* **1.** pp. of **choose.** —*adj.* **2.** selected from a number; preferred. **3.** *Theol.* elect.

Chosen (chō′sĕn′), *n.* Japanese name of **Korea.**

chosen people, the Israelites. Ex. 19, etc.

Chou (chō), *n.* a Chinese dynasty, beginning in legendary times and continuing into historical times. The traditional date for its foundation, 1122 B.C., cannot be verified; it ended *c.* 249 B.C.

Chou En-lai (chō′ ĕn lī′), born 1898, Chinese communist leader.

chough (chŭf), *n.* an Old World crow, *Pyrrhocorax pyrrhocorax*, of a glossy black colour, with red feet and beak. [ME *choghe.* Cf. OE *cēo*]

chouse (chous), *v.,* **choused, chousing,** *n. Archaic.* —*v.t.* **1.** to swindle; cheat; dupe (often fol. by *of* or *out of*). —*n.* **2.** a swindle. **3.** a swindler. **4.** a dupe. [var. of *chiaus*, ? t. Turk.: m. *chāush* official messenger]

chow (chou), *n.* **1.** Also, **chow-chow.** one of a Chinese breed of dogs of medium size, with a thick, even coat of brown or black hair and a black tongue. **2.** *Colloq.* food. **3.** *Austral., N.Z., Slang.* (offensively) a Chinese.

chow-chow (chou′chou′), *n.* **1.** a Chinese mixed fruit preserve. **2.** a mixed pickle in mustard (orig. East Indian). **3.** chow (def. 1). [Pidgin English]

Chow
(20 in. high at the shoulder)

chowder (chou′də), *n. U.S.* a kind of soup or stew made of clams, fish, or vegetables, with potatoes, onions, other ingredients and seasoning. [prob. t. F: m. *chaudière* cauldron, g. LL *caldāria*, der. *caldus, calidus* hot]

chow mein (chou′mān′), a dish of noodles mixed with shredded vegetables such as carrots, cabbage, mushrooms, etc., and with small quantities of meat and/or poultry. [t. Chinese: fried flour]

choux pastry (shōō), a very light pastry made with eggs, water, flour, and butter, used in making éclairs, etc.; cream puff pastry.

Chr., Christian.

chrematistic (krē′mə tĭs′tĭk), *adj.* of or pertaining to the acquisition of wealth. [t. Gk: m. s. *chrēmatistikós*] —**chrematistics,** *n.*

Chrestien de Troyes (*Fr.* krĕ tyăN də trwȧ′), *c.* 1140–*c.* 1191, French poet. Also, **Chrétien de Troyes.**

chrestomathy (krĕs tŏm′ə thĭ), *n., pl.* **-thies.** a collection of selected passages, esp. from a foreign language. —**chrestomathic** (krĕs′tō măth′ĭk), *adj.* [t. Gk: m. s. *chrēstomátheia*, lit., useful learning]

chrism (krĭz′əm), *n. Eccles.* **1.** a consecrated oil used by certain churches in the rites of baptism, confirmation, etc. **2.** consecrated oil generally. **3.** a sacramental anointing; the rite of confirmation, esp. in the Greek Church. Also, **chrisom.** [learned respelling of ME *crisme*, OE *crisma*, t. L: m. *chrisma*, t. Gk: unguent, unction] —**chris′mal,** *adj.*

chrismatory (krĭz′mə tə rĭ), *n., pl.* **-ries.** *Eccles.* a receptacle for the chrism. [t. ML: m. s. *chrismatōrium*]

chrisom (krĭz′əm), *n. Eccles.* **1.** chrism. **2.** *Obs.* a white cloth or robe formerly put on a child at baptism, and also at burial if the child died soon after baptism. [var. of CHRISM]

Christ (krīst), *n. Bible.* **1.** the Anointed; the Messiah expected by the Jews. **2.** Jesus of Nazareth, as fulfilling this expectation. [learned respelling of ME and OE *Crist*, t. L: m. s. *Christus*, t. Gk: m. *Christós* anointed, trans. of Heb. *māshīah* anointed, MESSIAH]

Christadelphian (krĭs′tə dĕl′fĭ ən, -fyən), *n.* **1.** a member of a small religious body, founded in America in 1833, believing in selective immortality. —*adj.* **2.** of or belonging to this body.

Christchurch (krīst′chûch′), *n.* **1.** a town in England, in SW Hampshire. 26,326 (1961). **2.** a city in New Zealand, near the E coast of South Island. 237,600 (est. 1964).

christcross (krĭs′krŏs′), *n. Archaic.* the figure or mark of a cross. Also, **crisscross.** [lit., Christ's cross]

christcross-row (krĭs′krŏs rō′), *n. Archaic or Dial.* the alphabet. Also, **crisscross-row.**

christen (krĭs′ən), *v.t.* **1.** to receive into the Christian Church by baptism; baptize. **2.** to give a name to at baptism. **3.** to name and dedicate; give a name to; name. **4.** *Colloq.* to make use of for the first time. [ME *cristene(n)*, OE *cristnian* make Christian (by baptism), der. *cristen* Christian, t. L: m. s. *Christiānus*]

Christendom (krĭs′ən dəm), *n.* **1.** Christians collectively. **2.** the Christian world. [ME and OE *cristendōm*, f. *cristen* Christian + -DOM]

christening (krĭs′ə nĭng, krĭs′nĭng), *n.* the ceremony of baptism, esp. as accompanied by the giving of the name to the infant baptized.

Christhood (krīst′hŏŏd), *n.* the condition of being the Christ.

Christian (krĭs′chən), *adj.* **1.** pertaining to or derived from Jesus Christ or his teachings. **2.** believing in or belonging to the religion of Jesus Christ. **3.** pertaining to Christianity or Christians. **4.** exhibiting a spirit proper to a follower of Jesus Christ; Christlike. **5.** *Colloq.* decent or respectable. **6.** *Colloq.* humane; not brutal. —*n.* **7.** one who believes in the sanctity of Jesus Christ; an adherent of Christianity. **8.** one who exemplifies in his life the teachings of Christ. **9.** *Colloq.* a decent or presentable person. **10.** *Colloq., Dial.* a human being as distinguished from an animal. [t. L: s. *Christiānus*]

Christian Brothers, a Roman Catholic religious order of laymen, founded in 1684 for the education of the poor (in full, **Brothers of the Christian Schools**).

Christian Era, the period since the assumed date of the birth of Jesus, adopted in Christian countries.

Christiania (krĭs′tĭ ä′nyə), *n.* **1.** former name of **Oslo. 2.** Also, **Christiania turn** or **Christy.** *Skiing.* a type of turn originating in Norway in which the body is swung around from a crouching position, in order to turn the skis into a new direction or to stop quickly.

Christianity (krĭs′tĭ ăn′ĭ tĭ), *n., pl.* **-ties. 1.** the Christian religion. **2.** Christian beliefs or practices; Christian quality or character. **3.** a particular Christian religious system. **4.** the state of being a Christian.

Christianize (krĭs′chə nīz′), *v.,* **-nized, -nizing.** —*v.t.* **1.** to make Christian. **2.** to imbue with Christian principles. —*v.i.* **3.** to become Christian. Also, **Christianise.** —**Chris′tianiza′tion,** *n.* —**Chris′tianiz′er,** *n.*

Christian-like (krĭs′chən līk′), *adj.* like or befitting a Christian.

Christianly (krĭs′chən lĭ), *adj.* **1.** Christian-like. —*adv.* **2.** in a Christian manner.

Christian name, the name given one at baptism, as distinguished from the family name; the personal name; forename.

Christiansand (*Norw.* krēs tē ȧn sȧn′), *n.* Kristiansand.

Christian Science, a system of religious teaching, based on the Scriptures, the most notable application of which is the treatment of disease by mental and spiritual means, founded in America about 1866 by Mrs Mary Baker Eddy. —**Christian Scientist.**

Christie (krĭs′tĭ), *n.* **Agatha (Mary Clarissa),** born 1891, English thriller-writer.

Christina (krĭs tē′nə), *n.* 1626–89, queen of Sweden 1632–54 (daughter of Gustavus Adolphus).

Christless (krīst′lĭs), *adj.* without Christ or the spirit of Christ. —**Christ′lessness,** *n.*

Christlike (krīst′līk′), *adj.* like Christ; showing the spirit of Christ. —**Christ′like′ness,** *n.*

Christly (krīst′lĭ), *adj.* **1.** of or like Christ. **2.** Christlike. —**Christ′liness,** *n.*

Christmas (krĭs′məs), *n.* **1.** the annual festival of the Christian Church commemorating the birth of Jesus: celebrated on December 25th. **2.** December 25th (**Christmas Day**), now generally observed as an occasion for gifts, greetings, etc. **3.** the season when this occurs. [ME *cristmasse*, OE *Cristes mæsse* mass of Christ. See -MAS]

Christmas box, a gift of money, traditionally given at Christmas to tradesmen, esp. dustmen, milkmen, etc.

Christmas Eve, the day preceding Christmas Day.

Christmas Island, 1. an island in the Indian Ocean, 223 mi. S of Java. 3382 pop. (1964); 62 sq. mi. **2.** one of the Gilbert and Ellice Islands, in the central Pacific: largest atoll in the Pacific. 30 mi. across.

Christmas pudding, a rich steamed or boiled pudding containing raisins, currants, lemon rind, spices, etc., traditionally eaten at Christmas; plum pudding.

Christmas rose, one of a variety of perennial, evergreen, ranunculaceous plants of S Europe and W Asia, *Helleborus niger*, which produces large white or pinkish flowers in January and February.

Christmastide (krĭs′məs tīd′), *n.* the season of Christmas. [f. CHRISTMAS + TIDE[1] time]

Christmas tree, a tree, usually fir, hung with decorations at Christmas.

Christoff (krĭs′tŏf), *n.* **Boris,** born 1919, Bulgarian bass opera-singer.

Christology (krĭs tŏl′ə jĭ, krīs-), *n.* a branch of theology concerned with definitions of the nature of Christ.

Christophe (*Fr.* krēs tôf′), *n.* **Henri** (*Fr.* äɴ rē′), 1767–1820, Negro general and king of Haiti, 1811–20.

Christopher (krĭs′tə fə), *n.* **Saint,** died A.D. 250?, Christian martyr: protector of travellers.

Christ's Hospital, a public school, founded in 1552, formerly in London, now at Horsham for boys and Hertford for girls; Bluecoat School.

Christ's-thorn (krīsts′thôn′), *n.* either of two Old World rhamnaceous spring shrubs *Paliurus aculeatus* or *Zizyphus spina-christi*, supposed to have been used for Christ's crown of thorns.

Christy (krĭs′tĭ), *n.* Christiania (def. 2).

-chroic, an adjectival word element indicating colour (of skin, plants, etc.). Cf. **-chroous.** [t. Gk: m. s. *chrōikós* coloured]

chrom-, 1. a word element referring to colour, as in *chromic, chromite.* **2.** *Chem.* **a.** a word element referring to chromium, as in *chromic, bichromate.* **b.** a combining form in chemistry used to distinguish a coloured compound from its colourless form. Also, **chromo-.** [def. 1, see -CHROME; def. 2, see CHROMIUM]

-chrom-, a word element synonymous with **chrom-,** as in *polychromatic.*

chroma (krō′mə), *n.* **1.** purity of a colour, or its freedom from white or grey. **2.** intensity of distinctive hue; saturation of a colour. [t. Gk: colour]

chromat-, var. of **chromato-** before vowels.

chromate (krō′māt, -mĭt), *n.* *Chem.* a salt of chromic acid which contains the divalent radical CrO_4.

chromatic (krə măt′ĭk), *adj.* **1.** pertaining to colour or colours. **2.** *Music.* **a.** involving a modification of the normal scale by the use of accidentals. **b.** progressing by semitone to a note having the same letter name, as from C to C sharp. [t. L: s. *chrōmaticus*, t. Gk: m. *chrōmatikós* relating to colour (chiefly in musical sense)] —**chromat′ically,** *adv.*

chromatic aberration, *Optics.* (of a lens system) the variation of either the focal length or the magnification, with different wavelengths of light, characterized by prismatic colouring at the edges of, and colour distortion within, the optical image.

chromaticism (krō măt′ĭ sĭz′əm), *n.* *Music.* the extending of the diatonic style of composition to include all the semitones of the scale.

chromatic notes, *Music.* notes outside the normal diatonic scale in which the piece or passage is written.

chromatics (krə măt′ĭks), *n.* the science of colours. Also, **chromatology** (krō′mə tŏl′ə jĭ). —**chromatist** (krō′mə tĭst), *n.*

chromatic scale, *Music.* a scale progressing entirely by semitones. See illus. under **scale.**

chromatid (krō′mə tĭd), *n.* *Biol.* one of two identical chromosomal strands into which a chromosome splits longitudinally preparatory to cell division.

chromatin (krō′mə tĭn), *n.* *Biol.* that portion of the animal or plant cell nucleus which readily takes on stains. See diag. under **cell.** [f. CHROMAT- + -IN[2]]

chromato-, 1. a word element referring to colour. **2.** a word element meaning 'chromatin'. [t. Gk, comb. form of *chrôma* colour]

chromatogram (krō′mə tə grăm′, krō măt′ə-), *n.* *Chem.* **1.** the column or paper strip on which some or all the constituents of a mixture have been adsorbed in column or paper chromatography. **2.** a graphical representation of the detector response, either against time or volume of carrier gas, in gas chromatography.

chromatography (krō′mə tŏg′rə fĭ), *n.* *Chem.* **1.** the separation of mixtures into their constituents by preferential adsorption by a solid such as a column of silica (**column chromatography**). **2.** gas chromatography. **3.** paper chromatography. [f. CHROMATO- + -GRAPHY] —**chromatographic** (krō′mə tə grăf′ĭk), *adj.*

chromatolysis (krō′mə tŏl′ĭ sĭs), *n.* *Biol., Pathol.* the dissolution and disintegration of chromatin.

chromatophore (krō′mə tə fô′), *n.* **1.** *Zool.* **a.** a pigmented body or cell, as one of those which through contraction and expansion produce a temporary colour in cuttlefishes, etc. **b.** a coloured mass of protoplasm. **2.** *Bot.* one of the plastids in plant cells. —**chromatophoric** (krō′mə tə fô′rĭk, -fŏ′rĭk), *adj.*

chrome (krōm), *n., v.,* **chromed, chroming.** —*n.* **1.** chromium, esp. as a source of various pigments, as chrome yellow and chrome green. **2.** *Dyeing.* the dichromate of potassium or sodium. —*v.t.* **3.** *Dyeing.* to subject to a bath of dichromate of potassium or sodium. [t. F, t. Gk: m. *chrôma* colour]

-chrome, a word element meaning 'colour', as in *polychrome.* [t. Gk: m. *chrôma*]

chrome alum, *Chem.* a dark violet double sulphate of chromium and potassium, $KCr(SO_4)_2.12H_2O$, crystallizing like common alum, and used in dyeing.

chrome green, the permanent green colour made from chromic oxide, or any similar pigment made largely from chromic oxide, employed in printing textiles, etc.; Guignet's green.

chrome red, a bright red pigment, $PbO.PbCrO_4$, consisting of the basic chromate of lead.

chrome steel, steel of great hardness and strength, containing chromium, carbon, and other elements. Also, **chromium steel.**

chrome yellow, a yellow or orange pigment, $PbCrO_4$, consisting of lead chromate.

chromic (krō′mĭk), *adj. Chem.* of or containing chromium, esp. in the trivalent state.

chromic acid, *Chem.* a hypothetical acid, H_2CrO_4, which exists only in solution and forms chromates.

chromite (krō′mīt), *n.* **1.** *Chem.* a salt of chromous acid. **2.** a common mineral, iron magnesium chromite, $(Fe, Mg)Cr_2O_4$: the principal ore of chromium. Also, **chrome iron ore.**

chromium (krō′myəm), *n. Chem.* a lustrous, hard, brittle metallic element occurring in compounds, which are used for making pigments in photography, to harden gelatine, as a mordant, etc.; also used in corrosion-resisting chromium plating. *Symbol:* Cr; *at. wt:* 51·996; *at. no.:* 24; *sp. gr.:* 7·1. [f. Gk *chrôm(a)* colour + -IUM]

chromium plating, a thin film of chromium deposited by electrolysis on other metals to give them corrosion resistance.

chromium steel, chrome steel.

chromo (krō′mō), *n., pl.* **-mos.** chromolithograph.

chromo-, var. of **chrom-,** used before consonants, as in **chromogen.**

chromogen (krō′mə jən), *n.* **1.** *Chem.* any substance found in organic fluids which forms coloured compounds when oxidized. **2.** *Dyeing.* a coloured compound which, though not a dye itself, can be converted into a dye.

chromogenic (krō′mə jĕn′ĭk), *adj.* **1.** producing colour. **2.** pertaining to chromogen or a chromogen. **3.** (of bacteria) forming some characteristic colour or pigment, usually valuable in identification.

chromolithograph (krō′mō lĭth′ə grăf′, -gräf′), *n.* a picture produced by chromolithography.

chromolithography (krō′mō lĭ thŏg′rə fĭ), *n.* the process of lithographing in colours. **—chromolithographer** (krō′mō lĭ thŏg′rə fə), *n.* **—chro′molith′ograph′ic,** *adj.*

chromomere (krō′mə mĭə′), *n. Biol.* one of the chromatin granules of a chromosome.

chromophore (krō′mə fô′), *n. Chem.* **1.** any chemical group which produces colour in a compound, as the azo group $-N=N-$. **2.** the structural layout of atoms which is found in many coloured organic compounds.

chromoplasm (krō′mə plăz′əm), *n. Biol.* chromatin.

chromoplast (krō′mə plăst′), *n. Bot.* a plastid, or specialized mass of protoplasm, containing colouring matter other than chlorophyll.

chromoprotein (krō′mō prō′tēn), *n. Biochem.* any coloured protein, as haemoglobin, chlorophyll, etc.

chromosome (krō′mə sōm′), *n. Biol.* any of several threadlike, rodlike, or beadlike bodies which contain the chromatin during the meiotic and the mitotic processes. [f. CHROMO- + -SOME[3]] **—chro′moso′mal,** *adj.*

chromosome number, *Biol.* the characteristic number of chromosomes for each biological species. In sex cells this number is haploid; in fertilized eggs it is diploid, one half coming from the egg, one half from the sperm. Cf. **polyploid.**

chromosphere (krō′mə sfĭə′), *n. Astron.* **1.** a scarlet, gaseous envelope surrounding the sun outside the photosphere, from which enormous masses of hydrogen and other gases are erupted. **2.** a gaseous envelope surrounding a star. **—chromospheric** (krō′mə sfĕ′rĭk), *adj.*

chromous (krō′məs), *adj. Chem.* containing divalent chromium.

chromyl (krō′mĭl, -mēl), *adj. Chem.* containing the divalent radical CrO_2.

chron-, a word element meaning 'time', as in *chronaxie.* Also, **chrono-.** [t. Gk, comb. form of *chrónos*]

Chron., *Bible.* Chronicles.

chron., **1.** chronological. **2.** chronology.

chronaxie (krō′năk sĭ), *n. Physiol.* the minimum time that a current of twice the threshold strength (that value below which no excitation occurs) must flow in order to excite a tissue. Also, **chronaxy.** [f. CHRON- + m. Gk *axía* value]

chronic (krŏn′ĭk), *adj.* **1.** inveterate; constant: *a chronic smoker.* **2.** continuing a long time: *chronic civil war.* **3.** having long had a disease, habit, or the like: *a chronic invalid.* **4.** (of disease) long-continued (opposed to *acute*). **5.** *Colloq.* very bad; deplorable. Also, **chron′ical.** [t. L: s. *chronicus,* t. Gk: m. *chronikós* concerning time] **—chron′ically,** *adv.* **—Syn. 1.** habitual, confirmed, hardened.

chronicle (krŏn′ĭ kl), *n., v.,* **-cled, -cling.** —*n.* **1.** a record of events in the order of time; a history. —*v.t.* **2.** to record in or as in a chronicle. [ME, t. AF, var. of OF *cronique,* t. ML: m. *chronica,* t. Gk: m. *chroniká* annals, neut. pl.] **—chron′icler,** *n.*

Chronicles (krŏn′ĭ klz), *n.* two historical books of the Old Testament, following Kings.

chrono-, var. of **chron-,** used before consonants, as in *chronogram.*

chronogram (krŏn′ə grăm′), *n.* **1.** an inscription or the like in which certain letters, usually distinguished from the others, express by their values as Roman numerals a date or epoch. **2.** a record made by a chronograph. **—chronogrammatic** (krŏn′ō grə măt′ĭk), *adj.*

chronograph (krŏn′ə grăf′, -gräf′), *n.* a clock-driven instrument for recording the exact instant of occurrences, or for measuring small intervals of time. **—chron′ograph′ic,** *adj.*

chronological (krŏn′ə lŏj′ĭ kl), *adj.* **1.** arranged in the order of time: *chronological tables.* **2.** pertaining to or in accordance with chronology: *chronological character.* Also, **chron′olog′ic. —chron′olog′ically,** *adv.*

chronologist (krə nŏl′ə jĭst), *n.* one versed in chronology. Also, **chronol′oger.**

chronology (krə nŏl′ə jĭ), *n., pl.* **-gies. 1.** a particular statement of the supposed or accepted order of past events. **2.** the science of arranging time in periods and ascertaining the dates and historical order of past events.

chronometer (krə nŏm′ĭ tə), *n.* a timekeeper with special mechanism for ensuring accuracy, for use in determining longitude at sea or for any purpose where very exact measurement of time is required. **—chronometric** (krŏn′ə mĕt′rĭk), **chron′omet′rical,** *adj.* **—chron′omet′rically,** *adv.*

chronometry (krə nŏm′ĭ trĭ), *n.* **1.** the art of measuring time accurately. **2.** the measuring of time by periods or divisions.

chronopher (krŏn′ə fə), *n. Radio.* an electrical apparatus for broadcasting time signals.

chronoscope (krŏn′ə skōp′), *n.* an instrument for measuring accurately very small intervals of time, as in determining the velocity of projectiles.

chronotron (krŏn′ə trŏn′), *n. Physics.* an electronic device for measuring the time interval between two events.

-chroous, -chroic. [suffix f. s. Gk *chróa* surface, colour + -OUS]

chrysalid (krĭs′ə lĭd), *Entomol.* —*n.* **1.** a chrysalis. —*adj.* **2.** of a chrysalis.

chrysalis (krĭs′ə lĭs), *n., pl.* **chrysalises, chrysalids, chrysalides** (krĭ săl′ĭ dēz′). the hard-shelled pupa of a moth or butterfly; an obtected pupa. [t. L: m. *chrȳsallis,* t. Gk: gold-coloured sheath of butterflies]

Chrysalis of swallowtail butterfly

chrysanthemum (krĭ săn′thə məm), *n.* **1.** any of the perennial composite plants constituting the genus *Chrysanthemum,* as *C. leucanthemum,* the oxeye daisy. **2.** any of many cultivated varieties of *C. morifolium,* a native of China, and of other species of *Chrysanthemum,* notable for the diversity of colour and size of their autumnal flowers. **3.** the flower of any such plant. [t. L, t. Gk: m. *chrȳsánthemon,* lit., golden flower]

Chryseis (krĭ sē′ĭs), *n. Gk Legend.* (in the *Iliad*) the beautiful daughter of Chryses, a priest of Apollo. She was captured and given to Agamemnon.

chryselephantine (krĭs′ĕl ĭ făn′tĭn), *adj.* overlaid with gold and ivory (used in describing objects of ancient Greece). [t. Gk: m. s. *chrȳselephántinos*]

chrysene (krī′sēn), *n. Chem.* a hydrocarbon, $C_{18}H_{12}$, which occurs in coal tar.

chrysoberyl (krĭs′ə bĕ′rĭl), *n.* a mineral, beryllium aluminate, $BeAl_2O_4$, occurring in green or yellow crystals, sometimes used as a gem. [t. L: m. s. *chrȳsobēryllus,* t. Gk: m. *chrȳsobḗryllos*]

chrysolite (krĭs′ə līt′), *n.* **1.** olivine. **2.** *Colloq.* yellow chrysoberyl. [ME *crisolite,* t. ML: m. *crīsolitus,* for L *chrȳsolithos,* t. Gk: a bright yellow stone (prob. topaz)]

chrysoprase (krĭs′ə prāz′), *n.* a nickel-stained, apple green chalcedony, much used in jewellery. [t. L: m. s. *chrȳsoprasus,* t. Gk: m. *chrȳsóprasos,* lit., gold leek; r. ME *crisopace,* t. OF]

Chrysostom (krĭs′əs təm), *n.* **Saint John,** A.D. 347?–407, archbishop of Constantinople.

chrysotile (krĭs′ə tĭl), *n.* *Mineral.* a fibrous variety of serpentine.

chthonian (thō′nyən), *adj.* *Chiefly Gk Myth.* dwelling in the earth; pertaining to the deities or spirits of the underworld. [f. s. Gk *chthónios* in the earth + -AN]

c.h.u., centigrade heat unit.

chub (chŭb), *n., pl.* **chubs,** (*esp. collectively*) **chub. 1.** a common freshwater fish, *Leuciscus cephalus,* of Europe, with a thick fusiform body. **2.** any of several allied fishes, as the *Semotilus atromaculatus* of America. **3.** any of several unrelated American fishes, esp. the tautog of the Atlantic and the deep-water whitefishes (*Coregonidae*) of the Great Lakes. [ME *chubbe*]

chubby (chŭb′ĭ), *adj.,* **-bier, -biest.** round and plump: *a chubby face, chubby cheeks.*

chuck[1] (chŭk), *v.t.* **1.** to pat or tap lightly, as under the chin. **2.** to throw with a quick motion, usually a short distance. **3.** *Slang.* to eject (fol. by *out*): *they chucked him out of the nightclub.* **4.** *Slang.* to resign from: *he's chucked his job.* **5. chuck it,** *Slang.* stop it. **6. chuck one's hand in,** to give up; refuse to go on. **7. chuck one's weight about,** to be overbearing; interfere forcefully and unwelcomely. —*n.* **8.** a light pat or tap, as under the chin. **9.** a toss; a short throw. **10.** *Slang.* dismissal. [prob. imit., but cf. F *choquer* knock]

chuck[2] (chŭk), *n.* **1.** Also, **chuck steak.** the cut of beef between the neck and the shoulder-blade. **2.** a block or log used as a chock. **3.** *Mach.* a mechanical device for holding tools or work in a machine: *lathe chuck.* [var. of CHOCK]

Simple chuck[2] (def. 3)

chuck[3] (chŭk), *v.i., v.t.* **1.** to cluck. —*n.* **2.** a clucking sound. **3.** *Archaic or Dial.* a term of endearment. [imit.]

chucker-out (chŭk′ər out′), *n.* *Slang.* one employed at a place of public entertainment to eject undesirable persons.

chuck-full (chŭk′fo͝ol′), *adj.* chock-full.

chuckle (chŭk′l), *v.,* **chuckled, chuckling,** *n.* —*v.i.* **1.** to laugh in a soft, amused manner, usually with satisfaction. **2.** to laugh to oneself. **3.** to cluck, as a fowl. —*n.* **4.** a soft, amused laugh, usually with satisfaction. **5.** *Obs.* the call of a hen to her young; a cluck. [freq. of CHUCK[3]] —**chuck′ler,** *n.* —**Syn. 4.** See **laugh.**

chucklehead (chŭk′l hĕd′), *n.* *Colloq.* a blockhead; fool. —**chuck′lehead′ed,** *adj.* —**chuck′lehead′edness,** *n.*

chuck steak, chuck[2] (def. 1).

chuck wagon, *Western U.S.* a wagon carrying provisions, stoves, etc., for cowboys, harvest hands, etc.

chuckwalla (chŭk′wŏl′ə), *n.* a fat-bodied iguanid lizard, *Sauromalus obesus,* found commonly in the south-western deserts of the U.S. [t. Mex. Sp.: m. *chacahuala*]

chuddar (chŭd′ə), *n.* a kind of fine, plain-coloured woollen shawl made in India. Also, **chuddah, chudder.** [t. Hind.: m. *chadar* square piece of cloth]

Chudskoe (*Russ.* cho͞ot skô′yə), *n.* a lake in the W Soviet Union in Europe, on the E boundary of the Estonian Republic. 93 mi. long; 356 sq. mi. Estonian, **Peipsi.** Formerly, **Peipus.**

chufa (cho͞o′fə), *n.* a perennial cyperaceous plant, *Cyperus esculentus,* grown in warm regions for its edible tubers. [t. Sp.]

chuff (chŭf), *adj.* *Obs.* fat-cheeked; chubby. [adj. use of obs. *chuff,* n., muzzle]

chuffed (chŭft), *adj.* *Slang.* pleased; delighted.

chug (chŭg), *n., v.,* **chugged, chugging.** —*n.* **1.** a short, dull explosive sound: *the steady chug of an engine.* —*v.i.* **2.** to make this sound. **3.** to move while making this sound: *the train chugged along.* [imit.]

Chu-Kiang (cho͞o′kyăng′), *n.* a river in SE China, forming a large estuary below Canton. ab. 100 mi. Also, **Canton River, Pearl River.**

chukker (chŭk′ə), *n.* *Polo.* one of the periods of play. Also, **chuk′ka.** [t. Hind.: m. *chakar*]

chum (chŭm), *n., v.,* **chummed, chumming.** —*n.* **1.** an intimate friend or companion: *boyhood chums.* **2.** a room-mate, as at college. —*v.i.* **3.** to associate intimately. **4.** to share the same room or rooms with another. [orig. uncert.]

chummy (chŭm′ĭ), *adj.,* **-mier, -miest.** intimate; sociable. —**chum′mily,** *adv.*

chump (chŭmp), *n.* **1.** *Colloq.* a blockhead or dolt. **2.** a short thick piece of wood. **3.** the thick blunt end of anything. **4.** *Slang.* the head. —**chump′ish,** *adj.*

chump chop, a chop, usually of mutton, lamb, or pork, cut from the tail end of the loin. Also, **loin chop.**

Chungjin (chŭng′jĭn′), *n.* a seaport in NE North Korea. 200,000 (est. 1963). Also, **Chongjin.**

Chungking (cho͝ong′kĭng′), *n.* a city in China, on the Yangtse, in Szechwan province. 2,165,000 (est. 1958).

chunk (chŭngk), *n.* **1.** a thick mass or lump of anything: *a chunk of bread.* **2.** *Colloq.* a thickset and strong person. **3.** *Colloq.* a strong and stoutly built horse or other animal. [nasalized var. of CHUCK[2], n.]

chunky (chŭng′kĭ), *adj.,* **-kier, -kiest. 1.** thick or stout; thickset; stocky. **2.** in a chunk or chunks. **3.** knitted in very thick wool: *a chunky sweater.* —**chunk′iness,** *n.*

Chur (*Ger.* ko͞or), *n.* a town in E Switzerland, capital of Grisons canton. 28,400 (est. 1966).

church (chûch), *n.* **1.** an edifice for public Christian worship. **2.** public worship of God in a church; church service. **3.** (*cap.*) the whole body of Christian believers. **4.** (*cap.*) any division of this body professing the same creed and acknowledging the same ecclesiastical authority; a Christian denomination: *the Methodist Church.* **5.** (*cap.*) that part of the whole Christian body, or of a particular denomination, belonging to the same city, country, nation, etc. **6.** a body of Christians worshipping in a particular building or constituting one congregation. **7.** the ecclesiastical organization or power as distinguished from the state. **8.** the clerical profession. **9.** a place of public worship of a non-Christian religion. **10.** (*sometimes cap.*) any non-Christian religious society, organization, or congregation: *the Jewish Church.* —*v.t.* **11.** to conduct or bring to church, esp. for special services. **12.** to perform a church service of thanksgiving for (a woman after childbirth). [ME *churche, chirche,* OE *cir(i)ce, cyrice* (c. G *Kirche*), ult. t. Gk: m. *kȳriakón* (*dôma*) Lord's (house)]

Church Army, a Church of England organization founded in 1882 on the pattern of the Salvation Army to assist the clergy in parochial work at a practical level.

Church Assembly, a consultative council of the Church of England established in 1919 and elected every five years. It debates the practical application and effects of higher decision.

church commissioner, a member of a body of trustees charged with the care of the finances of the Church of England, and the administration of its investments and properties.

churchgoer (chûch′gō′ə), *n.* one who attends church services. —**church′go′ing,** *n., adj.*

Churchill (chû′chĭl), *n.* **1. John.** See **Marlborough, Duke of. 2. Lord Randolph,** 1849–95, British statesman (father of Winston Churchill). **3. Sir Winston (Leonard Spencer),** 1874–1965, British statesman and writer: prime minister 1940–45 and 1951–55. **4.** a river in Canada, flowing from E Saskatchewan NE through Manitoba to Hudson Bay. ab. 1000 mi. **5.** a seaport and railway terminus on Hudson Bay at the mouth of this river.

churchless (chûch′lĭs), *adj.* **1.** without a church. **2.** not belonging to or attending any church.

churchlike (chûch′līk′), *adj.* resembling, or appropriate to, a church: *churchlike silence.*

churchly (chûch′lĭ), *adj.* of or appropriate for the church or a church; ecclesiastical. [OE *ciriclic*; f. CHURCH + -LY] —**church′liness,** *n.*

churchman (chûch′mən), *n., pl.* **-men. 1.** an ecclesiastic; a clergyman. **2.** an adherent or active supporter of a church. **3.** a member of the established church. —**church′manly,** *adj.* —**church′manship′,** *n.*

Church of Christ, Scientist, (official name of) Christian Science.

Church of England, the established Church in England, Catholic in faith and order but incorporating Protestant features, having the monarch as head and governed under Parliament by chambers of representatives drawn from the clergy and from the laity.

Church of Jesus Christ of Latter-day Saints, (official name of) the Mormon Church.

Church of Rome, Roman Catholic Church.

Church of Scotland, the established Church in Scotland, Presbyterian in constitution, and Calvinist in doctrine.

church parade, a parade of servicemen or scouts, guides, etc., before a church service.

church text, *Print.* Old English (def. 2).

churchward (chûch′wəd), *adj.* **1.** directed towards the church. —*adv.* **2.** churchwards.

churchwards (chûch′wədz), *adv.* towards the church. Also, **churchward.**

churchwarden (chûch′wô′dn), *n.* **1.** *C. of E.* a lay officer who looks after the secular affairs of the church, and who, in England, is the legal representative of the parish. **2.** *Colloq.* a clay tobacco pipe with a very long stem.

churchwoman (chûch′wo͝om′ən), *n., pl.* **-women.** a female member of a church, esp. of an Anglican church.

churchy (chû′chĭ), *adj.* obtrusively religious.

churchyard (chûch′yäd′), *n.* the yard or ground adjoining a church, often used as a graveyard.

churl (chûl), *n.* **1.** a peasant; a rustic. **2.** a rude, boorish, or surly person. **3.** a niggard; miser. **4.** *Eng. Hist.* a freeman of the lowest rank. [ME; OE *ceorl* freeman of the lowest rank, c. G *Kerl.* Cf. CARL]

churlish (chûʹlĭsh), *adj.* **1.** of a churl or churls. **2.** like a churl; boorish; rude; surly. **3.** niggardly; sordid. **4.** difficult to work or deal with, as soil. —**churlʹishly,** *adv.* —**churlʹishness,** *n.*

churn (chûn), *n.* **1.** a vessel or machine in which cream or milk is agitated to make butter. **2.** any of various similar vessels or machines. **3.** a large metal container for milk. —*v.t.* **4.** to stir or agitate in order to make into butter: *to churn cream.* **5.** to make by the agitation of cream: *to churn butter.* **6.** to shake or agitate with violence or continued motion. —*v.i.* **7.** to operate a churn. **8.** to move in agitation, as a liquid or any loose matter: *leaves churning.* [ME *chyrne,* OE *cyrin,* c. Icel. *kirna* tub, pail] —**churnʹer,** *n.*

churning (chûʹnĭng), *n.* **1.** the act of one that churns. **2.** the butter made at any one time.

churr (chû), *v.i., n.* chirr. [? var. of CHIRR]

chute[1] (shōōt), *n.* **1.** a channel, trough, tube, shaft, etc., for conveying water, grain, coal, etc., to a lower level; a shoot. **2.** a waterfall; a steep descent, as in a river; a rapid. **3.** an inclined board, with sides, down which a swimmer may slide into the water. **4.** a parachute. [b. F *chute* a fall (b. OF *cheue* and OE *cheoite,* both der. OF *cheoir* fall, g. L *cadere*) and E SHOOT]

chute[2] (shōōt), *n.* a steep slope, as for tobogganing. [Frenchified spelling of d. E *shoot, shute,* ME *shote* steep slope, akin to SHOOT v.]

Chu Teh (chōōʹtāʹ), born 1886, former leader of Chinese Communist army.

chutney (chŭtʹnĭ), *n., pl.* **-neys.** a sauce or relish of Indian origin compounded of both sweet and sour ingredients (fruits, herbs, etc.) with spices and other seasoning. Also, **chutnee.** [t. Hind.: m. *chatnī*]

chylaceous (kī lāʹshəs), *adj.* of or resembling chyle.

chyle (kīl), *n.* a milky fluid containing emulsified fat and other products of digestion, formed from the chyme in the small intestine and conveyed by the lacteals and the thoracic duct to the veins. [t. NL: m. s. *chȳlus,* t. Gk: m. *chȳlós* juice, chyle] —**chyʹlous,** *adj.*

chyme (kīm), *n.* the pulpy matter into which food is converted by gastric digestion. [t. L: m. s. *chȳmus,* t. Gk: m. *chȳmós* juice] —**chyʹmous,** *adj.*

chymistry (kĭmʹĭs trĭ), *n. Archaic.* chemistry. —**chymʹic,** *adj.* —**chymʹist,** *n.*

chymotrypsin (kīʹmō trĭpʹsĭn), *n. Biochem.* a proteolytic enzyme produced by the pancreas.

chymotrypsinogen (kīʹmō trĭp sĭnʹə jĭn), *n. Biochem.* the inactive precursor of chymotrypsin.

Cia., (Sp. *Compañía*) Company.

C.I.A., Central Intelligence Agency.

ciao (chou), *interj. Italian Colloq.* **1.** goodbye. **2.** hello. [It., alter. of *schiavo,* at your service]

Cibber (sĭbʹə), *n.* **Colley** (kŏlʹĭ), 1671–1757, English actor and dramatist.

Ciborium (def. 2)

ciborium (sĭ bôʹrĭ əm), *n., pl.* **-boria** (-bôʹrĭ ə). **1.** a permanent canopy placed over an altar; baldachin. **2.** any vessel designed to contain the consecrated bread or sacred wafers for the Eucharist. [t. ML: canopy, in L drinking cup, t. Gk: m. *kibṓrion* cup, seed vessel of the Egyptian bean]

cicada (sĭ käʹdə), *n., pl.* **-dae** (-dē), **-das.** any insect of the family *Cicadidae,* which comprises large homopterous insects noted for the shrill sound produced by the male by means of vibrating membranes or drums on the underside of the abdomen. [t. L]

Imago of cicada, *Magicicada septendecim*

cicala (sĭ käʹlə; *It.* chē käʹlä), *n., pl.* **-le** (*It.* -lĕ). cicada. [t. It. or L]

cicatricle (sĭkʹə trĭkʹl), *n.* **1.** *Embryol.* the small blastodisc on the yolk of an unincubated bird's egg. **2.** a cicatrix. [t. L: m. s. *cicātrīcula* a small scar]

cicatrix (sĭkʹə trĭks), *n., pl.* **cicatrices** (sĭkʹə trīʹsēz), **cicatrixes. 1.** the new tissue which forms over a wound or the like, and later contracts into a scar. **2.** *Bot.* the scar left by a fallen leaf, seed, etc. Also, **cicatrice** (sĭkʹə-trĭs). [t. L] —**cicatricial** (sĭkʹə trĭshʹəl), *adj.* —**cicatricose** (sĭkʹə trĭ kōsʹ), *adj.*

cicatrize (sĭkʹə trīzʹ), *v.,* **-trized, -trizing.** —*v.t.* **1.** to heal by inducing the formation of a cicatrix. —*v.i.* **2.** to become healed by the formation of a cicatrix. Also, **cicatrise.** —**cicʹatrizaʹtion,** *n.* —**cicʹatrizʹer,** *n.*

cicely (sĭsʹə lĭ), *n., pl.* **-lies.** a plant of the parsley family, *Myrrhis odorata* (the **sweet cicely**), grown for its pleasing smell and sometimes used as a potherb. [? t. L: m. s. *seselis,* t. Gk: kind of plant]

Cicero (sĭsʹə rōʹ), *n.* **Marcus Tullius** (mäʹkəs tōōʹlyəs), 106–43 B.C. Roman statesman, orator, and writer. Also, **Tully.**

cicerone (sĭsʹə rōʹnĭ, chĭchʹə-; *It.* chē chĕ rōʹnĕ), *n., pl.* **-ni** (*It.* -nē). a guide who shows and explains the antiquities, curiosities, etc., of a place. [t. It., t. L: abl. sing. of *Cicero* CICERO]

cichlid (sĭkʹlĭd), *n.* any of the *Cichlidae,* a family of spiny-rayed, freshwater fishes of South America, Africa, and southern Asia: often kept in home aquariums. [t. NL: s. *Cichlidae,* pl., der. Gk *kíchlē* kind of sea fish] —**cichloid** (sĭkʹloid), *n., adj.*

cicisbeo (chĭchʹĭz bāʹō; *It.* chē chēz bĕʹō), *n., pl.* **-bei** (*It.* -bĕʹē). a professed lover of a married woman. [t. It.]

C.I.D., Criminal Investigation Department.

Cid (sēd; *Sp.* thēd), *n.* **El (the)** (*'El Cid Campeador'*; *Rodrigo Díaz de Bivar*) 1040?–99, Spanish soldier and hero of the wars against the Moors. [t. Sp., t. Ar.: m. *sayyid* lord]

-cidal, adjective form of **-cide.** [f. -CIDE + -AL[1]]

-cide, a word element meaning 'killer' or 'act of killing'. [t. L: *-cīda* -killer and *-cīdium* act of killing; der. *caedere* to kill]

cider (sīʹdə), *n.* the expressed juice of apples (or formerly of some other fruit), used for drinking, either before fermentation (**sweet cider**) or after fermentation (**rough cider**), or for making applejack, vinegar, etc. Also, **cyder.** [ME *sidre,* t. OF, g. LL *sicera,* t. Gk: m. *síkera,* repr. Heb. *shēkār* strong drink]

cider-cup (sīʹdə kŭpʹ), *n.* a beverage made from sweetened cider and various flavourings.

ciderkin (sīʹdə kĭn), *n.* an inferior quality of cider. Also, **water cider.**

cider-press (sīʹdə prĕsʹ), *n.* a press for crushing apples for cider.

ci-devant (*Fr.* sē də väɴʹ), *adj. French.* former; late: *a ci-devant official.* [F: heretofore]

Cie, (F *Compagnie*) Company. Also, **cie.**

Cienfuegos (*Sp.* thyĕn fwĕʹgōs), *n.* a seaport in S Cuba. 99,530 (1960).

C.I.F., cost, insurance, and freight (included in the price quoted). Also, **c.i.f., c.f.i.**

cigar (sĭ gäʹ), *n.* a small, shaped roll of tobacco leaves prepared for smoking. [t. Sp.: m. *cigarro,* ? der. *cigarra* grasshopper, g. L *cicāla,* var. of *cicāda* CICADA]

cigar-cutter (sĭ gäʹkŭtʹə), *n.* an instrument for cutting the tips off cigars.

cigarette (sĭgʹə rĕtʹ), *n.* a roll of finely cut tobacco for smoking, usually enclosed in thin paper. [t. F, dim. of *cigare* CIGAR]

cigarette-holder (sĭgʹə rĕtʹhōlʹdə), *n.* a tubular mouthpiece, often having an ornate pattern, through which the smoke of a cigarette is drawn.

cilia (sĭlʹĭ ə), *n.pl., sing.* **cilium** (sĭlʹĭ əm). **1.** the eyelashes. **2.** *Zool.* short hairs on the surface of protozoans or of metazoan cells accomplishing locomotion or producing a current. **3.** *Bot.* minute, hairlike processes. [t. L, pl. of *cilium* eyelid, eyelash]

Flower with cilia

ciliary (sĭlʹyə rĭ), *adj.* **1.** denoting or pertaining to a delicate ring of tissue in the eye from which the lens is suspended by means of fine ligaments. See diag. under **eye. 2.** pertaining to cilia.

ciliate (sĭlʹĭ ĭt, -ātʹ), *n.* **1.** one of the *Ciliata,* a class of protozoans distinguished by the cilia on part or all of the body, among the most common of microscopic animals. —*adj.* **2.** Also, **cilʹiatʹed.** having cilia; fringed or surrounded with hairs.

cilice (sĭlʹĭs), *n.* **1.** a garment of haircloth; a hairshirt. **2.** haircloth. [t. F, t. L: m. s. *cilicium,* t. Gk: m. *kilíkion* coarse cloth made of (orig. Cilician) goat's hair; r. OE *cilic,* t. L (as above)]

Cilicia (sĭ lĭshʹĭ ə), *n.* an ancient country and Roman province in SE Asia Minor.

Cilician Gates (sĭ lĭshʹĭ ən), a narrow mountain pass in SE Asia Minor, leading from Cappadocia into Cilicia. Turkish, **Gülek Bogaz.**

ciliolate (sĭlʹĭ ə lĭt, -lātʹ), *adj.* furnished with minute cilia.

Cimabue (*It.* chē mä bōōʹĕ), *n.* **Giovanni** (*It.* jō vänʹnē), 1240?–1302?, Florentine painter.

Cimarron (sĭmʹə rōnʹ, sĭmʹə rōnʹ, -rŏnʹ), *n.* a river in the U.S. flowing from NE New Mexico E to the Arkansas river in Oklahoma. ab. 600 mi.

cimbalom (chĭmʹbə ləm), *n.* a Magyar dulcimer.

C.I. Mech. E., Companion of the Institute of Mechanical Engineers.

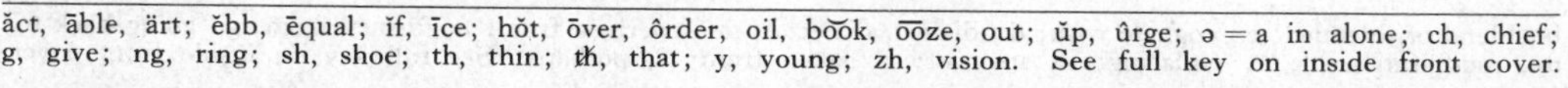

Ciment Fondu (*Fr.* sĕ mäN fôN dY′), *Trademark.* a rapid-hardening cement consisting mostly of calcium aluminate; bauxite cement.
cimex (sī′mĕks), *n., pl.* **cimices** (sĭm′ĭ sēz′). the bedbug (of the genus *Cimex*). [t. L: bug]
Cimmerian (sĭ mĭə′rĭ ən), *adj.* **1.** pertaining to or suggestive of a mythical western people said by Homer to dwell in perpetual darkness. **2.** very dark; gloomy. [f. s. L *Cimmerius* (t. Gk: m. *Kimmérios* (Odyssey XI 14)) + -AN]
Cimon (sī′mən), *n.* 507?–449 B.C., Athenian military and naval commander, and statesman: son of Miltiades.
C.-in-C., commander-in-chief.
cinch[1] (sĭnch), *Chiefly U.S.* —*n.* **1.** a strong girth for a saddle or pack. **2.** *Colloq.* a firm hold or tight grip. **3.** *Slang.* something certain or easy. —*v.t.* **4.** to gird with a cinch; gird or bind firmly. **5.** *Slang.* to seize on or make sure of. —*v.i.* **6.** to fix the saddle girth; tighten the cinch. [t. Sp.: m. *cincha*, g. L *cincta* girdle, der. L *cingere* gird]
cinch[2] (sĭnch), *n. Cards.* a variety of all fours. [? t. Sp.: m. *cinco* five]
cinchona (sĭng kō′nə), *n.* **1.** any of the rubiaceous trees or shrubs constituting the genus *Cinchona*, as *C. calisaya*, native in the Andes, cultivated there and in Java and India for their bark, which yields quinine and other alkaloids. **2.** the medicinal bark of such trees or shrubs; Peruvian bark. **3.** the drug prepared from this bark. [t. NL, named after the Countess of *Chinchón*, 1576–1639, wife of a Spanish viceroy of Peru] —**cinchonic** (sĭng-kŏn′ĭk), *adj.*
cinchonine (sĭng′kə nēn′), *n. Chem.* a colourless, crystalline alkaloid, $C_{19}H_{22}ON_2$, obtained from various species of the cinchona bark, used as an antiperiodic and quinine substitute.
cinchonism (sĭng′kə nĭz′əm), *n.* poisoning from cinchona or its alkaloids.
Cincinnati (sĭn′sĭ năt′ĭ), *n.* a city in the U.S., in SW Ohio, on the Ohio river. 502,550 (1960).
Cincinnatus (sĭn′sĭ nā′təs), *n.* **Lucius Quinctius** (lōō′-syəs kwĭngk′tĭ əs), 519?–439? B.C., Roman patriot. He was called from his farm to be dictator in 458 and 439 B.C. Each time he resigned his dictatorship and returned to his farm when the enemy was defeated.
cincinnus (sĭn sĭn′əs), *n.* a cymose inflorescence with short alternating internodes forming a coiled axis, as in forget-me-not or comfrey. See illus. under **inflorescence.**
cincture (sĭngk′chə), *n., v.,* **-tured, -turing.** —*n.* **1.** a belt or girdle. **2.** something surrounding or encompassing like a girdle; a surrounding border. **3.** the act of girding or encompassing. —*v.t.* **4.** to gird with or as with a cincture; encircle; encompass. [t. L: m. s. *cinctūra* girdle]
cinder (sĭn′də), *n.* **1.** a burnt-out or partially burnt piece of coal, wood, etc. **2.** (*pl.*) any residue of combustion; ashes. **3.** (*pl.*) *Geol.* coarse scoriae thrown out of volcanoes. —*v.t.* **4.** to reduce to cinders: *cindering flame.* [ME *cyndir, sindir*, OE *sinder* cinder, slag, c. G *Sinter*] —**cin′-dery,** *adj.*
Cinderella (sĭn′də rĕl′ə), *n.* **1.** the heroine of a well-known fairytale. **2.** any girl, esp. one of unrecognized beauty, who is forced to be a household drudge, or who, for the time being, is despised and oppressed.
Cinders (sĭn′dəz), *n. Colloq.* Cinderella.
cinder track, a path covered with small cinders, used in running races.
cine-, a word element meaning 'motion', used of films, etc., as in *cinecamera.* [comb. form f. Gk *kineîn* move]
cineaste (sĭn′ĭ ăst′), *n.* a devotee of the cinema. [t. F: m. *cinéaste*]
cinecamera (sĭn′ĭ kăm′ə rə, -kăm′rə), *n.* a camera used for taking moving films.
cinefilm (sĭn′ĭ fĭlm′), *n.* **1.** a type of film, usually 8 mm., used in a cinecamera, on which moving pictures are taken. **2.** the pictures so taken.
cinema (sĭn′ĭ mə), *n.* **1.** a theatre where films are shown. **2. the cinema,** films collectively. [short for CINEMATOGRAPH] —**cinematic** (sĭn′ĭ măt′ĭk), *adj.* —**cin′emat′-ically,** *adv.*
cinemagoer (sĭn′ĭ mə gō′ə), *n.* one who visits the cinema regularly. [modelled on THEATREGOER]
Cinemascope (sĭn′ĭ mə skōp′), *n. Trademark.* a film process using a single-lens camera or projector, an extra-wide screen, and a stereophonic arrangement of loud-speakers.
cinematize (sĭn′ĭ mə tīz′), *v.t., v.i.,* **-tized, -tizing.** cinematograph (def. 3). Also, **cinematise.**
cinematograph (sĭn′ĭ măt′ə grăf′, -gräf′), —*n.* **1.** a film projector. **2.** a film camera. —*v.t., v.i.* **3.** to take films (of). Also, **kinematograph.** [f. *cinemato-* (comb. form repr. Gk *kī́nēma* motion) + -GRAPH] —**cinematographer** (sĭn′ĭ mə tŏg′rə fə), *n.* —**cin′emat′ograph′ic,** *adj.* —**cin′ematog′raphy,** *n.*
cineol (sĭn′ĭ ōl′), *n. Chem.* a colourless liquid, $C_{10}H_{18}O$, a terpene ether found in eucalyptus and other essential oils and used in medicine; eucalyptol. Also, **cineole** (sĭn′ĭ ōl′). [t. NL: m. *oleum cinae* (reversed), oil of wormwood]
cine-projector (sĭn′ĭ prə jĕk′tə), *n.* a projector for cine-films.
Cinerama (sĭn′ə rä′mə), *n. Trademark.* a film process designed to produce a three-dimensional effect by using three cameras, set at different angles, to photograph separate overlapping images of each scene and project them on a large concave screen in conjunction with stereophonic sound.
cineraria (sĭn′ə rĕə′rĭ ə), *n.* any of various horticultural varieties of the asteraceous plant *Senecio cruentus*, a native of the Canary Islands, with heart-shaped leaves and clusters of flowers with white, blue, purple, red, or variegated rays. [t. NL, prop. fem. of L *cinerārius* pertaining to ashes (with reference to the soft white down on the leaves)]
cinerarium (sĭn′ə rĕə′rĭ əm), *n., pl.* **-raria** (-rĕə′rĭ ə). a place for depositing the ashes of the dead after cremation. [t. L] —**cinerary** (sĭn′ə rə rĭ), *adj.*
cinerator (sĭn′ə rā′tə), *n.* an incinerator.
cinereous (sĭ nĭə′rĭ əs), *adj.* **1.** in the state of ashes: *cinereous bodies.* **2.** resembling ashes. **3.** ashen; ash-coloured; greyish: *cinereous crow.* Also, **cineritious** (sĭn′ə rĭsh′əs). [t. L: m. *cinereus* ash-coloured]
cingulum (sĭng′gyŏŏ ləm), *n., pl.* **-la** (-lə). *Anat., Zool.* a belt, zone, or girdle-like part. [t. L: girdle] —**cingulate** (sĭng′gyŏŏ lĭt,-lāt′), **cin′gulat′ed,** *adj.*
Cinisello Balsamo (*It.* chē nē zĕl′lò bál′sá mò), a town in Italy, in Lombardy, near Milan. 60,188 (1966).
cinnabar (sĭn′ə bä′), *n.* **1.** a mineral, mercuric sulphide, occurring in red crystals or masses; the principal ore of mercury. It is very heavy (*sp. gr.* : 8·1). **2.** red mercuric sulphide, used as a pigment. **3.** bright red; vermilion. **4.** a large red European moth, *Hypocrita jacobaeae*, of the tiger moth (*Arctiidae*) family. [t. L: m. *cinnabaris*, t. Gk: m. *kinnábari*; of oriental orig.; r. ME *cynoper*, t. ML]
cinnamic (sĭ năm′ĭk), *adj.* of or obtained from cinnamon.
cinnamic acid, *Chem.* an unsaturated acid, $C_6H_5.CH.CH.COOH$, derived from cinnamon, balsams, etc.
cinnamon (sĭn′ə mən), *n.* **1.** the aromatic inner bark of any of several lauraceous trees of the genus *Cinnamomum* of the East Indies, etc., esp. **Ceylon cinnamon,** *C. zeylanicum*, much used as a spice, and **Saigon cinnamon,** *C. loureirii*, used in medicine as a cordial and carminative. **2.** a tree yielding cinnamon. **3.** any of various allied or similar trees. **4.** cassia bark. **5.** yellowish or reddish brown. [t. LL, t. Gk: m. *kínnamon*; r. ME *cynamome*, t. F: m. *cinnamome.* Ult. of Semitic orig.; cf. Heb. *qinnāmōn*]
cinnamon bear, the cinnamon-coloured variety of the black bear of North America, *Euarctos americanus.*
cinnamon stone, a light brown grossularite garnet.
cinque (sĭngk), *n.* the five at dice, cards, etc. [t. F; r. ME *cink*, t. OF, g. L *quinque* five]
cinquecentist (chĭng′kwĭ chĕn′tĭst), *n.* an Italian writer or artist of the 16th century.
cinquecento (chĭng′kwĭ chĕn′tō), *n.* the 16th century, with reference to Italy, esp. to the Italian art or literature of that period. [t. It.: five hundred, short for *mille cinquecento* one thousand five hundred]

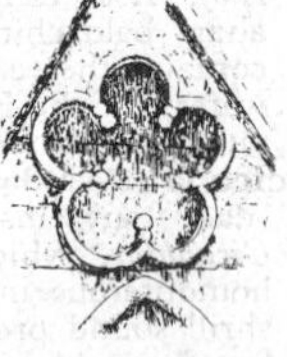
Cinquefoil (def. 2)

cinquefoil (sĭngk′foil′), *n.* **1.** any species of the rosaceous genus *Potentilla*, as the **creeping cinquefoil** (*P. reptans*) of Europe and the **silvery cinquefoil** (*P. argentea*) of North America. **2.** a decorative design or feature resembling the leaf of cinquefoil, as an architectural ornament or opening of a generally circular or rounded form divided into five lobes by cusps. **3.** *Her.* a five-leafed clover, used as a bearing. [ME *synkefoile*, through OF (unrecorded), g. L *quinquefolium*, f. *quinque* five + *folium* leaf]
Cinque Ports (sĭngk), an ancient association of maritime towns in Sussex and Kent: originally (1278) numbering five (Hastings, Romney, Hythe, Dover, and Sandwich) and later including Winchelsea, Rye, and several others, receiving special privileges for their part in the naval defence of England.
C.I.O., Congress of Industrial Organizations.
-cion, a suffix having the same function as **-tion,** as in *suspicion.* [t. L: s. *-cio*, f. *-c*, final vowel in verb stem, + *-io*, n. suffix. Cf. -SION, -TION]
cipher (sī′fə), *n.* **1.** an arithmetical symbol (0) which denotes nought, or no quantity or magnitude. **2.** any

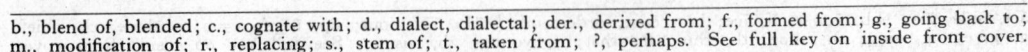

of the Arabic numerals or figures. **3.** Arabic numerical notation collectively. **4.** something of no value or importance. **5.** a person of no influence; a nonentity. **6.** a secret method of writing, as by a specially formed code of symbols. **7.** writing done by such a method. **8.** the key to a secret method of writing. **9.** a combination of letters, as the initials of a name, in one design; a monogram. **10.** *Music.* the mechanical failure of an organ pipe, causing continuous sounding. *—v.i.* **11.** to use figures or numerals arithmetically. **12.** (of an organ note) to sound continuously without being played. *—v.t.* **13.** to calculate numerically; figure. **14.** to write in, or as in, cipher. Also, **cypher.** [ME *siphre,* t. ML: m. *ciphra,* t. Ar.: m. *ṣifr,* lit., empty. Cf. ZERO]

cipolin (sĭp′ə lĭn), *n.* a variety of marble with alternate white and greenish zones and a laminated structure. Also, **cipollino** (*It.* chē pōl lē′nō). [t. F, t. It.: (m.) *cipollino* (so called from its layered structure), dim. of *cipolla* onion, g. L *cēpa*]

cir., (L *circa, circiter, circum*) about. Also, **circ.**

circa (sûr′kə), *prep., adv.* about (used esp. in approximate dates). *Abbrev.: c., c,* or *ca.* [t. L]

Circassia (sûr kăs′ĭ ə), *n.* a region NW of the Caucasus Mountains in the S Soviet Union in Europe, bordering on the Black Sea.

Circassian (sûr kăs′ĭ ən), *n.* **1.** a native or inhabitant of Circassia. **2.** a North Caucasian language. **3.** a light fabric originally made of mohair, now often of rayon.

Circe (sûr′sĭ), *n.* **1.** *Gk Legend.* the enchantress represented by Homer as turning the companions of Odysseus into swine by a magic drink. **2.** a dangerously or irresistibly fascinating woman. **—Circean** (sûr sē′ən), *adj.*

circinate (sûr′sĭ nāt′), *adj.* **1.** made round; ring-shaped. **2.** *Bot.* rolled up on the axis at the apex, as a leaf, etc. [t. L: m. s. *circinātus,* pp.] **—cir′cinate′ly,** *adv.*

Circinate fronds of a young fern

circle (sûr′kl), *n., v.,* **-cled, -cling.** *—n.* **1.** a closed plane curve which is at all points equidistant from a fixed point within it, called the centre. **2.** the portion of a plane bounded by such a curve. **3.** any circular object, formation, or arrangement. **4.** a ring; a circlet; crown. **5.** the ring of a circus. **6.** an upper section of seats in a theatre: *dress circle.* **7.** *Archaeol.* a ring of standing stones, usually originating in the Bronze Age and believed to have been used for ritual purposes. **8.** the area within which something acts, exerts influence, etc. **9.** *Hockey.* the semicircle in front of each goal into which the attacking player must have entered before shooting a goal; striking circle. **10.** a series ending where it began, and perpetually repeated: *the circle of the year.* **11.** *Logic.* an inconclusive form of reasoning in which unproved statements, or their equivalents, are used to prove each other; vicious circle. **12.** a complete series forming a connected whole; cycle: *the circle of the sciences.* **13.** a number of persons bound by a common tie; a coterie. **14.** an administrative division, esp. of a province. **15.** *Geog.* a parallel of latitude. **16.** *Astron.* **a.** the orbit of a heavenly body. **b.** an instrument for observing the transit of stars across the meridian of the observer. **17.** a sphere or orb. **18.** a ring of light in the sky; halo. *—v.t.* **19.** to enclose in a circle; surround: *the enemy circled the hill.* **20.** to move in a circle or circuit round: *he circled the house cautiously.* *—v.i.* **21.** to move in a circle. [t. L: m. s. *circulus,* dim. of *circus* circle, ring; r. ME *cercle,* t. OF] **—cir′cler,** *n.*

—**Syn.** 13. CIRCLE, CLUB, COTERIE, SET, SOCIETY are terms applied to more or less restricted social groups. A CIRCLE may be a pleasant little group meeting chiefly for conversation; in the plural it often suggests a whole section of society interested in one mode of life, occupation, etc.: *a sewing circle, a language circle, in theatrical circles.* CLUB implies an association with definite requirements for membership, fixed dues, and often a stated time of meeting: *an athletic club.* COTERIE suggests a little group closely and intimately associated because of great congeniality: *a literary coterie.* SET refers to a number of persons of similar background, upbringing, interests, etc., somewhat like a CLIQUE (see RING) but without disapproving connotations; it often implies wealth or interest in fashionable social activities: *the country club set.* A SOCIETY is a group associated to further common interests of a cultural or practical kind: *a humane society.*

circlet (sûr′klĭt), *n.* **1.** a small circle. **2.** a ring. **3.** a ring-shaped ornament, esp. for the head.

circling disease, a fatal infectious bacterial disease of cattle and sheep which damages the nervous system and often causes the afflicted animal to walk in circles.

circs (sûks), *n. Colloq.* circumstances.

circuit (sûr′kĭt), *n.* **1.** the act of going or moving round. **2.** a circular journey; a round. **3.** a roundabout journey or course. **4.** a periodical journey from place to place, to perform certain duties, as of judges to hold court or ministers to preach. **5.** the persons making such a journey. **6.** the route followed, places visited, or district covered by such a journey. **7.** the line going round or bounding any area or object; the distance about an area or object. **8.** the space within a bounding line. **9.** a number of theatres, cinemas, etc., under common control or visited in turn by the same actors, etc. **10.** *Elect.* **a.** the complete path of an electric current, including the generating apparatus or other source, or a distinct segment of the complete path. **b.** a more or less elaborately contrived arrangement of conductors, waveguides, electronic tubes, and other devices, for the investigation or utilization of electrical phenomena. **c.** the diagram of the connections of such apparatus. *—v.t.* **11.** to go or move round; make the circuit of. *—v.i.* **12.** to go or move in a circuit. [ME, t. L: s. *circuitus*]

circuit-breaker (sûr′kĭt brā′kə), *n. Elect.* a device for interrupting an electric circuit between separable contacts under normal or abnormal conditions.

circuitous (sə kyōō′ĭ təs), *adj.* roundabout; not direct: *they took a circuitous route to the house.* **—circu′itously,** *adv.* **—circu′itousness,** *n.*

circuit rider, *U.S.* a Methodist minister who rides from place to place to preach along a circuit.

circuitry (sûr′kĭ trĭ), *n.* any system of electrical circuits.

circuity (sə kyōō′ĭ tĭ), *n.* circuitous quality; roundabout character: *circuity of language or of a path.*

circular (sûr′kyŏŏ lə), *adj.* **1.** of or pertaining to a circle. **2.** having the form of a circle; round. **3.** moving in or forming a circle or a circuit. **4.** moving or occurring in a cycle or round. **5.** circuitous; roundabout; indirect. **6.** (of a letter, etc.) addressed to a number of persons or intended for general circulation. **7.** (of a velocity) required to maintain a body in a given circular orbit. *—n.* **8.** a letter, notice, advertisement, or statement for circulation among the general public for business or other purposes. [t. L: s. *circulāris,* der. L *circulus* circle; r. ME *circuler,* t. AF] **—circularity** (sûr′kyŏŏ lăr′ĭ tĭ), *n.* **—cir′cularly,** *adv.*

circularize (sûr′kyŏŏ lə rīz′), *v.t.,* **-rized, -rizing. 1.** to send circulars to. **2.** to circulate (a letter, pamphlet, or the like). **3.** to make circular. Also, **circularise. —cir′cularīza′tion,** *n.* **—cir′culariz′er,** *n.*

circular measure, the measurement of an angle in radians: 360 degrees = 2 pi radians; 1 radian = 57 degrees 17·7 minutes.

circular mil, a unit used principally for measuring the cross-sectional area of wires, being the area of a circle having the diameter of one mil.

circular saw, a saw consisting of a circular plate or disc with a toothed edge, which is rotated at high speed in machines for sawing logs, cutting timber, etc.

circular triangle, a triangle in which the sides are arcs of circles.

circulate (sûr′kyŏŏ lāt′), *v.,* **-lated, -lating.** *—v.i.* **1.** to move in a circle or circuit; move or pass through a circuit back to the starting point, as the blood in the body. **2.** to pass from place to place, from person to person, etc.; be disseminated or distributed. **3.** *Maths.* (of a decimal) to recur. *—v.t.* **4.** to cause to pass from place to place, person to person, etc.: *to circulate a rumour.* [t. L: m. s. *circulātus,* pp., made circular, gathered into a circle] **—cir′cula′tive,** *adj.* **—cir′cula′tor,** *n.* **—circulatory** (sûr′kyŏŏ lə tə rĭ, -lə trĭ), *adj.*

circulating capital, *Finance.* capital which has been used to acquire assets intended to be sold or resold at a profit (opposed to *fixed capital*).

circulating decimal, *Maths.* a recurring decimal.

circulating library, a commercially owned library which charges a fee for each book borrowed; subscription library.

circulating medium, 1. any coin or note passing, without endorsement, as a medium of exchange. **2.** such coins or notes collectively.

circulation (sûr′kyŏŏ lā′shən), *n.* **1.** the act of circulating or moving in a circle or circuit. **2.** the recurrent movement of the blood through the various vessels of the body. **3.** any similar circuit or passage, as of the sap in plants. **4.** the transmission or passage of anything from place to place, person to person, etc. **5.** the distribution of copies of a publication among readers. **6.** the number of copies of each issue of a newspaper, magazine, etc., distributed. **7.** coin, notes, bills, etc., in use as currency; currency.

circum-, a prefix referring to movement round or about motion on all sides, as in *circumvent, circumnavigate, circumference.* [t. L, prefix use of *circum,* adv. and prep., orig. acc. of *circus* circle, ring. See CIRCUS]

circumambient (sûr′kəm ăm′bĭ ənt), *adj.* surrounding; encompassing: *circumambient gloom.* **—cir′cumam′bience, cir′cumam′biency,** *n.*

circumambulate (sû′kəm ăm′byōō lāt′), *v.t., v.i.*, **-lated, -lating.** to walk or go about. —**cir′cumam′bula′tion,** *n.*

circumbendibus (sû′kəm bĕn′dĭ bōōs), *n.* (in humorous use) a roundabout way; a circumlocution.

circumcise (sû′kəm sīz′), *v.t.*, **-cised, -cising. 1.** to remove the foreskin of (males), esp. as a religious rite. **2.** to perform an analogous operation on (females). **3.** to purify spiritually. [ME *circumcise(n)*, t. L: m. s. *circumcīsus*, pp., cut around] —**cir′cumcis′er,** *n.*

circumcision (sû′kəm sĭzh′ən), *n.* **1.** the act or rite of circumcising. **2.** spiritual purification. **3. the circumcision,** the Jews, as the circumcised people of the Bible. **4.** (*cap.*) a church festival in honour of the circumcision of Jesus, observed on Jan. 1st. [ME *circumcisi(o)un*, t. L: m. s. *circumcisio*]

circumdenudation (sû′kəm dēn′yōō dā′shən), *n. Geog.* a process of erosion which leaves a hard rocky core exposed in the form of a mountain, etc.

circumference (sə kŭm′fə rəns), *n.* **1.** the outer boundary, esp. of a circular area. **2.** the length of such a boundary. **3.** the space within a bounding line. [t. L: m. s. *circumferentia*] —**circumferential** (sə kŭm′fə rĕn′shəl), *adj.*

circumflex (sû′kəm flĕks′), *adj.* **1.** denoting, or having a particular accent (ˆ, ˆ, ˜), indicating orig. a combination of rising and falling pitch (as in ancient Greek), later a long vowel (as in the French *bête*, earlier *beste*), quality of sound (as in phonetic notation), etc. **2.** bending or winding round. —*n.* **3.** the circumflex accent. —*v.t.* **4.** to bend around. [t. L: s. *circumflexus*, pp., bent round] —**circumflexion** (sû′kəm flĕk′shən), *n.*

circumfluent (sə kŭm′flōō ənt), *adj.* flowing round; encompassing: *two circumfluent rivers.* —**circum′fluence,** *n.*

circumfluous (sə kŭm′flōō əs), *adj.* **1.** flowing round; encompassing: *circumfluous tides.* **2.** surrounded by water. [t. L: m. *circumfluus* flowing round]

circumfuse (sû′kəm fyōōz′), *v.t.*, **-fused, -fusing. 1.** to pour round; diffuse. **2.** to surround as with a fluid; suffuse. [t. L: m. s. *circumfūsus*, pp., poured around] —**circumfusion** (sû′kəm fyōō′zhən), *n.*

circumjacent (sû′kəm jā′sənt), *adj.* lying round; surrounding: *the circumjacent parishes.*

circumlittoral (sû′kəm lĭt′ə rəl), *adj.* adjacent to the shoreline.

circumlocution (sû′kəm lə kyōō′ shən), *n.* **1.** a roundabout way of speaking; the use of too many words. **2.** a roundabout expression. [t. L: s. *circumlocūtio*] —**circumlocutory** (sû′kəm lŏk′yōō tə rĭ, -trĭ), *adj.*

circumlunar (sû′kəm lōō′nə), *adj.* around the moon: *circumlunar orbit.*

circumnavigate (sû′kəm năv′ĭ gāt′), *v.t.*, **-gated, -gating.** to sail round; make the circuit of by navigation: *he circumnavigated the world alone.* —**cir′cumnav′iga′tion,** *n.* —**cir′cumnav′iga′tor,** *n.*

circumnutate (sû′kəm nyōō′ tāt), *v.i.*, **-tated, -tating.** (of the apex of a stem or other growing part of a plant) to bend or move round in an irregular circular or elliptical path. —**cir′cumnuta′tion,** *n.*

circumpolar (sû′kəm pō′lə), *adj.* around one of the poles of the earth or of the heavens.

circumrotate (sû′kəm rō tāt′), *v.i.*, **-tated, -tating.** to rotate like a wheel.

circumscissile (sû′kəm sĭs′ĭl), *adj. Bot.* opening along a transverse circular line, as a seed vessel.

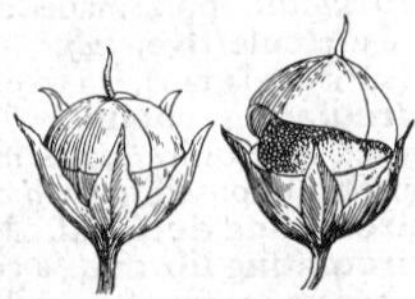

Circumscissile pod of pimpernel

circumscribe (sû′kəm skrīb′, sû′kəm skrīb′), *v.t.*, **-scribed, -scribing. 1.** to draw a line round; encircle; surround. **2.** to enclose within bounds; limit or confine, esp. narrowly. **3.** to mark off; define. **4.** *Geom.* **a.** to draw (a figure) round another figure so as to touch as many points as possible. **b.** (of a figure) to enclose (another figure) in this manner. [t. L: m. s. *circumscrībere* draw a line round, limit] —**cir′cumscrib′er,** *n.*

circumscription (sû′kəm skrĭp′shən), *n.* **1.** the act of circumscribing. **2.** circumscribed state; limitation. **3.** anything that circumscribes, surrounds, or encloses. **4.** periphery; outline. **5.** a circumscribed space. **6.** a circular inscription on a coin, seal, etc. **7.** *Archaic.* limitation of a meaning; definition. —**cir′cumscrip′tive,** *adj.*

circumsolar (sû′kəm sō′lə), *adj.* round the sun.

circumspect (sû′kəm spĕkt′), *adj.* **1.** watchful on all sides; cautious; prudent: *circumspect in behaviour.* **2.** well-considered: *circumspect ambition.* [late ME, t. L: s. *circumspectus*, pp., considerate, wary] —**cir′cumspect′ly,** *adv.* —**cir′cumspect′ness,** *n.*

circumspection (sû′kəm spĕk′shən), *n.* circumspect observation or action; caution; prudence.

circumspective (sû′kəm spĕk′tĭv), *adj.* given to or marked by circumspection; watchful; cautious: *a circumspective approach.*

circumstance (sû′kəm stəns), *n., v.*, **-stanced, -stancing.** —*n.* **1.** a condition, with respect to time, place, manner, agent, etc., which accompanies, determines, or modifies a fact or event. **2.** (*usually pl.*) the existing condition or state of affairs surrounding and affecting an agent: *forced by circumstances to do a thing.* **3.** an unessential accompaniment of any fact or event; a secondary or accessory matter; a minor detail. **4.** (*pl.*) the condition or state of a person with respect to material welfare: *a family in reduced circumstances.* **5.** an incident or occurrence: *his arrival was a fortunate circumstance.* **6.** detailed or circuitous narration; specification of particulars. **7.** *Archaic.* ceremonious accompaniment or display: *pomp and circumstance.* **8. in** or **under no circumstances,** never; regardless of events. **9. in** or **under the circumstances,** because of the conditions; such being the case. —*v.t.* **10.** to place in particular circumstances or relations. **11.** *Obs.* to furnish with details. **12.** *Obs.* to control or guide by circumstances. [ME, t. L: m. s. *circumstantia* surrounding condition] —**cir′cumstanced,** *adj.*

circumstantial (sû′kəm stăn′shəl), *adj.* **1.** of, pertaining to, or derived from circumstances: *circumstantial evidence.* **2.** of the nature of a circumstance or unessential accompaniment; secondary; incidental. **3.** dealing with or giving circumstances or details; detailed; particular. **4.** pertaining to conditions of material welfare: *circumstantial prosperity.* —**cir′cumstan′tially,** *adv.*

circumstantial evidence, proof of facts offered as evidence from which other facts are to be inferred (contrasted with *direct evidence*).

circumstantiality (sû′kəm stăn′shĭ ăl′ĭ tĭ), *n., pl.* **-ties. 1.** the quality of being circumstantial; minuteness; fullness of detail. **2.** a circumstance; a particular detail.

circumstantiate (sû′kəm stăn′shĭ āt′), *v.t.*, **-ated -ating. 1.** to set forth or support with circumstances or particulars. **2.** to describe fully or minutely. —**cir′cumstan′tia′tion,** *n.*

circumvallate (sû′kəm văl′āt), *adj., v.*, **-lated, -lating.** —*adj.* **1.** surrounded by, or as by, a rampart, etc. —*v.t.* **2.** to surround with, or as with, a rampart, etc. **3.** *Zool.* (of protozoa) to engulf (food) by surrounding it. [t. L: m. s. *circumvallātus*, pp., surrounded with a rampart] —**cir′cumvalla′tion,** *n.*

circumvent (sû′kəm vĕnt′), *v.t.* **1.** to surround or encompass as by strategem; entrap. **2.** to gain advantage over by artfulness or deception; outwit; overreach. **3.** to go round: *circumvent the bridge.* [t. L: s. *circumventus*, pp., surrounded] —**cir′cumvent′er, cir′cumven′tor,** *n.* —**cir′cumven′tion,** *n.* —**cir′cumven′tive,** *adj.*

circumvolution (sû′kəm və lōō′shən), *n.* **1.** the act of rolling or turning round. **2.** a single complete turn. **3.** a winding or folding about something. **4.** a fold so wound. **5.** a winding in a sinuous course; a sinuosity. **6.** roundabout course or procedure.

circumvolve (sû′kəm vŏlv′), *v.t., v.i.*, **-volved, -volving.** to revolve. [t. L: m. s. *circumvolvere* roll round]

circus (sû′kəs), *n.* **1.** a company of performers, animals, etc., esp. a travelling company. **2.** the performance itself. **3.** a circular arena surrounded by tiers of seats, for the exhibition of wild animals, acrobatic feats, etc. **4.** (in ancient Rome) a large, usually oblong, or oval, roofless enclosure, surrounded by tiers of seats rising one above another, for chariot races, public games, etc. **5.** anything like the Roman circus, as a natural amphitheatre, a circular range of houses as those built in the 18th century, etc. **6.** a flying circus. **7.** a place, originally circular, where several streets converge: *Piccadilly Circus.* **8.** uproar; a display of rowdy sport and behaviour. **9.** *Obs.* a circlet or ring. [t. L, t. Gk: m. *kírkos* ring]

Circus Maximus (măk′sĭ məs), the great Roman circus in the hollow between the Palatine and the Aventine.

ciré (sĭ′rā; *Fr.* sē rè′), *n.* **1.** a highly glazed surface produced on fabrics by subjecting them to certain heat treatments. **2.** a fabric having such a surface.

cirque (sûk), *n.* **1.** a circular space, esp. a natural amphitheatre, as in mountains. **2.** *Poetic.* a circle or ring of any kind. **3.** a circus. [t. F, t. L: m. s. *circus*]

cirrate (sĭ′rāt), *adj.* having cirri. [t. L: m. s. *cirrātus* curled, der. *cirrus* curl]

cirrhosis (sĭ rō′sĭs), *n. Pathol.* a disease of the liver characterized by increase of connective tissue and alteration in gross and microscopic make-up. [t. NL, f. m. s. Gk *kirrhós* tawny + *-osis* -OSIS] —**cirrhotic** (sĭ rŏt′ĭk), *adj.*

cirri (sĭ′rī), *n.* pl. of **cirrus.**

cirriped (sĭ′rĭ pĕd′), *n.* **1.** any of the *Cirripedia*, an order or group of crustaceans, typically having slender legs bearing bristles used in gathering food. —*adj.* **2.** having legs like cirri. **3.** pertaining to the *Cirripedia.* [t. NL: m. s. *Cirripedia*, pl.; f. *cirri-* CIRRO- + *-pedia* footed]

cirro-, a combining form of **cirrus.**

cirrocumulus (sĭ′rō kyōō′myōō ləs), *n. Meteorol.* a cloud of high altitude, consisting of small fleecy balls or flakes, often in rows or ripples.

cirrose (sĭ′rōs, sĭ rōs′), *adj.* **1.** having a cirrus or cirri. **2.** *Meteorol.* of the nature of cirrus clouds. Also, **cirrous** (sĭ′rəs).

cirrostratus (sĭ′rō strä′təs), *n. Meteorol.* a high veil-like cloud or sheet of haze, often giving rise to haloes round the sun and moon, sometimes very thin and only slightly whitening the blue of the sky. —**cir′rostra′tive,** *adj.*

cirrus (sĭ′rəs), *n., pl.* **cirri** (sĭ′rī). **1.** *Bot.* a tendril. **2.** *Zool.* a filament or slender appendage serving as a barbel, tentacle, foot, arm, etc. **3.** *Meteorol.* a variety of cloud having a thin, fleecy or filamentous appearance, normally occurring at great altitudes and consisting of minute ice crystals. [t. L: curl, tuft, fringe]

cirsoid (sû′soid), *adj.* varix-like; varicose. [t. Gk: m. s. *kirsoeidēs*]

cis-, **1.** a prefix denoting relative nearness (this side of), applied to time as well as space, as in *cisalpine*. Cf. **citra-.** **2.** *Chem.* See **cis-trans isomerism.** [t. L, prefix use of *cis*, prep.]

cisalpine (sĭs ăl′pīn), *adj.* on this (the Roman or south) side of the Alps.

cisatlantic (sĭs′ət lăn′tĭk), *adj.* on this (the speaker's or writer's) side of the Atlantic.

Ciscaucasia (sĭs′kô kā′zyə), *n.* that part of Caucasia north of the Caucasus Mountains.

cisco (sĭs′kō), *n., pl.* **-coes, -cos.** any of several North American species of whitefish of the genus *Leucichthys*, esp. *L. artedi*, the lake herring of the Great Lakes. [t. N Amer. Ind.]

cismontane (sĭs mŏn′tān), *adj.* on this side of the mountains.

cispadane (sĭs′pə dān′, sĭs pā′dān), *adj.* on this (the Roman or south) side of the river Po. [f. CIS- + m. s. L *Padānus* of the river Po]

cissoid (sĭs′oid), *Geom.* —*n.* **1.** a curve having a cusp at the origin and a point of inflection at infinity. —*adj.* **2.** included between the concave sides of two intersecting curves (opposed to *sistroid*): *a cissoid angle.* [t. Gk: m. s. *kissoeidēs* ivylike]

cissy (sĭs′ĭ), *n. Slang.* **1.** an effeminate man or boy. **2.** a timid or cowardly person. Also, **sissy.** [? der. SISTER]

cist[1] (sĭst), *n. Class. Antiq.* a box or chest, esp. for sacred utensils. [t. L: s. *cista*, t. Gk: m. *kistē* CHEST]

cist[2] (sĭst), *n.* a prehistoric sepulchral stone tomb or casket. [t. Welsh, t. L: s. *cista.* See CIST[1]]

cistaceous (sĭs tā′shəs), *adj.* belonging to the *Cistaceae*, or rockrose family of plants. [f. s. Gk *kístos* rockrose + -ACEOUS]

Cistercian (sĭs tû′shən), *n.* **1.** a member of an order of monks and nuns founded in 1098 at Cîteaux, near Dijon, France, under the rule of St Benedict. —*adj.* **2.** belonging to this order.

Cistercian Rule, an adaptation of the Benedictine Rule stressing contemplation and extreme asceticism.

cistern (sĭs′tən), *n.* **1.** a reservoir, tank, or vessel for holding water or other liquid. **2.** *Anat.* a reservoir or receptacle of some natural fluid of the body. [ME, t. L: s. *cisterna*, der. *cista* box]

cis-trans isomerism, *Chem.* a form of isomerism occurring in compounds which contain a double bond: like groups on the same side of the plan of the double bond are called the *cis*-form; like groups on opposite sides are called the *trans*-form.

cit., **1.** citation. **2.** cited. **3.** citizen.

citadel (sĭt′ə dl), *n.* **1.** a fortress in or near a city, intended to keep the inhabitants in subjection, or, in a siege, to form a final point of defence. **2.** any strongly fortified place; a stronghold. **3.** a heavily armoured structure on a warship. [t. F: m. *citadelle*, t. It.: m. *cittadella*, der. *città* CITY]

citation (sī tā′shən), *n.* **1.** the act of citing or quoting. **2.** the quoting of a passage, book, author, etc.; a reference to an authority or a precedent. **3.** a passage cited; a quotation. **4.** mention or enumeration. **5.** call or summons, esp. to appear in court. **6.** a document containing such a summons. **7.** *Mil.* mention of a soldier or unit, in orders, usually for gallantry: *Presidential citation.* [ME *citacion*, t. L: m. s. *citātio*] —**citatory** (sī′tə tə rĭ, -trĭ), *adj.*

cite (sīt), *v.t.,* **cited, citing.** **1.** to quote (a passage, book, author, etc.), esp. as an authority. **2.** to mention in support, proof, or confirmation; refer to as an example. **3.** to summon officially or authoritatively to appear in court. **4.** to summon or call; rouse to action: *cited to the field of battle.* **5.** to call to mind; mention: *citing my own praise.* **6.** *Mil.* to mention (a soldier, unit, etc.) in orders, as for gallantry. [late ME, t. L: m. *citāre*, freq. of *ciēre, cire*, move, excite, call] —**cit′able, cite′able,** *adj.*

cithara (sĭth′ə rə), *n.* kithara. [L form of KITHARA]

cither (sĭth′ə), *n.* cittern. Also, **cithern** (sĭth′ən). [t. L: m. s. *cithara* KITHARA]

citied (sĭt′ĭd), *adj.* **1.** occupied by a city or cities. **2.** formed into or like a city.

citified (sĭt′ĭ fīd′), *adj.* having city habits, fashions, etc.

citizen (sĭt′ĭ zən), *n.* **1.** a member, native or naturalized, of a state or nation (as distinguished from *alien*). **2.** a person owing allegiance to a government and entitled to its protection. **3.** an inhabitant of a city or town, esp. one entitled to its privileges or franchises. **4.** an inhabitant or denizen. **5.** a civilian (as distinguished from a soldier, police officer, etc.). [ME *citisein*, t. AF, var. of OF *citeain*, der. *cite* CITY] —**citizeness** (sĭt′ĭ zən-ĭs), *n. fem.*

citizen of the world, a person who is concerned about all nations, not just his own.

citizenry (sĭt′ĭ zən rĭ), *n., pl.* **-ries.** citizens collectively.

citizenship (sĭt′ĭ zən shĭp′), *n.* the status of a citizen, with its rights and duties.

citole (sĭt′ōl, sĭ tōl′), *n.* **1.** cittern. **2.** kithara.

citra-, a prefix synonymous with **cis-.** [t. L, repr. *citrā*, adv. and prep., akin to *cis.* See CIS-]

citral (sĭt′rəl), *n. Chem.* a liquid aldehyde, $C_9H_{15}CHO$, with a strong lemon-like smell, obtained from the oils of lemon, orange, etc., used in perfumery. [f. CITR(US) + AL(DEHYDE)]

citrate (sĭt′rāt, -rĭt, sī′trāt), *n. Chem.* a salt or ester of citric acid.

citreous (sĭt′rĭ əs), *adj.* lemon yellow; greenish yellow. [t. L: m. *citreus* of the citron tree]

citric acid (sĭt′rĭk), *Chem.* an organic acid containing three carboxyl groups, $C_6H_8O_7$, occurring in small amounts in almost all living cells as a component of the citric acid cycle, and in greater amounts in many fruits, especially in limes and lemons.

citric acid cycle, *Biochem.* a cyclic system of reactions, occurring in almost all living cells, whereby pyruvic acid is metabolized to carbon dioxide, and the energy thereby liberated is trapped as chemical energy for use in biosynthesis, etc.; tricarboxylic acid cycle.

citril finch (sĭt′rĭl), a small finch, *Carduelis citrinella*, an occasional visitor to the British Isles.

citrin (sĭt′rĭn), *n. Biochem.* vitamin P.

citrine (sĭt′rĭn), *adj.* **1.** pale yellow; lemon-coloured. —*n.* **2.** a pale yellow colour. **3.** a pellucid yellow variety of quartz. [ME, t. F: m. *citrin*, der. L *citrus* citron tree]

citron (sĭt′rən), *n.* **1.** a pale yellow fruit resembling the lemon but larger and with thicker rind, borne by a small tree or large bush, *Citrus medica*, allied to the lemon and lime. **2.** the tree itself. **3.** pale yellow. **4.** the rind of the fruit, candied or preserved. [t. F, t. It.: m. *citrone*, der. L *citrus* citron tree]

citronella (sĭt′rə nĕl′ə), *n.* a fragrant grass, *Andropogon* (*Cymbopogon*) *nardus*, of southern Asia, cultivated as the source of an oil (**citronella oil**) used in making liniment, perfume, and soap. [t. NL; named from its citron-like smell]

citronellal (sĭt′rə nĕl′ăl), *n.* a colourless, liquid aldehyde, $C_9H_{17}CHO$, found in essential oils, and used as a flavouring agent and in the perfume industry.

citron wood, **1.** the wood of the citron. **2.** the wood of the sandarac.

citrus (sĭt′rəs), *n.* **1.** any tree or shrub of the rutaceous genus *Citrus*, which includes the citron, lemon, lime, orange, grapefruit, etc. —*adj.* **2.** Also, **citrous.** of or pertaining to such trees or shrubs: *citrus fruit.* [t. L]

cittern (sĭt′ən), *n.* **1.** an old musical instrument, related to the guitar, having a flat pear-shaped soundbox and wire strings. **2.** a zither. Also, **cither, cithern, gittern, zittern.** [b. L *cithara* CITHARA and GITTERN]

Cittern

city (sĭt′ĭ), *n., pl.* **cities.** **1.** a borough on which the title of city has been conferred by the crown. **2.** a town which has, or has had a cathedral. **3.** a large or important town. **4. the city,** the part of London in which commercial and financial interests are chiefly centred. **5.** *U.S.* an incorporated municipality, usually governed by a mayor and a board of aldermen or councillors. **6.** *Canada.* a municipality of high rank, usually based on population. **7.** a city-state. **8.** the inhabitants of a city

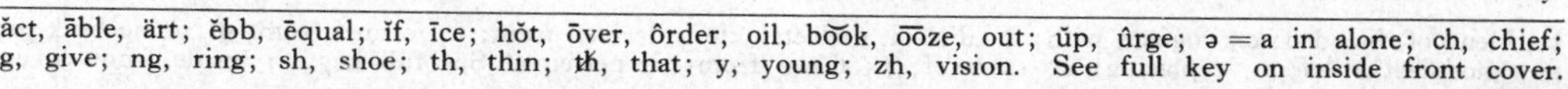

collectively. [ME *cite*, t. OF, g. L *cīvitas* citizenship, the state, a city]

city editor, (on a newspaper, etc.), the editor in charge of the financial and commercial news.

city father, one of the officials and prominent citizens of a city.

city hall, (in some cities, esp. in the U.S.) a building housing the administrative offices of a city; town hall.

city man, a financier; a person employed in the banking establishments of the city (def. 4).

city manager, *U.S.* a person not publicly elected but appointed by a city council to manage a city.

City of God, heaven.

City of Seven Hills, Rome.

city-state (sĭt′ĭ stāt′), *n.* a sovereign state consisting of an autonomous city with its dependencies.

Ciudad Bolívar (*Sp.* thyo͞o dȧd′bô lē′bär), a town in E Venezuela: a port on the Orinoco. 213,543 (1961). Formerly, **Angostura.**

Ciudad Juárez (*Sp.* thyo͞o dȧd′ KHwä′rĕth), a town in N Mexico, across the Rio Grande from El Paso, Texas. 385,082 (est. 1965).

civ., **1.** civil. **2.** civilian.

civet (sĭv′ĭt), *n.* **1.** a yellowish, unctuous substance with a strong musklike smell, obtained from a pouch in the genital region of civets and used in perfumery. **2.** any of the catlike, carnivorous mammals of southern Asia and Africa (family *Viverrinae*) having glands in the genital region that secrete civet. **3.** any of certain allied or similar animals, as the **palm civet.** Also, **civet cat** (for defs 2, 3). [t. F: m. *civette*, t. It.: m. *zibetto*, t. Ar.: m. *zabād*]

African civet, *Viverra civetta* (Total length 4 to 4½ ft, ab. 1 ft high)

civic (sĭv′ĭk), *adj.* **1.** of or pertaining to a city; municipal: *civic problems.* **2.** of or pertaining to citizenship; civil: *civic duties.* **3.** of citizens: *civic pride.* [t. L: s. *cīvicus*, der. *cīvis* citizen]

civic centre, an area where the chief public buildings of a town are grouped.

civics (sĭv′ĭks), *n.* **1.** the science of civic affairs. **2.** a school subject giving training in good citizenship.

civies (sĭv′ĭz), *n., pl. U.S. Colloq.* civvies.

civil (sĭv′əl), *adj.* **1.** of or consisting of citizens: *civil life, civil society.* **2.** of the commonwealth or state: *civil affairs.* **3.** of citizens in their ordinary capacity, or the ordinary life and affairs of citizens (distinguished from *military, ecclesiastical, etc.*). **4.** of the citizen as an individual: *civil liberty.* **5.** befitting a citizen: *a civil duty.* **6.** of, or in a condition of, social order or organized government; civilized. **7.** polite; courteous. **8.** not rude or discourteous. **9.** (of divisions of time) legally recognized in the ordinary affairs of life: *the civil year.* **10.** *Law.* **a.** of or in agreement with Roman civil law. **b.** of the civil law, as the medieval and modern law derived from the Roman system. **c.** pertaining to the private rights of individuals and to legal proceedings connected with these (distinguished from *criminal, military, or political*). [ME *civile*, t. L: m. s. *cīvīlis* pertaining to citizens]

—Syn. 7, 8. respectful, deferential, gracious, complaisant, suave, affable, urbane, courtly. CIVIL, AFFABLE, COURTEOUS, POLITE all imply avoidance of rudeness towards others. CIVIL suggests a minimum observance of social requirements. AFFABLE suggests ease of approach, often with a touch of condescension. COURTEOUS implies positive dignified, sincere, and thoughtful consideration for others. POLITE implies habitual courtesy, arising from a consciousness of one's training and the demands of 'good manners'. **—Ant. 7, 8.** boorish, churlish.

civil defence, the protection of a civilian population against military, esp. aerial, attack.

civil disobedience, a refusal, usually on political grounds, to obey laws, pay taxes, etc.

civil engineer, one versed in the design, construction, and maintenance of public works, such as roads, bridges, dams, canals, aqueducts, harbours, large buildings, etc.

civil engineering, the action, work, or profession of a civil engineer.

civilian (sĭ vĭl′yən), *n.* **1.** one engaged in civil pursuits (distinguished from a soldier, etc.) **2.** *Obs.* one versed in or studying the Roman or civil law. **—***adj.* **3.** relating to non-military life and activities.

civility (sĭ vĭl′ĭ tĭ), *n., pl.* **-ties. 1.** courtesy; politeness. **2.** a polite attention or expression. **3.** (*usually pl.*) polite conversation. **4.** *Archaic.* civilization; culture; good breeding.

civilization (sĭv′ĭ lĭ zā′shən), *n.* **1.** an advanced state of human society, in which a high level of art, science, religion, and government has been reached. **2.** those people or nations that have reached such a state. **3.** the type of culture, society, etc., of a specific group: *Greek civilization.* **4.** the act or process of civilizing. Also, **civilisation.**

civilize (sĭv′ĭ līz′), *v.t.,* **-lized, -lizing.** to make civil; bring out of a savage state; elevate in social and individual life; enlighten; refine. Also, **civilise.** [t. ML: m. s. *cīvīlizāre.* See CIVIL, -IZE] **—civ′iliz′able,** *adj.* **—civ′iliz′er,** *n.*

civilized (sĭv′ĭ līzd′), *adj.* **1.** having an advanced culture, society, etc. **2.** polite; well-bred; refined. **3.** of or pertaining to civilized people. Also, **civilised.**

civil law, 1. the laws of a state or nation regulating ordinary private matters (distinguished from criminal, military, or political matters). **2.** the body of law proper to the city or state of Rome. **3.** the systems of law derived from Roman law (distinguished from *common law, canon law*). **4.** the law of a state (distinguished from other kinds of law, as *international law*).

civil liberty, complete liberty of opinion, etc., restrained only as much as necessary for the public good.

civil list, the provision of money by Parliament for the monarch and his household.

civilly (sĭv′ĭ lĭ), *adv.* **1.** politely; considerately; gently. **2.** in accordance with civil law.

civil marriage, a marriage performed by a government official rather than a clergyman.

civil rights, 1. the personal rights of the individual in society. **2.** *U.S.* rights to personal liberty established by the 13th and 14th Amendments to the Constitution and other Congressional acts.

civil servant, a civil-service employee; a non-political non-judicial servant of the crown.

civil service, the administrative departments of a state collectively.

civil war, 1. a war between parties, regions, etc., within their own country. **2.** (*caps.*) the war in England between the Parliamentarians and Royalists (1642–52). **3.** (*caps.*) the American war between the North and the South (1861–65). **4.** (*caps.*) the Spanish Civil War (1936–39).

civism (sĭv′ĭz′əm), *n.* good citizenship.

civvies (sĭv′ĭz), *n.pl. Colloq.* civilian clothes (opposed to military dress). Also, *U.S.*, **civies.**

civvy (sĭv′ĭ), *n. Colloq.* civilian. Also, *U.S.*, **civy.**

civvy street, *Colloq.* civilian life.

C.J., court justice.

cl., 1. centilitre. **2.** class. **3.** classification. **4.** clause. **5.** clergyman. **6.** cloth.

clabber (klăb′ə), *n.* **1.** bonnyclabber. **—***v.i.* **2.** (of milk) to become thick in souring. [t. Irish: m. *clabar*, short for *bainne clabair* bonnyclabber, curds]

clachan (klăKH′ən), *n. Gaelic.* a small village or hamlet. [t. Gaelic, der. *clach* stone]

clack (klăk), *v.i.* **1.** to make a quick, sharp sound, or a succession of such sounds, as by striking or cracking. **2.** to talk rapidly and continuously, or with sharpness and abruptness; chatter. **3.** to cluck or cackle. **—***v.t.* **4.** to utter by clacking. **5.** to cause to clack. **—***n.* **6.** a clacking sound. **7.** something that clacks, as a rattle. **8.** rapid, continuous talk; chatter. **9.** *Slang.* the tongue. [ME *clacke(n)*; imit.] **—clack′er,** *n.*

Clack., Clackmannanshire.

clackbox (klăk′bŏks′), *n.* a box which contains a clack-valve.

Clackmannanshire (klăk măn′ən shiə′, -shə), *n.* a county in central Scotland. 41,391 pop. (1961); 55 sq. mi. *Co. town:* Alloa. Also, **Clackmannan** (klăk măn′ən).

clackvalve (klăk′vălv′), *n.* a simple non-return valve, as in a locomotive.

Clactonian (klăk tō′nyən, -nĭ ən), *adj.* of, pertaining to, or characteristic of a Lower Palaeolithic culture in England marked by the production of tools made from stone flakes. [named after CLACTON (-ON-SEA), where the tools were first unearthed + -IAN]

Clacton-on-Sea (klăk′tən ŏn sē′), *n.* a town in England, in Essex: seaside resort. 27,572 (1961).

clad (klăd), *v.* a pt. and pp. of **clothe.**

cladding (klăd′ĭng), *n.* **1.** a covering of any kind, esp. one attached to a building structure, a lock-gate, or the like. **2.** *Physics.* the process of covering a fuel element in a nuclear reactor with a thin layer of another metal, in order to prevent corrosion and the escape of fission products. **3.** *Obs.* clothing.

clado-, a word element meaning 'sprout,' 'branch'. Also, before vowels, **clad-.** [comb. from repr. Gk *kládos* sprout]

cladode (klăd′ōd), *n. Bot.* a leaf-like flattened branch or stem. Also, **cladophyll** (klăd′ə fĭl).

Cladode

claim (klām), *v.t.* **1.** to demand by or as by virtue of a right; demand as a right or as due. **2.** to assert, and demand the recognition of (a right, title, possession, etc.); assert one's right to. **3.** to assert or maintain as a fact. **4.** to require as due or fitting. **5.** to need, esp. to need deservingly. *—n.* **6.** a demand for something as due; an assertion of a right or alleged right. **7.** an assertion of something as a fact. **8.** a right to claim or demand; a just title to something. **9.** that which is claimed; a piece of public land to which formal claim is made for mining or other purposes. **10.** a payment demanded in accordance with an insurance policy, etc. [ME *claime(n)*, t. OF: m. *claimer*, *clamer*, g. L *clāmāre* call] —**claim′able,** *adj.* —**claim′er,** *n.* —**Syn. 1.** See **demand.** —**Ant. 3.** deny.

claimant (klā′mənt), *n.* one who makes a claim.

claiming race, a race in which horses are 'claimed' for a fixed amount prior to the running of the race.

Clair (*Fr.* klĕr), *n.* **René** (*Fr.* rə nė′), born 1898, French film director.

clairvoyance (klĕə voi′əns), *n.* **1.** the alleged power of seeing objects or actions beyond the natural range of the senses. **2.** quick intuitive knowledge of things; perception. [t. F]

clairvoyant (klĕə voi′ənt), *adj.* **1.** having the power of seeing objects or actions beyond the natural range of the senses. *—n.* **2.** a clairvoyant person. [t. F, f. *clair* clear + *voyant*, ppr. of *voir* see, g. L *vidēre*]

clam[1] (klăm), *n.*, *v.*, **clammed, clamming.** *—n.* **1.** any of various bivalve molluscs, esp. certain edible species, as *Venus mercenaria* (the **hard clam** or **round clam**) of the Atlantic coast of North America. **2.** *Colloq.* a secretive or silent person. *—v.i.* **3.** *U.S.* to gather or dig clams. [special use of CLAM[2], with reference to the shell]

clam[2] (klăm), *n.* **1.** a clamp[1] (def. 1). **2.** (*pl.*) pincers (def. 1). [ME; OE *clamm* band, bond]

clamant (klā′mənt), *adj.* **1.** clamorous. **2.** urgent. [t. L: s. *clāmans*, ppr., crying out]

clamatorial (klăm′ə tô′rĭ əl), *adj.* of or pertaining to the *Clamatores*, a large group of passerine birds with relatively simple vocal organs and little power of song, as the flycatchers. [f. s. NL *Clāmātores* (pl. of L *clāmātor* one who cries out) + -IAL]

clambake (klăm′bāk′), *n.* *U.S.* **1.** a picnic by the sea, at which the baking of clams (usually on hot stones under seaweed) is a main feature. **2.** *Slang.* any social gathering, esp. a very gay one. **3.** *Slang.* a bungled or unsuccessful performance or rehearsal.

clamber (klăm′bə), *v.i.*, *v.t.* **1.** to climb, using both feet and hands; climb with effort or difficulty. *—n.* **2.** a clambering. [ME *clambren*, *clameren*, irreg. formed freq. of CLIMB; cf. *clamb*, obs. pt. of CLIMB] —**clam′berer,** *n.*

clammy (klăm′ĭ), *adj.*, **-mier, -miest.** covered with a cold, sticky moisture; cold and damp. [? t. Flem.: m. *klammig* sticky; akin to OE *clǣman* anoint, smear] —**clam′miness,** *n.*

clamorous (klăm′ə rəs), *adj.* **1.** full of, marked by, or of the nature of clamour; vociferous; noisy. **2.** vigorous in demands or complaints. —**clam′orously,** *adv.* —**clam′orousness,** *n.*

clamour (klăm′ə), *n.* **1.** a loud outcry. **2.** a vehement expression of desire or dissatisfaction. **3.** popular outcry. **4.** any loud and continued noise. *—v.i.* **5.** to make a clamour; raise an outcry. *—v.t.* **6.** to drive, force, put, etc., by clamouring. **7.** to utter noisily. **8.** *Obs.* to disturb with clamour. Also, *U.S.*, **clamor.** [ME, t. OF, g. L *clāmor* a cry, shout] —**clam′ourer,** *n.* —**Syn. 1.** shouting, uproar. **2.** vociferation. **4.** See **noise.**

clamp[1] (klămp), *n.* **1.** a device, usually of some rigid material, for strengthening or supporting objects or fastening them together. **2.** an appliance with opposite sides or parts that may be screwed or otherwise brought together to hold or compress something. **3.** one of a pair of movable pieces, made of lead or other soft material, for covering the jaws of a vice and enabling it to grasp without bruising. **4.** *Naut.* **a.** a metal band in which the end of a derrick or the like is secured when not in use. **b.** a heavy timber acting as a bearer for a deckbeam in a wooden ship. *—v.t.* **5.** to fasten with or fix in a clamp. **6.** to press firmly. *—v.i.* **7. clamp down,** *Colloq.* to become more strict. [t. MD: m. *klampe* clamp, cleat]

Clamp (def. 2)

clamp[2] (klămp), *v.i.* **1.** to tread heavily; clump. *—n.* **2.** a heavy tread. [imit.]

clamp[3] (klămp), *n.* **1.** a stack of root vegetables, esp. potatoes, stored under earth. **2.** a pile of bricks for burning in the open air. *—v.t.* **3.** to stack (potatoes, etc.). [t. MD: m. *klamp*; akin to CLUMP]

clampdown (klămp′doun′), *n.* a sudden enforcement, restriction, or stoppage: *a clampdown on the sale of drugs.*

clamper (klăm′pə), *n.* **1.** *Dial.* **a.** a clamp. **b.** (*pl.*) pincers. **2.** an iron frame with sharp prongs, fastened to the sole of the shoe to prevent slipping on ice.

clamshell (klăm′shĕl′), *n.* **1.** the shell of a clam. **2.** *U.S.* a dredging bucket made of two similar pieces hinged together at one end. **3.** eyelid (def. 2).

clan (klăn), *n.* **1.** a group of families or households, as among the Scots, the heads of which claim descent from a common ancestor. **2.** a group of people of common descent. **3.** a clique, set, society, or party. **4.** *Anthrop.* **a.** a social unit in a tribe in which descent is reckoned in the maternal line. **b.** a group of people supposed to be descended from a common ancestor, descent being reckoned in the female line. [t. Gaelic: m. *clann* family, stock]

clandestine (klăn dĕs′tĭn), *adj.* secret; private; concealed (generally implying craft or deception): *a clandestine marriage.* [t. L: m. s. *clandestīnus*] —**clandes′tinely,** *adv.* —**clandes′tineness,** *n.*

clang (klăng), *v.i.* **1.** to give out a loud, resonant sound, as metal when struck; ring loudly or harshly. **2.** to emit a harsh cry, as geese. *—v.t.* **3.** to cause to resound or ring loudly. *—n.* **4.** a clanging sound. **5.** the harsh cry of some birds, esp. geese. [imit. Cf. L *clangere*]

clanger (klăng′ə), *n.* *Colloq.* a glaring error or mistake, as an embarrassing remark: *to drop a clanger.*

clangor (klăng′gə, klăng′ə), *n.* **1.** a loud, resonant sound, as of pieces of metal struck together or of a trumpet; a clang. **2.** clamorous noise. *—v.i.* **3.** to make a clangor; clang. Also, **clang′our.** [t. L] —**clang′orous,** *adj.* —**clang′orously,** *adv.*

clank (klăngk), *n.* **1.** a sharp, hard, metallic sound: *the clank of chains.* *—v.i.* **2.** to make such a sound. **3.** to move with such sounds. *—v.t.* **4.** to cause to resound sharply, as metal in collision. [t. D: m. *klank*]

clannish (klăn′ĭsh), *adj.* **1.** of, pertaining to, or characteristic of a clan. **2.** disposed to adhere closely, as the members of a clan. **3.** imbued with or influenced by the sentiments, prejudices, etc., peculiar to clans. —**clan′nishly,** *adv.* —**clan′nishness,** *n.*

clanship (klăn′shĭp), *n.* **1.** the system of clans; the association of families under a chieftain. **2.** a feeling of loyalty to a clan.

clansman (klănz′mən), *n.*, *pl.* **-men.** a member of a clan. —**clanswoman** (klănz′wo͝om′ən), *n. fem.*

clap[1] (klăp), *v.*, **clapped, clapping,** *n.* *—v.t.* **1.** to strike with a quick, smart blow, producing an abrupt, sharp sound; slap; pat. **2.** to strike together resoundingly, as the hands to express applause. **3.** to applaud in this manner. **4.** to flap (the wings). **5.** to put, place, apply, etc., promptly and effectively. **6. clap eyes on,** *Colloq.* to catch sight of. *—v.i.* **7.** to make an abrupt, sharp sound, as of bodies in collision. **8.** to move or strike with such a sound. **9.** to clap the hands, as in applause. *—n.* **10.** the act or sound of clapping. **11.** a resounding blow; a slap. **12.** a loud and abrupt or explosive noise, as of thunder. **13.** a sudden stroke, blow, or act. **14.** an applauding; applause. **15.** a clapper. **16.** *Obs.* a sudden mishap. [ME *clappen*, OE *clæppan*, c. D and LG *klappen*]

clap[2] (klăp), *n.* *Taboo Slang.* gonorrhoea, or any other venereal disease (usually prec. by *the*). [ult. der. MF *clapier* brothel]

clapboard (klăp′bôd′), *n.* **1.** a size of oak board used for making barrel staves and for wainscoting. **2.** *U.S.* weatherboard. *—adj.* **3.** of or pertaining to clapboard: *a clapboard roof.* *—v.t.* **4.** to cover with clapboards. [t. MD: m. *klapholt*, with BOARD for *-holt* wood]

clapnet (klăp′nĕt′), *n.* a net, as used by entomologists, which closes quickly when a string is pulled.

clapped (klăpt), *adj.* *Slang.* completely worn out (often fol. by *out*).

clapper (klăp′ə), *n.* **1.** one who or that which claps. **2.** the tongue of a bell. **3.** *Slang.* the tongue. **4.** any clapping contrivance. **5.** (*pl.*) clapper board.

clapperboard (klăp′ə bôd′), *n.* *Films.* a board showing details of a scene and having a clapper to mark the soundtrack audibly: shot at the beginning of a take for the editor's guidance.

clapper bridge, an ancient type of bridge made of large slabs of stone, some piled to make rough piers and longer ones laid across them to make a roadway.

clapperclaw (klăp′ə klô′), *v.t.* *Archaic or Dial.* **1.** to claw or scratch with the hand and nails. **2.** to revile.

claptrap (klăp′trăp′), *n.* **1.** any artifice or expedient for winning applause or impressing the public. **2.** pretentious but insincere or empty language.

claque (klăk), *n.* **1.** a set of hired applauders in a theatre. **2.** any group of persons ready to applaud from interested motives. [t. F, der. *claquer* clap]

clarabella (klă′rə bĕl′ə), *n.* an organ stop which gives soft, sweet tones. [f. L *clāra* (fem. of *clārus* clear) + *bella* (fem. of *bellus* beautiful)]

Clare (klěə), *n.* **1. John,** 1793–1864, English poet. **2.** a county in W Ireland, in Munster province. 73,702 pop. (1961); 1231 sq. mi. *Co. town:* Ennis.

clarence (klă′rəns), *n.* a closed four-wheeled carriage with a curved glass front and inside seats for four persons. [named after the Duke of *Clarence,* 1765–1837 (afterwards William IV of England)]

Clarence (klă′rəns), *n.* **1.** a river in N South Island, New Zealand. 130 mi. **2.** a river of Australia flowing S, SE, and then NE through N New South Wales into the Pacific Ocean. 295 mi.

Clarendon (klă′rən dən), *n.* **1. Edward Hyde, 1st Earl of,** 1609–74, English statesman and historian. **2. The Council of,** a council (1164) occasioned by the opposition of Thomas à Becket to Henry II. **3.** (*l.c.*) a condensed form of printing type, like roman in outline but with thicker lines.

claret (klă′rət), *n.* **1.** the red (orig. the light red or yellowish) table wine of Bordeaux, France. **2.** a similar wine made elsewhere, as **Australian claret. 3.** Also, **claret red.** a deep purplish red. **4.** *Slang.* blood. —*adj.* **5.** deep purplish red. [ME, t. OF: somewhat clear, light-coloured, dim. of *cler,* g. L *clārus* clear]

claret cup, an iced beverage made of claret with lemon juice, brandy (or other spirits), fruit, sugar, etc.

clarify (klă′rĭ fī′), *v.t., v.i.,* **-fied, -fying.** to make or become clear, pure, or intelligible. [ME *clarifie(n),* t. OF: m. *clarifier,* t. LL: m. *clārificāre*] —**clarification** (klă′rĭ fĭ kā′shən), *n.* —**clar′ifi′er,** *n.*

clarinet (klă′rĭ nět′), *n.* a wind instrument in the form of a cylindrical tube with a single reed attached to its mouthpiece. Also, **clarionet** (klă′rĭ ə nět′). [t. F: m. *clarinette,* dim. of *clarine* clarion] —**clar′inet′tist,** *n.*

clarino (klă rē′nō), *n.* **1.** the high register of the trumpet. **2.** a clarion. **3.** a 4-ft organ stop, giving a trumpet-like tone.

clarion (klă′rĭ ən), *adj.* **1.** clear and shrill. **2.** inspiring; rousing. —*n.* **3.** an old kind of small-bore trumpet used for high-sounding passages; Bach trumpet; clarino. **4.** *Poetic.* the sound of this instrument. **5.** any similar sound. **6.** a rousing call. [ME, t. ML: s. *clārio,* der. L *clārus* clear]

clarity (klă′rĭ tĭ), *n.* clearness: *clarity of thinking.* [t. L: m. s. *clāritas*; r. ME *clarte,* t. OF]

Clarinet

Clark cell (kläk), *n.* *Physics.* a standard primary cell producing 1·4328 volts at 15°C; consists of a mercury cathode and a zinc amalgam anode both dipping into a saturated solution of zinc sulphate.

Clarke Range (kläk), a mountain range in E Queensland, Australia. Highest point, Mt Dalrymple, 4190 ft.

clarkia (klä′kĭ ə, -kyə), *n.* any of the annual onagraceous plants belonging to the genus *Clarkia,* native of North America, but commonly cultivated elsewhere. [named after Captain William *Clark,* 1770–1838, U.S. explorer]

claro (klä′rō), *adj., n., pl.* **-ros.** —*adj.* **1.** (of cigars) light-coloured and, usually, mild. —*n.* **2.** such a cigar. [t. Sp., g. L *clārus* clear]

clart (klät), *v.t.* *Scot. and N Dial.* to smear or spot with something sticky or dirty. [orig. obscure] —**clar′ty,** *adj.*

clary (klěə′rĭ), *n., pl.* **claries.** any of several ornamental species of herbaceous plants of the labiate genus *Salvia,* as **meadow clary,** *S. pratensis.* [late ME *sclarreye,* r. OE *slarie.* Cf. OF *sclaree,* ML *sclarea*]

clash (klăsh), *v.i.* **1.** to make a loud, harsh noise. **2.** to collide, esp. noisily. **3.** to conflict; disagree. **4.** to coincide unfortunately (esp. of events). —*v.t.* **5.** to strike with a resounding or violent collision. **6.** to produce (sound, etc.) by, or as by, collision. —*n.* **7.** the noise of, or as of, a collision. **8.** a collision, esp. a noisy one. **9.** a conflict; opposition, esp. of views or interests. [b. CLAP and DASH] —**Syn. 9.** See **struggle.**

clasp (kläsp), *n.* **1.** a device, usually of metal, for fastening things or parts together; any fastening or connection; anything that clasps. **2.** a grasp; an embrace. **3.** a military decoration consisting of a small design of metal fixed on the ribbon which represents a medal that the bearer has been awarded, the clasp usually indicating an additional award. —*v.t.* **4.** to fasten with, or as with, a clasp. **5.** to furnish with a clasp. **6.** to take hold of with an enfolding grasp: *clasping hands.* [ME *claspe(n), clapse(n)*; orig. uncert.] —**Syn. 6.** grasp, clutch, hug.

clasper (kläs′pə), *n.* **1.** one who or that which clasps. **2.** *Zool.* a clasping organ.

clasp-knife (kläsp′nīf′), *n.* a knife with a blade (or blades) folding into the handle.

clasp-nail (kläsp′nāl′), *n.* a flat-headed nail that clasps the wood.

class (kläs), *n.* **1.** a number of persons or things, regarded as forming one group through the possession of similar qualities; a kind; sort. **2.** any division of persons or things according to rank or grade. **3.** (in universities) a division of candidates into groups, according to merit on the basis of final examinations for degrees. **4.** *Educ.* **a.** a group of pupils taught together. **b.** a period during which they are taught. **c.** *U.S.* a number of students in a school or university, pursuing the same course or graduated in the same year. **5.** *Sociol.* a social stratum sharing essential economic, political, or cultural characteristics, and having the same social position. **6.** the system of dividing society; caste. **7.** social rank, esp. high rank. **8.** *Chiefly U.S. Slang.* excellence; merit. **9.** a grade of accommodation in railway carriages, ships, aeroplanes, etc.: *first class.* **10.** drafted or conscripted soldiers, or men available for draft or conscription, all of whom were born in the same year. **11.** *Zool., Bot.* the usual major subdivision of a phylum or subphylum, commonly comprising a plurality of orders, as the *gastropods,* the *mammals,* the *angiosperms.* **12.** *Gram.* a form class. **13.** *Eccles.* classis. **14.** (in early Methodism) one of several small companies, each composed of about twelve members under a leader, into which each society or congregation was divided. —*v.t.* **15.** to arrange, place, or rate as to class: *to class justice with wisdom.* —*v.i.* **16.** to take or have a place in a particular class: *those who class as believers.* —*adj.* **17.** pertaining to a class, or class. **18.** *Slang.* of high class. [earlier *classe,* t. F, t. L: m. s. *classis* class (of people, etc.), army, fleet] —**class′able,** *adj.*

class., **1.** classic. **2.** classical. **3.** classification. **4.** classified.

class-conscious (kläs′kŏn′shəs), *adj.* **1.** acutely aware of belonging to a particular social class. **2.** showing hostility engendered by this feeling. —**class′-con′sciousness,** *n.*

class-distinction (kläs′dĭs tĭngk′shən), *n.* **1.** awareness of differences between social classes. **2.** criteria used in distinguishing between social classes.

classic (klăs′ĭk), *adj.* **1.** of the first or highest class or rank. **2.** serving as a standard, model, or guide. **3.** of or characteristic of Greek and Roman antiquity, esp. with reference to literature and art. **4.** in the style of the ancient Greek and Roman literature or art; classical. **5.** of, or adhering to, an established set of artistic or scientific standards and methods. **6.** of literary or historical renown. **7.** balanced, simple, austere; pertaining to classicism. —*n.* **8.** an author or a literary production of the first rank, esp. in Greek or Latin. **9.** (*pl.*) the literature of ancient Greece and Rome; the Greek and Latin languages. **10.** an artistic production of the highest class. **11.** one versed in the classics. **12.** one who adheres to classical rules and models. **13.** *Horseracing.* any of the five chief annual flat races for three-year-old horses in England; the Derby, the Oaks, the St Leger, the 1000-Guineas or the 2000-Guineas. [t. L: s. *classicus* pertaining to a class, of the first or highest class]

classical (klăs′ĭ kl), *adj.* **1.** classic. **2.** (*sometimes cap.*) in accordance with ancient Greek and Roman models in literature or art, or with later systems of principles modelled upon them. **3.** pertaining to or versed in the ancient classics. **4.** restrained and simple; affected by classicism. **5.** conforming to established taste or critical standards; adhering to traditional forms. **6.** (of music) following strict stylistic and rhythmic rules, esp. that composed before 1800 (opposed to *romantic*). **7.** (of music) composed with serious artistic intent, having a more than ephemeral appeal and usually taking one of several traditional forms, as concerto, symphony, etc. (opposed to *light*). **8.** teaching, or relating to, academic branches of knowledge (the humanities, general sciences, etc.), distinguished from technical subjects. **9.** *Eccles.* pertaining to a classis. —**classicality** (klăs′ĭ kăl′ĭ tĭ), *n.* —**clas′sically,** *adv.*

classical architecture, **1.** any architectural style distinguished by clarity and balance of design and plan, expressive of poise and dignity, and as a rule by the use of a Greek or Roman vocabulary. **2.** the architecture of Greek and Roman antiquity. **3.** the architectural style popular from 1770–1840, esp. in Europe, which sought to revive Greek and Roman architecture.

classical economics, a system of thought developed by Adam Smith and David Ricardo, according to which the wealth of nations is promoted by free competition with a minimum of government intervention and by division of labour (labour being the source of wealth).

classical physics, physics either before the quantum theory, of before the theory of relativity, or before both.

classicism (klăs′ĭ sĭz′əm), *n.* **1.** the principles of classical literature or art, or adherence to them. **2.** the classical style in literature or art, characterized esp. by attention to form with the general effect of regularity, simplicity, balance, proportion, and controlled emotion (contrasted with *romanticism*). **3.** a classical idiom or form. **4.** classical scholarship or learning. Also, **classicalism** (klăs′ĭ-kə lĭz′ əm).

classicist (klăs′ĭ sĭst), *n.* **1.** one who advocates the study of the ancient classics. **2.** an adherent of classicism in literature or art. **3.** an authority on Greek and Roman studies. Also, **classicalist** (klăs′ĭ kə lĭst).

classicize (klăs′ĭ sīz′), *v.*, **-cized, -cizing.** —*v.t.* **1.** to make classic. —*v.i.* **2.** to conform to the classic style. Also, **classicise.**

classification (klăs′ĭ fĭ kā′shən), *n.* **1.** the act or the result of classifying. **2.** *Zool.*, *Bot.* the assignment of plants and animals to groups within a system of categories distinguished by structure, origin, etc. The usual series of categories is phylum (in zoology) or division (in botany), class, order, family, genus, species, and variety. **3.** one of the several degrees (restricted, confidential, secret, top secret, etc.) of security protection for government documents, papers, etc. **4.** (in libraries, etc.) a system for arranging publications according to broad fields of knowledge and specific subjects within each field. —**classificatory** (klăs′ĭ fĭ kā′tə rĭ), *adj.*

classified (klăs′ĭ fīd′), *adj.* **1.** arranged or distributed in classes; placed according to class. **2.** (of military and other government information) placed in categories in relation to security risk. **3.** (of roads) having a classification number and receiving government financial assistance. **4.** (of football results) arranged in divisions.

classified ad, *Colloq.* a small newspaper advertisement, usually single-column, esp. one advertising a vacancy, an object for sale, etc.

classifier (klăs′ĭ fī′ə), *n.* **1.** one who or that which classifies. **2.** *Metall.*, *Mining.* a device for separating solids of different characteristics by controlled rates of settling.

classify (klăs′ĭ fī′), *v.t.* **-fied, -fying.** **1.** to arrange or distribute in classes; place according to class. **2.** to mark or otherwise declare (a document, paper, etc.) of value to an enemy, and limit and safeguard its handling and use. [f. L *classi(s)* CLASS + -FY] —**clas′sifi′able,** *adj.*

class inclusion, *Logic.* the relation between one class and a second when every object that belongs to the first class also belongs to the second. For example: the class of *men* is included in the class of *animals.*

classis (klăs′ĭs), *n.*, *pl.* **classes** (klăs′ēz). *Eccles. Obs.* (in certain Reformed churches) **1.** the organization of pastors and elders which governs a group of local churches; a presbytery. **2.** the group of churches governed by such an organization. [t. L. See CLASS]

class-list (kläs′lĭst′), *n.* a university list of final examination candidates, dividing them into classes according to merit.

classmate (kläs′māt′), *n.* a member of the same class, as at school.

class meaning, *Gram.* **1.** the meaning of a grammatical category or a form class, common to all forms showing the category or to all members of the form class, as in the meaning of possession common to all English nouns in the possessive case. **2.** that part of the meaning of a linguistic form which it has by virtue of membership in a particular form class, as the past tense meaning of *ate* (opposed to *lexical meaning*).

class resolution, a resolution passed by a specified class of shareholders.

classroom (kläs′ro͝om′, -ro͞om′), *n.* a room in a school, etc., in which classes meet.

class war, **1.** conflict between different classes in the community. **2.** (in Marxist thought) the struggle for political and economic power carried on between capitalists and workers.

classy (klä′sĭ), *adj. Slang.* of high class, rank, or grade; stylish; fine.

clastic (klăs′tĭk), *adj.* **1.** *Biol.* breaking up into fragments or separate portions; dividing into parts; causing or undergoing disruption or dissolution: *clastic action, the clastic pole of an ovum.* **2.** pertaining to an anatomical model made up of detachable pieces. **3.** *Geol.* denoting or pertaining to rock or rocks composed of fragments or particles of older rocks or previously existing solid matter; fragmental. [f. m. s. Gk *klastós* broken + -IC]

clathrate (klăth′rāt), *adj. Bot.* resembling a lattice; divided or marked like latticework. [t. L: m. s. *clāthrātus* having a lattice]

clathrate compound, *Chem.* a chemical compound in which one component is attached mechanically to another, rather than by a valency bond.

clatter (klăt′ə), *v.i.* **1.** to make a rattling sound, as of hard bodies striking rapidly together. **2.** to move rapidly with such a sound. **3.** to talk fast and noisily; chatter. —*v.t.* **4.** to cause to clatter. —*n.* **5.** a clattering noise; disturbance. **6.** noisy talk; din of voices. **7.** *Chiefly Scot.* idle talk; gossip. [ME *clatren*, OE *clatrian*, of imit. orig. Cf. D *klateren* rattle]

Claudel (*Fr.* klō dĕl′), *n.* **Paul Louis Charles** (*Fr.* pŏl lwē shárl′), 1868–1955, French diplomat, poet, and dramatist.

Claude Lorrain. See **Lorrain.**

claudication (klô dĭ kā′shən), *n.* a limp. [t. L: s. *claudicātio*, der. *claudus* lame]

Claudius (*Ger.* klou′dĭ o͞os), *n.* **Matthias** (*Ger.* mä tē′äs), 1740–1815, German poet.

Claudius I (klô′dyəs), 10 B.C.–A.D. 54, Roman emperor A.D. 41–54.

Claudius II (′*Gothicus*′), A.D. 214–70, Roman emperor A.D. 268–70.

clause (klôz). **1.** *Gram.* a group of words containing a subject and a predicate, forming part of a compound or complex sentence, or coextensive with a simple sentence. **2.** part of a written composition containing complete sense in itself, as a sentence or paragraph (in modern use commonly limited to such parts of legal documents, as of statutes, contracts, wills, etc.). [ME *claus*, t. ML: s. *clausa* in sense of L *clausula* clause] —**claus′al,** *adj.*

Clausewitz (*Ger.* klou′zə vĭts), *n.* **Karl von** (*Ger.* kärl fōn), 1780–1831, German army officer and author of books on military science.

Clausius (*Ger.* klou′zĭ o͞os), *n.* **Rudolf Julius** (*Ger.* ro͞o′dôlf yo͞o′lĭ o͞os), 1822–88, German physicist.

claustral (klôs′trəl), *adj.* cloistral; cloister-like. [t. LL: s. *claustrālis*, der. *claustrum* enclosure, CLOISTER]

claustrophobia (klôs′trə fō′byə), *n. Psychol.* a morbid dread of confined places. [t. NL, f. *claustro-* (comb. form repr. L *claustrum* enclosure) + *-phobia* -PHOBIA] —**claus′tropho′bic,** *adj.*

clavate (klā′vāt, -vĭt), *adj.* club-shaped. [t. L: m. s. *clāvātus*, pp., studded with nails; sense influenced by assoc. with L *clāva* club]

clave (klāv), *v. Archaic.* pt. of **cleave**[1].

clavecina (klăv′ĭ sē′nə), *n.* a harpsichord.

claver (klā′və, klä′-), *Scot.* —*n.* **1.** idle talk. —*v.i.* **2.** to talk idly; gossip.

clavicembalo (klăv′ĭ chĕm′bə lō′), *n.* a harpsichord; cembalo. [t. It.]

clavichord (klăv′ĭ kôd′), *n.* an ancient keyboard instrument, in which the strings were softly struck with metal blades vertically projecting from the rear ends of the keys. [t. ML: m. s. *clāvichordium*, f. L: *clāvi(s)* key + s. *chorda* string (see CHORD[1]) + *-ium* -IUM]

clavicle (klăv′ĭ kl), *n. Anat.*, *Zool.* **1.** a bone of the pectoral arch. **2.** (in man) either of two slender bones each articulating with the sternum and a scapula and forming the anterior part of a shoulder; the collarbone. See diag. under **shoulder.** [t. L: m. s. *clāvicula*, dim. of *clāvis* key] —**clavicular** (klə vĭk′yo͞o lə), *adj.*

clavicorn (klăv′ĭ kôn′), *adj.* **1.** having club-shaped antennae, as many beetles of the group *Clavicornia.* **2.** belonging to this group. —*n.* **3.** a clavicorn beetle. [t. NL: s. *clāvicornis*, f. *clāvi-* (comb. form repr. *clāva* club) + *-cornis* horned] —**clavicornate** (klăv′ĭ kô′nāt), *adj.*

clavier[1] (klăv′ĭ ə), *n.* the keyboard of a musical instrument. [t. F, der. L *clāvis* key]

clavier[2] (klə vĭə′, klăv′ĭ ə), *n.* any musical instrument with a keyboard, as a harpsichord, clavichord, piano, or organ. [t. G, t. F: keyboard]

claviform (klăv′ĭ fôm′), *adj.* club-shaped; clavate.

claw (klô), *n.* **1.** a sharp, usually curved, nail on the foot of an animal. **2.** *Obs.* the foot of an animal armed with such nails. **3.** any part or thing resembling a claw, as the cleft end of the head of a hammer. **4.** the pincers of some shellfish and insects. **5.** *Bot.* the narrow basal region of a petal or sepal found in some types of flowers. —*v.t.* **6.** to tear, scratch, seize, pull, etc., with or as with claws. **7.** to scratch fiercely, as to relieve itching. **8.** to make, bring, etc., by clawing: *claw a hole.* **9.** *Naut.* (of or in a sailing ship) to beat to windward to get away from a danger, a lee shore, etc. (often fol. by *off*). [ME *clawen*, OE *clawian*, der. *clawu*, n., c. G *Klaue*]

claw-foot (klô′fo͝ot′), *n. Pathol.* **a.** a condition in which the arch of the foot is abnormally high due to deformity of the metatarsal bones. **b.** a foot with such a deformity.

claw hammer, a hammer having a head with one end curved and cleft for drawing out nails.

clay (klā), *n.* **1.** a natural earthy material which is plastic when wet, consisting essentially of hydrated silicates of aluminium, and used for making bricks, pottery, etc. **2.** earth; mud. **3.** earth as the material from which the human body was originally formed. **4.** the human body. —*v.t.* **5.** to cover, mix or treat with clay. [ME; OE *clǣg*, c. D *klei* and G *Klei*] —**clayey** (klā′ĭ), *adj.* —**clay′ish,** *adj.*

Clay (klā), *n.* **Cassius** (kăs′yəs), (*Mohammed Ali*), born 1942, U.S. heavyweight boxer.
claybank (klā′băngk′), *n. U.S.* a yellow shade; dun; brownish yellow.
claymore (klā′mô′), *n.* **1.** a heavy two-edged sword formerly used by the Scottish Highlanders. **2.** a basket-hilted broadsword, often singled-edged, formerly used by Highlanders.
claypan (klā′păn′), *n. Austral.* a depression in the ground which retains water.
clay pigeon, a disc of baked clay or other material hurled into the air as a target to be shot at.
clay pipe, a tobacco pipe made of clay.
claystone (klā′stōn′), *n.* **1.** a deeply decomposed igneous rock. **2.** argillite.
claytonia (klā tō′nyə), *n.* any of the low, succulent portulacaceous herbs constituting the genus *Claytonia.* [named after Dr J. *Clayton,* 1685?–1773, American botanist]
-cle, var. of **-cule.** [t. L: m. *-culus, -cula, -culum*; in some words, t. F]
cleading (klē′dĭng), *n. Obs.* **1.** lagging. **2.** cladding.
clean (klēn), *adj.* **1.** free from dirt or filth; unsoiled; unstained. **2. a.** free from foreign or extraneous matter. **b.** *Physics, Chem.* free of radioactivity. **3.** free from defect or blemish. **4.** free from disease: *a clean bill of health.* **5.** unadulterated; pure. **6.** entirely (or almost so) without corrections; easily readable: *clean printer's proofs.* **7.** free from encumbrances or obstructions: *a clean harbour.* **8.** (of a ship) **a.** having its bottom free of marine growth, etc. **b.** having a clean bill of health. **9.** (of timber) free from knots. **10.** *Aerodynamics.* designed to create a wake of as little turbulence as possible. **11.** free from any form of defilement; morally pure; innocent; upright; honourable. **12.** free from dirty habits, as an animal. **13.** (among the Jews) **a.** (of persons) free from ceremonial defilement. **b.** (of animals, fowl, and fish) permissible to eat. **14.** neatly or evenly made or proportioned; shapely; trim. **15.** even; with a smooth edge or surface. **16.** free from awkwardness; not bungling; dexterous; adroit: *a clean boxer, a clean leap.* **17.** complete; perfect: *a clean sweep.* —*adv.* **18.** in a clean manner; cleanly. **19.** wholly; completely; quite. **20.** *Cricket.* (bowled) by a ball, which breaks the wicket without touching the batsman or his bat. **21. come clean,** to make a full confession. —*v.t.* **22.** to make clean. **23. clean out, a.** to rid of dirt, etc. **b.** to use up; exhaust. **c.** *U.S. Slang.* to drive out by force. **d.** *Colloq.* to empty or rid (a place) of occupants, contents, etc.: *clean out the larder.* **24. clean up, a.** to rid of dirt, etc. **b.** to put in order; tidy up. **c.** to finish up; reach the end of. **d.** *Colloq.* to make (money, or the like) as profit, gain, etc. —*v.i.* **25.** to perform or to undergo a process of cleaning. **26.** to get rid of dirt, etc. (fol. by *up*): *to clean up for dinner.* [ME *clene,* OE *clǣne* pure, clear, c. D and G *klein* small] —**clean′able,** *adj.* —**clean′ness,** *n.*
—**Syn. 1.** CLEAN, CLEAR, PURE refer to freedom from soiling, flaw, stain, or mixture. CLEAN refers esp. to freedom from soiling: *a clean dress.* CLEAR refers particularly to freedom from flaw or blemish: *a clear pane of glass.* PURE refers esp. to freedom from mixture or stain: *a pure metal, not diluted but pure and full strength.* **11.** unsullied, chaste, virtuous. **22.** scour, scrub, sweep, brush, wipe, mop, dust, wash, rinse, lave. CLEAN, CLEANSE refer to removing dirt or impurities. To CLEAN is the general word with no implication of method or means: *to clean windows, a kitchen, streets.* CLEANSE is often used in advertising English where CLEAN is meant; usually it is used of thorough cleaning by chemical or other technical process; figuratively it applies to moral or spiritual purification: *to cleanse parts of machinery, one's soul of guilt.* —**Ant. 1.** soiled. **11.** impure. **22.** soil.
clean-cut (klēn′kŭt′), *adj.* **1.** distinctly outlined. **2.** well-shaped. **3.** definite.
cleaner (klē′nə), *n.* **1.** one who or that which cleans. **2.** an apparatus or preparation for cleaning.
clean hands, 1. a clear conscience. **2.** *Law.* a suitor who is free from taint of fraud. —**clean-handed** (klēn′hăn′dĭd), *adj.*
cleanly (*adj.* klĕn′lĭ; *adv.* klēn′lĭ), *adj.,* **-lier, -liest,** *adv.* —*adj.* **1.** personally neat; careful to keep or make clean. **2.** habitually clean. **3.** *Obs.* cleansing; making clean. —*adv.* **4.** in a clean manner. —**cleanlily** (klĕn′lĭ lĭ), *adv.* —**cleanliness** (klĕn′lĭ nĭs), *n.*
cleanse (klĕnz), *v.t.,* **cleansed, cleansing. 1.** to make clean. **2.** to remove by, or as by, cleaning: *his leprosy was cleansed.* [ME *clense(n),* OE *clǣnsian,* der. *clǣne* clean] —**cleans′er,** *n.* —**Syn. 1.** See **clean.**
clean-shaven (klēn′shā′vən), *adj.* **1.** having all the hairs shaved off. **2.** having facial hair shaved off.
cleanskin (klēn′skĭn′), *n. Austral.* an unbranded animal.
Cleanthes (klĭ ăn′thēz), *n. c.* 300–*c.* 232 B.C., Greek Stoic philosopher.
clean-up (klēn′ŭp′), *n.* **1.** the act or process of cleaning up, esp. of gambling, vice, graft, etc. **2.** *Slang.* a very large profit.
clear (klĭə), *adj.* **1.** free from darkness, obscurity, or cloudiness; light. **2.** bright; shining. **3.** transparent; pellucid: *good, clear wine.* **4.** of a pure, even colour: *a clear complexion.* **5.** distinctly perceptible to the eye, ear, or mind; easily seen, heard or understood. **6.** distinct; evident; plain. **7.** free from confusion, uncertainty, or doubt. **8.** perceiving or discerning distinctly: *a clear thinker.* **9.** convinced; certain. **10.** free from guilt or blame; innocent. **11.** serene; calm; untroubled. **12.** free from obstructions or obstacles; open: *a clear space.* **13.** unentangled or disengaged; free; quit or rid (fol. by *of*). **14.** *Mil.* not in code; in plain language. **15.** having no parts that protrude, are rough, etc. **16.** freed or emptied of contents, cargo, etc. **17.** without limitation or qualification: *a clear victory.* **18.** without obligation or liability; free from debt. **19.** without deduction or diminution: *a clear £1000.* **20.** *Phonet.* light; palatal; resembling a front vowel in quality. **21.** *Obs.* illustrious. —*adv.* **22.** in a clear manner; clearly; distinctly; entirely. —*v.t.* **23.** to make clear; free from darkness, cloudiness, muddiness, indistinctness, confusion, uncertainty, obstruction, contents, entanglement, obligation, liability, etc. **24.** to free from imputation, esp. of guilt; prove or declare to be innocent. **25.** to pass or get over without entanglement or collision. **26.** to pay (a debt) in full. **27.** to pass (cheques, etc.) through a clearing house. **28.** to free (a person, etc.) from debt. **29.** to gain as clear profit: *to clear £1000 in a transaction.* **30.** to free (a ship, cargo, etc.) from legal detention at a port by satisfying the customs and other required condition. **31.** *Football, etc.* to get (the ball) away from the area of one's own goal. **32.** *Mil.* to decode.
—*v.i.* **33.** to become clear. **34.** (of a ship) **a.** to comply with the customs and other conditions legally imposed upon leaving or entering a port. **b.** to leave port after having complied with such conditions.
—*v.* **35.** Some special verb phrases are:
clear away, off, etc., **1.** to remove so as to leave something clear. **2.** to disappear; vanish.
clear out, 1. to empty; remove, in order to make clear. **2.** *Colloq.* to go away.
clear the air, 1. to relieve tension. **2.** to remove misunderstanding.
clear up, 1. to make clear. **2.** to solve; explain. **3.** to put in order; tidy up. **4.** to become brighter, lighter, etc.
—*n.* **36.** plain language; not code: *the orders were radioed in clear.* **37. in the clear,** free from the imputation of blame, censure, or the like. [ME *cler,* t. OF, g. L *clārus*] —**clear′able,** *adj.* —**clear′er,** *n.* —**Syn. 1.** See **clean. 3.** translucent, limpid, crystalline, diaphanous. **5.** intelligible, comprehensible. **6.** obvious, manifest, apparent. **7.** unmistakeable, unambiguous.
Clear (klĭə), *n.* an island in the Republic of Ireland off SW county Cork. The SW tip, **Cape Clear,** is the southernmost point of Ireland.
clearage (klĭə′rĭj), *n.* **1.** the act of clearing. **2.** a cleared space.
clearance (klĭə′rəns), *n.* **1.** the act of clearing. **2.** a clear space; a clearing. **3.** an intervening space, as between machine parts for free play. **4.** distance or extent of an object to be passed over or under. **5.** *Football, etc.* the act of getting the ball away from one's own goal area. **6.** *Banking.* an exchange of cheques and other commercial paper drawn on members of a clearing house, usually effected at a daily meeting of the members. **7.** *Naut.* **a.** the clearing of a ship at a port. **b.** the official certificate or papers (**clearance papers**) indicating this.
clearance sale, a sale to clear shop-soiled or out-of-date goods, etc.
Clearchus (klĭ ä′kəs), *n.* died 401 B.C., Spartan general.
clearcole (klĭə′kōl′), *n.* a size, or glue, containing whiting.
clear-cut (klĭə′kŭt′), *adj.* cut or formed with clearly defined outlines; distinctly defined.
clear-eyed (klĭər′īd′), *adj.* **1.** having clear, bright eyes; clear-sighted. **2.** mentally acute or discerning.
clear-headed (klĭə′hĕd′ĭd), *adj.* having or showing a clear head or understanding. —**clear′-head′edness,** *n.*
clearing (klĭə′rĭng), *n.* **1.** the act of one who or that which clears. **2.** a tract of cleared land, as in a forest. **3.** the mutual exchange between banks of cheques and drafts, and the settlement of the differences. **4.** (*pl.*) the total of claims settled at a clearing house.
clearing house, a place or institution where mutual claims and accounts are settled, as between banks.
clearing station, a military field hospital where first aid is given, before casualties are sent back to base hospitals. Also, **clearing hospital.**
clearly (klĭə′lĭ), *adv.* **1.** in a clear manner. **2.** undoubtedly.

—Syn. 1. CLEARLY, DEFINITELY, DISTINCTLY, EVIDENTLY imply the way in which something is plainly understood or understandable. CLEARLY suggests without doubt or obscurity: *expressed clearly.* DEFINITELY means explicitly, with precision: *definitely phrased.* DISTINCTLY means without blurring or confusion: *distinctly enunciated.* EVIDENTLY means patently, unquestionably: *evidently an error.*

clearness (klĭəʹnĭs), *n.* the state or quality of being clear; distinctness; plainness.
clear-sighted (klĭəʹsīʹtĭd), *adj.* having clear sight; having keen mental perception; discerning; perspicacious: *clear-sighted businessman, reason, etc.* —**clear′-sight′edly,** *adv.* —**clear′-sight′edness,** *n.*
clearskin (klĭəʹskĭn′), *n. Austral.* a cleanskin.
clear-starch (klĭəʹstäch′), *v.t., v.i.* to stiffen and dress (linen, etc) with clear or transparent (boiled) starch. —**clear′-starch′er,** *n.*
clearstory (klĭəʹstə rĭ), *n., pl.* **-ries.** clerestory.
clearway (klĭəʹwā′), *n.* a stretch of road on which motorists may stop only in an emergency.
clearwing (klĭəʹwĭng′), *n.* a moth with wings for the most part destitute of scales and transparent, esp. any of the family *Sesiidae,* many species of which are injurious to plants.
cleat (klēt), *n.* **1.** a small wedge-shaped block, as one fastened to a spar or the like as a support, etc. **2.** *Naut.* **a.** a piece of wood nailed down to secure something from slipping. **b.** a piece of wood or iron consisting of a bar with arms, to which ropes are belayed. **3.** a piece of wood or iron fastened across anything for support, security, etc. **4.** a piece of iron fastened under a shoe to preserve the sole. **5.** *Mining.* one of the main cleavage planes in a seam of coal, as **face cleat** (prominent), **butt cleat** (poor). —*v.t.* **6.** to supply or strengthen with cleats; fasten to or with a cleat. [ME *clete* wedge, c. D *kloot* ball. Cf. CLOT]

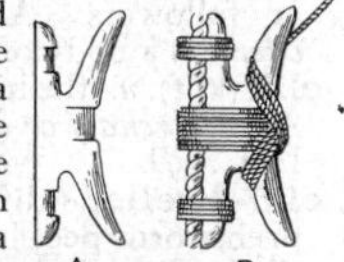

A, Cleat; B, Cleat, lashed to a stay on to which a rope is belayed

cleavable (klēʹvə bl), *adj.* that may be cleft or split.
cleavage (klēʹvĭj), *n.* **1.** the act of cleaving. **2.** (in rocks) a tendency to split, in certain directions. **3.** the state of being cleft or split; division. **4.** *Biol.* the total or partial division of the egg into smaller cells or blastomeres. **5.** *Crystall.* the tendency to break in certain definite directions, yielding more or less smooth surfaces. **6.** *Geol.* the splitting of a rock under pressure into slabs. **7.** *Chem.* the breaking down of a molecule or compound into simpler molecules or compounds. **8.** *Colloq.* the cleft between a woman's breasts. **9.** *Colloq.* that which is revealed by a woman's low-cut dress.
cleave[1] (klēv), *v.i.,* **cleaved** or (*Archaic*) **clave, cleaved, cleaving. 1.** to stick or adhere; cling or hold fast (fol. by *to*). **2.** to be attached or faithful (fol. by *to*). [ME *cleve(n),* OE *cleofian,* c. G *kleben*]
cleave[2] (klēv), *v.,* **cleft** or **cleaved** or **clove, cleft** or **cleaved** or **cloven, cleaving.** —*v.t.* **1.** to part by, or as by, a cutting blow, esp. along the grain or any other natural line of division. **2.** to split; rend apart; rive. **3.** to penetrate or pass through (air, water, etc.). **4.** to make by or as by cutting: *to cleave a path through the wilderness.* **5.** to separate or sever by, or as by, splitting. —*v.i.* **6.** to part or split, esp. along a natural line of division. **7.** to penetrate or pass (fol. by *through*). [ME *cleven,* OE *clēofan,* c. G *klieben.* Cf. Gk *glýphein* carve]
cleaver (klēʹvə), *n.* **1.** one who or that which cleaves. **2.** a heavy knife or long-bladed hatchet used by butchers for cutting up carcasses.
cleavers (klēʹvəz), *n. sing. and pl.* **1.** a rubiaceous plant, *Galium aparine,* with short hooked bristles by means of which it adheres to clothing, etc.; goosegrass; sticky willie. **2.** any of certain related species. [ME *clivre* (der. CLEAVE[1]), r. OE *clife*]
cleek (klēk), *n. Golf.* a club having an iron head with a long, narrow face. [akin to CLUTCH[1]]
Cleethorpes (klēʹthôps), *n.* a town in England, in Lincolnshire: seaside resort. 32,700 (1961).
clef (klĕf), *n. Music.* a symbol placed upon a stave to indicate the name and pitch of the notes corresponding to its lines and spaces. The **G clef** (or **treble clef**) indicates that the second line of the stave corresponds to the G next above middle C. The **F clef** (or **bass clef**) indicates that the fourth line of the stave corresponds to the F next below middle C. The **C clef** (or **alto clef**) indicates middle C on the third line of the stave. [t. F, g. L *clāvis* key]

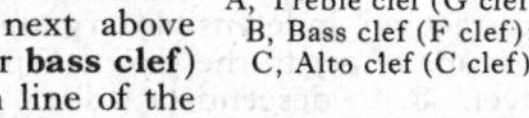

A, Treble clef (G clef); B, Bass clef (F clef); C, Alto clef (C clef)

cleft[1] (klĕft), *n.* **1.** a space or opening made by cleavage; a split. **2.** a division formed by cleaving. **3.** (in horses) a crack on the bend of the pastern. [ME *clift,* OE *geclyft* split, crack, fissure] —**Syn. 1.** fissure, crevice, crack.
cleft[2] (klĕft), *v.* **1.** a pt. and pp. of **cleave**[2]. —*adj.* **2.** cloven; split; divided. **3.** (of a leaf) having divisions formed by incisions or narrow sinuses which extend halfway, or more than halfway, to the midrib or the base.
cleft graft, *Hort.* the insertion of the wedge-shaped base of a scion into a cleft at the top of a stock.
cleft palate, a congenital defect of the palate in which a longitudinal fissure exists in the roof of the mouth.
cleg (klĕg), *n.* a horsefly. [ME, t. Scand.; cf. Icel. *kleggi*]
cleidoic (klī dōʹĭk), *adj. Embryol.* closed-up. Cleidoic eggs, as those of birds and insects, have little more than gaseous exchange with the environment. [f. m. Gk *kleidó(ein)* lock up + -IC]
Cleisthenes (klīsʹthĭ nēz′), *n.* fl. 508 B.C., Athenian statesman.
cleistogamy (klī stŏgʹə mĭ), *n. Bot.* the condition of having (usually in addition to the ordinary, fully developed flowers) small, inconspicuous flowers which do not open, but are pollinated from their own anthers, as in the case of some violets. [f. m. Gk *kleistó(s)* closed + -GAMY] —**cleistog′amous, cleistogamic** (klīʹstə gămʹĭk), *adj.*
clematis (klĕmʹə tĭs), *n.* any of the flowering vines or erect shrubs constituting the ranunculaceous genus *Clematis,* as *C. vitalba,* the traveller's joy of Europe and W Asia. [t. L, t. Gk: m. *klēmatís,* dim. of *klêma* vine branch]
Clemenceau (*Fr.* klė mäɴ sō′), *n.* **Georges Eugène Benjamin** (*Fr.* zhôrzh œ zhĕn′ bäɴ zhä mäɴ′), 1841–1929, French statesman, journalist, and physician: prime minister of France 1906–9 and 1917–20.
Clemens (klĕmʹənz), *n.* **Samuel Langhorne** (lăngʹhôn, lăngʹən). See **Twain, Mark.**
clement (klĕmʹənt), *adj.* **1.** mild or merciful in disposition; lenient; compassionate. **2.** (of the weather, etc.) mild or pleasant. [late ME, t. L: s. *clēmens*] —**clem′ently,** *adv.*
Clement (klĕmʹənt), *n.* the name adopted by 14 popes, esp.: **1. V** (*Bertrand de Got*), 1264–1314, pope 1305–14, who transferred the papacy to Avignon. **2. VII** (*Giulio de'Medici*), 1478?–1534, pope 1523–34 (nephew of Lorenzo de'Medici).
Clement of Alexandria, A.D. *c.* 150–*c.* 215, Greek Christian theologian and writer.
clench (klĕnch), *v.t.* **1.** to close (the hands, teeth, etc.) tightly. **2.** to grasp firmly; grip. **3.** to settle decisively; clinch. **4.** *Naut.* to clinch. —*n.* **5.** the act of clenching. **6.** a tight hold; grip. **7.** that which holds fast or clenches. **8.** *Naut.* a clinch. [ME *clench(en),* OE *-clencan* (in *beclencan* hold fast)]
cleome (klĭ ōʹmĭ), *n.* any of the numerous herbaceous or shrubby plants constituting the capparidaceous genus *Cleome,* mostly natives of tropical regions, and often bearing showy flowers. [t. NL, t. L, plant name]
Cleomenes III (klĭ ŏmʹĭ nēz′), *n.* died 220? B.C., king of Sparta 235?–220? B.C.
Cleon (klēʹŏn), *n.* died 422 B.C., Athenian general and political opponent of Pericles.
Cleopatra (klĭə päʹtrə, -pătʹrə), *n.* 69?–30 B.C., queen of Egypt 47–30 B.C. She saved her kingdom by winning the love of Julius Caesar and Mark Antony, but was defeated by Octavian. After her death by suicide, Egypt became a Roman province.
clepe (klēp), *v.t.,* **cleped** or **clept** (also **ycleped** or **yclept**), **cleping.** *Archaic.* to call; name (now chiefly in the pp. as *ycleped* or *yclept*). [ME *clepien,* OE *cleopian*]
clepsydra (klĕpʹsĭ drə), *n., pl.* **-dras, -drae** (-drē′). a device for measuring time by the regulated flow of water or mercury through a small aperture. [t. L, t. Gk: m. *klepsýdra*]
cleptomania (klĕp′tō māʹnyə), *n.* kleptomania. —**clep′-toma′niac′,** *n.*
clerestory (klĭəʹstə rĭ), *n., pl.* **-ries. 1.** the upper part of the nave, transepts, and choir of a building, esp. a church, perforated with a series of windows above the aisle roofs, and forming the chief source of light for the building. **2.** a similar raised construction in any other structure. Also, **clearstory.** [f. *cler-* CLEAR (def. 1) + m. F *estoré* built]
clergy (klûʹjĭ), *n., pl.* **-gies.** the body of men ordained for ministering in the Christian Church, as distinct from the laity. [ME *clergie,* t. OF, ult. der. LL *clēricus* CLERIC]

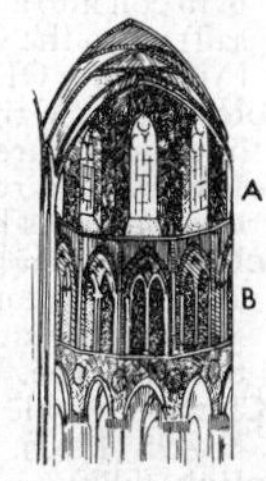

A, Clerestory; B, Triforium

clergyman (klûʹjĭ mən), *n., pl.* **-men. 1.** a

member of the clergy. **2.** an ordained Christian minister.
cleric (klĕr′ĭk), *n.* **1.** a member of the clergy. **2.** a member of a clerical party. —*adj.* **3.** pertaining to the clergy; clerical. [t. LL: s. *clēricus*, t. Gk: m. *klērikós*, der. *klêros* clergy, orig., lot, allotment]
clerical (klĕr′ĭ kl), *adj.* **1.** pertaining to a clerk or to clerks: *a clerical error.* **2.** of, pertaining to, or characteristic of the clergy or a clergyman. **3.** upholding the power or influence of the clergy in politics. —*n.* **4.** a cleric. **5.** (*pl.*) *Colloq.* clerical garments. **6.** a person or a party trying to extend the power of the church in government. [t. LL: s. *clēricālis*, der. *clēricus* clergyman] —**cler′ically,** *adv.*
clericalism (klĕr′ĭ kə lĭz′əm), *n.* **1.** clerical principles. **2.** clerical power or influence in politics. **3.** support of such power or influence. —**cler′icalist,** *n.*
clerihew (klĕr′ĭ hyo͞o′), *n.* a four-line jingle epitomizing a notable character. [named after E. *Clerihew* Bentley, 1875–1956, English journalist]
clerisy (klĕr′ĭ sĭ), *n.* learned men as a whole; the literati. [t. ML: m. s. *clēricia*]
clerk (kläk), *n.* **1.** one employed in an office, shop, etc., to keep records or accounts, attend to correspondence, etc. **2.** *U.S.* an assistant in business, esp. a retail salesman or saleswoman. **3.** one who keeps the records and performs the routine business of a court, legislature, board, etc. **4.** the administrative officer, and chief executive of a town or borough council. **5.** a builder's representative, responsible for the quality of the work on a building site: *clerk of the works.* **6.** *Chiefly Legal.* a clergyman; ecclesiastic. **7.** a layman charged with various minor ecclesiastical duties. **8.** *Archaic.* a person able to read, or to read and write. **9.** *Archaic.* a scholar. —*v.i.* **10.** to act or serve as a clerk. [ME; OE *clerc, cleric*, t. LL: s. *clēricus* CLERIC] —**clerk′ship′,** *n.*
clerkly (kläk′lĭ), *adj.*, **-lier, -liest,** *adv.* —*adj.* **1.** of a clerk or clerks. **2.** *Archaic.* scholarly. —*adv.* **3.** in the manner of a clerk. —**clerk′liness,** *n.*
Clerk-Maxwell (kläk′măks′wəl, -wĕl), *n.* **James,** 1831–1879, Scottish physicist.
clerk of the council, town clerk.
clerk of the works, one who is in charge of a construction works.
Clermont-Ferrand (*Fr.* klĕr mᴏɴ fĕ räɴ′), *n.* a town in central France, in Puy-de-Dôme department. 159,687 (1962).
cleveite (klē′vīt), *n.* a crystallized variety of uraninite. [named after P. T. *Cleve*, 1840–1905, Swedish chemist]
Cleveland (klēv′lənd), *n.* **1. (Stephen) Grover** (grō′və), 1837–1908, 22nd and 24th president of the U.S., 1885–89, 1893–97. **2.** a city in the U.S., in NE Ohio: a port on Lake Erie. 876,050 (1960).
clever (klĕv′ə), *adj.* **1.** bright mentally; having quick intelligence; able. **2.** dexterous or nimble with the hands or body. **3.** showing adroitness or ingenuity: *a clever remark, a clever device.* **4.** *Colloq.* superficially smart or bright; facile. **5.** *Colloq.* sly; cunning. **6.** *Dial. or U.S. Colloq.* suitable; convenient; satisfactory. **7.** *U.S. Colloq.* good-natured. **8.** *U.S. Dial.* in good health. **9.** *U.S. Dial.* handsome. [ME *cliver*; orig. uncert.] —**clev′erish,** *adj.* —**clev′erly,** *adv.* —**clev′erness,** *n.* —**Syn. 1.** ingenious, talented, quick-witted. **2.** skilful, adroit. —**Ant. 1.** stupid. **2.** clumsy.
clevis (klĕv′ĭs), *n.* a piece of metal, usually U-shaped, with a pin or bolt passing through holes at the two ends, as for attaching an implement to a drawbar for pulling. [akin to CLEAVE²]

C, Clevis

clew (klo͞o), *n.* **1.** a ball or skein of thread, yarn, etc. **2.** *Class. Myth.* a ball of thread unwound by Theseus to guide him through the labyrinth. **3.** a clue. **4.** (*pl. or sing.*) the rigging for a hammock. **5.** *Naut.* either lower corner of a square sail or the after lower corner of a fore-and-aft sail. —*v.t.* **6.** to coil into a ball. **7.** *Naut.* to haul (the lower corners of a sail) up to the yard by means of the clew lines (fol. by *up*). [ME *clewe*, OE *cleowen*, c. D *kluwen*]
clew iron, a ring in the corner of a sail to which the clew lines are secured.
clew line, a rope by which a clew of a square sail above the courses is hauled to the yard.
cliché (klē′shā; *Fr.* klē shĕ′), *n., pl.* **-chés** (-shāz; *Fr.* -shĕ′). a trite, stereotyped expression, idea, practice, etc., as *sadder but wiser*, or *strong as an ox.* [t. F, pp. of *clicher* to stereotype. Cf. G *Klitsch* doughy mass]
Clichy (*Fr.* klē shē′), *n.* a suburb of Paris, on the Seine. 56,495 (1962).
click (klĭk), *n.* **1.** a slight, sharp sound: *the click of a latch.* **2.** some clicking mechanism, as a detent or a pawl. **3.** *Phonet.* a speech sound produced by allowing air to flow suddenly into a partial vacuum in the mouth or in part of the mouth. —*v.i.* **4.** to emit or make a slight sharp sound, or series of such sounds, as by the cocking of a pistol. **5.** *Slang.* to make a success; make a hit. **6.** to fall into place or be understood: *his story suddenly clicked.* **7.** *Colloq.* to establish an immediate affinity, usually with a member of the opposite sex. —*v.t.* **7.** to cause to click; strike with a click. [imit. Cf. D *klikken*]
click beetle, an elaterid beetle that makes a clicking sound in springing up, as after having been laid on its back; snapping beetle.
clicker (klĭk′ə), *n.* **1.** one who or that which clicks. **2.** *Colloq.* a foreman in a printing works. **3.** *Colloq.* a foreman shoemaker.
client (klī′ənt), *n.* **1.** one who applies to a solicitor for advice or commits his cause or legal interests to a solicitor's management. **2.** one who employs or seeks advice from a professional adviser. **3.** a customer. **4.** (in ancient Rome) **a.** (orig.) a hereditary dependant of one of the nobility. **b.** a plebeian who lived under the patronage of a patrician. **4.** anyone under the patronage of another; a dependant. [ME, t. L: s. *cliens* retainer] —**cliental** (klī ĕn′tl), *adj.*
clientele (klē′ŏn tĕl′), *n.* **1.** the customers, clients, etc. (of a solicitor, businessman, etc.) as a whole. **2.** dependants or followers. Also, **clientage** (klī′ən tĭj). [t. L: m. *clientēla* a body of retainers]
cliff (klĭf), *n.* the high, steep face of a rocky mass; precipice. Also, *Archaic or Dial.*, **clift** (klĭft). [ME and OE *clif*, c. Icel. *klif*]
cliff-dweller (klĭf′dwĕl′ə), *n.* **1.** (*usually cap.*) one of a prehistoric people of the south-western U.S., ancestors of the Pueblo Indians, who built houses in caves or on ledges of the cliffs. **2.** one who dwells on a cliff. —**cliff′-dwel′ling,** *adj.*
cliff-hanging (klĭf′hăng′ĭng), *adj.* (of a film, novel, or the like) having as a characteristic crude, often melodramatic, suspense.
cliff swallow, a colonial bird, *Petrochelidon pyrrhonota*, of North America, so called because it attaches its bottle-shaped nests of mud to cliffs and walls.
cliffy (klĭf′ĭ), *adj.* having, or formed by, cliffs; craggy.
climacteric (klī măk′tə rĭk, klī′măk tĕ′rĭk), *adj.* **1.** pertaining to a critical period; crucial. —*n.* **2.** a year in which important changes in health, fortune, etc., are said to occur: *the grand climacteric* (*the sixty-third year*). **3.** *Physiol.* a period of decrease of reproductive activity in men and women, culminating, in women, in the menopause. **4.** any critical period. Also, **climacterical** (klī′măk tĕ′rĭ kl). [t. L: s. *clīmactēricus*, t. Gk: m. *klīmaktērikós* of the nature of a critical period]
climactic (klī măk′tĭk), *adj.* pertaining to or forming a climax: *climactic arrangement.* Also, **climac′tical.**
climate (klī′mĭt), *n.* **1.** the composite or generalization of weather conditions of a region, as temperature, pressure, humidity, precipitation, sunshine, cloudiness, and winds, throughout the year, averaged over a series of years. **2.** an area of a particular kind of climate. **3.** the general attitude and prevailing opinions of a group of people. [ME *climat*, t. LL: s. *clima*, t. Gk: m. *klíma* clime, zone, lit., slope (of the earth from equator to pole)] —**climatic** (klī măt′ĭk), *adj.* —**climat′ically,** *adv.*
climatology (klī′mə tŏl′ə jĭ), *n.* the science that deals with climates or climatic conditions. —**climatologic** (klī′mə tə lŏj′ĭk), **cli′matolog′ical,** *adj.* —**cli′matol′ogist,** *n.*
climax (klī′măks), *n.* **1.** the highest point of anything; the culmination. **2.** that point in the drama in which it is clear that the central motive will or will not be successful. **3.** *Rhet.* **a.** a figure consisting in a series of related ideas so arranged that each surpasses the preceding in force or intensity. **b.** (popularly) the last term or member of this figure. **4.** *Ecol.* that stage in the ecological succession or evolution of a plant-animal community, which is stable and self-perpetuating. —*v.i., v.t.* **5.** to reach, or bring to, the climax. [t. L, t. Gk: m. *klîmax* ladder, staircase, climax]
climb (klīm), *v.i.* **1.** to mount or ascend, esp. by using both hands and feet. **2.** to rise slowly by, or as by, continued effort. **3.** to slope upward. **4.** to ascend by twining or by means of tendrils, adhesive tissues, etc., as a plant. **5.** to rise, or attempt to rise, in social position. **6. climb down, a.** to descend, esp. by using both hands and feet. **b.** *Colloq.* to withdraw from an untenable position; retract an indefensible argument. —*v.t.* **7.** to ascend, go up, or get to the top of, esp. by the use of hands and feet. **8.** to descend (a ladder, pole, etc.), esp. by using both hands and feet (fol. by *down*). —*n.* **9.** a climbing; an ascent by climbing. **10.** a place to be climbed. [ME *climben*, OE *climban*, c. D and G *klimmen*] —**climb′able,** *adj.*

—**Syn.** **1.** CLIMB, ASCEND, MOUNT, SCALE imply a moving upwards. To CLIMB is to make one's way upwards with effort: *to climb a mountain.* ASCEND, in its literal meaning (to go up), is general; but it now usually suggests a gradual or stately movement, with or without effort, often to a considerable degree of altitude: *to ascend stairs.* MOUNT may be interchangeable with ascend, but also suggests climbing on top of or astride of: *to mount a platform, a horse.* SCALE, a more literary word, implies difficult or hazardous climbing up or over something: *to scale a summit.* —**Ant.** **1, 7.** descend.

climber (klī'mə), *n.* **1.** one who or that which climbs. **2.** a person who strives to associate with social superiors. **3.** a climbing plant. **4.** a spike attached to a shoe to assist in climbing telegraph poles, etc.

climbing fish, a small fish of India, *Anabas testudineus,* which is reputed to climb trees.

climbing irons, iron frames with spikes attached, worn on the feet or legs to help in climbing trees, etc.

clime (klīm), *n. Poetic.* **1.** a tract or region of the earth. **2.** climate. [t. L: m. *clima* CLIMATE]

clinandrium (klĭ năn'drĭ əm), *n., pl.* **-dria** (-drĭ ə). a cavity in the apex of the column in orchids, in which the anthers rest; the androclinium. [t. NL, f. s. Gk *klīnē* bed + s. Gk *anḗr* man + *-ium* -IUM]

clinch (klĭnch), *v.t.* **1.** to secure (a driven nail, etc.) by beating down the point. **2.** to fasten (work) together thus. **3.** to settle (a matter) decisively. **4.** *Naut.* to secure overlapping plates on the side of a ship with a fastening. —*v.i.* **5.** *Boxing, etc.* to engage in a clinch. **6.** to beat down the point of a nail, etc., in order to fasten something. —*n.* **7.** the act of clinching. **8.** *Boxing, etc.* the act or an instance of one or both contestants holding the other in such a way as to hinder his punches. **9.** *Slang.* an embrace or passionate kiss. **10.** a clinched nail or fastening. **11.** the clinched part of a nail, etc. **12.** *Naut.* a kind of half-hitch in which the end of the rope is fastened back by seizing or lashing to its main part. **13.** *Obs.* a pun. [later var. of CLENCH]

clincher (klĭnch'ə), *n.* **1.** one who or that which clinches. **2.** something decisive.

cline (klīn), *n. Biol.* a continuous, graded variation of an organism across its geographical or ecological range.

cling (klĭng), *v.,* **clung, clinging. 1.** to adhere closely; stick. **2.** to hold fast, as by grasping or embracing; cleave. **3.** to be or remain close. **4.** to remain attached (to an idea, hope, memory, etc.). **5.** *Obs.* to cohere. [ME *clingen,* OE *clingan* stick or draw together, shrivel] —**cling'er,** *n.* —**cling'ingly,** *adv.*

clingfish (klĭng'fĭsh'), *n., pl.* **-fishes,** (*esp. collectively*) **fish.** any fish of the family *Gobiesocidae,* all of which have a ventral sucking disc constructed from the pectoral as well as the pelvic fins. They use this disc to adhere tightly to rocks.

cling peach, a clingstone peach.

clingstone (klĭng'stōn'), *adj.* **1.** having a stone to which the pulp adheres closely, as certain peaches. —*n.* **2.** a clingstone peach.

clingy (klĭng'ĭ), *adj.* apt to cling; adhesive or tenacious.

clinic (klĭn'ĭk), *n.* **1.** a class of medical students which takes place in a hospital ward, where practical instruction in examining and treating patients is given. **2.** one of a number of out-patient sections of a hospital for the specialized treatment of particular conditions and diseases. **3.** any medical centre used for such treatments as X-rays, child care, vaccinations, etc. **4.** a hospital for private patients. [t. LL: s. *clīnicus* pertaining to a bed, t. Gk: m. *klīnikós*]

clinical (klĭn'ĭ kl), *adj.* **1.** pertaining to a clinic. **2.** pertaining to or used in a sickroom. **3.** pertaining to medical training carried out in a hospital. **4.** concerned with observation and treatment of disease in the patient (as distinguished from an artificial experiment). **5.** scientific; involving professional knowledge and not affected by the emotions: *he has a clinical attitude to even the most distressing cases.* **6.** administered on a sickbed or deathbed: *clinical conversion or baptism.* —**clin'ically,** *adv.*

clinical thermometer, an instrument used to determine the body temperature.

clinician (klĭ nish'ən), *n.* a physician who studies diseases at the bedside or is skilled in clinical methods.

clink[1] (klĭngk), *v.i., v.t.* **1.** to make, or cause to make, a light, sharp, ringing sound. **2.** to rhyme or jingle. **3.** to move with a clinking sound. —*n.* **4.** a clinking sound. **5.** a rhyme; jingle. **6.** the rather piercing cry of some birds, as the stonechat. [ME *clynk(e).* Cf. D *klinken*]

clink[2] (klĭngk), *n. Colloq.* a prison; jail. [appar. from *Clink* prison in Clink Street, Southwark, London]

clink[3] (klĭngk), *n.* a short, square, pointed steel bar, as used for breaking up road surfaces. [special use of CLINK[1]]

clinker[1] (klĭng'kə), *n.* **1.** a hard brick, used for paving, etc. **2.** a partially vitrified mass of brick. **3.** the scale of oxide formed on iron during forging. **4.** a mass of incombustible matter fused together, as in the burning of of coal. —*v.i.* **5.** to form clinkers in burning, as coal. [t. D: m. *klinker* kind of brick]

clinker[2] (klĭng'kə), *n.* **1.** one who or that which clinks. **2.** *Slang.* something first-rate or worthy of admiration. **3.** *Mountaineering.* a soft iron edge-nail for climbing-boots.

clinker[3] (klĭng'kə), *adj.* made of pieces, as boards or plates of metal, which overlap one another. Also, **clinker-built** (klĭng'kə bĭlt').

clinking (klĭng'kĭng), *adj., adv. Slang.* very fine.

clinkstone (klĭngk'stōn'), *n. Geol.* any of several varieties of phonolite which give out a ringing sound when struck.

clinometer (klī nŏm'ĭ tə, klĭ-), *n.* an instrument used to determine inclination or slope. [f. *clino-* (comb. form repr. L *-clīnāre* incline) + -METER[1]]

clinometric (klī'nə mĕt'rĭk), *adj.* **1.** (of crystals) having oblique angles between one or all axes. **2.** pertaining to or determined by a clinometer. Also, **cli'nomet'rical.**

clinostat (klī'nō stăt'), *n. Bot.* an apparatus for slowly rotating a plant so that all its sides are equally subjected to a unilateral stimulus, as light or gravity.

clinquant (klĭng'kənt), *adj.* **1.** glittering, esp. with tinsel; decked with garish finery. —*n.* **2.** imitation gold leaf; tinsel. **3.** *Obs.* false glitter. [t. F, ppr. of obs. *clinquer* clink, tinkle, glitter, t. D: m. *klinken*]

clint (klĭnt), *n.* a flat-topped ridge between furrows or grikes, caused by solution in a horizontal limestone surface.

clintonia (klĭn tō'nyə), *n.* any plant of the liliaceous genus *Clintonia,* comprising stemless perennial herbs with a few broad, ribbed, basal leaves, and white or greenish yellow flowers on a short peduncle. [t. NL; named after De Witt *Clinton* 1769–1828, U.S. politician]

Clio (klī'ō), *n. Class. Myth.* the Muse of history.

clip[1] (klĭp), *v.,* **clipped, clipping,** *n.* —*v.t.* **1.** to cut, or cut off or out, as with shears; trim by cutting. **2.** to cut or trim the hair or fleece of; shear. **3.** to pare the edge of (a coin). **4.** to punch a hole in (a ticket). **5.** to cut short; curtail. **6.** to omit sounds of (a word) in pronouncing. **7.** *Colloq.* to hit with a quick, sharp blow. —*v.i.* **8.** to clip or cut something; make the motion of clipping something. **9.** to move swiftly. **10.** *Archaic.* to fly rapidly. —*n.* **11.** the act of clipping. **12.** anything clipped off, esp. the wool shorn at a single shearing of sheep. **13.** the amount of wool shorn in one season. **14.** (*pl.*) shears. **15.** an excerpt from a film. **16.** *Colloq.* a quick, sharp blow or punch. **17.** *Colloq.* rate; pace: *at a rapid clip.* **18.** *Colloq.* general appearance; looks. [ME *clippen,* t. Scand.; cf. Icel. *klippa*]

clip[2] (klĭp), *n., v.,* **clipped, clipping.** —*n.* **1.** a device for gripping and holding tightly; a metal clasp, esp. one for papers, letters, etc. **2.** a flange on the upper surface of a horseshoe. **3.** a holder for ammunition ready for insertion into the magazine of certain weapons. **4.** *Archaic or Dial.* an embrace. —*v.t.* **5.** to grip tightly; hold together by pressure. **6.** to encircle; encompass. **7.** *Archaic or Dial.* to embrace or hug. [ME *clippe(n),* OE *clyppan* embrace]

clipjoint (klĭp'joint'), *n. Colloq.* a nightclub or restaurant where prices are exorbitant and customers are swindled.

clipper (klĭp'ə), *n.* **1.** one who or that which clips or cuts. **2.** (*often pl.*) a cutting tool, esp. shears. **3.** (*often pl.*) a tool with rotating or reciprocating knives for cutting hair. **4.** one that clips, or moves swiftly, as a horse. **5.** a sailing vessel built and rigged for speed. **6.** *Slang.* a first-rate person or thing.

clipper-built (klĭp'ə bĭlt'), *adj. Naut.* built on sharp, rakish lines conducive to fast sailing.

clippie (klĭp'ĭ), *n. Colloq.* a bus conductress.

clipping (klĭp'ĭng), *n.* **1.** the act of one who or that which clips. **2.** a piece clipped off or out. **3.** *U.S.* a cutting. —*adj.* **4.** that clips. **5.** *Colloq.* swift: *a clipping pace.* **6.** *Slang.* first-rate or excellent.

clique (klēk), *n., v.,* **cliqued, cliquing.** —*n.* **1.** a small set or coterie, esp. one that is snobbishly exclusive. —*v.i.* **2.** *Colloq.* to form, or associate in, a clique. [t. F, der. OF *cliquer* make a sharp sound. Cf. CLAQUE] —**Syn. 1.** See **ring**[1].

cliquey (klē'kĭ), *adj. Colloq.* cliquish. Also, **cli'quy.**

cliquish (klē'kĭsh), *adj.* of, pertaining to, or savouring of a clique: *a cliquish fashion.* —**cli'quishly,** *adv.* —**cli'quishness,** *n.*

clitellum (klĭ tĕl'əm), *n., pl.* **-tella** (-tĕl'ə). *Zool.* the glandular part of the epidermis which, in some oligochaete annelid worms, secretes the cocoon within which the eggs are deposited. [t. NL, m. L *clitellae* pack-saddle]

Clitheroe (klĭth'ə rō'), *n.* a town in England, in NE Lancashire. 12,147 (1961).

clitoris (klī′tə rĭs, klĭt′ə rĭs), *n. Anat.* the erectile organ of the vulva, homologous to the penis of the male. [t. NL, t. Gk: m. *kleitorís*, der. *kleíein* shut]

Clive (klīv), *n.* **Robert** (*Baron Clive of Plassey*), 1725–1774, British general and statesman in India. His victory in the Battle of Plassey in 1757 was important in giving Great Britain control of India.

cllr, councillor.

cloaca (klō ā′kə), *n., pl.* **-cae** (-kē). **1.** a sewer. **2.** a privy. **3.** a place or receptacle of moral filth. **4.** *Zool.* **a.** the common cavity into which the intestinal, urinary, and generative canals open in birds, reptiles, amphibians, many fishes, and certain mammals (*monotremes*). **b.** a similar cavity in invertebrates. [t. L, prob. der. *cluere* cleanse] —**cloa′cal,** *adj.*

cloak (klōk), *n.* **1.** a loose outer garment. **2.** that which covers or conceals; disguise; pretext. —*v.t.* **3.** to cover with, or as with a cloak. **4.** to hide; conceal. [ME *cloke*, t. OF, g. ML *cloc(c)a* cloak, orig. bell; ? of Celtic orig. See CLOCK[1]]

cloak-and-dagger (klōk′ən dăg′ə), *adj.* melodramatic; concerned with espionage, intrigue, etc.

cloakroom (klōk′ro͝om′, -ro͞om′), *n.* **1.** a room where cloaks, overcoats, etc., may be left temporarily. **2.** a lavatory.

cloanthite (klō ăn′thīt), *n.* chloanthite.

clobber[1] (klŏb′ə), *v.t. Slang.* to batter severely; maul. [? b. CLUB and SLOBBER]

clobber[2] (klŏb′ə), *n. Colloq.* clothes or gear. [alter. of CLOTHES]

clobber[3] (klŏb′ə), *n.* **1.** a paste used to cover cracks in leather. —*v.t.* **2.** to paint over existing decorations on (a ceramic piece). **3.** *Obs.* to mend. [t. Scot. Gaelic: m. *clābar* mud]

cloche (klŏsh), *n.* **1.** a bell-shaped or tunnel-like cover, as used to cover and protect young plants, usually made of glass. **2.** a woman's bell-shaped, close-fitting hat. [t. F: lit., bell. See CLOCK[1]]

clock[1] (klŏk), *n.* **1.** an instrument for measuring and indicating time, having pointers which move round on a dial to mark the hour, etc. **2.** such a timepiece not carried on the person (distinguished from a *watch*). **3.** *Colloq.* a mileometer. **4.** *Electronics.* a circuit producing regular pulses which control the speed of operation of a system. —*v.t.* **5.** to time, test, or ascertain by the clock. **6. clock in,** to register the time of arrival at a place of work. **7. clock out,** to register the time of departure from a place of work. [ME *clokke*, t. MD: m. *klocke* instrument for measuring time; cf. OE *clugge* bell, ONF *cloke*]

clock[2] (klŏk), *n.* an embroidered or woven ornament on each side of a stocking, extending from the ankle upwards. [orig. uncert.] —**clocked,** *adj.*

clock-golf (klŏk′gŏlf′), *n.* a putting game in which one or more of the players seek to hole a ball from twelve marked clock figures.

clockmaker (klŏk′mā′kə), *n.* a person who makes or repairs clocks.

clock-pulse (klŏk′pŭls′), *n. Electronics.* a regular electric pulse which controls the speed of operation of an electronic system.

clock-watcher (klŏk′wŏch′ə), *n.* an employee who spends much of the time longing for the end of the working day. —**clock′-watch′ing,** *n., adj.*

clockwise (klŏk′wīz′), *adv., adj.* in the direction of rotation of the hands of a clock.

clockwork (klŏk′wûk′), *n.* **1.** the mechanism of a clock. **2.** any mechanism similar to that of a clock. **3. like clockwork,** with perfect regularity or precision.

clod (klŏd), *n.* **1.** a lump or mass, esp. of earth or clay. **2.** earth; soil. **3.** anything earthy or base, as the body in comparison with the soul: *this corporeal clod.* **4.** a stupid person; blockhead; dolt. **5.** a part of the shoulder of beef. [ME *clodde*, OE *clodd* (in *clodhamer* fieldfare). Cf. CLOUD] —**clod′dish,** *adj.* —**clod′dishness,** *n.* —**clod′dy,** *adj.*

clodhopper (klŏd′hŏp′ə), *n.* **1.** a clumsy boor; rustic; bumpkin. **2.** (*pl.*) strong, heavy shoes.

clodhopping (klŏd′hŏp′ĭng), *adj.* loutish; boorish.

clodpoll (klŏd′pōl′), *n.* a blockhead; a stupid person. Also, **clodpole, clodpate** (klŏd′pāt′).

clog (klŏg), *v.,* **clogged, clogging,** *n.* —*v.t.* **1.** to encumber; hamper; hinder. **2.** to hinder or obstruct, esp. by sticky matter; choke up. —*v.i.* **3.** to become clogged, encumbered, or choked up. **4.** to stick; stick together. —*n.* **5.** anything that impedes motion or action; an encumbrance; a hindrance. **6.** a heavy block, as of wood, fastened to a man or beast to impede movement. **7.** a kind of shoe with a thick sole usually of wood. **8.** a similar but lighter shoe worn in the clog dance. **9.** a thick piece of wood. [ME *clog, clogge*; orig. uncert.] —**clog′gy,** *adj.*

clog dance, a dance performed with clogs to beat time to the music. —**clog′-danc′er,** *n.* —**clog′-danc′ing,** *n.*

cloisonné (klwä zŏn′ā; *Fr.* klwȧ zō nė′), *n.* **1.** enamelwork in which colour areas are separated by thin, metal bands fixed edgeways to the ground. —*adj.* **2.** of, pertaining to, or resembling cloisonné. [t. F, der. *cloison* partition]

cloister (klois′tə), *n.* **1.** a covered walk, esp. one adjoining a building, as a church, commonly running round an open court (garth) and opening on to it with an open arcade or colonnade. **2.** a place of religious seclusion; a monastery or nunnery; a convent. **3.** any quiet, secluded place. **4.** life in a monastery or nunnery. —*v.t.* **5.** to confine in a cloister or convent. **6.** to confine in retirement; seclude. **7.** to furnish with a cloister or covered walk. **8.** to convert into a cloister or convent. [ME *cloistre*, t. OF, b. *cloison* partition (cf. CLOISONNÉ) and L *claustrum* enclosed place] —**cloi′ster-like′,** *adj.* —**Syn. 2.** See **convent.**

cloistered (klois′təd), *adj.* solitary; retired from the world: *cloistered seclusion.*

cloister-garth (kloi′stə gäth′), *n.* See **garth** (def. 1).

cloistral (klois′trəl), *adj.* **1.** of, pertaining to, or living in a cloister. **2.** cloister-like: *a cloistral house.*

cloke (klōk), *n., v. Obs.* cloak.

Cloncurry (klŏn kŭ′rĭ), *n.* a river in Australia, flowing N through Queensland to join the Flinders river. 280 mi.

clone (klōn), *n., v.,* **cloned, cloning.** —*n.* **1.** *Biol.* the descendants or a descendant of an asexually produced individual, deriving from a single cell in an organism. **2.** *Hort.* a group of plants originating as parts of the same individual, from buds or cuttings. —*v.t., v.i.* **3.** to produce (descendants) asexually, from a single cell in an organism. Also, **clon** (klŏn, klōn). [t. Gk: m. *klṓn* slip, twig]

clonus (klō′nəs), *n. Pathol.* a rapid succession of flexion and extension of a group of muscles, usually signifying an affection of the brain or spinal cord. [t. NL, t. Gk: m. *klónos* commotion, turmoil] —**clonic** (klŏn′ĭk), *adj.* —**clonicity** (klō nĭs′ĭ tĭ), *n.*

Cloots (*Fr.* klōts), *n.* **Jean Baptiste du Val-de-Grâce** (*Fr.* zhäɴ bȧ tēst dʏ vȧl də grȧs′), **Baron de** ('*Anacharsis Clootz*'), 1755–94, Prussian leader in the French Revolution.

clop (klŏp), *n., v.,* **clopped, clopping.** —*n.* **1.** the sound made by a horse's hoofs. —*v.i.* **2.** to move with such a sound. [imit.]

close (*v.* klōz; *adj., adv.* klōs; *n.* klōz *for 46–50,* klōs *for 51–53*), *v.,* **closed, closing,** *adj.,* **closer, closest,** *adv., n.* —*v.t.* **1.** to stop or obstruct (a gap, entrance, aperture, etc.). **2.** to stop or obstruct the entrances, apertures, or gaps in. **3.** to shut in or surround on all sides; enclose; cover in. **4.** to refuse access to or passage across: *the authorities closed the border to tourists.* **5.** to bring together the parts of; join; unite: *to close the ranks of troops.* **6.** to bring to an end; to shut down, either temporarily or permanently: *to close a debate, to close a shop.* **7.** *Naut.* to come close to. —*v.i.* **8.** to become closed; shut. **9.** to come together; unite. **10.** to come close. **11.** to grapple; engage in close encounter (fol. by *with*). **12.** to come to terms (fol. by *with*). **13.** to agree (fol. by *on, upon*). **14.** to come to an end; terminate. **15.** *Stock Exchange.* to be worth at the end of a trading period. **16. close in,** to surround and approach (a place) gradually, as in making a capture. [ME *close(n)*, t. OF: m. *clos-*, s. *clore*, g. L *claudere* shut; r. OE *clȳsan*]

—*adj.* **17.** shut; shut tight; not open. **18.** shut in; enclosed. **19.** completely enclosing. **20.** without opening; with all openings covered or closed. **21.** confined; narrow: *close quarters.* **22.** lacking fresh or freely circulating air: *a close room.* **23.** heavy; oppressive: *a spell of close weather.* **24.** narrowly confined, as a prisoner. **25.** practising secrecy; secretive; reticent. **26.** parsimonious; stingy. **27.** scarce, as money. **28.** not open to public or general admission, competition, etc. **29.** under prohibition as to hunting or fishing: *a close season.* **30.** having the parts near together: *a close texture.* **31.** compact; condensed. **32.** near, or near together, in space, time, or relation: *in close contact.* **33.** *Ball Games.* characterized by short passes and cautious tactics: *they played a close game.* **34.** intimate; confidential: *close friendship.* **35.** based upon a strong uniting feeling of love, honour, etc.; *a close union of nations.* **36.** fitting tightly, as a cap. **37.** short; near the surface. **38.** not deviating from the subject under consideration: *close attention.* **39.** strict; searching; minute: *close investigation.* **40.** not deviating from a model or original: *a close translation.* **41.** nearly even or equal: *a close contest.* **42.** strictly logical: *close reasoning.* **43.** *Phonet.* pronounced with a relatively small opening above the tongue. *Beet* and *boot* have the closest English vowels. **44.** *Rare.* viscous; not volatile. —*adv.*

45. in a close manner; closely. [ME *clos*, t. F, g. L *clausus*, pp., shut]
—*n.* 46. the act of closing. 47. the end or conclusion. 48. *Music.* a cadence. 49. a junction; union. 50. a close encounter; a grapple. 51. an enclosed place; an enclosure; any piece of land held as private property. 52. an enclosure about or beside a building, cathedral, etc. 53. a narrow entry or alley, or a courtyard to which it leads. [(defs 46–50) n. use of v.; (defs 51–53) ME *clos*, t. F, g. L *clausum* enclosed place] —**closely** (klōs′lĭ), *adv.* —**closeness** (klōs′nĭs), *n.* —**closer** (klō′zə), *n.*

—**Syn.** 1. CLOSE, SHUT mean to cause something not to be open. CLOSE suggests blocking an opening or vacant place: *to close a breach in a wall.* The informal word SHUT refers esp. to blocking or barring openings intended for literal or figurative ingress and egress: *to shut a door, mouth, gate, etc.* 6. end, conclude, terminate, finish, complete. 22. unventilated, muggy. 26. penurious, miserly. 47. See **end**[1].

close call (klōs), *Colloq.* a narrow escape.

closed (klōzd), *adj.* 1. restricted or exclusive in any of various ways. 2. *Phonet.* (of syllables) ending with a consonant.

closed book, *Colloq.* 1. a subject about which one knows nothing. 2. a matter which has been completely finished.

closed chain, *Chem.* a linking of atoms in an organic molecule which may be represented by a structural formula which forms a ring or cycle.

closed circuit, a path along which electricity can flow.

closed-circuit television, a system of televising by wire to designated viewing sets, as within a factory for monitoring production operations, etc.

close-down (klōz′doun′), *n.* 1. a general stoppage of work. 2. the end of a period of broadcasting.

closed scholarship, a scholarship which may be competed for only by candidates fulfilling certain preconditions.

closed shop, a workshop, factory, or the like, in which the employer must call on a particular trade union to furnish employees.

close-fisted (klōs′fĭs′tĭd), *adj.* stingy; miserly.

close-grained (klōs′grānd′), *adj.* (of wood) having the grain close or fine in texture.

close harmony, a style of part-singing, chiefly heard in jazz, in which all the voices except the bass sing in octaves or tenths.

close-hauled (klōs′hôld′), *adj.* *Naut.* sailing as close to the wind as a vessel will sail, with sails trimmed as flat as possible.

close-lipped (klōs′lĭpt′), *adj.* not talking or revealing much.

close-order (klōs′ô′də), *adj.* *Mil.* (of drill) carried out with two paces between ranks, as in ceremonial duties.

close position (klōs), *Music.* arrangement of a chord so that the parts are as close together as possible.

close quarters (klōs), 1. a small, cramped place or position. 2. direct and close contact in a fight.

close shave (klōs), *Colloq.* a narrow escape.

closet (klŏz′ĭt), *n.* 1. a small room, enclosed recess, or cabinet for clothing, food, utensils, etc. 2. a small private room, esp. one for prayer, thought, etc. 3. a water closet; toilet. —*adj.* 4. suited for use or enjoyment in privacy: *a closet drama* (one to be read rather than acted). —*v.t.* 5. to shut up in a private room for a conference, interview, etc. [ME, t. OF, dim. of *clos*, g. L *clausum* enclosed place]

close thing (klōs), *Colloq.* a narrow escape.

close-up (klōs′ŭp′), *n.* 1. a picture taken at close range or with a long focal length lens, on a relatively large scale. 2. an intimate view or presentation of anything.

closing order, an order, made by a local authority, to close down a condemned property.

closing time, the end of the period in which alcoholic drinks may legally be sold in a public house.

clostridium (klŏs trĭd′ĭ əm), *n.* any of the group of spore-forming, anaerobic bacteria.

closure (klō′zhə), *n.*, *v.*, **-sured, -suring.** —*n.* 1. the act of closing or shutting. 2. the state of being closed. 3. a bringing to an end; conclusion. 4. a metal or plastic cap for a bottle. 5. *Obs.* that which closes or shuts. 6. *Obs.* that which encloses or shuts in; enclosure. 7. *Phonet.* an articulation which keeps the breath from moving outwards by closing the vocal tract at some point. 8. *Parl. Proc.* a method of closing a debate and causing an immediate vote to be taken on the question under discussion, as by moving the previous question. —*v.t.* 9. *Parl. Proc.* to end (a debate, etc.) by closure. [ME, t. OF, g. LL *clausura*, der. L *clausus*, pp., shut]

clot (klŏt), *n.*, *v.*, **clotted, clotting.** —*n.* 1. a mass or lump. 2. a semisolid mass, as of coagulated blood. 3. *Colloq.* a stupid person. —*v.i.* 4. to form into clots; coagulate. —*v.t.* 5. to cause to clot; cover with clots. [ME; OE *clott* lump, c. G *Klotz* block, log]

cloth (klŏth), *n.*, *pl.* **cloths** (klŏt͟hz; klŏths), *adj.* —*n.* 1. a fabric formed by weaving, felting, etc., from wool, hair, silk, flax, cotton, or other fibre, used for garments, upholstery, and many other purposes. 2. a piece of such a fabric for a particular purpose: *a tray cloth.* 3. *Theat.* a painted fabric used as a curtain or as scenery. 4. a particular profession, esp. that of a clergyman. 5. **the cloth,** the clergy. 6. *Naut.* one of several lengths of canvas, usually about two feet wide, which are stitched together to make a sail. 7. *Obs.* a garment; clothing. 8. *Obs.* a livery or customary garb, as of a trade or profession. —*adj.* 9. made of, covered with, or pertaining to cloth. [ME; OE *clath*, c. G *Kleid* garment]

clothe (klōt͟h), *v.t.*, **clothed** or **clad, clothing.** 1. to dress; attire. 2. to provide with clothing. 3. to cover with, or as with, clothing. 4. to endow; invest (as with meaning). 5. to conceal. [ME *clothen*, OE *clāthian*]

clothes (klōz, klōt͟hz), *n.pl.* 1. garments for the body; articles of dress; wearing apparel. 2. bedclothes. [orig., pl. of CLOTH] —**Syn.** 1. clothing, attire, raiment, vesture, costume, garb; vestments, habiliments.

clothes basket, 1. a basket in which soiled clothes are stored before washing. 2. a basket in which clothes are sent to and from the wash.

clothes hanger, a support for clothes, usually bow-shaped with a hook.

clothes horse, a frame on which to hang clothes, etc., esp. for drying.

clothes line, a rope on which to hang clothes, etc., to dry after being washed.

clothes moth, any of certain small moths whose larvae feed on wool, fur, etc.

clothes peg, a forked piece of wood or other device for hanging clothes on a line.

clothes press, 1. a receptacle for clothes, as a chest, wardrobe, or cupboard. 2. a device for pressing clothes.

clothes prop, a pole that holds up a clothes line.

clothier (klō′t͟hĭ ə), *n.* a maker or seller of cloth or clothes.

clothing (klō′t͟hĭng), *n.* 1. garments collectively; clothes; raiment; apparel. 2. a covering.

Clotho (klō′thō), *n.* *Gk Myth.* one of the three Fates. [t. L, t. Gk: m. *Klōthṓ*, lit., the spinner]

cloth of gold, a tissue of threads of gold and silk or wool.

clottish (klŏt′ĭsh), *adj.* *Colloq.* foolish; silly.

clotty (klŏt′ĭ), *adj.* 1. full of clots. 2. tending to clot. 3. *Colloq.* silly; stupid.

cloture (klō′chə), *n.* *U.S. Parl. Proc.* closure of a debate. [t. F, g. L *claustūra*, var. of *clausūra* CLOSURE]

cloud (kloud), *n.* 1. a visible collection of particles of water or ice suspended in the air, usually at an elevation above the earth's surface. 2. any similar mass, esp. of smoke or dust. 3. a dim or obscure area in something otherwise clear or transparent. 4. *Obs.* a patch or spot, differing in colour from the surrounding surface. 5. anything that obscures, darkens, or causes gloom, trouble, suspicion, disgrace, etc. 6. a great number of insects, birds, etc., flying together: *a cloud of locusts.* 7. a multitude; a crowd. 8. **have one's head in the clouds,** to be divorced from reality; be in a dreamlike state. 9. **in the clouds,** a. imaginary; unreal. b. impractical. —*v.t.* 10. to overspread or cover with, or as with, a cloud or clouds. 11. to overshadow; obscure; darken. 12. to make gloomy. 13. to place under suspicion, disgrace, etc. 14. to variegate with patches of another colour. —*v.i.* 15. to grow cloudy; become clouded. [ME *cloud(e)* rock, clod, cloud, OE *clūd* rock, hill; akin to CLOD]

—**Syn.** 9. CLOUD, FOG, HAZE, MIST differ somewhat in their figurative uses. CLOUD connotes esp. daydreaming: *his mind is in the clouds.* FOG and HAZE connote esp. bewilderment or confusion: *to go around in a fog (haze).* MIST has an emotional connotation and suggests tears: *a mist in one's eyes.*

cloudbank (kloud′băngk′), *n.* a thick mass of low cloud.

cloudberry (kloud′bə rĭ, -brĭ), *n.*, *pl.* **-ries.** 1. the orange-yellow edible fruit of *Rubus chamaemorus*, a small raspberry of the Northern Hemisphere. 2. the plant.

cloudburst (kloud′bûst′), *n.* a sudden and very heavy rainfall.

cloud-capped (kloud′kăpt′), *adj.* (of mountains, etc.) having the summit surrounded by clouds. Also, **cloud-capt.**

cloud chamber, *Physics.* a closed chamber containing saturated water vapour which indicates the presence of moving particles by the trails of water condensation which they produce. Also, **Wilson cloud chamber.**

cloud-cuckoo-land (kloud′ko͝ok′o͞o lănd′), *n.* a fanciful place of unrealistic notions.

cloudland (kloud′lănd′), *n.* a region of unreality, imagination, etc.; dreamland.

cloudless (kloud′lĭs), *adj.* without clouds; clear. —**cloud′lessly,** *adv.* —**cloud′lessness,** *n.*

cloudlet (kloud′lĭt), *n.* a little cloud.
cloud rack, a group of drifting clouds.
Clouds (kloudz), *n.* **Sea of,** a dark plain, *Mare Nubium,* in the third quadrant of the face of the moon.
cloud-topped (kloud′tŏpt′), *adj.* having the top covered with clouds.
cloudy (klou′dĭ), *adj.*, **cloudier, cloudiest. 1.** full of or overcast with clouds: *a cloudy sky.* **2.** of or like a cloud or clouds; pertaining to clouds. **3.** having cloud-like markings: *cloudy marble.* **4.** not clear or transparent: *a cloudy liquid.* **5.** obscure; indistinct: *cloudy notions.* **6.** darkened by gloom, trouble, etc.: *cloudy looks.* **7.** under suspicion, disgrace, etc.: *a cloudy reputation.* **—cloud′ily,** *adv.* **—cloud′iness,** *n.* **—Syn. 1.** overclouded, lowering.
clough (klŭf), *n. Dial.* a narrow valley; a ravine; a glen. [ME, OE *clōh,* c. OHG *klāh*]
Clough (klŭf), *n.* **Arthur Hugh,** 1819–61, English poet.
clout (klout), *n.* **1.** *Colloq.* a blow, esp. with the hand; a cuff. **2.** the mark shot at in archery. **3.** a shot that hits the mark. **4.** *Archaic or Dial.* a patch, or piece of cloth or other material used to mend something. **5.** *Archaic or Dial.* any worthless piece of cloth; a rag. **6.** *Dial.* an iron plate, on a shoe, plough, etc., to prolong wear. *—v.t.* **7.** *Colloq.* to strike, esp. with the hand; cuff. **8.** *Archaic or Dial.* to bandage. **9.** *Archaic or Dial.* to patch; mend. [ME; OE *clūt* piece of cloth or metal. Cf. CLOT]
clout nail, a nail with a large flat head used to stud or clout a surface.
clove[1] (klōv), *n.* **1.** the dried flower bud of a tropical myrtaceous tree, *Eugenia aromatica,* used whole or ground as a spice. **2.** the tree. [ME *clowe,* t. OF: m. *clou* (g. L *clāvus*), in *clou de girofle* nail of clove (see GILLYFLOWER), so called from the shape]
clove[2] (klōv), *n. Bot.* one of the small bulbs formed in the axils of the scales of a mother bulb, as in garlic. [ME; OE *clufu* clove, bulb, tuber, c. D *kloof* cleft]
clove[3] (klōv), *v.* pt. of **cleave**[2].
clove hitch, *Naut.* a form of hitch for fastening a rope about a spar, etc., in which two rounds of rope are crossed about the spar, with the ends of the rope issuing in opposite directions between the crossed parts.
cloven (klō′vən), *v.* **1.** pp. of **cleave**[2]. *—adj.* **2.** cleft; split; divided: *cloven feet or hoofs.* **3.** cleaved.
cloven-footed (klō′vən fo͝ot′ĭd), *adj.* **1.** having cloven feet. **2.** devilish; satanic.
cloven hoof, the figurative indication of Satan or evil temptation. Also, **cloven foot.**
cloven-hoofed (klō′vən ho͞oft′), *adj.* **1.** having split hoofs, once assumed to represent the halves of a single undivided hoof, as in cattle. **2.** devilish; satanic.
clove pink, a pink, *Dianthus caryophyllus,* with a spicy scent like that of cloves; a carnation.
clover (klō′və), *n.* **1.** any of various herbs of the fabaceous genus *Trifolium,* with trifoliolate leaves and dense flower heads, many species of which, as *T. pratense* (the common **red clover**), are cultivated as forage plants. **2. in clover,** in comfort or luxury. [ME *clovere,* OE *clāfre,* c. D *klaver*]
cloverleaf (klō′və lēf′), *n., pl.* **-leaves. 1.** the leaf of a clover. **2.** a road junction consisting of flyovers, underpasses, etc., forming the pattern of a four-leaf clover.
Clovis I (klō′vĭs; *Fr.* klō vēs′) (Ger. *Chlodwig*), A.D. 465?–511, king of the Franks A.D. 481–511: first of the Merovingian dynasty of Frankish kings.
clown (kloun), *n.* **1.** a jester or buffoon in a circus, pantomime, etc. **2.** a peasant; a rustic. **3.** a coarse, ill-bred person; a boor. *—v.i.* **4.** to act like a clown. [orig. uncert. Cf. Icel. *klunni* clumsy fellow] **—clown′ish,** *adj.* **—clown′ishly,** *adv.* **—clown′ishness,** *n.*
clownery (klou′nə rĭ), *n., pl.* **-eries. 1.** clownish behaviour. **2.** a clown's performance.
cloy (kloi), *v.t.* **1.** to weary by an excess of food, sweetness, pleasure, etc.; surfeit; satiate. *—v.i.* **2.** to cause to feel satiated or surfeited. [aphetic var. of obs. *acloy* to stop up, drive in a nail, ? t. MF: m. *encloyer,* der. *clou,* g. L *clāvus* nail] **—cloy′ingly,** *adv.* **—cloy′ingness,** *n.*
club (klŭb), *n., v.,* **clubbed, clubbing.** *—n.* **1.** a heavy stick, usually thicker at one end than at the other, suitable for a weapon; a cudgel. **2.** the butt end of a rifle. **3.** a stick or bat used to drive a ball, etc., in various games. **4.** a stick with a crooked head used in golf, etc. **5.** an Indian club. **6.** a group of persons organized for a social, literary, athletic, political, or other purpose, regulated by rules agreed by its members. **7.** *Insurance.* a friendly society. **8.** the building or rooms occupied by such a group. **9.** a black trifoliate figure on a playing card. **10.** a card bearing such figures. **11.** (*pl.*) the suit so marked. *—v.t.* **12.** to beat with, or as with, a club. **13.** to gather or form into a clublike mass. **14.** to unite; combine; join together. **15.** to contribute as one's share towards a joint expense; make up by joint contribution (often fol. by *up* or *together*). **16.** to defray by proportional shares: *to club the expense.* **17.** to invert (a rifle, etc.) so as to use as a club. *—v.i.* **18.** to combine or join together as for a common purpose. **19.** to gather into a mass. **20.** to contribute to a common fund. [ME *clubbe,* t. Scand.; cf. Icel. *klubba;* akin to CLUMP] **—Syn. 6.** society, association. See **circle.**
clubbable (klŭb′ə bl), *adj.* fit to be a member of a social club; sociable. Also, **clubable.**
club foot, 1. a deformed or distorted foot. **2.** the condition of such a foot; talipes. **—club′-foot′ed,** *adj.*
club hammer, a double-headed hammer.
club hand, 1. a deformed or distorted hand, similar in nature and causation to a club foot. **2.** the condition of such a hand.
clubhaul (klŭb′hôl′), *v.t. Naut.* to cause (a ship), in an emergency, to go on the other tack by letting go the lee anchor, and pulling on a hawser leading from the anchor to the lee quarter, the hawser being cut when the ship gathers way on the new tack.
clubhouse (klŭb′hous′), *n.* a building occupied by a club.
clubland (klŭb′lănd′), *n.* the district of a town where clubs, etc., are chiefly situated, esp. the West End of London.
clublaw (klŭb′lô′), *n. Colloq.* rule by the strongest; government by violence.
clubman (klŭb′mən), *n., pl.* **-men.** a member of a fashionable club. **—club′wom′an,** *n. fem.*
club moss, any plant of the genus *Lycopodium.*
clubroom (klŭb′ro͞om′), *n.* a room used by a club.
club rush, any of several perennial cyperaceous herbs of the genus *Scirpus,* as the widespread **sea club rush,** *S. maritimus.*
club sandwich, *U.S.* a sandwich of toast (usually three slices) with a filling of cold chicken, salad, etc.
cluck (klŭk), *v.i.* **1.** to utter the cry of a hen brooding or calling her chicks. **2.** to make a similar sound. *—v.t.* **3.** to call or utter by clucking: *clucking her sympathy.* *—n.* **4.** the sound uttered by a hen when brooding, or in calling her chicks. **5.** any clucking sound. [var. of *clock* (now Scot. and d.), OE *cloccian*]
clue (klo͞o), *n., v.,* **clued, cluing.** *—n.* **1.** anything that serves to guide or direct in the solution of a problem, mystery, etc. **2.** clew. *—v.t.* **3.** to clew. [var. of CLEW]
clueless (klo͞o′lĭs), *n. Colloq.* helpless; stupid.
Cluj (*Rum.* klo͞ozh), *n.* a city in NW Rumania. 167,011 (est. 1964). German, **Klausenburg.** Hungarian, **Kolozsvár.**
clumber (klŭm′bə), *n.* one of a breed of spaniels with short legs and long, heavy body, valued as retrievers. Also, **clumber spaniel.** [named after *Clumber,* estate of the Duke of Newcastle, in Nottinghamshire]

Clumber (1½ ft high)

clump (klŭmp), *n.* **1.** a cluster, esp. of trees, or other plants. **2.** *Bacteriol.* a cluster of agglutinated bacteria. **3.** a lump or mass. **4.** a clumping tread, sound, etc. **5.** a thick extra sole on a shoe. **6.** *Colloq.* a blow; a clout. *—v.i.* **7.** to walk heavily and clumsily. **8.** *Bacteriol.* to gather or be gathered into clumps. *—v.t.* **9.** to gather into or form a clump; mass. **10.** *Bacteriol.* to gather or form in clumps. **11.** *Colloq.* to strike; punch. [back-formation from *clumper* lump, OE *clympre*] **—clump′y, clump′ish,** *adj.*
clumsy (klŭm′zĭ), *adj.,* **-sier, -siest. 1.** awkward in movement or action; without skill or grace: *a clumsy workman.* **2.** awkwardly done or made; unwieldy; ill-contrived: *a clumsy apology.* [der. obs. v. *clumse* be benumbed with cold, t. Scand.; cf. Swed. *klummsen* benumbed] **—clum′sily,** *adv.* **—clum′siness,** *n.* **—Syn. 1.** ungraceful, ungainly, lumbering, lubberly. **2.** unhandy, unskilful, maladroit, inexpert, bungling.
clunch (klŭnch), *n.* a hard chalk formerly used in some districts for building.
clung (klŭng), *v.* pt. and pp. of **cling.**
Cluniac (klo͞o′nĭ ăk′), *n., adj.* (a monk or nun) of a branch of the Benedictines, originating at Cluny.
Cluny (*Fr.* klʏ nē′), *n.* a town in E France in Saône-et-Loire department: ruins of a famous Benedictine abbey. 3420 (est. 1964).
Cluny lace (klo͞o′nĭ), **1.** a lace made by hand with bobbins, originally in France. **2.** a machine lace copied from it.
clupeid (klo͞o′pĭ ĭd), *n.* **1.** any of the *Clupeidae,* a family of (chiefly) marine, teleostean fishes, including the herrings, sardines, menhaden, and shad. *—adj.* **2.** relating to the family *Clupeidae.* [t. NL: s. *Clupeidae,* pl., f. s. *Clupea* the herring genus (L *clupea* kind of small river fish) + *-idae* (see -ID[2])]

clupeoid (kloo͞ʹpĭ oidʹ), *adj.* **1.** herring-like. —*n.* **2.** any member of the *Isospondyli*, an order of fishes including the clupeids, salmon, smelts, etc.

cluse (kloo͞z), *n.* a narrow gorge cutting through a mountain ridge. [t. F, t. ML: m. *clusa*, L *cl(a)usa*, prop. pp. fem., closed]

cluster (klŭsʹtə), *n.* **1.** a number of things of the same kind, growing or held together; a bunch: *a cluster of grapes.* **2.** a group of things or persons near together. **3.** *Astron.* a group of stars which move together. **4.** *U.S. Army.* a small metal design placed on the ribbon representing an awarded medal, which indicates that the same medal has been awarded again (equivalent to British *bar*): *oak-leaf cluster.* —*v.t.* **5.** to gather into a cluster. **6.** to furnish or cover with clusters. —*v.i.* **7.** to form a cluster or clusters. [ME and OE, var. of *clyster* bunch] —**clusʹtery,** *adj.*

clustered column, a group of several pillars attached to each other to form a single unit.

cluster pine, the maritime pine.

clutch[1] (klŭch), *v.t.* **1.** to seize with, or as with, the hands or claws; snatch. **2.** to grip or hold tightly or firmly. —*v.i.* **3.** to try to seize or grasp (fol. by *at*). —*n.* **4.** the hand, claw, paw, etc., when grasping. **5.** (*usually pl.*) power of disposal or control; mastery: *in the clutches of an enemy.* **6.** the act of clutching; a snatch; a grasp. **7.** a tight grip or hold. **8.** a device for gripping something. **9.** a coupling or appliance by which working parts of machinery (as a pulley and a shaft) may be made to engage or disengage at will. [ME *clucche(n)*, var. of *clycche(n)*, OE *clyccan* crook or bend, close (the hand), clench] —**Syn. 1.** See **catch.**

clutch[2] (klŭch), *n.* **1.** a hatch of eggs; the number of eggs produced or incubated at one time. **2.** a brood of chickens. **3.** *Colloq.* a group; a bunch. —*v.t.* **4.** to hatch (chickens). [var. of d. *cletch*, akin to *cleck* hatch, t. Scand.; cf. Sw. *kläcka*]

Clutha (kloo͞ʹthə), *n.* a river in S South Island, New Zealand, flowing SE to the Pacific Ocean. 210 mi.

clutter (klŭtʹə), *v.t.* **1.** to heap, litter, or strew in a disorderly manner. —*v.i.* **2.** to run in disorder; move with bustle and confusion. **3.** to make a clatter. **4.** to speak so rapidly and inexactly that distortions of sound and phrasing result. —*n.* **5.** a disorderly heap or assemblage; litter. **6.** confusion; disorder. **7.** *Archaic or Dial.* confused noise; clatter. **8.** *Radio.* a jumble of unwanted radar signals. [var. of *clotter*, der. CLOT; associated with CLUSTER]

Clyde (klīd), *n.* **1.** a river in S Scotland, flowing into the Firth of Clyde: shipbuilding. 106 mi. **2. Firth of,** an inlet of the Atlantic, in SW Scotland. 64 mi. long.

Clydebank (klīdʹbăngkʹ), *n.* a burgh in SW Scotland, in Dunbarton, on the Clyde. 49,654 (1961).

Clydesdale (klīdzʹdālʹ), *n.* one of a breed of active, strong and hardy draught horses originally raised in Clydesdale, Scotland.

Clydesdale terrier, a variety of Skye terrier bred for smallness.

clypeate (klĭpʹĭ ātʹ, -ĭ ĭt), *adj.* shaped like a round shield or buckler. [t. L: m. s. *clypeātus*, pp., furnished with a shield]

clypeus (klĭpʹĭ əs), *n.*, *pl.* **clypei** (klĭpʹĭ īʹ). the area of the facial wall of an insect's head between the labrum and the front, usually separated from the latter by a groove. [t. L: prop., *clipeus* round shield] —**clypʹeal,** *adj.*

clyster (klĭsʹtə), *n.* *Med.* an enema. [ME *clister*, t. L: m. *clyster*, t. Gk: m. *klystḗr* syringe]

Clytemnestra (klīʹtĭm nĕsʹtrə), *n.* *Gk Legend.* the daughter of Tyndareus and Leda, wife of Agamemnon. See **Agamemnon, Aegisthus, Orestes.** Also, **Clytaemnestra.**

cm., centimetre; centimetres.

cmd, command. Also, **cmnd**

cmdr, commander.

C.M.G., Companion of the Order of St Michael and St George.

cml, commercial.

C.M.S., Church Missionary Society.

c/n, credit note.

C.N.D., Campaign for Nuclear Disarmament.

cnidarian (nī dēəʹrĭ ən, knī-), *n.* *Zool.* **1.** a member of the *Cnidaria*, a phylum of invertebrate animals belonging to the coelenterates and comprising the jellyfish, sea-anemones, and corals. —*adj.* **2.** belonging to the *Cnidaria.*

Cnidus (nīʹdəs), *n.* an ancient city of Caria, in SW Asia Minor: Athenian naval victory over the Spartans, 394 B.C.

Cnossus (nŏsʹəs), *n.* Knossos.

Cnut (kə nyoo͞tʹ), *n.* Canute.

co-, **1.** a prefix signifying association and accompanying action, occurring mainly before vowels and *h* and *gn*, as in *coadjutor, cohabit, cognate.* **2.** *Maths., Astron.* a prefix meaning 'complement of', as in *cosine, codeclination.* [t. L, var. of *com-* COM-]

Co, *Chem.* cobalt.

Co., **1.** company. **2.** county. Also, **co.**

C.O., **1.** commanding officer. **2.** conscientious objector.

c.o., **1.** care of. **2.** carried over. Also, **c/o.**

coach (kōch), *n.* **1.** a large, enclosed, four-wheeled carriage used esp. on state occasions. **2.** a stagecoach. **3.** a bus, esp. a single-decker, used for long distances or for sightseeing. **4.** a railway carriage. **5.** a person who trains athletes for games, a contest, etc. **6.** a private tutor who prepares a student for an examination. **7.** *Austral.* a tame beast used to decoy wild cattle. —*v.t.* **8.** to give instruction or advice to in the capacity of a coach. —*v.i.* **9.** to act as a coach. **10.** to study with or be instructed by a coach. [t. F: m. *coche*, ult. t. Hung.: m. *kocsi*]

coach-and-four (kōchʹən fôʹ), *n.* a coach drawn by four horses.

coachbox (kōchʹbŏksʹ), *n.* the driver's seat on a horse-drawn coach.

coachbuilder (kōchʹbĭlʹdə), *n.* one who makes the bodies of motor vehicles, railway carriages, etc.

coach-built (kōchʹbĭltʹ), *adj.* (of a vehicle, etc.) with bodywork specially built; custom-made.

coachdog (kōchʹdŏgʹ), *n.* Dalmatian (def. 4).

coacher (kōʹchə), *n.* **1.** one who coaches; a coach. **2.** a coach-horse.

coach-horn (kōchʹhônʹ), *n.* a post-horn.

coach-horse (kōchʹhôsʹ), *n.* a horse used or fitted to draw a coach.

coach-house (kōchʹhousʹ), *n.* an outhouse originally for carriages.

coachman (kōchʹmən), *n.*, *pl.* **-men.** a man employed to drive a coach or carriage. —**coachʹmanshipʹ,** *n.*

coachwork (kōchʹwûkʹ), *n.* the body of a motor car (as distinguished from the *chassis*, the *engine*, and the *upholstery*).

coaction (kō ăkʹshən), *n.* force or compulsion, either in restraining or in impelling. [t. F, t. L: s. *coactio*]

coactive (kō ăkʹtĭv), *adj.* compulsory; coercive. —**coacʹtively,** *adj.*

coadjutor (kō ăjʹoo͝ tə), *n.* **1.** an assistant. **2.** an assistant to a bishop or other ecclesiastic. **3.** a bishop who assists another bishop, with the right of succession. [t. LL: f. *co-* co- + *adjūtor* helper; r. ME *coadiutoure*, t. OF]

coadjutress (kō ăjʹoo͝ trĭs), *n.* a female coadjutor or assistant.

coadjutrix (kō ăjʹoo͝ trĭks), *n.*, *pl.* **coadjutrices** (kō ăjʹoo͝ trīʹsēz). coadjutress.

coadunate (kō ădʹyoo͝ nĭt, -nātʹ), *adj.* *Zool., Bot.* united by growth. [t. L: m. s. *coadūnātus*, pp., joined together] —**coadʹunaʹtion,** *n.*

coadventure (kōʹəd vĕnʹchə), *v.*, **-tured, -turing,** *n.* —*v.i.* **1.** to share in an adventure. —*n.* **2.** adventure in which two or more share. —**coʹadvenʹturer,** *n.*

coagulable (kō ăgʹyoo͝ lə bl), *adj.* capable of being coagulated: *this substance is highly coagulable.* —**coagʹulabilʹity,** *n.*

coagulant (kō ăgʹyoo͝ lənt), *n.* a substance that produces coagulation. [t. L: s. *coāgulans*, ppr., curdling]

coagulate (*v.* kō ăgʹ yoo͝ lātʹ; *adj.* kō ăgʹyoo͝ lĭt, -lātʹ), *v.*, **-lated, -lating,** *adj.* —*v.t., v.i.* **1.** to change from a fluid into a thickened mass; curdle; congeal. —*adj.* **2.** *Obs.* coagulated. [t. L: m. s. *coāgulātus*, pp., curdled] —**coagʹulaʹtion,** *n.* —**coagulative** (kō ăgʹyoo͝ lə tĭv), *adj.* —**coagʹulaʹtor,** *n.*

coagulum (kō ăgʹ yoo͝ ləm), *n.*, *pl.* **-la** (-lə). *Physiol., etc.* a clump, clot, curd, precipitate, or gel. [t. L: rennet]

coal (kōl), *n.* **1.** a black or dark brown combustible mineral substance consisting of carbonized vegetable matter, used as a fuel: **hard coal** (anthracite), **soft coal** (bituminous coal), **brown coal** (lignite). **2.** *Obs.* a piece of wood or other combustible substance either glowing, charred, or burned out. **3.** *Obs.* charcoal. **4. coals of fire, a.** good actions or the like in return for bad, giving rise to feelings of remorse. **b.** reproaches. **5. coals to Newcastle,** anything supplied unnecessarily. **6. take, haul, rake, etc., over the coals,** to scold; reprimand. —*v.t.* **7.** to burn to coal or charcoal. **8.** to provide with coal. —*v.i.* **9.** to take in coal for fuel. [ME *cole*, OE *col* live coal, c. G *Kohle*]

coal black, absolutely black; very black.

coalbunker (kōlʹbŭngʹkə), *n.* **1.** a small structure, usually of concrete, for storing coal. **2.** a space in a ship, etc., for storing coal.

coal cellar, a shed or cellar for storing coal.

coaldust (kōlʹdŭstʹ), *n.* finely powdered coal.

coaler (kōʹlə), *n.* a railway, ship, etc., used mainly to haul or supply coal.

coalesce (kōʹə lĕsʹ), *v.i.*, **-lesced, -lescing. 1.** to grow together or into one body. **2.** to unite so as to form one mass, community, etc. [t. L: m. s. *coalescere*] —**co'ales'cence,** *n.* —**co'ales'cent,** *adj.*

coalface (kōl'fās'), *n.* the part of the coal seam from which coal is cut.

coalfield (kōl'fēld'), *n.* an area containing coal deposits.

coalfish (kōl'fĭsh'), *n.* the saithe, a North Atlantic gadoid food fish, *Pollachius virens*, a species of pollack. [named from the colour of its back]

coal gas, 1. the gas formed by burning coal. **2.** a gas used for illuminating and heating, produced by distilling bituminous coal, and consisting chiefly of hydrogen, methane and carbon monoxide.

coal-heaver (kōl'hē'və), *n.* one who carries or shovels coal.

coal hod, 1. a hod for carrying coal. **2.** *U.S.* a coalscuttle.

coalhole (kōl'hōl'), *n.* **1.** a hole in a pavement through which coal is shot into a cellar. **2.** a small coal cellar.

coalhouse (kōl'hous'), *n.* a storage shed for coal.

coaling station (kō'lĭng), a place at which coal is supplied to ships, locomotives, etc.

Coalite (kōl'īt), *n. Trademark.* a smokeless fuel, manufactured by carbonizing coal at about 600°C; semicoke.

coalition (kō'ə lĭsh'ən), *n.* **1.** union into one body or mass; fusion. **2.** a combination or alliance, esp., a temporary one between persons, factions, states, etc. [t. ML: s. *coalitio*, der. L *coalescere* coalesce] —**co'ali'tionist,** *n.*

coalman (kōl'măn'), *n.* a man who delivers coal.

coal measures, *Geol.* **1.** coal-bearing strata. **2.** (*caps.*) a portion of the Carboniferous system, characterized by coal deposits.

coalmine (kōl'mīn'), *n.* a mine or pit from which coal is obtained. —**coal'-mi'ner,** *n.* —**coal'-mi'ning,** *n., adj.*

coal pit, 1. a pit where coal is dug. **2.** *U.S.* a place where charcoal is made.

coalsack (kōl'săk'), *n.* **1.** a sack for carrying coal. **2. Southern Coalsack,** a large dark space near the Southern Cross. **3. Northern Coalsack,** a dark space in the Milky Way in the northern constellation Cygnus.

coalscuttle (kōl'skŭt'l), *n.* a bucket in which coal is carried into, and kept in, a room.

coal tar, a thick, black, viscid liquid formed during the distillation of coal in the manufacture of coal gas and which upon further distillation yields benzene, anthracene, phenol, etc. (from which are derived a large number of dyes and synthetic compounds), and a final residuum (**coal-tar pitch**) which is used in making pavements, etc.

coal-tar creosote, impure phenol or carbolic acid, distinct from the creosote of wood tar.

coaltit (kōl'tĭt'), *n.* a black-headed tit, *Parus ater*, with a white patch on the nape of the neck.

coaly (kō'lĭ), *adj.* of, like, or containing coal.

coaming (kō'mĭng), *n.* **1.** a raised border round an opening in a deck, roof, or floor, designed to prevent water from running below. **2.** *Naut.* one of the pieces, esp. of the fore-and-aft pieces, of such a border.

coarctate (kō äk'tāt), *adj.* **1.** *Entomol.* denoting an insect pupa enclosed in the hardened cuticula (puparium) of a preceding larval instar. **2.** compressed; constricted. [t. L: m. s. *coarctātus*, pp., pressed together; r. ME *coartate*, t. L: m. s. *coartātus*, var. of *coarctātus*]

A B

Coarctate pupa
A, Lateral view;
B, Dorsal view

coarse (kôs), *adj.*, **coarser, coarsest. 1.** of inferior or faulty quality; not pure or choice; common; base: *coarse manners, a coarse lad.* **2.** composed of relatively large parts or particles: *coarse sand.* **3.** lacking in fineness or delicacy of texture, structure, etc. **4.** harsh. **5.** lacking delicacy of feeling, manner, etc.; not refined. **6.** (of screws) having the threads widely spaced. **7.** (of metals) unrefined. [adjectival var. of COURSE, n., with the sense of ordinary] —**coarse'ly,** *adv.* —**coarse'ness,** *n.* —**Syn. 5.** vulgar, gross, crass, indelicate, ribald.

coarse fish, any freshwater fish other than a member of the salmon family.

coarse-grained (kôs'grānd'), *adj.* **1.** having a coarse texture or grain. **2.** indelicate; crude; gross.

coarsen (kô'sən), *v.t., v.i.* to make or become coarse.

coast (kōst), *n.* **1.** the land next to the sea; the seashore. **2.** the region adjoining it. **3. the coast, a.** the seaside. **b.** (*cap.*) *U.S.* the region bordering on the Pacific Ocean. **4.** *Obs.* the boundary or border of a country. **5.** *U.S.* a hill or slope down which one may slide on a sledge. **6.** a slide or ride down a hill, etc. **7. the coast is clear,** the danger has gone. —*v.i.* **8.** to move along after effort has ceased; keep going on acquired momentum. **9.** to descend a hill, etc., as on a bicycle, without using pedals. **10.** to proceed or sail along, or sail from port to port of, a coast. **11.** to slide on a sledge down a snowy or icy hillside or incline. **12.** *Obs.* to proceed in a roundabout way. **13.** *Obs.* to go or pass (along, etc.). —*v.t.* **14.** *Archaic.* to proceed along the coast of. **15.** to go along or near to (a coast). **16.** *Obs.* to keep alongside of (a person moving). **17.** *Obs.* to go by the side or border of. [ME *coste*, t. OF, g. L *costa* rib, side] —**Syn. 1.** See **shore**[1].

coastal (kōs'tl), *adj.* of or at a coast: *coastal defence.*

coastal plain, *Phys. Geog.* lowland bordering a seacoast: the result of a relative fall in sea-level to expose part of a continental shelf, or deposition of sediment by rivers.

coaster (kōs'tə), *n.* **1.** one who or that which coasts. **2.** a vessel engaged in trading from port to port along a coast, usually of the same country. **3.** a bicycle incorporating into its freewheel a form of braking mechanism operating by back-pedalling. **4.** the brake itself. **5.** *U.S.* a type of sledge for sliding down icy slopes, etc. **6.** *U.S.* a roller-coaster. **7.** a tray, sometimes on wheels, for holding a decanter to be passed round a dining table. **8.** a small dish or mat placed under glasses, etc., to protect a table from moisture or heat.

coastguard (kōst'gäd'), *n.* **1.** (in Great Britain) a coastal police force, under the control of the Board of Trade, preventing smuggling, watching for ships in distress or danger, etc. **2.** any of various similar organizations elsewhere. **3.** a member of such an organization.

coastline (kōst'līn'), *n.* the outline or contour of a coast.

coastward (kōst'wəd), *adv.* **1.** Also, **coast'wards.** towards the coast. —*adj.* **2.** directed towards the coast: *coastward movement.*

coastwise (kōst'wīz'), *adv.* **1.** Also, **coastways** (kōst'wāz'). along the coast. —*adj.* **2.** following the coast: *coastwise drift.*

coat (kōt), *n.* **1.** an outer garment with sleeves; an overcoat, dress coat, etc. **2.** a natural integument or covering, as the hair, fur, or wool of an animal, the bark of a tree, or the skin of a fruit. **3.** anything that covers or conceals: *a coat of paint.* **4.** *Obs.* a garment indicating profession, class, etc. **5.** *Obs.* the profession, class, etc., so indicated. **6.** *Obs. or Dial.* a petticoat or skirt. —*v.t.* **7.** to cover or provide with a coat. **8.** to cover with a layer or coating; cover as a layer or coating does. [ME *cote*, t. OF, t. Gmc; cf. OS *cott* woollen coat, ML *cotta* kind of tunic] —**coat'less,** *adj.*

coat-armour (kōt'ä'mə), *n.* a coat of arms.

Coatbridge (kōt'brĭj'), *n.* a burgh in Scotland, in Lanarkshire. 53,946 (1961).

coat-card (kōt'käd'), *n. Obs.* a court card.

coated (kō'tĭd), *adj.* **1.** (of paper) having a highly polished coating applied to provide a smooth surface for printing. **2.** (of a fabric) having a plastic, paint, or pyroxylin coating, making it impervious to moisture. **3.** having a coat.

coatee (kō tē', kō'tē), *n.* a short coat.

coat-hanger (kōt'hăng'ə), *n.* a curved piece of wood, plastic, etc., with a hook attached, on which clothes are hung.

coat-hardie (kōt'hä'dĭ), *n.* a close-fitting medieval garment with long sleeves, for men or women. Also, **cote-hardie.**

coati (kō ä'tĭ), *n., pl.* **-tis.** any of the tropical American plantigrade carnivores constituting the genus *Nasua*, closely related to the raccoon, and having an elongated body, a long, ringed tail, and an attenuated, flexible snout. Also, **coati-mondi, coati-mundi** (kō ä'tĭ mŭn'dĭ). [t. Tupi]

Coati, *Nasua narica*
(3½ ft long, tail 18 in.)

coating (kō'tĭng), *n.* **1.** a layer of any substance spread over a surface. **2.** material for coats.

coat of arms, 1. a surcoat or tabard embroidered with heraldic devices, worn by medieval knights over their armour. **2.** the heraldic bearings of a person; a hatchment; an escutcheon. [trans. of F *cotte d'armes*]

coat of mail, *pl.* **coats of mail.** a hauberk; a defensive garment made of interlinked metal rings, overlapping metal plates, etc.

coat-tails (kōt'tālz'), *n.pl.* the divided, tapering skirts, or tails of a man's tail coat.

Coat of arms
(def. 2)

coauthor (kō ô'thə), *n.* a joint author.

coax (kōks), *v.t.* **1.** to influence by gentle persuasion, flattery, etc. **2.** to get or win by coaxing. **3.** *Obs.* to fondle. **4.** *Obs.* to befool. —*v.i.* **5.** to use gentle persuasion, etc. [der. obs. *cokes*, n., fool; of doubtful orig. Cf. COCKNEY] —**coax'er,** *n.* —**coax'ingly,** *adv.* —**Syn. 1.** wheedle, cajole, beguile inveigle, persuade.

coaxial (kō ăk′sĭ əl), *adj.* **1.** having a common axis or coincident axes. **2.** (of a cable) composed of an insulated central conductor with tubular stranded conductors laid over it concentrically and separated by layers of insulation. Also, **coaxal** (kō ăk′səl).

cob[1] (kŏb), *n.*, *v.*, **cobbed, cobbing.** —*n.* **1.** a corncob. **2.** a cobnut. **3.** a male swan. **4.** a short-legged, thickset horse. **5.** a horse with an unnaturally high gait. **6.** a small lump of coal, ore, etc. **7.** *Dial.* a man of importance; leader. **8.** *Dial.* a roundish mass, lump, or heap. **9.** a mixture of clay and straw, used as a building material. —*v.t.* **10.** to beat; strike. [ME; orig. obscure]

cob[2] (kŏb), *n.* a gull, esp. the great black-backed gull, *Larus marinus.* Also, **cobb.** [orig. unknown. Cf. D *kob*]

cobalamine (kō băl′ə mēn′), *n.* *Biochem.* vitamin B_{12}.

cobalt (kō′bôlt), *n.* **1.** *Chem.* a silver-white metallic element with a faint pinkish tinge, occurring in compounds the silicates of which afford important blue colouring substances for ceramics; also used in alloys, particularly in cobalt steel. *Symbol:* Co; *at. wt:* 58·9332; *at. no.:* 27; *sp. gr.:* 8·9 at 20°C. **2.** a blue pigment containing cobalt. **3.** the isotope, cobalt 60; used in the treatment of cancer. [t. G: m. *Kobalt*, var. of *Kobold* goblin]

cobalt bloom, the mineral erythrite, hydrous cobalt arsenate, $Co_3As_2O.8H_2O$, usually of a peach-red colour, and often occurring as a pulverulent encrustation.

cobalt blue, any of a number of pigments containing an oxide of cobalt.

cobaltic (kō bôl′tĭk), *adj.* *Chem.* of or containing cobalt, esp. in the trivalent state.

cobaltite (kō bôl′tīt, kō′bôl tīt′), *n.* an ore of cobalt, cobalt arsenic sulphide, CoAsS, silver-white with reddish tinge. Also, **cobaltine; cobalt glance.**

cobaltous (kō bôl′təs), *adj.* *Chem.* containing divalent cobalt.

cobber (kŏb′ə), *n.* *Austral., N.Z. Colloq.* mate; friend.

Cobbett (kŏb′ĭt), *n.* **William,** 1763–1835, English journalist and politician.

cobble (kŏb′l), *n.*, *v.*, **-bled, -bling.** —*n.* **1.** a cobblestone. **2.** (*pl.*) cob coal. **3.** a clumsily completed job of sewing, mending, etc. —*v.t.* **4.** to pave with cobblestones. **5.** to mend (shoes, etc.); patch. **6.** to put together roughly or clumsily. [? der. COB[1], def. 8]

cobbler (kŏb′lə), *n.* **1.** one who mends shoes. **2.** a clumsy workman. **3.** an iced drink made of wine, fruit, sugar, etc. **4.** *Austral., N.Z., Slang.* the last sheep to be shorn.

cobbler's punch, a hot punch made of beer, spices, etc.

cobblestone (kŏb′l stōn′), *n.* a naturally rounded stone, large enough for use in paving.

Cobden (kŏb′dən), *n.* **Richard,** 1804–65, English manufacturer, merchant, economist, and politician.

cobelligerent (kō′bĭ lĭj′ə rənt), *n.* **1.** a nation, state, or individual that cooperates with, but is not bound by a formal alliance to, another in carrying on war. —*adj.* **2.** relating to such cooperation.

Cóbh (kōv), *n.* a seaport in S Republic of Ireland; the port for Cork. 5266 (1961). Formerly, **Queenstown.**

Cobham (kŏb′əm), *n.* **John Oldcastle** (ōld′käs′əl), **Lord,** 1377–1417, English martyr: leader of a Lollard conspiracy.

coble (kō′bl, kŏb′l), *n.* a kind of flat-bottomed rowing or fishing boat. [ME; cf. OE *cuopl*, Welsh *ceubal*, ML *caupulus*]

Coblenz (kō blĕnts′; *Ger.* kō′blĕnts), *n.* former name of **Koblenz.**

cobloaf (kŏb′lōf′), *n.* a rounded loaf, not baked in a tin.

cobnut (kŏb′nŭt′), *n.* the hazelnut.

cobol (kō′bl), *n.* an autocode for writing computer programs of a business nature. [f. *co(mmon) b(usiness) o(riented) l(anguage)*]

cobra (kō′brə), *n.* any snake of the genus *Naja*, exceedingly venomous and characterized by the ability to dilate its neck so that it assumes a hoodlike form. [short for Pg. *cobra* (g. L *colubra* serpent) *de capello* hood snake]

cobra de capello (kō′brə dē kə pĕl′ō), *pl.* **cobras de capello.** a cobra, *Naja tripudians*, common in India.

Coburg (kō′bûg; *Ger.* kō′bo͝ork), *n.* **1.** a city in West Germany, in N Bavaria. 44,000 (est. 1966). **2.** (*l.c.*) an all-worsted fabric. **3.** (*l.c.*) an oval-shaped loaf of white bread.

cobweb (kŏb′wĕb′), *n.* **1.** a web or net spun by a spider to catch its prey. **2.** a single thread spun by a spider. **3.** anything fine-spun, flimsy, or unsubstantial. **4.** a network of plot or intrigue; an insidious snare. **5.** anything obscure or confused: *the cobwebs of early medieval scholarship.* [ME *coppeweb*, f. *coppe* spider (OE *-coppe* in *ātorcoppe* spider) + WEB] —**cob′webbed′,** *adj.* —**cob′-web′by,** *adj.*

coca (kō′kə), *n.* **1.** either of two shrubs, *Erythroxylon coca* and *Erythroxylon truxillense*, native in the Andes and cultivated in Java and elsewhere. **2.** their dried leaves, which are chewed for their stimulant properties and which yield cocaine and other alkaloids. [t. Quechua: m. *cuca*]

cocaine (kə kān′), *n.* *Chem., Pharm.* a bitter crystalline alkaloid, $C_{17}H_{21}NO_4$, obtained from coca leaves, used as a local anaesthetic. Also, **cocain.** [f. COCA + -INE[2]]

cocainism (kō kā′nĭz′əm, kə kā′n-), *n.* a morbid condition due to excessive or habitual use of cocaine.

coccid (kŏk′sĭd), *n.* any insect of the homopterous superfamily *Coccoidea*, including the scale insects, etc.

coccidioidomycosis (kŏk sĭd′ĭ oid ō mī kō′sĭs), *n.* a fungus infection characterized by infective granulomas formed in the viscera and the skin.

coccidiosis (kŏk sĭd′ĭ ō′sĭs), *n.* any one of a series of specific infectious diseases caused by epithelial protozoan parasites, which usually affect the intestines. The disease is known in birds, cattle, swine, sheep, and dogs; it rarely occurs in man.

coccus (kŏk′əs), *n.*, *pl.* **-ci** (-sī). **1.** *Bacteriol.* a spherical organism when free, slightly flattened when two or more form in apposition, as in the *Neissenia gonorrhoeae* or *N. meningitidis.* **2.** *Bot.* one of the carpels of a schizocarp. **3.** *Pharm.* cochineal. [t. NL, t. Gk: m. *kókkos* grain, seed] —**coccoid** (kŏk′oid), *adj.*

Cocci (def. 2)
A, Fruit composed of ten cocci;
B, Fruit composed of four cocci

coccyx (kŏk′sĭks), *n.*, *pl.* **coccyges** (kŏk sī′jēz). **1.** a small triangular bone forming the lower extremity of the spinal column in man, consisting of four ankylosed rudimentary vertebrae. See diag. under **spinal column.** **2.** a corresponding part in certain other animals. [t. L, t. Gk: m. *kókkyx* coccyx, orig., cuckoo] —**coccygeal** (kŏk sĭj′ĭ əl), *adj.*

Cochabamba (*Sp.* kō chä bäm′bä), *n.* a town in central Bolivia. 92,008 (1962); 8394 ft high.

cochin (kō′chĭn, kŏch′ĭn), *n.* (*sometimes cap.*) a breed of large domestic fowls, of Asiatic origin, resembling the brahma but slightly smaller. [named after COCHIN-CHINA]

Cochin (kō′chĭn′), *n.* **1.** a seaport in W Kerala near the SW extremity of India: the first European fort in India was built here by the Portuguese, 1503. 35,076 (1961). **2.** a former state in SW India, merged with Travancore in 1949; now part of Kerala.

Cochin-China (kō′chĭn chī′nə, kŏch′ĭn-), *n.* a former state in S French Indochina: now part of South Vietnam. French, **Cochinchine** (*Fr.* kō shăN shēn′).

cochineal (kŏch′ĭ nēl′, kŏch′ĭ nēl′), *n.* **1.** a red dye prepared from the dried bodies of the females of a scale insect, *Dactylopius coccus*, which lives on cacti of Mexico and other warm regions of Central America. **2.** the insect itself. **3.** the crimson colour of this dye. [t. F: m. *cochenille*, t. Sp.: m. *cochinilla*, orig. woodlouse, der. *cochino* pig]

cochlea (kŏk′lĭ ə), *n.*, *pl.* **-leae** (-lĭ ē′). a division, spiral in form, of the internal ear, in man and most other mammals. See diag. under **ear.** [t. L, t. Gk: m. *kochlíās* snail, something spiral] —**coch′lear,** *adj.*

cochleate (kŏk′lĭ āt′, -lĭ ĭt), *adj.* shaped like a snail shell; spiral. Also, **coch′leat′ed.** [t. L: m. s. *cochleātus*]

Cochran (kŏk′rən), *n.* **(Sir) C(harles) B(lake),** 1872–1951, English theatrical manager and producer.

cock[1] (kŏk), *n.* **1.** a male chicken. **2.** the male of any bird, esp. of the gallinaceous kind. **3.** the crowing of the cock. **4.** *Archaic.* the time of its crowing, in the early morning. **5.** a weathercock. **6.** a leader; chief person; ruling spirit. **7.** a device for permitting or arresting the flow of a liquid or gas from a receptacle or through a pipe; a tap or stop valve. **8.** (in a firearm) **a.** that part of the lock which by its fall or action causes the discharge; the hammer. **b.** the position into which the cock or hammer is brought by being drawn partly or completely back, preparatory to firing. See illus. under **flintlock.** **9.** the pointer or needle of a balance. **10.** *Curling.* the mark aimed at. —*v.t.* **11.** to pull back and set the cock or hammer of (a firearm) preparatory to firing. **12. cock a snook,** or **snoot,** *Colloq.* to put a thumb to the nose, in a contemptuous gesture. —*v.i.* **13.** to cock the firing mechanism of a gun. [ME *cok*, OE *cocc*, c. Icel. *kokkr*]

cock[2] (kŏk) *v.t.* **1.** to set or turn up or to one side, often in an assertive, jaunty, or significant manner. —*v.i.* **2.** to stand or stick up conspicuously. **3.** *Obs.* to strut; swagger; put on airs of importance. —*n.* **4.** the act of turning the head, a hat, etc., up or to one side in a jaunty or significant way. **5.** the position of anything thus placed. **6.** *Colloq.* a mate, friend, or fellow. **7.** *Taboo Slang.* the penis. [prob. special use of COCK[1]]

cock[3] (kŏk), *n.* **1.** a conical pile of hay, etc. —*v.t.* **2.** to

put (hay, etc.) in such piles. [ME. Cf. Norw. *kok* heap]
cockade (kŏ kād′), *n.* a knot of ribbon, rosette, etc., worn on the hat as a badge or a part of a uniform. [alter. of *cockard*, t. F: m. *cocarde*, der. *coq* cock] —**cockad′ed,** *adj.*
cock-a-doodle-doo (kŏk′ə do͞o′dl do͞o′), *n.*, *pl.* **-doos,** *v.* **-dooed, -dooing.** —*n.* **1.** the sound of the crowing of a cock. —*v.i.* **2.** to crow.
cock-a-hoop (kŏk′ə ho͞op′), *adj.* in a state of unrestrained joy or exultation.
Cockaigne (kŏ kān′), *n.* **1.** a mythical land of luxury and idleness. **2.** *Colloq.* London. Also, **Cockayne.** [ME *cokaigne*, t. OF, ? t. MLG: m. *kokenje* sugar cakes given to children at fairs]
cock-a-leekie (kŏk′ə lē′kĭ), *n.* *Scot.* a soup made from a fowl boiled with leeks, etc. Also, **cocky-leeky, cocka-leekie.**
cockalorum (kŏk′ə lô′rəm), *n.* *Colloq.* a self-important little man.
cock-and-bull story (kŏk′ən bo͝ol′), an absurd improbable story told as true.
cockatiel (kŏk′ə tēl′), *n.* a small, crested, long-tailed Australian parrot, *Nymphicus hollandicus*, common as a cagebird. Also, **cockateel.** [t. D: m. *kaketielje*. Cf. COCKATOO]
cockatoo (kŏk′ə to͞o′), *n.* **1.** any of the crested parrots constituting the genera *Cacatua*, *Callocephalon*, or *Calyptorhynchus*, forming the subfamily *Kakatoeinae*, of the East Indies, Australia, etc., often white, or white and yellow, pink, or red. **2.** *Austral.* a small farmer. [t. D: m. *kaketoe*, t. Malay: m. *kakatūa*]
cockatoo fence, *Austral.* a rough fence made of logs and branches.

Cockatoo, *Cacatua galerita* (13 in. long)

cockatrice (kŏk′ə trĭs, -trīs′), *n.* **1.** a mythical serpent with deadly glance, reputed to be hatched by a serpent from a cock's egg, and commonly represented with the head, legs, and wings of a cock and the body and tail of a serpent. **2.** a basilisk. **3.** *Bible.* an unidentified species of venomous serpent. [ME *cocatris*, t. OF, der. L *calcāre* tread; used to render Gk *ichneúmōn* ICHNEUMON; assoc. with COCK[1]]
Cockayne (kŏ kān′), *n.* Cockaigne.
cockboat (kŏk′bōt′), *n.* a small boat, esp. one used as a tender.
cockchafer (kŏk′chā′fə), *n.* any of certain scarabaeid beetles, esp. the European species, *Melolontha melolontha*, which is very destructive to forest trees. [f. COCK[1] (def. 6, with reference to size) + CHAFER]
Cockcroft (kŏk′krŏft′), *n.* **Sir John Douglas,** 1897–1967, English nuclear physicist.
cockcrow (kŏk′krō′), *n.* the time at which cocks crow; dawn. Also, **cock′crow′ing.**
cocked hat (kŏkt). **1.** a hat having the brim turned up on two or three sides, common in the 18th century. **2. knock into a cocked hat,** *Slang.* to damage or destroy completely; outdo, overcome, or defeat utterly.
cocker[1] (kŏk′ə), *n.* **1.** a cocker spaniel. **2.** one who promotes or patronizes cockfighting. [f. COCK[1], v. + -ER[1]]
cocker[2] (kŏk′ə), *v.t.* to pamper. [? freq. of obs. *cock*, v., ? orig. meaning make a cock of]
cockerel (kŏk′ə rəl, kŏk′rəl), *n.* a young domestic cock. [dim. of COCK[1]. See -REL]
Cockerell (kŏk′ə rəl, kŏk′rəl), *n.* **Christopher Sydney,** born 1910, English engineer: inventor of the hovercraft.
cocker spaniel, one of a breed of small spaniels trained for use in hunting or kept as pets.
cockeye (kŏk′ī′), *n.* an eye that squints, or is affected with strabismus. [f. COCK[2], v. + EYE]
cockeyed (kŏk′īd′), *adj.* **1.** having a squinting eye; cross-eyed. **2.** *Slang.* twisted or slanted to one side. **3.** *Slang.* foolish; absurd. **4.** *Slang.* drunk.

Cocker spaniel (11 in. high)

cockeyed bob, *W Austral. Slang.* a sudden storm or squall.
cockfight (kŏk′fīt′), *n.* a fight between gamecocks usually armed with spurs. —**cock′fight′ing,** *n.*, *adj.*
cockhorse (kŏk′hôs′), *n.* **1.** a child's rocking horse or hobbyhorse. **2. ride a cockhorse,** to be jubilant.
cockish (kŏk′ĭsh), *adj.* *Colloq.* cocklike; cocky. —**cock′ishly,** *adv.* —**cock′ishness,** *n.*
cockle (kŏk′l), *n.*, *v.*, **-led, -ling.** —*n.* **1.** any of the bivalve molluscs with somewhat heart-shaped, radially ribbed valves which constitute the genus *Cardium*, esp. *C. edule*, the common edible species of Europe. **2.** any of various allied or similar molluscs. **3.** cockleshell. **4.** a wrinkle; pucker. **5. cockles of the heart,** the inmost parts of the heart; the depths of one's emotions or feelings. **6.** a small shallow or light boat. **7.** a furnace; a stove. **8.** *U.S.* a small crisp sweet of sugar and flour, bearing a motto. —*v.i.* **9.** to contract into wrinkles; pucker. **10.** to rise into short, irregular waves. —*v.t.* **11.** to cause to wrinkle or pucker: *a book cockled by water.* [ME *cockille*, t. F: m. *coquille*, b. F *coque* shell and L *conchylium*, t. Gk: m. *konchýlion*, dim. of *kónchē* mussel or cockle, CONCH]
cockleboat (kŏk′l bōt′), *n.* a cockboat.
cocklebur (kŏk′l bû′), *n.* any plant of the composite genus *Xanthium*, comprising coarse weeds with spiny burs.
cockleshell (kŏk′l shĕl′), *n.* **1.** a shell of the cockle. **2.** a shell of some other mollusc, as the scallop. **3.** a small, light boat. **4.** *Hist.* the badge of a pilgrim.
cockloft (kŏk′lŏft′), *n.* a small upper loft; a small garret.
cockney (kŏk′nĭ), *n.*, *pl.* **-neys,** *adj.* —*n.* (*often cap.*) **1.** a native of London, especially of the East End (often with reference to one who has marked peculiarities of pronunciation and dialect). **2.** this pronunciation or dialect. **3.** *Obs.* a pampered child. **4.** *Obs.* a squeamish, affected, or effeminate person. —*adj.* **5.** of cockneys or their dialect. [ME *cockeney* cock's egg (i.e. malformed egg), f. *coken*, gen. pl. of *cok* cock + *ey*, OE *ǣg* egg] —**cock′neyish,** *adj.*
cockneydom (kŏk′nĭ dəm), *n.* **1.** the region of cockneys. **2.** cockneys collectively.
cockneyese (kŏk′nĭ ēz′), *n.* cockney dialect.
cockneyfy (kŏk′nĭ fī′), *v.t.*, **-fied, -fying.** to give a cockney character to. Also, **cocknify.**
cockneyism (kŏk′nĭ ĭz′əm), *n.* **1.** cockney quality or usage. **2.** a cockney peculiarity, as of speech.
cock-of-the-rock (kŏk′əv thə rŏk′), *n.* a brilliant orange-red bird of the genus *Rupicola* with the bill hidden by the frontal plumes, found in northern South America.
cock of the walk, one who asserts himself domineeringly, as the leader of a gang.
cockpit (kŏk′pĭt′), *n.* **1.** (in some aeroplanes) an enclosed space containing seats for the pilot and copilot. **2.** the driver's seat in a racing car. **3.** a recess aft, in the deck of a yacht or other boat, which provides a small amount of deck space at a lower level. **4.** *Hist.* a space below the waterline, in warships, used as quarters for certain officers and as a dressing station for the wounded. **5.** a pit or enclosed space for cockfights. **6.** a place where a contest is fought, or which has been the scene of many contests or battles: *Belgium, the cockpit of Europe.*
cockroach (kŏk′rōch′), *n.* any of various orthopterous insects of the family *Blattidae*, usually nocturnal, and having a flattened body, esp. the dark brown or black oriental roach (black beetle, *Blatta orientalis*). [f. COCK[1] + ROACH, popular analysis of Sp. *cucaracha*. Cf. popular *sparrow grass* for *asparagus*, etc.]
cockscomb (kŏks′kōm′), *n.* **1.** the comb or caruncle of a cock. **2.** the cap of a professional fool, resembling a cock's comb. **3.** an amaranthaceous garden plant, *Celosia cristata*, with flowers, commonly crimson or purple, in a broad spike somewhat resembling the comb of a cock. **4.** any of several other species of *Celosia*. **5.** a coxcomb.
cock's-foot (kŏks′fo͝ot′), *n.* a perennial grass, *Dactylis glomerata*, with inflorescences resembling a cock's foot, common in temperate regions.
cockshot (kŏk′shŏt′), *n.* **1.** *Colloq.* a throw at an object, esp. for amusement. **2.** an object set up to be shot at.
cockshut (kŏk′shŭt′), *n.* *Obs. or Dial.* the close of the day; evening; twilight.
cockshy (kŏk′shī′), *n.*, *pl.* **-shies. 1.** the act or sport of throwing missiles at a target. **2.** an object of attack.
cock sparrow, 1. a male sparrow. **2.** *Colloq.* a conceited little man.
cockspur (kŏk′spû′), *n.* an annual grass, *Echinochloa crus-galli*, widespread in warm temperate regions.
cocksure (kŏk′sho͝oə′, -shô′), *adj.* **1.** perfectly sure or certain; completely confident in one's own mind. **2.** too certain; overconfident. **3.** *Obs.* perfectly secure or safe. —**cock′sure′ness,** *n.* —**Ant. 1.** doubtful. **2.** cautious.
cockswain (kŏk′sən, -swān′), *n.* coxswain.
cocktail (kŏk′tāl′), *n.* **1.** any of various short mixed drinks, consisting typically of gin, whisky, or brandy, mixed with vermouth, fruit juices, etc., usually chilled and frequently sweetened. **2.** a portion of oysters, prawns, crabmeat, etc., served in a glass. **3.** a mixture of fruits served in a glass. **4.** an appetizer of fruit or tomato juice. **5.** a horse with a docked tail. **6.** a horse which is not thoroughbred. **7.** an ill-bred person passing as a gentleman. [orig. unknown]
cock-up (kŏk′ŭp′), *n.* **1.** *Print.* a letter rising above other letters; ascender. **2.** *Colloq.* a mess; a tangle.

cocky[1] (kŏk′ĭ), *adj.*, **cockier, cockiest.** *Colloq.* arrogantly smart; pertly self-assertive; conceited: *a cocky fellow, air, answer.* —**cock′ily,** *adv.* —**cock′iness,** *n.*

cocky[2] (kŏk′ĭ), *n. Austral., N.Z.* a small farmer.

cocky-leeky (kŏk′ĭ lē′kĭ), *n.* cock-a-leekie.

cockyolly bird (kŏk′ĭ ŏl′ĭ), a pet name for any small bird.

coco (kō′kō), *n., pl.* **-cos. 1.** a tall, slender tropical palm, *Cocos nucifera,* which produces the coconut; coconut palm. **2.** the coconut fruit or seed. Also, **cocoa.** [t. Sp., Pg.: grinning face]

cocoa[1] (kō′kō), *n.* **1.** the roasted, husked, and ground seeds of the cacao, *Theobroma cacao,* from which much of the fat has been removed. **2.** a beverage made from cocoa powder. **3.** brown; reddish brown. —*adj.* **4.** of or pertaining to cocoa. **5.** of the colour of cocoa. [var. of CACAO]

cocoa[2] (kō′kō), *n.* coco.

cocoa bean, the seed of the cacao tree.

cocoa butter, a fatty substance obtained from the seeds of the cacao, used in making soaps, cosmetics, etc. Also, **cacao butter.**

coconsciousness (kō kŏn′shəs nĭs), *n. Psychol.* mental processes dissociated from the main stream of thought or from the dominant personality integration. —**cocon′scious,** *adj.* —**cocon′sciously,** *adv.*

coconut (kō′kə nŭt′), *n.* the seed of the coconut palm, large, hard-shelled, lined with a white edible meat, and containing a milky liquid. Also, **cocoanut.**

coconut butter, a butter substitute made from the coconut.

coconut ice, a confection, usually pink or white, made from sugar, desiccated coconut, etc.

coconut matting, matting made from the tough outer fibres of the coconut husks.

coconut oil, a fatty oil extracted from coconuts and used in the preparation of soaps, cosmetics, etc.

coconut palm, coco (def. 1). Also, **coconut tree.**

coconut-shy (kō′kə nŭt shī′), *n.* a cockshy with coconuts as targets and prizes.

cocoon (kə ko͞on′), *n.* **1.** the silky envelope spun by the larvae of many insects, as silkworms, serving as a covering while they are in the chrysalis or pupal state. **2.** any of various similar protective coverings, as the silky case in which certain spiders enclose their eggs. —*v.t.* **3.** to enclose within a protective covering. [t. F: m. *cocon,* der. *coque* shell]

cocoplum (kō′kō plŭm′), *n.* a small rosaceous shrub of the Caribbean, *Chrysobalanus icaco,* with an edible fruit.

Cocos Islands (kō′kŏs, kō′kəs), an Australian group of 20 coral islands in the Indian Ocean. SW of Java. 664 pop. (1963); 1½ sq. mi. Also, **Keeling Islands.** See map under **East Indies.**

cocotte (kŏ kŏt′, kə-; *Fr.* kŏ kŏt′), *n.* a courtesan; immoral woman. [t. F: hen, der. *coq* rooster]

Cocteau (*Fr.* kŏk tō′), *n.* **Jean** (*Fr.* zhäɴ), 1889–1963, French poet, novelist, dramatist, critic, artist, and film director.

Cocytus (kō sī′təs), *n. Class. Myth.* a river of Hades, connected with the Acheron.

cod[1] (kŏd), *n., pl.* **cod. 1.** one of the most important North Atlantic food fishes, *Gadus callarias.* **2.** *U.S.* any of several other gadoid fishes, as the Pacific cod, *Gadus macrocephalus.* [ME; orig. uncert.]

cod[2] (kŏd), *n.* **1.** a bag or sack. **2.** *Dial.* a pod. **3.** *Taboo Obs.* the scrotum. [ME; OE *codd*]

cod[3] (kŏd), *v.t. Colloq.* to hoax; poke fun at.

Cod (kŏd), *n.* **Cape.** See **Cape Cod.**

C.O.D., 1. cash on delivery. **2.** *U.S.* collect on delivery. Also, **c.o.d.**

coda (kō′də), *n. Music.* a more or less independent passage, at the end of a composition, introduced to bring it to a satisfactory close. [t. It., g. L *cauda* tail]

coddle (kŏd′l), *v.t.,* **-dled, -dling. 1.** to boil gently; stew (fruit, etc.). **2.** to treat tenderly; nurse or tend indulgently; pamper. [var. of and v. use of *caudle* kind of gruel, t. ONF: m. *caudel,* g. ML *caldellum,* dim. of *cal(i)dum* hot drink, neut. of L *calidus* hot]

code (kōd), *n., v.,* **coded, coding.** —*n.* **1.** any systematic collection or digest of the existing laws of a country, or of those relating to a particular subject: *the Civil Code of France.* **2.** any system or collection of rules and regulations. **3.** a system of signals for communication by telegraph, heliograph, etc. **4.** a system of arbitrarily chosen words, etc., used for brevity or secrecy. **5.** a system of symbols for conveying information or instructions to an electronic computer. **6.** See **Justinian Code.** —*v.t.* **7.** to arrange in a code; enter in a code. **8.** to translate into a code. [ME, t. F, t. L: m. s. *cōdex.* See CODEX]

codeclination (kō′dĕk lĭ nā′shən), *n. Astron.* the complement of the declination.

codefendant (kō′dĭ fĕn′dənt), *n.* a joint defendant.

codeine (kō′dēn), *n. Chem., Pharm.* a white, crystalline, slightly bitter alkaloid, $C_{18}H_{21}NO_3H_2O$, obtained from opium, used in medicine as an analgesic, sedative, and hypnotic. Also, **codein** (kō′dĭ ĭn), **codeia** (kō dē′ə). [f. m. s. Gk *kṓdeia* head, poppyhead + -INE[2]]

Code Napoléon (*Fr.* kŏd nȧ pŏ lĕ ôɴ′), the body of French private law, the Civil Code, promulgated between 1804 and 1810.

codetta (kō dĕt′ə), *n. Italian.* a short coda.

codex (kō′dĕks), *n., pl.* **codices** (kō′dĭ sēz′, kŏd′ĭ-). a manuscript volume of an ancient classic, the Scriptures, etc. [t. L, earlier *caudex* tree trunk, book]

Codex Juris Canonici (kō′dĕks jo͞o′rĭs kə nŏn′ĭ sī′), *Rom. Cath. Ch.* an official collection of Church law. [L]

codfish (kŏd′fĭsh′), *n., pl.* **-fishes,** (*esp. collectively*) **-fish.** cod[1].

codger (kŏj′ə), *n. Colloq.* **1.** a mean, miserly person. **2.** an odd or peculiar (old) person: *a lovable old codger.* **3.** a fellow; a chap. [? var. of CADGER]

codices (kō′dĭ sēz, kŏd′ĭ-), *n. pl.* of **codex.**

codicil (kŏd′ĭ sĭl), *n.* **1.** a supplement to a will, containing an addition, explanation, modification, etc., of something in the will. **2.** some similar supplement. [t. L: m. s. *cōdicillus,* dim. of *cōdex.* See CODEX]

codicillary (kŏd′ĭ sĭl′ə rĭ), *adj.* of the nature of a codicil.

codification (kŏd′ĭ fĭ kā′shən, kō′dĭ-), *n.* **1.** the act or result of arranging in a code. **2.** *Law.* the reducing of unwritten customs or case law to statutory form.

codify (kŏd′ĭ fī′, kō′dĭ-), *v.t.,* **-fied, -fying. 1.** to reduce (laws, etc.) to a code. **2.** to digest; arrange in a systematic collection. [f. COD(E) + -(I)FY. Cf. F *codifier*] —**cod′ifi′er,** *n.*

codling[1] (kŏd′lĭng), *n.* **1.** any of several varieties of elongated apples, used for cooking purposes. **2.** the tree which bears codlings. **3.** an unripe, half-grown apple. Also, **codlin** (kŏd′lĭn). [ME *querdling,* f. *querd* (orig. unknown) + -LING[1]]

codling[2] (kŏd′lĭng), *n.* the young of the cod. [ME; f. cod[1] + -LING[1]]

codling moth, a small moth, *Carpocapsa pomonella,* whose caterpillar (larva) feeds on the pulp around the core of apples and other fruit. Also, **codlin moth.**

codlins-and-cream (kŏd′lĭnz ən krēm′), *n.* a tall perennial onagraceous herb with pink flowers, *Epilobium hirsutum,* common near water in temperate regions.

cod-liver oil (kŏd′lĭv′ə), a fixed oil, extracted from the liver of the common cod or of allied species, extensively used in medicine as a source of vitamins A and D.

codpiece (kŏd′pēs′), *n.* (in 15th- and 16th-century male costume) a bagged appendage to the front of tight-fitting hose or breeches, covering the genitals. [f. COD[2] + PIECE]

codswallop (kŏdz′wŏl′əp), *n. Slang.* rubbish or nonsense.

Cody (kō′dĭ), *n.* **William Frederick** (*'Buffalo Bill'*), 1846–1917, U.S. Army scout and showman.

co-ed (kō′ĕd′), *Colloq.* —*adj.* **1.** coeducational. —*n.* **2.** *U.S.* a female student in a coeducational institution, esp. in a college or university. Also, *Chiefly U.S.,* **coed.** [short for COEDUCATIONAL]

coedition (kō′ĭ dĭsh′ən), *n.* a book published simultaneously by two or more publishers in different countries.

coeditor (kō′ĕd′ĭ tə), *n.* a joint editor.

coeducation (kō′ĕd yo͝o kā′shən), *n.* joint education, esp. of both sexes in the same institution and classes. —**co′educa′tional,** *adj.*

coefficient (kō′ĭ fĭsh′ənt), *n.* **1.** that which acts together with another thing to produce a result. **2.** *Maths.* a number or quantity placed (generally) before and multiplying another quantity: *3 is the coefficient of* x *in* 3x. **3.** *Physics.* a quantity, constant for a given substance, body, or process under certain specified conditions, that serves as a measure of some one of its properties: *coefficient of friction.* —*adj.* **4.** cooperating.

coefficient of thermal conductivity, thermal conductivity.

coehorn (kō′hôn′), *n.* a small mortar for throwing grenades, used in the 18th century.

coelacanth (sē′lə kănth′), *n.* one of a group of fishes belonging to the suborder *Actinistia,* which, until a living specimen was caught in South African waters in 1938, were believed to have been extinct for 70 million years. [f. *coel-* (comb. form repr. Gk *koîlos* hollow) + *-acanth* (see ACANTHO-)]

-coele, a word element referring to some small cavity of the body. Also, **-cele, -coel.** [comb. form repr. Gk *koilía* belly and *koîlos* hollow]

coelenterate (sē lĕn′tə rāt′, -tə rĭt), *Zool.* —*n.* **1.** a member of the *Coelenterata,* a phylum of invertebrate animals that includes the hydras, jellyfishes, sea-anemones, corals, etc., and is characterized by a single internal cavity serving for digestion, excretion, and other functions. —*adj.* **2.** belonging to the *Coelenterata.* [f. COELENTER(ON) + -ATE[1]]

coelenteron (sē lĕn′tə rŏn′), *n., pl.* **-tera** (-tə rə). *Zool.* the body cavity of a coelenterate. [f. *coel-* (comb. form repr. Gk *koîlos* hollow) + Gk *énteron* intestine]

coeliac (sē′lĭ ăk′), *adj. Anat.* pertaining to the cavity of the abdomen. Also, **celiac.** [t. L: s. *coeliacus*, t. Gk: m. *koiliakós* of the belly]

Coelian (sē′lĭ ən), *n.* one of the Seven Hills of ancient Rome.

coelom (sē′ləm), *n. Zool.* the body cavity of a metazoan, as distinguished from the intestinal cavity. Also, **coelome** (sē′lōm), **celom.** [t. Gk: m. *koílōma* a hollow]

coemption (kō ĕmp′shən, -ĕm′shən), *n.* the buying up of the whole of a particular commodity, esp. in order to acquire a monopoly. [t. L: s. *coemptio*, der. *coemere* buy up]

coenaesthesia (sē′nĭs thē′zyə), *n. Psychol.* the general sense of life, the bodily consciousness, or the total impression from all contemporaneous organic sensations, as distinct from special and well-defined sensations, such as those of touch or sight. Also, **coenesthesia, cenesthesia, coenaesthesis** (sē′nĭs thē′sĭs), **coenesthesis, cenesthesis.** [f. COEN(O)- + AESTHESIA. Cf. ANAESTHESIA]

coeno-, a word element meaning 'common'. Also, **ceno,** (before a vowel) **coen-.** [t. Gk: m. *koino-*, comb. form of *koinós*]

coenobite (sē′nə bīt′), *n.* one of a religious order living in a convent or community. Also, **cenobite.** [t. LL: m. s. *coenobīta*, der. *coenobium*, t. Gk: m. *koinóbion* convent, neut. of *koinóbios* living in a community] —**coenobitic** (sē′nə bĭt′ĭk), **coe′nobit′ical,** *adj.* —**coenobitism** (sē′nə bī tĭz′əm), *n.*

coenobium (sē nō′bĭ əm), *n.* a colony of unicellular organisms.

coenocyte (sē′nə sīt′), *n. Biol.* an organism made up of many protoplasmic units enclosed by one cell wall, as in some algae and fungi.

coenosarc (sē′nō säk′), *n. Biol.* the common living tissue uniting the polyps of a compound zoophyte.

coenurus (sē nyŏŏə′rəs), *n.* the larva of a tapeworm of the genus *Multiceps*, in which a number of heads (**scoleces**) form in the bladder. One species causes gid in sheep. [t. NL, f. *coen-* COEN- + m. Gk *ourá* tail]

coenzyme (kō ĕn′zīm), *n. Biochem.* an organic nonprotein substance other than the substrate required by certain enzymes to produce their reactions.

coequal (kō ē′kwəl), *adj.* **1.** equal in rank, ability, etc. —*n.* **2.** a person or thing coequal with another. —**coequality** (kō′ĭ kwŏl′ĭ tĭ), *n.* —**coe′qually,** *adv.*

coerce (kō ûs′), *v.t.,* **-erced, -ercing. 1.** to restrain or constrain by force, law, or authority; force or compel, as to do something. **2.** to compel by forcible action: *coerce obedience.* [t. L: m. s. *coercēre* hold together] —**coer′cer,** *n.* —**coer′cible,** *adj.*

coercion (kō û′shən), *n.* **1.** the act or power of coercing; forcible constraint. **2.** government by force.

coercive (kō û′sĭv), *adj.* serving or tending to coerce. —**coer′cively,** *adv.* —**coer′civeness,** *n.*

coercive force, *Physics.* the strength of the magnetic field required to annul the residual magnetism in a ferromagnetic substance; coercivity.

coercivity (kō′û sĭv′ĭ tĭ), *n.* coercive force.

coessential (kō′ĭ sĕn′shəl), *adj.* united in essence; having the same essence or nature. —**coessentiality** (kō′ĭ sĕn′shĭ ăl′ĭ tĭ), **co′essen′tialness,** *n.* —**co′essen′tially,** *adv.*

coetaneous (kō′ĭ tā′nyəs), *adj.* of the same age or duration. [t. LL: m. *coaetāneus* of the same age]

coeternal (kō′ĭ tû′nəl), *adj.* equally eternal; existing with another eternally. —**co′eter′nally,** *adv.*

coeternity (kō′ĭ tû′nĭ tĭ), *n.* coexistence from eternity with another eternal being.

Coeur-d'Alene (kû′də lān′), *n.* **1.** a member of a North American Indian people of N Idaho. **2.** their language, part of the Salishan family. [named after Lake *Coeur d'Alene*, in N Idaho]

coeval (kō ē′vəl), *adj.* **1.** of the same age, date, or duration; equally old. **2.** contemporary; coincident. —*n.* **3.** a contemporary. **4.** one of the same age. [f. m. s. L *coaevus* of the same age + -AL[1]] —**coe′vally,** *adv.*

coexecutor (kō′ĭg zĕk′yŏŏ tə), *n.* a joint executor.

coexecutrix (kō′ĭg zĕk′yŏŏ trĭks), *n., pl.* **-executrices** (-ĭg zĕk′yŏŏ trī′sēz). a female coexecutor.

coexist (kō′ĭg zĭst′), *v.i.* to exist together or at the same time. —**co′exist′ence,** *n.* —**co′exist′ent,** *adj.*

coextend (kō′ĭk stĕnd′), *v.t., v.i.* to extend equally through the same space or duration. —**coextension** (kō′ĭk stĕn′shən), *n.*

coextensive (kō′ĭk stĕn′sĭv), *adj.* having equal or coincident extension. —**co′exten′sively,** *adv.*

cofactor (kō′făk′tə, kō făk′tə), *n.* an accompanying factor.

coffee (kŏf′ĭ), *n.* **1.** a beverage, consisting of a decoction or infusion of the roasted and ground or crushed seeds (**coffee beans**) of the two-seeded fruit (**coffee berry**) of *Coffea arabica* and other species of *Coffea*, rubiaceous trees and shrubs of tropical regions. **2.** the berry or seed of such plants. **3.** the tree or shrub itself. **4.** light brown. [t. Turk.: m. *qahveh*, t. Ar.: m. *qahwa*]

coffee bar, an establishment where coffee and other refreshments are served.

coffee break, a pause from work, usually in the middle of the morning for coffee, etc.

coffee house, a public room where coffee and other refreshments are supplied. London coffee houses formerly held a position similar to modern clubs.

coffeepot (kŏf′ĭ pŏt′), *n.* a container, with a spout or pouring lip, in which coffee is made or served.

coffee royal, coffee laced with rum.

coffee shop, 1. a shop which sells and/or serves coffee, tea, etc. **2.** *U.S.* a public room, as in a hotel, where coffee and food are served.

coffee stall, a movable barrow, stall, etc., from which hot beverages and refreshments are served in the streets, esp. at night.

coffee table, a small, low table, on which coffee may be served, magazines and ornaments arranged, etc.

coffee-table (kŏf′ĭ tā′bl), *adj.* of, pertaining to, or suitable for a coffee table, as books designed more for display than for reading.

coffee tree, any tree, as *Coffea arabica*, yielding coffee beans.

coffer (kŏf′ə), *n.* **1.** a box or chest, esp. one for valuables. **2.** (*pl.*) a treasury; funds. **3.** any of various boxlike enclosures, as a cofferdam. **4.** a canal lock chamber. **5.** a caisson, or watertight box. **6.** an ornamental sunken panel in a ceiling or soffit. —*v.t.* **7.** to deposit or lay up in or as in a coffer or chest. **8.** to ornament with coffers or sunken panels: *a coffered ceiling.* [ME *cofre*, t. OF: chest, g. L *cophinus* basket. See COFFIN]

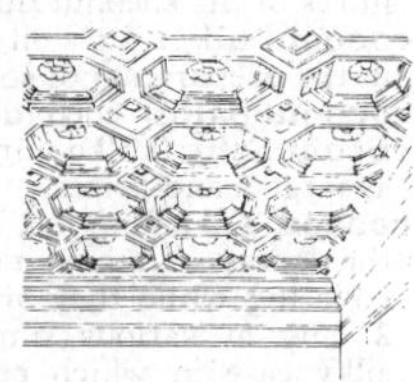
Coffers of a ceiling (def. 6)

cofferdam (kŏf′ə dăm′), *n.* a watertight enclosure constructed in rivers, etc., and then pumped dry so that bridge foundations, etc., may be constructed in the open.

coffin (kŏf′ĭn), *n.* **1.** the box or case in which a corpse is placed for burial. **2.** the part of a horse's foot containing the coffin bone. —*v.t.* **3.** to put or enclose in or as in a coffin. [ME *cofin*, t. OF: small basket, coffin, t. L: m. s. *cophinus*, t. Gk: m. *kóphinos* basket]

coffin bone, the terminal phalanx in the foot of the horse and allied animals, enclosed in the hoof.

coffle (kŏf′əl), *n.* a train of men or beasts, esp. of slaves, fastened together. [t. Ar.: m. *qāfila* caravan]

C. of E., Church of England.

C. of S., 1. Also, **C.O.S.** chief of staff. **2.** Church of Scotland.

cog[1] (kŏg), *n.* **1.** a tooth or projection (usually one of a series) on a wheel, etc., for transmitting motion to, or receiving motion from, a corresponding tooth or part with which it engages. **2.** a cogwheel. **3.** a person of little importance, in a large organization. **4.** *Carp.* a rectangular piece of wood let into notches in two adjacent timbers to prevent sliding. [ME *cogge*, akin to CUDGEL]

cog[2] (kŏg), *v.,* **cogged, cogging.** —*v.t.* **1.** to manipulate or load (dice) unfairly. —*v.i.* **2.** to cheat, esp. at dice. [orig. obscure]

cog., cognate.

cogency (kō′jən sĭ), *n.* power of proving or producing belief; convincing force.

cogent (kō′jənt), *adj.* compelling assent or belief; convincing; forcible: *a cogent reason.* [t. L: s. *cōgens*, ppr., forcing, collecting] —**co′gently,** *adv.*

cogitate (kŏj′ĭ tāt′), *v.,* **-tated, -tating.** —*v.i.* **1.** to think hard; ponder; meditate. —*v.t.* **2.** to think about; devise. [t. L: m. s. *cōgitātus*, pp.] —**cog′itat′or,** *n.*

cogitation (kŏj′ĭ tā′shən), *n.* **1.** meditation. **2.** the faculty of thinking. **3.** a thought; a design or plan.

cogitative (kŏj′ĭ tə tĭv), *adj.* **1.** meditating. **2.** given to meditation; thoughtful: *cogitative pause.* —**cog′itatively,** *adv.*

cogito, ergo sum (kŏg′ĭ tō û′gō sŏŏm′), *Latin.* I think, therefore I exist (the philosophical principle of Descartes).

cognac (kŏn′yăk; *Fr.* kō ñyăk′), *n.* **1.** (*often cap.*) the brandy distilled in and shipped from the legally delimited area surrounding the town of Cognac, France. 2. any brandy, esp. one made in France.

cognate (kŏg′nāt), *adj.* **1.** related by birth; of the same parentage, descent, etc. **2.** related in origin: *cognate languages, words, etc.* **3.** allied in nature or quality. —*n.* **4.** a person or thing cognate with another. [t. L: m. s. *cognātus*]

cognation (kŏg nā′shən), *n.* cognate relationship.

cognition (kŏg nĭsh′ən), *n.* **1.** the act or process of knowing; perception. **2.** the product of such a process; thing thus known, perceived, etc. **3.** *Obs.* knowledge. [ME, t. L: s. *cognitio* a getting to know] —**cognitive** (kŏg′nĭ tĭv), *adj.*

cognizable (kŏg′nĭ zə bl, kŏn′ĭ-), *adj.* **1.** capable of being perceived or known. **2.** within the jurisdiction of a court. Also, **cognisable.** —**cog′nizably,** *adv.*

cognizance (kŏg′nĭ zəns, kŏn′ĭ-), *n.* **1.** knowledge; notice; perception: *to have or take cognizance of a fact, remark, etc.* **2.** *Law.* **a.** judicial notice as taken by a court in dealing with a cause. **b.** the right of taking judicial notice, as possessed by a court. **c.** acknowledgement; admission, as a plea admitting the fact alleged in the declaration. **3.** the range or scope of knowledge, observation, etc. **4.** *Her.* a distinctive badge, etc., worn by retainers. Also, **cognisance.** [ME *conisance*, t. OF: m. *conoissance*, der. *conoistre*, g. L *cognoscere* come to know]

cognizant (kŏg′nĭ zənt, kŏn′ĭ-), *adj.* **1.** having cognizance; aware (fol. by *of*). **2.** competent to take judicial notice, as of causes. Also, **cognisant.**

cognize (kŏg′nīz, kŏg nīz′), *v.t.*, **-nized, -nizing.** to perceive; become conscious of; know. Also, **cognise.**

cognomen (kŏg nō′mĕn), *n., pl.* **-nomens, -nomina** (-nŏm′ĭ nə, -nō′mĭ nə). **1.** a surname. **2.** any name, esp. a nickname. **3.** the third and commonly the last name (in order) of a Roman citizen, indicating his house or family, as in 'Caius Julius *Caesar*'. [t. L] —**cognominal** (kŏg-nŏm′ĭ nəl, -nō′mĭ-), *adj.*

cognoscente (kŏn′yō shĕn′tĭ), *n., pl.* **-ti** (-tē). a person having a superior knowledge or critical appreciation in a particular branch of the arts; a connoisseur. Also, **conoscente.** [It., var. of *conoscente*, ppr. of *conoscere*, g. L *cognoscere* know]

cognoscible (kŏg nŏs′ĭ bl), *adj.* capable of being known. —**cognos′cibil′ity,** *n.*

cognovit (kŏg nō′vĭt), *n. Law.* (now superseded) an acknowledgement or confession by a defendant that the plaintiff's cause, or a part of it, is just, wherefore the defendant, to save expense, suffers judgement to be entered without trial. [t. L: he acknowledged]

cogon (kō′gōn), *n.* a tall, coarse grass, *Imperata cylindrica*, of the tropics and subtropics, furnishing an excellent material for thatching. [t. Sp., t. Tagalog]

cog railway, *Chiefly U.S.* a rack-railway.

cogwheel (kŏg′wēl′), *n.* a wheel with cogs, for transmitting or receiving motion. [late ME]

cohabit (kō hăb′ĭt), *v.i.* **1.** to live together as husband and wife. **2.** *Archaic.* to dwell or reside in company or in the same place. [t. LL: s. *cohabitāre* dwell with] —**cohab′itant,** **cohab′iter,** *n.* —**cohab′ita′tion,** *n.*

Cogwheels

coheir (kō ĕə′), *n.* a joint heir. —**coheir′ess,** *n. fem.*

cohere (kō hĭə′), *v.i.*, **-hered, -hering. 1.** to stick together; be united; hold fast, as parts of the same mass. **2.** to be naturally or logically connected. **3.** to agree; be congruous. [t. L: m. s. *cohaerēre* stick together] —**Syn. 1.** See **stick**[2].

coherence (kō hĭə′rəns), *n.* **1.** the act or state of cohering; cohesion. **2.** natural or logical connection. **3.** congruity; consistency. Also, **coher′ency.**

—**Syn.** 1, 2. COHERENCE, COHESION imply a sticking together. COHERENCE is more often applied figuratively, relating to the order and consistency of thought or of statements: *the coherence of a report.* COHESION usually applies to the literal sticking together of material things: *the cohesion of wood and glue in plywood.*

coherent (kō hĭə′rənt), *adj.* **1.** cohering; sticking together. **2.** having a natural or due agreement of parts; connected. **3.** consistent; logical. **4.** *Physics.* of electromagnetic radiation, esp. light having its waves in phase. —**coher′ently,** *adv.*

coherer (kō hĭə′rə), *n. Radio.* an obsolete device for detecting radio waves, usually a tube filled with a conducting substance in granular form, whose electrical resistance decreases when radio waves pass through it.

cohesion (kō hē′zhən), *n.* **1.** the act or state of cohering, uniting, or sticking together. **2.** *Physics.* the state or process by which the particles of a body or substance are bound together, esp. the attraction between the molecules of a liquid. **3.** *Bot.* the congenital union of one part with another. —**Syn. 1.** See **coherence.**

cohesive (kō hē′sĭv), *adj.* **1.** characterized by or causing cohesion. **2.** cohering; tending to cohere. —**cohe′sively,** *adv.* —**cohe′siveness,** *n.*

cohobate (kō′hō bāt′), *v.t.*, **-bated, -bating.** *Pharm.* to distil again from the same or a similar substance, as a distilled liquid poured back upon the matter remaining in the vessel, or upon another mass of similar matter. [t. ML: m. s. *cohobātus*, pp. of *cohobāre*; der. obs. med. term *cohob* of uncert. orig.]

cohort (kō′hôt), *n.* **1.** one of the ten divisions in an ancient Roman legion, numbering from 300 to 600 men. **2.** any group of warriors. **3.** any group or company. [t. L: s. *cohors* (orig. enclosure; see COURT)]

cohosh (kō′hŏsh, kō hŏsh′), *n.* either of two perennial herbs of the eastern U.S., the ranunculaceous *Cimicifuga racemosa* (**black cohosh**), or the berberidaceous *Caulophyllum thalictroides* (**blue cohosh**), both used medicinally. [t. Algonquian (Mass.): m. *kŭski* rough]

cohune (kō hōōn′), *n.* a pinnate-leaved palm, *Orbignya cohune*, native of Central America, bearing large nuts whose meat yields an oil resembling that of the coconut. Also, **cohune palm.**

C.O.I., Central Office of Information.

coif (koif), *n.* **1.** a hood-shaped cap worn under a veil, as by nuns. **2.** a close-fitting cap of various kinds, as one worn by European peasant women. **3.** a cap like the skullcap, retained until the common introduction of the wig, esp. as the headdress of barristers. **4.** *Obs.* the rank or position of a serjeant-at-law. —*v.t.* **5.** to cover or dress with, or as with, a coif. [ME, t. OF: m. *coife*, g. LL *cofea* cap; appar. of Gmc orig. (cf. MHG *kupfe* cap)]

coiffeur (kwä fû′; *Fr.* kwȧ fœr′), *n.* a hairdresser. [t. F, der *coiffer*. See COIFFURE]

coiffure (kwä fyōōə′; *Fr.* kwȧ fʏr′), *n.* **1.** a style of arranging or combing the hair. **2.** a head covering; headdress. [t. F, der. *coiffer*, lit., furnish with a coif]

coign (koin), *n.* a quoin. Also, **coigne.** [var. of COIN (def. 4)]

coign of vantage, a good position or place for observation or action.

coil[1] (koil), *v.t.* **1.** to wind into rings one above another; twist or wind spirally: *to coil a rope.* —*v.i.* **2.** to form rings, spirals, etc.; wind. **3.** to move in winding course. —*n.* **4.** a connected series of spirals or rings into which a rope or the like is wound. **5.** a single such ring. **6.** an arrangement of pipes, coiled or in a series, as in a radiator. **7.** *Elect.* **a.** a conductor, as a copper wire, wound up in a spiral or other form. **b.** a device composed essentially of such a conductor. **8.** *Philately.* **a.** a stamp issued in a roll, usually of 500 stamps, and usually perforated vertically or horizontally only. **b.** a roll of such stamps. [t. F: m. *cueillir* gather, g. a LL form r. L *colligere.* See COLLECT]

coil[2] (koil), *n.* **1.** disturbance; tumult; bustle. **2.** trouble. [orig. unknown]

coil ignition, *Motor Vehicles.* a system for supplying the sparking plugs of an internal-combustion engine with a high voltage from an induction coil rather than a magneto.

coil spring, *Mach.* a spring coiled helically. See illus. under **spring.**

Coimbatore (koim′bə tô′), *n.* a town in SW India, in Madras state. 286,305 (1961).

Coimbra (kō ĭm′brə; *Port.* kwẽm′brə), *n.* a town in central Portugal: university. 56,497 (1960).

coin (koin), *n.* **1.** a piece of metal stamped and issued by the authority of the government for use as money. **2.** such pieces collectively. **3. pay (someone) in his own coin,** to treat (someone) as he has treated others. **4.** *Archit.* a quoin. —*v.t.* **5.** to make (money) by stamping metal. **6.** to convert (metal) into money. **7.** *Colloq.* to make or gain (money) rapidly. **8.** to make; invent; fabricate: *to coin words.* —*v.i.* **9.** to counterfeit money, etc. [ME, t. F: wedge, corner, die, g. L *cuneus* wedge] —**coin′able,** *adj.* —**coin′er,** *n.*

coinage (koi′nĭj), *n.* **1.** the act, process, or right of making coins. **2.** that which is coined. **3.** coins collectively; the currency. **4.** the forming of new words. **5.** anything made, invented, or fabricated.

coin box, 1. a coin-operated telephone. **2.** any receptacle for coins, esp. for telephones. **3.** a callbox.

coincide (kō′ĭn sīd′), *v.i.*, **-cided, -ciding. 1.** to occupy the same place in space, the same point or period in time, or the same relative position. **2.** to correspond exactly (in nature, character, etc.). **3.** to agree or concur (in opinion, etc.). [t. ML: m. s. *coincidere*, f. L: *co-* co- + *incidere* fall on]

coincidence (kō ĭn′sĭ dəns), *n.* **1.** the condition or fact of coinciding. **2.** a striking occurrence of two or more events at one time apparently by mere chance. **3.** exact agreement in nature, character, etc.

coincidence circuit, *Physics.* an electronic circuit which

is so arranged that it will produce an output only if two or more input signals arrive simultaneously (or within a specified interval). Also, **coincidence gate.**
coincident (kō ĭn′sĭ dənt), *adj.* **1.** coinciding; occupying the same place or position. **2.** happening at the same time. **3.** exactly corresponding. **4.** in exact agreement (fol. by *with*). —**coin′cidently,** *adv.*
coincidental (kō ĭn′sĭ dĕn′tl), *adj.* showing or involving coincidence. —**coin′ciden′tally,** *adv.*
coinheritance (kō′ĭn hĕ′rĭ təns), *n.* joint inheritance. —**co′inher′itor,** *n.*
coinstantaneous (kō′ĭn stən tā′nyəs), *adj.* happening at the same time.
coinsurance (kō′ĭn shŏŏə′rəns, -shô′-), *n.* **1.** insurance jointly with another or others. **2.** a form of fire and various other forms of property insurance in which a person taking out insurance on property for less than its full value is regarded as a joint insurer and becomes jointly and proportionately responsible for losses. **3.** the method of distributing liability, in case of loss, among several insurers whose policies attach to the same risk.
coinsure (kō′ĭn shŏŏə′, -shô′), *v.t., v.i.,* **-sured, -suring.** to insure jointly with another or others; insure on the basis of coinsurance. —**co′insur′er,** *n.*
coir (koi′ə), *n.* the prepared fibre of the husk of the coconut fruit, used in making rope, matting, etc. [t. Malayalam: m. *kāyar* cord]
coital exanthema (kō′ĭ tl ĕk′săn thē′mə), a virus disease affecting horses and cattle characterized by the appearance of vesicles which later become pustules on the mucous membranes of the genital organs and neighbouring skin. It is transmitted by copulation.
coitus (kō′ĭ təs), *n.* sexual intercourse. Also, **coition** (kō ĭsh′ən). [t. L: s. *coitio*, der. *coīre* go together]
coitus interruptus (kō′ĭ təs ĭn tə rŭp′təs), (in sexual intercourse) withdrawal of the penis before orgasm, to avoid conception.
coke[1] (kōk), *n., v.,* **coked, coking.** —*n.* **1.** the solid product resulting from the distillation of coal in an oven or closed chamber, or by imperfect combustion: used as a fuel, in metallurgy, etc. It contains about 80 per cent carbon. —*v.t., v.i.* **2.** to convert into or become coke. [? var. of *colk* core]
coke[2] (kōk), *n. Slang.* cocaine. [short for COCAINE]
Coke (kŏŏk, kōk), *n.* **1. Sir Edward,** 1552–1634, English jurist. **2. Thomas William, Earl of Leicester,** 1754–1842, English agriculturist.
col (kŏl), *n.* **1.** *Phys. Geog.* a saddle or pass between two higher-standing parts of a mountain range or ridge. **2.** *Meteorol.* the region of relatively low pressure between two anticyclones. [t. F, g. L *collum* neck]
col-[1], variant of **com-**, by assimilation before *l*, as in *collateral.*
col-[2], variant of **colo-** before vowels, as in *colectomy.*
Col., **1.** Colombia. **2.** colonel. **3.** Colorado. **4.** Colossians.
col., column.
cola[1] (kō′lə), *n.* **1.** the cola nut. **2.** an extract prepared from it. **3.** the tree producing it. Also, **kola.** [Latinization of *Kola, Kolla, Goora*, in Negro languages of W Africa]
cola[2] (kō′lə), *n.* pl. of **colon.**
colander (kŭl′ən də, kŏl′-), *n.* a strainer for draining off liquids, esp. in cookery. Also, **cullender.** [cf. ML *cōlātōrium*, der. *cōlāre* strain]
cola nut, a brownish seed, about the size of a chestnut, produced by a sterculiaceous tree of western tropical Africa, the West Indies, and Brazil, *Cola acuminata*, and containing both caffeine and theobromine; used as a stimulant in soft drinks. Also, **kola nut.**
colatitude (kō lăt′ĭ tyŏŏd′), *n. Astron., Navig.* the complement of the latitude; the difference between a given latitude and 90°.
Colbert (*Fr.* kŏl bĕr′), *n.* **Jean Baptiste** (*Fr.* zhäɴ bȧ tēst′), 1619–83, French statesman and financier.
colcannon (kəl kăn′ən, kŏl′kăn′-), *n.* an Irish dish made of cabbage (or greens) and potatoes boiled and mashed together. [f. COLE + *-cannon* (of uncert. orig. and meaning)]
Colchester (kŏl′chĭs tə), *n.* a town in E England, in Essex. 67,450 (1961).
colchicine (kŏl′chĭ sēn′, -sĭn, kŏl′kĭ-), *n. Chem.* a yellow crystalline alkaloid, $C_{22}H_{25}NO_6$, obtained from colchicum. Used to obtain new agricultural and horticultural varieties because it causes abnormal division of some living cells with an increase in the number of chromosomes.
colchicum (kŏl′chĭ kəm, kŏl′kĭ-), *n.* **1.** any plant of the Old World liliaceous genus *Colchicum*, esp. *C. autumnale*, a crocus-like plant. **2.** the dried seeds or corms of this plant. **3.** a medicine or drug prepared from them, used esp. for gout. [t. L, t. Gk: m. *kolchikón*; appar. named after COLCHIS]
Colchis (kŏl′kĭs), *n.* the legendary land of Medea and the Golden Fleece.
colcothar (kŏl′kə thä′), *n.* the red oxide of iron, Fe_2O_3, which remains after heating ferrous sulphate: used as a pigment and polishing agent; rouge. [t. ML, t. Ar.: m. *qolqotār*]
cold (kōld), *adj.* **1.** having a temperature lower than the normal temperature of the body: *cold hands.* **2.** having a relatively low temperature; having little or no warmth: *a cold day.* **3.** producing or feeling, esp. in a high degree, a lack of warmth: *I am cold.* **4.** dead. **5.** *Colloq.* unconscious because of a severe blow, shock, etc. **6.** deficient in passion, emotion, enthusiasm, ardour, etc.: *cold reason.* **7.** not affectionate, cordial, or friendly; unresponsive: *a cold reply.* **8.** lacking sensual desire; frigid. **9.** failing to excite feeling or interest. **10.** imperturbable. **11.** depressing; dispiriting: *cold misgivings.* **12.** faint; weak: *a cold scent.* **13.** distant from the object of search. **14.** *Art.* blue in effect, or inclined towards blue in tone: *a picture cold in tone.* **15.** slow to absorb heat, as a soil containing a large amount of clay and hence retentive of moisture. **16. cold feet,** *Slang.* loss of courage or confidence for carrying out some undertaking. **17. in cold blood,** calmly; coolly and deliberately. **18. leave one cold,** to fail to affect one, as with enthusiasm, sympathy, etc.: *her ravings left him cold.* **19. throw cold water on,** to dampen enthusiasm of (a person), or for (a thing); discourage. —*n.* **20.** the relative absence of heat. **21.** the sensation produced by loss of heat from the body, as by contact with anything having a lower temperature than that of the body. **22.** an indisposition caused by a virus, characterized by catarrh, hoarseness, coughing, etc. **23. catch** or **take cold,** to suffer from such a cold. **24.** cold weather. **25. in the cold,** neglected; ignored. [ME; d. OE *cald*, r. OE *ceald*, c. G *kalt*. Cf. L *gelidus* icy] —**cold′ish,** *adj.* —**cold′ly,** *adv.* —**cold′ness,** *n.*
—**Syn. 2.** COLD, CHILL, CHILLING, CHILLY, COOL refer to various degrees of absence of heat. COLD refers to temperature possibly so low as to cause suffering: *cold water.* CHILL, now chiefly poetical, suggests a raw cold which causes shivering and numbness: *how bitter chill it was.* CHILLING carries a connotation of (killing) frost: *a chilling wind.* CHILLY is a weaker word, though it also connotes shivering and discomfort: *a chilly room.* COOL means merely somewhat cold, not warm: *cool and comfortable.* All have figurative uses. **6.** indifferent. —**Ant. 2.** hot. **6.** emotional.
Cold (kōld), *n.* **Sea of,** a dark plain, *Mare Frigoris*, in the first and second quadrant on the face of the moon.
cold-blooded (kōld′blŭd′ĭd), *adj.* **1.** without feeling; unsympathetic; cruel: *a cold-blooded murder.* **2.** sensitive to cold. **3.** designating or pertaining to animals, as fishes and reptiles, whose blood temperature ranges from the freezing point upwards, in accordance with the temperature of the surrounding medium. —**cold′-blood′edly,** *adv.* —**cold′-blood′edness,** *n.*
cold chisel, a strong steel chisel used on cold metal.
cold comfort, almost no consolation; negligible comfort.
cold cream, an emollient of oily and heavy consistency, used to soothe and cleanse the skin, esp. of the face and neck.
cold desert, the Greenland icecap.
cold feet, *Colloq.* loss of courage or confidence.
cold frame, a small glass-covered structure, and the bed of earth which it covers, used to protect plants.
cold front, *Meteorol.* **1.** the contact surface between two air-masses where the cooler mass is advancing against and under the warmer mass. **2.** the line of intersection of this surface with the surface of the earth.
cold-hearted (kōld′hä′tĭd), *adj.* lacking sympathy or feeling; indifferent; unkind.
cold pack, a cold towel, icebag, etc., applied to the body to reduce swelling, relieve pain, etc.
cold saw, a metal-cutting saw.
cold-short (kōld′shôt′), *adj. Metall.* brittle when at atmospheric temperature.
cold-shoulder (kōld′shōl′də), *v.t.* to ignore; show indifference to.
cold shut, *Metall.* an imperfectly fused junction of two streams of metal in a mould.
cold snap, a sudden period of cold weather.
cold sore, a vesicular eruption on the face often accompanying a cold or a febrile condition; herpes simplex.
cold steel, a sword, bayonet, etc.
cold storage, **1.** the storage of food, furs, etc., in an artificially cooled place. **2.** abeyance; indefinite postponement.
Coldstream Guards (kōld′strēm gädz′), a regiment of foot guards, forming part of the Household Brigade of the sovereign.
cold sweat, perspiration and coldness caused by fear, nervousness, etc.
cold war, intense economic and political rivalry just short of military conflict.

cold wave, **1.** *Meteorol.* a rapid and considerable fall in temperature, usually affecting a large area. **2.** a permanent wave in the hair set by chemicals.
cold-work (kōld′wûk′), *v.t.* to work (a metal, etc.) when it is in a solid or cold condition.
cole (kōl), *n.* any of various plants of the genus *Brassica*, esp. rape, *Brassica napus.* [ME *col(e)*, OE *cāl*, var. of *cāw(e)l*, t. L: m. s. *caulis* stalk, cabbage]
colectomy (kə lĕk′tə mĭ), *n., pl.* **-mies.** *Surg.* the removal of all or part of the colon or large intestine.
colemanite (kōl′mə nīt′), *n.* a mineral, hydrous calcium borate, $Ca_2B_6O_{11}.5H_2O$, occurring in colourless or milky white crystals. [named after W. T. *Coleman* of San Francisco, in whose mine it was found]
coleopteron (kŏl′ĭ ŏp′tə-rən), *n.* a coleopterous insect; a beetle. Also, **coleopteran.** [t. NL, t. Gk: m. *koleópteron,* adj. (neut.), sheath-winged]

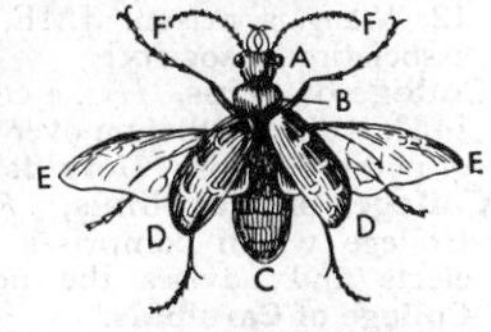

Coleopteron, *Cicindela campestris*
A, Head; B, Prothorax; C, Abdomen; D, Elytra; E, Wings; F, Antennae

coleopterous (kŏl′ĭ ŏp′tə-rəs), *adj.* belonging or pertaining to the order *Coleoptera*, the beetles. [t. Gk: m. *koleópteros* sheath-winged]
coleoptile (kŏl′ĭ ŏp′tĭl), *n.* *Bot.* (in grasses) the first leaf above the ground, forming a sheath round the stem tip. [t. NL: m. s. *coleoptilum*, f. Gk: m. *koleón* sheath + *ptílon* soft feathers, down]
coleorhiza (kŏl′ĭ ə rī′zə), *n., pl.* **-zae** (-zē). *Bot.* the sheath which envelops the radicle in certain plants, and which is penetrated by the root in germination. [t. NL, f. Gk: m. *koleó(s)* sheath + *rhíza* root]
Coleridge (kōl′rĭj), *n.* **Samuel Taylor,** 1772–1834, English poet, critic, and philosopher.
coleslaw (kōl′slô′), *n.* a salad of finely sliced white cabbage. [t. D: m. *koolsla*, f. *kool* cabbage + *sla*, m. *salade* salad]
Colet (kŏl′ĭt), *n.* **John,** 1467?–1519, English humanist; founder of St Paul's School, London.
Colette (*Fr.* kō lĕt′), *n.* (*Sidonie Gabrielle Claudine Colette*), 1873–1954, French novelist.
coleus (kō′lĭ əs), *n.* any plant of the menthaceous genus *Coleus*, of tropical Asia and Africa, species of which are cultivated for their showy, coloured foliage. [NL, t. Gk: m. *koleós* sheath (so called from the union of the filaments about the style)]
colewort (kōl′wût′), *n.* **1.** any plant of the genus *Brassica.* **2.** a collard.
coley (kō′lĭ, kŏl′ĭ), *n.* *Colloq.* (in fishmongers' usage) any of several edible fishes, esp. coalfish. [alter. of COALFISH]
colic (kŏl′ĭk), *Pathol., Vet. Sci.* —*n.* **1.** paroxysmal pain in the abdomen or bowels. —*adj.* **2.** pertaining to or affecting the colon or the bowels. [ME *colyke*, t. L: m. s. *cōlicus*, t. Gk: m. *kōlikós* pertaining to the colon] —**colicky** (kŏl′ĭ kĭ), *adj.*
colicroot (kŏl′ĭk ro͞ot′), *n.* either of two North American liliaceous herbs, *Aletris farinosa* and *A. aurea*, having small yellow or white flowers in a spikelike raceme, and a root reputed to relieve colic.
Coligny (*Fr.* kō lē nyē′), *n.* **Gaspard de** (*Fr.* gȧs pȧr′ də), 1519–72, French admiral and Huguenot leader. Also, **Coligni.**
-coline, -colous. [f. s. L *colere* inhabit + -INE[1]]
coliseum (kŏl′ĭ sĭəm′), *n.* **1.** an amphitheatre, stadium, large theatre, etc., for public meetings and entertainment. **2.** (*cap.*) Colosseum. [t. ML: COLOSSEUM]
colitis (kō lī′tĭs, kə-), *n.* *Pathol.* inflammation of the mucous membrane of the colon. [t. NL; see COL(ON), -ITIS]
Coll (kŏl), *n.* an island of the Inner Hebrides, Argyll, Scotland.
coll., **1.** collective. **2.** college. **3.** collegiate. **4.** colloquial.
collaborate (kə lăb′ə rāt′), *v.i.,* **-rated, -rating. 1.** to work, one with another; cooperate, as in literary work. **2.** to cooperate treacherously: *collaborating with the Nazis.* [t. LL: m. s. *collabōrātus*, pp.] —**collab′ora′tion,** *n.* —**collab′ora′tor, collab′ora′tionist.** *n.*
collage (kə läzh′, kō-; *Fr.* kō lȧzh′), *n.* an abstract composition employing various materials, such as newspaper clippings, fragments of advertisements, etc., with lines, colours, and design supplied by the artist. [F]
collagen (kŏl′ə jən), *n.* *Biochem.* the protein contained in connective tissue and bones which yields gelatine on boiling. [t. F: m. *collagène*, f. m. Gk *kólla* glue + *-gène* -GEN]
collapse (kə lăps′), *v.,* **-lapsed, -lapsing,** *n.* —*v.i.* **1.** to fall or cave in; crumble suddenly: *the roof collapsed.* **2.** to be made so that parts can be folded, placed, etc., together: *this card table collapses.* **3.** to break down; come to nothing; fail: *the project collapsed.* **4.** to lose strength, courage, etc., suddenly. **5.** *Pathol.* **a.** to sink into extreme weakness. **b.** (of lungs) to come into an airless state. —*v.t.* **6.** to cause to collapse. —*n.* **7.** a falling in or together. **8.** a sudden, complete failure; a breakdown. [t. L: m. s. *collapsus*, pp., fallen together] —**collaps′ible, collaps′able,** *adj.* —**collaps′ibil′ity,** *n.*
collar (kŏl′ə), *n.* **1.** anything worn or placed round the neck. **2.** the part of a shirt, blouse, coat, etc., round the neck, usually folded over. **3.** a close-fitting necklace or ornamental band of linen, velvet, or the like, worn by women round the neck. **4.** an ornamental necklace worn as insignia of an order of knighthood. **5.** a leather or metal band put round an animal's neck to restrain or identify it. **6.** part of a harness round the horse's neck that bears some of the weight of the load drawn. See illus. under **harness. 7.** *Bot.* the point of junction of the plumule and the radical. **8.** *Zool.* any of various markings, or structures, about the neck, suggesting a collar. **9.** a cut of bacon taken from the fore end. **10.** *Mach.* an enlargement encircling a rod or shaft, and serving usually as a holding or bearing piece. —*v.t.* **11.** to put a collar on; furnish with a collar. **12.** to seize by the collar or neck. **13.** *Slang.* to lay hold of, seize, or take. **14.** *Slang.* to gain a monopoly over: *to collar the market in wool.* [t. L: m. *collāre*, v., der. *collum* neck; r. ME *coler*, t. AF] —**col′larless,** *adj.*
collar-and-elbow (kŏl′ər ənd ĕl′bō), *n.* a style of wrestling in which the opponents grip each other by the collar and elbow, the first to relinquish his hold being deemed the loser.
collarbone (kŏl′ə bōn′), *n.* clavicle.
collard (kŏl′əd), *n.* a kind of cabbage, *Brassica oleracea*, var. *acephala*, cut before the hearts become hard. [var. of COLEWORT, with second element assimilated to -ARD]
collaret (kŏl′ə rĕt′), *n.* a woman's small collar or neckpiece of lace, embroidery, chiffon, fur, or other material. Also, **col′larette′.** [f. COLLAR + -ET, r. *colleret*, t. F: m. *collerette*, dim. of *collier* collar]
collar stud, a stud for fastening a collar to a shirt.
collate (kŏ lāt′, kə-), *v.t.,* **-lated, -lating. 1.** to compare (texts, statements, etc.) in order to note points of agreement or disagreement. **2.** *Bookbinding.* to verify the arrangement of, as the sheets of a book after they have been gathered, usually by inspecting the signature at the foot of the first page of each sheet. **3.** *Bibliog.* to verify the number and order of the sheets of (a volume) as a means of determining its completeness. **4.** *Eccles.* to present by collation, as to a benefice. [t. L: m. s. *collātus*, pp., brought together]
collateral (kŏ lăt′ə rəl), *adj.* **1.** situated at the side. **2.** running side by side. **3.** *Bot.* standing side by side. **4.** accompanying; attendant; auxiliary. **5.** additional; confirming: *collateral security.* **6.** secured by collateral: *a collateral loan.* **7.** aside from the main subject, course, etc.; secondary; indirect. **8.** descended from the same stock, but in a different line; not lineal. **9.** pertaining to those so descended. —*n.* **10.** security pledged for the payment of a loan. **11.** a collateral kinsman. [ME, t. ML: s. *collaterālis.* See COL-, LATERAL] —**collat′erally,** *adv.*
collation (kŏ lā′shən, kə-), *n.* **1.** the act of collating. **2.** description of the technical features of a book; volumes, size, pages, illustrations, etc. **3.** the presentation of a clergyman to a benefice, esp. by a bishop who is himself the patron or has acquired the patron's rights. **4.** a light meal which may be permitted on days of general fast. **5.** a light meal. **6.** the act of reading and conversing on the lives of the saints, or the Scriptures (a practice instituted in monasteries by St Benedict). [ME *collacion*, t. L: m. s. *collātio* a bringing together]
collative (kŏ lā′tĭv, kŏl′ə-), *adj.* **1.** collating. **2.** *Eccles.* presented by collation: *collative benefices.*
collator (kŏ lā′tə), *n.* **1.** one who or that which collates. **2.** *Computers.* a machine which interleaves two packs of punched cards so that those with the same control information are brought together.
colleague (kŏl′ēg), *n.* an associate in office, professional work, etc. [t. F: m. *collègue*, t. L: m. *collēga* one chosen with another] —**col′leagueship′,** *n.*
collect[1] (kə lĕkt′), *v.t.* **1.** to gather together; assemble. **2.** to accumulate; make a collection of. **3.** to gather money for contributions or debts, for charity, etc. **4.** to regain control of (one's thoughts, faculties, etc., or oneself). **5.** to fetch; call for and remove. **6.** *Rare.* to infer. —*v.i.* **7.** to gather together; assemble. **8.** to accumulate: *rainwater collecting in the drainpipe.* **9.** to gather or bring together books, stamps, coins, etc., usually as a hobby.

—*adj., adv.* **10.** *U.S.* to be paid for on delivery: *to send a telegram collect.* [t. L: s. *collectus*, pp., gathered together] —**collect′able, collect′ible,** *adj.* —**Syn. 1.** See **gather.**

collect[2] (kŏl′ĕkt), *n.* any of certain brief prayers used in Western churches as before the epistle in the communion service, and in Anglican churches, also in morning and evening prayers. [ME *collecte*, t. ML: m. *collecta* short prayer, orig., a gathering together. See COLLECT[1]]

collectanea (kŏl′ĕk tā′nyə), *n.pl.* collected passages; a miscellany; anthology. [t. L, neut. pl. of *collectāneus* collected]

collected (kə lĕk′tĭd), *adj.* having control of one's faculties; self-possessed. —**collect′edly,** *adv.* —**collect′edness,** *n.* —**Syn.** See **calm.**

collection (kə lĕk′shən), *n.* **1.** the act of collecting. **2.** the clearing of pillar-boxes by a paid official. **3.** that which is collected; a set of objects, specimens, writings, etc., gathered together. **4.** a sum of money collected, esp. for charity or church use. **5.** the gathering of such money. **6.** (*usually pl.*) a terminal or other examination conducted by the colleges of certain universities. —**Syn. 3.** accumulation, aggregation. [ME, t. L: s. *collectio*]

collective (kə lĕk′tĭv), *adj.* **1.** formed by collection. **2.** forming a collection or aggregate; aggregate; combined. **3.** pertaining to a group of individuals taken together. **4.** (of a fruit) formed by the coalescence of the pistils of several flowers, as the mulberry or the pineapple. —*n.* **5.** a collective noun. **6.** a collective body; aggregate. **7.** *Govt.* a unit of organization or the organization in a collectivist system. —**collec′tively,** *adv.*

collective agreement, 1. the contract, written or oral, made between an employer or employers and a union or unions on behalf of all the employees represented by the union or unions. **2.** the schedule of wages, rules, and working conditions agreed upon.

collective bargaining, the process by which wages, hours, rules, and working conditions are negotiated and agreed upon by a union with an employer for all the employees collectively whom it represents.

collective behaviour, *Sociol.* the concerted behaviour of individuals acting under the influence of one another.

collective farm, (in Communist countries) a farm formed of pooled smallholdings worked as a single unit.

collective noun, *Gram.* a noun that under the singular form expresses a grouping of individual objects or persons, as *herd, jury,* and *clergy.* The singular verb is used when the noun is thought of as naming a single unit, acting as one, as *family* in *his family is descended from Edward III.* The plural verb is used when the noun is thought of as composed of individuals who retain their separateness, as *my family are all at home.*

collective security, a policy or principle in international relations, designed to preserve world peace, according to which all countries collectively guarantee the security of individual countries, as by sanctions or multilateral alliances against an aggressor.

collective unconscious, (in psychology, esp. Jungian psychology) those elements in the individual's unconscious derived from the experiences of the race.

collectivism (kə lĕk′tĭ vĭz′əm), *n.* the socialist principle of control by the people collectively, or the state, of all means of production or economic activities. —**collec′tivist,** *n., adj.* —**collec′tivis′tic,** *adj.*

collectivity (kŏl′ĕk tĭv′ĭ tĭ), *n., pl.* **-ties. 1.** collective character. **2.** a collective whole. **3.** the people collectively.

collectivize (kə lĕk′tĭ vīz′), *v.t.,* **-vized, -vizing.** to organize (a people, industry, economy, etc.) according to the principles of collectivism. Also, **collectivise.** —**collec′tiviza′tion,** *n.*

collector (kə lĕk′tə), *n.* **1.** one who or that which collects. **2.** a person employed to collect debts, tickets, taxes, etc. **3.** one who collects books, paintings, stamps, shells, etc., as a hobby. **4.** (formerly in India) the chief official of a district. **5.** *Elect.* **a.** any device for collecting current from contact inductors. **b.** an electrode in a radio valve for collecting unwanted electrons or ions. **c.** an electrode in a transistor through which a primary flow of carriers leaves the inter-electrode region. [ME, t. LL] —**collec′torship′,** *n.*

collector electrode. See **klystron.**

colleen (kŏl′ēn, kŏ lēn′), *n. Irish.* a girl. [t. Irish: m. *cailín*]

college (kŏl′ĭj), *n.* **1.** (in Great Britain) a constituent unit of certain universities, sometimes residential, divided into faculties or the like, providing courses of instruction usually leading to the degree of bachelor. **2.** an institution for special or professional instruction, as in medicine, pharmacy, agriculture, music, etc., often part of a university. **3.** *U.S.* an institution of higher learning, esp. one not divided (like a university) into distinct schools and faculties, and affording a general or liberal education rather than technical or professional training. **4.** an endowed, self-governing association of scholars incorporated within a university, as at the universities of Oxford and Cambridge. **5.** a similar foundation outside a university. **6.** (in Great Britain) any of certain large public schools, or sometimes private schools. **7.** the building or buildings occupied by any of these educational institutions. **8.** (in French use) an institution for secondary education. **9.** an organized association of persons having certain powers and rights, and performing certain duties or engaged in a particular pursuit: *an electoral college.* **10.** a company; assembly. **11.** *Hist.* a body of clergy living together on a foundation for religious service, etc. **12.** *Slang.* a prison. [ME, t. OF, t. L: m. s. *collēgium* association, a society]

College of Arms, *Her.* a collegiate body, incorporated in 1483, with jurisdiction over armorial bearings and matters of pedigree. Also, **Heralds' College.**

College of Cardinals, *Rom. Cath. Ch.* the Sacred College which comprises all the cardinals and which elects and advises the pope. Official name, **Sacred College of Cardinals.**

College of Propaganda. See **propaganda** (def. 4).

college pudding, a baked or steamed suet or sponge pudding containing dried fruit.

colleger (kŏl′ĭ jə), *n.* (at Eton) a student supported by funds provided by the college.

collegial (kə lē′jĭ əl), *adj.* belonging or pertaining to a college.

collegian (kə lē jĭ ən), *n.* a member of a college.

collegiate (kə lē′jĭ ĭt), *adj.* **1.** of or pertaining to a college. **2.** of the nature of or constituted as a college. **3.** of a town containing a college.

collegiate church, 1. a church which is endowed for a chapter of canons (usually with a dean), but which has no bishop's see. **2.** (loosely) a chapel connected with a college. **3.** *U.S.* a church or group of churches under the general management of one consistory or session. **4.** *U.S.* a consolidation of formerly distinct churches under one or more pastors. **5.** (in Scotland) a church or congregation the active pastor of which is the colleague and successor of the emeritus pastor.

col legno (kŏl lā′nyō), *Music.* with the wood (of sound produced by players striking the strings of a bowed instrument with the wooden back of the bow). [It.]

collembolan (kə lĕm′bə lən), *n.* **1.** a member of the *Collembola*, an order of small wingless insects; springtail. —*adj.* **2.** belonging to the *Collembola*.

collenchyma (kə lĕng′kĭ mə), *n. Bot.* a layer of modified parenchyma consisting of cells which are thickened at the angles and commonly elongated. [NL, f. Gk: m. s. *kólla* glue + *énchyma* infusion]

collet (kŏl′ĭt), *n., v.,* **-leted, -leting.** —*n.* **1.** a collar or enclosing band. **2.** the enclosing rim within which a jewel is set. **3.** *Horol.* the tiny collar which supports the inner terminal of the hairspring. —*v.t.* **4.** to set in a collet: *colleted in gold.* [t. F, dim. of *col* neck, g. L *collum*]

collide (kə līd′), *v.i.,* **-lided, -liding. 1.** to come together with force; come into violent contact; crash: *the two cars collided.* **2.** to clash; conflict. [t. L: m. s. *collīdere*]

collie (kŏl′ĭ), *n.* a dog of any of certain intelligent varieties much used for tending sheep, esp. one of Scottish breed, usually with a heavy coat of long hair and a bushy tail. Also, **colly.**

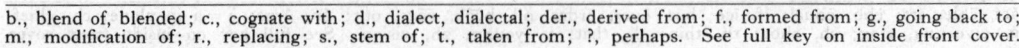

Collie
(2 ft high at the shoulder)

Collier (kŏl′ĭ ə), *n.* **Jeremy,** 1650–1726, English clergyman and author.

collier (kŏl′ĭ ə), *n.* **1.** a ship for carrying coal. **2.** a sailor in such a ship. **3.** a coal-miner. **4.** *Obs.* one who carries or sells coal.

colliery (kŏl′yə rĭ), *n., pl.* **-ries.** a coal mine, including all buildings and equipment.

colligate (kŏl′ĭ gāt′), *v.t.,* **-gated, -gating. 1.** to bind or fasten together. **2.** *Logic.* to bind (facts) together by a general description or by a hypothesis which applies to them all. [t. L: m. s. *colligātus*, pp., bound together] —**col′liga′tion,** *n.*

colligative properties (kə lĭg′ə tĭv), *n. Chem.* the properties of a solution which depend only on the concentration of dissolved particles (molecules or ions) and not on their nature, as osmotic pressure.

collimate (kŏl′ĭ māt′), *v.t.,* **-mated, -mating. 1.** to bring into line; make parallel. **2.** to adjust accurately the line of sight of (a telescope). [t. L: m. s. *collīmātus*, pp., var. (by false reading) of *collīneātus*, pp., brought into line with] —**col′lima′tion,** *n.*

collimator (kŏl′ĭ mā′tə), *n. Optics.* **1.** a small fixed telescope for use in collimating other instruments. **2. a.** a device for obtaining a parallel beam of light, consisting of a tube containing a convex lens at one end and an adjustable slit at the other; chiefly used in spectroscopes. **b.** the convex lens itself. **3.** (in radiology) an arrangement of absorbers for limiting a beam of radiation to the required dimensions.
collinear (kŏ lĭn′yə), *adj.* lying in the same straight line. [f. COL-[1] + LINEAR] —**collin′early,** *adv.*
Collingwood (kŏl′ĭng wŏŏd′), *n.* **1. Lord Cuthbert,** 1750–1810, English admiral. **2.** a town in SE Australia, near Melbourne. 25,413 (1961).
Collins (kŏl′inz), *n.* **1. Michael,** 1890–1922, Irish revolutionist and patriot. **2. William,** 1721–59, English poet. **3.** (**William**) **Wilkie,** 1824–89, English novelist.
collinsia (kə lĭn′sĭ ə, -zĭ ə), *n.* any of the scrophulariaceous herbs constituting the genus *Collinsia*, bearing whorled, (usually) particoloured flowers. [t. NL, named after Z. *Collins*, 1764–1831, American botanist]
collision (kə lĭzh′ən), *n.* **1.** the act of colliding; a coming violently into contact; crash. **2.** a clash; conflict. [late ME, t. LL: s. *collīsio*, der. L *collīdere* COLLIDE]
collision course, a course or path of a vehicle which, if unchanged, will cause a collision.
collocate (kŏl′ə kāt′), *v.t.*, **-cated, -cating. 1.** to set or place together. **2.** to arrange in proper order: *collocated events.* [t. L: m. s. *collocātus*, pp., set in a place]
collocation (kŏl′ə kā′shən), *n.* **1.** the act of collocating. **2.** the state or manner of being collocated. **3.** arrangement, esp. of words in a sentence.
collocutor (kə lŏk′yŏŏ tə), *n.* one who talks to another; one who takes part in a colloquy.
collodion (kə lō′dyən), *n.* soluble guncotton dissolved in a mixture of ether and alcohol, used to form a coating or film on wounds, photographic plates, etc. [f. Gk: m. s. *kollṓdēs* gluelike + *-ion*, suffix]
collogue (kŏ lōg′), *v.i.*, **-logued, -loguing.** *Dial.* to confer secretly; plot mischief; conspire. [t. L: m. s. *colloquī* converse. See COLLOQUY]
colloid (kŏl′oid), *n.* **1.** *Chem.* a substance present in solution in the colloidal state. **2.** *Med.* a homogeneous gelatinous substance occurring in some diseased states. [f. m. s. Gk *kólla* glue + -OID]
colloidal (kŏ loi′dl), *adj. Phys. Chem.* pertaining to, or of the nature of a colloid: *colloidal gold, silver, etc.*
colloidal graphite, finely ground graphite. When added to oil it reduces its surface tension but not its viscosity.
colloidal solution, *Chem.* a solution in which the solute is in the colloidal state; a sol.
colloidal state, *Chem.* a system of particles in a dispersion medium in which the particle diameters are between 10^{-5} and 10^{-7} cm., i.e. between a true molecular solution and a coarse suspension.
colloid mill, a high-speed mill capable of reducing a substance to a particle size of about 10^{-5} cm.
collop (kŏl′əp), *n. Dial.* **1.** a small slice of bacon or other meat. **2.** a small slice or piece of anything. **3.** a fold or roll of flesh on the body. [ME *colope, coloppe.* Cf. Sw. *kollops*, now *kalops*]
colloq., 1. colloquial. **2.** colloquialism. **3.** colloquially.
colloquial (kə lō′kwĭ əl), *adj.* **1.** characteristic of or appropriate to ordinary or familiar conversation rather than formal speech or writing. In standard English, *he hasn't got any* is colloquial, while *he has none* is formal. **2.** conversational. —**collo′quially,** *adv.*
—**Syn. 1, 2.** COLLOQUIAL, CONVERSATIONAL, INFORMAL refer to types of speech or to usages not on a formal level. COLLOQUIAL is often mistakenly used with a connotation of disapproval, as if it meant vulgar or 'bad' or 'incorrect' usage, whereas it is merely a familiar style more used in speaking than in writing. CONVERSATIONAL refers to a style used in the oral exchange of ideas, opinions, etc.: *an easy conversational style.* INFORMAL means without formality, without strict attention to set forms, unceremonious: *an informal manner of speaking.* —**Ant. 1, 2.** formal.
colloquialism (kə lō′kwĭ ə lĭz′əm), *n.* **1.** a colloquial expression. **2.** colloquial style or usage.
colloquium (kə lō′kwĭ əm), *n.* an informal conference or group discussion.
colloquy (kŏl′ə kwĭ), *n.*, *pl.* **-quies. 1.** a speaking together; a conversation. **2.** a conference. **3.** (in certain Reformed Churches) a governing body corresponding to a presbytery. **4.** a literary composition in dialogue form. [t. L: m. s. *colloquium* conversation] —**col′loquist,** *n.*
collotype (kŏl′ō tīp′), *n.* **1.** a photomechanical process of printing in ink from a gelatine plate. **2.** the plate. **3.** a print made from it. [f. *collo-* (comb. form repr. Gk *kólla* glue) + -TYPE]
collude (kə lōōd′), *v.i.*, **-luded, -luding. 1.** to act together through a secret understanding. **2.** to conspire in a fraud. [t. L: m. s. *collūdere* play with] —**collud′er,** *n.*
collunarium (kŏl′yŏŏ nĕə′rĭ əm), *n. Med.* a solution for application to the nose; nose drops. [t. NL, equiv. to s. L *colluere* wash + s. *nārēs* nostrils + *-ium* -IUM]
collusion (kə lōō′zhən), *n.* **1.** secret agreement for a fraudulent purpose; conspiracy. **2.** *Law.* a secret understanding between two or more persons prejudicial to another, or a secret understanding to appear as adversaries though in agreement: *collusion of husband and wife to obtain a divorce.* [ME, t. L: s. *collūsio* a playing together]
collusive (kə lōō′sĭv), *adj.* involving collusion; fraudulently concerted: *a collusive treaty.* —**collu′sively,** *adv.* —**collu′siveness,** *n.*
colly[1] (kŏl′ĭ), *v.*, **-lied, -lying,** *n. Archaic or Dial.* —*v.t.* **1.** to blacken as with coal dust; begrime. —*n.* **2.** grime; soot. [var. of *collow*, ME *colwen*, der. *col* COAL]
colly[2] (kŏl′ĭ), *n.*, *pl.* **-lies.** collie.
collyrium (kŏ lĭə′rĭ əm), *n.*, *pl.* **-lyria** (-lĭə′rĭ ə), **-lyriums.** *Med.* a solution for application to the eye; an eyewash. [t. L, t. Gk: m. *kollýrion* poultice, eye salve]
collywobbles (kŏl′ĭ wŏb′lz), *n. Colloq.* **1.** stomach-ache. **2.** diarrhoea. [f. alter. of COLIC + WOBBLE(S)]
Colmar (*Fr.* kŏl mȧr′), *n.* a town in NE France, the capital of Haut-Rhin department. 54,264 (1962).
Cöln (*Ger.* kœln), *n.* former German name of **Cologne.**
Colne (kōn), *n.* a town in England, in E Lancashire. 19,430 (1961).
colo-, a combining form of **colon**[2].
Colo., Colorado.
Colobus (kŏl′ə bəs), *n.* any of the primates of the genus *Colobus*, leaf-eating monkeys from tropical Africa.
colocynth (kŏl′ə sĭnth), *n.* **1.** a cucurbitaceous plant, *Citrullus colocynthis*, of the warmer parts of Asia, the Mediterranean region, etc., bearing a fruit with a bitter pulp which yields a purgative drug. **2.** the fruit. **3.** the drug. [t. L: m. *colocynthis*, t. Gk: m. *kolokynthis*]
cologne (kə lōn′), *n.* a perfumed toilet water; eau de Cologne. Also, **Cologne water.** [for *Cologne water* (made at COLOGNE, Germany, since 1709)]
Cologne (kə lōn′), *n.* a city in West Germany, in S North Rhine-Westphalia; formerly a member of the Hanseatic League. 861,000 (est. 1966). German, **Köln.** Formerly, **Cöln.** See map under **Hanseatic League.**
Colomb-Béchar (*Fr.* kŏ lôɴ bĕ shȧr′), *n.* a town in W Algeria. 27,000 (est. 1960). Also, **Béchar.**
Colombes (*Fr.* kŏ lôɴb′), *n.* a town in N France, in Hauts-de-Seine department. 76,918 (1962).
Colombia (kə lŏm′bĭ ə; *Sp.* kô lôm′byȧ), *n.* a republic in NW South America. 15,097,640 pop. (est. 1963); 439,828 sq. mi. *Cap.:* Bogotá. See map under **Caribbean.** —**Colom′bian,** *adj.*, *n.*
Colombo (kə lŭm′bō), *n.* a seaport in and the capital of Ceylon, on the W coast. 510,947 (1963). See map under **Ceylon.**
Colombo Plan, a plan for economic development in S and SE Asia, established 1950.
colon[1] (kō′lən), *n.*, *pl.* **-lons** *for 1*, **-la** (-lə) *for 2.* **1.** a point of punctuation (:) marking off a main portion of a sentence (intermediate in force between the semicolon and the period). **2.** *Class. Pros.* one of the members or sections of a rhythmical period, consisting of a sequence of from two to six feet united under a principal ictus or beat. [t. L, t. Gk: m. *kôlon* limb, member, clause]
colon[2] (kō′lən), *n.*, *pl.* **-lons, -la** (-lə). *Anat.* that portion of the large intestine which extends from the caecum to the rectum. See diag. under **intestine.** [ME, t. L, t. Gk: m. *kólon* food, colon]
colón (kŏ lŏn′; *Sp.* kô lôn′), *n.*, *pl.* **colons,** *Sp.* **colones** (*Sp.* kô lô′nĕs). **1.** the monetary unit of Costa Rica, equal to 100 centimos, and equivalent to about £0·0629 sterling. **2.** the monetary unit of El Salvador, equal to 100 centavos, and equivalent to £0·165 sterling. **3.** a banknote or coin of these denominations. [t. Amer. Sp.: lit., Columbus]
Colón (kŏ lŏn′; *Sp.* kô lôn′), *n.* a seaport in Panama at the Atlantic end of the Panama Canal. 59,598 (1960). See map under **Panama Canal.**
colonel (kûr′nəl), *n. Mil.* **1.** an officer ranking in the British Army between lieutenant colonel and brigadier, now no longer an executive rank. **2.** an equivalent rank in any other army. [earlier *coronel*, t. F: m. *coronnel*, var. of *colonnel*, t. It.: m. *colonnello*, dim. of *colonna* COLUMN] —**colo′nelcy, colo′nelship′,** *n.*
colonel-in-chief (kûr′nəl ĭn chēf′), *n.* an honorary colonel.
colonial (kə lō′nyəl), *adj.* **1.** of or pertaining to a colony or colonies, esp. the British colonies. **2.** of or pertaining to a colonist: *paternalism is part of the colonial outlook.* **3.** pertaining to the thirteen British colonies which became the United States of America, or to their period. **4.** *Ecol.* forming a colony. **5.** (*cap.*) *Archit.* of the American colonies; largely derived from contemporary English

styles, as Queen Anne, often translated into new building materials (brick, wood) and simpler forms. —*n.* **6.** an inhabitant of a colony. —**colo′nially,** *adv.*

colonial animals, 1. animals that live in a group. **2.** single-celled animals that live together as a single unit.

Colonial Development Corporation, a body, originally government-sponsored, established to assist colonial territories to develop their own resources.

colonialism (kə lō′nyə lĭz′əm), *n.* the policy of a nation seeking to extend or retain its authority over other peoples or territories.

colonic (kə lŏn′ĭk), *adj. Anat.* of or affecting the colon.

colonist (kŏl′ə nĭst), *n.* **1.** an inhabitant of a colony. **2.** a member of a colonizing expedition.

colonize (kŏl′ə nīz′), *v.*, **-nized, -nizing.** —*v.t.* **1.** to plant or establish a colony in; form into a colony; settle: *England colonized Australia.* —*v.i.* **2.** to form a colony. **3.** to settle in a colony. Also, **colonise.** —**col′oniza′tion,** *n.* —**col′oniz′er,** *n.*

colonnade (kŏl′ə nād′), *n.* **1.** *Archit.* a series of columns set at regular intervals, and usually supporting an entablature, a roof, or a series of arches. **2.** a long row of trees. [t. F, t. It.: m. *colonnato*, der. *colonna*, g. L *columna* COLUMN] —**col′onnad′ed,** *adj.*

colony (kŏl′ə nĭ), *n.*, *pl.* **-nies. 1.** a group of people who leave their native country to form in a new land a settlement subject to, or connected with, the parent state. **2.** the country or district settled or colonized. **3.** any people or territory separated from but subject to a ruling power. **4. the Colonies,** *U.S.* those British colonies that formed the original thirteen states of America: New Hampshire, Massachusetts, Rhode Island, Connecticut, New York, New Jersey, Pennsylvania, Delaware, Maryland, Virginia, North Carolina, South Carolina, and Georgia. **5.** a number of foreigners from a particular country living in a city or country, esp. in one locality: *the American colony in Paris.* **6.** any group of individuals of similar occupation, etc., usually living in a community of their own: *a colony of artists.* **7.** the district or quarter inhabited by such a group. **8.** an aggregation of bacteria growing together as the descendants of a single cell. **9.** *Ecol.* a group of animals or plants, of the same kind, coexisting in close association. [ME *colonie*, t. L: m. *colōnia*]

colophon (kŏl′ə fŏn′, -fən), *n.* **1.** an inscription at the close of a book, used esp. in the 15th and 16th centuries, giving the title, author, and other publication facts. **2.** a publisher's distinctive emblem. [t. LL, t. Gk: m. *kolophṓn* summit, finishing touch]

colophony (kŏ lŏf′ə nĭ), *n.* rosin. [t. L: m. s. *Colophōnia* (*resina*) (resin) of *Colophon* (Ionian city in Asia Minor)]

color (kŭl′ə), *n. U.S.* colour. —**col′ored,** *adj.* —**col′orer,** *n.* —**col′orful,** *adj.* —**col′ored,** *n.* —**col′orist,** *n.* —**col′orless,** *adj.*

colorable (kŭl′ə rə bl), *adj. U.S.* colourable. —**col′orabil′ity, col′orableness,** *n.*

colorado (kŏl′ə rä′dō), *adj.* (of cigars) of medium colour and strength. [t. Sp.: coloured, red]

Colorado (kŏl′ə rä′dō), *n.* **1.** a state in the W United States. 1,753,947 pop. (1960); 104,247 sq. mi. *Cap.:* Denver. *Abbrev.:* Colo. **2.** a river in the U.S. flowing from N Colorado into the Gulf of California: Grand Canyon; Boulder Dam. 1450 mi. **3.** a river in the U.S. flowing from W Texas SE to the Gulf of Mexico. 840 mi. —**Col′orad′an,** *adj.*, *n.*

Colorado beetle, a black and yellow beetle, *Leptinotarsa decemlineata*; a potato pest.

Colorado Desert, an arid region in the U.S., in SE California, including the Salton Sink. ab. 2000 sq. mi.

coloration (kŭl′ə rā′shən), *n.* colouring; appearance as to colour.

coloratura (kŏl′ə rə tŏŏ′rə), *n.* **1.** runs, trills, and other florid decorations in vocal music. **2.** music marked by this. **3.** a lyric soprano of high range who specializes in such music. Also, **colorature** (kŏl′ə rə tyŏŏ′). [t. It., der. *colorare* to colour, g. L *colōrāre*]

color guard, *U.S.* a colour party.

colorific (kŭl′ə rĭf′ĭk), *adj.* **1.** producing or imparting colour. **2.** pertaining to colour. [f COLO(U)R + -(I)FIC]

colorimeter (kŭl′ə rĭm′ĭ tə), *n.* an instrument for analysing colours into their components, as by measuring a given colour in terms of a standard colour, of a scale of colours, or of certain primary colours. [f. COLO(U)R + -(I)-METER[1]] —**colorimetric** (kŭl′ə rĭ mĕt′rĭk), **col′orimet′rical,** *adj.* —**col′orim′etry,** *n.*

colossal (kə lŏs′əl), *adj.* **1.** gigantic; huge; vast. **2.** like a colossus. —**colos′sally,** *adv.* —**Syn. 1.** See **gigantic.**

Colosseum (kŏl′ə sē′əm), *n.* **1.** an amphitheatre in Rome, the greatest in antiquity, begun by Vespasian and inaugurated (A.D. 80) by Titus. **2.** (*l.c.*) coliseum. [t. L, prop. neut. of *colossēus* colossal. Cf. COLOSSUS]

Colossian (kə lŏsh′ən), *n.* **1.** a native of or an inhabitant of **Colossae,** an ancient city of Phrygia, in Asia Minor. **2.** one of the Christians of Colossae, to whom Paul addressed one of his epistles. **3.** (*pl.*) the book of the New Testament called *The Epistle of Paul the Apostle to the Colossians.* —*adj.* **4.** of or pertaining to Colossae or its inhabitants.

colossus (kə lŏs′əs), *n.*, *pl.* **-lossi** (-lŏs′ī), **-lossuses. 1.** (*cap.*) the legendary bronze statue of Apollo at Rhodes. See **Seven Wonders of the World. 2.** any statue of gigantic size. **3.** anything colossal or gigantic. [ME, t. L, t. Gk: m. *kolossós*]

colostomy (kə lŏs′tə mĭ), *n.*, *pl.* **-mies.** *Surg.* incision of an artificial opening into the colon for drainage.

colostrum (kə lŏs′trəm), *n.* the milk secreted before and for a few days after parturition. [t. L]

colour (kŭl′ə), *n.* **1.** the evaluation by the visual sense of that quality of light (reflected or transmitted by a substance) which is basically determined by its spectral composition; that quality of a visual sensation distinct from form. Any colour may be expressed in terms of three factors: hue, chroma (purity or saturation), and brightness (or value). Generally the most obvious or striking feature of a colour is its hue, which gives it its name. The colour is qualified if necessary as pale, dark, dull, light, etc. **2.** complexion. **3.** a ruddy complexion. **4.** racial complexion other than white, esp. Negro. **5.** a blush. **6.** vivid or distinctive quality, as of literary work. **7.** details in description, customs, speech, habits, etc., of a place or period, included for the sake of realism: *a novel about the Reformation with much local colour.* **8.** that which is used for colouring: pigment; paint; dye. **9.** *Painting.* the general effect of all the hues entering into the composition of a picture. **10.** *Print.* the amount and quality of ink used. **11.** (*pl.*) any distinctive colour, symbol, badge, etc., of identification: *the colours of a school, jockey, etc.* **12.** (*pl.*) an award made to outstanding members of a school team: *cricket colours.* **13.** (*pl.*) **a.** a flag, ensign, etc., as of a military body or ship. **b.** *U.S. Navy.* the ceremony of hoisting the national flag at 8 a.m. and of lowering it at sunset. **14.** outward appearance or aspect; guise or show. **15.** a pretext. **16.** kind; sort; variety; general character. **17.** *Music.* timbre of sound. **18.** an apparent or prima-facie right or ground (esp. in legal sense): *to hold possession under colour of title.* **19.** *U.S.* a trace or particle of valuable mineral, esp. gold, as shown by washing auriferous gravel, etc. **20.** *Her.* heraldic tincture. **21. change colour,** to turn pale or red. **22. flying colours,** eclat. **23. give** or **lend colour,** to make probable or realistic. **24. join the colours,** to enlist in the army. **25. lose colour,** to turn pale. **26. nail one's colours to the mast,** to commit oneself to a party, action, etc. **27. off colour,** not well; indisposed. **28. show one's true colours,** to reveal one's true nature, opinions, etc. —*v.t.* **29.** to give or apply colour to; tinge; paint; dye. **30.** to cause to appear different from the reality. **31.** to give a special character or distinguishing quality to: *an account coloured by personal feelings.* —*v.i.* **32.** to take on or change colour. **33.** to flush; blush. Also, *U.S.*, **color.** [ME, t. OF, g. L *color*] —**col′ourer,** *n.*

colourable (kŭl′ə rə bl), *adj.* **1.** capable of being coloured. **2.** specious; plausible. **3.** pretended; deceptive. Also, *U.S.*, **colorable.** —**col′ourabil′ity, col′ourableness,** *n.* —**col′ourably,** *adv.*

colour-bar (kŭl′ə bä′), *n.* discrimination against people belonging wholly, or in part, to any race other than the white. Also, *U.S.*, **color line, color bar.**

colour-blindness (kŭl′ə blīnd′nĭs), *n.* defective colour perception, independent of the capacity for distinguishing light and shade, and form. Also, *U.S.*, **color-blindness.** —**col′our-blind′,** *adj.*

colourcast (kŭl′ə käst′), *n.*, *v.*, **-cast, -casting.** —*n.* **1.** a television programme broadcast in colour. —*v.t.*, *v.i.* **2.** to broadcast (television) in colour. Also, *U.S.*, **colorcast.**

colour company, *Mil.* a company carrying the flag of a battalion.

coloured (kŭl′əd), *adj.* **1.** having colour. **2.** belonging wholly or in part to, or pertaining to, some other race than the white, esp. to the Negro race. **3.** specious; deceptive: *a coloured statement.* **4.** influenced or biased. **5.** *Bot.* of some hue other than green. —*n.* **6.** any person of a race other than the white, esp. a Negro. **7.** Also, **Cape Coloured.** (in South Africa) a person of mixed blood. Also, *U.S.*, **colored.**

colour-filter (kŭl′ə fĭl′tə), *n.* (in photography, etc.) a filter for modifying the reproduction of colours. Also, *U.S.*, **color-filter.**

colourful (kŭl′ə fəl), *adj.* **1.** abounding in colour. **2.** richly picturesque: *a colourful historical period.* **3.** presenting or suggesting vivid or striking scenes. Also, *U.S.*, **col′orful.** —**col′ourfully,** *adv.* —**col′ourfulness,** *n.*

colouring (kŭl′ə rĭng), *n.* **1.** the act or method of applying colour. **2.** appearance as to colour. **3.** characteristic aspect or tone. **4.** specious appearance; show. **5.** a substance used to colour something. Also, *U.S.*, **coloring.**

colourist (kŭl′ə rĭst), *n.* **1.** a user of colour, as in painting. **2.** a painter who devotes himself specially to effects of colour. Also, *U.S.*, **colorist.** —**col′ouris′tic,** *adj.*

colourless (kŭl′ə lĭs), *adj.* **1.** without colour. **2.** pallid; dull in colour. **3.** without vividness or distinctive character: *a colourless description of the parade.* **4.** unbiased; neutral. Also, *U.S.*, **colorless.** —**col′ourlessly,** *adv.* —**col′ourlessness,** *n.*

colour party, *Mil.* a party of officers and N.C.O.s who carry and escort the colours.

colour-scheme (kŭl′ə skēm′), *n.* the overall colour conception in a design, plan, etc. Also, *U.S.*, **color-scheme.**

colour sergeant, a sergeant who has charge of battalion or regimental colours. Also, *U.S.*, **color sergeant.**

colourwash (kŭl′ə wŏsh′), *n.* coloured distemper. Also, *U.S.*, **colorwash.**

-colous, a word element indicating habitat. [f. s. L *colere* inhabit + -OUS]

colpitis (kŏl pī′tĭs), *n.* *Pathol.* vaginitis. [f. m. s. Gk *kólpos* bosom, womb + -ITIS]

colportage (kŏl′pô′tĭj; *Fr.* kŏl pŏr tȧzh′), *n.* the work of a colporteur. [f. F, der. *colporter* hawk, lit., carry on the neck, f. *col* neck + *porter* carry]

colporteur (kŏl′pô′tə; *Fr.* kŏl pŏr tœr′), *n.* **1.** a hawker of books, etc. **2.** one employed to travel about distributing Bibles, religious tracts, etc., gratuitously or at a low price. [t. F. See COLPORTAGE]

colt (kōlt), *n.* **1.** a young horse or animal of the horse kind, esp. a young male. **2.** a young or inexperienced person. **3.** *Naut.* a rope's end used in chastising. [ME and OE; cf. d. Sw. *kult* pig] —**colt′ish,** *adj.* —**colt′ishly,** *adv.* —**colt′ishness,** *n.*

Colt (kōlt), *n.* a type of revolver. [named after Samuel *Colt*, 1814–62, U.S. inventor]

colter (kōl′tə), *n.* coulter.

coltsfoot (kōlts′fo͝ot′), *n., pl.* **-foots.** a composite perennial, *Tussilago farfara*, native to Europe but widespread as a weed, formerly used in medicine.

colubrine (kŏl′yo͝o brīn′, -brĭn), *adj.* **1.** of or resembling a snake; snakelike. **2.** of or pertaining to the snake family *Colubridae* (or the subfamily *Colubrinae*). In older definitions this family included various venomous snakes as well as the great majority of non-venomous snakes. [t. L: m. s. *colubrīnus* like a serpent]

colugo (kə lo͞o′gō), *n., pl.* **-gos.** the flying lemur.

Colum (kŏl′əm), *n.* **Padraic** (pä′drĭk), born 1881, Irish poet.

Columba (kə lŭm′bə), *n.* **Saint,** A.D. 521–97, Irish missionary to Scotland.

columbarium (kŏl′əm bĕə′rĭ əm), *n., pl.* **-baria** (-bĕə′rĭ ə). **1.** a sepulchral vault or other structure with recesses in the walls to receive the ashes of the dead. **2.** one of the recesses. **3.** a dovecot. **4.** a hole in a wall, left for the insertion of the end of a beam. [t. L, orig., dovecot, der. *columba* dove]

Columbia (kə lŭm′bĭ ə), *n.* **1.** a city in the U.S., the capital of South Carolina, in the central part. 97,433 (1960). **2.** a river flowing from SE British Columbia along the boundary between Washington and Oregon into the Pacific. 1214 mi. **3.** America, or the United States, esp. as a feminine personification: *Columbia, the Gem of the Ocean.* **4.** *U.S.* a white-faced breed of sheep noted for its quick-growing lambs and heavy fleeces.

Columbian (kə lŭm′bĭ ən), *adj.* **1.** pertaining to America or the United States. **2.** pertaining to Columbus. [f. s. NL *Columbia* poetic name for America + -AN]

columbic (kə lŭm′bĭk), *adj.* *Chem.* niobic.

columbine[1] (kŏl′əm bīn′), *n.* any plant of the ranunculaceous genus *Aquilegia*, comprising erect branching herbs with handsome flowers, as *A. vulgaris* with blue flowers, which occurs on calcareous soils throughout temperate Europe and Asia. [ME, t. LL: m. *columbīna*, prop. fem. of L *columbīnus* dovelike; from the resemblance of the inverted flower to a cluster of doves]

columbine[2] (kŏl′əm bīn′), *adj.* **1.** of a dove. **2.** dovelike; dove-coloured. [ME *columbyn*, t. L: m. s. *columbīnus*]

Columbine (kŏl′əm bīn′), *n.* a female character in comedy (orig. the early Italian) and pantomime, the sweetheart of Harlequin. [t. It.: m. *Colombina*, der. *colomba* dove, g. L *columba*]

columbite (kə lŭm′bīt), *n.* a black, crystalline mineral, $FeNb_2O_6$, often containing manganese and tantalum. It is the principal ore of niobium. [f. COLUMB(IUM) + -ITE[1]]

columbium (kə lŭm′bĭ əm), *n.* *Chem.* former name for **niobium.** [t. NL, named after COLUMBIA the United States]

columbous (kə lŭm′bəs), *adj.* *Chem.* niobous.

Columbus (kə lŭm′bəs), *n.* **1. Christopher** (Sp. *Cristóbal Colón*; It. *Cristoforo Colombo*), 1446?–1506, Italian navigator in Spanish service: discoverer of America, 1492. **2.** a town in the U.S., the capital of Ohio, in the central part. 471,316 (1960). **3.** a town in the U.S., in W Georgia. 116,779 (1960).

columella (kŏl′yo͝o mĕl′ə), *n., pl.* **-mellae** (-mĕl′ē). *Anat., Zool., Bot.* a small column-like part; an axis. [t. L, dim. of *columna* COLUMN] —**col′umel′lar,** *adj.*

columelliform (kŏl′yo͝o mĕl′ĭ fôm′), *adj.* like a columella.

column (kŏl′əm), *n.* **1.** *Archit.* **a.** an upright shaft or body of greater length than thickness, usually serving as a support; a pillar. **b.** a vertical architectural member consisting typically of an approximately cylindrical shaft with a base and a capital. **2.** any column-like object, mass, or formation: *a column of smoke.* **3.** *Bot.* the upright cylindrical structure, formed by the union of stamens in an orchid. **4.** one of the two or more vertical rows of lines of type or printed matter of a page: *there are two columns on this page.* **5.** a perpendicular row of figures. **6.** a regular contribution to a newspaper, usually signed, and consisting of comment, news, etc. **7.** a journalistic department devoted to short articles, etc., of an entertaining or esp. readable kind, furnished by a particular editor or writer with or without the aid of contributors. **8.** a line of ships following one after the other. **9.** a formation of troops, narrow laterally and extended from front to rear. [t. L: s. *columna* pillar, post; t. ME *columpne*, t. OF] —**columned** (kŏl′əmd), *adj.*

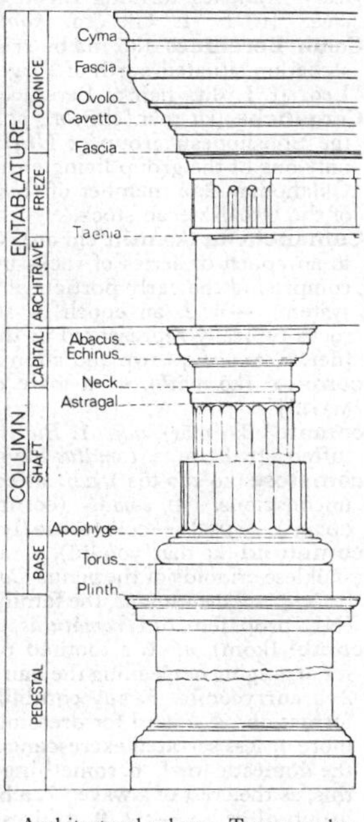

Architectural column, Tuscan order

—**Syn. 1.** COLUMN, PILLAR refer to upright supports in architectural structures. PILLAR is the general word: *the pillars supporting the roof.* A COLUMN is a particular kind of pillar, esp. one with three identifiable parts: shaft, base, and capital: *columns of the Corinthian style.*

columnar (kə lŭm′nə), *adj.* **1.** shaped like a column. **2.** printed, arranged, etc., in columns.

columniation (kə lŭm′nĭ ā′shən), *n.* **1.** the use of columns in a structure. **2.** *U.S.* the system of columns used in a structure.

columnist (kŏl′ə mĭst, -əm nĭst), *n.* the editor, writer, or organizer of a special column in a newspaper.

colure (kə lyo͝oə′, kō′lyo͝oə), *n.* *Astron.* either of two great circles of the celestial sphere intersecting each other at the poles, one passing through the equinoctial and the other through the solstitial points of the ecliptic. [t. L: m. s. *colūrus*, t. Gk: m. *kólouros* dock-tailed (the colures being cut off by the horizon)]

Colvin (kŏl′vĭn), *n.* **Sir Sidney,** 1845–1927, English literary and art critic.

Colwyn Bay (kŏl′wĭn bā′), a town in Wales, in Denbighshire. 23,090 (1961).

coly (kō′lĭ), *n.* any of the small birds of the African family *Coliidae*, having soft plumage, prominent crest, and pointed tail; mousebird.

colza (kŏl′zə), *n.* rapeseed. [t. F, t. D: m. *koolzaad* coleseed]

colza oil, rapeseed oil.

com-, a prefix meaning 'with', 'jointly', 'in combination' and (with intensive force) 'completely', occurring in this form before *p* and *b*, as in *compare*, and (by assimilation) before *m*, as in *commingle.* Cf. **co-** (def. 1). Also, **con-, col-, cor-.** [t. L: comb. form of *cum* with]

Com., **1.** commander. **2.** commission. **3.** commissioner. **4.** committee. **5.** commodore. **6.** Communist.

com., **1.** comedy. **2.** comic. **3.** commerce. **4.** common. **5.** commonly. **6.** communicate. **7.** community.

coma[1] (kō′mə), *n., pl.* **-mas.** a state of prolonged unconsciousness from which it is difficult or impossible to rouse a person, due to disease, injury, poison, etc.; stupor. [t. Gk: m. *kôma* deep sleep]

coma[2] (kō′mə), *n., pl.* **-mae** (-mē). **1.** *Astron.* the nebulous envelope round the nucleus of a comet. **2.** *Optics.* that aberration of optical systems by which rays of an oblique pencil cannot be brought to a sharp focus. **3.** *Bot.* a tuft of silky hairs at the end of a seed. **4.** the leafy branches forming the head of a tree. [t. L, t. Gk: m. *kómē* hair]

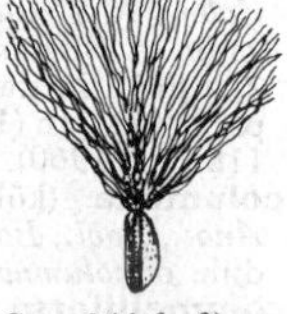

Coma² (def. 3) on seed of willowherb, *Chamaenerion angustifolium*

Coma Berenices (kō′mə bĕ′rī nī′sēz), a northern constellation situated north of Virgo and between Boötes and Leo. [t. L: lit., hair of Berenice]

Comanche (kə măn′chĭ), *n., pl.* **-ches. 1.** (*pl.*) a tribe of the Shoshonean group of North American Indians, the only one of the group living entirely on the plains, now in Oklahoma. **2.** a member of this tribe. **3.** their language, of the Uto-Aztecan stock.

Comanchean (kə măn′chĭ ən), *Geol.* —*adj.* **1.** pertaining to an epoch or series of rocks in parts of North America comprising the early portion of the Cretaceous period or system. —*n.* **2.** an epoch or series of early Cretaceous rocks typically represented in the Gulf of Mexico region. [der. *Comanche*, town and county in central Texas]

comate[1] (kō māt′), *n.* a mate or companion. [f. CO- + MATE[1]]

comate[2] (kō′māt), *adj.* **1.** *Bot.* having a coma. **2.** hairy; tufted. [t. L: m. s. *comātus* having long hair]

comatose (kō′mə tōs′), *adj.* affected with coma; lethargic; unconscious. [f. *comat-* (comb. form repr. Gk. *kôma* COMA[1]) + -OSE] —**com′atose′ly,** *adv.*

comatulid (kə măt′yōō lĭd), *n.* any of the free-swimming, stalkless crinoids of the genus *Comatula* or a related genus. [t. NL: s. *Comatulidae*, the family containing the *Comatula* (NL, prop. fem. of L *comātulus*, dim. of *comātus* COMATE[2])]

comb[1] (kōm), *n.* **1.** a toothed piece of bone, metal, etc., for arranging or cleaning the hair, or for keeping it in place. **2.** a currycomb. **3.** any comblike instrument, object, or formation. **4.** a card for dressing wool, etc. **5.** the fleshy, more or less serrated excrescence or growth on the head of the domestic fowl. **6.** something resembling or suggesting this, as the crest of a wave. **7.** a honeycomb, or any similar group of cells. —*v.t.* **8.** to dress (the hair, etc.) with, or as with, a comb. **9.** to card (wool). **10.** to scrape as with a comb. **11.** to search everywhere and with great thoroughness: *she combed the files for the missing letter.* —*v.i.* **12.** to roll over or break at the crest, as a wave. [OE *comb*, var. of *camb*, c. G *Kamm*]

comb[2] (kōōm), *n.* coomb[1].

comb., combining.

combat (*v., n.* kŏm′băt, kŭm′-, -bət; *v. also* kəm băt′), *v.,* **-bated, -bating,** *n.* —*v.t.* **1.** to fight or contend against; oppose vigorously. —*v.i.* **2.** to fight; battle; contend (fol. by *with* or *against*). —*n.* **3.** a fight between two men, armies, etc. [t. F, der. *combattre*, v., g. L *com-* COM- + *batt(u)ere* beat] —**combatable** (kŏm′băt ə bl, -bət-, kŭm′-, kəm băt′-), *adj.* —**com′bater,** *n.* —**Syn. 3.** struggle, conflict. See **fight.**

combatant (kŏm′bə tənt, kŭm′-), *n.* **1.** a person or group that fights. —*adj.* **2.** combating; fighting. **3.** disposed to combat.

combat fatigue, *Psychol.* battle fatigue.

combative (kŏm′bə tĭv, kŭm′-), *adj.* ready or inclined to fight; pugnacious. —**com′batively,** *adv.* —**com′bativeness,** *n.*

combe (kōōm), *n.* coomb[1].

combed yarn (kōmd), cotton or worsted yarn made of fibres laid parallel.

comber[1] (kō′mə), *n.* **1.** one who or that which combs. **2.** a long curling wave.

comber[2] (kŏm′bə), *n.* a sea-perch, *Serranus cabrilla*, with rows of comblike teeth, found in the Mediterranean and Red Sea. Also, **gaper.**

combination (kŏm′bĭ nā′shən), *n.* **1.** the act of combining. **2.** the state of being combined. **3.** a number of things combined. **4.** something formed by combining. **5.** a motorcycle with sidecar attached. **6.** an alliance of persons or parties. **7.** the set or series of numbers or letters used in setting the mechanism of a certain type of lock (**combination lock**) used on safes, etc. **8.** the parts of the mechanism operated by this. **9.** (*pl.*) a one-piece undergarment combining vest and pants, esp. with long legs and sleeves. **10.** *Maths.* **a.** the arrangement of a number of individuals into various groups, as *a*, *b*, and *c* into *ab*, *ac*, and *bc*. **b.** a group thus formed. **c.** a selection of a specified number of different objects from a larger specified number. The number of combinations of *n* objects taken *r* at a time is denoted by $^{n}C_{r}$. **11.** *Chem.* chemical union in which a new compound is formed. [t. LL: s. *combīnātio*] —**com′binational,** *adj.*

—**Syn. 3.** COMBINATION, COMPOSITE, COMPOUND all mean a union of individual parts. COMBINATION implies a grouping which is close but which may be easily dissolved. A COMPOSITE is a stronger union, in which the parts have become subordinate to a unity. COMPOUND implies a more or less complete merging of individual parts into an organic whole.

combination room, a common room for fellows or undergraduates at Cambridge University.

combinative (kŏm′bĭ nā′tĭv, kŏm′bĭ nə tĭv), *adj.* **1.** tending or serving to combine. **2.** pertaining to combination.

combinatorial analysis (kəm bī′nə tô′rĭ əl), *Maths.* the branch of mathematics which studies permutations, and combinations, etc.

combine (*v.* kəm bīn′; *n.* kŏm′bīn), *v.,* **-bined, -bining,** *n.* —*v.t.* **1.** to bring or join into a close union or whole; unite; associate; coalesce. **2.** to possess or exhibit in union. —*v.i.* **3.** to unite; coalesce. **4.** to unite for a common purpose; join forces. **5.** to enter into chemical union. —*n.* **6.** a combination. **7.** a combination of persons or groups for the furtherance of their political, commercial, or other interests. **8.** a combine harvester. [late ME *combyne(n)*, t. LL: m. *combīnāre* join together] —**combin′able,** *adj.* —**combin′er,** *n.* —**Syn. 1.** See **mix.**

combined operations, war operations carried out by cooperation of land, sea, and air forces.

combine harvester, a machine that simultaneously combines the operations of reaping, threshing, and winnowing corn.

combings (kō′mĭngz), *n.pl.* hairs removed with a comb.

combining form, *Gram.* a special form of a word used only in compounds, as *Anglo-* in *Anglophil* and *Anglo-French.*

comb jelly, ctenophore.

combo (kŏm′bō), *n. Colloq.* any small group of musicians playing jazz.

combust (kəm bŭst′), *adj. Astrol.* so near the sun as to be obscured by it. [ME, t. L: s. *combūstus*, pp., burned up]

combustible (kəm bŭs′tə bl), *adj.* **1.** capable of catching fire and burning; inflammable. **2.** easily excited. —*n.* **3.** a combustible substance. [t. LL: m. s. *combūstibilis*, der. L *combūstus*, pp. See COMBUST] —**combus′tibil′ity, combus′tibleness,** *n.*

combustion (kəm bŭs′chən), *n.* **1.** the act or process of burning. **2.** *Chem.* **a.** rapid oxidation accompanied by heat and usually light. **b.** chemical combination attended by heat and light. **c.** slow oxidation not accompanied by high temperature and light. **3.** violent excitement; tumult. —**combus′tive,** *adj.*

combustion chamber, *Mech.* the chamber in an engine where the fuel and oxidant are burnt.

combustion tube, a tube of hard glass in which a substance may be burnt in a current of air or oxygen (usually used in a furnace).

combustor (kəm bŭs′tə), *n.* the combustion chamber, fuel injection system, and igniter in a jet engine or ramjet.

comdg, commanding.

Comdr, commander.

Comdt, commandant.

come (kŭm), *v.,* **came, come, coming.** —*v.i.* **1.** to move towards the speaker or towards a particular place; approach. **2.** to arrive by movement or in course of progress; approach or arrive in time, succession, etc.: *when Christmas comes.* **3.** to move into view; appear: *the light comes and goes.* **4.** to extend; reach: *the dress comes to her knees.* **5.** to take place; occur; happen. **6.** to occur at a certain point, position, etc. **7.** to be available, produced, offered, etc.: *toothpaste comes in a tube.* **8.** to occur to the mind. **9.** to befall a person. **10.** to issue; emanate; be derived. **11.** to arrive or appear as a result: *this comes of carelessness.* **12.** to enter or be brought into a specified state or condition: *to come into use.* **13.** to enter into being or existence; be born. **14.** to become: *to come untied.* **15.** to turn out to be: *his dream came true.* **16.** (in the imperative, used to call attention, express remonstrance, etc.): *Come, that will do!* **17.** to germinate, as grain. **18.** *Taboo.* to have an orgasm. —*v.t.* **19.** *Slang.* to do; perform. **20.** *Colloq. or Slang.* to play the part of. **21.** Some special verb phrases are:

come about, 1. to arrive in due course; come to pass. **2.** *Naut.* to tack.

come across, 1. to meet with, esp. by chance. **2.** *Colloq.* to pay or give. **3.** to communicate successfully; to be understood.

come again, 1. to return. **2.** *Colloq.* to repeat.

come along, to make haste; hurry.

come at, 1. to reach. **2.** to rush at; attack.

come back, 1. to return, esp. in memory. **2.** to return to a former position or state.

come by, **1.** to obtain; acquire. **2.** to stop for a brief visit.
come clean, *Slang.* to confess.
come down, **1.** to lose wealth, rank, etc. **2.** to be handed down by tradition or inheritance. **3.** to leave a university. **4.** to travel, esp. from a town.
come down on, to scold; blame.
come down with, to become afflicted, esp. with a disease.
come forward, to offer one's services, etc.; volunteer.
come in, **1.** to enter. **2.** to arrive. **3.** to become useful, fashionable, etc. **4.** to finish in a race or competition.
come into, **1.** to get. **2.** to inherit.
come off, **1.** to happen; occur. **2.** to end. **3.** to reach the end; acquit oneself: *to come off with honours.* **4.** to become detached or unfastened.
come off it, *Slang.* to stop; lay aside (a pretentious attitude, etc.).
come on, **1.** to meet unexpectedly. **2.** to make progress; develop. **3.** to appear onstage. **4.** to begin; start. **5.** to hurry.
come out, **1.** to appear; be published. **2.** to be revealed; show itself. **3.** to make a debut in society, on the stage, etc. **4.** to emerge; reach the end.
come out with, **1.** to tell; say. **2.** to bring out; publish. **3.** to blurt out.
come over, to happen to; affect: *what's come over him?*
come round, **1.** to relent. **2.** to recover consciousness; revive. **3.** to change (an opinion, direction, etc.).
come through, **1.** to succeed; reach an end. **2.** to do as expected or hoped. **3.** to pass through.
come to, **1.** to recover consciousness. **2.** to amount to; equal. **3.** *Naut.* to take the way off a vessel, as by bringing her head into the wind, anchoring, etc.
come to light, to be found after a lapse of time.
come up, **1.** to arise; present itself. **2.** to come into residence at a school or university. **3.** to be presented for discussion or consideration. **4.** to arrive; travel, esp. to a town.
come up against, to meet difficulties or opposition.
come upon, to meet unexpectedly.
come up to, **1.** to equal. **2.** to approach; near.
come up with, **1.** to produce; supply. **2.** to present; propose.
[ME *comen*, OE *cuman*, c. G *kommen*] **—Syn.** **2.** See **arrive.** **—Ant.** **2.** leave, depart.

come-at-able (kŭm ăt′ə bl), *adj.* *Colloq.* accessible.

comeback (kŭm′băk′), *n.* **1.** *Colloq.* a return to a former position, prosperity, etc., as after a period of retirement. **2.** *Slang.* a retort; repartee. **3.** *Slang.* a ground for complaint.

Comecon (kŏm′ĭ kŏn′), *n.* a confederation of Communist countries founded in 1949, consisting of Albania (resigned 1961), Bulgaria, Czechoslovakia, Hungary, Poland, Rumania, the Soviet Union, East Germany, and Mongolia, to coordinate their economic development and exchange economic and technical experience for mutual aid. [*Co(uncil for) M(utual) Econ(omic Aid)*]

comedian (kə mē′dyən), *n.* **1.** an actor in comedy. **2.** a writer of comedy. **3.** a very amusing person. [f. m. COMEDY + -AN. Cf. F *comédien*]

Comédie Française (*Fr.* kŏ mė dē fräɴ sĕz′), the French national theatre; founded 1650.

comedienne (kə mē′dĭ ĕn′; *Fr.* kŏ mė dyĕn′), *n.* **1.** an actress in comedy. **2.** a professional female comic. [t. F, fem. of *comédien* comedian]

comedo (kŏm′ĭ dō′), *n.*, *pl.* **comedos, comedones** (kŏm′ĭ-dō′nēz). a blackhead (def. 1). [t. L: glutton]

comedown (kŭm′doun′), *n.* *Colloq.* an unexpected or humiliating descent from dignity, importance, or prosperity.

comedy (kŏm′ĭ dĭ), *n.*, *pl.* **-dies.** **1.** a play, film, etc., of light and humorous character, typically with a happy or cheerful ending; a drama in which the central motive of the play triumphs over circumstances and is therefore successful. **2.** that branch of the drama which concerns itself with this form of composition. **3.** the comic element of drama, of literature generally, or of life. **4.** any literary composition dealing with a theme suitable for comedy, or employing the methods of comedy. **5.** any comic or humorous incident or series of incidents. [ME *comedye*, t. ML: m. *cōmēdia*, L *cōmoedia*, t. Gk: m. *kōmōidia*, der. *kōmōidós* comedian, f. s. *kômos* mirth + *ōidós* singer]

comedy of errors, a series of mistakes, with a comic effect.

come-hither (kŭm′hĭth′ə), *adj.* deliberately alluring.

comely (kŭm′lĭ), *adj.*, **-lier, -liest.** **1.** pleasing in appearance; fair. **2.** proper; seemly; becoming. [ME; OE *cȳmlic*, f. *cȳme* comely + *lic.* See -LY, LIKE] **—come′liness,** *n.* **— Syn.** **1.** pretty, handsome, beautiful, good-looking, personable. **—Ant.** **1.** unattractive.

Comenius (kə mā′nyəs), *n.* **John Amos** (*Jan Amos Komensky*), 1592–1670, Moravian educational reformer and bishop.

come-on (kŭm′ŏn′), *n.* *U.S. Slang.* inducement; lure.

comer (kŭm′ə), *n.* **1.** one who or that which comes or has lately come. **2.** *U.S. Colloq.* one who or something that is coming on or promising well.

comestible (kə mĕs′tĭ bl), *adj.* **1.** edible; eatable. **—***n.* **2.** something edible; an article of food. [late ME, t. LL: m. s. *comestibilis*, der. L *comestus*, var. of *comēsus*, pp., eaten up]

comet (kŏm′ĭt), *n.* a celestial body moving about the sun in an elongated orbit, usually consisting of a central mass (the *nucleus*) surrounded by a misty envelope (the *coma*) which extends into a stream (the *tail*) in the direction away from the sun. [ME, t. L: s. *comēta*, t. Gk: m. *komḗtēs*, lit., long-haired] **—cometary** (kŏm′ĭ tə rĭ), *adj.* **—cometic** (kō mĕt′ĭk), *adj.*

comet-finder (kŏm′ĭt fīn′ də), *n.* a telescope of low power but with a wide field, used to search for comets. Also, **comet-seeker.**

comeuppance (kŭm′ŭp′əns), *n.* *Slang.* a well-deserved punishment or retribution.

comfit (kŭm′fĭt, kŏm′-), *n.* a sugar-coated sweet. [ME, t. OF, g. L *confectus*, pp., prepared]

comfiture (kŭm′fĭ tyŏŏə′), *n.* *Obs.* a confection; a preserve, as of fruit. Also, **confiture.** [ME, t. F, der. *confit* comfit, pp. of *confire* preserve, prepare, g. L *conficere*]

comfort (kŭm′fət), *v.t.* **1.** to soothe when in grief; console; cheer. **2.** to make physically comfortable. **3.** *Obs.* to aid; encourage. **—***n.* **4.** relief in affliction; consolation; solace. **5.** the feeling of relief or consolation. **6.** a person or thing that affords consolation. **7.** a cause or matter of relief or satisfaction. **8.** a state of ease, with freedom from pain and anxiety, and satisfaction of bodily wants. **9.** that which promotes such a state. **10.** *U.S.* a comforter; bedcover. **11.** *Obs.* strengthening aid; assistance. [ME *conforte(n)*, t. OF: m. *conforter*, g. L *confortāre* strengthen] **—com′fortingly,** *adv.* **—com′fortless,** *adj.* **—com′fortlessly,** *adv.* **com′fortlessness,** *n.*
—Syn. **1.** COMFORT, CONSOLE, RELIEVE, SOOTHE imply assuaging sorrow, worry, discomfort, or pain. To COMFORT is to lessen the sadness or sorrow of someone, and to strengthen by inspiring with hope and restoring a cheerful outlook: *to comfort a despairing person.* CONSOLE, a more formal word, means to make grief or distress seem lighter, by means of kindness and thoughtful attentions: *to console a bereaved parent.* RELIEVE means to lighten, lessen, or remove pain, trouble, discomfort, or hardship: *to relieve a needy person.* SOOTHE means to pacify or calm: *to soothe a child.* **8.** See **ease.**

comfortable (kŭmf′tə bl, kŭm′fə tə bl), *adj.* **1.** giving comfort, support, or consolation. **2.** producing or attended with comfort or ease of mind or body. **3.** being in a state of comfort or ease; easy and undisturbed. **4.** *Obs.* adequate. **5.** *Obs.* cheerful. **—***n.* **6.** *U.S.* a quilted bedcover. **—com′fortableness,** *n.* **—com′fortably,** *adv.*

comforter (kŭm′fə tə), *n.* **1.** one who or that which comforts. **2.** (*cap.*) the Holy Spirit. **3.** a woollen scarf for wrapping round the neck in cold weather. **4.** *U.S.* a quilted bedcover. **5.** *Chiefly U.S.* a baby's dummy. **6.** **Job's comforter,** one who professes to give comfort but who achieves the opposite result.

comfrey (kŭm′frĭ), *n.*, *pl.* **-freys.** any plant of the boraginaceous genus *Symphytum*, of Europe and Asia, as *S. officinale*, formerly used as a vulnerary. [ME *cumfirie*, t. ML: m. *cumfiria*, appar. var. of L *conferva*]

comfy (kŭm′fĭ), *adj.* *Colloq.* comfortable.

comic (kŏm′ĭk), *adj.* **1.** of, pertaining to, or of the nature of comedy, as distinct from tragedy. **2.** acting in or composing comedy. **3.** provoking laughter; humorous; funny; laughable. **—***n.* **4.** *Colloq.* a comic actor. **5.** *Colloq.* a comic periodical. **6.** (*pl.*) *U.S. Colloq.* comic strips. **7.** the amusing element in art, life, etc. [t. L: s. *cōmicus*, t. Gk: m. *kōmikós*]

comical (kŏm′ĭ kl), *adj.* **1.** provoking laughter, or amusing; funny. **2.** *Obs.* pertaining to or of the nature of comedy. **3.** *Colloq.* queer; odd; strange. **—com′ical′ity, com′icalness,** *n.* **—com′ically,** *adv.* **—Syn.** **1.** See **amusing.**

comice (kŏm′ĭs), *n.* a variety of pear. [t. F: short for *doyenne du comice*]

comic opera, a diverting opera with spoken dialogue and a happy ending.

comic strip, a series of drawings, in colour or black and white, relating a comic incident, an adventure story, etc.

Comines (*Fr.* kŏ mēn′), *n.* **Philippe de** (*Fr.* fē lēp′ də), 1445?–1511?, French historian and diplomat. Also, **Commines.**

Cominform (kŏm′ĭn fôm′), *n.* an organization (1947–56), established by the Communist parties of nine European countries for mutual advice and coordinated activity. [*Com(munist) Inform(ation Bureau)*]

coming (kŭm′ĭng), *n.* **1.** approach; arrival; advent. —*adj.* **2.** that comes; approaching. **3.** on the way to fame or success: *up and coming.*

Comintern (kŏm′ĭn tûn′), *n.* the Third Communist International, dissolved 1943; the organization of the Soviet Communist Party, headed by its Politburo, for extending world revolution. Also, **Komintern.** [*Com(munist) Intern(ational)*]

comitia (kə mĭsh′ĭ ə), *n. Rom Hist.* an assembly of the people convened to pass laws, nominate magistrates, etc. [t. L, pl. of *comitium* place of assembly] —**comitial** (kə mĭsh′əl), *adj.*

comity (kŏm′ĭ tĭ), *n., pl.* **-ties. 1.** courtesy; civility. **2.** *Internat. Law.* courtesy between nations, as in respect shown by one country for the laws, judicial decisions, and institutions of another. [t. L: m. s. *cōmitas* courtesy]

Comm., 1. commander. **2.** commerce. **3.** commission. **4.** committee. **5.** commodore. **6.** commonwealth. Also, **comm.**

comma (kŏm′ə), *n.* **1.** a mark of punctuation (,) used to indicate the smallest interruptions in continuity of thought or grammatical construction. **2.** *Class. Pros.* a fragment or smaller section of a colon. **3.** a comma butterfly. [t. L, t. Gk: m. *kómma* short clause]

comma bacillus, a slightly curved bacterium, *Vibrio cholerae,* which causes Asiatic cholera. It is contracted by eating or drinking contaminated food, and causes a violent form of dysentery.

comma butterfly, a nymphalid butterfly, *Polygonia c-album,* having a white, comma-shaped mark on the underside of the hind wings.

command (kə mänd′), *v.t.* **1.** to order or direct with authority. **2.** to require with authority; demand: *he commanded silence.* **3.** to have or exercise authority over; be in control over; be master of; have at one's bidding or disposal. **4.** to dominate by reason of location; overlook: *a hill commanding the sea.* **5.** to deserve and get (respect, sympathy, etc.). **6.** to have charge of and authority over (a military or naval unit or station). —*v.i.* **7.** to issue commands. **8.** to occupy a dominating position; look down upon or over a region, etc. —*n.* **9.** the act of commanding or ordering. **10.** an order given by a commander. **11.** *Mil.* **a.** an order given by an officer or N.C.O. to a military subordinate. **b.** a military formation exercising command over a specific geographical area, or (R.A.F.) over a specific function. **c.** a body of troops, etc., or an area, station, etc., under a commander. **12.** the possession or exercise of controlling authority. **13.** control; mastery; disposal. **14.** a royal invitation. **15.** power of dominating a region by reason of location; extent of view or outlook. [ME *comande(n),* t. OF: m. *comander,* g. LL *commandāre,* f. L *com-* COM- + *mandāre* enjoin] —**command′ingly,** *adv.* —**Syn. 1.** bid, enjoin, charge, instruct. See **direct. 3.** govern, control, manage. See **rule. 5.** exact, compel, secure. **10.** direction, bidding, injunction, charge.

commandant (kŏm′ən dănt′, -dänt′), *n.* the commanding officer of a place, group, etc.; a commander. [t. F, orig. ppr. of *commander* COMMAND]

commandeer (kŏm′ən dĭə′), *v.t.* **1.** to order or force into active military service. **2.** to seize (private property) for military or other public use. **3.** *Colloq.* to seize arbitrarily. [t. Afrikaans: s. *commandeeren,* t. F: m. *commander* command]

commander (kə män′də), *n.* **1.** one who commands. **2.** one who exercises authority; a leader; a chief officer. **3.** the chief commissioned officer (irrespective of rank) of a military unit. **4.** a naval officer ranking below a captain. **5.** an officer in charge of a district of the London metropolitan police, or having some other function. **6.** this rank. **7.** a rank in certain modern orders of knighthood. **8.** the chief officer of a commandery in the medieval orders of Knights Templar, Hospitallers, etc. —**command′ership′,** *n.*

commander-in-chief (kə män′dər ĭn chēf′), *n., pl.* **commanders-in-chief. 1.** an officer in supreme command of an army or armed forces. **2.** an officer in command of a particular part of an army or navy.

commandery (kə män′də rĭ), *n., pl.* **-ries. 1.** the office or district of a commander. **2.** (among certain medieval orders of knights) a district controlled by a commander.

command guidance, a system of missile guidance in which computed information transmitted to a missile causes it to follow a planned course.

commanding officer, an officer in command.

commandment (kə mänd′mənt), *n.* **1.** a command or mandate. **2.** any one of the precepts (the **Ten Commandments**) spoken by God to Israel (Exodus 20: Deut. 10) or delivered to Moses (Exodus 24:12 and 34) on Mount Sinai. **3.** *Obs.* the act, fact, or power of commanding.

commando (kə män′dō), *n., pl.* **-dos, -does. 1.** (in World War II) **a.** a special type of Allied military unit used for organized raids against Axis forces. **b.** a member of this unit. **2.** *S African.* an armed force raised by the Boers for service during the Boer War, 1899–1902. [t. Afrikaans, t. Pg.]

command performance, a performance of a play, etc., by royal command.

commeasurable (kə mĕzh′ə rə bl), *adj.* having the same measure; commensurate.

commeasure (kə mĕzh′ə), *v.t.,* **-ured, -uring.** to equal in measure; be coextensive with.

commedia dell'arte (*It.* kòm mĕ′dyȧ dĕl lȧr′tė), a stylized form of popular comedy developed in Italy in the 16th and 17th centuries, employing improvisations on traditional situations and characters, as Punch (Punchinello, Pierrot), Pantaloon, Columbine, and Harlequin. Cf. **harlequinade, pierrot, Punch and Judy.**

comme il faut (*Fr.* kŏm ēl fō′), *French.* as it should be; proper; properly.

commem., commemoration (def. 4).

commemorate (kə mĕm′ə rāt′), *v.t.* **-rated, -rating. 1.** to serve as a memento of. **2.** to honour the memory of by some solemnity or celebration. **3.** to make honourable mention of. [t. L: m. s. *commemorātus,* pp., brought to remembrance] —**commem′ora′tor,** *n.*

commemoration (kə mĕm′ə rā′shən), *n.* **1.** the act of commemorating. **2.** a service, celebration, etc., in memory of some person or event. **3.** a memorial. **4.** (at Oxford University) a celebration in memory of the founders and benefactors of a college. —**commem′ora′tional,** *adj.*

commemorative (kə mĕm′ə rə tĭv), *adj.* **1.** serving to commemorate. **2.** (of stamps, coins, etc.) issued to celebrate a particular historical event, in honour of a famous personage, etc. —*n.* **3.** anything that commemorates. —**commem′oratively,** *adv.*

commemoratory (kə mĕm′ə rə tə rĭ, -rə trĭ), *adj.* commemorative (def. 1).

commence (kə mĕns′), *v.i., v.t.,* **-menced, -mencing.** to begin; start. [ME *comence(n),* t. OF: m. *comencer,* g. LL *cominitiāre,* f. *com-* COM- + *initiāre* begin] —**commenc′er,** *n.* —**Syn.** See **begin.** —**Ant.** finish, end.

commencement (kə mĕns′mənt), *n.* **1.** the act or fact of commencing; beginning. **2.** *U.S.* (in universities, colleges, etc.) the ceremony of conferring degrees or granting diplomas at the end of the academic year. **3.** *U.S.* the day on which this takes place.

commend (kə mĕnd′), *v.t.* **1.** to present or mention as worthy of confidence, notice, kindness, etc.; recommend. **2.** to entrust; give in charge; deliver with confidence: *into Thy hands I commend my spirit.* **3.** *Archaic.* to recommend (a person) to the kind remembrance of another. [ME *commend(en),* t. L: m. *commendāre* commit. Cf. COMMAND] —**commend′able,** *adj.* —**commend′ableness,** *n.* —**commend′ably,** *adv.* —**Syn. 1.** praise, laud, extol. See **approve.**

commendam (kə mĕn′dăm), *n. Eccles.* **1.** the tenure of a benefice to be held until the appointment of a regular incumbent, the benefice being said to be held *in commendam.* **2.** a benefice so held. [t. ML, acc. sing. of *commenda,* as in *dare in commendam* give in trust]

commendation (kŏm′ĕn dā′shən), *n.* **1.** the act of commending; recommendation; praise. **2.** something that commends. **3.** (*pl.*) *Archaic or Obs.* complimentary greeting. —**Syn. 2.** eulogy, encomium.

commendatory (kə mĕn′də tə rĭ, -də trĭ), *adj.* **1.** serving to commend; approving; praising. **2.** holding a benefice in commendam. **3.** held in commendam.

commensal (kə mĕn′səl), *adj.* **1.** eating together at the same table. **2.** (of an animal or plant) living with, on, or in another, but neither one at the expense of the other (distinguished from *parasite*). —*n.* **3.** a companion at table. **4.** a commensal animal or plant. [t. ML: s. *commensālis,* f. L: *com-* COM- + *mensālis* belonging to the table] —**commen′salism,** *n.* —**commensality** (kŏm′ĕn săl′ĭ tĭ), *n.* —**commen′sally,** *adv.*

commensurable (kə mĕn′shə rə bl), *adj.* **1.** having a common measure or divisor. **2.** suitable in measure; proportionate. [t. LL: m. s. *commensūrābilis* having a common measure] —**commen′surabil′ity,** *n.* —**commen′surably,** *adv.*

commensurate (kə mĕn′shə rĭt), *adj.* **1.** having the same measure; of equal extent or duration. **2.** corresponding in amount, magnitude, or degree. **3.** proportionate. **4.** having a common measure; commensurable. [t. LL: m. s. *commensūrātus,* f. L: *com-* COM- + *mensūrātus,* pp., measured] —**commen′surately,** *adv.* —**commensuration** (kə mĕn′shə rā′shən), *n.*

comment (kŏm′ĕnt), *n.* **1.** a note in explanation, expansion, or criticism of a passage in a writing, book, etc.; an annotation. **2.** explanatory or critical matter added to a text. 3. a remark, observation, or criticism. —*v.i.* 4. to write explanatory or critical notes upon a text. 5. to make remarks. —*v.t.* 6. to make comments or remarks on; furnish with comments. [ME, t. LL: s. *commentum* exposition, L contrivance, invention, prop. pp. neut.] —**com′menter,** *n.* —**Syn. 3.** See **remark.**

commentary (kŏm′ən tə rĭ, -trĭ), *n., pl.* **-taries. 1.** a series of comments or annotations. **2.** an explanatory essay or treatise: *a commentary on the Bible.* **3.** anything serving to illustrate a point; comment. **4.** (*usually pl.*) a record of facts or events: *the Commentaries of Caesar.* —**commentarial** (kŏm′ən tēə′rĭ əl), *adj.*

commentator (kŏm′ən tā′tə), *n.* a writer or broadcaster who makes critical or explanatory remarks about news, events, etc. [t. L]

commerce (kŏm′ûs), *n.* **1.** interchange of goods or commodities, esp. on a large scale between different countries (**foreign commerce**) or between different parts of the same country (**domestic** or **internal commerce**); trade; business. **2.** social relations. **3.** sexual intercourse. **4.** *Obs.* intellectual interchange. [t. F, t. L: m. s. *commercium* trade] —**Syn. 1.** See **trade.**

commercial (kə mû′shəl), *adj.* **1.** of, or of the nature of, commerce. **2.** engaged in commerce. **3.** prepared merely for sale. **4.** not entirely or chemically pure: *commercial soda, etc.* —*n.* **5.** *Radio and Television.* **a.** an advertisement between radio or television programmes or during an interval in the programmes. **b.** *U.S.* a sponsored announcement or programme. **6.** a commercial traveller. —**commerciality** (kə mû′shĭ ăl′ĭ tĭ), *n.* —**commer′cially,** *adv.*

—**Syn. 1.** COMMERCIAL, MERCANTILE refer to the activities of business, industry, and trade. COMMERCIAL is the broader term, covering all the activities and relationships of industry and trade. In a derogatory sense it may mean such a preoccupation with the affairs of commerce as results in indifference to considerations other than wealth: *commercial treaties, relations, law, a merely commercial viewpoint.* MERCANTILE applies to the actual purchase and sale of goods, or to business transactions: *a mercantile house.*

commercial art, graphic art created specifically for commercial uses, esp. for advertising, illustrations in magazines or books, etc. —**commer′cial art′ist.**

commercial college, a college that trains people for careers in business.

commercialism (kə mû′shə lĭz′əm), *n.* **1.** the principles, methods, and practices of commerce. **2.** commercial spirit. **3.** a commercial custom or expression. —**commer′cialist,** *n.* —**commer′cialis′tic,** *adj.*

commercialize (kə mû′shə līz′), *v.t.,* **-lized, -lizing.** to make commercial in character, methods, or spirit; make a matter of profit. Also, **commercialise.** —**commer′cializa′tion,** *n.*

commercial paper, *Chiefly U.S.* negotiable paper, as drafts, bills of exchange, etc., given in the course of business.

commercial traveller, a travelling agent, esp. for a wholesale business house, who solicits orders for goods.

commere (kŏm′ĕə), *n.* a female compere. [t. F: m. *commère*]

Commie (kŏm′ĭ), *n.* (*also l.c.*) *Colloq.* Communist.

commination (kŏm′ĭ nā′shən), *n.* **1.** a threat of punishment or vengeance. **2.** a denunciation. **3.** (in the Church of England) a penitential office read on Ash Wednesday proclaiming God's anger and judgements against sinners. [late ME, t. L: s. *comminātio* a threatening] —**comminatory** (kŏm′ĭ nə tə rĭ, -trĭ), *adj.*

Commines (*Fr.* kŏ mĕn′), *n.* Comines.

commingle (kŏ mĭng′gl), *v.t., v.i.,* **-gled, -gling.** to mingle together; blend.

comminute (kŏm′ĭ nyōōt′), *v.t.,* **-nuted, -nuting.** to pulverize; triturate. [t. L: m. s. *comminūtus,* pp., made smaller] —**com′minu′tion,** *n.*

commiserate (kə mĭz′ə rāt′), *v.t.,* **-rated, -rating.** to feel or express sorrow or sympathy for; pity. [t. L: m. s. *commiserātus,* pp.] —**commis′era′tion,** *n.* —**commiserative** (kə mĭz′ə rə tĭv), *adj.* —**commis′eratively,** *adv.*

commissar (kŏm′ĭ sä′), *n.* head of a government department (commissariat) in any republic of the Soviet Union. [t. Russ: m. *kommisar,* t. F: m. *commissaire*]

commissariat (kŏm′ĭ sēə′rĭ ət), *n.* **1.** the department of an army charged with supplying provisions, etc. **2.** the organized method or manner by which food, equipment, transport, etc., is delivered to the armies. **3.** any of the governmental divisions of the Soviet Union. [t. F, der. *commissaire.* See COMMISSARY]

commissary (kŏm′ĭ sə rĭ), *n., pl.* **-saries. 1.** *Mil.* an officer of the commissariat. **2.** *U.S.* a store that supplies food and equipment, esp. in an army, mining camp, or lumber camp. **3.** one to whom some charge is committed by a superior power; a deputy. **4.** *Eccles.* an officer who, by delegation from the bishop, exercises spiritual jurisdiction in remote parts of a diocese, or is entrusted with the performance of duties of the bishop in his absence. **5.** (in the Soviet Union) a commissar. **6.** (in France) a police official, usually just below the police chief and mayor. [ME, t. ML: m. s. *commissārius,* der. L *commissus,* pp., committed] —**commissarial** (kŏm′ĭ sēə′rĭ əl), *adj.* —**com′missaryship′,** *n.*

commission (kə mĭsh′ən), *n.* **1.** the act of committing or giving in charge. **2.** an authoritative order, charge, or direction. **3.** authority granted for a particular action or function. **4.** a document or warrant granting authority to act in a given capacity or conferring a particular rank. **5.** a body of persons authoritatively charged with particular functions. **6.** the condition of being placed under special authoritative charge. **7.** the condition of anything in active service or use: *to be in or out of commission.* **8.** a task or matter committed to one's charge. **9.** authority to act as agent for another or others in commercial transactions. **10.** the committing or perpetrating of a crime, error, etc. **11.** that which is committed. **12.** a sum or percentage allowed to an agent, salesman, etc., for his services. **13.** the amount or percentage charged for exchanging money, collecting a bill, or the like. **14.** the position or rank of an officer in the army or navy: *to hold or resign a commission.* **15.** *Naval.* **a.** the condition of a ship ordered to active service, and supplied with a captain and crew. **b. put in** or **into commission,** to transfer (a ship) to active service. —*v.t.* **16.** to give a commission to. **17.** to authorize; send on a mission. **18.** to put (a ship, etc.) in commission. **19.** to give a commission or order for. [ME, t. L: s. *commissio* a committing]

commission agent, 1. Also, **commission merchant.** an agent who receives goods for sale on a commission basis, or who buys on this basis and has the goods delivered to a principal. **2.** a bookmaker (def. 2).

commissionaire (kə mĭsh′ə nēə′), *n.* **1.** a uniformed messenger or doorkeeper at a hotel, office, theatre, etc. **2.** a member of the Corps of Commissionaires.

commission day, *Law.* the opening day of assizes.

commissioned officer, an army, naval, or airforce officer holding rank by commission.

commissioner (kə mĭsh′ə nə), *n.* **1.** one commissioned to act officially; a member of a commission. **2.** a government official in charge of a department. **3.** *Slang.* a bookmaker (def. 2). —**commis′sionership′,** *n.*

commissure (kŏm′ĭ syŏŏə′), *n.* **1.** a joint; seam; suture. **2.** *Bot.* the joint or face by which one carpel coheres with another. **3.** *Anat., Zool.* a connecting band of nerve tissue, etc. [late ME, t. L: m. s. *commissūra* joining] —**commissural** (kə mĭs′yŏŏ rəl, kŏm′ĭ syŏŏə′rəl), *adj.*

A B

Botanical commissure AB, line of the commissural faces of the two carpels

commit (kə mĭt′), *v.t.,* **-mitted, -mitting. 1.** to give in trust or charge; entrust; consign. **2.** to consign for preservation: *to commit to writing, memory, etc.* **3.** to consign to custody: *to commit a person to jail.* **4.** to send troops into battle. **5.** to consign, esp. for safe-keeping; commend: *to commit one's soul to God.* **6.** to hand over for treatment, disposal, etc.: *to commit a manuscript to the flames.* **7.** *Parl. Proc.* to refer (a bill, etc.) to a committee for consideration. **8.** to do; perform; perpetrate: *to commit murder, an error, etc.* **9.** to bind by pledge or assurance; pledge. [ME *committe(n),* t. L: m. *committere* bring together, join, entrust] —**commit′table,** *adj.*

commitment (kə mĭt′mənt), *n.* **1.** the act of committing. **2.** the state of being committed. **3.** that to which one has committed oneself; a pledge. **4.** *Parl. Proc.* the act of referring or entrusting to a committee for consideration. **5.** consignment, as to prison. **6.** *Law.* a written order of a court directing that someone be confined to prison (formerly more often termed a *mittimus*). **7.** perpetration or commission, as of a crime. **8.** the act of committing, pledging, or engaging oneself. **9.** bargain (def. 3). Also, **commit′tal** for defs 1, 4, 5, 7, 8.

committee (kə mĭt′ĭ), *n.* **1.** a person or a group of persons elected or appointed from a larger body to investigate, report, or act in special cases. **2. standing committee,** a permanent committee, as of a legislature, society, etc., intended to consider all matters pertaining to a designated subject. **3.** *Law.* one to whom the care of a person (as a lunatic) or an estate was formerly entrusted. [t. AF, orig. pp., committed]

committeeman (kə mĭt′ĭ mən, -măn′), *n., pl.* **-men** (-mən, -mĕn′). a member of a committee. —**committeewoman** (kə mĭt′ĭ wŏŏm′ən), *n. fem.*

Committee of 100, (in Great Britain) a left-wing group,

originally headed by a committee having 100 members, formed to exert political and social pressure by means of civil disobedience for pacifist and allied objectives.

Committee of the Whole House, *Parl. Proc.* a legislative body, esp. the British House of Commons, meeting for informal debate and preliminary consideration of matters awaiting legislative action.

Committee of Ways and Means, *Parl. Proc.* (in Great Britain) a committee, esp. of the House of Commons, to whom financial matters are referred.

committee stage, *Parl. Proc.* the stage in the passage of a bill through parliament, between the second and third readings, when it is subjected to detailed discussion in committee.

commix (kō mĭks′), *v.t., v.i.* to mix together; blend.

commixture (kō mĭks′chə), *n.* a mixing together; the product of mixing; mixture. [t. L: m. s. *commixtūra*]

commode (kə mōd′), *n.* **1.** a piece of furniture containing drawers or shelves. **2.** a stand or cupboard containing a chamber-pot or washbasin. **3.** a large, high headdress worn by women about 1700. [t. F, t. L: m. s. *commodus* fit, convenient, useful]

commodious (kə mō′dyəs), *adj.* **1.** convenient and roomy; spacious: *a commodious harbour.* **2.** convenient or satisfactory for the purpose. [late ME, t. ML: m. s. *commodiōsus.* See COMMODE] **—commo′diously,** *adv.* **—commo′diousness,** *n.*

commodity (kə mŏd′ĭ tĭ), *n., pl.* **-ties. 1.** a thing that is of use or advantage. **2.** an article of trade or commerce. **3.** *Obs.* a quantity of goods.

commodore (kŏm′ə dô′), *n. Naval.* **1.** a naval officer next in rank below a rear admiral, usually in temporary command of a squadron. **2.** *Naval.* the senior captain when three or more ships of war are cruising in company. **3.** the senior captain of a line of merchant vessels. **4.** the president or head of a yacht club or boat club. **5.** the ship of a commodore. [earlier *commandore,* possibly t. D: m. *kommandeur,* t. F: m. *commandeur,* der. *commander* command]

Commodus (kŏm′ə dəs), *n.* **Lucius Aelius Aurelius** (lōō′syəs ē′lĭ əs ô rē′lĭ əs), A.D. 161–192, Roman emperor A.D. 180–192 (son and successor of Marcus Aurelius).

common (kŏm′ən), *adj.* **1.** belonging equally to, or shared alike by, two or more or all in question: *common property.* **2.** joint; united: *to make common cause against the enemy.* **3.** pertaining or belonging to the whole community; public: *common council.* **4.** generally or publicly known; notorious: *a common scold.* **5.** widespread; general; ordinary; *common knowledge.* **6.** of frequent occurrence; familiar; usual: *a common event, common salt.* **7.** hackneyed; trite. **8.** of mediocre or inferior quality; mean; low. **9.** coarse; vulgar: *common manners.* **10.** ordinary; having no rank, etc.: *common soldier, the common people.* **11.** *Anat.* denoting a trunk from which two or more arteries, veins, or nerves are given off: *the common carotid arteries.* **12.** *Pros.* (of a syllable) either long or short. *—n.* **13.** a tract of land owned or used in common, esp. by all the members of a community. **14. in common,** in joint possession, use, etc.; jointly. **15.** *Law.* the power, shared with other persons to enter on the land or waters of another, and to remove something therefrom, as by pasturing cattle, catching fish, etc. **16.** (*sometimes cap.*) *Eccles.* an office or form of service used on a festival of a particular kind. **17.** *Obs.* the community or public. **18.** *Obs.* the common people. [ME *comun,* t. OF, g. L *commūnis* common, general] **—com′monness,** *n.*

—Syn. 5. universal, prevalent, popular. See **general. 10.** COMMON, VULGAR, ORDINARY refer to the usual or most often experienced; often with derogatory connotations of cheapness or inferiority. COMMON means the accustomed or usually experienced; or the inferior, and the opposite of exclusive or aristocratic: *she is a common person.* VULGAR properly means belonging to, or characteristic of common people; it connotes low taste, coarseness, or ill-breeding: *the vulgar view of things, vulgar in manners and speech.* ORDINARY means what is to be expected in the usual order of things; or only average, or below average: *the quality is just ordinary.* **—Ant. 1.** individual. **6.** unusual.

commonable (kŏm′ə nə bl), *adj.* **1.** held in common, or subject to general use, as lands. **2.** that may be pastured on common land.

commonage (kŏm′ə nĭj), *n.* **1.** the use of anything in common, esp. of a pasture. **2.** the right to such use. **3.** the state of being held in common. **4.** that which is so held, as land. **5.** the commonalty.

commonalty (kŏm′ə nəl tĭ), *n., pl.* **-ties. 1.** the common people as distinguished from the nobility, etc. **2.** the members of an incorporated body.

common carrier, an individual or company, such as a railway or steamship line, which transports the public or goods for hire.

common core, *Educ.* those subjects in a British school curriculum which are compulsory.

common denominator, *Maths.* a number, usually the least, divisible by the denominators of a set of fractions.

common entrance examination, *Educ.* an examination taken by pupils at British preparatory schools for gaining admission to public schools.

commoner (kŏm′ə nə), *n.* **1.** one of the common people; a member of the commonalty. **2.** (at Oxford University, etc.) a student who pays for his commons, etc., and is not supported by any foundation. **3.** one who has a joint right in common land.

common factor, *Maths.* a number which is an exact divisor of two or more given numbers. Also, **common divisor.**

common fraction, *Maths.* a fraction having the numerator above and the denominator below a horizontal or diagonal line (as opposed to a *decimal fraction*).

common gender, *Gram.* (in a language having masculine and feminine gender) a class of nouns which change gender according to meaning.

common law, 1. the system of law originating in England, as distinct from the civil or Roman law and the canon or ecclesiastical law. **2.** the unwritten law, esp. of England, based on custom or court decision, as distinct from statute law. **3.** the law administered through the system of writs, as distinct from equity, admiralty, etc. **—com′mon-law′,** *adj.*

common logarithm, *Maths.* a logarithm using 10 as the base.

commonly (kŏm′ən lĭ), *adv.* **1.** usually; generally; ordinarily. **2.** in a common manner. **—Ant. 1.** rarely.

Common Market, the European Economic Community.

Common Marketeer, one who favours Britain's entry to the Common Market.

common measure, common time.

common multiple, *Maths.* a number divisible by two or more given numbers. The **least** (or **lowest**) **common multiple** is the smallest common multiple of a set of numbers.

common name, 1. a common noun. **2.** the vernacular name of a plant, animal, etc., as opposed to the name used in scientific classification.

common noun, *Gram.* (in English and some other languages) a noun that can be preceded by an article or other limiting modifier, in meaning applicable to any one or all the members of a class, as *man, men, city, cities,* in contrast to *Shakespeare, London.* Cf. **proper noun.**

common-or-garden (kŏm′ən ô gä′dn), *adj. Colloq.* ordinary.

commonplace (kŏm′ən plās′), *adj.* **1.** ordinary; uninteresting; without individuality: *a commonplace person.* **2.** trite; hackneyed: *a commonplace remark.* *—n.* **3.** a well-known, customary, or obvious remark; a trite or uninteresting saying. **4.** anything common, ordinary, or uninteresting. **5.** a place or passage in a book or writing noted as important for reference or quotation. [trans. of L *locus commūnis,* Gk (*koinós*) *topós* a stereotyped topic, argument, or passage in literature] **—com′monplace′ness,** *n.*

—Syn. 2. COMMONPLACE, BANAL, HACKNEYED, STEREOTYPED, TRITE describe words, remarks, and styles of expression, etc., which are lifeless and uninteresting. COMMONPLACE characterizes thought which is dull, ordinary, and platitudinous: *commonplace and boring.* That is BANAL which seems inane, insipid, and pointless: *a heavy and banal affirmation of the obvious.* HACKNEYED characterizes that which seems stale and worn out through overuse: *a hackneyed comparison.* STEREOTYPED emphasizes the fact that situations felt to be similar invariably call for the same thought in exactly the same form and the same words: *so stereotyped as to seem automatic.* TRITE describes that which was originally striking and apt, but which has become so well known and been so commonly used that all interest has been worn out of it: *true but trite.*

commonplace book, a book in which noteworthy passages, poems, comments, etc., are written.

common pleas, 1. the chief common-law court of civil jurisdiction, now merged in the Queen's Bench Division of the High Court. **2.** *U.S.* any of various courts of civil jurisdiction in several states.

common prayer, 1. the liturgy or public form of prayer prescribed by the Church of England to be used in all churches and chapels in public worship. **2.** (*cap.*) the Book of Common Prayer.

common room, (in schools and colleges) a sitting room for the use of the teaching staff, or, in some cases, of the students.

commons (kŏm′ənz), *n. pl.* **1.** the common people as distinguished from their rulers or a ruling class; the commonalty. **2.** the body of people not of noble birth or ennobled, as represented in England by the House of Commons. **3.** (*cap.*) the representatives of this body.

4. (*cap.*) the elective house of the parliament of Great Britain and Northern Ireland, Canada, and some of the other Commonwealth countries. **5.** food provided at a common table as in colleges. **6.** food or provisions in general.

common seal, the official seal used by a corporation.

common sense, sound practical sense; normal intelligence. —**com'mon-sense',** *adj.*

common shares, stock which ordinarily has no preference in the matter of dividends or assets and represents the residual ownership of a corporate business. Also, *U.S.*, **common stock.**

common time, *Music.* duple and quadruple rhythm. Also, **common measure.**

commonweal (kŏm'ən wēl'), *n.* **1.** the common welfare; the public good. **2.** *Archaic.* the body politic; a commonwealth.

commonwealth (kŏm'ən wĕlth'), *n.* **1.** the whole body of people of a nation or state; the body politic. **2.** (*cap.*) a federation of former colonies, esp. a member of the Commonwealth of Nations: *the Commonwealth of Australia.* **3.** (*cap.*) a self-governing territory associated with the U.S.; the official name of Puerto Rico. **4.** (*cap.*) the official designation of certain states of the U.S. **5.** (*cap.*) the English government from the abolition of the monarchy in 1649 until the establishment of the Protectorate in 1653. **6.** any body of persons united by some common interest. **7.** *Obs.* the public welfare. [f. COMMON + WEALTH]

Commonwealth Day, May 24th, the anniversary of Queen Victoria's birth, observed in many countries of the Commonwealth of Nations. Formerly, **Empire Day.**

Commonwealth of Nations, a community including the following independent nations and their dependencies bound together by a common allegiance to the British crown or by recognition of the British monarch as head of the Commonwealth: Australia, Botswana, Canada, Ceylon, Cyprus, Gambia, Ghana, Guyana, India, Jamaica, Kenya, Lesotho, Malawi, Malta, Malaysia, Mauritius, New Zealand, Nigeria, Pakistan, Sierra Leone, Singapore, Tanzania, Trinidad and Tobago, Uganda, United Kingdom, Zambia.

commotion (kə mō'shən), *n.* **1.** violent or tumultuous motion; agitation. **2.** political or social disturbance; sedition; insurrection. —**Syn. 1.** disturbance, disorder, turmoil, tumult, riot, turbulence. See **ado.**

commove (kŏ mo͞ov'), *v.t.*, **-moved, -moving.** to move violently; agitate; excite. [t. L: m. s. *commovēre*; r. ME *commoeve(n)*, t. F: m. *commouvoir*]

communal (kŏm'yo͝o nəl), *adj.* **1.** pertaining to a commune or a community. **2.** of or belonging to the people of a community: *communal land.* —**communally** (kŏm'yo͝o nə lĭ), *adv.*

communalism (kŏm'yo͝o nə lĭz'əm), *n.* a theory or system of government according to which each commune is virtually an independent state, and the nation merely a federation of such states. —**com'munalist,** *n.* —**com'munalis'tic,** *adj.*

communalize (kŏm'yo͝o nə līz'), *v.t.*, **-lized, -lizing.** to make communal; convert into municipal property. Also, **communalise.** —**com'munaliza'tion,** *n.* —**com'munaliz'er,** *n.*

Communard (kŏm'yo͝o näd'), *n.* (*often l.c.*) a member or supporter of the Paris Commune of 1871. [t. F]

commune[1] (*v.* kə myo͞on'; *n.* kŏm'yo͞on), *v.*, **-muned, -muning,** *n.* —*v.i.* **1.** to converse; talk together; interchange thoughts or feelings. —*n.* **2.** interchange of ideas or sentiments; friendly conversation. [ME *com(m)une(n)*, t. OF: m. *comuner* share, der. *comun* common]

commune[2] (kə myo͞on'), *v.i.*, **-muned, -muning.** *U.S.* to partake of the Eucharist. [ME *comunen*, t. OF: m. *communier*, g. L *commūnicāre* COMMUNICATE]

commune[3] (kŏm'yo͞on), *n.* **1.** the smallest administrative division in France, Italy, Switzerland, etc., governed by a mayor assisted by a municipal council. **2.** a similar division in some other country. **3.** any community organized for the protection and promotion of local interests, and subordinate to the state. **4.** the government or citizens of a commune. **5.** *Ethnol.* a representative group in primitive society. **6. the Commune, a.** a revolutionary committee which took the place of the municipality of Paris in the French Revolution of 1789, and soon usurped the supreme authority in the state. It was suppressed by the Convention in 1794. **b.** a socialist government of Paris from March 18th to May 27th, 1871. [t. F, fem. of *commun* common]

communicable (kə myo͞o'nĭ kə bl), *adj.* **1.** capable of being communicated. **2.** communicative. [t. ML: m. s. *commūnicābilis*] —**commu'nicabil'ity, commu'nicableness,** *n.* —**commu'nicably,** *adv.*

communicant (kə myo͞o'nĭ kənt), *n.* **1.** one who partakes, or is entitled to partake, of the Eucharist; a member of a church. **2.** one who communicates. —*adj.* **3.** communicating; imparting.

communicate (kə myo͞o'nĭ kāt'), *v.*, **-cated, -cating.** —*v.t.* **1.** to give to another as a partaker; impart; transmit. **2.** to impart knowledge of; make known. **3.** to administer the Eucharist to. **4.** *Archaic.* to share in or partake of. —*v.i.* **5.** to have interchange of thoughts. **6.** to have or form a connecting passage. **7.** to partake of the Eucharist. **8.** *Obs.* to take part or participate. [t. L: m. s. *commūnicātus*, pp., shared] —**commu'nica'tor,** *n.*

—**Syn. 1.** COMMUNICATE, IMPART denote giving to a person or thing a part or share of something, now usually something immaterial, as knowledge, thoughts, hopes, qualities, or properties. COMMUNICATE, the more common word, implies often an indirect or gradual transmission: *to communicate by means of letters, telegrams, etc., to communicate one's wishes to someone else.* IMPART usually implies directness of action: *to impart information.* —**Ant. 1.** withhold. **2.** conceal.

communication (kə myo͞o'nĭ kā'shən), *n.* **1.** the act or fact of communicating; transmission. **2.** the imparting or interchange of thoughts, opinions, or information by speech, writing, or signs. **3.** that which is communicated or imparted. **4.** a document or message imparting views, information, etc. **5.** passage, opportunity of passage, or a means of passage between places. **6.** (*pl.*) **a.** the means of transmitting information by telephone, telegraph, radio, television, etc. **b.** any means of sending military messages, orders, etc. **c.** routes and transportation for moving troops and supplies overseas, or in a theatre of operations.

communication cord, a cord or chain running the length of a train by which a passenger may signal to the driver to stop in an emergency.

communication satellite, *Radio, Aeron.* an artificial earth satellite used for relaying radio and television signals around the curved surface of the earth.

communicative (kə myo͞o'nĭ kə tĭv), *adj.* **1.** inclined to communicate or impart. **2.** talkative; not reserved. **3.** of or pertaining to communication. —**commu'nicatively,** *adv.* —**commu'nicativeness,** *n.*

communicatory (kə myo͞o'nĭ kə tə rĭ, -kə trĭ), *adj.* of or pertaining to communication.

communion (kə myo͞o'nyən), *n.* **1.** the act of sharing, or holding in common; participation. **2.** the state of things so held. **3.** association; fellowship. **4.** interchange of thoughts or interests; communication; intimate talk. **5.** *Eccles.* **a.** a body of persons having one common religious faith; a religious denomination. **b.** reception of the Eucharist. **c.** the celebration of the Lord's Supper; the Eucharist. [ME, t. L: s. *commūnio* fellowship]

communiqué (kə myo͞o'nĭ kā'), *n.* an official bulletin or communication, usually to the press or public. [t. F]

communism (kŏm'yo͝o nĭz'əm), *n.* **1.** a theory or system of social organization based on the holding of all property in common, actual ownership being ascribed to the community as a whole or to the state. **2.** a system of social organization in which all economic activity is conducted by a totalitarian state dominated by a single and self-perpetuating political party. **3.** communalism. [t. F: m. *communisme*, der. *commun.* See COMMON]

Communism (kŏm'yo͝o nĭz'əm), *n.* **Mount,** a mountain in the Soviet Union, in the Pamirs. 24,590 ft.

communist (kŏm'yo͝o nĭst), *n.* **1.** an advocate of communism. **2.** (*often cap.*) a person who belongs to the Communist Party, esp. the party in the Soviet Union. **3.** (*usually cap.*) a Communard. —*adj.* **4.** pertaining to communists or communism.

communistic (kŏm'yo͝o nĭs'tĭk), *adj.* **1.** *Chiefly U.S.* communist. **2.** tending towards or sympathizing with communism. —**com'munis'tically,** *adv.*

Communist Manifesto, a pamphlet (1848) by Karl Marx and Friedrich Engels: first statement of the principles of modern communism.

Communist Party, a political party professing the principles of communism.

communitarian (kə myo͞o'nĭ tĕə'rĭ ən), *n.* **1.** a member of a communistic community. **2.** an advocate of such a community.

community (kə myo͞o'nĭ tĭ), *n.*, *pl.* **-ties. 1.** a social group of any size whose members reside in a specific locality, share government, and have a cultural and historical heritage. **2. the community,** the public. **3.** *Eccles.* a group of men or women leading a common life according to a rule. **4.** *Ecol.* a group of organisms, both plant and animal, living together in an ecologically related fashion in a definite region: *an oak forest community.* **5.** joint possession, enjoyment, liability, etc.: *community of property.* **6.** similar character; agreement; identity:

community of interests. [t. L: m. s. *commūnitas*; r. ME *comunete*, t. OF]

community centre, a building in which members of a community meet for social or other purposes.

community chest, *U.S. and Can.* a fund for local welfare activities, raised by voluntary contributions.

community singing, organized singing at a public gathering.

communize (kŏm′yo͝o nīz′), *v.t.*, **-nized, -nizing. 1.** to make the property of the community. **2.** to make communist. Also, **communise.** —**com′muniza′tion,** *n.*

commutable (kə myo͞o′tə bl), *adj.* that may be commuted; exchangeable. —**commut′abil′ity,** *n.*

commutate (kŏm′yo͝o tāt′), *v.t.*, **-tated, -tating.** *Elect.* **1.** to reverse the direction of (a current or currents), as by a commutator. **2.** to convert (alternating current) into direct current by use of a commutator.

commutation (kŏm′yo͝o tā′shən), *n.* **1.** the act of substituting one thing for another; substitution; exchange. **2.** the substitution of one kind of payment for another. **3.** *U.S.* regular travel between home (usually distant) and work, generally using a season ticket. **4.** the changing of a penalty, etc., for another less severe. **5.** *Elect.* **a.** the act of reversing the direction of the current. **b.** the act of converting an alternating current into a direct current.

commutative (kə myo͞o′tə tĭv, kŏm′yo͝o tā′tĭv), *adj.* of or pertaining to commutation, exchange, substitution, or interchange.

commutative law, *Logic.* a law asserting that the order in which certain logical operations are performed is indifferent; in mathematics the two commutative laws are stated symbolically as: $a + b = b + a$ and $ab = ba$. For example: *Smith is ill or out of town* is equipollent with *Smith is out of town or ill.*

commutator (kŏm′yo͝o tā′tə), *n. Elect.* **1.** a device for reversing the direction of a current. **2.** (in a dynamo) a cylindrical ring or disc assembly of conducting members, individually insulated in a supporting structure with an exposed surface for contact with current-collecting brushes, and mounted on the armature shaft.

commute (kə myo͞ot′), *v.*, **-muted, -muting.** —*v.t.* **1.** to exchange for another or something else; give and take reciprocally; interchange. **2.** to change (one kind of payment) into or for another, as by substitution. **3.** to change (a penalty, etc.) for one less burdensome or severe. —*v.i.* **4.** to make substitution. **5.** to serve as a substitute. **6.** to make a collective payment, esp. of a reduced amount, as an equivalent for a number of payments. **7.** to travel regularly between home (usually distant) and work, generally using a season ticket. [t. L: m. s. *commūtāre* change wholly] —**commut′er,** *n.*

commuter belt, the area around a city from which workers commute.

Comnenus (kŏm nē′nəs), *n.* a dynasty of Byzantine emperors that ruled at Constantinople 1057?–1185, and at Trebizond in Asia Minor 1204–1461?

Como (kō′mō), *n.* **1. Lake,** a lake in N Italy, in Lombardy. 35 mi. long; 56 sq. mi. **2.** a town on this lake. 89,966 (1966).

Comorin (kŏm′ə rĭn), *n.* **Cape,** a cape at the S tip of India extending into the Indian Ocean.

Comoro Islands (kŏm′ə rō′), a group of French islands in the Mozambique Channel between N Madagascar and E Africa. 212,386 pop. (est. 1965); ab. 800 sq. mi. See map under **Mauritius.**

comose (kō′mōs, kō mōs′), *adj.* hairy; comate. [t. L: m. s. *comōsus* covered with hair]

comp., 1. comparative. **2.** compare. **3.** compilation. **4.** compiled. **5.** composition. **6.** compositor. **7.** compound.

compact[1] (*adj.*, *v.* kəm păkt′; *n.* kŏm′păkt), *adj.* **1.** joined or packed together; closely and firmly united; dense; solid. **2.** arranged within a relatively small space. **3.** expressed concisely; pithy; terse; not diffuse. **4.** composed or made (fol. by *of*). —*v.t.* **5.** to join or pack closely together; consolidate; condense. **6.** to make firm or stable. **7.** to form or make by close union or conjunction; make up or compose. **8.** *Metall.* to press (metallic and other powders) in a die. —*n.* **9.** a small case containing a mirror, face powder, a puff, and (sometimes) rouge. **10.** *Metall.* the moulded shape obtained after pressing metallic and other powders in a die. [t. L: s. *compactus*, pp., joined together] —**compact′ly,** *adv.* —**compact′ness,** *n.*

compact[2] (kŏm′păkt), *n.* an agreement between parties; a covenant; a contract. [t. L: s. *compactum*, prop. pp. neut., having agreed with] —**Syn.** treaty, pact. See **agreement.**

companion[1] (kəm păn′yən), *n.* **1.** one who accompanies or associates with another. **2.** a person, usually a woman, employed to accompany or assist another. **3.** a mate or match for a thing. **4.** a handbook; guide. **5.** a member of the lowest rank in an order of knighthood, or of a grade in an order. **6.** *Obs.* a fellow (used in contempt). —*v.t.* **7.** to be a companion to; accompany. [t. LL: s. *compānio* messmate, der. L *pānis* bread; r. ME *compainoun*, t. OF: m. *compaignon*] —**compan′ionless,** *adj.* —**Syn. 1.** mate, comrade, associate, partner. See **acquaintance.**

companion[2] (kəm păn′yən), *n.* **1.** a covering or hood over the top of a companionway. **2.** a companionway. [t. D: m. *kampanje* quarterdeck. Cf. It. *camera della campagna* storeroom]

companionable (kəm păn′yə nə bl), *adj.* fitted to be a companion; sociable. —**compan′ionableness,** *n.* —**compan′ionably,** *adv.*

companionate (kəm păn′yə nĭt), *adj. Obs.* of, by, or like companions.

companionate marriage, a suggested form of marriage without the traditional rights and obligations of the spouses and with a simplified divorce completely terminating the relationship of childless couples.

companion cell, *Bot.* a cell associated with a sieve tube and, collectively, forming one of the elements of phloem.

Companion of Honour, a member of an order instituted in Great Britain in 1917, with a membership restricted to sixty-five, awarded to those who have rendered conspicuous service to the nation.

companionship (kəm păn′yən shĭp′), *n.* association as companions; fellowship.

companionway (kəm păn′yən wā′), *n. Naut.* **1.** the space or shaft occupied by the steps leading down from the deck to a cabin. **2.** the steps themselves.

company (kŭm′pə nĭ), *n.*, *pl.* **-nies,** *v.*, **-nied, -nying.** —*n.* **1.** a number of individuals assembled or associated together; group of people. **2.** an assemblage of persons for social purposes. **3.** companionship; fellowship; association. **4.** a guest or guests. **5.** society collectively. **6.** a number of persons united or incorporated for joint action, esp. for business: *a publishing company.* **7.** the member or members of a firm not specifically named in the firm's title: *John Jones and Company.* **8.** a number of persons associated for the purpose of presenting theatrical productions, etc. **9.** a medieval trade guild. **10.** *Mil.* **a.** a subdivision of a regiment or battalion. **b.** any relatively small group of soldiers. **11.** *Naut.* a ship's crew, including the officers. **12. bear or keep company,** to associate or go with. **13. part company, a.** to cease association or friendship with. **b.** to leave or separate from (each other). —*v.i.* **14.** *Archaic.* to associate. —*v.t.* **15.** *Archaic.* to accompany. [ME *compaignie*, t. OF. See COMPANION[1]]

—**Syn. 1.** COMPANY, BAND, PARTY, TROOP refer to a group of people formally or informally associated. COMPANY is the general word and means any group of people: *a company of travellers.* BAND, used esp. of a band of musicians, suggests a relatively small group pursuing the same purpose or sharing a common fate: *a concert by a band, a band of survivors.* PARTY, except when used of a political group, usually implies an indefinite and temporary assemblage as for some common pursuit: *an exploring party.* TROOP, used specifically of a body of cavalry, usually implies a number of individuals organized as a unit: *a troop of cavalry.* **2.** assembly, gathering, concourse, crowd. **6.** firm, house, corporation, syndicate.

compar., comparative.

comparable (kŏm′pə rə bl, -prə bl), *adj.* **1.** capable of being compared. **2.** worthy of comparison. —**com′parableness,** *n.* —**com′parably,** *adv.*

comparative (kəm pă′rə tĭv), *adj.* **1.** of or pertaining to comparison. **2.** proceeding by or founded on comparison: *comparative anatomy.* **3.** estimated by comparison; not positive or absolute; relative. **4.** *Gram.* **a.** denoting the intermediate degree of the comparison of adjectives and adverbs. **b.** denoting the form of an adjective or adverb inflected to show this degree. **c.** having or pertaining to the function or meaning of this degree of comparison. —*n.* **5.** *Gram.* **a.** the comparative degree. **b.** a form in it, as English *lower* in contrast to *low* and *lowest*, *more gracious* in contrast to *gracious* and *most gracious.* —**compar′atively,** *adv.*

comparator (kŏm′pə rā′tə), *n.* any of various instruments for making comparisons, as of lengths or distances, tints of colours, etc.

compare (kəm pěə′), *v.*, **-pared, -paring,** *n.* —*v.t.* **1.** to represent as similar or analogous; liken (fol. by *to*). **2.** to note the similarities and differences of (fol. by *with*). **3.** to bring together for the purpose of noting points of likeness and difference: *to compare two pieces of cloth.* **4.** *Gram.* to form or display the degrees of comparison of (an adjective or adverb). **5. compare notes,** to exchange views, ideas, impressions, etc. —*v.i.* **6.** to bear comparison; be held equal. **7.** to vie. *—n.* **8.** comparison: *joy beyond compare.* [ME, t. F: m. s. *comparer,* g. L *comparāre,* lit., bring together] **—compar′er,** *n.*

—Syn. 1, 2. COMPARE, CONTRAST agree in placing together two or more things and examining them to discover characteristics, qualities, etc. To COMPARE means to examine in order to discover like or unlike characteristics. We compare things of the same class *with* each other; one of unlike classes *to* the other: *to compare one story with another, a man to a mountain.* To CONTRAST is to examine with an eye to differences; or to place together so that the differences are striking. We contrast one thing *with* another: *to contrast living conditions in peace and in war.*

comparison (kəm pă′rĭ sən), *n.* **1.** the act of comparing. **2.** the state of being compared. **3.** a likening; an illustration by similitude; a comparative estimate or statement. **4.** *Rhet.* the considering of two things with regard to some characteristic which is common to both, as the likening of a hero to a lion in courage. **5.** the capability of being compared or likened. **6.** *Gram.* **a.** that function of an adverb or adjective used to indicate degrees of superiority or inferiority in quality, quantity, or intensity. **b.** the patterns of formation involved therein. **c.** the degrees of a particular word, displayed in a fixed order, as *mild, milder, mildest, less mild, least mild.* [ME, t. OF: m. *comparaison,* g. L *comparātio,* der. *comparāre.* See COMPARE]

compartment (kəm pät′mənt), *n.* **1.** a part or space marked or partitioned off. **2.** a separate room, section, etc.: *the compartment of a railway carriage, a watertight compartment in a ship.* **3.** *Archit., Art.* an ornamental division of a larger design. *—v.t.* **4.** to divide into compartments. [t. F: m. *compartiment,* t. It.: m. *compartimento,* der. LL *compartīrī* divide]

compass (kŭm′pəs), *n.* **1.** an instrument for determining directions, consisting essentially of a freely moving magnetized needle indicating magnetic north and south. **2.** the enclosing line or limits of any area; measurement round. **3.** space within limits; area; extent; range; scope. **4.** the total range of notes of a voice or of a musical instrument. **5.** due or proper limits; moderate bounds. **6.** a passing round; a circuit; a detour. **7.** (*usually pl.*) an instrument for describing circles, measuring distances, etc., consisting generally of two movable legs hinged at one end. **8.** *Obs* a circle. *—v.t.* **9.** to go or move round; make the circuit of. **10.** to extend or stretch around; hem in; encircle. **11.** to attain or achieve; accomplish; obtain. **12.** to contrive; scheme. **13.** to make curved or circular. **14.** to grasp with the mind. [ME *compas,* t. OF, der. *compasser* divide exactly, ult. der. L *compassus* equal step] **—com′passable,** *adj.* **—Syn.** **3.** See **range.**

compass card, a circular card attached to the needle of a mariners' compass, on which the degrees or points indicating direction are marked.

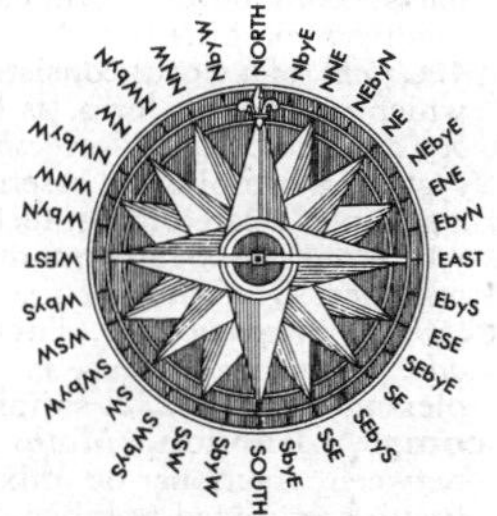

Compass card

compassion (kəm păsh′ən), *n.* **1.** a feeling of sorrow or pity for the sufferings or misfortunes of another; sympathy. *—v.t.* **2.** to have compassion for. [ME, t. LL: s. *compassio* sympathy] **—Syn.** **1.** ruth, commiseration, mercy.

compassionate (*adj.* kəm păsh′ə nĭt; *v.* kəm păsh′ə nāt′), *adj., v.,* **-nated, -nating.** *—adj.* **1.** having or showing compassion. **2.** on the grounds of compassion: *compassionate leave.* **3.** *Obs.* pitiable. *—v.t.* **4.** to have compassion for; pity. **—compas′sionately,** *adv.* **—compas′sionateness,** *n.* **—Syn.** **1.** pitying, sympathizing, sympathetic, tender, kind, merciful.

compass plane, *Carp.* a plane, usually of metal, capable of adjustment to convex or concave curves and used for smoothing curved timbers.

compass plant, any of various plants whose leaves tend to lie in a plane at right angles to the strongest light, hence usually north and south, esp. *Silphium laciniatum,* or *Lactuca* (wild lettuce).

compass saw, a narrow tapered handsaw used for cutting curves.

compatible (kəm păt′ə bl), *adj.* capable of existing together in harmony; such as to agree; consistent; congruous (usually fol. by *with*). [t. ML: m. s. *compatibilis,* der. LL *compati* suffer with] **—compat′ibil′ity, compat′ibleness,** *n.* **—compat′ibly,** *adv.*

compatriot (kəm păt′rĭ ət), *n.* **1.** a fellow countryman or fellow countrywoman. *—adj.* **2.** of the same country. [t. L: s. *compatriōta*] **—compat′riotism,** *n.*

compeer (kŏm′pĭə), *n.* **1.** an equal or peer; a comrade; an associate. *—v.t.* **2.** *Archaic.* to be the equal of; match. [ME *comper,* t. OF. See COM-, PEER]

compel (kəm pĕl′), *v.t.,* **-pelled, -pelling.** **1.** to force or drive, esp. to a course of action. **2.** to secure or bring about by force. **3.** to force to submit; subdue. **4.** to overpower. **5.** to drive together; unite by force; herd. [ME *compelle(n),* t. L: m. *compellere*] **—compel′lable,** *adj.* **—compel′ler,** *n.*

—Syn. 1. constrain, oblige, coerce. COMPEL, IMPEL agree in the idea of using (physical or other) force to cause something to be done. COMPEL means to constrain someone, in some way, to yield or to do what one wishes: *to compel a recalcitrant debtor to pay, fate compels men to face danger and trouble.* IMPEL may mean literally to push forward; but is usually applied figuratively, meaning to provide a strong motive or incentive towards a certain end: *wind impels a ship, curiosity impels me to speak.*

compellation (kŏm′pĕ lā′shən), *n.* **1.** the act or manner of addressing a person. **2.** form of address or designation; appellation. [t. L: s. *compellātio*]

compendious (kəm pĕn′dĭ əs), *adj.* containing the substance of a subject in a brief form; concise. [t. L: m. s. *compendiōsus* abridged] **—compen′diously,** *adv.* **—compen′diousness,** *n.*

compendium (kəm pĕn′dĭ əm), *n., pl.* **-diums, -dia** (-dĭ ə). a comprehensive summary of a subject; a concise treatise; an epitome. Also, **compend** (kŏm′pĕnd). [t. L: a saving, a short way]

compensate (kŏm′pĕn sāt′), *v.,* **-sated, -sating.** *—v.t.* **1.** to counterbalance; offset; make up for. **2.** to make up for something to (a person); recompense. **3.** *Mech.* to counterbalance (a force or the like); adjust or construct so as to offset or counterbalance variations or produce equilibrium. **4.** *U.S.* to change the gold content (of the monetary unit) to counterbalance price fluctuations and thereby stabilize its purchasing power. *—v.i.* **5.** to provide or be an equivalent; make up; make amends (fol. by *for*). [t. L: m. s. *compensātus,* pp., counterbalanced] **—com′pensa′tor,** *n.* **—Syn.** **2.** remunerate, reward, pay.

compensation (kŏm′pĕn sā′shən), *n.* **1.** the act of compensating. **2.** something given or received as an equivalent for services, debt, loss, suffering, etc.; indemnity. **3.** *Biol.* the improvement of any defect by the excessive development or action of another structure or organ of the same structure. **4.** *Psychol.* behaviour which compensates for some personal trait, as a weakness or inferiority. **—com′pensa′tional,** *adj.* **—Syn.** **2.** recompense, remuneration, payment, amends, reparation.

compensatory (kŏm′pĕn sā′tə rĭ, kəm pĕn′sə tə rĭ, -trĭ), *adj.* serving to compensate. Also, **compensative** (kŏm′pĕn sā′tĭv, kəm pĕn′sə tĭv).

compere (kŏm′pĕə), *n., v.,* **-pered, -pering.** *—n.* **1.** one who introduces and links the acts in an entertainment. *—v.t., v.i.* **2.** to act as a compere in (a show, etc.). See **commere.** [t. F: m. *compère*]

compete (kəm pēt′), *v.i.,* **-peted, -peting.** to contend with another for a prize, profit, etc.; engage in a contest; vie: *to compete in a race, in business, etc.* [t. L: m. s. *competere* contend for, (earlier) come together]

—Syn. COMPETE, CONTEND, CONTEST mean to strive to outdo or excel: they may apply to individuals or groups. COMPETE implies having a sense of rivalry and of striving to do one's best as well as to outdo another: *to compete for a prize.* CONTEND suggests opposition or disputing as well as rivalry: *to contend with an opponent, against obstacles.* CONTEST suggests struggling to gain or hold something, as well as contending or disputing: *to contest a position or ground (in battle), to contest a decision.*

competence (kŏm′pĭ təns), *n.* **1.** the quality of being competent; adequacy; due qualification or capacity. **2.** sufficiency; a sufficient quantity. **3.** an income sufficient to furnish the necessities of life, without great luxuries. **4.** *Law.* the quality or position of being legally competent; legal capacity or qualification (which presupposes the meeting of certain minimum requirements of age, soundness of mind, citizenship, or the like). **5.** *Embryol.* the sum total of possible reactions of any group of blastemic cells under varied external conditions.

competency (kŏm′pĭ tən sĭ), *n.* **1.** competence (defs 1–4). **2.** *Law.* (of a witness) eligibility to be sworn and testify (presupposing the meeting of requirements of ability to observe, remember, and recount).

competent (kŏm′pĭ tənt), *adj.* **1.** fitting, suitable, or sufficient for the purpose; adequate; properly qualified. **2.** rightfully belonging; permissible (fol. by *to*). **3.** *Law.* (of a witness, a party to a contract, etc.) having legal capacity or qualification. [t. L: s. *competens,* ppr., being fit] **—com′petently,** *adv.* **—Syn.** **1.** fit, qualified, capable, proficient. See **able.**

competition (kŏm′pĭ tĭsh′ən), *n.* **1.** the act of competing; rivalry. **2.** a contest for some prize or advantage. **3.** the rivalry between two or more business enterprises to secure the patronage of prospective buyers. **4.** a competitor or competitors. **5.** *Sociol.* rivalry for the purpose of obtaining some advantage over some other person or group, but not involving the destruction of that person or group. **6.** *Ecol.* the struggle among organisms, both of the same and of different species, for food, space, and other factors of existence. [t. L: s. *competītio*]

competitive (kəm pĕt′ĭ tĭv), *adj.* of, pertaining to, involving, or decided by competition: *a competitive examination.* Also, **competitory** (kəm pĕt′ĭ tə rĭ, -trĭ). —**compet′itively,** *adv.* —**compet′itiveness,** *n.*

competitor (kəm pĕt′ĭ tə), *n.* one who competes; a rival. —**competitress** (kəm pĕt′ĭ trĭs), *n. fem.* —**Syn.** See **opponent.**

Compiègne (*Fr.* kôɴ pyĕny′), *n.* a town in N France, in Oise department, on the river Oise: nearby were signed the armistices between the Allies and Germany, 1918, and between Germany and France, 1940. 28,415 (1962).

Compiègne

compilation (kŏm′pĭ lā′shən), *n.* **1.** the act of compiling: *the compilation of an index to a book.* **2.** something compiled, as a book.

compile (kəm pīl′), *v.t.*, **-piled, -piling. 1.** to put together (literary materials) in one book or work. **2.** to make (a book, etc.) of materials from various sources. [ME *compile(n)*, t. OF: m. *compiler*, g. L *compīlāre* snatch together and carry off]

compiler (kəm pī′lə), *n.* **1.** one who compiles. **2.** *Computers.* a computer program which translates autocode computer programs into the basic commands which activate the computer.

complacency (kəm plā′sən sĭ), *n., pl.* **-cies. 1.** a feeling of quiet pleasure; satisfaction; gratification; self-satisfaction. **2.** that which gives satisfaction; a cause of pleasure or joy; a comfort. **3.** *Obs.* friendly civility. **4.** *Obs.* a civil act. Also, **compla′cence.**

complacent (kəm plā′sənt), *adj.* **1.** pleased, esp. with oneself or one's own merits, advantages, etc.; self-satisfied. **2.** pleasant; complaisant. [t. L: s. *complacens*, ppr., pleasing] —**compla′cently,** *adv.*

complain (kəm plān′), *v.i.* **1.** to express grief, pain, uneasiness, censure, resentment, or dissatisfaction; find fault. **2.** to tell of one's pains, ailments, etc. **3.** to state a grievance; make a formal accusation. [ME *complayn(en)*, t. OF: m. *complaindre*, g. LL *complangere* lament] —**complain′er,** *n.* —**complain′ingly,** *adv.*

—**Syn. 1.** COMPLAIN, GRUMBLE, GROWL, MURMUR, WHINE are terms for expressing dissatisfaction or discomfort. To COMPLAIN is to protest against or lament a condition or cause of wrong, etc.: *to complain about high prices.* To GRUMBLE is to utter surly, ill-natured complaints half to oneself: *to grumble about the service.* To GROWL may express more anger than GRUMBLE: *to growl ungraciously in reply to a question.* To MURMUR is to complain in low or suppressed tones, and may indicate greater dissatisfaction than GRUMBLE: *to murmur against a government.* To WHINE is to complain or beg in a mean-spirited, objectionable way, using a nasal tone; whining often connotes persistence in begging or complaining: *to whine like a coward, like a spoilt child.* —**Ant. 1.** rejoice.

complainant (kəm plā′nənt), *n.* one who makes a complaint, as in a legal action.

complaint (kəm plānt′), *n.* **1.** an expression of grief, regret, pain, censure, resentment, or discontent; lament; fault-finding. **2.** a cause of grief, discontent, lamentation, etc. **3.** a cause of bodily pain or ailment; a malady. **4.** *Law.* the first pleading of the plaintiff in a civil action, stating his cause of action. [ME, t. OF: m. *complainte*, der. *complaindre.* See COMPLAIN]

complaisance (kəm plā′zəns), *n.* **1.** the quality of being complaisant. **2.** a complaisant act. [t. F]

complaisant (kəm plā′zənt), *adj.* disposed to please; obliging; agreeable; gracious; compliant. [t. F, ppr. of *complaire* please, g. L *complacēre*] —**complai′santly,** *adv.*

complement (*n.* kŏm′plĭ mənt; *v.* kŏm′plĭ mĕnt′), *n.* **1.** that which completes or makes perfect. **2.** the quantity or amount that completes anything. **3.** either of two parts or things needed to complete the whole. **4.** full quantity or amount; complete allowance. **5.** the full number of officers and crew required to man a ship. **6.** a word or words used to complete a grammatical construction, esp. in the predicate, as an object (*man* in *he saw the man*), predicate adjective (*tall* in *the tree is tall*), or predicate noun (*John* in *his name is John*). **7.** *Geom.* the angular amount needed to bring a given angle to a right angle. **8.** *Music.* the interval which added to a given interval completes an octave. **9.** *Immunol.* a thermolabile substance which is normally present in all sera. —*v.t.* **10.** to complete; form a complement to. [ME, t. L: s. *complēmentum* that which fills up, (later) fulfilment]

—**Syn. 10.** COMPLEMENT, SUPPLEMENT both mean to make an addition or additions to something. To COMPLEMENT is to provide something felt to be lacking or needed; it is often applied to putting together two things, each of which supplies what is lacking in the other, to make a complete whole: *two discussions from different points of view may complement each other.* To SUPPLEMENT is merely to add to; no lack or deficiency is implied nor is there an idea of a definite relationship between parts: *some additional remarks may supplement either discussion or both.*

complemental (kŏm′plĭ mĕn′tl), *adj.* complementary. —**com′plemen′tally,** *adv.*

complementarity (kŏm′plĭ mĕn tă′rĭ tĭ), *n.* *Physics.* a concept which acknowledges that different pieces of evidence relating to atomic systems, obtained under different conditions, cannot necessarily be understood by a single model: thus the concept of complementarity is necessary in order to accept the wave and particle models of an electron.

complementary (kŏm′plĭ mĕn′tə rĭ, -trĭ), *adj.* **1.** forming a complement; completing. **2.** complementing each other.

complementary angle, the complement of the given angle.

complementary cells, *Bot.* cells fitting loosely together in the lenticel.

complementary colour, either of two spectral colours which when mixed in ideal proportions produce white, as blue-green and red.

Complementary angles: Angle BCD, complement of angle ACB; Arc BD, complement of arc AB

complete (kəm plēt′), *adj., v.,* **-pleted, -pleting.** —*adj.* **1.** having all its parts or elements; whole; entire; full. **2.** finished; ended; concluded. **3.** thorough; consummate; perfect in kind or quality. **4.** *Archaic.* (of persons) accomplished; skilled; expert. —*v.t.* **5.** to make complete; make whole or entire. **6.** to make perfect. **7.** to bring to an end; finish; fulfil. [ME *compleet*, t. L: m. s. *complētus*, pp., filled up, completed] —**complete′ly,** *adv.* —**complete′ness,** *n.* —**complet′er,** *n.* —**comple′tive,** *adj.*

—**Syn. 1–3.** COMPLETE, ENTIRE, INTACT, PERFECT imply that there is no lack or defect, nor has any part been removed. COMPLETE implies that a certain unit has all its parts, fully developed or perfected; and may apply to a process or purpose carried to fulfilment: *a complete explanation.* ENTIRE means whole, having unbroken unity: *an entire book.* INTACT implies retaining completeness and original condition: *a parcel delivered intact.* PERFECT emphasizes not only completeness but also high quality and absence of defects or blemishes: *a perfect diamond.* **7.** consummate, accomplish, flower. —**Ant. 1.** partial. **3.** defective.

completion (kəm plē′shən), *n.* **1.** the act of completing. **2.** state of being completed. **3.** conclusion; fulfilment.

complex (kŏm′plĕks), *adj.* **1.** composed of interconnected parts; compound; composite. **2.** characterized by an involved combination of parts. **3.** complicated; intricate. **4.** *Gram.* (of a word) consisting of two parts, at least one of which is a bound form, as *boyish* (consisting of the word *boy* and the bound form *-ish*). —*n.* **5.** a complex whole or system; a complicated assembly of particulars. **6.** *Psychol.* a group of related ideas, feelings, memories, and impulses which operate together and may be repressed or inhibited together. **7.** *Colloq.* a fixed idea; an obsessing notion. [t. L: s. *complexus*, pp., having embraced] —**com′plexly,** *adv.* —**com′plexness,** *n.* —**Syn. 2, 3.** involved, perplexing. —**Ant. 2, 3.** simple.

complex fraction, *Maths.* a fraction expressing a ratio between fractions or mixed numbers, or between a fraction or mixed number and a whole number.

complexion (kəm plĕk′shən), *n.* **1.** the natural colour and appearance of the skin, esp. of the face. **2.** appearance; aspect; character. **3.** viewpoint; outlook. **4.** *Old Physiol.* constitution or nature of body and mind, regarded as the result of certain combined qualities. **5.** *Obs.* nature; disposition; temperament. [ME, t. LL: s. *complexio* constitution, in L combination] —**complex′ional,** *adj.*

complexity (kəm plĕk′sĭ tĭ), *n., pl.* **-ties. 1.** the state or quality of being complex; intricacy. **2.** something complex: *the motor car was a complexity far beyond her mechanical skill.*

complex number, *Maths.* a number consisting of a real part (x) and an imaginary part (iy), where x and y are both real and $i = \sqrt{-1}$.

complex sentence, a sentence containing one or more dependent clauses in addition to the main clause. For example: *When the clock strikes* (dependent clause), *it will be three o'clock* (main clause).

compliable (kəm plī′ə bl), *adj.* compliant. —**compli′ableness,** *n.* —**compli′ably,** *adv.*

compliance (kəm plī′əns), *n.* **1.** the act of complying; an acquiescing or yielding. **2.** *Obs.* a disposition to yield to others. **3.** base subservience. **4. in compliance with,** in keeping or accordance with. Also, **compli′ancy** for 1–3.

compliant (kəm plīʹ ənt), *adj.* complying; yielding; obliging: *they were uncomfortably compliant.* [f. m. COMPLY + -ANT] —**compliʹantly,** *adv.*

complicacy (kŏmʹplĭ kə sĭ), *n., pl.* **-cies. 1.** a complicated state. **2.** a complication.

complicate (*v.* kŏmʹplĭ kātʹ; *adj.* kŏmʹplĭ kĭt), *v.,* **-cated, -cating,** *adj.* —*v.t.* **1.** to make complex, intricate, or involved. **2.** to fold or twine together; combine intricately (fol. by *with*). —*adj.* **3.** complex; involved. **4.** *Bot.* folded upon itself: *a complicate embryo.* **5.** *Zool.* (of insects' wings) folded longitudinally one or more times. [t. L: m. s. *complicātus,* pp., folded together]

complicated (kŏmʹplĭ kāʹtĭd), *adj.* **1.** composed of interconnected parts; not simple; complex. **2.** consisting of many parts not easily separable; difficult to analyse, understand, explain, etc. —**comʹplicatʹedly,** *adv.* —**comʹplicatʹedness,** *n.*

complication (kŏmʹplĭ kāʹshən), *n.* **1.** the act of complicating. **2.** a complicated or involved state or condition. **3.** a complex combination of elements or things. **4.** a complicating element. **5.** *Pathol.* a concurrent disease or a fortuitous condition which aggravates the original disease.

complicity (kəm plĭsʹĭ tĭ), *n., pl.* **-ties. 1.** the state of being an accomplice; partnership in wrongdoing. **2.** complexity.

complier (kəm plīʹə), *n.* one who complies.

compliment (*n.* kŏmʹplĭ mənt; *v.* kŏmʹplĭ mĕntʹ), *n.* **1.** an expression of praise, commendation, or admiration: *he paid you a great compliment.* **2.** a formal act or expression of civility, respect, or regard: *the compliments of the season.* **3.** polite, esp. insincere, praise or commendation; flattery. **4.** a present; gift. —*v.t.* **5.** to pay a compliment to: *to compliment a woman on her new hat.* **6.** to show kindness or regard for by a gift or other favour: *he complimented us with tickets for the exhibition.* **7.** to congratulate; felicitate: *to compliment a prince on the birth of a son.* [t. F, t. It.: m. *complimento,* t. Sp.: m. *cumplimiento,* der. *cumplir* fulfil, ult. g. L *complēre*] —**Syn. 1.** praise, tribute. —**Ant. 1.** disparagement.

complimentary (kŏmʹplĭ mĕnʹtə rĭ, -trĭ), *adj.* **1.** of the nature of, conveying, or addressing a compliment. **2.** politely flattering. **3.** free: *a complimentary ticket.* —**comʹplimenʹtarily,** *adv.*

complin (kŏmʹplĭn), *n. Eccles.* the last of the seven canonical hours, or the service for it, orig. occurring after the evening meal, but now usually following immediately upon vespers. Also, **compline** (kŏmʹplĭn, -plīn). [ME *compelin,* var. of *cumplie,* t. OF, g. L *complēta* (*hōra*) completed (hour)]

complot (*n.* kŏmʹplŏt; *v.* kəm plŏtʹ), *n., v.,* **-plotted, -plotting.** —*n.* **1.** a joint plot; a conspiracy. —*v.t., v.i.* **2.** to plot together. [t. F: plot, OF concerted plan, also crowd, struggle; orig. uncert.] —**complotʹter,** *n.*

comply (kəm plīʹ), *v.i.,* **-plied, -plying. 1.** to act in accordance with wishes, requests, commands, requirements, conditions, etc. (fol. by *with*). **2.** *Obs.* to be courteous or conciliatory. [appar. t. It.: m. *complire* fulfil, complete, t. Sp.: m. *cumplir,* ult. g. L *complēre* COMPLETE; in part appar. affected by PLY] —**Syn. 1.** acquiesce, yield, conform, obey. —**Ant. 1.** refuse, resist.

compo (kŏmʹpō), *n., pl.* **-pos.** shortened form of *composition,* esp. as the name of various composite substances in industrial use.

component (kəm pōʹnənt), *adj.* **1.** composing; constituent. —*n.* **2.** a constituent part. **3.** *Mech.* one of the parts of a force, velocity, or the like, out of which the whole may be compounded or into which it may be resolved. [t. L: s. *compōnens,* ppr., composing] —**Syn. 2.** See **element.**

compony (kəm pōʹnĭ), *adj. Her.* composed of a single row of squares, metal and colour alternating. Also, **componé** (kəm pōʹnā; *Fr.* kôɴ pô nĕʹ). [ME; t. AF: pp., composed]

compo rations, *Mil.* highly concentrated compact food supplies given to soldiers in the field for emergency use; iron rations.

comport (kəm pôtʹ), *v.t.* **1.** to bear or conduct (oneself); behave. —*v.i.* **2.** to agree or accord; suit (fol. by *with*). [t. F: s. *comporter* bear, behave, g. L *comportāre* carry together]

comportment (kəm pôtʹmənt), *n.* bearing; demeanour; behaviour.

compose (kəm pōzʹ), *v.,* **-posed, -posing.** —*v.t.* **1.** to make or form by uniting parts or elements. **2.** to be the parts or elements of. **3.** to make up; constitute. **4.** to put or dispose in proper form or order. **5.** to arrange the parts or elements of (a picture, etc.). **6.** to devise and make (a literary or musical production). **7.** to arrange or settle, as a quarrel, etc. **8.** to bring (the body or mind) to a condition of repose, calmness, etc.; calm; quiet. **9.** *Print.* **a.** to set (type). **b.** to set the types for (an article, etc.). —*v.i.* **10.** to practise composition. **11.** to enter into composition. [late ME *compose(n),* t. OF: m. *composer* (see COM-, POSE[2]), but assoc. with derivatives of L *compōnere.* See COMPOSITE]

composed (kəm pōzdʹ), *adj.* calm; tranquil; serene. —**composedly** (kəm pōʹzĭd lĭ), *adv.* —**composʹedness,** *n.* —**Syn.** See **calm.** —**Ant.** agitated, perturbed.

composer (kəm pōʹzə), *n.* **1.** one who or that which composes. **2.** a writer of music. **3.** an author.

composing room, the room in which compositors work in a printing establishment.

composing stick, *Print.* a small (usually) metal tray of adjustable width, in which type is set.

composite (kŏmʹpə zĭt), *adj.* **1.** made up of various parts or elements; compound. **2.** *Bot.* belonging to the *Compositae,* a family of plants, including the daisy, dandelion, aster, etc., in which the florets are borne in a close head surrounded by a common involucre of bracts. **3.** (*cap.*) *Archit.* denoting or pertaining to a classical order in which capital and entablature combine features of the Corinthian and Ionic orders. —*n.* **4.** something composite; a compound. **5.** *Bot.* a composite plant. [t. L: m. s. *compositus,* pp. of *compōnere* put together, compound, compose] —**comʹpositely,** *adv.* —**comʹpositeness,** *n.* —**Syn. 4.** See **combination.**

composite number, *Maths.* a number exactly divisible by some number other than itself and unity.

composite photograph, a photograph obtained by combining two or more separate photographs.

composition (kŏmʹpə zĭshʹən), *n.* **1.** the act of combining parts or elements to form a whole. **2.** the manner in which such parts are combined. **3.** the resulting state or product. **4.** make-up; constitution. **5.** a compound or composite substance. **6.** *Fine Arts.* organization or grouping of the different parts of a work of art so as to achieve a unified whole. **7.** the art of putting words and sentences together in accordance with the rules of grammar and rhetoric: *Greek prose composition.* **8.** the act of producing a literary work. **9.** the art of composing music. **10.** the resulting production or work. **11.** a short essay written as a school exercise. **12.** *Gram.* the formation of compounds: *the composition of 'bootblack' from 'boot' and 'black'.* **13.** a settlement by mutual agreement. **14.** an agreement or compromise, esp. one by which a creditor (or group of creditors) accepts partial payment from a debtor. **15.** a sum of money so paid. **16.** *Print.* the setting up of type for printing.

composition of forces, *Mech.* the union or combination of two or more forces, velocities, or the like (called *components*) acting in the same or in different directions, into a single equivalent force, velocity, or the like (called the *resultant*).

compositor (kəm pŏzʹĭ tə), *n. Print.* typesetter.

compos mentis (kŏmʹpəs mĕnʹtĭs), *Latin.* sane.

compost (kŏmʹpŏst), *n.* **1.** a composition; compound. **2.** a mixture of various substances, as dung, dead leaves, etc., undergoing decay, used for fertilizing land. [ME, t. OF, g. L *compositus,* pp., compounded]

composure (kəm pōʹzhə), *n.* serene state of mind; calmness; tranquillity. —**Syn.** equability, calmness.

compotation (kŏmʹpə tāʹshən), *n.* a drinking or tippling together. [t. L: s. *compōtātio* drinking together]

compotator (kŏmʹpə tāʹtə), *n.* one who drinks or tipples with another. [t. LL]

compote (kŏmʹpŏt; *Fr.* kôɴ pŏtʹ), *n.* a preparation or dish of fruit stewed in a syrup. [t. F, in OF *composte,* g. L *compos(i)ta,* fem. of *compositus.* See COMPOSITE]

compound[1] (*adj. and n.* kŏmʹpound; *v.* kəm poundʹ), *adj.* **1.** composed of two or more parts, elements, or ingredients, or involving two or more actions, functions, etc.; composite. **2.** *Gram.* (of a word) consisting of two or more parts which are also words, but distinguished from a phrase by special phonetic features, in English often consisting of reduction of stress on one constituent, as in *housetop, blackberry,* historically also *cupboard, breakfast.* **3.** *Zool.* (of an animal) composed of a number of distinct individuals which are connected to form a united whole or colony.
—*n.* **4.** something formed by compounding or combining parts, elements, etc. **5.** *Chem.* a pure substance composed of two or more elements whose composition is constant. **6.** *Gram.* a compound word.
—*v.t.* **7.** to put together into a whole; combine. **8.** to make or form by combining parts, elements, etc.; construct. **9.** to make up or constitute. **10.** to settle or adjust by agreement, esp. for a reduced amount, as a debt. **11.** *Law.* to agree, for a consideration, not to prosecute or punish a wrongdoer for: *to compound a*

crime or felony. **12.** to pay (interest) on the accrued interest as well as the principal. **13.** *Elect.* to connect a portion of the field turns of (a direct-current dynamo) in series with the armature circuit.
—*v.i.* **14.** to make a bargain; come to terms; compromise. **15.** to settle a debt, etc., by compromise.
[ME *compoune(n)*, t. OF: m. *compondre*, g. L *compōnere* put together] —**compound′able,** *adj.* —**compound′er,** *n.* —**Syn. 4.** See **combination.**

compound[2] (kŏm′pound), *n.* **1.** (in Africa, India, and elsewhere) an enclosure containing a residence or other establishment of Europeans. **2.** (in South Africa and elsewhere) an enclosure in which African and other non-European labourers are housed during the term of their employment. **3.** any similar enclosure for native workmen. **4.** an enclosure in which prisoners of war are held. [cf. Malay *kampong* enclosure]

compound eye, an arthropod eye subdivided into many individual light-receptive elements, each including a lens, a transmitting apparatus, and retinal cells.

compound flower, the flower head of a composite plant.

compound fraction, *Maths.* a complex fraction or a fraction of a fraction.

compound fracture, a break in a bone such that the fracture line communicates with an open wound.

compound householder, a householder whose rates are included in his rent.

compound interest, interest paid, not only on the principal, but on the interest after it has periodically come due and, remaining unpaid, been added to the principal.

compound leaf, a leaf composed of a number of leaflets on a common stalk. It may be either digitately or pinnately compound, and the leaflets may be themselves compound.

Pinnately compound leaf

compound number, a quantity expressed in more than one denomination or unit, as the length 1 foot 6 inches.

compound sentence, a sentence having two or more coordinate independent clauses, usually joined by one or more conjunctions. For example: *the lightning flashed* (independent clause) *and* (conjunction) *the rain fell* (independent clause).

comprador (kŏm′prə dô′), *n.* (in China, etc.) a native agent or factotum, as of a foreign business house. Also, **compradore.** [t. Pg.: a buyer, purveyor]

comprehend (kŏm′prĭ hĕnd′), *v.t.* **1.** to understand the meaning or nature of; conceive; know. **2.** to take in or embrace; include; comprise. [ME, t. L: s. *comprehendere* seize] —**com′prehend′ible,** *adj.* —**com′prehend′ingly,** *adv.* —**Syn. 1.** See **know.** 2. See **include.**

comprehensible (kŏm′prĭ hĕn′sə bl), *adj.* capable of being comprehended; intelligible. —**com′prehen′sibil′ity, com′prehen′sibleness,** *n.* —**com′prehen′sibly,** *adv.*

comprehension (kŏm′prĭ hĕn′shən), *n.* **1.** the act or fact of comprehending. **2.** inclusion; comprehensiveness; perception or understanding. **3.** capacity of the mind to understand; power to grasp ideas; ability to know. **4.** *Logic.* the sum of all those attributes which make up the content of a given conception (distinguished from *extension* or *extent*). For example: *rational, sensible, moral, etc.,* form the comprehension of the conception *man.* [t. L: s. *comprehensio* a comprising]

comprehensive (kŏm′prĭ hĕn′sĭv), *adj.* **1.** comprehending; inclusive; comprehending much; of large scope. **2.** comprehending mentally; having a wide mental grasp. —**com′prehen′sively,** *adv.* —**com′prehen′siveness,** *n.* —**Syn. 1.** broad, wide, extensive, full.

comprehensive school, (in Great Britain) a large school providing all kinds of secondary education, esp. one replacing separate grammar and secondary modern schools.

compress (*v.* kəm prĕs′; *n.* kŏm′prĕs), *v.t.* **1.** to press together; force into less space. —*n.* **2.** *Med.* a soft pad of lint, linen, or the like, held in place by a bandage, used as a means of pressure or to supply moisture, cold, heat, or medication. **3.** an apparatus or establishment for compressing cotton bales, etc. [ME *compresse(n)*, t. L: m. *compressāre*] —**compress′ible,** *adj.* —**compress′ibil′ity,** *n.* —**Syn. 1.** condense, squeeze, constrict. See **contract.**

compressed (kəm prĕst′), *adj.* **1.** pressed into less space; condensed. **2.** pressed together. **3.** flattened. **4.** *Bot.* flattened laterally or along the length. **5.** *Zool.* narrow from side to side, and therefore of greater height than width. —**Ant. 1.** expanded.

compressed air, air, under a higher pressure than the atmosphere, the expansive force of which is used to operate drills, brakes, etc.

compression (kəm prĕsh′ən), *n.* **1.** the act of compressing. **2.** compressed state. **3.** (in internal-combustion engines) the reduction in volume and increase of pressure of the air or combustible mixture in the cylinder prior to ignition, produced by the motion of the piston towards the cylinder head after intake. Also, **compressure** (kəm prĕsh′ə) for 1, 2.

compression ratio, the ratio of the total volume enclosed in the cylinder of an internal-combustion engine, to the volume at the end of the compression stroke.

compressive (kəm prĕs′ĭv), *adj.* compressing; tending to compress. —**compres′sively,** *adv.*

compressor (kəm prĕs′ə), *n.* **1.** one who or that which compresses. **2.** *Anat.* a muscle that compresses some part of the body. **3.** *Surg.* an instrument for compressing a part of the body. **4.** any machine, as a pump, in which a gas is compressed so that its expansion may be utilized as a source of power. In refrigeration the compressor is used to compress the gas so that it can be condensed with water or air at prevailing temperatures. **5.** *Naut.* any of various devices for gripping and stopping an anchor cable. [t. L]

comprise (kəm prīz′), *v.t.,* **-prised, -prising. 1.** to comprehend; include; contain. **2.** to consist of; be composed of. [ME *comprise(n)*, t. F: m. *compris*, pp. of *comprendre*, g. L *compre(he)ndere* seize] —**compris′able,** *adj.* —**compris′al,** *n.* —**Syn. 1.** See **include.**

compromise (kŏm′prə mīz′), *n., v.,* **-mised, -mising.** —*n.* **1.** a settlement of differences by mutual concessions; an adjustment of conflicting claims, principles, etc., by yielding a part of each; arbitration. **2.** anything resulting from compromise. **3.** something intermediate between different things. **4.** an endangering, esp. of reputation; exposure to danger, suspicion, etc. —*v.t.* **5.** to settle by a compromise. **6.** to make liable to danger, suspicion, scandal, etc.; endanger the reputation of. **7.** to involve unfavourably; commit. **8.** *Obs.* to bind by bargain or agreement. **9.** *Obs.* to bring to terms. —*v.i.* **10.** to make a compromise. [ME, t. F: m. *compromis*, g. L *comprōmissum* a mutual promise to abide by a decision, prop. pp. neut.] —**com′promis′er,** *n.*

comptometer (kŏmp tŏm′ĭ tə), *n.* **1.** a high-speed adding and calculating machine. **2.** (*cap.*) a trademark for this machine.

Compton effect, *Physics.* the reduction in the energy of a photon after its interaction with a free or loosely bound electron. Part of the photon's energy is transferred to the electron (**Compton electron**) and part is redirected as a photon of reduced energy (**Compton scatter**). [named after A. H. *Compton*, 1892–1962, U.S. physicist]

comptroller (kən trō′lə), *n.* **1.** controller (def. 1). **2.** the financial officer and controller of a household, esp. of a royal household. [var. sp. of CONTROLLER] —**comptrol′lership′,** *n.*

compulsion (kəm pŭl′shən), *n.* **1.** the act of compelling; constraint; coercion. **2.** the state of being compelled. **3.** *Psychol.* **a.** a strong irrational impulse to carry out a given act. **b.** the act. [late ME, t. LL: s. *compulsio*]

compulsive (kəm pŭl′sĭv), *adj.* **1.** compulsory. **2.** *Chiefly Psychol.* pertaining to compulsion. —**compul′sively,** *adv.*

compulsory (kəm pŭl′sə rĭ), *adj.* **1.** using compulsion; compelling; constraining: *compulsory measures.* **2.** compelled; forced; obligatory. —**compul′sorily,** *adv.* —**compul′soriness,** *n.* —**Ant. 1, 2.** voluntary.

compunction (kəm pŭngk′shən), *n.* uneasiness of conscience or feelings; regret for wrongdoing or giving pain to another; contrition; remorse. [ME, t. LL: s. *compunctio* remorse]

compunctious (kəm pŭngk′shəs), *adj.* causing compunction; causing misgiving, regret, or remorse.

compurgation (kŏm′pû gā′shən), *n.* an early common-law method of trial (abolished 1833) in which the defendant was acquitted if a specified number of friends or neighbours would swear to his innocence or veracity. [t. LL: s. *compurgātio*, der. L *compurgāre* purify completely]

compurgator (kŏm′pû gā′tə), *n.* one who testifies to another's innocence or veracity.

computation (kŏm′pyŏŏ tā′shən), *n.* **1.** the act, process, or method of computing; calculation. **2.** a result of computing; the amount computed.

compute (kəm pyōōt′), *v.,* **-puted, -puting,** *n.* —*v.t.* **1.** to determine by calculation; reckon; calculate: *to compute the distance of the moon from the earth.* —*v.i.* **2.** to reckon; calculate. —*n.* **3.** computation; reckoning. [t. L: m. s. *computāre* reckon. Cf. COUNT[1]] —**comput′abil′ity,** *n.* —**Syn. 1.** estimate, count, figure.

computer (kəm pyōō′tə), *n.* **1.** one who computes.

2. an apparatus for performing mathematical computations electronically: an **analogue computer** represents quantities as voltages; a **digital computer** represents information by patterns of pulses.

computer program, a sequence of commands in autocode or machine language which will cause a computer to perform a desired calculation. Also, **computer programme.**

comrade (kŏm′rĭd, -răd), *n.* **1.** an associate in occupation or friendship; a close companion; a fellow; a mate. **2.** a fellow member of a political party (esp. a Communist Party), fraternal group, etc. [earlier *camerade,* t. F: m. *camarade,* t. Sp.: m. *camarada,* lit., group living in one room, der. *cámara* room, g. L *camera* CHAMBER] —**com′radeship′,** *n.*

comsat (kŏm′săt), *n.* communications satellite.

comstockery (kŭm′stŏk′ə rĭ, kŏm′-), *n. Chiefly U.S.* overzealous censorship of the fine arts and literature, often mistaking outspokenly honest works for salacious ones. [named after Anthony *Comstock,* 1844–1915, U.S. moralist]

Comte (kônt; *Fr.* kôɴt), *n.* **Auguste** (*Fr.* ō gYst′), 1798–1857, French philosopher, founder of positivism. —**Comtian** (kôn′tĭ ən), *adj.* —**Comtism** (kôn′tĭz′əm), *n.* —**Com′tist,** *n., adj.*

Comus (kō′məs), *n. Later Class. Myth.* a young god of revelry, represented by Milton as the son of Bacchus and Circe. [t. L, t. Gk: m. *kômos* revel]

con¹ (kŏn), *adv.* **1.** against a proposition, opinion, etc.; not pro (for). —*n.* **2.** the argument, arguer, or voter against (something). [short for L *contrā,* adv., in opposition, as prep., against]

con² (kŏn), *v.t.,* **conned, conning.** to learn; study; commit to memory; peruse or examine carefully. [var. of CAN, OE *can, con,* a finite form of *cunnan* know]

con³ (kŏn), *v.,* **conned, conning,** *n. Naut.* —*v.t.* **1.** to direct the steering of (a ship). —*n.* **2.** the station of the person who cons. **3.** the act of conning. [var. of obs. *cond,* short for *condue,* t. OF: m. *conduire* CONDUCT]

con⁴ (kŏn), *adj., n., v.,* **conned, conning.** *Slang.* —*adj.* **1.** confidence: *con game, con man.* —*n.* **2.** a confidence trick; swindle. —*v.t.* **3.** to swindle; defraud. [short for CONFIDENCE GAME or MAN]

con-, var. of **com-,** before consonants except *b, h, l, p, r, w,* as in *convene, condone,* and, by assimilation, before *n,* as in *connection.* Cf. **co-** (def. 1).

con., 1. conclusion. 2. consolidated. 3. (L *contra*) against.

Conakry (*Fr.* kō nȧ krē′), *n.* a seaport in and the capital of Guinea. 112,491 (1960). Also, **Konakry.**

con amore (kŏn′ ä mô′rĭ; *It.* kōn ȧ mō′rė), *Italian.* **1.** with love, tender enthusiasm, or zeal. **2.** *Music.* (as a direction) tenderly and lovingly.

conation (kō nā′shən), *n. Psychol.* that portion of mental life having to do with striving, embracing desire and volition. [t. L: s. *cōnātio* an endeavouring, effort]

conative (kŏn′ə tĭv, kō′nə-), *adj.* **1.** *Psychol.* pertaining to or of the nature of conation. **2.** *Gram.* expressing endeavour or effort: *a conative verb.*

conatus (kō nā′təs), *n., pl.* **-tus. 1.** an effort or striving. **2.** a force or tendency simulating a human effort. [t. L: effort, endeavour]

con brio (kŏn brē′ō; *It.* kōn brē′ō), *Music.* with vigour; vivaciously. [It.]

concatenate (kŏn kăt′ĭ nāt′), *v.,* **-nated, -nating,** *adj.* —*v.t.* **1.** to link together; unite in a series or chain. —*adj.* **2.** linked together as in a chain. [t. L: m. s. *concatēnātus,* pp.]

concatenation (kŏn kăt′ĭ nā′shən), *n.* **1.** the act of concatenating. **2.** the state of being concatenated; connection, as in a chain. **3.** a series of interconnected or interdependent things or events.

concave (kŏn kāv′), *adj., n., v.,* **-caved, -caving.** —*adj.* **1.** curved like the interior of a circle or hollow sphere; hollow and curved, esp. of optical lenses and mirrors. **2.** *Obs.* hollow. —*n.* **3.** a concave surface, part, line, etc. —*v.t.* **4.** to make concave. [t. L: m. s. *concavus*] —**concave′ly,** *adv.* —**concave′ness,** *n.* —**Ant. 1.** convex.

A B C

A, Concave or plano-concave lens; B, Biconcave lens; C, Concavo-convex lens

concavity (kŏn kăv′ĭ tĭ), *n., pl.* **-ties. 1.** the state of being concave. **2.** a concave surface or thing; a hollow; cavity.

concavo-concave (kŏn kā′vō kŏn kāv′), *adj.* biconcave.

concavo-convex (kŏn kā′vō kŏn vĕks′), *adj.* **1.** concave on one side and convex on the other. **2.** denoting or pertaining to a lens in which the concave face has a greater degree of curvature than the convex face, the lens being thinnest in the middle.

conceal (kən sēl′), *v.t.* **1.** to hide; withdraw or remove from observation; cover or keep from sight. **2.** to keep secret; forbear to disclose or divulge. [ME *concele(n),* t. OF: m. *conceler,* g. L *concēlāre* hide] —**conceal′able,** *adj.* —**conceal′er,** *n.* —**Syn. 1.** See **hide.**

concealment (kən sēl′mənt), *n.* **1.** the act of concealing. **2.** concealed state. **3.** a means or place of hiding.

concede (kən sēd′), *v.,* **-ceded, -ceding.** —*v.t.* **1.** to admit as true, just, or proper; admit. **2.** to grant as a right or privilege; yield. —*v.i.* **3.** to make concession; yield; admit. [t. L: m. s. *concēdere*] —**conced′edly,** *adv.* —**conced′er,** *n.* —**Ant. 1.** deny. **2.** refuse.

conceit (kən sēt′), *n.* **1.** an exaggerated estimate of one's own ability, importance, wit, etc. **2.** that which is conceived in the mind; a thought; an idea. **3.** imagination; fancy. **4.** a fancy; whim; a fanciful notion. **5.** a fanciful thought, idea, or expression, esp. of a strained or far-fetched nature. **6.** the use of such thoughts, ideas, etc., as a literary characteristic. **7.** *Archaic.* **a.** favourable opinion; esteem. **b.** personal opinion or estimation. **8.** *Obs.* the faculty of conceiving; apprehension. **9.** *Obs.* a fancy article. —*v.t.* **10.** to flatter (esp. oneself). **11.** to conceive mentally; apprehend. **12.** to imagine. **13.** *Archaic or Dial.* to take a fancy to; have a good opinion of. [ME *conceyte;* der. CONCEIVE, modelled on DECEIT] —**Syn. 1.** self-esteem, vanity, egotism. See **pride.** —**Ant. 1.** humility.

conceited (kən sē′tĭd), *adj.* **1.** having an exaggerated opinion of one's abilities, importance, etc. **2.** *Dial.* having an opinion. **3.** *Dial.* fanciful; whimsical. **4.** *Obs.* intelligent; clever. —**conceit′edly,** *adv.* —**conceit′edness,** *n.* —**Syn. 1.** vain, proud, egotistical.

conceivable (kən sē′və bl), *adj.* capable of being conceived; imaginable. —**conceiv′abil′ity, conceiv′ableness,** *n.* —**conceiv′ably,** *adv.*

conceive (kən sēv′), *v.,* **-ceived, -ceiving.** —*v.t.* **1.** to form (a notion, opinion, purpose, etc.). **2.** to form a notion or idea of; imagine. **3.** to apprehend in the mind; understand. **4.** to hold as an opinion; think; believe. **5.** to experience or entertain (a feeling). **6.** to express, as in words. **7.** to become pregnant with. —*v.i.* **8.** to form an idea; think (fol. by *of*). **9.** to become pregnant. [ME *conceive(n),* t. OF: m. *conceveir,* g. L *concipere* take in] —**conceiv′er,** *n.* —**Syn. 2, 8.** See **imagine.**

concent (kən sĕnt′), *n.* concord of sounds, voices, etc. [t. L: s. *concentus* a singing together]

concentrate (kŏn′sən trāt′), *v.,* **-trated, -trating,** *n., adj.* —*v.t.* **1.** to bring or draw to a common centre or point of union; cause to come close together; bring to bear on one point; direct towards one object; focus. **2.** to intensify the action of; make more intense, stronger, or purer by removing or reducing the proportion of what is foreign or inessential. **3.** *Chem.* to increase the strength of a solution, usually by evaporation. **4.** *Mining.* to separate (metal or ore) from rock, sand, etc., so as to improve the quality of the valuable portion. —*v.i.* **5.** to converge to a centre. **6.** to become more intense, stronger, or purer. **7.** to direct one's thoughts or actions towards one subject. —*n.* **8.** a concentrated form of something; a product of concentration. —*adj.* **9.** concentrated. [f. CON- + s. L *centrum* centre + -ATE¹] —**concentrative** (kŏn′sən trā′tĭv), *adj.* —**con′centra′tor,** *n.* —**Syn. 1.** See **contract.** —**Ant. 1.** radiate. **5.** diverge.

concentration (kŏn′sən trā′shən), *n.* **1.** the act of concentrating. **2.** concentrated state. **3.** exclusive attention to one object; close mental application. **4.** *Mil.* **a.** the assembling of military or naval forces in a particular area in preparation for further operations. **b.** a specified intensity and duration of artillery fire placed on a small area. **5.** something concentrated. **6.** *Chem.* (in a solution) a measure of the amount of dissolved substance contained per unit of volume.

concentration camp, a guarded enclosure for the detention or imprisonment of political prisoners, racial minority groups, refugees, etc., esp. any of the camps established by the Nazis before and during World War II for the confinement, persecution, and mass execution of prisoners.

concentre (kŏn sĕn′tə), *v.t., v.i.,* **-tred, -tring.** to bring or converge to a common centre; concentrate. Also, *U.S.,* **concenter.**

concentric (kən sĕn′trĭk), *adj.* having a common centre, as circles or spheres. Also, **concen′trical.** —**concen′trically,** *adv.* —**concentricity** (kŏn′sən trĭs′ĭ tĭ), *n.*

Concepción (*Sp.* kōn thėp thyōn′), *n.* a city in central Chile, near the mouth of the Bío-Bío. 167,468 (1960).

concept (kŏn′sĕpt), *n.* **1.** a general notion; the predicate of a (possible) judgement. **2.** a complex of characters. **3.** the immediate object of thought in simple apprehension. [t. L: s. *conceptus* a conceiving]

conceptacle (kən sĕp′tə kl), *n. Biol.* an organ or cavity enclosing reproductive bodies. [t. L: m. s. *conceptāculum* receptacle]

conception (kən sĕp′shən), *n.* **1.** the act of conceiving. **2.** the state of being conceived. **3.** fertilization; inception of pregnancy. **4.** that which is conceived. **5.** beginning; origination. **6.** the act or power of forming notions, ideas, or concepts. **7.** a notion; idea; concept. **8.** a design; plan. —**concep′tional,** *adj.* —**concep′tive,** *adj.*

conceptual (kən sĕp′tyŏŏ əl), *adj.* pertaining to the forming of concepts or to concepts. [t. ML: s. *conceptuālis*] —**concep′tually,** *adv.*

conceptualism (kən sĕp′tyŏŏ ə lĭz′əm), *n.* the philosophical doctrine, midway between nominalism and realism, that concepts enable the mind to grasp objective reality. It is often ambiguous as to the existence and status of universals. —**concep′tualist,** *n.* —**concep′tualis′tic,** *adj.*

conceptualize (kən sĕp′tyŏŏ ə līz′), *v.t.*, *v.i.*, **-lized, -lizing.** to hold, have, or form as a concept. Also, **conceptualise.**

concern (kən sûn′), *v.t.* **1.** to relate to; be connected with; be of interest or importance to; affect: *the problem concerns us all.* **2.** to interest, engage, or involve (used reflexively or in the passive, often fol. by *with* or *in*): *to concern oneself with a matter, to be concerned in a plot.* **3.** to disquiet or trouble (used in the passive): *to be concerned about a person's health.* —*n.* **4.** that which relates or pertains to one; business; affair. **5.** a matter that engages one's attention, interest, or care, or that affects one's welfare or happiness: *it's no concern of mine.* **6.** solicitude or anxiety. **7.** important relation or bearing. **8.** a commercial or manufacturing firm or establishment. **9.** *Colloq.* any material object or contrivance. [t. ML: s. *concernere* relate to, in LL mix, f. L: *con-* CON- + *cernere* separate, have respect to]

—**Syn. 6.** CONCERN, CARE, WORRY connote an uneasy and burdened state of mind. CONCERN implies an anxious sense of interest in, or responsibility for, something: *concern over a friend's misfortune.* CARE suggests a heaviness of spirit caused by dread, or by the constant pressure of burdensome demands: *poverty weighs one down with care.* WORRY is an active state of agitated uneasiness and restless apprehension: *he was disturbed by worry over the stock market.* —**Ant. 6.** indifference.

concerned (kən sûnd′), *adj.* **1.** interested. **2.** involved. **3.** troubled or anxious: *a concerned look.*

concerning (kən sû′nĭng), *prep.* relating to; regarding; about.

concernment (kən sûn′mənt), *n.* **1.** importance or moment. **2.** interest or participation. **3.** relation or bearing. **4.** anxiety or solicitude. **5.** a concern or affair. **6.** *Archaic.* a thing in which one is concerned.

concert (*n.* kŏn′sût, -sət; *v.* kən sût′), *n.* **1.** a public musical performance in which several singers or players, or both, participate. **2.** agreement of two or more in a design or plan; combined action; accord or harmony. —*v.t.* **3.** to contrive or arrange by agreement. **4.** to plan; devise. —*v.i.* **5.** to plan or act together. [t. F: s. *concerter*, t. It.: m. *concertare* be in accord, g. L *concertāre* contend; influenced in meaning by *consertus*, pp., joined]

concert A, the note to which concert performers tune their instruments.

concertante (kŏn′chə tăn′tĭ), *n.* *Music.* a composition for one or more solo instruments with an orchestra. [t. It.]

concerted (kən sû′tĭd), *adj.* **1.** contrived or arranged by agreement; prearranged; planned or devised: *concerted action.* **2.** *Music.* arranged in parts for several voices or instruments. —**concert′edly,** *adv.*

concert grand piano. See **piano** (def. 2).

concertina (kŏn′sə tē′nə), *n.*, *v.*, **-naed, -naing.** —*n.* **1.** a small hexagonal accordion. —*v.i.* **2.** to fold up or collapse like a concertina. [f. CONCERT + -INA]

Concertina

concertino (kŏn′chə tē′nō), *n.*, *pl.* **-ni** (-nē). a short concerto. [It.]

concertmaster (kŏn′sət mäs′tə), *n.* *U.S.* the leader, usually the first violinist, of an orchestra. Also, *German,* **Konzertmeister** (*Ger.* kŏn tsĕrt′mīs tər).

concerto (kən chû′tō; *It.* kŏn chĕr′tō), *n.*, *pl.* **-tos,** *It.* **-ti** (*It.* -tē). *Music.* a composition for one or more principal instruments, with orchestral accompaniment, now usually in symphonic form. [t. It.]

concert pitch, 1. the standard pitch to which all instruments are tuned, where the frequency of A is 440, at 68°F. **2.** *Colloq.* a state of complete readiness for an event.

concession (kən sĕsh′ən), *n.* **1.** the act of conceding or yielding, as a right or privilege, or as a point or fact in an argument. **2.** the thing or point yielded. **3.** something conceded by a government or a controlling authority, as a grant of land, a privilege, or a franchise. [t. L: s. *concessio*, der. *concēdere.* See CONCEDE]

concessionaire (kən sĕsh′ə nĕə′), *n.* one to whom a concession has been granted, as by a government. [t. F: m. *concessionnaire*]

concessionary (kən sĕsh′ə nə rĭ), *adj.*, *n.*, *pl.* **-ries.** —*adj.* **1.** pertaining to concession; of the nature of a concession. —*n.* **2.** a concessionaire.

concessive (kən sĕs′ĭv), *adj.* **1.** tending or serving to concede. **2.** *Gram.* expressing concession, as the English conjunction *though.* [t. L: m. s. *concessīvus*]

conch (kŏngk, kŏnch), *n.*, *pl.* **conchs** (kŏngks), **conches** (kŏn′chĭz). **1.** the spiral shell of a gastropod, often used as a trumpet. **2.** any of several marine gastropods, esp. *Strombus gigas.* **3.** the fabled shell trumpet of the Tritons. **4.** *Archit.* **a.** the concave surface of a dome or half-dome. **b.** apse. [t. L: s. *concha*, t. Gk: m. *kónchē* mussel or cockle, shell-like part or thing, external ear]

concha (kŏng′kə), *n.*, *pl.* **-chae** (-kē). **1.** *Anat.* a shell-like structure, esp. the external ear. See diag. under **ear.** **2.** *Archit.* a conch. [see CONCH]

conchie (kŏn′shĭ), *n.* conchy.

conchiferous (kŏng kĭf′ə rəs), *adj.* shell-bearing.

Conchobar (kŏng′kō wə, kŏn′ŏŏə), *n.* See **Deidre.**

conchoid (kŏng′koid), *n.* *Geom.* a plane curve such that if a straight line be drawn from a certain fixed point, called the pole of the curve, to the curve, the part of the line intersected between the curve and its asymptote is always equal to a fixed distance. [see CONCHOIDAL]

conchoidal (kŏng koi′dl), *adj.* **1.** pertaining to a conchoid. **2.** *Mineral.* having convex elevations and concave depressions like shells. [f. m. s. Gk *konchoeidḗs* shell-like + -AL[1]]

conchology (kŏng kŏl′ə jĭ), *n.* the branch of zoology dealing with molluscs. [f. *concho-* (t. Gk: m. *koncho-*, comb. form of *kónchē* mussel) + -LOGY] —**conchological** (kŏng′kə lŏj′ĭ kl), *adj.* —**conchol′ogist,** *n.*

conchy (kŏn′chĭ), *n.*, *pl.* **-chies.** *Slang.* conscientious objector. Also, **conchie, conshie, conshy.** [short for CONSCIENTIOUS]

concierge (kŏn′sĭ ĕəzh′; *Fr.* kôɴ syĕrzh′), *n.* **1.** (in France, etc.) one who has charge of the entrance of a building; a janitor or doorkeeper. **2.** *Obs.* a custodian or warden. [t. F]

conciliate (kən sĭl′ĭ āt′), *v.t.*, **-ated, -ating. 1.** to overcome the distrust or hostility of, by soothing or pacifying means; placate; win over. **2.** to win or gain (regard or favour). **3.** to render compatible; reconcile. [t. L: m. s. *conciliātus*, pp., brought together] —**concil′ia′tion,** *n.* —**concil′ia′tor,** *n.* —**Syn. 1.** propitiate. See **appease.**

conciliatory (kən sĭl′yə tə rĭ, -trĭ), *adj.* tending to conciliate: *a conciliatory manner.* Also, **conciliative** (kən sĭl′yə tĭv). —**concil′iatorily,** *adv.* —**concil′iatoriness,** *n.*

concinnity (kən sĭn′ĭ tĭ), *n.*, *pl.* **-ties. 1.** *Rhet.* **a.** a close harmony of tone as well as logic among the elements of a discourse. **b.** an instance of this effect. **2.** any harmonious adaptation of parts. [t. L: m. s. *concinnitas*, der. *concinnus* well put together]

concise (kən sīs′), *adj.* expressing much in few words; brief and comprehensive; succinct; terse: *a concise account.* [t. L: m. s. *concīsus*, pp., cut up or off] —**concise′ly,** *adv.*

conciseness (kən sīs′nĭs), *n.* the quality of being concise. —**Syn.** See **brevity.**

concision (kən sĭzh′ən), *n.* **1.** concise quality; brevity; terseness. **2.** a cutting up or off; mutilation.

conclave (kŏn′klāv, kŏng′-), *n.* **1.** any private meeting. **2.** the place in which the cardinals of the Roman Catholic Church meet in private for the election of a pope. **3.** the assembly or meeting of the cardinals for the election of a pope. **4.** the body of cardinals; the Sacred College. [ME, t. L: lockable place]

conclavist (kŏn′klā′vist, kŏng′-), *n.* either of two persons who attend upon a cardinal in conclave.

conclude (kən klōōd′), *v.*, **-cluded, -cluding.** —*v.t.* **1.** to bring to an end; finish; terminate: *to conclude a speech.* **2.** to say in conclusion. **3.** to bring to a decision or settlement; settle or arrange finally: *to conclude a treaty.* **4.** to determine by reasoning; deduce; infer. **5.** to decide, determine, or resolve. **6.** *Obs.* to shut up or enclose. **7.** *Obs.* to restrict or confine. —*v.i.* **8.** to come to an end; finish. **9.** to arrive at an opinion or judgement; come to a decision; decide. [ME *conclude(n)*, t. L: m. *conclūdere* shut up] —**conclud′er,** *n.*

conclusion (kən klōō′zhən), *n.* **1.** the end or close; the final part. **2.** the last main division of a discourse, containing a summing up of the points. **3.** a result, issue, or outcome: *a foregone conclusion.* **4.** final settlement or arrangement. **5.** final decision. **6.** a deduction or inference: *to jump to a conclusion.* **7.** *Logic.* a proposition concluded or inferred from the premises of an argument. **8.** *Law.* **a.** the effect of an act by which he who did it is bound not to do anything inconsistent therewith; an estoppel. **b.** the end of a pleading or conveyance. **9.** *Gram.* apodosis. **10. in conclusion,** finally. **11. try conclusions with,** to engage (a person) in a contest or struggle for victory or mastery. [ME, t. L: s. *conclūsio*] **—Syn. 1.** ending, termination, completion, finale. See **end.**

conclusive (kən klo͞o′sĭv), *adj.* serving to settle or decide a question; decisive; convincing: *conclusive evidence.* **—conclu′sively,** *adv.* **—conclu′siveness,** *n.*

concoct (kən kŏkt′), *v.t.* **1.** to make by combining ingredients, as in cookery: *to concoct a soup or a dinner.* **2.** to prepare; make up; contrive: *to concoct a story.* [t. L: s. *concoctus,* pp., cooked together, digested] **—concoc′ter, concoc′tor,** *n.* **—concoc′tive,** *adj.*

concoction (kən kŏk′shən), *n.* **1.** the act or process of concocting. **2.** something concocted. [t. L: s. *concoctio*]

concomitant (kən kŏm′ĭ tənt), *adj.* **1.** accompanying; concurrent; attending. **—***n.* **2.** a concomitant quality, circumstance, person, or thing. [t. LL: s. *concomitans,* ppr., accompanying] **—concom′itance, concom′itancy,** *n.* **—concom′itantly,** *adv.*

concord (kŏn′kôd, kŏng′-), *n.* **1.** agreement between persons; concurrence in opinions, sentiments, etc.; unanimity; accord. **2.** peace. **3.** a compact or treaty. **4.** agreement between things; mutual fitness; harmony. **5.** *Gram.* agreement. **6.** *Music.* consonance. [ME *concorde,* t. F, t. L: m. *concordia* agreement]

Concord (kŏng′kôd; *U.S.* kŏng′kərd), *n.* a town in the U.S., the capital of New Hampshire, in the S part. 28,991 (1960).

concordance (kən kô′dns), *n.* **1.** the state of being concordant; agreement; harmony. **2.** an alphabetical index of the principal words of a book, as of the Bible, with a reference to the passage in which each occurs and usually some part of the context. **3.** *U.S.* an alphabetical index of subjects or topics.

concordant (kən kô′dnt), *adj.* agreeing; harmonious. **—concord′antly,** *adv.*

concordat (kŏn kô′dăt), *n.* **1.** an agreement; a compact. **2.** an agreement between the pope and a secular government regarding the regulation of ecclesiastical matters. [t. F, t. ML: s. *concordātum,* prop. pp. neut. of L *concordāre* agree]

concourse (kŏn′kôs′, kŏng′-), *n.* **1.** a flocking together of people; a throng so drawn together; an assembly. **2.** an open space or main hall in a public building, esp. a railway station. **3.** *U.S.* grounds for racing, athletic sports, etc. **4.** a running or coming together; confluence. [ME *concours,* t. OF, g. L *concursus* running together]

concrescence (kən krĕs′əns), *n.* **1.** a growing together, as of parts, cells, etc.; coalescence. **2.** *Embryol.* the moving together and growing together of embryonic parts which give origin to the left and right halves of an embryo or of an organ. **3.** the fusion together of the roots of the upper second and third molar teeth by secondary cementum; false or pathological germination. [t. L: m. s. *concrescentia* a condensing]

concrete (kŏn′krēt *for 1–10, 13;* kən krēt′ *for 11, 12*), *adj., n., v.,* **-creted, -creting.** **—***adj.* **1.** constituting an actual thing or instance; real: *a concrete example.* **2.** pertaining to or concerned with realities or actual instances rather than abstractions; particular as opposed to general: *concrete ideas.* **3.** representing or applied to an actual substance or thing as opposed to an abstract quality: *a concrete noun.* **4.** made of concrete: *a concrete pavement.* **5.** formed by coalescence of separate particles into a mass; united in a coagulated, condensed, or solid state. **—***n.* **6.** a concrete idea or term; a concrete object or thing. **7.** a mass formed by coalescence or concretion of particles of matter. **8.** an artificial stonelike material used for foundations, etc., made by mixing cement, sand, and broken stones, etc., with water, and allowing the mixture to harden. **9.** this material strengthened by a system of embedded iron or steel bars, netting, or the like, used for building: *reinforced concrete.* **—***v.t.* **10.** to treat or lay with concrete. **11.** to form into a mass by coalescence of particles; render solid. **—***v.i.* **12.** to coalesce into a mass; become solid; harden. **13.** to use or apply concrete. [t. L: m. s. *concrētus,* pp., grown together, hardened] **—con′cretely,** *adv.* **—con′creteness,** *n.* **—concre′tive,** *adj.* **—concre′tively,** *adv.* **—Ant. 1, 2.** abstract.

concrete-mixer (kŏn′krēt mĭk′sə), *n.* a machine, usually with a rotating drum, in which aggregates, cement, and water are mixed to make concrete.

concrete music, a form of musical composition, using sounds both tonal and atonal produced by electrophonic means.

concretion (kən krē′shən), *n.* **1.** the act or process of concreting. **2.** *Obs.* the state of being concreted. **3.** a solid mass formed by or as by coalescence or cohesion. **4.** a calculus. **5.** a hard solid mass of foreign material in a cavity in the body or within an organism. **6.** the act of becoming solid or calcified. **7.** an adhesion of two parts. **8.** *Geol.* a rounded mass of mineral matter occurring in sandstone, clay, etc., often in concentric layers about a nucleus.

concretionary (kən krē′shə nə rĭ), *adj.* formed by concretion; consisting of concreted matter or masses.

concubinage (kŏn kyo͞o′bĭ nĭj), *n.* **1.** cohabitation without legal marriage. **2.** the condition of a concubine.

concubinary (kŏn kyo͞o′bĭ nə rĭ), *adj.* **1.** of a concubine. **2.** living in concubinage.

concubine (kŏng′kyo͝o bīn′, kŏn′-), *n.* **1.** a woman who cohabits with a man without being married to him. **2.** (among polygamous peoples) a secondary wife. [ME, t. L: m. *concubīna*]

concupiscence (kən kyo͞o′pĭ səns), *n.* **1.** sensual appetite; lust. **2.** eager or illicit desire.

concupiscent (kən kyo͞o′pĭ sənt), *adj.* **1.** eagerly desirous. **2.** lustful; sensual. [t. L: s. *concupiscens,* ppr.]

concur (kən kû′), *v.i.,* **-curred, -curring.** **1.** to accord in opinion; agree. **2.** to cooperate; combine; be associated. **3.** to coincide. **4.** to come together, as lines; unite. **5.** *Obs.* to run together. [late ME, t. L: m. s. *concurrere* run together] **—Syn. 1.** See **consent.**

concurrence (kən kŭ′rəns), *n.* **1.** the act of concurring. **2.** accordance in opinion; agreement. **3.** cooperation, as of agents or causes. **4.** simultaneous occurrence; coincidence. **5.** *Geom.* a point which is in three or more lines simultaneously. **6.** competition. Also, **concur′rency** for 1–4.

concurrent (kən kŭ′rənt), *adj.* **1.** occurring or existing together or side by side. **2.** acting in conjunction; cooperating. **3.** having equal authority or jurisdiction. **4.** accordant or agreeing. **5.** tending to or intersecting in the same point: *four concurrent lines.* **—***n.* **6.** something joint or contributory. **7.** *Rare.* a rival or competitor. **—concur′rently,** *adv.*

concuss (kən kŭs′), *v.t.* **1.** to injure the brain by concussion; to knock out. **2.** to strike or shake violently. **3.** to overawe; threaten.

concussion (kən kŭsh′ən), *n.* **1.** the act of shaking or shocking, as by a blow. **2.** shock occasioned by a blow or collision. **3.** *Pathol.* jarring of the brain, spinal cord, etc., from a blow, fall, etc. [t. L: s. *concussio* shock] **—concussive** (kən kŭs′ĭv), *adj.*

concyclic (kŏn sī′klĭk), *adj.* *Geom.* lying on the circumference of the same circle. **—concyclically** (kŏn-sī′klĭ kə lĭ, -klĭ klĭ), *adv.*

condé (*Fr.* kôɴ dĕ′), *n.* a creamed dessert made with rice, fruit and jam.

Condé (*Fr.* kôɴ dĕ′), *n.* **Louis II de Bourbon** (*Fr.* lwē, də bo͝or bôɴ′), **Prince de** (*'the Great Condé'*), 1621–86, French general.

condemn (kən dĕm′), *v.t.* **1.** to pronounce adverse judgement on; express strong disapproval of; censure. **2.** to afford occasion for convicting: *his very looks condemn him.* **3.** to pronounce to be guilty; sentence to punishment; doom. **4.** to judge or pronounce to be unfit for use or service: *the old ship was condemned.* **5.** to declare incurable. **6.** to compel or force into a certain state or action: *the injury to his leg condemned him to a life of inactivity.* **7.** *U.S. Law.* to acquire ownership of for a public purpose, under the right of eminent domain. [ME *condem(p)ne,* t. OF: m. *condem(p)ner,* g. L *condem(p)nāre*] **—condemnable** (kən dĕm′ə bl), *adj.* **—condemner** (kən dĕm′ə), *n.* **—condemn′ingly,** *adv.* **—Syn. 1.** See **blame.**

condemnation (kŏn′dĕm nā′shən), *n.* **1.** the act of condemning. **2.** strong censure; disapprobation; reproof. **3.** the state of being condemned. **4.** the cause or reason for condemning. **5.** *U.S.* the seizure (of property) for public use.

condemnatory (kən dĕm′nə tə rĭ, -trĭ), *adj.* serving to condemn.

condemned cell, a cell for prisoners sentenced to death.

condensable (kən dĕn′sə bl), *adj.* capable of being condensed. **—conden′sabil′ity,** *n.*

condensate (kən dĕn′sāt), *n.* something formed by condensation.

condensation (kŏn′dĕn sā′shən), *n.* **1.** the act of condensing. **2.** condensed state or form. **3.** a condensed mass. **4.** *Chem.* a reaction between two or more like or unlike organic molecules, leading to the formation of a larger molecule and the splitting out of a simple molecule such as water or alcohol. **5.** the act of reducing a gas or vapour to a liquid or solid form. **6.** *Psychoanal.* the representation of two or more ideas, memories, feelings, or impulses by one word or image, as in wit, slips, allegories, and dreams.

condensation pump, a diffusion pump.

condense (kən dĕns′), *v.*, **-densed, -densing.** —*v.t.* **1.** to make more dense or compact; reduce the volume or compass of. **2.** to reduce to another and denser form, as a gas or vapour to a liquid or solid state. **3.** to compress into fewer words; abridge. **4.** *Optics.* to concentrate light; focus a ray on to a smaller space. —*v.i.* **5.** to become liquid or solid, as a gas or vapour. [late ME, t. L: m. s. *condensāre* make thick] —**Syn. 1.** compress, concentrate. See **contract.** —**Ant. 1, 3.** expand.

condensed milk, milk reduced by evaporation to a thick consistency with sugar added.

condensed type, *Print.* a kind of type narrow in proportion to its height.

condenser (kən dĕn′sə), *n.* **1.** one who or that which condenses. **2.** an apparatus for condensing. **3.** *Chem.* any device for reducing gases or vapours to liquid or solid form. **4.** *Optics.* a lens or combination of lenses, used to gather and concentrate the rays of light and direct them upon the object. **5.** *Elect.* a capacitor.

condescend (kŏn′dĭ sĕnd′), *v.i.* **1.** to waive ceremony voluntarily and assume equality with an inferior. **2.** to stoop or deign (to do something). **3.** to behave as if one is conscious of descending from a superior position, rank, or dignity. **4.** *Obs.* to yield. **5.** *Obs.* to assent. [ME *condescende(n)*, t. F: m. *condescendre*, t. LL: m. *condēscendere* stoop] —**con′descend′ence,** *n.*

condescending (kŏn′dĭ sĕn′dĭng), *adj.* showing or implying a gracious descent from dignity; patronizing. —**con′descend′ingly,** *adv.*

condescension (kŏn′dĭ sĕn′shən), *n.* the act of condescending; gracious or patronizing complaisance.

condign (kən dīn′), *adj.* (chiefly of punishment, etc.) well-deserved; fitting; adequate. [ME *condigne*, t. F, t. L: m. *condignus* wholly worthy] —**condign′ly,** *adv.*

Condillac (*Fr.* kôɴ dē yȧk′), *n.* **Étienne Bonnot de** (*Fr.* ĕ tyĕn bŏ nô′ də), 1715–80, French philosopher.

condiment (kŏn′dĭ mənt), *n.* something used to give a special or additional flavour to food, as a sauce or seasoning. [t. L: s. *condīmentum* spice] —**condimental** (kŏn′dĭ mĕn′tl), *adj.*

condition (kən dĭsh′ən), *n.* **1.** particular mode of being of a person or thing; situation with respect to circumstances; existing state or case. **2.** state of health. **3.** fit or requisite state. **4.** social position. **5.** a restricting, limiting, or modifying circumstance. **6.** a circumstance indispensable to some result; a prerequisite; that on which something else is contingent. **7.** something demanded as an essential part of an agreement. **8.** *Law.* **a.** a stipulation in a contract making some liability contingent on the happening of a future uncertain event. **b.** the event. **9.** *Gram.* protasis. **10.** *Logic.* antecedent. **11. on condition that,** if; provided that. —*v.t.* **12.** to put in fit or proper state. **13.** to form or be a condition of; determine, limit, or restrict as a condition. **14.** to subject to something as a condition; make conditional (fol. by *on* or *upon*). **15.** to subject to particular conditions or circumstances. **16.** to test (a commodity) to ascertain its condition. **17.** to make it a condition; stipulate. **18.** *Psychol.* to cause a conditioned response in. —*v.i.* **19.** to make conditions. [ME *condicion*, t. L: s. *condicio* (erroneously *conditio*) agreement, stipulation, circumstances] —**condi′tioner,** *n.* —**Syn. 1.** See **state. 6.** prerequisite. **7.** requirement, proviso.

conditional (kən dĭsh′ə nəl), *adj.* **1.** imposing, containing, or depending on a condition or conditions; not absolute; made or granted on certain terms: *a conditional agreement, sale, etc.* **2.** *Gram.* (of a sentence, clause, or mood) involving or expressing a condition. For example: *If the suit is expensive* (conditional clause), *don't buy it.* **3.** *Logic.* **a.** (of a proposition) asserting that one state of affairs is or will be realized if some other state of affairs is realized, as in *if Smith is 21 years old, he is eligible to vote.* **b.** (of a syllogism) containing a conditional proposition as a premise. —*n.* **4.** (in certain languages) a mood, tense, or other category used in expressing conditions, often corresponding to an English verb preceded by *if: Spanish 'comería' (he would eat) is in the conditional.* —**conditionality** (kən dĭsh′ə năl′ĭ tĭ), *n.* —**condi′tionally,** *adv.*

conditional probability, *Statistics.* the probability of the occurrence of an event under the condition that only a portion of the cases or alternatives are to be considered.

conditioned (kən dĭsh′ənd), *adj.* existing under or subject to conditions. —**Ant.** free, absolute.

conditioned reflex, *Psychol.* an acquired response elicited by a stimulus, object, or situation other than that to which it is the natural or normal response. Also, **conditioned response.**

condole (kən dōl′), *v.*, **-doled, -doling.** —*v.i.* **1.** to express sympathy with one in affliction; grieve (fol. by *with*). —*v.t.* **2.** *Obs.* to grieve with. [t. LL: m. s. *condolēre* suffer greatly] —**condolatory** (kən dō′lə tə rĭ, -trĭ), *adj.* —**condol′er,** *n.* —**condol′ingly,** *adv.*

condolence (kən dō′ləns), *n.* expression of sympathy with a person in affliction. Also, **condole′ment.**

con dolore (kŏn′ dŏ lô′rĭ; *It.* kôn dô lô′rĕ), *Music.* sorrowfully. [It.]

condom (kŏn′dəm), *n.* a contraceptive device worn over the penis during intercourse; sheath (def. 6). [named after *Condom*, 18th-century English physician said to have devised it]

condominium (kŏn′də mĭn′ĭ əm), *n.* **1.** joint or concurrent dominion. **2.** *Internat. Law.* joint sovereignty over a territory by several foreign states. [t. NL, f. L: *con-* CON- + *dominium* lordship]

condonation (kŏn′dō nā′shən), *n.* the act of condoning.

condone (kən dōn′), *v.t.*, **-doned, -doning. 1.** to pardon or overlook (an offence). **2.** to cause the condonation of. **3.** to atone for; make up for. **4.** *Law.* to forgive, or act so as to imply forgiveness of (a violation of the marriage vow). [t. L: m. s. *condōnāre* give up] —**condon′er,** *n.*

condor (kŏn′dô), *n.* a large vulture of the New World, as the **Andean condor** (*Sarcorhamphus gryphus*) and **California condor** (*Gymnogyps californianus*). [t. Sp., t. Quechua: m. *cuntur*]

Andean condor, *Sarcorhamphus gryphus* (Total length 3½ ft, wingspan 9 ft)

Condorcet (*Fr.* kôɴ dŏr sĕ′), *n.* **Marie Jean Antoine Nicolas Caritat** (*Fr.* mȧ rē zhäɴ äɴ twȧn nē kō lȧ kȧ rē tȧ′), **Marquis de,** 1743–94, French mathematician and philosopher.

condottiere (kŏn′dŏ tyĕə′rĭ), *n.*, *pl.* **-ri** (-rē). (in Europe, esp. in the 14th and 15th centuries) a professional military commander or leader of mercenaries, in the service of states at war. [It.: leader, der. *condotto* mercenary (soldier), g. L *conductus*, pp., led together, hired]

conduce (kən dyōō s′), *v.i.*, **-duced, -ducing.** to lead or contribute to a result (fol. by *to*). [late ME, t. L: m. s. *condūcere* lead together, hire] —**Ant.** hinder.

conducive (kən dyōō′sĭv), *adj.* conducting; contributive; helpful (fol. by *to*). —**condu′civeness,** *n.*

conduct (*n.* kŏn′dŭkt; *v.* kən dŭkt′), *n.* **1.** personal behaviour; way of acting; deportment: *good conduct.* **2.** direction or management; execution: *the conduct of a business.* **3.** the act of conducting; guidance; escort. **4.** *Obs.* a guide; an escort. —*v.t.* **5.** to behave (oneself). **6.** to direct in action or course; manage; carry on: *to conduct a campaign.* **7.** to direct as leader: *to conduct an orchestra.* **8.** to lead or guide; escort. **9.** to serve as a channel or medium for (heat, electricity, sound, etc.). —*v.i.* **10.** to lead. **11.** to act as conductor. [t. LL: s. *conductus*, n., escort, der. L *condūcere* bring together; r. ME *conduyt*, t. OF: m. *conduit*] —**conduct′ible,** *adj.* —**conduct′ibil′ity,** *n.* —**Syn. 1.** See **behaviour. 6.** supervise, regulate. **8.** See **guide.**

conductance (kən dŭk′təns), *n.* *Elect.* the conducting power of a conductor; the reciprocal of *resistance* for direct current; the resistance divided by the square of *impedance* for alternating currents.

conduction (kən dŭk′shən), *n.* **1.** a conducting, as of water through a pipe. **2.** *Physics.* **a.** transmission through a conductor. **b.** conductivity. **3.** *Physiol.* the carrying of an impulse by a nerve or other tissue.

conductive (kən dŭk′tĭv), *adj.* having the property of conducting.

conductivity (kŏn′dŭk tĭv′ĭ tĭ), *n.*, *pl.* **-ties. 1.** *Physics.* the property or power of conducting heat, electricity, or sound. **2.** thermal conductivity. **3.** *Elect.* the conductance between opposite faces of a one centimetre cube of a given material (the reciprocal of *resistivity*).

conductor (kən dŭk′tə), *n.* **1.** one who conducts; a leader, guide, director, or manager. **2.** the person in charge of a public transport vehicle, who collects fares, issues tickets, etc. **3.** *U.S.* a railway guard. **4.** the director of an orchestra or chorus, who communicates to the performers by motions of a baton, etc., his interpretation of the music. **5.** that which conducts. **6.** a substance, body, or device that readily conducts heat, electricity, sound, etc. **7.** a lightning conductor. —**conduc′torship′,** *n.* —**conductress** (kən dŭk′trĭs), *n. fem.*

conductor rail, *Railways.* an exposed rail, usually laid alongside the running rails, for conducting the current to an electric train.

conduit (kŏn′dĭt, kŏn′dyo͞o ĭt), *n.* **1.** a pipe, tube, or the like, for conveying water or other fluid. **2.** some similar natural passage. **3.** *Elect.* a pipe that encases electrical wires or cables to protect them from damage. **4.** (formerly on tramways) an underground trough containing positive and negative conductor rails, from which current is collected by a plough (attached to the underside of the tram) which passes through a slot in the road surface. **5.** *Archaic.* a fountain. [ME *condit*, t. OF: m. *conduit*, g. LL *conductus*. See CONDUCT]

conduplicate (kŏn dyo͞o′plĭ kĭt), *adj. Bot.* (of a leaf in the bud) folded lengthways with the upper face of the blade within.

condyle (kŏn′dĭl), *n. Anat.* a rounded protuberance on a bone, serving to form an articulation with another bone. [t. F, t. L: m. s. *condylus*, t. Gk: m. *kóndylos* knuckle, bony knob] —**con′dylar,** *adj.*

condyloid (kŏn′dĭ loid′), *adj.* of or like a condyle.

condyloma (kŏn′dĭ lō′mə), *n., pl.* **-mata** (-mə tə). *Pathol.* a wartlike excrescence on the skin, usually in the region of the anus or genitals. [t. L, t. Gk: m. *kondýlōma*, der. *kóndylos* CONDYLE] —**condylomatous** (kŏn′dĭ lŏm′ə təs, -lō′mə-), *adj.*

Condy's fluid (kŏn′dĭz), a solution of sodium or calcium permanganate; used as a disinfectant. [named after Henry Bollman *Condy*, 19th-century English physician]

cone (kōn), *n., v.,* **coned, coning.** —*n.* **1.** *Geom.* a solid whose surface is generated by the straight lines joining a fixed point to the points of a plane curve whose plane does not contain the fixed point. When the plane curve is a circle and the fixed point lies on the perpendicular to the plane of the circle through its centre, the cone is a **right circular cone.** When the plane curve is a circle and the fixed point is not so situated, the cone is an **oblique circular cone. 2.** *Mach.* a mechanical part having the shape of a cone or conoid. **3.** *Bot.* **a.** the more or less conical multiple fruit of the pine, fir, etc., consisting of imbricated or valvate scales bearing naked ovules or seeds; a strobilus. **b.** a similar fruit, as in cycads, club mosses, etc. **4.** *Zool.* a light-sensitive nerve-cell present in the retina of most invertebrates. **5.** anything cone-shaped. **6.** the conical peak built up with the ejected material from a volcano. **7.** a cone-shaped vessel hoisted as a warning of bad weather. **8.** a conical container of wafer for a portion of ice-cream; cornet. —*v.t.* **9.** to shape like a cone or the segment of a cone. [t. L: m. s. *cōnus*, t. Gk: m. *kônos*]

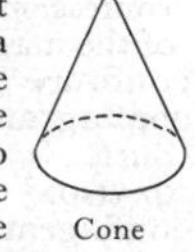
Cone

coneflower (kōn′flou′ə), *n.* **1.** a rudbeckia. **2.** any of various allied plants.

cone shell, any one of the chiefly tropical marine gastropods of the genus *Conus*, which has a smooth conical shell.

coney (kō′nĭ), *n., pl.* **-neys.** cony.

Coney Island (kō′nĭ), an island off New York: seaside resort and amusement centre. 5 mi. long.

conf., conference.

confab (kŏn′făb), *n., v.,* **-fabbed, -fabbing.** *Colloq.* —*n.* **1.** a confabulation. —*v.i.* **2.** to confabulate.

confabulate (kən făb′yo͞o lāt′), *v.i.,* **-lated, -lating.** to talk together; converse. [t. L: m. s. *confābulātus*, pp.] —**confab′ula′tion,** *n.*

confarreation (kŏn fă′rĭ ā′shən), *n.* (among the ancient Romans) the highest form of marriage, marked by the offering of a cake made of spelt. [t. L: s. *confarreātio*]

confect (*v.* kən fĕkt′, *n.* kŏn′fĕkt), *v.t.* **1.** *Obs.* to make up, compound, or prepare from ingredients or materials. **2.** *Obs.* to make into a preserve or confection. **3.** to construct, form, or make. —*n.* **4.** a preserved, crystallized, or other sweet confection; a comfit. [t. L: s. *confectus*, pp., put together]

confection (kən fĕk′shən), *n.* **1.** the process of compounding, preparing, or making. **2.** a sweet preparation (liquid or dry) of fruit or the like, as a preserve or sweetmeat. **3.** a sweet or bonbon. **4.** a medicinal preparation, now one made with the aid of sugar, honey, or syrup. **5.** a ready-made garment, esp. a woman's frilly garment. —*v.t.* **6.** to prepare as a confection. [ME, t. L: s. *confectio* a making ready]

confectionary (kən fĕk′shə nə rĭ), *n., pl.* **-aries,** *adj.* —*n.* **1.** a place where confections are kept or made. **2.** a confection or sweet. **3.** *Obs.* a confectioner. —*adj.* **4.** pertaining to or of the nature of confections or their making.

confectioner (kən fĕk′shə nə), *n.* one who makes or sells sweets, and sometimes ice-cream, cakes, etc.

confectioners' sugar, *U.S.* icing sugar.

confectionery (kən fĕk′shə nə rĭ), *n., pl.* **-eries. 1.** confections or sweets collectively. **2.** the work or business of a confectioner. **3.** a confectioner's shop.

confederacy (kən fĕd′ə rə sĭ, -fĕd′rə sĭ), *n., pl.* **-cies. 1.** an alliance of persons, parties, or states for some common purpose. **2.** a group of persons, parties, etc., united by such an alliance. **3.** a combination for unlawful purposes; a conspiracy. **4. the Confederacy,** the Confederate States of America.

confederate (*adj., n.* kən fĕd′ə rĭt, -fĕd′rĭt; *v.* kən fĕd′ə rāt′), *adj., n., v.,* **-rated, -rating.** —*adj.* **1.** united in a league or alliance, or a conspiracy. **2.** (*cap.*) denoting or pertaining to the Confederate States of America: *the Confederate army.* —*n.* **3.** one united with others in a confederacy; an ally. **4.** an accomplice. **5.** (*cap.*) an adherent of the Confederate States of America. —*v.t., v.i.* **6.** to unite in a league or alliance, or a conspiracy. [ME, t. LL: m. s. *confoederātus*, pp., united in a league]

Confederate States of America, the name assumed by the eleven Southern states which seceded from the American Union in 1860–61.

confederation (kən fĕd′ə rā′shən), *n.* **1.** the act of confederating. **2.** the state of being confederated. **3.** a league or alliance. **4.** a body of confederates, esp. of states more or less permanently united for common purposes. **5. the Confederation,** the union of the American colonies from 1781 to 1789 under the Articles of Confederation. —**Syn. 3.** See **alliance.**

Confederation of British Industry, an association of manufacturers whose aim is to encourage and protect British industry, to formulate industrial policy at home and overseas, and to act in an advisory capacity to member firms. *Abbrev.:* C.B.I.

confederative (kən fĕd′ə rə tĭv), *adj.* pertaining to a confederation.

confer (kən fû′), *v.t.,* **-ferred, -ferring.** —*v.t.* **1.** to bestow as a gift, favour, honour, etc. (fol. by *on* or *upon*). **2.** *Obs.* to compare. —*v.i.* **3.** consult together; compare opinions; carry on a discussion or deliberation. [t. L: s. *conferre* bring together] —**confer′ment,** *n.* —**confer′rable,** *adj.* —**confer′rer,** *n.* —**Syn. 1.** See **give. 3.** See **consult.**

conferee (kŏn′fû rē′), *n.* **1.** one on whom something is conferred. **2.** *U.S.* one who is conferred with or takes part in a conference. Also, **conferree.**

conference (kŏn′fə rəns), *n.* **1.** a meeting for consultation or discussion. **2.** the act of conferring or consulting together; consultation, esp. on an important or serious matter. **3.** *Eccles.* **a.** an official assembly of clergy, or of clergy and laymen, customary in many Christian denominations. **b.** a group of churches the representatives of which regularly meet in such an assembly. **4.** an act of conferring; a bestowal. **5.** *U.S. Sport.* an organization of teams. **6.** (*cap.*) a high-yielding variety of sweet, juicy pear. —**conferential** (kŏn′fə rĕn′shəl), *adj.* —**Syn. 1.** See **convention.**

conferva (kŏn fû′və), *n., pl.* **-vae** (-vē). *Obs.* any simple filamentous green alga. [t. L: kind of water plant] —**confervoid** (kŏn fû′void), *adj., n.*

confess (kən fĕs′), *v.t.* **1.** to acknowledge or avow: *to confess a secret, fault, crime, debt, etc.* **2.** to own or admit; admit the truth or validity of: *I must confess that I haven't read it.* **3.** to acknowledge one's belief in; declare adherence to. **4.** to declare (one's sins) or declare the sins of (oneself), esp. to a priest, for the obtaining of absolution. **5.** (of a priest) to hear the confession of. **6.** *Archaic.* to reveal by circumstances. —*v.i.* **7.** to make confession; plead guilty; own (fol. by *to*). **8.** to make confession of sins, esp. to a priest. [ME *confesse(n)*, t. LL: m. *confessāre*, der. L *confessus*, pp.] —**Syn. 1.** See **acknowledge.** —**Ant. 1.** conceal. **2.** deny.

confessedly (kən fĕs′ĭd lĭ), *adv.* by confession or acknowledgement; admittedly.

confession (kən fĕsh′ən), *n.* **1.** acknowledgement or avowal; admission or concession: *a confession of guilt.* **2.** acknowledgement of sin or sinfulness. **3.** a disclosing of sins to a priest to obtain forgiveness. **4.** that which is confessed. **5.** Also, **confession of faith.** a formal profession of belief and acceptance of church doctrines, as before being admitted to church membership. **6.** the tomb of a martyr or confessor, or the altar or shrine connected with it. [ME, t. L: s. *confessio*]

confessional (kən fĕsh′ə nəl), *adj.* **1.** of, or of the nature of, confession. —*n.* **2.** the place set apart for the hearing of confessions by a priest. **3.** the practice or institution of confession.

confessionary (kən fĕsh′ə nə rĭ), *adj.* of or pertaining to confession, esp. auricular confession of sins.

confessor (kən fĕs′ə), *n.* **1.** Also, **confesser.** one who confesses. **2.** a priest authorized to hear confessions. **3.** one who confesses and adheres to the Christian religion, esp. in spite of persecution and torture. **4. the Confessor,** Edward the Confessor.

confetti (kən fĕt′ĭ; *It.* kōn fĕt′tē), *n.pl., sing.* **-fetto** (*It.* -fĕt′tō). **1.** small bits of coloured paper, thrown at carnivals, weddings, etc. **2.** confections; bonbons. [t. It., pl. of *confetto* comfit]

confidant (kŏn′fĭ dănt′, kŏn′fĭ dănt′), *n.* one to whom secrets are confided or with whom intimate problems are discussed. [t. F, t. It.: m. *confidente*, t. L: m. s. *confidens*, ppr., trusting] —**con′fidante′**, *n. fem.*

confide (kən fīd′), *v.*, **-fided, -fiding.** —*v.i.* **1.** to show trust by imparting secrets (fol. by *in*). **2.** to have full trust: *confiding in that parting promise.* —*v.t.* **3.** to tell in assurance of secrecy. **4.** to entrust; commit to the charge, knowledge, or good faith of another. [late ME, t. L: m. s. *confidere* trust altogether] —**confid′er**, *n.*

confidence (kŏn′fĭ dəns), *n.* **1.** full trust; belief in the trustworthiness or reliability of a person or thing. **2.** *Politics.* the wish to retain the incumbent government in office, as shown by a vote on a particular issue: *the future of the government rests on a vote of confidence.* **3.** self-reliance, assurance, or boldness. **4.** presumption. **5.** certitude or assured expectation. **6.** a confidential communication; a secret. **7.** *Archaic.* a ground of trust. **8. in confidence,** as a secret or private matter, not to be divulged to others: *I told him in confidence.*

—**Syn.** **1.** See **trust.** **3.** CONFIDENCE, ASSURANCE both imply a faith in oneself. CONFIDENCE may imply trust in oneself or arrogant self-conceit. ASSURANCE implies even more sureness of oneself; this may be shown as undisturbed calm or as offensive boastfulness or headstrong conduct.

confidence limits, *Statistics.* a pair of numbers used to estimate a characteristic of a population from a sample, which are such that it can be stated with a specified probability that the pair of numbers calculated from a sample will include the value of the population characteristic between them.

confidence man, one who swindles by a confidence trick.

confidence trick, a swindle in which the victim's confidence is gained and he is then induced to part with money or property. Also, *U.S.*, **confidence game.** —**confidence trickster.**

confident (kŏn′fĭ dənt), *adj.* **1.** having strong belief or full assurance; sure: *confident of victory.* **2.** sure of oneself; bold: *a confident bearing.* **3.** overbold. **4.** *Obs.* trustful or confiding. —*n.* **5.** a confidant. —**con′fidently,** *adv.* —**Syn.** **1.** certain, positive. See **sure.**

confidential (kŏn′fĭ dĕn′shəl), *adj.* **1.** spoken or written in confidence; secret: *a confidential document.* **2.** betokening confidence or intimacy; imparting private matters: *a confidential tone.* **3.** enjoying another's confidence; entrusted with secrets or private affairs: *a confidential secretary.* —**confidentiality** (kŏn′fĭ dĕn′shĭ ăl′ĭ tĭ), **con′fiden′tialness,** *n.* —**con′fiden′tially,** *adv.* —**Syn.** **3.** See **familiar.**

confiding (kən fī′dĭng), *adj.* trustful; credulous or unsuspicious. —**confid′ingly,** *adv.* —**confid′ingness,** *n.*

configuration (kən fĭg′yŏŏ rā′shən), *n.* **1.** the relative disposition of the parts or elements of a thing. **2.** external form, as resulting from this; conformation. **3.** *Astron.* the relative position or aspect of heavenly bodies. **4.** *Physics, Chem.* the relative position in space of the atoms in a molecule. **5.** *Geog.* the horizontal outline and elevation of part of the earth's surface. [t. LL: s. *configūrātio*, der. L *configūrāre* shape after some pattern] —**config′ura′tional, configurative** (kən fĭg′yŏŏ rə tĭv), *adj.*

confine (kən fīn′ *for 1–3, 5, 6b*; kŏn′fīn *for 4, 6a*), *v.*, **-fined, -fining,** *n.* —*v.t.* **1.** to enclose within bounds; limit or restrict. **2.** to shut or keep in; imprison. **3.** to be in childbed, or be delivered of a child (used in the passive). —*n.* **4.** (*usually pl.*) a boundary or bound; a border or frontier. **5.** *Poetic.* confinement. **6.** *Obs.* **a.** (*usually pl.*) a region. **b.** a place of confinement. [t. F: m. s. *confiner*, t. It.: m. *confinare*, der. *confino* bordering, g. L *confīnis*] —**confin′er,** *n.* —**Syn.** **1.** circumscribe. —**Ant.** **1, 2.** free.

confinement (kən fīn′mənt), *n.* **1.** the act of confining. **2.** the state of being confined; imprisonment. **3.** the lying-in of a woman in childbirth. [t. F, der. *confiner* CONFINE, v.]

confirm (kən fûm′), *v.t.* **1.** to make certain or sure; corroborate; verify: *this confirmed my suspicions.* **2.** to make valid or binding by some formal or legal act; sanction; ratify: *to confirm an agreement, appointment, etc.* **3.** to make firm or more firm; add strength to: settle or establish firmly: *the news confirmed my resolution.* **4.** to strengthen (a person) in habit, resolution, opinion, etc. **5.** *Eccles.* to administer the rite of confirmation to. [t. L: s. *confirmāre* make firm; r. ME *conferme(n)*, t. OF: m. *confermer*] —**confirm′able,** *adj.* —**confirm′er;** *Law,* **confirmor** (kŏn′fû mô′, kən fû′mə), *n.* —**Syn.** **1.** substantiate, authenticate. —**Ant.** **1.** disprove. **2.** invalidate. **3.** shake.

confirmation (kŏn′fə mā′shən), *n.* **1.** the act of confirming. **2.** that which confirms, as a corroborative statement. **3.** *Eccles.* a rite administered to baptized persons, in some Churches as a sacrament for confirming and strengthening the recipient in the Christian faith, in others as a rite without sacramental character by which the recipient is admitted to full communion with the Church.

confirmatory (kən fû′mə tə rĭ, -trĭ), *adj.* serving to confirm; corroborative. Also, **confirm′ative.**

confirmed (kən fûmd′), *adj.* **1.** made firm; settled; ratified. **2.** made certain as regards truth or accuracy; corroborated. **3.** firmly established in a habit or condition; inveterate: *a confirmed drunkard.* **4.** made more resolute or more determined; strengthened. **5.** (of a disease) chronic.

confiscable (kən fĭs′kə bl), *adj.* liable to be confiscated.

confiscate (kŏn′fĭs kāt′), *v.*, **-cated, -cating,** *adj.* —*v.t.* **1.** to seize as forfeited to the public treasury; appropriate, by way of penalty, to public use. **2.** to seize as if by authority; appropriate summarily. —*adj.* **3.** confiscated. [t. L: m. s. *confiscātus*, pp., put away in a chest] —**con′fisca′tion,** *n.* —**con′fisca′tor,** *n.*

confiscatory (kən fĭs′kə tə rĭ, -trĭ), *adj.* characterized by or effecting confiscation.

confiteor (kŏn fĭt′ĭ ô′), *n.* *Rom. Cath. Ch.* a form of prayer beginning with 'Confiteor', in which a general confession of sinfulness is made, used at the beginning of the mass and on other occasions. [t. L: I confess]

confiture (kŏn′fĭ tyŏŏə′), *n.* *Obs.* comfiture.

conflagrate (kŏn′flə grāt′), *v.t., v.i.*, **-grated, -grating.** burn. [t. L: m. *conflagrātus*, pp., burnt. See CONFLAGRATION] —**conflagrant** (kən flā′grənt), *adj.*

conflagration (kŏn′flə grā′shən), *n.* a large and destructive fire. [t. L: s. *conflagrātio*] —**Syn.** See **flame.**

conflation (kən flā′shən), *n.* *Bibliog.* **1.** the combination of two variant texts into a new one. **2.** the result. [t. LL: s. *conflātio*, der. L *conflāre* blow together]

conflict (*v.* kən flĭkt′; *n.* kŏn′flĭkt), *v.i.* **1.** to come into collision; clash, or be in opposition or at variance; disagree. **2.** to contend; do battle. —*n.* **3.** a battle or struggle, esp. a prolonged struggle; strife. **4.** controversy; a quarrel: *conflicts between Church and state.* **5.** discord of action, feeling, or effect; antagonism, as of interests or principles: *a conflict of ideas.* **6.** a striking together; collision. [t. L: s. *conflictus*, pp., struck together] —**conflic′tion,** *n.* —**conflic′tive,** *adj.* —**Syn.** **3.** See **fight.** **5.** contention, opposition, variance. —**Ant.** **4.** accord.

confluence (kŏn′flŏŏ əns), *n.* **1.** a flowing together of two or more streams. **2.** the place of junction. **3.** the body of water so formed. **4.** a coming together of people or things. **5.** a throng; an assemblage. Also, **conflux** (kŏn′flŭks).

confluent (kŏn′flŏŏ ənt), *adj.* **1.** flowing or running together; blending into one. **2.** *Pathol.* **a.** running together: *confluent efflorescences.* **b.** characterized by confluent efflorescences: *confluent smallpox.* —*n.* **3.** one of two or more confluent streams. **4.** a tributary stream. [t. L: s. *confluens*, ppr., flowing together]

confocal (kŏn fō′kl), *adj.* *Maths.* having the same focus or foci.

conform (kən fôm′), *v.i.* **1.** to act in accord or harmony; comply (fol. by *to*). **2.** to become similar in form or character. **3.** to comply with the usages of the Established Church of England. —*v.t.* **4.** to make similar in form or character. **5.** to bring into correspondence or harmony. [ME *conforme(n)*, t. F: m. *conformer*, t. L: m. *conformāre* fashion] —**conform′er.** *n.* —**Syn.** **5.** adapt, adjust, accommodate. —**Ant.** **1, 3.** dissent. **2.** differ.

conformable (kən fô′mə bl), *adj.* **1.** corresponding in form or character; similar. **2.** exhibiting agreement or harmony (usually fol. by *to*). **3.** compliant, acquiescent, or submissive. **4.** *Geol.* (of strata or beds) having the same dip and strike as a result of successive depositions uninterrupted by crustal movement. —**conform′abil′ity, conform′ableness,** *n.* —**conform′ably,** *adv.*

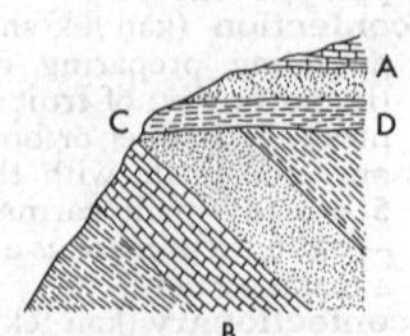

Conformable and unconformable strata
A and B, two sets of unconformable strata; CD, line of junction of A and B

conformance (kən fô′məns), *n.* the act of conforming; conformity.

conformation (kŏn′fô mā′shən), *n.* **1.** the manner of formation; structure; form. **2.** symmetrical disposition or arrangement of parts. **3.** the act of conforming; adaptation; adjustment. **4.** the state of being conformed.

conformist (kən fô′mĭst), *n.* **1.** one who conforms to a usage or practice. 2. one who conforms to the usages of the Established Church of England.

conformity (kən fô′mĭ tĭ), *n.*, *pl.* **-ties.** 1. correspondence in form or character; agreement, congruity, or accordance. 2. compliance or acquiescence. 3. compliance with the usages of the Church of England.

confound (kən found′; *for 8 usually* kŏn′found′), *v.t.* 1. to mingle so that the elements cannot be distinguished or separated. 2. to treat or regard erroneously as identical; mix or associate by mistake. 3. to throw into confusion or disorder: *confusion worse confounded.* 4. to perplex, as with sudden disturbance or surprise. 5. to refute in argument; contradict. 6. *Archaic.* to put to shame; abash. 7. *Archaic.* to defeat or overthrow; bring to ruin or naught. 8. (in mild imprecations) to damn: *confound it!* 9. *Obs.* to spend uselessly, or waste. [ME *confounde(n)*, t. OF: m. *confondre*, g. L *confundere* pour together, mix, confuse] —**confound′er,** *n.*

confounded (kən foun′dĭd), *adj.* 1. (used euphemistically) damned: *a confounded lie.* 2. discomfited; astonished. 3. *Colloq.* execrable; odious. —**confound′edly,** *adv.*

confraternity (kŏn′frə tû′nĭ tĭ), *n.*, *pl.* **-ties.** 1. a lay brotherhood devoted to some particular religious or charitable service. 2. a society or body of men united for some purpose or in some profession. [late ME *confraternite*, t. ML: m. s. *confrāternitas* brotherhood, der. *confrāter*. See CONFRÈRE]

confrère (kŏn′frĕə; *Fr.* kôɴ frĕr′), *n.* a fellow member of a profession, association, etc.; a colleague. [ME, t. F, trans. of ML *confrāter* colleague]

confront (kən frŭnt′), *v.t.* 1. to stand or come in front of; stand or meet facing; stand in the way of. 2. to face in hostility or defiance; oppose. 3. to set face to face. 4. to bring together for examination or comparison. [t. F: s. *confronter*, t. ML: m. s. *confrontārī*, f. L: *con-* CON- + s. *frons* forehead + *-ārī*, inf. ending] —**confrontation** (kŏn′frŭn tā′shən), **confront′ment,** *n.* —**confront′er,** *n.*

Confucius (kən fyo͞o′shyəs), *n.* (Chinese, *Kung-fu-tse*), 551–479 B.C., Chinese philosopher and teacher of principles of conduct. His highest standards of conduct were treating others as you wish to be treated, loyalty, intelligence, and the fullest development of the individual in the five chief relationships of life: ruler and subject, father and son, elder and younger brother, husband and wife, friend and friend. —**Confu′cian,** *adj.*, *n.* —**Confu′cianism,** *n.* —**Confu′cianist,** *n.*, *adj.*

confuse (kən fyo͞oz′), *v.t.*, **-fused, -fusing.** 1. to combine without order or clearness; jumble; render indistinct. 2. to throw into disorder. 3. to fail to distinguish between; associate by mistake; confound: *to confuse dates.* 4. to perplex or bewilder. 5. to disconcert or abash. 6. *Obs.* to bring to ruin or naught. [back-formation from *confused*, f. ME *confus* (t. F, t. L: s. *confūsus*, pp., confounded) + -ED²] —**confusedly** (kən fyo͞o′zĭd lĭ, -fyo͞ozd′lĭ), *adv.* —**confus′edness,** *n.* —**confus′ingly,** *adv.*

—**Syn.** 4. CONFUSE, DISCONCERT, EMBARRASS imply temporary interference with the clear working of the mind. To CONFUSE is to produce a general bewilderment: *to confuse by giving complicated directions.* To DISCONCERT is quickly or violently to disturb the mind by irritation, perplexities, etc., making it difficult to collect thoughts together: *to disconcert by asking irrelevant questions.* To EMBARRASS is to cause to be ill at ease or uncomfortable, so that judgement and presence of mind are lost: *to embarrass by treating with unexpected rudeness.* —**Ant.** 5. compose.

confusion (kən fyo͞o′zhən), *n.* 1. the state of being confused. 2. disorder. 3. lack of clearness or distinctness. 4. embarrassment or abashment. 5. perplexity; bewilderment. 6. *Psychol.* a disturbed mental state; a clouding of consciousness; disorientation. 7. *Archaic.* the act of confusing. 8. *Obs.* overthrow; defeat. [ME, t. L: s. *confūsio*] —**Syn.** 2. turmoil.

confutation (kŏn′fyo͞o tā′shən), *n.* 1. the act of confuting. 2. that which confutes. 3. (in classical rhetoric) the fourth section (of a speech), given over to direct refutation. —**confutative** (kən fyo͞o′tə tĭv), *adj.*

confute (kən fyo͞ot′), *v.t.*, **-futed, -futing.** 1. to prove to be false or defective; disprove: *to confute an argument.* 2. to prove to be wrong; convict of error by argument or proof: *to confute one's opponent.* 3. to confound or bring to naught. [t. L: m. s. *confūtāre*] —**confut′er,** *n.*

Cong., 1. Congregational. 2. Congregationalist. 3. Congress. 4. Congressional.

cong., 1. congregation. 2. congress.

conga (kŏng′gə), *n.* a Latin-American dance consisting of three steps forwards followed by a kick and usually performed by a group following a leader in a single column, each dancer clasping the waist of the person in front.

congé (kŏn′zhā; *Fr.* kôɴ zhĕ′), *n.* 1. leave to depart, or dismissal; leave or permission; leave-taking. 2. a bow or obeisance. 3. *Archit.* a type of concave moulding. [F. See CONGEE]

congeal (kən jēl′), *v.t.*, *v.i.* 1. to change from a fluid or soft to a solid or rigid state, as by freezing or cooling. 2. to stiffen or coagulate, as blood. 3. *U.S.* to make or become fixed, as sentiments, principles, etc. [ME *congele(n)*, t. L: m. *congelāre* cause to freeze together] —**congeal′able,** *adj.* —**congeal′er,** *n.* —**congeal′ment,** *n.*

congee (kŏn′jē), *n.*, *v.*, **-geed, -geeing.** *Obs.* —*n.* 1. congé. —*v.i.* 2. to take one's leave. 3. to bow. [ME *congye*, t. OF: m. *congie* (F *congé*), g. L *commeātus* a going to and fro, leave of absence]

congelation (kŏn′jĭ lā′shən), *n.* 1. the act or process of congealing. 2. the state of being congealed. 3. the product of congealing; a concretion; a coagulation. 4. formation of stalactites; crystallization.

congener (kŏn′jĭ nə), *n.* 1. one of the same kind or class. 2. a fellow member of a genus, as of plants or animals. [t. L: of the same kind]

congeneric (kŏn′jĭ nĕ′rĭk), *adj.* of the same kind or genus. Also, **congenerous** (kən jĕn′ə rəs).

congenial (kən jē′nyəl), *adj.* 1. suited or adapted in spirit, feeling, temper, etc.: *congenial companions.* 2. agreeable or pleasing; agreeing or suited in nature or character: *a congenial task.* [f. CON- + s. L *genius* spirit + -AL¹] —**congeniality** (kən jē′nĭ ăl′ĭ tĭ), *n.* —**congen′ially,** *adv.* —**Syn.** 1. kindred, sympathetic.

congenital (kən jĕn′ĭ tl), *adj.* existing at or from one's birth: *a congenital defect.* [f. s. L *congenitus* born together with + -AL¹] —**congen′itally,** *adv.*

conger (kŏng′gə), *n.* 1. a large marine eel, *Conger conger*, sometimes growing to a length of 10 feet, which is caught for food or sport along the coast of Europe. 2. any other species of the family *Congridae.* Also, **conger eel.** [ME *congre*, t. OF, g. L *conger*, *congrus*, t. Gk: m. *góngros*]

congeries (kŏn jĭə′rēz), *n. sing. and pl.* a collection of several particles or bodies in one mass; an assembly.

congest (kən jĕst′), *v.t.* 1. to fill to excess; overcrowd. 2. *Pathol.* to cause an unnatural accumulation of blood in the vessels of (an organ or part). 3. *Obs.* to heap together. —*v.i.* 4. to become congested. [t. L: s. *congestus*, pp., brought together] —**congest′ible,** *adj.* —**conges′tion,** *n.* —**conges′tive,** *adj.*

congius (kŏn′jĭ əs), *n.*, *pl.* **congii** (kŏn′jĭ ī′). 1. *Pharm.* a gallon. 2. an ancient Roman unit of liquid measure, equal to about 7 pints. [t. L]

Congleton (kŏng′gl tən), *n.* a town in England, in E Cheshire. 16,823 (1961).

conglobate (kŏng′glō bāt′), *adj.*, *v.*, **-bated, -bating.** —*adj.* 1. formed into a ball. —*v.t.*, *v.i.* 2. to collect or form into a ball or rounded mass. [t. L: m. s. *conglobātus*, pp.] —**con′globa′tion,** *n.*

conglobe (kŏn glōb′), *v.t.*, *v.i.*, **-globed, -globing.** to conglobate.

conglomerate (*adj.*, *n.* kən glŏm′ə rĭt; *v.* -ə rāt′), *n.*, *adj.*, *v.*, **-rated, -rating.** —*n.* 1. anything composed of heterogeneous materials or elements. 2. *Geol.* a rock consisting of rounded and waterworn pebbles, etc., embedded in a finer cementing material; consolidated gravel. —*adj.* 3. gathered into a rounded mass; consisting of parts so gathered; clustered. 4. *Geol.* of the nature of a conglomerate. —*v.t.* 5. to bring together into a cohering mass. 6. to gather into a ball or rounded mass. —*v.i.* 7. to collect or cluster together. [t. L: m. s. *conglomerātus*, pp., rolled together] —**conglomeratic** (kən glŏm′ə răt′ĭk), **conglomeritic** (-rĭt′ĭk), *adj.*

conglomeration (kən glŏm′ə rā′shən), *n.* 1. the act of conglomerating. 2. the state of being conglomerated. 3. a cohering mass; a cluster. 4. a heterogeneous combination.

conglutinate (kən glo͞o′tĭ nāt′), *v.*, **-nated, -nating,** *adj.* —*v.t.*, *v.i.* 1. to join or become joined as with glue. —*adj.* 2. conglutinated. [t. L: m. s. *conglūtinātus*, pp., glued together] —**conglu′tina′tion,** *n.* —**conglutinative** (kən glo͞o′tĭ nə tĭv), *adj.*

Congo (kŏng′gō), *n.* 1. **Democratic Republic of the.** Formerly, **Belgian Congo.** an independent republic in central Africa. 14,150,000 pop. (est. 1961); 905,063 sq. mi. *Cap.*: Kinshasa. 2. **Republic of.** Formerly, **Middle Congo.** a republic in Africa, W of this country: member of the French Community. 836,000 pop. (est. 1961); 139,000 sq. mi. *Cap.*: Brazzaville. 3. a river in central Africa, rising in the SE part of the Democratic Republic of the Congo, flowing in a wide arc through Kinshasa to the Atlantic. ab. 3000 mi. —**Congolese** (kŏng′gə lēz′), *adj.*, *n.*

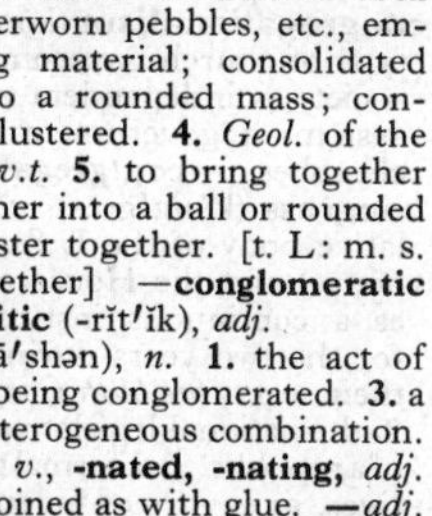

Congo

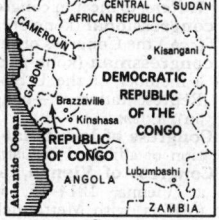

Congo colours, a group of azo dyes derived from benzidine which will dye cotton and other vegetable fibres without the aid of a mordant. Also, **Congo dyes.**

Congo Free State, former name of **Congo** (def. 1).

Congo red, one of the Congo colours, used esp. to dye cotton, etc., red. Since it is not acid-fast or light-fast, it is often used as a chemical indicator.

congo snake, either of two eel-shaped salamanders: 1. *Siren*, of the southern U.S., with small forelimbs but no hind ones. 2. *Amphiuma*, of the south-eastern U.S., having four minute limbs, and sometimes attaining a length of three feet. Also, **congo eel.**

congou (kŏng′go͞o), *n.* a kind of black tea from China. Also, **congo** (kŏng′gō). [t. Chinese: m. *kung-fu* labour]

congratulant (kən grăt′yo͞o lənt), *adj.* **1.** congratulating. —*n.* **2.** one who congratulates.

congratulate (kən grăt′yo͞o lāt′), *v.t.*, **-lated, -lating.** **1.** to express sympathetic joy to (a person), as on a happy occasion; compliment with expressions of sympathetic pleasure; felicitate. **2.** to consider (oneself) happy or fortunate. **3.** *Obs.* **a.** to express sympathetic joy or satisfaction at (an event, etc.). **b.** to salute. [t. L: m. s. *congrātulātus*, pp.] —**congrat′ula′tor,** *n.*

congratulation (kən grăt′yo͞o lā′shən), *n.* **1.** the act of congratulating. —*interj.* **2.** (*usually pl.*) (a congratulatory exclamation.).

congratulatory (kən grăt′yo͞o lə tə rĭ, -trĭ), *adj.* **1.** conveying congratulations. **2.** inclined to congratulate.

congregate (kŏng′grĭ gāt′), *v.*, **-gated, -gating,** *adj.* —*v.i.* **1.** to come together; assemble, esp. in large numbers. —*v.t.* **2.** to bring together in a crowd, body, or mass; assemble; collect. —*adj.* **3.** congregated; assembled. **4.** collective. [ME, t. L: m. s. *congregātus*, pp., collected into a flock] —**con′grega′tive,** *adj.* —**con′grega′tiveness,** *n.* —**con′grega′tor,** *n.*

congregation (kŏng′grĭ gā′shən), *n.* **1.** the act of congregating. **2.** a congregated body; an assemblage. **3.** an assembly of persons met for common religious worship. **4.** an organization formed for the purpose of providing for worship of God, religious education, and other church activities; a local church society. **5.** (in the Old Testament) the whole body of the Hebrews. **6.** (in the New Testament) the Christian Church in general. **7.** *Rom. Cath. Ch.* **a.** a committee of cardinals or other ecclesiastics. **b.** a community of men or women who observe the simple vows of poverty, chastity, and obedience: *Congregation of the Holy Cross.* **8.** a general assembly of members of a university, or such members who possess certain specified qualifications. **9.** (in colonial North America) a parish, town, or other settlement.

congregational (kŏng′grĭ gā′shə nəl), *adj.* **1.** of or pertaining to a congregation: *congregational singing.* **2.** (*cap.*) pertaining or adhering to a form of church government in which each congregation or local church acts as an independent, self-governing body, while maintaining fellowship with other like congregations.

congregationalism (kŏng′grĭ gā′shə nə lĭz′əm), *n.* **1.** the type of church government in which each local religious society is independent and self-governing. **2.** (*cap.*) the system of government and doctrine of Congregational churches. —**con′grega′tionalist,** *n., adj.*

congress (kŏng′grĕs), *n.* **1.** (*cap.*) **a.** the national legislative body of the U.S., consisting of the Senate (upper house) and the House of Representatives (lower house), as a continuous institution. **b.** this body as it exists for the two years during which the representatives hold their seats: *the 69th Congress.* **c.** the session of this body. **2.** the national legislative body of some other nations, esp. of a republic. **3.** a formal meeting or assembly of representatives, as envoys of independent states, for the discussion, arrangement, or promotion of some matter of common interest. **4.** the act of coming together; an encounter. **5.** social relations; converse. **6.** sexual intercourse. —*v.i.* **7.** *Rare.* to meet in congress. [t. L: s. *congressus* a meeting]

congressional (kŏng grĕsh′ə nəl), *adj.* of a congress, esp. (*cap.*) the Congress of the U.S.

congressman (kŏng′grĭs mən), *n., pl.* **-men.** (*often cap.*) a member of the U.S. Congress, esp. of the House of Representatives. —**congresswoman** (kŏng′grĭs wo͝om′-ən), *n. fem.*

Congress of Industrial Organizations, *U.S.* a federation of affiliated industrial trade unions. *Abbrev.*: CIO

Congress of Vienna, an international conference held at Vienna, 1814–15, after Napoleon I's banishment to Elba, with Metternich as the dominant figure, aimed at territorial resettlement and restoration to power of the crowned heads of Europe.

congress tart, a pastry case filled with jam and almond paste, topped with pastry strips.

Congreve (kŏng′grēv), *n.* **William,** 1670–1729, English dramatist.

congruence (kŏng′gro͞o əns), *n.* **1.** the fact or condition of agreeing; agreement. **2.** *Maths.* a relation between two numbers which give the same remainder when divided by a third number. —**con′gruency,** *n.*

congruent (kŏng′gro͞o ənt), *adj.* **1.** agreeing; accordant; congruous. **2.** *Maths.* pertaining to two numbers related by a congruence. **3.** *Geom.* coinciding exactly when superposed. [t. L: s. *congruens*, ppr., agreeing] —**con′gruently,** *adv.*

congruity (kən gro͞o′ĭ tĭ), *n., pl.* **-ties.** **1.** the state or quality of being congruous; agreement; harmony; appropriateness. **2.** (*usually pl.*) a point of agreement.

congruous (kŏng′gro͞o əs), *adj.* **1.** agreeing or harmonious in character; accordant; consonant; consistent (fol. by *with* or *to*). **2.** exhibiting harmony of parts. **3.** appropriate or fitting. [t. L: m. *congruus* fit] —**con′gruously,** *adv.* —**con′gruousness,** *n.*

conic (kŏn′ĭk), *adj.* **1.** Also, **con′ical.** having the form of, resembling, or pertaining to a cone. —*n.* **2.** *Maths.* a conic section. [t. Gk: m. s. *kōnikós* cone-shaped] —**con′ically,** *adv.*

conical projection, *Cartog.* a map projection based on the concept of projecting the earth's surface on a conical surface, which is then unrolled to a plane surface. Also, **conic projection.**

conics (kŏn′ĭks), *n.* the branch of mathematics dealing with conic sections.

conic section, **1.** *Maths.* a curve formed by the intersection of a plane with a right circular cone; an ellipse, a parabola, or a hyperbola. **2.** (*pl.*) the branch of mathematics dealing with these curves.

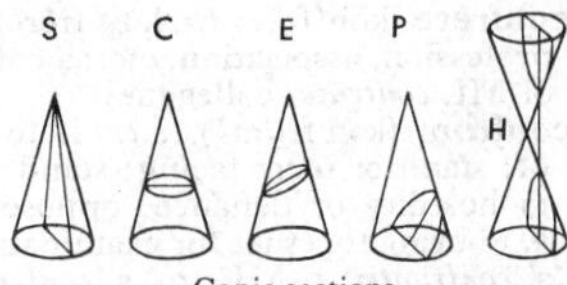

Conic sections

The two principal forms are fig. H, hyperbola, and fig. E, ellipse. Fig. P, parabola, is the intermediate case. The degenerate form of the hyperbola is a pair of straight lines, fig. S. Fig. C, circle, is a special case of the ellipse in which the plane becomes perpendicular to the axis of the cone.

conidiophore (kō nĭd′ĭ ə fô′), *n. Bot.* (in fungi) a special stalk or branch of the mycelium, bearing conidia. [f. *conidio-* (combining form of CONIDIUM) + -PHORE]

conidium (kō nĭd′ĭ əm), *n., pl.* **-nidia** (-nĭd′ĭ ə). *Bot.* (in fungi) an asexual spore formed by abstriction at the top of a hyphal branch, usually thin-walled and windborne. [NL, f. m. s. Gk *kónis* dust + dim. *-ium*] —**conid′ial, conid′ian,** *adj.*

conifer (kō′nĭ fə, kŏn′ĭ-), *n.* any of the (mostly evergreen) trees and shrubs producing naked seeds usually on cones, such as pine, spruce, and fir, constituting the gymnospermous order or group *Coniferales* or *Coniferae.* [t. L: cone-bearing]

coniferous (kə nĭf′ə rəs, kō-), *adj. Bot.* belonging or pertaining to the conifers.

coniform (kō′nĭ fôm′), *adj.* cone-shaped.

coniine (kō′nĭ ēn′, -ĭn, -nēn), *n. Chem.* a highly poisonous volatile alkaloid, $C_3H_7C_5H_9NH$, constituting the active principle of the poison hemlock. Also, **conin** (kō′nĭn), **conine** (kō′nēn, -nĭn). [f. CONI(UM) + -INE[2]]

Coniston (kŏn′ĭs tən), *n.* **Lake,** a lake in England, in N Lancashire. 5 mi. long. Also, **Coniston Water.**

conium (kō′nĭ əm), *n.* **1.** a plant of the umbelliferous genus *Conium*, esp. the poison hemlock, *Conium masculatum.* **2.** its extract as a drug. [t. L, t. Gk: m. *kṓneion* hemlock]

conj., **1.** conjugation. **2.** conjunction. **3.** conjunctive.

conjectural (kən jĕk′chə rəl), *adj.* **1.** of, of the nature of, or involving conjecture; problematical. **2.** given to making conjectures. —**conjec′turally,** *adv.*

conjecture (kən jĕk′chə), *n., v.*, **-tured, -turing.** —*n.* **1.** the formation or expression of an opinion without sufficient evidence for proof. **2.** an opinion so formed or expressed. **3.** *Obs.* the interpretation of signs or omens. —*v.t.* **4.** to conclude or suppose from grounds or evidence insufficient to ensure reliability. —*v.i.* **5.** *Archaic.* to form conjectures. [ME, t. L: m. *conjectūra* a throwing together, inference] —**conjec′turable,** *adj.* —**conjec′turably,** *adv.* —**conjec′turer,** *n.* —**Syn.** **2.** surmise, inference, supposition. **4.** suppose, presume. See **guess.**

conjoin (kən join′), *v.t., v.i.* to join together; unite; combine; associate. [ME *conjoigne(n)*, t. F: m. *conjoign-*, s. *conjoindre*, g. L *conjungere* join together] —**conjoin′er,** *n.* —**Ant.** disjoin.

conjoint (kən joint′), *adj.* **1.** joined together; united; combined; associated. **2.** pertaining to or formed by two or more in combination; joint. [t. F, pp. of *conjoindre*, g. L *conjungere* join together] —**conjoint′ly,** *adv.*

conjugal (kŏn′jo͞o gl), *adj.* concerning husband and wife; marital. [t. L: s. *conjugālis*, der. *conjunx* husband or wife] —**conjugality** (kŏn′jōō găl′ĭ tĭ), *n.* —**con′jugally,** *adv.*

conjugate (*v.* kŏn′jōō gāt′; *n.* kŏn′jōō gĭt, -gāt′), *v.,* **-gated, -gating,** *adj., n.* —*v.t.* **1.** *Gram.* **a.** to inflect (a verb). **b.** to recite or display all, or some subset of, the inflected forms of (a verb), in a fixed order: *conjugate the present tense verb 'be' as I am, you are, he is, we are, you are, they are.* **2.** *Obs.* to join together, esp. in marriage. —*v.i.* **3.** *Biol.* to unite temporarily. **4.** *Gram.* to be characterized by conjugation: *the Latin verb 'esse' does not conjugate in the passive voice.* —*adj.* **5.** joined together, esp. in a pair or pairs; coupled. **6.** *Bot.* (of a pinnate leaf) having only one pair of leaflets. **7.** (of words) having a common derivation. **8.** *U.S.* (of two leaves in a book) forming one sheet. **9.** *Maths.* (of two points, lines, etc.) so related as to be interchangeable in the enunciation of certain properties. **10.** *Optics.* (of two points on either side of a lens) so placed that an object placed at either will produce an image at the other. —*n.* **11.** one of a group of conjugate words. **12.** a conjugate number or axis. [t. L: m. s. *conjugātus*, pp., joined together, yoked] —**con′juga′tive,** *adj.*

conjugation (kŏn′jōō gā′shən), *n.* **1.** *Gram.* **a.** the inflection of verbs. **b.** the whole set of inflected forms of a verb, or the recital or display thereof in a fixed order: *the conjugation of the Latin verb 'amo' begins amō, amas, amat.* **c.** a class of verbs having similar sets of inflected forms, as the Latin *second conjugation.* **2.** the act of joining. **3.** the state of being joined together; union; conjunction. **4.** *Biol.* **a.** the sexual process in ciliate protozoans in which two animals adhere and exchange nuclear material through a temporary area of fusion. **b.** the temporary union or fusion of two cells or individuals, as in certain plants. —**con′juga′tional,** *adj.* —**con′juga′tionally,** *adv.*

conjunct (kən jŭngkt′, kŏn′jŭngkt), *adj.* **1.** conjoined; associate. **2.** formed by conjunction. **3.** *Gram.* **a.** occurring only in combination with an immediately preceding or following form of a particular class, and constituting with this form a single phonetic unit, as *'ll* in English *he'll,* and *n't* in *isn't.* **b.** (of a pronoun) having enclitic or proclitic form and occurring with a verb, as French *me, le, se.* **c.** pertaining to a word so characterized. [late ME, t. L: s. *conjunctus*, pp., joined together] —**conjunct′ly,** *adv.*

conjunction (kən jŭngk′shən), *n.* **1.** the act of conjoining; combination. **2.** the state of being conjoined; union; association. **3.** a combination of events or circumstances. **4.** *Gram.* **a.** (in some languages) one of the major form classes, or 'parts of speech', comprising words used to link together words, phrases, clauses, or sentences. **b.** such a word, as English *and* or *but.* **c.** any form of similar function or meaning. **5.** *Astron.* **a.** the meeting of heavenly bodies in the same longitude or right ascension. **b.** the situation of two or more heavenly bodies when their longitudes are the same. —**conjunc′tional,** *adj.* —**conjunc′tionally,** *adv.*

conjunctiva (kŏn′jŭngk tī′və), *n., pl.* **-vas, -vae** (-vē). *Anat.* the mucous membrane which lines the inner surface of the eyelids and is reflected over the forepart of the sclera and the cornea. See diag. under **eye.** [t. NL, short for *membrāna conjunctīva* membrane serving to connect] —**con′juncti′val,** *adj.*

conjunctive (kən jŭngk′tĭv), *adj.* **1.** connective. **2.** conjoined; joint. **3.** *Gram.* **a.** (of a mode) subjunctive. **b.** (of a pronoun) conjunct. **c.** of the nature of a conjunction. —*n.* **4.** *Gram.* a conjunctive word; a conjunction. —**conjunc′tively,** *adv.*

conjunctivitis (kən jŭngk′tĭ vī′tĭs), *n. Pathol.* inflammation of the conjunctiva. [t. NL. See CONJUNCTIVA, -ITIS]

conjuncture (kən jŭngk′chə), *n.* **1.** a combination of circumstances or affairs; a particular state of affairs. **2.** a critical state of affairs; a crisis. **3.** *Obs.* conjunction; meeting. [f. CON- + JUNCTURE]

conjuration (kŏn′jōō rā′shən), *n.* **1.** the act of calling on or invoking by a sacred name. **2.** an incantation; a spell or charm. **3.** supernatural accomplishment by invocation or spell. **4.** the practice of legerdemain. **5.** *Archaic.* supplication; solemn entreaty. **6.** *Obs.* a conspiracy.

conjure (kŭn′jə *for 1–3, 6–9, 11;* kən jōōə′ *for 4, 5, 10*), *v.,* **-jured, -juring.** —*v.t.* **1.** to call upon or command (a devil or spirit) by invocation or spell. **2.** to affect or influence by, or as by, invocation or spell. **3.** to effect, produce, bring, etc., by, or as by, magic. **4.** to appeal to solemnly or earnestly. **5.** to charge solemnly. **6. conjure up, a,** to call, raise up, or bring into existence by magic. **b.** to bring to mind or recall. —*v.i.* **7.** to call upon or command a devil or spirit by invocation or spell. **8.** to practise magic. **9.** to practise legerdemain. **10.** *Obs.* to conspire. **11. to conjure with,** likely to be influential if quoted; effective: *a name to conjure with.* [ME *conjure(n)*, t. OF: m. *conjurer*, t. L: m. s. *conjūrāre* swear together]

conjurer (kŭn′jə rə *for 1, 2;* kən jōōə′rə *for 3, 4*), *n.* **1.** one who conjures spirits or practises magic; magician. **2.** one who practises legerdemain; juggler. **3.** one who solemnly charges or entreats. **4.** one who is bound with others by oath. Also, **conjuror.**

conk (kŏngk), *n. Slang.* **1.** a nose. **2.** a blow; a violent stroke. —*v.t.* **3.** *Slang.* to hit or strike, esp. on the head. —*v.i.* **4. conk out, a.** *Colloq.* (of an engine) to break down. **b.** *Colloq.* to faint; collapse. **c.** *Slang.* to die. [prob. alter. of CONCH]

conker (kŏng′kə), *n.* **1.** *Colloq.* a horse chestnut. **2.** (*pl.*) a children's game in which one child swings a conker, which has been threaded on a string, in an attempt to break his opponent's conker. [d.: snail shell (with which the game was originally played)]

con-man (kŏn′măn′), *n. Slang.* a confidence man.

conn (kŏn), *v.t., n.* con³.

Conn (kŏn), *n.* **Lough,** a lake in the Republic of Ireland, in Co. Mayo. ab. 11 mi. long and 2 mi. wide.

Conn., Connecticut.

connate (kŏn′āt), *adj.* **1.** existing in a person or thing from birth or origin; inborn; congenital. **2.** associated in birth or origin. **3.** allied or agreeing in nature; cognate. **4.** *Biol.* congenitally or firmly united into one body. [t. LL: m. s. *connātus*, pp., born at the same time] —**con′nately,** *adv.* —**connation** (kŏ nā′shən), *n.*

connatural (kə năch′ə rəl), *adj.* **1.** belonging to a person or thing by nature or from birth or origin. **2.** of the same or like nature. [t. ML: s. *connātūrālis*] —**connat′urally,** *adv.*

Connaught (kŏn′ôt), *n.* a province in the NW Republic of Ireland. 419,465 pop. (1961); 6611 sq. mi. Irish, **Connacht** (kŏn′ət).

connect (kə nĕkt′), *v.t.* **1.** to bind or fasten together; join or unite; link. **2.** to establish communication between; put in communication (fol. by *with*). **3.** to associate or attach: *the pleasures connected with music.* **4.** to associate mentally. —*v.i.* **5.** to become connected; join or unite. **6.** (of trains, buses, etc.) to run so as to make connections (*with*). [t. L: s. *connectere*, var. of *cōnectere* join, tie] —**connect′edly,** *adv.* —**connect′er, connec′tor,** *n.* —**Syn. 1.** See **join.** —**Ant. 1.** divide. **3.** dissociate.

Connecticut (kə nĕt′ĭ kət), *n.* **1.** a state in the NE United States. 2,535,234 pop. (1960); 5009 sq. mi. *Cap.:* Hartford. *Abbrev.:* Conn. **2.** a river in the U.S. forming the boundary between Vermont and New Hampshire, flowing S through Massachusetts and Connecticut into Long Island Sound. 407 mi.

connecting rod, **1.** any rod or bar connecting movable parts. **2.** the rod connecting the crosshead to the crank in a steam-engine. **3.** the rod connecting the piston to the crankshaft in an internal-combustion engine.

connection (kə nĕk′shən), *n.* **1.** the act of connecting. **2.** the state of being connected. **3.** anything that connects; a connecting part. **4.** *Elect.* a joint between two conductors. **5.** association; relationship. **6.** a circle of friends or associates, or a member of such a circle. **7.** union in due order or sequence of words or ideas. **8.** contextual relation. **9.** the meeting of means of transport for transfer of passengers without delay. **10.** a person related to another or others, esp. by marriage or distant consanguinity. **11.** a body of persons connected as by political or religious ties. **12.** a religious denomination. **13.** a channel of communication. **14.** sexual intercourse. **15.** (*usually pl.*) influential friends, associates, relatives, etc. Also, **connexion.** [t. L: m. s. *connexio*] —**connec′tional,** *adj.* —**Syn. 1.** junction, conjunction, union. **3.** bond, tie, link, coupling. **5.** affiliation, alliance, combination. **10.** relation, relative, kinsman.

connective (kə nĕk′tĭv), *adj.* **1.** serving or tending to connect. —*n.* **2.** that which connects. **3.** *Gram.* a word used to connect words, phrases, clauses, and sentences, as a conjunction. **4.** *Bot.* the tissue joining the two cells of the anther. —**connec′tively,** *adv.* —**connectivity** (kŏn′ĕk tĭv′ĭ tĭ), *n.*

connective tissue, *Anat.* a tissue, usually of mesoblastic origin, which connects, supports, or surrounds other tissues, organs, etc., and occurs in various forms throughout the body.

Connemara (kŏn′ĭ mä′rə), *n.* **1.** a mountainous district in the Republic of Ireland, in W Co. Galway. **2.** a breed of small, sturdy pony, originally from Connemara.

conning tower (kŏn′ĭng), **1.** the superstructure on a submarine which acts as observation tower and main entrance to the interior. **2.** the low, dome-shaped, armoured pilot house of a warship, used esp. during battle.

connivance (kə nī′vəns), *n.* **1.** the act of conniving.

2. *Law.* intentional acquiescence by the petitioner in the adultery of the respondent; an absolute bar to divorce in England. Also, **connivence.**

connive (kə nīv′), *v.i.*, **-nived, -niving. 1.** to avoid noticing that which one should oppose or condemn but secretly approves; give aid to wrongdoing, etc., by forbearing to act or speak; be secretly accessory (fol. by *at*): *conniving at their escape.* **2.** to cooperate secretly (fol. by *with*). [t. L: s. *connīvēre*, var. of *cōnīvēre* shut the eyes] **—conniv′er,** *n.*

connivent (kə nī′vənt), *adj. Bot., Zool.* converging, as petals. [t. L: s. *connīvens*, ppr., winking at]

connoisseur (kŏn′ĭ sû′), *n.* one competent to pass critical judgements in an art, esp. one of the fine arts, or in matters of taste. [t. F (now *connaisseur*), der. *connaître*, older *connoître*, g. L *cognoscere* come to know]

connotation (kŏn′ə tā′shən), *n.* **1.** the act or fact of connoting. **2.** that which is connoted; secondary implied or associated meanings (as distinguished from *denotation*). **3.** *Logic.* the set of attributes constituting the meaning of a term, and thus determining the range of objects to which that term may be applied; comprehension; intension. **—connotative** (kŏn′ə tā′tĭv, kə nō′tə-), *adj.* **—con′nota′tively,** *adv.*

connote (kŏ nōt′), *v.t.*, **-noted, -noting. 1.** to denote secondarily; signify in addition to the primary meaning; imply. **2.** to involve as a condition or accompaniment. [t. ML: m. s. *connotāre* mark with, f. L: *con-* CON- + *notāre* mark. See NOTE, v.]

connubial (kə nyo͞o′byəl), *adj.* of marriage or wedlock; matrimonial; conjugal. [t. L: s. *connūbiālis*, der. *connūbium* marriage] **—connubiality** (kə nyo͞o′bĭ ăl′ĭ tĭ), *n.* **—connu′bially,** *adv.*

conoid (kō′noid), *adj.* **1.** Also, **conoi′dal.** resembling or approaching a cone in shape. **—*n.* 2.** a geometrical solid formed by the revolution of a conic section about one of its axes. [t. Gk: m. s. *kōnoeidḗs* cone-shaped]

conoscente (kŏn′ō shĕn′tĭ), *n., pl.* **-ti** (-tē). cognoscente.

conquer (kŏng′kə), *v.t.* **1.** to acquire by force of arms; win in war: *to conquer territories.* **2.** to overcome by force; subdue: *to conquer an enemy.* **3.** to gain or obtain by effort. **4.** to gain the victory over; surmount. **—*v.i.* 5.** to make conquests; gain the victory. [ME *conquere(n)*, t. OF: m. *conquerre*, g. L *conquaerere, conquīrere* seek for] **—con′querable,** *adj.* **—con′queringly,** *adv.* **—Syn. 2.** vanquish, overpower, overthrow, subjugate. See **defeat.**

conqueror (kŏng′kə rə), *n.* **1.** one who conquers. **2. the Conqueror,** William I of England.

conquest (kŏn′kwĕst, kŏng′-), *n.* **1.** the act of conquering. **2.** captivation, as of favour or affections. **3.** the condition of being conquered; vanquishment. **4.** territory acquired by conquering. **5.** a person whose favour or affections have been captivated. **6. the Conquest,** the conquering of England by William, Duke of Normandy, in 1066. [ME, t. OF: m. *conqueste*, fem. collective of *conquest*, pp. of *conquerre* conquer] **—Syn. 3.** See **victory.**

conquian (kŏng′kyən), *n.* a card game of the rummy family for two players. [orig. uncert.]

conquistador (kŏn kwĭs′tə dô′; *Sp.* kòn kēs tä dòr′), *n., pl.* **-dors,** *Sp.* **-dores** (-dòr′ĕs). one of the Spanish conquerors of Mexico and Peru in the 16th century. [t. Sp.]

Conrad (kŏn′răd), *n.* **Joseph** (*Teodor Józef Konrad Korzeniowski*), 1857–1924, British novelist, born of Polish parents. **—Conrad′ian,** *adj.*

consanguineous (kŏn′săng gwĭn′ĭ əs), *adj.* related by birth; akin. Also, **consanguine** (kŏn săng′gwĭn). [t. L: m. *consanguineus*] **—con′sanguin′eously,** *adv.*

consanguinity (kŏn′săng gwĭn′ĭ tĭ), *n.* **1.** relationship by blood; kinship. **2.** relationship or affinity.

conscience (kŏn′shəns), *n.* **1.** the internal recognition of right and wrong as regards one's actions and motives; the faculty which decides upon the moral quality of one's actions and motives, enjoining one to conformity with the moral law. **2.** conscientiousness. **3.** *Obs.* consciousness. **4.** *Obs.* inmost thought. **5. in (all) conscience, a.** in (all) reason and fairness; in truth. **b.** most certainly; assuredly. [ME, t. OF, t. L: m. s. *conscientia* joint knowledge] **—con′scienceless,** *adj.*

conscience clause, a clause or article in an act or law or the like, which relieves persons whose conscientious or religious scruples forbid their compliance with it.

conscience money, money paid to relieve the conscience, as for obligations previously evaded.

conscience-smitten (kŏn′shəns smĭt′n), *adj.* remorseful; disturbed by the knowledge of having acted wrongfully. Also, **conscience-stricken.**

conscientious (kŏn′shĭ ĕn′shəs), *adj.* controlled by or done according to conscience; scrupulous: *a conscientious judge, conscientious conduct.* **—con′scien′tiously,** *adv.* **—con′scien′tiousness,** *n.* **—Syn.** just, upright, honest, faithful, careful, particular, painstaking.

conscientious objector, one who, when called upon in time of war to fight for his country, refuses to do so because of conscientious scruples, as of religion, morality, etc.

conscionable (kŏn′shə nə bl), *adj.* conformable to conscience; just. **—con′scionably,** *adv.*

conscious (kŏn′shəs), *adj.* **1.** aware of one's own existence, sensations, cognitions, etc.; endowed with consciousness. **2.** inwardly sensible or awake to something: *conscious of one's own faults.* **3.** having the mental faculties awake. **4.** present to consciousness; known to oneself; felt: *conscious guilt.* **5.** aware of what one is doing: *a conscious liar.* **6.** aware of oneself; self-conscious. **7.** deliberate or intentional. **8.** *Obs.* inwardly sensible of wrongdoing. [t. L: m. *conscius* knowing] **—con′sciously,** *adv.*

—Syn. 2. CONSCIOUS, AWARE refer to an individual sense of recognition of something. CONSCIOUS implies to be awake or awakened to an inner realization of a fact, a truth, a condition, etc.: *he was conscious of an extreme weariness.* AWARE lays the emphasis on sense perceptions which lead to consciousness: *he was aware of the smell of tobacco.*

consciousness (kŏn′shəs nĭs), *n.* **1.** the state of being conscious. **2.** inward sensibility of something; knowledge of one's own existence, sensations, cognitions, etc. **3.** the thoughts and feelings, collectively, of an individual, or of an aggregate of people: *the moral consciousness of a nation.* **4.** activity of mental faculties: *to regain consciousness after fainting.*

conscribe (kən skrīb′), *v.t.*, **-scribed, -scribing. 1.** to enlist by conscription. **2.** to limit; circumscribe.

conscript (*adj., n.* kŏn′skrĭpt; *v.* kən skrĭpt′), *adj.* **1.** enrolled or formed by conscription: *a conscript soldier or army.* **—*n.* 2.** a recruit obtained by conscription. **—*v.t.* 3.** to enrol compulsorily for service in the armed forces. [t. L: s. *conscriptus*, pp., enrolled]

conscript fathers, 1. the senators of ancient Rome. **2.** any legislators.

conscription (kən skrĭp′shən), *n.* compulsory enrolment of men for service in the armed forces.

consecrate (kŏn′sĭ krāt′), *v.*, **-crated, -crating,** *adj.* **—*v.t.* 1.** to make or declare sacred; set apart or dedicate to the service of the Deity. **2. a.** to induct (a person) into high office by means of a religious rite. **b.** (in the Church of England) ordain (a bishop). **3.** to devote or dedicate to some purpose: *a life consecrated to science.* **4.** to make an object of veneration: *a custom consecrated by time.* **—*adj.* 5.** *Archaic.* consecrated; sacred. [ME, t. L: m. s. *consĕcrātus*, pp., dedicated] **—con′secra′tor,** *n.* **—consecratory** (kŏn′sĭ krā′tə rĭ), *adj.* **—Syn. 3.** devote. **4.** sanctify. **5.** See **holy.**

consecration (kŏn′sĭ krā′shən), *n.* **1.** the act of consecrating; dedication to the service and worship of God. **2.** the act of giving the sacramental character to the Eucharistic elements of bread and wine. **3.** ordination to a sacred office, esp. to the episcopate.

consecution (kŏn′sĭ kyo͞o′shən), *n.* **1.** succession; sequence. **2.** logical sequence; inference. [t. L: s. *consecūtio*, der. *consequī* follow after]

consecutive (kən sĕk′yo͝o tĭv), *adj.* **1.** following one another in uninterrupted succession; uninterrupted in course or succession; successive. **2.** marked by logical sequence. **3.** *Gram.* expressing consequence or result: *a consecutive clause.* **4.** *Music.* a succession of similar harmonic intervals. [t. F: m. *consécutif*, der. L *consecūtus*, pp., having followed after] **—consec′utively,** *adv.* **—consec′utiveness,** *n.* **—Syn. 1.** See **successive.**

consensual (kən sĕn′syo͝o əl), *adj.* **1.** formed or existing by mere consent: *a consensual contract.* **2.** *Physiol.* (of an action) involuntarily correlative with a voluntary action, as the contraction of the iris when the eye is opened. [f. L *consensu(s)* agreement + -AL[1]] **—consen′sually,** *adv.*

consensus (kən sĕn′səs), *n.* **1.** general agreement or concord. **2.** majority of opinion. [t. L: agreement]

consent (kən sĕnt′), *v.i.* **1.** to give assent; agree; comply or yield (fol. by *to* or infinitive). **2.** *Obs.* to agree in sentiment, opinion, etc.; be in harmony. **—*n.* 3.** assent; acquiescence; permission; compliance. **4.** agreement in sentiment, opinion, a course of action, etc.: *by common consent.* **5.** *Archaic.* accord; concord; harmony. **6. age of consent,** the age at which consent to certain acts, esp. sexual intercourse and marriage, is valid in law. [ME *consente(n)*, t. OF: m. *consentir*, g. L *consentīre* feel together] **—consent′er,** *n.* **—consen′tingly,** *adv.*

—Syn. 1. CONSENT, ASSENT, CONCUR imply agreeing with someone. CONSENT, applying to somewhat important matters, conveys an active and positive idea; it implies making a definite decision to comply with someone's expressed wish: *to consent to become* *engaged.* ASSENT conveys a more passive idea; it suggests agreeing intellectually or merely verbally with someone's assertion, request, etc.: *to assent to a speaker's theory, to a proposed arrangement.* To CONCUR is to show accord in matters of opinion, as of minds independently running along the same channels: *to concur in a judgement about an art exhibit.*

consentaneous (kŏn′sĕn tā′nyəs), *adj.* **1.** agreeing or accordant. **2.** done by common consent; unanimous. [t. L: m. *consentāneus* agreeing, fit] —**con′senta′neously,** *adv.* —**consentaneity** (kən sĕn′tə nē′ĭ tĭ), **con′senta′neousness,** *n.*

consentient (kən sĕn′shənt), *adj.* **1.** agreeing; accordant. **2.** acting in agreement or harmony. **3.** unanimous, as an opinion. —**consen′tience,** *n.*

consequence (kŏn′sĭ kwəns), *n.* **1.** the act or fact of following as an effect or result upon something antecedent. **2.** that which so follows; an effect or result. **3. in consequence,** as a result. **4.** the conclusion of an argument or inference. **5.** importance or significance: *a matter of no consequence.* **6.** importance in rank or position; distinction. —**Syn. 2.** outcome, issue, upshot, sequel. See **effect. 5.** moment, weight. See **importance.** —**Ant. 2.** cause.

consequences (kŏn′sĭ kwən sĭz), *n.pl., usually construed as sing.* a parlour game in which each participant contributes to a written story without knowing the rest of it, the object being to produce the utmost absurdity.

consequent (kŏn′sĭ kwənt), *adj.* **1.** following as an effect or result; resulting. **2.** following as a logical conclusion. **3.** logically consistent. **4.** *Geol.* (of a river) flowing in the direction of the original slope of the land. —*n.* **5.** anything that follows upon something else, with or without implication of causal relation. **6.** *Logic.* the second member of a conditional or hypothetical proposition, as the proposition expressed by the second clause in *If Jones is ill, he will remain indoors.* **7.** *Arith.* the second term of a ratio. [t. L: s. *consequens*, ppr.]

consequential (kŏn′sĭ kwĕn′shəl), *adj.* **1.** of the nature of a consequence; following as an effect or result, or as a logical conclusion or inference; consequent; resultant. **2.** self-important; pompous. **3.** logically consistent. **4.** of consequence or importance. —**con′sequen′tial′ity, con′sequen′tialness,** *n.* —**con′sequen′tially,** *adv.*

consequential loss insurance, an insurance policy indemnifying against contingent results of accident, esp. the cost of the hire of a car to replace one under repair or the cost of alternative accommodation after a fire.

consequently (kŏn′sĭ kwənt lĭ), *adv.* by way of consequence; in consequence of something; therefore. —**Syn.** See **therefore.**

conservable (kən sû′və bl), *adj.* capable of being conserved; preservable.

conservancy (kən sû′vən sĭ), *n., pl.* **-cies. 1.** (in England) a court or board with authority to preserve the fisheries, banks, etc., of a river. **2.** the official preservation of forests, etc. **3.** conservation of natural resources.

conservation (kŏn′sə vā′shən), *n.* **1.** the act of conserving; preservation. **2.** official supervision of rivers, forests, etc. [t. L: s. *conservātio*] —**con′serva′tional,** *adj.*

conservationist (kŏn′sə vā′shə nĭst), *n.* one who advocates or promotes conservation, esp. of the natural resources of a country.

conservation of mass and energy, *Physics.* the principle that in any system the total of the mass (matter) and energy remains constant.

conservatism (kən sû′və tĭz′əm), *n.* **1.** the disposition to preserve what is established; opposition to innovation or change. **2.** the principles and practices of political conservatives as (*cap.*) those of a Conservative Party.

conservative (kən sû′və tĭv), *adj.* **1.** disposed to preserve existing conditions, institutions, etc. **2.** cautious or moderate: *a conservative estimate.* **3.** traditional in style or manner. **4.** having the power or tendency to conserve; preservative. **5.** (*often cap.*) denoting or pertaining to a Conservative Party. —*n.* **6.** a person of conservative principles. **7.** (*often cap.*) a member of a Conservative Party in politics. **8.** a preservative. —**conserv′atively,** *adv.* —**conserv′ativeness,** *n.*

Conservative Party, 1. a political party in Great Britain, founded in the early 1830s as a successor to the Tory Party and characterized chiefly by a moderately progressive policy. **2.** (elsewhere) a party characterized by a tendency to oppose change in prevailing institutions, esp. those associated with capitalism.

conservatoire (kən sû′və twä′; *Fr.* kôN sĕr vȧ twȧr′), *n.* a place for instruction in music and theatrical arts; a school of music. [t. F]

conservator (kŏn′sə vā′tə, kən sû′və tə), *n.* **1.** one who conserves or preserves; a preserver. **2.** *Law.* a guardian; a custodian. **3.** one who has duties in conservancy (def. 1).

conservatory (kən sû′və trĭ), *n., pl.* **-tries,** *adj.* —*n.* **1.** a glass-covered house or room into which plants in bloom are brought from the greenhouse. **2.** *U.S.* a conservatoire. **3.** *Obs.* a place where things are preserved. —*adj.* **4.** serving or adapted to conserve; preservative.

conserve (*v.* kən sûv′; *n.* kŏn′sûv, kən sûv′), *v.,* **-served, -serving,** *n.* —*v.t.* **1.** to keep in a safe or sound state; preserve from loss, decay, waste, or injury; keep unimpaired. **2.** *Obs.* to preserve, as fruit, with sugar, etc. —*n.* **3.** (*often pl.*) a mixture of several fruits, cooked, with sugar, to a jamlike consistency. [ME, t. L: m. s. *conservāre* preserve] —**conserv′er,** *n.*

conshie (kŏn′shĭ), *Slang.* conchy. Also, **conshy.**

consider (kən sĭd′ə), *v.t.* **1.** to contemplate mentally; meditate or reflect on. **2.** to regard as or deem to be: *I consider him a rascal.* **3.** to think; suppose. **4.** to make allowance for. **5.** to pay attention to; regard: *he never considers others.* **6.** to regard with consideration or respect; hold in honour; respect. **7.** to think about (a position, purchase, etc.) with a view to accepting or buying. **8.** *Archaic.* to view attentively, or scrutinize. **9.** *Obs.* to recompense or remunerate. —*v.i.* **10.** to think deliberately or carefully; reflect. **11.** *Obs. or Archaic.* to look attentively. [ME *considere(n)*, t. L: s. *consīderāre* examine closely] —**Syn. 1.** ponder, deliberate, weigh, revolve. See **study.**

considerable (kən sĭd′ə rə bl), *adj.* **1.** worthy of consideration; important; of distinction. **2.** (of an amount, extent, etc.) worthy of consideration; fairly large or great. —*n.* **3.** *U.S. Colloq.* much; not a little: *he has done considerable for the community.* —**consid′erably,** *adv.*

considerate (kən sĭd′ə rĭt), *adj.* **1.** showing consideration or regard for another's circumstances, feelings, etc. **2.** marked by consideration or reflection; deliberate. **3.** *Archaic.* given to consideration or reflection; prudent. —**consid′erately,** *adv.* —**consid′erateness,** *n.* —**Syn. 1.** See **thoughtful.**

consideration (kən sĭd′ə rā′shən), *n.* **1.** the act of considering; meditation or deliberation. **2.** regard or account; something taken, or to be taken, into account. **3.** a thought or reflection. **4.** a recompense for service rendered, etc.; a compensation. **5.** *Law.* something which suffices to make an informal promise legally binding, usually something of value given in exchange for the promise. **6.** thoughtful or sympathetic regard or respect; thoughtfulness for others. **7.** importance or consequence. **8.** estimation; esteem. **9. in consideration of, a.** in view of. **b.** in return for. **10. take into consideration,** to consider; take into account. **11. under consideration,** being considered. —**Syn. 1.** contemplation, advisement, attention. **8.** See **honour.**

considering (kən sĭd′ə rĭng), *prep.* **1.** taking into account; in view of. —*adv.* **2.** with all things considered (used after the statement it modifies). —*conj.* **3.** taking into consideration that: *considering he is so young, he has achieved a great deal.*

consign (kən sīn′), *v.t.* **1.** to hand over or deliver formally; commit (fol. by *to*). **2.** to transfer to another's custody or charge; entrust. **3.** to set apart, as to a purpose or use. **4.** *Com.* **a.** to transmit, as by public carrier, esp. for sale or custody. **b.** to address for such transmission. **5.** *Obs* to mark with a sign or seal. —*v.i. Obs.* **6.** to yield or submit. **7.** to agree or assent. [t. F: m. *consigner*, t. L: m. *consignāre* furnish or mark with a seal] —**consign′able,** *adj.* —**consignation** (kŏn′sĭ nā′shən), *n.*

consignee (kŏn′sī nē′), *n.* the person or party to whom merchandise is consigned.

consignment (kən sīn′mənt), *n.* **1.** the act of consigning. **2.** that which is consigned. **3.** *Com.* **a.** property sent to an agent for sale, storage, or shipment. **b. on consignment,** (of goods) sent to an agent for sale, title being held by the consignor until they are sold.

consignor (kən sī′nə, kŏn′sī nô′), *n.* one who consigns goods, etc. Also, **consigner** (kən sī′nə).

consist (kən sĭst′), *v.i.* **1.** to be made up or composed (fol. by *of*). **2.** to be comprised or contained (fol. by *in*). **3.** to be compatible, consistent, or harmonious (fol. by *with*). **4.** *Obs.* to exist together or be capable of existing together. **5.** *Obs.* to stand together; be supported and maintained. [t. L: s. *consistere* place oneself]

—**Syn. 1, 2.** CONSIST OF, CONSIST IN are often confused. With CONSIST OF, parts, materials, or ingredients are spoken of: *bread consists of flour, yeast, etc.* With CONSIST IN, something resembling a definition is given: *cooperation consists in helping one another and in sharing losses or gains.*

consistency (kən sĭs′tən sĭ), *n., pl.* **-cies. 1.** material coherence with retention of form; solidity or firmness. **2.** degree of density or viscosity: *the consistency of cream.* **3.** constant adherence to the same principles, course, etc. **4.** agreement, harmony, or compatibility; agreement among themselves of the parts of a complex thing. Also, **consist′ence.**

consistent (kən sĭs′tənt), *adj.* **1.** agreeing or accordant; compatible; not self-opposed or self-contradictory. **2.** constantly adhering to the same principles, course, etc. **3.** *Obs.* holding firmly together; cohering. **4.** *Obs.* fixed; firm; solid. —**consist′ently,** *adv.* —**Syn. 1.** congruous, consonant, harmonious. —**Ant. 2.** contradictory.

consistory (kən sĭs′tə rĭ), *n., pl.* **-ries. 1.** any of various ecclesiastical councils or tribunals. **2.** the place where it meets. **3.** the meeting of any such body. **4.** *Rom. Cath. Ch.* an ecclesiastical senate, consisting of the whole body of cardinals, which deliberates upon the affairs of the Church. **5.** *C. of E.* a diocesan court held before the bishop or the bishop's chancellor or commissary in the cathedral church for the trial of ecclesiastical questions. **6.** (in certain Reformed Churches) the governing board of a local church or congregation. **7.** *Archaic.* an assembly or council. **8.** *Obs.* a council chamber. [ME *consistorie,* t. ONF, t. L: m. *consistōrium* place of assembly] —**consistorial** (kŏn′sĭs tô′rĭ əl), **con′sisto′rian,** *adj.*

consociate (*adj., n.* kən sō′shĭ ĭt, -āt′; *v.* kən sō′shĭ āt′), *adj., n., v.i.,* **-ated, -ating.** associate. [t. L: m. s. *consociātus,* pp.]

consociation (kən sō′sĭ ā′shən), *n.* **1.** the act or fact of associating together. **2.** fellowship; companionship. **3.** *Eccles.* a confederation of churches or religious societies.

consolation (kŏn′sə lā′shən), *n.* **1.** the act of consoling. **2.** the state of being consoled. **3.** one who or that which consoles. [ME, t. L: s. *consōlātio*] —**Syn. 3.** comfort, solace.

consolation prize, a prize, usually of little value, given to the loser, or runner-up, in a contest, etc.

consolatory (kən sŏl′ə tə rĭ, -trĭ), *adj.* affording consolation; consoling.

console[1] (kən sōl′), *v.t.,* **-soled, -soling.** to alleviate the grief or sorrow of; comfort; solace; cheer. [t. L: m. *consōlārī* comfort] —**consol′able,** *adj.* —**consol′er,** *n.* —**consol′ingly,** *adv.* —**Syn.** See **comfort.**

console[2] (kŏn′sōl), *n.* **1.** a desklike structure containing the keyboards, pedals, etc., of an organ, from which the organ is played. **2.** a desk on which are mounted the controls of an electrical or electronic system. **3.** a floor-model radio, television, or radiogram cabinet. **4.** a console table. **5.** *Archit.* an ornamental projection, as for supporting a cornice, bust, etc. [t. F; orig. uncert.]

console table, 1. a table supported by consoles or brackets fixed to a wall. **2.** a table, often with bracket-like legs, designed to fit against a wall.

consolidate (kən sŏl′ĭ dāt′), *v.,* **-dated, -dating,** *adj.* —*v.t.* **1.** to make solid or firm; solidify; strengthen: *to consolidate gains.* **2.** *Mil.* to strengthen by rearranging the position of ground combat troops after a successful attack. **3.** to bring together compactly in one mass or connected whole; unite; combine: *to consolidate two companies.* —*v.i.* **4.** to unite or combine. **5.** to become solid or firm. —*adj.* **6.** *Archaic.* consolidated. [t. L: m. s. *consolidātus,* pp., made solid] —**consol′ida′tor,** *n.*

consolidated fund, a fund made up by consolidating the yield of various taxes and other sources of public revenue, from which are paid the interest on the national debt, grants to the royal family, etc.

consolidation (kən sŏl′ĭ dā′shən), *n.* **1.** the act of consolidating; unification. **2.** the state of being consolidated; combination. **3.** a consolidated whole. **4.** *Law.* a statutory combination of two or more previous enactments.

consols (kŏn′sŏlz, kən sŏlz′), *n.pl.* the funded government securities of Great Britain, which originated in the consolidation in 1751 of various public securities, chiefly in the form of annuities, into a single debt issue without maturity. [short for *consolidated annuities*]

consommé (kən sŏm′ā, kŏn′sŏm ā′; *Fr.* kôɴ sŏ mė′), *n.* a clear soup made by boiling meat long and slowly in order to extract the nutritive properties. [t. F, prop. pp. of *consommer,* t. L: m. *consummāre* finish]

consonance (kŏn′sə nəns), *n.* **1.** accord or agreement. **2.** correspondence of sounds; harmony of sounds. **3.** *Music.* a simultaneous combination of notes conventionally accepted as being in a state of repose (opposite of *dissonance*). Also, **con′sonancy.**

consonant (kŏn′sə nənt), *n.* **1.** *Phonet.* **a.** (as a member of a syllable) a sound subordinated to another sound that has greater sonority; *w* and *g* in *wig* are subordinate to *i,* the sound of greatest sonority in the syllable, and by virtue of this subordination they are called consonants. **b.** (as a member of an articulation class) a sound made with more or less obstruction of the breath stream in its passage outwards, as the *l, s,* and *t* of *list,* each an example of a consonantal subclass: *l* is a *sonorant* (relatively slight obstruction), *s* a *fricative* (relatively great obstruction), and *t* a *stop* (complete obstruction). **2.** a letter which usually represents a consonant sound. —*adj.* **3.** in agreement; agreeable or accordant; consistent (fol. by *to* or *with*). **4.** corresponding in sound, as words. **5.** harmonious, as sounds. **6.** *Music.* constituting a consonance. **7.** consonantal. [ME, t. L: s. *consonans* sounding together] —**con′sonantly,** *adv.* —**Ant. 6.** dissonant.

consonantal (kŏn′sə năn′tl), *adj.* **1.** of, or of the nature of, a consonant. **2.** marked by consonant sounds.

consort (*n.* kŏn′sôt, *v.* kən sôt′), *n.* **1.** a husband or wife; a spouse, esp. of a reigning monarch. **2.** one vessel or ship accompanying another. **3.** *Obs.* a group of instruments or voices in harmony. **4.** *Obs.* a companion or partner. **5.** *Obs.* company or association. **6.** *Obs.* accord or agreement. **7.** *Obs.* harmony of sounds. —*v.i.* **8.** to associate; keep company. **9.** to agree or harmonize. —*v.t.* **10.** to associate. **11.** *Obs.* to accompany; espouse. **12.** *Obs.* to sound in harmony. [late ME, t. F: mate, t. L: s. *consors* partner, sharer, orig. adj., sharing]

consortium (kən sô′tyəm), *n., pl.* **-tia** (-tyə). **1.** a combination of financial institutions, capitalists, etc., for carrying into effect some financial operation requiring large resources of capital. **2.** an association or union. [t. L: partnership]

conspectus (kən spĕk′təs), *n.* **1.** a general or comprehensive view. **2.** a digest; a résumé. [t. L: survey]

conspicuous (kən spĭk′yo͞o əs), *adj.* **1.** easy to be seen. **2.** readily attracting the attention. [t. L: m. *conspicuus* visible, striking] —**conspic′uously,** *adv.* —**conspic′uousness,** *n.* —**Syn. 1.** visible, manifest, noticeable, clear, marked, salient. **2.** prominent, striking, noteworthy.

conspiracy (kən spĭ′rə sĭ), *n., pl.* **-cies. 1.** the act of conspiring. **2.** a combination of persons for an evil or unlawful purpose; a plot. **3.** *Law.* an agreement by two or more persons to commit a crime, fraud, or other wrongful act. **4.** any concurrence in action; combination in bringing about a given result. [f. CONSPIR(E) + -ACY] —**conspir′ator,** *n.* —**conspiratress** (kən spĭ′rə trĭs), *n. fem.*

conspire (kən spī′ə), *v.,* **-spired, -spiring.** —*v.i.* **1.** to agree together, esp. secretly, to do something reprehensible or illegal; combine for an evil or unlawful purpose. **2.** to act in combination; contribute jointly to a result. —*v.t.* **3.** to plot (something evil or unlawful). [ME *conspire(n),* t. L: m. *conspīrāre,* lit., breathe together] —**conspir′er,** *n.* —**conspir′ingly,** *adv.* —**Syn. 1.** complot, intrigue. See **plot**[1]. **2.** combine, concur, cooperate.

constable (kŭn′stə bl), *n.* **1.** any of various officers of the peace, as one who executes the processes of a justice of the peace. **2.** a police officer ranking below sergeant, the lowest in rank in a police force. **3.** the rank. **4.** an officer of high rank in medieval monarchies, usually the commander of all armed forces, particularly in the absence of the ruler. **5.** the keeper or governor of a royal fortress or castle. [ME *conestable,* t. OF, g. LL *comes stabulī* count of the stable, master of the horse] —**con′stableship′,** *n.*

Constable (kŭn′stə bl), *n.* **John,** 1776–1837, English landscape painter.

constabulary (kən stăb′yo͞o lə rĭ), *n., pl.* **-ries,** *adj.* —*n.* **1.** the body of constables of a district or locality. **2.** a body of officers of the peace organized on a military basis. —*adj.* **3.** pertaining to constables or their duties. [t. ML: m. s. *constabulāria*]

Constance (kŏn′stəns), *n.* **1. Lake.** German, **Bodensee.** a lake bounded by Germany, Austria, and Switzerland. 46 mi. long; 207 sq. mi. **2.** German, **Konstanz.** a town in West Germany, in S Baden-Württemberg, on this lake. Church council, 1414–18. 55,000 (est. 1963).

constancy (kŏn′stən sĭ), *n.* **1.** the quality of being constant; firmness or fortitude; faithfulness to a person or cause. **2.** invariability, uniformity, or regularity. [t. L: m. s. *constantia* firmness] —**Syn. 1.** steadfastness, fidelity, fealty, loyalty.

constant (kŏn′stənt), *adj.* **1.** invariable; uniform; always present. **2.** continuing without intermission. **3.** regularly recurrent; continual; persistent. **4.** steadfast, as in attachment; faithful. **5.** standing firm in mind or purpose; resolute. **6.** *Obs.* certain or confident. —*n.* **7.** something constant, invariable, or unchanging. **8.** *Physics.* a numerical quantity expressing a relation or value that remains unchanged under certain conditions. **9.** *Maths.* a quantity assumed to be unchanged throughout a given discussion. [ME, t. L: s. *constans,* ppr., standing firm] —**con′stantly,** *adv.* —**Syn. 2.** perpetual, unremitting, uninterrupted. **3.** incessant, ceaseless. See **continual. 4.** loyal, staunch, true. See **faithful. 5.** steady, unwavering, unshaken. —**Ant. 1.** changeable. **2.** fitful. **3.** sporadic. **4.** unreliable. **5.** wavering.

Constanța (kən stănt′sə; *Rum.* kón stán′tsá), *n.* a seaport in SE Rumania, on the Black Sea. 121,071 (est. 1964).
constantan (kŏn′stən tăn′), *n.* an alloy containing 60 per cent copper and 40 per cent nickel, used for electrical resistance heating and thermocouples. [f. CONSTANT + -AN]
Constant de Rebecque (*Fr.* kôɴ stäɴ də rə bĕk′), **Henri Benjamin** (*Fr.* äɴ rē băɴ zhä mäɴ′), (*Benjamin Constant*), 1767–1830, French statesman and author.
Constantine (kŏn′stən tīn′; *Fr.* kôɴ stäɴ tēn′), *n.* a city in NE Algeria. 223,000 (1960).
Constantine I (kŏn′stən tīn′), **1.** ('*the Great*'), A.D. 288?–337, Roman emperor A.D. 324–37: built Constantinople as new capital; made Christian worship lawful. **2.** 1868–1923, king of Greece 1913–17 and 1920–22.
Constantine II (kŏn′stən tīn′), born 1940, king of Greece since 1964, in exile since 1967. Official title, **Constantine XIII.**
Constantinople (kŏn′stăn tĭ nō′pl), *n.* a city built on the site of ancient Byzantium by Constantine the Great, A.D. 330: capital of the Eastern Roman Empire and later of the Ottoman Empire. See **Istanbul.**
constellate (kŏn′stĭ lāt′), *v.i., v.t.,* **-lated, -lating.** to cluster together, as stars in a constellation.
constellation (kŏn′stĭ lā′shən), *n.* **1.** *Astron.* **a.** any of various groups of stars to which definite names have been given, as Great Bear, Little Bear, Boötes, Cancer, Orion. **b.** a division of the heavens occupied by such a group. **2.** *Astrol.* **a.** the grouping or relative position of the stars as supposed to influence events, esp. at a person's birth. **b.** *Obs.* character as supposed to be determined by the stars. **3.** any brilliant assemblage. **4.** *Psychol.* a group of emotionally coloured ideas, mostly repressed. [ME, t. LL: s. *constellātio* group of stars]
conster (kŏn′stə), *v.t., v.i. Obs.* construe.
consternate (kŏn′stə nāt′), *v.t.,* **-nated, -nating.** to dismay; terrify (usually used in the passive).
consternation (kŏn′stə nā′shən), *n.* amazement and dread tending to confound the faculties; paralysing dismay. [t. L: s. *consternātio*] **—Syn.** bewilderment, alarm, terror, fear, panic. **—Ant.** equanimity.
constipate (kŏn′stĭ pāt′), *v.t.,* **-pated, -pating. 1.** to cause constipation in; make costive. **2.** *Obs.* to crowd or pack closely together. [t. L: m. s. *constīpātus*, pp., pressed together] **—con′stipat′ed,** *adj.*
constipation (kŏn′stĭ pā′shən), *n.* **1.** a condition of the bowels marked by defective or difficult evacuation. **2.** *Obs.* the act of crowding anything into a smaller compass; condensation.
constituency (kən stĭt′yōō ən sĭ), *n., pl.* **-cies. 1.** a body of constituents; the body of voters, or, loosely, of residents, in a district represented by an elected member of the legislature. **2.** the district itself. **3.** *U.S.* any body of supporters, customers, etc.; a clientele.
constituent (kən stĭt′yōō ənt), *adj.* **1.** serving to make up a thing; component; elementary: *constituent parts.* **2.** having power to frame or alter a political constitution or fundamental law (as distinguished from lawmaking power): *a constituent assembly.* **—***n.* **3.** a constituent element, material, etc.; a component. **4.** a voter, or (loosely) a resident, in a district represented by an elected official. **5.** a person who appoints, by power of attorney, another to act for him. **6.** *Gram.* an element that forms part of a construction. The **immediate constituents** are the largest parts (usually two) into which a construction is divisible, any or all of them sometimes further divisible into constituents of their own; the **ultimate constituents** are all the parts of a construction which are not further divisible. The sentence *John's hat looked slightly stained* has the immediate constituents *John's hat* (subject) and *looked slightly stained* (predicate), and the ultimate constituents *John, -'s, hat, look, -ed, slight, -ly, stain,* and *-ed.* [t. L: s. *constituens*, ppr., setting up] **—Syn. 3.** See **element.**
constitute (kŏn′stĭ tyōōt′), *v.t.,* **-tuted, -tuting. 1.** (of elements, etc.) to compose; form. **2.** to appoint to an office or function; make or create. **3.** to set up or found (an institution, etc.). **4.** to give legal form to (an assembly, court, etc.). **5.** *Obs.* to set up or establish (laws, etc.). **6.** to make up or form of elements, material, etc.; frame. **7.** *Obs.* to set or place. [t. L: m. s. *constitūtus*, pp., set up, established] **—con′stitut′er, con′stitu′tor,** *n.*
constitution (kŏn′stĭ tyōō′shən), *n.* **1.** the way in which anything is constituted; make-up or composition: *the physical constitution of the sun.* **2.** the physical character of the body as to strength, health, etc.: *a strong constitution.* **3.** character or condition of mind; disposition; temperament. **4.** the act of constituting; establishment. **5.** the state of being constituted; formation. **6.** any established arrangement or custom. **7.** the system of fundamental principles according to which a nation, state, etc., is governed: *the British constitution.* **8.** the document embodying these principles. [ME, t. L: s. *constitūtio*]
constitutional (kŏn′stĭ tyōō′shə nəl), *adj.* **1.** belonging to or inherent in a person's constitution of body or mind: *a constitutional weakness.* **2.** beneficial to, or designed to benefit, the bodily constitution: *a constitutional walk.* **3.** pertaining to the constitution or composition of a thing; essential. **4.** pertaining to, in accordance with, or subject to the constitution of a state, etc.: *a constitutional monarchy.* **5.** having the power of, or existing by virtue of and subject to, a constitution or fundamental organic law: *a constitutional government.* **6.** forming a part of, or authorized by, the constitution or fundamental organic law of a nation or state. **—***n.* **7.** a walk or other exercise taken for the benefit of the health. **—con′stitu′tionally,** *adv.*
constitutionalism (kŏn′stĭ tyōō′shə nə lĭz′əm), *n.* **1.** the principles of constitutional government, or adherence to them. **2.** constitutional rule or authority.
constitutionalist (kŏn′stĭ tyōō′shə nə lĭst), *n.* **1.** an adherent or advocate of constitutionalism, or of an existing constitution. **2.** a student of or writer on a political constitution.
constitutionality (kŏn′stĭ tyōō′shə năl′ĭ tĭ), *n.* **1.** the quality of being constitutional. **2.** accordance with the constitution of a state, etc. (as a measure or norm of law-making power).
constitutive (kŏn′stĭ tyōō′tĭv), *adj.* **1.** constituent; making a thing what it is; essential. **2.** having power to establish or appoint to an office. **—con′stitu′tively,** *adv.*
constrain (kən strān′), *v.t.* **1.** to force, compel, or oblige; bring about by compulsion: *to constrain obedience.* **2.** to confine forcibly, as by bonds. **3.** to repress or restrain. [ME *constreign(en)*, t. OF: m. *constreindre*, g. L *constringere* draw together] **—constrain′able,** *adj.* **—constrain′er,** *n.* **—Syn. 3.** check, bind, confine.
constrained (kən strānd′), *adj.* forced; cramped; restrained; stiff or unnatural: *a constrained smile or manner.* **—constrainedly** (kən strā′nĭd lĭ), *adv.*
constraint (kən strānt′), *n.* **1.** confinement or restriction. **2.** repression of natural feelings and impulses. **3.** unnatural restraint in manner, etc.; embarrassment. **4.** something that constrains. **5.** the act of constraining. **6.** the condition of being constrained. [ME *constreinte*, t. OF, prop. pp. fem. of *constreindre* CONSTRAIN]
constrict (kən strĭkt′), *v.t.* **1.** to draw together; compress; cause to contract or shrink. **2.** to restrict, or inhibit. [t. L: s. *constrictus*, pp., drawn together] **—Syn.** cramp, squeeze, bind, tighten. **—Ant.** expand.
constriction (kən strĭk′shən), *n.* **1.** the act of constricting. **2.** the state of being constricted. **3.** a constricted part. **4.** something that constricts.
constrictive (kən strĭk′tĭv), *adj.* **1.** constricting, or tending to constrict. **2.** pertaining to constriction.
constrictor (kən strĭk′tə), *n.* **1.** a snake that crushes its prey in its coils. **2.** *Anat.* a muscle that constricts a hollow part of the body, as the pharynx. **3.** one who or that which constricts. [t. NL]
constringe (kən strĭnj′), *v.,* **-stringed, -stringing. —***v.t.* **1.** to constrict; compress; cause to contract. **—***v.i.* **2.** to become close or dense. [t. L: m. s. *constringere.* Cf. CONSTRAIN]
constringent (kən strĭn′jənt), *adj.* **1.** constringing. **2.** causing constriction. **—constrin′gency,** *n.*
construct (*v.* kən strŭkt′, *n.* kŏn′strŭkt), *v.t.* **1.** to form by putting together parts; build; frame; devise. **2.** *Gram.* to put together words in syntactical arrangement. **3.** *Geom., etc.* to draw, as a figure, so as to fulfil given conditions. **—***n.* **4.** something constructed. **5.** a complex image or idea resulting from a synthesis by the mind. [t. L: s. *constructus*, pp., constructed, piled or put together] **—construct′or, construct′er,** *n.* **—Syn. 1.** erect, form. See **make.**
construction (kən strŭk′shən), *n.* **1.** the act or art of constructing. **2.** the way in which a thing is constructed; structure: *objects of similar construction.* **3.** that which is constructed; a structure. **4.** *Geom.* the drawing of lines to solve a problem or prove a proposition. **5.** *Gram.* **a.** the arrangement of two or more forms in a grammatical unit. Constructions involving bound forms are called morphological, as the bound forms *fif-* and *-teen* in *fifteen.* Those involving only free forms are called syntactic, as *the good man, in the house.* Cf. **bound form, free form. b.** a word or phrase consisting of two or more forms arranged in a particular way. **6.** explanation or interpretation, as of a law or a text, or of conduct or the like. **—construc′tional,** *adj.*
constructionist (kən strŭk′shə nĭst), *n.* one who construes or interprets, esp. laws or the like.
constructive (kən strŭk′tĭv), *adj.* **1.** constructing, or tending to construct: *constructive* (*as opposed to destructive*)

criticism. **2.** of, pertaining to, or of the nature of construction; structural. **3.** deduced by construction or interpretation; inferential: *constructive permission.* **4.** *Law.* not actually existing, but having the same legal effects as one that does: *a constructive possession.* —**construc′tively,** *adv.* —**construc′tiveness,** *n.*

constructivism (kən strŭk′tĭ vĭz′əm), *n.* a Russian art movement originating in Moscow just after World War I which emphasizes the machine in modern life. —**construc′tivist,** *n.*

construe (kən stro͞o′), *v.*, **-strued, -struing.** —*v.t.* **1.** to show the meaning or intention of; explain; interpret; put a particular interpretation on. **2.** to deduce by construction or interpretation; infer. **3.** to translate, esp. literally. **4.** to explain the syntax of: *in construing the sentence 'He caught a fish' one says 'he' is the subject, 'caught a fish' is the predicate, '(a) fish' is the direct object of the verb 'caught', etc.* **5.** to arrange or combine (words, etc.) syntactically. —*v.i.* **6.** to admit of grammatical analysis or interpretation. —*n.* **7.** the act of construing. [ME *construe(n)*, t. L: m. *construere* build up, pile together] —**constru′able,** *adj.* —**constru′abil′ity,** *n.* —**constru′er,** *n.*

consubstantial (kŏn′səb stăn′shəl), *adj.* of one and the same substance, essence, or nature. [t. LL: s. *consubstantiālis*, f. L: *con-* CON- + s. *substantia* substance + *-ālis* -AL[1]] —**consubstantiality** (kŏn′səb stăn′shĭ ăl′ĭ tĭ), *n.* —**con′substan′tially,** *adv.*

consubstantiate (kŏn′səb stăn′shĭ āt′), *v.*, **-ated, -ating.** —*v.i.* **1.** to profess the doctrine of consubstantiation. **2.** to become united in one common substance or nature. —*v.t.* **3.** to unite in one common substance or nature. **4.** to regard as so united. [t. ML: m. s. *consubstantiātus*, pp., identified in substance]

consubstantiation (kŏn′səb stăn′shĭ ā′shən), *n.* *Theol.* the doctrine that the substance of the body and blood of Christ coexist in and with the substance of bread and wine of the Eucharist.

consuetude (kŏn′swĭ tyo͞od′), *n.* custom, esp. as having legal force. [ME, t. L: m. *consuētūdo* custom]

consuetudinary (kŏn′swĭ tyo͞o′dĭ nə rĭ), *adj.* customary.

consul (kŏn′səl), *n.* **1.** an agent appointed by an independent state to reside in a foreign state and discharge certain administrative duties. **2.** either of the two chief magistrates of the ancient Roman republic. **3.** one of the three supreme magistrates of the French republic from 1799 to 1804. [t. L] —**consular** (kŏn′syo͝o lə), *adj.* —**con′sulship′,** *n.*

consular agent, **1.** a consular officer of one of the lower ranks. **2.** any consular officer.

consular invoice, an invoice, certified by the consul or consular officer of the country to which goods are being exported.

consulate (kŏn′syo͝o lĭt), *n.* **1.** the premises officially occupied by a consul. **2.** consulship. **3.** (*often cap.*) a government by consuls, as in France from 1799 to 1804. [t. L: m. s. *consulātus*]

consul general, a consular officer of the highest rank, as one stationed at a place of considerable commercial importance.

consult (kən sŭlt′), *v.t.* **1.** to seek counsel from; ask advice of. **2.** to refer to for information. **3.** to have regard for (a person's interest, convenience, etc.) in making plans. **4.** *Obs.* to meditate, plan, or contrive. —*v.i.* **5.** to consider or deliberate; take counsel; confer (fol. by *with*). —*n.* **6.** *Obs.* **a.** consultation. **b.** a council. [t. L: s. *consultāre*, freq. of *consulere* deliberate, take counsel. Cf. COUNSEL, n., CONSUL] —**consult′able,** *adj.* —**consult′er,** *n.*

—**Syn.** 1. CONSULT, CONFER imply talking over a situation or a subject with someone to decide points in doubt. To CONSULT is to seek from a presumably qualified personal or an impersonal source advice, opinion, etc.: *to consult an authority.* To CONFER is to interchange views in order to throw light on a subject under consideration: *the partners conferred concerning their business policy.*

consultant (kən sŭl′tənt), *n.* **1.** one who consults. **2.** one who gives professional or expert advice. **3.** *Med.* a medical or surgical specialist.

consultation (kŏn′səl tā′shən), *n.* **1.** the act of consulting; conference. **2.** a meeting for deliberation.

consultative (kən sŭl′tə tĭv), *adj.* of consultation; advisory. Also, **consultatory** (kən sŭl′tə tə rĭ, -trĭ).

consulting (kən sŭl′tĭng), *adj.* employed in giving professional advice, either to the public or to those practising the profession: *a consulting physician.*

consulting room, a room where a doctor interviews and examines patients.

consume (kən syo͞om′), *v.*, **-sumed, -suming.** —*v.t.* **1.** to destroy or expend by use; use up. **2.** to eat or drink up; devour. **3.** to destroy, as by decomposition or burning. **4.** to spend (money, time, etc.) wastefully. **5.** to absorb; engross. —*v.i.* **6.** to be consumed; suffer destruction; waste away. [ME *consume(n)*, t. L: m. *consūmere* take up completely] —**consum′able,** *adj.*, *n.* —**Syn.** **1.** exhaust, expend. **4.** squander, dissipate.

consumedly (kən syo͞o′mĭd lĭ), *adv.* excessively; extremely.

consumer (kən syo͞o′mə), *n.* **1.** one who or that which consumes. **2.** *Econ.* one who uses a commodity or service (opposed to *producer*).

consumer durables, *Econ.* consumer goods of a semi-permanent nature.

consumer goods, *Econ.* goods ready for consumption in satisfaction of human wants, as clothing, food, etc., and which are not utilized in any further production.

Consumers' Association, (in Great Britain) an association formed in 1951 to report on the comparative quality of goods and services available to the public.

consummate (*v.* kŏn′sə māt′, *adj.* kən sŭm′ĭt), *v.*, **-mated, -mating,** *adj.* —*v.t.* **1.** to bring to completion or perfection. **2.** to complete (a marriage) by sexual intercourse. —*adj.* **3.** complete or perfect; supremely qualified; of the highest quality. [late ME, t. L: m. s. *consummātus*, pp., brought to the highest degree] —**consum′mately,** *adv.* —**con′summa′tive,** *adj.* —**con′summa′tor,** *n.* —**Syn.** **1.** complete, perfect, fulfil, accomplish, achieve. **3.** excellent, finished, supreme.

consummation (kŏn′sə mā′shən), *n.* the act of consummating, or the state of being consummated; completion; perfection; fulfilment.

consumption (kən sŭmp′shən), *n.* **1.** the act of consuming; destruction or decay. **2.** destruction by use. **3.** the amount consumed. **4.** *Econ.* the using up of goods and services having an exchangeable value. **5.** *Pathol.* **a.** a wasting disease, esp. tuberculosis of the lungs. **b.** progressive wasting of the body. [ME, t. L: s. *consumptio* a wasting]

consumptive (kən sŭmp′tĭv), *adj.* **1.** tending to consume; destructive; wasteful. **2.** pertaining to consumption by use. **3.** *Pathol.* **a.** pertaining to or of the nature of consumption. **b.** disposed to or affected with consumption. —*n.* **4.** one who suffers from consumption. —**consump′tively,** *adv.* —**consump′tiveness,** *n.*

cont., **1.** containing. **2.** contents. **3.** continent. **4.** continental. **5.** continued.

contact (*n.* kŏn′tăkt; *v.* kŏn′tăkt, kən tăkt′), *n.* **1.** the state or fact of touching; a touching or meeting of bodies. **2.** immediate proximity or association. **3.** *Elect.* the moving part of a switch or relay which completes and breaks the circuit. **4.** *Maths.* a meeting of two curved surfaces so that they have a common tangent at the point where they meet. **5.** *Colloq.* a person through whom contact is established, often a business acquaintance. **6.** *Med.* **a.** one who has lately been exposed to an infected person. **b.** inflammation of the skin due to contact with an irritating agent. **7.** *Sociol.* **a.** a condition in which two or more individuals or groups are placed in communication with one another. **b. categoric contact,** acting towards one on the basis of the type or group of people he represents rather than on the basis of his personal make-up. **c. primary contact,** a contact characterized by intimacy and personal familiarity. **d. secondary contact,** a contact characterized by impersonal and detached interest on the part of the participants, such as between strangers. **e. sympathetic contact,** acting towards an individual on the basis of his personal or individual make-up instead of on the basis of his group membership. —*v.t.* **8.** to put or bring into contact. **9.** *Colloq.* to get in touch with (a person). —*v.i.* **10.** to enter into or be in contact. [t. L: s. *contactus* a touching]

contact-breaker (kŏn′tăkt brā′kə), *n.* *Elect.* any device for repeatedly making and breaking an electric circuit, esp. an electromagnetic device as used in an electric bell.

contact flight, *Aeron.* **1.** a flight in which the pilot always sees land or water over which he passes. **2.** navigation by ground observations only.

contact lenses, devices to aid defective vision inconspicuously, consisting of small lenses, usually of plastic, which cover the irises and are held in place by eye fluid.

contactor (kŏn′tăk′tə), *n.* *Elect.* a contact-breaker.

contact paper, *Photog.* sensitized paper on which a contact print is made.

contact print, *Photog.* a print made by placing a negative upon sensitized paper, and exposing to light.

contagion (kən tā′jən), *n.* **1.** the communication of disease by direct or indirect contact. **2.** a disease so communicated. **3.** the medium by which a contagious disease is transmitted. **4.** pestilential influence; hurtful contact or influence. **5.** the communication of any influence, as enthusiasm, from one to another. [ME, t. L: s. *contāgio* a contact]

contagious (kən tā′jəs), *adj.* **1.** communicable to other individuals, as a disease. **2.** carrying or spreading a disease. **3.** tending to spread from one to another: *panic is contagious.* [ME, t. LL: m. s. *contāgiōsus*] —**conta′giously,** *adv.* —**conta′giousness,** *n.*

—**Syn.** **3.** CONTAGIOUS, INFECTIOUS have scientific uses in which they are precisely defined; but in popular use in referring to disease the words are often confused. In popular figurative use, in which both may have some favourable connotations, they are differentiated to some extent. CONTAGIOUS emphasizes the rapidity with which the 'contagion' spreads from person to person: *contagious laughter ran through the hall.* INFECTIOUS suggests the pleasantly irresistible quality of the source of 'contagion': *his infectious enthusiasm stimulated applause.*

contain (kən tān′), *v.t.* **1.** to have within itself; hold within fixed limits. **2.** *Geom.* to form the boundary of. **3.** to be capable of holding; have capacity for. **4.** to have as contents or constituent parts; comprise; include. **5.** to keep within proper bounds; restrain: *to contain oneself or one's feelings.* **6.** (of an enemy force, hostile power, disease, etc.) to keep in check, confine within certain limits. **7.** *Maths.* to be divisible by, without a remainder. **8.** to be equal to: *a quart contains two pints.* [ME *conteine(n)*, t. OF: m. *contenir*, g. L *continēre* hold together, hold back] —**contain′able,** *adj.*

—**Syn.** **1.** CONTAIN, ACCOMMODATE, HOLD express the idea that something is so designed that something else can exist or be placed within it. CONTAIN refers to what is actually within a given container. HOLD emphasizes the idea of causing to remain in position, or keeping within bounds; it refers also to the greatest amount or number that can be kept within a given container. ACCOMMODATE means to contain comfortably or conveniently, or to meet the needs of a certain number. An aeroplane which ACCOMMODATES fifty passengers may be able to HOLD sixty, but at a given time may CONTAIN only thirty.

container (kən tā′nə), *n.* **1.** anything that contains or can contain, as a carton, box, crate, tin, etc. **2.** a box-shaped unit for carrying goods; its standardized size facilitates easy transference from one form of transport to another.

containerize (kən tā′nə rīz′), *v.t.*, **-rized, -rizing.** **1.** to send (goods) in containers. **2.** to convert (a goods-carrying system) to the use of containers. Also, **containerise.** —**contai′neriza′tion,** *n.*

containment (kən tān′mənt), *n.* **1.** the act or policy of preventing the expansion beyond certain limits of a hostile power, etc. **2.** *Physics.* the process of preventing the plasma in a controlled thermonuclear reaction from coming into contact with the walls of the containing vessel.

contam., contamination.

contaminate (*v.* kən tăm′ĭ nāt′; *adj.* -nĭt, -nāt′), *v.*, **-nated, -nating,** *adj.* —*v.t.* **1.** to render impure by contact or mixture. **2.** to render harmful or unusable by adding radioactive material to. **3.** *Bibliog.* (of variant versions of a text) to influence and cause corruption. —*adj.* **4.** *Archaic.* contaminated. [t. L: m. s. *contāminātus*, pp.] —**contaminative** (kən tăm′ĭ nə tĭv), *adj.* —**contam′ina′tor,** *n.* —**Syn.** **1.** defile, pollute, befoul, sully, taint, infect, poison, corrupt.

contamination (kən tăm′ĭ nā′shən), *n.* **1.** the act of contaminating. **2.** the state of being contaminated. **3.** something that contaminates. **4.** *Bibliog.* the corruption of a text by the influence of variant versions.

contango (kən tăng′gō), *n.*, *pl.* **-gos.** (on the Stock Exchange) a fee paid by the buyer of securities to the seller for deferring delivery until the next settling day (opposed to *backwardation*); continuation.

contango day, the day, two before settling day, on which contangos are fixed.

contd, continued.

conte (*Fr.* kôNt), *n.*, *pl.* **contes** (*Fr.* kôNt). a tale or short story, esp. of extraordinary and usually imaginary events. [t. F]

contemn (kən tĕm′), *v.t.* to treat disdainfully or scornfully; view with contempt. [t. L: s. *contemnere* despise] —**contemner, contemnor** (kən tĕm′nə, kən tĕm′ə), *n.*

contemplate (kŏn′tĕm plāt′), *v.*, **-plated, -plating.** —*v.t.* **1.** to look at or view with continued attention; observe thoughtfully. **2.** to consider attentively; reflect upon. **3.** to have as a purpose; intend. **4.** to have in view as a future event. —*v.i.* **5.** to think studiously; meditate; consider deliberately. [t. L: m. s. *contemplātus*, pp., having surveyed] —**con′templa′tor,** *n.* —**Syn.** **1.** observe, regard. **2.** design, plan.

contemplation (kŏn′tĕm plā′shən), *n.* **1.** the act of contemplating; thoughtful observation or consideration; reflection. **2.** religious meditation. **3.** purpose or intention. **4.** prospect or expectation.

contemplative (kŏn′tĕm plā′tĭv, kən tĕm′plə-), *adj.* **1.** given to or characterized by contemplation. —*n.* **2.** a person devoted to religious contemplation. —**con′templa′tively,** *adv.* —**con′templa′tiveness,** *n.* —**Syn.** thoughtful, reflective, meditative. —**Ant.** active.

contemporaneous (kən tĕm′pə rā′nyəs), *adj.* contemporary. [t. L: m. *contemporāneus*] —**contem′pora′neously,** *adv.* —**contem′pora′neousness,** *n.*

contemporary (kən tĕm′prə rĭ), *adj.*, *n.*, *pl.* **-raries.** —*adj.* **1.** belonging to the same time; existing or occurring at the same time. **2.** of the same age or date. **3.** of the present time. **4.** *Colloq.* in the most modern style; up-to-date. —*n.* **5.** one belonging to the same time or period with another or others. **6.** a person of the same age as another. [f. CON- + TEMPORARY] —**Syn.** **1.** coeval, coexistent.

contemporize (kən tĕm′pə rīz′), *v.*, **-rized, -rizing.** —*v.t.* **1.** to place in, or regard as belonging to, the same age or time. —*v.i.* **2.** *Rare.* to be contemporary. Also, **contemporise.**

contempt (kən tĕmpt′), *n.* **1.** the act of contemning or despising. **2.** the feeling with which one regards anything considered mean, vile, or worthless. **3.** the state of being despised; dishonour; disgrace. **4.** *Law.* **a.** disobedience to, or open disrespect of, the rules or orders of a court or legislature. **b.** an act showing this disrespect. [ME, t. L: s. *contemptus* scorn]

—**Syn.** **2.** CONTEMPT, DISDAIN, SCORN imply strong feelings of disapproval combined with disgust or derision. CONTEMPT is disapproval tinged with disgust for what seems mean, base, or worthless: *to feel contempt for a weakling.* DISDAIN is a feeling that something is beneath the level of one's own dignity or is unworthy of one's notice or acceptance: *disdain for crooked dealing.* SCORN denotes derisive, open, or undisguised contempt, as for a thing thought unworthy of considerate treatment: *scorn for attempted evasion of punishment by blaming others.* —**Ant.** **2.** respect.

contemptible (kən tĕmp′tə bl), *adj.* **1.** deserving of or held in contempt; despicable. **2.** *Obs.* contemptuous. —**contempt′ibil′ity, contempt′ibleness,** *n.* —**contempt′ibly,** *adv.* —**Syn.** **1.** mean, abject, low, base. —**Ant.** **1.** admirable.

Contemptibles (kən tĕmp′tə blz), *n.* **Old.** See **Old Contemptibles.**

contemptuous (kən tĕmp′tyo͝o əs), *adj.* manifesting or expressing contempt or disdain; scornful. [f. L *contemptu(s)* scorn + -OUS] —**contemp′tuously,** *adv.* —**contemp′tuousness,** *n.* —**Syn.** disdainful, sneering, insolent, arrogant, supercilious, haughty.

contend (kən tĕnd′), *v.i.* **1.** to struggle in opposition. **2.** to strive in rivalry; compete; vie. **3.** to strive in debate; dispute earnestly. —*v.t.* **4.** to assert or maintain earnestly. [t. L: s. *contendere* stretch out] —**contend′er,** *n.* —**Syn.** **1.** wrestle, grapple, battle, fight. **2.** See **compete.** **3.** argue, wrangle. —**Ant.** **3.** agree.

content[1] (kŏn′tĕnt), *n.* **1.** (*usually pl.*) that which is contained: *the contents of a cask, room, or book.* **2.** (*usually pl.*) the chapters or chief topics of a book or document; a list of such chapters or topics. **3.** substance or purport, as of a document. **4.** the sum of the attributes or notions composing a given conception; the substance or matter of cognition, etc. **5.** power of containing; capacity; volume. **6.** area; extent; size. **7.** the amount contained. [t. ML: s. *contentum* that which is contained, prop. pp. neut.]

content[2] (kən tĕnt′), *adj.* **1.** having the desires limited to what one has; satisfied. **2.** easy in mind. **3.** willing or resigned; assenting. —*v.t.* **4.** to make content. —*n.* **5.** the state or feeling of being contented; contentment. **6.** (in the House of Lords) an affirmative vote or voter (as opposed to *not-content*). [ME, t. L: s. *contentus* satisfied, prop. pp.] —**Syn.** **4.** appease, gratify. See **satisfy.**

contented (kən tĕn′tĭd), *adj.* satisfied, as with what one has or with something mentioned; content. —**content′edly,** *adv.* —**content′edness,** *n.*

contention (kən tĕn′shən), *n.* **1.** a struggling together in opposition; strife. **2.** a striving in rivalry; competition; a contest. **3.** strife in debate; a dispute; a controversy. **4.** a point contended for or affirmed in controversy. [ME, t. L: s. *contentio* strife] —**Syn.** **1.** struggle, conflict, combat. **3.** disagreement, dissension, debate, wrangle, altercation.

contentious (kən tĕn′shəs), *adj.* **1.** given to contention: *a contentious crew.* **2.** characterized by contention: *contentious issues.* **3.** *Law.* pertaining to causes between contending parties. [t. L: m. s. *contentiōsus*] —**conten′tiously,** *adv.* —**conten′tiousness,** *n.*

contentment (kən tĕnt′mənt), *n.* **1.** the state of being contented; satisfaction; ease of mind. **2.** *Archaic.* the act of contenting. —**Syn.** **1.** See **happiness.**

conterminous (kŏn tû′mĭ nəs), *adj.* **1.** having a common boundary; bordering; contiguous. **2.** meeting at their ends. **3.** having the same boundaries or limits; coextensive. Also, **conter′minal.** [t. L: m. *conterminus*] —**conter′minously,** *adv.*

contest (*n.* kŏn′tĕst; *v.* kən tĕst′), *n.* **1.** struggle for victory or superiority. **2.** conflict between competitors; a competition. **3.** strife in argument; dispute; controversy. —*v.t.* **4.** to struggle or fight for, as in battle. **5.** to argue against; dispute. **6.** to call in question. **7.** to contend for in rivalry. —*v.i.* **8.** to dispute; contend; compete. [t. F: s. *contester*, t. L: m. *contestārī* call to witness, bring a legal action] —**contest′able,** *adj.* —**contest′er,** *n.* —**Syn. 1.** See **fight. 2.** rivalry, match, tournament, game. **4.** See **compete. 5.** controvert, oppose. **6.** challenge. **7.** strive, compete, vie.

contestant (kən tĕs′tənt), *n.* **1.** one who takes part in a contest or competition. **2.** *U.S.* one who contests the result of an election. **3.** *U.S. Law.* the party who, in proceedings in the probate court, contests the validity of a will. [t. F, ppr. of *contester* contest, used as n.]

contestation (kŏn′tĕs tā′shən), *n.* **1.** the act of contesting. **2.** an assertion contended for.

context (kŏn′tĕkst), *n.* **1.** the parts of a discourse or writing which precede or follow, and are directly connected with, a given passage or word. **2.** the circumstances or facts that surround a particular situation, event, etc. [late ME, t. L: s. *contextus* connection]

contextual (kən tĕks′tŏŏ əl), *adj.* of or pertaining to the context; depending on the context. [f. L *contextu(s)* connection + -AL[1]] —**contex′tually,** *adv.*

contexture (kən tĕks′chə), *n.* **1.** the disposition and union of the constituent parts of anything; constitution; structure. **2.** an interwoven structure; a fabric. **3.** the act of weaving together. **4.** the fact or manner of being woven together. [t. F, der. L *contexere* weave together. See CON-, TEXTURE]

contiguity (kŏn′tĭ gyŏŏ′ĭ tĭ), *n., pl.* **-ties. 1.** the state of being contiguous. **2.** *Obs.* a series of things in continuous connection; a continuous mass or extent.

contiguous (kən tĭg′yŏŏ əs), *adj.* **1.** touching; in contact. **2.** in close proximity without actually touching; near. [t. L: m. *contiguus* touching] —**contig′uously,** *adv.* —**contig′uousness,** *n.*

continence (kŏn′tĭ nəns), *n.* **1.** self-restraint, esp. in regard to sexual activity; moderation; chastity. **2.** ability to exercise voluntary control over natural functions, esp. urinating and defecating. Also, **con′tinency.** [ME, t. L: m. s. *continentia*]

continent (kŏn′tĭ nənt), *n.* **1.** one of the main land masses of the globe, usually reckoned as seven in number (Europe, Asia, Africa, North America, South America, Australia, and Antarctica). **2.** the mainland (as distinguished from islands or peninsulas). **3. the Continent,** the mainland of Europe (as distinguished from the British Isles). **4.** a continuous tract or extent, as of land. **5.** *Archaic.* that which contains, holds, or comprises. —*adj.* **6.** exercising restraint in relation to the desires or passions; temperate. **7.** characterized by the ability to exercise control over natural impulses or functions; chaste. **8.** *Rare.* containing; being a container; capacious. **9.** *Obs.* restraining or restrictive. **10.** *Obs.* continuous; forming a continuous tract, as land. [ME, t. L: s. *continens*, pp., lit., holding together]

continental (kŏn′tĭ nĕn′tl), *adj.* **1.** of, or of the nature of, a continent. **2.** (*usually cap.*) of or pertaining to the mainland of Europe. **3.** (*cap.*) *U.S. Hist.* of the colonies during and immediately after the War of American Independence: *the Continental Congress.* —*n.* **4.** an inhabitant of a continent, esp. (*usually cap.*) of the mainland of Europe. **5.** (*cap.*) *U.S. Hist.* a soldier of the Continental army in the War of American Independence. **6.** *U.S. Hist.* a piece of paper money issued by the Continental Congress during the war.

continental climate, a type of climate associated with continental interiors, and characterized by extremely hot, sunny, summers, bitterly cold winters, and little rainfall, which occurs mainly in early summer.

Continental Congress, one of the two American legislative congresses during and after the War of American Independence, responsible for the Declaration of Independence and The Articles of Confederation.

continental divide, 1. a water parting between river systems that flow into opposite sides of a continent. **2.** (*caps.*) (in North America) the line of summits of the Rocky Mountains, separating streams flowing towards the Pacific from those flowing towards the Gulf of Mexico, and the Arctic Ocean.

continental drift, the supposed movement of the continents away from an original single land mass to their present position.

continental shelf, *Phys. Geog.* that portion of a continent submerged under relatively shallow sea, in contrast with the deep ocean basins from which it is separated by the relatively steep **continental slope.**

continently (kŏn′tĭ nənt lĭ), *adv.* in a continent manner.

contingence (kən tĭn′jəns), *n.* contact or tangency.

contingency (kən tĭn′jən sĭ), *n., pl.* **-cies. 1.** fortuitousness; uncertainty; dependence on chance or on the fulfilment of a condition. **2.** a contingent event; a chance, accident, or possibility, conditional on something uncertain. **3.** something incidental to a thing.

contingency table, *Statistics.* the frequency distribution for a two-way statistical classification.

contingent (kən tĭn′jənt), *adj.* **1.** dependent for existence, occurrence, character, etc., on something not yet certain; conditional (often fol. by *on* or *upon*). **2.** liable to happen or not; uncertain; possible. **3.** happening by chance or without known cause; fortuitous; accidental. **4.** *Logic.* (of a proposition) not involving any self-contradiction if denied, so that its truth or falsity can be established only by sensory observation (as opposed to *analytic* or *necessary* propositions). —*n.* **5.** the proportion that falls to one as a share to be contributed or furnished. **6.** a quota of troops furnished. **7.** any one of the representative groups composing an assemblage. **8.** something contingent; a contingency. [ME, t. L: s. *contingens*, ppr., touching, bordering on, reaching, befalling] —**contin′gently,** *adv.*

continual (kən tĭn′yŏŏ əl), *adj.* **1.** proceeding without interruption or cessation; continuous in time. **2.** of regular or frequent recurrence; often repeated; very frequent. [t. ML: s. *continuālis*; r. ME *continuel*, t. OF] —**Syn. 1, 2.** unceasing, ceaseless, incessant, uninterrupted, unremitting, constant. CONTINUAL, CONSTANT, CONTINUOUS, all refer to a succession of occurrences. CONTINUAL implies that successive recurrences are very close together, with only small breaks between them, or none at all: *continual misunderstanding between nations.* CONSTANT implies always recurring in the same way, under uniform conditions, with similar results, and the like: *constant repetition of the same mistakes.* CONTINUOUS emphasizes the idea that the succession is unbroken: *the continuous life of the universe.*

continually (kən tĭn′yŏŏ ə lĭ), *adv.* **1.** without cessation or intermission; unceasingly. **2.** very often; at regular or frequent intervals; habitually.

continuance (kən tĭn′yŏŏ əns), *n.* **1.** the act or fact of continuing; continuation. **2.** the remaining in the same place, condition, etc. **3.** *U.S.* a sequel. **4.** *Law.* adjournment of a step in a proceeding to a future day. [ME, t. OF, der. *continuer* CONTINUE]

continuant (kən tĭn′yŏŏ ənt), *n.* *Phonet.* a consonant, such as *f* or *m*, which may be prolonged without change of quality. [t. L: s. *continuans*, ppr., continuing]

continuation (kən tĭn′yŏŏ ā′shən), *n.* **1.** the act or fact of continuing or prolonging. **2.** the state of being continued. **3.** extension or carrying on to a further point: *the continuation of a road.* **4.** that by which anything is continued; a sequel, as to a story. **5.** contango.

continuation day, contango day.

continuation school, *U.S.* a school or college for further education.

continuative (kən tĭn′yŏŏ ə tĭv), *adj.* **1.** tending or serving to continue, or to cause continuation or prolongation. **2.** expressing continuance of thought. **3.** *Gram.* expressing a following event. In the sentence 'they arrested a suspect, who gave his name as John Smith' the second clause is a continuative clause. —*n.* **4.** something continuative. **5.** a continuative word or expression. **6.** a mood or aspect of a verb expressing that the action is viewed as a continuous development. **7.** a conjunction which connects a subordinate clause to a main clause. —**contin′uatively,** *adv.* —**contin′uativeness,** *n.*

continuator (kən tĭn′yŏŏ ā′tə), *n.* one who or that which continues: *the continuator of a story.*

continue (kən tĭn′yŏŏ), *v.,* **-ued, -uing.** —*v.i.* **1.** to go forwards or onwards in any course or action; keep on. **2.** to go on after suspension or interruption. **3.** to last or endure. **4.** to remain in a place; abide; stay. **5.** to remain in a particular state or capacity. —*v.t.* **6.** to go on with or persist in: *to continue an action.* **7.** to extend from one point to another in space; prolong. **8.** to carry on from the point of suspension or interruption: *to continue a narrative.* **9.** to say in continuation. **10.** to cause to last or endure; maintain or retain, as in a position. **11.** to carry over, postpone, or adjourn; keep pending, as a legal proceeding. [ME *continue(n)*, t. L: m. *continuāre* make continuous] —**contin′uable,** *adj.* —**contin′uer,** *n.*

—**Syn. 3.** CONTINUE, ENDURE, LAST, REMAIN imply existing uninterruptedly for an appreciable length of time. CONTINUE implies duration or existence without break or interruption: *the rain continued for two days.* ENDURE implies persistent continuance against influences that tend to weaken, undermine, or destroy: *brass endures through many years of wear.* LAST often applies to that which holds out to a desired end, fresh, unimpaired, or unexhausted, sometimes under conditions that tend to produce the opposite effect: *they had provisions enough to last all winter.* REMAIN is esp. applied to what continues without change in its essential state: *he remained a bachelor.*

continued fraction, a fraction whose denominator contains a fraction whose denominator contains a fraction, and so on, as

$$\cfrac{2}{7+\cfrac{1}{9+\cfrac{3}{4+\dots}}}$$

Also, **recurring fraction.**

continuity (kŏn′tĭ nyōō′ĭ tĭ), *n.*, *pl.* **-ties. 1.** the state or quality of being continuous. **2.** a continuous or connected whole. **3.** a film scenario giving the complete action, scenes, etc., in detail and in the order in which they are to be shown on the screen. **4.** the full version of a broadcast script, including spoken parts, linking comments, sound effects, etc.

continuity girl, *Films.* a girl employed to ensure complete consistency in a film.

continuo (kən tĭn′yŏŏ ō′), *n.* *Music.* a type of bass line accompaniment for a keyboard instrument.

continuous (kən tĭn′yŏŏ əs), *adj.* **1.** having the parts in immediate connection. **2.** uninterrupted in time; without cessation. **3.** *Gram.* progressive (def. 6). **—*n.* 4.** *Gram.* the progressive aspect of a verb. [t. L: m. *continuus* hanging together] **—contin′uously,** *adv.* **—contin′uousness,** *n.* **—Syn.** 2. See **continual.**

continuous creation, the cosmological theory that matter is being continuously created throughout the universe to compensate for its expansion, thus maintaining the universe in a steady state.

continuous current, direct current.

continuous waves, *Radio.* radiation which is not intermittent or broken up into damped wave-trains. *Abbrev.:* cw.

continuum (kən tĭn′yŏŏ əm), *n.*, *pl.* **-tinuums, -tinua** (-tĭn′yŏŏ ə). **1.** a continuous extent, series, or whole. **2.** *Maths.* an infinite set of objects such that between any two of them there is a third object: *the continuum of rational numbers.* **3. four-dimensional continuum,** *Physics.* (in the theory of relativity) the three dimensions of space and the dimension of time considered together.

conto (kŏn′tō; *Port.* kôn′tōō), *n.*, *pl.* **-tos** (-tōz; *Port.* -tōōsh). a Portuguese money of account in which large sums are calculated, equal to 1000 escudos. [t. Pg., g. L *computus* calculated]

contort (kən tôt′), *v.t.* to twist; bend or draw out of shape; distort. [t. L: s. *contortus*, pp., twisted] **—contortion** (kən tô′shən), *n.*

contortionist (kən tô′shə nĭst), *n.* **1.** one who performs gymnastic feats involving contorted postures. **2.** one who practices contortion: *a verbal contortionist.*

contour (kŏn′tŏŏə), *n.* **1.** the outline of a figure or body; the line that defines or bounds anything. **2.** a contour line. **—*v.t.* 3.** to mark with contour lines. **4.** to make or form the contour or outline of. **5.** to build (a road, etc.) in conformity to a contour. **—*adj.* 6.** *Agric.* of or used in a system of ploughing and sowing along the contour lines of the terrain, thereby preventing rainwater from washing away the topsoil. [t. F, t. It.: m. *contorno*, der. *contornare*, f. L: *con-* CON- + *tornāre* turn]

contour feathers, any of the feathers which form the surface plumage of a bird, apart from wings, tail, and specialized types, as filoplumes.

contour interval, the difference in elevation represented by each contour line on a map.

contour line, 1. a line joining points of equal elevation on a surface. **2.** the representation of such a line on a map.

contour map, a map on which irregularities of land surface are shown by contour lines, the relative spacing of the lines indicating the relative slope of the surface.

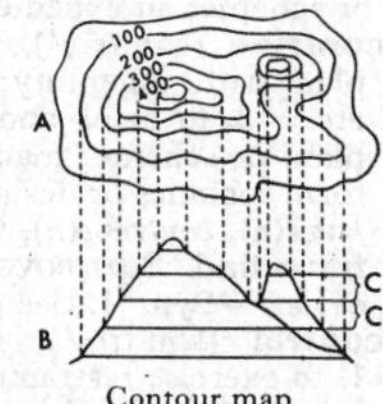

Contour map
A, Contour; B, Elevation; C, Contour interval

contr., 1. contracted. **2.** contraction. **3.** contrary.

contra-, a prefix meaning 'against', 'opposite', or 'opposing'. [t. L, prefix use of *contrā*, adv. and prep.]

contraband (kŏn′trə bănd′), *n.* **1.** anything prohibited by law from being imported or exported. **2.** goods imported or exported illegally. **3.** illegal or prohibited traffic; smuggling. **4.** *Internat. Law.* goods which neutrals cannot supply to one belligerent except at the risk of seizure and confiscation by the other **(contraband of war). 5.** *U.S.* (during the American Civil War) a fugitive Negro slave. **—*adj.* 6.** prohibited from export or import. [t. Sp.: m. *contrabando*; r. *counterband*, t. F: m. *contrebande*, t. It.: m. *contrabando*, f. *contra* against (g. L *contrā*) + *bando* proclamation (g. LL *bandum* BAN², n.)]

contrabandist (kŏn′trə băn′dĭst), *n.* a smuggler.

contrabass (kŏn′trə bās′), *Music.* **—*n.* 1.** (in any family of instruments) the member below the bass. **2.** (in the violin family) the double bass. **—*adj.* 3.** denoting such instruments: *a contrabass trombone.* **—contrabassist** (kŏn′trə bā′sĭst, -băs′ĭst), *n.*

contrabassoon (kŏn′trə bə sōōn′), *n.* a bassoon larger in size and an octave lower in pitch than the ordinary bassoon; a double bassoon.

contraception (kŏn′trə sĕp′shən), *n.* the prevention of conception by deliberate measures; birth control. [f. CONTRA- + (CON)CEPTION]

contraceptive (kŏn′trə sĕp′tĭv), *adj.* **1.** tending or serving to prevent conception or impregnation. **2.** pertaining to contraception. **—*n.* 3.** a contraceptive agent or device.

contraclockwise (kŏn′trə klŏk′wīz′), *adj.*, *adv.* *U.S.* anticlockwise.

contract (*n. and usually for v. 12* kŏn′trăkt; *otherwise v.* kən trăkt′), *n.* **1.** an agreement between two or more parties for the doing or not doing of some definite thing. **2.** an agreement enforceable by law. **3.** the writing containing such an agreement. **4.** the division of law dealing with contracts. **5.** the formal agreement of marriage; betrothal. **6.** Also, **contract bridge.** a modification of auction bridge in which the side which wins the bid can earn towards game only that number of tricks bid, all additional points being credited above the score line. **7.** (in auction or contract bridge) **a.** the highest bid. **b.** the number of tricks so bid. **—*v.t.* 8.** to draw together or into smaller compass; draw the parts of together: *to contract a muscle.* **9.** to wrinkle: *to contract the brows.* **10.** to shorten (a word, etc.) by combining or omitting some of its elements. **11.** to acquire, as by habit or contagion; incur, as a liability or obligation: *to contract a disease*; *to contract debts.* **12.** to settle or establish by agreement: *to contract an alliance.* **13.** to enter into (friendship, acquaintance, etc.). **14.** to betroth. **—*v.i.* 15.** to be drawn together or reduced in compass; become smaller; shrink. **16.** to enter into an agreement. [ME, t. LL: s. *contractus* agreement] **—contract′ible,** *adj.* **—contract′ibil′ity, contract′ibleness,** *n.*

—Syn. 1. See **agreement. 8.** reduce, shorten, lessen, narrow, shrivel, shrink. CONTRACT, COMPRESS, CONCENTRATE, CONDENSE imply retaining original content but reducing the amount of space occupied. CONTRACT means to cause to draw more closely together: *to contract a muscle.* COMPRESS suggests causing to become smaller by means of fairly uniform external pressure: *to compress gases into liquid form, clay into bricks.* CONCENTRATE implies causing to gather round a point, or eliminating non-essentials: *to concentrate troops near an objective, attention, strength.* CONDENSE implies increasing the compactness, or thickening the consistency of a homogeneous mass: *to condense milk.* **—Ant. 8.** expand.

contracted (kən trăk′tĭd), *adj.* **1.** drawn together; shrunken. **2.** abridged; (of a word) shortened by the elision of part of it. **—contract′edly,** *adv.* **—contract′edness,** *n.*

contractile (kən trăk′tīl), *adj.* capable of undergoing or of producing contraction. **—contractility** (kŏn′trăk tĭl′ĭ tĭ), *n.*

contraction (kən trăk′shən), *n.* **1.** the act of contracting. **2.** the state of being contracted. **3.** a shortened form of a word, etc., as *e'er* for *ever*, *can't* for *cannot.* **4.** *Physiol.* the change in a muscle by which it becomes thickened and shortened. [t. L: s. *contractio* a drawing together]

contractive (kən trăk′tĭv), *adj.* serving or tending to contract. **—contrac′tively,** *adv.* **—contrac′tiveness,** *n.*

contractor (kŏn′trăk′tə, kən trăk′tə), *n.* **1.** one who contracts to furnish supplies or perform work at a certain price or rate. **2.** one who or that which contracts. [t. LL]

contractual (kən trăk′tyŏŏ əl), *adj.* of, or of the nature of, a contract. [f. L *contractu(s)* contract + -AL¹]

contradance (kŏn′trə däns′), *n.* contredanse.

contradict (kŏn′trə dĭkt′), *v.t.* **1.** to assert the contrary or opposite of; deny directly and categorically. **2.** to deny the words or assertion of (a person). **3.** (of a statement, action, etc.) to be directly contrary to. **4.** *Obs.* to speak or declare against; oppose. **—*v.i.* 5.** to utter a contrary statement. [t. L: s. *contrādictus*, pp., said against] **—con′tradict′able,** *adj.* **—con′tradic′tor,** *n.* **—Syn. 1, 2.** gainsay, impugn, controvert, dispute. See **deny.**

contradiction (kŏn′trə dĭk′shən), *n.* **1.** the act of contradicting; gainsaying or opposition. **2.** assertion of the contrary or opposite; denial. **3.** a statement or proposition that contradicts or denies another or itself. **4.** direct opposition between things compared; inconsistency. **5.** a contradictory act, fact, etc. **6.** See **law of contradiction.**

contradictious (kŏn′trə dĭk′shəs), *adj.* **1.** inclined to contradict; disputatious. **2.** *Archaic.* self-contradictory. [f. CONTRADICTI(ON) + -OUS]

contradictive (kŏn′trə dĭk′tĭv), *adj.* tending to contradict; involving contradiction.

contradictory (kŏn′trə dĭk′tə rĭ), *adj., n., pl.* **-ries.** —*adj.* **1.** of the nature of a contradiction; asserting the contrary or opposite; contradicting each other; inconsistent. **2.** given to contradiction. —*n.* **3.** *Logic.* a proposition so related to a second that it is impossible for both to be true or both to be false. —**con′tradic′torily,** *adv.* —**con′tradic′toriness,** *n.* —**Syn. 1.** opposing, antagonistic, irreconcilable, paradoxical.

contradistinction (kŏn′trə dĭs tĭngk′shən), *n.* distinction by opposition or contrast: *plants and animals in contradistinction to man.* —**con′tradistinc′tive,** *adj.* —**con′tradistinc′tively,** *adv.*

contradistinguish (kŏn′trə dĭs tĭng′gwĭsh), *v.t.* to distinguish by contrasting opposite qualities.

contrail (kŏn′trāl′), *n.* vapour trail. [b. CON(DENSATION) + TRAIL]

contraindicate (kŏn′trə ĭn′dĭ kāt′), *v.t.,* **-cated, -cating.** *Med.* (of a symptom or condition) to give indication against the advisability of (a particular or usual remedy or treatment). —**contraindicant** (kŏn′trə ĭn′dĭ kənt), *n.* —**con′train′dica′tion,** *n.*

contralto (kən trăl′tō), *n., pl.* **-ti,** *adj. Music.* —*n.* **1.** the lowest female voice or voice part, intermediate between soprano and tenor. **2.** the alto, or highest male voice or voice part. **3.** a singer with a contralto voice. —*adj.* **4.** pertaining to the contralto or its compass. [t. It., f. *contra* against, counter to + *alto* high]

contraposition (kŏn′trə pə zĭsh′ən), *n.* **1.** placing opposite or against. **2.** opposition, antithesis, contrast. **3.** *Logic.* an immediate inference drawn from a given proposition by negating its terms and changing their order. —**contrapositive** (kŏn′trə pŏz′ĭ tĭv), *adj.*

contraption (kən trăp′shən), *n. Colloq.* a contrivance; a device.

contrapuntal (kŏn′trə pŭn′tl), *adj. Music.* **1.** of or pertaining to counterpoint. **2.** composed of two or more relatively independent melodies sounded together. [f. m. It. *contrappunto* counterpoint + -AL[1]] —**con′trapun′tally,** *adv.*

contrapuntist (kŏn′trə pŭn′tĭst), *n.* one skilled in the practice of counterpoint.

contrariety (kŏn′trə rī′ə tĭ), *n., pl.* **-ties. 1.** the state or quality of being contrary. **2.** something contrary or of opposite character; a contrary fact or statement. [t. LL: m. s. *contrārietas*]

contrarious (kən trĕə′rĭ əs), *adj. Now Rare.* **1.** perverse. **2.** adverse. [ME, t. ML: m. s. *contrāriōsus*]

contrariwise (kŏn′trə rĭ wīz′ *for 1, 2;* kən trĕə′rĭ wīz′ *for 3*), *adv.* **1.** in the opposite way. **2.** on the contrary. **3.** perversely.

contrary (kŏn′trə rĭ; *for 5 also* kən trĕə′rĭ), *adj., n., pl.* **-ries,** *adv.* —*adj.* **1.** opposite in nature or character; diametrically opposed; mutually opposed: *contrary to fact, contrary propositions.* **2.** opposite in direction or position. **3.** being the opposite one of two. **4.** untoward or unfavourable: *contrary winds.* **5.** perverse; self-willed. **6.** *Bot.* at right angles. —*n.* **7.** that which is contrary or opposite: *to prove the contrary of a statement.* **8.**. either of two contrary things. **9.** *Logic.* a proposition so related to a second that it is impossible for both to be true, though both may be false. For example: *all judges are male* is the contrary of *no judges are male.* **10. by contraries, a.** by way of opposition. **b.** contrary to expectation. **11. on the contrary,** in opposition to what has been stated. **12. to the contrary,** to the opposite or a different effect. —*adv.* **13.** contrarily; contrariwise. [ME *contrarie,* t. AF, t. L: m. *contrārius* opposite, hostile] —**con′trarily,** *adv.* —**con′trariness,** *n.*

—**Syn. 1.** contradictory, conflicting, discordant, counter. See **opposite. 4.** CONTRARY, ADVERSE both describe that which unfavourably opposes. CONTRAST conveys an idea of something impersonal and objective whose opposition happens to be unfavourable: *contrary winds.* ADVERSE suggests something more personally unfriendly or even hostile; it emphasizes the idea of the resulting misfortune to that which is opposed: *the judge rendered a decision adverse to the defendant.* **5.** intractable, refractory, obstinate, headstrong.

contrary motion, *Music.* melodic motion in which one part rises in pitch while the other descends, and vice versa.

contrast (*v.* kən träst′; *n.* kŏn′träst), *v.t.* **1.** to set in opposition in order to show unlikeness; compare by observing differences. **2.** to afford or form a contrast to; set off. —*v.i.* **3.** to exhibit unlikeness on comparison; form a contrast. —*n.* **4.** the act of contrasting. **5.** the state of being contrasted. **6.** a striking exhibition of unlikeness. **7.** something strikingly unlike. **8.** opposition or juxtaposition of different forms, lines, or colours in a work of art to intensify each other's properties and produce a more dynamic expression. **9.** *Photog.* the variation between light and dark areas of a print or negative. [t. F: s. *contraster,* t. It.: m. *contrastare,* g. LL: withstand, oppose] —**contrast′able,** *adj.* —**Syn. 1.** differentiate, discriminate, distinguish, oppose. See **compare.**

contrasty (kən träs′tĭ), *adj. Photog.* having coarse or sharp gradations of tone, esp. between dark and light areas (opposed to *soft*).

contravallation (kŏn′trə və lā′shən), *n. Fort.* a chain of redoubts and breastworks raised by besiegers about the place invested. [t. F: m. *contrevallation,* f. *contre-* CONTRA- + s. LL *vallātio* entrenchment]

contravene (kŏn′trə vēn′), *v.t.,* **-vened, -vening. 1.** to come or be in conflict with; go or act counter to; oppose. **2.** to violate, infringe, or transgress: *to contravene the law.* [t. L: m. s. *contrāvenīre* oppose] —**con′traven′er,** *n.*

contravention (kŏn′trə vĕn′shən), *n.* the act of contravening; action counter to something; violation.

contrayerva (kŏn′trə yû′və), *n.* the root of certain plants of the tropical American moraceous genus *Dorstenia,* esp. *D. contrayerva,* used as a stimulant, tonic, and diaphoretic. [t. Sp.: counter herb, antidote, f. L *contra-* CONTRA- + Sp. *yerva* herb]

contredanse (*Fr.* kôɴ trə däɴs′), *n.* **1.** a variation of the quadrille, in which the dancers face each other. **2.** a piece of music suitable for such a dance. Also, **contradance.** [F, mistranslation of COUNTRY DANCE]

contretemps (*Fr.* kôɴ trə täɴ′), *n., pl.* **-temps** (*Fr.* -täɴ′), **1.** an inopportune occurrence; an embarrassing mischance. **2.** *Fencing.* a feint made with the intention of producing a stop from the opponent. [t. F, respelling of *contretant,* g. OF *contrestant* opposing, ppr. of *contrester* oppose, g. L *contrāstāre*]

contribute (kən trĭb′yo͞ot), *v.,* **-uted, -uting.** —*v.t.* **1.** to give in common with others; give to a common stock or for a common purpose: *to contribute money, time, help.* **2.** to furnish to a magazine or journal. —*v.i.* **3.** to make contribution; furnish a contribution. [t. L: m. s. *contribūtus,* pp., brought together] —**contrib′utable,** *adj.* —**contrib′utive,** *adj.* —**contrib′utively,** *adv.* —**contrib′utiveness,** *n.*

contribution (kŏn′trĭ byo͞o′shən), *n.* **1.** the act of contributing. **2.** something contributed. **3.** an article contributed to a magazine or the like. **4.** an impost or levy. **5.** *U.S.* coinsurance. [ME, t. L: s. *contribūtio*]

contributor (kən trĭb′yo͞o tə), *n.* **1.** one who or that which contributes. **2.** one who contributes articles to a newspaper, magazine, or other joint literary work.

contributory (kən trĭb′yo͞o tə rĭ, -trĭ), *adj., n., pl.* **-ries.** —*adj.* **1.** pertaining to or of the nature of contribution; contributing. **2.** furnishing something towards a result: *contributory negligence.* **3.** subject to contribution or levy. —*n.* **4.** one who or that which contributes. **5.** a person liable to contribute to the assets of a company in the event of its being wound up.

contrite (kŏn′trīt), *adj.* **1.** broken in spirit by a sense of guilt; penitent: *a contrite sinner.* **2.** proceeding from contrition: *contrite tears.* [ME *contrit,* t. L: s. *contrītus,* pp., ground, worn down] —**con′tritely,** *adv.* —**con′triteness,** *n.*

contrition (kən trĭsh′ən), *n.* **1.** sincere penitence. **2.** *Theol.* sorrow for and detestation of sin with a true purpose of amendment, arising from a love of God for His own perfections (**perfect contrition**), or from some inferior motive, as fear of divine punishment (**imperfect contrition**). [ME, t. L: s. *contrītio*]

contrivance (kən trī′vəns), *n.* **1.** something contrived; a device, esp. a mechanical one. **2.** the act or manner of contriving; the faculty or power of contriving. **3.** a plan or scheme; an expedient.

contrive (kən trīv′), *v.,* **-trived, -triving.** —*v.t.* **1.** to plan with ingenuity; devise; invent. **2.** to plot (evil, etc.). **3.** to bring about or effect by a device, stratagem, plan, or scheme; manage (to do something). —*v.i.* **4.** to form schemes or designs; plan. **5.** *Obs.* to plot. [ME *contreve(n), controve(n),* t. OF: m. *controver,* f. *con-* CON- + *trover* find. See TROVER] —**contriv′able,** *adj.* —**contriv′er,** *n.* —**Syn. 1.** See **prepare.**

control (kən trōl′), *v.,* **-trolled, -trolling,** *n.* —*v.t.* **1.** to exercise restraint or direction over; dominate; command. **2.** to hold in check; curb. **3.** to test or verify (a scientific experiment) by a parallel experiment or other standard of comparison. **4.** *Obs.* to check or regulate (payments, etc.), orig. by means of a duplicate register. —*n.* **5.** the act or power of controlling; regulation; domination or command. **6.** check or restraint. **7.** something that serves to control; a check; a standard of comparison in scientific experimentation. **8.** a person who acts as a check; a controller. **9.** (*pl.*) a coordinated arrangement of devices for regulating and guiding a machine, as a motor, aeroplane, etc. **10.** *Motor Racing, etc.* that portion of the track which is not included in the timing. **11.** (in spiritualism) an agency believed to assist the medium at a seance.

12. *Philately.* an authenticating device printed on some stamps. [t. F: s. *contrôler*, in OF *contreroller*, der. *contrerolle* register. See COUNTER-, ROLL] —**control′lable,** *adj.* —**control′labil′ity,** *n.* —**control′ment,** *n.* —**Syn.** 1. manage, govern, rule. 5. See **authority.**

control chart, *Statistics.* a chart on which observations are plotted as ordinates in the order in which they are obtained, and on which **control lines** are constructed to indicate whether the population from which the observations are being drawn is remaining the same (used particularly in industrial quality control work).

control experiment, an experiment in which the variables are controlled so that the effects of varying one factor at a time may be observed.

controller (kən trō′lə), *n.* 1. one employed to check expenditures, etc.; a comptroller. 2. one who regulates, directs, or restrains. 3. a regulating mechanism. —**control′lership′,** *n.*

control rod, 1. *Physics.* a rod or tube, capable of moving up and down on its axis, which controls the rate of reaction in a nuclear reactor; made from a material containing a strong neutron absorber such as boron or cadmium. 2. *Radio.* the electrode in a radio valve, lying between the cathode and the anode, which controls the flow of current through the valve.

control room, a room, housing control equipment, as in a recording studio.

control stick, *Aeron.* a lever which, by tubes or cables, controls the ailerons and elevator of an aeroplane; joystick. Also, **control column.**

control tower, an airport building, usually tower-shaped, from which landing and take-off instructions are given.

control unit, *Computers.* the part of a digital computer which causes it to perform its program in the correct sequence.

controversial (kŏn′trə vû′shəl), *adj.* 1. of, or of the nature of, controversy; polemical. 2. subject to controversy; debatable. 3. given to controversy; disputatious. —**con′trover′sialist,** *n.* —**con′trover′sially,** *adv.*

controversy (kŏn′trə vû′sĭ, kən trŏv′ə sĭ), *n., pl.* **-sies.** 1. dispute, debate, or contention; disputation concerning a matter of opinion. 2. a dispute or contention. [t. L: m. s. *controversia* debate, contention] —**Syn.** 1. disagreement, altercation. 2. quarrel, wrangle. See **argument.**

controvert (kŏn′trə vût′, kŏn′trə vût′), *v.t.* 1. to contend against in discussion; dispute; deny; oppose. 2. to contend about in discussion; debate; discuss. —**con′trovert′er,** *n.* —**con′trovert′ible,** *adj.* —**con′trovert′ibly,** *adv.*

contumacious (kŏn′tyŏŏ mā′shəs), *adj.* stubbornly perverse or rebellious; wilfully and obstinately disobedient to authority. [f. m. CONTUMACY + -OUS] —**con′tuma′ciously,** *adv.* —**con′tuma′ciousness,** *n.*

contumacy (kŏn′tyŏŏ mə sĭ), *n., pl.* **-cies.** 1. stubborn perverseness or rebelliousness; wilful and obstinate resistance or disobedience to authority. 2. *Law.* wilful refusal to obey an order of a court. [ME *contumacie*, t. L: m. *contumācia*, der. *contumax* stubborn]

contumely (kŏn′tyŏŏ mĭ lĭ), *n., pl.* **-lies.** 1. insulting manifestation of contempt in words or actions; contemptuous or humiliating treatment. 2. a humiliating insult. [ME *contumelie*, t. L: m. *contumēlia*] —**contumelious** (kŏn′tyŏŏ mē′lyəs), *adj.* —**con′tume′liously,** *adv.* —**con′tume′liousness,** *n.*

contuse (kən tyŏŏz′), *v.t.,* **-tused, -tusing.** to injure as by a blow with a blunt instrument, without breaking the skin; bruise. [t. L: m. s. *contūsus*, pp., beaten together] —**contusive** (kən tyŏŏ′sĭv), *adj.*

contusion (kən tyŏŏ′zhən), *n.* an injury as from a blow with a blunt instrument, without breaking of the skin; a bruise.

conundrum (kə nŭn′drəm), *n.* 1. a riddle the answer to which involves a pun or play on words. 2. anything that puzzles. [orig. unknown]

conurbation (kŏn′û bā′shən), *n.* a large urban agglomeration formed by the growth and gradual merging of formerly separate towns. [f. CON- + s. L *urbs* city + -ATION]

conure (kŏn′yŏŏə), *n.* any small parrot of the genus *Aratinga* and some related genera. [t. NL: m. s. *Conurus* genus name, f. Gk: m. s. *kônos* cone + m. s. *ourás* tail]

convalesce (kŏn′və lĕs′), *v.i.,* **-lesced, -lescing.** to grow stronger after illness; make progress towards recovery of health. [t. L: m. s. *convalescere* grow strong]

convalescence (kŏn′və lĕs′əns), *n.* 1. the gradual recovery of health and strength after illness. 2. the period during which one is convalescing.

convalescent (kŏn′və lĕs′ənt), *adj.* 1. convalescing. 2. of or pertaining to convalescence or convalescents. —*n.* 3. a convalescent person.

convallariaceous (kŏn′və lēə′rĭ ā′shəs), *adj.* belonging to the *Convallariaceae*, a family of plants including the lily-of-the-valley, asparagus, etc. [f. s. NL *Convallaria* the lily-of-the-valley genus (der. L *convallis* valley enclosed on all sides) + -ACEOUS]

convection (kən vĕk′shən), *n.* 1. *Physics.* the transference of heat by the circulation or movement of the heated parts of a liquid or gas. 2. *Meteorol.* a mechanical process thermally produced involving the upward or downward transfer of a limited portion of the atmosphere. Convection is essential to the formation of many types of clouds. 3. conveyance. [t. LL: s. *convectio*, der. L *convehere* carry together] —**convec′tional,** *adj.* —**convec′tive,** *adj.* —**convec′tively,** *adv.*

convectional rain, rain formed from evaporated earth liquids on a hot day.

convector (kən vĕk′tə), *n.* a room-heating apparatus that warms and circulates the air passing over its heated elements.

convenance (kŏn′vĭ näns′; *Fr.* kôɴ və näɴs′), *n.* 1. suitability; expediency; propriety. 2. (*pl.*) the proprieties or conventionalities. [t. F: agreement, propriety, der. *convenir* agree, be fitting, g. L *convenīre* come together]

convene (kən vēn′), *v.,* **-vened, -vening.** —*v.i.* 1. to come together; assemble, usually for some public purpose. —*v.t.* 2. to cause to assemble; convoke. 3. to summon to appear, as before a judicial officer. [late ME, t. L: m. s. *convenīre* come together] —**conven′er,** *n.* —**Syn.** 1. congregate, meet, collect, gather.

convenience (kən vē′nyəns), *n.* 1. the quality of being convenient; suitability. 2. a situation of affairs or a time convenient for one: *to await one's convenience.* 3. advantage, as from something convenient: *a shelter for the convenience of travellers.* 4. anything convenient; an advantage; an accommodation; a convenient appliance, utensil, or the like. 5. a water closet or urinal; lavatory.

convenient (kən vē′nyənt), *adj.* 1. agreeable to the needs or purpose; well-suited with respect to facility or ease in use; favourable, easy, or comfortable for use. 2. at hand; easily accessible. 3. *Obs.* fitting or appropriate. [ME, t. L: s. *conveniens*, ppr., agreeing, suiting] —**conven′iently,** *adv.* —**Syn.** 1. suitable, adapted, serviceable.

convent (kŏn′vənt), *n.* 1. a community of persons devoted to religious life under a superior. 2. a society of monks, friars, or nuns. 3. (in popular usage) a society of nuns. 4. the building or buildings occupied by such a society; a monastery or nunnery. 5. a Roman Catholic or other school where children are taught by nuns. 6. (in popular usage) a nunnery. [t. L: s. *conventus* meeting, assembly, company, in ML convent; r. ME *covent*, t. AF]

conventicle (kən vĕn′tĭ kl), *n.* 1. a secret or unauthorized meeting, esp. for religious worship, as those held by Protestant dissenters in England when they were prohibited by law. 2. a place of meeting or assembly, esp. a Nonconformist meeting house. 3. *Obs.* a meeting or assembly. [ME, t. L: m. s. *conventiculum*, dim. of *conventus* meeting] —**conven′ticler,** *n.*

convention (kən vĕn′shən), *n.* 1. a meeting or assembly, esp. a formal assembly, as of representatives or delegates, for action on particular matters. 2. (in France) any of various national assemblies, esp. that from 1792 to 1795. 3. *U.S. Politics.* a representative party assembly to nominate candidates, etc. 4. an agreement, compact, or contract. 5. an international agreement, esp. one dealing with a specific matter, as postal service, copyright, arbitration, etc. 6. general agreement or consent; accepted usage, esp. as a standard of procedure. 7. conventionalism. 8. a rule, method, or practice established by general consent or usage. 9. *Bridge.* a. a bid or lead, which, if interpreted according to an agreed system and not taken at face value, yields information about the hand. b. the system. [t. L: s. *conventio* a meeting]

—**Syn.** 1. CONVENTION, ASSEMBLY, CONFERENCE, CONVOCATION name meetings for particular purposes. CONVENTION, a formal word, usually suggests a meeting of delegates representing political, church, social, or fraternal organizations. ASSEMBLY usually implies a meeting for a settled or customary purpose, as for discussion, legislation, or participation in a social function. CONFERENCE suggests a meeting for consultation and discussion about business or professional problems. CONVOCATION denotes an assembly, usually ecclesiastical or university, the members of which have been summoned for a special purpose. 8. custom, precedent.

conventional (kən vĕn′shə nəl), *adj.* 1. conforming or adhering to accepted standards, as of conduct or taste. 2. pertaining to convention or general agreement; established by general consent or accepted usage; arbitrarily determined: *conventional symbols.* 3. formal, rather than spontaneous or original: *conventional phraseology.* 4. *Art.* a. in accordance with accepted manner, model, or tradition. **b.** (of figurative art) represented in a generalized or simplified manner. **5.** of or pertaining to a convention, agreement, or compact. **6.** *Law.* resting on consent, express or implied. **7.** of or pertaining to a convention or assembly. **8.** *Colloq.* (of weapons or arms) not nuclear. —**conven′tionalist,** *n.* —**conven′tionally,** *adv.* —**Syn. 1.** See **formal.**

conventionalism (kən vĕn′shə nə lĭz′əm), *n.* **1.** adherence or the tendency to adhere to that which is conventional. **2.** something conventional.

conventionality (kən vĕn′shə năl′ĭ tĭ), *n., pl.* **-ties. 1.** conventional quality or character. **2.** adherence to convention. **3.** a conventional practice, principle, form, etc. **4. the conventionalities,** the conventional rules of propriety.

conventionalize (kən vĕn′shə nə līz′), *v.t.,* **-lized, -lizing. 1.** to make conventional. **2.** *Art.* to represent in a conventional manner. Also, **conventionalise.** —**conven′tionaliza′tion,** *n.*

conventual (kən vĕn′tyŏŏ əl), *adj.* **1.** of, belonging to, or characteristic of a convent. —*n.* **2.** (*cap.*) one of an order of Franciscan friars which in the 15th century was separated from the Observants, and which follows a mitigated rule. **3.** an inmate of a convent. [late ME, t. ML: s. *conventuālis,* der. *conventus* CONVENT]

converge (kən vûj′), *v.,* **-verged, -verging.** —*v.i.* **1.** to tend to meet in a point or line; incline towards each other, as lines which are not parallel. **2.** to tend to a common result, conclusion, etc. **3.** *Maths.* (of a sequence of numbers) to approach a single number, called the limit. —*v.t.* **4.** to cause to converge. [t. LL: m. s. *convergere* incline together]

convergence (kən vû′jəns), *n.* **1.** the act or fact of converging. **2.** convergent state or quality. **3.** degree of convergence, or point of convergence. **4.** *Physiol.* a turning of the eyes inwards to bear upon a near point. **5.** *Meteorol.* a condition brought about by a net flow of air into a given region. **6.** *Biol.* similarity of form or structure caused by environment rather than heredity. Also, **conver′gency** for 1–3. —**conver′gent,** *adj.*

convergent evolution, the appearance of apparently similar structures in organisms of different lines of descent.

conversable (kən vû′sə bl), *adj.* **1.** that may be conversed with, esp. easily and agreeably. **2.** able or disposed to converse. **3.** pertaining to or proper for conversation. —**convers′ableness,** *n.* —**convers′ably,** *adv.*

conversant (kən vû′sənt), *adj.* **1.** familiar by use or study (fol. by *with*): *conversant with a subject.* **2.** *Archaic.* having regular or frequent conversation; intimately associating; acquainted. [ME, t. L: s. *conversans,* ppr., associating with] —**conver′sance, conver′sancy,** *n.* —**conver′santly,** *adv.* —**Syn. 1.** versed, learned, skilled, practised, well-informed; proficient.

conversation (kŏn′və sā′shən), *n.* **1.** informal interchange of thoughts by spoken words; a talk or colloquy. **2.** an instance of this. **3.** *Obs.* association or social intercourse; intimate acquaintance. **4.** *Obs.* familiar acquaintance from using or studying. **5.** *Archaic.* behaviour, or manner of living. [ME, t. OF, t. L: s. *conversātio* frequent use, intercourse]

conversational (kŏn′və sā′shə nəl), *adj.* **1.** of, pertaining to, or characteristic of, conversation. **2.** able, or ready to converse; given to conversation. —**con′versa′tionally,** *adv.* —**Syn. 1.** See **colloquial.**

conversationalist (kŏn′və sā′shə nə lĭst), *n.* one given to or excelling in conversation.

conversational quality, (in public speaking and reading) a manner of utterance which sounds like spontaneous, direct communication.

conversation piece, 1. a type of painting esp. popular in England in the 18th century, showing a group of more or less fashionable people in an appropriate setting. **2.** *Theat.* a play emphasizing dialogue. **3.** an object that arouses comment because of some striking or unusual quality.

conversazione (kŏn′və săt′sĭ ō′nĭ; *It.* kôn vĕr sä tsyô′nĕ), *n., pl.* **-ziones** (-sĭ ō′nēz), *It.* **-zioni** (*It.* -tsyô′nē). *Italian.* **1.** a social gathering for conversation, etc., esp. on literary or scholarly subjects. **2.** a soiree given by a learned society, for demonstrations, exhibition of specimens, etc.

converse[1] (*v.* kən vûs′; *n.* kŏn′vûs), *v.,* **-versed, -versing,** *n.* —*v.i.* **1.** to talk informally with another; interchange thought by speech. **2.** to hold inward communion (fol. by *with*). —*n.* **3.** familiar discourse or talk; conversation. **4.** inward communion. [ME *converse(n),* t. OF: m. *converser,* g. L *conversārī* dwell or associate with] —**convers′er,** *n.* —**Syn. 1.** talk, chat. See **speak.**

converse[2] (kŏn′vûs), *adj.* **1.** turned about; opposite or contrary in direction or action. —*n.* **2.** a thing which is the opposite or contrary of another. **3.** *Logic.* **a.** a proposition obtained from another proposition by conversion. **b.** the relation between one term and a second when the second term is related in a certain manner to the first. For example: the relation *descendant of* is the converse of *ancestor of.* **4.** a group of words correlative with a preceding group but having a significant pair of terms interchanged. Example: *hot in winter but cold in summer* is the *converse* of *cold in winter but hot in summer.* [t. L: m. s. *conversus,* pp., turned about] —**conversely** (kŏn vûs′lĭ, kŏn′vûs-), *adv.*

conversion (kən vû′shən), *n.* **1.** the act of converting. **2.** the state of being converted. **3.** change in character, form, or function. **4.** spiritual change from sinfulness to righteousness. **5.** change from one religion, party, etc., to another. **6.** *Maths.* a change in the form or units of an expression. **7.** *Logic.* the transposition of the subject and the predicate of a proposition, in accordance with rules of syllogistic logic, so as to form a new proposition. For example: *no good man is unhappy* becomes by conversion *no unhappy man is good.* **8.** *Law.* **a.** unauthorized assumption and exercise of rights of ownership over personal property belonging to another. **b.** change from realty into personalty, or vice versa, as in sale or purchase of land, minerals, etc. **9.** *Rugby Football.* **a.** the act of converting a try. **b.** the try so converted. **10.** *Psychol.* the process by which a repressed psychic event, idea, feeling, memory, or impulse is represented by a bodily change or symptom, thus simulating physical illnesses or their symptoms. **11.** *Physics.* the process of converting fertile material into fissile material in a nuclear reactor. —**conver′sional, conversionary** (kən vû′shə nə rĭ), *adj.*

convert (*v.* kən vût′; *n.* kŏn′vût), *v.t.* **1.** to change into something of different form or properties; transmute; transform. **2.** *Chem.* to cause (a substance) to undergo a chemical change: *to convert sugar into alcohol.* **3.** to cause to adopt a different religion, party, opinion, etc., esp. one regarded as better. **4.** to change in character; cause to turn from an evil life to a righteous one. **5.** to turn to another or a particular use or purpose; divert from the proper or intended use. **6.** to appropriate wrongfully to one's own use. **7.** *Law.* to assume unlawful rights of ownership of (personal property). **8.** *Rugby Football.* to change (a try) into a goal by kicking the ball over the crossbar of the goalposts, scoring 5 points in all. **9.** *Logic.* to transpose the subject and predicate of (a proposition) by conversion. **10.** to exchange for an equivalent: *to convert banknotes into gold.* **11.** to change stocks or debentures into others of a different type. **12.** *Obs.* to invert or transpose. —*v.i.* **13.** *Rugby Football.* to score a goal from a try. —*n.* **14.** one who has been converted, as to a religion or an opinion. [ME *converte(n),* t. L: m. *convertere* turn about, change] —**Syn. 1.** See **transform. 14.** proselyte, neophyte, disciple.

converter (kən vû′tə), *n.* **1.** one who or that which converts. **2.** *Elect.* **a.** a device which changes alternating current to direct current or vice versa. **b.** a device which alters the frequency of signals. **3.** *Metall.* a Bessemer converter. **4.** Also, **converter reactor.** *Physics.* a nuclear reactor which produces fissile material from fertile material. **5.** *U.S.* one engaged in converting textile fabrics from the raw state into the finished product. Also, **convertor.**

convertible (kən vû′tə bl), *adj.* **1.** capable of being converted. **2.** (of a motor car) having a removable top. **3.** (of currency) capable of being exchanged at a fixed price. **4.** (of paper currency) capable of being exchanged for gold on demand to its full value at the issuing bank. —*n.* **5.** *Colloq.* a convertible motor car. —**convert′ibil′ity, convert′ibleness,** *n.* —**convert′ibly,** *adv.*

convertiplane (kən vû′tĭ plān′), *n.* an aircraft capable of both vertical flight (like a helicopter) and level forward flight as a conventional fixed-wing aircraft.

convertite (kŏn′və tīt′), *n. Archaic.* a convert, esp. a reformed prostitute.

convex (*adj.* kŏn vĕks′, kən-; *n.* kŏn′vĕks), *adj.* **1.** curved like a circle or sphere when viewed from without; bulging and curved; esp. of optical lenses and mirrors. —*n.* **2.** a convex surface, part, or thing. [t. L: s. *convexus* vaulted, arched; appar. earlier var. of *convectus,* pp., carried together] —**convex′ly,** *adv.*

A B C

A, Convex or plano-convex lens; B, Convexo-concave lens; C, Biconvex lens

convexity (kən vĕk′sĭ tĭ), *n., pl.* **-ties. 1.** the state of being convex. **2.** a convex surface or thing.

convexo-concave (kən vĕk′sō kŏn kāv′), *adj.* convex on one side and concave on the other.

convexo-convex (kən vĕk′sō kŏn vĕks′), *adj.* biconvex.

convexo-plane (kən vĕk′sō plān′), *adj.* plano-convex.

convey (kən vā′), *v.t.* **1.** to carry or transport from one place to another. **2.** to lead or conduct as a channel or medium; transmit. **3.** to communicate; impart; make known. **4.** *Law.* to transfer; pass the title to. **5.** *Obs.* to take away secretly. **6.** *Obs.* to steal. [ME *conveye(n)*, t. OF: m. *conveier*, f. *con-* CON- + *veier*, der. *veie*, g. L *via* way, journey] —**convey′able,** *adj.* —**Syn. 1.** See **carry.**

conveyance (kən vā′əns), *n.* **1.** the act of conveying; transmission; communication. **2.** a means of conveyance, esp. a vehicle; a carriage, motor car, etc. **3.** *Law.* **a.** the transfer of property from one person to another. **b.** the instrument or document by which this is effected.

conveyancer (kən vā′ən sə), *n.* a person engaged in conveyancing.

conveyancing (kən vā′ən sĭng), *n.* that branch of legal practice consisting of examining titles, giving opinions as to their validity, and preparing of deeds, etc., for the conveyance of property from one person to another.

conveyor (kən vā′ə), *n.* **1.** one who or that which conveys. **2.** a contrivance for transporting material, as from one part of a building to another. Also, **conveyer.**

conveyor belt, a flexible band passing about two or more wheels, etc., used to transport objects from one place to another, esp. in a factory.

convict (*v.*, *adj.* kən vĭkt′; *n.* kŏn′vĭkt), *v.t.* **1.** to prove or declare guilty of an offence, esp. after a legal trial: *to convict the prisoner of felony.* **2.** to impress with the sense of guilt. —*n.* **3.** a person proved or declared guilty of an offence. **4.** a person serving a prison sentence. —*adj.* **5.** *Archaic.* convicted. [ME, t. L: s. *convictus*, pp., overcome, convicted] —**convic′tive,** *adj.*

conviction (kən vĭk′shən), *n.* **1.** the act of convicting. **2.** the fact or state of being convicted. **3.** the act of convincing. **4.** the state of being convinced. **5.** a fixed or firm belief. —**convic′tional,** *adj.* —**Syn. 5.** See **belief.** —**Ant. 2.** doubt, uncertainty.

convince (kən vĭns′), *v.t.*, **-vinced, -vincing. 1.** to persuade by argument or proof; cause to believe in the truth of what is alleged (often fol. by *of*): *to convince a man of his errors.* **2.** *Obs.* to prove or find guilty. **3.** *Obs.* to overcome; vanquish. [t. L: m. s. *convincere* overcome by argument or proof, convict of error or crime, prove] —**convince′ment,** *n.* —**convinc′er,** *n.* —**convin′cible,** *adj.* —**convinc′ingly,** *adv.* —**convinc′ingness,** *n.* —**Syn. 1.** See **persuade.**

convivial (kən vĭv′ĭ əl), *adj.* **1.** fond of feasting, drinking, and merry company; jovial. **2.** of or befitting a feast; festive. **3.** agreeable; sociable; merry. [t. L: s. *convīviālis* pertaining to a feast] —**conviv′ialist,** *n.* —**conviv′ial′ity,** *n.* —**conviv′ially,** *adv.*

convocation (kŏn′və kā′shən), *n.* **1.** the act of convoking. **2.** the fact or state of being convoked. **3.** a group of persons met in answer to a summons; an assembly. **4.** *C. of E.* one of the two provincial synods or assemblies of the clergy. **5.** *U.S. Episc. Ch.* **a.** an assembly of the clergy of part of a diocese. **b.** the area represented at such an assembly. **6.** (*sometimes cap.*) a legislative assembly of graduates of certain British universities. [ME, t. L: s. *convocātio*] —**con′voca′tional,** *adj.* —**Syn. 3.** See **convention.**

convoke (kən vōk′), *v.t.*, **-voked, -voking.** to call together; summon to meet; assemble by summons. [t. L: m. s. *convocāre* call together] —**convok′er,** *n.*

convolute (kŏn′və lo͞ot′), *v.*, **-luted, -luting,** *adj.* —*v.t.* **1.** to coil up; form into a twisted shape. —*adj.* **2.** rolled up together, or one part over another. **3.** *Bot.* coiled up longitudinally, so that one margin is within the coil and the other without, as the petals of cotton. [t. L: m. s. *convolūtus*, pp., rolled together] —**con′volute′ly,** *adv.*

convolution (kŏn′və lo͞o′shən), *n.* **1.** a rolled up or coiled condition. **2.** a rolling or coiling together. **3.** a turn of anything coiled; whorl; sinuosity. **4.** *Anat.* one of the sinuous folds or ridges of the surface of the brain.

convolve (kən vŏlv′), *v.t.*, *v.i.*, **-volved, -volving.** to roll or wind together; coil; twist. [t. L: m. s. *convolvere* roll together]

convolvulaceous (kən vŏl′vyo͝o lā′shəs), *adj.* belonging to the *Convolvulaceae*, or morning-glory family of plants, including the convolvuluses, ipomoeas, etc.

convolvulus (kən vŏl′vyo͝o ləs), *n.*, *pl.* **-luses, -li** (-lī′). any plant of the genus *Convolvulus*, which comprises erect, twining, or prostrate herbs with trumpet-shaped flowers. See **morning-glory.** [t. L: bindweed]

convoy (kŏn′voi), *v.t.* **1.** to accompany or escort, now usually for protection: *a merchant ship convoyed by a destroyer.* —*n.* **2.** the act of convoying. **3.** the protection afforded by an escort. **4.** an armed force, warship, etc., that escorts, esp. for protection. **5.** a formation of ships, a train of vehicles, etc., usually accompanied by a protecting escort. **6.** any group of military vehicles travelling together under the same orders. [ME, t. F: s. *convoyer*, earlier *conveier* CONVEY] —**Syn. 1.** See **accompany.**

convulse (kən vŭls′), *v.t.*, **-vulsed, -vulsing. 1.** to shake violently; agitate. **2.** to cause to laugh violently. **3.** to cause to suffer violent muscular spasms; distort (the features) as by strong emotion. [t. L: m. s. *convulsus*, pp., shattered]

convulsion (kən vŭl′shən), *n.* **1.** *Pathol.* contortion of the body caused by violent muscular contractions of the extremities, trunk, and head. **2.** violent agitation or disturbance; commotion. **3.** a violent fit of laughter.

convulsionary (kən vŭl′shə nə rĭ), *adj.*, *n.*, *pl.* **-ries.** —*adj.* **1.** pertaining to, of the nature of, or affected with convulsion. —*n.* **2.** one who is subject to convulsions.

convulsive (kən vŭl′sĭv), *adj.* **1.** of the nature of or characterized by convulsions or spasms. **2.** producing or attended by convulsion: *convulsive rage.* —**convul′sively,** *adv.* —**convul′siveness,** *n.*

cony (kō′nĭ), *n.*, *pl.* **-nies. 1.** the fur of a rabbit, esp. when dyed to simulate more expensive furs. **2.** the daman or some other animal of the same genus. **3.** the pika. **4.** *Archaic.* a rabbit. Also, **coney.** [ME *cunin*, t. OF: m. *conil*, g. L *cunīculus* rabbit]

coo (ko͞o), *v.*, **cooed, cooing,** *n.* —*v.i.* **1.** to utter the soft, murmuring sound characteristic of pigeons or doves, or a similar sound. **2.** murmur or talk fondly or amorously. —*v.t.* **3.** to utter by cooing. —*n.* **4.** a cooing sound. —*interj.* **5.** *Slang.* (an exclamation of surprise or amazement.) [imit.] —**coo′er,** *n.* —**coo′ingly,** *adv.*

coobah (ko͞o′bä), *n.* a tree, *Acacia salicina*, of Australia, a small leguminous wattle with drooping branches and pale green foliage. [t. native Australian]

Cooch Behar (ko͞och′ bĭ hä′), **1.** a former state in NE India, in Bengal, now a part of West Bengal. **2.** a town in West Bengal. 41,922 (1961).

cooee (ko͞o′ĭ, ko͞o′ē), *n.*, *v.*, **cooeed, cooeeing.** —*n.* **1.** a prolonged, shrill, clear call or cry used as a signal by Australian aborigines and adopted by the settlers in the country. —*v.i.* **2.** to utter the call 'cooee'.

cooey (ko͞o′ĭ, ko͞o′ē), *n.*, *pl.* **cooeys,** *v.*, **cooeyed, cooeying.** cooee.

cook (ko͝ok), *v.t.* **1.** to prepare (food) by the action of heat, as by boiling, baking, roasting, etc. **2.** to subject (anything) to the action of heat. **3.** *Colloq.* to concoct; invent falsely; falsify (often fol. by *up*). **4.** *Slang.* to ruin; spoil. **5. cook one's goose,** to frustrate or spoil one's plans. —*v.i.* **6.** to prepare food by the action of heat. **7.** (of food) to undergo cooking. —*n.* **8.** one who cooks. **9.** one whose occupation is the preparation of food for the table. [ME; OE *cōc*, t. LL: m. s. *cocus*, L *coquus*]

Cook (ko͝ok), *n.* **1. Captain James,** 1728–79, English navigator and explorer; expeditions to S Pacific, Antarctic oceans, and coasts of Australia and New Zealand. **2. Thomas,** 1808–92, English pioneer of the tourist trade. **3. Mount.** Also, **Aorangi.** a mountain in New Zealand, on South Island; the highest point in New Zealand. 12,349 ft.

cookbook (ko͝ok′bo͝ok′), *n.* *Chiefly U.S.* a cookery book.

cooker (ko͝ok′ə), *n.* **1.** an appliance for cooking: *a pressure cooker.* **2.** an apparatus, portable or fixed, and in many forms, for cooking, commonly using coal, oil, gas, or electricity. **3.** *Colloq.* a variety of fruit, esp. of apples, suitable for cooking.

cookery (ko͝ok′ərĭ), *n.*, *pl.* **-eries. 1.** the art or practice of cooking. **2.** *Obs.* a place for cooking.

cookery book, a book containing recipes and instructions for cooking. Also, *Chiefly U.S.*, **cookbook.**

cookhouse (ko͝ok′hous′), *n.* a camp kitchen; an outdoor kitchen.

Cook Islands, a group of islands in the S Pacific, belonging to New Zealand. 19,214 pop. (1963); 99 sq. mi.

cookout (ko͝ok′out′), *n.* *U.S.* **1.** a barbecue party. **2.** a meal cooked at a barbecue.

Cook Strait, a strait between North and South Islands, in New Zealand. ab. 15 mi. wide at the narrowest point.

cooky (ko͝ok′ĭ), *n.*, *pl.* **cookies. 1.** *Scot.* a bun. **2.** *U.S.* a biscuit. **3.** *U.S. Slang.* a person: *a smart cookie.* Also, *U.S.*, **cookie.** [t. D: m. *koekie*, colloq. var. of *koekje*, dim. of *koek* cake]

cool (ko͞ol), *adj.* **1.** moderately cold; neither warm nor very cold. **2.** imparting or permitting a sensation of moderate coldness: *a cool dress.* **3.** not excited; calm; unmoved; not hasty; deliberate; aloof. **4.** deficient in ardour or enthusiasm. **5.** lacking in cordiality: *a cool reception.* **6.** calmly audacious or impudent. **7.** *Colloq.* (of a number or sum) without exaggeration or qualification: *a cool thousand.* **8.** (of colours) with green, blue, or violet predominating. **9.** (of jazz) controlled, subtle, and relaxed. **10.** *Colloq.* smart; up-to-date; fashionable. **11.** *Colloq.* attractive; excellent. —*adv.* **12.** *Colloq.* coolly. —*n.* **13.** that which is cool; the cool part, place, time, etc. **14.** coolness. —*v.i.* **15.** to become cool. **16.** to become less ardent, cordial, etc.; become more moderate. —*v.t.* **17.** to make cool; impart a sensation of coolness to. **18.** to lessen the ardour or intensity of; allay; calm; moderate. **19.** *U.S. Slang.* to kill. **20. cool off** or **cool down,** *Colloq.* to become calmer; to become more reasonable. **21. cool one's heels,** to be kept waiting. [ME, OE *cōl*; akin to COLD, CHILL] —**cool′ly,** *adv.* —**cool′ness,** *n.* —**Syn. 1.** See **cold. 3.** composed, collected; self-possessed. See **calm. 5.** indifferent, lukewarm.

coolabah (ko͞o′lə bä′), *n.* a tree, *Eucalyptus microtheca,* of Australia, having smooth bark and narrow leaves; found on inland rivers. Also, **coolibah.** [t. native Australian]

coolamon (ko͞o′lə mən), *n. Austral.* a basin-shaped wooden dish made and used by aborigines. [t. native Australian]

coolant (ko͞o′lənt), *n.* **1.** a substance, usually a liquid or gas, used to reduce the temperature of a system below a specified value by conducting away the heat evolved in the operation of the system, as the liquid in a motor-car cooling system. The coolant may be used to transfer heat to a power generator, as in a nuclear reactor. **2.** a lubricant which serves to dissipate the heat caused by friction. [f. COOL + -ANT]

cooler (ko͞o′lə), *n.* **1.** a container or apparatus for cooling or keeping cool: *a water-cooler.* **2.** anything that cools or makes cool; refrigerant. **3.** *Slang.* prison.

cool-headed (ko͞ol′hĕd′ĭd), *adj.* not easily excited; calm.

Coolidge (ko͞o′lĭj), *n.* **Calvin,** 1872–1933, 30th president of the U.S. 1923–29.

coolie (ko͞o′lĭ), *n.* **1.** (in India, China, etc.) an unskilled native labourer. **2.** (elsewhere) such a labourer employed for cheap service. [prob. var. of *kōlī*, name of tribe of Gujarat, but cf. Tamil *kūli* hire, wages]

cooling tower, a concrete or wooden structure used in industrial processes to cool water after it has passed through a condenser; so arranged that the maximum surface area of water is exposed to the atmosphere.

coolish (ko͞o′lĭsh), *adj.* somewhat cool.

cooly (ko͞o′lĭ), *n., pl.* **-lies.** coolie.

coom (ko͞om), *n. Chiefly Scot. and N Dial.* **1.** any of various kinds of dust as coaldust, soot, dust from a gristmill, sawdust, etc. **2.** grease from axles, bearings, etc. Also, **coomb.** [var. of CULM[1]]

coomb[1] (ko͞om), *n.* a narrow valley or deep hollow, esp. one enclosed on all sides but one. Also, **combe, comb.** [OE *cumb* valley, c. d. G *Kumme* trough; but cf. Welsh *cwm* valley]

coomb[2] (ko͞om), *n.* a measure of capacity equal to four bushels.

coon (ko͞on), *n.* **1.** a raccoon. **2.** *Colloq.* a sly fellow. **3.** *U.S. Slang.* (in contemptuous use) a Negro.

cooncan (ko͞on′kăn′), *n. U.S.* a card game of the rummy family for two players.

coon's age, *U.S. Slang.* a long time.

coontie (ko͞on′tĭ), *n.* **1.** either of two arrowroot plants, *Zamia integrifolia* or *Z. floridana* of Florida. **2.** the flour produced from its starch. [t. Seminole: m. *kunti* the flour]

coop (ko͞op), *n.* **1.** an enclosure, cage, or pen, usually with bars or wires on one side or more, in which fowls, etc., are confined for fattening, transportation, etc. **2.** a wicker basket used for catching fish. **3.** any small or narrow place. **3.** *Slang.* a prison. **4. fly the coop,** *U.S. Slang.* to escape from a prison, etc. —*v.t.* **5.** to place in, or as in, a coop; confine narrowly (often fol. by *up* or *in*). [ME *coupe*, *cupe*, OE *cȳpe* basket, c. LG *küpe*]

co-op (kō′ŏp), *n.* a cooperative shop, store, or society.

cooper (ko͞o′pə), *n.* **1.** one who makes or repairs vessels formed of staves and hoops, as casks, barrels, tubs, etc. —*v.t.* **2.** to make or repair (casks, barrels, etc.). —*v.i.* **3.** to work as a cooper. [ME *couper*, t. MD or MLG: m. *kuper*, t. VL: m. s. *cūpārius*, der. L *cūpa* cask]

Cooper (ko͞o′pə), *n.* **1. Anthony Ashley.** See **Shaftesbury. 2. James Fenimore** (fĕn′ĭ môr′), 1789–1851, U.S. novelist.

cooperage (ko͞o′pə rĭj), *n.* **1.** the work or business of a cooper. **2.** the place where it is carried on. **3.** the price paid for coopers' work.

cooperate (kō ŏp′ə rāt′), *v.i.*, **-rated, -rating. 1.** to work or act together or jointly; unite in producing an effect. **2.** to practise economic cooperation. [t. LL: m. s. *cooperātus*, pp., having worked together] —**coop′era′tor,** *n.*

cooperation (kō ŏp′ə rā′shən), *n.* **1.** the act or fact of cooperating; joint operation or action. **2.** *Econ.* the combination of persons for purposes of production, purchase, or distribution for their joint benefit: *producers' cooperation, consumers' cooperation.* **3.** *Sociol.* activity shared for mutual benefit. **4.** *Ecol.* the conscious or unconscious behaviour of organisms living together and producing a result which has survival value for them. —**coop′era′tionist,** *n.*

cooperative (kō ŏp′ə rə tĭv, -ŏp′rə tĭv), *adj.* **1.** cooperating. **2.** showing a willingness to cooperate; helpful. **3.** pertaining to economic cooperation: *a cooperative farm.* —*n.* **4.** a cooperative society or shop. **5.** a cooperative farm. —**coop′eratively,** *adv.* —**coop′erativeness,** *n.*

cooperative farm, 1. a farm which joins with others in the mutual use of marketing facilities, machinery, labour, etc. **2.** a farm owned by a cooperative society or one run on cooperative principles. **3.** a farm run on a communal basis, as a kibbutz. **4.** a collective farm.

Cooperative Party, a political party in Great Britain founded in 1917 and linked with the Labour Party, characterized by its promotion of economic and social cooperation.

cooperative society, a business undertaking owned and controlled by its members, and formed to provide them with work or with goods at advantageous prices: a **consumers' cooperative** is owned by its customers, and **producers' cooperative** by its workers.

Cooper Creek (ko͞o′pə), an irregularly flowing river of Australia in SW Queensland. In wet years it flows into Lake Eyre. Also, **Cooper River.**

coopery (ko͞o′pə rĭ), *n., pl.* **-ries. 1.** the work of a cooper. **2.** a cooper's shop. **3.** articles made by a cooper.

coopt (kō ŏpt′), *v.t.* to elect into a body by the votes of the existing members. [t. L: s. *cooptāre*] —**cooption** (kō ŏp′shən), **co′opta′tion,** *n.* —**cooptative** (kō ŏp′tə tĭv), *adj.*

coordinal (kō ô′dĭ nəl), *adj. Bot., Zool.* belonging to the same order.

coordinate (*adj., n.* kō ô′dĭ nĭt, -nāt′; *v.* kō ô′dĭ nāt′), *adj., n., v.*, **-nated, -nating.** —*adj.* **1.** of the same order or degree; equal in rank or importance. **2.** involving coordination. **3.** *Maths.* using or pertaining to systems of coordinates. —*n.* **4.** one who or that which is equal in rank or importance; an equal. **5.** *Maths.* any of the magnitudes which define the position of a point, line, or the like, by reference to a fixed figure, system of lines, etc. —*v.t.* **6.** to place or class in the same order, rank, division, etc. **7.** to place or arrange in due order or proper relative position. **8.** to combine in harmonious relation or action. —*v.i.* **9.** to become coordinate. **10.** to assume proper order or relation. **11.** to act in harmonious combination. [f. CO- + ORDINATE] —**coor′dinately,** *adv.* —**coor′dinateness,** *n.* —**coor′dinative,** *adj.* —**coor′dina′tor,** *n.*

coordinate geometry, analytical geometry.

coordination (kō ô′dĭ nā′shən), *n.* **1.** the act of coordinating. **2.** the state of being coordinated. **3.** due ordering or proper relation. **4.** harmonious combination.

Coorg (ko͞oəg), *n.* a former province in SW India, now a part of Mysore state. 1593 sq. mi. Also, **Kurg.**

Coos (ko͞os), *n.* any of several Penutian languages of Oregon.

coot (ko͞ot), *n.* **1.** any of the aquatic birds constituting the genus *Fulica,* characterized by lobate toes and short wings and tail, as the **common coot** (*F. atra*) of Europe. **2.** any of various other swimming or diving birds, as the scoter. **3.** *Colloq.* a fool; simpleton. [cf. D *koet*]

Coot, *Fulica atra* (15 in. long)

cootie (ko͞o′tĭ), *n. Chiefly U.S.* a body louse. [f. Malay *kutu* + -IE]

cop[1] (kŏp), *n., v.,* **copped, copping.** —*n.* **1.** *Slang.* a policeman. **2.** *Slang.* an arrest; a state of being caught. —*v.t.* **3.** *Slang.* to catch. **4.** *Slang.* to steal. **5. cop it,** *Slang.* to be punished: *you're going to cop it for saying that.* [OE *coppian* lop, steal]

cop[2] (kŏp), *n.* **1.** a conical mass of thread, etc., wound on a spindle. **2.** *Obs. or Dial.* the top or crest, esp. of a hill. [OE *cop, copp* top, summit. Cf. G *Kopf* head]

copacetic (kō′pə sĕt′ĭk, -sē′tĭk), *adj. U.S. Slang.* very good; absolutely satisfactory; all right: *if I get this job, everything will be copacetic.* Also, **copasetic, copesetic.** [orig. unknown]

copaiba (kō pī′bə), *n.* an oleoresin obtained from various tropical (chiefly South American) trees of the caesalpiniaceous genus *Copaiba,* used esp. as a stimulant and diuretic. Also, **copaiva.** [t. Sp., t. Guarani: m. *kupaiba*]

copal (kō′pl, -păl), *n.* a hard, lustrous resin yielded by various tropical trees, used chiefly in making varnishes. [t. Sp., t. Nahuatl: m. *kopalli* resin]

Copán (*Sp.* kō pän′), *n.* Santa Rosa de Copán.

coparcenary (kō pä′sĭ nə rĭ), *n. Law.* a special kind of joint ownership, esp. arising under common law upon the descent of real property to several female heirs. Also, **coparceny** (kō pä′sĭ nĭ).

coparcener (kō pä′sĭ nə), *n.* a member of a coparcenary. [f. CO- + PARCENER]

copartner (kō pät′ nə), *n.* a partner; an associate. —**co-part′nership′,** *n.*

cope[1] (kōp), *v.*, **coped, coping.** —*v.i.* **1.** to struggle or contend, esp. on fairly even terms or with a degree of success (fol. by *with*). **2.** *Archaic.* to have to do (fol. by *with*). —*v.t.* **3.** *Colloq.* to cope with. **4.** *Obs.* to meet in contest. [ME *coupe(n)*, t. F: m. *couper* strike, der. *coup* stroke, blow. See COUP, n.]

cope[2] (kōp), *n.*, *v.*, **coped, coping.** —*n.* **1.** a long mantle of silk or other material worn by ecclesiastics over the alb or surplice in processions and on other occasions. **2.** any cloaklike or canopy-like covering. **3.** the vault of heaven; the sky. **4.** *Archit.* a coping. —*v.t.* **5.** to furnish with or as with a cope or coping. [ME; OE *cāp* (in *cantel-cāp* cope), t. ML: s. *cāpa* cope]

A, Cope; B, Crosier

copeck (kō′ pĕk), *n.* kopeck.

Copenhagen (kō′ pən hā′ gən), *n.* a seaport in and the capital of Denmark, on the E coast of Zealand. 923,974 (1960); with suburbs, 1,348,454 (1960). Danish, **København.**

Copenhagen blue, grey-blue.

copepod (kō′ pə pŏd′), *n.* **1.** any of the *Copepoda*, a large order of (mostly) minute freshwater and marine crustaceans. —*adj.* **2.** pertaining to the *Copepoda.* [f. m. Gk *kṓpē* handle, oar + -POD]

coper (kō′ pə), *n.* a horse-dealer.

Copernicus (kō pû′ nĭ kəs, kə-), *n.* **Nicolaus** (nĭk′ ə lā′ əs), 1473–1543, Polish astronomer who promulgated the now accepted theory that the earth and the planets move about the sun (the **Copernican system**). Polish, **Kopernik.** —**Coper′nican,** *adj.*

copestone (kōp′ stōn′), *n.* coping stone.

copier (kŏp′ ĭ ə), *n.* one who or that which copies; a copyist.

copilot (kō′ pī′ lət), *n.* the assistant or second pilot in an aircraft.

coping (kō′ pĭng), *n.* the uppermost course of a wall or the like, usually made sloping so as to carry off water.

coping saw, a saw with a short, narrow blade held at both ends in a deeply recessed handle, for cutting curved shapes.

coping stone, 1. the top stone of a building or the like. **2.** a stone used for or in coping. **3.** the crown or completion. Also, **copestone.**

copious (kō′ pyəs), *adj.* **1.** large in quantity or number; abundant. **2.** having or yielding an abundant supply. **3.** exhibiting abundance or fullness, as of thoughts or words. [ME, t. L: m. s. *cōpiōsus* plentiful] —**co′piously,** *adv.* —**co′piousness.** *n.* —**Syn. 1.** plentiful, overflowing. See **ample.** —**Ant. 1.** scanty. **3.** meagre.

coplanar (kō plā′ nə), *adj. Maths.* (of figures) in the same plane.

Copland (kōp′ lənd), *n.* **Aaron** (ĕə′ rən), born 1900, U.S. composer.

Copley (kŏp′ lĭ), *n.* **John Singleton** (sĭng′ gl tən), 1738–1815, U.S. painter.

copolymer (kō pŏl′ ĭ mə), *n. Chem.* a compound made by polymerizing different compounds together.

copolymerize (kō pŏl′ ĭ mə rīz′), *v.t.*, *v.i.*, **-rized, -rizing.** to subject to or undergo a change analogous to polymerization, but with a union of unlike molecules. Also, **copolymerise.** —**copol′ymeriza′tion,** *n.*

Coppée (*Fr.* kō pė′), *n.* **François** (*Fr.* fräɴ swȧ′), 1842–1908, French poet, dramatist, and novelist.

copper[1] (kŏp′ ə), *n.* **1.** *Chem.* a malleable, ductile metallic element having a characteristic reddish brown colour. *Symbol:* Cu; *at. wt:* 65·54; *at. no.:* 29; *sp. gr.:* 8·92 at 20°C. **2.** a copper coin, as the English penny or half-penny or the U.S. cent. **3.** a container made of copper. **4.** a large vessel (formerly of copper) for boiling clothes. **5.** a metallic reddish brown. —*v.t.* **6.** to cover, coat, or sheathe with copper. **7.** *U.S. Slang.* to bet against, esp. in faro. —*adj.* **8.** made of copper. **9.** copper-coloured. **10.** pertaining to copper. [ME *coper*, OE *coper*, *copor* (c. G *Kupfer*), t. LL: m. s. *cuprum*, for L *aes Cyprium* Cyprian metal. See CYPRUS]

copper[2] (kŏp′ ə), *n. Slang.* a policeman. [see COP[1]]

copperas (kŏp′ ə rəs), *n.* ferrous sulphate. [ME *coperose.* Cf. OF *couperose*, t. ML: m. s. *(aqua) cuprōsa*, der. LL *cuprum.* See COPPER[1]]

copper beech, a variety of the beech, *Fagus sylvatica*, with reddish brown leaves.

copper-bottomed (kŏp′ ə bŏt′ əmd), *adj.* **1.** with bottom covered with copper. **2.** sound, esp. financially sound.

copperhead (kŏp′ ə hĕd′), *n.* **1.** a venomous snake, *Ancistrodon contortrix*, of the U.S., having a copper-coloured head and reaching a length of about 3 feet. **2.** (*cap.*) *U.S.* a Northern sympathizer with the South during the U.S. Civil War.

coppernob (kŏp′ ə nŏb′), *n. Colloq.* a red-headed person. Also, **cop′pertop′.**

copperplate (kŏp′ ə plāt′), *n.* **1.** a plate of polished copper on which a writing, picture, or design is made by engraving or etching. **2.** a print or an impression from such a plate. **3.** engraving or printing of this kind. **4.** an ornate, rounded style of handwriting, formerly much used in engravings. —*adj.* **5.** (of handwriting) ornate, rounded, and formal; in the style of copperplate. **6.** *Colloq.* polished; without blemish; neat; clear.

copper pyrites, chalcopyrite.

coppersmith (kŏp′ ə smĭth′), *n.* a worker in copper; one who manufactures copper utensils.

copper sulphate, blue vitriol.

copper uranite, torbernite. Also, **cupro-uranite.**

coppery (kŏp′ ə rĭ), *adj.* of, like, or containing copper.

coppice (kŏp′ ĭs), *n.* a wood, thicket, or plantation of small trees or bushes. Also, **copse.** [t. OF: m. *copeiz*, f. m. s. *couper* cut + *-eiz* (g. L *-ātīcium*)]

copra (kŏp′ rə), *n.* the dried kernel or meat of the coconut, from which coconut oil is pressed. [t. Pg., t. Malayalam: m. *koppara*, c. Hind. *khoprā* coconut]

copraemia (kŏp rē′ mĭ ə), *n. Pathol.* blood-poisoning due to absorption of faecal matter. Also, *Chiefly U.S.*, **copremia.** [f. *copr(o)-* (see COPROLITE) + -AEMIA]

coprolite (kŏp′ rə līt′), *n.* a roundish, stony mass consisting of petrified faecal matter of animals. [f. *copro-* (t. Gk: m. *kopro-*, comb. form of *kópros* dung) + -LITE]

coprology (kŏp rŏl′ ə jĭ), *n.* scatology (def. 3).

coprophagous (kŏp rŏf′ ə gəs), *adj.* feeding on dung, as certain beetles. [f. *copro-* (see COPROLITE) + -PHAGOUS]

coprophilia (kŏp′ rō fĭl′ ĭ ə, -yə), *n.* a morbid pleasure or interest in faeces, obscenity, or filth.

coprophobia (kŏp′ rō fō′ byə), *n.* a morbid fear of faeces.

copse (kŏps), *n.* coppice.

Copt (kŏpt), *n.* **1.** one of the natives of Egypt descended from the ancient Egyptians. **2.** an Egyptian Christian of the sect of the Monophysites. [t. Ar.: m. *qibt*, *qubt* the Copts, t. Coptic: m. *gyptios*, aphetic var. of Gk *Aigýptios* Egyptian]

copter (kŏp′ tə), *n. Colloq.* a helicopter.

Coptic (kŏp′ tĭk), *n.* **1.** the extinct language of Egypt which developed from ancient Egyptian, used liturgically by Egyptian Christians. —*adj.* **2.** of the Copts.

Coptic Church, the native Christian church in Egypt.

copula (kŏp′ yŏŏ lə), *n.*, *pl.* **-lae** (-lē′). **1.** something that connects or links together. **2.** *Gram.*, *Logic.* a word or set of words (in English the verb *be*) which acts as a connecting link between the subject and the predicate. [t. L: a band, bond] —**cop′ular,** *adj.*

copulate (*v.* kŏp′ yŏŏ lāt′; *adj.* kŏp′ yŏŏ lĭt), *v.*, **-lated, -lating,** *adj.* —*v.i.* **1.** to unite in sexual intercourse. —*adj.* **2.** *Obs.* joined. [t. L: m. s. *copulātus*, pp., coupled]

copulation (kŏp′ yŏŏ lā′ shən), *adj.* **1.** sexual union or intercourse. **2.** a joining together or coupling.

copulative (kŏp′ yŏŏ lə tĭv), *adj.* **1.** serving to unite or couple. **2.** involving or consisting of connected words or clauses. **3.** of the nature of a copula: *a copulative verb.* **4.** of or pertaining to copulation. —*n.* **5.** a copulative word. —**cop′ulatively,** *adv.*

copy (kŏp′ ĭ), *n.*, *pl.* **copies,** *v.*, **copied, copying.** —*n.* **1.** a transcript, reproduction, or imitation of an original. **2.** that which is to be transcribed, reproduced, or imitated. **3.** written, typed, or printed matter, or artwork, intended to be reproduced in print. **4.** paper, specially prepared for the writing of advertisements, etc., having guide lines to indicate margins and the number of spaces per line. **5.** one of the various examples or specimens of the same book, engraving, or the like. **6.** *Archaic.* an example of penmanship to be copied by a pupil. **7.** *Law.* (formerly) a transcript of the manorial court roll with entries of admissions of tenants to land. —*v.t.* **8.** to make a copy of; transcribe; reproduce: *to copy a set of figures.* **9.** to follow as a pattern or model; imitate. —*v.i.* **10.** to make a copy or copies. **11.** to make or do something in imitation of something else. **12.** to reproduce or make use of unfairly another's written work, as a fellow pupil's. [ME *copie*, t. F, t. L: m. *cōpia* plenty, ML transcript] —**Syn. 1.** duplicate. **8.** See **imitate.** —**Ant. 9.** originate.

copybook (kŏp′ ĭ bŏŏk′), *n.* **1.** a book in which copies are written or printed for learners to imitate. **2.** *U.S.* a book for or containing copies, as of documents. **3. blot one's copybook,** to spoil, damage or destroy one's reputation or record. —*adj.* **4.** (in some sports) according to the rules; excellent; conforming to established principles.

copycat (kŏp′ ĭ kăt′), *n. Slang.* **1.** a child who copies another's work. **2.** a slavish imitator.

copy desk, *Journalism.* the desk at which news stories, etc., are edited and prepared for printing.
copyhold (kŏp′ĭ hōld′), *n. Law.* **1.** (formerly) a type of ownership of land in England, evidenced by a copy of the manorial court roll establishing the title. **2.** (formerly) land held in this way.
copyholder (kŏp′ĭ hōl′də), *n.* **1.** one who or that which holds copy. **2.** a device for holding copy in its place, as on a printer's frame or on a typewriter. **3.** a proofreader's assistant who reads copy aloud, or follows it while proof is read, for the detection of deviations from it in proof. **4.** *Law.* one who holds an estate in copyhold.
copyist (kŏp′ĭ ĭst), *n.* **1.** a transcriber, esp. of documents. **2.** an imitator.
copyreader (kŏp′ĭ rē′də), *n. U.S.* a subeditor.
copyright (kŏp′ĭ rīt′), *n.* **1.** the exclusive right, granted by law for a certain term of years, to make and dispose of copies of, and otherwise to control, a literary, musical, or artistic work. *—adj.* **2.** protected by copyright. *—v.t.* **3.** to secure a copyright on. **—cop′yright′able,** *adj.* **—cop′yright′er,** *n.*
copywriter (kŏp′ĭ rī′tə), *n.* a writer of copy for advertisements or publicity releases.
Coquelin (*Fr.* kŏk lăɴ′), *n.* **Benoît Constant** (*Fr.* bə nwȧ kôɴ stäɴ′), 1841–1909, French actor.
coquet (kō kĕt′, kŏ kĕt′), *v.,* **-quetted, -quetting,** *adj., n.* *—v.i.* **1.** to trifle in love; flirt; play the coquette. **2.** to act without seriousness; trifle; dally. *—adj.* **3.** coquettish. *—n.* **4.** *Obs.* a male flirt. [t. F, dim. of *coq* cock]
coquetry (kō′kĭ trĭ, kŏk′ĭ trĭ), *n., pl.* **-tries. 1.** the behaviour or arts of a coquette; flirtation. **2.** trifling.
coquette (kō kĕt′, kŏ kĕt′), *n.* a woman who tries to gain the admiration and affections of men for mere self-gratification; a flirt. [t. F. See COQUET] **—coquet′tish,** *adj.* **—coquet′tishly,** *adv.* **—coquet′tishness,** *n.*
coquilla nut (kŏ kē′lyə), the elongated oval fruit or nut of a South American palm, *Attalea funifera*, having a very hard brown shell. [*coquilla*, t. Pg.: m. *coquilho*, dim. of *coco* coconut]
coquille (kŏ kē′), *n. Fencing.* a bell-shaped guard on a foil to protect and cushion the hand.
coquina (kŏ kē′nə), *n.* a soft, whitish rock made up of fragments of marine shells and coral, used to some extent as a building material. [t. Sp.: shellfish, cockle]
coquito (kŏ kē′tō), *n., pl.* **-tos.** a palm, *Jubaea spectabilis*, of Chile, bearing small edible nuts, which yield a sweet syrup. Also, **coquito palm.** [t. Sp., dim. of *coco* coconut]
cor (kô), *interj. Slang.* (an exclamation of surprise.)
cor-, var. of **com-** before *r*, as in *corrupt.*
Cor., 1. Corinthians. **2.** coroner.
cor., 1. corner. **2.** cornet. **3.** corpus. **4.** correct. **5.** corrected. **6.** correction. **7.** correspondence. **8.** correspondent. **9.** corresponding.
coraciiform (kŏ′rə sī′ĭ fôm′), *adj.* belonging or pertaining to the *Coraciiformes*, the order of birds that includes the kingfishers, motmots, rollers, bee-eaters, and hornbills. [f. s. NL *Coracia* genus of birds (der. Gk *kórax* raven) + -(I)FORM]
coracle (kŏ′rə kl), *n.* (in Wales and W England) a small boat, nearly or quite as broad as long, made like a basket. [t. Welsh: m. *corwgl, cwrwgl*, der. *corwg, cwrwg* carcass, boat]
coracoid (kŏ′rə koid′), *Anat., Zool. —adj.* **1.** pertaining to a bony process extending from the scapula towards the sternum in many vertebrates. *—n.* **2.** a coracoid bone. [t. Gk: m. s. *korakoeidḗs* raven-like]
coral (kŏ′rəl), *n.* **1.** the hard, calcareous (red, white, black, etc.) skeleton of any of various, mostly compound, marine coelenterate animals, the individual polyps of which come forth by budding. **2.** such skeletons collectively, as forming reefs, islands, etc. **3.** an animal of this kind. **4.** something made of coral, as an ornament, child's toy, etc. **5.** a reddish yellow; light yellowish red; pinkish yellow. **6.** the unimpregnated roe or eggs of the lobster, which when boiled assume the colour of red coral. *—adj.* **7.** made of coral: *a coral reef, coral ornament.* **8.** making coral: *a coral polyp.* **9.** resembling coral, esp. in colour. [ME, t. OF, g. L *corallum, coralium*, t. Gk: m. *korállion* red coral]
coral island, an island made from a coral reef.
coralfish (kŏ′rəl fĭsh′), *n.* any of various small, brightly coloured marine fish of coral reefs, as members of the *Chaetodontidae* family.
coralliferous (kŏ′rə lĭf′ə rəs), *adj.* containing or bearing coral; producing coral.
coralline (kŏ′rə līn′), *adj.* **1.** consisting of or containing deposits of calcium carbonate. **2.** coral-like. **3.** coral-coloured; reddish yellow; light yellowish red; pinkish yellow. *—n.* **4.** any alga having a red colour and impregnated with lime. **5.** any of various coral-like animals, or calcareous algae.
corallite (kŏ′rə līt′), *n.* a fossil coral.
coralloid (kŏ′rə loid′), *adj.* having the form or appearance of coral. Also, **cor′alloi′dal.**
coral reef, a reef or bank formed by the growth and deposit of coral polyps.
Coral Sea, a part of the S Pacific, partially enclosed by NE Australia, New Guinea, the Solomon Islands, and the New Hebrides.

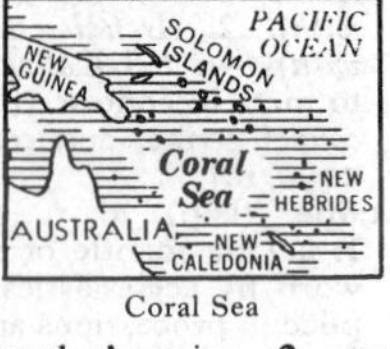

Coral Sea

coral snake, 1. any of the brilliantly coloured venomous snakes of the genus *Micrurus*, often with alternating black, yellow, and red rings, including forms found in the southern U.S. and tropical South America. **2.** any of the brightly coloured snakes of the genus *Aspidelaps* of Africa.
coral tree, any of several species of tropical leguminous trees or shrubs with showy red flowers belonging to the genus *Erythrina.*
coralwort (kŏ′rəl wût′), *n.* a creeping perennial cruciferous herb, *Dentaria bulbifera*, growing in beech woods on calcareous soils in Europe and W Asia.
cor anglais (kor′ŏng′glā), *Music.* the alto of the oboe family, richer in tone and a fifth lower than the oboe; English horn.

Cor anglais

corban (kô′băn), *n.* (among the ancient Jews) an offering of any kind made to God, one kind being in fulfilment of a vow. [t. Heb.: m. *qorbān*]
corbel (kô′bl), *n., v.,* **-belled, -belling,** or (*U.S.*) **-beled, -beling.** *Archit. —n.* **1.** a supporting projection of stone, wood, etc., on the face of a wall. *—v.t.* **2.** to furnish with or support by a corbel or corbels. [ME, t. OF, g. LL *corvellus*, dim. of L *corvus* raven]
corbelling (kô′bə lĭng), *n. Archit.* **1.** the construction of corbels. **2.** an overlapping arrangement of stones, etc., supported by corbels. Also, *U.S.,* **corbeling.**
corbie (kô′bĭ), *n. Scot.* a raven or crow. [ME *corbin*, t. OF, dim. of *corb* raven, g. L *corvus*]

Corbel (def. 1)

corbie gable, a crow-stepped gable.
corbie step, a crow step.
Corbusier (kô byōō′zĭ ā′; *Fr.* kŏr bʏ zyĕ′), *n.* See **Le Corbusier.**
Corcyra (kô sī′ə rə), *n.* ancient name of **Corfu** (def. 1).
cord (kôd), *n.* **1.** a string or small rope composed of several strands twisted or woven together. **2.** a hangman's rope. **3.** *U.S.* flex. **4.** *Anat.* a cordlike structure: *the spinal cord, the vocal cords.* **5.** a cordlike rib on the surface of cloth. **6.** a ribbed fabric, esp. corduroy. **7.** (*pl.*) *Slang.* corduroy breeches or trousers. **8.** any influence which binds, restrains, etc. **9.** a unit of volume used chiefly for fuel wood, now generally equal to 128 cubic feet, usually specified as 8 feet long, 4 feet wide, and 4 feet high. *—v.t.* **10.** to furnish with a cord. **11.** to bind or fasten with cords. **12.** to pile or stack up (wood) in cords. [ME *corde*, t. OF, g. L *chorda*, t. Gk: m. *chordḗ* gut. Cf. CHORD[1]]
cordage (kô′dĭj), *n.* **1.** cords or ropes collectively, esp. in a ship's rigging. **2.** a quantity of wood measured in cords.
cordate (kô′dāt), *adj.* **1.** heart-shaped, as a shell. **2.** (of leaves) heart-shaped with the attachment at the notched end. [t. NL: m. s. *cordātus*, der. L *cor* heart] **—cor′dately,** *adv.*
Corday d'Armont (*Fr.* kŏr dĕ dȧr môɴ′), (**Marie Anne**) **Charlotte** (*Fr.* mȧ rē ȧn shȧr lŏt′), 1768–93, French revolutionary who assassinated Marat.

Cordate leaf

corded (kô′dĭd), *adj.* **1.** furnished with, made of, having, or in the form of cords. **2.** ribbed, as a fabric. **3.** bound with cords. **4.** (of wood) stacked up in cords.
Cordelier (kô′dĭ lĭə′), *n.* **1.** a Franciscan friar (so called from his girdle of knotted cord). **2.** (*pl.*) a Parisian political club in the time of the French Revolution, which met in an old convent of the Cordeliers. **3.** (*l.c.*) *Her.* a knotted cord. [ME *cordilere*, t. F: m. *cordelier*, ult. der. *corde* CORD]
cord grass, any of various species of grasses of the genus

Spartina including the vigorous hybrid *S. x townsendii* common on tidal mud flats in many temperate regions.

cordial (kô′dyəl), *adj.* **1.** hearty; warmly friendly. **2.** invigorating the heart; stimulating. **3.** *Obs.* of the heart. —*n.* **4.** anything that invigorates or exhilarates. **5.** a strong, sweetened, aromatic alcoholic drink; a liqueur. **6.** a cordial or stimulating medicine. [ME, t. ML: s. *cordiālis*, der. L *cor* heart] —**cor′dially,** *adv.* —**cor′dialness,** *n.*

cordiality (kô′dĭ ăl′ĭ tĭ), *n.*, *pl.* **-ties.** **1.** cordial quality or feeling. **2.** an instance or expression of cordial feeling.

cordierite (kô′dĭ ə rīt′), *n.* a blue mineral, consisting of a silicate of magnesium, aluminium, and iron.

cordiform (kô′dĭ fôm′), *adj.* heart-shaped. [f. s. L *cor* heart + -(I)FORM]

cordillera (kô′dĭ lyĕə′rə), *n.* **1.** one of the mountain ranges in a mountain chain comprising a series of broadly parallel ranges. **2.** *U.S.* a chain of mountains, usually the principal mountain system or mountain axis of a large land mass. [t. Sp.: mountain chain, ult. der. L *chorda* rope] —**cor′dille′ran,** *adj.*

cordite (kô′dīt), *n.* a smokeless explosive composed of 30–58 per cent nitroglycerine, 65–37 per cent nitrocellulose, and 5–6 per cent mineral jelly. [f. CORD + -ITE[1]; so named from its cordlike or cylindrical form]

Cordoba (kô′də bə), *n.* **1.** Also, **Cordova** (kô′də və). a city in S Spain, on the Guadalquivir river, the capital of Spain under Moorish rule; famous cathedral. 215,454 (1965). **2.** a city in central Argentina. 589,153 (est. 1960). **3.** (*l.c.*) the Nicaraguan monetary unit, equal to 100 centavos, and equivalent to about £0·0505 sterling. **4.** a banknote of this value. *Abbrev.*: C$. Spanish, **Córdoba** (*Sp.* kôr′dō bä).

cordon (kô′dn), *n.* **1.** a cord or braid worn for ornament or as a fastening. **2.** a ribbon worn, usually diagonally across the breast, as a badge of a knightly or honorary order. **3.** a line of sentinels, military posts, or the like, enclosing or guarding a particular area. **4.** *Fort.* a projecting course of stone at the base of a parapet. **5.** *Archit.* a string-course. **6.** a fruit tree, with one branch or opposing branches trained to grow parallel with the ground. —*v.t.* **7.** to enclose or cut off with a cordon. [t. F, der. *corde* CORD]

cordon bleu (*Fr.* kŏr dôɴ blœ′), **1.** the sky-blue ribbon worn as a badge by knights of the highest order of French knighthood under the Bourbons. **2.** some similar high distinction, esp. in cookery. **3.** one entitled to wear the cordon bleu. **4.** any person of great distinction in his field, esp. a chef.

cordon rouge (*Fr.* kŏr dôɴ ro͞ozh′), **1.** an award made in Great Britain to cooks, chefs, and cookery writers of outstanding merit. **2.** (*caps.*) the society which makes such awards.

Cordovan (kô′də vən), *adj.* **1.** of Cordoba, Spain. **2.** (*l.c.*) designating or made of a leather made orig. at Cordoba, first of goatskin tanned and dressed, but later also of split horsehide, etc. —*n.* **3.** a native or inhabitant of Cordoba in Spain. **4.** (*l.c.*) cordovan leather.

corduroy (kô′də roi′, kô′də roi′), *n.* **1.** a cotton pile fabric with lengthwise cords or ridges. **2.** (*pl.*) trousers or breeches made of this. —*adj.* **3.** of or like corduroy. **4.** constructed of logs laid together transversely, as a road across swampy ground. —*v.t.* **5.** to form, as a road, by laying logs together transversely. **6.** to make a corduroy road over. [cf. obs. *duroy*, a kind of coarse woollen fabric]

cordwain (kôd′wān), *n.* *Archaic.* cordovan leather. [ME *corduan*, t. OF: m. *cordoan*, t. Sp.: m. *cordován*]

cordwainer (kôd′wā′nə), *n.* **1.** *Archaic.* a worker in cordovan leather. **2.** *Obs.* a shoemaker.

core (kô), *n.*, *v.*, **cored, coring.** —*n.* **1.** the central part of a fleshy fruit, containing the seeds. **2.** the central, innermost, or most essential part of anything. **3.** *Elect.* **a.** the piece of iron, bundle of iron wires, or the like, forming the central or inner portion of an electromagnet, induction coil, or the like. **b.** the armature core of a dynamo machine, consisting of the assembled armature laminations without the slot insulation or windings. **c.** a small ferrite ring used to store a binary digit of information by induced magnetism. **4.** *Foundry.* a body of sand, usually dry, placed in a mould to form openings or give shape to a casting. **5.** a cylinder of rock, soil, etc., cut out by boring. **6.** the inside wood of a tree. **7.** the base to which veneer woods are attached, usually of a soft or inexpensive wood. **8.** *Physics.* the inner part of a nuclear reactor consisting of the fuel and the moderator. **9.** *Geol.* the central mass of the earth, which is surrounded by the mantle, and is generally thought to consist of nickel iron, probably in the liquid state. —*v.t.* **10.** to remove the core of (fruit). **11.** to cut from the central part. [ME; orig. unknown] —**core′less,** *adj.*

Corea (kə rīə′), *n.* Korea.

coregent (kō rē′jənt), *n.* a joint regent.

coreligionist (kō′rĭ lĭj′ə nĭst), *n.* an adherent of the same religion as another.

corella (kŏ rĕl′ə), *n.* **1.** *Austral.* any of various birds of the genus *Kakatoë*, esp. the **little corella,** *K. sanguinea.* **2.** *Austral. Slang.* a sheep with wool hanging loose. [t. native Australian]

Corelli (kə rĕl′ĭ; *It.* kō rĕl′lē), *n.* **Arcangelo** (ä kăn′jĭ lō′; *It.* är kän′jĕ lō), 1653–1713, Italian composer and violinist.

coreopsis (kŏ′rĭ ŏp′sĭs), *n.* any plant of the composite genus *Coreopsis*, including familiar garden species with yellow, brownish, or particoloured (yellow and red) flowers. [t. NL, f. m. s. Gk *kóris* bug + *-opsis* -OPSIS; so called from the form of the seed]

corer (kô′rə), *n.* **1.** a knife for coring apples, etc. **2.** a hollow drill for extracting cores of rock, for samples, etc.

co-respondent (kō′rĭ spŏn′dənt), *n.* *Law.* a joint defendant, esp. in divorce proceedings, where one charged with adultery is made a joint defendant.

core store, *Computers.* a fast memory unit, consisting of an array of ferrite cores wired so that any desired core can be switched to one of two magnetic states by an electrical impulse.

corf (kôf), *n.*, *pl.*, **corves** (kôvz). a small wagon (formerly a wicker basket) for carrying ore, coal, etc., in mines. [t. MD, t. L: m. s. *corbis* basket]

Corfu (kô fo͞o′; *It.* kōr fo͞o′), *n.* **1.** Ancient, **Corcyra.** one of the Ionian Islands, off the NW coast of Greece. 101,555 pop. (1961); 229 sq. mi. **2.** a seaport on this island. 26,991 (1961). Greek, **Kerkyra.**

ALBANIA
Strait of Otranto
GREECE
CORFU
Ionian Sea

Corfu

corgi (kô′gĭ), *n.* a dog of either of two ancient Welsh breeds, having short legs, squat body, and erect ears, the **Cardigan** variety having a long tail and the **Pembroke** a short tail. Also, **Welsh corgi.**

coriaceous (kŏ′rĭ ā′shəs), *adj.* of or like leather. [t. LL: m. *coriāceus* leathern]

coriander (kŏ′rĭ ăn′də), *n.* **1.** a herbaceous plant, *Coriandrum sativum*, with aromatic seedlike fruit (**coriander seeds**) used in cookery and medicine. **2.** the fruit or seeds. [ME *coriandre*, t. F, t. L: m. *coriandrum*, t. Gk: m. *koríandron*, var. of *koríannon*]

Corinth (kŏ′rĭnth), *n.* **1.** an ancient city in Greece, strategically situated on the Isthmus of Corinth: notorious for its luxury. **2.** a port in the NE Peloponnesus, in S Greece NE of the site of ancient Corinth. **3. Gulf of.** Also, **Gulf of Lepanto.** an arm of the Ionian Sea, N of the Peloponnesus. **4. Isthmus of,** a narrow isthmus at the head of the Gulf of Corinth, connecting the Peloponnesus with central Greece: traversed by a ship canal.

Corinthian (kə rĭn′thĭ ən), *adj.* **1.** of Corinth, noted in ancient times for its artistic adornment, luxury, and licentiousness. **2.** luxurious; licentious. **3.** ornate, as literary style. **4.** *Archit.* designating or pertaining to one of the three Greek orders, distinguished by a bell-shaped capital with rows of acanthus leaves and a continuous frieze. See diag. under **order.** —*n.* **5.** a native or inhabitant of Corinth. **6.** (*pl.*) the two books or epistles of the New Testament addressed by St Paul to the Christian community at Corinth. **7.** a man of fashion. **8.** a man about town; a profligate. **9.** an amateur sportsman or yachtsman.

Coriolanus (kŏ′rĭ ə lā′nəs), *n.* **Gaius** (or **Gnaeus**) **Marcius** (gī′əs, *or* nē′əs, mä′syəs), a legendary Roman general of the 5th century B.C. who, in revenge for being exiled, led an army against Rome, but was turned back by the appeals of his mother and his wife.

corium (kô′rĭ əm), *n.*, *pl.* **coria** (kô′rĭ ə). *Anat.* the sensitive vascular layer of the skin, beneath the epidermis; the derma. [t. L: skin, hide, leather]

cork (kôk), *n.* **1.** the outer bark of the cork oak, used for making stoppers of bottles, floats, etc. **2.** something made of cork. **3.** a piece of cork, or other material (as rubber), used as a stopper for a bottle, etc. **4.** *Angling.* a small float to buoy up a fishing line or to indicate when a fish bites. **5.** *Bot.* an outer tissue of bark produced by and exterior to the phellogen. —*v.t.* **6.** to provide or fit with cork or a cork. **7.** to stop with, or as with, a cork (often fol. by *up*). **8.** to blacken with burnt cork. [t. Sp.: aphetic m. *alcorque* shoe with cork, t. Ar.: m. *al qorq*, t. L: m. *quercus* oak] —**cork′like′,** *adj.*

Cork (kôk), *n.* **1.** county in S Ireland, in Munster province. 330,443 pop. (1961); 2881 sq. mi. **2.** its county town: a seaport. 77,780 (1961).

corkage (kô′kĭj), *n.* a charge made by a restaurant, etc., for serving liquor not supplied by the house.

cork cambium, *Bot.* phellogen.

corked (kôkt), *adj.* **1.** stopped with a cork. **2.** (of wine) tasting of the cork; having the flavour spoilt by poor corking. **3.** blackened with burnt cork. **4.** *Slang.* drunk.

corker (kôʹkə), *n.* **1.** one who or that which corks. **2.** *Slang.* something that closes a discussion or settles a question. **3.** *Slang.* something striking or astonishing. **4.** *Slang.* something very good of its kind.

corking (kôʹkĭng), *adj. Slang.* excellent; fine.

cork oak, a species of oak tree, *Quercus suber*, found in Mediterranean countries, the bark of which yields cork.

corkscrew (kôkʹskro͞oʹ), *n.* **1.** an instrument consisting of a metal spiral with a sharp point and a transverse handle, used to draw corks from bottles. **2.** *Boxing.* a punch, which finishes with a turning motion of the wrist. —*adj.* **3.** resembling a corkscrew; helical; spiral. —*v.t., v.i.* **4.** to move in a spiral or zigzag course.

corkwing (kôkʹwĭngʹ), *n.* a small, colourful wrasse, *Labrus melops*, found in shallow water and rock pools along the southern coasts of the British Isles.

corkwood (kôkʹwo͝odʹ), *n.* **1.** a stout shrub or small tree, *Leitneria floridana*, a native of SE North America, with shining deciduous leaves, densely pubescent amenta, and a drupaceous fruit. **2.** any of certain trees and shrubs having a light and porous wood, as the balsa.

corky (kôʹkĭ), *adj.*, **corkier, corkiest. 1.** of the nature of cork; corklike. **2.** *Colloq.* buoyant, lively, or skittish. **3.** (of wine) corked (def. 2). —**corkʹiness,** *n.*

corm (kôm), *n. Bot.* an enlarged, fleshy bulblike base of a stem, as in the crocus. [t. NL: s. *cormus*, t. Gk: m. *kormós* tree trunk with boughs lopped off]

Corm of crocus

cormophyte (kôʹmə fītʹ), *n.* any of the *Cormophyta*, an old primary division or group of plants having an axis differentiated into stem and root, and including all phanerogams and the higher cryptogams. [f. *cormo-* (comb. form of CORM) + -PHYTE] —**cormophytic** (kôʹmə fĭtʹĭk), *adj.*

cormorant (kôʹmə rənt), *n.* **1.** any bird of the family *Phalacrocoracidae*, comprising large, voracious, totipalmate waterbirds with a long neck and a pouch under the beak in which captured fish are held, as *Phalacrocorax carbo*, a common species of America, Europe, and Asia. **2.** a greedy or rapacious person. —*adj.* **3.** greedy; rapacious; insatiable. [ME *cormoraunte*, t. OF: m. *cormoran*, *cormaran*, f. *corp* raven + *marenc* marine (der. *mer* sea)]

Crested cormorant, *Phalacrocorax auritus* (2½ ft long)

corn[1] (kôn), *n.* **1.** collectively, any edible grain, esp. wheat in England, oats in Scotland and Ireland, and maize in North America. **2.** the cereal plants still growing and containing the grain. **3.** a single seed of certain plants, esp. of cereal plants, as wheat, rye, barley, and maize. **4.** *U.S.* maize; Indian corn. **5.** a grain or hard particle, as of salt or sand. **6.** *U.S.* whisky made from Indian corn. **7.** *Colloq.* a trite or sentimental writing or style. —*v.t.* **8.** to granulate, as gunpowder. **9.** to preserve and season with salt in grains. **10.** to lay down in brine, as meat. **11.** to plant (land) with corn. **12.** to feed with corn. [ME and OE; c. G *Korn*, akin to L *grānum* GRAIN]

corn[2] (kôn), *n.* **1.** a horny induration or callosity of the epidermis, usually with a central core, caused by undue pressure or friction, esp. on the toes or feet. **2. tread on one's corns,** to hurt one's feelings. [t. OF: horn, g. L *cornū*]

cornaceous (kô nāʹshəs), *adj.* belonging to the *Cornaceae*, a family of plants, mostly shrubs and trees, including the dogwood, etc. [f. NL *cornāce(ae)* (der. L *cornus* cornel) + -OUS]

Corn Belt, a region in the Midwestern U.S., esp. Iowa, Illinois, and Indiana, excellent for growing maize and raising cattle.

corn-belt climate, the climate of the U.S. Corn Belt, found also in the Danube basin and N China.

cornbrash (kônʹbrăshʹ), *n. Geol.* thin limestone of the Oolite and Upper Jurassic, often with clay or sand admixture.

corn bread, *U.S.* a kind of bread made of maize meal.

corn cake, *U.S.* a cake made of maize meal.

corn-chandler (kônʹchänʹdlə), *n.* a retailer of grain.

corncob (kônʹkŏbʹ), *n.* **1.** the elongated woody core in which the grains of an ear of maize are embedded. **2.** a tobacco pipe with a bowl made of this.

corncockle (kônʹkŏkʹl), *n.* a caryophyllaceous annual, *Agrostemma githago*, bearing red or white flowers, common as a weed in cornfields.

corn colour, light yellow-gold. —**cornʹ-colʹoured,** *adj.*

corncrake (kônʹkrākʹ), *n.* the European land rail, *Crex crex*, a bird of the cornfields.

corncrib (kônʹkrĭbʹ), *n. U.S.* a ventilated structure used for the storage of maize on the cob.

corn-dodger (kônʹdŏjʹə), *n. Chiefly Southern U.S.* a kind of bread made of maize meal, fried or baked hard.

cornea (kôʹnĭ ə), *n., pl.* **-neas** (-nĭ əz); **-neae** (-nĭ ēʹ). *Anat.* the transparent anterior part of the external coat of the eye, covering the iris and the pupil, and continuous with the sclera. See diag. under **eye.** [t. L, fem. sing. of *corneus* horny] —**corʹneal,** *adj.*

corn earworm, *U.S.* the larva of a noctuid moth, *Heliothis armigera*, destructive to maize, cotton, and other plants; bollworm.

corned (kônd), *adj.* preserved or cured with salt: *corned beef.*

Corneille (kô nāʹ; *Fr.* kŏr nĕyʹ), *n.* **Pierre** (*Fr.* pyĕr), 1606–84, French dramatist and poet.

cornel (kôʹnəl), *n.* any of the trees or perennials constituting the genus *Cornus*, as *C.* (*Thelycrania*) *sanguinea*, the European dogwood. [t. G, t. ML: *cornolius* cornel tree, ult. der. L *cornus*]

Cornelia (kô nēʹlyə), *n.* died after 121 B.C., the mother of Tiberius and Gaius Gracchus, champions of the rights of the Roman people.

cornelian (kô nēʹlyən), *n.* a red or reddish variety of chalcedony, used in jewellery, etc. Also, **carnelian.** [ME *corneline*, t. OF, of uncert. orig. Cf. ML *cornelius*]

Cornelius (*Ger.* kŏr nĕʹlĭ o͝os), *n.* **Peter von** (*Ger.* pĕʹtər fōn), 1783–1867, German painter, esp. of historical frescoes.

cornemuse (kôʹnə myo͞ozʹ), *n.* an ancient instrument resembling the bagpipe. [ME, t. OF, back-formation from *cornemuser*, v., equiv. to *corne* HORN + *muser*, der. VL *musa* pipe]

corneous (kôʹnĭ əs), *adj.* consisting of a horny substance; horny. [t. L: m. *corneus* horny]

corner (kôʹnə), *n.* **1.** the meeting place of two converging lines or surfaces. **2.** the space between two converging lines or surfaces near their intersection; angle. **3.** a projecting angle. **4.** the place where two streets meet. **5.** an end; margin; edge. **6.** any narrow, secluded, or secret place. **7.** an awkward or embarrassing position, esp. one from which escape is impossible. **8.** any part, even the least or the most remote. **9.** *Finance.* a monopolizing or a monopoly of the available supply of a stock or commodity, to a point permitting control of price. **10.** a region; quarter: *all the corners of the earth.* **11.** a piece to protect the corner of anything. **12.** *Soccer, Hockey, etc.* a free kick or hit from the corner of the field taken by the attacking side when the ball has crossed the goal line after last being touched by a member of the defending side. **13.** *Boxing.* the space between the junction of two of the ropes, where the contestants rest between rounds. **14. cut corners, a.** to take short cuts habitually. **b.** to bypass an official procedure, or the like. **15. cut off a corner,** to take a short cut. **16. turn the corner,** to begin to get well. **17. round the corner,** very close; within walking distance. —*v.t.* **18.** to furnish with corners. **19.** to place in or drive into a corner. **20.** to force into an awkward or difficult position, or one from which escape is impossible. **21.** to form a corner in (a stock, etc.). —*v.i.* **22.** *U.S.* to meet in, or be situated on or at, a corner. **23.** to form a corner in a stock or commodity. **24.** in a motor vehicle, to turn a corner, esp. at speed. —*adj.* **25.** situated at a junction of two roads. **26.** made to be fitted or used in a corner. [ME, t. AF, var. of OF *cornere*, ult. der. L *cornū* horn, corner]

cornerstone (kôʹnə stōnʹ), *n.* **1.** a stone which lies at the corner of two walls, and serves to unite them, **2.** a stone built into a corner of the foundation of an important edifice as the actual or nominal starting point in building, usually laid with formal ceremonies, and often hollowed out and made the repository of documents, etc. **3.** something or someone of prime or fundamental importance.

cornerwise (kôʹnə wīzʹ), *adv.* **1.** with the corner in front. **2.** so as to form a corner. **3.** from corner to corner; diagonally. Also, **cornerways** (kôʹnə wāzʹ).

cornet (kôʹnĭt), *n.* **1.** a wind instrument of the trumpet class, with valves or pistons. **2.** a player of a cornet in an orchestra. **3.** an organ stop. **4.** a little cone of paper twisted at the end, used for enclosing sweets, groceries, etc. **5.** a cone, as for ice-cream. **6.** the large white head-

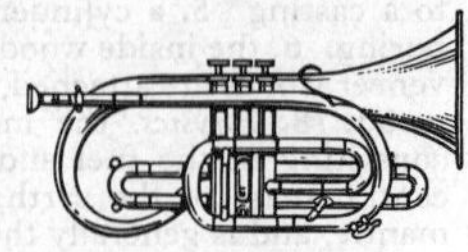
Cornet (def. 1)

dress worn by Sisters of Charity. **7.** a headdress formerly worn by women. **8.** (formerly) an officer in a troop of cavalry, who carried the colours. [ME *cornette*, t. OF: m. *cornet*, ult. der. L *cornū* horn]

cornet-à-pistons (kô′nĭt ə pĭs′tənz; *Fr.* kŏr nĕ ȧ pĕs tôN′), *n., pl.* **cornets-à-pistons** (kô′nĭts; *Fr.* kŏr nĕ zȧ pĕs tôN′). cornet. [t. F: cornet with pistons]

corn exchange, a meeting place or market in a large town, where traders or merchants interested in corn, transact their business.

corn-factor (kôn′făk′tə), *n.* a corn merchant.

cornfield (kôn′fēld′), *n.* a field in which corn is growing, or grows.

cornflakes (kôn′flāks′), *n.pl.* a breakfast cereal consisting of small toasted flakes made from maize and served with milk, sugar, etc.

cornflour (kôn′flou′ə), *n.* a starch, or a starchy flour made from maize, rice, or other grain, used for making puddings, etc.

cornflower (kôn′flou′ə), *n.* any of several plants growing in cornfields, as *Centaurea cyanus*, a composite plant with blue (varying to white) flowers, growing wild in Europe and often cultivated; bluebottle.

cornhusk (kôn′hŭsk′), *n. U.S.* the husk of an ear of maize.

cornice (kô′nĭs), *n., v.,* **-niced, -nicing.** *—n.* **1.** *Archit.* **a.** a horizontal moulded projection which crowns or finishes a wall, building, etc. **b.** the uppermost division of an entablature, resting on the frieze. See diag. under **column. 2.** the overhanging snow at the edge of a precipice. **3.** an overhanging crest of snow. **4.** the moulding or mouldings between the walls and ceiling of a room. **5.** any of the various other ornamental horizontal mouldings or bands, as for concealing hooks or rods from which curtains are hung or for supporting picture hooks. *—v.t.* **6.** to furnish or finish with, or as with, a cornice. [t. F, t. It., t. MGk: m. s. *korōnís* summit, Gk anything curved or bent]

corniculate (kô nĭk′yŏŏ lāt′, -lĭt), *adj.* resembling a small horn in appearance. [f. s. L *corniculus* little horn + -ATE¹]

Cornish (kô′nĭsh), *adj.* **1.** of Cornwall, its inhabitants, or the language formerly spoken by them. *—n.* **2.** the old Celtic language of Cornwall. **3.** the dialect of English now spoken in Cornwall. —**Cornishman** (kô′nĭsh mən), *n.*

cornland (kôn′lănd′), *n.* land suitable or appropriated for the cultivation of corn.

Corn Law, *Eng. Hist.* any one of a series of laws regulating the home and foreign grain trade, the last of which was repealed in 1846.

corn lily, any of several ornamental bulbous plants of the South African genus *Ixia*, family *Iridaceae*.

corn marigold, an erect annual composite herb with yellow flowers, *Chrysanthemum segetum*, a common weed of cultivated land throughout temperate regions.

corn meal, 1. oatmeal. **2.** *U.S.* meal made of maize or grain; Indian meal. —**corn′meal′,** *adj.*

cornopean (kô nō′pyən), *n.* an organ stop for a trumpet-like sound.

corn-picker (kôn′pĭk′ə), *n. U.S.* a machine for picking ears of maize from standing stalks and removing husks from the ears.

corn pit, *U.S.* an exchange devoted to trading in maize.

corn plaster, a resin plaster, containing salicylic acid, used to cure corns.

corn pone, *Southern U.S.* **1.** corn bread, esp. of a plain or simple kind. **2.** a cake or loaf of this.

corn poppy, the common poppy, *Papaver rhoeas*, bearing bright red flowers, since World War I the symbol of fallen soldiers. Also, **Flanders poppy.**

corn rose, 1. the common red poppy, *Papaver rhoeas*. **2.** the corncockle, *Agrostemma githago*.

corn salad, any of several plants of the genus *Valerianella*, esp. *V. olitoria* and *V. eriocarpa*, sometimes found wild in cornfields, and used for salad.

corn shock, a stack of upright cornstalks.

corn silk, the fresh styles and stigmas of *Zea mays*, used in medicine as a diuretic.

corn smut, a fungus, *Ustilago zeae*, growing on maize, formerly used medicinally.

cornstalk (kôn′stôk′), *n.* **1.** the stalk or stem of corn. **2.** *Austral.* a native Australian. **3.** *Colloq., esp. Austral.* a tall, thin man.

cornstarch (kôn′stăch′), *n. U.S.* cornflour.

corn syrup, *U.S.* syrup prepared from maize.

cornu (kô′nyŏŏ), *n., pl.* **-nua** (-nyŏŏ ə). a horn, esp. a process of bone resembling a horn. [t. L. See HORN]

cornucopia (kô′nyŏŏ kō′pyə), *n.* **1.** the mythical horn of the goat Amalthaea, which suckled Zeus, represented as overflowing with flowers, fruit, etc., and symbolizing plenty. **2.** an overflowing supply. **3.** a horn-shaped or conical receptacle or ornament. [t. LL, for L *cornū cōpiae* horn of plenty] —**cor′nuco′pian,** *adj.*

cornus (kô′nəs), *n.* a cornel. [t. L: dogwood tree]

cornuted (kô nyŏŏ′tĭd), *adj.* having horns.

Cornwall (kôn′wəl), *n.* a county in SW England. 342,301 pop. (1961); 1357 sq. mi. *Co. town:* Bodmin.

Cornwallis (kôn wŏl′ĭs), *n.* **Charles, 1st Marquess,** 1738–1805, English general and statesman: in the War of American Independence he surrendered to Washington at Yorktown, Virginia, October 19th, 1781.

corn whiskey, *U.S.* a type of whisky made from maize. Also, **corn whisky.**

corny¹ (kô′nĭ), *adj.,* **-nier, -niest. 1.** *Slang.* old-fashioned; lacking subtlety. **2.** *Slang.* sentimental; mawkish and of poor quality. **3.** of or abounding in corn.

corny² (kô′nĭ), *adj.* having corns (on the feet).

corody (kŏ′rə dĭ), *n., pl.* **-dies.** *Chiefly Hist.* **1.** an allowance, as of food, etc., for one's maintenance. **2.** the right to this. Also, **corrody.** [late ME, t. ML: m. s. *corrōdium*, var. of *corrēdium* provision. Cf. ARRAY]

corolla (kə rŏl′ə), *n. Bot.* the internal envelope or floral leaves of a flower, usually of delicate texture and of some colour other than green; the petals considered collectively. [t. L: garland, dim. of *corōna* crown]

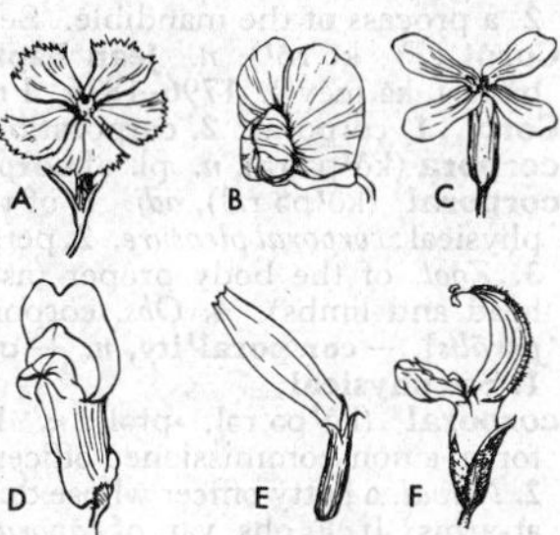

Corollas
Polypetalous corollas: A, Unguiculate; B, Papilionaceous; C, Cruciate; Gamopetalous corollas: D, Personate; E, Ligulate; F, Bilbiate

corollaceous (kŏ′rə lā′shəs), *adj. Bot.* having or resembling a corolla.

corollary (kə rŏl′ə rĭ), *n., pl.* **-ries. 1.** *Maths.* a proposition incidentally proved in proving another. **2.** an immediate or easily drawn consequence. **3.** a natural consequence or result. [ME *corolarie*, t. LL: m. *corollārium* corollary, L gift, orig. garland, der. L *corolla* garland]

Coromandel Coast (kŏ′rə măn′dl), that part of the coastline of SE India extending from Point Calimere (opposite the N end of Ceylon) to the mouth of the river Kistna.

corona (kə rō′nə), *n., pl.* **-nas, -nae** (-nē). **1.** a white or coloured circle of light seen round a luminous body, esp. the sun or moon (in meteorology, restricted to those circles due to the diffraction produced by thin clouds or mist). **2.** *Astron.* a faintly luminous envelope outside the sun's chromosphere, the inner part consisting of highly ionized elements. **3.** *Archit.* that part of a cornice supported by and projecting beyond the bed moulding. **4.** a type of circular chandelier, suspended from the roof of a church. **5.** *Anat.* the upper portion or crown of a part, as of the head. **6.** *Bot.* a crownlike appendage, esp. one on the inner side of a corolla, as in the narcissus. **7.** *Elect.* a discharge, frequently luminous, at the surface of a conductor, or between two conductors of the same transmission line, accompanied by ionization of the surrounding atmosphere and power loss; brush discharge. [t. L: garland, CROWN]

Corona Australis (kə rō′nə ŏ strā′lĭs), the Southern Crown, a southern constellation touching the southern part of Sagittarius. [t. L]

Corona Borealis (kə rō′nə bô′rĭ ā′lĭs), the Northern Crown, a northern constellation between Hercules and Boötes. [t. L]

coronach (kŏ′rə nək), *n.* (in Scotland and Ireland) a song or lamentation for the dead; a dirge. [t. Gaelic: m. *corranach* outcry, dirge]

coronal (kŏ′rə nəl *for 1, 2, 3, and 5*; kə rō′nəl *for 4*), *n.* **1.** *Anat.* the coronal suture. **2.** a crown; coronet. **3.** a garland. *—adj.* **4.** of or pertaining to a coronal. **5.** *Phonet.* retroflex. [t. LL: s. *corōnālis*]

coronal suture, *Anat.* a suture extending across the skull between the frontal bone and the parietal bones. See diag. under **cranium.**

coronary (kŏ′rə nə rĭ), *adj.* **1.** of or like a crown. **2.** *Anat.* **a.** encircling like a crown, as certain blood vessels. **b.** pertaining to the arteries which supply the heart tissues and which originate in the root of the aorta. *—n.* **3.** a coronary thrombosis. [t. L: m. s. *corōnārius*]

coronary thrombosis, *Pathol.* the occlusion of a coronary arterial branch by a blood clot within the vessel, usually at a site narrowed by arteriosclerosis.

coronate (kŏ′rə nāt′), *adj.* having or wearing a crown, coronet, or the like.

coronation (kŏ′rə nā′shən), *n.* the act or ceremony of investing a king, etc., with a crown.

coroner (kŏ′rə nə), *n.* an officer, as of a county or municipality, whose chief function is to investigate by inquest (often before a **coroner's jury**) any death not clearly due to natural causes. [ME, t. AF: m. *corouner* officer of the crown, der. *coroune.* See CROWN] —**cor′onership′,** *n.*

coronet (kŏ′rə nĭt), *n.* **1.** a small or inferior crown. **2.** an insignia for the head, worn by peers or members of nobility. **3.** a crownlike ornament for the head, as of gold or jewels. **4.** the lowest part of the pastern of a horse, just above the hoof. [t. OF: m. *coronete,* dim. of *corone* CROWN]

coroneted (kŏ′rə nĭ tĭd), *adj.* wearing, or entitled to wear, a coronet. Also, **coronetted.**

coronoid (kŏ′rə noid′), *adj.* **1.** crown-shaped; like a corona. **2.** *Anat.* beaklike. [f. Gk: m. s. *korṓnē* crow + m. s. *eîdos* form]

coronoid process, *Anat.* **1.** a projection from the ulna which articulates in the coronoid fossa of the humerus. **2.** a process of the mandible. See diag. under **mandible.**

Corot (*Fr.* kō rō′), *n.* **Jean Baptiste Camille** (*Fr.* zhäɴ bȧ tēst kȧ mēy′), 1796–1875, French landscape painter.

Corp., **1.** corporal. **2.** corporation. Also, **corp.**

corpora (kô′pə rə), *n.* pl. of **corpus.**

corporal[1] (kô′pə rəl), *adj.* **1.** of the human body; bodily; physical: *corporal pleasure.* **2.** personal: *corporal possession.* **3.** *Zool.* of the body proper (as distinguished from the head and limbs). **4.** *Obs.* corporeal. [ME, t. L: s. *corporālis*] —**cor′poral′ity,** *n.* —**cor′porally,** *adv.* —**Syn. 1.** See **physical.**

corporal[2] (kô′pə rəl, -prəl), *n.* **1.** (in the army and air-force) a non-commissioned officer ranking below sergeant. **2.** *Naval.* a petty officer whose duty is to assist the master-at-arms. [t. F, obs. var. of *caporal,* t. It.: m. *caporale,* der. *capo* (der. L *caput*) head] —**cor′poralship′,** *n.*

corporal[3] (kô′pə rəl), *n.* *Eccles.* a fine cloth, usually of linen, on which the consecrated elements are placed during the celebration of the Eucharist. [ME, t. ML: s. *corporālis, corporāle,* der. L *corpus* body]

corporal punishment, physical injury, esp. by flogging, inflicted on the body of one convicted of a crime or misdeed.

corporate (kô′pə rĭt, -prĭt), *adj.* **1.** forming a corporation. **2.** of a corporation. **3.** united in one body. **4.** pertaining to a united body, as of persons. [t. L: m. s. *corporātus,* pp., formed into a body] —**cor′porately,** *adv.*

corporation (kô′pə rā′shən), *n.* **1.** an association of individuals, created by law or under authority of law, having a continuous existence irrespective of that of its members, and powers and liabilities distinct from those of its members. **2.** (*cap.*) the principal officials of a borough, etc. **3.** any group of persons united, or regarded as united, in one body. **4.** *Slang.* the abdomen, esp. when large and prominent.

corporation tax, a tax imposed by Act of Parliament on the profits of limited companies (being any corporate or incorporated association), intended to separate the taxation of companies from that of individuals.

corporative (kô′pə rə tĭv, -prə tĭv), *adj.* **1.** of or pertaining to a corporation. **2.** *Pol. Econ.* of a political system under which the principal economic functions (banking, industry, labour, etc.) are organized as corporate unities.

corporator (kô′pə rā′tə), *n.* a member of a corporation, esp. one of the original members.

corporeal (kô pô′rĭ əl), *adj.* **1.** of the nature of the physical body; bodily. **2.** of the nature of matter; material; tangible: *corporeal property.* [f. s. L *corporeus* of the nature of body + -AL[1]] —**corpo′real′ity, corpo′realness,** *n.* —**corpo′really,** *adv.* —**Syn. 1.** See **physical.** —**Ant. 1.** spiritual. **2.** intangible.

corporeity (kô′pə rē′ĭ tĭ), *n.* material or physical nature or quality; materiality.

corposant (kô′pə zănt′), *n.* a light, due to atmospheric electricity, sometimes seen on the mastheads, yardarms, etc., of ships and on church towers, treetops, etc. [t. Pg.: m. *corpo santo* holy body (L *corpus sanctum*)]

corps (kô), *n., pl.* **corps** (kôz). **1.** a military unit of ground combat forces consisting of two or more divisions and other troops. **2.** a group so organized for a particular operation. **3.** a group of persons associated or acting together. **4.** *Obs.* corpse. [t. F. See CORPSE]

corps-à-corps (*Fr.* kŏr ȧ kŏr′), *n.* *Fencing.* any position in which two fencers are engaged in such a way that neither can use his weapon. [t. F: body to body]

corps area, *Mil.* the geographical area within which a corps commander exercises military responsibility.

corps de ballet (kô′ də băl′ā; *Fr.* kŏr də bȧ lĕ′), *French.* the dancers in a ballet company who perform as a group and have no solo parts.

corps Didot (*Fr.* kŏr dē dō′), *Print.* the continental European method of measuring type. [t. F: Didot body, named after François Ambroise *Didot,* 1730–1804, French printer]

corps diplomatique (kô′ dĭp′lō mă tēk′; *Fr.* kŏr dē plō-mȧ tēk′), *French.* the whole body of ambassadors and their staffs accredited to a state.

corpse (kôps), *n.* **1.** a dead body, usually of a human being. **2.** *Obs.* a living body. [ME *corps, cors,* t. OF, g. L *corpus* body] —**Syn. 1.** See **body.**

corpse-candle (kôps′kăn′dl), *n.* a flame seen hovering over a grave and believed to be an omen of death.

corpsman (kô′mən), *n., pl.* **-men. 1.** *U.S. Naval.* a hospital orderly. **2.** *U.S. Army.* a stretcher-bearer.

corps of commissionaires, an association of old soldiers and sailors, established 1859, for employment as messengers, doorkeepers, etc.

corpulence (kô′pyo͝o ləns), *n.* bulkiness or largeness of body; fatness; fleshiness; portliness. Also, **cor′pulency.** [late ME, t. F, t. L: m. s. *corpulentia*]

corpulent (kô′pyo͝o lənt), *adj.* large or bulky of body; portly; stout; fat. [ME, t. L: s. *corpulentus,* der. *corpus* body] —**cor′pulently,** *adv.*

corpus (kô′pəs), *n., pl.* **-pora** (-pə rə). **1.** the body of a man or animal. **2.** *Anat.* any of various bodies, masses, or parts of special character or function. **3.** a large or complete collection of writings, laws, etc. **4.** a principal or capital sum, as opposed to interest or income. [t. L]

corpus allatum (kô′pəs ə lā′təm), *pl.* **corpora allata** (kô′pə rə ə lā′tə). *Entomol.* one of a pair of small ductless, hormone-secreting glands in the head of an insect behind the brain. [NL: added body]

corpus callosum (kô′pəs kə lō′səm), *pl.* **corpora callosa** (kô′pə rə kə lō′sə). *Anat., Zool.* a great band of deeply situated transverse white fibres uniting the two halves of the cerebrum, peculiar to *Mammalia.* [NL: hard body]

corpus cardiacum (kô′pəs kä dī′ə kəm), *pl.* **corpora cardiaca** (kô′pə rə kä dī′ə kə). *Entomol.* one of a pair of small cellular bodies associated with the corpora allata in the back of an insect's head, generally attached to the aorta, probably organs of hormone secretion.

Corpus Christi (kô′pəs krĭs′tĭ), **1.** *Eccles.* a festival in honour of the Eucharist, kept on the Thursday after Trinity Sunday. **2.** a town in the U.S., in S Texas. 167,690 (1960). [t. L: body of Christ]

corpuscle (kô′pŭs′əl), *n.* **1.** *Physiol.* one of the minute bodies which form a constituent of the blood (**blood corpuscles,** both red and white), the lymph (**lymph corpuscles,** white only), etc. **2.** a minute body forming a more or less distinct part of an organism. **3.** *Physics, Chem.* a minute or elementary particle of matter, as an electron, proton, or atom. **4.** a minute particle. Also, **corpuscule** (kô pŭs′kyo͞ol). [t. L: m. s. *corpusculum,* dim. of *corpus* body] —**corpuscular** (kô pŭs′kyo͝o lə), *adj.*

corpus delicti (kô′pəs dĭ lĭk′tī), *Law.* the body of essential facts constituting a criminal offence. [L: body of the transgression]

corpus juris (kô′pəs jo͞oə′rĭs), a compilation of law or the collected law of a nation or state. [L]

Corpus Juris Canonici (kə nŏn′ĭ sī′), the collection of church law which remained in force until it was replaced in 1918 by the Codex Juris Canonici. [L]

Corpus Juris Civilis (sĭ vī′lĭs), the collective title (since the 17th century) of the whole legislation of Justinian Code, promulgated in the 6th century, as the Digest, the Institutes, the Code, and the Novels. [L]

corpus luteum (kô′pəs lo͞o′tĭ əm), *pl.* **corpora lutea** (kô′pə rə lo͞o′tĭ ə). *Anat.* a ductless gland developed within the ovary by the reorganization of a Graafian follicle following ovulation. [NL: yellow body]

corpus striatum (kô′pəs strī ā′təm), *pl.* **corpora striata** (kô′pə rə strī ā′tə). *Anat.* a mass of grey matter beneath the cortex and in front of the thalamus in each cerebral hemisphere. [NL: striped body]

corral (kŏ räl′), *n., v.,* **-ralled, -ralling.** —*n.* **1.** a pen or enclosure for horses, cattle, etc. **2.** an enclosure formed of wagons during an encampment, for defence against attack. —*v.t.* **3.** to confine in, or as in, a corral. **4.** *U.S. Colloq.* to seize; capture. **5.** to form (wagons) into a corral. [t. Sp.: enclosed yard, der. *corro* a ring]

corrasion (kə rā′zhən), *n.* *Phys. Geog.* erosion caused by loose material during its transportation, as windborne sand or riverborne pebbles.

correct (kə rĕkt′), *v.t.* **1.** to set right; remove the errors or faults of. **2.** to point out or mark the errors in. **3.** to admonish or rebuke in order to improve. **4.** to counteract the operation or effect of (something hurtful). **5.** *Maths, Physics., etc.* to alter or adjust so as to bring into accordance with a standard or with some required condition. —*adj.* **6.** conforming to fact or truth; free from error, accurate:

a correct statement. **7.** in accordance with an acknowledged or accepted standard; proper. [ME *correcte(n)*, t. L: m. s. *correctus*, pp., made straight, directed] **—correct′ly,** *adv.* **—correct′ness,** *n.* **—correc′tor,** *n.*
—Syn. 1. rectify, amend, emend, reform, remedy. **3.** discipline. See **punish. 6.** faultless, perfect, exact. CORRECT, ACCURATE, PRECISE imply conformity to fact, standard, or truth. A CORRECT statement is one free from error, mistakes, or faults. An ACCURATE statement is one which, as a result of an active effort to comprehend and verify, shows careful conformity to fact, truth, or spirit. A PRECISE statement shows scrupulously strict and detailed (sometimes excessive) conformity to fact. **—Ant. 6.** faulty, inaccurate. **7.** unconventional.

correction (kə rĕk′shən), *n.* **1.** the act of correcting. **2.** that which is substituted or proposed for what is wrong; an emendation. **3.** punishment; chastisement; discipline; reproof. **4.** *Maths, Physics., etc.* a subordinate quantity that has to be applied in order to ensure accuracy, as in the use of an instrument or the solution of a problem. **—correc′tional,** *adj.*

correctitude (kə rĕk′tĭ tyōōd′), *n.* correctness, esp. of manners and conduct. [f. CORRECT, v. + *-itude*, modelled on RECTITUDE]

corrective (kə rĕk′tĭv), *adj.* **1.** tending to correct; having the quality of correcting. **—***n.* **2.** a corrective agent. **—correc′tively,** *adv.*

corrective training, reformative imprisonment for persistent offenders of twenty-one or over, for periods of two to four years.

Correggio (*It.* kôr rĕd′jō), *n.* **Antonio Allegri da** (än tō′nyō äl lĕ′grē dä), 1494–1534, Italian painter.

Corregidor (kə rĕg′ĭ dô′; *Sp.* kôr rĕ KHĒ dôr′), *n.* a fortified island in Manila Bay, in the Philippine Islands. 2 sq. mi. See map under **Bataan.**

correlate (kŏ′rĭ lāt′), *v.*, **-lated, -lating,** *adj.*, *n.* **—***v.t.* **1.** to place in or bring into mutual or reciprocal relation; establish in orderly connection. **—***v.i.* **2.** to have a mutual or reciprocal relation; stand in correlation. **—***adj.* **3.** *Rare.* mutually or reciprocally related; correlated. **—***n.* **4.** either of two related things, esp. when one implies the other. [f. COR- + RELATE]

correlation (kŏ′rĭ lā′shən), *n.* **1.** mutual relation of two or more things, parts, etc. **2.** the act of correlating. **3.** the state of being correlated. **4.** *Statistics.* the degree of relationship of two attributes or measurements on the same group of elements. **5.** *Physiol.* the interdependence or reciprocal relations of organs or functions.

correlation coefficient, *Statistics.* the measure of correlation, called *r*, having the value +1 for perfect positive linear correlation, −1 for perfect negative linear correlation, and a value of 0 for a complete lack of correlation.

correlation ratio, *Statistics.* a mathematical measure of the correlation between two sets of values not linearly correlated.

correlative (kŏ rĕl′ə tĭv), *adj.* **1.** so related that each implies or complements the other. **2.** being in correlation; mutually related. **3.** having a mutual relation; answering to or complementing one another, as *either* and *or*, *where* and *there.* **4.** *Biol.* (of a typical structure of an organism) found in correlation with another. **—***n.* **5.** either of two things, as two terms, which are correlative. **6.** a correlative expression. **—correl′atively,** *adv.* **—correl′ativeness, correl′ativ′ity,** *n.*

correspond (kŏ′rĭ spŏnd′), *v.i.* **1.** to be in agreement or conformity (often fol. by *with* or *to*): *his words and actions do not correspond.* **2.** to be similar or analogous; be equivalent in function, position, amount, etc. (fol. by *to*): *the U.S. Congress corresponds to the British Parliament.* **3.** to communicate by exchange of letters. [t. ML: s. *correspondēre* f. L: *cor-* COR- + *rēspondēre* answer] **—cor′respond′ingly,** *adv.* **—Syn. 1.** harmonize, accord, match. See **agree.**

correspondence (kŏ′rĭ spŏn′dəns), *n.* **1.** Also, **cor′respond′ency.** the act or fact of corresponding. **2.** relation or similarity or analogy. **3.** agreement; conformity. **4.** communication by exchange of letters. **5.** letters that pass between correspondents.

correspondence course, a course of instruction conducted by a correspondence school.

correspondence school, a school which gives instruction by postal correspondence. Also, **correspondence college.**

correspondent (kŏ′rĭ spŏn′dənt), *n.* **1.** one who communicates by letters. **2.** one employed to contribute news, etc., regularly from a distant place. **3.** one who contributes letters to a newspaper. **4.** one who has regular business relations with another, esp. at a distance. **5.** a thing that corresponds to something else. **—***adj.* **6.** corresponding, having a relation of correspondence. **—cor′respond′ently,** *adv.*

corresponsive (kŏ′rĭ spŏn′sĭv), *adj.* responsive to effort or impulse, answering; corresponding.

Corrèze (*Fr.* kŏ rĕz′), *n.* a department in S central France. 237,926 pop. (1962); 2273 sq. mi. *Cap.:* Tulle.

Corrib (kŏ′rĭb), *n.* **Lough,** the largest lake in Ireland, lying between counties Galway and Mayo. 68 sq. mi.

corridor (kŏ′rĭ dô′), *n.* **1.** a gallery or passage connecting parts of a building. **2.** a passage into which several rooms or apartments open. **3.** a passageway on one side of a railway carriage into which the compartments open. **4.** a narrow tract of land forming a passageway, as one belonging to an inland country and affording an outlet to the sea: *the Polish Corridor.* [t. F: long passageway, t. It.: m. *corridore* covered way, t. Sp.: m. *corredor*, der. *correr* run, g. L *currere*]

corrie (kŏ′rĭ), *n.* *Geol. and Scot.* a circular hollow in the side of a hill or mountain, often containing a small lake. [t. Gaelic: m. *coire* cauldron]

Corriedale (kŏ′rĭ dāl′), *n.* a white-faced breed of sheep, orig. developed in New Zealand, noted for high-quality wool and good market lambs.

Corrientes (kŏ′rĭ ĕn′tēs; *Sp.* kôr ryĕn′tĕs), *n.* a city in NE Argentina: a port on the Paraná river. 112,725 (1965).

corrigendum (kŏ′rĭ jĕn′dəm), *n.*, *pl.* **-da** (-də). **1.** an error to be corrected, esp. an error in print. **2.** (*pl.*) a list of corrections of errors in a book, etc. [t. L, neut. ger. of *corrigere* correct]

corrigible (kŏ′rĭ jə bl), *adj.* **1.** capable of being corrected. **2.** submissive to correction. [t. LL: m. s. *corrigibilis*, der. L *corrigere* correct] **—cor′rigibil′ity,** *n.* **—cor′rigibly,** *adv.*

corrival (kə rī′vəl), *n.*, *adj.* rival. [t. L: s. *corrīvālis* joint rival]

corroborant (kə rŏb′ə rənt), *adj.* **1.** corroborating; confirming. **2.** strengthening, invigorating. **—***n.* **3.** something that corroborates or strengthens. **4.** *Obsolesc.* a strengthening medicine.

corroborate (*v.* kə rŏb′ə rāt′; *adj.* kə rŏb′ə rĭt), *v.*, **-rated, -rating,** *adj.* **—***v.t.* **1.** to make more certain; confirm. **—***adj.* **2.** *Archaic.* corroborated. [t. L: m. s. *corrōborātus*, pp., strengthened] **—corroborative** (kə rŏb′ə rə tĭv), **corroboratory** (kə rŏb′ə rə tə rĭ, -trĭ), *adj.* **—corrob′oratively,** *adv.* **—corrob′ora′tor,** *n.*

corroboration (kə rŏb′ə rā′shən), *n.* **1.** the act of corroborating. **2.** a corroboratory fact, statement, etc. **3.** *Law.* independent evidence which implicates a person accused of a crime, by connecting him with it.

corroboree (kə rŏb′ə rĭ), *n.* **1.** a native Australian assembly of sacred, festive, or warlike character. **2.** *Austral.* any large or noisy gathering. **3.** a disturbance; an uproar. [t. native Australian]

corrode (kə rōd′), *v.*, **-roded, -roding.** **—***v.t.* **1.** to eat away gradually as if by gnawing. **2.** *Chem.* to eat away the surface of a solid, esp. of metals, by chemical action. **3.** to impair; deteriorate: *jealousy corroded his whole being.* **—***v.i.* **4.** to become corroded. [t. L: m. s. *corrōdere* gnaw away] **—corrod′ible,** *adj.* **—Syn. 1.** gnaw, eat, consume. **4.** canker, rust, crumble.

corrody (kŏ′rə dĭ), *n.* corody.

corrosion (kə rō′zhən), *n.* **1.** the act or process of corroding. **2.** corroded condition. **3.** a product of corroding, as rust. [t. L: s. *corrōsio*]

corrosion fatigue, *Metall.* the failure of a metal under stress when it is exposed to corrosive attack.

corrosive (kə rō′sĭv), *adj.* **1.** having the quality of corroding, eating away, or consuming. **—***n.* **2.** something corrosive, as an acid, drug, etc. **—corro′sively,** *adv.* **—corro′siveness,** *n.*

corrosive sublimate, *Chem.* mercuric chloride.

corrugate (*v.* kŏ′rōō gāt′; *adj.* kŏ′rōō gĭt, -gāt′), *v.*, **-gated, -gating,** *adj.* **—***v.t., v.i.* **1.** to draw or bend into folds or alternate furrows and ridges. **2.** to wrinkle, as the skin, etc. **—***adj.* **3.** corrugated; wrinkled; furrowed. [t. L: m. s. *corrūgātus*, pp., wrinkled]

corrugated iron, a type of sheet iron or steel strengthened for use in construction by being formed into a series of alternating grooves and ridges and usually galvanized for weather resistance.

corrugated paper, heavy paper with alternating ridges and grooves, used for protecting packages, etc.

corrugation (kŏ′rōō gā′shən), *n.* **1.** the act of corrugating. **2.** the state of being corrugated. **3.** a wrinkle; fold; furrow; ridge.

corrupt (kə rŭpt′), *adj.* **1.** dishonest; without integrity; guilty of dishonesty, esp. involving bribery: *a corrupt judge.* **2.** debased in character; depraved; perverted; wicked; evil. **3.** putrid. **4.** infected; tainted. **5.** made bad by errors or alterations, as a text. **—***v.t.* **6.** to destroy the integrity of; cause to be dishonest, disloyal, etc., esp. by bribery. **7.** to lower morally; pervert; deprave. **8.** to infect; taint. **9.** to make putrid or putrescent. **10.** to alter (a language, text, etc.) for the worse; debase.

11. *Archaic.* to mar; spoil. **—*v.i.*** **12.** to become corrupt. [ME, t. L: s. *corruptus*, pp., broken in pieces, destroyed] **—corrupt′er,** *n.* **—corrup′tive,** *adj.* **—corrupt′ly,** *adv.* **—corrupt′ness,** *n.*

—Syn. 1. CORRUPT, DISHONEST, VENAL apply to one, esp. in public office, who acts on mercenary motives, without regard to honour, right, or justice. A CORRUPT politician is one originally honest who has succumbed to temptation and begun questionable practices. A DISHONEST politician is one lacking native integrity and trustworthiness. VENAL is a strongly opprobrious term; a VENAL politician is one so debased that he frankly sells his patronage. **6.** demoralize, bribe. **7.** debase. **8.** contaminate, pollute.

corruptible (kə rŭp′tə bl), *adj.* that may be corrupted. **—corrupt′ibil′ity, corrupt′ibleness,** *n.* **—corrupt′ibly,** *adv.*

corruption (kə rŭp′shən), *n.* **1.** the act of corrupting. **2.** the state of being corrupt. **3.** moral perversion; depravity. **4.** perversion of integrity. **5.** corrupt or dishonest proceedings. **6.** bribery. **7.** debasement, as of a language. **8.** a debased form of a word. **9.** putrefactive decay. **10.** any corrupting influence or agency. **—Syn. 4.** baseness, dishonesty. **9.** foulness, pollution.

corsage (kô säzh′), *n.* **1.** the body or waist of a dress; bodice. **2.** a small bouquet worn by a woman at the waist, on the shoulder, etc. [t. F, der. *cors* body. See CORSE]

corsair (kô′sēə), *n.* **1.** a privateer, esp. one of the Barbary Coast. **2.** a pirate. **3.** a fast vessel used for piracy. [t. F: m. *corsaire*, t. It.: m. *corsaro*, runner, g. LL *cursārius*, der. *cursus* COURSE]

corse (kôs), *n. Archaic.* corpse. [ME *cors*, t. OF, g. L *corpus* body]

corselet (kôs′lĭt), *n.* **1.** a supporting undergarment with very few or no bones, worn by women. **2.** a corslet. [t. F, dim. of OF *cors.* See CORSE]

corset (kô′sĭt), *n.* **1.** (*often pl.*) a shaped, close-fitting inner garment stiffened with whalebone or the like and capable of being tightened by lacing, enclosing the trunk and extending for a distance above and below the waistline, worn, chiefly by women, to give shape and support to the body; stays. **2.** *Obs.* a close-fitting outer body garment. [ME, t. F, dim. of OF *cors.* See CORSE]

corsetiere (kô′sĕt ĭ ēə′, kô sĕt′-), *n.* an expert trained in the fitting and selecting of corsets.

corsetry (kô′sĭ trĭ), *n.* **1.** the art of making corsets. **2.** corsets considered collectively.

Corsica (kô′sĭ kə), *n.* **1.** an island in the Mediterranean, SE of and forming a department of France. 275,467 pop. (1962); 3367 sq. mi. *Cap.:* Ajaccio. French, **Corse** (*Fr.* kôrs). See map under **Elba. 2.** See **Provence** (def. 2). **—Cor′sican,** *adj., n.*

corslet (kôs′lĭt), *n.* armour for the body, esp. the breastplate and back piece together. Also, **corselet.**

cortege (kô tāzh′), *n.* **1.** a train of attendants; retinue. **2.** a procession. Also, **cortège** (*Fr.* kŏr tĕzh′). [t. F, t. It.: m. *corteggio*, der. *corte* COURT]

Cortes (kô′tĕz; *Sp.* kȯr′tės), *n.* the two houses constituting the national legislative body of Spain, or those of Portugal. [t. Sp., Pg., pl. of *corte.* See COURT]

Cortés (kô′tĕz; *Sp.* kȯr tės′), *n.* **Hernando** or **Hernán** (*Sp.* ėr nän′dȯ *or* ėr nän′), 1485–1547, Spanish conqueror of Mexico. Also, **Cortez.**

C, Corslet of German or Flemish pikeman (1600)

cortex (kô′tĕks), *n., pl.* **-tices** (-tĭ sēz′). **1.** *Bot.* that portion of the stem between the epidermis and the vascular tissue; bark. **2.** *Anat., Zool.* **a.** the rind of an organ, such as the outer wall of the kidney. See diag. under **kidney. b.** the layer of grey matter which invests the surface of the cerebral hemispheres and the cerebellum. [t. L: bark, rind, shell]

cortical (kô′tĭ kl), *adj.* **1.** *Anat.* of, or of the nature of, cortex. **2.** *Physiol., Pathol.* due to the function or condition of the cerebral cortex. **3.** *Bot.* of the cortex. [t. NL: s. *corticālis.* See CORTEX] **—cor′tically,** *adv.*

corticate (kô′tĭ kĭt, -kāt′), *adj.* having a cortex. Also, **cor′ticat′ed.** [t. L: m. s. *corticātus* having bark]

Corticine (kô′tĭ sēn′), *n. Trademark.* a durable covering for floors, decks, etc.

corticosteroid (kô′tĭ kō stĕ′roid), *n. Biochem.* any of the steroid hormones secreted by the adrenal glands.

cortile (kô tē′lĭ), *n.* an enclosed courtyard, within or attached to a building, usually roofless. [t. It.]

cortisone (kô′tĭ sōn′, -zōn′), *n.* an adrenal-gland hormone, originally obtained by extraction from animal glands, now prepared synthetically from strophanthus or other plants: used in the treatment of arthritic ailments and many other diseases.

Cortona (kô tō′nə; *It.* kȯr tō′nȧ), *n.* **Pietro da** (*It.* (pyĕ′trȯ dȧ), 1596–1669, Italian architect and painter.

Coruña (*Sp.* kȯ rōō′nyȧ), *n.* **La,** Spanish name of **Corunna.**

corundum (kə rŭn′dəm), *n.* a common mineral, aluminium oxide, Al_2O_3, notable for its hardness (9 on the Mohs scale). Transparent varieties, including the ruby and sapphire, are prized gems; translucent varieties are used as abrasives. [t. Tamil: m. *kurundam*, t. Skt: m. *kuruvinda* ruby]

Corunna (kə rŭn′ə), *n.* a seaport in NW Spain; scene of British army victory and subsequent withdrawal by sea (1809). 182,212 (1965). Spanish, **La Coruña.**

coruscate (kŏ′rə skāt′), *v.i.*, **-cated, -cating.** to emit vivid flashes of light; sparkle; gleam. [t. L: m. s. *coruscātus*, pp., moved quickly, flashed]

coruscation (kŏ′rə skā′shən), *n.* **1.** the act of coruscating. **2.** a flashing or a flash of light.

corvée (kô′vā; *Fr.* kŏr vė′), *n.* **1.** labour, as on the repair of roads, exacted by a feudal lord. **2.** an obligation imposed on inhabitants of a district to perform services, as repair of roads, etc., for little or no remuneration. [F, ult. der. L *corrogāre* bring together by entreaty]

corves (kôvz), *n.* pl. of **corf.**

corvette (kô vĕt′), *n.* **1.** a warship of the old sailing class, having a flush deck and usually only one tier of guns. **2.** a small, lightly armed, fast vessel, used mostly for convoy escort, ranging between a destroyer and a gunboat in size. [t. F, ult. g. L *corbīta* ship of burden]

corvine (kô′vīn), *adj.* **1.** pertaining to or resembling a crow. **2.** belonging or pertaining to the *Corvidae*, a family of birds including the crows, ravens, jays, etc. [t. L: m. s. *corvinus*, der. *corvus* raven]

Corvus (kô′vəs), *n., gen.* **-vi** (-vī). a southern constellation between Virgo and Hydra. [t. L: raven]

Corybant (kŏ′rĭ bănt′), *n., pl.* **Corybants, Corybantes** (kŏ′rĭ băn′tēz). **1.** one of the spirits or secondary divinities fabled to form the train of the ancient goddess Cybele, following her over the mountains by torchlight with wild music and dancing. **2.** an ancient Phrygian priest of Cybele. [t. L: s. *Corybās*, t. Gk: m. *Korýbās*] **—Corybantian** (kŏ′rĭ băn′tyən), **Cor′yban′tic, Corybantine** (kŏ′rĭ băn′tĭn), *adj.*

corydalis (kə rĭd′ə lĭs), *n.* any plant of the papaveraceous genus *Corydalis* (*Capnoides*), comprising erect or climbing herbs with divided leaves, tuberous or fibrous roots, and very irregular spurred flowers. [NL, t. Gk: m. *korydallís* crested lark]

Corydon (kŏ′rĭ dən), *n.* (in pastoral literature) a name for a shepherd or rustic.

corymb (kŏ′rĭmb, -rĭm), *n. Bot.* a form of inflorescence resembling a raceme but having a relatively shorter rachis and longer lower pedicles, so that the flowers form a flat-topped or convex cluster, the outermost flowers being the first to expand. [t. L: s. *corymbus*, t. Gk: m. *kórymbos* top, cluster of fruit or flowers] **—cor′ymb-like′,** *adj.*

corymbose (kə rĭm′bōs), *adj.* characterized by or growing in corymbs; corymb-like. **—corym′bosely,** *adv.*

Corymb

coryphaeus (kŏ′rĭ fē′əs), *n., pl.* **-phaei** (-fē′ī). **1.** the leader of the chorus in the ancient Greek drama. **2.** (in modern use) the leader of an operatic chorus, or of any band of singers. [t. L, t. Gk: m. *koryphaîos* leader, head man]

coryphée (kŏ′rĭ fā′; *Fr.* kŏ rē fė′), *n.* (in ballet) a leading dancer other than one of the soloists. [t. F, t. L: m. s. *coryphaeus* CORYPHAEUS]

coryza (kə rī′zə), *n.* **1.** *Pathol.* acute inflammation of the mucous membrane of the nasal cavities; cold in the head. **2.** *Vet. Sci.* a contagious disease of birds, esp. poultry, characterized by the secretion of a thick mucus in the mouth and throat. [t. LL, t. Gk: m. *kóryza* catarrh]

cos[1] (kŏs), *n.* a kind of lettuce, with erect oblong heads and generally crisp leaves. Also, **cos lettuce.** [named after COS, whence it orig. came]

cos[2] (kŏs), *n. Maths.* cosine.

Cos (kŏs), *n.* one of the Dodecanese Islands, in the Aegean, off the SW coast of Turkey. 18,545 pop. (est. 1963); 111 sq. mi. Also, **Kos.**

C.O.S., chief of staff.

cosec (kō′sĕk), *n. Trig.* cosecant.

cosecant (kō sē′kənt), *n. Trig.* the secant of the complement, or the reciprocal of the sine, of a given angle or arc.

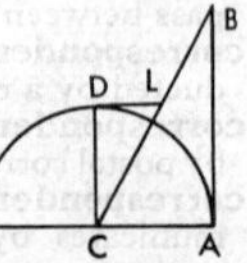

Cosecant
ACB being the angle, the ratio of LC to DC or AC is the cosecant; or, DC being equal to unity, it is the line LC

cosech (kō′sĕsh), *n. Maths.* hyperbolic cosecant. See **hyperbolic functions.**

coseismal (kō sīz′məl), *adj.* of, pertaining to, or being in a line, curve, etc., connecting or comprising points on the earth's surface at which an earthquake wave arrives simultaneously. Also, **coseis′mic.**

Cosenza (*It.* kȯ zĕn′tsȧ), *n.* a town in Italy, in Calabria. 89,938 (1966).

cosey (kō′zĭ), *adj.*, **-sier, -siest,** *n., pl.* **-seys.** cosy.

Cosgrave (kŏz′grāv′), *n.* **William Thomas,** born 1880, Irish political leader: president of the executive council of the Irish Free State, 1922–32.

cosh[1] (kŏsh), *n. Maths.* hyperbolic cosine. See **hyperbolic functions.**

cosh[2] (kŏsh), *n.* **1.** any instrument, usually flexible, used as a bludgeon. *—v.t.* **2.** to hit with a cosh.

cosher[1] (kŏsh′ə), *v.t.* to pamper. [t. Irish: m. *coisir* feast]

cosher[2] (kō′shə), *n., adj.* kosher.

cosignatory (kō sĭg′nə tə rĭ, -trĭ), *adj., n., pl.* **-eries.** *—adj.* **1.** signing jointly with another or others. *—n.* **2.** one who signs a document jointly with another or others.

cosinage (kŭz′ĭ nĭj), *n. Law.* consanguinity.

cosine (kō′sīn′), *n. Trig.* the sine of the complement of a given angle or arc. *Abbrev.*: cos.

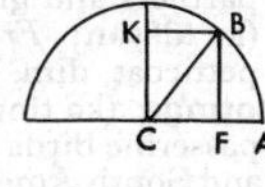

Cosine
ACB being the angle, the ratio of FC to BC or that of BK to CD, is the cosine; or, CD being equal to unity, it is the line BK

cos lettuce, cos.

cosm-, var. of **cosmo-,** before vowels.

cosmetic (kŏz mĕt′ĭk), *n.* **1.** a preparation for beautifying the complexion, skin, etc. *—adj.* **2.** serving to beautify; imparting or improving beauty, esp. of the complexion. [t. Gk: m. s. *kosmētikós* relating to adornment] **—cosmet′ically,** *adv.*

cosmetician (kŏz′mĭ tĭsh′ən), *n.* an expert in making, selling, or applying cosmetics.

cosmic (kŏz′mĭk), *adj.* **1.** of or pertaining to the cosmos: *cosmic philosophy.* **2.** characteristic of the cosmos or its phenomena; immeasurably extended in time and space; vast. **3.** forming a part of the material universe, esp. outside of the earth. **4.** orderly or harmonious. [t. Gk: m. s. *kosmikós* of the world] —**cos′mically,** *adv.*

cosmic dust, *Astron.* matter in fine particles collected by the earth from space, like meteorites.

cosmic radiation, radiation of extremely high penetrating power originating outside the earth's atmosphere, consisting principally of charged particles moving at nearly the velocity of light. The source of this radiation is not known, but some of it appears to emanate from the sun. Also, **cosmic rays.**

cosmism (kŏz′mĭz′əm), *n.* the philosophy of cosmic evolution. **—cos′mist,** *n.*

cosmo-, a word element representing **cosmos.**

cosmodrome (kŏz′mə drōm′), *n.* a space-vehicle launching site (used esp. of a Soviet one).

cosmogenic (kŏz′mə jĕn′ĭk), *adj. Physics, Astron.* produced by, or resulting from the action of, cosmic radiation.

cosmogony (kŏz mŏg′ə nĭ), *n., pl.* **-nies.** a theory or story of the genesis or origination of the universe. [t. Gk: m. s. *kosmogonía* creation of the world. See COSMO-, -GONY] **—cosmogonic** (kŏz′mə gŏn′ĭk), **cos′mogon′ical,** *adj.* **—cosmog′onist,** *n.*

cosmography (kŏz mŏg′rə fĭ), *n., pl.* **-phies. 1.** the science which describes and maps the main features of the heavens and the earth, embracing astronomy, geography, and geology. **2.** a description or representation of the universe in its main features. [t. Gk: m. s. *kosmographía* description of the world. See COSMO-, -GRAPHY] **—cosmog′rapher,** *n.* **—cosmographic** (kŏz′mə grăf′ĭk), **cos′mograph′ical,** *adj.*

cosmology (kŏz mŏl′ə jĭ), *n.* the branch of philosophy that concerns itself with the origin and general structure of the universe, its parts, elements, and laws, esp. with such characteristics as space, time, causality. **—cosmological** (kŏz′mə lŏj′ĭ kl), **cos′molog′ic,** *adj.* **—cosmol′ogist,** *n.*

cosmonaut (kŏz′mə nôt′), *n.* an astronaut, esp. a Soviet one. [f. COSMO- + s. Gk *nautílos* sailor]

cosmonautic (kŏz′mə nô′tĭk), *adj.* astronautic. Also, **cosmonautical. —cos′monaut′ically,** *adv.*

cosmonautics (kŏz′mə nô′tĭks), *n.* astronautics.

cosmopolitan (kŏz′mə pŏl′ĭ tn), *adj.* **1.** belonging to all parts of the world; not limited to one part of the social, political, commercial, or intellectual world. **2.** *Bot., Zool.* widely distributed over the globe. **3.** free from local, provincial, or national ideas, prejudices, or attachments; at home all over the world. **4.** of or characteristic of a cosmopolite. *—n.* **5.** one who is free from provincial or national prejudices; a citizen of the world. [f. COSMOPOLITE + -AN] **—cos′mopol′itanism,** *n.*

cosmopolite (kŏz mŏp′ə līt′), *n.* **1.** a citizen of the world; one who is cosmopolitan in his ideas or life. **2.** an animal or plant of worldwide distribution. [t. Gk: m. s. *kosmopolítēs* citizen of the world] **—cosmop′olitism,** *n.*

cosmorama (kŏz′mə rä′mə), *n.* an exhibition of pictures of different parts of the world. [f. COSM- + m. Gk *hórāma* view] **—cosmoramic** (kŏz′mə răm′ĭk), *adj.*

cosmos (kŏz′mŏs), *n.* **1.** the physical universe. **2.** the world or universe as an embodiment of order and harmony (as distinguished from *chaos*). **3.** a complete and harmonious system. **4.** order; harmony. **5.** any plant of the composite genus *Cosmos*, of tropical America, some species of which, as *C. bipinnatus* and *C. sulphureus*, are cultivated for their showy flowers. [t. NL, t. Gk: m. *kósmos* order, form, the world or universe as an ordered whole, ornament]

cosmosphere (kŏz′mə sfĭə′), *n.* a model for indicating the position of the earth with respect to the fixed stars at any given time; consisting of a hollow glass globe representing the celestial sphere containing within it a small sphere representing the earth.

cosmotron (kŏs′mə trŏn′), *n. Physics.* a type of proton accelerator used in nuclear physics.

COSPAR (kŏs′pä), *n.* an international committee established in 1948 to enable scientists to exploit satellites for research purposes, and to exchange data. [*co(mmittee on) spa(ce) r(esearch)*]

coss (kŏs), *n.* kos.

Cossack (kŏs′ăk), *n.* one of a people of the southern Soviet Union in Europe and adjoining parts of Asia, noted as horsemen or light cavalry. [t. Russ.: m. *kazak*, t. Turk.: m. *quzzāq* adventurer, freebooter]

cosset (kŏs′ĭt), *v.t.* **1.** to treat as a pet; pamper; coddle. *—n.* **2.** a lamb brought up by hand; a pet lamb. **3.** a pet of any kind. [cf. OE *cossetung* kissing]

cost (kŏst), *n., v.,* **cost, costing.** *—n.* **1.** the price paid to acquire, produce, accomplish, or maintain anything. **2.** a sacrifice, loss, or penalty: *to work at the cost of one's health.* **3.** outlay or expenditure of money, time, labour, trouble, etc. **4.** (*pl.*) *Law.* the sums which the successful party is usually entitled to recover for reimbursement of particular expenses incurred in the litigation. **5. at all costs,** or **at any cost,** regardless of the cost. *—v.t.* **6.** to require the expenditure of money, time, labour, etc., in exchange, purchase, or payment; be of the price of; be acquired in return for: *it cost five shillings.* **7.** to result in a particular sacrifice, loss, or penalty: *it may cost him his life.* **8.** to estimate or determine the cost of. *—v.i.* **9.** to estimate or determine costs. [ME, t. OF, der. *coster*, g. L *constāre* stand together] **—cost′less,** *adj.* **—Syn. 1.** charge, expense. See **price.**

costa (kŏs′tə), *n., pl.* **-tae** (-tē). **1.** a rib or riblike part. **2.** *Entomol.* **a.** a vein in the anterior part of the wing of certain insects. **b.** the anterior edge or border of the wing of such insects. **3.** the midrib of a leaf in mosses. **4.** a ridge. [t. L: rib, side]

Costa Brava (kŏs′tə brä′və; *Sp.* kȯs′tȧ brȧ′bȧ), *Spanish.* a coastal region in NE Spain, extending along the Mediterranean from Barcelona to the border with France: holiday resort.

cost accounting, 1. an accounting system indicating the cost items involved in production. **2.** the operation of such an accounting system. **—cost accountant.**

Costa del Sol (kŏs′tə dĕl sŏl′; *Sp.* kȯs′tȧ dĕl sȯl′), *Spanish.* a coastal region in S Spain, extending along the Mediterranean from Gibraltar to Almeria: holiday resort.

costal (kŏs′tl), *adj. Anat.* pertaining to the ribs or the side of the body: *costal nerves.* [t. LL: s. *costālis*]

co-star (kō′stä′), *v.,* **-starred, -starring,** *n. Theat., Films.* *—v.i.* **1.** to share star billing with another actor. *—n.* **2.** a star who does this.

costard (kŭs′təd), *n.* **1.** a large English apple with prominent ribs. **2.** the tree bearing this fruit. **3.** *Archaic.* the head. [t. AN, f. *cost(e)* rib (t. L: m. *costa*) + *-ard* -ARD]

Costa Rica (kŏs′tə rē′kə), a republic in Central America between Panama and Nicaragua. 1,302,829 pop. (1962); 19,238 sq. mi. *Cap.*: San José. **—Cos′ta Ri′can.**

costate (kŏs′tāt), *adj.* **1.** *Anat.* bearing ribs. **2.** (of mosses) having a midrib or costa.

costermonger (kŏs′tə mŭng′gə), *n.* a hawker of fruit, vegetables, fish, etc. Also, **cos′ter.** [earlier *costardmonger*, f. COSTARD + MONGER]

costive (kŏs′tĭv), *adj.* **1.** suffering from constipation; constipated. **2.** slow in action or in expressing ideas, opinions, etc. [t. OF, g. L *constīpātus*, pp. See CONSTIPATE] **—cos′tively,** *adv.* **—cos′tiveness,** *n.*

costly (kŏst′lĭ), *adj.,* **-lier, -liest. 1.** costing much; of great price or value. **2.** *Archaic.* lavish; extravagant. **—cost′liness,** *n.* **—Syn. 1.** dear, high-priced, valuable, sumptuous. See **expensive.**

costmary (kŏst′mĕə′rĭ), *n., pl.* **-maries.** a perennial plant, *Chrysanthemum balsamita*, with fragrant leaves, used in salads, to flavour ale, etc. [f. OE *cost* (t. L: s. *costus*, t. Gk: m. *kóstos* kind of aromatic plant) + MARY]

costo-, *Anat.*, *Zool.* a word element meaning 'rib', as in *costoscapular.* [comb. form repr. L *costa*]
costoclavicular (kŏs′tō klə vĭk′yŏŏ lə), *adj.* referring to both the ribs and the collarbone.
cost of living, the average retail prices of food, clothing, and other necessities paid by a person, family, etc., in order to live at their usual standard.
cost-of-living bonus, a bonus, paid to some workers, the sum of which depends on the rise in the cost of living as shown in the cost-of-living index.
cost-of-living index, an index compiled from official statistics which represents the monthly rise or fall in the cost of living in terms of points as compared with a selected earlier year. Official name, **index of retail prices.**
costoscapular (kŏs′tō skăp′yŏŏ lə), *adj. Anat.* pertaining to ribs and to the scapula.
cost-plus (kŏst′plŭs′), *n.* the cost of production plus an agreed rate of profit (often used as a basis of payment in government contracts).
cost price, 1. the price at which a merchant buys goods for resale. 2. the cost of production.
costrel (kŏs′trəl), *n.* a bottle of leather, earthenware, or wood, often of flattened form and commonly having an ear or ears to suspend it by, as from the waist. [ME, t. OF: m. *costerel*, appar. orig. a flask hung at the side, der. *coste* rib, side, g. L *costa.* See -REL]
costume (kŏs′tyōōm), *n.*, *v.*, **-tumed, -tuming.** —*n.* **1.** the style of dress, including ornaments and the way of wearing the hair, esp. that peculiar to a nation, class, or period. **2.** dress or garb belonging to another period, place, etc., as worn on the stage, at balls, etc. **3.** a set of garments, esp. a woman's two-piece suit or dress and jacket. **4.** fashion of dress appropriate to a particular occasion or season: *winter costume, swimming costume.* —*v.t.* **5.** to dress; furnish with a costume; provide appropriate dress for: *to costume a play.* [t. F, t. It.: habit, fashion, g. L *consuētūdo* custom] —**Syn. 1.** See **dress.**
costume jewellery, decorative jewellery of little monetary value.
costumier (kŏs tyōō′mĭ ə), *n.* one who makes or deals in costumes. Also, **costumer.**
cost unit, the basis of computing of costs: a unit of product, a unit of process, or the like.
cosy (kō′zĭ), *adj.*, **-sier, -siest,** *n.*, *pl.* **-sies.** —*adj.* **1.** snug; comfortable. —*n.* **2.** a padded covering for a teapot, boiled egg, etc., to retain the heat. Also, *U.S.*, **cozy.** [orig. Scot.; prob. t. Scand.; cf. Norw. *koselig*] —**co′sily,** *adv.* —**co′siness,** *n.*
cot[1] (kŏt), *n.* **1.** a child's bed with enclosed sides. **2.** a light portable bed, esp. one of canvas stretched on a frame. **3.** a light bedstead. **4.** *Naut.* a swinging bed made of canvas for officers, sick persons, etc. [t. Anglo-Ind., t. Hind.: m. *khāt*]
cot[2] (kŏt), *n.* **1.** a small house; cottage; hut. **2.** a small place of shelter or protection. **3.** *Dial.* a sheath; covering. [ME and OE; orig. unknown]
cot[3] (kŏt), *n. Trig.* cotangent.
cotan (kō′tăn), *n. Trig.* cotangent.
cotangent (kō tăn′jənt), *n. Trig.* the tangent of the complement, or the reciprocal of the tangent, of a given angle or arc. *Abbrev.:* cot or cotan. —**cotangential** (kō′tăn jĕn′shəl), *adj.*
cotanh (kō′thăn, kō′tănsh), *n. Maths.* hyperbolic cotangent.

Cotangent
ACB being the angle, the ratio of DL to DC, or that of AC to AH, is the cotangent; or, DC being taken as unity, it is the line DL

cote[1] (kōt), *n.* **1.** a shelter for doves, pigeons, sheep, etc. **2.** *N Dial.* a small house; cottage. [OE. See COT[2]]
cote[2] (kōt), *v.t.*, **coted, coting.** *Archaic.* to pass by; outstrip; surpass. [? var. of COAST, v.]
Côte d'Azur (*Fr.* kōt dȧ zʏr′), **1.** French name for the Riviera of S France. **2.** See **Provence** (def. 2).
Côte-d'Or (*Fr.* kōt dôr′), *n.* a department of E central France. 387,869 pop. (1962); 3393 sq. mi. *Cap.:* Dijon.
cote-hardie (kōt′hä′dĭ), *n.* coat-hardie.
cotemporaneous (kō tĕm′pə rā′nyəs), *adj.* contemporaneous.
cotemporary (kō tĕm′prə rĭ), *adj.*, *n.*, *pl.* **-raries.** contemporary.
cotenant (kō tĕn′ənt), *n.* a tenant in common with another or others; a joint tenant. —**coten′ancy,** *n.*
coterie (kō′tə rĭ), *n.* **1.** a group of persons who associate closely, esp. for social purposes. **2.** a clique. [t. F: set, association of people; earlier, cottars' tenure, der. OF *cotier* cottar. See COTTAR] —**Syn. 1.** See **circle.**
coterminous (kō tû′mĭ nəs), *adj.* conterminous.
Côtes-du-Nord (*Fr.* kōt dʏ nôr′), *n.* a department of W France. 501,923 pop. (1962); 2787 sq. mi. *Cap.:* Saint-Brieuc.
coth (kŏth), *n. Maths.* hyperbolic cotangent. See **hyperbolic functions.**
cothurnus (kō thû′nəs), *n.*, *pl.* **-ni** (-nī). the high, thick-soled shoe worn by ancient Greek and Roman tragic actors, often symbolic of tragedy. Also, **cothurn** (kō′thûn, kō thûn′). [t. L, t. Gk: m. *kóthornos*]
cotidal (kō tī′dl), *adj.* **1.** pertaining to a coincidence of tides. **2.** denoting a line connecting points where it is high tide at the same time.
cotillion (kə tĭl′yən), *n.* **1.** a lively French social dance, originated in the 18th century, for two, eight, or even more performers, and consisting of a variety of steps and figures. **2.** *U.S.* any of various dances of the quadrille kind. **3.** *U.S.* music arranged or played for these dances. **4.** *U.S.* a complex dance, or entertainment of dancing, consisting of picturesque or elaborate figures, with changing of partners and giving of favours; a german. Also, **cotillon** (kə tĭl′yən; *Fr.* kō tē yôɴ′). [t. F: m. *cotillon*, orig., petticoat, dim. of *cotte* coat]
cotinga (kə tĭng′gə), *n.* any of several chiefly tropical passerine birds of the family *Cotingidae* of North, Central, and South America. [t. NL, t. F, t. Tupi]
cotise (kŏt′ĭs, kō′tĭs), *n.*, *v.*, **-ised, -ising.** *Her.* —*n.* **1.** a narrow diminutive of a bend. —*v.t.* **2.** to border with cotises. [t. NF: m. *co(s)tice*, ult. der. L *costa* rib]
Cotman (kŏt′mən), *n.* **John Sell,** 1782–1842, English watercolour artist.
cotoneaster (kə tō′nĭ ăs′tə), *n.* any plant of the rosaceous evergreen genus *Cotoneaster*, some species of which, as *C. melanocarpa* and *C. tomentosa* are cultivated for their small white or pink flowers and their red or black berries. [NL, f. L: m. s. *cotōnium* quince + *-aster* -ASTER[2]]
Cotonou (*Fr.* kō tō nōō′), *n.* a seaport in Dahomey. 85,000 (est. 1963).
Cotopaxi (kŏt′ə păk′sĭ; *Sp.* kō tō päk′sē), *n.* a volcano in central Ecuador, in the Andes: the highest known active volcano in the world. 19,498 ft.
cotquean (kŏt′kwēn′), *n. Obs.* **1.** a coarse hussy. **2.** a man who busies himself with women's household affairs. [f. COT[2] + QUEAN]
Cotswold (kŏts′wōld′, -wəld), *n.* a breed of large sheep with long wool (so called from the Cotswolds).
Cotswolds (kŏts′wōldz′, -wəldz), *n.* a range of hills in SW England, in Gloucestershire: sheep farming. Highest point, Cleeve Cloud, 1083 ft. Also, **Cotswold Hills** or, *Archaic*, **Cotteswolds.**
cotta (kŏt′ə), *n. Eccles.* **1.** a surplice. **2.** a short surplice, with short sleeves or sleeveless, worn esp. by choristers. [t. ML. See COAT]
cottage (kŏt′ĭj), *n.* **1.** a small, humble house. **2.** a small country residence. **3.** *U.S.* a temporary residence at a holiday resort. [ME, var. of *cotage* (f. COT[2] + -AGE)]
cottage cheese, a kind of soft white cheese made of skimmed milk curds without rennet.
cottage hospital, a small, usually single-storeyed hospital.
cottage industries, industries, as knitting, pottery, and weaving, carried out in the home of the worker.
cottage loaf, a loaf made by placing a small round lump of dough on top of a larger round lump.
cottage piano, a small kind of upright piano.
cottage pie, shepherd's pie.
cottage pudding, a baked pudding containing dried fruit, glacé cherries, spice, and nuts; served with a sauce.
cottager (kŏt′ĭ jə), *n.* **1.** one who lives in a cottage. **2.** a labourer in a village or on a farm. **3.** *U.S.* a person having a private house at a holiday resort.
cottar (kŏt′ə), *n.* **1.** *Scot.* a person occupying a plot of land under a system similar to cottier tenure. **2.** *Irish.* cottier. **3.** a cottager. Also, **cot′ter.** [t. ML: m. s. *cotārius*, der. *cota*, Latinized form of COT[2]]
cotter (kŏt′ə), *n. Mech.* **1.** a pin, wedge, key, or the like, fitted or driven into an opening in order to secure something or hold parts together. **2.** cotter pin. [orig. uncert.]
cotter pin, *Mech.* a cotter having a split end which is spread after being pushed through a hole, to prevent the cotter from working loose.
Cottian Alps (kŏt′ĭ ən), a range of the Alps on the boundary between France and Italy. Highest peak, Monte Viso, 12,602 ft.
cottier (kŏt′ĭ ə), *n.* **1.** an Irish peasant holding a portion of land directly from the owner, the amount of rent being fixed not by custom or private agreement but by public competition (**cottier tenure**). **2.** a cottager (def. 1). [ME *cotier*, t. OF, der. *cote* cot, t. Gmc]
cotton (kŏt′n), *n.* **1.** a soft, white, downy substance, consisting of the hairs or fibres attached to the seeds of plants of the malvaceous genus *Gossypium*, used in making fabrics, thread, wadding, guncotton, etc. **2.** a plant yielding cotton, as *G. hirsutum* (**upland cotton**) or *G. barbadense* (**sea-island cotton**). **3.** such plants collec-

tively, as a cultivated crop. **4.** cloth, thread, etc., made of cotton. **5.** any soft, downy substance resembling cotton. but growing on some other plant. *—v.i.* **6.** *Colloq.* to make friends. **7.** *Colloq.* to become attached or friendly (fol. by *to* or *with*). **8.** *Colloq.* to get on together; agree. **9.** *Colloq.* to understand; perceive meaning or purpose (often fol. by *on*). **10.** *Obs.* to prosper or succeed. [ME *coton*, t. OF, t. It.: m. *cotone*, t. Ar.: m. *qutn*]

cottonade (kŏt′n ād′), *n.* an inferior cotton cloth, often used for making cheap pyjamas, etc.

cotton belt, that part of the southern U.S. where cotton is grown.

cotton cake, a mass of compressed cottonseed after the oil has been extracted, used to feed cattle, etc.

cotton flannel, Canton flannel.

cotton gin, a machine for separating the fibres of cotton from the seeds.

cotton grass, any of the rushlike cyperaceous plants constituting the genus *Eriophorum*, common in swampy places and bearing spikes resembling tufts of cotton.

cottonmouth (kŏt′n mouth′), *n.* the water-moccasin, a venomous snake of the southern U.S.

cotton-picker (kŏt′n pĭk′ə), *n.* a machine for removing ripe cotton fibre from the standing plant.

cotton print, cotton cloth with a printed design or pattern.

cottonseed (kŏt′n sēd′), *n., pl.* **-seeds,** (*esp. collectively*) **-seed.** the seed of the cotton plant, yielding an oil.

cottonseed meal, cotton cake.

cottonseed oil, a brown-yellow viscid oil, with a nutlike smell, obtained from the seed of the cotton plant, used in pharmacology and as an oil for salad dressing.

cottontail (kŏt′n tāl′), *n.* the common rabbit, *Sylvilagus floridanus*, of the U.S., having a fluffy white tail.

cotton waste, the refuse from manufacturing cotton, as used for cleaning machinery.

cottonweed (kŏt′n wēd′), *n.* a hairy, perennial, maritime composite, *Otanthus maritimus*, of W Europe and Mediterranean areas.

cottonwood (kŏt′n wo͝od′), *n.* any of several American species of poplar, as ***Populus deltoides***, with cotton-like tufts on the seeds.

cottonwool (kŏt′n wo͝ol′), *n.* **1.** raw cotton for surgical dressings and toilet purposes which has had its natural wax chemically removed. **2.** cotton in its raw state, as on the boll or gathered for use. **3.** *Colloq.* a protected and comfortable state or existence. *—adj.* **4.** made of cotton-wool. **5.** *Colloq.* protected and comfortable.

cottony (kŏt′n ĭ), *adj.* **1.** of or like cotton; soft. **2.** covered with a down or nap resembling cotton.

Coty (*Fr.* kō tē′), *n.* **René** (*Fr.* rə nė′), born 1882, president of France 1953–59.

cotyledon (kŏt′ĭ lē′dn), *n.* **1.** *Bot.* the primary or rudimentary leaf of the embryo of plants. See diag. under **hypocotyl.** **2.** *Zool.* a tuft or patch of villi on the placenta of most ruminants. [t. L: navelwort (a plant), t. Gk: m. *kotylēdṓn* any cup-shaped hollow] **—cot′yle′donal,** *adj.* **—cotyledonary** (kŏt′ĭ lē′də nə rĭ), *adj.*

coucal (ko͞o′kăl, ko͞o′kl), *n.* any of various long-tailed cuckoos, esp. of the genus *Centropus*, of Africa, Australia, and southern Asia. [t. F]

couch (kouch), *n.* **1.** a piece of furniture, for seating two to four people, with a back and sometimes armrests. **2.** a similar piece of upholstered furniture, without a back but with a headrest, as used by doctors for their patients. **3.** a bed or other place of rest; any place used for repose. **4.** the lair of a wild beast. **5.** the frame on which barley is spread to be malted. **6.** a coat of paint, etc. *—v.t.* **7.** to arrange or frame (words, a sentence, etc.); put into words; express. **8.** to express indirectly. **9.** to lower or bend down, as the head. **10.** *Archaic.* to lower (a spear, etc.) to a horizontal position, as for attack. **11.** to lay or put down; cause to lie down; lay or spread flat. **12.** to overlay; embroider with thread laid flat on a surface and caught down at intervals. **13.** *Obs.* to place or lodge; conceal. **14.** *Surg.* **a.** to remove (a cataract) by inserting a needle and pushing the opaque crystalline lens downwards in the vitreous humour below the axis of vision. **b.** to remove a cataract from (a person) in this manner. *—v.i.* **15.** to lie at rest; repose; recline. **16.** to crouch; bend; stoop. **17.** to lie in ambush; lurk. **18.** to lie in a heap for decomposition or fermentation, as leaves. [ME *couche(n)*, t. OF: m. *coucher*, g. L *collocāre* lay in its place]

couchant (kou′chənt), *adj.* **1.** lying down; crouching. **2.** *Her.* lying down, as of a lion. [t. F, ppr. of *coucher* lie]

couchette (ko͞o shĕt′), *n.* **1.** (in a railway carriage) a bunk for passengers to sleep on. **2.** a railway sleeping-car. [t. F]

couch-grass (kouch′gräs′, ko͞och′-), *n.* any of various grasses, esp. *Agropyron repens*, known chiefly as troublesome weeds, characterized by creeping rootstocks which spread rapidly; quitch. [var. of QUITCH GRASS]

couching (kou′chĭng), *n.* **1.** the act of one who or that which couches. **2.** a method of embroidering in which a thread, often heavy, laid upon the surface of the material, is caught down at intervals by stitches taken with another thread through the material. **3.** work so made.

Coué (ko͞o′ā; *Fr.* kwė), *n.* **Émile** (*Fr.* ė mĕl′), 1857–1926, French psychologist: advocate of autosuggestion.

cougar (ko͞o′gə), *n.* the puma. [t. F: m. *couguar*, t. NL: m. s. *cuguacuara*, repr. Tupi *çuaçu ara*, Guarani *guaçu ara*]

cough (kŏf), *v.i.* **1.** to expel the air from the lungs suddenly and with a characteristic noise. *—v.t.* **2.** to expel by coughing (fol. by *up* or *out*). **3. cough up,** *Slang.* to give; hand over. *—n.* **4.** the act or sound of coughing. **5.** an illness characterized by frequent coughing. [ME *coghen*, back-formation from OE *cohhetan* cough. Cf. G *keuchen* wheeze] **—cough′er,** *n.*

cough drop, a small medicinal lozenge for relieving a cough, sore throat, etc.

could (ko͝od), *v.* pt. of **can**[1]. [ME *coude*, OE *cūthe*; mod. *l* improperly inserted, after *would* and *should*]

couldn't (ko͝od′nt), contraction of *could not.*

couldst (ko͝odst), *v.* *Archaic or Poetic.* 2nd pers. sing. of **could.**

coulee (ko͞o′lā, -lĭ), *n.* **1.** a stream of lava. **2.** *Western North America.* a deep ravine or gulch, usually dry, which has been worn by running water. Also, *French,* **coulée** (*Fr.* ko͞o lė′). [t. F, der. *couler* flow, slide, g. L *colāre* strain]

coulisse (ko͞o lēs′), *n., pl.* **-lisses** (-lē′sĭz). **1.** a timber grooved for a frame to slide in it. **2.** (*pl.*) the wings in a theatre. **3.** an unofficial dealer on the Paris Exchange.

couloir (ko͞ol′wä), *n.* a steep gorge or gully on the side of a mountain. [F, der. *couler.* See COULEE]

coulomb (ko͞o′lŏm), *n.* the derived SI unit of electric charge, defined as the quantity of electricity. *Symbol:* C [named after C. A. de *Coulomb*, 1736–1806, French physicist]

coulomb force, the force between two electrically charged bodies. If the charges are of the same polarity the force is repulsive; if they are of opposite polarity the force is attractive.

Coulomb's Law, *Physics.* the attractive or repulsive force between two electrically charged bodies, or magnetic poles, is proportional to the product of the charges, or pole strengths, and inversely proportional to the square of the distance between them.

coulometer (ko͞o lŏm′ĭ tə), *n.* a voltameter. Also, **coulombmeter.**

Coulsdon (ko͞olz′dən), *n.* a district of the S outer London borough of Croydon.

coulter (kōl′tə), *n.* a sharp blade or wheel attached to the beam of a plough, used to cut the ground in advance of the ploughshare. Also, *Chiefly U.S.,* **colter.** [ME and OE *culter*, t. L: knife]

coumarin (ko͞o′mə rĭn), *n.* a white crystalline substance, with a vanilla-like smell, $C_9H_6O_2$, obtained from the tonka bean and certain other plants, or prepared synthetically, and used for flavouring and in perfumery. [t. F: m. *coumarine*, der. *coumarou*, repr. Tupi *kumarū* tonka-bean tree]

coumarone (ko͞o′mə rōn′), *n.* *Chem.* a stable, inert compound found in coal tar, $C_6H_4OC_2H_2$; polymerizes into coumarone resins which are used for varnishes, printing inks, etc.

council (koun′səl), *n.* **1.** an assembly of persons summoned or convened for consultation, deliberation, or advice. **2.** an ecclesiastical assembly for deciding matters of doctrine or discipline. **3.** (in the New Testament) the Sanhedrin or other body of authorities. **4.** a body of persons specially designated or selected to act in an advisory, administrative, or legislative capacity. **5.** (in many of the British crown colonies) a body assisting the governor in either an executive or a legislative capacity, or in both. **6.** the local administrative body of a town, county, parish, or city. [ME *counceil*, t. OF: m. *concile*, t. L: m. s. *concilium* assembly, union, but with sense affected by L *consilium* COUNSEL]

council board, the table round which a council meets for deliberations.

council chamber, the room where a council meets.

council estate, a group of council houses and other amenities within a clearly defined area.

council house, a dwelling house built and let at a subsidized rent, by the local governing authority (county council, urban district council, or rural district council).

Council of Europe, a confederation of European states, established in 1949 for the maintenance of civil liberties and the achievement of common objectives.

Council of Trent, the council of the Roman Catholic Church which met at Trent intermittently from 1545 to

1563, condemning the Reformation and defining church doctrines.
council of war, 1. a conference of high-ranking military or naval officers, usually to discuss major war problems and plans. 2. any conference to make important plans.
councillor (koun′sĭ lə), *n.* a member of a council. Also, *U.S.,* **councilor.** —**coun′cillorship′,** *n.*
council school, a school governed by a rural, urban, or county council.
counsel (koun′səl), *n., v.,* **-selled, -selling** or (*U.S.*) **-seled, -seling.** —*n.* **1.** advice; opinion or instruction given in directing the judgement or conduct of another. **2.** interchange of opinions as to future procedure; consultation; deliberation: *to take counsel with one's partners.* **3.** *Archaic.* wisdom; prudence. **4.** deliberate purpose; plan; design. **5.** a private or secret opinion or purpose: *to keep one's own counsel.* **6.** the barrister or barristers engaged in the direction of a cause in court; a legal adviser. **7.** *Theol.* one of the advisory declarations of Christ, considered as not universally binding but as given for aid in attaining greater moral perfection. **8. keep one's own counsel,** to keep secret one's opinion or plans. **9. counsel of perfection,** excellent but impracticable advice. —*v.t.* **10.** to give counsel to; advise. **11.** to urge the doing or adoption of; recommend (a plan, etc.). —*v.i.* **12.** to give counsel or advice. **13.** *Obs.* to take counsel. [ME *counseil,* t. OF, g. L *consilium* consultation, plan. Cf. COUNCIL] —**Syn. 1.** See **advice.**
counsellor (koun′sə lə), *n.* **1.** one who counsels; an adviser. **2.** *U.S. Law.* a lawyer, esp. a trial lawyer. **3.** an adviser, esp. a legal adviser, in an embassy or legation. Also, *U.S.,* **coun′selor.** —**coun′sellorship′,** *n.*
count[1] (kount), *v.t.* **1.** to check over one by one (the individuals of a collection) in order to ascertain their total number; enumerate. **2.** to reckon up; calculate; compute. **3.** to list or name the numerals up to. **4.** to include in a reckoning; take into account. **5.** to reckon to the credit of another; ascribe; impute. **6.** to esteem; consider. **7. count in,** to include. **8. count out, a.** to exclude: *count me out.* **b.** *Boxing.* to proclaim (one) the loser because of his inability to stand up before the referee has counted ten seconds. **c.** *Parl. Proc.* to adjourn (a sitting of the House of Commons) because of the lack of a quorum. —*v.i.* **9.** to count the items of a collection one by one in order to know the total. **10.** to list or name the numerals in order. **11.** to reckon numerically. **12.** to depend or rely (fol. by *on* or *upon*). **13.** to have a numerical value (as specified). **14.** to be accounted or worth: *a book which counts as a masterpiece.* **15.** to enter into consideration: *every effort counts.* **16.** to be worth; amount (fol. by *for*). **17.** to divide into groups by calling off numbers in order (fol. by *off*). **18.** *Obs.* to take account (fol. by *of*). —*n.* **19.** the act of counting; enumeration; reckoning; calculation. **20.** the number representing the result of a process of counting; the total number. **21.** an accounting. **22.** *Law.* a distinct charge or theory of action in a declaration or indictment. **23.** *Textiles.* the number of hanks of a length of cotton or worsted in 1 lb. **24.** *Boxing.* the calling aloud by the referee of ten seconds, while a boxer is unable to stand up, after which he is declared to have lost by a knockout. **25.** regard; notice; awareness. **26. on all counts,** in every respect. **27. out for the count,** *Colloq.* **a.** completely exhausted. **b.** unable to continue an activity. [ME *counte(n),* t. OF: m. *conter,* g. L *computāre* calculate, reckon] —**count′able,** *adj.*
count[2] (kount), *n.* (in some European countries) a nobleman corresponding in rank to the English earl. [t. AF: m. *counte,* g. L *comes* companion]
countdown (kount′doun′), *n.* the final check prior to the firing of a missile, detonation of an explosive, etc. With the precise moment of firing or detonation designated as zero, the days, hours, minutes, and seconds are counted backwards from the initiation of a project.
countenance (koun′tĭ nəns), *n., v.,* **-nanced, -nancing.** —*n.* **1.** aspect; appearance, esp. the look or expression of the face. **2.** the face; visage. **3.** composed expression of face. **4.** appearance of favour; encouragement; moral support. **5.** *Obs.* bearing; behaviour. **6. in countenance,** unabashed. **7. out of countenance,** visibly disconcerted, or abashed. —*v.t.* **8.** to give countenance or show favour to; encourage; support. **9.** to tolerate; permit. [ME, t. OF: m. *contenance* bearing, t. ML: m. s. *continentia* demeanour, L restraint] —**coun′tenancer,** *n.* —**Syn. 2.** See **face.**
counter[1] (koun′tə), *n.* **1.** a table or board on which money is counted, business is transacted, or goods are laid for examination. **2.** (in some restaurants, etc.) a long, narrow table with stools for customers along one side: food being served from the other. **3.** a counter tube. **4.** anything used in keeping account, as in games, esp. a round or otherwise shaped piece of metal, ivory, wood, or other material. **5.** an imitation coin or token. **6.** *Slang.* a piece of money. **7. under the counter, a.** in a manner other than that of an open and honest business transaction; clandestinely and often illegally. **b.** clandestine or reserved for favoured customers. [ME, t. AF: m. *counteour* counting house, counting table, der. OF *conter* COUNT[1]]
counter[2] (koun′tə), *n.* **1.** one who counts. **2.** an apparatus for counting revolutions or other movements. [f. COUNT[1] + -ER[1]]
counter[3] (koun′tə), *adv.* **1.** in the wrong way; contrary to the right course; in the reverse direction. **2.** contrary; in opposition (chiefly with *run* or *go*): *to run counter to the rules.* —*adj.* **3.** opposite; opposed; contrary. —*n.* **4.** that which is opposite or contrary to something else. **5.** a blow delivered in receiving or parrying another blow, as in boxing. **6.** *Fencing.* a circular parry. **7.** that portion of the stern of a boat or vessel extending from the waterline to the full outward swell. **8.** the piece of stiff leather forming the back of a shoe or boot round the heel. **9.** that part of a horse's breast which lies between the shoulders and under the neck. **10.** *Print.* any part of the face that is less than type-high and is therefore not inked. —*v.t.* **11.** to go counter to; oppose; controvert. **12.** to meet or answer (a move, blow, etc.) by another in return. —*v.i.* **13.** to make a counter or opposing move. **14.** to give a blow while receiving or parrying one, as in boxing. [t. F: m. *contre,* g. L *contrā,* adv. and prep., in opposition, against. Cf. COUNTER-[1]]
counter[4] (koun′tə), *n., v.t. Obs.* encounter.
counter-, 1. a combining form of **counter**[3], as in *counteract.* **2.** *Her.* a word element signifying opposition to the second element, as in contrary directions (*counter-rampant*), on two opposite sides (*counter-indented*), or having the tinctures reversed (*counter-ermine*). [see COUNTER[3]]
counteract (koun′tər ăkt′), *v.t.* to act in opposition to; frustrate by contrary action. —**coun′terac′tion,** *n.* —**coun′terac′tive,** *adj.* —**coun′terac′tively,** *adv.*
counterattack (koun′tə rə tăk′), *n.* **1.** an attack designed to counteract another attack; a responsive attack. **2.** *Mil.* an attack to regain an objective taken by an enemy. —*v.t., v.i.* **3.** to deliver a counterattack (to).
counterattraction (koun′tə rə trăk′shən), *n.* a rival or opposite attraction. —**coun′terattrac′tive,** *adj.*
counterbalance (*n.* koun′tə băl′əns; *v.* koun′tə băl′əns), *n., v.,* **-anced, -ancing.** —*n.* **1.** a weight balancing another weight; an equal weight, power, or influence acting in opposition; counterpoise. —*v.t.* **2.** to weight or act against with an equal weight or force.
counterblast (koun′tə bläst′), *n.* **1.** an opposing blast. **2.** an unrestrained and vigorously powerful response to an attacking statement; a denunciation.
counterbrace (koun′tə brās′), *v.t.,* **-braced, -bracing.** to brace the fore and main yards on opposite tacks to reduce the headway of a ship.
counterchange (koun′tə chānj′), *v.t.,* **-changed, -changing. 1.** to cause to change places, qualities, etc.; interchange. **2.** to diversify; chequer.
countercharge (koun′tə chäj′), *n., v.,* **-charged, -charging.** —*n.* **1.** a charge by an accused person against his accuser. **2.** *Mil.* a retaliatory charge. —*v.t.* **3.** to make an accusation against (one's accuser). **4.** *Mil.* to charge in retaliation.
countercheck (*n.* koun′tə chĕk′; *v.* koun′tə chĕk′), *n.* **1.** a check that opposes or restrains. **2.** a check controlling or confirming another check. —*v.t.* **3.** to oppose or restrain (some obstacle, etc.) by contrary action. **4.** to control or confirm by a second check.
counter cheque, a cheque available in a bank for the use of a customer in making a withdrawal from that bank.
counterclaim (koun′tə klām′), *n.* **1.** a claim set up against another claim. —*v.i.* **2.** to set up a counterclaim. —**coun′terclaim′ant,** *n.*

coun′terac′cusa′tion, *n.*
coun′tera′gent, *n.*
coun′terapproach′, *n.*
coun′terar′gument, *n.*
coun′terblow′, *n.*
coun′terbluff′, *n., v.i.*
coun′tercharm′, *n.*
coun′terdem′onstra′tion, *n.*
coun′terdrain′, *n.*
coun′terev′idence, *n.*
coun′terforce′, *n.*
coun′tergauge′, *n.*
coun′terguard′, *n.*
coun′terin′fluence, *n.*
coun′terinsur′gency, *n.*
coun′terinsur′gent, *n., adj.*
coun′termea′sure, *n.*
coun′termo′tion, *n.*
coun′termove′, *n., v.i.*
coun′termove′ment, *n.*
coun′terof′fer, *n.*
coun′tero′pening, *n.*
coun′terpace′, *n.*

counterclockwise (koun′tə klŏk′wīz′), *adj.*, *adv.* *U.S.* anticlockwise.

countercurrent (koun′tə kŭ′rənt), *n.* a current flowing in an opposite direction.

counterespionage (koun′tər ĕs′pĭ ə nĭj, -näzh′), *n.* the detection of enemy espionage.

counterfactual (koun′tə făk′tyŏŏ əl), *n. Logic.* a conditional statement, the first clause of which expresses something contrary to fact, as: *If I had known.*

counterfeit (koun′tə fĭt), *adj.* **1.** made to imitate, and pass for, something else; not genuine: *counterfeit coin.* **2.** pretended: *counterfeit grief.* —*n.* **3.** an imitation designed to pass as an original; a forgery. **4.** *Archaic.* a copy. **5.** *Obs.* a likeness; portrait. **6.** *Obs.* an impostor. —*v.t.* **7.** to make a counterfeit of; imitate fraudulently; forge. **8.** to resemble. **9.** to simulate. —*v.i.* **10.** to make counterfeits, as of money. **11.** to feign; dissemble. [ME *countrefet*, t. OF: m. *contrefait*, pp. of *contrefaire* imitate, der. *contre* CONTRA- + *faire* do (g. L *facere*)] —**coun′terfeit′er,** *n.* —**Syn. 1.** spurious. See **false. 2.** sham, feigned, simulated, fraudulent.

counterfoil (koun′tə foil′), *n.* a complementary part of a bank cheque, etc., which is retained by the issuer, and on which particulars are noted.

counterindemnity (koun′tə rĭn dĕm′nĭ tĭ), *n.* a document intended to secure against loss, given in exchange for an indemnity bond or guarantee.

counterintelligence (koun′te rĭn tĕl′ĭ jəns), *n.* **1.** the use of various devices, as codes, censorship, etc., to prevent an enemy obtaining information. **2.** the organization set up to carry this out.

counterirritant (koun′tər ĭ′rĭ tənt), *n. Med.* an agent for producing irritation in one part to counteract irritation or relieve pain or inflammation elsewhere. —**coun′terir′rita′tion,** *n.*

counterjumper (koun′tə jŭm′pə), *n. U.S. Slang.* a salesman at a counter.

countermand (koun′tə mänd′), *v.t.* **1.** to revoke (a command, order, etc.). **2.** to recall or stop by a contrary order. —*n.* **3.** a command, order, etc., revoking a previous one. [ME *countermaund(en)*, t. OF: m. *contremander*, f. *contre* CONTRA- + *mander* command, g. L *mandāre* enjoin]

countermarch (koun′tə mäch′), *n.* **1.** a march back again. **2.** a complete reversal of conduct or measures. —*v.i.* **3.** to turn about and march back along the same route; execute a countermarch. —*v.t.* **4.** to cause to countermarch.

countermark (koun′tə mäk′), *n.* **1.** a hallmark, put on standard metal by the London Goldsmiths' Company. **2.** a device stamped on a coin after minting. **3.** an additional mark put on a bale of goods belonging to several merchants so that it shall not be opened except in the presence of all of them. —*v.t.* **4.** to mark with a countermark.

countermine (*n.* koun′tə mīn′; *v.* koun′tə mīn′), *n.*, *v.*, **-mined, -mining.** —*n.* **1.** *Mil.* a mine intended to intercept or destroy an enemy's mine. **2.** a counterplot. —*v.t.* **3.** to oppose by a countermine. —*v.i.* **4.** to make a countermine. **5.** *Mil.* to destroy enemy mines.

counteroffensive (koun′tə rə fĕn′sĭv), *n. Mil.* an attack by an army against an enemy force which has been and may still be attacking.

counterpane (koun′tə pān′), *n.* a quilt or coverlet for a bed; a bedspread. [var. of obs. *counterpoint* cover, t. OF]

counterpart (koun′tə pät′), *n.* **1.** a copy; duplicate. **2.** a part that answers to another, as each part of a document executed in duplicate. **3.** one of two parts which fit each other; a thing that complements something else. **4.** a person or thing closely resembling another.

counterplot (koun′tə plŏt′), *n.*, *v.*, **-plotted, -plotting.** —*n.* **1.** a plot directed against another plot. **2.** a secondary theme in a play, or other literary work, usually as a contrast to or variation of the main theme. —*v.i.* **3.** to devise a counterplot; plot in opposition. —*v.t.* **4.** to plot against (a plot or plotter); frustrate by a counterplot.

counterpoint (koun′tə point′), *n. Music.* **1.** the art of combining melodies. **2.** the texture resulting from the combining of individual melodic lines. **3.** a melody composed to be combined with another melody. [t. F: m. *contrepoint*, t. ML: m. s. *(cantus) contrā punctus* (song) pointed against]

counterpoise (koun′tə poiz′), *n.*, *v.*, **-poised, -poising.** —*n.* **1.** a counterbalancing weight. **2.** any equal and opposing power or force. **3.** the state of being in equilibrium. **4.** an artificial earth plane used to increase the sensitivity of an aerial. —*v.t.* **5.** to balance by an opposing weight; counteract by an opposing force. **6.** to bring into equilibrium. **7.** *Archaic.* to weigh (one thing) against another. [ME *countrepeis*, t. OF, var. of *contrepois*, f. *contre* CONTRA- + *pois* weight (g. L *pensum*)]

counterpoison (koun′tə poi′zən), *n.* **1.** an agent for counteracting a poison; an antidote. **2.** an opposite poison.

counter-reformation (koun′tə rĕf′ə mā′shən), *n.* **1.** a reformation opposed to or counteracting a previous reformation. **2.** (*caps.*) the movement within the Roman Catholic Church which followed the Protestant Reformation of the 16th century.

counter-revolution (koun′tə rĕv′ə lōō′shən), *n.* **1.** a revolution against a government recently established by revolution. **2.** a political movement that resists revolutionary tendencies.

counter-revolutionary (koun′tə rĕv′ə lōō′shən rĭ), *n.*, *pl.* **-aries,** *adj.* —*n.* **1.** Also, **counter-revolutionist.** one who advocates or engages in a counter-revolution. —*adj.* **2.** characteristic of or resulting from a counter-revolution. **3.** opposing a revolution or revolutionary government.

counterscarp (koun′tə skäp′), *n. Fort.* **1.** the exterior slope or wall of the ditch of a fort, supporting the covered way. **2.** this slope with the covered way and glacis. [t. F: m. *contrescarpe*, t. It.: m. *contrascarpa*, f. *contra-* COUNTER- + *scarpa* slope of a wall]

countershading (koun′tə shā′dĭng), *n. Zool.* the development (on an animal) of dark colours on parts usually exposed to the sun and of light colours on parts usually shaded, esp. as serving for protection or concealment.

countershaft (koun′tə shäft′), *n. Mach.* an intermediate shaft driven from a main shaft.

countersign (*n.*, *v.* koun′tə sīn′; *v. also* koun′tə sīn′), *n.* **1.** *Mil.* a password given by authorized persons in passing through a guard. **2.** a sign used in reply to another sign. —*v.t.* **3.** to sign (a document) in addition to another signature, esp. in confirmation or authentication. [t. OF: m. *contresigne*, t. It.: m. *contrasegno*]

countersignature (koun′tə sĭg′nə chə), *n.* a signature added by way of countersigning.

countersink (koun′tə sĭngk′), *v.*, **-sunk, -sinking,** *n.* —*v.t.* **1.** to enlarge the upper part of (a hole or cavity), esp. by chamfering, to receive the cone-shaped head of a screw, bolt, etc. **2.** to cause (the head of a screw, bolt, etc.) to sink into a depression made for it, so as to be flush with or below the surface. —*n.* **3.** a tool for countersinking a hole. **4.** a countersunk hole.

counterstain (*n.* koun′tə stān′; *v.* koun′tə stān′), *n.* **1.** a stain applied to a microscopic specimen to distinguish even further parts not retaining a previous stain. —*v.t.* **2.** to treat (a specimen) with a counterstain. —*v.i.* **3.** to become counterstained; take a counterstain.

countersubject (koun′tə sŭb′jĭkt), *n. Music.* the formal accompaniment to the answer in a fugue.

countertenor (koun′tə tĕn′ə), *n. Music.* **1.** an adult male voice or voice part higher than the tenor. **2.** a singer with such a voice; a high tenor.

countertransference (koun′tə trănz′fə rəns, -frəns), *n. Psychiatry.* the transferring back to the analyst of the repressed feelings aroused by an analyst in a patient.

counter tube, *Physics.* a device, such as a Geiger counter, for counting ionizing events.

countervail (koun′tə vāl′, koun′tə vāl′), *v.t.* **1.** to act or avail against with equal power, force, or effect; counteract. **2.** to furnish an equivalent of or a compensation for; offset. **3.** *Archaic.* to equal. —*v.i.* **4.** to be of equal force in opposition; avail. [ME *countrevaile(n)*, t. AF: m. *countrevaloir*, f. *countre* against + *valoir* be strong, g. L *valēre*]

counterweigh (koun′tə wā′), *v.t.* to counterbalance.

counterweight (koun′tə wāt′), *n.* a counterbalancing weight; a counterpoise. —**coun′terweight′ed,** *adj.*

counterword (koun′tə wûd′), *n.* a word that has come to be used with a meaning less specific than it had originally, as 'awful', 'terrific', etc.

counterwork (*n.* koun′tə wûk′; *v.* koun′tə wûk′), *n.* **1.** opposing work or action; a work in opposition to another work. —*v.i.* **2.** to work in opposition. —*v.t.* **3.** to work in opposition to; hinder. —**coun′terwork′er,** *n.*

---

coun′terpale′, *n.*
coun′terparole′, *n.*
coun′terplea′, *n.*
coun′terplead′, *v.i.*, *v.t.*
coun′terpres′sure, *n.*
coun′terproduc′tive, *adj.*
coun′terproof′, *n.*
coun′terprop′agan′da, *n.*
coun′terpropos′al, *n.*
coun′terprop′osi′tion, *n.*
coun′terpunch′, *n.*, *v.t.*
coun′terseal′, *n.*, *v.t.*
coun′tersecur′ity, *n.*
coun′tersense′, *n.*
coun′tersig′nal, *n.*
coun′terstate′ment, *n.*
coun′terstroke′, *n.*
coun′terten′dency, *n.*
coun′terthrust′, *n.*, *v.t.*
coun′terturn′, *n.*
coun′tertype′, *n.*, *v.t.*
coun′terview′, *n.*
coun′tervote′, *n.*

---

countess (koun′tĭs), *n.* **1.** the wife or widow of a count in the nobility of continental Europe, or of an earl in the British peerage. **2.** a woman having the rank of a count or earl in her own right. [ME *contesse*, t. OF, g. LL *comitissa*, fem. of L *comes*. See COUNT²]
counting house, 1. (formerly) a building or room in a noble or merchant's household set aside for the transaction of business. **2.** an accounts office, as in some British firms.
counting room, a room used as a counting house.
countless (kount′lĭs), *adj.* incapable of being counted; innumerable: *the countless stars of the unbounded heavens.*
count palatine, *pl.* **counts palatine. 1.** a count of the Holy Roman Empire having independent judicial authority within his own domain. **2.** a count granted certain royal or imperial powers under the German emperors. **3.** an earl palatine.
countrified (kŭn′trĭ fīd′), *adj.* rustic or rural in appearance, conduct, etc. Also, **countryfied.**
country (kŭn′trĭ), *n., pl.* **-tries,** *adj.* **—n. 1.** a tract of land considered apart from geographical or political limits; region; district. **2.** any considerable territory demarcated by geographical conditions or by a distinctive population. **3.** the territory of a nation. **4.** a state. **5.** the people of a district, state, or nation. **6.** the public. **7.** the land of one's birth or citizenship. **8.** rural districts (as opposed to towns or cities). **9.** *Sport Colloq.* any part of the ground on which a sporting event takes place which is far from the main area of activity, as the outfield in cricket, or the part of the course away from the stands in horseracing. *—adj.* **10.** of the country; rural. **11.** rude; unpolished: *country manners.* **12.** of a country or one's own country. [ME *contree*, t. OF, g. LL *contrāta*, lit., what lies opposite, der. L *contrā* opposite to]
country club, a club in the country with a house, grounds, and facilities for outdoor sports, etc.
country cousin, a relative from the country to whom the sights and activities of a large city are novel and bewildering.
country dance, a dance of rural (or native) origin, as one in which partners in a group start by facing each other in two lines.
countryfied (kŭn′trĭ fīd′), *adj.* countrified.
country house, a large house in the country, esp. one part of an estate.
countryman (kŭn′trĭ mən), *n., pl.* **-men. 1.** a man of one's own country. **2.** a native or inhabitant of a particular region. **3.** a man who lives in the country. —**countrywoman** (kŭn′trĭ wo͝om′ən), *n. fem.* **—Syn. 1.** compatriot, fellow citizen. **3.** rustic, farmer.
country rock, *Geol.* the rock which surrounds and is penetrated by mineral or igneous intrusions.
country seat, a country estate, esp. a fine one, often one used for only part of the year.
countryside (kŭn′trĭ sīd′), *n.* **1.** a particular section of a country, esp. rural. **2.** its inhabitants.
country town, a small town in a rural district.
country-wide (kŭn′trĭ wīd′), *adj.* throughout the country.
county (koun′tĭ), *n., pl.* **-ties. 1.** one of the chief administrative divisions of a country or state, as in Great Britain and Ireland. **2.** the political unit next below the state in the U.S. **3.** one of the larger divisions, as for purposes of local administration, in Canada, New Zealand, etc. **4.** the inhabitants of a county. **5.** the landed gentry of a county. **6.** *Obs. or Hist.* the domain of a count or an earl. *—adj.* **7.** of or pertaining to a county. **8.** *Colloq.* belonging or pertaining to the county or landed gentry; upper-class. [ME *counte*, t. AF, var. of OF *conte*, der. *conte* COUNT²]
county borough, a borough of more than 100,000 inhabitants having some of the administrative power of a county.
county council, a body elected to administer the public affairs of a county.
county court, 1. a local inferior court of record for the trial of civil disputes. **2.** *U.S.* **a.** an administrative board in counties in some states. **b.** *Hist.* a judicial tribunal in some states with jurisdiction extending over one or more counties.
county palatine, the domain of a count or earl palatine.
county school, formerly, a school provided and wholly maintained by the local educational authority; now the name only is retained by some schools.
county seat, *U.S.* a county town.
county town, the town in which the public business of a county is transacted; formerly, but not necessarily now, the seat of administration of a county.
coup (ko͞o), *n., pl.* **coups** (ko͞oz; *Fr.* ko͞o). an unexpected and successful stroke. [t. F, in OF *colp*, g. LL *colpus* blow, for L *colaphus*, t. Gk: m. *kólaphos*]
coup de grâce (ko͞o′də gräs′; *Fr.* ko͞o də grás′), **1.** a deathblow, as a bullet in the head, to make sure an executed person is dead. **2.** a finishing stroke. [F: grace-stroke]
coup de main (*Fr.* ko͞o də măN′), *French.* a surprise attack. [F: hand-stroke]
coup d'état (ko͞o′dā tä′; *Fr.* ko͞o dĕ tȧ′), a sudden and decisive measure in politics, esp. one effecting a change of government illegally or by force. [F: lit., stroke of state]
coup de théâtre (*Fr.* ko͞o də tĕ ȧ′tr), *French.* **1.** a theatrical hit. **2.** a surprising or sensational trick.
coup d'oeil (*Fr.* ko͞o dœy′), *French.* a quick glance.
coupe (ko͞op), *n.* a chilled dessert consisting of fruit and ice-cream. [ME, t. OF, t. LL: m. s. *cuppa* cup]
coupé (ko͞o′pā), *n.* **1.** *Now Chiefly U.S.* an enclosed motor car with four seats and two doors, usually shorter than a saloon. **2.** a short four-wheeled closed carriage with (usually) a single cross-seat for two persons and with an outside seat for the driver. **3.** the end compartment in a diligence or railway carriage. [t. F, prop. pp. of *couper* cut]
couped (ko͞opt), *adj.* *Her.* cut off, as of a cross cut off so as not to touch the edge of the shield, or an animal, cut off at its chest.
Couperin (*Fr.* ko͞o prăN′), *n.* **François** (*Fr.* fräN swȧ′), 1668–1733, French composer.
Couperus (*Du.* ko͞o pĕ′rəs), *n.* **Louis** (lwē), 1863–1923, Dutch writer.
couple (kŭp′l), *n., v.,* **-led, -ling. —n. 1.** a combination of two; a pair. **2.** two of the same sort connected or considered together. **3.** a man and a woman united by marriage or betrothal, associated as partners in a dance, etc. **4.** *Mech.* a pair of equal, parallel forces acting in opposite directions and tending to produce rotation. **5.** a leash for holding two hounds together **6.** one of a pair of rafters or beams that meet at the top and are fixed at the bottom by a tie. *—v.t.* **7.** to fasten, link, or associate together in a pair or pairs. **8.** to join; connect. **9.** *Colloq.* to unite in matrimony. **10.** *Radio.* to join or associate by means of a coupler. **11.** to provide an electrical or magnetic link between (two or more wave circuits). *—v.i.* **12.** to join in a pair; unite. **13.** to copulate. [ME, t. OF: m. *cople*, g. L *copula* band, bond] **—Syn. 1.** See **pair.**
coupler (kŭp′lə), *n.* **1.** one who or that which couples, or links together. **2.** a device in an organ for connecting keys, manuals, or a manual and pedals, so that they are played together when one is played. **3.** *Radio.* a device for transferring electrical energy from one circuit to another, as a transformer which joins parts of a radio apparatus together by induction.
couplet (kŭp′lĭt), *n.* **1.** a pair of successive lines of verse, esp. such as rhyme together and are of the same length. **2.** a pair; couple. [t. F, dim. of *couple* COUPLE]
coupling (kŭp′lĭng), *n.* **1.** the act of one who or that which couples. **2.** any mechanical device for uniting or connecting parts or things. **3.** a device used in joining railway carriages, etc. **4.** *Elect.* **a.** the association of two circuits or systems in such a way that power may be transferred from one to the other. **b.** a device or expedient to ensure coupling. **5.** the part of the body between the tops of the shoulder-blades and the tops of the hip joints in a dog or horse.
coupon (ko͞o′pŏn), *n.* **1.** a separable part of a certificate, ticket, advertisement, etc., entitling the holder to something. **2.** one of a number of such parts calling for periodical payments on a bond. **3.** a separate ticket or the like, for a similar purpose. **4.** a printed entry form for football pools, newspaper competitions, etc. **5.** a detachable printed certificate, issued as a means of rationing commodities and goods to ensure fair distribution of short supplies. [t. F, der. *couper* cut]
courage (kŭ′rĭj), *n.* **1.** the quality of mind that enables one to encounter difficulties and danger with firmness or without fear; bravery. **2.** *Obs.* heart; mind; disposition. **3. have the courage of one's convictions,** to act consistently with one's opinions. [ME *corage*, t. OF, der. *cuer* heart, g. L *cor*]

—Syn. 1. fearlessness, dauntlessness, intrepidity, fortitude, pluck, heroism, daring, hardihood. COURAGE, BRAVERY, VALOUR, BRAVADO refer to qualities of spirit and conduct. COURAGE is that quality of mind which enables one to face dangers, difficulties, threats, pain, etc., without fear: *courage in the face of death.* BRAVERY implies true courage together with daring and an intrepid boldness: *bravery in a battle.* VALOUR implies continuous, active bravery in the face of personal danger and a noble and lofty quality of courage: *valour throughout a campaign, in fighting for the right.* BRAVADO is now usually a boastful and ostentatious pretence of courage or bravery: *empty bravado.* **—Ant. 1.** cowardice.

courageous (kə rā′jəs), *adj.* possessing or characterized by courage; brave; valiant. —**coura′geously,** *adv.* —**coura′geousness,** *n.* **—Syn.** See **brave.**
courante (ko͞o ränt′; *Fr.* ko͞o räNt′), *n.* **1.** an old-fashioned dance dating back to the 17th century characterized by a running or gliding step. **2.** a piece of music for or suited

to this dance. **3.** *Music.* a movement in the classical suite, following the allemande. Also, **courant.** [t. F, prop. fem. of *courant*, ppr. of *courir* run]

Courbet (*Fr.* ko͞or bĕ′), *n.* **Gustave** (*Fr.* gʏs tȧv′), 1819–77, French painter.

Courbevoie (*Fr.* ko͞or bə vwȧ′), *n.* a town in France, NW of Paris. 59,941 (1962).

courgette (ko͞oə zhĕt′; *Fr.* ko͞or zhĕt′), *n.* a small variety of vegetable marrow.

courier (ko͞oə′rĭ ə), *n.* **1.** a messenger sent in haste. **2.** a state messenger who carries government or embassy papers. **3.** a person employed to take charge of the arrangements of a journey. [t. F, t. It.: m. *corriere* runner, der. *corre* run, g. L *currĕre*; r. ME *corour*, t. OF: m. *coreor*, g. LL *curritor* runner]

Courland (ko͞oə′lənd), *n.* a former duchy on the Baltic: later a province of Russia, and in 1918 incorporated into Latvia. Also, **Kurland.**

course (kôs), *n.*, *v.*, **coursed, coursing.** —*n.* **1.** advance in a particular direction; onward movement. **2.** the path, route or channel along which anything moves: *the course of a stream, ship, etc.* **3.** the ground, water, etc., on which a race is run, sailed, etc. **4.** the continuous passage or progress through time or a succession of stages: *in the course of a year, a battle, etc.* **5.** customary manner of procedure; regular or natural order of events: *the course of a disease, argument, etc., a matter of course.* **6.** a mode of conduct; behaviour. **7.** a particular manner of proceeding: *try another course with him.* **8.** a systematized or prescribed series: *a course of studies, lectures, medical treatments, etc.* **9.** any one of the studies in such a series: *the first course in algebra.* **10.** a part of a meal served at one time: *the main course was steak.* **11.** *Naut.* **a.** the point of the compass towards which a ship sails. **b.** the lowest square sail on any mast of a square-rigged ship, identified as **fore course, main course,** etc. **12.** a continuous horizontal (or inclined) range of stones, bricks, or the like, in a wall, the face of a building, etc. **13.** *Textiles.* the row of stitches going across from side to side. **14.** (*often pl.*) the menses. **15.** a charge, as in tilting. **16.** pursuit of game with dogs. **17.** *Archaic.* a race. **18. in due course,** in the proper or natural order; at the right time. **19. of course, a.** certainly; obviously. **b.** in the natural order. —*v.t.* **20.** to run through or over. **21.** to chase; pursue. **22.** to hunt (game) with hounds, esp. by sight and not by scent. **23.** to cause (dogs) to pursue game.
—*v.i.* **24.** to follow a course; direct one's course. **25.** to run; move swiftly; race. **26.** to engage in coursing, in a hunt, a tilting match, etc.
[t. F; r. ME *cors*, t. OF, g. L *cursus* a running] —**Syn. 2.** way, road, track, passage. **5.** process, career. **7.** method, mode. **8.** sequence, succession.

courser[1] (kô′sə), *n.* **1.** one who or that which courses. **2.** a dog for coursing. [f. COURSE, v. + -ER[1]]

courser[2] (kô′sə), *n.* *Chiefly Poetic.* a swift horse. [ME, t. F: m. *coursier*, der. *cours* COURSE]

courser[3] (kô′sə), *n.* any of certain swift-footed, plover-like birds constituting the genus *Cursorius*, of the desert regions of Africa and Asia, as *C. cursor*, occasionally found also in Europe. [t. L: m. s. *cursōrius* fitted for running]

coursing (kô′sĭng), *n.* **1.** the act of one who or that which courses. **2.** the sport of pursuing hares, etc., with hounds that follow by sight rather than by scent.

court (kôt), *n.* **1.** an open space wholly or partly enclosed by a wall, buildings, etc. **2.** a large building within such a space. **3.** (at Cambridge university) a college quadrangle. **4.** a stately dwelling; manor house. **5.** a short street. **6.** a smooth, level area on which to play tennis, netball, etc. **7.** one of the divisions of such an area. **8.** the residence of a sovereign or other high dignitary; palace. **9.** the collective body of persons forming his retinue. **10.** a sovereign and his councillors as the political rulers of a state. **11.** a formal assembly held by a sovereign. **12.** homage paid, as to a sovereign. **13.** assiduous attention directed to gain favour, affection, etc.: *to pay court to a pretty woman.* **14.** *Law.* **a.** a place where justice is administered. **b.** a judicial tribunal duly constituted for the hearing and determination of cases. **c.** the judge or judges who sit in a court. **15.** the body of qualified members of a corporation, council, board, etc. **16.** a branch or lodge of a friendly society. **17. out of court, a.** without a hearing; privately. **b.** *Colloq.* out of the question; not to be considered. —*v.t.* **18.** to endeavour to win the favour of. **19.** to seek the affections of; woo. **20.** to attempt to gain (applause, favour, a decision, etc.). **21.** to hold out inducements to; invite. **22.** to provoke or risk provoking as a consequence of one's actions: *to court disaster.* —*v.i.* **23.** to seek another's love; woo. [ME, t. OF: m. *cort*, g. L *co(ho)rs* enclosure, also division of troops (see COHORT)]

court-bouillon (ko͞oət′bo͞o′yən), *n.* a fish stock.

court card, a king, queen, or knave in a pack of playing cards.

Court Circular, (in Great Britain) an official record of the daily activities of the Royal Family.

court dress, the formal costume worn on state or ceremonial occasions; for men it includes silk knee breeches and stockings.

courteous (kû′tyəs), *adj.* having or showing good manners; polite. [ME *curteis*, t. OF, der. *cort* COURT] —**cour′teously,** *adv.* —**cour′teousness,** *n.* —**Syn.** See **civil.** —**Ant.** rude.

courtesan (kô′tĭ zăn′), *n.* **1.** a court mistress. **2.** any prostitute. Also, **courtezan.** [t. F: m. *courtisane*, t. It.: m. *cortigiana* woman of the court, der. *corte* COURT]

courtesy (kû′tĭ sĭ), *n.*, *pl.* **-sies. 1.** excellence of manners or behaviour; politeness. **2.** a courteous act or expression. **3.** acquiescence; indulgence; consent: *a title by courtesy rather than by right.* **4.** *Archaic.* a curtsy. [ME *cortesie*, t. OF, der. *corteis* COURTEOUS] —**Syn. 1.** courteousness, civility, urbanity.

courtesy title, (in Great Britain) a title allowed by custom, as to the children of dukes.

court hand, a style of handwriting formerly used in the English law courts.

courthouse (kôt′hous′), *n.* **1.** a building in which courts of law are held. **2.** *U.S.* a county town.

courtier (kô′tyə), *n.* **1.** one in attendance at the court of a sovereign. **2.** one who seeks favour by obsequiousness.

court leet, leet[1].

courtly (kôt′lĭ), *adj.*, **-lier, -liest,** *adv.* —*adj.* **1.** polite; elegant; refined. **2.** flattering; obsequious. **3.** of the court of a sovereign. —*adv.* **4.** in the manner of courts; elegantly; flatteringly. —**court′liness,** *n.*

courtly love, a medieval concept originating in the courts of southern France, which idealized illicit love, prescribed a highly conventionalized code of conduct for lovers, and gave rise to an extensive literature on the subject.

court martial, *pl.* **court martials, courts martial.** a court consisting of naval, army, or airforce officers appointed by a commander to try charges of offence against martial law.

court-martial (kôt′mä′shəl), *v.t.*, **-tialled, -tialling** or (*U.S.*) **-tialed, -tialing.** to arraign and try by court martial.

Court of Appeal, *Law.* a branch of the supreme court of judicature, to which appeals may be sent from the High Court, judges in chamber, the county courts, etc.

Court of Cassation, the supreme court of appeal in some countries which deals only with points of law.

Court of Common Pleas, a common-law court, established in the thirteenth century, in which are heard chiefly actions by one subject against another.

Court of Exchequer. See **Exchequer** (def. 2c).

Court of Honour, the planning body of a girl guide company, composed of patrol leaders and guiders.

court of inquiry, a body of people appointed to ascertain facts or causes concerning a particular event, esp. a major accident.

Court of Session, the highest civil court in Scotland, which hears the most important civil cases and all matrimonial cases.

Court of St James's, the official name of the British royal court, so called from St James's Palace, the former scene of royal receptions.

court plaster, 1. (formerly) a black patch worn as adornment on the face by court ladies. **2.** cotton or other fabric coated on one side with an adhesive preparation, as of isinglass and glycerine, used for covering slight cuts, etc., on the skin.

Courtrai (*Fr.* ko͞or trĕ′), *n.* a town in W Belgium, on the river Lys: important medieval town. 43,984 (1962).

court roll, (formerly) a book in which an account of all the proceedings of a manorial court was entered by an authorized person.

courtroom (kôt′ro͞om′, -ro͝om′), *n.* a room in which the sessions of a law court are held.

courtship (kôt′shĭp), *n.* **1.** the wooing of a woman. **2.** solicitation, esp. of favours. **3.** *Obs.* courtly manners.

court shoe, a simply cut heeled shoe, without fastenings, for women. Also, **court.**

court tennis, *U.S.* real tennis.

courtyard (kôt′yäd′), *n.* a space enclosed by walls, next to or within a castle, large house, etc.

couscous (ko͞os′ko͞os), *n.* a Tunisian dish, made of steamed flour, etc., served with semolina, stewed lamb, and vegetables. [t. F, t. Ar.: m. *kuskus*, der. *kaskasa* to beat, pulverize]

cousin (kŭz′ən), *n.* **1.** the son or daughter of an uncle or aunt. **2.** one related by descent in a diverging line from a known common ancestor. The children of brothers and sisters are called **cousins, cousins-german, first cousins,** or **full cousins;** children of **first cousins** are called **second cousins,** etc. Often, however, the term **second cousin** is loosely applied to the son or daughter of a **cousin-german,** more properly called **a first cousin once removed.** 3. a kinsman or kinswoman. 4. a person or thing related to another by similar natures, languages, etc.: *our Canadian cousins.* 5. a term of address from one sovereign to another or to a great noble. [t. F, g. L *consobrinus* mother's sister's child: r. ME *cosin,* t. OF] **—cous′inhood′, cous′inship′,** *n.*

Cousin (*Fr.* kōō zăN′), *n.* **Victor** (*Fr.* vēk tōr′), 1792–1867, French philosopher and educational reformer.

cousin-german (kŭz′ən jû′mən), *n., pl.* **cousins-german.** a first cousin. See **cousin** (def. 2). [t. F: m. *cousin-germain.* See GERMAN, adj.]

cousinly (kŭz′ən lĭ), *adj.* **1.** like or befitting a cousin. *—adv.* **2.** in the manner of a cousin; as a cousin.

Cousteau (*Fr.* kōō stō′), *n.* **Jacques-Yves** (*Fr.* zhăk ēv′), born 1910, French undersea explorer.

couteau (*Fr.* kōō tō′), *n., pl.* **-teaux** (*Fr.* -tō′). a knife, esp. a large double-edged one formerly carried as a weapon. [F, in OF *coutel,* g. L *cultellus,* dim. of *culter* knife]

coutil (*Fr.* kōō tē′), *n.* a strong herringbone twill, used in the manufacture of surgical corsets.

couture (kōō tyōōə′; *Fr.* kōō tʏr′), *n.* the occupation of a couturier; dressmaking and designing considered together.

couturier (*Fr.* kōō tʏ ryĕ′), *n.* a person who designs, makes, and sells fashionable clothes for women. [F, der. *couture* sewing] **—couturière** (*Fr.* kōō tʏ ryĕr′), *n. fem.*

couvade (kōō väd′; *Fr.* -våd′), *n.* a practice among some primitive peoples by which, at the birth of a child, the father takes to bed and performs other acts natural rather to the mother. [t. F, der. *couver* brood, incubate. See COVEY]

Couve de Murville (*Fr.* kōōv də mʏr vĕl′), *n.* **(Jacques) Maurice** (*Fr.* zhăk mō rēs′), born 1907, French statesman, prime minister of France 1968–69.

covalency (kō vā′lən sĭ), *n. Chem.* the number of electron pairs that an atom can share with those which surround it. Also, *Chiefly U.S.,* **covalence** (kō vā′ləns).

covalent bond, *Chem.* a chemical bond formed by the sharing of a pair of electrons by two atoms.

cove[1] (kōv), *n., v.,* **coved, coving.** *—n.* **1.** a small indentation or recess in the shoreline of a sea, lake, or river. **2.** a sheltered nook. **3.** a hollow or recess in a mountain; cave; cavern. **4.** a recess with precipitous sides in the steep flank of a mountain. **5.** a sheltered area between woods or hills. **6.** *Archit.* a concavity; a concave moulding or member. *—v.t., v.i.* **7.** to form into a cove. [ME; OE *cofa* chamber, c. Icel. *kofi* hut]

cove[2] (kōv), *n. Slang.* a person; a fellow. [said to be t. Romany: m. *kova* creature]

coven (kŭv′ən), *n.* **1.** a gathering of witches. **2.** a company of thirteen witches. [var. of CONVENT]

covenant (kŭv′ə nənt), *n.* **1.** an agreement between two or more persons to do or refrain from doing some act; a compact; a contract. **2.** an incidental clause of agreement in such an agreement. **3.** (*cap.*) one of certain bonds of agreement signed by the Scottish Presbyterians for the defence or promotion of their religion, esp. the **National Covenant** of 1638, or the **Solemn League and Covenant** of 1643 (entered into with England). **4.** (in biblical usage) the agreement or engagement of God with man as set forth in the Old and New Testaments. **5.** *Law.* **a.** a formal agreement of legal validity, esp. one under seal. **b.** an early English form of action in suits involving sealed agreements. **6.** (*cap.*) in full, **Covenant of the League of Nations.** the 'Constitution' of the League of Nations, included as the first 26 articles in the Treaty of Versailles. *—v.i.* **7.** to enter into a covenant. *—v.t.* **8.** to agree to by covenant; stipulate. [ME, t. OF, der. *covenir,* g. L *convenire* agree]

covenanter (kŭv′ə nən tə), *n.* **1.** one who enters into a covenant. **2.** (*cap.*) an adherent of the National Covenant. See **covenant** (def. 3).

covenantor (kŭv′ə nən tə), *n. Law.* the party who is to perform the obligation expressed in a covenant.

covenant theology, federal theology.

Covent Garden (kŭv′ənt, kŏv′-), **1.** a district in central London, noted for its vegetable and flower market. **2.** a theatre in this district, first built in 1731; now the royal opera house and home of the Royal Ballet.

Coventry (kŏv′ən trĭ), *n.* **1.** a city in England, in N Warwickshire: industrial centre; cathedral. 305,060 (1961). **2. send to Coventry,** to refuse to associate or speak with.

cover (kŭv′ə), *v.t.* **1.** to put something over or upon, as for protection or concealment. **2.** to be or serve as a covering for; extend over; occupy the surface of. **3.** to put a cover or covering on; clothe. **4.** to put one's hat on (one's head). **5.** to bring upon or invest (oneself): *he covered himself with glory.* **6.** to shelter; protect; serve as a defence to. **7.** *Mil.* **a.** to be in line with by occupying a position directly before or behind. **b.** to protect (a soldier, force, or military position) during an expected period of ground combat by taking a position from which any hostile troops can be fired upon who might shoot at the soldier, force, or position. **8.** to take charge or responsibility for: *an assistant covered his post while he was ill.* **9.** to hide from view; screen. **10.** to spread thickly the surface of. **11.** to aim directly at, as with a pistol. **12.** to have within range, as a fortress does certain territory. **13.** to include; comprise; provide for; take in: *this book covers all common English words.* **14.** to suffice to defray or meet (a charge, expense, etc.); offset (an outlay, loss, liability, etc.). **15.** to deposit the equivalent of (money deposited), as in wagering; accept the conditions of (a bet, etc.). **16.** to act as reporter of (occurrences, performances, etc.), as for a newspaper, etc. **17.** to pass or travel over. **18.** (of a male animal) to copulate with. **19.** *Obs.* to brood or sit on eggs. *—v.i.* **20.** to serve as substitute for one who is absent: *she covered for the telephonist during lunch hour.* **21.** *Cards.* **a.** to play a card, laying it over a card previously played. **b.** to play a card higher than any previously played in the round. **22.** to lay a table for a meal. **23. cover up, a.** to cover completely; enfold. **b.** to attempt to conceal. **c.** *Boxing.* to position the arms so that the opponent's attack can hardly penetrate. *—n.* **24.** that which covers, as the lid of a vessel, the binding of a book, etc. **25.** protection; shelter; concealment. **26.** woods, underbrush, etc., serving to shelter and conceal wild animals or game; a covert. **27.** *Ecol.* vegetation which serves to protect or conceal animals, such as birds, from excessive sunlight or drying, as predators. **28.** something which veils, screens, or shuts from sight. **29.** a set of articles (plate, knife, fork, etc.) laid at table for one person. **30.** *Finance.* funds to cover liability or secure against risk of loss. **31.** *Philately.* **a.** an envelope or outer wrapping for mail. **b.** a letter folded so that the address may be placed on the outside and the missive posted. **32.** cover-point. **33. break cover,** to emerge, esp. suddenly, from a place of concealment. **34. take cover,** to seek shelter or safety. **35. under cover, a.** secret. **b.** secretly. **c.** within an envelope. [ME *cover(en),* t. OF: m. *covrir,* g. L *cooperire*] **—cov′erer,** *n.* **—cov′erless,** *adj.*

—Syn. 1. overlay, overspread, envelop, enwrap. **9.** cloak, conceal. **14.** compensate for. **25.** COVER, PROTECTION, SCREEN, SHELTER mean a defence against harm or danger, and a provision for safety. The main idea in COVER is that of concealment, as in darkness, in a wood, behind something, etc.: *keep under cover, take cover, the ground troops were left without cover when the airforce was withdrawn.* SCREEN refers especially to something behind which one can hide: *a heavy fire formed a screen for ground operations.* PROTECTION and SHELTER emphasize the idea of a guard or defence, a shield against injury or death. A PROTECTION is any such shield: *in World War II, an 'air cover' of aeroplanes acted as a protection for troops.* A SHELTER is something which covers over, and acts as a place of refuge: *an abandoned monastery acted as a shelter.*

coverage (kŭv′ə rĭj), *n.* **1.** the extent to which something is covered. **2.** *Insurance.* the total extent of risk, or the total number of risks, as fire, accident, etc., covered in a policy of insurance. **3.** *Finance.* the value of funds held to back up or meet liabilities. **4.** the reporting of an event or series of events in journals or other media. **5.** the members of the public considered together who may be reached through a specified means of communication.

coverall (kŭv′ə rôl′), *n.* (*usually pl.*) *U.S.* a boilersuit.

cover charge, an amount charged by a restaurant, night-club, etc., for service or entertainment.

cover crop, a crop, preferably leguminous, planted to keep nutrients from leaching, soil from eroding, and land from weeding over, as during the winter.

Coverdale (kŭv′ə dāl′), *n.* **Miles,** 1488–1569, English divine: translator of the Bible into English, 1535.

cover drive, *Cricket.* a drive which sends the ball towards or past cover-point.

covered wagon, *U.S.* a large wagon with a canvas top, esp. a prairie schooner.

covered way, 1. a roofed passage, with open sides, as between buildings. **2.** Also, **covert way.** *Fort.* a protective passage on a counterscarp.

cover girl, a girl pictured on the cover of a magazine.

cover glass, a thin piece of glass used to cover an object mounted on a slide for microscopic observation.

covering (kŭv′ə rĭng), *n.* **1.** something laid over or wrapped about a thing, esp. for concealment, protection, or warmth. **2.** *Com.* the operation of buying securities, etc., that one has sold short, in order to return them to the person from whom they were borrowed.

covering letter, a letter which explains or commends an accompanying parcel, person, etc.

coverlet (kŭv′ə lĭt), *n.* **1.** the outer covering of a bed; a bedspread. **2.** any covering or cover. Also, **coverlid** (kŭv′ə lĭd). [ME *coverlite,* t. AF: m. *covrelit,* f. OF *covre* COVER + *lit* bed]

Coverley (kŭv′ə lĭ), *n.* **1. Sir Roger de,** a literary figure representing the ideal of the early 18th-century squire in *The Spectator* by Addison and Steele. **2.** See **Sir Roger de Coverley.**

cover note, a document given by an insurance company or agent to the insured to provide temporary coverage until a policy is issued.

cover-point (kŭv′ə point′), *n.* **1.** *Cricket.* a fielding position between point and mid-off. **2.** *Lacrosse.* a position situated in front of point. **3.** a player in these positions.

covers., *Maths.* coversed sine.

coversed sine (kō′vûst), *Maths.* the versed sine of the complement of an angle or arc.

covert (kŭv′ət), *adj.* **1.** covered; sheltered. **2.** concealed; secret; disguised. **3.** *Law.* under cover or protection of a husband. **—*n.* 4.** a covering; cover. **5.** shelter; concealment; disguise; a hiding place. **6.** *Hunting.* a thicket giving shelter to wild animals or game. **7.** (*pl.*) *Ornith.* the smaller feathers that cover the bases of the large feathers of the wing and tail. **8.** covert cloth. [ME, t. OF, pp. of *covrir* COVER] **—cov′ertly,** *adv.* **—cov′ertness,** *n.*

covert cloth, a cotton or worsted fabric or twill weave. The warp is of ply yarns, one of which is light-coloured.

covert coat, a short, light overcoat.

coverture (kŭv′ə chə), *n.* **1.** a cover or covering; shelter; concealment. **2.** *Law.* the status of a married woman considered as under the protection and authority of her husband. [ME, t. OF]

covet (kŭv′ĭt), *v.t.* **1.** to desire inordinately, or without due regard to the rights of others; desire wrongfully. **2.** to wish for, esp. eagerly. **—*v.i.* 3.** to have an inordinate or wrongful desire. [ME *coveiten,* t. OF: m. *cuveitier,* ult. der. L *cupiditas* desire] **—cov′etable** *adj.* **—cov′eter,** *n.* **—Syn. 1.** See **envy.**

covetous (kŭv′ĭ təs), *adj.* **1.** inordinately or wrongly desirous. **2.** eagerly desirous. [ME, t. OF: m. *coveitos,* ult. der. L *cupiditas* desire] **—cov′etously,** *adv.* **—cov′etousness,** *n.* **—Syn. 1.** greedy, grasping, rapacious, avaricious.

covey (kŭv′ĭ), *n., pl.* **-eys. 1.** a brood or small flock of partridges or similar birds. **2.** a company; a group. [ME, t. OF: m. *covee,* der. *cover* incubate, g. L *cubāre* lie]

covin (kŭv′ĭn), *n.* **1.** *Obs. except Law.* a secret or collusive agreement between two or more to the prejudice of another. **2.** *Obs. or Archaic.* fraud. [ME, t. OF, ult. der. L *convenīre* agree]

coving (kō′vĭng). *n.* **1.** an arched or vaulted piece of building. **2.** the arching of a coved ceiling.

cow[1] (kou), *n., pl.* **cows,** (*Archaic*) **kine. 1.** the female of a bovine animal, esp. of the genus *Bos,* that has produced a calf and is usually over three years of age. **2.** the female of various other large animals, as the elephant, whale, etc. **3.** *Slang.* an ugly or bad-tempered woman. **4.** *Austral., N.Z. Slang.* anything objectionable, esp. in phrase: *a fair cow.* **5. till the cows come home,** for a long time; for ever. [ME; OE *cū,* c. G *Kuh*]

cow[2] (kou), *v.t.* to frighten with threats, etc.; intimidate. [t. Scand.; cf. Icel. *kūga* cow, tyrannize over]

cowage (kou′ĭj), *n.* **1.** the hairs on the pods of a tropical leguminous plant, *Stizolobium* (or *Mucuna*) *pruriens,* which cause intense itching; sometimes used as a vermifuge. **2.** the pods. **3.** the plants. Also, **cow-itch.** [t. Hind.: m. *kawānch*]

coward (kou′əd), *n.* **1.** one who lacks courage to meet danger or difficulty; one who is basely timid. **—*adj.* 2.** lacking courage; timid. **3.** proceeding from or expressive of fear or timidity: *a coward cry.* [ME, t. OF: m. *coart,* der. *coe* tail, g. L *cauda,* through comparison with an animal with its tail between its legs] **—Syn. 1.** craven, dastard, milksop.

Coward (kou′əd), *n.* **Noel** (nō′əl), born 1899, English author, actor, and composer.

cowardice (kou′ə dĭs), *n.* lack of courage to face danger, difficulty, opposition, etc. **—Syn.** dastardliness, pusillanimity, timidity.

cowardly (kou′əd lĭ), *adj.* **1.** lacking courage; basely timid. **2.** characteristic of or befitting a coward. **—*adv.* 3.** like a coward. **—cow′ardliness,** *n.*
—Syn. 1. craven, dastardly, pusillanimous, timorous, faint-hearted, white-livered, chicken-hearted. COWARDLY, TIMID refer to a lack of courage or self-confidence. COWARDLY means weakly and basely fearful in the presence of danger: *the cowardly wretch deserted his comrades in battle.* TIMID means lacking in boldness or self-confidence even when there is no danger present: *he was so timid he hardly spoke at all.* **—Ant. 1.** brave, self-confident.

cowbane (kou′bān′), *n.* any of several umbelliferous plants supposed to be poisonous to cattle, as the European water-hemlock, *Cicuta virosa.*

cowbell (kou′bĕl′), *n.* **1.** a bell hung round a cow's neck, to indicate her whereabouts. **2.** *U.S.* the bladder campion, *Silene latifolia.*

cowberry (kou′bə rĭ, -brĭ), *n., pl.* **-ries. 1.** the berry or fruit of any of various shrubs, as *Vaccinium vitis-idaea,* that grow in pastures. **2.** any of these shrubs.

cowbind (kou′bīnd′), *n.* either the black-berried white bryony, *Bryonia alba,* or the red-berried bryony, *B. dioica.*

cowbird (kou′bûd′), *n.* any of the American blackbirds of the genus *Molothrus,* esp. *M. ater* of North America (so called because they accompany cattle). Also, **cow blackbird, cow bunting.**

cowboy (kou′boi′), *n.* **1.** a boy in charge of cows. **2.** *U.S.* a man employed in the care of the cattle of a ranch, doing his work largely on horseback.

cowcatcher (kou′kăch′ə), *n.* *U.S.* a triangular frame at the front of a locomotive, etc., designed for clearing the track of obstructions.

cow-cocky (kou′kŏk′ĭ), *n.* *Austral., N.Z. Colloq.* a dairy farmer.

cower (kou′ə), *v.i.* **1.** to crouch in fear or shame. **2.** to bend with the knees and back; stand or squat in a bent position. [ME *couren,* t. Scand.; cf. Icel. *kūra* sit moping, doze, c. G *kauern* cower, crouch]

Cowes (kouz), *n.* a seaport on the Isle of Wight: annual sailing regatta. 16,974 (1961).

cowfish (kou′fĭsh′), *n., pl.* **-fishes,** (*esp. collectively*) **-fish. 1.** any of various marine fishes with hornlike projections over the eyes, as *Lactophrys tricornis,* found along the southern Atlantic coast of the U.S., to Panama, Brazil, etc.; trunkfish. **2.** a sirenian, as the manatee. **3.** any of various small cetaceans, as a porpoise or dolphin or the grampus, *Grampus griseus.*

cowgirl (kou′gûl′), *n.* a girl who assists in herding and handling cattle on a ranch.

cow hand, one employed on a cattle ranch; a cowboy.

cow heel, a dish consisting of a cow's or ox's hoof stewed to make an edible jelly.

cowherd (kou′hûd′), *n.* one whose occupation is the tending of cows.

cowhide (kou′hīd′), *n., v.,* **-hided, -hiding. —*n.* 1.** the hide of a cow. **2.** the leather made from it. **3.** *U.S.* a strong, flexible whip made of rawhide or of braided leather. **—*v.t.* 4.** *U.S.* to whip with a cowhide.

cowhouse (kou′hous′), *n.* a building in which cows are stalled; a byre.

cow-itch (kou′ĭch′), *n.* cowage.

cowl (koul), *n.* **1.** a hooded garment worn by monks. **2.** the hood of this garment. **3.** a hood-shaped covering for a chimney or ventilating shaft, to increase the draught. **4.** the forward part of the motor-car body supporting the rear of the bonnet and the windscreen, and housing the pedals and dashboard. **5.** *Aeron.* a cowling. **6.** a wire netting fastened to the top of the chimney of a steam locomotive, to prevent large sparks from being discharged. **—*v.t.* 7.** to put a monk's cowl on. **8.** to make a monk of. **9.** to cover with, or as with, a cowl. [ME *couel,* OE *cūle, cug(e)le,* t. LL: m. *cucullа* cowl, var. of L *cucullus* hood]

cowled (kould), *adj.* **1.** wearing a cowl. **2.** shaped like a cowl; cucullate.

Cowley (kou′lĭ), *n.* **Abraham,** 1618–67, English poet.

cowlick (kou′lĭk′), *n.* *U.S.* a tuft of hair turned up, usually over the forehead.

cowling (kou′lĭng), *n.* *Aeron.* a streamlined housing for an aircraft engine, usually forming a continuous line with the fuselage or wing.

cowman (kou′mən), *n., pl.* **-men. 1.** a farm labourer who takes care of cows. **2.** *Western U.S.* an owner of cattle; a ranchman.

coworker (kō wû′kə), *n.* fellow worker.

cow-parsley (kou′päs′lĭ), *n.* a biennial umbelliferous herb with white flowers, *Anthriscus sylvestris,* widespread in hedgerows.

cow-parsnip (kou′päs′nĭp), *n.* any plant of the umbelliferous genus *Heracleum,* as *H. spondylium,* of Europe, or *H. lanatum,* of North America.

cowpea (kou′pē′), *n.* **1.** an annual plant, *Vigna sinensis,* extensively cultivated for forage, soil improvement, etc., the seeds sometimes being used for human food. **2.** the seed.

Cowper (kōō′pə, kou′pə), *n.* **William,** 1731–1800, English poet.

Cowper's glands (kou′pəz, kōō′-), *Anat., Zool.* a pair of accessory prostate or urethral glands in males, which during sexual excitement pour a mucous secretion into the urethra. [named after Wm. *Cowper,* 1666–1709, English anatomist who discovered them]

cowpox (kou′pŏks′), *n.* an eruptive disease appearing on the teats and udders of cows in which small pustules form which contain a virus used in the vaccination of man against smallpox.
cowpuncher (kou′pŭn′chə), *n.* *U.S. Colloq.* a cowboy.
cowrie (kou′rĭ), *n.* **1.** the shell of any of the marine gastropods constituting the genus *Cypraea*, as that of *C. moneta*, a small shell with a fine gloss, used as money in certain parts of Asia and Africa, or that of *C. tigris*, a large, handsome shell often used as a mantel ornament. **2.** the animal itself. [t. Hind.: m. *kauri*]
cowry (kou′rĭ), *n.*, *pl.* **-ries.** cowrie.
cowshed (kou′shĕd′), *n.* a shed in which cows are stalled; a cowhouse; a byre.
cowskin (kou′skĭn′), *n.* **1.** the skin of a cow. **2.** the leather made from it.
cowslip (kou′slĭp′), *n.* **1.** an English primrose, *Primula officinalis* (*P. veris*), bearing yellow flowers. **2.** *U.S.* the kingcup. [OE, *cūslyppe* cowslime, var. of *cū-sloppe* (ME *couslop*) cow-slobber. Cf. OXLIP]
cow-wheat (kou′wēt′), *n.* any of the species of scrophulariaceous semiparasitic herbs of the genus *Melampyrum* as the common cow-wheat, *M. pratense*, of Europe and Asia.
cox (kŏks), *n.* **1.** the steersman of a boat, esp. in rowing; a coxswain. *—v.t., v.i.* **2.** to act as cox. **—cox′less,** *adj.*
Cox (kŏks), *n.* **David,** 1783–1859, English landscape painter.
coxa (kŏk′sə), *n.*, *pl.* **coxae** (kŏk′sē). **1.** *Anat.* **a.** the innominate bone. **b.** the joint of the hip. **2.** *Zool.* the first or proximal segment of the leg of insects and other arthropods. [t. L: hip] **—cox′al,** *adj.*

Leg of beetle (enlarged)
A, Coxa; B, Trochanter; C, Femur; D, Tibia; E, Tarsus

coxalgia (kŏk săl′jĭ ə), *n.* *Pathol.* pain in the hip. [NL; f. COX(A) + -ALGIA] **—coxal′gic,** *adj.*
coxcomb (kŏks′kōm′), *n.* **1.** a conceited dandy. **2.** *Bot.* cockscomb. **3.** *Obs.* the cap, resembling a cock's comb, formerly worn by professional fools. **4.** *Obs.* the head. [var. of *cock's comb*] **—coxcombical** (kŏks kŏm′ĭ kl, -kō′mĭ-), *adj.* **—Syn. 1.** fop, exquisite, beau, popinjay, jackanapes.
coxcombry (kŏks′kōm′rĭ), *n.*, *pl.* **-ries. 1.** the manners or behaviour of a coxcomb. **2.** a foppish trait.
Cox's orange pippin, a juicy, crisp variety of apple, with firm flesh and russet skin.
coxswain (kŏk′sən, -swān), *n.* **1.** the helmsman of a boat. **2.** (on a ship) one who has charge of a boat and its crew. Also, **cockswain.** [f. *cock* ship's boat + SWAIN servant]
coy (koi), *adj.* **1.** shy; modest (now usually of girls). **2.** affectedly shy or reserved. **3.** *Obs.* disdainful. **4.** *Obs.* quiet. *—v.i.* **5.** *Archaic.* to act in a coy manner. *—v.t.* **6.** *Obs.* to quiet; calm. **7.** *Obs.* to pat; caress. [ME, t. F: m. *coi*, earlier *quei*, g. L *quiētus* at rest] **—coy′ly,** *adv.* **—coy′ness,** n. **—Syn. 1.** retiring, diffident, bashful, demure.

Coyote, *Canis latrans* (3½ to 4 ft long)

coyote (koi′ōt, koi ōt′, koi ō′tĭ), *n.* **1.** a wild, wolf-like animal, *Canis latrans*, of western North America, noted for loud and prolonged howling at night; the prairie wolf. **2.** *Amer. Ind. Legend.* the culture hero and trickster of the American Indians of the West (sometimes human, sometimes animal). **3.** *U.S.* a contemptible person. [t. Mex. Sp., t. Nahuatl: m. *koyotl*]
coypu (koi′po͞o), *n.*, *pl.* **-pus,** (*esp. collectively*) **-pu.** a large aquatic rodent, *Myocastor* (or *Myopotamus*) *coypus*, yielding the fur nutria, originally from South America but later introduced into Europe, and now officially a pest. [t. Amer. Sp.: m. *coipu*, t. Araucanian: m. *koypu*]

Coypu, *Myocastor coypus* (Total length ab. 3 ft, tail 14 in.)

coz (kŭz), *n.* *Colloq.* cousin.
coze (kōz), *v.*, **cozed, cozing,** *n.* *Obs.* *—v.i.* **1.** to converse in a friendly way; chat. *—n.* **2.** a friendly talk; a chat. [t. F: m. s. *causer*]
cozen (kŭz′ən), *v.t.* to cheat; deceive; beguile. [orig. obscure] **—coz′ener,** *n.*
cozenage (kŭz′ə nĭj), *n.* **1.** the practice of cozening. **2.** the fact of being cozened. **3.** a fraud; a deception.
cozy (kō′zĭ), *adj.*, **-zier, -ziest,** *n.*, *pl.* **-zies.** *U.S.* cosy. **—co′zily,** *adv.* **—co′ziness,** *n.*
cp., compare.
C.P., 1. Chief Patriarch. **2.** Common Prayer. **3.** Communist party. **4.** Court of Probate.
c.p., candlepower.
C/P., charter party.
cpl, corporal.
c.p.o., chief petty officer.
c.p.s., cycles per second.
C.P.S., (L *Custos Privati Sigilli*) Keeper of the Privy Seal.
Cr, *Chem.* chromium.
cr., 1. credit. **2.** creditor.
crab[1] (krăb), *n.*, *v.*, **crabbed, crabbing.** *—n.* **1.** any of the stalk-eyed decapod crustaceans constituting the suborder *Brachyura* (**true crabs**) having a short, broad, more or less flattened body, the abdomen or so-called tail being small and folded under the thorax.

Crab, *Callinectes sapidus* (3 in. long)

2. any of various other crustaceans (as the **hermit crab**), or other animals (as the **horseshoe crab**), resembling the true crabs. **3.** (*cap.*) the zodiacal constellation or sign Cancer. **4.** an ill-tempered or grouchy person. **5.** any of various mechanical contrivances for hoisting or pulling. **6.** *Aeron.* the manoeuvre of crabbing. **7.** (*pl.*) a losing throw, as two aces, in the game of hazard. **8.** a crablouse. **9. catch a crab,** *Rowing.* to make a faulty stroke, as one in which the blade either enters the water at the wrong angle and sinks too deep, or is held at the wrong angle and fails to enter the water at all. *—v.i.* **10.** to move sideways. **11.** *Aeron.* (of an aircraft) to head partly into the crosswind to compensate for drift. **12.** to fish for crabs. *—v.t.* **13.** *Aeron.* to head (an aircraft) partly into the crosswind to compensate for drift. [ME *crabbe*, OE *crabba*, c. G *Krabbe*] **—crab′like′,** *adj.*
crab[2] (krăb), *n.* a crab-apple (fruit or tree). [ME *crabbe*, ? var. of d. *scrab* crab-apple. Cf. d. Sw. *skrabba*]
crab[3] (krăb), *v.*, **crabbed, crabbing.** *—v.i.* **1.** (of hawks) to claw each other. **2.** to find fault. *—v.t.* **3.** to claw, as a hawk. **4.** *Colloq.* to find fault with. **5.** *Colloq.* to spoil. [cf. MD *krabben* scratch, quarrel; akin to CRAB[1]]
crab-apple (krăb′ăp′l), *n.* **1.** a small, sour wild apple. **2.** any of various cultivated species and varieties of apple, small, sour, and astringent or slightly bitter, used for making jelly and preserves. **3.** any tree bearing such fruit.
Crabb (krăb), *n.* **George,** 1778–1851, English writer and philologist.
Crabbe (krăb), *n.* **George,** 1754–1832, English poet.
crabbed (krăb′ĭd), *adj.* **1.** perverse; contrary; grouchy; ill-natured; churlish; irritable. **2.** perplexing; intricate: *a crabbed author, writings, etc.* **3.** difficult to decipher, as handwriting. [ME; f. CRAB[1] + -ED[3]] **—crab′bedly,** *adv.* **—crab′bedness,** *n.*
crabber (krăb′ə), *n.* **1.** one who fishes for crabs. **2.** a boat used in fishing for crabs.
crabby (krăb′ĭ), *adj.*, **-bier, -biest.** crabbed (def. 1).
crabgrass (krăb′gräs′), *n.* an annual grass, *Digitaria sanguinalis*, common in cultivated and waste grounds. It is a weedy pest in lawns.
crablouse (krăb′lous′), *n.* a small wingless insect, *Phthirius pubis*, parasitic on man and other mammals and having its mouth parts adapted for biting.
crabstick (krăb′stĭk′), *n.* **1.** a stick, cane, or club made of wood, esp. of the crab-tree. **2.** an ill-tempered, crabbed person.
crab-tree (krăb′trē′), *n.* a tree which bears crab-apples.
crabwise (krăb′wīz′), *adv.* in the manner of a crab; (referring esp. to motion) sideways or diagonally. Also, **crabways** (krăb′wāz′).
crack (krăk), *v.i.* **1.** to make a sudden, sharp sound in, or as in, breaking; snap, as a whip. **2.** to break with a sudden, sharp sound. **3.** to break without complete separation of parts; become fissured. **4.** (of the voice) to break abruptly and discordantly, esp. into an upper register. **5.** to fail; give way. **6.** *Dial.* to brag; boast. **7.** *Chiefly Scot.* to chat; gossip.
—v.t. **8.** to cause to make a sudden sharp sound; make a snapping sound with (a whip, etc.); strike with a sharp noise. **9.** to break without complete separation of parts; break into fissures. **10.** to break with a sudden sharp sound. **11.** *Colloq.* to break into (a safe, vault, etc.). **12.** *Colloq.* to solve (a mystery, etc.). **13.** to open and drink (a bottle of wine, etc.). **14.** to damage; impair. **15.** to make unsound mentally. **16.** to make (the voice) harsh or unmanageable. **17.** to break with grief; affect deeply. **18.** to utter or tell, as a joke. **19.** *Obs.* to boast. **20.** to

subject to the process of cracking in the distillation of petroleum, etc.
—*v.* 21. Some special verb phrases are:
crack down, *Colloq.* to take severe measures, esp. in enforcing discipline.
crack on, 1. *Naut.* to hoist (sail) esp. in heavy weather. 2. *Chiefly Naut.* to pursue a course at high speed, esp. in adverse conditions.
crack up, 1. to suffer a physical, mental, or moral breakdown. 2. *Aeron.* to crash. 3. *Colloq.* to praise; extol. 4. to crash: *to crack up a plane.*
get cracking, *Slang.* to start an activity, esp. energetically.
—*n.* 22. a sudden, sharp noise, as of something breaking. 23. the snap of a whip, etc. 24. a shot, as with a rifle. 25. a resounding blow. 26. a break without complete separation of parts; a fissure; a flaw. 27. a slight opening, as one between door and doorpost. 28. a mental flaw. 29. a broken or changing tone of the voice. 30. *Mountaineering.* a cleft in rock, narrower than a chimney. 31. *Colloq.* a try; an opportunity or chance. 32. *Slang.* a joke; gibe. 33. *Colloq.* a moment; instant: *he was on his feet again in a crack.* 34. *Slang.* a burglary. 35. *Scot.* conversation; chat. 36. *Now Chiefly Dial.* loud talk; boasting.
—*adj.* 37. *Colloq.* of superior excellence; first-rate. [unexplained var. of obs. *crake* creak, OE *cracian* resound. See CREAK, CROAK, all prob. imit. in orig.] —**Syn.** 22. snap, report. 26. crevice, cranny, chink, cleft, interstice.
crackajack (krăk′ə jăk′), *n., adj.* crackerjack.
crackbrain (krăk′brān′), *n.* an insane person.
crackbrained (krăk′brānd′), *adj.* insane; crazy.
cracked (krăkt), *adj.* 1. broken. 2. broken without separation of parts; fissured. 3. damaged. 4. *Colloq.* mentally unsound. 5. broken in tone, as the voice.
cracker (krăk′ə), *n.* 1. a thin, crisp biscuit. 2. a kind of firework which explodes with a loud report, esp. a long paper or cardboard tube containing a fuse and several charges of explosive, bound into a concertina shape, which bounces at the explosion of each charge. 3. a small paper roll containing an explosive, and usually a small gift, motto, etc., and which explodes when pulled sharply at both ends. 4. *U.S.* one of a class of poor whites in parts of the south-eastern U.S. 5. *Obs. or Dial.* a boaster; a liar. 6. one who or that which cracks.
crackerjack (krăk′ə jăk′), *n. U.S. Slang.* 1. a person of marked ability; something exceptionally fine. —*adj.* 2. *Slang.* of marked ability; exceptionally fine. Also, **crackajack.**
crackers (krăk′əz), *adj. Colloq.* insane; crazy.
cracking (krăk′ĭng), *n.* 1. (in the distillation of petroleum or the like) the process of breaking down certain hydrocarbons into simpler ones of lower boiling points, by means of excess heat, distillation under pressure, etc., in order to give a greater yield of low-boiling products than could be obtained by simple distillation. —*adj.* 2. fast; vigorous: *a cracking pace.* 3. done with precision: *a cracking salute.* 4. *Colloq.* first-rate; fine; excellent.
crackle (krăk′l), *v.*, **-led, -ling,** *n.* —*v.i.* 1. to make slight, sudden, sharp noises, rapidly repeated. —*v.t.* 2. to cause to crackle. 3. to break with a crackling noise. —*n.* 4. the act of crackling. 5. a crackling noise. 6. a network of fine cracks, as in the glaze of some kinds of porcelain. 7. pottery ware with a network of fine cracks in the glaze. [freq. of CRACK]
crackleware (krăk′l wĕə′), *n.* crackle (def.7).
crackling (krăk′lĭng), *n.* 1. the making of slight cracking sounds rapidly repeated. 2. the crisp browned skin or rind of roast pork. 3. (*usually pl.*) *Dial.* the crisp residue left when fat, esp. that of pigs, is rendered.
crackly (krăk′lĭ), *adj.* apt to crackle.
cracknel (krăk′nəl), *n.* 1. a hard, brittle cake or biscuit. 2. (*pl.*) small bits of fat pork fried crisp. [ME *crakenelle*, appar. t. F: m. *craquelin*, t. MD: m. *crakelinc*]
crack of dawn, the first light of the day.
crack of doom, 1. the signal that announces the Day of Judgement. 2. the end of the world; doomsday.
crackpot (krăk′pŏt′), *Slang.* —*n.* 1. an eccentric or insane person. —*adj.* 2. eccentric; insane; impractical.
cracksman (krăks′mən), *n., pl.* **-men.** *Slang.* a burglar.
crack-up (krăk′ŭp′), *n.* 1. a crash; collision. 2. *Colloq.* a breakdown in health. 3. collapse; defeat.
Cracow (krăk′ou, krăk′ō, krăk′ŏf), *n.* a city in S Poland, on the Vistula: capital of Poland 1320–1609; formerly a member of the Hanseatic League. 513,000 (1964). Polish, **Kraków.** German, **Krakau.** See map under **Hanseatic League.**
-cracy, a noun termination meaning 'rule', 'government', 'governing body', as in *autocracy, bureaucracy.* [t. F: m. *-cratie*, ult. t. Gk: m. *-kratia*, der. *krátos* rule, strength]
cradle (krā′dl), *n., v.*, **-dled, -dling.** —*n.* 1. a little bed or cot for an infant, usually built on rockers. 2. the place where anything is nurtured during its early existence. 3. any of various contrivances similar to a child's cradle, as the framework on which a ship rests during construction or repair. 4. a frame that prevents the bedclothes touching an injured part of a bedridden patient. 5. a plank supported in a sling from above, on which a man may sit, or stand, to carry out work on a vertical surface, as the side of a building or ship. 6. a flat, movable framework with swivel wheels, on which a mechanic can lie while working beneath a motor vehicle. 7. *Agric.* a. a frame of wood with a row of long curved teeth projecting above and parallel to a scythe, for laying grain in bunches as it is cut. b. a scythe together with the cradle in which it is set. 8. a kind of box on rockers used by miners for washing auriferous gravel or sand to separate the gold. 9. an engraver's tool for laying mezzotint grounds. —*v.t.* 10. to place or rock in or as in a cradle. 11. to nurture during infancy. 12. to cut (grain) with a cradle. 13. to place in a ship's cradle. 14. to wash in a miner's cradle. 15. to receive or hold as a cradle. 16. *Lacrosse.* to hold (the ball) in the net of the crosse while running with it. —*v.i.* 17. to lie in, or as in, a cradle. 18. to cut grain with a cradle-scythe. [ME *cradel*, OE *cradol.* Cf. G *Kratte* basket] —**cra′dler,** *n.*
cradle-scythe (krā′dl sīth′), *n.* cradle (def. 7b).
cradlesong (krā′dl sŏng′), *n.* a lullaby.
cradling (krăd′lĭng), *n.* 1. *Archit.* a framework of wood, fixed round beams or columns to receive a casing. 2. *Lacrosse.* the technique of swinging the crosse while running so the ball is kept in the net.
craft (kräft), *n.* 1. skill; ingenuity; dexterity. 2. skill or art applied to bad purposes; cunning; deceit; guile. 3. an art, trade, or occupation requiring special skill, esp. manual skill; a handicraft. 4. the members of a trade or profession collectively; a guild. 5. (*construed as pl.*) boats, ships, and vessels collectively. 6. a single vessel. 7. (*construed as pl.*) aircraft collectively. 8. a single aircraft. [ME; OE *cræft*, c. G *Kraft*] —**Syn.** 2. craftiness, subtlety, artifice. See **cunning.**
craft guild, an association of people working in the same craft.
craftsman (kräfts′mən), *n., pl.* **-men.** 1. one who practices a craft; an artisan. 2. an artist. [f. *crafts* (poss. of CRAFT) + MAN] —**crafts′manship′,** *n.* —**Syn.** 1. artificer, mechanic, handicraftsman.
craft union, 1. a trade union whose members are all skilled craftsmen (opposed to unskilled or clerical workers). 2. *U.S.* a trade union composed only of people in the same craft.
crafty (kräf′tĭ), *adj.*, **-tier, -tiest.** 1. skilful in underhand or evil schemes; cunning, deceitful; sly. 2. *Archaic.* skilful; ingenious; dexterous. —**craft′ily,** *adv.* —**craft′iness,** *n.* —**Syn.** 1. artful, wily, insidious, tricky, designing, scheming, plotting.
crag[1] (krăg), *n.* 1. a steep, rugged rock; a rough, broken, projecting part of a rock. 2. (*cap.*) *Geol.* a deposit of shelly sands of Pliocene age found in East Anglia. [ME, t. Celtic; cf. Welsh *craig* rock] —**cragged** (krăg′ĭd), *adj.*
crag[2] (krăg), *n. Scot. and N Dial.* the neck; the throat; the craw. [t. MFlem.: m. *krage*]
crag-and-tail (krăg′ən tāl′), *n. Geog.* a hill or crag, of which one face has a steep slope and the other a gentle slope.
craggy (krăg′ĭ), *adj.*, **-gier, -giest.** 1. full of crags or broken rocks. 2. rugged; rough. —**crag′gily,** *adv.* —**crag′giness,** *n.*
cragsman (krăgz′mən), *n., pl.* **-men.** one accustomed to or skilled in climbing crags.
Craig (krăg), *n.* **Edward Gordon,** 1782–1966, English theatrical designer and illustrator.
Craigie (krā′gĭ), *n.* **Sir William A.,** 1867–1957, Scottish lexicographer.
Craik (krāk), *n.* **Dinah Maria Mulock** (myōō′ lŏk), 1826–87, English novelist and poet.
Craiova (*Rum.* krȧ yô′vȧ), *n.* a city in SW Rumania. 122,108 (est. 1964).
crake (krāk), *n.* 1. the corncrake. 2. any of several related or similar birds of the family *Rallidae.* 3. *N Dial.* a crow. [ME, t. Scand.; cf. Icel. *krāka*]
cram (krăm), *v.*, **crammed, cramming,** *n.* —*v.t.* 1. to fill (something) by force with more than it can conveniently hold. 2. to force or stuff (fol. by *into, down,* etc.). 3. to fill with or as with excess of food. 4. to prepare (a person), as for an examination, by hastily storing his memory with facts. 5. to get a knowledge of (a subject) by so preparing oneself. 6. *Slang.* to tell lies or exaggerated stories to. —*v.i.* 7. to eat greedily or to excess. 8. to study for an examination by hastily memorizing facts. —*n.* 9. the act or result of cramming. 10. a crammed state.

11. *Colloq.* a dense crowd. [OE *crammian*, der. *crimman* insert] **—Syn. 2.** stuff, crowd, pack, squeeze, compress, overcrowd.

crambo (krăm′bō), *n.* **1.** a game in which one person or side must find a rhyme to a word or a line of verse given by another. **2.** (in contemptuous use) rhyme. [earlier *crambe*, t. L: lit., cabbage, short for *crambē repetīta* repeated cabbage, dull rhyme]

cram-full (krăm′fo͝ol′), *adj.* full to the utmost; crammed: *a larder cram-full of food.*

crammer (krăm′ə), *n.* **1.** one who or that which crams. **2.** a school which prepares pupils for examinations by cramming them with facts in a short time. **3.** a pupil studying for an examination. **4.** a textbook from which facts may be crammed. **5.** an apparatus for forcibly feeding poultry to fatten them.

cramoisy (krăm′oi zĭ, -ə zĭ), *adj.* **1.** *Archaic.* crimson. *—n.* **2.** *Obs.* crimson cloth. Also, **cramesy.** [t. F: m. *cramoisi*, ult. t. Ar.: m. *qirmizī* CRIMSON]

cramp[1] (krămp), *n.* **1.** a sudden involuntary, persistent contraction of a muscle or a group of muscles, esp. of the extremities, sometimes associated with severe pain. **2.** *U.S.* (*often pl.*) piercing pains in the abdomen. **3. writer's cramp,** a professional or occupational disease involving some muscles of the fingers and hands. *—v.t.* **4.** to affect with, or as with, a cramp. [ME *crampe*, t. MD]

cramp[2] (krămp), *n.* **1.** a small metal bar with bent ends, for holding together planks, masonry, etc.; a cramp iron. **2.** a portable frame or tool with a movable part which can be screwed up to hold things together; clamp. **3.** anything that confines or restrains. **4.** a cramped state or part. *—v.t.* **5.** to fasten or hold with a cramp. **6.** to confine narrowly; restrict; restrain; hamper. **7. cramp one's style,** to hinder a person from showing his best abilities, etc. *—adj.* **8.** cramped. [t. MD: hook, clamp]

cramped (krămpt, krămt), *adj.* **1.** contracted; narrow. **2.** difficult to decipher or understand.

cramp iron, a cramp, or piece of iron with bent ends, for holding together pieces of stone, etc.

crampon (krăm′pən), *n.* **1.** a grappling iron, esp. one of a pair for raising heavy weights. **2.** *Mountaineering.* a spiked iron plate worn on the shoe to prevent slipping. [t. F, der. *crampe* (t. Gmc. See CRAMP[2])]

cran (krăn), *n.* a measure of capacity for fresh herrings by the barrel, equal to 37½ imperial gallons.

Cranach (*Ger.* krä′näKH), *n.* **Lucas** (*Ger.* lo͞o′käs), 1472–1553, German Renaissance painter and engraver.

cranage (krā′nĭj), *n.* **1.** the service performed by a crane, in docks etc. **2.** the charge made for the use of a crane.

cranberry (krăn′bə rĭ, -brĭ), *n., pl.* **-ries. 1.** the red, acid fruit or berry of any plant of the ericaceous genus *Vaccinium*, as *V. oxycoccus*, used in making sauce, jelly, etc. **2.** the plant itself. [t. LG: m. *kraanbere*; cf. G *Kran(ich)beere* craneberry. See CRANE]

crane (krān), *n., v.,* **craned, craning.** *—n.* **1.** any of a group of large wading birds (family *Gruidae*) with very long legs, bill, and neck, and elevated hind toe. **2.** (popularly) any of various similar birds of other families, as the great blue heron, *Ardea herodias.* **3.** a device for moving heavy weights, having two motions, one a direct lift and the other a horizontal movement, and consisting in one of its simplest forms of an upright post turning on its vertical axis and bearing a projecting arm on which the hoisting tackle is fitted. **4.** (*pl.*) *Naut.* supports of iron or timber at a vessel's side for stowing boats or spars upon. *—v.t.* **5.** to hoist, lower, or move by or as by a crane. **6.** to stretch (the neck) as a crane does. *—v.i.* **7.** to stretch out one's neck. **8.** *Colloq.* to hesitate at danger, difficulty, etc. **9.** *Hunting.* (of a horse) to pull up at a hedge and look over before jumping. [ME; OE *cran*, c. G *Kran*]

Crane (def. 1), *Grus grus* (45 in. long)

Crane (krān), *n.* **1. (Harold) Hart,** 1899–1932, U.S. writer. **2. Stephen,** 1871–1900, U.S. novelist, poet, and short-story writer.

cranefly (krān′flī′), *n.* any of the dipterous insects constituting the family *Tipulidae*, characterized by very long legs; the daddy-long-legs.

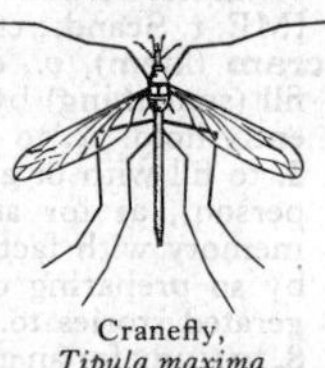

Cranefly, *Tipula maxima*

cranesbill (krānz′bĭl′), *n.* any plant of the genus *Geranium* (see **geranium**) with long, slender, beaked fruit. Also, **crane's-bill.** [f. CRANE('s) + BILL[2]; 16th cent. trans. of D *kranebek* geranium]

cranial (krā′nyəl), *adj.* of or pertaining to the cranium or skull. *—***cra′nially,** *adv.*

cranial index, *Anat.* the ratio of the greatest breadth of the skull to the greatest length from front to back, multiplied by 100.

craniate (krā′nĭ ĭt, -āt′), *adj.* **1.** having a cranium or skull. **2.** belonging to the *Craniata*, a primary division of vertebrates, comprising those which possess a skull and brain, and including the mammals, birds, reptiles, amphibians, and fishes. *—n.* **3.** a craniate animal.

cranio-, a combining form of **cranium.** Also, **crani-.**

craniol., craniology.

craniology (krā′nĭ ŏl′ə jĭ), *n.* the science that deals with the size, shape, and other characteristics of skulls. **—craniological** (krā′nĭ ə lŏj′ĭ kl), *adj.* **—cra′niol′ogist,** *n.*

craniom., craniometry.

craniometer (krā′nĭ ŏm′ĭ tə), *n.* an instrument for measuring the external dimensions of skulls.

craniometry (krā′nĭ ŏm′ĭ trĭ), *n.* the science of measuring skulls. **—craniometric** (krā′nĭ ə mĕt′rĭk), **cra′niomet′rical,** *adj.* **—cra′niom′etrist,** *n.*

craniotomy (krā′nĭ ŏt′ə mĭ), *n., pl.* **-mies.** *Surg.* the operation of opening the skull, usually for operations on the brain.

cranium (krā′nyəm), *n., pl.* **-nia** (-nyə). **1.** the skull of a vertebrate. **2.** that part of the skull which encloses the brain. [t. ML, t. Gk: m. *krānion*]

Human cranium (from above) F, Frontal, P, Parietal, O, Occipital bones; C, Coronal, S, Sagittal, L, Lambdoidal sutures

crank[1] (krăngk), *n.* **1.** *Mach.* a device for communicating motion, or for changing rotary motion into reciprocating motion, or vice versa, consisting in its simplest form of an arm projecting from, or secured at right angles at the end of, the axis or shaft which receives or imparts the motion. **2.** *Colloq.* an eccentric person, or one who holds stubbornly to eccentric views. **3.** *Colloq.* an eccentric notion. **4.** *U.S. Colloq.* an ill-tempered, grouchy person. **5.** a turn of speech; a verbal conceit. **6.** *Obs.* a winding path. *—v.t.* **7.** to bend into or make in the shape of a crank. **8.** to furnish with a crank. **9.** *Mach.* to cause (a shaft) to revolve by applying force to a crank; turn a crankshaft in (an internal-combustion engine) to start the engine. *—v.i.* **10.** to turn a crank, as in starting a motor-car engine. **11.** *Obs.* to twist, wind. *—adj.* **12.** unstable; shaky; unsteady. **13.** *Dial.* sickly. [ME *cranke*, OE *cranc*, in *crancstæf* weaving implement, crank]

crank[2] (krăngk), *adj.* liable to lurch or capsize, as a ship. [short for *crank-sided*; cf. D *krengd* careened]

crank[3] (krăngk), *adj. Obs. or Dial.* lively; in high spirits; cheerful. [ME; orig. unknown]

crankcase (krăngk′kās′), *n.* (in an internal-combustion engine) the housing which encloses the crankshaft, connecting rods, and allied parts.

crankle (krăng′kl), *n., v.t., v.i.,* **-kled, -kling.** bend; turn. [freq. of CRANK[1], v.]

crankous (krăng′kəs), *adj. Scot.* irritated; cranky.

crankpin (krăngk′pĭn′), *n. Mach.* a pin or cylinder at the outer end or part of a crank, as for holding a connecting rod.

crankshaft (krăngk′shäft′), *n. Mach.* a shaft driving or driven by a crank, esp. the main shaft of an engine which carries the cranks to which the connecting rods are attached.

cranky[1] (krăng′kĭ), *adj.,* **-kier, -kiest. 1.** eccentric; queer. **2.** ill-tempered; cross. **3.** shaky; unsteady; out of order. **4.** full of bends or windings; crooked. **5.** *Dial.* sickly; infirm. **—crank′ily,** *adv.* **—crank′iness,** *n.*

cranky[2] (krăng′kĭ), *adj.* liable to capsize.

Cranmer (krăn′mə), *n.* **Thomas,** 1489–1556, first Protestant Archbishop of Canterbury: a leader and martyr of the Protestant Reformation in England.

crannog (krăn′əg), *n.* an ancient Irish or Scottish lake dwelling, usually built on an artificial island. Also, **crannoge** (krăn′əj). [t. Irish, der. *crann* tree, beam]

cranny (krăn′ĭ), *n., pl.* **-nies.** a small, narrow opening (in a wall, rock, etc.); a chink; crevice; fissure. [ME *crany*, f. F *cran* fissure (der. *crener* cut away, g. L *crēnāre*) + -Y[2], dim. suffix] **—cran′nied,** *adj.*

cranreuch (krăn′rək), *n. Scot.* hoarfrost.

crap (krăp), *n., v.,* **crapped, crapping.** *Taboo Slang.* *—n.* **1.** excrement. **2.** nonsense; rubbish. **3.** junk; odds and ends. *—v.i.* **4.** to defecate. *—v.t.* **5.** *U.S.* to make a mess of; bungle (often fol. by *up*): *to crap a job up.* [late ME *crappe* chaff, t. MD]

crape (krāp), *n., v.t.,* **craped, craping.** crepe (esp. defs 3 and 4). [anglicized sp. of CREPE]

craps (krăps), *n. U.S.* a gambling game played with two dice, a modern and simplified form of hazard.

crapshooter (krăp′shōō′tə), *n. U.S.* a person who plays the game of craps.

crapulent (krăp′yŏŏ lənt), *adj.* sick from gross excess in drinking or eating. [t. L: s. *crāpulentus* drunk] —**crap′ulence,** *n.*

crapulous (krăp′yŏŏ ləs), *adj.* **1.** given to or characterized by gross excess in drinking or eating. **2.** suffering from or due to such excess. [t. LL: m. s. *crāpulōsus*, der. L *crāpula* intoxication] —**crap′ulousness,** *n.*

craquelure (krăk′ə lyŏŏə′), *n. Painting.* the fine hairlines that develop on old paintings. [t. F, der. *craqueler* CRACKLE]

crash[1] (krăsh), *v.t.* **1.** to break in pieces violently and noisily; shatter. **2.** to force or drive with violence and noise. **3.** *Colloq.* to come uninvited to (a party, etc.). **4.** *Colloq.* to enter without buying a ticket: *to crash the gate.* **5.** to cause (an aircraft) to make a landing in an abnormal manner, usually damaging or wrecking the aircraft. —*v.i.* **6.** to break or fall to pieces with noise. **7.** to make a loud, clattering noise, as of something dashed to pieces. **8.** to collapse or fail suddenly, as a financial enterprise. **9.** to move or go with a crash; strike with a crash. **10.** *Aeron.* to land in an abnormal manner, usually damaging or wrecking the apparatus. —*n.* **11.** a breaking or falling to pieces with loud noise. **12.** the shock of collision and breaking. **13.** a sudden and violent falling to ruin. **14.** a sudden collapse of a financial enterprise or the like. **15.** a sudden loud noise, as of something dashed to pieces; the sound of thunder, loud music, etc. **16.** *Aeron.* the act of crashing. —*adj.* **17.** *Colloq.* characterized by all-out, intensive effort, esp. to meet an emergency: *a crash programme.* [ME; b. CRAZE and MASH] —**crash′er,** *n.* —**Syn. 1.** smash. **14.** failure, ruin.

crash[2] (krăsh), *n.* **1.** a fabric of plain weave, made of rough, irregular, or lumpy yarns. It may be used as linen or cotton towelling, rayon dress fabric, etc. **2.** *U.S.* mull[3] (def. 2). [orig. unknown]

Crashaw (krăsh′ô), *n.* **Richard,** 1613?–49, English religious poet.

crash dive, a rapid dive by a submarine made at a steep angle, esp. to avoid attack on the surface.

crash-dive (krăsh′dīv′), *v.i., v.t.,* **-dived, -diving.** (of a submarine) to dive rapidly at a steep angle.

crash-helmet (krăsh′hĕl′mĭt), *n.* a helmet worn by motorcyclists, racing drivers and others, to protect the head in the event of a crash.

crashing (krăsh′ĭng), *adj. Colloq.* complete and utter: *a crashing bore.*

crash-land (krăsh′lănd′), *v.t., v.i.* to land (an aircraft) in an emergency in such a way that the minimum of damage is sustained; to make a controlled crash. —**crash′-land′ing,** *n.*

crasis (krā′sĭs), *n., pl.* **-ses** (-sēz). **1.** the mixture or blending of different elements in the constitution of the body; temperament. **2.** *Gram.* the mingling or combination of two vowels.

crass (krăs), *adj.* **1.** gross; stupid: *crass ignorance.* **2.** thick; coarse. [t. L: s. *crassus* solid, thick, dense, fat] —**crass′ly,** *adv.* —**crass′ness,** *n.*

crassitude (krăs′ĭ tyōōd′), *n.* **1.** gross ignorance or stupidity. **2.** thickness; grossness.

crassulaceous (krăs′yŏŏ lā′shəs), *adj.* belonging to the *Crassulaceae* family of plants, mostly fleshy or succulent herbs, including the houseleek, etc. [f. s. NL *Crassula* the typical genus (der. L *crassus* thick) + -ACEOUS]

Crassus (krăs′əs), *n.* **Marcus Licinius** (mä′kəs lĭ sĭn′ĭ əs), *c.* 115–53 B.C., Roman general: member of the first triumvirate.

-crat, a noun termination meaning 'ruler', 'member of a ruling body', 'advocate of a particular form of rule', as in *aristocrat, autocrat, democrat, plutocrat.* Cf. **-cracy.** [t. F: m. *-crate*, ult. t. Gk: m. *kratḗs* ruler]

cratch (krăch), *n. Archaic or Dial.* a crib to hold fodder; a manger. [ME *crecche*, t. OF: m. *creche*, t. Gmc]

crate (krāt), *n., v.,* **crated, crating.** —*n.* **1.** a box or framework, usually made of wooden slats, for packing and transporting fruit, furniture, etc. **2.** a basket of wickerwork, for the transportation of crockery, etc. **3.** the amount contained by or contents of a crate. **4.** *Colloq.* a motor vehicle, aeroplane, or the like, esp. a dilapidated one. —*v.t.* **5.** to put in a crate. [t. L: m. s. *crātis* wickerwork]

crater (krā′tə), *n.* **1.** the cup-shaped depression or cavity marking the orifice of a volcano. **2.** (in the surface of the earth, moon, etc.) a rounded hollow formed by the impact of a meteorite. **3.** (on the surface of the moon) a roughly circular depression, almost always containing a central mountain, and often shut in by mountainous walls. **4.** the hole or pit in the ground where a military mine, bomb, or shell has exploded. **5.** a large vessel or bowl used by the ancient Greeks and Romans, orig. for mixing wine with water. **6.** (*cap.*) *Astron.* a small southern constellation. —*v.i.* **7.** to form a crater or craters. —*v.t.* **8.** to make a crater or craters in. [t. L, t. Gk: m. *krātḗr*, orig. bowl for mixing wine and water] —**cra′terlike′,** *adj.* —**cra′terous,** *adj.*

craunch (krônch), *v.t., v.i., n.* crunch. [var. of *scranch*, *cranch.* Cf. D *schranzen* break]

cravat (krə văt′), *n.* a scarf worn round the neck; neckcloth. [t. F: m. *cravate*; so called because adopted from the Croats (F *Cravates*)]

crave (krāv), *v.,* **craved, craving.** —*v.t.* **1.** to long for or desire eagerly. **2.** to need greatly; require. **3.** to ask earnestly for (something); beg for. **4.** *Obs.* to ask (a person) earnestly for something or to do something. —*v.i.* **5.** to beg or plead (fol. by *for*). **6.** to long (fol. by *for* or *after*). [ME *craven*, OE *crafian.* Cf. Icel. *krefja* demand] —**crav′er,** *n.* —**crav′ingly,** *adv.* —**Syn. 1.** want, yearn for, hunger for. **4.** beg, beseech, entreat, implore.

craven (krā′vən), *adj.* **1.** cowardly; pusillanimous; mean-spirited. —*n.* **2.** a coward. —*v.t.* **3.** *Obs.* to make cowardly. [ME *cravant*, f. OF, b. *crav(anté)* overthrown and *(recre)ant* RECREANT] —**cra′venly,** *adv.* —**cra′venness,** *n.* —**Ant. 1.** brave.

craving (krā′vĭng), *n.* eager or urgent desire; longing; yearning. —**Syn.** See **desire.**

craw (krô), *n.* **1.** the crop of a bird or insect. **2.** the stomach of an animal. **3. stick in one's craw,** to irritate or annoy a person. [ME *crawe*, c. D *kraag* neck]

crawfish (krô′fĭsh′), *n., pl.* **-fishes,** (*esp. collectively*) **-fish.** *Chiefly U.S.* crayfish (esp. def. 2).

Crawford (krô′fəd), *n.* **Francis Marion,** 1854–1909, U.S. novelist, resident in Italy after 1885.

crawl[1] (krôl), *v.i.* **1.** to move by dragging the body along the ground, as a worm, or on the hands and knees, as a young child. **2.** to progress slowly, laboriously, or timorously: *the work crawled.* **3.** to go stealthily or abjectly. **4.** to behave abjectly. **5.** to be, or feel as if, overrun with crawling things. —*n.* **6.** the act of crawling; a slow, crawling motion. **7.** *Swimming.* a stroke in prone position characterized by alternate overarm movements and a continuous up and down kick. [ME, t. Scand.; cf. Dan. *kravle* creep] —**crawl′ingly,** *adv.*

—**Syn. 1.** CRAWL, CREEP refer to methods of moving with the body prone and close to the ground, like a reptile or snake. CREEP was formerly used for the movement of creatures without limbs, as worms, snakes, etc., but now CRAWL is more common. CRAWL alone is used for the movement of a child on hands and knees.

crawl[2] (krôl), *n.* an enclosure in shallow water on the seacoast, for confining fish, turtles, etc. [t. D: m. *kraal*, t. Sp.: m. *corral* CORRAL]

crawler (krô′lə), *n.* **1.** one who or that which crawls. **2.** a caterpillar (defs 2, 3, and 4). **3.** an abject flatterer. **4.** (*usually pl.*) rompers.

Crawley (krô′lĭ), *n.* a new town in England, in NE West Sussex. 60,717 (est. 1965).

crawly (krô′lĭ), *adj. Colloq.* that crawls; imparting the sensation of being overrun with crawling things; creepy.

crayfish (krā′fĭsh′), *n., pl.* **-fishes,** (*esp. collectively*) **-fish. 1.** any of numerous freshwater decapod crustaceans of the genera *Astacus* and *Cambarus*, closely related to the lobsters, but usually much smaller. **2.** any of several similar marine crustaceans, as *Palinurus vulgaris*, the spiny lobster. Also, *Chiefly U.S.*, **crawfish.** [alter. (by pop. etym.) of ME *crevice*, t. OF, t. OHG: m. *krebiz* crab]

Crayfish, *Astacus fluviatilis* (6 in. long)

Crayford (krā′fəd), *n.* a district of the SE outer London borough of Bexley.

crayon (krā′ən, -ŏn), *n., v.,* **-oned, -oning.** —*n.* **1.** a pointed stick or pencil of coloured wax, chalk, etc., used for drawing. **2.** a drawing in crayons. —*v.t.* **3.** to draw with a crayon or crayons. **4.** to sketch out (a plan, etc.). [t. F, der. *craie*, g. L *crēta* chalk] —**cray′oner, cray′onist,** *n.*

craze (krāz), *v.,* **crazed, crazing,** *n.* —*v.t.* **1.** to impair in intellect; make insane. **2.** *Archaic or Dial.* to weaken or impair (health, etc.). **3.** to make small cracks on the surface of (pottery, etc.); to crackle. **4.** *Obs.* to break. —*v.i.* **5.** to become insane. **6.** to become minutely cracked, as the glaze of pottery. **7.** to break; shatter. —*n.* **8.** a mania; a popular fashion, etc., usually short-lived; a rage. **9.** insanity; an insane condition. **10.** a minute crack in the glaze of pottery, etc. **11.** *Obs. or Dial.* a crack. [ME *crase(n)* break, t. Scand.; cf. Sw. *krasa*]

crazed (krāzd), *adj.* **1.** insane; demented. **2.** having small cracks in the glaze, as pottery.
crazy (krā′zĭ), *adj.*, **-zier, -ziest. 1.** demented; mad. **2.** eccentric; bizarre; unusual. **3.** unrealistic; impractical: *a crazy scheme.* **4.** *Colloq.* intensely enthusiastic or excited. **5.** likely to collapse, fall to pieces, or disintegrate. **6.** *Obs.* weak; infirm. **—cra′zily,** *adv.* **—cra′ziness,** *n.* **—Syn. 1.** crazed, deranged, lunatic. See **mad. 5.** rickety, shaky, tottering.
crazy bone, *U.S.* funny bone.
crazy paving, a pavement made up of slabs of various irregular shapes.
crazy quilt, *U.S.* a patchwork quilt made of irregular patches combined with little or no regard to pattern.
creak (krēk), *v.i.* **1.** to make a sharp, harsh, grating, or squeaking sound. **2.** to move with creaking. **—*v.t.* 3.** to cause to creak. **—*n.* 4.** a creaking sound. [ME *creken.* Cf. OE *crǣcettan*, var. of *crācettan* CROAK]
creaky (krē′kĭ), *adj.*, **-kier, -kiest.** creaking; apt to creak. **—creak′ily,** *adv.* **—creak′iness,** *n.*
cream (krēm), *n.* **1.** the fatty part of milk, which rises to the surface when the liquid is allowed to stand. **2.** any dish or delicacy made largely of cream or resembling cream. **3.** any creamlike substance, esp. various cosmetics. **4.** (*usually pl.*) a soft-centred confection of fondant or fudge coated with chocolate. **5.** a puree or soup containing cream or milk: *cream of tomato soup.* **6.** the best part of anything. **7.** yellowish white; light tint of yellow or buff. **—*v.i.* 8.** to form cream. **9.** to froth; foam. **—*v.t.* 10.** to work (butter and sugar, etc.) to a smooth, creamy mass. **11.** to prepare (chicken, oysters, vegetables, etc.) with cream, milk, or a cream sauce. **12.** to allow (milk) to form cream. **13.** to skim (milk). **14.** to separate as cream. **15.** to take the cream or best part of. **16.** to use a cosmetic cream on. **17.** to add cream to (coffee, or the like). **—*adj.* 18.** cream-coloured. [ME *creme*, t. F, g. LL *chrisma* CHRISM]
cream bun, a bun with a split containing cream.
cream cake, a cake or other confection with a cream filling.
cream cheese, a soft, white, smooth-textured, unripened cheese made of sweet milk and sometimes cream.
cream-coloured (krēm′kŭl′əd), *adj.* having a yellowish white colour. Also, *U.S.*, **cream-colored.**
creamcups (krēm′kŭps′), *n., pl.* **-cups.** a papaveraceous plant, *Platystemon californicus*, of California, bearing small pale yellow or cream-coloured flowers.
creamer (krē′mə), *n.* **1.** one who or that which creams. **2.** a small jug, pitcher, etc., for holding cream. **3.** a refrigerator in which milk is placed to facilitate the formation of cream. **4.** a vessel or apparatus for separating cream from milk.
creamery (krē′mə rĭ), *n., pl.* **-ries. 1.** an establishment engaged in the production of butter and cheese. **2.** a place for the sale of milk and its products. **3.** a place where milk is set to form cream.
cream horn, a confection consisting of a hollow cone of puff pastry filled with cream.
cream of tartar, purified and crystallized potassium bitartrate, used as a baking powder ingredient, etc. See **tartar** (def. 3).
cream puff, 1. a confection of choux pastry with a cream filling. **2.** *Colloq.* a weak person; an effeminate person; a cissy.
cream puff pastry, choux pastry.
cream sauce, a sauce made of cream or milk, flour, butter, etc.
cream soda, a soft drink made with vanilla-flavoured carbonated water.
creamy (krē′mĭ), *adj.*, **-mier, -miest. 1.** containing cream. **2.** resembling cream, as in appearance or consistency; soft and smooth. **3.** cream-coloured. **—cream′iness,** *n.*
creance (krē′əns), *n.* *Falconry.* a cord secured to the leg of a hawk to prevent escape during training. [ME, t. F: m. *créance*]
crease[1] (krēs), *n., v.*, **creased, creasing. —*n.* 1.** a line or mark produced in anything by folding; a fold; a ridge; a furrow. **2.** the sharp vertical ridge in the front and at the back of each leg of a pair of trousers, produced by pressing. **3.** *Cricket.* one of three lines marked near each wicket: **a. bowling crease,** beyond which the bowler may not advance when bowling. **b. popping crease,** 4 feet in front of it, at which the batsman stands when batting. **c. return crease,** marking the sideways limits of the bowler at each side of the bowling crease. **4.** *Ice Hockey.* a small rectangular area in front of each goal, into which an attacking player may skate only if he has the puck, if the puck is already within the area, or if the goalkeeper is absent. **5.** *Lacrosse.* a semicircle in front of each goal, which no attacking player may enter unless the ball is already within the area. **—*v.t.* 6.** to make a crease or creases in or on; wrinkle. **—*v.i.* 7.** to become creased. [orig. unknown] **—creas′er,** *n.* **—creas′y,** *adj.*
crease[2] (krēs), *n.* kris.
crease-resistant (krēs′rĭ zĭs′tənt), *adj.* (of a fabric) able to resist normal wrinkling.
create (krē āt′), *v.*, **-ated, -ating,** *adj.* **—*v.t.* 1.** to bring into being; cause to exist; produce. **2.** to evolve from one's own thought or imagination. **3.** to be the first to represent (a part or role). **4.** to make by investing with new character or functions; constitute; appoint: *to create a peer.* **5.** to be the cause or occasion of; give rise to. **—*v.i.* 6.** to be engaged, often ostentatiously, in creating something, as a work of art: *the painter was creating while we stood by.* **7.** *Colloq.* to make a fuss or an uproar. **—*adj.* 8.** *Poetic.* created. [t. L: m. s. *creātus*, pp. of *creāre* bring into being] **—Syn. 1.** originate, invent.
creatine (krē′ə tēn′, -tĭn), *n.* *Biochem.* an amino acid, $C_4H_9N_3O_2.H_2O$, found mainly in combined form as creatine phosphate, present as the phosphagen in the tissues of all vertebrates and some invertebrates.
creation (krē ā′shən), *n.* **1.** the act of creating. **2.** the fact of being created. **3. the Creation,** the original bringing into existence of the universe by the Deity. **4.** that which is created. **5.** the world; universe. **6.** creatures collectively. **7.** a product of inventive ingenuity; an original work, esp. of the imaginative faculty. **8.** a strikingly fashionable garment or hat, distinguished by its unique styling. **—crea′tional,** *adj.*
creationism (krē ā′shə nĭz′əm), *n.* **1.** the doctrine that God immediately creates out of nothing a new human soul for each individual born. Cf. **traducianism. 2.** the doctrine that matter and all things were created, substantially as they now exist, by the fiat of an omnipotent Creator, and not gradually evolved or developed. **—crea′tionist,** *n.*
creative (krē ā′tĭv), *adj.* **1.** having the quality or power of creating. **2.** resulting from originality of thought or expression. **3.** originative; productive (fol. by *of*). **—crea′tively,** *adv.* **—crea′tiveness,** *n.*
creativity (krē′ā tĭv′ĭ tĭ), *n.* **1.** the state or quality of being creative. **2.** creative ability.
creator (krē ā′tə), *n.* **1.** one who or that which creates. **2. the Creator,** God. **—crea′torship′,** *n.*
creatural (krē′chə rəl), *adj.* of, pertaining to, or of the nature of a creature or creatures.
creature (krē′chə), *n.* **1.** anything created, animate or inanimate. **2.** an animate being. **3.** an animal, as distinct from man. **4.** a human being (often used in contempt, commiseration, or endearment). **5.** a person owing his rise and fortune to another, or subject to the will or influence of another. **6.** *U.S. Colloq.* alcoholic drink, esp. whisky. [ME, t. OF, t. LL: m. *creātūra* a thing created]
creature comforts, material things which minister to bodily comfort; esp. food, alcoholic drink, etc.
creaturely (krē′chə lĭ), *adj.* creatural.
creche (krāsh), *n.* **1.** a nursery where children are cared for while their mothers work. **2.** a home for foundlings. **3.** a tableau of Mary, Joseph, and others round the crib of Jesus in the stable at Bethlehem, often built for display at Christmas. Also, *French*, **crèche** (*Fr.* krĕsh). [t. F, t. OHG: m. *kripja* crib]
Crécy (krĕs′ĭ; *Fr.* krė sē′), *n.* a village in N France: English victory over the French, 1346. Also, **Cressy.**
credence (krē′dns), *n.* **1.** belief: *to give credence to a statement.* **2.** something giving a claim to belief or confidence: *letter of credence.* **3.** Also, **credence table, credenza.** a small side table, shelf, or niche for holding articles used in the Eucharist service. [ME, t. ML: m. s. *crēdentia* belief, credit, sideboard, der. L *crēdens*, ppr., believing]
credendum (krĭ dĕn′dəm), *n., pl.* **-da** (-də). that which is to be believed; an article of faith. [L, neut. of *crēdendus*, gerundive of *crēdere* believe]
credent (krē′dnt), *adj.* **1.** believing. **2.** *Obs.* credible.
credential (krĭ dĕn′shəl), *n.* **1.** that which gives a title to belief or confidence. **2.** (*usually pl.*) a letter or other testimonial attesting the bearer's right to confidence or authority. **—*adj.* 3.** giving a title to belief or confidence. [f. s. ML *crēdentia* belief + -AL[1]]
credenza (krĭ dĕn′zə), *n.* credence (def. 3). [It., t. ML: m. *crēdentia.* See CREDENCE]
credibility gap, the difference between what is said, as by a politician, and what is actually meant or done.
credible (krĕd′ĭ bl), *adj.* **1.** capable of being believed; believable. **2.** worthy of belief or confidence; trustworthy. [ME, t. L: m. s. *crēdibilis*] **—cred′ibil′ity, cred′ibleness,** *n.* **—cred′ibly,** *adv.*
credit (krĕd′ĭt), *n.* **1.** belief; trust. **2.** influence or author-

ity resulting from the confidence of others or from one's reputation. **3.** trustworthiness; credibility. **4.** repute; reputation. **5.** favourable estimation. **6.** commendation or honour given for some action, quality, etc. **7.** a source of commendation or honour. **8.** the ascription or acknowledgement of something as due or properly attributable to a person, etc. **9.** *U.S. Educ.* **a.** official acceptance and recording of the work of a student in a particular course of study. **b.** a unit of a curriculum (short for **credit hour**): *he took the course for four credits.* **10.** time allowed for payment for goods, etc., obtained on trust. **11.** confidence in a purchaser's ability and intention to pay, displayed by entrusting him with goods, etc., without immediate payment. **12.** reputation of solvency and probity, entitling a person to be trusted in buying or borrowing. **13.** power to buy or borrow on trust. **14.** a sum of money due to a person; anything valuable standing on the credit side of an account. **15.** the balance in one's favour in an account. **16.** *Bookkeeping.* **a.** the acknowledgement or an entry of payment or value received, in an account. **b.** the side (right-hand) of an account on which such entries are made (opposed to *debit*). **c.** an entry, or the total shown, on the credit side. **17.** any deposit or sum against which one may draw. **18. on credit,** by deferred payment. **19. do someone credit.** Also, **do credit to someone.** be a source of honour or distinction to someone. *—v.t.* **20.** to believe; put confidence in; trust; have faith in. **21.** to reflect credit upon; do credit to; give reputation or honour to. **22.** to ascribe (something) to a person, etc.; make ascription of something to (a person, etc.) (fol. by *with*). **23. a.** *Bookkeeping.* to enter upon the credit side of an account; give credit for or to. **b.** to give the benefit of such an entry to (a person, etc.) **24.** *U.S. Educ.* to award educational credits to: *credited with three hours in history.* [t. F, t. It.: m. *credito*, g. L *creditus*, pp., believed]

—Syn. 12. CREDIT, REPUTE, REPUTATION, STANDING refer to one's status in the estimation of a community. CREDIT refers to business and financial status and the amount of money for which a man will be trusted: *his credit is excellent at all the shops.* REPUTE is particularly what is reported about someone, the favour in which he is held, etc.: *a man of fine repute among his acquaintances.* REPUTATION is the moral and other character commonly ascribed to someone: *of unblemished reputation.* STANDING is one's position in a community, or rank and condition in life: *a man of good standing and education.* **—Ant. 5.** disrepute.

creditable (krĕd′ĭ tə bl), *adj.* bringing credit, honour, reputation, or esteem. —**cred′itableness,** *n.* —**cred′itably,** *adv.* **—Syn.** praiseworthy, meritorious, estimable, honourable, reputable, respectable.

credit agency, an organization that investigates on behalf of a client the credit worthiness of the client's prospective customers.

credit card, 1. a card which identifies the holder as entitled to obtain without payment of cash, goods, food, services, etc., which are then charged to the holder's account. **2.** *U.S.* an account card.

credit insurance, insurance coverage designed to minimize loss to creditors when a debtor defaults.

credit life insurance, insurance guaranteeing payment of the unpaid portion of a loan, in the event of the debtor's death.

credit note, a note issued by a trader showing the amount of credit due to a customer, usually for goods to be taken in lieu of those returned.

creditor (krĕd′ĭ tə), *n.* **1.** one who gives credit in business transactions. **2.** one to whom money is due (opposed to *debtor*). **3.** *Bookkeeping.* credit (def. 16b, c).

credit rating, an estimation of the extent to which a customer can be granted credit, usually determined by a credit agency.

credit slip, a form completed and signed by a person when paying into the credit of an account.

credit squeeze, *Colloq.* **1.** restriction by a government of the amount of credit available to borrowers. **2.** the period during which the restrictions are in operation.

credit standing, reputation for meeting financial obligations.

credit transfer, a system by which credit is paid into a bank for transfer to the payee's account at another bank or branch.

credo (krē′dō, krā′dō), *n., pl.* **-dos. 1.** the Apostles' or the Nicene Creed. **2.** a musical setting of the creed, usually of the Nicene Creed. **3.** any creed or formula of belief. [t. L: I believe, the first word of the Apostles' and the Nicene Creeds in Latin]

credulity (krĭ dyo͞o′lĭ tĭ), *n.* a disposition, arising from weakness or ignorance, to believe too readily. [late ME *credulite*, t. L: m. s. *crēdulitas*]

credulous (krĕd′yo͝o ləs), *adj.* **1.** ready or disposed to believe, esp. on weak or insufficient evidence. **2.** marked by or arising from credulity. [t. L: m. *crēdulus* apt to believe] —**cred′ulously,** *adv.* —**cred′ulousness,** *n.* **—Syn. 1.** believing, trustful, unsuspecting, gullible.

Cree (krē), *n., pl.* **Cree, Crees. 1.** (*pl.*) an American Indian tribe belonging to the Algonquian linguistic stock, and situated in Manitoba, Saskatchewan, etc. **2.** a member of this tribe. [short for F *Kristinaux*, m. *Kinistenoag*, given as one of their own names]

creed (krēd), *n.* **1.** an authoritative formulated statement of the chief articles of Christian belief, as the **Apostles',** the **Nicene,** or the **Athanasian Creed. 2.** the Apostles' Creed. **3.** any formula of religious belief, as of a denomination. **4.** an accepted system of religious belief. **5.** any system of belief or of opinion. [ME *crede*, OE *crēda*, t. L: m. *crēdo* I believe. See CREDO] —**creed′al, cre′dal,** *adj.* —**creed′less,** *adj.*

creek (krēk), *n.* **1.** a narrow recess in the shore of the sea, a river, etc.; a small inlet or bay. **2.** *U.S., Can., and Austral.* a small stream, as a branch of a river. **3.** *Obs.* a narrow or winding passage. **4. up the creek,** *Slang.* in a predicament; in trouble. [ME *creke*, appar. north. var. of *crike* (short vowel), t. Scand.; cf. Icel. *kriki* crack, nook]

Creek (krēk), *n.* **1.** (*pl.*) a powerful confederacy of Muskhogean Indians which once occupied the greater part of Alabama and Georgia. **2.** an Indian of this confederacy. [so called because of numerous streams in Creek territory]

creel (krēl), *n.* **1.** a wickerwork basket, esp. one used by anglers for holding fish. **2.** a wickerwork trap to catch fish, lobsters, etc. **3.** a framework, esp. one for holding bobbins in a spinning machine. [ME *crele*, ? t. F: m. *creil*, ult. der. L *crātis* wickerwork. Cf. GRILLE]

creep (krēp), *v.,* **crept, creeping,** *n.* *—v.i.* **1.** to move with the body close to the ground, as a reptile or an insect. **2.** to move slowly, imperceptibly, or stealthily. **3.** to enter undetected; to sneak up behind. **4.** to move or behave timidly or servilely. **5.** *Colloq.* to cringe, flatter, or fawn. **6.** to move along very slowly, as a motor car in heavy traffic. **7.** to have a sensation as of something creeping over the skin. **8.** to grow along the ground, a wall, etc., as a plant, esp. a creeper (def. 3). **9.** *Naut.* to grapple (usually fol. by *for*). *—v.t.* **10.** *Poetic.* to creep along or over. **11. make one's flesh creep,** to frighten; repel. *—n.* **12.** the act of creeping. **13.** (*usually pl.*) a sensation as of something creeping over the skin. **14.** *Colloq.* one who fawns, cringes or flatters. **15.** *Colloq.* an unpleasant, obnoxious, or insignificant person. **16.** *Engineering.* the deformation of metal caused by heat or stress. **17.** *Geol.* the slow movement of earth or loose rock, etc. [ME *crepen*, OE *crēopan*, c. D *kruipen*] **—Syn. 1.** See **crawl.**

creeper (krē′pə), *n.* **1.** one who or that which creeps. **2.** (*pl.*) *U.S.* rompers. **3.** *Bot.* a plant which grows upon or just beneath the surface of the ground, or upon any other surface, sending out rootlets from the stem, as ivy and couch-grass. **4.** any of various birds that creep or climb about on trees, esp. the several species of the family *Certhiidae* of Europe and North America, as the tree creeper, *Certhia familiaris.* **5.** a grappling device for dragging a river, etc. **6.** a spiked piece of iron worn on the heel of the shoe to prevent slipping on ice, etc. **7.** (*pl.*) *Slang.* thick rubber-soled shoes. **8.** *Cricket.* a ball that moves along the ground instead of bouncing as expected.

creep feeder, an animal feeding pen constructed to admit young animals while excluding the larger ones.

creepie (krē′pĭ), *n.* *Dial.* a low stool.

creeping barrage, *Mil.* a barrage of slowly advancing artillery fire.

creeping bent grass, a grass, *Agrostis palustris*, cultivated in pastures in Europe and North America.

creeping Jenny, a prostrate perennial primulaceous herb with yellow flowers, *Lysimachia nummularia*, found growing in damp places throughout Europe and W Asia.

creeping Jesus, *Slang.* a slinking, fawning person.

creeping thistle, a perennial dioecious herb, *Cirsium arvense*, family *Compositae*, widespread in Europe and Asia; a naturalized troublesome weed in N America.

creepy (krē′pĭ), *adj.,* **-pier, -piest. 1.** that creeps, as an insect. **2.** having or causing a creeping sensation of the skin, as from horror: *a creepy silence.* —**creep′iness,** *n.*

creepy-crawly (krē′pĭ krô′lĭ), *Colloq.* *—n.* **1.** an insect. *—adj.* **2.** having or causing a creeping sensation.

creese (krēs), *n.* kris.

creesh (krēsh), *n., v.t.* *Scot.* grease. [t. OF: m. *cresse*, *craisse*, g. L *crassa*, fem. of *crassus* thick, fat]

Crefeld (krā′fĕld; *Ger.* krĕ′fĕlt), *n.* Krefeld.

cremate (krĭ māt′), *v.t.,* **-mated, -mating. 1.** to reduce (a corpse) to ashes by fire. **2.** to consume by fire; burn. [t. L: m. s. *cremātus*, pp., consumed by fire] —**crema′tion,** *n.*

cremationist (krĭ mā′shə nĭst), *n.* one who advocates cremation instead of burial of the dead.

cremator (krĭ mā′tə), *n.* **1.** one who cremates. **2.** a furnace for cremating corpses. **3.** an incinerator for rubbish, etc. [t. LL]
crematorium (krĕm′ə tô′rĭ əm), *n.* an establishment for cremating dead bodies.
crematory (krĕm′ə tə rĭ, trĭ), *adj., n., pl.* **-ries.** *—adj.* **1.** of or pertaining to cremation. *—n.* **2.** a crematorium.
crème (*Fr.* krĕm), *n. French.* **1.** cream. **2.** one of various liqueurs. [F. See CREAM]
crème de la crème (*Fr.* krĕm də lȧ krĕm′), *French.* the very best; the flower; the choicest part.
crème de menthe (*Fr.* krĕm də mäɴt′), *French.* liqueur flavoured with mint.
Cremnitz white (krĕm′nĭts), *Painting.* a white pigment based on lead carbonate.
cremocarp (krĕm′ō käp′), *n. Bot.* a dry fruit which splits vertically into two one-seeded portions, characteristic of the family *Umbelliferae.*
Cremona (krĭ mō′nə; *It.* krė mô′nȧ), *n.* **1.** a city in N Italy, on the river Po. 79,377 (1966). **2.** one of a class of violins of superior quality made there during the 16th, 17th, and 18th centuries.
crenate (krē′nāt), *adj.* having the margin notched or scalloped so as to form rounded teeth, as a leaf. Also, **cre′nated.** [t. NL: m. s. *crēnātus,* der. *crēna* notch] *—***cre′nately,** *adv.*

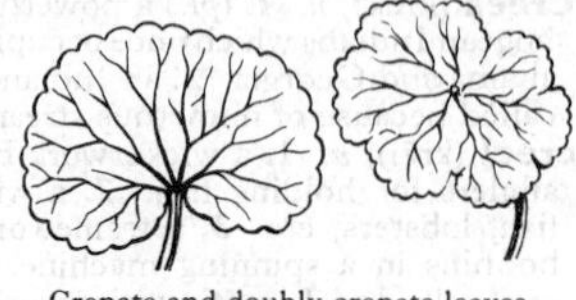
Crenate and doubly crenate leaves

crenation (krĭ nā′shən), *n.* **1.** a rounded projection or tooth, as on the margin of a leaf. **2.** crenate state.
crenature (krĕn′ə työŏə′, krē′nə-), *n.* **1.** a rounded tooth as of a crenate leaf. **2.** a notch between teeth.
crenel (krĕn′əl), *n., v.,* **-elled, -elling,** or (*U.S.*) **-eled, -eling.** *—n.* **1.** one of the open spaces between the merlons of a battlement. **2.** a crenature. *—v.t.* **3.** to crenellate. See illus. under **battlement.** Also, **crenelle.** [late ME, t. MF, dim. of *cren* notch. See CRENULATE]
crenellate (krĕn′ĭ lāt′), *v.t.,* **-lated, -lating.** **1.** to furnish with crenels or battlements. **2.** *Archit.* to form with square indentations as a moulding. Also, *U.S.,* **crenelate.** [f. s. F *créneler* (der. *crenel,* dim. of *cren* notch) + -ATE[1]] *—***cren′ellat′ed,** *adj.*
crenellation (krĕn′ĭ lā′shən), *n.* **1.** the act of crenellating. **2.** the state of being crenellated. **3.** a battlement. **4.** a notch; indentation. Also, *U.S.,* **crenelation.**
crenelle (krĭ nĕl′), *n., v.t.,* **-nelled, -nelling.** crenel.

Crenellated moulding

crenulate (krĕn′yŏŏ lāt′, -lĭt), *adj.* having the edge cut into very small scallops, as some leaves. Also, **cren′ulat′ed.** [t. NL: m. s. *crēnulātus,* der. *crēnula,* dim. of *crena* notch, t. OIt., g. L (unrecorded)]
crenulation (krĕn′yŏŏ lā′shən), *n.* **1.** a minute crenation. **2.** crenulate state.
creodont (krē′ə dŏnt′), *n.* any of the *Creodonta,* a group of primitive carnivorous mammals, characterized by small brains. Certain creodonts are regarded as the ancestors of the modern carnivores. [t. NL: s. *Creodonta* (pl.), f. Gk: m. *kréas* flesh + m. s. *odoús* tooth]
Creole (krē′ōl), *n.* **1.** (in the West Indies and Spanish America) one born in the region but of European, usually Spanish, ancestry. **2.** (in Louisiana and elsewhere) a person born in the region but of French ancestry. **3.** a person born in a place but of foreign ancestry, as distinguished from the aborigines and half-breeds. **4.** the French language of Louisiana, especially that spoken by white persons in New Orleans. **5.** (*l.c.*) a person of mixed Creole and Negro ancestry speaking a form of French or Spanish. **6.** (*l.c.*) a native-born Negro, as distinguished from a Negro brought from Africa. *—adj.* **7.** of, pertaining to, or characteristic of a Creole or the Creoles. **8.** (*l.c.*) of, belonging to, or characteristic of the Creoles: *a creole dialect, creole French.* **9.** bred or growing in a country, but of foreign origin, as an animal or plant. **10.** *Cookery.* denoting a sauce or dish made with stewed tomatoes, peppers, onions, etc. [t. F, t. Sp.: m. *criollo* native to the locality, t. Pg.: m. *crioulo,* der. *criar* bring up, g. L *creāre* create]
creolized (krē′ə līzd′), *adj.* (of a language) having become a jargon and then passed into use as a native language, as the English used by many Negroes of Guyana. Also, **creolised.**
Creon (krē′ŏn), *n. Gk Legend.* king of Thebes, after the fall of Oedipus. See **Antigone.**
creosol (krē′ə sŏl′), *n. Chem.* a colourless oily liquid, $C_8H_{10}O_2$, with an agreeable smell and burning taste, resembling carbolic acid; obtained from wood tar and guaiacum resin. [f. CREOS(OTE) + -OL[2]]
creosote (krĭə′sōt), *n., v.,* **-soted, -soting.** *—n.* **1.** an oily liquid with a burning taste and a penetrating smell, obtained by the distillation of wood tar, and used as a preservative and antiseptic. **2.** coal-tar creosote. *—v.t.* **3.** to treat with creosote. [f. *creo-* (comb. form repr. Gk *kréas* flesh) + m. Gk *sōtḗr* saviour] *—***creosotic** (krĭə sŏt′ĭk), *adj.*
creosote bush, a zygophyllaceous evergreen shrub, *Covillea tridentata* (or *Larrea mexicana*) of northern Mexico and adjacent regions, bearing resinous foliage with a strong smell of creosote.
crepe (krāp), *n., v.,* **creped, creping.** *—n.* **1.** a thin, light fabric of silk, cotton, or other fibre, with a finely crinkled or ridged surface. **2.** Also, **crepe paper.** thin paper wrinkled to resemble crepe. **3.** a black (or white) silk fabric, used for mourning veils, trimmings, etc. **4.** a band or piece of this material, as for a token of mourning. *—v.t.* **5.** to cover, clothe, or drape with crepe. Also, **crêpe, crape.** [t. F, g. L *crispus* curled]
crepe de Chine (krāp′ də shēn′), a light, soft silk or rayon fabric with minute surface irregularities. [t. F: China crepe]
crepe hair, false hair, usually plaited, used in theatrical make-up for beards, etc.
crepe rubber, a type of crude rubber, pressed into corrugated sheets, used especially for making shoe soles.
crepe suzette (krāp′sŏŏ zĕt′), a thin dessert pancake usually rolled and served with hot orange or tangerine sauce, often flavoured with curaçao or other liqueurs. French, **crêpe suzette** (*Fr.* krĕp sʏ zĕt′).
crepitant (krĕp′ĭ tənt), *adj.* crackling.
crepitate (krĕp′ĭ tāt′), *v.i.,* **-tated, -tating.** to make a crackling sound; crackle; rattle. [t. L: m. s. *crepitātus,* pp.] *—***crep′ita′tion,** *n.*
crept (krĕpt), *v.* pt. and pp. of **creep.**
crepuscular (krĭ pŭs′kyŏŏ lə), *adj.* **1.** of, pertaining to, or resembling twilight; dim; indistinct. **2.** *Zool.* appearing or flying in the twilight.
crepuscule (krĕp′əs kyŏŏl′), *n.* twilight; dusk. [t. F, t. L: m. *crepusculum*]
cres., **1.** *Music.* crescendo (def. 3). **2.** (*cap.*) crescent. Also, **cresc.**
crescendo (krĭ shĕn′dō; *It.* krėsh shĕn′dȯ), *n., pl.* **-dos** (-dōz), *It.* **-di** (-dē), *adj., adv.* *—n.* **1.** a gradual increase in force or loudness. **2.** *Music.* a crescendo passage. *—adj., adv.* **3.** gradually increasing in force or loudness. [It., ppr. of *crescere* increase, g. L *crescere*] *—***Ant.** **2.** diminuendo.
crescent (krĕs′ənt), *n.* **1. a.** the biconvex figure of the moon in its first quarter, or the similar figure of the moon in its last quarter, resembling a bow terminating in points. See diag. under **moon. b.** any of the similar aspects of Venus or Mercury when less than half of the illuminated hemisphere can be seen. **2.** a representation of this. **3.** the emblem of the Turkish Empire. **4.** the symbol of Turkish or Islamic power. **5.** any crescent-shaped object, as a roll of bread. **6.** *U.S.* a musical percussion instrument of Turkish origin used in military bands, consisting of a crescent-shaped metal plate hung with a set of little bells. **7.** a curved street. *—adj.* **8.** shaped like the moon in its first quarter. **9.** increasing; growing. [t. L: s. *crescens,* ppr., increasing; r. ME *cressant,* t. OF: m. *creissant* (later *croissant*), ppr.]
crescive (krĕs′ĭv), *adj.* increasing; growing.
cresol (krē′sŏl), *n. Chem.* any of three isolated methyl phenols, $CH_3C_6H_4OH$, occurring in coal tar and wood tar; obtained by the condensation of cresol with an aldehyde. [var. of CREOSOL]
Crespin (*Fr.* krĕs păɴ′), *n.* **Régine** (*Fr.* rė zhēn′), born 1927, French operatic soprano.
cress (krĕs), *n.* **1.** any of various plants of the mustard family with pungent-tasting leaves, often used for salad and as a garnish, esp. the **garden cress,** *Lepidium sativum.* **2.** any of various similar plants. [ME and OE *cresse,* c. G *Kresse*]
cresset (krĕs′ĭt), *n.* a metal cup often mounted on a pole or suspended from above, containing oil, pitch, etc., which is burnt for light or as a beacon. [ME, t. OF]

Cresset

Cressida (krĕs′ĭ də), *n.* a new character developed, in medieval adaptations of the story of the Trojan wars, out of Chryseis and Briseis and made the lover of the Trojan Troilus, who is deserted for the Greek Diomedes.
cressy (krĕs′ĭ), *adj.* abounding in cresses.
Cressy (krĕs′ĭ), *n.* Crécy.
crest (krĕst), *n.* **1.** a tuft or other natural

growth of the top of an animal's head, as the comb of a cock. **2.** anything resembling or suggesting such a tuft. **3.** the ridge of the neck of a horse, dog, etc. See illus. under **horse. 4.** the mane growing from this ridge. **5.** a plume or other ornament on the top of a helmet. **6.** a helmet. **7.** the apex of a helmet. **8.** *Her.* a figure borne above the escutcheon in a coat of arms, and also used separately as a distinguishing device. **9.** the head or top of anything. **10.** the highest part of a hill or mountain range. **11.** a ridge or ridgelike formation. **12.** *Anat.* a ridge along the surface of a bone. **13.** the foamy top of a wave. **14.** the highest or best of the kind. **15.** pride; high spirit; courage; daring. **16.** *Archit.* a cresting. *—v.t.* **17.** to furnish with a crest. **18.** to serve as a crest for; crown or top. **19.** to reach the crest or summit of (a hill, etc.). *—v.i.* **20.** to form or rise into a crest, as a wave. [ME *creste,* t. OF, g. L *crista* tuft] **—crest′ed,** *adj.* **—crest′less,** *adj.*

crested flycatcher, a North American flycatcher, *Myiarchus crinitus,* famous for its use of cast-off snakeskin as nest material.

crestfallen (krĕst′fô′lən), *adj.* **1.** dejected; dispirited; depressed. **2.** with drooping crest. **—crest′fall′enly,** *adv.* **—crest′fall′enness,** *n.*

cresting (krĕs′tĭng), *n.* *Archit.* the ornamental part which surmounts a roof ridge, wall, etc.

cretaceous (krĭ tā′shəs), *adj.* **1.** of the nature of, resembling, or containing chalk. **2.** (*cap.*) *Geol.* pertaining to a geological period or a system of rocks succeeding the Jurassic and preceding the Tertiary. *—n.* **3.** (*cap.*) *Geol.* the period or system comprising the youngest or uppermost part of the Mesozoic. [t. L: m. *crētāceus* chalklike]

Cretan (krē′tn), *adj.* **1.** of or pertaining to the island of Crete or its inhabitants. *—n.* **2.** a native or inhabitant of Crete, esp. one of the indigenous Greeks.

Crete (krēt), *n.* a Greek island in the Mediterranean, SE of Greece. 483,258 pop. (1961); 3235 sq. mi. *Cap.:* Canea. Also, **Candia.**

Crete

cretin (krē′tĭn), *n.* **1.** a person afflicted with cretinism. **2.** *Colloq.* a fool; a stupid person. [t. F, m. d. F. *crestin,* g. L *Christiānus* Christian] **—cre′tinous,** *adj.*

cretinism (krē′tĭ nĭz′əm), *n.* *Pathol.* a chronic disease, due to absence or deficiency of the normal thyroid secretion, characterized by physical deformity (often with goitre), dwarfism, and idiocy.

cretonne (krĕ tŏn′, krĕt′ŏn), *n.* a heavy cotton material in printed designs, used esp. for curtains and loose covers. [t. F, der. *Creton,* village in Normandy]

Creüsa (krĭ ōō′zə), *n.* *Gk Legend.* **1.** Also, **Glauce.** the bride of Jason, slain by the magic of the jealous Medea. **2.** a daughter of Priam and the wife of Aeneas, lost in the flight from Troy.

Creuse (*Fr.* krœz), *n.* a department in central France. 163,515 pop. (1962); 2165 sq. mi. *Cap.:* Guéret.

crevasse (krĭ văs′), *n., v.,* **-vassed, -vassing.** *—n.* **1.** a fissure or deep cleft in the ice of a glacier. **2.** *U.S.* a breach in an embankment or river bank. *—v.t.* **3.** to fissure with crevasses. [t. F. See CREVICE]

crevice (krĕv′ĭs), *n.* a crack forming an opening; a cleft; a rift; a fissure. [ME *crevace,* t. OF, der. *crever* burst, g. L *crepāre* crack] **—crev′iced,** *adj.*

crew[1] (krōō), *n.* **1.** a group of persons engaged upon a particular work; a gang. **2.** *Naut.* **a.** the company of men who man a ship or boat. **b.** the common sailors of a ship's company. **c.** a particular section of a ship's company. **3.** the persons manning an aircraft in flight. **4.** (often in derogatory use) a company; crowd. *—v.i., v.t.* **5.** to act as a member of a crew. [late ME *crue,* t. ONF: m. *creue* increase, ult. der. L *crescere* grow]

crew[2] (krōō), *v.* pt. of **crow**[2].

crew cut, a very closely cropped haircut.

Crewe (krōō), *n.* a town in England, in Cheshire. 53,195 (1961).

crewel (krōō′ĭl), *n.* a fine worsted yarn used for embroidery, etc. [late ME *crule,* of unknown orig.] **—crew′elwork′,** *n.*

crib (krĭb), *n., v.,* **cribbed, cribbing.** *—n.* **1.** a child's bed, usually oval, and often of wickerwork, lined and decorated with muslin, etc. **2.** a stall or pen for cattle. **3.** a rack or manger for fodder, as in a stable or house for cattle. **4.** a tableau of Mary, Joseph, and the others grouped round the holy crib in Bethlehem, often on display at Christmas. **5.** a small house. **6.** a small room. **7.** any confined space. **8.** *Slang.* a house, shop, etc. **9.** a wicker basket. **10.** any of various frameworks, as of logs or timber, used in construction work. **11.** the wooden lining on the inside of a mine shaft. **12.** a bin for storing grain, etc. **13.** *Colloq.* a petty theft, plagiarism, etc. **14.** *Colloq.* a translation or other illicit aid used by students. **15.** *Cribbage.* a set of cards made up by equal contributions from each player's hand, and belonging to the dealer. *—v.t.* **16.** to confine in, or as in, a crib. **17.** to provide with a crib or cribs. **18.** to line with timber or planking. **19.** *Colloq.* to pilfer or steal, as a passage from an author. *—v.i.* **20.** *Colloq.* to use a crib. **21.** to crib-bite. [ME *cribbe,* OE *crib(b),* c. G *Krippe*]

cribbage (krĭb′ĭj), *n.* a game at cards, basically for two, but also played by three, or four players, a characteristic feature of which is the crib. [f. CRIB + -AGE]

cribber (krĭb′ə), *n.* **1.** one who cribs. **2.** a horse that practises cribbing.

cribbing (krĭb′ĭng), *n.* **1.** Also, **crib-biting.** windsucking by horses, an injurious habit in which the animal bites his manger and in the process swallows air. **2.** *Mining.* **a.** timber lining, closely spaced, as in a shaft, etc. **b.** pieces of timber for lining a shaft, etc.

crib-bite (krĭb′bīt′), *v.i.,* **-bit, -bitten** or **-bit, -biting.** to practise cribbing, as a horse. **—crib′-bit′er,** *n.*

cribriform (krĭb′rĭ fôm′), *adj.* sievelike. Also, **cribrous** (krĭb′rəs). [f. s. L *crībrum* sieve + -(I)FORM]

cribwork (krĭb′wûk′), *n.* structural work consisting of layers of logs or beams one above another, with the logs of each layer at right angles to those below.

Crichton (krī′tn), *n.* **James** (*'the Admirable Crichton'*), 1560?–82, Scottish scholar, poet, and adventurer who spoke many languages.

crick (krĭk), *n.* **1.** a sharp, painful spasm of the muscles, as of the neck or back, making it difficult to move the part. *—v.t.* **2.** to give a crick or wrench to (the neck, etc.). [orig. uncert.]

cricket[1] (krĭk′ĭt), *n.* any of the orthopterous insects comprising the family *Gryllidae,* characterized by their long antennae, ability to leap, and the ability of the males to produce shrill sounds by friction of their leathery forewings. [ME *criket,* t. OF: m. *criquet;* ult. imit.]

cricket[2] (krĭk′ĭt), *n.* **1.** an open-air game played with ball, bats, and wickets, by two sides of eleven players each. **2.** *Colloq.* fair play: *his behaviour was not cricket.* *—v.i.* **3.** to play cricket. [cf. OF *criquet* stick] **—crick′eter,** *n.*

cricket[3] (krĭk′ĭt), *n.* a small, low stool. [orig. obscure]

cricoid (krī′koid), *Anat.* *—adj.* **1.** having the shape of a seal ring: applied to a cartilage at the lower part of the larynx. *—n.* **2.** the cricoid cartilage. [t. Gk: m. s. *krikoeidēs* ring-shaped]

crier (krī′ə), *n.* **1.** one who cries. **2.** a court or town official who makes public announcements. **3.** one who cries goods for sale in the streets; a hawker.

crikey (krī′kĭ), *interj.* *Slang.* (an expression of surprise; a mild oath.) Also, **cricky, crickey.**

crim., criminal.

crime (krīm), *n.* **1.** an act committed or an omission of duty, injurious to the public welfare, for which punishment is prescribed by law, imposed in a judicial proceeding usually brought in the name of the state. **2.** serious violation of human law: *steeped in crime.* **3.** any offence, esp. one of grave character. **4.** serious wrongdoing; sin. **5.** *Colloq.* a foolish or senseless act: *it's a crime to have to work so hard.* [ME, t. OF, t. L: m. s. *crīmen* offence]

—Syn. 2. CRIME, OFFENCE, SIN agree in meaning a breaking of law. CRIME usually means any serious violation of human laws: *the crime of treason, of robbery.* OFFENCE is used of an infraction of either human or divine law, and does not necessarily mean a serious one: *an offence leading to a jail sentence, an offence against morals.* SIN means a serious breaking of moral or divine law: *the sin of hating one's neighbour.*

Crimea (krī mĭə′), *n.* a large peninsula in the SW Soviet Union, separating the Black Sea from the Sea of Azov; formerly an autonomous republic of the Soviet Union, now part of the Ukraine. ab. 10,000 sq. mi. **—Crimean′,** *adj.*

Crimea

Crimean War, a war between Great Britain, France, Turkey, and Sardinia on one side, and Russia on the other, fought chiefly in the Crimea, 1853–56.

crime sheet, *Mil.* a list of offences against military law.

criminal (krĭm′ĭ nəl), *adj.* **1.** of or pertaining to crime or its punishment: *criminal law.* **2.** of the nature of or involving crime. **3.** guilty of crime. *—n.* **4.** a person guilty or convicted of a crime. [t. L: s. *crīminālis*] **—crim′inally,** *adv.* **—Syn. 2.** felonious, unlawful, illegal, nefarious, flagitious, iniquitous, wicked, sinful, wrong. **4.** convict, malefactor, evildoer, transgressor, culprit. **—Ant. 2.** lawful. **3.** innocent.

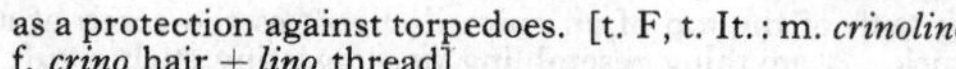

criminal conversation, *Obs. Law.* in old common law, a form of action by which a husband might recover damages against an adulterer.

criminality (krĭm′ĭ năl′ĭ tĭ), *n., pl.* **-ties. 1.** the quality of being criminal. **2.** a criminal act or practice.

criminate (krĭm′ĭ nāt′), *v.t.,* **-nated, -nating. 1.** to charge with a crime. **2.** to incriminate. **3.** to censure (an act, etc.) as criminal; condemn. [t. L: m. s. *crīminātus,* pp., accused] **—crim′ina′tion,** *n.*

criminative (krĭm′ĭ nə tĭv), *adj.* tending to or involving crimination; accusatory. Also, **criminatory** (krĭm′ĭ nə tə rĭ, -trĭ).

criminology (krĭm′ĭ nŏl′ə jĭ), *n.* the science dealing with the causes and treatment of crimes and criminals. [f. s. L *crīmen* crime + -(O)LOGY] **—criminological** (krĭm′ĭ nə lŏj′ĭ kl), *adj.* **—crim′inol′ogist,** *n.*

crimmer (krĭm′ə), *n.* krimmer.

crimp[1] (krĭmp), *v.t.* **1.** to press into small regular folds; frill; corrugate; make wavy. **2.** to curl (hair), esp. with a hot iron. **3.** to bend (leather) into shape. **4.** *Cookery.* to gash (the flesh of a live fish or of one just killed) with a knife to make it more crisp when cooked. **—***n.* **5.** the act of crimping. **6.** crimped condition or form. **7.** (*usually pl.*) something crimped, as a lock of hair. **8.** the waviness of wool fibres as naturally grown on sheep. **9.** a crease formed in sheet metal or plate metal to make the material less flexible, or for fastening purposes. **10. put a crimp in,** *U.S. Colloq.* to hinder. **—***adj.* **11.** crisp; brittle; easily crumbled. [ME *crympe(n),* OE *gecrympan* curl (der. *crump* crooked), c. LG *krūmpen,* Dan. *krympe* shrink] **—crimp′er,** *n.*

crimp[2] (krĭmp), *n.* **1.** an agent who procures seamen, soldiers, etc., for service, by inducing, swindling, or coercing them. **—***v.t.* **2.** to procure (seamen, soldiers, etc.) by such means. [special use of CRIMP[1]]

crimping iron, a heated iron, used to crimp hair or material.

crimple (krĭm′pl), *v.i., v.t.,* **-pled, -pling.** to wrinkle, crinkle, or curl. [freq. of CRIMP[1]]

Crimplene (krĭm′plēn), *n. Trademark.* a modified Terylene filament yarn, used for garments, and noted for its crease-resistant qualities.

crimpy (krĭm′pĭ), *adj.,* **-pier, -piest.** of a crimped form or appearance.

crimson (krĭm′zən), *adj.* **1.** deep purplish red. **2.** sanguinary. **—***n.* **3.** a crimson colour, pigment, or dye. **—***v.t.* **4.** to make crimson. **—***v.i.* **5.** to become crimson; to blush. [ME *cremesin,* t. early It.: m. *cremesino,* der. *chermisí,* or t. Sp.: m. *cremesin,* der. *carmesí*; both t. Ar.: m. *qirmizī*]

cringe (krĭnj), *v.,* **cringed, cringing,** *n.* **—***v.i.* **1.** to shrink, bend, or crouch, esp. from fear or servility; cower. **2.** to fawn. **—***n.* **2.** servile or fawning obeisance. [ME *crengen,* der. OE *cringan* yield, fall (in battle). See CRINKLE, CRANK] **—cring′er,** *n.* **—cring′ingly,** *adj.*

cringle (krĭng′gl), *n. Naut.* a ring or eye of rope or the like, esp. on the edge of a sail. It is usually made up round a metal thimble or grummet. [t. LG: m. *kringel,* dim. of *kring* circle, ring]

Cringle

crinite[1] (krī′nīt), *adj.* **1.** hairy. **2.** *Bot., Entomol.* having long hairs, or tufts of long, weak hairs. [t. L: m. s. *crīnītus,* pp., provided with hair]

crinite[2] (krī′nīt, krĭn′īt), *n.* a fossil crinoid. [f. m. s. Gk *krínon* lily + -ITE[1]]

crinkle (krĭng′kl), *v.,* **-kled, -kling,** *n.* **—***v.t., v.i.* **1.** to wind or turn in and out. **2.** to wrinkle; crimple; ripple. **3.** to make slight, sharp sounds; rustle. **—***n.* **4.** a turn or twist; a wrinkle; a ripple. **5.** a crinkling sound. [ME; freq. of OE *crincan* bend, yield. See CRINGE, CRANK] **—crin′kly,** *adj.*

crinkleroot (krĭng′kl ro͞ot′), *n.* any of several species of the North American cruciferous perennials (genus *Dentaria*), esp. *Dentaria diphylla.*

crinkum-crankum (krĭng′kəm krăng′kəm), *n. U.S. Colloq.* something full of twists and turns.

crinoid (krī′noid, krĭn′oid), *adj.* **1.** lily-like. **—***n.* **2.** one of the *Crinoidea,* a class of echinoderms with radiating arms usually borne mouth up on an attached stalk, including the sea-lilies, feather-stars and numerous fossil forms. [t. Gk: m. s. *krinoeidḗs* lily-like]

Unstalked crinoid, feather-star, *Antendon rosacea*

crinoline (krĭn′ə lĭn), *n.* **1.** a petticoat of horsehair and flax or other stiff material, formerly worn by women under a full dress skirt. **2.** a hoop skirt. **3.** stiff coarse cotton material for interlining. **4.** netting fitted round a ship as a protection against torpedoes. [t. F, t. It.: m. *crinolino,* f. *crino* hair + *lino* thread]

crinum (krī′nəm), *n.* any plant of the tropical and subtropical amaryllidaceous genus *Crinum,* comprising tall bulbous plants, usually with umbels of large, showy flowers. [NL, t. Gk: m. *krínon* lily]

criosphinx (krī′ə sfĭngks′), *n., pl.* **-sphinxes, -sphinges** (-sfĭn′jēz). a sphinx with the head of a ram. [f. m. Gk *krió(s)* ram + *sphinx* sphinx]

cripes (krīps), *interj.* (an expression of amazement, disgust, or the like.) [euphemistic var. of CHRIST]

cripple (krĭp′l), *n., v.,* **-pled, -pling. —***n.* **1.** one who is partially or wholly deprived of the use of one or more of his limbs; a lame person. **—***v.t.* **2.** to make a cripple of; lame. **3.** to disable; impair. [ME *cripel,* OE *crypel*; akin to CREEP] **—crip′pler,** *n.*

—Syn. 2, 3. CRIPPLE, DISABLE mean to injure permanently or temporarily, to a degree which interferes with normal activities. To CRIPPLE is to injure in such a way as to deprive of the use of a member, particularly a leg or arm: *a broken arm cripples but does not disable a judge.* DISABLE, a more general work, implies such illness, injury, or impairment as makes a person incapable of engaging in his normal activities: *disabled by an attack of malaria, by a wound.*

Cripple Creek, a town in central Colorado: gold rush, 1891. 614 (1960); 9600 ft above sea-level.

Cripps (krĭps), *n.* **Sir Stafford,** 1889–1952, British statesman and socialist leader.

Crises (krī′sēz), *n.* **Sea of,** a dark plain, *Mare Crisium,* in the first quadrant of the face of the moon.

crisis (krī′sĭs), *n., pl.* **-ses** (-sēz). **1.** a decisive or vitally important stage in the course of anything; a turning point; a critical time or occasion: *a political crisis, a business crisis.* **2.** the point in a play or story at which hostile elements are most tensely opposed to each other. **3.** *Pathol.* **a.** the point in the course of a disease at which a decisive change occurs, leading either to recovery or to death. **b.** the change itself. [t. L, t. Gk: m. *krísis* decision] **—Syn. 1.** climax, juncture, exigence, strait, pinch. See **emergency.**

crisp (krĭsp), *adj.* **1.** hard but easily breakable; brittle: *crisp toast.* **2.** firm and fresh: *crisp leaf of lettuce.* **3.** brisk; sharp; decided: *crisp manner, reply, etc.* **4.** lively; pithy; sparkling: *crisp repartee.* **5.** bracing; invigorating: *crisp air.* **6.** crinkled, wrinkled, or rippled, as skin or water. **7.** in small, stiff or firm curls; curly. **—***v.t., v.i.* **8.** to make or become crisp. **9.** to curl. **—***n.* **10.** a wafer of potato fried, dried, and usually served cold. **11.** something that is crisp: *burnt to a crisp.* [ME and OE, t. L: s. *crispus* curled] **—crisp′ly,** *adv.* **—crisp′ness,** *n.*

crispate (krĭs′pāt, -pĭt), *adj.* crisped or curled. Also, **cris′pated.** [t. L: m. s. *crispātus,* pp., curled]

crispation (krĭs pā′shən), *n.* **1.** the act of crisping or curling. **2.** the state of being crisped. **3.** a slight contraction or undulation.

crisper (krĭs′pə), *n.* one who or that which crisps, corrugates, or curls.

Crispi (*It.* krēs′pē), *n.* **Francesco** (*It.* från chĕ′skō), 1819–1901, prime minister of Italy 1887–91, and 1893–96.

Crispin (krĭs′pĭn), *n.* **1. Saint,** fl. 3rd century A.D., patron saint of shoemakers. **2.** (*l.c.*) a shoemaker.

crispy (krĭs′pĭ), *adj.,* **-pier, -piest. 1.** brittle; crisp. **2.** curly or wavy. **3.** brisk.

crissal (krĭs′əl), *adj.* of or pertaining to the crissum.

crisscross (krĭs′krŏs′), *adj.* **1.** in crossing lines; crossed; crossing; marked by crossings. **—***n.* **2.** a crisscross mark, pattern, etc. **—***adv.* **3.** in a crisscross manner; crosswise. **—***v.t., v.i.* **4.** to mark with or form crossing lines. [var. of CHRISTCROSS]

crisscross-row (krĭs′krŏs rō′), *n. Archaic or Dial.* christ-cross-row.

crissum (krĭs′əm), *n., pl.* **crissa** (krĭs′ə). *Ornith.* **1.** the region surrounding the cloacal opening beneath the tail of a bird. **2.** the feathers of this region collectively. [NL, der. L *crissāre* move the haunches]

cristate (krĭs′tāt), *adj.* **1.** having a crest; crested. **2.** forming a crest. Also, **cris′tated.** [t. L: m. s. *cristātus,* der. *crista* CREST]

Cristobal (krĭs tō′bl; *Sp.* krēs tō′bäl), *n.* a seaport in the Canal Zone at the Atlantic end of the Panama Canal, adjacent to Colón. 817 (1960). Also, **Cristóbal.**

criterion (krī tĭə′rĭ ən), *n., pl.* **-teria** (-tĭə′rĭ ə), **-terions.** a standard of judgement or criticism; an established rule or principle for testing anything. [t. Gk: m. *kritḗrion* test, standard] **—Syn.** See **standard.**

critic (krĭt′ĭk), *n.* **1.** a person skilled in judging the qualities or merits of some class of things, esp. of literary or artistic work. **2.** one who judges captiously or with severity; one who censures or finds fault. **3.** *Obs.* a critique. [t. L: s. *criticus,* t. Gk: m. *kritikós* skilled in judging, decisive, critical (as n., a critic)] **—Syn. 1.** re-

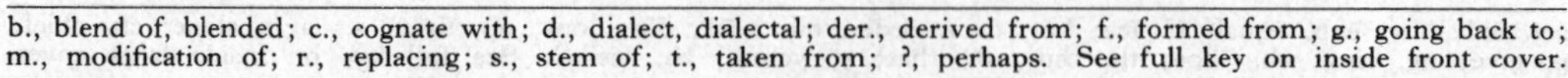

viewer, censor, judge, connoisseur. **2.** censurer, carper.

critical (krĭt′ĭ kl), *adj.* **1.** inclined to find fault or to judge with severity. **2.** occupied with or skilled in criticism. **3.** involving skilful judgement as to truth, merit, etc.; judicial: *a critical analysis.* **4.** of or pertaining to critics or criticism: *critical essays.* **5.** pertaining to, or of the nature of, a crisis; of decisive importance with respect to the outcome; crucial: *the critical moment.* **6.** involving suspense, risk, peril, etc.; dangerous: *a critical shortage.* **7.** *Physics.* denoting a constant value, as of temperature, frequency, etc., at which one or more related properties of a substance undergo an abrupt change: *critical pressure.* **8.** *Maths.* indicating a point at which some transition or change takes place. **9.** *Bot., Zool.* (of species) distinguished by slight or questionable differences; uncertain or difficult to determine. —**crit′ically,** *adv.* —**crit′icalness,** *n.* —**Syn. 1.** captious, censorious, carping, faultfinding, cavilling. **3.** discriminating, fastidious, nice, exact. **5.** decisive, climacteric. **6.** hazardous, precarious.

critical angle, 1. *Optics.* the limiting angle of incidence for total internal reflection. **2.** *Aeron.* the angle of attack at which there is a sudden change in the airflow round an aerofoil with subsequent decrease in lift and increase in drag.

critical constants, *Physics.* the critical temperature, pressure, density, and volume of a substance.

critical mass, *Physics.* the minimum quantity of fissile material necessary for a chain-reaction to take place.

critical-path analysis, *Computers.* a method of using a computer to predict bottlenecks in civil engineering projects, factory organization, etc.

critical philosophy, the mature philosophy of Kant, based on a critical examination of the faculty of knowledge.

critical pressure, *Physics.* the pressure of the saturated vapour of a substance at the critical temperature.

critical temperature, 1. *Physics.* (of a gas) the temperature above which a gas cannot be liquefied by pressure alone. **2.** *Metall.* the temperature at which certain changes occur in the crystalline structure of a metal. **3.** Also, **critical point.** the temperature at which magnetic materials lose their magnetic properties.

critical velocity, the velocity at which the flow of a fluid ceases to be streamline and becomes turbulent.

criticaster (krĭt′ĭ kăs′tə), *n.* an inferior or incompetent critic. [f. CRITIC + -ASTER[1]]

criticism (krĭt′ĭ sĭz′əm), *n.* **1.** the act or art of analysing and judging the quality of a literary or artistic work, etc.: *literary criticism.* **2.** the act of passing judgement as to the merits of something. **3.** the act of passing severe judgement; censure; faultfinding. **4.** a critical comment, article, or essay; a critique. **5.** any of various methods of investigating the origin, meaning, etc., of a book of the Bible: *higher criticism, historical criticism.* **6.** any of various methods of investigation with the purpose of establishing an authentic text corresponding as nearly as possible to an author's intended text: *verbal criticism.* —**Syn. 3.** stricture, animadversion, reflection. **4.** See **review.**

criticize (krĭt′ĭ sīz′), *v.*, **-cized, -cizing.** —*v.i.* **1.** to make judgements as to merits and faults. **2.** to find fault. —*v.t.* **3.** to judge or discuss the merits and faults of. **4.** to find fault with. Also, **criticise.** —**crit′iciz′able,** *adj.* —**crit′iciz′er,** *n.*

critique (krĭ tēk′), *n.* **1.** an article or essay criticizing a literary or other work: a review. **2.** the art or practice of criticism. [t. F, t. Gk: m. *kritikḗ* the critical art, prop. fem. of *kritikós*]

critter (krĭt′ə), *n. U.S. Dial.* creature.

croak (krōk), *v.i.* **1.** to utter a low, hoarse, dismal cry, as a frog or a raven. **2.** to speak with a low, hollow voice. **3.** to talk despondently; forebode evil; grumble. **4.** *Slang.* to die. —*v.t.* **5.** to utter or announce by croaking. **6.** *Slang.* to kill. —*n.* **7.** the act or sound of croaking. [late ME; back-formation from OE *crăcettan.* Cf. CREAK]

croaker (krō′kə), *n.* one who or that which croaks.

croaky (krō′kĭ), *adj.* making a croaking sound. —**croak′ily,** *adv.*

Croat (krō′ăt), *n.* **1.** a native or inhabitant of Croatia; a Croatian. **2.** Croatian (def. 3).

Croatia (krō ā′shyə), *n.* a constituent republic of Yugoslavia, in the NW part: a medieval kingdom; now corresponding to the former Austrian crownland of **Croatia and Slavonia.** 4,159,696 pop. (1961); 21,835 sq. mi. *Cap.:* Zagreb.

Croatia

Croatian (krō ā′shyən), *adj.* **1.** of or pertaining to Croatia, the Croats, or their language. —*n.* **2.** a Croat. **3.** Serbo-Croat.

Croce (*It.* krō′chė), *n.* **Benedetto** (*It.* bė nė dėt′tō), 1866–1952, Italian statesman, philosopher, and historian.

crochet (krō′shā, -shĭ), *n., v.,* **-cheted** (-shād, -shĭd), **-cheting** (-shā ĭng, -shĭ ĭng). —*n.* **1.** a kind of needlework done with a needle having at one end a small hook for drawing the thread or yarn into intertwined loops. **2.** the work or fabric so made. —*v.t., v.i.* **3.** to form by crochet. [t. F: hooked implement, dim. of OF *croche* hook]

crochet hook, a thin rodlike knitting needle, with a hook at one end, used to crochet.

crocidolite (krō sĭd′ə līt′), *n.* a mineral of the amphibole group, essentially a sodium iron silicate, occurring in fibres of a delicate blue colour, and appearing in altered form as the (golden brown) tiger's-eye or (dark blue) hawk's-eye. [f. *crocido-* (comb. form repr. Gk *krokís* nap, wool) + -LITE]

crock[1] (krŏk), *n.* **1.** an earthen pot, jar, or other vessel. **2.** a potsherd. **3.** *Dial.* a vessel of metal. [ME *crokke,* OE *croc(c), crocca* pot. Cf. Icel. *krukka* jug]

crock[2] (krŏk), *n.* **1.** an old ewe. **2.** an old worn-out horse. **3.** *Colloq.* a worn-out, decrepit old person. **4.** *Colloq.* an old motor car. —*v.i.* **5.** *Slang.* to get injured (often fol. by *up*). [akin to CRACK, v.]

crock[3] (krŏk), *Dial.* —*n.* **1.** soot; smut. —*v.t.* **2.** to soil with crock. [orig. uncert.]

crockery (krŏk′ə rĭ), *n.* **1.** crocks or earthen vessels collectively; earthenware. **2.** china in general, esp. as for domestic use.

crocket (krŏk′ĭt), *n. Archit.* a medieval ornament in the form of leafage curled out over a knot or knob; placed on the angles of the inclined sides of pinnacles, under cornices, etc. [ME *croket,* t. AF. See CROCHET]

Crockett (krŏk′ĭt), *n.* **David** (*Davy*), 1786–1836, American frontiersman and political figure, killed in the Texan defence of the Alamo.

crocodile (krŏk′ə dīl′), *n.* **1.** any of the large, thick-skinned reptiles, lizard-like in form, which constitute the genus *Crocodylus* (order *Crocodilia*), inhabiting the waters of tropical Africa, Asia, Australia, and America, esp. *C. niloticus* of the Nile. **2.** any animal of the order *Crocodilia,* including the alligators of America and the gavial of India. **3.** the skin of these animals, used for shoes, handbags, etc. **4.** one who makes a hypocritical show of sorrow. **5.** *Colloq.* a double file of persons, as schoolchildren out for a walk. [t. L: m. s. *crocodīlus,* t. Gk: m. *krokódeilos* lizard; r. ME *cocodrille,* t. OF]

Nile crocodile, *Crocodylus niloticus* (16 ft long)

crocodile bird, an African plover, *Pluvianus aegyptius,* which often sits upon basking crocodiles and feeds on their insect parasites.

crocodile clip, *Elect.* a terminal for temporary electrical connections with narrow jaws like those of a crocodile.

Crocodile River, 1. Limpopo. **2.** a river in the Republic of South Africa, flowing E through SE Transvaal to the Incomati river in Mozambique. ab. 175 mi.

crocodile tears, 1. false or insincere tears, as the tears said to be shed by crocodiles over those they devour. **2.** hypocritical show of sorrow.

crocodilian (krŏk′ə dĭl′yən), *n.* **1.** any of the *Crocodilia,* an order of reptiles including the crocodiles, alligators, etc. —*adj.* **2.** of or pertaining to the crocodile. **3.** pertaining to the crocodilians. **4.** hypocritical.

crocoite (krō′kō īt′), *n.* a mineral, lead chromate, $PbCrO_4$. Also, **crocoisite** (krō kō′ĭ sīt′, krō′kwə sīt′). [f. m. Gk *krokó(eis)* saffron-coloured + -ITE[1]]

crocus (krō′kəs), *n., pl.* **crocuses. 1.** any of the small bulbous plants constituting the iridaceous genus *Crocus,* much cultivated for their showy, solitary flowers. **2.** the flower or bulb of the crocus. **3.** a deep yellow; orangish yellow; saffron. **4.** a polishing powder consisting of iron oxide. [t. L, t. Gk: m. *krókos* saffron]

Croesus (krē′səs), *n.* **1.** died 546 B.C., king of Lydia 560–546 B.C., noted for his great wealth. **2.** a very rich man.

croft (krŏft), *n.* **1.** a small piece of enclosed ground for tillage, pasture, etc. **2.** a very small farm, as one worked by a Scottish crofter. [ME and OE. Cf. MD *kroft* field on high land]

crofter (krŏf′tə), *n.* one who rents or owns and works a croft, as in parts of Scotland or northern England.

croissant (krə wŭs′ŏng; *Fr.* krwȧ säɴ′), *n.* a roll of leavened dough or puff pastry, shaped into a crescent and baked.

Croix de Guerre (*Fr.* krwȧ də gĕr′), *n.* a French military award for heroism in battle.

Cro-Magnon (krō măn′yŏn; *Fr.* krō mȧ nyôɴ′), *adj. An-*

thropol. belonging to a prehistoric race of Europe, believed to be of the same species as modern man. Remains found in the cave of Cro-Magnon in Dordogne, in France, were characterized by a very long head, low face and orbits, and tall stature.

crombec (krŏm′bĕk), *n.* krombek.

Crome (krōm), *n.* **John,** 1768–1821, English landscape painter.

Cromer (krō′mə), *n.* **Evelyn Baring, 1st Earl of,** 1841–1917, English statesman and diplomat.

cromlech (krŏm′lĕk), *n. Archaeol.* **1.** a circle of upright stones or monoliths. **2.** a dolmen. [t. Welsh, f. *crom* bent, bowed + *llech* flat stone]

Crompton (krŏmp′tən), *n.* **Samuel,** 1753–1827, English inventor of the spinning mule.

Cromwell (krŏm′wəl, -wĕl), *n.* **1. Oliver,** 1599–1658, English general, Puritan statesman, and lord protector of the Commonwealth 1653–58. **2.** his son, **Richard,** 1626–1712, English soldier and politician, lord protector of the Commonwealth 1658–59. **3. Thomas** (*Earl of Essex*), 1485?–1540, English statesman.

crone (krōn), *n.* an old woman. [t. MD: m. *croonje,* t. ONF: m. *carogne* carcass]

Cronjé (krŏn′jĭ), *n.* **Piet Arnoldus** (pēt′ ä nŏl′dəs), 1835?–1911, Boer general.

Cronus (krō′nəs), *n. Gk Myth.* a Titan, son of Uranus and Gaea, who dethroned his father, and was dethroned by his own son Zeus. Saturn is his Roman counterpart. Also, **Cronos** (krō′nŏs), **Kronos.**

crony (krō′nĭ), *n., pl.* **-nies.** an intimate friend or companion. [earlier *chrony,* ? t. Gk: m. s. *chrónios* long-lasting, der. *chrónos* time]

crook[1] (kro͝ok), *n.* **1.** a bent or curved implement, piece, appendage, etc.; a hook; the hooked part of anything. **2.** an instrument or implement having a bent or curved part, as a shepherd's staff hooked at one end or as the crosier of a bishop or abbot. **3.** *Scot.* a pothook. **4.** the act of crooking or bending. **5.** any bend, turn, or curve. **6.** *Colloq.* a dishonest person, esp. a sharper, swindler, or thief. **7.** a device on some musical wind instruments for changing the pitch, consisting of a piece of tubing inserted into the main tube. **—*v.t.* 8.** to bend; curve; make a crook in. **—*v.i.* 9.** to bend; curve. [ME *crok(e),* t. Scand.; cf. Icel. *krōkr*]

crook[2] (kro͝ok), *adj. Austral., N.Z. Slang.* **1.** sick. **2.** bad; unfair.

crookback (kro͝ok′băk′), *n.* a hunchback. **—crook′-backed′,** *adj.*

crooked (kro͝ok′ĭd), *adj.* **1.** bent; not straight; curved. **2.** deformed. **3.** not straightforward or honest. [OE *gecrōcod*] **—crook′edly,** *adv.* **—crook′edness,** *n.* **—Syn. 1.** winding, devious, sinuous, flexuous, tortuous, spiral, twisted, askew, awry. **2.** misshapen. **3.** dishonest, unscrupulous, knavish, fraudulent. **—Ant. 1.** straight. **3.** honourable.

Crookes (kro͝oks), *n.* **Sir William,** 1832–1919, English chemist and physicist: discovered the element thallium and cathode rays.

Crookes dark space, *Physics.* the dark space in a vacuum tube between the cathode and the negative glow, occurring when pressure is very low. [named after Sir William CROOKES]

croon (kro͞on), *v.i.* **1.** to sing softly, esp. with exaggerated feeling. **2.** to utter a low murmuring sound. **3.** *Scot. and N Dial.* to lament; moan. **—*v.t.* 4.** to sing softly, esp. with exaggerated feeling. **—*n.* 5.** the act or sound of crooning. [late ME, t. MD: m. *krōnen* murmur] **—croon′er,** *n.*

crop (krŏp), *n., v.,* **cropped, cropping. —*n.* 1.** the cultivated produce of the ground, as grain or fruit, while growing or when gathered. **2.** the yield of such produce for a particular season. **3.** the yield of some other product in a season: *the lamb crop.* **4.** a supply produced. **5.** a collection or group of persons or things occurring together: *a crop of lies.* **6.** the stock or handle of a whip. **7.** a short riding whip with a loop instead of a lash. **8.** an entire tanned hide of an animal. **9.** the act of cropping. **10.** a mark produced by clipping the ears, as of an animal. **11.** a style of wearing the hair cut short. **12.** a head of hair so cut. **13.** an outcrop of a vein or seam. **14.** a special pouchlike enlargement of the gullet of many birds, in which food is held, and may undergo partial preparation for digestion. **15.** a digestive organ in other animals; the craw. **—*v.t.* 16.** to cut off or remove the head or top of (a plant, etc.). **17.** to cut off the ends or a part of. **18.** to cut short. **19.** to clip the ears, hair, etc., of. **20.** *Photog.* to cut off or mask the unwanted parts of (a print or negative). **21.** to cause to bear a crop or crops. **—*v.i.* 22.** to bear or yield a crop or crops. **23.** *Mining.* to come to the surface of the ground, as a vein of ore (usually fol. by *up* or *out*). **24.** to appear unintentionally or unexpectedly (fol.by *up* or *out*): *a new problem cropped up.* [ME and OE, c. G *Kropf*; orig. meaning protuberance. See CROUP[2]]

—Syn. 1. CROP, HARVEST, PRODUCE, YIELD refer to the return in food for men and animals obtained from land at the end of a season of growth. CROP, the term common in agricultural and commercial use, denotes the amount produced at one cutting or for one particular season: *the wheat crop, potato crop.* HARVEST denotes either the time of reaping and gathering, or the gathering, or that which is gathered: *the season of harvest; to bring in a harvest; a ripe harvest.* PRODUCE esp. denotes household vegetables: *produce from the fields and gardens was taken to market.* YIELD emphasizes what is given by the land in return for expenditure of time and labour: *there was a heavy yield of grain this year.*

crop-dust (krŏp′dŭst′), *v.t.* to subject arable land to crop-dusting.

crop-dusting (krŏp′dŭs′tĭng), *n.* the spraying of insecticides or fungicides on crops, usually by an aeroplane.

crop-eared (krŏp′ĭəd′), *adj.* **1.** having the ears cropped. **2.** having the hair cropped short, so that the ears are conspicuous.

cropper[1] (krŏp′ə), *n.* **1.** one who or that which crops. **2.** one who raises a crop. **3.** one who cultivates land for its owner in return for part of the crop. **4.** a plant which furnishes a crop. **5.** a machine that shears the nap of cloth. **6. come a cropper,** *Colloq.* **a.** to fall heavily, esp. from a horse. **b.** to fail; collapse, or be struck by misfortune.

cropper[2] (krŏp′ə), *n.* one of a breed of pigeons, having the power of distending their crops; a pouter.

croquet (krō′kā, -kĭ), *n., v.,* **-queted** (-kād, -kĭd), **-queting** (-kā ĭng, -kĭ ĭng). **—*n.* 1.** an outdoor game played by knocking wooden balls through a series of iron arches by means of mallets. **2.** (in this game) the act of driving away an opponent's ball by striking one's own when the two are in contact. **—*v.t.* 3.** to drive away (a ball) by a croquet. [t. d. F: hockey stick]

croquette (krō kĕt′, krŏ-), *n.* a small mass of minced meat or fish, or of rice, potato, or other material, often coated with beaten egg and breadcrumbs, and fried in deep fat. [t. F, der. *croquer* crunch]

crore (krô), *n. India.* ten million; one hundred lakhs: *a crore of rupees.* [t. Hind.: m. *k(a)rōr,* g. Prakrit *krodi*]

Crosby (krŏz′bĭ), *n.* a town in England, in SW Lancashire. 59,166 (1961).

crosier (krō′zhə), *n.* **1.** the pastoral staff of a bishop or an abbot, hooked at one end like a shepherd's crook. See illus. under **cope. 2.** *Bot.* the circinate young frond of a fern. Also, **crozier.** [short for *crosier-staff* staff carried by the *crosier* crossbearer (t. F: m. *crosier,* g. ML *crociārius* crookbearer)]

cross (krŏs), *n.* **1.** a structure consisting essentially of an upright and a transverse piece, upon which persons were formerly put to death. **2. the Cross,** the cross upon which Jesus died. **3.** a figure of the cross as a Christian emblem, badge, etc. **4.** the cross as the symbol of Christianity. **5.** a small cross with a human figure attached to it, as a representation of Jesus crucified; a crucifix. **6.** the sign of the cross made with the right hand as an act of devotion. **7.** a structure or monument sometimes in the form of a cross, set up for prayer, as a memorial, or a place where proclamations are read. **8.** the place in a town or village where such a monument stands or stood. **9.** any of various conventional representations or modifications of the Christian emblem as used symbolically or for ornament, as in heraldry, art, etc.: *a Latin, Greek, St George's, or Maltese cross.* **10.** the crucifixion of Jesus as the culmination of His redemptive mission. **11.** any suffering borne for Jesus' sake. **12.** the teaching of redemption gained by Jesus' death. **13.** Christian religion, or those who accept it; Christianity; Christendom. **14.** any object, figure, or mark resembling a cross, as two intersecting lines. **15.** such a mark made instead of a signature by a person unable to write. **16.** a four-way joint or connection used in pipe-fitting, the connections being at right angles. **17.** a crossing. **18.** a place of crossing. **19.** an opposing; thwarting. **20.** any misfortune; trouble. **21.** a crossing of animals or plants; a mixing of breeds. **22.** an animal, plant, breed, etc., produced by crossing; a crossbreed. **23.** something intermediate in character

A B C D E F G H I J K

Forms of crosses
A, Latin cross; B, Tau cross or St Anthony's cross; C, Cross of Calvary; D, Cross of Lorraine; E, Patriarchal cross; F, St Andrew's cross; G, Greek cross or St George's cross; H, Papal cross; I, Maltese cross; J, Jerusalem cross; K, Celtic cross

between two things. 24. *Slang.* a contest, the result of which is dishonestly arranged beforehand. 25. **the Southern Cross,** the constellation Crux. —*v.t.* 26. to make the sign of the cross upon or over, as in devotion. 27. to mark with a cross. 28. to cancel by marking with a cross or with a line or lines. 29. to place in the form of a cross or crosswise. 30. to put or draw (a line, etc.) across. 31. to mark (the face of a cheque) with two parallel lines with or without the words 'and company' or any abbreviation thereof, or with the name of a banking company, thereby restricting the cheque to negotiation through a bank. 32. to set (a yard, etc.) in position across a mast. 33. to lie or pass across; intersect. 34. to move, pass, or extend from one side to the other side of (a street, river, etc.). 35. to transport across something. 36. to meet and pass. 37. *Archaic.* to encounter. 38. to oppose; thwart. 39. *Biol.* to cause (members of different genera, species, breeds, varieties, or the like) to produce offspring; cross-fertilize. 40. **cross one's heart,** to pledge; promise; swear. 41. **cross one's mind,** to occur to one; come as an idea. 42. **cross one's t's and dot one's i's,** to pay punctilious attention to details. 43. **cross someone's palm with silver,** to give money to someone to tell one's fortune. —*v.i.* 44. to lie or be athwart; intersect. 45. to move, pass, extend from one side or place to another. 46. to meet and pass. 47. to interbreed. —*adj.* 48. lying or passing crosswise or across each other; athwart; transverse: *cross axes.* 49. involving interchange; reciprocal. 50. contrary; opposite. 51. adverse; unfavourable. 52. ill-humoured; snappish: *a cross word.* 53. crossbred; hybrid. 54. *Slang.* dishonest. [ME and OE *cros,* t. OIrish, t. L: m. *crux* (Icel. *kross,* also, t. OIrish or ? t. OE)] —**cross'ly,** *adv.* —**cross'ness,** *n.*

—**Syn.** 38. baffle, frustrate, foil, contradict. 52. petulant, fractious, irascible, waspish, crabbed, churlish, sulky, cantankerous. CROSS, ILL-NATURED, PEEVISH, SULLEN refer to being in a bad mood or ill temper. CROSS means temporarily in an irritable or fretful state, and sometimes somewhat angry: *a cross reply, cross and tired.* ILL-NATURED implies a more permanent condition, without definite cause, and means unpleasant, unkind, inclined to snarl or be spiteful: *an ill-natured dog, ill-natured spite.* PEEVISH means complaining and snappish: *a peevish and whining child.* SULLEN suggests a kind of glowering silent gloominess and means refusing to speak because of bad humour, anger, or a sense of injury or resentment: *sullen and vindictive.* —**Ant.** 38. aid. 52. good-natured.

cross-, a first element of compounds, modifying the second part, meaning: 1. going across: *crossroad.* 2. counter: *cross-examination.* 3. marked with a cross: *hot cross buns.* 4. cruciform: *crossbones,* etc.

cross-action (krŏs'ăk'shən), *n.* *Law.* the bringing by the defendant in an action of another action against the plaintiff in respect of the same subject matter.

cross-banding (krŏs'băn'dĭng), *n.* decorative banding on a piece of furniture, formed by laying the grain crosswise to the grain of the principal surface.

crossbar (krŏs'bä'), *n.* 1. a transverse bar, line, or stripe. 2. a transverse bar between goalposts, as in soccer, rugby football, etc. 3. a horizontal bar used in gymnastics. 4. (in athletics) the transverse bar that a high-jumper, pole-vaulter, etc., must clear.

crossbeam (krŏs'bēm'), *n.* a transverse beam.

cross-bearings (krŏs'bĕə'rĭngz), *n.pl.* compass bearings of two or more fixed points taken from a ship to determine its position.

cross-bedded (krŏs'bĕd'ĭd), *adj.* *Geol.* having irregular laminations, as strata of sandstone, inclining in various directions not coincident with the general stratification.

cross-bench (krŏs'bĕnch'), *n.* 1. one of a set of seats, as at the back of both houses of Parliament, for those who belong neither to the government nor to opposition parties. 2. a bench laid crosswise. —*adj.* 3. independent; impartial. —**cross'-ben'cher,** *n.*

crossbill (krŏs'bĭl'), *n.* any bird of the fringilline genus *Loxia,* characterized by mandibles curved so that the tips cross each other when the bill is closed.

crossbones (krŏs'bōnz'), *n.pl.* two bones placed crosswise, usually below a skull, symbolizing death.

crossbow (krŏs'bō'), *n.* an old weapon for shooting missiles, consisting of a bow fixed transversely on a stock having a groove or barrel to direct the missile. —**crossbowman** (krŏs'bō'mən), *n.*

crossbred (krŏs'brĕd'), *adj.* 1. produced by crossbreeding. —*n.* 2. an animal or group of animals produced by hybridization.

crossbreed (krŏs'brēd'), *v.,* **-bred, -breeding,** *n.* —*v.t.* 1. to produce (a hybrid) within a species, using two breeds or varieties. —*v.i.* 2. to undertake or engage in hybridizing, esp. within a single species. —*n.* 3. a crossbred.

cross-buttock (krŏs' bŭt'ək), *n.* *Wrestling.* a throw over the hip, using it as a fulcrum.

cross-channel (krŏs'chăn'əl), *adj.* that crosses the English Channel.

crosscheck (krŏs'chĕk'), *v.t.* to determine the accuracy of something by checking from different sources; to recheck.

cross-country (krŏs'kŭn'trĭ), *adj., adv.* 1. directed across fields or open country; not following the main roads. 2. from one end of the country to the other.

cross-current (krŏs'kŭ'rənt), *n.* a current, as in a stream, the sea, etc., moving across the main current.

crosscut (krŏs'kŭt'), *adj., n., v.,* **-cut, -cutting.** —*adj.* 1. made or used for cutting: *a crosscut saw.* 2. cut across or transversely. —*n.* 3. a direct course between two points, as one diagonal to a main way. 4. a transverse cut or course. 5. *Mining.* an underground passageway, usually from shaft to a vein of ore or across a vein of ore. —*v.t.* 6. to cut across.

crosscut chisel, a cold chisel.

crosscut file, a file with two intersecting rows of cuts.

crosscut saw, a saw used for sawing timber in a direction perpendicular to the axis of the tree.

crosse (krŏs), *n.* a long-handled racket used in the game of lacrosse. [t. F; of Gmc orig.]

cross-examine (krŏs'ĭg zăm'ĭn), *v.t.,* **-ined, -ining.** 1. to examine by questions intended to check a previous examination; examine closely or minutely. 2. to examine (a witness called by the opposing side), as for the purpose of disproving his testimony. —**cross-examination** (krŏs'-ĭg zăm'ĭ nā'shən), *n.* —**cross'-exam'iner,** *n.*

cross-eye (krŏs'ī'), *n.* strabismus, esp. the form in which both eyes turn towards the nose. —**cross'-eyed',** *adj.*

cross-fertilization (krŏs'fû'tĭ lī zā'shən), *n.* 1. *Biol.* the fertilization of an organism by the fusion of an egg from one individual with a sperm (or male gamete) of a different individual. 2. *Bot.* fertilization of one flower or plant by pollen from another (opposed to *self-fertilization*). Also, **cross-fertilisation.**

cross-fertilize (krŏs'fû'tĭ līz'), *v.t.,* **-lized, -lizing.** to cause the cross-fertilization of. Also, **cross-fertilise.**

cross-fire (krŏs'fī'ə), *n.* 1. a brisk exchange of words or opinions. 2. *Mil.* lines of fire from two or more positions, crossing one another, or a single one of such lines.

cross-garnet (krŏs'gä'nĭt), *n.* a T-shaped hinge. [CROSS + obs. *garnet,* ? der. ONF *carne,* t. L: m. *cardin-,* s. *cardo* hinge]

cross-gartered (krŏs'gä'təd), *adj.* *Archaic.* having garters crossed at the knees.

cross-grained (krŏs'grānd'), *adj.* 1. having the grain running transversely, or diagonally, or having an irregular or gnarled grain, as timber. 2. perverse; intractable. —*adv.* 3. across the grain; perversely. —**cross'-grain'-edness,** *n.*

cross-guard (krŏs'gäd'), *n.* the transverse guard of a sword set at right angles to the blade.

crosshair (krŏs'hĕə'), *n.* a fine wire or strand of spider's web or other material, crossing another or others in a focal plane of an optical instrument, serving to define a line of sight; crosswire.

crosshatch (krŏs'hăch'), *v.t.* to hatch or shade with two or more intersecting series of parallel lines. —**cross'-hatch'ing,** *n.*

crosshead (krŏs'hĕd'), *n.* 1. *Print.* a title or heading filling a line or group of lines the full width of the column. 2. the sliding and bearing member of a diesel, steam, or gas engine, between the piston rod and the connecting rod. 3. *Naut.* a crossbar fitted on top of the rudder post by which the rudder is turned. 4. the rod or beam across the head of any of various other mechanisms. —**cross'head'-ing,** *n.*

cross-index (krŏs'ĭn'dĕks), *n.* 1. a note, or a group of notes referring the reader to material elsewhere. —*v.t.* 2. to provide with cross-references. —*v.i.* 3. to contain cross-references; to refer to related material as in a book, etc.

crossing (krŏs'ĭng), *n.* 1. the act of one who or that which crosses. 2. a place where lines, tracks, etc., cross each other. 3. the intersection of nave and transept in a cruciform church. 4. a place at which a road, river, etc., may be crossed. 5. the act of opposing or thwarting; contradiction. 6. crossbreeding.

crossing over, *Biol.* the interchange of corresponding chromatid segments of homologous chromosomes with their linked genes.

crossjack (krŏs'jăk'; *Naut.* krŏj'ĭk), *n.* *Naut.* a square sail on the lower yard of a mizzenmast. See illus. under **sail.**

crosskick (krŏs'kĭk'), *Rugby Football.* —*v.i.* 1. to kick the ball across the field to be gathered by another player. —*n.* 2. such a kick.

cross-legged (krŏs′lĕg′ĭd, -lĕgd′), *adj.* having the legs crossed; having one leg placed across the other.

crosslet (krŏs′lĭt), *n. Chiefly Her.* a small cross.

crossness (krŏs′nĭs), *n.* the condition or quality of being cross or irritable.

crossopterygian (krŏ sŏp′tə rĭj′ĭ ən), *n.* **1.** any fish of the group *Crossopterygii*, all fossil except *Latimeria chalumnae*, supposed to be ancestral to amphibians and other land vertebrates. *—adj.* **2.** of or pertaining to any fish of this group.

crossover (krŏs′ō′və), *n.* **1.** the act of crossing over. **2.** *Biol.* a genotype resulting from crossing over. **3.** *Railways.* a system of points, usually connecting up and down tracks. **4.** a flyover.

crossover network, an audio circuit device in a radio or record player which sorts the impulses received and channels them into high- or low-frequency loudspeakers.

crosspatch (krŏs′păch′), *n. Colloq.* a cross person.

crosspiece (krŏs′pēs′), *n.* a piece of any material placed across something; a transverse piece.

cross-ply (krŏs′plī′), *adj.* (of a motor tyre) having the fabric cords stretched diagonally, thus bracing the tread.

cross-pollinate (krŏs′pŏl′ĭ nāt′), *v.t.*, **-nated, -nating.** cross-fertilize. —**cross′-pol′lina′tion,** *n.*

cross-purpose (krŏs′pûr′pəs), *n.* **1.** an opposing or contrary purpose. **2. be at cross-purposes,** to misunderstand another's, or each other's, purpose, or act under such a misunderstanding. **3.** (*pl.*) a kind of conversational game in which words are taken in different senses.

cross-question (krŏs′kwĕs′chən), *v.t.* **1.** to cross-examine. *—n.* **2.** a question asked by way of cross-examination.

cross-refer (krŏs′rĭ fû′), *v.t.*, *v.i.*, **-ferred, -ferring.** to refer by a cross-reference.

cross-reference (krŏs′rĕf′rəns), *n.*, *v.*, **-renced, -rencing.** *—n.* **1.** a reference from one part of a book, etc., to a word, item, etc., in another part. *—v.t.*, *v.i.* **2.** to cross-refer.

cross-relation (krŏs′rĭ lā′shən), *n. Music.* a false relation.

crossroad (krŏs′rōd′), *n.* **1.** a road that crosses another road, or one that runs transversely to main roads. **2.** a byroad. **3. a.** (*often pl., construed as sing.*) the place where roads intersect. **b.** (*usually pl.*) a stage at which a vital decision must be made.

crossruff (krŏs′rŭf′), *Whist, Bridge.* *—n.* **1.** a play in which each hand of a partnership trumps a different suit; a seesaw. *—v.t.*, *v.i.* **2.** to play by means of a crossruff.

cross-section (krŏs′sĕk′shən), *n.* **1.** a section made by a plane cutting anything transversely, esp. at right angles to the longest axis. See diag. under **section. 2.** a piece so cut off. **3.** the act of cutting anything across. **4.** a typical selection; a sample showing all characteristic parts, etc.: *a cross-section of British opinion.* **5.** *Survey.* a vertical section of the ground surface taken at right angles to a survey line. *—v.t.* **6.** to cut or make into a cross-section. —**cross′-sec′tional,** *adj.*

cross-staff (krŏs′stäf′), *n. Survey.* a surveyor's instrument, having two sights at right angles to each other and used for setting out right angles in the field.

cross-stitch (krŏs′stĭch′), *n.* **1.** a kind of stitching employing pairs of diagonal stitches of the same length crossing each other in the middle at right angles. *—v.t.*, *v.i.* **2.** to work in cross-stitch.

cross-street (krŏs′strēt′), *n.* a street crossing another street, or one running transversely to main streets.

cross-talk (krŏs′tôk′), *n.* **1.** *Electronics.* unwanted interference between two neighbouring circuits. **2.** *Parl. Proc.* an interchange of remarks across the house between members of different parties. **3.** rapid, witty dialogue.

cross-town (krŏs′toun′), *adj. U.S.* that runs across the town: *a cross-town bus.*

crosstree (krŏs′trē′), *n. Naut.* one of the horizontal transverse pieces of timber or metal fastened to the head of a lower mast or topmast in order to support the top, spread the shrouds, etc.

C, Crosstree

crossway (krŏs′wā′), *n.* a crossroad.

cross-wind (krŏs′wĭnd′), *n.* a wind blowing at right angles to the line of flight of an aircraft.

crosswire (krŏs′wī′ə), *n.* crosshair.

crosswise (krŏs′wīz′), *adv.* **1.** across; transversely. **2.** in the form of a cross. **3.** *U.S.* contrarily. Also, **crossways** (krŏs′wāz′).

crossword puzzle (krŏs′wûd′), a puzzle in which words corresponding to given meanings are to be supplied and fitted into a particular figure divided into spaces, the letters of the words being arranged across the figure, or vertically, or sometimes otherwise.

crosswort (krŏs′wût′), *n.* a rubiaceous perennial herb, *Galium cruciata*, with pale yellow flowers, of calcareous soils of Europe and Asia.

crotalin (krŏt′ə lĭn), *n.* **1.** *Biochem.* a preparation from the venom of the rattlesnakes *Crotalus horridus* and *C. adamanteus*, formerly used in the treatment of epilepsy. **2.** (*cap.*) a trademark for this preparation.

crotch (krŏch), *n.* **1.** a forked piece, part, support, etc. **2.** a forking or place of forking, as of the human body between the legs. **3.** the part of a pair of trousers, pants, etc., formed by the joining of the two legs. **4.** a piece of material, so used in the join. [var. of CRUTCH] —**crotched** (krŏcht), *adj.*

crotchet (krŏch′ĭt), *n.* **1.** a hooklike device or part. **2.** *Entomol.* a small hooklike process. **3.** a curved surgical instrument with a sharp hook. **4.** an odd fancy or whimsical notion. **5.** *Music.* a note having one quarter of the time value of a semibreve or half the value of a minim. See illus. under **note. 6.** *Obs.* a small hook. [ME *crochet*, t. OF. See CROCHET]

crotchety (krŏch′ĭ tĭ), *adj.* **1.** given to crotchets or odd fancies; full of crotchets. **2.** of the nature of a crotchet. **3.** *Colloq.* irritable, difficult, or cross. —**crotch′etiness,** *n.*

croton (krō′tn), *n.* **1.** any of the chiefly tropical euphorbiaceous plants constituting the genus *Croton*, many species of which, as *C. tiglium*, have important medicinal properties. **2.** (among florists) any plant of the related genus *Codiaeum* (or *Phyllaurea*) cultivated for the ornamental foliage. [NL, t. Gk: m. *krotṓn* a tick, also a plant having ticklike seeds]

crotonic acid (krō tŏn′ĭk), *Chem.* a colourless, crystalline compound, $CH_3CHCHCOOH$, used in organic synthesis.

croton oil, a powerful purgative oil from *Croton tiglium* (**croton-oil plant**), a euphorbiaceous shrub or tree of the East Indies.

crouch (krouch), *v.i.* **1.** to stoop or bend low. **2.** to bend close to the ground, as an animal preparing to spring, or shrinking with fear. **3.** to bow or stoop servilely; cringe. *—v.t.* **4.** to bend low. *—n.* **5.** the act of crouching; a stooping or bending low. [ME *crouche(n)*, t. OF: m. *crochir* become bent, der. *croche* hook]

crouchback (krouch′băk′), *Archaic.* *—n.* **1.** a crooked or hunched back. **2.** one who has a crooked back; a hunchback. *—adj.* **3.** having a hunched back.

croup^1 (kro͞op), *n. Pathol.* any affection of the larynx or trachea characterized by a hoarse cough and difficult breathing. [n. use of *croup*, v. (now dial.), cry hoarsely, b. CROAK and WHOOP]

croup^2 (kro͞op), *n.* the rump or buttocks of certain animals, esp. of a horse. Also, **croupe.** See illus. under **horse.** [ME *croupe*, t. F, t. Gmc; cf. CROP]

croupade (kro͞o pād′), *n.* in dressage, a leap in which a horse draws up its hind legs towards the belly.

croupier (kro͞o′pĭ ə; *Fr.* kro͞o pyė′), *n.* **1.** an attendant who collects and pays the money at a gaming table. **2.** one who at a public dinner sits at the lower end of the table as assistant chairman. [t. F; orig., one who rides behind on the croup of another's horse]

croupous (kro͞o′pəs), *adj. Pathol.* pertaining to, of the nature of, or resembling croup.

croupy (kro͞o′pĭ), *adj.* **1.** pertaining to or resembling croup. **2.** affected with croup.

crouse (kro͞os), *adj. Scot. and N Dial.* bold; brisk; lively. [ME *crus, crous(e)*, prob. t. Fris.: m. *krus* cocky, wild, etc.]

croustade (kro͞o städ′, kro͞o′städ), *n.* a shell or case of fried bread, pastry, mashed potatoes, etc., for filling with ragout or the like.

crouton (kro͞o′tŏn; *Fr.* kro͞o tôɴ′), *n.* a small piece of fried or toasted bread, used in soups, etc. [t. F, der. *croûte.* See CRUST]

crow^1 (krō), *n.* **1.** certain of the oscine birds constituting the genus *Corvus* (family *Corvidae*), with lustrous black plumage and a characteristic harsh cry of 'caw', as the **carrion crow** (*C. corone*) of Europe and the **American crow** (*C. brachyrhynchos*). **2.** certain birds of the family *Corvidae*, as the chough, or **Cornish crow,** *Pyrrhocorax graculus.* **3.** any of various similar birds of other families, as the **pied crow** of Australia. **4.** *Astron.* the southern constellation Corvus. **5.** a crowbar. **6. as the crow flies,** in a straight line. **7. eat crow,** *U.S.* to be forced to do or say something very unpleasant or humiliating. **8. have a crow to pluck with,** to have an unpleasant matter to discuss with. [ME; OE *crāwe.* See CROW^2, v.]

Carrion crow, *Corvus corone* (18 in. long)

crow^2 (krō), *v.*, **crowed** (or **crew** *for 1*), **crowed, crowing,** *n.* *—v.i.* **1.** to utter the characteristic cry of a cock. **2.** to utter an inarticulate cry of pleasure, as an infant does. **3.** to exult loudly; boast. —*n.* **4.** the characteristic cry of the cock. **5.** an inarticulate cry of pleasure. [ME *crowe(n)*, OE *crāwen*, c. D *kraaien*, G *krähen*; imit.]

Crow (krō), *n.* **1.** a North American Indian tribe, belonging to the Siouan linguistic stock, found in eastern Montana. **2.** a member of this tribe. **3.** a Siouan language closely related to Hidatsa. [trans. (through F *gens de corbeaux*) of their own name, *Absaroke* crow, sparrowhawk, or bird people]

crowbar (krō′bä′), *n.* a bar of iron, often with a wedge-shaped end, for use as a lever, etc.

crowberry (krō′bə rĭ, -brĭ), *n.*, *pl.* **-ries.** **1.** the insipid black or reddish berry of an evergreen heathlike shrub, *Empetrum nigrum*, of northern regions. **2.** the plant itself, of the family *Empetraceae*.

crow blackbird, any of several North American birds of the genus *Quiscalus* (family *Icteridae*), as *Q. quiscula*, the purple grackle, noted for iridescent black plumage and trough-shaped tails.

crowd[1] (kroud), *n.* **1.** a large number of persons gathered closely together; a throng. **2.** any large number of persons. **3.** people in general; the masses. **4.** any group or set of persons: *a jolly crowd.* **5.** a large number of things gathered or considered together. **6.** *Sociol.* a group of persons acting together only through temporary stimulus, having no past or future continuity. —*v.i.* **7.** to gather in large numbers; throng; swarm. **8.** to press forward; advance by pushing. —*v.t.* **9.** to push; shove. **10.** to press closely together; force into a confined space. **11.** to fill to excess; fill by crowding or pressing into. **12.** *U.S. Colloq.* to urge; press by solicitation; annoy by urging: *to crowd a debtor for immediate payment.* **13.** **crowd (on) sail,** *Naut.* to carry a press of sail. [ME *crowde(n)*, OE *crūdan*, c. MD *kruyden*]

—**Syn.** 1. CROWD, MULTITUDE, SWARM, THRONG, MOB are terms referring to large numbers of people. CROWD suggests a jostling, uncomfortable, and possibly disordered company: *a crowd gathered to listen to the speech.* MULTITUDE emphasizes the great number of persons or things but suggests that there is space enough for all: *a multitude of people at the market on Saturdays.* MOB and SWARM as used of people are usually contemptuous, suggesting a moving, restless, often noisy, crowd: *a swarm of dirty children played in the street.* THRONG suggests a company that presses together or forwards, often with some common aim: *the throng pushed forwards to see the cause of the excitement.* 10. pack, cram, squeeze, cramp.

crowd[2] (kroud), *n.* an ancient Celtic musical instrument related to the kithara, but bowed. Also, **crwth.** [ME *crowde*, t. Welsh: m. *crwth*]

crowded (krou′dĭd), *adj.* **1.** filled to excess; filled with a crowd; packed: *crowded streets.* **2.** uncomfortably close together: *crowded passengers on a bus.* —**crowd′edly,** *adv.* —**crowd′edness,** *n.*

crowfoot (krō′fŏŏt′), *n.*, *pl.* **-foots** for 1 and 2, **-feet** for 3 and 4. **1.** any plant of the genus *Ranunculus*, esp. one with divided leaves suggestive of a crow's foot; a buttercup. **2.** any of various other plants with leaves or other parts suggestive of a bird's foot, as certain species of the genus *Geranium.* **3.** caltrop. **4.** *Naut.* a device consisting of small diverging lines or cords rove through a block of wood, used for suspending awnings, etc.

crow garlic, an Old World liliaceous plant, *Allium vineale*, which often bears bulbils in place of flowers.

crowkeeper (krō′kē′pə), *n. Dial.* scarecrow.

crown (kroun), *n.* **1.** an ornamental wreath or garland for the head, conferred by the ancients as a mark of victory or distinction. **2.** honorary distinction; reward. **3.** a decorative fillet or covering for the head, worn as a symbol of sovereignty. **4.** the power or dominion of a sovereign. **5.** **the Crown,** the sovereign as head of the state, or the supreme governing power of a state under a monarchical government. **6.** any crownlike emblem or design, used in a heraldic crest, as a badge of rank in some armies, etc. **7.** a coin of several countries generally bearing a crown or a crowned head on the obverse. The commemoratively minted English crown is worth five shillings. **8.** a krone or a krona. **9.** a size of paper, 15 × 20 inches. **10.** something having the form of a crown, as the corona of a flower. **11.** *Bot.* **a.** the leaves and living branches of a tree. **b.** the point at which the root of a seed plant joins the stem. **c.** a circle of appendages on the throat of the corolla, etc.; corona. **12.** the top or highest part of anything, as of the head, a hat, a mountain, etc. **13.** the head itself: *he broke his crown.* **14.** the crest, as of a bird. **15.** *Dentistry.* **a.** that part of a tooth which is covered by enamel. **b.** an artificial substitute, as of gold or porcelain, for the crown of a tooth. **16.** *Rare.* the highest or most perfect state of anything. **17.** an exalting or chief attribute. **18.** the acme or supreme source of honour, excellence, beauty, etc. **19.** crown glass. **20.** *Naut.* the part of an anchor where the arms join the shank. **21.** the part of a cut gem above the girdle. —*v.t.* **22.** to place a crown or garland upon the head of. **23.** to invest with a regal crown, or with regal dignity and power. **24.** to honour as with a crown; reward; invest with honour, dignity, etc. **25.** to surmount as with a crown; surmount as a crown does. **26.** *Colloq.* to hit on the top of the head. **27.** to complete worthily; bring to a successful or effective conclusion. **28.** *Draughts.* to change (a piece) into a king, after it has safely reached the last row, by putting another piece on top of it. [ME *croune, coroune*, t. AF, g. L *corōna* garland, wreath, crown. Cf. CORONA] —**crown′er,** *n.*

crown agent, **1.** an agent for the crown in charge of the finances of a crown colony. **2.** (*caps.*) *Law.* (in Scotland) the solicitor to the department of the Lord Advocate.

crown cap, a clasping metal bottle cap, often lined with cork.

crown colony, a colony in which the crown has the entire control of legislation and administration, as distinguished from one having a constitution and representative government.

crown court, *Law.* a court of quarter sessions and assizes.

crown daisy, summer chrysanthemum.

crowner (krou′nə), *n. Obs. Dial.* coroner.

crown gall, a bacterial disease producing abnormal growths on fruit trees and other plants, caused by *Agrobacterium tumefaciens.*

crown glass, **1.** an optical glass of low dispersion and generally low refractive index. **2.** an old form of window glass formed by blowing a globe and whirling it into a disc: composed essentially of soda, lime, and silica.

crown graft, *Hort.* a graft in which the scion is inserted at the crown of the stock.

crown imperial, a liliaceous bulbous plant, *Fritillaria imperialis*, with an erect stem bearing a whorl of large pendulous flowers near the top.

crown jewels, the jewels used by the sovereign on state occasions.

crownland (kroun′lănd′), *n.* one of the provinces or great administrative divisions of the former empire of Austria-Hungary.

Crown land, land belonging to the Crown, the revenue from which goes to the reigning sovereign.

crownpiece (kroun′pēs′), *n.* **1.** a piece or part forming or fitting the crown or top of anything. **2.** crown (def. 7).

crown prince, the heir apparent of a monarch.

crown princess, **1.** the heiress apparent of a monarch. **2.** the wife of a crown prince.

crown saw, a rotary saw consisting of a hollow cylinder with teeth on its end or edge, as the surgeons' trephine.

crown wheel, **1.** the larger of the two wheels in a bevel gear. See illus. under **gear.** **2.** *Horol.* a wheel next to the winding knob, having two sets of teeth, one at right angles to its plane.

crown witness, a witness for the Crown in a criminal prosecution.

crownwork (kroun′wûk′), *n. Fort.* an outwork containing a central bastion with a curtain and demibastions, usually designed to cover some advantageous position.

crow's-foot (krōz′fŏŏt′), *n.*, *pl.* **-feet.** **1.** (*usually pl.*) a wrinkle at the outer corner of the eye. **2.** *Tailoring.* a three-pointed embroidered figure used as a finish.

crow's-nest (krōz′nĕst′), *n. Naut.* **1.** a box or shelter for the lookout man, secured near the top of a mast. **2.** a similar lookout station ashore.

crow step, one of a series of steps on the face of a gable, sometimes used instead of a slope. Also, **corbie step.**

crow-stepped gable, a gable with crow steps. Also, **corbie gable.**

Croydon (kroi′dn), *n.* a S outer London borough. 328,300 (1965).

croze (krōz), *n.* **1.** the groove at the ends of the staves of a barrel, cask, etc., into which the edge of the head fits. **2.** a tool for cutting such a groove. [cf. F *creux* groove]

crozier (krō′zhə), *n.* crosier.

C.R.P., (L *Calendarium Rotulorum Patentium*) Calendar of the Patent Rolls.

cruces (krōō′sēz), *n.* pl. of **crux.**

crucial (krōō′shəl), *adj.* **1.** involving a final and supreme decision; decisive; critical: *a crucial experiment.* **2.** severe; trying. **3.** of the form of a cross; cross-shaped. [f. *cruci-* (t. L, comb. form of *crux* cross) + -AL[1]] —**cru′cially,** *adv.*

cruciate (krōō′shĭ ĭt, -āt′), *adj.* **1.** cross-shaped. **2.** *Bot.* having the form of a cross with equal arms, as the flowers of mustard, etc. **3.** *Entomol.* crossing each other diagonally in repose, as the wings of an insect. [t. NL: m. s. *cruciātus*, der. L *crux* CROSS]

Cruciate flower

crucible (krōō′sĭ bl), *n.* **1.** a vessel of metal or refractory material employed for heating substances to high temperatures.

2. (in a metallurgical furnace) the hollow part at the bottom, in which molten metal collects. 3. a severe, searching test. [t. ML: m. s. *crucibulum* night lamp, melting pot; this ? m. *crucibolum* whale oil cruse (cf. L *bālaena* whale). See CRUSE]

crucible steel, steel made in a crucible, esp. a high-grade steel prepared by melting selected materials.

crucifer (kroo͞/sĭ fə), *n.* 1. one who carries a cross, as in ecclesiastical processions. 2. *Bot.* a cruciferous plant. [t. LL]

cruciferous (kroo͞ sĭf/ə rəs), *adj.* 1. bearing a cross. 2. *Bot.* belonging or pertaining to the family *Cruciferae* or *Brassicaceae*, whose members bear flowers having a crosslike, four-petalled corolla; brassicaceous. [f. LL *crucifer* cross-bearing + -OUS]

crucifix (kroo͞/sĭ fĭks), *n.* 1. a cross with the figure of Jesus crucified upon it. 2. any cross. [ME, t. LL: s. *crucifixus*, pp., fixed to a cross]

crucifixion (kroo͞/sĭ fĭk/shən), *n.* 1. the act of crucifying. 2. (*cap.*) the death of Jesus by exposure upon a cross. 3. a picture or other representation of this.

cruciform (kroo͞/sĭ fôm/), *adj.* cross-shaped. [f. s. L *crux* cross + -(I)FORM] —**cru/ciform/ly,** *adv.*

crucify (kroo͞/sĭ fī/), *v.t.*, **-fied, -fying.** 1. to put to death by nailing or binding the body to a cross. 2. to torment; treat with severity. 3. to subdue (passion, sin, etc.). [ME *crucifien*, t. OF: m. *crucifier*, t. LL: m. *crucifigere* fix to a cross. See -FY] —**cru/cifi/er,** *n.*

crud (krŭd), *v.t.*, *v.i.*, **crudded, crudding.** *Obs. or Dial.* to curd. [metathetic var. of CURD]

crude (kroo͞d), *adj.*, **cruder, crudest.** 1. in a raw or unprepared state; unrefined: *crude oil, sugar, etc.* 2. unripe; not mature. 3. lacking finish, polish, proper arrangement, or completeness: *a crude summary.* 4. lacking culture, refinement, tact, etc.: *crude persons, behaviour, speech,* etc. [ME, t. L: m. s. *crūdus* raw, crude, rough. Cf. CRUEL] —**crude/ly,** *adv.* —**crude/ness,** *n.* —**Syn.** 1. unfinished. See **raw.** 2. undeveloped. 3. unpolished. 4. uncouth, rough, rude, coarse, clumsy. —**Ant.** 4. cultivated.

crudity (kroo͞/dĭ tĭ), *n.*, *pl.* **-ties.** 1. the state or quality of being crude. 2. an instance of this; anything crude.

cruel (kroo͞/əl), *adj.* 1. disposed to inflict suffering; indifferent to, or taking pleasure in, the pain or distress of another; hard-hearted; pitiless. 2. causing, or marked by, great pain or distress: *a cruel remark.* [ME, t. OF, g. L *crūdēlis* hard, cruel, akin to *crudus* CRUDE] —**cru/elly,** *adv.* —**cru/elness,** *n.*

—**Syn.** 1. barbarous, bloodthirsty, ferocious, merciless, relentless, implacable. CRUEL, PITILESS, RUTHLESS, BRUTAL, SAVAGE imply readiness to cause pain to others, and being unmoved by their suffering. CRUEL implies willingness to cause pain, and indifference to suffering: *a cruel stepfather, cruel to animals.* PITILESS adds the idea of hard-heartedness and positive refusal to show compassion: *pitiless to captives, fate that seems pitiless.* RUTHLESS implies cruelty and unscrupulousness, letting nothing stand in one's way, and using any methods necessary: *ruthless in pressing an advantage, ruthless greed.* BRUTAL implies cruelty which takes the form of physical violence: *a brutal master.* SAVAGE suggests fierceness and brutality: *savage battles, jealousy.*

cruelty (kroo͞/əl tĭ), *n.*, *pl.* **-ties.** 1. the state or quality of being cruel. 2. cruel disposition or conduct. 3. a cruel act. —**Syn.** 1. harshness, brutality, ruthlessness, barbarity, inhumanity, atrocity. —**Ant.** 2, 3. kindness.

cruet (kroo͞/ĭt), *n.* 1. a set, on a stand, of containers for salt, pepper, and mustard or for vinegar and oil. 2. an individual container. 3. any of the contents. 4. *Eccles.* one of the vessels used in the celebration of the mass for holding wine or water. [ME, t. OF, dim. of *crue* pitcher, pot, t. Gmc; cf. G *Krug* pot]

Cruft's (krŭfts), *n.* an international dog show, founded 1886, held annually in London. [named after Charles *Cruft*, 1852–1938]

Cruickshank (kro͝ok/shăngk/), *n.* **George,** 1792–1878, English artist and caricaturist.

cruise (kroo͞z), *v.*, **cruised, cruising,** *n.* —*v.i.* 1. to sail to and fro, or from place to place, as in search of hostile ships, or for pleasure. 2. *Aeron.* to fly at practical rather than high speed, esp. at the speed which permits maximum operating efficiency. 3. *Colloq.* (of a car, aeroplane, etc.) to move along easily at a moderate speed. —*v.t.* 4. to cruise over. —*n.* 5. the act of cruising; a voyage made by cruising. [t. D: m. *kruisen* cross, cruise, der. *kruis* cross]

cruiser (kroo͞/zə), *n.* 1. one who or that which cruises, as a person or a ship. 2. one of a class of warships of medium tonnage, designed for high speed and long cruising radius. 3. a boat, usually power-driven, adapted for pleasure trips.

cruiserweight (kroo͞/zə wāt/), *n.* a boxer in the light-heavyweight group, weighing between 11 st. 10 lbs and 12 st. 10 lbs.

crumb (krŭm), *n.* 1. a small particle of bread, cake, etc., such as breaks or falls off. 2. a small particle or portion of anything. 3. the soft inner portion of bread (distinguished from *crust*). —*v.t.* 4. *Cookery.* to dress or prepare with breadcrumbs; to bread. 5. to break into crumbs or small fragments. Also, (formerly) **crum.** [ME *crumme*, OE *cruma*, akin to G *Krume*]

crumble (krŭm/bl), *v.*, **-bled, -bling,** *n.* —*v.t.* 1. to break into small fragments or crumbs. —*v.i.* 2. to fall into small pieces; break or part into small fragments. 3. to decay; disappear piecemeal. —*n.* 4. something crumbling or crumbled. 5. a sweet dish containing stewed fruit topped by a rubbed-in mixture of flour, fat, and sugar. [earlier *crimble*, freq. of OE *gecrymman* crumble (der. *cruma* crumb); assimilated in form to CRUMB]

crumbly (krŭm/blĭ), *adj.*, **-blier, -bliest.** apt to crumble; friable.

crumby (krŭm/ĭ), *adj.*, **-ier, -iest.** 1. full of crumbs. 2. soft.

crummy[1] (krŭm/ĭ), *adj.*, **-mier, -miest.** *Slang.* very inferior, mean, or shabby.

crummy[2] (krŭm/ĭ), *n.*, *pl.* **-mies.** a cow with crooked horns. Also, **crummie.** [der. obs. *crum* crooked, OE *crumb*, c. G *krumm*, adj.]

crump (krŭmp), *v.t.* 1. to crunch with the teeth. 2. to strike heavily. —*v.i.* 3. to make a crunching sound, as in walking over snow, or as snow when trodden on. —*n.* 4. a crunching sound. 5. *Colloq.* a heavy blow. 6. *Mil. Slang.* a large explosive shell. [imit.]

crumpet (krŭm/pĭt), *n.* 1. a kind of light, soft bread, cooked on a griddle or the like, and often toasted. 2. *Slang.* a sexually attractive girl or woman. [short for *crumpet cake* curled cake, ME *crompid*, pp. of obs. *crump*, var. of CRIMP]

crumple (krŭm/pl), *v.*, **-pled, -pling,** *n.* —*v.t.* 1. to draw or press into irregular folds; rumple; wrinkle. —*v.i.* 2. to contract into wrinkles; shrink; shrivel. 3. *Colloq.* to collapse; give way. —*n.* 4. an irregular fold or wrinkle produced by crumpling. [freq. of obs. *crump*, var. of CRIMP]

crunch (krŭnch), *v.t.* 1. to crush with the teeth; chew with a crushing noise. 2. to crush or grind noisily. —*v.i.* 3. to chew with a crushing sound. 4. to produce, or proceed with, a crushing noise. —*n.* 5. the act or sound of crunching. 6. *Slang.* a moment of crisis. [b. CRAUNCH and CRUSH]

crunode (kroo͞/nōd), *n.* *Maths.* a node (def. 5) at which the tangents to the two curves are real and distinct (opposed to *acnode*). [irreg. f. L *cru(x)* cross + NODE]

cruor (kroo͞/ô), *n.* coagulated blood, or that portion of the blood which forms the clot. [t. L: blood, gore]

crupper (krŭp/ə), *n.* 1. a leather strap on the back of the saddle of a harness, which passes in a loop under a horse's tail, to prevent the saddle from slipping forward. See illus. under **harness.** 2. the rump or buttocks of a horse. [ME *cropere*, t. OF, der. *crope.* See CROUP[2]]

crural (kro͝oə/rəl), *adj.* of or pertaining to the crus, or leg, or the hind limb. [t. L: s. *crūrālis*, der. *crūs* leg]

crus (krŭs), *n.*, *pl.* **crura** (kro͝oə/rə). 1. *Anat., Zool.* **a.** that part of the leg or hind limb between the femur or thigh and the ankle or tarsus; the shank. **b.** an elongated process, as of a bone or other structure. 2. any of various parts likened to a leg. [t. L: leg]

crusade (kroo͞ sād/), *n.*, *v.*, **-saded, -sading.** —*n.* 1. (*often cap.*) any of the military expeditions undertaken by the Christians of Europe in the 11th, 12th, and 13th centuries for the recovery of the Holy Land from the Muslims. 2. any war carried on under papal sanction. 3. any vigorous, aggressive movement for the defence or advancement of an idea, cause, etc. 4. a campaign to stimulate or increase Christian faith. Cf. **mission.** —*v.i.* 5. to go on or engage in a crusade. [b. earlier *crusada* (t. Sp.: m. *cruzada*) and *croisade* (t. F). See CROSS, -ADE[1]] —**crusad/er,** *n.*

crusado (kroo͞ sā/dō), *n.*, *pl.* **-does, -dos.** an early Portuguese coin of gold or silver, bearing the figure of a cross. [t. Pg.: m. *cruzado*, prop. pp. of *cruzar* mark with a cross. Cf. CRUSADE]

cruse (kroo͞z), *n.* an earthen pot, bottle, etc., for liquids. [t. MD]

crush (krŭsh), *v.t.* 1. to press and bruise between two hard bodies; squeeze out of shape or normal condition. 2. to break into small fragments or particles, as ore, stone, etc. 3. to force out by pressing or squeezing. 4. to put down, overpower, or subdue completely; overwhelm. 5. to oppress grievously. 6. *Archaic.* to drink (wine, etc.). —*v.i.* 7. to become crushed. 8. to advance with crushing; press or crowd forcibly. —*n.* 9. the act of crushing. 10. the state of being crushed. 11. *Colloq.* a great crowd; a crowded social gathering. 12. a beverage made by expressing the juice from fruit, as from oranges.

13. *Colloq.* **a.** an infatuation. **b.** the object of this infatuation. [ME *crusch(en)*, appar. t. OF: m. *croissir* crash, gnash, break, crush; prob. t. Gmc] —**crush′er,** *n.* —**Syn. 1.** crumple, rumple. **2.** shatter, pulverize, mash. See **break. 5.** quell, subdue, overcome.

Crusoe (kro͞o′sō), *n.* **Robinson,** the shipwrecked seaman in Defoe's novel *Robinson Crusoe* (1719), who lives adventurously for years on a small uninhabited island.

crust (krŭst), *n.* **1.** the hard outer portion of a loaf of bread (distinguished from *crumb*). **2.** a piece of this. **3.** the outside covering of a pie. **4.** any more or less hard external covering or coating. **5.** the hard outer shell or covering of an animal or plant. **6.** the exterior portion of the earth, accessible to examination. **7.** a scab or eschar. **8.** deposit from wine, as it ripens, on the interior of bottles, consisting of tartar and colouring matter. **9.** *Slang.* impertinence. —*v.t.* **10.** to cover with or as with a crust; encrust. **11.** to form (something) into a crust. —*v.i.* **12.** to form or contract a crust. **13.** to form into a crust. [ME, t. L: s. *crusta* rind; r. ME *crouste,* t. OF]

crustacean (krŭs tā′shyən), *adj.* **1.** belonging to the *Crustacea,* a class of (chiefly aquatic) arthropods, including the lobsters, shrimps, crabs, barnacles, woodlice, etc., commonly having the body covered with a hard shell or crust. —*n.* **2.** a crustacean animal.

crustaceous (krŭs tā′shyəs), *adj.* **1.** of the nature of or pertaining to a crust or shell. **2.** belonging to the *Crustacea.* **3.** having a hard covering or crust. [t. NL: m. *crustāceus* hard-shelled]

crustal (krŭs′tl), *adj.* of or pertaining to a crust, as that of the earth.

crusty (krŭs′tĭ), *adj.,* **crustier, crustiest. 1.** of the nature of or resembling a crust; having a crust. **2.** harsh; surly; crabbed: *crusty person, manner, remark, etc.* —**crust′ily,** *adv.* —**crust′iness,** *n.*

crutch (krŭch), *n.* **1.** a staff or support to assist a lame or infirm person in walking, now usually with a crosspiece at one end to fit under the armpit. **2.** any of various devices resembling this in shape or use. **3.** a forked support or part. **4.** a forked rest for the legs in side-saddle. **5.** the crotch of the human body. **6.** *Naut.* a forked support for the booms, when the sails are stowed. —*v.t.* **7.** to support on crutches; prop; sustain. [ME *crucche,* OE *crycc,* c. D *kruk* and G *Krücke.* Cf. CROOK]

crutched (krŭcht, krŭch′ĭd), *adj.* having or bearing a cross: *a crutched friar.*

crux (krŭks), *n., pl.* **cruxes, cruces** (kro͞o′sēz). **1.** a vital, basic, or decisive point. **2.** a cross. **3.** something that torments by its puzzling nature; a perplexing difficulty. [t. L: cross, torment, trouble]

Crux (krŭks), *n., gen.* **Crucis** (kro͞o′sĭs). *Astron.* the Southern Cross.

crux ansata (krŭks′ ăn sā′tə), a T-shaped cross with a loop at the top; ankh. [L: cross with a handle]

Cruz (*Sp.* kro͞oth), *n.* **Ramón de la** (*Sp.* rȧ mōn′ dė lȧ), 1731–94, Spanish playwright.

cruzeiro (kro͞o zē′ə′rō; *Port.* kro͞o zĕy′ro͞o), *n., pl.* **-ros. 1.** the monetary unit of Brazil, equal to 100 centavos, and equivalent to about £0·1538. **2.** a note or coin of this value. *Abbrev.*: Cr.$. [t. Pg., equiv. to *cruz* CROSS + *-eiro* -ER[2]]

crwth (kro͞oth), *n. Music.* crowd[2]. [t. Welsh]

cry (krī), *v.,* **cried, crying,** *n., pl.* **cries.** —*v.i.* **1.** to utter inarticulate sounds, esp. of lamentation, grief, or suffering, usually with tears. **2.** to weep; shed tears, with or without sound. **3.** to call loudly; shout. **4.** to give forth vocal sounds or characteristic calls, as animals; yelp; bark. —*v.t.* **5.** to utter or pronounce loudly; call out. **6.** to announce orally in public; sell by outcry. **7.** to beg for or implore in a loud voice. **8.** to disparage; belittle (fol. by *down*). **9.** to break a promise, agreement, etc. (fol. by *off*). **10.** to praise; extol (fol. by *up*). —*n.* **11.** the act or sound of crying; any loud utterance or exclamation; a shout, scream, or wail. **12.** clamour; outcry. **13.** an entreaty; appeal. **14.** *Obs.* an oral proclamation or announcement. **15.** a call of wares for sale, etc., as by a street vendor. **16.** public report. **17.** an opinion generally expressed. **18.** a battle cry. **19.** a political or party slogan. **20.** a fit of weeping. **21.** the utterance or call of an animal. **22.** a pack of hounds. **23. a far cry, a.** quite some distance; a long way. **b.** only remotely related; very different. [ME *crie(n),* t. OF: m. *crier,* g. L *quirītāre*] —**cry′ingly,** *adv.*

—**Syn. 1.** wail, bewail, weep, sob, squall, blubber, whimper, mewl, pule. **3.** clamour, vociferate, exclaim, ejaculate, bawl, scream, howl, yell, yowl. CRY, SHOUT, BELLOW, ROAR refer to kinds of loud articulate or inarticulate sounds. CRY is the general word: *to cry out.* To SHOUT is to raise the voice loudly in uttering words or other articulate sounds: *he shouted back to his companions.* BELLOW especially refers to the loud, deep cry of a bull, etc., or, somewhat in deprecation, to human utterance which suggests such a sound: *the speaker bellowed his answer.* ROAR refers to a deep, hoarse, rumbling or vibrant cry; it often implies tumultuous volume: *the crowd roared.* **6.** hawk. **11.** roar, howl, yell, whoop.

cry-baby (krī′bā′bĭ), *n., pl.* **-bies.** *Colloq.* one given to crying like a baby, or to weak display of injured feeling.

crying (krī′ĭng), *adj.* **1.** that cries; clamorous; wailing; weeping. **2.** demanding attention or remedy: *a crying evil.* —**Syn. 2.** flagrant, notorious, urgent.

cryo-, a word element meaning 'icy cold', 'frost', 'low temperature'. [t. Gk: m. *kryo-,* comb. form of *krýos*]

cryogen (krī′ə jən), *n.* a substance for producing low temperatures; a freezing mixture.

cryogenics (krī′ə jĕn′ĭks), *n. Physics.* that branch of physics concerned with the properties of materials at very low temperatures. —**cry′ogen′ic,** *adj.*

cryohydrate (krī′ō hī′drāt), *n.* a mixture of ice and another substance in definite proportions such that a minimum melting or freezing point is attained.

cryolite (krī′ə līt′), *n.* a mineral, sodium aluminium fluoride, Na_3AlF_6, occurring in white masses, used as a flux in the electrolytic production of aluminium and as an insecticide; Greenland spar.

cryometer (krī ŏm′ĭ tə), *n.* a thermometer for the measurement of low temperatures, as one containing alcohol instead of mercury.

cryoscope (krī′ə skōp′), *n. Physics.* an instrument for determining freezing and solidification points.

cryoscopic method (krī′ə skŏp′ĭk), *Chem.* a method of determining the molecular weight of a dissolved substance by measuring the depression of the freezing point produced by a known concentration.

cryoscopy (krī ŏs′kə pĭ), *n.* **1.** the determination of the freezing points of liquids or solutions, or of the lowering of the freezing points by dissolved substances. **2.** *Med.* the determination of the freezing points of certain bodily fluids, as urine, for diagnosis.

cryostat (krī′ə stăt′), *n.* an apparatus, usually automatic, maintaining a very low constant temperature.

cryotherapy (krī′ō thĕ′rə pĭ), *n. Med.* treatment by means of applications of ice.

cryotron (krī′ə trŏn′), *n. Physics.* a miniature switch which operates at the temperature of liquid helium and which depends on superconductivity.

crypt (krĭpt), *n.* **1.** a subterranean chamber or vault, esp. one beneath the main floor of a church, used as a burial place, etc. **2.** *Anat.* a slender pit or recess; a small glandular cavity. [t. L: s. *crypta,* t. Gk: m. *kryptḗ,* prop. fem. of *kryptós* hidden] —**crypt′al,** *adj.*

cryptic (krĭp′tĭk), *adj.* **1.** hidden; secret; occult. **2.** *Zool.* fitted for concealing. Also, **cryp′tical.** —**cryp′tically,** *adv.*

crypto-, a word element meaning 'hidden', as in *cryptoclastic.* Also, before vowels, **crypt-.** [comb. form repr. Gk *kryptós*]

cryptoclastic (krĭp′tō klăs′tĭk), *adj. Geol.* composed of fragments invisible to the unaided eye.

cryptocrystalline (krĭp′tō krĭs′tə līn′), *adj. Mineral.* indistinctly crystalline or consisting of very small crystals which cannot be easily distinguished.

cryptogam (krĭp′tō găm′), *n. Bot.* **1.** any of the *Cryptogamia,* an old primary division of plants comprising those without true flowers and seeds, as the ferns, mosses, and thallophytes. **2.** a plant without a true seed (opposed to *phanerogam*). [back-formation from NL *cryptogamia,* f. *crypto-* CRYPTO- + Gk *-gamia* married state] —**cryp′togam′ic, cryptogamous** (krĭp tŏg′ə məs), *adj.*

cryptogenic (krĭp′tō jĕn′ĭk), *adj.* of obscure or unknown origin, as a disease.

cryptogram (krĭp′tō grăm′), *n.* a message or writing in secret characters or otherwise occult; a cryptograph. —**cryp′togram′mic,** *adj.*

cryptograph (krĭp′tō grăf′, -grăf′), *n.* **1.** a cryptogram. **2.** a system of secret writing; a cipher. **3.** a device for translating text into cipher.

cryptography (krĭp tŏg′rə fĭ), *n.* **1.** the process or art of writing in secret characters or in cipher. **2.** anything so written. —**cryptog′rapher, cryptog′raphist,** *n.* —**cryptographic** (krĭp′tō grăf′ĭk), *adj.*

cryptonym (krĭp′tō nĭm), *n.* a secret name. [f. CRYPT- + Gk *ónym(a)* name]

cryptonymous (krĭp tŏn′ĭ məs), *adj.* anonymous.

cryptozoite (krĭp′tō zō′īt), *n. Zool., Med.* the phase in the development of malaria parasites in their vertebrate hosts during which they live in cells other than red corpuscles, as in the human liver.

cryst., crystallography. Also, **crystall.**

crystal (krĭs′tl), *n.* **1.** a clear, transparent mineral or glass resembling ice. **2.** the transparent form of crystallized quartz. **3.** *Chem., Mineral.* a solid body having a characteristic internal structure and enclosed by symmetrically arranged plane surfaces, intersecting at definite and characteristic angles. **4.** anything made of or resembling such a substance. **5.** a single grain or mass of a crystalline substance. **6.** glass of a high degree of brilliance. **7.** cut glass. **8.** the glass or plastic cover over the face of a watch. **9.** *Radio.* **a.** the piece of galena, carborundum, or the like, forming the essential part of a crystal detector. **b.** the crystal detector itself. **10.** a quartz crystal ground in the shape of a rectangular parallelepiped, which vibrates strongly at one frequency when electric voltages of that frequency are placed across opposite sides. It is used to control the frequency of an oscillator as, for example, the frequency of a radio transmitter. *—adj.* **11.** composed of crystal. **12.** resembling crystal; clear; transparent. **13.** *Radio.* pertaining to or employing a crystal detector. [ME *cristal,* t. OF; r. OE *cristalla,* t. L: m. *crystallum,* t. Gk: m. *krýstallos* ice, crystal] **—crys′tal-like′,** *adj.*

crystal detector, *Radio.* a device for rectifying the alternating currents in a receiving apparatus, consisting essentially of a crystal, as of galena or carborundum, permitting a current to pass freely in one direction only.

crystal face, one of the surfaces of a crystal.

crystal-gazing (krĭs′tl gā′zĭng), *n.* a steady staring at a crystal or glass ball or other clear object in order to arouse visual perceptions, as of distant happenings, the future, etc. **—crystal-gazer** (krĭs′tl gā′zə), *n.*

crystall-, var. of **crystallo-,** used before vowels.

crystall., crystallography.

crystal lattice. See **lattice** (def. 3).

crystalliferous (krĭs′tə lĭf′ə rəs), *adj.* bearing, containing, or yielding crystals. [f. s. L *crystallum* crystal + -(I)FEROUS]

crystalline (krĭs′tə lĭn′), *adj.* **1.** of or like crystal; clear; transparent. **2.** formed by crystallization. **3.** composed of crystals, as rocks. **4.** pertaining to crystals or their formation. [ult. t. Gk: m. *krystállinos*]

crystalline lens, *Anat.* a doubly convex, transparent, lenslike body in the eye, situated behind the iris and serving to focus the rays of light on the retina. See diag. under **eye.**

crystallite (krĭs′tə līt′), *n.* *Mineral.* a minute body in igneous rocks, marking an incipient stage in crystallization. [f. CRYSTALL- + -ITE[1]]

crystallization (krĭs′tə lī zā′shən), *n.* **1.** the act of crystallizing; the process of forming crystals. **2.** a crystallized body or formation. Also, **crystallisation.**

crystallize (krĭs′tə līz′), *v.,* **-lized, -lizing.** *—v.t.* **1.** to form into crystals; cause to assume crystalline form. **2.** to give definite or concrete form to. **3.** *Cookery.* to coat (fruit or flower petals) with sugar to give an attractive, edible finish. *—v.i.* **4.** to form crystals; become crystalline in form. **5.** to assume definite or concrete form. Also, **crystallise. —crys′talliz′able,** *adj.*

crystallo-, a word element meaning 'crystal', as in *crystallographic.* Also, before vowels, **crystall-.** [t. Gk: m. *krystallo-,* comb. form of *krýstallos*]

crystallographic (krĭs′tə lō grăf′ĭk), *adj.* of or pertaining to crystallography. Also, **crys′tallograph′ical. —crys′tallograph′ically,** *adv.*

crystallography (krĭs′tə lŏg′rə fĭ), *n.* the science dealing with crystallization and the forms and structure of crystals. **—crys′tallog′rapher,** *n.*

crystalloid (krĭs′tə loid′), *adj.* **1.** resembling a crystal; of the nature of a crystalloid. *—n.* **2.** a substance (usually crystallizable) which, when dissolved in a liquid, will diffuse readily through vegetable or animal membranes (contrasted with *colloid*). **3.** *Bot.* one of certain minute crystal-like granules of protein, found in the tissues of various seeds. [t. Gk: m. s. *krystalloeidḗs.* See CRYSTAL, -OID] **—crys′talloi′dal,** *adj.*

Crystal Palace, **1.** a vast structure of glass and iron, originally built at Hyde Park to house the Great Exhibition of 1851, removed to a site in S London in 1854, and burnt down in 1936. **2.** the site, on a hill in S London: sports centre. **3.** a district in S London.

crystal rectifier, *Radio.* a semiconducting crystal used as a rectifier: a semiconductor diode.

crystal set, *Radio.* a simple form of radio receiver based on a crystal detector.

crystal violet, a dye derived from rosaniline, used as an indicator in medicine and in Gram's method in bacteriology.

crystal vision, **1.** visual perception, as of distant happenings, the future, etc., supposed to be aroused by crystal-gazing. **2.** that which seems to be perceived.

C.S., **1.** (L *Custos Sigilli*) Keeper of the Seal. **2.** civil servant.

Cs, *Chem.* caesium.

C.S.I., Chartered Surveyors' Institution.

C.S.M., company sergeant major.

C-spring (sē′sprĭng′), *n.* cee-spring.

C.S.T., (in the U.S.) central standard time. Also, **CST, c.s.t.**

C.T., (in the U.S.) central time.

Ct, **1.** Connecticut. **2.** Count.

ct, **1.** cent. **2.** court.

cteno-, *Zool.* a word element referring to comblike scales, as in *ctenophore.* Also, before vowels, **cten-.** [t. Gk: m. *kteno-,* comb. form of *kteís* comb]

ctenoid (tē′noid, tĕn′oid), *adj.* *Zool.* **1.** comblike or pectinate; rough-edged. **2.** having rough-edged scales. [t. Gk: m. s. *ktenoeidḗs* comb-shaped]

ctenophoran (tĭ nŏf′ə rən), *n.* **1.** a member of the *Ctenophora,* a phylum of marine swimming invertebrates with rounded, oval or band-shaped gelatinous bodies and eight meridional rows of ciliated plates. *—adj.* **2.** of, belonging to, or pertaining to this phylum.

ctenophore (tĕn′ə fô′, tē′nə-), *n.* one of the ctenophorans or comb jellies.

Ctesiphon (tĕs′ĭ fŏn′), *n.* a ruined city in Iraq, on the Tigris, near Baghdad: an ancient capital of Parthia.

cts, cents.

Cu, *Chem.* cuprum; copper.

cu., cubic.

cub (kŭb), *n., v.,* **cubbed, cubbing.** *—n.* **1.** the young of certain animals, as the fox, bear, etc. **2.** (in humorous or contemptuous use) an awkward or uncouth youth. **3.** a novice or apprentice, esp. a cub reporter. **4.** a member of the junior division (ages 8–11) of the Scouts; wolf cub. *—v.i., v.t.* **5.** to give birth to (cubs). **6.** to hunt (fox cubs). [var. of COB] **—cub′bish,** *adj.* **—cub′bishness,** *n.*

Cuba (kyōō′bə; *Sp.* kōō′bȧ), *n.* a republic S of Florida: largest island in the West Indies. 6,900,000 pop. (est. 1961); 44,218 sq. mi. *Cap.:* Havana. See map under **Haiti. —Cu′ban,** *adj., n.*

cubage (kyōō′bĭj), *n.* cubature.

Cuba libre (kyōō′bə lē′brə), a drink consisting of rum and a cola drink.

Cuban heel, a high, uncurved heel on a boot or shoe.

cubature (kyōō′bə chə), *n.* **1.** the determination of the cubic contents of a thing. **2.** cubic contents. [der. L *cubus* cube, on model of QUADRATURE]

cubby (kŭb′ĭ), *n., pl.* **-bies.** a snug, confined place; a cubbyhole. [der. *cub* shed; cf. LG *kübje* shed]

cubbyhole (kŭb′ĭ hōl′), *n.* a small enclosed space.

cube (kyōōb), *n., v.,* **cubed, cubing.** *—n.* **1.** a solid bounded by six equal squares, the angle between any two adjacent faces being a right angle. **2.** a piece of anything of this form. **3.** *Arith., Alg.* the third power of a quantity: *the cube of 4 is 4 × 4 × 4, or 64.* *—v.t.* **4.** to make into a cube or cubes. **5.** to measure the cubic contents of. **6.** to raise to the third power; find the cube of. [t. L: m. s. *cubus,* t. Gk: m. *kýbos* die, cube]

cubeb (kyōō′bĕb), *n.* the spicy fruit or drupe of an East Indian piperaceous climbing shrub, *Piper cubeba,* dried in an unripe but fully grown state, and used in the treatment of urinary and bronchial disorders. [ME *quibibe,* t. F: m. *cubèbe,* ult. t. Ar.: m. *kabāba*]

cube root, the quantity of which a given quantity is the cube: *4 is the cube root of 64.*

cube sugar, granulated crystals of sugar formed into rough cubes by a heat-drying process.

cubic (kyōō′bĭk), *adj.* **1.** of three dimensions; solid, or pertaining to solid content: *a cubic foot* (the volume of a cube whose edges are each a foot long). **2.** having the form of a cube. **3.** *Arith., Alg., etc.,* being of the third power or degree. **4.** *Crystall.* belonging or pertaining to the isometric system of crystallization. Also, **cu′bical. —cu′bically,** *adv.* **—cu′bicalness,** *n.*

cubicle (kyōō′bĭ kl), *n.* **1.** a bedroom, esp. one of a number of small ones in a divided dormitory. **2.** any small space or compartment partitioned off. [t. L: m. s. *cubiculum* bedchamber]

cubic measure, **1.** the measurement of volume in cubic units. **2.** a system of such units, esp. that in which 1728 cubic inches = 1 cubic foot, 27 cubic feet = 1 cubic yard.

cubiculum (kyōō bĭk′yŏŏ ləm), *n., pl.* **-la** (-lə). *Archaeol.* a burial chamber, as in catacombs. [t. L: bedroom]

cubiform (kyōō′bĭ fôm′), *adj.* formed like a cube.

cubism (kyōō′bĭz′əm), *n.* (*sometimes cap.*) a modern French art movement, initiated in 1907, which aimed at the analysis of form through surface arrangement of planes, colours, and textures. **—cub′ist,** *n., adj.* **—cubistic** (kyōō bĭs′tĭk), *adj.* **—cubis′tically,** *adv.*

cubit (kyōō′bĭt), *n.* an ancient linear unit based on the length of the forearm, varying in extent, but usually between 18 and 22 inches. [ME, t. L: s. *cubitum* elbow, ell]

cuboid (kyōō′boid), *adj.* **1.** resembling a cube in form. **2.** *Anat.* denoting or pertaining to the outermost bone of the distal row of tarsal bones. *—n.* **3.** *Maths.* a rectangular parallelepiped. 4. *Anat.* the cuboid bone. **—cuboiʹdal,** *adj.*

cub reporter, *Colloq.* a reporter without experience.

cucking stool (kŭkʹĭng), a former instrument of punishment consisting of a chair in which an offender, esp. a common scold, was strapped, to be jeered at and pelted by the crowd, or, sometimes, to be ducked. [ME *cuking stol* mucking stool; *cucking,* ppr. of obs. v. *cuck* defecate (t. Scand.; cf. Icel. *kúka*)]

cuckold (kŭkʹld), *n.* **1.** the husband of an unfaithful wife. *—v.t.* **2.** to make a cuckold of (a husband). [ME *cokewold*; orig. uncert.]

cuckoldry (kŭkʹl drĭ), *n.* **1.** the act or fact of making a cuckold of one. **2.** the state of being a cuckold.

cuckoo (kŏŏkʹōō), *n., pl.* **-os,** *v.,* **-ooed, -ooing,** *adj.* *—n.* **1.** any bird of the family *Cuculidae,* esp. *Cuculus canorus,* a common European migratory bird noted for its characteristic call, and for its loss of the instinct to build a nest. The females lay their eggs in the nests of various 'host species', which rear the young cuckoos. **2.** the call of the cuckoo, or an imitation of it. **3.** a fool; simpleton. *—v.i.* **4.** to utter the call of the cuckoo or an imitation of it. *—v.t.* **5.** to repeat monotonously. *—adj.* **6.** *Slang.* crazy; silly; foolish. [ME *cucu* (imit. of its call). Cf. F *coucou,* G *Kuckuk*]

cuckoo clock, a clock which announces the hours by a sound like the call of the cuckoo.

cuckooflower (kŏŏkʹōō flouʹə), *n.* any of various plants, as the lady's-smock or the ragged robin.

cuckoopint (kŏŏkʹōō pīntʹ), *n.* a common European species of arum, *Arum maculatum*; wake-robin.

cuckoo-spit (kŏŏkʹōō spĭtʹ), *n.* **1.** a frothy secretion found on plants, exuded as a protective covering by the young of certain insects, as the froghoppers. **2.** an insect secreting this.

cuckoo wrasse, a common British fish, *Labrus mixtus,* with a marked colour difference between the male and the female.

cuculiform (kyŏŏ kyōōʹlĭ fômʹ), *adj.* pertaining to or resembling the order *Cuculiformes,* containing the cuckoos, roadrunners, etc. [f. s. L *cucūlus* cuckoo + -(I)FORM]

cucullate (kyōōʹkə lātʹ, -lĭt), *adj.* **1.** cowled; hooded. **2.** resembling a cowl or hood. Also, **cucullated** (kyōōʹkə lāʹtĭd). [t. LL: m. s. *cucullātus* hooded]

cucumber (kyōōʹkŭm bə), *n.* **1.** a creeping plant, *Cucumis sativus,* occurring in many cultivated forms, yielding a long fleshy fruit which is commonly eaten green as a salad and used for pickling. **2.** the fruit of this plant. **3.** any of various allied or similar plants or their fruits. [t. F (obs.): m. *cocombre,* g. s. L *cucumis*; r. ME *cucumer,* t. L: s. *cucumis*]

cucumber tree, 1. any of several American magnolias, esp. *Magnolia acuminata.* **2.** any of certain other trees, as an East Indian tree of the genus *Averrhoa.*

cucumiform (kyŏŏ kyōōʹmĭ fômʹ), *adj.* shaped like a cucumber; approximately cylindrical, with rounded or tapering ends. [f. L *cucumi(s)* cucumber + -FORM]

cucurbit (kyŏŏ kûʹbĭt), *n.* **1.** a gourd. **2.** any cucurbitaceous plant. [ME *cucurbite,* t. F, t. L: m. *cucurbita* gourd]

cucurbitaceous (kyŏŏ kûʹbĭ tāʹshəs), *adj.* belonging to the *Cucurbitaceae,* or gourd family of plants which includes the pumpkin, cucumber, muskmelon, watermelon, etc. [f. s. L *cucurbita* gourd + -ACEOUS]

Cúcuta (*Sp.* kōōʹkōō tȧ), *n.* a town in N Colombia. 175,336 (1964).

cud (kŭd), *n.* **1.** the portion of food which a ruminating animal returns from the first stomach to the mouth to chew a second time. **2. chew the cud,** to reflect; meditate. [ME; OE *cudu,* var. of *cwidu.* See QUID]

cudbear (kŭdʹbĕəʹ), *n.* a violet colouring matter obtained from various lichens, esp. *Lecanora tartarea.*

cuddle (kŭdʹl), *v.,* **-dled, -dling,** *n.* *—v.t.* **1.** to draw or hold close in an affectionate manner; hug tenderly; fondle. *—v.i.* **2.** to lie close and snug; nestle; curl up in going to sleep. *—n.* **3.** the act of cuddling; a hug; an embrace. [f. *couth,* adj., comfortable, friendly (OE *cūth* familiar) + *-le,* freq. suffix. Cf. FONDLE] **—cuddlesome** (kŭdʹl səm), **cudʹdly,** *adj.*

cuddy[1] (kŭdʹĭ), *n., pl.* **-dies. 1.** a small cabin on a ship or boat, esp. one under the poop. **2.** a small room; a cupboard. [orig. unknown]

cuddy[2] (kŭdʹĭ), *n., pl.* **-dies.** *Chiefly Scot.* **1.** a donkey. **2.** a stupid fellow. [orig. unknown]

cudgel (kŭjʹəl), *n., v.,* **-elled, -elling** or (*U.S.*) **-eled, -eling.** *—n.* **1.** a short, thick stick used as a weapon; a club. **2. take up the cudgels,** to engage in a contest. *—v.t.* **3.** to strike with a cudgel; beat. **4. cudgel one's brains,** to think hard. [ME *cuggel,* OE *cycgel,* akin to G *Kugel* ball] **—cudgʹeller;** *U.S.,* **cudgeler,** *n.*

cudgerie (kŭjʹə rĭ), *n.* **1.** an Australian rutaceous tree, *Flindersia schottina.* **2.** an Australian anacardiaceous tree, *Euroschinus falcatus.* [t. native Australian]

cudweed (kŭdʹwēdʹ), *n.* **1.** any of the woolly herbs constituting the composite genus *Gnaphalium.* **2.** any of various plants of allied genera.

cue[1] (kyōō), *n.* **1.** anything said or done on or behind the stage that is followed by a specific line or action: *each line of dialogue is a cue to the succeeding line; an offstage door slam was his cue to enter.* **2.** a hint; an intimation; a guiding suggestion. **3.** the part one is to play; a prescribed or necessary course of action. **4.** *Archaic.* humour; disposition. [? sp. of abbrev. *q.* or *qu.* for L *quando* when]

cue[2] (kyōō), *n., v.,* **cued, cuing.** *—n.* **1.** a long tapering rod, tipped with a soft leather pad, used to strike the ball in billiards, etc. **2.** a queue of hair. *—v.t.* **3.** to tie into a cue or tail. [var. of *queue,* t. F]

cue ball, *Billiards, etc.* the ball struck by the cue as distinguished from the other balls on the table.

cueist (kyōōʹĭst), *n.* a billiard-player.

Cuenca (*Sp.* kwĕnʹkȧ), *n.* a town in SW Ecuador. 60,021 (est. 1962).

cuesta (kwĕsʹtə), *n.* *Chiefly U.S.* a long low ridge presenting a relatively steep face or escarpment on one side and a long gentle slope on the other.

cuff[1] (kŭf), *n.* **1.** a fold, band, or variously shaped piece serving as a trimming or finish for the bottom of a sleeve. **2.** the part of a gauntlet or long glove that extends over the wrist. **3.** a separate or detachable band or piece of linen or other material worn about the wrist, inside or outside the sleeve. **4. off the cuff,** impromptu; extemporaneously; on the spur of the moment. [ME *cuffe, coffe* glove, mitten; orig. uncert.]

cuff[2] (kŭf), *v.t.* **1.** to strike with the open hand; beat; buffet. *—n.* **2.** a blow with the fist or the open hand; a buffet. **3.** a handcuff. [cf. Swed. *kuffa* thrust, push]

cufflink (kŭfʹlĭngkʹ), *n.* a link which fastens a shirt cuff.

cui bono (kwēʹbōnʹō), *Latin.* **1.** for whose benefit? **2.** for what use? of what good?

cuirass (kwĭ răsʹ), *n.* **1.** a piece of defensive armour for the body, combining a breastplate and a piece for the back. **2.** the breastplate alone. **3.** any similar covering, as the protective armour of a ship. **4.** *Zool.* a hard shell or other covering forming an indurated defensive shield. *—v.t.* **5.** to equip or cover with a cuirass. [t. F: m. *cuirasse,* b. *cuir(ie)* leather armour (der. *cuir,* g. L *corium* leather) and Pr. *(coir)assa* (g. LL *coriācea,* fem., made of leather)]

cuirassier (kwĭʹrə sĭəʹ), *n.* a cavalry soldier wearing a cuirass. [t. F]

cuisine (kwĭ zēnʹ), *n.* **1.** the kitchen; the culinary department of a house, hotel, etc. **2.** style of cooking; cookery. [t. F, g. L *cocīna, coquīna* kitchen. See KITCHEN]

cuisse (kwĭs), *n.* a piece of armour to protect the thigh Also, **cuish** (kwĭsh). See illus. under **armour.** [t. F: thigh, g. L *coxa* hip]

cuittle (kyōōʹtl), *v.t.,* **-tled, -tling.** *Scot.* to wheedle, cajole, or coax. Also, **cuiʹtle.**

Culbertson (kŭlʹbət sən), *n.* **Ely** (ēʹlĭ), 1893–1955, U.S. authority and writer on contract bridge.

culch (kŭlch), *n.* **1.** the stones, old shells, etc., forming an oyster bed and furnishing points of attachment for the spawn of oysters. **2.** the spawn. **3.** *Chiefly Dial.* rubbish; refuse. *—v.t.* **4.** to prepare (an oyster bed) with culch. Also, **cultch.** [cf. OF *culche* bed]

cul-de-sac (kŭlʹdə săkʹ, kŏŏlʹ-; *Fr.* kʏd sȧkʹ), *n.* **1.** saclike cavity, tube, or the like, open only at one end, as the caecum. **2.** a street, lane, etc., closed at one end; blind alley. **3.** *Mil.* the situation of a military force hemmed in on all sides except behind. [t. F: bottom of sack]

-cule, a diminutive suffix of nouns, as in *animalcule, molecule.* Also, **-cle.** [t. F, or t. L: m. *-culus, -cula, -culum*]

Culebra Cut (kōō lĕbʹrə; *Sp.* kōō lĕʹbrȧ), former name of **Gaillard Cut.**

culet (kyōōʹlĭt), *n.* **1.** the small flat face forming the bottom of a brilliant. **2.** the part of medieval armour protecting the back of the body below the waist. [t. F (obs.), dim. of *cul* bottom, g. L *cūlus.* Cf. F *culasse* culet]

culex (kyōōʹlĕks), *n., pl.* **-lices** (-lĭ sēzʹ), any mosquito of the genus *Culex,* including the common house mosquito, *Culex pipiens.* [t. L: a gnat]

Culgoa (kŭl gōʹə), *n.* a river in E Australia flowing SW through Queensland, then New South Wales to the river Darling. ab. 200 mi.

culicid (kyŏŏ lĭsʹĭd), *n.* **1.** any of the dipterous insects of the family *Culicidae*; a mosquito. *—adj.* **2.** belonging or pertaining to the *Culicidae.*

culinary (kŭlʹĭ nə rĭ), *adj.* pertaining to the kitchen or to cookery; used in cooking. [t. L: m. s. *culīnārius,* der. *culīna* kitchen]

Culion (ko͞o lyōn′), *n.* one of the Philippine Islands, in the W part of the group, N of Palawan: leper colony. 11,237 pop. (1963); 150 sq. mi.

cull[1] (kŭl), *v.t.* **1.** to choose; select; pick; gather the choice things or parts from. **2.** to collect; gather; pluck. —*n.* **3.** the act of culling. **4.** something culled, esp. an inferior animal withdrawn from a herd or flock. [ME *culle(n)*, t. OF: m. *coillir*, g. L *colligere* COLLECT]

cull[2] (kŭl), *n. Slang.* a fool; a dupe. [? short for CULLY]

cullender (kŭl′ĭn də), *n.* colander.

cullet (kŭl′ĭt), *n.* broken or waste glass suitable for remelting.

cullion (kŭl′yən), *n. Archaic.* a base or vile fellow. [ME *coillion*, t. F: m. *couillon*, der. L *cōleus* testicle]

Culloden (kə lŏd′n), *n.* a moor in Scotland, near Inverness; the decisive battle of the Second Jacobite Rebellion, 1746.

cully (kŭl′ĭ), *n., pl.* **-lies,** *v.,* **-lied, -lying.** *Archaic. Slang or Colloq.* —*n.* **1.** a dupe. **2.** a man or fellow. —*v.t.* **3.** to trick; cheat; dupe. [short for CULLION]

culm[1] (kŭlm), *n.* **1.** coal dust; slack. **2.** anthracite, esp. of inferior grade. **3.** (*cap.*) *Geol.* **a.** a series of Lower Carboniferous rocks, mainly developed in parts of Europe, mostly dark-coloured and siliceous. **b.** Also, **Culm Measures.** a series of similar rocks of the Carboniferous age in Devon and Cornwall. [var. of *coom* soot]

culm[2] (kŭlm), *n.* **1.** a stem or stalk, esp. the jointed and usually hollow stem of grasses. —*v.i.* **2.** to grow or develop into a culm. [t. L: s. *culmus* stalk. Cf. HAULM]

culmiferous (kŭl mĭf′ə rəs), *adj.* bearing culms.

culminant (kŭl′mĭ nənt), *adj.* culminating; topmost.

culminate (kŭl′mĭ nāt′), *v.i.,* **-nated, -nating. 1.** to reach the highest point, the summit, or highest development (usually fol. by *in*). **2.** *Astron.* (of a celestial body) to be on the meridian, or reach the highest or the lowest altitude. [t. LL: m. s. *culminātus*, pp., crowned]

culmination (kŭl′mĭ nā′shən), *n.* **1.** the act or fact of culminating. **2.** that in which anything culminates; the highest point; the acme. **3.** *Astron.* the position of a celestial body when it is on the meridian. —**Syn. 2.** climax, zenith, peak.

culottes (kyo͞o lŏts′; *Fr.* KY lŏt′), *n.pl.* a skirtlike garment, separated and sewn like trousers. [t. F]

culpable (kŭl′pə bl), *adj.* deserving blame or censure; blameworthy. [t. L: m. s. *culpābilis* blameworthy; r. ME *coupable*, t. OF] —**cul′pabil′ity, cul′pableness,** *n.* —**cul′pably,** *adv.* —**Syn.** censurable, reprehensible. —**Ant.** praiseworthy.

culprit (kŭl′prĭt), *n.* **1.** a person arraigned for an offence. **2.** one guilty of or responsible for a specified offence or fault. [orig. uncert.; traditionally explained as f. L *cul(pābilis)*, guilty + AF *pri(s)t* ready, i.e. the prosecution is ready to prove guilt]

cult (kŭlt), *n.* **1.** a particular system of religious worship, esp. with reference to its rites and ceremonies. **2.** an instance of an almost religious veneration for a person or thing, esp. as manifested by a body of admirers: *a cult of Napoleon.* **3.** the object of such devotion. **4.** *Sociol.* a group having an exclusive sacred ideology and a series of rites centring round their sacred symbols. **5.** a popular fashion; fad. [t. L: s. *cultus* care, worship]

cultch (kŭlch), *n., v.t.* culch.

cultigen (kŭl′tĭ jən), *n.* a plant found only in cultivation, the origin of which is not known with any certainty.

cultivable (kŭl′tĭ və bl), *adj.* capable of being cultivated. Also, **cultivatable** (kŭl′tĭ vā′tə bl). [t. F, der. *cultiver* cultivate] —**cul′tivabil′ity,** *n.*

cultivar (kŭl′tĭ vä′), *n.* a variety of plant that has been produced only under cultivation. [f. CULTI(VATED) + VAR(IETY)]

cultivate (kŭl′tĭ vāt′), *v.t.,* **-vated, -vating. 1.** to bestow labour upon (land) in raising crops; till; improve by husbandry. **2.** to use a cultivator on. **3.** to promote or improve the growth of (a plant, etc.) by labour and attention. **4.** to produce by culture. **5.** to develop or improve by education or training; train; refine. **6.** to promote the growth or development of (an art, science, etc.); foster. **7.** to devote oneself to (an art, etc.). **8.** to seek to promote or foster (friendship, etc.). **9.** to seek the acquaintance or friendship of (a person). [t. ML: m. s. *cultīvātus*, pp. of *cultīvāre;* der. *cultīvus* tilled, der. L *cultus*, pp. of *colere* till] —**Ant. 8.** neglect. **9.** ignore.

cultivated (kŭl′tĭ vā′tĭd), *adj.* **1.** subjected to cultivation. **2.** produced or improved by cultivation, as a plant. **3.** educated; refined; cultured.

cultivation (kŭl′tĭ vā′shən), *n.* **1.** the act or art of cultivating. **2.** the state of being cultivated. **3.** culture.

cultivator (kŭl′tĭ vā′tə), *n.* **1.** one who or that which cultivates. **2.** an implement for loosening the earth and destroying weeds when drawn between rows of growing plants.

cultrate (kŭl′trāt), *adj.* sharp-edged and pointed, as a leaf. Also, **cul′trated.** [t. L: m. s. *cultrātus*, der. *culter* knife]

cultural (kŭl′chə rəl), *adj.* of or pertaining to culture or cultivation. —**cul′turally,** *adv.*

Cultural Revolution, a movement in China, 1966–68, intended to preserve ideological and revolutionary enthusiasm, esp. among the young, for Mao Tse-Tung's revolution.

culture (kŭl′chə), *n., v.,* **-tured, -turing.** —*n.* **1.** the action or practice of cultivating the soil; tillage. **2.** the raising of plants or animals, esp. with a view to their improvement. **3.** the product or growth resulting from such cultivation. **4.** development or improvement by education or training. **5.** enlightenment or refinement resulting from such development. **6.** a particular state or stage of civilization, as in the case of a certain nation or period: *Greek culture.* **7.** *Sociol.* the sum total of ways of living built up by a group of human beings, which is transmitted from one generation to another. **8.** *Biol.* **a.** the cultivation of micro-organisms, as bacteria, or of tissues, for scientific study, medicinal use, etc. **b.** the product or growth resulting from such cultivation. —*v.t.* **9.** to subject to culture; cultivate. **10.** *Biol.* **a.** to develop (micro-organisms, tissues, etc.) in an artificial medium. **b.** to introduce (living material) into a culture medium. [ME, t. F, t. L: m. *cultūra* tending, cultivation] —**cul′tureless,** *adj.* —**Syn. 5.** See **education.**

culture complex, *Sociol.* a group of culture traits all interrelated and dominated by one essential trait: *political nationalism is a culture complex.*

cultured (kŭl′chəd), *adj.* **1.** cultivated; artificially nurtured or grown. **2.** enlightened; refined.

culture factor, *Sociol.* the whole of a culture at a given time as it affects further cultural development.

culture pattern, *Sociol.* a group of interrelated cultural traits of some continuity.

culturist (kŭl′chə rĭst), *n.* **1.** a cultivator. **2.** an advocate or devotee of culture.

cultus (kŭl′təs), *n.* a cult. [t. L]

culver (kŭl′və), *n.* a dove; a pigeon. [ME *colfre*, OE *culfre*]

culverin (kŭl′və rĭn), *n.* **1.** a medieval form of musket. **2.** a kind of heavy cannon, used in the 16th and 17th centuries. [t. F: m. *coulevrine*, der. *couleuvre*, g. L *colubra* serpent. Cf. COBRA]

Culver's root (kŭl′vəz), **1.** the root of a tall scrophulariaceous herb, *Veronica virginica*, used in medicine as a cathartic and emetic. **2.** the plant. Also, **Culver's physic.**

culvert (kŭl′vət), *n.* a drain or channel crossing under a road, etc.; a sewer; a conduit. [orig. uncert.]

cum (kŭm), *prep.* **1.** with; together with; including (used sometimes in financial phrases, as *cum dividend*, etc., which are often abbreviated simply *cum*). **2.** (in combination) serving a dual function as; the functions being indicated by the preceding and following elements: *the dwelling-cum-workshop was nearby.* [t. L]

Cumae (kyo͞o′mē), *n.* an ancient city on the coast of Campania, in SW Italy: reputedly the earliest Greek colony in Italy and Sicily. —**Cumae′an,** *adj.*

Cumaean sibyl, one of the legendary women of antiquity whose authority in matters of divination was acknowledged by the Romans.

Cumb., Cumberland.

cumber (kŭm′bə), *v.t.* **1.** to hinder; hamper. **2.** to overload; burden. **3.** to inconvenience; trouble. —*n.* **4.** hindrance. **5.** that which cumbers. **6.** *Archaic.* embarrassment; trouble. [t. MFlem.: m. *comber*, c. G *Kummer* trouble] —**cum′berer,** *n.*

Cumberland (kŭm′bə lənd), *n.* **1. William Augustus, Duke of,** 1721–65, 2nd son of George II; known as 'Butcher' after his cruel but effective defeat of the Young Pretender's rebellion at Culloden in 1746. **2.** a county in NW England. 294,162 pop. (1961); 1520 sq. mi. *Co. town:* Carlisle. *Abbrev.:* Cumb.

cumbersome (kŭm′bə səm), *adj.* **1.** burdensome; troublesome. **2.** unwieldy; clumsy. —**cum′bersomely,** *adv.* —**cum′bersomeness,** *n.*

cumbrance (kŭm′brəns), *n.* **1.** trouble. **2.** encumbrance.

Cumbrian Mountains (kŭm′brĭ ən), a range of low mountains forming the Lake District of Cumberland, Westmorland, and N Lancashire. Highest point, Scafell Pike, 3210 ft.

cumbrous (kŭm′brəs), *adj.* cumbersome. —**cum′brously,** *adv.* —**cum′brousness,** *n.*

cumin (kŭm′ĭn), *n.* **1.** a small apiaceous plant, *Cuminum cyminum*, bearing aromatic seedlike fruit used in cookery and medicine. **2.** the fruit or seeds. [ME *comin*, t. OF, t. L: m. s. *cuminum*, t. Gk: m. *kýminon*; r. OE *cymen*]

cum laude (kŭm lôʹdĭ, ko͝om louʹdā), *Latin.* with honour (used chiefly in American universities to grant the lowest of three special honours for above-average academic performance). See **magna cum laude** and **summa cum laude.**

cummer (kŭmʹə), *n. Scot.* **1.** a godmother. **2.** a female companion. **3.** a girl or woman. [Scot., ME *commare,* t. F: m. *commère,* g. LL *commāter.* See COM-, MATER]

cummerbund (kŭmʹə bŭndʹ), *n.* (in India and elsewhere) a shawl or sash worn as a belt. [t. Hind., Pers.: m. *kamarband* loin band]

Cummings (kŭmʹĭngz), *n.* **Edward Estlin** (ĕstʹlĭn) (*e e cummings*), 1894–1962, U.S. poet, writer, and painter.

cumquat (kŭmʹkwŏt), *n.* kumquat.

cumshaw (kŭmʹshô), *n.* (formerly in Chinese ports) a present; gratuity; tip. [t. Chinese: m. Amoy *kamsiā* for Mandarin *kan hsieh* grateful thanks]

cumulate (*v.* kyo͞oʹmyo͝o lātʹ; *adj.* kyo͞oʹmyo͝o lĭt, -lātʹ), *v.* **-lated, -lating,** *adj.* —*v.t.* **1.** to heap up; amass; accumulate. —*adj.* **2.** heaped up. [t. L: m. s. *cumulātus,* pp., heaped up]

cumulation (kyo͞oʹmyo͝o lāʹshən), *n.* **1.** the act of cumulating; accumulation. **2.** a heap; mass.

cumulative (kyo͞oʹmyo͝o lə tĭv), *adj.* **1.** increasing or growing by accumulation or successive additions. **2.** formed by or resulting from accumulation or the addition of successive parts or elements. **3.** *Finance.* of or pertaining to a dividend or interest which accumulates if not paid when due, and must be paid before those with an inferior claim to earnings can be paid. —**cuʹmulatively,** *adv.* —**cuʹmulativeness,** *n.*

cumulative evidence, 1. evidence of which the parts reinforce one another, producing an effect stronger than any part taken by itself. **2.** testimony repetitive of testimony earlier given.

cumulative voting, a system which gives each voter as many votes as there are persons to be elected from one representative district, allowing him to accumulate them on one candidate or to distribute them.

cumuliform (kyo͞oʹmyo͝o lĭ fômʹ), *adj.* having the appearance or character of cumulus clouds.

cumulonimbus (kyo͞oʹmyo͝o lō nĭmʹbəs), *n. Meteorol.* a heavy, tall mass of cloud whose summits rise in the form of mountains or towers, the upper parts having a fibrous texture characteristic of high clouds formed of ice crystals. This cloud is characteristic of thunderstorm conditions.

cumulous (kyo͞oʹmyo͝o ləs), *adj.* of the form of a cumulus (cloud); composed of cumuli.

cumulus (kyo͞oʹmyo͝o ləs), *n. pl.* **-li** (-līʹ), **1.** a heap; pile. **2.** *Meteorol.* a cloud with summit domelike or made up of rounded heaps, and with flat base, seen in fair weather and usually a brilliant white with a smooth, well-outlined structure.

cumulus fractus, *Meteorol.* a cumulus cloud that is ill-formed, ragged, usually small, and rapidly changing.

Cunaxa (kyo͞o năkʹsə), *n.* an ancient town in Babylonia, near the Euphrates: famous battle between Cyrus the Younger and Artaxerxes II, 401 B.C.

Cuneate leaf

cunctation (kŭngk tāʹshən), *n.* delay. [t. L: s. *cunctātio,* der. *cunctārī* delay] —**cunctative** (kŭngkʹtə tĭv), *adj.*

cunctator (kŭngk tāʹtə), *n.* a delayer. [t. L] —**cunctaʹtorshipʹ,** *n.*

cuneal (kyo͞oʹnĭ əl), *adj.* wedgelike; wedge-shaped. [f. s. L *cuneus* wedge + -AL[1]]

cuneate (kyo͞oʹnĭ ĭt, -ātʹ), *adj.* **1.** wedge-shaped. **2.** (of leaves) triangular and tapering to a point at the base. Also, **cuʹneatʹed.** [t. L: m. s. *cuneātus,* pp., made wedge-shaped]

cuneiform (kyo͞oʹnĭ fômʹ), *adj.* **1.** having the form of a wedge; wedge-shaped, as the characters anciently used in writing in Persia, Assyria, etc. **2.** denoting or pertaining to this kind of writing. **3.** *Anat.* denoting or pertaining to any of various wedge-shaped bones, as of the tarsus. —*n.* **4.** cuneiform characters or writing. **5.** a cuneiform bone. [f. s. L *cuneus* wedge + -(I)FORM]

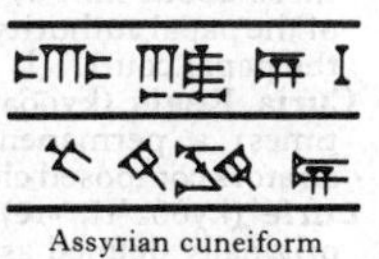
Assyrian cuneiform characters

Cuneo (*It.* ko͞oʹnĕ ō), *n.* a town in Italy, in Piedmont. 50,940 (1966).

cunnilinctus (kŭnʹĭ lĭngkʹtəs), *n.* oral stimulation of the female genitals. Also, **cunnilingus** (kŭnʹĭ lĭngʹgəs). [t. NL, f. L: *cunni-* comb. form of *cunnus* vulva + *linctus,* pp., licked]

cunning (kŭnʹĭng), *n.* **1.** ability; skill; expertness. **2.** skill employed in a crafty manner; skilfulness in deceiving; craftiness; guile. —*adj.* **3.** exhibiting or wrought with ingenuity. **4.** artfully subtle or shrewd; crafty; sly. **5.** *U.S. Colloq.* quaintly pleasing or attractive, as a child or something little. **6.** *Archaic.* skilful; expert. [ME; var. of OE *cunnung,* der. *cunnan* know (how). See CAN[1]] —**cunʹningly,** *adv.* —**cunʹningness,** *n.*

—**Syn. 2.** shrewdness, artfulness, wiliness, trickery, finesse, intrigue. CUNNING, ARTIFICE, CRAFT imply an inclination towards deceit, slyness, and trickery. CUNNING implies a shrewd, often instinctive skill in concealing or disguising the real purposes of one's actions: *not intelligence but a low kind of cunning.* An ARTIFICE is a clever, unscrupulous ruse, used to mislead others: *a successful artifice to conceal one's motives.* CRAFT suggests underhand methods and the use of deceptive devices and tricks to attain one's ends: *craft and deceitfulness in every act.* **4.** artful, wily, tricky, foxy.

cunt (kŭnt), *n. Taboo.* **1.** the vagina. **2.** *Slang.* a woman considered as a sexual object. **3.** (used derogatorily) any mean, unpleasant, foul, or despicable person. **4.** *Slang.* sexual intercourse.

cup (kŭp), *n., v.,* **cupped, cupping.** —*n.* **1.** a small, open container, esp. of porcelain or metal, used mainly to drink from. **2.** (*often cap.*) an ornamental cup or other article, esp. of precious metal, offered as a prize for a contest. **3.** the containing part of a goblet or the like. **4.** a cup with its contents. **5.** the quantity contained in a cup. **6.** an American unit of capacity equal in England to 8 fluid ounces. **7.** any of various beverages, as a mixture of wine and various ingredients: *claret cup.* **8.** the chalice used in the eucharist. **9.** the wine of the eucharist. **10.** something to be partaken of or endured, as suffering. **11.** (*pl.*) the drinking of alcoholic beverages. **12.** (*pl.*) a state of intoxication. **13.** any cuplike utensil, organ, part, cavity, etc. **14.** *Golf.* **a.** the metal receptacle within the hole. **b.** the hole itself. **15.** (*cap.*) *Astron.* the southern constellation Crater. **16.** a cupping glass. **17. in one's cups,** intoxicated; tipsy. —*v.t.* **18.** to take or place in or as in a cup: *he cupped his ear with the palm of his hand to hear better.* **19.** to form into the shape of a cup. **20.** to use a cupping glass on. [ME and OE *cuppe,* t. LL: m. *cuppa* cup, var. of L *cūpa* tub, cask] —**cupʹlikeʹ,** *adj.*

Cupar (ko͞oʹpə), *n.* a burgh in Scotland, the county town of Fife. 5495 (1961).

cupbearer (kŭpʹbĕəʹrə), *n.* an attendant who fills and hands the cups in which drink is served.

cupboard (kŭbʹəd), *n.* **1.** an enclosed recess of a room for storing foodstuffs, clothing, etc., usually having shelves, hooks or the like. **2.** a free-standing article of furniture for any of these or similar purposes. [ME, f. CUP + BOARD]

cupboard love, love inspired by considerations of material gain.

cupcake (kŭpʹkākʹ), *n.* a small cake baked in a cup-shaped pan.

cupel (kyo͞oʹpl, kyo͞o pĕlʹ), *n., v.,* **-pelled, -pelling** or (*U.S.*) **-peled, -peling,** *n.* **1.** a small cuplike porous vessel, usually made of bone ash, used in assaying, as for separating gold and silver from lead. **2.** a receptacle or furnace bottom in which silver is refined. —*v.t.* **3.** to heat or refine in a cupel. [t. F: m. *coupelle,* ult. der. LL *cuppa* CUP]

cupellation (kyo͞oʹpĭ lāʹshən), *n.* the process of separating noble metals, esp. gold and silver, from impurities by subjecting the impure metal to a blast of hot air in a cupel.

cup final, *Sport.* the final match in an eliminating contest, esp. the F.A. Cup competition, after which the winning team is awarded the cup as a symbol of victory.

cupful (kŭpʹfo͝olʹ), *n., pl.* **-fuls.** a quantity sufficient to fill a cup.

Cupid (kyo͞oʹpĭd), *n.* **1.** the Roman god of love, son of Venus, commonly represented as a winged boy with bow and arrows. See **Eros. 2.** (*l.c.*) a similar winged being or a representation of one, esp. as symbolical of love. [ME *Cupide,* t. L: m. *Cupīdo,* lit., desire, passion]

cupidity (kyo͞o pĭdʹĭ tĭ), *n.* eager or inordinate desire, esp. to possess something. [t. L: m. s. *cupiditas* passionate desire]

cup of tea, *Colloq.* a task, topic, person, or object, etc., well suited to one's experience, taste or liking: *that show wasn't my cup of tea.*

cupola (kyo͞oʹpə lə), *n.* **1.** a rounded vault or dome constituting, or built upon, a roof; a small domelike or tower-like structure on a roof. **2.** a dome of relatively small size, esp. when forming part of a minor or decorative element of a larger building. **3.** any of various domelike structures, organs, etc. **4.** *Metall.* a vertical, circular furnace for melting cast iron. It uses coke as a fuel, a flux, and a forced blast. [t. It.: dome, t. LL: m. *cūpula,* dim. of *cūpa* tub, cask]

cuppa (kŭpʹə), *n. Slang.* a cup of tea.

cupped (kŭpt), *adj.* hollowed out like a cup; cup-shaped.

cupper (kŭpʹə), *n.* one who performs the operation of cupping.

cupping (kŭp′ĭng), *n.* the process of drawing blood from the body by scarification and the application of a cupping glass, or by the application of a cupping glass without scarification, as for relieving internal congestion.
cupping glass, a glass vessel in which a partial vacuum is created, as by heat, used in cupping.
cupr-, a word element referring to copper. Also, before consonants, **cupri-, cupro-.** [t. L, comb. form of *cuprum*]
cuprammonium (kyo͞o′prə mō′nyəm), *n. Chem.* any cation containing copper and ammonia.
cupreous (kyo͞o′prĭ əs), *adj.* **1.** copper-coloured; metallic reddish brown. **2.** consisting of or containing copper; copper-like. [t. L: m. *cupreus* of copper]
cupric (kyo͞o′prĭk), *adj. Chem.* of or containing copper, esp. in the divalent state, as *cupric oxide,* CuO.
cupriferous (kyo͞o prĭf′ə rəs), *adj.* yielding copper.
cuprite (kyo͞o′prīt), *n.* a mineral, cuprous oxide, Cu_2O, occurring in red crystals and granular masses: an ore of copper.
cupronickel (kyo͞o′prō nĭk′l), *n.* **1.** an alloy of copper containing nickel. *—adj.* **2.** containing copper and nickel.
cupro-uranite (kyo͞o′prə yo͝oə′rə nīt′), *n.* copper uranite.
cuprous (kyo͞o′prəs), *adj. Chem.* containing monovalent copper, as *cuprous oxide,* Cu_2O.
cuprum (kyo͞o′prəm), *n.* copper. *Symbol:* Cu [t. L]
cup tie, *Sport.* a match between two teams in an eliminating contest for a cup, as the F.A. Cup.
cupule (kyo͞o′pyo͞ol), *n.* **1.** *Bot.* a cup-shaped involucre consisting of indurated, cohering bracts, as in the acorn. **2.** *Zool.* a small cup-shaped sucker or similar organ or part. [t. L: m. s. *cūpula,* dim. of *cūpa* tub, cup]

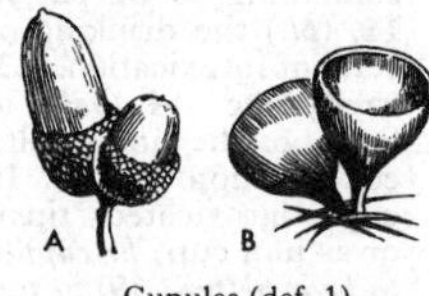

Cupules (def. 1)
A, of acorn; B, of fungus

cur (kû), *n.* **1.** a snarling, worthless, or outcast dog. **2.** a low, despicable person. [ME *curre;* imit.]
curable (kyo͝oə′rə bl), *adj.* that may be cured. *—***cur′abil′ity, cur′ableness,** *n.* *—***cur′ably,** *adv.*
Curaçao (kyo͝oə′rə sō′; *Du.* kʏ rȧ sôw′), *n.* **1.** the main island of the Netherlands Antilles, off the NW coast of Venezuela. 129,676 pop. (1963); 173 sq. mi. *Cap.:* Willemstad. **2.** (*l.c.*) a cordial or liqueur flavoured with the peel of the (bitter) **Curaçao orange.**
curacy (kyo͝oə′rə sĭ), *n., pl.* **-cies.** the office or position of a curate.
curagh (kŭ′rəKH, kŭ′rə), *n.* currach.
curare (kyo͞o rä′rĭ), *n.* **1.** a blackish resin-like substance from *Strychnos toxifera* and other tropical plants of the genus *Strychnos,* and from *Chondodendron tomentosum,* used by South American Indians for poisoning arrows, and employed in physiological experiments, etc., for arresting the action of the motor nerves. **2.** a plant yielding it. Also, **curari.** [t. Carib: m. *kurare*]
curassow (kyo͝oə′rə sō′), *n.* any of various large, arboreal, gallinaceous South and Central American birds belonging to the family *Cracidae,* somewhat resembling the turkey and sometimes domesticated. [named after the island of CURAÇAO]
curate (kyo͝oə′rĭt), *n.* **1.** a clergyman employed as assistant or deputy of a rector or vicar. **2.** *Archaic.* any ecclesiastic entrusted with the cure of souls, as a parish priest. [ME *curat,* t. ML: s. *cūrātus,* der. *cūra.* See CURÉ, n.]
curative (kyo͝oə′rə tĭv), *adj.* **1.** serving to cure or heal; pertaining to curing or remedial treatment; remedial. *—n.* **2.** a curative agent; a remedy. *—***cur′atively,** *adv.* *—***cur′ativeness,** *n.* *—***Ant. 1.** injurious.
curator (kyo͝oə rā′tə), *n.* **1.** the person in charge of a museum, art collection, etc.; a custodian. **2.** a manager; overseer; superintendent. **3.** a guardian, as of a minor, lunatic, etc. [t. L: overseer, guardian; r. ME *curatour,* t. AF] *—***curatorial** (kyo͝oə′rə tô′rĭ əl), *adj.* *—***cura′torship′,** *n.* *—***curatrix** (kyo͝oə rā′trĭks), *n., fem.*
curb (kûb), *n.* **1.** a chain or strap attached to the upper ends of the branches of a bit and passing under the horse's lower jaw, used in restraining the horse. **2.** anything that restrains or controls; a restraint; a check. **3.** an enclosing framework or border. **4.** *Chiefly U.S.* kerb (defs 1–4). **5.** *Vet. Sci.* a swelling on the lower part of the back of the hock of a horse, often causing lameness. *—v.t.* **6.** to control as with a curb; restrain; check. **7.** to put a curb on (a horse). **8.** *Chiefly U.S.* kerb (def. 5). [late ME, t. F: m. *courbe* curved, g. L *curvus* bent, crooked] *—***Syn. 6.** bridle, repress, control. See **check.**
curb bit, a bit for a horse, which, by slight effort, produces great pressure on the mouth for controlling the animal.
curbing (kû′bĭng), *n. Chiefly U.S.* kerbing.
curb roof, a roof with two slopes to each face, the lower being the steeper.

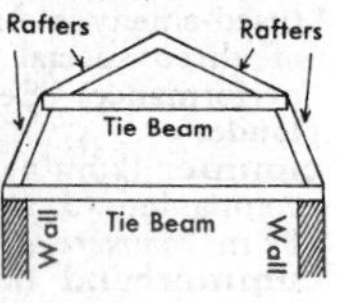

Diagram of a curb roof

curbstone (kûb′stōn′), *n. Chiefly U.S.* kerbstone.
curch (kûch), *n.* a kerchief.
curculio (kû kyo͞o′lĭ ō′), *n., pl.* **-lios.** any of certain snout-beetles or weevils of the family *Curculionidae,* as the **plum curculio,** *Conotrachelus nenuphar,* injurious to fruit. [t. L: weevil]
curcuma (kû′kyo͞o mə), *n.* any plant of the zingiberaceous genus *Curcuma,* of the East Indies, etc., as *C. longa* or *C. zedoaria,* the former yielding turmeric and the latter zedoary. [NL, t. Ar.: m. *kurkum* saffron, turmeric]
curd (kûd), *n.* **1.** (*often pl.*) a substance consisting of casein, etc., obtained from milk by coagulation, used for making into cheese or eaten as food. **2.** any substance resembling this. *—v.t., v.i.* **3.** to turn into curd; coagulate; congeal. [ME *crud.* Cf. CROWD[1]]
curd cheese, cottage cheese.
curdle (kû′dl), *v.t., v.i.,* **-dled, -dling. 1.** to change into curd; coagulate; congeal. **2. curdle the blood,** to terrify with horror or fear. [freq. of CURD]
curdy (kû′dĭ), *adj.* like curd; full of or containing curd; coagulated.
cure (kyo͝oə), *n., v.,* **cured, curing.** *—n.* **1.** a method or course of remedial treatment, as for disease. **2.** successful remedial treatment; restoration to health. **3.** a means of healing or curing; a remedy. **4.** the act or a method of curing meat, fish, etc. **5.** spiritual charge of the people in a certain district. **6.** the office or district of one exercising such oversight. *—v.t.* **7.** to restore to health. **8.** to relieve or rid of something troublesome or detrimental, as an illness, a bad habit, etc. **9.** to prepare (meat, fish, etc.) for preservation, by salting, drying, etc. *—v.i.* **10.** to effect a cure. **11.** to become cured. [ME, t. OF, g. L *cūra* care, treatment, concern, ML an ecclesiastical cure] *—***cure′less,** *adj.* *—***cure′lessly,** *adv.* *—***cur′er,** *n.*

*—***Syn. 8.** CURE, HEAL, REMEDY imply making well, whole, or right. CURE is especially applied to the eradication of disease or sickness: *to cure a fever, a headache.* HEAL suggests the making whole of wounds, sores, etc.: *to heal a cut or a burn.* REMEDY is a more general word which includes both the others and applies also to making wrongs right: *to remedy a mistake.*

curé (kyo͝oə′rā; *Fr.* kʏ rē′), *n.* (in French use) a parish priest. [t. F, g. VL *cūrātus.* See CURATE]
cure-all (kyo͝oə′rôl′), *n.* a cure for all ills; a panacea.
curettage (kyo͝oə rĕt′ĭj), *n.* the process of curetting. [t. F]
curette (kyo͝oə rĕt′), *n., v.,* **-retted, -retting.** *—n.* **1.** a scoop-shaped surgical instrument used for removing diseased tissue from body cavities such as the uterus, etc. *—v.t.* **2.** to scrape with a curette. [t. F, der. *curer* cleanse, g. L *curāre*]
curfew (kû′fyo͞o), *n.* **1.** the ringing of a bell at a fixed hour in the evening as a signal for covering or extinguishing fires, as practised in medieval Europe. **2.** the ringing of an evening bell as later practised. **3.** a regulation, as enforced during civil disturbances, which establishes strict controls on movement after nightfall. **4.** the time at which such a bell is rung or such a regulation enforced. **5.** the bell itself. [ME *corfew,* t. AF: m. *coeverfu,* var. of OF *cuevre-feu* cover-fire]
curia (kyo͝oə′rĭ ə), *n., pl.* **curiae** (kyo͝oə′rĭ ē′). **1.** one of the political subdivisions of each of the three tribes of ancient Roman citizens. **2.** the building in which such a division or group met, as for worship or public deliberation. **3.** the senate house in ancient Rome. **4.** the senate of ancient Italian towns. **5.** (*usually cap.*) the pope and those about him at Rome engaged in the administration of the papal authority (the **Curia Romana**). **6.** (*usually cap.*) the papal court. [L and ML] *—***cu′rial,** *adj.*
Curia Regis (kyo͝oə′rĭ ə rē′jĭs), *Eng. Hist.* (in Norman times) a permanent council of advisers and administrators composed chiefly of officers of the royal household.
curie (kyo͝oə′rĭ, -rē), *n. Physics.* a unit of radioactivity; originally defined as the quantity of radon in equilibrium with one gram of radium, but now defined as that quantity of a radioactive isotope which undergoes $3{\cdot}7 \times 10^{10}$ disintegrations per second. [named after Marie CURIE]
Curie (kyo͝oə′rĭ, -rē; *Fr.* kʏ rē′), *n.* **1. Marie,** 1867–1934, Polish physicist and chemist, in France: with her husband, discovered radium in 1898. **2. Pierre,** her husband, 1859–1906, French physicist and chemist.
curie point, *Physics.* the temperature at which a ferromagnetic substance becomes merely paramagnetic.
Curie's law, *Physics.* the law that the magnetic susceptibility of a substance is inversely proportional to the absolute temperature. [named after Pierre CURIE]

curio (kyŏŏə′rĭ ō′), *n., pl.* **curios.** any article, object of art, etc., valued as a curiosity. [short for CURIOSITY]

curiosa (kyŏŏə′rĭ ō′sə), *n.pl. Chiefly U.S.* books, pamphlets, etc., dealing with unusual subjects, esp. pornographic ones (a term used by booksellers and collectors); erotica. [t. L: curious (things)]

curiosity (kyŏŏə′rĭ ŏs′ĭ tĭ), *n., pl.* **-ties. 1.** the desire to learn or know about anything; inquisitiveness. **2.** curious or interesting quality, as from strangeness. **3.** a curious, rare, or novel thing. **4.** *Obs.* carefulness; fastidiousness. [t. L: m. s. *cūriōsitas*] **—Syn. 3.** curio, rarity, wonder, marvel, phenomenon, freak.

curious (kyŏŏə′rĭ əs), *adj.* **1.** desirous of learning or knowing; inquisitive. **2.** prying; meddlesome. **3.** *Archaic.* made or prepared with skill or art. **4.** marked by special care or pains, as an inquiry or investigation. **5.** exciting attention or interest because of strangeness or novelty. **6.** odd; eccentric. **7.** (of books) indelicate, indecent, or obscene. **8.** *Obs.* marked by intricacy or subtlety. [ME, t. OF: m. *curios*, g. L *cūriōsus* careful, inquiring, inquisitive] **—cu′riously,** *adv.* **—cu′riousness,** *n.*

—Syn. 1, 2. CURIOUS, INQUISITIVE, MEDDLESOME, PRYING refer to taking an undue (and petty) interest in others' affairs. CURIOUS implies a desire to know what is not properly one's concern: *curious about a neighbour's habits.* INQUISITIVE implies asking impertinent questions in an effort to satisfy curiosity: *inquisitive in asking about a neighbour's habits.* MEDDLESOME implies thrusting oneself into and taking an active part in other people's affairs (or handling their possessions) entirely unasked and unwelcomed: *a meddlesome aunt who tries to run the affairs of a family.* PRYING implies a meddlesome and persistent inquiring into others' affairs: *prying into the secrets of a business firm.* **5.** strange, unusual, singular, novel, rare.

Curitiba (kŏŏə′rĭ tē′bə; *Port.* kōō rē tē′bȧ), *n.* a city in S Brazil. 361,309 (1963). Also, **Curityba.**

curium (kyŏŏə′rĭ əm), *n. Chem.* an element not found in nature, but discovered in 1944 among the products of the bombardment of uranium and plutonium by very energetic helium ions. *Symbol:* Cm; *at. no.:* 96.

curl (kûl), *v.t.* **1.** to form into ringlets, as the hair. **2.** to form into a spiral or curved shape; coil. **3.** *Obs.* to adorn with, or as with, curls or ringlets. **4. curl one's lip,** to express disdain. *—v.i.* **5.** to form curls or ringlets, as the hair. **6.** to coil. **7.** to become curved or undulated. **8.** *Scot.* to play at curling. **9.** *Colloq.* to shrink away, as in horror or disgust: *the sight of blood always makes me curl.* **10. curl up,** to lie down comfortably: *to curl up with a good book.* *—n.* **11.** a ringlet or hair. **12.** anything of a spiral or curved shape. **13.** a coil. **14.** the act of curling. **15.** the state of being curled. **16.** any of various diseases of plants with which the leaves are distorted, fluted, or puffed because of unequal growth. [ME *crolled, crulled*, ppl. adj., t. MD or MFlem.]

curler (kû′lə), *n.* **1.** one who or that which curls. **2.** any of various types of rollers, etc., used by women to curl the hair. **3.** a player at curling.

curlew (kû′lyōō), *n.* **1.** any of several shorebirds of the genera *Numenius* and *Phaeopus*, with long slender downward curved bill, as the **common curlew** (*Numenius arquatus*) and the **stone curlew** (*Burhinus oedicnemus*). **2.** any of certain superficially similar birds. [ME *corlewe*, t. OF: m. *courlieu*; imit.]

Curlew, *Numenius arquatus* (Length 23 in.)

curlicue (kû′lĭ kyōō′), *n.* a fantastic curl or twist. Also **curlycue.**

curling (kû′lĭng), *n.* a game, common in Scotland, played on the ice, in which large, smooth, rounded stones are slid towards a mark called the tee.

curling iron, a rod of iron to be used when heated for curling the hair, which is twined around it. Also, **curling irons, curling tongs.**

curlpaper (kûl′pā′pə), *n.* a piece of paper on which a lock of hair is rolled up tightly, to remain until the hair has become fixed in a curl.

curly (kû′lĭ), *adj.*, **curlier, curliest. 1.** curling or tending to curl. **2.** having curls. **—curl′iness,** *n.*

curlyhead (kû′lĭ hĕd′), *n.* a person, esp. a child, with curly hair.

curmudgeon (kû mŭj′ən), *n.* an irascible, churlish, miserly fellow. **—curmudg′eonly,** *adj.*

curn (kûn), *n. Scot.* **1.** a grain. **2.** a small quantity or number. [? akin to KERNEL]

curr (kû), *v.i.* to make a low, murmuring sound, like the purring of a cat. [cf. Icel. *kurra* murmur]

currach (kŭ′rəKH, kŭ′rə), *n. Scot., Irish.* a coracle. Also, **curagh, cur′ragh.** [t. Gaelic or Irish: m. *curach.* Cf. Welsh *corwg*]

currajong (kŭ′rə jŏng′), *n.* kurrajong.

currant (kŭ′rənt), *n.* **1.** a small seedless raisin, produced chiefly in California and in the Levant, used in cookery, etc. **2.** the small, edible, acid, round fruit or berry of certain wild or cultivated shrubs of the genus *Ribes*, as *R. sativum* (**redcurrant** and **white currant**) and *R. nigrum* (**blackcurrant**). **3.** the shrub itself. **4.** any of various similar fruits or shrubs. [ME (*raysons of*) *Coraunte*, t. AF: m. (*raisins de*) *Corauntz* (raisins of) Corinth; so called because orig. from Corinth in Greece]

currawong (kŭ′rə wŏng′), *n.* any of the large black or grey Australian birds of the genus *Strepera.* [t. native Australian]

currency (kŭ′rən sĭ), *n., pl.* **-cies. 1.** that which is current as a medium of exchange; the money in actual use. **2.** the fact or quality of being passed on, as from person to person. **3.** general acceptance; prevalence; vogue. **4.** the fact or state of passing in time. **5.** circulation, as of coin. **6.** *Austral.* one born in Australia. **7.** *Obs. or Rare.* a running; flowing. *—adj.* **8.** *Austral.* born in Australia.

current (kŭ′rənt), *adj.* **1.** passing in time, or belonging to the time actually passing: *the current month.* **2.** passing from one to another; circulating, as coin. **3.** publicly reported or known. **4.** prevalent. **5.** generally accepted; in vogue. **6.** *Now Rare.* running or flowing. **7.** *Obs.* genuine; authentic. *—n.* **8.** a flowing; flow, as of a river. **9.** that which flows, as a stream. **10.** a portion of a large body of water, or of air, etc., moving in a certain direction. **11.** *Elect.* **a.** a movement or flow of electricity. **b.** the rate of flow, in amperes. **12.** course, as of time or events; the main course; the general tendency. [t. L: s. *currens*, ppr., running; r. ME *corant*, t. OF] **—cur′rently, adv.**

—Syn. 4. CURRENT, PRESENT, PREVAILING, PREVALENT, refer to something generally or commonly in use. That which is CURRENT is in general circulation or a matter of common knowledge or acceptance: *current usage in English.* PRESENT refers to that which is in general use now; it is more limited than CURRENT, as to time: *present customs.* That which is PREVAILING is that which has superseded others: *prevailing fashion.* That which is PREVALENT exists or is spread widely: *a prevalent idea.* **9.** See **stream. —Ant. 4.** obsolete. **5.** old-fashioned.

current account, a bank account which is subject to withdrawal by cheque at any time by the customer.

current assets, *Com.* cash and assets readily convertible into cash.

current collector, *Elect.* (on a tramcar, electric train, etc.) any device, as a pantograph (def. 2), for maintaining electrical contact between a contact conductor and the electrical circuit of the vehicle on which the collector is mounted.

current density, *Elect.* the rate of flow in amperes per unit of cross-sectional area at a given place in a conductor.

current expenses, regularly continuing expenditures for the maintenance and the carrying on of business.

current liabilities, *Com.* indebtedness maturing within one year; liabilities payable out of current assets.

curricle (kŭ′rĭ kl), *n.* a light, two-wheeled, open carriage drawn by two horses abreast. [t. L: m. s. *curriculum* a running, course, race, race chariot]

curriculum (kə rĭk′yōō ləm), *n., pl.* **-la** (-lə). **1.** the aggregate of courses of study given in a school, college, university, etc. **2.** the regular or a particular course of study in a school, college, etc. [t. L. See CURRICLE] **—curric′ular,** *adj.*

curriculum vitae (kə rĭk′yōō ləm vī′tē), a brief account of one's career to date.

currier (kŭ′rĭ ə), *n.* **1.** one who dresses and colours leather after it is tanned. **2.** one who curries (a horse, etc.). [ME *corier*, t. OF, g. L *coriārius* tanner]

curriery (kŭ′rĭ ə rĭ), *n., pl.* **-eries. 1.** the occupation or business of a currier. **2.** the place where it is carried on.

currish (kû′rĭsh), *adj.* **1.** of or pertaining to a cur. **2.** cur-like; snarling; quarrelsome. **3.** contemptible. **—cur′rishly,** *adv.* **—cur′rishness,** *n.*

curry[1] (kŭ′rĭ), *n., pl.* **-ries,** *v.,* **-ried, -rying. 1.** an Indian sauce or relish in many varieties, containing a mixture of spices, seeds, vegetables, fruits, etc., eaten with rice or combined with meat, fish, or other food. **2.** a dish prepared with a curry sauce or with curry powder. *—v.t.* **3.** to prepare (food) with a curry sauce or with curry powder. [t. Tamil: m. *kari* sauce]

curry[2] (kŭ′rĭ), *v.t.,* **-ried, -rying. 1.** to rub and clean (a horse, etc.) with a comb; currycomb. **2.** to dress (tanned hides) by soaking, scraping, beating, colouring, etc. **3.** to beat; thrash. **4. curry favour,** to seek favour by a show of kindness, courtesy, flattery, etc. [ME *cory*, t. OF: m. *coreer*, earlier *conreder* put in order, f. *con-* CON- + *-reder* make ready (ult. t. Gmc. See REDD)]

currycomb (kŭ′rĭ kōm′), *n.* **1.** a comb, usually with rows of metal teeth, for currying horses, etc. *—v.t.* **2.** to rub or clean with such a comb.

curry powder, a powdered preparation of spices and other ingredients, notably turmeric, used for making curry sauce or for seasoning food.

curse (kûs), *n.*, *v.*, **cursed** or **curst, cursing.** —*n.* **1.** the expression of a wish that evil, etc., befall another. **2.** an ecclesiastical censure or anathema. **3.** a profane oath. **4.** evil that has been invoked upon one. **5.** something accursed. **6.** the cause of evil, misfortune, or trouble. —*v.t.* **7.** to wish or invoke evil, calamity, injury, or destruction upon. **8.** to swear at. **9.** to blaspheme. **10.** to afflict with great evil. **11.** to excommunicate. —*v.i.* **12.** to utter curses; swear profanely. [ME *curs*, OE *cūrs*, der. *cūrsian*, v., curse, reprove (whence ME *cursen*), t. OIrish: m. s. *cūrsagim* I blame] —**curs′er,** *n.*

—**Syn. 1.** imprecation, execration, fulmination, malediction. **6.** bane, scourge, plague, affliction, torment. **7–9.** CURSE, BLASPHEME, SWEAR are often interchangeable in the sense of using profane language. However, CURSE is the general word for the heartfelt invoking or violent or angry calling down of evil on another: *they called down curses on their enemies.* To BLASPHEME is to speak contemptuously or with abuse of God or of sacred things: *to blaspheme openly.* To SWEAR is to use the name of God or of some holy person or thing as an exclamation to add force or show anger: *to swear in every sentence.* —**Ant. 7.** bless.

cursed (kû′sĭd, kûst), *adj.* **1.** under a curse; damned. **2.** deserving a curse; hateful; abominable. **3.** *Dial.* cantankerous; ill-tempered; cross. —**curs′edly,** *adj.* —**curs′edness,** *n.* —**Syn. 2.** damnable, execrable.

cursillo (ko͞oə sĭl′ō), *n.* *Rom. Cath. Ch.* (*often cap.*) a movement designed to relate spiritual strength to mundane problems, initiated by a three-day course of study and devotion, and continued through regular meetings.

cursive (kû′sĭv), *adj.* **1.** (of writing or printing type) in flowing strokes, with the letters joined together. —*n.* **2.** a cursive letter or printing type. [t. ML: m. s. *cursīvus*, der. L *cursus* a running] —**cur′sively,** *adv.*

cursor (kû′sə), *n.* a slider, as the transparent slider forming part of a slide rule on which are marked one or more reference lines.

cursorial (kû sô′rĭ əl), *adj.* *Zool.* **1.** adapted for running, as the feet and skeleton of dogs, horses, etc. **2.** having limbs adapted for running, as certain birds, insects, etc.

cursory (kû′sə rĭ), *adj.* going rapidly over something, without noticing details; hasty; superficial. [t. L: m. s. *cursōrius* pertaining to a runner or a race] —**cur′sorily,** *adv.* —**cur′soriness,** *n.*

curst (kûst), *v.* **1.** pt. and pp. of **curse.** —*adj.* **2.** cursed.

curt (kût), *adj.* **1.** short; shortened. **2.** brief in speech, etc. **3.** rudely brief in speech, manner, etc. [t. L: s. *curtus* cut short, clipped. Cf. SHORT] —**curt′ly,** *adv.* —**curt′ness,** *n.* —**Syn. 2.** See **blunt.**

curtail (kû tāl′), *v.t.* to cut short; cut off a part of; abridge; reduce; diminish. [var. (by assoc. with TAIL) of obs. *curtal*, v., dock. See CURTAL, adj.] —**curtail′er,** *n.* —**curtail′ment,** *n.* —**Syn.** lessen, dock. See **shorten.**

curtail step (kû′tāl), the first or bottom step of a stair, when it is finished in a curved line at its outer end.

curtain (kû′tn, -tĭn), *n.* **1.** a hanging piece of fabric used to shut out the light from a window, adorn a room, etc. **2.** *Theat.* **a.** a set of hanging drapery, etc., for concealing all or part of the set from the view of the audience. **b.** the act or time of raising or opening a curtain at the start of a performance. **c.** the fall of a curtain at the end of a scene or act. **3.** anything that shuts off, covers, or conceals: *a curtain of artillery fire.* **4.** *Archit.* a flat portion of a wall, connecting two towers, projecting structures, or the like. **5.** *Fort.* the part of a wall or rampart connecting two bastions, towers, or the like. See diag. under **bastion. 6.** (*pl.*) *Slang.* the end, esp. of a life. —*v.t.* **7.** to provide, shut off, conceal, or adorn with, or as with, a curtain. [ME *curtine*, t. OF, g. LL *cortina* curtain]

—**Syn. 1.** drapery, portiere, lambrequin, valance. CURTAIN, BLIND, SHADE, SHUTTER are covers for a window, to shut out light or keep persons from looking in. CURTAIN, BLIND, and SHADE may mean a cover, usually of cloth, which can be rolled up and down inside the window. CURTAIN, however, may also refer to a drapery at a window; and a Venetian BLIND consists of slats mounted on tapes for drawing up or down and varying the pitch of the slats. BLIND and SHUTTER may mean a cover made of two wooden frames with movable slats, attached by hinges outside a window and pulled together or opened at will. SHUTTERS may mean also a set of panels (wooden or iron) put up outside certain shops at closing time.

curtain call, the appearance of performers at the conclusion of a performance in response to the applause of the audience.

curtain lecture, a private scolding, esp. one by a wife to her husband.

curtain-raiser (kû′tn rā′zə), *n.* **1.** a short play acted before a main play. **2.** a prelude or foretaste of something.

curtain wall, *Building.* an exterior wall having no structural function.

curtal (kû′tl), *Obs. or Archaic.* —*adj.* **1.** wearing a short frock: *a curtal friar.* —*n.* **2.** anything docked or cut short. **3.** a 16th-century bassoon. [t. F: m. *courtault*, der. *court* short, g. L *curtus*]

curtana (kû tä′nə, -tā′nə), *n.* the pointless sword carried before monarchs of England at their coronation.

curtesy (kû′tĭ sĭ), *n.*, *pl.* **-sies.** *Law.* the life tenure formerly enjoyed by a husband in his wife's land inheritance after her death, provided they had issue able to inherit: *a tenancy by the curtesy.* [var. of COURTESY]

curtilage (kû′tĭ lĭj), *n.* *Law.* the area of land occupied by a dwelling and its yard and outbuildings, actually enclosed or considered as enclosed. [ME, t. AF, der. OF *courtil* little court. See COURT]

Curtin (kû′tn), *n.* **John,** 1885–1945, Australian statesman, prime minister 1941–45.

Curtius (*Ger.* ko͝or′tsē o͞os), *n.* **Ernst** (*Ger.* ĕrnst), 1814–96, German archaeologist and historian.

curtsey (kût′sĭ), *n.*, *pl.* **-seys,** *v.*, **-seyed, -seying.** curtsy.

curtsy (kût′sĭ), *n.*, *pl.* **-sies,** *v.*, **-sied, -sying.** —*n.* **1.** a bow by women in recognition or respect, consisting of bending the knees and lowering the body. —*v.i.* **2.** to make a curtsy. [var. of COURTESY]

curule (kyo͞oə′ro͞ol), *adj.* **1.** privileged to sit in a curule chair. **2.** of the highest rank.

curule chair, *Hist.* a folding seat with curved legs and no back, often ornamented with ivory, etc., used only by certain high officials of ancient Rome.

curvaceous (kû vā′shəs), *adj.* *Colloq.* (of a woman) having a full figure. [f. CURVE + -ACEOUS]

curvature (kû′və chə), *n.* **1.** the act of curving. **2.** curved condition, often abnormal: *curvature of the spine.* **3.** the degree of curving. **4.** something curved. **5.** *Maths.* a measure of the extent to which a line departs from being straight or a surface departs from being plane.

curve (kûv), *n.*, *v.*, **curved, curving,** *adj.* —*n.* **1.** a continuously bending line, without angles. **2.** a curving. **3.** any curved outline, form, thing, or part. **4.** a curved ruler used by draughtsmen. **5.** *Maths.* a collection of points whose coordinates are continuous functions of a single independent variable. —*v.t.*, *v.i.* **6.** to bend in a curve; take, or cause to take, the course of a curve. —*adj.* **7.** *Rare.* curved. [t. L: m. s. *curvus* bent, curved] —**curvedly** (kû′vĭd lĭ), *adv.* —**curv′edness,** *n.*

curvet (kû vĕt′), *n.*, *v.*, **-vetted, -vetting** or **-veted, -veting.** —*n.* **1.** a leap of a horse in which the forelegs are raised together and equally advanced, and then, as they are falling, the hindlegs are raised with a spring, so that all the legs are off the ground at once. —*v.i.* **2.** to leap in a curvet, as a horse; cause one's horse to do this. **3.** to leap and frisk. —*v.t.* **4.** to cause to make a curvet. [t. It.: m. *corvetta*, dim. of *corvo*, g. L *curvus* bent, curved]

curvi-, a combining form of **curve.**

curvilinear (kû′vĭ lĭn′ĭ ə), *adj.* **1.** consisting of or bounded by curved lines: *a curvilinear figure.* **2.** forming, or moving in a curved line. **3.** formed, or characterized by, curved lines. Also, **cur′vilin′eal.**

curvy (kû′vĭ), *adj.* having curves; curvaceous.

Curzon (kû′zən), *n.* **1. Clifford,** born 1907, English concert pianist. **2. George Nathaniel, 1st Marquess of Kedlestone** (kĕd′l stən, kĕl′stən), 1859–1925, British statesman: viceroy of India 1899–1905.

Cusco (*Sp.* ko͞os′kô), *n.* Cuzco.

cuscus (kŭs′kəs), *n.* any of several members of the phalanger family, esp. the largest of the Australian opossums, *Phalanger maculatus.*

cusec (kyo͞o′sĕk), *n.* one cubic foot per second (as a rate of flow).

Cush (kŭsh), *n.* *Bible.* **1.** the eldest son of Ham. Gen. 10:6. **2.** (probably) Upper Egypt and the neighbouring country.

cushat (kŭsh′ət), *n.* the woodpigeon or ringdove, *Columba palumbus*, of Europe. [OE *cūscote*]

cushion (ko͝osh′ən), *n.* **1.** a soft bag of cloth, leather, or rubber, filled with feathers, air, etc., used to sit, kneel, or lie on. **2.** anything similar in appearance or use. **3.** a pillow used in lacemaking. **4.** the elastic raised rim encircling the top of a billiard table. **5.** something to absorb or counteract a shock, jar, or jolt, as a body of air or steam. **6.** the air supporting a hovercraft. **7.** *Archit.* the cap of a column, shaped like a cushion, peculiar to Norman architecture. —*v.t.* **8.** to place on or support by a cushion. **9.** to furnish with a cushion or cushions. **10.** to cover or conceal with, or as with, a cushion. **11.** to lessen or soften the effects of. **12.** to check the motion of (a piston, etc.) by a cushion, as of steam. **13.** to form (steam, etc.) into a cushion. **14.** to suppress (complaints, etc.) quietly, as by ignoring. [ME *cushin*, t. OF: m. *coussin*, ? ult. der. L *culcita* cushion]

—**Syn. 1.** CUSHION, PILLOW agree in being cases filled with a material more or less resilient, intended to be used as supports for the body or parts of it. A CUSHION is a soft pad used to sit, lie, or kneel on, or to lean against: *a number of cushions on a sofa, cushions on pews in a church.* A PILLOW is a bag or case filled with feathers, down, or other soft material, usually to support the head: *to sleep with a pillow under one's head.*

Cushitic (ko͝o shĭt′ĭk), *n.* a group of Hamitic languages, including Somali and other languages of Somaliland and Ethiopia.

cushy (ko͝osh′ĭ), *adj.*, **cushier, cushiest.** *Slang.* easy; pleasant. [f. CUSH(ION) + -Y[1]]

cusp (kŭsp), *n.* **1.** a point; pointed end. **2.** *Anat., Zool., Bot.* a point, projection, or elevation, as on the crown of a tooth. **3.** *Geom.* a point where two branches of a curve meet, end, and are tangent; spinode. **4.** *Archit., etc.* a point or figure formed by the intersection of two small arcs or curved members, as one of the pointed projections sometimes decorating the internal curve of an arch or a traceried window. **5.** *Astron.* a point of a crescent, esp. of the moon. [t. L: m. *cuspis* point]

cusped (kŭspt), *adj.* having a cusp or cusps; cusplike. Also, **cuspate** (kŭs′pĭt, -pāt), **cus′pated.**

cuspid (kŭs′pĭd), *n.* a tooth with a single projection point or elevation; a canine tooth (*cuspid* is preferred for a human canine tooth). [t. L: s. *cuspis* point]

cuspidal (kŭs′pĭ dl). *adj.* of, like, or having a cusp; cuspidate.

cuspidate (kŭs′pĭ dāt′), *adj.* **1.** having a cusp or cusps. **2.** furnished with or ending in a sharp and stiff point or cusp: *cuspidate leaves, cuspidate tooth.* Also, **cus′pidat′ed.** [t. NL: m. s. *cuspidātus*, der. L *cuspis* point]

cuspidation (kŭs′pĭ dā′shən), *n.* decoration with cusps, as in architecture.

cuspidor (kŭs′pĭ dô′), *n. U.S.* a bowl used as a receptacle for spit. [t. Pg.: spitter, spittoon, der. *cuspir*, g. L *conspuere* spit upon]

cuss (kŭs), *Orig. U.S. Colloq.* —*n.* **1.** a curse. **2.** a person or animal: *a queer but likeable cuss.* —*v.t., v.i.* **3.** to curse. [early var. of CURSE]

cussed (kŭs′ĭd), *adj. Colloq.* **1.** cursed. **2.** obstinate; perverse. —**cuss′edly,** *adv.* —**cuss′edness,** *n.*

custard (kŭs′təd), *n.* a dish made of eggs and milk, sweetened and baked or boiled, or of boiled milk and sweetened flavoured cornflour. [earlier *crustarde* (with loss of first *-r-* by dissimilation), a kind of patty, der. OE *croste* CRUST]

custard-apple (kŭs′təd ăp′l), *n.* **1.** the fruit of any of a group of shrubs and trees, native in tropical America, and possessing soft edible pulp; often confined to the single species, *Annona reticulata.* **2.** the tree itself.

Custer (kŭs′tə), *n.* **George Armstrong,** 1839–76, U.S. general and Indian fighter.

custodial (kŭs tō′dyəl), *adj.* of or pertaining to custody.

custodian (kŭs tō′dyən), *n.* a person who has custody; a keeper; guardian. —**custo′dianship′,** *n.*

custody (kŭs′tə dĭ), *n., pl.* **-dies. 1.** keeping; guardianship; care: *in the custody of her father.* **2.** the keeping or charge of officers of the law: *the car was held in the custody of the police.* **3.** imprisonment: *he was taken into custody.* [t. L: m. s. *custōdia*]

—**Syn. 1, 2.** safekeeping, charge, watch. CUSTODY, KEEPING, POSSESSION imply a guardianship or care for something. CUSTODY denotes a strict keeping, as by a formally authorized and responsible guardian or keeper: *in the custody of the police.* KEEPING denotes having in one's care or charge, as for guarding or preservation: *in a bank for safekeeping.* POSSESSION means holding, ownership, or mastery: *leave it in possession of its owner.*

custom (kŭs′təm), *n.* **1.** a habitual practice; the usual way of acting in given circumstances. **2.** habits or usages collectively; convention. **3.** a long-continued habit which is so established that it has the force of law. **4.** such habits collectively. **5.** a customary tax, tribute, or service due by feudal tenants to their lord. **6.** *Sociol.* a group pattern of habitual activity usually transmitted from one generation to another. **7.** toll; duty. **8.** (*pl.*) customs duties. **9.** (*pl.*) the government department that collects these duties. **10.** habitual patronage of a particular shop, etc.; business patronage. **11.** customers or patrons collectively. **12.** the aggregate of customers. —*adj.* **13.** *U.S.* made specially for individual customers: *custom shoes.* **14.** dealing in things so made, or doing work to order: *a custom tailor.* [ME *custume*, t. OF, ult. g. L *consuētūdo* custom. See CONSUETUDE. Cf. COSTUME]

—**Syn. 1, 2.** CUSTOM, HABIT, PRACTICE mean an established way of doing things. CUSTOM, applied to a community or to an individual, implies a (more or less permanent) continuance of a social usage: *it is the custom to give gifts at Christmas time.* HABIT, applied particularly to an individual, implies such repetition of the same action as to develop a natural, spontaneous, or rooted tendency or inclination to perform it: *make a habit of reading the newspapers.* PRACTICE applies to a set of fixed habits or an ordered procedure in conducting activities: *secret practice of a cult.*

customable (kŭs′tə mə bl), *adj.* subject to customs or duties; dutiable.

customary (kŭs′tə mə rĭ, -təm rĭ), *adj., n., pl.* **-aries.** —*adj.* **1.** according to or depending on custom; usual; habitual. **2.** of or established by custom rather than law. **3.** *Law.* defined by long-continued practices: *the customary service due from land in a manor.* —*n.* **4.** a book or document containing the legal customs or customary laws of a locality. **5.** any body of such customs or laws. [t. ML: m. s. *customārius*, der. OF *custume* CUSTOM] —**cus′tomarily,** *adv.* —**cus′tomariness,** *n.* —**Syn. 1.** wonted, accustomed, conventional. See **usual.** —**Ant. 1.** uncommon.

custom-built (kŭs′təm bĭlt′), *adj. Chiefly U.S.* made to individual order: *a custom-built limousine.*

customer (kŭs′tə mə), *n.* **1.** one who purchases goods from another; a buyer; a patron. **2.** *Colloq.* a person one has to deal with; a fellow: *a queer customer.*

custom-made (kŭs′təm mād′), *adj. Chiefly U.S.* made to individual order: *custom-made shoes.*

customs duties, duties imposed by law on imported or, less commonly, exported goods.

customs house, a government office, often at a seaport, for collecting customs, clearing vessels, etc. Also, *Chiefly U.S.,* **custom house.**

customs union, an arrangement between independent nations or tariff areas to remove customs barriers between them and to adopt a uniform tariff policy.

custos (kŭs′tŏs), *n., pl.* **custodes** (kŭs tō′dēz). *Latin.* **1.** a custodian. **2.** a superior in the Franciscan order.

custos morum (kŭs′tŏs mô′rəm), *Latin.* a custodian or guardian of morals; censor.

custumal (kŭs′tyo͞o məl), *n.* customary. [t. ML: s. *custumālis*, Latinization of OF *costumel* customary]

cut (kŭt), *v.*, **cut, cutting,** *adj., n.* —*v.t.* **1.** to penetrate with, or as with, a sharp-edged instrument: *he cut his finger.* **2.** to strike sharply, as with a whip. **3.** to wound severely the feelings of. **4.** to divide with, or as with, a sharp-edged instrument; sever; carve: *to cut a rope, bread into slices, etc.* **5.** to hew or saw down; fell: *to cut timber.* **6.** to detach with, or as with, a sharp-edged instrument; separate from the main body; lop off. **7.** to reap; mow; harvest: *to cut grain or hay.* **8.** to trim by clipping, shearing, paring, or pruning: *to cut the hair or the nails.* **9.** to castrate. **10.** to intersect; cross: *one line cuts another at right angles.* **11.** to stop; halt the running of, as an engine, a liquid, etc. **12.** to abridge or shorten by omitting a part: *to cut a speech.* **13.** to lower; reduce; diminish (sometimes fol. by *down*): *to cut rates.* **14.** *Radio and Television.* to stop recording or transmitting (a scene, broadcast, etc.). **15.** *Films, Television, etc.* to edit (filmed material) by cutting and rearranging pieces of film. **16.** to make or fashion by cutting, as a statue, jewel, garment, etc. **17.** to hollow out; excavate; dig: *cut a trench.* **18.** *Colloq.* to renounce; give up. **19.** *Colloq.* to refuse to recognize socially. **20.** to perform or execute: *to cut a caper.* **21.** *Colloq.* to absent oneself from. **22.** *Cards.* **a.** to divide (a pack of cards) at random into two or more parts, by removing cards from the top. **b.** to take (a card) from a pack. **23.** *Sports.* to hit (a ball) either with the hand or some instrument so as to change its course and often to cause it to spin. **24.** *Cricket.* to strike and send off (a ball) on the off side, usually in a direction between cover and third man.

—*v.i.* **25.** to penetrate or divide something as with a sharp-edged instrument; make an incision: *the scissors cut well.* **26.** to admit of being cut, or turn out upon being cut. **27.** to pass, go, or come, esp. in the most direct way (fol. by *across, through, in,* etc.): *to cut across a field.* **28.** to strike sharply, as with a whip. **29.** (of the teeth) to grow through the gums. **30.** *Cards.* to cut the cards. **31.** *Radio and Television.* to stop filming or recording. **32.** *Slang.* to run away; make off. **33.** (of a horse) to interfere.

—*v.* **34.** Some special verb phrases are:

cut back, 1. to shorten by cutting off the end. **2.** (in a novel, film, etc.) to return suddenly to earlier events. **3.** *Football.* to reverse direction suddenly by moving in the diagonally opposite course.

cut down, 1. to bring down by cutting. **2.** to reduce, esp. expenses, costs, etc.

cut in, 1. to interrupt. **2.** (in traffic) to pull in dangerously soon after overtaking.

cut it fine, to leave only a narrow margin of error.

cut off, 1. to intercept. **2.** to interrupt. **3.** to bring to a sudden end. **4.** to shut out. **5.** to disinherit.

cut out, 1. to omit; delete; excise. **2.** to oust and replace; supplant (esp. a rival). **3.** to be fit for. **4.** to stop; cease. **5.** to plan or arrange; prepare. **6.** to fashion or shape; form; make. **7.** to move suddenly out of the lane or path in which one has been driving. **8.** *Print.* to remove the background from an illustration so that the

outline of the subject appears on an unprinted background. **9.** (of an electrical device) to switch off, as when overloaded.
cut teeth, to have the teeth grow through the gums.
cut up, 1. to cut into pieces. **2.** *Colloq.* to criticize severely. **3.** *Colloq.* to upset or cause distress to.
cut up rough, to behave badly; become unpleasant.
—*adj.* **35.** that has been subjected to cutting; divided into pieces by cutting; detached by cutting: *cut flowers.* **36.** *Bot.* incised; cleft. **37.** fashioned by cutting; having the surface shaped or ornamented by grinding and polishing: *cut glass.* **38.** reduced by, or as by, cutting: *cut rates.* **39.** *Slang.* drunk. **40. cut and dried, a.** fixed or settled in advance. **b.** lacking freshness or spontaneity.
—*n.* **41.** the act of cutting; a stroke or a blow as with a knife, whip, etc. **42.** a piece cut off, esp. of meat. **43.** *Butchering.* part of an animal usually cut as one piece. **44.** *Colloq.* share: *his cut was 20 per cent.* **45.** *Chiefly U.S.* quantity cut, esp. of timber. **46.** the result of cutting, as an incision, wound, etc.; a passage, channel, etc., made by cutting or digging. **47.** manner or fashion in which anything is cut. **48.** style; manner; kind. **49.** a passage or course straight across: *a short cut.* **50.** an excision or omission of a part. **51.** a part excised or omitted. **52.** a reduction in price, salary, etc. **53.** an act, speech, etc., which wounds the feelings. **54.** an engraved block or plate used for printing, or an impression from it. **55.** *Colloq.* a refusal to recognize an acquaintance. **56.** *Sports.* **a.** the act of cutting a ball. **b.** the spin of the ball. **57.** *Cards.* a cutting of the cards. **58.** one of several pieces of straw, paper, etc., used in drawing lots. **59. a cut above,** *Colloq.* somewhat superior to another in some respect. [ME *cutten, kytten, kitten*; akin to d. Sw. *kata* cut]
—Syn. 1. gash, slash, slit, lance. **4.** cleave, sunder, bisect. CUT, CHOP, HACK, HEW, refer to giving a sharp blow or stroke. CUT is a general word for this: *to cut the grass.* To CHOP is to cut by giving repeated blows with something sharp, for example, an axe. To CHOP and to HEW are practically interchangeable, but CHOP may refer to a more or less undirected action; whereas HEW, more formal, suggests keeping to a definite purpose: *to chop or hew down a tree, to hew to a line.* To HACK is to cut or chop roughly and unevenly: *hack off a limb.* **46.** gash, slash, slit.

cutaneous (kyōō tā′nyəs), *adj.* of, pertaining to, or affecting the skin. [t. ML: m. *cutāneus*, der. L *cutis* skin]

cutaway (kŭt′ə wā′), *adj.* **1.** (of a coat) having the skirt cut away from the waist in front in a curve. **—***n.* **2.** a cutaway coat.

cutback (kŭt′băk′), *n.* **1.** reduction to an earlier rate, as in production. **2.** *U.S.* flashback.

cutch (kŭch), *n.* catechu.

Cutch (kŭch), *n.* **1.** Also, **Kutch.** a former state in western India, now part of Bombay State. 8461 sq. mi. *Former cap.:* Bhuj. **2. Rann of** (răn), a large salt marsh NE of this state. ab. 9000 sq. mi.

cutcherry (kə chĕ′rĭ), *n.* **1.** *India.* a public administrative or judicial office. **2.** any administrative office. Also, **cutchery** (kŭch′ə rĭ). [t. Hind.: m. *kacherī*]

cute (kyōōt), *adj.*, **cuter, cutest. 1.** *Colloq.* pleasingly pretty or dainty. **2.** *Archaic or Dial.* clever; shrewd. [aphetic var. of ACUTE] **—cute′ly,** *adv.* **—cute′ness,** *n.*

cut glass, glass ornamented or shaped by cutting or grinding with abrasive wheels. **—cut′glass′,** *adj.*

cut-grass (kŭt′gräs′), *n.* any of various grasses with blades having rough edges, esp. grasses of the genus *Leersia*, as *Leersia oryzoides*, a perennial grass growing in wet places.

Cuthbert (kŭth′bət), *n.* **Saint,** died A.D. 687, English monk and bishop.

cuticle (kyōō′tĭ kl), *n.* **1.** the epidermis. **2.** a superficial integument, membrane, or the like. **3.** the non-living epidermis which surrounds the edges of the fingernail or toenail. **4.** *Bot.* a very thin hyaline film covering the surface of plants, and derived from the outer surfaces of the epidermal cells. [t. L: m. s. *cutīcula*, dim. of *cutis* skin] **—cuticular** (kyōō tĭk′yōō lə), *adj.*

cuticula (kyōō tĭk′yōō lə), *n.*, *pl.* **-lae** (-lē′). the outer non-cellular layer of the arthropod integument, composed of a mixture of chitin and protein, but commonly containing other hardening substances. [t. L: skin]

cutin (kyōō′tĭn), *n.* a transparent waxy substance constituting together with cellulose the cuticle of plants. [f. s. L *cutis* skin + -IN[2]]

cutinize (kyōō′tĭ nīz′), *v.t., v.i.*, **-nized, -nizing.** to make into or become cutin. Also, **cutinise. —cu′tiniza′tion,** *n.*

cutis (kyōō′tĭs), *n.* *Latin.* the corium or true skin, beneath the epidermis. Also, **cutis vera** (vĭə′rə).

cutlass (kŭt′ləs), *n.* a short, heavy, slightly curved sword, formerly used esp. at sea. [t. F: m. *coutelas*, ult. der. L *cultellus* small knife]

cutler (kŭt′lə), *n.* one who makes, sells, or repairs knives and other cutting instruments. [ME *coteler*, t. F: m. *coutelier*, der. *coutel* small knife, g. L *cultellus*]

cutlery (kŭt′lə rĭ), *n.* **1.** the art or business of a cutler. **2.** cutting instruments collectively, esp. those for dinner-table use. [t. F: m. *coutelerie.* See CUTLER]

cutlet (kŭt′lĭt), *n.* a cut of meat for grilling, frying, or roasting, containing a rib and cut from the neck of veal or mutton. [t. F: m. *côtelette*, double dim. of *côte* rib, g. L *costa*]

cut-off (kŭt′ŏf′), *n.* **1.** a cutting off, or something that cuts off; a shorter passage or way. **2.** oxbow (def. 2). **3.** the arresting of the passage of steam or working fluid to the cylinder of an engine, or the mechanism effecting it. **4.** the negative bias which has to be applied to the control grid of a radio valve in order to reduce the anode current to zero.

cut-out (kŭt′out′), *n.* **1.** something cut out from something else. **2.** *Elect.* an automatic device (usually electromagnetic or thermal) for breaking an electric circuit when the current exceeds the predetermined value. **3.** *Print.* an illustration whose subject appears on an unprinted background.

cut-out box, a box containing cut-outs.

cut-price (kŭt′prīs′), *adj.* **1.** (of goods) for sale at a price lower than the suggested retail price. **2.** (of a shop, etc.) dealing in such goods.

cutpurse (kŭt′pûs′), *n.* **1.** (formerly) one who steals by cutting purses from the girdle. **2.** a pickpocket.

cut rate, a price, fare, or rate below the standard charge. **—cut′-rate′,** *adj.*

Cuttack (kŭ tăk′), *n.* a town in India, in E Orissa. 146,303 (1961).

cutter (kŭt′ə), *n.* **1.** one who or that which cuts. **2.** a small sailing boat with one mast, a bowsprit, a gaff, and a boom. **3.** a medium-sized boat for rowing or sailing, or a launch, belonging to a warship. **4.** a light-armed government vessel (**revenue cutter**), used to prevent smuggling and enforce customs regulations.

cutthroat (kŭt′thrōt′), *n.* **1.** one who cuts throats; a murderer. **2.** a cutthroat razor. **—***adj.* **3.** murderous. **4.** (of a razor) having an open blade. **5.** relentless: *cutthroat competition.* **6.** pertaining to a game participated in by three or more persons, each acting and scoring as an individual.

cutting (kŭt′ĭng), *n.* **1.** the act of one who or that which cuts. **2.** something cut off. **3.** *Hort.* a piece of plant, commonly a root, shoot, or leaf, cut from a plant to reproduce an entire new plant. **4.** a piece clipped out of a newspaper; a clipping. **5.** something produced by cutting; an excavation through high ground, as in constructing a road, etc. **—***adj.* **6.** that cuts; penetrating or dividing by, or as by, a cut. **7.** piercing, as a wind. **8.** wounding the feelings severely; sarcastic. **—cut′tingly,** *adv.* **—Syn. 7.** sharp, keen, incisive, trenchant. **8.** caustic, biting, mordant.

cuttlebone (kŭt′l bōn′), *n.* the calcareous internal shell or plate of true cuttlefishes, used to make powder for polishing, and fed to canaries to supply the necessary lime, etc.

cuttlefish (kŭt′l fĭsh′), *n.*, *pl.* **-fishes,** (*esp. collectively*) **-fish.** any of various decapod dibranchiate cephalopods, esp. of the genus *Sepia*, having sucker-bearing arms and the power of ejecting a black, inklike fluid when pursued. Also, **cut′tle.** [f. *cuttle* (ME *codulle*, OE *cudele* cuttlefish; akin to COD[1]) + FISH]

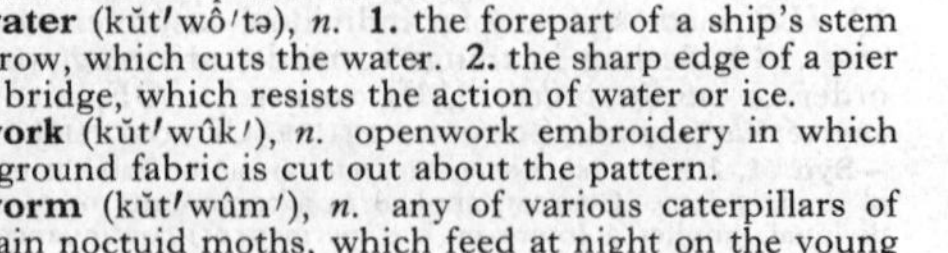

Cuttlefish, *Sepia officinialis* (5 in. long)

cutty (kŭt′ĭ), *adj.*, *n.*, **-ties.** *Chiefly Scot.* **—***adj.* **1.** cut short; short. **2.** testy. **—***n.* **3.** a short spoon. **4.** a short-stemmed tobacco pipe. **5.** an immoral girl or woman. [der. CUT, v.]

Cutty Sark (kŭt′ĭ säk′), a famous three-masted tea clipper built in 1869 and now docked permanently at Greenwich.

cutty stool, *Scot.* **1.** a low stool. **2.** a seat in old churches, where offenders against chastity, or other delinquents, sat and received public rebuke.

cutwater (kŭt′wô′tə), *n.* **1.** the forepart of a ship's stem or prow, which cuts the water. **2.** the sharp edge of a pier of a bridge, which resists the action of water or ice.

cutwork (kŭt′wûk′), *n.* openwork embroidery in which the ground fabric is cut out about the pattern.

cutworm (kŭt′wûm′), *n.* any of various caterpillars of certain noctuid moths, which feed at night on the young plants of corn, cabbage, etc., cutting them off at or near the ground.

Cuvier (kyōō′vĭ ā′; *Fr.* kY vyė′), *n.* **Georges Léopold Chrétien Frédéric Dagobert** (*Fr.* zhŏrzh lė ō pŏl krė tyăN frė dė rĕk dȧ gō bĕr′), **Baron,** 1769–1832, French naturalist: founder of the science of palaeontology.

Cuvilliés (*Fr.* kY vē lyė′), *n.* **François de** (*Fr.* frăN swȧ′də)

1695–1768, a baroque architect of French origin who worked mainly in Bavaria.

Cuxhaven (ko͝oks′hä′vən; *Ger.* ko͝oks hä′fən), *n.* a seaport in N West Germany at the mouth of the Elbe. 47,000 (est. 1963).

Cuyp (kīp; *Du.* kœyp), *n.* **Aalbert** (*Du.* äl′bĕrt), 1620?–91, Dutch painter. Also, **Kuyp.**

Cuzco (*Sp.* ko͞os′kȯ), *n.* a city in S Peru: ancient Inca ruins. 78,289 (1961). Also, **Cusco.**

C.V., *Bible.* Common Version,

c.v.d., cash against documents.

C.V.O., Commander of the (Royal) Victorian Order.

Cwmbran (ko͞om′brän′), *n.* a new town in England, in Monmouthshire. 35,860 (1965).

c.w.o., cash with order.

cwt, hundredweight.

-cy, **1.** a suffix of abstract nouns, paired usually with adjectives ending in *-t, -te, -tic,* especially *-nt* (like the pair *-ant, -ance*), as *democracy, accuracy, expediency, necromancy,* also paired with other adjectives, as *fallacy,* or with a noun, as *lunacy,* sometimes forming (in extended suffixes) action nouns, as *vacancy* (*vacate*), *occupancy* (*occupy*). **2.** a suffix of nouns denoting a rank or dignity, sometimes attached to the stem of a word rather than the word itself, as *captaincy, colonelcy, magistracy.* [repr. F *-cie, -tie,* L *-cia, -tia,* Gk *-kia, -keia, -tia, -teia*]

cyan-[1], var. of **cyano-**[1], usually before vowels and *h,* as in *cyanamide.*

cyan-[2], var. of **cyano-**[2], before vowels.

cyan-[3], var. of **cyano-**[3], before vowels.

cyanamide (sī′ə nə mīd′, sī ăn′ə mīd′), *n. Chem.* **1.** a white crystalline compound, H_2NCN, obtainable by the action of ammonia on cyanogen chloride or from calcium cyanamide. **2.** an ester or salt of this substance. Also, **cyanamid** (sī′ə nə mĭd, sī ăn′ə mĭd). [f. CYAN(O)-[1] + AMIDE]

cyanate (sī′ə nāt′), *n. Chem.* a salt of cyanic acid.

cyanic (sī ăn′ĭk), *adj.* **1.** blue (applied esp. to a series of colours in flowers, including the blues and colours tending towards blue). **2.** containing, of, or belonging to cyanogen. [f. CYAN(O)-[1] + -IC]

cyanic acid, *Chem.* a poisonous compound, $HOCN$, isomeric with fulminic acid, but unstable except at low temperatures.

cyanide (sī′ə nīd′), *n., v.,* **-nided, -niding.** —*n.* Also, **cyanid** (sī′ə nĭd). **1.** a salt of hydrocyanic acid, as *potassium cyanide,* KCN. —*v.t.* **2.** to treat with a cyanide, as an ore in the process of extracting gold.

cyanide hardening, *Metall.* the introduction of carbon and nitrogen into the surface of steel by heating it in contact with molten cyanides; a form of case-hardening.

cyanide process, *Metall.* a process for extracting gold from its ores, by dissolving in potassium cyanide, reducing the resulting aurocyanide with zinc, filtering off the product and subjecting it to cupellation.

cyanine (sī′ə nēn′), *n.* any of several groups of dyes which make silver halide photographic plates sensitive to a colour range. Also, **cyanin** (sī′ə nĭn).

cyanite (sī′ə nīt′), *n.* a mineral aluminium silicate, Al_2SiO_5, occurring in blue or greenish bladed crystals, used as a refractory. Also, **kyanite.** [f. CYAN(O)-[1] + -ITE[1]]

cyano-[1], a word element indicating dark blue colouring. Also, **cyan-**[1]. [t. Gk: m. *kyano-,* comb. form of *kýanos* dark blue]

cyano-[2], a combining form of **cyanide.** Also, **cyan-**[2].

cyano-[3], *Chem.* a word element referring to the cyanogen group, CN. Also, **cyan-**[3]. [comb. form repr. CYANOGEN]

cyanogen (sī ăn′ə jĭn), *n.* **1.** a poisonous, inflammable gas, C_2N_2. **2.** a univalent radical, CN. [f. CYANO-[2] + -GEN]

cyanohydrin (sī′ə nō hī′drĭn), *n.* one of a class of organic compounds which have both the CN and the OH radicals linked to the same carbon atom.

cyanosis (sī′ə nō′sĭs), *n. Pathol.* blueness or lividness of the skin, as from imperfectly oxygenated blood. Also, **cyanopathy** (sī′ə nŏp′ə thĭ). [NL, t. Gk: m. *kyánōsis* dark blue colour] —**cyanotic** (sī′ə nŏt′ĭk), *adj.*

cyanotype (sī ăn′ə tīp′), *n.* **1.** a process of photographic printing with ferric salts producing blue lines on a white background, used chiefly in printing tracings. **2.** a print made by such a process. [f. CYANO-[1] + -TYPE]

cyanuric acid (sī′ə nyo͝o′rĭk), *Chem.* a white, crystalline acid, $C_3H_3O_3N_3.2H_2O$, obtained by heating urea or by decomposing cyanogen chloride with water. [f. CYAN-[2] + URIC]

cyathiform (sī′ə thĭ fôm′, sī ăth′-), *adj.* shaped like a cup; widened at the top.

Cybele (sĭb′ĭ lĭ), *n.* a great nature goddess of Phrygia and Asia Minor whose worship was carried to Greece and Rome ('the Great Mother of the Gods').

cybernetics (sī′bə nĕt′ĭks), *n.* the scientific study of those methods of control and communication which are common to living organisms and machines, esp. as applied to the analysis of the operations of machines such as computers. [f. s. Gk *kybernḗtēs* helmsman + -ICS] —**cy′bernet′ic,** *adj.*

cycad (sī′kăd), *n.* any of the *Cycadales,* an order of gymnospermous plants intermediate in appearance between ferns and the palms, many species having a thick unbranched columnar trunk bearing a crown of large leathery pinnate leaves. [t. NL: s. *Cycas* the typical genus, t. Gk: m. *kýkās,* late spelling var. of *kóikās,* acc. pl. of *kóïx* kind of palm]

cycadaceous (sĭk′ə dā′shəs), *adj.* belonging or pertaining to the *Cycadales.* See **cycad.**

cycl-, a word element meaning 'cycle', used especially in the chemical terminology of cyclic compounds, also in referring to wheel turns. Also, **cyclo-.** [t. Gk: m. *kykl-,* comb. form of *kýklos* ring, circle, wheel]

Cyclades (sĭk′lə dēz′), *n.pl.* a group of Greek Islands in the S Aegean. 99,931 pop. (1961); 1023 sq. mi.

cyclamate (sī′klə māt′), *n.* any of a group of artificial sweeteners, sometimes used as food additives.

cyclamen (sĭk′lə mən, -mĕn′), *n.* any plant of the primulaceous genus *Cyclamen,* which have tuberous rootstocks and nodding white, purple, pink, or crimson flowers with reflexed petals. [t. NL, t. Gk: m. s. *kykláminos*]

cycle (sī′kl), *n., v.,* **-cled, -cling.** —*n.* **1.** a round of years or a recurring period of time, esp. one in which certain events or phenomena repeat themselves in the same order and at the same intervals. **2.** any round of operations or events; a series which returns upon itself; any complete course or series. **3.** any long period of years; an age. **4.** a series of poetic or prose narratives about some mythical or heroic theme: *the Arthurian cycle.* **5.** any group of poems or songs about a central event, figure, etc. **6.** the aggregate of legendary or traditional matter with a common mythical or heroic theme. **7.** a bicycle, tricycle, etc. **8.** a period pertaining to the recurrence of astronomical phenomena. **9.** *Physics.* **a.** a sequence of changes at the end of which the initial situation has been re-established. **b.** one of a succession of similar sequences of events or values. **c.** a complete or double alternation or reversal of an alternating electric current. **10.** bicycle. —*v.i.* **11.** to ride or travel by a bicycle, etc. **12.** to move or revolve in cycles; pass through cycles. [t. L: m. s. *cyclus,* t. Gk: m. *kýklos* ring, circle]

cyclic (sī′klĭk, sĭk′lĭk), *adj.* **1.** of or pertaining to a cycle or cycles; revolving or recurring in cycles; characterized by recurrence in cycles. **2.** of or belonging to a cycle of heroic or mythical poems or prose narratives. **3.** *Geom.* (of a figure) one which can be inscribed in a circle: *cyclic quadrilateral.* **4.** *Chem.* of or denoting a compound whose structural formula contains a closed chain or ring of atoms. **5.** *Bot.* **a.** arranged in whorls, as the parts of a flower. **b.** (of a flower) having the parts so arranged. Also, **cy′clical.** [t. L: s. *cyclicus,* t. Gk: m. *kyklikós* circular] —**cy′clically,** *adv.*

cyclist (sī′klĭst), *n.* one who rides or travels by a bicycle, tricycle, etc. Also, *U.S.,* **cy′cler.**

cyclo-, var. of **cycl-,** before consonants, as in *cyclograph.*

cyclograph (sī′klō grăf′, -gräf′), *n.* **1.** *Elect.* an instrument in which the position of a beam of light, or a cathode ray, is controlled by two forces at right angles to each other, such that a closed figure is produced on a screen. **2.** arcograph.

cyclohexane (sī′klō hĕk′ sān, sĭk′lō-), *n. Chem.* a colourless, hydrocarbon, ring compound, C_6H_{12}, composed of six methylene radicals (CH_2) united by single bonds. It is made by hydrogenation of benzene, and also occurs in some petroleum oils.

cycloid (sī′kloid), *adj.* **1.** resembling a circle; circular. **2.** (of fishes' scales) smooth-edged, more or less circular in form, with concentric striations. **3.** having such scales, as a fish. **4.** *Psychol.* (of a personality type) characterized by variations of mood between excitement and depression. —*n.* **5.** a cycloid fish. **6.** *Geom.* a curve generated by a point on the circumference of a circle which rolls, without slipping, on a straight line in its plane. [t. Gk: m. s. *kykloeidḗs* like a circle] —**cycloi′dal,** *adj.*

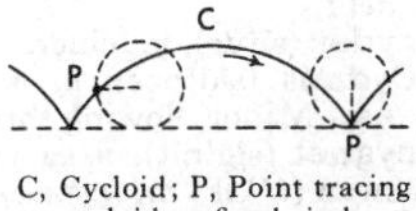

C, Cycloid; P, Point tracing cycloid on fixed circle

cyclometer (sī klŏm′ĭ tə), *n.* **1.** an instrument which measures circular arcs. **2.** a device for recording the revolutions of a wheel and hence the distance traversed by a wheeled vehicle, esp. a bicycle.

cyclonal (sī klō′nəl), *adj.* of or like a cyclone.

cyclone (sī′klōn), *n. Meteorol.* **1.** an atmospheric pressure system characterized by relatively low pressure at its centre, and by anticlockwise wind motion in the northern hemisphere, clockwise in the southern. **2.** a tropical hurricane, esp. in the Indian Ocean. [t. Gk: m. s. *kyklôn,* ppr., moving in a circle] —**cyclonic** (sī klŏn′ĭk), **cyclon′-ical,** *adj.* —**cyclon′ically,** *adv.*

cyclonite (sī′klə nīt′), *n. Chem.* a colourless crystalline solid, $(CH_2N.NO_2)_3$, used as an explosive; hexogen; RDX.

cyclonoscope (sī klō′nə skōp′), *n.* a device for determining the centre of a cyclone.

Cyclopean (sī′klō pē′ən, sī klō′pyən), *adj.* **1.** of or characteristic of the Cyclops. **2.** (*sometimes l.c.*) gigantic; vast. **3.** *Archit.* of, like, or denoting an early style of masonry employing massive stones, more or less irregular in shape.

cyclopedia (sī′klō pē′dyə), *n.* a book having articles on subjects from all or certain branches of knowledge; an encyclopedia. Also, **cyclopaedia.** [aphetic var. of EN-CYCLOPEDIA] —**cy′clope′dist,** *n.*

cyclopedic (sī′klō pē′dĭk), *adj.* like a cyclopedia in character or contents; broad and varied; exhaustive. Also, **cyclopaedic.** —**cy′clope′dically,** *adv.*

cyclopentane (sī′klō pĕn′tān, sĭk′lō-), *n. Chem.* a colourless liquid, C_5H_{10}, derived from some petroleums.

cycloplegia (sī′klō plē′jĭ ə, sĭk′lō-), *n. Pathol.* paralysis of the intraocular muscles.

cyclopropane (sī′klō prō′pān, sĭk′lō-), *n. Chem.* a colourless gas, C_3H_6, used as an anaesthetic.

Cyclops (sī′klŏps), *n., pl.* **Cyclopes** (sī klō′pēz), **Cyclopses** (sī′klŏp′sĭz). **1.** *Gk Myth.* one of a race of lawless giants with only one eye, which was circular and in the middle of the forehead, said to have forged thunderbolts for Zeus and to have assisted Hephaestus (Vulcan) in his workshops. **2.** Antigonus. [t. L, t. Gk: m. *Kýklōps,* lit., round-eyed]

cyclorama (sī′klō rä′mə), *n.* **1.** a pictorial representation, in natural perspective, of a landscape, a battle, etc., on the inner wall of a cylindrical room or hall, the spectators occupying a position in the centre. **2.** *Theat.* a curved wall or backcloth at the back of a stage used to create the impression of unlimited space or distance, or for lighting effects. [f. CYCL- + Gk (*h*)*órama* view] —**cycloramic** (sī′klō răm′ĭk), *adj.*

cyclostomatous (sī′klō stŏm′ə təs, -stō′mə-, sĭk′lə-), *adj.* **1.** having a circular mouth. **2.** belonging or pertaining to the *Cyclostomata.* See **cyclostome.** Also, **cyclostomate** (sī klŏs′tə mĭt, -māt′).

cyclostome (sī′klə stōm′, sĭk′lə-), *adj.* **1.** belonging or pertaining to the *Cyclostomata,* a group or class of eel-like aquatic vertebrates (the lampreys and hagfishes), characterized by pouchlike gills and a circular suctorial mouth without hinged jaws. **2.** having a circular mouth. —*n.* **3.** a cyclostome vertebrate; a lamprey or a hagfish. [f. CYCLO- + m. Gk *stóma* mouth]

cyclostyle (sī′klə stīl′), *n.* **1.** a manifolding device consisting of a kind of pen with a small toothed wheel at the end which cuts minute holes in a specially prepared paper stretched over a smooth surface, thus forming a stencil from which copies are printed. —*v.t.* **2.** to use a cyclostyle.

cyclothymia (sī′klō thī′mĭ ə, sĭk′lō-), *n. Psychol.* a mild manic-depressive psychosis involving recurring cycles of exhilaration and depression. [f. CYCLO- + Gk *-thymia* -mindedness (der. *thymós* mind)] —**cy′clothy′mic,** *adj.*

cyclothymiac (sī′klō thī′mĭ ăk′, sĭk′lō-), *n.* a person affected with cyclothymia.

cyclotron (sī′klə trŏn′), *n. Physics.* a device for imparting very high speed to electrified particles by successive electric impulses at high frequency, space requirements and applied voltage being kept relatively low by causing the particles to move in spiral paths in a strong magnetic field.

cyder (sī′də), *n.* cider.

Cydnus (sĭd′nəs), *n.* a historic river of Cilicia, in SE Asia Minor, flowing through ancient Tarsus.

cygnet (sĭg′nĭt), *n.* a young swan. [ME, f. s. L *cygnus* swan (t. Gk: m. *kýknos*) + -ET]

Cygnus (sĭg′nəs), *n., gen.* **-ni** (-nī). *Astron.* a northern constellation containing the star Deneb. [t. L: swan]

cyl., cylinder.

cylinder (sĭl′ĭn də), *n.* **1.** *Geom.* a solid which may be conceived as generated by the revolution of a rectangle about one of its sides (a **right circular cylinder**). **2.** a similar solid in which the elements of the curved surface are oblique to the circular bases (**oblique circular cylinder**). **3.** any solid bounded by two parallel planes and a curved surface generated by a moving straight line which intersects a given curve and is always parallel to its original position. **4.** a curved surface generated in this manner. **5.** any cylinder-like object or part, whether solid or hollow. **6.** the rotating part of a revolver, which contains the chambers for the cartridges. **7.** the body of a pump. **8.** the chamber in an engine in which the working medium acts upon the piston. **9.** *Bldg Trades.* a closed circular tank for storing hot water to be drawn off through taps. **10.** (in certain printing presses) **a.** a rotating cylinder which produces the impression, under which a flat forme to be printed from passes. **b.** either of two cylinders, one carrying a curved form or plate to be printed from, which rotate against each other in opposite directions. **11.** *Archaeol.* a cylindrical or somewhat barrel-shaped stone or clay object, bearing a cuneiform inscription or a carved design, worn by the Babylonians, Assyrians, and kindred peoples as a seal and amulet. —*v.t.* **12.** to furnish with a cylinder or cylinders. **13.** to subject to the action of a cylinder or cylinders. [t. L: m. s. *cylindrus,* t. Gk: m. *kýlindros* roller, cylinder] —**cyl′inder-like′,** *adj.*

Right circular cylinder

cylinder block, the casting in which the cylinders of an internal-combustion engine are contained.

cylinder head, a detachable portion of an engine fastened securely to the cylinder block containing all or a portion of the combustion chamber.

cylinder lock, a lock for an entrance door, opened by key from the outside and by a knob from the inside.

cylinder press. See **press**[1] (def. 32a).

cylindrical (sĭ lĭn′drĭ kl), *adj.* of, pertaining to, or of the form of a cylinder. Also, **cylin′dric.** —**cylin′drically,** *adv.*

cylindrical projection, *Cartog.* a kind of map projection in which the earth's surface is projected on to a surrounding cylinder, which is then opened out.

cylindrite (sĭl′ĭn drīt′), *n.* a mineral composed of a complex sulphide of lead, antimony, and tin which has a cylindrical habit.

cylindroid (sĭl′ĭn droid′), *n.* **1.** a solid having the form of a cylinder with equal and parallel elliptical bases. —*adj.* **2.** resembling a cylinder. [t. Gk: m. s. *kylindroeidēs* cylinder-like. See -OID]

cylix (sī′lĭks), *n., pl.* **cylices** (sī′lĭ sēz′). *Gk Antiq.* a shallow drinking cup, usually with a stem and foot, and two handles; kylix. [t. Gk: m. *kýlix*]

Cyllenian (sĭ lē′nyən), *adj.* pertaining to Mount Cyllene, in Arcadia, Greece, or to the god Hermes, reputed to have been born there.

cyma (sī′mə), *n., pl.* **-mae** (-mē), **-mas** (-məz). **1.** *Archit.* a projecting moulding whose profile is a compound bi-concave curve. It is called a **cyma recta** when the projective part is concave and a **cyma reversa** when the projecting portion is convex. See diag. under **column. 2.** *Bot.* a cyme. [NL, t. Gk: m. *kŷma* something swollen, wave, waved moulding, sprout]

cymar (sĭ mä′), *n.* a loose, light jacket or robe worn by women, fashionable in the 17th and 18th centuries. Also, **simar.** [var. sp. of SIMAR]

cymatium (sĭ mā′ tyəm), *n., pl.* **-tia** (-tyə). *Archit.* the capping moulding of a cornice, placed above the corona commonly having a cyma recta as its most important feature. [t. L, t. Gk: m. *kymátion,* dim. of *kŷma* wave]

cymbal (sĭm′bl), *n.* one of a pair of concave plates of brass or bronze which are struck together to produce a sharp ringing sound. [OE, t. L: s. *cymbalum,* t. Gk: m. *kýmbalon,* der. *kýmbē* cup, bowl] —**cym′balist,** *n.*

cymbalo (sĭm′bə lō′), *n.* dulcimer.

cyme (sīm), *n. Bot.* **1.** an inflorescence in which the primary axis bears a single terminal flower which develops first, the inflorescence being continued by secondary, tertiary, and other axes. **2.** a flat or convex inflorescence of this type. [t. L: m. s. *cȳma* sprout, t. Gk: m. *kŷma.* See CYMA]

A B

Cymes

A, of houseleek;

B, of forget-me-not

cymene (sī′mēn), *n. Chem.* a liquid hydrocarbon, $C_{10}H_{14}$, with a pleasant smell, occurring in the volatile oil of the common cumin, *Cuminum cyminum,* and existing in three isomeric forms, *ortho-, meta-,* and *para-cymene.* [f. *cym-* (comb. form repr. Gk *kýminon* cumin) + -ENE]

cymo-, a word element meaning 'wave'. [t. Gk: m. *kymo-,* comb. form of *kŷma* wave, embryo, sprout]

cymograph (sī′mə grăf′, -gräf′), *n.* kymograph.

cymophane (sī′mə fān′), *n.* chrysoberyl. —**cymophanous** (sī mŏf′ə nəs), *adj.*

cymose (sīʹmōs, sī mōsʹ), *adj. Bot.* **1.** bearing a cyme or cymes. **2.** of or of the nature of a cyme. [t. L: m. s. *cȳmōsus* full of shoots. See CYME] —**cyʹmosely,** *adv.*

Cymric (kĭmʹrĭk), *adj.* **1.** pertaining to the Cymry. —*n.* **2.** Welsh (the language). Also, **Kymric.** [f. m. Welsh *Cymru* Wales or *Cymry* the Welsh + -IC]

Cymry (kĭmʹrĭ), *n.pl.* the Welsh, or the branch of the Celtic race to which the Welsh belong, comprising also the Cornish people and the Bretons. Also, **Kymry.** [t. Welsh, pl. *Cymro* Welshman. Cf. Welsh *Cymru* Wales]

cynic (sĭnʹĭk), *n.* **1.** a sneering faultfinder; one who doubts or denies the goodness of human motives, and who often displays his attitude by sneers, sarcasm, etc. **2.** (*cap.*) one of a sect of Greek philosophers founded by Antisthenes of Athens (born about 444 B.C.), who sought to develop the ethical teachings of Socrates. The chief doctrines of the Cynics were that virtue is the only good, that the essence of virtue is self-control, and that surrender to any external influence is beneath the dignity of man. —*adj.* **3.** cynical. **4.** (*cap.*) of or pertaining to the Cynics or their doctrines. **5.** of or pertaining to the Dog Star: *the cynic year.* [t. L: s. *cynicus,* t. Gk: m. *kynikós* doglike, churlish, Cynic]

cynical (sĭnʹĭ kl), *adj.* **1.** like or characteristic of a cynic; distrusting the motives of others. **2.** (*cap.*) cynic (def. 4). —**cynʹically,** *adv.*

—**Syn. 1.** CYNICAL, PESSIMISTIC, SARCASTIC, SATIRICAL, imply holding a low opinion of mankind. CYNICAL suggests a disbelief in the sincerity of human motives: *cynical about honesty.* PESSIMISTIC implies a more or less habitual disposition to look on the dark side of things, and to believe that the worst will happen: *pessimistic as to the future.* SARCASTIC refers to sneering or making cutting jibes: *sarcastic about a profession of faith.* SATIRICAL suggests expressing scorn or ridicule: *satirical about the way in which actions and protestations differ.* —**Ant. 1.** optimistic.

cynicism (sĭnʹĭ sĭzʹəm), *n.* **1.** cynical disposition or character. **2.** a cynical remark. **3.** (*cap.*) the doctrines or practices of the Cynics.

cynocephalus (sīʹnō sĕfʹə ləs), *n., pl.* **-cephali** (-sĕfʹə līʹ). any mammal of the genus *Cynocephalus,* of SE Asia, as the flying lemur or colugo. **2.** the dog-faced baboon. **3.** any of a mythical race of dog-headed men.

cynosure (sĭnʹə zyo͞oəʹ), *n.* **1.** something that strongly attracts attention by its brilliance, etc.: *the cynosure of all eyes.* **2.** something serving for guidance or direction. **3.** (*cap.*) the constellation of the Little Bear. **4.** (*cap.*) the Pole Star. [t. L: m. s. *Cynosūra,* t. Gk: m. *Kynósoura,* lit., dog's tail]

Cynthia (sĭnʹthĭ ə), *n.* **1.** Artemis (Diana). **2.** *Poetic.* the moon, the emblem of Artemis (Diana).

cyperaceous (sīʹpə rāʹshəs), *adj.* pertaining or belonging to, or resembling, the *Cyperaceae* or the sedge family of monocotyledonous plants, with solid, often triangular, stems and small, coriaceous, achenial fruit. [f. s. NL *Cyperus* the typical genus (t. Gk: m. *kýpeiros* kind of marsh plant) + -ACEOUS]

cyphel (sīʹfəl), *n.* mossy cyphel.

cypher (sīʹfə), *n., v.i., v.t.* cipher.

cy pres (sēʹ prāʹ), *Law.* **1.** as near as practicable. **2. doctrine of cy pres,** an equitable doctrine (applicable only to cases of charitable trusts or donations) which, in place of an impossible or illegal condition, limitation, or object, allows the nearest practicable one to be substituted. Also, **cypres.** [t. late AF: as nearly]

cypress[1] (sīʹprəs), *n.* **1.** any of the evergreen trees constituting the coniferous genus *Cupressus,* distinguished by dark green scalelike, overlapping leaves, often a very slender tree with a durable wood. **2.** any of various other allied coniferous trees as *Chamaecyparis, Taxodium* (**bald cypress**), etc. **3.** any of various other plants in some way resembling the true cypress, as *Gilia coronopifolia* (**standing cypress**), a tall, slender, herb of the U.S. **4.** the wood of these trees. [t. LL: s. *cypressus,* t. Gk: m. *kypárissos*; r. ME *cipres,* t. OF]

cypress[2] (sīʹprəs), *n. Obs.* a fine, thin fabric resembling lawn or crepe, which was formerly much used in black for mourning garments, etc. Also, **cyprus.** [ME *cipres,* prob. t. OF; appar. named from CYPRUS]

cypress vine, a convolvulaceous garden plant, *Quamoclit pennata,* with finely parted leaves and scarlet or white tubular flowers.

Cyprian (sĭpʹrĭ ən), *adj.* **1.** pertaining to Cyprus, famous as a centre for the worship of Aphrodite (Venus). **2.** lewd; licentious. —*n.* **3.** a native or inhabitant of Cyprus. **4.** a lewd person, esp. a prostitute. [f. s. L *Cyprius* (t. Gk: m. *Kýprios* of Cyprus) + -AN]

Cyprian (sĭpʹrĭ ən), *n.* **Saint,** A.D. 200?–258, a bishop of Carthage, writer, and martyr.

cyprinid (sĭ prīʹnĭd, sĭpʹrĭ nĭd), *n.* **1.** any fish belonging to the *Cyprinidae,* or minnow family. —*adj.* **2.** carplike in form or structure.

cyprinodont (sĭ prĭnʹə dŏntʹ, sĭ prīʹnə-), *n.* any of the *Cyprinodontidae,* a family of small soft-finned fishes, mostly inhabiting the fresh and brackish waters of North America, including the killifishes, certain top minnows, the guppy, etc. [f. s. Gk *kyprînos* carp + s. *odoús* tooth]

cyprinoid (sĭpʹrĭ noidʹ, sĭ prīʹnoid), *adj.* **1.** resembling a carp; belonging to the *Cyprinoidea,* a group of fishes including the carps, suckers, loaches, etc. —*n.* **2.** a cyprinoid fish. [f. s. Gk *kyprînos* carp + -OID]

Cypriot (sĭpʹrĭ ət), *n.* **1.** a native or inhabitant of Cyprus. **2.** the Greek dialect of Cyprus. —*adj.* **3.** Cyprian. Also, **Cypriote** (sĭpʹrĭ ōtʹ). [t. Gk: m. s. *Kypriṓtēs*]

cypripedium (sĭpʹrĭ pēʹdyəm), *n.* any plant of the genus *Cypripedium,* comprising orchids having large flowers with a protruding saclike labellum; a lady's-slipper. [NL, f. L *Cypri(s)* Venus + s. L *pēs* foot + -IUM]

cyprus (sīʹprəs), *n. Obs.* cypress[2].

Cyprus (sīʹprəs), *n.* an island republic in the Mediterranean, S of Turkey, and a member of the Commonwealth of Nations. 584,000 pop. (est. 1962); 3572 sq. mi. *Cap.:* Nicosia.

cypsela (sĭpʹsĭ lə), *n., pl.* **-lae** (-lēʹ). *Bot.* an achene with an adherent calyx, as in the composite plants. [NL, t. Gk: m. *kypsélē* hollow vessel]

Cyrenaic (sīʹə rə nāʹĭk, sīʹrə-), *adj.* **1.** of or pertaining to Cyrenaica, or its chief city, Cyrene. **2.** denoting or pertaining to a school of hedonistic philosophy founded by Aristippus of Cyrene, who taught that pleasure is the only rational aim of life. —*n.* **3.** a native or inhabitant of Cyrenaica. **4.** a disciple of the Cyrenaic school of philosophy.

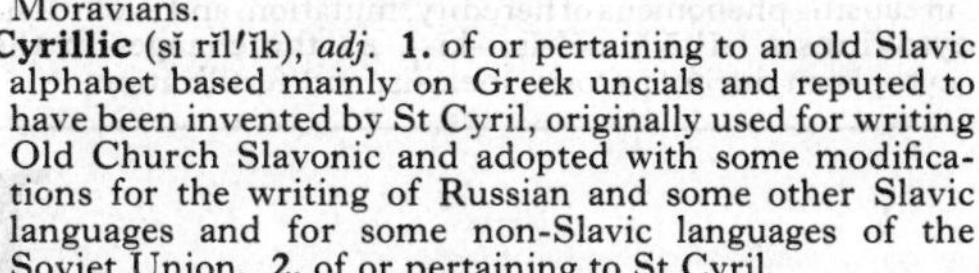

Cyrenaica

Cyrenaica (sīʹə rə nāʹĭ kə, sīʹrə-), *n.* an ancient region in N Africa, W of Egypt. Also, **Barca.**

Cyrene (sī rēʹnĭ), *n.* an ancient Greek city and colony in Cyrenaica, in N Africa.

Cyril (sĭʹrĭl), *n.* **Saint** ('Apostle of the Slavs'), A.D. 827–869, Greek missionary to the Moravians.

Cyrillic (sĭ rĭlʹĭk), *adj.* **1.** of or pertaining to an old Slavic alphabet based mainly on Greek uncials and reputed to have been invented by St Cyril, originally used for writing Old Church Slavonic and adopted with some modifications for the writing of Russian and some other Slavic languages and for some non-Slavic languages of the Soviet Union. **2.** of or pertaining to St Cyril.

cyrto-, a word element meaning 'curved.' [t. Gk: m. *kyrto-,* comb. form of *kyrtós*]

Cyrus (sīʹə rəs), *n.* **1.** ('*the Elder*' or '*the Great*'), died 529 B.C., king of Persia 558?–529 B.C.; founder of Persian Empire. **2.** ('*The Younger*'), died 401 B.C., Persian satrap: led army (including 10,000 Greeks) against his brother, Artaxerxes II, Persian king.

cyst (sĭst), *n.* **1.** *Pathol.* a closed bladder-like sac formed in animal tissues, containing fluid or semifluid morbid matter. **2.** a bladder, sac, or vesicle. **3.** *Bot.* **a.** a spore-like cell with a resistant protective wall. **b.** a cell or cavity enclosing reproductive bodies, etc. **4.** *Zool.* **a.** a sac, usually spherical, surrounding an animal that has passed into a dormant condition. **b.** such a sac plus the contained animal. [t. NL: s. *cystis,* t. Gk: m. *kýstis* bladder, bag, pouch]

cyst-, a combining form representing **cyst.** Also, **cysti-, cysto-.**

-cyst, a terminal combining form of **cyst.**

cystectomy (sĭs tĕkʹtə mĭ), *n., pl.* **-mies.** *Surg.* excision of a cyst or bladder, usually the urinary bladder.

cysteine (sĭsʹtĭ ēnʹ, -ĭn), *n. Chem.* an amino acid $HSCH_2CH(NH_2)COOH$, occurring in proteins.

cysti-, var. of **cyst-,** as in *cysticercoid.*

cystic (sĭsʹtĭk), *adj.* **1.** pertaining to, of the nature of, or having a cyst or cysts; encysted. **2.** *Anat.* belonging to or relating to the urinary bladder or the gall bladder.

cysticercoid (sĭsʹtĭ sûʹkoid), *n. Biol.* the larva of certain tapeworms, developing in insects, etc., in which a single head forms without a spacious bladder around it.

cysticercus (sĭsʹtĭ sûʹkəs), *n., pl.* **-cerci** (-sûʹsī). *Biol.* the bladder worm larva of certain tapeworms, with a single head (scolex) formed in a large bladder. [NL, f. Gk: m. *kysti-* CYSTI- + m. *kérkos* tail]

cystic fibrosis, *Pathol.* a hereditary, chronic disease of the pancreas, lungs, etc., beginning in infancy, in which there is difficulty in breathing and an inability to digest.

cystine (sĭsʹtēn, -tĭn), *n. Biochem.* one of the important sulphur-containing amino acids, $SCH_2CH(NH_2)COOH$, found in proteins, esp. hair, wool, and horn.

cystitis (sĭs tīʹtĭs), *n. Pathol.* inflammation of the urinary bladder.

cysto-, var. of **cyst-,** before consonants, as in *cystoscope.*
cystocarp (sĭs′tə kăp′), *n.* the mass of carpospores formed as a result of fertilization in red algae (*Rhodophyta*), with or without a special envelope (pericarp).
cystocoele (sĭs′tə sēl′), *n. Pathol.* hernia in which the urinary bladder protrudes into the vagina.
cystoid (sĭs′toid), *adj.* **1.** resembling a cyst but having no enclosing capsule. —*n.* **2.** a cystlike formation.
cystolith (sĭs′tə lĭth), *n. Bot.* a mass of calcium carbonate on the cellulose wall.
cystoscope (sĭs′tə skōp′), *n. Med.* a slender, cylindrical instrument for examining the interior of the urinary bladder and for the introduction of medication therein.
cystotomy (sĭs tŏt′ə mĭ), *n., pl.* **-mies.** *Surg.* the operation of cutting into the urinary bladder.
cytaster (sī tăs′tə, sī′tăs′-), *n. Biol.* aster.
-cyte, a word element referring to cells or corpuscles, as in *leucocyte.* [comb. form repr. Gk *kýtos* container]
Cythera (sĭ thĭə′rə), *n.* one of the Ionian Islands, off the S coast of Greece. 7930 pop. (est. 1963); 108 sq. mi. Also, **Kythera.**
Cytherea (sĭth′ə rē′ə), *n. Gk Myth.* a surname of Aphrodite or Venus. —**Cyth′ere′an,** *adj.*
cytidine (sĭt′ĭ dīn′), *n. Biochem.* a compound of cytosine and ribose, present in all living cells, mainly in combined form, esp. in ribonucleic acids.
cytidylic acid, *Biochem.* the monophosphate of cytidine, present in all living cells, mainly in combined form, esp. in ribonucleic acids.
cytisine, *Biochem.* a highly toxic alkaloid, $C_{11}H_{14}N_2O$, obtained from the seeds of *Cystisus laburnum.*
cyto-, a word element referring to cells, as in *cytogenesis.* Also, before vowels, **cyt-.** [t. Gk: m. *kyto-*, comb. form of *kýtos* container]
cytochrome (sī′tə krōm′), *n. Biochem.* any of a group of haemoproteins, occurring widely in living cells, all of which take part in biological oxidations.
cytogenesis (sī′tō jĕn′ĭ sĭs), *n.* the genesis and differentiation of cells.
cytogenetics (sī′tō jĭ nĕt′ĭks), *n.* the part played by cells in causing phenomena of heredity, mutation, and evolution.
cytokinesis (sī′tō kĭ nē′sĭs, -kī-), *n.* the changes in the cytoplasm during mitosis, meiosis, and fertilization.
cytology (sī tŏl′ə jĭ), *n.* the scientific study of cells, esp. their formation, structure, and functions. —**cytol′ogist,** *n.*
cytolysis (sī tŏl′ĭ sĭs), *n. Physiol.* the dissolution or degeneration of cells.
cyton (sī′tŏn), *n.* the body of a nerve cell.
cytoplasm (sī′tō plăz′əm), *n. Biol.* the living substance or protoplasm of a cell exclusive of the nucleus. See diag. under **cell.** Also, **cytoplast** (sī′tō plăst′). —**cy′toplas′mic,** *adj.*
cytosine (sī′tə sĭn), *n. Biochem.* a pyrimidine base, $C_4H_5N_3O$, present in all living cells, mainly in combined form, as in nucleic acids.
Cyzicus (sĭz′ĭ kəs), *n.* an ancient city of Mysia, in NW Asia Minor, on a peninsula in the Sea of Marmara.
czar (zä), *n.* tsar. —**czardom** (zä′dəm), *n.*
czardas (chä′dăsh), *n.* a Hungarian national dance in two movements, one slow and the other fast. [t. Hung.: m. *csárdás*]
czarevitch (zä′rĭ vĭch), *n.* tsarevich.
czarevna (zä rĕv′nə), *n.* tsarevna.
czarina (zä rē′nə), *n.* tsarina.
czarism (zä′rĭz′əm), *n.* tsarism.
czaritza (zä rĭt′sə), *n.* tsaritsa.
Czech (chĕk), *n.* **1.** a member of the most westerly branch of the Slavs, comprising the Bohemians (or Czechs proper), the Moravians, and the Slovaks. **2.** the language of Bohemia and Moravia, a Slavic language similar to Slovak. —*adj.* **3.** of or pertaining to the Czechs or their language. **4.** Czechoslovak.
Czech., Czechoslovakia. Also, **Czechosl.**
Czechoslovak (chĕk′ō slō′văk), *n.* **1.** a member of the branch of the Slavic race comprising the Czechs proper, the Slovaks, etc. —*adj.* **2.** of or pertaining to the Czechoslovaks.
Czechoslovakia (chĕk′ō slō văk′ĭ ə), *n.* a republic in central Europe. 13,970,000 pop. (est. 1963); 49,379 sq. mi. (1938). *Cap.:* Prague. See map under **Bohemia.** —**Czech′oslovak′ian,** *adj., n.*
Czernowitz (*Ger.* chĕr′nȯ vĭts), *n.* German name of **Chernovtsy.**
Czestochowa (*Pol.* chĕɴ stō ᴋʜō′vȧ), *n.* a city in S Poland. 173,000 (1964).

D

D, d (dē), *n., pl.* **D's** or **Ds, d's** or **ds. 1.** the fourth letter of the English alphabet. **2.** (used as a symbol) the fourth in order; the fourth in a series. **3.** *Music.* **a.** the second degree of the scale of C, or the fourth degree of the scale of A minor. **b.** a written or printed note representing this tone. **c.** a key, string, or pipe tuned to this note. **d.** (in solmization) the second note of the scale, called **re.**
D, 1. Roman numeral for 500. **2.** *Chem.* deuterium. **3.** Dutch.
D., 1. December. **2.** *Physics.* density. **3.** Dutch. **4.** Duke. **5.** (L *Deus*) God.
d., 1. date. **2.** daughter. **3.** degree (def. 10). **4.** delete. **5.** (L *denarius*) penny or (L *denarii*) pence. **6.** *Physics.* density. **7.** *Chem.* dextro-. **8.** dialect. **9.** dialectal. **10.** diameter. **11.** died. **12.** *U.S.* dime. **13.** dividend. **14.** dollar. **15.** dose.
'd, contraction of: **1.** had. **2.** would.
d.a., 1. deposit account. **2.** delayed action (bomb).
D.A., *U.S.* District Attorney.
dab[1] (dăb), *v.,* **dabbed, dabbing,** *n.* —*v.t.* **1.** to tap lightly, as with the hand. **2.** to pat or tap gently, as with some soft or moist substance. **3.** to apply (a substance) by light strokes. —*v.i.* **4.** to touch lightly; peck. —*n.* **5.** a quick or light blow; a pat, as with the hand or something soft. **6.** a small moist lump or mass. **7.** a small quantity. **8.** a dab hand. **9.** (*pl.*) *Slang.* fingerprints. [ME. Cf. Norw. *dabba* tap with the foot, G *Tappe* footprint]
dab[2] (dăb), *n.* **1.** a European flatfish, *Limanda limanda.* **2.** a sand-dab or other small flatfish. [orig. unknown]
dabber (dăb′ə), *n.* **1.** one who or that which dabs. **2.** a pad for applying ink, etc., used by printers and engravers.
dabble (dăb′l), *v.,* **-bled, -bling.** —*v.t.* **1.** to wet slightly or repeatedly in or with a liquid; splash; spatter. —*v.i.* **2.** to play in water, as with the hands or feet. **3.** to do anything in a slight or superficial manner: *to dabble in literature.* [t. Flem.: m. s. *dabbelen*] —**dab′bler,** *n.*
dabchick (dăb′chĭk′), *n.* a small diving bird, esp. the little grebe, *Podiceps fluviatilis,* of Europe, or the pied-billed grebe, *Podilymbus podiceps,* of America.
dab hand, *Colloq.* a person particularly skilled (usually fol. by *at*).
dabster (dăb′stə), *n. Dial.* an expert.
da capo (dä kä′pō), *Music.* from the beginning (a direction to repeat). [It.]
Dacca (dăk′ə), *n.* the principal city of East Pakistan, in E Bengal. 556,712 (1961).
dace (dās), *n., pl.* **dace. 1.** a small freshwater cyprinoid fish, *Leuciscus leuciscus,* of Europe, with a stout, fusiform body. **2.** any of several similar or related fishes of the U.S. [ME *darse,* t. OF: m. *dars* DART]
dacha (dăch′ə; *Russ.* dȧ′chə), *n.* a country villa (in Russia). [t. Russ.]
Dachau (*Ger.* dȧ′ᴋʜou), *n.* a Nazi concentration camp, the scene of mass murders, in S Germany, near Munich.
dachshund (dăks′ho͝ond′; *Ger.* dȧᴋʜs′ho͝ont), *n.* one of a German breed of small dogs with a long body and very short legs. [t. G: f. *Dachs* badger + *Hund* dog]

Dachshund (8 in. high at shoulder)

Dacia (dā′syə), *n.* an ancient kingdom and later a Roman province in S Europe between the Carpathian Mountains and the Danube, corresponding generally to modern Rumania and adjacent regions. —**Dacian** (dā′syən), *adj., n.*
dacker (dăk′ə), *v.i. Scot. and N Dial.* to saunter; loiter.
dacoit (də koit′), *n.* one of a class of robbers in India and Burma, who plunder in bands. [t. Hind.: m. *dākāit,* der. *dākā* gang robbery]
dacoity (də koi′tĭ), *n.* gang robbery in India and Burma. [t. Hind.: m. *dākāiti*]
Dacron (dā′krŏn), *n. Trademark.* a strong synthetic textile fibre resistant to creases.

dactyl (dăk′tĭl), *n.* **1.** *Zool.* a digit. **2.** *Pros.* a foot of three syllables, one long followed by two short, or in modern verse, one accented followed by two unaccented (¯ ˘ ˘), as in 'Gĕntlȳ ănd hūmănlȳ'. [ME *dactile*, t. L: m. s. *dactylus*, t. Gk: m. *dáktylos* finger or toe, date (see DATE²), metrical foot]
dactylic (dăk tĭl′ĭk), *adj.* **1.** of or characterized by dactyls. **2.** of a dactyl. —*n.* **3.** a dactylic verse.
dactylology (dăk′tĭ lŏl′ə jĭ), *n.* the art of communicating ideas by signs made with the fingers, as in a manual alphabet used by the deaf.
dad¹ (dăd), *n.* (in childish or familiar use) father. [earlier *dadde*, nursery substitute for FATHER]
dad² (dăd), *n.*, *v.*, **dadded, dadding.** *Scot. and N Dial.* —*n.* **1.** a blow. **2.** a large piece, of or as of bread, etc. —*v.t.* **3.** to strike; beat.
dadaism (dä′də ĭz′əm), *n.* a movement in art, literature, etc., which flourished during and just after World War I. It attempted to discredit all previous art by using the incongruous and the accidental. Also, **dada** (dä′də). [t. F: m. *Dadaisme*, der. *Dada*, title of a review] —**da′dist,** *n.*, *adj.*
Daddah (*Fr.* dȧ dȧ′), *n.* **Moktar Ould** (*Fr.* mŏk tȧr ōōl′), born 1925, president of the Republic of Mauritania since 1961.
daddy (dăd′ĭ), *n.*, *pl.* **-dies.** (in childish or familiar use) dad; father.
daddy-long-legs (dăd ĭ lŏng′lĕgz′), *n. sing. and pl.* **1.** a cranefly. **2.** *U.S.* a harvestman.
dado (dā′dō), *n.*, *pl.* **-dos, -does. 1.** *Archit.* the part of a pedestal between the base and the cornice or cap. **2.** the lower broad part of an interior wall finished in wallpaper, a fabric, paint, or the like. **3.** a strip of patterned wallpaper just below the picture rail; the frieze. [t. It.: die, cube, pedestal, g. L *dātus*. See DIE²]

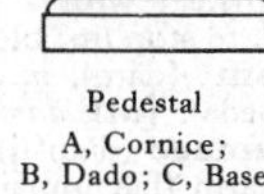

Pedestal
A, Cornice; B, Dado; C, Base

daedal (dē′dl), *adj. Chiefly Poetic.* **1.** skilful or ingenious. **2.** showing skill or artistic cunning. **3.** diversified. [t. L: s. *daedalus* skilful, t. Gk: m. *daídalos*]
Daedalus (dē′də ləs), *n. Gk Myth.* an Athenian architect who built the labyrinth for Minos and made wings for himself and his son Icarus. [t. L, t. Gk: m. *Daídalos*, lit., the cunning worker] —**Daedalian, Daedalean** (dĭ dā′lĭ ən, -dā′lyən), *adj.*
daemon (dē′mən), *n.* **1.** *Gk Myth.* **a.** a god. **b.** a subordinate deity, as the genius of a place or a man's attendant spirit. **2.** a demon. Also, **daimon.** [t. L, t. Gk: m. *daímōn*] —**daemonic** (dē mŏn′ĭk), *adj.*
daff¹ (dăf), *v.i. Scot.* to make sport; dally; play. [prop. play the fool, v. use of d. *daff* a fool; akin to DAFT]
daff² (dăf), *v.t. Obs. or Dial.* **1.** to turn or thrust aside. **2.** to doff. [var. of DOFF]
daffodil (dăf′ə dĭl), *n.* **1.** a plant, *Narcissus pseudonarcissus*, with single or double yellow nodding flowers, blooming in the spring; Lent lily. **2.** any plant of the genus *Narcissus*. **3.** light or pale yellow. [unexplained var. of ME *affodille*, t. VL: m. *affodillus*, var. of *asphodelus*, t. Gk: m. *asphódelos*]
daffodilly (dăf′ə dĭl′ĭ), *n.*, *pl.* **-lies.** *Poetic.* daffodil (defs 1, 2). Also, **daffadowndilly** (dăf′ə doun dĭl′ĭ), **daf′fydowndil′ly.**
daffy (dăf′ĭ), *adj.*, **daffier, daffiest.** *Colloq. or Dial.* silly; weak-minded; crazy. [cf. DAFF¹]
daft (däft), *adj.* **1.** simple or foolish. **2.** insane; crazy. **3.** *Scot.* frolicsome. [ME *daffte*, OE *gedæfte* mild, meek. Cf. DEFT] —**daft′ly,** *adv.* —**daft′ness,** *n.*
daftie (däf′tĭ), *n. Dial. or Colloq.* a daft person.
dag¹ (dăg), *n. Obs.* a daglock. [ME *dagge*; orig. uncert.]
dag² (dăg), *n.* an old form of heavy pistol. [orig. uncert.]
da Gama (də gä′mə; *Port.* ᵺə gə′mə), **Vasco.** See **Gama.**
Dagan (dä′gən), *n.* the Babylonian earth god.
Dagenham (dăg′ə nəm), *n.* a district of London, now part of the outer London boroughs of Barking and Newham: motor-vehicle manufacturing.
dagga (dä′gə, dä′KHə), *n. S African.* wild hemp, *Cannabis indica.* [t. Afrikaans]
dagger (dăg′ə), *n.* **1.** a short-edged and pointed weapon, like a small sword, used for thrusting and stabbing. **2.** *Print.* a mark (†) used for references, etc.; the obelisk. **3. look daggers,** to cast angry, threatening, or vengeful glances. —*v.t.* **4.** to stab with a dagger. **5.** *Print.* to mark with a dagger. [ME, der. obs. *dag* pierce, stab]
daggle (dăg′l), *v.t.*, *v.i.*, **-gled, -gling.** *Obs.* to drag or trail through mud, water, etc.; draggle. [freq. of d. *dag* bemire. See DAG¹]
daglock (dăg′lŏk′), *n.* a lock of wool on a sheep that hangs and drags in the wet. [see DAGGLE, LOCK²]
Dago (dā′gō), *n.*, *pl.* **-gos, -goes.** *Slang.* (in contemptuous use) **1.** an Italian. **2.** a Spaniard. **3.** a Portuguese. [said to be t. Sp.: m. *Diego* James]
Dagö (*Dan.* dȧ′gœ), *n.* Danish name of **Hiiumaa.**
dagoba (dä′gə bə), *n.* a dome-shaped memorial alleged to contain relics of Buddha or a Buddhist saint.
Dagon (dā′gŏn), *n.* the national god of the Philistines, represented as half man and half fish, originally a fish god and later the god of corn and grain. [t. L, t. Gk, t. Heb.: m. *dāghōn* little fish]
daguerreotype (də gĕr′rō tīp′), *n.*, *v.*, **-typed, -typing.** —*n.* **1.** an early photographic process (invented in 1839) in which the impression was made on a silver surface sensitized to the action of light by iodine, and then developed by mercury vapour. **2.** a picture so made. —*v.t.* **3.** to photograph by this process. [named after L. J. M. *Daguerre*, 1789–1851, French inventor. See -TYPE] —**daguerre′otyp′er, daguerre′otyp′ist,** *n.*
dahabeah (dä′hə bē′ə), *n.* a kind of houseboat or passenger boat, used on the Nile. Also, **da′habee′yah, da′habi′ya.** [t. Ar.: m. *dhahabīyah*, lit., the golden]
dahlia (dā′lyə), *n.* **1.** any plant of the composite genus *Dahlia*, native in Mexico and Central America, widely cultivated for its showy, variously coloured flowers. **2.** the flower or tuberous root of a dahlia. [t. NL; named after A. *Dahl*, died 1789, Swedish botanist]
Dahomey (də hō′mĭ; *Fr.* dȧ ō mĕ′), *n.* a republic in W Africa: independent member of the French Community. 2,050,000 pop. (1963); 44,290 sq. mi. *Cap.:* Porto Novo. See map under **Nigeria.** —**Dahoman** (də hō′mən), *adj.*, *n.*
Dáil Eireann (dīl′ĕə′rən), the lower house of parliament of the Republic of Ireland. See **Oireachtas.** Also, **Dáil.** [Irish: *dáil* assembly + *éireann*, gen. of *éire* Erin]
daily (dā′lĭ), *adj.*, *n.*, *pl.* **-lies,** *adv.* —*adj.* **1.** of, done, occurring, or issued each day or each weekday. —*n.* **2.** a newspaper appearing each day or each weekday. **3.** a servant, usually female, who comes to work every day. —*adv.* **4.** every day; day by day: *she phoned the hospital daily.*
daimen (dā′mĭn), *adj. Scot.* rare; occasional.
daimio (dī′myō), *n.*, *pl.* **-mio, -mios. 1.** the class of greater nobles in Japanese feudalism. Often the damio were descendants of younger sons of emperors. **2.** a member of this class. Also, **daimyo.** [t. Jap., f. Chinese: *dai* great + *mio* name]
Daimler (dām′lə; *Ger.* dīm′lər), *n.* **Gottlieb** (*Ger.* gŏt′lēp), 1839–90, German engineer and motor-car manufacturer.
daimon (dī′mŏn), *n.* daemon. [see DEMON]
Dai Nippon (dī′ nĭp′ŏn), Greater Japan. Once the watchword of Japanese expansionists, it is now against the law to use *Dai Nippon* in Japan. See **Japan.**
dainty (dān′tĭ), *adj.*, **-tier, -tiest,** *n.*, *pl.* **-ties.** —*adj.* **1.** of delicate beauty or charm; exquisite. **2.** pleasing to the palate; toothsome; delicious: *dainty food.* **3.** particular in discrimination or taste; fastidious. **4.** too particular; squeamish. —*n.* **5.** something delicious to the taste; a delicacy. [ME *deinte*, t. OF, g. L *dignitas* worthiness] —**dain′tily,** *adv.* —**dain′tiness,** *n.* —**Syn. 1.** See **delicate. 3.** See **particular. 4.** finical, overnice.
daiquiri (dī′kĭ rĭ, dăk′ĭ rĭ), *n.*, *pl.* **-ris.** a vigorously shaken cocktail consisting of rum, lime juice, sugar, and ice.
Dairen (dī rĕn′), *n.* a seaport in NE China in Liaoning province. 1,508,000 (est. 1957). Chinese, **Talien.**
dairy (dĕə′rĭ), *n.*, *pl.* **dairies,** *adj.* —*n.* **1.** a place, as a room or building, where milk and cream are kept and made into butter and cheese. **2.** a shop or company that sells milk, butter, etc. **3.** the business of producing milk, butter, and cheese. **4.** a dairy farm. **5.** the cows on a farm. —*adj.* **6.** pertaining to or made in a dairy. [ME *deierie*, f. *dei* female servant, dairymaid (OE *dǣge* breadmaker) + *-erie* -ERY]
dairy cattle, cows raised mainly for their milk.
dairy farm, a farm devoted chiefly to the production of milk and the manufacture of butter and cheese.
dairying (dĕə′rĭ ĭng), *n.* the business of a dairy.
dairymaid (dĕə′rĭ mād′), *n.* a female servant employed in a dairy.
dairyman (dĕə′rĭ măn′), *n.*, *pl.* **-men. 1.** an employee in a dairy. **2.** *Chiefly U.S.* an owner or manager of a dairy.
dairywoman (dĕə′rĭ wŏŏm′ən), *n.*, *pl.* **-men.** a female dairyman.
dais (dā′ĭs, dās), *n.* a raised platform, as at the end of a room, for a throne, seats of honour, a lecturer's desk, etc. [ME *deis*, t. OF, g. LL *discus* table, L disc, dish. See DISCUS]
daisy (dā′zĭ), *n.*, *pl.* **-sies,** *adj.* —*n.* **1.** any of various composite plants, as the European *Bellis perennis* or *Chrysanthemum leucanthemum* (the N American **oxeye**

daisy) whose flower heads have a yellow disc and white rays. **2.** *Slang.* something fine or first-rate. **—*adj.* 3.** *Slang.* fine; first-class; excellent; first-rate. [ME *dayesye,* OE *daegesēage* day's eye] **—dai′sied,** *adj.*

daisy-chain (dā′zĭ chān′), *n.* a garland of daisies joined together by interlinked stems.

daisy-cutter (dā′zĭ kŭt′ə), *n. Colloq.* (in cricket, football, tennis, etc.) a ball which, after being struck or kicked, skims along near the ground.

dak (däk), *n.* (in India) **1.** transport by relays of men or horses. **2.** the mail. Also, **dawk.** [t. Hind.]

Dakar (dăk′ə; *Fr.* dȧ kär′), *n.* a seaport in and the capital of Senegal; formerly capital of French West Africa. 75,000 pop. (est. 1962); 68 sq. mi.

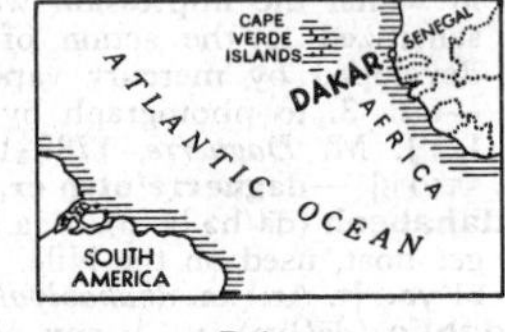

Dakar

Dakin's solution (dā′kĭnz), a liquid antiseptic, an approximately neutral solution containing about 0·5 per cent of sodium hypochlorite, used in treating infected wounds. [named after H. D. *Dakin,* 1880–1952, English chemist, the originator]

Dakota (də kō′tə), *n.* **1.** a former territory in the United States: divided into the states of North Dakota and South Dakota, 1889. **2.** North Dakota or South Dakota. **3.** a Sioux Indian. **4.** a division of the Siouan stock of North American Indians, whose former habitat was in and near North and South Dakota. **5.** any of several Siouan languages. **—Dako′tan,** *adj., n.*

Daladier (*Fr.* dȧ lȧ dyĕ′), *n.* **Édouard** (*Fr.* ĕ dwȧr′), born 1884, prime minister of France, 1933, 1934, and 1938–40.

Dalai Lama (dăl′ī lä′mə), the Grand Lama, formerly the chief pontiff and governmental ruler of Tibet, believed to be a reincarnation of previous Dalai Lamas. [t. Tibetan: *dalai* lit., ocean + *lama* priest]

dale (dāl), *n.* **1.** a vale; valley. **2.** *Phys. Geog.* a small, open, river valley partly enclosed by low hills. [ME; OE *dæl,* c. G *Tal*]

d'Alembert (*Fr.* dȧ läɴ bĕr′), *n.* **Jean le Rond.** See **Alembert.**

dalesman (dālz′mən), *n., pl.* **-men.** a person living in a dale, esp. in the northern counties of England.

Dalhousie (dăl hou′zĭ), *n.* **1. George Ramsay, 9th Earl of,** 1770–1838, British general: governor of the Canadian colonies 1819–28. **2. James Andrew Broun Ramsay** (răm′zĭ), **1st Marquess and 10th Earl of,** 1812–60, British statesman: governor-general of India 1848–56.

Dali (dä′lĭ), *n.* **Salvador** (săl′ və dô′; *Sp.* sȧl bȧ dôr′), born 1904, Spanish surrealist painter.

Dallas (dăl′əs), *n.* a city in the U.S., in NE Texas; President Kennedy assassinated here in 1963. 679,684 (1960).

dalles (dălz), *n.pl. Western U.S.* **1.** the precipice on either side of a deep ravine or canyon. **2.** rapids flowing over a flat rock bottom in a narrowed portion of a river, esp. (*cap.*) the rapids of the Columbia river. [t. Canadian F, special use of F *dalle* gutter, t. Gmc; cf. OE *dæl* gorge, DALE]

dalliance (dăl′ĭ əns), *n.* **1.** a trifling away of time; dawdling **2.** amorous toying; flirtation. [ME; f. DALLY + -ANCE]

dally (dăl′ĭ), *v.,* **-lied, -lying.** **—*v.i.* 1.** to sport or play, esp. amorously. **2.** to play mockingly; trifle: *dally with danger.* **3.** to waste time; loiter; delay. **—*v.t.* 4.** to waste (time) (fol. by *away*). [ME *daly(en),* t. OF: m. *dalier* talk; ? of Gmc orig.] **—dal′lier,** *n.* **—dal′lyingly,** *adv.* **—Syn. 3.** See **loiter.** **—Ant. 3.** hasten.

Dalmatia

Dalmatia (dăl mā′shyə), *n.* a region in W Yugoslavia, along the E coast of the Adriatic.

Dalmatian (dăl mā′shyən), *adj.* **1.** of or pertaining to Dalmatia or its people. **—*n.* 2.** an inhabitant of Dalmatia, esp. a member of the native Slavic-speaking race. **3.** a Romance language formerly spoken in Dalmatia, now extinct. **4.** one of a breed of dogs resembling the pointer, of a white colour profusely marked with small black or liver-coloured spots; coach dog.

Dalmatian (def. 4) (19 to 23 in. high at the shoulder)

dalmatic (dăl măt′ĭk), *n.* **1.** an ecclesiastical vestment worn over the alb by a deacon or bishop, as at the celebration of the mass. **2.** a similar robe worn by kings and emperors at their coronation. [t. L: s. *dalmatica,* prop. fem. of *Dalmaticus* Dalmatian]

Daloa (*Fr.* dȧ lō ȧ′), *n.* a town in Ivory Coast. 32,000 (est. 1964).

Dalrymple (dăl rĭm′pl, dăl′rĭm′-), *n.* **Sir James** (*1st Viscount Stair*), 1619–95, Scottish jurist.

dal segno (dăl sĕn′yō; *It.* dȧl sĕn′nyȯ), *Music.* go back to the sign and repeat (a direction). [It.]

Dalton (dôl′tən), *n.* **1. Hugh, Baron,** 1887–1962, English politician. **2. John,** 1766–1844, English chemist and physicist.

daltonism (dôl′tə nĭz′əm), *n.* colour blindness; esp. inability to distinguish red from green. [named after John DALTON, who was so afflicted]

Dalton's atomic theory, *Chem.* the theory that matter is composed of indivisible particles called atoms; the atoms of any particular element being identical in all respects, but differing from those of other elements in their weight. Compounds are formed by the combination of different elements in simple numerical proportions. Although refined by modern discoveries this theory forms the basis of chemistry. [named after John DALTON]

Dalton System, a method of progressive education, whereby students contract to carry through on their own responsibility the year's work as divided up into monthly assignments. [from use in *Dalton* (Massachusetts) high schools]

Daly (dā′lĭ), *n.* **River,** a river in N Australia flowing NW through Northern Territory to the Timor Sea. Near its mouth is the **Daly River Reserve.** ab. 200 mi.

dam[1] (dăm), *n., v.,* **dammed, damming.** **—*n.* 1.** a barrier to obstruct the flow of water, esp. one of earth, masonry, etc., built across a stream. **2.** a body of water confined by a dam. **3.** any barrier resembling a dam. **—*v.t.* 4.** to furnish with a dam; obstruct or confine with a dam. **5.** to stop up; block up. [ME, c. G *Damm*]

dam[2] (dăm), *n.* a female parent (used esp. of quadrupeds). [ME *dam(me),* var. of DAME]

damage (dăm′ĭj), *n., v.,* **-aged, -aging.** **—*n.* 1.** injury or harm that impairs value or usefulness. **2.** (*pl.*) *Law.* the estimated money equivalent for detriment or injury sustained. **3.** *Colloq.* cost; expense. **—*v.t.* 4.** to cause damage to; injure or harm; impair the usefulness of. **—*v.i.* 5.** to suffer damage. [ME, t. OF: f. *dam* (g. L *damnum* harm, loss) + *-age* -AGE] **—dam′ageable,** *adj.* **—dam′ageabil′ity,** *n.* **—dam′ager,** *n.* **—dam′agingly,** *adv.*

—Syn. 1. DAMAGE, DETRIMENT, HARM, MISCHIEF refer to injuries of various kinds. DAMAGE is the kind of injury (or the effect of injury) which directly impairs appearance, value, usefulness, soundness, etc.: *fire causes damage to property, property suffers damage.* DETRIMENT is a falling off from an original condition as the result of damage, depreciation, devaluation, etc.: *detriment to health because of illness, to property because of neglect.* HARM is the kind of injury which connotes sorrow or a sense of evil; it may denote either physical hurt or mental, moral, or spiritual injury: *bodily harm, harm to one's self-confidence.* MISCHIEF may be damage, harm, trouble, or misfortune caused by a person esp. if maliciously: *an enemy who would do one mischief.*

daman (dăm′ən), *n.* **1.** a small mammal, *Procavia syriaca,* of the order *Hyracoidea,* inhabiting Syria, Palestine, etc. (the *cony* of the English Bible). **2.** any hyrax. [t. Ar.: short for *daman isrāīl* lamb of Israel]

Daman (dä män′), *n.* **1.** a union territory in W India, formerly a district of Portuguese India; annexed by India December, 1961. 23,093 pop. (1961); 176 sq. mi. **2.** the capital of this territory. 22,390 (1961). Portuguese, **Damão** (*Port.* də mᴀwɴ′).

Damanhur (dä′mən ho͝or′), *n.* a town in N Egypt, near Alexandria. 126,000 (est. 1960).

Damaraland (də mä′rə lănd′), *n.* a region in the central part of South-West Africa.

Damascene (dăm′ə sēn′, dăm′ə sēn′), *adj., n., v.,* **-scened, -scening.** **—*adj.* 1.** of or pertaining to the city of Damascus. **2.** (*l.c.*) of or pertaining to the art of damascening. **—*n.* 3.** an inhabitant of Damascus. **4.** (*l.c.*) work or patterns produced by damascening. **—*v.t.* 5.** (*l.c.*) to produce wavy lines on, as in the welding of iron and steel in the swords of Damascus. **6.** (*l.c.*) to ornament (objects of iron and steel) by inlaying with precious metals, or by etching. Also, **damaskeen** for defs 5 and 6. [ME, t. L: m. s. *Damascēnus,* t. Gk: m. *Damaskēnós* of Damascus]

Damascus (də măs′kəs, -mäs′-), *n.* the capital of Syria, in the SW part: reputed to be the oldest continuously existing city in the world. 630,063 (est. 1964).

Damascus steel, a kind of steel with a wavy or variegated pattern, originally made in the Near East, chiefly at Damascus, and used for making sword blades.

damask (dăm′əsk), *n.* **1.** a reversible fabric of linen, silk, cotton, or wool, woven with patterns. **2.** the table linen of this material. **3.** Damascus steel. **4.** the peculiar pattern or wavy appearance on its surface. **5.** the pink colour of the damask rose. *—adj.* **6.** made of or like damask: *damask cloth.* **7.** pink (like the damask rose). *—v.t.* **8.** to damascene. **9.** to weave or adorn with elaborate design, as in damask cloth. [ME *damaske*, t. L: m. *Damascus*, t. Gk: m. *Damaskós* Damascus]

damaskeen (dăm′ə skēn′), *v.t.* damascene.

damask rose, a fragrant pink rose, *Rosa damascena.*

dame (dām), *n.* **1.** a form of address to any woman of rank or authority. **2.** the legal title of the wife of a knight or baronet. **3.** (since 1917) the distinctive title employed before the name of a woman who holds the Order of the British Empire. **4.** *Chiefly U.S. Slang.* a woman. **5.** *Archaic.* the mistress of a household. **6.** *Archaic.* a woman of rank or authority, as a female ruler. **7.** *Hist.* the mistress of a school. **8.** a comic representation of an old woman in a pantomime, usually played by a man. **9.** the keeper, male or female, of a boarding house at Eton college. **10.** the title given to Benedictine nuns who have made their solemn profession. See **dom.** [ME, t. OF, g. L *domina* mistress, lady]

dame school, *Hist.* a small school for young children, conducted by a woman.

dame's violet, a branched cruciferous herb, *Hesperis matronalis*, with scented white or violet flowers, a native of Europe and Asia.

Damien de Veuster (*Fr.* dà myăɴ də vœs tĕr′), **Joseph** (*Fr.* zhô zĕf′), known as **Father Damien** (dā′myən), 1840–89, Belgian Roman Catholic missionary to the lepers of Molokai.

Damietta (dăm′ĭ ĕt′ə), *n.* a town in NE Egypt, in the Nile delta. 72,000 (1960). Arabic, **Dumyat.**

dammar (dăm′ə), *n.* **1.** a copal-like resin chiefly from dipterocarpaceous trees of southern Asia, esp. Malaya and Sumatra, much used for making colourless varnish. **2.** any of various similar resins from trees of other families. Also, **dammer.** [t. Malay: m. *damar* resin]

damn (dăm), *v.t.* **1.** to declare (something) to be bad, unfit, invalid, or illegal. **2.** to condemn as a failure: *damn a play.* **3.** to bring condemnation upon; ruin. **4.** to doom to eternal punishment, or condemn to hell. **5.** to swear at or curse, using the word 'damn'. **6. as near as damn it,** *Colloq.* as near as conceivably possible. *—n.* **7.** a negligible amount: *not worth a damn.* *—interj.* **8.** (an expression of anger, annoyance, or emphasis.) [ME *damne(n)*, t. OF: m. *damner*, t. L: m. *damnāre* condemn, doom]

damnable (dăm′nə bl), *adj.* **1.** worthy of damnation. **2.** detestable, abominable, or outrageous. **3.** hateful, annoying. **—dam′nableness,** *n.* **—dam′nably,** *adv.*

damnation (dăm nā′shən), *n.* **1.** act of damning. **2.** state of being damned. **3.** a cause or occasion of being damned. **4.** *Theol.* sin as incurring or deserving eternal punishment. *—interj.* **5.** (the noun 'damnation', used as an oath expressing anger, disappointment, etc.)

damnatory (dăm′nə tə rĭ, -trĭ), *adj.* conveying or occasioning condemnation; damning.

damned (dămd), *adj.* **1.** condemned, esp. to eternal punishment. **2.** detestable. *—adv.* **3.** extremely, very.

damnedest (dăm′dĭst), *n. Colloq.* the limit of personal effort, or an object's or element's natural function: *to do one's damnedest.*

damnify (dăm′nĭ fī′), *v.t.*, **-fied, -fying.** *Law.* to cause loss or damage to. [t. AF: m. *damnifier*, t. L: m. *damnificāre* injure]

damning (dăm′ĭng), *adj.* that damns or condemns; incrimination. **—damn′ingly,** *adv.*

Damocles (dăm′ə klēz′), *n. Class. Legend.* a flatterer, who, having extolled the happiness of Dionysius, tyrant of Syracuse, was placed at a banquet with a sword suspended over his head by a single hair, to show him the perilous nature of that happiness. **—Damoclean** (dăm′ə-klē′ən), *adj.*

Damon (dā′mən), *n. Class. Legend.* a Syracusan who barely escaped suffering the death penalty as voluntary hostage for his friend Pythias.

damosel (dăm′ə zĕl′), *n. Archaic.* damsel. Also, **dam′-oiselle′, dam′ozel′.**

damp (dămp), *adj.* **1.** moderately wet; moist. **2.** *Archaic.* dejected. *—n.* **3.** moisture; humidity; moist air. **4.** a noxious or stifling vapour or gas, esp. in a mine. **5.** depression of spirits; dejection. **6.** a check or discouragement. *—v.t.* **7.** to make damp; moisten. **8.** to check or retard the energy, action, etc., of. **9.** to stifle or suffocate; extinguish. **10.** *Acoustics, Music.* to check or retard the action of (a vibrating string, etc.); dull; deaden. **11.** to furnish (esp. pianos) with a damper or dampers. **12.** *Physics.* to cause a decrease in amplitude of (successive oscillations or waves). [ME *domp*, t. MFlem.: vapour, c. G *Dampf* steam] **—damp′ish,** *adj.* **—damp′ly,** *adv.* **—damp′ness,** *n.*

—Syn. 1. DAMP, HUMID, MOIST mean slightly wet. DAMP usually implies slight and extraneous wetness, generally undesirable or unpleasant unless the result of intention: *a damp cellar, to put a damp cloth on a patient's forehead.* HUMID is a literary or scientific word, applied to that which is so permeated with moisture that the moisture seems a part of it, esp. unpleasant dampness in the air in either hot or cold weather: *the air is oppressively humid today.* MOIST denotes that which is slightly wet, naturally or properly: *moist ground, leather.* **—Ant. 1.** dry.

dampcourse (dămp′kôs′), *n.* a horizontal layer of impervious material laid in a wall to stop moisture rising. Also, **damp-proof course.**

dampen (dăm′pən), *v.t.* **1.** to make damp; moisten. **2.** to dull or deaden; depress. *—v.i.* **3.** to become damp. **—damp′ener,** *n.*

damper (dăm′pə), *n.* **1.** one who or that which damps. **2.** a movable plate for regulating the draught in a stove, furnace, etc. **3.** *Music.* **a.** a device in stringed keyboard instruments to deaden the vibration of the strings. **b.** the mute of a brass instrument, as a horn. **4.** *Elect.* an attachment to keep the indicator of a measuring instrument from oscillating excessively, usually a set of vanes in an air space or fluid, or a short-circuited winding in a magnetic field. **5.** *Chiefly Austral., N.Z.* a cake made from flour and water, baked in ashes.

Dampier (dăm′pĭ ə, dăm′pyə), *n.* **William,** 1652–1715, English navigator, explorer, writer, and pirate.

Dampier Land, a peninsula of N Western Australia, W of King Sound.

damping-off (dăm′pĭng ŏf′), *n.* a disease of plants, esp. seedlings, caused by various fungi, mainly *Pythium debaryanum*, which spread rapidly under conditions of excessive moisture.

damp-proof (dămp′pro͞of), *adj.* **1.** resistant to damp. *—v.t.* **2.** to make resistant to damp.

damsel (dăm′zəl), *n. Archaic.* a young woman; a girl; a maiden, originally one of gentle or noble birth. [ME *dameisele*, t. OF, ult. der. L *domina* mistress, lady. See DAME]

damsel fly, any of the more fragile, slow-flying insects of the order *Odonata*, distinguished from the dragonflies by having the wings closed while at rest.

damson (dăm′zən), *n.* **1.** the small dark blue or purple fruit of a plum, *Prunus institiia*, introduced into Europe from Asia Minor. **2.** the tree bearing it. [ME *damascene*, repr. L (*prunum*) *damascēnum* (plum) of Damascus. See DAMASCENE]

damson cheese, a thick, viscous conserve made of pulped and sieved damsons and sugar.

Dan[1] (dăn), *n.* **1.** one of the twelve sons of Jacob. Gen. 30:6. **2.** one of the twelve Hebrew tribes. Josh. 19:40. **3.** a city at the northern end of Palestine; hence, the common phrase **from Dan to Beersheba** (the two limits of Palestine). Judges 20:1. [t. Heb.]

Dan[2] (dăn), *n. Archaic.* a title of honour, equivalent to *master* or *sir*: *Dan Chaucer, Dan Cupid.* [ME, t. OF, g. L *dominus* master, lord]

Dan[3] (dăn), *n. Judo.* **1.** one of the grades into which experienced judo contestants are divided: *there are twelve Dans, but the highest ever achieved is tenth Dan.* **2.** a contestant who has achieved such a grade.

Dan., **1.** Daniel. **2.** Danish.

Dana (dā′nə), *n.* **1. Charles Anderson,** 1819–97, U.S. journalist. **2. James Dwight,** 1813–95, U.S. geologist and mineralogist. **3. Richard Henry,** 1815–82, U.S. lawyer and writer.

Danaë (dăn′ĭ ē′), *n. Gk Legend.* a maiden imprisoned in a brazen tower by her father Acrisius, King of Argos. Visited by Zeus in the form of a shower of gold, she became the mother of Perseus.

Danaides (də nā′ĭ dēz′), *n. pl. Gk Myth.* daughters of Danaüs, who for killing their husbands were condemned in Hades to pour water for ever into a perforated or bottomless vessel. **—Danaidean** (dăn′ĭ ĭd′ĭ ən, dăn′ĭ ə-dē′ən), *adj.*

Da Nang (dä′ năng′), a seaport and U.S. military base in NE South Vietnam. 109,000 (est. 1967). Formerly, **Tourane.**

Danaüs (dăn′ĭ əs), *n. Gk Myth.* the ruler of Argos who married his daughters, the Danaides, to their fifty cousins, the sons of Aegyptus, but made them slay their husbands on the wedding night.

dance (däns), *v.*, **danced, dancing,** *n.* *—v.i.* **1.** to move with the feet or body rhythmically, esp. to music. **2.** to leap, skip, etc., as from excitement or emotion; move nimbly or quickly. **3.** to bob up and down. *—v.t.* **4.** to perform or take part in (a dance). **5.** to cause to dance. **6.** to cause to be in a specified condition by dancing. **7. dance attendance,** to attend constantly or solicitously.

8. dance on air, *Slang.* to be hanged. —*n.* **9.** a successive group of rhythmical steps, generally executed to music. **10.** an act or round of dancing. **11.** a social gathering for dancing; ball. **12.** a piece of music suited in rhythm to a particular form of dancing. **13.** a series of apparently rhythmic movements as performed by some insects or birds, etc. **14.** *Colloq.* a troubled or difficult life or period of life: *to lead someone a dance.* [ME *daunse(n)*, t. OF: m. *danser*; prob. of Gmc orig.] —**dance′able,** *adj.* —**danc′ingly,** *adv.*

dance band, a band which plays music for dancing.

dance hall, a large public hall in which dances may be held.

dance of death, a symbolic dance in which a skeleton Death leads people to their graves. Also, **danse macabre.**

dancer (dän′sə), *n.* **1.** one who dances. **2.** one who dances professionally, as on the stage.

dancette (dän sět′), *n.* **1.** *Her.* a fesse with three indentations. **2.** *Archit.* a zigzag or chevron moulding.

d. and c., dilatation and curettage: a surgical method for the removal of tissue from the uterus by scraping.

dandelion (dăn′dĭ lī′ən), *n.* **1.** a common composite plant, *Taraxacum officinale*, abundant as a weed, characterized by deeply toothed or notched leaves and golden yellow flowers. **2.** any other plant of the genus *Taraxacum.* [t. F: m. *dent de lion* lion's tooth (with allusion to the toothed leaves)]

dandelion clock, the seed-head of the dandelion. It is said that the number of puffs needed to blow all the seeds off will give the hour of the day.

dander[1] (dăn′də), *n.* *U.S. Colloq.* anger or temper. [? fig. use of *dander* DANDRUFF; or fig. use of *dander* ferment]

dander[2] (dăn′də), *Scot.* —*n.* **1.** a stroll. —*v.i.* **2.** to stroll.

Dandie Dinmont (dăn′dĭ dĭn′mŏnt), one of a breed of small terriers with a long body, short legs, and a pepper- or mustard-coloured coat. [from *Dandie* (Andrew) *Dinmont*, in Scott's '*Guy Mannering*', said to own the progenitors]

dandify (dăn′dĭ fī′), *v.t.*, **-fied, -fying.** to make dandy-like or foppish; dress like a dandy. —**dan′difica′tion,** *n.*

dandiprat (dăn′dĭ prăt′), *n.* **1.** *Hist.* a 16th-century English coin worth 1½d. **2.** *Archaic.* a child, esp. a diminutive one. **3.** *Archaic.* an insignificant or silly person.

dandle (dăn′dl), *v.t.*, **-dled, -dling.** **1.** to move lightly up and down, as a child on the knees or in the arms. **2.** to pet. [? t. Scand.; cf. Faeroese *danda* dandle] —**dan′dler,** *n.*

dandruff (dăn′drəf), *n.* a scurf which forms on the scalp and comes off in small scales. Also, **dandriff** (dăn′drĭf). [orig. unknown]

dandy[1] (dăn′dĭ), *n.*, *pl.* **-dies,** *adj.*, **-dier, -diest.** —*n.* **1.** a man who is excessively concerned about clothes and appearance; a fop. **2.** *U.S. Colloq.* something very fine or first rate. **3.** *Naut.* a yawl with a jigger mast abaft on which a mizzen lugsail is set. —*adj.* **4.** foppish. **5.** *U.S. Colloq.* fine; first-rate. [? special use of *Dandy*, var. of *Andy* (Andrew)] —**dan′dyish,** *adj.* —**dan′dyism,** *n.*

dandy[2] (dăn′dĭ), *n.* (in the West Indies) dengue. Also, **dandy fever.**

dandy-brush (dăn′dĭ brŭsh′), *n.* a stiff brush used for grooming horses, made of split whalebone, vegetable fibre, or the like.

dandy-roller (dăn′dĭ rō′lə), *n.* a roller used in making some kinds of paper and in impressing watermarks. Also, **dandy-roll.**

Dane[1] (dān), *n.* **1.** a native or inhabitant of Denmark. **2.** a person of Danish descent. **3.** *Hist.* any of the Northmen or Vikings who invaded and occupied England in the ninth to eleventh centuries. [appar. back-formation from OE *Dænemarc* Denmark; *Dene*, pl., the Danes; cf. Icel. *Danir*]

Dane[2] (dān), *n.* **Clemence** (*Winifred Ashton*), died 1965, English novelist and playwright.

danegeld (dān′gĕld′, -gĕlt′), *n.* *Hist.* **1.** a tax raised in England in the tenth century to buy off Danish invaders. **2.** a Norman land tax.

Danelaw (dān′lô′), *n.* **1.** the body of laws in force in that part of England which the Danes occupied in the ninth century. **2.** that part of England under this law. Also, **Danelagh** (dān′lô′). [f. DANE + LAW; r. OE *Denalagu* law of the Danes]

danewort (dān′wûrt′), *n.* a stout, perennial caprifoliaceous herb, *Sambucus ebulus*, with serrated leaves and white flowers, widespread in Europe and Asia.

danger (dān′jə), *n.* **1.** liability or exposure to harm or injury; risk; peril. **2.** an instance or cause of peril. **3.** the position (of a signal, etc.) indicating danger: *although the signal was at danger, the train did not stop.* **4.** *Obs.* power; jurisdiction; domain. [ME *daunger*, t. OF: m. *dangier*, g. LL deriv. of *dominium* lordship]

—**Syn. 1.** DANGER, HAZARD, PERIL, JEOPARDY imply some evil or harm which one may encounter. DANGER is the general word for liability to all kinds of injury or evil consequences, either near at hand and certain, or remote and doubtful: *to be in danger of catching cold or of being killed.* HAZARD suggests a danger which one can foresee and may not be able to avoid: *there are hazards in any military operation.* PERIL usually denotes great and imminent danger: *the passengers on the disabled ship were in great peril.* JEOPARDY, a less common word, has essentially the same meaning as PERIL, but emphasizes possible exposure to the chances of a situation: *to save his friend he put his life in jeopardy.* —**Ant. 1.** safety.

dangerous (dān′jə rəs), *adj.* full of danger or risk; causing danger; perilous; hazardous; unsafe. —**dan′gerously,** *adv.* —**dan′gerousness,** *n.*

dangle (dăng′gl), *v.*, **-gled, -gling,** *n.* —*v.i.* **1.** to hang loosely with a swaying motion. **2.** *Colloq.* to be hanged. **3.** to hang about or follow a person, as if seeking favour. —*v.t.* **4.** to cause to dangle; hold or carry swaying loosely. —*n.* **5.** the act of dangling. **6.** something that dangles. [t. Scand.; cf. Dan. *dangle* dangle, bob up and down] —**dan′gler,** *n.*

dangling participle, *Gram.* misrelated participle.

Daniel (dăn′yəl), *n.* **1.** *Bible.* **a.** a Jewish captive and prophet living in Babylon. **b.** a canonical book in the Old Testament. **2. Samuel,** 1562–1619, English poet and historian. [t. Heb.: m. *Dānī'ēl*]

Daniell cell, *Physics.* a primary cell producing 1·1 volts; consisting of a zinc anode standing in dilute sulphuric acid, and a copper cathode standing in copper sulphate, the two electrolytes being separated by a porous pot. [named after John *Daniell*, 1790–1845, English physicist]

Danish (dā′nĭsh), *adj.* **1.** of or pertaining to the Danes, their country, or their language. —*n.* **2.** a Germanic language, the language of Denmark, closely related to Norwegian, Swedish, and Icelandic.

Danish pastry, a confection of sweet yeast dough containing egg and milk, cut into crescents, turnovers, triangles, etc., and filled with almond paste, apple, apricots, lemon curd, sweetened cream cheese, etc., before cooking.

Danite (dăn′īt), *n.* **1.** *Bible.* a descendant of Dan. Judges 13:2. **2.** a member of an alleged secret order of Mormons supposed to have been formed about 1837.

dank (dăngk), *adj.* unpleasantly moist or humid; damp. [cf. Sw. *dank* marshy place, Icel. *dökk* pool] —**dank′ly,** *adv.* —**dank′ness,** *n.*

danke schön (*Ger.* dàng′kə shœn′), *German.* thank you very much.

d'Annunzio (*It.* dàn nōōn′tsyō), *n.* **Gabriele** (*It.* gà-bryĕ′lĕ), 1863–1938, Italian author and soldier. Also, **D'Annunzio.**

Dano-Norwegian (dā nō′ nô wē′jən), *n.* a literary and urban language of Norway, based on Danish; Riksmål.

danse macabre (*Fr.* däNs mà kà′br), *French.* dance of death.

danseur (*Fr.* däN sœr′), *n.* a male ballet dancer. [t. F, der. *danser* DANCE]

danseuse (*Fr.* däN sœz′), *n.*, *pl.* **-seuses** (*Fr.* -sœz′). a female ballet dancer. [t. F, fem. of *danseur*]

Dante (dăn′tĭ; *It.* dàn′tĕ), *n.* (*Dante Alighieri*), 1265–1321, Italian poet: author of the *Divine Comedy.*

Dantean (dăn′tĭ ən, dăn tē′ən), *adj.* **1.** of Dante or his writings. **2.** Dantesque. —*n.* **3.** a scholar devoted to the study of Dante.

Dantesque (dăn′tĕsk′), *adj.* in the style of Dante; characterized by impressive elevation of style combined with deep solemnity or sombreness of feeling.

Danton (dăn′tən; *Fr.* däN tôN′), *n.* **Georges Jacques** (*Fr.* zhôrzh zhàk′), 1759–94, French revolutionary leader.

Danube (dăn′yōōb), *n.* a river in Europe, flowing from SW West Germany E to the Black Sea. 1725 mi. German, **Donau.** Hungarian, **Duna.** —**Danubian** (dă nyōō′byən), *adj.*

Danzig (dăn′sĭg; *Ger.* dàn′tsĭKH), *n.* **1.** a seaport, formerly a member of the Hanseatic League, in N Poland, on the **Bay of Danzig,** an inlet of the Baltic. See map under **Hanseatic League. 2. Free City of,** a former self-governing territory including the seaport of Danzig, constituted by the treaty of Versailles, 1920: a part of Germany 1939–45; now in Poland. Polish, **Gdańsk.**

dap[1] (dăp), *v.i.*, **dapped, dapping.** **1.** to fish by letting the bait fall lightly on the water. **2.** to dip lightly or suddenly into water. **3.** to bounce on, or as on, the surface of water. [ME *dop.* Cf. DIP]

dap[2] (dăp), *n.* *Bldg Trades.* a groove to receive connectors; occasionally, a notch.

Daphne (dăf′nĭ), *n.* **1.** *Gk Myth.* a nymph who, pursued by Apollo, was saved by being changed into a laurel tree. **2.** (*l.c.*) **a.** the laurel, *Laurus nobilis.* **b.** any plant of the thymelaeaceous genus *Daphne*, of Europe and Asia, comprising small shrubs of which some species, as *D.*

mezereum, are cultivated for their fragrant flowers. [t. L, t. Gk: laurel]

daphnia (dăf′nyə), *n.* any member of the genus *Daphnia*, of small freshwater crustaceans, or of one of several closely related genera; water-flea.

Daphnis (dăf′nĭs), *n. Gk Myth.* a son of Hermes by a nymph: the inventor of pastoral poetry.

Daphnis and Chloë (klō′ĭ), two lovers in pastoral literature, esp. in a Greek romance attributed to Longus.

dapper (dăp′ə), *adj.* **1.** neat; trim; smart. **2.** small and active. [late ME *dapyr* pretty, elegant; cf. G *tapfer* brave.] **—dap′perly,** *adv.* **—dap′perness,** *n.*

dapple (dăp′l), *n., adj., v.,* **-pled, -pling.** **—***n.* **1.** mottled marking, as of an animal's skin or coat. **2.** an animal with a mottled skin or coat. **—***adj.* **3.** dappled; spotted: *a dapple horse.* **—***v.t., v.i.* **4.** to mark or become marked with spots. [orig. uncert. Cf. Icel. *depill* spot, dot]

dapple-bay (dăp′l bā′), *adj.* bay with ill-defined mottling of a darker shade.

dappled (dăp′ld), *adj.* having spots of different colours or shades; spotted.

dapple-grey (dăp′l grā′), *adj.* grey with ill-defined mottling of a darker shade.

Darbhanga (dä bŭng′ə), *n.* a town in India, in N Bihar. 103,016 (1961).

d'Arblay (där′blā; *Fr.* dȧr blĕ′), *n.* See **Burney.**

Darby (dä′bĭ), *n.* **Abraham,** 1677–1717, English pioneer ironmaster.

Darby and Joan (dä′bĭ ən jōn′), the typical 'old married couple' happily leading a life of placid domesticity.

Darbyites (dä′bĭ īts′), *n. pl.* Plymouth Brethren.

Dardan (dä′dn), *adj., n.* Trojan. Also, **Dardanian** (dä dā′nyən). [t. L: m. s. *Dardanius*, t. Gk: m. *Dardánios*]

Dardanelles (dä′də nĕlz′), *n. pl.* the strait between European and Asiatic Turkey, connecting the Aegean with the Sea of Marmara. 40 mi. long; 1–5 mi. wide. Ancient, **Hellespont.**

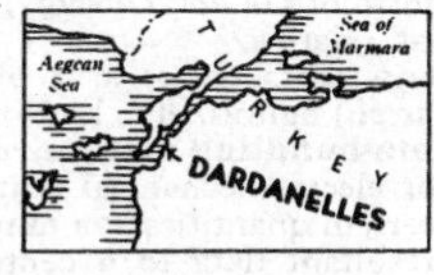

Dardanelles

Dardanus (dä′də nəs), *n.* the mythical ancestor of the Trojans.

dare (dĕə), *v.,* **dared** or (*Dial.*) **durst, dared** (p. subj. often *dare*), **daring,** *n.* **—***v.i.* **1.** to have the necessary courage or boldness for something; be bold enough. **2. dare say,** to assume as probable; have no doubt. **—***v.t.* **3.** to have the necessary courage for; venture on. **4.** to meet defiantly. **5.** to challenge or provoke to action, esp. by doubting one's courage; defy: *to dare a man to fight.* **—***n.* **6.** *Colloq.* a challenge, as to some dangerous act. [ME *dar*, OE *dear(r)*, 1st and 3rd pers. sing. pres. ind. of *durran*; akin to OHG *giturran*] **—dar′er,** *n.*

—Syn. 1. DARE, VENTURE imply involvement in risks and dangers. DARE emphasizes the state of mind that makes one willing to meet danger: *he dared to do what he knew was right.* VENTURE emphasizes the act of doing something which involves risk: *he ventured into deep water.*

daredevil (dĕə′dĕv′əl), *n.* **1.** a recklessly daring person. **—***adj.* **2.** recklessly daring.

daredevilry (dĕə′dĕv′əl rĭ), *n.* recklessness; venturesomeness. Also, *U.S.*, **daredeviltry** (dĕə′dĕv′əl trĭ).

Dar-es-Salaam (dä′rĭs sə läm′), *n.* a seaport in and the capital of Tanzania. 150,000 (est. 1964).

darg (däg), *n.* **1.** *Scot. and N Dial.* a day's work. **2.** *Austral.* a fixed or definite amount of work. [ME *dawerk*, OE *dægweorc* day-work]

daric (dă′rĭk), *n.* the gold coin unit of ancient Persia. [t. Gk: m. s. *dāreikós*; ult. t. Pers.]

Darien (dĕə′rĭ ən, dă′rĭ ən; *Sp.* dȧ ryĕn′), *n.* **1. Gulf of,** an arm of the Caribbean between the NE coast of Panama and Colombia. **2. Isthmus of,** former name of the **Isthmus of Panama.**

daring (dĕə′rĭng), *n.* **1.** adventurous courage; boldness. **—***adj.* **2.** that dares; bold; intrepid; adventurous. **—dar′ingly,** *adv.* **—dar′ingness,** *n.* **—Syn. 2.** dauntless, undaunted, venturesome, audacious. **—Ant. 1.** caution.

Dario (*Sp.* dȧ rē′ō), *n.* **Rubén** (*Sp.* ro͞o bĕn′) (*Félix Rubén Garcia-Sarmiento*), 1867–1916, Nicaraguan poet.

dariole (dă′rĭ ōl′), *n. Cookery.* **1.** a type of small, cup-shaped mould. **2.** a type of small cake. [ME, t. F]

Darius I (də rī′əs) (*'the Great', Darius Hystaspis*), 558?–486? B.C., king of Persia 521–486? B.C.

Darius II, died 404 B.C., king of Persia 424–404 B.C.

Darius III, died 330 B.C., king of Persia 336–330 B.C.

Darjeeling (dä jē′lĭng), *n.* **1.** a town in NE India, in W Bengal: mountain resort. 40,700 (1961). **2.** Also, **Darjeeling tea.** a high-quality tea grown in the mountains around Darjeeling.

dark (däk), *adj.* **1.** without light; with very little light: *a dark room.* **2.** radiating or reflecting little light: *a dark colour.* **3.** approaching black in hue: *a dark brown.* **4.** not pale or fair: *a dark complexion.* **5.** gloomy; cheerless; dismal. **6.** sullen; frowning. **7.** evil; wicked: *dark thoughts.* **8.** destitute of knowledge or culture; unenlightened. **9.** hard to understand; obscure. **10.** hidden; secret. **11.** silent; reticent. **12.** *Phonet.* (of *l* sounds) resembling a back vowel in quality: *English l is darker than French l.* **—***n.* **13.** absence of light; darkness. **14.** night; nightfall. **15.** a dark place. **16.** a dark colour. **17.** obscurity. **18.** secrecy. **19.** ignorance: *in the dark.* **—***v.t., v.i. Obs.* **20.** to darken. [ME *derk*, OE *deorc*. Cf. MHG *terken*] **—dark′ish,** *adj.*

—Syn. 1. DARK, DIM, GLOOMY, MURKY refer to absence or insufficiency of light. DARK implies a more or less complete absence of light: *a dark night.* DIM implies faintness of light or indistinctness of form (resulting from the lack of light or from imperfect vision): *a dim outline.* GLOOMY means cloudy, badly lit, dusky: *a gloomy hall.* MURKY implies a thick, cloudy, or misty darkness: *a murky cave.* **4.** dusky, swarthy, black. **9.** recondite, abstruse. **—Ant. 2.** bright. **5.** cheerful. **6.** pleasant. **9.** clear.

Dark Ages, 1. the time in history from about A.D. 476 to about A.D. 1000. **2.** (occasionally) the whole of the Middle Ages, from about A.D. 476 to the Renaissance.

Dark Continent, The, Africa: so called because it was formerly so little known.

darken (dä′kən), *v.t.* **1.** to make dark or darker; make obscure. **2.** to make less white or clear in colour. **3.** to make gloomy; sadden. **4.** to make blind. **—***v.i.* **5.** to become dark or darker. **6.** to become obscure. **7.** to become less white or clear in colour. **8.** to grow clouded, as with gloom or anger. **9.** to become blind. **—dark′ener,** *n.*

darkey (dä′kĭ), *n., pl.* **darkeys.** darky.

Darkhan (dä kän′), *n.* a city in Mongolia. 25,000 (est. 1966).

dark horse, 1. a racehorse, competitor, etc., about whom little is known or who unexpectedly wins. **2.** a person whose capabilities may be greater than they are known to be. **3.** *U.S.* a person unexpectedly nominated, esp. in a political convention.

dark lantern, a lantern whose light can be obscured by a dark slide or cover at the opening.

darkle (dä′kl), *v.i.,* **-kled, -kling. 1.** to appear dark; show indistinctly. **2.** to grow dark, gloomy, etc. [backformation from DARKLING, adv., taken as ppr.]

darkling (däk′lĭng), *Poetic.* **—***adv.* **1.** in the dark. **—***adj.* **2.** being or occurring in the dark; dark; obscure. [f. DARK + -LING[2]]

darkly (däk′lĭ), *adv.* **1.** so as to appear dark. **2.** mysteriously; threateningly. **3.** *Archaic.* imperfectly; faintly.

darkness (däk′nĭs), *n.* **1.** the state or quality of being dark. **2.** absence or deficiency of light. **3.** wickedness or evil. **4.** obscurity; concealment. **5.** blindness; ignorance.

darkroom (däk′ro͞om′, -ro͝om′), *n. Photog.* a room from which the actinic rays of light have been excluded: used in making, handling, and developing film, etc.

darksome (däk′səm), *adj. Poetic.* dark; darkish.

darky (dä′kĭ), *n., pl.* **darkies.** *Colloq.* (often offensive) a Negro. Also, **darkey.**

Darlan (*Fr.* dȧr län′), *n.* **Jean Louis Xavier François** (*Fr.* zhän lwē zȧ vyė frän swȧ′), 1881–1942, French admiral and politician.

darling (dä′lĭng), *n.* **1.** a person very dear to another; person dearly loved. **2.** a person or thing in great favour. **—***adj.* **3.** very dear; dearly loved. **4.** favourite. [ME *derling*, OE *dēorling*, f. *dēore* dear + -LING[1]]

Darling (dä′lĭng), *n.* **1. Grace,** 1815–42, English daughter of a lighthouse-keeper, who rescued shipwrecked sailors. **2.** the longest river in Australia, flowing SW through New South Wales to the Murray river. Its course is known by several names: Severn, Dumaresq, Macintyre, Barwon, and Darling. From the source of the Severn to the Murray, ab. 1700 mi.

Darling Downs, a rich wheat-growing area of SE Queensland, Australia, about 100 miles W of Brisbane.

Darling Range, a range of hills in SW Western Australia. Highest point, Mt Cooke, 1910 ft.

Darlington (dä′lĭng tən), *n.* a market town and county borough in England, in co. Durham. 84,320 (1964).

Darmstadt (däm′stăt; *Ger.* dȧrm′shtȧt), *n.* a town in West Germany, in S Hesse: former capital of Hesse. 139,058 (1963).

darn[1] (dän), *v.t.* **1.** to mend (clothes, etc., or a rent or hole) with rows of stitches, sometimes with crossing and interwoven rows to fill up a gap. **—***n.* **2.** a darned place in a garment, etc. **3.** the act of darning. [? ME *dernen*, OE *dernan* hide] **—darn′er,** *n.* **—Syn. 1.** See **mend.**

darn[2] (dän), *Colloq.* **—***adj., adv.* **1.** darned. **—***v.t.* **2.** to confound; curse. **—***n.* **3. not give a darn,** to be utterly indifferent. **—***interj.* **4.** (a mild expletive.) [var. of DAMN]

darned (dänd), *Colloq.* —*adj.* **1.** confounded; blessed. —*adv.* **2.** extremely; remarkably.

darnel (däʹnəl), *n.* an annual grass, *Lolium temulentum*, found as a weed in grain fields. [ME. Cf. d. F *darnelle*, prob. of Gmc orig.]

darning (däʹnĭng), *n.* **1.** the act of one who darns. **2.** the result produced. **3.** articles darned or to be darned.

darning needle, **1.** a long needle with a large eye used in darning. **2.** *Dial.* a dragonfly.

Darnley (dänʹlĭ), *n.* **Henry Stewart** or **Stuart, Lord,** 1545–1567, Scottish nobleman; the second husband of Mary, Queen of Scots; father of James I of England.

darraign (də rānʹ), *v.t.* deraign.

Darran Range (dăʹrən), a mountain range in New Zealand, in S South Island. Highest peak, Mount Tutoko, 9042 ft.

dart (dät), *n.* **1.** a long, slender, pointed, missile weapon propelled by the hand or otherwise. **2.** something resembling such a weapon, as the sting of an insect. **3.** act of darting; a sudden, swift movement. **4.** (*pl.*) a game in which a pointed missile is thrown at a dartboard. **5.** a seam that is used where a wedge-shaped piece has been cut out to adjust the fit of a garment. —*v.i.* **6.** to move swiftly; spring or start suddenly and run swiftly. —*v.t.* **7.** to throw or thrust suddenly and rapidly. **8.** to throw with a sudden thrust, as a dart. [ME, t. OF, t. Gmc] —**darʹtingly,** *adv.* —**Syn. 6.** dash, bolt.

dartboard (dätʹbôdʹ), *n.* the target in the game of darts, marked with concentric circles divided into segments, and having a bull's-eye at the centre.

darter (däʹtə), *n.* **1.** one who or that which darts or moves swiftly. **2.** a snakebird.

Dartford (dätʹfəd), *n.* a town in England, in Kent, on the Thames. 46,700 (1965).

Dartford Tunnel, a tunnel under the Thames between Dartford and Purfleet: the lowest crossing point.

dartle (däʹtl), *v.t., v.i.,* **-tled, -tling.** to dart or shoot forth repeatedly. [freq. of DART]

Dartmoor (dätʹmo͝oəʹ), *n.* a rocky plateau in SW England, in Devonshire: National Park. Highest point, High Willhays, 2038 ft.

Dartmouth (dätʹməth), *n.* **1.** a seaport in England, in Devonshire. 5757 (1961). **2.** the Royal Naval Training College situated there. **3.** a private men's college at Hanover, New Hampshire, U.S.A., founded in 1769.

Darton (däʹtn), *n.* a town in England, in the S West Riding of Yorkshire. 14,111 (1961).

Darwen (däʹwĭn), *n.* a town in England, in NE Lancashire. 29,475 (1961).

Darwin (däʹwĭn), *n.* **1. Charles,** 1809–82, English naturalist. **2.** his grandfather, **Erasmus,** 1731–1802, English naturalist and poet. **3.** a town in N Australia, capital of Northern Territory. 15,218 (1964).

Darwinian (dä wĭnʹĭ ən), *adj.* **1.** pertaining to Charles Darwin or his doctrines. —*n.* **2.** a follower of Charles Darwin; one who accepts Darwinism.

Darwinism (däʹwĭ nĭzʹəm), *n.* the body of biological doctrine maintained by Charles Darwin respecting the origin of species as derived by descent, with variation, from parent forms, through the natural selection of those best adapted to survive in the struggle for existence. —**Darʹwinist,** *n., adj.* —**Darwinite** (däʹwĭ nītʹ), *n.*

dash[1] (dăsh), *v.t.* **1.** to strike violently, esp. so as to break to pieces. **2.** to throw or thrust violently or suddenly. **3.** to splash violently; bespatter (with water, mud, etc.). **4.** to apply roughly as by splashing. **5.** to throw something into so as to produce a mixture; mix; adulterate: *to dash wine with water.* **6.** to ruin or frustrate (hopes, plans, etc.). **7.** to depress or dispirit. **8.** to confound or abash. **9.** to write, make, sketch, etc., hastily (usually fol. by *off* or *down*). —*v.i.* **10.** to strike with violence. **11.** to move with violence; rush. —*n.* **12.** a violent and rapid blow or stroke. **13.** a check or discouragement. **14.** the throwing or splashing of water, etc., against a thing. **15.** the sound of splashing. **16.** a small quantity of anything thrown into or mixed with something else: *a dash of salt, a dash of pink.* **17.** a hasty stroke, esp. of a pen. **18.** a horizontal line (—) used in writing and printing as a mark of punctuation to indicate an abrupt break or pause in a sentence, to begin and end a parenthetic clause, as an indication of omission of letters, words, etc., as a dividing line between distinct portions of matter, and for other purposes. **19.** *Music.* the sign placed above or below a note to indicate that it is to be played staccato. **20.** *Maths.* an acute accent, used in algebra and in lettering diagrams as a discrimination mark; prime. **21.** an impetuous movement; a rush; a sudden onset. **22.** *Athletics.* a short race or sprint decided in one attempt, not in heats: *a hundred-yard dash.* **23.** spirited action; vigour in action or style. **24.** a dashboard. **25.** *Teleg.* a signal of longer duration than a dot, used in groups of dots and dashes to represent letters, as in morse code. **26. cut a dash,** to create a brilliant impression. [ME *dasche(n)*, c. Dan. *daske* slap, flap] —**Syn. 11.** dart, bolt. See **rush**[1]. **16.** pinch, bit; touch, tinge.

dash[2] (dăsh), *v.t.* **1.** to confound. —*interj.* **2.** (a mild expletive.)

dashboard (dăshʹbôdʹ), *n.* **1.** the instrument board of a motor car or an aeroplane. **2.** (formerly) a panel on the front of a vehicle, to prevent mud splashing.

dasheen (dă shēnʹ), *n.* the taro plant, *Colocasia esculenta*, native in tropical Asia, grown in the tropics for its edible tubers. [t. F: m. *de Chine* of China]

dasher (dăshʹə), *n.* **1.** one who or that which dashes. **2.** the plunger of a churn. **3.** *Colloq.* a spirited person.

dashing (dăshʹĭng), *adj.* **1.** impetuous; spirited; lively. **2.** brilliant; showy; stylish. —**dashʹingly,** *adv.*

dashpot (dăshʹpŏtʹ), *n. Mech.* a device for damping vibrations, consisting of a piston attached to the part whose movements are to be damped and fitted into a cylinder containing a fluid such as oil.

dashy (dăshʹĭ), *adj.* showy; stylish; dashing.

dassie (dăsʹĭ), *n. S African.* the hyrax, *Procavia capensis.* [t. Afrikaans: f. D *das* badger + *-ie* hypocoristic suffix]

dastard (dăsʹtəd), *n.* **1.** a mean, sneaking coward. —*adj.* **2.** mean and sneaking; cowardly. [ME; f. *dast* (? var. of *dazed*, pp. of DAZE) + -ARD]

dastardly (dăsʹtəd lĭ), *adj., adv.* cowardly; meanly base; sneaking. —**dasʹtardliness,** *n.*

dasyure (dăsʹĭ yo͝oəʹ), *n.* **1.** any of the small, spotted, carnivorous marsupials constituting the genus *Dasyurus* and related genera, native in Australia, Tasmania, etc. **2.** any of several related animals, as the Tasmanian devil or ursine dasyure. [t. NL: m.s. *Dasyūrus*, f. *dasy-* (comb. form of Gk *dasýs* shaggy) + *-ūrus* (m. Gk *ourá* tail)]

dat., dative.

data (dāʹtə, däʹtə), *n.* **1.** pl. of **datum. 2.** (*construed as sing. or pl.*) figures, etc., known or available; information.

data-handling system, a system consisting of electronic or electromechanical units which automatically measure certain quantities at a number of points, and transmit the resultant data to a central location for display or for automatic processing.

datal (dāʹtl), *adj.* chronological; pertaining to a date (of historical documents).

data processing. See **automatic data processing.**

datary (dāʹtə rĭ), *n., pl.* **-ries.** *Rom. Cath. Ch.* **1.** an officer, now cardinal, at the head of a certain office or department of the Curia who investigates the fitness of candidates for benefices in the gift of the papal see. **2.** this office or department. [t. ML: m.s. *datārius* (the officer), *datāria* (the office), der. *data* DATE[1]]

date[1] (dāt), *n., v.,* **dated, dating.** —*n.* **1.** a particular point or period of time when something happens or happened. **2.** an inscription on a writing, coin, etc., that shows the time, or time and place, of writing, casting, delivery, etc. **3.** the time or period of an event or to which anything belongs. **4.** the time during which anything lasts; duration. **5.** *Colloq.* an appointment made for a particular time. **6.** *Colloq.* a person, usually of the opposite sex, with whom one has a social appointment. **7. to date,** to the present time. —*v.i.* **8.** to have a date: *the letter dates from 1873.* **9.** to belong to a particular period; have its origin. **10.** to reckon from some point in time. **11.** *Colloq.* to go out on dates (def. 5) with a person or persons of the opposite sex. —*v.t.* **12.** to mark or furnish with a date. **13.** to ascertain or fix the date or time of; assign a date or time to. **14.** to show to be of a certain age, old-fashioned, or out of date: *that dress dates you.* **15.** *Colloq.* to make a date (def. 5) with. [ME, t. F, t. ML: m. *data*, prop. pp. fem. of L *dare* give] —**datʹer,** *n.*

date[2] (dāt), *n.* **1.** the oblong, fleshy fruit of the date palm, a staple food in northern Africa, Arabia, etc., and an important export. **2.** the date palm. [ME, t. OF, g. L *dactylus*, t. Gk: m. *dáktylos* date, orig. finger]

dateless (dātʹlĭs), *adj.* **1.** without a date; undated. **2.** endless. **3.** so old as to be undatable. **4.** of permanent interest regardless of age.

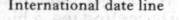

International date line

date line, **1.** a line in a letter, newspaper article, or the like, giving the date (and often the place) of origin. **2.** Also, **international date line.** a line, theoretically coinciding with the meridian of 180° from Greenwich, the regions on either side of which are counted as differing by one day in their calendar dates.

date palm, the species of palm, *Phoenix dactylifera*, which bears dates, having a stem up to 60 feet high terminating in a crown of pinnate leaves.

date plum, a small tree from China and the Himalaya region, *Diospyros lotus*, family *Ebenaceae*, having small yellow or bluish fruit.

date stamp, a device for stamping dates, esp. on postal matter.

dative (dā′tĭv), *Gram.* —*adj.* **1.** denoting a case, in some inflected languages, having as one function indication of the indirect object of a verb. —*n.* **2.** the dative case. **3.** a word or form in that case, as Latin *regi* in *regi haec dicite* meaning *tell this to the king.* [ME, t. L: m. s. *datīvus* of or pertaining to giving] —**datival** (də tī′vəl), *adj.* —**da′tively,** *adv.*

dative bond, *Chem.* a type of covalent bond in which both the electrons forming the bond are donated by the same atom; coordinate bond.

dato (dä′tō; *Sp.* dȧ′tō), *n., pl.* **-tos** (-tōz; *Sp.* -tōs). **1.** (in the Philippines) a native chief. **2.** the headman of a barrio or tribe in the East Indies. Also, **dat′to.** [t. Malay: m. *dātoq* title of respect]

datum (dā′təm, dä′təm), *n., pl.* **-ta** (-tə). **1.** any proposition assumed or given, from which conclusions may be drawn. **2.** (*often pl.*) any fact assumed to be a matter of direct observation. [t. L: given (pp. neut.)]

datum plane, level, line, etc., *Survey., Civ. Eng., etc.* a plane, level, line, etc., from which heights and depths are calculated or measured.

datura (də tyŏŏə′rə), *n.* any plant of the solanaceous genus *Datura*, the species of which have funnel-shaped flowers, prickly pods, and narcotic properties. [NL, t. Hind.: m. *dhatūra*, native name of the plant]

dau., daughter.

daub (dôb), *v.t.* **1.** to cover or coat with soft, adhesive matter, such as plaster, mud, etc. **2.** to spread (plaster, mud, etc.) on or over something. **3.** to smear, soil, or defile. **4.** to paint unskilfully. —*v.i.* **5.** to daub something. **6.** to paint unskilfully. —*n.* **7.** material, esp. of an inferior kind, for daubing walls, etc. **8.** anything daubed on. **9.** the act of daubing. **10.** a crude, inartistic painting. [ME *daube(n)*, t. OF: m. *dauber*, g. L *dealbāre* whiten, plaster] —**daub′er,** *n.*

daubery (dô′bə rĭ), *n.* unskilful painting or work. Also, **daubry** (dô′brĭ).

Daubigny (*Fr.* dō bē nyē′), *n.* **Charles François** (*Fr.* shȧrl fräN swȧ′), 1817–78, French landscape painter.

Daudet (*Fr.* dō dĕ′), *n.* **1. Alphonse** (*Fr.* ȧl fôNs′), 1840–97, French novelist. **2. Léon** (*Fr.* lĕ ôN′), 1867–1942, French journalist and novelist; son of Alphonse.

Daugava (dou′gä vä′), *n.* Lettish name of **Dvina.**

Daugavpils (dou′găf pēls′), *n.* a city in the W Soviet Union, in the Latvian Republic. 74,000 (1964). Russian, **Dvinsk.** German, **Dünaburg.**

daughter (dô′tə), *n.* **1.** a female child or person in relation to her parents. **2.** any female descendant. **3.** one related as if by the ties binding daughter to parent: *daughter of the church.* **4.** anything (personified as female) considered with respect to its origin. —*adj.* **5.** denoting first-generation offspring or offshoot, irrespective of sex: *daughter cell.* [var. of ME *doughter*, OE *dohtor*, c. G *Tochter*, Gk *thygátēr*]

daughter-in-law (dô′tə rĭn lô′), *n., pl.* **daughters-in-law.** the wife of one's son.

daughterly (dô′tə lĭ), *adj.* pertaining to, befitting, or like a daughter. —**daugh′terliness,** *n.*

Daughters of the American Revolution, The, a U.S. patriotic society of women descended from Americans of the period of the War of Independence, which was organized in 1890.

Daumier (*Fr.* dō myĕ′), *n.* **Honoré** (*Fr.* ō nō rĕ′), 1808–79, French lithographer, painter, and sculptor.

daunt (dônt), *v.t.* **1.** to overcome with fear; intimidate. **2.** to lessen the courage of; dishearten. [ME *daunte(n)*, t. OF: m. *danter*, ult. der. L *domāre* tame, subdue] —**Syn. 1.** overawe. **2.** discourage, dispirit.

dauntless (dônt′lĭs), *adj.* not to be daunted; fearless; intrepid; bold. —**daunt′lessly,** *adv.* —**daunt′lessness,** *n.* —**Syn.** daring, courageous, indomitable.

dauphin (dô′fĭn; *Fr.* dō făN′), *n.* the distinctive title of the eldest son of the king of France, from 1349 to 1830. [t. F, appar. orig. a proper name used as a surname; often identified with L *delphīnus* dolphin]

Dauphiné (dō′fĭ nā′; *Fr.* dō fē nĕ′), *n.* an old province in SE France.

dauphiness (dô′fĭn ĭs), *n.* the wife of the dauphin. Also, **dauphine** (dô′fĭn, -fēn; *Fr.* dō fēn′).

daut (dôt, dät), *v.t. Scot.* to fondle; caress. Also, **dawt.**

Davao (dä vou′), *n.* a seaport in the Philippines, on Mindanao. 225,712 (1960).

D'Avenant (dăv′ĭ nənt), *n.* **Sir William,** 1606–68, English dramatist and poet. Also, **Dav′enant.**

davenport (dăv′ən pôt′), *n.* **1.** a small ornamental writing table. **2.** *U.S.* a large sofa, as one convertible into a bed.

David (dā′vĭd *for 1, 2; Fr.* dȧ vēd′ *for 3*), *n.* **1.** fl. *c.* 1000 B.C., the second king of the Hebrews, successor to Saul: united tribes of Israel into a nation with the capital at Jerusalem. **2. Saint** (*Saint Dewi*), died A.D. 601?, Welsh bishop: patron saint of Wales. **3. Jacques Louis** (*Fr.* zhȧk lwē′), 1748–1825, French painter. [t. Heb.: m. *Dāwīd*]

David I (dā′vĭd), 1084–1153, king of Scotland 1124–53.

David II, 1324–71, king of Scotland 1329–71.

David d'Angers (*Fr.* dȧ vēd däN zhĕ′), (*Pierre Jean David*), 1788–1856, French sculptor.

Davies (dā′vĭs, -vēz), *n.* **1. Sir Henry Walford,** 1869–1941, English composer and organist. **2. William Henry,** 1871–1940, English poet.

da Vignola. See **Vignola.**

da Vinci. See **Leonardo.**

Davis (dā′vĭs), *n.* **1. Colin,** born 1927, English conductor. **2. Jefferson,** 1808–89, U.S. statesman: president of the Confederate States of America 1861–65. **3. John,** 1550?–1605, English navigator and explorer.

Davis apparatus, a device to enable occupants to escape from a disabled submarine; an escape lock.

Davis Cup, international lawn tennis trophy.

Davis Strait, a strait between Canada and Greenland, connecting Baffin Bay and the Atlantic. 200–500 mi. wide. See map under **Baffin Bay.**

davit (dăv′ĭt, dā′vĭt), *n. Naut.* a projecting piece of wood or iron (frequently one of a pair) on the side or stern of a vessel, fitted with a tackle, etc., for raising, lowering, or suspending a small boat, anchor, or other weight. [ME *daviot*, t. AF, appar. dim. of *Davi* David]

D, Davit

Davos (*Ger.* dȧ′vōs), *n.* a winter sports resort in Switzerland. 10,000 (est. 1965).

Davout (*Fr.* dȧ vōō′), *n.* **Louis Nicholas** (*Fr.* lwē nē kō lȧ′) (*Duke of Auerstädt and Prince of Eckmühl*), 1770–1823, marshal of France: one of Napoleon's leading generals.

Davy (dā′vĭ), *n.* **Sir Humphry,** 1778–1829, English chemist.

Davy Jones (dā′vĭ jōnz′), *Naut.* the spirit of the sea; the sailors' devil.

Davy Jones's locker, 1. the ocean's bottom, esp. as the grave of all who perish at sea. **2.** the ocean.

Davy lamp, an early safety lamp for miners.

daw (dô), *n.* a jackdaw. [ME *dawe.* Cf. OHG *tāha*]

dawdle (dô′dl), *v.,* **-dled, -dling.** —*v.i.* **1.** to waste time; idle; trifle. **2.** to walk slowly or lag behind others. —*v.t.* **3.** to waste (time) by trifling (usually fol. by *away*). [? var. of *daddle* TODDLE] —**daw′dler,** *n.* —**Syn. 1.** See **loiter.**

Dawes (dôz), *n.* **Charles Gates,** 1865–1951, U.S. financier and diplomat: vice-president of the U.S. 1925–29.

dawk (dôk, däk), *n.* dak.

Dawley (dô′lĭ), *n.* a new town in England, in E Shropshire. 21,500 (est. 1965).

dawn (dôn), *n.* **1.** the first appearance of daylight in the morning. **2.** the beginning or rise of anything; advent. —*v.i.* **3.** to begin to grow light in the morning. **4.** to begin to open or develop. **5.** to begin to be perceived (fol. by *on* or *upon*): *the idea dawned on him.* [ME *dawen-* (in *dawening* dawn), appar. t. Scand.; cf. Icel. *dögun* dawn] —**dawn′ing,** *n.* —**Syn. 1.** daybreak, sunrise.

Dawson (dô′sən), *n.* **1. Sir John William,** 1820–99, Canadian geologist. **2.** a town in NW Canada at the confluence of the Yukon and Klondike rivers: former capital of Yukon Territory. 881 (1961). See map under **Klondike.**

Dawson Creek, a town in W Canada, at the SE terminus of the Alaska Highway. 10,946 (est. 1964).

dawt (dôt), *v.t. Scot.* daut.

Dax (*Fr.* dȧks), *n.* a town in SW France, in Landes department: mineral hot springs. 18,422 (1962).

day (dā), *n.* **1.** the interval of light between two successive nights; the time between sunrise and sunset. **2.** the light of day; daylight. **3.** *Astron.* **a.** the period during which the earth (or a heavenly body) makes one revolution on its axis. **b.** the average length of this interval, twenty-four hours (**mean solar day**). **c.** the interval of time which elapses between two consecutive returns of the same terrestrial meridian to the sun (**solar day**). **d.** a period reckoned from midnight to midnight and equivalent in length to the mean solar day (**civil day**), as contrasted with a similar period reckoned from noon to noon (**astronomical day**). **e.** the interval of time between the meridional transits of a star, specifically the first point of Aries (**sidereal day**), four minutes shorter than the solar day. **4.** the portion of a day allotted to working: *an eight-hour day.* **5.** a day as a point or unit of time, or on which something occurs. **6.** a day assigned to a particular purpose or observance: *New Year's Day.* **7.** a day of contest, or the contest itself: *to win the day.* **8.** (*often pl.*) a particular time or period: *the present day, in days of old.* **9.** (*often pl.*) period of life or activity. **10.** period of power or influence. **11. call it a day,** to bring an activity to a close, either temporarily or permanently. **12. day by day,** daily. **13. day in, day out,** for an undetermined succession of days. *—adj.* **14.** *Mining.* (of a level of coal) near the surface. [ME; OE *dæg*, c. G *Tag*]

Dayak (dī′ăk), *n.* Dyak.

day bed, 1. a narrow bed convertible to a couch by day. **2.** chaise longue.

day blindness, nyctalopia (def. 2).

day boarder, a pupil who lives at home but attends a school designed mainly or partly for boarders.

daybook (dā′bo͝ok′), *n.* **1.** *Bookkeeping.* a book in which the transactions of the day are entered in the order of their occurrence. **2.** a diary.

dayboy (dā′boi′), *n.* a boy who attends school during the day but who lives at home (opposed to *boarder*).

daybreak (dā′brāk′), *n.* the first appearance of light in the morning; dawn.

day coach, *U.S.* an ordinary railway passenger coach, as distinguished from a sleeper.

daydream (dā′drēm′), *n.* **1.** a visionary fancy indulged in while awake; reverie. *—v.i.* **2.** to indulge in daydreams. **—day′dream′er,** *n.*

dayfly (dā′flī′), *n., pl.* **-flies.** mayfly.

daygirl (dā′gûl′), *n.* a girl who attends school during the day but who lives at home (opposed to *boarder*).

day labour, work, generally unskilled, paid for by the day.

day labourer, an unskilled worker paid by the day.

Day-Lewis (dā′lo͞o′ĭs), *n.* **C(ecil),** born 1904, English poet.

daylight (dā′līt′), *n.* **1.** the light of day. **2.** openness; publicity. **3.** daytime. **4.** daybreak.

daylight factor, *Physics.* the intensity of light in lumens per square foot on a horizontal surface inside a building, expressed as a fraction of the intensity when the same horizontal surface is in the open under a sky of uniform brightness.

daylight-saving (dā′līt sā′vĭng), *n.* **1.** time one or more hours later than the standard time for a country or community, usually used during summer months to give more hours of daylight to the working day. *—adj.* **2.** of or pertaining to such time.

day lily, 1. any plant of the liliaceous genus *Hemerocallis*, with yellow or orange flowers which commonly last only for a day. **2.** any plant of the liliaceous genus *Niobe* (or *Funkia*), with white or blue flowers. **3.** the flower of any of these plants.

daylong (dā′lŏng′), *adj.* lasting the whole day.

day nursery, a nursery for the care of small children during the day, esp. while their mothers are at work.

Day of Atonement, a Jewish fast day, Yom Kippur.

Day of Judgement, the day of the Last Judgement, at the end of the world.

day of reckoning, 1. the time when one has to pay for one's actions, fulfil one's obligations, etc. **2.** (*cap.*) Day of Judgement.

day release, *Educ.* a system in Britain allowing a worker to attend a technical college course one or more days a week.

days (dāz), *adv. Now Colloq.* during or in the day regularly.

day school, 1. a private school for pupils living outside the school (distinguished from *boarding school*). **2.** a school held in the daytime (distinguished from *night school*). **3.** a school held on weekdays (distinguished from *Sunday school*).

day shift, 1. a work period during the day, esp. the shift between 7 a.m. and 2.30 p.m. in mining. **2.** the group of workers working this shift.

daysman (dāz′mən), *n., pl.* **-men.** *Archaic.* an umpire; mediator. [f. *day's* (poss. of DAY) + MAN]

days of grace, days (commonly three) allowed by law or custom for payment after a bill or note falls due.

dayspring (dā′sprĭng′), *n. Poetic.* dawn; daybreak.

daystar (dā′stä′), *n.* **1.** the morning star. **2.** *Poetic.* the sun.

daytime (dā′tīm′), *n.* the time between sunrise and sunset.

Dayton (dā′tn), *n.* a city in the U.S., in SW Ohio. 262,332 (1960).

Daytona Beach (dā tō′nə), a town in the U.S., in NE Florida: seaside resort. 37,395 (1960).

daze (dāz), *v.,* **dazed, dazing,** *n. —v.t.* **1.** to stun or stupefy with a blow, a shock, etc. **2.** to confuse; bewilder; dazzle. *—n.* **3.** a dazed condition. [ME *dase(n)*, t. Scand.; cf. Dan. *dase* doze, mope] **—dazedly** (dā′zĭd lĭ), *adv.*

dazzle (dăz′əl), *v.,* **-zled, -zling,** *n. —v.t.* **1.** to overpower or dim (the vision) by intense light. **2.** to bewilder by brilliancy or display of any kind. *—v.i.* **3.** to be overpowered by light. **4.** to excite admiration by brilliance. *—n.* **5.** the act or fact of dazzling. **6.** bewildering brightness. [freq. of DAZE] **—daz′zler,** *n.* **—daz′zlingly,** *adv.*

db., decibel; decibels.

D.B.E., Dame (Commander of the Order) of the British Empire.

dbl., double.

D.C., 1. *Music.* da capo. **2.** Also, **d.c.** *Elect.* direct current. **3.** District of Columbia.

D.C.L., Doctor of Civil Law.

D.C.M., Distinguished Conduct Medal; officially, Medal for Distinguished Conduct in the Field.

D.C.V.O., Dame Commander of the (Royal) Victorian Order.

D.D., Doctor of Divinity.

D-day (dē′dā′), *n.* the day, usually unspecified, set for the beginning of a previously planned attack, esp. the day (6th June 1944) of the Allied invasion of Normandy.

DDT, a very powerful insecticide, p,p′-dichlorodiphenyltrichloroethane.

de (də), *prep.* from; of: much used in French personal names, orig. to indicate place of origin. Also, **De;** before vowels, **D′, d′.**

de-, a prefix meaning: **1.** privation and separation, as in *dehorn, dethrone, detrain.* **2.** negation, as in *demerit, derange.* **3.** descent, as in *degrade, deduce.* **4.** reversal, as in *deactivate.* **5.** intensity, as in *decompound.* [ME, t. L, repr. *de*, prep., from, away from, of, out of, etc.; in some words t. F, g. L *de-*, or g. L *dis-* (see DIS-[1])]

deacon (dē′kən), *n.* **1.** (in hierarchical churches) a member of the clerical order next below that of priest. **2.** (in other churches) an appointed or elected officer having variously defined duties. [ME *deacon, deken*, OE *dēacon, diacon*, t. LL: s. *diāconus*, t. Gk: m. *diākonos* servant, minister, deacon] **—dea′conship′,** *n.*

deaconess (dē′kən ĭs), *n.* **1.** (in certain Protestant churches) one of an order of women who carry on educational, hospital, or social work. **2.** a woman elected by a church to assist the clergy.

deaconry (dē′kən rĭ), *n., pl.* **-ries. 1.** the office of a deacon. **2.** deacons collectively.

deactivate (dē′ăk′tĭ vāt′), *v.t.,* **-vated, -vating. 1.** *Phys. Chem.* to return an activated atom, molecule, or substance to its normal state. **2.** *Chem.* to make less active; to return an activated substance (esp. a catalyst) to its normal state. **3.** *Physics.* to lose radioactivity. **—de′activa′tion** *n.*

dead (dĕd), *adj.* **1.** no longer living; deprived of life. **2.** not endowed with life; inanimate: *dead matter.* **3.** resembling death: *a dead sleep.* **4.** bereft of sensation; insensible; numb: *dead to all sense of shame.* **5.** no longer in existence or use: *dead languages.* **6.** *Law.* deprived of civil rights so that one is in the state of civil death, esp. deprived of the rights of property. **7.** without spiritual life or vigour. **8.** *Colloq.* very tired; exhausted. **9.** infertile; barren. **10.** deprived of or lacking animation, motion, force, vigour, or any other characteristic quality: *dead air, water, machinery, affections, etc.* **11.** extinguished: *a dead fire.* **12.** tasteless or flat, as alcoholic drink. **13.** not glossy, bright, or brilliant. **14.** without resonance: *a dead sound.* **15.** without resilience or bounce: *a dead tennis ball.* **16.** closed at one end: *a dead street.* **17.** dull or inactive: *a dead market.* **18.** complete; absolute: *dead loss, dead silence.* **19.** sure; unerring: *a dead shot.* **20.** direct; straight: *a dead line.* **21.** unproductive: *dead capital.* **22.** *Sport.* out of play: *a dead ball.* **23.** having been used or rejected, as type set up or copy for printing. **24.** *Elect.* **a.** free from any electric connection to a source of potential difference and from electric charge. **b.** not having a potential different from that of the earth. **25.** *Mil.* (of land) not visible; hidden, as by undulations: *dead ground.* **26. dead from the neck up,** *Colloq.* lacking intelligence; stupid. *—n.* **27.** one who is dead. **28.** (usually preceded by *the*) dead persons collectively. **29.** the period of greatest darkness, coldness, etc.: *the dead of night.* *—adv.* **30.** absolutely; completely: *dead right.* **31.** with abrupt and complete stoppage of motion, etc.: *he stopped dead.* **32.** directly; exactly; diametrically: *the wind was dead ahead.* [ME *deed*, OE *dēad*, c. G *tot*; orig. pp. See DIE] **—dead′ness,** *n.*

—Syn. 1. DEAD, DECEASED, EXTINCT, LIFELESS refer to something which does not have (or appear to have) life. DEAD is usually applied to that which had life but from which life is now gone:

dead trees, animals; they recovered the dead bodies. DECEASED, a more formal word than DEAD, is applied to human beings who no longer have life: *a deceased member of the church.* EXTINCT is applied esp. to a race, species, or the like, no member of which is any longer alive: *mastodons are now extinct.* LIFELESS is applied to what may or may not have had life but which does not have it (or appear to have it) now: *the lifeless body of a child was taken out of the water, minerals consist of lifeless materials.* **4.** unfeeling, indifferent, callous. **10.** still, motionless, inert, inoperative. **—Ant.** 1. living, alive.

dead-ball line (dĕd′bôl′), *Rugby Football.* a line 10 yards behind the goal line, running parallel to it, beyond which the ball passes out of play.

dead beat, 1. *Slang.* a loafer; sponger. **2.** *Colloq.* a beatnik.

deadbeat (dĕd′bēt′), *adj. Physics, etc.* **1.** free from oscillation or recoil; aperiodic. **2.** having an index needle that comes to a stop with little or no oscillation.

dead-beat (dĕd′bēt′), *adj. Colloq.* **1.** very tired; exhausted. **2.** disreputable; socially undesirable.

dead centre, 1. (in a reciprocating engine or pump) either of two positions of the crank in which the connecting rod has no power to turn it, occurring when the crank and connecting rod are in the same plane, at each end of a stroke. **Top** (or **inner**) **dead centre** is the position of the piston when it is at the top of its stroke; **bottom** (or **outer**) **dead centre** is the position of the piston at the bottom of its stroke. **2.** *Mach.* a stationary centre which holds the work, as the tailstock of a lathe.

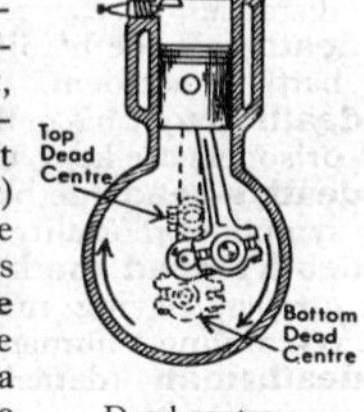

Dead centre

deaden (dĕd′n), *v.t.* **1.** to make less sensitive, active, energetic, or forcible; dull; weaken: *to deaden sound, the force of a ball, the senses.* **2.** to lessen the velocity of; retard. **3.** to make impervious to sound, as a floor. *—v.i.* **4.** to become dead. —**dead′ener,** *n.*

dead end, a cul-de-sac.

dead-end (dĕd′ĕnd′), *adj.* **1.** leading nowhere. **2.** offering no future: *dead-end job.* **3.** having no apparent hopes or future, as a juvenile delinquent: *dead-end kid.*

deadening (dĕd′n ĭng), *n.* **1.** a device or material employed to deaden or render dull. **2.** a device or material preventing the transmission of sound. *—adj.* **3.** dulling or rendering less sensitive, as pain, light, sound, etc.

deadeye (dĕd′ī′), *n.* **1.** *Naut.* a round, laterally flattened block encircled by a rope or an iron band and pierced with three holes. **2.** *Slang.* an accurate shot; marksman.

deadfall (dĕd′fôl′), *n.* a trap, esp. for large game, in which a weight falls upon and crushes the prey.

dead freight, the sum paid for that part of a vessel not occupied by cargo when the whole vessel is chartered.

dead hand, *Law.* mortmain.

deadhead (dĕd′hĕd′), *n. U.S. Colloq.* one who attends a theatre, rides in a public vehicle, etc., without payment.

dead heat, a heat or race in which two or more competitors finish together.

dead letter, 1. a law, ordinance, etc., which has lost its force, though not formally repealed or abolished. **2.** a letter which lies unclaimed for a certain time at a post office, or which, because of faulty address, etc., cannot be delivered. Such letters are sent to and handled in a special division or department (**dead-letter office**) of the post office. —**dead′-let′ter,** *adj.*

Deadeyes

deadlight (dĕd′līt′), *n. Naut.* **1.** a strong wooden or iron shutter for a cabin window or porthole, to prevent water from entering. **2.** a thick pane of glass set in the hull or deck to admit light.

deadline (dĕd′līn′), *n.* **1.** a line or limit that must not be passed. **2.** the latest time for finishing something.

dead load, a load that is permanent and immovable, as the weight of a bridge.

deadlock (dĕd′lŏk′), *n.* **1.** a state of affairs in which progress is impossible; complete standstill. *—v.t.* **2.** to bring to a deadlock. *—v.i.* **3.** to come to a deadlock.

deadly (dĕd′lĭ), *adj.*, **-lier, -liest,** *adv. —adj.* **1.** causing or tending to cause death; fatal: *a deadly poison.* **2.** aiming to kill or destroy; implacable: *a deadly enemy.* **3.** involving spiritual death: *a deadly sin.* **4.** like death: *a deadly pallor.* **5.** excessive: *deadly haste.* *—adv.* **6.** in a manner resembling or suggesting death: *deadly pale.* **7.** *Colloq.* excessively: *deadly dull.* —**dead′liness,** *n.* **—Syn. 1.** See **fatal.**

deadly nightshade, the belladonna.

deadly sins, pride, covetousness, lust, anger, gluttony, envy, and sloth.

dead man's handle, a handle for controlling the speed of an electric train or other vehicle which requires the constant pressure of the driver's hand to maintain the current supply.

dead man's pedal, a pedal which operates as a dead man's handle.

dead march, a piece of solemn music for a funeral procession, esp. one played at a military funeral.

dead men's fingers, 1. the gills of a lobster or crab. **2.** the soft coral *Alcyonium digitatum*, of European coastal waters. **3.** any of various species of orchid, esp. the European *Orchis latifolia* and *O. maculata.* Also, **dead man's fingers.**

deadnettle (dĕd′nĕt′l), *n.* any plant of the genus *Lamium*, superficially like the nettle in appearance, but stingless.

dead pan, *U.S. Colloq.* a deadpan expression or person.

deadpan (dĕd′păn′), *adj. Colloq.* **1.** (of a person or his face) completely lacking expression or reaction. **2.** said without any indication in the speaker's manner or expression that he is aware of the force or implication of what is said: *deadpan humour.*

dead point, dead centre.

dead reckoning, *Navig.* **1.** the calculation of a ship's, aircraft's, or other vehicle's position without astronomical observations, by means of the distances sailed on the various courses as shown by the log and compass, with corrections for currents, etc. **2.** position as so calculated.

Dead Sea, a salt lake between Israel and Jordan: the lowest lake in the world. 46 mi. long; 10 mi. wide; 1293 feet below sea-level. See map under **Bethlehem.**

Dead Sea scrolls, a collection of ancient Hebrew and Aramaic scriptural manuscripts dating from 2nd century B.C. to A.D. 70, found in caves NW of the Dead Sea, in 1947 and 1952.

dead shore, one of a set of vertical posts supporting masonry while an opening is made through it.

dead-stick landing (dĕd′stĭk′), *Aeron.* a landing made with a dead engine.

dead time, *Elect.* (in a circuit) the interval time after the circuit has responded to a stimulus during which it cannot respond to a second stimulus.

dead weight, 1. the heavy, unrelieved weight of anything inert. **2.** a heavy or oppressive burden. **3.** *Naut.* the difference in weight, displacement, etc., between a ship or other vehicle when loaded and when empty.

deadwood (dĕd′wŏŏd′), *n.* **1.** the dead branches on a tree; dead branches or trees. **2.** anything useless. **3.** *Naut.* a wooden wedge at the keel of a yacht.

deaf (dĕf), *adj.* **1.** lacking or deprived of the sense of hearing, wholly or partially; unable to hear. **2.** refusing to listen; heedless; inattentive: *deaf to advice, turn a deaf ear to a plea.* *—n.* **3. the deaf,** people unable to hear. [ME *deef*, OE *dēaf*, c. G *taub*] —**deaf′ly,** *adv.* —**deaf′ness,** *n.*

deaf-aid (dĕf′ād′), *n.* an electrical or other device used by the deaf to improve their hearing; hearing aid.

deafen (dĕf′ən), *v.t.* **1.** to make deaf. **2.** to stun with noise. **3.** to render (a sound) inaudible, esp. by a louder sound. —**deaf′eningly,** *adv.*

deaf-mute (dĕf′myōōt′), *n.* a person who is deaf and dumb, esp. one in whom inability to speak is due to congenital or early deafness.

deal[1] (dēl), *v.*, **dealt, dealing,** *n.* *—v.i.* **1.** to occupy oneself or itself (fol. by *with* or *in*): *deal with the first question, botany deals with the study of plants.* **2.** to take action with respect to a thing or person (usually fol. by *with*): *law courts must deal with lawbreakers.* **3.** to conduct oneself towards persons: *deal fairly.* **4.** to trade or do business: *to deal with a firm, to deal in an article.* **5.** to distribute, esp. the cards required in a game. *—v.t.* **6.** to give to one as his share; apportion (often fol. by *out*). **7.** to distribute among a number of recipients, as the cards required in a game. **8.** *Cards.* to give a player (a specific card) in dealing. **9.** to deliver (blows, etc.). *—n.* **10.** *Colloq.* a business transaction. **11.** a bargain or arrangement for mutual advantage, as in commerce or politics, often a secret or underhand one. **12.** treatment; arrangement: *a raw deal, a fair deal.* **13.** a quantity, amount, extent, or degree. **14.** an indefinite but large amount or extent: *a deal of money.* **15.** act of dealing or distributing. **16.** *Cards.* **a.** the distribution to the players of the cards in a game. **b.** the set of cards in one's hand. **c.** the turn of a player to deal. **d.** the period of time during which a deal is played. **17.** *Obs.* portion or share. [ME *delen*, OE *dǣlan* (c. G *teilen*, etc.), der. *dǣl* part (c. G *Teil*)] **—Syn. 6.** allot, assign.

deal[2] (dēl), *n.* **1.** a board or plank, esp. of fir or pine, in Britain usually 9 inches wide and 6 feet long, and less than 3 inches thick; in the U.S. and Canada, 11 inches wide, 12 feet long, 2 inches thick. **2.** such boards collectively. **3.** fir or pine wood. *—adj.* **4.** made of fir or pine wood. **5.** in the form of deal (def. 1). [ME *dele*, t. MLG or MD]

Deal (dēl), *n.* a town in England, in E Kent: seaside resort. 24,815 (1961).

dealer (dē′lə), *n.* **1.** one who buys and sells articles without altering their condition; trader or merchant. **2.** *Cards.* the player distributing the cards.

dealfish (dēl′fĭsh′), *n., pl.* **-fishes,** (*esp. collectively*) **-fish.** any of the deep-sea fishes constituting the genus *Trachypterus,* characterized by a long, compressed, tapelike body. [f. DEAL[2] + FISH]

dealing (dē′lĭng), *n.* **1.** (*usually pl.*) relations; trading: *business dealings.* **2.** conduct in relation to others; treatment: *honest dealing.*

dealt (dĕlt), *v.* pt. and pp. of **deal**[1].

dean[1] (dēn), *n.* **1.** *Educ.* **a.** the official, usually a member of the teaching staff, in charge of undergraduates, internal organization, etc., at a university, college, or a similar institute of learning. **b.** the head of a medical school, university faculty, or the like. **c.** *U.S.* a college or university official in charge of personnel, students, etc. **2.** *Eccles.* **a.** the head of the chapter of a cathedral or a collegiate church. **b.** any of various other ecclesiastical dignitaries, as the head of a division of a diocese. **3.** the senior member, in length of service, of any body; father. [ME *deen,* t. OF: m. *deien,* g. LL *decānus* chief of ten] **—dean′ship,** *n.*

dean[2] (dēn), *n.* dene.

Dean (dēn), *n.* **Forest of,** an area in England, in W Gloucestershire, formerly a royal forest.

deanery (dē′nə rĭ), *n., pl.* **-eries.** **1.** the office, jurisdiction, or district of a dean. **2.** the residence of a dean.

dear[1] (dĭə), *adj.* **1.** beloved or loved: *a dear friend of mine.* **2.** (in the salutation of a letter) highly esteemed: *Dear Sirs.* **3.** precious in one's regard: *our dearest possessions.* **4.** high-priced; expensive. **5.** charging high prices. **6.** high; excessive: *a dear price to pay.* **7.** *Obs.* worthy. **—*n.*** **8.** one who is dear. **9.** a beloved one (often used in direct address): *my dear.* **—*adv.*** **10.** dearly; fondly. **11.** at a high price. **—*interj.*** **12.** (an exclamation of surprise, distress, etc.) [ME *dere,* OE *dēore,* c. G *teuer*] **—dear′ly** *adv.* **—dear′ness,** *n.* **—Syn. 4.** See **expensive. —Ant. 4.** cheap.

dear[2] (dĭə), *adj. Archaic.* hard; grievous. Also, **dere.** [ME *dere,* OE *dēor*; cf. Icel. *dȳr* difficult, rigorous]

Dearborn (dĭə′bən, -bôn′), *n.* **1.** a city in the U.S., in SE Michigan, near Detroit. 112,007 (1960). **2. Fort,** a former U.S. fort on the site of Chicago, 1803–37.

dearth (dûth), *n.* **1.** scarcity or scanty supply; lack. **2.** scarcity and dearness of food; famine. [ME *derthe.* See DEAR[2], -TH[1]]

deary (dĭə′rĭ), *n., pl.* **dearies.** (esp. as an affectionate or colloquial term of address by an elderly woman) dear; darling. Also, **dearie.**

deasil (dĕs′əl, dĕsh′əl), *adv. Scot.* clockwise. [t. Gaelic: m. *deiseil* to the right, ult. c. L *dexter*]

death (dĕth), *n.* **1.** the act of dying; the end of life; the total and permanent cessation of the vital functions of an animal or plant. **2.** (*often cap.*) the annihilating power personified, usually represented as a skeleton: '*O Death, where is thy sting?*' **3.** the state of being dead: *to lie still in death.* **4.** extinction; destruction: *it will mean the death of our hopes.* **5.** the time at which a person dies: *the letters may be published after my death.* **6.** manner of dying: *a hero's death.* **7.** loss or deprivation of civil life. **8.** loss or absence of spiritual life. **9.** bloodshed or murder. **10.** a cause or occasion of death: *you'll be the death of me.* **11.** a pestilence: *the black death.* **12. at death's door,** in danger of death; gravely ill. **13. do to death, a.** to kill. **b.** to repeat until hackneyed. **14. in at the death, a.** *Hunting.* present when the hunted animal is caught and killed. **b.** present at the climax or conclusion of a series of events or a situation. **15. put to death,** to kill; execute. **16. sick to death,** *Colloq.* irritated or annoyed to an extreme degree. [ME *deeth,* OE *dēath,* c. G *Tod*] **—Syn. 1.** decease, demise, passing, departure.

death-adder (dĕth′ăd′ə), *n.* a venomous viper-like snake, *Acanthopis antarcticus,* of Australasia, having a stout body and broad head.

deathbed (dĕth′bĕd′), *n.* **1.** the bed on which a person dies. **2.** the last few hours before death.

death bell, the bell that announces a death.

deathblow (dĕth′blō′), *n.* a blow causing death.

death cell, a building or part of a prison in which persons condemned to death await execution.

death certificate, a certificate issued compulsorily on the death of each person, signed by a qualified medical practitioner to certify death and its cause if known.

death cup, 1. a poisonous toadstool of the genus *Amanita,* part of which persists around the base of the stipe as a definite membranous cup. **2.** the cup.

death duty, (*usually pl.*) a tax paid upon the inheritance of property.

deathful (dĕth′fəl), *adj.* **1.** fatal. **2.** deathlike.

death knell, 1. death bell. **2.** the harbinger of the death or destruction of a person or thing. **3.** anything which precipitates the end of a plan or action.

deathless (dĕth′lĭs), *adj.* **1.** not subject to death; immortal. **2.** perpetual. **—death′lessly,** *adv.* **—death′lessness,** *n.*

deathlike (dĕth′līk′), *adj.* resembling death.

deathly (dĕth′lĭ), *adj.* **1.** causing death; deadly; fatal. **2.** like death. **3.** *Poetic.* of death. **—*adv.*** **4.** in the manner of death. **5.** very; utterly: *deathly afraid.* [ME *dethlich,* OE *dēathlīc*]

death mask, a cast of a person's face taken after death.

death rate, the number of deaths per unit (usually 1000) of population in a given place and time.

death-rattle (dĕth′răt′l), *n.* a sound sometimes produced in the throat immediately before death, caused by the passage of air through collected mucus.

death ray, a hypothetical ray able to destroy life from a distance.

death-roll (dĕth′rōl′), *n.* a list of persons killed, as in a battle or accident.

death row, *Colloq.* the group of cells in which condemned prisoners are kept, esp. in the U.S.

death's-head (dĕths′hĕd′), *n.* a human skull, esp. as a symbol of mortality.

death's-head moth, a European hawkmoth, *Acherontia atropos,* having markings on the back of the thorax resembling a human skull.

deathsman (dĕths′mən), *n., pl.* **-men.** *Archaic.* an executioner.

deathtrap (dĕth′trăp′), *n.* a structure or situation involving imminent risk of death.

Death Valley, an arid basin in E California; lowest land in the Western Hemisphere. 276 ft below sea-level.

death warrant, 1. an official order authorizing the execution of the sentence of death. **2.** anything which ends hope, expectation, etc.

deathwatch (dĕth′wŏch′), *n.* **1.** a vigil beside a dying or dead person. **2.** a guard set over a condemned person before execution.

deathwatch beetle, any of certain beetles of the family *Anobiidae* which infest timbers, esp. in Europe. The ticking sound caused by their heads tapping against wood was thought to presage death.

death-wish (dĕth′wĭsh′), *n.* the desire, esp. subconscious, for one's own death, or sometimes for the death of another.

deathy (dĕth′ĭ), *adj., adv. Rare.* deathly.

Deauville (dō′vēl; *Fr.* dō vēl′), *n.* a coastal resort in NW France, in Calvados department, S of Le Havre. 5239 (1962).

deave (dēv), *v.t.,* **deaved, deaving.** *Dial.* to make deaf; deafen. [ME *deve,* OE *dēafian*]

deb., **1.** debenture. **2.** debutante.

debacle (dā bä′kl, dĭ-), *n.* **1.** a general break-up or rout; sudden overthrow or collapse; overwhelming disaster. **2.** a breaking up of ice in a river. **3.** a violent rush of waters. Also, *French,* **débâcle** (*Fr.* dė bȧ′kl). [t. F, der. *débâcler* unbar, clear, f. *dé-* DIS-[1] + *bâcler* bar (der. L *baculum* stick, rod)]

debag (dē băg′), *v.t.,* **-bagged, -bagging.** *Colloq.* to remove the trousers of, as a joke or punishment.

debar (dĭ bä′), *v.t.,* **-barred, -barring. 1.** to bar out or exclude from a place or condition. **2.** to prevent or prohibit (an action, etc.). [t. F: m. s. *débarrer,* OF *desbarrer,* f. *des-* DIS-[1] + *barrer* BAR[1], v.] **—debar′ment,** *n.* **—Syn. 1.** See **exclude. 2.** interdict, hinder. **—Ant. 1.** admit. **2.** permit.

debark (dĭ bäk′), *v.t., v.i.* to disembark. [t. F: m. s. *débarquer,* der. *dé-* DIS-[1] + *barque* BARQUE[3]] **—debarkation** (dē′bä kā′shən), *n.*

debase (dĭ bās′), *v.t.,* **-based, -basing. 1.** to reduce in quality or value; adulterate. **2.** to lower in rank or dignity. [f. DE- + obs. *base* (aphetic var. of ABASE)] **—debase′ment,** *n.* **—debas′er,** *n.* **—debas′ingly,** *adv.* **—Syn. 1.** lower, vitiate, corrupt, deteriorate.

debatable (dĭ bā′tə bl), *adj.* **1.** capable of being debated. **2.** in dispute. Also, **debateable**

debate (dĭ bāt′), *n., v.,* **-bated, -bating. —*n.*** **1.** a discussion, esp. of a public question in an assembly. **2.** deliberation; consideration. **3.** a systematic contest of speakers in which two opposing points of view of a proposition are advanced. **4.** *Obs.* strife; contention. **—*v.i.*** **5.** to engage in discussion, esp. in a legislative or public assembly. **6.** to deliberate; consider; discuss or argue. **7.** *Obs.* to fight; quarrel. **—*v.t.*** **8.** to discuss or argue (a question), as in a public assembly. **9.** to dispute about. **10.** to deliberate upon; consider. **11.** *Archaic.* to contend for or over. [ME *debate(n),* t. OF: m. *debatre,*

f. *de-* DE- + *batre* BEAT] —**debat′er,** *n.* —**Syn. 1.** argument, controversy, disputation. **6.** See **argue.**

debauch (dĭ bôch′), *v.t.* **1.** to corrupt by sensuality, intemperance, etc.; seduce. **2.** to corrupt or pervert; deprave. **3.** *Obs.* to lead away, as from allegiance or duty. —*v.i.* **4.** to indulge in a debauch. —*n.* **5.** a period of debauchery. **6.** debauchery. [t. F: s. *débaucher,* OF *desbaucher* seduce from duty] —**debauched′,** *adj.* —**debauch′er,** *n.* —**debauch′ment,** *n.*

debauchee (dĕb′ô chē′, -shē′), *n.* one addicted to excessive indulgence in sensual pleasures; one given to debauchery. [t. F: m. *débauché,* pp. of *débaucher* DEBAUCH]

debauchery (dĭ bô′chə rĭ), *n., pl.* **-eries. 1.** excessive indulgence in sensual pleasures; intemperance. **2.** *Obs.* seduction from virtue, allegiance, or duty.

de bene esse (dā′ bĕn′ĭ ĕs′ĭ), *Law.* (of evidence) valid for the time being, but to be considered more fully later.

debenture (dĭ bĕn′chə), *n.* **1.** a note or certificate acknowledging a debt, as given by an incorporated company; a bond or one of a series of bonds. **2.** a deed containing a charge or mortgage on a company's assets; a mortgage debenture. **3.** a certificate of drawback issued at a customs house. [t. L: m. *dēbentur* there are owing]

debenture stock, a series or group of debentures for a single debt.

debilitate (dĭ bĭl′ĭ tāt′), *v.t.,* **-tated, -tating.** to make weak or feeble; weaken; enfeeble. [t. L: m. s. *dēbilitātus,* pp., weakened] —**debil′ita′tion,** *n.* —**debilitative** (dĭ bĭl′ĭ-tə tĭv), *adj.*

debility (dĭ bĭl′ĭ tĭ), *n., pl.* **-ties. 1.** the state of being weak or feeble; weakness. **2.** *Pathol.* a condition of the body in which the vital functions are feebly discharged. [ME *debylite,* t. L: m. s. *dēbilitas* weakness]

debit (dĕb′ĭt), *n.* **1.** the recording of an entry of debt in an account. **2.** *Bookkeeping.* **a.** that which is entered in an account as a debt; a recorded item of debt. **b.** any entry, or the total shown, on the debit side. **c.** the side (left side) of an account on which such entries are made (opposed to *credit*). —*v.t.* **3.** to charge with a debt. **4.** to charge as a debt. **5.** *Bookkeeping.* to enter upon the debit side of an account. [t. L: s. *dēbitum* something owed. See DEBT]

de Blank (də blăngk′), **Joost.** See **Blank.**

debonair (dĕb′ə nėə′), *adj.* **1.** of pleasant manners; courteous. **2.** gay; sprightly. Also, **deb′onaire′, deb′onnaire′.** [ME *debonere,* t. OF: m. *debonaire,* orig. phrase *de bon aire* of good disposition] —**deb′onair′ly,** *adv.* —**deb′onair′ness,** *n.*

de bonne grace (*Fr.* də bŏn grȧs′), *French.* graciously.

Deborah (dĕb′ə rə), *n. Bible.* a prophetess and judge of Israel. Judges 4, 5.

debouch (dĭ bouch′), *v.i.* **1.** to march out from a narrow or confined place into open country, as a body of troops. 2. *Phys. Geog.* **a.** to emerge from a relatively narrow valley upon an open plain: *a river or glacier debouches on the plains.* **b.** to flow from a small valley into a larger one. **3.** to issue; emerge. —*n.* **4.** débouché. [t. F: m. s. *déboucher,* der. *dé-* DIS-[1] + *bouche* mouth (g. L *bucca* cheek, mouth)]

débouché (*Fr.* dė bo͞o shė′), *n. French.* **1.** *Fort.* an opening in works for passing troops. **2.** an outlet; an exit.

debouchment (dĭ bouch′mənt), *n.* **1.** the act or fact of debouching. **2.** a mouth or outlet, as of a river or pass.

Debrecen (*Hung.* dĕ′brĕ tsĕn), *n.* a city in E Hungary. 137,000 (1960).

debrief (dē′brēf′), *v.t. Orig. U.S.* to interrogate (a soldier, astronaut, diplomat, etc.) on return from a mission in order to assess the conduct and results of the mission. —**de′brief′ing,** *n.*

debris (dā′brē, dĕb′rē), *n.* **1.** the remains of anything broken down or destroyed; ruins; fragments; rubbish. **2.** *Geol.* an accumulation of loose fragments of rock, etc. Also, **dé′bris.** [t. F: m. *débris,* der. OF *debrisier* break down, f. *de-* DE- + *brisier* break (cf. BRUISE)]

de Broglie (*Fr.* də brŏy′). See **Broglie.**

Debs (dĕbz), *n.* **Eugene Victor,** 1855–1926, U.S. labour leader; Socialist candidate for president 1900, 1904, 1908, 1912, and 1920.

debt (dĕt), *n.* **1.** that which is owed; that which one person is bound to pay to or perform for another. **2.** a liability or obligation to pay or render something. **3.** the condition of being under such an obligation. **4.** *Theol.* an offence requiring reparation; a sin; a trespass. **5. bad debt,** a debt of which there is no prospect of payment. [ME *det,* t. OF: m. *dete,* g. L *dēbitum* (thing) owed, prop. pp. neut.] —**Syn. 1.** obligation, duty, due.

debt of honour, a debt which is not legally recoverable, as a gambling debt.

debtor (dĕt′ə), *n.* one who is in debt or under obligations to another (opposed to *creditor*).

debug (dē bŭg′), *v.t.,* **-bugged, -bugging.** *Colloq.* **1.** to detect and remove faults in (an electronic system). **2.** to detect and remove electronic listening devices from (a room or the like).

debunk (dē bŭngk′), *v.t. Colloq.* to strip of false sentiments, opinions, etc., about.

debus (dē′bŭs′), *v.i., v.t.,* **-bussed, -bussing.** *Chiefly Mil.* to get out of or take out of a bus or other vehicle serving as a bus. [DE- + BUS]

Debussy (də bo͞o′sĭ; *Fr.* də bʏ sē′), *n.* **Claude Achille** (*Fr.* klōd ȧ shēl′), 1862–1918, French composer.

debut (dā′bo͞o, dā′byo͞o, dĕb′yo͞o), *n.* **1.** a first public appearance on a stage, on television, etc. **2.** a formal introduction and entrance into society. **3.** the beginning of a professional career, etc. Also, *French,* **début** (*Fr.* dė bʏ′). [t. F, der. *débuter* make the first stroke in a game, make one's first appearance, der. *dé-* DE- + *but* goal, mark]

debutante (dĕb′yo͞o tänt′, -tănt′), *n.* a girl making a debut, esp. into society. Also, *French,* **débutante** (*Fr.* dė bʏ tänt′). [t. F, fem. ppr. of *débuter.* See DEBUT] —**deb′utant′,** *n. masc.*

dec-, var. of **deca-.**

Dec., December.

dec., 1. deceased. **2.** decimetre. **3.** declension. **4.** decrease. **5.** decrescendo.

deca-, a word element meaning 'ten', specialized in the metric system so that *deca-* (deka-) gives the multiplication by 10, *deci-* the division by 10; e.g. *decalitre* (610·25 cu. in.), *litre* (61·025 cu. in), *decilitre* (6·10 cu. in.). Cf. **deci-.** [t. Gk: m. *deka-,* comb. form of *déka* ten]

decade (dĕk′ād), *n.* **1.** a period of ten years. **2.** a group, set, or series of ten. [t. F, t. L: m. s. *decas,* t. Gk: m. *dekás* a group of ten] —**decad′al,** *adj.*

decadence (dĕk′ə dəns), *n.* the act or process of falling into an inferior condition or state, esp. moral; decay; deterioration. Also, **decadency** (dĕk′ə dən sĭ). [t. F, ult. der. L *dē* DE- + *cadere* fall] —**Syn.** decline, degeneration, retrogression.

decadent (dĕk′ə dənt), *adj.* **1.** deteriorating, as morally or aesthetically. **2.** of or like the Decadents. —*n.* **3.** one who is decadent. **4.** (*often cap.*) one of a group of French (and other) writers and artists towards the end of the 19th century whose work was characterized by great refinement or subtlety of style with a marked tendency towards the artificial and abnormal. [der. DECADENCE] —**de′cadently,** *adv.*

decagon (dĕk′ə gən), *n. Geom.* a polygon having 10 angles and 10 sides. [t. ML: s. *decagōnum.* See DECA-, -GON] —**decagonal** (dĭ kăg′ə nəl), *adj.*

Decagon

decagram (dĕk′ə grăm′), *n. Metric System.* a unit of 10 grams, equivalent to 0·3527 ounce avoirdupois. Also, **dec′agramme′.** [t. F: m. *decagramme.* See DECA-, GRAM]

decahedron (dĕk′ə hē′drən), *n., pl.* **-drons, -dra** (-drə). *Geom.* a solid figure having 10 faces. —**decahedral** (dĕk′ə hē′drəl), *adj.*

decal (dĭ kăl′), *n.* **1.** the art or process of transferring pictures or designs from specially prepared paper to wood, metal, china, glass, etc. **2.** the paper bearing such a picture or design. —*v.t.* **3.** to transfer (a design) on to such a surface. [short for DECALCOMANIA]

decalcify (dē kăl′sĭ fī′), *v.t.,* **-fied, -fying.** to deprive (esp. a bone) of lime or calcareous matter. —**decalcification** (dē kăl′sĭ fĭ kā′shən), *n.*

decalcomania (dĭ kăl′kə mā′nyə), *n.* decal. [t. F: m. *décalcomanie,* f. *décalco-* (repr. *décalquer* transfer a tracing of) + *manie* MANIA]

decalescence (dē′kə lĕs′əns), *n.* (in the heating of iron) the sudden absorption of heat observed as it passes a certain temperature. —**de′cales′cent,** *adj.*

decalitre (dĕk′ə lē′tə), *n. Metric System.* a unit of 10 litres, equivalent to 2·1998 gallons or 2·64 U.S. gallons. Also, **dekalitre**; *esp. U.S.,* **dec′alit′er.** [t. F. See DECA-, LITRE]

Decalogue (dĕk′ə lŏg′), *n.* (*sometimes l.c.*) the Ten Commandments. Ex. 20:2–17. [ME *decaloge,* t. LL: m. s. *decalogus,* t. MGk: m. *dekálogos,* f. *déka* ten + *lógos* word]

Decameron (dĭ kăm′ə rən), *n.* **The,** a collection of 100 tales (1353) by Boccaccio. [t. It.: m. *Decamerone,* f. Gk *déka* ten + *hēmerōn* (gen. pl.) of days; the book being divided into ten days on each of which ten tales are told]

decametre (dĕk′ə mē′tə), *n. Metric System.* a measure of length equal to 10 metres. Also, **dekametre**; *esp. U.S.,* **dec′ame′ter.** [t. F: m. *décamètre.* See DECA-, METRE]

decamp (dĭ kămp′), *v.i.* **1.** to depart from a camp; break camp. **2.** to depart quickly, secretly, or unceremoniously. [t. F: m. s. *décamper,* f. *dé-* DIS-[1] + *camper* encamp] —**decamp′ment,** *n.*

decanal (dĭ kā′nəl), *adj.* **1.** of or pertaining to a dean or his office. —*n.* **2.** the decani. [f. ML *decānus* dean + -AL[1]] —**decanally** (dĭ kā′nə lĭ), *adv.*

decane (dĕk′ān), *n. Chem.* a hydrocarbon, $C_{10}H_{22}$, of the methane series, occurring in several isomeric forms.

decani (dĭ kā′nī), *n.* the portion of a cathedral choir on the south or dean's side. [t. ML: gen. of *decānus* dean]

decant (dĭ kănt′), *v.t.* **1.** to pour off gently, as liquor, without disturbing the sediment. **2.** to pour from one container into another. [t. ML: m. s. *dēcanthāre.* See DE-, CANT[2]] —**decantation** (dē′kăn tā′shən), *n.*

decanter (dĭ kăn′tə), *n.* **1.** a bottle used for decanting. **2.** a vessel, usually an ornamental bottle, from which wine, water, etc., are served at table.

decapitate (dĭ kăp′ĭ tāt′), *v.t.*, **-tated, -tating.** to cut off the head of; behead; kill by beheading. [t. ML: m. s. *dēcapitātus*, pp. of *dēcapitāre*, der. L *caput* head] —**de-cap′ita′tion,** *n.* —**decap′ita′tor,** *n.*

decapod (dĕk′ə pŏd′), *n.* **1.** any crustacean of the order *Decapoda*, including crabs, lobsters, crayfish, prawns, shrimps, etc., characterized by their five pairs of walking legs. **2.** any ten-armed dibranchiate cephalopod, as the cuttlefish, squid, etc. —*adj.* **3.** belonging to the *Decapoda.* **4.** having ten limbs. —**decapodous** (dĭ kăp′ə dəs), *adj.*

Decapolis (dĭ kăp′ ə lĭs), *n.* a region in NE part of ancient Palestine, the site of a first-century B.C. confederacy of ten cities. See map under **Jericho.**

decarb., decarbonization.

decarbonize (dē kä′bə nīz′), *v.t.*, **-nized, -nizing.** to remove the carbon deposit from the walls of the combustion chamber and piston head of an internal-combustion engine. Also, **decarbonise.** —**decar′boniza′tion,** *n.*

decarburize (dē kä′byŏŏə rīz′), *v.t.*, **-rized, -rizing.** *Metall.* to remove carbon from the surface of molten steel. Also, **decarburise.** —**decar′buriza′tion,** *n.*

decare (dĕk′ĕə, dē kĕə′), *n. Metric System.* a unit of area equal to 10 ares.

decartelize (dē kä′tə līz′), *v.t.*, **-lized, -lizing.** to break up or dissolve (a cartel, def. 1). Also, **decartelise.** —**decar′teliza′tion,** *n.*

decastere (dĕk′ə stĭə′), *n. Metric System.* a unit of volume equal to 10 steres.

decasualize (dē kăzh′yŏŏ ə līz′), *v.t.*, **-lized, -lizing.** **1.** to reduce or eliminate the employment of casual labour in (a firm, industry, etc.). **2.** to change the status of (a casual worker), as to permanent employment. Also, **decasualise.** —**decas′ualiza′tion,** *n.*

decasyllabic (dĕk′ə sĭ lăb′ĭk), *adj.* **1.** having ten syllables. —*n.* **2.** (*pl.*) decasyllabic verse.

decasyllable (dĕk′ə sĭl′ə bl), *n.* a line or verse of ten syllables.

decathlon (dĭ kăth′lŏn), *n.* an athletic contest comprising ten different events, and won by the contestant having the highest total score. [f. DECA- + Gk *âthlon* contest]

Decatur (dĭ kā′tə), *n.* **Stephen,** 1779–1820, U.S. naval officer.

decay (dĭ kā′), *v.i.* **1.** to fall away from a state of excellence, prosperity, health, etc.; deteriorate; decline. **2.** to become decomposed; rot. **3.** *Physics.* **a.** (of a radioactive substance) to transform into a daughter product. **b.** (of an elementary particle) to transform into a more stable particle. **4.** *Electronics.* (of a current or voltage) to fall away after the source of energy has been removed from the circuit. —*v.t.* **5.** to cause to decay. —*n.* **6.** a gradual falling into an inferior condition; progressive decline. **7.** loss of strength, health, intellect, etc. **8.** decomposition; rotting. **9.** *Physics.* the disintegration of a radioactive substance or the transformation of an elementary particle into one of greater stability. **10.** *Electronics.* the falling away of a current or voltage after the source of energy has been removed from the circuit. **11.** *Obs.* a wasting disease, esp. consumption. [ME *decay(en)*, t. OF: m. s. *decair*, f. *de-* DE- + *cair* (g. L *cadere* fall)]

—**Syn. 2.** DECAY, DECOMPOSE, DISINTEGRATE, ROT, PUTREFY, imply a deterioration or falling away from a sound condition. DECAY implies either entire or partial dissolution or deterioration by progressive natural changes: *teeth decay.* DECOMPOSE suggests the reducing of a substance, through natural change or human agency, to its component elements: *moisture makes some chemical compounds decompose.* DISINTEGRATE emphasizes the breaking up, going to pieces, or wearing away of anything, so that its original wholeness is impaired: *rocks disintegrate.* PUTREFY and ROT are stronger words than DECAY and are esp. applied to decaying matter which may or may not emit offensive smells. PUTREFY is usually applied to animal matter: *putrefying flesh*; ROT to vegetable matter: *potatoes rot.* **6.** deterioration, decadence, impairment, dilapidation.

Decca (dĕk′ə), *n. Trademark.* a short-range marine and aviation radio navigation aid.

Deccan (dĕk′ən), *n.* **1.** the entire peninsula of India S of the Narbada river. **2.** the plateau region between the Narbada and Kistna rivers.

decease (dĭ sēs′), *n., v.*, **-ceased, -ceasing.** —*n.* **1.** departure from life; death. —*v.i.* **2.** to depart from life; die. [ME *deces*, t. OF, t. L: m. s. *dēcessus* departure, death] —**Syn. 2.** See **die**[1].

deceased (dĭ sēst′), *adj.* **1.** dead. —*n.* **2. the deceased,** the dead person. —**Syn. 1.** See **dead.**

decedent (dĭ sē′dnt), *n. Now Chiefly U.S. Law.* a deceased person. [t. L: s. *dēcēdens*, ppr., departing]

deceit (dĭ sēt′), *n.* **1.** the act or practice of deceiving; concealment or perversion of the truth for the purpose of misleading; fraud; cheating. **2.** an act or device intended to deceive; a trick; stratagem. **3.** deceiving quality; falseness. [ME *deceite*, t. OF, der. *deceveir* DECEIVE]

—**Syn. 1.** DECEIT, GUILE, HYPOCRISY imply (usually) deliberate attempts to mislead someone. DECEIT is the habit or practice of intentionally concealing or perverting the truth for the purpose of misleading: *honest and without deceit.* GUILE implies craftiness in the use of deceit: *using guile and trickery to attain one's ends.* HYPOCRISY is the pretended possession of those qualities which would make others believe in one's sincerity, goodness, etc.: *her concern was sheer hypocrisy.* —**Ant. 3.** honesty, sincerity.

deceitful (dĭ sēt′fəl), *adj.* **1.** full of deceit; given to deceiving. **2.** misleading; fraudulent; deceptive. —**deceit′fully,** *adv.* —**deceit′fulness,** *n.* —**Syn. 1.** insincere, disingenuous, false, hollow.

deceive (dĭ sēv′), *v.*, **-ceived, -ceiving.** —*v.t.* **1.** to mislead by a false appearance or statement; delude. **2.** to be unfaithful to; commit adultery against. **3.** *Obs.* to beguile or while away (time, etc.). —*v.i.* **4.** to practise deceit; act deceitfully. [ME *deceyve(n)*, t. OF: m. *deceveir*, g. L *dēcipere* catch, ensnare, deceive] —**deceiv′able,** *adj.* —**deceiv′ableness, deceiv′abil′ity,** *n.* —**deceiv′ably,** *adv.* —**deceiv′er,** *n.* —**deceiv′ingly,** *adv.* —**Syn. 1.** See **cheat.** cozen, dupe, fool, gull, hoodwink, trick, defraud, outwit, entrap, ensnare, betray, bamboozle.

decelerate (dē sĕl′ə rāt′), *v.t., v.i.*, **-rated, -rating.** to decrease in velocity. [f. DE- + (AC)CELERATE] —**decel′era′tion,** *n.* —**decel′era′tor,** *n.*

December (dĭ sĕm′bə), *n.* the twelfth month of the year, containing 31 days. [t. L: the tenth month of the early Roman year; r. ME *decembre*, t. OF]

Decembrist (dĭ sĕm′brĭst), *n. Russian Hist.* a participant in the conspiracy and insurrection against the Tsar Nicholas on his accession in December, 1825.

decemvir (dĭ sĕm′və), *n., pl.* **-virs, -viri** (-vĭ rē′). **1.** a member of a permanent board or a special commission of ten members in ancient Rome, esp. the commission appointed to draw up Rome's first code of law. **2.** a member of any council or ruling body of ten. [t. L, orig. pl., *decemvirī*, f. *decem* ten + *virī* men] —**decem′viral,** *adj.*

decemvirate (dĭ sĕm′vĭ rĭt), *n.* **1.** a body of decemvirs. **2.** the office or government of decemvirs.

decency (dē′sən sĭ), *n., pl.* **-cies. 1.** the state or quality of being decent. **2.** conformity to the recognized standards of propriety, good taste, modesty, etc. **3.** something decent or proper. **4.** (*pl.*) the requirements or observances of decent life or conduct.

decennary (dĭ sĕn′ə rĭ), *n., pl.* **-ries.** a decennium. [f. s. L *decennis* of ten years + -ARY[1]]

decennial (dĭ sĕn′yəl), *adj.* **1.** of or for ten years. **2.** occurring every ten years. —*n.* **3.** a decennial anniversary. **4.** its celebration. —**decen′nially,** *adv.*

decennium (dĭ sĕn′yəm), *n., pl.* **-cenniums, -cennia** (-sĕn′yə). a period of ten years; a decade. [t. L, der. *decennis* of ten years]

decent (dē′sənt), *adj.* **1.** fitting; appropriate. **2.** conforming to recognized standards of propriety, good taste, modesty, etc., as in behaviour or speech. **3.** respectable; worthy: *a decent family.* **4.** of seemly appearance: *decent clothes; are you decent?* **5.** fair; tolerable; passable: *a decent wage.* **6.** *Colloq.* kind; obliging: *thanks, that's frightfully decent of you.* [t. L: s. *decens*, ppr., fitting] —**de′cently,** *adv.* —**de′centness,** *n.* —**Syn. 2.** seemly, proper, decorous.

decentralize (dē′sĕn′trə līz′), *v.t.*, **-lized, -lizing.** to undo the centralization of (administrative powers, etc.) Also, **decentralise.** —**decen′traliza′tion,** *n.*

decentre (dē sĕn′tə), *v.t.*, **-tred, -tring. 1.** to put out of centre. **2.** to make eccentric. Also, *U.S.*, **decenter.**

deception (dĭ sĕp′shən), *n.* **1.** the act of deceiving. **2.** the state of being deceived. **3.** something that deceives or is intended to deceive; an artifice; a sham; a cheat. [ME *decepcioun*, t. LL: m. s. *dēceptio*, der. L *dēcipere* DECEIVE] —**Syn. 3.** imposture, treachery, subterfuge, stratagem, ruse, hoax, fraud. See **trick.**

deceptive (dĭ sĕp′tĭv), *adj.* apt or tending to deceive. [t. NL: m. s. *dēceptīvus*] —**decep′tively,** *adv.* —**decep′tiveness,** *n.* —**Syn.** misleading, delusive, fallacious, specious, false.

decerebrate (dē sĕ′rĭ brāt), *v.t.*, **-brated, -brating.** *Surg.* to interrupt the connection between the brain or a part of the brain and the nervous system.

decerebration (dē sĕ′rĭ brā′shən), *n.* *Surg.* **1.** the interruption of the paths of connection between the brain and the rest of the nervous system. **2.** interruption of the brain's influence on the nervous system by spinal cord transection.

decern (dĭ sûn′), *v.t.* **1.** *Scot. Law.* to decree by judicial sentence. **2.** to discern. [t. L: s. *dēcernere* decide, decree]

deci-, a word element meaning 'ten', specialized in the metric system so that *deci-* gives division by 10, e.g. *decilitre* (6·102 cu. in.), *litre* (61·02 cu. in.). See **deca-.** [comb. form repr. L *decem* ten, *decimus* tenth]

deciare (dĕs′ĭ ĕə′), *n.* *Metric System.* a unit of area equal to one tenth of an are.

decibel (dĕs′ĭ bĕl′), *n.* *Physics.* the unit of power ratio equal to one tenth of a bel.

decide (dĭ sīd′), *v.*, **-cided, -ciding.** —*v.t.* **1.** to determine or settle (a question, controversy, struggle, etc.) by giving victory to one side. **2.** to adjust or settle (anything in dispute or doubt). **3.** to bring (a person) to a decision. —*v.i.* **4.** to settle something in dispute or doubt. **5.** to pronounce a judgement; come to a conclusion. [ME *decide(n)*, t. L: m. *dēcīdere* cut off, determine] —**decid′able,** *adj.*

—**Syn. 1.** DECIDE, RESOLVE, DETERMINE imply setting upon a purpose and being able to adhere to it. To DECIDE is to make up one's mind as to what shall be done and the way to do it: *he decided to go today.* To RESOLVE is usually positively or actively to show firmness of purpose: *he resolved to go out into the blizzard alone.* To DETERMINE is to make up one's mind and then doggedly, and sometimes obstinately, to stick to a fixed or settled purpose: *determined to maintain his position at all costs.*

decided (dĭ sī′dĭd), *adj.* **1.** free from ambiguity; unquestionable; unmistakable. **2.** free from hesitation or wavering; resolute; determined. —**decid′edly,** *adv.* —**decid′edness,** *n.* —**Syn. 1.** undeniable, indisputable, positive, certain, emphatic, pronounced.

decider (dĭ sī′də), *n.* **1.** one who or that which decides. **2.** a decisive action, event, or the like. **3.** an extra race or game to decide a previously level contest.

decidua (dĭ sĭd′yo͞o ə), *n.* *Embryol.* the inner mucosal lining of the uterus which in some mammals is cast off at parturition. [NL, prop. fem. of L *dēciduus.* See DECIDUOUS] —**decid′ual,** *adj.*

deciduous (dĭ sĭd′yo͞o əs), *adj.* **1.** shedding the leaves annually, as trees, shrubs, etc. **2.** falling off or shed at a particular season, stage of growth, etc., as leaves, horns, teeth, etc. **3.** not permanent; transitory. [t. L: m. *dēciduus* falling down] —**decid′uously,** *adv.* —**decid′uousness,** *n.*

decigram (dĕs′ĭ grăm′), *n.* *Metric System.* a unit of weight of one tenth of a gram, equivalent to 1·543 grains. Also, **dec′igramme′.** [t. F: m. *décigramme.* See DECI-, GRAM]

decile (dĕs′ĭl), *n.* *Statistics.* one of the values of a variable which divides its distribution into ten groups having equal frequencies. [f. L *dec(em)* ten + -ILE]

decilitre (dĕs′ĭ lē′tə), *n.* *Metric System.* a unit of capacity of one tenth of a litre, equivalent to 6·102 cubic inches, or 3·5196 British fluid ounces. Also, *esp. U.S.*, **dec′ili′ter.** [t. F: m. *décilitre.* See DECI-, LITRE]

decillion (dĭ sĭl′yən), *n.* **1.** (in England and Germany) a cardinal number represented by one followed by 60 zeros. **2.** (in the U.S. and France) a cardinal number represented by one followed by 33 zeros. —*adj.* **3.** amounting to one decillion in number. [f. DECI- + (M)ILLION] —**decil′lionth,** *adj.*, *n.*

decimal (dĕs′ĭ məl), *adj.* **1.** pertaining to tenths, or to the number ten. **2.** proceeding by tens: *a decimal system.* —*n.* **3.** a decimal fraction. [f. s. L *decimus* tenth + -AL[1]] —**dec′imally,** *adv.*

decimal classification, (in libraries) a system of classifying books into ten main subject-classes, with further subdivision by tens in these classes, the divisions being represented by the numbers of a decimal system.

decimal fraction, a fraction whose denominator is some power of ten, usually indicated by a dot (the **decimal point**) written before the numerator: as $0·4 = \frac{4}{10}$; $0·126 = \frac{126}{1000}$.

decimalize (dĕs′ĭ mə līz′), *v.t.*, **-lized, -lizing.** to reduce to a decimal system. Also, **decimalise.** —**dec′imaliza′tion,** *n.*

decimal system, any system of counting or measurement whose units are powers of ten.

decimate (dĕs′ĭ māt′), *v.t.*, **-mated, -mating. 1.** to destroy a great number or proportion of. **2.** to select by lot and kill every tenth man of. **3.** *Obs.* to take a tenth of or from. [t. L: m. s. *decimātus*, pp.] —**dec′ima′tion,** *n.* —**dec′ima′tor,** *n.*

decimetre (dĕs′ĭ mē′tə), *n.* *Metric System.* a unit of length of one tenth of a metre. Also, *esp. U.S.*, **dec′ime′ter.** [t. F: m. *décimètre.* See DECI-, -METRE[1]]

Děčín (*Cz.* dyĕ′chēn), *n.* a town in NW Czechoslovakia. 41,000 (est. 1965).

decinormal (dĕs′ĭ nô′məl), *adj.* *Chem.* (of a solution) containing one tenth of the equivalent weight of the constituent in question in one litre of solution.

decipher (dĭ sī′fə), *v.t.* **1.** to make out the meaning of (poor or partially obliterated writing, etc.). **2.** to discover the meaning of (anything obscure or difficult to trace or understand). **3.** to interpret by the use of a key, as something written in cipher. **4.** *Obs.* to depict. —**deci′pherable,** *adj.* —**deci′pherer,** *n.* —**deci′pherment,** *n.*

decision (dĭ sĭzh′ən), *n.* **1.** the act of deciding; determination (of a question or doubt). **2.** a judgement, as one formally pronounced by a court. **3.** a making up of one's mind. **4.** that which is decided; a resolution. **5.** the quality of being decided; firmness, as of character. [t. L: s. *dēcīsio* a cutting down, decision]

decisive (dĭ sī′sĭv), *adj.* **1.** having the power or quality of determining; putting an end to controversy: *a decisive fact, test, etc.* **2.** characterized by or displaying decision; resolute; determined. —**deci′sively,** *adv.* —**deci′siveness,** *n.* —**Syn. 1.** conclusive, final.

decistere (dĕs′ĭ stĭə′), *n.* *Metric System.* a unit of volume equal to one tenth of a stere.

deck (dĕk), *n.* **1.** a horizontal platform extending from side to side of a ship or of part of a ship, forming a covering for the space below and itself serving as a floor. **2.** any platform or part suggesting the deck of a ship. **3.** a floor, platform or tier, as in a bus or bridge. **4.** the horizontal platform on or in a tape-recorder, gramophone, or the like, above which the turntable or spools revolve, and which often incorporates some of the controls. **5.** *Now Chiefly U.S.* a pack of playing cards. **6.** *Slang.* the ground floor. **7. clear the decks, a.** *Naut.* to prepare for combat, as by removing from the deck all unnecessary gear. **b.** *Colloq.* to prepare for action of any kind. **8. hit the deck,** *Slang.* **a.** to fall to the ground or floor. **b.** to rise from bed. —*v.t.* **9.** to clothe or attire in something ornamental; array. **10.** *Naut.* to furnish with or as with a deck, as a vessel. [t. MD: s. *decken* cover, c. G *decken*] —**Syn. 9.** bedeck, garnish, trim, bedizen.

deck cargo, *Naut.* cargo carried on an open deck of a ship.

deckchair (dĕk′chĕə′), *n.* a portable folding chair with back and seat of canvas or similar material, often in one piece.

decker (dĕk′ə), *n.* **1.** one who or that which decks. **2.** a ship, vehicle, etc., having a certain number of decks: *a three-decker.*

deckhand (dĕk′hănd′), *n.* *Naut.* any sailor, over the age of seventeen, who has served at sea for at least twelve months.

deck head, *Naut.* the underneath of any deck in the compartment below.

deckhouse (dĕk′hous′), *n.* *Naut.* a large cabin erected on the deck of a ship for any purpose.

decking (dĕk′ĭng), *n.* **1.** the material, or a unit or units of the material, composing a deck or roof. **2.** material, as waterproofed paper, for forming a cover or deck. **3.** a flat roof. **4.** the deck of a jetty or quay. **5.** adornment or embellishment.

deckle (dĕk′l), *n.* **1.** (in paper making) a frame which forms the paper pulp, fixing the size of a sheet of paper. **2.** deckle edge. [t. G: m. *Deckel*, dim. of *Decke* cover]

deckle edge, the untrimmed edge of handmade paper, formerly much used for ornamental effect in fine books.

deckle-edged (dĕk′l ĕjd′), *adj.* having a deckle edge.

deck officer, *Naut.* **1.** an officer in charge on deck. **2.** a watch-keeping officer on the bridge.

deck quoit, one of a set of rope or rubber rings thrown in any of various games known as **deck quoits,** as on the deck of a ship.

deck tennis, any of several games adapted from tennis for playing in the confined space of a ship's deck.

decl., declension.

declaim (dĭ klām′), *v.i.* **1.** to speak aloud rhetorically; make a formal speech. **2.** to inveigh (fol. by *against*). **3.** to speak or write for oratorical effect, without sincerity or sound argument. —*v.t.* **4.** to utter aloud in a rhetorical manner. [ME *declame(n)*, t. L: m. *dēclāmāre* cry aloud] —**declaim′er,** *n.*

declamation (dĕk′lə mā′shən), *n.* **1.** the act or art of declaiming. **2.** an exercise in oratory or elocution. **3.** speech or writing for oratorical effect. **4.** *Music.* the proper enunciation of the words, as in recitative.

declamatory (dĭ klăm′ə tə rĭ, -trĭ), *adj.* **1.** pertaining to or characterized by declamation. **2.** merely rhetorical; stilted.

declarable (dĭ klēə′rə bl), *adj.* **1.** capable of being declared or proved. **2.** (of goods, etc.) required by law to be declared at customs; dutiable.

declarant (dĭ klēə′rənt), *n.* one who makes a declaration, esp. a legal declaration.

declaration (dĕk′lə rā′shən), *n.* **1.** a positive, explicit, or formal statement, announcement, etc. **2.** a proclamation: *a declaration of war.* **3.** that which is proclaimed. **4.** the document embodying the proclamation. **5.** a statement of goods, etc., liable to duty. **6.** *Law.* the decision of a court or judge on a question of law or rights, esp. in Chancery. **7.** *Law Obs.* **a.** the formal statement in which a plaintiff presents his claim in an action. **b.** a complaint. **8.** *Cricket.* the voluntary closure of an innings before all ten wickets have fallen. **9.** *Cards.* **a.** *Bridge.* a bid, esp. the successful bid. **b.** the statement during the game of the points earned by a player, in bezique or other games.

Declaration of Independence, *U.S. Hist.* **1.** the public act by which the Second Continental Congress, on July 4th, 1776, declared the colonies to be free and independent of Great Britain. **2.** the document embodying it.

Declaration of Rights, *Eng. Hist.* the statement of rights and liberties of the people accepted by William and Mary on taking the throne in 1688.

declarative (dĭ klă′rə tĭv), *adj.* serving to declare, make clear, or explain; declaratory. —**decla′ratively,** *adv.*

declaratory (dĭ klă′rə tə rĭ, -trĭ), *adj.* serving to explain rather than pronounce: *the court gave a declaratory judgement, Parliament passed a declaratory act.* —**declaratorily** (dĭ klă′rə tə rĭ lĭ, -trĭ lĭ), *adv.*

declare (dĭ klēə′), *v.*, **-clared, -claring.** —*v.t.* **1.** to make known, esp. in explicit or formal terms. **2.** to announce officially; proclaim. **3.** to state emphatically; affirm. **4.** to manifest; reveal. **5.** to make due statement of (dutiable goods, etc.). **6.** to make (a dividend) payable. **7.** *Bridge.* to signify (a certain suit) as trumps or to establish the bid at no-trump. —*v.i.* **8.** to make a declaration. **9.** to proclaim oneself. **10.** *Cricket.* to close an innings voluntarily before all ten wickets have fallen. [ME *declar(en)*, t. L: m. *dēclārāre* make clear] —**declar′er,** *n.*

—**Syn. 3.** DECLARE, AFFIRM, ASSERT, PROTEST imply making something known emphatically, openly, or formally. To DECLARE is to make known, sometimes in the face of actual or potential contradiction: *to declare someone the winner of a contest.* To AFFIRM is to make a statement based on one's reputation for knowledge or veracity, or so related to a generally recognized truth that denial is not likely: *to affirm the necessity of high standards.* To ASSERT is to state boldly, usually without other proof than personal authority or conviction: *to assert that the climate is changing.* To PROTEST is to affirm publicly, as if in the face of doubt: *to protest that a newspaper account is misleading.*

declared (dĭ klēəd′), *adj.* avowed; professed. —**declaredly** (dĭ klēə′rĭd lĭ), *adv.*

declass (dē′kläs′), *v.t.* to remove or degrade from one's class (social or other).

déclassé (*Fr.* dė klȧ sė′), *adj.* fallen or lowered in social rank, class, etc. —**déclassée′,** *adj. fem.*

declassify (dē′klăs′ĭ fī′), *v.t.* to remove the classification (def. 3) from; take off the security list.

declension (dĭ klĕn′shən), *n.* **1.** *Gram.* **a.** the inflection of nouns, and of words similarly inflected, for categories such as case and number. Example (Latin): *puella, puellam, puellae, puellae, etc.* **b.** the whole set of inflected forms of such a word, or the recital thereof in a fixed order. **c.** a class of such words having similar sets of inflected forms, as the Latin *second declension.* **2.** an act or instance of declining. **3.** a bending, sloping, or moving downward. **4.** deterioration; decline. **5.** deviation, as from a standard. [irreg. t. L: m. s. *dēclīnātio* a bending aside, inflection, prob. modelled on *descensio* descent] —**declen′sional,** *adj.*

declinate (dĕk′lĭ nāt′, -nĭt), *adj. Chiefly Bot.* having a downward curve; bending away, as from the horizontal.

declination (dĕk′lĭ nā′shən), *n.* **1.** *Astron.* the angular distance of a heavenly body from the celestial equator, measured on a great circle passing through the celestial pole and the body. **2.** Also, **magnetic declination, variation.** the horizontal angle between the direction of true north and magnetic north at any place. **3.** a bending, sloping, or moving downward. **4.** *Now Chiefly U.S.* deterioration; decline. **5.** *Now U.S.* a swerving or deviating, as from a standard. **6.** *Obs.* a polite refusal.

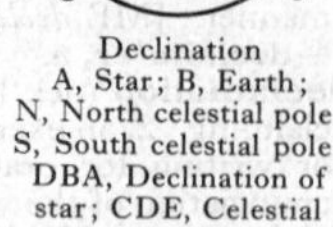

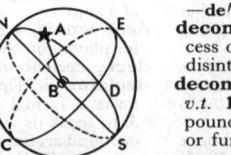

Declination
A, Star; B, Earth; N, North celestial pole; S, South celestial pole; DBA, Declination of star; CDE, Celestial equator

declinatory (dĭ klī′nə tə rĭ, -trĭ), *adj.* expressing refusal; implying declination.

declinature (dĭ klī′nə chə), *n.* the act or fact of refusing.

decline (dĭ klīn′), *v.*, **-clined, -clining,** *n.* —*v.t.* **1.** to withhold consent to do, enter upon, or accept; refuse: *he declined to say more about it, he declined the offer with thanks.* **2.** to cause to slope or incline downward. **3.** *Gram.* **a.** to inflect (a noun, pronoun, or adjective). In Latin, *puella* is declined *puella, puellam, puellae, puellae, puellā* in the five cases of the singular. **b.** to recite or display all, or some subset, of the inflected forms of a noun, pronoun, or adjective in a fixed order. —*v.i.* **4.** to express courteous refusal; refuse. **5.** to bend or slant down; slope or trend downward; descend. **6.** to draw towards the close, as the day. **7.** to fail in strength, vigour, character, value, etc.; deteriorate. **8.** *Gram.* to be characterized by declension. —*n.* **9.** a downward incline or slope. **10.** a failing or gradual loss, as in strength, character, value, etc.; deterioration; diminution. **11.** progress downwards or towards a close, as of the sun or the day. **12.** a gradual diminution of the physical powers, as in later life or in disease. **13.** the last part or phase. [ME *decline(n)*, t. OF: m. *decliner*, t. L: m. *dēclīnāre* bend from, avoid, inflect] —**declin′able,** *adj.* —**declin′er,** *n.* —**Syn. 1.** reject. See **refuse**[1]. **7.** degenerate, decay. **10.** retrogression, degeneration.

declinometer (dĕk′lĭ nŏm′ĭ tə), *n.* an instrument for measuring magnetic declination. [f. *declino-* (comb. form repr. L *dēclīnāre* bend from) + -METER[1]]

declivitous (dĭ klĭv′ĭ təs), *adj.* rather steep.

declivity (dĭ klĭv′ĭ tĭ), *n.*, *pl.* **-ties.** a downward slope, as of ground (opposed to *acclivity*). [t. L: m. s. *dēclīvitas* slope]

declivous (dĭ klī′vəs), *adj.* sloping downwards.

declutch (dē klŭch′), *v.i. Motor Vehicles.* to disengage the clutch.

decoct (dĭ kŏkt′), *v.t.* to boil (a medicinal substance, etc.) in water, etc.; to extract the essence or principles. [t. L: s. *dēcoctus*, pp., boiled down]

decoction (dĭ kŏk′shən), *n.* **1.** the act of boiling in water, in order to extract the peculiar properties or virtues. **2.** an extract obtained by decocting. **3.** water in which a substance, usually animal or vegetable, has been boiled, and which thus contains the constituents or principles of the substance soluble in boiling water.

decode (dē kōd′), *v.t.*, **-coded, -coding.** to translate from code into the original language or form. —**decod′er,** *n.*

decoke (dē kōk′), *v.*, **-coked, -coking,** *n. Colloq.* —*v.t.* **1.** to decarbonize. —*n.* **2.** decarbonization. [f. DE- + COKE]

decollate (dĭ kŏl′āt), *v.t.*, **-lated, -lating.** to behead; decapitate. [t. L: m. s. *dēcollātus*, pp., beheaded] —**decollation** (dē′kŏ lā′shən), *n.* —**de′colla′tor,** *n.*

décolletage (dā′kŏl täzh′; *Fr.* dė kŏl tȧzh′), *n.* **1.** the neckline of a dress cut low in the front and across the shoulders. **2.** a décolleté garment or dress. [F, der. *décolleter.* See DÉCOLLETÉ]

décolleté (dā kŏl′tā; *Fr.* dė kŏl tė′), *adj.* **1.** (of a garment) low-necked. **2.** wearing a low-necked garment. [t. F, pp. of *décolleter* bare the neck of, ult. der. *col.* neck]

decolonize (dē′kŏl′ə nīz′), *v.t.*, **-nized, -nizing.** to release from the status of a colony; to grant self-government or independence to. Also, **decolonise.** —**decol′oniza′tion,** *n.*

decolorant (dē kŭl′ə rənt), *adj.* **1.** having the property of removing colour; bleaching. —*n.* **2.** a decolorant substance or agent.

decolorize (dē kŭl′ə rīz′), *v.t.*, **-ized, -izing.** decolour. Also, **decolorise.** —**decol′oriza′tion,** *n.* —**decol′oriz′er,** *n.*

decolour (dē kŭl′ə), *v.t.* to deprive of colour; bleach. Also, *U.S.*, **decol′or.** [t. L: m. *dēcolōrāre* deprive of colour] —**de′colora′tion,** *n.*

decompose (dē′kəm pōz′), *v.t.*, *v.i.*, **-posed, -posing.** **1.** to separate or resolve into constituent parts or elements; disintegrate. **2.** to rot; putrefy. [t. F: s. *décomposer*, f. *dé-* DIS-[1] + *composer* COMPOSE] —**de′compos′able,** *adj.* —**de′compos′er,** *n.* —**Syn. 2.** See **decay.**

decomposition (dē′kŏm pə zĭsh′ən), *n.* **1.** the act or process of decomposing. **2.** the state of being decomposed; disintegration; decay.

decompound (dē′kəm pound′), *v.t.* **1.** (of things already compound) to compound a second or further time. **2.** to decompose. —*adj.* **3.** *Bot.* divided into compound divisions. **4.** composed of things which are themselves compound.

Decompound leaf

decompress (dē′kəm prĕs′), *v.t.*, *v.i.* to undergo or cause to undergo decompression.

decompression (dē′kəm prĕsh′ən, *n.* **1.** the act or process

b., blend of, blended; c., cognate with; d., dialect, dialectal; der., derived from; f., formed from; g., going back to; m., modification of; r., replacing; s., stem of; t., taken from; ?, perhaps. See full key on inside front cover.

of relieving pressure. **2.** the gradual return of persons, as divers or construction workers, to normal atmospheric pressure after working in deep water or in air under compression.

decompression chamber, a chamber in which the pressure can be varied, in which persons who have been subjected to abnormal pressure remain while returning gradually to atmospheric pressure.

decompression sickness, caisson disease.

deconsecrate (dē kŏn′sĭ krāt′), *v.t.*, **-crated, crating.** to deprive of sanctity acquired through consecration; secularize.

decontaminate (dē′kən tăm′ĭ nāt′), *v.t.*, **-nated, -nating.** to make (any object or area) safe for unprotected personnel by absorbing, making harmless, or destroying chemicals with which they have been in contact. **—de′contam′ina′tion,** *n.*

decontrol (dē′kən trōl′), *v.*, **-trolled, -trolling,** *n.* *—v.t.* **1.** to remove controls, or from control. *—n.* **2.** removal of control.

decor (dā′kô), *n.* **1.** decoration in general. **2.** a style of decoration. **3.** *Theat.* scenic decoration; scenery. *French,* **décor** (*Fr.* dė kôr′). [t. F, der. *décorer* decorate, t. L: m. *decorāre*]

decorate (dĕk′ə rāt′), *v.*, **-rated, -rating.** *—v.t.* **1.** to furnish or deck with something becoming or ornamental; embellish. **2.** to plan and execute the design, wallpaper, etc., and sometimes the furnishings of (a house, room, or the like). **3.** to confer distinction upon by a badge, a medal of honour, etc. *—v.i.* **4.** to be engaged in executing the decoration of a house, room, etc. [t. L: m. s. *decorātus,* pp.]

Decorated style, *Archit.* the second style of English pointed architecture, in use from the end of the thirteenth to the beginning of the fifteenth century.

decoration (dĕk′ə rā′shən), *n.* **1.** the act of decorating. **2.** adornment; embellishment. **3.** the style in which a house, room, etc., is decorated. **4.** a badge of an order, medal, etc., conferred and worn as a mark of honour.

decorative (dĕk′ə rə tĭv, dĕk′rə tĭv), *adj.* serving or tending to decorate. **—dec′oratively,** *adv.* **—dec′orativeness,** *n.*

decorator (dĕk′ə rā′tə), *n.* **1.** one who decorates. **2.** one who professionally decorates houses or buildings, particularly their interior.

decorous (dĕk′ə rəs), *adj.* characterized by propriety in conduct, manners, appearance, character, etc. [t. L: m. *decōrus* becoming, seemly] **—dec′orously,** *adv.* **—dec′orousness,** *n.* **—Syn.** proper, seemly, becoming, decent, sedate, conventional. **—Ant.** undignified.

decorticate (dē kô′tĭ kāt′), *v.t.*, **-cated, -cating.** to remove the bark, husk, or outer covering from. [t. L: m. s. *dēcorticātus,* pp.] **—decor′tica′tion,** *n.* **—decor′tica′tor,** *n.*

decorum (dĭ kô′rəm), *n.* **1.** propriety of behaviour, speech, dress, etc. **2.** that which is proper or seemly; fitness; congruity; propriety. **3.** an observance or requirement of polite society. [t. L, prop. neut. of *decōrus* DECOROUS] **—Syn. 1.** See **etiquette.**

decouple (dē kŭp′l), *v.t.* *Electronics.* to reduce unwanted interference in a system or between two parts of a system.

decoy (*n.* dĭ koi′, dē′koi; *v.* dĭ koi′), *n.* **1.** one who entices or allures, as into a trap, danger, etc. **2.** anything used as a lure. **3.** a trained bird or other animal used to entice game into a trap or within gunshot. **4.** an image of a bird used for the same purpose. **5.** a pond into which wild fowl are lured to permit their capture. *—v.t.* **6.** to lure by or as by a decoy. [var. of *coy* (now d.), both t. D: m. (*de*) *kooi* (the) cage, t. L: m. s. *cavea* CAGE] **—decoy′er,** *n.*

decrease (*v.* dĭ krēs′; *n.* dē′krēs, dĭ krēs′), *v.*, **-creased, -creasing,** *n.* *—v.i.* **1.** to diminish gradually in extent, quantity, strength, power, etc. *—v.t.* **2.** to make less; cause to diminish. *—n.* **3.** a process of growing less, or the resulting condition; gradual diminution. **4.** the amount by which a thing is lessened. [ME *decrese(n),* t. OF: m. *decreiss-,* g. L *dēcrescere* grow less] **—decreas′ingly,** *adv.*

—Syn. 1. wane, lessen, fall off, decline, contract, abate. DECREASE, DIMINISH, DWINDLE, SHRINK imply becoming smaller or less in amount. DECREASE commonly implies a gradual and sustained reduction, esp. of bulk, size, volume, or quantity, often from some imperceptible, cause or inherent process: *the swelling decreased daily.* DIMINISH usually implies the action of some external cause which keeps taking away: *disease caused the number of troops to diminish steadily.* DWINDLE implies an undesirable reduction by degrees, resulting in attenuation: *his followers dwindled to a mere handful.* SHRINK esp. implies contraction through an inherent property under specific conditions: *many fabrics shrink when wet.* **3.** abatement, reduction, decline. **—Ant. 1.** increase, expand.

decree (dĭ krē′), *n.*, *v.*, **-creed, -creeing.** *—n.* **1.** an ordinance or edict promulgated by civil or other authority. **2.** *Law.* a judicial decision or order. **3.** *Theol.* one of the eternal purposes of God, by which events are foreordained. *—v.t., v.i.* **4.** to ordain or decide by decree. [ME *decre,* t. OF, var. of *decret,* t. L: s. *dēcrētum,* prop. pp. neut.]

decree absolute, *Law.* See **absolute** (def. 9).

decree nisi (nī′sī), *Law.* a decree of divorce that will become absolute at a later date, unless cause is shown within six months why it should not.

decrement (dĕk′rĭ mənt), *n.* **1.** the process or fact of decreasing; gradual diminution. **2.** the amount lost by diminution. **3.** *Maths.* a negative increment.

decrepit (dĭ krĕp′ĭt), *adj.* broken down or weakened by old age; feeble; infirm. [t. L: s. *dēcrepitus,* lit., broken down] **—decrep′itly,** *adv.* **—Syn.** See **weak. —Ant.** vigorous.

decrepitate (dĭ krĕp′ĭ tāt′), *v.*, **-tated, -tating.** *—v.t.* **1.** to roast or calcine (salt, etc.) so as to cause crackling or until crackling ceases. *—v.i.* **2.** to make a crackling noise, as salt in roasting. [t. NL: m. s. *dēcrepitātus* crackled down] **—decrep′ita′tion,** *n.*

decrepitude (dĭ krĕp′ĭ tyōōd′), *n.* decrepit condition; feebleness, esp. from old age.

decresc., *Music.* decrescendo.

decrescendo (dē′krĭ shĕn′dō; *It.* dė krĕsh shĕn′dȯ), *adj.*, *n.*, *pl.* **-dos.** *Music.* *—adj., adv.* **1.** gradually reducing force of loudness; diminuendo (opposed to *crescendo*). *—n.* **2.** a gradual reduction in force or loudness. **3.** a decrescendo passage. [t. It., ger. of *decrescere* DECREASE]

decrescent (dĭ krĕs′ənt), *adj.* **1.** decreasing. **2.** waning, as the moon. [t. L: s. *dēcrescens,* ppr., decreasing]

decretal (dĭ krē′tl), *adj.* **1.** pertaining to, of the nature of, or containing a decree or decrees. *—n.* **2.** a papal document authoritatively determining some point of doctrine or church law. **3. Decretals,** the body or collection of such decrees as a part of the canon law. [ME *decretale,* t. ML, ult. der. L *dēcrētum* DECREE]

decretist (dĭ krē′tĭst), *n.* (in medieval universities) **1.** a student in the faculty of law. **2.** a student of the Decretals; one versed in the canon law.

decretive (dĭ krē′tĭv), *adj.* having the force of a decree; pertaining to a decree.

decretory (dĕk′rə tə rĭ, -trĭ), *adj.* **1.** pertaining to or following a decree. **2.** established by a decree; judicial.

decrial (dĭ krī′əl), *n.* the act of decrying; disparagement.

decry (dĭ krī′), *v.t.*, **-cried, -crying. 1.** to speak disparagingly of; censure as faulty or worthless. **2.** to condemn or depreciate by proclamation, as foreign or obsolete coins. [t. F: m. *décrier,* f. *dé-* DIS-[1] + *crier* CRY] **—decri′er,** *n.* **—Syn. 1.** belittle, disparage, discredit.

decuman (dĕk′yōō mən), *adj.* **1.** large or immense, as a wave. **2.** every tenth in a series. [t. L: s. *decumānus,* var. of *decimānus* of the tenth, large (from the notion that every tenth wave is a large one)]

decumbent (dĭ kŭm′bənt), *adj.* **1.** lying down; recumbent. **2.** *Bot.* (of stems, branches, etc.) lying or trailing on the ground with the extremity tending to ascend. [t. L: s. *dēcumbens,* ppr.] **—decum′bence, decum′bency,** *n.* **—decum′bently,** *adv.*

decuple (dĕk′yōō pl), *adj.*, *n.*, *v.*, **-pled, -pling.** *—adj.* **1.** tenfold; ten times as great. *—n.* **2.** a tenfold quantity or multiple. *—v.t.* **3.** to make ten times as great. [t. F, t. L: m. *decuplus* tenfold]

decurion (dĭ kyōō′rĭ ən), *n.* **1.** *Rom. Hist.* the head of a decury. **2.** a member of the senate of an ancient Roman colony or municipality. [ME, t. L: s. *decurio*]

decurrent (dĭ kŭ′rənt), *adj.* *Bot.* extending down the stem below the place of insertion, as certain leaves. [t. L: s. *dēcurrens,* ppr., running down] **—decur′rently,** *adv.*

Decurrent leaf of thistle

decury (dĕk′yōōə rĭ), *n.*, *pl.* **-ries. 1.** *Rom. Hist.* a division of a larger unit, nominally comprising ten persons, but often more than ten. **2.** a division, group, or class. [t. L: m. s. *decuria* a company of ten]

decussate (*v.* dĭ kŭs′āt, dĕk′ə sāt′; *adj.* dĭ kŭs′āt, -ĭt), *v.*, **-sated, -sating,** *adj.* *—v.t., v.i.* **1.** to cross in the form of the letter X: intersect. *—adj.* **2.** in the form of the letter X; crossed; intersected. **3.** *Bot.* (of leaves, etc.) arranged along the stem in pairs, each pair at right angles to the pair next above or below. [t. L: m. s. *decussātus,* pp., divided in the form of an X] **—decuss′ately,** *adv.* **—decussation** (dē′kə sā′shən, dĕk′ə-), *n.*

dedans (dĭ dănz′; *Fr.* də dăɴ′), *n.* an open gallery at the service end of a real-tennis court.

Dede Agach (*Turk.* dĕ dĕ′ăch), former name of **Alexandroupolis.**

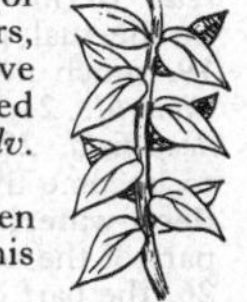

Decussate leaf

dedicate (dĕd′ĭ kāt′), *v.*, **-cated, -cating,** *adj.* —*v.t.* **1.** to set apart and consecrate to a deity or to a sacred purpose. **2.** to give up wholly or earnestly, as to some person or end; set apart or appropriate. **3.** to inscribe or address (a book, piece of music, etc.) to a patron, friend, etc., as in testimony of respect or affection. —*adj.* **4.** *Archaic.* consecrated. [t. L: m. s. *dēdicātus*, pp., proclaimed, devoted] —**ded′ica′tor,** *n.*

dedicated (dĕd′ĭ kā′tĭd), *adj.* wholly committed to something, as an ideal, way of life, etc.: *a dedicated socialist, a dedicated lexicographer.*

dedication (dĕd′ĭ kā′shən), *n.* **1.** the act of dedicating. **2.** the fact of being dedicated. **3.** an inscription prefixed or attached to a book, etc., dedicating it to some person.

dedicatory (dĕd′ĭ kā′tə rĭ, dĕd′ĭ kə tə rĭ, -trĭ), *adj.* of or pertaining to dedication; serving as a dedication. Also, **dedicative** (dĕd′ĭ kā′tĭv).

deduce (dĭ dyōōs′), *v.t.*, **-duced, -ducing. 1.** to derive as a conclusion from something known or assumed; infer. **2.** to trace the derivation of; trace the course of. [t. L: m. s. *dedūcere* lead down, derive] —**deduc′ible,** *adj.*

deduct (dĭ dŭkt′), *v.t.* to take away, as from a sum or amount. [t. L: s. *dēductus*, pp., led down, withdrawn] —**deduct′able, deduct′ible,** *adj.* —**Syn.** See **subtract.**

deduction (dĭ dŭk′shən), *n.* **1.** the act of deducting; subtraction; abatement. **2.** that which is deducted. **3.** the process of drawing a conclusion from something known or assumed. **4.** *Logic.* inference by reasoning from generals to particulars (opposed to *induction*).

deductive (dĭ dŭk′tĭv), *adj.* based on inference from accepted principles; reasoning by deduction. —**deduc′tively,** *adv.*

—**Syn.** DEDUCTIVE, INDUCTIVE, often confused, are not properly synonyms. They do agree in referring to processes of (formal or informal) reasoning, but the processes they describe are of opposite kinds. In DEDUCTIVE reasoning, an accepted general statement (true or false) is applied to an individual case; if formally, by the method of syllogism: *all dogs are animals; this is a dog; therefore this is an animal.* In INDUCTIVE reasoning, a set of individual cases is studied by the experimental method, and, from the observations made, a general principle is formed: *every metal I have tested expands when heated; therefore I can expect all metals to expand when heated.* When the general premise in deductive reasoning is true, the deduction from it will be certain for all possible instances. The principle formed in inductive reasoning is a workable theory but would be certain only when all possible instances had been examined.

Dee (dē), *n.* **1.** a river in NE Scotland, flowing into the North Sea at Aberdeen. 90 mi. **2.** a river in N Wales and W England, flowing into Liverpool Bay. 70 mi. **3.** a river of Kirkcudbrightshire, Scotland, flowing into the Solway Firth. 50 mi.

deed (dēd), *n.* **1.** that which is done, performed, or accomplished; an act. **2.** an exploit or achievement. **3.** action or performance, often as contrasted with words. **4.** *Law.* a writing or document signed, sealed and delivered to effect a conveyance, esp. of real property. —*v.t.* **5.** *U.S.* to convey or transfer by deed. [ME *dede*, OE *dēd*, var. of *dǣd*, c. G *Tat.* See DO[1]] —**deed′less,** *adj.* —**Syn. 2.** See **achievement.**

deed poll, a deed in the form of a declaration to all the world of the grantor's act and intention, as, for example, to change his name.

deem (dēm), *v.i.* **1.** to form or have an opinion; judge; think. —*v.t.* **2.** to hold as an opinion; think; regard. [ME *demen*, OE *dēman*, c. Goth. *dōmjan.* See DOOM] —**Syn. 1.** See **think**[1].

deemster (dēm′stə), *n.* one of the justices of the Isle of Man. Also, **dempster.** —**deem′stership′,** *n.*

deep (dēp), *adj.* **1.** extending far downwards, inwards, or backwards. **2.** having a specified dimension downwards, inwards, or backwards: *a tank 8 feet deep.* **3.** situated far or a certain distance down, in, or back. **4.** extending far in width; broad: *a deep border.* **5.** outside the solar system: *deep space.* **6.** extending or advancing far down: *a deep dive.* **7.** coming from far down: *a deep breath.* **8.** lying below a surface. **9.** difficult to penetrate or understand; abstruse. **10.** not superficial; profound. **11.** grave or serious. **12.** heartfelt: *deep sorrow or prayer.* **13.** absorbing: *deep study.* **14.** great in measure; intense: *deep sleep.* **15.** (of colours) intense; dark and vivid: *a deep red.* **16.** low in pitch, as sound. **17.** having penetrating intellectual powers. **18.** profoundly cunning or artful. **19.** much involved: *deep in debt.* **20.** absorbed: *deep in thought.* **21.** *Cricket.* relatively far from the wicket: *the deep field.* **22. go off the deep end, a.** to get into a dither; to become hysterical. **b.** *U.S.* to go to extremes. **23. in deep water,** in trouble or difficulties. —*n.* **24.** the deep part of the sea, a river, etc. **25.** any deep space or place. **26.** the part of greatest intensity, as of winter. **27.** *Naut.* the depth in fathoms between two successive marks on a lead line. **28. the deep,** *Poetic.* the sea or ocean. —*adv.* **29.** to or at a considerable or specified depth. **30.** far on (in time). **31.** profoundly; intensely. [ME *depe*, OE *dēop*, c. G *tief.* See DIP, *v.*] —**deep′ly,** *adv.* —**deep′ness,** *n.* —**Syn. 9.** recondite, mysterious, obscure.

deep-dyed (dēp′dīd′), *adj.* (usually pejorative) thoroughgoing; unmitigated.

deepen (dē′pən), *vt.*, *v.i.* to make or become deep or deeper. —**deep′ener,** *n.*

deep-freeze (dēp′frēz′), *n.*, *v.*, **-froze, -frozen, -freezing.** —*n.* **1.** a locker or compartment in which food is stored at a low temperature; freezer. —*v.t.* **2.** to store or freeze in a deep-freeze.

deep-frier (dēp′frī′ə), *n.* a pan containing sufficient fat for deep-frying, and usually a wire-mesh basket for holding the food being cooked. Also, **deep-fryer.**

deep-fry (dēp′frī′), *v.t.*, **-fried, -frying.** to fry in a sufficient quantity of fat or oil to cover the food being cooked.

deep-laid (dēp′lād′), *adj.* carefully, cunningly, or secretly made: *deep-laid plot.*

deep-litter (dēp′lĭt′ə), *n.* a structure with a floor of peat or similar material in which hens are kept.

deep-rooted (dēp′rōō′tĭd), *adj.* deeply rooted; firmly implanted.

deep-sea (dēp′sē′), *adj.* of, pertaining to, or in the deeper parts of the sea.

deep-seated (dēp′sē′tĭd), *adj.* firmly implanted.

Deep South, the south-eastern part of the U.S., esp. those states which formed the original Confederacy in the Civil War.

deer (dĭə), *n.*, *pl.* **deer. 1.** any animal of the family *Cervidae*, comprising ruminants most of which have solid deciduous horns or antlers (usually the male only), as *Cervus elaphus* of Europe. **2.** any of the smaller species of this family, as distinguished from the moose, elk, etc. [ME *dere*, OE *dēor*, c. G *Tier* beast]

Roe deer, *Capreolus capreolus* (2½ ft high at shoulder)

deergrass (dĭə′gräs′), *n.* a tufted cyperaceous perennial, *Trichophorum caespitosum*, common in wet peaty situations throughout N temperate regions.

deerhound (dĭə′hound′), *n.* one of a Scottish breed of dogs, allied to and resembling the greyhound but larger and having a shaggy coat.

Scottish deerhound (2½ ft high at shoulder)

deerlick (dĭə′lĭk′), *n.* a spot of ground, naturally or artificially salty, where deer come to nibble or lick the earth.

deer-mouse (dĭə′mous′), *n.* any of several species of mice (family *Cricetidae*), esp. the widely distributed white-footed mouse, *Peromyscus leucopus*, of North America.

deer-park (dĭə′päk′), *n.* a park in which deer are kept.

deerskin (dĭə′skĭn′), *n.* **1.** the skin of a deer. **2.** leather made from this. **3.** a garment made of such leather. —*adj.* **4.** made of deerskin.

deerstalker (dĭə′stô′kə), *n.* **1.** one who stalks deer. **2.** a sportsman's helmet-shaped hat, having peaks back and front and earflaps. —**deer′stalk′ing,** *n.*

def., 1. defective. **2.** defendant. **3.** deferred. **4.** defined. **5.** definite. **6.** definition.

deface (dĭ fās′), *v.t.*, **-faced, -facing. 1.** to mar the face or appearance of; disfigure. **2.** to blot out; obliterate; efface. [ME *deface(n)*, t. F (obs.): m. *defacer*, earlier *desfacier*, der. *des-* DIS-[1] + *face* FACE] —**deface′able,** *adj.* —**deface′ment,** *n.* —**defac′er,** *n.* —**Syn. 1.** See **mar.**

de facto (dē făk′tō), **1.** in fact; in reality. **2.** actually existing, whether with or without right (opposed to *de jure*). [L: from the fact]

defalcate (dē′făl kāt′), *v.i.*, **-cated, -cating.** *Law.* to be guilty of defalcation. [t. ML: m. s. *dēfalcātus*, pp.] —**de′falca′tor,** *n.*

defalcation (dē′făl kā′shən), *n.* *Law.* **1.** misappropriation of money, etc., held by a trustee or other fiduciary. **2.** the sum misappropriated.

defamation (dĕf′ə mā′shən), *n.* the wrong of injuring another's reputation without good reason or justification; calumny; slander or libel.

defamatory (dĭ făm′ə tə rĭ, -trĭ), *adj.* containing defamation; injurious to reputation; slanderous. —**defamatorily** (dĭ făm′ə tə rĭ lĭ, -trĭ lĭ), *adv.*

defame (dĭ fām′), *v.t.*, **-famed, -faming.** **1.** to attack the good name or reputation of, as by uttering or publishing maliciously anything injurious; slander; libel; calumniate. **2.** *Archaic.* to disgrace. **3.** *Obs.* to accuse. [ME *defamen*, t. ML: m. *dēfāmāre*; r. ME *diffamen*, t. OF: m. *diffamer*, t. L: m. *diffāmāre*] —**defam′er,** *n.*

default (dĭ fôlt′), *n.* **1.** failure to act; neglect. **2.** failure to meet financial obligations. **3.** *Law.* failure to perform an act or obligation legally required, esp. to appear in court or to plead at a time assigned. **4.** failure to participate in or complete anything, as a scheduled match. **5.** want; lack; absence: *owing to default of water.* —*v.i.* **6.** to fail in fulfilling or satisfying an engagement, claim, or obligation. **7.** to fail to meet financial engagements, or to account properly for money, etc., in one's care. **8.** *Law.* to fail to appear in court. **9. a.** to fail to participate in or complete anything, as a match. **b.** to lose a match by default. —*v.t.* **10.** to fail to perform or pay. **11.** to declare to be in default, esp. legally. **12.** *Law.* to lose by failure to appear in court. **13.** *Sport.* **a.** to fail to compete in (a game, race, etc.). **b.** to lose by default. [ME *defaute*, t. OF, der. *defaillir*, after *faute* and *faillir*. See FAULT]

defaulter (dĭ fôl′tə), *n.* **1.** one who defaults, or fails to fulfil an obligation, esp. a legal or financial one. **2.** a soldier convicted summarily of a minor offence and sentenced to restriction of privileges.

defeasance (dĭ fē′zəns), *n. Law.* **1.** a rendering null and void. **2.** a condition on the performance of which a deed or other instrument is defeated or rendered void. **3.** a collateral deed or other writing embodying such a condition. [ME *defesance*, t. OF, der. *defesant*, ppr. of *de(s)-faire* undo. See DEFEAT]

defeasible (dĭ fē′zə bl), *adj.* that may be annulled or terminated. —**defea′sibleness, defea′sibil′ity,** *n.*

defeat (dĭ fēt′), *v.t.* **1.** to overcome in a contest, battle, etc.; vanquish; win or achieve victory over. **2.** to frustrate; thwart. **3.** *Law.* to annul. **4.** *Archaic.* to deprive of something expected. —*n.* **5.** the act of overcoming in a contest. **6.** an overthrow; vanquishment. **7.** a bringing to naught; frustration. **8.** *Obs.* undoing; destruction; ruin. [ME *defete(n)*, t. OF: m. *de(s)fait*, pp. of *desfaire* undo, f. *des-* DIS-[1] + *faire* (g. L *facere* do)] —**defeat′er,** *n.*

—**Syn. 1.** DEFEAT, CONQUER, OVERCOME, SUBDUE imply gaining a victory or control over an opponent. DEFEAT suggests temporarily, and often permanently, beating or frustrating: *to defeat an enemy in battle.* CONQUER, more formal, implies finally gaining control over, usually after a series of efforts or against systematic resistance: *to conquer a country, one's inclinations.* OVERCOME emphasizes surmounting difficulties in prevailing over an antagonist: *to overcome opposition, bad habits.* SUBDUE means to conquer so completely that the spirit of resistance is broken: *to subdue an uprising or a rebellious spirit.*

defeatism (dĭ fē′tĭz′əm), *n.* the attitude, policy, or conduct of those who admit or expect defeat, usually resulting from a premature decision that further struggle or effort is futile. —**defeat′ist,** *n., adj.*

defeature[1] (dē fē′chə), *n., v.,* **-featured, -featuring.** *Archaic.* —*n.* **1.** disfigurement. —*v.t.* **2.** to disfigure. [DE- + FEATURE]

defeature[2] (dĭ fē′chə), *n. Obs.* defeat; ruin. [t. OF: m. *deffaiture.* See DEFEAT]

defecate (dĕf′ĭ kāt′), *v.,* **-cated, -cating.** —*v.t.* **1.** to clear of dregs, impurities, etc.; purify; refine. —*v.i.* **2.** to become clear of dregs, impurities, etc. **3.** to void excrement. [t. L: m. s. *dēfaecātus*, pp., cleansed from dregs] —**def′eca′tion,** *n.* —**def′eca′tor,** *n.*

defect (*n.* dĭ fĕkt′, dē′fĕkt; *v.* dĭ fĕkt′), *n.* **1.** a falling short; a fault or imperfection. **2.** want or lack, esp. of something essential to perfection or completeness; deficiency. **3.** *Chem.* a discontinuity in the structure of a crystal. —*v.i.* **4.** to desert a country, cause, etc. [t. L: s. *dēfectus* want, defect] —**defec′tor,** *n.*

—**Syn. 1.** DEFECT, BLEMISH, FLAW refer to faults which detract from perfection. DEFECT is the general word for any kind of shortcoming or imperfection, whether literal or figurative: *a defect in eyesight, in character, in a plan.* A BLEMISH is usually a defect on a surface, which mars the appearance: *a mole or scar on a cheek (or a scratch on a table) is a blemish.* FLAW is applied to a defect in quality, caused by imperfect structure (as in a diamond) or brought about during manufacture (as in texture of cloth, in tensile strength of metals, in clearness of glass, etc.).

defection (dĭ fĕk′shən), *n.* **1.** a falling away from allegiance, duty, virtue; desertion; backsliding; apostasy. **2.** failure; lack. —**Ant. 1.** loyalty.

defective (dĭ fĕk′tĭv), *adj.* **1.** having a defect; faulty; imperfect. **2.** *Psychol.* characterized by subnormal intelligence or behaviour. **3.** *Gram.* (of an inflected word or its inflection) lacking one or more of the inflected forms proper to most words of the same class in the language, as English *must* (which occurs only in the present tense). —*n.* **4.** one who or that which is defective. —**defec′tively,** *adv.* —**defec′tiveness,** *n.* —**Ant. 1.** perfect, complete.

defence (dĭ fĕns′), *n.* **1.** resistance against attack; protection. **2.** something that defends, esp. a fortification. **3.** the defending of a cause or the like by speech, argument, etc. **4.** a speech, argument, etc., in vindication. **5.** *Law.* **a.** the denial or pleading of the defendant in answer to the claim or charge against him. **b.** the proceedings adopted by a defendant, or his legal agents, for defending himself. **c.** a defendant and his legal agents collectively. **6.** *Sport.* **a.** the practice or art of defending oneself or one's goal against attack, as in fencing, boxing, soccer, etc. **b.** the players in a team collectively whose primary function is to defend the goal, etc. **c.** a plan or system of defending. Also, *U.S.*, **defense.** [ME, t. OF, t. LL: m. *dēfensa* prohibition, der. L *dēfendere* ward off; r. ME *defens*, t. OF, t. L: s. *dēfensum* (thing) forbidden, prop. pp. of *dēfendere*] —**defence′less,** *adj.* —**defence′lessly,** *adv.* —**defence′lessness,** *n.*

defence mechanism, 1. *Physiol.* organic activity, as the formation of an antitoxin, as a defensive measure. **2.** *Psychoanal.* a group of unconscious processes which oppose the entrance into consciousness or the acting out of unacceptable or painful ideas and impulses.

defend (dĭ fĕnd′), *v.t.* **1.** to ward off attack from; guard against assault or injury (fol. by *from* or *against*). **2.** to maintain by argument, evidence, etc.; uphold. **3.** to contest (a legal charge, claim, etc.). **4.** to act as counsel for (an accused man). —*v.i.* **5.** *Law.* to enter or make a defence. [ME *defende(n)*, t. OF: m. *defendre*, g. L *dēfendere* ward off] —**defend′able,** *adj.* —**defend′er,** *n.*

—**Syn. 1.** garrison, fortify, shield, shelter, screen. DEFEND, GUARD, PRESERVE, PROTECT all mean to keep safe. To DEFEND is to strive to keep safe by resisting attack: *to defend (a position) in battle, to defend one's country.* To GUARD is to watch over in order to keep safe: *to guard a camp, a secret.* To PRESERVE is to keep safe in the midst of danger, either in a single instance or continuously: *to preserve a city, a spirit of conciliation.* To PROTECT is to keep safe by interposing a shield or barrier: *to protect books by means of heavy paper covers, the reputation of a friend.* —**Ant. 1.** attack.

defendant (dĭ fĕn′dənt), *n.* **1.** *Law.* the party against whom a claim or charge is brought in a proceeding. —*adj.* **2.** *Obs.* defensive.

Defender of the Faith. See **Fidei Defensor.**

defenestrate (dē fĕn′ĭ strāt′), *v.t.*, **-strated, -strating.** to throw out of a window. [back-formation from DEFENESTRATION]

defenestration (dē fĕn′ĭ strā′shən), *n.* the act of throwing out of a window. [f. DE- + s. L *fenestra* window + -ATION]

defense (dĭ fĕns′), *n. U.S.* defence.

defensible (dĭ fĕn′sĭ bl), *adj.* **1.** capable of being defended against assault or injury. **2.** capable of being defended in argument; justifiable. —**defen′sibil′ity, defen′sibleness,** *n.* —**defen′sibly,** *adv.*

defensive (dĭ fĕn′sĭv), *adj.* **1.** serving to defend; protective: *defensive armour.* **2.** made or carried on for the purpose of resisting attack. **3.** of or pertaining to defence: *a defensive attitude.* —*n.* **4.** something that serves to defend. **5.** defensive position or attitude. —**defen′sively,** *adv.* —**defen′siveness,** *n.*

defer[1] (dĭ fû′), *v.,* **-ferred, -ferring.** —*v.t.* **1.** to put off (action, etc.) to a future time. —*v.i.* **2.** to put off action; delay. [ME *differre(n)*, t. L: m. *differre* delay. See DIFFER] —**defer′rer,** *n.*

—**Syn. 1.** DEFER, DELAY, POSTPONE imply keeping something from occurring until a future time. To DEFER is to decide deliberately to do something later on: *to defer making a decision, a payment.* To DELAY is sometimes equivalent to DEFER, but usually it is to act in a dilatory manner and thus lay something aside until some indefinite future time: *to delay one's departure, answering a letter.* To POSTPONE a thing is to defer it to (usually) some particular time in the future, with the intention of beginning or resuming it then; the word is esp. used of official business, formal meetings, or the like: *to postpone an election.* —**Ant. 1.** accelerate.

defer[2] (dĭ fû′), *v.i.*, **-ferred, -ferring.** to yield in judgement or opinion (fol. by *to*). [t. F: s. *déférer*, t. L: m. *deferre* carry from or down, report, accuse]

deference (dĕf′ə rəns), *n.* **1.** submission or yielding to the judgement, opinion, will, etc., of another. **2.** respectful or courteous regard: *in deference to his wishes.*

deferent[1] (dĕf′ə rənt), *adj.* deferential. [t. L: s. *dēferens*, ppr., bringing down]

deferent[2] (dĕf′ə rənt), *adj. Anat.* **1.** conveying away. **2.** pertaining to the vas deferens, the deferent duct of the testes. [See DEFERENT[1], DEFER[2]]

deferential (dĕf′ə rĕn′shəl), *adj.* marked by or showing deference; respectful. —**def′eren′tially,** *adv.*

deferment (dĭ fû′mənt), *n.* the act of deferring or putting off; postponement.

deferred (dĭ fûd′), *adj.* **1.** postponed or delayed, as property rights which do not vest until some future event has occurred. **2.** suspended or held back for a period: *deferred interest account of shareholders.*

deferred shares, shares in a company which rank after the ordinary shares in the distribution of dividends.
defiance (dĭ fī′əns), *n.* **1.** a daring or bold resistance to authority or to any opposing force. **2.** open disregard: *in defiance of criticism.* **3.** a challenge to meet in combat or contest.
defiant (dĭ fī′ənt), *adj.* characterized by defiance, bold opposition, or antagonism. [t. F, ppr. of *défier* DEFY] —**defi′antly,** *adv.* —**defi′antness,** *n.* —**Syn.** insubordinate, contumacious, refractory, recalcitrant, rebellious, insolent. —**Ant.** obedient.
deficiency (dĭ fĭsh′ən sĭ), *n., pl.* **-cies. 1.** the state or fact of being deficient; lack; incompleteness; insufficiency. **2.** the amount lacked; a deficit.
deficiency disease, an illness due to an insufficient supply of one or more essential dietary constituents.
deficient (dĭ fĭsh′ənt), *adj.* **1.** lacking some element or characteristic; defective. **2.** insufficient; inadequate. [t. L: s. *dēficiens,* ppr., wanting] —**defi′ciently,** *adv.*
deficit (dĕf′ĭ sĭt, dĭ fĭs′ĭt), *n.* the amount by which a sum of money falls short of the required amount. [t. L: there is wanting] —**Ant.** surplus.
de fide (dē fī′dĭ), *Latin.* of the faith (used to describe a teaching of the Roman Catholic Church in which belief is obligatory).
defier (dĭ fī′ə), *n.* one who defies.
defilade (dĕf′ĭ lād′), *v.,* **-laded, -lading,** *n. Fort.* —*v.t.* **1.** to arrange the plan and profile of (a fortification) so as to protect its lines from enfilading fire and its interior from plunging or reverse fire. —*n.* **2.** the act or operation of defilading. [t. F, der. *défiler,* orig., unthread, f. *dé-* DIS- + *(en)filer* thread (ult. der. L *filum* a thread)]
defile[1] (dĭ fīl′), *v.t.,* **-filed, -filing. 1.** to make foul, dirty, or unclean; pollute; taint. **2.** to violate the chastity of. **3.** to make ceremonially unclean; desecrate. **4.** to sully (a reputation, etc.). [alter. of *befile* (OE *befȳlan* befoul)] —**defile′ment,** *n.* —**defil′er,** *n.*
defile[2] (dĭ fīl′, dē′fīl), *n., v.,* **-filed, -filing.** —*n.* **1.** any narrow passage, esp. between mountains. —*v.i.* **2.** to march in a line, or by files; file off. [t. F, n. use of pp. of *défiler* file off]
define (dĭ fīn′), *v.t.,* **-fined, -fining. 1.** to state or set forth the meaning of (a word, phrase, etc.). **2.** to explain the nature or essential qualities of; describe. **3.** to determine or fix the boundaries or extent of. **4.** to make clear the outline or form of. **5.** to fix or lay down definitely; specify distinctly. [ME *deffyne(n),* t. F: m. *définir,* t. L: m. *dēfīnīre* limit, determine, explain, terminate] —**defin′able,** *adj.* —**defin′abil′ity,** *n.* —**defin′ably,** *adv.* —**defin′er,** *n.*
defining clause, restrictive clause.
definite (dĕf′ĭ nĭt), *adj.* **1.** clearly defined or determined; not vague or general; fixed; precise; exact. **2.** having fixed limits; bounded with precision. **3.** defining; limiting. **4.** *Colloq.* certain; sure: *he was quite definite about his intentions.* **5.** *Bot.* (of an inflorescence) determinate. [t. L: m. s. *dēfīnītus,* pp., limited, determined] —**def′initely,** *adv.* —**def′initeness,** *n.* —**Syn. 2.** certain, clear, express. —**Ant. 1.** confused.
definite article, the article, as English *the,* which classes as identified the noun it modifies.
definition (dĕf′ĭ nĭsh′ən), *n.* **1.** the act of defining or making definite or clear. **2.** the formal statement of the meaning or signification of a word, phrase, etc. **3.** the condition of being definite. **4.** *Optics.* sharpness of the image formed by an optical system. **5.** *Electronics.* the accuracy of sound reproduction through a receiver, or picture reproduction in a television receiver.
definitive (dĭ fĭn′ĭ tĭv), *adj.* **1.** having the function of deciding or settling; determining; conclusive; final. **2.** serving to fix or specify definitely. **3.** having its fixed and final form. —*n.* **4.** a defining or limiting word, as an article, a demonstrative, or the like. —**defin′itively,** *adv.* —**defin′itiveness,** *n.*
definitude (dĭ fĭn′ĭ tyo͞od′), *n.* definiteness; exactitude; precision.
deflagrate (dĕf′lə grāt′, dē′flə-), *v.t., v.i.,* **-grated, -grating.** to burn, esp. suddenly and violently. [t. L: m. s. *dēflagrātus,* pp.] —**def′lagra′tion,** *n.*
deflate (dē flāt′), *v.t.,* **-flated, -flating. 1.** to release the air or gas from (something inflated, as a tyre). **2.** to reduce (currency, prices, etc.) from an inflated condition. **3.** to reduce in esteem, esp. self-esteem (a person or a person's ego). [t. L: m. s. *dēflātus,* pp., blown off]
deflation (dē flā′shən), *n.* **1.** the act of deflating. **2.** an abnormal decline in the level of commodity prices, esp. one not accompanied by an equal reduction in the costs of production. —**deflationary** (dē flā′shə nə rĭ, -shən rĭ), *adj.* —**defla′tionist,** *n., adj.*
deflect (dĭ flĕkt′), *v.t., v.i.* to bend or turn aside; turn from a true course or right line; swerve. [t. L: s. *dēflectere*] —**deflec′tor,** *n.*
deflection (dĭ flĕk′shən), *n.* **1.** the act of deflecting. **2.** the state of being deflected. **3.** amount of deviation. **4.** *Physics.* the deviation or swing of the indicator of an instrument from the position taken as zero. **5.** *Optics.* the bending of rays of light from a straight line. Also, **deflex′ion.**
deflective (dĭ flĕk′tĭv), *adj.* causing deflection.
defloration (dē′flô rā′shən), *n.* the act of deflowering. [ME *defloracion,* t. LL: m. s. *dēflōrātio*]
deflower (dē flou′ə), *v.t.* **1.** to deprive or strip of flowers. **2.** to deprive (a woman) of virginity; ravish. **3.** to despoil of beauty, freshness, sanctity, etc. [f. DE- + FLOWER, r. ME *deflore(n),* t. OF: m. *desflorer* remove the flower(s) from, ravish] —**deflow′erer,** *n.*
defluxion (dĭ flŭk′shən), *n. Pathol.* a copious discharge of fluid matter, as in catarrh.
Defoe (dĭ fō′), *n.* **Daniel,** 1661?–1731, English novelist and essayist.
defoliate (dē fō′lĭ āt′), *v.,* **-ated, -ating,** *adj.* —*v.t.* **1.** to strip or deprive (a tree, etc.) of leaves. —*v.i.* **2.** to lose leaves. —*adj.* **3.** having lost its leaves, as a tree; defoliated. [t. ML: m. s. *dēfoliātus,* pp., of *dēfoliāre,* der. L *folium* leaf] —**defo′lia′tion,** *n.*
deforce (dĭ fôs′), *v.t.,* **-forced, -forcing.** *Law.* to withhold (something) by force or violence, as from the rightful owner. [t. AF: s. *deforcer,* f. *de-* DE- + *forcer* FORCE, v.] —**deforce′ment,** *n.*
deforciant (dĭ fô′shənt), *n. Law.* one who deforces.
deforest (dē fŏ′rĭst), *v.t.* to divest of forests or trees. —**defor′esta′tion,** *n.* —**defor′ester,** *n.*
De Forest (də fŏ′rĭst), **Lee,** 1873–1961, U.S. inventor.
deform[1] (dĭ fôm′), *v.t.* **1.** to mar the natural form or shape of; put out of shape; disfigure. **2.** to make ugly, ungraceful, or displeasing; mar the beauty of; spoil. **3.** to change the form of; transform. **4.** *Mech.* to subject to deformation. [ME, t. L: s. *dēformāre* disfigure] —**deform′er,** *n.* —**Syn. 1.** See **mar.**
deform[2] (dĭ fôm′), *adj. Archaic.* deformed; ugly. [ME *defourme,* t. L: m. *dēformis* misshapen]
deformable (dĭ fô′mə bl), *adj.* capable of being deformed. —**deform′abil′ity,** *n.*
deformation (dē′fô mā′shən), *n.* **1.** the act of deforming; distortion; disfigurement. **2.** the result of deforming; change of form, esp. for the worse. **3.** *Mech.* a change in the shape or dimensions of a body resulting from stress; strain. **4.** an altered form.
deformed (dĭ fômd′), *adj.* **1.** having the form changed, with loss of beauty, etc.; misshapen; disfigured. **2.** hateful; offensive. —**deformedly** (dĭ fô′mĭd lĭ), *adv.* —**Syn. 1.** malformed, crippled.
deformity (dĭ fô′mĭ tĭ), *n., pl.* **-ties. 1.** the quality or state of being deformed, disfigured, or misshapen. **2.** *Pathol.* an abnormally formed part of the body, etc. **3.** a deformed person or thing. **4.** hatefulness; ugliness.
defraud (dĭ frôd′), *v.t.* to deprive of a right or property by fraud; cheat. [ME *defraude(n),* t. L: m. *dēfraudāre.* Cf. FRAUD] —**de′frauda′tion,** *n.* —**defraud′er,** *n.*
defray (dĭ frā′), *v.t.* to bear or pay (the costs, expenses, etc.). [t. F: s. *défrayer,* OF *desfraier* pay costs, der. *des-* DIS-[1] + *frai* cost, of Gmc origin] —**defray′able,** *adj.* —**defray′er,** *n.*
defrayal (dĭ frā′əl), *n.* payment of charges or expenses. Also, **defray′ment.**
defrock (dē′frŏk′), *v.t.* to unfrock.
defrost (dē frŏst′), *v.t.* **1.** to remove the frost or ice from. **2.** to cause (food, etc.) to thaw, as by removing from a refrigerator. —*v.i.* **3.** to thaw; to become free of frost and ice. —**defrost′er,** *n.*
deft (dĕft), *adj.* dexterous; nimble; skilful; clever. [ME; var. of DAFT] —**deft′ly,** *adv.* —**deft′ness,** *n.*
defunct (dĭ fŭngkt′), *adj.* **1.** deceased; dead; extinct. **2.** no longer operative; not in use. —*n.* **3. the defunct, a.** the dead person. **b.** dead people collectively. [t. L: s. *dēfunctus,* pp., discharged, finished] —**defunct′ness,** *n.*
defunctive (dĭ fŭngk′tĭv), *adj.* of or pertaining to the dead; funereal.
defy (dĭ fī′), *v.,* **-fied, -fying,** *n., pl.* **-fies.** —*v.t.* **1.** to challenge the power of; resist boldly or openly. **2.** to offer effective resistance to: *a fort which defies attacks.* **3.** to challenge (one) to do something deemed impossible. **4.** *Archaic.* to challenge to a combat or contest. —*n.* **5.** *Obs. except in U.S.* a challenge; a defiance. [ME *defye(n),* t. OF: m. *defier,* f. *de-* DE- + *fier* (g. L *fīdere* trust)] —**Syn. 1.** dare, brave, flout, scorn.
deg., degree; degrees.
dégagé (*Fr.* dė gȧ zhė′), *adj.* **1.** unconstrained; easy, as in manner. **2.** disinterested. [F, pp. of *dégager* disengage, put at ease]

degas (dĭ găs′), *v.t.*, **-gassed, -gassing. 1.** to free from gas. **2.** to treat with chemical agents to destroy a gas or its harmful properties. **3.** to complete the evacuation of gases in (a radio valve).

Degas (dā′gä; *Fr.* də gá′), *n.* **Hilaire Germain Edgar** (*Fr.* ē lĕr zhĕr măɴ ĕd gár′), 1834–1917, French painter.

de Gaulle (də gôl′; *Fr.* də gōl′), **Charles André Joseph Marie** (*Fr.* shàrl äɴ drė zhō zĕf märē′), 1890–1970, French general and statesman: president of France 1959–69.

degauss (dē′gous′, -gôs′), *v.t.* to demagnetize, esp. to neutralize a ship's magnetic field as a protection against magnetic mines. [f. DE- + *gauss* (from K. F. GAUSS)]

degeneracy (dĭ jĕn′ə rə sĭ), *n.* a degenerate state or character; degeneration.

degenerate (*v.* dĭ jĕn′ə rāt′; *adj., n.* dĭ jĕn′ə rĭt), *v.*, **-rated, -rating,** *adj., n.* —*v.i.* **1.** to decline in physical, mental, or moral qualities; deteriorate. **2.** *Biol.* to revert to a less highly organized or simpler type. —*adj.* **3.** having declined in physical or moral qualities; deteriorated; degraded: *a degenerate king.* **4.** having lost, or become impaired with respect to, the qualities proper to the race or kind: *a degenerate plant.* **5.** characterized by or associated with degeneracy: *degenerate times.* **6.** *Physics., Astron.* (of a gas) having its constituent atomic nuclei and electrons packed too closely together to permit the evolution of nuclear energy, as in white dwarf stars. —*n.* **7.** one who has retrogressed from a normal type or standard, as in morals or character. **8.** one exhibiting morbid physical and mental traits or tendencies, esp. from birth. [t. L: m. s. *dēgenerātus*, pp., departed from its race] —**degen′erately,** *adv.* —**degen′erateness,** *n.*

degeneration (dĭ jĕn′ə rā′shən), *n.* **1.** the process of degenerating. **2.** the state of being degenerate. **3.** *Biol.* reversion to a less highly organized or a simpler type. **4.** *Pathol.* **a.** a process by which a tissue deteriorates, loses functional activity, and may become converted into or replaced by other kinds of tissue. **b.** the morbid condition produced by such a process.

degenerative (dĭ jĕn′ə rə tĭv), *adj.* **1.** tending to degenerate. **2.** characterized by degeneration.

deglutinate (dĭ glo͞o′tĭ nāt′), *v.t.*, **-nated, -nating.** to extract the gluten from. [t. L: m. s. *dēglūtinātus*, pp., unglued]

deglutition (dē′glo͞o tĭsh′ən), *n.* *Physiol.* the act or process of swallowing. [der. *deglute* swallow down (now obs.), t. L: m. s. *dēglūtire*]

degradation (dĕg′rə dā′shən), *n.* **1.** the act of degrading. **2.** the state of being degraded. **3.** *Phys. Geog.* the wearing down of the land by the action of water, wind, or ice; erosion. **4.** *Chem.* the breakdown of a complex compound into simple ones, esp. the conversion of a sucrose into a compound with one less carbon atom. —**Syn. 2.** humiliation, disgrace, dishonour, debasement.

degrade (dĭ grād′), *v.t.*, **-graded, -grading. 1.** to reduce from a higher to a lower rank, degree, etc.; deprive of office, rank, degree, or title as a punishment. **2.** to lower in character or quality; debase; deprave. **3.** to lower in dignity or estimation; bring into contempt. **4.** to reduce in amount, strength, intensity, etc. **5.** *Phys. Geog.* to wear down by erosion, as hills (opposed to *aggrade*). [ME *degrade(n)*, t. ecclesiastical LL: m. *dēgradāre* reduce in rank, der. L *gradus* GRADE] —**degrad′er,** *n.* —**Syn. 1.** demote, depose. **3.** humiliate, disgrace, dishonour. See **humble.** —**Ant 1.** promote. **2.** uplift.

degraded (dĭ grā′dĭd), *adj.* debased; degenerate. —**degrad′edly,** *adv.* —**degrad′edness,** *n.*

degrading (dĭ grā′dĭng), *adj.* that degrades; debasing: *degrading obsequiousness.* —**degrad′ingly,** *adv.* —**degrad′ingness,** *n.*

degrease (dē′grēs′), *v.t.*, **-greased, -greasing.** to remove grease from; cleanse of grease.

degree (dĭ grē′), *n.* **1.** a step or stage in an ascending or descending scale, or in a course or process. **2.** *Genetics, etc.* a certain distance or remove in the line of descent, determining the proximity of blood. **3.** a stage in a scale of rank or dignity; relative rank, station, etc. **4.** a stage in a scale of intensity or amount: *to the last degree.* **5.** *Geom., etc.* the 360th part of a complete angle or turn (often indicated by the sign °, as 45°). **6.** *Alg.* the sum of the exponents of the variables in an algebraic expression: x^3 *and* $2x^2y$ *are terms of degree three.* **7.** a unit in the measurement of temperature. **8.** a unit on an arbitrary scale of measurement. **9.** *Geog., Astron.* a line or point on the earth or in the celestial sphere whose position is fixed by its angular distance measured in degrees from the equator (equinoctial) or a given meridian. **10.** a qualification conferred by a university for successful work, as judged by examination, or as an honorary recognition of achievement. **11.** *Gram.* one of the three parallel formations (positive, comparative, and superlative) of adjectives and adverbs, showing differences in quality, quantity, or intensity in the attribute referred to, as English *low, lower, lowest.* **12.** *Music.* **a.** the interval from one note to another on a stave. **b.** one of the eight progressive intervals from the tonic in an octave. **13.** *Law.* a relative measure of criminal responsibility. **14.** *Obs.* a step, as of a stair. **15. by degrees,** gradually. **16. to a degree,** to an undefined but considerable extent. [ME *degre*, t. OF, f. *de-* DE- + *gre*, g. L *gradus* step, degree, GRADE]

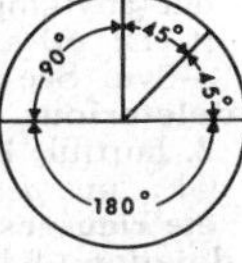

Degrees (def. 5) of a circle

degrees of freedom, *Chem.* **1.** the least number of variables which must be determined in order to define the state of a system in the phase-rule. **2.** the number of independent ways in which a molecule can possess translational, vibrational, or rotational energies.

De Groot (də grōt′; *Du.* də KHrōt′), **Huig** (*Du.* hœyKH). See **Grotius.**

degum (dē′gŭm′), *v.t.*, **-gummed, -gumming.** to free from gum.

degust (dĭ gŭst′), *v.t., v.i.* *Obs.* to taste. [t. L: s. *dēgustāre*] —**de′gusta′tion,** *n.*

de gustibus non est disputandum (dā go͝os′tĭ bo͝os nŏn′ ĕst dĭs′pyo͞o tăn′do͝om), *Latin.* there is no disputing about tastes.

de Havilland (də hăv′ĭ lənd), **Sir Geoffrey,** 1882–1965, British aircraft designer and manufacturer.

dehisce (dĭ hĭs′), *v.i.*, **-hisced, -hiscing.** to gape; burst open, as capsules of plants. [t. L: m. s. *dēhiscere*]

dehiscence (dĭ hĭs′əns), *n.* **1.** *Bot.* the natural bursting open to capsules, fruits, anthers, etc., for the discharge of their contents. **2.** *Biol.* the release of materials by the splitting open of an organ or tissue.

dehiscent (dĭ hĭs′ənt), *adj.* gaping open; characterized by dehiscence.

Dehiwala (dā′ wə lə), *n.* a town in SW Ceylon, near Colombo. 111,013 (1963).

de Hooch (*Du.* də hōKH′). See **Hooch.**

dehorn (dē hôn′), *v.t.* to deprive (cattle) of horns. —**dehorn′er,** *n.*

dehort (dĭ hôt′), *v.t., v.i.* *Archaic.* to seek to dissuade. [t. L: s. *dēhortārī*] —**de′horta′tion,** *n.* —**dehortative** (dĭ hô′tə tĭv), **dehortatory** (dĭ hô′tə tə rĭ), *adj., n.* —**dehort′er,** *n.*

Dehra Dun (dĕə′rə do͞on′), a town in India, in NW Uttar Pradesh. 126,918 (1961).

dehumanize (dē hyo͞o′mə nīz′), *v.t.*, **-nized, -nizing.** to deprive of human character. Also, **dehumanise.** —**dehu′maniza′tion,** *n.*

dehumidify (dē′hyo͞o mĭd′ĭ fī′), *v.t.*, **-fied, -fying.** to remove moisture from. —**de′humid′ifica′tion,** *n.* —**de′humid′ifi′er,** *n.*

dehydrate (dē hī′drāt), *v.*, **-drated, -drating.** —*v.t.* **1.** to deprive (a chemical compound) of water or the elements of water. **2.** to free (vegetables, etc.) from moisture for preservation. **3.** to remove water or moisture from (the body or a tissue). —*v.i.* **4.** to lose water or moisture. [f. DE- + HYDR- + -ATE[1]] —**de′hydra′tion,** *n.* —**Syn. 2.** See **evaporate.**

dehydrogenase (dē hī′drə jə nās′), *n.* *Biochem.* any enzyme that catalyses the dehydrogenation of a substrate.

dehydrogenize (dē hī′drə jə nīz′), *v.t.*, **-nized, -nizing.** *Chem.* to remove hydrogen from (a compound). Also, **dehydrogenise, dehydrogenate** (dē hī′drə jə nāt′). —**dehy′drogena′tion, dehydrogenization** (dē hī′drə jə nī zā′shən), *n.*

dehypnotize (dē′hĭp′nə tīz′), *v.t.*, **-tized, -tizing.** to bring out of the hypnotic state. Also, **dehypnotise.**

Deianira (dē′ə nī′ə rə), *n.* *Gk Legend.* a sister of Meleager and wife of Hercules, whom she unwittingly killed by giving him a shirt dipped in the poisonous blood of Nessus.

de-ice (dē′īs′), *v.t.*, **-iced, -icing.** to free or keep free of ice.

de-icer (dē′ī′sə), *n.* a mechanical or exhaust-heat device preventing or removing ice formation.

deicide (dē′ĭ sīd′), *n.* **1.** one who kills a god. **2.** the killing of a god. [f. s. L *deus* god + (I)CIDE] —**de′ici′dal,** *adj.*

deictic (dīk′tĭk), *adj.* **1.** *Logic.* proving directly. **2.** *Gram.* pointing; demonstrative. [t. Gk: m. s. *deiktikós*] —**deic′tically,** *adv.*

deid (dēd), *adj.* *Scot.* dead.

deific (dē ĭf′ĭk), *adj.* making divine; deifying. [t. LL: s. *deificus* god-making, sacred]

deification (dē′ĭ fĭ kā′shən), *n.* **1.** the act of deifying. **2.** the state of being deified. **3.** a deified embodiment.

deiform (dē′ĭ fôm′), *adj.* godlike; divine. [t. ML: s. *deiformis*, der. L *deus* god. See -FORM]

deify (dē′ĭ fī′), *v.t.*, **-fied, -fying. 1.** to make a god of;

exalt to the rank of a deity. **2.** to adore or regard as a deity: *to deify prudence.* [ME *deify(en)*, t. OF: m. *deifier*, t. LL: m. *deificāre*] **—de′ifi′er,** *n.*

deign (dān), *v.i.* **1.** to think fit or in accordance with one's dignity; condescend. *—v.t.* **2.** to condescend to give or grant: *deigning no reply.* **3.** *Obs.* to condescend to accept. [ME *deine(n)*, t. OF: m. *deignier*, g. L *dignārī* deem worthy]

Dei gratia (dā′ē grä′tĭ ä′), *Latin.* by the grace of God.

deil (dēl), *n. Scot.* devil.

Deïphobus (dē ĭf′ə bəs), *n. Gk Legend.* a son of Priam and Hecuba, who married Helen after the death of Paris and was slain by Menelaus.

deipnosophist (dīp nŏs′ə fĭst), *n.* a master of the art of dining, esp. of conversation at table. [t. Gk: s. *deipnosophistaí* (pl.) kitchen-sophists, title of a work by Athenaeus (?228 A.D.)]

Deirdre (dĭə′drĭ), *n.* heroine of an Irish legend: raised to be the wife of King Conchobar of Ulster, she fell in love with one of the sons of Usnach and escaped with him and his brothers to Scotland. Conchobar had the brothers killed and Deirdre killed herself, fulfilling a prenatal prophecy that she would bring sorrow and death. Deirdre is often used as a symbol for Ireland.

Deir-ez-Zor (dĕə′ rĕz zô′), *n.* a town in E Syria. 59,757 (1962).

deism (dē′ĭz′əm), *n.* **1.** belief in the existence of a God on the evidence of reason and nature only, with rejection of supernatural revelation (distinguished from *theism*). **2.** belief in a God who created the world but has since remained indifferent to his creation (distinguished from *atheism, pantheism,* and *theism*). [f. s. L *deus* god + -ISM]

deist (dē′ĭst), *n.* one who believes in deism. **—deis′tic, deis′tical,** *adj.* **—deis′tically,** *adv.*

deity (dē′ĭ tĭ), *n., pl.* **-ties. 1.** a god or goddess. **2.** divine character or nature. **3.** the estate or rank of a god. **4.** the character or nature of the Supreme Being. **5. the Deity,** God. [ME *deite*, t. OF, t. LL: m. s. *deitās*]

déjà vu (dā′zhä vyōō′; *Fr.* dė zhȧ vʏ′), *French.* **1.** the sense or illusion of having previously experienced something actually being encountered for the first time. **2.** unoriginal; trite.

deject (dĭ jĕkt′), *v.t.* **1.** to depress the spirits of; dispirit; dishearten. *—adj.* **2.** *Archaic.* dejected; downcast. [t. L: s. *dējectus*, pp., thrown down]

dejecta (dĭ jĕk′tə), *n.pl.* excrements.

dejected (dĭ jĕk′tĭd), *adj.* depressed in spirits; disheartened; low-spirited. **—deject′edly,** *adv.* **—deject′edness,** *n.* **—Syn.** discouraged, despondent, dispirited, downhearted. See **sad.** **—Ant.** gay.

dejection (dĭ jĕk′shən), *n.* depression or lowness of spirits. **—Ant.** exhilaration.

déjeuner (dā′zhə nā′; *Fr.* dė zhœ nė′), *n.* **1.** breakfast. **2.** (in Continental use) lunch. [F, orig. inf., OF *desjeuner* break one's fast, der. *des-* DIS-[1] + *jeun* fasting, g. L *jējūnus* jejune]

de jure (dē jŏŏə′rĭ), *Latin.* by right; according to law.

dek-, var. of **dec-.**

deka-, var. of **deca-.**

deki-, var. of **deci-.**

Dekker (dĕk′ə), *n.* **Thomas,** 1570?–1645?, English dramatist.

dekko (dĕk′ō), *n., pl.* **-kos.** *Slang.* a look or view. [t. Hind.: m. *dekho* look!]

Del., Delaware.

del., delegate.

Delacroix (*Fr.* də lȧ krwȧ′), *n.* **Ferdinand Victor Eugène** (*Fr.* fĕr dē näN vĕk tŏr œ zhĕn′), 1798?–1863, French painter.

Delagoa Bay (dĕl′ə gō′ə), an inlet of the Indian Ocean in S Mozambique. 55 mi. long.

delaine (də lān′), *n.* a thin woollen fabric, often having a printed pattern; mousseline de laine.

de la Mare (dĕl′ə mĕə′), **Walter (John),** 1873–1956, English poet and novelist.

delaminate (dē lăm′ ĭ nāt′), *v.i.,* **-nated, -nating.** to split into laminae or thin layers.

delamination (dē lăm′ĭ nā′shən), *n.* **1.** a splitting apart into layers. **2.** *Embryol.* the separation of a primitive blastoderm into two layers of cells.

delate (dĭ lāt′), *v.t.,* **-lated, -lating. 1.** to inform against; denounce or accuse. **2.** to relate or report (an offence, etc.). [t. L: m. s. *dēlātus*, pp., carried from or down, reported, accused] **—dela′tion,** *n.* **—dela′tor,** *n.*

Delavigne (*Fr.* də lȧ vēny′), *n.* **Jean François Casimir** (*Fr.* zhäN fräN swȧ kȧ zē mēr′), 1793–1843, French poet and dramatist.

Delaware (dĕl′ə wĕə′), *n.* **1.** a state in the eastern United States, on the Atlantic coast. 446,292 pop. (1960); 2057 sq. mi. *Cap.:* Dover. *Abbrev.:* Del. **2.** a river flowing from SE New York along the boundary between Pennsylvania and New Jersey into Delaware Bay. 296 mi. **3.** a member of a group of North American Indians, formerly occupying the drainage basin of the Delaware river and the greater part of New Jersey. **4.** a member of this group. **5.** their language, of the Algonquian stock. **6.** See **De La Warr.** [named after Baron DE LA WARR] **—Delawarean** (dĕl′ə wĕə′rĭ ən), *adj., n.*

Delaware Bay, an estuary between E Delaware and S New Jersey. ab. 70 mi. long.

De La Warr (dĕl′ə wĕə′), **Thomas West, Baron,** 1577–1618, first English colonial governor of Virginia. Also, **Del′aware′.**

delay (dĭ lā′), *v.t.* **1.** to put off to a later time; defer; postpone. **2.** to impede the progress of; retard; hinder. *—v.i.* **3.** to put off action; linger; loiter: *Don't delay!* *—n.* **4.** the act of delaying; procrastination; loitering. **5.** an instance of being delayed. **6.** *Electronics.* **a.** the time interval required for a signal to propagate through a circuit. **b.** a circuit whose sole function is to delay a signal by a fixed amount of time. [ME *delaie(n)*, t. OF: m. *delaier* put off, b. L *dīlātāre* (freq. of L *differre* DEFER[1]) and L var. (unrecorded) of *dēliquāre* strain, clear off] **—delay′er,** *n.* **—Syn. 1.** See **defer. 5.** deferment, postponement, respite.

delayed action, (of an explosive projectile) designed to explode some time after hitting the target or being otherwise primed.

delayed neutron, *Physics.* a neutron, resulting from a nuclear fission, which is emitted after a measurable time-delay.

delaying action, any action taken whose purpose is to gain time, esp. a military action delaying the advance of a superior enemy force by withdrawing while inflicting the maximum damage possible without becoming involved in decisive combat.

delay line, *Electronics.* a device which introduces a delay into a signal path.

del credere (dĕl krĕd′ə rĭ), a guarantee by a commission agent of the solvency of a purchaser, for which an extra commission is paid.

dele (dē′lĭ), *v.,* **deled, deleing,** *n., pl.* **deles** (dē′lēz). *Print.* *—v.t.* **1.** (usually imperative) to take out; omit; delete (generally represented by a symbol). *—n.* **2.** the symbol meaning delete. [t. L]

delectable (dĭ lĕk′tə bl), *adj.* delightful; highly pleasing; enjoyable. [ME, t. L: m. s. *dēlectābilis*] **—delec′tableness, delec′tabil′ity,** *n.* **—delec′tably,** *adv.* **—Ant.** disagreeable, distasteful.

delectate (dĭ lĕk′tāt), *v.t.,* **-tated, -tating.** to please; charm; delight. [t. L: m. s. *dēlectātus*, pp. delighted]

delectation (dē′lĕk tā′shən), *n.* delight.

Deledda (*It.* dė lĕd′dȧ), *n.* **Grazia** (*It.* grȧt′tsyȧ), 1875–1936, Italian novelist.

delegacy (dĕl′ĭ gə sĭ), *n., pl.* **-cies. 1.** the position or commission of a delegate. **2.** the sending or appointing of a delegate. **3.** a body of delegates. **4.** (at English universities) a standing committee for certain duties.

delegate (*n.* dĕl′ĭ gāt′, -gĭt; *v.* dĕl′ĭ gāt′), *n., v.,* **-gated, -gating.** *—n.* **1.** one delegated to act for or represent another or others; a deputy; a representative, as at a conference, or the like. **2.** *U.S. Govt.* **a.** the representative of a Territory in the House of Representatives of the U.S. **b.** a member of the lower house of the state legislatures of Maryland, Virginia, and West Virginia. *—v.t.* **3.** to send or appoint (a person) as deputy or representative. **4.** to commit (powers, functions, etc.) to another as agent or deputy. [t. L: m. s. *dēlēgātus*, pp., sent, deputed] **—Syn. 4.** depute, entrust.

delegation (dĕl′ĭ gā′shən), *n.* **1.** the act of delegating. **2.** the fact of being delegated. **3.** any group of delegates. **4.** *U.S.* the body of delegates chosen to represent a political unit in an assembly.

delenda (dĭ lĕn′də), *n.pl.* matter which is to be deleted. [t. L, neut. gerundive of *dēlēre* to delete]

de Lesseps (*Fr.* də lĕ sĕps′). See **Lesseps.**

delete (dĭ lēt′), *v.t.,* **-leted, -leting.** to strike out or take out (anything written or printed); cancel; erase; expunge. [t. L: m. s. *dēlētus*, pp., done away with, destroyed] **—Syn.** See **cancel.**

deleterious (dĕl′ĭ tĭə′rĭ əs), *adj.* **1.** injurious to health. **2.** hurtful; harmful; injurious. [t. NL: m. *dēlētērius*, t. Gk: m. *dēlētérios*] **—del′ete′riously,** *adv.* **—del′ete′riousness,** *n.* **—Ant. 2.** beneficial.

deletion (dĭ lē′shən), *n.* **1.** the act of deleting. **2.** the fact of being deleted. **3.** a deleted passage. [t. L: s. *dēlētio*]

delft (dĕlft), *n.* **1.** a kind of glazed earthenware decorated in colours, esp. in blue, made at Delft. **2.** any pottery resembling this. Also, **delf** (dĕlf), **delft′ware′.**

Delft (dĕlft), *n.* a town in W Netherlands. 76,760 (1965).

Delgado (dĕl gä′dō), *n.* **Cape,** a cape at the NE extremity of Mozambique.

Delhi (dĕl′ĭ), *n.* **1.** a centrally administered territory in N India. 2,658,612 pop. (1961); 574 sq. mi. **2.** the capital of this territory; former capital of the old Mogul Empire. Delhi was the administrative headquarters of British India from 1912 until 1929, when New Delhi became the capital. 2,061,758 (1961).

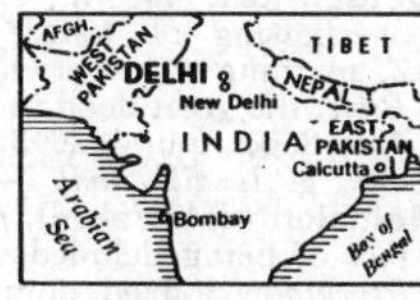

Delhi (def. 2)

Delian (dē′lyən), *adj.* **1.** pertaining to Delos. —*n.* **2.** a native or inhabitant of Delos.

deliberate (*adj.* dĭ lĭb′ə rĭt; *v.* dĭ lĭb′ə rāt′), *adj., v.,* **-rated, -rating.** —*adj.* **1.** carefully weighed or considered; studied; intentional. **2.** characterized by deliberation; careful or slow in deciding. **3.** leisurely in movement or action; slow; unhurried. —*v.t.* **4.** to weigh in the mind; consider: *to deliberate a question, a proposition, etc.* —*v.i.* **5.** to think carefully or attentively; reflect. **6.** to consult or confer formally. [t. L: m. s. *dēlīberātus*, pp., weighed well] —**delib′erately,** *adv.* —**delib′erateness,** *n.* —**delib′era′tor,** *n.*

—**Syn. 1.** DELIBERATE, INTENTIONAL, PREMEDITATED, VOLUNTARY refer to something not happening by chance. DELIBERATE is applied to what is not done hastily but with full realization of what one is doing: *a deliberate attempt to evade justice.* INTENTIONAL is applied to what is definitely intended, or done on purpose: *an intentional omission.* PREMEDITATED is applied to what has been planned in advance: *a premeditated crime.* VOLUNTARY is applied to what is done by a definite exercise of the will and not because of outward pressures: *a voluntary enlistment.* **2.** thoughtful, circumspect, cautious. **3.** See **slow. 5.** weigh, ponder, cogitate. —**Ant. 1.** accidental. **2.** impulsive, precipitate.

deliberation (dĭ lĭb′ə rā′shən), *n.* **1.** careful consideration before decision. **2.** formal consultation or discussion. **3.** deliberate quality; leisureliness of movement or action; slowness.

deliberative (dĭ lĭb′ə rə tĭv), *adj.* **1.** having the function of deliberating, as a legislative assembly. **2.** having to do with policy; dealing with the wisdom and expediency of a proposal: *a deliberative speech.* —**delib′eratively,** *adv.* —**delib′erativeness,** *n.*

Delibes (*Fr.* də lēb′), *n.* **Clément Philibert Léo** (*Fr.* klĕ mäɴ fē lē bĕr lė ō′), 1836–91, French composer.

delicacy (dĕl′ĭ kə sĭ), *n., pl.* **-cies. 1.** fineness of texture, quality, etc.; softness: *the delicacy of lace.* **2.** something delightful or pleasing, esp. to the palate. **3.** fineness of perception or feeling; sensitiveness. **4.** the quality of requiring or involving great care or tact: *negotiations of great delicacy.* **5.** nicety of action or operation; minute accuracy: *a surgeon's delicacy of touch.* **6.** fineness of feeling with regard to what is fitting, proper, etc. **7.** bodily weakness; liability to sickness. **8.** gratification; luxury. —**Ant. 1, 2.** coarseness.

delicate (dĕl′ĭ kĭt), *adj.* **1.** fine in texture, quality, construction, etc. **2.** dainty or choice, as food. **3.** soft or faint, as colour. **4.** so fine or slight as to be scarcely perceptible; subtle. **5.** easily damaged; fragile. **6.** requiring great care, caution, or tact. **7.** fine or exquisite in action or execution: *a delicate instrument.* **8.** regardful of what is becoming, proper, etc., or of the feelings of others. **9.** exquisite or refined in perception or feeling; sensitive. **10.** distinguishing subtle differences. **11.** *Obs.* fastidious. **12.** *Obs.* luxurious or voluptuous. —*n.* **13.** *Archaic.* a delicacy; a dainty. **14.** *Obs.* a luxury. [ME, t. L: m. s. *dēlicātus* delightful, luxurious, soft; akin to DELICIOUS] —**del′icately,** *adv.* —**del′icateness,** *n.*

—**Syn. 1.** DELICATE, DAINTY, EXQUISITE imply beauty such as belongs to rich surroundings or which needs careful treatment. DELICATE, used of an object, suggests fragility, small size, and often very fine workmanship: *a delicate piece of carving.* DAINTY, in concrete references, suggests a smallness, gracefulness, and beauty which forbid rough handling; there is a connotation of attractiveness: *a dainty handkerchief;* of persons, it refers to fastidious sensibilities: *dainty in eating habits.* EXQUISITE suggests an outstanding beauty, daintiness, and elegance, or a discriminating sensitivity and ability to perceive fine distinctions: *an exquisite face, an exquisite sense of humour.* **5.** tender, frail. **6.** critical, precarious. **7.** exact, precise, accurate. —**Ant. 1, 2.** coarse.

delicatessen (dĕl′ĭ kə tĕs′ən), *n.* **1.** (*construed as sing.*) a shop selling chiefly foreign foods, delicacies, and foods difficult to obtain. **2.** (*construed as pl.*) the foods sold. [t. G: pl. of *Delikatesse* delicacy, t. F]

delicious (dĭ lĭsh′əs), *adj.* **1.** highly pleasing to the senses, esp. to taste or smell. **2.** pleasing in the highest degree; delightful. —*n.* **3.** (*cap.*) a variety of eating apple; Golden Delicious. [ME, t. OF, t. LL: m. s. *dēliciōsus*, der. L *dēlicia* delight] —**deli′ciously,** *adv.* —**deli′ciousness,** *n.*

—**Syn. 1.** DELICIOUS, LUSCIOUS refers to that which is especially agreeable to the senses. That which is DELICIOUS is highly agreeable to the taste (or sometimes to the smell): *a delicious meal.* LUSCIOUS implies such a luxuriant fullness or ripeness as to make an object sweet and rich, sometimes to excess; it is often used in transferred or humorous senses: *a luscious banana, a luscious beauty, luscious music.* —**Ant. 1.** tasteless, insipid.

delict (dĭ lĭkt′, dē′lĭkt), *n.* **1.** *Civil Law.* a legal offence. **2.** *Rom. Law.* a civil wrong permitting compensation or punitive damages. [t. L: s. *dēlictum* fault, orig. pp. neut.]

delight (dĭ līt′), *n.* **1.** a high degree of pleasure or enjoyment; joy; rapture. **2.** something that gives great pleasure. —*v.t.* **3.** to give great pleasure, satisfaction, or enjoyment to; please highly. —*v.i.* **4.** to have great pleasure; take pleasure (fol. by *in* or an infinitive). [erroneous 16th-cent. sp., after *light*, r. ME *delit*, t. OF: der. *delitier*, g. L *dēlectāre*, freq. of *dēlicere* allure] —**delight′er,** *n.* —**Syn. 1.** enjoyment, transport, delectation. See **pleasure.** —**Ant. 1.** distress. **2.** disappointment.

delighted (dĭ lī′tĭd), *adj.* **1.** highly pleased. **2.** *Obs.* delightful. —**delight′edly,** *adv.* —**delight′edness,** *n.*

delightful (dĭ līt′fəl), *adj.* affording delight; highly pleasing. —**delight′fully,** *adv.* —**delight′fulness,** *n.* —**Syn.** pleasurable, enjoyable; charming, enchanting, delectable, agreeable. —**Ant.** obnoxious.

delightsome (dĭ līt′səm), *adj. Archaic.* delightful. —**delight′somely,** *adv.* —**delight′someness,** *n.*

Delilah (dĭ lī′lə), *n.* **1.** *Bible.* Samson's mistress, who betrayed him to the Philistines. Judges 16. **2.** a seductive and treacherous woman.

delimit (dĭ lĭm′ĭt), *v.t.* to fix or mark the limits of; demarcate. [t. F: s. *délimiter*, t. L: m. *dēlīmitāre*] —**delim′ita′tion,** *n.* —**delimitative** (dĭ lĭm′ĭ tə tĭv), *adj.*

delineable (dĭ lĭn′ĭ ə bl), *adj.* that can be delineated.

delineate (dĭ lĭn′ĭ āt′), *v.t.,* **-ated, -ating. 1.** to trace the outline of; sketch or trace in outline; represent pictorially. **2.** to portray in words; describe. [t. L: m. s. *dēlīneātus*, pp., sketched out]

delineation (dĭ lĭn′ĭ ā′shən), *n.* **1.** the act or process of delineating. **2.** a chart or diagram; a sketch; a rough draft. **3.** a description. —**delineative** (dĭ lĭn′ĭ ə tĭv), *adj.*

delineator (dĭ lĭn′ĭ ā′tə), *n.* **1.** one who or that which delineates. **2.** a tailor's pattern which can be adjusted for cutting garments of different sizes.

delineavit (dĭ lĭn′ĭ ā′vĭt), *Latin.* he (or she) drew (this).

delinquency (dĭ lĭng′kwən sĭ), *n., pl.* **-cies. 1.** failure in or neglect of duty or obligation; fault; guilt. **2.** a misdeed or offence, esp. by a young person. **3.** delinquent behaviour or character.

delinquent (dĭ lĭng′kwənt), *adj.* **1.** failing in or neglectful of a duty or obligation; guilty of a misdeed or offence. **2.** of or pertaining to delinquents: *delinquent taxes.* —*n.* **3.** one who is delinquent, esp. a young person: *juvenile delinquent.* [t. L: s. *dēlinquens*, ppr.] —**delin′quently,** *adv.*

deliquesce (dĕl′ĭ kwĕs′), *v.i.,* **-quesced, -quescing. 1.** to melt away. **2.** to become liquid by absorbing moisture from the air, as certain salts. **3.** *Bot.* to form many small divisions or branches. [t. L: m. s. *dēliquescere* melt away]

deliquescence (dĕl′ĭ kwĕs′əns), *n.* **1.** the act or process of deliquescing. **2.** the liquid when something deliquesces. —**del′iques′cent,** *adj.*

deliration (dĕl′ĭ rā′shən), *n. Obs.* mental derangement; raving; delirium. [t. L: s. *dēlīrātio*]

delirious (dĭ lĭə′rĭ əs), *adj.* **1.** *Pathol.* affected with delirium. **2.** characteristic of delirium. **3.** wild with excitement, enthusiasm, etc. —**delir′iously,** *adv.* —**delir′iousness,** *n.*

delirium (dĭ lĭ′rĭ əm), *n., pl.* **-liriums, -liria** (-lĭ′rĭ ə). **1.** a more or less temporary disorder of the mental faculties, as in fevers, disturbances of consciousness, or intoxication, characterized by restlessness, excitement, delusions, hallucinations, etc. **2.** a state of violent excitement or emotion. [t. L, der. *dēlīrāre* be deranged, lit., go out of the furrow]

delirium tremens (trē′mĕnz), a violent restlessness due to excessive indulgence in alcohol, characterized by trembling, terrifying visual hallucinations, etc. [NL: trembling delirium]

delitescent (dĕl′ĭ tĕs′ənt), *adj.* concealed. [t. L: s. *dēlitescens*, ppr.] —**del′ites′cence,** *n.*

Delius (dē′lyəs), *n.* **Frederick,** 1862–1934, English composer.

deliver (dĭ lĭv′ə), *v.t.* **1.** to give up or surrender; give into another's possession or keeping. **2.** to carry and pass over (letters, goods, etc.) to the intended recipient or recipients. **3.** to direct; cast; cause to move in a certain direction: *the bowler delivers the ball to the batsman.* **4.** to strike: *to deliver a blow.* **5.** to give forth or produce: *our mines are still delivering 192 million tons of coal each year.* **6.** to give forth in words; utter or pronounce: *to deliver a verdict.* **7.** to bring forth (young); give birth to. **8.** to assist (a female) in giving birth. **9.** to assist at the birth of. **10.** to disburden (oneself) of thoughts, opinions, etc. **11.** to set free; liberate. **12.** to release or save: *deliver us from evil.* **13.** *U.S.* to bring (votes) to the support of a candidate or cause. **14.** *Obs.* to make known; assert. *—v.i.* **15.** to make a delivery or deliveries. **16.** to give birth. **17.** to provide a delivery service. *—adj.* **18.** *Obs. or Archaic.* agile; active; quick. [ME *delivre(n)*, t. F: m. *délivrer*, g. LL *dēlīberāre* set free] **—deliv′erable,** *adj.* **—deliv′erer,** *n.* **—Syn. 1.** hand over, transfer, cede. **6.** communicate, impart. **11.** free, emancipate. **12.** redeem, rescue.

deliverance (dĭ lĭv′ə rəns), *n.* **1.** the act of delivering. **2.** the fact of being delivered. **3.** a thought or judgement expressed; a formal or authoritative pronouncement.

deliverly (dĭ lĭv′ə lĭ), *adv. Archaic.* quickly; deftly.

delivery (dĭ lĭv′ə rĭ), *n., pl.* **-eries. 1.** the delivering of letters, goods, etc. **2.** a giving up or handing over; surrender. **3.** the utterance or enunciation of words. **4.** vocal and bodily behaviour during the presentation of a speech. **5.** the act or manner of giving or sending forth, as of a ball by the bowler in cricket. **6.** release or rescue. **7.** the being delivered of, or giving birth to a child; parturition. **8.** something delivered. **9.** *Com.* a shipment of goods from the seller to the buyer. **10.** *Law.* an act sometimes essential to a legally effective transfer of property: *a delivery of deed.*

dell (dĕl), *n.* a small valley; a vale, esp. a wooded one. [ME *delle*, OE *dell*; akin to DALE]

della Robbia (*It.* dĕl lä rôb′byä), **Luca** (*It.* lo͞o′kä). See **Robbia.**

Delmenhorst (*Ger.* dĕl′mən hŏrst), *n.* a town in West Germany, in N central Lower Saxony. 61,800 (est. 1966).

del Monaco (*It.* dĕl mŏn′ä kō), **Mario** (*It.* mä′ryō), born 1919, Italian operatic tenor.

delocalize (dē lō′kə līz′), *v.t.,* **-lized, -lizing.** to remove from the proper or usual locality. Also, **delocalise. —delo′caliza′tion,** *n.*

Delorme (*Fr.* də lŏrm′), *n.* **Philibert** (*Fr.* fē lē bĕr′), c. 1510–70, French architect.

Delos (dē′lŏs), *n.* a tiny Greek island in the Cyclades, in the SW Aegean: the site of an oracle of Apollo.

de los Angeles (də lŏs ăn′jĭ lĭs), **Victoria** (vĭk tô′rĭ ə), born 1923, Spanish soprano.

delouse (dē lous′, -louz′), *v.t.,* **-loused, -lousing.** to free of lice; remove lice from.

Delphi (dĕl′fī), *n.* an ancient city in central Greece, in Phocis: the site of an oracle of Apollo.

Delphic (dĕl′fĭk), *adj.* **1.** pertaining to Delphi, to the temple and oracle of Apollo there, or to Apollo himself. **2.** ambiguous. Also, **Delphian** (dĕl′fĭ ən). [t. L: s. *Delphicus*, t. Gk: m. *Delphikós*]

Delphic oracle, the oracle of the temple of Apollo at Delphi which often gave ambiguous answers.

delphinine (dĕl′fĭ nēn′, -nĭn), *n. Chem.* a bitter, poisonous, crystalline alkaloid obtained from various species of delphinium, esp. *Delphinium staphisagria.* [f. DELPHIN(IUM) + -INE[2]]

delphinium (dĕl fĭn′ĭ əm), *n.* any of numerous garden varieties of ranunculaceous plants of the genus *Delphinium*, having handsome, usually blue, irregular flowers; larkspur. [t. NL, t. Gk: m. *delphínion* larkspur, dim. of *delphín* dolphin; so called from the shape of the nectary]

Delphinus (dĕl fī′nəs), *n., gen.* **-ni** (-nī). *Astron.* the Dolphin, a northern constellation between Aquila and Pegasus. [t. L: dolphin]

Del Sarto (dĕl sä′tō), **Andrea** (ăn′drĭ ə). See **Sarto.**

delta (dĕl′tə), *n.* **1.** the fourth letter (Δ, δ, = English *D, d*) of the Greek alphabet. **2.** anything triangular, like the Greek capital Δ. **3.** a nearly flat plain of alluvial deposit between diverging branches of the mouth of a river, often, though not necessarily, triangular: *the delta of the Nile.*

deltaic (dĕl tā′ĭk), *adj.* **1.** forming a delta. **2.** having a delta. **3.** like a delta; fan-shaped.

delta iron, *Metall.* the allotropic form of iron consisting of body-centred cubic crystals which, when pure, exists between approx. 1400°C and the melting point.

delta ray, *Physics.* an electron knocked out of an atom by a fast-moving ionized particle.

delta wing, *Aeron.* an approximately triangular swept-back aircraft wing.

deltoid (dĕl′toid), *n.* **1.** a large triangular muscle covering the joint of the shoulder and serving to raise the arm away from the side of the body. *—adj.* **2.** triangular. [t. Gk: m. s. *deltoeidḗs* delta-shaped]

Deltoid leaf

delude (dĭ lo͞od′), *v.t.* **-luded, -luding. 1.** to mislead the mind or judgement of; deceive. **2.** *Obs.* to cheat the hopes of. **3.** *Obs.* to elude; evade. [t. L: m. s. *dēlūdere* play false] **—delud′er,** *n.* **—Syn. 1.** beguile, cozen, dupe, cheat.

deluge (dĕl′yo͞oj), *n., v.,* **-uged, -uging.** *—n.* **1.** a great overflowing of water; inundation; flood; downpour. **2.** anything that overwhelms like a flood. **3. the Deluge,** *Bible.* the great flood in the days of Noah. Gen. 7. *—v.t.* **4.** to flood; inundate. **5.** to overrun; overwhelm. [ME, t. OF, g. L *dīluvium*] **—Syn. 1.** See **flood.**

delusion (dĭ lo͞o′zhən), *n.* **1.** the act of deluding. **2.** the fact of being deluded. **3.** a false belief or opinion. **4.** *Psychiatry.* a fixed, dominating, or persistent false mental conception resistant to reason with regard to actual things or matters of fact: *a paranoiac delusion.* **—delu′sional,** *adj.* **—Syn. 2.** See **illusion.**

delusive (dĭ lo͞o′sĭv), *adj.* **1.** tending to delude; deceptive. **2.** of the nature of a delusion; false; unreal. Also, **delusory** (dĭ lo͞o′sə rĭ). **—delu′sively,** *adv.* **—delu′siveness,** *n.*

de luxe (də lo͝oks′, lŭks′; *Fr.* də lʏks′), of special elegance, sumptuousness, or fineness. [F: of luxury]

delve (dĕlv), *v.,* **delved, delving.** *—v.i.* **1.** to carry on intensive or thorough research for information, etc. **2.** to dip; slope suddenly. **3.** *Archaic or Dial.* to dig, as with a spade. *—v.t.* **4.** *Archaic or Dial.* to dig. **5.** *Archaic.* to obtain by digging. [ME *delve(n)*, OE *delfan*, c. D *delven*] **—delv′er,** *n.*

Dem., 1. Democrat. 2. Democratic.

demagnetize (dē măg′nə tīz′), *v.t.,* **-tized, -tizing.** to remove magnetic properties from. Also, **demagnetise. —demag′netiza′tion,** *n.* **—demag′netiz′er,** *n.*

demagogic (dĕm′ə gŏg′ĭk), *adj.* **1.** characteristic of a demagogue. **2.** of a demagogue. Also, **dem′agog′ical.**

demagogue (dĕm′ə gŏg′), *n.* **1.** a leader who uses the passions or prejudices of the populace for his own interests; an unprincipled popular orator or agitator. **2.** (historically) a leader of the people. Also, *U.S.*, **demagog.** [t. Gk: m. s. *dēmagōgós*, f. s. *dēmos* people + *agōgós* leader]

demagoguery (dĕm′ə gŏg′ə rĭ), *n.* the methods or practices of a demagogue.

demagoguism (dĕm′ə gŏg′ĭz əm), *n.* demagoguery. Also, **dem′agog′ism.**

demagogy (dĕm′ə gŏg′ĭ), *n.* **1.** demagoguery. **2.** the character of a demagogue. **3.** a body of demagogues.

demand (dĭ mănd′), *v.t.* **1.** to ask for with authority; claim as a right: *to demand something of or from a person.* **2.** to ask for peremptorily or urgently. **3.** to call for or require as just, proper, or necessary: *a task which demands patience.* **4.** *Law.* to lay formal legal claim to. *—v.i.* **5.** to make a demand; inquire or ask. *—n.* **6.** the act of demanding. **7.** that which is demanded. **8.** an urgent or pressing requirement: *demands upon one's time.* **9.** an inquiry or question. **10.** a requisition; a legal claim. **11.** the state of being in request for purchase or use: *an article in great demand.* **12.** *Econ.* **a.** the desire to purchase and possess, coupled with the power of purchasing. **b.** the quantity of any goods which buyers will take at a particular price. See **supply. 13. on demand,** subject to payment upon presentation and demand. [t. F: s. *demander*, g. L *dēmandāre* give in charge, entrust, ML demand] **—demand′able,** *adj.* **—demand′er,** *n.*

—Syn. 1. DEMAND, CLAIM, REQUIRE imply making an authoritative request. To DEMAND is to ask in a bold, authoritative way: *to demand an explanation.* To CLAIM is to assert a right to something: *he claimed it as his due.* To REQUIRE is to ask for something as being necessary; to compel: *the Army requires absolute obedience.*

demandant (dĭ măn′dənt), *n. Law.* **1.** the plaintiff in a real action. **2.** any plaintiff.

demand bill, draft, or **note,** a bill of exchange, note, etc., payable on demand or presentation.

demarcate (dē′mä kāt′), *v.t.,* **-cated, -cating. 1.** to mark off the boundaries of. **2.** to separate distinctly. [back-formation from DEMARCATION]

demarcation (dē′mä kā′shən), *n.* **1.** the marking off of the boundaries of something. **2.** a division between things, esp. the division between types of work carried out by members of different trade unions. **3.** separation by distinct boundaries. **4.** the defining of boundaries. Also, **de′marka′tion.** [Latinization of Sp. *demarcación*, der. *demarcar* mark out the bounds of]

démarche (dā′mäsh; *Fr.* dė mȧrsh′), *n. French.* **1.** a plan or mode of procedure. **2.** a change in a course of action. **3.** a diplomatic representation made to a foreign government. [F, der. *démarcher* march]

dematerialize (dē′mə tĭə′rĭ ə līz′), *v.t., v.i.,* **-lized, -lizing.** to deprive of or lose material character. Also, **dematerialise. —de′mate′rializa′tion,** *n.*

Demavend (dĕm′ə vĕnd′), *n.* a mountain peak of the Elburz Mountains in N Iran. 18,606 ft.

deme (dēm), *n.* one of the administrative divisions of ancient Attica and of modern Greece. [t. Gk: m. s. *dêmos* district, country, people, commons]

demean[1] (dĭ mēn′), *v.t.* to lower in dignity or standing; debase. [f. DE- + MEAN[2], modelled on DEBASE]

demean[2] (dĭ mēn′), *v.t.* to conduct or behave (oneself) in a specified manner. [ME *demene(n)*, t. OF: m. *demener*, f. *de-* DE- + *mener* lead, g. L *mināre* drive]

demeanour (dĭ mē′nə), *n.* conduct; behaviour; bearing. Also, *U.S.*, **demeanor.** [ME *demenure*, der. *demene(n)* DEMEAN[2], v.]

dement (dĭ mĕnt′), *v.t.* to drive mad or insane. [t. L: s. *dēmentāre* deprive of mind]

demented (dĭ mĕn′tĭd), *adj.* out of one's mind; crazed; insane; affected with dementia. —**dement′edly,** *adv.* —**dement′edness,** *n.*

dementia (dĭ mĕn′shə, -shĭ ə), *n. Pathol., Psychol.* a state of mental disorder characterized by impairment or loss of the mental powers; commonly an end result of several mental or other diseases. [t. L: madness]

dementia praecox (prē′kŏks), *Pathol., Psychol.* a form of insanity usually occurring or beginning at puberty and characterized by introversion, dissociation, and odd, distorted behaviour. [t. L: precocious insanity]

demerara (dĕm′ə rĕə′rə), *n.* a brown crystallized cane sugar from the West Indies and nearby countries. [from *Demerara* a region in Guyana, where it was originally chiefly produced]

demerit (dē mĕ′rĭt, dē′mĕ′rĭt), *n.* **1.** censurable or punishable quality; fault. **2.** *U.S.* a mark against a person for misconduct or deficiency. **3.** *Obs.* merit or desert. [t. L: s. *dēmeritum* (in ML, fault), prop. pp. neut. of *dēmerērī* deserve (esp. well)]

demersal (dĭ mû′səl), *adj. Zool.* found at or near the sea bottom. [f. s. L *dēmersus*, pp., submerged + -AL[2]]

demesne (dĭ mān′, -mēn′), *n.* **1.** possession (of land) as one's own. **2.** an estate possessed, or in the actual possession or use of the owner. **3.** the land attached to a manor house, reserved for the owner's use. **4.** the dominion or territory of a sovereign or state; a domain. **5.** a district; region. [ME *demeyne*, t. AF. See DOMAIN]

Demeter (dĭ mē′tə), *n. Gk Myth.* the goddess of the fruitful earth, protectress of social order and marriage, identified by the Romans with Ceres. [t. L, t. Gk]

demi-, a prefix meaning: **1.** half, as in *demiquaver*. **2.** inferior, as in *demigod*. [t. F: repr. *demi*, adj. (also n. and adv.), g. L *dīmedius*, r. *dīmidius* half]

demibastion (dĕm′ĭ băs′tĭ ən), *n. Fort.* a work consisting of half a bastion, and hence having one face and one flank.

demigod (dĕm′ĭ gŏd′), *n.* **1.** one partly divine and partly human; an inferior deity. **2.** a deified mortal. —**demigoddess** (dĕm′ĭ gŏd′ĭs), *n. fem.*

demijohn (dĕm′ĭ jŏn′), *n.* a large small-necked bottle, usually cased in wickerwork. [t. F: m. *damejeanne*, appar. a popular name, Dame Jane]

demilitarize (dē mĭl′ĭ tə rīz′), *v.t.*, **-rized, -rizing. 1.** to deprive of military character; free from militarism. **2.** to place under civil instead of military control. Also, **demilitarise.** —**demil′itariza′tion,** *n.*

demilune (dĕm′ĭ lo͞on′, -lyo͞on′), *n.* anything crescent-shaped, esp. an outwork of a fortification resembling a bastion.

demimondaine (dĕm′ĭ mŏn′dān; *Fr.* də mē mōɴ dĕn′), *n.* a woman of the demimonde. [t. F]

demimonde (dĕm′ĭ mŏnd′; *Fr.* də mē mōɴd′), *n.* the world or class of women who have become socially declassed, or of doubtful reputation and standing. [t. F: lit., half-world]

demipique (dĕm′ĭ pēk′), *n.* an 18th-century saddle having a peak about half the height of earlier styles. [f. DEMI- + *pique* (pseudo-F sp. of PEAK)]

demirelief (dĕm′ĭ rĭ lēf′), *n.* mezzo-rilievo.

demirep (dĕm′ĭ rĕp′), *n.* a woman of doubtful or compromised reputation. [short for *demi-reputation*]

demise (dĭ mīz′), *n., v.*, **-mised, -mising.** —*n.* **1.** death or decease. **2.** *Law.* **a.** a death or decease occasioning the transfer of an estate. **b.** a conveyance or transfer of an estate. **3.** *Govt.* transfer of sovereignty, as by the death or deposition of the sovereign. —*v.t.* **4.** *Law.* to transfer (an estate, etc.) for a limited time; lease. **5.** *Govt.* to transfer (sovereignty), as by the death or abdication of the sovereign. —*v.i.* **6.** *Law.* to pass by bequest, inheritance, or succession to the Crown. [t. OF, prop. pp. fem. of *desmettre* send or put away. See DEMIT] —**demis′able,** *adj.*

demisemiquaver (dĕm′ĭ sĕm′ĭ kwā′və), *n. Music.* a note having half the time value of a semiquaver. See illus. under **note.**

demission (dĭ mĭsh′ən), *n.* **1.** abdication. **2.** *Rare.* dismissal. [t. F. Cf. L *dīmissio* a sending away]

demit (dĭ mĭt′), *v.*, **-mitted, -mitting.** *Chiefly Scot.* —*v.t.* **1.** to give up, as a dignity or office; resign. **2.** *Archaic.* to dismiss. —*v.i.* **3.** to resign. [b. F *démettre* send or put away and L *dīmittere* send away]

demitasse (dĕm′ĭ tăs′; *Fr.* də mē tȧs′), *n.* a small cup for serving black coffee after dinner. [t. F: half cup]

demiurge (dĕm′ĭ ûj′, dē′mĭ-), *n.* **1.** *Philos.* **a.** (in Platonic philosophy) the artificer of the world. **b.** (in the Gnostic and certain other systems) a supernatural being imagined as creating or fashioning the world in subordination to the Supreme Being, and sometimes regarded as the originator of evil. **2.** (in many states of ancient Greece) a public official or magistrate. [t. Gk: m. s. *dēmiourgós* worker for the people, artificer, maker] —**demiurgeous** (dĕm′ĭ û′jəs, dē′mĭ-), **dem′iur′gic,** *adj.* —**dem′iur′gically,** *adv.*

demivolt (dĕm′ĭ vŏlt′), *n.* a half-turn made by a horse with the forelegs raised. Also, **dem′ivolte′.** [t. F: m. *demi-volte.* See DEMI-, VOLT[1]]

demo (dĕm′ō), *n. Colloq.* a demonstration.

demo-, a word element meaning 'people', 'population', 'common people'. [t. Gk, comb. form of *dêmos* DEMOS]

demob (dē mŏb′), *n., v.*, **-mobbed, -mobbing.** *Colloq.* —*n.* **1.** demobilization. —*v.t.* **2.** to discharge (a soldier) from the army. [short for DEMOBILIZE]

demobilize (dē mō′bĭ līz′), *v.*, **-lized, -lizing.** —*v.t.* **1.** to disband (an army, etc.). —*v.i.* **2.** (of an army or its members) to disband. Also, **demobilise.** —**demo′biliza′tion,** *n.*

democracy (dĭ mŏk′rə sĭ), *n., pl.* **-cies. 1.** government by the people; a form of government in which the supreme power is vested in the people and exercised by them or by their elected agents under a free electoral system. **2.** a state having such a form of government. **3.** (in a restricted sense) a state in which the supreme power is vested in the people and exercised directly by them rather than by elected representatives. See **republic. 4.** a state of society characterized by formal equality of rights and privileges. **5.** political or social equality; democratic spirit. **6.** the common people of a community as distinguished from any privileged class; the common people with respect to their political power. **7.** (*cap.*) *U.S. Pol.* **a.** the principles of the Democratic Party. **b.** the members of this party collectively. [t. F: m. *démocratie*, ult. t. Gk: m. s. *dēmokratía* popular government, f. *dēmo-* DEMO- + *-kratía* rule, authority]

democrat (dĕm′ə krăt′), *n.* **1.** an advocate of democracy. **2.** one who maintains the political or social equality of men. **3.** (*cap.*) *U.S. Pol.* a member of the Democratic Party.

democratic (dĕm′ə krăt′ĭk), *adj.* **1.** pertaining to or of the nature of democracy or a democracy. **2.** pertaining to or characterized by the principle of political or social equality for all. **3.** advocating or upholding democracy. **4.** (*cap.*) *U.S. Pol.* of, pertaining to, or characteristic of the Democratic Party. Also, **dem′ocrat′ical.** —**dem′ocrat′ically,** *adv.*

democratize (dĭ mŏk′rə tīz′), *v.t., v.i.*, **-tized, -tizing.** to make or become democratic. Also, **democratise.** —**democ′ratiza′tion,** *n.*

Democritus (dĭ mŏk′rĭ təs), *n.* ('*the Laughing Philosopher*'), *c.* 460–*c.* 370 B.C., Greek philosopher.

demoded (dē mō′dĭd), *adj.* no longer in fashion.

demodulate (dē mŏd′yo͞o lāt′), *v.t.*, **-lated, -lating.** *Radio.* to separate (a signal) from the carrier wave in a radio receiver. —**demod′ula′tion,** *n.*

Demogorgon (dē′mō gô′gən), *n.* a vague, mysterious, infernal power or divinity of ancient mythology, variously represented, as an object of awe or fear. [t. LL, t. Gk. See DEMO-, GORGON]

demography (dĭ mŏg′rə fĭ), *n.* the science of vital and social statistics, as of the births, deaths, diseases, marriages, etc., of populations. —**demog′rapher, demog′raphist,** *n.* —**demographic** (dē′mə grăf′ĭk, dĕm′ə-), **de′mograph′ical,** *adj.* —**de′mograph′ically,** *adv.*

demoiselle (də mwä zĕl′; *Fr.* də mwȧ zĕl′), *n.* **1.** a damsel. **2.** the Numidian crane, *Anthropoides virgo*, of northern Africa, Asia, and Europe, having long white plumes behind the eyes. **3.** any of various slender-bodied dragonflies. [F]

demolish (dĭ mŏl′ĭsh), *v.t.* **1.** to throw or pull down (a building, etc.); reduce to ruins. **2.** to put an end to; destroy; ruin utterly; lay waste. [t. F: m. *démoliss-*, s. *démolir*, t. L: m. *dēmōlīrī* throw down, destroy] —**demol′isher,** *n.* —**demol′ishment,** *n.* —**Syn. 2.** See **destroy.** —**Ant. 2.** restore.

demolition (dĕm′ə lĭsh′ən, dē′mə-), *n.* **1.** the act of demolishing. **2.** the state of being demolished; destruction.

demon (dē′mən), *n.* **1.** an evil spirit; a devil. **2.** an evil passion or influence. **3.** an atrociously wicked or cruel person. **4.** a person of great energy, etc. **5.** daemon. [(defs 1–4) used for L *daemonium*, t. Gk: m. *daimónion* thing of divine nature (in Jewish and Christian writers, evil spirit); (def. 5) t. L: m. *daemon* spirit, evil spirit, t. Gk: m. *daímōn* tutelary divinity, evil spirit]

demon-, a word element meaning 'demon'. [t. Gk, comb. form of *daímōn*]

demonetize (dē mŭn′ĭ tīz′), *v.t.*, **-tized, -tizing. 1.** to divest of value, as the monetary standard. **2.** to withdraw from use as money. Also, **demonetise.** —**demon′etiza′tion,** *n.*

demoniac (dĭ mō′nĭ ăk′), *adj.* Also, **demoniacal** (dē′mə nī′ə kl). **1.** of, pertaining to, or like a demon. **2.** possessed by an evil spirit; raging; frantic. —*n.* **3.** one seemingly possessed by a demon or evil spirit. [ME *demoniak*, t. LL: m. s. *daemoniacus*, t. Gk: m. *daimoniakós*] —**demoniacally** (dē′mə nī′ĭ kə lĭ, -klĭ), *adv.* —**Ant. 1.** angelic.

demonian (dē mō′nyən), *adj.* pertaining to or of the nature of a demon.

demonic (dē mŏn′ĭk), *adj.* **1.** of, pertaining to, or of the nature of a demon. **2.** inspired as if by a demon, indwelling spirit, or genius. [t. L: m. s. *daemonicus*, t. Gk: m. *daimonikós*]

demonism (dē′mə nĭz′əm), *n.* **1.** belief in demons. **2.** worship of demons. **3.** demonology. —**de′monist,** *n.*

demonize (dē′mə nīz′), *v.t.*, **-nized, -nizing. 1.** to turn into or make like a demon. **2.** to subject to the influence of demons. Also, **demonise.**

demono-, var. of **demon-,** before consonants.

demonolater (dē′mə nŏl′ə tə), *n.* a demon worshipper.

demonolatry (dē′mə nŏl′ə trĭ), *n.* the worship of demons.

demonology (dē′mə nŏl′ə jĭ), *n.* the study of demons or of beliefs about demons. —**de′monol′ogist,** *n.*

demonstrable (dĭ mŏn′strə bl, dĕm′ən-), *adj.* capable of being demonstrated. —**demon′strabil′ity, demon′strableness,** *n.* —**demon′strably,** *adv.*

demonstrant (dĭ mŏn′strənt), *n.* demonstrator.

demonstrate (dĕm′ən strāt′), *v.*, **-strated, -strating.** —*v.t.* **1.** to make evident by arguments or reasoning; prove. **2.** to describe and explain with the help of specimens or by experiment. **3.** to manifest or exhibit. —*v.i.* **4.** to make, give, or take part in, a demonstration. **5.** *Mil.* to attack or make a show of force to deceive the enemy. [t. L: m. s. *dēmonstrātus*, pp., showed, proved]

demonstration (dĕm′ən strā′shən), *n.* **1.** the proving of anything conclusively, as by arguments, reasoning, evidence, etc. **2.** proof, or anything serving as a proof. **3.** a description or explanation, as of a process, given with the help of specimens or by experiment. **4.** the act of exhibiting and explaining an article or commodity by way of advertising it. **5.** an exhibition, as of feeling; a display; manifestation. **6.** a public exhibition of sympathy, opposition, etc., as a parade or mass meeting. **7.** a show of military force or of offensive operations, made to deceive the enemy. **8.** *Maths.* a logical presentation of the way in which given assumptions imply a certain result. —**dem′onstra′tional,** *adj.* —**dem′onstra′tionist,** *n.*

demonstrative (dĭ mŏn′strə tĭv), *adj.* **1.** characterized by or given to open exhibition or expression of the feelings, etc. **2.** serving to demonstrate; explanatory or illustrative. **3.** serving to prove the truth of anything; indubitably conclusive. **4.** *Gram.* indicating or specifying the thing referred to. —*n.* **5.** *Gram.* a demonstrative word, as *this* or *there.* —**demon′stratively,** *adv.* —**demon′strativeness,** *n.*

demonstrator (dĕm′ən strā′tə), *n.* **1.** one who or that which demonstrates. **2.** Also, **demonstrant.** one who takes part in a public demonstration. **3.** one who explains or teaches by practical demonstrations; (in some university faculties) a lecturer. **4.** one who shows the use and application (of a product, etc.) to prospective customers.

demoralize (dĭ mŏ′rə līz′), *v.t.*, **-lized, -lizing. 1.** to corrupt or undermine the morals of. **2.** to deprive (a person, a body of soldiers, etc.) of spirit, courage, discipline, etc. **3.** to reduce to a state of weakness or disorder. Also, **demoralise.** [t. F: m. s. *démoraliser*] —**demor′aliza′tion,** *n.* —**demor′aliz′er,** *n.*

de mortuis nil nisi bonum (dā mô′tyŏŏ is nĭl′ nē′sĭ bŏn′ŏŏm), *Latin.* of the dead (say) nothing but good.

demos (dē′mŏs), *n.* **1.** the people or commons of an ancient Greek state. **2.** the common people; the populace. [t. Gk: district, people]

Demosthenes (dĭ mŏs′thə nēz′), *n.* 384?–322 B.C., Athenian statesman and orator. —**Dem′osthen′ic,** *adj.*

demote (dĭ mōt′), *v.t.*, **-moted, -moting.** to reduce to a lower grade or class (opposed to *promote*). [f. DE- + *mote*, modelled on PROMOTE] —**demo′tion,** *n.*

demotic (dĭ mŏt′ĭk), *adj.* **1.** of or pertaining to the common people; popular. **2.** of or pertaining to the ancient Egyptian handwriting of ordinary life, a simplified form of the hieratic characters. **3.** of or pertaining to the Modern Greek vernacular. —*n.* **4.** the demotic script of ancient Egypt. **5.** (*cap.*) the Modern Greek vernacular. [t. Gk: m. s. *dēmotikós* popular, plebeian]

demount (dē mount′), *v.t.* to remove from its mounting, setting, or place of support, as a gun. —**demount′able,** *adj.*

dempster (dĕmp′stə), *n.* deemster.

demulcent (dĭ mŭl′sənt), *adj.* **1.** soothing or mollifying, as a medicinal substance. —*n.* **2.** a demulcent (often mucilaginous) substance or agent, as for soothing or protecting an irritated mucous membrane. [t. L: s. *dēmulcens*, ppr., stroking down, softening]

demulsify (dē mŭl′sĭ fī′), *v.t.*, **-fied, -fying.** *Phys. Chem.* to break down (an emulsion) into separate substances, incapable of re-forming the same emulsion.

demur (dĭ mû′), *v.*, **-murred, -murring,** *n.* —*v.i.* **1.** to make objection; take exception; object. **2.** *Law.* to interpose a demurrer. **3.** *Obs.* to linger; hesitate. —*n.* **4.** the act of making objection. **5.** an objection raised. **6.** *Obs., Law.* a demurrer. **7.** *Obs.* hesitation. [ME *demeore(n)*, t. OF: m. *demeurer*, g. L *dēmorārī* linger] —**Ant. 1.** agree, accede.

demure (dĭ myŏŏ′), *adj.*, **-murer, -murest. 1.** affectedly or unnaturally modest, decorous, or prim. **2.** sober; serious; sedate; decorous. [ME, der. OF *meur* grave, ripe, g. L *mātūrus* MATURE] —**demure′ly,** *adv.* —**demure′ness,** *n.* —**Syn. 1.** See **modest.**

demurrage (dĭ mŭ′rĭj), *n.* *Com.* **1.** the detention of a vessel, as in loading or unloading, beyond the time agreed upon. **2.** the similar detention of a railway wagon, etc. **3.** a charge for such detention. **4.** a charge made by the Bank of England in exchanging gold or notes for bullion.

demurral (dĭ mû′rəl), *n.* the act of demurring; demur.

demurrer (dĭ mû′rə *for 1*; dĭ mŭ′rə *for 2 and 3*), *n.* **1.** one who demurs; an objector. **2.** *Law.* a pleading in effect that even if the facts are as alleged by the opposite party, they do not sustain the contention based on them. **3.** an objection or demur. [t. AF, var. of OF *demourer.* See DEMUR]

demy (dĭ mī′), *n.*, *pl.* **-mies. 1.** a foundation scholar at Magdalen College, Oxford (so called because orig. receiving half the allowance of a fellow). **2.** a particular size of paper, 22 × 17 inches for printing; 20 × 15 inches for writing, or (U.S.) 21 × 16 inches. [free form of DEMI-, with change of final *i* to *y* in accordance with rules of English spelling]

demyelization (dē′mī′ĭ lī zā′shən), *n.* *Physiol.* a process in which the myelin is lost from nervous tissue. Also, **demyelisation, demyelination** (dē′mī′ĭ lĭ nā′shən).

demythologize (dē′mĭth ŏl′ə jīz), *v.t.*, **-gized, -gizing. 1.** to divest (a writing, person, work of art, etc.) of its legendary or mythological character. **2.** to present (a religious system) in rational terms. Also, **demythologise.**

den (dĕn), *n.*, *v.*, **denned, denning.** —*n.* **1.** a secluded place, as a cave, serving as the habitation of a wild beast. **2.** a cave as a place of shelter, concealment, etc. **3.** a squalid or vile abode or place: *dens of misery.* **4.** a cosy or secluded room for personal use. —*v.i.* **5.** to live in or as in a den. [ME; OE *denn.* Cf. early mod. D *denne* floor, cave, den, G *Tenne* floor]

Den., Denmark.

denarius (dĭ nēə′rĭ əs), *n.*, *pl.* **-narii** (-nēə′rĭ ī′). **1.** a Roman silver coin of varying intrinsic value. **2.** (in English monetary reckoning) a penny, hence *d.* [t. L, orig. adj., containing ten (asses). See DENARY]

denary (dē′nə rĭ), *adj.* **1.** containing ten; tenfold. **2.** proceeding by tens; decimal. [t. L: m. s. *dēnārius* containing ten, der. *dēnī* ten at a time]

denationalize (dē năsh′ə nə līz′), *v.t.*, **-lized, -lizing. 1.** to deprive of national status, attachments, or characteristics. **2.** to return (an industry, etc.) from state to private ownership. Also, **denationalise.** —**dena′tionaliza′tion,** *n.*

denaturalize (dē năch′rə līz′), *v.t.*, **-lized, -lizing. 1.** to deprive of the original nature; make unnatural. **2.** to deprive of the rights and privileges of citizenship or of naturalization. Also, **denaturalise.** —**denat′uraliza′tion,** *n.*

denature (dē nā′chə), *v.t.*, **-tured, -turing. 1.** to deprive (something) of its peculiar nature. **2.** to render (alcohol, etc.) unfit for drinking or eating by adding a poisonous substance without altering the usefulness for other purposes. **3.** *Biochem.* to treat (a protein, etc.) by chemical or physical means so as to alter its original state. **4.** to render (a fissile material) unsuitable for use in a nuclear weapon by adding another isotope to it. —**dena′turant,** *n.* —**dena′tura′tion,** *n.*

denaturize (dē nā′chə rīz′), *v.t.*, **-rized, -rizing.** to denature. Also, **denaturise.** —**dena′turiza′tion,** *n.*

denazify (dē nät′sĭ fī), *v.t.*, **-fied, -fying.** to rid of Nazism or Nazi influences. —**dena′zifica′tion,** *n.*
Denb., Denbighshire.
Denbigh (dĕn′bĭ), *n.* **1.** Denbighshire. **2.** a town in N Wales, the county town of Denbighshire. 8044 (1961).
Denbighshire (dĕn′bĭ shĭə′, -shə), *n.* a county in N Wales. 173,843 pop. (1961); 669 sq. mi. *Co. town:* Denbigh. *Abbrev.:* Denb. Also, **Den′bigh.**
dendr-, var. of **dendro-,** before vowels.
dendriform (dĕn′drĭ fôm′), *adj.* treelike in form. [DENDR- + -(I)FORM]
dendrite (dĕn′drīt), *n.* **1.** *Geol.* **a.** a branching figure or marking, resembling moss or a shrub or tree in form, found on or in certain stones or minerals, and due to the presence of a foreign material. **b.** any arborescent crystalline growth. **2.** *Anat., Physiol.* the branching portion of a neurone which picks up the stimulus and transmits it to the cyton. See diag. under **nerve cell.** [t. Gk: m. s. *dendrítēs* of a tree]

Dendrite (def. 1a)

dendritic (dĕn drĭt′ĭk), *adj.* **1.** formed or marked like a dendrite. **2.** of a branching form; arborescent. Also, **dendrit′ical.** —**dendrit′ically,** *adv.*
dendro-, a word element meaning 'tree', as in *dendrology.* [t. Gk, comb. form of *déndron*]
dendrobates (dĕn drŏb′ə tēz′), *n.* any member of the *Dendrobates,* a S American genus of frogs whose glands exude a poison used by Indians for poisoning their arrowheads; the poison-arrow frog.
dendroid (dĕn′droid), *adj.* treelike; branching like a tree; arborescent. Also, **dendroi′dal.** [t. Gk: m. s. *dendroeidḗs* treelike]
dendrolatry (dĕn drŏl′ə trĭ), *n.* the worship of trees.
dendrology (dĕn drŏl′ə jĭ), *n.* the part of botany that treats of trees and shrubs. —**dendrological** (dĕn′drə lŏj′ĭ kl), **dendrologous** (dĕn drŏl′ə gəs), *adj.* —**dendrologist** (dĕn drŏl′ə jĭst), *n.*
-dendron, a word element meaning 'tree', as in *rhododendron.* [repr. Gk *déndron* tree]
dene (dēn), *n.* a bare sandy tract or low sandhill near the sea. Also, **dean.** [ME; orig. uncert.]
Deneb (dĕn′ĕb), *n.* *Astron.* a star of the first magnitude in the constellation Cygnus. [t. Ar.: m. *dhanab* tail]
Denebola (dĭ nĕb′ə lə), *n.* a star at the tail of the constellation Leo.
denegation (dĕn′ĭ gā′shən), *n.* denial; contradiction. [t. LL: s. *dēnegātio*]
dengue (dĕng′gĭ), *n.* *Pathol.* an infectious, eruptive, usually epidemic, fever of warm climates, characterized esp. by severe pains in the joints and muscles; breakbone fever. [t. Sp., t. Swahili: m. *dinga* cramp]
Den Haag (*Du.* dĕn hȧKH′), Dutch name for **The Hague.**
Denham (dĕn′əm), *n.* **Sir John,** 1615–69, English poet.
Den Helder (*Du.* dĕn hĕl′dər), a town in the Netherlands, in North Holland. 53,583 (1965).
denial (dĭ nī′əl), *n.* **1.** a contradiction of a statement, etc. **2.** refusal to believe a doctrine, etc. **3.** disbelief in the existence or reality of a thing. **4.** the refusal of a claim, request, etc., or of a person making a request. **5.** refusal to recognize or acknowledge; a disowning or disavowal. **6.** self-denial. [f. DENY + -AL[3]]
denier[1] (dĭ nī′ə), *n.* one who denies. [ME; f. DENY + -ER[1]]
denier[2] (dĕn′ĭ ā′ *for 1;* dĭ nĭə′ *for 2; Fr.* də nyĕ′), *n.* **1.** a unit of weight used to indicate the fineness of silk, nylon, etc. **2.** *Obs.* a French coin varying in value with time and locality. [ME, t. OF, g. L *dēnārius* DENARIUS]
denigrate (dĕn′ĭ grāt′), *v.t.*, **-grated, -grating. 1.** to sully; defame. **2.** to blacken. [t. L: m. s. *dēnigrātus,* pp., blackened] —**den′igra′tion,** *n.* —**den′igra′tor,** *n.*
denim (dĕn′ĭm), *n.* **1.** a heavy twilled cotton for overalls, trousers, etc. **2.** a similar fabric of a finer quality used to cover cushions, etc. **3.** (*pl.*) *Colloq.* denim trousers or overalls. [t. F: short for *serge de Nîmes* serge of NÎMES]
Denis (dĕn′ĭs; *Fr.* də nē′), *n.* **Saint,** died A.D. 280?, first bishop of Paris; patron saint of France. Also, **Denys.**
denitrify (dē nī′trĭ fī′), *v.t.*, **-fied, -fying.** to reduce (nitrates) to nitrites, ammonia, and free nitrogen, as in soil by micro-organisms. —**deni′trifica′tion,** *n.*
denizen (dĕn′ĭ zən), *n.* **1.** an inhabitant; resident. **2.** an alien admitted to residence and to certain rights of citizenship in a country. **3.** anything adapted to a new place, condition, etc., as a naturalized foreign word, or an animal or plant not indigenous to a place but successfully naturalized. —*v.t.* **4.** to make a denizen of. [ME *deynseyn,* t. AF: m. *deinzein,* der. AF *deinz* within, g. L *dē intus*]
Denmark (dĕn′mäk), *n.* a kingdom in N Europe, on Jutland peninsula and the adjacent islands. 4,636,700 pop. (est. 1962); 16,576 sq. mi. *Cap.:* Copenhagen.
Denmark Strait, a strait between Iceland and Greenland. 130 mi. wide.
Dennis (dĕn′ĭs), *n.* **John,** 1657–1734, English critic and dramatist.
denom., denomination.
denominate (dĭ nŏm′ĭ nāt′), *v.t.*, **-nated, -nating.** to give a name to, esp. to call by a specific name. [t. L: m. s. *dēnōminātus,* pp.]
denomination (dĭ nŏm′ĭ nā′shən), *n.* **1.** a name or designation, esp. one for a class of things. **2.** a class or kind of persons or things distinguished by a specific name. **3.** a religious group. **4.** the act of denominating. **5.** one of the grades or degrees in a series of designations of quantity, value, measure, weight, etc.: *money of small denominations.*
denominational (dĭ nŏm′ĭ nā′shə nəl), *adj.* of or pertaining to a particular religious body or sect; sectarian. —**denom′ina′tionally,** *adv.*
denominationalism (dĭ nŏm′ĭ nā′shə nə lĭz′əm), *n.* denominational or sectarian spirit or policy; the tendency to divide into denominations or sects. —**denom′ina′tionalist,** *n.*
denominative (dĭ nŏm′ĭ nə tĭv), *adj.* **1.** conferring or constituting a distinctive denomination or name. **2.** *Gram.* (esp. of verbs) formed from a noun, as English *to man* from the noun *man.* —*n.* **3.** *Gram.* a denominative verb or other word.
denominator (dĭ nŏm′ĭ nā′tə), *n.* **1.** *Maths.* that term of a fraction (usually under the line) which shows the number of equal parts into which the unit is divided; a divisor placed under a dividend. **2.** one who or that which denominates or from which a name is derived.
denotation (dē′nō tā′shən), *n.* **1.** the meaning of a term when it identifies something by naming it (distinguished from *connotation*). **2.** the act or fact of denoting; indication. **3.** something that denotes; a mark; symbol. **4.** *Logic.* the class of particulars to which a term is applicable.
denotative (dĭ nō′tə tĭv), *adj.* having power to denote. —**deno′tatively,** *adv.*
denote (dĭ nōt′), *v.t.*, **-noted, -noting. 1.** to be a mark or sign of; indicate: *a quick pulse often denotes fever.* **2.** to be a name or designation for. **3.** to represent by a symbol; stand as a symbol for. **4.** to impress with a denoting stamp. [t. F: m. s. *dénoter,* t. L: m. *dēnotāre* mark out] —**denot′able,** *adj.*
denoting stamp, a revenue stamp on a document showing the amount of stamp duty paid on a corresponding document.
denouement (dā nōō′mŏng), *n.* **1.** the final disentangling of the intricacies of a plot, as of a drama or novel. **2.** the place in the plot at which this occurs. **3.** outcome; solution. Also, *French,* **dénouement** (*Fr.* dė nōō mäɴ′). [t. F, der. *dénouer* untie, f. *de(s)-* DE- + *nouer,* g. L *nodāre* knot, tie]
denounce (dĭ nouns′), *v.t.*, **-nounced, -nouncing. 1.** to condemn openly; assail with censure. **2.** to make formal accusation against; inform against. **3.** to give formal notice of the termination of (a treaty, etc.). **4.** *Archaic.* to announce or proclaim (something evil). **5.** *Obs.* to portend. [ME *denounse(n),* t. OF: m. *denoncier,* g. L *dēnuntiāre* threaten] —**denounce′ment,** *n.* —**denounc′er,** *n.* —**Ant. 1.** praise.
de novo (dē nō′vō), *Latin.* from the beginning; anew.
dense (dĕns), *adj.*, **denser, densest. 1.** having the component parts closely compacted together; compact: *a dense forest, dense population.* **2.** thickheaded; obtuse; stupid. **3.** intense: *dense ignorance.* **4.** *Photog.* (of a developed negative) relatively opaque; transmitting little light. [t. L: m. s. *densus* thick, thickly set] —**dense′ly,** *adv.* —**dense′ness,** *n.*
densimeter (dĕn sĭm′ĭ tə), *n.* *Chem., Physics.* any instrument for measuring density.
densitometer (dĕn′sĭ tŏm′ĭ tə), *n.* *Photog.* an instrument for measuring the density of negatives.
density (dĕn′sĭ tĭ), *n., pl.* **-ties. 1.** the state or quality of being dense; compactness; closely set or crowded condition. **2.** stupidity. **3.** *Physics.* the mass per unit of volume. **4.** *Elect.* **a.** the quantity of electricity per unit of volume at a point in space, or the quantity per unit of area at a point on a surface. **b.** current density. **5.** *Photog.* the opacity of any medium, esp. of a photographic plate or negative, which is often expressed logarithmically.
dent[1] (dĕnt), *n.* **1.** a hollow or depression in a surface, as from a blow. —*v.t.* **2.** to make a dent in or on; indent. **3.** to impress as a dent. —*v.i.* **4.** to sink in, making a dent. **5.** to become indented. [ME *dente;* var. of DINT]
dent[2] (dĕnt), *n.* a toothlike projection, as a tooth of a gearwheel. [t. F, g. L *dens* tooth]
dent., **1.** dentist. **2.** dentistry.

dental (dĕn′tl), *adj.* **1.** of or pertaining to the teeth. **2.** of or pertaining to dentistry. **3.** *Phonet.* **a.** with the tongue tip touching or near the upper front teeth, as French *t*. **b.** alveolar, as English alveolar *t*. —*n.* **4.** *Phonet.* a dental sound. [t. ML: s. *dentālis*, der. L *dens* tooth]

dentary (dĕn′tə rĭ), *n.* one of the pair of bones in the lower jaw of some vertebrates, usually bearing teeth.

dentate (dĕn′tāt), *adj. Bot., Zool.* having a toothed margin, or toothlike projections or processes. [t. L: m. s. *dentātus*, der. *dens* tooth] —**den′tately,** *adv.*

dentation (dĕn tā′shən), *n. Bot., Zool.* **1.** a dentate state or form. **2.** an angular projection of a margin.

denti-, a word element meaning 'tooth', as in *dentiform*. Also, before vowels, **dent-**. [t. L, comb. form of *dens*]

denticle (dĕn′tĭ kl), *n.* a small tooth or toothlike part. [ME, t. L: m. s. *denticulus*, dim. of *dens* tooth]

Dentate leaf

denticulate (dĕn tĭk′yōō lĭt, -lāt′), *adj.* **1.** *Bot., Zool.* finely dentate, as a leaf. **2.** *Archit.* having dentils. Also, **dentic′ulat′ed.** —**dentic′ulately,** *adv.*

denticulation (dĕn tĭk′yōō lā′shən), *n.* **1.** a denticulate state or form. **2.** a denticle. **3.** a series of denticles.

dentiform (dĕn′tĭ fôm′), *adj.* having the form of a tooth.

dentifrice (dĕn′tĭ frĭs), *n.* a powder, paste, or other preparation for cleaning the teeth. [t. F, t. L: m. s. *dentifricium* tooth powder. See DENTI-, FRICTION]

dentil (dĕn′tĭl), *n. Archit.* one of a series of small rectangular blocks arranged like a row of teeth, as in the lower part of a cornice. [t. F: m. *dentille* (obs.), fem. dim. of *dent* tooth]

dentilabial (dĕn′tĭ lā′byəl), *adj., n.* labiodental.

dentilingual (dĕn′tĭ lĭng′gwəl), *adj.* **1.** (of speech sounds) uttered with the tongue at the teeth, as the *th* in *thin* and *this*. —*n.* **2.** a dentilingual sound.

dentine (dĕn′tēn), *n. Anat.* the hard calcareous tissue beneath the enamel of the crown of the tooth and beneath the cementum of the root of the tooth. It contains less organic substance than cementum or bone and forms the greatest part of a tooth. Also, *Chiefly U.S.*, **dentin** (dĕn′tĭn). See diag. under **tooth.** [f. DENT- + -INE[2]] —**den′tinal,** *adj.*

dentiphone (dĕn′tĭ fōn′), *n.* an instrument held against the teeth to assist hearing by transmitting sound vibrations to the auditory nerve.

dentirostral (dĕn′tĭ rŏs′trəl), *adj. Ornith.* having a toothlike or notched projection on the bill.

dentist (dĕn′tĭst), *n.* one whose profession is dentistry. [t. F: m. *dentiste*, der. *dent* tooth]

dentistry (dĕn′tĭs trĭ), *n.* the science or art dealing with the prevention and treatment of oral disease, esp. in relation to the health of the body as a whole, and including such operations as the filling and crowning of teeth, the construction of dentures, etc.

dentition (dĕn tĭsh′ən), *n.* **1.** the growing of teeth; teething. **2.** the kind, number, and arrangement of the teeth of an animal, including man. [t. L: s. *dentītio* teething]

Denton (dĕn′tən), *n.* a town in England, in E Lancashire, near Manchester. 31,086 (1961).

D'Entrecasteaux Islands (dän trə käs tō′), a group of islands SE of New Guinea belonging to Australia: part of the territory of Papua.

denture (dĕn′chə), *n.* an artificial restoration of several teeth (**partial denture**) or of all the teeth of either jaw (**full denture**). [t. F, der. *dent* tooth]

denudate (dĕn′yōō dāt′, dĭ nyōō′dāt), *v.*, **-dated, -dating,** *adj.* —*v.t.* **1.** to denude. —*adj.* **2.** denuded; bare.

denudation (dĕn′yōō dā′shən, dē′nyōō-), *n.* **1.** the act of denuding. **2.** denuded or bare condition. **3.** *Geol.* the laying bare of rock by erosive processes.

denude (dĭ nyōōd′), *v.t.*, **-nuded, -nuding. 1.** to make naked or bare; strip. **2.** *Geol.* to subject to denudation. [t. L: m. s. *dēnūdāre* lay bare]

denunciate (dĭ nŭn′sĭ āt′), *v.t., v.i.*, **-ated, -ating.** to denounce; condemn openly. [t. L: m. s. *dēnuntiātus*, pp.] —**denun′cia′tor,** *n.*

denunciation (dĭ nŭn′sĭ ā′shən), *n.* **1.** a denouncing as evil; open and vehement condemnation. **2.** *Obs.* an accusation of crime before a public prosecutor or tribunal. **3.** notice of the termination of an international agreement or part thereof. **4.** announcement of impending evil; threat; warning.

denunciatory (dĭ nŭn′syə tə rĭ, -trĭ), *adj.* characterized by or given to denunciation. Also, **denunciative** (dĭ nŭn′syə tĭv). —**denun′cia′tor,** *n.*

Denver (dĕn′və), *n.* a city in the U.S., the capital of Colorado, in the central part. 493,887 (1960).

deny (dĭ nī′), *v.t.*, **-nied, -nying. 1.** to assert the negative of; declare not to be true: *I deny the charge, I deny he has done it.* **2.** to refuse to believe (a doctrine, etc.); reject as false or erroneous. **3.** to refuse to grant (a claim, request, etc.): *he denied me this, I was denied this.* **4.** to refuse to recognize or acknowledge; disown; disavow; repudiate. **5.** to refuse access to (one visited). **6.** *Obs.* to refuse to accept. **7.** *Obs.* to refuse (to do something). **8. deny oneself,** to exercise self-denial. [ME *denye(n)*, t. F: m. *dénier*, g. L *dēnegāre*] —**deni′able,** *adj.*

—**Syn. 1.** dispute, controvert, oppose, gainsay. DENY, CONTRADICT both imply objecting to or arguing against something. To DENY is to say that something is not true, or that it would not hold in practice: *to deny an allegation.* To CONTRADICT is to declare that the contrary is true: *to contradict a statement.* —**Ant. 1.** admit. **2.** accept. **3.** allow.

Denys (dĕn′ĭs; *Fr.* də nē′), *n.* **Saint.** See **Denis.**

deodand (dē′ō dănd′), *n. Eng. Law.* (formerly) an animal or article which, having been the immediate occasion of the death of a human being, was forfeited to the Crown to be applied to pious uses. [t. ML: s. *deōdandum* a thing to be given to God, f. L: dat. of *deus* god + neut. gerundive of *dare* give]

deodar (dē′ō dä′), *n.* a species of cedar, *Cedrus deodara*, a large Himalayan tree valued for its beauty and for its durable wood. [t. Hind., g. Skt *devadāru* wood of the gods]

deodorant (dē ō′də rənt), *n.* **1.** an agent for destroying odours. **2.** a substance, often combined with an antiperspirant, for inhibiting or masking perspiration or other bodily odours. —*adj.* **3.** capable of destroying odours.

deodorize (dē ō′də rīz′), *v.t.*, **-rized, -rizing.** to deprive of odour, esp. of the fetid smell arising from impurities. Also, **deodorise.** —**deo′doriza′tion,** *n.* —**deo′doriz′er,** *n.*

Deo favente (dā′ō fä vĕn′tĭ), *Latin.* God favouring (befriending, protecting).

Deo gratias (dā′ō grä′tĭ äs′), *Latin.* thanks be to God.

Deo juvante (dā′ō yōō văn′tĭ), *Latin.* God helping; if God gives aid.

deontology (dē′ŏn tŏl′ə jĭ), *n.* the science of duty or moral obligation; ethics. [f. Gk: s. *déon* that which is binding or needful (prop. ppr. neut. of *deîn* bind) + (O)LOGY] —**deontological** (dĭ ŏn′tə lŏj′ĭ kl), *adj.* —**de′ontol′ogist,** *n.*

Deo volente (dā′ō vŏ lĕn′tĭ), *Latin.* God willing (it); if God wills it.

deoxidize (dē ŏk′sĭ dīz′), *v.t.*, **-dized, -dizing.** to remove oxygen from; reduce from the state of an oxide. Also, **deoxidise.** —**deox′idiza′tion,** *n.* —**deox′idiz′er,** *n.*

deoxygenate (dē ŏk′sĭ jĭ nāt′), *v.t.*, **-nated, -nating.** to remove oxygen from. —**deox′ygena′tion,** *n.*

deoxygenize (dē ŏk′sĭ jĭ nīz′), *v.t.*, **-nized, -nizing.** to deoxygenate. Also, **deoxygenise.**

deoxyribonucleic acid (dē ŏk′sĭ rī′bō nyōō klā′ĭk), *Biochem.* one of a class of large molecules which are found in the nuclei of cells and in viruses and which are responsible for the transference of genetic characteristics, usually consisting of two interwoven helical chains of polynucleotides, the sugar of which is 2-deoxy-D-ribose. Also, **desoxyribonucleic acid.** *Abbrev.*: DNA.

deoxyribose (dē ŏk′sĭ rī′bōs), *n. Chem.* a pentose sugar, $C_5H_{10}O_4$, present in combined form in deoxyribonucleic acids.

dep., 1. department. **2.** departs. **3.** deponent. **4.** departure. **5.** deputy.

depart (dĭ pät′), *v.i.* **1.** to go away, as from a place; take one's leave. **2.** to turn aside or away; diverge; deviate (fol. by *from*). **3.** to pass away, as from life or existence. —*v.t.* **4.** to go away from or leave: *rare*, except in *to depart this life.* —*n.* **5.** *Obs.* departure; death. [ME *departe(n)*, t. OF: m. *departir*, f. *de-* DE- + *partir* leave, divide (g. L *partīre*)]

—**Syn. 1.** DEPART, RETIRE, RETREAT, WITHDRAW imply leaving a place. DEPART is a somewhat literary word, implying going away from a definite place: *to depart on a journey.* RETIRE emphasizes the reason or purpose for absenting oneself or drawing back from a place: *to retire from a position (in battle).* RETREAT implies a necessary withdrawal, esp. as a result of adverse fortune in war: *to retreat to secondary lines of defence.* WITHDRAW suggests leaving some specific place or situation, usually for some definite and often unpleasant reason: *to withdraw from a hopeless task.* —**Ant. 1.** arrive.

departed (dĭ pä′tĭd), *adj.* **1.** deceased; dead. **2.** gone; past. —*n.* **3. the departed, a.** the dead person. **b.** the dead collectively.

department (dĭ pät′mənt), *n.* **1.** a distinct part of anything arranged in divisions; a division of a complex whole or organized system. **2.** a division of official business or duties or functions. **3.** one of the (large) districts into which a country, as France, is divided for administrative purposes. **4.** one of the principal branches of a governmental organization. **5.** one of the sections of a school, college, or university dealing with a particular field of knowledge: *the department of English.* **6.** a section of a retail store selling a particular class or kind of goods. **7.** a sphere or province of activity, knowledge or responsibility. —**departmental** (dē′pät mĕn′tl), *adj.* —**de′partmen′tally,** *adv.*

departmentalism (dē′pät mĕn′tə lĭz′əm), *n.* **1.** division into departments. **2.** advocacy of or strict adherence to such a division.

departmentalize (dē′pät mĕn′tə līz′), *v.t.*, **-lized, -lizing.** to divide into departments. Also, **departmentalise.**

department store, a large retail shop selling a variety of goods in different departments.

departure (dĭ pä′chə), *n.* **1.** a going away; a setting out or starting. **2.** divergence or deviation. **3.** *Naut.* **a.** the distance due east or west made by a ship when sailing on any course. **b.** the bearing or position of a point from which a vessel commences dead reckoning. **4.** *Archaic.* decease or death.

depasture (dē päs′chə), *v.*, **-tured, -turing.** —*v.t.* **1.** to consume the produce of (land) as pasture. **2.** to pasture (cattle). —*v.i.* **3.** to graze.

depend (dĭ pĕnd′), *v.i.* **1.** to rely; trust: *you may depend on the accuracy of the report.* **2.** to rely for support, maintenance, help, etc.: *children depend on their parents.* **3.** to be conditioned or contingent: *it depends upon himself, his efforts, his knowledge.* **4.** *Gram.* (of a word or other linguistic form) to be subordinate (to another linguistic form in the same construction). **5.** to hang down; be suspended. **6.** to be undetermined or pending. [ME *depend(en)*, t. OF: m. *dependre*, t. L: m. *dēpendēre* hang upon]

dependable (dĭ pĕn′də bl), *adj.* that may be depended on; reliable; trustworthy. —**depend′abil′ity, depend′ableness,** *n.* —**depend′ably,** *adv.*

dependant (dĭ pĕn′dənt), *n.* Also, **dependent. 1.** one who depends on or looks to another for support, favour, etc. **2.** a person to whom one contributes all or a major amount of necessary financial support. **3.** a retainer; servant. —*adj.* **3.** dependent.

dependence (dĭ pĕn′dəns), *n.* **1.** the state of depending for aid, support, etc. **2.** reliance; confidence; trust. **3.** the state of being conditional or contingent on something; natural or logical sequence. **4.** subordination or subjection: *the dependence of the church upon the state.* **5.** an object of reliance or trust.

dependency (dĭ pĕn′dən sĭ), *n.*, *pl.* **-cies. 1.** the state of being dependent; dependence. **2.** something dependent or subordinate; an appurtenance. **3.** an outbuilding or annexe. **4.** a subject territory which is not an integral part of the ruling country.

dependent (dĭ pĕn′dənt), *adj.* Also, **dependant. 1.** depending on something else for aid, support, etc. **2.** conditioned; contingent. **3.** subordinate; subject. **4.** (of linguistic forms) not used in isolation; used only in connection with other forms. **5.** hanging down; pendent. —*n.* **6.** dependant.

dependent variable, *Maths.* a variable expressed as a function of other more basic variables called independent variables.

depersonalize (dē pûs′nə līz′), *v.t.*, **-lized, -lizing. 1.** to make impersonal. **2.** *Psychiatry.* to cause to lose the reality of one's own personality; to deprive of personality or individuality. Also, **depersonalise.** —**deper′sonaliza′tion,** *n.*

depict (dĭ pĭkt′), *v.t.* **1.** to represent by or as by painting; portray; delineate. **2.** to represent in words; describe. [t. L: s. *dēpictus*, pp., portrayed] —**depict′er,** *n.* —**depic′tion,** *n.* —**depic′tive,** *adj.*

—**Syn. 1, 2.** DEPICT, PORTRAY, SKETCH imply an actual reproduction of an object or scene by colours or lines, or by words. DEPICT emphasizes vividness of detail: *to depict the confusion of departure.* PORTRAY emphasizes faithful representation: *could not portray the anguish of the exiles.* SKETCH suggests a drawing in which only the outlines of the most prominent features or fundamental facts are given, often in a preparatory way: *to sketch a scene so that it can later be painted, to sketch the plans for a community development.*

depicture (dĭ pĭk′chə), *v.t.*, **-tured, -turing.** to picture; depict.

depilate (dĕp′ĭ lāt′), *v.t.*, **-lated, -lating.** to remove the hair from. [t. L: m. s. *dēpilātus*, pp.] —**dep′ila′tion,** *n.*

depilatory (dĭ pĭl′ə tə rĭ, -trĭ), *adj.*, *n.*, *pl.* **-ries.** —*adj.* **1.** capable of removing hair. —*n.* **2.** a depilatory agent.

deplete (dĭ plēt′), *v.t.*, **-pleted, -pleting. 1.** to deprive of that which fills; decrease the fullness of; reduce the stock or amount of. **2.** *Med.* to empty or relieve (overcharged vessels, etc.), as by blood-letting or purging. [t. L: m. s. *dēplētus*, pp., emptied out] —**deple′tion,** *n.* —**deple′tive, depletory** (dĭ plē′tə rĭ), *adj.*

depleted (dĭ plē′tĭd), *adj.* *Physics.* (of a substance) containing less of a particular isotope than is normal, esp. (of a nuclear fuel) containing fewer fissile isotopes than natural uranium.

deplorable (dĭ plô′rə bl), *adj.* **1.** causing or being a subject for grief or regret; sad; lamentable. **2.** causing or being a subject for censure or reproach; bad; wretched. —**deplor′ableness, deplor′abil′ity,** *n.* —**deplor′ably,** *adv.*

deplore (dĭ plô′), *v.t.*, **-plored, -ploring.** to feel or express deep grief for or in regard to; regret deeply. [t. L: m. s. *dēplōrāre* bewail] —**deplor′er,** *n.* —**deplor′ingly,** *adv.* —**Syn.** lament, bemoan, bewail.

deploy (dĭ ploi′), *Mil.* —*v.t.* **1.** to spread out (troops or military units) and form an extended front. —*v.i.* **2.** to spread out with extended front. [t. F: s. *déployer*, f. *dé-* DIS-[1] + *ployer*, g. L *plicāre* fold] —**deploy′ment,** *n.*

deplume (dē plo͞om′), *v.t.*, **-plumed, -pluming. 1.** to deprive of feathers; pluck. **2.** to strip of honour, wealth, etc. [t. F: m. s. *déplumer*, der. *dé-* DIS-[1] + *plume* (g. L *plūma* feather)] —**de′pluma′tion,** *n.*

depolarize (dē pō′lə rīz′), *v.t.*, **-rized, -rizing.** to deprive of polarity or polarization. Also, **depolarise.** —**depo′lariza′tion,** *n.* —**depo′lariz′er,** *n.*

depone (dĭ pōn′), *v.t.*, *v.i.*, **-poned, -poning.** to testify under oath; depose. [t. L: m. s. *dēpōnere* put away or down, ML testify. See DEPOSIT]

deponent (dĭ pō′nənt), *adj.* **1.** *Gk and Lat. Gram.* (of a verb) appearing only in the passive (or Greek middle) voice forms, but with active meaning. —*n.* **2.** *Law.* one who testifies under oath, esp. in writing. **3.** *Gk and Lat. Gram.* a deponent verb: *a Latin form such as* loqui *is a deponent.* [t. L: s. *dēpōnens*, ppr., laying aside, depositing, ML testifying]

depopulate (*v.* dē pŏp′yo͞o lāt′; *adj.* dē pŏp′yo͞o lĭt, -lāt′), *v.*, **-lated, -lating,** *adj.* —*v.t.* **1.** to deprive of inhabitants, wholly or in part, as by destruction or expulsion. —*adj.* **2.** *Archaic.* depopulated. [t. L: m. s. *dēpopulātus*, pp., having laid waste] —**depop′ula′tion,** *n.* —**depop′ula′tor,** *n.*

deport (dĭ pôt′), *v.t.* **1.** to transport forcibly, as to a penal colony or a place of exile. **2.** to expel (an undesirable alien) from a country; banish. **3.** to bear, conduct, or behave (oneself) in a particular manner. —*n.* **4.** *Obs.* deportment. [t. F: s. *déporter*, g. L *deportāre* carry away, transport, banish oneself]

deportation (dē′pô tā′shən), *n.* the lawful expulsion of undesirable aliens and other persons from a state.

deportee (dē′pô tē′), *n.* **1.** one who is deported, as from a country. **2.** a person awaiting deportation. [f. DEPORT, V. + -EE]

deportment (dĭ pôt′mənt), *n.* **1.** manner of bearing; carriage. **2.** demeanour; conduct; behaviour. —**Syn. 2.** See **behaviour.**

deposal (dĭ pō′zəl), *n.* deposition, as from office.

depose (dĭ pōz′), *v.*, **-posed, -posing.** —*v.t.* **1.** to remove from office or position, esp. high office. **2.** to declare or testify, esp. under oath, usually in writing. —*v.i.* **3.** to bear witness; give sworn testimony, esp. in writing. [ME *depose(n)*, t. OF: m. *deposer* put down, f. *de-* DE- + *poser* POSE[1]] —**depos′able,** *adj.* —**depos′er,** *n.*

deposit (dĭ pŏz′ĭt), *v.t.* **1.** to put or lay down; place; put. **2.** to throw down or precipitate: *soil deposited by a river.* **3.** to place for safekeeping or in trust. **4.** to give as security or in part payment. —*n.* **5.** anything laid or thrown down, as matter precipitated from a fluid; sediment. **6.** a coating of metal deposited by an electric current. **7.** an accumulation, or occurrence, of ore, oil, etc., of any form or nature. **8.** anything laid away or entrusted to another for safekeeping. **9.** money placed in a bank. **10.** anything given as security or in part payment. [t. L: s. *dēpositus*, pp., put away or down, deposited, ML testified. See DEPONE] —**Syn. 5.** precipitate, deposition.

deposit account, a bank account opened for the purpose of saving money and earning interest, as opposed to a current account.

depositary (dĭ pŏz′ĭ tə rĭ, -trĭ), *n.*, *pl.* **-taries. 1.** one to whom anything is given in trust. **2.** a depository.

deposition (dĕp′ə zĭsh′ən, dē′pə-), *n.* **1.** removal from an office or position. **2.** the act of depositing. **3.** that which is deposited. **4.** *Law.* **a.** the giving of testimony under oath. **b.** the testimony so given. **c.** a statement under oath, taken down in writing, which may be used in court in place of the production of the witness. **5.** (*cap.*) **a.** the removal of Christ's body from the Cross. **b.** a representation of this.

depositor (dĭ pŏz′ĭ tə), *n.* **1.** one who or that which deposits. **2.** one who deposits money in a bank.

depository (dĭ pŏz′ĭ tə rĭ, -trĭ), *n.*, *pl.* **-ries. 1.** a place where anything is deposited or stored for safekeeping; a storehouse. **2.** a depositary; trustee.

deposit receipt, a written acknowledgement by a bank that it has received from a person named a specified sum as a deposit.
depot (dĕp′ō), *n.* **1.** *Mil.* **a.** a place to which supplies and materials are shipped and stored for distribution. **b.** a place where recruits receive their first training. **2.** a depository; storehouse. **3.** a garage where buses or trams are kept. **4.** *U.S.* a railway station. [t. F: m. *dépôt*, g. L *dēpositum* DEPOSIT, n.]
deprave (dĭ prāv′), *v.t.*, **-praved, -praving. 1.** to make bad or worse; vitiate; corrupt. **2.** *Obs.* to defame. [ME *deprave(n)*, t. L: m. *dēprāvāre* pervert] **—depravation** (dĕp′rə vā′shən), *n.* **—deprav′er,** *n.*
depraved (dĭ prāvd′), *adj.* corrupt or perverted, esp. morally; wicked. **—Syn.** See **immoral.**
depravity (dĭ prăv′ĭ tĭ), *n., pl.* **-ties. 1.** the state of being depraved. **2.** a depraved act or practice. **3.** *Theol.* the innate sinfulness of man.
deprecate (dĕp′rĭ kāt′), *v.t.*, **-cated, -cating. 1.** to express earnest disapproval of; urge reasons against; protest against (a scheme, purpose, etc.). **2.** *Archaic.* to pray for deliverance from. [t. L: m. s. *dēprecātus*, pp., having prayed against] **—dep′recat′ingly,** *adv.* **—dep′reca′tion,** *n.* **—dep′reca′tor,** *n.*
deprecative (dĕp′rĭ kā′tĭv), *adj.* deprecatory. **—dep′reca′tively,** *adv.*
deprecatory (dĕp′rĭ kā′tə rĭ), *adj.* **1.** of the nature of deprecation; expressing deprecation. **2.** apologetic; expressing apology. **—dep′reca′torily,** *adv.*
depreciate (dĭ prē′shĭ āt′), *v.*, **-ated, -ating.** *—v.t.* **1.** to reduce the purchasing value of (money). **2.** to lessen the value of. **3.** to represent as of little value or merit; belittle. *—v.i.* **4.** to decline in value. [t. LL: m. s. *dēpretiātus* (ML *dēpreciātus*) undervalued] **—depre′ciat′ingly,** *adv.* **—depre′cia′tor,** *n.*
depreciation (dĭ prē′shĭ ā′shən), *n.* **1.** decrease in value due to wear and tear, decay, decline in price, etc. **2.** a decrease in the purchasing or exchange value of money. **3.** a lowering in estimation; disparagement.
depreciatory (dĭ prē′shyə tə rĭ, -trĭ), *adj.* tending to depreciate. Also, **depreciative** (dĭ prē′shyə tĭv).
depredate (dĕp′rĭ dāt′), *v.*, **-dated, -dating.** *—v.t.* **1.** to prey upon; plunder; lay waste. *—v.i.* **2.** to prey; make depredations. [t. L: m. s. *dēpraedātus*, pp., having pillaged] **—dep′reda′tor,** *n.* **—depredatory** (dĕp′rĭ-dā′tə rĭ, dĭ prĕd′ĭ tə rĭ, -trĭ), *adj.*
depredation (dĕp′rĭ dā′shən), *n.* a preying upon or plundering; robbery; ravage.
depress (dĭ prĕs′), *v.t.* **1.** to lower in spirits; deject; dispirit. **2.** to lower in force, vigour, etc.; weaken; make dull. **3.** to lower in amount or value. **4.** to put into a lower position: *to depress the muzzle of a gun.* **5.** to press down. **6.** *Music.* to lower in pitch. [ME *depresse(n)*, t. OF: m. *depresser*, der. L *dēpressus*, pp., pressed down] **—depress′ible,** *adj.* **—depress′ingly,** *adv.* **—Syn. 1.** See **oppress. —Ant. 4.** raise, elevate.
depressant (dĭ prĕs′ənt), *Med.* *—adj.* **1.** having the quality of depressing or lowering the vital activities; sedative. *—n.* **2.** a sedative.
depressed (dĭ prĕst′), *adj.* **1.** dejected; downcast. **2.** pressed down; lower than the general surface. **3.** lowered in force, amount, etc. **4.** *Bot., Zool.* flattened down; broader than high. **5.** economically backward. **—Syn. 1.** See **sad.**
depressed area, a region where unemployment and a low standard of living prevail.
depression (dĭ prĕsh′ən), *n.* **1.** the act of depressing. **2.** the state of being depressed. **3.** a depressed or sunken place or part; a hollow. **4.** dejection of spirits. **5.** *Psychol.* a morbid condition of emotional dejection and withdrawal; sadness greater and more prolonged than that warranted by any objective reason. **6.** dullness or inactivity, as of trade. **7.** a period during which there is a general slump in economic activities. **8.** *Pathol.* a low state of vital powers or functional activity. **9.** *Astron., etc.* angular distance below the horizon. **10.** *Survey.* the angle between the line from an observer to an object below him and a horizontal line. **11.** *Meteorol.* an area of low atmospheric pressure. [ME, t. L: s. *dēpressio*] **—Syn. 4.** discouragement, despondency, gloom.
depressive (dĭ prĕs′ĭv), *adj.* **1.** tending to depress. **2.** characterized by depression, esp. mental depression. **—depres′sively,** *adv.* **—depres′siveness,** *n.*
depressomotor (dĭ prĕs′ō mō′tə), *adj.* *Physiol., Med.* causing a retardation of motor activity: *depressomotor nerves.*
depressor (dĭ prĕs′ə), *n.* **1.** one who or that which depresses. **2.** *Physiol., Anat.* **a.** a muscle that draws down a part. **b.** Also, **depressor nerve.** a nerve from the aorta to the centres controlling heart rate and blood pressure. **3.** *Surg.* an instrument for pressing down a protruding part.
deprivation (dĕp′rĭ vā′shən), *n.* **1.** the act of depriving. **2.** the fact of being deprived. **3.** dispossession; loss; bereavement. Also, **deprival** (dĭ prī′vəl).
deprive (dĭ prīv′), *v.t.*, **-prived, -priving. 1.** to divest of something possessed or enjoyed; dispossess; strip; bereave. **2.** to keep (a person, etc.) from possessing or enjoying something withheld. **3.** to remove (an ecclesiastic) from a benefice; to remove from office. [ME *deprive(n)*, t. OF: m. *depriver*, der. *priver*, g. L *prīvāre* deprive] **—depriv′able,** *adj.* **—depriv′er,** *n.* **—Syn. 1.** See **strip**[1].
de profundis (dā′prŏ fŏŏn′dĭs), *Latin.* out of the depths (of sorrow, despair, etc.).
depside (dĕp′sīd, -sĭd), *n.* *Chem.* any of a group of esters formed from two or more phenol carboxylic acid molecules. [f. s. Gk *dépsein* tan + -IDE]
dept, department.
Deptford (dĕt′fəd), *n.* a district of the S Inner London borough of Lewisham.
Deptford pink, a caryophyllaceous annual, *Dianthus armeria*, found in Europe and Asia and having pale red flowers.
depth (dĕpth), *n.* **1.** measure or distance downwards, inwards, or backwards. **2.** deepness, as of water, suited to or safe for a person or thing. **3.** abstruseness, as of a subject. **4.** gravity; seriousness. **5.** emotional profundity: *depth of woe.* **6.** (*pl.*) a low intellectual or moral condition. **7.** intensity, as of silence, colour, etc. **8.** lowness of pitch. **9.** extent of intellectual penetration, sagacity, or profundity. **10.** (*usually pl.*) a deep part or place, as of the sea. **11.** an unfathomable space, or abyss. **12.** the remotest or extreme part, as of space. **13.** a deep or underlying region, as of feeling. **14.** the part of greatest intensity, as of night or winter. **15. beyond** or **out of one's depth, a.** in water too deep for one to touch the bottom. **b.** beyond one's capacity or understanding. **16. in depth,** intensely, thoroughly. [ME *depth(e)*, f. *dep-* (OE *dēop* DEEP) + -TH[1]] **—Ant. 2.** shallowness. **9.** superficiality.
depth charge, a bomb dropped or thrown into the water from a ship or aeroplane which explodes on reaching a certain depth, used to destroy submarines, etc.
depth of field, *Optics.* the range of distances along the axis of a camera or other optical instrument, in which an object will produce a reasonably clear image. Also, **depth of focus.**
depurate (dĕp′yŏŏ rāt′), *v.t., v.i.*, **-rated, -rating.** to make or become free from impurities; purify; cleanse. [t. ML: m. s. *dēpūrātus*, pp.] **—dep′ura′tion,** *n.* **—dep′ura′tor,** *n.*
depurative (dĕp′yŏŏ rā′tĭv, dĕp′yŏŏ rə tĭv), *adj.* **1.** serving to depurate; purifying. *—n.* **2.** a depurative agent or substance.
deputation (dĕp′yŏŏ tā′shən), *n.* **1.** appointment to represent or act for another or others. **2.** the person or (usually) body of persons so appointed or authorized. Cf. *U.S.* **delegation** (def. 4).
depute (dĭ pyŏŏt′), *v.t.*, **-puted, -puting. 1.** to appoint as one's substitute or agent. **2.** to assign (a charge, etc.) to a deputy. [ME *depute(n)*, t. OF: m. *deputer*, t. LL: m. *dēputāre* destine, allot, in L count as, reckon]
deputize (dĕp′yŏŏ tīz′), *v.*, **-tized, -tizing.** *—v.t.* **1.** to appoint as a deputy. *—v.i.* **2.** *Colloq.* to act as a deputy. Also, **deputise.**
deputy (dĕp′yŏŏ tĭ), *n., pl.* **-ties,** *adj.* *—n.* **1.** a person appointed or authorized to act for another or others. **2.** a person appointed or elected as assistant to a public official as an alderman or (U.S.) a sheriff, serving as successor in the event of a vacancy. **3.** a person representing a constituency in any of certain legislative bodies, as in the French Chamber of Deputies. *—adj.* **4.** acting as deputy for another. [ME *depute*, t. OF, prop. pp. of *deputer* DEPUTE]
deputy commander, 1. an officer in the London metropolitan police force ranking above chief superintendent and below commander. **2.** the rank.
De Quincey (də kwĭn′sĭ), **Thomas,** 1785–1859, English essayist.
der., 1. derivation. **2.** derivative. **3.** derived.
deracinate (dĭ răs′ĭ nāt′), *v.t.*, **-nated, -nating.** to pull up by the roots; uproot; extirpate; eradicate. [f. s. F *déraciner* (der. *dé-* DIS-[1] + *racine*, der. L *rādix* root) + -ATE[1]] **—derac′ina′tion,** *n.*
deraign (dĭ rān′), *v.t.* **1.** *Law. Obs.* **a.** to dispute or contest (a claim, etc., of another). **b.** to maintain or vindicate a claim to (something). **2.** *Hist.* to dispose troops for (battle). Also, **darraign.** [ME *dereyne(n)*, t. OF: m. *deraisnier* render an account, f. *de-* DE- + *raisnier* discourse, der. *raison*, g. L *ratio* reckoning. Cf. ARRAIGN] **—deraign′ment,** *n.*

derail (dĭ rāl′), *v.t.* **1.** to cause (a train, etc.) to run off the rails. —*v.i.* **2.** (of a train, etc.) to run off the rails of a track. [t. F: m. *dérailler*, der. *dé-* DIS-[1] + *rail* rail, t. E. See RAIL[1]] —**derail′ment,** *n.*

Derain (*Fr.* də răɴ′), *n.* **André** (*Fr.* äɴ drė′), 1880–1954, French painter.

derange (dĭ rānj′), *v.t.*, **-ranged, -ranging. 1.** to throw into disorder; disarrange. **2.** to disturb the condition, action, or functions of. **3.** to unsettle the reason of; make insane. [t. F: m. s. *déranger*, OF *desrengier*, f. *des-* DIS-[1] + *rengier* RANGE, v.]

deranged (dĭ rānjd′), *adj.* **1.** disordered. **2.** insane.

derangement (dĭ rānj′mənt), *n.* **1.** the act of deranging. **2.** disarrangement; disorder. **3.** mental disorder; insanity.

deray (dĭ rā′), *n.* *Archaic or Dial.* disorderly merrymaking. [ME *derai*, t. OF: m. *desrei*, der. *desreer* put out of order, der. *des-* DIS-[1] + *rei* order. Cf. ARRAY, v.]

Derbent (*Russ.* dĭr byĕnt′), *n.* a seaport in the SE Soviet Union in Europe, on the Caspian Sea. 38,000 (1959).

Derby (dä′bĭ; *U.S.* dû′bĭ, dûr′bĭ *for def. 6*), *n.*, *pl.* **-bies. 1. Edward George Geoffrey Smith Stanley, 14th Earl of,** 1799–1869, British statesman: prime minister 1852; 1858–59; 1866–68. **2.** a county borough in central England: the county town of Derbyshire, 132,408 (1961). **3.** Derbyshire. **4.** a horserace, founded 1780, run annually at Epsom Downs. **5.** some other important race, of horses, aeroplanes, footrunners, etc. **6.** (*l.c.*) *U.S.* a stiff felt hat with rounded crown and brim, worn chiefly by men. Cf. **bowler. 7.** a pale, bone-coloured close-textured cheese. **8. local Derby,** any sporting contest between teams from the same area.

Derbys., Derbyshire.

Derbyshire (dä′bĭ shĭə′, -shə), *n.* a county in central England. 877,548 pop. (1961); 1006 sq. mi. *Co. town:* Derby. *Abbrev.:* Derbys. Also, **Derby.**

dere (dĭə), *adj. Archaic.* dear[2].

de règle (*Fr.* də rĕ′gl), *French.* according to rule; following a pattern, principle, or law.

derelict (dĕ′rĭ lĭkt), *adj.* **1.** left or abandoned, as by the owner or guardian (said esp. of a ship abandoned at sea). **2.** neglected; dilapidated. —*n.* **3.** personal property abandoned or thrown away by the owner. **4.** a ship abandoned at sea. **5.** a person forsaken or abandoned, esp. by society. **6.** *Law.* land left dry by a change of the waterline. [t. L: s. *dērelictus*, pp., forsaken utterly]

dereliction (dĕ′rĭ lĭk′shən), *n.* **1.** culpable neglect, as of duty; delinquency; fault. **2.** the act of abandoning. **3.** the state of being abandoned. **4.** *Law.* **a.** a leaving dry of land by recession of the waterline. **b.** the land thus left dry. —**Syn. 1.** See **neglect.**

derequisition (dē rĕk′wĭ zĭsh′ən), *n.* **1.** the return from military to civilian control. —*v.t., v.i.* **2.** to return to civilian control.

de rerum natura (dā rēə′ro͝om nă to͞oə′rä), *Latin.* on the nature of things.

Derg (dûg), *n.* **1. Lough,** the largest and lowest lake on the Shannon river, Republic of Ireland, dividing County Tipperary from Galway and Clare. 24 mi. long and averaging 2 mi. in width. **2. Lough,** a small lake in County Donegal, Republic of Ireland.

deride (dĭ rīd′), *v.t.*, **-rided, -riding.** to laugh at in contempt; scoff or jeer at; mock. [t. L: m. s. *dērīdēre* laugh] —**derid′er,** *n.* —**derid′ingly,** *adv.* —**Syn.** taunt, flout, gibe, banter, rally. See **ridicule.**

de rigueur (*Fr.* də rē gœr′), *French.* strictly required, as by etiquette or usage.

derisible (dĭ rĭz′ĭ bl), *adj.* subject to or worthy of derision.

derision (dĭ rĭzh′ən), *n.* **1.** the act of deriding; ridicule; mockery. **2.** an object of ridicule. [t. L: s. *dērīsio*]

derisive (dĭ rī′sĭv), *adj.* characterized by derision; ridiculing; mocking. Also, **derisory** (dĭ rī′sə rĭ). —**deri′sively,** *adv.* —**deri′siveness,** *n.*

deriv., **1.** derivation. **2.** derivative. **3.** derive. **4.** derived.

derivate (dĕ′rĭ vĭt, -vāt′), *n.* **1.** something derived; a derivative. —*adj.* **2.** derived.

derivation (dĕ′rĭ vā′shən), *n.* **1.** the act of deriving. **2.** the fact of being derived. **3.** origination or origin. **4.** that which is derived; derivative. **5.** *Maths.* (of a theorem) **a.** development. **b.** differentiation. **6.** *Gram.* **a.** the process of composing new words by the addition of prefixes or suffixes to already existing root words, as *atomic* from *atom*, *hardness* from *hard.* **b.** the systematic description of such processes in a particular language, as contrasted with *inflection* which consists of adding prefixes, infixes, or suffixes to make a different form of the same word: *hardness* is an example of derivation; *harder* of inflection. **c.** such processes collectively or in general. **7.** *Gram.* the process of tracing a word back to its earliest known form. —**der′iva′tional,** *adj.*

derivative (dĭ rĭv′ə tĭv), *adj.* **1.** derived. **2.** not original or primitive; secondary. —*n.* **3.** something derived or derivative. **4.** *Gram.* a form derived from another: *atomic* is a derivative of *atom.* **5.** *Chem.* a substance or compound obtained from, or regarded as derived from, another substance or compound. **6.** *Maths.* the limit of the ratio of the increment of a function to the increment of a variable in it, as the latter becomes 0. —**deriv′atively,** *adv.*

derive (dĭ rīv′), *v.*, **-rived, -riving.** —*v.t.* **1.** to receive or obtain from a source or origin (fol. by *from*). **2.** to trace, as from a source or origin. **3.** to obtain by reasoning; deduce. **4.** *Chem.* to produce (a compound) from another compound by replacement of elements or radicals. **5.** *Obs.* to bring or direct (fol. by *to, on, upon*, etc.). —*v.i.* **6.** to come from a source; originate. [t. F: m. s. *dériver*, t. L: m. *dērīvāre* lead off] —**deriv′able,** *adj.* —**deriv′er,** *n.*

derived unit, *Physics, etc.* any unit derived from primary units of length, time, mass, etc.

-derm, a word element meaning 'skin', as in *endoderm.* [t. Gk: s. *-dermos*, etc., having skin, skinned]

derma (dû′mə), *n.* *Anat., Zool.* **1.** the corium or true skin, beneath the epidermis. **2.** the skin in general. [NL, t. Gk: skin] —**der′mal,** *adj.*

dermatitis (dû′mə tī′tĭs), *n.* *Pathol.* inflammation of the skin.

dermato-, a word element meaning 'skin', as in *dermatology.* Also, **derm-, dermat-, dermo-.** [t. Gk, comb. form of *dérma*]

dermatogen (də măt′ə jən, dû′mə tō′jən), *n.* *Bot.* a thin layer of meristem in embryos and growing ends of stems and roots, which give rise to the epidermis.

dermatographia (dû′mə tō grăf′yə, -grăf′ĭ ə), *n.* *Med.* a condition in which touching or lightly scratching the skin causes raised reddish marks. Also, **dermatographism** (dû′mə tō grăf′ĭz′əm), **der′mogra′phia, der′mogra′phism.**

dermatoid (dû′mə toid′), *adj.* resembling skin; skinlike.

dermatology (dû′mə tŏl′ə jĭ), *n.* the science of the skin and its diseases. —**dermatological** (dû′mə tə lŏj′ĭ kl), *adj.* —**der′matol′ogist,** *n.*

dermatome (dû′mə tōm′), *n.* **1.** *Anat.* an area of the skin that is supplied with the nerve fibres of a single posterior, spinal root. **2.** *Surg.* a mechanical instrument for cutting thin sections of skin for grafting. **3.** *Embryol.* the part of a mesodermal somite contributing to the development of the dermis. —**der′matom′ic,** *adj.*

dermatophyte (dû′mə tō fīt′), *n.* *Pathol., Vet. Sci.* any fungus parasitic on the skin and causing a skin disease, as ringworm.

dermatoplasty (dû′mə tō plăs′tĭ), *n.* plastic surgery of the skin. See **skin grafting.**

dermatosis (dû′mə tō′sĭs), *n.*, *pl.* **-toses** (-tō′sēz). *Pathol.* any disease of the skin.

dermis (dû′mĭs), *n.* *Anat., Zool.* derma. [NL; abstracted from EPIDERMIS] —**der′mic,** *adj.*

dermoid (dû′moid), *adj.* **1.** skinlike; dermatoid. **2.** *Pathol.* a congenital cyst containing hair, skin, teeth, etc.

dernier (*Fr.* dĕr nyė′), *adj.* last; final; ultimate. [F]

dernier cri (*Fr.* dĕr nyė krē′), *French.* **1.** the last word. **2.** the latest fashion.

derogate (*v.* dĕ′rə gāt′; *adj.* dĕ′rə gĭt, -gāt′), *v.*, **-gated, -gating,** *adj.* —*v.i.* **1.** to detract, as from authority, estimation, etc. (fol. by *from*). **2.** to fall away in character or conduct; degenerate (fol. by *from*). —*v.t.* **3.** *Archaic.* to take away (something) from a thing so as to impair it. —*adj.* **4.** *Obs. or Archaic.* debased. [t. L: m. s. *dērogātus*, pp., repealed, taken or detracted from] —**der′oga′tion,** *n.*

derogative (dĭ rŏg′ə tĭv), *adj.* lessening; belittling; derogatory. —**derog′atively,** *adv.*

derogatory (dĭ rŏg′ə tə rĭ, -trĭ), *adj.* tending to derogate or detract, as from authority or estimation; disparaging; depreciatory. —**derog′atorily,** *adv.* —**derog′atoriness,** *n.*

derrick (dĕ′rĭk), *n.* **1.** any of various devices for lifting and moving heavy weights. **2.** the tower-like framework over an oil-well or the like. **3.** a crane, usually stationary, carrying lifting tackle at the end of a boom or jib. —*v.t.* **4.** to move (the jib of a crane). [named after *Derrick*, a hangman at Tyburn, London, about 1600]

derring-do (dĕ′rĭng do͞o′), *n.* *Pseudoarchaic.* daring deeds; heroic daring. [ME *dorryng don* daring to do; erroneously taken as n. phrase by Spenser]

derringer (dĕ′rĭn jə), *n.* *U.S.* a short-barrelled pistol of large calibre. [named after the inventor]

derris (dĕ′rĭs), *n.* an East Indian leguminous plant, *Derris elliptica* and allied species, the roots of which contain rotenone and are used as an insecticide.

derry (dĕ′rĭ), *n.* a meaningless refrain or chorus in old songs. Also, **derry-down** (dĕ′rĭ doun′).

Derry (dĕ′rĭ), *n.* Londonderry.
der Tag (*Ger.* der täk′), *German.* the day: used by German nationalists to refer to the day on which Germany would begin the 'Drang nach Osten'; later, the day on which she would undertake a plan of conquest.
derv (dûv), *n.* diesel engine fuel oil. [short for *d(iesel) e(ngined) r(oad) v(ehicle)*]
dervish (dû′vĭsh), *n.* a member of any of various Muslim ascetic orders, some of which carry on ecstatic observances, such as violent dancing and pirouetting (**dancing, spinning,** or **whirling dervishes**) or vociferous chanting or shouting (**howling dervishes**). [t. Turk., t. Pers.: m. *darvīsh* religious mendicant]
Derwent (dû′wənt), *n.* **1.** a river in Cumberland flowing N and W through Derwentwater to Solway Firth. 35 mi. **2.** a river in Derbyshire flowing SE to the Trent. 60 mi. **3.** a river in Durham flowing NE to the Tyne. 30 mi. **4.** a river in Yorkshire flowing S to the Ouse. 60 mi. **5.** a river in Tasmania flowing SE to the Tasman Sea. 120 mi.
Derwentwater (dû′wənt wô′tə), *n.* **Lake,** a lake in Cumberland. 3 mi. long; 1 mi. wide.
Desaix de Veygoux (*Fr.* də sĕ də vĕ go͞o′), **Louis Charles Antoine** (*Fr.* lwē shärl äɴ twän′), 1768–1800, French general.
desalinate (dē săl′ĭ nāt′), *v.t.*, **-nated, -nating.** to subject (sea water) to a process of desalination. Also, **desalinize.**
desalination (dē săl′ĭ nā′shən), *n.* the process of removing the dissolved salts from sea water so that it becomes suitable for drinking water or for agricultural irrigation. Also, **desal′iniza′tion.**
desalinize (dē săl′ĭ nīz′), *v.t.* **-nized, -nizing.** to desalinate. Also, **desalinise.**
descant (*n.* dĕs′kănt; *v.* dĕs kănt′, dĭs-), *n.* **1.** *Music.* **a.** a melody or counterpoint accompanying a simple musical theme and usually written above it. **b.** (in part music) the soprano. **c.** a song or melody. **2.** a variation upon anything; comment on a subject. *—v.i.* **3.** *Music.* to sing. **4.** to make comments; discourse at length and with variety. Also, **discant.** [ME, t. ONF, f. *des-* DES-[1] + *cant* (g. L *cantus* song)] **—descant′er,** *n.*
Descartes (*Fr.* dė kart′), *n.* **René** (*Fr.* rə nė′), 1596–1650, French philosopher and mathematician.
descend (dĭ sĕnd′), *v.i.* **1.** to move or pass from a higher to a lower place; go or come down; fall; sink. **2.** to pass from higher to lower in any scale. **3.** to go from generals to particulars. **4.** to slope or tend downward. **5.** to come down by transmission, as from ancestors. **6.** to be derived by birth or extraction. **7.** to come down in a hostile manner, as an army: *to descend upon the enemy.* **8.** to approach or pounce upon, esp. in a greedy or hasty manner (fol. by *on* or *upon*). **9.** to come down from a certain intellectual, moral, or social standard: *he would never descend to baseness.* **10.** *Astron.* to move towards the horizon, or towards the south, as a star. *—v.t.* **11.** to move or lead downwards upon or along; go down. [ME *descend(en)*, t. OF: m. *descendre*, g. L *dēscendere*]
descendant (dĭ sĕn′dənt), *n.* **1.** one descended from an ancestor; an offspring, near or remote. *—adj.* **2.** descendent. [t. F, ppr. of *descendre* DESCEND]
descendent (dĭ sĕn′dənt), *adj.* **1.** descending; going or coming down. **2.** descending from an ancestor. [t. L: s. *dēscendens*, ppr., descending]
descender (dĭ sĕn′də), *n.* **1.** one who or that which descends. **2.** *Print.* the part of such letters as *p, q, j,* and *y* that goes below the body of most lower-case letters.
descendeur (*Fr.* dĕ säɴ dœr′), *n.* *Mountaineering.* a small metal device for controlling a climber's rate of descent in abseil. [t. F]
descendible (dĭ sĕn′də bl), *adj.* capable of being transmitted by inheritance. Also, **descend′able.**
descension (dĭ sĕn′shən), *n.* *Now Rare.* descent.
descent (dĭ sĕnt′), *n.* **1.** the act or fact of descending. **2.** a downward inclination or slope. **3.** a passage or stairway leading down. **4.** derivation from an ancestor; extraction; lineage. **5.** any passing from higher to lower in degree or state. **6.** a sudden incursion or attack. **7.** *Law.* transmission of real property by intestate succession. [ME, t. OF: m. *descente*, der. *descendre* DESCEND] **—Syn. 1.** falling, sinking. **2.** decline, grade, declivity.
Deschamps (*Fr.* dė shäɴ′), *n.* **Eustache** (*Fr.* œs tȧsh′), 1340?–1407?, French poet.
Deschutes (dā sho͞ot′), *n.* a river flowing from the Cascade Range in central Oregon N to the Columbia river. ab. 250 mi.
describe (dĭ skrīb′), *v.t.*, **-scribed, -scribing. 1.** to set forth in written or spoken words; give an account of: *to describe a scene, a person, etc.* **2.** *Geom.* to draw or trace, as an arc. [t. L: m. s. *dēscrībere* copy off, sketch off, describe] **—describ′able,** *adj.* **—describ′er,** *n.*
—Syn. 1. DESCRIBE, NARRATE agree in the idea of giving an account of something. To DESCRIBE is to convey an image or impression in words designed to reveal the appearance, nature, attributes, etc., of the thing described. The word applies primarily to what exists in space (by extension, to what occurs in time) and often implies the vividness of personal observation: *to describe a scene, a sensation, a character, a room.* To NARRATE is to recount the occurrence of something, usually by giving the details of an event or events in the order of their happening. NARRATE thus applies only to that which happens in time: *to narrate an incident.*
description (dĭ skrĭp′shən), *n.* **1.** representation by written or spoken words; a statement that describes. **2.** sort; kind; variety: *persons of that description.* **3.** *Geom.* the act of describing a figure. [ME, t. L: s. *dēscriptiō*]
descriptive (dĭ skrĭp′tĭv), *adj.* **1.** having the quality of describing; characterized by description. **2.** *Gram.* **a.** (of an adjective) expressing a quality of the noun it modifies (opposed to *limiting* or *demonstrative*), as *fresh* in *fresh milk.* **b.** (of any other expression) acting like such an adjective. **—descrip′tively,** *adv.* **—descrip′tiveness,** *n.*
descriptive clause, a relative clause, in English writing usually set off in commas, which describes or supplements, but does not identify, the antecedent; nonrestrictive clause. In 'this year, *which has been dry,* is bad for crops' the italicized part is a descriptive clause (opposed to *restrictive clause*).
descriptive geometry, 1. the theory of making projections of any accurately defined figure such that from them can be deduced not only its projective, but also its metrical, properties. **2.** geometry in general, treated by means of projections.
descriptive science, a science which classifies and describes the material in a particular field (usually opposed to *explanatory science,* which gives causes).
descry (dĭ skrī′), *v.t.*, **-scried, -scrying. 1.** to make out (something distant or unclear) by looking; espy: *the lookout descried land.* **2.** to discover; perceive; detect. [ME *descry(en)*, appar. t. OF: m. *descrier* proclaim. See DECRY] **—descri′er,** *n.*
desecrate (dĕs′ĭ krāt′), *v.t.*, **-crated, -crating.** to divest of sacred or hallowed character or office; divert from a sacred to a profane purpose; treat with sacrilege; profane. [f. DE- + *-secrate*, modelled on CONSECRATE] **—des′ecra′ter, des′ecra′tor,** *n.* **—des′ecra′tion,** *n.*
desegregate (dē sĕg′rĭ gāt′), *v.t., v.i.*, **-gated, -gating.** to eliminate racial segregation from (schools and other public places or institutions).
desegregation (dē′sĕg rĭ gā′shən), *n.* the process of eliminating racial segregation in schools, public places, railways, the armed forces, etc.
desensitize (dē sĕn′sĭ tīz′), *v.t.*, **-tized, -tizing. 1.** to lessen the sensitiveness of. **2.** *Physiol.* to eliminate the natural or acquired reactivity or sensitivity of (an animal, organ, tissue, etc.) to an external stimulus, as an allergen. **3.** *Photog.* to make less sensitive or wholly insensitive to light, as the emulsion on a film. Also, **desensitise. —desen′sitiza′tion,** *n.* **—desen′sitiz′er,** *n.*
desert[1] (dĕz′ət), *n.* **1.** an area so deficient in moisture as to support only a sparse, widely spaced vegetation, or none at all. **2.** any area in which few forms of life can exist because of lack of water, permanent frost, or absence of soil. **3.** any place lacking in something. *—adj.* **4.** of, pertaining to, or like a desert; desolate; barren. [ME, t. OF, t. L (Eccl.): s. *dēsertum*, prop. neut. pp. *of dēserere* abandon, forsake]
—Syn. 1. DESERT, WASTE, WILDERNESS refer to areas which are uninhabitated. DESERT emphasizes lack of water; it refers to a dry, barren, treeless region, usually sandy: *an oasis in a desert, the Sahara Desert.* WASTE emphasizes lack of inhabitants and of cultivation; it is used of wild, barren land, but fig. the word is also applied to turbulent seas: *a desolate waste, a terrifying waste of water.* WILDERNESS emphasizes the difficulty of finding one's way, whether because of barrenness or of luxuriant vegetation; it is also applied to the ocean, especially in stormy weather: *a trackless wilderness.*
desert[2] (dĭ zût′), *v.t.* **1.** to leave (a person, place, etc.) without intending to return; to abandon or forsake; *he deserted his wife.* **2.** (of a soldier or sailor) to leave or run away from (the service, duty, etc.) with the intention of never returning. **3.** to fail (one): *all hope deserted him.* *—v.i.* **4.** (esp. of a soldier or sailor) to forsake one's duty, etc. [t. F: m. s. *déserter*, t. LL: m. *dēsertāre*, freq. of L *dēserere*] **—desert′er,** *n.*
—Syn. 1. DESERT, ABANDON, FORSAKE mean to leave behind one persons, places, or things. DESERT implies intentionally violating an oath, formal obligation, or duty: *to desert one's home and family.* ABANDON suggests giving up wholly and finally, whether of necessity, unwillingly or through shirking responsibilities: *to abandon a hopeless task.* FORSAKE has emotional connotations, since it implies violating obligations of affection or association: *to forsake a noble cause.*
desert[3] (dĭ zût′), *n.* **1.** that which is deserved; a due reward or punishment. **2.** worthiness of reward or

punishment; merit or demerit. **3.** the fact of deserving well; merit; a virtue. [ME, t. OF: m. *deserte*, der. *deservir* DESERVE] **—Syn. 3.** See **merit.**

deserted (dĭ zû′tĭd), *adj.* **1.** abandoned; forsaken; uninhabited. **2.** lonely; unfrequented.

desertion (dĭ zû′shən), *n.* **1.** the act of deserting. **2.** the state of being deserted. **3.** *Law.* wilful abandonment, esp. of one's wife or husband without consent, in violation of legal or moral obligation.

desert rat, 1. a jerboa. **2.** *Mil. Colloq.* a member of the British 7th armoured division who fought in N Africa, 1941–42. [def. 2 from the divisional sign, a jerboa]

deserve (dĭ zûv′), *v.*, **-served, -serving.** *—v.t.* **1.** to merit (reward, punishment, esteem, etc.) in return for actions, qualities, etc. *—v.i.* **2.** to be worthy of recompense. [ME *deserve(n)*, t. OF: m. *deservir*, g. L *dēservīre* serve zealously] **—deserv′er,** *n.*

deservedly (dĭ zû′vĭd lĭ), *adv.* justly; according to desert, whether of good or evil.

deserving (dĭ zû′vĭng), *adj.* worthy of reward, praise, or help; meritorious (often fol. by *of*). **—deserv′ingly,** *adv.* **—deserv′ingness,** *n.*

desexualize (dē sĕk′syo͞o ə līz′), *v.t.*, **-lized, -lizing.** to deprive of sexual characteristics or quality. Also, **desexualise.**

déshabillé (dā′ză bē′ā; *Fr.* dė zȧ bē yė′), *adj.* in dishabille. [t. F]

desiccant (dĕs′ĭ kənt), *adj.* **1.** desiccating or drying, as a medicine. *—n.* **2.** a desiccant substance or agent.

desiccate (dĕs′ĭ kāt′), *v.*, **-cated, -cating.** *—v.t.* **1.** to dry thoroughly; dry up. **2.** to preserve by depriving of moisture, as foods. *—v.i.* **3.** to become dry. [t. L: m. s. *dēsiccātus*, pp., completely dried] **—des′icca′tion,** *n.* **—desiccative** (dĕs′ĭ kə tĭv, də sĭk′ə tĭv), *adj.*, *n.*

desiccated (dĕs′ĭ kā′tĭd), *adj.* dehydrated or powdered: *desiccated milk or soup.*

desiccator (dĕs′ĭ kā′tə), *n.* **1.** one who or that which desiccates. **2.** an apparatus for drying fruit, milk, etc., or for absorbing the moisture present in a chemical substance, etc.

desiderata (dĭ zĭd′ə rā′tə), *n.* pl. of **desideratum.**

desiderate (dĭ zĭd′ə rāt′), *v.t.*, **-rated, -rating.** to feel a desire for; long for; feel the want of. [t. L: m. s. *dēsīderātus*, pp., longed for] **—desid′era′tion,** *n.*

desiderative (dĭ zĭd′ə rə tĭv), *adj.* **1.** having or expressing desire. **2.** *Gram.* (of a verb derived from another) expressing desire to perform the action denoted by the underlying verb. Example: Sanskrit *véda*, he knows; *vi-vid-is-ati*, he wishes to know. *—n.* **3.** *Gram.* a desiderative verb.

desideratum (dĭ zĭd′ə rā′təm), *n.*, *pl.* **-ta** (-tə). something wanted or needed. [t. L, prop. pp. neut.]

design (dĭ zīn′), *v.t.* **1.** to prepare the preliminary sketch or the plans for (a work to be executed). **2.** to plan or fashion artistically or skilfully. **3.** to intend for a definite purpose. **4.** to form or conceive in the mind; contrive; plan: *he is designing a plan to enlarge his garden.* **5.** *Obs.* to mark out, as by a sign; indicate. *—v.i.* **6.** to make drawings, preliminary sketches, or plans. **7.** to plan and fashion a work of art, etc. *—n.* **8.** an outline, sketch, or plan, as of a work of art, an edifice, or a machine to be executed or constructed. **9.** the combination of details or features of a picture, building, etc.; the pattern or device of artistic work. **10.** the art of designing: *a school of design.* **11.** a plan; a project; a scheme. **12.** a hostile plan; crafty scheme. **13.** the end in view; intention; purpose. **14.** evil or selfish intention: *have designs on* (*or against*) *a person.* **15.** adaptation of means to a preconceived end. **16.** an artistic work. **17. by design,** deliberately. [t. F: s. *désigner* designate, t. L: m. *dēsignāre* mark out] **—Syn. 11.** See **plan.**

designate (*v.* dĕz′ĭg nāt′; *adj.* dĕz′ĭg nĭt, -nāt′), *v.*, **-nated, -nating,** *adj.* *—v.t.* **1.** to mark or point out; indicate; show; specify. **2.** to name; entitle; style. **3.** to nominate or select for a duty, office, purpose, etc.; appoint; assign. *—adj.* **4.** appointed to an office but not yet in possession of it; designated. [t. L: m. s. *dēsignātus*, pp., marked out] **—des′igna′tive,** *adj.* **—des′igna′tor,** *n.*

designation (dĕz′ĭg nā′shən), *n.* **1.** the act of designating. **2.** the fact of being designated. **3.** that which designates; a name. **4.** nomination; appointment.

designedly (dĭ zī′nĭd lĭ), *adv.* by design; purposely.

designer (dĭ zī′nə), *n.* **1.** one who devises or executes designs, as for works of art, decorative patterns, dresses, machines, etc. **2.** a schemer or intriguer.

designing (dĭ zī′nĭng), *adj.* **1.** contriving schemes; artful. **2.** showing forethought. *—n.* **3.** the act or art of making designs. **—design′ingly,** *adv.* **—Syn. 1.** wily, cunning, crafty, tricky, sly.

designment (dĭ zīn′mənt), *n.* *Obs.* designation; design.

desinence (dĕs′ĭ nəns), *n.* **1.** termination or ending, as a line of verse. **2.** *Gram.* an ending or suffix of a word.

desirable (dĭ zī′ə rə bl), *adj.* **1.** worthy to be desired; pleasing, excellent, or fine. **2.** arousing desire: *a desirable woman.* **3.** advisable: *a desirable course of action.* *—n.* **4.** one who or that which is desirable. **—desir′abil′ity, desir′ableness,** *n.* **—desir′ably,** *adv.*

desire (dĭ zī′ə), *v.*, **-sired, -siring,** *n.* *—v.t.* **1.** to wish or long for; crave; want. **2.** to express a wish to obtain; ask for; request: *the king desired that he should return.* *—n.* **3.** a longing or craving. **4.** an expressed wish; request. **5.** something desired. **6.** sexual appetite; lust. [ME *desire(n)*, t. OF: m. *desirer*, g. L *dēsīderāre* want] **—desir′er,** *n.*

—Syn. 1. See **wish. 3.** DESIRE, CRAVING, LONGING, YEARNING suggest feelings which impel one to the attainment or possession of something. DESIRE is a strong feeling, worthy or unworthy, that impels to the attainment or possession of something which is (in reality or imagination) within reach: *a desire for success.* CRAVING implies a deep and imperative wish for something, based on a sense of need and hunger (lit. or fig.): *a craving for food, companionship.* A LONGING is an intense wish, generally repeated or enduring, for something that is at the moment beyond reach but may be attainable at some future time: *a longing to visit France.* YEARNING suggests persistent, uneasy, and sometimes wistful or tender longing: *a yearning for home.* **—Ant. 3.** indifference.

desirous (dĭ zī′ə rəs), *adj.* having or characterized by desire; desiring.

desist (dĭ zĭst′), *v.i.* to cease, as from some action or proceeding; stop. [t. OF: s. *desister*, t. L: m. *dēsistere* leave off] **—desist′ance, desist′ence,** *n.*

desk (dĕsk), *n.* **1.** a table specially adapted for convenience in writing or reading, sometimes made with a sloping top, and generally fitted with drawers and compartments. **2.** a frame for supporting a book from which the service is read in a church. **3.** a pulpit. **4.** a music-stand. **5.** a section of the editorial office of a newspaper with responsibilities for a particular branch of the newspaper's activities. [ME *deske*, t. It.: m. *desco*, g. L *discus* disc, dish, ML table]

deskwork (dĕsk′wûk′), *n.* **1.** work done at a desk. **2.** habitual writing, as that of a clerk or an author.

D. ès L., (F *Docteur ès Lettres*) Doctor of Letters.

desman (dĕs′mən), *n.*, *pl.* **-mans.** either of two aquatic insectivorous mammals, related to shrews, *Myogale moschata* of SE Russia, and *M. pyrenaica* of the Pyrenees. [t. Sw.: short for *desman-ratta* muskrat]

desmid (dĕs′mĭd), *n.* any of the microscopic freshwater algae belonging to the family *Desmidiaceae.* [t. NL: m. s. *Desmidium*, typical genus, dim. of Gk *desmós* band, chain] **—desmid′ian,** *adj.*

desmitis (dĕs′mī tĭs), *n.* *Pathol.* inflammation of a ligament. [t. NL, f. Gk s. *desmós* (see DESMID) + *-itis* -ITIS]

desmoid (dĕs′moid), *adj.* *Anat.* **1.** resembling a fascia or fibrous sheet. **2.** resembling a ligament; ligamentous. *—n.* **3.** *Pathol.* a firm and tough tumour of woven fibrous tissue. [f. s. Gk *desmós* band, chain, ligament + -OID]

Des Moines (də moin′, də moinz′), **1.** a city in the U.S., the capital of Iowa, in the central part, on the Des Moines river. 208,982 (1960). **2.** a river flowing from SW Minnesota, SE through Iowa to the Mississippi. ab. 530 mi.

Desmoulins (*Fr.* dė mo͞o lăN′), *n.* **(Lucie Simplice) Camille (Benoît)** (*Fr.* ly sē săN plēs kȧ mēy bə nwȧ′), 1760–94, one of the leaders of the French Revolution.

desolate (*adj.* dĕs′ə lĭt; *v.* dĕs′ə lāt′), *adj.*, *v.*, **-lated, -lating.** *—adj.* **1.** barren or laid waste; devastated. **2.** deprived or destitute of inhabitants; deserted. **3.** left alone; lonely. **4.** having the feeling of being abandoned by friends or by hope. **5.** dreary; dismal. *—v.t.* **6.** to lay waste; devastate. **7.** to deprive of inhabitants; depopulate. **8.** to make disconsolate. **9.** to forsake or abandon. [ME, t. L: m. s. *dēsōlātus*, pp., left alone, forsaken] **—des′olat′er, des′ola′tor,** *n.* **—des′olately,** *adv.* **—des′olateness,** *n.*

—Syn. 4. miserable, wretched, woebegone. DESOLATE, DISCONSOLATE, FORLORN suggest one who is in a sad and wretched condition. The DESOLATE person or place gives a feeling or impression of isolation or of being deprived of human consolation, relationships, or presence: *desolate and despairing.* The DISCONSOLATE person is aware of the efforts of others to console and comfort him, but is unable to be relieved or cheered by them: *she remained disconsolate even in the midst of friends.* The FORLORN person has the feeling or gives the impression of being lost, deserted, or forsaken by friends: *wretched and forlorn in a strange city.*

desolation (dĕs′ə lā′shən), *n.* **1.** the act of desolating. **2.** the state of being desolated. **3.** depopulation. **4.** devastation; ruin. **5.** dreariness; barrenness. **6.** deprivation of companionship or comfort; loneliness; disconsolateness. **7.** a desolate place. [ME, t. L: s. *dēsōlātiō*]

De Soto (də sō′tō; *Sp.* dė sō′tō), **Hernando** or **Fernando**

(*Sp.* er nän′dō or fer nän′dō), 1500?–42, Spanish soldier-explorer in America: reached the Mississippi river, 1541.

desoxyribonucleic acid (dĕs ŏk′sĭ rī′bō nyōō klā′ĭk), *Biochem.* deoxyribonucleic acid.

despair (dĭ spâr′), *n.* **1.** loss of hope; hopelessness. **2.** that which causes hopelessness; that of which there is no hope (fol. by *of*): *to despair of humanity.* [ME *despeir(en)*, t. OF: m. s. *desperer*, g. L *dēspērāre* be without hope]
—**Syn. 1.** DESPAIR, DESPERATION, DESPONDENCY, DISCOURAGEMENT, HOPELESSNESS refer to a state of mind caused by circumstances which seem too much to cope with. DESPAIR suggests total loss or abandonment of hope, which may be passive or may drive one to furious efforts, even if at random: *in the depths of despair, courage born of despair.* DESPERATION is usually an active state, the abandonment of hope impelling to a furious struggle against adverse circumstances, with utter disregard of consequences: *an act of desperation when everything else had failed.* DESPONDENCY is usually a temporary state of deep gloom and disheartenment: *a spell of despondency.* DISCOURAGEMENT is a temporary loss of courage, hope, and ambition because of obstacles, frustrations, etc.: *his optimism resisted all discouragements.* HOPELESSNESS is a loss of hope so complete as to result in a more or less permanent state of passive despair: *a state of hopelessness and apathy.*

despairing (dĭ spâr′ĭng), *adj.* **1.** given to despair or hopelessness. **2.** indicating despair. —**despair′ingly,** *adv.* —**Syn. 1.** See **hopeless.** —**Ant. 1.** hopeful.

despatch (dĭs păch′), *v.t., v.i., n.* dispatch. —**despatch′er,** *n.*

desperado (dĕs′pə rä′dō), *n., pl.* **-does, -dos.** a desperate or reckless criminal; one ready for any desperate deed. [prob. refashioning of *desperate* after Sp. words in *-ado.* Cf. OSp. *desperado*, g. L *dēspērātus* DESPERATE]

desperate (dĕs′pə rĭt, -prĭt), *adj.* **1.** reckless from despair; ready to run any risk. **2.** characterized by the recklessness of despair. **3.** leaving little or no hope; very serious or dangerous. **4.** extremely bad. **5.** extreme or excessive. **6.** having no hope. **7.** moved by a feeling of hopelessness. **8.** undertaken as a last resort. [late ME, t. L: m. s. *dēspērātus*, pp., given up] —**des′perately,** *adv.* —**des′perateness,** *n.* —**Syn. 3.** See **hopeless.** —**Ant. 1.** cautious.

desperation (dĕs′pə rā′shən), *n.* **1.** the state of being desperate; the recklessness of despair. **2.** the act or fact of despairing; despair. —**Syn. 1.** See **despair.**

despicable (dĕs′pĭ kə bl), *adj.* that is to be despised; contemptible. [t. LL: m. s. *dēspicābilis*, der. L *dēspicārī* despise] —**des′picabil′ity, des′picableness,** *n.* —**des′picably,** *adv.* —**Syn.** worthless, base, vile. —**Ant.** admirable.

despise (dĭ spīz′), *v.t.*, **-spised, -spising.** to look down upon, as in contempt; scorn; disdain. [ME *despise(n)*, t. OF: m. *despis-*, s. *despire*, g. L *dēspicere* look down upon, despise] —**despis′er,** *n.* —**Ant.** admire.

despite (dĭ spīt′), *prep., n., v.*, **-spited, -spiting.** —*prep.* **1.** in spite of; notwithstanding. —*n.* **2.** contemptuous treatment; insult. **3.** *Archaic.* malice, hatred, or spite. **4. in despite of,** in contempt or defiance of; in spite of; notwithstanding. —*v.t.* **5.** *Obs.* to offend; vex; spite. [orig. *in despite of*; ME *despit*, t. OF, g. L *despectus* a looking down upon] —**Syn. 1.** See **notwithstanding.**

despiteful (dĭ spīt′fəl), *adj.* *Archaic.* contemptuous; malicious; spiteful. —**despite′fully,** *adv.* —**despite′fulness,** *n.*

despiteous (dĕs pĭt′ĭ əs), *adj.* *Archaic.* **1.** malicious; spiteful. **2.** contemptuous. —**despit′eously,** *adv.*

despoil (dĭ spoil′), *v.t.* to strip of possessions; rob; plunder; pillage. [ME *despoile(n)*, t. OF: m. *despoillier*, g. L *dēspoliāre* plunder, rob] —**despoil′er,** *n.* —**despoil′ment,** *n.*

despoliation (dĭ spō′lĭ ā′shən), *n.* **1.** the act of despoiling. **2.** the fact of being despoiled.

despond (dĭ spŏnd′), *v.i.* **1.** to lose heart, courage, or hope. —*n.* **2.** *Archaic.* despondency. [t. L: s. *dēspondēre* promise, give up, lose (heart)] —**despond′ingly,** *adv.*

despondency (dĭ spŏn′dən sĭ), *n.* a state of being despondent; depression of spirits from loss of courage or hope; dejection. Also, **despond′ence.** —**Syn.** discouragement, melancholy, gloom, desperation. See **despair.**

despondent (dĭ spŏn′dənt), *adj.* desponding; depressed or dejected. [t. L: s. *dēspondens*, ppr., giving up, despairing] —**despond′ently,** *adv.* —**Syn.** discouraged, disheartened, downhearted, melancholy, low-spirited. See **hopeless.** —**Ant.** hopeful.

despot (dĕs′pŏt), *n.* **1.** an absolute ruler; an autocrat. **2.** a tyrant or oppressor. **3.** *Hist.* master or lord (a title of autocratic rulers, esp. the late Roman and Byzantine Emperors). [t. Gk: s. *despótēs* master]

despotic (dĕs pŏt′ĭk), *adj.* of, pertaining to, or of the nature of a despot or despotism; autocratic; arbitrary; tyrannical. —**despot′ically,** *adv.*

despotism (dĕs′pə tĭz′əm), *n.* **1.** the rule of a despot; the exercise of absolute authority. **2.** an absolute or autocratic government. **3.** absolute power or control; tyranny. **4.** a country ruled by a despot.

Des Prés (*Fr.* dĕ prĕ′), **Josquin** (*Fr.* zhôs kăN′), 1445?–1521, Flemish composer. Also, **Deprès, Deprez.**

despumate (dĭ spyōō′māt, dĕs′pyōō māt′), *v.*, **-mated, -mating.** —*v.t.* **1.** to skim. —*v.i.* **2.** to throw off froth, scum, or impurities. [t. L: m. s. *dēspūmātus*, pp., skimmed] —**des′puma′tion,** *n.*

desquamate (dĕs′kwə māt′), *v.i.*, **-mated, -mating.** *Pathol.* to come off in scales, as the skin in certain diseases; peel off. [t. L: m. s. *dēsquāmātus*, pp., scaled off] —**des′quama′tion,** *n.* —**desquamatory** (dĕs kwăm′ə tə rĭ, -trĭ), *adj.*

D. ès S., (F. *Docteur ès Sciences*) Doctor of Sciences.

Dessau (*Ger.* dĕs′ou), *n.* a town in East Germany, formerly capital of Anhalt. 95,682 (1965).

dessert (dĭ zûrt′), *n.* **1.** a final course of a meal including pies, puddings, etc. **2.** a serving of fruits, or some sweet confection, at the end of a meal. [t. F, der. *desservir* clear the table, f. *des-* DIS-[1] + *servīre* serve]

dessertspoon (dĭ zûrt′spōōn′), *n.* a spoon intermediate in size between a tablespoon and a teaspoon.

dessertspoonful (dĭ zûrt′spōōn fōōl′), *n.* as much as a dessertspoon can hold, equal to about two teaspoonfuls.

dessiatine (dĕs′yə tēn′), *n.* a Russian unit of land measure equal to 2·7 acres. [t. Russ.: m. *desyatīna*, lit., tithe, tenth]

Dessie (dĕs′ĭ), *n.* a town in N central Ethiopia. 43,000 (est. 1962).

de-Stalinize (dē stä′lĭ nīz′), *v.t.*, **-nized, -nizing.** to remove the influence of Stalin from. Also, **de-Stalinise.** —**de-Sta′liniza′tion,** *n.*

desterilize (dē stĕ′rĭ līz′), *v.t.*, **-lized, -lizing. 1.** to make unsterile. **2.** *U.S.* to utilize an idle fund or commodity, as when a nation issues currency against gold previously unused. Also, **desterilise.**

Desterro (*Port.* dĕs tĕr′rō), *n.* former name of **Florianópolis.**

destination (dĕs′tĭ nā′shən), *n.* **1.** the predetermined end of a journey or voyage. **2.** the purpose for which anything is destined; ultimate end or design.

destine (dĕs′tĭn), *v.t.*, **-tined, -tining. 1.** to set apart for a particular use, purpose, etc.; design; intend. **2.** to appoint or ordain beforehand, as by divine decree; foreordain; predetermine. [ME *destenen*, t. OF: m. *destiner*, t. L: m. *dēstināre* make fast, establish, appoint]

destined (dĕs′tĭnd), *adj.* **1.** bound for a certain destination. **2.** designed; intended. **3.** predetermined.

destiny (dĕs′tĭ nĭ), *n., pl.* **-nies. 1.** that which is to happen to a particular person or thing; one's lot or fortune. **2.** the predetermined course of events. **3.** the power or agency which determines the course of events. **4.** (*cap.*) this power personified or represented as a goddess. **5. the Destinies,** the Fates. [ME *destinee*, t. OF, der. *destiner* DESTINE] —**Syn. 2.** See **fate.**

destitute (dĕs′tĭ tyōōt′), *adj.* **1.** bereft of means or resources; lacking the means of subsistence. **2.** deprived or devoid of (something) (fol. by *of*). **3.** *Obs.* abandoned or deserted. [ME, t. L: m. s. *dēstitūtus*, pp., put away, abandoned] —**des′titute′ness,** *n.* —**Syn. 1.** needy, poor, indigent, penniless, poverty-stricken.

destitution (dĕs′tĭ tyōō′shən), *n.* **1.** want of the means of subsistence; utter poverty. **2.** deprivation. [ME, t. L: s. *dēstitūtiō*] —**Syn. 1.** See **poverty.** —**Ant. 1.** affluence.

destrier (dĕs′trĭ ə), *n.* *Archaic.* a warhorse; a charger. [ME *destrer*, t. AF, var. of OF *destrier*, g. LL *dextrārius*, lit., (horse) led at the right hand]

destroy (dĭ stroi′), *v.t.* **1.** to reduce to pieces or to a useless form; ruin; spoil; consume; demolish. **2.** to put an end to; extinguish. **3.** to kill; slay. **4.** to render ineffective; nullify; invalidate. [ME *destruy(en)*, t. OF: m. *destruire*, g. LL var. of L *dēstruere* pull down, destroy] —**destroy′able,** *adj.*
—**Syn. 1.** DESTROY, DEMOLISH, RAZE imply reducing a thing to uselessness. To DESTROY is to reduce something to nothingness or to take away its powers and functions so that restoration is impossible; the action is usually violent or sudden, but may be gradual and slow, esp. when it entails a reversal of natural processes: *fire destroys a building, disease destroys tissues.* To DEMOLISH is to destroy an organized body or structure by complete separation of parts: *to demolish a machine.* To RAZE is to lay level with the ground: *to raze a fortress.* —**Ant. 1.** construct. **2.** establish. **3.** save. **4.** preserve.

destroyer (dĭ stroi′ə), *n.* **1.** one who or that which destroys. **2.** a small, fast warship, originally designed to destroy torpedo boats.

destruct (dĭ strŭkt′), *n.* the deliberate destruction of a rocket or the like before completion of its mission.

destructible (dĭ strŭk′tə bl), *adj.* that may be destroyed; liable to destruction. —**destruct′ibil′ity, destruct′ibleness,** *n.*

destruction (dĭ strŭk′shən), *n.* **1.** the act of destroying. **2.** the fact or condition of being destroyed; demolition; annihilation. **3.** a cause or means of destroying. [ME, t. L: s. *dēstructio*] **—Syn. 1.** extinction, extermination. See **ruin.**

destructionist (dĭ strŭk′shə nĭst), *n.* an advocate of the destruction of an existing political institution or the like.

destructive (dĭ strŭk′tĭv), *adj.* **1.** tending to destroy; causing destruction (fol. by *of* or *to*). **2.** tending to overthrow, disprove, or discredit: *destructive criticism.* **—***n.* **3.** a destructive agent or force. **—destruc′tively,** *adv.* **—destruc′tiveness, destructivity** (dē′strŭk tĭv′ĭ tĭ), *n.* **—Syn. 1.** ruinous, baleful, pernicious, deleterious.

destructive distillation, *Chem.* the destruction or decomposition of a substance, as wood, coal, etc., by heat in a closed vessel, and the collection of the volatile matters evolved.

destructor (dĭ strŭk′tə), *n.* a furnace for the burning of refuse; an incinerator. [t. LL, der. L *dēstruere* destroy]

desuetude (dĕs′wĭ tyo͞od′, dĭ syo͞o′ĭ tyo͞od′), *n.* the state of being no longer used or practised. [t. F, t. L: m. *dēsuētūdo*]

desultory (dĕs′əl tə rĭ, -trĭ), *adj.* **1.** veering about from one thing to another; disconnected, unmethodical, or fitful: *desultory reading or conversation.* **2.** random: *a desultory thought.* [t. L: m. s. *dēsultōrius* of a leaper, superficial] **—des′ultorily,** *adv.* **—des′ultoriness,** *n.* **—Ant. 1.** methodical. **2.** pertinent.

detach (dĭ tăch′), *v.t.* **1.** to unfasten and separate; disengage; disunite. **2.** to send away (a regiment, ship, etc.) on a special mission: *men were detached to defend the pass.* [t. F: s. *détacher*, der. OF *tache* (g. Rom. *tacca*) nail. Cf. ATTACH] **—detach′able,** *adj.* **—detach′abil′ity,** *n.* **—detach′er,** *n.*

detached (dĭ tăcht′), *adj.* **1.** standing apart; separate; unattached (usually applied to houses): *he lives in a detached house.* **2.** not interested; unconcerned; aloof. **3.** objective; unbiased.

detachment (dĭ tăch′mənt), *n.* **1.** the act of detaching. **2.** the condition of being detached. **3.** a state of aloofness, as from worldly affairs or from the concerns of others. **4.** freedom from prejudice or partiality. **5.** the act of sending out a detached force of troops or naval ships. **6.** something detached, as a number of troops separated from a main force for some special combat or other task.

detail (dĭ tāl′, dē′tāl), *n.* **1.** an individual or minute part; an item or particular. **2.** particulars collectively; minutiae. **3.** a dealing with or treating part by part or item by item. **4.** fine, intricate decoration. **5.** a detail drawing. **6.** any small section of a larger structure considered as a unit. **7.** a reproduction of a part or section of something, esp. a work of art, often enlarged. **8.** *Mil.* **a.** detailing or telling off, as of a small force or an officer, for a special service. **b.** the party or person so selected. **c.** a particular assignment of duty. **9.** *Archaic.* a narrative or report of particulars. **10. in detail,** circumstantially; item by item. **—***v.t.* **11.** to relate or report in particulars; tell fully and distinctly. **12.** *Mil.* to order or appoint for some particular duty, as a patrol, a guard, etc. **13.** to decorate with fine, intricate designs. [t. F, der. *détailler* cut in pieces, retail]

detail drawing, a drawing, on a relatively large scale, of a part of a building, machine, etc., with dimensions or other information for use in construction.

detain (dĭ tān′), *v.t.* **1.** to keep from proceeding; keep waiting; delay. **2.** to keep under restraint or in custody. **3.** to keep back or withhold, as from a person. [late ME *detaine(n)*, t. OF: m. *detenir*, t. L: m. *dētinēre* keep back] **—detain′ment,** *n.* **—Syn. 1.** retard, stop.

detainee (dē′tā nē′), *n.* one who is detained or held prisoner or in custody without trial.

detainer (dĭ tā′nə), *n.* **1.** one who or that which detains. **2.** *Law.* the wrongful detaining or withholding of what belongs to another. **3.** *Law.* a writ for the further detention of a person already in custody. [t. AF: m. *detener*, var. of OF *detenir*]

detect (dĭ tĕkt′), *v.t.* **1.** to discover or notice (a person) in the performance of some act: *to detect someone in a dishonest act.* **2.** to find out the action or character of: *to detect a hypocrite.* **3.** to discover the presence, existence, or fact of. **4.** *Radio.* to subject to the action of a detector. [t. L: s. *dētectus*, pp., discovered, uncovered] **—detect′able, detect′ible,** *adj.* **—Syn. 3.** See **learn.**

detectaphone (dĭ tĕk′tə fōn′), *n.* a device for tapping telephone conversations.

detection (dĭ tĕk′shən), *n.* **1.** the act of detecting. **2.** the fact of being detected. **3.** discovery, as of error or crime. **4.** *Radio.* **a.** rectification of alternating currents in a radio receiver. **b.** the conversion of an alternating carrier wave or current into a direct pulsating current equivalent to the transmitted signal; demodulation.

detective (dĭ tĕk′tĭv), *n.* **1.** a member of the police force or a private investigator whose job it is to obtain information and evidence, as of offences against the law. **—***adj.* **2.** pertaining to detection or detectives: *a detective story.* **3.** serving to detect; detecting.

detector (dĭ tĕk′tə), *n.* **1.** one who or that which detects. **2.** *Radio.* **a.** a device for detecting electric oscillations or waves. **b.** a device, as a crystal detector or a radio valve, which rectifies the alternating currents in a radio receiver. [t. LL]

detent (dĭ tĕnt′), *n.* a piece of a mechanism which, when disengaged, releases the operating power, or by which the action is prevented or checked; a catch, as in a lock, clock, etc.; a pawl. [t. F: m. *détente*, der. *détendre* relax, f. *dé-* DIS-[1] + *tendre* (g. L *tendere* stretch)]

détente (dā tŏnt′, *Fr.* dĕ täɴt′), *n.* a relaxing, as of international tension. [F]

detention (dĭ tĕn′shən), *n.* **1.** the act of detaining. **2.** the state of being detained. **3.** a keeping in custody; confinement. **4.** a keeping in (of a pupil) after school hours as a form of punishment. **5.** the withholding of what belongs to or is claimed by another.

detention centre, a form of prison to which offenders between the ages of 14 and 21 may be committed.

deter (dĭ tû′), *v.t.*, **-terred, -terring.** to discourage or restrain (one) from acting or proceeding through fear, doubt, etc. [t. L: m. s. *dēterrēre* frighten from] **—deter′ment,** *n.* **—Syn.** dissuade, hinder, prevent, stop.

deterge (dĭ tûj′), *v.t.*, **-terged, -terging. 1.** to wipe away. **2.** to cleanse by removing foul or morbid matter, as from a wound. [t. L: m. s. *dētergēre* wipe off]

detergence (dĭ tû′jəns), *n.* cleansing or purging power. Also, **deter′gency.**

detergent (dĭ tû′jənt), *adj.* **1.** cleansing; purging. **—***n.* **2. a.** any cleaning agent, including soap. **b.** one of a group of synthetic, organic cleaning agents with surface-active properties which, unlike soap, is not produced from fats or oils.

deteriorate (dĭ tĭə′rĭ ə rāt′), *v.t., v.i.*, **-rated, -rating.** to make or become worse; make or become lower in character or quality. [t. L: m. s. *dēteriōrātus*, pp.] **—dete′riora′tion,** *n.* **—dete′riorative,** *adj.*

determinable (dĭ tû′mĭ nə bl), *adj.* **1.** capable of being determined. **2.** *Law.* subject to termination.

determinant (dĭ tû′mĭ nənt), *adj.* **1.** serving to determine; determining. **—***n.* **2.** a determining agent or factor. **3.** *Maths.* an algebraic expression in the elements of any square matrix used in solving linear systems of equations.

determinate (dĭ tû′mĭ nĭt), *adj.* **1.** having defined limits; definite. **2.** settled; positive. **3.** determined upon; conclusive; final. **4.** determined; resolute. **5.** *Bot.* (of an inflorescence) having the primary and each secondary axis ending in a flower or bud, thus preventing further elongation. [ME, t. L: m. s. *dētermīnātus*, pp., determined] **—deter′minately,** *adv.* **—deter′minateness,** *n.*

determination (dĭ tû′mĭ nā′shən), *n.* **1.** the act of coming to a decision; the fixing or settling of a purpose. **2.** ascertainment, as after observation or investigation. **3.** a result ascertained; a solution. **4.** the settlement of a dispute, etc., by authoritative decision. **5.** the decision arrived at or pronounced. **6.** the quality of being determined or resolute; firmness of purpose. **7.** a fixed purpose or intention. **8.** the fixing or settling of amount, limit, character, etc. **9.** fixed direction or tendency towards some object or end. **10.** *Chiefly Law.* conclusion or termination. **11.** *Embryol.* the fixation of the nature of morphological differentiation in a group of cells before actual, visible differentiation. **12.** *Logic.* the rendering of a notion more definite by the addition of differentiating characters.

determinative (dĭ tû′mĭ nə tĭv), *adj.* **1.** serving to determine; determining. **—***n.* **2.** something that determines. **3.** (in hieroglyphics) an ideographic sign attached to a word as an indication of its meaning. **—deter′minatively,** *adv.* **—deter′minativeness,** *n.*

determine (dĭ tû′mĭn), *v.*, **-mined, -mining. —***v.t.* **1.** to settle or decide (a dispute, question, etc.) by an authoritative decision. **2.** to conclude or ascertain, as after reasoning, observation, etc. **3.** *Geom.* to fix the position of. **4.** to fix or decide causally; condition: *demand determines supply.* **5.** to give direction or tendency to; impel. **6.** *Logic.* to limit, as an idea, by adding differentiating characters. **7.** *Chiefly Law.* to put an end to; terminate. **8.** to lead or bring (a person) to a decision: *it finally determined him to do it.* **9.** to decide upon. **—***v.i.* **10.** to come to a decision or resolution; decide. **11.** *Chiefly Law.* to come to an end. [ME *determine(n)*, t. OF: m. *determiner*, t. L: m. *dētermināre* limit] **—deter′miner,** *n.* **—Syn. 1.** See **decide.**

determined (dĭ tû′mĭnd), *adj.* **1.** resolute; unflinching; firm. **2.** decided; settled; resolved. **—deter′minedly,**

adv. —**deter′minedness,** *n.* —**Syn. 1.** staunch, inflexible, unfaltering, unwavering.

determinism (dĭ tû′mĭ nĭz′əm), *n.* the doctrine that neither outside events nor human choices are uncaused, but are the results of antecedent conditions, physical or psychological. —**deter′minist,** *n., adj.* —**deter′minis′tic,** *adj.*

deterrent (dĭ tĕ′rənt), *adj.* **1.** deterring; restraining. —*n.* **2.** something that deters or is expected to deter, esp. a nuclear weapon. —**deter′rence,** *n.*

detersive (dĭ tû′sĭv), *adj.* **1.** detergent. —*n.* **2.** a detersive agent or medicine.

detest (dĭ tĕst′), *v.t.* to feel abhorrence of; hate; dislike intensely. [t. F: s. *détester*, t. L: m. *dētestārī*, lit., curse while calling a deity to witness] —**detest′er,** *n.* —**Syn.** abhor, loathe, abominate. See **hate.**

detestable (dĭ tĕs′tə bl), *adj.* deserving to be detested; abominable; hateful. —**detest′abil′ity, detest′ableness,** *n.* —**detest′ably,** *adv.* —**Syn.** execrable, abhorrent, loathsome, odious, vile.

detestation (dē′tĕs tā′shən), *n.* **1.** abhorrence; hatred. **2.** a person or thing detested.

dethrone (dĭ thrōn′), *v.t.,* **-throned, -throning.** to remove from the throne; depose. —**dethrone′ment,** *n.* —**dethron′er,** *n.*

detinue (dĕt′ĭ nyōō′), *n. Law.* an old common-law form of action to recover possession or the value of articles of personal property wrongfully detained. [t. OF: m. *detenue* detention, orig. pp. fem. of *detenir* DETAIN]

detonate (dĕt′ə nāt′), *v.i., v.t.,* **-nated, -nating.** to explode, esp. with great noise, suddenness, or violence. [t. L: m. s. *dētonātus*, pp., thundered forth]

detonating gas, electrolytic gas.

detonation (dĕt′ə nā′shən), *n.* **1.** the act of detonating. **2.** an explosion. **3. a.** *Chem.* very rapid combustion which occurs in a shock wave. **b.** the combustion reactions which cause knocking or pinking in an internal-combustion engine. **c.** the accompanying knocking or pinking sound.

detonator (dĕt′ə nā′tə), *n.* **1.** a device, as a percussion cap or an explosive, used to make another substance explode. **2.** something that explodes.

detour (dā′tōōə, dē′-), *n.* **1.** a roundabout or circuitous way or course, esp. one used temporarily instead of the main route. —*v.i.* **2.** to make a detour; go by way of a detour. —*v.t.* **3.** to cause to make a detour; send by way of a detour. Also, *French,* **détour** (*Fr.* dė tōōr′). [t. F, der. *détourner* turn aside, f. *dé-* DIS-[1] + *tourner* turn]

detract (dĭ trăkt′), *v.t.* **1.** to take away (a part); abate (fol. by *from*). **2.** to draw away or divert. —*v.i.* **3.** to take away a part, as from quality, value, or reputation. [t. L: s. *dētractus*, pp., drawn away or down] —**detrac′tingly,** *adv.* —**detrac′tor,** *n.*

detraction (dĭ trăk′shən), *n.* the act of detracting, or of disparaging or belittling the reputation or worth of a person. —**Syn.** defamation, vilification.

detractive (dĭ trăk′tĭv), *adj.* tending or seeking to detract; depreciative. Also, **detractory** (dĭ trăk′tə rĭ). —**detrac′tively,** *adv.*

detrain (dē trān′), *v.i., v.t. Chiefly Mil.* to discharge or alight from a railway train. —**detrain′ment,** *n.*

detribalize (dē trī′bə līz′), *v.t.,* **-lized, -lizing.** to cause to relinquish tribal allegiances or customs, mainly through contact with different cultures. Also, **detribalise.**

detriment (dĕt′rĭ mənt), *n.* **1.** loss, damage, or injury. **2.** a cause of loss or damage. [t. L: s. *dētrīmentum* loss, damage] —**Syn. 1.** harm, hurt, impairment, disadvantage, prejudice. See **damage.**

detrimental (dĕt′rĭ mĕn′tl), *adj.* causing detriment; injurious; prejudicial. —**det′rimen′tally,** *adv.*

detrital (dĭ trī′tl), *adj.* composed of detritus.

detrition (dĭ trĭsh′ən), *n.* act of wearing away by rubbing.

detritus (dĭ trī′təs), *n.* **1.** *Geol.* particles of rock or other material worn or broken away from a mass, as by the action of water or glacial ice. **2.** any disintegrated material; debris. [t. L: a rubbing away]

Detroit (dĭ troit′), *n.* a city in the U.S., in SE Michigan, on the Detroit river. 1,670,144 (1960).

de trop (də trō′; *Fr.* də trō′), *French.* **1.** too much; too many. **2.** in the way; not wanted.

detrude (dĭ trōōd′), *v.t.,* **-truded, -truding. 1.** to thrust out or away. **2.** to thrust or force down. [t. L: m. s. *dētrūdere*]

detruncate (dē trŭng′kāt), *v.t.,* **-cated, -cating.** to reduce by cutting off a part; cut down. [t. L: m. s. *dētruncātus*, pp.] —**de′trunca′tion,** *n.*

detrusion (dĭ trōō′zhən), *n.* the act of detruding. [t. LL: s. *dētrūsio*, der. L *dētrūdere* thrust away]

detumescence (dē′tyōō mĕs′əns), *n.* subsidence of swelling. [t. L: der. *dētumescere* cease to swell. See TUMESCENCE]

Deucalion (dyōō kā′lyən), *n. Gk Legend.* a son of Prometheus. He survived the deluge with his wife Pyrrha, and became the ancestor of the renewed human race.

deuce[1] (dyōōs), *n.* **1.** *Cards, Dice.* a card, or the side of a dice, having two pips. **2.** *Tennis, etc.* a juncture in a game at which the scores are level and either player or pair, must score two consecutive points in order to win the game. [t. OF: m. *deus*, g. L *duōs*, acc. of *duo* two]

deuce[2] (dyōōs), *n. Colloq.* bad luck; the mischief; the devil (used in mild imprecations and exclamations). [special use of *deuce*, prob. t. LG: m. *de duus!* the deuce, an unlucky throw at dice. Cf. G *der Daus!*]

deuced (dyōō′sĭd; dyōōst), *Colloq.* —*adj.* **1.** confounded; excessive. —*adv.* **2.** Also, **deu′cedly.** confoundedly; excessively.

Deurne (*Flem.* dœr′nə), *n.* a town in N Belgium. 72,144 (est. 1964).

deus ex machina (dā′ōōs ĕks măk′ĭ nə), *Latin.* an improbable, artificial, or unmotivated device for unravelling a plot, esp. in drama. [L: god from a machine]

Deus Misereatur (dā′ōōs mē′zē rĭ ä′tōōə), *Latin.* (May) God have mercy; God be merciful (title of Psalm 67).

Deus vult (dā′ōōs vōōlt′), *Latin.* God wills (it) (cry of the Crusaders).

deut-, var. of **deuto-,** before vowels.

Deut., Deuteronomy.

deuter-, a form of **deutero-** (def. 1) before a vowel.

deuterium (dyōō tĭə′rĭ əm), *n. Chem.* an isotope of hydrogen, having twice the mass of ordinary hydrogen; heavy hydrogen. *Symbol:* D; *at. no.:* 1; *at. wt.:* 2·01. [NL, t. Gk: m. *deutereîon*, neut. sing. of *deutereîos*, adj., having second place]

deuterium oxide, *Chem.* heavy water, D_2O.

deutero-, a word element: **1.** meaning 'second' or 'later', as in *deuterogamy.* **2.** *Chem.* indicating the presence of deuterium. [t. Gk, comb. form of *deúteros* second]

deuterocanonical books (dyōō′tə rō kə nŏn′ĭ kl), the books of the Bible regarded by the Roman Catholic Church as canonical but not universally acknowledged as such in the early church, including, in the Old Testament, most of the Protestant Apocrypha.

deuterogamy (dyōō′tə rŏg′ə mĭ), *n.* a second marriage, after the death or divorce of a first husband or wife. [t. Gk: m. s. *deuterogamía* second marriage] —**deu′terog′amist,** *n.*

deuteron (dyōō′tə rŏn′), *n. Physics.* a deuterium nucleus, a particle with one positive charge.

Deuteronomist (dyōō′tə rŏn′ə mĭst), *n.* the author or part-author of the book of Deuteronomy.

Deuteronomy (dyōō′tə rŏn′ə mĭ), *n. Bible.* the fifth book of the Pentateuch, containing a second statement of the Mosaic law. [t. LL: m. s. *Deuteronomium*, t. Gk: m. *Deuteronómion* the second law] —**Deuteronomic** (dyōō′tə rə nŏm′ĭk), *adj.*

deuto-, **1.** var. of **deutero-. 2.** *Chem.* a prefix denoting the second in a series. Also, **deut-.**

deutoplasm (dyōō′tə plăz′əm), *n. Embryol.* that part of the ovocyte which furnishes the nourishment of the embryo.

Deutsche Mark (doich; *Ger.* dŏʏ′chə), **1.** the monetary unit of West Germany since 1948, equal to 100 pfennigs, and equivalent to about £0·104. **2.** a cupronickel coin of this value. *Abbrev.:* DM.

Deutsches Reich (*Ger.* dŏʏ′chəs rīKH′), former official name of **Germany.**

Deutschland (*Ger.* dŏʏch′länt), *n.* German for **Germany.**

deutzia (dyōōt′sĭ ə), *n.* any saxifragaceous shrub of the genus *Deutzia*, having mostly white, pink, or purplish flowers. [named after Jan *Deutz*, 1743–88?, Dutch naturalist]

Deux-Sèvres (*Fr.* dœ sĕ′vr), *n.* a department in W France. 321,118 pop. (1962); 2338 sq. mi. *Cap.:* Niort.

deva (dā′və), *n. Hindu Myth.* a god or divinity; one of an order of good spirits. [t. Skt]

De Valera (də və lĕə′rə, -lĭə′rə), **Eamon** (ā′mən), born 1882, Irish statesman: president of Executive Council of Irish Free State, 1932–37; prime minister of Ireland 1937–48, 1951–54, 1957–59; president from 1959.

de Valois (də văl′wä), **Dame Ninette** (nĕ′nĕt), born 1898, English ballet dancer and choreographer.

devaluate (dē văl′yōō āt′), *v.t.,* **-ated, -ating. 1.** to deprive of value; reduce the value of. **2.** to devalue. [f. DE- + VALUE, n. + -ATE[1]]

devaluation (dē văl′yōō ā′shən), *n.* **1.** an official lowering of the legal exchange value of a country's currency. **2.** a reduction of value, importance, etc.

devalue (dē văl′yōō), *v.t.,* **-valued, -valuing.** to lower the legal value of (a currency); devaluate.

Devanagari (dā′və nä′gə rĭ), *n.* the alphabetical script in which Sanskrit is usually written, also employed for Hindi, and, in a modified form, other modern languages of

India. [t. Skt: lit., Nagari (an alphabet of India) of the gods]

devastate (dĕv′ə stāt′), *v.t.*, **-stated, -stating.** to lay waste; ravage; render desolate. [t. L: m. s. *dēvastātus*, pp.]

devastating (dĕv′ə stā′tĭng), *adj.* **1.** tending or threatening to devastate. **2.** *Colloq.* (of a remark, description, etc.) highly effective.

devastation (dĕv′ə stā′shən), *n.* **1.** act of devastating; destruction. **2.** devastated state; desolation.

de Vega (*Sp.* dĕ vĕ′gä), **Lope** (*Sp.* lō′pĕ) (*Lope Félix de Vega Carpio*), 1562–1635, Spanish dramatist and poet.

develop (dĭ vĕl′əp), *v.t.* **1.** to bring out the capabilities or possibilities of; bring to a more advanced or effective state. **2.** to cause to grow or expand. **3.** to elaborate or expand in detail. **4.** to bring into being or activity; generate; evolve. **5.** to build on (land). **6.** *Biol.* to cause to go through the process of natural evolution from a previous and lower stage, or from an embryonic state to a later and more complex or perfect one. **7.** *Maths.* **a.** to express in an extended form, as in a series. **b.** to unroll on to a plane surface. **8.** *Music.* to unfold, by various technical means, the inherent possibilities of (a theme). **9.** *Photog.* **a.** to render visible (the latent image) in the exposed sensitized film of a photographic plate, etc. **b.** to treat (a photographic plate, etc.) with chemical agents so as to bring out the latent image. **10.** *Chess.* to bring a piece into a useful position. *—v.i.* **11.** to grow into a more mature or advanced state; advance; expand. **12.** to come gradually into existence or operation; be evolved. **13.** to be disclosed; become evident or manifest. **14.** *Biol.* to undergo differentiation in ontogeny or progress in phylogeny. **15.** to undergo developing, as a photographic plate. Also, **devel′ope.** [t. F: m. s. *développer*, f. *dé-* DIS-[1] + m. *voluper* wrap. Cf. ENVELOP] —**devel′opable,** *adj.*

developer (dĭ vĕl′ə pə), *n.* **1.** one who or that which develops. **2.** *Photog.* the reducing agent or solution used to develop a photographic film or plate.

development (dĭ vĕl′əp mənt), *n.* **1.** the act, process or result of developing. **2.** a developed state, form, or product. **3.** evolution, growth, expansion. **4.** a fact or circumstance bringing about a new situation. **5.** *Music.* the part of a movement or composition in which a theme or themes are developed. —**devel′opmen′tal,** *adj.* —**devel′opmen′tally,** *adv.* —**Syn. 1.** expansion, elaboration, growth, evolution. **2.** maturity, ripeness.

development area, a region of high unemployment where government encouragement is given to the establishment of new industry.

Deventer (*Du.* dĕ′vən tər), *n.* a town in the Netherlands, in SW Overijssel. 59,204 (1965).

Devereux (dĕv′ə rōō′), *n.* **Robert.** See **Essex.**

devest (dĭ vĕst′), *v.t.* **1.** *Law.* to divest. **2.** *Obs.* to undress. [MF: s. *devester*, var. of OF *desvestir*, f. *des-* DIS-[1] + *vestir*, g. L *vestīre* clothe. See DIVEST]

Devi (dā′vē), *n.* *Hinduism.* a female deity. [t. Skt]

deviant (dē′vĭ ənt), *adj.* **1.** deviating from an accepted norm. *—n.* **2.** one who or that which deviates markedly from an accepted norm.

deviate (dē′vĭ āt′), *v.*, **-ated, -ating,** *adj.*, *n.* *—v.i.* **1.** to turn aside (from a way or course). **2.** to depart or swerve, as from a procedure, course of action, or acceptable standard. **3.** to digress as from a line of thought or reasoning. *—v.t.* **4.** to cause to swerve; turn aside. *—adj.*, *n.* **5.** *Chiefly U.S.* deviant. [t. LL: m. s. *dēviātus*, pp. of *dēviāre*, der. L *de-* DE- + *via* way] —**de′via′tor,** *n.*

—**Syn. 1.** DEVIATE, DIGRESS, DIVERGE, SWERVE imply turning or going aside from a path. To DEVIATE is to turn or wander, often by slight degrees, from what is considered the most direct or desirable approach to a given physical, intellectual, or moral end: *fear caused him to deviate from the truth.* To DIGRESS is primarily to wander from the main theme or topic in writing or speaking, esp. for explanation or illustration: *some authors digress to relate entertaining episodes.* Two paths DIVERGE when they proceed from a common point in such directions that the distance between them increases: *the sides of an angle diverge from a common point, their interests gradually diverged.* To SWERVE is to make a sudden or sharp turn from a line or course (and then, often, return to it): *the car swerved to avoid striking a pedestrian.*

deviation (dē′vĭ ā′shən), *n.* **1.** the act of deviating; divergence. **2.** departure from an accepted standard. **3.** *Statistics.* the difference between one of a set of values and the mean of the set. **4.** *Navig.* the error of a ship's magnetic compass due to local magnetism; the angle between the compass meridian and the magnetic meridian.

deviationist (dē′vĭ ā′shə nĭst), *n.* (chiefly in Communist ideology) one who departs from accepted party policies or practices. —**de′via′tionism,** *n.*

device (dĭ vīs′), *n.* **1.** an invention or contrivance. **2.** a plan or scheme for effecting a purpose. **3.** a crafty scheme; a trick. **4.** an artistic figure or design used as a heraldic bearing (often accompanied by a motto), or as an emblem, badge, trademark, or the like. **5.** a motto. **6.** (*pl.*) will; desire; inclination: *left to his own devices.* **7.** something artistically or fancifully designed. **8.** *Archaic.* the act or faculty of planning, contriving, or inventing. [b. ME *devis* division, discourse and *devise* heraldic device, will, both t. OF, g. L *dīvīsus, -a*, pp., divided] —**Syn. 3.** wile, ruse, artifice, shift.

devil (dĕv′əl), *n.*, *v.*, **-illed, -illing** or (*U.S.*) **-iled, -iling.** *—n.* **1.** *Theol.* **a.** (*sometimes cap.*) the supreme spirit of evil; Satan. **b.** a subordinate evil spirit at enmity with God, and having power to afflict man both with bodily disease and with spiritual corruption. **2.** an atrociously wicked, cruel, or ill-tempered person. **3.** a person of great cleverness, energy, or recklessness. **4.** the errand boy or the youngest apprentice in a printing office. **5.** *Colloq.* a person, usually one in unfortunate circumstances. **6.** *Law.* a junior counsel working without a fee. **7.** a hack writer. **8.** *Colloq.* fighting spirit. **9.** any of various mechanical devices, as a machine for tearing rags, etc. **10.** any of various portable furnaces or braziers. **11. the devil!** (an emphatic expletive or mild oath used to express disgust, anger, astonishment, negation, etc.) **12. between the devil and the deep blue sea,** faced with two equally distasteful alternatives. **13. devil of a,** *Colloq.* extremely difficult. **14. give the devil his due,** to do justice to or give deserved credit to an unpleasant or disliked person. **15. the devil to pay,** serious trouble to be faced. **16. go to the devil, a.** to fail completely; be ruined. **b.** to become depraved. **c.** an expletive expressing annoyance, disgust, impatience, etc. **17. let the devil take the hindmost,** to leave the least fortunate to suffer unpleasant consequences; abandon or leave to one's fate. **18. play the (very) devil with,** to ruin; do great harm to. **19. raise the devil,** to make a commotion. **20. speak** or **talk of the devil,** here comes the person who has been the subject of conversation. *—v.t.* **21.** *Colloq.* to harass, torment or pester. **22.** *Cookery.* to prepare food esp. by grilling with hot spices. **23.** to tear (rags, cloth, etc.) with a devil (def. 9). *—v.i.* **24.** to do work, esp. hackwork, for a lawyer or literary man; perform arduous or unpaid work or without recognition of one's services. [ME *devel*, OE *deofol*, t. L: m. s. *diabolus*, t. Gk: m. *diábolos* Satan, orig. slanderer]

devilfish (dĕv′əl fĭsh′), *n.*, *pl.* **-fishes,** (*esp. collectively*) **-fish. 1.** any of various marine animals, as the manta rays. **2.** any of various large cephalopods, as the octopus. **3.** batfish. **4.** angler (def. 2).

Devilfish, *Mantana hamiltoni* (Total length 20 ft, tail 6 ft, width 20 ft)

devilish (dĕv′əl ĭsh, dĕv′lĭsh), *adj.* **1.** of, like, or befitting a devil; diabolical; fiendish. **2.** *Colloq.* excessive; very great. *—adv.* **3.** *Colloq.* excessively; extremely. —**dev′ilishly,** *adv.* —**dev′ilishness,** *n.* —**Syn. 1.** satanic, demoniac, infernal, diabolical.

devilkin (dĕv′əl kĭn), *n.* a little devil; an imp.

devil-may-care (dĕv′əl mā kĕə′), *adj.* reckless; careless; happy-go-lucky.

devilment (dĕv′əl mənt), *n.* devilish action or conduct; mischief.

devilry (dĕv′əl rĭ), *n.*, *pl.* **-ries. 1.** wicked or reckless mischief. **2.** extreme wickedness. **3.** mischievous or wicked behaviour. **4.** diabolic magic or art. **5.** demonology. Also, **dev′iltry.**

devil's advocate. 1. an advocate of an opposing or bad cause, esp. for the sake of argument. **2.** *Rom. Cath. Ch.* a person appointed to present the arguments against a proposed canonization as a saint. [trans. of L *advocātus diabolī*]

devil's-bit scabious, a perennial dipsacaceous herb, *Succisa pratensis*, with dense heads of small mauve flowers, common in grassy places throughout Europe and W Asia.

devil's darning needle, dragonfly.

devil's food cake, a rich, chocolate cake.

Devil's Island, one of the Safety Islands, off the coast of French Guiana: former French penal colony. French, **Île du Diable.**

devil's punchbowl, a deep hollow in a hillside.

devil's tattoo, a meaningless beating or drumming with the hands or feet.

deviltry (dĕv′əl trĭ), *n.*, *pl.* **-tries.** devilry.

devious (dē′vyəs), *adj.* **1.** departing from the direct way; circuitous. **2.** out of the way; remote. **3.** departing from the accepted way; roundabout. **4.** not straightforward; tricky; deceptive; deceitful. [t. L: m. *dēvius* out of the way] —**de′viously,** *adv.* —**de′viousness,** *n.*

devisable (dĭ vī′zə bl), *adj.* **1.** capable of being invented or contrived. **2.** *Law.* capable of being bequeathed or assigned by will.

devisal (dĭ vī′zəl), *n.* the act of devising; contrivance.

devise (dĭ vīz′), *v.*, **-vised, -vising,** *n.* —*v.t.* **1.** to order or arrange the plan of; think out; plan; contrive; invent. **2.** *Law.* to assign or transmit (property, esp. real property) by will. **3.** *Obs.* to conceive or imagine. —*v.i.* **4.** to form a plan; contrive. —*n.* **5.** *Law.* **a.** the act of disposing of property, esp. real property, by will. **b.** a will or clause in a will disposing of property, esp. real property. **c.** the property disposed of. [ME *devise(n)*, t. OF: m. *deviser*, g. LL freq. of L *dīvidere* separate] —**devis′er,** *n.* —**Syn. 1.** See **prepare.**

devisee (dĭ vī′zē′, dĕv′ĭ zē′), *n.* *Law.* one to whom a devise is made.

devisor (dĭ vī′zə), *n.* *Law.* one who makes a devise.

devitalize (dē vī′tə līz′), *v.t.*, **-lized, -lizing.** to deprive of vitality or vital properties; make lifeless or weak. Also, **devitalise.** —**devi′taliza′tion,** *n.* —**Ant.** invigorate.

devitrify (dē vĭt′rĭ fī′), *v.t.* **1.** to deprive, wholly or partly, of vitreous character or properties, esp. to process glass so that it develops a minute crystalline structure, with a corresponding loss of transparency. —*v.i.* **2.** *Geol.* (of glass, igneous rocks) to crystallize into dull crypto-crystalline rocks. —**devit′rifica′tion,** *n.*

devocalize (dē vō′kə līz′), *v.t.*, **-lized, -lizing.** *Phonet.* to unvoice. Also, **devocalise.** —**devo′caliza′tion,** *n.*

devoid (dĭ void′), *adj.* empty, not possessing, free from, void, or destitute (fol. by *of*). [orig. pp. of obs. *devoid*, v., t. OF: m. *desvuidier* empty out, f. *des-* DIS-[1] + *vuidier* empty, void, v.]

devoir (dəv′wä; *Fr.* də vwȧr′), *n.* **1.** an act of civility or respect. **2.** (*pl.*) respects or compliments. **3.** *Archaic.* duty. [t. F, orig. inf., g. L *dēbēre* owe]

devolution (dē′və lo͞o′shən), *n.* **1.** the act or fact of devolving; passage onward from stage to stage. **2.** the passing on to a successor of an unexercised right. **3.** *Law.* the passing of property, as upon death or bankruptcy. **4.** *Biol.* degeneration; retrograde evolution (opposed to *evolution*). **5.** the transfer or delegation of power or authority.

devolve (dĭ vŏlv′), *v.*, **-volved, -volving.** —*v.t.* **1.** to transfer or delegate (a duty, responsibility, etc.) to or upon another; pass on. **2.** *Law.* to pass by inheritance or legal succession. **3.** *Archaic.* to roll downward; roll. —*v.i.* **4.** to fall as a duty or responsibility on a person. **5.** to be transferred or passed on from one to another. **6.** *Archaic.* to roll down. [t. L: m. s. *dēvolvere* roll down] —**devolve′-ment,** *n.*

Devon (dĕv′ən), *n.* **1.** one of a breed of cattle, usually red, originating in Devonshire. **2.** Devonshire.

Devonian (dĕ vō′nyən), *adj.* **1.** *Geol.* pertaining to a geological period or a system of rocks following the Silurian and preceding the Carboniferous. **2.** of or pertaining to Devonshire. —*n.* **3.** *Geol.* the Devonian period or system.

Devonshire (dĕv′ən shĭə′, -shə), *n.* a county in SW England. 822,906 pop. (1961); 2612 sq. mi. *Co. town:* Exeter. Also, **Devon.**

Devonshire cream, cream prepared by scalding milk; clotted cream.

devote (dĭ vōt′), *v.*, **-voted, -voting,** *adj.* —*v.t.* **1.** to give up or appropriate to or concentrate on a particular pursuit, occupation, purpose, cause, person, etc.: *devoting himself to science, evenings devoted to reading.* **2.** to appropriate by or as by a vow; set apart or dedicate by a solemn or formal act; consecrate. **3.** *Archaic.* to pronounce a curse upon; doom. —*adj.* **4.** *Archaic.* devoted. [t. L: m. s. *dēvōtus*, pp., vowed]

devoted (dĭ vō′tĭd), *adj.* **1.** zealous or ardent in attachment: *a devoted friend.* **2.** dedicated; consecrated. **3.** *Archaic.* accursed or doomed. —**devot′edly,** *adv.* —**devot′edness,** *n.*

devotee (dĕv′ə tē′), *n.* **1.** one ardently devoted to anything; an enthusiast. **2.** one zealously or fanatically devoted to religion.

devotement (dĭ vōt′mənt), *n.* devotion; dedication.

devotion (dĭ vō′shən), *n.* **1.** dedication; consecration. **2.** earnest attachment to a cause, person, etc. **3.** a giving over or appropriating to any purpose, cause, etc. **4.** *Theol.* the ready will to perform what belongs to the service of God. **5.** (*often pl.*) *Eccles.* religious observance or worship; a form of prayer or worship for special use. [ME, t. L: s. *dēvōtio*] —**Syn. 2.** See **love.**

devotional (dĭ vō′shə nəl), *adj.* characterized by devotion; used in devotions. —**devo′tionally,** *adv.*

devour (dĭ vou′ə), *v.t.* **1.** to swallow or eat up voraciously or ravenously. **2.** to consume destructively, recklessly, or wantonly. **3.** to swallow up or engulf. **4.** to take in greedily with the senses or intellect. **5.** to absorb or engross wholly: *devoured by fears.* [ME *devoure(n)*, t. OF: m. *devorer*, t. L: m. *dēvorāre* swallow down] —**devour′er,** *n.* —**devour′ingly,** *adv.*

devout (dĭ vout′), *adj.* **1.** devoted to divine worship or service; pious; religious. **2.** expressing devotion or piety: *devout prayer.* **3.** earnest or sincere; hearty. [ME, t. OF: m. *devot*, t. L: s. *dēvōtus*, pp., devoted] —**devout′ly,** *adv.* —**devout′ness,** *n.* —**Syn. 1.** See **religious.**

De Vries (*Du.*, *Flem.* də vrēs′), **1. Hans Vredeman** (*Flem.* hŏns′ vrĕ də mŏn), 1527–?1604, Flemish designer. **2. Hugo** (*Du.* hʏ′ KHō), 1848–1935, Dutch botanist: developed mutation theory of evolution.

dew (dyo͞o), *n.* **1.** moisture condensed from the atmosphere, esp. at night, and deposited in the form of small drops upon any cool surface. **2.** something likened to dew, as serving to refresh or as suggestive of morning. **3.** moisture in small drops on a surface, as tears, perspiration, etc. —*v.t.* **4.** to wet with or as with dew. [ME; OE *dēaw*, c. G *Tau*] —**dew′less,** *adj.*

Dew (dyo͞o), *n.* **Bay of,** a dark plain, *Sinus Roris*, in the second quadrant of the face of the moon.

dewan (dĭ wän′), *n.* (in India) any of certain officials, as a finance minister or a state prime minister. Also, **diwan.** [t. Hind; minister (of state), t. Pers.: m. *dēvan* register. See DIVAN]

Dewar (dyo͞o′ə), *n.* **Sir James,** 1842–1923, Scottish chemist and physicist.

Dewar flask, *Physics, Trademark.* a double-walled silvered-glass flask in which the space between the walls is evacuated. Used for storing liquids at a low temperature, esp. liquid air. [named after Sir James DEWAR, its inventor]

dewberry (dyo͞o′bə rĭ, -brĭ), *n.*, *pl.* **-ries. 1.** the fruit of *Rubus caesius.* **2.** (in North America) the fruit of several species of running, trailing blackberries, principally *Rubus flagellaris.* **3.** a plant bearing either fruit.

dewclaw (dyo͞o′klô′), *n.* **1.** a functionless inner claw or digit in the foot of some dogs, not reaching the ground in walking. **2.** an analogous false hoof of deer, pigs, etc.

D, Dewclaw on the foot of a terrier

dewdrop (dyo͞o′drŏp′), *n.* **1.** a drop of dew. **2.** *Colloq.* a drop at the end of a person's nose.

De Wet (*Afrik.* də vĕt′), **Christian Rudolph** (*Afrik.* krĭs′tē ȧn rʏ′dŏlf), 1854–1922, Boer general and politician.

Dewey (dyo͞o′ĭ), *n.* **1. George,** 1837–1917, U.S. admiral: defeated Spanish fleet in Manila Bay in the Spanish-American War. **2. John,** 1859–1952, U.S. philosopher. **3. Thomas E(dmund),** born 1902, U.S. lawyer and politician.

Dewey decimal classification. See **decimal classification.** [named after Melvil *Dewey*, 1851–1931, U.S. librarian]

De Witt (*Du.* də vĭt′), **Jan** (*Du.* yŏn), 1625–72, Dutch statesman.

dewlap (dyo͞o′lăp′), *n.* **1.** a pendulous fold of skin under the throat of cattle. **2.** any similar part, as the loose skin under the throat of some dogs, the wattle of fowls, etc. **3.** any loose skin on the human throat. [f. *dew*, of uncert. meaning + *lap*, OE *læppa* pendulous piece. Cf. Dan. *doglæp*] —**dew′lapped′,** *adj.*

DEW line (dyo͞o), a 3000-mile-long network of radar stations north of the Arctic Circle that provides the U.S. government and its allies with advance warning of the approach of hostile aircraft, missiles, etc. [*d(istant) e(arly) w(arning)*]

dewpoint (dyo͞o′point′), *n.* the temperature of the air at which dew begins to be deposited; the temperature at which a given sample of air will have a relative humidity of 100 per cent.

dewpond (dyo͞o′pŏnd′), *n.* a shallow pond containing rainwater, found on higher chalk downs esp. in S England.

Dewsbury (dyo͞oz′bə rĭ, -brĭ), *n.* a county borough in England in the W Riding of Yorkshire. 52,963 (1961).

dewy (dyo͞o′ĭ), *adj.*, **dewier, dewiest. 1.** moist with or as with dew. **2.** having the quality of dew: *dewy tears.* **3.** *Poetic.* falling gently, or refreshing like dew: *dewy sleep.* **4.** of dew. —**dew′ily,** *adv.* —**dew′iness,** *n.*

dewy-eyed (dyo͞o′ĭ īd′), *adj.* credulous; naive; trusting.

Dexadrine (dĕks′ə drēn′), *n.* *Trademark.* Dexamphetamine.

Dexamphetamine (dĕks′ăm fĕt′ə mēn′), *n.* *Trademark.* dextroamphetamine. Also, **Dexadrine.**

dexter (dĕks′tə), *adj.* **1.** on the right side; right. **2.** *Her.* situated to the right of the bearer and hence to the left of the spectator (opposed to *sinister*). **3.** *Obs.* favourable. [t. L: right, favourable]

dexterity (dĕks tĕ′rĭ tĭ), *n.* **1.** adroitness or skill in using the hands or body. **2.** mental adroitness or skill; cleverness. **3.** right-handedness. [f. DEXTER + -(I)TY[2]]

dexterous (dĕks′trəs), *adj.* **1.** skilful or adroit in the use of the hands or body. **2.** having mental adroitness or skill;

clever. **3.** done with dexterity. **4.** right-handed. Also, **dextrous.** —**dex′terously,** *adv.* —**dex′terousness,** *n.* —**Syn. 1.** adroit, deft, nimble, skilful. —**Ant. 1.** clumsy. **2.** inept. **3.** awkward.

dextral (dĕks′trəl), *adj.* **1.** of, pertaining to, or on the right-hand side; right (opposed to *sinistral*). **2.** right-handed. **3.** *Zool.* (of certain shells) coiling from left to right. —**dex′trally,** *adv.* —**dextral′ity,** *n.*

dextran (dĕks′trən), *n. Chem.* a white gummy material, produced from milk, molasses, etc., by bacterial action. [f. DEXTR(O)- + -AN(E)]

dextrin (dĕks′trĭn), *n. Chem.* a soluble gummy substance formed from starch by the action of heat, acids, or ferments, occurring in various forms and having dextrorotatory properties, used chiefly as a thickening agent in printing inks and food, substitute for gum arabic and as a mucilage; starch-gum. Also, **dextrine** (dĕks′trĭn, -trēn). [t. F: m. *dextrine*, der. L *dexter* right]

dextro (dĕks′trō), *adj. Chem.* turning clockwise.

dextro-, a word element meaning: **1.** right. **2.** *Chem.* turning clockwise. Also, **dextr-.** [t. L, comb. form of *dexter* right]

dextroamphetamine (dĕks′trō ăm fĕt′ə mēn′), *n. Chem.* a white, crystalline, water-soluble solid, $C_6H_5CH_2CH(NH_2)CH_3$, used in the treatment of obesity.

dextroglucose (dĕks′trō gloo͞′kōs), *n. Chem.* d-glucose. See **glucose.**

dextrogyrate (dĕks′trō jī′ə rĭt, -rāt′), *adj. Optics, Crystall., etc.* causing to turn towards the right hand: *a dextrogyrate crystal.*

dextrorotation (dĕks′trō rō tā′shən), *n. Optics, Chem., etc.* a turning of the plane of polarization of light to the right.

dextrorotatory (dĕks′trō rō′tə tə rĭ), *adj. Optics, Chem., etc.* turning the plane of polarization of light to the right, as certain crystals and compounds. Also, **dextrorotary** (dĕks′-trō rō′tə rĭ).

dextrorse (dĕks′trôs, dĕks trôs′), *adj. Bot.* rising spirally from left to right (from a point of view at the centre of the spiral), as a stem (opposed to *sinistrorse*). Also, **dextror′sal.** [t. L: m. s. *dextrorsum* towards the right] —**dex′trorsely,** *adv.*

Dextrorse stem

dextrose (dĕks′trōs), *n. Chem.* dextroglucose, commercially obtainable from starch by acid hydrolysis. See **glucose.** [f. DEXTR(O)- + (GLUC)OSE]

dextrous (dĕks′trəs), *adj.* dexterous. —**dex′trously,** *adv.* —**dex′trousness,** *n.*

dey (dā), *n.* **1.** the title of the governor of Algiers before the French conquest in 1830. **2.** a title sometimes borne by the former rulers of Tunis and Tripoli. [t. F, t. Turk.: m. *dāī*, orig., maternal uncle]

Dezful (dĕz foo͞l′), *n.* Dizful.

Dezhnev (*Russ.* dĭzh nyôf′), *n.* **Cape,** a cape in the NE Soviet Union in Asia, on the Bering Strait: the north-easternmost point of Asia. Also, **East Cape.**

dezincification (dē zĭng′kĭ fĭ kā′shən), *n. Metall.* a process of corrosion in which the zinc of copper-zinc alloys becomes absorbed by the environment.

D/F, direction finding.

D.F., (L *Defensor Fidei*) Defender of the Faith.

D.F.C., Distinguished Flying Cross.

D.F.M., Distinguished Flying Medal.

dg., decigramme; decigrammes.

d-glucose (dē′gloo͞′kōs), *n. Chem.* dextroglucose. See **glucose.**

Dhahran (dä rän′), *n.* a town in E Saudi Arabia; oil centre. 75,000 (est. 1952).

dharma (dä′mə), *n.* (in Hinduism and Buddhism) **1.** essential quality or character. **2.** law, esp. religious law. **3.** conformity to law; propriety. **4.** virtue. **5.** religion. **6.** the doctrine or teaching of the Buddha. [Skt: decree, custom]

Dhaulagiri (dou′lə gĭə′rĭ), *n.* a peak of the Himalayas, in W central Nepal. 26,826 ft.

dhobi (dō′bĭ), *n.* an Indian washerman or laundry-boy. [t. Hind.]

dhole (dōl), *n.* an Indian wild dog, a fierce, red-coated species, *Cuon rutilus*, hunting in packs, and capable of running down large game. [orig. unknown]

dhoti (dō′tĭ), *n., pl.* **-tis.** a nether garment worn by male Hindus. Also, **dhooti** (doo͞′tĭ). [t. Hind.]

dhow (dou), *n.* an Arab coasting vessel, usually lateen-rigged.

Di, *Chem.* didymium.

di-¹, a prefix of Greek origin, meaning 'twice', 'doubly', 'two', freely used (like *bi-*) as an English formative, as in *dicotyledon*, *dipolar*, and in many chemical terms, as *diatomic*, *disulphide*. Also, **dis-².** Cf. **mono-.** [t. Gk, repr. *dis* twice, doubly; akin to Gk *dýo* two. See BI-]

di-², var. of **dis-¹,** before *b, d, l, m, n, r, s,* and *v*, and sometimes *g* and *j*, as in *divide*.

di-³, var. of **dia-,** before vowels, as in *diocese, diorama.*

dia-, a prefix of learned words meaning: **1.** passing through, as in *diathermy*. **2.** thoroughly; completely, as in *diagnosis*. **3.** going apart, as in *dialysis*. **4.** opposed in moment, as in *diamagnetism*. Also, **di-³.** [t. Gk, repr. *diá*, prep., through, between, across, by, of; akin to *dýo* two, and *di-* DI-¹]

diabase (dī′ə bās′), *n.* **1.** a dark igneous rock consisting essentially of augite and felspar, an altered dolerite. **2.** *U.S.* a dark igneous rock occurring as minor intrusives composed essentially of labradorite and pyroxene. **3.** *Obs.* diorite. [t. F, f. *dia-* (erron. for *di-* two) + *base* BASE¹] —**di′aba′sic,** *adj.*

diabetes (dī′ə bē′tĭs, -tēz), *n. Pathol.* **1.** a disease in which the ability of the body to use sugar is impaired and sugar appears abnormally in the urine (**diabetes mellitus**). **2.** a disease in which there is a persistent abnormal amount of urine (**diabetes insipidus**). [t. NL, t. Gk: lit., a passer through]

diabetic (dī′ə bĕt′ĭk), *adj.* **1.** of or pertaining to diabetes. **2.** having diabetes. —*n.* **3.** a person who has diabetes.

diablerie (dĭ ä′blə rĭ; *Fr.* dyȧ blə rē′), *n.* **1.** diabolic magic or art; sorcery. **2.** the domain or realm of devils. **3.** the lore of devils; demonology. **4.** reckless mischief; devilry. Also, **dia′blery.** [t. F, der. *diable* DEVIL]

diabolic (dī′ə bŏl′ĭk), *adj.* **1.** having the qualities of a devil; fiendish; outrageously wicked: *a diabolic plot.* **2.** pertaining to or actuated by the devil or a devil. **3.** *Colloq.* difficult; unpleasant; very bad. Also, **di′abol′ical** (esp. for def. 3). [t. LL: s. *diabolicus*, t. Gk: m. *diabolikós*] —**di′abol′ically,** *adv.* —**di′abol′icalness,** *n.*

diabolism (dī ăb′ə lĭz′əm), *n.* **1.** *Theol.* **a.** action aided or caused by the devil; sorcery; witchcraft. **b.** the character or condition of a devil. **c.** doctrine concerning devils; belief in or worship of devils. **2.** action befitting the devil; devilry. —**diab′olist,** *n.*

diabolize (dī ăb′ə līz′), *v.t.,* **-lized, -lizing. 1.** to make diabolical or devilish. **2.** to represent as diabolical. **3.** to subject to diabolical influences. Also, **diabolise.**

diabolo (dĭ ăb′ə lō′), *n.* **1.** a game in which a top is spun, thrown and caught by or balanced on and whirled along a string attached to two sticks, held one in each hand. **2.** the top itself.

diacaustic (dī′ə kôs′tĭk, -kŏs′-), *Maths., Optics.* —*adj.* **1.** denoting a caustic surface or curve formed by refraction of light. See **catacaustic.** —*n.* **2.** a diacaustic surface or curve.

diachylon (dī ăk′ĭ lŏn′), *n.* an adhesive plaster consisting essentially of lead oxide and oil. Also, **diachylum** (dī ăk′ĭ ləm). [t. L, t. Gk: m. *dià chȳlôn* (something) made of juices; also Latinized as *diachȳlum*, whence E sp. with *-um*; r. ME *diaculon*, t. ML, and ME *diaquilon*, t. F, both g. L *diachȳlōn*]

diacid (dī ăs′ĭd), *adj. Chem.* **1.** capable of combining with two molecules of a monobasic acid. **2.** (of an acid or a salt) having two replaceable hydrogen atoms.

diaconal (dī ăk′ə nəl), *adj.* pertaining to a deacon. [t. LL: s. *diāconālis*, der. *diāconus* DEACON]

diaconate (dī ăk′ə nĭt, -nāt′), *n.* **1.** the office or dignity of a deacon. **2.** a body of deacons. **3.** the period during which a deacon holds office.

diaconicon (dī′ə kŏn′ĭ kən), *n., pl.* **-ca** (-kə). a sacristy in an Eastern or Early Christian church. [t. MGk: m. *diākonikón*, neut. of *diākonikós*, adj., of a DEACON]

diacritic (dī′ə krĭt′ĭk), *n.* **1.** a diacritical mark, point, or sign. —*adj.* **2.** diacritical. **3.** *Med.* diagnostic. [t. Gk: m. s. *diakritikós* that separates or distinguishes]

diacritical (dī′ə krĭt′ĭ kl), *adj.* **1.** serving to distinguish; distinctive. **2.** capable of distinguishing. **3.** denoting a mark, point, or sign added or attached to a letter or character to distinguish it from another of similar form, to give it a particular phonetic value, to indicate stress, etc. —**di′acrit′ically,** *adv.*

diactinic (dī′ăk tĭn′ĭk), *adj. Photog., etc.* capable of transmitting the actinic rays of light. —**diac′tinism,** *n.*

diadelphous (dī′ə dĕl′fəs), *adj. Bot.* **1.** (of stamens) united into two sets by their filaments. **2.** (of plants) having the stamens so united. [f. DI-¹ + s. Gk *adelphós* brother + -OUS]

diadem (dī′ə dĕm′), *n.* **1.** a crown. **2.** a cloth headband, sometimes adorned with jewels, formerly worn by oriental kings. **3.** royal dignity or authority. —*v.t.* **4.** to adorn with, or as if with, a diadem; crown. [t. L: m. *diadēma*, t. Gk: fillet, band; r. ME *dyademe*, t. OF]

diadem spider, the common garden spider, *Araneus diademata*, of Europe and N Asia.

Diadochi (dī ăd′ə kī′), *n. pl.* the Macedonian generals of Alexander the Great who, after his death, divided up his empire among themselves. [t. NL, t. Gk: m. *diádochoi*, pl. of *diádochos* successor (n. use of adj.)]

diaeresis (dī ĭə′rĭ sĭs), *n.*, *pl.* **-ses** (-sēz′). dieresis.

diag., diagram.

diageotropic (dī′ə jīə trŏp′ĭk), *adj. Bot.* growing at right angles to the direction of gravity. —**di′ageotrop′ically,** *adv.* —**diageotropism** (dī′ə jĭ ŏt′rə pĭz′əm), *n.*

Diaghilev (dĭ ăg′ĭ lĕf′), *n.* **Sergei Pavlovich** (sĕə gā′ păv′lə vĭch), 1872–1929, Russian ballet producer and art critic.

diagnose (dī′əg nōz), *v.t., v.i.,* **-nosed, -nosing.** to make a diagnosis of (a case, disease, etc.).

diagnosis (dī′əg nō′sĭs), *n.*, *pl.* **-ses** (-sēz). **1.** *Med.* **a.** the process of determining by examination the nature and circumstances of a diseased condition. **b.** the decision reached from such an examination. **2.** *Biol.* scientific determination; a description which classifies precisely. **3.** any analogous examination or analysis. [t. NL, t. Gk: a distinguishing]

diagnostic (dī′əg nŏs′tĭk), *adj.* **1.** pertaining to a diagnosis. **2.** having value in diagnosis. —*n.* **3.** diagnosis (def. 1 a, b). **4.** a symptom or characteristic of value in diagnosis. [t. Gk: m. s. *diagnōstikós*] —**di′agnos′tically,** *adv.*

diagnostician (dī′əg nŏs tĭsh′ən), *n.* an expert or specialist in making diagnoses.

diagnostics (dī′əg nŏs′tĭks), *n.* the art or science of diagnosis. [pl. of DIAGNOSTIC]

diagonal (dī ăg′ə nəl), *adj.* **1.** *Maths.* **a.** connecting, as a straight line, two non-adjacent angles or vertices of a quadrilateral, polygon, or polyhedron. **b.** extending, as a plane, from one edge of a solid figure to an opposite edge. **2.** having an oblique direction. **3.** having oblique lines, ridges, etc. —*n.* **4.** a diagonal line or plane. **5.** a diagonal row, plank, part, etc. **6.** diagonal cloth. [t. L: s. *diagōnālis*, der. Gk *diagṓnios* from angle to angle] —**diag′onally,** *adv.*

diagonal cloth, a twilled fabric with a diagonal weave.

diagram (dī′ə grăm′), *n., v.,* **-grammed, -gramming** or (*esp. U.S.*) **-gramed, -graming.** —*n.* **1.** a figure, or set of lines, marks, etc., to accompany a geometrical demonstration, give the outlines or general features of an object, show the course or results of a process, etc. **2.** a drawing or plan that outlines and explains, the parts, operation, etc., of something. **3.** a chart, plan, or scheme. —*v.t.* **4.** to represent by a diagram; make a diagram of. [t. L: m. *diagramma*, t. Gk: that which is marked out by lines]

diagrammatic (dī′ə grə măt′ĭk), *adj.* **1.** in the form of a diagram. **2.** pertaining to diagrams. Also, **di′agrammat′ical.** —**di′agrammat′ically,** *adv.*

diagrammatize (dī′ə grăm′ə tīz′), *v.t.,* **-tized, tizing.** to diagram (def. 4). Also, **diagrammatise.**

diagraph (dī′ə grăf′, -gräf′), *n.* **1.** a device for drawing, used in reproducing outlines, plans, etc., mechanically on any desired scale. **2.** a combined protractor and scale. [t. F: m. *diagraphe*, t. Gk: m. *digraphḗ* marking out by lines. See DIAGRAM]

diakinesis (dī′ə kĭ nē′sĭs, -kī-), *n. Biol.* the prophase of the first meiotic division of a spermatocyte or ovocyte. [NL, f. *dia-* DIA- + Gk *kī́nēsis* movement]

dial (dī′əl, dīl), *n., v.,* **dialled, dialling** or (*esp. U.S.*) **dialed, dialing.** —*n.* **1.** a face upon which time is indicated by hands, pointers, or shadows. **2.** a plate or disc with graduations or figures, as for the indication of pressure, number of revolutions, etc., as by the movements of a pointer. **3.** a rotatable plate or disc used for tuning a radio station in or out. **4.** a plate or disc with letters and numbers, used in making telephone connections. **5.** *Mining.* a compass used for underground surveying. **6.** *Slang.* the human face. —*v.t.* **7.** to measure with or as with a dial. **8.** to regulate, select, or tune in by means of a dial, as on a radio. **9.** to indicate on a telephone dial. **10.** to call by means of a telephone dial. **11.** *Mining.* to survey with the aid of a dial (def. 5) or compass. —*v.i.* **12.** to use a telephone dial. [ME, t. ML: s. *diālis* daily, der. L *dies* day]

dial., **1.** dialect. **2.** dialectal.

dialect (dī′ə lĕkt′), *n.* **1.** the language of a particular district or class, esp. as distinguished from the standard language, as a provincial or rural substandard form of a language. **2.** a special variety or branch of a language, as Afrikaans if considered as a branch of Dutch. **3.** a language considered as one of a number of related languages: *the Roman dialects.* [t. L: s. *dialectus*, t. Gk: m. *diálektos* discourse, language, dialect] —**Syn. 3.** See **language.**

dialectal (dī′ə lĕk′tl), *adj.* **1.** of a dialect. **2.** characteristic of a dialect. —**di′alec′tally,** *adv.*

dialectic (dī′ə lĕk′tĭk), *adj.* **1.** of, pertaining to, or of the nature of logical argumentation. **2.** dialectal. —*n.* **3.** the art or practice of logical discussion as employed in investigating the truth of a theory or opinion. **4.** logical argumentation. **5.** (*often pl.*) **a.** logic or a branch of logic. **b.** any formal system of reasoning or thought. **6.** See **Hegelian dialectic. 7.** dialectical materialism. **8.** (in Kantian philosophy) the use of the principles of understanding in an attempt to determine objects beyond the limits of experience. [t. L: s. *dialectica*, t. Gk m. *dialektikḗ* (*technḗ*) argumentative (art); r. ME *dialetike*, t. OF]

dialectical (dī′ə lĕk′tĭ kl), *adj.* **1.** of or pertaining to the Hegelian dialectic. **2.** dialectal.

dialectical materialism, a theory of reality developed chiefly by Karl Marx, combining elements of traditional materialist philosophy and the method of Hegelian dialectic. —**dialectical materialist.**

dialectician (dī′ə lĕk tĭsh′ən), *n.* **1.** one skilled in dialectic; a logician. **2.** one who studies dialects.

dialecticism (dī′ə lĕk′tĭ sĭz′əm), *n.* **1.** dialectal speech or influence. **2.** a dialectal word or expression.

dialectics (dī′ə lĕk′tĭks), *n.* dialectic (def. 5).

dialectology (dī′ə lĕk tŏl′ə jĭ), *n.* the study of dialects.

dial gauge, *Eng.* an instrument in which small displacements of a plunger are indicated on a dial.

dialling (dī′ə lĭng, dī′lĭng), *n.* **1.** the art of constructing sundials. **2.** the measurement of time by means of dials. **3.** surveying by means of a dial. Also, *U.S.*, **dialing.**

dialling code, *Teleph.* a sequence of numbers or letters preceding the subscriber's number, indicating the area or exchange.

dialling tone, (in a dial telephone) a sound which indicates that the line is ready for dialling. Also, *U.S.*, **dial tone.**

dialogism (dī ăl′ə jĭz′əm), *n.* the discussion of a subject in an imaginary dialogue. [t. Gk: s. *dialogismós* consideration]

dialogist (dī ăl′ə jĭst), *n.* **1.** a speaker in a dialogue. **2.** a writer of dialogue. —**dialogistic** (dī′ə lō jĭs′tĭk), *adj.*

dialogize (dī ăl′ə jīz′), *v.i.,* **-gized, -gizing.** *Now Chiefly U.S.* to carry on a dialogue. Also, **dialogise, dialoguize** (dī ăl′ə gīz′), **dialoguise.** [t. Gk: m. s. *dialogízesthai* converse]

dialogue (dī′ə lŏg′), *n., v.,* **-logued, -loguing.** —*n.* **1.** conversation between two or more persons. **2.** the conversation between characters in a novel, drama, etc. **3.** an exchange of ideas or opinions on a particular issue. **4.** a literary work in the form of a conversation. —*v.i.* **5.** to carry on a dialogue; converse. —*v.t.* **6.** to put into the form of a dialogue. Also, *U.S.*, **dialog.** [t. F, t. L: m. s. *dialogus*, t. Gk: m. *diálogos*; r. ME *dialoge*, t. OF] —**di′alogu′er,** *n.*

dialyse (dī′ə līz′), *v.t.,* **-lysed, -lysing** or (*esp. U.S.*) **-lyzed, -lyzing.** *Phys. Chem.* to subject to dialysis; separate or procure by dialysis. —**di′alys′er,** *n.*

dialysis (dī ăl′ĭ sĭs), *n.*, *pl.* **-ses** (-sēz′). *Phys. Chem.* the separation of crystalloids from colloids in a solution by diffusion through a membrane. [t. Gk: separation, dissolution]

diam., diameter.

diamagnetic (dī′ə măg nĕt′ĭk), *adj.* denoting or pertaining to a class of substances, as bismuth and copper, whose permeability is less than that of a vacuum. In a magnetic field their induced magnetism is in a direction opposite to that of iron (opposed to *paramagnetic* and *ferromagnetic*). —**di′amagnet′ically,** *adv.* —**diamagnetism** (dī′ə măg′nĭ tĭz′əm), *n.*

diamanté (dī′ə măn′tĭ, dĭə-), *n.* **1.** a fabric made to sparkle by covering with glittering particles. —*adj.* **2.** (of a fabric) sparkling. [F, orig. adj.]

diamantiferous (dī′ə măn tĭf′ə rəs), *adj.* containing diamonds. Also, **diamondiferous.** [see DIAMOND, -FEROUS]

Diamantina (dĭə′măn tē′nə), *n.* a river of Australia flowing SW through Queensland joining with the Georgina to form the Warburton river. ab. 560 mi.

diameter (dī ăm′ĭ tə), *n.* **1.** *Geom.* **a.** a straight line passing through the centre of a circle or sphere and terminated at each end by the circumference or surface. **b.** a straight line passing from side to side of any figure or body, through its centre. **2.** the length of such a line; thickness. [ME *diametre*, t. OF, t. L: m. s. *diametros*, t. Gk: diagonal, diameter]

diametral (dī ăm′ĭ trəl), *adj.* **1.** of a diameter. **2.** forming a diameter. —**diam′etrally,** *adv.*

diametrical (dī′ə mĕt′rĭ kl), *adj.* **1.** pertaining to a diameter; along a diameter. **2.** direct; complete; absolute: *diametrical opposites.* Also, **di′amet′ric.** —**di′amet′rically,** *adv.*

diamine (dī′ə mēn′, -mĭn, dī′ə mēn′), *n. Chem.* a compound containing two NH_2 radicals.

diamond (dī′ə mənd), *n.* **1.** a pure or nearly pure form of carbon, crystallized in the isometric system, of extreme hardness and, when used as a precious stone, of great brilliancy. **2.** a piece of this stone. **3.** a tool provided with an uncut diamond, used for cutting glass. **4.** *Geom.* an equilateral quadrilateral, esp. as placed with its diagonals vertical and horizontal; a lozenge or rhombus. **5.** *Cards.* **a.** a red lozenge-shaped figure on a playing card. **b.** a card of the suit bearing such figures. **c.** (*pl.*) the suit. **6.** *U.S.* a baseball field or the space enclosed within the baselines. **7.** a 4½-point type of a size between gem and pearl. **8. diamond cut diamond,** an encounter between two persons equally matched in skill or ruthlessness. —*adj.* **9.** made of or with a diamond or diamonds. **10.** indicating the 75th, or sometimes the 60th, event of a series, as a wedding anniversary. **11.** shaped like a diamond (def. 4). —*v.t.* **12.** to adorn with or as with diamonds. [ME *diamant*, t. OF, t. LL: s. *diamas*, alter. of L *adamas* adamant, diamond. See ADAMANT]

diamondback (dī′ə mənd băk′), *n.* a common venomous rattlesnake, *Crotalus adamantus*, of the southern U.S. Also, **diamondback rattlesnake.**

diamondback moth, a moth, *Plutella maculipennis*, the male of which has diamond-shaped yellow spots on the wing; the larvae breed on leaves of *Cruciferae* and are therefore a major pest.

diamond beetle, one of the weevil genus, *Entimus*, of Brazil, noted for its bright iridescent coloration.

diamond drill, a drill having a hollow, cylindrical bit set with diamonds, used for obtaining cores of rock samples for geological or mineralogical examination.

diamond dust, pulverized diamonds, used as an abrasive.

diamond point, **1.** a tool tipped with diamond, used in engraving. **2.** (*pl.*) the set of points where two lines of rails intersect obliquely without communicating.

diamond saw, a circular saw, with carbonadoes set in its perimeter, used for cutting stone.

diamorphine (dī′ə mô′fēn), *n.* *Pharm.* heroin.

Diana (dī ăn′ə), *n.* **1.** an ancient Italian deity, goddess of the moon and of hunting, and protectress of women, identified by the Romans with the Greek Artemis. **2.** the moon personified as a goddess.

diandrous (dī ăn′drəs), *adj.* *Bot.* **1.** (of a flower) having two stamens. **2.** (of a plant) having flowers with two stamens. [t. NL: m. *diandrus*. See DI-[1], ADAMANT]

dianoetic (dī′ə nō ĕt′ĭk), *adj.* pertaining to thought or reasoning, esp. discursive reasoning. [t. Gk: s. *dianoētikós* pertaining to thinking]

dianthus (dī ăn′thəs), *n.* any plant of the caryophyllaceous genus *Dianthus*, as the carnation or the sweet william. [NL, f. Gk: *Di(ós)* of Zeus + m. *ánthos* flower]

diapason (dī′ə pā′zən, -sən), *n.* *Music.* **1.** a melody or strain. **2.** the compass of a voice or instrument. **3.** a fixed standard of pitch. **4.** either of two principal timbres or stops of a pipe organ: **a.** the **open diapason,** giving full, majestic tones. **b.** the **stopped diapason,** giving powerful flutelike tones. **5.** any of several other organ stops. **6.** a tuning fork. [t. L, t. Gk, short for *dià pasôn chordôn symphōnía* concord through all notes (of the scale)] —**diapasonic** (dī′ə pā zŏn′ĭk, -sŏn′-), *adj.*

diapause (dī′ə pôz′), *n.* *Zool.* **1.** a period of quiescence during the development of insects, etc. **2.** a sexually quiescent period in an adult insect.

diaper (dī′ə pə), *n.* **1.** *U.S.* a baby's napkin. **2.** a linen or cotton fabric with a woven pattern of small constantly repeated figures, as diamonds. **3.** such a pattern (originally used in medieval weaving of silk and gold), used as a decoration for walls, etc. —*v.t.* **4.** to ornament with a diaper-like pattern. [ME *diapre*, t. OF, var. of *diaspre*, ult. t. MGk: m. *diaspros* pure white]

diaphaneity (dī′ə fə nē′ĭ tĭ), *n.* transparency.

diaphanous (dī ăf′ə nəs), *adj.* transparent; translucent. [t. ML: m. *diaphanus*, t. Gk: m. *diaphanḗs*] —**diaph′anously,** *adv.* —**diaph′anousness,** *n.*

diaphoresis (dī′ə fə rē′sĭs), *n.* *Med.* perspiration, esp. when artificially produced. [t. LL, t. Gk: a sweat]

diaphoretic (dī′ə fə rĕt′ĭk), *Med.* —*adj.* **1.** producing perspiration. —*n.* **2.** a diaphoretic medicine.

diaphragm (dī′ə frăm′), *n.* **1.** *Anat.* **a.** a muscular, membranous or ligamentous wall separating two cavities or limiting a cavity. **b.** the partition separating the thoracic cavity from the abdominal cavity in mammals. **2.** *Phys. Chem., etc.* **a.** a porous plate separating two liquids, as in a galvanic cell. **b.** a semi-permeable membrane or the like. **3.** a vibrating membrane or disc, as in a telephone or microphone. **4.** pessary (def. 3). **5.** *Optics.* a ring, or a plate pierced with a circular hole so arranged as to fall in the axis of the instrument, used in optical instruments to control the amount of light entering the instrument, as in a camera or a telescope. **6.** *Civ. Eng.* a plate for strengthening metal-framed constructions. [t. LL: m. *diaphragma*, t. Gk: midriff, barrier]

diaphragmatic (dī′ə frăg măt′ĭk), *adj.* **1.** of the diaphragm. **2.** like a diaphragm. —**di′aphragmat′ically,** *adv.*

diaphysis (dī ăf′ĭ sĭs), *n.*, *pl.* **-ses** (-sēz′). *Anat.* the shaft of a long bone. [NL, t. Gk: a growing through] —**diaphysial** (dī′ə fĭz′ĭ əl), *adj.*

diapophysis (dī′ə pŏf′ĭ sĭs), *n.*, *pl.* **-ses** (-sēz′). *Anat.*, *Zool.* the transverse process proper of a vertebra. [NL. See DI-[3], APOPHYSIS] —**diapophysial** (dī′ăp ə fĭz′ĭ əl), *adj.*

Diarbekr (*Turk.* dē yär′bĕk ĭr), *n.* Diyarbekir.

diarchy (dī′ä′kĭ), *n.*, *pl.* **-chies.** government or a government in which power is vested in two rulers or authorities. Also, **dyarchy.** [f. DI-[1] + m. s. Gk *archía* rule] —**di′ar′-chal, di′ar′chic,** *adj.*

diarist (dī′ə rĭst), *n.* one who keeps a diary.

diarrhoea (dī′ə rĭə′), *n.* *Pathol.* an intestinal disorder characterized by morbid frequency and fluidity of faecal evacuations. Also, **di′arrhea′.** [t. LL, t. Gk: m. *diárrhoia* a flowing through] —**di′arrhoeal′, di′arrhoe′ic,** *adj.*

diarthrosis (dī′ä thrō′sĭs), *n.*, *pl.* **-ses** (-sēz). *Anat.* a type of articulation which permits movement in any direction, the opposing bones being held in opposition. [NL, t. Gk: division by joints. See DIA-, ARTHROSIS] —**diarthrodial** (dī′ä thrō′dĭ əl), *adj.*

diary (dī′ə rĭ), *n.*, *pl.* **-ries.** **1.** a daily record, esp. of the writer's own experiences or observations. **2.** a book for keeping such a record, or for noting appointments and engagements. [t. L: m. s. *diārium* daily allowance, journal]

Dias (dē′əs; *Port.* dē′əsh), *n.* **Bartholomeu** (*Port.* bȧr-tȯ lȯ mė′ōō), *c.* 1450–1500, Portuguese navigator and discoverer of the Cape of Good Hope. Also, **Diaz.**

Diaspora (dī ăs′pə rə), *n.* **1.** the whole body of Jews living scattered among the Gentiles after the Babylonian captivity. **2.** (among the early Jewish Christians) the body of Jewish Christians outside Palestine. **3.** the dispersion of the Jews. [t. Gk: a scattering]

diaspore (dī′ə spô′), *n.* a mineral, aluminium hydroxide, $HAlO_2$, occurring in crystals, or more usually in lamellar or scaly masses.

diastase (dī′ə stās′), *n.* *Biochem.* an enzyme (amylase) present in germinated barley, potatoes, etc., which converts starch into dextrin and maltose. [t. F, t. Gk: m. *diástasis* separation]

diastatic (dī′ə stăt′ĭk), *adj.* *Biochem.* **1.** pertaining to diastase; having the properties of diastase: *diastatic action.* **2.** *Med.*, *Physiol.* of or pertaining to diastasis. Also, **diastasic** (dī′ə stā′sĭk). [t. Gk: m. s. *diastatikós* separating]

diaster (dī ăs′tə), *n.* *Biol.* a stage in mitosis at which the chromosomes, after their division and separation, are grouped near the poles of the spindle. [f. DI-[1] + -ASTER[2]] —**dias′tral,** *adj.*

diastole (dī ăs′tə lĭ), *n.* **1.** *Physiol.*, *etc.* the normal rhythmical dilatation of the heart, esp. that of the ventricles. **2.** *Pros.* the lengthening of a syllable regularly short, esp. before a pause or at the ictus. [t. LL, t. Gk: a putting asunder, dilatation, lengthening] —**diastolic** (dī′ə stŏl′ĭk), *adj.* pertaining to or produced by diastole.

diastrophism (dī ăs′trə fĭz′əm), *n.* *Geol.* **1.** the action of the forces which cause the earth's crust to be deformed, producing continents, mountains, changes of level, etc. **2.** any such deformation. [f. s. Gk *diastrophe* distortion + -ISM] —**diastrophic** (dī′ə strŏf′ĭk), *adj.*

diatessaron (dī′ə tĕs′ə rŏn′), *n.* **1.** *Bible.* a harmony of the four Gospels, arranged to form a single narrative. **2.** *Gk and Medieval Music.* the interval of a fourth. [t. L, t. Gk: the interval of a fourth (lit., made of four, or up to four)]

diathermancy (dī′ə thû′mən sĭ), *n.* *Physics.* the property of transmitting radiant heat; quality of being diathermanous. [t. F: m. *diathermansie*, f. *dia-* DIA- + m. s. Gk *thérmansis* heating]

diathermanous (dī′ə thû′mə nəs), *adj.* *Physics.* permeable to radiant heat.

diathermic (dī′ə thû′mĭk), *adj.* **1.** *Med.* pertaining to diathermy. **2.** *Physics.* diathermanous. [t. F: m. *diathermique*, f. *dia-* DIA- + s. Gk *thérmē* heat + *-ique* -IC]

diathermy (dī′ə thû′mĭ), *n.* *Med.* the production of heat in body tissues by high currents for therapeutic purposes. Also, **diathermia** (dī′ə thû′mĭ ə).

diathesis (dī ăth′ĭ sĭs), *n.*, *pl.* **-eses** (-ĭ sēz′). *Pathol.* a constitutional predisposition or tendency, as to a particular disease or affection. [NL, t. Gk arrangement, disposition] —**diathetic** (dī′ə thĕt′ĭk), *adj.*

diatom (dī′ə təm, -tŏm′), *n.* any of numerous microscopic, unicellular, marine or freshwater algae having siliceous cell walls. [t. NL: m. *Diatoma*, a genus of diatoms, der. LGk *diátomos,* verbal adj. of Gk *diatémnein* cut through]

diatomaceous (dī′ə tə mā′shəs), *adj.* consisting of or containing diatoms or their fossil remains.

diatomaceous earth, a fine siliceous earth composed chiefly of cell walls of diatoms: used in filtration, as an abrasive, etc.; kieselguhr. Also, **diatomite** (dī ăt′ə mīt′).

diatomic (dī′ə tŏm′ĭk), *adj. Chem.* **1.** having two atoms in the molecule. **2.** containing two replaceable atoms or groups; bivalent.

diatonic (dī′ə tŏn′ĭk), *adj. Music.* involving only the tones, intervals, or harmonies of a major or minor scale without chromatic alteration. [t. LL: s. *diatonicus,* t. Gk: m. *diatonikós,* for *diátonos*] —**di′aton′ically,** *adv.*

diatribe (dī′ə trīb′), *n.* a bitter and violent denunciation, attack, or criticism. [t. L: m. s. *diatriba,* t. Gk: m. *diatribḗ* pastime, study, discourse]

diatropism (dī ăt′rə pĭz′əm), *n. Bot.* the tendency of some plant organs to take a transverse position to the line of action of an outside stimulus. —**diatropic** (dī′ə-trŏp′ĭk), *adj.*

Diaz (dē′əs; *Port.* dē′əsh), *n.* **Bartholomeu.** See **Dias.**

Díaz (*Sp.* dē′äth), *n.* **Porfirio** (*Sp.* pȯr fē′ryȯ), 1830–1915, president of Mexico 1877–80, 1884–1911.

Díaz de Bivar (*Sp.* dē′äth dė bē bär′), **Rodrigo** (*Sp.* (rȯ drē′gȯ). See **Cid, El.**

Díaz del Castillo (*Sp.* dē′äth dėl käs tē′lyȯ), **Bernal** *Sp.* bėr näl′), 1492–1581, Spanish soldier-historian of the conquest of Mexico.

diazine (dī′ə zēn′, dī ăz′ēn, -ĭn), *n. Chem.* any of a group of three isomeric hydrocarbons, $C_4H_4N_2$, containing a ring of four carbon and two nitrogen atoms. Also, **diazin** (dī′ə zĭn, dī ăz′ĭn).

diazo-, *Chem.* a combining form denoting a diazo compound. [f. DI-[1] + AZO-]

diazo compound (dī ăz′ō), a compound containing a group of two nitrogen atoms, N_2, united with one hydrocarbon radical or with one hydrocarbon radical and another atom or group of atoms.

diazole (dī′ə zōl′, dī ăz′ōl), *n. Chem.* any of a group of organic compounds containing three carbon and two nitrogen atoms arranged in a ring.

diazomethane (dī ăz′ō mē′thān), *n. Chem.* an odourless, yellow gas, CH_2N_2, which is poisonous, used as a methylating agent in organic syntheses.

diazonium salts, *Chem.* a group of salts formed by the combination of the diazonium radical (Ar.N ≡ N-, where Ar. is an aryl group) and an acid radical, important intermediates in the manufacture of dyes.

Díaz Ordaz (*Sp.* dē′äth ȯr′däth), **Gustavo** (*Sp.* gōōs tä′-bȯ), born 1911, Mexican politician: president since 1964.

diazotization (dī ăz′ə tĭ zā′shən), *n.* the preparation of a diazo compound, as by treating an amine with nitrous acid. Also, **diazotisation.**

diazotize (dī ăz′ə tīz′), *v.t.,* **-tized, -tizing.** *Chem.* to treat so as to convert into a diazonium salt. Also, **diazotise.**

dib[1] (dĭb), *v.i.,* **dibbed, dibbing.** to fish by letting the bait bob lightly on the water. [b. DIP and BOB[1]]

dib[2] (dĭb), *n.* jack[1] (def. 7).

dibasic (dī bā′sĭk), *adj. Chem.* **1.** containing two replaceable or ionizable hydrogen atoms, as *dibasic acid.* **2.** having two univalent, basic atoms, as *dibasic sodium phosphate,* Na_2HPO_4.

dibber (dĭb′ə), *n.* a dibble.

dibble (dĭb′l), *n., v.,* **-bled, -bling.** —*n.* **1.** an implement for making holes in the ground for planting seeds, bulbs, etc. —*v.t.* **2.** to make a hole in (the ground) with or as with a dibble. [? akin to DIB] —**dibb′ler,** *n.*

dibranchiate (dī brăng′kĭ ĭt, -kĭ āt′), *Zool.* —*adj.* **1.** belonging or pertaining to the *Dibranchiata,* a subclass or order of cephalopods with two gills, including the decapods and octopods. —*n.* **2.** a dibranchiate cephalopod. [t. NL: m. s. *Dibranchiāta,* pl. See DI-[1], BRANCHIATE]

dicarboxylic acid (dī kä′bŏk sĭl′ĭk), *Chem.* any of the organic compounds which have two carboxyl radicals, -COOH.

dicast (dĭk′ăst), *n.* (in ancient Athens) one of 6000 citizens over 30 years old, eligible to be chosen annually by lot to sit as judges. [t. Gk: s. *dikastḗs* juryman] —**dicas′-tic,** *adj.*

dicastery (dĭ kăs′tə rĭ), *n., pl.* **-teries.** (in ancient Athens) **1.** a court of dicasts. **2.** the location of the court. [t. Gk: m. s. *dikastḗrion* a hall of justice]

dice (dīs), *n. pl., sing.* **die,** *v.,* **diced, dicing.** —*n.* **1.** small cubes of plastic, ivory, bone, or wood, marked on each side with a different number of spots (1 to 6), usually used in pairs in games of chance or in gambling. **2.** any of various games, esp. gambling games, played by shaking the dice (in the cupped hand or in a receptacle) and throwing them on to a flat surface. **3.** any small cubes. —*v.t.* **4.** to cut into small cubes. **5.** to decorate with cube-like figures. —*v.i.* **6.** to play at dice. **7.** *Colloq.* to act dangerously or take a risk. [see DIE[2]] —**dic′er,** *n.*

dicentra (dī sĕn′trə), *n.* any of the plants constituting the genus *Dicentra* (or *Bikukulla*), characterized by racemes of drooping flowers, as the Dutchman's-breeches or the bleeding heart. [NL, t. Gk: m. *díkentros* with two stings or points]

dicephalous (dī sĕf′ə ləs), *adj.* having two heads. [t. Gk: m. *diképhalos*]

dicey (dī′sĭ), *adj. Colloq.* dangerous; risky; tricky.

Dicey (dī′sĭ), *n.* **Albert Venn,** 1835–1922, English jurist.

dichasium (dī kā′zĭ əm), *n., pl.* **-sia** (-zĭ ə). *Bot.* a form of cymose inflorescence in which each axis produces a pair of lateral axes. [NL, f. s. Gk *díchasis* division + -IUM] —**dicha′sial,** *adj.*

dichlamydeous (dī′klə mĭd′ē əs), *adj.* (of a flower) having both a calyx and a corolla.

dichlorodifluoromethane (dī klô′rō dī flōōə′rō mē′-thān), *n. Chem.* a colourless, non-inflammable gas, CCl_2F_2, used as a refrigerant, and as a propellant in aerosols and fire-extinguishers.

dichlorodiphenyl-trichloroethane (dī klô′rō dī fĕn′ĭl-trī klô′rō ē′thān), *n. Chem.* a white powdery compound having a faint, pleasant smell, used as a contact insecticide: commonly known as DDT.

dichloromethane (dī klô′rō mē′thān), *n. Chem.* a colourless liquid, CH_2Cl_2, used as an industrial solvent; methylene chloride.

dicho-, a word element meaning in 'two parts', 'in pairs'. [t. Gk, comb. form of *dícha* in two, asunder]

dichogamous (dī kŏg′ə məs), *adj. Bot.* having the stamens and pistils maturing at different times (thus preventing self-fertilization), as a monoclinous flower (opposed to *homogamous*). Also, **dichogamic** (dī′kō-găm′ĭk).

dichogamy (dī kŏg′ə mĭ), *n.* dichogamous condition.

dichotomize (dī kŏt′ə mīz′), *v.t., v.i.,* **-mized, -mizing.** **1.** to divide or separate into two parts. **2.** to divide into pairs. Also, **dichotomise.** —**dichot′omist,** *n.* —**dichot′-omiza′tion,** *n.*

dichotomous (dī kŏt′ə məs), *adj.* divided or dividing into two parts. Cf. **dichotomy.** Also, **dichotomic** (dī′kō-tŏm′ĭk). —**dichot′omously,** *adv.*

dichotomy (dī kŏt′ə mĭ), *n., pl.* **-mies.** **1.** division into two parts or into twos; subdivision into halves or pairs. **2.** *Logic.* classification by division, or by successive subdivision, into two groups or sections. **3.** *Bot.* a mode of branching by constant bifurcation as in some stems, in veins of leaves, etc. **4.** *Astron.* the phase of the moon, or of an inferior planet, when half of its disc is visible. [t. Gk: m. s. *dichotomia* a cutting in two]

Dichotomy (def. 3)

dichroic (dī krō′ĭk), *adj.* **1.** characterized by dichroism: *a dichroic crystal.* **2.** dichromatic. Also, **dichroitic** (dī′krō ĭt′ĭk). [f. s. Gk *díchroos* of two colours + -IC]

dichroism (dī′krō ĭz′əm), *n.* **1.** *Crystall.* a property possessed by many doubly refracting crystals of exhibiting different colours when viewed in different directions. **2.** *Chem.* the exhibition of essentially different colours by certain solutions in different degrees of dilution or concentration. [f. s. Gk *díchroos* of two colours + -ISM]

dichromate (dī krō′māt, -mĭt), *n. Chem.* a salt of a hypothetical acid, $H_2Cr_2O_7$, as *potassium dichromate,* $K_2Cr_2O_7$.

dichromatic (dī′krō măt′ĭk), *adj.* **1.** having or showing two colours; dichromic. **2.** of or having dichromatism (def. 2). **3.** *Zool.* exhibiting two colour phases within a species not due to age or season. [f. DI-[1] + m. s. Gk *chrōmatikós* pertaining to colour]

dichromaticism (dī′krō măt′ĭ sĭz′əm), *n.* dichroism (def. 1).

dichromatism (dī krō′mə tĭz′əm), *n.* **1.** dichromatic condition. **2.** dichromic condition of vision.

dichromic[1] (dī krō′mĭk), *adj.* of or embracing two colours only. [f. s. Gk *díchrōmos* two-coloured + -IC]

dichromic[2] (dī krō′mĭk), *adj. Chem.* of a compound containing two atoms of chromium. [f. DI-[1] + CHROM(IUM) + -IC]

dichromic acid, *Chem.* the hypothetical acid, $H_2Cr_2O_7$, from which the dichromates (sometimes called bichromates) are derived.

dichromic vision, *Pathol.* colour-blindness in which only two of the three primary colours are perceived.

dichroscope (dī′krə skōp′), *n. Crystall.* an instrument for testing the dichroism (or pleochroism) of crystals. [f. s. Gk *díchroos* of two colours + -SCOPE]

dicing (dī′sĭng), *n.* **1.** gambling or playing dice. **2.** ornamentation, esp. of leather, with squares or diamonds.
dick (dĭk), *n. Slang.* **1.** a detective. **2.** *Taboo.* the penis. **3.** a person: *clever dick.*
dickens (dĭk′ĭnz), *n., interj.* (prec. by *the*) devil; deuce (often used in exclamations and as a mild imprecation).
Dickens (dĭk′ĭnz), *n.* **Charles (John Huffam)** (hŭf′əm), 1812–70, English novelist. —**Dickensian** (dĭ kĕn′zĭ ən), *adj.*
dicker[1] (dĭk′ə), *n. Hist.* a quantity of ten, esp. hides or skins. [ME *dyker*; ult. akin to DECURY]
dicker[2] (dĭk′ə), *Chiefly U.S.* —*v.i., v.t.* **1.** to trade by barter or by petty bargaining; haggle. **2.** *U.S. Politics* to try to arrange matters by mutual bargaining. —*n.* **3.** a petty bargain; barter. **4.** *U.S. Politics.* a deal. [? v. use of DICKER[1]]
dickey (dĭk′ĭ), *n., pl.* **-eys.** dicky.
Dickinson (dĭk′ĭn sən), *n.* **Emily,** 1830–86, U.S. poet.
dicky[1] (dĭk′ĭ), *n., pl.* **-ies. 1.** a detachable shirt front, or (*U.S.*) blouse front. **2.** a pinafore or apron. **3.** a donkey, esp. a male. **4.** *Obs.* a small additional seat at the outside or back of a vehicle; rumble seat. Also, **dickey, dick′ie.** [application of *Dicky*, dim. of *Dick*, proper name]
dicky[2] (dĭk′ĭ), *adj. Colloq.* **1.** unsteady, shaky; in bad health; in poor condition. **2.** difficult; untenable: *a dicky position.*
dickybird (dĭk′ĭ bûd′), *n.* (childish) a bird.
diclinous (dī′klĭ nəs, dī klī′-), *adj. Bot.* **1.** (of a plant species, etc.) having the stamens and the pistils in separate flowers, either on the same plant or on different plants; either monoecious or dioecious. **2.** (of a flower) having only stamens or only pistils; unisexual. [f. DI-[1] + m. s. Gk *klīnē* bed + -OUS]
dicotyledon (dī kŏt′ĭ lē′dn, dī′kŏt-), *n.* **1.** a plant with two cotyledons. **2.** a member of the group *Dicotyledones*, one of the two subclasses of angiospermous plants, characterized by producing seeds with two cotyledons or seed leaves, and by an exogenous mode of growth. Cf. **monocotyledon.**
dicotyledonous (dī kŏt′ĭ lē′də nəs, dī′kŏt-), *adj.* having two cotyledons; belonging or pertaining to the *Dicotyledones.* See **dicotyledon** (def. 2).
dicoumarin (dī ko͞o′mə rĭn), *n.* a drug occurring in spoiled clover and also synthesized, used to prevent the coagulation of blood and in the treatment of arterial thrombosis. [f. DI-[1] + COUMARIN]
dicrotic (dī krŏt′ĭk), *adj. Physiol.* **1.** having two arterial beats for one heartbeat, as certain pulses. **2.** pertaining to such a pulse. [f. m. s. Gk *díkrotos* double-beating + -IC] —**dicrotism** (dī′krə tĭz′əm), *n.*
dict., 1. dictation. **2.** dictator. **3.** dictionary.
dicta (dĭk′tə), *n.* a pl. of **dictum.**
Dictaphone (dĭk′tə fōn′), *n. Trademark.* an instrument that records and reproduces dictation. [f. DICTA(TE) + -PHONE]
dictate (*v.* dĭk tāt′; *n.* dĭk′tāt), *v.,* **-tated, -tating,** *n.* —*v.t.* **1.** to say or read aloud (something) to be taken down in writing or recorded mechanically. **2.** to prescribe positively; command with authority. —*v.i.* **3.** to say or read aloud something to be taken down. **4.** to give orders. —*n.* **5.** an authoritative order or command. **6.** a guiding or ruling principle, requirement, etc. [t. L: m. s. *dictātus*, pp., pronounced, dictated, composed, prescribed]
dictation (dĭk tā′shən), *n.* **1.** the act of dictating for reproduction in writing, etc. **2.** words dictated, or taken down as dictated. **3.** the act of commanding positively or authoritatively. **4.** something commanded.
dictator (dĭk tā′tə), *n.* **1.** a person exercising absolute power, esp. one who assumes absolute control in a government without hereditary right or the free consent of the people. **2.** (in ancient Rome) a person constitutionally invested with supreme authority during a crisis, the regular magistracy being subordinated to him until the crisis was met. **3.** a person who authoritatively prescribes conduct, usage, etc.; a domineering or overbearing person. [t. L] —**dictatress** (dĭk tā′trĭs), **dictatrix** (dĭk′tə trĭks), *n. fem.*
dictatorial (dĭk′tə tô′rĭ əl), *adj.* **1.** of or pertaining to a dictator or a dictatorship. **2.** appropriate to, or characteristic of, a dictator; absolute; unlimited. **3.** inclined to dictate or command; imperious; overbearing: *a dictatorial tone.* Also, **dictatory.** —**dic′tato′rially,** *adv.* —**dic′tato′rialness,** *n.*
dictatorship (dĭk tā′tə shĭp′), *n.* **1.** a country, government, or the form of government in which absolute authority is exercised by a dictator. **2.** absolute or imperious power. **3.** the office or position held by a dictator. **4.** the period of a dictator's tenure of office. Also, **dictature** (dĭk′tə chə).
dictatorship of the proletariat, (in Marxist theory) a period of absolute rule by the proletariat, leading to the establishment of a classless society.
diction (dĭk′shən), *n.* **1.** style of speaking or writing as dependent upon choice of words: *good diction, a Latin diction.* **2.** the degree of distinctness with which speech sounds are uttered; enunciation. [t. L: s. *dictio* saying]
—**Syn. 1.** DICTION, PHRASEOLOGY, WORDING refer to the means and the manner of expressing ideas. DICTION usually implies a high level of usage; it refers chiefly to the choice of words, their arrangement, and the force, accuracy, and distinction with which they are used: *the speaker was distinguished for his excellent diction, poetic diction.* PHRASEOLOGY refers more to the manner of combining the words into related groups, and esp. to the peculiar or distinctive manner in which certain technical, scientific, and professional ideas are expressed: *legal phraseology.* WORDING refers to the exact words or phraseology used to convey thought: *the wording of a will.*
dictionary (dĭk′shən rĭ), *n., pl.* **-aries. 1.** a book containing a selection of the words of a language, usually arranged alphabetically, with explanations of their meanings, pronunciations, etymologies, and other information concerning them, expressed either in the same or in another language; a lexicon; a glossary. **2.** a book giving information on particular subjects or a particular class of words, names or facts, usually under alphabetically arranged headings: *a biographical dictionary.* [t. ML: m. s. *dictiōnārium*, lit., a word-book, der. LL *dictio* word. See DICTION]
dictograph (dĭk′tə grăf′, -gräf′), *n.* **1.** a telephonic device with a highly sensitive transmitter obviating the necessity of a mouthpiece, much used for secretly listening to conversations or obtaining a record of them. **2.** (*cap.*) a trademark for this device. [f. s. L *dictum* something said + -(O)GRAPH]
dictum (dĭk′təm), *n., pl.* **-ta** (-tə), **-tums. 1.** an authoritative pronouncement; judicial assertion. **2.** a saying; maxim. **3.** obiter dictum. [t. L: something said, a saying, a command, prop. pp. neut. of *dīcere* say]
dicyandiamide (dī sī′ən dī ăm′ĭd), *n. Chem.* a polymerization product of cyanamide, $(H_2NCN)_2$, used in the manufacture of plastics and resins and as a chemical intermediate.
did (dĭd), *v.* pt. of **do.**
Didache (dĭd′ə kē′), *n.* a Christian treatise of the second century, called more fully 'The Teaching of the Twelve Apostles'. [t. Gk: teaching]
didactic (dī dăk′tĭk), *adj.* **1.** intended for instruction; instructive: *didactic poetry.* **2.** inclined to teach or lecture others too much: *a didactic old lady.* [t. Gk: m. s. *didaktikós* apt at teaching] —**didac′tically,** *adv.* —**didac′ticism,** *n.*
didactics (dĭ dăk′tĭks), *n.* the art or science of teaching.
didapper (dī′dăp′ə), *n.* a dabchick. [for *divedapper*]
diddle (dĭd′l), *v.t.,* **-dled, -dling.** *Slang.* to cheat; swindle; victimize. [orig. uncert.] —**did′dler,** *n.*
Diderot (*Fr.* dē drō′), *n.* **Denis** (*Fr.* də nē′), 1713–84, French philosopher, critic, and encyclopedist.
didgeridoo (dĭj′ə rĭ do͞o′), *n. Austral.* a musical wind instrument of the N Australian aborigines, consisting of a hollow pipe about five feet long, emitting a resonant sound. [t. native Australian]
didn't (dĭd′nt), contraction of *did not.*
dido (dī′dō), *n., pl.* **-does.** *Slang.* a prank; an antic. [orig. uncert.]
Dido (dī′dō), *n.* the legendary queen of Carthage who killed herself when abandoned by Aeneas.
Didot body, corps Didot.
didst (dĭdst), *v. Archaic or Poetic.* 2nd pers. sing. pt. of **do.**
didymium (dī dĭm′ĭ əm, dĭ-), *n. Chem.* a mixture of neodymium and praseodymium, formerly supposed to be an element (and called the 'twin brother of lanthanum'). [NL, f. s. Gk *didymos* twin + *-ium* -IUM]
didymous (dĭd′ĭ məs), *adj. Bot.* occurring in pairs; paired; twin. [t. Gk: m. *didymos* double, twin]
die[1] (dī), *v.i.,* **died, dying. 1.** to cease to live; undergo the complete and permanent cessation of all vital functions. **2.** (of something inanimate) to cease to exist: *the secret died with him.* **3.** to lose force, strength, or active qualities: *traditions die slowly.* **4.** to cease to function; stop: *the engine died.* **5.** to pass gradually; fade or subside gradually (usually fol. by *away, out,* or *down*): *the storm slowly died down.* **6.** *Theol.* to lose spiritual life. **7.** to faint or languish. **8.** to suffer as if dying. **9.** to pine with desire, love, longing, etc. **10.** *Colloq.* to desire or want keenly or greatly: *I'm dying for a drink.* **11. die away,** (of a sound) to become weaker or fainter and then cease: *the music gradually died away.* **12. die back,** (of a plant, etc.) to wither from the top downwards to the stem or root. **13. die down, a.** to become calm or quiet; subside. **b.** (of a plant, etc.) to die above the ground, leaving only the root. **14. die hard,**

a. to die only after a bitter struggle. b. to cling stubbornly to a belief, theory, etc.; refuse to yield. **15. die off,** to die one after another until the number is greatly reduced. **16. die out,** to become extinct; disappear. [early ME *deghen*, c. Icel. *deyja*. Cf. DEAD, DEATH]

—**Syn.** **1, 2.** DIE, DECEASE, PASS AWAY (PASS ON), PERISH mean to relinquish life. To DIE is to become dead from any cause and in any circumstances. It is the simplest, plainest and most direct word for this idea, and is used fig. of anything that has once displayed activity: *an echo, flame, storm, rumour dies.* DECEASE, now almost entirely a legal term, refers only to the death of a human being: *a person deceases.* PASS AWAY (or PASS ON) is a commonly used euphemism implying a continuation of life after death: *Grandpa has passed away (passed on).* PERISH, a more literary term, implies death under harsh circumstances such as hunger, cold, neglect, etc.; fig. PERISH connotes utter extinction: *hardship caused many pioneers to perish.*

die² (dī), *n., pl.* **dies** for 1, 2, 4, **dice** for 3; *v.,* **died, dieing.** —*n.* **1.** *Mach.* **a.** any of various devices for cutting or forming material in a press or a stamping or forging machine. **b.** a hollow device of steel, often composed of several pieces to be fitted into a stock, for cutting the threads of bolts, etc. **c.** one of the separate pieces of such a device. **d.** a steel block or plate with small conical holes through which wire, plastic rods, etc., are drawn. **2.** an engraved stamp for impressing a design, etc., upon some softer material, as in coining money. **3.** sing. of **dice.** **4.** *Archit.* the dado of a pedestal, esp. when cubical. **5. the die is cast,** the decision has been irrevocably made. —*v.t.* **6.** to impress, shape, or cut with a die. [ME *de*, t. OF, g. L *datum*, orig. pp. neut., lit., given (appar. in sense of given by fortune)]

die-casting (dī′käs′tĭng), *Metall.* —*n.* **1.** a process in which metal is forced into metallic moulds under hydraulic pressure. **2.** an article made by this process. —*adj.* **3.** of or pertaining to this process.

diecious (dī ē′shəs), *adj. U.S. Bot.* dioecious.

Diefenbaker (dē′fən bā′kə), *n.* **John George,** born 1895, prime minister of Canada 1957–63.

Diégo-Suarez (*Fr.* dyė gō sʏ ȧ rĕz′), *n.* a seaport in N Malagasy Republic. 32,064 (1964).

diehard (dī′häd′), *n.* **1.** one who resists vigorously to the last, esp. a bigoted conservative. —*adj.* **2.** resisting vigorously to the last.

dielectric (dī′ĭ lĕk′trĭk), *Elect.* —*adj.* **1.** non-conducting. **2.** conveying electric effects otherwise than by conduction, as a medium through which electricity acts in the process of induction. —*n.* **3.** a dielectric substance. [f. DI-³ + ELECTRIC] —**di′elec′trically,** *adv.*

dielectric constant, *Elect.* the ratio of the capacitance of a capacitator when its plates are separated by the given dielectric, to the capacitance when its plates are separated by air.

dielectric heating, *Elect.* a form of heating in which a non-conductor is heated by being subjected to an alternating electric field.

Dien Bien Phu (dyĕn′byĕn fo͞o′), a village in SW Tonkin, North Vietnam: the site of a French military post besieged and captured by the Vietminh in 1954.

diencephalon (dī′ĕn sĕf′ə lŏn′), *n. Anat.* the posterior section of the prosencephalon; the interbrain or middle brain; thalamencephalon. [f. DI-³ + ENCEPHALON]

-dienes, *Chem.* a suffix designating a compound containing two double bonds. [f. DI-¹ + -ENE + -*s* (pl.)]

Dientzenhofer (*Ger.* dĕn′tsən hō fər), *n.* **1. Christian** (*Ger.* krĭs′tē ȧn) or **Christoph** (*Ger.* krĭs′tŏf), 1655–1722, Bavarian Baroque architect. **2.** his son, **Kilian Ignaz** (*Ger.* kē′lē ȧn ĭg′näts), 1689–1751, Bavarian Baroque architect.

Dieppe (dĭ ĕp′; *Fr.* dyĕp), *n.* a seaport in N France, on the English Channel. 30,327 (1962).

dieresis (dī ĭə′rĭ sĭs), *n., pl.* **-ses** (-sēz′). **1.** the separation of two adjacent vowels. **2.** a sign (¨) placed over the second of two adjacent vowels to indicate separate pronunciation, as in *Alcinoüs*. **3.** *Pros.* the division made in a line of verse by coincidence of the end of a foot and the end of a word. Also, **diaeresis.** [t. L, t. Gk: m. *diaíresis* separation, division]

dies (dī′ēz *or, esp. in Church Latin,* dē′ās), *n., sing. and pl. Latin.* day.

Diesel (dē′zəl), *n.* **1. Rudolf** (ro͞o′dŏlf), 1858–1913, German engineer who invented the diesel engine. **2.** (*often l.c.*) a diesel engine. **3.** (*often l.c.*) a locomotove, lorry, ship, or the like, driven by a diesel engine. **4.** (*often l.c.*) diesel oil.

diesel cycle, *Mach.* an engine cycle, usually 4 strokes, as intake, compression, power, and exhaust, in which ignition occurs at constant pressure, and heat is rejected at constant volume.

diesel-electric (dē′zəl ĭ lĕk′trĭk), *adj.* having an electric motor powered by a diesel engine.

diesel engine, (*sometimes cap.*) an ignition-compression type of internal-combustion engine in which fuel oil is sprayed into the cylinder after the air in it has been compressed to about 1000° F, thus causing the ignition of the oil, at substantially constant pressure. Also, **diesel motor.** [named after Rudolf DIESEL]

diesel oil, gas oil.

die-sinker (dī′sĭngk′ə), *n.* an engraver of dies for stamping or embossing. —**die′-sink′ing,** *n.*

Dies Irae (dē′āz ĭə′rī), *Latin.* a famous medieval Latin hymn on the Day of Judgement (commonly ascribed to Thomas of Celano, a Franciscan of the first half of the 13th century), sung or recited in the mass for the dead. [ML: day of wrath (the first words of the hymn)]

diesis (dī′ĭ sĭs), *n., pl.* **-ses** (-sēz′). **1.** *Music.* the difference between a major and a minor semitone. **2.** *Print.* the mark ‡; double dagger. [t. L, t. Gk: a sending through]

dies non (dī′ēz nŏn′), *Law.* a day on which no courts can be held or no legal business transacted. [short for L *dies nōn jūridicus* a day not juridical]

diestock (dī′stŏk′), *n. Mach.* a device for holding the dies used in cutting threads on a rod or pipe.

diet¹ (dī′ət), *n., v.,* **-eted, -eting.** —*n.* **1.** food considered in terms of its qualities, composition, and its effects on health: *milk is a wholesome article of diet.* **2.** a particular selection of food, esp. as prescribed to improve the physical condition, regulate weight, or cure a disease. **3.** the usual or regular food or foods a person eats most frequently. **4.** anything that is habitually provided. —*v.t.* **5.** to regulate the food of, esp. in order to improve the physical condition or regulate weight. —*v.i.* **6.** to select or limit the food one eats to improve one's physical condition or lose weight. [ME *diete*, t. OF, t. L: m. *diaeta*, t. Gk: m. *díaita* way of living, diet] —**di′eter,** *n.*

diet² (dī′ət), *n.* a formal assembly for discussing or acting upon public or state affairs, as (formerly) the general assembly of the estates of the Holy Roman Empire, the German Reichstag, Japan, etc. [late ME, t. ML: m. s. *diēta*, *diaeta* public assembly, appar. the same word as L *diaeta* (see DIET¹), with sense affected by L *dies* day]

dietarian (dī′ə tēə′rĭ ən), *n.* one who strictly follows a prescribed diet.

dietary (dī′ə tə rĭ, -trĭ), *adj., n., pl.* **-taries.** —*adj.* **1.** pertaining to diet: *dietary laws.* —*n.* **2.** a regulated allowance of food. **3.** a system or course of diet.

dietetic (dī′ĭ tĕt′ĭk), *adj.* pertaining to diet or to regulation of the use of food. Also, **di′etet′ical.** [t. L: m. s. *diaetēticus*, t. Gk: m. *diaitētikós*] —**di′etet′ically,** *adv.*

dietetics (dī′ĭ tĕt′ĭks), *n.* the art or science concerned with the regulation of diet.

diethylstilboestrol (dī ĕth′ĭl stĭl bēs′trŏl), *n. Chem.* a synthetic substance, $[HOC_6H_4C(C_2H_5)_2=]_2$, not itself an oestrogen but having a more potent oestrogenic activity than oestrone: used in the treatment of menopausal symptoms, etc.

dietist (dī′ə tĭst), *n.* an authority on diet.

dietitian (dī′ĭ tĭsh′ən), *n.* one versed in the regulation of diet, or in the planning or supervision of meals. Also, **di′etic′ian.** [der. DIET¹, modelled on PHYSICIAN]

Dietrich (dē′trĭk; *Ger.* dē′trĭKH), *n.* **Marlene** (mä′lē nĭ, mä lē′nĭ; *Ger.* mȧr lė′nə), born 1904, U.S. actress and singer, born in Germany.

Dieu avec nous (*Fr.* dyœ ȧ vĕk no͞o′), *French.* God with us.

Dieu et mon droit (*Fr.* dyœ ė mōN drwȧ′), *French.* God and my right (motto on the royal arms of England).

diff., 1. difference. 2. different.

differ (dĭf′ə), *v.i.* **1.** to be unlike, dissimilar, or distinct in nature or qualities (*often* fol. by from). **2.** to disagree in opinion, belief, etc.; be at variance (often fol. by *with* or *from*). **3.** *Obs.* to dispute. [t. F: s. *différer*, t. L: m. *differre* bear apart, put off, delay (see DEFER¹), be different]

difference (dĭf′rəns), *n., v.,* **-enced, -encing.** —*n.* **1.** the state or relation of being different; dissimilarity. **2.** an instance or point of unlikeness or dissimilarity. **3.** a significant change in or effect upon a situation. **4.** a distinguishing characteristic; distinctive quality or feature. **5.** the degree in which one person or thing differs from another. **6.** the act of distinguishing; discrimination; distinction. **7.** a disagreement in opinion; dispute; quarrel. **8.** *Maths.* the amount by which one quantity is greater or less than another. **9.** *Logic.* a differentia. **10.** *Her.* the descent of a younger branch from the main line of a family. **11. split the difference, a.** to compromise. **b.** to divide the remainder equally. —*v.t.* **12.** to cause or constitute a difference in or between; make different. **13.** to perceive the difference in or between; discriminate. **14.** *Her.* to make an addition (to a coat of arms) to identify a particular branch of a family. [ME, OE, t. L: m. s. *differentia*]

—**Syn.** 1. DIFFERENCE, DISCREPANCY, DISPARITY, DISSIMILARITY imply perceivable unlikeness, variation, or diversity. DIFFERENCE refers to a complete or partial lack of identity or a degree of unlikeness: *a difference of opinion, a difference of six inches.* DISCREPANCY usually refers to the difference or inconsistency between things that should agree, balance, or harmonize: *a discrepancy between the statements of two witnesses.* DISPARITY implies inequality, often where a greater approximation to equality might reasonably be expected: *a great disparity between the ages of husband and wife.* DISSIMILARITY indicates an essential lack of resemblance between things in some respect comparable: *a dissimilarity between the customs in Asia and in America.* 6. See **distinction.** —**Ant.** 1. likeness, similarity.

different (dĭf′rənt), *adj.* 1. differing in character; having unlike qualities; dissimilar. 2. not identical; separate or distinct. 3. various; several. 4. unusual; not ordinary; striking. [ME, t. OF, t. L: s. *differens,* ppr. of *differre.* See DIFFER] —**dif′ferently,** *adv.* —**Syn.** 1. unlike, diverse, divergent, altered, changed. 2. sundry, divers, miscellaneous. See **various.**

differentia (dĭf′ə rĕn′shĭ ə), *n., pl.* **-tiae** (-shĭ ē′). *Logic.* the character or attribute by which one species is distinguished from all others of the same genus. [t. L: difference]

differentiable (dĭf′ə rĕn′shyə bl), *adj.* capable of being differentiated.

differential (dĭf′ə rĕn′shəl), *adj.* 1. of or pertaining to difference or diversity. 2. constituting a difference; distinguishing; distinctive: *a differential feature.* 3. exhibiting or depending upon a difference or distinction. 4. *Physics, Mach., etc.* pertaining to or involving the difference of two or more motions, forces, etc.: *a differential gear.* 5. *Maths.* pertaining to or involving differentials. —*n.* 6. *Mach.* an epicyclic train of gears designed to permit two or more shafts to revolve at different speeds when driven by a third shaft; esp. a set of gears in a motor car which permit the driving wheels to revolve at different speeds when the car is turning. 7. *Elect.* a coil of wire in which the polar action produced is opposite to that of another coil. 8. *Maths.* (of a function) a linear form whose coefficients are the derivatives of the function with respect to its arguments. 9. *Com.* a. the difference involved in a differential rate. b. differential rate. [t. ML: s. *differentiālis,* der. L *differentia* DIFFERENCE] —**dif′feren′tially,** *adv.*

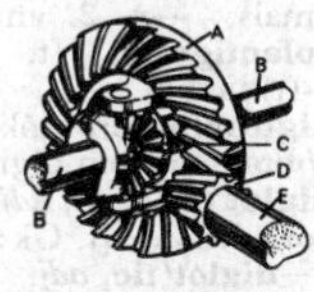

Differential (def. 6)
A, Ring gear; B, Axle; C, Pinion gear; D, Driveshaft gear; E, Driveshaft

differential calculus, the branch of mathematics which treats of differentials and derivatives.

differential coefficient, *Maths.* the derivative of a function with respect to one of its arguments.

differential equation, *Maths.* an equation involving differentials or derivatives.

differential gear, *Mach.* 1. differential (def. 6). 2. any of various analogous arrangements of gears.

differential quotient, derivative (def. 6).

differential rate, a special lower rate, as one charged by one of two or more competing businesses.

differential thermometer, a thermometer with two linked bulbs, for measuring changes in temperature.

differential windlass, *Mach.* a windlass with a barrel composed of two parts of different diameter, its power being determined by the difference in the two diameters.

differentiate (dĭf′ə rĕn′shĭ āt), *v.,* **-ated, -ating.** —*v.t.* 1. to mark off by differences; distinguish; alter; change. 2. to perceive the difference in or between; discriminate. 3. to make different by modification, as a biological species. 4. *Maths.* to obtain the differential or the derivative of. —*v.i.* 5. to become unlike or dissimilar; change in character. 6. to make a distinction; discriminate. 7. *Biol.* (of cells or tissues) to change from relatively generalized to specialized kinds, during development. —**dif′feren′tia′tion,** *n.* —**dif′feren′tia′tor,** *n.* —**Syn.** 1. See **distinguish.**

difficile (dĭf′ĭ sēl′; *Fr.* dē fē sēl′), *adj.* hard to deal with, get on with, please, or satisfy; difficult. [t. F, t. L: m. *difficilis* hard to do]

difficult (dĭf′ĭ klt), *adj.* 1. hard to do, perform, or accomplish; not easy; requiring much effort: *a difficult task.* 2. hard to understand or solve: *a difficult problem.* 3. hard to deal with or get on with. 4. hard to please or induce. 5. disadvantageous; hampering; involving hardships. [back-formation from DIFFICULTY] —**dif′ficultly,** *adv.* —**Syn.** 1. See **hard.** —**Ant.** 1. easy. 2. simple.

difficulty (dĭf′ĭ kl tĭ), *n., pl.* **-ties.** 1. the fact or condition of being difficult. 2. (*often pl.*) an embarrassing situation, esp. of financial affairs. 3. a trouble. 4. a cause of trouble or embarrassment. 5. reluctance; unwillingness. 6. a demur; objection. 7. that which is hard to do, understand, or surmount. [ME *difficulte,* t. L: m. s. *difficultas*] —**Syn.** 2. dilemma, predicament, quandary.

diffidence (dĭf′ĭ dəns), *n.* 1. lack of confidence in one's own ability, worth, or fitness; timidity; shyness. 2. restraint or reserve in manner, conduct, etc.

diffident (dĭf′ĭ dənt), *adj.* 1. lacking confidence in one's own ability, worth or fitness; timid; shy. 2. restrained or reserved in manner, conduct, etc. 3. *Rare.* distrustful. [t. L: s. *diffīdens,* ppr., mistrusting] —**dif′fidently,** *adv.* —**Syn.** 1. See **shy**[1]. —**Ant.** 1. self-confident.

diffluent (dĭf′lōō ənt), *adj.* tending to flow apart; readily dissolving. [t. L: s. *diffluens,* ppr., flowing away] —**dif′fluence,** *n.*

diffract (dĭ frăkt′), *v.t.* to break up or bend by diffraction. [t. L: s. *diffractus,* pp., broken in pieces]

diffraction (dĭ frăk′shən), *n. Physics.* 1. a modification that light or other radiation undergoes when it passes by the edge of an opaque body, or is sent through small apertures, resulting in the formation of a series of light and dark bands, prismatic colours, or spectra. This effect is an interference phenomenon due to the wave nature of radiation. 2. the analogous modification produced upon soundwaves when passing by the edge of a building or other large body.

diffraction grating, *Physics.* a band of equidistant parallel lines (from 10,000 to 30,000 or more to the inch), ruled on a surface of glass or polished metal, used for obtaining optical spectra.

diffractive (dĭ frăk′tĭv), *adj.* causing or pertaining to diffraction. —**diffrac′tively,** *adv.* —**diffrac′tiveness,** *n.*

diffuse (*v.* dĭ fyōōz′; *adj.* dĭ fyōōs′), *v.,* **-fused, -fusing,** *adj.* —*v.t.* 1. to pour out and spread, as a fluid. 2. to spread or scatter widely or thinly; disseminate. 3. *Physics.* to spread by diffusion. —*v.i.* 4. to spread. 5. *Physics.* to intermingle or pass by diffusion. —*adj.* 6. characterized by great length or discursiveness in speech or writing; wordy. 7. widely spread or scattered; dispersed. 8. *Bot.* widely or loosely spreading. [ME, t. L: m. s. *diffūsus,* pp., poured out] —**diffusely** (dĭ fyōōs′lĭ), *adv.* —**diffuse′ness,** *n.*

diffused (dĭ fyōōzd′), *adj.* 1. spread widely. 2. (of lighting) distributed evenly, without glare. —**diffus′edly,** *adv.*

diffuser (dĭ fyōō′zə), *n.* 1. one who or that which diffuses. 2. (in any of various machines or mechanical systems, as centrifugal pumps or compressors) a device for utilizing part of the kinetic energy of a fluid passing through a machine by gradually increasing the cross-sectional area of the channel or chamber through which it flows so as to decrease its speed and increase its pressure. 3. (in a lighting fixture) any of a variety of translucent materials for filtering glare from the light source. 4. a pierced plate or similar device for distributing compressed air for aeration of sewerage. 5. a wedge or cone placed in front of an open-diaphragm loudspeaker to avoid focusing of the high-frequency soundwaves. 6. *Photog.* a frame enclosing a fine silk or lightly ground glass screen which can be placed over the lens of a camera to soften the lighting. Also, **diffusor.**

diffusible (dĭ fyōō′zə bl), *adj.* capable of being diffused. —**diffusibility** (dĭ fyōō′zə bĭl′ĭ tĭ), *n.*

diffusion (dĭ fyōō′zhən), *n.* 1. the act of diffusing. 2. the state of being diffused. 3. diffuseness or prolixity of speech or writing. 4. *Physics.* a. the gradual permeation of any region by a fluid, owing to the thermal agitation of its particles or molecules. b. the process of being scattered. See **scatter** (def. 3). 5. *Anthropol., Sociol.* the transmission of elements from one culture to another.

diffusion pump, a pump for obtaining a high vacuum in which mercury or oil is forced through an orifice; gas molecules from the vessel to be exhausted diffuse through the mercury or oil vapour around the orifice and are entrained by the issuing jet; condensation pump.

diffusive (dĭ fyōō′sĭv), *adj.* 1. tending to diffuse. 2. characterized by diffusion. 3. diffuse; prolix. —**diffu′sively,** *adv.* —**diffu′siveness,** *n.*

diffusivity (dĭf′yōō sĭv′ĭ tĭ), *n. Physics.* the property of a substance indicative of the rate at which a thermal disturbance will be transmitted.

dig (dĭg), *v.,* **dug** or **digged, digging,** *n.* —*v.i.* 1. to break up, turn over, or remove earth, etc., as with a spade; make an excavation. 2. to make one's way by, or as by, digging. —*v.t.* 3. to break up and turn over, or penetrate and loosen (the ground) with a spade, etc. (often fol. by *up*). 4. to make (a hole, tunnel, etc.) by removing material. 5. to obtain or remove by digging (often fol. by *up* or *out*). 6. to find or discover by effort or search. 7. to thrust, plunge, or force (fol. by *into*): *he dug his heel into the* *ground.* **8.** *Slang.* **a.** to understand or find to one's taste. **b.** to take notice of; pay attention to. **9. dig in, a.** *Mil.* to dig trenches, as in order to defend a position in battle. **b.** to maintain one's position or opinion firmly. **c.** *Colloq.* to apply oneself vigorously. **10. dig into,** *Colloq.* to apply oneself vigorously to (work, eating, etc.). **11. dig out, dig up, a.** to discover in the course of digging. **b.** *Slang.* to discover, find, reveal. —*n.* **12.** thrust; poke. **13.** a cutting, sarcastic remark. **14.** an archaeological site undergoing excavation. **15.** *U.S. Slang.* a diligent student. **16.** (*pl.*) lodgings. [ME *diggen*, prob. t. F: m. *diguer*, of Gmc orig.]

dig., digest.

digamma (dī găm′ə), *n.* a letter of the Greek alphabet, but early in disuse, corresponding in form to *F* and having much the same sound as English *w.* [t. L, t. Gk: f. *di-* DI-¹ + *gámma* gamma; from its likeness to two gammas (Γ) one above the other]

digamy (dĭg′ə mĭ), *n.* second marriage; the practice of marrying again after the death or divorce of the first spouse. [t. LL: m. s. *digamia*, t. Gk] —**dig′amous,** *adj.*

digastric (dī găs′trĭk), *adj.* **1.** *Anat.* having two fleshy bellies with an intervening tendinous part, as certain muscles. —*n.* **2.** a muscle of the lower jaw (so called because in man it has two bellies).

digenesis (dī jĕn′ĭ sĭs), *n.* *Zool.* reproduction in alternate generations by different processes, one sexual and one asexual. —**digenetic** (dī′jĭ nĕt′ĭk), *adj.*

digest (*v.* dĭ jĕst′, dī-; *n.* dī′jĕst), *v.t.* **1.** to prepare (food) in the alimentary canal for assimilation into the system. **2.** to promote the digestion of (food). **3.** to assimilate mentally; obtain mental nourishment or improvement from. **4.** to arrange methodically in the mind; think over: *to digest a plan.* **5.** to bear with patience; endure. **6.** to arrange in convenient or methodical order; reduce to a system; classify. **7.** to condense, abridge, or summarize. **8.** *Chem.* to keep (a substance) in contact with a liquid to soften or to disintegrate it. —*v.i.* **9.** to digest food. **10.** to undergo digestion, as food. —*n.* **11.** a collection or summary, esp. of literary, historical, legal, or scientific matter, often classified or condensed. **12.** *Law.* **a.** a systematic abstract of some body of law. **b. the Digest,** a collection in fifty books, of excerpts compiled by order of Justinian in the sixth century, the largest part of the Corpus Juris Civilis; the Pandects. [ME, t. L: s. *dīgestus*, pp. separated, arranged, dissolved] —**digest′edly,** *adv.* —**digest′edness,** *n.* —**Syn. 11.** See **summary.**

digestant (dĭ jĕs′tənt, dī-), *n.* *Med.* an agent that promotes digestion.

digester (dĭ jĕs′tə, dī-), *n.* **1.** one who or that which digests. **2.** an apparatus in which substances are reduced or prepared by moisture and heat, chemical action, etc.

digestible (dĭ jĕs′tə bl, dī-), *adj.* capable of being digested; easily digested. —**digest′ibil′ity, digest′ibleness,** *n.* —**digest′ibly,** *adv.*

digestion (dĭ jĕs′chən, dī-), *n.* **1.** the process by which food is digested. **2.** the function or power of digesting food. **3.** the act of digesting. **4.** the resulting state.

digestive (dĭ jĕs′tĭv, dī-), *adj.* **1.** serving for or pertaining to digestion; having the function of digesting food. **2.** promoting digestion. —*n.* **3.** an agent or medicine promoting digestion. —**diges′tively,** *adv.*

digestive biscuit, a biscuit made from wholemeal flour.

digger (dĭg′ə), *n.* **1.** a person or an animal that digs. **2.** a miner, esp. a gold-miner. **3.** a tool, part of a machine, etc., for digging. **4.** (*cap.*) any one of several Indian tribes of western North America, who subsist largely on roots dug from the ground. **5.** (*cap.*) *Slang.* an Australian or New Zealand soldier (used also as a term of address).

digger wasp, any of the solitary wasps of the family *Sphecidae* which excavate holes in the ground and provision them with caterpillars, etc.

diggings (dĭg′ĭngz), *n. pl.* **1.** a place where digging is carried on. **2.** a mining operation or locality. **3.** that which is dug out. **4.** *Colloq.* living quarters; lodgings.

dight (dīt), *v.t.*, **dight** or **dighted, dighting.** *Archaic.* **1.** to make ready; prepare. **2.** to equip; furnish. **3.** to dress; adorn. **4.** *Dial.* to clean. [ME *dighte(n)*, OE *dihtan* compose, arrange, t. L: m. *dictāre* DICTATE. Cf. G *dichten* compose, Icel. *dikta* to write Latin]

digit (dĭj′ĭt), *n.* **1.** a finger or toe. **2.** the breadth of a finger used as a unit of linear measure, usually equal to three-quarters of an inch. **3.** any of the Arabic figures 0, 1 . . . 9. **4.** *Astron.* the twelfth part of the diameter of the sun or moon. [t. L: s. *digitus* finger, toe]

digital (dĭj′ĭ tl), *adj.* **1.** of or pertaining to a digit. **2.** resembling a digit or finger. **3.** having digits or digit-like parts. —*n.* **4.** one of the keys or finger levers of instruments of the organ or piano class.

digital computer. See **computer.**

digitalin (dĭj′ĭ tā′lĭn), *n.* *Pharm.* **1.** a glucoside obtained from digitalis. **2.** any of several extracts of mixtures of glucosides obtained from digitalis.

digitalis (dĭj′ĭ tā′lĭs), *n.* **1.** any plant of the scrophulariaceous genus *Digitalis*, esp. the common foxglove, *D. purpurea.* **2.** the dried leaves of the common foxglove, used in medicine, esp. as a heart stimulant. [NL, the genus name (after G name *Fingerhut* thimble; from the shape of the corolla), special use of L *digitālis* pertaining to the finger]

digitalism (dĭj′ĭ tə lĭz′əm), *n.* *Pathol.* the morbid result of overconsumption of digitalis.

digitate (dĭj′ĭ tāt′), *adj.* **1.** *Zool.* having digits or digit-like processes. **2.** *Bot.* having radiating divisions or leaflets resembling the fingers of a hand. **3.** like a digit or finger. Also, **dig′itat′ed.** —**dig′itate′ly,** *adv.*

Digitate leaf

digitation (dĭj′ĭ tā′shən), *n.* *Biol.* **1.** digitate formation. **2.** a digit-like process or division.

digitiform (dĭj′ĭ tĭ fôm′), *adj.* finger-like.

digitigrade (dĭj′ĭ tĭ grād′), *Zool.* —*adj.* **1.** walking on the toes, as most quadruped mammals. —*n.* **2.** an animal that walks on its toes. See **plantigrade.** [t. F, f. s. L *digitus* finger + -(*i*)*grade* -(I)GRADE]

digitoxin (dĭj′ĭ tŏk′sĭn), *n.* *Pharm.* a cardiac glucoside obtained from digitalis.

diglot (dī′glŏt), *adj.* **1.** bilingual. —*n.* **2.** a bilingual book or edition. [t. Gk: m. s. *díglōttos* speaking two languages] —**diglot′tic,** *adj.*

Digne (*Fr.* dēny), *n.* a town in SE France, capital of Basses-Alpes department. 13,660 (1967).

dignified (dĭg′nĭ fīd′), *adj.* marked by dignity of aspect or manner; noble; stately: *dignified conduct.* —**dig′nified′ly,** *adv.* —**Syn.** stately, grave, august.

dignify (dĭg′nĭ fī′), *v.t.*, **-fied, -fying. 1.** to confer honour or dignity upon; honour; ennoble. **2.** to give high-sounding title or name to; confer unmerited distinction upon. [t. ML: m. s. *dignificāre*, f. L: *digni-* worthy + *-ficāre* make]

dignitary (dĭg′nĭ tə rĭ, -trĭ), *n.*, *pl.* **-taries.** one who holds a high rank or office, esp. in the church.

dignity (dĭg′nĭ tĭ), *n.*, *pl.* **-ties. 1.** nobility of manner or style; stateliness; gravity. **2.** nobleness or elevation of mind; worthiness: *dignity of sentiments.* **3.** honourable place; elevated rank. **4.** degree of excellence, either in estimation or in the order of nature: *man is superior in dignity to brutes.* **5.** relative standing; rank. **6.** a high office or title. **7.** the person holding it. **8.** *Astrol.* a position within a sign which lends a heightened influence to a planet. [t. L: m. s. *dignitas* worthiness, rank; r. ME *dignete*, t. OF]

digraph (dī′grăf, -gräf), *n.* a pair of letters representing a single speech sound, as *ea* in *meat*, or *th* in *path.*

digress (dī grĕs′), *v.i.* **1.** to deviate or wander away from the main purpose in speaking or writing, or from the principal line of argument, study, etc. **2.** *Archaic.* to turn aside. [t. L: s. *dīgressus*, pp., having departed] —**digres′ser,** *n.* —**Syn. 1.** See **deviate.**

digression (dī grĕsh′ən), *n.* **1.** the act of digressing. **2.** a portion of a discourse, etc., deviating from the main theme. —**digres′sional,** *adj.*

digressive (dī grĕs′ĭv), *adj.* tending to digress; departing from the main subject. —**digres′sively,** *adv.* —**digres′siveness,** *n.*

digs (dĭgz), *n. pl.* *Colloq.* living quarters; lodgings; diggings.

dihedral (dī hē′drəl), *adj.* *Maths.* **1.** having, or formed by, two planes: *a dihedral angle.* **2.** pertaining to or having a dihedral angle or angles. —*n.* **3.** Also, **dihedral angle.** *Maths.* the figure made by two planes which intersect. **4.** *Aeron.* the angle at which the right and left wings of an aeroplane or the like are inclined upwards or downwards with reference to the centre section. [f. DI-¹ + s. Gk *hédra* seat, base + -AL¹]

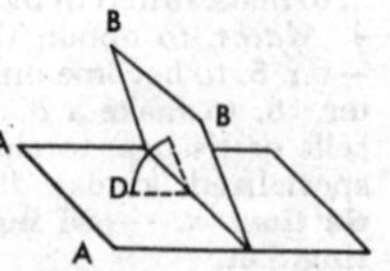

D, Dihedral angle included between planes AA and BB

dihedron (dī hē′drən, -hĕd′rən), *n.* dihedral (def. 3).

Dijon (*Fr.* dē zhôN′), *n.* a town in E France, in Côte-d'Or department. 153,699 (1962).

dik-dik (dĭk′dĭk′), *n.* any diminutive antelope of the genera *Madoqua* and *Rhynchotragus*, native to eastern and south-western Africa. [? t. some Cushitic language]

dike (dīk), *n.*, *v.*, **diked, diking.** *Now Chiefly U.S.* dyke. —**dik′er,** *n.*

diketone (dī kē′tōn), *n. Chem.* a compound containing two CO groups.

dikkop (dĭk′ŏp), *n. S African.* **1.** the stone curlew, *Burhinus capensis.* **2.** the goby. [t. Afrikaans: f. *dik* THICK + *kop* head]

dilacerate (dĭ lăs′ə rāt′, dī-), *v.t.*, **-ated, -ating.** to rend asunder; tear in pieces. [t. L: m. s. *dīlacerātus*, pp.] —**dilac′era′tion,** *n.*

dilapidate (dĭ lăp′ĭ dāt′), *v.*, **-dated, -dating.** —*v.t.* **1.** to bring (a building, etc.) into a ruinous condition, as by misuse or neglect. **2.** to squander; waste. —*v.i.* **3.** to fall into ruin or decay. [t. L: m. s. *dīlapidātus*, pp., thrown away, lit., scattered (orig. referring to stones)]

dilapidated (dĭ lăp′ĭ dā′tĭd), *adj.* reduced to, or fallen into, ruin or decay.

dilapidation (dĭ lăp′ĭ dā′shən), *n.* **1.** a state of ruin or decay; the process of becoming or causing to become dilapidated. **2.** (*pl.*) *Law.* the extent of the repairs necessary to premises at the end of a tenancy. **3.** the wearing away of rocks as a result of natural causes.

dilatant (dī lā′tnt, dĭ-), *adj.* **1.** dilating; expanding. —*n.* **2.** dilator (def. 3). —**dilat′ancy,** *n.*

dilatation (dĭl′ə tā′shən, dī′lə-), *n.* **1.** the act of dilating. **2.** the state of being dilated. **3.** a dilated formation or part. **4.** *Pathol.* **a.** an abnormal enlargement of an aperture or a canal of the body, or one made for the purposes of surgical or medical treatment. **b.** a restoration to normal potency of an abnormally small body opening or passageway, as the anus or oesophagus.

dilate (dī lāt′, dĭ-), *v.*, **-lated, -lating.** —*v.t.* **1.** to make wider or larger; cause to expand. —*v.i.* **2.** to spread out; expand. **3.** to speak at length; expatiate (fol. by *upon* or *on* or used absolutely). [t. L: m. s. *dīlātāre* spread out] —**dilat′able,** *adj.* —**dilat′abil′ity,** *n.* —**Syn. 1.** See **expand.** —**Ant. 1.** narrow.

dilation (dī lā′shən, dĭ-), *n.* dilatation.

dilative (dī lā′tĭv, dĭ-), *adj.* serving or tending to dilate.

dilatometer (dĭl′ə tŏm′ĭ tə), *n.* an instrument for measuring the expansion of substances.

dilator (dī lā′tə, dĭ-), *n.* **1.** one who or that which dilates. **2.** *Anat.* a muscle that dilates some cavity of the body. **3.** *Surg.* an instrument for dilating body canals, orifices, or cavities. Also, **dil′ata′tor.**

dilatory (dĭl′ə tə rĭ, -trĭ), *adj.* **1.** inclined to delay or procrastinate; slow; tardy; not prompt. **2.** intended to bring about delay, gain time, or defer decision: *a dilatory strategy.* [t. L: m. s. *dīlātōrius*, der. *dīlātor* delayer] —**dil′atorily,** *adv.* —**dil′atoriness,** *n.*

dildo (dĭl′dō), *n.*, *pl.* **-dos.** *Taboo.* an artificial erect penis. Also, **dildoe.**

dilemma (dĭ lĕm′ə, dī-), *n.* **1.** a situation requiring a choice between equally undesirable alternatives; an embarrassing or perplexing situation. **2.** *Logic.* a form of argument in which two or more alternatives (**the horns of the dilemma**) are presented, each of which is indicated to have consequences (usually unfavourable) for the one who must choose. [t. LL, t. Gk: double proposition] —**dilemmatic** (dĭl′ĭ măt′ĭk, dī′lĭ-), *adj.* —**Syn. 1.** See **predicament.**

dilettante (dĭl′ĭ tăn′tĭ), *n.*, *pl.* **-ti** (-tĭ), **-tes,** *adj.* —*n.* **1.** one who pursues an art or science desultorily or merely for amusement; a dabbler. **2.** a lover of an art or science, esp. of a fine art. —*adj.* **3.** of or pertaining to dilettantes. [t. It., prop. ppr. of *dilettare*, g. L *dēlectāre* DELIGHT, v.] —**dil′ettan′tish,** *adj.*

dilettantism (dĭl′ĭ tăn′tĭz′əm), *n.* the practice or characteristics of a dilettante. Also, **dilettanteism** (dĭl′ĭ tăn′tĭ ĭz′əm).

Dili (*Port.* dē lē′), *n.* a seaport in and the capital of Timor. 7000 (est. 1960).

diligence[1] (dĭl′ĭ jəns), *n.* **1.** constant and earnest effort to accomplish what is undertaken; persistent exertion of body or mind. **2.** *Obs.* care; caution. [ME, t. L: m. *dīligentia*] —**Syn. 1.** application, industry, assiduity, perseverance or persistence.

diligence[2] (dĭl′ĭ jəns; *Fr.* dē lē zhäNs′), *n.* a public stagecoach, esp. in France. [t. F: short for *carrosse de diligence* speed coach]

Diligence[2]

diligent (dĭl′ĭ jənt), *adj.* **1.** constant and persistent in an effort to accomplish something. **2.** pursued with persevering attention; painstaking. [ME, t. L: s. *dīligens*, prop. ppr., choosing, liking] —**dil′igently,** *adv.* —**Syn. 1.** industrious, assiduous. See **busy. 2.** persevering, indefatigable, untiring, unremitting.

dill (dĭl), *n.* **1.** an apiaceous plant, *Anethum graveolens*, bearing a seedlike fruit used in medicine and for flavouring pickles, etc. **2.** its aromatic seeds or leaves. [ME *dille, dile*, OE *dile-*; akin to G *Dill(e)*, Sw. *dill*]

dill pickle, a pickled cucumber flavoured with dill.

dill water, a medicinal drink prepared from dill.

dilly (dĭl′ĭ), *n. Austral.* **1.** a bag of twisted grass or fibre. **2.** any small bag for carrying food or personal belongings. [t. native Australian]

dillybag (dĭl′ĭ băg′), *n. Austral.* dilly.

dillydally (dĭl′ĭ dăl′ĭ), *v.i.*, **-dallied, -dallying.** to waste time, esp. by indecision; trifle; loiter. [dissimilated reduplication of DALLY. Cf. SHILLYSHALLY]

diluent (dĭl′yo͞o ənt), *adj.* **1.** diluting; serving for dilution. —*n.* **2.** a diluting substance, esp. one that dilutes the blood. [t. L: s. *dīluens*, ppr., washing away]

dilute (dī lyo͞ot′), *v.*, **-luted, -luting,** *adj.* —*v.t.* **1.** to make thinner or weaker by the addition of water or the like. **2.** to make (a colour, etc.) fainter. **3.** to reduce the strength, force, or efficiency of by admixture. **4.** to increase the proportion (in a labour force) of unskilled to skilled. —*v.i.* **5.** to become diluted. —*adj.* **6.** reduced in strength, as a chemical by admixture; weak: *a dilute solution.* [t. L: m. s. *dīlūtus*, pp., washed to pieces, dissolved, diluted] —**di′lutee′,** *n.* —**dilu′ter,** *n.*

dilution (dī lo͞o′shən), *n.* **1.** the act of diluting. **2.** the state of being diluted. **3.** something diluted; a diluted form of anything. **4.** *Chem.* the reciprocal of concentration: the volume of solvent (usually in litres) in which a unit quantity (usually a gram-molecule) of solute is dissolved.

diluvial (dĭ lo͞o′vyəl, dī-), *adj.* **1.** pertaining to a deluge or flood, esp. the flood described in Genesis. **2.** *Geol.* pertaining to or consisting of diluvium. Also, **dilu′vian.** [t. L: s. *dīluviālis*]

diluvium (dĭ lo͞o′vyəm, dī-), *n.*, *pl.* **-via** (-vyə). *Geol.* a coarse superficial deposit formerly attributed to a general deluge but now regarded as glacial drift. [t. L: deluge]

dim (dĭm), *adj.*, **dimmer, dimmest,** *v.*, **dimmed, dimming.** —*adj.* **1.** not bright; obscure from lack of light; somewhat dark: *a dim room.* **2.** not clearly seen; indistinct: *a dim object.* **3.** not clear to the mind; vague: *a dim idea.* **4.** not brilliant; dull in lustre: *a dim colour.* **5.** faint: *a dim sound.* **6.** not seeing clearly: *eyes dim with tears.* **7.** not clearly understanding. **8.** disparaging; adverse: *to take a dim view.* **9.** *Colloq.* (of a person), stupid; lacking in intelligence. —*v.t.* **10.** to make dim. —*v.i.* **11.** to become or grow dim. [ME *dim(e)*, OE *dim(m)*, c. OFris. *dim*, Icel. *dimmr*] —**dim′ly,** *adv.* —**dim′ness,** *n.* —**Syn. 1.** See **dark. 10.** darken, cloud. **11.** blur, dull, fade.

dim., **1.** diminuendo. **2.** diminutive. Also, **dimin.**

dime (dīm), *n.* a silver coin of the U.S., of the value of 10 cents or $\frac{1}{10}$ dollar. [ME, t. OF, var. of *disme*, g. L *decima* tenth part, tithe, prop. fem. of *decimus* tenth]

dime novel, *U.S.* a cheap and usually sensational novel.

dimension (dĭ mĕn′shən), *n.* **1.** magnitude measured in a particular direction, or along a diameter or principal axis. **2.** (*usually pl.*) measure; extent; size; magnitude; scope; importance. **2.** *Alg.* the number of factors in a term. [t. L: s. *dīmensio* a measuring] —**dimen′sional,** *adj.* —**dimen′sionless,** *adj.*

dimer (dī′mə), *n. Chem.* a substance composed of molecules formed from two molecules of a monomer.

dimercaprol (dī′mû kăp′rŏl), *n. Chem.* a colourless, oily, viscous liquid, $CH_2(SH)CH(SH)CH_2OH$, used as an antidote to lewisite, and in treating bismuth, gold, mercury, and arsenic poisoning. [alter. of *di-mercapto-propanol*]

dimerous (dĭm′ə rəs), *adj.* **1.** consisting of or divided into two parts. **2.** *Bot.* (of flowers) having two members in each whorl. [f. s. Gk *dimerḗs* bipartite + -OUS] —**dim′erism,** *n.*

Dimerous flower

dimeter (dĭm′ĭ tə), *n. Pros.* a verse or line of two measures or feet. For example: *He is gone on the mountain,|He is lost to the forest.* [t. LL, t. Gk: m. s. *dimetros* of two measures]

dimidiate (*v.* dĭ mĭd′ĭ āt′; *adj.* dĭ mĭd′ĭ ĭt), *v.*, **-ated, -ating,** *adj.* —*v.t.* **1.** to divide into halves; reduce to half. —*adj.* **2.** divided into halves. **3.** *Biol.* having only one side or one half fully developed. [t. L: m. s. *dīmidiātus*, pp., halved]

diminish (dĭ mĭn′ĭsh), *v.t.* **1.** to make, or cause to seem, smaller; lessen; reduce. **2.** *Archit., etc.* to cause to taper. **3.** *Music.* to make smaller by a semitone than the corresponding perfect or minor interval. **4.** to detract from; disparage. —*v.i.* **5.** to lessen; decrease. [b. earlier *diminue* (t. ML: m. s. *dīminuere*, for L *dēminuere* make smaller) and MINISH] —**dimin′ishable,** *adj.* —**dimin′ishingly,** *adv.* —**Syn. 1.** See **decrease. 5.** subside, ebb, dwindle, shrink, abate.

diminished responsibility, *Law.* limitation of a person's criminal responsibility in doing or being a party to the killing of another on the ground of mental weakness or abnormality.

diminishing returns, *Econ.* the fact, often stated as a law or principle, that as any factor in production (as labour, capital, etc.) is increased, the output per unit factor will eventually decrease.

diminuendo (dĭ mĭn′yo͞o ĕn′dō; *It.* dē mē nwĕn′dȯ), *adj.*, *n.*, *pl.* **-dos** (-dōz; *It.* -dȯs). *Music.* —*adj.* **1.** gradually reducing in force or loudness; decrescendo (opposed to *crescendo*). —*n.* **2.** a gradual reduction of force or loudness. **3.** a diminuendo passage. *Symbol*: > [t. It., ppr. of *diminuire*. See DIMINISH]

diminution (dĭm′ĭ nyo͞o′shən), *n.* **1.** the act, fact or process of diminishing; lessening; reduction. **2.** *Music.* the repetition or imitation of a subject or theme in notes of shorter duration than those first used. [ME *diminucion*, t. AF: m. *diminuciun*, t. L: m. s. *dīminūtio*]

diminutive (dĭ mĭn′yo͞o tĭv), *adj.* **1.** small; little; tiny: *a diminutive house.* **2.** *Gram.* pertaining to or productive of a form denoting smallness, familiarity, affection, or triviality, as the suffix *-let*, in *droplet* from *drop*. —*n.* **3.** a small thing or person. **4.** *Gram.* a diminutive element or formation. **5.** *Her.* a charge smaller in length or breadth than the usual. [ME, t. ML: m. s. *dīminutīvus*, der. L *dī-*, *dēminutis*, pp., lessened] —**dimin′utively,** *adj.* —**dimin′utiveness,** *n.* —**Syn. 1.** See **little.**

dimissory letter (dĭ mĭs′ə rĭ), a letter issued by a bishop, abbot, etc., permitting a subject to be ordained by another bishop. Also, **dim′isso′rial letter.** [ME *dymyssories* (pl.), t. L: m. (*litterae*) *dimissōriae* dimissory (letter), der. *dīmissus*, pp., sent away]

Dimitrov (*Bulg.* dē mē′trȯf), *n.* **Georgi** (*Bulg.* gė ŏr′gē), 1882–1949, Bulgarian political leader; prime minister 1946–49.

Dimitrovo (*Bulg.* dē mē′trȯ vȯ), *n.* a town in W Bulgaria. 82,601 (1964). Formerly, **Pernik.**

dimity (dĭm′ĭ tĭ), *n.*, *pl.* **-ties.** a thin cotton fabric, white, dyed, or printed, woven with a stripe or check of heavier yarn. [late ME *demyt*, t. It.: m. *dimito* coarse cotton, t. Gk: m. *dímitos* of double thread]

dimmer (dĭm′ə), *n.* **1.** one who or that which dims. **2.** a rheostat, or similar device, by which the intensity of illumination, especially in stage lighting, is varied.

dimorph (dī′môf), *n.* *Crystall.* either of the two forms assumed by a dimorphous substance.

dimorphism (dī mô′fĭz′əm), *n.* **1.** *Zool.* the occurrence of two forms distinct in structure, coloration, etc., among animals of the same species. **2.** *Bot.* the occurrence of two different forms of flowers, leaves, etc., on the same plant or on distinct plants of the same species. **3.** *Crystall.* the property of some substances of crystallizing in two chemically identical but crystallographically distinct forms.

Dimorphism (def. 2) Submerged and floating leaves of water crowfoot, *Ranunculus aquatilis*

dimorphous (dī mô′fəs), *adj.* exhibiting dimorphism. Also, **dimor′phic.** [t. Gk: m. *dímorphos*]

dim-out (dĭm′out′), *n.* *U.S.* a reduction or concealment of night lighting, as of a city, a ship, etc., to make it less visible from the air or sea; blackout (def. 1).

dimple (dĭm′pl), *n.*, *v.*, **-pled, -pling.** —*n.* **1.** a small natural hollow, permanent or transient, in some soft part of the human body, esp. one produced in the cheek in smiling. **2.** any slight depression like this. —*v.t.* **3.** to mark with, or as with, dimples; produce dimples in. —*v.i.* **4.** to form dimples. [ME *dympull*, c. MHG *tümpfil* pool] —**dim′ply,** *adj.*

dimwit (dĭm′wĭt′), *n.* *Slang.* a stupid or slow-thinking person. —**dim′-wit′ted,** *adj.*

din (dĭn), *n.*, *v.*, **dinned, dinning.** —*n.* **1.** a loud, confused noise; a continued loud or tumultuous sound; noisy clamour. —*v.t.* **2.** to assail with din. **3.** to sound or utter with clamour or persistent repetition. —*v.i.* **4.** to make a din. [ME *din(e)*, OE *dyne*, *dynn*, c. Icel. *dynr*] —**Syn. 1.** hubbub, uproar, racket. See **noise.**

dinar (dē′nä), *n.* **1.** any of the monetary units of Iraq, Jordan, or Kuwait, equal to 1000 fils, and equivalent to about £0·857 sterling. *Abbrevs.*: I.D.; J.D.; K.D. **2.** a banknote of this value. **3.** the monetary unit of Tunisia, equal to 1000 millimes, and equivalent to about £0·794 sterling. **4.** a banknote of this value. **5.** the monetary unit of Yugoslavia, equal to 100 paras, and equivalent to about £0·033 sterling. **6.** a banknote or coin of this value. **7.** an Iranian unit of currency, equal to one hundredth part of a rial. **8.** a coin of this value. **9.** any of various oriental coins, esp. gold coins of ancient Arab governments. [t. Ar. and Pers., t. LGk: m. s. *dēnárion*, t. L: m. *dēnārius* DENARIUS]

Dinaric Alps (dĭ nă′rĭk), a mountain range in W Yugoslavia: a part of the E Alpine system.

dindle (dĭn′dl), *v.t.*, *v.i.*, **-dled, -dling,** *n.* *Scot. and N Dial.* dinnle; tingle or thrill.

dine (dīn), *v.*, **dined, dining,** *n.* —*v.i.* **1.** to eat the principal meal of the day; have dinner. **2.** to take any meal. **3. dine out,** to eat dinner away from home. —*v.t.* **4.** to entertain at dinner. —*n.* **5.** *Obs.* dinner. [ME *dine(n)*, t. F: m. *dîner*, g. LL *disjējūnāre* breakfast]

diner (dī′nə), *n.* **1.** one who dines. **2.** *U.S.* a railway restaurant car. **3.** a restaurant built like such a car. **4.** *Colloq.* a dining room.

Dinesen (dĭn′ĭ sən), *n.* **Isak** (ī′zək) (*Baroness Karen Blixen* (*Finecke*)), 1885–1962, Danish author.

dinette (dī nĕt′), *n.* a part of a kitchen or other room set apart for meals.

ding (dĭng), *v.i.*, *v.t.* **1.** to sound, as a bell; ring, esp. with wearisome continuance. **2.** *Colloq.* to keep repeating; impress by reiteration. —*n.* **3.** the sound of a bell or the like. [imit.]

Dingaan (dĭng′gän), *n.* died 1840, king of the Zulus 1828–40.

ding-dong (dĭng′dŏng′), *n.* **1.** the sound of a bell. **2.** any similar sound of repeated strokes. —*adj.* **3.** repeated in succession or alternation. **4.** *Colloq.* vigorously fought with alternating success: *a ding-dong contest.* [imit.]

dingey (dĭng′gĭ), *n.*, *pl.* **-geys.** dinghy.

dinghy (dĭng′gĭ), *n.*, *pl.* **-ghies. 1.** a small rowing or sailing boat or ship's tender. **2.** an inflatable rubber boat for aircraft. **3.** any of various boats for rowing or sailing used in the East Indies. Also, **dingey, dingy, dinky.** [t. Hind.: m. *dīngī*]

dingle (dĭng′gl), *n.* *Chiefly Poetic and Dial.* a deep narrow cleft between hills; a shady dell.

dingo (dĭng′gō), *n.*, *pl.* **-goes.** a wolf-like wild dog, *Canis dingo*, of Australia, believed to have been introduced by the aborigines. [t. native Australian]

Dingo, *Canis dingo* (Total length 3½ ft, tail 14 in., 21 in. high at the shoulder)

Dingwall (dĭng′wôl′), *n.* a burgh in Scotland, the county town of Ross and Cromarty. 3752 (1961).

dingy¹ (dĭn′jĭ), *adj.*, **-gier, -giest.** of a dark, dull, or dirty colour or aspect; lacking brightness or freshness; shabby; disreputable. [orig. uncert.] —**din′gily,** *adv.* —**din′giness,** *n.*

dingy² (dĭng′gĭ), *n.*, *pl.* **-gies.** dinghy.

dining car, restaurant car.

dining hall, a large room, as at a college or other institution where dinner and other meals are eaten.

dining room, a room in which dinner and other meals are taken.

dining table, a table on which meals, esp. the more formal meals, are served.

dinitrobenzene (dī nī′trō bĕn′zēn, -bĕn zēn′), *n.* *Chem.* one of three isomeric compounds, $C_6H_4(NO_2)_2$, the most important of which is made by nitration of benzene or nitrobenzene and used in the manufacture of azo dyes.

dink (dĭngk), *Scot.* —*adj.* **1.** neatly dressed. —*v.t.* **2.** to deck; array. [? nasalized var. of *decked* adorned]

Dinka (dĭng′kə), *n.*, *pl.* **-kas,** (*esp. collectively*) **-ka. 1.** a member of a Negroid people of the Sudan. **2.** this people. **3.** their language.

dinkum (dĭng′kəm), *Austral. Colloq.* —*adj.* **1.** true; honest; genuine. —*adv.* **2.** truly.

dinky (dĭngk′ĭ), *adj.*, **dinkier, dinkiest,** *n.*, *pl.* **dinkies.** *Colloq.* —*adj.* **1.** of small size. **2.** neat; dainty; smart. —*n.* **3.** dinghy.

dinner (dĭn′ə), *n.* **1.** the main meal, taken either about noon or in the evening. **2.** a formal meal in honour of some person or occasion. [ME *diner*, t. F, orig. inf. See DINE] —**din′nerless,** *adj.*

dinner-dance (dĭn′ə däns′), *n.* a social function at which dinner is served and dancing takes place.

dinner jacket, a jacket for semi-formal wear by men.

dinnertime (dĭn′ə tīm′), *n.* **1.** the time in the evening when dinner is eaten. **2.** lunchtime. —*adj.* **3.** denoting, pertaining to, or taking place at either of these times.

dinnle (dĭn′əl), *v.t.*, *v.i.*, **-led, -ling,** *n.* *Scot. and N Dial.* tingle; thrill. Also, **dindle.**

dino-, a word element meaning 'terrible', as in *dinothere*. [t. Gk: m. *deino-*, comb. form of *deinós*]

dinoceras (dī nŏs′ə rəs), *n.* *Palaeontol.* any member of an extinct genus, *Dinoceras*, comprising the huge horned ungulate mammals of the Eocene of North America. [t. NL, f. *dino-* DINO- + m. Gk *kéras* horn]

dinosaur (dīʹnə sôʹ), *n. Palaeontol.* any member of extinct groups of Mesozoic reptiles, mostly of gigantic size, known in modern classifications as the *Saurischia* and the *Ornithischia*. [t. NL: s. *dīnosaurus*. See DINO-, -SAUR]

Dinosaur, *Triceratops elatus* (Ab. 29 ft long)

dinosaurian (dīʹnə sôʹrĭ ən), *adj.* **1.** pertaining to or of the nature of a dinosaur.

dinothere (dīʹnə thĭəʹ), *n. Palaeontol.* any animal of the extinct genus *Dinotherium*, comprising elephant-like mammals of the later Tertiary of Europe and Asia, characterized by downward curving tusks in the lower jaw. [t. NL: m. s. *dinotherium*, f. *dino-* DINO- + m. Gk *thērion* wild beast]

Dinslaken (*Ger.* dĭnsʹlä kən), *n.* a town in West Germany, in E North Rhine-Westphalia. 50,700 (est. 1966).

dint (dĭnt), *n.* **1.** force; power: *by dint of argument.* **2.** a dent. **3.** *Obs.* a blow; stroke. —*v.t.* **4.** to make a dint or dints in. **5.** to impress or drive in with force. [ME; OE *dynt*, c. Icel. *dyntr*] —**dintʹless,** *adj.*

diocesan (dī ŏsʹĭ sən), *adj.* **1.** of or pertaining to a diocese. —*n.* **2.** one of the clergy or people of a diocese. **3.** the bishop in charge of a diocese.

diocese (dīʹə sĭs), *n.* the district, with its population, falling under the pastoral care of a bishop. [ME *diocise*, t. OF, t. ML: m. *diocēsis*, for L *dioecēsis* district, t. Gk: m. *dioíkēsis* housekeeping, administration, province, diocese]

Diocletian (dīʹə klēʹshən), *n.* A.D. 245–313, Roman emperor, A.D. 284–305.

diode (dīʹōd), *n. Electronics.* a device consisting of an anode and cathode whose volt-ampere characteristics are asymmetric. [f. DI-[1] + -ODE[2]]

Diodorus Siculus (dīʹə dôʹrəs sĭkʹyōō ləs), late 1st century B.C. Greek historian.

dioecious (dī ēʹshəs), *adj. Biol.* (esp. of plants) having the male and female organs in separate and distinct individuals; having separate sexes. [f. s. NL *dioecia* genus name (f. Gk: *di-* DI-[1] + m. s. *oikíon* little house) + -OUS]

diœstrum (dī ēsʹtrəm), *n.* the period between the rutting periods, esp. of female animals. [NL. See DI-[1], OESTRUM]

Diogenes (dī ŏjʹĭ nēzʹ), *n. c.* 412–*c.* 323 B.C., Greek Cynic philosopher.

Diomedes (dīʹə mēʹdēz), *n. Gk Legend.* the son of Tydeus and the next in prowess to Achilles among the Greeks before Troy. Also, **Diomede** (dīʹə mēdʹ), **Diomed** (dīʹə mĕdʹ). [t. L, t. Gk]

Dionysia (dīʹə nĭzʹĭ ə), *n. pl. Gk Antiq.* the orgiastic and dramatic festivals in honour of Dionysus or Bacchus, celebrated periodically in various parts of Greece, esp. those in Attica, out of which Greek comedy and tragedy developed. [t. L, t. Gk]

Dionysiac (dīʹə nĭzʹĭ ăkʹ), *adj.* pertaining to the Dionysia or to Dionysus; Bacchic. —**Dionysiacally** (dīʹə nĭ zīʹĭ kə lĭ), *adv.*

Dionysian (dīʹə nĭzʹĭ ən), *adj.* **1.** pertaining to Dionysus or Bacchus. **2.** (*l.c.*) wild; orgiastic.

Dionysius (dīʹə nĭsʹĭ əs), *n.* (*the Elder*), 430?–367 B.C., ruler of the ancient Greek city of Syracuse, in Sicily.

Dionysius Exiguus (ĕg zĭgʹyōō əs), fl. A.D. 530, Scythian monk and scholar: believed to have founded the system of reckoning dates as before or after the birth of Christ.

Dionysius of Halicarnassus, died 7? B.C., Greek rhetorician and historian, in Rome.

Dionysus (dīʹə nīʹsəs), *n. Gk Myth.* the youthful and beautiful god of wine and the drama, identified with the Roman god Bacchus. Also, **Dionysos.**

diopside (dī ŏpʹsīd, -sĭd), *n. Mineral.* a common variety of pyroxene, occurring in various colours, usually in crystals. [t. F, f. *di-* DI-[1] + m. s. Gk *ópsis* appearance]

dioptase (dī ŏpʹtās), *n.* a mineral, hydrous copper silicate, $CuSiO_3H_2O$, occurring in emerald green crystals; emerald copper. [t. F, f. Gk: *di-* DI-[3] + m. s. *optasia* view]

dioptometer (dīʹŏp tŏmʹĭ tə), *n.* an instrument for measuring the eye's refraction.

dioptre (dī ŏpʹtə), *n. Optics.* the refractive power of a lens whose focal length is one metre. Also, *U.S.*, **diopter.** [t. L: m. s. *dioptra*, t. Gk: kind of levelling instrument]

dioptric (dī ŏpʹtrĭk), *adj.* **1.** *Optics.* pertaining to dioptrics: *dioptric images.* **2.** *Ophthalm.* assisting vision by refractive correction. Also, **diopʹtrical.** [t. Gk: s. *dioptrikós* pertaining to the use of the *dióptra*. See DIOPTRE] —**diopʹtrically,** *adv.*

dioptrics (dī ŏpʹtrĭks), *n.* the branch of geometrical optics dealing with the formation of images by lenses.

Dior (dēʹô; *Fr.* dyŏr), *n.* **Christian** (*Fr.* krēs tyäNʹ), 1905–57, French couturier.

diorama (dīʹə räʹmə), *n.* **1.** a miniature scene reproduced in three dimensions with the aid of lights, colours, etc. **2.** a spectacular picture, partly translucent, for exhibition through an aperture, made more realistic by various illuminating devices. **3.** a building where such scenes or pictures are exhibited. [t. F, f. *di-* DI-[3] + Gk (*h*)*órama* view] —**dioramic** (dīʹə rămʹĭk), *adj.*

Diori (*Fr.* dyŏ rēʹ), *n.* **Hamani** (*Fr.* à mà nēʹ), born 1916, president of Niger since 1960.

diorite (dīʹə rītʹ), *n.* a granular igneous rock consisting essentially of plagioclase felspar and hornblende. [t. F, f. Gk *dior*(*ízein*) distinguish + *-ite* -ITE[1]] —**dioritic** (dīʹə rĭtʹĭk), *adj.*

Dioscuri (dīʹŏs kyōōʹrĭ), *n. pl.* Castor and Pollux.

diosmose (dī ŏsʹmōs, -ŏzʹ-), *v.t.*, **-mosed, -mosing.** osmose. —**diosmosis** (dīʹŏs mōʹsĭs, dīʹŏz-), *n.*

dioxan (dī ŏkʹsən), *n. Chem.* a colourless liquid, a cyclic ether with a faint, pleasant smell, $C_4H_8O_2$, used in the varnish and silk industries and as a dehydrator in histology. Also, **dioxane** (dī ŏkʹsān).

dioxide (dī ŏkʹsīd), *n. Chem.* **1.** an oxide containing two atoms of oxygen per molecule, as *manganese dioxide*, MnO_2. **2.** (loosely) peroxide. [f. DI-[1] + OXIDE]

dip (dĭp), *v.*, **dipped, dipping,** *n.* —*v.t.* **1.** to plunge temporarily into a liquid, as to wet or to take up some of the liquid. **2.** to raise or take up by a dipping action; lift by bailing or scooping: *to dip water out of a boat.* **3.** to lower and raise: *to dip a flag in salutation.* **4.** to baptize by immersion. **5.** to immerse (a sheep, etc.) in a solution to destroy germs, parasites, or the like. **6.** to make (a candle) by repeatedly dipping a wick into melted tallow. **7.** to moisten or wet as if by immersion. **8.** to direct (motor-car headlights) downwards, as to avoid dazzling oncoming drivers. —*v.i.* **9.** to plunge into water or other liquid and emerge quickly. **10.** to plunge the hand, a dipper, etc., into water, etc., esp. in order to remove something. **11.** to sink or drop down, as if plunging into water. **12.** to incline or slope downwards. **13.** to engage slightly in a subject. **14.** to read here and there in a book. **15. dip into one's pocket,** to spend money; pay. —*n.* **16.** the act of dipping; a plunge into water, etc. **17.** that which is taken up by dipping. **18.** a liquid into which something is dipped. **19.** a lowering momentarily; a sinking down. **20.** a soft savoury mixture into which potato crisps, sticks of celery, or the like, are dipped before being eaten, usually served with cocktails. **21.** downward extension, inclination, or slope. **22.** the amount of such extension. **23.** a hollow or depression in the land. **24.** *Geol.*, *Mining.* the downward inclination of a stratum or vein, referred to a horizontal plane; inclination. **25.** *Survey.* the angular amount by which the horizon lies below the level of the eye. **26.** the angle which a freely poised magnetic needle makes with the plane of the horizon; inclination. **27.** a short downward plunge of an aeroplane or the like. **28.** *Colloq.* a short swim. **29.** a candle made by repeatedly dipping a wick into melted tallow. **30.** *Gymnastics.* an exercise on parallel bars in which a person bends his elbows until his chin is on a level with the bars, then elevates himself by straightening out his arms. **31.** Also, **dipper.** *Slang.* a pickpocket. [ME *dippe*(*n*), OE *dyppan*; akin to G *taufen* baptize, and DEEP]

—**Syn. 1.** DIP, IMMERSE, PLUNGE refer literally to putting something into water (or any liquid). To DIP is to put down into a liquid quickly or partially and lift out again: *to dip a finger into water to test the temperature.* IMMERSE denotes a gradual lowering into a liquid until covered by it, sometimes for a moment only (as in one mode of baptism): *to immerse meat in salt water.* PLUNGE adds a suggestion of force or suddenness to the action of dipping: *to plunge a chicken into boiling water before stripping off the feathers.*

dipartite (dī päʹtīt), *adj.* divided into several parts.

dip circle, an instrument for measuring dip (def. 26); consisting of a magnetized needle mounted on a horizontal axis, the angle being measured on a circular scale calibrated in degrees.

dipetalous (dī pĕtʹə ləs), *adj. Bot.* bipetalous.

diphase (dīʹfāzʹ), *adj. Elect.* having two phases. Also, **diphasic** (dī fāʹzĭk).

diphenyl (dī fēnʹĭl, -fĕʹnĭl), *n. Chem.* biphenyl.

diphenylamine (dī fēnʹĭl ə mēnʹ, -ămʹĭn, -fēʹnĭl-), *n. Chem.* an aromatic crystalline benzene derivative, $(C_6H_5)_2$-NH, used in the preparation of various dyes, as a reagent for oxidizing agents, and as a stabilizer in nitrocellulose propellants.

diphosgene (dī fŏsʹjēn), *n. Chem.* a poison gas, ClCOO-CCl_3, used in World War I.

diphtheria (dĭf thĭəʹrĭ ə), *n. Pathol.* a febrile infectious disease caused by a specific bacillus and characterized by the formation of a false membrane in the air passages, esp. the throat. [NL, f. s. Gk *diphthéra* skin, leather + *-ia*, noun suffix]

diphtheritic (dĭfʹthə rĭtʹĭk), *adj. Pathol.* **1.** pertaining to diphtheria. 2. affected by diphtheria. Also, **diphtherial** (dĭf thĭə′rĭ əl), **diphtheric** (dĭf thĕ′rĭk).

diphtheroid (dĭf′thə roid′), *adj. Pathol.* resembling diphtheria.

diphthong (dĭf′thŏng), *n.* **1.** a composite speech sound made up of two vowels, one sonantal, the other consonantal, as *ei* in *vein*. **2.** a digraph or ligature representing a vowel, as *æ* or *œ*. [t. LL: s. *diphthongus*, t. Gk: m. *díphthongos*, lit., having two sounds] —**diphthon′gal,** *adj.*

diphthongize (dĭf′thŏng gīz′), *v.*, **-ized, -izing.** —*v.t.* **1.** to change into or pronounce as a diphthong. —*v.i.* **2.** to become a diphthong. Also, **diphthongise.** —**diph′thongiza′tion,** *n.*

diphyllous (dī fĭl′əs), *adj. Bot.* having two leaves.

diphyodont (dĭf′ĭ ō dŏnt′), *adj. Zool.* having two successive sets of teeth, as most mammals. [f. s. Gk *diphyḗs* double + -ODONT]

diplex (dī′plĕks), *adj.* denoting or pertaining to a system of telegraphic or radio communication for sending two messages simultaneously in the same direction over a single wire or communications channel. [f. DI-[1] + *-plex*, modelled on DUPLEX] —**di′plex′er,** *n.*

diplo-, a word element referring to pairs, doubles, as in *diplocardiac*. Also, before vowels, **dipl-.** [t. Gk, comb. form of *diplóos* twofold]

diplocardiac (dĭp′lō kä′dĭ ăk′), *adj. Zool.* pertaining to a condition whereby the right and left sides of the heart are somewhat or completely divided.

diplococcus (dĭp′lō kŏk′əs), *n.*, *pl.* **-cocci** (-kŏk′sī). *Bacteriol.* any of certain bacterial species whose organisms occur in pairs, as in *diplococcus pneumoniae*, etc. [NL. See DIPLO-, COCCUS]

diplodocus (dĭ plŏd′ə kəs), *n. Palaeontol.* any animal of the extinct genus *Diplodocus*, comprising gigantic dinosaurs of the upper Jurassic of western North America. [NL, f. *diplo-* DIPLO- + m. Gk *dokós* beam]

diploe (dĭp′lō ē′), *n. Anat.* the cancellate bony tissue between the hard inner and outer walls of the bones of the cranium. [t. Gk: a fold]

diploid (dĭp′loid), *adj.* **1.** double. **2.** *Biol.* having two similar complements of chromosomes. —*n.* **3.** *Biol.* an organism or cell with double the basic (haploid) number of chromosomes. **4.** *Crystall.* a solid belonging to the isometric system, with 24 trapezoidal planes.

diploma (dĭ plō′mə), *n.*, *pl.* **-mas,** *v.*, **-maed, -maing.** —*n.* **1.** a document as one stating a candidate's success in an examination or some other qualification, etc., usually of a lower standard or more specialized character than a degree. **2.** a public or official document. —*v.t.* **3.** to furnish with a diploma. [t. L, t. Gk: paper folded double, letter of recommendation, licence, etc.]

diplomacy (dĭ plō′mə sĭ), *n.*, *pl.* **-cies. 1.** the conduct by government officials of negotiations and other relations between states. **2.** the science of conducting such negotiations. **3.** skill in managing any negotiations; artful management. [t. F: m. *diplomatie* (with *t* pron. as *s*), der. *diplomate* diplomat]

diplomat (dĭp′lə măt′), *n.* one employed or skilled in diplomacy; a diplomatist.

diplomate (dĭp′lə māt′), *n.* one who has received a diploma; esp. a doctor, engineer, etc., who has been certified as a specialist by a board within his profession. [f. DIPLOM(A) + -ATE]

diplomatic (dĭp′lə măt′ĭk), *adj.* **1.** of, pertaining to, or engaged in diplomacy. **2.** skilled in diplomacy; tactful. **3.** of or pertaining to diplomatics. —**dip′lomat′ically,** *adv.*

—**Syn.** 2. DIPLOMATIC, POLITIC, TACTFUL imply ability to avoid offending others or hurting their feelings, esp. in situations where this is important. DIPLOMATIC suggests a smoothness and skill in handling others, usually in such a way as to attain one's own ends and yet avoid any unpleasantness or opposition: *by diplomatic conduct he avoided antagonizing anyone.* POLITIC emphasizes expediency or prudence in looking out for one's own interests, thus knowing how to treat people of different types and on different occasions: *a truth which it is not politic to insist on.* TACTFUL suggests a nice touch in the handling of delicate matters or situations, and, unlike the other two, often suggests a sincere desire not to hurt the feelings of others: *a tactful hint.* —**Ant.** 2. blunt, blundering, tactless.

diplomatic corps, the body of diplomats accredited to and resident at a court or capital. Also, **diplomatic body.**

diplomatic immunity, the immunity from local jurisdiction, taxation, etc., which is the privilege of official representatives of a foreign state.

diplomatics (dĭp′lə măt′ĭks), *n.* the phase of palaeography devoted to ancient documents.

diplomatist (dĭ plō′mə tĭst), *n.* **1.** a diplomat. **2.** one who is astute and tactful in any negotiation.

diplopia (dĭ plō′pyə), *n. Ophthalm.* a morbid condition of vision in which a single object appears double. [NL. See DIPL-, -OPIA] —**diplopic** (dĭ plŏp′ĭk), *adj.*

diplopod (dĭp′lə pŏd′), *adj.* **1.** of or pertaining to the *Diplopoda*, a class of arthropods having tracheae, consisting of the millipedes. —*n.* **2.** any member of the *Diplopoda*; a millipede. [f. DIPLO- + -POD]

diplosis (dĭ plō′sĭs), *n. Biol.* the doubling of the chromosome number by the union of the haploid sets in the union of gametes. [t. Gk: a doubling]

diplostemonous (dĭp′lō stē′mə nəs, -stĕm′ə-), *adj. Bot.* having two series of stamens, or twice as many stamens as petals.

dip needle, a dipping needle.

dipnoan (dĭp nō′ən), *adj.* **1.** belonging or pertaining to the *Dipnoi*, a class or group of fishes having both gills and lungs. —*n.* **2.** a dipnoan fish. [f. NL: s. *Dipnoi*, pl., genus type (t. Gk: m. *dípnoos* (sing.) having two breathing apertures) + -AN]

dipody (dĭp′ə dĭ), *n.*, *pl.* **-dies.** *Pros.* a group of two feet.

dipole (dī′pōl′), *n. Physics, Phys. Chem.* **1.** a pair of equal and opposite electric charges or magnetic poles, forces, etc., as on the surfaces of a body or in a molecule. **2.** a molecule having the effective centre of the positive and negative charges separated. —**dipo′lar,** *adj.*

dipper (dĭp′ə), *n.* **1.** one who or that which dips. **2.** a container with a handle, used to dip liquids. **3.** (*cap.*) *Chiefly U.S. Astron.* **a.** Also, **Big Dipper.** the Plough. **b.** Also, **Little Dipper.** a star group in Ursa Minor. **4.** any of various diving birds, esp. of the genus *Cinclus*, as *C. aquaticus*, the common European water ouzel. —**dipperful** (dĭp′ə fo͝ol′), *n.*

dipping needle, a simple form of dip circle. Also, **dip needle.**

dipsacaceous (dĭp′sə kā′shəs), *adj.* belonging to the *Dipsacaceae*, or teasel family of plants. [f. s. NL *Dipsacus*, typical genus (t. Gk: m. *dípsakos* teasel) + ACEOUS]

dipso (dĭp′sō), *Colloq.* —*n.* **1.** a dipsomaniac. —*adj.* **2.** dipsomaniacal.

dipsomania (dĭp′sō mā′nyə), *n.* an irresistible, generally periodic, craving for intoxicating drink. [NL, f. Gk: *dípso(s)* thirst + *mania* MANIA]

dipsomaniac (dĭp′sō mā′nĭ ăk′), *n.* one who suffers from an irresistible and insatiable craving for intoxicants. —**dipsomaniacal** (dĭp′sō mə nī′ə kl), *adj.* —**Syn.** See **drunkard.**

dip stick, a stick or rod inserted into a tank or motor-car sump to measure the level of liquid which it contains.

dipteral (dĭp′tə rəl), *adj.* **1.** *Archit.* having two rows of columns on all sides. **2.** *Biol.* dipterous.

dipteran (dĭp′tə rən), *adj.* **1.** dipterous. —*n.* **2.** a dipterous insect.

dipterocarpaceous (dĭp′tə rō kä pā′shəs), *adj.* belonging to the *Dipterocarpaceae*, a family of trees, chiefly of tropical Asia.

dipterous (dĭp′tə rəs), *adj.* **1.** *Entomol.* belonging or pertaining to the order *Diptera*, that includes the common houseflies, gnats, mosquitoes, etc., characterized typically by a single pair of membranous wings. **2.** *Bot.* having two winglike appendages, as seeds, stems, etc. [t. NL: m. *dīpterus* two-winged, t. Gk: m. *dípteros*]

diptych (dĭp′tĭk), *n.* **1.** a hinged two-leaved tablet used by the ancients for writing on with the stylus. **2.** a pair of pictures or carvings on two panels hinged together. [t. LL: s. *diptycha*, neut. pl., double-folded, t. Gk]

Dirac (dĭ răk′), *n.* **Paul Adrien Maurice** (pôl′ā′drĭ ən mŏ′rĭs), born 1902, English physicist.

dirdum (dĭə′dəm, dû′-), *n. Scot. and N Dial.* blame.

dire (dī′ə), *adj.*, **direr, direst.** causing or attended with great fear or suffering; dreadful; awful: *a dire calamity.* [t. L: m. s. *dīrus*] —**dire′ly,** *adv.* —**dire′ness,** *n.*

direct (dĭ rĕkt′, dī-), *v.t.* **1.** to guide with advice; regulate the course of; conduct; manage; control. **2.** to give authoritative instructions to; command; order or ordain (something): *I directed him to do it, or that he do it.* **3.** to tell or show (a person) the way to a place, etc. **4.** to organize and supervise the artistic production of a play or film. **5.** to point or aim towards a place or an object; cause to move, act, or work towards a certain object or end. **6.** to address (words, etc.) to a person. **7.** to mark (a letter, etc.) as intended for or sent to a particular person. —*v.i.* **8.** to act as a guide or director. **9.** to give commands or orders. —*adj.* **10.** proceeding in a straight line or by the shortest course; straight; undeviating; not oblique. **11.** proceeding in an unbroken line of descent; lineal, not collateral. **12.** following the natural order, as in mathematics. **13.** without intervening agency; immediate; personal. **14.** going straight to the point; straightforward; downright. **15.** absolute; exact: *the direct contrary.* **16.** *Gram.* (of quotation or speech) consisting exactly of the words originally used (opposed to *reported*). Example: *He said 'I am coming'.* **17.** *Govt.* of or by action of voters, which takes effect without any intervening agency such as representatives. **18.** *Elect.* of or pertaining to direct current. **19.** *Astron.* **a.** moving in an orbit in the same direction as the earth in its revolution round the sun. **b.** appearing to move in the zodiac according to the natural order of the signs, or from west to east (opposed to *retrograde*). **20.** *Dyeing.* working without the use of a mordant; substantive. *—adv.* **21.** in a direct manner; directly; straight. [ME *direct(en)*, t. L: s. *dīrectus*, pp.] **—direct′ness,** *n.*

—Syn. 1. See **guide. 2.** DIRECT, ORDER, COMMAND mean to issue instructions. DIRECT suggests also giving explanations or advice; the emphasis is not on the authority of the director, but on steps necessary for the accomplishing of a purpose. ORDER connotes a personal relationship, in which one in a superior position imperatively instructs a subordinate (or subordinates) to do something. COMMAND, less personal and, often, less specific in detail suggests greater formality; and, sometimes, a more fixed authority on the part of the superior. **13.** DIRECT, IMMEDIATE imply relationships which are readily observed. A DIRECT result is one which is easily traceable to its cause or causes; there may be a number of steps in between, but the line from one to another is unbroken, simple, and quite evident. An IMMEDIATE result is one in which there is no medium or step (or practically none) intervening between cause and result; these are consecutive or side by side, so that it is possible to pass at once from one to the other. **—Ant. 14.** devious.

direct action, any method of directly pitting the strength of organized workers or any other large group against employers or capitalists or government, as by strikes, picketing, sabotage, working strictly to rule, civil disobedience, etc. **—direct-actionist** (dĭ rĕkt′ăk′shə nĭst), *n.*

direct carving, *Sculpture.* the art of carving directly in stone or wood without a finished model as a guide or template.

direct current, *Elect.* a relatively steady current in one direction in a circuit; a continuous stream of electrons through a conductor. Cf. **alternating current.**

direct evidence, evidence of a witness who testifies to the truth of the fact to be proved (contrasted with *circumstantial evidence*).

direct-grant school (dĭ rĕkt′ gränt′, dī-), (in Great Britain) a private school which receives money from the Ministry of Education on the understanding that it accepts a certain number of pupils without fee.

direct heating, the heating of a room by means of a heat source within that room.

direction (dĭ rĕk′shən, dī-), *n.* **1.** the act of directing, pointing, aiming, etc. **2.** the line along which anything lies, faces, moves, etc., with reference to the point or region towards which it is directed. **3.** the point or region itself. **4.** a line of action, tendency, etc. **5.** guidance; instruction. **6.** order; command. **7.** management; control. **8.** a directorate. **9.** the superscription on a letter, etc., giving the name and address of the intended recipient. **10.** *Theat.* decisions in a stage or film production as to stage business, speaking of lines, lighting, and general presentation. **11.** *Music.* a symbol or phrase in a score which indicates the correct tempo, style of performance, mood, etc. **—Syn. 4.** See **tendency.**

directional (dĭ rĕk′shə nəl, dī-), *adj.* **1.** of or pertaining to direction in space. **2.** *Radio.* adapted for determining the direction of signals received, or for transmitting signals in a given direction: *a directional antenna.*

direction-finder (dĭ rĕk′shən fīn′də), *n.* *Radio.* a contrivance on a receiver usually based on a loop antenna rotating on a vertical axis, which ascertains the direction of incoming radio waves.

directive (dĭ rĕk′tĭv, dī-), *adj.* **1.** serving to direct; directing. *—n.* **2.** an authoritative instruction or direction.

direct labour, the direct employment of labour in the building industry by the promoter of the work instead of through a contractor.

directly (dĭ rĕkt′lĭ, dī-), *adv.* **1.** in a direct line, way, or manner; straight. **2.** without delay; immediately. **3.** presently. **4.** absolutely; exactly; precisely. *—conj.* **5.** as soon as: *directly he arrived, he mentioned the subject.* **—Syn. 2.** See **immediately.**

direct method, a method of teaching a foreign language without reference to the learner's native tongue.

direct object, (in English and some other languages) the person or thing upon which the action of the verb is expended or towards which it is directed, in English expressed by a noun or pronoun without a preposition and generally coming after the verb. Example: *he hit the horse* has *the horse* as the direct object.

Directoire (*Fr.* dē rĕk twȧr′), *n.* **1.** *French Hist.* the French Directory. See **Directory.** *—adj.* **2.** (of costume) in the style of the period of the French Directory.

director (dĭ rĕk′tə, dī-), *n.* **1.** one who or that which directs. **2.** *Com.* one of a body of persons chosen to control or govern the affairs of a company or corporation. **3.** the manager of the interpretative aspects of a stage or film production who supervises such elements as the acting, photography, etc. **4.** *Mil.* a device used in field-gunnery for measuring angles in the horizontal and vertical planes. **—direc′torship′,** *n.* **—directress** (dĭ rĕk′trĭs, dī-), **direc′trix,** *n. fem.*

directorate (dĭ rĕk′tə rĭt, dī-), *n.* **1.** the office of a director. **2.** a body of directors.

directorial (dĭ rĕk′tô′rĭ əl, dī′rĕk-), *adj.* pertaining to a director or directorate.

Director of Public Prosecutions. See **Public Prosecutor.**

directory (dĭ rĕk′tə rĭ, -trĭ), *n., pl.* **-ries,** *adj.* *—n.* **1.** a book or the like containing an alphabetical list of the names and addresses of people in a city, district, building, etc., or of a particular class of persons, etc. **2.** a book containing an alphabetical list of telephone subscribers and their numbers. **3.** a book of directions. **4. the Directory,** *French Hist.* the body of five directors forming the executives of France from 1795 to 1799. *—adj.* **5.** serving to direct; directing. [(defs 1, 2, 3, 5) t. L: m. s. *dīrectōrius* that directs (ML *dīrectōrium*, n.); (def. 4) t. F: m. *Directoire*, t. L, etc.]

directrix (dĭ rĕk′trĭks, dī-), *n., pl.* **directrices** (dĭ rĕk′trĭ sēz′, dī-). **1.** *Maths.* a fixed line used in the description of a curve or surface. See diag. under **parabola. 2.** a directress. [t. NL]

direct tax, *Govt.* a tax demanded from the very persons who will bear the burden of it (not reimbursing themselves at the expense of others), as a selective employment tax or an income tax.

direct wave, *Radio.* ground wave. Also, **direct ray.**

Dire-Dawa (dī′rĭ dou′ə), *n.* a town in E Ethiopia. 30,000 (est. 1962).

direful (dī′ə fo͝ol), *adj.* dreadful; awful; terrible. **—dire′fully,** *adv.* **—dire′fulness,** *n.*

direttissimo (dĭ′rĭ tĭs′ĭ mō′), *n.* *Mountaineering.* a straight or nearly straight route up a mountain face, regardless of difficulty. [It: most direct]

dirge (dûj), *n.* **1.** a funeral song or tune, or one expressing mourning. **2.** *Eccles.* the office of the dead, or the funeral service as sung. [t. L, syncopated var. of *dīrige* (impv. of *dīrigere* direct), first word of the antiphon sung in the L office of the dead]

dirhem (dīə hĕm′), *n.* **1.** an ancient silver coin of the Arabs and others, usually equal to $\frac{1}{10}$ dinar. **2.** Also, **dirham.** the unit of Moroccan currency, equal to 100 francs, and equivalent to about £0·0823. **3.** a silver or nickel coin of this value. *Abbrev.:* Dh.

dirigible (dĭ rĭj′ĭ bl), *n.* **1.** an airship. *—adj.* **2.** that may be controlled, directed, or steered. [f. s. L *dīrigere* DIRECT, v. + -IBLE]

diriment (dĭ′rĭ mənt), *adj.* **1.** that renders absolutely void; nullifying. **2.** *Rom. Cath. Ch.* rendering marriage null and void from the very beginning. [t. L: s. *dirimens*, ppr., separating, breaking off]

dirk (dûk), *n.* **1.** a stabbing weapon; a dagger, esp. as used in the Highlands of Scotland. *—v.t.* **2.** to stab with a dirk. [orig. unknown]

dirl (dīəl, dûl), *v.i.* *Scot.* to vibrate; shake.

dirndl (dûn′dl), *n.* **1.** a type of woman's dress with full skirt and close-fitting bodice, commonly of colourful and strikingly patterned material, derived from Tyrolean peasant use. **2.** a skirt in such a style. [t. d. G: girl]

dirt (dût), *n.* **1.** any foul or filthy substance, as dust, excrement, mud, etc. **2.** *Dial.* earth or soil, esp. when loose. **3.** something vile, mean, or worthless. **4.** moral filth; vileness. **5.** abusive or scurrilous language. **6.** unsavoury or malicious gossip. **7.** *Mining.* **a.** crude broken ore or waste. **b.** (in placer mining) the material from which the gold is separated by washing. **8. do (someone) dirt,** *Colloq.* to behave unfairly or wrongly towards (someone). **9. eat dirt,** to accept insult without complaint. *—adj.* **10.** consisting of dirt: *a dirt road.* [metathetic var. of ME *drit*, t. Scand.; cf. Icel. *drit* excrement]

dirt-cheap (dût′chēp′), *adj.* very inexpensive.

dirt track, an oval or circular track surfaced with cinders, used for motor-cycle speedway racing.

dirty (dû′tĭ), *adj.*, **dirtier, dirtiest,** *v.* **dirtied, dirtying.** *—adj.* **1.** soiled with dirt; foul; unclean. **2.** imparting dirt; soiling. **3.** vile; mean. **4.** morally unclean; indecent. **5.** *Sport.* characterized by rough, unfair play, frequent fouls, etc. **6.** (of devices capable of producing nuclear reactions) having the quality of generating unwanted radioactive by-products: *a dirty bomb.* **7.** stormy; squally, as the weather: *it looks dirty to windward.* **8.** appearing as if soiled; dark-coloured; dingy. *—v.t., v.i.* **9.** to make or become dirty. *—n.* **10. do the dirty on,** *Colloq.* to behave unfairly or wrongly towards. **—dirt′ily,** *adv.* **—dirt′iness,** *n.*

—Syn. 1. DIRTY, FILTHY, FOUL, SQUALID refer to that which is not clean. DIRTY is applied to that which is filled or covered with dirt so that it is unclean or defiled: *dirty streets, dirty clothes.* FILTHY is an emphatic word suggesting that which is offensively defiled or is excessively soiled or dirty: *a filthy hovel.* FOUL implies an uncleanness that is grossly offensive to the senses: *a foul smell.* SQUALID, applied usually to dwellings or surroundings, implies dirtiness that results from the slovenly indifference often associated with poverty: *a whole family living in one squalid room.* **4.** obscene, nasty.

Dis (dĭs), *n. Rom. Myth.* **1.** the god of the lower world, Pluto. **2.** the infernal world.

dis-[1], a prefix of Latin origin meaning 'apart', 'asunder', 'away', 'utterly', or having a privative, negative, or reversing force (see **de-** and **un-**[2]), used freely, esp. with these latter significations, as an English formative, as in *disability, disaffirm, disbar, disbelief, discontent, disentangle, dishearten, disinfect, dislike, disown, disrelish.* Also, **di-**. [t. L (akin to L *bis*, Gk *dis* twice); before *f*, *dif-*; before some consonants, *di-*; often r. obs. *des-*, t. OF]

dis-[2], var. of **di-**[1], as in *dissyllable.*

disability (dĭs′ə bĭl′ĭ tĭ), *n., pl.* **-ties. 1.** lack of competent power, strength, or physical or mental ability; incapacity. **2.** to make legally incapable; disqualify. **—disa′blement,**

—Syn. 1. DISABILITY, INABILITY imply a lack of power or ability. A DISABILITY is some disqualifying deprivation or loss of power, physical or other: *excused drill because of a physical disability; a temporary disability.* INABILITY is a want of ability, usually because of an inherent lack of talent, power, etc.: *inability to sing.*

disability clause, *Life Assurance.* a clause whereby a policy belonging to a totally and permanently disabled policyholder remains in full force and effect without payment of additional premiums, often providing for periodic payment of money to the assured during the period of disability.

disable (dĭs ā′bl), *v.t.*, **-bled, -bling. 1.** to make unable; weaken or destroy the capability of; cripple; incapacitate. **2.** to make legally incapable; disqualify. **—disa′blement,** *n.* **—Syn. 1.** See **cripple.**

disabuse (dĭs′ə byōōz′), *v.t.*, **-bused, -busing.** to free from deception or error; set right. [f. DIS-[1] + ABUSE, v.]

disaccharide (dī săk′ə rīd′, -rĭd), *n. Chem.* any of a group of carbohydrates, as sucrose or lactose, which hydrolyse into two simple sugars (monosaccharides). [f. DI-[1] + SACCHARIDE]

disaccord (dĭs′ə kôd′), *v.i.* **1.** to disagree. **—***n.* **2.** disagreement.

disaccredit (dĭs′ə krĕd′ĭt), *v.t.* take away the credentials of; cause to be no longer authorized.

disaccustom (dĭs′ə kŭs′təm), *v.t.* to cause to lose a habit.

disadvantage (dĭs′əd vän′tĭj), *n., v.*, **-taged, -taging. —***n.* **1.** absence or deprivation of advantage; any unfavourable circumstance or condition. **2.** injury to interest, reputation, credit, profit, etc.; loss. **—***v.t.* **3.** to subject to disadvantage. **—Syn. 1.** drawback, inconvenience, hindrance. **2.** detriment, hurt, harm, damage.

disadvantageous (dĭs ăd′vän tā′jəs, dĭs′ăd-), *adj.* attended with disadvantage; unfavourable; detrimental. **—disad′vanta′geously,** *adv.* **—disad′vanta′geousness,** *n.*

disaffect (dĭs′ə fĕkt′), *v.t.* to alienate the affection of; make ill-affected, discontented, or disloyal.

disaffection (dĭs′ə fĕk′shən), *n.* absence or alienation of affection or goodwill; estrangement; disloyalty.

disaffirm (dĭs′ə fûm′), *v.t.* **1.** to deny; contradict. **2.** *Law.* to annul; reverse; repudiate. **—dis′affirm′ance, disaffirmation** (dĭs′ăf ə mā′shən, dĭs ăf′ə-), *n.*

disafforest (dĭs′ə fŏ′rĭst), *v.t.* **1.** to reduce from the legal status of a forest to that of common land. **2.** to strip of forests. [t. ML: s. *disafforestāre*] **—dis′affor′esta′tion, dis′affor′estment,** *n.*

disagree (dĭs′ə grē′), *v.i.*, **-greed, -greeing. 1.** to fail to agree; differ (fol. by *with*): *the conclusions disagree with the facts.* **2.** to differ in opinion; dissent. **3.** to quarrel. **4.** to conflict in action or effect: *food that disagrees with one.*

disagreeable (dĭs′ə grĭə′bl), *adj.* **1.** contrary to one's taste or liking; unpleasant; offensive; repugnant. **2.** unpleasant in manner or nature; unamiable. **—dis′agree′ableness,** *n.* **—dis′agree′ably,** *adv.*

disagreement (dĭs′ə grē′mənt), *n.* **1.** the act, state, or fact of disagreeing. **2.** lack of agreement; diversity; unlikeness. **3.** difference of opinion; dissent. **4.** dissension; quarrel. **5.** unwholesome action or effect, as of food.

disallow (dĭs′ə lou′), *v.t.* **1.** to refuse to allow. **2.** to refuse to admit the truth or validity of. **—dis′allow′able,** *adj.* **—dis′allow′ance,** *n.*

disannul (dĭs′ə nŭl′), *v.t.*, **-nulled, -nulling.** to annul utterly; make void. [f. DIS-[1] (intensive) + ANNUL] **—dis′annul′ment,** *n.*

disanoint (dĭs′ə noint′), *v.t.* to invalidate the consecration of.

disappear (dĭs′ə pĭə′), *v.i.* **1.** to cease to appear or be seen; vanish from sight. **2.** to cease to exist or be known; pass away; end gradually. **3.** *Colloq.* to go away; depart. **—Syn. 1.** DISAPPEAR, FADE, VANISH suggest that something passes from sight. DISAPPEAR is used of whatever suddenly or gradually goes out of sight: *we watched him turn down a side street and then disappear.* FADE suggests a (complete or partial) disappearance that proceeds gradually and often by means of a blending into something else: *colours in the sky at sunrise quickly fade.* VANISH suggests complete, generally rapid, and often mysterious disappearance: *a mirage can vanish as suddenly as it appeared.*

disappearance (dĭs′ə pĭə′rəns), *n.* the act of disappearing; a ceasing to appear or to exist.

disappoint (dĭs′ə point′), *v.t.* **1.** to fail to fulfil the expectations or wishes of (a person): *his conduct disappointed us.* **2.** to defeat the fulfilment of (hopes, plans, etc.); thwart; frustrate. [t. OF: m. *desappointer*, f. *des-* DIS-[1] + *appointer* APPOINT] **—dis′appoint′er,** *n.* **—dis′appoint′ingly,** *adv.*

disappointment (dĭs′ə point′mənt), *n.* **1.** the act or fact of disappointing: *he has lost hope because of frequent disappointments.* **2.** state or feeling of being disappointed: *great was his disappointment.* **3.** something that disappoints: *the play was a disappointment.* **—Syn. 1.** failure, defeat, frustration. **2.** mortification, frustration.

Disappointment (dĭs′ə point′mənt), *n.* **Lake,** a salt lake in central Western Australia lying across the Tropic of Capricorn. ab. 100 sq. mi.

disapprobation (dĭs′ăp rō bā′shən), *n.* disapproval. **—dis′appro′bative,** *adj.* **—dis′appro′batory,** *adj.*

disapproval (dĭs′ə prōō′vəl), *n.* the act or state of disapproving; a condemnatory feeling or utterance; censure. **—Syn.** disapprobation, dislike, condemnation.

disapprove (dĭs′ə prōōv′), *v.*, **-proved, -proving. —***v.t.* **1.** to think wrong or reprehensible; censure or condemn in opinion. **2.** to withhold approval from; decline to sanction: *the court disapproved the verdict.* **—***v.i.* **3.** to have an unfavourable opinion (fol. by *of*). **—dis′approv′er,** *n.* **—dis′approv′ingly,** *adv.* **—Ant. 1.** praise.

disarm (dĭs äm′), *v.t.* **1.** to deprive of arms. **2.** to deprive of means of attack or defence. **3.** to divest of hostility, suspicion, etc.; make friendly. **—***v.i.* **4.** to lay down arms. **5.** (of a country) to reduce or limit the size, equipment, armament, etc., of the army, navy, or air forces. [t. OF: m. s. *desarmer*, f. *des-* DIS-[1] + *armer* ARM[2]] **—disarm′er,** *n.*

disarmament (dĭs ä′mə mənt), *n.* **1.** the act of disarming. **2.** the state of being disarmed, as in fencing. **3.** the reduction or limitation of the size, equipment, armament, etc., of the army, navy, or air forces.

disarming (dĭs ä′mĭng), *adj.* removing or likely to remove antagonism, suspicion, or the like. **—disarm′ingly,** *adv.*

disarrange (dĭs′ə rānj′), *v.t.*, **-ranged, -ranging.** to disturb the arrangement of; disorder; unsettle. **—dis′arrange′ment,** *n.* **—dis′arrang′er,** *n.*

disarray (dĭs′ə rā′), *v.t.* **1.** to put out of array or order; throw into disorder. **2.** to undress. **—***n.* **3.** disorder; confusion. **4.** disorder of apparel; disorderly dress.

disarthria (dĭs ä′thrĭ ə), *n. Pathol.* a disease of the central nervous system, causing difficulty in articulating words.

disarticulate (dĭs′ä tĭk′yōō lāt′), *v.t., v.i.*, **-lated, -lating.** to take or come apart at the joints. **—dis′artic′ula′tion,** *n.* **—dis′artic′ula′tor,** *n.*

disassemble (dĭs′ə sĕm′bl), *v.t.*, **-bled, -bling.** to take apart.

disassembly (dĭs′ə sĕm′blĭ), *n.* **1.** the act of disassembling. **2.** state of being disassembled.

disassociate (dĭs′ə sō′shĭ āt′), *v.t.*, **-ated, -ating.** to dissociate. **—dis′asso′cia′tion,** *n.*

disaster (dĭ zäs′tə), *n.* **1.** any unfortunate event; esp. a sudden or great misfortune. **2.** *Obs.* an unfavourable aspect of a star or planet. [t. It.: m. *disastro*, der. *disastrato* not having a (lucky) star, f. *dis-* DIS-[1] + *astr(o)* star + *-ato*, prop., ppl. ending]

—Syn. 1. mischance, misfortune, misadventure, blow, reverse. DISASTER, CALAMITY, CATASTROPHE refer to adverse happenings occurring often suddenly and unexpectedly. A DISASTER may be caused by carelessness, negligence, bad judgement, and the like; or by natural forces, as a hurricane, flood, etc.: *a railway disaster.* CALAMITY suggests great affliction, either personal or general; the emphasis is on the grief or sorrow caused: *the calamity of losing a dear child.* CATASTROPHE refers esp. to the tragic outcome of a personal or a public situation; the emphasis is on the destruction or irreplaceable loss: *the catastrophe of a defeat in battle.*

disastrous (dĭ zäs′trəs), *adj.* **1.** causing great distress or injury; ruinous; unfortunate; calamitous. **2.** *Archaic.* foreboding disaster. **—disas′trously,** *adv.* **—disas′trousness,** *n.*

disavow (dĭs′ə vou′), *v.t.* to disclaim knowledge of, connection with, or responsibility for; disown; repudiate. [ME *desavoue(n)*, t. OF: m. *desavouer*, f. *des-* DIS-[1] + *avouer* AVOW] **—dis′avow′er,** *n.*

disavowal (dĭs′ə vou′əl), *n.* a disowning; repudiation; denial.

disband (dĭs bănd′), *v.t.* **1.** to break up or disorganize (a band or company); dissolve (a military force) by dismissing from service. —*v.i.* **2.** to break up, as a band or company. [t. MF: m. *desbander*, f. *des-* DIS-[1] + *bander* tie] —**disband′ment,** *n.* —**Syn. 1.** demobilize, dissolve, disperse.

disbar (dĭs bä′), *v.t.*, **-barred, -barring.** *Law.* to expel from the legal profession or from the bar. [f. DIS-[1] + BAR[1]] —**disbar′ment,** *n.*

disbosom (dĭs bo͝oz′əm), *v.t. Archaic.* to make known; reveal; confess.

disbranch (dĭs bränch′), *v.t.* **1.** to deprive of branches, as a tree. **2.** to cut or break off, as a branch.

disbud (dĭs bŭd′), *v.t.*, **-budded, -budding.** to remove leaf or flower buds from (a plant, etc.), to improve the quality or shape of what remains.

disburden (dĭs bû′dn), *v.t.* **1.** to remove a burden from; rid of a burden. **2.** to relieve of anything oppressive or annoying. **3.** to get rid of (a burden); discharge. —*v.i.* **4.** to unload a burden. —**disbur′denment,** *n.*

disburse (dĭs bûs′), *v.t.*, **-bursed, -bursing.** to pay out (money); expend. [t. OF: m. *desbourser*, f. *des-* DIS-[1] + *bourse* purse (g. LL *bursa.* See BURSA)] —**disburs′able,** *adj.* —**disburs′er,** *n.* —**Syn.** See **spend.**

disbursement (dĭs bûs′mənt), *n.* **1.** the act of disbursing. **2.** that which is disbursed; money expended.

disburthen (dĭs bû′t͟hən), *v.t., v.i. Archaic.* to disburden.

disc (dĭsk), *n.* **1.** any thin, flat, circular plate or object. **2.** a round, flat area. **3.** the apparently flat surface of the sun, etc. **4.** a gramophone record. **5.** a disc brake. **6.** *Archaic.* a discus. **7.** *Bot., Zool., etc.* any of various roundish, flat structures or parts. **8.** *Bot.* (in the daisy and other composite plants) the central portion of the flower head, composed of tubular florets. **9.** *Anat., Zool.* **a. interarticular disc,** a plate of cartilage interposed between the articulating ends of bones. **b. intervertebral disc,** the plate of fibrocartilage interposed between the bodies of adjacent vertebrae. —*v.t.* **10.** to prepare (soil) with a disc harrow. Also, *Chiefly U.S.*, **disk.** [t. L: s. *discus* DISCUS] —**dis′cal,** *adj.* —**disc′like′,** *adj.*

disc., 1. discount. 2. discovered.

discalced (dĭs kălst′), *adj.* without shoes; unshod; barefooted: specif. applied to a branch of the Carmelite monks known as **Discalceati** (the barefooted). Also, **discalceate** (dĭs kăl′sĭ ĭt, -āt′).

discant (*n.* dĭs′kănt; *v.* dĭs kănt′), *n., v.i., v.t.* descant.

discard (*v.* dĭs käd′; *n.* dĭs′käd′), *v.t.* **1.** to cast aside; reject; dismiss, esp. from use. **2.** *Cards.* **a.** to throw out (a card or cards) from one's hand. **b.** to play (a card, not a trump, of a different suit from that of the card led). —*v.i.* **3.** *Cards.* to discard a card or cards. —*n.* **4.** the act of discarding. **5.** one who or that which is cast out or rejected. **6.** *Cards.* the card or cards discarded. —**discard′er,** *n.* —**Syn. 1.** See **reject.** —**Ant. 1.** retain.

discase (dĭs kās′), *v.t.*, **-cased, -casing.** to take the case or covering from; uncase.

disc brake, a brake, commonly used on the road wheels of motor cars and the landing wheels of aircraft, in which friction is obtained by the action of pads on a flat disc attached to the rotating part to be slowed down.

discept (dĭ sĕpt′), *v.i.* to dispute. [t. L: s. *disceptāre* contend] —**dis′cepta′tion,** *n.*

discern (dĭ sûn′), *v.t.* **1.** to perceive by the sight or some other sense or by the intellect; see, recognize, or apprehend clearly. **2.** to distinguish mentally; recognize as distinct or different; discriminate: *he discerns good and bad, good from bad.* —*v.i.* **3.** to distinguish or discriminate. [ME *discerne(n)*, t. F: m. *discerner*, t. L: m. *discernere*] —**discern′er,** *n.* —**Syn. 1.** See **notice.**

discernible (dĭ sû′nə bl), *adj.* capable of being discerned; distinguishable. —**discern′ibleness,** *n.* —**discern′ibly,** *adv.*

discerning (dĭ sû′nĭng), *adj.* showing discernment; discriminating. —**discern′ingly,** *adv.*

discernment (dĭ sûn′mənt), *n.* **1.** faculty of discerning; discrimination; acuteness of judgement. **2.** the act of discerning.

discharge (dĭs chäj′; *n. also* dĭs′chäj′), *v.*, **-charged, -charging,** *n.* —*v.t.* **1.** to relieve of a charge or load; unload (a ship, etc.). **2.** to remove, send forth, or get rid of (a charge, lead, etc.). **3.** to fire; shoot: *discharge a gun, bow, bullet, etc.* **4.** to pour forth, as water. **5.** to relieve oneself of (an obligation, etc.). **6.** to relieve of obligation, responsibility, etc. **7.** to fulfil, perform, or execute (a duty, function, etc.). **8.** to relieve or deprive of office, employment, etc.; dismiss from service. **9.** to send away or allow to go (fol. by *from*). **10.** to pay (a debt). **11.** *Law.* to release, as bail or a defendant. **12.** *Elect.* to rid (something) of a charge of electricity. **13.** *Dyeing.* to free from a dye, as by chemical bleaching. —*v.i.* **14.** to get rid of a burden or load. **15.** to deliver a charge or load. **16.** to come or pour forth. **17.** to blur; run. **18.** *Elect.* to lose, or give up, a charge of electricity. —*n.* **19.** the act of discharging a ship, load, etc. **20.** act of firing a missile weapon, as a bow by drawing and releasing the string, or a gun by exploding the charge of powder. **21.** a sending or coming forth, as of water from a pipe; ejection; emission. **22.** rate or amount of issue. **23.** something discharged or emitted. **24.** a relieving or ridding, or a getting rid, of something of the nature of a charge. **25.** *Law.* **a.** acquittal or exoneration. **b.** annulment, as of a court order. **c.** freeing of one held under legal process. **26.** a relieving or being relieved of obligation or liability; the fulfilling of an obligation. **27.** the payment of a debt. **28.** release or dismissal from office, employment, etc. **29.** a certificate of release, as from obligation or liability. **30.** *Elect.* **a.** the withdrawing or transference of an electric charge. **b.** the equalization of the difference of potential between two terminals or the like. [ME *descharge(n)*, t. OF: m. *deschargier.* See DIS-[1], CHARGE] —**discharge′able,** *adj.* —**discharg′er,** *n.* —**Syn. 4.** eject, expel, emit, exude. **6.** See **release. 7.** See **perform. 10.** settle, liquidate. **26.** fulfilment, execution, performance.

disc harrow, a harrow having a number of sharp-edged concave discs set at such an angle that as the machine is drawn along they pulverize and turn the soil, and destroy weeds.

disci-, a combining form of **disc.**

discifloral (dĭs′ĭ flô′rəl), *adj. Bot.* having flowers in which the receptacle is expanded into a conspicuous disc.

disciple (dĭ sī′pl), *n., v.*, **discipled, discipling.** —*n.* **1.** one of the twelve personal followers of Jesus Christ. **2.** any follower of Christ. **3.** an adherent of the doctrines of another; a follower. —*v.t.* **4.** *Archaic.* to convert into a disciple. **5.** *Obs.* to teach; train. [ME, t. OF, t. L: m. s. *discipulus*; r. ME *deciple*, t. OF; r. OE *discipul*, t. L (as above)] —**disci′pleship′,** *n.* —**Syn. 3.** See **pupil**[1].

Disciples of Christ, a denomination of Christians, founded in the U.S. in the early part of the 19th century by Alexander Campbell (1788–1866), which seeking the unity of all Christians, rejects all creeds, accepts the Bible as a sufficient rule of faith and practice, and administers baptism by immersion.

disciplinable (dĭs′ĭ plĭn′ə bl), *adj.* **1.** subject to or meriting correction. **2.** capable of being instructed.

disciplinal (dĭs′ĭ plī′nəl, dĭs′ĭ plĭ nəl), *adj.* of, pertaining to, or of the nature of discipline.

disciplinant (dĭs′ĭ plĭ nənt), *n.* **1.** one who subjects himself to discipline. **2.** (*cap.*) *Eccles.* a member of a former Spanish religious order who scourged themselves publicly and inflicted upon themselves other severe tortures.

disciplinarian (dĭs′ĭ plĭ nĕə′rĭ ən), *n.* **1.** one who enforces or advocates discipline. —*adj.* **2.** disciplinary.

disciplinary (dĭs′ĭ plĭn′ə rĭ), *adj.* of or for discipline; promoting discipline.

discipline (dĭs′ĭ plĭn), *n., v.*, **-plined, -plining.** —*n.* **1.** training to act in accordance with rules; drill: *military discipline.* **2.** instruction and exercise designed to train to proper conduct or action. **3.** punishment inflicted by way of correction and training. **4.** the training effect of experience, adversity, etc. **5.** subjection to rules of conduct of behaviour; a state of order maintained by training and control: *good discipline in an army.* **6.** a set or system of rules and regulations. **7.** *Eccles.* the system of government regulating the practice of a church as distinguished from its doctrine. **8.** a branch of instruction or learning. —*v.t.* **9.** to train by instruction and exercise; drill. **10.** to bring to a state of order and obedience by training and control. **11.** to subject to discipline or punishment; correct; chastise. [ME, t. L: m. *disciplīna* instruction] —**dis′cipliner,** *n.* —**Syn. 11.** See **punish.**

disc jockey, one who comperes radio or television programmes of gramophone records.

disclaim (dĭs klām′), *v.t.* **1.** to repudiate or deny interest in or connection with; disavow; disown: *disclaiming all participation.* **2.** *Law.* to renounce a claim or right to. **3.** to reject the claims or authority of. —*v.i.* **4.** *Law.* to renounce or repudiate a legal claim or right. **5.** *Obs.* to disavow interest. [t. AF: s. *disclaimer*, *desclamer*, f. *des-* DIS-[1] + *clamer* CLAIM]

disclaimer (dĭs klā′mə), *n.* **1.** the act of disclaiming; the renouncing, repudiating, or denying of a claim; disavowal. **2.** one who disclaims. [t. AF]

disclamation (dĭs′klə mā′shən), *n.* the act of disclaiming; renunciation; disavowal.

disclose (dĭs klōz′), *v.*, **-closed, -closing,** *n.* —*v.t.* **1.** to cause to appear; allow to be seen; make known; reveal: *to disclose a plot.* **2.** to uncover; lay open to view. **3.** *Obs.* to open up; unfold. —*n.* **4.** *Obs.* disclosure. [ME *disclose(n)*, *desclose(n)*, t. OF: m. *desclos-*, s. *desclore* unclose,

f. *des-* DIS-[1] + *clore* (g. L *claudere* CLOSE)] —**disclos′er,** *n.* —**Syn. 1.** See **reveal.**

disclosure (dĭs klō′zhə), *n.* **1.** the act of disclosing; exposure; revelation. **2.** that which is disclosed; a revelation.

discobolus (dĭs kŏb′ə ləs), *n., pl.* **-li** (-lī′). *Class. Antiq.* a thrower of the discus. [t. L, t. Gk: m. *diskobólos*]

discoid (dĭs′koid), *adj.* **1.** having the form of a discus or disc; flat and circular. **2.** *Bot.* (of a composite flower) consisting of a disc only, without rays. —*n.* **3.** something in the form of a disc. [t. LL: s. *discoidēs*, t. Gk: m. *diskoeidēs*]

discoidal (dĭs koi′dl), *adj.* discoid.

discoloration (dĭs kŭl′ə rā′shən), *n.* **1.** the act or fact of discolouring. **2.** the state of being discoloured. **3.** a discoloured marking; a stain. Also, **discol′ourment.**

discolour (dĭs kŭl′ə), *v.t.* **1.** to change the colour of; spoil the colour of; stain. —*v.i.* **2.** to change colour; become faded or stained. Also, *U.S.*, **discol′or.** [ME *discolour(en)*, t. OF: m. *descolorer*, der. L: *dis-* DIS-[1] + *color* colour]

discomfit (dĭs kŭm′fĭt), *v.t.* **1.** to defeat utterly; rout. **2.** to frustrate the plans of; thwart; foil. **3.** to throw into perplexity and dejection; disconcert. —*n.* **4.** *Obs.* rout; defeat. [ME, t. OF: m. *desconfit*, pp. of *desconfire*, f. *des-* DIS-[1] + *confire* make, accomplish (g. L *conficere*)]

discomfiture (dĭs kŭm′fĭ chə), *n.* **1.** defeat in battle; rout. **2.** frustration of hopes or plans. **3.** disconcertion; confusion.

discomfort (dĭs kŭm′fət), *n.* **1.** absence of comfort or pleasure; uneasiness; disturbance of peace; pain. **2.** anything that disturbs the comfort. —*v.t.* **3.** to disturb the comfort or happiness of; make uncomfortable or uneasy. [ME *discomfort(en)*, t. OF: m. *desconforter*, f. *des-* DIS-[1] + *conforter* COMFORT]

discomfortable (dĭs kŭmf′tə bl), *adj. Archaic.* **1.** uncomfortable; uneasy. **2.** discomforting.

discommend (dĭs′kə mĕnd′), *v.t.* **1.** to express disapproval of. **2.** to bring into disfavour. —**dis′commend′able,** *adj.* —**discommendation** (dĭs′kŏ mĕn dā′shən), *n.* —**dis′commend′er,** *n.*

discommode (dĭs′kə mōd′), *v.t.*, **-moded, -moding.** to put to inconvenience; trouble; incommode. [f. DIS-[1] + m. s. L *commodāre* make fit]

discommodity (dĭs′kə mŏd′ĭ tĭ), *n., pl.* **-ties. 1.** inconvenience; disadvantageous. **2.** a source of inconvenience or trouble; disadvantage.

discommon (dĭs kŏm′ən), *v.t.* **1.** (at Oxford and Cambridge) to prohibit (a tradesman or townsman who has violated the regulations of the university) from dealing with the undergraduates. **2.** *Law.* to deprive of the character of a common, as by enclosing a piece of land. [f. DIS-[1] + obs. *common*, v., participate, associate]

discompose (dĭs′kəm pōz′), *v.t.*, **-posed, -posing. 1.** to bring into disorder; disarrange; unsettle. **2.** to disturb the composure of; agitate; perturb. —**dis′compos′edly,** *adv.* —**dis′compos′ingly,** *adv.*

discomposure (dĭs′kəm pō′zhə), *n.* the state of being discomposed; disorder; agitation; perturbation.

disconcert (dĭs′kən sût′), *v.t.* **1.** to disturb the self-possession of; confuse; perturb; ruffle. **2.** to throw into disorder or confusion; disarrange. —**dis′concert′ingly,** *adv.* —**dis′concer′tion, dis′concert′ment,** *n.* —**Syn. 1.** See **confuse.**

disconcerted (dĭs′kən sû′tĭd), *adj.* confused; abashed. —**dis′concert′edly,** *adv.* —**dis′concert′edness,** *n.*

disconformity (dĭs′kən fô′mĭ tĭ), *n., pl.* **-ties. 1.** the lack of conformity; refusal or failure to conform. **2.** *Geol.* the surface of a division between parallel rock strata, indicating interruption of sedimentation (a type of unconformity).

disconnect (dĭs′kə nĕkt′), *v.t.* to sever or interrupt the connection of or between; detach.

disconnected (dĭs′kə nĕk′tĭd), *adj.* **1.** disjointed; broken. **2.** incoherent. —**dis′connect′edly,** *adv.* —**dis′connect′edness,** *n.*

disconnection (dĭs′kə nĕk′shən), *n.* **1.** the act of disconnecting. **2.** the state of being disconnected; lack of union. Also, **dis′connex′ion.**

disconsolate (dĭs kŏn′sə lĭt), *adj.* **1.** without consolation or solace; unhappy; inconsolable. **2.** characterized by or causing discomfort; cheerless; gloomy. [t. ML: m. s. *disconsōlātus*, f. *dis-* DIS-[1] + L *consōlātus*, pp., having consoled] —**discon′solately,** *adv.* —**disconsolation** (dĭs kŏn′sə lā′shən), **discon′solateness,** *n.* —**Syn. 1.** See **desolate.**

discontent (dĭs′kən tĕnt′), *adj.* **1.** not content; dissatisfied; discontented. —*n.* **2.** Also, **dis′content′ment.** lack of content; dissatisfaction. **3.** *Archaic.* a malcontent. —*v.t.* **4.** to deprive of content; dissatisfy; displease. —**Syn. 2.** uneasiness, inquietude, restlessness, displeasure. See **dissatisfaction.**

discontented (dĭs′kən tĕn′tĭd), *adj.* uneasy in mind; dissatisfied; restlessly unhappy. —**dis′content′edly,** *adv.* —**dis′content′edness,** *n.*

discontinuance (dĭs′kən tĭn′yŏŏ əns), *n.* **1.** lack of continued connection or cohesion of parts; lack of union; disruption. **2.** *Law.* the termination of a suit by the act of the plaintiff, as by notice in writing, or by neglect to take the proper adjournments to keep it pending.

discontinuation (dĭs′kən tĭn′yŏŏ ā′shən), *n.* breach or interruption of continuity or unity.

discontinue (dĭs′kən tĭn′yŏŏ), *v.*, **-tinued, -tinuing.** —*v.t.* **1.** to cause to cease; put an end to. **2.** to cease to take, use, etc.: *to discontinue a newspaper.* **3.** *Law.* to terminate or abandon (a suit, etc). —*v.i.* **4.** to come to an end or stop; cease; desist. —**dis′contin′uer,** *n.* —**Syn. 1.** See **interrupt.** —**Ant. 1.** resume.

discontinuity (dĭs′kŏn tĭ nyōō′ĭ tĭ), *n.* lack of continuity, uninterrupted connection, or cohesion.

discontinuous (dĭs′kən tĭn′yŏŏ əs), *adj.* not continuous; broken; interrupted; intermittent. —**dis′contin′uously,** *adv.* —**dis′contin′uousness,** *n.*

discophil (dĭs′kə fĭl), *n.* one who studies and collects gramophone records, esp. rare ones or a particular type of record. Also, **discophile** (dĭs′kə fīl′).

discord (*n.* dĭs′kôd; *v.* dĭs kôd′), *n.* **1.** lack of concord or harmony between persons or things; disagreement of relations. **2.** difference of opinions. **3.** strife; dispute; war. **4.** *Music.* an inharmonious combination of musical notes sounded together. **5.** any confused or harsh noise; dissonance. —*v.i.* **6.** to disagree. [ME *discord(en)*, t. OF: m. *discorder*, t. L: m. *discordāre* be at variance]

discordance (dĭs kô′dns), *n.* discordant character; disagreement; discord. Also, **discord′ancy.**

discordant (dĭs kô′dnt), *adj.* **1.** being at variance; disagreeing; incongruous: *discordant opinions.* **2.** disagreeable to the ear; dissonant; harsh. —**discord′antly,** *adv.*

discotheque (dĭs′kə tĕk′), *n.* a place of public entertainment or a club in which patrons may dance to recorded music. Also, **discothèque** (*Fr.* dĕs kŏ tĕk′). [t. F]

discount (*v.* dĭs′kount, dĭs kount′; *n.* dĭs′kount), *v.t.* **1.** to deduct, as a certain amount in settling a bill; make a reduction of. **2.** to advance money with deduction of interest on (not immediately payable). **3.** to purchase or sell (a bill or note) before maturity at a reduction based on the interest for the time it still has to run. **4.** to leave out of account; disregard. **5.** to make a deduction from; allow for exaggeration in (a statement, etc.). **6.** to take (an event, etc.) into account in advance, esp. with loss of value, effectiveness, etc. —*v.i.* **7.** to advance money after deduction of interest. —*n.* **8.** the act of discounting. **9.** amount deducted for prompt payment or other special reason. **10.** any deduction from the nominal value. **11.** the amount of interest obtained by one who discounts. **12. at a discount, a.** *Com.* below par. **b.** in low esteem or regard. **c.** not in demand. [t. OF: m. *desconter*, f. *des-* DIS-[1] + *conter* COUNT[1]] —**discount′able,** *adj.* —**dis′counter,** *n.*

discount broker, a merchant who cashes bills of exchange at a discount, or lends money at a discount on securities. Also, **bill broker.**

discountenance (dĭs koun′tĭ nəns), *v.*, **-nanced, -nancing,** *n.* —*v.t.* **1.** to put out of countenance; disconcert; abash. **2.** to show disapproval of; treat with disfavour. —*n.* **3.** disapproval. [t. F (obs.): m. *descontenancer*, f. *des-* DIS-[1] + *contenancer* COUNTENANCE, V.]

discount house, 1. the place of business of a discount broker. **2.** *U.S.* a store selling practically all its merchandise at a price often considerably below the usual or advertised retail price.

discount rate, *Finance.* rate of interest charged by a banker for discounting bills of exchange.

discourage (dĭs kŭ′rĭj), *v.t.*, **-raged, -raging. 1.** to deprive of courage; dishearten; dispirit. **2.** to dissuade (fol. by *from*). **3.** to obstruct by opposition or difficulty; hinder: *low prices discourage industry.* **4.** to express disapproval of: *to discourage the expression of enthusiasm.* [t. OF: m. *descoragier*, der. *des-* DIS-[1] + *corage* COURAGE] —**discour′ager,** *n.* —**discour′agingly,** *adv.*

—**Syn. 1.** daunt, depress, deject, overawe, cow, abash. DISCOURAGE, DISMAY, INTIMIDATE may imply the attempt to dishearten or frighten one so as to prevent some action, or any further action. To DISCOURAGE is to dishearten by expressing disapproval or by suggesting that a contemplated action or course will probably fail: *he was discouraged from giving up his job.* To DISMAY is to dishearten completely, by the disclosure of unsuspected facts, so that the action contemplated seems useless or dangerous: *to dismay a prosecutor by revealing his brother's connection with a crime.* To INTIMIDATE is to frighten, as by threats of force, violence, or dire consequences: *to intimidate a witness.* —**Ant. 1.** encourage.

discouragement (dĭs kŭʹrĭj mənt), *n.* **1.** the act of discouraging. **2.** the state of being discouraged. **3.** something that discourages. **—Syn. 2.** depression, dejection, hopelessness. See **despair. 3.** deterrent, damper.

discourse (*n.* dĭsʹkôs, dĭs kôsʹ; *v.* dĭs kôsʹ), *n., v.,* **-coursed, -coursing.** **—***n.* **1.** communication of thought by words; talk; conversation. **2.** a formal discussion of a subject in speech or writing, as a dissertation, treatise, sermon, etc. **—***v.i.* **3.** to communicate thoughts orally; talk; converse. **4.** to treat of a subject formally in speech or writing. **—***v.t.* **5.** to utter or give forth (musical sounds). [ME *discours,* t. F, t. L: m. s. *discursus*] **—discoursʹer,** *n.*

discourteous (dĭs kûʹtyəs), *adj.* lacking courtesy; impolite; uncivil; rude. **—discourʹteously,** *adv.* **—discourʹteousness,** *n.*

discourtesy (dĭs kûʹtĭ sĭ), *n., pl.* **-sies. 1.** lack or breach of courtesy; incivility; rudeness. **2.** a discourteous or impolite act.

discover (dĭs kŭvʹə), *v.t.* **1.** to get knowledge of, learn of, or find out; gain sight or knowledge of (something previously unseen or unknown). **2.** *Archaic.* to act so as to manifest unconsciously or unintentionally; betray. **3.** *Archaic.* to make known; reveal. [ME *discover(en),* t. OF: m. *descovrir,* f. *des-* DIS-¹ + *covrir* COVER] **—discovʹerable,** *adj.* **—discovʹerer,** *n.*

—Syn. 1. detect, espy, descry, discern, ascertain, unearth, ferret out, notice. DISCOVER, INVENT, ORIGINATE suggest bringing to light something previously unknown. To DISCOVER may be to find something which had previously been in existence but had hitherto been unknown: *to discover a new continent, a planet, electricity;* it may also refer to devising a new use for something already known: *to discover how to use steam in engine propulsion.* To INVENT is to make or create something new, esp. something ingeniously devised to perform mechanical operations: *to invent a device for detecting radioactivity.* To ORIGINATE is to begin something new, esp. new ideas, methods, etc.: *to originate a religious or political movement. the use of deep-freezing units.* See **learn.**

discovert (dĭs kŭvʹət), *adj. Law.* (of a woman) not covert; not under the protection of a husband. [t. OF: m. *descovert,* pp. of *descouvrir* DISCOVER] **—discovʹerture,** *n.*

discovery (dĭs kŭvʹə rĭ), *n., pl.* **-eries. 1.** the act of discovering. **2.** something discovered. **3.** *Law.* compulsory disclosure, as of facts or documents. **4.** (*cap.*) the ship in which Captain Scott sailed to the South Pole in 1912; now moored on the Thames embankment.

Discovery Inlet, an inlet of the Ross Sea, Antarctica.

discredit (dĭs krĕdʹĭt), *v.t.* **1.** to injure the credit or reputation of. **2.** to show to be undeserving of credit or belief; destroy confidence in. **3.** to give no credit to; disbelieve: *the report is discredited.* **—***n.* **4.** loss or lack of belief, of confidence; disbelief; distrust. **5.** loss or lack of repute or esteem; disrepute. **6.** something that damages a good reputation. [f. DIS-¹ + CREDIT, V.]

discreditable (dĭs krĕdʹĭ tə bl), *adj.* such as to bring discredit; disgraceful. **—discredʹitably,** *adv.*

discreet (dĭs krētʹ), *adj.* wise or judicious in avoiding mistakes or faults; prudent; circumspect; cautious; not rash. [ME *discret,* t. OF, t. L: s. *discrētus,* pp., separated] **—discreetʹly,** *adv.* **—discreetʹness,** *n.* **—Syn.** See **careful.**

discrepancy (dĭs krĕpʹən sĭ), *n., pl.* **-cies. 1.** the state or quality of being discrepant; difference; inconsistency. **2.** an instance of difference or inconsistency. Also, **discrepʹance. —Syn. 1.** See **difference.**

discrepant (dĭs krĕpʹənt), *adj.* differing; disagreeing; discordant; inconsistent. [t. L: s. *discrepans,* ppr., being discordant] **—discrepʹantly,** *adv.*

discrete (dĭs krētʹ), *adj.* **1.** detached from others; separate; distinct. **2.** consisting of or characterized by distinct or individual parts; discontinuous. [t. L: m. s. *discrētus* separated] **—discreteʹly,** *adv.* **—discreteʹness,** *n.*

discretion (dĭs krĕshʹən), *n.* **1.** power or right of deciding, or of acting according to one's own judgement; freedom of judgement or choice. **2.** the quality of being discreet; discernment of what is judicious or expedient, esp. with reference to one's own actions or speech; prudence. **3. at discretion,** as one wishes or decides.

discretional (dĭs krĕshʹə nəl), *adj.* discretionary. **—discreʹtionally,** *adv.*

discretionary (dĭs krĕshʹə nə rĭ, -ən rĭ), *adj.* **1.** subject or left to one's discretion. **2.** of or pertaining to discretion.

discriminate (*v.* dĭs krĭmʹĭ nātʹ; *adj.* dĭs krĭmʹĭ nĭt), *v.,* **-nated, -nating,** *adj.* **—***v.i* **1.** to make a distinction, as in favour of or against a person or thing: *to discriminate against a minority.* **2.** to note or observe a difference; distinguish accurately: *to discriminate between things.* **3.** *Electronics.* to extract a desired frequency from unwanted frequency components in a radio signal. **—***v.t.* **4.** to make or constitute a distinction in or between; differentiate: *to discriminate one thing from another.* **5.** to note or distinguish as different. **6.** *Electronics.* to extract (a desired frequency) from unwanted frequency components in a radio signal. **—***adj.* **7.** marked by discrimination; making nice distinctions. [t. L: m. s. *discrīminātus,* pp., divided, distinguished] **—discrimʹinately,** *adv.* **—discrimʹinaʹtor,** *n.* **—Syn. 4.** See **distinguish.**

discriminating (dĭs krĭmʹĭ nāʹtĭng), *adj.* **1.** differentiating; distinctive. **2.** perceiving differences or distinctions with nicety; possessing discrimination. **3.** differential, as a tariff. **—discrimʹinaʹtingly,** *adv.*

discrimination (dĭs krĭmʹĭ nāʹshən), *n.* **1.** the act of discriminating. **2.** the resulting state. **3.** the making of a difference in particular cases, as in favour of or against a person or thing. **4.** the power of making nice distinctions; discriminating judgement. **5.** *Archaic.* something that serves to differentiate. **6.** *Electronics.* the extraction of a desired frequency from a signal containing many frequencies, esp. in radio receivers.

discriminative (dĭs krĭmʹĭ nə tĭv), *adj.* **1.** that marks distinction; constituting a difference; characteristic: *the discriminative features of men.* **2.** making distinctions; discriminating. **3.** (of a tariff, etc.) differential. Also, **discriminatory** (dĭs krĭmʹĭ nə tə rĭ, -trĭ). **—discrimʹinatively,** *adv.*

discrown (dĭs krounʹ), *v.t.* to deprive of a crown.

discursive (dĭs kûʹsĭv), *adj.* **1.** passing rapidly or irregularly from one subject to another; rambling; digressive. **2.** proceeding by reasoning or argument; not intuitive. **—discurʹsively,** *adv.* **—discurʹsiveness,** *n.* **—discurʹsion,** *n.*

discus (dĭsʹkəs), *n., pl.* **discuses, disci** (dĭsʹī). *Athletics.* **1.** a circular stone or metal plate for throwing, as among the ancient Greeks and Romans. **2.** a similar object, thrown by modern athletes, usually made of wood rimmed with metal. **3.** the exercise or competition of throwing it. [t. L, t. Gk: m. *dískos* discus, disc, DISH]

discuss (dĭs kŭsʹ), *v.t.* **1.** to examine by argument; sift the considerations for and against; debate; talk over. **2.** (in humorous use) to try the quality of (food or drink) by consuming. **3.** *Civil Law.* **a.** to collect a debt from (the person primarily liable) before proceeding against the person secondarily liable. **b.** to execute against the moveable property of (a debtor) before proceeding against his immoveable property, as land. **4.** *Obs.* to make known; reveal. [ME *discusse(n),* t. L: m. s. *discussus,* pp., struck asunder] **—discussʹer,** *n.* **—discussʹible, discussʹable,** *adj.* **—Syn. 1.** reason, deliberate. See **argue.**

discussion (dĭs kŭshʹən), *n.* the act of discussing; critical examination by argument; debate.

disc wheel, a spokeless vehicular wheel, esp. on motor cars, having a heavy, circular disc of pressed steel mounted on the hub and supporting the tyre rim on its outer edge.

disdain (dĭs dānʹ), *v.t.* **1.** to look upon or treat with contempt; despise; scorn. **2.** to think unworthy of notice, performance, etc.; consider beneath oneself. **—***n.* **3.** a feeling of contempt for anything regarded as unworthy; haughty contempt; scorn. [ME *desdaine(n),* t. OF: m. *desdeignier,* f. *des-* DIS-¹ + *deignier* DEIGN] **—Syn. 3.** contemptuousness, haughtiness, arrogance, superciliousness, contumely. See **contempt.**

disdainful (dĭs dānʹfəl), *adj.* full of or showing disdain; scornful. **—disdainʹfully,** *adv.* **—disdainʹfulness,** *n.* **—Syn.** contemptuous, haughty, supercilious, contumelious.

disease (dĭ zēzʹ), *n., v.,* **-seased, -seasing. —***n.* **1.** a morbid condition of the body, or of some organ or part; illness; sickness; ailment. **2.** a similar disorder in plants. **3.** any deranged or depraved condition, as of the mind, affairs, etc. **—***v.t.* **4.** to affect with disease; make ill. [ME *disese,* t. OF: m. *desaise,* f. *des-* DIS-¹ + *aise* EASE]

—Syn. 1. DISEASE, AFFECTION, DISORDER, MALADY imply a deviation of the body, or an organ of it, from health or normality. DISEASE and MALADY apply to organic deviations involving structural change. A DISEASE is a serious, active, prolonged, and deep-rooted condition. A MALADY is a lingering, chronic disease, usually painful and often fatal. An AFFECTION is a seriously abnormal state of body or mind, esp. one that interferes with their functions. A DISORDER is usually a physical or mental derangement, frequently a slight or transitory one. **—Ant. 1.** health. **4.** cure.

disembark (dĭsʹĭm bäkʹ), *v.t., v.i.* to put or go on shore from a ship; land. **—disembarkation** (dĭsʹĕm bä kāʹshən), *n.*

disembarrass (dĭsʹĭm băʹrəs), *v.t.* **1.** to free from embarrassment. **2.** to relieve; rid. **3.** to disentangle; extricate. **—disʹembarʹrassment,** *n.*

disembody (dĭsʹĭm bŏdʹĭ), *v.t.,* **-bodied, -bodying.** to divest (a soul, etc.) of the body. **—disʹembodʹiment,** *n.*

disembogue (dĭsʹĭm bōgʹ), *v.,* **-bogued, -boguing. —***v.i.* **1.** to empty or discharge by pouring forth the contents. **2.** (of a river, stream, etc.) to flow out or discharge at the mouth. **3.** *Geol.* to debouch. **—***v.t.* **4.** to discharge; cast forth. [t. Sp.: m. *desembocar,* f. *des-* DIS-¹ + *embocar* enter by the mouth, f. *en-* in- + *boca* mouth (g. L *bucca*)] —**dis′embogue′ment,** *n.*

disembosom (dĭs′ĭm bo͝oz′əm), *v.t.* **1.** to reveal; divulge. **2.** to relieve (oneself) of a secret.

disembowel (dĭs′ĭm bou′əl), *v.t.*, **-elled, -elling** or (*U.S.*) **-eled, -eling.** to remove the bowels or entrails from; eviscerate. —**dis′embow′elment,** *n.*

disembroil (dĭs′ĭm broil′), *v.t.* to free from embroilment, entanglement, or confusion.

disenable (dĭs′ĭ nā′bl), *v.t.*, **-bled, -bling.** to deprive of ability; make unable; prevent.

disenchant (dĭs′ĭn chănt′), *v.t.* to free from enchantment; disillusion. —**dis′enchant′er,** *n.* —**dis′enchant′ment,** *n.*

disencumber (dĭs′ĭn kŭm′bə), *v.t.* to free from encumbrance; disburden.

disendow (dĭs′ĭn dou′), *v.t.* to deprive of endowment, esp. a church. —**dis′endow′er,** *n.* —**dis′endow′ment,** *n.*

disenfranchise (dĭs′ĭn frăn′chīz), *v.t.*, **-chised, -chising.** to disfranchise. —**disenfranchisement** (dĭs′ĭn frăn′chĭz-mənt), *n.*

disengage (dĭs′ĭn gāj′), *v.*, **-gaged, -gaging.** —*v.t.* **1.** to release from attachment or connection; loosen; unfasten. **2.** to free from engagement, pledge, obligation, etc. **3.** *Mil.* to break off action with (an enemy). —*v.i.* **4.** to become disengaged; free onself.

disengagement (dĭs′ĭn gāj′mənt), *n.* **1.** the act or process of disengaging, or state of being disengaged. **2.** freedom from obligation or occupation; leisure.

disentail (dĭs′ĭn tāl′), *v.t.* *Law.* to free (an estate) from entail. —**dis′entail′ment,** *n.*

disentangle (dĭs′ĭn tăng′gl), *v.t.*, *v.i.*, **-gled, -gling.** to free or become free from entanglement; untangle; extricate (fol. by *from*). —**dis′entan′glement,** *n.*

disenthral (dĭs′ĭn thrôl′), *v.t.*, **-thralled, -thralling.** to free from thraldom. Also, **disenthrall.** —**dis′enthral′-ment,** *n.*

disenthrone (dĭs′ĭn thrōn′), *v.t.*, **-throned, -throning.** to dethrone. —**dis′enthrone′ment,** *n.*

disentitle (dĭs′ĭn tī′tl), *v.t.*, **-tled, -tling.** to deprive of title or right.

disentomb (dĭs′ĭn to͞om′), *v.t.* to take from the tomb; disinter. —**dis′entomb′ment,** *n.*

disentrance (dĭs′ĭn träns′), *v.t.*, **-tranced, -trancing.** to bring out of an entranced condition. —**dis′entrance′-ment,** *n.*

disentwine (dĭs′ĭn twīn′), *v.t.*, *v.i.*, **-twined, -twining.** to bring or come out of an entwined or intertwined state; untwine.

disepalous (dī sĕp′ə ləs), *adj.* *Bot.* having two sepals.

disestablish (dĭs′ĭs tăb′lĭsh), *v.t.* **1.** to deprive of the character of being established. **2.** to withdraw exclusive state recognition or support from (a church). —**dis′-estab′lishment,** *n.*

disestablishmentarian (dĭs′ĭs tăb′lĭsh mən tĕə′rĭ ən), *n.* **1.** one who favours the disestablishment of the state church. —*adj.* **2.** of, pertaining to, or in favour of the disestablishment of the state church. —**dis′estab′-lishmenta′rianis′m,** *n.*

disesteem (dĭs′ĭs tēm′), *v.t.* **1.** to hold in low esteem; think slightingly of. —*n.* **2.** lack of esteem; disregard.

diseur (dē zû′; *Fr.* dē zœr′), *n.* a professional public entertainer who talks, recites, etc. [t. F: one who tells, says] —**diseuse** (dē zûz′; *Fr.* dē zœz′), *n. fem.*

disfavour (dĭs fā′və), *n.* **1.** unfavourable regard; displeasure; disesteem: *the minister incurred the king's disfavour.* **2.** lack of favour; state of being regarded unfavourably: *in disfavour at court.* **3.** an act of disregard, dislike, or unkindness: *to dispense disfavours.* —*v.t.* **4.** to regard or treat with disfavour. Also, *U.S.*, **disfa′vor.**

disfeature (dĭs fē′chə), *v.t.*, **-tured, -turing.** to mar the features of; disfigure. —**disfea′turement,** *n.*

disfigure (dĭs fĭg′ə), *v.t.*, **-ured, -uring. 1.** to mar the figure, appearance, or beauty of; deform; deface. **2.** to mar the effect or excellence of. [ME *disfigure(n)*, t. OF: m. *desfigurer*, f. *des-* DIS-[1] + *figurer*, der. *figure* FIGURE, n.] —**disfig′urer,** *n.* —**Syn. 1.** See **mar.**

disfigurement (dĭs fĭg′ə mənt), *n.* **1.** the act of disfiguring. **2.** disfigured condition. **3.** something that disfigures. Also, **disfiguration** (dĭs fĭg′yo͞o rā′shən).

disforest (dĭs fŏ′rĭst), *v.t.* *Law.* to disafforest. —**dis-for′esta′tion,** *n.*

disfranchise (dĭs frăn′chīz), *v.t.*, **-chised, -chising. 1.** to deprive (persons) of rights of citizenship, as of the right to vote. **2.** to deprive of a franchise, privilege, or right. —**disfranchisement** (dĭs frăn′chĭz mənt), *n.*

disfrock (dĭs frŏk′), *v.t.* *Eccles.* to unfrock.

disfurnish (dĭs fû′nĭsh), *v.t.* to deprive of something with which a person or thing is furnished; strip. —**dis-fur′nishment,** *n.*

disgorge (dĭs gôj′), *v.*, **-gorged, -gorging.** —*v.t.* **1.** to eject or throw out from or as from the gorge or throat; to vomit; discharge. **2.** to give up unwillingly. —*v.i.* **3.** to disgorge something. [late ME, t. OF: m. *desgorger*, f. *des-* DIS-[1] + *gorge* throat] —**disgorge′ment,** *n.* —**dis-gorg′er,** *n.*

disgrace (dĭs grās′), *n.*, *v.*, **-graced, -gracing.** —*n.* **1.** the state of being in dishonour; ignominy; shame. **2.** a cause of shame or reproach; that which dishonours. **3.** the state of being out of favour; exclusion from favour, confidence, or trust. —*v.t.* **4.** to bring or reflect shame or reproach upon. **5.** to dismiss with discredit; put out of grace or favour; treat with disfavour. [t. F, t. It.: m. *disgrazia*. See DIS-[1], GRACE] —**disgrac′er,** *n.*

—**Syn. 1.** DISGRACE, DISHONOUR, IGNOMINY, INFAMY imply a very low position in the opinion of others. DISGRACE implies the disfavour, with a greater or less degree of reproachful disapprobation, of others: *he brought disgrace on his family, to be in disgrace.* DISHONOUR implies a stain on honour or honourable reputation; it relates esp. to the conduct of the person himself: *he preferred death to dishonour.* IGNOMINY is disgrace in which one's situation invites contempt: *the ignominy of being discovered cheating.* INFAMY is shameful notoriety, or baseness of action or character which is widely known and recognized: *the children never outlived the father's infamy.* —**Ant. 1.** honour.

disgraceful (dĭs grās′fəl), *adj.* bringing or deserving disgrace; shameful; dishonourable; disreputable. —**dis-grace′fully,** *adv.* —**disgrace′fulness,** *n.*

disgruntle (dĭs grŭn′tl), *v.t.*, **-tled, -tling.** to put into a state of sulky dissatisfaction; make discontent. [f. DIS-[1] + *gruntle*, freq. of GRUNT] —**disgrun′tlement,** *n.*

disguise (dĭs gīz′), *v.*, **-guised, -guising,** *n.* —*v.t.* **1.** to change the guise or appearance of so as to conceal identity or to mislead; conceal the identity of by means of a misleading garb, etc. **2.** to conceal or cover up the real state or character of by a counterfeit form or appearance; misrepresent: *to disguise one's intentions.* —*n.* **3.** that which disguises; something that serves or is intended for concealment of identity, character, or quality; a deceptive covering, condition, manner, etc. **4.** the make-up, mask or costume of an entertainer. **5.** the act of disguising. **6.** the state of being disguised. [ME *desgise(n)*, t. OF: m. *desguiser*, f. *des-* DIS-[1] + *guise* GUISE] —**disguis′able,** *adj.* —**disguis′edly,** *adv.* —**disguis′er,** *n.*

disgust (dĭs gŭst′), *v.t.* **1.** to cause nausea or loathing in. **2.** to offend the good taste, moral sense, etc., of; cause aversion or impatient dissatisfaction in. —*n.* **3.** strong distaste; nausea; loathing. **4.** repugnance caused by something offensive; strong aversion; impatient dissatisfaction. [t. MF: m. *desgouster*, f. *des-* DIS-[1] + *gouster* taste, relish] —**disgust′edly,** *adv.* —**Syn. 4.** See **dislike.**

disgustful (dĭs gŭst′fəl), *adj.* causing disgust; nauseous; offensive. —**disgust′fully,** *adv.*

disgusting (dĭs gŭs′tĭng), *adj.* causing disgust; offensive to the physical, moral, or aesthetic taste. —**disgust′ingly,** *adv.* —**Syn.** loathsome, sickening, nauseous, repulsive, revolting.

dish (dĭsh), *n.* **1.** an open, more or less shallow container of pottery, glass, metal, wood, etc., used for various purposes, esp. for holding or serving food. **2.** any container used at table. **3.** that which is served or contained in a dish. **4.** a particular article or preparation of food. **5.** as much as a dish will hold; a dishful. **6.** anything like a dish in form or use. **7.** concave state, or the degree of concavity, as of a wheel. **8.** *Electronics.* a parabolic reflector for transmitting or receiving radio or radar signals. **9.** *Slang.* an attractive girl or man. —*v.t.* **10.** to put into or serve in a dish, as food (often fol. by *up*): *to dish up food.* **11.** to fashion like a dish; make concave. **12.** *Slang.* to defeat; frustrate; cheat. **13. dish out,** to distribute; share out. [ME; OE *disc* dish, plate, bowl (cf. G *Tisch* table), t. L: *discus* dish, DISCUS]

dishabille (dĭs′ă bēl′), *n.* **1.** the state of being undressed, partly dressed, or dressed negligently or carelessly. **2.** a garment worn in undress. **3.** a loose morning dress. [t. F: m. *déshabillé*, prop. pp. of *deshabiller* undress, f. *dés-* DIS-[1] + *habiller* dress]

dishabituate (dĭs′hə bĭt′yo͞o āt′), *v.t.*, **-ated, -ating.** to cause to be no longer habituated or accustomed.

dishallow (dĭs hăl′ō), *v.t.* to profane; desecrate.

disharmonious (dĭs′hä mō′nyəs), *adj.* inharmonious; discordant.

disharmonize (dĭs′hä′mə nīz′), *v.t.*, *v.i.*, **-nized, -nizing.** to make or be inharmonious. Also, **disharmonise.**

disharmony (dĭs′hä′mə nĭ), *n.*, *pl.* **-nies. 1.** discord. **2.** something discordant.

dishcloth (dĭsh′klŏth′), *n.* a cloth for use in washing dishes. Also, **dishclout** (dĭsh′klout′).

dishearten (dĭs hä′tn), *v.t.* to depress the spirits of; discourage. —**disheart′eningly,** *adv.* —**disheart′en-ment,** *n.*

dished (dĭsht), *adj.* **1.** concave: *a dished face.* **2.** *Slang.*

defeated; frustrated; cheated. **3.** (of parallel wheels) farther apart at the top than at the bottom.

dishelm (dĭs hĕlm′), *v.t., v.i. Archaic.* to divest of, or take off, the helmet.

disherit (dĭs hĕ′rĭt), *v.t. Obs. or Rare.* to disinherit.

dishevel (dĭ shĕv′əl), *v.t.*, **-elled, -elling** or (*U.S.*) **-eled, -eling.** to let down (the hair); let hang in loose disorder. [ME *dischevelen*, t. OF: m. *descheveler*, der. *des-* DIS-[1] + *chevel* hair (g. L *capillus*)] —**dishev′elment,** *n.*

dishevelled (dĭ shĕv′əld), *adj.* **1.** hanging loosely or in disorder; unkempt: *dishevelled hair.* **2.** untidy; disarranged: *dishevelled appearance.* Also, *U.S.*, **disheveled.**

dishful (dĭsh′fo͝ol′), *n.* the amount contained in a dish.

dishonest (dĭs ŏn′ĭst), *adj.* **1.** not honest; disposed to lie, cheat, or steal: *a dishonest person.* **2.** proceeding from or exhibiting lack of honesty; fraudulent. —**dishon′estly,** *adv.* —**Syn. 1.** unscrupulous, knavish, thievish. See **corrupt.**

dishonesty (dĭs ŏn′ĭs tĭ), *n., pl.* **-ties. 1.** lack of honesty; a disposition to lie, cheat, or steal. **2.** a dishonest act; a fraud; theft.

dishonour (dĭs ŏn′ə), *n.* **1.** lack of honour; dishonourable character or conduct. **2.** disgrace; ignominy; shame. **3.** an indignity; insult. **4.** a cause of shame; a disgrace. **5.** *Com.* failure or refusal of the drawee or acceptor of a bill of exchange or cheque to accept it, or, if it is accepted, to honour his liability by payment. —*v.t.* **6.** to deprive of honour; disgrace; bring reproach or shame on. **7.** *Com.* to fail or refuse to honour (a draft, etc.) by payment. Also, *U.S.*, **dishon′or.** [ME *dishonour*, t. OF: m. *deshonor*, f. *des-* DIS-[1] + *honor* honour (t. L)] —**dishon′ourer,** *n.* —**Syn. 2.** See **disgrace.**

dishonourable (dĭs ŏn′ə rə bl, -ŏn′rə bl), *adj.* **1.** showing lack of honour; ignoble; base; disgraceful; shameful: *a dishonourable act.* **2.** having no honour or good repute: *a dishonourable man.* Also, *U.S.*, **dishon′orable.** —**dishon′ourableness,** *n.* —**dishon′ourably,** *adv.* —**Syn. 2.** infamous, unscrupulous, unprincipled.

dishwasher (dĭsh′wŏsh′ə), *n.* **1.** one who washes dishes, plates, etc. **2.** an electric machine which automatically washes and sometimes dries dishes, plates, etc.

dishwater (dĭsh′wô′tə), *n.* water in which dishes are, or have been, washed.

dishy (dĭsh′ĭ), *adj. Slang.* (of persons or things) attractive.

disillusion (dĭs′ĭ lo͞o′zhən), *v.t.* **1.** to free from illusion; disenchant. —*n.* **2.** a freeing or a being freed from illusion; disenchantment. —**dis′illu′sionment,** *n.* —**disillusive** (dĭs′ĭ lo͞o′sĭv), *adj.*

disillusionize (dĭs′ĭ lo͞o′zhə nīz′), *v.t.*, **-nized, -nizing.** *Chiefly U.S.* to disillusion. Also, **disillusionise.**

disimpassioned (dĭs′ĭm păsh′ənd), *adj.* calm; dispassionate; passionless.

disimprison (dĭs′ĭm prĭz′ən), *v.t.* to release from imprisonment. —**dis′impris′onment,** *n.*

disincentive (dĭs′ĭn sĕn′tĭv), *n.* **1.** anything that deters from action, etc. —*adj.* **2.** discouraging, as from action; disheartening.

disinclination (dĭs′ĭnk lĭ nā′shən), *n.* the absence of inclination; averseness; distaste; unwillingness.

disincline (dĭs′ĭn klīn′), *v.t., v.i.*, **-clined, -clining.** to make or be averse or indisposed.

disinfect (dĭs′ĭn fĕkt′), *v.t.* to cleanse (rooms, clothing, etc.) from infection; destroy disease germs in. —**dis′infec′tor,** *n.*

disinfectant (dĭs′ĭn fĕk′tənt), *n.* **1.** any chemical agent that destroys bacteria. —*adj.* **2.** disinfecting.

disinfection (dĭs′ĭn fĕk′shən), *n.* the process of disinfecting.

disinfest (dĭs′ĭn fĕst′), *v.t.* to rid of vermin, especially lice or rats. —**dis′infesta′tion,** *n.*

disingenuous (dĭs′ĭn jĕn′yo͞o əs), *adj.* not ingenuous; lacking in frankness, candour, or sincerity; insincere: *disingenuous persons.* —**dis′ingen′uously,** *adv.* —**dis′ingen′uousness,** *n.*

disinherit (dĭs′ĭn hĕ′rĭt), *v.t.* **1.** *Law.* to exclude from inheritance (an heir or a next of kin). **2.** to deprive of the right to inherit. —**dis′inher′itance,** *n.*

disintegrate (dĭs ĭn′tĭ grāt′), *v.*, **-grated, -grating.** —*v.t.* **1.** to reduce to particles, fragments, or parts; break up or destroy the cohesion of: *rocks are disintegrated by frost and rain.* —*v.i.* **2.** to separate into its component parts; break up. **3.** (of a person) to lose one's judgement, memory, mental grasp, etc., as through senility. **4.** *Physics.* to decay (def. 3). —**disintegrable** (dĭs ĭn′tĭ grə bl), *adj.* —**disin′tegra′tion,** *n.* —**disin′tegra′tor,** *n.* —**Syn. 2.** See **decay.**

disinter (dĭs′ĭn tû′), *v.t.*, **-terred, -terring. 1.** to take out of the place of interment; exhume; unearth. **2.** to bring from obscurity into view. —**dis′inter′ment,** *n.*

disinterest (dĭs ĭn′trĭst), *n.* **1.** absence of interest; indifference. —*v.t.* **2.** to divest of interest or concern.

disinterested (dĭs ĭn′trĭstĭd), *adj.* **1.** unbiased by personal interest or advantage; not influenced by selfish motives. **2.** *Colloq.* uninterested. —**disin′terestedly,** *adv.* —**disin′terestedness,** *n.*

—**Syn. 1.** DISINTERESTED, UNINTERESTED are not properly synonyms. DISINTERESTED stresses lack of prejudice or of selfish interests: *a disinterested report.* UNINTERESTED suggests aloofness and indifference: *completely uninterested and taking no part in proceedings.* See **fair**[1]

disject (dĭs jĕkt′), *v.t.* to cast asunder; scatter; disperse. [t. L: s. *disjectus*, pp., thrown asunder]

disjecta membra (dĭs jĕk′tə mĕm′brə), *Latin.* scattered members; disjointed portions or parts.

disjoin (dĭs join′), *v.t.* **1.** to undo or prevent the junction or union of; disunite; separate. —*v.i.* **2.** to become disunited; separate. [ME *desjoyne(n)*, t. OF: m. *desjoindre*, g. L *disjungere*]

disjoint (dĭs joint′), *v.t.* **1.** to separate or disconnect the joints or joinings of. **2.** to put out of order; derange. —*v.i.* **3.** to come apart. **4.** to be dislocated; to put out of joint. —*adj.* **5.** *Obs.* disjointed; out of joint. [t. OF: m. *desjoint*, pp. of *desjoindre*, g. L *disjungere*]

disjointed (dĭs join′tĭd), *adj.* **1.** having the joints or connections separated: *a disjointed fowl.* **2.** disconnected; incoherent: *a disjointed discourse.* —**disjoint′edly,** *adv.* —**disjoint′edness,** *n.*

disjunct (dĭs jŭngkt′), *adj.* **1.** disjointed; separated. **2.** *Music.* progressing melodically by intervals larger than a second. **3.** *Entomol.* having the head, thorax, and abdomen separated by deep constrictions. [t. L: s. *disjunctus*, pp., disjoined]

disjunction (dĭs jŭngk′shən), *n.* **1.** the act of disjoining. **2.** the state of being disjoined. **3.** *Logic.* **a.** a proposition in which two (or more) alternatives are asserted, only one of which can be true. **b.** the relation between the terms of such a proposition.

disjunctive (dĭs jŭngk′tĭv), *adj.* **1.** serving or tending to disjoin; separating; dividing; distinguishing. **2.** *Gram.* **a.** syntactically setting two or more expressions in opposition to each other, as *but* in *poor but happy*, or expressing an alternative, as *or* in *this or that.* **b.** not syntactically dependent upon some particular expression. **3.** *Logic.* characterizing propositions which are disjunctions. —*n.* **4.** a statement, etc., involving alternatives. **5.** *Gram.* a disjunctive word. —**disjunc′tively,** *adv.*

disjuncture (dĭs jŭngk′chə), *n.* **1.** the act of disjoining. **2.** the state of being disjoined.

disjune (dĭs jo͞on′), *n. Scot. Obs.* breakfast.

disk (dĭsk), *n. Chiefly U.S.* disc.

dislike (dĭs līk′), *v.*, **-liked, -liking,** *n.* —*v.t.* **1.** not to like; regard with displeasure or aversion: *I dislike him, I dislike having to work.* —*n.* **2.** the feeling of disliking; distaste: *I have taken a strong dislike to him.* —**dislike′able,** *adj.*

—**Syn. 2.** disrelish. DISLIKE, DISGUST, DISTASTE, REPUGNANCE imply antipathy towards something. DISLIKE is a general word, the strength of the feeling being indicated by the context. It expresses a positive (not necessarily strong), sometimes inherent or permanent feeling of antipathy for something: *to have a dislike for crowds, for someone, for noise.* DISGUST is a very strong word, expressing a feeling of loathing for what is offensive to the physical taste or to the feelings and sensibilities: *the taste of spoilt food fills one with disgust, to feel disgust at seeing snobbery and ostentation.* DISTASTE, though etymologically equal to DISGUST, is weaker; it implies a more or less settled dislike for what is naturally uncongenial or has been made so by association: *to have distaste for certain foods, for hard work, for unconventional art or music.* REPUGNANCE is a strong feeling of aversion for, and antagonism towards, something: *to feel repugnance for (or towards) murderers or their crimes.*

dislimn (dĭs lĭm′), *v.t. Archaic.* to obliterate (a picture); efface.

dislocate (dĭs′lə kāt′), *v.t.*, **-cated, -cating. 1.** to put out of place; displace; put out of proper relative position. **2.** *Surg.* to put out of joint or out of position, as a limb or an organ. **3.** to throw out of order; derange; upset; disorder. [t. ML: m. s. *dislocātus*, pp. of *dislocāre*, f. L: *dis-* DIS-[1] + *locāre* place]

dislocation (dĭs′lə kā′shən), *n.* **1.** the act of dislocating. **2.** the state of being dislocated. **3.** a dislocated joint. **4.** *Geol.* a fault. **5.** *Crystall.* a line defect in a crystal.

dislodge (dĭs lŏj′), *v.*, **-lodged, -lodging.** —*v.t.* **1.** to remove or drive from a place of rest or lodgement; drive from a position occupied. —*v.i.* **2.** to go from a place of lodgement. —**dislodge′ment,** *n.*

disloyal (dĭs loi′əl), *adj.* not loyal; false to one's obligations or allegiance; faithless; treacherous. [t. OF: m. *desloial*, f. *des-* DIS-[1] + *loial* law-abiding (g. L *lēgālis*)] —**disloy′ally,** *adv.* —**Syn.** unfaithful, false, perfidious, traitorous, treasonable. —**Ant.** constant.

disloyalty (dĭs loi′əl tĭ), *n., pl.* **-ties. 1.** the quality of being disloyal; unfaithfulness. **2.** violation of allegiance or duty, as to a government. **3.** a disloyal act.

—**Syn.** **1.** Disloyalty, perfidy, treachery, treason imply betrayal of trust, and esp. traitorous acts against one's country or its government. Disloyalty applies to any violation of loyalty, whether to a person, a cause, or one's country, and whether in thought or in deeds: *to suspect disloyalty in a friend.* Perfidy implies deliberate breaking of faith or of one's pledges and promises, on which others are relying: *it is an act of perfidy to cheat innocent persons.* Treachery implies being secretly traitorous but seeming friendly and loyal: *in treachery deceit is added to disloyalty.* Treason is definitely wishing harm to one's country or government, and performing overt acts to help its enemies: *an act of help to a hostile power is treason.*

dismal (dĭz′məl), *adj.* **1.** causing gloom or dejection; gloomy; dreary; cheerless; melancholy. **2.** terrible; dreadful. **3.** *Now Rare.* disastrous; calamitous. **4.** *Obs.* evil; unlucky. —*n.* **5.** (*usually pl.*) *Colloq.* gloom; melancholy; dumps: *in the dismals.* **6.** something dismal. **7.** any of certain tracts of swampy land along or near the southern Atlantic coast of the U.S. [ME *dismall*; orig. uncert.] —**dis′mally,** *adv.* —**dis′malness,** *n.* —**Ant. 1.** gay.

dismantle (dĭs măn′tl), *v.t.*, **-tled, -tling. 1.** to deprive or strip of apparatus, furniture, equipments, defences, etc.: *to dismantle a ship or a fortress.* **2.** to pull down; take apart; take to pieces. **3.** to divest of dress, covering, etc. [t. F (obs.): m. s. *desmanteler.* See dis-[1], mantle] —**disman′tlement,** *n.*

dismast (dĭs măst′), *v.t.* to deprive of masts; break off the masts of. —**dismast′ment,** *n.*

dismay (dĭs mā′), *v.t.* **1.** to break down the courage of utterly, as by sudden danger or trouble; dishearten utterly; daunt. —*n.* **2.** sudden or complete loss of courage; utter disheartenment. [ME *desmaien*, prob. t. OF; cf. OF *esmaier* dismay] —**Syn. 1.** appal, terrify, horrify, frighten, disconcert. See **discourage. 2.** consternation, terror, panic, horror, fear.

dismember (dĭs mĕm′bə), *v.t.* **1.** to deprive of members or limbs; divide limb from limb. **2.** to separate into parts; divide and distribute the parts of (a kingdom, etc.). [ME *dismembre(n)*, t. OF: m. *desmembrer*, der. *des-* dis-[1] + *membre* member] —**dismem′berer,** *n.* —**dismem′berment,** *n.*

dismiss (dĭs mĭs′), *v.t.* **1.** to direct or allow (an assembly of persons, etc.) to disperse. **2.** to bid or allow (a person) to go; give permission to depart. **3.** to send forth (a thing); let go. **4.** to discharge or remove, as from office or service. **5.** to discard or reject. **6.** to put off or away; lay aside; esp. to put aside from consideration. **7.** to have done with (a subject) after summary treatment. **8.** *Law.* to put out of court, as a complaint or appeal. —*n.* **9.** *Mil.* a command for soldiers to drop out of their ranks and disperse. [t. ML: m. s. *dismissus*, pp., sent away, for L *dismissus*] —**dismiss′ible,** *adj.* —**Syn. 2.** See **release.** —**Ant. 5.** accept.

dismissal (dĭs mĭs′əl), *n.* **1.** the act of dismissing. **2.** state of being dismissed. **3.** a spoken or written order of discharge. Also, **dismission** (dĭs mĭsh′ən).

dismissive (dĭs mĭs′ĭv), *adj.* **1.** expressing dismissal, disregard, or rejection. **2.** expressing contempt.

dismissory (dĭs mĭs′ə rĭ), *adj.* expressing dismissal, disregard or rejection.

dismount (dĭs mount′), *v.i.* **1.** to get off or alight from a horse, bicycle, etc. —*v.t.* **2.** to bring or throw down, as from a horse; unhorse. **3.** to remove (a thing) from its mounting, support, setting, etc. **4.** to take (a piece of mechanism) to pieces. —*n.* **5.** the act or manner of dismounting. —**dismount′able,** *adj.*

disnature (dĭs nā′chə), *v.t.*, **-tured, -turing.** to deprive of its proper nature; make unnatural.

Disney (dĭz′nĭ), *n.* **Walt(er E.),** 1901–66, U.S. film producer, esp. of animated cartoons.

disobedience (dĭs′ə bē′dyəns), *n.* lack of obedience; neglect or refusal to obey.

disobedient (dĭs′ə bē′dyənt), *adj.* neglecting or refusing to obey; refractory. —**dis′obe′diently,** *adv.* —**Syn.** insubordinate, contumacious, defiant.

disobey (dĭs′ə bā′), *v.t.*, *v.i.* to neglect or refuse to obey. [ME *disobey(en)*, t. OF: m. *desobeir*, f. *des-* dis-[1] + *obeir* obey] —**dis′obey′er,** *n.* —**Syn.** violate, disregard, defy.

disoblige (dĭs′ə blīj′), *v.t.*, **-bliged, -bliging. 1.** to refuse or neglect to oblige; act contrary to the desire or convenience of; fail to accommodate. **2.** to give offence to; affront. **3.** *Obs. or Dial.* to incommode; put to inconvenience. —**dis′oblig′ing,** *adj.* —**dis′oblig′ingly,** *adv.* —**dis′oblig′ingness,** *n.*

disoperation (dĭs ŏp′ə rā′shən), *n. Ecol.* the conscious or unconscious behaviour of organisms living together and producing a result which is disadvantageous or harmful to the organisms concerned.

disorder (dĭs ô′də), *n.* **1.** lack of order or regular arrangement; disarrangement; confusion. **2.** an irregularity. **3.** breach of order; disorderly conduct; a public disturbance. **4.** a derangement of physical or mental health or functions. —*v.t.* **5.** to destroy the order or regular arrangement of; disarrange. **6.** to derange the physical or mental health or functions of.

—**Syn. 1.** disorderliness, disarray, jumble, litter, clutter. **3.** Disorder, brawl, disturbance, uproar are disruptions or interruptions of a peaceful situation. Disorder refers to unrest within a city and to any scene in which there is confusion or fighting among individuals or groups: *the police went to a scene of disorder.* A brawl is a noisy, unseemly quarrel, usually in a public place: *a tavern brawl.* A disturbance is disorder of such size as to inconvenience many people: *to cause a disturbance.* An uproar is a tumult, a bustle and clamour of many voices, often because of a disturbance: *a mighty uproar.* **4.** ailment, malady. See **disease.**

disordered (dĭs ô′dəd), *adj.* **1.** in confusion. **2.** mentally ill.

disorderly (dĭs ô′də lĭ), *adj.* **1.** characterized by disorder; irregular; untidy; confused. **2.** unruly; turbulent; tumultuous. **3.** *Law.* violating, or opposed to, constituted order; contrary to public order or morality. —*adv.* **4.** without order, rule, or method; irregularly; confusedly. —**disor′derliness,** *n.*

disorderly conduct, *Law.* any of various petty disdemeanours, generally including nuisances, breaches of the peace, offensive or immoral conduct in public, etc.

disorderly house, 1. a house of prostitution; brothel. **2.** a gambling place.

disorderly person, *Law.* **1.** a person guilty of disorderly conduct. **2.** a person guilty of a separate offence including loitering in public, vagrancy, etc.

disorganization (dĭs ô′gə nī zā′shən), *n.* **1.** a breaking up of order or system; disunion or disruption of constituent parts. **2.** the absence of organization or orderly arrangement; disarrangement; disorder. Also, **disorganisation.**

disorganize (dĭs ô′gə nīz′), *v.t.*, **-nized, -nizing.** to destroy the organization, systematic arrangement, or orderly connection of; throw into confusion or disorder. Also, **disorganise.** —**disor′ganiz′er,** *n.*

disorientate (dĭs ô′rĭ ən tāt′), *v.t.*, **-tated, -tating. 1.** to confuse as to direction. **2.** to turn away from east. **3.** to perplex; to confuse. Also, **disorient.** —**dis′orienta′tion,** *n.*

disown (dĭs ōn′), *v.t.* to refuse to acknowledge as belonging or pertaining to oneself; deny the ownership of or responsibility for; repudiate; renounce. —**disown′er,** *n.* —**disown′ment,** *n.*

disparage (dĭs păr′ĭj), *v.t.*, **-raged, -raging. 1.** to bring reproach or discredit upon; lower the estimation of. **2.** to speak of or treat slightingly; depreciate; belittle. [ME *desparage(n)*, t. OF: m. *desparagier* match equally, der. *des-* dis-[1] + *parage* equality, der. *parer* equalize (g. L *pariāre*)] —**dispar′ager,** *n.* —**dispar′agingly,** *adv.*

disparagement (dĭs păr′ĭj mənt), *n.* **1.** the act of disparaging. **2.** something that causes loss of dignity or reputation.

disparate (dĭs′pə rĭt), *adj.* distinct in kind; essentially different; dissimilar; unlike; having no common genus. [t. L: m. s. *disparātus*, pp., separated] —**dis′parately,** *adv.* —**dis′parateness,** *n.*

disparity (dĭs păr′ĭ tĭ), *n.*, *pl.* **-ties.** lack of similarity or equality; inequality; difference: *a disparity in age, rank, condition, etc.* —**Syn.** See **difference.**

dispart (dĭs păt′), *v.t.*, *v.i.* to part asunder; separate; divide into parts. [appar. t. It.: s. *dispartire* part, separate, divide, g. L] —**dispart′ment,** *n.*

dispassion (dĭs păsh′ən), *n.* freedom from passion; unemotional state or quality.

dispassionate (dĭs păsh′ən ĭt), *adj.* free from or unaffected by passion; devoid of personal feeling or bias; impartial; calm: *a dispassionate critic.* —**dispas′sionately,** *adv.* —**dispas′sionateness,** *n.*

dispatch (dĭs păch′), *v.t.* **1.** to send off; put under way: *to dispatch a messenger, telegram, etc.* **2.** *Rare.* to dismiss (a person), as after an audience. **3.** to put to death; kill. **4.** to transact or dispose of (business, etc.) promptly or speedily; execute quickly; settle. —*v.i.* **5.** *Archaic.* to hasten; be quick. **6.** *Obs.* to settle a matter. —*n.* **7.** the sending off of a messenger, letter, etc., to a destination. **8.** *Obs.* dismissal of a person after the transaction of his business. **9.** a putting to death; killing. **10.** prompt or speedy transaction, as of business. **11.** expeditious performance, promptitude, or speed: *proceed with all possible dispatch.* **12.** *Com.* **a.** a method of effecting a speedy delivery of goods. **b.** a conveyance or organization for the expeditious transmission of merchandise, etc. **13.** a written message sent in haste. **14.** a state paper as a diplomatic or military communication, sent by special messenger. **15. mentioned in dispatches,** named in military reports for special bravery or acts of service. **16.** *Journalism.* a news account transmitted by a reporter to his newspaper or other agency. **17.** a telegram. Also,

despatch. [t. It.: m. *dispacciare* hasten, speed, or t. Sp.: m. *despachar*] —**dispatch′er,** *n.*

dispatch box, a sealed and locked box in which confidential government papers are carried by special messengers.

dispatch case, a briefcase.

dispatch note, **1.** a notification sent in advance of a parcel to notify the recipient of its pending arrival. **2.** a document attached to a parcel to be sent abroad, containing details of the contents.

dispatch rider, *Chiefly Mil.* an official messenger who carries dispatches by motorcycle.

dispel (dĭs pĕl′), *v.*, **-pelled, -pelling.** —*v.t.* **1.** to drive off in various directions; scatter; disperse; dissipate: *to dispel vapours, fear, etc.* —*v.i.* **2.** to be scattered; melt away. [t. L: m. s. *dispellere* drive asunder] —**dispel′ler,** *n.* —**Syn.** See **scatter.** —**Ant.** gather.

dispend (dĭs pĕnd′), *v.t. Archaic.* to pay out; expend; spend. [ME *despende(n)*, t. OF: m. *despendre*, g. L *dispendere* weigh out]

dispensable (dĭs pĕn′sə bl), *adj.* **1.** that may be dispensed with or done without; unimportant. **2.** capable of being dispensed or administered. **3.** admitting of dispensation, as an offence or a sin. **4.** that may be declared not binding. —**dispen′sabil′ity,** *n.*

dispensary (dĭs pĕn′sə rĭ, -srĭ), *n., pl.* **-saries.** **1.** a place where something is dispensed, esp. medicines. **2.** a charitable or public institution where medicines are furnished and medical advice is given gratuitously or for a small fee.

dispensation (dĭs′pĕn sā′shən), *n.* **1.** the act of dispensing; distribution; administration; management. **2.** that which is distributed or given out. **3.** a certain order, system, or arrangement. **4.** *Theol.* **a.** the divine ordering of the affairs of the world. **b.** an appointment or arrangement, as by God. **c.** a divinely appointed order or system: *the old, Mosaic, or Jewish dispensation; the new, gospel, or Christian dispensation.* **5.** a dispensing with, doing away with, or doing without something. **6.** *Rom. Cath. Ch.* **a.** the relaxation of a law by a competent superior in a specific case directly affecting physical matters. **b.** the document containing this. —**dis′pensa′tional,** *adj.*

dispensator (dĭs′pĕn sā′tə), *n.* one who dispenses; a distributor; an administrator.

dispensatory (dĭs pĕn′sə tə rĭ, -trĭ), *n., pl.* **-ries.** a book in which the composition, preparation, and uses of medicinal substances are described; a non-official pharmacopoeia.

dispense (dĭs pĕns′), *v.*, **-pensed, -pensing,** *n.* —*v.t.* **1.** to deal out; distribute: *to dispense justice, wisdom, etc.* **2.** to administer (laws, etc.). **3.** *Pharm.* to put up and distribute (medicine), esp. on prescription. **4.** *Rom. Cath. Ch.* to grant a dispensation to, for, or from. —*v.i.* **5.** to grant dispensation. **6.** **dispense with, a.** to do without; forgo. **b.** to do away with (a need, etc.). **c.** to grant exemption from (a law, promise, etc.). —*n.* **7.** *Obs.* dispensation. [ME *dispense(n)*, t. OF: m. *dispenser*, t. L: m. *dispensāre* weigh out, freq. of L *dispendere*] —**dispens′er,** *n.* —**Syn. 1.** See **distribute.**

dispeople (dĭs pē′pl), *v.t.*, **-pled, -pling.** to deprive of people; depopulate.

dispermous (dī spû′məs), *adj. Bot.* two-seeded.

dispersal (dĭs pû′səl), *n.* dispersion (defs 1 and 2).

disperse (dĭs pûs′), *v.*, **-persed, -persing.** —*v.t.* **1.** to scatter abroad; send or drive off in various directions. **2.** to spread; diffuse: *the wise disperse knowledge.* **3.** to dispel; cause to vanish: *the fog is dispersed.* —*v.i.* **4.** to separate and move apart in different directions without order or regularity; become scattered: *the company dispersed at 10 o'clock.* **5.** to be dispelled; be scattered out of sight; vanish. [t. F: m. s. *disperser*, ult. der. L *dispersus*, pp., scattered] —**dispers′edly,** *adv.* —**dispers′er,** *n.* —**Syn. 1.** See **scatter.**

disperse phase, *Chem.* the suspended particles in a colloidal solution.

dispersion (dĭs pû′shən), *n.* **1.** the act of dispersing. **2.** the state of being dispersed. **3.** *Optics.* **a.** (of glass or other transparent substance) the variation of the refractive index with the wavelength of light increasing as the wavelength decreases. It is responsible for prism spectra. **b.** the separation of white or complex light into its constituent colours. **4.** *Statistics.* the scattering of values of a variable round the mean or median of a distribution. **5.** *Chem.* a system of dispersed particles suspended in a fluid. **6.** *Electronics.* the scattering of electromagnetic radiation in a medium which affects the higher frequencies present more than the lower ones. **7.** (*cap.*) the Diaspora.

dispersion error, *Mil.* the distance of one shot from the centre of impact.

dispersion medium, *Chem.* the solvent in a colloidal solution.

dispersive (dĭs pû′sĭv), *adj.* serving or tending to disperse.

dispirit (dĭ spĭ′rĭt), *v.t.* to deprive of spirit; depress the spirits of; discourage; dishearten. —**dispir′ited,** *adj.* —**dispir′itedly,** *adv.* —**dispir′itedness,** *n.* —**dispir′iting,** *adj.* —**dispir′itingly,** *adv.*

dispiteous (dĭs pĭt′yəs), *adj. Archaic.* cruel; pitiless.

displace (dĭs plās′), *v.t.*, **-placed, -placing.** **1.** to put out of the usual or proper place: *to displace a bone.* **2.** to take the place of; replace. **3.** to remove from a position, office, etc. **4.** *Obs.* to banish; remove. —**displace′able,** *adj.*

—**Syn. 1.** DISPLACE, MISPLACE mean to put something in a different place from where it should be. To DISPLACE means to move from its place more or less permanently, often referring to people: *the chairman was displaced from office.* To MISPLACE is to put an object, usually an easily portable one, in a wrong place, so that it is difficult to find: *papers that belonged in the safe were misplaced and temporarily lost.*

displaced person, a person removed from his homeland as a prisoner or slave labourer or driven from it by an invasion.

displacement (dĭs plās′mənt), *n.* **1.** the act of displacing. **2.** the state of being displaced. **3.** *Physics.* **a.** the displacing or replacing of one thing by another, as of water by something immersed or floating in it. **b.** the weight or the volume of fluid displaced by a floating or submerged body, equivalent to the weight of the floating body or to the volume of the submerged body. **4.** *Mach.* (of a cylinder) the volume swept out by the piston. **5.** *Geol.* offset of rocks due to movement along a fault. **6.** *Psychoanal.* the transfer of an emotion from the object about which it was originally experienced to another object.

displacement ton. See **ton**[1] (def. 4).

displacer (dĭs plā′sə), *n.* **1.** one who or that which displaces. **2.** plum (def. 8).

displant (dĭs plänt′), *v.t. Obs.* **1.** to dislodge. **2.** to transplant.

display (dĭs plā′), *v.t.* **1.** to show; exhibit; make visible: *to display a flag.* **2.** to reveal; betray: *to display fear.* **3.** to unfold; open out; spread out: *to display a sail.* **4.** to show ostentatiously. **5.** *Print.* to give special prominence to (words, etc.) by choice and arrangement of type, etc. —*n.* **6.** the act of displaying; exhibition; show: *a display of goods, skill, etc.* **7.** an ostentatious show: *a vulgar display of wealth.* **8.** *Print.* **a.** the giving of prominence to particular words, etc., by the choice and arrangement of types and position, as in an advertisement, headline, or news story. **b.** printed matter thus displayed. **9.** *Electronics.* an electronic system capable of representing information visibly, as on a cathode ray tube. [ME *desplay(en)*, t. OF: m. *despleier, desploier* DEPLOY] —**display′er,** *n.*

—**Syn. 1.** DISPLAY, EVINCE, EXHIBIT, MANIFEST mean to show or bring to the attention of another or others. To DISPLAY is literally to spread something out so that it may be most completely and favourably seen: *to display goods for sale.* To EXHIBIT is to put something in plain view and usually in a favourable position for particular observation: *to exhibit the best flowers at a special show.* They may both be used of showing (off) one's qualities or feelings: *he displayed his wit, his ignorance; he exhibited great surprise.* To EVINCE and to MANIFEST have only this latter reference, MANIFEST being the stronger word: *to evince or manifest surprise, interest, sympathy.* **4.** flourish, flaunt, parade, air. **6.** See **show.** —**Ant. 1.** conceal.

displease (dĭs plēz′), *v.*, **-pleased, -pleasing.** —*v.t.* **1.** to cause dissatisfaction or dislike to; offend; annoy. —*v.i.* **2.** to be unpleasant; cause displeasure. —**displeas′ingly,** *adv.*

displeasure (dĭs plĕzh′ə), *n., v.*, **-ured, -uring.** —*n.* **1.** dissatisfaction; annoyance; anger. **2.** *Archaic.* discomfort, uneasiness, or pain. **3.** *Archaic.* a cause of offence, annoyance, or injury. —*v.t.* **4.** *Archaic.* to displease. —**Syn. 1.** See **dissatisfaction.**

displode (dĭs plōd′), *v.t., v.i.*, **-ploded, -ploding.** *Obs.* to explode. [t. L: m. s. *displōdere* burst asunder]

displume (dĭs plo͞om′), *v.t.*, **-plumed, -pluming.** **1.** to strip of plumes; deplume. **2.** to strip of honours.

disport (dĭs pôt′), *v.t.* **1.** to divert or amuse (oneself); exercise or display (oneself) in a sportive manner. —*v.i.* **2.** to divert oneself; sport. —*n.* **3.** *Archaic.* diversion; amusement; play; sport. [ME *desporte(n)*, t. OF: m. *desporter, deporter*, f. *des-* DIS-[1], *de-* DE- + *porter* carry (g. L *portāre*)]

disposable (dĭs pō′zə bl), *adj.* capable of being disposed of; subject to disposal; inclined.

disposable income, that part of a person's income which remains after the deduction of income tax, etc.

disposal (dĭs pō′zəl), *n.* **1.** the act of disposing, or of disposing of, something; arrangement. **2.** a disposing of as by gift or sale; bestowal or assignment. **3.** power or right to dispose of a thing; control: *left to his disposal.*

dispose (dĭs pōz′), *v.*, **-posed, -posing,** *n.* —*v.t.* **1.** to put in a particular or the proper order or arrangement; adjust by arranging the parts. **2.** to put in a particular or suitable place. **3.** to give a tendency or inclination to; incline. **4.** *Archaic.* to make fit or ready; prepare. —*v.i.* **5.** to arrange or decide matters. **6.** *Obs.* to make terms. **7. dispose of, a.** to deal with definitely; get rid of. **b.** to make over or part with, as by gift or sale. —*n.* **8.** *Archaic.* disposition; habit. **9.** *Obs.* arrangement; regulation; disposal. [ME *dispose(n)*, t. OF: m. *disposer*, f. *dis-* DIS-[1] + *poser* POSE[1], but assoc. with derivs. of L *dispōnere* (cf. DISPOSITION)] —**dispos′er,** *n.*

disposed (dĭs pōzd′), *adj.* inclined or minded, esp. favourably (usually fol. by *to* or infinitive).

disposition (dĭs′pə zĭsh′ən), *n.* **1.** mental or moral constitution; turn of mind. **2.** mental inclination; willingness. **3.** physical inclination or tendency. **4.** arrangement, as of troops or buildings. **5.** final settlement of a matter. **6.** *Archaic.* regulation; appointment; dispensation. **7.** bestowal, as by gift or sale. **8.** power to dispose of a thing; control. [t. L: s. *dispositio*] —**dis′posi′tional,** *adj.*

—**Syn. 1.** DISPOSITION, TEMPER, TEMPERAMENT refer to the aspects and habits of mind which one displays over a length of time. DISPOSITION is the natural or prevailing aspect of one's mind as shown in behaviour and in relationships with others: *a happy disposition, a selfish disposition.* TEMPER sometimes denotes the essential quality of one's nature: *a temper of iron;* usually it has to do with propensity towards anger: *an even temper, a quick or hot temper.* TEMPERAMENT suggests the delicate balance of one's emotions, the disturbance of which determines one's moods: *an artistic temperament, an unstable temperament.*

dispossess (dĭs′pə zĕs′), *v.t.* to put (a person) out of possession, esp. of real property; oust. —**dis′posses′sion,** *n.* —**dis′posses′sor,** *n.* —**dispossessory** (dĭs′pə zĕs′ə rĭ), *adj.* —**Syn.** See **strip**[1].

disposure (dĭs pō′zhə), *n.* disposal; disposition.

dispraise (dĭs prāz′), *v.*, **-praised, -praising,** *n.* —*v.t.* **1.** to speak of as undeserving; censure; disparage. —*n.* **2.** act of dispraising; censure. —**disprais′er,** *n.* —**disprais′ingly,** *adv.*

dispread (dĭ sprĕd′), *v.t., v.i.*, **-spread, -spreading.** *Archaic.* to spread out; extend.

disprize (dĭs prīz′), *v.t.*, **-prized, -prizing.** *Archaic.* to hold in small esteem; disdain.

disproof (dĭs proof′), *n.* the act of disproving; proof to the contrary; refutation.

disproportion (dĭs′prə pô′shən), *n.* **1.** lack of proportion; want of due relation, as in size, number, etc. **2.** something out of proportion. —*v.t.* **3.** to make disproportionate. —**dis′propor′tionable,** *adj.* —**dis′propor′tionableness,** *n.* —**dis′propor′tionably,** *adv.*

disproportional (dĭs′prə pô′shə nəl), *adj.* disproportionate. —**dis′propor′tionally,** *adv.*

disproportionate (dĭs′prə pô′shə nĭt), *adj.* not proportionate; out of proportion, as in size, number, etc. —**dis′propor′tionately,** *adv.* —**dis′propor′tionateness,** *n.*

disprove (dĭs proov′), *v.t.*, **-proved, -proving.** to prove (an assertion, claim, etc.) to be false or wrong; refute; invalidate. [ME *disprove(n)*, t. OF: m. *desprover*, f. des- DIS-[1] + *prover.* PROVE] —**disprov′able,** *adj.* —**disprov′al,** *n.*

disputable (dĭs pyoo′tə bl, dĭs′pyoo tə bl), *adj.* that may be disputed; liable to be called in question; questionable. —**disput′abil′ity, disput′ableness′,** *n.* —**disput′ably,** *adv.*

disputant (dĭs pyoo′tənt, dĭs′pyoo tənt), *adj.* **1.** disputing. —*n.* **2.** one who disputes; a debater.

disputation (dĭs′pyoo tā′shən), *n.* **1.** the act of disputing or debating; verbal controversy; a discussion or debate. **2.** an academic exercise consisting of the arguing of a thesis between its maintainer and his opponents. **3.** *Obs.* conversation.

disputatious (dĭs′pyoo tā′shəs), *adj.* given to disputation; argumentative; contentious. Also, **disputative** (dĭs pyoo′tə tĭv). —**dis′puta′tiously,** *adv.* —**dis′puta′tiousness,** *n.*

dispute (dĭs pyoot′; *n. sometimes* dĭs′pyoot), *v.*, **-puted, -puting,** *n.* —*v.i.* **1.** to engage in argument or discussion. **2.** to argue vehemently; wrangle or quarrel. —*v.t.* **3.** to argue or debate about; discuss. **4.** to argue against; call in question. **5.** to quarrel or fight about; contest. **6.** to strive against; oppose: *to dispute an advance.* —*n.* **7.** argumentation; verbal contention; a debate or controversy; a quarrel. [ME, t. L: m. s. *disputāre;* r. ME *despute(n)*, t. OF] —**disput′er,** *n.* —**Syn. 7.** See **argument.**

disqualification (dĭs kwŏl′ĭ fĭ kā′shən), *n.* **1.** the act of disqualifying. **2.** the state of being disqualified. **3.** something that disqualifies.

disqualify (dĭs kwŏl′ĭ fī′), *v.*, **-fied, -fying.** —*v.t.* **1.** to deprive of qualification or fitness; render unfit; incapacitate. **2.** to deprive of legal or other rights or privileges; pronounce unqualified. **3.** *Sport.* to deprive of the right to engage or compete in a match because the rules have been broken.

disquiet (dĭs kwī′ət), *v.t.* **1.** to deprive of quiet, rest, or peace; disturb; make uneasy. —*n.* **2.** lack of quiet; disturbance; unrest; uneasiness. —*adj.* **3.** *Rare.* unquiet; uneasy. —**disqui′etly,** *adv.*

disquieting (dĭs kwī′ə tĭng), *adj.* causing disquiet; disturbing.

disquietude (dĭs kwī′ĭ tyood′), *n.* a state of disquiet; uneasiness.

disquisition (dĭs′kwĭ zĭsh′ən), *n.* a formal discourse or treatise in which a subject is examined and discussed; a dissertation. [t. L: s. *disquisitio* inquiry]

Disraeli (dĭz rā′lĭ), *n.* **Benjamin** (*Earl of Beaconsfield*), 1804–81, British statesman and novelist: prime minister 1868, 1874–80.

disrate (dĭs rāt′), *v.t.*, **-rated, -rating.** *Naut.* to reduce to a lower rating, as a petty officer, or a non-commissioned officer of marines. Cf. **degrade.**

disregard (dĭs′rĭ gäd′), *v.t.* **1.** to pay no attention to; leave out of consideration. **2.** to treat without due regard, respect, or attentiveness. —*n.* **3.** lack of regard or attention; neglect. **4.** lack of due or respectful regard. —**dis′regard′er,** *n.* —**Syn. 2.** See **slight.**

disregardful (dĭs′rĭ gäd′fəl), *adj.* neglectful; careless.

disrelish (dĭs rĕl′ĭsh), *v.t.* **1.** to have a distaste for; dislike. —*n.* **2.** distaste; dislike.

disremember (dĭs′rĭ mĕm′bə), *v.t., v.i. Colloq.* to fail to remember; forget.

disrepair (dĭs′rĭ pĕə′), *n.* the state of being out of repair; impaired condition.

disreputable (dĭs rĕp′yoo tə bl), *adj.* **1.** not reputable; having a bad reputation. **2.** discreditable; dishonourable. —**disrep′utabil′ity, disrep′utableness,** *n.* —**disrep′utably,** *adv.*

disrepute (dĭs′rĭ pyoot′), *n.* ill repute; discredit (usually prec. by *in, into*): *that policy is in disrepute; this would bring the administration of justice into disrepute.* Also, *Archaic,* **disreputation** (dĭs rĕp′yoo tā′shən).

disrespect (dĭs′rĭ spĕkt′), *n.* **1.** lack of respect; disesteem; rudeness. —*v.t.* **2.** to regard or treat without respect; regard or treat with contempt or rudeness.

disrespectable (dĭs′rĭ spĕk′tə bl), *adj.* not respectable. —**dis′respect′abil′ity,** *n.*

disrespectful (dĭs′rĭ spĕkt′fəl), *adj.* characterized by disrespect; having or showing disrespect. —**dis′respect′fully,** *adv.* —**dis′respect′fulness,** *n.* —**Syn.** discourteous, uncivil, impolite, rude, impudent.

disrobe (dĭs rōb′), *v.t., v.i.*, **-robed, -robing. 1.** to undress. **2.** to divest of official robes; remove from office. —**disrobe′ment,** *n.* —**disrob′er,** *n.*

disroot (dĭs root′), *v.t.* to uproot; dislodge.

disrupt (dĭs rŭpt′), *v.t., v.i.* **1.** to break or rend asunder; break up. —*adj.* **2.** disrupted; rent asunder. [t. L: s. *disruptus*, pp.] —**disrupt′er, disrup′tor,** *n.*

disruption (dĭs rŭp′shən), *n.* **1.** forcible separation or division into parts. **2.** a disrupted condition.

disruptive (dĭs rŭp′tĭv), *adj.* disrupting; pertaining to disruption.

disruptive discharge, *Elect.* the sudden and large increase in current through an insulating medium due to complete failure of the medium under electrostatic stress.

disrupture (dĭs rŭp′chə), *v.t.*, **-tured, -turing.** *Rare.* to disrupt.

dissatisfaction (dĭs′săt ĭs făk′shən), *n.* lack of satisfaction; state of not being satisfied.

—**Syn.** DISSATISFACTION, DISCONTENT, DISPLEASURE imply a sense of dislike for, or unhappiness in, one's surroundings and a wish for other conditions. DISSATISFACTION results from contemplating what falls short of one's wishes or expectations, and is usually only temporary: *dissatisfaction with results of an afternoon's work.* DISCONTENT is a sense of lack, and a general feeling of uneasy dislike for the conditions of one's life, which colours one's entire outlook: *feeling a continual vague discontent.* DISPLEASURE, a more positive word, suggests a certain amount of anger as well as dissatisfaction: *displeasure at being kept waiting.*

dissatisfactory (dĭs′săt ĭs făk′tə rĭ, -trĭ), *adj.* causing dissatisfaction.

dissatisfied (dĭs săt′ĭs fīd′), *adj.* **1.** discontented; not pleased; offended. **2.** showing dissatisfaction: *a dissatisfied look.* —**dissat′isfied′ly,** *adv.*

dissatisfy (dĭs săt′ĭs fī′), *v.t.*, **-fied, -fying.** to make ill satisfied, ill pleased, or discontented.

disseat (dĭs sēt′), *v.t.* to unseat.

dissect (dĭ sĕkt′), *v.t.* **1.** to cut apart (an animal body, plant, etc.) to examine the structure, relation of parts, or the like. **2.** to examine minutely part by part; analyse. [t. L: s. *dissectus*, pp., cut asunder] —**dissec′tible,** *adj.* —**dissec′tor,** *n.*

dissected (dĭ sĕk′tĭd), *adj.* **1.** *Bot.* deeply cut into numerous segments, as a leaf. **2.** *Phys. Geog.* cut up by many closely spaced valleys, as a plateau. **3.** *Geog.* (of a map) cut into sections and mounted on linen, enabling it to be folded and carried without damage.

dissection (dĭ sĕk′shən), *n.* **1.** the act of dissecting. **2.** something that has been dissected.

disseise (dĭs sēz′), *v.t.*, **-seised, -seising.** *Law.* to deprive (a person) of seisin, or of the possession, of a freehold interest in land, esp. wrongfully or by force; oust. Also, **disseize.** [ME *disseyse(n)*, t. AF: m. *disseisir* dispossess, f. *dis-* DIS-¹ + *saisir* SEIZE] —**dissei′sor,** *n.*

disseisee (dĭs′sē zē′, dĭs sē′zē′), *n.* one who is disseised. Also, **dis′seizee′.**

disseisin (dĭs sē′zĭn), *n.* *Law.* **1.** the act of disseising. **2.** the state of being disseised. Also, **dissei′zin.** [ME *dysseysyne*, t. AF: m. *disseisine*, f. *dis-* DIS-¹ + *saisine* possession, SEISIN]

dissemblance¹ (dĭ sĕm′bləns), *n.* *Archaic.* dissimilarity; unlikeness. [t. OF: m. *dessemblance*, der. *dessembler* be unlike, f. *des-* DIS-¹ + *sembler* seem (g. L *simulāre*)]

dissemblance² (dĭ sĕm′bləns), *n.* *Archaic.* dissembling; dissimulation. [f. DISSEMBLE + -ANCE]

dissemble (dĭ sĕm′bl), *v.*, **-bled, -bling.** —*v.t.* **1.** to give a false semblance to; conceal the real nature of. **2.** to put on the appearance of; feign. **3.** *Archaic.* to let pass unnoticed; ignore. —*v.i.* **4.** to conceal one's motives, etc., under some pretence; speak or act hypocritically. [f. DIS-¹ + *-semble*, modelled on RESEMBLE] —**dissem′bler,** *n.* —**dissem′blingly,** *adv.*

disseminate (dĭ sĕm′ĭ nāt′), *v.t.*, **-nated, -nating.** to scatter, as seed in sowing; spread abroad; diffuse; promulgate. [t. L: m. s. *dissēminātus*, pp.] —**dissem′ina′tion,** *n.* —**dissem′inative,** *adj.* —**dissem′ina′tor,** *n.*

disseminated sclerosis, multiple sclerosis.

dissension (dĭ sĕn′shən), *n.* **1.** violent disagreement; discord; a contention or quarrel. **2.** difference in sentiment or opinion; disagreement.

dissent (dĭ sĕnt′), *v.i.* **1.** to differ in sentiment or opinion; disagree; withhold assent (fol. by *from*). **2.** to differ in religious opinion; reject the doctrines or authority of an established church. —*n.* **3.** difference in sentiment or opinion. **4.** separation from an established church; nonconformity. [ME *dissente(n)*, t. L: m. *dissentīre* differ in opinion] —**dissent′ing,** *adj.* —**dissent′ingly,** *adv.*

—**Syn.** 3. DISSENT, DISSIDENCE mean disagreement with the majority opinion. DISSENT, formerly much the same as DISSIDENCE, has come to suggest not only strong dissatisfaction but possibly also a determined opposition. If DISSENTERS withdraw from a group, they continue to oppose it. DISSIDENCE may express either withholding of agreement or open disagreement. DISSIDENTS may withdraw from a group but, if so, they are more likely merely to go their own way.

dissenter (dĭ sĕn′tə), *n.* **1.** one who dissents in any matter; one who disagrees with any opinion. **2.** (*sometimes cap.*) a person, now esp. a Protestant, who dissents from the established church.

dissentient (dĭ sĕn′shənt), *adj.* **1.** dissenting, esp. from the opinion of the majority. —*n.* **2.** one who dissents. —**dissen′tience,** *n.*

dissentious (dĭ sĕn′shəs), *adj.* contentious; quarrelsome.

dissepiment (dĭ sĕp′ĭ mənt), *n.* **1.** a partition or septum. **2.** *Bot.* one of the partitions formed within ovaries and fruits by the coherence of the sides of the constituent carpels. [t. L: m. s. *dissaepimentum* that which separates] —**dissep′imen′tal,** *adj.*

D, Dissepiment

dissert (dĭ sût′), *v.i.* *Obs. or Rare.* to discourse on a subject. [t. L: s. *dissertus*, pp., examined, discussed]

dissertate (dĭs′ə tāt′), *v.i.*, **-tated, -tating.** to treat of a subject in discourse; make a dissertation. [t. L: m. s. *dissertātus*, pp., discussed] —**dis′serta′tor,** *n.*

dissertation (dĭs′ə tā′shən), *n.* **1.** a written essay, treatise, or thesis, esp. one written by a candidate for a doctorate. **2.** a formal discourse. —**dis′serta′tional,** *adj.*

disserve (dĭs sûv′), *v.t.*, **-served, -serving.** to serve ill; do an ill turn to.

disservice (dĭs sû′vĭs), *n.* harm; injury; an ill turn. —**disser′viceable,** *adj.*

dissever (dĭ sĕv′ə), *v.t.* **1.** to sever; separate. **2.** to divide into parts. —*v.i.* **3.** to part; separate. —**dissev′erance, dissev′erment, dissev′era′tion,** *n.*

dissidence (dĭs′ĭ dəns), *n.* disagreement. —**Syn.** See **dissent.**

dissident (dĭs′ĭ dənt), *adj.* **1.** differing; disagreeing; dissenting. —*n.* **2.** one who differs; a dissenter. [t. L: s. *dissidens*, ppr., differing, sitting apart]

dissilient (dĭ sĭl′ĭ ənt), *adj.* flying or bursting asunder. [t. L: s. *dissiliens*, ppr.] —**dissil′ience, dissil′iency,** *n.*

dissimilar (dĭ sĭm′ĭ lə), *adj.* not similar; unlike; different. —**dissim′ilarly,** *adv.*

dissimilarity (dĭs′ĭ mĭ lă′rĭ tĭ), *n.*, *pl.* **-ties.** **1.** unlikeness; difference. **2.** a point of difference. —**Syn.** **1.** See **difference.**

dissimilate (dĭ sĭm′ĭ lāt′), *v.t.*, **-lated, -lating.** *Phonet.* to change (a speech sound) so that it is less like another sound in a neighbouring syllable, as in *marble*, which derives from the French *marbre.* —**dissimilative** (dĭ sĭm′ĭ lə tĭv), *adj.*

dissimilation (dĭs′ĭ mĭ lā′shən), *n.* **1.** a making or becoming unlike. **2.** *Phonet.* the act or process of dissimilating speech sounds. **3.** *Biol.* catabolism.

dissimilitude (dĭs′ĭ mĭl′ĭ tyōōd′), *n.* **1.** unlikeness; difference. **2.** a point of difference.

dissimulate (dĭ sĭm′yōō lāt′), *v.*, **-lated, -lating.** —*v.t.* **1.** to disguise or conceal under a false semblance; dissemble. —*v.i.* **2.** to use dissimulation; dissemble. [t. L: m. s. *dissimulātus*, pp.] —**dissimulative** (dĭ sĭm′yōō lə tĭv), *adj.* —**dissim′ula′tor,** *n.*

dissimulation (dĭ sĭm′yōō lā′shən), *n.* **1.** the act of dissimulating; feigning; hypocrisy. **2.** *Psychiatry.* the ability or the tendency to appear mentally normal when actually suffering from disorder: a characteristic of the paranoiac. Cf. **simulation.**

dissipate (dĭs′ĭ pāt′), *v.*, **-pated, -pating.** —*v.t.* **1.** to scatter in various directions; disperse; dispel; disintegrate. **2.** to scatter wastefully or extravagantly; squander. —*v.i.* **3.** to become scattered or dispersed; be dispelled; disintegrate. **4.** to indulge in extravagant, intemperate, or dissolute pleasure; practise dissipation. [t. L: m. s. *dissipātus*, pp., scattered, demolished] —**dis′sipa′ter,** *n.* —**dis′sipa′tive,** *adj.* —**Syn.** **1.** See **scatter.**

dissipated (dĭs′ĭ pā′tĭd), *adj.* **1.** indulging in or characterized by excessive devotion to pleasure; intemperate; dissolute. **2.** dispersed; scattered; dispelled. —**dis′sipa′tedly,** *adv.* —**dis′sipa′tedness,** *n.*

dissipation (dĭs′ĭ pā′shən), *n.* **1.** the act of dissipating. **2.** the state of being dissipated; dispersing; disintegration. **3.** a wasting by misuse. **4.** mental distraction; a diversion. **5.** dissolute mode of living; intemperance or debauchery.

dissociable (dĭ sō′shyə bl, -shə bl), *adj.* **1.** capable of being dissociated; separable. **2.** unsociable. **3.** incongruous; not reconcilable.

dissocial (dĭ sō′shəl), *adj.* unsocial; disinclined to or unsuitable for society.

dissocialize (dĭs sō′shə līz′), *v.t.* to make unsociable. Also, **dissocialise.**

dissociate (dĭ sō′shĭ āt′), *v.*, **-ated, -ating.** —*v.t.* **1.** to sever the association of; disunite; separate. **2.** *Chem.* to subject to dissociation. —*v.i.* **3.** to withdraw from association. **4.** *Chem.* to undergo dissociation. [t. L: m. s. *dissociātus*, pp.] —**dissociative** (dĭ sō′shyə tĭv), *adj.*

dissociation (dĭ sō′sĭ ā′shən), *n.* **1.** the act of dissociating. **2.** the state of being dissociated; disunion. **3.** *Phys. Chem.* **a.** the reversible resolution or decomposition of a complex substance into simpler constituents, due to variation in the physical conditions, as when water gradually decomposes into hydrogen and oxygen under great heat, in such a way that when the temperature is lowered the liberated elements recombine to form water. **b.** electrolytic dissociation. **4.** *Psychiatry.* the splitting off of certain mental processes from the main body of consciousness, with varying degrees of autonomy resulting.

dissoluble (dĭ sŏl′yōō bl), *adj.* capable of being dissolved. —**dissol′ubil′ity, dissol′ubleness,** *n.*

dissolute (dĭs′ə lōōt′), *adj.* indifferent to moral restraints; given over to dissipation; licentious. [t. L: m.s. *dissolūtus*, pp., loosened] —**dis′solute′ly,** *adv.* —**dis′solute′ness,** *n.*

dissolution (dĭs′ə lōō′shən), *n.* **1.** the act of resolving into parts or elements. **2.** the resulting state. **3.** the undoing or breaking up of a tie, bond, union, etc. **4.** the breaking up of an assembly or organization; dismissal; dispersal. **5.** *Govt.* an order issued by the head of the state terminating a parliament and necessitating a new election. **6.** death or decease. **7.** a bringing or coming to an end; destruction. **8.** the legal termination of business activity, including the distribution of assets and the fixing of liabilities. **9.** *Chem.* solution in a liquid substance. —**dis′solu′tive,** *adj.*

dissolve (dĭ zŏlv′), *v.*, **-solved, -solving,** *n.* —*v.t.* **1.** to make a solution of in a solvent. **2.** to undo (a tie or bond); break up (a connection, union, etc.). **3.** to break up (an assembly or organization); dismiss; disperse. **4.** *Govt.* to order the termination of Parliament, in Great Britain done at five-year intervals, or less if the government is defeated. **5.** to bring to an end; destroy; dispel. **6.** to resolve into parts or elements; disintegrate. **7.** to destroy the binding power of: *dissolve a spell.* **8.** *Law.* to deprive of force; annul: *to dissolve a marriage or injunction.* —*v.i.* **9.** to become dissolved, as in a solvent. **10.** to break up or disperse. **11.** to lose force or strength; lose binding force. **12.** to disappear gradually; fade from sight or apprehension. **13.** *Films.* to fade out one shot while simultaneously fading in the next shot, overlapping the two shots during the process. *—n.* **14.** *Films.* a scene made by dissolving. [ME *dissolve(n)*, t. L: m. *dissolvere* loosen, disunite] **—dissol′vabil′ity, dissol′vableness,** *n.* **—dissol′vable,** *adj.* **—dissol′ver,** *n.*

dissolvent (dĭ zŏl′ vənt), *adj., n.* solvent.

dissonance (dĭs′ə nəns), *n.* **1.** an inharmonious or harsh sound; discord. **2.** *Music.* a simultaneous combination of notes conventionally accepted as being in a state of unrest and needing resolution (opposed to *consonance*). **3.** disagreement or incongruity. Also, **dis′sonancy.**

dissonant (dĭs′ə nənt), *adj.* **1.** disagreeing or harsh in sound; discordant. **2.** out of harmony; incongruous; at variance. [t. L: s. *dissonans*, ppr., disagreeing in sound] **—dis′sonantly,** *adv.*

dissuade (dĭ swād′), *v.t.*, **-suaded, -suading. 1.** to deter by advice or persuasion; persuade not to do something (fol. by *from*): *dissuade him from leaving home.* **2.** to advise or urge against (an action, etc.). [t. L: m. s. *dissuādēre* advise against] **—dissuad′er,** *n.*

dissuasion (dĭ swā′zhən), *n.* the act of dissuading.

dissuasive (dĭ swā′sĭv), *adj.* tending to dissuade. **—dissua′sively,** *adv.*

dissymmetry (dĭ sĭm′ĭ trĭ), *n.* **1.** absence of symmetry. **2.** symmetry between two objects disposed in opposite directions. **—dissymmetric** (dĭs′ĭ mĕt′rĭk), **dis′symmet′rical,** *adj.*

dist., 1. distance. **2.** distinguish. **3.** distinguished. **4.** district.

distaff (dĭs′tăf), *n.* **1.** a staff with a cleft end, formerly used for holding the wool, flax, etc., from which the thread was drawn in spinning by hand. **2.** an analogous part of a spinning wheel, for holding flax to be spun. **3.** the female sex. **4.** a female heir; a woman. [ME *distaf*, OE *distæf*, f. *dis-*, akin to LG *diesse* bunch of flax on a distaff (cf. DIZEN) + *stæf* STAFF]

distaff side, the female side of a family.

distain (dĭ stān′), *v.t. Archaic.* to discolour; stain; sully. [ME *disteyne(n)*, t. OF: m. *desteindre*, f. *des-* DIS-[1] + *teindre* wet, dye (g. L *tingere*)]

distal (dĭs′tl), *adj.* situated away from the point of origin or attachment, as of a limb or bone; terminal (opposed to *proximal*). [f. DIST(ANT) + -AL[1]] **—dis′tally,** *adj.*

distance (dĭs′təns), *n., v.*, **-tanced, -tancing.** *—n.* **1.** the extent of space intervening between things or points. **2.** the state or fact of being distant, as of one thing from another; remoteness. **3.** the interval between two points of time. **4.** progress; advance: *our business has come a good distance in a year.* **5.** remoteness in any respect. **6.** a distant point, place or region. **7.** the distant part of a landscape, etc. **8.** reserve or aloofness; one's proper degree of aloofness: *to keep one's distance.* **9.** *Horseracing, etc.* the official length, usually measured in furlongs, to be run. **10.** *Obs.* disagreement or dissension; a quarrel. *—v.t.* **11.** to leave behind at a distance, as at a race; surpass. **12.** to place at a distance. **13.** to cause to appear distant.

distant (dĭs′tənt), *adj.* **1.** far off or apart in space; not near at hand; remote (fol. by *from*). **2.** separate or apart in space: *a place a mile distant.* **3.** apart or far off in time. **4.** far apart in any respect: *a distant relative.* **5.** reserved; not familiar or cordial. **6.** to a distance: *a distant journey.* [t. F, t. L: s. *distans*, ppr., being distant, standing apart] **—dis′tantly,** *adv.*

distant signal, *Railways.* a preliminary signal which shows how the next signal along the line, the home signal, is set.

distaste (dĭs tāst′), *n., v.*, **-tasted, -tasting.** *—n.* **1.** dislike; disinclination. **2.** disrelish for food or drink. *—v.t.* **3.** *Archaic.* to dislike. **—Syn. 1.** aversion, repugnance, disgust. See **dislike.**

distasteful (dĭs tāst′fəl), *adj.* **1.** causing dislike. **2.** unpleasant to the taste. **—distaste′fully,** *adv.* **—distaste′fulness,** *n.* **—Syn. 1.** disagreeable, displeasing, offensive, repugnant, repulsive. **2.** unpalatable, unsavoury.

distemper[1] (dĭs tĕm′pə), *n.* **1.** *Vet. Sci.* **a.** a specific infectious disease of young dogs caused by a filterable virus. **b.** a disease of horses; strangles. **c.** (formerly) any of several diseases characterized by fever and catarrhal symptoms. **2.** deranged condition of mind or body; a disorder or disease. **3.** disorder or disturbance. **4.** ill humour; discontent. *—v.t.* **5.** to derange physically or mentally. [ME *distempre(n)*, t. ML: m. *distemperāre.* See DIS-[1], TEMPER]

distemper[2] (dĭs tĕm′pə), *n.* **1.** a water paint used for the decoration of interior walls and ceilings, esp. one in which the binding medium consists essentially of glue, casein, or a similar sizing material. *—v.t.* **2.** to paint with distemper. [t. OF: m. *destemprer*, f. *des-* DIS-[1] + *temprer* dilute, soak (g. L *temperāre*)]

distemperature (dĭs tĕm′prə chə), *n. Archaic.* distempered or disordered condition; disturbance of health, mind, or temper.

distend (dĭs tĕnd′), *v.t., v.i.* **1.** to stretch apart or asunder; stretch out. **2.** to expand by stretching, as something hollow or elastic. [t. L: s. *distendere*] **—Syn. 2.** See **expand.**

distensible (dĭs tĕn′sə bl), *adj.* capable of being distended. **—disten′sibil′ity,** *n.*

distension (dĭs tĕn′shən), *n.* **1.** the act of distending. **2.** the state of being distended. Also, **disten′tion.**

distent (dĭs tĕnt′), *adj. Obs.* distended. [t. L: s. *distentus*, pp.]

distich (dĭs′tĭk), *n. Pros.* **1.** a group of two lines of verse, usually making complete sense; a couplet. **2.** a rhyming couplet. [t. L: s. *distichon*, t. Gk, neut. of *dístichos* of two rows or lines] **—dis′tichal,** *adj.*

distichous (dĭs′tĭ kəs), *adj. Bot.* arranged alternately in two vertical rows on opposite sides of an axis, as leaves. See illus. under **alternate.** [t. L: m. *distichus* of two rows. See DISTICH] **—dis′tichously,** *adv.*

distil (dĭs tĭl′), *v.*, **-tilled, -tilling.** *—v.t.* **1.** to subject to a process of vaporization and subsequent condensation, as for purification or concentration. **2.** to extract the volatile components of by distillation; transform by distillation. **3.** to extract or obtain by distillation. **4.** to drive (*off* or *out*) by distillation. **5.** to let fall in drops; give forth in or as in drops. *—v.i.* **6.** to undergo distillation. **7.** to become vaporized and then condensed in distillation. **8.** to drop, pass, or condense as a distillate. **9.** to fall in drops; trickle; exude. Also, *U.S.*, **distill.** [ME *distille(n)*, t. L: m. *distillāre*, var. of *dēstillāre* drip down] **—distill′able,** *adj.*

distillate (dĭs′tĭ lĭt, -lāt′), *n.* the product obtained from the condensation of vapours in distillation.

distillation (dĭs′tĭ lā′shən), *n.* **1.** the volatilization or evaporation and subsequent condensation of a liquid, as when water is boiled in a retort and the steam is condensed in a cool receiver. **2.** the purification or concentration of a substance; the obtaining of the essence or volatile properties contained in it, or the separation of one substance from another, by such a process. **3.** a product of distilling; a distillate. **4.** the act or process of distilling. **5.** the fact of being distilled. **—distillatory** (dĭs tĭl′ə tə rĭ, -trĭ), *adj.*

distilled (dĭs tĭld′), *adj.* obtained or produced by distillation.

distiller (dĭs tĭl′ə), *n.* **1.** an apparatus for distilling, as a condenser, or esp., one for distillation of salt water at sea. **2.** one whose business it is to extract alcoholic spirits by distillation.

distillery (dĭs tĭl′ə rĭ), *n., pl.* **-eries.** a place or establishment where distilling, esp. the distilling of alcoholic spirits, is carried on.

distilment (dĭs tĭl′mənt), *n.* **1.** the act or process of distilling. **2.** the product of distilling. Also, *U.S.*, **distillment.**

distinct (dĭs tĭngkt′), *adj.* **1.** distinguished as not being the same; not identical; separate (fol. by *from* or used absolutely). **2.** different in nature or qualities; dissimilar. **3.** clear to the senses or intellect; plain; definite; unmistakeable. **4.** distinguishing clearly, as the vision. **5.** notable, unusually good: *his book is a distinct enrichment of our literature.* **6.** pronounced; effective: *he has a distinct advantage over his competitors.* **7.** *Archaic.* decorated or adorned. [ME, t. L: s. *distinctus*, pp., separated] **—distinct′ness,** *n.* **—Syn. 1.** See **various.**

distinction (dĭs tĭngk′shən), *n.* **1.** a marking off or distinguishing as different. **2.** the recognizing or noting of differences; discrimination. **3.** a discrimination made between things as different. **4.** the condition of being different; a difference. **5.** a distinguishing characteristic. **6.** a distinguishing or treating with special attention or favour. **7.** a mark of special favour. **8.** marked superiority; note; eminence. **9.** (in certain examinations) the highest awarded grade. **10.** distinguished appearance. **11.** division.

—Syn. 3. DISTINCTION and DIFFERENCE may both refer to perceivable dissimilarities and, in this meaning, may be used interchangeably: *there is a distinction (difference) between the two.* DISTINCTION, however, usually suggests the perception of dissimilarity, as the result of analysis and discrimination (*a carefully made distinction between two treatments of the same theme*) whereas DIFFERENCE refers only to the condition of being dissimilar: *the differences between Gothic and Roman architecture.* 'A distinction without a difference' is a way of referring to an artificial or false discrimination. **7.** See **honour. —Ant. 4.** resemblance.

distinctive (dĭs tĭngk′tĭv), *adj.* distinguishing; serving to distinguish; characteristic. **—distinc′tively,** *adv.* **—distinc′tiveness,** *n.*

distinctly (dĭs tĭngkt′lĭ), *adv.* **1.** a distinct manner; clearly. **2.** without doubt; unmistakably. **—Syn. 1.** See **clearly.**

distingué (dĭs tăng′gā; *Fr.* dēs tăN gĕ′), *adj.* distinguished; having an air of distinction. [F, pp. of *distinguer* distinguish] —**distin′guée,** *adj. fem.*

distinguish (dĭs tĭng′gwĭsh), *v.t.* **1.** to mark off as different (fol. by *from*). **2.** to recognize as distinct or different; discriminate. **3.** to perceive clearly by sight or other sense; discern; recognize. **4.** to serve to separate as different; be a distinctive characteristic of; characterize. **5.** to make prominent, conspicuous, or eminent: *to distinguish oneself in battle.* **6.** to divide into classes; classify. **7.** *Archaic.* to single out for or honour with special attention. —*v.i.* **8.** to indicate or show a difference (fol. by *between*). **9.** to recognize or note differences; discriminate. [f. s. L *distinguere* separate, distinguish + -ISH[2], modelled on EXTINGUISH] —**distin′guishable,** *adj.* —**distin′guishableness,** *n.* —**distin′guishably,** *adv.* —**distin′guisher,** *n.* —**distin′guishingly,** *adv.*

—**Syn.** 2. DISTINGUISH, DIFFERENTIATE, DISCRIMINATE suggest a positive attempt to analyse characteristic features or qualities of things. To DISTINGUISH is to recognize the characteristic features belonging to a thing: *to distinguish a light cruiser from a heavy cruiser.* To DISCRIMINATE is to perceive the particular, nice, or exact differences between things, to determine wherein these differences consist, and to estimate their significance: *to discriminate prejudiced from unprejudiced testimony.* To DIFFERENTIATE is especially to point out exactly and in detail the differences (usually) between two things: *the symptoms of some diseases are so similar that it is hard to differentiate one from another.* —**Ant.** 2. confuse.

distinguished (dĭs tĭng′gwĭsht), *adj.* **1.** conspicuous; marked. **2.** noted; eminent; famous. **3.** having an air of distinction; distingué. —**Syn.** 2. See **famous.**

distort (dĭs tôt′), *v.t.* **1.** to twist awry or out of shape; make crooked or deformed. **2.** to pervert; misrepresent. **3.** *Electronics.* to change (a signal wave-form) so that the information is degraded. [t. L: s. *distortus*, pp.] —**distort′ed,** *adj.* —**distort′edly,** *adv.* —**distort′edness,** *n.* —**distort′er,** *n.*

distortion (dĭs tô′shən), *n.* **1.** the act of distorting. **2.** the state of being distorted. **3.** anything distorted. **4.** *Electronics.* a change in the wave-form of a signal which degrades the information. —**distor′tional,** *adj.*

distract (dĭs trăkt′), *v.t.* **1.** to draw away or divert, as the mind or attention. **2.** to divide (the mind, attention, etc.) between objects. **3.** to entertain; amuse; divert. **4.** to disturb or trouble greatly in mind. **5.** to rend by dissension or strife. —*adj.* **6.** *Archaic.* distracted. [t. L: s. *distractus*, pp., pulled asunder. Cf. DISTRAUGHT] —**distract′ed,** *adj.* —**distract′edly,** *adv.* —**distract′er,** *n.* —**distract′ing,** *adj.* —**distract′ingly,** *adv.*

distraction (dĭs trăk′shən), *n.* **1.** the act of distracting. **2.** the state of being distracted. **3.** amusement; recreation; entertainment. **4.** violent disturbance of mind; mental derangement or madness. **5.** division or disorder due to dissension; tumult.

distractive (dĭs trăk′tĭv), *adj.* tending to distract.

distrain (dĭs trān′), *Law.* —*v.t.* **1.** to constrain by seizing and holding goods, etc., in pledge for rent, damages, etc., or in order to obtain satisfaction of a claim. **2.** to levy a distress upon. —*v.i.* **3.** to levy a distress. [ME *destreyne(n)*, t. OF: m. *destreindre* constrain, g. L *distringere* draw asunder, detain, hinder] —**distrain′able,** *adj.* —**distrain′ment,** *n.* —**distrain′er, distrain′or,** *n.*

distraint (dĭs trānt′), *n.* *Law.* an act of distraining; a distress.

distrait (dĭs trā′; *Fr.* dēs trĕ′), *adj.* abstracted in thought; absent-minded. [t. F, pp. of *distraire*, g. L *distrahere* pull asunder. See DISTRACT] —**distraite** (dĭs trāt′; *Fr.* dēs-trĕt′), *adj., fem.*

distraught (dĭs trôt′), *adj.* **1.** distracted; bewildered; deeply agitated. **2.** crazed. [var. of obs. *distract*, adj., by assoc. with *straught*, pp. of STRETCH]

distress (dĭs trĕs′), *n.* **1.** great pain, anxiety, or sorrow; acute suffering; affliction; trouble. **2.** acute poverty; physical exhaustion. **3.** a state of extreme necessity. **4.** *Naut.* the state of a ship requiring immediate assistance, as because of accident. **5.** *Law.* **a.** an act of distraining; the legal seizure and detention of the goods of another as security or satisfaction for debt, etc. **b.** the thing seized in distraining. —*v.t.* **6.** to afflict with pain, anxiety, or sorrow; trouble sorely; worry; bother. **7.** to subject to pressure, stress, or strain; embarrass or exhaust by strain. **8.** to constrain. [ME *destresse*, t. OF: m. *destrece*, der. L *districtus*, pp., distrained] —**distress′ing,** *adj.* —**distress′ingly,** *adv.* —**Syn.** 1. grief, agony, anguish, misery. See **sorrow.**

distress call, **1.** an international code sign inferring that the sender is in danger or difficulty, as *Mayday* or *SOS*. **2.** any communication indicating distress: *the police sent out a distress call for blood donors.*

distressed area, a region where unemployment and a low standard of living prevail.

distressful (dĭs trĕs′fəl), *adj.* **1.** causing or involving distress. **2.** full of distress; feeling or indicating distress. —**distress′fully,** *adv.* —**distress′fulness,** *n.*

distress rocket, a rocket used to make a distress signal.

distress signal, a signal by persons in danger summoning aid and indicating their position by rocket, radio code, flag, or any other means.

distributary (dĭs trĭb′yŏŏ tə rĭ, -trĭ), *n.* **1.** a branch of a distributing system. **2.** a branch of a river flowing from the main river and not rejoining it, as in a delta.

distribute (dĭs trĭb′yŏŏt), *v.t.*, **-uted, -uting.** **1.** to divide and bestow in shares; deal out; allot. **2.** to disperse through a space or over an area; spread; scatter. **3.** to divide into parts of distinct character. **4.** to divide into classes: *these plants are distributed into 22 classes.* **5.** *Print.* to separate the type that has been used for printing and replace in its proper compartments. **6.** *Logic.* to employ (a term) so as to refer to all the individuals denoted by it: *the term 'men' is distributed in 'all men are mortal' but not in 'some men are old'.* [t. L: m. s. *distribūtus*, pp.] —**distrib′utable,** *adj.*

—**Syn.** 1. assign, mete, apportion. DISTRIBUTE, DISPENSE, apply to giving out something. DISTRIBUTE implies apportioned, individualized, and, often, personal giving, esp. of something that is definite or limited in amount or number: *the prizes were distributed among ten winners.* DISPENSE formerly implied indiscriminate, general, and liberal giving, esp. of something that was more or less indefinite or unmeasured in amount: *to dispense largess.* It now applies chiefly to giving according to need or deserts, from an organized and official source: *to dispense medicines and food to the victims, justice to criminals.*

distributee (dĭs trĭb′yŏŏ tē′), *n.* *U.S. Law.* a person who shares in the estate of one deceased; beneficiary.

distribution (dĭs′trĭ byŏŏ′shən), *n.* **1.** the act of distributing. **2.** the state or manner of being distributed. **3.** arrangement; classification. **4.** that which is distributed. **5.** the places where things of any particular category occur: *the distribution of coniferous forests in the world.* **6.** the transporting, marketing, merchandising, and selling of a product. **7.** *Econ.* **a.** the division of the aggregate income of any society among its members, or among the factors of production. **b.** the system of dispersing goods throughout a community. **8.** *Statistics.* a set of values or measurements of a set of elements, each measurement being associated with an element. —**dis′tribu′tional,** *adj.*

distribution curve, *Statistics.* the curve or line of a graph whose axes or data are based upon a specific frequency distribution. See **frequency distribution.**

distributive (dĭs trĭb′yŏŏ tĭv), *adj.* **1.** that distributes; characterized by or pertaining to distribution. **2.** *Gram.* treating the members of a group individually, as the adjectives *each* and *every*. **3.** *Logic.* (of a term) distributed in a given proposition. —*n.* **4.** a distributive word or expression. —**distrib′utively,** *adv.* —**distrib′utiveness,** *n.*

distributor (dĭs trĭb′yŏŏ tə), *n.* **1.** one who or that which distributes. **2.** *Com.* one engaged in the general distribution or marketing of some article or class of goods. **3.** *Mach.* a device in a multicylinder engine which distributes the igniting voltage to the sparking plugs in a definite sequence. Also, **distributer.**

district (dĭs′trĭkt), *n.* **1.** a division of territory marked off for administrative, ecclesiastical, or other purposes. **2.** a region or locality. **3.** a subdivision of a town, city, or county, often reflecting old and now non-existent boundaries. —*v.t.* **4.** *U.S.* to divide into districts. [t. ML: s. *districtus* territory under jurisdiction, special use of L *districtus*, pp., constrained]

district attorney, *U.S.* the public prosecutor for a specific district.

district commissioner, a representative of government or a magistrate with semi-judicial powers in a colony. Also, **district officer.**

district council, the council of an urban or rural district.

district nurse, a nurse employed by a local authority to visit and treat patients in their own homes.

District of Columbia, an area in the E United States coextensive with the federal capital, Washington: governed by Congress. 763,957 pop. (1960); 69 sq. mi. *Abbrev.:* D.C.

district surveyor, an officer, usually a qualified surveyor, employed by a local authority to supervise all new buildings, alterations, etc.

distrust (dĭs trŭst′), *v.t.* **1.** to feel distrust of; regard with doubt or suspicion. —*n.* **2.** lack of trust; doubt; suspicion. —**distrust′er,** *n.* —**Syn.** 2. See **suspicion.**

distrustful (dĭs trŭst′fəl), *adj.* full of distrust; doubtful; suspicious. —**distrust′fully,** *adv.* —**distrust′fulness,** *n.*

disturb (dĭs tûb′), *v.t.* **1.** to interrupt the quiet, rest, or peace of. **2.** to interfere with; interrupt; hinder. **3.** to throw into commotion or disorder; agitate; disorder; disarrange; unsettle. **4.** to perplex; trouble. [t. L: s.

disturbāre throw into disorder, disturb] —**disturb′er,** *n.* —**disturb′ingly,** *adv.*
disturbance (dĭs tû′bəns), *n.* **1.** the act of disturbing. **2.** the state of being disturbed. **3.** an instance of this; a commotion. **4.** something that disturbs. **5.** an outbreak of disorder; a breach of public peace. **6.** *Geol.* a mountain-making crustal movement of moderate intensity and somewhat restricted in geographic extent. **7.** *Law.* infringement of an incorporeal right. —**Syn. 2.** perturbation. See **agitation. 5.** confusion, tumult, riot. See **disorder.**
disulphate (dī sŭl′fāt), *n.* **1.** *Chem.* a salt of pyrosulphuric acid, as *sodium disulphate,* $Na_2S_2O_7$. See **pyro-. 2.** bisulphate. Also, *U.S.,* **disulfate.** [f. DI- + SULPHATE]
disulphide (dī sŭl′fīd), *n.* *Chem.* a sulphide containing two atoms of sulphur, as *carbon disulphide,* CS_2. Also, *U.S.,* **disulfide.**
disulphuric (dī′sŭl fyŏŏə′rĭk), *n.* *Chem.* pyrosulphuric. See **pyro-.** Also, *U.S.,* **disulfuric.**
disunion (dĭs yōō′nyən), *n.* **1.** severance of union; separation; disjunction. **2.** lack of union; dissension.
disunite (dĭs′yōō nīt′), *v.,* **-nited, -niting.** —*v.t.* **1.** to sever the union of; separate; disjoin. **2.** to set at variance, or alienate. —*v.i.* **3.** to part; fall asunder.
disunity (dĭs yōō′nĭ tĭ), *n., pl.* **-ties.** lack of unity.
disuse (*n.* dĭs yōōs′; *v.* dĭs yōōz′), *n., v.,* **-used, -using.** —*n.* **1.** discontinuance of use or practice. —*v.t.* **2.** to cease to use.
disutility (dĭs′yōō tĭl′ĭ tĭ), *n.* the quality of causing inconvenience or harm; injuriousness.
disvalue (dĭs văl′yōō), *v.t.,* **-ued, -uing.** *Rare.* to depreciate; disparage.
disyllable (dī sĭl′ə bl), *n.* a word of two syllables, as *virtue.* [t. L: m. s. *disyllabus,* t. Gk: m. *disýllabos.* See SYLLABLE] —**disyllabic** (dĭs′ĭ lăb′ĭk), *adj.* —**disyllabification** (dĭs′ĭ lăb′ĭ fĭ kā′shən), *n.* —**disyllabism** (dī-sĭl′ə bĭz′əm), *n.*
disyoke (dĭs yōk′), *v.t.,* **-yoked, -yoking.** to free from or as from a yoke.
dita (dē′tə), *n.* an apocynaceous shrub or tree, *Alstonia scholaris,* of Old World tropics with large, glossy, whorled leaves.
ditch (dĭch), *n.* **1.** a long, narrow hollow made in the earth by digging, as one for draining or irrigating land; a trench. **2.** any open passage or trench, as a natural channel or waterway. **3.** the border of a bowling green. **4. last ditch,** *Colloq.* the last defence; utmost extremity. —*v.t.* **5.** to dig a ditch or ditches in. **6.** *U.S.* to cause to be thrown into or as into a ditch, as a motor car in a crash. **7.** *Slang.* to get rid of; get away from. **8.** *Slang.* to crash-land (an aeroplane), esp. in the sea. —*v.i.* **9.** *Slang.* to crash-land an aeroplane. [ME *dich,* OE *dīc,* c. G *Teich.* See DIKE] —**ditch′er,** *n.*
ditheism (dī′thē ĭz′əm), *n.* *Relig.* **1.** the doctrine of, or belief in, two supreme gods. **2.** belief in the existence of two independent antagonistic principles, one good and the other evil. [f. DI-¹ + s. Gk *theós* god + -ISM] —**di′theist,** *n.* —**di′theis′tic,** *adj.*
dither (dĭth′ə), *n.* **1.** a trembling; vibration. **2.** *Colloq.* a state of trembling excitement or vacillation. —*v.i.* **3.** to be vacillating; uncertain. **4.** *Chiefly Dial.* to tremble with excitement or fear. [var. of *didder,* ME *diddir;* orig. obscure. Cf. DODDER]
dithionous (dī thī′ə nəs), *adj.* *Chem.* hyposulphurous. [f. DI-¹ + m. Gk *theîon* sulphur + -OUS]
dithyramb (dĭth′ĭ răm′, -rămb′), *n.* **1.** a choral song or hymn of vehement or wild character and usually irregular in form, orig. in honour of Dionysus or Bacchus. **2.** any poem or other composition having similar characteristics. [t. L: s. *dīthyrambus,* t. Gk: m. *dithýrambos*]
dithyrambic (dĭth′ĭ răm′bĭk), *adj.* **1.** of, pertaining to, or of the nature of a dithyramb. **2.** wildly irregular in form. **3.** wildly enthusiastic.
dittander (dĭ tăn′də), *n.* a perennial cruciferous herb, *Lepidium latifolium,* found mainly in coastal regions of Europe and formerly used as a condiment.
dittany (dĭt′ə nĭ), *n., pl.* **-nies. 1.** a labiate plant, *Origanum dictamnus* (**dittany of Crete**), formerly in high repute for its alleged medicinal virtues. **2.** a labiate plant, *Cunila origanoides,* of North America, bearing clusters of purplish flowers. **3.** a rutaceous plant, *Dictamnus albus,* cultivated for its showy flowers. [ME *ditonye,* der. OF *ditan,* g. L *dictamnus,* t. Gk: m. *diktamnon,* said to be so called from Mount *Dicte* in Crete, where it abounded]
ditto (dĭt′ō), *n., pl.* **-tos,** *adv., v.,* **-toed, -toing.** —*n.* **1.** the aforesaid; the same (used in accounts, lists, etc., to avoid repetition). *Symbol:* ,, ; *abbrev.:* do. **2.** the same thing repeated. **3.** *Colloq.* a duplicate or copy. —*adv.* **4.** as already stated; likewise. —*v.t.* **5.** to duplicate; copy. [t. It.: said, aforesaid, g. L *dictus,* pp., said]
dittography (dĭ tŏg′rə fĭ), *n.* **1.** unintentional repetition of one or more symbols in writing, as in copying a manuscript. **2.** the resulting passage or reading. [f. Gk *dittó(s)* double + -GRAPHY] —**dittographic** (dĭt′ə grăf′ĭk), *adj.*
ditto marks, two small marks (,,) indicating the repetition of something, usually placed beneath the thing repeated.
ditty (dĭt′ĭ), *n., pl.* **-ties. 1.** a poem intended to be sung. **2.** a short, simple song. [ME *dite,* t. OF, g. L *dictātum* thing composed or recited]
ditty-bag (dĭt′ĭ băg′), *n.* a bag used by sailors to hold sewing implements and other necessaries.
ditty-box (dĭt′ĭ bŏks′), *n.* a small box used as a ditty-bag.
diuresis (dī′yōō rē′sĭs), *n.* *Pathol.* excessive discharge of urine. [NL, f. Gk: *di-* DI-³ + *oúrēsis* urination]
diuretic (dī′yōō rĕt′ĭk), *Med.* —*adj.* **1.** increasing the volume of the urine, as a medicinal substance. —*n.* **2.** a diuretic medicine or agent. [t. LL: s. *diūrēticus* promoting urine, t. Gk: m. *diourētikós*]
diurnal (dī û′nəl), *adj.* **1.** of or pertaining to each day; daily. **2.** of or belonging to the daytime. **3.** *Bot.* showing a periodic alteration of condition with day and night, as certain flowers which open by day and close by night. **4.** active by day, as certain birds and insects. —*n.* **5.** *Liturgy.* a service-book containing offices for the daily hours of prayer. **6.** *Archaic.* a diary. **7.** *Archaic.* a daily or other newspaper. [t. LL: s. *diurnālis* daily] —**diur′nally,** *n.*
diurnal parallax. See **parallax** (def. 2).
div., 1. divide. **2.** divided. **3.** divine. **4.** dividend. **5.** division. **6.** divisor.
diva (dē′və), *n., pl.* **-vas, -ve** (-vĭ). a distinguished female singer; a prima donna. [t. It., t. L: goddess]
divagate (dī′və gāt′), *v.i.,* **-gated, -gating. 1.** to wander; stray. **2.** to digress in speech. [t. L: m. s. *divagātus,* pp., having wandered] —**di′vaga′tion,** *n.*
divalent (dī vā′lənt, dī′vā′lənt), *adj.* *Chem.* having a valency of two, as the ferrous ion, Fe^{++}.
divan (dĭ văn′), *n.* **1.** a low bed with no headboard or tailboard. **2.** a sofa or couch. **3.** a long, cushioned seat against a wall, as in Middle Eastern countries. **4.** (formerly) a council of state in Turkey and other Middle Eastern countries. **5.** any council, committee, or commission. **6.** (formerly in the Middle East) **a.** a council chamber, judgement hall, audience chamber, or bureau of state. **b.** a large building used for some public purpose, as a customs house. **7.** a smoking room, as in connection with a tobacco shop. **8.** *Obs.* a collection of oriental lyric verse, esp. poems by one author. [t. Turk., t. Pers.: m. *dēvān* (now *dīwān*)]
divaricate (*v.* dī văr′rĭ kāt′; *adj.* dī văr′rĭ kĭt, -kāt′), *v.,* **-cated, -cating,** *adj.* —*v.i., v.t.* **1.** to spread apart; branch; diverge. **2.** *Bot., Zool.* to branch at a wide angle. —*adj.* **3.** spread apart; widely divergent. **4.** *Bot., Zool.* branching at a wide angle. [t. L: m. s. *dīvāricātus,* pp., spread apart] —**divar′icately,** *adv.* —**divar′ica′tion,** *n.* —**divar′ica′tor,** *n.*
dive (dīv), *v.,* **dived** or (*U.S. Colloq.*) **dove, dived, diving,** *n.* —*v.i.* **1.** to plunge, esp. head first, as into water. **2.** to go below the surface of the water, as a submarine. **3.** to plunge deeply. **4.** *Aeron.* (of an aeroplane) to plunge downward at a greater angle than when gliding. **5.** to penetrate suddenly into anything, as with the hand. **6.** to dart. **7.** to enter deeply into (a subject, business, etc.). —*n.* **8.** the act of diving. **9.** *Colloq.* a disreputable place, as for drinking, gambling, etc., esp. a cellar or basement. [ME *dive(n)* dive, dip, OE *dȳfan,* v.t., dip (causative of *dūfan,* v.i., dive, sink), c. Icel. *dȳfa* dip]
dive-bomb (dīv′bŏm′), *v.t., v.i.* *Aeron.* to bomb by diving at a steep angle so that the pilot sights the target through his gun sights and releases the bombs just before pulling out.
dive-bomber (dīv′bŏm′ə), *n.* an aeroplane of the pursuit type which drops its bombs while diving at the target.
diver (dī′və), *n.* **1.** one who or that which dives. **2.** one who makes a business of diving, as for pearl oysters, to examine sunken vessels, etc. **3.** any of various birds which habitually dive, as loons, grebes, etc.
diverge (dī vûj′), *v.i.,* **-verged, -verging. 1.** to move or lie in different directions from a common point; branch off. **2.** to differ in opinion or character; deviate. **3.** to digress, from a plan, discussion, etc. [t. NL: m. s. *dīvergere,* f. L *dī-* DIS-¹ + *vergere* incline, VERGE²] —**Syn. 2.** See **deviate.**
divergence (dī vû′jəns), *n.* **1.** the act, fact, or amount of diverging. **2.** *Meteorol.* a condition brought about by a net flow of air from a given region. Also, **divergency** (dī vû′jən sĭ).
divergent (dī vû′jənt), *adj.* **1.** diverging; deviating. **2.** pertaining to divergence. —**diver′gently,** *adv.*

divers (dī′ vəz), *adj.* several, sundry (sometimes used pronominally): *divers of them.* [ME, t. OF, g. L *dīversus*, pp., lit., turned different ways]

diverse (dī vûs′, dī′ vûs), *adj.* **1.** of a different kind, form, character, etc.; unlike. **2.** of various kinds or forms; multiform. [var. of DIVERS, but now assoc. more directly with L *dīversus*] —**diverse′ly,** *adv.* —**diverse′ness,** *n.* —**Syn. 2.** See **various.**

diversification (dī vû′sī fī kā′shən), *n.* **1.** the state or act of diversifying. **2.** the art of manufacturing a number of different articles; selling a number of different goods, or putting money into a number of different investments in order to diminish the effects of a possible financial failure of one part.

diversified (dī vû′sī fīd′), *adj.* **1.** distinguished by various forms, or by a variety of objects. **2.** varied; distributed among several types: *diversified investments.*

diversiform (dī vû′sī fôm′), *adj.* differing in form; of various forms. [f. s. L *dīversus* various + -(I)FORM]

diversify (dī vû′sī fī′), *v.t.*, **-fied, -fying. 1.** to make diverse, as in form or character; give variety or diversity to; variegate. **2.** to vary (investments); invest in different types of (securities). [t. F: m. *diversifier*, t. ML: m. s. *dīversificāre*, f. L *dīversi-* diverse + *-ficāre* make] —**diver′sifi′able,** *adj.*

diversion (dī vû′shən), *n.* **1.** the act of diverting or turning aside, as from a course. **2.** a compulsory detour on a road or motorway, to avoid an obstacle, bottleneck, etc. **3.** distraction from business, care, etc.; recreation; entertainment; amusement; a pastime. **4.** *Mil.* a feint intended to draw off attention from the point of main attack. —**diver′sionary,** *adj.*

diversity (dī vû′sī tī), *n., pl.* **-ties. 1.** the state or fact of being diverse; difference; unlikeness. **2.** variety; multiformity. **3.** a point of difference.

divert (dī vût′), *v.t.* **1.** to turn aside or from a path or course; deflect. **2.** to set (traffic) on a detour. **3.** to draw off to a different object, purpose, etc. **4.** to distract from serious occupation; entertain or amuse. [t. OF: s. *divertir*, t. L: m. *dīvertere* turn aside, separate] —**divert′er,** *n.* —**divert′ible,** *adj.* —**Syn. 4.** See **amuse.**

diverticulum (dī′və tĭk′yŏŏ ləm), *n., pl.* **-la** (-lə). *Anat.* a blind tubular sac or process, branching off from a canal or cavity. [L: byway] —**di′vertic′ular,** *adj.*

divertimento (dĭ vû′tĭ mĕn′tō), *n., pl.* **-ti** (-tē). *Music.* an instrumental composition in several movements, light and diverting in character; a potpourri. [It.]

diverting (dī vû′tĭng), *adj.* that diverts; entertaining; amusing. —**divert′ingly,** *adv.*

divertissement (*Fr.* dē vĕr tēs mäɴ′), *n.* **1.** a diversion or entertainment. **2.** *Music.* a divertimento. **3.** a short ballet or other performance given between or in the course of acts or longer pieces. **4.** a series of such performances. [F, der. *divertiss-*, s. of *divertir* DIVERT]

divertive (dī vû′tĭv), *adj.* diverting; amusing.

Dives (dī′vēz), *n.* **1.** *Bible.* the rich man of the parable in Luke 16:19–31. **2.** any rich man. [L: rich, rich man]

divest (dī vĕst′), *v.t.* **1.** to strip of clothing, etc.; disrobe. **2.** to strip or deprive of anything; dispossess. **3.** *Law.* to take away or alienate (property, etc.). [t. ML: s. *dīvestīre*, var. of *disvestīre* (Latinization of OF *desvestir*)] —**Syn. 2.** See **strip**[2].

divestible (dī vĕs′tĭ bl), *adj.* capable of being divested, as an estate in land.

divestiture (dī vĕs′tĭ chə), *n.* **1.** the act of divesting. **2.** the state of being divested. Also, **divest′ment, divesture** (dī vĕs′chə).

dividable (dĭ vī′də bl), *adj.* divisible.

divide (dĭ vīd′), *v.*, **-vided, -viding,** *n.* —*v.t.* **1.** to separate into parts. **2.** to separate or part from each other or from something else; sunder; cut off. **3.** to deal out in parts; apportion; share. **4.** to separate in opinion or feeling; cause to disagree. **5.** to distinguish the kinds of; classify. **6.** *Maths.* **a.** to separate into equal parts by the process of division. **b.** to be a divisor of, without a remainder. **c.** to graduate (a rule, etc.). **7.** *Parl. Proc.* to separate (a legislature, etc.) into two groups in ascertaining the vote on a question. —*v.i.* **8.** to become divided or separated. **9.** to share something with others. **10.** to branch; diverge; fork. **11.** *Maths.* to go through the process of division. **12.** *Parl. Proc.* to vote by separating into two groups. —*n.* **13.** *Colloq.* act of dividing; a division. **14.** *U.S. Phys. Geog.* a watershed. [ME *divide(n)*, t. L: m. *dīvidere* force asunder, cleave, part, distribute] —**Syn. 1.** See **separate.**

divided (dĭ vī′dĭd), *adj.* **1.** separated; separate; disunited; shared. **2.** *Bot.* (of a leaf) cut into distinct portions by incisions extending to the midrib or the base.

divide et impera (dĭv′ĭ dā′ ĕt ĭm′pə rä′), *Latin.* divide and rule (political maxim of Machiavelli, etc.).

dividend (dĭv′ĭ dĕnd′), *n.* **1.** *Maths.* a number to be divided by another number (the divisor). **2.** *Law.* a sum out of an insolvent estate to be divided among the creditors. **3.** *Finance.* **a.** a pro-rata share in an amount to be distributed. **b.** a sum of money paid to shareholders of a company or trading concern out of earnings. **c.** interest payable on public funds. **4.** a percentage of the purchasing money spent over a period in a cooperative store, etc., returned to the purchaser at the end of that period. **5.** a payment to creditors and shareholders in a liquidated company. **6.** *Insurance.* a distribution of profit by a company to an assured. **7.** a share of anything divided. [t. L: s. *dīvidendum* (thing) to be divided, neut. ger. of *dīvidere* DIVIDE]

dividend cover, *Com.* the number of times that the declared dividend is covered by a company's net profit.

dividend warrant, *Com.* an order issued by a company in favour of a shareholder for payment of the dividend due to him.

divider (dĭ vī′də), *n.* **1.** one who or that which divides. **2.** (*pl.*) a pair of compasses as used for dividing lines, measuring, etc.

divi-divi (dĭv′ĭ dĭv′ĭ), *n.* **1.** a shrub or small tree, *Caesalpinia coriaria*, of tropical America, the astringent pods of which are much used in tanning and dyeing. **2.** the related species. **3.** the pods of either plant. [t. Carib or Galibi]

dividual (dĭ vĭd′yŏŏ əl), *adj. Archaic.* **1.** divisible or divided. **2.** separate; distinct. **3.** distributed; shared. [f. s. L *dīviduus* divisible + -AL[1]] —**divid′ually,** *adv.*

divination (dĭv′ĭ nā′shən), *n.* **1.** the discovering of what is obscure or the foretelling of future events, as by supernatural means. **2.** augury; a prophecy. **3.** instinctive prevision. [t. L: s. *dīvīnātio*, der. *dīvīnāre* DIVINE, v.] —**divinatory** (dĭ vĭn′ə tə rĭ, -trĭ), *adj.*

divine (dĭ vīn′), *adj., n., v.*, **-vined, -vining.** —*adj.* **1.** of or pertaining to a god, esp. the Supreme Being. **2.** addressed or appropriated to God; religious; sacred. **3.** proceeding from God. **4.** godlike; characteristic of or befitting a deity. **5.** heavenly; celestial. **6.** being a god, or God. **7.** pertaining to divinity or theology. **8.** of superhuman or surpassing excellence. **9.** *Colloq.* excellent. —*n.* **10.** one versed in divinity; a theologian. **11.** a priest or clergyman. —*v.t.* **12.** to discover (water, metal, etc.) by a divining rod. **13.** to discover or declare (something obscure or future), as by supernatural means; prophesy. **14.** to perceive by intuition or insight; conjecture. **15.** *Obs. or Archaic.* to portend. —*v.i.* **16.** to use or practise divination; prophesy. **17.** to have perception by intuition or insight; conjecture. [ME, t. L: m. s. *dīvīnus*; r. ME *devine*, t. OF] —**divine′ly,** *adv.* —**divine′ness,** *n.*

diviner (dĭ vī′nə), *n.* **1.** one who divines; a soothsayer; a prophet; a conjecturer. **2.** one who searches for and finds hidden water, metal, or oil, by means of a divining rod.

divine right of kings, the right to rule derived directly from God, not from the consent of the people.

diving beetle, any of the predacious beetles that constitute the family *Dytiscidae*, adapted for swimming and diving.

diving bell, a hollow vessel filled with air under pressure, in which persons may work under water.

diving board, a plank or board placed beside or projecting over a swimming pool at a certain height from which swimmers may dive.

diving suit, a watertight garment, consisting of a rubber or metal body covering and a helmet with an air-supply line attached, worn by divers. Also, **diving dress.**

divining rod, a rod used in divining, esp. a forked stick, commonly of hazel, said to tremble or move when held by some people over a spot where water, metal, etc., is underground.

divinity (dĭ vĭn′ĭ tĭ), *n., pl.* **-ties. 1.** the quality of being divine; divine nature. **2.** deity; godhood. **3.** a divine being; God. **4. the Divinity,** the Deity. **5.** a deity below God but above man. **6.** the science of divine things; theology. **7.** godlike character; supreme excellence.

divinize (dĭv′ĭ nīz′), *v.t.*, **-nized, -nizing.** to make divine; deify Also, **divinise.** —**div′iniza′tion,** *n.*

divisibility (dĭ vĭz′ĭ bĭl′ĭ tĭ), *n.* **1.** capability of being divided. **2.** *Maths.* the capacity of being exactly divided, without remainder.

divisible (dĭ vĭz′ə bl), *adj.* capable of being divided. —**divis′ibleness,** *n.* —**divis′ibly,** *adv.*

division (dĭ vĭzh′ən), *n.* **1.** the act of dividing; partition. **2.** the state of being divided. **3.** a distribution; a sharing-out. **4.** *Maths.* the operation inverse to multiplication; the finding of a quantity (the quotient) which, when multiplied by a given quantity (the divisor) gives another given quantity (the dividend). **5.** something that divides; a dividing line or mark. **6.** one of the parts into which a thing is divided; a section. **7.** separation by difference of opinion or feeling; disagreement; dissension. **8.** *Bot.* one of the major groupings of the plant kingdom. **9.** *Govt.* the separation of the members of a legislature, etc., into two groups, in taking a vote. **10.** one of the parts into which a country or an organization is divided for political, administrative, judicial, military, or other purposes. **11.** a semi-independent, but ultimately subordinate administrative unit in industry or government. **12.** *Sport.* a category or section containing all teams or competitors divided according to weight, skill, age, or some other criterion. **13.** *Mil.* a major administrative and tactical formation, larger than a regiment or brigade, and smaller than a corps. It is usually commanded by a major general. [t. L: s. *dīvīsio;* r. ME *devisioun,* t. OF] **—divis′ional, divis′ionary,** *adj.* **—divis′ionally,** *adv.*

—Syn. 1. separation, apportionment, allotment, distribution. DIVISION, PARTITION suggest the operation of dividing into parts or of one part from another. DIVISION usually means little more than the marking off or separation of a whole into parts. PARTITION often adds the idea of sharing, of an allotting or assigning of parts following division: *partition of an estate of a country.*

divisionism (dĭ vĭzh′ə nĭz′əm), *n.* pointillism.

division sign, the symbol (÷) placed between two expressions, denoting division of the first by the second.

divisive (dĭ vī′sĭv), *adj.* **1.** forming or expressing division or distribution. **2.** creating division or discord. **—divi′sively,** *adv.* **—divi′siveness,** *n.*

divisor (dĭ vī′zə), *n. Maths.* **1.** a number by which another number (the dividend) is divided. **2.** a number contained in another given number a certain number of times, without a remainder.

divorce (dĭ vôs′), *n., v.,* **-vorced, -vorcing.** *—n.* **1.** the dissolution of the marriage contract. **2.** any formal separation of man and wife according to established custom. **3.** a complete separation of any kind. *—v.t.* **4.** to separate; cut off. [ME *divors,* t. F: m. *divorce,* g. L *dīvortium* separation, dissolution] **—divorce′able,** *adj.* **—divorc′er,** *n.*

divorcé (dĭ vô′sā), *n.* a divorced man. [t. F, prop. pp. of *divorcer*] **—divor′cée,** *n. fem.*

divorcee (dĭ vô′sē′), *n.* a divorced person.

divorcement (dĭ vôs′mənt), *n.* divorce.

divot (dĭv′ət), *n.* **1.** *Golf, Cricket, etc.* a piece of turf cut out with a club or bat in making a stroke. **2.** *Scot.* a piece of turf; a sod.

divulgate (dĭ vŭl′gāt), *v.t.,* **-gated, -gating.** to make publicly known; publish. [t. L: m. s. *dīvulgātus,* pp., divulged] **—divul′ga′ter, divul′ga′tor,** *n.* **—divulgation** (dĭv′ŭl gā′shən), *n.*

divulge (dĭ vŭlj′), *v.t.,* **-vulged, -vulging.** to disclose or reveal (something private, secret, or previously unknown). [t. L: m. s. *dīvulgāre* make common] **—divulge′ment,** *n.* **—divulg′er,** *n.* **—Syn. 1.** See **reveal.**

divulgence (dĭ vŭl′jəns), *n.* a divulging.

divulsion (dĭ vŭl′shən), *n.* a tearing asunder; violent separation. [t. F, t. L: s. *dīvulsio*] **—divulsive** (dĭ vŭl′sĭv), *adj.*

diwan (dĭ wän′), *n.* dewan. [see DIVAN]

dixie (dĭk′sĭ), *n. Mil. Slang.* **1.** a large iron pot in which stew, tea, or the like is made. **2.** a mess tin. [t. Hind.: m. *degachī*]

Dixie (dĭk′sĭ), *n.* **1.** Also, **Dixie Land.** the southern states of the United States. **2.** any of several songs with this name. [orig. uncert.]

Dixiecrat (dĭk′sĭ krăt′), *n. U.S.* a member of a minority in the Democratic party, consisting of Democrats living in the southern states. [f. DIXIE + (DEMO)CRAT]

Dixieland (dĭk′sĭ lănd′), *n. Jazz.* a style of composition and performance characterized by vigorous improvisation.

Diyarbekir (*Turk.* dē yär′bĕk ĭr), *n.* a town in SE Turkey, on the Tigris river. 80,645 (1960). Also, **Diarbekr.**

dizen (dī′zən), *v.t. Archaic.* to deck with gaudy clothes or finery; bedizen. [akin to *dis-* in DISTAFF] **—diz′enment,** *n.*

Dizful (dĭz fōōl′), *n.* a town in SW Iran. 60,874 (est. 1964). Also, **Dezful.**

dizzy (dĭz′ĭ), *adj.,* **-zier, -ziest,** *v.,* **-zied, -zying.** *—adj.* **1.** affected with a sensation of whirling, with tendency to fall; giddy; vertiginous. **2.** bewildered; confused. **3.** causing giddiness: *a dizzy height.* **4.** heedless; thoughtless. **5.** *Colloq.* foolish or stupid. *—v.t.* **6.** to make dizzy. [ME and OE *dysig* foolish, c. LG *düsig* stupefied] **—diz′zily,** *adv.* **—diz′ziness,** *n.*

d.j., **1.** dinner jacket. **2.** disc jockey.

Djakarta (jə kä′tə), *n.* a seaport in and the capital of Indonesia, on the NW coast of Java. 2,973,052 (est. 1961). Also, **Jacarta, Jakarta.** Formerly, **Batavia.**

Djambi (jăm′bĭ), *n.* a town in Indonesia, in central Sumatra. 113,080 (1961).

Djerba (jû′bə), *n.* an island off the coast of Tunisia: fruit production; holiday resort; the lotus-eaters' island of Greek mythology. 198 sq. mi.

Djibouti (jĭ bōō′tĭ), *n.* a seaport in and the capital of French Somaliland, on the Gulf of Aden. 41,200 (est. 1963). Also, **Jibuti.**

djinn (jĭn), *n.* jinn.

D.L., Deputy Lieutenant.

dl., decilitre.

D. Lit., (L *Doctor Literarum*) Doctor of Literature.

D. Litt., (L *Doctor Litterarum*) Doctor of Letters.

DM, Deutsche Mark.

dm., decimetre.

D. Mus., Doctor of Music.

DNA, *Biochem.* deoxyribonucleic acid.

Dneprodzerzhinsk (*Russ.* dnĭ prə dzĭr zhĭnsk′), *n.* a city in SE Soviet Union in Europe, on the Dnieper. 218,000 (est. 1965).

Dnepropetrovsk (*Russ.* dnĭ prə pĭ trôfsk′), *n.* a city in the SE Soviet Union in Europe, on the Dnieper. 774,000 (est. 1965). Formerly, **Ekaterinoslav.**

Dnieper (dnē′pə), *n.* a river in the W Soviet Union, flowing S to the Black Sea. ab. 1400 mi. Russian, **Dnepr** (*Russ.* dnyĕ′pr).

Dniester (dnē′stə), *n.* a river flowing from the Carpathian Mountains in the SW Soviet Union SE to the Black Sea. ab. 800 mi. Russian, **Dnestr** (*Russ.* dnyĕs′tr). Rumanian, **Nistru.**

do[1] (dōō), *v., pres. sing.* 1 **do,** 2 **do** or (*Archaic*) **doest** or **dost,** 3 **does** or (*Archaic*) **doeth** or **doth;** *pl.* **do;** pt. **did;** pp. **done;** ppr. **doing;** *n.* *—v.t.* **1.** to perform (acts, duty, penance, a problem, a part, etc.). **2.** to execute (a piece or amount of work, etc.). **3.** to accomplish; finish. **4.** to put forth; exert: *do your best.* **5.** to be the cause of (good, harm, credit, etc.); bring about; effect. **6.** to render (homage, justice, etc.). **7.** to deal with (anything) as the case may require: *to do (cook) meat, do (wash) the dishes.* **8.** to cover; traverse: *we did thirty miles today.* **9.** to travel at a specified speed: *the car was doing 50 m.p.h.* **10.** to serve a period of time in an office, prison, etc. **11.** to make; create; form: *she will do your portrait.* **12.** to study: *he is doing German.* **13.** to visit as a tourist or sightseer: *they did Spain last year.* **14.** *Colloq.* to serve; suffice for: *this will do us for the present.* **15.** *Colloq.* to provide; prepare: *this pub does lunches.* **16.** *Slang.* to cheat or swindle. **17.** *Slang.* **a.** to treat violently; beat up. **b.** *Taboo.* to have sexual intercourse with. *—v.i.* **18.** to act, esp. effectively; be in action. **19.** to behave or proceed (wisely, etc.). **20.** to get along or fare (well or ill); manage (with; without, etc.). **21.** to be as to health: *how do you do?* **22.** to serve or be satisfactory, as for the purpose; suffice; be enough: *will this do?* **23.** to deal; treat (fol. by *by*): *to do well by a man.* *—aux.v.* **24.** (used without special meaning in interrogative, negative, and inverted constructions, in imperatives with *you* or *thou* expressed, and occasionally as a metric expedient in verse): *do you think so? I don't agree.* **25.** (used to lend emphasis to a principal verb): *do come!* **26.** (used to avoid repetition of a full verb or verb expression): *I think as you do. Did you see him? I did.* *—v.* **27.** Some special verb phrases are:

can or **could do with,** to require or be likely to benefit from: *I could do with more sleep.*

do away with, 1. to put an end to; abolish. **2.** to kill.

do down, *Slang.* to get the better of; cheat.

do for, 1. to accomplish the defeat, ruin, death, etc., of. **2.** *Colloq.* to cook and keep house for. **3.** to provide or manage for. **4.** *Slang.* to charge with a certain offence: *I've been done for speeding again.*

do in, *Slang.* **1.** to kill; murder. **2.** to exhaust; tire out. **3.** to ruin.

do one proud, *Colloq.* to treat lavishly.

do or die, to make a supreme effort.

do out of, *Slang.* to deprive, cheat, or swindle of.

do over, 1. to redecorate; renovate: *to do a room over.* **2.** *Slang.* to assault.

do time, to serve a term in prison.

do up, 1. to wrap and tie up. **2.** to fasten. **3.** to comb out and pin up (hair). **4.** to renovate. **5.** to dress up, esp. in fancy costume.

do without, 1. to dispense with; give up: *to do without luxuries.* **2.** to manage without; get along in the absence of: *the shop was closed, so we had to do without sweets.*

have to do with, to be connected with: *smoking has a lot to do with cancer.*

make do, to get along with the resources available.

—n. **28.** *Dial.* ado; action; work. **29.** *Slang.* a swindle. **30.** *Colloq.* a festivity or treat: *we're having a big do next week.* **31.** rules: customs, etc.: *dos and don'ts.* [ME; OE *dōn,* c. D *doen,* G *tun;* akin to L *-dere,* Gk *tithénai*]

—Syn. 3. DO, ACCOMPLISH, ACHIEVE mean to bring some action to a conclusion. Do is the general word, carrying no implication of success or failure: *he did a great deal of hard work.* ACCOMPLISH and ACHIEVE both have a connotation of successful completion of an undertaking. ACCOMPLISH emphasizes attaining a desired purpose through effort, skill, and perseverance: *to accomplish what one has hoped for.* ACHIEVE emphasizes accomplishing something important, excellent, or great: *to achieve a beneficial service for mankind.*

do² (dō), *n. Music.* **1.** the syllable used for the first note or keynote of a diatonic scale. **2.** (sometimes) the note C. See **ut** and **sol-fa**. Also, **doh.** [see GAMUT]

do., ditto.

doab (dō′əb), *n.* an alluvial tract of land between two adjacent rivers; esp. that between the Ganges and the Jumna rivers.

doable (do͞o′ə bl), *adj.* that may be done.

do-all (do͞o′ôl′), *n.* a factotum.

doat (dōt), *v.i.* dote.

dobbin (dŏb′ĭn), *n.* **1.** a name for a horse, esp. a quiet, plodding horse for farm work or family use. **2.** a horse of this kind. [var. of *Robin*, familiar var. of *Robert*, man's name]

dobby (dŏb′ĭ), *n., pl.* **-bies.** *Dial.* a sprite or goblin.

Doberman pinscher (dō′bə mən pĭn′shə), a breed of large smooth-coated terriers, usually black-and-tan or brown, with long forelegs, and wide hindquarters.

Doberman pinscher (24 to 27 in. high at the shoulder)

Dobrich (*Bulg.* dôb′rĕch), *n.* former name of **Tolbuhin.**

Dobruja (dŏ bro͞oj′ə; *Bulg.* dô′bro͞o-jà), *n.* **1.** an administrative region in SE Rumania. 521,000 pop. (est. 1964); 6120 sq. mi. **2.** a region in NE Bulgaria; 2970 sq. mi. Rumanian, **Dobrogea** (*Rum.* dô brô′jyä).

dobson (dŏb′sən), *n.* **1.** a large, membranous-winged insect, *Corydalis cornutus*, possessing greatly elongated and hornlike mandibles. **2.** its large aquatic larva, the hellgrammite. [orig. uncert.]

Dobson (dŏb′sən), *n.* **(Henry) Austin,** 1840–1921, English poet, biographer, and essayist.

doc., *pl.* **docs. 1.** document. **2.** doctor.

docent (dō sĕnt′; *Ger.* dô tsĕnt′), *n.* **1.** (in Germany and U.S.) Privat-docent. **2.** *U.S.* a college or university lecturer. [t. L: s. *docens*, ppr., teaching. Cf. G *Privat-docent*] **—do′centship′,** *n.*

docile (dō′sīl), *adj.* **1.** readily trained or taught; teachable. **2.** easily managed or handled; tractable. [late ME, t. L: m. s. *docilis*] **—doc′ilely,** *adv.* **—docility** (dō sĭl′ĭ tĭ), *n.*

dock¹ (dŏk), *n.* **1.** a wharf. **2.** the space or waterway between two piers or wharves, as for receiving a ship while in port. **3.** such a waterway, enclosed or open, together with the surrounding piers, wharves, etc. **4.** dry dock. **5.** scene dock. *—v.t.* **6.** to bring into a dock; lay up in a dock. **7.** to put into a dry dock for repairs, cleaning, or painting. **8.** *Aerospace.* to close and lock (one spacecraft) into another while in orbit. *—v.i.* **9.** to come or go into a dock or dry dock. **10.** *Aerospace.* to close and lock two spacecraft together in orbit. [cf. D *dok*; orig. uncert.]

dock² (dŏk), *n.* **1.** the solid or fleshy part of an animal's tail, as distinguished from the hair. **2.** the part of a tail left after cutting or clipping. *—v.t.* **3.** to cut off the end of (a tail, etc.). **4.** to deduct a part from (wages, etc.). **5.** to cut short the tail of. **6.** to deduct from the wages of. [ME *dok*, OE *-docca*, in *fingerdocca* finger muscle]

dock³ (dŏk), *n.* an enclosed place in a courtroom where the accused is placed during trial. [cf. Flem. *dok* cage]

dock⁴ (dŏk), *n.* **1.** any of various plants of the polygonaceous genus *Rumex*, as *R. crispus* (**curled dock**) and *R. obtusifolius* (**broad-leaved dock**), mostly troublesome weeds with long taproots. **2.** any of various other plants, mostly coarse weeds. [ME *dokke*, OE *docce*, c. MD *docke*]

dockage¹ (dŏk′ĭj), *n.* **1.** a charge for the use of a dock. **2.** docking accommodations. **3.** act of docking a vessel. [f. DOCK¹ + -AGE]

dockage² (dŏk′ĭj), *n.* **1.** curtailment; deduction, as from wages. **2.** waste material in wheat and other grains which is easily removed. [f. DOCK² + -AGE]

dock-dues (dŏk′dyo͞oz′), *n.* payments for use of a dock; dockage.

docker¹ (dŏk′ə), *n.* a man employed on the wharves of a port, as in loading and unloading vessels; a dock labourer. [f. DOCK¹ + -ER¹]

docker² (dŏk′ə), *n.* one who or that which docks, cuts short, or cuts off. [f. DOCK² + -ER¹]

docket (dŏk′ĭt), *n., v.,* **-eted, -eting.** *—n.* **1.** an official memorandum or entry of proceedings in a legal cause, or a register of such entries. **2.** the abstract of the contents of proposed letters patent. **3.** *U.S.* the list of business to be transacted by court or assembly; the agenda; a list of projects or cases awaiting action. **4.** *U.S.* a list of causes in court for trials, or the names of the parties who have causes pending. **5.** *U.S.* a writing on a letter or document, stating its contents; any statement of particulars attached to a package, etc.; a label or ticket. **6.** a warrant certifying payment of customs duty. *—v.t.* **7.** *Law.* to make an abstract or summary of the heads of, as a document; abstract and enter in a book: *judgements regularly docketed.* **8.** to endorse (a letter, etc.) with a memorandum. [ME *doket*; orig. obscure]

docking (dŏk′ĭng), *n. Aerospace.* the technique of closing and locking together of two or more spacecraft in orbit.

dock labourer, a docker.

dockland (dŏk′lănd′), *n.* the part of the town around the docks in a large port, generally poor and working-class in character, where warehouses, sailors' lodgings, etc., are situated.

dockyard (dŏk′yäd′), *n.* a naval establishment containing docks, shops, warehouses, etc., where ships are repaired, fitted out, and built.

doctor (dŏk′tə), *n.* **1.** a person licensed to practise medicine, or some branch of medicine; a physician or medical practitioner other than a surgeon. **2.** a person who has received the highest degree conferred by a faculty of a university. **3.** (*cap.*) a conventional title of respect for such a person. **4.** the academic title possessed by such a person, orig. implying qualification to teach, now generally based on at least three years of advanced study and research beyond the bachelor's degree. **5.** a man of great learning. **6.** any of various mechanical contrivances for particular purposes. **7. Doctor of the Church,** one of the few great teachers who have had a major formative influence on orthodox Christian thinking: *St Augustine is considered a Doctor of the Church.* *—v.t.* **8.** to treat medicinally. **9.** *Colloq.* to repair or mend. **10.** *Colloq.* to tamper with; falsify; adulterate. *—v.i.* **11.** to practise medicine. [t. L: teacher; r. ME *doctour*, t. OF] **—doc′toral,** *adj.* **—doctoress, doctress** (dŏk′trĭs), (*Rare*) *n. fem.*

doctorate (dŏk′tə rĭt, -trĭt), *n.* the degree of doctor.

doctor fish, tench.

Doctors' Commons, a building in London; until the College was dissolved under the Probate Act, 1857, it was the dining hall of the College of Doctors of Civil Law; later it housed ecclesiastical and Admiralty courts which applied primarily civil law.

doctorship (dŏk′tə shĭp′), *n.* **1.** a doctorate. **2.** the position, function, or character of a doctor.

doctrinaire (dŏk′trĭ nĕə′), *n.* **1.** one who tries to apply some doctrine or theory without a sufficient regard to practical considerations; an impractical theorist. *—adj.* **2.** dogmatic about others' acceptance of one's ideas. **3.** theoretic and unpractical. **4.** of a doctrinaire. [t. F, der. *doctrine* DOCTRINE] **—doc′trinar′ism,** *n.* **—doc′trinar′ian,** *n.*

doctrinal (dŏk trī′nəl), *adj.* of, pertaining to, or concerned with, doctrine. **—doctri′nally,** *adv.*

doctrine (dŏk′trĭn), *n.* **1.** a particular principle taught or advocated. **2.** that which is taught; teachings collectively. **3.** a body or system of teachings relating to a particular subject. [ME, t. F, t. L: m. *doctrīna* teaching, learning] **—doc′trinism,** *n.* **—Syn. 1.** tenet, dogma, theory, precept, belief.

document (*n.* dŏk′yo͝o mənt; *v.* dŏk′yo͝o mĕnt′), *n.* **1.** a written or printed paper furnishing information or evidence, a legal or official paper. **2.** *Obs.* evidence; proof. *—v.t.* **3.** to furnish with documents, evidence, or the like. **4.** to support by documentary evidence. **5.** *Obs.* to instruct. [ME, t. L: s. *documentum* lesson, example]

documentary (dŏk′yo͝o mĕn′tə rĭ, -trĭ), *adj., n., pl.* **-ries.** *—adj.* **1.** Also, **documental** (dŏk′yo͝o mĕn′tl). pertaining to, consisting of, or derived from documents. *—n.* **2.** *Television, Films.* a film, usually non-fiction, in which the elements of dramatic conflict are provided by ideas, political or economic forces, etc.

documentary bill, a bill of exchange to which are attached various documents, as a policy of insurance, invoice, etc.

documentary credit, a credit established by a banker at the request of an importer, under which the banker lends his name as drawee of bills of exchange covering the cost of goods sold to the importer, such bills to be accompanied by shipping documents.

documentation (dŏk′yo͝o mĕn tā′shən), *n.* **1.** the use of documentary evidence. **2.** a furnishing with documents.

dodder¹ (dŏd′ə), *v.i.* to shake; tremble; totter. [cf. DITHER, TOTTER etc.] **—dod′derer,** *n.* **—dod′dery,** *adj.*

dodder² (dŏd′ə), *n.* any of the leafless parasitic plants comprising the genus *Cuscuta*, with yellowish, reddish, or white threadlike stems that twine about clover, flax, etc. [ME *doder*, c. G *Dotter*]

doddered (dŏd′əd), *adj.* infirm; feeble.

doddering (dŏd′ə rĭng), *adj.* that dodders; shaking; tottering; senile.

dodeca-, a word element meaning 'twelve'. Also, before vowels, **dodec-.** [t. Gk: m. *dōdeka-*, comb. form of *dōdeka*]

dodecagon (dō dĕk′ə gən), *n. Geom.* a polygon having twelve angles and twelve sides. [t. Gk: s. *dōdekágōnon.* See DODECA-, -GON] —**dodecagonal** (dō′dĕ kăg′-ə nəl), *adj.*

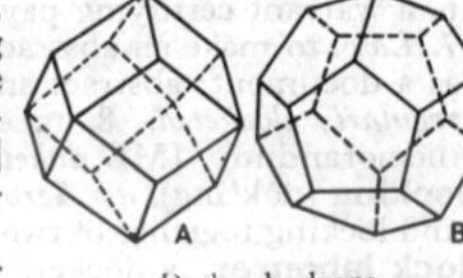

Dodecahedrons
A, Rhombic; B, Pentagonal

dodecahedron (dō′dĕk ə-hē′drən), *n., pl.* **-drons, -dra** (-drə). *Geom.* a solid figure having twelve faces. [t. Gk: m. *dōdekáedron*] —**do′decahe′dral,** *adj.*

Dodecanese Islands (dō′dĭk ə nēz′), a group of twelve Greek islands in the Aegean, off the SW coast of Turkey: belonging to Italy 1911–45. 122,346 pop. (1961); 1035 sq. mi.

dodecaphonic (dō′dĕk ə fŏn′ĭk), *adj. Music.* pertaining to serial music; twelve-tone. —**do′decaphon′ist,** *n.* —**do′decaphon′y,** *n.*

dodge (dŏj), *v.,* **dodged, dodging,** *n.* —*v.i.* **1.** to move aside or change position suddenly, as to avoid a blow or to get behind something. **2.** to use evasive methods; prevaricate. —*v.i.* **3.** (in change-ringing), the ringing of a bell one place out of its regular ascending or descending order. —*v.t.* **4.** to elude by a sudden shift of position or by strategy. —*n.* **5.** an act of dodging; a spring aside. **6.** *Colloq.* an ingenious expedient or contrivance; a shifty trick. [orig. uncert.] —**Syn. 2.** equivocate, quibble. **4.** evade, elude.

Dodge City, a town in the U.S., in SW Kansas, on the Arkansas river: it was an important frontier town and railhead on the old Santa Fe route. 13,520 (1960).

dodgem (dŏj′əm), *n.* a small, low-powered, electrically driven vehicle driven on a special rink at funfairs, etc., for the amusement of bumping other dodgems. [? b. DODGE + THEM]

dodger (dŏj′ə), *n.* **1.** one who dodges. **2.** a shifty person. **3.** *U.S.* a small handbill. **4.** *Naut.* a sheltering screen on a ship's bridge, made of canvas and light timber.

Dodgson (dŏj′sən), *n.* **Charles Lutwidge** (lŭt′wĭj). See **Carroll, Lewis.**

dodgy (dŏj′ĭ), *adj.* **1.** artful. **2.** *Slang.* difficult; awkward; tricky.

dodo (dō′dō), *n., pl.* **-does, -dos. 1.** a clumsy flightless bird of the genera *Raphus* and *Pezophaps*, about the size of a goose, related to the pigeons, formerly inhabiting the islands of Mauritius, Réunion, and Rodriguez, but extinct since the advent of European settlers. **2.** *Colloq.* a silly or slow-witted person. [t. Pg.: m. *doudo* silly]

Dodo, *Raphus solitarius* (Ab. 3 ft long)

Dodona (dō dō′nə), *n.* an ancient town in NW Greece, in Epirus: site of a famous oracle of Zeus. —**Dodonaean, Dodonean** (dō′dō nē′ən), *adj.*

doe (dō), *n.* the female of the deer, antelope, goat, rabbit, and certain other animals. [ME *do*, OE *dā*. Cf. L *dāma, damma* deer]

Doe (dō), *n.* **John,** a name referring to an avowedly fictitious person, used esp. as a 19th-century legal fiction for the plaintiff in actions of ejectment.

Doenitz (*Ger.* dœ′nĭts), *n.* **Karl** (*Ger.* kårl), born 1892, German admiral: German head of state for 3 weeks after Hitler's death, 1945. Also, **Dönitz.**

Doe of roe deer, *Capreolus capreolus* (Ab. 2½ ft high at the shoulder)

doer (dōō′ə), *n.* one who or that which does something; a performer; an actor.

does (dŭz), *v.* 3rd pers. sing. pres. ind. of **do**[1].

Doesburg (*Du.* dōōs′bʏʀkh), *n.* **Theo van,** 1883–1931, Dutch painter and architectural designer.

doeskin (dō′skĭn′), *n.* **1.** the skin of a doe. **2.** leather made from this. **3.** (*pl.*) gloves made of sheepskin. **4.** a smoothly finished, closely woven, finely twilled woollen cloth.

doesn't (dŭz′nt), contraction of *does not.*

doeth (dōō′ĭth), *v. Archaic.* (now only in poetic or liturgical use) 3rd pers. sing. pres. of **do**[1].

doff (dŏf), *v.t.* **1.** to put or take off, as dress. **2.** to remove (the hat) in salutation. **3.** to throw off; get rid of. [contr. of *do off.* Cf. DON[2]] —**doff′er,** *n.*

dog (dŏg), *n., v.,* **dogged, dogging.** —*n.* **1.** a domesticated carnivore, *Canis familiaris*, bred in a great many varieties. **2.** any animal belonging to the same family, *Canidae*, including the wolves, jackals, foxes, etc. **3.** the male of such an animal (opposed to *bitch*). **4.** any of various animals suggesting the dog, as the prairie dog. **5.** a despicable fellow. **6.** a fellow in general: *a gay dog.* **7.** (*cap.*) *Astron.* either of two constellations, Canis Major (**Great Dog**) and Canis Minor (**Little Dog**), situated near Orion. **8.** *Mech.* any of various mechanical devices, as for gripping or holding something. **9.** an andiron. **10. to go to the dogs,** *Colloq.* to go to ruin. **11.** (*pl.*) *Colloq.* greyhound racing. **12.** (*pl.*) *Slang.* feet. **13. dressed like a dog's dinner,** *Slang.* dressed ultra-fashionably; dressed stylishly. **14. hot dog,** *Orig. U.S.* a frankfurter in a roll. **15. lame dog,** an unfortunate person; a helpless person. **16. lead a dog's life,** to have a harassed existence; to be continuously unhappy. **17. let sleeping dogs lie,** to refrain from action which might alter the existing situation. **18. put on the dog,** *U.S. Colloq.* to behave pretentiously; put on airs. —*v.t.* **19.** to follow or track like a dog, esp. with hostile intent; hound. **20.** to drive or chase with a dog or dogs. [ME *dogge*, OE *docga*; orig. unknown]

dogbane (dŏg′bān′), *n.* any plant of the genus *Apocynum*, esp. *A. androsaemifolium*, a perennial herb abounding in an acrid milky juice and having an intensely bitter root that has been used in medicine.

dogberry[1] (dŏg′bĕ′rĭ, -bə rĭ, -brĭ), *n.* **1.** (*cap.*) a foolish constable in Shakespeare's *Much Ado About Nothing.* **2.** any ignorant and blundering official. —**dog′ber′ryism,** *n.*

dogberry[2] (dŏg′bĕ′rĭ, -bə rĭ, -brĭ), *n., pl.* **-ries. 1.** the berry or fruit of any of various plants, as the European dogwood, *Thelycrania sanguinea*, or the N American chokeberry, *Aronia arbutifolia.* **2.** the plant itself. **3.** any of several plants, esp. the dogrose, bearberry, and guelder-rose.

dogcart (dŏg′kăt′), *n.* **1.** a light, two-wheeled vehicle for ordinary driving, with two transverse seats back to back. **2.** a cart drawn by dogs.

dog-collar (dŏg′kŏl′ə), *n.* **1.** a collar to identify or control a dog. **2.** a stiff collar, fastened behind, worn by certain clergymen or priests; a clerical collar.

dog days, a sultry part of the summer supposed to occur about the time of the heliacal rising of one of the Dog Stars, now often reckoned from July 3rd to Aug. 11th.

doge (dōj), *n.* the chief magistrate of the old republics of Venice and Genoa. [t. It. (Venetian), g. L *dux* leader] —**doge′ship,** *n.*

dog-ear (dŏg′ĭə′), *n.* **1.** the corner of a page in a book folded over like a dog's ear, as by careless use or to mark a place. —*v.t.* **2.** to disfigure with dog-ears. —**dog′-eared′,** *adj.*

dog-fancier (dŏg′făn′sĭ ə), *n.* **1.** a breeder or seller of dogs. **2.** an expert or connoisseur of dogs.

dog fennel, mayweed.

dogfight (dŏg′fīt′), *n.* **1.** a fierce fight between two dogs. **2.** a violent engagement of fighter planes at close quarters. **3.** any rough-and-tumble physical battle.

dogfish (dŏg′fĭsh′), *n., pl.* **-fishes,** (*esp. collectively*) **-fish. 1.** any of various small sharks, as the spiny dogfish, *Squalus acanthias*, common on both coasts of the northern Atlantic and destructive to food fishes, and the smooth dogfishes (genus *Mustelus*). **2.** any of various other fishes, as the bowfin.

dog fox, a male fox.

dogged (dŏg′ĭd), *adj.* having the pertinacity of a dog; obstinate. [f. DOG + -ED[3]. Cf. CRABBED] —**dog′gedly,** *adv.* —**dog′gedness,** *n.* —**Syn.** mulish, persistent, inflexible, unyielding. See **stubborn.**

dogger (dŏg′ə), *n.* **1.** a two-masted Dutch fishing vessel with a blunt bow, used in the North Sea. **2.** *Geol.* a concretion of ironstone or silica in sands and clays. **3.** (*cap.*) *Geol.* the Middle Jurassic of Europe. [ME *doggere.* Cf. Icel. *dugga* small fishing vessel]

Dogger Bank (dŏg′ə), an extensive shoal in the North Sea, ab. 70 mi. E of N England: fishing grounds; naval battle 1915. 36–120 ft deep. [said to be named from DOGGER or from MD *dogger* trawler]

doggerel (dŏg′ə rəl), *adj.* **1.** (of verse) comic or burlesque, and usually loose or irregular in measure. **2.** rude; crude; poor. —*n.* **3.** doggerel verse. Also, **dogrel** (dŏg′rəl). [ME; orig. uncert.]

doggery (dŏg′ə rĭ), *n., pl.* **-eries. 1.** doggish behaviour or conduct; mean or mischievous action. **2.** dogs collectively. **3.** rabble; canaille.

doggish (dŏg′ĭsh), *adj.* **1.** canine. **2.** surly. —**dog′gishly,** *adv.* —**dog′gishness,** *n.*

doggo (dŏg′ō), *adv.* **1.** *Colloq.* out of sight. **2. lie doggo,** to hide; remain in concealment.

doggone (dŏg′ŏn), *adj., adv. U.S. Slang.* darned.

doggy (dŏg′ĭ), *n., pl.* **-gies,** *adj.,* **-gier, -giest.** —*n.* **1.** a little dog. **2.** a pet term for any dog. —*adj.* **3.** of or pertaining to a dog. **4.** fond of dogs. **5.** pretentious; ostentatious. Also, **dog′gie.**

doghole (dŏg′hōl′), *n.* a wretched house or dwelling. Also, **doghouse.**

doghouse (dŏg′hous′), *n.* **1.** a kennel. **2.** a doghole. **3. in the doghouse,** in disfavour.

dogie (dō′gĭ), *n. Western U.S.* a motherless calf in a cattle herd.

dog in the manger, a person who, like the dog in the fable, churlishly keeps something of no particular use to himself so that others cannot use it.

dog Latin, mongrel or spurious Latin.

dogma (dŏg′mə), *n., pl.* **-mas, -mata** (-mə tə). **1.** a system of principles or tenets, as of a church. **2.** a tenet or doctrine authoritatively laid down, as by a church. **3.** prescribed doctrine. **4.** a settled opinion; a belief; a principle. [t. L, t. Gk]

dogmatic (dŏg măt′ĭk), *adj.* **1.** of, pertaining to, or of the nature of a dogma or dogmas; doctrinal. **2.** asserting opinions in an authoritative, positive, or arrogant manner; positive; opinionated. Also, **dogmat′ical.** —**dogmat′ically,** *adv.*

dogmatics (dŏg măt′ĭks), *n.* the science which treats of the arrangement and statement of religious doctrines, esp. of the doctrines received in and taught by the Christian church; doctrinal theology.

dogmatism (dŏg′mə tĭz′əm), *n.* dogmatic character; authoritative, positive, or arrogant assertion of opinions.

dogmatist (dŏg′mə tĭst), *n.* **1.** one who asserts positively his own opinions; a dogmatic person. **2.** one who lays down dogmas.

dogmatize (dŏg′mə tīz′), *v.,* **-tized, -tizing.** —*v.i.* **1.** to make dogmatic assertions; speak or write dogmatically. —*v.t.* **2.** to assert or deliver as a dogma. Also, **dogmatise.** [t. ML: m. s. *dogmatizāre,* t. Gk: m. *dogmatízein*] —**dog′matiza′tion,** *n.* —**dog′matiz′er,** *n.*

do-gooder (do͞o′go͝od′ə), *n. Colloq.* a well-intentioned, but often clumsy social reformer.

dog paddle, a simple, very slow swimming stroke, in which the arms and legs are flicked below water.

dogrose (dŏg′rōz′), *n.* a common species of wild rose, *Rosa canina,* having delicate pink flowers.

dogsbody (dŏgz′bŏd′ĭ), *n. Colloq.* an overworked drudge, esp. one who is imposed on.

dogshore (dŏg′shô′), *n. Naut.* one of the timbers holding a small vessel temporarily before launching.

dog's mercury, a euphorbiaceous creeping perennial, *Mercuralis perennis,* with small unisexual flowers, common in woods of Europe and SW Asia.

dog's-tail (dŏgz′tāl′), *n.* any grass of the Old World genus *Cynosurus,* the species of which have the spikes fringed on one side only, esp. *C. cristatus* (**crested dog's-tail**). Also, **dog's-tail grass.**

Dog Star, 1. the bright star Sirius, in Canis Major. **2.** the bright star Procyon, in Canis Minor.

dogstick (dŏg′stĭk′), *n.* a sprag (def. 1).

dog's-tongue (dŏgz′tŭng′), *n.* hound's-tongue.

dog's-tooth grass (dŏgz′to͞oth′), Bermuda grass.

dog-tired (dŏg′tī′əd), *adj.* very tired.

dogtooth (dŏg′to͞oth′), *n., pl.* **-teeth** (-tēth′). **1.** a canine tooth. **2.** *Archit.* a toothlike medieval ornament, or a moulding cut in projecting teeth.

dogtooth violet, 1. a bulbous liliaceous plant, *Erythronium dens-canis,* of Europe, bearing purple flowers. **2.** any of several American plants of the same genus. Also, **dog's-tooth violet, dogviolet.**

dogtrot (dŏg′trŏt′), *n.* a gentle trot, like that of a dog.

dogvane (dŏg′vān′), *n. Naut.* a small vane, composed of bunting or the like, set on the weather gunwale of a vessel to show the direction of the wind.

dogwatch (dŏg′wŏch′), *n. Naut.* either of two short watches on shipboard, from 4 to 6 p.m. and from 6 to 8 p.m.

dogwhelk (dŏg′wĕlk′), *n.* any of several whelks of the class *Gastropoda,* esp. the **common dog whelk,** *Nucella lapillus,* widely distributed in coastal waters of the British Isles.

dogwood (dŏg′wo͝od′), *n.* **1.** any tree or shrub of the genus *Thelycrania* (*Cornus*), esp. *T. sanguinea,* a deciduous shrub of calcareous soil in Europe (family *Cornaceae*). **2.** the wood of any such tree.

Doha (dō′hä, dō′ə), *n.* a town in and capital of Qatar.

Dohnányi (dŏk nä′nyĭ; *Hung.* dȯh′nȧ nyĕ), *n.* **Ernö** (*Hung.* ĕr′nœ) or **Ernst von** (*Hung.* ĕrnst′ vŏn), 1877–1960, Hungarian pianist and composer.

doiled (doild), *adj. Scot.* stupid; foolish; crazed.

doily (doi′lĭ), *n., pl.* **-lies. 1.** a small ornamental mat, as of embroidery or lace, paper or plastic; often placed under cakes, sandwiches, etc., on a plate. **2.** *Archaic.* a small ornamental napkin used at table at dessert, etc. [named after a 17th-century draper of London]

doing (do͞o′ĭng), *n.* **1.** action; performance; execution. **2.** (*pl.*) deeds; proceedings.

doited (doi′tĭd, -tĭt), *adj. Scot.* enfeebled in mind, esp. by age; childish.

do-it-yourself (do͞o′ĭt yô sĕlf′), *adj. Colloq.* of or designed for use by amateurs without special training: *a do-it-yourself kit for building a radio.* —**do′-it-yourself′er,** *n.*

dol., dollar.

dolabriform (dō lăb′rĭ fôm′), *adj. Bot., Zool.* shaped like an axe or a cleaver. [f. s. L *dolābra* pickaxe, axe + -(I)FORM]

Dolabriform leaf

dolce (dŏl′chĭ), *Music.* —*adj.* **1.** sweet; soft. —*n.* **2.** an instruction to the performer that the music is to be executed softly and sweetly. **3.** a soft-toned organ stop. [It.: sweet, g. L *dulcis*]

dolce vita (dŏl′chĭ vē′tə; *It.* dȯl′chė vē′tȧ), *Italian.* sweet life; life dedicated to the pursuit of pleasure.

doldrum (dŏl′drəm), *n.* **1.** (*pl.*) *Naut.* **a.** the region of relatively calm winds near the equator. **b.** the calms or weather variations characteristic of those parts. **2.** (*often pl.*) dullness or low spirits. [orig. uncert.]

dole[1] (dōl), *n., v.,* **doled, doling.** —*n.* **1.** a portion of money, food, etc., given, esp. in charity or for maintenance. **2.** a dealing out or distributing, esp. in charity. **3.** a form of payment to the unemployed instituted by the British government in 1918. **4.** any similar payment by a government to an unemployed person. **5. go** or **be on the dole,** to receive such payments. **6.** *Archaic.* one's fate or destiny. —*v.t.* **7.** to distribute in charity. **8.** to give out sparingly or in small quantities (fol. by *out*). [ME; OE *dāl* part, portion. See DEAL[1]]

dole[2] (dōl), *n. Archaic.* grief or sorrow; lamentation. [ME *dol, doel,* t. OF, ult. der. L *dolēre* grieve]

doleful (dōl′fəl), *adj.* full of grief; sorrowful; gloomy. —**dole′fully,** *adv.* —**dole′fulness,** *n.*

dolerite (dŏl′ə rīt′), *n.* **1.** a coarse-grained variety of basalt. **2.** any of various other igneous rocks, as diabase. **3.** any igneous rock resembling basalt whose composition cannot be determined without microscopic examination. [t. F, f. s. Gk *dolerós* deceptive + -ITE[1]] —**doleritic** (dŏl′ə rĭt′ĭk), *adj.*

dolesome (dōl′səm), *adj. Rare.* doleful.

dolichocephalic (dŏl′ĭ kō sĭ făl′ĭk), *adj. Anat.* **1.** long-headed; having a breadth of head small in proportion to the length from front to back (opposed to *brachycephalic*). **2.** having a cephalic index of 76 or less. Also, **dolichocephalous** (dŏl′ĭ kō sĕf′ə ləs). [f. Gk *dolichó(s)* long + m. s. Gk *kephalḗ* head + -IC] —**dolichocephalism** (dŏl′ĭ kō sĕf′ə lĭz′əm), *n.* —**dol′ichoceph′aly,** *n.*

dolichocranic (dŏl′ĭ kō krā′nĭk), *adj. Anat.* **1.** long-skulled; having a breadth of skull small in proportion to length from front to back (opposed to *brachycranic*). **2.** having a cranial index of 75 or less.

doline (dŏl′ēn), *n.* a shallow depression, either funnel- or saucer-shaped, and having its floor covered by cultivated soil, formed by solution in mountain limestone country. Also, **dolina** (dŏ lē′nə). [t. Serbo-Croat: m. *dolina*]

doll (dŏl), *n.* **1.** a toy puppet representing a child or other human being; a child's toy baby. **2.** a pretty but expressionless or unintelligent woman. **3.** *Slang.* an attractive woman, esp. one who is young. —*v.t., v.i.* **4.** *Slang.* to dress in a smart or showy manner (fol. by *up*). [from *Doll, Dolly* for *Dorothy,* woman's name] —**doll′ish,** *adj.* —**doll′ishly,** *adv.* —**doll′ishness,** *n.*

dollar (dŏl′ə), *n.* **1.** the monetary unit of the U.S., equal to 100 cents, and equivalent to £0·417 sterling. *Symbol:* $. **2.** a coin of this value, or a paper note having a corresponding legal value. **3.** any of various units and coins or notes elsewhere, as in Canada, Australia, etc. **4.** the English name for the German thaler, a large silver coin of varying value, current in various German states from the 16th century. **5.** any of various similar coins, as the Spanish or Mexican peso. **6.** Levant dollar. **7.** *Slang.* five shillings. [earlier *daler,* t. LG, and early mod. D, c. HG *Thaler,* for *Joachimsthaler* coin of Joachimsthal, town in Bohemia where they were coined]

dollar area, those countries in which the U.S. dollar is the international unit of currency.

dollar diplomacy, *U.S.* **1.** diplomacy dictated by financial interest. **2.** diplomacy in the field of foreign relations employing financial means to increase another country's security, or increase political power in another country. **3.** a government policy of promoting the business interests of its citizens in other countries.

dollarfish (dŏl′ə fĭsh′), *n., pl.* **-fishes,** (*esp. collectively*) **-fish.** the moonfish.

dollar premium, the amount paid for investment dollars in order to purchase U.S. stocks and shares.
Dollfuss (*Ger.* dŏl′fo͞os), *n.* **Engelbert** (*Ger.* ĕng′əl bĕrt), 1892–1934, Austrian statesman: premier 1932–34.
dollop (dŏl′əp), *n. Colloq.* a lump; a mass.
doll's house, a toy house for dolls. Also, *U.S.*, **dollhouse.**
dolly (dŏl′ĭ), *n., pl.* **dollies. 1.** a child's name for a doll. **2.** a low truck with small wheels for moving loads too heavy to be carried by hand. **3.** *Mach.* a tool for receiving and holding the head of a rivet while the other end is being headed. **4.** *Bldg Trades.* an extension piece placed on the head of a pile while being driven. **5.** an apparatus for jerking clothes about while washing. **6.** *S African.* an early form of stamping machine for breaking up gold-bearing rock. **7.** *Cricket.* a ball delivered by the bowler in a deceptive manner so that it seems to be slow and hang in the air. **8.** *Cricket.* a simple catch from a high-lobbed ball. **9.** *Films, Television.* a small mobile platform for carrying cameras, directors, etc., and often running on tracks. **10.** *Slang.* a girl, esp. a young attractive one who is not particularly intelligent. *—v.i.* **11.** *Films, Television.* to move the dolly forwards or backwards while photographing.
dolly mixture, a variety of miniature sweets especially for children.
dolly tub, 1. a wooden vat used for washing mineral ore. **2.** a similar container used by housewives for washing clothes.
Dolly Varden (dŏl′ĭ vä′dn), **1.** a style of gay-flowered print gown. **2.** a broad-brimmed, flower-trimmed hat, formerly worn by women. [named after a character in Dickens's '*Barnaby Rudge*']
dolman (dŏl′mən), *n., pl.* **-mans. 1.** a woman's mantle with capelike arm pieces instead of sleeves. **2.** a long outer robe worn by Turks. **3.** a hussar's jacket, worn over the shoulder like a cape, with one or both sleeves hanging loosely. [ult. t. Turk.: m. *dōlāmān*]
dolman sleeve, a sleeve tapering to the wrist from a wide armhole, used in women's clothes.
dolmen (dŏl′mĕn), *n. Archaeol.* a structure usually regarded as a tomb, consisting of two or more large upright stones set with a space between and capped by a horizontal stone. Cf. **cromlech.** [t. F, made up by F writers as if from Breton *taol, tol* table + *men* stone]

Dolmen

Dolmetsch (dŏl′mĕch), *n.* **Arnold,** 1858–1940, English musician, born in France: revived some ancient musical instruments.
dolomite (dŏl′ə mīt′), *n.* **1.** a very common mineral, calcium magnesium carbonate, $CaMg(CO_3)_2$, occurring in crystals and in masses (called **dolomite marble** when coarse-grained); pearl spar. **2.** a rock consisting essentially or largely of this mineral. [named after D. G. de *Dolomieu*, 1750–1801, French geologist] —**dolomitic** (dŏl′ə mĭt′ĭk), *adj.*
Dolomites (dŏl′ə mīts′), *n.pl.* a mountain range in N Italy: a part of the Alpine system. Highest peak, Marmolada, 10,965 feet. Also, **Dolomite Alps.**
doloroso (dŏl′ə rō′sō; *It.* dô lô rô′sô), *adj. Music.* soft and pathetic; plaintive. [It.]
dolorous (dŏl′ə rəs), *adj.* full of, expressing, or causing pain or sorrow; distressed; grievous; mournful. —**dol′orously,** *adv.* —**dol′orousness,** *n.*
dolour (dō′lə), *n. Archaic.* sorrow or grief. Also, *U.S.*, **dolor.** [ME *doloure*, t. OF: m. *dolour*, g. L *dolor* pain, grief]
dolphin (dŏl′fĭn), *n.* **1.** any of various cetaceans of the family *Delphinidae*, some of which are commonly called porpoises, esp. *Delphinus delphis*, which has a long, sharp nose and abounds in the Mediterranean and the temperate Atlantic. **2.** a large, thin-bodied ocean fish, *Coryphaena hippurus* or *C. equisetis*, notable for its rapid colour change on death. **3.** *Naut.* a post, pile cluster, or buoy to which to moor a vessel. **4.** (*cap.*) *Astron.* the northern constellation Delphinus. [ME *dalphyne*, t. OF: m. *daulphin*, g. L *delphīnus*, t. Gk: m. s. *delphis*. Cf. DAUPHIN]

Dolphin, *Delphinus delphis* (Ab. 7½ ft long)

dolphin striker, *Naut.* a martingale (def. 2).
dolt (dōlt), *n.* a dull, stupid fellow; a blockhead. —**dolt′ish,** *adj.* —**dolt′ishly,** *adv.* —**dolt′ishness,** *n.*
dom (dŏm), *n.* **1.** (*often cap.*) the title of a monk in some orders, esp. the Benedictines. **2** (formerly) a title of nobility in Portugal.
-dom, a noun suffix meaning: **1.** domain, as in *kingdom.* **2.** collection of persons, as in *officialdom.* **3.** rank or station, as in *earldom.* **4.** general condition, as in *freedom.* [OE *-dōm*, suffix, repr. *dōm*, n. See DOOM]
dom., 1. domestic. **2.** domain.
domain (də mān′), *n.* **1.** *Law.* ultimate ownership and control over the use of land. **2.** an estate; any land held in possession. **3.** a territory under rule or influence; a realm. **4.** a field of action, thought, etc.: *the domain of commerce or of science.* **5.** the scope or range of any sphere of personal knowledge. **6.** a region with specific characteristics, types of growth, animal life, etc. **7.** *Physics.* a small region of a ferromagnetic substance in which the constituent atoms or molecules have a common polarity. **8.** *Maths.* the set of values assigned to the independent variables of a function. [t. F: m. *domaine*, OF *demeine* (see DEMESNE), g. L *dominicum*, orig. neut. of *dominicus* of a lord]
dome (dōm), *n., v.,* **domed, doming.** *—n.* **1.** *Archit.* **a.** a large, hemispherical, approximately hemispherical, or spheroidal vault, its form produced by rotating an arch on its vertical radius. **b.** a roof of domical shape. **c.** a vault or curved roof on a polygonal plan, as an octagonal dome. **2.** a large, impressive, or fanciful structure. **3.** anything shaped like a dome. **4.** *Crystall.* a form whose planes intersect the vertical axis but are parallel to one of the lateral axes. **5.** *Colloq.* a person's head. *—v.t.* **6.** to cover with or as with a dome. **7.** to shape like a dome. *—v.i.* **8.** to rise or swell as a dome. [t. L: m. s. *domus* house; partly through F *dôme* cathedral church, t. It.: m. *duomo* cupola, dome, t. Pr.: m. *doma* cupola, t. Gk: house] —**dome′like′,** *adj.*
Domesday Book (do͞omz′ dā′), a record of a survey of the lands of England made by order of William the Conqueror about 1086, giving ownership, extent, value, etc., of the properties. Also, **Doomsday Book.**
domestic (də mĕs′tĭk), *adj.* **1.** of or pertaining to the home, the household, or household affairs. **2.** devoted to home life or affairs. **3.** living with man; tame: *domestic animals.* **4.** of or pertaining to one's own or a particular country as apart from other countries. **5.** belonging, existing, or produced within a country; not foreign: *domestic trade.* *—n.* **6.** a hired household servant. **7.** (*pl.*) home manufacturers or goods. [t. L: s. *domesticus* belonging to the household] —**domes′tically,** *adv.*
domesticate (də mĕs′tĭ kāt′), *v.,* **-cated, -cating.** *—v.t.* **1.** to convert to domestic uses; tame. **2.** to attach to home life or affairs. **3.** to cause to be or feel at home; naturalize. *—v.i.* **4.** *Obs.* to be domestic. —**domes′tica′tion,** *n.* —**domes′tica′tor,** *n.*
domesticity (dō′mĕs tĭs′ĭ tĭ), *n., pl.* **-ties. 1.** the state of being domesticated; domestic or home life. **2.** (*pl.*) domestic affairs; home conditions and arrangements.
domestic science, the academic study of cookery, needlework, and housework.
domical (dō′mĭ kl, dŏm′ĭ kl), *adj.* **1.** domelike. **2.** having a dome or domes. —**dom′ically,** *adv.*
domicile (dŏm′ĭ sīl′), *n.; v.,* **-ciled, -ciling.** *—n.* **1.** a place of residence; an abode; a house or home. **2.** *Law.* a permanent legal residence. **3.** *Com.* a place at which a bill of exchange is made payable other than the acceptor's private or business address. *—v.t.* **4.** to establish in a domicile. *—v.i.* **5.** to have one's domicile; dwell (fol. by *at, in,* etc.). **6.** to name the place at which a bill of exchange will be payable. [t. F, t. L: m. s. *domicilium* habitation, dwelling]
domiciliary (dŏm′ĭ sĭl′yə rĭ), *adj.* of or pertaining to a domicile.
domiciliate (dŏm′ĭ sĭl′ĭ āt′), *v.t., v.i.,* **-ated, -ating.** domicile. —**dom′icil′ia′tion,** *n.*
dominance (dŏm′ĭ nəns), *n.* **1.** rule; control; authority; ascendancy. **2.** the condition of being dominant. Also, **dom′inancy.**
dominant (dŏm′ĭ nənt), *adj.* **1.** ruling; governing; controlling; most influential. **2.** occupying a commanding position: *the dominant points of the globe.* **3.** main; major; chief: *shipbuilding is the dominant industry in Barrow-in-Furness.* **4.** *Genetics.* pertaining to or exhibiting a dominant, as opposed to a recessive. **5.** *Music.* pertaining to or based on the dominant: *the dominant chord.* *—n.* **6.** *Genetics.* a hereditary character resulting from a gene with a greater biochemical activity than another, termed the recessive. The dominant masks the recessive. **7.** *Music.* the fifth note of a scale. [t. F, t. L: s. *dominans*, ppr.] —**dom′inantly,** *adv.*

—Syn. 1. prevailing, principal. DOMINANT, PREDOMINANT, PARAMOUNT, PRE-EMINENT describe something outstanding. DOMINANT describes that which is most influential or important: *the dominant characteristics of monkeys.* PREDOMINANT describes that which is dominant over all others, or is more widely prevalent: *curiosity is the predominant characteristic of monkeys.* PARAMOUNT applies to that which is first in rank or order: *safety is of paramount importance.* PRE-EMINENT applies to a prominence based on recognition of excellence: *his work was of pre-eminent quality.*

dominant tenement, *Law.* land in favour of which an easement or other servitude exists over another's land (the **servient tenement**). Also, **dominant estate.**

dominate (dŏm′ĭ nāt′), *v.*, **-nated, -nating.** —*v.t.* **1.** to rule over; govern; control. **2.** to tower above; overshadow. —*v.i.* **3.** to rule; exercise control; predominate. **4.** to occupy a commanding position. [t. L: m. s. *dominātus*, pp.] —**dom′ina′tor,** *n.*

domination (dŏm′ĭ nā′shən), *n.* **1.** the act of dominating. **2.** rule or sway, often arbitrary. **3.** (*pl.*) an order of angels. See **angel** (def. 1).

dominative (dŏm′ĭ nə tĭv), *adj.* dominating; controlling.

domine (dŏm′ə nĭ), *n. Obs.* lord; master (used as a title of address). [vocative of L *dominus* master]

domine, dirige nos (dŏm′ĭ nā′, dĭ′rĭ gā′ nōs′), *Latin.* Master, guide us (motto of the City of London).

domineer (dŏm′ĭ nĭə′), *v.i., v.t.* **1.** to rule arbitrarily; tyrannize. **2.** to command haughtily; behave arrogantly. **3.** to tower (over or above). [t. D: m. s. *domineren*, t. F: m. *dominer*, t. L: m. *dominārī* rule]

domineering (dŏm′ĭ nĭə′rĭng), *adj.* inclined to domineer; overbearing; tyrannical. —**dom′ineer′ingly,** *adv.* —**dom′ineer′ingness,** *n.*

Dominic (dŏm′ĭ nĭk), *n.* **Saint** (*Domingo de Guzmán*), 1170–1221, Spanish priest: founder of the Dominican order.

Dominica (dŏm′ĭ nē′kə), *n.* a British colony in the West Indies in the Windward Island group. 59,916 pop. (1960); 305 sq. mi. *Cap.:* Roseau.

dominical (də mĭn′ĭ kl), *adj.* **1.** of or pertaining to Jesus Christ as Lord. **2.** of or pertaining to the Lord's Day, or Sunday. [t. ML: s. *dominicālis* of or pertaining to the Lord or the Lord's Day (ML *dominica*), der. L *dominicus* belonging to a lord or (LL) the Lord]

dominical letter, any one of the seven letters *A* to *G* used in calendars to mark the Sundays throughout a particular year, and serving primarily to aid in determining the date of Easter.

Dominican (də mĭn′ĭ kən), *adj.* **1.** of or pertaining to St Dominic (1170–1221), or to the mendicant religious order founded by him. **2.** of or pertaining to the Dominican Republic. **3.** of or pertaining to Dominica. —*n.* **4.** a member of the order of St Dominic; a Black Friar. **5.** a native or inhabitant of the Dominican Republic. **6.** a native or inhabitant of Dominica. [t. Eccl. L: s. *Dominicānus*, der. Saint DOMINIC(US)]

Dominican Republic, a republic in the West Indies, occupying the E part of the island of Hispaniola. 3,007,941 (est. 1961); 19,129 sq. mi. *Cap.:* Santo Domingo. See map under **Haiti.** Also, **Santo Domingo.**

dominie (dŏm′ĭ nĭ), *n.* **1.** *Chiefly Scot.* a schoolmaster. **2.** *U.S.* a clergyman, pastor, or parson (a title used specifically in the Reformed Church in America). [t. L: m. *domine*, vocative of *dominus* master, lord]

dominion (də mĭn′yən), *n.* **1.** the power or right of governing and controlling; sovereign authority. **2.** rule or sway; control or influence. **3.** a territory, usually of considerable size, in which a single rulership holds sway. **4.** lands or domains subject to sovereignty or control. **5.** a territory constituting a self-governing commonwealth and being one of a number of such territories united in a community of nations, or empire (formerly applied to self-governing divisions of the British Empire, as Canada, New Zealand, etc.). **6.** (*pl.*) *Theol.* domination (def. 3). [ME, t. F (obs.), der. L *dominium* lordship, ownership]

Dominion Day, (in Canada) a legal holiday, July 1st, celebrating Canada's formation as a dominion on July 1st, 1867.

Dominion Register, a branch register of members of a company resident in a dominion.

dominium (də mĭn′ĭ əm), *n. Law.* complete power to use, to enjoy, and to dispose of property at will. [t. L. See DOMINION]

domino[1] (dŏm′ĭ nō′), *n., pl.* **-noes, -nos. 1.** a large, loose cloak, usually hooded, worn with a small mask by persons in masquerade. **2.** the mask. **3.** a person wearing such dress. [t. Sp., t. L, dative of *dominus* master]

domino[2] (dŏm′ĭ nō′), *n., pl.* **-noes. 1.** (*pl. construed as sing.*) any of various games played with flat, oblong pieces of ivory, bone, or wood, the face of which is divided into two parts, each left blank or marked with pips, usually from one to six. **2.** one of these pieces. [orig. unknown]

Dominus vobiscum (dŏm′ĭ nŏŏs vō bĭs′kŏŏm), *Latin.* the Lord (be or is) with you.

Domitian (də mĭsh′ĭ ən), *n.* A.D. 51–96, Roman emperor A.D. 81–96.

domra (dŏm′rə), *n.* a Russian folk-instrument, usually with three strings, which are plucked.

Domremy-la-Pucelle (*Fr.* dôɴ rē mē là pʏ sĕl′), *n.* a village in NE France: birthplace of Joan of Arc. Also, **Domremy′.**

don[1] (dŏn), *n.* **1.** (*cap.*) Mr; Sir (a Spanish title prefixed to a man's Christian name). **2.** a Spanish lord or gentleman. **3.** a person of great importance. **4.** (in universities) a head, fellow, or tutor of a college. [t. Sp., g. L *dominus* master, lord]

don[2] (dŏn), *v.t.*, **donned, donning.** to put on (clothing, etc.). [contr. of *do on.* Cf. DOFF]

Don (dŏn), *n.* **1.** a river flowing from the central Soviet Union in Europe S through a wide arc to the Sea of Azov. ab. 1300 mi. See map under **Volgograd. 2.** a river in NE Scotland, in Aberdeenshire, flowing E to the North Sea. 62 mi. **3.** a river in central England, in S Yorkshire, flowing NE to the Humber estuary. 60 mi.

dona (*Port.* dô′nə), *n.* Portuguese form of **doña.**

doña (dŏn′yə; *Sp.* dô′nyä), *n.* (in Spanish use) **1.** a lady. **2.** (*cap.*) a title of respect for a lady. [Sp., g. L *domina* lady, mistress. See DON[1]]

Donar (*Ger.* dô′när), *n. German Myth.* the god of thunder. [OHG, c. OE *thunor*, Icel. *Thōr*, G *Donner*]

donary (dō′nə rĭ), *n.* a votive offering; a thing given to sacred use.

donate (dō nāt′), *v.i., v.t.*, **-nated, -nating.** to present as a gift; make a gift or donation of, as to a fund or cause. [back-formation from DONATION] —**dona′tor,** *n.*

Donatello (dŏn′ə tĕl′ō; *It.* dô nä tĕl′lô), *n.* (*Donato di Betto Bardi*), *c.* 1386–1466, Italian sculptor. Also, **Donato** (*It.* dô nä′tô).

donatio mortis causa (dō nä′tĭ ō mô′tĭs kou′sä), a gift of personal property made by a person on the point of death, in contemplation of death, which takes effect when he dies. [L]

donation (dō nā′shən), *n.* **1.** the act of presenting something as a gift. **2.** a gift, as to a fund; a contribution. [t. L: s. *dōnātio*, der. *dōnāre* give] —**Syn. 2.** See **present**[2].

Donatist (dō′nə tĭst), *n.* one of a Christian sect which arose in northern Africa in A.D. 311, and which maintained that it constituted the whole and only true church and that the baptisms and ordinations of the orthodox clergy were invalid. [f. DONAT(US) + -IST] —**Don′atism,** *n.*

donative (dō′nə tĭv), *n.* **1.** a gift or donation; a largess. —*adj.* **2.** of the nature of a donation; vested or vesting by donation.

Donatus (dō nā′təs), *n.* fl. A.D. *c.* 315, bishop of Casae Nigrae in Numidia and leader of a heretical group of African Christians, the Donatists.

Donau (*Ger.* dô′nou), *n.* German name of the **Danube.**

Doncaster (dŏng′kəs tə), *n.* a county borough in central England, in the S West Riding of Yorkshire. 87,100 (est. 1964).

done (dŭn), *v.* **1.** pp. of **do**[1]. **2. have** or **be done with,** to finish relations or connections with. —*adj.* **3.** executed; completed; finished; settled. **4.** cooked. **5.** worn out; used up. **6.** in conformity with fashion and good taste: *it isn't done.* **7. done for,** *Colloq.* **a.** dead. **b.** close to death. **c.** utterly exhausted. **d.** deprived of one's means of livelihood, etc.; ruined. **8. done in,** *Colloq.* very tired; exhausted. **9. done out,** *Colloq.* cheated; tricked (fol. by *of*). **10. done up,** *Colloq.* **a.** dressed smartly. **b.** finished; ruined. —*interj.* **11.** agreed; settled.

donee (dō nē′), *n. Law.* **1.** one to whom a gift is made. **2.** one who has a power of appointment in property. [f. DON(OR) + -EE]

Donegal (dŏn′ĭ gôl′, dŏn′ĭ gôl′), *n.* a county in NW Republic of Ireland. 113,842 pop. (1961); 1865 sq. mi. *Co. town:* Lifford.

Donegal Bay, a bay between counties Donegal and Sligo, Ireland. ab. 30 mi. across.

Donets (*Russ.* dä nyĕts′), *n.* **1.** a river in the SE Soviet Union in Europe, flowing SE to the Don river. ab. 660 mi. See map under **Ukraine. 2.** Also, **Donets Basin.** an area S of this river, in the E Ukrainian Republic: important coal mining region and recently developed industrial area. 9650 sq. mi.

Donetsk (*Russ.* dä nyĕtsk′), *n.* a city in the SE Soviet Union in Europe, in the Donets Basin. 809,000 (est. 1965). Formerly, (until 1918) **Yuzovka**; (1918–35) **Stalin**; (1935–62) **Stalino.**

dong (dŏng), *n.* **1.** a monetary unit of N Vietnam, equal to 10 háo, and equivalent to £0·113 sterling. **2.** a banknote of this value.

donga (dŏng′gə), *n. S African.* a dried-out watercourse. [t. Zulu: m. *udonga*]

Dönitz (*Ger.* dœ′nĭts), *n.* **Karl.** See **Doenitz.**

Donizetti (dŏn′ĭ zĕt′ĭ; *It.* dō nĕd dzĕt′tē), *n.* **Gaetano** (*It.* gä ĕ tä′nō), 1797–1848, Italian operatic composer.

donjon (dŭn′jən, dŏn′-), *n.* the inner tower, keep, or stronghold of a castle. [archaic var. of DUNGEON]

Don Juan (dŏn′jo͞o′ən; *Sp.* dōn KHwän′), **1.** a legendary Spanish nobleman of dissolute life. **2.** any libertine or rake.

donkey (dŏng′kĭ), *n., pl.* **-keys,** *adj.* —*n.* **1.** the ass. **2.** a stupid, silly, or obstinate person. —*adj.* **3.** *Mach.* auxiliary: *donkey pump.* [? familiar var. of *Duncan,* man's name.]

donkey engine, a small, usually subsidiary, steam engine.

donkey jacket, 1. a hip-length thick jacket, in the style of a reefer, but usually with a leather or imitation leather panel across the shoulders. **2.** a reefer.

donkey's years, a long time.

donkey work, *Colloq.* drudgery; hard, tedious work.

donna (dŏn′ə; *It.* dŏn′nä), *n.* (in Italian use) **1.** a lady. **2.** (*cap.*) a title of respect for a lady. [It., g. L *domina* lady, mistress. See DON[1]]

donnard (dŏn′əd), *adj. Chiefly Scot.* stunned; dazed. Also, **donnered** (dŏn′əd). [var. of *donnered,* f. Scot. v. *donner* stupefy (e.g., with a blow or loud noise) + -ED[2]]

Donne (dŭn), *n.* **John,** 1573–1631, English poet and clergyman.

donnish (dŏn′ĭsh), *adj.* resembling or characteristic of a university don; stuffy or pedantic. —**don′nishly,** *adv.* —**don′nishness,** *n.*

Donnybrook Fair (dŏn′ĭ bro͝ok′), **1.** a fair which until 1855 was held annually at Donnybrook, Dublin, and which was famous for rioting and dissipation. **2.** any debauched or riotous occasion.

Donoghue (dŏn′ə hyo͞o′, dŏn′ə gyo͞o′), *n.* **Stephen** (*Steve*), 1884–1945, English jockey.

donor (dō′nə), *n.* **1.** one who gives or donates. **2.** *Med.* a person or animal furnishing blood for transfusion. **3.** *Law.* one who gives property by gift, legacy, or devise, or who confers a power of appointment. **4.** *Chem.* the atom which supplies both electrons in a dative bond. **5.** *Physics.* an imperfection in a semiconductor which causes conduction by electrons. [ME *donour,* t. AF, der. *doner* give, g. L *dōnāre*]

Don Quixote (dŏn′kwĭk′sət; *Sp.* dōn kē KHō′tē), the hero of a romance (1605 and 1615) by Cervantes, who was inspired by lofty and chivalrous but impractical ideals.

donsie (dŏn′sĭ), *adj. Scot.* unlucky. Also, **don′sy.**

don't (dōnt), contraction of *do not.*

donzel (dŏn′zəl), *n. Archaic.* a young gentleman not yet knighted; a squire; a page. [t. It.: m. *donzello,* t. Pr.: m. *donsel,* g. LL *domnicellus,* dim. of L *dominus* master]

donzella (dŏn zĕl′ə), *n. Archaic.* a young lady of noble birth.

doodad (do͞o′dăd), *n. Colloq.* any trifling ornament or bit of decorative finery.

doodle (do͞o′dl), *v.t., v.i.,* **-dled, -dling,** *n.* —*v.t., v.i.* **1.** to draw or scribble idly. —*n.* **2.** a scribbled design, figure, etc., drawn idly.

doodlebug[1] (do͞o′dl bŭg′), *n. U.S. Dial.* an antlion larva. [f. *doodle* simpleton (cf. LG *dudeltopf*) + BUG]

doodlebug[2] (do͞o′dl bŭg′), *n.* **1.** a divining rod or similar device supposedly useful in locating water, oil, minerals, etc., underground. **2.** *Colloq.* a buzzbomb. [appar. special uses of DOODLEBUG[1]]

dooly (do͞o′lĭ), *n., pl.* **-lies.** a kind of litter used in India. Also, **doo′lie.** [t. Hind.: m. *dōlī* litter]

doom (do͞om), *n.* **1.** fate or destiny, esp. adverse fate. **2.** ruin; death. **3.** a judgement, decision, or sentence, esp. an unfavourable one. **4.** (*sometimes cap.*) the Last Judgement, at the end of the world. —*v.t.* **5.** to destine, esp. to an adverse fate. **6.** to pronounce judgement against; condemn. **7.** to ordain or fix as a sentence or fate. [ME *dome,* OE *dōm* judgement, sentence, law, authority, c. OHG *tuom,* Icel. *dōmr,* Goth. *dōms,* orig., that which is put or set; akin to DO, v, -DOM, suffix] —**Syn. 1.** See **fate.**

dooms (do͞omz), *adv. Scot. and N Dial.* very; extremely.

doomsday (do͞omz′dā′), *n.* **1.** the day of the Last Judgement, at the end of the world. **2.** any day of sentence or condemnation. [ME *domes dai,* OE *dōmes dæg* day of judgement]

Doomsday Book, Domesday Book.

Doon (do͞on), *n.* a river in SW Scotland, in Ayrshire, flowing NW to the Firth of Clyde. ab. 30 mi.

door (dô), *n.* **1.** a movable barrier of wood or other material, commonly turning on hinges or sliding in a groove, for closing and opening a passage or opening into a building, room, cupboard, etc. **2.** a doorway. **3.** the building, etc., to which a door belongs: *two doors down the street.* **4.** any means of approach or access, or of exit. **5. lay at the door of,** to attribute to; to impute blame for. **6. next door to, a.** in the next house to. **b.** very near; bordering upon. **7. out of doors,** in the open air; outside a building. **8. show one the door,** to dismiss from the house; turn out. [ME *dore,* OE *duru.* Cf. G *Tür,* Icel. *dyrr,* also OE *dor* gate, c. G *Tor*; akin to L *foris,* Gk *thýra*]

doorbell (dô′bĕl′), *n.* a bell at a door or connected with a door, rung by persons outside seeking admittance.

doorframe (dô′frām′), *n.* the surrounds of a door, including a lintel and two jambs.

doorhandle (dô′hăn′dl), *n.* a handle, upon which pressure is applied in order to release the latch to open a door.

doorjamb (dô′jăm′), *n.* a side or vertical piece of a door supporting the lintel.

doorkeeper (dô′kē′pə), *n.* **1.** one who keeps or guards a door or entrance. **2.** a porter.

doorknob (dô′nŏb′), *n.* a knob, the turning of which releases the latch to open a door.

doorknocker (dô′nŏk′ə), *n.* a knocker on or near a door, used by persons outside to gain admittance.

doorman (dô′măn′, -mən), *n., pl.* **-men** (-mĕn′, -mən). a commissionaire.

doormat (dô′măt′), *n.* **1.** a mat, placed in front of a door, for scraping mud or dirt from shoes. **2.** *Colloq.* an uncomplaining person who meekly accepts ill-treatment or bullying.

doormoney (dô′mŭn′ĭ), *n.* a payment made for admission to a place of entertainment.

Doorn (*Du.* dōrn), *n.* a village in the central Netherlands, in Utrecht Province, SE of Utrecht: the residence of Wilhelm II of Germany after his abdication. 9357 (1964).

doornail (dô′nāl′), *n.* **1.** a large-headed nail formerly used for strengthening or ornamenting doors. **2. dead as a doornail,** dead beyond any doubt.

doornboom (do͝oən′bo͞om′, dôn′-), *n.* a southern African leguminous shrub, *Acacia karroo,* frequently planted for hedges and stabilizing sand, the bark of which is used in tanning. [t. D: thorn-tree]

doorplate (dô′plāt′), *n.* a plate on the door of a house or room, bearing a name, number, or the like.

doorpost (dô′pōst′), *n.* the jamb or upright sidepiece of a doorway.

doorsill (dô′sĭl′), *n.* the sill of a doorway.

doorstep (dô′stĕp′), *n.* **1.** a step at a door, raised above the level of the ground outside; one of a series of steps leading from the ground to a door. **2.** *Colloq.* an extremely thick slice of bread.

doorstopper (dô′stŏp′ə), *n.* **1.** a device, often heavy, to keep a door open. **2.** a device, often rubber or plastic, to prevent a door from hitting a wall. Also, **door′stop′.**

door-to-door (dô′tə dô′), *adj.* **1.** direct from one specified point to another: *door-to-door delivery.* **2.** making direct contact with customers or the like in their homes: *a door-to-door salesman.*

doorway (dô′wā′), *n.* **1.** the passage or opening into a building, room, etc., closed and opened by a door. **2.** the means of access; the start of something.

dop (dŏp), *n. S African Colloq.* **1.** a tot of some alcoholic drink. **2.** a cheap, strong, rough brandy made from the grapeskins left over from wine-production. [t. Afrikaans]

dope (dōp), *n., v.,* **doped, doping.** —*n.* **1.** any thick liquid or pasty preparation, as a sauce, lubricant, etc. **2.** an absorbent material used to absorb and hold a liquid, as in the manufacture of dynamite. **3.** *Aeron.* **a.** any of various varnish-like products for coating the cloth fabric of aeroplane wings or the like, in order to make it waterproof, stronger, etc. **b.** a similar product used to coat the fabric of a balloon to reduce gas leakage. **4.** *Slang.* a molasses-like preparation of opium used for smoking. **5.** *Slang.* any stupefying drug. **6.** *Slang.* a person under the influence, or addicted to the use, of drugs. **7.** *Slang.* a stimulating drug, as one illegally given to a racehorse to induce greater speed. **8.** *Slang.* information or data. **9.** *Slang.* a stupid person. —*v.t.* **10.** *Slang.* to affect with dope or drugs. [t. D: m. *doop* a dipping, sauce, der. *doopen* dip, baptize. See DIP] —**dop′er,** *n.*

dope fiend, *Slang.* a person addicted to drugs, esp. narcotics.

dopey (dō′pĭ), *adj.,* **dopier, dopiest.** *Slang.* **1.** affected by or as by a stupefying drug. **2.** slow-witted; stupid. Also, **dop′y.**

Doppelgänger (dŏp′l gĕng′ə), *n.* an apparitional double or counterpart of a living person. Also, **doubleganger.** [G: double-goer. Cf. D *Dubbelganger*]

Doppler effect (dŏp′lə), *Physics.* the apparent change in frequency and wavelength of a train of sound or light waves if the distance between the source and the receiver is changing. [named after C. J. *Doppler,* 1803–53, Austrian physicist]

dor[1] (dô), *n.* a common European dung beetle, *Geotrupes stercorarius.* Also, **dorr, dorbeetle** (dô′bē′tl), **dorr-beetle.** [ME *dor(r)e,* OE *dora*]

dor[2] (dô), *n. Obs.* scoff; mockery. [cf. Icel. *dār* scoff]

DORA, Defence of the Realm Act (August 1914).

Dorado (də rä′dō), *n. Astron.* the southern constellation, Goldfish or Swordfish, near Volans.

Dorati (dŏ rä′tĭ; *Hung.* dô′rȧ tē), *n.* **Antal** (*Hung.* ŏn′tŏl), born 1906, U.S. conductor born in Hungary.

Dorcas (dô′kəs), *n.* a Christian woman at Joppa who made clothing for the poor. Acts 9:36–41.

Dorcas society, a society of women of a church whose work it is to provide clothing for the poor.

Dorchester (dô′chĭs tə), *n.* a town in S England, the county town of Dorset. 12,750 (est. 1962).

Dordogne (*Fr.* dŏr dŏny′), *n.* **1.** a department in SW France. 375,455 pop. (1962); 3561 sq. mi. *Cap.:* Périgueux. **2.** a river in SW France, flowing W to the Gironde estuary. ab. 300 mi.

Dordrecht (*Du.* dôr′drĕKHt), *n.* a town in SW Netherlands, in South Holland province, on the Waal. 88,031 (1965). Also, **Dort.**

Dore (*Fr.* dŏr), *n.* **Monts** (*Fr.* mōN), a group of mountains in central France. Highest peak, 6188 ft.

Doré (*Fr.* dŏ rĕ′), *n.* **Paul Gustave** (*Fr.* pŏl gYs tȧv′), 1832?–83, French illustrator and artist.

Dorian (dô′rĭ ən), *adj.* **1.** of or pertaining to Doris, a division of ancient Greece, or the race named from it, one of the principal divisions of the ancient Greeks. —*n.* **2.** a Dorian Greek. [f. s. L *Dōrius* (t. Gk: m. *Dṓrios* Dorian) + -AN]

Dorian mode, *Music.* a scale, represented by the white keys of a keyboard instrument, beginning on D.

Doric (dŏ′rĭk), *adj.* **1.** of or pertaining to Doris, its inhabitants, or their dialect. **2.** rustic, as a dialect. **3.** *Archit.* denoting or pertaining to the simplest of the three Greek orders, distinguished by low proportions, shaft without base, saucer-shaped capital (echinus) and frieze of metopes and triglyphs. See illus. under **order.** —*n.* **4.** a dialect of ancient Greek. [t. L: s. *Dōricus*, t. Gk: m. *Dōrikós*]

Doris (dô′rĭs), *n.* an ancient region in central Greece.

Dorking (dô′kĭng), *n.* **1.** a town in England, in central Surrey, near London. 22,604 (1961). **2.** a breed of domestic fowls characterized by a long, low, full body and having five toes on each foot, esp. valued for the table.

dorm (dôm), *n. Colloq.* a dormitory.

dormancy (dô′mən sĭ), *n.* the state of being dormant.

dormant (dô′mənt), *adj.* **1.** lying asleep or as if asleep; inactive as in sleep; torpid. **2.** in a state of rest or inactivity; quiescent; inoperative; in abeyance. **3.** (of a volcano) not erupting. **4.** *Bot.* temporarily inactive: *dormant buds, dormant seeds.* **5.** *Her.* (of an animal) lying down with its head on its forepaws, as if asleep. [ME t. OF, ppr. of *dormir*, g. L *dormīre* sleep, be inactive] —**Syn. 1.** See **inactive.**

dormer (dô′mə), *n.* **1.** Also, **dormer window.** a vertical window in a projection built out from a sloping roof. **2.** the whole projecting structure. [orig., a sleeping chamber; cf. OF *dormeor*, g. L *dormītōrium* DORMITORY]

Dormer

dormered (dô′məd), *adj.* having dormer windows.

dormient (dô′mĭ ənt), *adj.* sleeping; dormant. [t. L: s. *dormiens*, ppr.]

dormitory (dô′mĭ trĭ), *n., pl.* **-tories. 1.** a room for sleeping, usually large and containing many beds, sometimes in cubicles, for the inmates of a school or other institution. **2.** a mental or spiritual resting-place. **3.** Also, **dormitory suburb.** a suburb in which a high proportion of the inhabitants are commuters. **4.** *U.S.* a building containing a number of sleeping rooms. [t. L: m. s. *dormītōrium*, prop. neut. of *dormitōrius* of sleeping]

dormouse (dô′mous′), *n., pl.* **-mice** (-mīs′). any of the small, furry-tailed Old World rodents which constitute the family *Gliridae*, resembling small squirrels in appearance and habits. [? f. DOR(MANT) + MOUSE]

dormy (dô′mĭ), *adj. Golf.* (of a player or side) being in the lead by as many holes as are still to be played.

Dormouse, *Muscardinus avellanarius* (Total length 5½ to 6 in.)

Dornoch (dô′nŏk), *n.* a burgh in Scotland, the county town of Sutherland. 933 (1961).

dorp (dôp), *n.* a village; a hamlet. [t. D. See THORP]

Dorpat (*Ger.* dŏr′pȧt), *n.* German name of **Tartu.**

dorr (dô), *n.* dor[1].

dorsal (dô′səl), *adj.* **1.** *Zool.* of, pertaining to, or situated on the back, as of an organ or part: *dorsal nerves.* **2.** *Bot.* pertaining to the surface away from the axis, as of a leaf; abaxial. [t. ML: s. *dorsālis*, der. L *dorsum* back] —**dor′sally,** *adv.*

dorsal fin, the fin or finlike integumentary expansion generally developed on the back of aquatic vertebrates.

dorsel (dô′səl), *n.* dossal.

Dorset (dô′sĭt), *n.* **1. Thomas Sackville, 1st Earl of,** 1536–1608, English statesman and poet. **2.** Dorsetshire.

Dorsetshire (dô′sĭt shĭə′, -shə), *n.* a county in S England. 309,176 pop. (1961); 973 sq. mi. *Co. town:* Dorchester. Also, **Dorset.**

dorsi-, a combining form of **dorsal, dorsum,** as in *dorsiferous.* Also, **dorso-.**

dorsiferous (dô sĭf′ə rəs), *adj. Bot.* borne on the back, as the sori on most ferns.

dorsiventral (dô′sĭ vĕn′trəl), *adj.* **1.** *Bot.* having distinct dorsal and ventral sides, as most foliage leaves. **2.** *Zool.* dorsoventral.

dorsoventral (dô′sō vĕn′trəl), *adj.* **1.** *Zool.* pertaining to the dorsal and ventral aspects of the body; extending from the dorsal to the ventral side: *the dorsoventral axis.* **2.** *Bot.* dorsiventral.

dorsum (dô′səm), *n., pl.* **-sa** (-sə). *Anat., Zool.* **1.** the back, as of the body. **2.** the back or outer surface of an organ, part, etc. [t. L]

Dort (*Du.* dôrt), *n.* Dordrecht.

Dorticas (dô′tĭ kəs), *n.* **Osvaldo** (ŏz văl′dō), born 1919, president of Cuba since 1959.

Dortmund (dôt′mənd; *Ger.* dŏrt′mŏŏnt), *n.* a city in West Germany, in central North Rhine-Westphalia. 657,100 (est. 1966).

dorty (dô′tĭ), *adj. Scot.* sullen; sulky; pettish; ill-humoured.

dory[1] (dô′rĭ), *n., pl.* **-ries.** *U.S.* a boat with a narrow, flat bottom, high ends, and flaring sides. [first used in W Indies; native Central Amer. name for a dugout]

dory[2] (dô′rĭ), *n., pl.* **-ries. 1.** a flattened, deep-bodied, spiny-rayed, marine food fish, *Zeus faber* (the **John Dory**), found both in European and in Australian seas. **2.** any of several related species. [ME *dore*, t. F: m. *dorée*, lit., gilded]

dos-à-dos (*Fr.* dŏ zȧ dŏ′; *n. in country dancing usually* dō′sĭ dō′), *adv., n., pl.* **-dos** (*Fr.* -dŏ′; -dōz′). —*adv.* **1.** back to back. —*n.* **2.** *Dancing.* an evolution in reels, etc., in which two persons advance, pass round each other back to back, and return to their places. [F]

dosage (dō′sĭj), *n.* **1.** the administration of medicine in doses. **2.** the amount of a medicine to be given. **3.** the sugar syrup added to champagne to produce secondary fermentation or to sweeten it. **4.** *Physics.* dose (def. 3).

dose (dōs), *n., v.,* **dosed, dosing.** —*n.* **1.** a quantity of medicine prescribed to be taken at one time. **2.** a definite quantity of anything analogous to medicine, esp. of something nauseous or disagreeable. **3.** *Physics.* the amount of ionizing radiation absorbed by a given quantity of material; usually measured in *rads*; dosage. —*v.t.* **4.** to administer in or apportion for doses. **5.** to give doses to. [t. F, t. ML: m. s. *dosis*, t. Gk: giving, portion, dose]

dosimeter (dō sĭm′ĭ tə), *n.* **1.** an apparatus for measuring minute quantities of liquid; a drop meter. **2.** an instrument for measuring doses of ionizing radiation (esp. X-rays). Also, **dosemeter.**

dosimetry (dō sĭm′ĭ trĭ), *n.* **1.** the measurement of the doses of medicines. **2.** the measurement of doses of ionizing radiation (esp. X-rays). —**dosimetric** (dō′sĭmĕt′rĭk), *adj.*

Dos Passos (dəs păs′əs), **John Roderigo** (rŏd rē′gō), born 1896, U.S. novelist and playwright.

doss (dŏs), *Slang.* —*n.* **1.** a place to sleep, esp. in a cheap lodging house. **2.** sleep. —*v.i.* **3.** to sleep in a dosshouse. **4.** to make a temporary sleeping place for onself (often fol. by *down*). [prob. t. F: m. *dos* back, through LL, g. L *dorsum*]

dossal (dŏs′əl), *n.* **1.** Also, **dorsel.** an ornamental hanging placed at the back of an altar or at the sides of the chancel. **2.** *Archaic.* dosser[1] (def. 2). Also, **dos′sel.** [t. ML: s. *dossālis* for *dorsālis*, L *dorsuālis* of the back]

dosser[1] (dŏs′ə), *n.* **1.** a basket for carrying objects on the back; a pannier. **2.** an ornamental covering for the back of a seat, esp. a throne, etc. **3.** a hanging sometimes richly embroidered for the walls of a hall or for the back or sides of a chancel. [ME *doser*, t. OF: m. *dossier*, der. *dos* back, g. L *dorsum*]

dosser[2] (dŏs′ə), *n.* one who sleeps in a dosshouse.

dosshouse (dŏs′hous′), *n.* a cheap lodging house; usually for men only.

dossier (dŏs′ĭ ā′, -ĭ ə; *Fr.* dŏ syĕ′), *n.* a bundle of documents on the same subject. [t. F. See DOSSER]

dossil (dŏs′ĭl), *n.* a plug of lint for a wound; a folded bandage used as a compress.

dost (dŭst), *v. Archaic.* 2nd pers. sing. pres. ind. of **do**[1].

Dostoevski (dŏs′toi ĕf′skĭ; *Russ.* də stȧ yĕf′skĭy), *n.* **Feodor Mikhailovich** (*Russ.* fĭ ô′dər mĭ KHȧy′lə vĭch), 1821–81, Russian novelist and short-story writer. Also, **Dos′toyev′sky.** —**Dos′toev′skian,** *adj.*

dot[1] (dŏt), *n., v.,* **dotted, dotting.** —*n.* **1.** a minute or small spot on a surface; a speck. **2.** a small, roundish mark made with or as with a pen. **3.** anything relatively small or specklike. **4.** *Music.* **a.** a point placed after a note or rest, to indicate that the duration of the note or rest is to be increased one half. A double dot further increases the duration by one half the value of the single dot. **b.** a point placed under or over a note to indicate that it is to be played staccato, i.e., shortened. **5.** *Teleg.* a signal of shorter duration than a dash, used in groups of dots, dashes, and spaces, to represent letters in a Morse or a similar code. **6.** a full stop; a decimal point. **7. in the year dot,** *Colloq.* long ago. **8. on the dot,** *Colloq.* punctual; exactly on time. —*v.t.* **9.** to mark with or as with a dot or dots. **10.** to stud or diversify, as dots do. **11.** to place like dots. **12.** *Slang.* to hit; punch. —*v.i.* **13.** to make a dot or dots. **14. dot and carry one,** *Colloq.* **a.** to walk with a limp. **b.** (in simple mathematics) to set down the unit and carry over the tens to the next column. **15. dot one's i's and cross one's t's,** *Colloq.* to be meticulous; to particularize minutely. [OE *dott* head of a boil. Cf. D *dot* kind of knot] —**dot′ter,** *n.*

dot[2] (dŏt; *Fr.* dŏt), *n. Civil Law.* dowry. [t. F, t. L: s. *dōs*] —**dotal** (dō′tl), *adj.*

dotage (dō′tĭj), *n.* **1.** feebleness of mind, esp. resulting from old age; senility. **2.** excessive fondness; foolish affection. [f. DOTE, v. + -AGE]

dotard (dō′təd), *n.* one who is weak-minded, esp. from old age.

dote (dōt), *v.i.,* **doted, doting. 1.** to bestow excessive love or fondness (fol. by *on* or *upon*). **2.** to be weak-minded, esp. from old age. Also, **doat.** [ME *doten,* c. MD *doten.* Cf. D *dutten* doze, dote, Icel. *dotta* nod from sleep, MHG *totzen* take a nap] —**dot′er,** *n.*

doth (dŭth), *v. Archaic.* 3rd per. sing. pres. ind. of **do**[1].

doting (dō′tĭng), *adj.* **1.** extravagantly fond. **2.** weak-minded, esp. from old age. —**dot′ingly,** *adv.*

dotterel (dŏt′rəl), *n.* **1.** a plover, *Eudromias morinellus,* of Europe and Asia, which allows itself to be approached and readily taken. **2.** *Dial.* a dotard or silly fellow. Also, **dottrel** (dŏt′rəl). [f. DOTE + -REL]

dottle (dŏt′l), *n.* the plug of half-smoked tobacco in the bottom of a pipe after smoking. Also, **dot′tel.** [dim. of DOT[1]]

dotty (dŏt′ĭ), *adj.,* **-tier, -tiest. 1.** *Colloq.* crazy; eccentric. **2.** *Colloq. or Dial.* feeble or unsteady in gait. **3.** marked with dots; placed like dots. [f. DOT[1], n. + -Y[1]]

Dou (*Du.* dôw), *n.* **Gerard** (*Du.* KHĕ′rŏrt), 1613–75, Dutch painter. Also, **Dow.**

Douai (dōō′ā; *Fr.* dwĕ), *n.* a town in N France. 50,104 (1962). Also, **Douay.**

Douala (dōō ä′lə), *n.* a seaport in Cameroun. 150,000 (est. 1964). Also, **Duala.**

Douay Bible (dōō′ā), an English translation of the Bible, from the Latin Vulgate, prepared by Roman Catholic scholars, the Old Testament being published at Douay (Douai) in France, in 1609–10, and the New Testament at Rheims, in 1582. Also, **Douay Version.**

double (dŭb′l), *adj., n., v.,* **-led, -ling,** *adv.* —*adj.* **1.** twice as great, heavy, strong, etc.: *double pay, a double portion.* **2.** twofold in form, size, amount, extent, etc.; of extra size or weight: *a double blanket.* **3.** composed of two like parts or members; paired: *a double cherry.* **4.** *Bot.* (of flowers) having the number of petals largely increased. **5.** (of musical instruments) producing a tone an octave lower than the notes indicate. **6.** twofold in character, meaning, or conduct; ambiguous: *a double interpretation.* **7.** deceitful; hypocritical; insincere. **8.** folded over once; folded in two; doubled. **9.** duple, as time or rhythm. **10.** *Print.* **a.** denoting a size of paper of twice the area of the size specified: *double crown.* **b.** a doublet (def. 5). —*n.* **11.** a twofold size or amount; twice as much. **12.** a duplicate; a counterpart. **13.** a sudden backward turn or bend. **14.** a shift or artifice. **15.** *Eccles.* one of the more important feasts of the year: so called because the antiphon is doubled, i.e., sung in full before each psalm as well as after (except for little hours). **16.** *Films, etc.* a substitute actor who takes another's place, as in difficult or dangerous scenes. **17.** *Theat.* an actor with two parts in one play. **18.** *Music, Rare.* a variation. **19.** *Mil.* double time. **20.** *Tennis.* two successive faults in serving. **21.** (*pl.*) a game in which there are two players on each side. **22.** (in bridge or other card games) a challenge by an opponent that declarer cannot fulfil his contract, increasing the points to be won or lost. **23.** *Bridge.* **a.** a hand which warrants such a challenge. **b.** a conventional bid informing partner that a player's hand is of certain strength. **24.** (in darts) **a.** a narrow space between two parallel circles on the outer edge of a dartboard. **b.** a throw which places a dart there. **25.** a bet on two horses, in different races, any winnings and the stake from the first bet being placed on the second horse. **26. at the double,** *Colloq.* **a.** in double time. **b.** fast; quickly; at a run. —*v.t.* **27.** to make double or twice as great: *to double a sum, size, etc.* **28.** *Films, etc.* to act as a double or substitute for another actor. **29.** to be or have twice as much as. **30.** to bend or fold with one part upon another (often fol. by *over, up, back,* etc.). **31.** to clench (the fist). **32.** to sail or go round: *to double Cape Horn.* **33.** to couple; associate. **34.** *Music.* to reduplicate by means of a note in another part, either at the unison or at an octave above or below. **35.** *Bridge.* **a.** to increase (the points) to be won or lost on a declaration. **b.** to make increased, as a bid. —*v.i.* **36.** to become double. **37.** to double a stake in gambling or the like (often fol. by *up*). **38.** to bend or fold (often fol. by *up*). **39.** to turn back on a course (often fol. by *back*). **40.** to share quarters, etc. (fol. by *up*). **41.** *Mil.* to march at the double-time pace. **42.** to serve in two capacities, as: **a.** *Theat.* to play two stage roles in a small company. **b.** *Music.* to play two instruments in a band. **43.** *Bridge.* to become increased, as a bid. —*adv.* **44.** twofold; doubly. [ME, t. OF: m. *duble,* g. L *duplus*] —**dou′bleness,** *n.* —**dou′bler,** *n.*

double-acting (dŭb′l ăk′tĭng), *adj.* (of any reciprocating machine or implement) acting effectively in both directions (distinguished from *single-acting*).

double-banked (dŭb′l băngkt′), *adj.* **1.** having two rowers at each oar. **2.** having two tiers of oars, one above the other, in ancient vessels. **3.** carrying guns on two decks.

double bar, *Music.* a double vertical line on a stave indicating the conclusion of a piece of music or a subdivision of it. See illus. under **bar.**

double-barrelled (dŭb′l bă′rəld), *adj.* **1.** having two barrels, as a gun. **2.** serving a double purpose. **3.** (of a surname) having two elements hyphenated. Also, *U.S.,* **double-barreled.**

double bass, *Music.* **1.** Also, **double-bass viol.** the largest instrument of the violin family, now usually having four strings (sometimes three), played resting vertically on the floor; the violone. **2.** contrabass.

double bassoon, *Music.* a bassoon an octave lower in pitch than the ordinary bassoon: the largest and deepest-toned instrument of the oboe class.

double boiler, *U.S.* double saucepan.

double bond, *Chem.* two covalent bonds linking two atoms of a molecule together; characteristic of unsaturated organic compounds.

double-breasted (dŭb′l brĕs′tĭd), *adj.* (of a garment) overlapping sufficiently to form two thicknesses of considerable width on the breast. See **single-breasted.**

double-check (dŭb′l chĕk′), *v.t., v.i.* to check twice or again; recheck. —**dou′ble-check′,** *n.*

double chin, a fold of fat beneath the chin.

double cloth, a fabric woven of two sets of yarns, as double-faced coating or Jacquard blanket.

double-cross (dŭb′l krŏs′), *v.t. Slang.* to prove treacherous to; betray. —**dou′ble-cross′er,** *n.*

double dagger, a mark (‡) used for references, etc.; the diesis.

double-dealing (dŭb′l dē′lĭng), *n.* **1.** duplicity. —*adj.* **2.** using duplicity; treacherous. —**dou′ble-deal′er,** *n.*

double-decker (dŭb′l dĕk′ə), *n.* something with two decks, tiers, or the like, as a ship with two decks above the waterline, or a bus or tram having a second floor for passengers.

double-declutch (dŭb′l dē klŭch′), *v.i. Motor Vehicles.* to change gear, by moving first into neutral and then into the desired gear, releasing the clutch-pedal between each movement.

double decomposition, *Chem.* a chemical reaction between two compounds in which both decompose and two new compounds are formed; metathesis.

double-dutch (dŭb′l dŭch′), *n. Colloq.* nonsense; gibberish; incomprehensible speech.

double-dyed (dŭb′l dīd′), *adj.* **1.** dyed twice. **2.** deeply imbued with guilt.

double eagle, **1.** an eagle with two heads, as represented in the old arms of Russia and Austria. **2.** a U.S. gold coin worth two eagles, or $20.

double-edged (dŭb′l ĕjd′), *adj.* **1.** having two cutting edges. **2.** acting both ways: *a double-edged charge.*

double elephant, a special size of ledger paper, 27 × 40 inches.

double entendre (*Fr.* dōō blän tän′dr), **1.** a double meaning. **2.** a word or expression with two meanings, one often indelicate. [F (obs.)]

double entry, *Bookkeeping.* a method in which each transaction is entered twice in the ledger, once to the debit of one account, and once to the credit of another. Cf. **single entry.**

double exposure, *Photog.* **1.** the taking of two pictures on one frame of film. **2.** a photograph so obtained; two pictures superimposed, thus making one photograph.

double-faced (dŭb′l fāst′), *adj.* **1.** practising duplicity; hypocritical. **2.** having two faces or aspects.

double-fault (dŭb′l fôlt′), *n.* (in tennis and squash) two serving faults in succession, resulting in the loss of a point to the server.

double-feature (dŭb′l fē′chə), *n. Films.* a cinema programme in which two full-length films are shown.

double first, **1.** (at Cambridge and some other universities) a first-class honours degree gained in two parts of a course in one subject. **2.** (at Oxford and some other universities) a first-class honours degree gained in two subjects. **3.** one who has achieved this.

double flat, *Music.* **1.** a symbol (♭♭) that lowers a note by two semitones. **2.** a note marked and affected by this symbol.

double glazing, glazing in which two layers of glass are separated by a dead air space.

double Gloucester, an orange-coloured, velvet-textured cheese, similar in flavour to Cheddar.

double helical gear, herringbone gear.

double-hung (dŭb′hŭng′), *adj. Bldg Trades.* of a window) having two sashes, each balanced by sash cords and weights in order to move up and down to open and close the window.

double-jointed (dŭb′l join′tĭd), *adj.* having unusually flexible joints which enable the appendages and spine to curve in extraordinary ways.

double-lock (dŭb′l lŏk′), *v.t.* to turn a key in a lock twice, so as to shoot a second bolt.

double magnum, a wine bottle four times the normal size.

double-minded (dŭb′l mīn′dĭd), *adj.* wavering or undecided in mind. —**dou′ble-mind′edness,** *n.*

doubleness (dŭb′l nĭs), *n.* **1.** the quality or condition of being double. **2.** deception or dissimulation.

double option, *Finance.* a privilege consisting of a put and a call combined, giving the holder the right, at his option, either of delivering a certain amount of stock, etc., at a specified price, or of buying a certain amount of stock, etc., at another specified price within a stipulated period.

double or quits, *Colloq.* **1.** a bet in which a debtor stands to double his debt if he loses or be excused if he wins. **2.** any of various gambling games based on this principle.

double-page spread (dŭb′l pāj′), a pair of facing pages of a book, magazine, or the like, viewed as a whole.

double-park (dŭb′l päk′), *v.t., v.i.* to park (a car) alongside another, making a double row along the kerb.

double-quick (dŭb′l kwĭk′), *adj.* **1.** very quick or rapid. —*adv.* **2.** in a quick or rapid manner. —*n.* **3.** double time.

double-reed (dŭb′l rēd′), *adj. Music.* of or pertaining to wind instruments producing sounds through two reeds fastened and beating together, as the oboe.

double refraction, *Physics.* the separation of a ray of light into two unequally refracted rays, as in passing through certain crystals.

double salt, *Chem.* a salt which crystallizes as a single substance, but when dissolved ionizes as two distinct salts.

double saucepan, a pair of interlocking pans, the bottom one containing water which while boiling gently heats the food in the upper pan.

double-sharp, *Music.* **1.** a symbol (𝄪) that raises a note by two semitones. **2.** a note marked and affected by this symbol.

double standard, a moral code more lenient for men than for women.

double star, *Astron.* two stars so near to each other in the sky that they appear as one under certain conditions. **Optical double stars** are two stars at greatly different distances but nearly in line with each other and the observer. **Physical double stars** or **binary stars** are a physical system whose two components are at nearly the same distance from the earth.

double-stop (dŭb′l stŏp′), *v.t., v.i. Music.* to play simultaneously two stopped notes (on a stringed instrument).

doublet (dŭb′lĭt), *n.* **1.** a close-fitting outer body garment, with or without sleeves, formerly worn by men. **2.** a pair of like things; a couple. **3.** one of a pair of like things; a duplicate. **4.** one of two words in the same language, representing the same original, as the English *coy* and *quiet*, one taken from Old French, the other from Latin. **5.** *Print.* an unintentional repetition in printed matter or proof. **6.** (*pl.*) two dice on each of which the same number of spots turns up at a throw. **7.** *Jewellery.* a counterfeit gem made by the welding of two pieces of a different nature, usually a garnet top with a coloured glass base. [ME, t. OF: f. *double* DOUBLE adj. + *-et* -ET]

Doublets (def. 1); Elizabethan

double take, a second look, either literally or figuratively given to a person, event, etc., whose significance had not been completely grasped at first.

doubletalk (dŭb′l tôk′), *n. Colloq.* **1.** speech using nonsense syllables together with words in a rapid patter. **2.** evasive or ambiguous language.

doublethink (dŭb′l thĭngk′), *n.* the ability to accept two contradictory facts simultaneously, and to discipline the mind to ignore the conflict between them.

double-throw (dŭb′l thrō′), *adj.* (of a switch) capable of engaging with two alternative sets of fixed contacts.

double time, **1.** double wages paid to persons who remain at work on certain occasions, such as public holidays, etc. **2.** *U.S. Army.* the fastest rate of marching troops, a slow jog in which 180 paces, each of 3 feet, are taken in a minute. **3.** a slow run by troops in step. **4.** *Colloq.* a run at any speed.

double-time (dŭb′l tīm′), *v.,* **-timed, -timing.** *U.S.* —*v.t.* **1.** to cause to march in double time. —*v.i.* **2.** to march in double time. **3.** to move or run at double time.

double-tongue (dŭb′l tŭng′), *v.i.,* **-tongued, -tonguing.** *Music.* (in playing the flute, cornet, etc.) to apply the tongue rapidly to the teeth and the hard palate alternately, so as to ensure a brilliant execution of a staccato passage.

double-tongued (dŭb′l tŭngd′), *adj.* deceitful.

doubloon (dŭb lo͞on′), *n.* a former Spanish gold coin. [t. F: m. *doublon*, or t. Sp.: m. *doblón*, aug. of *doble* DOUBLE, adj.]

doublure (*Fr.* do͞o blʏr′), *n.* an ornamental lining of a book cover. [F, der. *doubler* to line, DOUBLE]

doubly (dŭb′lĭ), *adv.* **1.** in a double manner, measure, or degree. **2.** in two ways. **3.** *Obs. or Archaic.* with duplicity.

Doubs (*Fr.* do͞o), *n.* **1.** a department in E France. 384,881 pop. (1962); 2031 sq. mi. *Cap.:* Besançon. **2.** a river in E France, flowing into the Saône river. ab. 270 mi.

doubt (dout), *v.t.* **1.** to be uncertain in opinion about; hold questionable; hesitate to believe. **2.** to distrust. **3.** *Archaic.* to fear; suspect. —*v.i.* **4.** to feel uncertainty as to something; be undecided in opinion or belief. —*n.* **5.** undecidedness of opinion or belief; a feeling of uncertainty. **6.** distrust; suspicion. **7.** a state of affairs such as to occasion uncertainty. **8.** *Obs.* fear; dread. **9. beyond a shadow of doubt,** for certain; definitely. **10. in doubt,** in uncertainty; in suspense. **11. no doubt, a.** probably. **b.** certainly. **12. without doubt,** without question; certainly. [ME *douten*, t. OF: m. *douter*, g. L *dubitāre* hesitate, doubt] —**doubt′able,** *adj.* —**doubt′er,** *n.* —**doubt′ingly,** *adv.* —**Syn. 1.** distrust, mistrust, suspect, question. **5.** faltering, indecision, irresolution, hesitation, hesitancy, vacillation.

doubtful (dout′fəl), *adj.* **1.** admitting of or causing doubt; uncertain; ambiguous. **2.** of uncertain issue. **3.** of questionable character. **4.** undecided in opinion or belief; hesitating. —**doubt′fully,** *adv.* —**doubt′fulness,** *n.*

—**Syn. 2.** undetermined, unsettled, indecisive, dubious. **4.** irresolute, vacillating. DOUBTFUL, DUBIOUS, INCREDULOUS, SCEPTICAL imply reluctance or unwillingness to be convinced. To be DOUBTFUL about something is to feel that it is open to question or that more evidence is needed to prove it: *to be doubtful about the statements of witnesses.* DUBIOUS implies greater vacillation, vagueness, or suspicion: *dubious about suggested methods of manufacture, about future plans.* INCREDULOUS means actively unwilling or reluctant to believe, usually in a given situation: *incredulous at the good news.* SCEPTICAL implies a general disposition to doubt or question: *sceptical of human progress.* —**Ant. 1.** certain.

doubting Thomas, one who refuses to believe without proof. See John 20:24–29.

doubtless (dout′lĭs), *adv.* **1.** without doubt; unquestionably. **2.** probably or presumably. —*adj.* **3.** free from doubt or uncertainty. —**doubt′lessly,** *adv.* —**doubt′lessness,** *n.*

douc (do͝ok), *n.* a colourful leaf-eating monkey, *Pygathrix nemaus*, of forest regions of SE Asia. Also, **douc langur.**

douce (do͞os), *adj. Scot. and N Eng.* quiet, sedate, or modest. [ME, t. OF, g. L *dulcis* sweet] —**douce′ly,** *adv.* —**douce′ness,** *n.*

douceur (*Fr.* do͞o sœr′), *n.* **1.** a gratuity, fee, or tip. **2.** a conciliatory gift or bribe. **3.** *Obs.* sweetness; agreeableness. [F, der. *douce* (fem.) sweet, g. L *dulcis*]

douche (do͞osh), *n., v.,* **douched, douching.** —*n.* **1.** a jet or current of water applied to a body part, organ, or cavity for medicinal, hygienic, or contraceptive purposes. **2.** the application of such a jet. **3.** an instrument for administering it. **4.** a bath administered by such a jet. —*v.t.* **5.** to apply a douche to; douse. —*v.i.* **6.** to receive a douche. [t. F, t. It.: m. *doccia* conduit, shower, ult. der. L *dūcere* lead]

dough (dō), *n.* **1.** flour or meal combined with water, milk, etc., in a mass for baking into bread, cake, etc.; paste of bread. **2.** any soft, pasty mass. **3.** *Slang.* money. [ME *dogh*, OE *dāh*, c. D *deeg*, G *Teig*]

doughboy (dō′boi′), *n.* **1.** *U.S. Colloq.* an infantryman. **2.** a rounded lump of dough boiled or steamed as a dumpling.

doughnut (dō′nŭt′), *n.* **1.** a small cake of sweetened or, sometimes, of unsweetened dough fried in deep fat. **2.** Also, **donut.** *Physics.* the toroidal vacuum chamber of a particle accelerator. [f. DOUGH + NUT, in allusion to the original shape]

dought (dout), *v.* pt. of **dow.**

doughty (dou′tĭ), *adj.*, **-tier, -tiest.** strong; hardy; valiant. [ME; OE *dohtig*, unexplained var. of *dyhtig*, der. *dugan* be good, avail, c. G *tüchtig*] —**dough′tily,** *adv.* —**dough′tiness,** *n.*

Doughty (dou′tĭ), *n.* **Charles Montagu** (mŏn′tə gyōō′), 1843–1926, English traveller and author.

doughy (dō′ĭ), *adj.*, **doughier, doughiest.** of or like dough; half-baked; soft and heavy; pallid and flabby.

Douglas (dŭg′ləs), *n.* **1. Clifford Hugh,** 1879–1952, English social economist. **2. Gavin,** *c.* 1475–1522, Scottish poet. **3. Sir James** (*'the Black Douglas'*), *c.* 1286–1330, Scottish military leader. **4.** the capital of the Isle of Man: resort. 18,837 (1961).

Douglas fir, a coniferous tree, *Pseudotsuga taxifolia* (*P. mucronata* or *P. douglasii*), of western North America, often over 200 feet high, and yielding a strong, durable timber. Also, **Douglas pine, Douglas spruce.** [named after David *Douglas*, 1798–1834, Scottish botanist and traveller]

Douglas-Home (dŭg′ləs hyōōm′), *n.* **Sir Alexander Frederick** (*Alec*), formerly **14th Earl of Home,** born 1903, British statesman: prime minister 1963–64.

Douglas Scale, the international sea and swell scale. [from the originator, Sir Henry Percy *Douglas*, 1876–1939, director of British Naval Meteorological Service]

Doukhobors (dōō′kō bôz′), *n.* Dukhobors.

douma (dōō′mə), *n.* duma.

Doumergue (*Fr.* dōō mĕrg′), *n.* **Gaston** (*Fr.* găs tôN′), 1863–1937, French statesman: president of France 1924–1931.

doum-palm (dōōm′päm′), *n.* any African palm of the genus *Hyphaene* which has branched stems and fan-shaped leaves, esp. the Egyptian *H. thebaica* with a hard wood used for making implements.

dour (dŏŏə), *adj.* **1.** sullen; gloomy; sour. **2.** *Scot.* hard; severe; stern. **3.** *Scot.* obstinate; stubborn. [ME *dowre*, t. L: m. s. *dūrus* hard] —**dour′ly,** *adv.* —**dour′ness,** *n.*

doura (dŏŏə′rə), *n.* durra. Also, **dou′rah.**

dourine (dŏŏə′rēn), *n.* *Vet. Sci.* an infectious disease of horses, affecting chiefly the genitals and hind legs, caused by a protozoan parasite, *Trypanosoma equiperdum.* [t. F: m. *dourin*]

Douro (dŏŏə′rō; *Port.* dō′rōō), *n.* a river flowing from N Spain W through N Portugal to the Atlantic. ab. 500 mi. Spanish, **Duero.**

douroucouli (dōō′rōō kōō′lĭ), *n.*, *pl.* **-lis.** the night ape or owl monkey, *Aotus trivergatus*; native of Central and South America, the only true monkey that is nocturnal.

douse (dous), *v.*, **doused, dousing.** —*v.t.* **1.** to plunge into water or the like; drench: *to douse someone with water.* **2.** *Slang.* to put out or extinguish (a light). **3.** *Colloq.* to take off or doff. **4.** *Naut.* to lower in haste, as a sail; slacken suddenly. —*v.i.* **5.** to plunge or be plunged into a liquid. —*n.* **6.** *Chiefly Dial.* a stroke or blow. Also, **dowse.** [orig. obscure] —**dous′er,** *n.*

douzepers (dōōz′pĕəz′), *n.pl.*, *sing.* **douzeper** (dōōz′pĕə′). **1.** *French Legend.* the twelve peers or paladins represented in old romances as attendants of Charlemagne. **2.** *French Hist.* twelve great spiritual and temporal peers of France, taken to represent those of Charlemagne. [ME *dusze pers*, *duspers*, t. OF: m. *douze pers* twelve peers]

dove (dŭv), *n.* **1.** any bird of the pigeon family (*Columbidae*), as the collared dove, *Streptopelia risoria.* **2.** (in literature) this bird as the symbol of innocence, gentleness, and tenderness. **3.** (*cap.*) *Theol.* the Holy Ghost. **4.** an innocent, gentle, or tender person. **5.** a politician or political adviser who favours conciliatory policies as a solution to armed conflict. **6.** *Colloq.* a term of endearment. [ME; OE *dūfe-*, c. D *duif*, G *Taube*, Icel. *dūfa*, Goth. *dubō* dove, lit., diver; akin to DIVE, v.]

dove colour (dŭv), a warm grey with a slight purplish or pinkish tint. —**dove′-col′oured,** *adj.*

dovecot (dŭv′kŏt′), *n.* a structure, usually at a height above the ground, for domestic pigeons. Also, **dovecote** (dŭv′kōt′).

dovedale moss, a small saxifragaceous perennial, *Saxifraga hypnoides*, found mainly in stony places on hills and mountains of the British Isles.

dovelike (dŭv′līk′), *adj.* like a dove; innocent; tender.

Dover (dō′və), *n.* **1.** a seaport in SE England, in E Kent, nearest to the coast of France. 35,650 (est. 1962). See map under **Dunkirk. 2. Strait of,** a strait between England and France, connecting the English Channel with the North Sea. Least width, 20 mi. French, **Pas de Calais. 3.** a town in the U.S., capital of Delaware. 7250 (1960).

Dover's powder, *Med.* a powder containing ipecacuanha and opium, used as an anodyne, diaphoretic, and antispasmodic. [named after Dr Thomas *Dover*, 1660–1742, English physician]

dovetail (dŭv′tāl′), *n.* **1.** *Carp.* a joint or fastening formed by one or more tenons and mortises spread in the shape of a dove's tail. —*v.t.*, *v.i.* **2.** *Carp.* to join or fit together by means of a dovetail or dovetails. **3.** to join or fit together compactly or harmoniously.

Dovetail joint

dovish (dŭv′ĭsh), *adj.* (of a politician or political adviser) conciliatory, favouring peaceful solutions.

dow (dou, dō), *v.i.*, **dowed** or **dought** (dout), **dowing.** *Scot. and N Dial.* **1.** to be able. **2.** to do well, or thrive. [ME *dowen*, *doghen*, OE *dugan*, c. G *taugen.* Cf. DOUGHTY]

Dow (*Du.* dôw), *n.* **Gerard** (*Du.* KHé′rŏrt). See **Dou.**

dow., dowager.

dowable (dou′ə bl), *adj.* *Law.* entitled to dower.

dowager (dou′ə jə), *n.* **1.** a woman who holds some title or property from her deceased husband, esp. the widow of a king, duke, or the like; often added to her title to distinguish her from the wife of the present king, duke, or the like. **2.** *Colloq.* a dignified elderly lady. —*adj.* **3.** like, pertaining to, or characteristic of a dowager. [t. MF: m. *douagiere*, der. *douage* dower, der. *douer* endow, g. L *dōtāre*]

Dowden (dou′dn), *n.* **Edward,** 1843–1913, Irish critic and poet.

dowdy (dou′dĭ), *adj.*, **-dier, -diest,** *n.*, *pl.* **-dies.** —*adj.* **1.** ill-dressed; not trim, smart, or stylish. —*n.* **2.** an ill-dressed woman. [earlier *dowd*, ME *doude*; orig. obscure] —**dow′dily,** *adv.* —**dow′diness,** *n.* —**dow′dyish,** *adj.* —**Syn. 1.** frumpy, shabby.

dowel (dou′əl), *n.*, *v.*, **-elled, -elling** or (*U.S.*) **-eled, -eling.** *Carp.* —*n.* **1.** Also, **dowel pin.** a pin, usually round, fitting into corresponding holes in two adjacent pieces to prevent slipping or to align the two pieces. —*v.t.* **2.** to reinforce with dowels; furnish with dowels. [cf. G *Döbel* peg, plug, pin]

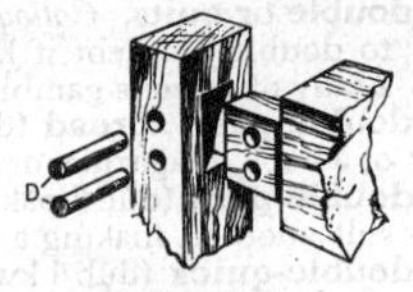

D, Dowel pins

dowel screw, a wood screw with a thread at each end, used esp. for picture frames.

dower (dou′ə), *n.* **1.** *Law.* the portion of a deceased husband's real property allowed by the law to his widow for her life. **2.** dowry (def. 1). **3.** a natural gift or endowment. —*v.t.* **4.** to provide with a dower or dowry. **5.** to give as a dower or dowry. [ME, t. OF: m. *douaire*, g. LL *dōtārium*, der. L *dōs* dowry] —**dow′erless,** *adj.*

dower house, 1. a house set apart for a widow, often a small house on her deceased husband's estate. **2.** any small house, once on the estate of a country-house.

dowery (dou′ə rĭ), *n.*, *pl.* **-eries.** dowry.

dowf (douf, dōōf), *adj.* *Scot. and N Dial.* dull; stupid.

dowie (dou′ĭ, dō′ĭ), *adj.* *Scot. and N Dial.* dull; melancholy; dismal. Also, **dowy.**

Dow-Jones index, the U.S. stock exchange equivalent of the *Financial Times* industrial share index.

Dowland (dou′lənd), *n.* **John,** 1563–1626, English composer and lutenist.

dowlas (dou′ləs), *n.* **1.** a coarse linen fabric originally used for clothing in the 16th century. **2.** a rough cotton fabric often used for roller towels and cheap sheets. [named after *Daoulas*, village in Brittany]

down[1] (doun), *adv.* **1.** from higher to lower; in descending direction or order; into or in a lower position or condition. **2.** on or to the ground. **3.** to a point of submission, inactivity, etc. **4.** to or in a position spoken of as lower, as the south, the country, a business district, etc. **5.** to or at a low point, degree, rate, pitch, volume, etc. **6.** from an earlier to a later time. **7.** from a greater to a less bulk, degree of consistency, strength, etc.: *to boil down syrup.*

8. in due position or state: *to settle down to work.* 9. on paper or in a book: *to write down.* 10. in cash; at once: *to pay £40 down.* 11. *Colloq.* to prison: *he was sent down for three years.* 12. *Colloq.* in a prostrate, depressed, or degraded condition. 13. **down with,** towards a lower position or total abolition. *—prep.* 14. to, towards, or at a lower place on or in: *down the stairs.* 15. to, towards, near, or at a lower station, condition, or rank in. 16. away from the source, origin, etc., of: *down the river.* 17. in the same course or direction as: *to sail down the wind.* 18. *Dial or Colloq.* towards or at: *down home.* *—adj.* 19. downwards; going or directed downwards. 20. travelling away from a terminus. 21. confined to bed through illness. 22. not in activity or operation.: *the wind is down.* 23. *Colloq.* in prison: *he is down for a few months.* 24. being a portion of the full price of an article bought on an instalment plan or mortgage, etc., that is paid at the time of purchase. 25. losing or having lost money at gambling: *he was £10 down after a day at the races.* 26. *Games.* losing or behind an opponent by a specified number of points, holes, etc. 27. **down and out, a.** *Colloq.* without friend, money, or prospects. **b.** *Boxing.* knocked out. 28. **down in the mouth,** *Colloq.* discouraged; depressed. 29. **down at heel,** *Colloq.* poor; shabby; seedy. 30. **down on,** over-severe; unnecessarily ready to detect faults and punish harshly. 31. **down on one's luck,** *Colloq.* suffering a period of poverty, destitution, etc. 32. **down to earth,** *Colloq.* practical; realistic.

—n. 33. a downward movement; a descent. 34. a reverse: *the ups and downs of fortune.* 35. *Colloq.* a grudge; a feeling of hostility: *he has a down on me.* *—v.t.* 36. to put or throw down; subdue. 37. *Colloq.* to drink down: *to down a tankard of ale.* 38. **down tools,** *Colloq.* (of workers) to cease to work, as in starting a strike.

—v.i. 39. to go down; fall.

—interj. 40. (a command, esp. to a dog, to cease jumping, etc.): *down, Rover!* 41. (a command to take cover, or duck). [ME *doune*, late OE *dūne*, aphetic var. of *adūne*, earlier *of dūne* from (the) hill. See DOWN[3]]

down[2] (doun), *n.* 1. the first feathering of young birds. 2. the soft under-plumage of birds as distinct from the contour feathers. 3. a soft hairy growth as the hair on the human face when first beginning to appear. 4. *Bot.* **a.** a fine soft pubescence upon plants and some fruits. **b.** the light feather pappus or coma upon seeds by which they are borne upon the wind, as in the dandelion and thistle. [ME *downe*, t. Scand.; cf. Icel. *dūnn*]

down[3] (doun), *n.* 1. (*usually pl.*) (esp. in S and SE England) open, rolling, upland country with fairly smooth slopes usually covered with grass. 2. *Archaic.* a hill; a sand hill or dune. [ME; OE *dūn* hill, c. OD *dūna.* See DUNE. Not connected with O Irish *dūn* walled town]

Down (doun), *n.* a county in SE Northern Ireland. 266,939 pop. (1961); 952 sq. mi. *Co. town:* Downpatrick.

down-and-out (doun′ ənd out′), *n.* *Colloq.* a person, usually of disreputable appearance, without friends, money, or prospects.

down-beat (doun′bēt′), *n.* *Music.* 1. a downward movement of the conductor's baton indicating the first beat of the bar. 2. the first beat of a bar.

down-bow (doun′bō′), *n.* *Music.* (in bowing on a stringed instrument) a stroke bringing the tip of the bow towards the strings, indicated in scores by the symbol ⌐ (opposed to *up-bow*).

downcast (doun′käst′), *adj.* 1. directed downwards, as the eyes. 2. dejected in spirit; depressed. *—n.* 3. *Rare.* overthrow or ruin. 4. Also, **downcast shaft.** a shaft down which air passes, as into a mine. 5. *Geol., Mining.* the downthrow of a fault.

downcome (doun′kŭm′), *n.* 1. descent; downfall. 2. a downcomer.

downcomer (doun′kŭm′ə), *n.* a pipe, tube or passage for conducting material downwards.

down draught, a descending current of air.

downfall (doun′fôl′), *n.* 1. descent to a lower position or standing; overthrow; ruin. 2. a cause of this. 3. a fall, as of rain or snow. 4. *U.S.* a kind of trap or deadfall, in which a weight or missile falls upon the prey. **—down′fall′en,** *adj.*

downgrade (doun′grād′), *v.*, **-graded, -grading,** *n., adj., adv.* *—v.t.* 1. to assign (a person, job or the like) to a lower status, usually with a smaller salary. *—n. U.S.* 2. a downward slope. 3. **on the downgrade,** heading for poverty, ruin, etc. *—adj., adv. U.S.* 4. downhill.

downhaul (doun′hôl′), *n.* *Naut.* a rope for hauling down a sail.

downhearted (doun′hä′tĭd), *adj.* dejected; depressed; discouraged. **—down′heart′edly,** *adv.* **—down′heart′edness,** *n.* **—Syn.** downcast, despondent.

downhill (doun′hĭl′), *adv.* 1. down the slope of a hill; downwards into a deteriorating or declining position, condition, etc. *—adj.* 2. going or tending downwards on or as on a hill.

Downing (dou′nĭng), *n.* **Andrew Jackson,** 1815–52, American landscape designer and architect.

Downing Street (dou′nĭng), 1. a short street in Westminster: usual residence of the British prime minister at No. 10; other important government offices here. 2. *Colloq.* the British prime minister and cabinet.

downland (doun′lănd′), *n.* hilly pasture; esp. the rolling grasslands of Australia and New Zealand.

down line, a railway line running from the terminus.

Downpatrick (doun′păt′rĭk), *n.* a town in Northern Ireland, the county town of Down. 4219 (1961).

down payment, the initial deposit on a purchase made on an instalment plan or mortgage.

downpipe (doun′pīp′), *n.* a pipe for conveying rainwater from roofs to the drain or the ground.

downpour (doun′pô′), *n.* a heavy, continuous fall of water, rain, etc.

downright (doun′rīt′), *adj.* 1. thorough; absolute; out-and-out. 2. direct; straightforward. 3. *Archaic.* directed straight downwards: *a downright blow.* *—adv.* 4. completely or thoroughly: *he is downright angry.* **—down′right′ly,** *adv.* **—down′right′ness,** *n.*

downrush (doun′rŭsh′), *n.* a rapid descent as of gas, water, etc.

Downs (dounz), *n.pl.* **The,** 1. low ranges of ridges in S and SE England. 2. a roadstead in the Strait of Dover, between the SE tip of England and Goodwin Sands.

downspout (doun′spout′), *n.* downpipe.

Down's syndrome, Mongolism.

downstage (doun′stāj′), *Theat.* *—adv.* 1. at or towards the front of the stage. *—adj.* 2. pertaining to the front of the stage. *—n.* 3. the front of a stage.

downstairs (doun′stĕəz′), *adv.* 1. down the stairs. 2. to or on a lower floor. *—adj.* 3. Also, **down′stair′.** pertaining to or situated on a lower floor. *—n.* 4. the lower floor of a house.

downstream (doun′strēm′), *adv.* 1. with or in the direction of the current of a stream. *—adj.* 2. farther down a stream; moving with the current.

downswing (doun′swĭng′), *n.* 1. *Golf.* in driving a ball, the downward swing of a golf club. 2. the often thicker downward line made by a pen in writing.

downthrow (doun′thrō′), *n.* 1. a throwing down or being thrown down; an overthrow. 2. *Geol.* the downward displacement of strata by a fault.

down town, *U.S.* the business section of a city.

downtown (doun′toun′), *U.S.* *—adv.* 1. to or in the business section of a city. *—adj.* 2. of, pertaining to, or situated in the business section of a city.

down train, a train travelling away from a terminus.

downtrodden (doun′trŏd′n), *adj.* trodden down; trampled upon; tyrannized over. Also, **down′trod′.**

down-under (doun′ŭn′də), *Colloq.* *—n.* 1. Australia. *—adv.* 2. to Australia.

downward (doun′wəd), *adj.* 1. moving or tending to a lower place or condition. 2. descending or deriving from a head, source, or beginning. *—adv.* 3. downwards. **—down′wardly,** *adv.* **—down′wardness,** *n.*

downwards (doun′wədz), *adv.* 1. from a higher to a lower place or condition. 2. down from a head, source, or beginning. 3. from more ancient times to the present day. Also, **downward.**

downwash (doun′wŏsh′), *n.* *Aeron.* the air deflected downwards by an aerofoil.

downwind (doun′wĭnd′), *adv.* 1. in the direction of the wind; with the wind. 2. towards the leeward side. *—adj.* 3. going downwind. 4. situated leeward.

downy (dou′nĭ), *adj.*, **downier, downiest.** 1. of the nature of or resembling down; fluffy; soft. 2. made of down. 3. covered with down. 4. soft; soothing; calm. **—down′iness,** *n.*

downy mildew, fungi belonging to the family *Peronosporaceae*, all of which are obligate parasites of vascular plants, as *Plasmopara viticola*, downy mildew of grapes.

dowry (dou′ə rĭ), *n., pl.* **-ries.** 1. the money, goods, or estate which a woman brings to her husband at marriage; dot. 2. any gift or reward given to or for a bride by a man in consideration for the marriage. 3. *Obs.* a widow's dower. 4. a natural gift or endowment; talent: *a noble dowry.* Also, **dowery.** [ME *dowerie*, t. AF. See DOWER]

dowsabel (do͞o′sə bĕl′); *n.* *Obs.* sweetheart. [var. of *Dulcibella*, woman's name]

dowse[1] (dous), *v.t., v.i.*, **dowsed, dowsing.** douse. **—dows′er,** *n.*

dowse[2] (douz), *v.i.*, **dowsed, dowsing.** to search for subterranean supplies of water, ore, etc., by the aid of a divining rod. [orig. unknown] **—dows′er,** *n.*

dowsing rod, a divining rod.
Dowson (dou′sən), *n.* **Ernest,** 1867–1900, English poet.
dowy (dou′ĭ, dō′ĭ), *adj.* dowie.
doxology (dŏk sŏl′ə jĭ), *n., pl.* **-gies.** a hymn or form of words containing an ascription of praise to God, as the Gloria in Excelsis (**great doxology** or **greater doxology**), the Gloria Patri (**lesser doxology**), or the metrical formula beginning 'Praise God from whom all blessings flow'. [t. ML: m. s. *doxologia,* t. Gk: a praising] **—doxological** (dŏk′sə lŏj′ĭ kl), *adj.* **—dox′olog′ically,** *adv.*
doxy[1] (dŏk′sĭ), *n., pl.* **doxies. 1.** opinion; doctrine. **2.** religious views. Also, **dox′ie.** [abstracted from ORTHODOXY, HETERODOXY, etc.]
doxy[2] (dŏk′sĭ), *n., pl.* **doxies.** *Archaic Slang.* a mistress or paramour; a prostitute. [f. MFlem. *docke* doll + *-sy,* affectionate dim. suffix]
doyen (doi′ən; *Fr.* dwȧ yăɴ′), *n.* the senior member of a body, class, profession, etc. [F. See DEAN] **—doyenne** (*Fr.* dwȧ yĕn′), *n. fem.*
Doyle (doil), *n.* **Sir Arthur Conan,** 1859–1930, British author of detective stories and historical romances.
doz., dozen; dozens.
doze (dōz), *v.,* **dozed, dozing,** *n.* **—***v.i.* **1.** to sleep lightly or fitfully. **2.** to fall into a light sleep unintentionally (often fol. by *off*). **3.** to be dull or half asleep. **—***v.t.* **4.** to pass or spend (time) in drowsiness (often fol. by *away*). **—***n.* **5.** a light or fitful sleep. [cf. OE *dwǣsian* become stupid, Dan. *döse* make dull, heavy, drowsy] **—doz′er,** *n.*
dozen[1] (dŭz′ən), *n., pl.* **dozen, dozens. 1.** a group of twelve units or things. **2. daily dozen,** daily physical exercises. [ME *dozein,* t. OF: m. *dozeine,* der. *douze* twelve, g. L *duodecim*]
dozen[2] (dō′zən), *v.t. Scot.* to stun. [? akin to DOZE]
dozenth (dŭz′ənth), *adj.* twelfth.
dozy (dō′zĭ), *adj.,* **dozier, doziest.** drowsy; half asleep. **—doz′ily,** *adv.* **—doz′iness,** *n.*
D.P., displaced person. Also, **DP.**
D.Phil., Doctor of Philosophy. Also, **D.Ph., Ph.D.**
D.P.H., 1. Department of Public Health. **2.** Diploma in Public Health.
dpt, 1. department. **2.** deponent.
D.P.W., Department of Public Works.
Dr, 1. Doctor. **2.** debtor. **3.** Drive (in street names).
dr., 1. dram; drams. **2.** drachm. **3.** drawer.
drab[1] (drăb), *adj.,* **drabber, drabbest,** *n.* **—***adj.* **1.** having a dull grey colour. **2.** dull; cheerless. **—***n.* **3.** dull grey; dull brownish or yellowish grey. [t. F. m. *drap* cloth. See DRAPE] **—drab′ly,** *adv.* **—drab′ness,** *n.*
drab[2] (drăb), *n., v.,* **drabbed, drabbing. —***n.* **1.** a dirty, untidy woman; a slattern. **2.** a prostitute. **—***v.i.* **3.** to associate with drabs. [? t. LG or D. Cf. D *drab* dregs, LG *drabbe* mire. Cf. also d. E *drabbletail* slattern (with DRABBLE, v.) and its synonym *draggletail*]
drabbet (drăb′ĭt), *n.* a coarse drab linen fabric used for making tea-towels, etc. [f. DRAB[1] + -ET]
drabble (drăb′l), *v.t., v.i.,* **-bled, -bling.** to draggle; make or become wet and dirty. [ME *drabelen,* ? t. LG]
dracaena (drə sē′nə), *n.* **1.** any tree of the liliaceous genus *Dracaena,* natives of tropical regions. **2.** any tree of the closely related genus *Cordyline.* [NL, t. Gk: m. *drákaina* she-dragon]
drachm (drăm), *n.* **1.** a unit of apothecaries' weight, equal to 60 grains, ⅛ ounce. **2.** a drachma. [t. L: s. *drachma,* t. Gk: m. *drachmḗ* an Attic weight and coin]
drachma (drăk′mə), *n., pl.* **-mas, -mae** (-mē). **1.** the monetary unit of modern Greece, equal to 100 lepta, and equivalent to about £0·014. **2.** a coin of this value. **3.** the principal silver coin of the ancient Greeks, varying in weight and value. **4.** a small ancient Greek weight, approximately corresponding to the apothecaries' drachm. [t. L, t. Gk: m. *drachmḗ,* lit., handful]
Draco[1] (drā′kō), *n., gen.* **Draconis** (drā kō′nĭs). a northern circumpolar constellation between Ursa Major and Cepheus. [t. L, t. Gk: m. *drákōn* serpent]
Draco[2] (drā′kō), *n.* fl. 7th century B.C., Athenian statesman noted for the severity of his code of laws.
draco lizard, any of the lizards of the genus *Draco,* esp. *D. volans,* the flying dragon of Malaysia, which has wings like membranes enabling it to glide from tree to tree, etc.
Draconian (drā kō′nyən), *adj.* **1.** of, like, or pertaining to Draco, or his laws. **2.** (*sometimes l.c.*) harsh; rigorous; severe. **—Draco′nianism,** *n.*
draconic (drā kŏn′ĭk), *adj.* of or like a dragon. [f. s. L *draco* DRAGON + -IC]
Draconic (drā kŏn′ĭk), *adj.* Draconian. **—Dracon′ically,** *adv.*
draff (drăf), *n.* refuse, esp. of malt after brewing; lees; dregs. **—draff′y,** *adj.*
draft (drăft), *n.* **1.** a drawing, sketch, or design. **2.** a first or preliminary form of any writing, subject to revision and copying. **3.** the act of drawing; delineation. **4.** *U.S.* the taking of supplies, forces, money, etc., from a given source. **5.** *Chiefly U.S.* conscription. **6.** (formerly) a selection of persons already in service, to be sent from one post or organization to another, in either the army or the navy; a detachment. **7.** a written order drawn by one person upon another; a writing directing the payment of money on account of the drawer; a bill of exchange. **8.** a drain or demand made on anything. **9.** *Foundry.* the slight taper given to a pattern so that it may be drawn from the sand without injury to the mould. **10.** *Masonry.* the narrow band worked along the margin or margins of a rough-faced stone, so that it can be accurately placed. **11.** the sectional area of the openings in a turbine wheel or in a sluice gate. **12.** *Obs.* an allowance for waste of goods sold by weight. **13.** *Chiefly U.S.* draught (esp. defs 3 and 4).
—*v.t.* **14.** to draw the outlines or plan of, or sketch. **15.** to draw up in written form, as a first draft. **16.** *U.S.* to conscript. **17.** *Masonry.* to cut a draft on. [ME *draht,* later *draught, droft* (cf. OE *droht* pull, draught), verbal abstract of *draw* (OE *dragan*), c. G *Tracht.* See DRAUGHT] **—draft′er,** *n.*
draftee (drăf tē′), *n. U.S.* a conscript.
drafting yard, *Austral., N.Z.* a yard in which sheep or cattle are sorted.
draftsman (drăfts′mən), *n., pl.* **-men. 1.** one who draws up documents. **2.** draughtsman (defs 1 and 2). **—drafts′-manship′,** *n.*
draft tube, the flared passage leading vertically from a water turbine to its tailrace.
drag (drăg), *v.,* **dragged, dragging,** *n.* **—***v.t.* **1.** to draw with force, effort, or difficulty; pull heavily or slowly along; haul; trail. **2.** to search with a drag, grapnel, or the like. **3.** to bring (*in*) or introduce, as an irrelevant matter. **4.** to protract or pass tediously (often fol. by *out* or *on*). **5. drag one's feet,** to hang back deliberately; be recalcitrant. **—***v.i.* **6.** to be drawn or hauled along. **7.** to trail on the ground. **8.** to move heavily or with effort. **9.** to proceed or pass with tedious slowness. **10.** to use a drag or grapnel; dredge. **—***n.* **11.** something used by or for dragging, as a dragnet or a dredge. **12.** a grapnel, net, or other apparatus dragged through water in searching, as for dead bodies. **13.** *Agric.* a heavy harrow. **14.** a four-horse sporting and passenger coach with seats inside and on top. **15.** a metal shoe to receive a wheel of heavy wagons and serve as a wheel lock on steep grades. **16.** anything that retards progress. **17.** act of dragging. **18.** slow, laborious movement or procedure; retardation. **19.** *Aeron.* the force due to the relative airflow exerted on an aeroplane or other body tending to reduce its forward motion. **20.** *Hunting.* **a.** the scent or trail of a fox, etc. **b.** something, as aniseed, dragged over the ground to leave an artificial scent. **c.** a hunt with such a scent. **21.** *Angling.* **a.** a brake on a fishing reel. **b.** the sideways pull on a fishline as caused by a cross current. **22.** *Slang.* somebody or something that is extremely boring. **23.** *Colloq.* a puff or a pull on a cigarette. **24.** *Slang.* women's clothes, worn by men; transvestite costume. **25.** *U.S. Slang.* influence: *he has a drag with the managing director.* [late ME; cf. MLG *dragge* grapnel] **—Syn. 1.** See **draw.**
drag-anchor (drăg′ăn′kə). *n. Naut.* sea-anchor.
dragée (*Fr.* drȧ zhē′), *n. French.* **1.** a sweetmeat in the form of a sugar-coated fruit or nut, or containing medicine, drugs, etc. **2.** a small edible decorative silver ball.
draggle (drăg′l), *v.,* **-gled, -gling. —***v.t.* **1.** to soil by dragging over damp ground or in the mud. **—***v.i.* **2.** to hang trailing; become draggled. **3.** to follow slowly; straggle. [f. DRAG + *-le,* freq. suffix]
draggletail (drăg′l tāl′), *n.* a bedraggled or untidy person; slut; slattern.
draggletailed (drăg′l tāld′), *adj.* having the garments draggled as from trailing in the wet and dirt.
draghound (drăg′hound′), *n.* a hound trained to follow a drag or artificial scent.
drag hunt, a hunt with a drag or artificial scent.
dragline (drăg′līn′), *n.* a dragrope (def. 2).
draglink (drăg′lĭngk′), *n. Mach.* a link for connecting the cranks of two shafts.
dragnet (drăg′nĕt′), *n.* **1.** a net to be drawn along the bottom of a river, pond, etc., or along the ground, to catch something. **2.** anything that serves to catch or drag in, as a police system.
dragoman (drăg′ō mən), *n., pl.* **-mans, -men.** (in Middle Eastern countries) a professional interpreter. [t. F, t. LGk: m. *dragoúmanos,* t. Ar.: m. *targumān* interpreter. Cf. TARGUM]
dragon (drăg′ən), *n.* **1.** a mythical monster variously represented, generally as a huge winged reptile with crested head and terrible claws, and often spouting fire.

2. *Now Rare.* a huge serpent or snake. 3. (in the Bible) a large serpent, a crocodile, a great marine animal, or a jackal. 4. a name for Satan. 5. a fierce, violent person. 6. a severely watchful woman; a duenna. 7. any of the small flying lizards of the East Indian region. 8. *Obs.* a short musket, carried by a dragoon (def. 2) in the 16th and 17th centuries. 9. (*cap.*) *Astron.* the northern constellation Draco. [ME, t. OF, g. L *draco*, t. Gk: m. *drákōn* serpent] —**dragoness** (drăg′ə nĭs), *n.fem.* —**drag′onish,** *adj.*

dragonet (drăg′ə nĭt), *n.* 1. a little or young dragon. 2. any fish of the genus *Callionymus*, comprising small shore fishes which are often brightly coloured. [ME, t. OF, dim. of *dragon* DRAGON]

dragonfly (drăg′ən flī′), *n.*, *pl.* **-flies.** any of the larger, harmless insects of the order *Odonata*, feeding on mosquitoes and other insects. Their immature forms are aquatic.

Dragonfly, *Libellula trimaculata* (Length ab. 1¾ in.)

dragonnade (drăg′ə nād′), *n.* 1. one of a series of persecutions of French Protestants, under Louis XIV, by dragoons quartered upon them. 2. any persecution with the aid of troops. [t. F, der. *dragon* DRAGOON]

dragon's blood, 1. a red resin exuding from the fruit of *Daemonorops* (or *Calamus*) *draco*, a palm of the Malay Archipelago, formerly used in medicine, but now chiefly in the preparation of varnishes, etc. 2. any of various similar resins from other trees.

dragon's head, any plant of the labiate genus *Dracocephalum*, esp. *D. grandiflorum.*

dragon tree, a liliaceous tree, *Dracaena draco*, of the Canary Islands, yielding a variety of dragon's blood.

dragoon (drə go͞on′), *n.* 1. a cavalryman of a particular type, as in the British Army. 2. *Obs.* a mounted infantryman armed with a short musket. —*v.t.* 3. to set dragoons or soldiers upon; to persecute by armed force; to oppress; harass. 4. to force by rigorous and oppressive measures; coerce. [t. F: m. *dragon* dragoon (orig., dragon), referring first to the hammer of a pistol, then to the firearm and then to the troops carrying it]

dragrope (drăg′rōp′), *n.* 1. a rope for dragging something, as a piece of artillery. 2. a rope dragging from something, as the guide rope from a balloon.

dragsail (drăg′sāl′), *n. Naut.* sea-anchor. Also, **dragsheet** (drăg′shēt′).

drain (drān), *v.t.* 1. to draw off gradually, as a liquid; remove by degrees, as by filtration. 2. to draw off or take away completely. 3. to withdraw liquid gradually from; make empty or dry by drawing off liquid. 4. to deprive of possessions, resources, etc., by gradual withdrawal; exhaust. —*v.i.* 5. to flow off gradually. 6. to become empty or dry by the gradual flowing off of moisture. —*n.* 7. that by which anything is drained, as a pipe or conduit. 8. *Surg.* a material or appliance for maintaining the opening of a wound to permit free exit of fluid contents. 9. gradual or continuous outflow, withdrawal, or expenditure. 10. the cause of a continual outflow, withdrawal, or expenditure. 11. act of draining. 12. *Colloq.* a small drink. 13. **go down the drain,** *Colloq.* a. to be wasted. b. to become worthless. [OE *drēnian*, *drēahnian* drain, strain out; akin to DRY] —**drain′able,** *adj.* —**drain′er,** *n.*

drainage (drā′nĭj), *n.* 1. the act or process of draining. 2. a system of drains, artificial or natural. 3. drainage basin. 4. that which is drained off. 5. *Surg.* the draining of body fluids (bile, urine, etc.) or of pus and other morbid products from a wound.

drainage basin, the entire area drained by a river and all its tributaries. Also, **drainage area.**

draining-board (drā′nĭng bôd′), *n.* a gently sloping board, etc., usually having runnels, beside a sink on which crockery is placed after washing to dry.

drainless (drān′lĭs), *adj. Poetic.* inexhaustible.

drainpipe (drān′pīp′), *n.* 1. a pipe receiving the discharge of waste pipes and soil pipes. 2. (*pl.*) *Slang.* tight, narrow trousers.

drake[1] (drāk), *n.* the male of any bird of the duck kind. [ME, c. d. G *draak*; cf. OHG *an(u)trahho*]

drake[2] (drāk), *n. Obs.* 1. a dragon. 2. a small kind of cannon. [ME; OE *draca*, t. L: m. *draco* DRAGON]

Drake (drāk), *n.* 1. **Sir Francis,** *c.* 1540–96, English buccaneer, circumnavigator of the globe, and admiral.

Drakensberg (drăk′ənz bûg′), *n.* a mountain range in the E part of the Republic of South Africa. ab. 600 mi. long; highest peak, Thabantshonyana (in Lesotho), 11,425 ft. Also, **Quanthlamba.**

dram (drăm), *n.*, *v.*, **drammed, dramming.** —*n.* 1. $\frac{1}{16}$ ounce avoirdupois weight (27·34 grains). 2. *U.S.* drachm (def. 1). 3. a fluid dram. 4. a small drink of liquor. 5. a small quantity of anything. —*v.i.* 6. *Archaic.* to drink drams; tipple. —*v.t.* 7. to ply with drink. [ME *drame*, t. OF, g. L *drachma* DRACHMA]

drama (drä′mə), *n.* 1. a composition in prose or verse presenting in dialogue or pantomime a story involving conflict or contrast of character, esp. one intended to be acted on the stage; a play. 2. the branch of literature having such compositions as its subject; dramatic art or representation. 3. that art which deals with plays from their writing to their final production. 4. any series of events having dramatic interest or results. [t. LL: a play, t. Gk: deed, play]

Dramamine (drăm′ə mēn′), *n. Trademark. Pharm.* a synthetic antihistamine, used in the treatment of allergic disorders and as a preventive for seasickness and airsickness.

dramatic (drə măt′ĭk), *adj.* 1. of or pertaining to the drama. 2. employing the form or manner of the drama. 3. characteristic of or appropriate to the drama; involving conflict or contrast. Also, *Rare,* **dramat′ical.** —**dramat′ically,** *adv.*

dramatic irony, irony[1] (def. 4).

dramatics (drə măt′ĭks), *n.* 1. (*construed as sing. or pl.*) the art of producing or acting dramas. 2. (*construed as pl.*) dramatic productions, esp. by amateurs. 3. (*construed as pl.*) dramatic behaviour.

dramatis personae (drä′mə tĭs pû sō′nī), *Latin.* the persons or characters in a drama.

dramatist (drăm′ə tĭst), *n.* a writer of dramas or dramatic poetry; a playwright.

dramatization (drăm′ə tī zā′zhən), *n.* 1. the act of dramatizing. 2. construction or representation in dramatic form. 3. a dramatized version, of another form of literature or of historic facts. Also, **dramatisation.**

dramatize (drăm′ə tīz′), *v.t.*, **-tized, -tizing.** 1. to put into dramatic form. 2. to express or represent dramatically: *he dramatizes his woes.* Also, **dramatise.** —**dram′atiz′er,** *n.*

dramaturge (drăm′ə tûj′), *n.* dramatist. Also, **dram′atur′gist.**

dramaturgy (drăm′ə tû′jĭ), *n.* 1. the science of dramatic composition. 2. the dramatic art. 3. dramatic representation. [t. Gk: m. s. *drāmatourgía* composition of dramas] —**dram′atur′gic, dram′atur′gical,** *adj.*

Drammen (*Norw.* drȧ′mən), *n.* a seaport in S Norway. 46,904 (1965).

dram. pers., dramatis personae.

dramshop (drăm′shŏp′), *n. Archaic.* a bar or room in licensed premises.

Drancy (*Fr.* dräN sē′), *n.* a town in N France, in Seine department. 65,890 (1962).

Drang nach Osten (*Ger.* drȧng′nȧKH ŏs′tən), *German.* drive to the east: the German imperialistic foreign policy of extending influence to the east and south.

drank (drăngk), *v.* pt. and former pp. of **drink.**

drape (drāp), *v.*, **draped, draping,** *n.* —*v.t.* 1. to cover or hang with cloth or some fabric, esp. in graceful folds; adorn with drapery. 2. to adjust (hangings, clothing, etc.) in graceful folds. 3. *Colloq.* to position in a casual manner: *he draped his legs over the arms of the chair.* —*v.i.* 4. to fall in folds, as drapery. —*n.* 5. manner or style of hanging. 6. (*pl.*) curtains. [t. F: m. s. *draper*, der. *drap* cloth, g. LL *drappus*]

draper (drā′pə), *n.* a dealer in textiles and cloth goods, etc. [ME, t. AF, var. of F *drapier*]

drapery (drā′pə rĭ), *n.*, *pl.* **-peries.** 1. cloths or textile fabrics collectively. 2. the business of a draper. 3. coverings, hangings, clothing, etc., of some fabric, esp. as arranged in loose, graceful folds. 4. *Art.* hangings, clothing, etc., so arranged as represented in sculpture or painting. —**dra′peried,** *adj.*

drastic (drăs′tĭk), *adj.* acting with force or violence; violent. [t. Gk: m. s. *drastikós* efficacious] —**dras′tically,** *adv.*

drat (drăt), *v.*, **dratted, dratting,** *interj.* —*v.t.* 1. *Colloq.* to confound; to damn. —*interj.* 2. (a mild exclamation of vexation.)

dratted (drăt′ĭd), *adj. Colloq. or Dial.* confounded.

draught (dräft), *n.* 1. a current of air, esp. in a room, chimney, stove, or any enclosed space. 2. a device for regulating the flow of air in a stove, fireplace, etc. 3. an act of drawing or pulling, or that which is drawn; a pull; haul. 4. an animal, or team of animals used to pull a load. 5. the drawing of a liquid from its receptacle, as of ale from a cask. 6. drinking, or a drink. 7. an amount drunk as a continuous act. 8. a dose of medicine. 9. a catch or take of fish. 10. a. the action of displacing water with a vessel. b. the depth of water a vessel needs to float it. 11. (*pl. construed as sing.*) a game played by two people each with twelve pieces on a chequered board. 12. one of the pieces in this game. 13. **feel the draught,** *Colloq.* feel or be

harmed by conditions becoming unfavourable. **14.** draft (esp. defs 1–3).
—*adj.* **15.** being on draught; drawn as required; draught ale. **16.** used or suited for drawing loads. [ME *draht*, c. D *dragt*, G *Tracht*, Icel. *drāttr*. See DRAFT]

draughtboard (dräft′bôd′), *n.* a board marked off into sixty-four squares of two alternating colours, on which draughts and chess are played. Also, **draughtsboard.**

draughtsman (dräfts′mən), *n.*, *pl.* **-men. 1.** one who draws sketches, plans, or designs. **2.** one employed in making mechanical drawings, as of machines, structures, etc. **3.** draftsman (def. 1). **4.** one of the pieces used in draughts, usually a small coloured disc. —**draughts′manship′**, *n.*

draughty (dräf′tĭ), *adj.*, **draughtier, draughtiest.** characterized by or causing draughts of air. —**draught′iness,** *n.*

Drava (drä′və), *n.* a river flowing from S Austria, along a portion of the boundary between Hungary and SE Yugoslavia into the Danube. ab. 450 mi. Also, **Drave** (drä′və). German, **Drau** (*Ger.* drou).

drave (drāv), *v. Archaic.* pt. of **drive.**

Dravidian (drə vĭd′ĭ ən), *n.* **1.** a great linguistic family of India, including Tamil, Telugu, Kanarese, and Malayalam, and, in Baluchistan, Brahui. It is wholly distinct from Indo-European. **2.** a member of a race of people speaking these languages, occupying much of southern India and parts of Ceylon. —*adj.* **3.** Also, **Dravid′ic.** of or pertaining to this people or their language.

draw (drô), *v.*, **drew, drawn, drawing,** *n.* —*v.t.* **1.** to cause to come in a particular direction as by a pulling force; pull; drag; lead (often fol. by *along, away, in, out, off*, etc.). **2.** to bring or take out, as from a receptacle, or source: *to draw water, blood, tears, teeth.* **3.** to bring towards oneself or itself, as by inherent force or influence; attract. **4.** to pick or choose at random. **5. a.** to be dealt or take a card from the pack. **b.** *Bridge.* to remove trumps, or outstanding cards of a given suit, from an opponent's hand. **6.** to sketch in lines or words; delineate; depict: *to draw a picture.* **7.** to mark out; trace. **8.** to frame or formulate, as a distinction. **9.** to take in, as by sucking or inhaling. **10.** to get; derive; deduce: *to draw a conclusion.* **11.** to disembowel (a fowl, etc.). **12.** to drain (a pond, etc.) by a channel, etc. **13.** to pull out to full or greater length; stretch: make by attenuating, as wire. **14.** to wrinkle or shrink by contraction. **15.** *Med.* to digest and cause to discharge: *to draw an abscess by a poultice.* **16.** *Naut.* (of a boat) to displace (a certain depth of water). **17.** *Sport.* to leave (a contest) undecided. **18.** *Billiards.* to cause to recoil after impact, as if pulled back. **19.** to search (covert) for game. **20.** *Cricket.* to play (a ball) with the bat held at such an angle as to deflect the ball between the wicket and the legs. **21.** *Curling.* to toss (the stone) gently. **22.** (of tea) to infuse.
—*v.i.* **23.** to exert a pulling, moving, or attracting force: *a sail draws by being filled with wind and properly trimmed.* **24.** to be drawn; move as under a pulling force (often fol. by *on, off, out*, etc.): *the day draws near.* **25.** to take out a sword, pistol, etc., for action (often fol. by *on*). **26.** to use or practise the art of tracing figures; practise drawing. **27.** to shrink or contract. **28.** *Med.* to act as an irritant or to cause blisters. **29.** to produce or have a draught of air, etc., as in a pipe or flue. **30.** *Games.* to leave a contest undecided. **31.** *Hunting.* **a.** (of a hound) to advance carefully towards the game, after indicating it by pointing. **b.** (of a hound) to follow the game animal by its scent.
—*v.* **32.** Some special verb phrases are:
draw on, 1. to approach; to near. **2.** to clothe; to pull on a garment. **3.** to call on or make a demand on: to draw on supplies, etc. **4.** to make a levy or call on for money, supplies, etc.
draw out, 1. to extract. **2.** to lengthen or prolong. **3.** to encourage or persuade somebody to talk.
draw the line, *Colloq.* **1.** to fix a limit. **2.** to decline.
draw the teeth of, *Colloq.* to render harmless.
draw up, 1. to bring to, or come to a halt. **2.** to prepare, or set out a document, plan, etc. **3.** to arrange, esp. in military formation.
—*n.* **33.** the act of drawing. **34.** something that draws or attracts. **35.** that which is drawn, as a lot. **36.** *Sport.* a drawn or undecided contest. **37.** *U.S. Phys. Geog.* a small natural ditch or drain, usually the upper part of a stream valley. **38.** *Lacrosse.* the starting or restarting movement of a game, in which the crosses of two opposing players are pulled apart, having previously been placed back to back with the ball between them.
[ME *drawen*, OE *dragan*, c. Icel. *draga* draw, G *tragen* carry, bear. Cf. DRAG]
—**Syn. 1.** DRAW, DRAG, HAUL, PULL imply causing movement of an object by exerting force upon it. To DRAW is to move by a force, in the direction from which the force is exerted: *a magnet draws iron to it, horses draw a wagon.* To DRAG is to draw with greater force, necessary to overcome friction between the object drawn and the surface on which it rests: *to drag a sledge to the top of a hill, a heavy piece of furniture across a room.* To HAUL is to transport a heavy object slowly by mechanical force or with sustained effort: *to haul a piano up to the seventh floor, to haul a large boat across a portage.* To PULL is to draw or tug, exerting varying amounts of force according to the effort needed: *to pull out an eyelash, to pull fighting dogs apart.* —**Ant. 1.** push.

drawback (drô′băk′), *n.* **1.** a hindrance or disadvantage. **2.** *Com.* an amount paid back from a charge made. **3.** *Govt.* refund of excise or import duty, as when imported goods are re-exported. See **rebate**[1].

drawbar (drô′bä′), *n. Railways.* a metal rod or bar for connecting a locomotive and the carriages or trucks.

drawbore (drô′bô′), *v.*, **-bored, -boring,** *n. Carp.* —*v.t.* **1.** to bore a hole (in a tenon) slightly out of alignment, so that when a pin is driven in, the mortised and tenoned parts are drawn snugly together. —*n.* **2.** a hole thus made.

drawbridge (drô′brĭj′), *n.* a bridge of which the whole or a part may be drawn up or aside to prevent access or to leave a passage open for boats, etc.

drawee (drô ē′), *n. Finance.* one on whom an order, draft, or bill of exchange is drawn.

drawer (drô *for 1, 2;* drô′ə *for 3–5*), *n.* **1.** a sliding compartment, as in a piece of furniture, that may be drawn out in order to get access to it. **2.** (*pl.*) a garment for the lower part of the body, with a separate portion for each leg; underpants. **3.** one who or that which draws. **4.** *Finance.* one who draws an order, draft, or bill of exchange. **5.** *Archaic.* a tapster.

drawing (drô′ĭng), *n.* **1.** the act of a person or thing that draws. **2.** representation by lines; delineation of form without reference to colour. **3.** a sketch, plan, or design, esp. one made with pen, pencil, or crayon. **4.** the art of making these.

drawing account, *U.S. Banking, etc.* current account.

drawing-board (drô′ĭng bôd′), *n.* a rectangular board to which paper can be placed or tacked for drawing on.

drawing card, *U.S.* an entertainer, act, etc., that can be relied upon to produce a large audience.

drawing paper, a rough-surfaced paper, particularly suited to pencil, crayon or charcoal drawing, as its surface gives a grained effect.

drawing-pin (drô′ĭng pĭn′), *n.* a short broad-headed tack designed to be pushed in by the thumb. Also, *U.S.*, **thumbtack.**

drawing room, 1. a room for the reception and entertainment of visitors; a living room. **2.** a formal reception, esp. at court. **3.** *U.S.* a private compartment in a railway carriage. [f. obs. *drawing* withdrawing + ROOM]

drawknife (drô′nīf′), *n. Carp., etc.* a knife with a handle at each end at right angles to the blade, used by drawing over a surface.

Drawknife

drawl (drôl), *v.t., v.i.* **1.** to say or speak with slow, lingering utterance. —*n.* **2.** the act or utterance of one who drawls. [appar. a freq. form connected with DRAW. Cf. D *dralen*, LG *drauеln* loiter] —**drawl′er,** *n.* —**drawl′ingly,** *adv.* —**drawl′y,** *adj.*

drawn (drôn), *v.* **1.** pp. of **draw.** —*adj.* **2.** haggard; tired; tense. **3.** pulled together; closed. **4.** equal in score, as a game. **5.** eviscerated, as a fowl. **6.** (of a weapon) unsheathed.

drawn butter sauce, *U.S.* a sauce of melted butter, flour, seasonings, and hot water.

drawnet (drô′nĕt′), *n.* a net with a drawstring in various weights and meshes, used for trapping animals.

drawn-thread work, ornamental work done by drawing threads from a fabric, the remaining portions usually being formed into lacelike patterns by needlework. Also, **drawn work.**

drawplate (drô′plāt′), *n. Mach.* a die plate with conical holes through which to draw wire and thus to regulate its size and shape.

drawshave (drô′shāv′), *n. Carp., etc.* drawknife.

drawsheet (drô′shēt′), *n.* a sheet that can be pulled from under a patient in bed.

drawstring (drô′strĭng′), *n.* a string, cord, etc., which tightens or closes an opening, as of a bag, clothing, etc., when one or both ends are pulled.

draw table, a table with one or more leaves which slide out to form an extension.

drawtube (drô′tyo͞ob′), *n.* a tube sliding within another tube, as the tube carrying the eyepiece in a microscope.

draw-well (drô′wĕl′), *n.* a well from which water is drawn by a bucket suspended by a rope.

dray (drā), *n.* **1.** a low, strong cart without fixed sides, for carrying heavy loads. **2.** a sledge. **3.** a drey. —*v.t.* **4.** to convey on a dray. [ME *draye* sledge without wheels.

Cf. OE *dræg-* in *drægnett* dragnet, der. OE *dragan* draw]

drayage (drā′ĭj), *n.* **1.** conveyance by dray. **2.** a charge made for it.

dray-horse (drā′hôs′), *n.* a strong carthorse; a powerful horse used to draw a dray.

drayman (drā′mən), *n., pl.* **-men.** a man who drives a dray.

Drayton (drā′tn), *n.* **Michael,** 1563–1631, English poet.

dread (drĕd), *v.t.* **1.** to fear greatly; be in shrinking apprehension or expectation of: *to dread death.* **2.** *Obs.* to hold in respectful awe. —*v.i.* **3.** *Obs.* to be in great fear. —*n.* **4.** terror or apprehension as to something future; great fear. **5.** deep awe or reverence. **6.** a person or thing dreaded. —*adj.* **7.** greatly feared; frightful; terrible. **8.** held in awe; revered. [ME *drede(n)*, OE *drǣdan*, aphetic var. of *adrǣdan, ondrǣdan*, c. OHG *intrātan* fear] —**Syn. 4.** See **fear.** —**Ant. 1.** welcome.

dreadful (drĕd′fəl), *adj.* **1.** causing great dread, fear, or terror; terrible: *a dreadful storm.* **2.** venerable; awe-inspiring. **3.** *Colloq.* extremely bad, unpleasant, ugly, great, etc. —*n. Colloq.* **4.** Also, **penny-dreadful.** a cheap, lurid story, as of crime or adventure. **5.** a periodical given to highly sensational matter. —**dread′fully,** *adv.* —**dread′fulness,** *n.* —**Syn. 1.** frightful, dire.

dreadnought (drĕd′nôt′), *n.* **1.** a type of battleship with the main battery consisting of heavy-calibre guns in turrets: so called from the British battleship, *Dreadnought*, launched in 1906, the first of the type. **2.** one who fears nothing. **3.** an outer garment of heavy woollen cloth. **4.** *Slang.* a heavyweight boxer. Also, **dread′naught′.**

dream (drēm), *n., v.,* **dreamed** or **dreamt, dreaming.** —*n.* **1.** a succession of images or ideas present in the mind during sleep. **2.** the sleeping state in which this occurs. **3.** an object seen in a dream. **4.** an involuntary vision occurring to one awake: *a waking dream.* **5.** a vision voluntarily indulged in while awake; daydream; reverie. **6.** a wild or vain fancy. **7.** something or somebody of an unreal beauty or charm. **8.** a hope; an inspiration; an aim. —*v.i.* **9.** to have a dream or dreams. **10.** to indulge in daydreams or reveries. **11.** to think or conceive of something in a very remote way (fol. by *of*). —*v.t.* **12.** to see or imagine in sleep or in a vision. **13.** to imagine as if in a dream; fancy; suppose. **14.** to pass or spend (time, etc.) in dreaming (often fol. by *away*). **15. dream up,** *Colloq.* to invent; to form or plan an idea in the imagination. [ME *dreem* dream, OE *drēam* mirth, noise; change of meaning prob. due to Scand. influence. Cf. Icel. *draumr* dream] —**dream′er,** *n.* —**dream′ful,** *adj.* —**dream′ingly,** *adv.* —**dream′less,** *adj.* —**dream′lessly,** *adv.* —**dream′lessness,** *n.* —**dream′like′,** *adj.*

dreamboat (drēm′bōt′), *n. Slang.* **1.** an overwhelmingly attractive member of the opposite sex. **2.** anything greatly desired.

dreamland (drēm′lănd′), *n.* the land of imagination or fancy; the region of reverie.

Dreams (drēmz), *n.* **Lake of,** a dark plain, *Lacus Somniorum*, in the first quadrant of the face of the moon.

dreamt (drĕmt), *v.* a pt. and pp. of **dream.**

dreamtime (drēm′tīm′), *n. Austral.* the Aboriginal concept of the Creation.

dream world, the world of fancy, rather than of objective reality.

dreamy (drē′mĭ), *adj.,* **dreamier, dreamiest. 1.** full of dreams; characterized by or causing dreams. **2.** of the nature of or characteristic of dreams; visionary. **3.** vague; dim. **4.** soothing; quiet; gentle. **5.** *Colloq.* marvellous; extremely pleasing. —**dream′ily,** *adv.* —**dream′iness,** *n.*

dreary (drĭə′rĭ), *adj.,* **drearier, dreariest. 1.** causing sadness or gloom. **2.** dull. **3.** *Archaic.* sad; sorrowful. Also, *Poetic,* **drear.** [ME *drery*, OE *drēorig* gory, cruel, sad] —**drear′ily,** *adv.* —**drear′iness,** *n.* —**drearisome** (drĭə′rĭ səm), *adj.* —**Syn. 1.** gloomy, dismal, drear, cheerless. **2.** tedious, monotonous, wearisome.

dredge[1] (drĕj), *n., v.,* **dredged, dredging.** —*n.* **1.** a dragnet or other contrivance for gathering material or objects from the bed of a river, etc. **2.** any of various powerful machines for dredging up or removing earth, etc., as from the bottom of a river, by means of a scoop, a series of buckets, a suction pipe, or the like. —*v.t.* **3.** to clear out with a dredge; remove sand, silt, mud, etc., from the bottom of. **4.** to take, catch, or gather with a dredge; obtain or remove by a dredge. —*v.i.* **5.** to use a dredge. [late ME *dreg*, akin to OE *dragan* DRAW]

dredge[2] (drĕj), *v.t.,* **dredged, dredging.** *Cookery.* to sprinkle or coat with some powdered substance, esp. flour. [appar. v. use of *dredge* mixed grain]

dredger[1] (drĕj′ə), *n.* **1.** a machine for dredging. **2.** one who uses a dredge. **3.** a barge, boat, etc., equipped for dredging.

dredger[2] (drĕj′ə), *n.* a container with a perforated top for sprinkling flour, etc. [f. DREDGE[2] + -ER[1]]

dredging machine, dredge[1] (def. 2).

dree (drē), *v.,* **dreed, dreeing,** *adj.* —*v.t.* **1.** *Scot. and N Dial.* to suffer; endure. —*adj.* **2.** Also, **dreegh** (drēKH), **dreigh** (drēKH), **driegh.** *N Dial.* tedious; dreary. [ME; OE *drēogan* endure]

dreg (drĕg), *n.* **1.** (*usually pl.*) the sediment of wine or other drink; lees; grounds. **2.** (*usually pl.*) any waste or worthless residue. **3.** a small remnant or quantity. [ME, t. Scand.; cf. Icel. *dreggjar* dregs] —**dreg′gy,** *adj.*

Dreibund (*Ger.* drī′bo͝ont), *n.* **1.** the alliance between Germany, Austria-Hungary, and Italy, formed in 1882 and continuing until the withdrawal of Italy in May, 1915. **2.** (*l.c. or cap.*) a triple alliance. [G: f. *drei* three + *Bund* alliance]

Dreiser (drī′sə), *n.* **Theodore,** 1871–1945, U.S. novelist.

drench (drĕnch), *v.t.* **1.** to wet thoroughly; steep; soak: *garments drenched with rain, swords drenched in blood.* **2.** *Archaic.* to cause to drink. **3.** *Vet. Sci.* to administer a draught of medicine to (an animal), esp. by force: *to drench a horse.* —*n.* **4.** the act of drenching. **5.** something that drenches: *a drench of rain.* **6.** a preparation for drenching or steeping. **7.** *Obs.* a large drink or draught. **8.** a draught of medicine, esp. one administered to an animal by force. [ME *drenche(n)*, OE *drencan*, causative of *drincan* drink] —**drench′er,** *n.* —**Syn. 1.** See **wet.**

Drenthe (*Du.* drĕn′tə), *n.* a province in E Netherlands. 329,992 pop. (est. 1963); 1028 sq. mi. *Cap.:* Assen.

Dresden (drĕz′dən; *Ger.* drĕs′dən), *n.* **1.** a city in S East Germany, on the Elbe. 503,859 (1964). See map under **Saxony. 2.** a kind of fine china originally from Dresden.

dress (drĕs), *n., adj., v.,* **dressed** or **drest, dressing.** —*n.* **1.** the chief outer garment worn by women, consisting of a skirt and a bodice, made either separately or together. **2.** clothing; apparel; garb. **3.** fine clothes; formal costume: *full dress.* **4.** outer covering, as the plumage of birds. —*adj.* **5.** of or for a dress or dresses. **6.** of or for a formal occasion: *a dress suit.* —*v.t.* **7.** to equip with clothing, ornaments, etc.; deck; attire. **8.** to put formal or evening clothes on. **9.** to arrange a display in; ornament or adorn: *to dress a shop window.* **10.** to prepare (fowl, game, skins, fabrics, timber, stone, ore, etc.) by special processes. **11.** to comb out and do up (hair). **12.** to cultivate (land, etc.). **13.** to treat (wounds or sores). **14.** to make straight; bring (troops) into line: *to dress ranks.* **15.** *Colloq.* to scold; thrash (fol. by *down*). **16. dress ship,** *Naut.* to decorate a ship by hoisting lines of flags running the full length of the ship. —*v.i.* **17.** to clothe or attire oneself, esp. in formal or evening clothes: *she is dressing for dinner.* **18.** to come into line, as troops. **19. dress up, a.** to put on best clothes. **b.** to put on fancy dress, costume, or guise. [ME *dres(en)*, t. OF: m. *dresser* arrange, ult. der. L *directus* straight. See DIRECT, v.]

—**Syn. 1.** DRESS, COSTUME, GOWN refer to the outer garment of women. DRESS is the general term, esp. for a garment such as is used not only for covering but for adornment: *a black dress, a summer dress, a becoming dress.* COSTUME is used of the style of dress appropriate to some occasion, purpose, period, or character, esp. as used on the stage, at balls, at court, or the like: *an eighteenth-century costume, an appropriate costume for the country, costumes worn at an important social event.* GOWN is usually applied to a dress more expensive and elegant than the ordinary, to be worn on a special occasion: *a wedding gown, an evening gown.* **2.** clothes, garments, vestments. **7.** clothe, apparel, array, robe.

dressage (drĕs′äzh), *n.* the art and training of a horse in obedience, deportment, and responses.

dress circle, a circular or curving division of seats in a theatre, cinema, etc., usually the first gallery above the floor, orig. set apart for spectators in evening dress.

dress coat, a man's close-fitting evening coat, with open front and with the skirts cut away over the hips.

dresser[1] (drĕs′ə), *n.* **1.** one who dresses. **2.** one employed to help to dress actors, etc., at a theatre. **3.** any of several tools or devices used in dressing materials. **4.** an assistant to a surgeon. **5.** a window-dresser. [f. DRESS + -ER[1]]

dresser[2] (drĕs′ə), *n.* **1.** a kitchen sideboard with a set of shelves and drawers for dishes and cooking utensils. **2.** *Obs.* a table or sideboard on which food is dressed for serving. [ME *dressour*, t. OF: m. *dresseur*, der. *dresser* DRESS]

dress goods, cloth or material for dresses.

dressing (drĕs′ĭng), *n.* **1.** the act of one who or that which dresses. **2.** that with which something is dressed. **3.** a sauce for food: *salad dressing.* **4.** stuffing for a fowl. **5.** an application for a wound. **6.** manure, compost, or other fertilizers for land. **7.** (*usually pl.*) *Archit.* worked or dressed stones, esp. those around window or door openings or at the angle of a building. **8.** the grooming of a horse.

dressing-down (drĕs′ĭng doun′), *n. Colloq.* **1.** a severe reprimand; scolding. **2.** a thrashing; beating.

dressing-gown (drĕs′ĭng goun′), *n.* a loose gown or robe generally worn over night attire.

dressing-room (drĕs′ĭng ro͝om′, -ro͞om′), *n.* a room for use in getting dressed, esp. backstage in a theatre.
dressing station, *Mil.* a post or centre close to the combat area, which gives first aid to the wounded.
dressing-table (drĕs′ĭng tā′bl), *n.* **1.** a table or stand, usually surmounted by a mirror, for use in making the toilet. **2.** a small desklike table, with drawers beneath often screened by curtains.
dressmaker (drĕs′mā′kə), *n.* one whose occupation is the making of women's dresses, coats, etc. **—dress′-mak′ing,** *n.*
dress rehearsal, a rehearsal of a play in costume and with scenery, properties, and lights arranged and operated as for a performance; the final rehearsal.
dress shield, a pad worn under the arms beneath the clothing to keep perspiration from showing or staining.
dress suit, a man's suit of evening clothes.
drest (drĕst), *v. Archaic.* a pt. and pp. of **dress.**
drew (dro͞o), *v.* pt. of **draw.**
drey (drā), *n.* a squirrel's nest. Also, **dray.**
Dreyer (drī′ə; *Dan.* drȧ′yər), *n.* **Carl Theodore** (*Dan.* kȧrl tĕ′ô dōr), 1889–1968, Danish film director.
Dreyfus (drā′fəs, drī′-; *Fr.* drĕ fʏs′), *n.* **Alfred** (ăl′frĭd; *Fr.* ăl frĕd′), 1859–1935, French army officer (Jewish), convicted of treason in 1894 and 1899, but proved innocent in 1906.
dribble (drĭb′l), *v.*, **-bled, -bling,** *n.* **—*v.i.*** **1.** to fall or flow in drops or small quantities; trickle. **2.** to drivel; slaver. **3.** *Soccer, Hockey, etc.* to advance a ball by a series of short kicks or pushes. **4.** (in netball and basketball) to move about a court while bouncing a ball. **—*v.t.*** **5.** to let fall in drops. **6.** *Sport.* **a.** (in soccer, hockey, etc.) to move (the ball) along by a rapid succession of short kicks, pushes, or hits. **b.** (in netball and basketball) to bounce a ball. **—*n.*** **7.** a small trickling stream. **8.** a drop. **9.** a small quantity of anything. **10.** *Sport.* the act of dribbling. **11.** *Scot.* a drizzle. [freq. of obs. *drib* drip, in some senses influenced by DRIVEL] **—drib′bler,** *n.*
driblet (drĭb′lĭt), *n.* **1.** a small portion or part. **2.** a small or petty sum. Also, **drib′blet.** [f. DRIBBLE + -ET]
dribs and drabs, small and often irregular amounts.
dried (drīd), *v.* pt. and pp. of **dry.**
driegh (drēᴋʜ), *adj.* dree.
drier (drī′ə), *adj.* **1.** compar. of **dry.** **—*n.*** Also, **dryer.** **2.** one who or that which dries. **3.** any substance added to paints, varnishes, etc., to make them dry quickly. **4.** a mechanical contrivance for removing moisture.
driest (drī′ĭst), *adj.* superl. of **dry.**
drift (drĭft), *n.* **1.** a driving movement or force; impulse; impetus; pressure. **2.** *Navig.* movement or course under the impulse of water currents, wind, etc. **3.** *Phys. Geog.* a broad and shallow current which advances at a rate of ten or fifteen miles a day, like that which crosses the middle Atlantic. **4.** *Naut.* the direction and distance that a ship is carried by a current at sea. **5.** *Aeron.* deviation of an aircraft from a set course, due to cross-winds. **6.** the course of anything; tendency; aim: *the drift of an argument.* **7.** something driven, or formed by driving. **8.** a heap of any matter driven together: *a drift of snow.* **9.** *Geol.* **a.** a deposit of detritus. **b.** the deposit of a continental ice-sheet. **10.** the state or process of being driven. **11.** Also, **drift bolt.** a tapering steel rod, used to bring two holes into alignment for riveting or bolting. **12.** *Mach.* a round, tapering piece of steel for enlarging holes in metal, or for bringing holes in line to receive rivets, etc. **13.** *Civ. Eng.* a secondary tunnel between two main tunnels or shafts. **14.** *Mining.* an approximately horizontal passageway in underground mining, etc. **15.** (in South Africa) **a.** a river ford. **b.** a sudden dip in a road across which water may flow at times. **—*v.i.*** **16.** to be carried along by currents of water or air, or by the force of circumstances. **17.** to wander aimlessly. **18.** to be driven into heaps: *drifting sand.* **—*v.t.*** **19.** to carry along: *the current drifted the boat to sea.* **20.** to drive into heaps: *drifted snow.* [ME *drift* act of driving, verbal abstract from OE *drīfan* drive] **—drift′er,** *n.*
driftage (drĭf′tĭj), *n.* **1.** the action or amount of drifting. **2.** drifted matter. **3.** *Naut.* the amount of deviation from a ship's course due to leeway. **4.** windage.
drift anchor, a sea-anchor or drag.
drift bolt, drift (def. 11).
drifter (drĭf′tə), *n.* **1.** one who or that which drifts. **2.** *Colloq.* a shiftless person. **3.** a fishing boat that uses a driftnet.
drift ice, detached floating ice in masses which drift with the wind or ocean currents, as in the polar seas.
drift meter, *Aeron.* an instrument for measuring the drift of aircraft.
drift mining, mining by means of horizontal tunnels or drifts, as against the use of vertical shafts.
driftnet (drĭft′nĕt′), *n.* a fine-mesh fishing net, weighted at the bottom, and supported with floats at the top, which drifts with the tide or current.
drift sail, a sail dropped in the sea and used as a sea anchor, to help lessen the drift of a ship in a storm.
drift tube, *Radio.* a conducting enclosure, usually cylindrical, held at a constant potential so that electrons or charged particles within will experience no force, and hence no change in velocity. See **klystron.**
driftway (drĭft′wā′), *n.* a road or track along which cattle, etc., may be driven.
driftwood (drĭft′wo͝od′), *n.* wood floating on, or cast ashore by, the water.
drifty (drĭf′tĭ), *adj.* of the nature of, or characterized by, drifts.
drill[1] (drĭl), *n.* **1.** a tool or machine for drilling or boring cylindrical holes. **2.** *Mil.* **a.** training in formal marching or other precise military or naval movements. **b.** an exercise in such training: *gun drill.* **3.** any strict, methodical training, instrument, or exercise. **4.** *Colloq.* correct procedure; routine. **5.** a gastropod, *Urosalpinx cinera,* destructive to oysters. **—*v.t.*** **6.** to pierce or bore a hole in (anything). **7.** to make (a hole) by boring. **8.** *Mil.* to instruct and exercise in formation marching and movement, the carrying of arms during formal marching, and the formal handling of arms for ceremonies and guard work. **9.** to impart (knowledge) by strict training or discipline. **—*v.i.*** **10.** to pierce or bore with a drill. **11.** to go through exercise in military or other training. [t. D: m. *drillen* bore, drill] **—drill′able,** *adj.* **—drill′er,** *n.* **—Syn. 3.** See **exercise.**
drill[2] (drĭl), *n.* **1.** a small furrow made in the soil in which to sow seeds. **2.** a machine for sowing in rows and for covering the seeds when sown. **3.** a row of seeds or plants thus sown. **—*v.t.*** **4.** to sow (seed) or raise (crops) in drills. **5.** to plant (ground) in drills. [orig. uncert.] **—drill′er,** *n.*
drill[3] (drĭl), *n.* strong twilled cotton for a variety of uses. [short for DRILLING[2], t. G: triplet, confused with *Drillich* ticking (f. *dri* three + *-lich*), t. L: m. s. *trilix* with three threads, *tri-* being translated]
drill[4] (drĭl), *n.* a baboon, *Papio leucophaeus,* of western Africa, smaller than the mandrill. [orig. unknown]
drilling[1] (drĭl′ĭng), *n.* the act of a person or thing that drills. [f. DRILL[1], v. + -ING[1]]
drilling[2] (drĭl′ĭng), *n.* drill[3].
drillmaster (drĭl′mäs′tə), *n.* one who trains others in anything, esp. in a mechanical manner.
drill press, *Mach.* a machine tool for boring holes with a drill or drills.
drill sergeant, a sergeant specially employed in instructing drill.
drill team, a team of drilled men, trained in ceremonial drill for exhibitions, etc.
drily (drī′lĭ), *adv.* dryly.
Drin (*Alban.* drĕn), *n.* a river flowing from S Yugoslavia through N Albania into the Adriatic. 180 mi.
Drina (*Serb.* drē′nȧ), *n.* a river in central Yugoslavia, flowing N to the Sava river. 160 mi.
drink (drĭngk), *v.*, **drank** (formerly also **drunk**); **drunk** (sometimes **drank,** formerly or as pred. adj. **drunken**); **drinking;** *n.* **—*v.i.*** **1.** to swallow water or other liquid; imbibe. **2.** to imbibe alcoholic beverages, esp. habitually or to excess; tipple. **3.** to salute in drinking; drink in honour of (fol. by *to*). **—*v.t.*** **4.** to swallow (a liquid). **5.** to take in (a liquid) in any manner; absorb. **6.** to take in through the senses, esp. with eagerness and pleasure. **7.** to swallow the contents of (a cup, etc.). **8.** to drink in honour of or with good wishes for: *to drink one's health.* **—*n.*** **9.** any liquid which is swallowed to quench thirst, for nourishment, etc.; a beverage. **10.** alcoholic liquor. **11.** excessive indulgence in alcoholic liquor. **12.** a draught of liquid; a potion. **13. the drink,** *Slang.* the sea or a large lake. [ME *drinke(n)*, OE *drincan*, c. G *trinken*]
—Syn. 1. DRINK, IMBIBE, SIP refer to swallowing liquids. DRINK is the general word: *to drink coffee.* IMBIBE is more formal and today is hardly used in reference to actual drinking except facetiously; it is used figuratively in the meaning to absorb: *to imbibe culture.* SIP implies drinking little by little, at short, succeeding intervals, often in a delicate, toying, or idle manner: *sip a cup of broth.*
drinkable (drĭngk′ə bl), *adj.* **1.** that may be drunk; suitable for drinking. **—*n.*** **2.** (*usually pl.*) something drinkable; a liquid for drinking.
drinker (drĭngk′ə), *n.* **1.** one who drinks. **2.** one who drinks alcoholic liquors habitually or to excess.
drinking fountain, a fountain, often ornamental, which ejects water suitable for drinking.
drinking song, a hearty song often in praise of liquor, suitable to be sung by a group engaged in friendly drinking.
drinking water, water suitable to be drunk by humans without boiling first.

Drinkwater (drĭngk′wô′tə), *n.* **John,** 1882–1937, English poet, dramatist, and critic.

drip (drĭp), *v.*, **dripped** or **dript, dripping,** *n.* —*v.i.* **1.** to let fall drops; shed drops. **2.** to fall in drops, as a liquid. —*v.t.* **3.** to let fall in drops. —*n.* **4.** the act of dripping. **5.** the liquid that drips. **6.** the sound made by the fall of liquid drops. **7.** *Archit.* **a.** a projecting part of a cornice or the like, so shaped as to throw off rainwater and thus protect the parts below. **b.** a projecting metal strip having the same function. **8.** *Colloq.* an insipid or colourless person; a fool. [late ME *dryppe*, t. Scand.: cf. Dan. *dryppe*]

drip-dry (drĭp′drī′), *adj.*, *v.*, **-dried, -drying.** —*adj.* **1.** (of a fabric) drying in its desired shape, when hung dripping wet after being rinsed. —*v.t.* **2.** to hang a fabric article after rinsing, while still dripping wet, and allow it to dry and assume its desired shape with no ironing. —*v.i.* **3.** (of a fabric) to dry in this way.

drip-feed (drĭp′fēd′), *n.*, *v.*, **-fed, -feeding.** —*n.* **1.** nourishment given via a tube into the stomach or a vein. —*v.t.* **2.** to feed by such means.

dripping (drĭp′ĭng), *n.* **1.** the act of anything that drips. **2.** (*often pl.*) the liquid that drips. **3.** fat exuded from meat in cooking and used as shortening, for making gravy, or for basting.

dripping pan, a pan used under roasting meat to receive the dripping.

drippy (drĭp′ĭ), *adj.* *Colloq.* (of a person) colourless; insipid.

dripstone (drĭp′stōn′), *n.* **1.** *Archit.* a projecting stone moulding or cornice for throwing off rainwater. **2.** calcium carbonate, $CaCo_3$, occurring in the form of stalactites and stalagmites.

drive (drīv), *v.*, **drove** or (*Archaic*) **drave; driven; driving;** *n.* —*v.t.* **1.** to send along, away, off, in, out, back, etc., by compulsion; force along: *to drive someone to desperation, out of one's senses, to do something.* **2.** to overwork; overtask. **3.** to cause and guide the movement of (an animal, vehicle, etc.). **4.** to convey in a vehicle. **5.** to keep (machinery) going. **6.** to impel; constrain; urge; compel. **7.** to carry (business, a bargain, etc.) vigorously through. **8.** *Mining, etc.* to excavate horizontally (or nearly so). **9.** *Tennis, Cricket, Golf, etc.* to knock or throw (the ball) very swiftly. **10.** *Hunting.* to chase (game). —*v.i.* **11.** to go along before an impelling force; be impelled: *the ship drove before the wind.* **12.** to rush or dash violently. **13.** to make an effort to reach or obtain; aim (fol. by *at*): *the idea he was driving at, what is he driving at?* **14.** to act as driver. **15.** to go or travel in a driven vehicle: *to drive away, back, in, out, from, to, etc.* —*n.* **16.** the act of driving. **17.** an impelling along, as of game, cattle, or floating logs, in a particular direction. **18.** the animals, logs, etc., thus driven. **19.** *Psychol.* a source of motivation: *the sex drive.* **20.** *Sport.* propelling or forcible stroke. **21.** a vigorous onset or onward course. **22.** a strong military offensive. **23.** a united effort to accomplish some purpose, esp. to raise money for a government loan or for some charity. **24.** vigorous pressure or effort, as in business. **25.** energy and initiative. **26.** a trip in a driven vehicle. **27.** a road for driving, esp. a private access road to a private house. **28.** *Mach.* a driving mechanism, as of a motor car: *gear drive, chain drive.* **29.** *Motor Vehicles.* point or points of power application to the roadway: *front drive, rear drive, four-wheel drive.* **30.** *Com. Slang.* an attempt to force down the market price of a commodity by offering a quantity at a low price. **31.** *Tennis, Cricket, Golf, etc.* the knocking of a ball very swiftly. —*adj.* **32.** pertaining to a part of a machine used in its propulsion. [ME *driven*, OE *drīfan*, c. G *treiben*]
—**Syn. 1.** push, force. **15.** DRIVE, RIDE are used interchangeably to mean taking a trip in a private horse-drawn vehicle or a motor car. These two words are not synonyms in other connections. To DRIVE is to guide or steer the progress of a vehicle: *to drive a bus, a lorry, a motor car, a horse, oxen.* To RIDE is to sit on the back of, and be carried about by, an animal; or to be carried as a passenger in a vehicle: *to ride a horse, in a train, on a bus, on a public conveyance.* **24.** energy. —**Ant. 1.** lead.

drive-in (drīv′ĭn′), *n.* *U.S.* a cinema, cafe, etc., catering to customers who remain in their cars.

drivel (drĭv′əl), *v.*, **-elled, -elling** or (*U.S.*) **-eled, -eling,** *n.* —*v.i.* **1.** to let saliva flow from the mouth or mucus from the nose; slaver. **2.** to issue like spittle. **3.** to talk childishly or idiotically. **4.** to act foolishly. —*v.t.* **5.** to utter childishly or idiotically. **6.** to waste foolishly. —*n.* **7.** childish, idiotic, or silly talk; twaddle. **8.** *Rare.* saliva flowing from the mouth, or mucus from the nose; slaver. [ME *dryvele, drevel(en)*, OE *dreflian*] —**driv′eller,** *n.*

driven (drĭv′ən), *v.* pp. of **drive.**

driver (drī′və), *n.* **1.** one who or that which drives. **2.** one who drives an animal or animals, a vehicle, etc.; coachman, drover, chauffeur, etc. **3.** one whose job is to drive and control railway engines. **4.** *Mach.* a part that transmits force or motion. **5.** *Golf.* a club (No. 1 wood), with a long shaft, used for making long shots, as from the tee. —**driv′erless,** *adj.*

driver ant, any of the ants of the subfamily *Dorylinae*, occurring in tropical Africa and America, which live in temporary nests and travel as vast armies in long files, preying on other animals, chiefly insects. See **army ant.**

driveway (drīv′wā′), *n.* a passage along which vehicles may be driven, esp. outside a private house.

driving (drī′vĭng), *adj.* **1.** (of a person) effective in eliciting work from others; energetic. **2.** violent; having tremendous force. **3.** relaying or transmitting power.

driving licence, a permit, issued by a licensing authority, allowing one to drive certain vehicles on public roads.

driving test, a test of the fitness and ability of a person to drive a vehicle on public roads.

driving wheel, 1. *Mach.* a main wheel which communicates motion to others. **2.** one of the propelling wheels of a locomotive; any wheel used to transform the force of the locomotive cylinder into tractive effort. **3.** one of the road wheels of a motor vehicle which transmits the drive.

drizzle (drĭz′əl), *v.*, **-zled, -zling,** *n.* —*v.i.* **1.** to rain gently and steadily in fine drops; sprinkle. —*n.* **2.** a very light rain; mist. **3.** *Meteorol.* precipitation consisting of numerous, minute droplets of water less than $\frac{1}{50}$ inch in diameter. [possibly dim. and freq. form of rare ME *dresen*, OE *drēosan* fall] —**drizz′ly,** *adj.*

Drogheda (droi′ĭ də), *n.* a seaport in NE Republic of Ireland, in Louth, near the mouth of the Boyne river: town captured and the inhabitants massacred by Cromwell, 1649. 16,800 (est. 1961).

drogue (drōg), *n.* **1.** a bucket-like contrivance used as a sea-anchor. **2.** *Aerospace.* a small parachute used to pull out the main canopy of a parachute brake.

droit (droit; *Fr.* drwȧ), *n.* **1.** a legal right or claim. **2.** that to which one has a legal right or claim. **3.** *Finance.* duty; custom. **4.** *Obs.* the body of rules constituting the law. [t. F, g. Rom. *dērectum*, r. L *dīrectum* right, prop. neut. of L *dīrectus* straight. See DIRECT, adj.]

droll (drōl), *adj.* **1.** amusingly queer; comical; waggish. —*n.* **2.** *Rare.* a waggish fellow; a jester; a buffoon. —*v.i.* **3.** to play the droll or buffoon; jest; joke. [t. F: m. *drôle*, t. MD: m. *drolle* little man] —**droll′ness,** *n.* —**drol′ly,** *adv.* —**Syn. 1.** See **amusing.**

drollery (drō′lə rĭ), *n.*, *pl.* **-eries. 1.** something amusingly queer or funny. **2.** a jest; a facetious tale. **3.** droll quality; humour. **4.** the action or behaviour of a buffoon or wag; jesting. **5.** *Obs.* a comic picture. **6.** *Obs.* a puppet show.

drome (drōm), *n.* *Colloq.* an aerodrome. Also, **'drome.**

Drôme (*Fr.* drōm), *n.* a department in SE France. 304,227 pop. (1962); 2533 sq. mi. *Cap.*: Valence.

-drome, a word element meaning 'running', 'course', 'racecourse', as in *hippodrome.* [comb. form repr. Gk *drómos*]

dromedary (drŭm′ə də rĭ, -drĭ), *n.*, *pl.* **-daries.** the one-humped or Arabian camel, *Camelus dromedarius*, light swift types of which are bred for riding and racing. [ME *dromedarye*, t. LL: m. *dromedārius* (sc. *camēlus*), der. L *dromas* dromedary, t. Gk: running]

Dromedary, *Camelus dromedarius* (6 ft high at the shoulder)

dromond (drŏm′ənd, drŭm′-), *n.* a large, fast-sailing vessel of the Middle Ages. [ME *dromon*, t. LL: s. *dromo*, t. LGk: m. *drómōn* light vessel, der. *Gk drómos* a running]

dromos (drŏm′ŏs), *n.* **1.** a passage or entrance-way, as to an ancient subterranean tomb. **2.** a racecourse or track in ancient Greece. [t. Gk]

-dromous, an adjective termination corresponding to **-drome.** [f. -DROME + -OUS]

drone[1] (drōn), *n.* **1.** the male of the honey bee and other bees, stingless and making no honey. See illus. under **bee. 2.** one who lives on the labour of others; an idler; a sluggard. **3.** a remotely controlled mechanism, as a radio-controlled aeroplane or boat. [earlier *dron(e)*, *drowne*, early ME *dron*, var. of ME and OE *dran* (cf. G *Drohne*)] —**dron′ish,** *adj.*

drone[2] (drōn), *v.*, **droned, droning,** *n.* —*v.i.* **1.** to make a dull, continued, monotonous sound; hum; buzz. **2.** to speak in a monotonous tone. —*v.t.* **3.** to say in a dull, monotonous tone. —*n.* **4.** *Music.* **a.** a continuous low tone produced by the bass pipes or bass strings of musical instruments. **b.** the pipes (esp. of the bagpipe) or strings producing this tone. **c.** a bagpipe equipped with such pipes. 5. a monotonous tone; a humming; a buzzing. 6. a monotonous speaker. [cf. DRONE[1]; akin to ME *droun* roar] **—dron′ingly,** *adv.*

drongo (drŏng′gō), *n., pl.* **-gos.** any of the oscine passerine birds of the African and Asiatic family *Dicruridae*, usually black in colour, with long forked tails, and insectivorous habits. [t. Malagasy]

dronkgras (drŏngk′gräs′), *n.* any of various poisonous grasses of southern Africa, esp. *Melica decumbens*, which have a semi-paralysing effect on cattle. [t. Afrikaans: lit., drunk grass]

drool (drōōl), *v., n. Colloq.* drivel. [contr. of DRIVEL]

droop (drōōp), *v.i.* **1.** to sink, bend, or hang down, as from weakness or exhaustion. **2.** *Poetic.* to sink; descend, as the sun. **3.** to fall into a state of physical weakness; flag; fail. **4.** to lose spirit or courage. *—v.t.* **5.** to let sink or drop. *—n.* **6.** a drooping. [ME *droupe(n)*, t. Scand.; cf. Icel. *drūpa*; akin to DROP] **—droop′ingly,** *adv.* **—droop′y,** *adj.* **—Syn. 1.** flag, languish.

drop (drŏp), *n., v.,* **dropped** or **dropt, dropping.** *—n.* **1.** a small quantity of liquid which falls or is produced in a more or less spherical mass; a liquid globule. **2.** the quantity of liquid contained in such a mass. **3.** a very small quantity of liquid. **4.** a minute quantity of anything. **5.** (*usually pl.*) liquid medicine given in drops. **6.** something like or likened to a drop. **7.** a lozenge (confection). **8.** a pendant. **9.** act of dropping; fall; descent. **10.** the distance or depth to which anything drops. **11.** a steep slope. **12.** a fall in degree, amount, value, etc.: *a drop in price.* **13.** that which drops or is used for dropping. **14.** a drop curtain. **15.** a trapdoor. **16.** gallows. **17. a.** a stick of parachutists. **b.** a descent by parachute. **18.** *Naut.* the vertical length of a course. See **hoist. 19. get** or **have the drop on,** *U.S. Colloq.* **a.** to pull and aim a gun, etc., before an antagonist can. **b.** to get or have at a disadvantage.
—v.i. **20.** to fall in globules or small portions, as water or other liquid: *rain drops from the clouds.* **21.** to fall vertically like a drop; have an abrupt descent. **22.** to sink to the ground as if inanimate. **23.** to fall wounded, dead, etc. **24.** to come to an end; cease; lapse: *there the matter dropped.* **25.** to withdraw; disappear (fol. by *out*). **26.** to squat or crouch, as a dog at the sight of game. **27.** to fall lower in condition, degree, etc.; sink: *the prices dropped sharply.* **28.** to pass without effort into some condition: *to drop asleep, drop into the habit of doing it.* **29.** to move down gently, as with the tide or a light wind. **30.** to fall or move (*back, behind, to the rear,* etc.). **31.** to come or go casually or unexpectedly into a place; to visit informally (fol. by *in, by,* etc.): *he dropped in on us occasionally.* **32.** (of an unborn child) to change position in the womb so that the head becomes engaged before labour. **33.** (of animals) to give birth. **34. drop astern,** *Naut.* to pass or move towards the stern; move back; let another vessel pass ahead. **35. drop off, a.** to decrease; decline: *sales have dropped off.* **b.** to fall asleep.
—v.t. **36.** to let fall in drops or small portions: *drop a tear.* **37.** *Archaic.* to sprinkle with or as with drops. **38.** to let fall; allow to sink to a lower position; lower: *to drop anchor.* **39.** to give birth to (young). **40.** to utter or express casually or incidentally, as a hint. **41.** to send or post (a note, etc.): *drop me a line.* **42.** to bring to the ground by a blow or shot. **43.** to set down, as from a ship, car, etc. **44.** to omit (a letter or syllable) in pronunciation or writing: *he dropped his h's.* **45.** to lengthen by lowering: *to drop a hem.* **46.** to lower (the voice) in pitch or loudness. **47.** to cease to keep up or have to do with: *I dropped the subject.* **48.** to cease to employ; to dismiss. **49.** *Rugby Football, etc.* to score (a goal) by a drop kick. **50.** *Naut.* to outdistance; pass out of sight of. **51.** *U.S. Cookery.* to poach.
[ME *drope*, OE *dropa*, c. Icel. *dropi*]

drop ceiling, a false ceiling suspended below the real ceiling for acoustic or architectural reasons or to give space for service pipes.

drop curtain, *Theat.* a curtain which is lowered into position from the flies.

drop-forge (drŏp′fôj′), *v.t.,* **-forged, -forging.** *Metall.* to forge by the impact of a falling mass or weight, the hot piece of metal usually being placed between dies and subjected to the blow of a drop hammer or the like.

drop forging, *Metall.* a drop-forged forging.

drop goal, *Rugby Football.* a goal scored by a drop kick.

drop hammer, an apparatus for forging, etc., in which a heavy weight is made to drop on the metal to be worked, which is placed on an anvil or in dies.

drop kick, *Rugby Football.* a kick given the ball as it rises from the ground after being dropped by the kicker.

drop-kick (drŏp′kĭk′), *v.i., v.t. Rugby Football.* to give a drop kick (to). **—drop′-kick′er,** *n.*

drop leaf, *Furnit.* an extension attached to the end or side of a table and folded vertically when not needed. **—drop′-leaf′,** *adj.*

droplet (drŏp′lĭt), *n.* a little drop.

droplight (drŏp′līt′), *n.* an electric lamp connected with a fixture above by a tube or wire which enables it to be brought down to a lower level.

drop meter, dosimeter (def. 1).

drop-out (drŏp′out′), *n.* **1.** *Rugby Football.* a kick-off by a drop kick. **2.** Also, **dropout.** *U.S.* one, as a student, who fails to complete a course.

dropper (drŏp′ə), *n.* **1.** one who or that which drops. **2.** a glass tube with an elastic cap at one end and a small orifice at the other, for drawing in a liquid and expelling it in drops; medicine dropper.

dropping (drŏp′ĭng), *n.* **1.** act of one who or that which drops. **2.** that which drops or falls in drops. **3.** (*pl.*) dung of animals.

drop scene, 1. a drop curtain. **2.** a final scene in an act or play.

drop scone, a scone made by dropping batter from a spoon on to a greased baking tin or griddle for cooking.

drop shipment, *Com.* an order shipped by a seller to the customer or his distributor, as a shipment by a manufacturer to a retailer that is invoiced to a wholesaler.

drop shot, 1. shot made in a shot tower. **2.** *Tennis.* a stroke which causes a ball to fall abruptly after clearing the net. **3.** a ball so played.

dropsical (drŏp′sĭ kl), *adj.* of, like, or affected with dropsy. **—drop′sically,** *adv.*

dropsy (drŏp′sĭ), *n. Pathol.* an excessive accumulation of serous fluid in a serous cavity or in the subcutaneous cellular tissue. [ME *(y)dropesie*, t. OF: m. *idropisie*, t. L: m. s. *hydrōpsis*, der. Gk *hýdrōps*] **—dropsied** (drŏp′sĭd), *adj.*

dropt (drŏpt), *v.* pt. and pp. of **drop.**

drop window, (drŏp′wĭn′dō), *n.* a sash window descending completely into a space below the sill.

dropwort (drŏp′wût′), *n.* a European rosaceous herb, *Filipendula vulgaris*, bearing small, scentless, white or reddish flowers.

droshky (drŏsh′kĭ), *n., pl.* **-kies. 1.** a light, low, four-wheeled, open vehicle, used in Russia, in which the passengers sit astride or sideways on a long, narrow bench. **2.** any of various other vehicles, as the ordinary carriage, used elsewhere. Also, **drosky** (drŏs′kĭ). [t. Russ.: m. *drozhki*, dim. of *drogi* wagon]

drosometer (drŏ sŏm′ĭ tə), *n.* an instrument for measuring the amount of dew formed on a surface.

drosophila (drŏ sŏf′ĭ lə), *n., pl.* **-lae** (-lē′). a fly of the genus *Drosophila*, esp. *D. melanogaster*, which is widely used in laboratory studies of heredity. [NL, f. Gk: *dróso(s)* dew + *phila*, fem. of *phílos* loving]

dross (drŏs), *n.* **1.** *Metall.* a waste product taken off molten metal during smelting, essentially metallic in character. **2.** waste matter; refuse. [ME and OE *drōs*, c. MD *droes* dregs. Cf. G *Drusen* dregs, husks] **—dross′y,** *adj.* **—dross′iness,** *n.*

Droste-Hülshoff (*Ger.* drŏs′tə hʏls′hŏf), *n.* **Annette von** (*Ger.* ä nĕt′ə fŏn), 1797–1848, German poet.

drought (drout), *n.* **1.** dry weather; lack of rain. **2.** *Archaic.* scarcity. **3.** *Dial.* thirst. Also, **drouth** (drouth). [ME *drought(h)*, etc., OE *drūgath*, akin to *drȳge* dry]

droughty (drou′tĭ), *adj.* **1.** dry. **2.** lacking rain. **3.** *Dial.* thirsty. Also, **drouthy** (drou′thĭ).

drouk (drōōk), *v.t. Scot.* to drench; wet thoroughly. [t. Scand.; cf. Icel. *drukna* be drowned]

drove[1] (drōv), *v.* pt. of **drive.**

drove[2] (drōv), *n., v.,* **droved, droving.** *—n.* **1.** a number of oxen, sheep, or swine driven in a group; herd; flock. **2.** a large crowd of human beings, esp. in motion. **3.** *Bldg Trades.* **a.** Also, **drove chisel.** a stonemason's chisel, from two to four inches broad, used in making droved work. **b.** drove work. **4.** a road along which animals are driven. *—v.t., v.i.* **5.** to drive or deal in (cattle) as a drover. **6.** *Bldg Trades.* to work or smooth (stone, etc.) as with a stonemason's drove. [ME; OE *drāf* act of driving, herd, company. See DRIVE] **—Syn. 1.** See **flock**[4].

drover (drō′və), *n.* **1.** one who drives cattle, sheep, etc., to market. **2.** a dealer in cattle.

drove work, *Bldg Trades.* the surface of stone worked with a drove.

drown (droun), *v.i.* **1.** to be suffocated by immersion in water or other liquid. *—v.t.* **2.** to suffocate (a person, etc.) by immersion in water or other liquid. **3.** to destroy; get rid of. **4.** to flood; inundate. **5.** to overwhelm as by a flood; overpower. **6.** to make inaudible; muffle; obscure. [var. of obs. *drunken*, OE *druncnian*; ME *drounne* shows loss of *c* between the nasals; length of nasal later shifted to vowel]

drowned valley, a submerged valley, flooded by sea or lake.
drowse (drouz), *v.*, **drowsed, drowsing,** *n.* —*v.i.* **1.** to be sleepy; be half asleep. **2.** to be dull or sluggish. —*v.t.* **3.** to make sleepy. **4.** to pass or spend (time) in drowsing. —*n.* **5.** a sleepy condition; state of being half asleep. [OE *drūsian* droop, become sluggish]
drowsihead (drou′zĭ hĕd′), *n. Archaic.* drowsiness.
drowsy (drou′zĭ), *adj.*, **-sier, -siest. 1.** inclined to sleep; half asleep. **2.** marked by or resulting from sleepiness. **3.** dull; sluggish. **4.** inducing sleepiness. —**drow′sily,** *adv.* —**drow′siness,** *n.*
drub (drŭb), *v.*, **drubbed, drubbing,** *n.* —*v.t.* **1.** to beat with a stick or the like; cudgel; flog; thrash: *to drub something into or out of a person.* **2.** to defeat decisively. **3.** to stamp (the feet). —*n.* **4.** a blow with a stick or the like. [? t. Ar.: m. *darb* stroke] —**drub′ber,** *n.*
drubbing (drŭb′ĭng), *n.* a beating; a decisive defeat.
drudge (drŭj), *n.*, *v.*, **drudged, drudging.** —*n.* **1.** one who labours at servile or uninteresting tasks; a hard toiler. —*v.i.* **2.** to perform servile, distasteful, or hard work. [OE *Drycg-* bearer (in proper name); akin to DREE] —**drudg′er,** *n.* —**drudg′ingly,** *adv.*
drudgery (drŭj′ə rĭ), *n.*, *pl.* **-eries.** tedious, hard, or uninteresting work. —**Syn.** See **work.**
drug (drŭg), *n.*, *v.*, **drugged, drugging.** —*n.* **1.** a chemical substance given with the intention of preventing or curing disease or otherwise enhancing the physical or mental welfare of men or animals. **2.** a habit-forming medicinal substance; a narcotic. **3.** (formerly) any ingredient used in chemistry, pharmacy, dyeing, or the like. **4.** a commodity that is overabundant, or in excess of demand, in the market. —*v.t.* **5.** to mix (food or drink) with a drug, esp. a narcotic or poisonous drug. **6.** to stupefy or poison with a drug. **7.** to administer anything nauseous to; surfeit. [ME *drogges* (pl.), t. OF: m. *drogue*, ? t. D: m. *drog* dry thing]
drugget (drŭg′ĭt), *n.* **1.** a rug from India made of coarse hair with cotton or jute. **2.** *Obs.* a fabric woven wholly or partly of wool, used for clothing. [t. F: m. *droguet*, der. *drogue* drug, cheap article]
druggist (drŭg′ĭst), *n. U.S.* a pharmacist; dispensing chemist.
drugstore (drŭg′stô′), *n. U.S.* a chemist's shop where cigarettes, light meals, etc., are also sold.
Druid (drōō′ĭd), *n.* (*often l.c.*) **1.** one of an order of priests or ministers of religion among the ancient Celts of Gaul, Britain, and Ireland. **2.** a member of one of several modern movements to revive druidism, which meet seasonally in special costume to conduct their ceremonies. **3.** an official at an eisteddfod. [t. F: m. *druide*, t. L: m. *druidae*, pl.] —**Druidess** (drōō′ĭ dĭs), *n. fem.* —**druid′ic, druid′ical,** *adj.*
druidism (drōō′ĭ dĭz′əm), *n.* the religion or rites of the Druids.
drum[1] (drŭm), *n.*, *v.*, **drummed, drumming.** —*n.* **1.** a musical instrument consisting of a hollow body covered at one or both ends with a tightly stretched membrane, or head, which is struck with the hand, a stick, or a pair of sticks. **2.** any hollow tree or similar device used in this way. **3.** the sound produced by either of these. **4.** any noise suggestive of it. **5.** one who plays the drum. **6.** a natural organ by which an animal produces a loud or bass sound. **7.** something resembling a drum in shape or structure, or in the noise it produces. **8.** *Archit.* the supporting wall, circular in plan, upon which a dome sits. **9.** *Archit.* one section of a circular column. **10.** *Anat.*, *Zool.* the eardrum or tympanic membrane. **11.** a cylindrical part of a machine. **12.** a magnetic drum. **13.** a cylindrical box or receptacle. **14.** *Austral. Slang.* a swag. **15.** drumfish. **16.** *Obs.* an assembly of fashionable people at a private house in the evening. —*v.i.* **17.** to beat or play a drum. **18.** to beat on anything rhythmically. **19.** to make a sound like that of a drum; resound. **20.** (of partridges and other birds) to produce a sound resembling drumming. —*v.t.* **21.** to beat rhythmically; perform (a tune) by drumming. **22.** to call or summon by, or as by, beating a drum. **23.** to drive or force by persistent repetition: *to drum an idea into someone.* **24.** (formerly) to expel or dismiss in disgrace to the beat of a drum (fol. by *out*). **25.** to solicit or obtain (trade, customers, etc.) (often fol. by *up*). [back-formation from *drumslade* drummer, t. LG: m. *trommelslag* drumbeat (confused in E with *trommelslager* drummer); E *d-* ? by assoc. with *dub-a-dub* sound made in beating a drum]
drum[2] (drŭm), *n. Irish, Scot.* a long, narrow hill or ridge. [t. Irish and Gaelic: m. *druim* back, ridge]
drumbeat (drŭm′bēt′), *n.* the sound of a drum.
drumble (drŭm′bl, drŭm′əl), *v.i.*, **-bled, -bling.** *Obs. or Dial.* to move sluggishly.
drumfire (drŭm′fī′ə), *n.* gunfire so heavy and continuous as to sound like the beating of drums.
drumfish (drŭm′fĭsh′), *n.*, *pl.* **-fishes,** (*esp. collectively*) **-fish.** any of various American sciaenoid fishes producing a drumming sound, as *Pogonias cromis.*
drumhead (drŭm′hĕd′), *n.* **1.** the membrane stretched upon a drum. **2.** the top part of a capstan.
drumhead court martial, a court martial held (orig. round an upturned drum for a table) for the summary trial of charges of offences committed during military operations.
drumlin (drŭm′lĭn), *n. Geol.* a long narrow, or oval, smoothly rounded hill of unstratified glacial drift. [? var. of *drumling*, dim. of DRUM[2]]
drumly (drŭm′lĭ), *adj. Scot.* troubled; gloomy.
drum-major (drŭm′mā′jə), *n.* a person (in the army usually of the rank of sergeant major) in command of a corps of drums, who also commands both the band and corps of drums on parade.
drum-majorette (drŭm′mā′jə rĕt′), *n. Chiefly U.S.* a girl who marches in front of a band in a parade twisting a baton.
drummer (drŭm′ə), *n.* **1.** one who plays a drum. **2.** *U.S.* a commercial traveller or travelling salesman.
drumstick (drŭm′stĭk′), *n.* **1.** a stick for beating a drum. **2.** the lower part of the leg of a cooked chicken, duck, turkey, etc.
drunk (drŭngk), *pred. adj.* **1.** intoxicated with, or as with, strong drink: *drunk with joy, success.* —*n. Colloq.* **2.** a drunken person. **3.** a spree; a drinking party. —*v.* **4.** pp. and former pt. of **drink.**
drunkard (drŭngk′əd), *n.* one who is frequently drunk.
—**Syn.** sot. DRUNKARD, INEBRIATE, DIPSOMANIAC are terms for a person who drinks alcoholic drink habitually. DRUNKARD connotes wilful indulgence to excess. INEBRIATE is a more formal word. DIPSOMANIAC is the term for a person who, because of some psychological or physiological illness, has an irresistible craving for drink. The dipsomaniac is popularly called an ALCOHOLIC.
drunken (drŭngk′ən), *adj.* **1.** intoxicated; drunk. **2.** given to drunkenness. **3.** pertaining to, proceeding from, or marked by intoxication: *a drunken quarrel.* —**drunk′enly,** *adv.* —**drunk′enness,** *n.* —**Syn. 1.** inebriated, tipsy.
drupaceous (drōō pā′shəs), *adj. Bot.* **1.** resembling or relating to a drupe; consisting of drupes. **2.** producing drupes: *drupaceous trees.*
drupe (drōōp), *n. Bot.* a fruit, as the peach, cherry, plum, etc., consisting of an outer skin (epicarp), a (generally) pulpy and succulent layer (mesocarp), and a hard and woody inner shell or stone (endocarp) which encloses usually a single seed. [t. NL: m. s. *drūpa* drupe, L *drūpa*, *druppa* overripe olive, t. Gk: m. *drýppa*]
drupelet (drōōp′lĭt), *n. Bot.* a little drupe, as one of the individual pericarps composing the blackberry. Also, **drupel** (drōō′pl).
Drury Lane (drōōə′rĭ), a street in central London, famous for its theatres.
druse (drōōz), *n.* **1.** *Geol.* a crust of small crystals which forms on the surface of a rock or mineral. **2.** *Bot.* a mass of small crystals of sodium oxalate which forms around some plant cells. [t. F, t. G: *Druse* weathered ore]
Druse (drōōz), *n.* one of a fanatical and warlike people and religious sect of Syria. [t. Ar.: m. *Durūz*, pl.] —**Drusian, Drusean** (drōō′zĭ ən), *adj.*
Drusus (drōō′səs), *n.* **Nero Claudius** (nīə′rō klô′dyəs) ('*Germanicus*'), 38–9 B.C., Roman general.
dry (drī), *adj.*, **drier, driest,** *v.*, **dried, drying,** *n.*, *pl.* **dries.** —*adj.* **1.** free from moisture; not moist; not wet. **2.** having little or no rain: *a dry climate or season.* **3.** characterized by absence, deficiency, or failure of natural or ordinary moisture. **4.** not under, in, or on water: *dry land.* **5.** not yielding water or other liquid: *a dry well.* **6.** not yielding milk: *a dry cow.* **7.** free from tears: *dry eyes.* **8.** wiped or drained away; evaporated: *a dry river.* **9.** desiring drink; thirsty. **10.** causing thirst: *dry work.* **11.** without butter or the like: *dry toast.* **12.** (of a biscuit) not sweet. **13.** *Art.* hard and formal in outline, or lacking mellowness and warmth in colour. **14.** *Bldg Trades.* (of an interior wall, ceiling, etc.) finished without the use of plastering. **15.** plain; bald; unadorned: *dry facts.* **16.** dull; uninteresting: *a dry subject.* **17.** humorous or sarcastic in an unemotional or impersonal way: *dry humour.* **18.** indifferent; cold; unemotional: *a dry answer.* **19.** (of wines) not sweet. **20.** of or pertaining to non-liquid substances or commodities: *dry measure.* **21.** *Colloq.* characterized by or favouring prohibition of the manufacture and sale of alcoholic liquor for use as beverages: *a dry ship.* —*v.t.* **22.** to make dry; free from moisture: *dry your eyes.* —*v.i.* **23.** to become dry; lose moisture. **24. dry up, a.** to become completely dry. **b.** to become intellectually barren. **c.** *Colloq.* to stop talking. —*n.* **25.** a dry state,

condition, or place. **26.** *U.S. Colloq.* a prohibitionist. [ME *drie*, OE *drȳge*, akin to LG *drög*, G *trocken*] —**dry′ly, drily,** *adv.* —**dry′ness,** *n.*

—**Syn. 1.** DRY, ARID both mean without moisture. DRY is the general word indicating absence of water or freedom from moisture (which may be favourable): *dry well, dry clothes or land.* ARID suggests great or intense dryness in a region or climate, esp. such as results in bareness or in barrenness: *arid tracts of desert.* **22.** See **evaporate.** —**Ant. 1.** wet.

dryad (drī′əd, -ăd), *n., pl.* **-ads, -ades** (-ə dēz′). *Gk Myth.* (*often cap.*) a deity or nymph of the woods; a nymph supposed to reside in trees or preside over woods. [t. L: s. *Dryas* (pl. *Dryades*), t. Gk, der. *drŷs* tree, oak] —**dryadic** (drī ăd′ĭk), *adj.*

dryasdust (drī′əz dŭst′), *n.* one who deals with dry, uninteresting subjects; a dull pedant. —**dry′asdust′,** *adj.*

dry battery, *Elect.* a dry cell, or voltaic battery consisting of a number of dry cells.

dry-blow (drī′blō′), *v.i. Austral.* to separate gold from other material by winnowing.

dry cell, *Elect.* a primary cell in which the electrolyte exists in the form of a paste or is absorbed in a porous medium, or is otherwise restrained from flowing from its original position.

dry-clean (drī′klēn′), *v.t.* to clean (garments, etc.) with benzine, chemical solvents, etc., rather than water. —**dry′-clean′er,** *n.*

dry-cleaning (drī′klē′nĭng), *n.* **1.** the process of cleaning (garments, etc.) with benzene, chemical solvents, etc. **2.** the articles cleaned by this process.

Dryden (drī′dn), *n.* **John,** 1631–1700, English poet, dramatist, and critic.

dry dock, 1. a basin-like structure from which the water can be removed after the entrance of a ship: used when making repairs on a ship's bottom, etc. **2.** a floating structure which may be partially submerged to permit a vessel to enter, and then raised to lift the vessel out of the water for repairs, etc.

dry-dock (drī′dŏk′), *v.t.* **1.** to place in a dry dock. —*v.i.* **2.** to go into dry dock.

dryer (drī′ə), *n.* drier.

dry farming, a mode of farming practised in regions of slight or insufficient rainfall, depending largely upon tillage methods which render the soil more receptive of moisture and reduce evaporation. —**dry farmer.**

dry-fly fishing (drī′flī′), fishing with an artificial fly in such a manner that the fly floats on the surface of the water.

dry goods, textile fabrics and related articles of trade, as distinct from groceries, hardware, etc.

dry ice, 1. solid carbon dioxide, having a temperature of 109°F below zero at atmospheric pressure. **2.** (*cap.*) a trademark for this substance.

drying oil, an animal or vegetable oil which hardens to a tough film when a thin layer is exposed to the air.

dry kiln, an oven for the controlled drying of cut wood.

dry law, *U.S.* a law prohibiting general use of intoxicating liquors.

dry measure, the system of units of capacity ordinarily used in measuring dry commodities, as grain, fruit, etc. In Great Britain, 2 pints = 1 quart, 4 quarts = 1 gallon, 8 gallons = 1 bushel, and 8 bushels = 1 quarter. In the U.S., 8 quarts = 1 peck, and 4 pecks = 1 bushel of 2150·42 cubic inches.

dry nurse, a nurse who takes care of a child but does not suckle it.

dry-nurse (drī′nûs′), *v.t.,* **-nursed, -nursing.** to act as a dry nurse to.

dry plate, *Photog.* a glass plate coated with a sensitive emulsion of silver bromide and silver iodide in gelatine, upon which a negative or positive can be produced by exposure (as in a camera) and development.

dry point, 1. a stout, sharp-pointed needle used for ploughing into copper plates to produce furrows with raised edges that print with a fuzzy, velvety black. **2.** the process of engraving in this way. **3.** an engraving so made.

dry rot, 1. a decay of seasoned timber causing it to become brittle and to crumble to a dry powder, due to various fungi. **2.** any of various diseases of vegetables in which the dead tissue is dry, caused in timber by *Merulius lacrymans*; in potatoes by *Fusarium caeruleum*; and in swedes, turnips, etc., by *Phoma lingam.*

drysalter (drī′sôl′tə), *n.* **1.** a dealer in certain chemical products as gums, dyes, etc. **2.** *Obs.* a dealer in salted meats, pickles, sauces, etc. —**dry′sal′tery,** *n.*

dry-shod (drī′shŏd′), *adj.* having or keeping the shoes dry.

dry-stone wall (drī′stōn′), a rubble or stone wall built without mortar. Also, **dry wall.**

Dry Tortugas (drī′ tô to͞o′gəz), a group of ten small islands at the N entrance to the Gulf of Mexico: a part of Florida; the site of Fort Jefferson.

Ds, *Chem. Obs.* symbol for dysprosium. See **Dy.**

D.S., *Music.* dal segno.

D.Sc., Doctor of Science.

D.S.M., Distinguished Service Medal.

D.S.O., Distinguished Service Order.

D.S.T., Daylight Saving Time.

d.t., delirium tremens. Also, **d.t.'s.**

D. Th., Doctor of Theology. Also, **D. Theol.**

Du., 1. Duke. **2.** Dutch.

duad (dyo͞o′ăd), *n.* a group of two. [b. DUAL and DYAD]

dual (dyo͞o′əl), *adj.* **1.** of or pertaining to two. **2.** composed or consisting of two parts; twofold; double: *dual ownership, dual controls on a plane.* **3.** *Gram.* (in some languages) designating a number category which implies two persons or things. —*n.* **4.** *Gram.* **a.** the dual number. **b.** a form therein, as Greek *anthrṓpō* two men, nominative dual of *ánthrōpos* man, cf. *ánthrōpoi* three or more men, or Old English *git* 'you two' as contrasted with *ge*, 'you' referring to three or more. [t. L: s. *duālis* containing two] —**du′ally,** *adv.*

Duala (do͞o ä′lə), *n.* Douala.

Dual Alliance, 1. the alliance formed in 1891–94 between France and Russia, lasting until the Bolshevik revolution in 1917. **2.** the alliance between Germany and Austria, 1879–1918, more frequently called the Austro-German alliance.

dual carriageway, a major road on which the lanes of traffic moving in opposite directions are separated as by a strip of grass, trees, etc.

dualism (dyo͞o′ə lĭz′əm), *n.* **1.** the state of being dual or consisting of two parts; division into two. **2.** *Philos.* a theory holding that there are two, and only two, basic and irreducible principles, as mind and body. **3.** *Theol.* **a.** the doctrine that there are two independent divine beings or eternal principles, one good and the other evil. **b.** the belief that man embodies two parts, such as body and soul. —**du′alist,** *n.*

dualistic (dyo͞o′ə lĭs′tĭk), *adj.* **1.** of, pertaining to, or of the nature of dualism. **2.** dual. —**du′alis′tically,** *adv.*

duality (dyo͞o ăl′ĭ tĭ), *n.* dual state or quality.

Dual Monarchy, the kingdom of Austria-Hungary, 1867–1918.

dual-purpose (dyo͞o′əl pû′pəs), *adj.* **1.** serving two functions. **2.** (of cattle) bred for two purposes, as beef and milk.

dub[1] (dŭb), *v.t.,* **dubbed, dubbing. 1.** to strike lightly with a sword in the ceremony of conferring knighthood; make, or designate as, a knight: *the king dubbed him knight.* **2.** to invest with any dignity or title; style; name; call: *he dubbed me quack.* **3.** to strike, cut, rub, etc., to make smooth, or of an equal surface: *to dub leather, timber.* **4.** to dress (a fly) for fishing. [ME *dubben*, OE *dubbian*, c. Icel. *dubba* equip, dub; akin to DOWEL]

dub[2] (dŭb), *v.,* **dubbed, dubbing,** *n.* —*v.t., v.i.* **1.** to thrust; poke. —*n.* **2.** a thrust; poke. **3.** a drumbeat. [see DUB[1]. Cf. LG *dubben* thrust, beat]

dub[3] (dŭb), *v.,* **dubbed, dubbing,** *n. Films.* —*v.t.* **1.** to change the soundtrack of (a film) or to add sounds, as in substituting a dialogue in another language. —*v.i.* **2.** to dub a film, soundtrack, etc. —*n.* **3.** the new sounds added. [shortened form of DOUBLE]

dub[4] (dŭb), *n. Scot. and N Dial.* a pool of water; a puddle. [orig. uncert.]

Dubai (do͞o bī′), *n.* See **Trucial States.**

Du Barry (dyo͞o bă′rĭ; *Fr.* dʏ bȧ rē′), **Comtesse** (born *Marie Jeanne Bécu*), 1746–93, mistress of Louis XV of France.

dubbing[1] (dŭb′ĭng), *n.* the conferring of knighthood; accolade.

dubbing[2] (dŭb′ĭng), *n.* **1.** alteration of, or addition to, the soundtrack of a film. **2.** the new sounds thus added.

dubbing[3] (dŭb′ĭng), *n.* a preparation of oil and tallow used for softening and waterproofing leather. Also, **dubbin.**

Dubček (*Cz.* do͞ob′chĕk), *n.* **Alexandr** (*Cz.* ȧl′ĕk sán dr), born 1921, Czechoslovak statesman, first secretary of the Communist Party 1968–69.

Du Bellay (*Fr.* dʏ bĕl lĕ′), **Joachim** (*Fr.* zhȯ ȧ shăɴ′), 1522–60, French poet.

dubiety (dyo͞o bī′ə tĭ), *n., pl.* **-ties. 1.** doubtfulness; doubt. **2.** a matter of doubt. Also, **dubiosity** (dyo͞o′bĭ-ŏs′ĭ tĭ), *n.*

dubious (dyo͞o′byəs), *adj.* **1.** doubtful; marked by or occasioning doubt: *a dubious question.* **2.** of doubtful quality or propriety; questionable: *a dubious transaction, a dubious compliment.* **3.** of uncertain outcome: *in dubious battle.* **4.** wavering or hesitating in opinion; inclined to doubt. [t. L: m. s. *dubiōsus* doubtful] —**du′biously,** *adv.* —**du′biousness,** *n.* —**Syn. 1.** See **doubtful.**

dubitable (dyo͞o′bĭ tə bl), *adj.* that may be doubted; doubtful; uncertain. —**du′bitably,** *adv.*

dubitation (dyo͞o′bĭ tā′shən), *n.* doubt. [t. L: s. *dubitātio*, der. *dubitāre* doubt]

dubitative (dyo͞o′bĭ tə tĭv), *adj.* **1.** doubting; doubtful. **2.** expressing doubt. [t. LL: m. s. *dubitātīvus* doubtful] —**du′bitatively,** *adv.*

Dublin (dŭb′lĭn), *n.* **1.** the capital of Ireland, in the E part. 537,488 (1961). **2.** a county in the E Republic of Ireland. 718,338 pop. (1961); 356 sq. mi. *Co. town:* Dublin.

Dubrovnik (dyo͞o brŏv′nĭk; *Serb.* do͞o′brôv nēk), *n.* a seaport in SW Yugoslavia, on the Adriatic. 21,000 (1960). Italian, **Ragusa.**

duc (*Fr.* dʏk), *n. French.* duke.

ducal (dyo͞o′kl), *adj.* of or pertaining to a duke. [t. LL: s. *ducālis*, der. *dux* leader. See DUKE] —**du′cally,** *adv.*

ducat (dŭk′ət), *n.* **1.** any of various gold coins formerly in wide use in European countries. **2.** an old silver coin of varying value; an old Venetian money of account. **3.** (*pl.*) *Slang.* money; cash. [ME, t. F, t. It.: m. *ducato* a coin (orig. one issued in 1140 by Roger II of Sicily as Duke of Apulia), also duchy, der. *duca* DUKE]

duce (do͞o′chĭ), *n.* **1.** leader. **2. il Duce,** the leader (applied esp. to Benito Mussolini as head of the Fascist Italian state). [It., g. L *dux* leader]

Duchamp (*Fr.* dʏ shäɴ′), *n.* **Marcel** (*Fr.* mȧr sĕl′), 1887–1968, French pioneer of modern art.

duchess (dŭch′ĭs), *n.* **1.** the wife or widow of a duke. **2.** *Hist.* a woman who holds in her own right the sovereignty or titles of a duchy. **3.** *Slang.* a woman of showy demeanour or appearance. [ME *duchesse*, t. F, der. *duc* DUKE]

duchy (dŭch′ĭ), *n., pl.* **duchies.** the territory ruled by a duke or duchess. [ME *duche*, t. OF, der. *duc* DUKE]

duck[1] (dŭk), *n.* **1.** any of numerous wild or domesticated web-footed swimming birds of the family *Anatidae*, esp. of the genus *Anas* and allied genera, characterized by a broad, flat bill, short legs, and depressed body. **2.** the female of this fowl, as distinguished from the male (or drake). **3.** the flesh of a duck, eaten as food. **4.** *Colloq.* a darling; pet. [ME *duk*, *doke*, OE *dūce*, lit., diver; akin to DUCK[2], v.]

duck[2] (dŭk), *v.i.* **1.** to plunge the whole body or the head momentarily under water. **2.** to stoop suddenly; bob. **3.** to avoid a blow, unpleasant task, etc. —*v.t.* **4.** to plunge or dip in water momentarily. **5.** to lower (the head, etc.) suddenly. **6.** to avoid (a blow, unpleasant task, etc.). —*n.* **7.** the act of ducking. [ME *duke*, *douke*, c. MLG *duken*, G *tauchen* dive] —**Syn. 1.** dive, dip, souse. **2.** bow, dodge.

duck[3] (dŭk), *n.* **1.** heavy plain cotton fabric for tents, clothing, bags, mechanical uses, etc., in many weights and widths. **2.** (*pl.*) clothes, esp. trousers, made of it. [t. D: m. *doek* cloth, c. G *Tuch*]

duck[4] (dŭk), *n.* (in World War II) a military vehicle for amphibious use. [from *DUKW*, its code name]

duck[5] (dŭk), *n. Cricket Slang.* a batsman's score of nought. Also, **duck's egg.**

duck-billed platypus (dŭk′-bĭld′), a small, aquatic, egg-laying monotreme mammal *Ornithorhynchus anatinus*, of Australia and Tasmania, having webbed feet and the muzzle like the beak of a duck. Also, **duck-bill** (dŭk′bĭl′).

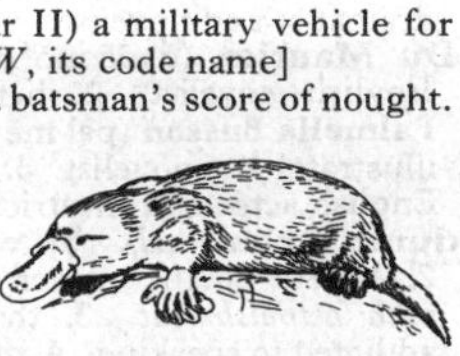

Duck-billed platypus, *Ornithorhynchus anatinus* (2 ft long, tail 4 to 5 in.)

duckboard (dŭk′bôd′), *n.* a board, or a section or structure of boarding, laid as a floor or track over wet or muddy ground, as for military use.

duck call, *Hunting.* a tubular device into which a hunter blows to imitate the quack of a duck.

ducker[1] (dŭk′ə), *n.* one who or that which ducks. [f. DUCK[2] + -ER[1]]

ducker[2] (dŭk′ə), *n.* **1.** one who breeds ducks. **2.** one who hunts ducks. [f. DUCK[1] + -ER]

duck hawk, the American peregrine falcon, *Falco peregrinus anatum*, well known for its speed and audacity.

ducking stool, a stool or chair in which common scolds were formerly punished by being tied and plunged into water. See **cucking stool.**

duckling (dŭk′lĭng), *n.* a young duck.

ducks and drakes, 1. (*construed as sing.*) a pastime consisting in throwing shells, flat stones, etc., over the surface of water so as to strike and rebound repeatedly. **2. make ducks and drakes of, play (at) ducks and drakes with,** to handle recklessly; squander.

Ducking stool

duckweed (dŭk′wēd′), *n.* any member of the family *Lemnaceae*, esp. of the genus *Lemna*, comprising small aquatic plants which float free on still water. [so called because it is eaten by ducks]

ducky (dŭk′ĭ), *adj., n., pl.* **duckies.** *Colloq.* —*adj.* **1.** dear; darling. —*n.* **2.** darling; dear; pet. Also, **duckie.**

duct (dŭkt), *n.* **1.** any tube, canal, or conduit by which fluid or other substances are conducted or conveyed. **2.** *Anat.*, *Zool.* a tube, canal, or vessel conveying a body fluid, esp. a glandular secretion or excretion. **3.** *Bot.* a cavity or vessel formed by elongated cells or by many cells. **4.** *Elect.* a pipe for enclosing electric cables. [t. L: s. *ductus* leading, conduct, conduit]

ductile (dŭk′tīl), *adj.* **1.** capable of being hammered out thin, as certain metals; malleable. **2.** capable of being drawn out into wire or threads, as gold. **3.** able to stand deformation under a load without fracture. **4.** capable of being moulded or shaped; plastic. **5.** susceptible; compliant; tractable. [ME *ductil*, t. L: s. *ductilis* that may be led] —**ductility** (dŭk tĭl′ĭ tĭ), *n.*

ductless gland (dŭkt′lĭs), *Anat.*, *Zool.* a gland which possesses no excretory duct, but whose secretion is absorbed directly into the blood or lymph, as the thyroid, adrenals, pituitary gland, and parathyroids.

dud[1] (dŭd), *n. Colloq.* **1.** *Obs.* an article of clothing. **2.** clothes; (often) old or ragged clothes. **3.** belongings in general. [ME *dudde*, akin to LG *dudel* a coarse sackcloth]

dud[2] (dŭd), *Colloq.* —*n.* **1.** any thing or person that proves a failure. **2.** *Mil.* a shell that fails to explode after being fired. —*adj.* **3.** useless; defective. [? special use of DUD[1]]

duddy (dŭd′ĭ), *adj. Scot.* ragged; tattered.

dude (dyo͞od), *n. Chiefly U.S. Colloq.* **1.** an affected or fastidious man; fop. **2.** a person brought up in a large city. **3.** a city-dweller holidaying on a ranch.

dudeen (do͞o dēn′), *n. Irish.* a short clay tobacco pipe.

dude ranch, *U.S.* a ranch operated also as a holiday resort.

Dudevant (*Fr.* dʏd väɴ′), *n.* **Amandine Lucile Aurore** (*Fr.* ȧ mäɴ dēn lʏ sēl ō rōr′). See **Sand, George.**

dudgeon[1] (dŭj′ən), *n.* a feeling of offence or resentment; anger: *we left in high dudgeon.* [orig. unknown]

dudgeon[2] (dŭj′ən), *n.* **1.** *Obs.* a kind of wood used esp. for the handles of knives, daggers, etc. **2.** *Obs.* a handle or hilt made of this wood. **3.** *Archaic.* a dagger having such a hilt. [t. AF: m. *digeon*, ult. orig. unknown]

Dudley (dŭd′lĭ), *n.* **1. Robert, Earl of Leicester,** 1532?–88, English statesman and favourite of Queen Elizabeth. **2.** a town in England, in Worcestershire, near Birmingham. 63,880 (est. 1964).

Dudok (*Du.* dʏ′dôk), *n.* **William Marinus,** born 1884, Dutch architect.

due (dyo͞o), *adj.* **1.** immediately payable. **2.** owing, irrespective of whether the time of payment has arrived. **3.** rightful; proper; fitting: *due care, in due time.* **4.** adequate; sufficient: *a due margin for delay.* **5.** attributable, as to a cause: *a delay due to an accident.* **6.** under engagement as to time; expected to be ready, be present, or arrive. —*n.* **7.** that which is due or owed. **8.** (*usually pl.*) a payment due, as a charge, a fee, etc. **9. give a person his due,** to ascribe proper credit to. —*adv.* **10.** directly or straight: *a due east course.* **11.** *Archaic.* duly. [ME *dew*, t. OF: m. *deü*, orig. pp. of *devoir*, g. L *dēbēre* owe]

duel (dyo͞o′əl), *n., v.,* **-elled, -elling** or (*U.S.*) **-eled, -eling.** —*n.* **1.** a prearranged combat between two persons, fought with deadly weapons according to an accepted code of procedure, esp. to settle a private quarrel. **2.** any contest between two persons or parties. —*v.i.* **3.** to fight in a duel. [t. ML: m. s. *duellum* a combat between two] —**du′eller, du′ellist,** *n.*

duello (dyo͞o ĕl′ō), *n., pl.* **-los. 1.** the practice or skill of duelling. **2.** the code of rules regulating it. [t. It.]

duenna (dyo͞o ĕn′ə), *n.* **1.** (in Spain and Portugal) an older woman serving as escort or protector of a young lady. **2.** a governess; chaperon. [t. Sp.: m. *dueña*, g. L *domina* mistress]

Duero (*Sp.* dwĕ′rō), *n.* Spanish name of **Douro.**

duet (dyo͞o′ĕt), *n. Music.* a composition for two voices or performers. [t. It.: m. *duetto*, dim. of *duo* two] —**duet′-tist,** *n.*

duff[1] (dŭf), *n.* **1.** a kind of organic surface consisting of matted peaty materials in forested soils. **2.** coal dust. [fig. use of DUFF[2]]

duff[2] (dŭf), *n.* a flour pudding boiled, or sometimes steamed, in a bag. [var. of DOUGH]

duff[3] (dŭf), *v.t.* **1.** to recondition or change the appearance of (esp. old or stolen goods). **2.** *Austral.*, *Colloq.* to steal (usually cattle). **3.** *Golf.* to strike (a ball) clumsily by hitting the ground behind the ball. [back-formation from DUFFER]

duffel (dŭf′əl), *n.* a coarse woollen cloth having a thick nap. Also, **duffle.** [after *Duffel*, town near Antwerp]

duffel bag, a cylindrical canvas bag used for carrying personal effects. Also, **duffle bag.**

duffel coat, a heavy woollen coat, knee-length or three-quarter-length, usually with a hood and toggles. Also, **duffle coat.**

duffer (dŭf′ə), *n.* **1.** one who duffs. **2.** a plodding, stupid, or incompetent person. **3.** *Slang.* anything inferior, counterfeit, or useless. **4.** *Slang or Dial.* a pedlar, esp. one who sells cheap, flashy goods as valuable. [Scot. d. *dowfart,* c. ON *daufr* deaf]

Dufy (*Fr.* dʏ fē′), *n.* **Raoul** (*Fr.* rȧ o͞ol′), 1877–1953, French artist.

dug[1] (dŭg), *v.* pt. and pp. of **dig.**

dug[2] (dŭg), *n.* the mamma or the nipple of a female. [cf. Sw. *dägga,* Dan. *dægge* suckle]

Dugdale (dŭg′dāl′), *n.* **Sir William,** 1605–86, English antiquary.

dugong (do͞o′gŏng), *n.* the only member of the sirenian genus *Dugong,* a large herbivorous aquatic mammal of East Indian and other waters, characterized by a fishlike body, flipper-like forelimbs, no hind limbs, and a rounded, paddle-like tail. [t. Malay: m. *dūyong*]

Dugong, *Dugong dugon* (8 to 10 ft long)

dugout (dŭg′out′), *n.* **1.** a rough shelter or dwelling formed by an excavation in the ground or in the face of a bank. **2.** a boat made by hollowing out a log. **3.** *Colloq.* a retired person who has been recalled to employment.

Du Guesclin (*Fr.* dʏ gė klăɴ′), **Bertrand** (*Fr.* bĕr träɴ′), *c.* 1320–80, French military leader, constable of France.

Duhamel (*Fr.* dʏ ȧ mĕl′), *n.* **Georges** (*Fr.* zhôrzh), 1884–1966, French novelist, poet, and essayist.

duiker (dī′kə), *n.* **1.** Also, **duyker, duikerbok** (dī′kə bŏk′). any of the small African antelopes with spikelike horns (usually on the males only). They plunge through and under bushes instead of leaping over them. They are included in two genera, *Cephalophus* and *Sylvicapra.* **2.** any of various seabirds of southern Africa, family *Sulidae,* having all four toes webbed, that dive into the sea. **3.** tropicbird. [t. Afrikaans: diver]

Duisburg (*Ger.* dʏs′bo͝ork), *n.* a city in West Germany, in W North Rhine-Westphalia, at the junction of the Rhine and Ruhr rivers: the largest river port in Europe; formerly the two cities of Duisburg and Hamborn. 484,000 (est. 1966).

duke (dyo͞ok), *n.* **1.** a sovereign prince, the ruler of a small state called a duchy. **2.** (in Great Britain) a nobleman of the highest rank after that of a prince and ranking next above marquess. **3.** a nobleman of corresponding rank in certain other countries. **4.** (*chiefly pl.*) *Slang.* the hand or fist. [ME *duc,* t. OF, t. L: s. *dux* leader, ML duke]

dukedom (dyo͞ok′dəm), *n.* **1.** the state or territory ruled by a duke. **2.** the office or rank of a duke.

Dukhobors (do͞o′kō bôz′), *n.pl.* a Russian Christian religious sect of peasants, dating from the 18th century. A number of them, under persecution, migrated to Canada in 1899. [t. Russ.: m. *Dukhobortsy* spirit wrestlers, contenders against the Holy Spirit]

Dukinfield (dŭk′ĭn fēld′), *n.* a town in England, in Cheshire. 17,316 (1961).

dulce et decorum est pro patria mori (do͞ol′kā ĕt dā kô′ro͞om ĕst′prō păt′rĭ ä mô′rē), *Latin.* sweet and fitting it is to die for one's country.

dulcet (dŭl′sĭt), *adj.* **1.** agreeable to the feelings, the eye, or, esp., the ear; pleasing; soothing; melodious. **2.** *Archaic.* sweet to the taste or smell. —*n.* **3.** an organ stop resembling the dulciana, but an octave higher. [ME *doucet,* t. OF, dim. of *dous* sweet, g. L *dulcis*]

dulciana (dŭl′sĭ ăn′ə), *n.* an organ stop having metal pipes, and giving thin, incisive, somewhat stringlike tones. [NL, der. L *dulcis* sweet]

dulcify (dŭl′sĭ fī′), *v.t.,* **-fied, -fying.** **1.** to make more agreeable; mollify; appease. **2.** to sweeten. [t. LL: m. s. *dulcificāre,* f. L: *dulci-* sweet + *-ficāre* make] —**dul′ci-fica′tion,** *n.*

dulcimer (dŭl′sĭ mə), *n. Music.* **1.** a trapezoidal zither with metal strings struck by light hammers; a cembalo; a cymbalo. **2.** *U.S.* a modern folk instrument related to the guitar and plucked with the fingers. [late ME *dowcemer,* t. OF: m. *doulcemer,* var. of *doulcemele.* See DOUCE]

Dulcimer

dulcinea (dŭl′sĭ nĭə′; *Sp.* do͞ol thē nė′ȧ), *n.* a ladylove; a sweetheart. [from *Dulcinea* (der. Sp. *dulce,* g. L *dulcis* sweet), name given by Don Quixote, in Cervantes's romance, to his peasant ladylove]

dulia (dyo͞o lī′ə), *n. Rom. Cath. Theol.* veneration and invocation given to saints as the servants of God and friends of God. See **hyperdulia** and **latria.** [t. ML, t. Gk: m. *douleía* servitude, service]

dull (dŭl), *adj.* **1.** slow of understanding; obtuse; stupid. **2.** lacking keenness of perception in the senses or feelings; insensible; unfeeling. **3.** not intense or acute: *a dull pain.* **4.** slow in motion or action; not brisk; sluggish. **5.** listless; spiritless. **6.** causing ennui or depression; tedious; uninteresting: *a dull sermon.* **7.** not sharp; blunt: *a dull knife.* **8.** having very little depth of colour; lacking in richness or intensity of colour. **9.** not bright, intense, or clear; dim: *a dull day or sound.* —*v.t., v.i.* **10.** to make or become dull. [ME *dul, dull;* akin to OE *dol* foolish, stupid, G *toll* mad] —**dull′ish,** *adj.* —**dull′ness, dul′ness,** *n.* —**dul′ly,** *adv.*

—**Syn.** 1. DULL, BLUNTED, SLOW, STUPID are applied figuratively to mental qualities. DULL implies obtuseness, inability to receive clear impressions, lack of imagination: *a dull child.* BLUNTED implies loss of original keenness of intelligence through disease, sad experience, and the like: *blunted wits or faculties.* SLOW applies to a sluggish intellect not able rapidly to take in or understand, though its eventual action may be good: *a slow mind.* STUPID implies slowness of mental processes, but also applies to lack of intelligence, wisdom, prudence, etc.: *a stupid person, thing to do.* 7. DULL, BLUNT refer to the edge or point of an instrument, tool, or the like. DULL implies a lack or a loss of keenness or sharpness: *a dull razor or saw.* BLUNT may mean the same or may refer to an edge or point not intended to be keen or sharp: *a blunt pen, a blunt foil.* —**Ant.** 1. keen. 7. sharp.

dullard (dŭl′əd), *n.* a dull or stupid person. [f. DULL, adj. + -ARD]

Dulles (dŭl′ĭs), *n.* **John Foster,** 1888–1959, U.S. statesman; secretary of state 1953–59.

Dulong and Petit's Law, *Physics.* the law which states that for a solid element the product of the atomic weight and the specific heat is approximately equal to 6·4 calories per gram-atom. [named after P. L. *Dulong,* 1785–1838, and A. T. *Petit,* 1791–1820, French physicists]

dulse (dŭls), *n.* coarse, edible, red seaweed, *Rhodymenia palmata.* [t. Irish and Gaelic: m. *duileasg*]

Duluth (dyo͞o lo͞oth′), *n.* a city in the U.S., in E Minnesota: a port on Lake Superior. 106,884 (1960).

duly (dyo͞o′lĭ), *adv.* **1.** in a due manner; properly; fitly. **2.** in due season; punctually. **3.** adequately.

duma (do͞o′mä), *n.* (in Russia prior to 1917) **1.** a council or official assembly. **2.** (*cap.*) an elective legislative assembly, constituting the lower house of parliament, which was established in 1905 by Nicholas II. Also, **douma.** [t. Russ.]

Dumas (*Fr.* dʏ mȧ′), *n.* **1. Alexandre** (*Fr.* ȧ lĕk säɴ′dr) (*Dumas père*), 1802–70, French novelist and dramatist. **2.** his son, **Alexandre** (*Dumas fils*), 1824–95, French dramatist and novelist.

Du Maurier (dyo͞o mŏ′rĭ ā′), **1. Daphne,** born 1907, English novelist. **2.** her grandfather, **George Louis Palmella Busson** (păl mĕ lə byo͞o′sən), 1834–96, English illustrator and novelist. **3.** his son, **Sir Gerald,** 1873–1934, English actor and theatrical manager.

dumb (dŭm), *adj.* **1.** without the power of speech. **2.** bereft of the power of speech temporarily: *dumb with astonishment.* **3.** that does not speak, or is little addicted to speaking. **4.** made, done, etc., without speech. **5.** lacking some usual property, characteristic, etc.: *dumb ague.* **6.** stupid; dull-witted. [OE, c. G *dumm* stupid] —**dumb′ly,** *adv.* —**dumb′ness,** *n.*

—**Syn.** 1, 2, DUMB, MUTE, SPEECHLESS, VOICELESS describe a condition in which speech is absent. DUMB was originally used to refer to persons unable to speak; it is now also applied to the inability of animals to speak: *the child was dumb, the dumb animals in the field.* The term MUTE is applied to persons who, usually because of congenital deafness, have never learnt to talk: *with training most mutes learn to speak well enough to be understood.* Either of the foregoing terms or SPEECHLESS may describe a temporary inability to speak, caused by emotion, etc.: *dumb with amazement, mute with terror, left speechless by surprise.* VOICELESS means literally having no voice, either from natural causes or from injury: *fish are voiceless, removal of the larynx left him voiceless.*

dumb ague, an irregular form of intermittent malarial fever, lacking the usual chill.

Dumbarton (dŭm bä′tn), *n.* **1.** a burgh in Scotland, the county town of Dunbarton on the river Clyde: shipbuilding. 26,461 (est. 1962). **2.** Dunbarton.

dumbbell (dŭm′bĕl′), *n.* gymnasium hand apparatus made of wood or metal, consisting of two balls joined by a bar-like handle, used as weights, usually in pairs.

dumbfound (dŭm found′), *v.t.* to strike dumb with amazement. Also, **dumfound′.** [appar. b. DUMB and CONFOUND] —**dumfound′er,** *n.*

dumb show, 1. a part of a dramatic representation given in pantomime, common in the early English drama. **2.** gesture without speech.

dumb waiter, 1. a small stand placed near a dining table. **2.** a large revolving tray for food, placed at the centre of the table. **3.** a conveyor consisting of a framework with shelves, drawn up and down in a shaft.

dumdum (dŭm′dŭm′), *n.* a kind of hollow-nosed bullet that expands on impact, inflicting a severe wound. Also, **dumdum bullet.** [named after DUM-DUM]

Dum-Dum (dŭm′dŭm′), *n.* a town in India, in W Bengal, near Calcutta: former ammunition factory. 111,284 (1961).

Dumf., Dumfriesshire.

Dumfries (dŭm frēs′), *n.* a burgh in Scotland, the county town of Dumfriesshire. 27,042 (est. 1962).

Dumfriesshire (dŭm frēs′shĭə′, -shə), *n.* a county in S Scotland. 88,472 pop. (est. 1964); 1074 sq. mi. *Co. town:* Dumfries. *Abbrev.:* Dumf. Also, **Dumfries.**

dummy (dŭm′ĭ), *n., pl.* **-mies,** *adj.* —*n.* **1.** an imitation or copy of something, as for display, to indicate appearance, exhibit clothing, etc. **2.** *Colloq.* a stupid person; dolt. **3.** one who has nothing to say or who takes no active part in affairs. **4.** one put forward to act for others while ostensibly acting for himself. **5.** a dumb person; a mute. **6.** *Cards.* **a.** (in bridge) the dealer's partner whose hand is exposed and played by the dealer. **b.** the cards so exposed. **c.** a game so played. **d.** an imaginary player represented by an exposed hand which is played by and serves as partner to one of the players. **7.** a rubber teat, etc., given to a baby to suck. **8.** *Print.* sheets folded and made up to show the size, shape, form, sequence, and general style of a contemplated piece of printing. —*adj.* **9.** put forward to act for others while ostensibly acting for oneself. **10.** counterfeit; sham; imitation. **11.** *Cards.* played with a dummy. [f. DUMB + -Y[3]]

dumortierite (dyo͞o mô′tĭ ə rīt′), *n.* a mineral, aluminium borosilicate, used in making refractories. [named after Eugène *Dumortier*, 19th-century French palaeontologist. See -ITE[1]]

dump[1] (dŭmp), *v.t.* **1.** to throw down in a mass; fling down or drop heavily. **2.** to empty out, as from a cart by tilting. **3.** to get rid of; hand over to somebody else. **4.** *Com.* **a.** to put (goods) on the market in large quantities and at a low price, esp. to a large or favoured buyer. **b.** to market (goods) thus in a foreign country, as at a price below that charged in the home country. —*v.i.* **5.** to fall or drop down suddenly. **6.** to unload. **7.** to offer for sale at a low price, esp. to offer low prices to favoured buyers. —*n.* **8.** anything, as rubbish, dumped or thrown down. **9.** a place where it is deposited. **10.** *Mil.* a collection of ammunition, stores, etc., deposited at some point, as near a battle front, to be distributed for use. **11.** the act of dumping. **12.** *Mining.* **a.** a runway or embankment, equipped with tripping devices, from which low-grade ore, rock, etc., are dumped. **b.** the pile of ore so dumped. **13.** *Colloq.* a place, house, or town that is poorly kept up. [ME, t. Scand.; cf. Dan. *dumpe* fall plump]

dump[2] (dŭmp), *n.* **1.** (*now only pl.*) *Colloq.* a dull, gloomy state of mind. **2.** *Obs.* a plaintive melody. **3.** *Obs.* a tune. **4.** *Obs.* a slow dance with a peculiar rhythm. [orig. obscure. Cf. MD *domp* haze]

dump[3] (dŭmp), *n. Dial.* a clumsy leaden counter used by boys in games. [orig. uncert.; ? akin to DUMPY[2]]

dumper (dŭmp′ə), *n.* **1.** one who or that which dumps. **2.** *Austral., Surfing.* a wave that rears up and crashes down, throwing surfers.

dumpish (dŭmp′ĭsh), *adj.* depressed; sad. —**dump′ishly,** *adv.* —**dump′ishness,** *n.*

dumpling (dŭmp′lĭng), *n.* **1.** a rounded mass of steamed dough (often served with stewed meat, etc.). **2.** a kind of pudding consisting of a wrapping of dough enclosing an apple or other fruit, and boiled or baked. **3.** *Colloq.* a short and stout person or animal. [history obscure; ? orig. *lumpling* (f. LUMP[1] + -LING[1]), with *d-* by dissimilation]

dump-truck (dŭmp′trŭk′), *n.* a lorry whose body can be tilted to discharge the contents. Also, **dum′per-truck′.**

dumpy[1] (dŭmp′ĭ), *adj.,* **dumpier, dumpiest.** dumpish; dejected; sulky. [f. DUMP[2] + -Y[1]]

dumpy[2] (dŭmp′ĭ), *adj.,* **dumpier, dumpiest.** short and stout; squat: *a dumpy woman.* [? akin to DUMPLING] —**dump′ily,** *adv.* —**dump′iness,** *n.*

dumpy level, *Survey.* an instrument consisting of a spirit level mounted under and parallel to a telescope, the latter being rigidly attached to its supports.

dum spiro, spero (do͝om spī′ə rō spē′rō), *Latin.* while I breathe, I hope.

dum vivimus, vivamus (do͝om vĭv′ĭ mo͝os, vĭ vä′mo͝os), *Latin.* while we are living, let us live (to the full).

Dumyat (do͝om yăt′), *n.* Arabic name of **Damietta.**

dun[1] (dŭn), *v.,* **dunned, dunning,** *n.* —*v.t.* **1.** to make repeated and insistent demands upon, esp. for the payment of a debt. —*n.* **2.** one who duns; an importunate creditor. **3.** a demand for payment, esp. a written one. [special use of obs. *dun* din, t. Scand.; cf. Icel. *duna* boom, roar]

dun[2] (dŭn), *adj.* **1.** dull or greyish brown. **2.** dark; gloomy. —*n.* **3.** dun colour. **4.** a mayfly. **5.** a dun fly. **6.** a dun-coloured horse. [ME *dun(ne)*, OE *dunn*, c. OS *dun* reddish brown]

Duna (*Hung.* do͞o′nŏ), *n.* Hungarian name of **Danube.**

Düna (*Ger.* dʏ′nä), *n.* German name of **Dvina.**

Dünaburg (*Ger.* dʏ′nä bo͝ork′), *n.* German name of **Daugavpils.**

Dunb., Dunbarton.

Dunbar (dŭn bä′), *n.* **1. William,** 1465?–1530?, Scottish poet. **2.** a town in SE Scotland at the mouth of the Firth of Forth: Cromwell defeated the Scots here, 1650. 3926 (est. 1962).

Dunbarton (dŭn bä′tn), *n.* a county in W Scotland. 184,546 (1961); 241 sq. mi. *Cap.:* Dumbarton. *Abbrev.:* Dunb. Also, **Dunbartonshire.**

Dunbartonshire (dŭn bä′tn shĭə′, -shə), *n.* **1.** Dunbarton. **2.** Dumbarton.

Duncan (dŭng′kən), *n.* **1. I,** died 1040, king of Scotland 1034–40, murdered by Macbeth. **2. Isadora** (ĭz′ə dô′rə), 1878–1927, U.S. dancer.

Duncan Phyfe (dŭng′kən fīf′), of or like the furniture designed by Duncan Phyfe.

dunce (dŭns), *n.* a dull-witted or stupid person; a dolt. [from John DUNS SCOTUS; his system was attacked as foolish by the humanists] —**Syn.** dullard, numbskull, blockhead, ignoramus, simpleton, nincompoop, ninny.

dunce cap, a tall paper cone formerly put on the head of a slow or lazy student. Also, **dunce's cap.**

dunch (dunch), *n. Scot. and N Dial.* a jog; shove.

Dundalk (dŭn dôk′), *n.* a seaport in the Republic of Ireland, capital of Co. Louth. 19,706 (1961).

Dundalk Bay (dŭn dôk′ bā′), a small bay on the E coast of Co. Louth, Republic of Ireland. ab. 7 mi. across.

Dundee (dŭn dē′), *n.* a seaport in E Scotland, in Angus, on the Firth of Tay. 182,959 (1961).

Dundee cake, a fruit cake decorated with almonds.

dunderhead (dŭn′də hĕd′), *n.* a dunce; blockhead. Also, **dunderpate** (dŭn′də pāt′). —**dun′derhead′ed,** *adj.*

dundreary (dŭn drĭə′rĭ), *n., pl.* **-ries.** (*usually pl.*) long side-whiskers worn without a beard.

dune (dyo͞on), *n.* a sand hill or sand ridge formed by the wind, usually in desert regions or near lakes and oceans. [t. F, t. MD, c. OE *dūn.* See DOWN[3]]

Dunedin (dŭ nē′dĭn), *n.* a seaport in New Zealand, on South Island. 77,500 (est. 1965).

Dunfermline (dŭn fûm′lĭn), *n.* a burgh in E Scotland, in the county of Fife. 49,555 (est. 1964).

dun fly, *Angling.* a dun-coloured artificial fly attached to the leader to mimic the larval stage of certain flies.

dung (dŭng), *n.* **1.** manure; excrement, esp. of animals. —*v.t.* **2.** to manure (ground) with, or as with, dung. [ME *dunge*, OE *dung*, c. G *Dung*] —**dung′y,** *adj.*

dungaree (dŭng′gə rē′), *n.* **1.** a coarse cotton fabric of East Indian origin, used esp. for sailors' clothing. **2.** (*pl.*) work clothes, overalls, etc., made of this fabric. [t. Hind.: m. *dungrī*]

dung beetle, any of various scarabaeid beetles that feed upon or breed in dung, as the sacred Egyptian scarab *Scarabaeus sacer.*

dungeon (dŭn′jən), *n.* any strong, close cell, esp. underground; donjon. [ME, t. OF: m. *donjon*, g. LL *dominio* dominion, tower, der. L *dominus* master, lord]

dunghill (dŭng′hĭl′), *n.* **1.** a heap of dung. **2.** a mean or vile place, abode, condition, or person.

duniewassal (do͞o′nĭ wŏs′əl), *n.* a gentleman, esp. of secondary rank, among the Highlanders of Scotland; a cadet of a ranking family. [t. Gaelic: m. *duine uasal* gentleman (f. *duine* man + *uasal* of good birth)]

dunk (dŭngk), *v.t., v.i.* to dip (biscuits, etc.) into coffee, milk, etc. [t. G: s. *dunken*, var. of *tunken* dip] —**dunk′er,** *n.*

Dunker (dŭngk′ə), *n.* a popular name for a member of the German Baptist Brethren, now chiefly in America, characterized by their Baptist practices, opposition to legal oaths and military service and by simplicity of life. Also, **Dunkard** (dŭngk′əd). [var. of *Tunker*, t. G, der. *tunken* dip; with reference to baptism by immersion]

Dunkirk (dŭn kûk′), *n.* **1.** Also, *French,* **Dunkerque** (*Fr.* dœɴ kĕrk′). a seaport in N France: scene of the evacuation under German fire of the British expeditionary force of over 330,000 men May 29th–June 4th, 1940. 28,388 (1962). **2.** (*l.c.*) a desperate situation demanding decisive action.

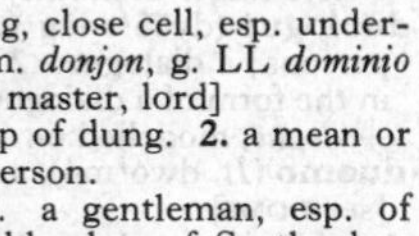

Dunkirk

dunlin (dŭn′lĭn), *n.* a widely distributed sandpiper, *Erolia alpina,* which breeds in northern parts of the northern hemisphere, esp. the red-backed sandpiper, *E. a. sakhalina.* [d. var. of *dunling,* f. DUN[2] + -LING[1]]
dunlop (dŭn′lŏp), *n.* a pressed Scottish cheese, creamy white in colour and having a mild flavour and creamy texture.
dunnage (dŭn′ĭj), *n.* **1.** baggage or personal effects. **2.** *Naut.* loose material laid beneath or wedged among cargo to prevent injury from water or chafing: *dried brush for dunnage.* [t. D: m. *dunnetjes* loosely together]
Dunnet Head (dŭn′ĭt), a promontory of Caithness and the most northerly point of Scotland.
dunnock (dŭn′ək), *n.* the common hedge sparrow, *Prunella modularis,* of Europe. [f. DUN[2] + -OCK]
Dunois (*Fr.* dʏ nwȧ′), *n.* **Jean** (*Fr.* zhäɴ), **Comte de** ('*Bastard of Orleans*'), *c.* 1403–68, French military leader, relieved by Joan of Arc and her troops when besieged at Orleans.
Duns (dŭnz), *n.* a burgh in Scotland, the county town of Berwick. 1838 (1961).
Dunsany (dŭn sā′nĭ), *n.* **Edward John Moreton Drax Plunkett, 18th Baron,** 1878–1957, Irish dramatist and writer of tales.
Dunsinane (dŭn′sĭ nān′), *n.* a hill in central Scotland, NE of Perth: a ruined fort on its summit is traditionally called Macbeth's Castle. 1012 ft.
Duns Scotus (dŭnz′ skō′təs), **John,** *c.* 1265–*c.* 1308, Irish or Scottish scholastic theologian in England.
Dunstable (dŭn′stə bl), *n.* a town in England, in Bedfordshire. 25,645 (1961).
Dunstan (dŭn′stən), *n.* **Saint,** A.D. *c.* 910 or *c.* 925–988, archbishop of Canterbury and statesman.
dunt (dŭnt, dōōnt), *Scot. Dial.* —*n.* **1.** a hard blow making a dull sound. **2.** a wound from such a blow. —*v.t., v.i.* **3.** to strike or knock with a dull sound. [var. of DINT. Cf. Swed. *dunt* dint]
duo (dyōō′ō), *n., pl.* **duos, dui** (dyōō′ē), **1.** *Music.* a duet. **2.** a pair of singers, entertainers, etc. [t. It., t. L: two]
duo-, a word element meaning 'two', as in *duologue.* [t. L, comb. form of *duo*]
duodecimal (dyōō′ō dĕs′ĭ məl), *adj.* **1.** pertaining to twelfths, or to the number twelve. **2.** proceeding by twelves. —*n.* **3.** one of a system of numerals the base of which is twelve. **4.** one of twelve equal parts. [f. L: s. *duodecimus* twelfth + -AL[1]] —**du′odec′imally,** *adv.*
duodecimo (dyōō′ō dĕs′ĭ mō′), *n., pl.* **-mos,** *adj.* —*n.* **1.** a book size (about 5 × 7½ inches) determined by printing on sheets folded to form twelve leaves or twenty-four pages. *Abbrev.:* 12mo or 12°. —*adj.* **2.** in duodecimo. [t. L: (*in*) *duodecimō* in twelfth]
duoden-, a combining form representing **duodenum,** as in *duodenitis.* Also, **duodeno-.**
duodenal (dyōō′ō dē′nəl), *adj.* of or pertaining to the duodenum.
duodenary (dyōō′ō dē′nə rĭ), *adj.* duodecimal. [t. L: m. s. *duodēnārius* containing twelve]
duodenitis (dyōō′ō dĭ nī′tĭs), *n. Pathol.* inflammation of the duodenum.
duodenum (dyōō′ō dē′nəm), *n. Anat., Zool.* the first portion of the small intestine, from the stomach to the jejunum. See diag. under **intestine.** [t. ML, der. L *duodēnī* twelve each; so called from its length, about twelve finger breadths]
duologue (dyōō′ə lŏg′), *n.* **1.** a conversation between two persons; a dialogue. **2.** a dramatic performance or piece in the form of a dialogue limited to two speakers. [f. DUO- + *-logue,* modelled on MONOLOGUE]
duomo (*It.* dwô′mô), *n., pl.* **-mi** (-mē). *Italian.* cathedral. [see DOME]
dup (dŭp), *v.t.,* **dupped, dupping.** *Archaic or Dial.* to open (a door or gate). [contr. of *do up*]
dup., duplicate.
dupe (dyōōp), *n., v.,* **duped, duping.** —*n.* **1.** a person who is imposed upon or deceived; a gull. —*v.t.* **2.** to make a dupe of; deceive; delude; trick. [t. F: prop., hoopoe, g. L *upupa*] —**dup′able,** *adj.* —**dup′abil′ity,** *n.* —**dup′er,** *n.*
dupery (dyōō′pə rĭ), *n., pl.* **-eries. 1.** the act or practice of duping. **2.** the state of one who is duped.
duple (dyōō′pl), *adj.* double; twofold. [t. L: m. s. *duplus* double]
Dupleix (*Fr.* dʏ plĕks′), *n.* **Joseph Francois** (*Fr.* zhô zĕf fräɴ swȧ′), **Marquis,** 1697–1763, French colonial governor in India 1742–54.
Duplessis-Mornay (*Fr.* dʏ plĕ sē mŏr nĕ′), *n.* Mornay.
duplet (dyōō′plĭt), *n. Chem.* a pair of electrons, shared between two atoms, forming a covalent bond.
duple time, *Music.* characterized by two beats to the bar.
duplex (dyōō′plĕks), *adj.* **1.** twofold; double. **2.** *Mach.* including two identical working parts in a single framework, though one could operate alone. —*n.* **3.** duplex house. [t. L: f. *du(o)* two + *-plex,* der. *plicāre* fold] —**duplex′ity,** *n.*
duplexer (dyōō′plĕks′ə), *n.* a radio system which permits simultaneous transmission and reception of signals.
duplex house, *U.S.* a two-family house, as a semidetached.
duplicate (*adj., n.* dyōō′plĭ kĭt; *v.* dyōō′plĭ kāt′), *adj., n., v.,* **-cated, -cating.** —*adj.* **1.** exactly like or corresponding to something else. **2.** double; consisting of or existing in two corresponding parts. **3.** *Cards.* denoting a game in which a team tries for the best result on hands also played by competing partnerships: *duplicate bridge.* —*n.* **4.** a copy exactly like an original. **5.** anything corresponding in all respects to something else. **6.** *Cards.* a duplicate game. **7. in duplicate,** in two copies, exactly alike. —*v.t.* **8.** to make an exact copy of; repeat. **9.** to double; make twofold. [t. L: m. s. *duplicātus,* pp., doubled] —**duplicative** (dyōō′plĭ kə tĭv), *adj.* —**Syn. 4.** facsimile, replica, reproduction. **8.** See **imitate.**
duplication (dyōō′plĭ kā′shən), *n.* **1.** the act of duplicating. **2.** the state of being duplicated. **3.** a duplicate. **4.** *Obs.* a folding or doubling, as of a membrane.
duplicator (dyōō′plĭ kā′tə), *n.* a machine for making duplicates.
duplicity (dyōō plĭs′ĭ tĭ), *n., pl.* deceitfulness in speech or conduct; speaking or acting in two different ways concerning the same matter with intent to deceive; double-dealing. [t. LL: m. s. *duplicitas* doubleness, der. L *duplex.* See DUPLEX] —**Syn.** guile, hypocrisy, deception, dissimulation. —**Ant.** straightforwardness.
Du Pont (dyōō′pŏnt, dyōō pŏnt′; *Fr.* dʏ pôɴ′), U.S. industrialist family, founded by **Éleuthère Irénée** (*Fr.* ė lœ tĕr ē rė nė′), 1771–1834.
du Pré (dyōō prā′), **Jacqueline,** born 1945, English cellist.
Dupré (*Fr.* dʏ prė′), *n.* **Jules** (*Fr.* zhʏl), 1812–89, French landscape painter.
Duque de Caxias (*Braz.* dōō′kė dė kə shē′ás), a town in SE Brazil. 173,077 (1960).
Duquesne (*Fr.* dʏ kĕn′), *n.* **Abraham** (*Fr.* ȧ brȧ ȧm′), **Marquis,** 1610–88, French naval commander.
dura (dyŏŏə′rə), *n.* dura mater. —**du′ral,** *adj.*
durable (dyŏŏə′rə bl), *adj.* having the quality of lasting or enduring; not easily worn out, decayed, etc. [ME, t. L: m. s. *dūrābilis* lasting. See DURE[2]] —**du′rabil′ity, du′rableness,** *n.* —**du′rably,** *adv.* —**Syn.** permanent. —**Ant.** weak, transitory.
duralumin (dyŏŏ răl′yŏŏ mĭn), *n.* **1.** an aluminium-based alloy containing copper, manganese, and, sometimes, magnesium. It may be hardened and strengthened by heat treatment and was one of the first successful lightweight high-strength alloys: originally used in aircraft construction. **2.** (*cap.*) a trademark for this alloy. [f. s. L *dūrus* hard + ALUMIN(IUM)]
dura mater (dyŏŏə′rə mā′tə), *Anat.* the tough, fibrous membrane forming the outermost of the three coverings of the brain and spinal cord. See **arachnoid** and **pia mater.** Also, **dura.** [t. ML: lit., hard mother]
duramen (dyŏŏ rā′mĕn), *n. Bot.* the hard central wood, or heartwood, of an exogenous tree. [t. L: hardness, a hardened vine branch]
durance (dyŏŏə′rəns), *n.* **1.** forced confinement; imprisonment. **2.** *Archaic.* duration. **3.** *Archaic.* endurance. [late ME, t. MF: duration, der. *durer,* g. L *dūrāre* last]
Durango (dyŏŏə răng′gō; *Sp.* dōō rán′gô), *n.* a town in N Mexico. 124,472 (est. 1965).
durante vita (dyŏŏə răn′tā vē′tä), *Latin.* during life.
duration (dyŏŏ rā′shən), *n.* **1.** continuance in time. **2.** the length of time anything continues. [ME, t. LL: s. *dūrātio,* der. L *dūrāre* last]
durative (dyŏŏə′rə tĭv), *adj. Gram.* denoting a verb aspect, as in Russian, expressing incompleted, or continued, action, etc. Compare English *beat* which implies duration or continued action with *strike,* also *walk,* durative, with *step.*
Durazzo (*It.* dōō rát′tsô), *n.* a seaport in W Albania, on the Adriatic: important ancient city. 45,935 (est. 1964). Albanian, **Durrës.**
Durban (dû′bən), *n.* a seaport in the E part of the Republic of South Africa, in Natal. 681,492 (1960).
durbar (dû′bä), *n.* (in India before 1947) **1.** the court of a native ruler. **2.** a public audience or levee held by a native prince or a British governor or viceroy; an official reception. **3.** the hall or place of audience. **4.** the audience itself. [t. Hind., Pers.: m. *darbār* court]
dure[1] (dyŏŏə), *adj. Archaic.* hard; severe. [ME *dur,* t. OF, g. L *dūrus* hard. Cf. DOUR]
dure[2] (dyŏŏə), *v.i., v.t.,* **dured, during.** *Archaic.* endure. [ME *dure(n),* t. F: m. *durer,* g. L *dūrāre* endure]
Düren (*Ger.* dʏ′rən), *n.* a town in West Germany, in SW North Rhine-Westphalia. 53,700 (est. 1966).

Dürer (*Ger.* dʏ′rər), *n.* **Albrecht** (*Ger.* äl′brĕKHt) or **Albert** (*Ger.* äl′bĕrt), 1471–1528, German painter and engraver.

duress (dyo͝oə rĕs′), *n.* **1.** constraint; compulsion. **2.** forcible restraint of liberty; imprisonment. **3.** *Law.* such constraint or coercion as will render void a contract or other legal act entered or performed under its influence. [ME *duresse*, t. OF, g. L *dūritia* hardness]

Durham (dŭ′rəm), *n.* **1.** a county in NE England. 1,515,643 pop. (1961); 1015 sq. mi. **2.** its county town: university, founded 1832. 22,010 (est. 1962). **3.** one of a breed of beef cattle originating in Durham, at one time known as good milkers, but now bred largely for meat production.

durian (dyo͝oə′rĭ ən), *n.* **1.** the edible fruit, with a hard, prickly rind, of a tree, *Durio zibethinus*, of south-eastern Asia. It has an unusual flavour and smell. **2.** the tree itself. Also, **du′rion.** [t. Malay, der. *duri* thorn]

during (dyo͝oə′rĭng), *prep.* **1.** throughout the continuance of. **2.** in the course of. [orig. ppr. of DURE[2]]

Durkheim (dûk′hīm, *Fr.* dʏr kĕm′), *n.* **Émile** (*Fr.* (ė mēl′), 1858–1917, French sociologist and philosopher.

durmast (dû′mäst), *n.* a European oak, *Quercus petraea*, with a heavy, elastic wood highly valued by the builder and the cabinet-maker.

duro (*Sp.* do͞o′rò), *n.*, *pl.* **-ros** (*Sp.* -ròs). the Spanish silver dollar. [t. Sp., for *peso duro* hard piastre]

durra (dŭ′rə), *n.* a type of grain sorghum with slender stalks, cultivated in Asia, etc.; Indian millet; Guinea corn. Also, **doura, dourah.** [t. Ar.: m. *dhura*]

Durrell (dŭ′rəl), *n.* **Lawrence** (**George**), born 1912, English novelist and poet.

Dürrenmatt (*Ger.* dʏ′rən mȧt), *n.* **Friedrich** (*Ger.* frē′drĭKH), born 1921, Swiss novelist and playwright.

Durrës (*Alb.* do͞or′rəs), *n.* Albanian name of **Durazzo.**

durst (dûst), *v.* a pt. of **dare.**

durum wheat (dyo͝oə′rəm), an important species or variety of wheat, *Triticum durum*, the flour from which is largely used for macaroni, etc. Also, **durum.** [i.e. hard wheat. See DURE[1]]

Duse (*It.* do͞o′zė), *n.* **Eleonora** (*It.* ė lė ó nó′rȧ) (*Signora Checchi*), 1859–1924, Italian actress.

dusk (dŭsk), *n.* **1.** partial darkness; a state between light and darkness; twilight; shade; gloom. **2.** the darker stage of twilight. —*adj.* **3.** dark; tending to darkness. —*v.t.*, *v.i.* **4.** to make or become dusk; darken. [metathetic var. of OE *dux*, *dox* dark, c. L *fuscus* dark brown] —**dusk′-ish,** *adj.*

dusky (dŭs′kĭ), *adj.* **duskier, duskiest. 1.** somewhat dark; dark-coloured. **2.** deficient in light; dim. **3.** gloomy. —**dusk′ily,** *adv.* —**dusk′iness,** *n.*

—**Syn. 1.** DUSKY, SWARTHY both mean dark in colour. They differ more in application than in meaning. DUSKY suggests shadiness or a veiled and dim light, as well as darkness of colouring: *dusky twilight shadows, a dusky grove, a dusky Ethiopian.* SWARTHY, which usually denotes a greater degree of darkness or blackness, is used only of the complexion: *a swarthy skin.*

Düsseldorf (do͝os′əl dôf′; *Ger.* dʏ′səl dŏrf), *n.* a city in W West Germany: a port on the Rhine and capital of North Rhine-Westphalia, in the central part. 698,400 (est. 1966).

dust (dŭst), *n.* **1.** earth or other matter in fine, dry particles. **2.** any finely powdered substance, as sawdust. **3.** a cloud of finely powdered earth or other matter in the air. **4.** that to which anything, as the human body, is reduced by disintegration or decay. **5.** the mortal body of man. **6.** *Archaic.* a single particle or grain. **7.** ashes, refuse, etc. **8.** a low or humble condition. **9.** anything worthless. **10.** gold dust. **11.** *Slang.* money; cash. **12.** disturbance; turmoil. **13. bite the dust,** to be killed or wounded. **14. kick up a dust,** *Colloq.* make a fuss; cause a disturbance. **15. lick the dust, a.** to be killed or wounded. **b.** to grovel; humble oneself abjectly. **16. shake the dust off one's feet,** to depart with scorn. **17. throw dust in one's eyes,** to mislead. —*v.t.* **18.** to free from dust; wipe the dust from: *to dust* (*or dust off*) *the table.* **19.** to sprinkle with dust or powder: *to dust plants with powder.* **20.** to strew or sprinkle as dust: *dust powder over plants.* **21.** to soil with dust; make dusty. —*v.i.* **22.** to wipe dust from a table, room, etc. **23.** to become dusty. [ME *doust*, OE *dūst*, c. G *Dunst* vapour] —**dust′less,** *adj.*

dustbin (dŭst′bĭn′), *n.* a receptacle for household rubbish. Also, *U.S.*, **ash can.**

dust bowl, an area subject to dust storms.

dustcart (dŭst′kät′), *n.* a lorry in which household rubbish is collected from dustbins and taken away.

dustcoat (dŭst′kōt′), *n.* a long, light overgarment worn to protect clothing from dust. Also, *U.S.*, **duster.**

dustcover (dŭst′kŭv′ə), *n.* a dustsheet.

dust devil, a miniature whirlwind of considerable intensity that picks up dust and rubbish and carries it some distance into the air.

duster (dŭs′tə), *n.* **1.** one who or that which dusts. **2.** cloth, brush, etc., for removing dust. **3.** an apparatus for sprinkling dust or powder on something. **4.** *U.S.* a dust coat.

dusting (dŭs′tĭng), *n.* **1.** a light coating, as of powder. **2.** *Colloq.* a beating; thrashing.

dust jacket, a jacket (def. 3) for a book. Also, **dust cover.**

dustman (dŭst′mən), *n.*, *pl.* **-men** (-mən). **1.** one employed to remove household rubbish. **2.** *Colloq.* a personification of sleep. See **sandman.**

dustpan (dŭst′păn′), *n.* a shovel-like utensil with a short handle into which dust is swept for removal.

dustproof (dŭst′pro͞of′), *adj.* impervious to dust.

dustsheet (dŭst′shēt′), *n.* a large cloth or sheet placed over furniture to protect it from dust.

dust-shot (dŭst′shŏt′), *n.* the smallest size of shot for a shotgun.

dust storm, a storm of wind which raises dense masses of dust into the air, as in a desert region.

dust-up (dŭst′ŭp′), *n.* *Colloq.* a commotion; fight; scuffle.

dusty (dŭs′tĭ), *adj.*, **dustier, dustiest. 1.** filled, covered, or clouded with dust. **2.** of the nature of dust; powdery. **3.** of the colour of dust; grey. **4. not so dusty,** *Colloq.* not too bad; quite good. —**dust′ily,** *adv.* —**dust′iness,** *n.*

dusty miller, a creeping perennial caryophyllaceous herb, *Cerastium tomentosum*, covered with dense white hairs, a native of SE Europe commonly grown in rock gardens; snow-in-summer.

dutch (dŭch), *n.* *Slang.* wife. [shortened form of DUCHESS]

Dutch (dŭch), *adj.* **1.** of, pertaining to, or characteristic of the natives or inhabitants of the Netherlands or Holland, or their country or language. **2.** *Archaic or U.S. Slang.* German; Teutonic. **3.** *U.S.* of or pertaining to the Pennsylvania Dutch. **4. go Dutch,** *Colloq.* to have each person pay his or her own expenses. —*n.* **5. the Dutch, a.** the people of the Netherlands or Holland. **b.** *U.S. Slang.* the German people. **6.** *U.S.* the Pennsylvania Dutch. **7.** a Germanic language, the language of the Netherlands. **8.** *Obs.* the German language. [t. MD: m. *dutsch* German, Dutch, c. G *deutsch* German, orig., popular, national, trans. of L *vulgāris* vernacular]

Dutch auction, an auction in which the price is gradually lowered until a bid is made.

Dutch barn, a steel-framed building without walls and with a curved roof, often used for storing hay on farms.

Dutch Borneo, former name for the southern and larger part of the island of Borneo: now part of Indonesia.

Dutch cap, pessary (def. 3).

Dutch cheese, 1. a small, globular, hard cheese made from skimmed milk. **2.** cottage cheese.

Dutch clover, the common white clover.

Dutch courage, courage inspired by alcoholic drink.

Dutch door, a door consisting of two units horizontally divided so that while the upper part is open the lower can be closed and act as a barrier.

Dutch East Indies, a former name for the Republic of Indonesia.

Dutch gold, an alloy of copper and zinc in the form of thin sheets, used as a cheap imitation of gold leaf. Also, **Dutch foil, Dutch leaf, Dutch metal.**

Dutch Guiana, Surinam.

Dutch liquid, ethylene dichloride.

Dutchman (dŭch′mən), *n.*, *pl.* **-men. 1.** a native or inhabitant of Holland. **2.** *Carp., etc.* a piece or wedge inserted to hide the fault in a badly made joint, stop an opening, etc., **3.** *Obs.* a German.

Dutchman's-breeches (dŭch′mənz brĭch′ĭz), *n. sing. and pl.* a delicate herb, *Dicentra* (or *Bicuculla*) *cucullaria*, with pale yellow, two-spurred flowers.

Dutchman's-pipe (dŭch′mənz pīp′), *n.* an aristolochiaceous climbing vine, *Aristolochia sipho*, with large leaves and flowers of a curved form suggesting a tobacco pipe.

Dutchman's-pipe, *Aristolochia sipho*

Dutch New Guinea. See **West Irian.** Also, **Netherlands New Guinea.**

Dutch oven, a container with a hole to admit heat, used as an improvised oven.

Dutch rush, a widespread horsetail, *Equisetum hyemale*, the long, scarcely branched siliceous stems of which were formerly used for scouring pots and pans.

Dutch treat, a meal or entertainment in which each person pays for himself.

Dutch uncle, a person who criticizes or reproves with unsparing severity and frankness.

Dutch West Indies, former name of **Netherlands Antilles.**

duteous (dyōō′tyəs), *adj.* dutiful; obedient; submissive. —**du′teously,** *adv.* —**du′teousness,** *n.*

dutiable (dyōō′tyə bl), *adj.* subject to duty, as imported goods.

dutiful (dyōō′tĭ fəl), *adj.* **1.** performing the duties required of one; obedient: *a dutiful child.* **2.** required by duty; proceeding from or expressive of a sense of duty: *dutiful attention.* —**du′tifully,** *adv.* —**du′tifulness,** *n.* —**Syn. 1.** respectful, docile, submissive.

duty (dyōō′tĭ), *n., pl.* **-ties. 1.** that which one is bound to do by moral or legal obligation. **2.** the binding or obligatory force of that which is morally right; moral obligation. **3.** action required by one's position or occupation; office; function: *the duties of a soldier or clergyman.* **4.** the conduct due to a superior; homage; respect. **5.** an act of respect, or an expression of respectful consideration. **6.** a specific or *ad valorem* levy imposed by law on the import, export, sale, or manufacture of goods, the transference of property, the legal recognition of deeds and documents, etc. **7.** a payment, service, etc., imposed and enforceable by law or custom. **8.** *Mach.* **a.** the amount of work done by an engine per unit amount of fuel consumed. **b.** the measure of effectiveness of any machine. **9.** *Agric.* the amount of water necessary to provide for the crop in a given area. **10. do duty for,** be a substitute for; serve the same function as. **11. off duty,** not at work. **12. on duty,** at work. [ME *duete,* t. AF, der. *du, due* DUE]
—**Syn. 1.** DUTY, OBLIGATION refer to what one feels bound to do. DUTY is what one performs, or avoids doing, in fulfilment of the permanent dictates of conscience, piety, right, or law: *duty to one's country, one's duty to tell the truth, to raise children properly.* An OBLIGATION is what one is bound to do to fulfil the dictates of usage, custom, or propriety, and to carry out a particular, specific, and often personal promise or agreement: *financial or social obligations.*

duty-free (dyōō′tĭ frē′), *adj.* free of customs duty.

duumvir (dyōō ŭm′və), *n., pl.* **-virs, -viri** (-vĭ rē′). *Rom. Hist.* one of two officers or magistrates jointly exercising the same public function. [t. L: back-formation from *duum virum,* gen. pl., of two men]

duumvirate (dyōō ŭm′vĭ rĭt), *n.* **1.** a union of two men in the same office, as in ancient Rome. **2.** the office or government of two such persons.

Duvalier (*Fr.* dʏ vȧ lyĕ′), *n.* **Dr François** (*Fr.* fräɴ swȧ′), born 1907, dictator of Haiti since 1957.

duvet (dyōō′vā), *n.* any of various things stuffed with down, as a kind of quilt, or a climbing-jacket. [t. F]

duvetyn (dyōō′və tēn′), *n.* a napped fabric, in a twilled or plain weave, of cotton, wool, silk, or rayon. Also, **du′vetine′, du′vetyne′.** [t. F: f. *duvet* DUVET + *-yn*-INE²]

D.V., Deo volente.

dvandva (dvän′dvä, də vän′də vä′), *Gram.* —*adj.* **1.** denoting a compound word neither element of which is subordinate to the other, as *bittersweet, Anglo-Saxon.* —*n.* **2.** a dvandva compound. [t. Skt: nasalized reduplication of *dva* TWO]

Dvina (*Russ.* dvyĭ nȧ′), *n.* **1.** Lettish, **Daugava.** German, **Düna.** a river in the W Soviet Union, flowing NW to the Baltic at Riga, ab. 640 mi. **2. Northern,** a river in the N Soviet Union in Europe, flowing NW to **Dvina Bay** (Gulf of Archangel), an arm of the White Sea. ab. 470 mi.

Dvinsk (*Russ.* dvĕnsk), *n.* Russian name of **Daugavpils.**

Dvořák (*Cz.* dvŏ′rzhȧk), *n.* **Antonín** (*Cz.* ȧn′tŏ nyĕn), 1841–1904, Czech composer.

dwaal (dwäl), *n.* *S African Colloq.* the state of being bemused or abstracted; a daze. [t. Afrikaans: der. *dwaal,* v., to wander]

dwale (dwāl), *n.* the deadly nightshade, *Atropa belladonna.*

dwarf (dwôf), *n.* **1.** a human being much below the ordinary stature or size; a pygmy. **2.** an animal or plant much below the ordinary size of its kind or species. **3.** *Myth.* a small, manlike being, commonly associated with elves and goblins. —*adj.* **4.** of unusually small stature or size; diminutive. —*v.t.* **5.** to cause to appear or seem small in size, extent, character, etc. **6.** to make dwarf or dwarfish; prevent the due development of. —*v.i.* **7.** to become stunted or smaller. [ME *dwerf,* OE *dweorg,* c. D *dwerg,* G *Zwerg*] —**Syn. 1.** See **midget.**

dwarf cornel, a small cornaceous perennial herb, *Chamaepericlymenum suecium,* of the arctic and mountains of the northern hemisphere.

dwarfish (dwôf′ĭsh), *adj.* like a dwarf; below the ordinary stature or size; diminutive. —**dwarf′ishly,** *adv.* —**dwarf′ishness,** *n.* —**Syn.** pygmy, tiny, stunted, atrophied, runty.

dwarf mallow, a European herb, *Malva neglecta,* with roundish leaves and small pinkish white flowers.

dwarf star, *Astron.* a star of relatively small volume and low luminosity, but often of high density.

dwell (dwĕl), *v.,* **dwelt** or **dwelled, dwelling,** *n.* —*v.i.* **1.** to abide as a permanent resident. **2.** to continue for a time. **3.** to linger over in thought, speech, or writing; to emphasize (often fol. by *on* or *upon*): *to dwell upon a subject, a point in argument.* —*n.* **4.** *Mach.* a pause occurring regularly when a machine is in operation. **5.** a flat part on a cam which, during part of the cycle, keeps a part in a specific position. [ME *dwellen* delay, tarry, abide, OE *dwellan, dwelian* lead astray, hinder, delay, c. Icel. *dvelja*] —**dwell′er,** *n.* —**Syn. 1.** stay, reside, live.

dwelling (dwĕl′ĭng), *n.* **1.** a place of residence or abode; a house. **2.** continued or habitual residence. —**Syn. 1.** See **house.**

dwelling house, a house occupied, or intended to be occupied, as a residence.

dwelling place, a place of residence or abode.

dwelt (dwĕlt), *v.* pt. and pp. of **dwell.**

dwindle (dwĭn′dl), *v.,* **-dled, -dling.** —*v.i.* **1.** to become smaller and smaller; shrink; waste away: *his vast fortune has dwindled away.* **2.** to fall away, as in quality; degenerate. —*v.t.* **3.** to make smaller and smaller; cause to shrink: *failing health dwindles ambition.* [dim. of DWINE] —**Syn. 1.** diminish, decline. See **decrease.** —**Ant. 1.** increase. **3.** magnify.

dwine (dwīn), *v.i.,* **dwined, dwining.** *Archaic or Dial.* to waste away; fade. [OE *dwīnan* languish]

dwt, pennyweight. [f. *d,* for DENARIUS (see def. 2) + *wt* weight]

Dy, *Chem.* dysprosium.

dyad (dī′ăd), *n.* **1.** a group of two; a couple. **2.** *Biol.* **a.** a secondary morphological unit, consisting of two monads: *chromosome dyad.* **b.** the double chromosomes resulting from the splitting of a tetrad. **3.** *Chem.* an element, atom, or radical having a valency of two. —*adj.* **4.** dyadic. [t. LL: s. *dyas,* t. Gk: the number two]

dyadic (dī ăd′ĭk), *adj.* of two parts; pertaining to the number two.

Dyak (dī′ăk), *n.* a member of a wild inland people of Borneo, notorious as head-hunters, of the same stock as the Malays. Also, **Dayak.**

dyarchy (dī′ä′kĭ), *n., pl.* **-chies.** diarchy. —**dyar′chic, dyar′chical,** *adj.*

dye (dī), *n., v.,* **dyed, dyeing.** —*n.* **1.** a colouring material or matter. **2.** a liquid containing colouring matter for imparting a particular hue to cloth, etc. **3.** colour or hue, esp. as produced by dyeing. **4. of the deepest** or **blackest dye,** of the worst kind. [ME *die,* OE *dēag*] —*v.t.* **5.** to colour or stain; treat with a dye; colour (cloth, etc.) by soaking in a liquid containing colouring matter: *to dye cloth red.* **6.** to impart (colour) by means of a dye. —*v.i.* **7.** to impart colour, as a dye: *this brand dyes well.* **8.** to become coloured when treated with a dye: *this cloth dyes easily.* [ME *dien,* OE *dēagian*] —**dy′er,** *n.*

dyed-in-the-wool (dīd′ĭn thə wŏŏl′), *adj.* **1.** dyed before weaving. **2.** through-and-through; complete; inveterate: *a dyed-in-the-wool Republican.*

dyeing (dī′ĭng), *n.* process of colouring fibres, yarns, or fabrics.

dyer's greenweed, a small papilionaceous shrub, *Genista tinctoria,* with yellow flowers and yielding a yellow dye, widespread in rough grassland in Europe and W Asia.

dyer's rocket, a biennial resedaceous herb, *Reseda luteola,* with long spikes of yellowish or green flowers, widespread in Europe and W Asia and formerly cultivated for a yellow dye it contains.

dyestuff (dī′stŭf′), *n.* a material yielding, or used as, a dye.

dyewood (dī′wood′), *n.* any wood yielding a colouring matter used for dyeing.

dying (dī′ĭng), *adj.* **1.** ceasing to live; approaching death: *a dying man.* **2.** pertaining to or associated with death: *a dying hour.* **3.** given, uttered, or manifested just before death: *dying words.* **4.** drawing to a close: *the dying year.* —*n.* **5.** death.

dyke (dīk), *n., v.,* **dyked, dyking.** —*n.* **1.** an embankment for restraining the waters of the sea or a river. **2.** a ditch. **3.** a ridge or bank of earth as thrown up in excavating. **4.** a causeway. **5.** *Dial.* a low wall or fence, esp. of earth or stone, for dividing or enclosing land. **6.** an obstacle; barrier. **7.** *Geol.* **a.** a long, narrow, cross-cutting mass of igneous or eruptive rock intruded into a fissure in older rock. **b.** a similar mass of rock composed of other kinds of material, as sandstone. —*v.t.* **8.** to furnish or drain with a dyke. **9.** to enclose, restrain, or protect by a dyke: *to dyke a tract of land.* Also, **dike.** [ME, t. Scand.; cf. Icel. *dīk, dīki* ditch; akin to DITCH]

dyn., dynamics. Also, **dynam.**

dyna-, a word element referring to power, as in *dynameter.* Also, **dynam-.** [t. Gk, comb. form of *dýnamis* power, *dýnasthai* be able]

dynameter (dī năm′ĭ tə), *n.* *Optics.* an instrument for determining the magnifying power of telescopes. [f. DYNA- + -METER[1]; or shortened form of DYNAMOMETER]

dynamic (dī năm′ĭk), *adj.* **1.** of or pertaining to force not in equilibrium (opposed to *static*) or to force in any state. **2.** pertaining to dynamics. **3.** pertaining to or characterized by energy or effective action; active; forceful. Also, **dynam′ical.** [t. Gk: m. s. *dynamikós* powerful] **—dynam′ically,** *adv.*

dynamics (dī năm′ĭks), *n.* **1.** *Physics.* the branch of mechanics concerned with those forces which cause or affect the motion of bodies. **2.** the science or principles of forces acting in any field. **3.** (*construed as pl.*) the forces, physical or moral, at work in any field. **4.** *Music.* (*construed as pl.*) the variations in the volume of sound.

dynamic similarity, a principle whereby model aeroplanes, ships, and hydraulic structures are operated for test purposes under conditions exactly simulating full-scale performance.

dynamism (dī′nə mĭz′əm), *n.* **1.** *Philos.* a view or doctrine, typified by Leibnitz, that all phenomena are grounded in a force that is immanent in them. **2.** dynamic personality. **—dy′namist,** *n.* **—dy′namis′tic,** *adj.*

dynamite (dī′nə mīt′), *n., v.,* **-mited, -miting.** **—***n.* **1.** a high explosive consisting of nitroglycerine mixed with some absorbent substance such as kieselguhr. **2.** *Colloq.* anything or anyone potentially dangerous and liable to cause trouble. **—***v.t.* **3.** to blow up, shatter, or destroy with dynamite. **4.** to mine or charge with dynamite. **—dynamitic** (dī′nə mĭt′ĭk), *adj.*

dynamiter (dī′nə mī′tə), *n.* one who uses dynamite, esp. for revolutionary purposes. Also, **dy′namit′ist.**

dynamo (dī′nə mō′), *n., pl.* **-mos.** **1.** any rotating machine in which mechanical energy is converted into electrical energy, esp. a direct current generator. **2.** *Colloq.* a forceful, energetic person.

dynamo-, var. of **dyna-,** as in *dynamometer.*

dynamoelectric (dī′nə mō ĭ lĕk′trĭk), *adj.* pertaining to the conversion of mechanical energy into electric energy, or vice versa: *a dynamoelectric machine.* Also, **dy′namo-elec′trical.**

dynamometer (dī′nə mŏm′ĭ tə), *n.* a device for measuring force or power. [f. DYNAMO + -METER[1]]

dynamometry (dī′nə mŏm′ĭ trĭ), *n.* the study or practice of the construction or use of dynamometers. **—dynamometric** (dī′nə mō mĕt′rĭk), **dy′namomet′rical,** *adj.*

dynamotor (dī′nə mō′tə), *n.* a machine which combines both motor and generator action in one magnetic field either with two armatures or with one armature having two separate windings.

dynast (dĭn′əst, dīn′ăst), *n.* a ruler or potentate, esp. a hereditary ruler. [t. L: s. *dynastēs,* t. Gk: lord, chief]

dynasty (dĭn′əs tĭ), *n., pl.* **-ties.** **1.** a sequence of rulers from the same family or stock: *the Ming dynasty in China.* **2.** the rule of such a sequence. **—dynastic** (dī năs′tĭk), **dynas′tical,** *adj.* **—dynas′tically,** *adv.*

dynatron (dī′nə trŏn′), *n.* *Electronics.* a radio valve consisting of three electrodes, in which as the plate voltage increases there is a decrease in the plate current because of emission of electrons from the plate. It is frequently used as an oscillator in radio.

dyne (dīn), *n.* *Physics.* the unit of force in the centimetre-gram-second system; that force which will impart to a mass of the gram an acceleration of one centimetre per second per second. [t. F, f. Gk: m. *dýnamis* force]

dys-, a prefix, esp. medical, indicating difficulty, poor condition, as in *dysphoria.* [t. Gk: hard, bad, unlucky; akin to Skt *dus-, dur-,* OE *tō-,* HG *zer-*]

dysentery (dĭs′ən trĭ), *n.* *Pathol.* an infectious disease marked by inflammation and ulceration of the lower part of the bowels, with diarrhoea that becomes mucous and haemorrhagic. [t. L: m. s. *dysenteria,* t. Gk: r. ME *dissenterie,* t. OF] **—dysenteric** (dĭs′ən tĕ′rĭk), *adj.*

dysfunction (dĭs fŭngk′shən), *n.* *Med.* malfunctioning, as of a structure of the body.

dysgenic (dĭs jĕn′ĭk), *adj.* pertaining to or causing degeneration in the type of offspring produced (opposed to *eugenic*).

dysgenics (dĭs jĕn′ĭks), *n.* *Biol.* the study of the operation of factors that cause degeneration in offspring.

dyslogistic (dĭs′lə jĭs′tĭk), *adj.* conveying disapproval or censure; opprobrious; not eulogistic. [f. DYS- + (EU)LOGISTIC] **—dys′logis′tically,** *adv.*

dysmenorrhoea (dĭs′mĕn ə rĭə′, dĭs mĕn′ə rĭə′), *n.* *Med.* painful menstruation. Also, *Chiefly U.S.,* **dysmenorrhea.**

Dyson (dī′sən), *n.* **Sir George,** 1883–1964, English composer.

dyspareunia (dĭs′pə rōō′nĭ ə), *n.* *Med.* painful intercourse.

dyspepsia (dĭs pĕp′sĭ ə), *n.* deranged or impaired digestion; indigestion (opposed to *eupepsia*). Also, **dyspepsy** (dĭs pĕp′sĭ). [t. L, t. Gk]

dyspeptic (dĭs pĕp′tĭk), *adj.* **1.** pertaining to, subject to, or suffering from dyspepsia. **2.** morbidly gloomy or pessimistic. **—***n.* **3.** a person subject to or suffering from dyspepsia. Also, **dyspep′tical.** **—dyspep′tically,** *adv.*

dysphagia (dĭs fā′jĭ ə), *n.* *Pathol.* difficulty in swallowing. **—dysphagic** (dĭs făj′ĭk), *adj.*

dysphonia (dĭs fō′nyə), *n.* disturbance of the normal functioning in the production of sound. [NL, t. Gk: roughness of sound] **—dysphonic** (dĭs fŏn′ĭk), *adj.*

dysphoria (dĭs fô′rĭ ə), *n.* *Pathol.* a state of dissatisfaction, anxiety, restlessness, or fidgeting. [NL, t. Gk: agitation]

dyspnoea (dĭsp nē′ə), *n.* *Pathol.* difficult or laboured breathing (opposed to *eupnoea*). Also, *Chiefly U.S.,* **dyspne′a.** [t. L, t. Gk: m. *dýspnoia* difficulty of breathing] **—dyspnoe′al, dyspnoe′ic,** *adj.*

dysprosium (dĭs prō′sĭ əm), *n.* *Chem.* a rare-earth metallic element found in small amounts in certain minerals together with other rare earths. *Symbol:* Dy; *at. wt:* 162·50; *at. no.:* 66. [NL, der. Gk *dysprósitos* hard to get at]

dysuria (dĭs yŏŏə′rĭ ə), *n.* *Pathol.* difficult or painful urination. [t. LL, t. Gk: m. *dysouría*]

Dyushambe (*Russ.* dyŏŏ shăm′bĭ), *n.* a city in the SW Soviet Union in Asia: capital of the Tadzhik Republic. 316,000 (est. 1965). Formerly (1929–61), **Stalinabad.**

dz., dozen; dozens.

Dzerzinsk (*Russ.* dzĭr zhĭnsk′), *n.* a city in the central Soviet Union, in Europe. 180,000 (est. 1963).

Dzugashvili (*Russ.* jŏŏ găsh vē′lĭ), *n.* See **Stalin.**

E

E, e (ē), *n., pl.* **E's** or **Es, e's** or **es.** **1.** the fifth letter of the English alphabet. **2.** *Music.* **a.** the third degree in the scale of C major or the fifth in the relative minor scale of A minor. **b.** a written or printed note representing this tone. **c.** a string, key, or pipe, tuned to this note. **d.** (in solmization) the third note of the scale, called **mi.**

E, 1. east. **2.** eastern. **3.** English. **4.** excellent.

e, 1. *Maths.* a transcendental constant equal to 2·7182818 . . ., used as the base of natural logarithms. **2.** erg.

e-, var. of **ex-**[1], used in words of Latin orig. before consonants except *c, f, p, q, s,* and *t,* as in *emit.*

E., 1. Earl. **2.** east. **3.** eastern. **4.** English.

e., 1. eldest. **2.** entrance.

ea., each.

each (ēch), *adj.* **1.** every, of two or more considered individually or one by one: *each stone in the building.* **—***pron.* **2.** each one: *each went his way.* **—***adv.* **3.** apiece: *they cost a shilling each.* [ME *ech(e),* etc., OE *ǣlc,* etc., f. *ā* ever + (*ge*)*līc* like, c. OHG *ēo-gilīh*]

—Syn. 1. EACH, EVERY are alike in having a distributive meaning. Of two or more members composing a (usually) definite aggregate, EACH directs attention to the separate members in turn: *each child* (of those considered and enumerated) *received a large apple.* EVERY emphasizes the idea of inclusiveness or universality; it is also used of an indefinite number, all being regarded singly and separately: *every child present received an apple* (no child was omitted); *every child* (of all in existence) *likes to play.*

each other, each the other: *they struck each other;* that is, they struck, *each* striking the *other:* used also (like *one another*) as a compound reciprocal pronoun in oblique cases: *they struck at each other.*

each way, (of a bet in horseracing, etc.) staked on a place (second or third) as well as on a win.

eager (ē′gə), *adj.* **1.** keen or ardent in desire or feeling; impatiently longing: *I am eager for or about it, eager to do it.* **2.** characterized by great earnestness: *an eager look.* **3.** *Obs.* keen; sharp; biting. [ME *egre,* t. OF: m. *aigre,* g. L *ācer* sharp] **—ea′gerly,** *adv.* **—ea′gerness,** *n.* **—Syn. 1.** fervent, zealous, enthusiastic.

eager beaver, *Colloq.* a diligent and zealous person; one over-eager for work.

eagle (ē′gl), *n.* **1.** any of certain large diurnal birds of prey of the falcon family, esp. the **golden eagle,** *Aquila chry-*

saëtos, of the northern hemisphere, and the **bald eagle,** *Haliaetus leucocephalus*, of North America, noted for their size, strength, powerful flight, and keenness of vision. **2.** a figure or representation of an eagle, much used as an emblem: *the Roman eagle.* **3.** a standard, seal, etc., bearing such a figure, esp. the standard of the ancient Roman army. **4.** a lectern in the shape of an eagle. **5.** (*cap.*) *Astron.* the northern constellation Aquila. **6.** *Golf.* a score two below par on any but par-three holes. **7.** a gold coin of the U.S., of the value of ten dollars, having a figure of an eagle on the reverse. [ME *egle*, t. OF, g. L *aquila*]

eagle-eyed (ē′gl īd′), *adj.* sharp-sighted.

eagle-hawk (ē′gl hôk′), *v.i.* *Austral.* to pluck wool from a dead sheep.

eagle owl, a large, rapacious owl, *Bubo bubo*, of Europe.

eaglet (ē′glĭt), *n.* a young eagle. [t. F: m. *aiglette*, dim. of *aigle* EAGLE]

eaglewood (ē′gl wŏŏd′), *n.* a thymeleaceous tree from India and Malaysia, *Aquilaria agallocha*, the wood of which yields a resin used as a perfume. [trans. of Pg. *pão d'aguila* wood of agalloch, by confusion with Pg. *águia* eagle]

eagre (ā′gə), *n.* bore³. [f. OE: *ēa* river + *gār* storm]

ealdorman (ôl′də mən), *n.* *Early Eng. Hist.* **1.** a chief. **2.** (later) the chief magistrate of a country or group of countries.

Ealing (ē′lĭng), *n.* a W outer London borough. 303,800 (1965).

EAM, National Liberation Front, a Greek underground resistance movement of World War II and political coalition in various left-wing groups.

E. & O.E., errors and omissions excepted.

ear¹ (ɪə), *n.* **1.** the organ of hearing, in man and mammals usually consisting of three parts (**external ear, middle ear,** and **internal ear**). **2.** the external part alone. **3.** the sense of hearing. **4.** nice perception of the differences of sound; esp. sensitiveness to the quality and correctness of musical sounds: *an ear for music.* **5.** attention; heed, esp. favourable attention: *gain a person's ear.* **6.** any object resembling or suggestive of the external ear, as the handle of a pitcher or the part of a bell by which it is hung. **7.** *Journalism.* either of the small spaces or boxes in the upper corners of the front page of a newspaper, containing displayed matter, as an indication of the edition, an advertisement, etc. **8. be all ears,** to listen attentively. **9. by ear,** without dependence upon or reference to written music. **10. fall on deaf ears,** to pass unheeded. **11. have an ear to the ground,** to be well informed about gossip or trends. **12. go in one ear and out the other,** to be heard but ignored; to make no impression. **13. set by the ears,** to cause to disagree or quarrel. **14. turn a deaf ear,** to refuse to help or consider helping. **15. up to one's ears,** deeply involved; extremely busy. **16. wet behind the ears,** naive; immature. [ME *ere*, OE *ēare*, c. G *Ohr*; akin to L *auris*, Gk *oûs*] —**ear′less,** *adj.* —**ear′like′,** *adj.*

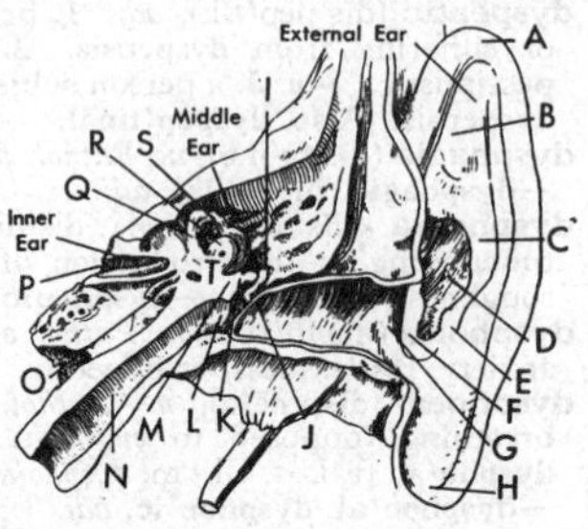

Transverse section of a human ear
External ear: A, Helix; B, Fossa of antihelix; C, Antihelix; D, Concha; E, Antitragus; F, Tragus; G, External auditory meatus; H, Lobe.
Middle ear: I, Incus; J, Tympanic membrane; K, Malleus; L, Tympanum; M, Stapes; N, Eustachian tube.
Inner ear: O, Cochlea; P, Internal auditory meatus; Q, R, S, Anterior, external, posterior, semicircular canals; T, Vestibule

ear² (ɪə), *n.* **1.** that part of a cereal plant, as wheat, barley, etc., which contains the flowers and hence the fruit, grains, or kernels. —*v.i.* **2.** to form or put forth ears. [ME *ere*, OE *ēar*, c. G *Ähre*]

earache (ɪər′āk′), *n.* pain in the ear; otalgia.

eardrop (ɪə′drŏp′), *n.* an earring with a pendant.

eardrum (ɪə′drŭm), *n.* the tympanic membrane.

eared (ɪəd), *adj.* having ears or earlike appendages, as **eared owls** (having earlike feathers), **eared seals** (having outer ears as contrasted with those which do not).

earflap (ɪə′flăp′), *n.* one of a pair of pieces attached to a cap, for covering the ears in cold weather.

earful (ɪə′fŏŏl′), *n.* *Colloq.* **1.** a quantity of oral advice, esp. unsolicited advice. **2.** a stern rebuke, esp. lengthy or abusive.

earing (ɪə′rĭng), *n.* a small rope attached to a cringle of a sail and used in reefing, etc. [appar. f. EAR¹ + -ING¹]

earl (ûl), *n.* **1.** a British nobleman of a rank next below that of marquess and next above that of viscount. *Earl* is now a title unconnected with territorial jurisdiction. After the Norman Conquest earls were for a time called counts; the wife of an earl is a countess. **2.** (before the Norman Conquest) the governor of one of the great divisions of England, as Wessex, Mercia, etc. [ME *erl*, OE *eorl* (c. Icel. *jarl* JARL), orig., man, warrior, esp. one of good birth (contrasted with *ceorl* simple freeman, CHURL)]

earlap (ɪə′lăp′), *n.* **1.** earflap. **2.** the lobe of the ear. **3.** the whole external ear.

earldom (ûl′dəm), *n.* **1.** the rank or title of an earl. **2.** *Obs.* the territory or jurisdiction of an earl.

Earl Marshal, an officer of state, the president and supervisor of the College of Heralds.

earl palatine, *pl.* **earls palatine.** *Hist.* an earl of England having royal powers and independent judicial authority within his county. Also, **count palatine.**

early (û′lĭ), *adv.*, **-lier, -liest,** *adj.* —*adv.* **1.** in or during the first part of some division of time, or of some course or series: *early in the year.* **2.** before the usual or appointed time; in good time: *come early.* **3.** far back in time. **4. early on,** after very little time has elapsed; before the main part of a project, game, etc., has been completed. —*adj.* **5.** occurring in the first part of some division of time, or of some course or series: *an early hour.* **6.** occurring before the usual or appointed time: *an early dinner.* **7.** belonging to a period far back in time: *early English architecture.* **8.** occurring in the near future: *an early reply.* [ME *erli*, etc., OE *ǣrlīce* (f. *ǣr* soon + *-līce* -LY)] —**ear′liness,** *n.* —**Ant. 1.** late.

early bird, *Colloq.* **1.** a person who gets up early. **2.** a person who arrives before others.

early blight, a fungus disease of potatoes caused by *Alternana solani* which produces a toxic antibiotic alternaric acid.

early closing, the observance of a weekly half-holiday in shops.

early English, pertaining to or belonging to the earliest style of English Gothic architecture, characterized by the use of pointed arches and narrow openings.

early warning system, *Electronics.* a radar system intended to give warning of the approach of hostile bombers or guided missiles.

earmark (ɪə′mäk′), *n.* **1.** a mark of identification made on the ear of an animal. **2.** any identifying or distinguishing mark or characteristic. —*v.t.* **3.** to mark with an earmark. **4.** to set aside for a specific purpose or use: *to earmark goods for export.*

ear-minded (ɪə′mīn′dĭd), *adj.* *Psychol.* responding strongly to auditory stimuli or showing a preference for them. —**ear′mind′edness,** *n.*

earmuff (ɪə′mŭf′), *n.* one of a pair of adjustable coverings for protecting the ears in cold weather.

earn¹ (ûn), *v.t.* **1.** to gain by labour or service: *to earn one's living.* **2.** to merit as compensation, as for service; deserve: *to receive more than one has earned.* **3.** to get as one's desert or due: *to earn a reputation for honesty.* **4.** to gain as due return or profit: *defence bonds earn interest.* **5.** to bring or procure as deserved: *fair dealing earns confidence.* [ME *ernie(n)*, OE *earnian*; akin to OHG *arnēn* earn] —**earn′er,** *n.* —**Syn. 1.** See **gain¹.**

earn² (ûn), *v.i.*, *v.t.* *Obs.* to yearn. [OE *eornian* murmur (? var. of *geornian*). See YEARN]

earnest¹ (û′nĭst), *adj.* **1.** serious in intention, purpose, or effort; sincerely zealous: *an earnest worker.* **2.** showing depth and sincerity of feeling: *earnest words.* **3.** having serious importance, or demanding serious attention: *'Life is real! Life is earnest!'* —*n.* **4.** seriousness, as of intention or purpose, as opposed to jest, play, or trifling: *in earnest.* [ME *erneste*, OE *eornost*, c. D and G *ernst*] —**ear′nestly,** *adv.* —**ear′nestness,** *n.*

—**Syn. 1.** EARNEST, RESOLUTE, SERIOUS, SINCERE imply having qualities of depth, firmness, and stability. EARNEST implies having a purpose and being steadily and soberly eager in pursuing it: *an earnest student.* RESOLUTE adds somewhat more of a quality of determination; one who is resolute is very difficult to sway or to turn aside from a purpose: *resolute in defending the right.* SERIOUS implies having depth and a soberness of attitude which contrasts with gaiety and frivolity; it may include the qualities of both earnestness and resolution: *serious and thoughtful.* SINCERE suggests genuineness, trustworthiness, and absence of deceit: *a sincere interest in his well-being.* —**Ant. 1.** frivolous.

earnest² (û′nĭst), *n.* **1.** a portion of something, given or done in advance as a pledge of the remainder. **2.** *Law.* earnest money. **3.** anything that gives pledge, promise, assurance, or indication of what is to follow. [ME *ernes*, alter. of earlier *erles* (orig., a pl. form, t. OF; see ARLES), appar. by assoc. with suffix *-ness*]

earnest money, *Law.* money given to bind a contract.

earning (û′nĭng), *n.* **1.** the act of one who earns. **2.** (*pl.*)

money earned; wages; profits. [ME *erning*, OE *earnung*]

earphone (ĭə′fōn′), *n.* a small device for converting electric signals into soundwaves, so designed that it is meant to fit into the ear or to be held close to it, so that only the wearer hears the signals.

earpiece (ĭə′pēs′), *n.* the earphone of a telephone receiver or the like.

ear-piercing (ĭə′pĭə′sĭng), *adj.* shrill; extremely harsh to the ears.

earplug (ĭə′plŭg′), *n.* a piece of soft material, as wax, inserted into the outer ear to keep out water, noise, etc.

earring (ĭə′rĭng′), *n.* a ring or other ornament worn in or on the lobe of the ear.

ear shell, abalone.

earshot (ĭə′shŏt′), *n.* reach or range of hearing.

ear-splitting (ĭə′splĭt′ĭng), *adj.* shrill; extremely harsh to the ears.

ear stone, an otolith.

earth (ûth), *n.* **1.** (*often cap.*) the planet which we inhabit, the third in order from the sun, having an equatorial diameter of 7926 miles and a mass of $5{\cdot}98 \times 10^{24}$ kilograms. Its period of revolution is 365·256 days, its mean distance from the sun 92,960,000 miles. It has one natural satellite, the moon. **2.** the inhabitants of this planet: *the whole earth rejoiced.* **3.** this planet as the habitation of man, often in contrast to heaven and hell. **4.** the surface of this planet. **5.** the solid matter of this planet; the dry land; the ground. **6.** the softer part of the land, as distinguished from rock; soil: *draw the earth up around the plant.* **7.** the hole of a burrowing animal. **8.** any hole in the ground where a fox seeks shelter when being chased. **9.** worldly matters, as distinguished from spiritual. **10.** *Chem.* any of several metallic oxides which are not easily reduced, as alumina, zirconia, etc. Cf. **alkaline earths** and **rare earths. 11.** *Elect.* **a.** a conducting connection between an electric circuit or equipment and the earth or some similar large conducting body. **b.** the terminal to which the earthing connection is attached. **12.** *Obs.* a land or country. **13. on earth,** (used as an intensive): *what on earth are you doing?* **14. run to earth, a.** *Hunting.* to pursue (an animal) to its burrow or hole. **b.** to hunt down; track down. *—v.t.* **15.** *Elect.* to establish an earth for (a device, circuit, etc.); join (a conductor) to earth. [ME *erthe*, OE *eorthe*, c. G *Erde*]

—Syn. 3. EARTH, GLOBE, WORLD are terms applied to the planet on which we dwell. EARTH is used esp. in speaking of a condition of existence contrasted with that in heaven or hell: *those who are yet on earth.* GLOBE formerly emphasized merely the roundness of the earth: *to circumnavigate the globe.* It is now coming to be used more like WORLD, with especial application to the inhabitants of the earth and their activities, interests, and concerns. In this sense, both GLOBE and WORLD are more inclusive than EARTH and are used more abstractly: *people all over the globe, the future of the world, One World.*

earthborn (ûth′bôn′), *adj.* **1.** born or sprung from the earth; of earthly origin. **2.** mortal.

earthbound (ûth′bound′), *adj.* **1.** firmly fixed in the earth. **2.** having only earthly interests.

earth closet, **1.** a closet in which earth is used as the deodorizing agent. **2.** a dry privy, midden, or bucket closet.

earthen (û′thən), *adj.* **1.** composed of earth. **2.** made of baked clay.

earthenware (û′thən wēə′), *n.* **1.** earthen pottery; vessels, etc., of baked or hardened clay. **2.** the material of such vessels (usually the coarse, opaque varieties, the finer, translucent kinds being called *porcelain*).

earthgod (ûth′gŏd′), *n.* a god associated with or identified with the earth, usually as a deity of fertility.

earthgoddess (ûth′gŏd′ĭs), *n.* a goddess associated with or identified with the earth, usually as a deity of fertility.

earth-house (ûth′hous′), *n.* an ancient underground dwelling or storehouse, esp. one from early Celtic times.

earth inductor compass, *Aeron.* a compass actuated by induction from the earth's magnetic field.

earthiness (û′thĭ nĭs), *n.* **1.** earthy nature or properties. **2.** the quality of being down to earth or direct.

earthlight (ûth′līt′), *n.* *Astron.* earthshine.

earthling (ûth′lĭng), *n.* **1.** an inhabitant of earth; a mortal. **2.** one attached to earthly or worldly things.

earthly (ûth′lĭ), *adj.*, **-lier, -liest. 1.** of or pertaining to the earth, esp. as opposed to heaven; worldly. **2.** possible or conceivable: *no earthly use.* [ME *erthly*, OE *eorthlic*] **—earth′liness,** *n.*

—Syn. 1. EARTHLY, TERRESTRIAL, WORLDLY, MUNDANE refer to that which is concerned with the earth literally or figuratively. EARTHLY now almost always implies a contrast to that which is heavenly: *earthly pleasures, our earthly home.* TERRESTRIAL, the dignified Latin equivalent of EARTHLY, applies to the earth as a planet or to the land as opposed to the water, and is contrasted with that which is celestial: *terrestrial areas, the terrestrial globe.* WORLDLY is commonly used in the derogatory sense of being devoted to the vanities, cares, advantages, or gains of this present life to the exclusion of spiritual interests or the life to come: *worldly success, worldly standards.* MUNDANE, a formal Latin word, equivalent to WORLDLY, especially suggests that which is bound to the earth, is not exalted, and therefore is commonplace: *mundane affairs, pursuits, etc.*

earth magnetism, terrestrial magnetism.

earthman (ûth′măn′), *n.* a native of the planet earth (used chiefly in science fiction).

earthmother (ûth′mŭth′ə), *n.* an earth-goddess considered as the source and spiritual mother of all living things.

earthnut (ûth′nŭt′), *n.* a slender umbelliferous perennial, *Conopodium majus*, with an edible underground tuber, of W Europe.

earth pillar, *Geol.* a column of soft earthy material, capped by a stone or boulder which has protected it from complete erosion.

earthquake (ûth′kwāk′), *n.* tremors or earth movements in the earth's crust when fracturing rocks send out a series of three distinct sets of shock waves (earthquake waves); they are tectonic in origin and may accompany volcanic activity.

earth return, *Electronics.* an electrical path which completes a circuit through the earth, or through a body at the same potential as the earth.

earth satellite, *Aerospace.* **1.** a man-made satellite (def. 5) which orbits the earth. **2.** the moon.

earth-shaking (ûth′shā′kĭng), *adj.* of the greatest importance; tending to cause great upheaval.

earthshine (ûth′shīn′), *n.* *Astron.* the faint light on the part of the moon not illuminated by the sun, due to the light which the earth reflects on the moon. Also, **earthlight.**

earthstar (ûth′stä′), *n.* a fungus of the genus *Geaster*, with an outer covering which splits into the form of a star.

earthward (ûth′wəd), *adj.* **1.** directed towards the earth. *—adv.* **2.** earthwards.

earthwards (ûth′wədz), *adv.* towards the earth. Also, **earthward.**

earth wax, *Chem.* ozocerite.

earthwolf (ûth′wo͝olf′), *n.* aardwolf.

earthwork (ûth′wûk′), *n.* **1.** the excavating and embanking of earth involved in engineering construction. **2.** *Mil.* a construction formed chiefly of earth, used in both defensive and offensive operations.

earthworm (ûth′wûm′), *n.* **1.** any one of numerous annelid worms that burrow in soil and feed on soil and decaying organic matter. **2.** a mean or grovelling person.

earthy (û′thĭ), *adj.*, **earthier, earthiest. 1.** of the nature of or consisting of earth or soil. **2.** characteristic of earth: *an earthy smell.* **3.** worldly. **4.** coarse or unrefined. **5.** direct; robust; unaffected.

ear trumpet, a device for collecting and intensifying sounds, held to the ear as an aid in defective hearing.

earwax (ĭə′wăks′), *n.* cerumen.

earwig (ĭə′wĭg′), *n.*, *v.*, **-wigged, -wigging.** *—n.* **1.** any insect of the order *Dermaptera*, characterized by the forceps or pincers at the end of the abdomen. These harmless insects were popularly supposed to injure the human ear. *—v.t.* **2.** to fill the mind of with prejudice by insinuations. [ME *erwyge*, OE *ēarwicga* ear insect]

earwitness (ĭə′wĭt′nĭs), *n.* **1.** one who can give testimony of something heard. *—adj.* **2.** delivered by an earwitness.

ease (ēz), *n.*, *v.*, **eased, easing.** *—n.* **1.** freedom from labour, pain, or physical annoyance of any kind; tranquil rest; comfort: *to take one's ease.* **2.** freedom from concern, anxiety, or solicitude; a quiet state of mind: *be at ease.* **3.** freedom from difficulty or great labour; facility: *it can be done with ease.* **4.** freedom from stiffness, constraint, or formality; unaffectedness: *ease of manner, at ease with others.* **5. at ease,** *Mil.* a position of rest in which soldiers may relax, but may not leave their place or talk. *—v.t.* **6.** to give rest or relief to; make comfortable. **7.** to free from anxiety or care: *to ease one's mind.* **8.** to mitigate, lighten, or lessen: *to ease the pain.* **9.** to release from pressure, tension, or the like: *to ease off a rope.* **10.** to render less difficult; facilitate. **11.** to move slowly and with great care. **12.** *Naut.* **a.** to bring (the helm) slowly towards midships. **b.** to give (a ship) leeward helm or trim sails so as to present the bow to a wave. *—v.i.* **13.** to reduce severity, pressure, tension, etc. (often fol. by *off* or *up*). **14.** to become less painful, burdensome, etc. **15.** to move with great care (often fol. by *along*). [ME *eise*, t. OF: m. *aise*, g. LL *adjacens* near]

—Syn. 1. EASE, COMFORT refer to a sense of relaxation or of well-being. EASE implies a relaxed condition with an absence of effort or pressure: *a life of ease, ease after the day's work.* COMFORT suggests a sense of well-being, along with ease, which produces a quiet happiness and contentment: *comfort in one's old age.* 7. tranquillize, soothe. 8. alleviate, assuage, allay. **—Ant.** 1. discomfort. 2. anxiety. 3. effort.

easeful (ēz′fəl), *adj.* comfortable; quiet; peaceful; restful. —**ease′fully,** *adv.* —**ease′fulness,** *n.*

easel (ē′zəl), *n.* a frame in the form of a tripod, for supporting an artist's canvas, a blackboard, or the like. [t. D: m. *ezel*, c. G *Esel* easel, lit., ass; akin to ASS]

easement (ēz′mənt), *n.* **1.** an easing; relief. **2.** something that gives ease; a convenience. **3.** *Law.* a right held by one person to make use of the land of another.

easer (ē′zə), *n.* one who or that which eases.

easily (ē′zĭ lĭ), *adv.* **1.** in an easy manner; with ease; without trouble. **2.** beyond question: *easily the best.* **3.** probably; likely.

easiness (ē′zĭ nĭs), *n.* **1.** the quality or condition of being easy. **2.** ease of manner; carelessness; indifference.

east (ēst), *n.* **1.** a cardinal point of the compass (90 degrees to the right of north), corresponding to the point where the sun is seen to rise. **2.** the direction in which this point lies. **3.** (*l.c. or cap.*) a quarter or territory situated in this direction. **4. the East, a.** the parts of Asia collectively (as lying east of Europe) where civilization has existed from early times, including Asia Minor, Syria, Arabia, India, China, etc.; the Orient. **b.** the countries collectively of Asia and Eastern Europe under Communist government. **c.** the whole eastern or Atlantic portion of the United States, esp. that north of Maryland. **d.** New England. —*adj.* **5.** directed or proceeding towards the east. **6.** coming from the east: *an east wind.* **7.** lying towards or situated in the east: *the east side.* **8.** *Eccles.* towards the altar as situated with respect to the nave. —*adv.* **9.** towards or in the east: *he went east.* **10.** from the east. [ME *est*, OE *ēast*, c. MHG *ōst*, G *Osten*, *n.* See EASTER]

East Anglia (ăng′glĭ ə), an early English kingdom in SE Britain; modern Norfolk and Suffolk. See map under **Mercia.**

Eastaway (ēs′tə wā′), *n.* **Edward.** See **Thomas, Edward.**

East Bengal, a state in Pakistan, formerly part of the Indian province of Bengal; now coextensive with East Pakistan. See **Bengal.**

East Berlin, the capital of East Germany, in the E central part, forming the eastern part of Berlin (the former **Soviet sector**). 1,061,218 (est. 1962). See **Berlin.**

eastbound (ēst′bound′), *adj.* travelling towards the east.

Eastbourne (ēst′bôn′), *n.* a coastal resort in S England, in East Sussex. 53,530 (1964).

east by north, *Navig., Survey.* 11°15′ (one point) north of east; 78° 45′ from due north. *Abbrev.:* E by N. See diag. under **compass card.**

east by south, *Navig., Survey.* 11° 15′ (one point) south of east; 101° 15′ from due south. *Abbrev.:* E by S. See diag. under **compass card.**

East Cape. See **Dezhnev, Cape.**

East China Sea, a part of the N Pacific, bounded by China, Korea, Japan, the Ryukyus, and Taiwan.

East End, a large, thickly populated part of E London: traditionally a working-class district. —**East Ender.**

Easter (ēs′tə), *n.* **1.** an annual Christian festival in commemoration of the resurrection of Jesus Christ, observed on the first Sunday after the full moon that occurs on or next after March 21. **2.** Also, **Easter Day, Easter Sunday.** the day on which this festival is celebrated. **3.** Eastertide. **4.** Easter term. [ME *ester*, OE *ēastre*, pl. *ēastron* (c. G *Ostern*, pl.), orig., name of goddess; akin to L *aurora* dawn, Gk *eōs*. Cf. EAST]

Easter egg, a coloured egg, or imitation of one, used at Easter as a gift or decoration.

Easter Island, an island in the S Pacific, ab. 2000 mi. W of and belonging to Chile: stone monuments. 45 sq. mi. Native name, **Rapa Nui.**

Easter-ledges (ēs′tə lĕj′ĭz), *n.* (*construed as sing. or pl.*) a perennial polygonaceous herb, *Polygonum bistorta*, the young leaves of which are used to make **Easter-ledge pudding** in the Lake District.

easterling (ēs′tə lĭng), *n.* a native of some country lying eastwards of another.

easterly (ēs′tə lĭ), *adj.* **1.** moving, directed, or situated towards the east: *an easterly course.* **2.** coming from the east: *an easterly wind.* —*adv.* **3.** towards the east. **4.** from the east.

Easter Monday, the day after Easter.

eastern (ēs′tən), *adj.* **1.** lying towards or situated in the east: *the eastern side of a town.* **2.** directed or proceeding towards the east: *an eastern route.* **3.** coming from the east: *an eastern wind.* **4.** (*usually cap.*) of or pertaining to the East: *the Eastern Church.* **5.** (*sometimes cap.*) oriental. [ME *esterne*, OE *ēasterne*]

Eastern Church, 1. the Christian Church of the countries formerly comprising the Eastern Roman Empire. **2.** any body of Christians owing allegiance to the Orthodox Church and observing the Greek rite rather than the Roman.

easterner (ēs′tə nə), *n.* (*often cap.*) a native or inhabitant of an eastern area, esp. of the eastern U.S.

Eastern Ghats. See **Ghats.**

Eastern Hemisphere, the part of the world lying E of the Greenwich Meridian, including Asia, Africa, Australia, and Europe.

easternmost (ēs′tən mōst′), *adj.* farthest east.

Eastern Nigeria, one of the four main regions of Nigeria: as **Biafra,** independent April 1967–Jan. 1970.

Eastern Roman Empire, the eastern division of the Roman Empire and, after A.D. 476, the Roman Empire with its capital at Constantinople. Also, **Eastern Empire.**

Eastern Time, one of the four standard time zones in the U.S. lying on the 75th meridian, five hours behind **Greenwich Mean Time** and one hour ahead of **Central Time.**

Easter term, an English law sitting and (at some universities, etc.) university term, between variable dates, but usually beginning in April and ending in May or June.

Eastertide (ēs′tə tīd′), *n.* **1.** Easter time. **2.** the week ushered in by and following Easter. **3.** the fifty days between Easter and Whitsuntide.

East Germany, a country in central Europe, formed after World War II as the Soviet zone of occupation. 17,181,085 pop. (1963); 41,535 sq. mi. *Cap.:* Berlin. Also, **Soviet Zone.** Official name, **German Democratic Republic.**

East Grinstead (grĭn′stĭd, -stĕd), a town in England, in N East Sussex. 15,421 (1961).

East Ham, a district of E London, in the outer London borough of Newham.

East India Company, 1. a company chartered by the British government to trade between India and Britain, 1600–1874. **2.** one of several similar companies of other European countries: Dutch (1602–1798); French (1664–1769); Danish (1729–1801).

East Indiaman, a large, armed sailing vessel of the East India Company.

East Indies, 1. a collective name of the two large peninsulas (India and Indochina) of SE Asia, together with the Malay Archipelago. **2.** the Malay Archipelago. **3.** Indonesia. Also, **East India.** —**East Indian.**

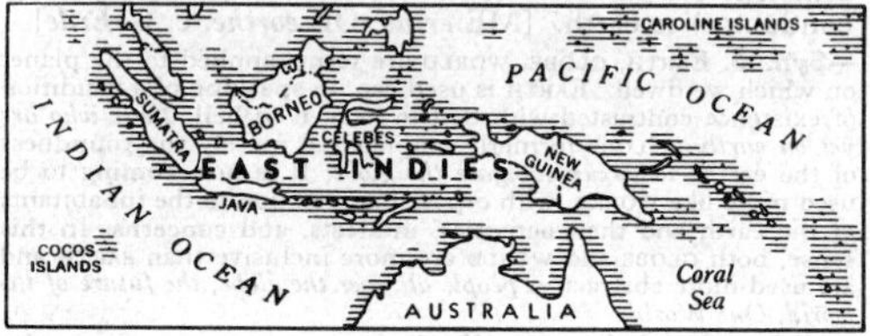

East Indies (def. 2)

easting (ēs′tĭng), *n.* **1.** eastward movement or deviation. **2.** the distance due east made on any course tending eastwards.

East Kilbride (kĭl brīd′), a town in Scotland, in N Lanark: new town, 1947. 31,972 (1961).

Eastleigh (ēst′lē), *n.* a town in England, in S Hampshire. 36,642 (1961).

East London, a seaport in the Republic of South Africa, in SE Cape of Good Hope province. with suburbs, 116,056 (1960).

East Lothian (lō′thyən), a county in SE Scotland. 52,653 pop. (1962); 267 sq. mi. *Co. town:* Haddington. Also, **Haddington.**

Eastman (ēst′mən), *n.* **George,** 1854–1932, U.S. inventor (in the field of photography) and philanthropist.

east-north-east (ēst′nôth′ēst′), *Navig., Survey.* —*n.* **1.** the point of the compass midway between east and north-east; 67° 30′ from north. —*adj.* **2.** lying or situated in this direction. —*adv.* **3.** to, in, or from this direction. *Abbrev.:* ENE. Also, *esp. Naut.*, **east-nor′-east** (ēst′nôr ēst′).

East Pakistan, a province of Pakistan, north of the Bay of Bengal. 50,840,235 pop. (1961); 54,501 sq. mi. *Cap.:* Dacca. See **Pakistan.**

East Prussia, a former province in NE Germany: until 1939 it was an exclave separated from Germany by the Polish Corridor; now divided between Poland and the Soviet Union. (Prior to the annexation of the Polish Corridor) 2,186,413 pop. (1939); 14,283 sq. mi. *Cap.:* Königsberg. German, **Ostpreussen.**

East Retford (rĕt′fəd), a town in England, in N Nottinghamshire. 17,792 (1961).

East Riding, an administrative division of Yorkshire. 527,292 pop. (1961); 1172 sq. mi. *Chief town:* Beverley.

east-south-east (ēst′south′ēst′), *Navig., Survey.* —*n.*

1. the point of the compass midway between east and south-east; 112° 30′ from north. —*adj.* **2.** lying or situated in this direction. —*adv.* **3.** to, in, or from this direction. *Abbrev.*: ESE. Also, *esp. Naut.*, **east-sou′-east** (ēst′sou ēst′).

East Suffolk, an administrative division of Suffolk. 342,696 pop. (1961); 871 sq. mi. *Chief town:* Ipswich.

East Sussex, an administrative division of Sussex. 664,669 pop. (1961); 829 sq. mi. *Chief town:* Lewes.

eastward (ēst′wəd), *adj.* **1.** moving, bearing, facing, or situated towards the east. —*adv.* **2.** eastwards.

eastwardly (ēst′wəd lĭ), *adj.* **1.** having an eastward direction or situation. **2.** coming from the east: *an eastwardly wind.* —*adv.* **3.** towards the east. **4.** from the east.

eastwards (ēst′wədz), *adv.* towards the east. Also, **eastward.**

easy (ē′zĭ), *adj.*, **easier, easiest,** *adv.*, *v.* **easied, easying.** —*adj.* **1.** not difficult; requiring no great labour or effort: *easy to read, an easy victory.* **2.** free from pain, discomfort, worry, or care: *he is resting easier this morning, easy in one's mind.* **3.** conducive to ease or comfort: *an easy stance.* **4.** fond of or given to ease; easygoing. **5.** not harsh or strict; lenient: *an easy master.* **6.** not burdensome or oppressive: *easy terms.* **7.** not difficult to influence; compliant. **8.** free from formality, constraint, or embarrassment: *easy style or manners.* **9.** not tight; fitting loosely: *an easy fit.* **10.** not forced or hurried; moderate: *an easy pace.* **11.** *Com.* **a.** (of a commodity) not difficult to obtain; in plentiful supply and (often) weak in price. **b.** (of the market) not characterized by eager demand. —*adv.* **12.** *Colloq.* in an easy manner; comfortably: *to go easy, take it easy.* —*v.i.*, *v.t.* **13.** *Rowing.* to cease rowing; stop the motion of (the oars). [ME *aisie*, t. OF, pp. of *aisier* EASE, v.] —**Syn. 2.** tranquil, untroubled, comfortable, contented. **8.** smooth, unconstrained. —**Ant. 1.** difficult.

easychair (ē′zĭ chēə′), *n.* an armchair in which to relax at ease.

easygoing (ē′zĭ gō′ĭng), *adj.* **1.** taking matters in an easy way; comfortably unconcerned. **2.** going easily, as a horse.

eat (ēt), *v.*, **ate** (ĕt, āt) or (*Archaic*) **eat** (ĕt, ēt); **eaten** (ē′tn) or (*Archaic*) **eat** (ĕt, ēt); **eating;** *n.* —*v.t.* **1.** to take into the mouth and swallow for nourishment; esp. to masticate and swallow, as solid food. **2.** to consume by or as by devouring. **3.** to ravage or devastate. **4.** to wear or waste away; corrode. **5.** to make (a hole, passage, etc.) as by gnawing or corrosion. **6.** *Colloq.* to cause to worry; trouble: *what's eating you?* **7. eat one's heart out,** to pine. **8. eat one's terms,** to study at the bar. **9. eat one's words,** to take back what one has said. —*v.i.* **10.** to consume food; take a meal. **11.** to make a way as by gnawing or corrosion. **12.** to be eatable; taste: *these pears eat well.* —*n.* **13.** (*pl.*) *Slang.* food. [ME *eten*, OE *etan*, c. G *essen*, akin to L *edere*, Gk *édein*]

eatable (ē′tə bl), *adj.* **1.** edible. —*n.* **2.** (*usually pl.*) an article of food.

eater (ē′tə), *n.* **1.** one who or that which eats. **2.** *Colloq.* a fruit suitable for eating, esp. raw.

eath (ēth), *Obs. or Dial.* —*adj.* **1.** easy. **2.** comfortable; free from pain. —*adv.* **3.** easily. [ME *ethe*, OE *ēathe* adv.]

eating (ē′tĭng), *n.* **1.** the act of one who or that which eats. **2.** food with reference to the quality perceived when eaten: *this fish is delicious eating.* —*adj.* **3.** suitable to be eaten, esp. raw.

eating house, a cafe or restaurant, esp. a cheap one.

eau (*Fr.* ȯ), *n.*, *pl.* **eaux** (ȯ), *French.* water. [F, g. L *aqua*]

eau de Cologne (ō′ də kə lōn′), **1.** cologne. **2.** (*cap.*) a trademark for a certain type of cologne. [F]

eau de Javelle (*Fr.* ȯ′də zhȧ vĕl′), *French.* Javel water.

eau de Nil (ō′də nēl′), a dull green colour. [F: lit., water of the Nile]

eau de vie (ō′də vē′; *Fr.* ȯd vē′), *French.* brandy, esp. the coarser and less purified varieties. [F: lit., water of life]

eaves (ēvz), *n.pl.* the overhanging lower edge of a roof. [ME *eves*, OE *efes*, c. OHG *obisa* hall]

eavesdrop (ēvz′drŏp′), *v.i.*, **-dropped, -dropping.** to listen clandestinely. [lit., be on the *eavesdrop* (of a house), earlier *eavesdrip* ground on which falls the drip from the eaves, OE *yfesdrype*] —**eaves′drop′per,** *n.*

ebb (ĕb), *n.* **1.** the reflux or falling of the tide (opposed to *flood* and *flow*). **2.** a flowing backwards or away; decline or decay. **3.** a point of decline: *his fortunes were at a low ebb.* —*v.i.* **4.** to flow back or away, as the water of a tide (opposed to *flow*). **5.** to decline or decay; waste or fade away: *his life is ebbing.* [ME *ebbe*, OE *ebba*, c. D *ebbe*, *eb*] —**Syn. 4.** subside, abate. **5.** sink, wane.

ebb tide, the reflux of the tide; the retiring tide.

Ebbw Vale (ĕb′o͞o vāl′), a town in NW Monmouthshire: coalmining, iron and tinplate industry. 28,350 (est. 1962).

Ebert (*Ger.* ē′bərt), *n.* **Friedrich** (*Ger.* frē′drĭKH), 1871–1925, first president of Germany, 1919–25.

ebionism (ĕb′ĭ ə nĭz′əm), *n.* an early Christian heresy which held Jesus to be the expected Messiah of the Jews.

ebionite (ĕb′ĭ ə nīt′), *n.* a believer in ebionism. [t. LL: m. s. *ebionita*, t. Heb. *ebyōn* poor, ? one poor in spirit]

Eblis (ĕb′lĭs), *n.* *Islamic Myth.* an evil spirit or devil, the chief of the wicked jinn. [t. Ar.: m. *Iblīs*, t. Gk: m. *diábolos* (see DEVIL); dropping of *di-* through confusion with Aram. *di-* of]

E-boat (ē′bōt′), *n.* a very fast unarmoured motor boat armed with torpedoes and guns. [short for *enemy boat*]

ebonist (ĕb′ə nĭst), *n.* a worker in ebony.

ebonite (ĕb′ə nīt′), *n.* vulcanite. [f. EBON(Y) + -ITE[1]]

ebonize (ĕb′ə nīz′), *v.t.*, **-nized, -nizing.** to stain or finish in imitation of ebony. Also, **ebonise.**

ebony (ĕb′ə nĭ), *n.*, *pl.* **-onies,** *adj.* —*n.* **1.** a hard, heavy, durable wood, most highly prized when black, from various tropical trees of the genus *Diospyros*, as *D. ebenum* of southern India and Ceylon, used for cabinetwork, etc. **2.** any tree yielding such wood. **3.** any of various similar woods or trees. —*adj.* **4.** made of ebony. **5.** like ebony; black. Also, *Poetic*, **eb′on.** [ME *hebenyf*, irreg. t. L: m. s. *hebeninus*, t. Gk: m. *ebéninos* made of ebony]

Eboracum (ē bŏ′rə kəm, ē′bô rä′kəm), *n.* ancient name of **York** (def. 4).

ebracteate (ĭ brăk′tĭ āt′, -tĭ ĭt), *adj.* *Bot.* without bracts.

ebracteolate (ĭ brăk′tĭ ə lāt′, -lĭt), *adj.* without bracteoles.

ebriety (ĭ brī′ə tĭ), *n.* the habit or state of drunkenness.

Ebro (ē′brō; *Sp.* ē′brȯ), *n.* a river flowing from N Spain SE to the Mediterranean. ab. 470 mi.

ebullience (ĭ bŭl′yəns), *n.* **1.** a boiling over; overflow. **2.** fervour; enthusiasm; excitement. Also, **ebul′liency.**

ebullient (ĭ bŭl′yənt), *adj.* **1.** seething or overflowing with fervour, enthusiasm, excitement, etc. **2.** boiling; bubbling like a boiling liquid. [t. L: s. *ēbulliens*, ppr., boiling out or up] —**ebul′liently,** *adv.*

ebullioscopy (ĭ bŭl′ĭ ŏs′kə pĭ), *n.* *Chem.* the method of determining the molecular weight of a substance by observing the boiling point of a solvent in which it is dissolved.

ebullition (ĕb′ə lĭsh′ən), *n.* **1.** a seething or overflowing, as of passion or feeling; an outburst: *ebullition of feeling.* **2.** an ebullient state. **3.** the act or process of boiling. **4.** a rushing forth of water, lava, etc., in a state of agitation. [t. L: s. *ēbullītio*]

eburnation (ē′bə nā′shən, ĕb′ə-), *n.* *Pathol.* a morbid change in bone, by which it becomes hard and dense, like ivory. [f. s. L *eburnus* of ivory + -ATION]

eburnean (ĭ bû′nĭ ən), *adj.* of or like ivory.

ec-, var. of **ex-**[3], before consonants, as in *eccentric.*

écarté (ā kä′tā; *Fr.* ē kȧr tē′), *n.* a game at cards for two persons. [t. F, prop. pp. of *écarter* discard]

Ecbatana (ĕk băt′ə nə), *n.* an ancient city in W Asia, the capital of ancient Media. Modern, **Hamadan.**

ecbolic (ĕk bŏl′ĭk), *adj.* *Med.* promoting labour; oxytocic.

ecce homo (ĕk′ā hō′mō), *Latin.* **1.** 'Behold the man!'—the words with which Pilate presented Christ, crowned with thorns, to his accusers. John 19:5. **2.** *Art.* a representation of Christ crowned with thorns.

eccentric (ĭk sĕn′trĭk), *adj.* **1.** deviating from the recognized or usual character, practice, etc.; irregular; peculiar; odd; queer: *eccentric conduct, an eccentric person.* **2.** not having the same centre, as two circles or spheres of which one is within the other or which intersect; not concentric. **3.** not situated in the centre, as an axis. **4.** *Mach.* having the axis or support away from the centre, as a wheel. **5.** *Astron.* deviating from a circular form, as an orbit. —*n.* **6.** one who or that which is unusual, peculiar, odd. **7.** *Mach.* a device for converting circular into reciprocating rectilinear motion, consisting of a disc fixed somewhat out of centre to a revolving shaft, and working freely in a surrounding collar (**eccentric strap**), to which a rod (**eccentric rod**) is attached. [t. LL: s. *eccentricus*, t. Gk: m. *ékkentros* out of the centre] —**eccen′trically,** *adv.* —**Ant. 1.** normal, ordinary.

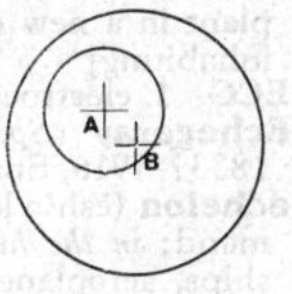

A B

Eccentric circles
A, Centre of small circle; B, Centre of large circle

eccentricity (ĕk′sĕn trĭs′ĭ tĭ), *n.*, *pl.* **-ties. 1.** an oddity or peculiarity, as of conduct. **2.** the quality of being eccentric. **3.** the amount by which anything is eccentric. **4.** *Mach.* the throw of an eccentric. **5.** *Maths.* the ratio of the distance from a point on a conic to a focus and the distance from that point to a directive. —**Syn. 2.** queerness, freakishness, aberration.

ecce signum (ĕk′ā sĭg′nōōm), *Latin.* behold the sign (or proof).
ecchymosis (ĕk′ĭ mō′sĭs), *n., pl.* **-ses** (-sēz). *Pathol.* a discoloration due to extravasation of blood, as in a bruise. [NL, t. Gk: m. *ekchýmōsis*, der. *ekchymoûsthai* extravasate blood] —**ecchymosed** (ĕk′ĭ mōzd′, -mōst′), **ecchymotic** (ĕk′ĭ mŏt′ĭk), *adj.*
Eccl., Ecclesiastes. Also, **Eccles.**
eccl., ecclesiastical. Also, **eccles.**
Eccles (ĕk′lz), *n.* a town in England, in S Lancashire. 43,173 (1961).
Eccles cake, a kind of flat cake with a dried fruit and spice filling.
ecclesia (ĭ klē′zyə), *n., pl.* **-siae** (-zĭ ē′). **1.** an assembly, esp. the popular assembly of ancient Athens. **2.** a congregation; a church. [t. L: assembly of the people, LL church, t. Gk: m. *ekklēsía*]
ecclesiarch (ĭ klē′zĭ äk′), *n.* **1.** a prince of the church, esp. in the Eastern Roman Empire. **2.** *Orthodox Church.* a sacristan.
ecclesiast (ĭ klē′zĭ ăst′), *n.* **1.** *Archaic.* an ecclesiastic. **2.** (*cap.*) the author of the Book of Ecclesiastes; the Preacher.
Ecclesiastes (ĭ klē′zĭ ăs′tēz), *n.* a book of the Old Testament traditionally ascribed to Solomon. [t. LL, t. Gk: lit., preacher]
ecclesiastic (ĭ klē′zĭ ăs′tĭk), *n.* **1.** a clergyman, or person in orders. —*adj.* **2.** ecclesiastical. [t. LL: s. *ecclēsiasticus*, t. Gk: m. *ekklēsiastikós* of the assembly or church]
ecclesiastical (ĭ klē′zĭ ăs′tĭ kl), *adj.* of or pertaining to the church or the clergy; churchly; clerical; not secular; not lay: *ecclesiastical discipline, affairs, ecclesiastical courts.* —**eccle′sias′tically,** *adv.*
ecclesiasticism (ĭ klē′zĭ ăs′tĭ sĭz′əm), *n.* **1.** ecclesiastical principles, practices, or spirit. **2.** devotion to the principles or interests of the church.
Ecclesiasticus (ĭ klē′zĭ ăs′tĭ kəs), *n.* the book of the Apocrypha called also 'The Wisdom of Jesus, the Son of Sirach'. [t. LL. See ECCLESIASTIC]
ecclesiolatry (ĭ klē′zĭ ŏl′ə trĭ), *n.* worship of the church; excessive reverence for churchly forms and traditions. [f. ECCLESI(A) + -(O)LATRY]
ecclesiology (ĭ klē′zĭ ŏl′ə jĭ), *n.* **1.** the science of church architecture and decoration. **2.** the study of church history and doctrine. [f. ECCLESI(A) + -(O)LOGY] —**ecclesiologic** (ĭ klē′zĭ ə lŏj′ĭk), **eccle′siolog′ical,** *adj.* —**eccle′siol′ogist,** *n.*
Ecclus., Ecclesiasticus (Apocrypha).
eccrinology (ĕk′rĭ nŏl′ə jĭ), *n.* the branch of physiology relating to secretions.
eccrisis (ĕk′rĭ sĭs), *n. Physiol.* the expulsion of waste matter from the body.
eccritic (ĕ krĭt′ĭk), *Physiol.* —*adj.* **1.** having the property of expelling waste matter. —*n.* **2.** something, as a medicine, that causes eccrisis.
ecdemic (ĕk dĕm′ĭk), *adj.* denoting or pertaining to a disease that originates outside the area in which it occurs (opposed to *epidemic* and *endemic*).
ecdysis (ĕk′dĭ sĭs), *n., pl.* **-ses** (-sēz′). the shedding or casting off of an outer coat or integument by snakes, crustaceans, etc. [NL, t. Gk: m. *ékdysis* a getting out]
ecesis (ĭ sē′sĭs), *n. Ecol.* the establishment of an immigrant plant in a new environment. [NL, t. Gk: m. *oíkēsis* an inhabiting]
ECG, 1. electrocardiogram. **2.** electrocardiograph.
Echegaray (*Sp.* ĕ chĕ gä räy′), *n.* **José** (*Sp.* KHō sĕ′), 1833?–1916, Spanish dramatist and statesman.
echelon (ĕsh′ə lŏn′; *Fr.* ĕsh lôɴ′), *n.* **1.** a level of command: *in the higher echelons.* **2.** a formation of troops, ships, aeroplanes, etc., in which groups are disposed in parallel lines, each to the right or left of the one in front, so that the whole presents the appearance of steps. **3.** one of the groups of a command so disposed. **4.** any step-like formation, esp. of people in movement. **5.** Also, **echelon grating.** *Physics.* a type of diffraction grating used in spectroscopy when high resolution is required: consists of a series of plates of equal thickness arranged in stepwise formation with a constant offset. —*v.t., v.i.* **6.** to form in echelon. [t. F: lit., ladder rung, der. *échelle* ladder, g. L *scāla* SCALE]
echidna (ĭ kĭd′nə), *n., pl.,* **-nas, -nae** (-nē). any of the spine-covered insectivorous monotreme mammals with claws and a slender snout, occurring in two genera, the curved-beaked echidna, *Zaglossus* (or *Proechidna*), of New Guinea, and the smaller, straight-beaked echidna, *Tachyglossus*, about 10 in. long, represented by several species in Australia, Tasmania, and southern New Guinea; spiny anteater. [NL, t. Gk: viper]

Echidna, *Tachyglossus aculeatus* (Ab. 10 in. long)

echinate (ĕk′ĭ nāt′), *adj.* spiny; bristly. Also, **ech′inat′ed.**
echinoccus (ĭ kī′nō kŏk′əs), *n. Pathol.* the bladder worm stage of the dog tapeworm.
echinoderm (ĭ kī′nə dûm′, ĕk′ĭ nə-), *n.* any of the *Echinodermata*, a phylum of marine animals such as starfishes, sea-urchins, sea-cucumbers, etc., having a radiating arrangement of parts and a body wall stiffened by calcareous pieces that may protrude as spines. [t. NL: m. *Echinodermata.* See ECHINUS, -DERM]
echinodermatous (ĭ kī′nō dû′mə təs), *adj.* belonging to or pertaining to the echinoderms.
echinoid (ĭ kī′noid, ĕk′ĭ noid′), *adj.* **1.** belonging to the *Echinoidea*, a class of echinoderms of rounded form covered with projecting spines, including the sea-urchins, etc. **2.** resembling a sea-urchin. —*n.* **3.** one of the *Echinoidea*; a sea-urchin. [f. ECHINU(S) + -OID]
echinus (ĭ kī′nəs), *n., pl.* **-ni** (-nī). **1.** a sea-urchin of the genus *Echinus.* **2.** *Archit.* a rounded moulding, as that supporting the abacus of a Doric capital. See diag. under **column.** [t. L, t. Gk: m. *echinos*, orig., hedgehog]
echo (ĕk′ō), *n., pl.* **echoes,** *v.,* **echoed, echoing.** —*n.* **1.** a repetition of sound, produced by the reflection of soundwaves from an obstructing surface. **2.** a sound heard again near its source, after reflection. **3.** any repetition or close imitation, as of the ideas or opinions of another. **4.** one who reflects or imitates another. **5.** a sympathetic response, as to sentiments expressed. **6.** (*cap.*) **a.** the personification of echo. **b.** *Class. Myth.* a mountain nymph who pined away for love of the beautiful youth Narcissus until only her voice remained. **7.** *Music.* **a.** a part (**echo organ**) or stop (**echo stop**) of a large organ for the production of echo-like effects. **b.** the manual controlling this. **8.** *Cards.* (esp. in bridge or whist) a signal, as by a card played, to a partner that the player wishes the suit continued. **9.** *Electronics.* the reflection of a radio wave such as is used in radar or the like. —*v.i.* **10.** to emit an echo; resound with an echo. **11.** to be repeated by or as by an echo. —*v.t.* **12.** to repeat by or as by an echo; emit an echo of: *the hall echoes even faint sounds.* **13.** to repeat or imitate the words, sentiments, etc., of (a person). **14.** to repeat or imitate (words, sentiments, etc.). [t. L, t. Gk: sound, echo] —**ech′oer,** *n.* —**ech′oless,** *adj.* —**ech′o-like′,** *adj.* —**Syn. 10, 12.** reverberate.
echo chamber, a room with sound-reflective walls, or a device, for creating echoes; used in sound recording, etc.
echoic (ĕ kō′ĭk), *adj.* **1.** echo-like. **2.** onomatopoeic.
echoism (ĕk′ō ĭz′əm), *n.* onomatopoeia.
echolalia (ĕk′ō lā′lyə), *n. Psychol.* an immediate, involuntary, and senseless repetition of words heard, occurring in some types of mental derangement. —**echolalic** (ĕk′ō lăl′ĭk), *adj.*
echolocation (ĕk′ō lō kā′shən), *n. Electronics.* the general method of locating objects by determining the time for an echo to return and the direction from which it returns, either by radar or by sonar.
echopraxia (ĕk′ō prăk′sĭ ə), *n. Psychol.* an immediate, involuntary, and senseless repetition of the movements of others, occurring in some types of mental derangement. Also, **echopraxis** (ĕk′ō prăk′sĭs). —**echopractic** (ĕk′ō-prăk′tĭk), *adj.*
echo ranging, a method of locating solid underwater objects by measuring the time required for the echo of a pulse of soundwaves to return to the point of observation.
echo sounder, a device for measuring the depth of water below a ship by observing the time taken for a pulse of soundwaves to reach the seabed and for its echo to return; sonar.
echo sounding, 1. a method of measuring the depth of water below a ship by the use of an echo sounder. **2.** a measurement so obtained.
echt (ĕkt; *Ger.* ĕKHt), *adj. German.* real; authentic; genuine.
Eckhart (*Ger.* ĕk′härt), *n.* **Johannes** (*Ger.* yō hä′nəs) ('*Meister Eckhart*'), *c.* 1260–1327?, the founder of German mysticism.
Eckington (ĕk′ĭng tən), *n.* a town in England, in NE Derbyshire. 14,614 (1961).
eclair (ā′klĕə), *n.* a light, finger-shaped cake having a cream or custard filling and coated with an icing. Also, *French,* **éclair** (*Fr.* ĕ klĕr′). [t. F: lit., lightning, der. *éclairer* lighten. Cf. L *exclārāre*]
éclaircissement (*Fr.* ĕ klĕr sēs mäɴ′), *n. French.* a clearing up of something obscure; an explanation.
eclampsia (ĭ klămp′sĭ ə), *n. Pathol.* a form of convulsions, esp. of a recurrent nature, as during pregnancy or

parturition. [NL, der. Gk *eklámpein* shine forth] —**eclamptic** (ĭ klămp′tĭk), *adj.*

eclat (ā′klä), *n.* **1.** brilliance of success, reputation, etc.: *the eclat of a great achievement.* **2.** ostentatious or elaborate display. **3.** applause; acclaim. Also, *French,* **éclat** (*Fr.* ė klȧ′). [t. F: fragment, also burst (of light, etc.)]

eclectic (ĕk lĕk′tĭk), *adj.* **1.** selecting; choosing from various sources. **2.** made up of what is selected from diverse sources. **3.** not following any one system, as of philosophy, medicine, etc., but selecting and using whatever is considered best in all systems. —*n.* **4.** one who follows an eclectic method, as in philosophy. [t. Gk: m. s. *eklektikós* selective] —**eclec′tically,** *adv.*

eclecticism (ĕk lĕk′tĭ sĭz′əm), *n.* **1.** the use or advocacy of an eclectic method. **2.** an eclectic system.

eclipse (ĭ klĭps′), *n., v.,* **eclipsed, eclipsing.** —*n.* **1.** *Astron.* **a.** the obscuration of the light of a satellite by the intervention of its primary planet between it and the sun, as in a **lunar eclipse** when the moon is partially or wholly within the earth's shadow. **b. solar eclipse,** the interception of the light of the sun by the intervention of the moon between it and the observer. **c.** (in an eclipsing binary system) the partial or complete interception of the light of one component by the other. **2.** any obscuration of light. **3.** any obscuration or overshadowing; loss of brilliance or splendour. —*v.t.* **4.** to cause to suffer eclipse: *the moon eclipses the sun.* **5.** to cast a shadow upon; obscure; darken. **6.** to make dim by comparison; surpass. [ME, t. OF, t. L: m. s. *eclipsis,* t. Gk: m. *ékleipsis,* lit., a failing] —**eclip′ser,** *n.*

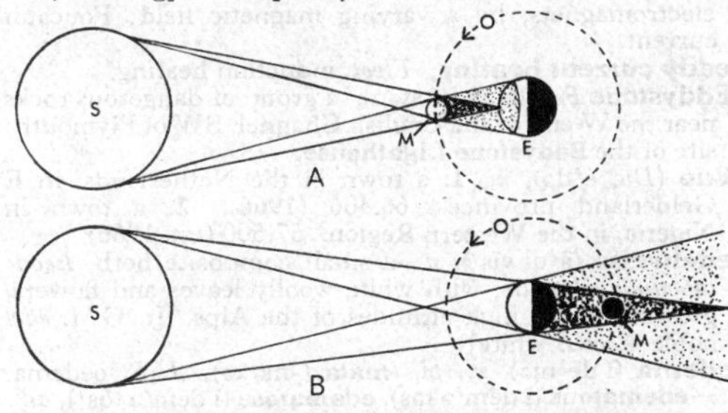

A, Solar eclipse; B, Lunar eclipse; S, Sun; E, Earth; M, Moon; O, Orbit of moon

eclipsing variable, *Astron.* a variable star whose changes in brightness are caused by periodic eclipses of two stars in a binary system.

ecliptic (ĭ klĭp′tĭk), *n.* **1.** the great circle formed by the intersection of the plane of the earth's orbit with the celestial sphere; the apparent annual path of the sun in the heavens. **2.** an analogous great circle on a terrestrial globe. —*adj.* Also, **eclip′tical. 3.** pertaining to an eclipse. **4.** pertaining to the ecliptic. [t. L: s. *eclīpticus,* t. Gk: m. *ekleiptikós* of or caused by an eclipse. See ECLIPSE] —**eclip′tically,** *adv.*

Diagram of ecliptic A, Ecliptic; B, Celestial equator; C, Orbit of earth; D, Sun

eclogite (ĕk′lə jīt′), *n.* a rock consisting of granular aggregate of green pyroxene and red garnet, often also containing cyanite, silvery mica, quartz, and pyrite. [f. s. Gk *eklogḗ* selection + -ITE[1]]

eclogue (ĕk′lŏg), *n.* a short poem, esp. pastoral or idyllic. [t. L: m. *ecloga,* t. Gk: m. *eklogḗ* a selection]

ecol., ecology.

école (*Fr.* ė kôl′), *n. French.* school.

ecology (ē kŏl′ə jĭ), *n.* **1.** the branch of biology which treats of the relations between organisms and their environment; bionomics. **2.** the branch of sociology concerned with the spacing of people and of institutions and their resulting interdependence. [f. m. Gk *oîko(s)* house + -LOGY] —**ecological** (ē′kə lŏj′ĭ kl), **ec′olog′ic,** *adj.* —**ec′olog′ically,** *adv.* —**ecologist** (ē kŏl′ə jĭst), *n.*

econ., **1.** economic. **2.** economics. **3.** economy.

econometrics (ĭ kŏn′ə mĕt′rĭks), *n.* the analysis by statistical and mathematical methods of economic data, theories, etc. —**econ′omet′ric, econ′omet′rical,** *adj.* —**econometrician** (ĭ kŏn′ə mə trĭsh′ən), **econ′omet′rist,** *n.*

economic (ē′kə nŏm′ĭk, ĕk′ə-), *adj.* **1.** pertaining to the production, distribution, and use of income and wealth. **2.** of or pertaining to the science of economics. **3.** pertaining to an economy, or system of organization or operation, esp. of the process of production. **4.** pertaining to the means of living; utilitarian: *economic entomology, botany, etc.* **5.** *Colloq.* economical. **6.** *Colloq.* cheap. [t. L: m. s. *oeconomicus,* t. Gk: m. *oikonomikós,* der. *oikonomía.* See ECONOMY]

economical (ē′kə nŏm′ĭ kl, ĕk′ə-), *adj.* **1.** avoiding waste or extravagance; thrifty. **2.** economic.

—**Syn. 1.** sparing, provident. ECONOMICAL, THRIFTY, FRUGAL imply careful and sparing use of resources. ECONOMICAL implies prudent planning in the disposition of resources so as to avoid unnecessary waste or expense: *economical in budgeting household expenditures.* THRIFTY is a stronger word than ECONOMICAL, and adds to it the idea of industry and successful management: *a thrifty housewife looking for bargains.* FRUGAL emphasizes being sparing, sometimes excessively sparing, esp. in such matters as food, dress, or the like: *frugal almost to the point of being stingy.* —**Ant. 1.** wasteful, lavish.

economically (ē′kə nŏm′ĭk lĭ, ĕk′ə-), *adv.* **1.** with economy; with frugality or moderation. **2.** as regards the efficient use of income and wealth.

economics (ē′kə nŏm′ĭks, ĕk′ə-), *n.* **1.** the science treating of the production, distribution, and consumption of goods and services, or the material welfare of mankind; political economy. **2.** (*construed as pl.*) economically significant aspects.

economist (ĭ kŏn′ə mĭst), *n.* **1.** one versed in the science of economics. **2.** an economical person.

economize (ĭ kŏn′ə mīz′), *v.,* **-mized, -mizing.** —*v.t.* **1.** to manage economically; use sparingly or frugally. —*v.i.* **2.** to practise economy; avoid waste or extravagance. Also, **econ′omise′.** —**econ′omiza′tion,** *n.* —**econ′omiz′er,** *n.*

economy (ĭ kŏn′ə mĭ), *n., pl.* **-mies. 1.** thrifty management; frugality in the expenditure or consumption of money, materials, etc. **2.** an act or means of thrifty saving; a saving. **3.** the management, or science of management, of the resources of a community, etc., with a view to productiveness and avoidance of waste: *national economy.* **4.** the disposition or regulation of the parts or functions of any organic whole; an organized system or method. **5.** the efficient, sparing, and concise use of something: *economy of effort.* **6.** *Theol.* **a.** the divine plan for man, his creation, redemption, final beatitude. **b.** the method of divine administration, as at a particular time or for a particular race. **7.** *Archaic.* the management of household affairs. [t. L: m. s. *oeconomia,* t. Gk: m. *oikonomía* management of a household or of the state] —**Syn. 1.** thriftiness, thrift, saving.

écossaise (ĕk′ŏ sĕz′, ā′kŏ-), *n.* **1.** a kind of country dance in quick 2/4 time. **2.** the music for such a dance. [F: Scottish (fem.)]

ecotone (ē′kə tōn′), *n.* the transition zone between two different plant communities, as that between forest and prairie. [f. Gk: m. *oîko(s)* home + m. s. *tónos* stress]

ecotype (ē′kə tīp′, ĕk′ə-), *n. Ecol.* a subspecies which has become specially adapted to certain environmental conditions.

écraseur (ā′krä zû′; *Fr.* ė krȧ zœr′), *n.* a surgical instrument used in an operation where haemorrhage is feared, as in removing certain types of tumours, consisting of a chain or wire loop which is gradually tightened. [t. F, der. *écraser* crush]

ecru (ĕk′rōō, ā′krōō), *adj.* **1.** very light brown in colour, as raw silk, unbleached linen, etc. —*n.* **2.** ecru colour. Also, *French,* **écru** (*Fr.* ė krʏ′). [F: raw, unbleached, f. *é-* thoroughly (g. L *ex-* EX-[1]) + *cru* raw, g. L *crūdus*]

ECSC, European Coal and Steel Community.

ecstasy (ĕk′stə sĭ), *n., pl.* **-sies. 1.** overpowering emotion or exaltation; a sudden access of intense feeling. **2.** rapturous delight. **3.** the frenzy of poetic inspiration. **4.** mental transport or rapture from the contemplation of divine things. [ME *extasie,* t. OF, t. ML: m. *extasis,* t. Gk: m. *ékstasis* extension] —**Syn. 1.** rapture.

ecstatic (ĕk stăt′ĭk), *adj.* **1.** of, pertaining to, or characterized by ecstasy. **2.** subject to or in a state of ecstasy; transported; rapturous. —*n.* **3.** one subject to fits of ecstasy. **4.** (*pl.*) ecstatic transports; raptures. —**ecstat′ically,** *adv.*

ECT, electroconvulsive therapy.

ecthlipsis (ĕk thlĭp′sĭs), *n., pl.* **-ses** (-sēz). the suppression of a sound, esp. (in Latin prosody) of a final syllable ending in *m* before a vowel or *h.*

ecthyma (ĕk′thĭ mə), *n. Vet. Sci.* a contagious virus disease of sheep and goats marked by vesicular and pustular lesions on the lips, and occasionally affecting man; sore mouth.

ecto-, a prefix (chiefly in biological words) meaning 'outside', 'outer', 'external', 'lying upon' (opposed to *endo- ento-*), as in *ectoderm.* [t. Gk: m. *ekto-,* comb. form of *ektós* outside]

ectoblast (ĕk′tō blăst′), *n. Embryol.* the prospective ectoderm, before the separation of the germ layers. —**ec′toblas′tic,** *adj.*

ectoderm (ĕk′tō dûm′), *n. Embryol.* the outer germ layer in the embryo of any metazoan. —ec′toder′mal, ec′toder′mic, *adj.*

ectogenous (ĕk tŏj′ĭ nəs), *adj.* (of bacteria) able to live and develop outside the host. —**ectogenesis** (ĕk′tō jĕn′ĭ sĭs), *n.*

ectomere (ĕk′tō mĭə′), *n. Embryol.* any one of the blastomeres which participate in the development of the ectoderm.

ectomorph (ĕk′tə môf′), *n. Physiol.* a person of ectomorphic type.

ectomorphic (ĕk′tə mô′fĭk), *adj. Physiol.* having a thinly built body characterized by the relative prominence of structures developed from the embryonic ectoderm (distinguished from *endomorphic, mesomorphic*).

-ectomy, a combining form attached to the name of a part of the body and producing a word meaning an operation for the excision of that part. [f. *ec-* (t. Gk: m. *ek-*, prefix form of *ek, ex-* out of) + -TOMY]

ectoparasite (ĕk′tō păr′ə sīt′), *n.* an external parasite (opposed to *endoparasite*).

ectopia (ĕk tō′pyə), *n. Pathol.* the morbid displacement of parts.

ectopic (ĕk tŏp′ĭk), *adj. Pathol.* in an abnormal position or place, as in pregnancy outside the womb, talipes, etc. [f. Gk *éktop(os)* displaced + -IC]

ectoplasm (ĕk′tə plăz′əm), *n.* **1.** *Biol.* the outer portion of the cytoplasm in the cell of a protozoan or vegetable cell (opposed to *endoplasm*). **2.** *Spiritualism.* the supposed emanation from the body of a medium. —**ec′toplas′mic,** *adj.*

ectosarc (ĕk′tə säk′), *n. Biol.* the ectoplasm of a protozoan (opposed to *endosarc*).

ectosteal (ĕk′tō stēl′), *adj. Anat.* pertaining to or situated on the outside of the bone.

ectostosis (ĕk′tŏs tō′sĭs), *n. Anat.* the ossification of cartilage proceeding from without inward. [NL; f. ECT(O)- + *ostosis* as in EXOSTOSIS]

ectotrophic (ĕk′tō trŏf′ĭk, -trō′fĭk), *adj. Bot.* of, denoting, or pertaining to a type of mycorrhizal association, found particularly in forest trees, in which the fungal hyphae form a dense layer on the surface of the roots.

ectozoon (ĕc′tō zō′ŏn), *n., pl.* **-zoa** (-zō′ə). epizoon.

ectype (ĕk′tīp′), *n.* a reproduction or copy (opposed to *prototype*). [t. Gk: m. s. *éktypos* wrought in relief, formed in outline] —**ectypal** (ĕk′tĭ pl), *adj.*

écu (*Fr.* ĕ kʏ′), *n., pl.* **écus** (ĕ kʏ′), *French.* **1.** the shield carried by a mounted man-at-arms in the Middle Ages. **2.** any of several gold and silver coins of France from the 14th century until 1794. [F: orig., shield, g. L *scūtum*]

Ecua., Ecuador.

Ecuador (ĕk′wə dô′), *n.* a republic in NW South America. 4,585,472 pop. (est. 1962); 104,510 sq. mi. *Cap.:* Quito. See map under **Galápagos Islands.** —**Ec′uado′rian,** *adj., n.*

ecumenical (ē′kyŏŏ mĕn′ĭ kl), *adj.* **1.** general; universal. **2.** pertaining to the whole Christian Church. **3.** tending or intended to promote Christian unity, esp. the unification of all Christian Churches: *the ecumenical movement.* Also, **ec′umen′ic, œcumenical.** [f. (m.) s. LL *oecumenicus* (t. Gk: m. *oikoumenikós* general, universal) + -AL[1]] —**ec′umen′ically,** *adv.*

Ecumenical Council, *Rom. Cath. Ch.* a conclave representative of the entire Church convened at a specific date and place to consider important questions of dogma and practice and to reach a conclusion binding upon the entire Church.

ecumenicalism (ē′kyŏŏ mĕn′ĭ kə lĭz′əm), *n.* the doctrines and practices of the ecumenical movement, esp. among Protestants in the 19th and 20th centuries.

eczema (ĕk′sĭ mə), *n. Pathol.* an inflammatory disease of the skin attended with itching and the exudation of serous matter. [t. NL, t. Gk: a cutaneous eruption] —**eczematous** (ĕk sĕm′ə təs), *adj.*

-ed[1], a suffix forming the past tense, as in *he crossed the river.* [OE *-de, -ede, -ode, -ade*]

-ed[2], a suffix forming: **1.** the past participle, as in *he had crossed the river.* **2.** participial adjectives indicating a condition or quality resulting from the action of the verb, as *inflated balloons.* [OE *-ed, -od, -ad*]

-ed[3], a suffix serving to form adjectives from nouns, as *bearded, moneyed, tender-hearted.* [OE *-ede*]

ed., 1. edited. **2.** edition. **3.** *pl.* **eds.** editor.

edacious (ĭ dā′shəs), *adj.* devouring; voracious; consuming. [f. EDACI(TY) + -OUS] —**eda′ciously,** *adv.* —**eda′ciousness,** *n.*

edacity (ĭ dăs′ĭ tĭ), *n.* good appetite. [t. L: m. s. *edācitas* gluttony]

Edam (ē′dăm; *Du.* ĕ dŏm′), *n.* a hard, round, fine-flavoured yellow cheese, usually coloured red on the outside.

edaphic (ĭ dăf′ĭk), *adj. Ecol.* due to soil or topography rather than climate. [f. s. Gk *édaphos* bottom + -IC] —**edaph′ically,** *adv.*

EDC, (formerly) European Defence Community.

Edda (ĕd′ə), *n., pl.* **Eddas. 1. Elder** or **Poetic** or **Verse Edda,** a collection of old Icelandic poems on mythical and religious subjects, erroneously ascribed to Saemund Sigfusson (about 1055–1133). **2. Younger** or **Prose Edda,** an old Icelandic work, compiled and partly written by Snorri Sturluson (1179–1241), containing ancient myths and legends of Scandinavia, rules and theories of verse-making, poems, etc. [t. Icel.] —**Eddaic** (ĕ dā′ĭk), **Ed′dic,** *adj.*

Eddington (ĕd′ĭng tən), *n.* **Sir Arthur Stanley,** 1882–1944, English astronomer, physicist, and author.

eddish (ĕd′ĭsh), *n. Obs. or Dial.* grass pasture.

eddo (ĕd′ō), *n., pl.* **eddoes** (ĕd′ōz). the edible root of the taro, or of any of several related plants; dasheen. [? t. Ibo: m. *edè*]

eddy (ĕd′ĭ), *n., pl.* **eddies,** *v.,* **eddied, eddying.** —*n.* **1.** a current at variance with the main current in a stream of liquid or gas, esp. one having a rotary or whirling motion. **2.** any similar current, as of air, dust, fog, etc. —*v.i., v.t.* **3.** to move or whirl in eddies. [f. OE: *ed-* turning + *ēa* stream. Cf. Icel. *idha*]

Eddy (ĕd′ĭ), *n.* **Mrs Mary Baker** (*Mrs Glover, Mrs Patterson*), 1821–1910, U.S. religious leader: founder of the Christian Science Church.

eddy current, *Elect.* an electric current induced in a mass of conducting material, esp. the iron cores of electromagnets, by a varying magnetic field; Foucault current.

eddy current heating, *Elect.* induction heating.

Eddystone Rocks (ĕd′ĭ stən), a group of dangerous rocks near the W end of the English Channel, SW of Plymouth: site of the **Eddystone Lighthouse.**

Ede (*Du.* ė′də), *n.* **1.** a town in the Netherlands, in E Gelderland province. 66,406 (1966). **2.** a town in Nigeria, in the Western Region. 57,500 (est. 1966).

edelweiss (ā′dl vīs′), *n.* a small composite herb, *Leontopodium alpinum,* with white woolly leaves and flowers, growing in the high altitudes of the Alps. [t. G: f. *edel* noble + *weiss* white]

edema (ĭ dē′mə), *n., pl.* **-mata** (-mə tə). *U.S.* oedema. —**edematous** (ĭ dĕm′ə təs), **edamatose** (ĭ dĕm′ə tōs′), *adj.*

Eden (ē′dn), *n.* **(Robert) Anthony** (*Earl of Avon*), born 1897, British foreign minister 1935–38, 1940–45, 1951–55; prime minister 1955–57.

Eden (ē′dn), *n.* **1.** the garden which was the first home of Adam and Eve. **2.** any delightful region or abode. **3.** a state of perfect happiness. [t. Heb.: lit., pleasure, delight] —**Edenic** (ē dĕn′ĭk), *adj.*

edentate (ē dĕn′tāt), *adj.* **1.** belonging or pertaining to the *Edentata,* an order of New World mammals, comprising the armadillos, the sloths, and the South American anteaters. **2.** toothless. —*n.* **3.** an edentate mammal. [t. L: m. s. *ēdentātus,* pp., deprived of teeth]

EDES, Hellenic National Democratic Army, a conservative Greek resistance coalition in World War II.

Edessa (ĭ dĕs′ə), *n.* an ancient city in NW Mesopotamia, an early centre of Christianity; the capital of a principality under the Crusaders. Modern, **Urfa.**

Edgar (ĕd′gə), *n.* A.D. 944–975, king of Northumbria and Mercia 957–975, king of Wessex 959–975. Also, **Eadgar.**

Edgar Atheling (ĕd′gər ăth′ĭ lĭng), 1050?–1125?, grandson of Edmund II; Saxon pretender to the throne of England from 1066.

edge (ĕj), *n., v.,* **edged, edging.** —*n.* **1.** the border or part adjacent to a line of division; a brim or margin: *the horizon's edge.* **2.** a brink or verge: *the edge of a precipice.* **3.** one of the narrow surfaces of a thin, flat object: *a book with gilt edges.* **4.** the line in which two surfaces of a solid object meet: *the edge of a box.* **5.** the thin, sharp side of the blade of a cutting instrument or weapon. **6.** the sharpness proper to a blade. **7.** sharpness or keenness of language, argument, appetite, desire, etc. **8.** *Dial.* a hill or cliff. **9. have the edge,** *Colloq.* to have the advantage (usually fol. by *on* or *over*). **10. on edge, a.** acutely uncomfortable or sensitive: *nerves on edge, to set the teeth on edge.* **b.** eager or impatient. —*v.t.* **11.** to put an edge on; sharpen. **12.** to machine to a straight line or a desired curve. **13.** to provide with an edge or border; border. **14.** to move edgeways; move or force gradually: *to edge one's way through a crowd, to edge a rival off the track.* —*v.i.* **15.** to move edgeways; advance gradually. [ME *egge,* OE *ecg,* c. G *Ecke,* Icel. *egg;* akin to L *aciēs* edge, point] —**edged,** *adj.* —**edge′less,** *adj.* —**edg′er,** *n.*

—**Syn. 1.** EDGE, BORDER, MARGIN refer to a boundary. An EDGE is the boundary line of a surface or plane: *the edge of a table.* BORDER is the boundary of a surface or the strip adjacent to it, inside or out: *a border of lace.* MARGIN is a limited strip, generally unoccupied, at the extremity of an area: *the margin of a page.*

edgebone (ĕj′bōn′), *n.* the aitchbone.

Edgehill (ĕj′hĭl′), *n.* a hill in England, in S Warwickshire: first battle of Civil War, 1642.

edge tool, a tool with a cutting edge.

edgeways (ĕj′wāz′), *adv.* **1.** with the edge forwards; in the direction of the edge. **2. get a word in edgeways,** to succeed in forcing one's way into an animated conversation or in making a remark when a voluble person is for a moment silent. Also, **edgewise** (ĕj′wīz′).

Edgeworth (ĕj′wûth′), *n.* **Maria,** 1767–1849, English novelist.

edging (ĕj′ĭng), *n.* **1.** the act of one who edges. **2.** something that serves for an edge; trimming for edges.

Edgware (ĕj′wĕə′), *n.* a NW suburb of London, in the outer borough of Barnet.

edgy (ĕj′ĭ), *adj.* **1.** sharp-edged; sharply defined, as outlines. **2.** on edge; irritable. **—edg′iness,** *n.*

edh (ĕth), *n.* eth.

edible (ĕd′ĭ bl), *adj.* **1.** fit to be eaten as food; eatable; esculent. **—***n.* **2.** (*usually pl.*) anything edible; an eatable. [t. LL: m. s. *edibilis,* der. L *edere* eat] **—ed′ibil′ity, ed′ibleness,** *n.*

edict (ē′dĭkt), *n.* **1.** a decree issued by a sovereign or other authority. **2.** any authoritative proclamation or command. [t. L: s. *ēdictum,* prop. pp. neut., declared, proclaimed; r. ME *edit,* t. OF] **—edic′tal,** *adj.* **—edic′tally,** *adv.*

edification (ĕd′ĭ fĭ kā′shən), *n.* **1.** the act of edifying. **2.** the state of being edified. **3.** moral improvement. **—ed′ifica′tory,** *adj.*

edifice (ĕd′ĭ fĭs), *n.* a building, esp. one of large size or imposing appearance: *a spacious edifice of brick.* [t. F, t. L: m. s. *aedificium* building] **—edificial** (ĕd′ĭ fĭsh′əl), *adj.* **—Syn.** See **building.**

edify (ĕd′ĭ fī′), *v.t.,* **-fied, -fying.** to build up or increase the faith, morality, etc., of; instruct or benefit, esp. morally. [ME *edifie(n),* t. OF: m. *edifier,* t. L: m. s. *aedificāre* build] **—ed′ifi′er,** *n.* **—ed′ify′ingly,** *adv.*

edile (ē′dīl), *n.* aedile.

Edinburgh (ĕd′ĭn bə rə, -brə), *n.* **1. Prince Philip, Duke of,** born 1921, husband of Queen Elizabeth II. **2.** the capital of Scotland and county town of Midlothian, in the N part. 468,378 (1961). **3.** former name of **Midlothian.**

Edirne (*Turk.* ĕ dĕr′nĕ), *n.* a city in European Turkey. 46,264 (1965). Formerly, **Adrianople.**

Edison (ĕd′ĭ sən), *n.* **Thomas Alva** (ăl′və), 1847–1931, U.S. inventor, esp. of electrical devices.

Edison accumulator, an accumulator in which the positive plate is nickel hydroxide and the negative plate is iron; the electrolyte is a 20 per cent solution of potassium hydroxide; Ni-Fe accumulator.

edit (ĕd′ĭt), *v.t.* **1.** to supervise or direct the preparation of (a newspaper, magazine, etc.); act as editor of; direct the policies of. **2.** to collect, prepare, and arrange (materials) for publication. **3.** to revise and correct. **4.** to make (a cinema or television film, sound recording, or any part of a film or recording) from rushes, by cutting and arranging them, synchronizing soundtrack, etc. [partly t. L: s. *ēditus,* pp., given forth; partly back-formation from EDITOR]

edit., 1. edited. 2. edition. 3. editor.

edition (ĭ dĭsh′ ən), *n.* **1.** one of a number of printings of the same book, newspaper, etc., issued at different times, and differing from another by alterations, additions, etc. (as distinguished from *impression*). **2.** the format in which a literary work is published: *a one-volume edition of Shakespeare.* **3.** the whole number of impressions or copies of a book, newspaper, etc., printed from one set of type at one time. **4.** *Colloq.* any version of anything, esp. one resembling an earlier version. [t. L: s. *ēditio*]

editor (ĕd′ĭ tə), *n.* **1.** one who edits written material for publication. **2.** a person responsible for the content of a newspaper, magazine, or the like, usually one who presents his opinion or comment in the name of the paper. **3.** a person responsible for one aspect of a newspaper's activities: *fashion editor.* **4.** a person responsible for the content and sometimes the policy of the publications of a publishing house. **5.** one who edits films, recordings, etc. [t. L]

editorial (ĕd′ĭ tô′rĭ əl), *n.* **1.** an article, in a newspaper or the like, presenting the opinion or comment of an editor or a leader-writer in the name of the paper; a leader (def. 5). **—***adj.* **2.** of or pertaining to an editor. **3.** written by an editor.

editorialize (ĕd′ĭ tô′rĭ ə līz′), *v.i.,* **-lized, -lizing.** to set forth one's position or opinion on some subject in, or as if in, an editorial. Also, **editorialise.**

editorially (ĕd′ĭ tô′rĭ ə lĭ), *adv.* **1.** in an editorial manner; as an editor does. **2.** in an editorial.

editorship (ĕd′ĭ tə shĭp′), *n.* **1.** the office or function of an editor. **2.** editorial direction.

Edmonton (ĕd′mən tən), *n.* **1.** a city in SW Canada: the capital of Alberta; Alberta university founded 1906. 357,696 (1965). **2.** a district of the N outer London borough of Enfield.

Edmund I (ĕd′mənd), A.D. 921?–946, king of England 940–946.

Edmund II (′*Ironside*′), A.D. 980?–1016, king of England in 1016.

Edom (ē′dəm), *n.* **1.** Esau, the brother of Jacob. **2.** Greek, **Idumaea** or **Idumea.** an ancient region between the Dead Sea and the Gulf of Aqaba, bordering ancient Palestine. **3.** the nation living there.

Edomite (ē′də mīt′), *n.* a descendant of Esau or Edom. Num. 20:14–21.

EDP, Electronic Data Processing.

eds, editors.

E.D.T., Eastern daylight time. Also, **e.d.t.**

educ., 1. educated. 2. education. 3. educational.

educable (ĕd′yo͝o kə bl), *adj.* capable of being educated. **—ed′ucabil′ity,** *n.*

educate (ĕd′yo͝o kāt′), *v.t.,* **-cated, -cating. 1.** to develop the faculties and powers of by teaching, instruction, or schooling; qualify by instruction or training for a particular calling, practice, etc.; train: *to educate someone for something or to do something.* **2.** to provide education for; send to school. **3.** to develop or train (the ear, taste, etc.). [t. L: m. s. *ēducātus,* pp., brought up, trained, educated] **—Syn. 1.** teach, instruct, school, drill, indoctrinate.

educated (ĕd′yo͝o kā′tĭd), *adj.* **1.** having undergone education. **2.** characterized by or displaying qualities of culture and learning.

education (ĕd′yo͝o kā′shən), *n.* **1.** the act or process of educating; the imparting or acquisition of knowledge, skill, etc.; systematic instruction or training. **2.** the result produced by instruction, training, or study. **3.** the science or art of teaching; pedagogics.

—Syn. 1. instruction, schooling, tuition. EDUCATION, TRAINING imply a discipline and development by means of study and learning. EDUCATION is the development of the special and general abilities of the mind (learning to know): *a liberal education.* TRAINING is practical education (learning to do) or practice, usually under supervision, in some art, trade, or profession: *training in art, teacher training.* **2.** learning, knowledge, enlightenment. EDUCATION, CULTURE are often used interchangeably to mean the results of schooling. EDUCATION, however, suggests chiefly the information acquired. CULTURE is a mode of thought and feeling encouraged by education (the process and the acquirement). It suggests an aspiration towards, and an appreciation of, high intellectual and aesthetic ideals: *the level of culture in a country depends upon the education of its people.*

educational (ĕd′yo͝o kā′shə nəl), *adj.* **1.** pertaining to education. **2.** tending to educate. **—ed′uca′tionally,** *adv.*

educationist (ĕd′yo͝o kā′shə nĭst), *n.* an expert in theories and methods of education. Also, **ed′uca′tionalist.**

educative (ĕd′yo͝o kə tĭv), *adj.* **1.** serving to educate: *educative knowledge.* **2.** pertaining to education: *the educative process.*

educator (ĕd′yo͝o kā′tə), *n.* one who or that which educates; a teacher. [t. L]

educatory (ĕd′yo͝o kə trĭ, ĕd′yo͝o kā′tə rĭ), *adj.* serving to educate.

educe (ĭ dyo͞os′), *v.t.,* **educed, educing.** to draw forth or bring out; elicit; develop. [t. L: m. s. *ēdūcere* lead forth, bring up] **—educ′ible,** *adj.*

educt (ē′dŭkt), *n.* **1.** something educed. **2.** *Chem.* one substance extracted unchanged from another (distinguished from a *product*). [t. L: s. *ēductus,* pp., educed]

eduction (ĭ dŭk′shən), *n.* **1.** the act of educing. **2.** something educed. **3.** *Mech.* the exhaust from a steam engine, or sometimes from an internal-combustion engine.

eductive (ĭ dŭk′tĭv), *adj.* serving to educe.

eductor (ĭ dŭk′tə), *n.* one who or that which educes.

edulcorate (ĭ dul′kə rāt′), *v.t.,* **-rated, -rating.** *Chem., Obs.* to free from acids, salts, or impurities by washing; purify. [t. L: m. s. *ēdulcorātus,* pp., sweetened] **—edul′cora′tion,** *n.*

Edward (ĕd′wəd), *n.* **1.** (′*the Black Prince*′), Prince of Wales 1330–76; English military commander (son of Edward III). **2.** a lake in central Africa between Uganda and the Republic of the Congo: a headwater of the Nile. ab. 830 sq. mi.

Edward I (′*Edward Longshanks*′), 1239–1307, king of England 1272–1307 (son of Henry III).

Edward II, 1284–1327, king of England 1307–27 (son of Edward I).

Edward III, 1312–77, king of England 1327–77 (son of Edward II).

Edward IV, 1442–83, king of England 1461–70 and 1471–83 (successor of Henry VI, son of Richard, Duke of York, and first king of the house of York).

Edward V, 1470–83, king of England in 1483; murdered in the Tower of London (son of Edward IV).

Edward VI, 1537–53, king of England 1547–53 (son of Henry VIII and Jane Seymour).

Edward VII (*Albert Edward*), 1841–1910, king of England England 1901–10 (son of Queen Victoria).

Edward VIII (*Duke of Windsor*), born 1894, king of England in 1936 (son of George V and brother of George VI).

Edwardian (ĕd wô′dyən), *adj.* pertaining to the time of Edward VII, a period now often regarded as ornate, opulent, and leisurely. **—Edward′ianism,** *n.*

Edwards (ĕd′wədz), *n.* **Jonathan,** 1703–58, colonial American clergyman and metaphysician.

Edward the Confessor, *c.* 1004–66, king of England 1042–66.

Edwin (ĕd′wĭn), *n.* *c.* 585–633, king of Northumbria 617–33.

-ee, a suffix of nouns denoting one who is the object of some action, or undergoes or receives something (often as opposed to the person acting), as in *assignee, donee, employee.* [t. F: m. -*é*, pp. ending, g. L -*ātus* -ATE¹]

E.E., Early English.

e.e., errors excepted.

EEC, European Economic Community; the Common Market.

EEG, 1. electroencephalogram. **2.** electroencephalograph.

eel (ēl), *n.* **1.** an elongate, snakelike, apodal fish, esp. of the genus *Anguilla*, as *A. anguilla*, of European fresh waters. **2.** any of several similar but unrelated fishes, as the lamprey. [ME *ele*, d. OE *ēl*, r. OE *ǣl*, c. D *aal*, G *Aal*] **—eel′-like′,** *adj.*

eelgrass (ēl′gräs′), *n.* any of several marine or sweet-water plants with ribbon-like leaves, as *Zostera marina* and *Vallisneria spiralis.*

eelpout (ēl′pout′), *n.* **1.** any of the blenny-like marine fishes constituting the family *Zoarcidae.* **2.** the burbot. [OE *ǣlepūte*]

eelspear (ēl′spĭə′), *n.* a broad-pronged instrument used for catching eels.

eelworm (ēl′wûm′), *n.* any small nematode worm of the family *Anguillulidae*, including the minute vinegar eel, *Anguillula aceti.*

eely (ē′lĭ), *adj.* eel-like; wriggling.

e'en¹ (ēn), *adv. Poetic.* even.

e'en² (ēn), *n. Poetic.* evening.

e'er (ēə), *adv. Poetic.* ever.

-eer, a suffix of nouns denoting one who is concerned with, or employed in connection with, or busies himself with something, as in *auctioneer, engineer, profiteer.* Also, **-ier.** [t. F: m. -*ier*, g. L -*ārius.* See -ARY¹ and -ER²]

eerie (ĭə′rĭ), *adj.*, **eerier, eeriest.** inspiring fear; weird, strange, or uncanny. [ME *eri*, d. var. of obs. *argh*, OE *earg* cowardly, c. G *arg* bad] **—ee′rily,** *adv.* **—ee′riness,** *n.* **—Syn. 1.** See **weird.**

eery (ĭə′rĭ), *adj.*, **eerier, eeriest.** eerie.

ef-, var. of **ex-** (by assimilation) before *f*, as in *efferent.*

effable (ĕf′ə bl), *adj.* utterable; expressible.

efface (ĭ fās′), *v.t.*, **effaced, effacing. 1.** to wipe out; destroy; do away with: *to efface a memory.* **2.** to rub out, erase, or obliterate (outlines, traces, inscriptions, etc.). **3.** to make inconspicuous or not noticeable: *to efface oneself.* [late ME, t. F: m. s. *effacer*, der. *ef-* (g. L *ex-* EX-¹) + *face* FACE] **—efface′able,** *adj.* **—efface′ment,** *n.* **—effac′er,** *n.*

effect (ĭ fĕkt′), *n.* **1.** that which is produced by some agency or cause; a result; a consequence: *the effect of heat.* **2.** power to produce results; efficacy; force; validity; weight: *of no effect.* **3.** the state of being operative; operation or execution; accomplishment or fulfilment: *to bring a plan into effect.* **4.** a mental impression produced, as by a painting, speech, etc. **5.** the result intended; purport or intent; tenor or significance: *he wrote to that effect.* **6.** *Theat.* a sight, sound, or occasionally smell simulated by artificial means to give a particular impression in a theatre. **7.** (*pl.*) goods; movables; personal property. **8. for effect,** for the sake of a desired impression. **9. in effect, a.** in fact or reality. **b.** in operation, as a law. **10. take effect,** to operate or begin to operate. *—v.t.* **11.** to produce as an effect; bring about; accomplish; make happen. **12.** to produce or make. [ME, t. L: s. *effectus*, der. *efficere* bring about] **—effect′er,** *n.* **—effect′ible,** *adj.*

—Syn. 1. EFFECT, CONSEQUENCE(S), RESULT refer to something produced by an action or a cause. An EFFECT is that which is produced, usually more or less immediately and directly: *the effect of morphine is to produce sleep,* or *morphine produces the effect of sleep.* A CONSEQUENCE, something that follows naturally or logically, as in a train of events or sequence of time, is less intimately connected with its cause than is an effect: *punishment is the consequence of disobedience, take the consequences.* A RESULT may be near or remote, and often is the sum of effects or consequences as making an end or final outcome: *the English language is the result of the fusion of many different elements.* **7.** See **property. 11.** accomplish, achieve, realize, fulfil. See **affect.**

effective (ĭ fĕk′tĭv), *adj.* **1.** serving to effect the purpose; producing the intended or expected result: *effective measures, effective steps towards peace.* **2.** actually in effect: *the law becomes effective at midnight.* **3.** producing a striking impression; striking: *an effective picture.* *—n.* **4.** a soldier or sailor fit for duty or active service. **5.** the effective total of a military force. **—effec′tively,** *adv.* **—effec′tiveness,** *n.*

—Syn. 1. capable, competent. EFFECTIVE, EFFECTUAL, EFFICACIOUS, EFFICIENT refer to that which is able to produce a (desired) effect. EFFECTIVE is applied to that which has the power to, or which actually does, produce an (often lasting) effect: *an effective action, remedy, speech.* EFFECTUAL is used esp. of that which produces the effect desired or intended, or a decisive result: *the bombardment effectually silenced the enemy.* EFFICACIOUS suggests the capability of achieving a certain end, a capability often manifested only when actually employed: *an efficacious plan, medicine.* EFFICIENT (applied also to persons) is the most active of these words, and implies the skilful use of energy or industry to accomplish desired results with little waste of effort: *efficient methods, an efficient manager.* **—Ant. 1.** futile.

effective resistance, *Elect.* the resistance of a conductor to alternating current; in addition to d.c. resistance it includes any losses caused by the current and is expressed as the ratio of the total loss to the square of the r.m.s. of the current.

effector (ĭ fĕk′tə), *n.* **1.** *Physiol.* an organ tissue or cell that carries out a response to a nerve impulse, such as a muscle or gland. **2.** effecter. [t. L]

effectual (ĭ fĕk′tyŏŏ əl), *adj.* **1.** producing, or capable of producing, an intended effect; adequate. **2.** valid or binding, as an agreement or document. [t. LL: s. *effectuālis*] **—effec′tual′ity, effec′tualness,** *n.* **—effec′tually,** *adv.* **—Syn. 1.** See **effective.**

effectuate (ĭ fĕk′tyŏŏ āt′), *v.t.*, **-ated, -ating.** to bring about; effect. [t. LL: s. *effectuātus.* See -ATE¹] **—effec′tua′tion,** *n.*

effeminacy (ĭ fĕm′ĭ nə sĭ), *n.* the state or quality of being effeminate.

effeminate (ĭ fĕm′ĭ nĭt), *adj.* **1.** soft or delicate to an unmanly degree in traits, tastes, habits, etc.; womanish. **2.** characterized by unmanly softness, delicacy, self-indulgence, etc.: *an effeminate life.* [t. L: m. s. *effēminātus*, pp., made womanish] **—effem′inately,** *adv.* **—effem′inateness,** *n.* **—Syn. 1.** See **female.**

effeminize (ĭ fĕm′ĭ nīz′), *v.t.* to make effeminate. Also, **effeminise.**

effendi (ĕ fĕn′dĭ), *n.*, *pl.* **-dis.** (formerly) a Turkish title of respect for government officials, etc. [t. Turk.: m. *efendī*, t. Gk: m. *authéntēs* master, actual doer. See AUTHENTIC]

efferent (ĕf′ə rənt), *adj. Anat., Physiol.* carrying away (opposed to *afferent*): *efferent impulses from the brain.* [t. L: s. *efferens*, ppr., bringing out, raising]

effervesce (ĕf′ə vĕs′), *v.i.*, **-vesced, -vescing. 1.** to give off bubbles of gas, as fermenting liquors; bubble and hiss. **2.** to issue forth in bubbles. **3.** to exhibit fervour, excitement, liveliness, etc. [t. L: m. s. *effervescere* boil up] **—ef′ferves′cence, ef′ferves′cency,** *n.* **—ef′ferves′cible,** *adj.*

effervescent (ĕf′ə vĕs′ənt), *adj.* **1.** effervescing; bubbling. **2.** gay; lively; sparkling. **—ef′ferves′cently,** *adv.*

effete (ĭ fēt′), *adj.* **1.** that has lost its vigour or energy; exhausted; worn out. **2.** unable to produce. [t. L: m. s. *effētus* exhausted] **—effete′ly,** *adv.* **—effete′ness,** *n.*

efficacious (ĕf′ĭ kā′shəs), *adj.* having or showing efficacy; effective as a means, measure, remedy, etc. [f. s. L *efficācia* efficacy + -OUS] **—ef′fica′ciously,** *adv.* **—ef′fica′ciousness,** *n.* **—Syn.** See **effective.**

efficacy (ĕf′ĭ kə sĭ), *n.*, *pl.* **-cies.** capacity for serving to produce effects; effectiveness. [t. L: m. s. *efficācia*]

efficiency (ĭ fĭsh′ən sĭ), *n.*, *pl.* **-cies. 1.** the fact or quality of being efficient; competency in performance. **2.** the ratio of the work done or energy developed by a machine, engine, etc., to the energy supplied to it.

efficient (ĭ fĭsh′ənt), *adj.* **1.** adequate in operation or performance; having and using the requisite knowledge, skill, and industry; competent; capable. **2.** producing an effect, as a cause; causative. *—n.* **3.** *Obs.* one who or that which produces an effect. [t. L: s. *efficiens*, ppr., accomplishing] **—effi′ciently,** *adv.* **—Syn. 1.** effectual, competent, capable. See **effective.**

effigies (ĕ fĭj′ĭ ēz′), *n. Archaic.* effigy. [L. See EFFIGY]

effigy (ĕf′ĭ jĭ), *n.*, *pl.* **-gies. 1.** a representation or image, esp. sculptured, as on a monument. **2.** a representation of an obnoxious person. **3. burn** or **hang in effigy,** to burn or hang an image of a person as an expression of public indignation, ridicule, or hatred. [t. F: m. *effigie*, t. L: m. *effigies* copy of an object]

effloresce (ĕf′lô rĕs′), *v.i.*, **-resced, -rescing. 1.** to burst into bloom; blossom. **2.** *Chem.* (of a crystal) to change on the surface to a powder, upon exposure to air, as a result of loss of water or crystallization. **3.** *Mineral.* (of a rock or mineral) to become encrusted with fine-grain crystals as a result of evaporation or chemical change. [t. L: m. s. *efflōrescere* blossom]

efflorescence (ĕf′lô rĕs′əns), *n.* **1.** the state or a period of flowering. **2.** *Chem., Mineral.* **a.** the act or process of efflorescing. **b.** the resulting powdery substance or encrustation. **3.** *Pathol.* a rash or eruption.

efflorescent (ĕf′lô rĕs′ənt), *adj.* **1.** efflorescing; blossoming. **2.** *Chem., Mineral.* **a.** subject to efflorescence. **b.** covered with or forming an efflorescence. [t. L: s. *efflōrescens*, ppr.]

effluence (ĕf′lo͞o əns), *n.* **1.** outward flow; efflux. **2.** something that flows out; an emanation. [coinage modelled on *affluence*. See EFFLUENT]

effluent (ĕf′lo͞o ənt), *adj.* **1.** flowing out or forth. —*n.* **2.** that which flows out or forth; outflow. **3.** a stream flowing out of another stream, a lake, etc. **4.** the outflow from sewage during purification. **5.** liquid industrial waste. **6.** the radioactive waste from nuclear power stations, etc. [t. L: s. *effluens*, ppr.]

effluvium (ĕ flo͞o′vyəm), *n., pl.* **-via** (-vyə), **-viums.** a slight or invisible exhalation or vapour, esp. one that is disagreeable or noxious. [t. L: a flowing out] —**efflu′vial,** *adj.*

efflux (ĕf′lŭks), *n.* **1.** outward flow, as of water. **2.** that which flows out; an effluence. **3.** *Aeron.* the mixture of combustion products and air which constitutes the propulsive gases in a jet or rocket engine.

Effner (*Ger.* ĕf′nər), *n.* **Joseph** (*Ger.* yō′zĕf), 1687–1745, German architect.

effort (ĕf′ət), *n.* **1.** exertion of power, physical or mental: *an effort to reform.* **2.** a strenuous attempt. **3.** something done by exertion; an achievement, as in literature or art. **4.** *Mech. Eng.* a measured amount of force exerted on a mechanism, e.g. a lever. [t. F, der. OF *esforcier*, der. *es-* (g. L *ex-* EX-[1]) + *force* strength, ult. der. L *fortis* strong] —**ef′fortful,** *adj.*

—**Syn. 1.** EFFORT, APPLICATION, ENDEAVOUR, EXERTION imply actions directed or force expended towards a definite end. EFFORT is an expenditure of energy to accomplish some (usually single and definite) object: *he made an effort to control himself.* APPLICATION is continuous effort plus careful attention: *constant application to duties.* ENDEAVOUR means a continued and sustained series of efforts to achieve some, often worthy and difficult, end: *a constant endeavour to be useful.* EXERTION is the vigorous and often strenuous expenditure of energy, frequently without conscious reference to a definite end: *out of breath from exertion.*

effortless (ĕf′ət lĭs), *adj.* **1.** requiring or involving no effort; easy. **2.** making no effort; passive. —**ef′fortlessly,** *adv.* —**ef′fortlessness,** *n.*

effrontery (ĭ frŭn′tə rĭ), *n., pl.* **-teries.** shameless or impudent boldness; barefaced audacity. [t. F: m. *effronterie*, der. OF *esfronte* shameless, f. *es-* (g. L *ex-* EX-[1]) + *front* brow (g. s. L *frons*) + *-e* -ed]

effulge (ĭ fŭlj′), *v.t., v.i.*, **-fulged, -fulging.** to shine or send forth brilliantly. [t. L: m. s. *effulgēre* shine forth]

effulgent (ĭ fŭl′jənt), *adj.* shining forth brilliantly; radiant. —**efful′gence,** *n.* —**efful′gently,** *adv.*

effuse (*v.* ĕ fyo͞oz′; *adj.* ĕ fyo͞os′), *v.*, **-fused, -fusing,** *adj.* —*v.t.* **1.** to pour out or forth; shed; disseminate. —*v.i.* **2.** to exude. **3.** *Physics.* (of gas) to flow gradually through porous material or one or more tiny apertures. —*adj.* **4.** *Bot.* spread out loosely. **5.** (of certain shells) having the lips separated by a gap or groove. [t. L: m. s. *effūsus*, pp., poured forth]

effusion (ĭ fyo͞o′zhən), *n.* **1.** the act of effusing or pouring forth. **2.** that which is effused. **3.** unrestrained expression of feelings, etc.: *poetic effusions.* **4.** *Pathol.* **a.** the escape of a fluid from its natural vessels into a body cavity. **b.** the fluid which escapes.

effusive (ĭ fyo͞o′sĭv), *adj.* **1.** unduly demonstrative; without reserve: *effusive emotion, an effusive person.* **2.** *Geol.* denoting or pertaining to igneous rocks which have solidified near or on the surface of the earth (opposed to *plutonic*). —**effu′sively,** *adv.* —**effu′siveness,** *n.*

eft[1] (ĕft), *n. Dial.* the common newt in its land stage. [ME *evete*, OE *efete*. See NEWT]

eft[2] (ĕft), *adv. Archaic.* **1.** again. **2.** afterwards. [OE, akin to AFT]

EFTA (ĕf′tə), *n.* European Free Trade Association.

eftsoon (ĕft so͞on′), *adv. Archaic.* **1.** soon afterwards. **2.** again. **3.** forthwith. Also, **eftsoons′.** [ME *eftsone*, OE *eftsōna*, f. EFT[2] + *sōna* at once]

Eg., 1. Egypt. **2.** Egyptian.

e.g., (L *exempli gratia*) for example.

egad (ĭ găd′, ē-), *interj. Obs.* (an expletive or mild oath): *egad, that's true.* [alter. of *A God* oh God!]

egalitarian (ĭ găl′ĭ tĕə′rĭ ən), *adj.* **1.** asserting the equality of all men. —*n.* **2.** one who asserts the equality of all men. [der. F *égal* EQUAL; r. EQUALITARIAN] —**egal′itar′ianism,** *n.*

égalité (*Fr.* ĕ gȧ lē tĕ′), *n. French.* equality.

Egbert (ĕg′bût), *n.* died A.D. 839?, king of the West Saxons in England A.D. 802–39: first overlord of England and Wales A.D. 829–39.

Egeria (ĭ jĭə′rĭ ə), *n.* **1.** *Rom. Legend.* a nymph who instructed King Numa in religious worship. **2.** a woman counsellor.

egest (ē jĕst′), *v.t.* to discharge, as from the body; void (opposed to *ingest*). [t. L: s. *ēgestus*, pp., brought out] —**eges′tive,** *adj.*

egesta (ē jĕs′tə), *n.pl.* matter egested from the body, as excrement. [t. L, neut. pl. of *ēgestus*, pp., brought out]

egestion (ē jĕs′chən), *n.* the process of egesting; the voiding of the refuse of digestion.

egg[1] (ĕg), *n.* **1.** the roundish reproductive body produced by the female of animals, consisting of the female reproductive cell and its envelopes. The envelopes may be albumen jelly, membranes, egg case, or shell, according to species. **2.** the body of this sort produced by birds, esp. the domestic hen. **3.** anything resembling a hen's egg. **4.** Also, **egg cell.** *Biol.* the ovum or female reproductive cell. **5. bad egg,** a person of reprehensible character. **6. in the egg,** in the planning stages. **7. put all one's eggs in one basket,** to devote all one's resources to or risk all one's possessions, etc., on a single undertaking. **8. tread on eggs,** to be very cautious. —*v.t.* **9.** to prepare (food) by dipping in beaten egg. [t. Scand. (cf. Icel. *egg*); r. ME *ey*, OE *ǣg*, c. G *Ei.* Cf. L *ōvum*, Gk *ōión*]

egg[2] (ĕg), *v.t.* to incite or urge; encourage (usually fol. by *on*). [t. Scand.; cf. Icel. *eggja*, der. *egg* EDGE]

egg and dart, egg and tongue, egg and anchor, an egg-shaped ornament alternating with a dart-like, tonguelike, or anchor-like ornament, used to enrich a moulding.

Egg-and-dart moulding

egg-and-spoon race, a race in which contestants have to pick up an egg in a spoon and balance it while running.

eggbound (ĕg′bound′), *adj.* unable to expel an egg. —**egg′bind′ing,** *n.*

eggcosy (ĕg′kō′zĭ), *n.* a little hood to put over a boiled egg to keep it warm until it is eaten.

eggcup (ĕg′kŭp′), *n.* a small cup for holding a boiled egg upright as at a table.

egger (ĕg′ə), *n.* any of various species of moths of the family *Lasiocampidae*, as the **oak egger,** *Lasiocampa quercus*, which occurs in Britain. Also, **eggar.**

egg-flip (ĕg′flĭp′), *n.* eggnog.

egghead (ĕg′hĕd′), *n. Colloq.* an intellectual.

eggnog (ĕg′nŏg′), *n.* a drink made of eggs, milk, sugar, spice, and, usually, wine, beer, or spirits. Also, **egg′nog′gin.** [f. EGG + *nog* strong ale]

eggplant (ĕg′plănt′), *n.* aubergine.

egg-shaped (ĕg′shāpt′), *adj.* having elongated rounded (oval) form, esp. with one end broader than the other.

eggshell (ĕg′shĕl′), *n.* **1.** the shell of an egg in birds, consisting of keratin fibres and calcite crystals. **2.** a pale yellow colour. —*adj.* **3.** like an eggshell; thin and delicate; very brittle. **4.** (of a paint) having an almost mat finish resembling the surface texture of an eggshell; having very little gloss. **5.** pale yellow.

eggshell china, very thin, translucent porcelain.

eggslice (ĕg′slīs′), *n.* a utensil for removing fried eggs, etc., from a pan.

eggspoon (ĕg′spo͞on′), *n.* a spoon for eating boiled eggs, smaller than a teaspoon.

eggtimer (ĕg′tī′mə), *n.* a small hourglass running for about three minutes, used to time the boiling of an egg.

egg tooth, a calcareous point on the tip of the beak or upper jaw, by which an unhatched bird or reptile breaks through the eggshell on hatching.

eggwhisk (ĕg′wĭsk′), *n.* a utensil for beating eggs, whipping cream, etc.

eggwhite (ĕg′wīt′), *n.* the white of an egg; albumen.

Egham (ĕg′əm), *n.* a town in England, in N Surrey. 30,553 (1961).

egis (ē′jĭs), *n.* aegis.

eglantine (ĕg′lən tīn′), *n.* **1.** the sweetbrier, *Rosa eglanteria.* **2.** the Austrian brier, *Rosa foetida.* Also, *Archaic,* **eglatere** (ĕg′lə tĭə′). [ME *eglentine*, t. F: m. *églantine*, der. OF *aiglent* sweetbrier, ult. der. L *acus* needle]

Egmont (ĕg′mŏnt), *n.* **1. Mount,** an extinct volcano in

W North Island, New Zealand. 8260 ft. **2. Cape,** a headland on the W coast of North Island, New Zealand.

ego (ē′gō, ĕg′ō), *n., pl.* **egos. 1.** the 'I' or self of any person; a person as thinking, feeling, and willing, and distinguishing itself from the selves of others and from objects of its thought. **2.** (*often cap.*) *Philos.* **a.** the enduring and conscious element which knows experience. **b.** (in Scholasticism) the complete man comprising both body and soul. **3.** *Psychoanal.* that part of the psychic apparatus which experiences the outside world and reacts to it, thus mediating between the primitive drives of the id and the demands of the social and physical environment. **4.** *Colloq.* conceit; egotism. [t. L: I]

egocentric (ē′gō sĕn′trĭk, ĕg′ō-), *adj.* **1.** having or regarding self as the centre of all things, esp. as applied to the known world. **2.** self-centred. —*n.* **3.** an egocentric person. —**egocentricity** (ē′gō sĕn trĭs′ĭ tĭ, ĕg′ō-), *n.*

ego ideal, *Psychoanal.* a more or less conscious criterion of personal excellence towards which an individual strives. It is derived from a composite image of the characteristics of persons (initially the parents) with whom the individual identifies himself.

egoism (ē′gō ĭz′əm, ĕg′ō-), *n.* **1.** the habit of valuing everything only in reference to one's personal interest; pure selfishness. **2.** egotism or self-conceit. **3.** *Ethics.* the doctrine that the individual and his self-interest are the basis of all behaviour. [f. EGO + -ISM] —**Syn. 1.** See **egotism.** —**Ant. 1.** altruism.

egoist (ē′gō ĭst, ĕg′ō-), *n.* **1.** a self-centred or selfish person. **2.** an egotist. **3.** an adherent of the metaphysical principle of the ego or self; a solipsist. [f. EGO + -IST] —**e′gois′tic, e′gois′tical,** *adj.* —**e′gois′tically,** *adv.*

egomania (ē′gō mā′nyə, ĕg′ō-), *n.* morbid egotism. —**e′goma′niac,** *n.*

egotism (ē′gə tĭz′əm, ĕg′ə-), *n.* **1.** the habit of talking too much about oneself; self-conceit; boastfulness. **2.** selfishness. [f. EGO + hiatus-filling *-t-* + -ISM]

—**Syn. 1.** EGOTISM, EGOISM refer to preoccupation with one's ego or self; the two words are often confused. EGOTISM is the common word for obtrusive and excessive reference to and emphasis upon oneself and one's own importance, in conversation and writing, often to the extent of monopolizing attention and showing disregard for others' opinions: *his egotism alienated all his friends.* EGOISM, a less common word, is used especially in philosophy, ethics, or metaphysics, where it emphasizes the importance of self in relation to other things: ***sufficient egoism to understand one's place in the universe.*** —**Ant. 1.** humility.

egotist (ē′gə tĭst, ĕg′ə-), *n.* **1.** a conceited, boastful person. **2.** an egoist. —**e′gotis′tic, e′gotis′tical,** *adj.* —**e′gotis′tically,** *adv.*

egregious (ĭ grē′jəs, -jĭ əs), *adj.* **1.** remarkably or extraordinarily flagrant: *an egregious lie, an egregious fool.* **2.** *Obs.* distinguished or eminent. [t. L: m. *ēgregius* distinguished, lit., (standing) out from the herd] —**egre′giously,** *adv.* —**egre′giousness,** *n.*

egress (ē′grĕs), *n.* **1.** the act of going or passing out, esp. from an enclosed place. **2.** a means or place of going out; an exit. **3.** the right of going out. **4.** *Astron.* emersion (def. 2). [t. L: s. *ēgressus,* der. *ēgredī* go out]

egression (ĭ grĕsh′ən), *n.* a going out; egress.

egret (ē′grĭt), *n.* **1.** any of various herons, as the great white heron, *Casmerodius albus,* of Europe and America and the **snowy egret,** *Leucophoyxt thula* of North America, bearing in the breeding season tufts of long plumes. **2.** the plume of an egret; aigrette. **3.** the feathery pappus of the dandelion, thistle, and other plants; aigrette. [ME *egrete,* t. OF, var. of *aigrette*]

Egret, *Casmerodius albus egretta* (2 ft long)

Egypt (ē′jĭpt), *n.* **1.** Official name, **United Arab Republic.** a republic in NE Africa. 27,963,000 pop. (est. 1963); 386,198 sq. mi. *Cap.:* Cairo. **2.** a former kingdom in NE Africa: divided into **Lower Egypt** (the Nile Delta) and **Upper Egypt** (from near Cairo S to the Sudan).

Egypt., Egyptian.

Egyptian (ĭ jĭp′shən), *adj.* **1.** of or pertaining to Egypt or its people: *Egyptian architecture.* **2.** of or pertaining to the gipsies. —*n.* **3.** a native or inhabitant of Egypt. **4.** a gipsy. **5.** the language of the ancient Egyptians, an extinct Hamitic language.

Egyptology (ē′jĭp tŏl′ə jĭ), *n.* the science or study of Egyptian antiquities. —**Egyptological** (ĭ jĭp′tə lŏj′ĭ kl), *adj.* —**E′gyptol′ogist,** *n.*

eh (ā), *interj.* (an interrogative utterance, sometimes expressing surprise or doubt): *wasn't it lucky, eh?*

E H F, *Radio.* extremely high frequency.

Ehrenbreitstein (ĕə′rən brīt′shtīn), *n.* a Roman fortress overlooking the Rhine at Koblenz.

Ehrenburg (ĕ′rən bûg′; *Russ.* ė′rən bo͝ork), *n.* **Ilya Grigorievich** (*Russ.* ē′lyə grĭ gô′ryĭ vĭch), 1891–1967, Soviet author.

Ehrlich (*Ger.* ėr′lĭkh), *n.* **Paul** (*Ger.* poul), 1854–1915, German physician, bacteriologist, and chemist.

Eichendorff (*Ger.* īkh′ən dŏrf), *n.* **Joseph Freiherr von** (*Ger.* yō′zĕf frī′hĕr fōn), 1788–1857, German poet, author, and critic.

eider (ī′də), *n.* **1.** eider duck. **2.** eiderdown. [t. Sw. or G, ult. t. Icel. (see EIDERDOWN)]

eiderdown (ī′də doun′), *n.* **1.** down or soft feathers from the breast of the eider duck. **2.** a heavy quilt, properly one filled with eiderdown (def. 1). **3.** *U.S.* a fabric of cotton with wool nap. [ult. t. Icel.: m. *ǣdardūn* (18th-century spelling) down of the eider (gen. sing.); spelling *eider-* follows (18th century) Sw. or G, repr. Icel. *ǣ* with *ei*]

eider duck, any of several large sea-ducks of the genus *Somateria* and allied genera of the Northern Hemisphere, generally black and white, and yielding eiderdown.

Eider duck, *Somateria mollissima* (2 ft long)

eidetic (ī dĕt′ĭk), *adj.* of, pertaining to, constituting or having a vivid and persistent type of imagery or memory, esp. during childhood.

eidolon (ī dō′lŏn), *n., pl.* **-la** (-lə). an image; a phantom; an apparition. [t. Gk: image. Cf. IDOL]

Eiffel (ī′fəl; *Fr.* ĕ fĕl′), *n.* **Gustave Alexandre** (*Fr.* gʏs tȧv ȧ lĕk sȧN′dr), 1832–1923, French engineer and designer.

Eiffel Tower (ī′fəl), a tower of skeletal iron construction in Paris: built for the exhibition of 1889. 984 ft. high.

Eiger (*Ger.* ī′gər), *n.* a mountain in Switzerland, in the Bernese Oberland. 13,042 ft.

eight (āt), *n.* **1.** a cardinal number, seven plus one. **2.** a symbol for this number, as 8 or VIII. **3.** a set of this many persons or things. **4.** a playing card bearing eight pips. **5.** *Rowing.* **a.** a crew of eight oarsmen. **b.** a racing boat for a crew of eight and a cox. —*adj.* **6.** amounting to eight in number. [ME *eighte, ehte,* OE *eahta,* c. D and G *acht;* akin to L *octō,* Gk *oktō*]

eighteen (ā′tēn′), *n.* **1.** a cardinal number, ten plus eight. **2.** a symbol for this number, as 18 or XVIII. —*adj.* **3.** amounting to eighteen in number. [ME *ehtetene,* OE *eahtatēne.* See EIGHT, -TEEN] —**eighteenth** (ā′tēnth′), *adj., n.*

eighteenmo (ā tēn′mō), *n.* octodecimo.

eightfold (āt′fōld′), *adj.* **1.** comprising eight parts or members; eight times as great or as much. —*adv.* **2.** in eightfold measure.

eighth (ātth), *adj.* **1.** next after the seventh. **2.** being one of eight equal parts. —*n.* **3.** the eighth number of a series. **4.** an eighth part. **5.** *Music.* an octave.

eighth note, *Music. U.S.* a quaver.

eightpence (āt′pəns), *n.* eight pennies.

eightpenny (āt′pə nĭ), *adj.* **1.** of the amount or value of eightpence. —*n.* **2.** something purchased for eightpence, esp. a journey by public transport.

Eights (āts), *n.pl. Rowing.* the annual bumping races held in the summer term on four consecutive days (formerly six), by the Oxford colleges. Also, **Eights week, Summer Eights.**

eightsome (āt′səm), *n.* **1.** *Rare.* a group of eight things or persons. **2.** Also, **eightsome reel.** a lively Scottish reel in which eight or a multiple of eight persons dance together.

eightvo (āt′vō), *n., pl.* **-vos,** *adj. Bookbinding.* octavo.

eighty (ā′tĭ), *n., pl.* **eighties,** *adj.* —*n.* **1.** a cardinal number, ten times eight. **2.** a symbol for this number, as 80 or LXXX or XXC. **3.** (*pl.*) the numbers from 80 to 89 of a series, esp. with reference to the years of a person's age, or the years of a century, esp. the nineteenth. —*adj.* **4.** amounting to eighty in number. [ME *eighteti,* OE *eahtatig*] —**eightieth** (ā′tĭ ĭth), *adj., n.*

eikon (ī′kŏn), *n.* icon.

Eilat (ī′lăt), *n.* a port in S Israel, at the head of the Gulf of Aqaba. 11,000 (est. 1968). Also, **Elath.**

Eindhoven (īnd′hō′vən; *Du.* ĕynt′hō və), *n.* a city in S Netherlands, in North Brabant province. 178,336 (1965).

einkorn (īn′kôn′), *n.* a species of wheat, *Triticum monococcum,* cultivated by Neolithic man and still grown on rocky mountainous ground in S Europe.

Einstein (īn′stīn; *Ger.* īn′shtīn), *n.* **Albert** (ăl′bət; *Ger.* ăl′bĕrt), 1879–1955, German physicist who formulated the theory of relativity; became a U.S. citizen in 1940. —**Einstein′ian,** *adj.*

einsteinium (īn stī′nĭ əm), *n. Chem.* a synthetic, radioactive, metallic element. *Symbol*: Es; *at. no.*: 99. [f. Albert EINSTEIN + -IUM]

Einstein shift, *Physics., Astron.* a slight displacement, towards the red, of lines of the spectrum of the sun and other dense stars due to their gravitational field: originally predicted by Einstein.

Einstein theory. See **relativity.**

Eire (ĕə′rə), *n.* former name (1937–49) of the **Republic of Ireland**; still its official Gaelic name.

Eisenach (*Ger.* ī′zə näKH), *n.* a town in East Germany, in Thuringia. 50,000 (est. 1963).

Eisenhower (ī′zən hou′ə), *n.* **Dwight David,** 1890–1969, 34th president of the United States, 1953–61: U.S. general, supreme commander of Allied Expeditionary Forces 1943–45.

Eisenstadt (*Ger.* ī′zən shtät′), *n.* a town in Austria, the capital of Burgenland. 7200 (est. 1968).

Eisenstein (ī′zən stīn′), *n.* **Sergei Mikhailovich** (*Russ.* sĭr gyĕy′ mĭ KHäy′lə vĭch), 1898–1948, Soviet film director.

Eisk (*Russ.* yĕsk), *n.* a seaport in the SW Soviet Union, on the Sea of Azov. 49,280 (est. 1946). Also, **Yeisk.**

eisteddfod (ī stĕth′vŏd), *n., pl.* **eisteddfods, eisteddfodau** (ī stĕth′vŏd′ī). **1.** (*cap.*) a congress of Welsh bards and minstrels. **2.** any competitive music festival, esp. of folk songs. [t. Welsh: session, der. *eistedd* sit]

either (ī′thə), *adj.* **1.** one or the other of two: *you may sit at either end of the table.* **2.** each of the two; the one and the other: *there are trees on either side of the river.* —*pron.* **3.** one or the other; not both: *take either; either is correct.* —*conj.* **4.** (used as one of two coordinate alternatives): *either come or write.* —*adv.* **5.** (used after negative sentences coordinated by *and, or, nor*): *he is not fond of parties and I am not either* (or *not I either*), *I am going and nobody can prevent it either;* after a neg. sub. clause: *if you do not come, he will not come either.* [ME; OE *ǣgther*, contr. of *ǣghwæther* each of two, both, f. *ā* always + *gehwæther* each of two. See WHETHER]

ejaculate (ĭ jăk′yŏŏ lāt′), *v.t.*, **-lated, -lating.** **1.** to utter suddenly and briefly; exclaim. **2.** to eject suddenly and swiftly; discharge. [t. L: m. s. *ējaculātus*, pp., having cast out] —**ejac′ula′tor,** *n.*

ejaculation (ĭ jăk′yŏŏ lā′shən), *n.* **1.** an abrupt, exclamatory utterance. **2.** the act of ejaculating. **3.** *Physiol.* the rhythmic discharge of seminal fluid from the male passages; an emission.

ejaculatory (ĭ jăk′yŏŏ lə tə rĭ, -trĭ), *adj.* **1.** pertaining to or of the nature of an ejaculation or exclamatory utterance. **2.** *Physiol.* pertaining to ejaculation. Also, **ejaculative** (ĭ jăk′yŏŏ lə tĭv).

eject (*v.* ĭ jĕkt′; *n.* ē′jĕkt), *v.t.* **1.** to drive or force out; expel, as from a place or position. **2.** to dismiss, as from office, occupancy, etc. **3.** to evict, as from property. —*n.* **4.** *Psychol.* something whose existence is inferred as a reality, but which is outside of, and inaccessible to, the consciousness of the one making the inference. [t. L: s. *ējectus*, pp. thrown out]

ejecta (ĭ jĕk′tə), *n.pl.* matter ejected, as from a volcano in eruption. [t. L, neut. pl. of *ējectus.* See EJECT]

ejection (ĭ jĕk′shən), *n.* **1.** the act of ejecting. **2.** the state of being ejected. **3.** something ejected, as lava.

ejection capsule, *Aeron.* a portion of an aircraft which can be fired clear in an emergency so that it can descend by parachute; usually consists of all or part of the cockpit or cabin.

ejection seat, *Aeron.* a seat designed to be catapulted from an aircraft (usually by explosives) with its occupant, in the case of an emergency. Also, **ejector seat.**

ejective (ĭ jĕk′tĭv), *adj.* **1.** serving to eject. **2.** *Phonet.* (of a stop or fricative) produced with air compressed above the closed glottis. —*n.* **3.** *Phonet.* an ejective stop or fricative.

ejectment (ĭ jĕkt′mənt), *n.* **1.** the act of ejecting. **2.** *Law.* an action for the recovery of land wherein the title of real property may be tried and the possession recovered, wherever the party claiming has a right of entry (abolished 1852).

ejector (ĭ jĕk′tə), *n.* **1.** one who or that which ejects. **2.** the mechanism in a firearm or gun which, after firing, throws out the empty cartridge or shell from the weapon.

Ekaterinburg (*Russ.* yĭ kə tĭ rĭn bŏŏrk′), *n.* former name of **Sverdlovsk.**

Ekaterinodar (*Russ.* yĭ kə tĭ rĭ nä där′), *n.* former name of **Krasnodar.**

Ekaterinoslav (*Russ.* yĭ kə tĭ rĭ näs läf′), *n.* former name of **Dnepropetrovsk.**

eke[1] (ēk), *v.t.*, **eked, eking.** **1.** *Archaic.* to increase; enlarge; lengthen. **2. eke out, a.** to supply what is lacking to; supplement. **b.** to contrive to make (a living) or support (existence) by various makeshifts. [var. of obs. *ēche*, OE *ēcan*, with *k* from obs. n. *eke* addition (OE *ēaca*). Cf. *ēacen* augmented. Akin to Icel. *auka*, Goth. *aukan*, L *augēre* increase]

eke[2] (ēk), *adv., conj. Archaic.* also. [ME *eek*, d. OE *ēc*; r. OE *ēac*, c. G *auch*]

elaborate (*adj.* ĭ lăb′ə rĭt; *v.* ĭ lăb′ə rāt′), *adj., v.*, **-rated, -rating.** —*adj.* **1.** worked out with great care and nicety of detail; executed with great minuteness: *elaborate preparations, care, etc.* —*v.t.* **2.** to work out carefully or minutely; work up to perfection. **3.** to produce or develop by labour. **4.** *Physiol.* to convert (food, plasma, etc.) by means of chemical processes into a substance more suitable for use within the body. —*v.i.* **5.** to add details in writing, speaking, etc.; give additional or fuller treatment (fol. by *on* or *upon*): *to elaborate upon a theme or an idea.* [t. L: m. s. *ēlabōrātus*, pp., worked out] —**elab′orately,** *adv.* —**elab′orateness,** *n.* —**elaborative** (ĭ lăb′ə rə tĭv), *adj.* —**elab′ora′tor,** *n.*

—**Syn. 1.** perfected, painstaking. ELABORATE, LABOURED, STUDIED apply to that which is worked out in great detail. That which is ELABORATE is characterized by great, sometimes even excessive, nicety or minuteness of detail: *elaborate preparations for a banquet, an elaborate apology.* That which is LABOURED is marked by excessive, often forced or uninspired, effort: *a laboured explanation, style of writing.* That which is STUDIED is accomplished with care and deliberation, and is done purposely, sometimes even having been rehearsed: *a studied pose.* —**Ant. 1.** simple.

elaboration (ĭ lăb′ə rā′shən), *n.* **1.** the act of elaborating. **2.** the state of being elaborated; elaborateness. **3.** something elaborated. **4.** *Physiol.* the process by which substances are built up in the bodies of animals or plants.

Elagabalus (ĕl′ə găb′ə ləs, ē′lə-), *n.* (*Varius Avitus Bassanius, 'Marcus Aurelius Antoninus'*), A.D. 205?–222, Roman emperor A.D. 218–222. Also, **Heliogabalus.**

Elaine (ĭ lān′), *n.* the name of several characters in Arthurian legends, notably: **1.** the 'lily maid of Astolat' who pined and died for Lancelot. **2.** the half-sister of Arthur and mother of his son Modred. **3.** the daughter of King Pelles and mother of Sir Galahad.

El Aiún (*Sp.* ĕl ä yōōn′), the capital of Spanish Sahara.

El Alamein (ĕl ăl′ə mān′), a town on the N coast of Egypt, ab. 70 mi. W of Alexandria: decisive British victory over the German Afrika Korps, October 1942.

Elam (ē′ləm), *n.* an ancient country E of Babylonia and N of the Persian Gulf. *Cap.*: Susa. —**Elamite** (ē′lə mīt′), *n., adj.*

elan (ĕ lŏn′), *n.* dash; impetuous ardour. Also, *French,* **élan** (*Fr.* è läN′). [t. F, der. *élancer* hurl, rush forth]

eland (ē′lənd), *n.* a large, heavily built antelope, *Taurotragus oryx*, of southern and eastern Africa. [t. Afrikaans, special use of D *eland* elk, t. G: m. *Elend*, t. Lithuanian: m. *élnis* elk]

Eland, *Taurotragus oryx* (5½ ft high at shoulder, 11½ ft long)

élan vital (*Fr.* è läN vē tȧl′), *French.* (esp. in Bergsonian philosophy) the creative force within an organism, which is able to build physical form and to produce growth and necessary or desirable adaptations. [F: lit., living force]

elapid (ĕl′ə pĭd), *n.* **1.** any snake of the family *Elapidae*, which includes the cobras, mambas, and coral snakes characterized by fixed venomous fangs at the front of the jaw. Members of the family are found in Africa, tropical Asia, Australia, and America. —*adj.* **2.** of or pertaining to the *Elapidae.*

elapse (ĭ lăps′), *v.*, **elapsed, elapsing,** *n.* —*v.i.* **1.** (of time) to slip by or pass away. —*n.* **2.** the passing (of time); lapse. [t. L: m. s. *ēlapsus*, pp.]

E.L.A.S., Hellenic People's Army of Liberation, the military organization of the EAM: powerful Greek resistance force in World War II. Also, **Elas** (ĕl′äs).

elasmobranch (ĭ lăs′mə brăngk′, ĭ lăz′-), *adj.* **1.** of the *Elasmobranchii*, the group of vertebrates including the sharks and rays, with cartilaginous skeletons and five to seven pairs of gill openings. —*n.* **2.** an elasmobranch fish. [t. NL: m. s. *Elasmobranchii*, pl., f. Gk: *elasmó(s)* metal plate + *bránchia* gills]

elastance (ĭ lăs′təns), *n. Elect.* the reciprocal of capacitance.

elastic (ĭ lăs′tĭk), *adj.* **1.** having the property of recovering shape after deformation, as solids. **2.** spontaneously expansive, as gases. **3.** flexible, yielding, or accommodating: *an elastic conscience.* **4.** springing back or rebounding; springy: *an elastic step.* **5.** readily recovering from depression or exhaustion; buoyant: *an elastic temperament.* —*n.* **6.** webbing, or material in the form of a band, made elastic with strips of rubber. **7.** a piece of this material.

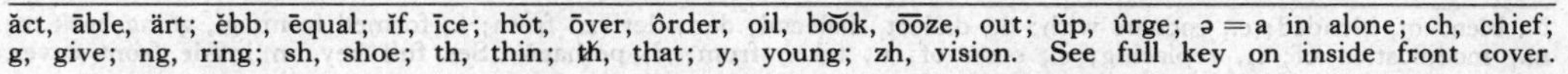

8. *U.S.* a rubber band. [t. NL: s. *elasticus*, t. Gk: m. *elastikós* propulsive] —**elas′tically,** *adv.*

elastic band, a rubber band.

elastic bitumen, elaterite.

elastic collision, *Physics.* **1.** an ideal collision between bodies in which their total kinetic energy before collision equals their total kinetic energy after collision. **2.** a collision between a particle and an atomic nucleus in which the nucleus is neither broken up nor excited.

elasticity (ĭ lăs′tĭs′ĭ tĭ, ē′lăs-), *n.* **1.** the state or quality of being elastic. **2.** flexibility: *elasticity of meaning.* **3.** buoyancy; ability to resist or overcome depression.

elasticize (ĭ lăs′tĭ sīz′), *v.t.*, **-cized, -cizing.** to weave with elastic thread or make with elastic sections. Also, **elasticise.**

elastic limit, *Physics.* the limiting value of the stress which can be applied to a body, or substance, without causing its permanent deformation.

elastin (ĭ lăs′tĭn), *n.* *Biochem.* a protein constituting the basic substance of elastic tissue. [f. ELAST(IC) + -IN[2]]

elastomer (ĭ lăs′tə mə), *n.* *Chem.* an elastic, rubber-like substance occurring naturally (natural rubber) or produced synthetically (butyl rubber, neoprene, etc.). [f. ELAST(IC) + -O- + Gk *mér(os)* part] —**elastomeric** (ĭ-lăs′tə mĕ′rĭk), *adj.*

Elastoplast (ĭ lăs′tə pläst′), *n.* *Trademark.* an adhesive plaster for covering superficial wounds.

elate (ĭ lāt′), *v.*, **elated, elating,** *adj.* —*v.t.* **1.** to put in high spirits; make proud. —*adj.* **2.** elated. [ME, t. L: m. s. *ēlātus*, pp., brought out, raised, exalted]

elated (ĭ lā′tĭd), *adj.* in high spirits; proud; jubilant. —**elat′edly,** *adv.* —**elat′edness,** *n.*

elater (ĕl′ə tə), *n.* **1.** *Bot.* an elastic filament serving to disperse spores. **2.** *Zool.* elaterid. [NL, t. Gk: driver]

elaterid (ĭ lăt′ə rĭd), *n.* **1.** any of the click beetles constituting the family *Elateridae*, most of which have the power of springing up when laid on their backs. —*adj.* **2.** of or pertaining to the *Elateridae.*

elaterin (ĭ lăt′ə rĭn), *n.* *Chem.* a white crystalline substance obtained from and constituting the active principle of elaterium, used as a cathartic.

elaterite (ĭ lăt′ə rīt′), *n.* a brownish, elastic, rubber-like, naturally occurring asphalt. Also, **elastic bitumen, mineral caoutchouc.**

elaterium (ĕl′ə tĭə′rĭ əm), *n.* a cathartic obtained from the juice of *Ecballium elaterium*, the squirting cucumber. [t. L; t. Gk.: m. *elatḗrion* an opening medicine]

Elath (ī′lăt), *n.* Eilat.

elation (ĭ lā′shən), *n.* exaltation of spirit, as from joy or pride; exultant gladness; high spirits.

Elazig (*Turk.* ĕ lä zĭ′), *n.* a town in E central Turkey. Also, **Elaziz.**

Elba (ĕl′bə), *n.* an Italian island in the Mediterranean between Corsica and Italy: the scene of Napoleon's first exile, 1814–15. 32,200 pop. (est. 1962); 94 sq. mi.

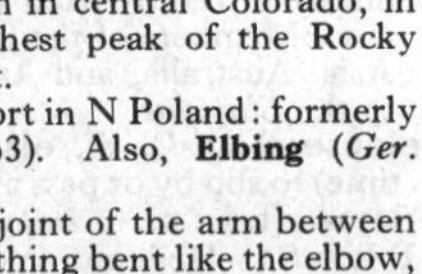

Elba

Elbe (ĕlb; *Ger.* ĕl′bə), *n.* a river flowing from W Czechoslovakia NW through East Germany and West Germany to the North Sea near Hamburg. 725 mi.

Elberfeld (*Ger.* ĕl′bər fĕlt), *n.* See **Wuppertal.**

Elbert Peak (ĕl′bət), a mountain in central Colorado, in the Sawatch range; second highest peak of the Rocky Mountains in the U.S. 14,431 ft.

Elbląg (*Pol.* ĕl′blŏngk), *n.* a seaport in N Poland: formerly in Germany. 83,200 (est. 1963). Also, **Elbing** (*Ger.* ĕl′bĭng).

elbow (ĕl′bō), *n.* **1.** the bend or joint of the arm between upper arm and forearm. **2.** something bent like the elbow, as a sharp turn in a road or river, or a piece of pipe bent at an angle. **3. at one's elbow,** near at hand. **4. out at elbows** or **out at the elbow,** ragged or impoverished. **5. up to the elbows,** very busy with; wholly engaged or engrossed. —*v.t.* **6.** to push with or as with the elbow; jostle. **7.** to make (one's way) by so pushing. —*v.i.* **8.** to elbow one's way. [ME *elbowe*, OE *elneboga*, c. G *Ellenbogen*, orig. arm bow. See ELL[2], BOW[1]]

elbow grease, vigorous, continuous exertion; hard physical labour.

elbow-room (ĕl′bō ro͞om′), *n.* sufficient room or scope.

Elbrus (*Russ.* ĭly bro͞os′), *n.* a mountain in the S Soviet Union in Europe, in the Caucasus Mountains: the highest peak in Europe. 18,481 ft. Also, **Elbruz.**

Elburz Mountains (*Pers.* ăl bōrz′), a mountain range in N Iran, along the S coast of the Caspian Sea. Highest peak, Mt Demavend, 18,606 ft.

Elche (*Sp.* ĕl′chĕ), *n.* a town in E Spain. 72,706 (1959).

El Cid Campeador (*Sp.* ĕl thēd′ käm pĕ á dōr′). See **Cid.**

eld (ĕld), *n.* *Archaic.* **1.** age. **2.** old age. **3.** antiquity. [ME *elde*, OE *eld(o)*, der. *eald, ald* OLD]

elder[1] (ĕl′də), *adj.* **1.** older. **2.** senior: *an elder officer.* **3.** earlier: *in elder times.* —*n.* **4.** a person who is older than oneself; one's senior. **5.** an aged person. **6.** one of the older and more influential men of a tribe or community, often a chief or ruler. **7.** a presbyter. **8.** (in certain Protestant churches) a governing officer, often with teaching or pastoral functions. **9.** (in the Mormon Church) one holding the higher or Melchizedek priesthood. [ME; OE *eldra*, etc. (compar. of *ald, eald* OLD), c. G *älter*] —**eld′ership′,** *n.* —**Syn. 1.** See **older.**

elder[2] (ĕl′də), *n.* any plant of the caprifoliaceous genus *Sambucus*, which comprises shrubs and small trees bearing clusters of small white or light-coloured flowers and a blackish or red fruit, *Alnus glutinosa*, of Europe. [ME *eldre, elrene, ellerne*, OE *ellærn*, c. MLG *ellern, elderne*]

elderberry (ĕl′də bĕ′rĭ), *n.*, *pl.* **-ries. 1.** the drupaceous fruit of the elder, used in making wine, jelly, etc. **2.** elder[2].

Elder Brethren, the governing members of Trinity House.

elderly (ĕl′də lĭ), *adj.* **1.** somewhat old; between middle and old age. **2.** of or pertaining to persons in later life. —**eld′erliness,** *n.* —**Syn. 1.** See **old.**

elder statesman, *pl.* **-men. 1.** an influential elderly citizen whose advice is sought, especially on major national problems. **2.** (*pl.*) (in Japan) a group of senior statesmen, with no legal status, and no defined membership, who towards the end of the Meiji era were a powerful influence on government policy; the genro.

eldest (ĕl′dĭst), *adj.* oldest: now surviving only in *the eldest brother, sister,* and *eldest hand.* [OE *eldest(a)*, superl. of *ald, eald* OLD, c. G *ältest(e)*]

eldest hand, *Cards.* the player on the dealer's left.

ELDO, European Launcher Development Organization, formed by the U.K., Italy, West Germany, France, Belgium, the Netherlands, and Australia in 1961 to develop a European spacecraft launcher and satellite.

El Dorado (ĕl′ dō rä′dō), **1.** a legendary treasure city of South America, sought by the early Spanish explorers. **2.** any place of reputed fabulous wealth. [t. Sp.: the gilded]

eldritch (ĕl′drĭch), *adj.* *Orig. Scot.* weird; unearthly.

Elea (ē′lĭ ə), *n.* an ancient Greek city in SW Italy.

Eleanor of Aquitaine (ĕl′ĭ nə), 1122?–1204, queen of Henry II of England.

Eleatic (ĕl′ĭ ăt′ĭk), *adj.* **1.** pertaining to Elea. **2.** pertaining to the philosophical system founded by Xenophanes of Colophon, who resided in Elea, whose doctrines are developments of the conception of the universal unity of being. —*n.* **3.** an Eleatic philosopher. [t. L: s. *Eleāticus*, der. *Elea* ELEA] —**El′eat′icism,** *n.*

elecampane (ĕl′ĭ kăm pān′), *n.* a composite plant, *Inula helenium*, with large yellow flowers and aromatic leaves and root. [earlier *elena* (OE *elene*) *campana*, for ML *enula* (in L *inula*) *campāna*, prob., inula of the fields]

elect (ĭ lĕkt′), *v.t.* **1.** to select by vote, as for an office. **2.** to determine in favour of (a course of action, etc.). **3.** to pick out or choose. **4.** *Theol.* (of God) to select for divine mercy or favour, esp. for salvation. —*adj.* **5.** selected for an office, but not yet inducted (usually after the noun): *the governor-elect.* **6.** picked out; chosen. **7.** select or choice. **8.** *Theol.* chosen by God, esp. for eternal life. —*n.* **9.** a person or the persons chosen or worthy to be chosen. **10.** *Theol.* those chosen by God, esp. for eternal life. [late ME, t. L: s. *ēlectus*, pp., chosen, picked out] —**Syn. 3.** See **choose.**

elect., **1.** electric. **2.** electrical. **3.** electricity. Also, **elec.**

election (ĭ lĕk′shən), *n.* **1.** the selection of a person or persons for office by vote. **2.** a public vote upon a proposition submitted. **3.** the act of electing. **4.** *Theol.* the choice by God of individuals, as for a particular work, or esp. for salvation of eternal life. —**Syn. 3.** choice.

electioneer (ĭ lĕk′shə nĭə′), *v.i.* to work for the success of a candidate, party, etc., in an election. —**elec′tioneer′er,** *n.* —**elec′tioneer′ing,** *adj.*, *n.*

elective (ĭ lĕk′tĭv), *adj.* **1.** pertaining to the principle of electing to office, etc. **2.** appointed by election, as an officer. **3.** bestowed by or derived from election, as an office. **4.** having the power of electing to office, etc., as a body of persons. **5.** *U.S.* open to choice; optional; not required: *an elective subject in high school or college.* **6.** *Chem.* selecting for combination or action: *elective attraction* (tendency to combine with certain substances in preference to others). —*n.* **7.** *U.S.* an optional study; a study which a student may select from among alternatives. —**elec′tively,** *adv.* —**elec′tiveness, electivity** (ē′lĕk tĭv′ĭ tĭ), *n.*

elector (ĭ lĕk′tə), *n.* **1.** one who elects or may elect, esp. a

qualified voter. 2. *U.S.* a member of the electoral college. 3. (*usually cap.*) (in the Holy Roman Empire) one of the princes entitled to elect the emperor. —**elec′torship′,** *n.*
electoral (ĭ lĕk′tə rəl), *adj.* 1. pertaining to electors or election. 2. consisting of electors.
electoral college, *U.S.* a body of electors chosen by voters in each state to elect the president and vice-president of the United States.
electoral register, a register of all persons entitled to vote in a constituency. Also, **electoral roll.**
electorate (ĭ lĕk′tə rĭt), *n.* 1. the body of persons entitled to vote in an election. 2. the dignity or territory of an elector of the Holy Roman Empire.
electr-, var. of **electro-,** before vowels, as in *electrode.*
Electra (ĭ lĕk′trə), *n. Gk Legend.* the daughter of Agamemnon and Clytemnestra. She incited her brother Orestes to avenge the murder of his father.
Electra complex, *Psychol.* the unresolved desire of a daughter for sexual gratification from her father.
electress (ĭ lĕk′trĭs), *n.* 1. a female elector. 2. the wife or widow of an elector of the Holy Roman Empire.
electric (ĭ lĕk′trĭk), *adj.* 1. pertaining to, derived from, produced by, or involving electricity: *an electric current, an electric shock.* 2. producing, transmitting, or operated by electric currents: *an electric bell.* 3. electrifying; thrilling; exciting; stirring. [t. NL: s. *ēlectricus,* der. L *ēlectrum,* t. Gk: m. *ḗlektron* amber (as a substance that develops electricity under friction)]
electrical (ĭ lĕk′trĭ kl), *adj.* 1. electric. 2. concerned with electricity: *an electrical engineer.* —**elec′trically,** *adv.*
electrical engineer, one who practises electrical engineering.
electrical engineering, the branch of engineering concerned with the design, construction, and maintenance of electrical machinery, power transmission equipment, and communication systems.
electrical storm, a thunderstorm.
electric blanket, a blanket containing an electric heating element, usually thermostatically controlled.
electric blue, a steely blue colour.
electric cell. See **cell** (def. 7).
electric chair, 1. an electrified chair used in some states of the U.S. to execute criminals. 2. the electrocution.
electric charge. See **charge** (def. 33).
electric current, a flow of electricity. See **current** (def. 11).
electric eel, a fish, *Electrophorus electricus,* of eel-like form, having the power of giving strong electric discharges. It is found in the fresh waters of northern South America, and is sometimes over 6 feet long.
electric eye, a photoelectric cell.
electric field, a condition of space in the vicinity of an electric charge, or a moving magnet which manifests itself as a force on an electric charge within that space.
electric furnace, a furnace in which the heat required is produced through electricity.
electric guitar, a guitar with a device attached to its bridge for transmitting the sounds produced through an amplifier to a loudspeaker.
electrician (ĭ lĕk′trĭsh′ən, ē′lĕk-), *n.* 1. one who installs, operates, maintains, or repairs electrical devices. 2. a student of the science of electricity.
electric intensity, the strength of an electric field at any given point; electric field strength.
electricity (ĭ lĕk′trĭs′ĭ tĭ, ē′lĕk-), *n.* 1. an agency producing various physical phenomena, as attraction and repulsion, luminous and heating effects, shock to the body, chemical decomposition, etc., which were originally thought to be caused by a kind of fluid, but are now regarded as being due to the presence and movements of electrons, protons, and other electrically charged particles. 2. the science dealing with this agency. 3. electric current.
electric organ, 1. *Zool.* an anatomical feature in certain fishes, as the electric eel, which generates and discharges electricity, mainly for defensive purposes. 2. *Music.* **a.** electronic organ. **b.** a pipe organ which is operated electrically.
electric ray, a ray of the family *Torpedinidae* which possesses a peculiar organ enabling it to stun its prey with electric shock.
electric shock. See **shock**[1] (def. 5).
electrify (ĭ lĕk′trĭ fī′), *v.t.,* **-fied, -fying.** 1. to charge with or subject to electricity; to apply electricity to. 2. to equip for the use of electric power, as a railway. 3. to startle greatly; excite or thrill: *to electrify an audience.* [f. ELECTR(IC) + -(I)FY] —**elec′trifi′able,** *adj.* —**elec′trifica′tion,** *n.* —**elec′trifi′er,** *n.*
electrize (ĭ lĕk′trīz), *v.t.,* **-trized, -trizing.** *Obs.* electrify (defs 1, 2). Also, **electrise.** —**elec′triza′tion,** *n.* —**elec′triz′er,** *n.*
electro (ĭ lĕk′trō), *n., pl.* **-tros.** 1. electroplate. 2. electrotype.
electro-, a word meaning 'pertaining to or caused by electricity', as in *electromagnet, electrotype, electrochemistry, electrolysis, electrocute.* Also, **electr-.** [t. Gk: m. *ēlektro-,* comb. form of *ḗlektron* amber]
electroanalysis (ĭ lĕk′trō ə năl′ĭ sĭs), *n.* chemical analysis by electrolysis. —**elec′troan′alyt′ic,** *adj.*
electrobiology (ĭ lĕk′trō bī ŏl′ə jĭ), *n.* the science of electrical phenomena in living organisms.
electrocardiogram (ĭ lĕk′trō kä′dĭ ə grăm′), *n.* the graphic record produced by an electrocardiograph. *Abbrev.:* ECG. Also, **cardiogram.** [f. ELECTRO- + CARDIO- + -GRAM[1]]
electrocardiograph (ĭ lĕk′trō kä′dĭ ə grăf′, -gräf′), *n.* a device which detects and records the minute differences in potential caused by heart action and occurring between different parts of the body: used in the diagnosis of heart disease. *Abbrev.:* ECG. Also, **cardiograph.** [f. ELECTRO- + CARDIO- + -GRAPH] —**elec′trocar′diograph′ic,** *adj.* —**elec′trocar′diograph′ically,** *adv.* —**electrocardiography** (ĭ lĕk′trō kä′dĭ ŏg′rə fĭ), *n.*
electrochemical equivalent, *Chem.* the mass of a substance liberated or deposited during electrolysis by 1 coulomb, usually expressed in grams.
electrochemical series, *Chem.* electromotive series.
electrochemistry (ĭ lĕk′trō kĕm′ĭs trĭ), *n.* the branch of chemistry that deals with the chemical changes produced by electricity and the production of electricity by chemical changes. —**electrochemical** (ĭ lĕk′trō kĕm′ĭ kl), *adj.* —**elec′trochem′ically,** *adv.* —**elec′trochem′ist,** *n.*
electroconvulsive therapy, *Psychiatry.* a type of therapy in which an electric shock is administered to the brain, used in the treatment of depression, etc. *Abbrev.:* ECT.
electrocute (ĭ lĕk′trə kyo͞ot′), *v.t.,* **-cuted, -cuting.** 1. to kill by electricity. 2. (in the U.S.) to execute (a criminal) by electricity. [f. ELECTRO- + *-cute* in EXECUTE] —**elec′trocu′tion,** *n.*
electrode (ĭ lĕk′trōd), *n. Elect.* a conductor belonging to the class of metallic conductors, but not necessarily a metal, through which a current enters or leaves an electrolytic cell, arc generator, radio valve, gaseous discharge tube, or any conductor of the non-metallic class. [f. ELECTR(O)- + -ODE[2]]
electrodeposit (ĭ lĕk′trō dĭ pŏz′ĭt), *v.t.* 1. to deposit (a metal, etc.) by electrolysis. —*n.* 2. a deposit, as of metal, produced by electrolysis.
electrodynamic (ĭ lĕk′trō dī năm′ĭk), *adj.* 1. pertaining to the force of electricity in motion. 2. pertaining to electrodynamics. Also, **elec′trodynam′ical.**
electrodynamics (ĭ lĕk′trō dī năm′ĭks), *n.* the branch of electricity that deals with the mutual action of electric currents and the interaction of currents and magnets.
electrodynamometer (ĭ lĕk′trō dī′nə mŏm′ĭ tə), *n.* an instrument in which the mechanical reactions between two parts of the same circuit are used for detecting or measuring an electric current.
electroencephalogram (ĭ lĕk′trō ĕn sĕf′ə lə grăm′), *n.* the graphic record produced by an electroencephalograph. *Abbrev.:* EEG. [f. ELECTRO- + ENCEPHALO- + -GRAM[1]]
electroencephalograph (ĭ lĕk′trō ĕn sĕf′ə lə grăf′, -gräf′), *n.* a device which detects and records the electrical activity of the brain. *Abbrev.:* EEG. [f. ELECTRO- + ENCEPHALO- + -GRAPH] —**elec′troenceph′alograph′ic,** *adj.* —**elec′troenceph′alograph′ically,** *adv.* —**electroencephalography** (ĭ lĕk′trō ĕn sĕf′ə lŏg′rə fĭ), *n.*
electroextraction (ĭ lĕk′trō ĭk străk′shən), *n.* the recovery of a metal from a solution of its salts by electrolysis.
electroform (ĭ lĕk′trə fôm′), *v.t.* to produce or reproduce (metallic articles) by electrodeposition. —**electroforming** (ĭ lĕk′trə fô′mĭng), *n.*
electrograph (ĭ lĕk′trō grăf′, -gräf′), *n.* 1. a curve automatically traced, forming a record of the indications of an electrometer. 2. an apparatus for engraving metal plates on cylinders used in printing. 3. an apparatus used to transmit pictures, etc., electrically. —**elec′trograph′ic,** *adj.* —**elec′trograph′ically,** *adv.* —**electrography** (ĭ lĕk′trŏg′rə fĭ, ē′lĕk-), *n.*
electrokinetics (ĭ lĕk′trō kĭ nĕt′ĭks, -kī-), *n.* the branch of electricity that deals with currents. —**elec′trokinet′ic,** *adj.*
electrolier (ĭ lĕk′trō lĭə′), *n.* a chandelier for electric lamps. [f. ELECTRO- + *-lier* in CHANDELIER]
electroluminescence (ĭ lĕk′trō lo͞o′mĭ nĕs′əns), *n.* the property of emitting light on activation by an alternating current. —**elec′trolu′mines′cent,** *adj.*
electrolyse (ĭ lĕk′trō līz′), *v.t.,* **-lysed, -lysing.** to decompose by electrolysis. Also, *U.S.,* **electrolyze.** —**elec′trolysa′tion,** *n.* —**elec′trolys′er,** *n.*
electrolysis (ĭ lĕk′trŏl′ĭ sĭs), *n.* 1. the decomposition of a

chemical compound by an electric current. **2.** *Surg.* the destruction of tumours, hair roots, etc., by an electric current.

electrolyte (ĭ lĕk′trō līt′), *n.* **1.** *Elect.* a conducting medium in which the flow of current is accompanied by the movement of matter. **2.** *Chem.* any substance which dissociates into ions when dissolved in a suitable medium or when melted, thus forming a conductor of electricity.

electrolytic (ĭ lĕk′trō lĭt′ĭk), *adj.* **1.** pertaining to or derived by electrolysis. **2.** pertaining to an electrolyte. Also, **elec′trolyt′ical.** —**elec′trolyt′ically,** *adv.*

electrolytic capacitor, *Elect.* a capacitor of fixed capacitance in which one electrode consists of a metal foil coated with a thin layer of the metal oxide, and the other electrode is a non-corrosive salt solution or paste. Also, **electrolytic condenser.**

electrolytic cell. See **cell** (def. 8).

electrolytic dissociation, the separation of the molecule of an electrolyte into its constituent atoms.

electrolytic gas, a gas produced by the electrolysis of water, consisting of a mixture of hydrogen and oxygen in the ratio 2:1 by volume; detonating gas.

electrolytic rectifier, *Elect.* a rectifier consisting of an electrolytic cell which depends for its action on the properties of certain metals and electrolytes to allow current to flow only in one direction.

electromagnet (ĭ lĕk′trō măg′nĭt), *n.* a device consisting of an iron or steel core which is magnetized by electric current in a coil which surrounds it.

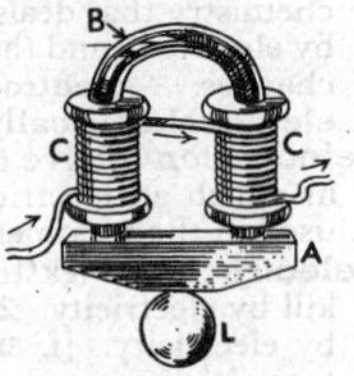

Electromagnet
A, Armature; B, Core; C, Coil carrying current; L, Load

electromagnetic (ĭ lĕk′trō măg nĕt′ĭk), *adj.* **1.** pertaining to an electromagnet. **2.** pertaining to electromagnetism. —**elec′tromag net′ically,** *adv.*

electromagnetic induction, *Elect.* the induction of an electromotive force in a circuit by a change in the magnetic flux linked with it.

electromagnetic pump, *Physics.* a pump used for liquid metals; consists of a flattened tube placed between the poles of an electromagnet. When a current is passed through the liquid metal in the tube it is subjected to a force along the axis of the tube.

electromagnetic radiation, *Physics.* radiation consisting of electromagnetic waves.

electromagnetic spectrum, *Physics.* the whole range of frequencies over which electromagnetic waves can be propagated, ranging from radio waves to cosmic radiation and including light.

electromagnetic tape, magnetic tape.

electromagnetic unit, *Physics.* a unit in a system of units within the c.g.s. system, used for measuring electric currents and magnetization, based on the unit magnetic pole which repels a similar pole placed 1 cm. distant with a force of 1 dyne. *Abbrev.:* emu, E.M.U.

electromagnetic wave, *Physics.* a moving disturbance in space produced by the acceleration of an electric charge; consisting of an electric field and a magnetic field at right-angles to each other, both moving at the same velocity in a direction at right angles to the plane of the two fields.

electromagnetism (ĭ lĕk′trō măg′nə tĭz′əm), *n.* **1.** the phenomena collectively resting upon the relations between electric currents and magnetism. **2.** the science that deals with these relations.

electromechanical (ĭ lĕk′trō mĭ kăn′ĭ kl), *adj.* containing both electrical and mechanical elements.

electrometallurgy (ĭ lĕk′trō mĕt′ə lûr′jĭ, -mĭ tăl′ə jĭ), *n.* the refining of metals and ores by an electric current. —**elec′tromet′allur′gical,** *adj.* —**elec′tromet′allur′gist,** *n.*

electrometer (ĭ lĕk′trŏm′ĭ tə, ē′lĕk-), *n.* an instrument for detecting or measuring a potential difference by means of the mechanical forces exerted between electrically charged bodies. —**electrometric** (ĭ lĕk′trō mĕt′rĭk), **elec′tromet′rical,** *adj.* —**elec′tromet′rically,** *adv.*

electromotive (ĭ lĕk′trō mō′tĭv), *adj.* pertaining to, producing, or tending to produce a flow of electricity.

electromotive force, the amount of energy supplied to an electric circuit in one second by a voltaic cell, dynamo, or other source of electrical energy when one ampere of current flows in the circuit. *Abbrev.:* e.m.f., E.M.F., emf.

electromotive series, *Chem.* the metals arranged in the order in which they will replace each other from their salts. Hydrogen is also included, and metals above hydrogen in the series will liberate it from acids. Also, **electrochemical series.**

electromotor (ĭ lĕk′trō mō′tə), *n.* electric motor.

electron (ĭ lĕk′trŏn), *n.* *Physics, Chem.* an elementary particle which is a constituent of all atoms: it has a minute mass of $9{\cdot}1083 \times 10^{-28}$ grams. It is also the unit of negative electric charge, having a charge of $1{\cdot}602 \times 10^{-19}$ coulombs; negatron. The positively charged electron is called a *positron.* [f. ELECTR(IC) + (ON)]

electron beam, a stream of electrons.

electronegative (ĭ lĕk′trō nĕg′ə tĭv), *adj.* *Physics, Chem.* **1.** containing negative electricity; tending to pass to the positive pole in electrolysis. **2.** assuming negative potential when in contact with a dissimilar substance. **3.** non-metallic.

electron gun, *Television.* the cathode in a cathode-ray tube which emits electrons, and the surrounding electrostatic or electromagnetic apparatus which controls and focuses the electron stream.

electronic (ĭ lĕk′trŏn′ĭk, ē′lĕk-), *adj.* **1.** of or pertaining to electrons. **2.** of, pertaining to, or concerned with electronics or any devices or systems based on electronics.

electronic computer. See **computer.**

electronic data processing, the use of digital computers to handle information. *Abbrev.:* EDP.

electronic music, electrophonic music.

electronic organ, organ (def. 1b).

electronics (ĭ lĕk′trŏn′ĭks, ē′lĕk-), *n.* the investigation and application of phenomena involving the movement of electrons in valves and semiconductors.

electron lens, a combination of static or varying electric and magnetic fields used to focus streams of electrons in a manner similar to that of an optical lens.

electron micrograph, a photograph of an object or collection of objects obtained with an electron microscope.

electron microscope, a microscope of extremely high power which uses beams of electrons focused by electron lenses instead of rays of light, the magnified image being formed on a fluorescent screen or recorded on a photographic plate. Its magnification is substantially greater than that of any optical microscope.

electron probe microanalysis, *Chem., Physics.* a method of analysing tiny quantities of a substance by bombarding it with a narrow beam of electrons and examining the resulting X-ray emission spectrum.

electron spin resonance spectroscopy, *Chem., Physics.* a method of locating electrons within a molecule and so providing information about the molecule's structure. It depends on a property of paramagnetic substances which results from their unpaired electrons.

electron tube, *U.S. Electronics.* valve (def. 7).

electronuclear machine (ĭ lĕk′trō nyōō′klĭ ə), a device for the production of very high energy beams of particles (protons, electrons, etc.) by acceleration in electric and magnetic fields. Examples are the cyclotron, synchrotron, cosmotron, etc.

electron-volt (ĭ lĕk′trŏn vōlt′), *n.* *Physics.* the energy acquired by an electron accelerating through a potential difference of one volt. *Abbrev.:* eV, ev.

electrophonic (ĭ lĕk′trō fŏn′ĭk), *adj.* (of musical instruments) based on oscillating electric currents. —**elec′trophon′ically,** *adv.*

electrophonic music, music produced by electrophonic means, which may include organized non-musical sounds. Also, **electronic music.**

electrophoresis (ĭ lĕk′trō fə rē′sĭs), *n.* *Physics, Chem.* the motion of colloidal particles suspended in a fluid medium, under the influence of an electric field. [f. ELECTRO- + Gk *phórēsis* a carrying]

electrophorus (ĭ lĕk′trŏf′ə rəs, ē′lĕk-), *n., pl.* **-ri** (-rī′). an instrument for generating static electricity by means of induction. [NL. See ELECTRO-, -PHOROUS]

electroplate (ĭ lĕk′trō plāt′), *v.,* **-plated, -plating,** *n.* —*v.t.* **1.** to plate or coat with a metal by electrolysis. —*n.* **2.** electroplated articles or ware. —**elec′troplat′er,** *n.* —**elec′troplat′ing,** *n.*

electropositive (ĭ lĕk′trō pŏz′ĭ tĭv), *adj.* *Physics, Chem.* **1.** containing positive electricity; tending to pass to the negative pole in electrolysis. **2.** assuming positive potential when in contact with another substance. **3.** basic, as an element or radical.

electroscope (ĭ lĕk′trə skōp′), *n.* a device for detecting the presence of electricity, and whether it is positive or negative, by means of electric attraction and repulsion. —**electroscopic** (ĭ lĕk′trə skŏp′ĭk), *adj.*

electrostatic (ĭ lĕk′trō stăt′ĭk), *adj.* *Elect.* of or pertaining to static electricity.

electrostatic generator, *Physics.* a machine for the production of charges at high potential, such as the Wimshurst machine and the Van de Graaff generator.

electrostatic precipitation, a method of removing small particles of dust, smoke, oil, etc., from a gas, esp. air, by first giving the particles an electrostatic charge and then passing the gas between two charged plates to which the particles are attracted.

electrostatics (ĭ lĕk′trō stăt′ĭks), *n.* the science of static electricity.

electrostatic unit, *Physics.* a unit in a system of units, within the c.g.s. system, based on the unit of charge, which is defined as that quantity of electricity which will repel an equal quantity 1 cm. distant with a force of 1 dyne. *Abbrev.*: e.s.u., E.S.U., esu.

electrostriction (ĭ lĕk′trō strĭk′shən), *n. Physics.* the elastic deformation of a dielectric when placed in an electric field.

electrotherapeutics (ĭ lĕk′trō thĕ′rə pyōō′tĭks), *n.* therapeutics based upon the curative use of electricity. **—elec′trother′apeu′tic, elec′trother′apeu′tical,** *adj.*

electrotherapist (ĭ lĕk′trō thĕ′rə pĭst), *n.* one versed in electrotherapeutics. Also, **electrotherapeutist** (ĭ lĕk′trō-thĕ′rə pyōō′tĭst).

electrotherapy (ĭ lĕk′trō thĕ′rə pĭ), *n.* treatment of diseases by means of electricity; electrotherapeutics.

electrotonus (ĭ lĕk′trŏt′ə nəs, ē′lĕk-), *n. Physiol.* the altered state of a nerve during the passage of an electric current through it. [NL, f. Gk: *ēlektro-* ELECTRO- + m. *tónos* tension] **—electrotonic** (ĭ lĕk′trō tŏn′ĭk), *adj.*

electrotype (ĭ lĕk′trō tīp′), *n., v.,* **-typed, -typing.** **—*n.*** **1.** a facsimile, for use in printing, of a block of type, an engraving, or the like, consisting of a thin shell of metal (copper or nickel), deposited by electrolytic action in a wax, lead, or plastic mould of the original and backed with lead alloy. **—*v.t.*** **2.** to make an electrotype or electrotypes of. **—elec′trotyp′er,** *n.*

electrovalency (ĭ lĕk′trō vā′lən sĭ), *n. Chem.* **1.** the valency of an ion; equal to the number of electrons lost or gained by an atom. **2.** a type of chemical bond in which an electron migrates from one atom to another, the resulting ions being held together by electrostatic attraction; electrovalent bond; ionic bond; polar bond. Also, *U.S.*, **elec′trova′lence. —elec′trova′lent,** *adj.*

electrum (ĭ lĕk′trəm), *n.* an amber-coloured alloy of gold and silver known to the ancients. [t. L, t. Gk: m. *ēlektron* amber, also gold-silver alloy. See ELECTRIC]

electuary (ĭ lĕk′tyōō ə rĭ), *n., pl.* **-aries.** a medicine composed usually of a powder mixed into a pasty mass with syrup or honey. [ME, t. LL: m. s. *ēlectuārium.* Cf. Gk *ekleiktón* electuary, der. *ekleíchein* lick up (in passive, be taken as an electuary)]

eleemosynary (ĕl′ĭ ē mŏs′ĭ nə rĭ), *adj.* **1.** of or pertaining to alms, charity, or charitable donations; charitable. **2.** derived from or provided by charity. **3.** dependent on or supported by charity. [t. ML: m. s. *eleēmosynārius*, der. LL *eleēmosyna* alms. See ALMS]

elegance (ĕl′ĭ gəns), *n.* **1.** elegant quality: *elegance of dress.* **2.** something elegant; a refinement.

elegancy (ĕl′ĭ gən sĭ), *n., pl.* **-cies.** elegance.

elegant (ĕl′ĭ gənt), *adj.* **1.** tastefully fine or luxurious in dress, manners, etc.: *elegant furnishings.* **2.** gracefully refined, as in tastes, habits, literary style, etc. **3.** nice, choice, or pleasingly superior in quality or kind, as a contrivance, preparation, or process. **4.** *Colloq.* excellent; fine; superior. [t. L: s. *ēlegans* fastidious, nice, fine, elegant] **—el′egantly,** *adv.* **—Syn. 1.** See **fine**[1].

elegiac (ĕl′ĭ jī′ək), *adj.* Also, **el′egi′acal. 1.** *Class. Pros.* denoting a distich the first line of which is a dactylic hexameter and the second a pentameter, or a verse differing from the hexameter by suppression of the arsis or metrically unaccented part of the third and the sixth foot. **2.** belonging to an elegy or to elegy; having to do with elegies. **3.** expressing sorrow or lamentation: *elegiac strains.* **—*n.*** **4.** an elegiac or distich verse. **5.** a poem or poems in such distichs or verses. [t. LL: s. *elegīacus*, t. Gk: m. *elegeiakós*]

elegist (ĕl′ĭ jĭst), *n.* the author of an elegy.

elegit (ĭ lē′jĭt), *n. Law.* a writ of execution against a judgement debtor's goods or property held by the judgement creditor until payment of the debt (abolished in Great Britain 1956). [L: he has chosen]

elegize (ĕl′ĭ jīz′), *v.,* **-gized, -gizing. —*v.t.*** **1.** to lament in or as in an elegy. **—*v.i.*** **2.** to compose an elegy. Also, **elegise.**

elegy (ĕl′ĭ jĭ), *n., pl.* **-gies. 1.** a mournful, melancholy, or plaintive poem, esp. a funeral song or a lament for the dead, as Milton's *Lycidas.* **2.** poetry or a poem written in elegiac meter. **3.** *Music.* a sad or funeral composition, vocal or instrumental, whether actually commemorative or not. [t. L: m. s. *elegīa*, t. Gk: m. *elegeía*, prop. neut. pl. of *elegeîos* elegiac, der. *élegos* lament]

elem., 1. elementary. **2.** elements.

element (ĕl′ĭ mənt), *n.* **1.** a component or constituent part of a whole. **2.** (*pl.*) the rudimentary principles of an art, science, etc.: *the elements of grammar.* **3.** one of the simple substances, usually earth, water, air, and fire, regarded by Aristotle as constituting the material universe. **4.** one of these four substances regarded as the natural habitat of something. **5.** the sphere or environment adapted to any person or thing: *to be in one's element.* **6.** (*pl.*) atmospheric agencies or forces: *exposed to the elements.* **7.** *Chem.* one of a class of substances which consist entirely of atoms of the same atomic number; 103 such substances are now recognized. **8.** *Maths.* **a.** an infinitesimal part of a given quantity, similar in nature to it. **b.** any entity that satisfies the conditions of belonging to a class of objects, such as one of a number of objects arranged in a symmetrical or regular figure. **9.** *Geom.* one of the points, lines, planes, or other geometrical forms, of which a figure is composed. **10.** *Astron.* any of the data required for the solution of a problem: *the elements of a planetary orbit*, which determine the orientation, size, and shape of the orbit, and the position of the planet in the orbit at any time. **11.** *Elect.* **a.** the resistance wire, and the former to which it is attached, of an electric heater or other domestic appliance containing a heating unit. **b.** one of the electrodes of a cell or radio valve. **12.** *Gram.* any word, group of words, or part of a word, which recurs in various contexts in a language with relatively constant meaning. **13.** (*pl.*) the bread and wine used in the Eucharist. [ME, t. L: s. *elementum* a first principle, rudiment]

—Syn. 1. ELEMENT, COMPONENT, CONSTITUENT, INGREDIENT refer to the units which build up substances and compounds or mixtures. ELEMENT denotes a fundamental, ultimate part: *the elements of matter, of a discussion.* COMPONENT and CONSTITUENT denote that which goes into the making of a compound, COMPONENT suggesting one of a number of parts, and CONSTITUENT an active and necessary participation: *iron and carbon as components of steel; hydrogen and oxygen the constituents of water.* INGREDIENT denotes something essential or non-essential which enters into a mixture or compound: *the ingredients of a cake.*

elemental (ĕl′ĭ mĕn′tl), *adj.* **1.** of the nature of an ultimate constituent; simple; uncompounded. **2.** pertaining to rudiments or first principles. **3.** of, pertaining to, or of the nature of the four elements or any one of them. **4.** pertaining to the agencies, forces, or phenomena of physical nature: *elemental gods, elemental worship.* **5.** comparable to the great forces of nature, as with reference to their power: *elemental grandeur.* **6.** pertaining to chemical elements. **—el′emen′tally,** *adv.*

elementary (ĕl′ĭ mĕn′tə rĭ, -trĭ), *adj.* **1.** pertaining to or dealing with elements, rudiments, or first principles: *elementary education, an elementary grammar.* **2.** of the nature of an ultimate constituent; simple or uncompounded. **3.** pertaining to the four elements or to the great forces of nature; elemental. **—el′emen′tarily,** *adv.* **—el′emen′tariness,** *n.*

—Syn. 1. ELEMENTARY, PRIMARY, RUDIMENTARY refer to what is basic and fundamental. ELEMENTARY refers to the introductory, simple, easy facts, steps, or parts of a subject which must necessarily be learnt first in order to understand succeeding ones: *elementary facts about geography, elementary arithmetic.* PRIMARY may mean much the same as ELEMENTARY; however, it usually emphasizes the idea of what comes first even more than that of simplicity: *the primary school is for younger children.* RUDIMENTARY applies to what is undeveloped or imperfect: *a rudimentary form of government.*

elementary particle, *Physics.* any of a class of entities which used to be thought to be the indivisible units of which all matter is composed. It is now known that some elementary particles are compounds of others; fundamental particle; ultimate particle.

elementary school, *Obs. in Great Britain.* a primary school.

elemi (ĕl′ĭ mĭ), *n., pl.* **-mis.** any of various fragrant resins used in medicine, varnish making, etc. [cf. F *élémi*, Sp. *elemí*, t. Ar.: m. *allāmi*]

elenchus (ĭ lĕng′kəs), *n., pl.* **-chi** (-kī). **1.** a logical refutation; an argument which refutes another argument by proving the contrary of its conclusion. **2.** a false refutation; a sophistical argument. [t. L, t. Gk: m. *élenchos* cross-examination] **—elenctic** (ĭ lĕngk′tĭk), *adj.*

eleoptene (ĕl′ĭ ŏp′tēn), *n. Chem.* the liquid portion of volatile oils (opposed to the solid part, *stearoptene*). [f. Gk: m. *élaio(n)* oil + m. s. *ptēnós* winged, volatile]

African elephant, *Loxodonta africana* (10 ft high at the shoulder)

elephant (ĕl′ĭ fənt), *n., pl.* **-phants,** (*esp. collectively*) **-phant. 1.** any of the large five-toed mammals, with long prehensile trunk or proboscis and long tusks of ivory, constituting the family *Eliphantidae*, comprising species of two existing genera, *Elephas* and *Loxodonta*, esp. *Elephas maximus*, of India and neighbouring regions, with comparatively small ears, *Loxodonta africana*, of Africa, with large, flapping ears. **2. a.** a size of printing paper, 20 × 27 inches. **b.** a size of writing paper, 23 × 28 inches. **c.** a size of wrapping paper, 24 × 34 inches. **3.** See **white elephant. 4.** See **pink elephant.** [t. L: s. *elephantus*, also s. *elephās*, t. Gk: m. *eléphas* elephant, ivory; r. ME *olifaunt*, t. OF: m. *olifant*] —**el′ephan′toid,** *adj.*

Indian elephant, *Elephas maximus* (9 ft high at the shoulder)

elephantiasis (ĕl′ĭ fən tī′ə sĭs, -făn-), *n. Pathol.* a chronic disease, due to lymphatic obstruction, characterized by enormous enlargement of the parts affected. [t. L, t. Gk, der. *eléphas* elephant]

elephantine (ĕl′ĭ făn′tīn), *adj.* **1.** pertaining to or resembling an elephant. **2.** huge; ponderous; clumsy.

elephant seal, either of two species of large seal of the genus *Mirounga*: *M. leomina* of the subantarctic islands, and *M. angustirostris* of NW North America.

elephant's-ear (ĕl′ĭ fənts ĭə′), *n.* **1.** the taro. **2.** any species of *Begonia*.

elephant shrew, a shrew, *Elephantulus rogeti*, of N, S, and E Africa, having a long snout.

Eleusinia (ĕl′yŏŏ sĭn′ĭ ə), *n. Gk Antiq.* the famous mysteries and festival celebrated at Eleusis and later Athens and elsewhere, in honour of Demeter (Ceres). —**El′eusin′ian,** *adj.*

Eleusis (ĭ lyōō′sĭs), *n.* a city in ancient Greece, in Attica.

elevate (ĕl′ĭ vāt′), *v.*, **-vated, -vating,** *adj.* —*v.t.* **1.** to move or raise to a higher place or position; lift up. **2.** to raise to a higher state or station; exalt. **3.** to raise the spirits of; put in high spirits. —*adj.* **4.** *Archaic.* raised; elevated. [ME *elevat*, t. L: s. *ēlevātus*, pp.]

—**Syn. 2.** ELEVATE, ENHANCE, EXALT, HEIGHTEN mean to raise or make higher in some respect. To ELEVATE is to raise something to a relatively higher level, position, or state: *to elevate the living standards of a group.* To ENHANCE is to add to the attractions or desirability of something: *landscaping enhances the beauty of the grounds, paved streets enhance the value of property.* To EXALT is to raise very high in rank, character, estimation, mood, etc.: *a king is exalted above his subjects.* To HEIGHTEN is to increase in strength or intensity: *to heighten one's powers of concentration.* —**Ant. 2.** lower.

elevated (ĕl′ĭ vā′tĭd), *adj.* **1.** raised, esp. above the ground: *an elevated platform.* **2.** exalted or noble: *elevated thoughts.* **3.** elated; joyful. **4.** *Colloq.* slightly drunk.

elevation (ĕl′ĭ vā′shən), *n.* **1.** altitude above sea or ground level. **2.** an elevated place; an eminence. **3.** loftiness; grandeur or dignity; nobleness. **4.** the act of elevating. **5.** the state of being elevated. **6.** *Archit.* **a.** a drawing or design which represents an object or structure as being projected geometrically on a vertical plane parallel to its chief dimension. **b.** one of the external faces of a building; façade. **7.** *Survey.* the angle between the line from an observer to an object above him and a horizontal line. **8.** the ability of a dancer to stay in the air while executing a step. **9.** *Rom. Cath. Ch.* (*usually cap.*) the lifting up of the bread and wine after consecration by the priest, in the view of the congregation. —**Syn. 2.** See **height.**

elevator (ĕl′ĭ vā′tə), *n.* **1.** one who or that which elevates or raises. **2.** a mechanical device for raising articles. **3.** *U.S.* a lift (def. 20). **4.** a building for storing grain, the grain being handled by means of mechanical lifting and conveying devices. **5.** a hinged horizontal plane on an aeroplane, etc., used to control the longitudinal inclination, generally placed at the tail end of the fuselage. **6.** *Anat.* a muscle for raising part of the body. [t. LL]

eleven (ĭ lĕv′ən), *n.* **1.** a cardinal number, ten plus one. **2.** a symbol for this number, as 11 and XI. **3.** a set of this many persons or things. **4.** a team of eleven players, as in soccer, cricket, hockey, etc. —*adj.* **5.** amounting to eleven in number. [ME *elleven(e)*, etc., OE *ellefne, endleofan*, etc., lit., one left (after counting ten). Cf. OHG *einlif*, MHG *eilf*, G *elf*] —**elev′enth,** *adj.*, *n.*

elevenpence (ĭ lĕv′ən pəns), *n.* eleven pennies.

elevenpenny (ĭ lĕv′ən pə nĭ), *adj.* **1.** of the amount or value of elevenpence. —*n.* **2.** something purchased for elevenpence.

eleven-plus (ĭ lĕv′ən plŭs′), *n.* an examination taken in England by many primary schoolchildren at the age of about eleven, the result of which determines the type of state secondary education for which they are eligible.

elevenses (ĭ lĕv′ən zĭz), *n. Colloq.* a light mid-morning snack, usually taken at about 11 o'clock.

eleventh hour, the last possible moment for doing something. —**eleventh-hour** (ĭ lĕv′ənth ou′ə), *adj.*

elevon (ĕl′ĭ vŏn′), *n. Aeronautics.* an aircraft control surface, usually on tailless aircraft, combining the functions of an aileron and an elevator. [b. ELEV(ATOR) + (AILER)ON]

elf (ĕlf), *n.*, *pl.* **elves** (ĕlvz). **1.** one of a class of imaginary beings, esp. from mountainous regions, with magical powers, given to capricious interference in human affairs, and usually imagined to be a diminutive being in human form; a sprite; a fairy. **2.** a dwarf or a small child. **3.** a small, mischievous person. [ME, back-formation from *elven*, OE *elfen* nymph (feminine elf), repr. OE *ælf*, c. G *Alp* nightmare (def. 3), incubus] —**elf′-like′,** *adj.* —**Syn. 1.** See **fairy.**

El Faiyum (ĕl′fī yōōm′), a town in N Egypt; archaeological, esp. Roman, remains. 102,000 (est. 1960). Also, **El Fayum, Faiyum.**

elfchild (ĕlf′chīld′), *n.* a changeling.

El Ferrol (*Sp.* ĕl fĕr rōl′), a seaport in NW Spain: naval arsenal and dockyard. 79,593 (1965). Also, **Ferrol.**

elfin (ĕl′fĭn), *adj.* **1.** of or like elves. **2.** small and mischievous. —*n.* **3.** an elf.

elfish (ĕl′fĭsh), *adj.* **1.** elf-like. **2.** small and mischievous. Also, **elvish.** —**elf′ishly,** *adv.* —**elf′ishness,** *n.* —**Syn.** impish.

elflock (ĕlf′lŏk′), *n.* a tangled lock of hair.

Elgar (ĕl′gə, -gä), *n.* **Sir Edward,** 1857–1934, English composer.

Elgin (ĕl′gĭn), *n.* former name of **Moray.**

Elgin marbles (ĕl′gĭn), Greek sculpture of the 5th century B.C., originally on the Parthenon in Athens, and supposedly sculptured under the direction of Phidias: now in the British Museum in London. [after Thomas Bruce, 7th Earl of *Elgin* (1766–1841), who arranged for the collection to be brought from Athens to London]

El Giza (ĕl gē′zə), a town in N Egypt, near Cairo: the pyramids and the Sphinx are situated nearby. 250,000 (est. 1960). Also, **El Gi′zeh, Giza,** or **Gizeh.**

Elgon (ĕl′gən), *n.* an isolated volcanic mountain in E Africa, on the borders of Uganda and Kenya. 14,176 ft.

El Greco (ĕl grĕk′ō; *Sp.* ĕl grĕ′kō), ('*the Greek*') (*Domenikos Theotocopoulos*), 1541–1614, Spanish painter, born in Crete.

El Hasa (ĕl hä′sə), Hasa.

Eli (ē′lī), *n. Bible.* a Hebrew judge and high priest. I Sam. 1–3. [t. Heb.: m. *'Elī*]

Elia (ē′lĭ ə), *n.* pen-name of Charles Lamb. —**E′lian,** *adj.*

Elias (ĭ lī′əs), *n.* (in the New Testament) Elijah. Matt. 16:14, etc.

elicit (ĭ lĭs′ĭt), *v.t.* to draw or bring out or forth; educe; evoke: *to elicit the truth.* [t. L: s. *ēlicitus*, pp.] —**elic′ita′tion,** *n.* —**elic′itor,** *n.*

elide (ĭ līd′), *v.t.*, **elided, eliding. 1.** to omit (a vowel, consonant, or syllable) in pronunciation. **2.** *Obs.* to suppress. **3.** *Scots. Law.* to annul or quash. [t. L: m. s. *ēlīdere* crush out]

eligibility (ĕl′ĭ jə bĭl′ĭ tĭ), *n.* **1.** worthiness or fitness to be chosen. **2.** legal qualification for election or appointment.

eligible (ĕl′ĭ jə bl), *adj.* **1.** fit or proper to be chosen; worthy of choice; desirable. **2.** legally qualified to be elected or appointed to office. [t. F, der. L *ēligere* pick out] —**el′igibly,** *adv.*

Elijah (ĭ lī′jə), *n.* a great Hebrew prophet of the 9th century B.C. I Kings 17, II Kings 2.

eliminate (ĭ lĭm′ĭ nāt′), *v.t.*, **-nated, -nating. 1.** to get rid of; expel; remove: *to eliminate errors.* **2.** to omit as irrelevant or unimportant; ignore. **3.** *Physiol.* to void or expel from an organism. **4.** *Maths.* to remove (a quantity) from an equation by elimination. [t. L: m. s. *ēlīminātus*, pp., turned out of doors] —**elim′inabil′ity,** *n.* —**elim′inable,** *adj.* —**eliminative** (ĭ lĭm′ĭ nə tĭv), *adj.* —**elim′ina′tor,** *n.* —**elim′inatory,** *adj.* —**Syn. 1.** See **exclude.** —**Ant. 2.** include.

elimination (ĭ lĭm′ĭ nā′shən), *n.* **1.** the act of eliminating. **2.** the state of being eliminated. **3.** *Maths.* the process of solving a system of linear equations by a procedure in which variables are successively removed.

Elinvar (ĕl′ĭn vä′), *n. Trademark.* a steel containing nickel and chromium, used in hairsprings of watches owing to its low thermal expansion, its rust-resistance and its magnetic properties.

Eliot (ĕl′yət), *n.* **1. George** (*Mary Ann Evans*), 1819–80, English novelist. **2. John** ('*the Apostle of the Indians*'), 1604–90, colonial American missionary. **3. Sir John,** 1592–1632, English statesman. **4. T(homas) S(tearns),** 1888–1965, British poet, critic, and essayist, born in the U.S.

Elis (ē′lĭs), *n.* **1.** an ancient country in W Greece, in the Peloponnesus: site of the ancient Olympic games. **2.** the capital of this country.

Elisabethville (ĭ lĭz′ə bəth vĭl), *n.* former name of **Lubumbashi.**

Elisavetgrad (*Russ.* yĭ lĭ zä vyĕt′grət), *n.* former name of **Kirovograd.**

Elisavetpol (*Russ.* yĭ lĭ zä vyĕt′pəly), *n.* former name of **Kirovabad.**

Elisha (ĭ lī′shə), *n.* a Hebrew prophet of the 9th century B.C., the successor of Elijah. II Kings 3–9.

elision (ĭ lĭzh′ən), *n.* the omission of a vowel, consonant, or syllable in writing or pronunciation. [t. L: s. *ēlīsio* a striking out]

elisor (ĕl′ĭ zə), *n.* *Law. Obsolesc.* a person named by the court to choose a jury when the jury returned by the sheriff and that returned by the coroner have been successfully challenged.

elite (ĭ lēt′, ā-), *n.* **1.** the choice or best part, as of a body or class of persons. **2.** a small type, approximately 10-point, used in typewriters and having 12 characters to the inch. Also, *French,* **élite** (*Fr.* ė lĕt′). [t. F, der. *élire* choose, g. L *ēligere*]

elixir (ĭ lĭk′sə), *n.* **1.** an alchemic preparation formerly believed to be capable of transmuting base metals into gold, or of prolonging life: *elixir vitae,* or *elixir of life.* **2.** a sovereign remedy; panacea; cure-all. **3.** the quintessence or absolute embodiment of anything. **4.** *Pharm.* **a.** a tincture with more than one base, or some similar compound medicine. **b.** an aromatic, sweetened alcoholic liquid containing medicinal agents, or used as a vehicle for them. [ME, t. ML, t. Ar.: m. *el, al* the + *iksīr* philosopher's stone, prob. t. LGk: m. *xḗrion* a drying powder for wounds]

Elizabeth (ĭ lĭz′ə bəth), *n.* **1. I,** 1533–1603, queen of England 1558–1603 (successor of Mary I; daughter of Henry VIII and Anne Boleyn). **2. II,** born 1926, queen of England since 1952; daughter of George VI. **3.** ('*Carmen Sylva*') 1843–1916, queen of Rumania 1881–1914, and author. **4.** (in the New Testament) the mother of John the Baptist. Luke 1:5–25. **5.** a town in the U.S., in NE New Jersey. 107,698 (1960). **6.** a town in S South Australia. 35,200 (est. 1964).

Elizabethan (ĭ lĭz′ə bē′thən), *adj.* **1.** of or pertaining to Elizabeth I, queen of England, or to her times. —*n.* **2.** one who lived in England during the Elizabethan period, esp. a poet or dramatist.

elk (ĕlk), *n., pl.* **elks,** (*esp. collectively*) **elk. 1.** the largest existing European and Asiatic deer, *Alces alces,* the male of which has large palmate antlers. See **moose. 2.** (in America) the wapiti. **3.** a pliable leather used for sports shoes, made orig. of elk hide but now of calfskin or cowhide tanned and smoked to resemble elk hide. [appar. f. OE *ealh* elk (c. G *Elch*) + *-k* suffix. Cf. OE *cranoc* crane (not dim.) L *alces,* Gk *álkē* elk, of Gmc orig.]

Elk, *Alces alces* (Ab. 6 ft high at the shoulder)

El Kerak (ĕl kĕ′răk), a town in W Jordan. 50,000 (est. 1965).

elkhorn fern (ĕlk′hôn′), stag's-horn fern.

elkhound (ĕlk′hound′), *n.* one of a large, strong breed of dogs with a thick grey coat, originally a Norwegian hunting dog. Also, **Norwegian elkhound.**

ell[1] (ĕl), *n.* *U.S.* an extension to a building, usually at right angles to one end. Also, **el.** [from the shape of the letter L]

ell[2] (ĕl), *n.* a measure of length, now little used, varying in different countries: in Great Britain equal to 45 inches. [ME and OE *eln,* c. D *el,* G *Elle*; orig. meaning arm, forearm (see ELBOW), and akin to L *ulna,* Gk *ōlénē*]

Elland (ĕl′ənd), *n.* a town in England, in the West Riding of Yorkshire, near Halifax. 18,353 (1961).

Ellesmere (ĕlz′mĭə′), *n.* **Lake,** a tidal lake in E South Island, New Zealand. 70 sq. mi.

Ellesmere Island, a large island in the Arctic Ocean, NW of Greenland: a part of the Canadian Northwest Territories. ab. 76,600 sq. mi.

Ellesmere Port, a seaport in England, in NW Cheshire, on the Manchester Ship Canal: docks and oil refinery. 44,681 (1961).

Ellice Islands (ĕl′ĭs), a group of islands in the central Pacific, S of the equator: a part of the British colony of Gilbert and Ellice islands. 5120 pop. (1962); 16½ sq. mi. Also, **Lagoon Islands.**

Ellington (ĕl′ĭng tən), *n.* **Edward Kennedy** ('*Duke*'), born 1899, U.S. jazz composer, pianist, and conductor.

ellipse (ĭ lĭps′), *n.* *Geom.* a plane curve such that the sums of the distances of each point in its periphery from two fixed points, the foci, are equal. It is a conic section formed by the intersection of a right circular cone by a plane which cuts obliquely the axis and the opposite sides of the cone. See diag. under **conic section.** [t. L: m. s. *ellipsis.* See ELLIPSIS]

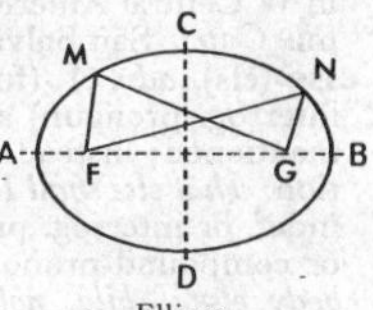

Ellipse
AB, CD, Axes of ellipse; F, G, Foci. FM + GM equals FN + GN, M and N being any points in the curve

ellipsis (ĭ lĭp′sĭs), *n., pl.* **-ses** (-sēz). **1.** *Gram.* the omission from a sentence of a word or words which would complete or clarify the construction. **2.** *Print.* a mark or marks as ——, . . ., * * *, to indicate an omission or suppression of letters or words. [t. L, t. Gk: m. *élleipsis* omission]

ellipsoid (ĭ lĭp′soid), *Geom.* —*n.* **1.** a solid figure all plane sections of which are ellipses or circles. —*adj.* **2.** ellipsoidal.

ellipsoidal (ĭ lĭp′soi′dl, ĕl′ĭp-), *adj.* pertaining to, or having the form of, an ellipsoid.

elliptical (ĭ lĭp′tĭ kl), *adj.* **1.** pertaining to or having the form of an ellipse. **2.** pertaining to or marked by grammatical ellipses. **3.** extremely or excessively concise or condensed. Also, **ellip′tic.**

elliptically (ĭ lĭp′tĭ kə lĭ), *adv.* **1.** in the form of an ellipse. **2.** in an elliptical manner; with an ellipsis.

ellipticity (ĭ lĭp′tĭs′ĭ tĭ, ĕl′ĭp-), *n.* the degree of divergence of an ellipse from the circle.

Ellis (ĕl′ĭs), *n.* **1. Alexander John** (orig. *Alexander John Sharpe*), 1814–90, English phonetician and mathematician. **2. (Henry) Havelock** (hăv′lŏk′), 1859–1939, English psychologist and writer.

Ellore (ĕ lô′), *n.* a town in India, in NE Andhra Pradesh. 108,321 (1961). Also, **Eluru.**

elm (ĕlm), *n.* **1.** any of the trees of the genus *Ulmus,* as *U. procera* (**English elm**), *U. americana* (**white** or **American elm**), *U. fulva* (**slippery elm**), etc., some of which are widely cultivated for shade and ornament. **2.** the wood of such a tree. [ME and OE, c. OHG *elm*; akin to Icel. *álmr,* L *ulmus*]

Elman (ĕl′mən), *n.* **Mischa** (mē′shə), 1891–1967, U.S. violinist, born in Russia.

El Mansura (ĕl′măn so͞o′rə), a town in NE Egypt, in the Nile Delta: defeat of the Crusaders by the Mamelukes 1250. 146,700 (est. 1959). Also, **Mansura.**

El Misti (*Sp.* ėl mēs′tē), a volcanic mountain in S Peru, in the Andes. 19,200 ft. Also, **Misti.**

elmy (ĕl′mĭ), *adj.* abounding in or consisting of elms.

El Obeid (ĕl ō′bā ĭd), a town in central Sudan: victory of the Mahdi over the Egyptians 1883. 52,372 (1956).

elocution (ĕl′ə kyo͞o′shən), *n.* **1.** manner of speaking or reading in public. **2.** *Speech.* the study and practice of delivery, including the management of voice and gesture. [t. L: s. *ēlocūtio* a speaking out] —**elocutionary** (ĕl′ə kyo͞o′shə nə rĭ, -kyo͞osh′nə rĭ), *adj.* —**el′ocu′tionist,** *n.*

Elohim (ĕ lō′hĭm), *n.* the Hebrew word for God, often used in Hebrew text of the Old Testament. [t. Heb.: m. *elōhīm,* prop. pl. of *elōh* god, but often taken as sing.]

Elohist (ĕ lō′hĭst), *n.* the writer (or writers) of one of the major strands or sources of the Hexateuch in which God is characteristically referred to as Elohim instead of Yahweh (Jehovah). See **Yahwist.** —**Elohistic** (ĕl′ō hĭs′tĭk), *adj.*

eloign (ĭ loin′), *v.t.* to remove (oneself) to a distance. Also, **eloin′.** [t. AF: m. s. *esloignier,* der. OF *es-* (See EX-[1]) + *loign* far away (g. L *longē*)]

elongate (ē′lŏng gāt′), *v.,* **-gated, -gating,** *adj.* —*v.t.* **1.** to draw out to greater length; lengthen; extend. —*v.i.* **2.** to increase in length. —*adj.* **3.** elongated. [f. LL: m. s. *ēlongātus,* pp., removed, prolonged]

elongation (ē′lŏng gā′shən), *n.* **1.** the act of elongating. **2.** the state of being elongated. **3.** that which is elongated; an elongated part. **4.** *Astron.* the angular distance measured from the earth, between a planet or the moon and the sun, or between a satellite and the planet about which it revolves.

elope (ĭ lōp′), *v.i.,* **eloped, eloping. 1.** to run away with a lover, usually in order to marry without parental consent. **2.** to abscond or escape. [ME **alopen,* f. *a-* A-[3] + *lopen* LOPE. Cf. AF *aloper* ravish (a woman), elope (with a man)] —**elope′ment,** *n.* —**elop′er,** *n.*

eloquence (ĕl′ə kwəns), *n.* **1.** the action, practice, or art of using language with fluency, power, and aptness. **2.** eloquent language or discourse: *a flow of eloquence.*

eloquent (ĕl′ə kwənt), *adj.* **1.** having or exercising the power of fluent, forcible, and appropriate speech: *an eloquent orator.* **2.** characterized by forcible and appropriate expression: *an eloquent speech.* **3.** movingly expressive: *eloquent looks.* [ME, t. L: s. *ēloquens,* ppr., speaking out] —**el′oquently,** *adv.*

El Paso (ĕl păs′ō), a city in the U.S., in W Texas, on the Rio Grande. 276,687 (1960).

El Salvador (ĕl săl′və dô′; *Sp.* ĕl säl bä dôr′), a republic in W Central America. 2,510,984 pop. (1961); 13,176 sq. mi. *Cap.*: San Salvador. Also, **Salvador.**

else (ĕls), *adv.* **1.** (following as an appositive an indef. or interrog. pronoun) **a.** other than the person or the thing mentioned; instead: *somebody else; who else?* **b.** in addition: *what else shall I do? who else is going?* **2.** (following an indef. or interrog. pronoun and forming with it an indef. or compound pronoun with inflection at the end): *somebody else's child, nobody else's business, whose else* (older usage) or now usually *who else's child could it be?* **3.** otherwise: *run, else* (or *or else*) *you will be late.* [ME and OE *elles* (c. OHG *elles*) adv. gen. of a pre-E word, c. L *alius* other]

Elsene (*Flem.* ĕl′sə nə), *n.* Flemish name of **Ixelles.**

Elsevier (ĕl′zə vĭə′, -və), *n., adj.* Elzevir.

elsewhere (ĕls′wĕə′), *adv.* somewhere else; in or to some other place.

Elsinore (ĕl′sĭ nô′, ĕl′sĭ nô′), *n.* Helsingör.

Elstree (ĕls′trē′), *n.* a town in England, in S Hertfordshire: film studios. 24,782 (1961).

Eluard (*Fr.* ĕ ly är′), *n.* **Paul** (*Fr.* pŏl), 1895–1952, French poet.

elucidate (ĭ lo͞o′sĭ dāt′), *v.t.,* **-dated, -dating.** to make lucid or clear; throw light upon; explain. [t. LL: m. s. *ēlūcidātus,* pp., made light] —**elu′cida′tion,** *n.* —**elu′cida′tive, elu′cida′tory,** *adj.* —**elu′cida′tor,** *n.* —**Syn.** See **explain.**

elude (ĭ lo͞od′), *v.t.,* **eluded, eluding. 1.** to avoid or escape by dexterity or artifice: *to elude pursuit.* **2.** to slip away from; evade: *to elude vigilance.* **3.** *Obs.* to escape the mind; baffle. [t. L: m. s. *ēlūdere* finish play, deceive] —**elud′er,** *n.* —**Syn. 1.** shun, dodge. See **escape. 3.** foil, frustrate.

Elul (ĕ lo͞ol′), *n.* (in the Jewish calendar) the twelfth month of the civil year and the sixth of the ecclesiastical year. [t. Heb.]

Eluru (ĕ lô′), *n.* Ellore.

elusion (ĭ lo͞o′zhən), *n.* the act of eluding; evasion; clever escape. [t. ML: s. *ēlūsio.* See ELUDE]

elusive (ĭ lo͞o′sĭv), *adj.* **1.** eluding clear perception or complete mental grasp; hard to express or define. **2.** dexterously evasive. Also, **elusory** (ĭ lo͞o′sə rĭ). —**elu′sively,** *adv.* —**elu′siveness,** *n.*

elutriate (ĭ lo͞o′trĭ āt′), *v.t.,* **-ated, -ating. 1.** to purify by washing and straining or decanting. **2.** to separate the light and heavy particles of by suspending in a current of water or air. [t. L: m. s. *ēlūtriātus,* pp.] —**elu′tria′tor,** *n.* —**elu′tria′tion,** *n.*

eluvium (ĭ lo͞o′vyəm), *n., pl.* **-via** (-vyə). *Geol.* a deposit of soil, dust, etc., originating in the place where found as through decomposition of rock (distinguished from *alluvium*). [NL, der. L *ēluere* wash out] —**elu′vial,** *adj.*

elvan (ĕl′vən), *n. Geol.* a granular, igneous rock found most often in dykes and composed essentially of quartz and orthoclase. Also, **elvanite** (ĕl′və nīt).

elver (ĕl′və), *n.* a young eel, particularly when running up a stream from the ocean. [var. of *eel-fare* (f. EEL + FARE) passage of young eels up a river]

elves (ĕlvz), *n.* pl. of **elf.**

elvish (ĕl′vĭsh), *adj.* elfish. —**elv′ishly,** *adv.*

Ely (ē′lĭ), *n.* **Isle of,** a former administrative division of Cambridgeshire.

Elyot (ĕl′ĭ ət, -yət), *n.* **Sir Thomas,** *c.* 1490–1546, English scholar and diplomat.

Elysée (*Fr.* ĕ lē zĕ′), *n.* a palace in Paris: the official residence of the president of France.

Elysian (ĭ lĭz′ĭ ən), *adj.* **1.** pertaining to, or resembling, Elysium. **2.** blissful; delightful.

Elysium (ĭ lĭz′ĭ əm), *n.* **1.** Also, **Elysian fields.** *Gk. Myth.* the abode of the blessed after death. **2.** any similarly conceived abode or state of the dead. **3.** any place or state of perfect happiness. [t. L, t. Gk: short for *Elýsion* (*pedíon*) Elysian (plain or field)]

elytra (ĕl′ĭ trə), *n.* pl. of **elytron, elytrum.**

elytral (ĕl′ĭ trəl), *adj.* of or pertaining to an elytron.

elytriform (ĕ lĭt′rĭ fôm′), *adj.* shaped like an elytron.

elytroid (ĕl′ĭ troid′), *adj.* like an elytron.

elytron (ĕl′ĭ trŏn′), *n., pl.* **-tra** (-trə). one of the pair of hardened forewings of certain insects, as beetles, forming a protective covering for the posterior wings. [NL, t. Gk: cover, sheath]

elytrous (ĕl′ĭ trəs), *adj.* having elytra.

elytrum (ĕl′ĭ trəm), *n., pl.* **-tra** (-trə). elytron.

Elzevir (ĕl′zə vĭə′, -və), *n.* **1. Louis,** *c.* 1540–1617, founder of a Dutch printing firm at Leyden, carried on by his son, **Bonaventure,** 1583–1652, and his grandson, **Abraham** (nephew of Bonaventure), 1592–1652. **2.** a book produced by the Elzevir printing house. **3.** a style of printing type with firm hairlines and stubby serifs. —*adj.* **4.** of or pertaining to the Elzevir family, famous for their small editions of the classics. **5.** indicating the type originated by this family. Also, **Elsevier, Elzevier.** —**Elzevirian** (ĕl′zə vĭə′rĭ ən), *adj.*

em[1] (ĕm), *n., pl.* **ems. 1.** the letter M, m. **2.** *Print.* the square of any size of type (orig. the portion of a line occupied by the letter M), used as the unit of measurement for printed matter. **3. em pica,** about one sixth of an inch, generally used as the unit of measurement in printing. —*adj.* **4.** having the size of an em: *em quad.* [name of the letter M]

em[2] (əm), *pron. pl. Colloq.* them (occurs only in unstressed position). Also, **'em.** [ME *hem,* dat. and acc. pl. of HE; now taken for weak form of THEM]

em-[1], var. of **en-**[1], before *b, p,* and sometimes *m,* as in *embalm.* Cf. **im-**[1].

em-[2], var. of **en-**[2], before *b, m, p, ph,* as in *embolism, emphasis.*

Em., *Chem.* emanation (def. 3).

emaciate (ĭ mā′shĭ āt′), *v.t.,* **-ated, -ating.** to make lean by a gradual wasting away of flesh. [t. L: m. s. *ēmaciātus,* pp.]

emaciation (ĭ mā′sĭ ā′shən), *n.* abnormal thinness, caused by lack of nutrition or by disease.

emanate (ĕm′ə nāt′), *v.i.,* **-nated, -nating.** to flow out, issue, or proceed as from a source or origin; come forth; originate. [t. L: m. s. *ēmānātus,* pp.] —**emanative** (ĕm′ə nə tĭv), **emanatory** (ĕm′ə nā′tə rĭ, -trĭ), *adj.* —**Syn.** See **emerge.**

emanation (ĕm′ə nā′shən), *n.* **1.** the act or fact of emanating. **2.** something that emanates. **3.** *Chem.* a gaseous product of radioactive disintegration including radon, thoron, and actinon; emanon.

emancipate (ĭ măn′sĭ pāt′), *v.t.,* **-pated, -pating. 1.** to free from restraint of any kind, esp. the inhibitions of tradition. **2.** to free (a slave). **3.** *Roman and Civil Law.* to terminate paternal control over. [t. L: m. s. *ēmancipātus,* pp.] —**eman′cipa′tive,** *adj.*

emancipation (ĭ măn′sĭ pā′shən), *n.* **1.** the act of emancipating. **2.** the fact of being emancipated; freedom. —**eman′cipa′tionist,** *n.*

emancipator (ĭ măn′sĭ pā′tə), *n.* one who emancipates. [t. LL]

emancipist (ĭ măn′sĭ pĭst), *n.* **1.** an emancipationist. **2.** *Austral. Hist.* a convict who has completed his sentence.

emanon (ĕm′ə nŏn′), *n.* emanation (def. 3).

emarginate (ĭ mä′jĭ nāt′), *adj.* **1.** notched at the margin. **2.** *Bot.* notched at the apex, as a petal or leaf. Also, **emar′ginat′ed.** [t. L: m. s. *ēmarginātus,* pp., deprived of an edge]

Emarginate leaves

emasculate (*v.* ĭ măs′kyo͝o lāt′; *adj.* ĭ măs′kyo͝o lĭt, -lāt′), *v.,* **-lated, -lating,** *adj.* —*v.t.* **1.** to castrate. **2.** to deprive of strength or vigour; weaken; render effeminate. —*adj.* **3.** emasculated; effeminate. [t. L: m. s. *ēmasculātus,* pp.] —**emas′cula′tion,** *n.* —**emas′cula′tor,** *n.* —**emasculatory** (ĭ măs′kyo͝o lə tə rĭ, -trĭ), **emas′culative,** *adj.*

embalm (ĭm bäm′), *v.t.* **1.** to treat (a dead body) with balsams, spices, etc., or (now usually) with drugs or chemicals, in order to preserve from decay. **2.** to preserve from oblivion; keep in memory. **3.** *Poetic.* to impart a balmy fragrance to. [ME *enbaume(n),* t. F: m. *embaumer,* der. *em-* EM-[1] + *baume* BALM] —**embalm′er,** *n.* —**embalm′ment,** *n.*

embank (ĭm băngk′), *v.t.* to enclose, confine, or protect with a bank, mound, dyke, or the like.

embankment (ĭm băngk′mənt), *n.* **1.** a bank, mound, dyke, or the like, raised to hold back water, carry a road, etc. **2.** the act of embanking.

embarcation (ĕm′bä kā′shən), *n.* embarkation.

embargo (ĕm bä′gō), *n., pl.* **-goes,** *v.,* **-goed, -going.** —*n.* **1.** an order of a government prohibiting the movement of merchant vessels from or into its ports. **2.** any restriction imposed upon commerce by law. **3.** a restraint or hindrance; a prohibition. —*v.t.* **4.** to impose an embargo on. [t. Sp., der. *embargar* restrain, ult. der. Rom. *barra* BAR[1]]

embark (ĭm bäk′), *v.i.* **1.** to board a ship, as for a voyage. **2.** to engage in an enterprise, business, etc. —*v.t.* **3.** to put or receive on board a ship. **4.** to involve (a person) in an enterprise; venture or invest (money, etc.) in an enterprise. [t. F: m. s. *embarquer,* der. *em-* EM-[1] (g. L *in-*) + *barque* BARQUE]

embarkation (ĕm′bä kā′shən), *n.* the act or process of embarking. Also, **embarcation.**

embarrass (ĭm bă′rəs), *v.t.* **1.** to disconcert; abash; make uncomfortable, self-conscious, etc.; confuse. **2.** to make difficult or intricate, as a question or problem; complicate. **3.** to put obstacles or difficulties in the way of; impede.

4. to beset with financial difficulties; burden with debt. —*v.i.* 5. to become disconcerted, abashed. [t. F: s. *embarrasser*, lit., block, obstruct, der. *embarras* obstacle] —**embar′rassing,** *adj.* —**embar′rassingly,** *adv.* —**Syn.** 1. discompose, discomfit, chagrin. See **confuse.** 3. hamper, hinder.

embarrassment (ĭm bă′rəs mənt), *n.* 1. embarrassed state; disconcertion; abashment. 2. the act of embarrassing. 3. that which embarrasses. 4. superabundance; excess. —**Syn.** 1. perplexity, discomposure, mortification, chagrin.

embassador (ĕm băs′ə də), *n. Obs.* ambassador.

embassy (ĕm′bə sĭ), *n., pl.* **-sies.** 1. a body of persons entrusted with a mission to a sovereign or government; an ambassador and his staff. 2. the official headquarters of an ambassador. 3. the function or office of an ambassador. 4. *Obs.* the sending of ambassadors. 5. *Colloq.* the body of persons sent on any undertaking. [var. of *ambassy*, t. MF: m. *ambassée*, ult. der. LL *ambactia* office]

embattle[1] (ĭm băt′l), *v.t.,* **-tled, -tling.** 1. to arrange in order of battle; prepare for battle; arm. 2. *Archaic.* to fortify (a town, etc.). [ME *embataile(n)*, t. OF: m. *embataillier*, der. *em-* EM-[1] + *bataille* BATTLE[1]]

embattle[2] (ĭm băt′l), *v.t.,* **-tled, -tling.** to furnish with battlements. [f. EM-[1] + BATTLE[2]]

embay (ĭm bā′), *v.t.* to enclose in or as in a bay; surround.

embayment (ĭm bā′mənt), *n.* 1. a bay. 2. *Phys. Geog.* the process by which a bay is formed.

embed (ĭm bĕd′), *v.t.,* **-bedded, -bedding.** 1. to fix firmly in a surrounding mass. 2. to lay in or as in a bed. Also, **imbed.** —**embed′ment,** *n.*

embellish (ĭm bĕl′ĭsh), *v.t.* 1. to beautify by or as by ornamentation; ornament; adorn. 2. to enhance (a statement or narrative) with fictitious additions; embroider. [ME *embelyss(en)*, t. OF: m. *embelliss-*, s. *embellir*, der. *em-* EM-[1] + *bel* handsome] —**embel′lisher,** *n.* —**Syn.** 1. decorate, garnish, bedeck, embroider.

embellishment (ĭm bĕl′ĭsh mənt), *n.* 1. an ornament or decoration. 2. a fictitious addition, as in a statement. 3. the act of embellishing. 4. *Music.* any pattern of decorative notes unessential to the implied harmony.

ember[1] (ĕm′bə), *n.* 1. a small live coal, brand of wood, etc., as in a dying fire. 2. (*pl.*) the smouldering remains of a fire. [ME *eemer, emeri*, OE *ǣmerge*, c. Icel. *eimyrja*]

ember[2] (ĕm′bə), *adj.* pertaining to the three-day period of prayer and fasting that comes once in each season. See **Ember days.** [ME *ymber* (attrib.), OE *ymbren*, special use of OE *ymbrene, ymbryne* circuit, course, f. *ymb* around + *ryne* a running]

Ember days, a quarterly season of fasting and prayer (the Wednesday, Friday, and Saturday after the first Sunday in Lent, after Whitsunday, after Sept. 14th, and after Dec. 13th) observed in the Roman Catholic and other Western churches.

Ember week, a week in which Ember days occur.

embezzle (ĭm bĕz′əl), *v.t.,* **-zled, -zling.** to appropriate fraudulently to one's own use, as money or property entrusted to one's possession. [ME *enbesyl(en)*, t. AF: m. *enbesiler*, f. *en-* EM-[1] + *beseler* destroy, dissipate] —**embez′zlement,** *n.* —**embez′zler,** *n.*

embitter (ĭm bĭt′ə), *v.t.* to make bitter or more bitter. —**embit′terer,** *n.* —**embit′terment,** *n.*

emblaze[1] (ĭm blāz′), *v.t. Archaic.* 1. to illuminate; light up. 2. to kindle.

emblaze[2] (ĭm blāz′), *v.t.* 1. to adorn with heraldic devices. 2. *Archaic.* to celebrate; render famous.

emblazon (ĭm blā′zən), *v.t.* 1. to portray or inscribe on or as on a heraldic shield; to embellish or decorate. 2. to proclaim; celebrate or extol. —**embla′zoner,** *n.*

emblazonment (ĭm blā′zən mənt), *n.* 1. the act of emblazoning. 2. that which is emblazoned.

emblazonry (ĭm blā′zən rĭ), *n.* 1. the act or art of emblazoning; heraldic decoration. 2. brilliant representation or embellishment.

emblem (ĕm′bləm), *n.* 1. an object, or a representation of it, symbolizing a quality, state, class of persons, etc.; a symbol. 2. an allegorical drawing or picture, often with explanatory writing. [t. L: m. *emblēma* inlaid work, ornamentation, t. Gk: an insertion] —**Syn.** 1. token, sign, figure, image, device, badge.

emblematic (ĕm′blə măt′ĭk), *adj.* pertaining to, of the nature of, or serving as an emblem; symbolic. Also, **em′blemat′ical.** —**em′blemat′ically,** *adv.*

emblematist (ĕm blĕm′ə tĭst), *n.* a designer, maker, or user of emblems.

emblematize (ĕm blĕm′ə tīz′), *v.t.,* **-tized, -tizing.** to serve as an emblem of; represent by an emblem. Also, **emblematise.**

emblements (ĕm′bl mənts), *n. pl. Law.* the products or profits of land which has been sown or planted. [t. AF: m. *emblaement*, der. *emblaer*, der. *em-* EM-[1] + *blé* grain (t. Gmc. Cf. MD *blaad*, OE *blǣd*)]

emblemize (ĕm′blə mīz′), *v.t.,* **-mized, -mizing.** to represent by an emblem; emblematize. Also, **emblemise.**

embodiment (ĭm bŏd′ĭ mənt), *n.* 1. the act of embodying 2. the state of being embodied. 3. that in which something is embodied; an incarnation. 4. something embodied.

embody (ĭm bŏd′ĭ), *v.t.,* **-bodied, -bodying.** 1. to invest with a body, as a spirit; incarnate; make corporeal. 2. to give a concrete form to; express or exemplify (ideas, etc.) in concrete form. 3. to collect into or include in a body; organize; incorporate. 4. to embrace or comprise.

embolden (ĭm bōl′dən), *v.t.* to make bold or more bold; hearten or encourage. —**embold′ener,** *n.*

embolectomy (ĕm′bə lĕk′tə mĭ), *n., pl.* **-mies.** the removal of an embolus from an artery, which it is obstructing, by surgery. [f. EMBOL(US) + -ECTOMY]

embolic (ĕm bŏl′ĭk), *adj.* 1. *Pathol.* pertaining to an embolus or to embolism. 2. *Embryol.* developing inwardly: related to a process of invagination.

embolism (ĕm′bə lĭz′əm), *n.* 1. intercalation, as of a day in a year. 2. a period of time intercalated. 3. an extension and elaboration of the last petition in the Lord's Prayer, as in the canon of the Roman Catholic liturgy. 4. *Pathol.* the occlusion of a blood vessel by an embolus. [t. LL: s. *embolismus* intercalation, der. Gk *embállein* throw in. See EMBLEM] —**em′bolis′mic,** *adj.*

embolus (ĕm′bə ləs), *n., pl.* **-li** (-lī′). *Pathol.* undissolved material carried by the blood current and impacted in some part of the vascular system, as thrombi or fragments of thrombi, tissue fragments, clumps of bacteria, protozoan parasites, fat globules, gas bubbles. [t. L: piston, t. Gk: m. *émbolos* peg, stopper]

emboly (ĕm′bə lĭ), *n. Pathol.* a gradual embedding of one part into another, as in the formation of certain gastrulae. [t. Gk: m. *embolē* throwing in, invasion]

embonpoint (*Fr.* äɴ bôɴ pwăɴ′), *n. French.* exaggerated plumpness; stoutness. [F: lit., in good condition]

embosom (ĭm bo͝oz′əm), *v.t.* 1. to enfold, envelop, or enclose. 2. to take into or hold in the bosom; embrace. 3. to cherish; foster.

emboss (ĭm bŏs′), *v.t.* 1. to raise or represent surface designs in relief. 2. to cause to bulge out; make protuberant; make umbonate. 3. to raise a design on a fabric by pressing. 4. to cover or ornament with bosses or studs. [ME *embosse(n)*, t. OF: m. *embocer* swell in protuberances, der. *em-* EM-[1] + *boce* swelling, BOSS[2]] —**emboss′er,** *n.* —**emboss′ment,** *n.*

embouchure (ŏm′bo͞o sho͞o′; *Fr.* äɴ bo͞o shʏr′), *n.* 1. the mouth of a river. 2. the opening out of a valley into a plain. 3. *Music.* **a.** the mouthpiece of a wind instrument, esp. when of metal. **b.** the adjustment of a player's mouth to such a mouthpiece. [t. F, der. *emboucher* put into the mouth, discharge by a mouth or outlet, der. *em-* EM-[1] + *bouche* mouth (g. L *bucca* cheek, mouth)]

embowel (ĭm bou′əl), *v.t.,* **-elled, -elling** or (*U.S.*) **-eled, -eling.** to disembowel.

embower (ĭm bou′ə), *v.t., v.i.* to shelter in or as in a bower; cover or surround with foliage.

embrace (ĭm brās′), *v.,* **-braced, -bracing,** *n.* —*v.t.* 1. to take or clasp in the arms; press to the bosom; hug. 2. to take or receive (an idea, etc.) gladly or eagerly; accept willingly. 3. to avail oneself of (an opportunity, etc.). 4. to adopt (a profession, a religion, etc.). 5. to take in with the eye or the mind. 6. to encircle; surround; enclose. 7. to include or contain. —*v.i.* 8. to join in an embrace. —*n.* 9. an act of embracing; a hug. [ME *enbrace(n)*, t. OF: m. *embracier*, der. *em-* EM-[1] + *bras* arm (g. L *bracchium*)] —**embrace′able,** *adj.* —**embrace′ment,** *n.* —**embrac′er,** *n.* —**embrac′ive,** *adj.* —**Syn.** 2. adopt, espouse. 7. comprise, comprehend. See **include.**

embraceor (ĭm brā′sə), *n. Law.* a person guilty of embracery. Also, **embracer.**

embracery (ĭm brā′sə rĭ), *n., pl.* **-eries.** *Law.* the offence of attempting to influence a judge or jury corruptly. [ME *embracerie*, der. OF *embraser* instigate, lit., set fire to]

embranchment (ĭm brănch′mənt), *n.* 1. a branching or ramification. 2. a branch.

embrangle (ĭm brăng′gl), *v.t.,* **-gled, -gling.** to confuse; entangle; perplex. Also, **imbrangle.** [EM-[1] + *brangle* (b. BRAWL and WRANGLE)] —**embran′glement,** *n.*

embrasure (ĭm brā′zhə), *n.* 1. an opening in a wall or parapet through which a gun may be fired, constructed with sides which flare outward. See diag. under **bartizan.** 2. *Archit.* an enlargement of the aperture of a door or window, at the inside face of the wall, by means of splayed sides. [t. F, der. *embraser, ébraser* to splay (an opening)]

embrocate (ĕm′brō kāt′), *v.t.,* **-cated, -cating.** to moisten and rub with a liniment or lotion. [t. ML: m. s. *embrocātus*, pp. of *embrocāre*, der. LL *embrocha*, t. Gk: m. *embrochḗ* lotion]

embrocation (ĕm′brō kā′shən), *n.* **1.** the act of embrocating a bruised or diseased part of the body. **2.** the liquid for this; a liniment or lotion.

embroider (ĭm broi′də), *v.t.* **1.** to decorate with ornamental needlework. **2.** to produce or form in needlework. **3.** to adorn or embellish rhetorically, esp. with fictitious additions. —*v.i.* **4.** to do embroidery. **5.** to provide rhetorical embellishment, esp. by fictitious additions. [appar. f. EM-¹ + BROIDER] —**embroi′derer,** *n.*

embroidery (ĭm broi′də rĭ), *n.*, *pl.* **-deries. 1.** the art of working, with a needle, raised and ornamental designs in threads of silk, cotton, gold, silver, or other material, upon any woven fabric, leather, paper, etc. **2.** embroidered work or ornamentation. **3.** *Colloq.* embellishment by invented or exaggerated detail.

embroil (ĭm broil′), *v.t.* **1.** to bring into a state of discord; involve in contention or strife. **2.** to throw into confusion; complicate. [t. F: m. *embrouiller*, f. *em-* EM-¹ + *brouiller* BROIL¹] —**embroil′er,** *n.* —**embroil′ment,** *n.*

embrown (ĭm broun′), *v.t.*, *v.i.* to make or become brown or dark.

embrute (ĭm bro͞ot′), *v.t.*, *v.i.* imbrute.

embryectomy (ĕm′brĭ ĕk′tə mĭ), *n.*, *pl.* **-mies.** removal of an embryo by surgery. [f. EMBRY(O) + -ECTOMY]

embryo (ĕm′brĭ ō′), *n.*, *pl.* **-os. 1.** an organism in the earlier stages of its development, as before emergence from the egg or before metamorphosis. **2.** (among mammals and other viviparous animals) a young animal during its earlier stages within the mother's body (including, in man, the developmental stages up to the end of the seventh week). **3.** *Bot.* the rudimentary plant usually contained in the seed. **4.** the beginning or rudimentary stage of anything. —*adj.* **5.** embryonic. [t. ML, t. Gk: m. *émbryon*]

embryogeny (ĕm′brĭ ŏj′ĭ nĭ), *n.* the formation and development of the embryo, as a subject of scientific study. Also, **embryogenesis** (ĕm′brĭ ō jĕn′ĭ sĭs). [f. EMBRYO + -GENY] —**embryogenetic** (ĕm′brĭ ō jĭ nĕt′ĭk), *adj.*

embryol., embryology.

embryology (ĕm′brĭ ŏl′ə jĭ), *n.* the science of the embryo, its genesis, development, etc. [f. EMBRYO + -LOGY] —**embryological** (ĕm′brĭ ə lŏj′ĭ kl), **em′bryolog′ic,** *adj.* —**em′bryol′ogist,** *n.*

embryonic (ĕm′brĭ ŏn′ĭk), *adj.* **1.** pertaining to or in the state of an embryo. **2.** rudimentary; undeveloped. Also, **embryonal** (ĕm′brĭ ə nəl).

embryo sac, *Bot.* the megaspore of a seed-bearing plant, being situated within the ovule, giving rise to the endosperm or supposed female prothallium, and forming the cell in which the embryo is developed.

embryotomy (ĕm′brĭ ŏt′ə mĭ), *n.* the dismemberment of a foetus to effect an otherwise impossible delivery.

embryulcia (ĕm′brĭ ŭl′sĭ ə), *n.* the mechanical removal of an embryo or foetus from the uterus.

embus (ĭm bŭs′), *v.i.*, *v.t.*, **-bussed, -bussing.** *Chiefly Mil.* to put into or get into a bus or the like. [EM-¹ + BUS]

Emden (*Ger.* ĕm′dən), *n.* a seaport in NW West Germany. 46,000 (1964).

emeer (ĕ mĭə′), *n.* emir.

emend (ĭ mĕnd′), *v.t.* **1.** to free from faults or errors; correct. **2.** to amend (a text) by removing errors. [t. L: s. *ēmendāre* correct] —**emend′able,** *adj.*

emendate (ē′mĕn dāt′), *v.t.*, **-dated, -dating.** to emend (a text). —**emendator** (ē′mĕn dā′tə), *n.*

emendation (ē′mĕn dā′shən), *n.* **1.** a correction. **2.** the act of emending. —**emendatory** (ĭ mĕn′də tə rĭ, -trĭ), *adj.*

emerald (ĕm′ə rəld, ĕm′rəld), *n.* **1.** a rare green variety of beryl, highly valued as a gem. **2.** clear bright green. **3.** a printing type (6½ point) of a size between nonpareil and minion. —*adj.* **4.** having a clear, bright green colour. [ME *emeraude*, t. OF, g. L *smaragdus* a green precious stone, t. Gk.: m. *smáragdos*]

emerald copper, dioptase.

Emerald Isle, Ireland.

emerge (ĭ mûj′), *v.i.*, **emerged, emerging. 1.** to rise or come forth from or as from water or other liquid. **2.** to come forth into view or notice, as from concealment or obscurity. **3.** to come up or arise, as a question or difficulty. [t. L: m. s. *ēmergere* rise out]

—**Syn. 2.** EMERGE, EMANATE, ISSUE mean to come forth from a place or source. EMERGE is used of coming forth from something that envelops or encloses, from a place shut off from view, or from concealment, obscurity, retirement, or the like, into sight and notice: *the sun emerges from behind the clouds.* EMANATE is used esp. of intangible or immaterial things, as light, vapour, ideas, news, etc., spreading or streaming from a source: *rumours often emanate from irresponsible persons.* ISSUE is most often used of a number of persons, a mass of matter, or a volume of smoke, sound, or the like, coming forth through any outlet or outlets: *the crowd issued from the building.*

emergence (ĭ mû′jəns), *n.* **1.** the act or fact of emerging. **2.** an outgrowth, as a prickle, on the surface of an organ.

emergency (ĭ mû′jən sĭ), *n.*, *pl.* **-cies.** an unforeseen occurrence; a sudden and urgent occasion for action. [t. L: m. s. *ēmergentia* a coming up]

—**Syn.** EMERGENCY, CRISIS, STRAITS refer to situations in which quick action and judgement are necessary, though they may not avert undesirable consequences. An EMERGENCY is a situation demanding immediate action: *a power failure created an emergency in hospitals.* A CRISIS is a vital or decisive turning point in a condition or state of affairs, and everything depends on the outcome of it: *help arrived when affairs had reached a crisis.* STRAIT (usually plural) suggests a pressing situation, often one of need or want, which usually makes necessary some difficult alternative or choice: *the family was in desperate straits for food and clothing.*

emergent (ĭ mû′jənt), *adj.* **1.** emerging; rising from a liquid or other surrounding medium. **2.** (of a nation) recently independent or newly formed as a political entity, and generally in an early stage of economic development. **3.** coming into view or notice; issuing. **4.** arising casually or unexpectedly. **5.** calling for immediate action; urgent. —**emer′gently,** *adv.*

emergent evolution, *Biol.*, *Philos.* the origin of entirely new properties at certain critical stages or levels in the course of evolution, e.g. the origin of multicellular organisms, of nervous systems, psychic processes, etc.

emeritus (ĭ mĕ′rĭ təs), *adj.*, *n.*, *pl.* **-ti** (-tī′, -tē′). —*adj.* **1.** retired or honourably discharged from active duty because of age, infirmity, or long service, but retained on the rolls: *a professor emeritus.* —*n.* **2.** an emeritus professor, etc. [t. L: pp., having served out one's time]

emersed (ĭ mûst′), *adj.* **1.** having emerged. **2.** *Bot.* risen or standing out of water, surrounding leaves, etc. [f. s. L *ēmersus*, pp., emerged + -ED²]

emersion (ĭ mû′shən), *n.* **1.** the act or fact of emerging; emergence. **2.** *Astron.* the reappearance of a heavenly body after an eclipse or occultation. [modelled on IMMERSION (see def. 6)]

Emerson (ĕm′ə sən), *n.* **Ralph Waldo,** 1803–82, U.S. essayist and poet. —**Emersonian** (ĕm′ə sō′nyən), *adj.*

emery (ĕm′ə rĭ), *n.* a granular mineral substance consisting typically of corundum mixed with magnetite or haematite, used powdered, crushed, or consolidated for grinding and polishing. [t. F: m. *émeri*, der. Gk *smêris*]

emery board, a small stiff strip, as of cardboard, or wood, covered with crushed emery and used to file fingernails.

emery cloth, emery-coated cloth used as an abrasive.

emery paper, emery-coated paper used as an abrasive.

emery wheel, a wheel for grinding or polishing, consisting mostly of or faced with emery.

emesis (ĕm′ĭ sĭs), *n.* *Pathol.* vomiting. [NL, t. Gk]

emetic (ĭ mĕt′ĭk), *adj.* **1.** inducing vomiting, as a medicinal substance. —*n.* **2.** an emetic medicine or agent. [t. L: s. *emeticus*, t. Gk: m. *emetikós*]

emetine (ĕm′ə tēn′, -tĭn), *n.* *Chem.* a colourless crystalline, or white powdery substance, $C_{29}H_{40}N_2O_4$, principal ingredient of ipecacuanha, a specific against amoebic dysentery. Also, **emetin** (em′ə tĭn). [f. s. Gk *émetos* vomiting + -INE²]

emeu (ē′myo͞o), *n.* emu.

e.m.f., electromotive force. Also, **E.M.F., emf.**

-emia, var. of **-aemia,** as in *hyperemia.*

emigrant (ĕm′ĭ grənt), *n.* **1.** one who emigrates, as from a native land. —*adj.* **2.** emigrating. [t. L: s. *ēmigrans*, ppr.]

emigrate (ĕm′ĭ grāt′), *v.i.*, **-grated, -grating.** to leave one country or region to settle in another; migrate. [t. L: m. s. *ēmigrātus*, pp.] —**Syn.** See **migrate.**

emigration (ĕm′ĭ grā′shən), *n.* **1.** the act of emigrating. **2.** a body of emigrants; emigrants collectively. —**em′igra′tional,** *adj.*

émigré (ĕm′ĭ grā′; *Fr.* ė mē grė′), *n.*, *pl.* **-grés** (-grāz′; *Fr.* -grė′). **1.** an emigrant, esp. one who flees from his native land to escape political persecution. **2.** a person who fled from France because of opposition to or fear of the revolution that began in 1789. [F, pp. of *émigrer*, t. L: m. *ēmigrāre* emigrate]

Emilia (ĭ mē′lyə; *It.* ė mē′lyȧ), *n.* an administrative region in N Italy. 3,646,507 pop. (1961); 8547 sq. mi. Official name, **Emilia-Romagna** (ĭ mē′lyə rō mä′nyə; *It.* ė mē′lyȧ rō mȧn′nyȧ). *Cap.:* Bologna.

eminence (ĕm′ĭ nəns), *n.* **1.** high station, rank, or repute. **2.** a high place or part; a hill or elevation; height. **3.** (*cap.*) *Rom. Cath. Ch.* the title of honour of a cardinal: *your Eminence.* —**Syn. 1.** distinction, prominence, celebrity, renown.

éminence grise (*Fr.* ė mē näNs′grēz′), *French.* a person who wields power unseen and unofficially, usually through another, official person; grey eminence.

eminency (ĕm′ĭ nən sĭ), *n.*, *pl.* **-cies.** *Rare.* eminence.

eminent (ĕm′ĭ nənt), *adj.* **1.** high in station, rank, or repute; distinguished. **2.** conspicuous, signal, or noteworthy: *eminent services, eminent fairness.* **3.** lofty; high. **4.** prominent; projecting; protruding. [t. L: s. *ēminens*, ppr., standing out] —**em′inently,** *adv.* —**Syn. 1.** prominent, celebrated, renowned, illustrious. See **famous. 2.** noted; noteworthy. —**Ant. 1.** unknown.

eminent domain, *Law.* the dominion of the sovereign power over all property within the state, by which it can appropriate private property for public use, compensation being given in return.

emir (ĕ mĭə′), *n.* **1.** a Muslim or Arabian chieftain or prince. **2.** a title of honour of the descendants of Mohammed. **3.** a former title of certain Turkish officials. Also, **emeer.** [var. of AMIR]

emissary (ĕm′ĭ sə rĭ, -ĭs rĭ), *n., pl.* **-saries. 1.** an agent sent on a mission. **2.** an agent sent on a mission of a secret nature. [t. L: m. s. *ēmissārius* sent out (adj.), scout (n.)]

emission (ĭ mĭsh′ən), *n.* **1.** the act of emitting. **2.** that which is emitted; a discharge; an emanation. **3.** the act of issuing. **4.** *Electronics.* a measure of the number of electrons emitted by the heated filament or cathode of a vacuum tube. **5.** a discharge of fluid from the body: specifically a discharge of semen. **6.** the fluid discharged. [t. L: s. *ēmissio*]

emission spectrum, *Physics.* the spectrum observed when light or other electromagnetic radiation coming directly from a source is examined with a spectroscope.

emissive (ĭ mĭs′ĭv), *adj.* **1.** serving to emit. **2.** pertaining to emission.

emissivity (ĭm′ĭ sĭv′ĭ tĭ, ĕm′ĭ-), *n. Thermodynamics.* the relative ability of a surface to emit radiant energy compared to an ideal black body at the same temperature and with the same area.

emit (ĭ mĭt′), *v.t.*, **emitted, emitting. 1.** to send forth; give out or forth (liquid, light, heat, sound, etc.); discharge. **2.** to issue, as an order or a decree. **3.** to issue formally for circulation. **4.** to utter, as opinions. [t. L: m. s. *ēmittere* send out] —**Syn. 1.** vent, exhale, exude, expel, eject.

emittance (ĭ mĭt′ns), *n. Optics.* the luminous flux emitted by a source per unit area; luminous emittance.

emitter (ĭ mĭt′ə), *n.* **1.** one who or that which emits. **2.** *Electronics.* an electrode that emits charge, especially in a transistor.

Emmanuel (ĭ măn′yo͞o əl), *n.* Christ. See **Immanuel.**

Emmen (*Du.* ĕm′ə), *n.* a town in the Netherlands, in Drenthe province. 73,008 (1965).

emmenagogue (ĭ mĕn′ə gŏg′, ĭ mē′nə-), *n.* a medicine that promotes the menstrual discharge. [f. Gk *émmēn(a)* menses + -AGOGUE] —**emmen′agog′ic,** *adj.*

Emmenthaler (ĕm′ən tä′lə; *Ger.* ĕ′mən tȧ lər), *n.* a firm, pale yellow or whitish cheese containing many holes, made usually from cows' milk half skimmed. Also, **Em′mental′, Em′menta′ler, Em′menthal′.** [named after *Emmenthal*, a valley in Switzerland; see -ER[1]]

emmer (ĕm′ə), *n.* a form of wheat, *Triticum dicoccum*, cultivated in the Mediterranean region since Neolithic times and still grown in mountainous regions of Europe to a limited extent.

emmet (ĕm′ĭt), *n. Archaic or Dial.* an ant.

Emmet (ĕm′ĭt), *n.* **Robert,** 1778–1803, Irish patriot.

emmetropia (ĕm′ĭ trō′pyə), *n.* the normal refractive condition of the eye, in which the rays of light are accurately focused on the retina. [NL, f. Gk: s. *émmetros* in measure + *-ōpia* eye state] —**emmetropic** (ĕm′ĭ trŏp′ĭk), *adj.*

emolliate (ĭ mŏl′ĭ āt′), *v.t.*, **-ated, -ating. 1.** to soften. **2.** to render effeminate. —**emollition** (ĕm′ə lĭsh′ən), *n.*

emollient (ĭ mŏl′yənt), *adj.* **1.** having the power of softening or relaxing living tissues, as a medicinal substance; soothing, esp. to the skin. —*n.* **2.** *Med.* an emollient medicine or agent. [t. L: s. *ēmolliens*, ppr.]

emolument (ĭ mŏl′yo͞o mənt), *n.* profit arising from office or employment; compensation for services; salary or fees. [t. L: (m.) s. *ēmolumentum, ēmolimentum* profit]

emote (ĭ mōt′), *v.i.*, **emoted, emoting.** *Colloq.* **1.** to show or affect emotion. **2.** to behave theatrically; to act a part, esp. without talent. [back-formation from EMOTION]

emotion (ĭ mō′shən), *n.* **1.** an affective state of consciousness in which joy, sorrow, fear, hate, or the like, is experienced (distinguished from cognitive and volitional states of consciousness). **2.** any of the feelings of joy, sorrow, fear, hate, love, etc. **3.** a state of agitation of the feelings actuated by experiencing fear, joy, etc. [t. L: s. *ēmōtio*, der. *ēmōtus*, pp., moved out, stirred up] —**emo′tionless,** *adj.* —**Syn. 1.** See **feeling.**

emotional (ĭ mō′shə nəl), *adj.* **1.** pertaining to emotion or the emotions. **2.** subject to or easily affected by emotion. **3.** appealing to the emotions. **4.** effected or determined by emotion rather than reason: *an emotional decision.* —**emo′tionally,** *adv.*

emotionalism (ĭ mō′shə nə lĭz′əm), *n.* **1.** emotional character. **2.** appeal to the emotions. **3.** tendency to emotion, esp. morbid emotion. **4.** expression of emotion.

emotionalist (ĭ mō′shə nəl ĭst), *n.* **1.** one who appeals to the emotions, esp. unduly. **2.** one easily affected by emotion. **3.** *Philos.* one who bases conduct or the theory of conduct upon feelings.

emotionality (ĭ mō′shə năl′ĭ tĭ), *n.* emotional state or quality.

emotionalize (ĭ mō′shə nə līz′), *v.t.*, **-lized, -lizing.** to make emotional; treat as a matter of emotion. Also, **emotionalise.**

emotive (ĭ mō′tĭv), *adj.* **1.** characterized by or pertaining to emotion. **2.** exciting emotion. —**emo′tively,** *adv.* —**emo′tiveness, emotivity** (ē′mō tĭv′ĭ tĭ), *n.*

Emp., 1. Emperor. **2.** Empire. **3.** Empress.

empale (ĭm pāl′), *v.t.*, **-paled, -paling.** impale.

empanel (ĭm păn′əl), *v.t.*, **-elled, -elling** or (*U.S.*) **-eled, -eling.** to enter on a panel or list for jury duty. Also, **impanel.** —**empan′elment,** *n.*

empathy (ĕm′pə thĭ), *n. Psychol.* mental entering into the feeling or spirit of a person or thing; appreciative perception or understanding. [t. Gk: m. s. *empátheia.* Cf. G *Einfühlung*, lit., infeeling] —**empathic** (ĕm păth′ĭk), *adj.* —**empath′ically,** *adv.*

Empedocles (ĕm pĕd′ə klēz′), *n. c.* 490–*c.* 430 B.C., Greek philosopher and statesman.

empennage (ĕm pĕn′ĭj; *Fr.* äɴ pĕ nȧzh′), *n.* the rear part of an aeroplane or airship, usually comprising stabilizer, elevator, vertical fin, and rudder. [t. F, der. *empenner*, v., feather, der. *em-* EM-[1] + *penne* (g. L *penna* feather)]

emperor (ĕm′pə rə), *n.* **1.** the sovereign or supreme ruler of an empire. **2.** a title of dignity given to certain kings who were or are not rulers of empires. **3.** a size of drawing or writing paper, 48 × 72 inches. [ME *emperour(e)*, t. OF: m. *empereor*, g. L *imperātor* ruler] —**em′perorship′,** *n.*

emperor moth, a large moth, *Saturnia pavonia*, of the family *Saturnidae*, found in Britain and Europe, having prominent eyelike markings on each wing.

emperor penguins, the largest of the penguins, *Aptenodykes forster*, family *Spheniscidae*, of the Antarctic.

empery (ĕm′pə rĭ), *n., pl.* **-peries.** *Poetic.* **1.** absolute dominion; empire. **2.** the territory of an emperor. [ME *emperie*, t. OF, der. *emperer* to rule, g. L *imperāre*]

emphasis (ĕm′fə sĭs), *n., pl.* **-ses** (-sēz′). **1.** stress laid upon, or importance or significance attached to, anything. **2.** anything upon which great stress is laid. **3.** *Rhet.* **a.** special and significant stress of voice laid on particular words or syllables. **b.** stress laid on particular words, by means of position, repetition, or other indication. **4.** intensity or force of expression, action, etc. **5.** prominence, as of outline. [t. L, t. Gk]

emphasize (ĕm′fə sīz′), *v.t.*, **-sized, -sizing.** to give emphasis to; lay stress upon; stress. Also, **emphasise.**

emphatic (ĭm făt′ĭk), *adj.* **1.** uttered, or to be uttered, with emphasis; strongly expressive. **2.** using emphasis in speech or action. **3.** forcibly significant; strongly marked; striking. **4.** *Phonet.* having a secondary velar articulation, as certain dental consonants in Arabic. —*n.* **5.** *Phonet.* an emphatic consonant. [t. Gk: m. s. *emphatikós*, var. of *emphantikós* expressive] —**emphat′ically,** *adv.* —**Syn. 3.** positive, energetic, forcible, pronounced.

emphysema (ĕm′fĭ sē′mə), *n. Pathol., Vet. Sci.* abnormal distension of an organ or a part of the body with air or other gas. [NL, t. Gk: inflation] —**emphysematous** (ĕm′fĭ-sĕm′ə təs, -sē′mə-), *adj.*

empire (ĕm′pī ə), *n.* **1.** an aggregate of nations or peoples ruled over by an emperor or other powerful sovereign or government; usually a territory of greater extent than a kingdom ruled by a single sovereign: *the Roman empire.* **2.** a government under an emperor: *the first French empire.* **3.** supreme power in governing; imperial power; sovereignty. **4.** supreme control; absolute sway. **5.** (*cap.*) either of two periods of monarchy in France: **First Empire,** 1804–15, Napoleon I; **Second Empire,** 1852–70, Napoleon III. **6.** *Colloq.* a large and powerful enterprise or group of enterprises controlled by a single person or group of people. —*adj.* **7.** (*cap.*) developed or in vogue during the First Empire (1804–15): applied esp. to certain styles of interior decoration, furniture, etc., and of women's dress (implying esp. a high waistline, with skirts hanging straight and loose). [ME, t. F, g. L *imperium* a command, authority, realm] —**Syn. 3.** dominion, rule.

Empire Day, former name for **Commonwealth Day.**

empiric (ĕm pĭ′rĭk), *n.* **1.** anyone who follows an empirical method. **2.** a quack; a charlatan. —*adj.* **3.** empirical. [t. L: s. *empiricus*, t. Gk: m. *empeirikós*, der. *empeiría* experience]

empirical (ĕm pĭrʹĭ kl), *adj.* **1.** derived from or guided by experience or experiment. **2.** depending upon experience or observation alone, without using science or theory, esp. in medicine. —**emprʹically,** *adv.*

empirical formula, **1.** *Chem.* a chemical formula indicating the number of each kind of atom in the molecule, as CH_2O. **2.** any mathematical or engineering formula which is obtained on the basis of experimental results rather than pure theory.

empiricism (ĕm pĭrʹĭ sĭzʹəm), *n.* **1.** empirical method or practice. **2.** *Philos.* the doctrine that all knowledge is derived from experience. **3.** undue reliance upon experience; quackery. **4.** an empirical conclusion. —**empirʹicist,** *n., adj.*

emplacement (ĭm plāsʹmənt), *n.* **1.** *Fort.* the space, platform, or the like for a gun or battery and its accessories. **2.** a putting in place or position; location.

employ (ĭm ploiʹ), *v.t.* **1.** to use the services of (a person); have or keep in one's service; keep busy or at work: *this factory employs thousands of men.* **2.** to make use of (an instrument, means, etc.); use; apply. **3.** to occupy or devote (time, energies, etc.): *I employ my spare time in reading.* —*n.* **4.** employment; service: *to be in someone's employ.* [t. F: s. *employer*, g. L *implicāre* enfold] —**employʹable,** *adj.* —**Syn. 1.** engage, hire. —**Ant. 1.** discharge.

employee (ĕm ploiʹē, ĕmʹploi ēʹ), *n.* a person working for another person or a business firm for pay. Also, **employʹe, employʹé.** [f. EMPLOY, V. + -EE; r. *employe*, t. F, pp. of *employer* employ] —**Syn.** See **servant.**

employer (ĭm ploiʹə), *n.* one who employs, esp. for wages.

employment (ĭm ploiʹmənt), *n.* **1.** the act of employing. **2.** the state of being employed; employ; services. **3.** that on which one is employed; work; occupation; business.

employment exchange, a government office for finding employment for the unemployed and for paying unemployment benefits. Also, **labour exchange.**

empoison (ĭm poiʹzən), *v.t.* **1.** to corrupt. **2.** *Obs.* to poison. [ME *empoyson(en)*, t. F: m. *empoisoner*, der. *em-* EM-[1] + *poison* POISON]

emporium (ĕm pôʹrĭ əm), *n., pl.* **-poriums, -poria** (-pôʹrĭ ə). **1.** a place, town, or city of important commerce, esp. a principal centre of trade. **2.** a large store selling a great variety of articles. [t. L, t. Gk: m. *empórion* a trading place]

empoverish (ĭm pŏvʹə rĭsh), *v.t. Obs.* impoverish.

empower (ĭm pouʹə), *v.t.* **1.** to give power or authority to; authorize: *I empowered him to make the deal for me.* **2.** to enable or permit. —**empowʹerment,** *n.* —**Syn. 1.** warrant, commission, license, qualify.

empress (ĕmʹprĭs), *n.* **1.** a woman ruler of an empire. **2.** the consort of an emperor. **3.** a supreme or sovereign ruler: *empress of the seas.* [ME *empresse*, t. OF: (m.) *emper(er)esse*, r. *empereris*, g. L *imperātrix*].

empressement (*Fr.* äN prĕs mäNʹ), *n. French.* display of cordiality.

emprise (ĕm prīzʹ), *n. Archaic.* **1.** an adventurous enterprise. **2.** knightly daring or prowess. [ME, t. OF, n. use of fem. pp. of *emprendre* undertake, f. *em-* EM-[1] + *prendre* take (g. L *prehendere*)]

Empson (ĕmpʹsən), *n.* **William,** born 1906, English poet and critic.

empty (ĕmpʹtĭ), *adj.,* **-tier, -tiest,** *v.,* **-tied, -tying,** *n., pl.* **-ties.** —*adj.* **1.** containing nothing; void of the usual or appropriate contents: *an empty bottle.* **2.** vacant; unoccupied: *an empty house.* **3.** without burden or load: *an empty wagon.* **4.** destitute of some quality or qualities; devoid (fol. by *of*): *a life now as empty of happiness as it was full of it.* **5.** without force, effect, or significance; unsatisfactory; meaningless: *empty compliments, empty pleasures.* **6.** *Colloq.* hungry. **7.** without knowledge or sense; frivolous; foolish. **8.** *Colloq.* drained of emotion; spent. —*v.t.* **9.** to make empty; deprive of contents; discharge the contents of: *to empty a bucket.* **10.** to discharge (contents): *empty the water out of a bucket.* —*v.i.* **11.** to become empty: *the room emptied rapidly after the lecture.* **12.** to discharge contents, as a river: *the river empties into the sea.* —*n.* **13.** *Colloq.* something empty, as a bottle, can, or the like. [ME; OE *æmtig*, var. of *ǣmettig*, f. s. *ǣmetta* leisure + *-ig* -Y[1]] —**empʹtily,** *adv.* —**empʹtiness,** *n.*

—**Syn. 1.** EMPTY, VACANT, BLANK, VOID denote absence of content or contents. EMPTY means without appropriate or accustomed contents: *empty barrel, the house is empty* (has no furnishings). VACANT is usually applied to that which is temporarily unoccupied: *vacant chair, house* (uninhabited). BLANK applies to surfaces free from any marks or lacking appropriate markings, openings, etc.: *blank paper, wall.* VOID means empty in the highest degree: *void of all understanding.* **5.** hollow, delusive, vain. **9.** unload, unburden. —**Ant. 1.** full.

empty-handed (ĕmpʹtĭ hănʹdĭd), *adj.* **1.** having nothing in the hands. **2.** bringing or taking nothing; having gained nothing.

empty-headed (ĕmpʹtĭ hĕdʹĭd), *adj.* brainless; foolish.

empurple (ĕm pûʹpl), *v.t.,* **-pled, -pling.** to tinge or colour with purple.

empyema (ĕmʹpī ēʹmə), *n. Pathol.* a collection of pus in some cavity of the body, esp. in the pleural cavity. [NL, t. Gk: suppuration] —**emʹpyeʹmic,** *adj.*

empyreal (ĕmʹpī rēʹəl), *adj.* **1.** pertaining to the highest heaven; empyrean. **2.** pertaining to the sky; celestial. **3.** formed of pure fire or light. [f. s. LL *empyreus* (t. Gk: m. *empýrios* fiery) + -AL[1]]

empyrean (ĕmʹpī rēʹən), *n.* **1.** the highest heaven, supposed by the ancients to contain the pure element of fire. **2.** the visible heavens; the firmament. —*adj.* **3.** empyreal.

emu (ēʹmyo͞o), *n.* either of two large, flightless, three-toed Australian birds of the ratite genus *Dromiceius*, *D. novae-hollandiae* and *D. diemenianus*, closely related to the ostrich, but smaller. The latter species is now extinct. Also, **emeu.** [t. Moluccan: m. *emeu* cassowary]

Emu, *Dromiceius novaehollandiae* (Length ab. 6 ft)

E.M.U., electromagnetic unit. Also, **emu.**

emulate (*v.* ĕmʹyo͞o lātʹ; *adj.* emʹyo͞o lĭt), *v.,* **-lated, -lating,** *adj.* —*v.t.* **1.** to try to equal or excel; imitate with effort to equal or surpass. **2.** to rival with some degree of success. —*adj.* **3.** *Obs.* emulous. [t. L: m. s. *aemulātus*, pp., having rivalled] —**emulative** (ĕmʹyo͞o lə tĭv), *adj.* —**emʹulaʹtor,** *n.*

emulation (ĕmʹyo͞o lāʹshən), *n.* **1.** effort or desire to equal or excel others. **2.** *Obs.* jealous rivalry. —**Syn. 1.** competition, rivalry.

emulous (ĕmʹyo͞o ləs), *adj.* **1.** desirous of equalling or excelling; filled with emulation. **2.** arising from or of the nature of emulation, as actions, etc. **3.** *Obs.* jealous; envious. [t. L: m. *aemulus*] —**emʹulously,** *adv.* —**emʹulousness,** *n.*

emulsify (ĭ mŭlʹsĭ fīʹ), *v.t.,* **-fied, -fying.** to make into an emulsion. —**emulʹsificaʹtion,** *n.* —**emulʹsifiʹer,** *n.*

emulsion (ĭ mŭlʹshən), *n.* **1.** a liquid preparation of the colour and consistency of milk. **2.** *Phys. Chem.* any colloidal suspension of a liquid in another liquid. **3.** *Pharm.* a liquid preparation consisting of minute particles of an oily, fatty, resinous, or other substance held in suspension in an aqueous fluid by means of a gum or other viscous matter. **4.** *Photog.* the light-sensitive layer on a photographic film, plate, or paper, consisting of one or more of the silver halides in gelatine. [t. NL: s. *ēmulsio*, der. L *ēmulsus*, pp., milked out] —**emulʹsive,** *adj.*

emulsion paint, a paint in which the pigment is dispersed in an emulsion, or an emulsion-like dispersion of an organic binding material in water.

emulsoid (ĭ mŭlʹsoid), *n.* a sol in which the disperse phase is a liquid.

emunctory (ĭ mŭngkʹtə rĭ), *n., pl.* **-ries,** *adj.* —*n.* **1.** a part or organ of the body, as the skin, a kidney, etc., carrying off waste products. —*adj.* **2.** excretory. [t. NL: m. s. *ēmunctōrium*, L a pair of snuffers]

emu wren, a small, brown, warbler-like bird, *Stipiturus malacurus*, of Australia and New Zealand, with long, loosely barbed tail feathers, similar to those of the emu.

en (ĕn), *n.* **1.** the letter N, n. **2.** *Print.* half of the width of an em; N quad.

en-[1], a prefix meaning primarily 'in', 'into', first occurring in words from French, but now used freely as an English formative: **1.** with the old concrete force of putting the object into or on something or of bringing the object into the specified condition, often serving to form transitive verbs from nouns or adjectives, as in *enable, enact, endear, engulf, enshrine, enslave.* **2.** prefixed to verbs, to make them transitive, or, if already transitive, to give them the transitive sign, as in *enkindle, entwine, engild, engird, engrave, enshield.* Also, **em-**[1]. Cf. **in-**[2], **im-**[1]. [t. F, g. L *in-*, repr. *in*, prep., in, into, on, to]

en-[2], a prefix representing Greek *en-*, corresponding to **en-**[1] and occurring chiefly in combinations already formed in Greek, as *energy, enthusiasm.* Also, **em-**[2].

-en[1], a suffix, forming transitive and intransitive verbs from adjectives, as in *fasten, harden, sweeten,* or from nouns, as in *heighten, lengthen, strengthen.* [abstracted from old verbs like *fasten* (contrast *listen*, where *-en* has kept its non-morphemic character)]

-en[2], a suffix of adjectives indicating 'material', 'appearance', as in *ashen, golden, oaken.* [OE]

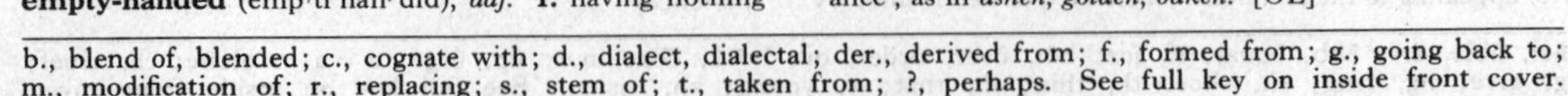
b., blend of, blended; c., cognate with; d., dialect, dialectal; der., derived from; f., formed from; g., going back to; m., modification of; r., replacing; s., stem of; t., taken from; ?, perhaps. See full key on inside front cover.

-en[3], a suffix used to mark the past participle in many strong and some weak verbs, as in *taken, proven.* [OE]
-en[4], a suffix forming the plural of some nouns, as in *brethren, children, oxen,* and other words, now mostly archaic, as *eyen, hosen.* [ME; OE *-an,* case ending of weak nouns, as in *oxan,* oblique sing. and nom. and acc. pl. of *oxa* ox]
-en[5], a diminutive suffix, as in *maiden, kitten,* etc. [OE]
enable (ĭ nā′bl), *v.t.,* **-bled, -bling. 1.** to make able; give power, means, or ability to; make competent; authorize: *this will enable him to do it.* **2.** to make possible or easy.
enabling (ĭ nā′blĭng), *adj.* (of an act, statute, or bill) enabling a person or a company to do something otherwise illegal.
enact (ĭ năkt′), *v.t.* **1.** to make into an act or statute. **2.** to ordain; decree. **3.** to represent on or as on the stage; act the part of: *to enact Hamlet.* **—enac′tor,** *n.*
enactive (ĭ năk′tĭv), *adj.* having power to enact or establish, as a law.
enactment (ĭ năkt′mənt), *n.* **1.** the act of enacting. **2.** the state or fact of being enacted. **3.** that which is enacted; a law; a statute. **4.** a section or part of a section in an act.
enactory (ĭ năk′tə rĭ), *adj. Law.* of or pertaining to an enactment which creates new rights and obligations.
enallage (ĭn ăl′ə jĭ), *n. Rhet.* the substitution of one grammatical form for another. [t. Gk]
enamel (ĭ năm′əl), *n., v.,* **-elled, -elling** or (*U.S.*) **-eled, -eling. —***n.* **1.** a glassy substance, usually opaque, applied by fusion to the surface of metal, pottery, etc., as an ornament or for protection. **2.** any of various enamel-like varnishes, paints, etc. **3.** any enamel-like surface with a bright lustre. **4.** an artistic work executed in enamel. **5.** *Anat., Zool.* the hard, glossy, calcareous outer structure of the crowns of the teeth, containing only a slight amount of organic substance. See diagram under **tooth. 6.** a coating applied to the nails to create a smooth and glossy surface, and often to colour them. **—***v.t.* **7.** to inlay or overlay with enamel. **8.** to form an enamel-like surface upon: *to enamel metal.* **9.** to decorate as with enamel; variegate with colours. [ME *enamayl,* t. AF, f. *en-* EN-[1] + *amayl,* OF *esmail,* c. It. *smalto* SMALT; akin to SMELT[1]] **—enam′eller,** *n.* **—enam′ellist,** *n.* **—enam′elwork′,** *n.*
enamelling (ĭ năm′ə lĭng), *n.* **1.** the act or work of one who enamels. **2.** a decoration or coating of enamel. Also, *U.S.,* **enameling.**
enamour (ĭ năm′ə), *v.t.* to inflame with love; charm; captivate (usually passive fol. by *of*): *to be enamoured of a lady.* Also, *U.S.,* **enam′or.** [ME *enamor(en),* t. OF: m. *enamourer,* der. *en-* EN-[1] + *amour* (g. L *amor* love)] **—Syn.** fascinate, bewitch.
enantiomorphism (ĭ năn′tĭ ō mô′fĭz′əm), *n. Crystall.* the property of certain substances which exist in two crystalline forms, one being a mirror image of the other. **—enan′tiomor′phic, enan′tiomor′phous,** *adj.*
enantiosis (ĭ năn′tĭ ō′sĭs), *n. Rhetoric.* a form of words in which the meaning to be conveyed is the opposite of what is stated. Cf. **irony.** [t. Gk]
enantiotropy (ĭ năn′tĭ ŏt′rə pĭ), *n. Crystall.* the property of certain substances which exist in two crystalline forms, one being stable below a certain temperature, the other above it. **—enantiotropic** (ĭ năn′tĭ ə trŏp′ĭk), *adj.*
enargite (ĭ nä′jīt, ĕn′ə jīt′), *n.* a mineral used as a source of copper, consisting of a copper and arsenic sulphide, Cu_3AsS_4; occurs as black orthorhombic crystals.
enarthrosis (ĕn′ä thrō′sĭs), *n., pl.* **-ses** (-sēz). *Anat.* a joint, as at the shoulder, in which a convex end of one bone is socketed in a concavity of another; a ball-and-socket joint. [NL, t. Gk: jointing in] **—en′arthro′dial,** *adj.*
en bloc (ŏn blŏk′; *Fr.* äN blŏk′), *French.* as a whole.
en brochette (*Fr.* äN brŏ shĕt′), *French.* See **brochette** (def. 2).
en brosse (*Fr.* äN brŏs′), *French.* (of hair) cut short and standing up stiffly. [F: lit., as a brush]
enc., 1. enclosed. **2.** enclosure.
encaenia (ĕn sē′nyə), *n.pl.* **1.** festive ceremonies commemorating the founding of a city or the consecration of a church. **2.** (*cap.*) ceremonies at Oxford University in honour of founders and benefactors. [t. L, t. Gk: m. *enkaínia* consecration feast]
encage (ĭn kāj′), *v.t.,* **-caged, -caging.** to confine in or as in a cage; coop up.
encamp (ĭn kămp′), *v.i., v.t.* to settle or lodge in a camp.
encampment (ĭn kămp′mənt), *n.* **1.** the act of encamping; lodgement in a camp. **2.** the place or quarters occupied in camping; a camp.
encapsulate (ĭn kăp′syŏŏ lāt′), *v.t., v.i.,* **-lated, -lating.** to enclose in or as in a capsule. **—encap′sula′tion,** *n.*
encarnalize (ĭn kä′nə līz′), *v.t.,* **-lized, -lizing.** to invest with a carnal or fleshly form. Also, **encarnalise.**
encase (ĭn kās′), *v.t.,* **-cased, -casing.** to enclose in or as in a case. Also, **incase.** [f. EN-[1] + CASE[2]] **—encase′ment,** *n.*
en casserole (*Fr.* äN kȧs rŏl′), *French.* See **casserole** (def. 4).
encaustic (ĕn kôs′tĭk), *adj.* **1.** painted with wax colours fixed with heat, or with any process in which colours are burnt in. **—***n.* **2.** a work of art produced by an encaustic process. [t. L: s. *encausticus* of burning in, t. Gk: m. *enkaustikós*]
-ence, a noun suffix equivalent to **-ance,** and corresponding to **-ent** in adjectives, as in *abstinence, consistence, dependence, difference.* [t. F, alter. of *-ance* -ANCE by etymological assoc. with L *-entia* noun suffix]
enceinte[1] (ŏn sănt′; *Fr.* äN săNt′), *adj.* pregnant; with child. [F, g. LL *incincta,* pp. fem., ungirt]
enceinte[2] (ŏn sănt′; *Fr.* äN săNt′), *n.* **1.** a wall or enclosure, as of a fortified place. **2.** the place enclosed. [F, der. *enceindre,* g. L *incingere* enclose, as with a girdle]
encephalic (ĕn′sĭ făl′ĭk), *adj.* of or pertaining to the encephalon or brain.
encephalitis (ĕn′sĕf ə lī′tĭs), *n. Pathol.* inflammation of the substance of the brain. [NL: see ENCEPHAL(O)-, -ITIS] **—encephalitic** (ĕn′sĕf ə lĭt′ĭk), *adj.*
encephalitis lethargica (lĭ thä′jĭ kə), *Pathol.* sleeping sickness.
encephalo-, a word element meaning 'brain', as in *encephalomyelitis.* Also, **encephal-.** [t. Gk: m. *enkephalo-,* comb. form of *enképhalos*]
encephalogram (ĕn sĕf′ə lə grăm′), *n. Med.* an X-ray photograph of the ventricles and subarachnoid space of the brain.
encephalograph (ĕn′sĕf′ə lə grăf′, -gräf), *n. Med.* **1.** an encephalogram. **2.** an electroencephalograph. [ENCEPHALO- + -GRAPH]
encephalography (ĕn′sĕf ə lŏg′rə fĭ, ĕn sĕf′ə-), *n.* the production of encephalograms after the introduction of air or oxygen into the ventricles and subarachnoid space by means of a lumbar or asternal puncture.
encephaloma (ĕn′sĕf ə lō′mə), *n., pl.* **-mata** (-mə tə). *Pathol.* **1.** a brain tumour. **2.** hernia of the brain.
encephalomyelitis (ĕn sĕf′ə lō mī′ə lī′tĭs), *n. Pathol., Vet. Sci.* any of several inflammatory diseases of the brain.
encephalon (ĕn sĕf′ə lŏn′), *n., pl.* **-la** (-lə). the brain. [NL, t. Gk:.(neut.) within the head, as n., the brain]
encephalopathy (ĕn′sĕf ə lŏp′ə thĭ, ĕn sĕf′ə-), *n. Pathol.* any degenerative disease of the brain.
encephalosis (ĕn′sĕf ə lō′sĭs, ĕn sĕf′ə-), *n. Pathol.* **1.** any organic disease of the brain. **2.** a degenerative, as opposed to an inflammatory, disease of the brain.
encephalotomy (ĕn sĕf′ə lŏt′ə mĭ), *n. Surg.* a surgical incision of the brain.
enchain (ĭn chān′), *v.t.* **1.** to fasten with or as with a chain or chains; fetter; restrain. **2.** to hold fast, as the attention. [ME *encheinen,* t. OF: m. *enchainer,* der. *en-* EN-[1] + *chaine* CHAIN] **—enchain′ment,** *n.*
enchant (ĭn chänt′), *v.t.* **1.** to subject to magical influence; cast a spell over; bewitch. **2.** to impart a magic quality or effect to. **3.** to delight in a high degree; charm. [ME *enchaunt(en),* t. OF: m. *enchanter,* g. L *incantāre* chant a magic formula against] **—Syn. 3.** fascinate, captivate, enrapture, transport.
enchanter (ĭn chän′tə), *n.* **1.** one who enchants. **2.** a magician.
enchanter's nightshade, any of several species of the N temperate onagraceous perennial herbs belonging to the genus *Circaea,* as the **common enchanter's nightshade,** *C. lutetiana.*
enchanting (ĭn chän′tĭng), *adj.* charming; bewitching. **—enchant′ingly,** *adv.*
enchantment (ĭn chänt′mənt), *n.* **1.** the act or art of enchanting. **2.** that which enchants. **—Syn. 1.** magic, sorcery, fascination, witchery. **2.** spell, charm.
enchantress (ĭn chän′trĭs), *n.* **1.** a woman who enchants; a sorceress. **2.** a fascinating woman.
enchase (ĭn chās′), *v.t.,* **-chased, -chasing. 1.** to place (gems) in an ornamental setting. **2.** to decorate with inlay, embossing, or engraving. [t. F: m. *enchâsser,* der. *en-* EN-[1] + *châsse* shrine (g. L *capsa* box). See CASE[2]]
enchiridion (ĕn′kī rĭd′ĭ ən), *n., pl.* **-ridions, -ridia** (-rĭd′ĭ ə). a handbook; a manual. [t. Gk: f. *en-* EN-[2] + m. *cheír* hand + *-idion,* dim. suffix]
enchondroma (ĕn′kən drō′mə), *n., pl.* **-mata** (-mə tə), **-dromas.** *Pathol.* a tumour which consists essentially of cartilage. [f. EN-[2] + s. Gk *chóndros* cartilage + -OMA] **—enchondromatous** (ĕn′kən drŏm′ə təs, -drō′mə-), *adj.*
enchorial (ĕn kô′rĭ əl), *adj.* (esp. of demotic writing) belonging to or used in a particular country; native; domestic. Also, **enchoric** (ĕn kô′rĭk, -kŏ′rĭk). [f. s. Gk *enchṓrios* in or of a country + -AL[1]]

encincture (ĭn sĭngk′chə), *v.*, **-tured, -turing,** *n.* —*v.t.* **1.** to girdle; surround or encompass as with a girdle. —*n.* **2.** the act or fact of being encompassed.

encircle (ĭn sûr′kl), *v.t.*, **-cled, -cling. 1.** to form a circle round; surround; encompass. **2.** to make a circling movement about; make the circuit of. —**encir′clement,** *n.* —**Syn. 1.** environ, gird, enfold, enclose.

encl., 1. enclosed. **2.** enclosure.

en clair (*Fr.* äN klĕr′), *French.* (of telegrams, etc.) in everyday language; not in code.

enclasp (ĭn kläsp′), *v.t.* to hold in or as in a clasp or embrace.

enclave (ĕn′klāv; *Fr.* äN kläv′), *n.* a country, or, esp., an outlying portion of a country, entirely or mostly surrounded by the territory of another country. [t. F, der. *enclaver* shut in, g. Rom. *inclāvāre*]

enclitic (ĭn klĭt′ĭk), *adj.* **1.** (of a word) so closely connected with a preceding word as to have no independent accent. —*n.* **2.** an enclitic word, as *que* (and) in Latin: *arma virumque,* arms and the man. [t. LL: s. *encliticus,* t. Gk: m. *enklitikós,* lit., leaning on] —**enclit′ically,** *adv.*

enclose (ĭn klōz′), *v.t.*, **-closed, -closing. 1.** to shut in; close in on all sides. **2.** to surround as with a fence or wall: *to enclose land.* **3.** to insert in the same envelope, etc., with the main letter, etc.: *he enclosed a cheque.* **4.** to contain (the thing transmitted): *his letter enclosed a cheque.* Also, *Law or Archaic,* **inclose.** [f. EN-[1] + CLOSE, v., after OF *enclos,* pp. of *enclore*] —**Syn. 1.** surround, encircle, encompass.

enclosure (ĭn klō′zhə), *n.* **1.** the act of enclosing. **2.** the separation and appropriation of land, especially of common land, by means of a fence. **3.** a tract of land surrounded by a fence. **4.** that which encloses, as a fence or wall. **5.** that which is enclosed, as a paper sent in a letter. **6.** *Sports.* a section of a ground reserved for spectators, or for a certain section of the spectators. Also, *Law or Archaic,* **inclosure.**

encolpion (ĕn kŏl′pĭ ən), *n.*, *pl.* **-pia** (-pĭ ə), a reliquary, cross, or the like, worn on the breast of bishops of the Eastern Church. [t. MGk, n. use of Gk adj. *enkólpios* in the bosom, der. *kólpos* bosom]

encomiast (ĕn kō′mĭ ăst′), *n.* one who utters or writes an encomium; a eulogist. [t. Gk: s. *enkōmiastḗs*]

encomiastic (ĕn kō′mĭ ăs′tĭk), *adj.* eulogistic. Also, **enco′mias′tical.**

encomium (ĕn kō′myəm), *n.*, *pl.* **-miums, -mia** (-myə). a formal expression of praise; a eulogy. [t. L, t. Gk: m. *enkṓmion* eulogy, prop. neut. of *enkṓmios* belonging to a Bacchic revel]

encompass (ĭn kŭm′pəs), *v.t.* **1.** to form a circle about; encircle; surround. **2.** to enclose; contain. **3.** *Obs.* to outwit. —**encom′passment,** *n.*

encore (ŏng′kô), *interj.*, *n.*, *v.*, **-cored, -coring.** —*interj.* **1.** again; once more (used by an audience in calling for a repetition of a song, etc., or for an additional number or piece). —*n.* **2.** a demand, as by applause, for a repetition of a song, etc., or for an additional number or piece. **3.** that which is given in response to such a demand. —*v.t.* **4.** to call for a repetition of. **5.** to call for an encore from (a performer). [t. F: still, yet, besides, g. L *hanc hōram* within this hour]

encounter (ĭn koun′tə), *v.t.* **1.** to come upon; meet with, esp. unexpectedly. **2.** to meet with or contend against (difficulties, opposition, etc.). **3.** to meet (a person, military force, etc.) in conflict. —*v.i.* **4.** *Obs.* to meet, esp. in conflict. —*n.* **5.** a meeting with a person or thing, esp. casually or unexpectedly. **6.** a meeting in conflict or opposition; a battle; a combat. **7.** *Obs.* manner of meeting; behaviour. [ME *encountre(n),* t. OF: m. *encontrer,* g. LL *incontrāre,* der. L *in-* IN-[2] + *contrā* against] —**Syn. 6.** conflict, skirmish.

encourage (ĭn kŭ′rĭj), *v.t.*, **-raged, -raging. 1.** to inspire with courage, spirit, or confidence. **2.** to stimulate by assistance, approval, etc. [ME *encorage(n),* t. OF: m. *encoragier,* der. *en-* EN-[1] + *corage* COURAGE] —**encour′ager,** *n.* —**encour′agingly,** *adv.* —**Syn. 1.** inspirit, embolden, hearten. **2.** urge, abet, second; foment, promote, advance, foster. —**Ant. 1.** dishearten.

encouragement (ĭn kŭ′rĭj mənt), *n.* **1.** the act of encouraging. **2.** the state of being encouraged. **3.** that which encourages. —**Ant. 1.** disapproval. **2.** depression.

encrimson (ĕn krĭm′zən), *v.t.* to make crimson.

encrinite (ĕn′krĭ nīt′), *n.* **1.** a fossil crinoid. **2.** any crinoid. [f. EN-[2] + m. s. Gk *krínon* lily + -ITE[1]]

encroach (ĭn krōch′), *v.i.* **1.** to advance beyond proper limits; make gradual inroads. **2.** to trespass upon the property or rights of another, esp. stealthily or by gradual advances. [ME *encroche(n),* t. OF: m. *encrochier,* der. *en-* EN-[1] + *croc* hook] —**encroach′er,** *n.* —**encroach′ingly,** *adv.* —**Syn. 1, 2.** See **trespass.**

encroachment (ĭn krōch′mənt), *n.* **1.** the act of encroaching. **2.** anything taken by encroaching.

encrust (ĭn krŭst′), *v.t.* **1.** to cover or line with a crust or hard coating. **2.** to form into a crust. **3.** to deposit as a crust. —*v.i.* **4.** to form a crust. Also, **incrust.** [t. L: m. s. *incrustāre*]

encrustation (ĕn′krŭs tā′shən), *n.* **1.** an encrusting or being encrusted. **2.** a crust or coat of anything on the surface of a body; a covering, coating, or scale. **3.** the inlaying or addition of enriching materials on a surface. **4.** the inlaid or added enriching materials to a surface or an object. Also, **incrustation.**

encumber (ĭn kŭm′bə), *v.t.* **1.** to impede or hamper; retard; embarrass. **2.** to block up or fill with what is obstructive or superfluous. **3.** to burden with obligations, debt, etc. **4.** to burden or impede with or as with parcels, etc. Also, **incumber.** [ME *encombre(n),* t. OF: m. *encombrer,* der. *en-* EN-[1] + *combre* barrier (g. LL *combrus,* t. Gallic: m. *comberos* a bringing together)] —**Syn. 3.** oppress, overload.

encumbrance (ĭn kŭm′brəns), *n.* **1.** that which encumbers; something useless or superfluous; a burden; a hindrance. **2.** a dependent person, esp. a child. **3.** *Law.* a burden or claim on property, as a mortgage. Also, **incumbrance.**

encumbrancer (ĭn kŭm′brən sə), *n.* *Law.* one who holds an encumbrance.

-ency, a noun suffix, equivalent to **-ence,** as in *consistency, dependency, exigency.* [t. L: m. s. *-entia*]

ency., encyclopedia. Also, **encyc.**

encyclical (ĕn sĭk′lĭ kl), *n.* **1.** a letter addressed by the Pope to all the bishops of the world in communion with the Holy See. —*adj.* **2.** intended for wide or general circulation; general. Also, **encyc′lic.** [f. s. LL *encyclicus* (r. L *encyclius,* t. Gk: m. *enkýklios* circular, general) + -AL[1]]

encyclopedia (ĕn sī′klō pē′dyə), *n.* **1.** a work treating separately various topics from all branches of knowledge, usually in alphabetical arrangement. **2.** a work treating exhaustively one art or science, esp. in articles arranged alphabetically; a cyclopedia. **3.** (*cap.*) the French work edited by Diderot and D'Alembert, published in the 18th century, distinguished by its advanced or radical character. Also, **encyclopaedia.** [t. LL, t. pseudo-Gk (occurring in mss. of Quintilian, Pliny, and Galen): m. *enkyklopaideía,* for *enkýklios paideía* general education, complete round or course of learning. See ENCYCLIC, CYCLOPEDIA]

encyclopedic (ĕn sī′klō pē′dĭk), *adj.* **1.** pertaining to or of the nature of an encyclopedia; relating to all branches of knowledge. **2.** embracing all or much human learning. Also, **encyclopaedic.**

encyclopedism (ĕn sī′klō pē′dĭz əm), *n.* **1.** encyclopedic learning. **2.** (*often cap.*) the doctrines and influence of the Encyclopedists. Also, **encyclopaedism.**

encyclopedist (ĕn sī′klō pē′dĭst), *n.* **1.** a compiler of or contributor to an encyclopedia. **2.** (*often cap.*) one of the collaborators in the French Encyclopedia. Also, **encyclopaedist.**

encyst (ĕn sĭst′), *v.t.*, *v.i.* *Biol.* to enclose or become enclosed in a cyst. —**encyst′ment, en′cysta′tion,** *n.*

end[1] (ĕnd), *n.* **1.** an extremity of anything that is longer than it is broad: *the end of a street, rope, rod, etc.* **2.** an extreme or farthermost part of anything extended in space: *the ends of the earth.* **3.** anything that bounds an object at one of its extremities; a limit. **4.** a place or section adjacent to an extremity or limit: *at the far end of the room.* **5.** the act of coming to an end; termination. **6.** the concluding part. **7.** a purpose or aim: *to gain one's end.* **8.** the object for which a thing exists: *the happiness of the people is the end of government.* **9.** issue or result. **10.** termination of existence; death. **11.** a cause of death, destruction, or ruin. **12.** a remnant or fragment: *odds and ends.* **13.** a part or share of something: *her end of the work.* **14.** a district or locality, esp. part of a town: *the West End.* **15.** *Cricket.* a wicket: *the batting end, the bowling end.* **16.** *Football, etc.* the half of the field which is defended by one team and attacked by the other. **17.** *Slang.* the worst possible; the limit of badness, incompetence, or the like. **18. at a loose end,** Also, **at loose ends. a.** unoccupied; with nothing to do. **b.** in disorder. **19. end on,** with the end facing, or next to. **20. end to end,** (of two objects) having the ends adjacent. **21. go off the deep end,** *Colloq.* to become violently agitated; lose control of emotions. **22. in the end,** as an outcome; at last; finally. **23. keep one's end up,** *Colloq.* **a.** to be in control of a situation, job, etc. **b.** to defend or preserve one's own interests. **24. make (both) ends meet,** to keep expenditure within one's means. **25. no end,** *Colloq.* very much; greatly. **26. on end, a.** upright. **b.** continuously. —*v.t.*

27. to bring to an end or natural conclusion. **28.** to put an end to by force. **29.** to form the end of. —*v.i.* **30.** to come to an end; terminate; cease: *he ended by settling down.* **31.** to issue or result: *extravagance ends in want.* **32.** *Colloq.* to reach a final condition, circumstance, goal (often fol. by *up*): *you'll end up in prison.* [ME and OE *ende*, c. G *Ende*. See AND] —**end′er,** *n.*
—**Syn.** **3.** tip, bound, limit, terminus. **5.** END, CLOSE, CONCLUSION, FINISH, OUTCOME refer to the termination of something. END implies a natural termination, completion of an action or process, or attainment of purpose: *the end of a day, of a race, to some good end.* CLOSE implies a planned rounding off of something in process: *the close of a conference.* CONCLUSION suggests a decision or arrangement: *all evidence leads to this conclusion, the conclusion of peace terms.* FINISH emphasizes completion of something begun: *a fight to the finish.* OUTCOME suggests the issue of something which was in doubt: *the outcome of a game.* **6.** finale, peroration. **7.** See **aim.** **9.** outcome, consequence. **10.** destruction, extermination, annihilation, ruin. **27.** conclude, finish, complete, terminate. **28.** close, stop, discontinue. —**Ant.** **5.** beginning, start. **27.** begin.

end[2] (ĕnd), *v.t.* *Now Dial.* to put (wheat, hay, etc.) into a barn, stack, etc. [? var. of *inn* to lodge, der. INN]

end-, var. of **endo-,** before vowels, as in *endamoeba.*

endamage (ĕn dăm′ĭj), *v.t.*, **-aged, -aging.** to damage. —**endam′agement,** *n.*

endamoeba (ĕn′də mē′bə), *n.* a protozoan, genus *Endamoeba*, one species of which causes dysentery and liver abscess. Also, *U.S.*, **en′dame′ba.** [f. END- + AMOEBA]

endanger (ĭn dān′jə), *v.t.* to expose to danger; imperil. —**endan′german,** *n.*

endarch (ĕnd′äk′), *adj.* *Bot.* denoting a strand or cylinder of primary xylem in a stem or root with the protoxylem on its inner edge.

end-blown (ĕnd′blōn′), *adj.* (of a flute) having a mouthpiece at the end of the tube, so that the player's breath is directed into the instrument.

endear (ĭn dĭə′), *v.t.* **1.** to make dear, esteemed, or beloved: *he endeared himself to his mother.* **2.** *Obs.* to make costly. —**endear′ingly,** *adv.*

endearment (ĭn dĭə′mənt), *n.* **1.** the act of endearing. **2.** the state of being endeared. **3.** an action or utterance manifesting affection; a caress or an affectionate term.

endeavour (ĭn dĕv′ə), *v.i.* **1.** to exert oneself to do or effect something; make an effort; strive. —*v.t.* **2.** to attempt; try: *he endeavours to keep things nice about his place.* —*n.* **3.** a strenuous effort; an attempt. Also, *U.S.*, **endeav′or.** [ME *endever(en)*, der. EN-[1] + DEVOIR. Cf. F *en devoir* in duty] —**endeav′ourer,** *n.* —**Syn.** **1, 2.** struggle, labour, essay, undertake, seek, aim. See **try.** **3.** exertion, struggle, essay. See **effort.**

endemic (ĕn dĕm′ĭk), *adj.* **1.** Also, **endem′ical.** peculiar to a particular people or locality, as a disease. —*n.* **2.** an endemic disease. [f. s. Gk *éndēmos* belonging to a people + -IC] —**endem′ically,** *adv.* —**endemism** (ĕn′də mĭz′əm), **endemicity** (ĕn′də mĭs′ĭ tĭ), *n.*

endenizen (ĭn dĕn′ĭ zən), *v.t.* to make a denizen or citizen of; enfranchise.

Enderby Land (ĕn′də bĭ), a part of the coast of Antarctica, E of Queen Maud Land: discovered 1831.

endermic (ĕn dû′mĭk), *adj.* acting through the skin, as a medicine. [f. EN-[2] + DERM(A) + -IC]

en déshabillé (*Fr.* äɴ dĕ zȧ bē yĕ′), *French.* in dishabille or undress.

endgame (ĕnd′gām′), *n.* *Chess.* the final stage of a game, played with few surviving pieces, leading to checkmate or stalemate.

ending (ĕn′dĭng), *n.* **1.** a bringing or coming to an end; termination; close. **2.** the final or concluding part. **3.** death. **4.** *Gram.* an inflectional morpheme at the end of a word form, as *-s* in *cuts.* **5.** (in popular use) any final word part, as the *-ow* of *widow.* [ME; OE *endung*]

endive (ĕn′dĭv; *Fr.* äɴ dēv′), *n.* a composite plant, *Cichorium endivia*, with finely divided curled leaves, used for salad. [ME, t. F, t. ML: m. s. *endivia*, t. MGk: m. *endiui*, t. L: m. *intibus, intibum*]

endless (ĕnd′lĭs), *adj.* **1.** having no end, limit, or conclusion; boundless; infinite; interminable; incessant. **2.** made continuous, as by joining the two ends of a single length: *an endless chain or belt.* —**end′lessly,** *adv.* —**end′lessness,** *n.* —**Syn.** **1.** limitless, illimitable, immeasurable, unending, unceasing, continuous, continual, perpetual, everlasting. See **eternal.**

endlong (ĕnd′lŏng′), *adv.* *Archaic or Dial.* **1.** lengthwise. **2.** on end. [ME *endelong*, t. OE *andlang* ALONG]

endman (ĕnd′măn′), *n.* **1.** a man at one end of a row or line. **2.** a man at either end of the line of performers of a minstrel troupe, who plays on the bones or tambourine and carries on humorous dialogue with the interlocutor.

endmost (ĕnd′mōst′), *adj.* farthest.

endo-, a word element meaning 'internal', as in *endocardial.* Also, **end-.** [t. Gk, comb. form of *éndon* within]

endoblast (ĕn′dō blăst′), *n.* *Embryol.* the prospective endoderm; the blastemic cells which are to form the endoderm. —**en′doblas′tic,** *adj.*

endocardial (ĕn′dō kä′dĭ əl), *adj.* **1.** within the heart; intracardiac. **2.** pertaining to the endocardium.

endocarditis (ĕn′dō kä dī′tĭs), *n.* *Pathol.* inflammation of the endocardium. [NL; f. ENDOCARD(IUM) + -ITIS] —**endocarditic** (ĕn′dō kä dĭt′ĭk), *adj.*

endocardium (ĕn′dō kä′dĭ əm), *n.* *Anat.* the delicate serous membrane which lines the cavities of the heart and aids in forming the valves by duplication. [NL: f. *endo-* ENDO- + *cardium* (comb. form repr. Gk *kardía* heart)]

endocarp (ĕn′dō käp′), *n.* *Bot.* the inner layer of a pericarp, as the stone of certain fruits.

Fruit of peach A, Endocarp; B, Epicarp; C, Mesocarp; ABC, Pericarp

endocentric (ĕn′dō sĕn′trĭk), *adj.* *Gram.* having the same function in a sentence as one of its immediate constituents. *Cold water* is an endocentric construction since it functions in the same way as would the noun *water.* Cf. **exocentric.**

endocrine (ĕn′dō krīn′), *n.* **1.** an endocrine gland or organ. **2.** an internal secretion. —*adj.* **3.** of or pertaining to the endocrine glands or their secretions: *endocrine function.* [f. ENDO- + m. s. Gk *krínein* separate] —**endocrinal** (ĕn′dō krī′nəl), **endocrinic** (ĕn′dō krĭn′ĭk), **endocrinous** (ĕn dŏk′rĭ nəs), *adj.*

endocrine gland, any of various glands or organs (as the thyroid gland, suprarenal bodies, pituitary body, etc.) which produce certain important internal secretions (products given up directly to the blood or lymph) acting upon particular organs, and which, through improper functioning, may cause grave disorders or death; ductless gland.

endocrinology (ĕn′dō krī nŏl′ə jĭ, -krĭ-), *n.* the science that deals with the endocrine glands, esp. in their relation to bodily changes. —**en′docrinol′ogist,** *n.*

endoderm (ĕn′dō dûm′), *n.* *Embryol.* the inner germ layer in the embryo of a metazoan. Also, **entoderm.** —**en′doder′mal, en′doder′mic,** *adj.*

endodermis (ĕn′dō dû′mĭs), *n.* *Bot.* a specialized uniseriate layer of cells delimiting the stele of vascular plants.

endoergic (ĕn′dō û′jĭk), *adj.* *Physics.* (of a process or reaction, esp. a nuclear one) consuming energy; endothermic.

endogamous (ĕn dŏg′ə məs), *adj.* **1.** marrying customarily within the tribe or other social unit. **2.** pertaining to such marriage (opposed to *exogamous*). Also, **endogamic** (ĕn′dō găm′ĭk).

endogamy (ĕn dŏg′ə mĭ), *n.* marriage within the tribe or other social unit, a custom among some savage peoples (opposed to *exogamy*).

endogen (ĕn′dō jĕn′), *n.* *Bot.* any plant of the obsolete class *Endogenae*, including the monocotyledons, whose stems were erroneously supposed to grow from within.

endogenous (ĕn dŏj′ĭ nəs), *adj.* **1.** growing or proceeding from within; originating within. **2.** *Anat.* autogenous. —**endog′enously,** *adv.*

endolymph (ĕn′dō lĭmf′), *n.* *Anat.* the fluid contained within the membranous labyrinth of the ear.

endometriosis (ĕn′dō mē′trĭ ō′sĭs), *n.* *Pathol.* the presence of uterine lining in other organs, most commonly the ovary, characterized by cyst formation, adhesions, and menstrual pain. —**en′dome′trial,** *adj.*

endometritis (ĕn′dō mĭ trī′tĭs), *n.* *Pathol.* inflammation of the lining of the uterus.

endometrium (ĕn′dō mē′trĭ əm), *n.*, *pl.* **-tria** (-trĭ ə). *Anat.* the mucous membrane lining the uterus.

endomorph (ĕn′dō môf′), *n.* **1.** *Mineral.* a mineral enclosed within another mineral (opposed to *perimorph*). **2.** *Physiol.* a person of endomorphic type.

endomorphic (ĕn′dō mô′fĭk), *adj.* **1.** *Mineral.* occurring in the form of an endomorph. **2.** *Mineral.* of or relating to endomorphs. **3.** *Mineral* taking place within a rock mass. **4.** *Physiol.* having a heavily built body characterized by the relative prominence of structures developed from the embryonic endoderm (distinguished from *ectomorphic, mesomorphic*).

endomorphism (ĕn′dō mô′fĭz′əm), *n.* *Mineral.* a change brought about within the mass of an intrusive igneous rock.

endoparasite (ĕn′dō păr′ə sīt′), *n.* an internal parasite (opposed to *ectoparasite*).

endoperidium (ĕn′dō pĭ rĭd′ĭ əm), *n.* *Bot.* See **peridium.**

endophyte (ĕn′dō fīt′), *n.* *Bot.* a plant living within an animal or another plant, usually as a parasite.

endoplasm (ĕn′dō plăz′əm), *n.* *Biol.* the inner portion of the cytoplasm in the cell of a protozoan or vegetable cell (opposed to *ectoplasm*). —**en′doplas′mic,** *adj.*

endopleura (ĕn′dō plo͞o′rə), *n.* the inner coat of a seed, the tegmen.

end organ, *Physiol.* one of several specialized structures found at the peripheral end of sensory or motor nerve fibres.

endorse (ĭn dôs′), *v.t.*, **-dorsed, -dorsing. 1.** to approve, support, or sustain: *to endorse a statement.* **2.** to write (something) on the back of a document, etc. **3.** to sign one's name on (a commercial document or other instrument). **4.** to designate (another) as payee by one's endorsement. **5.** to acknowledge (payment) by placing one's signature on a bill, draft, etc. **6.** to add a modifying statement to (a document). **7.** to record a conviction for a motoring offence on (a driving licence). Also, **indorse.** [partial Latinization of ME *endosse*, t. OF: m. *endosser*, der. *en-* on + *dos* (g. L *dorsum* back)] —**endors′able,** *adj.* —**endors′er,** *n.*

endorsee (ĭn′dô′sē′, ĕn′dô-), *n.* one to whom a negotiable document is endorsed. Also, **indorsee.**

endorsement (ĭn dôs′mənt), *n.* **1.** approval or sanction. **2.** the placing of one's signature, etc., on a document. **3.** the signature, etc., placed on the reverse of a commercial document which assigns the interest therein to another. **4.** *Insurance.* a clause under which the stated coverage of an insurance policy may be altered. **5.** any statement subsequently added to a document to indicate some modification of its original terms. **6.** the record of a conviction for a motoring offence placed on a driving licence.

endosarc (ĕn′dō säk′), *n. Biol.* the endoplasm of a protozoan (opposed to *ectosarc*).

endoscope (ĕn′dō skōp′), *n. Med.* a slender tubular instrument used to examine the interior of a body cavity or hollow viscus. —**endoscopic** (ĕn′dō skŏp′ĭk), *adj.* —**endoscopy** (en dŏs′kə pĭ), *n.*

endoskeleton (ĕn′dō skĕl′ĭ tən), *n. Anat.* the internal skeleton or framework of the body of an animal (opposed to *exoskeleton*). —**en′doskel′etal,** *adj.*

endosmosis (ĕn′dŏs mō′sĭs, -dŏz-), *n. Phys. Chem.* **1.** osmosis from without inwards. **2.** (in osmosis) the flow of that fluid which passes with the greater rapidity into the other (opposed to *exosmosis*). [NL] —**endosmotic** (ĕn′dŏs mŏt′ĭk, -dŏz-), *adj.* —**en′dosmot′ically,** *adv.*

endosperm (ĕn′dō spûm′), *n. Bot.* nutritive matter in seed plant ovules, derived from the embryo sac. See diag. under **seed.** —**en′dosper′mic,** *adj.*

endospore (ĕn′dō spô′), *n.* **1.** *Bot.* the inner coat of a spore. **2.** *Bacteriol.* a spore formed within a cell of a rod-shaped organism. **3.** a fungal spore formed within a reproductive structure, i.e. an endogenous spore. —**endosporous** (ĕn dŏs′pə rəs, ĕn′dō spô′rəs), *adj.*

endosteum (ĕn dŏs′tĭ əm), *n., pl.* **-tea** (-tĭ ə). *Anat.* the vascular membrane lining the medullary cavity of a bone. [NL, f. Gk: *end-* END- + m. *ostéon* bone]

endostosis (ĕn′dŏs tō′sĭs), *n. Anat.* bone formation beginning in the substance of cartilage. [f. END(O)- + OSTOSIS]

endothecium (ĕn′dō thē′shĭ əm, -sĭ əm), *n., pl.* **-cia** (-shĭ ə, -sĭ ə). *Bot.* **1.** the sub-epidermal cell layer of an anther which causes it to open when mature, often having special thickenings. **2.** the inner tissues of bryophyte capsules which give rise to the spores and other structures. [NL, f. Gk: *endo-* ENDO- + m. *thēkíon* little case]

endothelial (ĕn′dō thē′lĭ əl), *adj.* pertaining to endothelium.

endothelioid (ĕn′dō thē′lĭ oid′), *adj.* resembling endothelium.

endothelioma (ĕn′dō thē′lĭ ō′mə), *n., pl.* **-mata** (-mə tə), **-mas.** *Pathol.* a tumour (malignant or benign) originating from the endothelium. [f. ENDOTHELI(UM) + -OMA]

endothelium (ĕn′dō thē′lĭ əm), *n., pl.* **-lia** (-lĭ ə). *Anat.* the tissue which lines blood vessels, lymphatics, serous cavities, and the like: a form of epithelium (in the broad sense). [NL, f. Gk: *endo-* ENDO- + s. *thēlḗ* nipple + m. *-ion*]

endothermic (ĕn′dō thû′mĭk), *adj.* denoting or pertaining to a chemical change which is accompanied by an absorption of heat (opposed to *exothermic*).

endotoxin (ĕn′dō tŏk′sĭn), *n.* the toxic protoplasm of an organism which is liberated and causes its toxic action when the organism dies and disintegrates, as in *Eberthella typhi*, the causative agent of typhoid fever.

endotrophic (ĕn′dō trŏf′ĭk, -trō′fĭk), *adj. Bot.* of, denoting, or pertaining to a type of mycorrhizal association, as found in orchids, in which the fungal hyphae occur within the root tissue.

endow (ĭn dou′), *v.t.* **1.** to provide with a permanent fund or source of income: *to endow a college.* **2.** to furnish as with some gift, faculty, or quality; equip: *Nature has endowed him with great ability.* **3.** *Archaic.* to provide with a dower. [ME *endow(en)*, t. OF: m. *endouer*, f. *en-* EN-[1] + *douer*, g. L *dōtāre* endow] —**endow′er,** *n.*

endowment (ĭn dou′mənt), *n.* **1.** the act of endowing. **2.** that with which an institution, person, etc., is endowed, as property or funds. **3.** (*usually pl.*) an attribute of mind or body; a gift of nature. —**Syn. 3.** capacity, talent, faculties.

endowment insurance, a form of insurance providing for the payment of a fixed sum to the insured person at a specified time, or to his heirs, or a person designated, should he die before the time named.

endpaper (ĕnd′pā′pə), *n. Bookbinding.* a sheet of strong paper, half of which is pasted on to the inside of the cover, the other half forming the flyleaf.

end point, *Chem.* the point in a volumetric titration denoting the completion of a reaction, usually marked by a change in colour of an indicator.

end product, final or resulting product.

endue (ĭn dyo͞o′), *v.t.*, **-dued, -duing. 1.** to invest or endow with some gift, quality, or faculty: *endued with life.* **2.** to put on; assume. **3.** to clothe (fol. by *with*). Also, **indue.** [ME *endew(en)*, t. OF: m. *enduire*, g. L *indūcere* lead into, confused with L *induere* put on]

endurable (ĭn dyo͝o′rə bl), *adj.* that may be endured. —**endur′ableness,** *n.* —**endur′ably,** *adv.* —**Syn.** bearable, tolerable.

endurance (ĭn dyo͝o′rəns), *n.* **1.** the fact or power of enduring or bearing anything. **2.** lasting quality; duration. **3.** something endured, as a hardship. —**Syn. 1.** See **patience.**

endurance limit, (in fatigue testing) the maximum stress which a material will withstand without breaking.

endure (ĭn dyo͝o′), *v.*, **-dured, -during.** —*v.t.* **1.** to hold out against; sustain without impairment or yielding; undergo. **2.** to bear without resistance or with patience; tolerate: *I cannot endure to listen to that any longer.* —*v.i.* **3.** to continue to exist; last. **4.** to support adverse force or influence of any kind; suffer without yielding; suffer patiently. **5.** to retain a certain stature; maintain recognition of merit. [ME *endure(n)*, t. OF: m. *endurer*, g. L *indūrāre* harden, ML endure] —**Syn. 2.** experience, stand. See **bear**[1]. **3.** abide, remain, persist. See **continue.**

enduring (ĭn dyo͝o′rĭng), *adj.* **1.** lasting; permanent. **2.** long-suffering; patient. —**endur′ingly,** *adv.* —**endur′ingness,** *n.*

endways (ĕnd′wāz′), *adv.* **1.** on end. **2.** with the end upwards or forwards. **3.** towards the ends or end; lengthways. **4.** end to end. Also, **endwise** (ĕnd′wīz′).

Endymion (ĕn dĭm′ĭ ən), *n. Gk Myth.* a beautiful youth whom Selene caressed as he slept.

ENE, east-north-east. Also, **E.N.E.**

-ene, 1. a noun suffix used in chemistry, in names of hydrocarbons, as *anthracene, benzene, naphthalene*, specif. those of the olefine or ethylene series, as *butylene.* **2.** a generalized suffix used in trademarks for substances, often implying synthetic manufacture. [special use of *-ene*, adj. suffix (as in *terrene*), t. L: m. s. *-ēnus* (in Gk *-ēnos*)]

enema (ĕn′ĭ mə), *n., pl.* **enemas, enemata** (ĭ nĕm′ə tə). *Med.* **1.** a fluid injected into the rectum. **2.** an instrument for doing this. **3.** the injection of the fluid. [t. Gk: injection, clyster]

enemy (ĕn′ə mĭ), *n., pl.* **-mies,** *adj.* —*n.* **1.** one who cherishes hatred or harmful designs against another; an adversary or opponent. **2.** an armed foe; an opposing military force. **3.** a hostile nation or state. **4.** a subject of such a state. **5.** something harmful or prejudicial. **6. the Enemy,** the Devil. —*adj.* **7.** belonging to a hostile power or to any of its nationals: *enemy property.* **8.** *Obs.* inimical; ill-disposed. [ME, t. OF: m. *enemi*, g. L *inimīcus* unfriendly, hostile]

—**Syn. 1.** ENEMY, FOE refer to a dangerous public or personal adversary. ENEMY emphasizes the idea of hostility: *to overcome the enemy, a bitter enemy.* FOE, a more literary word, may be used interchangeably with ENEMY, but emphasizes somewhat more the danger to be feared from such a one: *deadly foe, arch foe of mankind (the Devil).* —**Ant. 1.** friend. **2.** ally.

energetic (ĕn′ə jĕt′ĭk), *adj.* **1.** possessing or exhibiting energy; forcible; vigorous. **2.** powerful in action or effect; effective. [t. Gk: m. s. *energētikós* active] —**en′erget′ically,** *adv.* —**Syn. 1.** See **active.** —**Ant. 1.** listless.

energetics (ĕn′ə jĕt′ĭks), *n.* the science of the laws of energy. [pl. of ENERGETIC. See -ICS]

energize (ĕn′ə jīz′), *v.*, **-gized, -gizing.** —*v.t.* **1.** to give energy to; rouse into activity. —*v.i.* **2.** to be in operation; put forth energy. Also, **energise.** —**en′ergiz′er,** *n.*

energumen (ĕn′û gyo͞o′mĕn), *n.* **1.** one possessed by an evil spirit; a demoniac. **2.** a fanatical enthusiast. [t. LL: s. *energūmenus*, t. Gk: m. *energoúmenos*, ppr. pass. of *energeîn* operate, influence]

energy (ĕn′ə jĭ), *n.*, *pl.* **-gies. 1.** capacity or habit of vigorous activity. **2.** the actual exertion of power; operation; activity. **3.** power as exerted. **4.** ability to produce action or effect. **5.** vigour or forcefulness of expression. **6.** *Physics.* the property of a system which diminishes, when the system does work on any other system, by an amount equal to the work so done. [t. LL: m. s. *energīa*, t. Gk: m. *enérgeia* agency, force] **—Syn. 1.** vigour, force, potency, zeal, push.

energy level, *Physics.* one of a number of quantized energy states in which a nucleus, atom, or molecule can exist. Transitions between different levels involve the loss or gain of a finite quantity of energy. Also, **energy state.**

enervate (*v.* ĕn′ə vāt′; *adj.* ĭ nû′vĭt), *v.*, **-vated, -vating,** *adj.* **—***v.t.* **1.** to deprive of nerve, force, or strength; destroy the vigour of; weaken. **—***adj.* **2.** enervated. [t. L: m. s. *ēnervātus*, pp.] **—en′erva′tion,** *n.* **—en′erva′tor,** *n.* **—en′erva′tive,** *adj.*

enface (ĭn fās′), *v.t.*, **-faced, -facing. 1.** to write, print, or stamp something on the face of (a note, draft, etc.). **2.** to write, print, or stamp (something) on the face of a note, draft, etc. **—enface′ment,** *n.*

en famille (*Fr.* äɴ fá mēy′), *French.* in the family.

enfant terrible (*Fr.* äɴ fäɴ tĕ rē′bl), *French.* **1.** a child that makes embarrassing remarks. **2.** an indiscreet and irresponsible person. [F: lit., terrible child]

enfeeble (ĭn fē′bl), *v.t.*, **-bled, -bling.** to make feeble; weaken. [ME *enfeble(n)*, t. OF: m. *enfeblir*, der. *en-* EN-[1] + *feble* FEEBLE] **—enfee′blement,** *n.* **—enfee′bler,** *n.*

enfeoff (ĭn fĕf′), *v.t.* **1.** to invest with a fief or fee. **2.** to give as a fief. **3.** to surrender. [ME *enfeoffe(n)*, t. AF: m. *enfeoffer*. See EN-[1], FIEF] **—enfeoff′ment,** *n.*

en fête (*Fr.* äɴ fĕt′), *French.* in festivity; in gala attire.

enfetter (ĕn fĕt′ə), *v.t.* to bind with or as with fetters.

Enfield (ĕn′fēld′), *n.* **1.** a N outer borough of London. 271,600 (1965). **2.** any of various rifles made at the Royal Small Arms Factory at Enfield.

enfilade (ĕn′fĭ lād′), *n.*, *v.*, **-laded, -lading.** *Mil.* **—***n.* **1.** a situation of works, troops, etc., making them subject to a sweeping fire from along the length of a line of troops, a trench, a battery, etc. **2.** the fire thus directed. **—***v.t.* **3.** to attack with an enfilade. [t. F, der. *enfiler* to thread, string, go through, rake with fire, der. *en-* EN-[1] + *fil* a thread]

enfold (ĭn fōld′), *v.t.* **1.** to wrap up; envelope: *enfolded in a magic mantle.* **2.** to clasp; embrace. **3.** to surround with or as with folds. **4.** to form into a fold or folds: *a cambium layer deeply enfolded where it extends downwards.* Also, **infold. —enfold′er,** *n.* **—enfold′ment,** *n.*

enforce (ĭn fôs′), *v.t.*, **-forced, -forcing. 1.** to put or keep in force; compel obedience to: *to enforce laws or rules.* **2.** to obtain (payment, obedience, etc.) by force or compulsion. **3.** to impose (a course of action) upon a person. **4.** to support (a demand, etc.) by force. **5.** to impress or urge (an argument, etc.) forcibly; lay stress upon. [ME *enforce(n)*, t. OF: m. *enforcier*, ult. der. L *in-* IN-[1] + *fortis* strong] **—enforce′able,** *adj.* **—enforcedly** (ĭn fô′sĭd lĭ), *adv.* **—enforc′er,** *n.*

enforcement (ĭn fôs′mənt), *n.* **1.** the act or process of enforcing. **2.** *Archaic.* that which enforces.

enfranchise (ĭn frăn′chīz), *v.t.*, **-chised, -chising. 1.** to grant a franchise to; admit to citizenship, esp. to the right of voting. **2.** *Law.* to invest with the right of being represented in Parliament. **3.** to set free; liberate, as from slavery. [t. MF: m. *enfranchiss-*, s. *enfranchir*, der. *en-* EN-[1] + *franc* free, FRANK] **—enfranchisement** (ĭn frăn′chĭz mənt), *n.* **—enfran′chis′er,** *n.*

Eng., 1. England. 2. English.

eng., 1. engine. 2. engineer. 3. engineering. 4. engraved. 5. engraver. 6. engraving.

Engadine (ĕng′gə dēn′), *n.* the valley of the Inn river in E Switzerland: resorts. ab. 60 mi. long.

engage (ĭn gāj′), *v.*, **-gaged, -gaging. —***v.t.* **1.** to occupy the attention or efforts of (a person, etc.): *he engaged her in conversation.* **2.** to secure for aid, employment, use, etc.; hire: *to engage a workman, to engage a room.* **3.** to attract and hold fast: *to engage the attention, interest, etc.* **4.** to reserve or secure. **5.** to attract or please: *his good nature engages everybody to him.* **6.** to bind as by pledge, promise, contract, or oath; make liable: *he engaged, verbally or in writing, to do it.* **7.** to betroth (usually used in the passive). **8.** to bring (troops) into conflict; enter into conflict with: *our army engaged the enemy.* **9.** *Mech.* to cause to become interlocked; interlock with. **10.** *Archaic.* to entangle or involve. **11.** *Archaic.* to attach or secure. **—***v.i.* **12.** to occupy oneself; become involved: *to engage in business, politics.* **13.** to take employment. **14.** to pledge one's word; assume an obligation. **15.** to cross weapons; enter into conflict. **16.** *Mech.* to interlock. [t. F: s. *engager*, der. *en-* EN-[1] + *gage* pledge, GAGE[1]] **—engag′er,** *n.* **—Ant. 2.** discharge. **9.** release.

engaged (ĭn gājd′), *adj.* **1.** busy or occupied; involved. **2.** under engagement; pledged. **3.** betrothed. **4.** entered into conflict with. **5.** *Mech.* **a.** interlocked. **b.** (of wheels) in gear with each other. **6.** *Archit.* secured to, or (actually or apparently) partly sunk into, something else, as a column with respect to a wall.

engagement (ĭn gāj′mənt), *n.* **1.** the act of engaging. **2.** the state of being engaged. **3.** a pledge; an obligation or agreement. **4.** betrothal. **5.** employment, or a period or post of employment. **6.** an appointment or arrangement, often of a business nature. **7.** an encounter, conflict, or battle. **8.** *Mech.* the act or state of interlocking. **9.** (*pl.*) *Com.* financial obligations. **—Syn. 3.** contract, promise.

engagement ring, a ring given in token of an engagement by a man to his fiancée; it is usually worn on the third finger of the left hand.

engaging (ĭn gā′jĭng), *adj.* winning; attractive; pleasing. **—engag′ingly,** *adv.* **—engag′ingness,** *n.*

engarland (ĭn gä′lənd), *v.t.* encircle with a garland.

Engels (*Ger.* ĕng′əls *for 1*; *Russ.* ĕn′gĭlys *for 2*), *n.* **1. Friedrich** (*Ger.* frē′drĭKH), 1820–95, German socialist writer in England, associated with Karl Marx. **2.** a town in the E Soviet Union in Europe, on the Volga. 106,000 (est. 1963).

engender (ĭn jĕn′də), *v.t.* **1.** to produce, cause, or give rise to: *hatred engenders violence.* **2.** to beget; procreate. **—***v.i.* **3.** to be produced or caused; come into existence. [ME *engendre(n)*, t. OF: m. *engendrer*, g. L *ingenerāre* beget] **—engen′derer,** *n.* **—engen′derment,** *n.* **—Syn. 1.** create, occasion, excite, stir up.

Enghien, d' (*Fr.* däɴ găɴ′; *Flem.* -gyăɴ′), *n.* **Duc** (*Louis Antoine Henry de Bourbon-Condé*), 1772–1804, French prince, executed by Napoleon I.

engin., engineering.

engine (ĕn′jĭn), *n.* **1.** any mechanism or machine designed to convert energy into mechanical work: *a steam engine, internal-combustion engine, etc.* **2.** a railway locomotive. **3.** any mechanical contrivance. **4.** a machine or instrument used in warfare, as a battering ram, catapult, piece of artillery, etc. **5.** *Obs.* an instrument of torture, esp. the rack. [ME *engin*, t. OF, g. L *ingenium* nature, invention]

engine-driver (ĕn′jĭn drī′və), *n.* one who drives a locomotive.

engineer (ĕn′jĭ nĭə′), *n.* **1.** one versed in the design, construction, and use of engines or machines, or in any of the various branches of engineering: *a mechanical engineer, an electrical, civil, etc., engineer.* **2.** one who manages a ship's engines. **3.** a member of the armed forces especially trained in engineering work. **4.** a skilful manager. **5.** *U.S.* an engine-driver. **—***v.t.* **6.** to plan, construct, or manage as an engineer. **7.** to arrange, manage or carry through by skilful or artful contrivance.

engineering (ĕn′jĭ nĭə′rĭng), *n.* **1.** the art or science of making practical application of the knowledge of pure sciences such as physics, chemistry, biology, etc. **2.** the action, work, or profession of an engineer. **3.** skilful or artful contrivance; manoeuvring.

engineer officer, *Naut.* a marine officer in charge of the engines on a ship, usually a watchkeeping officer in the engine-room.

engineer's chain. See **chain** (def. 9).

engine-house (ĕn′jĭn hous′), *n.* a building in which an engine is kept.

engine-room (ĕn′jĭn ro͝om′, -ro͞om′), *n.* **1.** the room in a vessel in which a ship's engines are situated. **2.** any room housing an engine.

engine-room artificer, *Naval.* a junior officer whose duty is to assist the engineer officer.

enginery (ĕn′jĭn rĭ), *n.* **1.** engines collectively. **2.** engines of war. **3.** skilful or artful contrivance.

engine turning, the engraving of any symmetrical pattern on a metallic surface by machinery.

engird (ĭn gûd′), *v.t.*, **-girt** or **-girded, -girding.** to encircle; encompass.

engirdle (ĭn gû′dl), *v.t.*, **-dled, -dling.** to engird.

englacial (ĭn glā′syəl), *adj.* *Geol.* **1.** within the ice of a glacier. **2.** believed to have been formerly within the ice of a glacier or ice-sheet: *englacial debris.*

englacial stream, *Phys. Geog.* a stream of melt-water which flows through a tunnel within an ice-sheet or glacier.

England (ĭng′glənd), *n.* the largest division of the United Kingdom, occupying all of the island of Great Britain except Scotland and Wales. 43,460,525 pop. (1961); 50,327 sq. mi. *Cap.:* London. Latin, **Anglia.** [ME *Engeland*, OE *Englaland* land of the English]

Englander (ĭng′glən də), *n.* **1.** *Rare.* a native of England.

2. little Englander, *Colloq.* an opponent of imperialism, esp. one advocating isolationist policies in the late 19th century.

English (ĭng′glĭsh), *adj.* **1.** of, pertaining to, or characteristic of England or its inhabitants, institutions, etc. **2.** belonging or pertaining to, or spoken or written in, the English language. —*n.* **3.** the people of England collectively, esp. as distinguished from the Scots, Welsh, and Irish. **4.** the Germanic language of the British Isles, widespread and standard also in the U.S. and most of the countries belonging to the Commonwealth of Nations, historically termed Old English or Anglo-Saxon (to 1150), Middle English (to 1450) and Modern English. **5.** (*l.c.*) *U.S.* side (def. 15). **6.** a printing type (14 point) of a size between pica and two-line brevier. **7.** straightforward and simple language. —*v.t.* **8.** to translate into English. **9.** to adopt (a foreign word) into English. **10.** (*l.c.*) *U.S. Billiards.* to impart english or side to (a ball). [ME; OE *Englisc*, der. *Engle*, *Angle* the English. See ANGLE]

English bond, a common arrangement of brickwork in which alternate courses of bricks are headers and stretchers, i.e., they show the short ends or the long faces of the bricks. Cf. **Flemish bond.**

English Channel, an arm of the Atlantic between England and France, connected with the North Sea by the Strait of Dover. ab. 350 mi. long; 20–100 mi. wide.

English horn, *U.S.* cor anglais.

Englishism (ĭng′glĭ shĭz′əm), *n.* a linguistic usage peculiar to English as spoken in England.

Englishman (ĭng′glĭsh mən), *n.*, *pl.* **-men. 1.** a native or a naturalized citizen of England. **2.** an English ship.

Englishness (ĭng′glĭsh nĭs), *n.* the quality of being English.

English Pale. See **pale** (def. 6).

Englishry (ĭng′glĭsh rĭ), *n.* **1.** the state of being English. **2.** a population that is English or of English descent.

English setter, one of a breed of long-haired gun dogs, usually tan-and-white, white with liver flecks, or pure white, with a rangy body.

English setter
(2 ft high at shoulder)

English springer spaniel, one of the two breeds of springer spaniel, slightly larger than the Welsh springer spaniel, and having a black-and-white or liver-and-white coat.

Englishwoman (ĭng′glĭsh wo͝om′ən), *n.*, *pl.* **-women.** a woman who is a native or citizen of England.

engorge (ĭn gôj′), *v.t.*, **-gorged, -gorging. 1.** to swallow greedily; glut or gorge. **2.** *Pathol.* to congest with blood. [t. F: m. s. *engorger*, der. *en-* EN-[1] + *gorge* GORGE] —**engorge′ment,** *n.*

engr., 1. engineer. 2. engraved. 3. engraver.

engraft (ĭn gräft′), *v.t.* to insert, as a scion of one tree or plant into another, for propagation: *to engraft a peach on a plum.* Also, **ingraft.** —**engraftation** (ĕn′gräf tā′shən), *n.* —**engraft′ment,** *n.*

engrail (ĭn grāl′), *v.t.* **1.** to ornament the edge of with curved indentations. **2.** (on a coin or medal) to form the decorative margin of a ring of dots. [ME *engrele(n)*, t. OF: m. *engresler*, der. *en-* EN-[1] + *gresle* hail] —**engrail′ment,** *n.*

engrain (ĭn grān′), *v.t.*, *adj.* ingrain. [ME, f. EN-[1] + GRAIN. Cf. F *en graine* where *graine* means cochineal dye]

engram (ĕn′grăm), *n.* **1.** *Biol.* the durable mark caused by a stimulus upon protoplasm. **2.** *Psychol.* trace[1] (def. 5).

engrave (ĭn grāv′), *v.t.*, **-graved, -graving. 1.** to chase (letters, designs, etc.) on a hard surface, as of metal, stone, or the end grain of wood. **2.** to print from such a surface. **3.** to mark or ornament with incised letters, designs, etc. **4.** to impress deeply; infix. [f. EN-[1] + GRAVE[3], v., modelled on F *engraver*] —**engrav′er,** *n.*

engraving (ĭn grā′vĭng), *n.* **1.** the act or art of one who or that which engraves. **2.** the art of forming designs by cutting, corrosion by acids, a photographic process, etc., on the surface of metal plates or of blocks of wood, etc., for the purpose of taking off impressions or prints of the design so formed. **3.** the design engraved. **4.** an engraved plate or block. **5.** an impression or print from this.

engross (ĭn grōs′), *v.t.* **1.** to occupy wholly, as the mind or attention; absorb. **2.** to write or copy in a fair, large hand or in a formal manner, as a public document or record. **3.** to acquire the whole of (a commodity), in order to control the market; monopolize. [ME *engross(en)*, t. AF: m. *engrosser* write large; also t. OF, der. *en gros* in large quantities, g. L *in-* IN-[2] + LL *grossus* thick, GROSS] —**engross′er,** *n.*

engrossing (ĭn grō′sĭng), *adj.* **1.** fully occupying the mind or attention; absorbing. **2.** acquiring overall control; monopolizing. —**engross′ingly,** *adv.*

engrossment (ĭn grōs′mənt), *n.* **1.** the act of engrossing. **2.** an engrossed copy of a document.

engulf (ĭn gŭlf′), *v.t.* **1.** to swallow up in or as in a gulf. **2.** to plunge or immerse. Also, **ingulf.** —**engulf′ment,** *n.*

enhance (ĭn häns′), *v.t.*, **-hanced, -hancing. 1.** to raise to a higher degree; intensify; magnify. **2.** to raise the value or price of. [ME *enhaunce(n)*, t. AF: m. *enhauncer*, nasalized var. of OF *enhaucier*, f. *en-* EN-[1] + *haucier* raise. See HAWSER] —**enhance′ment,** *n.* —**enhanc′er,** *n.* —**enhanc′ive,** *adj.* —**Syn. 2.** See **elevate.** —**Ant. 1.** diminish. **2.** reduce.

enharmonic (ĕn′hä mŏn′ĭk), *adj. Music.* having the same pitch in the tempered scale but written in different notation, as G-sharp and A-flat. [t. LL: s. *enharmonicus* in accord, t. Gk: m. *enarmonikós*] —**en′harmon′ically,** *adv.*

enigma (ĭ nĭg′mə), *n.* **1.** somebody or something puzzling or inexplicable. **2.** a saying, question, picture, etc., containing a hidden meaning; a riddle. [t. L: m. *aenigma*, t. Gk: m. *aínigma* riddle] —**Syn. 1.** See **puzzle.**

enigmatic (ĕn′ĭg măt′ĭk), *adj.* resembling an enigma; perplexing; mysterious. Also, **en′igmat′ical.** —**en′igmat′ically,** *adv.*

enisle (ĭ nīl′), *v.t.*, **-isled, -isling.** *Poetic.* **1.** to make an island of. **2.** to place on an island. **3.** to isolate.

enjambment (ĭn jăm′mənt; *Fr.* äɴ zhäɴb mäɴ′), *n. Pros.* the running on of the thought from one line or couplet to the next. Also, **enjambe′ment.** [t. F: m. *enjambement*, der. *enjamber* stride over, project, der. *en-* EN-[1] + *jambe* leg]

enjoin (ĭn join′), *v.t.* **1.** to order or direct (a person, etc.) to do something; prescribe (a course of action, etc.) with authority or emphasis. **2.** *Law.* to prohibit or restrain by an injunction. [ME *enjoyn(en)*, t. OF: m. *enjoindre*, g. L *injungere* join into or to, impose, enjoin] —**enjoin′er,** *n.* —**enjoin′ment,** *n.* —**Syn. 1.** charge.

enjoy (ĭn joi′), *v.t.* **1.** to experience with joy; take pleasure in. **2.** to have and use with satisfaction; have the benefit of. **3.** to find or experience pleasure for (oneself). **4.** to undergo (an improvement). **5.** to have sexual intercourse with (a woman). [ME *enjoye(n)*, t. OF: m. *enjoir*, f. *en-* EN-[1] + *joir* JOY, v.] —**enjoy′er,** *n.*

enjoyable (ĭn joi′ə bl), *adj.* that may be enjoyed; affording enjoyment. —**enjoy′ableness,** *n.* —**enjoy′ably,** *adv.*

enjoyment (ĭn joi′mənt), *n.* **1.** the possession, use, or occupancy of anything with satisfaction or pleasure. **2.** a particular form or source of pleasure. **3.** *Law.* the exercise of a right: *the enjoyment of an estate.* —**Syn. 1.** delight, delectation, gratification. See **pleasure.**

Enkalon (ĕng′kə lŏn′), *n. Trademark.* a type of nylon.

enkindle (ĭn kĭn′dl), *v.t.*, *v.i.*, **-dled, -dling.** to kindle into flame, ardour, activity, etc. —**enkin′dler,** *n.*

enl., enlarged.

enlace (ĭn lās′), *v.t.*, **-laced, -lacing. 1.** to bind or encircle as with a lace or cord. **2.** to interlace; intertwine. [ME *enlase(n)*, t. F: m. *enlacer*, f. *en-* EN-[1] + *lacier* LACE, v.] —**enlace′ment,** *n.*

enlarge (ĭn läj′), *v.*, **-larged, -larging.** —*v.t.* **1.** to make larger; increase in extent, bulk, or quantity; add to. **2.** to increase the capacity or scope of; expand. **3.** *Photog.* to make (a print) larger than the negative, by projection printing. —*v.i.* **4.** to grow larger; increase; expand. **5.** to speak or write at large; expatiate: *to enlarge upon a point.* [ME *enlargen*, t. OF: m. *enlarger*, der. *en-* EN-[1] + *large* LARGE] —**enlarge′able,** *adj.* —**enlarg′er,** *n.* —**Syn. 1.** extend, augment, amplify, dilate. See **increase.** —**Ant. 1.** diminish. **2.** contract.

enlargement (ĭn läj′mənt), *n.* **1.** the act of enlarging; increase; expansion; amplification. **2.** anything, as a photograph, that is an enlarged form of something else. **3.** anything that enlarges something else; an addition.

enlighten (ĭn lī′tn), *v.t.* **1.** to give intellectual or spiritual light to; instruct; impart knowledge to. **2.** *Archaic and Poetic.* to shed light upon. —**enlight′ener,** *n.* —**enlight′eningly,** *adv.* —**Syn. 1.** illumine, edify, teach, inform.

enlightened (ĭn lī′tnd), *adj.* **1.** instructed; well-informed; not bound by prejudice and superstition. **2.** tempered with reason: *enlightened despotism.*

enlightenment (ĭn lī′tn mənt), *n.* **1.** the act of enlightening. **2.** the state of being enlightened. **3. the Enlightenment,** an 18th-century philosophical movement characterized by rationalism. **4.** (in Hinduism and Buddhism) the condition that revelation brings to the believer who has striven for its attainment, making him henceforth separated from the rest of mankind.

enlist (ĭn lĭst′), *v.i.* **1.** to engage for military or naval service by enrolling after mutual agreement. **2.** to enter into some cause, enterprise, etc. —*v.t.* 3. to engage for military or naval service. 4. to secure (a person, services, etc.) for some cause, enterprise, etc. —**enlist′er,** *n.*

enlisted man, *U.S.* a serviceman who is not a commissioned officer or a warrant officer, or cadet.

enlistment (ĭn lĭst′mənt), *n.* the act of enlisting; state of being enlisted.

enliven (ĭn lī′vən), *v.t.* 1. to make vigorous or active; invigorate. 2. to make sprightly, gay, or cheerful; brighten. [f. obs. *enlive* enliven (der. EN-[1] + LIVE, adj.) + -EN[1]] —**enliv′ener,** *n.* —**enliv′enment,** *n.* —**Syn.** 1. animate, inspirit, vivify, stimulate, quicken. 2. exhilarate, gladden. See **cheer.** —**Ant.** 2. depress.

en masse (ŏn măs′; *Fr.* äɴ màs′), *French.* in a mass or body; all together.

enmesh (ĭn mĕsh′), *v.t.* to catch, as in a net; entangle. Also, **immesh, inmesh.** —**enmesh′ment,** *n.*

enmity (ĕn′mĭ tĭ), *n., pl.* **-ties.** a feeling or condition of hostility; hatred; ill will; animosity; antagonism. [ME *enemyte,* t. OF: m. *ennemistie,* der. L *inimīcus* enemy]

ennead (ĕn′ĭ ăd′), *n.* 1. a group of nine persons or things. 2. (*cap.*) a group of nine gods in Egyptian religion. [t. Gk: s. *enneás,* der. *ennéa* nine] —**en′nead′ic,** *adj.*

enneagon (ĕn′ĭ ə gən), *n.* nonagon.

Ennis (ĕn′ĭs), *n.* a town in W Republic of Ireland; county town of Clare. 5699 (1961).

Enniskillen (ĕn′ĭs kĭl′ĭn), *n.* a town in Northern Ireland, the county town of Fermanagh. 7438 (1961).

Ennius (ĕn′ĭ əs), *n.* **Quintus** (kwĭn′təs), 239–169? B.C., Roman poet.

ennoble (ĭ nō′bl), *v.t.,* **-bled, -bling.** 1. to elevate in degree, excellence, or respect; dignify; exalt. 2. to confer a title of nobility on. —**enno′blement,** *n.* —**enno′bler,** *n.*

ennui (ŏn′wē; *Fr.* äɴ nwē′), *n.* a feeling of weariness and discontent resulting from satiety or lack of interest; boredom. [t. F, g. L *in odiō.* See ANNOY, n.]

Enoch (ē′nŏk), *n. Bible.* 1. the father of Methuselah. Gen. 5: 18–24. 2. the eldest son of Cain. Gen. 4: 17, 18.

enol (ē′nŏl), *n. Chem.* an organic compound containing a hydroxyl group attached to a doubly linked carbon atom, as in C = C–OH. [appar. f. Gk (*h*)*én* (neut. of *heîs* one) + -OL[1]] —**enolic** (ē nŏl′ĭk), *adj.*

enormity (ĭ nô′mĭ tĭ), *n., pl.* **-ties.** 1. enormousness; hugeness of size, scope, extent, etc. 2. outrageous or heinous character; atrociousness: *the enormity of his offences.* 3. something outrageous or heinous, as an offence. [t. L: m. s. *ēnormitas* hugeness, irregularity]

enormous (ĭ nô′məs), *adj.* 1. greatly exceeding the common size, extent, etc.; huge; immense. 2. outrageous or atrocious: *enormous wickedness.* [t. L: m. *ēnormis* huge] —**enor′mously,** *adv.* —**enor′mousness,** *n.* —**Syn.** 1. vast, colossal, gigantic, mammoth, prodigious, stupendous. See **huge.**

Enos (ē′nŏs), *n. Bible.* the son of Seth. Gen. 5: 6.

enosis (ĕn′ō sĭs), *n. Greek.* the demand by Greek Cypriots for the political union of Cyprus with Greece. [MGk: union]

enough (ĭ nŭf′), *adj.* 1. adequate for the want or need; sufficient for the purpose or to satisfy desire: *I've had enough of it, noise enough to wake the dead.* —*n.* 2. an adequate quantity or number; a sufficiency. —*adv.* 3. in a quantity or degree that answers a purpose or satisfies a need or desire; sufficiently. 4. fully or quite: *ready enough.* 5. tolerably or passably: *he sings well enough.* —*interj.* 6. it (or that) is enough! [ME *enogh,* OE *genōh,* c. G *genug*]

enounce (ĭ nouns′), *v.t.,* **enounced, enouncing.** 1. to announce, declare, or proclaim. 2. to state definitely, as a proposition. 3. to utter or pronounce, as words. [t. F: m. s. *énoncer,* t. L: m. *ēnuntiāre*] —**enounce′ment,** *n.*

enow (ĭ nou′; *formerly* ĭ nō′), *adj., adv. Archaic.* enough. [ME; OE *genōg*(*e*) ENOUGH]

en passant (*Fr.* äɴ pà säɴ′), *French.* 1. in passing; by the way. 2. *Chess.* a rule according to which a pawn, after making the optional initial move over two squares, may be taken by an adversary's pawn, which makes the capture exactly as if the initial move had been over only one square.

enplane (ĕn plān′), *v.i.,* **-planed, -planing.** *Chiefly Mil.* to enter an aeroplane.

enprint (ĕn′prĭnt′), *n. Photog.* the smallest size of enlarged print commercially available. [f. *en*(*larged*) *print*]

en prise (*Fr.* äɴ prēz′), *French.* (in chess) in line for capture; likely to be captured.

enquire (ĭn kwī′ə), *v.,* **-quired, -quiring.** —*v.i.* 1. to seek information by questioning; ask. —*v.t.* 2. to seek to learn by asking. Also, *Chiefly U.S.,* **inquire.** —**enquir′er,** *n.*

—**Syn.** 2. ENQUIRE, ASK, QUESTION imply that a person (or persons) addresses another (or others) to obtain information. ASK is the general word: *ask what time it is.* ENQUIRE is more formal and always implies asking about something specific: *enquire about a rumour.* To QUESTION implies repetition and persistence in asking; it often applies to legal examination or investigation: *question the survivor of an accident.* —**Ant.** 1. tell.

enquiry (ĭn kwī′ə rĭ), *n., pl.* **-quiries.** 1. a seeking for truth, information, or knowledge. 2. a question or query. Also, *Chiefly U.S.,* **inquiry.**

enrage (ĭn rāj′), *v.t.,* **-raged, -raging.** to put into a rage; infuriate. [t. MF: m. s. *enrager,* der. *en-* EN-[1] + *rage* RAGE]

—**Syn.** ENRAGE, INCENSE, INFURIATE imply stirring to violent anger. To ENRAGE is to provoke a display of wrath: *enrage him by deliberate and continual injustice.* To INCENSE is to inflame with indignation or anger; the connotation is serious provocation present or prolonged: *to incense one by making insulting remarks.* To INFURIATE is to arouse suddenly to fury or fierce and vehement anger: *infuriate him by a false accusation.* —**Ant.** appease, pacify.

en rapport (*Fr.* äɴ rà pŏr′), *French.* in sympathy or accord; in agreement; congenial.

enrapt (ĭn răpt′), *adj.* rapt; transported; enraptured.

enrapture (ĭn răp′chə), *v.t.,* **-tured, -turing.** to move to rapture; delight beyond measure.

enregister (ĭn rĕj′ĭs tə), *v.t.* to register; record; enrol.

enrich (ĭn rĭch′), *v.t.* 1. to supply with riches, wealth, abundant or valuable possessions, etc.: *commerce enriches a nation.* 2. to supply with abundance of anything desirable: *to enrich the mind with knowledge.* 3. to adorn; make splendid with costly decoration. 4. to make finer in quality as by supplying desirable elements or ingredients: *to enrich bread or soil.* 5. to enhance; make finer in flavour, colour, or significance. 6. *Physics.* to increase the abundance of a particular isotope in a mixture of isotopes, esp. of a fissile isotope in a nuclear fuel. [ME *enrich*(*en*), t. OF: m. *enrichir,* der. *en-* EN-[1] + *riche* RICH]

enrichment (ĭn rĭch′mənt), *n.* 1. the act of enriching. 2. the state of being enriched. 3. something that enriches.

enrobe (ĭn rōb′), *v.t.,* **-robed, -robing.** to dress; attire.

enrol (ĭn rōl′), *v.t.,* **-rolled, -rolling.** 1. to write (a name) or insert the name of (a person) in a roll or register; place upon a list. 2. to enlist (oneself). 3. to put in a record; record. 4. to roll or wrap up. —*v.i.* 5. to enrol oneself. Also, *Chiefly U.S.,* **enroll.** [ME *enroll*(*en*), t. OF: m. *enroller,* der. *en-* EN-[1] + *rolle* ROLL, n.] —**enroll′er,** *n.*

enrolment (ĭn rōl′mənt), *n.* 1. the act of enrolling; process of being enrolled. 2. the number of persons enrolled, as for a course or in a school. Also, *Chiefly U.S.,* **enrollment.**

enroot (ĭn ro͞ot′), *v.t.* 1. to fix by the root. 2. to fix fast; implant deeply.

en route (ŏn ro͞ot′; *Fr.* äɴ ro͞ot′), on the way. [F]

ens (ĕnz), *n., pl.* **entia** (ĕn′shĭ ə). *Metaphys.* being, considered in the abstract. [t. LL, ppr. neut. of *esse* be]

Ens., Ensign.

ENSA (ĕn′sə), *n.* Entertainments National Services Association.

ensample (ĕn säm′pl), *n. Archaic.* example.

ensanguine (ĭn săng′gwĭn), *v.t.,* **-guined, -guining.** to stain or cover with or as with blood. [f. EN-[1] + SANGUINE]

Enschede (*Du.* ĕns′KHə dė), *n.* a town in the Netherlands, in Overijssel province. 134,281 (1965).

ensconce (ĭn skŏns′), *v.t.,* **-sconced, -sconcing.** 1. to cover or shelter; hide securely. 2. to settle securely or snugly: *ensconced in an armchair.* [f. EN-[1] + SCONCE[2]]

ensemble (ŏn sŏm′bl; *Fr.* äɴ säɴ′bl), *n.* 1. all the parts of a thing taken together, so that each part is considered only in relation to the whole. 2. the entire costume of an individual, esp. when all the parts are in harmony. 3. the general effect, as of a work of art. 4. *Music.* **a.** the united performance of the full number of singers, musicians, etc. **b.** the group so performing: *a string ensemble.* 5. a group of supporting singers, actors, dancers, etc., in a theatrical production. —*adv.* 6. *Obs.* together. [ME, t. F, g. LL *insimul* at the same time]

enshrine (ĭn shrīn′), *v.t.,* **-shrined, -shrining.** 1. to enclose in or as in a shrine. 2. to cherish as sacred. Also, **inshrine.** —**enshrine′ment,** *n.*

enshroud (ĭn shroud′), *v.t.* to shroud; conceal.

ensiform (ĕn′sĭ fôm′), *adj. Biol.* sword-shaped; xiphoid. [f. L *ensi*(*s*) sword + -FORM]

ensign (ĕn′sīn; *Naval for 1* ĕn′sən), *n.* 1. a flag or banner, as of a nation. 2. a badge of office or authority. 3. any sign, token, or emblem. 4. a standard-bearer, esp. one (formerly) in the British Army. 5. (formerly) the lowest commissioned rank in the British infantry. 6. *U.S. Naval.* the lowest ranking commissioned officer. [ME *ensaigne* t. OF: m. *enseigne,* g. L *insignia* INSIGNIA] —**en′signship′,** **en′signcy,** *n.*

ensilage (ĕn′sĭ lĭj), *n.*, *v.*, **-laged, -laging.** —*n.* **1.** the preservation of green fodder in a silo or pit. **2.** fodder thus preserved. —*v.t.* **3.** ensile. [t. F, der. *ensiler* ENSILE]

ensile (ĕn sīl′, ĕn′sīl), *v.t.*, **-siled, -siling. 1.** to preserve (green fodder) in a silo. **2.** to make into ensilage. [t. F: m. s. *ensiler*, t. Sp.: *ensilar*, der. *en-* EN-[1] + *silo* SILO]

enslave (ĭn slāv′), *v.t.*, **-slaved, -slaving.** to make a slave of; reduce to slavery. —**enslave′ment,** *n.* —**en-slav′er,** *n.*

ensnare (ĭn snĕə′), *v.t.*, **-snared, -snaring.** to capture in, or involve as in, a snare. —**ensnare′ment,** *n.* —**en-snar′er,** *n.* —**Syn.** entrap, entangle, enmesh. —**Ant.** release.

ensoul (ĭn sōl′), *v.t.* **1.** to endow with a soul. **2.** to put or cherish in the soul. Also, **insoul.**

ensphere (ĭn sfĭə′), *v.t.*, **-sphered, -sphering. 1.** to enclose in or as in a sphere. **2.** to make or form into a sphere. Also, **insphere.**

enstatite (ĕn′stə tīt′), *n.* a mineral of the pyroxene group consisting of magnesium silicate, occurring as an important constituent of basic igneous rocks. [f. s. Gk *enstátēs* adversary + -ITE[1]; so called because of its refractory nature]

ensue (ĭn syōō′), *v.i.*, **-sued, -suing. 1.** to follow in order; come afterwards, esp. in immediate succession. **2.** to follow as a consequence; result. [ME *ensewe(n)*, t. OF: m. *ensuivre*, g. L *insequī* follow close upon] —**Syn. 1, 2.** See **follow.** —**Ant. 2.** cause.

en suite (*Fr.* äɴ swēt′), *French.* in succession; in a series or set.

ensure (ĭn shōōə′, -shô′), *v.t.*, **-sured, -suring. 1.** to secure, or bring surely, as to a person: *this letter will ensure you a hearing.* **2.** to make sure or certain to come, occur, etc.: *measures to ensure the success of an undertaking.* **3.** to make secure or safe, as from harm. **4.** *Obsolesc.* to insure. [ME *ensure(n)*, t. AF: m. *ensurer*, der. *en-* EN-[1] + OF *seur* SURE]

enswathe (ĭn swāth′), *v.t.*, **-swathed, -swathing.** to swathe. Also, **inswathe.** —**enswathe′ment,** *n.*

E.N.T., *Med.* Ear, Nose, and Throat.

-ent, a suffix equivalent to **-ant,** in adjectives and nouns, as in *ardent, dependent, different, expedient.* [t. L: stem ending of ppr. in vbs. of conjugations 2, 3, 4]

entablature (ĕn tăb′lə chə), *n.* **1.** that part of a classic architectural order which rests horizontally upon the columns and consists of the architrave, frieze, and cornice. See diag. under **column. 2.** a similar part in other constructions. [t. It.: m. *intavolatura*, der. *intavolare* board up]

entail (ĭn tāl′), *v.t.* **1.** to bring on or involve by necessity or consequences: *a loss entailing no regret.* **2.** to impose as a burden. **3.** to limit the inheritance of (a landed estate) to a specified line of heirs, so that it cannot be alienated, devised, or bequeathed. **4.** to cause (anything) to descend to a fixed series of possessors. —*n.* **5.** the act of entailing. **6.** the state of being entailed. **7.** any predetermined order of succession, as to an office. **8.** that which is entailed, as an estate. **9.** the rule of descent settled for an estate. [f. EN-[1] + TAIL[2]] —**entail′er,** *n.* —**entail′ment,** *n.*

entangle (ĭn tăng′gl), *v.t.*, **-gled, -gling. 1.** to make tangled; complicate (usually used in the passive). **2.** to involve in anything like a tangle; ensnare; enmesh. **3.** to involve in difficulties; embarrass; perplex. —**en-tang′ler,** *n.* —**Syn. 3.** bewilder, confuse. See **involve.**

entanglement (ĭn tăng′gl mənt), *n.* **1.** the act of entangling. **2.** the state of being entangled. **3.** that which entangles; a snare; an embarrassment; a complication.

entasis (ĕn′tə sĭs), *n. Archit.* the swelling or outward curve of the shaft of a column. [t. NL, t. Gk: a stretching]

Entebbe (ĕn tĕb′ĭ), *n.* a town in S Uganda, on Lake Victoria. 10,941 (1959).

entelechy (ĕn tĕl′ĭ kĭ), *n.*, *pl.* **-chies. 1.** a realization or actuality as opposed to a potentiality. **2.** (in vitalist philosophy) the vital force or principle directing growth and life. [t. LL: m. s. *entelechīa*, t. Gk, der. *en télei échein* be in fulfilment or completion]

entellus (ĕn tĕl′əs), *n.* the sacred monkey or langur of India, *Semnopithecus entellus*, having a long tail, a beard, and a caplike growth of hair. [NL; appar. named after *Entellus*, character (elderly man) in Virgil's *Aeneid*]

entente (ŏn tŏnt′; *Fr.* äɴ täɴt′), *n.* **1.** understanding. **2.** the parties to an understanding. [F]

entente cordiale (*Fr.* äɴ täɴt kŏr dyȧl′), *French.* a friendly understanding, esp. between two governments.

enter (ĕn′tə), *v.i.* **1.** to come or go in. **2.** to make an entrance, as on the stage. **3.** to be admitted. **4.** to make a beginning (often fol. by *on* or *upon*). **5. enter into, a.** to take an interest or part in; engage in. **b.** to take up the consideration of (a subject); investigate. **c.** to sympathize with (a person's feelings, etc.). **d.** to assume the obligation of. **e.** to become a party to. **f.** to make a beginning in. **g.** to form a constituent part or ingredient of: *lead enters into the composition of pewter.* **h.** to penetrate; plunge deeply into. **i.** to go into a specific state: *enter into a state of hypnosis.* —*v.t.* **6.** to come or go into. **7.** to penetrate or pierce: *the bullet entered the flesh.* **8.** to put in or insert: *to enter a wedge.* **9.** to become a member of, or join. **10.** to cause to be admitted, as into a school, competition, etc. **11.** to make a beginning of or in, or begin upon; engage or become involved in. **12.** to make a record of; record or register. **13.** *Law.* **a.** to place in regular form before a court, as a writ. **b.** to occupy or to take possession of (lands); make an entrance, entry, ingress in, under claim of a right to possession. **14.** to register formally; submit; put forward: *to enter an objection.* **15.** to report (a vessel, etc.) at the customs house. [ME *entre(n)*, t. OF: *entrer*, g. L *intrāre* go into] —**en′terable,** *adj.* —**en′terer,** *n.* —**Ant. 1.** leave. **8.** remove.

enteric (ĕn tĕ′rĭk), *adj.* **1.** pertaining to the enteron; intestinal. **2.** typhoid. [t. Gk: m. s. *enterikós*, der. *énteron* intestine]

enteric fever, typhoid fever.

enteritis (ĕn′tə rī′tĭs), *n. Pathol.* inflammation of the intestines.

entero-, a word element meaning 'intestine', as in *enterotoxaemia.* [t. Gk, comb. form of *énteron*]

enteron (ĕn′tə rŏn′), *n.*, *pl.* **-tera** (-tə rə). *Anat., Zool.* the alimentary canal; the digestive tract. [NL, t. Gk: intestine]

enterostomy (ĕn′tə rŏs′tə mĭ), *n.*, *pl.* **-mies.** *Surg.* the making of an artificial opening into the small intestine, which opens on to the abdominal wall, for feeding or drainage.

enterotoxaemia (ĕn′tə rō tŏk sē′myə), *n. Vet. Sci.* a disease of sheep caused by severe systematic poisoning from bacterial toxins in the intestinal tract. Also, *U.S.*, **enterotoxemia.**

enterprise (ĕn′tə prīz′), *n.* **1.** a project undertaken or to be undertaken, esp. one that is of some importance or that requires boldness or energy. **2.** engagement in such projects. **3.** boldness or readiness in undertaking, adventurous spirit, or energy. **4.** a company organized for commercial purposes. [ME, t. OF: m. *entreprise*, der. *entreprendre* take in hand, f. *entre* INTER- + *prendre* seize, take (g. L *prehendere*)] —**Syn. 1.** plan, undertaking, venture.

enterpriser (ĕn′tə prī′zə), *n.* one who undertakes an enterprise.

enterprising (ĕn′tə prī′zĭng), *adj.* ready to undertake projects of importance or difficulty, or untried schemes; energetic and daring in carrying out any undertaking. —**en′terpris′ingly,** *adv.* —**Syn.** See **ambitious.** —**Ant.** timid.

entertain (ĕn′tə tān′), *v.t.* **1.** to hold the attention of agreeably; divert; amuse. **2.** to receive as a guest, esp. at one's table; show hospitality to. **3.** to give admittance or reception to. **4.** to admit into the mind; consider. **5.** to hold in the mind; harbour; cherish. **6.** *Archaic.* to maintain or keep up. —*v.i.* **7.** to exercise hospitality; entertain company; provide entertainment for guests. [late ME *entertene(n)*, t. F: m. *entretenir*, f. *entre-* INTER- + *tenir* (g. L *tenēre* hold)] —**Syn. 1.** See **amuse.**

entertainer (ĕn′tə tā′nə), *n.* **1.** one who entertains. **2.** a singer, reciter, or the like, who gives, or takes part in, public entertainments.

entertaining (ĕn′tə tā′nĭng), *adj.* affording entertainment; amusing; diverting. —**en′tertain′ingly,** *adv.* —**en′tertain′ingess,** *n.*

entertainment (ĕn′tə tān′mənt), *n.* **1.** the act of entertaining; agreeable occupation for the mind; diversion, or amusement. **2.** something affording diversion or amusement, esp. an exhibition or performance of some kind. **3.** hospitable provision for the wants of guests. **4.** *Obs.* maintenance in service.

enthalpy (ĕn′thəl pĭ, ĕn thăl′pĭ), *n. Physics.* a thermodynamic property of a substance or system equal to the sum of its internal energy and the product of its pressure and volume; heat content; total heat. *Symbol:* H.

enthetic (ĕn thĕt′ĭk), *adj.* introduced from without, as diseases propagated by inoculation. [t. Gk: m. s. *enthetikós* fit for implanting]

enthral (ĭn thrôl′), *v.t.*, **-thralled, -thralling. 1.** to captivate; charm. **2.** to put or hold in thraldom; subjugate. Also, *Chiefly U.S.*, **enthrall.** —**enthrall′er,** *n.* —**enthral′ment,** *U.S.*, **enthrallment,** *n.*

enthrall (ĭn thrôl′), *v.t. Chiefly U.S.* enthral. —**en-thrall′er,** *n.* —**enthrall′ment,** *n.*

enthrone (ĭn thrōn′), *v.t.*, **-throned, -throning. 1.** to place on or as on a throne. **2.** to invest with sovereign or

episcopal authority. 3. to exalt. —**enthrone′ment, enthronization** (ĭn thrō′nī zā′shən), *n.*
enthuse (ĭn thyo͞oz′), *v.*, **-thused, -thusing.** —*v.i.* 1. to become enthusiastic; show enthusiasm. —*v.t.* 2. to move to enthusiasm. [back-formation from ENTHUSIASM]
enthusiasm (ĭn thyo͞o′zĭ ăz′əm), *n.* 1. absorbing or controlling possession of the mind by any interest or pursuit; lively interest. 2. *Archaic.* extravagant religious emotion. [t. LL: s. *enthūsiasmus*, t. Gk: m. *enthousiasmós*] —**Syn.** 1. eagerness, warmth, fervour, zeal, ardour. —**Ant.** 1. indifference.
enthusiast (ĭn thyo͞o′zĭ ăst′), *n.* 1. one who is filled with enthusiasm for some principle, pursuit, etc.; a person of ardent zeal. 2. a religious visionary or fanatic. —**Syn.** 1. zealot, devotee.
enthusiastic (ĭn thyo͞o′zĭ ăs′tĭk), *adj.* 1. full of or characterized by enthusiasm; ardent. 2. pertaining to or of the nature of enthusiasm. —**enthu′sias′tically,** *adv.* —**Syn.** 1. zealous, eager, fervent, passionate.
enthymeme (ĕn′thĭ mēm′), *n. Logic.* a syllogism in which one premise is unexpressed. [t. L: m. s. *enthȳmēma*, t. Gk: thought, argument] —**en′thymemat′ic, en′thymemat′ical,** *adj.*
entice (ĭn tīs′), *v.t.*, **-ticed, -ticing.** to draw on by exciting hope or desire; allure; inveigle. [ME *entyce(n)*, t. OF: m. *enticier* incite, der. L *titio* firebrand] —**entic′er,** *n.* —**entic′ingly,** *adv.* —**Syn.** lure, attract, decoy, tempt.
enticement (ĭn tīs′mənt), *n.* 1. the act or practice of enticing, esp. to evil. 2. the state of being enticed. 3. that which entices; an allurement.
entire (ĭn tī′ə), *adj.* 1. having all the parts or elements; whole; complete. 2. not broken, mutilated, or decayed; intact. 3. unimpaired or undiminished. 4. being wholly of one piece; undivided; continuous. 5. *Bot.* without notches or indentations, as leaves. 6. full or thorough: *entire freedom of choice.* 7. not gelded: *an entire horse.* 8. *Obs.* wholly of one kind; unmixed or pure. —*n.* 9. the whole; entirety. 10. an entire horse; a stallion. 11. a kind of malt liquor; porter. [ME *enter*, t. OF: m. *entier*, g. L *integrum*, acc. of *integer* untouched, whole] —**entire′ness,** *n.* —**Syn.** 1. See **complete.** —**Ant.** 1. partial. 2. defective.
entirely (ĭn tī′ə lĭ), *adv.* 1. wholly or fully; completely or unreservedly. 2. solely or exclusively.
entirety (ĭn tī′ə rĭ tĭ), *n.*, *pl.* **-ties.** 1. the state of being entire; completeness. 2. that which is entire; the whole.
entitle (ĭn tī′tl), *v.t.*, **-tled, -tling.** 1. to give (a person or thing) a title, right, or claim to something; furnish with grounds for laying claim. 2. to call by a particular title or name; name. 3. to designate (a person) by an honorary title. [ME *entitle(n)*, t. OF: m. *entituler*, t. LL: m. *intitulāre*, der. L *in-* IN-[2] + *titulus* TITLE]
entity (ĕn′tĭ tĭ), *n.*, *pl.* **-ties.** 1. something that has a real existence; a thing. 2. being or existence. 3. essential nature. [t. LL: m. s. *entitas*]
ento-, var. of **endo-.** [t. Gk: comb. form of *entós* within]
entoblast (ĕn′tō blăst′), *n. Embryol.* 1. entoderm. 2. hypoblast.
entoderm (ĕn′tō dûm′), *n.* endoderm.
entoil (ĭn toil′), *v.t. Archaic.* to take in toils; ensnare.
entom., entomology. Also, **entomol.**
entomb (ĭn to͞om′), *v.t.* 1. to place in a tomb; bury; inter. 2. to serve as a tomb for. [t. OF: s. *entomber*, der. *en-* EN-[1] + *tombe* TOMB] —**entomb′ment,** *n.*
entomic (ĕn tŏm′ĭk), *adj.* of or pertaining to insects.
entomo-, a word element meaning 'insect'. Also, before vowels, **entom-.** [comb. form repr. Gk *éntomos*, lit., cut up, in neut. pl., insects]
entomologize (ĕn′tə mŏl′ə jīz′), *v.i.*, **-gized, -gizing.** 1. to study entomology. 2. to gather entomological specimens. Also, **entomologise.**
entomology (ĕn′tə mŏl′ə jĭ), *n.* the branch of zoology that treats of insects. —**entomological** (ĕn′tə mə lŏj′ĭ kl), **en′tomolog′ic,** *adj.* —**en′tomolog′ically,** *adv.* —**en′tomol′ogist,** *n.*
entomophagous (ĕn′tə mŏf′ə gəs), *adj.* feeding on insects; insectivorous.
entomophilous (ĕn′tə mŏf′ĭ ləs), *adj.* (of a plant) pollinated by insects. —**en′tomoph′ily,** *n.*
entomostracan (ĕn′tə mŏs′trə kən), *adj.* 1. belonging to the *Entomostraca*, a subclass of mostly small crustaceans. —*n.* 2. an entomostracan crustacean. [f. ENTOM(O)- + m. s. Gk *óstrakon* shell + -AN] —**en′tomos′tracous,** *adj.*
entophyte (ĕn′tō fīt′), *n. Bot.* a plant growing within an animal or another plant, usually as a parasite. [f. ENTO- + -PHYTE] —**entophytic** (ĕn′tō fĭt′ĭk), *adj.*
entopic (ĕn tŏp′ĭk), *adj. Anat.* occurring in the usual place.
entoptic (ĕn tŏp′tĭk), *adj.* lying or originating within the eyeball.
entotic (ĕn tŏt′ĭk), *adj.* of or pertaining to the interior of the ear.
entourage (ŏn′to͞o räzh′; *Fr.* äɴ to͞o ràzh′), *n.* 1. attendants, as of a person of rank. 2. surroundings; environment. [t. F, der. *entourer* surround. See EN-[1], TOUR]
entozoa (ĕn′tō zō′ə), *n.pl.*, *sing.* **-zoon** (-zō′ŏn). *Biol.* animals, esp. intestinal worms, living as parasites within the body of another animal. —**en′tozo′an,** *adj.*, *n.*
entozoic (ĕn′tō zō′ĭk), *adj. Biol.* living parasitically within the body of an animal.
entr'acte (ŏn′trăkt; *Fr.* äɴ tràkt′), *n.* 1. the interval between two consecutive acts of a theatrical or operatic performance. 2. a performance, as of music or dancing, given during such an interval. 3. a piece of music or the like for such a performance. [t. F: between-act]
entrails (ĕn′trālz), *n.pl.* 1. the internal parts of the trunk of an animal body. 2. the intestines or bowels. 3. the internal parts of anything. [ME *entraile*, t. F: m. *entrailles*, g. LL *intrālia* intestines, der. L *inter* within]
entrain (ĭn trān′), *v.t.*, *v.i.* to put or go aboard a train. —**entrain′ment,** *n.*
entrammel (ĭn trăm′əl), *v.t.* to trammel; fetter; entangle.
entrance[1] (ĕn′trəns), *n.* 1. the act of entering, as into a place or upon new duties. 2. a point or place of entering; an opening or passage for entering. 3. power or liberty of entering; admission. 4. *Theat.* the moment, or place in the script, at which an actor comes on the stage. [t. OF, der. *entrer* ENTER]
—**Syn.** 1. entry, ingress. 3. ENTRANCE, ADMITTANCE, ADMISSION refer to the possibility of entering a place. ENTRANCE suggests the possibility of entering without supervision or permission: *entrance is by the side door.* ADMITTANCE refers to the act of admitting or allowing entry: *to gain admittance to a building.* ADMISSION suggests entering by permission, special right or privilege, by ticket, and the like: *admission to a concert or football match.*
entrance[2] (ĭn träns′), *v.t.*, **-tranced, -trancing.** 1. to fill with delight or wonder; enrapture. 2. to put into a trance. [f. EN-[1] + TRANCE, v.] —**entrance′ment,** *n.* —**entranc′ingly,** *adv.*
entrant (ĕn′trənt), *n.* 1. one who enters. 2. a new member, as of an association, a university, etc. 3. a competitor in a contest. [t. F, ppr. of *entrer* ENTER]
entrap (ĭn trăp′), *v.t.*, **-trapped, -trapping.** 1. to catch in or as in a trap; ensnare. 2. to bring unawares into difficulty or danger. 3. to draw into contradiction or damaging admission. [t. OF: s. *entraper*, der. *en-* EN-[1] + *trape* trap] —**entrap′ment,** *n.* —**entrap′per,** *n.*
entreasure (ĭn trĕzh′ə), *v.t.*, **-ured, -uring.** to lay up in or as in a treasury.
entreat (ĭn trēt′), *v.t.* 1. to make supplication to (a person); beseech; implore: *to entreat a person for something.* 2. to ask earnestly for (something). —*v.i.* 3. to make an earnest request or petition. Also, **intreat.** [ME *entrete(n)*, t. OF: m. *entraitier*, f. *en-* EN-[1] + *traitier* TREAT] —**entreat′ingly,** *adv.* —**Syn.** 1. See **appeal.**
entreaty (ĭn trē′tĭ), *n.*, *pl.* **-treaties.** earnest request or petition; supplication. —**Syn.** appeal, suit, plea.
entrechat (*Fr.* äɴ trə shá′), *n.* (in ballet) a jump during which the dancer crosses his feet a number of times while in the air. [F, t. It.: m. (*capriola*) *intrecciata* complicated (caper), der. *in-* IN-[2] + *treccia* tress, plait]
entrecôte (*Fr.* äɴ trə kót′), *n. French.* a steak cut from between the ribs.
entree (ŏn′trā), *n.* 1. any food other than a roast, served as the main course. 2. a dish served at dinner before the main course or between the regular courses. 3. the right or privilege of entering. Also, *French,* **entrée** (*Fr.* äɴ trė′). [t. F. See ENTRY]
entremets (ŏn′trə mā′; *Fr.* äɴ trə mĕ′), *n.*, *pl.* **-mets** (-māz′; *Fr.* -mĕ′). *French.* a dish served at dinner between the principal courses or with the roast; a side dish. [F: lit., between-dish]
entrench (ĭn trĕnch′), *v.t.* 1. to dig trenches for defensive purposes around (oneself, a military position, etc.). 2. to place in a position of strength; establish firmly: *the soldiers entrenched themselves behind a thick concrete wall.* 3. to establish so strongly or securely as to make any change very difficult: *the clauses concerning human rights are entrenched in the new constitution.* —*v.i.* 4. to dig in. 5. to trench or encroach; trespass; infringe (fol. by *on* or *upon*): *to entrench on the domain or rights of another.* 6. to verge (fol. by *on* or *upon*): *proceedings entrenching on impiety.* Also, **intrench.** —**entrench′er,** *n.*
entrenchment (ĭn trĕnch′mənt), *n.* 1. the act of entrenching. 2. an entrenched position. 3. (*usually pl.*) an earth breastwork or ditch for protection against enemy fire. Also, **intrenchment.**
entre nous (*Fr.* äɴ trə no͞o′), *French.* between ourselves; confidentially.
entrepot (ŏn′trə pō′), *n.* 1. a warehouse. 2. a commercial centre for the collection, distribution, and transshipment

of goods. Also, *French*, **entrepôt** (*Fr.* äɴ trə pō′). [t. F, der. OF *entreposer* store up, f. *entre-* INTER- + *poser* place (g. L *pausāre* rest)]

entrepreneur (ŏn′trə prə nû′; *Fr.* äɴ trə prə nœr′), *n.* **1.** one who organizes and manages any enterprise, esp. one involving considerable risk. **2.** an employer of productive labour; a contractor. [t. F, der. *entreprendre* undertake. See ENTERPRISE]

entresol (ŏn′trə sŏl′; *Fr.* äɴ trə sŏl′), *n.* *Archit.* a low storey between two other storeys of greater height, usually one immediately above the chief or ground floor; a mezzanine. [t. F: between-floor]

entropy (ĕn′trə pĭ), *n.* *Physics.* a measure of the unavailable energy in a thermodynamic system; it may also be regarded as a measure of the state of disorder of a system. A change of entropy in a reversible process is the ratio of heat absorbed to the absolute temperature. *Symbol*: S. [f. Gk: *en-* EN-[2] + m. *tropē* transformation]

entrust (ĭn trŭst′), *v.t.* **1.** to invest with a trust or responsibility; charge with a specified office or duty involving trust. **2.** to commit (something) in trust (*to*); confide, as for care, use, or performance: *to entrust a secret, money, powers, or work to another.* **3.** to commit as if with trust or confidence: *to entrust one's life to a frayed rope.* Also, **intrust.** —**entrust′ment,** *n.*

entry (ĕn′trĭ), *n., pl.* **-tries. 1.** an act of entering; entrance. **2.** a place of ingress or entrance, esp. an entrance hall or vestibule. **3.** permission or right of entry; access. **4.** the act of entering or recording something in a book, register, list, etc. **5.** the statement, etc., so entered or recorded. **6.** one entered in a contest or competition. **7.** *Law.* the act of taking possession of lands or tenements by entering or setting foot on them. **8.** the giving of an account of a ship's cargo at a customs house, to obtain permission to land the goods. **9.** *Bookkeeping.* **a.** See **double entry. b.** See **single entry.** [ME *entree*, t. F, der. *entrer* ENTER]

entwine (ĭn twīn′), *v.t., v.i.,* **-twined, -twining.** to twine with, about, around, or together. Also, **intwine.** —**entwine′ment,** *n.*

entwist (ĭn twĭst′), *v.t.* to twist together or about. Also, **intwist.**

enucleate (*v.* ĭ nyōō′klĭ āt′; *adj.* ĭ nyōō′klĭ ĭt, -klĭ āt′), *v.t.,* **-ated, -ating,** *adj.* —*v.t.* **1.** *Biol.* to deprive of the nucleus. **2.** to remove (a kernel, tumour, eyeball, etc.) from its enveloping cover. **3.** to bring out; disclose. —*adj.* **4.** having no nucleus. [t. L: m. s. *ēnucleātus*, pp.] —**enu′clea′tion,** *n.*

Enugu (ĕ nōō′gōō), *n.* a town in S Nigeria, in the Eastern Region. 62,764 (1953).

enumerate (ĭ nyōō′mə rāt′), *v.t.,* **-rated, -rating. 1.** to mention separately as if in counting; name one by one; specify as in a list. **2.** to ascertain the number of; count. [t. L: m. s. *ēnumerātus*, pp., counted out] —**enumerative** (ĭ nyōō′mə rə tĭv), *adj.* —**enu′mera′tor,** *n.* —**Syn. 1.** recapitulate, recount, rehearse.

enumeration (ĭ nyōō′mə rā′shən), *n.* **1.** the act of enumerating. **2.** a catalogue or list.

enunciate (ĭ nŭn′sĭ āt′), *v.,* **-ated, -ating.** —*v.t.* **1.** to utter or pronounce (words, etc.), esp. in a particular manner: *he enunciates his words distinctly.* **2.** to state or declare definitely, as a theory. **3.** to announce or proclaim. —*v.i.* **4.** to pronounce words, esp. in an articulate or a particular manner. [t. L: m. s. *ēnuntiātus*, pp.] —**enunciable** (ĭ nŭn′sĭ ə bl), *adj.* —**enun′ciabil′ity,** *n.* —**enun′ciatively,** *adv.* —**enun′cia′tor,** *n.*

enunciation (ĭ nŭn′sĭ ā′shən), *n.* **1.** the act or the manner of enunciating. **2.** utterance or pronunciation. **3.** a formal announcement; a formal statement, as of a proposition, doctrine.

enure (ĭ nyŏŏə′), *v.t., v.i.,* **-ured, -uring.** inure.

enuresis (ĕn′yŏŏ rē′sĭs), *n.* *Pathol.* incontinence or involuntary discharge of urine; bed-wetting. [NL, der. Gk *enourein* make water in] —**en′uret′ic,** *adj.*

envelop (*for 5* ĕn′vĭ lōp′, ŏn′-; *otherwise* ĭn vĕl′əp), *v.,* **-oped, -oping,** *n.* —*v.t.* **1.** to wrap up in or as in a covering. **2.** to serve as a wrapping or covering for. **3.** to surround entirely. **4.** to obscure or conceal. —*n.* **5.** envelope. [ME *envolupe(n)*, t. OF: m. *envoluper*, f. *en-* EN-[1] + *voluper* wrap. Cf. DEVELOP] —**envel′oper,** *n.* —**Syn. 1.** enfold, cover, hide, conceal. **3.** encompass, enclose.

envelope (ĕn′vĭ lōp′, ŏn′-), *n.* **1.** a cover for a letter or the like, usually so made that it can be sealed or fastened. **2.** that which envelops; a wrapper, integument, or surrounding cover. **3.** *Bot.* a surrounding or enclosing part, as of leaves. **4.** *Geom.* a curve or surface tangent to each member of a family of curves or surfaces. **5.** the fabric structure enclosing the gasbag of a balloon or airship. **6.** the gasbag itself. **7.** *Electronics.* the airtight glass or metal container of a vacuum tube. [t. F: m. *enveloppe*]

envelopment (ĭn vĕl′əp mənt), *n.* **1.** the act of enveloping. **2.** the state of being enveloped. **3.** a wrapping or covering.

envenom (ĭn vĕn′əm), *v.t.* **1.** to impregnate with venom; make poisonous. **2.** to embitter. [ME *envenime(n)*, t. OF: m. *envenimer*, der. *en-* EN-[1] + *venim* VENOM]

Enver Pasha (ĕn′və pä′shə), 1881–1922, Turkish soldier and statesman.

enviable (ĕn′vĭ ə bl), *adj.* that is to be envied; worthy to be envied; highly desirable. —**en′viableness,** *n.* —**en′viably,** *adv.*

envious (ĕn′vĭ əs), *adj.* **1.** full of, feeling, or expressing envy: *envious of a person's success, an envious attack.* **2.** *Obs.* emulous. [ME, t. AF, var. of OF *envieus*, der. *envie* ENVY] —**en′viously,** *adv.* —**en′viousness,** *n.*

environ (ĭn vī′ə rən), *v.t.* to form a circle or ring round; surround; envelop. [ME *environ(en)*, t. F: m. *environner*, der. *environ* around]

environment (ĭn vī′ə rən mənt), *n.* **1.** the aggregate of surrounding things, conditions, or influences. **2.** the act of environing. **3.** the state of being environed. **4.** that which environs. —**envi′ronmen′tal,** *adj.*

environs (ĭn vī′ə rənz, ĕn′vĭ rənz), *n.pl.* immediate neighbourhood; surrounding parts or districts, as of a city; outskirts; suburbs. [t. F]

envisage (ĭn vĭz′ĭj), *v.t.,* **-aged, -aging. 1.** to contemplate; visualize. **2.** to look in the face of; face. [t. F: m. s. *envisager*, der. *en-* EN-[1] + *visage* VISAGE] —**envis′agement,** *n.*

envision (ĭn vĭzh′ən), *v.t.* to picture mentally, esp. some future event or events.

envoy[1] (ĕn′voi), *n.* **1.** a diplomatic agent of the second rank, next in dignity after an ambassador, commonly called minister (title in full: **envoy extraordinary and minister plenipotentiary**). **2.** a diplomatic agent. **3.** any accredited messenger or representative. [t. F: m. *envoyé*, prop. pp. of *envoyer* send. See ENVOY[2]]

envoy[2] (ĕn′voi), *n.* **1.** *Pros.* a short stanza concluding a poem in certain archaic metrical forms. **2.** a postscript to a poetical or prose composition, sometimes serving as a dedication. Also, **en′voi.** [ME *envoye*, t. OF, der. *envoier* send, der. *en voie* on the way]

envy (ĕn′vĭ), *n., pl.* **-vies,** *v.,* **-vied, -vying.** —*n.* **1.** a feeling of discontent or mortification, usually with ill will, at seeing another's superiority, advantages, or success. **2.** desire for some advantage possessed by another. **3.** an object of envious feeling. **4.** *Obs.* ill will. —*v.t.* **5.** to regard with envy; be envious of. —*v.i.* **6.** *Obs.* to be affected with envy. [ME *envie*, t. OF, g. L *invidia*] —**en′vier,** *n.* —**en′vyingly,** *adv.*

—**Syn. 5.** ENVY, BEGRUDGE, COVET refer to one's attitude concerning the possessions or attainments of others. To ENVY is to feel resentful, spiteful, and unhappy because someone else possesses, or has achieved, what one wishes oneself to possess, or to have achieved: *to envy the wealthy, a girl's beauty, an honest man's reputation.* To BEGRUDGE is simply to be unwilling that another should have the possessions, honours, or credit he deserves: *to begrudge a man a reward for heroism.* To COVET is to long jealously to possess what someone else possesses: *I covet your silverware.*

enwall (ĕn wôl′), *v.t.* to enclose with a wall.

enweave (ĭn wēv′), *v.t.,* **-wove** or **-weaved; -woven** or **-weaved; -weaving. 1.** to weave in or together. **2.** to introduce into or as into a fabric in weaving. **3.** to combine or diversify with something woven in. Also, **inweave.**

enwind (ĭn wīnd′), *v.t.,* **-wound, -winding.** to wind or coil about; encircle. Also, **inwind.**

enwomb (ĭn wōōm′), *v.t.* to enclose in or as in the womb.

enwrap (ĭn răp′), *v.t.,* **-wrapped, -wrapping. 1.** to wrap or envelop in something: *enwrapped in leaves.* **2.** to wrap in slumber, etc.: *enwrapped in fond desire.* **3.** to absorb or engross in thought, etc. Also, **inwrap.**

enwreathe (ĭn rēth′), *v.t.,* **-wreathed, -wreathing.** to surround with or as if with a wreath. Also, **inwreathe.**

Enzedder (ĕn zĕd′ə), *n.* *Colloq.* a New Zealander.

Enzensberger (*Ger.* ĕn′tsəns bĕr gər), *n.* **Hans Magnus** (*Ger.* häns mäg′nŏŏs), born 1929, German poet and essayist.

enzootic (ĕn′zō ŏt′ĭk), *adj.* **1.** (of diseases) prevailing among or afflicting animals in a particular locality. Cf. **endemic.** —*n.* **2.** an enzootic disease. [f. EN-[2] + ZO(O)- + -OTIC, modelled on EPIZOOTIC]

enzymatic (ĕn′zī măt′ĭk, -zĭ-), *adj.* of or pertaining to an enzyme. Also, **enzy′mic.**

enzyme (ĕn′zīm), *n.* any of various complex organic substances, as pepsin, originating from living cells, and capable of producing by catalytic action certain chemical changes, as digestion, in organic substances. [t. MGk: m. s. *énzymos* leavened, f. *en-* EN-[2] + Gk *zýmē* leaven]

enzymogen (ĕn zī′mə jən), *n.* *Biochem.* any of various inactive precursors which can be converted into an enzyme; zymogen (def. 1).

enzymogenesis (ĕn zī′mə jĕn′ĭ sĭs), *n.* **1.** *Biochem.* the conversion of an enzymogen into an enzyme; zymogenesis. **2.** *Biochem.* biosynthesis of enzymes in general.

enzymogenic (ĕn zī′mə jĕn′ĭk), *adj. Biochem.* of or pertaining to an enzymogen.

enzymology (ĕn′zī mŏl′ə jĭ), *n. Biochem.* the science that treats of enzymes and their properties; zymology. —**en′zymolog′ical,** *adj.* —**en′zymol′ogist,** *n.*

enzymolysis (ĕn′zī mŏl′ĭ sĭs), *n. Biochem.* fermentation or other lytic reactions produced by an enzyme; zymolysis (def. 2). —**enzymolytic** (ĕn′zī mə lĭt′ĭk), *adj.*

eo-, a word element meaning 'early', 'primeval', as in *Eocene.* [t. Gk, comb. form of *ēṓs* dawn]

Eocene (ē′ō sēn′), *adj.* **1.** pertaining to the second principal subdivision of the Tertiary period or system. —*n.* **2.** an early Tertiary epoch or series succeeding Palaeocene and preceding Oligocene.

Eogene (ē′ō jēn′), *adj. Geol.* **1.** pertaining to a division of the Tertiary period or system that comprises Palaeocene, Eocene, and Oligocene. —*n.* **2.** the time or rocks representing the earlier half of the Tertiary period or system.

eohippus (ē′ō hĭp′əs), *n.* a horse of a fossil genus, *Eohippus,* from the Lower Eocene of the western U.S., the oldest type of the family *Equidae,* about as large as a fox, with four complete toes on each forefoot and three hoofed toes on each hindfoot. [NL, f. Gk: *ēō-* EO- + m. *híppos* horse]

EOKA (ā ō′kə), *n.* the national liberation organization of Cypriots, formed to fight for the independence of Cyprus, 1955–59.

Eolian (ē ō′lyən), *adj., n.* Aeolian.

Eolic (ē ŏl′ĭk), *n., adj.* Aeolic.

eolith (ē′ō lĭth), *n.* a crude flint implement characteristic of the earliest stage of human culture, shaped by, rather than for, use.

eolithic (ē′ō lĭth′ĭk), *adj.* denoting or pertaining to the earliest stage of human culture, characterized by the use of amorphous stone implements.

e.o.m., *Chiefly Com.* end of the month.

eon (ē′ən, ē′ŏn), *n.* aeon.

eonism (ī′ə′nĭz′əm), *n. Psychiatry.* the adoption of female clothing, mannerisms, etc., by a man; transvestism. [named after the Chevalier d'*Eon* (d. 1810), Frenchman who dressed as a woman]

Eos (ē′ŏs), *n.* the Greek goddess of the dawn, identified with the Roman Aurora.

eosin (ē′ō sĭn), *n.* **1.** a coal-tar product, $C_{20}H_8O_5Br_4$, used for dyeing silk, etc., rose red. **2.** any of a variety of eosin-like dyes. Also, **eosine** (ē′ō sĭn, -sēn′). [f. Gk *ēṓs* dawn + -IN²] —**e′osin-like′,** *adj.*

eosinophil (ē′ō sĭn′ə fĭl), *n. Anat.* a cell containing granules staining with acid dyes, whose numbers increase in allergic diseases and certain parasitic infections. Also, **eosinophile.** [f. EOSIN + -(O)PHIL(E)]

-eous, var. of **-ous,** occurring in adjectives taken from Latin or derived from Latin nouns. [t. L: m. *-eus*]

Eozoic (ē′ō zō′ĭk), *n.* a division of pre-Cambrian time and rocks characterized by the dawn of life on the earth. [f. EO- + ZO(O)- + -IC]

EP (ē′pē′), *adj.* **1.** denoting a gramophone record impressed with microgrooves that revolves at 45 r.p.m. —*n.* **2.** such a record. [initials of *extended play*]

ep-, var. of **epi-,** before vowels, as in *epaxial.*

Ep., Epistle.

epact (ē′păkt), *n.* **1.** the excess in days of a solar year over a lunar year. **2.** the age in days of the calendar moon at the beginning of the year (Jan. 1st). [t. LL: s. *epacta,* t. Gk: m. *epaktḗ,* prop. fem. of *epaktós,* vbl. adj., added]

epagoge (ĕp′ə gō′jĭ), *n. Logic.* the induction of a general proposition from particular propositions. [t. Gk *epagōgḗ* argument by induction] —**epagogic** (ĕp′ə gŏj′ĭk), *adj.*

Epaminondas (ē păm′ĭ nŏn′dăs), *n. c.* 418–362 B.C., general and statesman of ancient Thebes in Greece.

eparch (ĕp′ärk), *n.* **1.** the prefect or governor of an eparchy. **2.** *Greek Orthodox Church.* a bishop or metropolitan of an eparchy. [t. Gk: s. *éparchos* commander]

eparchy (ĕp′är′kĭ), *n., pl.* **-chies. 1.** (in modern Greece) one of the administrative subdivisions of a province. **2.** (in ancient Greece) a province. **3.** *Greek Orthodox Church.* a diocese or archdiocese. —**epar′chial,** *adj.*

epaulet (ĕp′ə lĕt′ -lĭt), *n.* an ornamental shoulder piece worn on uniforms, chiefly by military and naval officers. Also, **ep′aulette′.** [t. F: m. *épaulette,* der. *épaule* shoulder, g. L *spatula* blade]

epaxial (ĕp ăk′sĭ əl), *adj. Anat.* above or posterior to an axis. —**epax′ially,** *adv.*

épée (ĕp′ā; *Fr.* ė pė′), *n. Fencing.* a long, narrow weapon with blunted edges and a sharp point. [F, g. L *spatha,* t. Gk: m. *spáthē* blade]

épéeist (ĕp′ā ĭst), *n. Fencing.* one who uses an épée.

epeirogeny (ĕp′ī rŏj′ĭ nĭ), *n. Geol.* vertical or tilting movement of the earth's crust, generally affecting broad areas of a continent. Also, **epeirogenesis, epirogeny.** [f. Gk *ḗpeiro(s)* land, mainland, continent + -GENY] —**epeirogenic** (ĭ pī′rō jĕn′ĭk), *adj.*

epencephalon (ĕp′ĕn sĕf′ə lŏn′), *n., pl.* **-la** (-lə). *Anat.* the hindbrain. —**epencephalic** (ĕp′ĕn sĭ făl′ĭk), *adj.*

epenthesis (ĕ pĕn′thĭ sĭs), *n., pl.* **-ses** (-sēz′). (in linguistic process) the insertion of one or more sounds in the middle of a word, as the schwa in the substandard pronunciation (ĕl′əm) of *elm.* [t. LL, t. Gk: insertion] —**epenthetic** (ĕp′ĕn thĕt′ĭk), *adj.*

epergne (ĭ pûn′), *n.* an ornamental piece for the centre of a dinner table, often elaborate in design, for holding fruit, flowers, etc. [? t. F: m. *épargne* saving, treasury]

epexegesis (ĕ pĕk′sĭ jē′sĭs), *n. Rhet.* **1.** the addition of a word or words to explain a preceding word or sentence. **2.** the word or words so added.

epexegetic (ĕ pĕk′sĭ jĕt′ĭk), *adj.* of or like an epexegesis. Also, **epex′eget′ical.** —**epex′eget′ically,** *adv.*

eph-, var. of **epi-,** before an aspirate, as in *ephemera.*

Eph., Ephesians.

ephah (ē′fə), *n.* a Hebrew unit of dry measure, equal to about a bushel. Also, **e′pha.** [t. Heb.]

ephebe (ĭ fēb′, ĕf′ēb), *n.* (among the ancient Greeks) a youth just entering upon manhood or just enrolled as a citizen. [t. Gk: m. *éphēbos*] —**ephe′bic,** *adj.*

ephedrine (ĭ fĕd′rĭn; *Chem.* ĕf′ĭ drēn′, -drĭn), *n. Pharm.* a crystalline alkaloid, $C_{10}H_{15}NO$, found in some plants of the genus *Ephedra,* used esp. for colds, asthma, and hay fever. Also, **ephedrin** (ĭ fĕd′rĭn; *Chem.* ĕf′ĭ drĭn). [f. s. NL *ephedra* (L horsetail, a plant, t. Gk) + -INE²]

ephemera (ĭ fĕm′ə rə), *n., pl.* **-eras, -erae** (-ə rē′). **1.** anything short-lived or transitory. **2.** an ephemerid. [t. NL, orig., pl. of *ephḗmeron* (t. Gk, neut. sing. of *ephḗmeros* of or for only one day), but now treated as sing.]

ephemeral (ĭ fĕm′ə rəl), *adj.* **1.** lasting only a day or a very short time; short-lived; transitory. —*n.* **2.** an ephemeral entity, as certain insects. —**ephem′erally,** *adv.* —**Syn. 1.** fleeting, evanescent, transient.

ephemerid (ĭ fĕm′ə rĭd), *n.* a mayfly. [t. NL: s. *Ephēmeridae.* See EPHEMERA]

ephemeris (ĭ fĕm′ə rĭs), *n., pl.* **ephemerides** (ĕf′ĭ mĕ′rĭdēz′). **1.** a table showing the positions of a heavenly body on a number of dates in an orderly sequence. **2.** an astronomical almanac containing such tables. **3.** *Obs.* an almanac or calendar. [t. L, t. Gk: diary, calendar, record]

ephemeris time, *Astron.* time measured by the orbital motions of the earth, the moon, and the planets. The **ephemeris second** is the fundamental unit and is defined as a precise fraction of the tropical year 1900.

ephemeron (ĭ fĕm′ə rŏn′), *n., pl.* **-era** (-ə rə), **-erons.** anything short-lived or ephemeral. [t. Gk: a short-lived insect. See EPHEMERA]

Ephes., Ephesians.

Ephesian (ĭ fē′zhyən), *adj.* **1.** of or pertaining to Ephesus. —*n.* **2.** a native or inhabitant of Ephesus. **3.** (*pl.*) the book of the New Testament called in full *The Epistle of Paul the Apostle to the Ephesians.*

Ephesus (ĕf′ĭ səs), *n.* an ancient city in W Asia Minor, S of Smyrna: famous Temple of Artemis (Diana).

ephod (ē′fŏd), *n.* a kind of Hebrew priestly vestment, esp. that worn by the high priest. [t. Heb.; in some passages appar. meaning 'idol']

ephor (ĕf′ô), *n., pl.* **-ors, -ori** (-ə rī′). one of a body of magistrates in various ancient Dorian states, esp. at Sparta, where a body of five was annually elected by the people. [t. Gk: s. *éphoros* overseer] —**eph′oral,** *adj.*

Ephraim (ē′frā ĭm), *n. Old Testament.* **1.** the younger son of Joseph. Gen. 41:52. **2.** the tribe of Israel traditionally descended from him. Gen. 48:1, etc. **3.** the Kingdom of Israel. [t. Heb.]

epi-, a prefix meaning 'on', 'to', 'against', sometimes used as an English formative, chiefly in scientific words, as *epiblast, epicalyx, epizoon.* Also, **ep-, eph-.** [t. Gk, repr. *epí,* prep. and adv., *ep-* before vowel, *eph-* before rough breathing]

epiblast (ĕp′ĭ blăst′), *n. Embryol.* the outer layer of a gastrula, consisting of ectoblast and various portions of mesoblast and endoblast, according to species. —**ep′iblas′tic,** *adj.*

epiboly (ĭ pĭb′ə lĭ), *n. Embryol.* the development of one part so that it surrounds another. [t. Gk: m. *epibolḗ* a throwing on] —**epibolic** (ĕp′ĭ bŏl′ĭk), *adj.*

epic (ĕp′ĭk), *adj.* Also, **ep′ical. 1.** denoting or pertaining to poetic composition in which a series of heroic achievements or events, usually of a hero, is dealt with at length as a continuous narrative in elevated style:

Homer's Iliad is an epic poem. **2.** resembling or suggesting such poetry. **3.** heroic; imposing; impressive. *—n.* **4.** an epic poem. **5.** any novel or film resembling an epic, esp. one dealing with the adventures and achievements of a single individual. **6.** something worthy to form the subject of an epic: *the epic of the defence of Stalingrad.* **7.** Also, **Homeric.** (*cap.*) the Greek dialect represented in the *Iliad* and the *Odyssey.* [t. L: s. *epicus,* t. Gk: m. *epikós,* der. *épos* EPOS] **—ep′ically,** *adv.* **—ep′ic-like′,** *adj.*

epicalyx (ĕp′ĭ kā′lĭks, -kăl′ĭks), *n., pl.* **-calyxes, -calyces** (-kăl′ĭ sēz′, -kā′lĭ-). *Bot.* an involucre resembling an outer calyx, as in the mallow.

A, Epicalyx; B, Calyx

epicanthus (ĕp′ĭ kăn′thəs), *n., pl.* **-thi** (-thī). *Anat.* a fold of skin extending from the eyelid over the inner canthus of the eye, characteristic in members of the Mongolian race. **—ep′ican′thic,** *adj.*

epicardium (ĕp′ĭ kä′dĭ əm), *n., pl.* **-dia** (-dĭ ə). *Anat.* the inner serous layer of the pericardium, lying directly upon the heart. [t. NL: f. *epi-* EPI- + *-cardium* (comb. form repr. Gk *kardía* heart)] **—ep′icar′dial,** *adj.*

epicarp (ĕp′ĭ käp′), *n. Bot.* the outermost layer of a pericarp, as the rind or peel of certain fruits. See diag. under **endocarp.**

epicedium (ĕp′ĭ sē′dyəm), *n., pl.* **-cedia** (-sē′dyə). a funeral song. [t. L, t. Gk: m. *epikḗdeion,* prop. neut. adj., of or for a funeral] **—ep′ice′dial, ep′ice′dian,** *adj.*

epicene (ĕp′ĭ sēn′), *adj.* **1.** belonging to, or partaking of the characteristics of, both sexes. **2.** (of Greek and Latin nouns) of the same gender class regardless of the sex of the being referred to, as Latin *vulpēs,* fox or vixen, always grammatically feminine. *—n.* **3.** an epicene person. [t.L:m. s. *epicoenus,* t. Gk: m. *epíkoinos* common]

epicentre (ĕp′ĭ sĕn′tə), *n. Geol.* a point from which earthquake waves seem to go out, directly above the true centre of disturbance. Also, **epicentrum** (ĕp′ĭ sĕn′trəm), *U.S.,* **epicenter.** [t. NL: m. *epicentrum,* t. Gk: m. *epíkentros* on the centre] **—ep′icen′tral,** *adj.*

epicist (ĕp′ĭ sĭst), *n.* a writer of epic poetry.

epicotyl (ĕp′ĭ kŏt′ĭl), *n. Bot.* (in the embryo of a plant) that part of the stem above the cotyledons.

epicritic (ĕp′ĭ krĭt′ĭk), *adj. Physiol.* referring or pertaining to cutaneous nerve fibres perceiving fine sensational variations, or to such perception (opposed to *protopathic*). [t. Gk: m. s. *epikritikós* determining]

Epictetus (ĕp′ĭk tē′təs), *n.* A.D. 60?–120?, Greek Stoic philosopher, who taught in Rome.

epicure (ĕp′ĭ kyo͝o′), *n.* **1.** one who cultivates a refined taste, as in food, drink, art, music, etc. **2.** one given up to sensuous enjoyment. [orig. anglicized form of EPICURUS] **—Syn. 1.** gastronome, gourmet, gourmand.

epicurean (ĕp′ĭ kyo͝o rē′ən), *adj.* **1.** given or adapted to luxury, or indulgence in sensuous pleasures; of luxurious tastes or habits, esp. in eating and drinking. **2.** fit for an epicure. **3.** (*cap.*) of Epicurus or Epicureanism. *—n.* **4.** one devoted to the pursuit of pleasure or luxury; an epicure. **5.** (*cap*) a disciple of Epicurus.

Epicureanism (ĕp′ĭ kyo͝o rē′ə nĭz′əm), *n.* **1.** the philosophical system of Epicurus, or attachment to his doctrines, the chief of which were that the external world resulted from a fortuitous concourse of atoms, and that the highest good in life is pleasure, which consists in freedom from disturbance or pain. **2.** (*l.c.*) epicurean indulgence or habits. Also, **Epicurism** (ĕp′ĭ kyo͝o rĭz′əm).

Epicurus (ĕp′ĭ kyo͝o′rəs), *n.* 342?–270 B.C., Greek philosopher.

epicycle (ĕp′ĭ sī′kl), *n.* **1.** a small circle the centre of which moves round in the circumference of a larger circle, used in Ptolemaic astronomy to account for observed periodic irregularities in planetary motions. **2.** *Maths.* a circle which rolls (externally or internally), without slipping, on another circle, generating an epicycloid or a hypocycloid. [t. LL: m. s. *epicyclus,* t. Gk: m. *epikýklos*]

epicyclic (ĕp′ĭ sī′klĭk, -sĭk′lĭk), *adj.* of or pertaining to an epicycle. Also, **ep′icy′clical.**

epicyclic train, *Mach.* any train of gears the axes of the wheels of which revolve around a common centre. Also, **epicyclic gear.**

epicycloid (ĕp′ĭ sī′kloid), *n. Geom.* a curve generated by the motion of a point on the circumference of a circle which rolls externally, without slipping, on a fixed circle. **—ep′icycloi′dal,** *adj.*

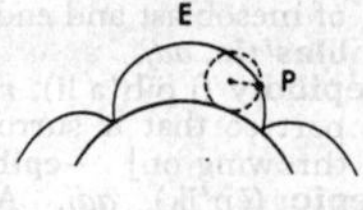

E, Epicycloid; P, Point tracing epicycloid on fixed circle

epicycloidal gear, one of the wheels in an epicyclic train. Also, **epicycloidal wheel.**

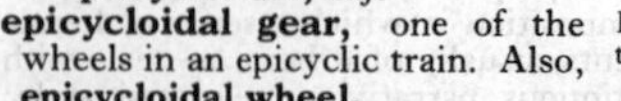

epideictic (ĕp′ĭ dīk′tĭk), *adj. Rhet.* displaying the skill of the speaker: *epideictic orations.* Also, **epidictic.** [t. Gk: m. s. *epideiktikós* displaying]

epidemic (ĕp′ĭ dĕm′ĭk), *adj.* **1.** Also, **ep′idem′ical.** affecting at the same time a large number of people in a locality, and spreading from person to person, as a disease not permanently prevalent there. *—n.* **2.** a temporary prevalence of a disease. [der. obs. *epidemy,* t. LL: m. s. *epidēmia,* t. Gk: prevalence of an epidemic] **—ep′idem′ical,** *adj.* **—ep′idem′ically,** *adv.* **—epidemicity** (ĕp′ĭ də mĭs′ĭ tĭ), *n.*

epidemiology (ĕp′ĭ dē′mĭ ŏl′ə jĭ), *n.* the branch of medicine dealing with epidemic diseases. **—epidemiological** (ĕp′ĭ dē′mĭ ə lŏj′ĭ kl), *adj.* **—ep′ide′miol′ogist,** *n.*

epidermis (ĕp′ĭ dû′mĭs), *n.* **1.** *Anat.* the outer, nonvascular, non-sensitive layer of the skin, covering the true skin or corium (dermis). **2.** *Zool.* the outermost living layer of an animal, usually composed of one or more layers of cells. **3.** *Bot.* the superficial cell layer of the primary regions of vascular plants. [t. LL, t. Gk: outer skin] **—ep′ider′mal, ep′ider′mic,** *adj.*

epidermoid (ĕp′ĭ dû′moid), *adj.* resembling epidermis. Also, **ep′idermoi′dal.**

epidiascope (ĕp′ĭ dī′ə skōp′), *n.* a projector for throwing an enlarged image of either an opaque object or a transparency on a screen.

epidictic (ĕp′ĭ dĭk′tĭk), *adj.* epideictic.

epididymis (ĕp′ĭ dĭd′ĭ mĭs), *n., pl.* **-didymides** (-dĭ dĭm′ĭ dēz′). *Anat.* an elongated organ applied to the posterior surface of a testis, in which the spermatozoa ripen: chiefly the convoluted beginning of the deferent duct. [NL, t. Gk] **—ep′idid′ymal,** *adj.*

epidote (ĕp′ĭ dōt′), *n.* a mineral, calcium aluminium iron silicate, $Ca_2(Al, Fe)_3Si_3O_{12}(OH)$, occurring in yellowish green prismatic crystals. [t. F, der. Gk *epididónai* increase] **—epidotic** (ĕp′ĭ dŏt′ĭk), *adj.*

epifocal (ĕp′ĭ fō′kl), *adj. Geol.* epicentral.

epigamic (ĕp′ĭ găm′ĭk), *adj. Zool.* tending to attract the opposite sex during the mating season, as the colours of certain birds.

epigastric (ĕp′ĭ găs′trĭk), *adj. Anat.* lying upon, distributed over, or pertaining to, the abdomen or the stomach.

epigastrium (ĕp′ĭ găs′trĭ əm), *n. Anat.* the upper and median part of the abdomen, lying over the stomach. [NL, t. Gk: m. *epigástrion* (neut.) over the belly]

epigeal (ĕp′ĭ jē′əl), *adj.* **1.** *Entomol.* living near the surface of the ground, as on low herbs or on other surface vegetation. **2.** *Bot.* epigeous. Also, **ep′ige′an.** [f. EPIGE(OUS) + -AL[1]]

epigene (ĕp′ĭ jēn′), *adj. Geol.* formed or originating on the earth's surface (opposed to *hypogene*). [t. F, t. Gk: m. s. *epigenḗs* growing after or later]

epigenesis (ĕp′ĭ jĕn′ĭ sĭs), *n.* **1.** *Biol.* a theoretical concept of generation according to which the embryo is formed by a series of new formations or successive differentiations (opposed to *preformation*). **2.** *Geol.* the processes of ore deposition effective during a period subsequent to the original formation of the enclosing rock. **—ep′igen′esist, epigenist** (ĭ pĭj′ĭ nĭst), *n.* **—epigenetic** (ĕp′ĭ jĭ nĕt′ĭk), *adj.* **—ep′igenet′ically,** *adv.*

epigenous (ĭ pĭj′ĭ nəs), *adj. Bot.* growing on the surface, esp. the upper surface, as fungi on leaves.

epigeous (ĕp′ĭ jē′əs), *adj. Bot.* **1.** growing on or close to the ground. **2.** (of cotyledons) lifted above ground in germination. [t. Gk: m. *epígeios* on earth]

epiglottis (ĕp′ĭ glŏt′ĭs), *n. Anat.* a thin, valvelike cartilaginous structure that covers the glottis during swallowing, preventing the entrance of food and drink into the larynx. See diag. under **larynx.** [t. NL, t. Gk] **—ep′iglott′al, ep′iglott′ic,** *adj.*

epigone (ĕp′ĭ gōn′), *n.* an inferior imitator or follower of an important writer, painter, etc. Also, **epigon.** [t. L: m. s. *epigonus,* t. Gk: m. *epígonos* born afterwards]

Epigoni (ĭ pĭg′ə nī′), *n.pl.* See **Seven against Thebes.**

epigram (ĕp′ĭ grăm′), *n.* **1.** any witty, ingenious, or pointed saying tersely expressed. **2.** epigrammatic expression. **3.** a short poem dealing concisely with a single subject, usually ending with a witty or ingenious turn of thought, and often satirical. [t. L: m. *epigramma,* t. Gk: an inscription]

epigrammatic (ĕp′ĭ grə măt′ĭk), *adj.* **1.** of or like an epigram; terse and ingenious in expression. **2.** given to epigrams. **—ep′igrammat′ically,** *adv.*

epigrammatism (ĕp′ĭ grăm′ə tĭz′əm), *n.* epigrammatic character or style.

epigrammatist (ĕp′ĭ grăm′ə tĭst), *n.* a maker of epigrams.

epigrammatize (ĕp′ĭ grăm′ə tīz′), *v.t., v.i.,* **-tized, -tizing.** to express by epigrams, or make epigrams. Also, **epigrammatise.**

epigraph (ĕp′ĭ grăf′, -gräf′), *n.* **1.** an inscription, esp.

on a building, statue, or the like. **2.** an apposite quotation at the beginning of a book, chapter, etc. [t. Gk: s. *epigraphḗ*]

epigraphic (ĕp′ĭ grăf′ĭk), *adj.* **1.** pertaining to epigraphs. **2.** pertaining to epigraphy. Also, **ep′igraph′ical.** **—ep′i-graph′ically,** *adv.*

epigraphy (ĭ pĭg′rə fĭ), *n.* **1.** the study or science of epigraphs or inscriptions. **2.** inscriptions collectively. **—epig′raphist, epig′rapher,** *n.*

epigynous (ĭ pĭj′ĭ nəs), *adj. Bot.* (of flowers) having the sepals, petals, and stamens inserted above the ovary. [f. EPI- + m. s. Gk *gynḗ* woman, female + -OUS]

epigyny (ĭ pĭj′ĭ nĭ), *n.* an epigynous condition.

Epigynous flower
A, Style; B, Stigma; C, Sepal; D, Ovary; P, Petal; S, Stamen

epilate (ĕp′ĭ lāt′), *v.t.*, **-lated, -lating.** to pluck out, remove (hair); depilate. **—ep′ila′tion,** *n.* **—ep′ila′tor,** *n.*

epilepsy (ĕp′ĭ lĕp′sĭ), *n. Pathol.* a nervous disease usually characterized by convulsions and almost always by loss of consciousness. [t. LL: m. s. *epilēpsia*, t. Gk: lit., a seizure]

epileptic (ĕp′ĭ lĕp′tĭk), *adj.* **1.** pertaining to epilepsy: *epileptic state.* **—***n.* **2.** one affected with epilepsy. **—ep′i-lep′tically,** *adv.*

epileptoid (ĕp′ĭ lĕp′toid), *adj.* resembling epilepsy. Also, **epileptiform** (ĕp′ĭ lĕp′tĭ fôm′).

epilogist (ĭ pĭl′ə jĭst), *n.* the writer or speaker of an epilogue.

epilogue (ĕp′ĭ lŏg′), *n.* **1.** a speech, usually in verse, by one of the actors after the conclusion of a play. **2.** the person or persons speaking this. **3.** a concluding part added to a literary work. **4.** the final programme, esp. one with a religious content, of a day's broadcasting on radio or television. [t. F, t. L: m. s. *epilogus*, t. Gk: m. *epílogos* a conclusion]

epimer (ĕp′ĭ mə), *n. Chem.* either of a pair of isomeric aldose compounds which differ from each other in the positions of H and OH group. Also, **ep′imeride′.** **—epimeric** (ĕp′ĭ mĕ′rĭk), *adj.*

epimerize (ĕp′ĭ mə rīz′), *v.t.*, **-rized, -rizing.** to convert into an epimer. Also, **epimerise.**

Epimetheus (ĕp′ĭ mē′thĭ əs), *n. Gk Myth.* the brother of Prometheus and husband of Pandora.

epimorphosis (ĕp′ĭ mô fō′sĭs), *n. Zool.* a form of development in segmented animals in which body segmentation is completed before hatching.

epinasty (ĕp′ĭ năs′tĭ), *n. Bot.* (esp. of leaves) increased growth on the upper surface of an organ or part, causing it to bend downwards. [f. EPI- + s. Gk *nastós* pressed close, compact + -Y[3]] **—ep′inas′tic,** *adj.* **—ep′inast′ically,** *adv.*

epinephrine (ĕp′ĭ nĕf′rĭn, -rēn), *n. Biochem., Med.* adrenaline. Also, **epinephrin** (ĕp′ĭ nĕf′rĭn). [f. EPI- + s. Gk *nephrós* kidney + -INE[2]]

epineurium (ĕp′ĭ nyōō′rĭ əm), *n., pl.* **-neuria** (-nyōō′rĭ ə). *Anat.* the dense sheath of connective tissue which surrounds the trunk of a nerve. [NL, f. Gk: *epi-* EPI- + m. *neûron* sinew, tendon]

epipetalous (ĕp′ĭ pĕt′ə ləs), *adj. Bot.* (of stamens) inserted on the petals and appearing to originate from them.

Epiph., Epiphany.

Epiphany (ĭ pĭf′ə nĭ), *n., pl.* **-nies.** **1.** a Christian festival, observed on Jan. 6th, commemorating the manifestation of Christ to the Gentiles in the persons of the Magi. **2.** (*l.c.*) an appearance or manifestation, esp. of a deity. [ME *epiphanie*, t. LL: m. *epiphania*, t. LGk: the Epiphany, ult. der. *epiphaínein* manifest]

epiphenomenalism (ĕp′ĭ fĭ nŏm′ĭ nə lĭz′əm), *n. Philos.* automatism (def. 2).

epiphenomenon (ĕp′ĭ fĭ nŏm′ĭ nən), *n., pl.* **-na** (-nə). **1.** *Pathol.* a secondary or additional symptom or complication arising during the course of a malady. **2.** any secondary phenomenon.

epiphyll (ĕp′ĭ fĭl), *n. Bot.* an epiphyte that grows on the surface, esp. the upper surface, of leaves, as a lichen. **—ep′iphyl′lous,** *adj.*

epiphysis (ĭ pĭf′ĭ sĭs), *n., pl.* **-ses** (-sēz′). *Anat.* **1.** a part or process of a bone which is separated from the main body of the bone by a layer of cartilage, and which finally becomes united with the bone through further ossification. **2.** the pineal body of the brain. [NL, t. Gk: an outgrowth] **—epiphysial** (ĕp′ĭ fĭz′ĭ əl), *adj.*

epiphyte (ĕp′ĭ fīt′), *n. Bot.* a plant which grows upon another but does not get food, water, or minerals from it; an air plant or aerophyte. **—epiphytic** (ĕp′ĭ fĭt′ĭk), **ep′iphyt′ical,** *adj.* **—ep′iphyt′ically,** *adv.*

epiphytotic (ĕp′ĭ fī tŏt′ĭk), *adj.* (of a disease or parasite) epidemic on plants. [f. EPI- + -PHYTE + -OTIC]

epiploon (ĭ pĭp′lō ən), *n. Anat.* the great omentum. **—ep′iplo′ic,** *adj.*

epirogeny (ĕp′ĭ rŏj′ĭ nĭ), *n.* epeirogeny. **—epirogenic** (ĭ pī′rō jĕn′ĭk), *adj.*

Epirus (ĭ pī′ə rəs), *n.* **1.** a country of ancient Greece, corresponding to what is now NW Greece and S Albania. **2.** a modern region in NW Greece. 352,604 pop. (1961); 3573 sq. mi.

Epis., Episcopal. Also, **Episc.**

episcopacy (ĭ pĭs′kə pə sĭ), *n., pl.* **-cies.** **1.** government of the church by bishops; church government in which there are three distinct orders of ministers, namely bishops, priests or presbyters, and deacons. **2.** the office or incumbency of a bishop. **3.** the order of bishops.

episcopal (ĭ pĭs′kə pl), *adj.* **1.** pertaining to a bishop. **2.** (*sometimes cap.*) based on or recognizing a governing order of bishops: *the Methodist Episcopal Church.* **3.** (*cap.*) designating the Anglican Church or some branch of it: *the Protestant Episcopal Church in the U.S.* [t. LL: s. *epīscopālis*, der. *epīscopus* BISHOP] **—epis′copally,** *adv.*

Episcopalian (ĭ pĭs′kə pā′lyən), *adj.* **1.** pertaining or adhering to the Episcopal Church (of the Anglican communion). **2.** (*l.c.*) pertaining or adhering to the episcopal form of church government. **—***n.* **3.** a member of the Episcopal Church. **4.** (*l.c.*) an adherent of the episcopal system of church government. **—Epis′copa′lianism,** *n.*

episcopalism (ĭ pĭs′kə pə lĭz′əm), *n.* the theory of church polity according to which the supreme ecclesiastical authority is vested in the episcopal order as a whole, and not in any individual except by delegation.

episcopate (ĭ pĭs′kə pĭt, -pāt′), *n.* **1.** the office and dignity of a bishop; a bishopric. **2.** the order or body of bishops. **3.** the incumbency of a bishop.

episcopize (ĭ pĭs′kə pīz′), *v.*, **-pized, -pizing.** **—***v.t.* **1.** to make a bishop of. **2.** to convert to Episcopalianism. **—***v.i.* **3.** to act as a bishop. Also, **episcopise.**

episode (ĕp′ĭ sōd′), *n.* **1.** an incident in the course of a series of events, in a person's life or experience, etc. **2.** an incidental narrative or digression in the course of a story, poem, or other writing. **3.** any of a number of loosely connected but generally related scenes or stories comprising a literary work. **4.** a part in an old Greek tragedy between two choric songs. **5.** *Music.* an intermediate or digressive passage, esp. in a contrapuntal composition. **6.** (in radio, television, etc.) any of the separate programmes constituting a serial. [t. Gk: m. s. *epeisódion* a parenthetic addition, prop. neut. of *epeisódios* coming in besides] **—Syn. 1.** See **event.**

episodic (ĕp′ĭ sŏd′ĭk), *adj.* **1.** pertaining to or of the nature of an episode; incidental. **2.** divided into separate or loosely connected parts: *an episodic novel.* Also, **ep′isod′ical.** **—ep′isod′ically,** *adv.*

epispastic (ĕp′ĭ spăs′tĭk), *adj.* **1.** raising a blister. **—***n.* **2.** a blistering agent; a vesicatory. [t. Gk: m. s. *epispastikós*, lit., drawing towards]

epistasis (ĭ pĭs′tə sĭs), *n. Med.* **1.** suppression of a secretion or discharge. **2.** a film which forms on the surface of urine after it has been left standing for some time. [t. Gk] **—epistatic** (ĕp′ĭ stăt′ĭk), *adj.*

epistaxis (ĕp′ĭ stăk′sĭs), *n. Pathol.* bleeding from the nose. [NL, der. Gk *epistázein* drop on]

epistemology (ĭ pĭs′tĭ mŏl′ə jĭ), *n.* the branch of philosophy which investigates the origin, nature, methods, and limits of human knowledge. [f. s. Gk *epistḗmē* knowledge + -(O)LOGY] **—epistemological** (ĭ pĭs′tĭ mə lŏj′ĭ kl), *adj.* **—epis′temolog′ically,** *adv.* **—epis′temol′ogist,** *n.*

episternum (ĕp′ĭ stû′nəm), *n., pl.* **-na** (-nə). **1.** *Anat.* the manubrium. **2.** *Entomol.* the principal anterior subdivision of a thoracic pleuron. **—ep′ister′nal,** *adj., n.*

epistle (ĭ pĭs′əl), *n.* **1.** a written communication; a letter, esp. one of formal or didactic character. **2.** (*usually cap.*) one of the apostolic letters found in the New Testament. **3.** (*often cap.*) an extract, usually from one of the Epistles of the New Testament, forming part of the Eucharistic service in certain churches. [ME; OE *epistol*, t. L: s. *epistola*, t. Gk: m. *epistolḗ* message, letter]

epistler (ĭ pĭs′lə, ĭ pĭst′lə), *n.* **1.** a writer of an epistle. **2.** the one who reads the epistle in the Eucharistic service. Also, **epistoler** (ĭ pĭs′tə lə), **epis′tolist.**

epistle side, the right-hand side of a church facing the altar. Cf. **gospel side.**

epistolary (ĭ pĭs′tə lə rĭ), *adj.* **1.** contained in or carried on by letters. **2.** of or pertaining to letters. Also, **epis′tolatory.**

epistyle (ĕp′ĭ stīl′), *n. Archit.* an architrave. [t. L: m. s. *epistȳlium*, t. Gk: m. *epistýlion*]

epitaph (ĕp′ĭ tăf′, -täf′), *n.* **1.** a commemorative inscription on a tomb or mortuary monument. **2.** any brief writing resembling such an inscription. [ME *epitaphe*, t. L: m. s. *epitaphium*, t. Gk: m. *epitáphion* funeral oration, neut. *of epitáphios* over or at a tomb] —**epitaphic** (ĕp′ĭ tăf′ĭk), *adj.* —**ep′itaph′ist,** *n.*

epitasis (ĭ pĭt′ə sĭs), *n.* (in ancient drama) the main part of the play, following the protasis. [t. L, t. Gk]

epithalamion (ĕp′ĭ thə lā′myən), *n., pl.* **-mia** (-myə). epithalamium.

epithalamium (ĕp′ĭ thə lā′myəm), *n., pl.* **-miums, -mia** (-myə). a nuptial song or poem; a poem in honour of a bride and bridegroom. [t. L, t. Gk: m. *epithalámion* (neut. adj.) nuptial] —**epithalamic** (ĕp′ĭ thə lăm′ĭk), *adj.*

epithelial (ĕp′ĭ thē′lyəl), *adj.* pertaining to epithelium.

epithelioid (ĕp′ĭ thē′lĭ oid′), *adj.* resembling epithelium.

epithelioma (ĕp′ĭ thē′lĭ ō′mə), *n., pl.* **-mata** (-mə tə), **-mas.** *Pathol.* a cancer or malignant growth consisting chiefly of epithelial cells. [NL; f. EPITHELI(UM) + -OMA] —**ep′ithelio′matous,** *adj.*

epithelium (ĕp′ĭ thē′lyəm), *n., pl.* **-liums, -lia** (-lyə). *Biol.* any tissue which covers a surface, or lines a cavity or the like, and which performs protective, secreting, or other functions, as the epidermis, the lining of blood vessels, etc. [NL, f. Gk: *epi-* EPI- + m. *thēlḗ* nipple + m. *-ion*, dim. suffix]

epithermal (ĕp′ĭ thû′məl), *adj. Physics.* having energy slightly above the energy of thermal agitation and comparable with chemical bond energies.

epithet (ĕp′ĭ thĕt′), *n.* **1.** an adjective or other term applied to a person or thing to express an attribute, as in Alexander *the Great.* **2.** a meaningful name. [t. L: s. *epitheton*, t. Gk, prop. neut. of *epíthetos* added] —**ep′ithet′ic, ep′ithet′ical,** *adj.*

epitome (ĭ pĭt′ə mĭ), *n.* **1.** a summary or condensed account, esp. of a literary work; an abstract. **2.** a condensed representation or typical characteristic of something: *the epitome of all mankind.* [t. L, t. Gk, der. *epitémnein* cut into, abridge] —**ep′itom′ic, ep′itom′ical,** *adj.*

epitomist (ĭ pĭt′ə mĭst), *n.* one who makes an epitome.

epitomize (ĭ pĭt′ə mīz′), *v.t.,* **-mized, -mizing. 1.** to make an epitome of. **2.** to contain in small compass. Also, **epitomise.** —**epit′omiz′er,** *n.*

epitrachelion (ĕp′ĭ trə kē′lyən), *n.* a stole worn by priests and bishops of the Greek Orthodox Church.

epizoic (ĕp′ĭ zō′ĭk), *adj. Zool.* externally parasitic.

epizoon (ĕp′ĭ zō′ŏn), *n., pl.* **-zoa** (-zō′ə). an external parasite; an ectozoon. [f. EPI- + ZOON]

epizootic (ĕp′ĭ zō ŏt′ĭk), *Vet. Sci.* —*adj.* **1.** (of diseases) prevalent temporarily among animals. —*n.* **2.** an epizootic disease. [f. EPI- + ZO(O)- + -OTIC. Cf. F *épizootique*] —**ep′izoot′ically,** *adv.*

epizooty (ĕp′ĭ zō′ə tĭ), *n., pl.* **-ties.** an epizootic disease.

e pluribus unum (ā plo͝o′rĭ bo͝os o͞o′no͝om), *Latin.* one out of many (motto of the United States).

epoch (ē′pŏk), *n.* **1.** a particular period of time as marked by distinctive character, events, etc. **2.** the beginning of any distinctive period in the history of anything. **3.** a point of time distinguished by a particular event, or state of affairs. **4.** *Geol.* the main division of a geological period, representing the time required for making a geological series. **5.** *Astron.* **a.** an arbitrarily fixed instant of time or date (usually the beginning of a century or half-century) used as a reference in giving the elements of a planetary orbit or the like. **b.** the mean longitude of a planet as seen from the sun at such an instant or date. [t. ML: s. *epocha*, t. Gk: m. *epochḗ* check, pause, position, epoch] —**Syn. 1.** See **age.**

epochal (ĕp′ŏk′l), *adj.* **1.** of or pertaining to an epoch or epochs. **2.** of the nature of an epoch. **3.** epoch-making.

epoch-making (ē′pŏk mā′kĭng), *adj.* opening a new era, as in human history, thought, or knowledge: *an epoch-making discovery.*

epode (ĕp′ōd), *n. Class. Pros.* **1.** a kind of lyric poem, invented by Archilochus (about 650 B.C.), in which a long verse is followed by a short one. **2.** the part of a lyric ode following the strophe and antistrophe. [t. F, t. L: m. s. *epōdos*, t. Gk: m. *epōidós* after song, incantation]

eponym (ĕp′ō nĭm), *n.* **1.** a person, real or imaginary, from whom a tribe, place, institution, etc., takes, or is supposed to take, its name, as *Britons* from *Brut* (supposed to be the grandson of Aeneas). **2.** any official in ancient times whose name was used to designate his year of office. [t. Gk: s. *epṓnymon* (neut.) named after] —**ep′onym′ic,** *adj.*

eponymous (ĭ pŏn′ĭ məs), *adj.* giving one's name to a tribe, place, etc. [t. Gk: m. *epṓnymos*]

eponymy (ĭ pŏn′ĭ mĭ), *n.* the derivation of names from eponyms. [t. Gk : m. s. *epōnymía* surname]

épopée (ĕp′ō pē′; *Fr.* ė pô pė′), *n.* **1.** an epic. **2.** epic poetry. Also, **epopoeia** (ĕp′ō pē′ə). [t. F, t. Gk: m. *epopoiia* epic poetry]

epos (ĕp′ŏs), *n.* **1.** an epic. **2.** epic poetry. **3.** a body of poems, transmitted orally, dealing with the traditions of a people, esp. poems treating parts of a common epic theme. **4.** a series of events worthy of treatment in epic poetry. [t. L, t. Gk: word, tale, song; pl. epic poetry]

epoxy (ĭ pŏk′sĭ), *adj., n., pl.* **epoxies.** *Chem.* —*adj.* **1.** containing an oxygen atom that bridges two connected atoms, as in *epoxy ethene.* —*n.* **2.** Also **epoxy** or **epoxide resin.** any of a class of substances derived by polymerization from certain viscous liquid or brittle solid compounds, used chiefly in adhesives, coatings, electrical insulation, solder mix, and in the casting of tools and dyes. [f. EPI- + OXY-[2]]

Epping Forest (ĕp′ĭng), a former royal forest in E England, at one time nearly coextensive with Essex: now a park NE of London. $8\frac{3}{4}$ sq. mi.

EPR, ethylene-propylene rubber.

epsilon (ĕp′sĭ lŏn′, ĕp sī′lən), *n.* the fifth letter (E, ε, English short E, e) of the Greek alphabet. [t. Gk: *è psilón* e simple]

Epsom (ĕp′səm), *n.* a town in SE England, in Surrey: site of **Epsom Downs,** a famous racecourse where the annual Derby is held. 71,159 (1961).

Epsom salts, hydrated magnesium sulphate, used as a cathartic, etc. [so called because first prepared from the water of the mineral springs at EPSOM]

Epstein (ĕp′stīn), *n.* **Sir Jacob,** 1880–1959, British Jewish sculptor, born in New York of Russian–Polish parents.

E.P.T., excess-profits tax.

eq., **1.** equal. **2.** equation. **3.** equivalent.

equable (ĕk′wə bl), *adj.* **1.** free from variations; uniform, as motion or temperature. **2.** uniform in operation or effect, as laws. **3.** tranquil, even, or not easily disturbed, as the mind. [t. L: m. s. *aequābilis* that can be made equal] —**eq′uabil′ity, eq′uableness,** *n.* —**eq′uably,** *adv.* —**Syn. 1, 3.** See **even.** —**Ant. 1.** variable.

equal (ē′kwəl), *adj., n., v.,* **equalled, equalling** or (*U.S.*) **equaled, equaling.** —*adj.* **1.** as great as another (fol. by *to* or *with*): *the velocity of sound is not equal to that of light.* **2.** like or alike in quantity, degree, value, etc.; of the same rank, ability, merit, etc. **3.** evenly proportioned or balanced: *an equal mixture, an equal contest.* **4.** uniform in operation or effect: *equal laws.* **5.** adequate or sufficient in quantity or degree: *the supply is equal to the demand.* **6.** having adequate powers, ability, or means: *he was not equal to the task.* **7.** level, as a plain. **8.** *Archaic.* tranquil or undisturbed. **9.** *Archaic.* impartial or equitable. —*n.* **10.** one who or that which is equal. —*v.t.* **11.** to be or become equal to; match. **12.** to make or do something equal to. **13.** to recompense fully. **14.** *Archaic.* to make equal; equalize. [t. L: m. s. *aequālis* like, equal]

—**Syn. 2.** proportionate, commensurate, coordinate, correspondent. EQUAL, EQUIVALENT, TANTAMOUNT imply a correspondence between two or more things. EQUAL indicates a correspondence in all respects, unless a particular respect (or respects) is stated or implied: *one hundred pence is equal to one pound* (that is, in purchasing power, which is implied). EQUIVALENT indicates a correspondence in one or more respects, but not in all: *an egg is said to be the equivalent of a pound of meat* (that is, in nutritive value). TANTAMOUNT, a word of limited application, is used esp. of immaterial things which are equivalent to such an extent as to be practically identical: *the prisoner's refusal to answer was tantamount to an admission of guilt.* **4.** even, uniform, regular, unvarying. **10.** peer, compeer, match, mate. —**Ant. 1, 3, 4.** unequal. **2.** different. **5.** disproportionate. **6.** inadequate.

equalitarian (ĭ kwŏl′ĭ tĕə′rĭ ən), *adj.* **1.** pertaining or adhering to the doctrine of equality among men; egalitarian. —*n.* **2.** one who adheres to the doctrine of equality among men. —**equal′itar′ianism,** *n.*

equality (ĭ kwŏl′ĭ tĭ), *n., pl.* **-ties. 1.** the state of being equal; correspondence in quality, degree, value, rank, ability, etc. **2.** uniform character, as of motion or surface.

equalize (ē′kwə līz′), *v.t.,* **-ized, -izing. 1.** to make equal: *to equalize tax burdens.* **2.** to make uniform. **3.** *Sport.* to reach a score equal to that of an opponent. Also, **equalise.** —**e′qualiza′tion,** *n.*

equalizer (ē′kwə lī′zə), *n.* **1.** one who or that which equalizes. **2.** any of various devices or appliances for equalizing strains, pressures, etc. **3.** *Elect.* an electrical connection established between two points in a network to secure some constant relation between the two points, as potential, impedance, etc. Also, **equaliser.**

equally (ē′kwə lĭ), *adv.* in an equal manner or degree.

equanimity (ē′kwə nĭm′ĭ tĭ, ĕk′wə-), *n.* evenness of mind or temper; calmness; composure. [t. L: m. s. *aequanimitas*, der. *aequanimis* of an even mind]

equate (ĭ kwāt′), *v.t.,* **equated, equating. 1.** to state the equality of or between; put in the form of an equation.

2. to reduce to an average; make such correction or allowance in as will reduce to a common standard of comparison. **3.** to regard, treat, or represent as equivalent. [t. L: m. s. *aequātus*, pp., made equal]

equation (ĭ kwā′zhən, -shən), *n.* **1.** the act of making equal; equalization. **2.** equally balanced state; equilibrium. **3.** *Maths.* **a.** an expression of, or a proposition asserting, the equality of two quantities, employing the sign = between them. **b.** a mathematical formula interpreted as a question asking for what values of a variable two expressions in that variable are equal, as $3x^2 - 2x + 4 = 0$. **4.** *Chem.* a symbolic representation of a reaction. **5.** See **personal equation.** —**equa′tional,** *adj.*

equator (ĭ kwā′tə), *n.* **1.** that great circle of a sphere or any heavenly body which has a centre at each pole and lies equidistant between them, its plane being perpendicular to the axis of the sphere or heavenly body. **2.** the great circle of the earth, equidistant from the North and South Poles. **3.** a circle separating a surface into two congruent parts. [ME, t. LL: m. *aequātor*, lit., equalizer (of day and night, as when the sun is on the equator)]

equatorial (ĕk′wə tô′rĭ əl), *adj.* **1.** of, pertaining to, or near an equator, esp. the equator of the earth. **2.** of or like the regions at the earth's equator: *equatorial vegetation.* —*n.* **3.** a telescope mounting having two axes of motion, one parallel to the earth's axis, and one at right angles to it. **4.** *Aerospace.* an orbit in the plane of the equator.

equatorial climate, a type of climate characterized by consistently high temperatures and rainfall throughout the year; roughly between latitudes 5°N and 5°S.

Equatorial Guinea, a Spanish autonomous region in W Africa, comprising the provinces of Rio Muni and Fernando Po. 272,000 pop. (est. 1965); 10,830 sq. mi. *Cap.*: Santa Isabel.

equerry (ĭ kwĕ′rĭ), *n., pl.* **-ries. 1.** an officer of a royal or similar household, charged with the care of the horses. **2.** an officer who attends on the British sovereign. [t. F: m. *écurie*, OF *escuirie*, der. *escuier* SQUIRE]

equestrian (ĭ kwĕs′trĭ ən), *adj.* **1.** of or pertaining to horsemen or horsemanship. **2.** mounted on horseback. **3.** of or pertaining to the Roman equites: *the equestrian order.* **4.** representing a person on horseback: *an equestrian statue.* **5.** pertaining to or composed of knights. —*n.* **6.** a rider or performer on horseback. [f. L *equestri(s)* of a horseman + -AN] —**eques′trianism,** *n.*

equestrienne (ĭ kwĕs′trĭ ĕn′), *n.* a female rider or performer on horseback. [pseudo-F fem. of EQUESTRIAN]

equi-, a word element meaning 'equal', as in *equidistant, equivalent.* [comb. form repr. L *aequus* equal]

equiangular (ē′kwĭ ăng′gyŏŏ lə), *adj.* having all the angles equal.

equidistance (ē′kwĭ dĭs′təns), *n.* equal distance.

equidistant (ē′kwĭ dĭs′tənt), *adj.* equally distant. —**e′quidis′tantly,** *adv.*

equilateral (ē′kwĭ lăt′ə rəl), *adj.* **1.** having all the sides equal. —*n.* **2.** a figure having all its sides equal. **3.** a side equivalent, or equal to others. [t. LL: m. s. *aequilaterālis*] —**e′quilat′erally,** *adv.*

60°

Equilateral triangle

equilibrant (ĭ kwĭl′ĭ brənt), *n.* *Physics.* a counterbalancing force or system of forces.

equilibrate (ē′kwĭ lī′brāt, ĭ kwĭl′ĭ brāt′), *v.*, **-brated, -brating.** —*v.t.* **1.** to balance equally; keep in equipoise or equilibrium. **2.** to be in equilibrium with; counterpoise. —*v.i.* **3.** to balance. [t. LL: m. s. *aequilībrātus* in equilibrium, f. L: *aequi-* EQUI- + *lībrātus* balanced] —**equilibration** (ē′kwĭ lī brā′shən, ĭ kwĭl′ĭ-), *n.* —**equilibrator** (ĭ kwĭl′ĭ brā′tə), *n.*

equilibrist (ĭ kwĭl′ĭ brĭst), *n.* one who practises balancing in unnatural positions and hazardous movements, as a rope-dancer. [f. EQUILIBR(IUM) + -IST] —**equil′ibris′tic,** *adj.*

equilibrium (ē′kwĭ lĭb′rĭ əm), *n.* **1.** a state of rest due to the action of forces that counteract each other. **2.** equal balance between any powers, influences, etc.; equality of effect. **3.** mental or emotional balance; equilibrium. **4.** *Chem.* the condition obtaining when a chemical reaction and its reverse reaction proceed at equal rates. [t. L: m. *aequilībrium*, f. *aequi-* EQUI- + s. *lībra* balance + *-ium* -IUM]

equimolecular (ē′kwĭ mə lĕk′yŏŏ lə), *adj.* *Chem.* containing equal numbers of molecules.

equine (ĕk′wīn), *adj.* **1.** of or resembling a horse. —*n.* **2.** a horse. [t. L: m. s. *equīnus*, der. *equus* horse] —**equi′nity,** *n.*

equinoctial (ē′kwĭ nŏk′shəl), *adj.* **1.** pertaining to an equinox or the equinoxes, or to the equality of day and night. **2.** pertaining to the celestial equator. **3.** occurring at or about the time of an equinox: *an equinoctial storm.* **4.** *Bot.* (of a flower) opening regularly at a certain hour. —*n.* **5.** equinoctial line. **6.** a gale or storm at or near the time of an equinox. [ME, t. L: m. s. *aequinoctiālis*, der. *aequinoctium* EQUINOX]

equinoctial line, the celestial equator. Also, **equinoctial circle.**

equinoctial point, either of the two points in which the celestial equator and the ecliptic intersect each other, reached by the sun's centre at the equinoxes.

equinox (ē′kwĭ nŏks′), *n.* **1.** the time when the sun crosses the plane of the earth's equator, making night and day all over the earth of equal length, occurring about March 21st (**vernal equinox**) and Sept. 22nd (**autumnal equinox**). **2.** either of the equinoctial points. [t. ML: m. s. *equinoxium*, L *aequinoctium* equality between day and night]

equip (ĭ kwĭp′), *v.t.*, **equipped, equipping. 1.** to furnish or provide with whatever is needed for services or for any undertaking; to fit out, as a ship. **2.** to dress out; array. [t. F: m. *équipper*, OF *esquiper*, prob. t. Scand.; cf. Icel. *skipa* put in order, arrange, man (a ship, etc.)] —**equip′per,** *n.* —**Syn. 1.** See **furnish.**

equipage (ĕk′wĭ pĭj), *n.* **1.** a carriage. **2.** a completely equipped carriage, with horses and servants. **3.** outfit, as of a ship, an army, or a soldier; equipment. **4.** a set of small household articles, as of china. **5.** a collection of articles for personal ornament or use.

equipment (ĭ kwĭp′mənt), *n.* **1.** anything used in or provided for equipping. **2.** the act of equipping. **3.** the state of being equipped. **4.** a person's knowledge and skill necessary for a task, etc.: *a man's equipment for the law, for medicine.* **5.** a collection of necessary implements (such as tools). —**Syn. 1.** apparatus, paraphernalia.

equipoise (ĕk′wĭ poiz′), *n.* **1.** an equal distribution of weight; even balance; equilibrium. **2.** a counterpoise.

equipollent (ē′kwĭ pŏl′ənt), *adj.* **1.** equal in power, effect, etc.; equivalent. **2.** *Logic.* (of two propositions, etc.) logically deducible from each other, as 'All men are mortal' and 'No men are immortal'. —*n.* **3.** an equivalent. [t. L: m. s. *aequipollens* of equal value] —**e′quipol′lence, e′quipol′lency,** *n.*

equiponderance (ē′kwĭ pŏn′də rəns), *n.* equality of weight; equipoise. Also, **e′quipon′derancy.** —**e′quipon′derant,** *adj.*

equiponderate (ē′kwĭ pŏn′də rāt′), *v.t.*, **-ated, -ating.** to equal or offset in weight, force, importance, etc.; counterbalance. [t. ML: m. s. *aequiponderātus*, pp. of *aequiponderāre*, f. L: *aequi-* EQUI- + *ponderāre* weigh]

equipotent (ē′kwĭ pō′tənt), *adj.* equal in power.

equipotential (ē′kwĭ pə tĕn′shəl), *adj.* *Physics.* of the same potential.

equisetum (ĕk′wĭ sē′təm), *n., pl.* **-tums, -ta** (-tə). any plant of the genus *Equisetum*; a horsetail or scouring rush. [NL, m. L *equisaetum*, f. *equi-* horse + m. *saeta* bristle] —**eq′uiset′ic,** *adj.*

equitable (ĕk′wĭ tə bl), *adj.* **1.** characterized by equity or fairness; just and right; fair; reasonable. **2.** *Law.* pertaining to or valid in equity, as distinguished from the common law. —**eq′uitableness,** *n.* —**eq′uitably,** *adv.*

equitant (ĕk′wĭ tənt), *adj.* *Bot.* straddling or overlapping, as leaves whose bases overlap the leaves above or within them. [t. L: s. *equitans*, ppr., riding]

equitation (ĕk′wĭ tā′shən), *n.* the act or art of riding a horse. [t. L: s. *equitātio*, der. *equitāre* ride]

equites (ĕk′wĭ tēz′), *n.pl.* **1.** (in ancient Rome) **a.** the mounted military units; the cavalry. **b.** the equestrian order of knights. **2.** (later) a privileged or imperial class. [t. L, pl. of *eques* a horseman, knight]

equity (ĕk′wĭ tĭ), *n., pl.* **-ties. 1.** the quality of being fair or impartial; fairness: impartiality. **2.** that which is fair and just. **3.** *Law.* **a.** the application of the dictates of conscience or the principles of natural justice to the settlement of controversies. **b.** a system of jurisprudence or a body of doctrines and rules developed in England and followed in the United States, serving to supplement and remedy the limitations and the inflexibility of the common law. **c.** an equitable right or claim. **d.** an equity of redemption. **4.** the interest of a shareholder of common stock in a company. **5.** (*pl.*) stocks and shares not bearing fixed interest. **6.** the amount by which the market value of a debtor's securities exceeds his indebtedness. **7.** (*cap.*) (in Great Britain) the actors' trade union. [ME *equite*, t. L: m. s. *aequitas* equality, justice]

equity of redemption, the equitable right of a mortgagor to redeem the mortgaged property by paying the debt, even after default in payment of the sum owed.

equiv., equivalent.

equivalence (ĭ kwĭv′ə ləns), *n.* **1.** the state or fact of being equivalent; equality in value, force, significance, etc. **2.** *Chem.* the quality of having equal valency. Also, **equiv′alency.**

equivalent (ĭ kwĭv′ə lənt), *adj.* **1.** equal in value, measure, force, effect, significance, etc. **2.** corresponding in position, function, etc. **3.** *Geom.* having the same extent, as a triangle and a square of equal area. **4.** *Chem.* having the same capacity to combine or reach chemically. —*n.* **5.** that which is equivalent. [ME, t. LL: s. *aequivalens*, ppr., having equal power] —**equiv′alently,** *adv.* —**Syn. 1.** See **equal.**

equivalent weight, *Chem.* the weight of an element, radical, or compound which will combine with, or replace, 1·00797 grams of hydrogen or 8 grams of oxygen: for an element, the atomic weight divided by the valency.

equivocal (ĭ kwĭv′ə kl), *adj.* **1.** of uncertain significance; not determined: *an equivocal attitude.* **2.** of doubtful nature or character; questionable; dubious; suspicious. **3.** having different meanings equally possible, as a word or phrase; susceptible of double interpretation; ambiguous. [f. ME *equivoc* (t. LL: m. s. *aequivocus* ambiguous) + -AL[1]] —**equiv′ocally,** *adv.* —**equiv′ocalness,** *n.* —**Syn. 3.** See **ambiguous.**

equivocate (ĭ kwĭv′ə kāt′), *v.i.*, **-cated, -cating.** to use equivocal or ambiguous expressions, esp. in order to mislead; prevaricate. [back-formation from EQUIVOCATION] —**equiv′ocat′ingly,** *adv.* —**equiv′oca′tor,** *n.* —**equivocatory** (ĭ kwĭv′ə kə tə rĭ, -trĭ), *adj.*

equivocation (ĭ kwĭv′ə kā′shən), *n.* **1.** the use of equivocal or ambiguous expressions, esp. in order to mislead; prevarication. **2.** an equivocal or ambiguous expression; equivoque. **3.** *Logic.* a fallacy depending on the double meaning of a word. [ME, t. LL: m. s. *aequivocātio*]

equivoque (ĕk′wĭ vōk′), *n.* **1.** an equivocal term; an ambiguous expression. **2.** a play upon words; a pun. **3.** double meaning; ambiguity. Also, **equivoke.** [t. F, r. ME *equivoc.* See EQUIVOCAL]

er (ə, û), *interj.* (the written representation of an inarticulate sound made by a speaker when hesitating.)

-er[1], a suffix: **1.** forming nouns designating persons from the object of their occupation or labour, as in *hatter, tiler, tinner, moonshiner*, or from their place of origin or abode, as in *Icelander, southerner, villager*, or designating either persons or things from some special characteristic or circumstances, as in *six-footer, three-master, teetotaller, fiver, tenner.* **2.** serving as the regular English formative of agent nouns (being attached to verbs of any origin), as in *bearer, creeper, employer, harvester, teacher, theorizer.* [OE *-ere*, c. G *-er*, etc.; akin to L *-ārius*]

-er[2], a suffix of nouns denoting persons or things concerned or connected with something, as in *butler, grocer, officer, garner.* [ME, t. AF, OF: *-er, -ier*, g. L *-ārius*, neut. *-ārium.* Cf. -ARY[1]]

-er[3], a termination of certain nouns denoting action or process, as in *dinner, rejoinder, remainder, trover.* [t. F: orig. sign of inf.]

-er[4], a suffix forming the comparative degree of adjectives, as in *harder, smaller.* [OE *-ra, -re*, c. G *-er*]

-er[5], a suffix forming the comparative degree of adverbs, as in *faster.* [OE *-or*, c. OHG *-or*, G *-er*]

-er[6], a suffix forming frequentative verbs, as *flicker, flutter, glimmer, patter.* [OE *-r-*, c. G *-(e)r-*]

Er., *Chem.* erbium.

E.R., 1. East Riding (Yorkshire). **2.** (L *Eduardus Rex*) King Edward. **3.** (L *Elizabeth Regina*) Queen Elizabeth.

era (ĭə′rə), *n.* **1.** a period of time marked by distinctive character, events, etc.: *an era of progress.* **2.** the period of time to which anything belongs or is to be assigned. **3.** a system of chronological notation reckoned from a given date. **4.** a period during which years are numbered and dates reckoned from a particular point of time in the past: *the Christian era.* **5.** a point of time from which succeeding years are numbered, as at the beginning of a system of chronology. **6.** a date or an event forming the beginning of any distinctive period. **7.** *Geol.* a major division of geological time: *Palaeozoic era.* [t. LL, var. of *aera* number or epoch by which reckoning is made, era, prob. the same word as L *aera* counters, pl. of *aes* copper, bronze] —**Syn. 1.** See **age.**

E.R.A., engine-room artificer.

eradiate (ĭ rā′dĭ āt′), *v.i., v.t.*, **-ated, -ating.** to radiate.

eradiation (ĭ rā′dĭ ā′shən), *n.* the act or process of shooting forth (light rays, etc); radiation.

eradicable (ĭ răd′ĭ kə bl), *adj.* that may be eradicated.

eradicate (ĭ răd′ĭ kāt′), *v.t.*, **-cated, -cating. 1.** to remove or destroy utterly; extirpate. **2.** to pull up by the roots. [t. L, m. s. *ērādicātus*, pp. rooted out] —**erad′ica′tion,** *n.* —**eradicative** (ĭ răd′ĭ kə tĭv), *adj.* —**erad′ica′tor,** *n.* —**Syn. 1.** See **abolish.**

erase (ĭ rāz′), *v.t.*, **erased, erasing. 1.** to rub or scrape out, as letters or characters written, engraved, etc.; efface. **2.** to obliterate material recorded on an electromagnetic tape by demagnetizing it. [t. L: m. s. *ērāsus*, pp., scratched out] —**eras′able,** *adj.* —**erasion** (ĭ rā′zhən), *n.* —**Syn. 1.** expunge, obliterate. See **cancel.**

eraser (ĭ rā′zə), *n.* **1.** an instrument, as a piece of rubber or cloth, for erasing marks made with pen, pencil, chalk, etc. **2.** one who or that which erases.

Erasmus (ĭ răz′məs), *n.* **Desiderius** (dĕz′ĭ dĭə′rĭ əs) (*Gerhard Gerhards*), 1466?–1536, Dutch humanist, scholar, and theologian.

Erastian (ĭ răs′tĭ ən), *adj.* **1.** pertaining to Thomas Erastus, or to his doctrines, advocating the supremacy of the state in ecclesiastical matters. —*n.* **2.** an advocate of the doctrines of Erastus. —**Eras′tianism,** *n.*

Erastus (ĭ răs′təs; *Ger.* ĕ rás′to͝os), *n.* **Thomas** (tŏm′əs; *Ger.* tō′más), 1524–83, Swiss–German theologian.

erasure (ĭ rā′zhə), *n.* **1.** the act of erasing. **2.** a place where something has been erased.

Erato (ĕ′rə tō′), *n.* *Gk Myth.* the Muse of love poetry. [t. L, t. Gk: lit., lovesome]

Eratosthenes (ĕ′rə tŏs′thĭ nēz′), *n.* 276?–195? B.C., Greek mathematician and astronomer, at Alexandria.

erbium (û′bĭ əm), *n.* *Chem.* a rare-earth metallic element, having pink salts. *Symbol:* Er; *at. wt:* 167·26; *at. no.:* 68. [t. NL: f. (*Ytt*)*erb*(*y*) (see YTTERBIUM) + *-ium* -IUM]

ere (ĕə), *prep., conj.* *Archaic.* before. [ME; OE *ǣr, ēr* (c. G *eher*), comparative of OE *ār* soon, early, c. Goth. *air.* See ERST, EARLY]

Erebus (ĕ′rĭ bəs), *n.* **1.** *Class. Myth.* the god of darkness, son of Chaos and brother of Night. **2.** a place of darkness between earth and Hades; the lower world. **3. Mount,** a volcano on Ross Island, in Antarctica. ab. 13,370 ft.

Erechtheum (ĕ′rĕk thē′əm), *n.* a temple of Ionic order on the Acropolis of Athens, built *c.* 420 B.C., and one of the most perfect examples of Greek architecture, notable for its porches of different height, supported by caryatids.

erect (ĭ rĕkt′), *adj.* **1.** upright in position or posture: *to stand or sit erect* **2.** raised or directed upwards: *a dog with ears erect.* **3.** *Bot.* vertical throughout; not spreading or declined: *an erect stem, an erect leaf or ovule.* **4.** *Optics.* (of an image) having the same position as the object; not inverted. —*v.t.* **5.** to build; construct; raise: *to erect a house.* **6.** to raise and set in an upright or perpendicular position: *to erect a telegraph pole.* **7.** *Geom.* to draw or construct (a line or figure) upon a given line, base, or the like. **8.** *Optics.* to change (an inverted image) to a normal position. **9.** to form (fol. by *into*): *to erect a territory into a state.* **10.** to set up or establish, as an institution; found. **11.** *Mach.* to assemble; make ready for use. [ME, t. L: s. *ērectus*, pp., set upright, built] —**erect′able,** *adj.* —**erect′er,** *n.* —**erect′ly,** *adv.* —**erect′ness,** *n.* —**Syn. 1.** standing, vertical. See **upright. 6.** upraise.

erectile (ĭ rĕk′tīl), *adj.* **1.** capable of being erected or set upright. **2.** *Anat.* susceptible of being distended with blood and becoming rigid, as tissue. —**erectility** (ĭ rĕk′tĭl′ĭ tĭ, ē′rĕk-), *n.*

erection (ĭ rĕk′shən), *n.* **1.** the act of erecting. **2.** the state of being erected. **3.** something erected, as a building or other structure. **4.** *Physiol.* a distended and rigid state of an organ or part containing erectile tissue.

erective (ĭ rĕk′tĭv), *adj.* tending to erect.

erector (ĭ rĕk′tə), *n.* **1.** one who or that which erects; erecter. **2.** *Anat.* a muscle which erects the body or one of its parts.

erelong (ĕə′lŏng′), *adv.* *Archaic.* before long; soon.

eremite (ĕ′rĭ mīt′), *n.* a religious solitary; a hermit. [ME, t. LL: m. *erēmīta*, t. Gk: m. *erēmítēs* HERMIT] —**eremitic** (ĕ′rĭ mĭt′ĭk), **er′emit′ical, eremitish** (ĕ′rĭmī′tĭsh), *adj.* —**eremitism** (e′rĭ mī tĭz′əm), *n.*

erenow (ĕə′nou′), *adv.* *Archaic.* before this time.

erepsin (ĭ rĕp′sĭn), *n.* *Biochem.* a mixture of proteolytic enzymes, consisting mainly of peptidases, produced by the wall of the small intestine of vertebrates.

erethism (ĕ′rĭ thĭz′əm), *n.* *Physiol.* an unusual or excessive degree of irritability or stimulation in an organ or tissue. [t. Gk: s. *erethismós* irritation] —**er′ethis′mic, er′ethist′ic, er′ethit′ic,** *adj.*

Erevan (*Russ.* yĭ rĭ văn′), *n.* Yerevan.

erewhile (ĕə wīl′), *adv.* *Archaic.* formerly.

erf (ĕəf), *n., pl.* **erven** (ĕə′vən), **erwe** (ĕə′və), **erfs.** *S African.* a plot of ground, the ownership of which may entail irrigation rights (**water erf**), or not (**dry erf**). [t. Afrikaans, t. D: lit., inheritance]

Erfurt (*Ger.* ĕr′fo͝ort), *n.* a town in SW East Germany. 189,770 (1964).

erg[1] (ûg), *n.* *Physics.* the unit of work or energy in the c.g.s. system, being the work done by a force of one dyne when its point of application moves through a distance of one centimetre. [t. Gk: s. *érgon* work. See WORK, n.]

erg[2] (ûg), *n.* *Geol.* any vast area covered with sand, as parts of the Sahara Desert. [t. F, ult. t. Hamitic]

ergo (û′gō), *conj., adv.* *Latin.* therefore; consequently.

ergograph (û′gə grăf′, -gräf′), *n.* an instrument that measures and records the amount of work done when a muscle contracts.

ergonomics (û′gə nŏm′ĭks), *n.* the study of the engineering aspects of the relationship between human workers and their working environment.

ergosterol (û gŏs′tə rōl′), *n. Biochem.* a sterol, $C_{28}H_{43}OH$, derived from ergot and contained in yeast and in small amounts in the fats of animals, converted into vitamin D by exposure to ultraviolet rays. [f. ERGO(T) + STEROL]

ergot (û′gət, -gŏt), *n.* **1.** a disease of rye and other cereals, due to a fungus (in rye, *Claviceps purpurea*) which replaces the grain by a long, hard, hornlike, dark-coloured body. **2.** a body so produced. **3.** the sclerotium of *C. purpurea*, developed on rye plants, and used medicinally as a haemostatic, etc. [t. F, in OF *argot* cock's spur]

ergotine (û′gə tĭn), *n.* a solid preparation or ergot obtained by precipitating the aqueous extract with alcohol and evaporating the filtrate.

ergotism (û′gə tĭz′əm), *n.* a disease due to eating food prepared from rye, etc., affected with ergot.

Erhard (ĕə′hät; *Ger.* ĕr′hȧrt), *n.* **Ludwig** (*Ger.* lōōt′vĭkh), born 1897, German statesman: federal chancellor of West Germany 1963–66.

eric (ĕ′rĭk), *n. Hist.* the fine paid by a murderer to his victim's family or friends in old Irish Law. Also, **eriach, erick.** [t. Ir.: m. *eiric*]

ericaceous (ĕ′rĭ kā′shəs), *adj.* belonging to the *Ericaceae*, or heath family of plants, which includes the heath, arbutus, azalea, rhododendron, American laurel, etc. [f. m. s. NL *Ericāceae* (der. *Erica* the heath genus, t. Gk: m. *ereikē* heath) + -OUS]

Ericsson (ĕ′rĭk sən), *n.* **1. John,** 1803–89, Swedish–American engineer and inventor. **2. Leif** (lēf; *Icel.* lĕyf), fl. A.D. 1000, a Scandinavian navigator (son of Eric the Red); probable discoverer of 'Vinland' or Nova Scotia.

Eric the Red (ĕ′rĭk), born about A.D. 950, Norseman who discovered Greenland about A.D. 982 and later colonized it. Also, **Eric.**

Eridanus (ĕ rĭd′ə nəs), *n. Astron.* a large southern constellation, also visible in the northern hemisphere, between Cetus and Orion, containing the bright star Achernar.

Erie (ĭə′rĭ), *n.* **1. Lake,** one of the five Great Lakes, between the U.S. and Canada: the southernmost and shallowest of the group. 239 mi. long; 9940 sq. mi. **2.** a port in the U.S., in NW Pennsylvania on Lake Erie. 138,440 (1960). **3.** a member of a tribe of American Indians formerly living along the southern shore of Lake Erie.

erigeron (ĭ rĭj′ə rən, -rĭg′-), *n.* any plant of the composite genus *Erigeron*, with flower heads resembling those of the asters but having narrower and usually more numerous (white or purple) rays. [t. L, t. Gk: groundsel]

Erin (ĭə′rĭn, ĕə′rĭn), *n. Poetic.* Ireland. [t. OIrish: m. *Erinn*, dat. of *Eriu*, later *Eire* Ireland]

erinaceous (ĕ′rĭ nā′shəs), *adj.* of the hedgehog kind or family.

eringo (ĭ rĭng′gō), *n.* eryngo.

Erinoid (ĕ′rĭ noid′), *n. Trademark.* a thermoplastic material made from casein and formaldehyde.

Erinys (ĭ rĭn′ĭs, ĭ rī′nĭs), *n., pl.* **Erinyes** (ĭ rĭn′ĭ ēz′). *Gk Myth.* one of the Furies.

Eris (ĕ′rĭs), *n. Gk Myth.* the goddess of discord, sister of Ares. See **apple of discord.**

eristic (ĕ rĭs′tĭk), *adj.* **1.** Also, **erist′ical.** pertaining to controversy or disputation; controversial. —*n.* **2.** one who engages in disputation; controversialist. **3.** the art of disputation. [t. Gk: m. s. *eristikós*, der. *erízein* wrangle]

Eritrea (ĕ′rĭ trā′ə; *It.* ĕ rē trĕ′ȧ), *n.* a former Italian colony in NE Africa, on the Red Sea: now an autonomous province federated with Ethiopia. 1,422,300 pop. (est. 1962); 47,076 sq. mi. *Cap.*: Asmara. —**Er′itre′an,** *adj., n.*

erk (ûk), *n. Slang.* **1.** a lower-deck naval rating. **2.** an aircraftman, the lowest rank in the Royal Air Force.

Erlander (*Sw.* är lȧn′dər), *n.* **Tage Fritiof** (*Sw.* tä′gə frē′tyŏf), born 1901, Swedish statesman: prime minister since 1946.

Erlangen (*Ger.* ĕr′lȧng ən), *n.* a town in SW West Germany. 80,300 (est. 1966).

Erlenmeyer flask (*Ger.* ĕr′lən mī′ər), a flat-bottomed, conical flask with a narrow neck, widely used in chemical laboratories. [named after E. *Erlenmeyer*, died 1909, German chemist]

erlking (ûl′kĭng′), *n.* (in German and Scandinavian mythology) a spirit or personified natural power which works mischief, esp. to children. [repr. G *Erlkönig* alderking, itself a mistrans. of Dan. *ellerkonge*, var. of *elverkonge* king of the elves]

ermine (û′mĭn), *n., pl.* **-mines,** (*esp. collectively*) **-mine. 1.** an Old World weasel, *Mustela erminea*, which turns white in winter. The brown summer phase is called the stoat. **2.** *U.S.* any of a number of weasels that are white in winter. **3.** the lustrous white winter fur of the ermine, having a black tail tip. **4.** the rank, office, or dignity of a king, nobleman, or judge, esp. one who wears a robe trimmed with ermine on ceremonial occasions. [ME, t. OF: m. (*h*)*ermine*, t. Gmc; cf. OHG *harmīn* pertaining to the ermine]

Ermine, *Mustela erminea* (Ab. 1 ft long)

ermined (û′mĭnd), *adj.* covered or adorned with ermine.

-ern, adj. suffix occurring in *northern*, etc. [ME and OE *-erne*, c. OHG *-rōni* (as in *nordrōni* northern)]

Ernakulam (ĕə nä′kōō ləm), *n.* a town in India, in central Kerala. 117,253 (1961).

erne (ûn), *n.* a sea-eagle. Also, **ern.** [ME; OE *earn*, c. MLG *arn* eagle]

Erne (ûn), *n.* **Lough** (lŏk, lŏkh), a lake of County Fermanagh, Northern Ireland, divided into **Upper Lough Erne** and **Lower Lough Erne,** together about 40 mi. long and averaging 5 mi. in width.

Ernie (û nĭ), *n.* (in Great Britain) Electronic Random Number Indicator Equipment; a computer used for selecting premium-bond prize-winning numbers.

Ernst (ûnst; *Ger.* ĕrnst), *n.* **Max** (măks; *Ger.* mȧks), born 1891, German painter.

erode (ĭ rōd′), *v.t.,* **eroded, eroding. 1.** to eat out or away; destroy by slow consumption. **2.** to form (a channel, etc.) by eating or wearing away (used esp. in geology, to denote the action of all the forces of nature that wear away the earth's surface). [t. L: m. s. *ērōdere* gnaw off]

erodent (ĭ rō′dnt), *adj.* eroding; erosive: *the erodent power of wind.*

erogenous (ĭ rŏj′ĭ nəs), *adj.* arousing or tending to arouse sexual desire. Also, **erogenic** (ĕ′rə jĕn′ĭk). —**erogeneity** (ĕ′rə jĭ nē′ĭ tĭ), *n.*

Eros (ĭə′rŏs, ĕ′rŏs), *n.* the Greek god of love, identified by the Romans with Cupid. [t. L, t. Gk: lit., love]

erose (ĭ rōs′), *adj.* **1.** uneven as if gnawed away. **2.** *Bot.* having the margin irregularly incised as if gnawed, as a leaf. [t. L: m. s. *ērōsus*, pp., gnawed off]

erosion (ĭ rō′zhən), *n.* **1.** the act of eroding. **2.** the state of being eroded. **3.** the process by which the surface of the earth is worn away by the action of water, glaciers, winds, waves, etc.

Erosion
Section of stratified rock bent into a low anticline by erosion

erosive (ĭ rō′sĭv), *adj.* serving to erode; causing erosion.

erotic (ĭ rŏt′ĭk), *adj.* **1.** of or pertaining to sexual love; amatory. **2.** arousing or satisfying sexual desire. **3.** subject to or marked by strong sexual desires. —*n.* **4.** an erotic poem. **5.** an erotic person. [t. Gk: m. s. *erōtikós* pertaining to love. See EROS] —**erot′ically,** *adv.*

erotica (ĭ rŏt′ĭ kə), *n.* literature or art dealing with sexual love.

eroticism (ĭ rŏt′ĭ sĭz′əm), *n.* **1.** erotic character or tendency. **2.** *Psychol.* morbid sexual desires or instincts.

erotism (ĕ′rə tĭz′əm), *n. Psychol.* the arousal and satisfaction of sexual desires.

erotomania (ĭ rŏt′ō mā′nyə), *n. Psychol.* abnormally strong or persistent sexual desire. —**erot′oma′niac,** *n.*

err (û), *v.i.* **1.** to go astray in thought or belief; be mistaken; be incorrect. **2.** to go astray morally; sin. **3.** to deviate from the true course, aim, or purpose. [ME *erre(n)*, t. OF: m. *errer*, t. L: m. *errāre* wander]

errand (ĕ′rənd), *n.* **1.** a trip to convey a message or execute a commission; a short journey for a specific purpose: *he was sent on an errand.* **2.** a special business entrusted to a messenger; a commission. **3.** the purpose of any trip or journey: *his errand was to bribe the chieftain into releasing the captives.* [ME; OE *ærende*, c. OHG *ārunti*. Cf. OE *ār* messenger]

errant (ĕ′rənt), *adj.* **1.** journeying or travelling, as a medieval knight in quest of adventure; roving adventurously. **2.** deviating from the regular or proper course; erring. **3.** moving in an aimless or quickly changing manner. [ME *erraunte*, t. F: m. *errant*, prop. ppr. of *errer*, OF *esrer* travel (g. VL *iterāre* journey), but b. with F *errant*, ppr. of *errer* ERR] —**er′rantly,** *adv.*

errantry (ĕ′rən trĭ), *n., pl.* **-tries.** conduct or performance like that of a knight-errant.

errare humanum est (ĕ rä′rĭ hōō mä′nōōm ĕst′), *Latin.* to err is human.

errata (ĭ rä′tə), *n.* pl. of **erratum.**

erratic (ĭ răt′ĭk), *adj.* **1.** deviating from the proper or usual course in conduct or opinion; eccentric. **2.** having no certain course; wandering; not fixed: *erratic winds.* **3.** *Geol.* **a.** (of boulders, etc.) transported from the original site to an unusual location, as by glacial action. **b.** pertaining to such boulders, etc. —*n.* **4.** an erratic or eccentric person. **5.** *Geol.* an erratic boulder or block of rock. [ME, t. L: s. *errāticus*, der. *errāre* wander, ERR] —**errat′ically,** *adv.*

erratum (ĭ rā′təm), *n.*, *pl.* **-ta** (-tə). an error in writing or printing. [t. L: prop. pp. neut., erred]

errhine (ĕ′rīn, ĕ′rĭn), *Med.* —*adj.* **1.** designed to be snuffed into the nose. **2.** occasioning discharges from the nose. —*n.* **3.** a medicine to be snuffed up the nostrils to promote sneezing and increased discharges. [t. NL: m. s. *errhīnum*, t. Gk: m. *érrhīnon*, der. *en-* EN-² + *rhís* nose]

erring (ûr′rĭng), *adj.* **1.** going astray; in error; wrong. **2.** sinning. —**err′ingly,** *adv.*

erron., **1.** erroneous. **2.** erroneously.

erroneous (ĭ rō′nyəs), *adj.* **1.** containing error; mistaken; incorrect. **2.** *Obs. or Archaic.* straying from the right. [ME, t. L: m. *errōneus* straying] —**erro′neously,** *adv.* —**erro′neousness,** *n.* —**Syn. 1.** inaccurate, wrong, untrue, false.

error (ĕ′rə), *n.* **1.** deviation from accuracy or correctness; a mistake, as in action, speech, etc. **2.** belief in something untrue, the holding of mistaken opinions. **3.** the condition of believing what is not true: *in error about the date.* **4.** a moral offence; wrongdoing. **5.** *Maths., etc.* the difference between the observed or approximately determined value and the true value of a quantity. [t. L: r. ME *errour*, t. OF] —**er′rorless,** *adj.* —**Syn. 1.** blunder, slip, oversight. See **mistake.**

error of closure, *Survey.* **1.** the amount by which a closed traverse fails to satisfy the requirements of a true mathematical figure, as the length of line joining the true and computed position of the same point. **2.** the ratio of this linear error to the perimeter of the traverse. **3.** (for angles) the amount by which the sum of the observed angles fails to equal the true sum. **4.** (in levelling) the amount by which an elevation determined by a series of levels fails to agree with an established elevation.

ersatz (ĕə′zăts, û′-), *adj.* **1.** serving as a substitute: *an ersatz meat dish made of aubergine and oatmeal.* —*n.* **2.** a substitute. [t. G]

Erse (ûs), *n.* **1.** Gaelic, esp. Scottish Gaelic. —*adj.* **2.** of or pertaining to the Celts in the Highlands of Scotland, of their language. [Scot. var. of IRISH]

Erskine (û′skĭn), *n.* **John,** 1695–1768, Scottish writer on law.

erst (ûst), *adv. Archaic.* before the present time; formerly. [ME; OE *ǣrst*, syncopated var. of *ǣrest* (c. G *erst*), superl. of *ǣr*. See ERE]

erstwhile (ûst′wīl′), *adj.* **1.** former: *erstwhile enemies.* —*adv.* **2.** *Archaic.* formerly; erst.

erubescent (ĕ′ro͞o bĕs′ənt), *adj.* becoming red or reddish; blushing. [t. L: s. *ērubescens*, ppr., reddening] —**e′rubes′cence,** *n.*

eruct (ĭ rŭkt′), *v.t., v.i.* **1.** to belch forth, as wind from the stomach. **2.** to emit or issue violently, as matter from a volcano. [t. L: s. *ēructāre* belch forth]

eructate (ĭ rŭk′tāt), *v.t., v.i.,* **-tated, -tating.** eruct. —**eructation** (ĭ rŭk′tā′shən, ē′rŭk-), *n.*

erudite (ĕ′ro͞o dīt′), *adj.* characterized by erudition; learned or scholarly: *an erudite professor, an erudite commentary.* [t. L: m. s. *ērudītus*, pp., instructed] —**e′rudite′ly,** *adv.* —**e′rudite′ness,** *n.*

erudition (ĕ′ro͞o dĭsh′ən), *n.* acquired knowledge, esp. in literature, languages, history, etc.; learning; scholarship. —**Syn.** See **learning.**

erumpent (ĭ rŭm′pənt), *adj.* **1.** bursting forth. **2.** *Bot.* prominent, as if bursting through the epidermis.

erupt (ĭ rŭpt′), *v.i.* **1.** to burst forth, as volcanic matter. **2.** (of a volcano, geyser, etc.) to eject matter. **3.** (of teeth) to break through surrounding hard and soft tissues and become visible in the mouth. **4.** to break out suddenly or violently, as if from restraint. **5.** to break out with or as with a skin rash. —*v.t.* **6.** to cause to burst forth. **7.** (of a volcano, etc.) to eject (matter). [t. L: s. *ēruptus*, pp.] —**erup′tible,** *adj.*

eruption (ĭ rŭp′shən), *n.* **1.** an issuing forth suddenly and violently; an outburst; an outbreak. **2.** *Geol.* the ejection of molten rock, water, etc., as from a volcano, geyser, etc. **3.** that which is erupted or ejected, as molten rock, etc. **4.** *Pathol.* **a.** the breaking out of a rash or the like. **b.** a rash or exanthema. [t. L: s. *ēruptio*] —**erup′tional,** *adj.*

eruptive (ĭ rŭp′tĭv), *adj.* **1.** bursting forth, or tending to burst forth. **2.** pertaining to or of the nature of an eruption. **3.** *Geol.* (of rocks) formed by the eruption of molten material. **4.** *Pathol.* causing or attended with an eruption or rash. —*n.* **5.** *Geol.* an eruptive rock.

Ervine (û′vĭn), *n.* **St John (Greer)** (sĭn′ jən grĭə′), 1883–1971. Irish dramatist and novelist.

-ery, a suffix of nouns denoting occupation, business, calling, or condition, place or establishment, goods or products, things collectively, qualities, actions, etc., as in *archery, bakery, cutlery, fishery, grocery, nunnery, pottery, finery, foolery, prudery, scenery, tracery, trickery, witchery.* [ME, t. OF: m. *-erie*, f. *-ier* -ER² + *-ie* -Y³]

Erymanthian boar (ĕ′rĭ măn′thĭ ən), *Gk Legend.* a savage beast fabled to have infested Arcadia and to have been caught by Hercules.

eryngo (ĭ rĭng′gō), *n.*, *pl.* **-goes.** any plant of the umbelliferous genus *Eryngium*, consisting of coarse herbs, as *E. maritimum*, the sea holly. Also, **eringo.** [t. It.: m. *eringio*, der. L *ēryngion*, t. Gk., dim. of *ḗryngos*]

erysipelas (ĕ′rĭ sĭp′ĭ ləs), *n. Pathol.* an acute, febrile, infectious disease, due to a specific streptococcus, and characterized by diffusely spreading, deep red inflammation of the skin or mucous membranes. [t. L, t. Gk; r. ME *herisipila*, etc., t. ML] —**erysipelatous** (ĕ′rĭ sĭ-pĕl′ə təs), *adj.*

erysipeloid (ĕ′rĭ sĭp′ĭ loid′), *n. Pathol.* a disease of man contracted by contact with the bacillus *Erysipelothrix rhusiopathiae* that causes erysipelas in swine: characterized by a painful local ulcer, generally on one of the hands.

erythema (ĕ′rĭ thē′mə), *n. Pathol.* abnormal redness of the skin due to local congestion, as in inflammation. [NL, t. Gk: redness or flush] —**erythematic** (ĕ′rĭ thĭ-măt′ĭk), **erythematous** (ĕ′rĭ thē′mə təs), *adj.*

erythrism (ĭ rĭth′rĭz′əm), *n.* abnormal redness, as of plumage or hair. —**erythrismal** (ĕ′rĭ thrĭz′məl), *adj.*

erythrite (ĭ rĭth′rīt), *n.* **1.** cobalt bloom. **2.** erythritol.

erythritol (ĭ rĭth′rĭ tŏl′), *n. Chem.* a tetrahydric crystalline alcohol $(CH_2OHCHOH)_2$, related to carbohydrates, derived from certain lichens.

erythro-, a word element meaning 'red', as in *erythrocyte.* Also, **erythr-.** [t. Gk, comb. form of *erythrós*]

erythroblast (ĭ rĭth′rō blăst′), *n. Anat.* a nucleated cell in the bone marrow from which red blood cells develop.

erythrocyte (ĭ rĭth′rō sīt′), *n. Anat.* one of the red corpuscles of the blood.

erythrocytometer (ĭ rĭth′rō sī tŏm′ĭ tə), *n.* a laboratory instrument using the light diffraction principle to measure the diameter of red cells (or other microscopic particles) in a thin film.

erythroderma (ĭ rĭth′rō dû′mə), *n. Pathol.* abnormal redness of skin.

erythrogenesis (ĭ rĭth′rō jĕn′ĭ sĭs), *n. Physiol.* the production of erythrocytes; erythropoiesis.

erythromycin (ĭ rĭth′rō mī′sĭn), *n. Med.* an antibiotic effective against diseases caused by bacteria, including several against which penicillin is ineffective. Its use is reserved for the treatment of resistant staphylococcal infections.

erythrophobia (ĭ rĭth′rō fō′byə), *n.* **1.** *Pathol.* morbid flushing. **2.** *Psychol.* morbid aversion to red.

erythropoiesis (ĭ rĭth′rō poi ē′sĭs), *n. Physiol.* the formation of erythrocytes. —**eryth′ropoiet′ic,** *adj.*

Erz Gebirge (*Ger.* ĕrts′gə bĭr gə), a mountain range on the boundary between East Germany and NW Czechoslovakia. Highest point, Keilberg, 4080 ft. See map under **Moravian Gate.**

Erzurum (*Turk.* ĕr′zo͞o ro͞om), *n.* a town in NE Turkey. 90,069 (1960). Also, **Er′zerum.**

es-. For words with initial **es-**, see also **aes-** and **oes-.**

-es, a variant of **-s²** and **-s³** after *s, z, ch, sh*, and in those nouns ending in *-f* which have *-v-* in the plural. Cf. **-ies.**

Esau (ē′sô), *n. Bible.* a son of Isaac, the elder twin brother of Jacob, to whom he sold his birthright. Gen. 25:21–25.

Esbjerg (*Dan.* ĕs′byĕr), *n.* a seaport in SW Denmark. 55,171 (1960).

Esbo (*Sw.* ĕs′bo͞o), *n.* Swedish name of **Espoo.**

escadrille (ĕs′kə drĭl′; *Fr.* ĕs kȧ drēy′), *n.* **1.** a small naval squadron. **2.** *U.S.* a squadron or divisional unit of aeroplanes: *the Lafayette Escadrille of World War I.* [t. F, t. Sp.: m. *escadrilla*, dim. of *escuadra* squadron, t. It.: m. *squadra* square, der. *squadrare* to square, g. L *exquadrāre*]

escalade (ĕs′kə lād′), *n.*, *v.*, **-laded, -lading.** —*n.* **1.** a scaling or mounting by means of ladders, esp. in an assault upon a fortified place. —*v.t.* **2.** to mount, pass, or enter by means of ladders. [t. F, t. It.: m. *scalata*, der. *scalare* climb, der. *scala* steps, SCALE³] —**es′calad′er,** *n.*

escalate (ĕs′kə lāt′), *v.t., v.i.,* **-lated, -lating.** to increase in intensity, magnitude, etc.; increase by stages. [back-formation from ESCALATOR] —**es′cala′tion,** *n.*

escalator (ĕs′kə lā′tə), *n.* a continuously moving staircase for carrying passengers up or down. [b. ESCALADE and ELEVATOR]

escalator clause, a provision in a contract allowing for an adjustment up or down under specific conditions, as in the cost of living in a wage agreement.

escallop (ĕs kŏl′əp, ĕs kăl′-), *n.* **1.** *Her.* a decoration in the form of a scallop-shell. —*v.t.* **2.** to scallop (def. 7).

escalope (ĕs′kə lŏp′), *n.* a thin slice of veal, pork, or beef coated in egg and breadcrumbs and fried.

escapade (ĕs′kə pād′, ĕs′kə pād′), *n.* **1.** a reckless proceeding; a wild prank. **2.** an escape from confinement or restraint. [t. F, t. Sp.: m. *escapada*, der. *escapar* escape, or t. It.: m. *scappata* (der. *scappare*)]

escape (ĭs kāp′), *v.*, **-caped, -caping,** *n.* —*v.i.* **1.** to slip or get away, as from confinement or restraint; gain or regain liberty. **2.** to slip away from pursuit or peril; avoid capture, punishment, or any threatened evil. **3.** to issue from a confining enclosure, as a fluid. **4.** *Bot.* (of an introduced plant) to grow wild. —*v.t.* **5.** to slip away from or elude (pursuers, captors, etc.). **6.** to succeed in avoiding (any threatened or possible danger or evil). **7.** to elude (notice, search, etc.). **8.** to fail to be noticed or recollected by (a person). **9.** to slip from (a person) inadvertently, as a remark. —*n.* **10.** an act or instance of escaping. **11.** the fact of having escaped. **12.** a means of escaping: *a fire escape.* **13.** avoidance of reality. **14.** leakage, as of water, gas, etc. **15.** *Bot.* a plant originally cultivated, now growing wild. [ME *escape(n)*, t. ONF: m. *escaper*, der. L: *ex-* EX-¹ + *cappa* cloak] —**escap′able,** *adj.* —**escap′ee′,** *n.* —**escape′less,** *adj.* —**escap′er,** *n.*

—**Syn. 1.** flee, abscond, decamp. **5.** shun, fly. ESCAPE, ELUDE, EVADE mean to keep free of something. To ESCAPE is to succeed in keeping away from danger, pursuit, observation, etc.: *to escape punishment.* To ELUDE implies slipping through an apparently tight net, thus avoiding, often by a narrow margin, whatever threatens; it implies, also, using vigilance, adroitness, dexterity, or slyness, so as to baffle or foil: *a fox managed to elude the hounds.* To EVADE is to turn aside from or go out of reach of a person or thing (at least temporarily), usually by using artifice or stratagem to direct attention elsewhere: *to evade the issue.* See **avoid.**

escape lock, Davis apparatus.

escape mechanism, *Psychol.* a means of avoiding unpleasant realities, as daydreaming.

escapement (ĭs kāp′mənt), *n.* **1.** *Archaic.* **a.** an act of escaping. **b.** a way of escape; an outlet. **2.** *Horol.* the portion of a watch or clock which measures beats and controls the speed of the time train. **3.** a mechanism consisting of a notched wheel and ratchet for regulating the motion of a typewriter carriage.

Escapements (def. 2) A, Anchor escapement; B, Deadbeat escapement

escape velocity, *Aerospace.* the minimum velocity that a body needs in order to overcome the gravitational field of a planet or satellite.

escape wheel, *Horol.* a revolving toothed wheel which transmits impulses to a vibrating fork. Also, **scapewheel.**

escapism (ĭs kā′pĭz′əm), *n.* the avoidance of reality by absorption of the mind in entertainment, or in an imaginative situation, activity, etc. —**escap′ist,** *adj.*, *n.*

escapology (ĕs′kə pŏl′ə jĭ), *n.* the technique of escaping from a confining device, prison, etc. —**es′capol′ogist,** *n.*

escargot (*Fr.* ĕs kȧr gō′), *n. French.* an edible snail.

escarp (ĭs kärp′), *n.* **1.** *Fort.* the inner slope or wall of the ditch surrounding a rampart. **2.** any similar steep slope. —*v.t.* **3.** to make into an escarp; give a steep slope to; furnish with escarps. [t. F: m. *escarpe*, t. It.: m. *scarpa*, of Gmc orig. See SHARP, and cf. SCARP]

escarpment (ĭs kärp′mənt), *n.* **1.** a long, cliff-like ridge of rock, or the like, commonly formed by faulting or fracturing of the earth's crust. **2.** ground cut into an escarp about a fortification or defensive position.

Escaut (*Fr.* ĕs kō′), *n.* French name of **Scheldt.**

-esce, a suffix of verbs meaning to begin to be or do something, become, grow, or be somewhat (as indicated by the rest of the word), as in *convalesce, putresce.* [t. L: m. s. *-escere*, with inchoative force]

-escence, a suffix of nouns denoting action or process, change, state, or condition, etc., and corresponding to verbs ending in *-esce* or adjectives ending in *-escent*, as in *convalescence, deliquescence, luminescence, recrudescence.* [t. L: m. s. *-escentia.* See -ESCE, -ENCE]

-escent, a suffix of adjectives meaning beginning to be or do something, becoming or being somewhat (as indicated), as in *convalescent, deliquescent, recrudescent*: often associated with verbs ending in *-esce* or nouns ending in *-escence.* [t. L: s. *-escens*, ppr. ending]

eschalot (ĕsh′ə lŏt′, ĕsh′ə lŏt′), *n.* shallot.

eschar (ĕs′kä), *n. Pathol.* a hard crust or scab, as from a burn. [t. LL: s. *eschara*, t. Gk: hearth, scar]

escharotic (ĕs′kə rŏt′ĭk), *Med.* —*adj.* **1.** producing an eschar, as a medicinal substance; caustic. —*n.* **2.** a caustic application. [t. LL: s. *escharōticus*, t. Gk: m. *escharōtikós*]

eschatology (ĕs′kə tŏl′ə jĭ), *n. Theol.* **1.** the doctrines of the last or final things, as death, the judgement, the future state, etc. **2.** the branch of theology dealing with them. [f. Gk *éschato(s)* last + -LOGY] —**eschatological** (ĕs′kətə lŏj′ĭ kl), *adj.* —**es′chatol′ogist,** *n.*

escheat (ĭs chēt′), *n. Law.* **1.** the reversion of property to the owner or to the crown when there is a failure of persons legally qualified to inherit or to claim. **2.** property or a possession which reverts by escheat. **3.** the right to take property subject to escheat. —*v.i.* **4.** to revert by escheat, as to the crown or the state. —*v.t.* **5.** to make an escheat of; confiscate. [ME *eschette*, t. OF, der. *escheoir* fall to one's share, f. *es-* EX-¹ + *cheoir* (g. L *cadere* fall)] —**escheat′able,** *adj.* —**escheat′ment,** *n.*

escheatage (ĭs chē′tĭj), *n.* the right of succeeding to an escheat.

escheator (ĭs chē′tə), *n.* an officer in charge of escheats.

Eschenbach (*Ger.* ĕsh′ən bȧKH), *n.* See **Wolfram von Eschenbach.**

eschew (ĭs chōō′), *v.t.* to abstain from; shun; avoid: *to eschew evil.* [ME *eschewen*, t. OF: m. *eschiver*, ult. t. Gmc; cf. SHY and see SKEW] —**eschew′al,** *n.* —**eschew′er,** *n.*

eschscholtzia (ĭs kŏl′shə), *n. Bot.* a genus of papaveraceous herbs of western North America, esp. the commonly cultivated Californian poppy.

Escorial (ĕs′kō rĭ äl′, ĕs kô′rĭ əl; *Sp.* ĕs kō ryäl′), *n.* a famous building in central Spain, 27 miles NW of Madrid, containing a monastery, palace, church, and mausoleum of the Spanish sovereigns: erected 1563–84. Also, **Escurial.** [t. Sp.: lit., a refuse heap, der. *escoria*, t. L: m. *scōria*]

escort (*n.* ĕs′kôt; *v.* ĭs kôt′), *n.* **1.** a body of persons, or a single person, ship or ships, etc., accompanying another or others for protection, guidance, or courtesy. **2.** an armed guard. **3.** protection, safeguard, or guidance on a journey. —*v.t.* **4.** to attend or accompany as an escort. [t. F: m. *escorta*, t. It.: m. *scorta*, der. *scorgere* guide, f. *s-* (g. L *ex-*) + *-corgere* (g. L *corrigere* correct)] —**Syn. 4.** conduct, usher, guard, convoy. See **accompany.**

escribe (ĭ skrīb′), *v.t.*, **escribed, escribing.** *Geom.* to draw (a circle) touching one side of a triangle externally and the other two sides internally.

escritoire (ĕs′krĭ twä′), *n.* a writing desk. [t. F, g. LL *scriptōria*, for *scriptōrium.* See SCRIPTORIUM]

escrow (ĕs′krō, ĕs krō′), *n. Law.* a contract, deed, bond, or other written agreement deposited with a third person, by whom it is to be delivered to the grantee or promisee on the fulfilment of some condition. [t. AF: m. *escrowe*, OF *escroe* piece of cloth, parchment, SCROLL; of Gmc orig.; akin to SHRED]

escuage (ĕs′kyōō ĭj), *n. Feudal Law.* scutage. [t. AF, der. OF *escu*, g. L *scūtum* shield]

escudo (ĕs kōō′dō; *Port.* ĭsh kōō′dōō), *n.*, *pl.* **-dos** (-dōz; *Port.* -dōōs). **1.** the monetary unit of Portugal, equal to 100 centavos, and equivalent to about £0·0145 sterling. *Abbrev.:* Esc. 1$00. **2.** a coin of this value. **3.** the monetary unit of Chile, equivalent to about £0·066 sterling. *Abbrev.:* E. **4.** a banknote of this value. **5.** any of various former gold and silver coins of Spain, Spanish America, and Portugal. [t. Sp., Pg., g. L *scūtum* shield. Cf. ECU, SCUDO]

escuerzo (ĕs kwĕə′zō), *n.* a large frog of the genus *Ceratophrys* living in and around the Amazon basin.

esculent (ĕs′kyōō lənt), *adj.* **1.** suitable for use as food; edible. —*n.* **2.** something edible, esp. a vegetable. [t. L: s. *ēsculentus* good to eat]

Escurial (ĕs kyōōə′rĭ äl′, ĕs kyōōə′rĭ əl). *n.* Escorial.

escutcheon (ĭs kŭch′ən), *n.* **1.** the shield or shield-shaped surface, on which armorial bearings are depicted. **2. blot on the escutcheon,** a stain on one's honour or reputation. **3.** a plate for protecting the keyhole of a door, or to which the handle is attached. **4.** the panel on a ship's stern bearing her name. [t. ONF: m. *escuchon*, ult. der. L *scūtum* shield] —**escutch′eoned,** *adj.*

Escutcheon A, Dexter chief; B, Middle chief; C, Sinister chief; D, Honour point; E, Fess point; F, Nombril point; G, Dexter base; H, Middle base; I, Sinister base

escutcheon of pretence, an escutcheon bearing the family arms of an heiress placed in the centre of her husband's coat of arms.

Esd., Esdras (Apocrypha).

Esdraelon (ĕz′drā ē′lŏn), *n.* a plain in N Palestine (now in Israel): the site of many ancient battles. Also, **Plain of Jezreel.** See **Megiddo.**

Esdras (ĕz′drăs), *n.* either of the first two books of the Apocrypha.

-ese, a noun and adjective suffix referring to locality, nationality, language, literary style, etc., as in *Bengalese, journalese.* [t. OF: m. *-eis,* g. L *-ēnsis*]

ESE, east-south-east. Also, **E.S.E.**

Esher (ē′shə), *n.* a town in England, in Surrey. 60,610 (1961).

Eshkol (ĕsh′kŏl), *n.* **Levi** (lē′vī), 1895–1969, prime minister of Israel 1963–69.

esker (ĕs′kə), *n. Geol.* a serpentine ridge of gravelly and sandy drift, believed to have been formed by streams under or in glacial ice; ås. Also, **eskar** (ĕs′kä, -kə). [t. Irish: m. *eiscir*]

Eskilstuna (*Sw.* ĕs′kēl stʏ nä), *n.* a town in SE Sweden. 62,428 (1964).

Eskimo (ĕs′kĭ mō′), *n., pl.* **-mos, -mo,** *adj.* —*n.* **1.** one of a race or people, characterized by short stature, muscular build, light brown complexion, and broad, flat face, inhabiting areas of Greenland, northern Canada, Alaska, and north-eastern Siberia. **2.** their language, of Eskimoan stock. —*adj.* **3.** of or pertaining to the Eskimos or their language. Also, **Esquimau.** [t. Dan., t. F: m. *Esquimaux* (pl.), t. N Amer. Ind.: m. Algonquian name for the people, meaning eaters of raw flesh; cf. Abnaki *eskimantsiš,* Ojibwa *aškimek.* Cf. *Innuit* men, name applied by Eskimos to themselves]

Eskimoan (ĕs′kĭ mō′ən), *adj.* **1.** of or pertaining to the Eskimos or their language. —*n.* **2.** a linguistic stock including Eskimo and Aleut. Also, **Es′kimau′an.**

Eskimo dog, one of a breed of strong dogs used by the Eskimos to draw sledges.

Eskisehir (*Turk.* ĕs kē′shĕ hēr), *n.* a town in W Turkey. 153,096 (1960). Also, **Eskishehir.**

ESN, educationally subnormal: a term applied to children considerably below the median intelligence.

esophageal (ē sŏf′ə jē′əl), *adj. U.S.* oesophageal.

esophagus (ē sŏf′ə gəs), *n., pl.* **-gi** (-gī′). *U.S.* oesophagus.

esoteric (ĕs′ō tĕ′rĭk), *adj.* **1.** understood by or meant for a select few; profound; recondite. **2.** belonging to the select few. **3.** private; secret; confidential. **4.** (of philosophical doctrine, etc.) intended to be communicated only to the initiated (orig. applied to certain writings of Aristotle, and afterwards to the secret teachings of Pythagoras). [t. Gk: m. s. *esōterikós* inner] —**es′oter′ically,** *adv.* —**es′oter′icism, esotery** (ĕs′ə tə rĭ), *n.*

ESP, extrasensory perception; perception or communication outside of normal sensory activity, as in telepathy and clairvoyance. Also, **e.s.p.**

esp., especially.

espadrille (ĕs′pə drĭl′), *n.* a rope-soled sandal. [t. F, t. Pr.: m. *espardilho,* dim. of *espart* ESPARTO]

espalier (ĭs păl′yə), *n.* **1.** a trellis or framework on which fruit trees or shrubs are trained to grow flat. **2.** a tree or plants so trained. —*v.t.* **3.** to train on an espalier. **4.** to furnish with an espalier. [t. F, t. It.: m. *spalliera* support, der. *spalia* shoulder]

España (*Sp.* ĕs pä′nyä), *n.* Spanish name of **Spain.**

Espartero (*Sp.* ĕs pär tĕ′rō), *n.* **Joaquín Baldomero** (*Sp.* KHwä kēn′ bäl dō mĕ′rō), 1792–1879, Spanish general and statesman.

esparto (ĕs pä′tō), *n.* any of several grasses, esp. *Stipa tenacissima,* of S Europe and N Africa, used for making paper, cordage, etc. Also, **esparto grass.** [t. Sp., g. L *spartum,* t. Gk: m. *spárton* a rope made of *spártos* a broomlike plant]

espec., especially.

especial (ĭs pĕsh′əl), *adj.* **1.** special; exceptional; outstanding: *of no especial importance, an especial friend.* **2.** of a particular kind, or peculiar to a particular one: *your especial case.* [ME, t. OF, t. L: m. s. *speciālis* pertaining to a particular kind]

especially (ĭs pĕsh′ə lĭ), *adv.* particularly; principally; unusually: *be especially watchful.*

—**Syn.** ESPECIALLY, CHIEFLY, PARTICULARLY, PRINCIPALLY refer to those cases of a class or kind which seem to be significant. ESPECIALLY and PARTICULARLY single out the most prominent case or example (often in order to particularize a general statement): *winter is especially severe on old people; corn grows well in Lincolnshire, particularly in the south.* CHIEFLY and PRINCIPALLY imply that the general statement applies to a majority of the cases in question, and have a somewhat comparative force: *owls fly chiefly at night, crime occurs principally in large cities.*

esperance (ĕs′pə rəns), *n. Obs.* hope. [ME *esperaunce,* t. OF: m. *esperance,* der. *esperer,* g. L *spērāre* hope]

Esperanto (ĕs′pə răn′tō), *n.* an artificial language invented in 1887 by L. L. Zamenhof and intended for international auxiliary use. It is based on the commonest words in the most important European languages. [t. Sp.: m. *esperanza* hope, used by Zamenhof as a pseudonym] —**Es′peran′tist,** *n., adj.*

espial (ĭs pī′əl), *n.* **1.** the act of spying or espying. **2.** keeping watch; observation.

espiègle (*Fr.* ĕs pyĕ′gl), *adj. French.* roguish; playful. [F, alter. of *Ulespiegel,* t. D or G: m. (TILL) *Uilenspiegel* or EULENSPIEGEL]

espièglerie (*Fr.* ĕs pyĕ glə rē′), *n. French.* a roguish or playful trick. [F, der. *espiègle* ESPIEGLE]

espionage (ĕs′pĭ ə nĭj, ĭ spī′-, ĕs′pĭ ə näzh′, ĕs′pĭ ə näzh′), *n.* **1.** the practice of spying on others. **2.** the systematic use of spies by a government to discover the military and political secrets of other nations. [t. F: m. *espionnage,* der. *espionner* spy upon, der. *espion* spy, t. It.: m. *spione,* aug. of *spia,* t. Gmc; cf. G *spähen* to scout, reconnoitre]

esplanade (ĕs′plə nād′), *n.* any open, level space serving for public walks or drives, esp. one by the sea. [t. F, t. Sp.: m. *esplanada,* der. *esplanar,* g. L *explānāre* to level]

Espoo (*Finn.* ĕs′pô), *n.* a town in Finland, 10 mi. W of Helsinki. 74,741 (1965). Swedish, **Esbo.**

espousal (ĭs pou′zəl), *n.* **1.** adoption or advocacy, as of a cause or principle. **2.** (*sometimes pl.*) a marriage (or sometimes an engagement) ceremony. [ME *espousaile,* t. OF, g. L *spōnsālia,* neut. pl. of *spōnsālis* pertaining to betrothal]

espouse (ĭs pouz′), *v.t.,* **-poused, -pousing. 1.** to make one's own, adopt, or embrace, as a cause. **2.** to take in marriage; marry. **3.** *Obs.* to give (a woman) in marriage. [t. MF: m. s. *espouser,* g. L *spōnsāre* betroth, espouse] —**espous′er,** *n.*

espresso (ĕs prĕs′ō), *n.* coffee made by forcing live steam under pressure or boiling water through ground coffee beans.

espresso bar, a coffee bar serving espresso coffee.

esprit (ĕs′prē; *Fr.* ĕs prē′), *n. French.* wit; sprightliness; lively intelligence. [F, t. L: m. s. *spīritus* SPIRIT]

esprit de corps (ĕs′prē də kô′; *Fr.* ĕs prēd kŏr′), *French.* a sense of union and of common interests and responsibilities, as developed among a group of persons associated together.

espy (ĭs pī′), *v.t.,* **-pied, -pying.** to see at a distance; catch sight of; detect. [ME *espy(en),* t. OF: m. *espier,* ult. t. Gmc; cf. G *spähen* to scout, reconnoitre] —**espi′er,** *n.* —**Syn.** discern, descry, discover, perceive, make out (def. 3).

Esq., Esquire.

-esque, an adjective suffix indicating style, manner, or distinctive character, as in *arabesque, picturesque, statuesque.* [t. F, t. It.: m. *-esco;* of Gmc orig. Cf. -ISH[1]]

Esquiline (ĕs′kwĭ līn′), *n.* one of the Seven Hills on which ancient Rome was built. [t. L: m. s. *Esquilīnus* (sc. *mons* hill)]

Esquimau (ĕs′kĭ mō′), *n., pl.* **-maux** (-mō′, -mōz′), *adj.* Eskimo. [t. F]

esquire (ĭs kwī′ə), *n., v.,* **-quired, -quiring.** —*n.* **1.** a polite title (usually abbreviated to *Esq.*) after a man's last name (*Mr* or *Dr* is omitted when it is used): *John Smith, Esq.* **2.** (in the Middle Ages) a squire, or aspirant to knighthood, attendant upon a knight. **3.** a man belonging to the order of English gentry ranking next below a knight. **4.** *Archaic.* an English country squire. —*v.t.* **5.** to raise to the rank of esquire. **6.** to address as 'Esquire'. [ME *esquier,* t. OF, g. LL *scūtārius* shield-bearer, der. L *scūtum* shield]

ESRO (ĕz′rō), *n.* European Space Research Organization.

ess (ĕs), *n.* **1.** the letter S, s. **2.** something shaped like an S.

-ess, a suffix forming distinctively feminine nouns, as *countess, hostess, lioness.* [t. F: m. *-esse,* g. L *-issa,* t. Gk]

essay (*n.* ĕs′ā for *1;* ĕs′ā, ĕ sā′ *for 2, 3; v.* ĕ sā′), *n.* **1.** a short literary composition on a particular subject. **2.** an effort to perform or accomplish something; an attempt. **3.** *Obs.* a tentative effort. —*v.t.* **4.** to try; attempt. **5.** to put to the test; make trial of. [t. MF: m. *essai,* g. LL *exagium* a weighing. Cf ASSAY] —**essay′er,** *n.* —**es′sayis′tic,** *adj.*

essayist (ĕs′ā ĭst), *n.* **1.** a writer of essays. **2.** *Rare.* one who makes essays or trials.

esse (ĕs′ĭ), *n. Latin.* being; existence. [L: to be]

Esseg (*Ger.* ĕ′sĕk), *n.* German name of **Osijek.**

Essen (*Ger.* ĕs′ən), *n.* a city in W West Germany: the chief city of the Ruhr; Krupp works. 721,200 (est. 1966).

essence (ĕs′əns), *n.* **1.** that by which a thing is what it is; intrinsic nature; important elements or features of a thing. **2.** a substance obtained from a plant, drug, or the like, by distillation or other process, and containing its characteristic properties in concentrated form. **3.** an alcoholic solution of an essential oil. **4.** a perfume. **5.** *Philos.* the inward nature, true substance, or constitution of anything. **6.** something that is, esp. a spiritual or immaterial entity. [ME, t. L: m. s. *essentia*]

Essene (ĕs′ēn, ĕ sēn′), *n.* one of an ascetic, celibate brotherhood of Jews in ancient Palestine, first appearing in the 2nd century B.C. [sing. of *Essenes,* Anglicized form of L *Essēnī*, pl., t. Gk: m. *Essēnoi*] —**Essenian** (ĕ sē′nyən), **Essenic** (ĕ sĕn′ĭk), *adj.*

essenhout (ĕs′ən hout′, -hōt′), *n.* a meliaceous timber tree, *Ekebergia capensis*, of southern Africa; Cape ash. [t. Afrikaans: ash wood]

essential (ĭ sĕn′shəl), *adj.* **1.** absolutely necessary; indispensable: *discipline is essential in an army.* **2.** pertaining to or constituting the essence of a thing. **3.** having the nature of an essence of a plant, etc. **4.** being such by its very nature, or in the highest sense: *essential happiness, essential poetry.* —*n.* **5.** an indispensable element; a chief point: *concentrate on essentials rather than details.* [ME, t. LL: s. *essentiālis.* See ESSENCE] —**essen′tially,** *adv.* —**essen′tialness,** *n.*

—**Syn. 1.** fundamental, basic, inherent, intrinsic. See **necessary. 2.** ESSENTIAL, INHERENT, INTRINSIC refer to that which is in the natural composition of a thing. ESSENTIAL suggests that which is in the very essence or constitution of a thing: *oxygen and hydrogen are the essential elements of water.* INHERENT means inborn or fixed from the beginning as a permanent quality or constituent of a thing: *properties inherent in iron.* INTRINSIC implies belonging to the nature of a thing itself, and comprised within it, without regard to external considerations or accidentally added properties: *the intrinsic value of diamonds.* —**Ant. 2.** accidental, extrinsic.

essentiality (ĭ sĕn′shĭ ăl′ĭ tĭ), *n.*, *pl.* **-ties. 1.** the quality of being essential; essential character. **2.** an essential element or point.

essential oil, any of a class of oils obtained from plants, possessing the smell and other properties of the plant, and volatilizing completely when heated: used in making perfumes, flavours, etc.

Essequibo (ĕs′ĭ kē′bō), *n.* a river flowing from S Guyana N to the Atlantic. ab. 550 mi.

Essex (ĕs′ĭks), *n.* **1. Robert Devereux** (dĕv′ə ro͞o′), **Earl of,** 1566–1601, English soldier; favourite of Queen Elizabeth I. **2.** a county in SE England. 2,888,058 pop. (1961); 1528 sq. mi. *Co. town:* Chelmsford.

Esslingen (*Ger.* ĕs′lĭng ən), *n.* a town in SW West Germany, on the river Neckar. 83,900 (est. 1966).

essonite (ĕs′ə nīt′), *n.* hessonite.

Essone (*Fr.* ĕ sŏn′), *n.* a department in N central France. 565,000 pop. (est. 1965); 700 sq. mi. *Cap.:* Évry.

-est, a suffix forming the superlative degree of adjectives and adverbs, as in *warmest, fastest, soonest.* [OE *-est, -ost.* Cf. Gk *-isto-*]

est., 1. established. 2. estate. 3. estimated. 4. estuary.

E.S.T., (in the U.S.) eastern standard time. Also, **EST, e.s.t.**

estab., established.

establish (ĭs tăb′lĭsh), *v.t.* **1.** to set up on a firm or permanent basis; institute; found: *to establish a government, a business, a university, etc.* **2.** to settle or install in a position, business, etc.: *to establish one's son in business.* **3.** to settle (oneself) as if permanently. **4.** to cause to be permanently accepted: *to establish a custom or a precedent.* **5.** to show to be valid or well grounded; prove: *to establish a fact, theory, claim, etc.* **6.** to appoint or ordain for permanence, as a law; fix unalterably. **7.** to set up or bring about permanently: *establish order.* **8.** to make (a church) a national or state institution. **9.** *Cards.* to obtain control of (a suit) so that one can win all the subsequent tricks in that suit. [ME *establisse(n)*, t. OF: m. *establiss-*, s. *establir*, g. L *stabilire* make stable] —**estab′lisher,** *n.* —**Syn. 1.** form, organize. See **fix. 5.** verify, substantiate.

established church, a church recognized and sometimes partly supported by the state, as (*caps*) the Church of England.

establishment (ĭs tăb′lĭsh mənt), *n.* **1.** the act of establishing. **2.** the state or fact of being established. **3.** something established; a constituted order or system. **4. the Establishment,** a loosely defined grouping of people in a community whose joint opinions and values have a strong influence on the existing power structure of the community. **5.** a household; a place of residence with everything connected with it. **6.** the building and equipment occupied by a business concern. **7.** a permanent civil, military, or other force or organization. **8.** institution. **9.** the recognition by the state of a church as the state church. **10.** the church so recognized, esp. the Church of England. **11.** *Archaic.* fixed allowance or income.

establishmentarian (ĭs tăb′lĭsh mən tēə′rĭ ən), *adj.* **1.** advocating and maintaining the principle of an established church, esp. the Church of England. —*n.* **2.** one who supports, or is an adherent of the established church.

Estaing, d' (*Fr.* dĕs tăN′), *n.* **Charles Hector** (*Fr.* shàrl ĕk tōr′), **Comte,** 1729–94, French admiral.

estaminet (*Fr.* ĕs tà mē nĕ′), *n. French.* a bar; café; bistro. [F, t. Walloon: m. *staminé*, der *stamon* post, t. Gmc; cf. G *Stamm* STEM]

estancia (ĭs tăn′syə; *Sp.* ĕs tän′thyä), *n.* (in Spanish America) a landed estate; a cattle farm.

estate (ĭs tāt′), *n.*, *v.*, **-tated, -tating.** —*n.* **1.** a piece of landed property, esp. one of large extent: *to have an estate in the country.* **2.** *Law.* **a.** property or possessions. **b.** the legal position or status of an owner, considered with respect to his property in land or other things. **c.** the degree or quantity of interest which a person has in land with respect to the nature of the right, its duration, or its relation to the rights of others. **d.** interest, ownership, or property in land or other things. **e.** the property of a deceased person, a bankrupt, etc., viewed as an aggregate. **3.** a housing development. **4.** an industrial development area; a trading estate. **5.** period or condition of life: *to attain to man's estate.* **6.** a political or social group or class, as in France, the clergy, nobles, and commons, or in England, the lords spiritual, lords temporal, and commons (the three **estates of the realm**). **7.** condition or circumstances with reference to worldly prosperity, estimation, etc.; social status or rank. **8.** high rank or dignity. **9.** *Archaic.* pomp or state. —*v.t.* **10.** *Now Rare or Obs.* to establish in or as in an estate. [ME, t. OF: m. *estat*, t. L: m. s. *status.* See STATE] —**Syn. 1.** See **property.**

estate agent, 1. one who acts as an intermediary between the buyer and the seller of properties, houses, land, etc. **2.** land agent.

estate car, a motor car with an enlarged body, sometimes made partly of wood, providing extra space for luggage, etc., behind the rear seats, and having additional doors which open at the back.

estate duty, death duty.

Estates General, *French Hist.* the States-General.

esteem (ĭs tēm′), *v.t.* **1.** to regard as valuable; regard highly or favourably: *I esteem him highly.* **2.** to consider as of a certain value; regard: *I esteem it worthless.* **3.** to set a value on; value: *to esteem lightly.* —*n.* **4.** favourable opinion or judgement; respect or regard: *to hold a person or thing in high esteem.* **5.** *Archaic.* opinion or judgement of merit or demerit; estimation. [late ME *estyme(n)*, t. MF: m. *estimer*, t. L: m. s. *aestimāre.* See ESTIMATE, and cf. AIM] —**Syn. 1.** prize, honour, revere. See **appreciate. 4.** favour, admiration, honour, reverence, veneration. See **respect.** —**Ant. 1.** disdain.

ester (ĕs′tə), *n. Chem.* a compound formed by the reaction between an acid and an alcohol with the elimination of a molecule of water. [coined by L. Gmelin, 1788–1853, German chemist]

esterase (ĕs′tə rās′), *n. Biochem.* any ferment of enzyme which saponifies an ester.

ester gum, a hard resin obtained by esterifying rosin, or other natural gums, with a polyhydric alcohol (esp. glycerol); used in the manufacture of paints and varnishes.

esterify (ĕs tĕ′rĭ fī′), *v.t.*, *v.i.*, **-fied, -fying.** *Chem.* to convert into an ester. —**ester′ifica′tion,** *n.*

Esth., 1. Esther. 2. Esthonia.

Esther (ĕs′tə), *n.* one of the books of the Old Testament, named from its principal character. [t. L (Vulgate), t. Gk (Septuagint), t. Heb. See ISHTAR]

esthesia (ēs thē′zyə), *n. U.S.* aesthesia.

esthesis (ēs thē′sĭs), *n. U.S.* aesthesis.

esthete (ēs′thēt), *n. U.S.* aesthete.

esthetic (ēs thĕt′ĭk), *adj. U.S.* aesthetic.

esthetician (ēs′thĭ tĭsh′ən), *n. U.S.* aesthetician.

estheticism (ēs thĕt′ĭ sĭz′əm), *n. U.S.* aestheticism.

esthetics (ēs thĕt′ĭks), *n. U.S.* aesthetics.

Esthonia (ĕs tō′nyə), *n.* Estonia. —**Estho′nian,** *adj.*, *n.*

Estienne (*Fr.* ĕs tyĕn′), *n.* a French printing firm famous for its scholarship, founded by **Henri** (*Fr.* äN rē′), 1460?–1520, and carried on by his son **Robert** (*Fr.* rŏ bĕr′), 1503–59, and by his grandson **Henri,** 1528–98.

estimable (ĕs′tĭ mə bl), *adj.* **1.** worthy of esteem; deserving respect. **2.** capable of being estimated. —**es′timableness,** *n.* —**es′timably,** *adv.* —**Syn. 1.** reputable, respectable, worthy, meritorious. —**Ant. 1.** contemptible.

estimate (*v.* ĕs′tĭ māt′; *n.* ĕs′tĭ mĭt), *v.*, **-mated, -mating,** *n.* —*v.t.* **1.** to form an approximate judgement or opinion regarding the value, amount, size, weight, etc., of; calculate approximately. **2.** to form an opinion of; judge. —*v.i.* **3.** to submit approximate figures, as of the cost of work to be done. —*n.* **4.** an approximate judgement or calculation, as of the value, amount, etc., of something. **5.** a judgement or opinion, as of the qualities of a person or thing; estimation or judgement. **6.** an approximate statement of what would be charged for certain work to be done, submitted by one ready to undertake the work. [t. L: m. s. *aestimātus*, pp., valued, rated. Cf. ESTEEM] —**es′tima′tor,** *n.* —**Syn. 1.** compute, count, reckon, gauge.

estimation (ĕs′tĭ mā′shən), *n.* **1.** judgement or opinion: *in my estimation.* **2.** esteem; respect: *to hold in high estimation.* **3.** approximate calculation; estimate: *to make* *an estimation of one's resources.* **—Syn. 1.** appreciation, regard, honour, veneration.

estimative (ĕs′tĭ mə tĭv), *adj.* **1.** capable of estimating. **2.** based upon or pertaining to estimation.

estipulate (ĭ stĭp′yo͝o lĭt, -lāt′), *adj.* exstipulate.

estival (ēs tī′vəl, ĕs′tĭ vəl), *adj. Chiefly U.S.* aestival.

estivate (ĕs′tĭ vāt′, ēs′-), *v.i.*, **-vated, -vating.** *Chiefly U.S.* aestivate.

estivation (ĕs′tĭ vā′shən, ēs′-), *n. Chiefly U.S.* aestivation.

estoc (ĕs′tŏk, ĕs tŏk′), *n.* a short stabbing sword. [ME, t. OF]

Eston (ĕs′tən), *n.* a town in England, in the N North Riding of Yorkshire. 37,160 (1961).

Estonia (ĕs tō′nyə), *n.* a constituent republic of the Soviet Union, on the Baltic, S of the Gulf of Finland; formerly an independent republic 1918–40. 1,244,000 pop. (1963); 18,300 sq. mi. *Cap.:* Tallinn. Also, **Esthonia.** Official name, **Estonian Soviet Socialist Republic.** See map under **Memel.**

Estonian (ĕs tō′nyən), *adj.* **1.** of or pertaining to Estonia and its people. *—n.* **2.** one of a Finnish people inhabiting Estonia, Livonia, and other districts of Russia. **3.** the Finno-Ugric language of Estonia, very closely related to Finnish. Also, **Esthonian.**

estop (ĭs tŏp′), *v.t.*, **-topped, -topping. 1.** *Law.* to hinder or prevent by estoppel. **2.** *Archaic.* to stop. [t. OF: m. *estoper* stop up, AF *estopper* (in law), der. OF *estoupe*, g. L *stuppa* tow. Cf. STOP, v.]

estoppage (ĭs tŏp′ĭj), *n.* condition of being estopped.

estoppel (ĭs tŏp′l), *n. Law.* a bar or impediment preventing a party from asserting a fact or a claim inconsistent with a position he previously took, either by conduct or words, esp. where a representation has been relied or acted upon by others. [cf. OF *estoupail* stopper, der. *estouper* ESTOP]

estovers (ĕs tō′vəz), *n.pl. Law.* necessaries allowed by law, as wood and timber to a tenant, alimony to a wife, etc. [t. AF: necessities, prop. *estover*, inf., be necessary, g. Rom. *estopēre*, der. L *est opus* it is necessary]

estradiol (ĕs′trə dī′ŏl, ēs′-), *n. U.S.* oestradiol.

estragon (ĕs′trə gŏn′), *n.* tarragon.

estrange (ĭ strānj′), *v.t.*, **estranged, estranging. 1.** to turn away in feeling or affection; alienate the affections of. **2.** to remove to or keep (usually oneself) at a distance. **3.** to divert from the original use or possessor. [late ME, t. MF: m. *estrangier*, g. L *extrāneāre*, der. *extrāneus* foreign. See STRANGE] **—estrange′ment,** *n.* **—estrang′er,** *n.*

estrapade (ĕs′trə pād′), *n.* an attempt by a horse to throw its rider by rearing and kicking.

estray (ĭs trā′), *n.* **1.** anything strayed away. **2.** *Law.* a domestic animal, as a horse or a sheep, found wandering or without an owner. *—v.i.* **3.** *Archaic.* to stray. [t. AF. See STRAY, v.]

estreat (ĭs trēt′), *Law. —n.* **1.** a true copy or extract of an original writing or record, as of a fine. *—v.t.* **2.** to make an estreat of (a fine, etc.) for prosecution. **3.** to levy (fines) under an estreat; exact (anything) by way of fine or levy. [t. AF: m. *estrete*, var. of *estraite*, prop. fem. pp. of *estraire*, g. L *extrahere.* See EXTRACT]

Estremadura (ĕs′trĭ mə do͞o′rə), *n.* a region in W Spain, formerly a province. Spanish, **Extremadura** (*Sp.* ĕs trĕ mä do͞o′rä).

estriol (ĕs′trĭ ŏl′, ēs′-), *n. U.S.* oestriol.

estrogen, (ĕs′trə jən, ēs′-), *n. U.S.* oestrogen. **—es′trogen′ic,** *adj.*

estrone (ĕs′trōn, ēs′-), *n. U.S.* oestrone.

estrous (ĕs′trəs, ēs′-), *adj. U.S.* oestrous.

estrous cycle, *U.S.* oestrous cycle.

estrus (ĕs′trəs, ēs′-), *n. U.S.* oestrus.

estuarine (ĕs′tyo͝o ə rīn, -rīn′), *adj.* **1.** formed in an estuary. **2.** found in estuaries.

estuary (ĕs′tyo͝o ə rĭ), *n.*, *pl.* **-aries. 1.** that part of the mouth or lower course of a river in which its current meets the sea's tides, and is subject to their effects. **2.** an arm or inlet of the sea. [t. L: m. s. *aestuārium*, der. *aestus* a heaving motion, surge, tide] **—estuarial** (ĕs′tyo͝o ĕə′rĭ əl), *adj.*

e.s.u., *Physics.* See **electrostatic unit.** Also, **E.S.U., esu.**

esurient (ĭ syo͝oə′rĭ ənt), *adj.* hungry; greedy. [t. L: s. *ēsuriens*, ppr., desiring to eat] **—esu′rience, esu′riency,** *n.* **—esu′riently,** *adv.*

Et, *Chem.* ethyl.

-et, a noun suffix having properly a diminutive force (now lost in many words), as in *islet, bullet, facet, midget, owlet, plummet.* [t. OF: *-et* masc., *-ette* fem.]

E.T., (in the U.S.) eastern time.

eta (ē′tə), *n.* the seventh letter (Η, η, English long E, e) of the Greek alphabet.

E.T.A., estimated time of arrival.

etagère (*Fr.* ĕ tȧ zhĕr′), *n. French.* a series of open shelves for bric-a-brac, etc.

et al., **1.** (L *et alibī*) and elsewhere. **2.** (L *et aliī*) and others.

etalon (ĕt′ə lŏn′), *n. Physics.* an interferometer used for studying the hyperfine structure of atomic spectra; the interference effect is produced by multiple reflection between fixed, parallel, half-silvered glass or quartz plates. [t. F: MF *estalon* standard, der. OF *estal* place, ult. t. Gmc; cf. STALL]

etc., et cetera.

et cetera (ĭt sĕt′rə), *Latin.* and others; and so forth; and so on (used to indicate that more of the same sort or class might have been mentioned, but for shortness are omitted). *Abbrev.:* etc. [L, *et cētera* (sometimes *caetera*) and the rest]

etcetera (ĭt sĕt′rə), *n.*, *pl.* **-ras. 1.** other things or persons unspecified. **2.** (*pl.*) extras or sundries.

etch (ĕch), *v.t.* **1.** to cut, bite, or corrode with an acid or the like; engrave (metals, etc.) with an acid or the like, esp. to form a design in furrows which when charged with ink will give an impression on paper. **2.** to produce or copy by this method, as on copper. **3.** to portray or outline clearly (a character, features, etc.). **4.** to fix in the memory; to root firmly in the mind. **5.** to cut, as a geographical feature, by erosion, etc. *—v.i.* **6.** to practise the art of etching. [t. D: m. *etsen*, t. G: m. *ätzen* feed, corrode, etch; akin to EAT] **—etch′er,** *n.*

etching (ĕch′ĭng), *n.* **1.** a process of making designs or pictures on a metal plate, glass, etc., by the corrosion of an acid instead of by a burin. **2.** an impression, as on paper, taken from an etched plate. **3.** the design produced. **4.** the plate on which such a design is etched.

Eteocles (ĭ tē′ə klēz′, ĕt′ĭ ə klēz′), *n. Gk Legend.* a son of Oedipus, and brother of Polynices, by whom he was slain. His breach of an agreement made with his brother led to the expedition of the Seven against Thebes.

eternal (ĭ tû′nəl), *adj.* **1.** lasting throughout eternity; without beginning or end: *eternal life.* **2.** perpetual; ceaseless: *eternal quarrelling, chatter, etc.* **3.** enduring; immutable: *eternal principles.* **4.** *Metaphys.* existing outside of all relations of time; not subject to change. *—n.* **5.** that which is eternal. **6. the Eternal,** God. [ME, t. LL: m. s. *aeternālis*, der. L *aeternus.* See ETERNE] **—eter′nally,** *adv.* **—eter′nalness,** *n.*

—Syn. 1. ETERNAL, ENDLESS, EVERLASTING, PERPETUAL imply lasting or going on without ceasing. That which is ETERNAL is, by its nature, without beginning or ending: *God, the eternal father.* That which is ENDLESS never stops but goes on continuously as if in a circle: *an endless succession of years.* That which is EVERLASTING will endure through all future time: *a promise of everlasting life.* PERPETUAL implies continuous renewal and lasting as far into the future as one can foresee: *perpetual strife between nations.* **3.** timeless, immortal, deathless, undying. **—Ant. 2.** temporary.

Eternal City, the, Rome.

eternalize (ĭ tû′nə līz′), *v.t.*, **-lized, -lizing. 1.** to make eternal. **2.** to immortalize. Also, **eternalise.**

eternal triangle, *Colloq.* the relationship of husband, wife, and mistress or lover, considered as a constantly recurring social phenomenon.

eterne (ĭ tûn′), *adj. Archaic.* eternal. [ME, t. OF, t. L: m. s. *aeternus*, for *aeviternus* eternal]

eternity (ĭ tû′nĭ tĭ), *n.*, *pl.* **-ties. 1.** infinite time; duration without beginning or end. **2.** eternal existence, esp. as contrasted with mortal life. **3.** an endless or seemingly endless period of time. [ME *eternite*, t. OF, t. L: m. s. *aeternitas*, der. *aeternus.* See ETERNE]

eternize (ē tû′nīz), *v.t.*, **-nized, -nizing. 1.** to make eternal; perpetuate. **2.** to immortalize. Also, **eternise.**

etesian (ĭ tē′zhyən), *adj.* recurring annually (applied to certain Mediterranean winds). [f. s. L *etēsius* (t. Gk: m. *etḗsios*, lit., annual) + -AN]

eth (ĕth), *n.* the name of a letter formerly used in the English alphabet, and still used in Icelandic and in phonetic alphabets. It is a crossed *d* in form, and represents (1) in Old English, both unvoiced and voiced *th*; (2) in present use, the voiced *th* only. See **thorn** (def. 5). Also, **edh.**

-eth[1], an ending of the third person singular present indicative of verbs, now occurring only in archaic forms or used in solemn or poetic language, as in *doeth* or *doth, hath, hopeth, sitteth.* [OE *-eth, -ath, -oth, -th*; akin to L *-t*]

-eth[2], the form of *-th*, the ordinal suffix, after a vowel, as in *twentieth, thirtieth*, etc. See **-th**[2].

Eth., Ethiopia.

ethane (ē′thān), *n. Chem.* an odourless, gaseous hydrocarbon, C_2H_6, of the methane series, present in illuminating gas and crude petroleum. [f. ETH(ER) + -ANE]

ethanol (ē′thə nŏl′), *n. Chem.* ethyl alcohol. [f. ETHANE(E) + -OL[1]]

ethanolamine (ē′thə nŏl′ə mēn′), *n. Chem.* one of a group of compounds derived from ethyl alcohol and amino groups: **monoethanolamine,** $NH_2CH_2CH_2OH$, **diethonolamine,** $NH(CH_2CH_2OH)_2$, and **triethanolamine,** $N(CH_2CH_2OH)_3$, are all used as solvents and in the manufacture of detergents.

Ethelbert (ĕth′əl bût′), *n.* 552–616, king of Kent 560–616.

Ethelred II (ĕth′əl rĕd′) (*'the Unready'*), 968?–1016, king of the English 978–1016.

ethene (ĕth′ēn), *n. Chem.* ethylene.

ethenoid plastics (ĕth′ĭ noid′), a group of thermoplastic resins containing a double bond; usually includes acrylic, styrene and vinyl resins.

ether (ē′thə), *n.* **1.** *Chem.* **a.** a highly volatile and inflammable colourless liquid (**ethyl ether**), $(C_2H_5)_2O$, obtained by the action of sulphuric acid on alcohol, and used as a solvent and anaesthetic; sulphuric ether; diethyl ether. **b.** one of a class of organic compounds in which any two organic radicals are attached directly to oxygen, having the general formula R_2O, as ethyl ether $(C_2H_5)_2O$. **2.** the upper regions of space; the clear sky; the heavens. **3.** the medium supposed by the ancients to fill the upper regions. **4.** an all-pervading medium postulated for the transmission of light, heat, etc., by the older elastic solid theory. Also, **aether** (for defs 2–4). [t. L: m. *aether*, t. Gk: m. *aithḗr* upper air, sky]

ethereal (ĭ thĭə′rĭ əl), *adj.* **1.** light, airy or tenuous. **2.** extremely delicate or refined: *ethereal beauty.* **3.** heavenly or celestial. **4.** of the ether or upper regions of space. **5.** *Chem.* pertaining to, containing, or resembling ethyl ether. Also, **aethereal** (for defs 1–4). —**ethe′real′ity, ethe′realness,** *n.* —**ethe′really,** *adv.*

etherealize (ĭ thĭə′rĭ ə līz′), *v.t.*, **-lized, -lizing.** to make ethereal. Also, **etherealise.** —**ethe′really,** *adv.*

Etherege (ĕth′ə rĭj), *n.* **Sir George,** 1635?–91, English dramatist.

etherify (ē′thə rĭ fī′, ē thĕ′rĭ fī′), *v.t.*, **-fied, -fying.** *Chem.* to convert into an ether. —**ether′ifica′tion,** *n.*

etherize (ē′thə rīz′), *v.t.*, **-rized, -rizing.** *Chiefly U.S.* to put under the influence of ether. Also, **etherise.** —**e′theriza′tion,** *n.* —**e′theriz′er,** *n.*

ethic (ĕth′ĭk), *adj.* **1.** pertaining to morals; ethical. —*n.* **2.** *Rare.* ethics. [t. L: s. *ēthicus*, t. Gk: m. *ēthikós* of morals, moral]

ethical (ĕth′ĭ kl), *adj.* **1.** pertaining to or dealing with morals or the principles of morality; pertaining to right and wrong in conduct. **2.** in accordance with the rules or standards for right conduct or practice, esp. the standards of a profession: *it is not considered ethical for doctors to advertise.* —**eth′ically,** *adv.* —**eth′icalness,** *n.*

ethicize (ĕth′ĭ sīz′), *v.t.*, **-cized, -cizing.** to make ethical; treat or regard as ethical. Also, **ethicise.**

ethics (ĕth′ĭks), *n.pl.* **1.** a system of moral principles, by which human actions and proposals may be judged good or bad or right or wrong. **2.** the rules of conduct recognized in respect of a particular class of human actions: *medical ethics.* **3.** moral principles, as of an individual. —**Syn. 2.** See **moral.**

ethine (ĕth′īn), *n. Chem.* acetylene. Also, **ethyne.**

Ethiop (ē′thĭ ŏp′), *adj., n.* Ethiopian. [t. L: s. *Aethiops*, t. Gk: m. *Aithíops*]

Ethiopia (ē′thĭ ō′pyə), *n.* **1.** Also, **Abyssinia.** a kingdom in E Africa: formerly a part of Italian East Africa, 1936–41. 21,461,700 pop. (est. 1962); 409,266 sq. mi. Present boundaries include Eritrea. *Cap.*: Addis Ababa. **2.** an ancient region in NE Africa, bordering on Egypt and the Red Sea.

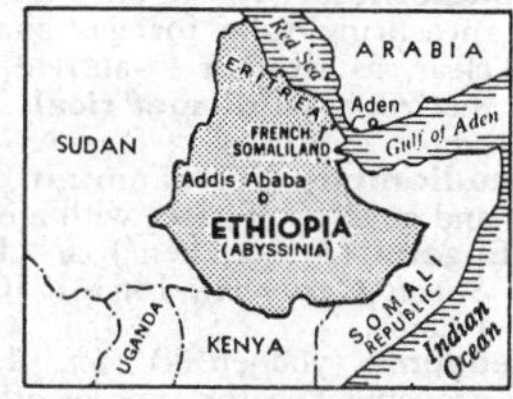

Ethiopia (def. 1)

Ethiopian (ē′thĭ ō′pyən), *adj.* **1.** pertaining to Ethiopia or to its inhabitants. **2.** *Archaic.* Negro. **3.** *Archaic.* belonging to Africa south of the Tropic of Cancer. —*n.* **4.** a native of Ethiopia. **5.** *Ethnol.* a member of the Ethiopian race, one of the five racial divisions originally recognized, including the African Negro and Negrito. **6.** *Archaic.* a Negro.

Ethiopic (ē′thĭ ŏp′ĭk, -ō′pĭk), *adj.* **1.** Ethiopian. —*n.* **2.** the ancient Semitic language of Ethiopia.

ethmoid (ĕth′moid), *Anat.* —*adj.* **1.** designating or pertaining to a bone of the skull at the root of the nose, containing numerous perforations for the filaments of the olfactory nerve. —*n.* **2.** the ethmoid bone. [t. Gk: m. s. *ethmoeidḗs* sievelike] —**ethmoi′dal,** *adj.*

ethnarch (ĕth′näk), *n.* the ruler of a people, tribe, or nation. [t. Gk: s. *ethnárchēs*. See ETHNO-, -ARCH]

ethnarchy (ĕth′nä′kĭ), *n., pl.* **-chies.** the government, office, or jurisdiction of an ethnarch.

ethnic (ĕth′nĭk), *adj.* **1.** pertaining to or peculiar to a population, esp. to a speech group, loosely also to a race. **2.** referring to the origin, classification, characteristics, etc., of such groups. **3.** pertaining to nations not Jewish or Christian; heathen or pagan: *ancient ethnic revels.* Also, **eth′nical.** [ME, t. LL: s. *ethnicus*, t. Gk: m. *ethnikós* national, gentile, heathen, der. *éthnos* nation] —**eth′nically,** *adv.*

ethnic group, *Sociol.* a group of people, racially or historically related, having a common and distinctive culture.

ethno-, a word element meaning 'race', 'nation', as in *ethnology.* [t. Gk, comb. form of *éthnos*]

ethnocentrism (ĕth′nō sĕn′trĭz′əm), *n. Orig. U.S. Sociol.* the belief in the inherent superiority of one's own group and culture accompanied by a feeling of contempt for other groups and cultures. —**eth′nocen′tric,** *adj.*

ethnog., ethnography.

ethnogeny (ĕth nŏj′ĭ nĭ), *n. Anthropol.* the branch of ethnology which studies the origin of distinctive populations or races.

ethnography (ĕth nŏg′rə fĭ), *n.* **1.** the scientific description and classification of the various cultural and racial groups of mankind. **2.** ethnology, esp. as descriptive. —**ethnog′rapher,** *n.* —**ethnographic** (ĕth′nə grăf′ĭk), **eth′nograph′ical,** *adj.* —**eth′nograph′ically,** *adv.*

ethnol., **1.** ethnological. **2.** ethnology.

ethnology (ĕth nŏl′ə jĭ), *n.* the science that treats of the distinctive subdivisions of mankind, their origin, relations, speech, institutions, etc. —**ethnological** (ĕth′nə lŏj′ĭ kl), **eth′nolog′ic,** *adj.* —**eth′nolog′ically,** *adv.* —**ethnol′ogist,** *n.*

ethology (ĭ thŏl′ə jĭ), *n.* the scientific study of the behaviour of animals in relation to their normal environments. —**ethologic** (ĕth′ə lŏj′ĭk), **eth′olog′ical,** *adj.* —**eth′olog′ically,** *adv.*

ethos (ē′thŏs), *n.* **1.** character or disposition. **2.** *Sociol.* the fundamental spiritual characteristics of a culture. **3.** *Art.* the inherent quality of a work which produces, or is fitted to produce, a high moral impression, noble, dignified, and universal (opposed to *pathos*). [t. NL, t. Gk: character]

ethyl (ĕth′ĭl), *n.* **1.** *Chem.* a univalent radical, C_2H_5, from ethane. **2.** a type of anti-knock fluid, containing lead tetraethyl and other ingredients for a more even combustion. **3.** petrol to which this fluid has been added. [f. ETH(ER) + -YL] —**ethylic** (ĭ thĭl′ĭk), *adj.*

ethyl acetate, *Chem.* a colourless liquid with a fruity smell, $CH_3COOC_2H_5$; used as a solvent for paints and varnishes, as a flavouring and in perfume.

ethyl alcohol. See **alcohol.**

ethylate (ĕth′ĭ lāt′), *v.*, **-lated, -lating,** *n. Chem.* —*v.t.* **1.** to introduce one or more ethyl radicals into (a compound). —*n.* **2.** a metallic derivative of ethyl alcohol, as potassium ethylate (KOC_2H_5).

ethyl carbamate, *Chem.* urethane.

ethylene (ĕth′ĭ lēn′), *n. Chem.* a colourless, inflammable gas, C_2H_4, with an unpleasant smell, the first member of the ethylene series. Also, **ethene.**

ethylene dichloride, *Chem.* a colourless oily liquid, $C_2H_4Cl_2$, extensively used as a solvent and in the synthesis of vinyl chloride; Dutch liquid.

ethylene glycol, *Chem.* glycol.

ethylene group, *Chem.* the bivalent radical, $-CH_2CH_2-$, derived from ethylene or ethane.

ethylene-propylene rubber, a fully saturated, stereoregular, synthetic rubber made by the polymerization of approximately equal proportions of ethylene and propylene. *Abbrev.*: EPR.

ethylene series, *Chem.* a series of unsaturated aliphatic hydrocarbons having one double bond, with the general formula, C_nH_{2n}.

ethyl ether. See **ether** (def. 1a).

ethyl nitrate, *Chem.* a colourless, explosive liquid, $C_2H_5ONO_2$, used in organic synthesis. Also, **nitric ether.**

ethyl nitrite, *Chem.* a colourless, volatile liquid, C_2H_5ONO, used in medicine and in organic synthesis. Also, **nitrous ether.**

ethyne (ĕth′īn), *n. Chem.* ethine.

ethynyl group, (ĕ thī′nĭl), *Chem.* the univalent group, $HC{\equiv}C-$, derived from acetylene.

etiolate (ē′tĭ ō lāt′), *v.*, **-lated, -lating.** —*v.t.* **1.** to cause (a plant) to whiten by excluding light. —*v.i.* **2.** (of plants) to whiten through lack of light. [f. s. F *étioler* blanch + -ATE[1]] —**e′tiola′tion,** *n.*

etiology (ē′tĭ ŏl′ə jĭ), *n. U.S.* aetiology.

etiquette (ĕt′ĭ kĕt′, ĕt′ĭ kĕt′), *n.* **1.** conventional requirements as to social behaviour; proprieties of conduct as established in any class or community or for any occasion.

2. a prescribed or accepted code of usage in matters of ceremony, as at a court or in official or other formal observances. 3. conventional and accepted standards and practices in certain professions, as medicine. [t. F, in OF *estiquette* TICKET, of Gmc orig.; cf. STICK²]
—**Syn.** 1. ETIQUETTE, DECORUM, PROPRIETY imply observance of the formal requirements governing behaviour in polite society. ETIQUETTE refers to conventional forms and usages: *the rules of etiquette.* DECORUM suggests dignity and a sense of what is becoming or appropriate for a person of good breeding: *a fine sense of decorum.* PROPRIETY (usually plural) implies established conventions of morals and good taste: *she never fails to observe the proprieties.*

Etna (ĕt′nə), *n.* 1. Also, **Aetna. Mount,** an active volcano in E Sicily. 10,758 ft. 2. (*l.c.*) a small vessel for heating liquids, consisting of a cup for the liquid with a fixed saucer surrounding it in which alcohol is burnt.

Eton (ē′tn), *n.* a town in England, in S Buckinghamshire, on the Thames; the site of Eton College. 3901 (1961).

Eton collar, a broad stiff collar folded outside an Eton jacket.

Eton College, a boys' public school founded in 1440 by Henry VI.

Etonian (ē tō′nyən), *n.* 1. one who is or has been a pupil at Eton College. —*adj.* 2. of or pertaining to Eton College.

Eton jacket, 1. a boy's short jacket reaching to the waist, as worn by students at Eton College. 2. a similar short jacket worn by women.

Eton jacket

Etruria (ĭ trŏŏə′rĭ ə), *n.* an ancient country in W Italy, between the Arno and the Tiber and roughly corresponding to modern Tuscany.

Etruscan (ĭ trŭs′kən), *adj.* 1. pertaining to Etruria, its inhabitants, civilization, art, or language. —*n.* 2. an inhabitant of ancient Etruria. 3. the extinct language of Etruria. Also, **Etrurian** (ĭ trŏŏə′rĭ ən). [f. s. L *Etruscus* of Etruria + -AN]

Etruscology (ē′trŭs kŏl′ə jĭ), *n.* the scientific study of ancient Etruscan civilization. —**E′truscol′ogist,** *n.*

et seq., *pl.* **et seqq., et sqq.** (L *et sequens*) and the following.

et sic de similibus (ĕt sĭk′ dā sĭ mĭl′ĭ bŏŏs), *Latin.* and thus concerning (all) similar (ones).

-ette, a noun suffix, the feminine form of *-et*, occurring esp.: 1. with the original diminutive force, as in *cigarette.* 2. as a distinctively feminine ending, as in *coquette*, and various colloquial formations, as *usherette.* 3. in trademarks of imitations or substitutes, as in *leatherette.* [t. F, fem. of *-et* -ET]

et tu, Brute! (ĕt tōō′ brōō′tā), *Latin.* and thou, Brutus! (reproachful exclamation of Julius Caesar on seeing his friend Brutus among his assassins).

étude (ā′tyōōd; *Fr.* ĕ tʏd′), *n. Music.* 1. a composition intended mainly for the practice of some point of technique. 2. a composition performed for its aesthetic appeal which also embodies a specific technical exercise. [F. See STUDY, n.]

etui (ĕ twē′), *n.*, *pl.* **etuis.** a small case, esp. one for small objects, as needles, toilet articles, etc. Also, *Chiefly U.S.*, **etwee.** [t. F: m. *étui*, der. OF *etuier* keep, g. L *studiāre* care for]

etym., 1. etymological. 2. etymology. Also, **etymol.**

etymologize (ĕt′ĭ mŏl′ə jīz′), *v.*, **-gized, -gizing.** —*v.t.* 1. to trace the history of (a word). —*v.i.* 2. to study etymology. 3. to give or suggest the etymology of words. Also, **etymologise.**

etymology (ĕt′ĭ mŏl′ə jĭ), *n.*, *pl.* **-gies.** 1. the study of historical linguistic change, esp. as applied to individual words. 2. an account of the history of a particular word. 3. the derivation of a word. [t. L: m. s. *etymologia*, t. Gk. See ETYMON, -LOGY] —**etymological** (ĕt′ĭ mə lŏj′ĭ kl), **et′ymolog′ic,** *adj.* —**et′ymolog′ically,** *adv.* —**et′ymol′ogist,** *n.*

etymon (ĕt′ĭ mŏn′), *n.*, *pl.* **-mons, -ma** (-mə). a primary linguistic form, from which derivatives are formed. [t. L, t. Gk: the original sense, form, or element of a word, prop. neut. of *étymos* true, real]

Etzel (ĕt′səl), *n. German Legend.* Attila.

Eu, *Chem.* europium.

eu-, a prefix meaning 'good', 'well', occurring chiefly in words of Greek origin, as in *eupepsia.* [t. Gk, comb. form of *eús*, adj., good, neut. *eú* (used as adv., well)]

Euboea (yōō bē′ə), *n.* an island in the Aegean, off the E coast of, and belonging to, Greece. 165,758 pop. (1961); 1586 sq. mi. *Cap.:* Chalcis. Modern Greek, **Evvoia.** Also, **Negropont.** See map under **Thermopylae.** —**Euboean′,** *adj.*, *n.*

eucaine (yōō kān′), *n. Chem.* 1. a crystalline organic compound used as a local anaesthetic as a substitute for cocaine, $C_{19}H_{27}NO_4$ (**alpha-eucaine**). 2. a similar but less used compound, $C_{15}H_{21}NO_2$ (**beta-eucaine**); benzamine; betacaine. [f. EU- + (CO)CAINE]

eucalyptol (yōō′kə lĭp′tōl), *n. Chem.* cineol. [f. EUCALYPT(US) + -OL²]

eucalyptus (yōō′kə lĭp′təs), *n.*, *pl.* **-tuses, -ti** (-tī). any member of the myrtaceous genus *Eucalyptus*, including many tall trees, esp. the blue gum, *E. globulus*, native in and around Australia and cultivated elsewhere, which yields a valuable timber and bears leaves containing an oil used in medicine, as a germicide and expectorant. Also, **eucalypt** (yōō′kə lĭpt). [t. NL, f. *eu-* EU- + m. Gk *kalyptós* covered (with allusion to the cap covering the buds)]

eucharis (yōō′kə rĭs), *n.* any of the amaryllidaceous plants constituting the South American genus *Eucharis*, some of which are cultivated for their large, fragrant white flowers. [NL, t. Gk: pleasing]

Eucharist (yōō′kə rĭst), *n.* 1. the sacrament of the Lord's Supper; the communion; the sacrifice of the mass. 2. the consecrated elements of the Lord's Supper, esp. the bread. 3. (*l.c.*) the giving of thanks; thanksgiving. [t. LL: m. s. *eucharistia*, t. Gk: gratefulness, thanksgiving, the eucharist] —**Eu′charis′tic, Eu′charis′tical,** *adj.* —**Eu′charis′tically,** *adv.*

euchre (yōō′kə), *n.*, *v.*, **-chred, -chring.** *U.S.* —*n.* 1. *Cards.* a game played usually by two, three, or four persons, with the 32 (or 28 or 24) highest cards in the pack. 2. an instance of euchring or being euchred. —*v.t.* 3. to get the better of (an opponent) in a hand at euchre by his failure to win three tricks after having made the trump. 4. *Colloq.* to outwit; get the better of, as by scheming (usually fol. by *out*). [orig. uncert.]

Eucken (*Ger.* oʏ′kən), *n.* **Rudolph Cristoph** (*Ger.* rōō′dŏlf krĭs′tŏf), 1846–1916, German philosopher.

euclase (yōō′klās), *n.* a green or blue mineral, beryllium aluminium silicate, $HBeAl(SiO_5)$, occurring in prismatic crystals. [t. F, f. *eu-* EU- + m. s. Gk *klásis* a breaking]

Euclid (yōō′klĭd), *n.* 1. fl. *c.* 300 B.C., Greek geometrician of Alexandria. 2. the works of Euclid, esp. his treatise on geometry. 3. Euclidean geometry.

Euclidean (yōō klĭd′ĭ ən), *adj.* of or pertaining to Euclid, or adopting his postulates: *Euclidean geometry.* Also, **Euclid′ian.**

eudemon (yōō dē′mən), *n.* a good demon or spirit. Also, **eudae′mon.** [t. Gk: m. *eudaímōn* happy, f. *eu-* EU- + *daímōn* spirit, destiny]

eudemonia (yōō′dĭ mō′nyə), *n.* 1. happiness; welfare. 2. (in Aristotelian philosophy) happiness as the result of an active life governed by reason. Also, **eu′daemo′nia.** [t. Gk: m. *eudaimonia*]

eudemonic (yōō′dĭ mŏn′ĭk), *adj.* 1. pertaining or conducive to happiness. 2. pertaining to endemonics. Also, **eu′daemon′ic.**

eudemonics (yōō′dĭ mŏn′ĭks), *n.* 1. the science of happiness. 2. eudemonism. Also, **eu′daemon′ics.**

eudemonism (yōō dē′mə nĭz′əm), *n.* the system of ethics which holds that the basis of moral obligations lies in their relation to the production of happiness. Also, **eudae′monism.** [f. EUDEMON(IA) + -ISM] —**eude′monist,** *n.* —**eude′monis′tic, eude′monis′tical,** *adj.*

eudiometer (yōō′dĭ ŏm′ĭ tə), *n. Chem.* a graduated glass measuring tube for gas analysis. [f. Gk *eúdio(s)* fine, clear, as weather + -METER¹] —**eudiometric** (yōō′dĭ ə-mĕt′rĭk), **eu′diomet′rical,** *adj.* —**eu′diomet′rically,** *adv.*

eudiometry (yōō′dĭ ŏm′ĭ trĭ), *n. Chem.* the measurement and analysis of gases with a eudiometer.

Eugène (*Fr.* œ zhĕn′), *n.* **Prince** (*François Eugène de Savoie-Carignan*), 1663–1736, Austrian general, born in France.

eugenic (yōō jĕn′ĭk), *adj.* 1. of or bringing about improvement in the type of offspring produced. 2. having good inherited characteristics. Also, **eugen′ical.** [f. s. Gk *eugenḗs* well born + -IC] —**eugen′ically,** *adv.*

eugenicist (yōō jĕn′ĭ sĭst), *n.* 1. a specialist in eugenics. 2. an advocate of eugenic measures. Also, **eugenist** (yōō′jə nĭst).

eugenics (yōō jĕn′ĭks), *n.* 1. the science of improving the qualities of the human race, esp. the careful selection of parents. 2. the science of improving offspring.

Eugénie (*Fr.* œ zhĕ nē′), *n.* **Empress** (*Marie Eugénie de Montijo de Guzmán*), 1826–1920, empress of France, born in Spain (wife of Napoleon III).

eugenol (yōō′jĭ nōl′), *n. Chem.* a colourless, aromatic, oily compound, $C_{10}H_{12}O_2$, contained in certain essential oils, as that of cloves. [f. NL *Eugen(ia)* genus of myrtaceous plants + -OL²]

euglena (yōō glē′nə), *n.* a green type of flagellate protozoan of the genus *Euglena*, with one flagellum and a red eyespot, much used for class and experimental study.

euhemerism (yōō hē′mə rĭz′əm), *n.* 1. the theory held by Euhemerus that polytheistic mythology arose out of the deification of dead heroes. **2.** mythological interpretation which reduces the gods to the level of distinguished men; the derivation of mythology from history. —**euhe′merist,** *n.* —**euhe′meris′tic,** *adj.* —**euhe′meris′tically,** *adv.*

euhemerize (yo͞o hē′mə rīz′), *v.t., v.i.,* **-rized, -rizing.** to treat or explain (myths) by euhemerism. Also, **euhemerise.**

Euhemerus (yo͞o hē′mə rəs), *n.* fl. *c.* 300 B.C., Greek writer. See **euhemerism.**

eulachon (yo͞o′lə kŏn′), *n.* candlefish.

Eulenspiegel (*Ger.* ŏʏ′lən shpē gəl), *n.* See **Till Eulenspiegel.**

Euler (*Ger.* ŏʏ′lə), *n.* **Leonhard** (*Ger.* lĕ′ŏn härt), 1707–1783, Swiss mathematician.

eulogia (yo͞o lō′jĭ ə), *n. Eccles.* the unconsecrated bread not needed in the Eucharist, but blessed and distributed among those members of the congregation who did not commune. This custom still exists in the Greek Church. [t. Eccl. L, t. Gk. See EULOGY]

eulogist (yo͞o′lə jĭst), *n.* one who eulogizes.

eulogistic (yo͞o′lə jĭs′tĭk), *adj.* pertaining to or containing eulogy; laudatory. Also, **eu′logis′tical.** —**eu′logis′tically,** *adv.*

eulogium (yo͞o lō′jĭ əm), *n., pl.* **-giums, -gia** (-jĭ ə). **1.** eulogy. **2.** eulogistic language. [t. ML. See EULOGY]

eulogize (yo͞o′lə jīz′), *v.t.,* **-gized, -gizing.** to praise highly; speak or write a eulogy about. Also, **eulogise.** —**eu′logiz′er,** *n.* —**Syn.** extol, laud, commend, panegyrize.

eulogy (yo͞o′lə jĭ), *n., pl.* **-gies. 1.** a speech or writing in praise of a person or thing, esp. a set oration in honour of a deceased person. **2.** high praise or commendation. [t. ML: m. s. *eulogium,* var. of *eulogia* (t. Gk: praise), by assoc. with *ēlogium* short saying]

Eumenides (yo͞o mĕn′ĭ dēz′), *n.pl. Class. Myth.* a euphemistic name for the Furies or Erinyes. [t. L, t. Gk: lit., the gracious goddesses]

eunuch (yo͞o′nək), *n.* a castrated man, esp. one formerly employed as a harem attendant or officer of state by oriental rulers. [ME *eunuchus,* t. L, t. Gk: m. *eunoûchos* chamber attendant]

euonymus (yo͞o ŏn′ĭ məs), *n.* any of the widespread genus *Euonymus,* of shrubs and small trees, of northern temperate regions, usually bearing crimson or rose-coloured capsules which on opening disclose the seed. Also, **evonymus.** [NL, t. Gk: m. *euṓnymos* spindle tree, lit., of good name]

eupatorium (yo͞o′pə tô′rĭ əm), *n.* any plant of the large composite genus *Eupatorium,* mostly American, with heads of white or purplish flowers; several species are cultivated. [NL, t. Gk: m. *eupatórion*; named after Mithridates *Eupator,* king of Pontus, 120?–63 B.C.]

eupatrid (yo͞o păt′rĭd), *n., pl.* **-patridae, -patrids. 1.** one of the hereditary aristocrats of ancient Athens and other states of Greece, who at one time formed the ruling class. **2.** any aristocrat or patrician. [t. NL, t. Gk: s. *eupatrídēs*]

Eupen and Malmédy (*Ger.* ŏʏ′pən; *Fr.* œ pĕn′, mál mė dē′), two districts on the Belgian–German border: ceded to Belgium 1919; reannexed to Germany 1940; now in Belgium.

eupepsia (yo͞o pĕp′sĭ ə), *n.* good digestion (opposed to *dyspepsia*). Also, **eupepsy** (yo͞o pĕp′sĭ). [t. NL, t. Gk: good digestion] —**eupeptic** (yo͞o pĕp′tĭk), *adj.*

euph., 1. euphemism. 2. euphemistic.

euphemism (yo͞o′fĭ mĭz′əm), *n.* **1.** the substitution of a mild, indirect, or vague expression for a harsh or blunt one. **2.** the expression so substituted: '*To pass away*' *is a euphemism for* '*to die*'. [t. Gk: s. *euphēmismós,* der. *euphēmízein* use fair words] —**eu′phemist,** *n.* —**eu′phemis′tic, eu′phemis′tical,** *adj.* —**eu′phemis′tically,** *adv.*

euphemize (yo͞o′fĭ mīz′), *v.,* **-mized, -mizing.** —*v.t.* **1.** to refer to by means of euphemism. —*v.i.* **2.** to employ euphemism. Also, **euphemise.**

euphonic (yo͞o fŏn′ĭk), *adj.* pertaining to or characterized by euphony. Also, **euphon′ical.** —**euphon′ically,** *adv.* —**euphon′icalness,** *n.*

euphonious (yo͞o fō′nyəs), *adj.* characterized by euphony, well-sounding; agreeable to the ear. —**eupho′niously,** *adv.* —**eupho′niousness,** *n.*

euphonium (yo͞o fō′nyəm), *n. Music.* a tenor tuba mainly used in brass bands. [t. NL, der. Gk *eúphōnos* well-sounding]

euphonize (yo͞o′fə nīz′), *v.t.,* **-nized, -nizing.** to make euphonious. Also, **euphonise.**

euphony (yo͞o′fə nĭ), *n., pl.* **-nies. 1.** agreeableness of sound; pleasing effect to the ear, esp. of speech sounds as uttered or as combined in utterance. **2.** a tendency to change speech sounds for ease and economy of utterance: a former explanation of phonetic change. [t. LL: m. s. *euphōnia,* t. Gk, der. *eúphōnos* well-sounding]

euphorbia (yo͞o fô′byə), *n.* any of the plants of the widespread genus *Euphorbia* which vary greatly, but consist mostly of herbs and shrubs with an acrid milky juice; a spurge. [ME *euforbia,* for L *euphorbea* an African plant; named after *Euphorbus,* a Greek physician]

euphorbiaceous (yo͞o fô′bĭ ā′shəs), *adj.* belonging to the *Euphorbiaceae,* or spurge family of plants, which includes the spurges, cascarilla, castor oil, and cassava plants.

euphoria (yo͞o fō′rĭ ə), *n. Psychol.* a feeling or state of well-being, esp. one of unnatural elation. [t. NL, t. Gk, der. *eúphoros* bearing well] —**euphoric** (yo͞o fō′rĭk), *adj.*

euphotic zone (yo͞o fō′tĭk), the zone, about 110 yards deep from the surface of the sea, in which enough light penetrates to allow active photosynthesis.

euphrasy (yo͞o′frə sĭ), *n.* eyebright, *Euphrasia officinalis.* [late ME, t. ML: m. s. *euphrasia,* t. Gk: delight]

Euphrates (yo͞o frā′tēz), *n.* a river flowing from E Turkey through Syria and Iraq, joining the Tigris to form the Shatt-al-Arab near the Persian Gulf. 1700 mi.

euphroe (yo͞o′frō, yo͞o′vrō), *n. Naut.* an oblong or oval piece of wood perforated with holes through which small lines are rove, forming a crowfoot, from which an awning is suspended. Also, **uphroe.** [t. D: pseudo-learned spelling of *juffrouw,* lit., young woman]

Euphrosyne (yo͞o frŏz′ĭ nē′), *n. Gk Myth.* one of the Graces.

euphuism (yo͞o′fyo͞o ĭz′əm), *n.* **1.** an affected style in imitation of that of Lyly, author of *Euphues, Anatomy of Wit* (1579) and *Euphues and his England* (1580), fashionable in England about the end of the 16th century, characterized chiefly by long series of antitheses, frequent similes relating to myths and natural history, alliteration, etc. **2.** any similar ornate style of writing or speaking; high-flown language. **3.** an instance of such style or language. —**eu′phuist,** *n.* —**eu′phuis′tic, eu′phuis′tical,** *adj.* —**eu′phuis′tically,** *adv.*

euplastic (yo͞o plăs′tĭk), *adj. Physiol.* capable of being transformed into organized tissue. [f. s. Gk *eúplastos* easy to mould + -IC]

euploid (yo͞o′ploid), *adj.* having each of the different chromosomes of the set present in the same number; an exact multiple of the haploid chromosome number.

eupnoea (yo͞op nĭə′), *n. Pathol.* easy or normal breathing (opposed to *dyspnoea*). [NL, t. Gk: m. *eúpnoia,* der. *eúpnoos* breathing well]

Eur., 1. Europe. 2. European.

Eurasia (yo͞oə rā′zhyə, -shyə), *n.* Europe and Asia considered as a whole.

Eurasian (yo͞oə rā′zhyən, -shyən), *adj.* **1.** pertaining to Europe and Asia taken together. **2.** of mixed European and Asian descent. —*n.* **3.** a person one of whose parents is European and the other Asian.

Euratom (yo͞oə răt′əm), *n.* a European organization formed in 1958 by Belgium, France, Italy, Luxembourg, the Netherlands, and West Germany, for coordinating nuclear research for peaceful purposes.

Eure (*Fr.* œr), *n.* a department in NW France. 361,904 pop. (1962); 2331 sq. mi. *Cap.*: Évreux.

eureka (yo͞oə rē′kə), *interj.* **1.** I have found (it): the reputed exclamation of Archimedes when, after long study, he discovered a method of detecting the amount of alloy in the crown of the king of Syracuse. **2.** an exclamation of triumph at a discovery or supposed discovery. [t. Gk: m. *heúrēka*]

Eure-et-Loire (*Fr.* œr ė lwȧr′), *n.* a department in central France. 277,546 pop. (1962); 2293 sq. mi. *Cap.*: Chartres.

eurhythmic (yo͞o rĭth′mĭk), *adj.* **1.** characterized by a pleasing rhythm; harmoniously ordered or proportioned. **2.** of or pertaining to eurhythmics. Also, **eurythmic.**

eurhythmics (yo͞o rĭth′mĭks), *n.* the art of interpreting in bodily movements the rhythm of musical compositions, with the aim of developing the sense of rhythm and symmetry; invented by Émile Jacques-Dalcroze. Also, **eurythmics.**

eurhythmy (yo͞o rĭth′mĭ), *n.* rhythmical movement or order; harmonious proportion. Also, **eurythmy.** [t. Gk: m. s. *eurhythmía* rhythmical order]

Euripides (yo͞oə rĭp′ĭ dēz′), *n.* 480?–406? B.C., Athenian tragic poet.

euripus (yo͞oə rī′pəs), *n., pl.* **-pi** (-pī). a strait, esp. one in which the flow of water in both directions is violent, as (*cap.*) that between the island of Euboea and Boeotia in Greece. [t. L, t. Gk: m. *eúripos,* f. *eu-* EU- + m. *rhīpḗ* impetus, rush]

Euroclydon (yo͞oə rŏk′lĭ dŏn′), *n.* a stormy north-east or north-north-east wind. [t. Gk: m. *euroklýdōn*]

Eurodollar (yo͞o′rō dŏl′ə), *n.* (*sometimes l.c.*) an international currency medium used to float United States securities by raising finance in European currencies.

Europa (yo͞oə rō′pə), *n.* *Gk Myth.* sister of Cadmus borne to Crete by Zeus disguised in the form of a white bull; the mother by him of Rhadamanthys, Minos, and Sarpedon. [t. L, t. Gk: m. *Eurṓpē*]

Europe (yo͞oə′rəp), *n.* a continent in the W part of Eurasia, separated from Asia by the Ural Mountains on the E and the Caucasus Mountains and the Black and Caspian seas on the SE. In British usage, *Europe* sometimes contrasts with *England* or the *British Isles.* 417,000,000 pop. excluding the Soviet Union (est. 1963); ab. 3,754,000 sq. mi.

European (yo͞oə′rə pīən′), *adj.* **1.** pertaining to Europe or its inhabitants. **2.** native to or derived from Europe. —*n.* **3.** a native or inhabitant of Europe. **4.** a person of European descent or connections. **5.** one who favours Britain's entry to the European Economic Community; a Common Marketeer.

European Atomic Energy Community. See **Euratom.**

European Coal and Steel Community, an association established in 1952 for the pooling of coal, iron and steel production in Belgium, France, Italy, Luxembourg, the Netherlands and West Germany. *Abbrev.:* ECSC.

European Economic Community, an association created in 1958 to abolish internal tariffs among member countries and establish a common external tariff, by Belgium, France, Italy, Luxembourg, the Netherlands, and West Germany; the Common Market. *Abbrev.:* EEC.

European Free Trade Association, an association established in 1960 by Austria, Denmark, Norway, Portugal, Sweden, Switzerland, and the United Kingdom, to eliminate customs duties, and quantitative restrictions on industrial products traded between its members. *Abbrev.:* EFTA.

Europeanism (yo͞o′rə pīə′nĭz′əm), *n.* **1.** European characteristics, ideas, methods, sympathies, etc. **2.** a European trait or practice.

Europeanize (yo͞oə′rə pīə′nīz), *v.t.*, **-nized, -nizing.** to make European. Also, **Europeanise.** —**Eu′ropea′niza′tion,** *n.*

European plan, *U.S.* that method of conducting a hotel according to which the fixed charge per day covers only lodging and service.

European Recovery Programme. See **Marshall Plan.**

European Space Research Organization, an organization formed by twelve European countries in 1960, to carry out scientific research in the upper atmosphere and in space. *Abbrev.:* ESRO.

europium (yo͞oə rō′pyəm), *n.* *Chem.* a rare-earth metallic element with light pink salts. *Symbol:* Eu; *at. wt:* 151·96; *at. no.:* 63. [t. NL, der. L *Eurōpa* Europe]

Europort (yo͞oə′rə pôt′), *n.* a town in the Netherlands, near Rotterdam; Common Market port for super-tankers. Dutch, **Europoort** (*Du.* œy′rō po͞ort).

Eurovision (yo͞oə′rō vĭzh′ən), *n.* a system for exchanging programmes and programme materials between twenty-two television organizations in fifteen countries of western Europe.

Eurus (yo͞oə′rəs), *n.* *Class. Myth.* the easterly or south-easterly wind personified. [t. L, t. Gk: m. *Eûros*]

eury-, a word element meaning 'broad', as in *eurypterid.* [t. Gk, comb. form of *eurýs*]

Euryale (yo͞oə rī′ə lĭ), *n.* *Gk Myth.* one of the Gorgons.

Eurydice (yo͞oə rĭd′ĭ sĭ), *n.* *Gk Myth.* the wife of Orpheus, permitted by Pluto to follow her husband out of Hades, but lost to him because he disobediently looked back at her. See **Orpheus.**

eurypterid (yo͞oə rĭp′tə rĭd), *n.* *Palaeontol.* any of the *Eurypterida,* a group of Palaeozoic arthropods resembling in some respects the horseshoe crabs. [t. NL: s. *Eurypterida,* pl., f. Gk *eury-* EURY- + s. Gk *pterón* wing + *-ida* (see -ID[2])]

Eurystheus (yo͞oə rĭs′thĭ əs), *n.* *Gk Myth.* a king of Mycenae: imposed twelve labours upon Hercules.

eurythmic (yo͞o rĭth′mĭk), *adj.* eurhythmic. —**euryth′mics,** *n.* —**euryth′my,** *n.*

Eusebius (yo͞o sē′byəs), *n.* (*Eusebius Pamphili*), A.D. 260?–340?, Christian bishop in Caesarea and historian of the early Christian church. —**Euse′bian,** *adj.*

eusol (yo͞o′sŏl), *n.* an antiseptic solution obtained from chlorinated lime and boric acid. [f. *E(dinburgh) U(niversity) S(olution) O(f) L(ime)*]

eusporangiate (yo͞o′spô răn′jĭ ĭt), *adj.* *Bot.* having sporangia derived from a group of cells.

Eustachian tube (yo͞o stā′shyən), *Anat.* a canal extending from the middle ear to the pharynx; auditory canal. See diag. under **ear.** [*Eustachian,* f. EUSTACHI(O) + -AN]

Eustachio (*It.* ĕ o͞o stä′kyō), *n.* **Bartolommeo** (*It.* bär-tō lôm mĕ′ō), (*Eustachius*), died 1574, Italian anatomist.

eustatic movement, *Geol.* a major change in sea-level due to an increase or decrease in the volume of water in the seas, which may be caused by the melting of ice-sheets; no movement of the land is involved. Also, **eustatic change.**

eutaxy (yo͞o′tăk′sĭ), *n.* good or right order. [t. F: m. *eutaxie,* t. Gk: m. *eutaxía* good arrangement]

eutectic (yo͞o tĕk′tĭk), *adj.* *Chem.* **1.** of greatest fusibility: said of an alloy or mixture whose melting point is lower than that of any other alloy or mixture of the same ingredients. **2.** denoting or pertaining to such a mixture or its properties: *a eutectic melting point.* —*n.* **3.** a eutectic substance. [f. s. Gk *eútēktos* easily melted + -IC]

eutectoid (yo͞o tĕk′toid), *adj.* **1.** resembling a eutectic. —*n.* **2.** eutectoid alloy. [f. EUTECT(IC) + -OID]

Euterpe (yo͞o tû′pĭ), *n.* *Class. Myth.* the Muse of music and lyric poetry. —**Euter′pean,** *adj.* [t. L, t. Gk: lit., well-pleasing]

euthanasia (yo͞o thə nā′zyə), *n.* **1.** painless death. **2.** the putting of a person to death painlessly, esp. a person suffering from an incurable and painful disease. [t. NL, t. Gk: an easy death]

euthenics (yo͞o thĕn′ĭks), *n.* the science of bettering the environment or living conditions, esp. to improve the race. [f. s. Gk *euthēnía* plenty, well-being + -ICS]

eutherian (yo͞o thĭə′rĭ ən), *adj.* belonging to the most highly evolved group of mammals, in which the young are nourished before birth by means of a placenta.

Eutopia (yo͞o tō′pyə), *n.* a place of ideal well-being. [f. Gk EU- + *-topia,* der. *tópos* place, modelled on UTOPIA]

euxenite (yo͞ok′sĭ nīt′), *n.* a brownish black mineral of complex composition, containing yttrium, columbium, titanium, uranium, etc. [f. s. Gk *eúxenos* hospitable (in allusion to its many constituents) + -ITE[1]]

Euxine Sea (yo͞ok′sīn), Black Sea.

eV, electron-volt. Also, **ev.**

e.v.a., (in space travel) extra-vehicular activity.

evacuant (ĭ văk′yo͞o ənt), *Med.* —*adj.* **1.** evacuating; promoting evacuation, esp. from the bowels. —*n.* **2.** an evacuant medicine or agent.

evacuate (ĭ văk′yo͞o āt′), *v.*, **-ated, -ating.** —*v.t.* **1.** to leave empty; vacate. **2.** to move (persons or things) from a threatened place, disaster area, etc., to a place of greater safety. **3.** *Mil.* **a.** to remove (troops, wounded soldiers, inhabitants, etc.) from a place. **b.** to withdraw from or quit (a town, fort, etc., which has been occupied). **4.** *Physiol.* to discharge or eject as through the excretory passages, esp. from the bowels. **5.** *Physics, Chem.* to pump out, creating a vacuum; exhaust: *the apparatus was evacuated before being filled with oxygen.* —*v.i.* **6.** to leave a town because of air-raid threats, etc.: *they evacuated when the air raids began.* [t. L: m. s. *ēvacuātus,* pp., emptied out] —**evac′ua′tor,** *n.*

evacuation (ĭ văk′yo͞o ā′shən), *n.* **1.** the act or process of evacuating. **2.** the condition of being evacuated. **3.** a making empty of contents; expulsion, as of contents. **4.** *Physiol.* discharge, as of waste matter through the excretory passages, esp. from the bowels. **5.** that which is evacuated or discharged. **6.** the removal of persons or things from a disaster or danger area, etc., to a place of greater safety. **7.** *Mil.* **a.** clearance by removal of troops, etc. **b.** the withdrawal or removal of troops, wounded soldiers, inhabitants, etc. —**evacuative** (ĭ văk′yo͞o ə tĭv), *adj.*

evacuee (ĭ văk′yo͞o ē′), *n.* a person who is withdrawn or removed from a place of danger.

evade (ĭ vād′), *v.*, **evaded, evading.** —*v.t.* **1.** to escape from by trickery or cleverness: *evade pursuit.* **2.** to get round by trickery: *evade the law, the rules.* **3.** to avoid doing or fulfilling: *evade a duty, obligation, etc.* **4.** to avoid answering directly: *evade a question.* **5.** to baffle; elude: *a word that evades definition, the solution evaded him.* —*v.i.* **6.** to practise evasion. [t. L: m. s. *ēvādere* pass over, go out] —**evad′able, evad′ible,** *adj.* —**evad′er,** *n.* —**evad′ingly,** *adv.* —**Syn. 1.** avoid, shun, dodge. **3.** See **escape. 6.** prevaricate.

evaginate (ĭ văj′ĭ nāt′), *v.t.*, **-nated, -nating.** to turn inside out, or cause to protrude by eversion, as a tubular organ. [t. L: m. s. *ēvāgīnātus,* pp., unsheathed] —**evag′ina′tion,** *n.*

evaluate (ĭ văl′yo͞o āt′), *v.t.*, **-ated, -ating. 1.** to ascertain the value or amount of; appraise carefully. **2.** *Maths.* to ascertain the numerical value of. [f. s. F *évaluer* (der. OF *value,* pp. of *valoir* be worth, g. L *valēre*) + -ATE[1]] —**eval′ua′tion,** *n.*

evanesce (ĕv′ə nĕs′), *v.i.*, **-nesced, -nescing.** to disappear gradually; vanish; fade away. [t. L: m. s. *ēvānescere*] —**ev′anes′cence,** *n.*

evanescent (ĕv′ə nĕs′ənt), *adj.* **1.** vanishing; passing away; fleeting. **2.** tending to become imperceptible; scarcely perceptible. —**ev′anes′cently,** *adv.*

Evang., Evangelical.
evangel[1] (ĭ vănˊjəl), *n.* **1.** the good tidings of the redemption of the world through Jesus Christ; the gospel. **2.** (*usually cap.*) any of the four Gospels. **3.** doctrine taken as a guide or regarded as of prime importance. [t. LL: m. s. *ēvangelium,* t. Gk: m. *euangélion* good tidings; r. ME *evangile,* t. OF]
evangel[2] (ĭ vănˊjəl), *n.* an evangelist. [t. Gk: m. s. *euángelos* good messenger]
evangelical (ēˊvăn jĕlˊĭ kl), *adj.* **1.** pertaining to the gospel and its teachings. **2.** related to those Christian bodies which emphasize the teachings and authority of the Scriptures, in opposition to that of the church itself or of reason. **3.** pertaining to certain movements in the 18th and 19th centuries which stressed the importance of personal experience of guilt for sin, and of reconciliation to God through Christ. **4.** evangelistic. *—n.* **5.** an adherent of evangelical doctrines or a member of an evangelical church or party, esp. of the Low Church party in the Church of England. **—eˊvangelˊically,** *adv.*
evangelicalism (ēˊvăn jĕlˊĭ kə lĭzˊəm), *n.* **1.** evangelical doctrines or principles. **2.** adherence to them, or to an evangelical church or party.
evangelism (ĭ vănˊjĭ lĭzˊəm), *n.* **1.** the preaching or promulgation of the gospel; the work of an evangelist. **2.** evangelicalism.
evangelist (ĭ vănˊjĭ lĭst), *n.* **1.** a preacher of the gospel. **2.** (*cap.*) any of the writers (Matthew, Mark, Luke, and John) of the four Gospels. **3.** one of a class of teachers in the early church, next in rank after apostles and prophets. **4.** a revivalist. **5.** an occasional or itinerant preacher. **6.** (*cap.*) *Mormon Ch.* a patriarch.
evangelistic (ĭ vănˊjĭ lĭsˊtĭk), *adj.* **1.** pertaining to evangelists, or preachers of the gospel. **2.** evangelical. **3.** seeking to evangelize; striving to convert sinners. **4.** designed or fitted to evangelize. **5.** (*often cap.*) of or pertaining to the four Evangelists. **—evanˊgelisˊtically,** *adv.*
evangelize (ĭ vănˊjĭ līzˊ), *v.,* **-lized, -lizing.** *—v.t.* **1.** to preach the gospel to. **2.** to convert to Christianity. *—v.i.* **3.** to preach the gospel; act as an evangelist. Also, **evangelise. —evanˊgelizaˊtion,** *n.* **—evanˊgelizˊer,** *n.*
evanish (ĭ vănˊĭsh), *v.i. Archaic.* **1.** to vanish or disappear. **2.** to cease to be. **—evanˊishment,** *n.*
Evans (ĕvˊənz), *n.* **1. Sir Arthur John,** 1851–1941, English archaeologist. **2. Dame Edith,** born 1888, English actress. **3. Geraint Llewellyn,** born 1922, Welsh operatic baritone. **4. Mary Ann** (*Mrs J. W. Cross*). See **Eliot, George.**
Evansville (ĕvˊənz vĭl), *n.* a town in the U.S., in Indiana. 141,543 (1960).
evaporable (ĭ văpˊə rə bl), *adj.* capable of being converted to gas by evaporation. **—evapˊorabilˊity,** *n.*
evaporate (ĭ văpˊə rātˊ), *v.,* **-rated, -rating.** *—v.i.* **1.** to turn to vapour; pass off in vapour. **2.** to give off moisture. **3.** to disappear; vanish; fade: *as soon as his situation became clear to him, his hopes quickly evaporated.* *—v.t.* **4.** to convert into a gaseous state or vapour; drive off or extract in the form of vapour. **5.** to extract moisture or liquid from, as by heat, so as to make dry or to reduce to a denser state: *to evaporate fruit.* **6.** to cause to fade or disappear. [t. LL: m. s. *ēvapōrātus,* pp., dispersed in vapour] **—evapˊoraˊtor,** *n.*
—Syn. 5. EVAPORATE, DEHYDRATE, DRY mean to abstract moisture from. TO EVAPORATE is to remove moisture by means of heat, and thus to produce condensation or shrivelling: *to evaporate milk, sliced apples.* TO DEHYDRATE is to remove all vestiges of moisture by means of a mechanical process: *to dehydrate foods makes them easier to preserve and to transport.* TO DRY is the general word, but may also mean to wipe moisture off the surface or to withdraw moisture by exposure to air or heat; the object dried is restored to its condition before it became wet: *to dry a dish, clothes.*
evaporated milk, thick, unsweetened, tinned milk made by removing some of the water from whole milk.
evaporation (ĭ văpˊə rāˊshən), *n.* **1.** the act or process of evaporating. **2.** the state of being evaporated. **3.** matter, or the quantity of matter, evaporated or passed off in vapour. **—evaporative** (ĭ văpˊə rə tĭv), *adj.*
evasion (ĭ vāˊzhən), *n.* **1.** the act of escaping something by trickery or cleverness: *evasion of one's duty, responsibilities, etc.* **2.** the avoiding of an argument, accusation, question, or the like, as by a subterfuge. **3.** a means of evading; a subterfuge; an excuse or trick to avoid or get round something. **4.** tax evasion. [late ME, t. LL: s. *ēvāsio*] **—Syn. 1.** avoidance, dodging. **2.** prevarication, equivocation, quibbling.
evasive (ĭ vāˊsĭv), *adj.* **1.** tending or seeking to evade; characterized by evasion: *an evasive answer.* **2.** elusive or evanescent. **—evaˊsively,** *adv.* **—evaˊsiveness,** *n.*
Evatt (ĕvˊət), *n.* **Herbert Vere,** 1894–1965, Australian lawyer and statesman.
eve (ēv), *n.* **1.** the evening, or often the day, before a church festival, and hence before any date or event. **2.** the period just preceding any event, etc.: *the eve of a revolution.* **3.** *Archaic.* the evening. [var. of EVEN[2]]
Eve (ēv), *n. Bible.* the first woman. Gen. 3:20. [ME; OE *Efe,* t. L: m. *Eva,* t. Gk (Septuagint), t. Heb.: m. *hawwāh,* explained as 'mother of the living' (*hāy*), but meaning uncert.]
evection (ĭ vĕkˊshən), *n. Astron.* a periodic inequality in the moon's motion caused by the attraction of the sun. [t. L: s. *ēvectio,* der. *ēvehere* carry forth or up] **—evecˊtional,** *adj.*
Evelyn (ēvˊlĭn, ĕvˊlĭn), *n.* **John,** 1620–1706, English diarist.
even[1] (ēˊvən), *adj.* **1.** level; flat; without irregularities; smooth: *an even surface, even country.* **2.** on the same level; in the same plane or line; parallel: *even with the ground.* **3.** free from variations or fluctuations; regular: *even motion.* **4.** uniform in action, character, or quality: *an even colour, to hold an even course.* **5.** equal in measure or quantity: *even quantities of two substances.* **6.** same: *letters of even date.* **7.** divisible by 2: thus, 2, 4, 6, 8, 10, and 12 are *even* numbers (opposed to *odd,* as 1, 3, etc.). **8.** denoted by such a number: *the even pages of a book.* **9.** exactly expressible in integers, or in tens, hundreds, etc., without fractional parts: *an even mile, an even hundred.* **10.** exactly balanced on each side; equally divided. **11.** leaving no balance of debt on either side, as accounts; square, as one person with another. **12.** calm; placid; not easily excited or angered: *an even temper.* **13.** equitable, impartial, or fair: *an even bargain, an even chance.*
—adv. **14.** evenly. **15.** still; yet (used to emphasize a comparative): *even more suitable.* **16.** (used to suggest that something mentioned as a possibility constitutes an extreme case, or one that might not be expected): *the slightest noise, even, disturbs him; even if he goes, he may not take part.* **17.** just: *even now.* **18.** fully or quite: *even to death.* **19.** indeed (used as an intensive for stressing identity or truth of something): *he is willing, even eager, to do it.* **20.** *Archaic.* exactly or precisely: *it was even so.* **21. break even,** to have one's credits or profits equal one's debits or losses. **22. get even,** to get one's revenge; square accounts.
—v.t. **23.** to make even; level; smooth. **24.** to place in an even state as to claim or obligation; balance: *to even, or even up, accounts.*
—v.i. **25.** to become even: *after Bristol, the road evens out.* [ME; OE *efen,* c. G *eben*] **—eˊvener,** *n.* **—eˊvenly,** *adv.* **—eˊvenness,** *n.*
—Syn. 1. See **level. 3.** EVEN, EQUABLE, UNIFORM imply a steady sameness. EVEN implies freedom from inequalities or irregularities: *even breathing, an even flow.* EQUABLE suggests the inherent quality of regularity or, in a non-material reference, that of being well-balanced, not easily disturbed, and impartial in judgement: *an equable temperament.* UNIFORM emphasizes sameness and conformity to a standard: *uniform height or practice.* **—Ant. 1.** irregular, changeable.
even[2] (ēˊvən), *n. Archaic.* evening; eve. [ME; OE *ēfen, ǣfen;* akin to G *Abend*]
evenfall (ēˊvən fôlˊ), *n. Archaic.* the beginning of evening.
even-handed (ēˊvən hănˊdĭd), *adj.* impartial; equitable: *even-handed justice.* **—eˊven-handˊedness,** *n.*
evening (ēvˊnĭng), *n.* **1.** the latter part of the day and early part of the night. **2.** the period from sunset to bedtime. **3.** any concluding or declining period: *the evening of life.* **4.** an evening's reception or entertainment. **5.** *Southern U.S.* the time between noon and dark, including afternoon and twilight. *—adj.* **6.** of or pertaining to evening. **7.** occurring or seen in the evening. [ME; OE *ǣfnung,* der. *ǣfnian* draw towards evening] **—Syn. 1.** eventide, dusk, twilight, gloaming, nightfall.
evening class, a class, held after normal working hours, often maintained by a local authority, providing further education at a low fee.
evening dress, formal evening clothes.
evening gown, a woman's formal or semi-formal dress, esp. one with a floor-length skirt.
Evening Prayer, (*sometimes l.c.*) Evensong.
evening primrose, 1. a plant, *Oenothera biennis,* family *Onagraceae,* with yellow flowers that open at nightfall. **2.** any of various plants of the same or related genera.
evenings (ēvˊnĭngz), *adv. Now Colloq.* during or in the evening regularly.
evening star, a bright planet seen in the west after sunset, esp. Venus.
even-minded (ēˊvən mīnˊdĭd), *adj.* not easily ruffled, disturbed, prejudiced, etc.; calm; equable. **—eˊven-mindˊedness,** *n.*
even money, *Betting.* **1.** an equal sum bet by each backer. **2.** paying out as winnings (of a bet) the same amount as staked.

evens (ē′vənz), *adv.* **1.** (of a bet staked) evenly; with even money. —*n.* **2.** (*usually construed as sing.*) even money.
Evensong (ē′vən sŏng′), *n.* **1.** *C. of E.* a form of worship appointed to be said or sung at evening; Evening Prayer. **2.** *Rom. Cath. Ch.* vespers. **3.** *Archaic.* evening. [ME; OE *ǣfensang*, f. *ǣfen* evening + *sang* song]
event (ĭ vĕnt′), *n.* **1.** anything that happens or is regarded as happening; an occurrence, esp. one of some importance. **2.** the fact of happening (chiefly in the phrase *in the event of*). **3.** the outcome, issue, or result of anything (chiefly in the phrase *after the event*). **4.** *Philos.* something which occurs in a certain place during a particular interval of time. **5.** *Sport.* each of the items in a programme of one sport or a number of sports. **6. at all events** or **in any event,** whatever happens; in any case. [t. L: s. *ēventus* occurrence, issue] —**event′less,** *adj.*
—**Syn. 1.** happening, affair, case, circumstance. EVENT, EPISODE, INCIDENT, OCCURRENCE are terms for a happening. An EVENT is usually an important happening, esp. one that comes out of and is connected with previous happenings: *historical events.* An EPISODE is one of a progressive series of happenings, frequently distinct from the main course of events but arising naturally from them and having a continuity and interest of its own: *an episode in one's life.* An INCIDENT is usually a happening which takes place in connection with an event or a series of events of greater importance: *an amusing incident in a play.* An OCCURRENCE is something (usually of an ordinary nature) that happens, having no particular connection with (or causation by) antecedent happenings: *his arrival was an unexpected occurrence.*
even-tempered (ē′vən tĕm′pəd), *adj.* not easily ruffled or disturbed; calm.
eventful (ĭ vĕnt′fəl), *adj.* **1.** full of events or incidents, esp. of a striking character: *an eventful period.* **2.** having important issues or results; momentous. —**event′fully,** *adv.* —**event′fulness,** *n.*
eventide (ē′vən tīd′), *n. Archaic.* evening.
eventu-, a word element meaning 'event'. [comb. form repr. L *eventus*]
eventual (ĭ vĕn′tyo͞o əl), *adj.* **1.** pertaining to the event or issue; consequent; ultimate. **2.** depending upon uncertain events; contingent.
eventuality (ĭ vĕn′tyo͞o ăl′ĭ tĭ), *n., pl.* **-ties. 1.** a contingent event; a possible occurrence or circumstance. **2.** the state or fact of being eventual; contingent character.
eventually (ĭ vĕn′tyo͞o ə lĭ), *adv.* finally; ultimately.
eventuate (ĭ vĕn′tyo͞o āt′), *v.i.,* **-ated, -ating. 1.** to have issue; result. **2.** to come about. —**even′tua′tion,** *n.*
ever (ĕv′ə), *adv.* **1.** at all times: *he is ever ready to excuse himself.* **2.** continuously: *ever since then.* **3.** at any time: *did you ever see anything like it?* **4.** (with emphatic force, in various idiomatic constructions and phrases) in any possible case; by any chance; at all: *how ever did you manage to do it?* **5. ever and again** or **ever and anon,** every now and then; continually. **6. ever so,** to whatever extent or degree; greatly; exceedingly: *ever so long, be he ever so bold.* **7. for ever,** for eternity; eternally; always; continually. **8. for ever and a day,** for ever; eternally. [ME; OE *ǣfre*, prob. akin to *ā* ever. See AY[1]] —**Syn. 1.** eternally, perpetually, constantly. See **always.**
Everard (ĕv′ə räd′), *n.* **Cape,** a promontory at the extreme E end of the coast of Victoria, Australia: lighthouse.
Everest (ĕv′ə rĭst), *n.* **Mount,** a peak of the Himalayas, in E Nepal: highest mountain in the world. 29,028 ft.

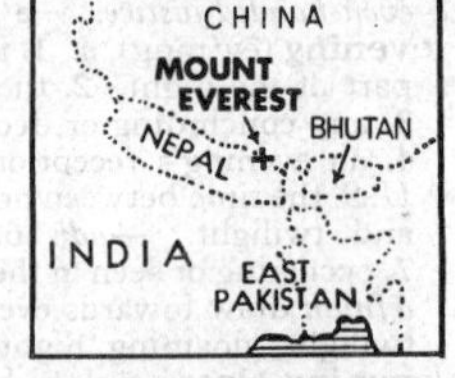

Mount Everest

everglade (ĕv′ə glād′), *n. Southern U.S.* a tract of low, swampy land characterized by clumps of tall grass and numerous branching waterways.
Everglades (ĕv′ə glādz′), *n.pl.* a swampy and partly forested region in the U.S., S Florida, mostly S of Lake Okeechobee. Over 5000 sq. mi.
evergreen (ĕv′ə grēn′), *adj.* **1.** (of trees, shrubs, etc.) having green leaves throughout the entire year, the leaves of the past season not being shed until after the new foliage has been completely formed. **2.** (of leaves) belonging to such a tree, shrub, etc. —*n.* **3.** an evergreen plant. **4.** (*pl.*) evergreen twigs or branches used for decoration.
everlasting (ĕv′ə läs′tĭng), *adj.* **1.** lasting for ever; eternal. **2.** lasting or continuing indefinitely. **3.** incessant; constantly recurring. **4.** wearisome: *to tire of someone's everlasting puns.* —*n.* **5.** eternal duration; eternity. **6. the Everlasting,** the Eternal Being; God. **7.** Also, **everlasting flower.** any of various plants or flowers which retain their shape, colour, etc., when dried, as certain species of the composite genus *Helichrysum*, and various species of cudweed, genus *Gnaphalium.* —**ev′erlast′ingly,** *adv.* —**ev′erlast′ingness,** *n.* —**Syn. 1.** See **eternal.**
everlasting flower, the immortelle.
evermore (ĕv′ə mô′), *adv.* **1.** always, for ever; eternally (often prec. by *for*). **2.** at all times; continually.
eversible (ĭ vû′sə bl), *adj.* capable of being everted.
eversion (ĭ vû′shən), *n.* a turning or being turned outwards, or inside out.
evert (ĭ vût′), *v.t.* to turn outwards, or inside out. [t. L: s. *ēvertere* overturn]
every (ĕv′rĭ), *adj.* **1.** each (referring one by one to all the members of an aggregate): *we go there every day, be sure to remember every word he says.* **2.** all possible; the greatest possible degree of: *every prospect of success.* **3. every bit,** *Colloq.* in every respect; in all points: *every bit as good.* **4. every now and then** or **every now and again** or **every once in a while,** occasionally; from time to time. **5. every other,** every second; every alternate. [ME *every*, *everich*, etc., OE *ǣfre ǣlc* EVER EACH] —**Syn. 1.** See **each.**
everybody (ĕv′rĭ bŏd′ĭ), *pron.* every person.
everyday (ĕv′rĭ dā′), *adj.* **1.** of or pertaining to every day; daily: *an everyday occurrence.* **2.** of or for ordinary days, as contrasted with Sundays or special occasions: *everyday clothes.* **3.** such as is met with every day; ordinary; commonplace: *an everyday scene.*
Everyman (ĕv′rĭ măn′), *n.* **1.** a 15th-century English morality play translated from the Dutch *Elkerlijk.* **2.** (*often l.c.*) a common or ordinary man. —*pron.* **3.** (*l.c.*) everybody; every person.
everyone (ĕv′rĭ wŭn′, -wən), *pron.* every person; everybody. Also, **every one.**
everything (ĕv′rĭ thĭng′), *pron.* **1.** every thing or particular of an aggregate or total; all. **2.** something extremely important: *this news means everything to us.*
everyway (ĕv′rĭ wā′), *adv.* in every way; in every direction, manner, or respect.
everywhere (ĕv′rĭ wēə′), *adv.* in every place or part; in all places.
Evesham (ēv′shəm), *n.* a town in England, in SE Worcestershire: fruit-growing; battle 1265. 12,608 (1961).
Eve's pudding, a baked sponge pudding with a fruit foundation.
evict (ĭ vĭkt′), *v.t.* **1.** to expel (a person, esp. a tenant) from land, a building, etc., by legal process. **2.** to recover (property, etc.) by virtue of superior legal title. [t. L: s. *ēvictus*, pp., overcome completely, (property) recovered by judicial decision] —**evic′tion,** *n.* —**evic′tor,** *n.*
evidence (ĕv′ĭ dəns), *n., v.,* **-denced, -dencing.** —*n.* **1.** ground for belief; that which tends to prove or disprove something; proof. **2.** something that makes evident; an indication or sign. **3.** *Law.* the data, in the form of testimony of witnesses, or of documents or other objects (such as a photograph, a revolver, etc.) identified by witnesses, offered to the court or jury in proof of the facts at issue. **4. in evidence,** in a situation to be readily seen; plainly visible; conspicuous. **5. turn queen's, king's,** or **state's evidence,** (of an accomplice in a crime) to become a witness for the prosecution against the others involved. —*v.t.* **6.** to make evident or clear; show clearly; manifest. **7.** to support by evidence.
—**Syn. 3.** information, deposition, affidavit. EVIDENCE, EXHIBIT, TESTIMONY, PROOF refer to information furnished in a legal investigation to support a contention. EVIDENCE is any information so given, whether furnished by witnesses or derived from documents or from any other source: *hearsay evidence is not admitted in a trial.* An EXHIBIT in law is a document or article which is presented in court as evidence: *the signed contract is Exhibit A.* TESTIMONY is usually evidence given by witnesses under oath: *the jury listened carefully to the testimony.* PROOF is evidence that is so complete and convincing as to put a conclusion beyond reasonable doubt: *proof of the innocence of the accused.*
evident (ĕv′ĭ dənt), *adj.* plain or clear to the sight or understanding: *an evident mistake.* [t. L: s. *ēvidens*] —**Syn.** obvious, manifest, palpable, patent, unmistakeable. See **apparent.**
evidential (ĕv′ĭ dĕn′shəl), *adj.* of or having the nature of, serving as, or based on evidence. —**ev′iden′tially,** *adv.*
evidentiary (ĕv′ĭ dĕn′shə rĭ), *adj.* **1.** of or pertaining to evidence. **2.** furnishing or constituting evidence.
evidently (ĕv′ĭ dənt lĭ), *adv.* obviously; apparently. —**Syn.** See **clearly.**
evil (ē′vəl), *adj.* **1.** violating or inconsistent with the moral law; wicked: *evil deeds, an evil life.* **2.** harmful; injurious: *evil laws.* **3.** characterized or accompanied by misfortune or suffering; unfortunate; disastrous: *to be fallen on evil days.* **4.** due to (actual or imputed) bad character or conduct: *an evil reputation.* **5.** characterized by anger, irascibility, etc. **6. the evil one,** the devil; Satan. —*n.* **7.** that which is evil; evil quality, intention, or conduct: *to choose the lesser of two evils.* **8.** (*sometimes cap.*) the force which governs and brings about wickedness and sin. **9.** that part of someone or something that is wicked. **10.** harm; mischief; misfortune: *to wish one evil.* **11.** any-

thing causing injury or harm. 12. a disease: *king's evil* (scrofula). —*adv.* 13. in an evil manner; badly; ill: *it went evil with his house.* [ME; OE *yfel*, c. G *übel*] —**e′villy,** *adv.* —**e′vilness,** *n.* —**Syn.** 1. sinful, iniquitous, depraved, vicious, corrupt, immoral. See **bad**[1]. 7. wickedness, depravity, iniquity, unrighteousness. 10. disaster, calamity. —**Ant.** 1. righteous.

evildoer (ē′vəl do͞o′ə), *n.* one who does evil. —**e′vildo′ing,** *adj., n.*

evil eye, the power superstitiously attributed to certain persons of inflicting injury or bad luck by a look. —**e′vil-eyed′,** *adj.*

evil-minded (ē′vəl mīn′dĭd), *adj.* 1. having an evil mind; malignant. 2. excessively sex-minded.

evince (ĭ vĭns′), *v.t.*, **evinced, evincing.** 1. to show clearly; make evident or manifest; prove. 2. to reveal the possession of (a quality, trait, etc.). [t. L: m. s. *ēvincere* overcome completely, prove, demonstrate] —**evin′cible,** *adj.* —**Syn.** 1. See **display.**

evincive (ĭ vĭn′sĭv), *adj.* serving to evince; indicative.

eviscerate (ĭ vĭs′ə rāt′), *v.*, **-rated, -rating,** *adj.* —*v.t.* 1. to disembowel. 2. to deprive of vital or essential parts. —*adj.* 3. *Surg.* disembowelled. [t. L: m. s. *ēviscerātus*, pp., disembowelled] —**evis′cera′tion,** *n.*

evitable (ĕv′ĭ tə bl), *adj.* avoidable. [t. L: m. s. *ēvītābilis* avoidable]

evite (ĭ vīt′), *v.t.*, **evited, eviting.** *Archaic.* to avoid; shun. [t. L: m. s. *ēvītāre*]

evocable (ĕv′ə kə bl), *adj.* that may be evoked.

evocate (ĕv′ə kāt′), *v.t.*, **-cated, -cating.** to call up, as from the dead.

evocation (ĕv′ə kā′shən), *n.* 1. the act of evoking; a calling forth. 2. *French Law.* withdrawing a case from an inferior court. [t. L: s. *ēvocātio*, der. *ēvocāre* call forth]

evocative (ĭ vŏk′ə tĭv), *adj.* tending to evoke.

evocator (ĕv′ə kā′tə), *n.* 1. *Embryol.* a morphogenic substance, or a piece of tissue, generally not living, which contains morphogenic substances. 2. one who evokes, esp., one who calls up spirits.

evoke (ĭ vōk′), *v.t.*, **evoked, evoking.** 1. to call up, or produce (memories, feelings, etc.): *to evoke a memory, a smile, etc.* 2. to provoke, or elicit. 3. to call up; cause to appear; summon: *to evoke a spirit from the dead.* [t. L: m. s. *ēvocāre* call forth] —**evok′er,** *n.*

evolute (ē′və lo͞ot′), *n.* *Geom.* the locus of the centres of curvature of, or the envelope of the normals to, another curve (called the *involute*). [t. L: m. s. *ēvolūtus*, pp., rolled out]

ABC, Evolute of parabolic arc OPQ

evolution (ē′və lo͞o′shən), *n.* 1. any process of formation or growth; development: *the evolution of man, the drama, the aeroplane, etc.* 2. something evolved; a product. 3. *Biol.* the continuous genetic adaptation of organisms or species to the environment by the integrating agencies of selection, hybridization, inbreeding, and mutation. 4. a motion incomplete in itself, but combining with coordinated motions to produce a single action, as in a machine. 5. an evolving or giving off of gas, heat, etc. 6. *Maths.* the extraction of roots from powers (the inverse of *involution*). [t. L: s. *ēvolūtio*, der. *ēvolvere* roll out] —**ev′olu′tional,** *adj.* —**ev′olu′tionally,** *adv.*

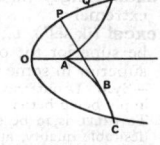

evolutionary (ē′və lo͞osh′nə rĭ), *adj.* 1. pertaining to evolution or development; developmental: *the evolutionary origin of species.* 2. in accordance with the theory of evolution. 3. pertaining to or performing evolutions.

evolutionist (ē′və lo͞o′shə nĭst), *n.* a believer in the doctrine of evolution.

evolutionistic (ē′və lo͞o′shə nĭs′tĭk), *adj.* 1. tending to support the theory of evolution. 2. tending to cause evolution.

evolve (ĭ vŏlv′), *v.*, **evolved, evolving.** —*v.t.* 1. to develop gradually: *to evolve a scheme, a plan, a theory, etc.* 2. *Biol.* to develop, as by a process of differentiation, to a more highly organized condition. 3. to give off or emit, as smells, vapours, etc. —*v.i.* 4. to come forth gradually into being; develop; undergo evolution. [t. L: m. s. *ēvolvere* roll out, unroll, unfold] —**evolv′able,** *adj.* —**evolve′ment,** *n.* —**evolv′er,** *n.*

evonymus (ĕv ŏn′ĭ məs), *n.* euonymus.

Évreux (*Fr.* ė vrœ′), *n.* a town in NW France, capital of Eure department. 40,200 (est. 1962).

evulsion (ĭ vŭl′shən), *n.* 1. the act of plucking or pulling out; forcible extraction. 2. the forcible tearing away of a part. [t. L: s. *ēvulsio*, der. *ēvellere* pluck out]

Evvoia (*Gk* ĕ′vyȧ), *n.* modern Greek name of **Euboea.**

ewe (yo͞o), *n.* a female sheep. [ME and OE, c. D *ooi*; akin to L *ovis*, Gk *óis*, Skt *avi* sheep]

Ewe (ĕ′wĕ), *n.* 1. a language of West Africa, spoken in parts of Togo and Ghana. 2. the people speaking this language.

ewe lamb, 1. a young female sheep. 2. *Colloq.* a favourite or loved daughter or other person.

ewe-neck (yo͞o′nĕk′), *n.* a thin hollow neck, low in front of the shoulder, as of a horse or other animal. —**ewe′-necked′,** *adj.*

ewer (yo͞o′ə), *n.* 1. a pitcher with a wide spout, esp. one to hold water for ablutions. 2. *Decorative Art.* a vessel having a spout and a handle; esp., a tall, slender vessel with a base. [ME, t. AF. g. L *aquāria* vessel for water]

Ewer and basin

ex[1] (ĕks), *prep.* 1. *Finance.* without, not including, or without the right to have: *ex dividend, ex interest, ex rights.* 2. *Com.* out of; free out of: *ex warehouse, ex ship, etc.* (free of charges until the time of removal out of the warehouse, ship, etc.). —*n.* 3. *Slang.* one's former husband or wife. 4. *Slang.* one's former boy friend or girl friend. [t. L. See EX-[1]]

ex[2] (ĕks), *n.* the letter X, x.

ex-[1], a prefix meaning 'out of', 'from', and hence 'utterly', 'thoroughly', and sometimes serving to impart a privative or negative force or to indicate a former title, status, etc.; freely used as an English formative, as in *exstipulate, exterritorial*, and esp. in such combinations as *ex-president* (former president), *ex-member, ex-wife*; occurring before vowels and *c, p, q, s, t*. Also, **e-, ef-.** [t. L, comb. form of *ex, ē*, prep., out of, from, beyond]

ex-[2], var. of **exo-.**

ex-[3], a prefix identical in meaning with **ex-**[1], occurring before vowels in words of Greek origin, as in *exarch, exegis.* Also, **ec-.** [t. Gk, also before consonants *ek-* EC-; becoming *ec-* in L derivatives]

Ex., Exodus.

ex., 1. examination. 2. examined. 3. example. 4. except. 5. exception. 6. exchange. 7. excursion. 8. executed. 9. executive.

exacerbate (ĕks ăs′ə bāt′), *v.t.*, **-bated, -bating.** 1. to increase the bitterness or violence of (disease, ill feeling, etc.); aggravate. 2. to embitter the feelings of (a person); irritate; exasperate. [t. L: m. s. *exacerbātus*, pp., irritated]

exacerbation (ĕks ăs′ə bā′shən), *n.* 1. the action of exacerbating; the condition of being exacerbated. 2. *Med.* a paroxysmal increase in severity.

exact (ĭg zăkt′), *adj.* 1. strictly accurate or correct: *an exact likeness, description, or translation.* 2. precise, as opposed to approximate: *the exact sum due, the exact date.* 3. admitting of no deviation, as laws, discipline, etc.; strict or rigorous. 4. characterized by or using strict accuracy or precision: *exact instruments, an exact thinker.* —*v.t.* 5. to call for, demand, or require: *to exact obedience, respect.* 6. to force or compel the payment, yielding, or performance of: *to exact money, tribute, etc.* [t. L: s. *exactus*, pp., forced out, required, measured by a standard] —**exact′able,** *adj.* —**exact′er, exac′tor,** *n.* —**exact′ness,** *n.* —**Syn.** 3. rigid, severe. 4. methodical, careful, punctilious. 5. force, compel. 6. extort, wrest, wring. See **extract.**

exacting (ĭg zăk′tĭng), *adj.* 1. severe or rigid in demands or requirements, as a person. 2. requiring close application, as a task. 3. given to or characterized by exaction; extortionate. —**exact′ingly,** *adv.* —**exact′ingness,** *n.*

exaction (ĭg zăk′shən), *n.* 1. the act of exacting; extortion. 2. something exacted.

exactitude (ĭg zăk′tĭ tyo͝od′), *n.* the quality of being exact; exactness; preciseness; accuracy.

exactly (ĭg zăkt′lĭ), *adv.* 1. in an exact manner; precisely, according to rule, measure, fact, etc., accurately. 2. just: *she does exactly as she likes.* 3. quite so; that's right.

exact science, a science (such as mathematics) which permits of accurate analysis.

exaggerate (ĭg zăj′ə rāt′), *v.*, **-rated, -rating.** —*v.t.* 1. to magnify beyond the limits of truth; overstate; represent disproportionately: *to exaggerate one's importance, the difficulties of a situation, the size of one's house, etc.* 2. to increase or enlarge abnormally. —*v.i.* 3. to employ exaggeration, as in speech or writing: *a person who is always exaggerating.* [t. L: m. s. *exaggerātus*, pp., heaped up] —**exag′gerat′ingly,** *adv.* —**exag′gera′tor,** *n.* —**Ant.** 1. minimize.

exaggerated (ĭg zăj′ə rā′tĭd), *adj.* 1. unduly magnified: *to have an exaggerated opinion of oneself.* 2. abnormally increased or enlarged: *a heart greatly exaggerated by disease.* —**exag′gerat′edly,** *adv.*

exaggeration (ĭg zăj′ə rā′shən), *n.* 1. the act of exaggerating. 2. the state of being exaggerated. 3. an exaggerated statement.

exaggerative (ĭg zăj′ə rə tĭv), *adj.* given to or characterized by exaggeration. Also, **exaggeratory** (ĭg zăj′ə rə trĭ, -ə rā′tə rĭ).

exalt (ĭg zôlt′), *v.t.* **1.** to elevate in rank, honour, power, character, quality, etc.: *exalted to the position of president.* **2.** to praise; extol: *to exalt someone to the skies.* **3.** *Obs.* to elate, as with pride or joy. **4.** to stimulate, as the imagination. **5.** to intensify, as a colour. **6.** *Archaic.* to raise up. [t. L: s. *exaltāre* lift up] —**exalter,** *n.* —**Syn. 1.** promote, dignify. See **elevate. 2.** glorify. —**Ant. 1.** humble. **2.** depreciate.

exaltation (ĕg′zôl tā′shən), *n.* **1.** the act of exalting. **2.** the state of being exalted. **3.** elation of mind, or feeling, sometimes abnormal or morbid in character; rapture. **4.** *Astrol.* the position of a planet in the zodiac in which it is considered to exert its greatest influence.

exalted (ĭg zôl′tĭd), *adj.* **1.** elevated, as in rank or character; of high station: *an exalted personage.* **2.** noble or elevated, lofty: *an exalted style.* **3.** rapturously excited. —**exalt′edly,** *adv.* —**exalt′edness,** *n.* —**Syn. 1.** sublime, grand.

exam (ĭg zăm′), *n. Colloq.* an examination.

exam., **1.** examination. **2.** examined. **3.** examinee. **4.** examiner.

examen (ĭg zā′mĕn), *n. Eccles.* an examination, as of conscience. [t. L: a weighing, consideration]

examinant (ĭg zăm′ĭ nənt), *n.* an examiner.

examination (ĭg zăm′ĭ nā′shən), *n.* **1.** the act of examining; inspection; inquiry; investigation. **2.** the state of being examined. **3.** the act or process of testing pupils, candidates, etc., as by questions. **4.** the test itself; list of questions asked. **5.** the statements, etc., made by one examined. **6.** *Law.* formal interrogation. [t. L: s. *exāminātio*] —**exam′ina′tional,** *adj.*

—**Syn. 1.** EXAMINATION, INSPECTION, SCRUTINY refer to a scanning of something. An EXAMINATION may mean a careful noting of details or may mean little more than a casual glance over something: *a thorough examination of the plumbing revealed a defective pipe.* An INSPECTION is a formal and official examination: *an inspection of records, a military inspection.* SCRUTINY implies a critical and minutely detailed examination: *his workmanship would not stand close scrutiny.* See **investigation.**

examine (ĭg zăm′ĭn), *v.t.,* **-ined, -ining. 1.** to inspect or scrutinize carefully; inquire into or investigate. **2.** to test the knowledge, reactions, or qualifications of (a pupil, candidate, etc.), as by questions or assigned tasks. **3.** to subject to legal inquisition; put to question in regard to conduct or to knowledge of facts; interrogate: *to examine a witness or a suspected person.* [ME *examine(n),* t. F: m. *examiner,* t. L: m. *exāmināre* weigh accurately, test] —**exam′inable,** *adj.* —**exam′iner,** *n.* —**Syn. 1.** search, probe, explore. **2.** catechize.

examinee (ĭg zăm′ĭ nē′), *n.* one who is examined.

example (ĭg zäm′pl), *n., v.,* **-pled, -pling.** —*n.* **1.** one of a number of things, or a part of something, taken to show the character of the whole. **2.** something to be imitated; a pattern or model: *to set a good example.* **3.** an instance serving for illustration; a specimen. **4.** an instance illustrating a rule or method, as a mathematical problem proposed for solution. **5.** an instance, esp. of punishment, serving for a warning; a warning. **6.** a precedent; a parallel case: *an action without example.* —*v.t.* **7.** to give or be an example of (chiefly in pp.). [ME, t. OF: m. *essample,* g. L *exempla,* pl. of *exemplum*]

—**Syn. 1.** EXAMPLE, SAMPLE, SPECIMEN refer to an individual phenomenon taken as representative of a type, or to a part representative of the whole. EXAMPLE is used of an object, activity, condition, etc., which is assumed to illustrate a certain principle, law, or standard: *a good example of baroque architecture.* SAMPLE, used mainly with a concrete reference, refers to a small portion of a substance, or to a single representative of a group or type, which is intended to show what the rest of the substance, or the group, is like: *a sample of yarn.* SPECIMEN usually suggests that the 'sample' chosen is intended to serve a scientific or technical purpose: *a blood specimen, zoological specimens.* **2.** See **ideal. 3.** See **case**[1].

exanimate (ĭg zăn′ĭ mĭt, -māt′), *adj.* **1.** inanimate or lifeless. **2.** spiritless; disheartened. [t. L: m. s. *exanimātus,* pp., deprived of breath, life, or spirit] —**exan′ima′tion,** *n.*

ex animo (ĕks ăn′ĭ mō′), *Latin.* from the heart; sincerely.

exanthema (ĕk′săn thē′mə), *n., pl.* **-themata** (-thē′mə tə). **1.** *Pathol.* an eruption or rash on the skin, esp. one attended with fever. **2.** See **vesicular exanthema.** [t. LL, t. Gk: a bursting into flower] —**exanthematic** (ĕk săn′thĭmăt′ĭk), **exanthematous** (ĕk′săn thē′mə təs), *adj.*

exarch[1] (ĕk′säk), *n.* **1.** (in the Eastern Church) **a.** a patriarch's deputy. **b.** (formerly), a bishop ranking below a patriarch and above a metropolitan. **c.** (orig.) patriarch. **2.** the ruler of a province in the Byzantine Empire. [t. LL: s. *exarchus,* t. Gk: m. *éxarchos* leader]

exarch[2] (ĕk′säk), *adj. Bot.* denoting or pertaining to a strand or cylinder of primary xylem in a stem or root with the protoxylem on its outer edge. [f. EX-[2] + Gk *archē* beginning]

exarchate (ĕk′sä kāt′, ĕk sä′kāt), *n.* the office, jurisdiction, or province of an exarch.

exasperate (ĭg zäs′pə rāt′), *v.t.,* **-rated, -rating. 1.** to irritate to a high degree; annoy extremely; infuriate. —*adj.* **2.** *Bot.* tough, with hard projecting points. [t. L: m. s. *exasperātus,* pp., roughened] —**exas′perat′edly,** *adv.* —**exas′perat′ingly,** *adv.* —**exas′perat′or,** *n.* —**Syn. 1.** exacerbate, incense, anger. See **irritate.** —**Ant. 1.** mollify.

exasperation (ĭg zäs′pə rā′shən), *n.* **1.** the act of exasperating; provocation. **2.** the state of being exasperated; irritation; extreme annoyance.

Exc., Excellency.

exc., **1.** except. **2.** exception. **3.** excursion.

Excalibur (ĕks kăl′ĭ bə), *n.* the magic sword of King Arthur.

ex cathedra (ĕks′kə thē′drə), *Latin.* from the seat of authority; with authority. [t. L: from the chair] —**ex′cathe′dra,** *adj.*

excaudate (ĕks kô′dāt), *adj. Zool.* tailless; destitute of a tail or tail-like process.

excavate (ĕks′kə vāt′), *v.t.,* **-vated, -vating. 1.** to make hollow by removing the inner part; make a hole or cavity in; form into a hollow, as by digging. **2.** to make (a hole, tunnel, etc.) by removing material. **3.** to dig or scoop out (earth, etc.). **4.** to expose or lay bare by digging; unearth: *to excavate an ancient city.* [t. L: m. s. *excavātus,* pp., hollowed out]

excavation (ĕks′kə vā′shən), *n.* **1.** the act of excavating. **2.** a hole or cavity made by excavating. **3.** the site of archaeological investigation by digging. —**Syn. 2.** See **hole.**

excavator (ĕks′kə vā′tə), *n.* **1.** one who or that which excavates. **2.** a power-driven machine for digging, moving, or transporting loose gravel, sand, or soil.

exceed (ĭk sēd′), *v.t.* **1.** to go beyond the bounds or limits of: *to exceed one's powers.* **2.** to go beyond in quantity, degree, rate, etc.: *to exceed the speed limit.* **3.** to surpass; be superior to; excel. —*v.i.* **4.** to be greater, as in quantity or degree. **5.** to surpass others, excel, or be superior. [ME *excede(n),* t. F: m. *excéder,* t. L: m. *excēdere* go out] —**exceed′er,** *n.* —**Syn. 1.** overstep, transcend.

exceeding (ĭk sē′dĭng), *adj.* **1.** extraordinary; excessive. —*adv.* **2.** *Archaic,* exceedingly.

exceedingly (ĭk sē′dĭng lĭ), *adv.* to an unusual degree; extremely.

excel (ĭk sĕl′), *v.,* **-celled, -celling.** —*v.t.* **1.** to surpass; be superior to; outdo. —*v.i.* **2.** to surpass others or be superior in some respect. [t. L: m. s. *excellere*]

—**Syn. 1.** outstrip, eclipse, transcend. EXCEL, OUTDO, SURPASS imply being better than others or being superior in achievement. To EXCEL is to be superior to others in some (usually) good or desirable quality, attainment, or performance: *to excel at playing chess.* To OUTDO is to make more successful effort than others: *to outdo competitors in the high jump.* To SURPASS is to go beyond others (who are definitely pointed out) esp. in a contest as to quality or ability: *to surpass one's fellow students in examinations.*

excellence (ĕk′sə ləns), *n.* **1.** the fact or state of excelling; superiority; eminence. **2.** an excellent quality or feature. **3.** (*usually cap.*) Excellency (def. 1). —**Syn. 1.** pre-eminence, transcendence. **2.** merit, virtue.

excellency (ĕk′sə lən sĭ), *n., pl.* **-cies. 1.** (*usually cap.*) a title of honour given to certain high officials, as governors and ambassadors. **2.** (*usually cap.*) a person so entitled. **3.** excellence. [t. L: m. s. *excellentia*]

excellent (ĕk′sə lənt), *adj.* **1.** possessing excellence or superior merit; remarkably good. **2.** *Obs.* extraordinary; superior. [ME, t. L: s. *excellens,* ppr.] —**ex′cellently,** *adv.* —**Syn. 1.** worthy, estimable, choice, fine, first-rate.

excelsior (ĕk sĕl′sĭ ô′), *n.* **1.** a printing type (3 point) smaller than brilliant. **2.** *U.S.* woodwool. [t. L, compar. of *excelsus* high, prop. pp., risen above others]

except[1] (ĭk sĕpt′), *prep.* **1.** with the exclusion of; excluding; save; but: *they were all there except me.* —*conj.* **2.** with the exception (that): *parallel cases except that A is younger than B.* **3.** otherwise than; but (fol. by an adv., phrase, or clause): *well fortified except here.* **4.** *Archaic.* unless. [t. L: s. *exceptus,* pp., taken out]

—**Syn. 1.** EXCEPT (more rarely EXCEPTING), BUT, SAVE point out something excluded from a general statement. EXCEPT emphasizes the excluding: *take any number except 12.* BUT merely states the exclusion: *we ate all but one.* SAVE is now mainly found in poetic use: *nothing in sight save sky and sea.*

except[2] (ĭk sĕpt′), *v.t.* **1.** to exclude; leave out: *present company excepted.* —*v.i.* **2.** to object: *to except against a statement, a witness, etc.* [ME *excepte(n),* t. F: m. *excepter,* der. L *exceptus,* pp.]

excepting (ĭk sĕp′tĭng), *prep.* **1.** excluding; barring; saving; except. —*conj.* **2.** *Archaic.* except; unless; save. —**Syn. 1.** See **except**[1].

exception (ĭk sĕpʹshən), *n.* **1.** the act of excepting. **2.** the fact of being excepted. **3.** something excepted; an instance or case not conforming to the general rule. **4.** an adverse criticism, esp. on a particular point; opposition of opinion; objection; demurral: *a statement liable to exception.* **5. take exception, a.** to make objection; demur with respect to something (usually fol. by *to*). **b.** to take offence (often fol. by *at*). [t. L: s. *exceptio*]

exceptionable (ĭk sĕpʹshə nə bl), *adj.* liable to exception or objection; objectionable. —**excepʹtionableness,** *n.* —**excepʹtionably,** *adv.*

exceptional (ĭk sĕpʹshə nəl), *adj.* forming an exception or unusual instance; unusual; extraordinary. —**excepʹtionally,** *adv.* —**excepʹtionalness,** *n.* —**Syn.** uncommon, peculiar, singular, superior. See **irregular.** —**Ant.** average.

exceptive (ĭk sĕpʹtĭv), *adj.* **1.** that excepts; making an exception. **2.** disposed to take exception; objecting.

excerpt (*n.* ĕkʹsûpt; *v.* ĕk sûptʹ), *n.* **1.** a passage taken out of a book or the like; an extract. —*v.t.* **2.** to take out (a passage) from a book or the like; extract. [t. L: s. *excerptus,* pp., picked out] —**excerpʹtion,** *n.*

excess (*n.* ĭk sĕsʹ; *adj.* ĕkʹsĕs, ĭk sĕsʹ), *n.* **1.** the fact of exceeding something else in amount or degree. **2.** the amount or degree by which one thing exceeds another. **3.** an extreme or excessive amount or degree; superabundance: *have an excess of energy.* **4.** a going beyond ordinary or proper limits. **5.** immoderate indulgence; intemperance in eating and drinking. —*adj.* **6.** more than or above what is necessary, usual, or specified; extra: *excess baggage, excess profits.* [ME *excesse,* t. L: m. *excessus* a departure] —**Syn. 3.** surplus, surplusage. —**Ant. 3.** deficiency.

excess charge, a charge, not a fine, imposed on a vehicle left at a parking meter longer than the time paid for.

excessive (ĭk sĕsʹĭv), *adj.* exceeding the usual or proper limit or degree; characterized by excess: *excessive charges, excessive indulgence.* —**excesʹsively,** *adv.* —**excesʹsiveness,** *n.* —**Syn.** immoderate, extravagant, extreme, inordinate, exorbitant.

excess-profits tax (ĕkʹsĕs prŏfʹĭts), a tax on the profits of a company in excess of the average profits for a number of base years, or of a specified rate of return on capital.

exch., 1. exchange. **2.** exchequer.

exchange (ĭks chānjʹ), *v.,* **-changed, -changing,** *n.* —*v.t.* **1.** to part with for some equivalent; give up (something) for something else. **2.** to replace by another or something else; change for another: *to exchange a purchase.* **3.** to give and receive reciprocally; interchange: *to exchange blows, gifts, etc.* **4.** to part with in return for some equivalent; transfer for a recompense; barter: *to exchange dollars for pounds.* **5.** *Chess.* to capture (an enemy piece) in return for a capture by the opponent generally of a piece or pieces of equal value. —*v.i.* **6.** to make an exchange. **7.** to pass or be taken in exchange or as an equivalent. —*n.* **8.** the act or process of exchanging: *an exchange of gifts, prisoners of war, etc.* **9.** that which is given or received in exchange or substitution for something else: *the car was a fair exchange.* **10.** a place for buying and selling commodities, securities, etc., typically open only to members. **11.** a central office or central station: *a telephone exchange.* **12.** the method or system by which debits and credits in different places are settled without the actual transference of money, by means of documents representing money values. **13.** the discharge of obligations in different places by the transfer of credits. **14.** the reciprocal transference of equivalent sums of money, as in the currencies of two different countries. **15.** the giving or receiving of a sum of money in one place for a bill ordering the payment of an equivalent sum in another. **16.** the varying rate or sum, in one currency, given for a fixed sum in another currency; rate of exchange. **17.** the amount of the difference in value between two or more currencies, or between the values of the same currency at two or more places. **18.** the cheques, drafts, etc., exchanged at a clearing house. **19.** *Chess.* the reciprocal capture of pieces, generally of equal value, in a single series of moves. **20.** transfusion (def. 2a). **21.** employment exchange. [ME *eschaunge,* t. AF, g. LL *excambium*] —**exchangʹer,** *n.* —**Syn. 1.** interchange, commute, barter, trade, swap. **8.** interchange, trade, traffic.

exchangeable (ĭks chānʹjə bl), *adj.* that can be exchanged. —**exchangeʹabilʹity,** *n.*

—**Syn.** EXCHANGEABLE, INTERCHANGEABLE apply to something which may replace something else. That is EXCHANGEABLE which may be taken or sent back to the place at which it was purchased, to be exchanged for money, credit, or other purchases to the amount of the original purchase: *these dishes are exchangeable if you find they are not satisfactory.* INTERCHANGEABLE applies to those things which are capable of being reciprocally put in each other's place: *standard parts are interchangeable.*

exchange force, *Physics.* **1.** strong nuclear force; a force which holds the nucleons together within an atomic nucleus as a result of the exchange of mesons. **2.** a force which occurs in ferromagnetic materials causing the alignment of all the individual magnetic moments of large groups of atoms.

exchange rate, rate of exchange.

exchequer (ĭks chĕkʹə), *n.* **1.** a treasury, as of a state or nation. **2.** (in Great Britain) **a.** (*often cap.*) the government department in charge of the public revenues. **b.** (formerly) an office which administered the royal revenues and determined all cases affecting them. **c.** (*cap.*) an ancient common-law court of civil jurisdiction (**Court of Exchequer**) in which all cases affecting the revenues of the crown were tried, now merged in the Queen's Bench Division of the High Court. **3.** *Colloq.* funds; finances. [ME *escheker,* t. OF: m. *eschequier* chess board (so called with reference to the table-cover marked with squares on which accounts were reckoned with counters). See CHEQUER]

exchequer bill, a promissory note issued by the government, first used in Britain in 1696 and now superseded by a Treasury bill.

excide (ĭk sīdʹ), *v.t.,* **-cided, -ciding.** to cut out; excise.

excipient (ĭk sĭpʹĭ ənt), *n. Pharm.* a more or less inert substance, as sugar, jelly, etc., used as the medium or vehicle for the administration of an active medicine. [t. L: s. *excipiens,* ppr., taking out]

excisable[1] (ĕk sīʹzə bl), *adj.* subject to excise duty.

excisable[2] (ĕk sīʹzə bl), *adj.* capable of being excised or cut out.

excise[1] (*n.* ĕk sīzʹ, ĕkʹsīz; *v.* ĕk sīzʹ), *n., v.,* **-cised, -cising.** —*n.* **1.** an inland tax or duty on certain commodities, as spirits, tobacco, etc., levied on their manufacture, sale, or consumption within the country. **2.** a tax levied for a licence to carry on certain employments, pursue certain sports, etc. **3.** that branch of the civil service which collects excise duties. —*v.t.* **4.** to impose an excise on. [t. MD: m. *excijs,* t. OF: m. *acceis* a tax, ult. der. LL *accēnsāre* tax] —**excision** (ĕk sĭzhʹən), *n.*

excise[2] (ĕk sīzʹ), *v.t.,* **-cised, -cising. 1.** to expunge, as a passage or sentence. **2.** to cut out or off, as a tumour. [t. L: m. s. *excīsus,* pp., cut out]

exciseman (ĕk sīzʹmănʹ), *n., pl.* **-men.** an officer who collects excise taxes and enforces excise laws.

excitability (ĭk sīʹtə bĭlʹĭ tĭ), *n.* **1.** the quality of being excitable. **2.** *Physiol.* irritability.

excitable (ĭk sīʹtə bl), *adj.* capable of being excited; easily excited. —**excitʹableness,** *n.* —**excitʹably,** *adv.* —**Syn.** emotional, passionate, fiery. —**Ant.** placid.

excitant (ĭk sīʹtnt, ĕkʹsĭ tənt), *adj.* **1.** exciting; stimulating. —*n.* **2.** *Physiol.* something that excites; a stimulant.

excitation (ĕkʹsĭ tāʹshən), *n.* **1.** the act of exciting. **2.** means of exciting; that which excites. **3.** the state of being excited. **4.** *Elect.* the relative strength of the magnetic field in a dynamo: *normal excitation.* **5.** *Physics.* a process in which an atom, nucleus, or molecule is raised to a higher energy state than normal.

excitative (ĭk sīʹtə tĭv), *adj.* tending to excite. Also, **excitatory** (ĭk sīʹtə tə rĭ, -trĭ).

excite (ĭk sītʹ), *v.t.,* **-cited, -citing. 1.** to arouse or stir up the feelings of: *to excite jealousy or hatred.* **2.** to cause; awaken: *to excite interest or curiosity.* **3.** to stir to action; stir up: *to excite a dog.* **4.** *Physiol.* to stimulate: *to excite a nerve.* **5.** *Elect.* to produce electric activity or a magnetic field in: *to excite a dynamo.* **6.** *Physics.* to raise (an atom, nucleus, or molecule) to a higher energy state than the normal. [ME *excite(n),* t. L: m. s. *excitāre,* freq. of *exciēre* call forth, rouse] —**Syn. 1.** stir, arouse, awaken, stimulate, animate, kindle, inflame. **3.** provoke. —**Ant. 1.** soothe.

excited (ĭk sīʹtĭd), *adj.* **1.** stirred emotionally; agitated. **2.** stimulated to activity; brisk. **3.** *Physics.* (of an atom or nucleus) in a state of higher energy than the normal state. —**excitʹedly,** *adv.* —**Syn. 1.** ruffled, discomposed, stormy, perturbed, impassioned.

excitement (ĭk sītʹmənt), *n.* **1.** an excited state or condition. **2.** something that excites. —**Syn. 1.** perturbation, commotion, ado. See **agitation.**

exciter (ĭk sīʹtə), *n.* **1.** one who or that which excites. **2.** *Elect.* an auxiliary generator which supplies energy for the excitation of another electric machine.

exciting (ĭk sīʹtĭng), *adj.* producing excitement; stirring. —**excitʹingly,** *adv.*

exciton (ĕkʹsĭ tŏnʹ), *n. Physics.* a non-conducting, nonlocalized electron state in a semiconductor which can be regarded as a combination of an electron and a hole.

excitor (ĭk sīʹtə, -tô), *n.* **1.** *Physiol.* a nerve whose stimulation excites greater action. **2.** exciter.

excl., excluding.

exclaim (ĭk sklām′), *v.i.* **1.** to cry out or speak suddenly and vehemently, as in surprise, strong emotion, protest, etc. —*v.t.* **2.** to cry out; say loudly or vehemently. [earlier *exclame*, t. L: m. s. *exclāmāre* call out] —**exclaim′er,** *n.*

exclam., **1.** exclamation. **2.** exclamatory.

exclamation (ĕks′klə mā′shən), *n.* **1.** the act of exclaiming; an outcry; a loud complaint or protest. **2.** an interjection. —**Syn. 1.** cry, ejaculation.

exclamation mark, 1. a punctuation mark (!) used after an exclamation. **2.** a road sign bearing a symbol resembling this mark, placed to give advance warning of some hazard. Also, **exclamation point.**

exclamatory (ĭks klăm′ə tə rĭ, -trĭ), *adj.* **1.** using, containing, or expressing exclamation. **2.** pertaining to exclamation. —**exclam′atorily,** *adv.*

exclave (ĕks′klāv), *n.* a part of a country separated from it geographically and surrounded by alien territory: *West Berlin is an exclave of West Germany.* [f. EX-[1] + *-clave* of ENCLAVE]

exclude (ĭk sklōōd′), *v.t.*, **-cluded, -cluding. 1.** to shut or keep out; prevent the entrance of. **2.** to shut out from consideration, privilege, etc. **3.** to expel and keep out; thrust out; eject. [ME *exclude(n)*, t. L: m. *exclūdere*] —**exclud′able,** *adj.* —**exclud′er,** *n.*

—**Syn. 2.** EXCLUDE, DEBAR, ELIMINATE mean to remove from a certain place, or from consideration in a particular situation. To EXCLUDE is to set aside as unwanted, unusable, etc.: *words excluded from polite conversation.* To DEBAR is to prohibit, esp. in a legal sense, from a place or from the enjoyment of privileges, rights, or the like: *to debar all candidates lacking the necessary preparation.* To ELIMINATE is to select and remove, esp. as irrelevant, unnecessary, or undesirable: *to eliminate such objections.* —**Ant. 2.** admit.

excluded middle, law of, *Logic.* the law which states that a proposition is either true or false, or that a thing either has or does not have a given property.

exclusion (ĭk sklōō′zhən), *n.* **1.** the act of excluding. **2.** the state of being excluded. **3.** *Physiol.* a keeping apart; the blocking of an entrance. [t. L: s. *exclūsio*]

exclusion clause, *Insurance.* a clause in a policy stipulating risks not covered in the policy.

exclusionism (ĭk sklōō′zhə nĭz′əm), *n.* the principle, policy, or practice of exclusion, as from rights or privileges. —**exclu′sionist,** *n.*

exclusion principle, *Physics.* the principle that no two electrons, protons, or neutrons in a given system can be characterized by the same set of quantum numbers. Also, **Pauli's exclusion principle.**

exclusive (ĭk sklōō′sĭv), *adj.* **1.** not admitting of something else; incompatible: *mutually exclusive ideas.* **2.** excluding from consideration or account: *from 100 to 121 exclusive* (excluding 100 and 121, and including from 101 to 120). **3.** limited to the object or objects designated: *exclusive attention to business.* **4.** shutting out all others from a part or share: *an exclusive grant.* **5.** shutting out all other activities: *an exclusive occupation.* **6.** in which no others have a share: *exclusive information.* **7.** single or sole: *the exclusive means of communication between two places.* **8.** available through only one channel of marketing. **9.** disposed to resist the admission of outsiders to association, intimacy, etc.: *an exclusive clique.* **10.** *Colloq.* fashionable: *an exclusive club.* **11.** *Logic.* excluding all except what is specified: *an exclusive proposition.* [t. ML: m. s. *exclūsīvus*, pp., excluded] —**exclu′sively,** *adv.* —**exclu′siveness,** *n.* —**Syn. 9.** select, narrow, clannish, snobbish.

Exclusive Brethren, a small and strict Protestant sect whose beliefs emphasize the salvation of the individual and place stringent restrictions upon his contact with all others.

exclusory (ĭk sklōō′zə rĭ), *adj.* having the power or function of excluding; exclusive.

excogitate (ĕks kŏj′ĭ tāt′), *v.t.*, **-tated, -tating.** to think out; devise; invent. [t. L: m. s. *excōgitātus*, pp., found out by thinking] —**excog′ita′tion,** *n.* —**excogitative** (ĕks kŏj′ĭ tə tĭv), *adj.* —**excog′ita′tor,** *n.*

excommunicable (ĕks′kə myōō′nĭ kə bl), *adj.* **1.** liable or deserving to be excommunicated, as a person. **2.** punishable by excommunication, as an offence.

excommunicate (ĕks′kə myōō′nĭ kāt′), *v.*, **-cated, -cating,** *n., adj.* —*v.t.* **1.** to cut off from communion or membership, esp. from the sacraments and fellowship of the church by ecclesiastical sentence. —*n.* **2.** an excommunicated person. —*adj.* **3.** excommunicated. [t. LL: m. s. *excommūnicātus*, pp., lit., put out of the community] —**ex′commu′nica′tor,** *n.*

excommunication (ĕks′kə myōō′nĭ kā′shən), *n.* **1.** the act of excommunicating. **2.** the state of being excommunicated. **3.** the ecclesiastical sentence by which a person is excommunicated.

excommunicative (ĕks′kə myōō′nĭ kə tĭv), *adj.* disposed or serving to excommunicate.

excommunicatory (ĕks′kə myōō′nĭ kə tə rĭ, -trĭ), *adj.* relating to or causing excommunication.

ex contracta, *Latin.* from or arising out of a contract.

excoriate (ĭk skô′rĭ āt′), *v.t.*, **-ated, -ating. 1.** to strip off or remove the skin from. **2.** to flay verbally; denounce; censure. [t. L: m. s. *excoriātus*, pp. of *excoriāre* strip off the hide]

excoriation (ĭk skô′rĭ ā′shən), *n.* **1.** the act of excoriating. **2.** the state of being excoriated. **3.** an excoriated place on the body.

excorticate (ĭks kô′tĭ kāt′), *n.* to remove the mark, husk or outer covering from; decorticate. —**excor′tica′tion,** *n.*

excrement (ĕks′krĭ mənt), *n.* waste matter discharged from the body, esp. the faeces. [t. L: s. *excrēmentum* what is evacuated] —**excremental** (ĕks′krĭ mĕn′tl), *adj.* —**ex′cremen′tally,** *adv.*

excrementitious (ĕks′krĭ mĕn tĭsh′əs), *adj.* of or like excrement. —**ex′crementit′iously,** *adv.*

excrescence (ĭk skrĕs′əns), *n.* **1.** abnormal growth or increase. **2.** an abnormal outgrowth, usually harmless, on an animal or vegetable body. **3.** a normal outgrowth, such as hair. **4.** any disfiguring addition.

excrescency (ĭk skrĕs′ən sĭ), *n., pl.* **-cies.** the state of being excrescent.

excrescent (ĭk skrĕs′ənt), *adj.* **1.** growing abnormally out of something else; superfluous. **2.** *Phonet.* added without grammatical or historical justification, as the *t* in against (ME *ageyns*). [t. L: s. *excrescens*, ppr., growing out]

excreta (ĭk skrē′tə), *n.pl.* excreted matter, as sweat, urine, etc. [t. L, neut. pl. of *excrētus*, pp., separated] —**excre′tal,** *adj.*

excrete (ĭk skrēt′), *v.t.*, **-creted, -creting.** to separate and eliminate from an organic body; separate and expel from the blood or tissues, as waste or harmful matters. [t. L: m. s. *excrētus*, pp., sifted out, discharged] —**excre′tive,** *adj.*

excretion (ĭk skrē′shən), *n.* **1.** the act of excreting. **2.** the substance excreted, as sweat or urine, or certain plant products.

excretory (ĭk skrē′tə rĭ), *adj.* pertaining to or concerned in excretion; having this function of excreting.

excruciate (ĭk skrōō′shĭ āt′), *v.t.*, **-ated, -ating.** to inflict severe pain upon; torture. [t. L: m. s. *excruciātus*, pp., tortured greatly]

excruciating (ĭk skrōō′shĭ ā′tĭng), *adj.* extremely painful; causing extreme suffering; torturing. —**excru′ciat′ingly,** *adv.*

excruciation (ĭk skrōō′shĭ ā′shən), *n.* **1.** the act of excruciating. **2.** the state of being excruciated. **3.** an instance of this; torture.

exculpate (ĕks′kŭl pāt′, ĭk skŭl′pāt), *v.t.*, **-pated, -pating.** to clear from a charge of guilt or fault; free from blame; vindicate. [f. EX-[1] + s. L *culpa* fault, blame + -ATE[1]] —**exculpable** (ĭk skŭl′pə bl), *adj.* —**ex′culpa′tion,** *n.*

exculpatory (ĭk skŭl′pə tə rĭ, -trĭ), *adj.* tending to clear from a charge of fault or guilt.

excurrent (ĕks kŭ′rənt), *adj.* **1.** running out or forth. **2.** *Zool.* giving passage outwards; affording exit: *the excurrent canal of certain sponges.* **3.** *Bot.* **a.** having the axis prolonged so as to form an undivided main stem or trunk, as the stem of the spruce. **b.** projecting beyond the apex, as the midrib in certain leaves. [t. L: s. *excurrens*, ppr., running out]

excurse (ĭk skûs′), *v.i.*, **-cursed, -cursing. 1.** to go on an excursion. **2.** to digress; wander.

excursion (ĭk skû′shən), *n.* **1.** a short journey or trip to some point for a special purpose, with the intention of speedy return: *a pleasure excursion, a scientific excursion.* **2.** a trip in a coach, train, etc., at a reduced rate: *weekend excursions to seashore or mountain resorts.* **3.** the persons who make such a journey. **4.** deviation or digression. **5.** *Physics.* the departure of a body from its mean position or proper course. **6.** *Mach.* **a.** the range of stroke of any moving part. **b.** the stroke itself. **7.** *Obs.* a sally or raid. [t. L: s. *excursio* a running out]

—**Syn. 2.** EXCURSION, JAUNT, TOUR are trips made primarily for pleasure. An EXCURSION is a short trip, usually no more than a day's outing, made usually by a number of people, as a result of special inducements (low fare, a special event, etc.): *an excursion at reduced rates.* JAUNT is a familiar term for a short, agreeable trip, now esp. by motor car: *take a little jaunt to the country.* A TOUR is a planned trip to celebrated places, to see interesting scenery, etc.: *a tour of Europe.*

excursionist (ĭk skû′shə nĭst), *n.* one who goes on an excursion.

excursion ticket, a return ticket for off-peak travel at a reduced rate, as to a resort, etc.

excursive (ĭk skû′sĭv), *adj.* **1.** given to making excursions; wandering; digressive. **2.** of the nature of an excursion; rambling; desultory. —**excur′sively,** *adv.* —**excur′siveness,** *n.*

excursus (ěks kûr′səs), *n.*, *pl.* **-suses, -sus. 1.** a detailed discussion of some point in a book (usually added as an appendix). **2.** an incidental discussion, or digression, as in a narrative. [t. L, der. *excurrere* run out]

excusatory (ĭk skyoo͞′zə tə rĭ, -trĭ), *adj.* serving or intended to excuse.

excuse (*v.* ĭk skyoo͞z′; *n.* ĭk skyoo͞s′), *v.*, **-scused, -scusing,** *n.* **—***v.t.* **1.** to regard or judge with indulgence; pardon or forgive; overlook (a fault, etc.). **2.** to offer an apology for; apologize for; seek to remove the blame of. **3.** to serve as an apology or justification for; justify: *ignorance of the law excuses no man.* **4. a.** to release from an obligation or duty: *to be excused from attending a meeting.* **b.** to allow to leave a place, or cease an activity: *to be excused from the room.* **5.** to seek or obtain exemption or release for (oneself): *to excuse oneself from duty.* **6.** to refrain from exacting; remit; dispense with: *to excuse a fine.* **—***n.* **7.** that which is offered as a reason for being excused; a plea offered in extenuation of a fault, or for release from an obligation, etc. **8.** something serving to excuse; a ground or reason for excusing. **9.** the act of excusing. **10.** a pretext or subterfuge. **11.** an inferior or inadequate example of something specified: *she was shabbily dressed and wearing a poor excuse for a hat.* [ME *excuse(n)*, t. L: m. *excūsāre* allege in excuse] **—excus′able,** *adj.* **—excus′ableness,** *n.* **—excus′ably,** *adv.* **—excus′al,** *n.* **—excuse′less,** *adj.* **—excus′er,** *n.* **—excus′ive,** *adj.*

—Syn. 1. EXCUSE, FORGIVE, PARDON imply being lenient or giving up the wish to punish. EXCUSE means to overlook some (usually) slight offence, because of circumstance, realization that it was unintentional, or the like: *to excuse bad manners.* FORGIVE is applied to excusing more serious offences: the person wronged not only overlooks the offence but harbours no ill feeling against the offender: *to forgive and forget.* PARDON usually applies to a specific act of lenience or mercy by an official or superior in remitting all or the remainder of the punishment that belongs to a serious offence or crime: *the king was asked to pardon the condemned criminal.* **3.** extenuate, palliate. **7.** EXCUSE, APOLOGY both imply an explanation of some failure or failing. EXCUSE implies a desire to avoid punishment or rebuke. APOLOGY usually implies acknowledgement that one has been, at least seemingly, in the wrong; it may aim at setting matters right by either alleging extenuating circumstances, or expressing regret for an error. **—Ant. 1.** blame, punish.

ex delicto (ěks′dĭ lĭk′tō), from or arising out of an offence or tort.

ex-directory (ěks′ dĭ rěk′tə rĭ), *adj., adv.* omitted from a telephone directory and not disclosed to enquirers: *an ex-directory telephone number*; *to go ex-directory.*

ex dividend, without dividend; the buyer of the stock being not entitled to the dividend.

exeat (ěk′sĭ ăt′), *n.* formal leave of absence, esp. for a student to leave a college when his presence there would normally be required. [L: 3rd pers. pres. subjunctive of *exīre* to go out]

exec., 1. executive. **2.** executor.

execrable (ěk′sĭ krə bl), *adj.* **1.** deserving to be execrated; detestable; abominable. **2.** *Colloq.* very bad: *an execrable pun.* **—ex′ecrably,** *adv.*

execrate (ěk′sĭ krāt′), *v.*, **-crated, -crating. —***v.t.* **1.** to detest utterly; abhor; abominate. **2.** to curse; imprecate evil upon. **—***v.i.* **3.** to utter curses. [t. L: m. s. *ex(s)ecrātus*, pp., having cursed] **—ex′ecra′tor,** *n.*

execration (ěk′sĭ krā′shən), *n.* **1.** the act of execrating. **2.** a curse or imprecation. **3.** the object execrated; a thing held in abomination.

execrative (ěk′sĭ krā′tĭv), *adj.* **1.** pertaining to or characterized by execration. **2.** prone to execrate. **—ex′ecrat′ively,** *adv.*

execratory (ěk′sĭ krā′tə rĭ), *adj.* **1.** pertaining to execration. **2.** having the nature of or containing an execration.

executant (ĭg zěk′yoo͝ tənt), *n.* one who executes or performs, esp. musically.

execute (ěk′sĭ kyoo͞t′), *v.t.*, **-cuted, -cuting. 1.** to carry out; accomplish: *to execute a plan or order.* **2.** to perform or do: *to execute a manoeuvre or gymnastic feat.* **3.** to inflict capital punishment on; put to death according to law. **4.** to produce in accordance with a plan or design: *to execute a statue or a picture.* **5.** to perform or play (a piece of music). **6.** *Law.* **a.** to give effect or force to (a law, decree, judicial sentence, etc.); carry out the terms of (a will). **b.** to carry out the terms of (a will). **c.** to transact or carry through (a contract, mortgage, etc.) in the manner prescribed by law; complete and give validity to (a legal instrument) by fulfilling the legal requirements, as by signing, sealing, etc. [ME *execute(n)*, t. ML: m. *executāre*, der. L *ex(s)ecūtus*, pp., having followed out] **—ex′ecut′able,** *adj.* **—ex′ecut′er,** *n.* **—Syn. 2.** See **perform. 3.** See **kill**[1]. **6. a.** administer, enforce.

execution (ěk′sĭ kyoo͞′shən), *n.* **1.** the act or process of executing. **2.** the state or fact of being executed. **3.** the infliction of capital punishment, or, formerly, of any legal punishment. **4.** the process of performing a judgement or sentence of a court. **5.** mode or style of performance; technical skill, as in music. **6.** effective action, esp. of weapons, or the result attained by it (usually prec. by *do*): *every shot did execution.* **7.** *Law.* a judicial writ directing the enforcement of a judgement.

executioner (ěk′sĭ kyoo͞′shə nə), *n.* **1.** one who executes. **2.** an official who inflicts capital punishment in pursuance of a legal warrant.

executive (ĭg zěk′yoo͝ tĭv), *adj.* **1.** suited for execution or carrying into effect; of the kind requisite for practical performance or direction: *executive ability.* **2.** charged with or pertaining to execution of laws, or administration of affairs. **3.** designed for or used by executives: *an executive aircraft.* **—***n.* **4.** a person or body having administrative authority, as in a company. **5.** *Chiefly U.S.* the person or persons in whom the supreme executive power of a government is vested. **6.** *Chiefly U.S.* the executive branch of a government. **—exec′utively,** *adv.*

Executive Mansion, (in the U.S.) the official residence of the President at Washington, D.C. (the White House), or of the governor of one of the states.

executive order, (*usually cap.*) an order issued by the President of the U.S. to the army, navy, or other part of the executive branch of the government.

executor (ĭg zěk′yoo͝ tə), *n.* **1.** one who executes, or carries out, performs, fulfils, etc. **2.** *Law.* a person named by a testator in his will to carry out the provisions of his will. [ME *executour*, t. AF, t. L: m. s. *ex(s)ecūtor*, lit., one who follows out] **—executorial** (ĭg zěk′yoo͝ tô′rĭ əl), *adj.* **—exec′utorship′,** *n.*

executory (ĭg zěk′yoo͝ tə rĭ, -trĭ), *adj.* **1.** executive. **2.** *Law.* that remains to be carried into effect.

executrix (ĭg zěk′yoo͝ trĭks′), *n.*, *pl.* **executrices** (ĭg zěk′yoo͝ trī′sēz). *Law.* a female executor.

exedra (ěk′sĭ drə, ěk sē′drə), *n.* a semicircular or rectangular recess with raised seats originating in classical architecture.

exegesis (ěk′sĭ jē′sĭs), *n.*, *pl.* **-ses** (-sēz). critical explanation or interpretation, esp. of Scripture. [t. NL, t. Gk: explanation]

exegete (ěk′sĭ jēt′), *n.* one skilled in exegesis.

exegetic (ěk′sĭ jět′ĭk), *adj.* pertaining to exegesis; expository. Also, **ex′eget′ical.** [t. Gk: s. *exēgētikós* explanatory] **—ex′eget′ically,** *adv.*

exegetics (ěk′sĭ jět′ĭks), *n.* the science of exegesis; exegetical theology.

exemplar (ĭg zěm′plə, -plä), *n.* **1.** a model or pattern to be copied or imitated. **2.** an example; typical instance. **3.** an original or archetype. **4.** a copy of a book or text. [t. L: copy, model; r. ME *exemplaire*, t. OF]

exemplary (ĭg zěm′plə rĭ), *adj.* **1.** worthy of imitation; commendable: *exemplary conduct.* **2.** such as may serve as a warning: *an exemplary penalty.* **3.** serving as a model or pattern. **4.** serving as an illustration or specimen; illustrative; typical. **5.** of, pertaining to, or consisting of exempla. **—exem′plarily,** *adv.* **—exem′plariness,** *n.*

exemplification (ĭg zěm′plĭ fĭ kā′shən), *n.* **1.** the act of exemplifying. **2.** that which exemplifies; an illustration or example. **3.** *Law.* an attested copy of a document, under official seal.

exemplificative (ĭg zěm′plĭ fĭ kā′tĭv), *adj.* serving to exemplify.

exemplify (ĭg zěm′plĭ fī′), *v.t.*, **-fied, -fying. 1.** to show or illustrate by example. **2.** to furnish, or serve as, an example of. **3.** *Law.* to transcribe or copy; make an attested copy of (a document) under seal. [ME *exemplyfy(en)*, t. ML: m. s. *exemplificāre*, f. L: *exempli-* example + *ficāre* make] **—exem′plifi′er,** *n.*

exempli gratia (ĭg zěm′plī grā′tĭ ä′), *Latin.* for the sake of example; for example. *Abbrev.*: e.g.

exemplum (ĭg zěm′pləm), *n.*, *pl.* **-pla** (-plə). **1.** an anecdote designed to point a moral, esp. in a medieval sermon. **2.** an example.

exempt (ĭg zěmpt′), *v.t.* **1.** to free from an obligation or liability to which others are subject; release: *to exempt someone from military service, from an examination,* etc. **—***adj.* **2.** released from, or not subject to, an obligation, liability, etc.: *exempt from taxes.* **—***n.* **3.** one who is exempt from, or not subject to, an obligation, duty, etc. **4.** exon. [ME, t. L: s. *exemptus*, pp.] **—exemp′tible,** *adj.*

exemption (ĭg zěmp′shən), *n.* **1.** the act of exempting. **2.** the state of being exempted; immunity.

—Syn. 2. EXEMPTION, IMMUNITY, IMPUNITY imply special privilege or freedom from requirements imposed upon others. EXEMPTION implies release or privileged freedom from sharing with others some (usually arbitrarily imposed) duty, tax, etc.: *exemption from military service.* IMMUNITY implies freedom from a penalty or from some natural or common liability, esp. one that is disagreeable or threatening: *immunity from disease.* IMPUNITY (limited mainly to the fixed expression *with impunity*) primarily suggests freedom from punishment: *the police were so inefficient that crimes were committed with impunity.* —**Ant.** 2. liability.

exenterate (*v.* ĭg zĕn′tə rāt′; *adj.* ĭg zĕn′tə rāt′, -rĭt), *v.*, **-rated, -rating,** *adj.* —*v.t.* **1.** to remove the contents of; disembowel; eviscerate. —*adj.* **2.** disembowelled.

exequatur (ĕk′sĭ kwā′tə), *n.* **1.** a written recognition of a consul by the government of the state in which he is stationed authorizing him to exercise his powers. **2.** an authorization granted by a secular ruler for the publication of papal bulls or other ecclesiastical enactments to give them binding force. [t. L: let him execute]

exequy (ĕk′sĭ kwĭ), *n.*, *pl.* **-quies** (-kwĭz). a funeral rite or ceremony. [ME *exequies* (pl.), t. OF, t. L: m. *exequiae* funeral procession] —**exe′quial,** *adj.*

exercise (ĕk′sə sīz′), *n.*, *v.*, **-cised, -cising.** —*n.* **1.** bodily or mental exertion, esp. for the sake of training or improvement. **2.** something done or performed as a means of practice or training, to improve a specific skill or to acquire competence in a particular field: *exercises in French grammar, exercises for the piano.* **3.** a putting into action, use, operation, or effect: *the exercise of caution or care, the exercise of willpower.* **4.** a composition or work of art executed for practice or to illustrate a specific technical point. **5.** a literary, artistic, or musical performance of technical rather than aesthetic value. **6.** a written school task. **7.** (*pl.*) military drill or manoeuvres. **8.** (*often pl.*) *U.S.* a ceremony; formal proceeding. **9.** a religious observance or act of worship. **10.** an academic disputation. —*v.t.* **11.** to put through exercises, or forms of practice or exertion, designed to train, develop, condition, etc.: *to exercise troops, a horse, the voice, etc.* **12.** to put (faculties, rights, etc.) into action, practice, or use: *to exercise one's strength, one's sight, etc.* **13.** to use or display in one's action or procedure: *to exercise caution, patience, judgement.* **14.** to make use of (one's privileges, powers, etc.): *to exercise one's rights.* **15.** to discharge (a function); perform: *to exercise the duties of one's office.* **16.** to have as an effect: *to exercise an influence on someone.* **17.** to worry; make uneasy; annoy: *to be much exercised about one's health.* —*v.i.* **18.** to go through exercises; take bodily exercise. [ME *exercise*, t. OF, g. L *exercitium*] —**ex′ercis′able,** *adj.* —**ex′ercis′er,** *n.*

—**Syn.** 2. EXERCISE, DRILL, PRACTICE refer to activities undertaken for training in some skill. An EXERCISE may be either physical or mental, and may be more or less irregular in time and varied in kind: *an exercise in arithmetic.* DRILL is disciplined repetition of set exercises, often performed in a group, directed by a leader: *military drill.* PRACTICE is methodical exercise, usually characterized by much repetition, with a view to becoming perfect in some operation or pursuit and to acquiring further skills: *even great musicians require constant practice.* 3. employment, application. 11. discipline. 13. employ, apply, exert.

exercitation (ĭg zû′sĭ tā′shən), *n.* **1.** exercise or exertion, as of faculties or powers. **2.** practice or training. **3.** a performance. **4.** a disquisition or discourse. [ME *exercitacion*, t. L: m. s. *exercitātio* exercise, practice]

exergue (ĕk sûg′), *n.* *Numismatics.* the space below the base line on a coin or medal. [t. F, f. Gk: *ex-* EX-[3] + m. s. *érgon* work] —**exerg′ual,** *adj.*

exert (ĭg zût′), *v.t.* **1.** to put forth, as power; exercise, as ability or influence; put into vigorous action. **2. exert oneself,** to put forth one's powers; use one's efforts; strive. [t. L: s. *ex(s)ertus*, pp.] —**exer′tive,** *adj.*

exertion (ĭg zû′shən), *n.* **1.** vigorous action or effort. **2.** an effort. **3.** exercise, as of power or faculties. **4.** an instance of this. —**Syn.** 1. endeavour, struggle, attempt. See **effort.**

Exeter (ĕk′sĭ tə), *n.* a city in SW England, in Devonshire: cathedral; university founded 1955. 80,215 (1961).

exeunt (ĕk′sĭ ŭnt′), *Latin.* they (or the persons named) go out (instruction for actors in plays).

exeunt omnes (ĕk′sĭ ŭnt ŏm′nāz), *Latin.* all go out; all go offstage (used in plays).

exfoliate (ĕks fō′lĭ āt′), *v.*, **-ated, -ating.** —*v.t.* **1.** to throw off in scales. —*v.i.* **2.** to throw off scales or flakes; peel off in thin fragments: *the exfoliating bark of a tree.* **3.** *Geol.* **a.** to split or swell into a scaly aggregate, as certain minerals when heated. **b.** to separate into rudely concentric layers or sheets, as certain rocks during weathering. **4.** *Surg.* to separate and come off in scales, as scaling skin or any structure separating in flakes. [t. LL: m. s. *exfoliātus*, pp., stripped of leaves] —**exfoliative** (ĕks-fō′lĭ ə tĭv), *adj.*

exfoliation (ĕks fō′lĭ ā′shən), *n.* **1.** the act or process of exfoliating. **2.** the state of being exfoliated. **3.** that which is exfoliated, or scaled off.

ex gratia (ĕks′ grā′shə), (of something granted) as a favour and not because of a legal obligation.

exhalant (ĕks hā′lənt, ĭg zā′lənt), *adj.* **1.** exhaling; emitting. —*n.* **2.** that which exhales.

exhalation (ĕks′hə lā′shən, ĕk′sə-), *n.* **1.** the act of exhaling. **2.** that which is exhaled; a vapour; an emanation.

exhale (ĕks hāl′, ĭg zāl′), *v.*, **-haled, -haling.** —*v.i.* **1.** to emit breath or vapour. **2.** to pass off as vapour; pass off as an effluence. —*v.t.* **3.** to breathe out; emit (air, etc.). **4.** to give off as vapour. **5.** to draw out as a vapour or effluence; evaporate. [ME *exhale(n)*, t. F: m. *exhaler*, t. L: m. *exhālāre* breathe out] —**exhal′able,** *adj.*

exhaust (ĭg zôst′), *v.t.* **1.** to empty by drawing out the contents. **2.** to create a vacuum in. **3.** to draw out or drain off; draw or drain off completely. **4.** to use up or consume completely; expend the whole of. **5.** to drain of strength or energy, wear out, or fatigue greatly, as a person: *I have exhausted myself working.* **6.** to draw out all that is essential in (a subject, topic, etc.); treat or study thoroughly. **7.** to deprive wholly of useful or essential properties, possessions, resources, etc. **8.** to deprive of ingredients by the use of solvents, as a drug. **9.** to destroy the fertility of (soil), as by intensive cultivation. —*v.i.* **10.** to pass out or escape, as spent steam from the cylinder of an engine. —*n.* **11.** *Mach.* the escape of the gases from the cylinder of an engine after expansion. **12.** the steam or gases ejected. **13.** the parts of an engine through which the exhaust is ejected. [t. L: s. *exhaustus*, pp., drained out] —**exhaust′er,** *n.* —**exhaust′ible,** *adj.* —**exhaust′ibil′ity,** *n.* —**Syn.** 5. tire, enervate, prostrate. See **tired**[1]. —**Ant.** 5. invigorate.

exhaust fan, the fan in a ventilation system used to remove vitiated or excess air.

exhaustion (ĭg zôs′chən), *n.* **1.** the act or process of exhausting. **2.** the state of being exhausted. **3.** extreme weakness or fatigue. —**Syn.** 3. weariness, lassitude.

exhaustive (ĭg zôs′tĭv), *adj.* **1.** exhausting a subject, topic, etc.; comprehensive; thorough. **2.** tending to exhaust or drain, as of resources or strength. —**exhaus′tively,** *adv.* —**exhaus′tiveness,** *n.*

exhaustless (ĭg zôst′lĭs), *adj.* inexhaustible. —**exhaust′-lessly,** *adv.* —**exhaust′lessness,** *n.*

exhaust pipe, a pipe for releasing waste gases from an internal-combustion engine.

exhibit (ĭg zĭb′ĭt), *v.t.* **1.** to offer or expose to view; present for inspection. **2.** to manifest or display: *to exhibit anger.* **3.** to place on show: *to exhibit paintings.* **4.** *Law.* to submit (a document, etc.) in evidence in a court of law. **5.** *Med.* to administer (a remedy, etc.). —*v.i.* **6.** to make or give an exhibition; present something to public view. —*n.* **7.** an exhibiting or exhibition. **8.** that which is exhibited. **9.** an object or a collection of objects shown in an exhibition, fair, etc. **10.** *Law.* a document or other object exhibited in court and referred to and identified in written evidence. [t. L: s. *exhibitus*, pp.] —**exhib′itor, exhib′iter,** *n.* —**Syn.** 1. See **display.** 2. evince, disclose, betray. 8, 10. See **evidence.** —**Ant.** 2. conceal.

exhibition (ĕk′sĭ bĭsh′ən), *n.* **1.** an exhibiting, showing, or presenting to view. **2.** a public display of feats of skill, athletic prowess, etc. **3.** a public show or display. **4.** *Med.* administration, as of a remedy. **5.** an allowance or grant made to a student at a university, usually upon the result of a competitive examination. **6. make an exhibition of oneself,** to behave foolishly or so as to excite ridicule.

exhibitioner (ĕk′sĭ bĭsh′ə nə), *n.* a student who receives an exhibition (def. 5).

exhibitionism (ĕk′sĭ bĭsh′ə nĭz′əm), *n.* **1.** a tendency to display one's abilities or to behave in such a way as to attract attention. **2.** *Psychiatry.* an abnormal tendency to make a display of oneself: in a more severe form with exposure of the genitals.

exhibitionist (ĕk′sĭ bĭsh′ə nĭst), *n.* **1.** one who desires to make an exhibition of himself or his powers, personality, etc. **2.** *Psychiatry.* one affected with the compulsions of exhibitionism. —**ex′hibi′tionis′tic,** *adj.*

exhibitive (ĭg zĭb′ĭ tĭv), *adj.* serving for exhibition; tending to exhibit.

exhibitory (ĭg zĭb′ĭ tə rĭ, -trĭ), *adj.* pertaining to or intended for exhibition or display.

exhilarant (ĭg zĭl′ə rənt), *adj.* **1.** exhilarating. —*n.* **2.** something that exhilarates.

exhilarate (ĭg zĭl′ə rāt′), *v.t.*, **-rated, -rating.** **1.** to make cheerful or merry. **2.** to enliven; stimulate; invigorate. [t. L: m. s. *exhilarātus*, pp.] —**exhil′arat′ing,** *adj.* —**exhil′arat′ingly,** *adv.* —**exhil′ara′tor,** *n.* —**Syn.** 1. cheer, gladden, enliven, animate, inspirit.

exhilaration (ĭg zĭl′ə rā′shən), *n.* **1.** exhilarated condition or feeling. **2.** the act of exhilarating. —**Syn.** 1. animation, joyousness, gaiety, jollity, hilarity.

exhilarative (ĭg zĭl′ə rə tĭv), *adj.* tending to exhilarate. Also, **exhilaratory** (ĭg zĭl′ə rə tə rĭ, -trĭ).

exhort (ĭg zôt′), *v.t.* **1.** to urge, advise, or caution earnestly; admonish urgently. —*v.i.* **2.** to make exhortation; give admonition. [ME *exhort(en)*, t. L: m. *exhortārī* urge, encourage] —**exhort′er,** *n.*

exhortation (ĕg′zô tā′shən), *n.* **1.** the act or process of exhorting. **2.** an utterance, discourse, or address conveying urgent advice or recommendations.

exhortative (ĭg zô′tə tĭv), *adj.* **1.** serving or intended to exhort. **2.** pertaining to exhortation. Also, **exhortatory** (ĭg zô′tə tə rĭ, -trĭ).

exhume (ĕks hyōōm′), *v.t.*, **-humed, -huming.** to dig (something buried, esp. a dead body) out of the earth; disinter. [t. ML: m. s. *exhumāre*, der. L *ex-* EX-[1] + *humus* earth, ground] —**exhumation** (ĕks′hyōō mā′shən), *n.* —**exhum′er,** *n.*

exigeant (ĕk′sĭ jənt; *Fr.* ĕg zē zhäN′), *adj.* exigent. —**exigeante** (*Fr.* ĕg zē zhäNt′), *adj. fem.*

exigency (ĕk′sĭ jən sĭ, ĭg zĭj′ən sĭ), *n., pl.* **-cies. 1.** exigent state of character; urgency. **2.** (*usually pl.*) a circumstance that renders prompt action necessary; the need, demand, or requirement of a particular occasion. **3.** a case or situation which demands prompt action or remedy; an emergency. Also, **ex′igence.**

exigent (ĕk′sĭ jənt), *adj.* **1.** requiring immediate action or aid; urgent; pressing. **2.** requiring a great deal, or more than is reasonable. [t. L: s. *exigens*, ppr., requiring, lit., driving out] —**ex′igently,** *adv.*

exigible (ĕk′sĭ jə bl), *adj.* that may be exacted; requirable.

exiguous (ĭg zĭg′yōō əs), *adj.* scanty; small; slender. [t. L: m. *exiguus*] —**exiguity** (ĕk′sĭ gyōō′ĭ tĭ), **exig′uousness,** *n.* —**exig′uously,** *adv.*

exile (ĕg′zīl, ĕk′sīl), *n., v.*, **-iled, -iling.** —*n.* **1.** prolonged separation from one's country or home, as by stress of circumstances. **2.** anyone separated from his country or home. **3.** expulsion from one's native land by authoritative decree. **4.** the fact or state of such expulsion. **5.** a person banished from his native land. **6. the Exile,** the Babylonian captivity of the Jews in the 6th century B.C. —*v.t.* **7.** to separate from country, home, etc. **8.** to expel or banish (a person) from his country; expatriate. [ME *exil*, t. OF, t. L: m. s. *ex(s)ilium* banishment]

exilic (ĕg zĭl′ĭk, ĕk sĭl′ĭk), *adj.* pertaining to exile, as that of the Jews in Babylon. Also, **exil′ian.**

eximious (ĕg zĭm′ĭ əs), *adj. Archaic.* distinguished; eminent; excellent. [t. L: m. *eximius* select]

ex int., ex (without) interest.

exist (ĭg zĭst′), *v.i.* **1.** to have actual being; be. **2.** to have life or animation; live. **3.** to continue to be or to live. **4.** to have being in a specified place or under certain conditions; be found; occur. [t. L: s. *ex(s)istere* stand forth, arise, be]

existence (ĭg zĭs′təns), *n.* **1.** the state or fact of existing; being. **2.** continuance in being or life; life: *a struggle for existence.* **3.** mode of existing. **4.** all that exists. **5.** something that exists, an entity, or a being.

existent (ĭg zĭs′tənt), *adj.* **1.** existing; having existence. **2.** now existing. —*n.* **3.** one who or that which exists.

existential (ĕg′zĭs tĕn′shəl), *adj.* **1.** pertaining to existence. **2.** *Philos.* of or pertaining to existentialism. **3.** *Logic.* (of a proposition) predicative of existence. —**ex′isten′tially,** *adv.*

existentialism (ĕg′zĭs tĕn′shə lĭz′əm), *n.* any of a group of doctrines, some theistic, some atheistic, deriving from Kierkegaard, which stress the importance of existence, as such, and of the freedom and responsibility of the finite human individual. —**ex′isten′tialist,** *adj., n.*

existential psychology, 1. a school of psychology based on the study of introspective data as themselves existing. **2.** the psychological aspect of existentialism.

exit (ĕg′zĭt, ĕk′sĭt), *n.* **1.** a way or passage out. **2.** a going out or away; a departure: *to make one's exit.* **3.** the departure of a player from the stage as part of the action of a play. —*v.i.* **4.** he (or she, or the person named) goes out (used in the text of plays, with reference to an actor). **5.** to depart; go away. **6.** to die. [special use of stage direction *exit* he goes out, influenced by assoc. with L *exitus* a going out]

ex lib., ex libris.

ex libris (ĕks lī′brĭs), *pl.* **-bris** *for 2. Latin.* **1.** from the library (of) (a phrase inscribed in or on a book, before the name of the owner). **2.** an inscription in or on a book, to indicate the owner; a bookplate.

ex-librist (ĕks lī′brĭst), *n.* a collector of bookplates. —**ex-li′brism,** *n.*

Exmoor (ĕks′mōōə′, -mô′), *n.* a high moorland in SW England, in Somersetshire and Devonshire: a national park. Highest point, Dunkery Beacon, 1707 ft. Also, **Exmoor Forest.**

ex nihilo nihil fit (ĕks nē′hĭ lō nē′hĭl fĭt′), *Latin.* (only) nothing is created from nothing; that is, all that exists has always existed.

exo-, a prefix meaning 'external'. Also, **ex-**[2]. [t. Gk: outside]

exocarp (ĕk′sō kärp′), *n. Bot.* epicarp.

exocentric (ĕk′sō sĕn′trĭk), *adj. Gram.* not having the same function in a sentence as any one of its immediate constituents. *In the garden* is an exocentric construction, since it does not function in the same way as the noun *garden.* Cf. **endocentric.**

Exod., Exodus.

exodermis (ĕk′sō dû′mĭs), *n. Bot.* the outer layer or layers of the cortex of primary roots which become suberized after the epidermis has been lost.

exodontia (ĕk′sō dŏn′tyə), *n.* the branch of dentistry dealing with the extraction of teeth. Also, **ex′odon′tics.** [NL, f. Gk: *ex-* EX-[3] + s. *odoús* tooth + *-ia* -IA. Cf. Gk *exodontízomai* have one's teeth removed] —**ex′odon′tist,** *n.*

exodus (ĕk′sə dəs), *n.* **1.** a going out; a departure or emigration, usually of a large number of people. **2.** (*often cap.*) the departure of the Israelites from Egypt under Moses. **3.** (*cap.*) the second book of the Old Testament, containing an account of this departure. [ME, t. L, t. Gk: m. *éxodos* a going out]

exoergic (ĕk′sō û′jĭk), *adj. Physics.* (of a process or reaction) giving off energy, esp. of a nuclear process; exothermic.

ex off., ex officio.

ex officio (ĕks′ə fĭsh′ĭ ō′, -fĭs′ĭ ō′), by virtue of office or official position. —**ex-officio,** *adj.* [t. L: from office]

exogamy (ĕk sŏg′ə mĭ), *n.* **1.** the custom of marrying outside the tribe or blood group (opposed to *endogamy*). **2.** *Biol.* the union of gametes of unrelated parents. —**exogamous** (ĕk sŏg′ə məs), **exogamic** (ĕk′sō găm′ĭk), *adj.*

exogen (ĕk′sō jĕn′), *n. Bot.* any plant of the obsolete class *Exogenae*, including the dicotyledons. [t. F: m. *exogène.* See EXO-, -GEN]

exogenous (ĕk sŏj′ĭ nəs), *adj.* **1.** having its origin external; derived externally. **2.** *Bot.* **a.** (of plants, as the dicotyledons) having stems which grow by the addition of an annual layer of wood to the outside beneath the bark. **b.** pertaining to plants having such stems. **c.** belonging to the exogens. **3.** *Physiol., Biochem.* of or denoting the metabolic assimilation of proteins, in which the elimination of nitrogenous catabolites is in direct proportion to the amount of protein taken in. [t. NL: m. *exōgenus* growing on the outside. See EXO-, -GENOUS] —**exog′enously,** *adv.*

exon (ĕk′sŏn), *n.* an officer of the Yeomen of the Guard. Also, **exempt.**

exonerate (ĭg zŏn′ə rāt′), *v.t.*, **-rated, -rating. 1.** to clear, as of a charge; free from blame; exculpate. **2.** to relieve, as from an obligation, duty, or task. [t. L: m. s. *exonerātus*, pp., disburdened] —**exon′era′tion,** *n.* —**exonerative** (ĭg zŏn′ə rə tĭv), *adj.* —**exon′era′tor,** *n.* —**Syn. 1.** See **absolve.**

exoperidium (ĕks′ō pĭ rĭd′ĭ əm), *n. Bot.* See **peridium.**

exophthalmos (ĕk′sŏf thăl′mŏs), *n. Pathol.* protrusion of the eyeball from the orbit, caused by disease or injury. Also, **exophthalmus** (ĕk′sŏf thăl′məs), **exophthalmia** (ĕk′sŏf thăl′mĭ ə). [NL, t. Gk: as adj., with prominent eyes] —**ex′ophthal′mic,** *adj.*

exopleura (ĕk′sō plōō′rə), *n. Bot.* the outer seedcoat; the testa.

exorable (ĕk′sə rə bl), *adj.* susceptible of being persuaded or moved by entreaty. [t. L: m. s. *exōrābilis*] —**ex′orabil′ity,** *n.*

exorbitance (ĭg zô′bĭ təns), *n.* the quality of being exorbitant; excessiveness. Also, **exor′bitancy.**

exorbitant (ĭg zô′bĭ tənt), *adj.* exceeding the bounds of custom, propriety, or reason, esp. in amount or extent: *to charge an exorbitant price for something.* [t. LL: s. *exorbitans*, ppr., going out of the track] —**exor′bitantly,** *adv.* —**Syn.** inordinate, excessive, extravagant, unreasonable, unconscionable. —**Ant.** fair.

exorcism (ĕk′sô sĭz′əm), *n.* **1.** the act or process of exorcising. **2.** the ceremony or the formula used.

exorcist (ĕk′sô sĭst), *n.* **1.** one who exorcizes. **2.** *Rom. Cath. Ch.* a member of one of the minor orders.

exorcize (ĕk′sô sīz′), *v.t.*, **-cized, -cizing. 1.** to seek to expel (an evil spirit) by adjuration or religious or solemn ceremonies. **2.** to deliver (a person, place, etc.) from evil spirits or malignant influences. Also, **ex′orcise′.** [t. LL: m. s. *exorcizāre*, t. Gk: m. *exorkízein*] —**ex′orcize′ment,** *n.* —**ex′orciz′er,** *n.*

exordium (ĕk sô′dyəm), *n., pl.* **-diums, -dia** (-dyə). **1.** the beginning of anything. **2.** the introductory part of an oration or discourse. [t. L: a beginning] —**exor′dial,** *adj.*

exoskeleton (ĕk′sō skĕl′ĭ tən), *n. Zool.* an external protective covering or integument, esp. when hard, as the shell of crustaceans, the scales and plates of fishes, etc. (opposed to *endoskeleton*). —**ex′oskel′etal,** *adj.*

exosmosis (ĕk′sŏs mō′sĭs, ĕk′sŏz-), *n. Phys. Chem., etc.* **1.** osmosis from within outwards. **2.** (in osmosis) the flow of that fluid which passes with the lesser rapidity into the other (opposed to *endosmosis*). Also, **exosmose** (ĕk′sŏs mōs′, ĕk′sŏz-). [f. EX-³ + OSMOSIS] —**exosmotic** (ĕk′sŏs mŏt′ĭk, ĕk′sŏz-), **exosmic** (ĕk sŏs′mĭk, -sŏz′-), *adj.*

exosphere (ĕk′sō sfĭə′), *n.* the outermost region of the atmosphere where collisions between molecular particles are so rare that only the force of gravity will return escaping molecules to the upper atmosphere.

exospore (ĕk′sō spô′), *n. Bot.* the outer coat of a spore.

exostosis (ĕk′sŏs tō′sĭs), *n.*, *pl.* **-ses** (-sēz). *Pathol.* the morbid formation of bone, or a morbid bony growth, on a bone. [NL, t. Gk: outgrowth of bone]

exoteric (ĕk′sō tĕ′rĭk), *adj.* **1.** suitable for or communicated to the general public. **2.** not belonging or pertaining to the inner or select circle, as of disciples. **3.** popular; simple; commonplace. **4.** of or pertaining to the outside; exterior; external. [t. LL: s. *exōtericus* external, t. Gk: m. *exōterikós*] —**ex′oter′ically,** *adv.* —**ex′oter′icism,** *n.*

exothermic (ĕk′sō thû′mĭk), *adj. Chem.* denoting or pertaining to a chemical change which is accompanied by a liberation of heat (opposed to *endothermic*).

exotic (ĭg zŏt′ĭk), *adj.* **1.** of foreign origin or character; not native; introduced from abroad, but not fully naturalized or acclimatized. **2.** *Colloq.* strikingly unusual or colourful in appearance or effect; strange; exciting. —*n.* **3.** anything exotic, as a plant. [t. L: s. *exōticus*, t. Gk: m. *exōtikós* foreign, alien] —**exot′ically,** *adv.*

exoticism (ĭg zŏt′ĭ sĭz′əm), *n.* **1.** tendency to adopt what is exotic. **2.** exotic quality or character. **3.** anything exotic, as a foreign word or idiom.

exotoxin (ĕk′sō tŏk′sĭn), *n. Bacteriol.* a toxin secreted during the life of an organism, either in the body tissues or in food. The organism itself is non-toxic.

exp., **1.** expenses. **2.** expired. **3.** export. **4.** exportation. **5.** exported. **6.** exporter. **7.** express.

expand (ĭk spănd′), *v.t.* **1.** to increase in extent, size, volume, scope, etc.: *heat expands metal.* **2.** to spread or stretch out; unfold: *a bird expands its wings.* **3.** to express in fuller form or greater detail; develop: *to expand a short story into a novel.* —*v.i.* **4.** to increase or grow in extent, bulk, scope, etc.: *most metals expand with heat, the mind expands with experience.* **5.** to spread out; unfold; develop: *the buds had not yet expanded.* [t. L: s. *expandere* spread out] —**expand′er,** *n.*

—**Syn. 1.** extend, swell, enlarge. EXPAND, DILATE, DISTEND, INFLATE imply becoming larger and filling more space. To EXPAND is to spread out, usually in every direction, so as to occupy more space or have more capacity: *to expand one's chest.* To DILATE is esp. to increase the width or circumference, and applies to space enclosed within confines or to hollow bodies: *to dilate the pupils of the eyes.* To DISTEND is to stretch, often beyond the point of natural expansion: *to distend an artery.* To INFLATE is to blow out or swell a hollow body with air or gas of some kind: *to inflate a balloon.* **2.** spread, unfurl. —**Ant. 1.** contract.

expanded (ĭk spăn′dĭd), *adj.* **1.** increased in area, bulk, or volume; enlarged. **2.** spread out; extended. **3.** (of printing type) wider than usual for its height.

expanded metal, sheet metal which has been cut and stretched so that it forms a network giving greater rigidity than wire netting.

expanse (ĭk spăns′), *n.* **1.** that which is spread out, esp. over a large area. **2.** an uninterrupted space or area; a wide extent of anything: *an expanse of water, of sky, etc.* **3.** expansion; extension.

expansible (ĭk spăn′sə bl), *adj.* capable of being expanded. —**expan′sibil′ity,** *n.*

expansile (ĭk spăn′sĭl), *adj.* **1.** capable of expanding; such as to expand. **2.** pertaining to expansion.

expansion (ĭk spăn′shən), *n.* **1.** the act of expanding. **2.** the state of being expanded. **3.** the amount or degree of expanding. **4.** an expanded, dilated, or enlarged portion or form of a thing. **5.** anything spread out; an expanse. **6.** *Maths.* the development at length of an expression indicated in a contracted form. **7.** *Mach.* that part of the operation of an engine in which the volume of the working medium increases and its pressure decreases. [t. LL: s. *expansio*]

expansionism (ĭk spăn′shə nĭz′əm), *n.* the policy of expansion, esp. of territorial expansion. —**expan′sionist,** *n.*

expansive (ĭk spăn′sĭv), *adj.* **1.** tending to expand or capable of expanding. **2.** causing expansion. **3.** having a wide range or extent; comprehensive; extensive. **4.** (of a person's character, or speech) effusive, unrestrained, free, or open. **5.** *Psychiatry.* marked by an abnormal euphoristic state and by delusions of grandeur. —**expan′sively,** *adv.* —**expan′siveness,** *n.*

ex parte (ĕks′ pä′tĭ), *Latin.* from or on one side only, as in a controversy; in the interest of one party.

expatiate (ĭk spā′shĭ āt′), *v.i.*, **-ated, -ating.** **1.** to enlarge in discourse or writing; be copious in description or discussion: *to expatiate upon a theme.* **2.** to move or wander about intellectually, imaginatively, etc., without restraint. [t. L: m. s. *ex(s)patiātus*, pp., extended, spread out] —**expa′tia′tion,** *n.* —**expa′tia′tor,** *n.*

expatriate (*v.* ĕks păt′rĭ āt′; *adj.*, *n.* ĕks păt′rĭ ĭt, -rĭ āt′), *v.*, **-ated, -ating,** *adj.*, *n.* —*v.t.* **1.** to banish (a person) from his native country. **2.** to withdraw (oneself) from residence in one's native country. **3.** to withdraw (oneself) from allegiance to one's country. —*adj.* **4.** expatriated; exiled. —*n.* **5.** an expatriated person. [t. LL: m. s. *expatriātus*, pp.] —**expat′ria′tion,** *n.*

expect (ĭk spĕkt′), *v.t.* **1.** to look forward to; regard as likely to happen; anticipate the occurrence or the coming of: *I expect to do it, I expect him to come, that he will come.* **2.** to look for with reason or justification: *we cannot expect obedience, expect him to do that.* —*v.i.* **3.** *Colloq.* to suppose or surmise. **4.** *Colloq.* to be pregnant: *my wife is expecting again.* [t. L: s. *ex(s)pectāre* look for]

—**Syn. 1.** EXPECT, ANTICIPATE, HOPE, AWAIT all imply looking to some future event. EXPECT implies confidently believing, usually for good reasons, that an event will occur: *to expect a visit from a friend.* ANTICIPATE is to look forward eagerly to an event and even to picture it: *to anticipate seeing a play.* HOPE implies a wish that an event may take place and an expectation that it will: *to hope for the best.* AWAIT (WAIT FOR) implies being alert and ready, whether for good or evil: *to await news after a cyclone.*

expectancy (ĭk spĕk′tən sĭ), *n.*, *pl.* **-cies.** **1.** the quality or state of expecting; expectation; anticipatory belief or desire. **2.** the state of being expected. **3.** an object of expectation; something expected. Also, **expec′tance.**

expectant (ĭk spĕk′tənt), *adj.* **1.** having expectations; expecting. **2.** expecting the birth of a child: *an expectant mother.* **3.** characterized by expectations. **4.** expected or anticipated; prospective. —*n.* **5.** one who expects; one who waits in expectation. —**expec′tantly,** *adv.*

expectation (ĕk′spĕk tā′shən), *n.* **1.** the act of expecting. **2.** the state of expecting: *wait in expectation.* **3.** the state of being expected. **4.** an expectant mental attitude. **5.** something expected; a thing looked forward to. **6.** (*often pl.*) a prospect of future good or profit: *to have great expectations.* **7.** the degree of probability of the occurrence of something. —**Syn. 2, 4.** expectancy, anticipation, hope, trust.

expectation of life, the average duration of life beyond a person's attained age, as shown by mortality tables.

expectative (ĭk spĕk′tə tĭv), *adj.* **1.** of or pertaining to expectation. **2.** characterized by expectation.

expectorant (ĭk spĕk′tə rənt), *Med.* —*adj.* **1.** promoting expectoration from the respiratory tract. —*n.* **2.** an expectorant medicine.

expectorate (ĭk spĕk′tə rāt′), *v.*, **-rated, -rating.** —*v.t.* **1.** to eject or expel (phlegm, etc.) from the throat or lungs by coughing or hawking and spitting; spit. —*v.i.* **2.** to spit. [t. L: m. s. *expectorātus*, pp., banished from the breast] —**expec′tora′tor,** *n.*

expectoration (ĭk spĕk′tə rā′shən), *n.* **1.** the act of expectorating. **2.** matter that is expectorated.

ex pede Herculem (ĕks pĕd′ā hû′kyo͝o lĕm′), *Latin.* from the foot (we may know) Hercules; from a part or sample we may judge the whole.

expediency (ĭk spē′dyən sĭ), *n.*, *pl.* **-cies.** **1.** the quality of being expedient; advantageousness; advisability. **2.** a regard for what is politic or advantageous rather than for what is right or just; a sense of self-interest. **3.** something expedient. Also, **expe′dience.**

expedient (ĭk spē′dyənt), *adj.* **1.** tending to promote some proposed or desired object; fit or suitable for the purpose; proper in the circumstances: *it is expedient that you go.* **2.** conducive to advantage or interest, as opposed to right. **3.** acting in accordance with expediency. —*n.* **4.** a means to an end. **5.** a means devised or employed in an exigency; a resource; a shift: *to resort to expedients to achieve one's purpose.* [ME, t. L: s. *expediens*, ppr., dispatching] —**expe′diently,** *adv.* —**Syn. 1.** advantageous, profitable, advisable. **5.** device, contrivance.

expediential (ĭk spē′dĭ ĕn′shəl), *adj.* pertaining to or regulated by expediency.

expedite (ĕks′pĭ dīt′), *v.*, **-dited, -diting,** *adj.* —*v.t.* **1.** to speed up the progress of; hasten: *to expedite matters.* **2.** to accomplish promptly, as a piece of business; dispatch. **3.** to issue officially, as a document. —*adj.* **4.** *Obs.* ready; alert. [t. L: m. s. *expedītus*, pp., extricated, helped forwards, sent off or dispatched] —**ex′pedit′er,** *n.* —**Syn. 1.** quicken, speed, push. —**Ant. 1.** delay.

expedition (ĕks′pĭ dĭsh′ən), *n.* **1.** an excursion, journey, or voyage made for some specific purpose, as of war or exploration. **2.** the body of persons or ships, etc., engaged in it. **3.** promptness or speed in accomplishing something. —**Syn. 1.** See **trip. 3.** haste, quickness, dispatch.

expeditionary (ĕks′pĭ dĭsh′ə nə rĭ, -dĭsh′nə rĭ), *adj.* pertaining to or composing an expedition: *an expeditionary force.*

expeditious (ĕks′pĭ dĭsh′əs), *adj.* characterized by promptness; quick. **—ex′pedi′tiously,** *adv.* **—ex′pedi′tiousness,** *n.*

expel (ĭk spĕl′), *v.t.*, **-pelled, -pelling. 1.** to drive or force out or away; discharge or eject: *to expel air from the lungs, an invader from a country.* **2.** to cut off from membership or relations: *to expel a pupil from a school.* [ME *expelle(n)*, t. L: m. *expellere* drive out] **—expel′lable,** *adj.* **—expellee** (ĕk′spĕl ē′), *n.* **—expel′ler,** *n.* **—Syn. 2.** oust, dismiss.

expellant (ĭk spĕl′ənt), *adj.* **1.** expelling or having the power to expel. **—***n.* **2.** an expellant medicine. Also, **expel′lent.**

expend (ĭk spĕnd′), *v.t.* **1.** to use up: *to expend energy, time, care, etc., on something.* **2.** to pay out; disburse; spend. [t. L: s. *expendere* weigh out, pay out] **—expend′er,** *n.* **—Syn. 1.** See **spend.**

expendable (ĭk spĕn′də bl), *adj.* **1.** capable of being expended. **2.** (of an item of equipment or supply) normally consumed in use. **3.** *Mil.* (of men, equipment, etc.) capable of being sacrificed to achieve an objective.

expenditure (ĭk spĕn′dĭ chə), *n.* **1.** the act of expending; disbursement; consumption. **2.** that which is expended; expense.

expense (ĭk spĕns′), *n.* **1.** cost or charge. **2.** a cause or occasion of spending: *owning a car is a great expense.* **3.** the act of expending; expenditure. **4.** loss or injury due to any detracting cause (prec. by *at*): *quantity at the expense of quality.* **5.** (*pl.*) *Com.* **a.** charges incurred in the execution of an undertaking or commission. **b.** money paid as reimbursement for such charges: *to receive a salary and expenses.* [ME, t. AF, t. LL: m. *expensa*, prop. pp. fem., paid or weighed out] **—Syn. 1.** See **price.**

expense account, a record of expenditure incurred by an employee in the course of business to be refunded by the employer or claimed against tax.

expensive (ĭk spĕn′sĭv), *adj.* entailing great expense; costly. **—expen′sively,** *adv.* **—expen′siveness,** *n.*

—Syn. EXPENSIVE, COSTLY, DEAR apply to that which is higher in price than the average person's usual purchases. EXPENSIVE is applied to whatever entails (usually considerable) expense; it suggests a price beyond a thing's worth and beyond what the person can properly afford to pay: *an expensive motor car.* COSTLY implies that the price is a large sum, usually because of the fineness, preciousness, etc., of the object: *a costly jewel.* DEAR is commonly applied to that which is selling beyond its usual or just price: *buy cheap and sell dear.* **—Ant.** cheap.

experience (ĭk spĭə′rĭ əns), *n.*, *v.*, **-enced, -encing. —***n.* **1.** a particular instance of personally encountering or undergoing something: *a strange experience.* **2.** the process or fact of personally observing, encountering, or undergoing something: *business experience.* **3.** the observing, encountering, or undergoing of things generally as they occur in the course of time: *to learn from experience, the range of human experience.* **4.** knowledge or practical wisdom gained from what one has observed, encountered, or undergone: *men of experience.* **5.** *Philos.* the totality of the cognitions given by perception; all that is perceived, understood, and remembered. **—***v.t.* **6.** to have experience of; meet with; undergo; feel. **7.** to learn by experience. [ME, t. OF, t. L: m. s. *experientia* trial, proof, knowledge]

—Syn. 6. EXPERIENCE, UNDERGO refer to encountering situations, conditions, etc., in life, or to having certain sensations, feelings. EXPERIENCE implies being affected by what one meets with (pleasant or unpleasant), so that to a greater or less degree one suffers a change: *to experience a change of heart, bitter disappointment.* UNDERGO usually refers to the bearing or enduring of something hard, difficult, disagreeable, or dangerous: *to undergo severe hardships, an operation.*

experienced (ĭk spĭə′rĭ ənst), *adj.* **1.** having had experience. **2.** having learned through experience; taught by experience. **3.** wise or skilful through experience: *an experienced teacher, general, etc.* **—Syn. 3.** skilled, expert, practised, veteran.

experience table, *Insurance.* actuarial tables. See **mortality table.**

experiential (ĭk spĭə′rĭ ĕn′shəl), *adj.* pertaining to or derived from experience. **—expe′rien′tially,** *adv.*

experientialism (ĭk spĭə′rĭ ĕn′shə lĭz′əm), *n. Philos.* a doctrine that maintains that all knowledge is derived from experience. **—expe′rien′tialist,** *n.*

experiment (*n.* ĭk spĕ′rĭ mənt; *v.* -mĕnt′), *n.* **1.** a test or trial; a tentative procedure; an act or operation for the purpose of discovering something unknown or testing a principle, supposition, etc.: *a chemical experiment.* **2.** the conducting of such operations; experimentation: *a product that is the result of long experiment.* **3.** *Obs.* experience. **—***v.i.* **4.** to try or test in order to find something out: *to experiment with drugs in order to find a cure for a certain disease.* [ME, t. L: s. *experīmentum* a trial, test] **—exper′iment′er,** *n.* **—Syn. 1.** See **trial.**

experimental (ĭk spĕ′rĭ mĕn′tl), *adj.* **1.** pertaining to, derived from, or founded on experiment: *an experimental science.* **2.** based on or derived from experience; empirical: *experimental religion.* **3.** of the nature of an experiment; tentative. **4.** functioning as an experiment or used as a means of experimentation: *an experimental aeroplane, an experimental theatre.* **—exper′imen′talist,** *n.* **—exper′imen′tally,** *adv.*

experimentalism (ĭk spĕ′rĭ mĕn′tə lĭz′əm), *n.* systematic reliance upon experimentation; empiricism.

experimentation (ĭk spĕ′rĭ mĕn tā′shən), *n.* the act or practice of making experiments; the process of experimenting.

expert (ĕks′pût), *n.* **1.** a person who has special skill or knowledge in some particular field; a specialist; authority: *a language expert, an expert on mining.* **—***adj.* **2.** possessing special skill or knowledge; trained by practice; skilful or skilled (often fol. by *in* or *at*): *an expert driver, to be expert at driving a car.* **3.** pertaining to, coming from, or characteristic of an expert: *expert work, expert advice.* [ME, t. L: s. *expertus*, pp., having tried] **—ex′pertly,** *adv.* **—ex′pertness,** *n.* **—Syn. 1.** authority, specialist, connoisseur, master. **2.** experienced, trained, proficient, dexterous, adroit. See **skilful. —Ant. 1.** novice. **2.** clumsy.

expertise (ĕk′spû tēz′), *n.* expert skill or knowledge; expertness.

expiable (ĕks′pĭ ə bl), *adj.* that may be expiated.

expiate (ĕks′pĭ āt′), *v.t.*, **-ated, -ating.** to atone for; make amends or reparation for. [t. L: m. s. *expiātus*, pp.] **—ex′pia′tor,** *n.*

expiation (ĕks′pĭ ā′shən), *n.* **1.** the act of expiating. **2.** the means by which atonement or reparation is made; atonement.

expiatory (ĕks′pĭ ə tə rĭ, -trĭ), *adj.* able to make atonement or expiation; offered by way of expiation.

expiration (ĕk′spə rā′shən, ĕk′spĭ rā′-), *n.* **1.** a coming to an end; termination; close. **2.** the act of expiring, or breathing out; emission of air from the lungs. **3.** *Obs.* death.

expiratory (ĭk spī′ə rə tə rĭ, -trĭ), *adj.* pertaining to the expiration of air from the lungs.

expire (ĭk spī′ə), *v.*, **-pired, -piring. —***v.i.* **1.** to come to an end; terminate. **2.** to die out, as a fire. **3.** to emit the last breath; die. **—***v.t.* **4.** to breathe out; emit (air) from the lungs. **5.** to emit or eject. [ME *expire(n)*, t. F: *expirer*, t. L: m. *ex(s)pīrāre* breathe out] **—expir′er,** *n.*

expiry (ĭk spī′ə rĭ), *n.*, *pl.* **-ries.** expiration.

explain (ĭk splān′), *v.t.* **1.** to make plain or clear; render intelligible: *to explain an obscure point.* **2.** to make known in detail: *to explain how to do something, to explain a process.* **3.** to assign a meaning to; interpret. **4.** to make clear the cause or reason of; account for. **5.** to dispel (difficulties, etc.) by explanation; nullify the significance, or the apparent significance, of (words, facts, occurrences, etc.) by explanation (fol. by *away*). **—***v.i.* **6.** to give an explanation. [t. L: m. s. *explānāre* make plain, flatten out] **—explain′able,** *adj.* **—explain′er,** *n.*

—Syn. 1. EXPLAIN, ELUCIDATE, EXPOUND, INTERPRET imply making the meaning of something clear or understandable. To EXPLAIN is to make plain, clear, or intelligible something that is not known or understood: *to explain a theory or a problem.* To ELUCIDATE is to throw light on what before was dark and obscure, usually by illustration and commentary and sometimes by elaborate explanation: *they asked him to elucidate his statement.* To EXPOUND is to give a methodical, detailed, scholarly explanation of something, usually Scriptures, doctrines, or philosophy: *to expound the doctrine of free will.* To INTERPRET is to give the meaning of something by paraphrase, by translation, or by an explanation (sometimes involving one's personal opinion and therefore original), which is often of a systematic and detailed nature: *to interpret a poem or a symbol.*

explanation (ĕk′splə nā′shən), *n.* **1.** the act or process of explaining. **2.** that which explains; a statement made to clarify something and make it understandable; an exposition. **3.** a meaning or interpretation: *to find an explanation of a mystery.* **4.** a mutual declaration of the meaning of words spoken, actions, motives, etc., with a view to adjusting a misunderstanding or reconciling differences. [t. L: s. *explānātio*] **—Syn. 1.** elucidation, explication, exposition, definition, interpretation. **3.** solution, key, answer.

explanatory (ĭk splăn′ə tə rĭ, -trĭ), *adj.* serving to explain. Also, **explan′ative. —explan′atorily,** *adv.*

explant (ĕks plänt′), *v.t.* **1.** to take living material from an animal or plant and place it in a culture medium. **—***n.* **2.** a piece of explanted tissue. [f. EX-[1] + PLANT]

expletive (ĕk splē′tĭv), *adj.* **1.** Also, **expletory** (ĕk splē′tə rĭ). added merely to fill out a sentence or line, give emphasis, etc. **—***n.* **2.** an expletive syllable, word, or phrase. **3.** an interjectory word or expression, frequently profane; an exclamatory oath. [t. LL: m. s. *explētīvus* serving to fill out] **—exple′tively,** *adv.*

explicable (ĕks′plĭ kə bl), *adj.* capable of being explained.

explicate (ĕks′plĭ kāt′), *v.t.*, **-cated, -cating.** **1.** to develop (a principle, etc.). **2.** to make plain or clear; explain; interpret. [t. L: m. s. *explicātus*, pp., unfolded]

explication (ĕks′plĭ kā′shən), *n.* **1.** the act of explicating. **2.** an explanation; interpretation.

explicative (ĭk splĭk′ə tĭv), *adj.* explanatory; interpretative. Also, **explic′atory.**

explicit (ĭk splĭs′ĭt), *adj.* **1.** leaving nothing merely implied; clearly expressed; unequivocal: *an explicit statement, instruction, etc.* **2.** clearly developed or formulated: *explicit knowledge or belief.* **3.** definite and unreserved in expression; outspoken: *he was quite explicit on that point.* **4.** *Maths.* (of a function) having the dependent variable expressed directly in terms of the independent variables. See **implicit** (def. 4). [t. L: s. *explicitus*, var. of *explicātus*, pp., unfolded] —**explic′itly,** *adv.* —**explic′itness,** *n.* —**Syn. 1.** express, definite, precise, exact, unambiguous. —**Ant. 1.** vague.

explode (ĭk splōd′), *v.*, **-ploded, -ploding.** —*v.i.* **1.** to expand with force and noise because of rapid chemical change or decomposition, as gunpowder, nitroglycerine, etc. **2.** to burst, fly into pieces, or break up violently with a loud report, as a boiler from excessive pressure of steam. **3.** to burst forth violently, esp. with noise, laughter, violent speech, etc. **4.** *Phonet.* (of stop consonants) to end with a plosion so that the end of the consonant is audible, as *t* in *ten.* —*v.t.* **5.** to cause (gunpowder, a boiler, etc.) to explode. **6.** to cause to be rejected; destroy the reputation of; discredit or disprove: *to explode a theory.* **7.** *Phonet.* to end with a plosion. **8.** *Obs.* to drive (a player, play, etc.) from the stage by loud expressions of disapprobation. [t. L: m. s. *explōdere* drive out by clapping] —**explod′er,** *n.*

exploit[1] (ĕks′ploit), *n.* a striking or notable deed; a feat; a spirited or heroic act. [ME *esploit*, t. OF, g. L *explicitum*, pp. neut., unfolded] —**Syn.** See **achievement.**

exploit[2] (ĭk sploit′), *v.t.* **1.** to turn to practical account; utilize for profit, esp. natural resources. **2.** to use selfishly for one's own ends. [ME *expleiten*, t. OF: m. *expleiter*, g. L *explicāre* unfold] —**exploit′able,** *adj.* —**exploitative** (ĭk sploi′tə tĭv), *adj.*

exploitation (ĕks′ploi tā′shən), *n.* **1.** utilization for profit. **2.** selfish utilization.

exploiter (ĭk sploi′tə), *n.* one who exploits.

exploration (ĕks′plô rā′shən), *n.* **1.** the act of exploring. **2.** the investigation of unknown regions.

exploratory (ĭk splô′rə tə rĭ, -trĭ, -splŏ′-), *adj.* **1.** pertaining to or concerned with exploration. **2.** inclined to make explorations. Also, **explor′ative.**

explore (ĭk splô′), *v.*, **-plored, -ploring.** —*v.t.* **1.** to traverse or range over (a region, etc.) for the purpose of discovery. **2.** to look into closely; scrutinize; examine. **3.** *Surg.* to investigate, esp. mechanically, as with a probe. **4.** *Obs.* to search for; search out. —*v.i.* **5.** to engage in exploration. [t. L: m. s. *explōrāre*]

explorer (ĭk splô′rə), *n.* **1.** one who or that which explores, esp., one who investigates unknown regions. **2.** any instrument used in exploring or sounding a wound, or a cavity in a tooth, etc.

explosion (ĭk splō′zhən), *n.* **1.** the act of exploding; a violent expansion or bursting with noise, as of gunpowder or a boiler. **2.** the noise itself. **3.** a violent outburst of laughter, anger, etc. **4.** any sudden, rapid, or large increase: *the population explosion.* **5.** the burning of fuel with air in an internal-combustion engine. **6.** *Phonet.* plosion. [t. L: s. *explōsio* a driving off by clapping]

explosive (ĭk splō′sĭv), *adj.* **1.** tending or serving to explode: *an explosive substance.* **2.** pertaining to or of the nature of an explosion. **3.** *Phonet.* plosive. —*n.* **4.** an explosive agent or substance, as dynamite. **5.** *Phonet.* a plosive. —**explo′sively,** *adv.* —**explo′siveness,** *n.*

explosive rivet, a rivet containing a small explosive charge for expanding the shank in positions which would otherwise be inaccessible.

exponent (ĭk spō′nənt), *n.* **1.** one who or that which expounds, explains, or interprets. **2.** one who or that which stands as a representative, type, or symbol of something: *the exponent of democratic principles.* **3.** *Maths.* a symbol placed above and at the right of another symbol (the base), to denote to what power the latter is to be raised, as in x^3. [t. L: s. *expōnens*, ppr., putting forth]

exponential (ĕks′pō nĕn′shəl), *adj.* **1.** of or pertaining to an exponent or exponents. **2.** *Maths.* **a.** of or pertaining to the constant *e*. **b.** having the unknown quantity or variable as an exponent. —*n.* **3.** *Maths.* an exponential quantity or function, esp. the constant *e* raised to the power of a given expression containing a variable.

exponential horn, a loudspeaker horn whose cross-sectional area increases exponentially with the distance from the throat.

exponible (ĭk spō′nə bl), *adj.* *Logic.* (esp. of an obscure proposition) admitting or requiring exposition.

export (*v.* ĭk spôt′, ĕks′pôt; *n.* ĕks′pôt), *v.t.* **1.** to send (commodities) to other countries or places for sale, exchange, etc. —*n.* **2.** the act of exporting; exportation. **3.** that which is exported; an article exported. —*adj.* **4.** of or pertaining to the export of goods or to exportable goods. [t. L: s. *exportāre* carry away] —**export′able,** *adj.* —**export′er,** *n.*

exportation (ĕks′pô tā′shən), *n.* **1.** the act of exporting; the sending of commodities out of a country, typically in trade. **2.** *U.S.* something exported.

exposal (ĭk spō′zəl), *n.* exposure.

expose (ĭk spōz′), *v.t.*, **-posed, -posing.** **1.** to lay open to danger, attack, harm, etc.: *to expose soldiers to gunfire, to expose one's character to attack.* **2.** to lay open to something specified: *to expose oneself to misunderstanding.* **3.** to uncover or bare to the air, cold, etc., *to expose one's head to the rain.* **4.** to present to view; exhibit; display: *the beggar who exposes his sores.* **5.** to make known, disclose, or reveal (intentions, secrets, etc.). **6.** to reveal or unmask (crime, fraud, an imposter, etc.). **7.** to hold up to public reprehension or ridicule (fault, folly, a fool, etc.). **8.** to leave in an unsheltered or open place, as (in primitive societies) an unwanted child to die. **9.** *Photog.* to subject (a plate, film or paper) to the action of light or other actinic rays. [t. OF: m. s. *exposer*, f. *ex-* EX-[1] + *poser* put (see POSE), but assoc. with deriv. of L *expōnere* set forth] —**expos′er,** *n.* —**Syn. 1.** subject (to), endanger, imperil, jeopardize. **5.** uncover, unveil, betray. —**Ant. 2.** protect (from). **5.** conceal.

exposé (ĕks pō′zā; *Fr.* ĕk spō zē′), *n.* **1.** a formal explanation or exposition. **2.** an exposure, as of something discreditable. [t. F, orig. pp. of *exposer* expose]

exposed (ĭk spōzd′), *adj.* **1.** left or being without shelter or protection; vulnerable; open to attack. **2.** laid open to view; unconcealed. —**exposedness** (ĭk spō′zĭd nĭs), *n.*

exposition (ĕks′pə zĭsh′ən), *n.* **1.** an exhibition or show, as of the products of art and manufacture. **2.** an act of expounding, setting forth, or explaining. **3.** a detailed statement or explanation; an explanatory treatise. **4.** the act of presenting to view; display. **5.** exposure (def. 7). **6.** the state of being exposed. **7.** *Music.* that part of a fugue or a sonata form, in which the subject or main themes are initially stated. —**Syn. 3.** explanation, elucidation, commentary.

expositor (ĭk spŏz′ĭ tə), *n.* one who expounds, or gives an exposition. [t. L; r. ME *exposit(o)ur*, t. AF]

expository (ĭk spŏz′ĭ tə rĭ, -trĭ), *adj.* serving to expound, set forth, or explain. Also, **expos′itive.**

ex post facto (ĕks′ pōst′ făk′tō), *Latin.* from or by subsequent action; subsequently; retrospectively.

ex post facto law, one passed after an alleged crime has been committed which, if applied in the case of an accused person, would work to his disadvantage.

expostulate (ĭk spŏs′tyŏŏ lāt′), *v.i.*, **-lated, -lating.** to reason earnestly with a person against something he intends to do or has done; remonstrate (*on*, or *upon*): *to expostulate with him on* (*or about*) *the impropriety.* [t. L: m. s. *expostulātus*, pp.] —**expos′tulat′ingly,** *adv.* —**expos′tula′tor,** *n.*

expostulation (ĭk spŏs′tyŏŏ lā′shən), *n.* **1.** the act of expostulating; remonstrance; earnest and kindly protest. **2.** an expostulatory remark or address.

expostulatory (ĭk spŏs′tyŏŏ lə tə rĭ, -trĭ), *adj.* expostulating; conveying expostulation. Also, **expos′tulative.**

exposure (ĭk spō′zhə), *n.* **1.** the act of exposing. **2.** disclosure, as of something private or secret. **3.** revealing or unmasking, as of crime, fraud, an imposter, etc. **4.** presentation to view, esp. in an open or public manner. **5.** a laying open or subjecting to the action or influence of something: *exposure to the weather, to danger, or to ridicule.* **6.** *Photog.* **a.** the act of presenting a sensitive material as film, plate, or paper, to the action of light or other actinic rays. **b.** the duration of this exposure. **7.** a putting out without shelter or protection, as of an abandoned child. **8.** a state of being exposed. **9.** situation with regard to sunlight or wind; aspect: *a southern exposure.* **10.** something exposed, as to view; an exposed surface. [f. EXPOS(E) + -URE] —**Syn. 2.** divulgement, revelation, exposé.

exposure meter, *Photog.* an instrument which measures the light intensity and indicates the proper exposure for a given scene. Also, **light meter.**

expound (ĭk spound′), *v.t.* **1.** to set forth or state in detail: *to expound theories, principles, etc.* **2.** to explain; interpret. [ME *expoune(n)*, *expounde(n)*, t. OF: m. *espondre*, g. L *expōnere* put out, expose, set forth, explain] —**expound′er,** *n.* —**Syn. 2.** See **explain.**

ex-president (ĕks′prĕz′ĭ dənt), *n.* a former president.

express (ĭk sprĕs′), *v.t.* **1.** to put (thought) into words:

to express an idea clearly. **2.** to show, manifest, or reveal: *to express one's feelings.* **3.** to set forth the opinions, feelings, etc., of (oneself), as in speaking, writing, painting. **4.** to represent by a symbol, character, figure, or formula. **5.** to press or squeeze out: *to express the juice of grapes.* **6.** to exude or emit (a liquid, smell, or the like) as if under pressure. **7.** *Chiefly U.S.* to send express: *to express a package or merchandise.* —*adj.* **8.** clearly indicated; distinctly stated (rather than implied); definite; explicit; plain. **9.** special; particular; definite: *an express purpose.* **10.** duly or exactly formed or represented: *an express image.* **11.** pertaining to an express: *an express agency.* **12.** specially direct or fast, as a train, etc. —*adv.* **13.** by express; by express train or messenger; unusually fast. **14.** specially; for a particular purpose. —*n.* **15.** an express train or, occasionally, a long-distance motor coach. **16.** a messenger or a message specially sent. **17.** a system or method for the speedy dispatch of parcels, money, etc.: *to send a parcel by express.* **18.** a company engaged in this business. **19.** that which is sent by express. [ME *expresse*, t. L: m. s. *expressus*, pp., pressed out, described] —**ex-press'er,** *n.* —**express'ible,** *adj.* —**Syn. 1.** utter, declare, state. **4.** indicate, designate. —**Ant. 1.** imply.

expressage (ĭk sprĕs'ĭj), *n.* **1.** the business of transmitting parcels, money, etc., by express. **2.** the charge for such transmission.

express delivery, rapid delivery by special messenger.

expression (ĭk sprĕsh'ən), *n.* **1.** the act of expressing or setting forth in words: *the expression of opinions, facts, etc.* **2.** a particular word, phrase, or form of words: *archaic expressions.* **3.** the manner or form in which a thing is expressed in words; wording; phrasing. **4.** the power of expressing in words: *joy beyond expression.* **5.** indication of feeling, spirit, character, etc., as on the face, in the voice, or in artistic execution. **6.** a look or intonation as expressing feeling, etc.: *a sad expression.* **7.** the quality or power of expressing feeling, etc.: *a face that lacks expression.* **8.** the act of expressing or representing, as by symbols. **9.** *Maths.* a symbol or a combination of symbols serving to express something. **10.** the act of expressing or pressing out. —**expres'sionless,** *adj.* —**Syn. 1.** utterance, declaration, assertion, statement. **2.** phrase, term. **3.** language, diction, phraseology. **5.** manifestation, sign. **6.** aspect, air.

expressionism (ĭk sprĕsh'ə nĭz'əm), *n.* a theory of art, esp. that originating in Europe about the time of World War I, which emphasizes free expression of the artist's emotional reactions rather than the representation of the natural appearance of objects. —**expres'sionist,** *n., adj.* —**expres'sionis'tic,** *adj.*

expressive (ĭk sprĕs'ĭv), *adj.* **1.** serving to express; indicative of power to express: *a look expressive of gratitude.* **2.** full of expression, as the face or voice. **3.** of, pertaining to, or concerned with expression. —**ex-pres'sively,** *adv.* —**expres'siveness,** *n.*

—**Syn. 1.** EXPRESSIVE, MEANING, SIGNIFICANT, SUGGESTIVE imply the conveying of a thought, indicating an attitude of mind, or the like, by words or otherwise. EXPRESSIVE suggests conveying or being capable of conveying a thought, intention, emotion, etc., in an effective or vivid manner: *an expressive shrug.* MEANING and SIGNIFICANT imply an underlying and unexpressed thought whose existence is plainly shown although its precise nature is left to conjecture. MEANING implies a more secret and intimate understanding between the persons involved: *meaning looks passed between them.* SIGNIFICANT suggests calling the attention of a person or persons to a happening which is important in some way to them or to others: *on hearing this statement, he gave the officers a significant glance.* SUGGESTIVE implies an indirect or covert conveying of a meaning, sometimes mentally stimulating, sometimes verging on impropriety or indecency: *a suggestive story or remark.*

express letter, a letter sent by special delivery.

expressly (ĭk sprĕs'lĭ), *adv.* **1.** in an express manner; explicitly. **2.** for the express purpose; specially.

expressway (ĭk sprĕs'wā'), *n.* *U.S.* a road designed for high-speed traffic; motorway.

expropriate (ĕks prō'prĭ āt'), *v.t.*, **-ated, -ating. 1.** to take, esp. for public use by the right of eminent domain, thus divesting the title of the private owner. **2.** to dispossess (a person) of ownership. [t. LL: m. s. *expropriātus*, pp., deprived of property, der. L *ex-* EX-[1] + *proprium* property] —**expro'pria'tion,** *n.* —**expro'pria'tor,** *n.*

expugnable (ĕks pŭg'nə bl), *adj.* capable of being overcome, defeated, conquered, etc.

expulsion (ĭk spŭl'shən), *n.* **1.** the act of driving out or expelling. **2.** the state of being expelled. [t. L: s. *expulsio*]

expulsive (ĭk spŭl'sĭv), *adj.* tending or serving to expel.

expunction (ĭk spŭngk'shən), *n.* the act of expunging; an erasure. [f. s. L *expunctus*, pp., struck out + -ION]

expunge (ĭk spŭnj'), *v.t.*, **-punged, -punging. 1.** to strike or blot out; erase; obliterate. **2.** to efface; wipe out or destroy. [t. L: m. s. *expungere* prick out, strike out] —**expung'er,** *n.*

expurgate (ĕks'pû gāt'), *v.t.*, **-gated, -gating. 1.** to amend by removing offensive or objectionable matter: *to expurgate a book.* **2.** to purge or cleanse. [t. L: m. s. *expurgātus*, pp., purged] —**ex'purga'tion,** *n.* —**ex'purga'tor,** *n.*

expurgatorial (ĕks pû'gə tô'rĭ əl), *adj.* pertaining to an expurgator or to expurgation.

expurgatory (ĕks pû'gə tə rĭ, -trĭ), *adj.* serving to expurgate; of or pertaining to expurgation.

exquisite (ĕks'kwĭ zĭt, ĭk skwĭz'ĭt), *adj.* **1.** of peculiar beauty or charm, or rare and appealing excellence, as a face, a flower, colouring, music, poetry, etc. **2.** extraordinarily fine, admirable, or consummate. **3.** intense, acute, or keen, as pleasure, pain, etc. **4.** keenly or delicately sensitive or responsive: *an exquisite ear for music.* **5.** of rare excellence of production or execution, as works of art, workmanship, or the artist or worker. **6.** of peculiar refinement or elegance, as taste, manners, etc., or persons. **7.** *Obs.* carefully sought out, chosen, ascertained, devised, etc. —*n.* **8.** a person, esp. a man, who is too much concerned about his clothes, etc.; a dandy; a coxcomb. [ME, t. L: m. s. *exquisītus*, pp., sought out] —**ex'quisitely,** *adv.* —**ex'quisiteness,** *n.* —**Syn. 1.** dainty, beautiful, elegant, rare. See **delicate. 2.** perfect, matchless. See **fine**[1]. —**Ant. 1.** gross. **2.** ordinary.

exsanguination (ĭks săng'gwĭ nā'shən), *n.* *Med.* **1.** expulsion of blood from a part. **2.** the state of being deprived of blood. —**exsan'guinous,** *adj.*

exsanguine (ĭks săng'gwĭn), *adj.* anaemic.

exscind (ĕk sĭnd'), *v.t.* to cut out or off. [t. L: s. *exscindere*]

exsect (ĕk sĕkt'), *v.t.* to cut out. [t. L: s. *exsectus*, pp.] —**exsec'tion,** *n.*

exsert (ĕks sûrt'), *v.t.* **1.** to thrust out. —*adj.* **2.** exserted. [t. L: s. *exsertus*, pp., put forth] —**exser'tion,** *n.*

exserted (ĕks sû'tĭd), *adj.* *Biol.* projecting beyond the surrounding parts, as a stamen.

exsertile (ĕks sû'tĭl), *adj.* *Biol.* capable of being exserted or protruded.

ex-service (ĕks'sû'vĭs), *adj.* having formerly served in the armed forces.

ex-serviceman (ĕks'sû'vĭs măn'), *n., pl.* **-men** (-mĕn'). one who has served in one of the armed services, esp. during wartime.

exsiccate (ĕk'sĭ kāt'), *v.t.*, **-cated, -cating. 1.** to dry or remove the moisture from, as a substance. **2.** to dry up, as moisture. [t. L: m. s. *exsiccātus*, pp.] —**ex'sicca'tion,** *n.* —**exsiccative** (ĕk'sĭ kə tĭv), *adj.* —**ex'sicca'tor,** *n.*

exstipulate (ĕks stĭp'yŏŏ lĭt, -lāt'), *adj.* *Bot.* without stipules. Also, **estipulate.**

ext., 1. extension. **2.** external. **3.** extinct. **4.** extra.

extant (ĕk stănt'), *adj.* **1.** in existence; still existing; not destroyed or lost. **2.** *Archaic.* standing out; protruding. [t. L: s. *ex(s)tans*, ppr., standing out]

extemporal (ĭk stĕm'pə rəl), *adj.* *Obs. or Archaic.* extemporaneous; extempore. [t. L: s. *extemporālis*]

extemporaneous (ĭk stĕm'pə rā'nyəs), *adj.* **1.** done or spoken extempore; impromptu: *an extemporaneous speech.* **2.** speaking or performing extempore. **3.** made for the occasion, as a shelter. [t. LL: m. *extemporāneus*, r. L *extemporālis*] —**extem'pora'neously,** *adv.* —**extem'pora'neousness,** *n.*

—**Syn. 1.** EXTEMPORANEOUS (EXTEMPORARY, EXTEMPORE), IMPROMPTU, IMPROVISED are used of (artistic) expression given without preparation or based on only partial preparation. EXTEMPORANEOUS, though often used interchangeably with IMPROMPTU, is applied esp. to an unmemorized speech given from an outline or notes: *an extemporaneous discussion.* IMPROMPTU is applied to a performance (poem, song, etc.) delivered without preparation and at a moment's notice: *called upon without warning, she nevertheless gave an excellent impromptu speech.* IMPROVISED is applied to that which is composed (recited, sung, acted) on a particular occasion, and is made up, at least in part, as one goes along: *an improvised piano accompaniment.* —**Ant. 1.** memorized, prepared.

extemporary (ĭk stĕm'pə rə rĭ, -prə rĭ), *adj.* **1.** extemporaneous; extempore. **2.** *Obs.* sudden; unexpected. —**extem'porarily,** *adv.* —**extem'porariness,** *n.* —**Syn. 1.** See **extemporaneous.**

extempore (ĭk stĕm'pə rĭ), *adv.* **1.** on the spur of the moment; without premeditation or preparation; offhand. **2.** without notes: *to speak extempore.* **3.** (of musical performance) by improvisation. —*adj.* **4.** extemporaneous; impromptu. [t. L: *ex tempore*, lit., out of the time] —**Syn. 4.** See **extemporaneous.**

extemporize (ĭk stĕm'pə rīz'), *v.*, **-rized, -rizing.** —*v.i.* **1.** to speak extempore. **2.** to sing, or play an instrument, composing the music as one proceeds; improvise. —*v.t.* **3.** to make or devise for the occasion. **4.** *Music.* to compose while playing; improvise. Also, **extemporise.** —**extem'poriza'tion,** *n.* —**extem'poriz'er,** *n.*

extend (ĭk stĕnd'), *v.t.* **1.** to stretch out; draw out to the full length. **2.** to stretch, draw, or arrange in a given direction, or so as to reach a particular point, as a cord or a line of troops. **3.** to stretch forth or hold out, as the arm or hand. **4.** to place at full length, esp. horizontally, as the body, limbs, etc. **5.** to increase the length or duration of; lengthen; prolong. **6.** to stretch out in various or all directions; expand; spread out in area. **7.** to enlarge the scope of, or make more comprehensive, as operations or influence. **8.** to hold forth as an offer or grant; offer; grant; give. **9.** *Finance.* to postpone (the payment of a debt) beyond the time originally agreed upon. **10.** *Com.* to transfer (figures) from one column to another in bookkeeping, invoices, etc. **11.** *Law.* **a.** to assess or value. **b.** to make a seizure or levy upon, as land, by a writ of extent. **12.** *Obs.* to take by seizure. **13.** *Obs.* to exaggerate. —*v.i.* **14.** to be or become extended; stretch out; to be continued in length or duration, or in various or all directions. **15.** to reach, as to a particular point. **16.** to increase in length, area, scope, etc. [ME *extend(en)*, t. L: m. *extendere*] —**extend'ible, extend'able,** *adj.* —**Syn.** **5.** prolong, protract, continue. See **lengthen.** **6.** spread, enlarge, widen. **8.** bestow, impart.

extended (ĭk stĕn'dĭd), *adj.* **1.** stretched out. **2.** continued or prolonged. **3.** spread out. **4.** widespread or extensive; having extension or spatial magnitude. **5.** outstretched. **6.** *Print.* (of type) expanded. —**extend'edly,** *adv.*

extender (ĭk stĕn'də), *n.* **1.** an inorganic powder added to paints to improve film formation and to minimize settlement on storage. **2.** a substance added to synthetic resins, glues, or elastomers either to reduce their cost or to some extent to modify their properties.

extensible (ĭk stĕn'sə bl), *adj.* capable of being extended. —**exten'sibil'ity, exten'sibleness,** *n.*

extensile (ĕk stĕn'sĭl), *adj. Chiefly Zool., Anat.* capable of being extended; adapted for stretching out; extensible; protrusible.

extensimeter (ĕks'tĕn sĭm'ĭ tə), *n.* extensometer.

extension (ĭk stĕn'shən), *n.* **1.** the act of extending. **2.** the state of being extended. **3.** that by which something is extended; a prolongation, as an addition to a house. **4.** something extended; an extended object or space. **5.** range of extending; degree of extensiveness; extent. **6.** an extra telephone connected to the same line as a main telephone. **7.** *Com.* a written engagement on the part of a creditor, allowing a debtor further time to pay a debt. **8.** *Physics., etc.* that property of a body by which it occupies a portion of space. **9.** *Anat.* **a.** the act of straightening a limb. **b.** the position which a limb assumes when it is straightened. **10.** *Logic.* the class of things to which a term is applicable; denotation: *the extension of the term 'man' consists of the class of such individuals as 'Socrates', 'Plato', 'Aristotle', etc.* **11.** *Gram.* a word or words added to a subject or predicate in order to amplify it. [t. L: s. *extensio*] —**exten'sional,** *adj.* —**exten'sionally,** *adv.* —**Syn.** **1.** stretching, expansion, enlargement. —**Ant.** **1.** contraction.

extension course, (in many universities and colleges) a course of study for persons not regularly enrolled as students, frequently provided through evening classes or by correspondence.

extensity (ĭk stĕn'sĭ tĭ), *n.* **1.** the quality of having extension. **2.** *Psychol.* that attribute of sensation from which the perception of extension is developed.

extensive (ĭk stĕn'sĭv), *adj.* **1.** of great extent; wide; broad; covering a great area; large in amount: *an extensive forest, an extensive influence.* **2.** far-reaching; comprehensive; thorough; lengthy; detailed: *extensive knowledge, extensive enquiries.* **3.** of or having extension. **4.** pertaining to a system of agriculture involving the use or cultivation of large areas of land (as where land is cheap) with a minimum of labour and expense (opposed to *intensive*). —**exten'sively,** *adv.* —**exten'siveness,** *n.* —**Syn.** **1.** extended, large, spacious, ample, vast. —**Ant.** **1.** limited.

extensometer (ĕks'tĕn sŏm'ĭ tə), *n. Mach.* an apparatus for measuring minute degrees of expansion, contraction, or deformation. Also, **extensimeter.** [f. s. L *extensus*, pp., extended + -(O)METER[1]]

extensor (ĭk stĕn'sə, -sô), *n.* a muscle which serves to extend or straighten a part of the body (opposed to *flexor*). [t. LL: one who or that which stretches]

extent (ĭk stĕnt'), *n.* **1.** the space or degree to which a thing extends; length, area, or volume: *the extent of a line, to the full extent of his power.* **2.** something extended; an extended space; a particular length, area, or volume; something having extension. **3.** *Eng. Law.* **a.** a writ to recover debts of record due to the crown, under which land, etc., may be seized. **b.** a seizure made under such a writ. **4.** *U.S. Law.* a writ, or a levy, by which a creditor has his debtor's lands valued and transferred to himself, absolutely or for a term of years. **5.** *Hist.* assessment or valuation, as of land. **6.** *Logic.* extension (def. 10). [ME *extente*, t. AF, ult. der. L *extendere* extend] —**Syn.** **1.** magnitude, measure, amount, scope, compass, range, expanse, stretch, reach. See **size.**

extenuate (ĕk stĕn'yo͞o āt'), *v.t.*, **-ated, -ating.** **1.** to represent (fault, offence, etc.) as less serious: *to extenuate a crime.* **2.** to serve to make (fault, offence, etc.) seem less serious: *extenuating circumstances.* **3.** to underestimate, underrate, or make light of. **4.** *Archaic.* **a.** to make thin, lean, or emaciated. **b.** to reduce the consistence or density of. [t. L: m. s. *extenuātus*, pp., made thin] —**exten'ua'tingly,** *adv.*—**extenuative** (ĕk stĕn'yo͞o ə tĭv), *adj.* —**exten'ua'tor,** *n.*

extenuation (ĕk stĕn'yo͞o ā'shən), *n.* **1.** the act of extenuating. **2.** the state of being extenuated. **3.** that which extenuates; a partial excuse.

extenuatory (ĕk stĕn'yo͞o ə te rĭ, -trĭ), *adj.* tending to extenuate; characterized by extenuation.

exterior (ĭk stĭə'rĭ ə), *adj.* **1.** outer; being on the outer side: *the exterior side or surface, exterior decorations.* **2.** situated or being outside; pertaining to or connected with what is outside: *the exterior possessions of a country.* **3.** *Geom.* (of an angle) outer, as an angle formed outside two parallel lines when cut by a third line. See diag. under **interior.** —*n.* **4.** the outer surface or part; the outside; outward form or appearance. **5.** (*pl.*) externals. **6.** *Films.* a sequence shot out-of-doors. [t. L, compar. of *exter, exterus* outer, outward] —**exteriority** (ĭk stĭə'rĭ ŏ'rĭ tĭ), *n.* —**exte'riorly,** *adv.* —**Syn.** **1.** outward, outside. **2.** outlying, extraneous. —**Ant.** **1.** interior.

exterminate (ĭk stû'mĭ nāt'), *v.t.*, **-nated, -nating.** to get rid of by destroying; destroy totally; extirpate. [t. L: m. s. *exterminātus*, pp., driven beyond the boundaries] —**exterminable** (ĭk stû'mĭ nə bl), *adj.* —**exter'mina'tion,** *n.* —**exter'mina'tor,** *n.* —**Syn.** eradicate, abolish, annihilate.

exterminatory (ĭk stû'mĭ nə tə rĭ, -trĭ), *adj.* serving or tending to exterminate. Also, **exterminative** (ĭk stû'mĭ nə tĭv).

extern (ĕks'tûn, ĭk stûn'), *n.* a person connected with an institution but not residing in it. Also, **externe.** [t. L: s. *externus* outward]

external (ĭk stû'nəl), *adj.* **1.** of or pertaining to the outside or outer part; outer. **2.** to be applied to the outside of a body, as a remedy. **3.** situated or being outside something; acting or coming from without. **4.** pertaining to the outward or visible appearance or show: *external acts of worship.* **5.** pertaining to or concerned with what is outside or foreign: *external commerce.* **6.** *Zool., Anat.* on the side farthest away from the body, from the median line, or from the centre of a radially symmetrical form. **7.** *Metaphys.* belonging or pertaining to the world of things, considered as independent of the perceiving mind. **8.** *Educ.* studying or studied outside the confines of a university or similar institution, and not subject to its discipline: *an external degree.* —*n.* **9.** the outside; outer surface. **10.** that which is external. **11.** (*pl.*) external or non-essential features, circumstances, etc.: *the externals of religion.* [f. EXTERN + -AL[1]] —**exter'nally,** *adv.*

external-combustion (ĭk stû'nəl kəm bŭs'chən), *adj.* of or pertaining to an engine in which the ignition of the fuel mixture takes place outside the engine cylinder (as distinct from an *internal-combustion engine*).

externalism (ĭk stû'nə lĭz'əm), *n.* attention or devotion to externals; excessive attention to externals, esp. in religion. —**exter'nalist,** *n.*

externality (ĕk'stû năl'ĭ tĭ), *n.*, *pl.* **-ties.** **1.** the state or quality of being external. **2.** something external; an outward feature. **3.** excessive attention to externals.

externalize (ĭk stû'nə līz'), *v.t.*, **-lized, -lizing.** to make external; embody in an outward form. Also, **externalise.** —**exter'naliza'tion,** *n.*

externat (ĭks tû'năt), *n.* a day school. [t. F. Cf. EXTERN]

exteroceptive (ĕk'stə rō sĕp'tĭv), *adj. Physiol.* pertaining to exteroceptors, the stimuli impinging upon them, and the nerve impulses initiated by them. [f. *extero-* (comb. form of L *exterus* exterior) + *-ceptive*, as in RECEPTIVE]

exteroceptor (ĕk'stə rō sĕp'tə), *n. Physiol.* a sense organ, as the nose, eyes, ears, or skin, responding to and conveying stimuli from the external environment. [f. *extero-* + -CEPTOR. See EXTEROCEPTIVE]

exterritorial (ĕks'tĕ rĭ tô'rĭ əl), *adj.* extraterritorial. —**exter'rito'rial'ity,** *n.* —**ex'territo'rially,** *adv.*

extinct (ĭk stĭngkt'), *adj.* **1.** extinguished; quenched; having ceased eruption, as a volcano. **2.** obsolete, as an institution. **3.** having come to an end; without a living representative, as a species. [ME *extincte*, t. L: m. s. *extinctus*, pp., destroyed, put out] —**Syn.** **3.** See **dead.**

extinction (ĭk stĭngk'shən), *n.* **1.** the act of extinguishing.

2. the fact of being extinguished; condition of being extinct. 3. suppression; abolition; annihilation. 4. *Biol.* a becoming extinct; a coming to an end or dying out.

extinction meter, *Photog.* an exposure meter in which the reading is made by attenuating the light from the object until the image on a ground-glass screen just becomes indistinguishable.

extinctive (ĭk stĭngk′tĭv), *adj.* tending or serving to extinguish.

extinguish (ĭk stĭng′gwĭsh), *v.t.* **1.** to put out (a fire, light, etc.); put out the flame of (something burning or alight). **2.** to put an end to or bring to an end; wipe out of existence: *to extinguish a hope, a life, etc.* **3.** to obscure or eclipse, as by superior brilliancy. **4.** *Law.* to discharge (a debt), as by payment. [f. s. L *ex(s)tinguere* put out, quench, destroy + -ISH²] —**extin′guishable,** *adj.* —**extin′guishment,** *n.*

extinguisher (ĭk stĭng′gwĭ shə), *n.* **1.** one who or that which extinguishes. **2.** any of various portable apparatuses for extinguishing fire: *a chemical extinguisher.*

extirpate (ĕk′stû pāt′), *v.t.,* **-pated, -pating. 1.** to remove utterly; destroy totally; exterminate; do away with. **2.** to pull up by the roots; root up. [t. L: m. s. *ex(s)tirpātus,* pp., rooted out] —**ex′tirpa′tion,** *n.* —**ex′tirpa′tive,** *adj.* —**ex′tirpa′tor,** *n.*

extol (ĭk stŏl′), *v.t.,* **-tolled, -tolling.** to praise highly; laud; eulogize. Also, **extoll.** [t. L: m. s. *extollere,* lit., lift out or up] —**extol′ler,** *n.* —**extol′ment,** *n.* —**Syn.** commend, glorify. —**Ant.** disparage.

extort (ĭk stôt′), *v.t.* **1.** to wrest or wring (something) from a person by violence, intimidation, or abuse of authority; obtain (money, information, etc.) by force, torture, threat, or the like. **2.** to take illegally under cover of office. [t. L: s. *extortus,* pp., twisted or wrested out] —**extort′er,** *n.* —**extor′tive,** *adj.* —**Syn. 1.** See **extract.**

extortion (ĭk stô′shən), *n.* **1.** the act of extorting. **2.** *Law.* the crime of obtaining money or other things of value under colour of office, when none is due or not so much is due, or before it is due. **3.** oppressive or illegal exaction, as of excessive price or interest. **4.** anything extorted. [ME, t. L: s. *extortio*]

extortionary (ĭk stô′shə nə rĭ), *adj.* characterized by or given to extortion.

extortionate (ĭk stô′shə nĭt), *adj.* **1.** exorbitant; grossly excessive: *extortionate prices.* **2.** characterized by extortion, as persons. —**extor′tionately,** *adv.*

extortioner (ĭk stô′shə nə), *n.* one who practises extortion. Also, **extor′tionist.**

extra (ĕks′trə), *adj.* **1.** beyond or more than what is usual, expected, or necessary; additional: *an extra edition of a newspaper, an extra price.* **2.** larger or better than what is usual: *an extra binding.* —*n.* **3.** something extra or additional. **4.** an additional expense. **5.** an edition of a newspaper other than the regular edition or editions. **6.** *U.S.* something of superior quality. **7.** *Films.* a person hired by the day to play a minor part, as a member of a mob or crowd. **8.** *U.S.* an additional worker. **9.** (*usually pl.*) *Cricket.* a score or run not made from the bat, as a bye or a wide. —*adv.* **10.** in excess of the usual or specified amount: *an extra high price.* **11.** beyond the ordinary degree; unusually; uncommonly: *done extra well.* [prob. orig. short for EXTRAORDINARY. Cf. EXTRA-]

extra-, a prefix meaning 'outside', 'beyond', 'besides', freely used as an English formative, as in *extrajudicial, extraterritorial,* and many other words mostly self-explanatory, as *extra-atmospheric,* etc. Also, **extro-.** [t. L, comb. form of *extrā,* adv. and prep., outside (of), without]

extrabold (ĕks′trə bōld′), *n. Print.* unusually heavy bold face.

extracanonical (ĕks′trə kə nŏn′ĭ kl), *adj. Eccles.* not included in the canon of Scripture.

extracellular (ĕks′trə sĕl′yŏŏ lə), *adj. Biol.* outside a cell or cells.

extra-condensed (ĕks′trə kən dĕnst′), *adj. Print.* (of type) having an extremely narrow face.

extra cover, *Cricket.* **1.** the position of a fielder between mid-off and cover-point. **2.** a fielder occupying this position. Also, **extra cover-point.**

extract (*v.* ĭk străkt′; *n.* ĕks′trăkt), *v.t.* **1.** to draw forth or get out by force: *to extract a tooth.* **2.** to deduce (a doctrine, principle, etc.). **3.** to derive or obtain (pleasure, comfort, etc.) from a particular source. **4.** to take or copy out (matter from a book, etc.), or make excerpts from (the book, etc.). **5.** to extort (information, money, etc.). **6.** to separate or obtain (a juice, ingredient, principle, etc.) from a mixture by pressure, distillation, treatment with solvents, or the like. **7.** *Metall.* to separate a metal from its ore by any process. **8.** *Maths.* to determine (the root of a quantity). —*n.* **9.** something extracted. **10.** a passage taken from a book, etc.; an excerpt; a quotation. **11.** a solution or preparation containing the active principles of a drug, plant juice, or the like. **12.** a solid or viscid substance extracted from a drug, plant, or the like. [t. L: s. *extractus,* pp., drawn out] —**extract′able, extract′ible,** *adj.*

—**Syn. 1.** pull out, pry out. **5.** evoke, educe, draw out, elicit. EXTRACT, EXACT, EXTORT, WREST imply using force to remove something. To EXTRACT is to draw forth something as by pulling, importuning, and the like: *to extract a confession by using third-degree methods.* To EXACT is to impose a penalty, or to obtain by force or authority, something to which one lays claim: *to exact payment, obedience.* To EXTORT is usually to wring something by intimidation or threats from an unwilling person: *to extort money by threats of blackmail.* To WREST is to take by force or violence in spite of active resistance: *the courageous minority wrested the power from their oppressors.* **6.** withdraw, distil.

extraction (ĭk străk′shən), *n.* **1.** the act of extracting. **2.** the state or fact of being extracted. **3.** descent or lineage. **4.** something extracted; an extract.

extractive (ĭk străk′tĭv), *adj.* **1.** tending or serving to extract. **2.** that may be extracted. **3.** of or of the nature of an extract. —*n.* **4.** something extracted.

extractor (ĭk străk′tə), *n.* **1.** a person or a thing that extracts. **2.** the mechanism in a firearm or cannon which, after firing, pulls an empty or unfired cartridge or shell case out of the chamber of the weapon and brings it into place for action by the ejector.

extracurricular (ĕks′trə kə rĭk′yŏŏ lə), *adj.* outside the regular curriculum.

extraditable (ĕks′trə dī′tə bl), *adj.* **1.** capable of being extradited; subject to extradition. **2.** capable of incurring extradition.

extradite (ĕks′trə dīt′), *v.t.,* **-dited, -diting. 1.** to give up (a fugitive or prisoner) to another nation or authority. **2.** to obtain the extradition of. [back-formation from EXTRADITION]

extradition (ĕks′trə dĭsh′ən), *n.* the surrender of a fugitive from justice or a prisoner by one state or authority to another. [t. F, f. L: *ex-* EX-¹ + s. *trāditio* a giving over]

extrados (ĕks trā′dŏs), *n. Archit.* the exterior curve or surface of an arch or vault. See diag. under **arch.** [t. F, f. L *extra-* EXTRA- + F *dos* back (g. L *dorsum*)]

extragalactic (ĕks′trə gə lăk′tĭk), *adj. Astron.* outside the galaxy.

extrajudicial (ĕks′trə jŏŏ dĭsh′əl), *adj.* outside the normal course of judicial procedure; beyond the action or authority of a court. —**ex′trajudi′cially,** *adv.*

extramarital (ĕks′trə mă′rĭ tl), *adj.* of or pertaining to sexual relations with someone other than one's spouse.

extrametrical (ĕks′trə mĕt′rĭ kl), *adj. Pros.* containing more syllables than those required by the meter.

extramundane (ĕks′trə mŭn′dān), *adj.* beyond our world or the material universe.

extramural (ĕks′trə myŏŏə′rəl), *adj.* **1.** outside the walls or boundaries, as of a city or town. **2.** outside the confines of a university; connected with a university but not under its direct control: *extramural studies, extramural activities.*

extraneous (ĭk strā′nyəs), *adj.* introduced or coming from without; not belonging or proper to a thing; external; foreign; not essential. [t. L: m. *extrāneus* that is without, foreign] —**extra′neously,** *adv.* —**extra′neousness,** *n.* —**Syn.** extrinsic, adventitious, alien.

extraordinary (ĭk strô′dn rĭ), *adj.* **1.** beyond what is ordinary; out of the regular or established order: *extraordinary power or expenses.* **2.** exceptional in character, amount, extent, degree, etc.; unusual; remarkable: *extraordinary weather, weight, speed, an extraordinary man or book.* **3.** (of officials, etc.) outside of, additional to, or ranking below an ordinary one: *an extraordinary professor.* [t. L: m. s. *extrāordinārius* out of the common order]—**extraor′dinarily,** *adv.* —**extraor′dinariness,** *n.* —**Syn. 2.** uncommon, exceptional, singular, rare, phenomenal.

extraordinary ray, *Physics.* the part of a doubly refracted ray which does not obey the ordinary laws of refraction. See **ordinary ray.**

extrapolate (ĕks trăp′ə lāt′), *v.,* **-lated, -lating.** —*v.t.* **1.** *Statistics.* to estimate a quantity which depends on one or more variables by extending the variables beyond their established ranges. **2.** to infer (what is not known) from that which is known; conjecture. —*v.i.* **3.** to perform extrapolation. [f. EXTRA- + *-polate* of INTERPOLATE] —**extrapolation** (ĕks trăp′ə lā′shən), *n.*

extraprofessional (ĕks′trə prə fĕsh′ən əl), *adj.* outside ordinary limits of professional interest or duty.

extrasensory (ĕks′trə sĕn′sə rĭ), *adj.* outside the normal sense perception.

extraterrestrial (ĕks′trə tĭ rĕs′trĭ əl), *adj.* outside or originating outside the earth.

extraterritorial (ĕks′trə tĕ′rĭ tô′rĭ əl), *adj.* **1.** beyond local territorial jurisdiction, as the status of persons resident in a country but not subject to its laws. **2.** pertaining to such persons. Also, **exterritorial.** [f. NL *extrā territōri(um)* outside the domain + -AL¹] —**ex'-trater'rito'rially,** *adv.*

extraterritoriality (ěks'trə tě'rĭ tô'rĭ ăl'ĭ tĭ), *n.* the possession or exercise of political rights by a foreign power within a state having its own government.

extrauterine (ěks'trə yōō'tə rĭn'), *adj.* being beyond or outside the uterus.

extravagance (ĭk străv'ĭ gəns), *n.* **1.** excessive expenditure or outlay of money. **2.** an instance of this. **3.** unrestrained or fantastic excess, as of actions, opinions, etc. **4.** an extravagant action, notion, etc. —**Syn. 3.** lavishness, profusion. —**Ant. 1.** frugality.

extravagancy (ĭk străv'ĭ gən sĭ), *n., pl.* **-cies.** extravagance.

extravagant (ĭk străv'ĭ gənt), *adj.* **1.** going beyond prudence or necessity in expenditure; wasteful: *an extravagant person.* **2.** excessively high; exorbitant: *extravagant expenses or prices.* **3.** exceeding the bounds of reason, as actions, demands, opinions, passions, etc. **4.** exceedingly elaborate; flamboyant: *an extravagant dress.* **5.** *Obs.* wandering beyond bounds. [ME, t. ML: s. *extrāvagans*, ppr. of *extrāvagārī* wander beyond, f. L *extrā-* EXTRA- + *vagārī* wander] —**extrav'agantly,** *adv.* —**extrav'agantness,** *n.* —**Syn. 2.** immoderate, excessive, inordinate. **3.** fantastic, wild. —**Ant. 3.** reasonable.

extravaganza (ĭk străv'ə găn'zə), *n.* **1.** a musical or dramatic composition, as comic opera or musical comedy, marked by wildness and irregularity in form and feeling and elaborateness in staging and costume. **2.** extravagant behaviour or speech. [b. EXTRAVAGANCE and It. *stravaganza* queer behaviour]

extravagate (ĭk străv'ə gāt'), *v.i.*, **-gated, -gating. 1.** to wander beyond bounds; stray; roam at will. **2.** to go beyond the bounds of propriety or reason.

extravasate (ĭk străv'ə sāt'), *v.*, **-sated, -sating.** —*v.t.* **1.** *Pathol.* to force out from the proper vessels, as blood, esp. so as to diffuse through the surrounding tissues. **2.** *Geol.* to pour forth, as lava from a subterranean source in a molten state. —*v.i.* **3.** *Pathol.* to be extravasated, as blood. **4.** *Geol.* to pour forth lava, etc. —*n.* **5.** *Pathol.* the extravasated material; extravasation. [f. EXTRA + L *vās* vessel + -ATE¹]

extravasation (ĭk străv'ə sā'shən), *n.* **1.** the act of extravasating. **2.** the matter extravasated.

extravascular (ěks'trə văs'kyōō lə), *adj. Anat.* situated outside a blood vessel or vessels.

extraversion (ěks'trə vû'shən), *n. Psychol.* extroversion.

extravert (ěks'trə vût'), *n. Psychol.* extrovert.

Extremadura (ěs'trĭ mə dōōə'rə; *Sp.* ěs trě mä dōō'rä), *n.* Estremadura.

extreme (ĭk strēm'), *adj.*, **-tremer, -tremist,** *n.* —*adj.* **1.** of a character or kind farthest removed from the ordinary or average: *an extreme case, extreme measures.* **2.** utmost or exceedingly great in degree: *extreme joy.* **3.** farthest from the centre or middle; outermost; endmost. **4.** farthest, utmost, or very far in any direction. **5.** going to the utmost lengths, or exceeding the bounds of moderation: *extreme fashions.* **6.** going to the utmost or very great lengths in action, habit, opinion, etc.: *an extreme socialist.* **7.** last or final: *extreme unction.* —*n.* **8.** the utmost or highest degree, or a very high degree: *showy in the extreme, or to an extreme.* **9.** one of two things as remote or different from each other as possible: *the extremes of joy and grief.* **10.** the farthest or utmost length, or an excessive length, beyond the ordinary or average: *to go to extremes in dress.* **11.** *Maths.* the first or the last term, as of a proportion or series. **12.** *Logic.* the subject or the predicate of the conclusion of a syllogism; either of two terms which are separated in the premises and brought together in the conclusion. **13.** *Obs. or Rare.* the utmost point, or extremity of something. [ME, t. L: m. s. *extrēmus*, superl. of *exter* outer, outward] —**extreme'-ness,** *n.* —**Syn. 6.** immoderate, excessive, fanatical, uncompromising. See **radical.** —**Ant. 6.** lukewarm.

extremely (ĭk strēm'lĭ), *adv.* in an extreme degree; exceedingly.

extremely high frequency, *Radio.* a radio frequency of between 30,000 and 300,000 megacycles per second. *Abbrev.:* EHF.

extreme unction, *Rom. Cath. Ch.* a sacrament in which a dying person is anointed with oil by a priest for the health of his soul and body.

extremism (ĭk strē'mĭz'əm), *n.* a tendency or disposition to go to extremes, esp. in political matters.

extremist (ĭk strē'mĭst), *n.* **1.** one who goes to extremes, esp. in political matters. **2.** a supporter of extreme doctrines or practices. —*adj.* **3.** belonging or pertaining to extremists.

extremity (ĭk strěm'ĭ tĭ), *n., pl.* **-ties. 1.** the extreme or terminal point, limit, or part of something. **2.** a limb of the body. **3.** (*chiefly pl.*) the end part of a limb, as a hand or foot. **4.** (*often pl.*) a condition, or circumstances, of extreme need, distress, etc. **5.** the utmost or any extreme degree: *the extremity of joy.* **6.** (*chiefly pl.*) an extreme measure: *to be forced to extremities.* **7.** extreme character, as of views. **8.** (*chiefly pl.*) a person's last moments. —**Syn. 1.** end, termination, extreme, verge, border, boundary.

extricable (ěks'trĭ kə bl), *adj.* that may be extricated.

extricate (ěks'trĭ kāt'), *v.t.*, **-cated, -cating. 1.** to disentangle; disengage; free: *to extricate one from a dangerous or embarrassing situation.* **2.** to liberate (gas, etc.) from combination, as in a chemical process. [t. L: m. s. *extrīcātus*, pp., disentangled] —**ex'trica'tion,** *n.*

extrinsic (ěks trĭn'sĭk), *adj.* **1.** extraneous; not inherent; unessential. **2.** being outside a thing; outward or external; operating or coming from without. **3.** *Anat.* (of certain muscles, nerves, etc.) originating outside the anatomical limits of a part. Also, **extrin'sical.** [f. EX-¹ + (IN)TRINSIC. Cf. F *extrinsèque*, adj., L *extrinsecus*, adv.] —**extrin'-sically,** *adv.*

extro-, var. of **extra-** (used to contrast with **intro-**).

extrorse (ěks trôs'), *adj. Bot.* turned or facing outwards, as anthers which open towards the perianth. [t. LL: m. s. *extrorsus* in an outward direction] —**extrorse'ly,** *adv.*

extroversion (ěks'trə vû'shən), *n.* **1.** Also, **extraversion.** *Psychol.* interest directed outwards or to things outside the self (opposed to *introversion*). **2.** *Pathol.* a turning inside out, as of the eyelids or of the bladder. **3.** the act of extroverting. **4.** an extroverted state.

extrovert (ěks'trə vût'), *Psychol.* —*n.* **1.** one characterized by extroversion; a person concerned chiefly with what is external or objective (opposed to *introvert*). —*adj.* **2.** marked by extroversion. —*v.t.* **3.** to direct (the mind, etc.) outwards, or to things outside the self. Also, **extravert.** [f. EXTRO- + s. L *vertere* turn. See INTROVERT]

extrude (ĭk strōōd'), *v.*, **-truded, -truding.** —*v.t.* **1.** to thrust out; force or press out; expel. **2.** (in moulding or making metals, plastics, etc.) to form into a desired cross-sectional shape by ejecting through a shaped opening: *to extrude tubing.* —*v.i.* **3.** to protrude. [t. L: m. s. *extrūdere* thrust out] —**extrusion** (ĭk strōō'zhən), *n.*

extrusive (ĭk strōō'sĭv), *adj.* **1.** tending to extrude. **2.** pertaining to extrusion. **3.** *Geol.* **a.** (of rocks) having been forced out in a molten or plastic condition at the surface of the earth. **b.** denoting or pertaining to volcanic rocks.

exuberance (ĭg zyōō'bə rəns), *n.* **1.** Also, **exu'berancy.** the state of being exuberant. **2.** an instance of this. —**Syn. 1.** superabundance, excess, copiousness, profusion, luxuriance, lavishness. —**Ant. 1.** scarcity.

exuberant (ĭg zyōō'bə rənt), *adj.* **1.** lavish; effusive: *an exuberant welcome.* **2.** full of vigour; abounding in high spirits: *the soldiers were exuberant after their victory.* **3.** profuse in growth or production; luxuriant; superabundant: *exuberant vegetation.* [t. L: s. *exūberans*, ppr., being fruitful] —**exu'berantly,** *adv.* —**Syn. 3.** copious, rank. —**Ant. 3.** sparse.

exuberate (ĭg zyōō'bə rāt'), *v.i.*, **-rated, -rating.** to be exuberant; superabound; overflow.

exudate (ěks'yōō dāt'), *n.* a substance exuded; exudation.

exudation (ěks'yōō dā'shən), *n.* **1.** the act of exuding. **2.** that which is exuded. **3.** a sweatlike issue or discharge through pores or small openings. —**exudative** (ĭg zyōō'də-tĭv), *adj.*

exude (ĭg zyōōd'), *v.*, **-uded, -uding.** —*v.i.* **1.** to come out gradually in drops like sweat through pores or small openings; ooze out. —*v.t.* **2.** to send out like sweat; emit through pores or small openings. [t. L: m. s. *ex(s)udāre*]

exult (ĭg zŭlt'), *v.i.* **1.** to show or feel a lively or triumphant joy; rejoice exceedingly; be highly elated; be jubilant (fol. by *in, at, over,* or an infinitive): *he exulted to find that he had won.* **2.** *Obs.* to leap, esp. for joy. [t. L: s. *ex(s)ultāre*, freq. of *exsilīre* leap out or up] —**exult'ingly,** *adv.*

exultant (ĭg zŭl'tənt), *adj.* exulting; highly elated; triumphant. —**exult'antly,** *adv.*

exultation (ĕg'zŭl tā'shən), *n.* the act of exulting; lively or triumphant joy, as over success or victory. Also, **exult'ance, exultancy** (ĭg zŭl'tən sĭ).

exuviae (ĭg zyōō'vĭ ē'), *n.pl.* the cast skins, shells, or other coverings of animals. [t. L: garments stripped off, skins of animals] —**exu'vial,** *adj.*

exuviate (ĭg zyōō'vĭ āt'), *v.i., v.t.*, **-ated, -ating.** to cast off or shed (exuviae); to moult. —**exu'via'tion,** *n.*

ex voto (ěks'vō'tō), *Latin.* from, or in pursuance of, a vow.

-ey¹, var. of **-y¹**, used esp. after *y*, as in *clayey.*

-ey², var. of **-y²**, used esp. after *y.*

Eyadema (*Fr.* ĕ yȧ dĕ mȧ′), *n.* **Étienne** (*Fr.* ĕ tyĕn′), born 1937, president of Togo since 1967.

eyalet (ā′yə lĕt′), *n.* vilayet.

eyas (ī′əs), *n.* a nestling. [ME, var. of *nyas, nias* (*a nyas* being taken as *an eyas*), t. F: m. *niais* a nestling, der. L *nīdus* nest]

Eyck (īk; *Flem.* ĕyk), *n.* **1. Hubert** or **Huybrecht Van** (*Flem.* hʏbərt *or* hœy′brĕkʜt vŏn), 1366–1426, Flemish painter. **2.** his brother, **Jan Van** (*Flem.* yŏn vŏn), (*Jan van Brugge*), 1385?–1440, Flemish painter.

eye (ī), *n., pl.* **eyes** or (*Archaic*) **eyen** or **eyne;** *v.,* **eyed, eyeing** or **eying.** —*n.* **1.** the origin of sight or vision. **2.** all the structures situated within or near the orbit which assist the organ of vision. **3.** this organ with respect to the colour of the iris: *blue eyes.* **4.** the region surrounding the eye: *a black eye.* **5.** sight; vision. **6.** power of seeing; appreciative or discriminating visual perception: *an eye for colour.* **7.** (*often pl.*) look, glance, or gaze: *to cast one's eye on a thing.* **8.** (*often pl.*) attentive look, close observation, or watch: *to keep an eye on a person, to be all eyes.* **9.** regard, respect, view, aim, or intention: *to have an eye to one's own advantage, with an eye to winning favour.* **10.** (*often pl.*) manner or way of looking at a thing, estimation, or opinion: *in the eyes of the law.* **11.** mental view: *in my mind's eye.* **12.** a centre of light, intelligence, influence, etc. **13.** something resembling or suggesting the eye in appearance, shape, etc., as the bud of a tuber, the central spot of a target, the lens of a camera, one of the round spots on the tail feathers of a peacock, the hole of a needle, a hole pierced in a thing for the insertion of some object, a metal or other ring as for a rope to pass through, or the loop into which a hook is inserted (forming together with the hood a **hook and eye**). **14.** *Meteorol.* the central region of low pressure in a tropical hurricane, where calm conditions prevail, often with clear skies. **15.** *Naut.* the precise direction from which the wind is blowing. **16.** *Naut.* the foremost part of the bows of a ship. **17.** Some special noun phrases are:

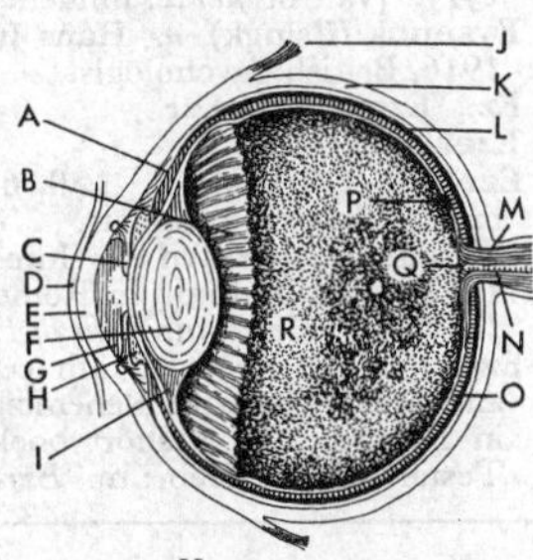

Human eye
A, Ciliary muscle; B, Ciliary processes; C, Iris; D, Conjunctiva; E, Cornea; F, Crystalline lens; G, Anterior chamber; H, Posterior chamber; I, Suspensory ligament; J, Ocular muscles; K, Sclera; L, Choroid; M, Optic nerve; N, Retinal artery; O, Retina; P, Yellow spot; Q, Blind spot; R, Vitreous humour

all my eye, *Slang.* nonsense.
an eye for an eye, repayment in kind, as revenge for an injustice.
before (under) one's very eyes, in one's presence.
catch someone's eye, to attract someone's attention.
cry one's eyes out, to weep copiously.
do in the eye, *Slang.* to take advantage of, cheat, swindle.
easy on the eye, attractive to look at.
eye of the day, the sun.
get one's eye in, (in cricket and other ball games) to be able, through practice, to follow the movement of the ball; to adapt oneself to, become accustomed to.
give someone the glad eye, to look amorously at.
have an eye for, to be discerning, be a good judge of.
have eyes only for, a. to look at nothing else but. **b.** to desire nothing else but.
in the public eye, often seen in public, well known.
keep an eye out for, to be watchful, be on the lookout for.
keep one's eyes open (skinned), to be especially watchful.
lay, clap, or **set eyes on,** to catch sight of; see.
make eyes at, to gaze flirtatiously at.
make someone open his eyes, to astonish, cause to stare in surprise.
mind your eye, *Colloq.* take care, look out.
open the eyes of, to make (a person) aware of the truth of something or of something previously unknown; to enlighten.
pipe one's eye, to weep.
run one's eye over, to glance at briefly.
see eye to eye, to have the same opinion; agree.
see with half an eye, to see easily, realize immediately.
shut or **close one's eyes to,** to refuse to see, disregard.
sight for sore eyes, a welcome sight, an agreeable surprise.
turn a blind eye on or **to,** to pretend not to see, ignore.
up to the eyes in, very busy with; deeply involved.
with one's eyes open, fully aware of potential risks.

—*v.t.* **18.** to fix the eyes upon; view. **19.** to observe or watch narrowly. **20.** to make an eye in: *to eye a needle.* —*v.i.* **21.** *Obs.* to appear to the eye. [ME; OE *ēge*, d. var. of *ēage*, c. G *Auge*. Cf. L *oculus*]

eyeball (ī′bôl′), *n.* the ball or globe of the eye.

eyebath (ī′bäth′), *n.* a vessel specially shaped for applying lotion to or bathing the eye. Also, **eyecup.**

eyebeam (ī′bēm′), *n.* a beam or glance of the eye.

eye bolt, *Naut.* an iron bar with a hole at one end, fixed to the deck or side of a ship and used to secure ropes.

eyebright (ī′brīt′), *n.* **1.** any of various scrophulariaceous herbs of the genus *Euphrasia*, as *E. officinalis* of Europe, formerly used for diseases of the eye. **2.** scarlet pimpernel.

eyebrow (ī′brou′), *n.* **1.** the arch or ridge forming the upper part of the orbit of the eye. **2.** the fringe of hair growing upon it.

eye-catching (ī′kăch′ĭng), *adj.* attracting attention; attractive or noticeable. —**eye′-catch′er,** *n.*

eyed (īd), *adj.* **1.** having eyes. **2.** having eyelike spots.

eyeful (ī′fo͝ol′), *n.* **1.** an amount of dust, etc., blown or thrown into the eye. **2.** as much as one wants to see or as much as the eye can take in at a glance. **3.** *Colloq.* a person of striking appearance, esp. a beautiful woman.

eyeglass (ī′gläs′), *n.* **1.** the eyepiece of an optical instrument; an ocular. **2.** an eyebath. **3.** glass (def. 4).

eyehole (ī′hōl′), *n.* **1.** eye socket. **2.** a hole to look through, as in a mask or a curtain. **3.** a circular opening for the insertion of a pin, hook, rope, etc.

eyelash (ī′lăsh′), *n.* one of the short, thick, curved hairs growing as a fringe on the edge of an eyelid.

eyeless (ī′lĭs), *adj.* **1.** lacking eyes. **2.** blind.

eyelet (ī′lĭt), *n.* **1.** a small, typically round hole, esp. one finished at the edge, as in cloth or leather, for the passage of a lace or cord, or in embroidery, for ornament. **2.** a metal ring for lining a small hole. **3.** an eyehole in a wall, mask, etc. **4.** a small eye. —*v.t.* **5.** to make eyelets (holes) in. **6.** to insert metal eyelets in. [ME *oilet*, t. F: m. *œillet*, dim. of *œil* eye]

eyeleteer (ī′lĭ tĭə′), *n.* a small pointed instrument for making eyelet holes.

eyelid (ī′lĭd′), *n.* **1.** the movable lid of skin which serves to cover and uncover the eyeball. **2.** the movable parts at the exhaust end of a jet engine designed to alter the direction of the exhaust flow. Also, **clamshell.**

eyen (ī′ən), *n. Archaic.* pl. of **eye.**

eye-opener (ī′ōp′nə), *n.* **1.** something that causes the eyes to open, as an enlightening or startling disclosure or experience. **2.** *Colloq.* an alcoholic drink, esp. one taken early in the day.

eyepiece (ī′pēs′), *n.* (in an optical instrument) the lens or combination of lenses to which the eye is applied.

eye rhyme, a rhyme in which two words are similar in spelling rather than sound: *a tough with a cough.*

eye-servant (ī′sû′vənt), *n. Archaic.* a servant or other who attends to his duty only when watched by his employer. Also, **eye′-serv′er.**

eye-service (ī′sû′vĭs), *n.* **1.** homage paid with the eyes; admiring looks. **2.** *Archaic.* service performed only under the eye or watch of the employer.

eyeshade (ī′shād′), *n.* a visor worn over the head or forehead to protect the eyes from overhead light.

eye shadow, a cosmetic material applied to the eyelids.

eyeshot (ī′shŏt′), *n.* **1.** range of vision; view. **2.** a glance.

eyesight (ī′sīt′), *n.* **1.** the power or faculty or seeing. **2.** the action or fact of seeing. **3.** the range of the eye.

eye socket, the socket or orbit of the eye.

eyesome (ī′səm), *adj.* pleasant to look at.

eyesore (ī′sô′), *n.* something unpleasant to look at: *the broken window was an eyesore to the neighbours.*

eye splice, a splice made in a rope by turning back one end and interweaving it with the main body of the rope so as to form a loop.

eyespot (ī′spŏt′), *n. Zool.* **1.** a sensory organ of lower animals, having a light-perceiving function. **2.** an eyelike spot, as on the tail of a peacock.

eyes right or **left,** *Mil.* the command given to turn the head and eyes to the right or to the left as a salute while marching in formation.

eyestalk (ī′stôk′), *n. Zool.* the stalk or peduncle upon which the eye is borne in lobsters, shrimps, etc.

eyestone (ī′stōn′), *n.* a small calcareous body, flat on one side and convex on the other, passed between the eye and the eyelid to bring out cinders, etc.

eyestrain (ī′strān′), *n.* a sensation of discomfort produced in the eyes by their excessive or faulty use.

eyetooth (ī′to͞oth′), *n., pl.* **-teeth** (-tēth′). **1.** a canine tooth, esp. of the upper jaw (so named from its position under the eye). **2. cut one's eyeteeth,** to become old and experienced enough to understand things.

eyewash (ī′wŏsh′), *n.* **1.** Also, **eyewater** (ī′wô′tə). a lotion for the eyes. **2.** *Slang.* a deception intended to mislead a person into thinking something is good or correct. **3.** *Slang.* nonsense.

eyewink (ī′wĭngk′), *n.* **1.** a wink of the eye. **2.** a look or glance.

eyewinker (ī′wĭng′kə), *n.* eyelash.

eyewitness (ī′wĭt′nĭs), *n.* **1.** one who actually beholds some act or occurrence, and hence can give testimony concerning it. *—adj.* **2.** given by an eyewitness.

eyne (īn), *n.* *Archaic.* pl. of **eye.**

eyot (āt, ā′ət), *n.* ait.

eyra (ēə′rə, ī′ə rə), *n.* jaguarondi. [t. Tupi]

eyre (ēə), *n.* **1.** a journey in a circuit. **2.** *Old Eng. Law.* (Between 1176 and the late 13th century) **a.** a journey made by judges to hold court throughout a circuit, under royal commission. **b. justices in eyre,** the judges holding the commission. **c.** the court held by justices in eyre. [ME, t. OF: m. *eire* journey, circuit, der. *errer,* v., journey, g. LL *iterāre*]

Eyre (ēə), *n.* **1. Creek,** an intermittent stream in Australia flowing south through Queensland, formed by the junction of the Georgina and Hamilton rivers and terminating in **Goyder Lagoon.** In wet seasons it unites with the Diamantina to form the Warburton. **2. Lake,** a salt lake in South Australia, the largest lake in Australia. 3200 sq. mi. **3. Peninsula,** a promontory on the South Australian coast between the Great Australian Bight and Spencer Gulf.

eyrie (ĭə′rĭ, ēə′rĭ, ī′ə rĭ), *n.* **1.** the nest of a bird of prey, as an eagle or a hawk. **2.** a lofty nest of any large bird. **3.** an elevated habitation or situation. Also, **aerie, aery, eyry.** [var. of AERIE, influenced by ME *ey* egg]

Eysenck (ī′sĭngk), *n.* **Hans Jurgen** (hănz′ yŏŏ′gən), born 1916, British psychologist.

Ez., Ezra. Also, **Ezr.**

Ezek., Ezekiel.

Ezekiel (ĭ zē′kyəl), *n.* **1.** fl. 6th century B.C., one of the major Hebrew prophets. **2.** the 26th book of the Old Testament, written by him. **3. Moses Jacob,** 1844–1917, U.S. sculptor in Rome. [t. Gk (Septuagint): m. *Iezekiēl,* t. Heb.: m. *Yeḥezqēl*; r. *Ezechiel,* t. L (Vulgate)]

Ezra (ĕz′rə), *n.* **1.** fl. 5th century B.C., Hebrew scribe and priest who with Nehemiah led the revival of Judaism in Palestine. **2.** a short book of chronicles of the Old Testament. [t. Heb.: m. *'Ezrā*]

F, f (ĕf), *n., pl.* **F's** or **Fs, f's** or **fs. 1.** the sixth letter of the English alphabet. **2.** the sixth in order or in a series. **3.** *Music.* **a.** the fourth degree in the scale of C major or the sixth in the relative scale of A minor. **b.** a printed or written note indicating this tone. **c.** a string, key, or pipe tuned to this note. **d.** (in solmization) the fourth note of the scale of C, called fa.

F, 1. Fahrenheit. **2.** *Elect.* farad. **3.** *Maths.* field. **4.** *Genetics.* (with a subscript number following) a generation of filial offspring from a given parent: F_1 is the first generation of offspring, F_2 is the second, etc. **5.** *Chem.* fluorine. **6.** French. **7.** *Maths.* function (of).

F, *Photog.* See **f number.** Also, **f, F:, f:, F/, f/.**

f., 1. *Music.* forte. **2.** *Maths.* function (of). **3.** *Elect.* farad. **4.** fathom. **5.** female. **6.** feminine. **7.** fluid (ounce). **8.** (*pl.* **ff.**) folio. **9.** following. **10.** formed from. **11.** franc. **12.** (euphemistic for) any of various vulgar, taboo, or obscene words beginning with f.

fa (fä), *n.* *Music.* the syllable used for the fourth note of a scale. Also, **fah.** [see GAMUT]

F.A., Football Association. See **F.A. Cup.**

fabaceous (fə bā′shəs), *adj.* *Bot.* belonging to the *Fabaceae,* or bean family of plants, sometimes included in the *Leguminosae,* including many herbs, shrubs, and trees, as the bean, pea, lentil, gorse, broom, etc., which bear seeds in pods or legumes. [t. L: m. *fabāceus,* der. *faba* bean]

Fabergé (făb′ĕə zhā′), *n.* gold and enamel ware made in St Petersburg, Russia, in the late 19th and early 20th centuries. [named after Peter Carl *Fabergé,* 1846–1920, Russian jeweller]

Fabian (fā′byən), *adj.* **1.** avoiding battle; purposely delaying; cautiously dilatory: *Fabian policy.* See **Fabius Maximus. 2.** of the Fabian Society. *—n.* **3.** a member of or sympathizer with the Fabian Society. **—Fa′bianism,** *n.* **—Fa′bianist,** *n., adj.*

Fabian Society, a socialist society founded in England in 1884 favouring the gradual spread of socialism by peaceful means.

Fabius Maximus (fā′byəs măk′sĭ məs), **Quintus** (kwĭn′təs) (*'Cunctator'*), died 203 B.C., Roman general who harassed Hannibal's army without risking a pitched battle.

fable (fā′bl), *n., v.,* **-bled, -bling.** *—n.* **1.** a short tale to teach a moral, often with animals or inanimate objects as characters; apologue: *the fable of the tortoise and the hare.* **2.** a story not founded on fact. **3.** a story about supernatural or extraordinary persons or incidents; a legend. **4.** legends or myths collectively: *classical fable.* **5.** an untruth; a falsehood. **6.** *Archaic.* the plot of an epic, a dramatic poem, or a play. **7.** *Archaic.* idle talk: *old wives' fables.* *—v.i.* **8.** to tell or write fables. **9.** to speak falsely; lie. *—v.t.* **10.** to invent (stories); talk about as if true. [ME *fabul,* t. L: s. *fābula* narrative] **—fa′bler,** *n.* **—Syn. 1.** See **legend.**

fabled (fā′bld), *adj.* **1.** celebrated as fables; mythical; legendary: *fabled goddess of the wood.* **2.** having no real existence; fictitious: *fabled chest of gold.*

fabliau (făb′lĭ ō′; *Fr.* fȧ blē ō′), *n., pl.* **-aux** (-ōz′; *Fr.* -ō′). one of the short metrical tales of the medieval French poets, usually rough and humorous. [t. F, orig. d., dim. of *fable* FABLE]

Fabre (fä′brə; *Fr.* fȧ′br), *n.* **Jean Henri** (*Fr.* zhäɴ äɴ rē′), 1823–1915, French entomologist and popular writer on insect life.

fabric (făb′rĭk), *n.* **1.** a cloth made by weaving, knitting, or felting fibres: *woollen fabrics.* **2.** the texture of the woven, knitted, or felted material: *cloths of different fabric.* **3.** framework; structure: *fabric of society.* **4.** a building; edifice. **5.** the method of construction. [late ME *fabrike,* t. L: m. s. *fabrica* workshop, art, fabric]

fabricant (făb′rĭ kənt), *n.* a maker; artisan.

fabricate (făb′rĭ kāt′), *v.t.,* **-cated, -cating. 1.** to make by art and labour; construct. **2.** to make by assembling standard parts or sections. **3.** to devise or invent (a legend, lie, etc.). **4.** to fake; forge (a document). [t. L: m. s. *fabricātus,* pp., having made] **—fab′rica′tor,** *n.* **—Syn. 1.** See **manufacture.**

fabrication (făb′rĭ kā′shən), *n.* **1.** the process of fabricating; manufacture. **2.** something fabricated, esp. an untruthful statement. **—Syn. 2.** See **fiction.**

fabulist (făb′yŏŏ lĭst), *n.* **1.** a person who invents or relates fables. **2.** a liar.

fabulous (făb′yŏŏ ləs), *adj.* **1.** almost unbelievable: *a fabulous price.* **2.** *Colloq.* wonderful; exceptionally pleasing. **3.** told about in fables; not true or real: *the fabulous exploits of Hercules.* **4.** known about only through myths or legends: *the fabulous age in Greek history.* **5.** based on fables. [t. L: m. s. *fābulōsus*] **—fab′ulously,** *adv.* **—fab′ulousness,** *n.* **—Syn. 1.** incredible, amazing, astonishing. **3.** fabled, fictitious, imaginary. **—Ant. 1.** moderate. **3.** historical.

faburden (făb′ə dən), *n.* *Music.* **1.** an ancient compositional style employing three voices harmonizing in fourths and sixths. **2.** harmony in progressions of parallel sixths.

fac., 1. facsimile. **2.** factor. **3.** factory.

facade (fə säd′, fă-), *n.* **1.** *Archit.* a face or front, or the principal face, of a building. **2.** an appearance, esp. a misleading one: *behind his facade of benevolence he hides a cruel nature.* Also, **façade** (*Fr.* fȧ sȧd′). [t. F, der. *face,* after It. *facciata,* der. *faccia* FACE]

F.A.C.C.A., Fellow of the Association of Certified and Corporate Accountants.

face (fās), *n., v.,* **faced, facing.** *—n.* **1.** the front part of the head, from the forehead to the chin. **2.** sight; presence: *to one's face.* **3.** a look or expression on the face: *sad face.* **4.** an expression, indicating ridicule, disgust, etc.: *to make faces.* **5.** *Colloq.* boldness; impudence: *to have the face to ask.* **6.** outward appearance: *old problems with new faces.* **7.** outward show; pretence: *to put a good face on a matter.* **8.** good name; prestige: *to save one's face, lose face.* **9.** (of a document) the manifest sense or express terms. **10.** the geographic characteristics or general appearance (of a land surface). **11.** the surface: *face of the earth.* **12.** the side or part of a side upon which the use of a thing depends: *the face of a cloth, document, playing card, watch, etc.* **13.** the most

important side; the front: *the face of a building, arch, etc.* **14.** the acting, striking, or working surface of an implement, tool, bat, club, etc. **15.** *Geom.* any one of the bounding surfaces of a solid figure: *a cube has six faces.* **16.** *Mining.* the front or end of a drift or excavation, where the material is being or was last mined. **17.** *Print.* **a.** the working surface of a type, plate, etc. See diag. under **type. b.** the style or appearance of type; typeface: *broad or narrow face.* **18.** *Fort.* either of the two outer sides which form the salient angle of a bastion or the like. See diag. under **bastion. 19.** *Crystall.* crystal face. **20. face to face, a.** opposite. **b.** confronted (*with*): *to come face to face with death.* **21. in (the) face of, a.** notwithstanding: *in the face of many obstacles.* **b.** when confronted with: *to keep up prices in the face of a falling market.* **22. look one in the face,** to meet without fear or embarrassment. **23. on the face of it,** to all appearances; seemingly. **24. set one's face against,** to oppose implacably. **25. show one's face,** to make an appearance; be seen.
—*v.t.* **26.** to look towards: *face the light.* **27.** to have the front towards or in the direction of: *the statue faces the park.* **28.** to meet face to face; confront: *faced with a problem.* **29.** to confront with impudence: *to face a thing out.* **30.** to oppose confidently or defiantly: *to face fearful odds.* **31.** to cover or partly cover with a different material in front: *a brick house faced with wood.* **32.** to cover some part of (a garment) with another material. **33.** to turn the face of (a playing card) upwards. **34.** to dress or smooth the surface of (a stone, etc.). **35.** *Now Chiefly U.S.* to cause (soldiers) to turn to the right, left, or in the opposite direction. **36.** *Ice Hockey.* (of the referee) to put (the puck) in play by dropping it between two opposing players. **37. face it out,** to ignore or defy blame, hostility, etc. **38. face (one) out, a.** to stare out. **b.** to cause (another) to concede by adhering consistently to a particular version.
—*v.i.* **39.** to be turned (often fol. by *to, towards*). **40.** to be placed (fol. by *on, to, towards*). **41.** *Now Chiefly U.S.* to turn to the right, left, or in the opposite direction. **42. face off,** *Ice Hockey.* to start play by dropping the puck between two opposing players. **43. face up to,** to meet courageously; acknowledge and act to deal with.
[ME, t. F, g. VL *facia*, r. L *facies* form, face] **—face′able,** *adj.*

—Syn. 1. FACE, COUNTENANCE, VISAGE, PHYSIOGNOMY refer to the front of the (usually human) head. The FACE is the combination of the features: *a face with broad cheekbones.* COUNTENANCE, a more formal word, denotes the face as it is affected by or reveals the state of mind, and hence often signifies the look or expression on the face: *an expressive countenance.* VISAGE, still more formal, refers to the face as seen in a certain aspect, esp. as revealing seriousness or severity: *a stern visage.* PHYSIOGNOMY is a learned word, relating to the typical or racial characters of the features: *he had the physiognomy of an Oriental.*

face-ache (fās′āk′), *n.* **1.** facial pains; neuralgia. **2.** *Colloq.* extreme ugliness. **3.** *Colloq.* an extremely ugly person.

face-card (fās′käd′), *n.* a court card.

face-centred (fās′sĕn′təd), *adj. Crystall.* (of a crystal structure) having atomic or ionic centres at the middle of the faces of each cubic cell as well as at the corners (distinguished from *body-centred*).

facecloth (fās′klŏth′), *n.* **1.** a small towel or face flannel. **2.** a cloth used to cover the face of a dead person.

face edge, a working edge.

face flannel, a small piece of flannel or similar material used for washing the face, hands, etc.

face gear, *Mech.* a gearwheel in which the teeth are on the face of the wheel instead of around its edge.

faceguard (fās′gäd′), *n. Fencing, etc.* a mask to protect the face.

faceless (fās′lĭs), *adj.* **1.** having no face. **2.** without discernible individuality; anonymous: *faceless officials.* **—face′lessness,** *n.*

facelift (fās′lĭft′), *n.* **1.** a session or course of plastic surgery on the face for the elimination of wrinkles, etc. **2.** any improvement in appearance: *to give an ancient building a facelift.* **—face′lif′ting,** *n., adj.*

face-off (fās′ŏf′), *n. Ice Hockey.* the process by which play is commenced, in which the referee drops the puck between two opposing players.

face-pack (fās′păk′), *n.* a paste or cream used by women to improve the complexion and free the skin from impurities.

face-plate (fās′plāt′), *n.* a circular plate, which may be attached to the mandrel of a lathe, provided with slots and holes for securing work of an irregular shape.

face powder, a cosmetic powder used by women on the face.

facer (fā′sə), *n.* **1.** one who or that which faces, esp. a cutter for smoothing a surface. See **face** (defs 31, 34). **2.** *Colloq.* a sudden and severe check; a disconcerting difficulty, problem, etc. **3.** *Colloq.* a blow in the face.

face-saver (fās′sā′və), *n.* one who or that which saves one's prestige. **—face′-sa′ving,** *adj.*

face side, a working face.

facet (fās′ĭt), *n., v.,* **-eted, -eting.** **—***n.* **1.** one of the small plane polished surfaces of a cut gem. **2.** aspect; phase: *a facet of the mind.* **3.** *Archit.* a filled-in flute sometimes seen at the bottom of columnar shafts. **4.** *Zool.* one of the corneal lenses of a compound arthropod eye. **—***v.t.* **5.** to cut facets on. [t. F: m. *facette,* dim. of *face* FACE]

Compound eye of a housefly showing facets (highly magnified)

facete (fə sēt′), *adj. Archaic.* facetious; witty. [t. L: m. s. *facētus* fine, elegant, witty]

facetiae (fə sē′shĭ ē′), *n.pl.* **1.** amusing writings or witty remarks. **2.** coarsely witty books. [t. L, pl. of *facētia* a witticism. See FACETE]

facetious (fə sē′shəs), *adj.* **1.** intended to be amusing: *his facetious remarks are often merely offensive.* **2.** trying to be amusing: *a facetious person.* **3.** *Obs.* pleasantly humorous. [f. FACETI(AE) + -OUS] **—face′tiously,** *adv.* **—face′tiousness,** *n.* **—Syn. 1.** See **humorous.**

face value, 1. par value; the value stated on the face of a financial instrument or document. **2.** apparent value: *accept promises at face value.*

facial (fā′shəl), *adj.* **1.** of the face: *facial expression.* **2.** for the face: *a facial cream.* **—***n.* **3.** *Colloq.* a massage or treatment for the face. **—fa′cially,** *adv.*

facial angle, *Ethnol., etc.* the angle formed on the face of a skull by a line from nasion to prosthion at its intersection with Reid's base-line.

facial index, *Ethnol., etc.* the ratio of the breadth of a face to its height.

-facient, a suffix forming adjectives meaning 'that makes or causes (something)' and nouns meaning 'one that makes or causes (something)', as in *absorbefacient,* n. and adj. [t. L: s. *faciens,* ppr., doing, making]

facies (fā′shĭ ēz′), *n.* **1.** *Med.* the face or facial expression. **2.** general appearance. **3.** *Geol.* the composite nature of sedimentary deposits, including texture, faunal content, etc., reflecting the conditions and environment of their origin. [t. L]

facile (fās′īl), *adj.* **1.** moving, acting, working, proceeding, etc., with ease: *a facile hand, tongue, pen, etc.* **2.** easily done, performed, used, etc.: *a facile victory, method, etc.* **3.** easy or unconstrained, as manners or persons; affable, agreeable, or complaisant; easily influenced. **4.** glib: *a facile expression.* [t. L: m. s. *facilis* easy to do, easy] **—fac′ilely,** *adv.* **—fac′ileness,** *n.*

facile princeps (făk′ĭ lā prĭn′kĕps), *Latin.* easily the first or best.

facilis descensus Averni (făk′ĭ lĭs dēs kĕn′so͞os ă vû′nī), *Latin.* (the) descent to hell is easy; it is easy to take the downward path. Virgil, *Aeneid,* 6, 126.

facilitate (fə sĭl′ĭ tāt′), *v.t.,* **-tated, -tating. 1.** to make easier or less difficult; help forward (an action, a process, etc.). **2.** *Archaic.* to assist the progress of (a person).

facilitation (fə sĭl′ĭ tā′shən), *n.* **1.** the act or process of facilitating. **2.** *Psychol.* the tendency of a stimulus to reinforce another stimulus.

facility (fə sĭl′ĭ tĭ), *n., pl.* **-ties. 1.** something that makes possible the easier performance of any action; advantage: *transport facilities, to afford someone every facility for doing something.* **2.** freedom from difficulty; ease: *facility of understanding.* **3.** readiness because of skill or practice; dexterity: *compose with great facility.* **4.** an easy-flowing manner: *facility of style.* **5.** ready compliance. **6.** a rocket base for non-military missiles. [t. L: m. s. *facilitas.* See FACILE]

facing (fā′sĭng), *n.* **1.** a covering in front, for ornament, protection, etc., as an outer layer of different stone forming the face of a wall. **2.** material applied on the edge of a garment for ornament or protection. **3.** (*pl.*) coverings of a different colour applied on the collar, cuffs, or other parts of a uniform coat. **4.** *Chiefly U.S. Mil.* the act of turning to face in a given direction in response to a command.

facing tool, a lathe tool for smoothing a plane surface at right angles to the axis of rotation.

facinorous (fə sĭn′ə rəs), *adj. Archaic.* atrociously wicked. [t. L: m. s. *facinorōsus,* der. *facinus* (bad) deed]

facsim., facsimile.

facsimile (făk sĭm′ĭ lĭ), *n., adj., v.,* **-led, -leing.** **—***n.* **1.** an exact copy. **2.** *Radio.* **a.** a method of transmitting pictures by radio telegraph. See **phototelegraphy. b.** a picture so sent. **—***adj.* **3.** of a facsimile. **4.** producing facsimiles. **—***v.t.* **5.** to reproduce in facsimile; make a facsimile of. [f. L: *fac,* impv., make + *simile* (neut.) like]

fact (făkt), *n.* **1.** what has really happened or is the case;

truth; reality: *in fact rather than theory, the fact of the matter is.* 2. something known to have happened; a truth known by actual experience or observation: *scientists working with facts.* 3. something said to be true or supposed to have happened: *the facts are as follows.* 4. *Law.* a. an actual or alleged physical or mental event or existence, as distinguished from a legal effect or consequence. Thus, whether certain words were spoken is *a question of fact*; whether, if spoken, they constituted a binding promise, is usually *a question of law.* b. an evil deed (now only in certain legal phrases): *before the fact, after the fact.* 5. **in fact,** really; indeed. [t. L: s. *factum* (thing) done, prop. pp. neut.]

fact-finding (făkt′fīn′dĭng), *adj.* engaged in determining facts.

factice (făk′tĭs), *n.* a rubber-like substance produced by vulcanizing vegetable oils with sulphur or sulphur chloride. [t. F, t. L: m. s. *factītius* artificial]

faction (făk′shən), *n.* 1. a smaller group of people within a larger group, often one using unscrupulous methods to accomplish selfish purposes. 2. party strife or intrigue: *faction has no regard for national interests.* [t. L: s. *factio* a doing or making, action, party] —**fac′tionary, fac′tionist,** *n.*

factional (făk′shə nəl), *adj.* of a faction or factions; self-interested; partisan. —**fac′tionalism,** *n.*

factious (făk′shəs), *adj.* 1. acting only in the interests of a group or faction: *factious opposition.* 2. caused by factional spirit or strife: *factious quarrels.* [t. L: m. s. *factiōsus*] —**fac′tiously,** *adv.* —**fac′tiousness,** *n.*

factitious (făk tĭsh′əs), *adj.* 1. artificial; not spontaneous or natural: *a factitious value, factitious enthusiasm.* 2. made; manufactured. [t. L: m. *factītius* made by art] —**facti′tiously,** *adv.* —**facti′tiousness,** *n.*

factitive (făk′tĭ tĭv), *adj. Gram.* designating verbs which convey the idea of making or rendering according to order or specification; such verbs are accompanied not only by the direct object but by an additional word indicating the result of the process. For example: They *made* him their *ruler*; to *paint* the house *red.* [t. NL: m. s. *factitīvus*, der. L *factitāre* declare (a person) to be, freq. of *facere* do, make] —**fac′titively,** *adv.*

fact of life, 1. an event, development, situation, etc., which must be faced as an unalterable reality in life. 2. **facts of life,** the details concerning sexual behaviour and reproduction, esp. as explained to children.

factor (făk′tə), *n.* 1. one of the elements that contribute to bring about any given result. 2. *Maths.* one of two or more numbers, algebraic expressions, or the like, which when multiplied together produce a given product; a divisor: *6 and 3 are factors of 18.* 3. *Genetics.* a gene, allele, or determiner for hereditary characters. 4. one who acts, or transacts business, for another. 5. an agent entrusted with the possession of goods for sale. 6. *Now only Scot.* the steward or bailiff of an estate. [t. L: doer, maker] —**fac′torship′,** *n.*

factorage (făk′tə rĭj), *n.* 1. the action or business of a factor. 2. the allowance or commission paid to a factor.

factorial (făk tô′rĭ əl), *n.* 1. *Maths.* the product of an integer multiplied by all the lower integers: *the factorial of 4 (written 4! or* $\underline{4|}$*) is* $4 \times 3 \times 2 \times 1 = 24$. —*adj.* 2. *Maths.* of or pertaining to factors or factorials. 3. of or pertaining to a factor or a factory.

factoring (făk′tə rĭng), *n. Com.* the business of purchasing and collecting accounts receivable.

factorize (făk′tə rīz′), *v.t.*, **-rized, -rizing.** *Maths.* to resolve into factors. Also, **factorise.** —**fac′toriza′tion,** *n.*

factor of safety, the ratio between the maximum stress that a structural part can withstand and the safe permissible stress which it may be expected to experience in use.

factory (făk′tə rĭ, făk′trĭ), *n., pl.* **-ries.** 1. a building or group of buildings, usually with equipment, where goods are manufactured. 2. (formerly) an establishment for factors and merchants carrying on business in a foreign country. [t. ML: m. s. *factōria*, der. L *factor*] —**fac′tory-like′,** *adj.* —**Syn.** 1. manufactory, mill, workshop.

Factory Acts, any of various laws relating to working conditions in factories, esp. those passed in Britain in the early 19th century.

factory ship, a whaling ship equipped to process killed whales and to store and transport the oil and by-products.

factotum (făk tō′təm), *n.* one employed to do all kinds of work for another. [t. ML, f. L *fac*, impv., do + *tōtum* (neut.) all]

factual (făk′tyo͞o əl), *adj.* pertaining to facts; of the nature of fact; real. —**fac′tually,** *adv.* —**fac′tualness,** *n.*

factum (făk′təm), *n. Law.* 1. a thing done; a deed. 2. (in Canada) a summary of the facts of a case.

facture (făk′chə), *n.* 1. the act, process, or manner of making anything; construction. 2. the thing made. [ME, t. L: m. s. *factūra*, der. *facere* do, make]

facula (făk′yo͞o lə), *n., pl.* **-lae** (-lē′). *Astron.* one of the irregular patches on the sun's disc, brighter than the general surface. [t. L, dim. of *fax* torch] —**fac′ular,** *adj.*

facultative (făk′l tə tĭv), *adj.* 1. conferring a faculty, privilege, or permission, or the power of doing or not doing something: *a facultative enactment.* 2. left to one's option or choice; optional. 3. that may or may not take place; that may or may not assume a specified character. 4. *Biol., Bacteriol.* having the capacity to live under more than one specific set of environmental conditions, as an animal or plant that can lead either a parasitic or a non-parasitic life (opposed to *obligate*).

faculty (făk′l tĭ), *n., pl.* **-ties.** 1. an ability, natural or acquired, for a particular kind of action. 2. one of the powers of the mind, as memory, reason, speech, etc.: *the mental faculties, be in full possession of all one's faculties.* 3. an inherent capability of the body: *the faculties of sight and hearing.* 4. *U.S.* executive ability; efficiency. 5. *Educ.* a. one of the departments of learning, as theology, medicine, or law, in a university. b. the teaching body, sometimes with the students, in any of these departments. c. *U.S.* the entire teaching and administrative force of a university or other educational institution. 6. the members of a learned profession, esp. the medical profession. 7. a power or privilege conferred. 8. *Eccles.* a dispensation, licence, or authorization. [ME *faculte*, t. L: m. s. *facultas* ability, means] —**Syn.** 1. capacity, capability, aptitude, knack, turn, talent. See **ability.**

F.A. Cup, a cup awarded annually to the winners of a knock-out competition, open to all member clubs of the Football Association.

fad (făd), *n.* a temporary, usually irrational, pursuit, fashion, etc., by numbers of people of some action that excites attention and has prestige. [n. use of d. *fad*, v., be busy about trifles, itself back-formation from obs. *faddle*, v., fondle. Cf. FIDDLE, v., and FIDDLE-FADDLE]

faddish (făd′ĭsh), *adj.* 1. resembling a fad. 2. given to fads. —**fad′dishness,** *n.*

faddist (făd′ĭst), *n.* one who has a fad or is given to fads.

faddy (făd′ĭ), *adj.*, **-dier, -diest.** faddish.

fade (fād), *v.*, **faded, fading.** —*v.i.* 1. to lose freshness, vigour, strength, or health: *the flower faded.* 2. to lose brightness or vividness, as light or colour. 3. to disappear or die gradually (often fol. by *away* or *out*): *a fading smile, sound, etc.* 4. *Television, Radio, Films.* to cause sound and/or vision gradually and progressively to increase (fol. by *in*) or decrease (fol. by *out*). 5. (of radio signals) to lose strength due to interference phenomena. —*v.t.* 6. to cause to fade: *sunshine faded the tapestry.* [ME *fade(n)*, t. OF: m. *fader*, der. *fade* pale, weak, g. b. L *vapidus* flat and *fatuus* insipid] —**fad′er,** *n.* —**Syn.** 1. wither, droop, languish. 2. blanch, bleach, pale. 3. See **disappear.**

fade-in (fād′ĭn′), *n. Television, Radio, Films.* a technique used to open a scene, consisting of the progressive introduction of sound and/or vision.

fadeless (fād′lĭs), *adj.* unfading. —**fade′lessly,** *adv.*

fade-out (fād′out′), *n.* 1. *Television, Radio, Films.* a technique used to close a scene, consisting of the gradual loss of sound and/or vision. 2. a disappearance, esp. a gradual one.

fadge (făj), *v.i.*, **fadged, fadging.** *Obs. or Dial.* 1. to fit; suit; agree. 2. to succeed; thrive. [akin to OE *gefægen* glad]

faeces (fē′sēz), *n.pl.* 1. waste matter discharged from the intestines; excrement. 2. dregs; sediment. Also, *Chiefly U.S.*, **feces.** [t. L: pl. of *faex* dregs] —**faecal** (fē′kl), *adj.*

Faenza (*It.* fä ĕn′tsä), *n.* a town in N Italy, in Emilia, SE of Bologna. 53,615 (1962).

faerie (fā′ə rĭ, fēə′rĭ), *n.* 1. fairyland. 2. *Archaic.* a fairy. —*adj.* 3. *Archaic.* fairy. Also, **faery.** [var. of FAIRY]

Faeroes (fēə′rōz), *n.pl.* a group of 21 islands in the N Atlantic between Great Britain and Iceland, belonging to Denmark but having extensive home rule. 34,596 pop. (1960); 540 sq. mi. *Cap.*: Thorshavn. Also, **Faeroe Islands, Faroe Islands.** Danish, **Faeröerne** (*Dan.* fĕr′-œ ər nə).

Faeroese (fēə′rō ēz′), *n., pl.* **-ese,** *adj.* —*n.* 1. an inhabitant of the Faeroes. 2. the language spoken there, closely related to Icelandic. —*adj.* 3. of or pertaining to the Faeroes, the people, or their language. Also, **Faroese.**

faery (fā′ə rĭ, fēə′rĭ), *n., pl.* **-ries,** *adj.* faerie.

Fafnir (fäf′nĭə, fäv′-), *n.* (in the Icelandic version of the Siegfried story) the guardian dragon of the Nibelungs' hoard, slain by Sigurd. [Icel.]

fag (făg), *v.*, **fagged, fagging,** *n.* —*v.i.* 1. to work till wearied; work hard: *to fag away at French.* 2. to act as a fag. —*v.t.* 3. to tire by labour; exhaust (often fol. by *out*):

we were fagged out. **4.** to make a fag of. —*n.* **5.** drudgery; toil. **6.** a younger boy at a public school required to perform certain services for an older pupil. **7.** a drudge. **8.** a fag-end, as of cloth. **9.** *Slang.* a cigarette. **10.** *U.S. Slang.* a homosexual. [special use of obs. *fag*, n., flap, which occurs only in expression *fag feathers*, ? for *wag feathers* by allit. assimilation; cf. FIELDFARE]

fagaceous (fə gā′shəs), *adj.* belonging to the *Fagaceae*, or beech family of trees and shrubs, which includes the beech, chestnut, oak, etc. [f. m. s. NL *Făgāceae* genus type (der. L *fāgus* beech) + -OUS]

fag-end (făg′ĕnd′), *n.* **1.** the last part or very end of something, esp. a remnant. **2.** the unfinished end of a piece of cloth. **3.** the stub of a finished cigarette.

faggot (făg′ət), *n.* **1.** a bundle of sticks, twigs, or small branches, etc., bound together, used for fuel, as a fascine for revetment, etc. **2.** a bundle of pieces of iron or steel to be welded. **3.** a bundle or bunch of anything. **4.** a ball of chopped meat, esp. pork offal, mixed with herbs, bread, or oats, etc., and eaten fried. —*v.t.* **5.** to bind or make into a faggot. **6.** to ornament with faggoting. Also, *U.S.*, **fagot.** [ME, t. OF; orig. uncert.]

faggoting (făg′ə tĭng), *n.* a type of decorative joining used to combine cloth or lace. Also, *U.S.*, **fagoting.**

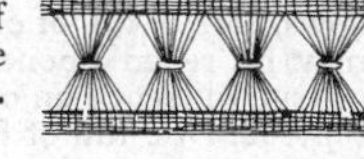
Faggoting

fagotto (fə gŏt′ō), *n.* *Italian.* bassoon. —**fagot′tist,** *n.*

fah (fä), *n.* *Music.* fa.

fahlband (fäl′bănd′; *Ger.* fäl′bänt), *n.* *Mining.* a belt or zone of rock impregnated with metallic sulphides. [G: f. *fahl* ash-coloured + *Band* band, stripe]

Fahr., Fahrenheit (thermometer).

Fahrenheit (făr′ən hīt′; *Ger.* fä′rən hīt), *adj.* **1.** denoting or pertaining to a thermometric scale in which the melting point of ice is 32 degrees above the zero, and the boiling point of water 212 degrees above the zero. See illus. under **thermometer.** —*n.* **2.** the Fahrenheit scale. **3. Gabriel Daniel** (*Ger.* gä′brē ĕl dä′nē ĕl), 1686–1736, German physicist who devised this scale and introduced the use of mercury in thermometers.

Faial (*Port.* fə yäl′), *n.* an island in the Azores, in the N Atlantic. 21,000 pop. (est. 1963); 66 sq. mi.

faible (fā′bl), *n.* foible (def. 2).

faïence (fī äns′; *Fr.* fä yäɴs′), *n.* glazed earthenware or pottery, esp. a fine variety with highly coloured designs. [t. F, orig. pottery of FAENZA]

fail (fāl), *v.i.* **1.** to come short or be wanting in action, detail, or result; disappoint or prove lacking in what is attempted, expected, desired, or approved. **2.** to be or become deficient or lacking; fall short; be insufficient or absent: *our supplies failed.* **3.** to fall off; dwindle; pass or die away. **4.** to lose strength or vigour; become weaker. **5.** to become unable to meet one's engagements, especially one's debts or business obligations; become insolvent or bankrupt. —*v.t.* **6.** to neglect to perform or observe: *he failed to come.* **7.** to prove of no use or help to, as some expected or usual resource: *his friends failed him, words failed him.* **8.** to take (an examination, etc.) without passing. **9.** to declare (a person) unsuccessful in a test, course of study, etc. —*n.* **10. without fail,** for certain; with certainty. [ME *faile(n)*, t. OF: m. *faillir*, g. var. of L *faller* deceive, disappoint] —**Syn. 4.** decline, sink, wane. **7.** desert, forsake. —**Ant. 4.** improve. **7.** support.

failing (fā′lĭng), *n.* **1.** the act or state of one who or that which fails; failure. **2.** a defect; shortcoming; weakness. —*prep.* **3.** in the absence or default of: *failing payment, we shall sue.* —**fail′ingly,** *adv.* —**Syn. 2.** See **fault.**

faille (fāl; *Fr.* fäy), *n.* a soft, transversely ribbed silk or rayon fabric. [t. F]

fail-safe (fāl′sāf′), *adj.* ensuring safety in the event of failure or accident: *a fail-safe system.*

Failsworth (fālz′wûth′), *n.* a town in England, in SE Lancashire. 19,805 (1961).

failure (fā′lyə), *n.* **1.** an act of failing; a proving unsuccessful; lack of success: *his effort ended in failure, the campaign was a failure.* **2.** non-performance of something due or required: *a failure to do what one has promised, a failure to appear.* **3.** running short; insufficiency: *failure of crops, of supplies.* **4.** loss of strength, vigour, etc.: *the failure of health.* **5.** the condition of being bankrupt by reason of insolvency. **6.** a becoming insolvent or bankrupt: *the failure of a bank.* **7.** one who or that which proves unsuccessful. [t. AF: m. *failer*, orig. inf., var. of OF *faillir* FAIL] —**Syn. 2.** neglect, omission, dereliction. **4.** decline, decay, deterioration.

fain (fān), *adv.* *Archaic.* **1.** gladly; willingly (only with *would*, fol. by simple infinitive): *I would fain be with you.* —*adj.* **2.** content; willing (fol. by an infinitive). **3.** constrained; obliged. **4.** glad; pleased. **5.** desirous; eager. [ME; OE *fægn*, var. of *fægen.* Cf. Icel. *feginn* glad]

faineant (fā′nĭ ənt), *adj.* **1.** that does nothing; idle; indolent. —*n.* **2.** an idler. Also, *French*, **fainéant** (*Fr.* fĕ nĕ äɴ′). [t. F; f. s. *faire* do + *néant* nothing] —**fai′neance,** *n.*

fains (fānz), *interj.* *Schoolboy Slang.* **1.** (a disclaimer: opposed to *bags*). **2.** pax (a call for a truce in children's games). Also, **fainites** (fā′nīts), **faynights.**

faint (fānt), *adj.* **1.** lacking brightness, vividness, clearness, loudness, strength, etc.: *a faint light, colour, resemblance.* **2.** feeble; half-hearted: *faint resistance, faint praise.* **3.** feeling weak, dizzy, or exhausted; about to swoon: *faint with hunger.* **4.** lacking courage; cowardly; timorous: *faint heart.* —*v.i.* **5.** to lose consciousness temporarily; swoon. **6.** *Now Rare.* to lose brightness, vividness, etc. **7.** *Archaic.* to grow weak; lose spirit or courage. —*n.* **8.** temporary loss of consciousness; a swoon. [ME *faint*, *feint*, t. OF: feigned, hypocritical, sluggish, spiritless, pp. of *feindre* FEIGN] —**faint′er,** *n.* —**faint′ish,** *adj.* —**faint′ly,** *adv.* —**faint′ness,** *n.* —**Syn. 1.** indistinct, ill-defined, dim, faded. **2.** faltering, irresolute, weak. **3.** feeble, languid.

faint-hearted (fānt′hä′tĭd), *adj.* lacking courage; cowardly; timorous. —**faint′-heart′edly,** *adv.* —**faint′-heart′edness,** *n.*

fair[1] (fĕə), *adj.* **1.** free from bias, dishonesty, or injustice: *a fair decision or judge.* **2.** that is legitimately sought, pursued, done, given, etc.; proper under the rules: *fair game, stroke, hit, etc.* **3.** moderately good, large, or satisfactory; not undesirable, but not excellent: *a fair income, appearance, reputation.* **4.** marked by favouring conditions; likely; promising: *in a fair way to succeed.* **5.** *Meteorol.* **a.** (of the sky) bright; sunny; cloudless to half-cloudy. **b.** (of the weather) fine; with no aspect of rain, snow, or hail; not stormy. **6.** unobstructed; not blocked up. **7.** without irregularity or unevenness: *a fair surface.* **8.** free from blemish, imperfection, or anything that impairs the appearance, quality, or character: *a fair copy.* **9.** clear; easy to read: *fair handwriting.* **10.** of a light hue; not dark: *fair skin.* **11.** beautiful; pleasing in appearance; attractive. **12.** seemingly good or sincere but not so: *fair promises.* **13.** courteous; civil: *fair words.* **14. fair and square,** honest; just; straightforward (cf. def. 20). **15. in a fair way to,** likely to; on the way to: *you're in a fair way to become an alcoholic, the amount you drink.* —*adv.* **16.** in a fair manner: *he doesn't play fair.* **17.** straight; directly, as in aiming or hitting. **18.** favourably; auspiciously: *to bid fair, speak fair.* **19.** *Colloq.* completely: *I was fair flabbergasted.* **20. fair and square, a.** directly; accurately: *I hit him fair and square on the chin.* **b.** honestly; justly; straightforwardly. —*n.* **21.** *Archaic.* that which is fair. **22.** *Archaic.* a woman. **23.** *Archaic.* a beloved woman, sweetheart. —*v.t.* **24.** *Shipbuilding.* to adjust or test the lines of curve of a hull, design, etc. **25.** *Obs.* to make fair. —*v.i.* **26.** *Dial.* (of the weather) to clear. [ME; OE *fæger*, c. OHG *fagar*] —**fair′ness,** *n.*

—**Syn. 1.** unbiased, equitable, just, honest. FAIR, IMPARTIAL, DISINTERESTED, UNPREJUDICED refer to lack of bias in opinions, judgements, etc. FAIR implies the treating of all sides alike, justly and equitably: *fair play.* IMPARTIAL, like fair, implies showing no more favour to one side than another, but suggests particularly a judicial consideration of a case: *an impartial judge.* DISINTERESTED implies a fairness arising particularly from lack of desire to obtain a selfish advantage: *the motives of her guardian were entirely disinterested.* UNPREJUDICED means not influenced or swayed by bias, or by prejudice caused by irrelevant considerations: *an unprejudiced decision.* **3.** passable, tolerable, average, middling. **8.** clean, spotless, pure, untarnished, unsullied. **9.** legible, distinct. **10.** blond, pale. **11.** pretty, comely, lovely.

fair[2] (fĕə), *n.* **1.** an amusement show, orig. as accompanying a sale of livestock; now usually travelling from place to place, having sideshows, merry-go-rounds, dodgems, etc. **2.** a periodic gathering of buyers and sellers, as of livestock, books, antiques, etc., in an appointed place. **3.** an exhibition, esp. an international one, for the display of national industrial and other achievements: *the Leipzig Fair, World's Fair.* [ME *feire*, t. OF, g. L *fēria* holiday]

Fairbairn (fĕə′bĕən′), *n.* **Sir William,** 1789–1874, Scottish engineer.

Fairbanks (fĕə′băngks′), *n.* **1.** a town in the U.S., in central Alaska, on the Tanana river. 13,311 (1960). See map under **Yukon. 2. Douglas,** 1883–1939, U.S. film actor.

fair copy, 1. a copy of a document made after final correction. **2.** the condition of such a copy.

Fairfax (fĕə′făks), *n.* **1. Thomas, 3rd Baron,** 1612–71, English general and commander-in-chief of the Parliamentarian army against Charles I in the Civil War. **2. Thomas, 6th Baron,** 1692–1782, English colonist in Virginia.

fair game, a legitimate, suitable, or likely subject of attack.

fairground (fĕə′ground′), *n.* (*often pl.*) a place where fairs, etc., are held.

fair-haired (fēə′hēəd′), *adj.* **1.** having light-coloured hair. **2.** *U.S. Colloq.* blue-eyed; favourite.

fairing[1] (fēə′rĭng), *n.* an exterior part of an aeroplane, motorcycle, or the like, which reduces eddying and resulting drag. [f. FAIR[1], adj. (def. 7) + -ING[1]]

fairing[2] (fēə′rĭng), *n. Archaic.* a gift, esp. one given at or bought at a fair. [f. FAIR[2] + -ING[1]]

fairish (fēə′rĭsh), *adj.* moderately good, large, or well.

Fair Isle, an intricate pattern knitted with Shetland wool in many colours, embellishing a neutral-coloured garment at the neck, waist, or cuffs. [named after an island midway between Shetland and Orkney]

fairlead (fēə′lēd′), *n. Naut.* a fitting such as a ring, thimble, or block, or a strip of board with holes in it, through which running rigging is passed to be guided and kept clear of obstructions and chafing. Also, **fair′-lead′-er.** [f. FAIR[1], adj. (def. 7) + LEAD[1]]

fairly (fēə′lĭ), *adv.* **1.** in a fair manner; justly; impartially. **2.** moderately; tolerably: *fairly good.* **3.** actually; completely: *the wheels fairly spun.* **4.** properly; legitimately. **5.** clearly; distinctly. **6.** *Obs.* softly. **7.** *Obs.* courteously.

fair-minded (fēə′mīn′dĭd), *adj.* fair in mind or judgement; impartial; unprejudiced: *a wise and fair-minded judge.* **—fair′-mind′edness,** *n.*

fair play, 1. *Sport.* play according to the rules. **2.** *Colloq.* action conforming to generally accepted ideas of what is fair or acceptable, in competition, etc.

fair sex, women.

fair-spoken (fēə′spō′kən), *adj.* courteous, civil, or plausible in speech; smooth-tongued.

fair to middling, *Colloq.* tolerably good in appearance or quality; so-so.

fair trade, 1. the imposition of duties on imports from foreign countries in direct proportion to the duties imposed by those countries on home exports. **2.** *U.S.* resale price maintenance.

fair-trade (fēə′trād′), *v.,* **-traded, -trading,** *adj., adv.* *U.S.* **—***v.t.* **1.** to market a product subject to resale price maintenance. **—***adj., adv.* **2.** by way of resale price maintenance.

fairway (fēə′wā′), *n.* **1.** an unobstructed passage or way. **2.** *Golf.* that part of the links between tees and putting greens where the grass is kept short. **3.** *Naut.* **a.** (in a harbour, river, etc.) the navigable portion or channel for vessels. **b.** the usual course taken by vessels.

fair-weather (fēə′wĕth′ə), *adj.* **1.** for fair weather only. **2.** weakening or failing in time of trouble: *he was surrounded by fair-weather friends.*

fairy (fēə′rĭ), *n., pl.* **-ries,** *adj.* **—***n.* **1.** one of a class of supernatural beings, generally conceived as of diminutive human form, having magical powers capriciously exercised for good or evil in human affairs. **2.** such beings collectively. **3.** *Slang.* an effeminate male, usually a homosexual. **—***adj.* **4.** having to do with fairies. **5.** of the nature of a fairy; fairy-like. [ME, t. OF: m. *faerie,* der. *fae* FAY[1]] **—fair′y-like′,** *adj.*

—Syn. 1. leprechaun. FAIRY, BROWNIE, ELF, SPRITE are terms for imaginary beings usually less than human size thought to be helpful or harmful to mankind. FAIRY is the most general name for such beings: *a good fairy as a godmother, misadventures caused by an evil fairy.* A BROWNIE is a good-natured tiny man who appears usually at night to do household tasks: *perhaps the brownies will come and help us tonight.* ELF suggests a young, mischievous or roguish fairy: *that child is a perfect little elf.* SPRITE suggests a fairy of pleasing appearance, older than an elf, to be admired for ease and lightness of movement; it may, however, be impish or even hostile: *a dainty sprite.*

fairy cake, a decorated, individual sponge cake.

fairy godmother, any benefactress, as one who by magic befriended Cinderella.

fairyhood (fēə′rĭ hŏŏd′), *n.* **1.** fairy state or nature. **2.** fairies collectively.

fairyism (fēə′rĭ ĭz′əm), *n.* **1.** fairy-like quality. **2.** belief in fairies.

fairyland (fēə′rĭ lănd′), *n.* **1.** the imaginary realm of the fairies. **2.** any enchanting, beautiful region.

fairy lights, small coloured electric lights or candles, used to illuminate gardens or distributed around a Christmas tree for decoration.

fairy penguin, a small penguin, *Eudyptula minor,* the only one to breed in Australia.

fairy ring, a circle formed on the grass in a field by the growth of certain fungi, formerly supposed to be caused by fairies in their dances.

fairy shrimp, a crustacean of the genus *Chirocephalus,* primitive in the retention on the body segments of unspecialized appendages.

fairytale (fēə′rĭ tāl′), *n.* **1.** a story about fairies. **2.** a statement or account of something imaginary or incredible. **—***adj.* **3.** pertaining to or likely to occur in a fairytale; unreal.

Faisal (fī′səl), *n.* born 1904, king of Saudi Arabia since 1964.

Faisal I, 1885–1933, king of Syria in 1920; king of Iraq 1921–33. Also, **Feisal, Feisul.**

Faisal II, 1935–58, king of Iraq 1953–58.

fait accompli (*Fr.* fĕ tȧ kôɴ plē′), *French.* an accomplished fact; a thing already done.

faith (fāth), *n.* **1.** confidence or trust in a person or thing. **2.** belief which is not based on proof. **3.** belief in the doctrines or teachings of religion. **4.** the doctrines which are or should be believed. **5.** a system of religious belief: *the Christian faith, the Jewish faith.* **6.** the obligation of loyalty or fidelity (to a person, promise, engagement, etc.): *to keep or break faith with.* **7.** the observance of this obligation: *to act in good or bad faith.* **8.** *Theol.* that trust in God and in his promises as made through Christ by which man is justified or saved. **9. in faith,** *Archaic.* in truth; indeed. [ME, t. OF: m. *feit,* g. L *fides*] **—Syn. 5.** doctrine, tenet, creed, dogma, persuasion, religion.

faith cure, faith-healing.

faithful (fāth′fəl), *adj.* **1.** strict or thorough in the performance of duty. **2.** true to one's word, promises, vows, etc. **3.** full of or showing loyalty or fidelity. **4.** that may be relied upon, trusted, or believed. **5.** adhering or true to fact or an original: *a faithful account, a faithful copy.* **6.** *Obs.* full of faith; believing. **—***n.* **7.** the body of loyal members of any party or group. **8. the faithful,** the believers, esp. **a.** the believing members of the Christian Church or of some branch of it. **b.** the adherents of the Muslim faith. **—faith′fully,** *adv.* **—faith′fulness,** *n.*

—Syn. 1. true, devoted, staunch. **3.** FAITHFUL, CONSTANT, LOYAL imply qualities of stability, dependability, and devotion. FAITHFUL implies long-continued and steadfast fidelity to whatever one is bound to by a pledge, duty, or obligation: *a faithful friend.* CONSTANT suggests firmness and steadfastness in attachment: *a constant loyalty.* LOYAL implies unswerving allegiance to a person, organization, cause, or idea: *loyal to one's associates.* **4.** trustworthy, trusty, reliable. **5.** accurate, precise, exact.

faith-healer (fāth′hē′lə), *n.* one who claims to effect healing by religious faith.

faith-healing (fāth′hē′lĭng), *n.* **1.** the practice of attempting to cure disease by prayer and religious faith. **2.** an instance of this.

faithless (fāth′lĭs), *adj.* **1.** not adhering to allegiance, promises, vows, or duty: *a faithless wife or servant.* **2.** that cannot be relied on or trusted: *faithless coward.* **3.** without trust or belief. **4.** without religious faith. **5.** (among Christians) without Christian faith. **—faith′-lessly,** *adv.* **—faith′lessness,** *n.* **—Syn. 1.** false, inconstant, fickle; disloyal, perfidious, treacherous.

Faiyum (fī yōōm′), *n.* El Faiyum.

fake[1] (fāk), *v.,* **faked, faking,** *n., adj. Colloq.* **—***v.t.* **1.** to get up, prepare, or make (something specious, deceptive, or fraudulent). **2.** to conceal the defects of, usually in order to deceive. **3.** to pretend; simulate: *to fake illness.* **—***v.i.* **4.** to fake something; pretend. **5.** *Theat., Jazz.* to improvise. **—***n.* **6.** something faked up; anything made to appear otherwise than it actually is. **7.** one who fakes. **—***adj.* **8.** designed to deceive or cheat. [orig. obscure; ? var. of obs. *feak, feague,* t. D: m. *vegen* furbish up]

fake[2] (fāk), *n., v.,* **faked, faking.** *Naut.* **—***n.* **1.** one of the rings or windings of a coiled cable or hawser. **—***v.t.* **2.** to lay (a rope, cable, etc.) in a coil to prepare it for running. [orig. obscure]

faker (fā′kə), *n. Colloq.* **1.** one who fakes. **2.** *U.S.* a petty swindler. **3.** *U.S.* a pedlar or street vendor.

fakir (fā′kĭə), *n.* **1.** a Muslim or Hindu religious ascetic or mendicant monk. **2.** a member of any Islamic religious order. Also, **fakeer.** [t. Ar.: m. *faqīr* poor]

fa-la (fä lä′), *n.* **1.** a text or refrain in old songs. **2.** a kind of part-song or madrigal of the 16th and 17th centuries. Also, **fal la.**

Falange (făl′ănj; *Sp.* fä län′ĸhĕ), *n.* the Spanish Fascist party founded in 1933 by José Antonio Primo de Rivera and subsequently united by General Franco with other right-wing groups into a single political party. [Sp., t. Gk: m. *phálanx,* the infantry formation of Philip of Macedon, instrumental in the defeat of the Greek democracies]

Falangist (fə lăn′jĭst), *n.* a member of the Falange. **—Falan′gism,** *n.*

falbala (făl′bə lə), *n.* a flounce; a furbelow. [t. F; orig. uncert.]

falcate (făl′kāt), *adj.* hooked; curved like a scythe or sickle; falciform: *a falcate part or organ.* [t. L: m. s. *falcātus,* der. *falx* sickle]

falchion (fôl′chən, -shən), *n.* **1.** a broad, short sword having a convex edge curving sharply to the point. **2.** *Archaic.* any sword. [t. It.: m. *falcione* (der. *falce* sickle, g. L *falx*); r. ME *fauchoun,* t. OF]

falciform (făl′sĭ fôm′), *adj.* sickle-shaped; falcate. [f. s. L *falx* sickle + -(I)FORM]

falcon (fôl′kən, fô′kən), *n.* **1.** any of various diurnal birds of prey of the family *Falconidae*, esp. of the genus *Falco*, as the **peregrine falcon** (*F. peregrinus*), having long, pointed wings and a notched bill, and taking its quarry as it moves. **2.** any of various hawks used in falconry, and trained to hunt other birds and game (properly, the female only, the male being known as a *tercel*). **3.** an old kind of cannon. [t. LL: s. *falco* (der. L *falx* sickle); r. ME *faucon*, t. OF]

Peregrine falcon, *Falco peregrinus* (Length up to 18 in.)

falconer (fôl′kə nə, fô′kə-), *n.* **1.** one who hunts with falcons; one who follows the sport of hawking. **2.** one who breeds and trains hawks for hunting.

falconet[1] (fôl′kə nĕt′, fô′kə-), *n.* any of several very small Asiatic birds of prey principally of the genus *Microhierax*. [f. FALCON + -ET]

falconet[2] (fôl′kə nĕt′, fô′kə-), *n.* an old kind of light cannon. [t. It.: m. *falconetto*, dim. of *falcone* FALCON]

falcon-gentle (fôl′kən jĕn′tl, fô′kən-), *n.* **1.** the female of the peregrine falcon. **2.** any female falcon. [trans. of F *faucon gentil*]

falconiform (făl kō′nĭ fôm′), *adj. Ornith.* of or belonging to the family *Falconidae*, which includes falcons, hawks, etc. [f. FALCON + -(I)FORM]

falconine (făl′kə nīn′), *adj.* of, belonging to, or resembling the family *Falconiformes* or the falcons; falconiform.

falconry (fôl′kən rĭ, fô′-), *n.* **1.** the art of training falcons to attack wild fowl or game. **2.** the sport of hawking.

falderal (făl′də răl′), *n.* **1.** meaningless syllables forming the refrain of various old songs. **2.** mere nonsense. **3.** a trifle; gewgaw. Also, **falderol** (făl′də rŏl′), **folderol.**

faldstool (fôld′sto͞ol′), *n.* **1.** a chair or seat, orig. one capable of being folded, used by a bishop or other prelate when officiating in his own church away from the throne, or in a church not his own. **2.** a movable folding stool or desk at which worshippers kneel during certain acts of devotion. **3.** such a stool placed at the south side of the altar, at which the kings or queens of England kneel at their coronation. **4.** a desk at which the litany is said or sung. [OE *fealdestōl*, c. OHG *faltistuol* folding chair. See FOLD[1], STOOL]

Falernian (fə lûr′nĭ ən), *adj.* of or pertaining to a district in Italy near Capua, famous in Roman times for its wine.

Falieri (*It.* fä lyĕ′rē), *n.* **Marino** (*It.* mä rē′nô), *c.* 1278–1355, doge of Venice in 1354.

Falkenhayn (*Ger.* fäl′kən hīn), *n.* **Erich von** (*Ger.* ĕ′rĭKH fōn), 1861–1922, German general of World War I.

Falkirk (fôl′kûk), *n.* a burgh in central Scotland, in Stirlingshire: site of the defeat of the Scots under Wallace by the English, 1298. 38,043 (1961).

Falkland Islands (fôk′lənd), **1.** a group of about 200 islands in the S Atlantic, ab. 300 mi. E of the Strait of Magellan; the British defeated the Germans in a naval battle near here, 1914. **2.** a British crown colony comprising East Falkland and West Falkland Islands and adjacent small islands; South Georgia Island, and the South Sandwich group. 2132 pop. (1963); 6430 sq. mi. *Cap.:* Stanley. **—Falkland Islander.**

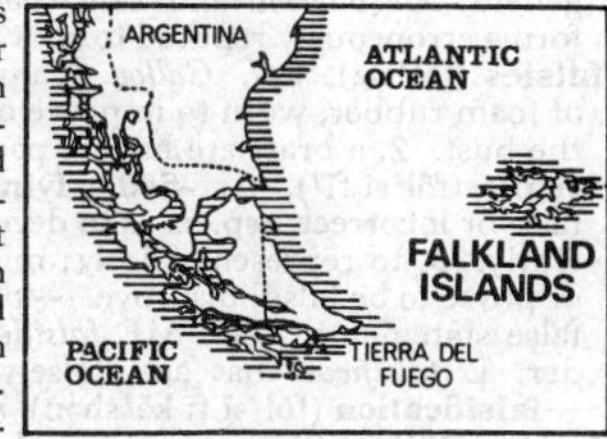

Falkland Islands

Falkland Islands Dependencies, a group of islands in the S Atlantic and Graham Land in Antarctica, all of which formed part of the Falkland Islands colony until March 1962 when the South Shetlands, South Orkneys, and Graham Land were made into a separate colony, British Antarctic Territory.

Falkner (fôk′nə), *n.* **William.** See **Faulkner.**

fall (fôl), *v.*, **fell, fallen, falling,** *n.* **—***v.i.* **1.** to descend from a higher to a lower place or position through loss or lack of support; drop. **2.** to come down suddenly from a standing or erect position: *to fall on one's knees.* **3.** to become less or lower: *the temperature fell ten degrees.* **4.** to hang down; extend downwards: *her hair falls from her shoulders.* **5.** to be cast down, as the eyes. **6.** to succumb to temptation. **7.** to lose high position, dignity, character, etc. **8.** to succumb to attack: *the city fell to the enemy.* **9.** to be overthrown, as a government. **10.** to drop down wounded or dead; be slain: *to fall in battle.* **11.** to pass into some condition or relation: *to fall asleep, in love, into ruin.* **12.** to become: *to fall sick, lame, vacant, due.* **13.** to become pregnant. **14.** to come as if by dropping, as stillness, night, etc. **15.** to come by lot or chance: *their choice fell upon him.* **16.** to come by chance into a particular position: *to fall among thieves.* **17.** to come to pass; occur; happen: *Christmas falls on a Monday this year.* **18.** to have proper place: *the accent falls on the first syllable.* **19.** come by right: *the inheritance fell to the only surviving relative.* **20.** (of speech, etc.) to issue or proceed: *the words that fall from his lips.* **21.** to be naturally divisible (fol. by *into*). **22.** to lose animation, as the face. **23.** to slope, as land. **24.** to be directed, as light, sight, etc., on something. **25.** to come down in fragments, as a building. **—***v.* **26.** Some special verb phrases are:

fall away, 1. to withdraw support or allegiance. **2.** to decline; decay; perish. **3.** to lose flesh; become lean.

fall back, to recede; give way; retreat.

fall back on, 1. *Mil.* to retreat to. **2.** to have recourse to.

fall behind, to slacken in pace or progress; lag: *to fall behind in work, payments, etc.*

fall down, *Colloq.* to fail: *to fall down on the job.*

fall flat, to fail to have a desired effect: *his jokes fell flat.*

fall for, *Colloq.* **1.** to be deceived by. **2.** to fall in love with.

fall foul, 1. to come into collision, as ships; become entangled. **2.** to come into conflict; have trouble. **3.** to make an attack.

fall in, 1. to sink inwards; fall to pieces inwardly. **2.** to take one's proper place in line, as a soldier. **3.** to agree.

fall in with, 1. to meet and become acquainted with. **2.** to agree to.

fall off, 1. to drop off. **2.** to separate or withdraw. **3.** to become estranged; withdraw from allegiance. **4.** to decline in vigour, interest, etc. **5.** to decrease in number, amount, intensity, etc.; diminish. **6.** *Naut.* to deviate from the course to which the head of the ship was directed; fall to leeward.

fall on or **upon, 1.** to assault; attack. **2.** to light upon; chance upon.

fall on one's feet, to emerge from a difficult or adverse situation without serious harm.

fall out, 1. to drop out of one's place in line, as a soldier. **2.** to disagree; quarrel. **3.** to occur; happen; turn out.

fall over oneself, to become confused in attempting to take some action.

fall short, 1. to fail to reach a particular amount, degree, standard, etc. **2.** to prove insufficient; give out.

fall through, to come to naught; fail; miscarry.

fall to, 1. to betake or apply oneself; begin: *to fall to work, argument, blows, etc.* **2.** to begin to eat.

fall under, to be classed as; be included in.

—*n.* **27.** the act of falling, or dropping from a higher to a lower place or position; descent, as of rain, snow, etc. **28.** the quantity that descends. **29.** a becoming less; a lowering; a sinking to a lower level. **30.** the distance through which anything falls. **31.** (*usually pl.*) a cataract or waterfall. **32.** downward slope or declivity. **33.** a falling from an erect position, as to the ground: *to have a bad fall.* **34.** a hanging down. **35.** a succumbing to temptation; lapse into sin. **36.** (*often cap.*) *Theol.* the lapse of mankind into a state of natural or innate sinfulness through the transgression of Adam and Eve: *the fall of man.* **37.** surrender or capture, as of a city. **38.** proper place: *the fall of an accent on a syllable.* **39.** *Wrestling.* **a.** the fact or a method of being thrown on one's back by an opponent and held down with both shoulders on the canvas for a specific period of time, usually a count of three; a pinfall. **b.** a bout, or one of the best of three victories which go to make up a bout: *to try a fall.* **40.** a loosely hanging veil or the like. **41.** *Mach., etc.* the part of the rope of a tackle to which the power is applied in hoisting. **42.** (*pl.*) *Naut.* the apparatus used in lowering or hoisting a ship's boat. **43.** *Hunting.* a deadfall. **44.** *Chiefly U.S.* autumn. [ME *falle(n)*, OE *feallan*, c. G *fallen*]

fal la, fa-la.

Falla (*Sp.* fä′lyä), *n.* **Manuel de** (*Sp.* mä nwĕl′ dĕ), 1876–1946, Spanish composer.

fallacious (fə lā′shəs), *adj.* **1.** deceptive: *fallacious evidence.* **2.** containing a fallacy; logically unsound: *fallacious arguments, etc.* **3.** disappointing; delusive: *a fallacious peace.* **—falla′ciously,** *adv.* **—falla′ciousness,** *n.*

fallacy (făl′ə sĭ), *n., pl.* **-cies. 1.** a deceptive, misleading, or false notion, belief, etc.: *a popular fallacy.* **2.** a misleading or unsound argument. **3.** deceptive, misleading, or false nature. **4.** *Logic.* any of various types of erroneous reasoning that render arguments logically unsound. **5.** *Obs.* deception. [ME *falacye*, t. L: m. *fallācia* deceit; r. ME *fallace*, t. OF]

fallal (făl′lăl′), *n.* **1.** a bit of finery; a showy article of

dress. **2.** a piece of ribbon, worn with streaming ends as an ornament in the 17th century. *—adj.* **3.** *Obs.* finicky; foppish; trifling. [? var. of FALBALA]
fallalery (făl′lăl′ə rĭ), *n.* fallals collectively; finery.
fallen (fô′lən), *v.* **1.** pp. of **fall.** *—adj.* **2.** that has dropped or come down from a higher place or level, or from an upright position. **3.** on the ground; prostrate; down flat. **4.** degraded: *a fallen woman.* **5.** overthrown; destroyed: *a fallen city.* **6.** dead: *fallen in battle.*
faller (fô′lə), *n.* **1.** one who or that which falls. **2.** any of various devices that operate by falling.
fall guy, *U.S. Slang.* an easy victim; scapegoat.
fallible (făl′ĭ bl), *adj.* **1.** liable to be deceived or mistaken; liable to err. **2.** liable to be erroneous or false. [t. ML: m. s. *fallibilis,* der. L *fallere* deceive] **—fal′libil′ity, fal′libleness,** *n.* **—fal′libly,** *adv.*
falling sickness, *Archaic.* epilepsy.
falling star, an incandescent meteor; a shooting star.
fall line, *Geog.* a line denoting the edge of a plateau or highland area where near-parallel rivers descend to a lowland by falls or rapids; it is often marked by a series of industrial centres where waterfalls have been tapped for power.
Fallopian tubes (fə lō′pyən), *Anat., Zool.* the uterine tubes, a pair of slender oviducts leading from the body cavity to the uterus, for transport and fertilization of ova. [named after Gabriello *Fallopio,* 1523–62, Italian anatomist]
fall-out (fôl′out′), *n.* **1.** the descent of airborne particles of dust, soot, or, more particularly, of radioactive materials resulting from a nuclear explosion. **2.** the radioactive particles themselves.
fallow[1] (făl′ō), *adj.* **1.** ploughed and left unseeded for a season or more; uncultivated. *—n.* **2.** land that has lain unseeded for a season or more after ploughing and harrowing. **3.** the method of allowing land to lie for a season or more untilled in order to increase its productivity. *—v.t.* **4.** to make (land) fallow for agricultural purposes. [ME *falwe,* OE *fealga,* pl., fallow land] **—fal′lowness,** *n.*
fallow[2] (făl′ō), *adj.* pale yellow; light brown; dun. [ME *fal(o)we,* OE *fealu,* c. G *fahl, falb* fallow]
fallow deer, a deer, *Dama dama,* of Europe and Asia, with a fallow or yellowish coat.

Fallow deer, *Dama dama* (3 ft high, antlers up to 2½ ft)

Fall River, a seaport in the U.S. in SE Massachusetts, on an arm of Narragansett Bay. 99,942 (1960).
Falmouth (făl′məth), *n.* a fishing port in SW England, in Cornwall. 15,427 (1961).
false (fôls), *adj.,* **falser, falsest,** *adv.* *—adj.* **1.** not true or correct; erroneous: *a false statement or accusation.* **2.** uttering or declaring what is untrue: *false prophets, a false witness.* **3.** deceitful; treacherous; faithless: *a false friend.* **4.** deceptive; used to deceive or mislead: *false weights, to give a false impression.* **5.** not genuine; *a false signature, false diamonds, false teeth.* **6.** substitute or supplementary, esp. temporarily: *false supports for a bridge.* **7.** *Biol.* improperly so called, as from deceptive resemblance to something that properly bears the name: *the false acacia.* **8.** not properly adjusted, as a balance. **9.** inaccurate in pitch, as a musical note. *—adv.* **10. play one false,** to behave disloyally towards a person. [ME and OE *fals,* t. L: s. *falsus* feigned, deceptive, false, orig. pp] **—false′ly,** *adv.* **—false′ness,** *n.*

—Syn. 1. mistaken, incorrect, wrong, untrue. 2. untruthful, lying, mendacious. 3. insincere, hypocritical, disingenuous, disloyal, unfaithful, inconstant, recreant, perfidious, traitorous. 4. misleading, fallacious. 5. artificial, spurious, bogus, forged. FALSE, SHAM, COUNTERFEIT agree in referring to something that is not genuine. FALSE is used mainly of imitations of concrete objects; it often implies an intent to deceive: *false teeth, false hair.* SHAM is rarely used of concrete objects and has nearly always the suggestion of intent to deceive: *sham title, sham tears.* COUNTERFEIT always has the implication of cheating; it is used particularly of spurious imitation of coins, paper money, etc.

false acacia, the locust tree, *Robinia pseudoacacia.*
false alarm, anything that gives rise to unfounded alarm or other expectations.
False Bay, an indentation of the Atlantic Ocean in the Republic of South Africa, in SW Cape Province, E of the Cape of Good Hope. ab. 16 mi. long and 16 mi. wide.
false bottom, a horizontal partition in the lower part of a box, trunk, etc., esp. one forming a secret section.
false brome, any grass of the genus *Brachypodium* as the **slender false brome,** *B. sylvaticum,* widespread in temperate Europe and Asia.
false card, *Bridge.* a card played to deceive an opponent about the nature of one's hand.
false-card (fôls′käd′), *v.i.* *Bridge.* to play a false card.
false cirrus, *Meteorol.* cirrus-like clouds found over thunder clouds.
false cleavers, a rubiaceous annual herb, *Galium spurium,* closely resembling the commoner cleavers, *G. aparine.*
false colours, 1. another nation's flag. **2.** deceptive appearance; pretence.
false dawn, zodiacal light appearing before sunrise.
false face, a mask.
false-hearted (fôls′hä′tĭd), *adj.* having a false or treacherous heart; deceitful; perfidious.
falsehood (fôls′ho͝od′), *n.* **1.** lack of conformity to truth or fact. **2.** something false; an untrue idea, belief, etc. **3.** a false statement; a lie. **4.** the act of lying or making false statements. **5.** *Obs.* deception.

—Syn. 3. FALSEHOOD, FIB, LIE, UNTRUTH refer to something untrue or incorrect. A FALSEHOOD is a statement that distorts or suppresses the truth, in order to deceive: *to tell a falsehood about one's ancestry, in order to escape punishment.* A FIB denotes a trivial falsehood, and is often used to characterize that which is not strictly true: *a polite fib.* A LIE is a more vicious falsehood: *to tell a lie about one's neighbour.* An UNTRUTH is an incorrect statement, either intentionally misleading (less harsh, however, than falsehood or lie) or arising from misunderstanding or ignorance: *I'm afraid you are telling an untruth.* 4. untruthfulness, inveracity, mendacity. **—Ant.** 3. truth.

false horizon, artificial horizon.
false imprisonment, *Law.* the imprisonment of a person contrary to law.
false keel, a narrow extension of the keel, to protect a ship's bottom and reduce the leeway.
false labour, *Med.* painful contractions of the uterus prior to actual labour.
false position, a situation in which a person's motives are liable to be misconstrued.
false pretences, *Law.* the obtaining of money or property by the use of false representations, forged documents, or similar illegal device.
false quantity, *Pros.* (in scansion) a vowel of a length other than that needed for the rhythmic pattern.
false relation, *Music.* the relationship between two clashing semitones occurring in parts simultaneously or in immediate succession, where each note is part of a musically coherent melodic line.
false ribs, *Anat.* the five lower pairs of ribs, which are not attached to the sternum.
false stage, *Theat.* a stage built above the actual stage.
false start, *Athletics, etc.* a start in which one or more competitors cross the starting line, etc., before the signal is given.
false step, 1. a stumble. **2.** an unwise act.
false teeth, a set of removable dentures.
falsetto (fôl sĕt′ō), *n., pl.* **-tos,** *adj., adv.* *—n.* **1.** an unnaturally or artificially high-pitched voice or register, esp. in a man. **2.** one who sings with such a voice. *—adj.* **3.** of, or having the quality and compass of, such a voice. **4.** singing in a falsetto. *—adv.* **5.** in a falsetto: *to speak falsetto.* [t. It., dim. of *falso* FALSE]
false vampire, a bat of either of the two Old World genera, *Megaderma* and *Macroderma,* large carnivorous forms erroneously reputed to suck blood.
falsies (fôl′sĭz), *n.pl.* *Colloq.* **1.** imitation breasts, usually of foam rubber, worn to improve or enlarge the outline of the bust. **2.** a brassiere having padded cups.
falsify (fôl′sĭ fī′), *v.,* **-fied, -fying.** *—v.t.* **1.** to make false or incorrect, esp. so as to deceive. **2.** to alter fraudulently. **3.** to represent falsely; misrepresent. **4.** to show or prove to be false; disprove. *—v.i.* **5.** *Now U.S.* to make false statements. [late ME *falsifie,* t. LL: m. *falsificāre,* der. L *falsificus* that acts falsely] **—fal′sifi′able,** *adj.* **—falsification** (fôl′sĭ fĭ kā′shən), *n.* **—fal′sifi′er,** *n.*
falsity (fôl′sĭ tĭ), *n., pl.* **-ties. 1.** the quality of being false; incorrectness; untruthfulness; treachery. **2.** something false; a falsehood. [t. L: m. s. *falsitas;* r. ME *falste,* t. OF: m. *falsete*]
Falstaff (fôl′stäf′), *n.* the jovial fat knight of brazen assurance and few scruples in Shakespeare's *Henry IV* and *Merry Wives of Windsor.* **—Falstaffian** (fôl stä′fyən), *adj.*
Falster (*Dan.* fäls′dər), *n.* an island in SE Denmark. 46,662 pop. (1960); 198 sq. mi.
faltboat (fält′bōt′), *n.* a folding boat similar to a kayak but more easily carried about. Also, **foldboat.** [t. G: part trans. of *Faltboot*]
falter (fôl′tə), *v.i.* **1.** to hesitate or waver in action, purpose, etc.; give way. **2.** to speak hesitatingly or brokenly. **3.** to become unsteady in movement, as a person, an animal, or the legs, steps, etc.: *with faltering steps.* *—v.t.* **4.** to utter hesitatingly or brokenly. *—n.* **5.** the act of faltering; an unsteadiness of gait, voice, action,

etc. 6. a faltering sound. [ME, ? t. Scand.; cf. Icel. *faltrask*, refl., be cumbered] —**fal′teringly,** *adv.* —**Syn.** **1.** vacillate. **2.** stammer, stutter.

falx (fălks), *n., pl.* **falces** (făl′sēz). *Anat.* a sickle-shaped part or process, as of the dura mater.

F.A.M., Free and Accepted Masons. Also, **F. & A.M.**

Famagusta (făm′ə gōōs′tə), *n.* a seaport on the E coast of Cyprus. 38,000 (est. 1964).

fame (fām), *n., v.,* **famed, faming.** —*n.* **1.** widespread reputation, esp. of a favourable character: *literary fame, to seek fame.* **2.** reputation; common estimation; opinion generally held. —*v.t.* **3.** to spread the fame of; make famous: *a place famed throughout the world.* [ME, t. obs. F, t. L: m. *fāma* report, fame] —**fame′less,** *adj.* —**Syn.** **1.** repute, notoriety, celebrity, renown, eminence, honour, glory. —**Ant.** **1.** obscurity; ignominy.

famed (fāmd), *adj.* famous.

familial (fə mĭl′yəl), *adj.* **1.** of or pertaining to a family. **2.** appearing in individuals by heredity: *a familial disease.*

familiar (fə mĭl′yə), *adj.* **1.** commonly or generally known or seen: *a familiar sight, a sight familiar to us all.* **2.** well-acquainted; thoroughly conversant: *to be familiar with a subject, book, method, tool, etc.* **3.** easy; informal; unceremonious; unconstrained: *to write in a familiar style.* **4.** closely intimate: *a familiar friend, to be on familiar terms.* **5.** unduly intimate; taking liberties; presuming. **6.** domesticated; tame. **7.** *Rare.* of or pertaining to a family or household. —*n.* **8.** a familiar friend or associate. **9.** a familiar spirit. **10.** *Rom. Cath. Ch.* **a.** an officer of the Inquisition, employed to arrest accused or suspected persons. **b.** one who belongs to the household of the pope or of a bishop, rendering domestic though not menial service. [t. L: s. *familiāris* belonging to a household; r. ME *familier*, t. OF] —**famil′iarly,** *adv.*

—**Syn.** **1.** common, well-known, frequent. **4.** close, friendly, fraternal. FAMILIAR, CONFIDENTIAL, INTIMATE suggest a long association between persons. FAMILIAR means well acquainted with another person: *a familiar friend.* CONFIDENTIAL suggests a sense of mutual trust which extends to the sharing of confidences and secrets: *a confidential adviser.* INTIMATE suggests close acquaintance or connection, often based on interest, sympathy, or affection: *intimate and affectionate letters.* **5.** free, forward, intrusive, bold. —**Ant.** **1.** strange. **2.** unacquainted. **5.** well-bred.

familiarity (fə mĭl′ĭ ăr′rĭ tĭ), *n., pl.* **-ties.** **1.** close acquaintance; thorough knowledge of (a thing, subject, etc.). **2.** undue intimacy; freedom of behaviour justified only by the most intimate friendly relations. **3.** (*often pl.*) an instance or manifestation of such freedom, as in action or speech. **4.** absence of formality or ceremony: *to be on terms of familiarity with someone.* —**Syn.** **2.** liberty, disrespect. **4.** informality, unconstraint.

familiarize (fə mĭl′yə rīz′), *v.,* **-rized, -rizing.** —*v.t.* **1.** to make (a person) familiarly acquainted or conversant, as with something. **2.** to make (something) well known; bring into common knowledge or use. **3.** *Rare.* to make familiar; establish (a person) in friendly intimacy. —*v.i.* **4.** *Obs.* to associate in a familiar way. Also, **familiarise.** —**famil′iariza′tion,** *n.*

familiar spirit, a supernatural spirit or demon supposed to attend on or serve a person.

family (făm′ĭ lĭ, făm′lĭ), *n., pl.* **-lies.** **1.** parents and their children, whether dwelling together or not. **2.** one's children collectively. **3.** any group of persons closely related by blood, as parents, children, uncles, aunts, and cousins. **4.** all those persons descended from a common progenitor. **5.** descent, esp. good or noble descent: *young men of family.* **6.** the group of persons who form a household under one head, including parents, children, servants, etc. **7.** the staff, or body of assistants, of an official. **8.** *Biol.* the usual major subdivision of an order or suborder, commonly comprising several genera: as *Equidae* (horses), *Formicidae* (the ants), *Orchidaceae* (the orchids). Names of animal families end in *-idae*, of plant families in *-aceae.* **9.** any group of related things. **10.** (in the classification of languages) a number of languages all of which are more closely related to each other than any of them are to any language outside the group, usually a major grouping admitting of subdivisions: *English is of the Indo-European family.* —*adj.* **11.** of, pertaining to, or used by a family. **12. in the family way,** *Colloq.* pregnant. [ME *familie*, t. L: m. s. *familia* the servants of a household, household, family]

family allowance, (in Britain) a weekly allowance paid for the second and for every subsequent child.

family Bible, a large Bible kept in one family for generations, usually with pages on which are recorded family events, as births, marriages, and deaths.

family circle, the closely related members of a family as a group: *a scandal known only within the family circle.*

family doctor, a general practitioner, esp. considered as the consultant and adviser of a family.

family man, a man who has or wishes to have a family.

family name, **1.** the hereditary surname of a family. **2.** a frequent Christian, or first name, in a family.

family planning, the regulation of the number of children born into a family by the use of contraceptives.

family skeleton, a hidden source of shame to a family.

family tree, a genealogical chart showing the ancestry, descent, and relationship of the members of a family.

famine (făm′ĭn), *n.* **1.** extreme and general scarcity of food. **2.** any extreme and general scarcity. **3.** extreme hunger; starvation. [ME, t. F, der. *faim* hunger, g. L *fames*]

famish (făm′ĭsh), *v.t., v.i. Archaic.* **1.** to suffer, or cause to suffer, extreme hunger; starve. **2.** to starve to death. [f. ME *fame(n)* famish (ult. der. L *fames* hunger) + -ISH²] —**fam′ishment,** *n.*

famished (făm′ĭsht), *adj.* very hungry. —**Syn.** See **hungry.**

famous (fā′məs), *adj.* **1.** celebrated in fame or public report; renowned; well known: *a famous victory.* **2.** *Colloq.* first-rate; excellent. **3.** *Obs.* notorious (in an unfavourable sense). [ME, t. AF, t. L: m. s. *fāmōsus*, der. *fāma* fame] —**fa′mously,** *adv.* —**fa′mousness,** *n.*

—**Syn.** **1.** famed, notable. FAMOUS, CELEBRATED, EMINENT, DISTINGUISHED, ILLUSTRIOUS, refer to someone or something widely and favourably known. FAMOUS is the general word: *a famous lighthouse.* CELEBRATED originally referred to something commemorated, but now usually refers to someone or something widely known for conspicuous merit, services, etc.: *a celebrated writer.* EMINENT implies high standing among one's contemporaries, esp. one's own profession or craft: *an eminent physician.* DISTINGUISHED adds to *eminent* the idea of honours conferred more or less publicly: *a distinguished scientist.* ILLUSTRIOUS is now mainly a literary word, implying glory as well as fame; it is sometimes used sarcastically: *your illustrious ancestor.* —**Ant.** **1.** unknown, obscure.

famulus (făm′yōō ləs), *n., pl.* **-li** (-lī′). *Hist.* a servant or attendant, esp. of a scholar or a magician. [t. L]

fan¹ (făn), *n., v.,* **fanned, fanning.** —*n.* **1.** any device for causing a current of air by the movement of a broad surface or a number of such surfaces. **2.** an object of feathers, leaves, paper, cloth, etc., for causing a cooling current of air. **3.** anything resembling such an implement, as the tail of a bird. **4.** any of various devices consisting essentially of a series of radiating vanes or blades attached to and revolving with a central hublike portion, and used to produce a current of air. **5.** a series of revolving blades supplying air for winnowing or cleaning grain. —*v.t.* **6.** to move or agitate (the air) with, or as with, a fan. **7.** to cause air to blow upon, as from a fan; cool or refresh with, or as with, a fan. **8.** to stir to activity with, or as with, a fan: *fan a flame, emotions, etc.* **9.** (of a breeze, etc.) to blow upon, as if driven by a fan. **10.** to spread out like a fan. **11.** *Agric.* to winnow, esp. by an artificial current of air. —*v.i.* **12.** to spread out like a fan (fol. by *out*). [ME; OE *fann*, t. L: m. s. *vannus* fan for winnowing grain] —**fan′like′,** *adj.*

fan² (făn), *n. Colloq.* an enthusiastic devotee or follower: *a football fan, a film fan.* [short for FANATIC]

Fanagalo (făn′ə gə lō′, fă′nə-), *n.* a Bantu pidgin, widely used in southern Africa. [t. Zulu: lit., like this]

fanatic (fə năt′ĭk), *n.* **1.** a person with an extreme and unreasoning enthusiasm or zeal, esp. in religious matters. —*adj.* **2.** fanatical. [t. L: s. *fānāticus* pertaining to a temple, inspired by a divinity, frantic]

fanatical (fə năt′ĭ kl), *adj.* **1.** actuated or characterized by an extreme, unreasoning enthusiasm or zeal, esp. in religious matters. **2.** pertaining to or characteristic of a fanatic. —**fanat′ically,** *adv.* —**Syn.** **1.** See **intolerant.** **2.** See **radical.**

fanaticism (fə năt′ĭ sĭz′əm), *n.* fanatical character, spirit, or conduct.

fanaticize (fə năt′ĭ sīz′), *v.,* **-cized, -cizing.** —*v.t.* **1.** to make fanatical. —*v.i.* **2.** to act with or show fanaticism. Also, **fanaticise.**

fancied (făn′sĭd), *adj.* **1.** imaginary: *fancied grievances.* **2.** expected to achieve something, as winning a race: *a much-fancied horse.*

fancier (făn′sĭ ə), *n.* **1.** a person having a liking for or interest in something, as some class of animals or plants. **2.** one who breeds and sells birds, dogs, etc. **3.** one who is under the influence of his fancy.

fanciful (făn′sĭ fəl), *adj.* **1.** exhibiting fancy; quaint or odd in appearance: *a fanciful design.* **2.** suggested by fancy; imaginary; unreal. **3.** led by fancy rather than by reason and experience; whimsical: *a fanciful mind.* —**fan′cifully,** *adv.* —**fan′cifulness,** *n.*

fanciless (făn′sĭ lĭs), *adj.* without fancy or imagination.

fan club, a club, usually consisting mainly of young people, having as its purpose the adulation of a well-known personality or group in the entertainment industry.

fancy (făn′sĭ), *n., pl.* **-cies,** *adj.,* **-cier, -ciest,** *v.,* **-cied, -cying,** *interj.* —*n.* **1.** imagination, esp. as exercised in a capricious or desultory manner. **2.** the faculty of creating illustrative or decorative imagery, as in poetical or literary composition, as distinct from the power of producing ideal creations consistent with reality (imagination). **3.** a mental image or conception. **4.** an idea or opinion with little foundation; a hallucination. **5.** a caprice; whim; vagary. **6.** capricious preference; inclination; a liking: *to take a fancy to something.* **7.** critical judgement; taste. **8.** the breeding of animals to develop points of beauty or excellence. **9.** people collectively with a deep and particular interest in something, esp. a sport. **10.** a fancy cake. **11.** *Obs.* love. —*adj.* **12.** adapted to please the taste or fancy; of delicate or refined quality: *fancy goods, fruits, etc.* **13.** ornamental. **14.** imaginative. **15.** depending on fancy or caprice; whimsical; irregular. **16.** bred to develop points of beauty or excellence, as an animal. —*v.t.* **17.** to form a conception of; picture to oneself: *fancy living with him all your life!* **18.** to believe without being sure or certain. **19.** to take a liking to; like. **20.** to place one's hopes or expectations on: *I fancy him for our next M.P.* **21.** to breed to develop a special type of animal. **22. fancy oneself,** *Colloq.* to hold an excessively good opinion of one's own merits. —*interj.* **23.** (an expression of mild surprise). [contr. of FANTASY]

—**Syn. 2.** FANCY, FANTASY, IMAGINATION refer to qualities in literary or other artistic composition. The creations of FANCY are casual, whimsical, and often amusing, being at once less profound and less inspirational than those of imagination: *letting one's fancy play freely on a subject, an impish fancy.* FANTASY now usually suggests an unrestrained or extravagant fancy, bordering on caprice: *the use of fantasy in art brings strange results.* The name and concept of creative IMAGINATION are less than two hundred years old; previously only the *reproductive* aspect had been recognized, hardly to be distinguished from memory. 'Creative imagination' suggests that the memories of sights and experiences may so blend in the mind of the writer or artist as to produce something that has never existed before—often a hitherto unperceived vision of the realities of life: *to use imagination in portraying character and action.*

fancy cake, a small cake, esp. of sponge, with an elaborate topping of icing, etc.

fancy dress, 1. dress chosen in accordance with the wearer's fancy, for wear at a ball or the like, as that characteristic of a particular period or place, class of persons, or historical or fictitious character. **2.** any bizarre or unusual costume.

fancy-dress ball (făn′sĭ drĕs′), a ball at which fancy dress is worn.

fancy-free (făn′sĭ frē′), *adj.* free from any influence, esp. that of love.

fancy man, *Slang.* **1.** a pimp. **2.** a lover.

fancy woman, *Slang.* **1.** a mistress. **2.** a prostitute.

fancywork (făn′sĭ wûrk′), *n.* ornamental needlework.

fandango (făn dăng′gō), *n., pl.* **-gos. 1.** a lively Spanish or Latin-American dance in triple time. **2.** a piece of music for such a dance or with its rhythm. **3.** *Now U.S.* a ball or dance. [t. Sp., from W Ind.]

fan delta, *Phys. Geog.* a partially submerged alluvial fan at the mouth of a river.

fane (fān), *n. Archaic.* **1.** a temple. **2.** a church. [t. L: m. s. *fānum* temple]

Faneuil Hall, a market house and hall in Boston, Massachusetts, called 'the Cradle of Liberty' because it was used as a meeting place by American patriots before and during the War of American Independence.

Fanfani (făn fä′nĭ; *It.* fän fä′nē), *n.* **Amintore** (*It.* ä mēn′tō rĕ), born 1908, Italian statesman: prime minister 1958–63.

fanfare (făn′fēə′), *n.* **1.** a flourish or short air played on trumpets or the like. **2.** an ostentatious flourish or parade. [t. F, der. *fanfarer* blow a fanfare, der. s. *fanfaron* FANFARON]

fanfaron (făn′fə rŏn′), *n.* **1.** a braggart. **2.** a fanfare. [t. F, t. Sp.: m. *fanfarrón*, der. Ar. *farfâr* talkative]

fanfaronade (făn′fə rə näd′), *n.* bragging; bravado; bluster. [t. F: m. *fanfaronnade*, t. Sp.: m. *fanfarronada*, der. *fanfarrón* FANFARON]

fanfold (făn′fōld′), *n.* a pad of invoice forms made up so that each form is followed by carbon and flimsy paper for making copies.

fang (făng), *n.* **1.** one of the long, sharp, hollow or grooved teeth of a snake, by which venom is injected. **2.** a canine tooth. **3.** the root of a tooth. **4.** a doglike tooth. **5.** a pointed tapering part of a thing. **6.** *Mach.* a tang of a tool. **7.** one of the chelicerae of a spider. —*v.t.* **8.** *Obs.* to seize. [ME and OE, c. G *Fang* something caught] —**fanged** (făngd), *adj.* —**fang′less,** *adj.* —**fang′like′,** *adj.*

Head of rattlesnake F, Fang; P, Poison sac; M, Muscle

fangle (făng′gl), *n. Obs.* a fashion: *new fangles of dress.* See **newfangled.**

fanion (făn′yən), *n.* a small flag used to mark surveying stations.

fanlight (făn′līt′), *n.* a fan-shaped or other window above a door or other opening.

fan mail, adulatory letters received by a well-known personality in the entertainment industry.

fanner (făn′ə), *n.* one who or that which fans.

fanning mill, *U.S.* a winnowing machine.

fanny (făn′ĭ), *n., pl.* **-nies.** *Slang.* **1.** the buttocks. **2.** *Taboo.* the female pudenda.

fanon (făn′ən), *n. Eccles.* **1.** a maniple. **2.** a striped scarf-like vestment worn by the pope over the alb when celebrating solemn pontifical mass. [ME, t. F, t. ML: s. *fano*, t. OHG: flag, cloth, c. VANE]

fan palm, any palm with fan-shaped leaves, as the talipot and numerous others.

fantail (făn′tāl′), *n.* **1.** a tail, end, or part shaped like a fan. **2.** a fancy breed of domestic pigeons with a fan-shaped tail. **3.** any of various small birds having fanlike tails, as the Old World flycatchers of the genus *Rhipidura* and the American wood warblers of the genus *Euthlypis.* **4.** an artificially bred variety of goldfish with double anal and caudal fins. **5.** *Archit.* **a.** a member, or piece of a construction, having the shape of a fan. **b.** a substructure of radiating supports, as of an arch. **6.** a gas burner with a fan-shaped jet. **7.** an auxiliary sail on a windmill for turning it into the wind.

fan-tan (făn′tăn′), *n. Cards.* a Chinese gambling game in which a pile of coins or counters is placed under a bowl and bets are made on what the remainder will be after they have been divided by four. [t. Chinese (Mandarin): m. *fan t'an* repeated divisions]

fantasia (făn tā′zyə, făn′tə zīə′), *n.* **1.** *Music.* **a.** a composition in fanciful or irregular rather than strict form or style. **b.** a potpourri of well-known airs arranged with interludes and florid decorations. **2.** a literary work that is not curbed by a fixed plan. [t. It., g. L *phantasia.* See FANTASY]

fantasm (făn′tăz′əm), *n.* phantasm.

fantast (făn′tăst), *n.* a visionary.

fantastic (făn tăs′tĭk), *adj.* **1.** odd, quaint, eccentric, or grotesque in conception, design, character, movement, etc.: *fantastic ornaments.* **2.** fanciful or capricious, as persons or their ideas, actions, etc. **3.** imaginary; groundless; not real: *fantastic fears.* **4.** extravagantly fanciful; irrational: *fantastic reasons.* **5.** incredibly great: *a fantastic sum of money.* **6.** grossly impractical: *a fantastic scheme.* **7.** *Colloq.* very good; fine; wonderful: *a fantastic pop song.* Also, **fantas′tical.** [ME *fantastik*, t. ML: m. s. *fantasticus* imaginary, LL *phantasticus*, t. Gk: m. *phantastikós* able to present (to the mind)] —**fantas′tically,** *adv.* —**fantas′ticalness, fantas′tical′ity.** *n.*

fantasy (făn′tə sĭ, -zĭ), *n., pl.* **-sies. 1.** imagination, esp. when unrestrained. **2.** the forming of grotesque mental images. **3.** a mental image, esp. when grotesque. **4.** *Psychol.* an imaginative sequence fulfilling a psychological need; a daydream. **5.** a hallucination. **6.** a supposition based on no solid foundation; a visionary idea. **7.** caprice; whim. **8.** an ingenious or odd thought, design, or invention. **9.** *Music, Lit.* a fantasia. Also, **phantasy.** [ME *fantasie*, t. OF, t. L: m. *phantasia* idea, fancy, t. Gk: impression, image] —**Syn. 1.** See **fancy.**

Fanti (făn′tĭ), *n., pl.* **Fanti. 1.** a people of Ghana. **2.** a member of this people. **3.** their language, a literary language of W Africa.

fantoccini (făn′tə chē′nĭ), *n.pl.* **1.** puppets operated by concealed wires or strings. **2.** dramatic representations in which they are used. [t. It., pl. of *fantoccino*, dim. of *fantoccio* puppet, der. *fante* boy, g. L *infans* child]

fan tracery, *Archit.* tracery which rises from a capital or a corbel and diverges like the folds of a fan, spreading over the surface of a vault.

fan vaulting, *Archit.* a complicated mode of roofing, in which the vault is covered by ribs and veins of tracery, diverging from a single point.

fanwise (făn′wīz′), *adj.* in the shape of an open fan.

fan-worm (făn′wûm′), *n.* any of several tube-living polychaete worms having feathery gills. Also, **feather-worm.**

F.A.N.Y., First Aid Nursing Yeomanry.

FAO, Food and Agriculture Organization.

far (fä), *adv., adj.,* **further** or (esp. defs 1, 6–8) **farther, furthest** or (esp. defs 1, 6–8) **farthest.** —*adv.* **1.** at or to a great distance; a long way off; to a remote point: *far ahead.* **2.** to or at a remote time, etc.: *to see far into the future.* **3.** to a great degree; very much: *far better, worse,*

different. **4.** at or to a definite distance, point of progress, or degree. **5.** Some special adverb phrases are:
as far as, to the distance, extent, or degree that.
by far, very much.
far and away, very much.
far and near, over great distances.
far and wide, over great distances.
far be it from me, I do not wish or dare.
far gone, 1. in an advanced or extreme state. **2.** *Colloq.* extremely mad. **3.** *Colloq.* extremely drunk.
far out, extremely unconventional.
few and far between, rare; infrequent.
go far, 1. to be successful; do much. **2.** to tend greatly.
how far, to what distance, extent, or degree.
in so far, to such an extent.
so far, 1. up to now. **2.** up to a certain point, extent, etc.
so far so good, no trouble yet.
—*adj.* **6.** at a great distance; remote in place. **7.** extending to a great distance. **8.** more distant of the two: *the far side.* **9.** remote in time, degree, scope, purpose, etc. **10.** greatly different or apart. **11. a far cry,** a great difference. [ME *far, fer,* etc., OE *feor,* c. OHG *fer*; akin to Gk *pérā* further] —**far′ness,** *n.*

farad (fă′rəd), *n. Elect.* the derived SI unit of capacitance, equivalent to one coulomb per volt: a capacitance of one farad requires a charge of one coulomb to raise its potential by one volt. *Symbol.*: F [named after FARADAY]

Faraday (fă′rə dī, -dā′), *n.* **1.** a unit of quantity used in electrolysis, equal to about 96,500 coulombs. **2. Michael,** 1791–1867, English physicist and chemist: discoverer of electromagnetic induction.

Faraday effect, *Physics.* the rotation of the plane of polarization of plane-polarized light on traversing an isotropic, transparent medium placed in a magnetic field which processes a component in the direction of the light ray. Also applies to other electromagnetic radiation.

Faraday's law, *Chem.* either of two laws relating to electrolysis which state that: **1.** the chemical action of an electric current is proportional to the quantity of electricity passing. **2.** the weight of substances liberated or deposited by a given quantity of electricity is proportional to their chemical equivalents.

faradic (fə răd′ĭk), *adj. Elect.* of or pertaining to induction or the phenomena connected with it. [var. of *faradaic,* der. FARADAY]

faradism (fă′rə dĭz′əm), *n.* **1.** induced electricity. **2.** *Med.* its application for therapeutic purposes.

faradize (fă′rə dīz′), *v.t.*, **-dized, -dizing.** *Med., Now Chiefly U.S.* to give faradic stimulation to (a muscle). Also, **faradise.** —**far′adiza′tion,** *n.* —**far′adiz′er,** *n.*

faradmeter (fă′rəd mē′tə), *n. Elect.* an instrument for measuring capacitance.

farand (fă′rənd), *adj.* farrand.

farandole (fă′rən dōl′; *Fr.* fȧ rä̃n dōl′), *n.* **1.** a lively dance, of Provençal origin, in which all the dancers join hands and execute various figures. **2.** the music for this dance. [t. F, t. Pr.: m. *farandoulo,* prob. f. *fa* make + *roundelo* round dance, ult. der. L *rotundus* round]

faraway (fä′rə wā′), *adj.* **1.** distant; remote. **2.** abstracted or dreamy, as a look.

farce (fäs), *n., v.,* **farced, farcing.** —*n.* **1.** a light, humorous play in which the plot depends upon situation rather than character. **2.** that branch of drama which is concerned with this form of composition. **3.** foolish show; mockery; a ridiculous sham. **4.** *Obs.* forcemeat. —*v.t. Obs.* **5.** to season (a speech or composition), as with scraps of wit. **6.** to stuff. [ME *farse(n),* t. F: m. *farcir,* g. L *farcire* stuff]

farcemeat (fäs′mēt′), *n. Cookery.* forcemeat.

farceur (*Fr.* fȧr sœr′), *n. French.* **1.** a writer or player of farces. **2.** a joker or wag. —**farceuse** (*Fr.* fȧr sœz′), *n. fem.*

farci (fä′sē; *Fr.* fȧr sē′), *adj. Cookery.* stuffed. [t. F]

farcical (fä′sĭ kl), *adj.* **1.** pertaining to or of the nature of farce. **2.** resembling farce; ludicrous; absurd. —**far′-cical′ity, far′cicalness,** *n.* —**far′cically,** *adv.*

farcify (fä′sĭ fī′), *v.t.*, **-fied, -fying.** to turn into a farce; make a mockery of.

farcy (fä′sĭ), *n. Vet. Sci.* a form of the disease glanders, chiefly affecting the superficial lymphatics and the skin of horses and mules. [var. of *farcin,* t. F, g. L *farcīminum* disease of horses]

farcy bud, *Vet. Sci.* an ulcerated swelling, produced in farcy. Also, **farcy button.**

fard (fäd), *Obs.* —*n.* **1.** cosmetic paint for the face. —*v.t.* **2.** to paint with fard. **3.** to embellish or gloss over.

fardel (fä′dl), *n. Archaic.* a bundle; a burden. [ME, t. OF, dim. of *farde* pack, t. Ar.: m. *farda* bundle]

fare (fĕə), *n., v.,* **fared, faring.** —*n.* **1.** the price of conveyance or passage. **2.** the person or persons who pay to be conveyed in a vehicle. **3.** food. **4.** *Archaic.* state of things. —*v.i.* **5.** to be entertained, esp. with food and drink. **6.** to experience good or bad fortune, treatment, etc.; get on: *he fared well.* **7.** to go; turn out; happen (used impersonally): *it fared ill with him.* **8.** *Archaic.* to go; travel. [ME *fare(n),* OE *faran,* c. G *fahren*; akin to Gk *perân* pass, *póros* passage] —**far′er,** *n.* —**Syn. 3.** See **food.**

Far East, the countries of E and SE Asia: China, Japan, Korea, Thailand, etc.

Far Eastern Region, former name of **Khabarovsk** (def. 1).

Fareham (fĕə′rəm), *n.* a town in England, in S Hampshire. 58,308 (1961).

fare stage, stage (def. 8).

farewell (fĕə′wĕl′), *interj.* **1.** goodbye; adieu; may you fare well. —*n.* **2.** an expression of good wishes at parting. **3.** leave-taking; departure: *a fond farewell.* —*adj.* **4.** parting; valedictory: *a farewell sermon or performance.* [orig. two words, *fare well.* See FARE, v.]

Farewell (fĕə′wĕl′), *n.* **Cape, 1.** the most southerly tip of Greenland. **2.** the most northerly tip of South Island, New Zealand.

farfel (fä′fəl), *n., pl.* **-fel.** *Jewish Cookery.* small pellets or crumbs of some solid foodstuff such as matzos or noodles. [t. Yiddish, t. MHG: m. *vanelen* noodles]

far-fetched (fä′fĕcht′), *adj.* remotely connected; forced; strained: *a far-fetched example.*

far-flung (fä′flŭng′), *adj.* flung or extending over a great distance: *our far-flung battle line.*

farina (fə rī′nə), *n.* **1.** flour or meal made from cereal grains, cooked as cereal or used in puddings, etc. **2.** starch. **3.** pollen. [t. L, der. *far* spelt]

farinaceous (fă′rĭ nā′shəs), *adj.* **1.** consisting or made of flour or meal, as food. **2.** containing or yielding starch, as seeds. **3.** mealy in appearance or nature.

farinose (fă′rĭ nōs′), *adj.* **1.** yielding farina. **2.** resembling farina. **3.** covered with a mealy powder.

farl (fäl), *n.* a thin cake, orig. quadrant-shaped, of flour or oatmeal. [contracted form of ME *fardel* quarter, repr. OE *fēortha dæl* fourth part]

farm (fäm), *n.* **1.** a tract of land devoted to agriculture. **2.** a farmhouse. **3.** a tract of land or water devoted to some other industry, esp. the raising of livestock, fish, etc.: *a chicken farm, an oyster farm.* **4.** the system, method, or act of collecting revenue by letting out a territory in districts. **5.** *Rare.* a country or district let out for the collection of revenue. **6.** a fixed amount accepted from a person in lieu of taxes or the like which he is authorized to collect. **7.** *Eng. Hist.* **a.** the rent or income from leased property or rights such as lands or revenues. **b.** the state of leased properties or rights; a lease; possession under lease. **8.** *Obs.* a fixed yearly amount payable in the form of rent, taxes, or the like. —*v.t.* **9.** to cultivate (land). **10.** to raise (livestock, fish, etc.) on a farm (def. 3). **11.** to take the proceeds or profits of (a tax, undertaking, etc.) on paying a fixed sum. **12.** to let or lease (taxes, revenues, an enterprise, etc.) to another for a fixed sum or a percentage (often fol. by *out*). **13.** to let or lease the labour or services of (a person) for hire. **14.** to contract for the maintenance of (a person, institution, etc.). —*v.i.* **15.** to cultivate the soil; operate a farm. [ME *ferme,* t. F, der. *fermer* fix, g. L *firmāre*] —**farm′able,** *adj.*

farmer (fä′mə), *n.* **1.** one who farms; one who cultivates land or operates a farm. **2.** one who undertakes some service, as the care of children, at a fixed price. **3.** one who undertakes the collection of taxes, etc., paying a fixed sum for the privilege of retaining them.

farmer-general (fä′mə jĕn′ə rəl, -jĕn′rəl), *n., pl.* **farmers-general.** (in France, under the old monarchy) a member of a company of capitalists that farmed certain taxes. [trans. of F *fermier-général*]

farmers' cooperative, an organization of farmers for marketing their products or buying supplies.

farmery (fä′mə rĭ), *n., pl.* **-ries.** the buildings, yards, etc., of a farm.

farmhand (fäm′hănd′), *n.* a person who works on a farm.

farmhouse (fäm′hous′), *n.* **1.** the chief house on a farm, usually where the owner or tenant lives and from which the farm is managed. **2.** Also, **farmhouse loaf.** a rectangular loaf of white bread.

farming (fä′mĭng), *n.* **1.** the business of operating a farm. **2.** the practice of letting or leasing taxes, revenue, etc., for collection. **3.** the business of collecting taxes. —*adj.* **4.** of, for, or pertaining to farms: *farming skills.*

farmland (fäm′lănd′), *n.* land subject to or suitable for farming.

farmstead (fäm′stĕd′), *n.* a farm with its buildings.

farmyard (fäm′yäd′), *n.* **1.** a yard or enclosure surrounded by or connected with farm buildings. —*adj.* **2.** of, belonging to, or suitable for a farmyard: *farmyard animals.*

Farnborough (fän′bə rə, -brə), *n.* a town in England, in Hampshire: RAF station. 31,011 (1961).

Farnese (*It.* fär nė′sė), *n.* **Alessandro** (*It.* ä lės sän′drō), **Duke of Parma,** 1545–92, Italian general, statesman, and diplomat in the service of Philip II of Spain.

farnesol (fä′nĭ sŏl′), *n. Chem.* an extract, $C_{15}H_{25}OH$, from the flowers of the acacia, cassia oil, etc., used in the perfume industry.

Farnham (fä′nəm), *n.* a town in England, in W Surrey. 26,927 (1961).

Far North, the arctic regions.

Farnworth (fän′wûth′), *n.* a town in England, in S Lancashire. 27,502 (1961).

faro (fēə′rō), *n. Cards.* a gambling game in which the players bet on the cards of the dealer's or banker's pack; common in the U.S. [alter. of PHARAOH]

Faroe Islands (fēə′rō), Faeroes.

Faroese (fēə′rō ēz′), *n., pl.* **-ese.** Faeroese.

far-off (fär′ŏf′), *adj.* distant; remote.

farouche (fə rōōsh′; *Fr.* fä rōōsh′), *adj. French.* **1.** fierce. **2.** unsociable; shy. **3.** sullen. [F, alter. of *farasche*, g. L *forasticus* foreign, der. *foras* outside]

Farouk (fə rōōk′), *n.* 1920–65, king of Egypt from 1936 to his abdication in 1952. Also, **Faruk.**

Farquhar (fä′kwə, -kə), *n.* **George,** 1678–1707, Irish writer of comedies.

farraginous (fə răj′ĭ nəs), *adj.* formed of various materials; confused. [f. s. L *farrāgo* mixed fodder + -OUS]

farrago (fə rä′gō), *n., pl.* **-goes.** a confused mixture; a hotchpotch; a medley: *a farrago of doubts, fears, hopes, wishes.* [t. L: mixed fodder, medley]

farrand (fă′rənd), *adj.* having a specific nature or appearance. Also, **farand.** [ME *farand* comely, orig. ppr. (N d.) of FARE, v.]

far-reaching (fä′rē′chĭng), *adj.* extending far in influence, effect, etc.

farrier (fă′rĭ ə), *n.* **1.** a blacksmith who shoes horses. **2.** a doctor for horses; a veterinary surgeon. **3.** *Mil.* an NCO specially trained in shoeing horses and minor veterinary duties. [t. MF: m. *ferrier*, g. L *ferrārius*, der. *ferrum* iron]

farriery (fă′rĭ ə rĭ), *n., pl.* **-ries.** the art or the establishment of a farrier.

farrow[1] (fă′rō), *n.* **1.** a litter of pigs. —*v.t.* **2.** (of swine) to bring forth (young). —*v.i.* **3.** to produce a litter of pigs. [ME *far*, OE *fearh*; akin to G *Ferkel* piglet, L *porcus*]

farrow[2] (fă′rō), *adj.* (of a cow) not pregnant. [orig. uncert. Cf. Flem. *verwekoe* barren cow]

far-seeing (fä′sē′ĭng), *adj.* **1.** having foresight; sagacious; discerning. **2.** able to see far; far-sighted.

far-sighted (fä′sī′tĭd), *adj.* **1.** seeing to a great distance. **2.** seeing objects at a distance more clearly than those near at hand; long-sighted; hypermetropic. **3.** foreseeing future results wisely: *a far-sighted statesman.* —**far′-sight′edly,** *adv.* —**far′-sight′edness,** *n.*

fart (fät), *Taboo.* —*n.* **1.** an emission of wind from the anus, esp. an audible one. —*v.i.* **2.** to emit wind from the anus. **3.** *Slang.* to behave stupidly or waste time (fol. by *around* or *about*). [ME *ferten*, OE *feortan*, c. OHG *ferzan*]

farther (fä′thə), *compar. of* **far.** —*adv.* **1.** at or to a greater distance. **2.** at or to a more advanced point. **3.** to a greater degree or extent; further. **4.** additionally; further. —*adj.* **5.** more distant or remote. **6.** extending or tending to greater distance. **7.** additional; further. [ME *ferther*; orig. var. of *further*, but now taken as an irreg. formed compar. (prop. *farrer*) of *far*, with superl. *farthest*]

farthermost (fä′thə mōst′), *adj.* most distant or remote; farthest.

farthest (fä′thĭst), *superl. of* **far.** —*adj.* **1.** most distant or remote. **2.** longest. —*adv.* **3.** to or at the greatest distance. [ME *ferthest*, orig. var. of *furthest.* See FARTHER]

farthing (fä′thĭng), *n.* **1.** a former British coin of bronze, worth one quarter of a penny, which ceased to be legal tender from January 1st, 1961. **2.** something of very small value. [ME *ferthing*, OE *fēorthung*, der. *fēortha* fourth]

farthingale (fä′thĭng gāl′), *n.* a kind of hoop skirt or framework for expanding a woman's skirt, worn in the 16th and 17th centuries. [t. MF: m. *verdugale*, t. Sp.: m. *verdugado*, der. *verdugo* shoot, rod]

Farthingale (Elizabethan)

Faruk (fə rōōk′), *n.* Farouk.

Far West, *U.S.* the area of the Rocky Mountains and the Pacific Coast.

F.A.S., free alongside ship (which see). Also, **f.a.s.**

fasces (făs′ēz), *n.pl., sing.* **fascis.** a bundle of rods containing an axe with the blade projecting, borne before Roman magistrates as an emblem of official power, adopted by the Italian Fascist party. [t. L, pl. of *fascis* bundle] —**fascial** (făsh′ĭ əl), *adj.*

Fasces

fascia (*Med.* făsh′ĭ ə; *otherwise* fā′shə), *n., pl.* **fasciae** (făsh′ĭ ē′). **1.** a band or fillet. **2.** the instrument panel of a motor vehicle. **3.** a long band above a shop front, usually bearing the name of the shop, etc. **4.** *Archit.* **a.** a long, flat member or band. **b.** a triple horizontal division of an architrave in Ionic, Corinthian, and composite orders. See diag. under **column.** **5.** *Anat., Zool.* **a.** a band or sheath of connective tissue investing, supporting, or binding together internal organs or parts of the body. **b.** tissue of this kind. **6.** *Chiefly Zool.* a distinctly marked band of colour. [t. L: band] —**fas′cial,** *adj.*

fasciate (făsh′ĭ āt′), *adj.* **1.** bound with a band, fillet, or bandage. **2.** *Bot.* **a.** compressed into a band or bundle. **b.** grown together, as stems. **3.** *Zool.* **a.** composed of bundles. **b.** bound together in a bundle. **c.** marked with a band or bands. Also, **fas′ciat′ed.** [t. L: m. s. *fasciātus*, pp., enveloped with bands]

fasciation (făsh′ĭ ā′shən), *n.* **1.** the act or an instance of binding up. **2.** *Bot.* an abnormality of growth resulting in the fusion of several stems to form a flat plate. **3.** the process of becoming fasciate. **4.** the resulting state.

fascicle (făs′ĭ kl), *n.* **1.** a small bundle. **2.** a part of a printed work; a number of printed or written sheets bound together, as an instalment for convenience in publication. **3.** *Bot.* a close cluster, as of flowers or leaves. **4.** *Anat.* a small bundle of fibres within a nerve or the central nervous system. [t. L: m. s. *fasciculus*, dim. of *fascis* bundle] —**fas′cicled,** *adj.*

fascicular (fə sĭk′yōō lə), *adj.* pertaining to or forming a fascicle; fasciculate.

fasciculate (fə sĭk′yōō lĭt, -lāt′), *adj.* arranged in a fascicle or fascicles. Also, **fascic′ulat′ed.** —**fascic′ulately,** *adv.*

fasciculation (fə sĭk′yōō lā′shən), *n.* **1.** fascicular condition. **2.** spontaneous contractions of a number of muscle fibres supplied by a single motor nerve filament.

fascicule (făs′ĭ kyōōl′), *n.* a fascicle, esp. of a book. [t. L: m. s. *fasciculus* little bundle]

fasciculus (fə sĭk′yōō ləs), *n., pl.* **-li** (-lī′). **1.** a fascicle, as of nerve or muscle fibres. **2.** a fascicle of a book. [t. L: little bundle]

fascinate (făs′ĭ nāt′), *v.t.,* **-nated, -nating. 1.** to attract and hold irresistibly by delightful qualities. **2.** to deprive of the power of resistance or movement, as through terror. **3.** *Obs.* to bewitch. **4.** *Obs.* to cast under a spell by a look. —*v.i.* **5.** to hold the attention. [t. L: m. s. *fascinātus*, pp., enchanted] —**Syn. 1.** bewitch, charm, enchant, entrance, enrapture, captivate, allure, infatuate, enamour. —**Ant. 1.** repel.

fascinating (făs′ĭ nā′tĭng), *adj.* bewitching; captivating; of overwhelming interest: *a fascinating idea.* —**fas′cinat′ingly,** *adv.*

fascination (făs′ĭ nā′shən), *n.* **1.** the act of fascinating. **2.** the state of being fascinated. **3.** fascinating quality; powerful attraction; charm.

fascinator (făs′ĭ nā′tə), *n.* **1.** one who or that which fascinates. **2.** a kind of scarf of crochet work, lace, etc., narrowing towards the ends, worn as a head covering.

fascine (fă sēn′, fə-), *n.* **1.** a faggot. **2.** a long bundle of sticks bound together, used in building earthworks and batteries, in strengthening ramparts, as a protective facing for river banks, etc. [t. F, t. L: m. *fascīna* bundle of sticks]

fascis (făs′ĭs), *n.* sing. of **fasces.**

fascism (făsh′ĭz′əm), *n.* **1.** (*often cap.*) a governmental system with strong centralized power, permitting no opposition or cricitism, controlling all affairs of the nation (industrial, commercial, etc.), emphasizing an aggressive nationalism, and (often) anticommunist. **2.** (*often cap.*) the philosophy, principles, or methods of fascism. **3.** (*cap.*) a fascist movement, esp. the one established in Italy by Mussolini in 1922, whence its influence spread to Germany and elsewhere; dissolved in Italy in 1943. **4.** *Colloq.* (pejoratively) any extreme right-wing ideology, esp. one involving racialism. [t. It.: m. *Fascismo*, der. *fascio* group, bundle, g. s. L *fascis* bundle (of sticks, as lictors' emblem). See FASCES]

fascist (făsh′ĭst), *n.* **1.** anyone who believes in or sympathizes with fascism. **2.** a member of a fascist movement or party, esp. (*cap.*) in Italy. **3.** *Colloq.* a dictatorial person. **4.** *Colloq.* anyone with extreme right-wing views, esp. with regard to race. —*adj.* **5.** of or like fascism or fascists.

Fascisti (fă shĭs′tē; *It.* fä shē′stē), *n.pl. Italian.* Fascists.

fash (făsh), *n., v.t., v.i. Scot.* trouble; worry. [t. F: m. s. *fâcher*]

fashion (făsh′ən), *n.* **1.** a prevailing custom or style of dress, etiquette, procedure, etc.: *the latest fashion in hats.* **2.** conventional usage in dress, manners, etc., esp. of polite society, or conformity to it: *dictates of fashion, out of fashion.* **3.** fashionable people collectively. **4.** manner; way; mode: *in a warlike fashion.* **5.** the make or form of anything. **6.** a kind; sort. **7.** *Obs.* workmanship. **8.** *Obs.* the act or process of making. **9. after** or **in a fashion,** in some manner or other, but not particularly well. —*v.t.* **10.** to give a particular shape or form to; make. **11.** to accommodate; adapt: *doctrines fashioned to the varying hour.* **12.** *Obs.* to contrive; manage. —*adj.* **13.** pertaining to or displaying new fashions in clothes, etc. [ME *facioun*, t. OF: m. *façon*, g. s. L *factio* a doing or making]

—**Syn. 1.** fad, rage, craze. FASHION, STYLE, VOGUE imply popularity or widespread acceptance of manners, customs, dress, etc. FASHION is that which characterizes or distinguishes the habits, manners, dress, etc., of a period or group: *the fashions of the eighteenth century.* STYLE is sometimes the equivalent of FASHION, but also denotes conformance to a prevalent standard: *to be in style, a chair in the Queen Anne style.* VOGUE suggests the temporary popularity of certain fashions: *this year's vogue in popular music.* **5.** shape, cut, pattern. **10.** frame, construct, mould.

fashionable (făsh′nə bl), *adj.* **1.** observant of or conforming to the fashion. **2.** of, characteristic of, or patronized by the world of fashion. —*n.* **3.** a fashionable person. —**fash′ionableness,** *n.* —**fash′ionably,** *adv.*

fashioner (făsh′ə nə), *n.* **1.** one who fashions, forms, or gives shape to anything. **2.** *Obs.* a tailor or modiste.

fashion plate, 1. a pictorial design showing a prevailing or new mode of dress. **2.** *Colloq.* a person who wears the latest style in dress.

Fashoda (fə shō′də), *n.* a town in the SE Sudan, on the White Nile: British and French colonial interests came into conflict here in the 'Fashoda incident', 1898. Now called **Kodok.**

fast[1] (fäst), *adj.* **1.** moving or able to move quickly; quick; swift; rapid: *a fast horse.* **2.** done in comparatively little time: *a fast race, fast work.* **3.** indicating a time in advance of the correct time, as a clock. **4.** adapted to or productive of rapid movement: *a fast track.* **5.** extremely energetic and active, esp. in pursuing pleasure immoderately or without restraint, as a person. **6.** characterized by such energy or pursuit of pleasure, as a mode of life. **7.** resistant: *acid-fast.* **8.** firmly fixed in place; not easily moved; securely attached. **9.** that cannot escape or be extricated. **10.** firmly tied, as a knot. **11.** closed and made secure, as a door. **12.** such as to hold securely: *to lay fast hold on a thing.* **13.** firm in adherence: *fast friends.* **14.** permanent; lasting: *a fast colour.* **15.** deep or sound, as sleep. **16.** deceptive, insincere, inconstant, or unreliable. **17.** *Photog.* permitting very short exposure, as by having a wide shutter opening or high film sensitivity: *a fast lens or film.* **18.** (of the surface of a cricket pitch, racecourse, etc.) hard and dry, and therefore conducive to fast movement. **19. pull a fast one,** *Slang.* to act unfairly or deceitfully. —*adv.* **20.** tightly: *to hold fast.* **21.** soundly: *fast asleep.* **22.** quickly, swiftly, or rapidly. **23.** in quick succession. **24.** in an energetic or dissipated way. **25.** *Archaic.* close; near: *fast by.* **26. play fast and loose with,** to behave in an inconsiderate, inconstant, or irresponsible manner towards. —*n.* **27.** something that fastens, as a rope that holds a ship to its moorings. [ME; OE *fæst*, c. D *vast*, Icel. *fastr* fast, firm] —**Syn. 1, 2.** fleet, speedy. See **quick. 6.** dissipated, dissolute, profligate, immoral. **8.** secure, tight. **13.** loyal, faithful, steadfast. **20.** fixedly, firmly, tenaciously. —**Ant. 1, 2.** slow. **6.** well-behaved. **8.** loose.

fast[2] (fäst), *v.i.* **1.** to abstain from all food. **2.** to eat only sparingly or of certain kinds of food, esp. as a religious observance. —*n.* **3.** a fasting; an abstinence from food, or a limiting of one's food, esp. when voluntary and as a religious observance. **4.** a day or period of fasting. [ME *faste(n)*, OE *fæstan*, c. G *fasten*] —**fast′er,** *n.*

fastback (fäst′băk′), *adj.* **1.** (of the rear of a car) designed to give the best aerodynamic flow; sloping uniformly from the back of the roof to a point above the bumper. —*n.* **2.** the rear of a car so designed. **3.** a car having such features.

fast day, a day on which fasting is observed, esp. such a day appointed by some ecclesiastical or civil authority.

fasten (fä′sən), *v.t.* **1.** to make fast; fix firmly or securely in place or position; attach securely to something else. **2.** to make secure, as an article of dress with buttons, clasps, etc., or a door with a lock, bolt, etc. **3.** to enclose securely, as a person or an animal (fol. by *in*). **4.** to attach by any connecting agency: *to fasten a nickname or a crime upon one.* **5.** to direct (the eyes, thoughts, etc.) intently. —*v.i.* **6.** to become fast, fixed, or firm. **7.** to take firm hold; seize (usually fol. by *on*). **8.** (of the eyes, thoughts, etc.) to be directed intently. [ME *fasten(en)*, *fastne(n)*, OE *fæstnian*, der. *fæst*, adj., FAST] —**fas′tener,** *n.* —**Syn. 2.** attach, connect, link, hook, clasp, clinch, rivet, clamp, secure, bind, tie, tether.

fastening (fäs′nĭng), *n.* something that fastens, as a lock or clasp.

fastidious (făs tĭd′ĭ əs), *adj.* hard to please; excessively critical: *a fastidious taste.* [t. L: m. s. *fastīdiōsus*, der. *fastīdium* loathing, disgust] —**fastid′iously,** *adv.* —**fastid′iousness,** *n.* —**Syn.** See **particular.**

fastigiate (făs tĭj′ĭ ĭt, -āt′), *adj.* **1.** rising to a pointed top. **2.** *Zool.* joined together in a tapering adhering group. **3.** *Bot.* **a.** erect and parallel, as branches. **b.** having such branches. Also, **fastig′iat′ed.** [f. s. L *fastīgium* gable top, summit, slope + -ATE[1]]

fastness (fäst′nĭs), *n.* **1.** a secure or fortified place. **2.** the state of being fixed or firm. **3.** the state of being rapid. **4.** the quality of being energetic or dissipated.

fast neutron, *Physics.* a neutron arising from nuclear fission which has lost little energy by collision and therefore travels through space very rapidly; a neutron with energy in excess of about 0·1 meV.

fast reactor, *Physics.* a nuclear reactor in which most of the fissions are caused by fast neutrons.

fat (făt), *adj.*, **fatter, fattest,** *n., v.*, **fatted, fatting.** —*adj.* **1.** having much flesh other than muscle; fleshy; corpulent; obese. **2.** having much edible flesh; well-fattened: *to kill a fat lamb.* **3.** consisting of, resembling, or containing fat. **4.** abounding in a particular element: *fat pine* (pine rich in resin). **5.** (of paint) having a comparatively high oil content. **6.** fertile, as land. **7.** profitable, as an office. **8.** affording good opportunities: *a fat profit.* **9.** thick; broad; extended. **10.** plentiful. **11.** plentifully supplied. **12.** dull; stupid. **13. a fat chance,** *Slang.* little or no chance. **14. a fat lot,** *Slang.* little or nothing. —*n.* **15.** any of several white or yellowish substances, greasy to the touch, forming the chief part of the adipose tissue of animals and also found in plants. When pure, the fats are odourless, tasteless, and colourless, and may be either solid or liquid. They are insoluble in water or cold alcohol but easily soluble in ether, chloroform, or benzene. They are compound esters of various fatty acids with glycerol, the pure fats being composed of carbon, hydrogen, and oxygen. **16.** animal tissue containing much of this substance. **17.** the richest or best part of anything. **18.** especially profitable or advantageous work. **19.** action or lines in a dramatic part which permit an actor to display his abilities. **20.** *Print.* matter that is easily and profitably composed. **21. chew the fat,** *Slang.* to grumble or bear a grudge. **22. live on one's fat,** to consume reserves; live on capital. **23. the fat is in the fire,** an irrevocable (and often disastrous) step has been taken, resulting in dire consequences. **24. the fat of the land,** great luxury. —*v.t., v.i.* **25.** to make or become fat; fatten. [ME; OE *fætt*, orig. pp., fatted, c. G *Feist*] —**fat′less,** *adj.* —**fat′like′,** *adj.* —**Syn. 1.** corpulent, obese, adipose, chubby, pudgy. See **stout. 3.** oily, greasy. **7.** lucrative, remunerative. —**Ant. 1.** thin. **7.** ill-paying.

fatal (fā′tl), *adj.* **1.** causing death: *a fatal accident.* **2.** causing destruction or ruin: *an action that is fatal to the success of a project.* **3.** decisively important; fateful: *the fatal day finally arrived.* **4.** influencing fate: *the fatal sisters.* **5.** proceeding from or decreed by fate; inevitable. **6.** *Obs.* doomed. **7.** *Obs.* prophetic. [ME, t. L: s. *fātālis* of or belonging to fate] —**fa′talness,** *n.*

—**Syn. 1.** FATAL, DEADLY, MORTAL refer to something which has caused or is capable of causing death. FATAL may refer to either the future or the past; in either case, it emphasizes inevitability and the inescapable—the disastrous, whether death or dire misfortune: *the accident was fatal, such a mistake would be fatal.* DEADLY looks to the future, and suggests that which is likely to cause death (though not inevitably so): *a deadly poison, disease.* MORTAL looks to the past, and refers to death which has actually occurred: *he received a mortal wound, the disease proved to be mortal.*

fatalism (fā′tə lĭz′əm), *n.* **1.** *Philos.* the doctrine that all events are subject to fate or inevitable predetermination. **2.** the acceptance of all things and events as inevitable; submission to fate. —**fa′talist,** *n.* —**fa′talis′tic,** *adj.* —**fa′talis′tically,** *adv.*

fatality (fə tăl′ĭ tĭ), *n., pl.* **-ties. 1.** a disaster resulting in death; a calamity or misfortune. **2.** one who is killed in an accident or disaster. **3.** the quality of causing death or disaster; deadliness; a fatal influence. **4.** predetermined liability to disaster. **5.** the quality of being predetermined by or subject to fate. **6.** the fate or destiny of a person or thing. **7.** a fixed, unalterably predetermined course of things.

fatally (fā′tə lĭ), *adv.* **1.** in a manner leading to death or disaster. **2.** by a decree of fate or destiny; by inevitable predetermination.

Fata Morgana (fä′tə mô gä′nə), **1.** a mirage seen esp. in the Strait of Messina, formerly attributed to fairy agency. **2.** Morgan le Fay. [t. It.: fairy Morgana. See FAY[1]]

fate (fāt), *n.*, *v.*, **fated, fating.** —*n.* **1.** fortune; lot; destiny. **2.** a divine decree or a fixed sentence by which the order of things is prescribed. **3.** that which is inevitably predetermined; destiny. **4.** a prophetic declaration of what must be. **5.** death, destruction, or ruin. —*v.t.* **6.** to predetermine as by the decree of fate; destine (now only in the passive). [ME, t. L: m. s. *fātum* a prophetic declaration, fate, prop. pp. neut., (thing) said]

—**Syn. 1.** FATE, DESTINY, DOOM refer to the idea of a fortune, usually adverse, which is predetermined and inescapable. The three words are frequently interchangeable. FATE stresses the irrationality and impersonal character of events: *it was Napoleon's fate to be exiled.* The word is often lightly used, however: *it was my fate to meet him that very afternoon.* DESTINY emphasizes the idea of an unalterable course of events, and is often used of a propitious fortune: *a man of destiny; it was his destiny, to save his nation.* DOOM esp. applies to the final ending, always unhappy or terrible, brought about by destiny or fate: *he met his doom bravely.*

fated (fā′tĭd), *adj.* **1.** subject to, guided by, or predetermined by fate. **2.** destined. **3.** doomed.

fateful (fāt′fəl), *adj.* **1.** involving momentous consequences; decisively important. **2.** fatal, deadly, or disastrous. **3.** controlled by irresistible destiny. **4.** prophetic; ominous. —**fate′fully,** *adv.* —**fate′fulness,** *n.*

Fates (fāts), *n.pl. Class. Myth.* the three goddesses of destiny. Clotho spins the thread of life, Lachesis measures it, and Atropos severs it.

fathead (făt′hĕd′), *n.* a stupid person. —**fat′head′ed,** *adj.*

fat-hen (făt′hĕn′), *n.* a common chenopodiaceous annual weed, *Chenopodium album*, with dark green mealy leaves, widespread in temperate regions.

father (fä′thə), *n.* **1.** a male parent. **2.** any male ancestor, esp. the founder of a race, family, or line. **3.** *Colloq.* a father-in-law, stepfather, or adoptive father. **4.** one who exercises paternal care over another; a fatherly protector or provider: *a father to the poor.* **5.** a title of respect for an old man. **6.** the oldest or sometimes chief member of a society, profession, etc. **7.** one of the leading men of a city, etc. **8.** a person or thing who originates or establishes something. **9.** (*cap.*) *Theol.* the Supreme Being and Creator; God. **10. the Father,** the first person of the Trinity. **11.** any of the chief early Christian writers, whose works are the main sources for the history, doctrines, and observances of the Church in the early ages. **12.** *Eccles.* **a.** (*often cap.*) a title of reverence, as for Church dignitaries, officers of monasteries, monks, confessors, and priests. **b.** a person bearing this title. **13.** (*pl.*) *Rom. Hist.* conscript fathers. —*v.t.* **14.** to beget. **15.** to originate; be the author of. **16.** to act as a father towards. **17.** to acknowledge oneself the father of. **18.** to assume as one's own; take the responsibility of. **19.** to charge with the begetting of. [ME *fader*, OE *fæder*, c. G *Vater*; akin to L *pater*, Gk *patḗr*]

Father Christmas, Santa Claus.

father confessor, *Eccles.* a confessor.

father-figure (fä′thə fĭg′ə), *n.* **1.** *Psychol.* a man for whom a person feels some or all of the emotions typically felt by a child for its natural father. **2.** *Colloq.* any elderly man of impressive presence.

fatherhood (fä′thə hŏŏd′), *n.* the state of being a father.

father-in-law (fä′thə rĭn lô′), *n.*, *pl.* **fathers-in-law. 1.** the father of one's husband or wife. **2.** *Colloq.* a stepfather.

fatherland (fä′thə lănd′), *n.* **1.** one's native country. **2.** the land of one's ancestors.

father-lasher (fä′thə lăsh′ə), *n.* a short-spined sea-scorpion, *Cottus scorpius*, common on W coasts of the British Isles.

fatherless (fä′thə lĭs), *adj.* **1.** without a living father. **2.** without a known or legally responsible father.

fatherly (fä′thə lĭ), *adj.* **1.** of, like, or befitting a father. —*adv.* **2.** in the manner of a father. —**fa′therliness,** *n.*

—**Syn. 1.** FATHERLY, PATERNAL refer to the relationship of a male parent to his children. FATHERLY has emotional connotations; it always suggests a kind, protective, tender, or forbearing attitude: *fatherly advice.* PATERNAL may suggest a kindly, more proprietary attitude: *paternal interest*; but it may also be used objectively, as a legal and official term: *his paternal grandmother, paternal estate.*

fathom (făth′əm), *n.*, *pl.* **fathoms,** (*esp. collectively*) **fathom,** *v.* —*n.* **1.** a unit of depth equal to 6 ft, used in nautical measurements. **2.** *Mining.* **a.** a depth of 6 ft. **b.** the volume of a 6-ft cube. **3.** a timber measure equal to 216 cu. ft. —*v.t.* **4.** to reach in depth by measurement in fathoms; sound; try the depth of; penetrate to or find the bottom or extent of. **5.** to measure the depth of by sounding. **6.** to penetrate to the bottom of; understand thoroughly. [ME *fathme*, OE *fæthm*, c. G *Faden*; akin to Gk *pétalos* spreading] —**fath′omable,** *adj.* —**fath′omer,** *n.*

fathometer (fə thŏm′ĭ tə), *n.* an instrument for measuring the depth of water; depends on measurement of the time taken for a sound to reach the seabed and for its echo to return.

fathomless (făth′əm lĭs), *adj.* impossible to fathom. —**fath′omlessly,** *adv.*

fatidic (fā tĭd′ĭk, fə-), *adj.* prophetic. Also, **fatid′ical.** [t. L: s. *fātidicus* prophesying]

fatigable (făt′ĭ gə bl), *adj.* easily fatigued or tired.

fatigue (fə tēg′), *n.*, *v.*, **-tigued, -tiguing,** *adj.* —*n.* **1.** weariness from bodily or mental exertion. **2.** a cause of weariness; labour; exertion. **3.** *Physiol.* temporary diminution of the excitability or functioning of organs, tissues, or cells after excessive exertion or stimulation. **4.** *Mech.* the weakening of material subjected to stress, esp. a continued series of stresses. **5.** Also, **fatigue duty.** *Mil.* **a.** labour of a generally non-military kind done by soldiers, such as cleaning up an area, or digging drainage ditches, or raking up leaves. **b.** the state of being engaged in such labour: *on fatigue.* **c.** (*pl.*) fatigue dress. —*v.t.* **6.** to weary with bodily or mental exertion; exhaust the strength of. —*adj.* **7.** of or pertaining to fatigue: *fatigue detail.* [t. F, der. *fatiguer*, t. L: m. *fatīgāre* tire] —**fatigue′less,** *adj.*

fatigued (fə tēgd′), *adj.* wearied. —**Syn.** See **tired**[1].

fatigue dress, a soldier's uniform for fatigue duty.

fatigue life, the number of applications of a given stress which a sample of material will withstand before failing.

fatigue party, a group of soldiers on fatigue.

fatigue test, a test made on a sample of a material to determine the range of alternating stress which it will withstand before failing.

Fatima (făt′ĭ mə, fä′tĭ mə), *n.* **1.** A.D. *c.* 606–632, daughter of Mohammed. **2.** the seventh and last wife of Bluebeard, popularly a symbol for feminine curiosity.

Fátima (făt′ĭ mə), *n.* a village in central Portugal, north of Lisbon: Roman Catholic shrine.

Fatimid (făt′ĭ mĭd), *n.* **1.** caliph of the North African dynasty, 909–1171, claiming descent from Fatima (def. 1) and Ali. **2.** Also, **Fatimite** (făt′ĭ mīt′). any descendant of Fatima and Ali.

fatling (făt′lĭng), *n.* a young animal, as a calf or a lamb, fattened for slaughter. [f. FAT + -LING[1]]

fatly (făt′lĭ), *adv.* **1.** in a fat manner; plumply. **2.** clumsily. **3.** plentifully; richly; profitably.

fat mouse, any of the short-tailed mice of the genus *Steatomys* of southern Africa, eaten by the Africans as a delicacy.

fatness (făt′nĭs), *n.* **1.** condition of being fat. **2.** corpulence. **3.** oiliness. **4.** richness; fertility.

fat-soluble (făt′sŏl′yŏŏ bl), *adj. Chem.* soluble in oils or fats.

fatten (făt′n), *v.t.* **1.** to make fat. **2.** to feed for slaughter. **3.** to enrich; make fertile. **4.** *Poker.* to increase the number of chips in (a pot). —*v.i.* **5.** *Now Chiefly U.S.* to grow fat. —**fat′tener,** *n.*

fattish (făt′ĭsh), *adj.* somewhat fat.

fatty (făt′ĭ), *adj.*, **-tier, -tiest,** *n.* —*adj.* **1.** consisting of, containing, or resembling fat: *fatty tissue.* **2.** *Pathol.* characterized by overproduction or excessive accumulation of fat. —*n.* **3.** *Colloq.* a fat person: *he's a real fatty.* —**fat′tiness,** *n.*

fatty acid, *Chem.* any of a class of aliphatic acids, esp. one such as palmitic, stearic, oleic, etc., present as glycerides in animal and vegetable fats and oils.

fatty degeneration, *Med.* deterioration of the cells of the body accompanied by the formation of fat globules within the diseased cells.

fatty tumour, lipoma.

fatuitous (fə tyŏŏ′ĭ təs), *adj.* characterized by fatuity.

fatuity (fə tyŏŏ′ĭ tĭ), *n.*, *pl.* **-ties. 1.** foolishness; complacent stupidity. **2.** something foolish. [t. L: m. s. *fatuitas*]

fatuous (făt′yŏŏ əs), *adj.* **1.** foolish, esp. in an unconscious, complacent manner; silly. **2.** unreal; illusory. [t. L: m. *fatuus*] —**fat′uously,** *adv.* —**fat′uousness,** *n.* —**Syn. 1.** See **foolish.**

fat-witted (făt′wĭt′ĭd), *adj.* dull; stupid.

faubourg (fō′bŏŏəg; *Fr.* fō bŏŏr′), *n.* a part of a city outside (or once outside) the walls; suburb. [t. F]

faucal (fô′kl), *adj.* **1.** pertaining to the fauces or opening of the throat. **2.** *Phonet.* **a.** (of the explosion of a stop) produced by lowering the velum: the *t* of *button* has faucal explosion if no vowel is pronounced before the *n.* **b.** laryngeal. [f. s. L *fauces* throat + -AL[1]]

fauces (fô′sēz), *n.pl. Anat.* the cavity at the back of the mouth, leading into the pharynx. [t. L] —**faucial** (fô′shəl), *adj.*

faucet (fô′sĭt), *n. Now Chiefly U.S.* any device for controlling the flow of liquid from a pipe or the like by opening or closing an orifice; a tap; a cock. [ME, t. OF: m. *fausset,* der. *fausser* force in, damage, g. L *falsāre* falsify]

faugh (fô), *interj.* (an exclamation of disgust.)

Faulkner (fôk′nə), *n.* **William,** 1897–1962, U.S. novelist, short-story writer, and poet. Also, **Falkner.**

fault (fôlt), *n.* **1.** a defect or imperfection; a flaw; a failing. **2.** an error or mistake. **3.** a misdeed or transgression. **4.** delinquency; culpability; cause for blame. **5.** *Geol., Mining.* a break in the continuity of a body of rock or of a vein, with dislocation along the plane of fracture. **6.** *Elect.* a partial or total local failure, in the insulation or continuity of a conductor, or in the functioning of an electric system. **7.** *Tennis etc.* **a.** a failure to serve the ball legitimately within the prescribed limits. **b.** a ball which when served does not land in the proper section of the opponent's court. **8.** *Show-jumping.* a scoring unit used in recording improper execution of jumps by contestants. **9.** *Hunting.* a break in the line of scent; a losing of the scent. **10.** *Obs.* lack; want. **11. at fault, a.** open to censure; blamable. **b.** puzzled; astray. **c.** (of hounds) unable to pick up a lost scent. **12. in fault,** open to censure; blamable. **13. find fault,** find something wrong; complain. **14. to a fault,** excessively. —*v.i.* **15.** *Geol.* to undergo a fault or faults. **16.** to commit a fault. —*v.t.* **17.** *Geol.* to cause a fault in. **18.** to find fault with, blame, or censure. [ME *faute,* t. OF, g. LL *fallita,* der. L *fallere* deceive]

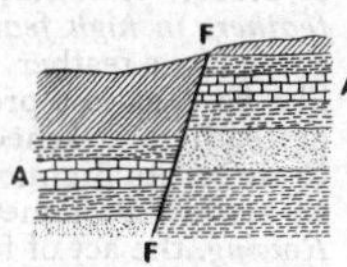

Fault (def. 5) Section of strata displaced by a fault: F, Fault line; A and A, Former continuous mass of rock

—**Syn. 1.** FAULT, FAILING, FOIBLE, WEAKNESS, VICE imply moral shortcomings or imperfections in a person. FAULT is the common word used to refer to any of the average shortcomings of a person; when it is used, condemnation is not necessarily implied: *of his many faults the greatest is vanity.* FOIBLE, FAILING, WEAKNESS all tend to excuse the person referred to. Of these, FOIBLE is the mildest, suggesting a weak point that is slight and often amusing, manifesting itself in eccentricity rather than in wrongdoing: *the foibles of artists.* WEAKNESS suggests that the person in question is unable to control a particular impulse, and gives way to self-indulgence: *a weakness for pretty women.* FAILING is closely akin to FAULT, except that it is particularly applied to humanity at large, suggesting common, often venial, shortcomings: *procrastination and making excuses are common failings.* VICE (which may also apply to a sin in itself, apart from a person: *the vice of gambling*) is the strongest term, and designates a habit that is truly evil and corrupt: *he is unruly, but has few vices.* —**Ant. 1.** virtue, merit.

fault-finder (fôlt′fīn′də), *n.* one who finds fault; one who complains or objects.

fault-finding (fôlt′fīn′dĭng), *n.* **1.** the act of pointing out faults; carping; picking flaws. —*adj.* **2.** given to finding fault; disposed to complain or object.

faultless (fôlt′lĭs), *adj.* without fault or defect; perfect. —**fault′lessly,** *adv.* —**fault′lessness,** *n.*

fault plane, *Geol.* the plane of fracture in a fault.

faulty (fôl′tĭ), *adj.,* **faultier, faultiest. 1.** having faults or defects: *faulty workmanship.* **2.** *Rare.* of the nature of a fault; morally blamable: *whatever is faulty with the Church.* **3.** *Obs.* culpable; at fault. —**fault′ily,** *adv.* —**fault′iness,** *n.* —**Syn. 1.** defective, imperfect, wrong, incomplete. **2.** blameworthy, reprehensible, censurable.

faun (fôn), *n. Rom. Myth.* one of a class of rural deities represented as men with the ears, horns, and tail, and later also the hind legs, of a goat. [ME. See FAUNUS] —**faun′like′,** *adj.*

fauna (fô′nə), *n., pl.* **-nas, -nae. 1.** the animals of a given region or period, taken collectively (as distinguished from the plants or *flora*). **2.** a treatise on the animals of a given region or period. [NL, special use of *Fauna,* name of sister of FAUNUS] —**fau′nal,** *adj.*

Fauntleroy (fônt′lə roi′), *n.* **Little Lord** (*Cedric Errol Fauntleroy*), an overdressed and simperingly virtuous child. [hero of '*Little Lord Fauntleroy*', a novel (1886) by Frances Hodgson Burnett]

Faunus (fô′nəs), *n. Rom. Relig.* a woodland deity, identified with Pan. [t. L]

Faure (*Fr.* fōr), *n.* **François Félix** (*Fr.* fräɴ swȧ fē lēks′), 1841–99, president of the French Third Republic, 1895–99.

Fauré (*Fr.* fō rē′), *n.* **Gabriel Urbain** (*Fr.* gȧ brē ĕl ʏr băɴ′), 1845–1924, French composer and teacher.

Faust (foust), *n.* the chief character in a famous German story; he is represented as selling his soul to the devil for power or knowledge. —**Faust′ian,** *adj.*

faute de mieux (fōt′ də myû′; *Fr.* fōt də myœ′), *French.* for want of anything better.

fauteuil (fō′tû ĭ; *Fr.* fō tœy′), *n. French.* an easy chair.

Fauve (fōv), *n.* **1.** one of a group of French painters from 1905, including Matisse, whose work is concerned with the expressionist possibilities of colour. —*adj.* **2.** of or pertaining to this group or a member of it, or the style. [t. F: lit., wild beast] —**Fauv′ism,** *n.* —**Fauv′ist,** *n., adj.*

fauxbourdon (făb′ə dən), *n. Music.* faburden.

faux pas (fō′pä), *pl.* **faux pas** (fō′päz, -pä). *French.* a false step; a slip in manners; a breach of etiquette.

faveolate (fə vē′ə lāt′), *adj.* honeycombed; alveolate; pitted. [f. s. NL *faveolus* (dim. of L *favus* honeycomb) + -ATE[1]]

favonian (fə vō′nyən), *adj.* **1.** of or pertaining to the west wind. **2.** mild; favourable; propitious. [t. L: s. *favōniānus,* der. *Favōnius* the west wind]

favorite son, *U.S. Politics.* a candidate for national office proposed by a local or state delegation, with local rather than national support: *Iowa's governor stood as a favorite son in the Democratic primaries for the presidency.* Also, *Brit.,* **favourite son.**

favour (fā′və), *n.* **1.** a kind act; something done or granted out of goodwill, rather than from justice or for remuneration: *ask a favour.* **2.** kindness; kind approval. **3.** a state of being approved, or held in regard: *in favour, out of favour.* **4.** excessive kindness; unfair partiality: *show undue favour to someone.* **5.** a gift bestowed as a token of goodwill, kind regard, love, etc. **6.** a ribbon, badge, etc., worn in evidence of goodwill or loyalty. **7.** (*pl.*) consent to sexual intimacy. **8.** *Obs.* a letter, esp. a commercial one. **9. in favour of, a.** in support of; on the side of. **b.** to the advantage of. **c.** (of a cheque, etc.) payable to. —*v.t.* **10.** to regard with favour. **11.** to have a preference for; treat with partiality. **12.** to show favour to; oblige. **13.** to be favourable to; facilitate. **14.** *Now Rare.* to deal with gently: *favour a lame leg.* **15.** to aid or support. **16.** *Chiefly U.S.* to resemble: *he favours his father.* Also, *U.S.,* **favor.** [ME, t. OF, g. L *favor*] —**fa′vourer,** *n.* —**fa′vouringly,** *adv.* —**fa′vourless,** *adj.*

—**Syn. 2.** FAVOUR, GOODWILL imply a kindly regard or friendly disposition shown by an individual or group. FAVOUR may be merely an attitude of mind: *to look with favour on a proposal.* GOODWILL is more active and leads often to outward manifestations of friendly approval: *by frequent applause the audience showed its goodwill towards the speaker.* —**Ant. 2.** animosity, malice.

favourable (fā′və rə bl, -vrə bl), *adj.* **1.** affording aid, advantage, or convenience: *a favourable position.* **2.** manifesting favour; inclined to aid or approve. **3.** (of an answer) granting what is desired. **4.** promising well: *the signs are favourable.* Also, *U.S.,* **favorable.** —**fa′vourableness,** *n.* —**fa′vourably,** *adv.*

favoured (fā′vəd), *adj.* **1.** regarded or treated with favour. **2.** enjoying special advantages. **3.** of specified appearance: *ill-favoured.* Also, *U.S.,* **favored.**

favourite (fā′və rĭt, -vrĭt), *n.* **1.** a person or thing regarded with special favour or preference. **2.** *Sport.* a competitor considered likely to win. **3.** a person treated with special (esp. undue) favour, as by a ruler. —*adj.* **4.** regarded with particular favour or preference: *a favourite child.* Also, *U.S.,* **favorite.** [t. F: m. *favorit,* var. of *favori,* t. It.: m. *favorito,* ult. der. *favore* favour, g. L *favor*]

favouritism (fā′və rĭ tĭz′əm, -vrĭ-), *n.* **1.** the favouring of one person or group over others having equal claims. **2.** the state of being a favourite. Also, *U.S.,* **favoritism.**

Fawkes (fôks), *n.* **Guy,** 1570–1606, English conspirator and leader in the Gunpowder Plot to blow up the Houses of Parliament.

fawn[1] (fôn), *n.* **1.** a young deer. **2.** a buck or doe of the first year. **3.** a fawn colour. —*adj.* **4.** light yellowish brown. —*v.i.* **5.** (of deer) to bring forth young. [ME *foun,* t. OF: m. *faon,* ult. der. L *fētus* offspring, young] —**fawn′like′,** *adj.*

Fawn of Virginia deer, *Odocoileus virginianus*

fawn[2] (fôn), *v.i.* **1.** to seek notice or favour by servile demeanour. **2.** to show fondness by crouching, wagging the tail, licking the hand, etc. (said esp. of dogs). [ME *faghne(n),* OE *fagnian,* var. of *fægnian* rejoice, fawn, der. *fægen* glad, fain] —**fawn′er,** *n.* —**fawn′ingly,** *adv.*

fay[1] (fā), *n.* a fairy. [ME, t. OF: m. *fae, fee,* g. L *fāta* the Fates, pl. of *fātum* FATE]

fay[2] (fā), *v.t., v.i.* to fit, esp. together closely, as timbers in shipbuilding. [ME *feien, fey,* OE *fēgan,* c. G *fügen*]

fay[3] (fā), *n. Archaic.* faith. [ME *fei,* t. OF. See FAITH]

Fayal (*Port.* fə yàl′), *n.* Faial.

fayalite (fā′ə līt′, fī ä′līt), *n.* a black, greenish, or brownish mineral of the olivine group, ferrous orthosilicate, Fe_2SiO_4; iron olivine. [f. FAYAL + -ITE[1]]

faynights (fā′nīts), *interj.* fains.
faze (fāz), *v.t.*, **fazed, fazing.** *U.S. Colloq.* to disturb; discomfit; daunt. [var. of FEEZE]
FBA, Fellow of the British Academy.
FBI, **1.** *U.S.* Federal Bureau of Investigation. **2.** (formerly) Federation of British Industries.
F.C., Football Club.
F.C.A., Fellow of the Institute of Chartered Accountants.
F.C.I.S., Fellow of the Chartered Institute of Secretaries.
F clef, *Music.* a bass clef. See illus. under **clef.**
fcp, foolscap.
fcs, francs.
F.C.W.A., Fellow of the Institute of Cost and Works Accountants.
F.D., Fidei Defensor.
Fe, *Chem.* (L *ferrum*) iron.
feal (fēl), *adj. Archaic.* faithful; loyal. [back-formation from FEALTY]
fealty (fē′əl tĭ), *n., pl.* **-ties. 1.** *Hist.* **a.** fidelity to a lord. **b.** the obligation or the engagement to be faithful to a lord, usually sworn to by the vassal. **2.** *Archaic.* fidelity; faithfulness. [ME *feaute*, t. OF, g. s. L *fidēlitas* fidelity]
fear (fĭə), *n.* **1.** a painful feeling of impending danger, evil, trouble, etc.; the feeling or condition of being afraid. **2.** a specific instance of such a feeling. **3.** anxiety; solicitude. **4.** reverential awe, esp. towards God. **5.** a cause for fear. **6. for fear of,** in order to avoid or prevent. **7. no fear!** *Colloq.* certainly not. **—*v.t.*** **8.** to regard with fear; be afraid of. **9.** to have reverential awe of. **10.** *Archaic.* to be afraid (used reflexively). **11.** *Archaic and Dial.* to frighten. **—*v.i.*** **12.** to have fear; be afraid. [ME *fere*, OE *fǣr* sudden attack, sudden danger, c. OS *fār* ambush; akin to G *Gefahr* danger] **—fear′er,** *n.*

—Syn. 1. apprehension, consternation, dismay, terror, fright, panic. FEAR, ALARM, DREAD all imply a painful emotion experienced when one is confronted by threatening danger or evil. ALARM implies an agitation of the feelings caused by awakening to imminent danger; it names a feeling of fright or panic: *he started up in alarm.* FEAR and DREAD usually refer more to a condition or state than to an event. FEAR is often applied to an attitude towards something which, when experienced, will cause the sensation of fright: *fear of falling.* DREAD suggests an attitude of anticipating something, usually a particular event, which, when experienced, will be disagreeable rather than frightening: *she lives in dread of losing her money.* (The same is often true of FEAR, when used in a negative statement: *she has no fear she'll lose her money.*)

fearful (fĭə′fəl), *adj.* **1.** causing, or apt to cause, fear. **2.** feeling fear, dread, or solicitude: *I am fearful of him doing it,* or *lest he should do it.* **3.** full of awe or reverence. **4.** showing or caused by fear. **5.** *Colloq.* extremely bad, large, etc. **—fear′fully,** *adv.* **—fear′fulness,** *n.*
fearless (fĭə′lĭs), *adj.* without fear; bold. **—fear′lessly,** *adv.* **—fear′lessness,** *n.* **—Syn.** See **brave.**
fearnought (fĭə′nôt′), *n.* a kind of stout woollen cloth. Also, **fearnaught.**
fearsome (fĭə′səm), *adj.* **1.** causing fear. **2.** afraid; timid. **—fear′somely,** *adv.* **—fear′someness,** *n.*
feasible (fē′zə bl), *adj.* **1.** capable of being done, effected, or accomplished: *a feasible plan.* **2.** suitable: *a road feasible for travel.* **3.** likely; probable: *a feasible theory.* [ME *fesable*, t. OF, der. *faire*, g. L *facere* do, make] **—fea′sibil′ity, fea′sibleness,** *n.* **—fea′sibly,** *adv.* **—Syn. 1.** See **possible.**
feast (fēst), *n.* **1.** a periodical celebration, or day or time of celebration, of religious or other character, in commemoration of some event or person, or having some other special significance: *feasts of the Church, the medieval feast of fools, the Chinese feast of lanterns.* **2.** a sumptuous entertainment or meal for many guests. **3.** any rich or abundant meal. **4.** something highly agreeable. **—*v.i.*** **5.** to have, or partake of, a feast; eat sumptuously. **6.** to dwell with gratification or delight, as on a picture. **—*v.t.*** **7.** to provide or entertain with a feast. **8.** to gratify; delight. [ME *feste*, t. OF, g. L *festa*, fem. sing. of *festus* festal] **—feast′er,** *n.* **—feas′ting,** *n.*

—Syn. 2. FEAST, BANQUET imply large social events, with an abundance of food. A FEAST is a meal with a plenteous supply of food and drink for a large company: *to provide a feast for all company employees.* A BANQUET is an elaborate feast for a formal and ceremonious occasion: *the main speaker at a banquet.*

feast-day (fēst′dā′), *n.* a day on which a religious feast is celebrated.
feastful (fēst′fəl), *adj.* festive; joyful.
Feast of Weeks, Pentecost (def. 2).
feat[1] (fēt), *n.* **1.** a noteworthy or extraordinary act or achievement, usually displaying boldness, skill, etc. **2.** an action; deed. [ME *fait*, t. OF, g. L *factum* (thing) done, prop. pp. neut.] **—Syn. 1.** See **achievement.**
feat[2] (fēt), *adj. Archaic.* **1.** apt; skilful; dexterous. **2.** suitable. **3.** neat. [ME *fete*, appar. t. OF: m. *fait*, pp. of *faire*, g. L *facere* do, make]

feather (fĕth′ə), *n.* **1.** one of the epidermal appendages which together constitute the plumage of birds, being typically made up of a hard, tubelike portion (the quill) attached to the body of the bird, which passes into a thinner, stemlike distal portion (the rachis) bearing a series of slender processes (barbs) which unite in a bladelike structure (web) on each side. **2.** plumage. **3.** attire. **4.** condition, as of health, spirits, etc.: *in fine feather, in high feather.* **5.** kind or character. **6.** something like a feather, as a tuft or fringe of hair. **7.** a featherlike flaw, as in a precious stone. **8.** *Archery.* **a.** a feather or feathers attached to the nock (rear) end of an arrow to direct its flight. **b.** the feathered end or string end of an arrow. **9.** something very light, weak, or small. **10.** *Rowing.* the act of feathering. **11. a feather in one's cap,** a mark of distinction; an honour. **12. make the feathers fly,** to cause confusion. **13. show the white feather,** to show cowardice. **—*v.t.*** **14.** to provide with feathers, as an arrow. **15.** to clothe or cover with, or as with, feathers. **16.** *Rowing.* to turn (an oar) after a stroke so that the blade becomes nearly horizontal, and hold it thus as it is moved back into position for the next stroke. **17.** *Aeron.* to stop (an engine) and hold its propeller in a position that offers least wind resistance. **18. feather one's nest,** to provide for or enrich oneself. **—*v.i.*** **19.** to grow feathers. **20.** to be or become feathery in appearance. **21.** to move like feathers. **22.** *Rowing.* to feather an oar. **23.** *Shooting.* to shoot feathers off (a bird) without killing it. [ME and OE *fether*, c. G *Feder*; akin to Gk *pterón* wing] **—feath′erless,** *adj.* **—feath′er-like′,** *adj.*
featherbed (*n., v.* fĕth′ə bĕd′; *v.* also fĕth′ə bĕd′), *n., v.*, **-bedded, -bedding. —*n.*** **1.** a mattress filled with feathers. **2.** luxury; a pampered state generally. **—*v.t.*** **3.** to pamper; shield from hardship. **4.** to subsidize. **5.** to limit the work done in (a factory, industry, etc.) in order to avoid dismissing redundant workers.
featherbone (fĕth′ə bōn′), *n.* a substitute for whalebone, made from the quills of domestic fowls.
featherbrain (fĕth′ə brān′), *n.* an irresponsible or weak-minded person. **—feath′er-brained′,** *adj.*
feather duster, a brush of feathers, used for dusting.
feathered (fĕth′əd), *adj.* **1.** clothed, covered, or provided with feathers. **2.** winged; swift.
feather-edge (fĕth′ər ĕj′), *n.* **1.** an edge which thins out like a feather. **2.** the thinner edge of a wedge-shaped board or plank. **—feath′er-edged′,** *adj.*
feather-grass (fĕth′ə gräs′), *n.* a densely tufted grass, *Stipa pennata*, of Europe and Asia, the dried feathery inflorescences of which are used for ornament.
featherhead (fĕth′ə hĕd′), *n.* **1.** a silly or light-headed person. **2.** a light or empty head. **—feath′er-head′ed,** *adj.*
feathering (fĕth′ə rĭng), *n.* **1.** plumage; a feather-like fringe. **2.** *Music.* a very light and delicate use of the violin bow.
feather-star (fĕth′ə stä′), *n.* a sea-lily or crinoid.
featherstitch (fĕth′ə stĭch′), *n.* **1.** an embroidery stitch producing work in which a succession of branches extend alternately on each side of a central stem. **—*v.t.*** **2.** to ornament by featherstitch.
Featherstone (fĕth′ə stən), *n.* a town in England, in the West Riding of Yorkshire. 14,633 (1961).
feather-veined (fĕth′ə vānd′), *adj. Bot.* (of a leaf) having a series of veins branching from each side of the midrib towards the margin.
featherweight (fĕth′ə wāt′), *n.* **1.** a boxer or other contestant lighter in weight than a lightweight (less than 9 st., and in professional boxing over 8 st. 6 lbs, in amateur boxing over 8 st. 7 lbs. **2.** a very light or insignificant person or thing. **—*adj.*** **3.** belonging to the class of featherweights. **4.** trifling; slight.
feather-weighted (fĕth′ə wā′tĭd), *adj.* (of a racehorse) assigned the least weight by the handicapper.
feather-worm (fĕth′ə wûm′), *n.* a fan worm. Also, **feather-duster worm.**
feathery (fĕth′ə rĭ), *adj.* **1.** clothed or covered with feathers; feathered. **2.** resembling feathers; light; airy; unsubstantial. **—feath′eriness,** *n.*
featly (fēt′lĭ), *adv. Archaic.* **1.** in a feat manner; fitly. **2.** skilfully; nimbly. **3.** neatly; elegantly. [f. FEAT[2] + -LY] **—feat′liness,** *n.*
feature (fē′chə), *n., v.*, **-tured, -turing. —*n.*** **1.** any part of the face, as the nose, chin, etc. **2.** (*pl.*) the face. **3.** the form or cast of the face. **4.** a prominent or conspicuous part or characteristic. **5.** the main film in a cinema programme. **6.** a special article, column, cartoon, etc., in a newspaper or magazine. **7.** a non-fiction radio or television programme designed to entertain and inform. **8.** *Obs. or Archaic.* make, form, or shape. **—*v.t.*** **9.** to be a feature or distinctive mark of. **10.** to make a feature of, or give prominence to: *to feature a story or picture in*

a newspaper. **11.** *Theat.* to present; give prominence to. **12.** to delineate the features of; depict; outline. **13.** *Dial.* to resemble in features. [ME *feture*, t. OF, g. L *factūra* making, formation]

—**Syn. 4.** FEATURE, CHARACTERISTIC, PECULIARITY refer to a distinctive trait of an individual, or of a class. FEATURE suggests an outstanding or marked property which attracts attention: *complete harmony was a feature of the conference.* CHARACTERISTIC means a distinguishing mark or quality (or one of such) always associated in one's mind with a particular person or thing: *defiance is one of his characteristics, arrogance is a characteristic of bad consciences.* PECULIARITY means that distinct or unusual characteristic which marks off an individual in the class to which he (or it) belongs: (among flowers) *the arrangement of the petals is a peculiarity of pansies.*

featured (fē′chəd), *adj.* **1.** made a feature of; given prominence; presented. **2.** having features, or a certain cast of features. **3.** *Obs.* formed; fashioned.

featureless (fē′chə lĭs), *adj.* without distinctive features; uninteresting.

feature story, *Journalism.* a story printed for reasons other than its news value.

feaze[1] (fēz), *v.t.*, *v.i.*, **feazed, feazing.** *Obs.* to unravel. [t. LG: m. *fāsen.* Cf. OE *fæs* fringe]

feaze[2] (fēz, fāz), *n.*, *v.i.*, *v.t.*, **feazed, feazing.** feeze.

Feb., February.

febri-, a word element meaning 'fever', as in *febrifuge.* [t. L, comb. form of *febris*]

febricity (fĭ brĭs′ĭ tĭ), *n.* feverishness.

febricula (fĭ brĭk′yŏŏ lə), *n.* a slight and short fever, especially when of obscure causation. [t. L, dim. of *febris* fever]

febrifacient (fĕb′rĭ fā′shənt), *adj.* **1.** producing fever. —*n.* **2.** something that produces fever.

febriferous (fĭ brĭf′ə rəs), *adj.* **1.** producing fever. **2.** carrying fever.

febrific (fĭ brĭf′ĭk), *adj.* producing or marked by fever. [f. FEBRI- + -FIC]

febrifugal (fĭ brĭf′yŏŏ gl, fĕb′rĭ fyōō′gl), *adj.* of or like a febrifuge.

febrifuge (fĕb′rĭ fyōōj′), *adj.* **1.** serving to dispel or reduce fever, as a medicine; antifebrile. —*n.* **2.** a febrifuge medicine or agent. **3.** a cooling drink. [t. F, t. L: m. s. *febrifugia*, f. *febri-* FEBRI- + *-fugia* -FUGE]

febrile (fē′brīl), *adj.* pertaining to or marked by fever; feverish. [t. L: m. s. *febrīlis* pertaining to fever]

February (fĕb′rōō ə rĭ), *n.* the second month of the year, containing ordinarily 28 days, in leap years 29. [t. L: m. s. *Februārius*, der. *februa*, pl., the Roman festival of purification, celebrated Feb. 15th; r. ME *feverer*, t. OF, and OE *Februarius*, t. L]

fec., fecit.

feces (fē′sēz), *n.pl. Chiefly U.S.* faeces. —**fecal** (fē′kl), *adj.*

Fechner (*Ger.* fĕKH′nər), *n.* **Gustav Theodor** (*Ger.* gōōs′täf tē′ō dōr), 1801–87, German physicist, psychologist, and philosopher.

fecit (fā′kĭt), *v. Latin.* he (or she) made (it, as a work of art).

feck (fĕk), *n. Scot. and N Dial.* **1.** effect; efficacy; value. **2.** amount. [var. of *fect*, aphetic var. of EFFECT]

feckless (fĕk′lĭs), *adj. Orig. Scot. and N Dial.* **1.** ineffective; feeble. **2.** spiritless; worthless. —**feck′lessly,** *adv.* —**feck′lessness,** *n.*

fecula (fĕk′yŏŏ lə), *n.*, *pl.* **-lae** (-lē′). starch obtained by washing the comminuted roots, grains, or other parts of plants. [t. L: m. *faecula* crust of wine, dim. of *faex* dregs]

feculent (fĕk′yŏŏ lənt), *adj.* abounding in dregs or foul matter; turbid; muddy; foul. [t. L: s. *faeculentus* abounding in dregs, impure] —**fec′ulence,** *n.*

fecund (fē′kənd, fĕk′ənd), *adj.* capable of producing offspring, or fruit, vegetation, etc., in abundance; prolific; fruitful; productive. [t. L: s. *fēcundus* fruitful; r. ME *fecounde*, t. OF: m. *fecond*]

fecundate (fē′kən dāt′, fĕk′ən-), *v.t.*, **-dated, -dating.** **1.** to make prolific or fruitful. **2.** *Biol.* to impregnate. [t. L: m. s. *fēcundātus*, pp., made fruitful] —**fe′cunda′tion,** *n.*

fecundity (fĭ kŭn′dĭ tĭ), *n.* **1.** the quality of being fecund; the capacity, esp. in female animals, of producing young in great numbers. **2.** fruitfulness or fertility, as of the earth. **3.** capacity of abundant production: *fecundity of imagination.*

fed (fĕd), *v.* pt. and pp. of **feed.**

Fed., Federal.

federacy (fĕd′ə rə sĭ), *n.* a confederacy.

federal (fĕd′ə rəl), *adj.* **1.** of or pertaining to a compact or a league, esp. a league between nations or states. **2. a.** pertaining to or of the nature of a union of states under a central government distinct from the individual governments of the separate states: *the federal government of the U.S.* **b.** favouring a strong central government in such a union. **c.** pertaining to such a central government: *federal offices.* **3.** (*cap.*) *U.S. Hist.* **a.** noting or pertaining to a party in early U.S. history advocating a strong central government. **b.** (in the Civil War) pertaining to or supporting the Union government. **c.** relating to, or adhering to, the support of the Constitution. —*n.* **4.** an advocate of federation or federalism. **5.** (*cap.*) *U.S. Hist.* **a.** a Federalist. **b.** an adherent of the Union government during the Civil War; a Unionist. **c.** a soldier in the Federal army. [earlier *foederal*, f. s. L *foedus* compact, league (akin to *fides* faith) + -AL[1]] —**fed′erally,** *adv.*

Federal Bureau of Investigation, a U.S. federal agency charged with investigations for the attorney general of the U.S. and safeguarding national security. *Abbrev.*: FBI.

Federal Capital Territory, former name of **Australian Capital Territory.**

federal district, a district in which the national government of a country is situated, esp. one in Latin America.

federalism (fĕd′ə rə lĭz′əm), *n.* **1.** the federal principle of government. **2.** (*cap.*) *U.S. Hist.* the principles of the Federalist Party.

federalist (fĕd′ə rə lĭst), *n.* **1.** an advocate of federalism. **2.** (*cap.*) *U.S. Hist.* a member or supporter of the Federalist Party. —*adj.* **3.** Also, **fed′eralis′tic.** of Federalism or the Federalists.

Federalist Party, *U.S. Hist.* **1.** a political group that favoured the adoption by the states of the Constitution (1787–89). **2.** a political party in early U.S. history advocating a strong central government. Also, **Federal Party.**

federalize (fĕd′ə rə līz′), *v.t.*, **-lized, -lizing.** to make federal; unite in a federal union, as different states. Also, **federalise.** —**fed′eraliza′tion,** *n.*

Federal Republic of Germany. Official name of **West Germany.**

Federal Reserve System, a system of banks (**Federal Reserve Banks**) in the U.S., forming 12 districts under the control of a central board of governors (**Federal Reserve Board**) and 12 central banks, which regulate the making of loans, the amount of reserves, etc., of member banks, and, in general, attempt to adjust banking practices to the needs of the nation's industry and agriculture; similar in function to the Bank of England.

federal theology, a theological system based on the idea of two covenants between God and man—of Works and of Grace. Also, **covenant theology.**

federate (*v.* fĕd′ə rāt′; *adj.* fĕd′ə rĭt), *v.*, **-rated, -rating,** *adj.* —*v.t.*, *v.i.* **1.** to unite in a league or federation. **2.** to organize on a federal basis. —*adj.* **3.** federate; allied: *federate nations.* [t. L: m. s. *foederātus*, pp., leagued together]

Federated Malay States, a former federation of four native states in Malaya. See **Malaya.**

federation (fĕd′ə rā′shən), *n.* **1.** the act of federating, or uniting in a league. **2.** the formation of a political unity, with a central government, out of a number of separate states, etc., each of which retains control of its own internal affairs. **3.** a league or confederacy. **4.** a federated body formed by a number of states, societies, etc., each retaining control of its own internal affairs.

Federation of Malaysia. See **Malaysia.**

Federation of Rhodesia and Nyasaland. See **Rhodesia and Nyasaland, Federation of.**

Federation of South Arabia. See **South Arabia, Federation of.**

Federation of the West Indies. See **West Indies, Federation of.**

federative (fĕd′ə rə tĭv), *adj.* **1.** pertaining to or of the nature of a federation. **2.** inclined to federate. —**fed′eratively,** *adv.*

fedora (fĭ dô′rə), *n. U.S.* a trilby. [said to be from '*Fédora*', drama by Sardou]

fee (fē), *n.*, *v.*, **feed, feeing.** —*n.* **1.** a payment for services: *a doctor's fee.* **2.** a sum paid for a privilege: *an admission fee.* **3.** a charge allowed by law for the service of a public officer. **4.** *Obs.* a gratuity; tip. **5.** *Law.* **a.** an estate of inheritance in land, either absolute and without limitation to any particular class of heirs (**fee simple**) or limited to a particular class of heirs (**fee tail**). **b.** an estate in land held of a feudal lord on condition of the performing of certain services. **c.** a territory held in fee. **6. hold in fee, a.** to have full ownership in (land, etc.). **b.** *Poetic.* to have absolute mastery over: *Once did she hold the gorgeous East in fee.* —*v.t.* **7.** to give a fee to. **8.** *Chiefly Scot.* to hire; employ. [ME, t. AF; of Gmc orig.] —**fee′less,** *adj.*

feeble (fē′bl), *adj.*, **-bler, -blest.** **1.** physically weak, as from age, sickness, etc. **2.** weak intellectually or morally: *a feeble mind.* **3.** lacking in volume, loudness, brightness, distinctness, etc.: *a feeble voice, light.* **4.** lacking in force, strength, or effectiveness: *feeble resistance, arguments, barriers.* [ME *feble*, t. OF, g. L *flēbilis* lamentable] —**fee′bleness,** *n.* —**fee′blish,** *adj.* —**fee′bly,** *adv.* —**Syn. 1.** infirm, frail, sickly. See **weak.**

feeble-minded (fē′bl mīn′dĭd), *adj.* **1.** feeble in intellect; lacking the normal mental powers, generally with an IQ between 50 and 70. **2.** lacking firmness of mind. —**fee′ble-mind′edness,** *n.*

feed (fēd), *v.*, **fed, feeding,** *n.* —*v.t.* **1.** to give food to; supply with nourishment. **2.** to provide with the requisite materials for development, maintenance, or operation. **3.** to yield, or serve as, food for. **4.** to provide as food. **5.** to furnish for consumption. **6.** to satisfy; minister to; gratify. **7.** to supply for maintenance or to be operated upon, as to a machine. **8.** to use (land) as pasture. **9.** *Colloq.* to provide cues to (an actor, esp. a comedian). **10. be fed up,** *Colloq.* to have had more than enough of something. —*v.i.* **11.** to take food; eat; graze. **12.** to be nourished or gratified; subsist. —*n.* **13.** food, esp. for babies or cattle, etc. **14.** an allowance of such food. **15.** *Colloq.* a meal. **16.** an act of feeding. **17.** the act or process of feeding a furnace, machine, etc. **18.** the material, or the amount of it, so fed or supplied. **19.** a feeding mechanism. **20.** the rate of advance of a cutting mechanism, as a drill or cutting tool. **21.** *Theat. Colloq.* a cue to an actor, esp. a comedian. [ME *fede(n)*, OE *fēdan*, akin to OE *fōda* FOOD]

—**Syn. 13.** FEED, FODDER, FORAGE, PROVENDER mean food for animals. FEED is the general word: *pig feed, chickenfeed.* FODDER is esp. applied to dry or green feed, as opposed to pasturage, fed to horses, cattle, etc.: *fodder for winter feeding.* FORAGE is food which an animal obtains (usually grass, leaves, etc.) by searching about for it: *lost cattle can usually live on forage.* PROVENDER denotes dry feed, such as hay, oats, or corn.

feedback (fēd′băk′), *n.* **1.** the returning of a part of the output of any system, esp. a mechanical or biological one, as input, esp. for correction or control purposes. **2.** *Electronics.* the return of part of the energy of the anode circuit of a radio valve to the grid circuit, either to oppose the input (**negative feedback**) or to reinforce it (**positive feedback**). **3.** *Radio.* the input of a signal into a microphone from the output of the same system, usually causing a high-pitched screech. —*adj.* **4.** of, involving, or denoting a feedback.

feeder (fē′də), *n.* **1.** one who or that which supplies food or feeds something. **2.** one who or that which takes food or nourishment. **3.** a person or device that feeds a machine, printing press, etc. **4.** a tributary stream, a secondary road, a branch of a railway or airline system, etc. **5.** *Elect.* a conductor, or group of conductors, connecting primary equipment in an electric power system. **6.** *Chiefly U.S.* a bib (def. 1).

feedpipe (fēd′pīp′), *n.* a pipe for supplying material, as fuel, to machines.

feedwater (fēd′wô′tə), *n.* water which has been treated to remove impurities, for feeding to a boiler to be converted into steam.

feel (fēl), *v.*, **felt, feeling,** *n.* —*v.t.* **1.** to perceive or examine by touch. **2.** to have a sensation (other than sight, hearing, taste, and smell) of. **3.** to find or pursue (one's way) by touching, groping, or cautious moves. **4.** to be or become conscious of. **5.** to be emotionally affected by: *to feel one's disgrace keenly.* **6.** to experience the effects of: *the whole region felt the storm.* **7.** to have a particular sensation or impression of (fol. by an adjunct or complement): *to feel oneself slighted.* **8.** to have a general or thorough conviction of. —*v.i.* **9.** to have perception by touch or by any nerves of sensation other than those of sight, hearing, taste, and smell. **10.** to make examination by touch; grope. **11.** to have mental sensations or emotions. **12.** to be consciously, in emotion, opinion, etc.: *to feel happy, angry, sure.* **13.** to have sympathy or compassion (fol. by *with* or *for*). **14.** to have a sensation of being: *to feel warm, free.* **15.** to seem in the impression produced: *how does it feel to be rich?* **16. feel like,** to have a desire or inclination for. **17. to feel oneself,** to be in one's usual mental or physical state. **18. feel up to,** *Colloq.* to be well enough to be capable of; to be able to cope with. —*n.* **19.** a quality of an object that is perceived by feeling or touching: *a soapy feel.* **20.** an act of feeling. **21.** a sensation of something felt; a vague mental impression or feeling. **22.** the sense of touch: *soft to the feel.* [ME *fele(n)*, OE *fēlan*, c. G *fühlen*]

feeler (fē′lə), *n.* **1.** one who or that which feels. **2.** a proposal, remark, hint, etc., designed to bring out the opinions or purposes of others. **3.** *Zool.* an organ of touch, as an antenna or a tentacle. **4.** (*pl.*) feeler gauge.

feeler gauge, a gauge consisting of thin strips of steel of known thickness fixed like penknife blades; used for measuring small distances, as the gap in a sparking plug. Also, **fee′lers.**

feeling (fē′lĭng), *n.* **1.** the function or the power of perceiving by touch; physical sensation not connected with sight, hearing, taste, or smell. **2.** a particular sensation of this kind: *a feeling of warmth, pain, or drowsiness.* **3.** *Psychol.* consciousness itself without regard to thought or a perceived object, as excitement–calm, strain–relaxation. **4.** a consciousness or impression: *a feeling of inferiority.* **5.** an intuition or premonition: *a feeling that something is going to happen.* **6.** an emotion: *a feeling of joy, sorrow, fear.* **7.** capacity for emotion; pity. **8.** a sentiment; opinion: *to have a feeling that something will succeed, the general feeling was in favour of the proposal.* **9.** Also, **bad feeling, ill feeling.** bitterness; collective or mutual hostility or ill will: *there is a certain amount of feeling between them; there was bad feeling over his promotion.* **10.** (*pl.*) sensibilities; susceptibilities: *to hurt one's feelings.* **11.** fine emotional endowment. **12.** *Music, etc.* **a.** emotional or sympathetic perception revealed by an artist in his work. **b.** the general impression conveyed by a work. **c.** sympathetic appreciation, as of music. —*adj.* **13.** that feels; sentient; sensitive, as nerves. **14.** accessible to emotion; sympathetic: *a feeling heart.* **15.** indicating emotion: *a feeling retort.* —**feel′ingly,** *adv.*

—**Syn. 6.** FEELING, EMOTION, PASSION, SENTIMENT refer to pleasurable or painful sensations experienced when one is stirred to sympathy, anger, fear, love, grief, etc. FEELING is a general term for a subjective point of view as well as for specific sensations: *to be guided by feeling rather than by facts, a feeling of sadness, of rejoicing.* EMOTION is applied to an intensified feeling: *agitated by emotion.* PASSION is strong or violent emotion, often so overpowering that it masters the mind or judgement: *stirred to a passion of anger.* SENTIMENT is a mixture of thought and feeling, esp. refined or tender feeling: *recollections are often coloured by sentiment.*

fee simple. See **fee** (def. 5a).

feet (fēt), *n.* pl. of **foot.** —**feet′less,** *adj.*

fee tail. See **fee** (def. 5a).

feeze (fēz, fāz), *n.*, *v.*, **feezed, feezing.** *Obs. or Dial.* —*n.* **1.** a rush; a violent impact. **2.** *U.S.* a state of vexation or worry. —*v.i.* **3.** to fret; worry. —*v.t.* **4.** to disturb. **5.** to beat; flog. Also, **feaze.** [ME *fese(n)*, OE *fēs(i)an* drive, c. Sw. *fösa*]

Fehling's solution (fā′lĭngz), *Chem.* a solution of copper sulphate and Rochelle salt in alkali, which is used for the detection and quantitative estimation of sugars and other reducing agents. [named after Hermann *Fehling*, 1812–85, German chemist]

feign (fān), *v.t.* **1.** to invent fictitiously or deceptively, as a story or an excuse. **2.** to represent fictitiously; put on an appearance of: *to feign sickness.* **3.** to imitate deceptively: *to feign another's voice.* —*v.i.* **4.** to make believe; pretend: *she feigns to be ill.* [ME *feigne(n)*, t. OF: m. *feign-*, s. *feindre*, g. L *fingere* form, conceive, devise] —**feign′er,** *n.* —**feign′ingly,** *adv.* —**Syn. 4.** See **pretend.**

feigned (fānd), *adj.* **1.** pretended; sham; counterfeit. **2.** assumed, as a name. **3.** disguised, as a voice. **4.** fictitiously invented. —**feignedly** (fā′nĭd lĭ), *adv.*

feint[1] (fānt), *n.* **1.** a movement made with the object of deceiving an adversary; appearance of aiming at one part or point when another is the real object of attack. **2.** a feigned or assumed appearance. —*v.i.* **3.** to make a feint. [t. F: m. *feinte*, der. *feindre* FEIGN]

feint[2] (fānt), *Print.* —*n.* **1.** the lightest weight of line used in printing ruled paper. —*adj.*, *adv.* **2.** (ruled) with a line of such weight. [var. of FAINT]

feints (fānts), *n.pl.* the impure spirit which comes over first and last in distilling whisky, etc.

Feisal (fī′səl), *n.* Faisal. Also, **Feisul.**

feist (fīst), *n.* *U.S. Dial.* a small dog.

feisty (fī′stĭ), *adj.* *U.S. Colloq.* snappy; irritable.

feldspar (fĕld′spä′, fĕl′-), *n.* felspar.

felicific (fē′lĭ sĭf′ĭk), *adj.* making happy; productive of happiness. [t. L: s. *fēlīcificus* making happy]

felicitate (fĭ lĭs′ĭ tāt′), *v.*, **-tated, -tating,** *adj.* —*v.t.* **1.** to compliment upon a happy event; congratulate: *to felicitate a friend on his good fortune.* **2.** *Archaic.* to make happy. —*adj.* **3.** *Obs.* made happy. [t. LL: m. s. *fēlīcitātus*, pp. of *fēlīcitāre* make happy, der. L *fēlix* happy] —**felic′ita′tor,** *n.*

felicitation (fĭ lĭs′ĭ tā′shən), *n.* expression of good wishes; congratulation.

felicitous (fĭ lĭs′ĭ təs), *adj.* **1.** apt or appropriate, as action, manner, or expression. **2.** apt in manner or expression, as a person. —**felic′itously,** *adv.* —**felic′itousness,** *n.*

felicity (fĭ lĭs′ĭ tĭ), *n.*, *pl.* **-ties.** **1.** the state of being happy, esp. in a high degree. **2.** an instance of this. **3.** a source of happiness. **4.** a skilful faculty: *felicity of expression.* **5.** an instance or display of this. **6.** *Archaic.*

good fortune. [ME *felicite*, t. L: m. s. *fēlīcitas* happiness] **—Syn. 1.** See **happiness.**

felid (fē′lĭd), *n.* one of the cat family, *Felidae.*

feline (fē′līn), *adj.* **1.** belonging or pertaining to the cat family, *Felidae*, which includes, besides the domestic cat, the lions, tigers, leopards, lynxes, jaguars, etc. **2.** catlike; characteristic of animals of the cat family: *feline softness of step.* **3.** sly; spiteful; stealthy; treacherous. **—***n.* **4.** an animal of the cat family. [t. L: m. s. *fēlīnus* of a cat] **—fe′linely,** *adv.* **—fe′lineness, felinity** (fĭ lĭn′ĭ tĭ), *n.*

feline agranulocytosis, *Vet. Sci.* a highly fatal, contagious virus disease of domestic cats characterized by fever, somnolence, and diarrhoea; distemper.

Felixstowe (fē′lĭk stō′), *n.* a seaport in England, in East Suffolk. 17,354 (1961).

fell[1] (fĕl), *v.* pt. of **fall.**

fell[2] (fĕl), *v.t.* **1.** to cause to fall; knock, strike, or cut down: *to fell an elephant, a tree, etc.* **2.** *Sewing.* to finish (a seam) by sewing the edge down flat. **—***n.* **3.** *U.S. Lumbering.* the timber cut down in one season. **4.** *Sewing.* a seam finished by felling. [ME *felle(n)*, OE *fellan*, causative of *feallan* fall] **—fell′er,** *n.*

fell[3] (fĕl), *adj.* **1.** fierce; cruel; dreadful. **2.** destructive; deadly: *fell poison or disease.* [ME, t. OF: m. *fel* base. See FELON[1]] **—fell′ness,** *n.*

fell[4] (fĕl), *n.* the skin or hide of an animal; a pelt. [ME and OE, c. G *Fell;* akin to L *pellis* skin]

fell[5] (fĕl), *n. Scot. and N Dial.* a stretch of elevated waste land or pasture; a down. [ME, t. Scand.; cf. Icel. *fiall* mountain]

fellable (fĕl′ə bl), *adj.* capable of being or fit to be felled.

fellah (fĕl′ə), *n., pl.* **fellahs** or **fellahin, fellaheen** (fĕl′ə hēn′). a native peasant or labourer in Egypt, Syria, etc. [t. Ar.: husbandman]

fellation (fĭ lā′shən), *n.* oral stimulation of the male genitals. Also, **fellatio** (fĭ lā′shĭ ō′). [t. L]

Felling (fĕl′ĭng), *n.* a town in England, in E Durham. 35,602 (1961).

Fellini (fĕ lē′nĭ; *It.* fĕl lē′nē), *n.* **Federico** (*It.* fĕ dĕ rē′kō), born 1920, Italian film director.

fellmonger (fĕl′mŭng′gə), *n.* a dealer in skins or hides of animals, esp. sheepskins.

felloe (fĕl′ō), *n.* the circular rim, or a part of the rim of a wheel, into which the outer ends of the spokes are inserted. Also, **felly.** [ME *fely, felwe*, OE *felg*, c. G *Felge*]

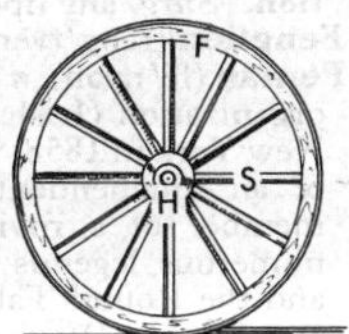

F, Felloe; S, Spoke; H, Hub

fellow (fĕl′ō), *n.* **1.** *Colloq.* a man; boy. **2.** *Colloq.* suitor. **3.** *Colloq.* a person. **4.** a person of small worth or no esteem. **5.** a companion; comrade. **6.** one belonging to the same class; an equal; peer. **7.** one of a pair; a mate or match. **8.** (*usually cap.*) a member of any of certain learned or professional societies: *a Fellow of the British Academy.* **9.** *Educ.* **a.** a member of the corporation or board of trustees of certain universities or colleges. **b.** an incorporated member of a college, entitled to certain privileges. **c.** *Chiefly U.S.* a postgraduate research student in a college or university, granted a special allowance. **10.** *Obs.* a partner. **—***v.t.* **11.** to make, or represent as, equal with another. **12.** to produce a fellow to; match. **—***adj.* **13.** belonging to the same class or group; united by the same occupation, interests, etc.; being in the same condition: *fellow students, citizens, etc., fellow sufferers.* [ME *felowe, felawe*, late OE *fēolaga*, t. Scand.; cf. Icel. *fēlagi* companion (f. *fē* money + *-lagi* one who lays (something) down)]

fellow creature, a creature produced by the same Creator (now used chiefly of human beings): *he was ashamed of his fellow creatures.*

fellow feeling, 1. sympathetic feeling; sympathy. **2.** sense of joint interest.

fellow servants, *Law.* workers engaged by the same employer.

fellowship (fĕl′ō shĭp′), *n., v.,* **-shipped, -shipping. —***n.* **1.** the condition or relation of being a fellow. **2.** community of interest, feeling, etc. **3.** communion, as between members of the same church. **4.** friendliness. **5.** an association of persons having similar tastes, interests, etc. **6.** a company; a guild or corporation. **7.** *Educ.* **a.** the body of fellows in a college or university. **b.** the position or emoluments of a fellow of a university, etc., or the sum of money he receives. **c.** a foundation for the maintenance of a fellow in a college or university. **—***v.t.* **8.** *Chiefly U.S.* to admit to fellowship, esp. religious fellowship. **—***v.i.* **9.** *Chiefly U.S.* to join in fellowship, esp. religious fellowship.

fellow traveller, 1. one who travels in company with another. **2.** a non-member who supports or sympathizes with a party, usually the Communist Party.

felly[1] (fĕl′ĭ), *n., pl.* **-lies.** felloe.

felly[2] (fĕl′lĭ), *adv. Archaic.* in a fell manner; fiercely; ruthlessly. [f. FELL[3] + -(L)Y]

felo-de-se (fē′lō dē sē′, fĕl′ō-), *n., pl.* **felones-de-se** (fĕl′ō nēz′dē sē′) or **felos-de-se** (fē′lōz dē sē′, fĕl′ōz-). *Latin.* **1.** one who commits suicide. **2.** suicide. [Anglo-L: a felon with respect to oneself]

felon[1] (fĕl′ən), *n.* **1.** *Law.* one who has committed a felony. **2.** *Obs.* a wicked person. **—***adj.* **3.** *Archaic.* wicked; malicious; treacherous. [ME *felun*, t. OF: m. *felon* base, der. L *fellāre* to suck (obscene)]

felon[2] (fĕl′ən), *n. Pathol.* an acute and painful inflammation of the deeper tissues of a finger or toe, usually near the nail: a form of whitlow. [orig. uncert.]

felonious (fĭ lō′nyəs), *adj.* **1.** *Law.* pertaining to, of the nature of, or involving a felony. **2.** *Now Rare.* wicked; base. **—felo′niously,** *adv.* **—felo′niousness,** *n.*

felonry (fĕl′ən rĭ), *n.* **1.** the whole body or class of felons. **2.** the convict population of a penal colony.

felony (fĕl′ə nĭ), *n., pl.* **-nies.** *Law.* **1.** any of various indictable offences, as murder, burglary, etc., of graver character than those called misdemeanours. **2.** (in early English law) any crime punishable by loss of life or member and forfeiture of goods and chattels, and which could be prosecuted by appeal.

felsite (fĕl′sīt), *n.* a dense, igneous rock consisting typically of felspar and quartz, both of which may appear as phenocrysts. [f. FELS(PAR) + -ITE[1]] **—felsitic** (fĕl sĭt′ĭk), *adj.*

felspar (fĕl′spä′), *n.* any of a group of minerals, principally aluminosilicates of potassium, sodium, and calcium, and characterized by two cleavages at nearly right angles. They are among the most important constituents of igneous rocks. Also, **feldspar.** [half-taken, half-translated from G *Feldspath*] **—felspathic** (fĕld spăth′ĭk, fĕl-), *adj.*

felspathose (fĕl′ spă thōs′), *adj. Mineral.* of, pertaining to, consisting of, or containing felspar.

felt[1] (fĕlt), *v.* pt. and pp. of **feel.**

felt[2] (fĕlt), *n.* **1.** a non-woven fabric of wool, fur, or hair, matted together by pressure. **2.** any matted fabric or material. **—***adj.* **3.** pertaining to or made of felt. **—***v.t.* **4.** to make into felt; mat or press together. **5.** to cover with, or as with felt. **—***v.i.* **6.** to become matted together. [ME and OE; akin to G *Filz.* See FILTER]

felting (fĕl′tĭng), *n.* **1.** felted material. **2.** the act or process of making felt. **3.** the materials of which felt is made.

felucca (fĕ lŭk′ə), *n.* a long, narrow vessel propelled by oars or lateen sails, or both, used in the Mediterranean. [t. It., t. Ar.]

Felucca

felwort (fĕl′wût′), *n.* a gentianaceous biennial herb with purple flowers, *Gentianella amarella*, widespread on non-acid grassland in Europe and SW China.

fem., feminine.

female (fē′māl), *n.* **1.** a human being of the sex which conceives and brings forth young; a woman or girl. **2.** any animal of corresponding sex. **3.** *Bot.* a pistillate plant. **—***adj.* **4.** belonging to the sex which brings forth young, or any division or group corresponding to it. **5.** pertaining to or characteristic of this sex; feminine. **6.** composed of females: *a female cricket team.* **7.** *Bot.* **a.** designating or pertaining to a plant or its reproductive structure which produces or contains elements that need fertilization. **b.** (of seed plants) pistillate. **8.** *Mech.* designating some part, etc., into which a corresponding part fits: *a female outlet.* **9.** *Obs.* womanish; weakly. [ME *female* (a form due to assoc. with *male*), var. of *femelle*, t. OF, g. L *fēmella*, dim. of *fēmina* woman]

—Syn. 1. See **woman. 5.** FEMALE, EFFEMINATE, FEMININE refer to attributes of women. FEMALE, referring to anything not male, is the scientific word, and was once the general word, to designate one of the two sexes: *female organs in a plant or animal, a female seminary.* EFFEMINATE is applied reproachfully or contemptuously to qualities which, when possessed by men, are unmanly and weak, though these same qualities might be proper and becoming in women: *effeminate gestures, an effeminate voice.* FEMININE, corresponding to *masculine*, applies to the attributes particularly appropriate to women, esp. the softer and more delicate qualities. The word is seldom used merely to denote sex, and, if applied to men, suggests the delicacy and weakness of women: *a feminine point of view, features.* **—Ant. 5.** male, masculine.

female rhyme, *Pros.* feminine rhyme.

feme (fĕm), *n. Law.* a woman or wife. [t. AF, g. L *fēmina* woman, wife; cf. F *femme*]

feme covert (kŭv′ət), *Law.* a married woman. [t. AF: a woman covered, i.e., protected]

feme sole (sōl), *Law.* **1.** an unmarried woman, whether spinster, widow, or divorcee. **2.** a married woman who is independent of her husband with respect to property. [t. AF: a woman alone]

femineity (fĕm′ĭ nē′ĭ tĭ), *n.* feminine nature; womanliness. Also, **femality** (fĭ măl′ĭ tĭ), **feminality** (fĕm′ĭ năl′ĭ tĭ). [f. s. L *fēmineus* feminine + -ITY]

feminie (fĕm′ĭ nĭ), *n. Archaic.* women collectively. [ME, t. OF, der. L *fēmina* woman]

feminin (fĕm′ĭ nĭn), *n. Biochem.* oestrone.

feminine (fĕm′ĭ nĭn), *adj.* **1.** pertaining to a woman. **2.** like a woman; weak; gentle. **3.** effeminate. **4.** belonging to the female sex. **5.** *Gram.* denoting or pertaining to one of the three genders of Latin, Greek, German, etc., or one of the two of French, Spanish, etc., including most nouns denoting females (e.g. in Latin *puella* 'girl' and in German *Frau* 'woman' are feminine) and other nouns (e.g. in Latin *stella* 'star' and in German *Zeit* 'time'). —*n.* **6.** *Gram.* **a.** the feminine gender. **b.** a noun of that gender. **c.** another element marking that gender, as *la* (the feminine article in French and Spanish). [ME, t. L: m. s. *fēmininus*, der. *fēmina* woman] —**fem′ininely,** *adv.* —**fem′inineness,** *n.* —**Syn. 2.** See **female.**

feminine cadence, *Music.* a cadence in which the final chord falls on a weak beat.

feminine ending, 1. *Pros.* an ending in which a line closes with an extra unaccented syllable in addition to the normal accented syllable. **2.** *Gram.* a termination or final syllable marking a feminine word: *'-ā' in Latin is a feminine ending for the ablative case in the singular.*

feminine rhyme, *Pros.* a rhyme of two syllables of which the second is unstressed: *motion, notion* (double rhyme), or of three syllables of which the second and third are unstressed: *fortunate, importunate* (triple rhyme).

femininity (fĕm′ĭ nĭn′ĭ tĭ), *n.* **1.** the quality of being feminine; womanliness: *she kept her femininity even when wearing greasy overalls.* **2.** women collectively. Also, **feminity** (fĭ mĭn′ĭ tĭ).

feminism (fĕm′ĭ nĭz′əm), *n.* **1.** advocation of the extension of the activities of women in social and political life. **2.** feminine character. —**fem′inist,** *n., adj.* —**fem′inis′tic,** *adj.*

feminize (fĕm′ĭ nīz′), *v.t., v.i.,* **-nized, -nizing.** to make or become feminine. Also, **feminise.** —**fem′iniza′tion,** *n.*

femme (făm; *Fr.* fȧm), *n.* **1.** *French.* woman. **2.** the more passive or feminine partner in a lesbian relationship.

femme de chambre (*Fr.* fȧm də shäN′br), *French.* **1.** a lady's maid. **2.** a chambermaid.

femme fatale (*Fr.* fȧm fȧ tȧl′), *French.* an extremely alluring woman, esp. one who leads men into disastrous situations.

femoral (fĕm′ə rəl), *adj.* of or pertaining to the thigh or femur. [f. s. L *femur* thigh + -AL[1]]

femto- (fĕm′tō), a prefix denoting one thousand million millionth; 10^{-15}. [der. Dan. *femten* fifteen]

femur (fē′mə), *n., pl.* **femurs, femora** (fĕm′ə rə). **1.** *Anat.* a bone in the limb of an animal extending from the pelvis to the knee; the thighbone. See diag. under **skeleton. 2.** *Entomol.* the third segment of an insect's leg (counting from the base), situated between the trochanter and the tibia. See diag. under **coxa.** [t. L: thigh]

fen (fĕn), *n.* **1.** low land covered wholly or partially with water; boggy land; a marsh. **2. the Fens,** a marshy region W and S of The Wash, in E England. [ME and OE, c. Icel. *fen* quagmire]

fence (fĕns), *n., v.,* **fenced, fencing.** —*n.* **1.** an enclosure or barrier, usually of wire or wood, as around or along a field, garden, etc. **2.** the act, practice, or art of fencing; swordplay. **3.** skill in argument, repartee, etc. **4. a.** a person who receives and disposes of stolen goods. **b.** *Slang.* the place of business of such a person. **5.** *Mach.* a guard or guide, as for regulating the movements of a tool or machine. **6.** *Aeron.* a projection on the wing of an aeroplane, parallel to the airstream, to prevent air flowing along the span. **7.** an obstacle to be jumped in show-jumping or steeplechasing. **8.** *Obs.* a means of defence; a bulwark. **9. on the fence,** undecided or neutral. —*v.t.* **10.** to enclose by some barrier, thus asserting exclusive right to possession. **11.** to separate by, or as by, a fence or fences. **12.** *Archaic.* to ward off; keep out. **13.** to defend; protect; guard. —*v.i.* **14.** to use a sword, foil, etc., in defence and attack, or in exercise or exhibition of skill in that art. **15.** to parry arguments; strive to evade giving direct answers. **16.** (of a horse) to leap over a fence. **17.** *Slang.* to receive stolen goods. **18.** *Obs.* to raise a defence. [aphetic var. of DEFENCE] —**fence′less,** *adj.* —**fence′lessness,** *n.* —**fence′like′,** *adj.*

fencer (fĕn′sə), *n.* **1.** one who fences. **2.** one who practises the art of fencing with a sword, foil, etc. **3.** *Austral.* a maker or mender of fences. **4.** a horse trained to jump.

fencible (fĕn′sə bl), *n.* **1.** *Archaic.* a soldier enlisted for defensive service in his own country only. —*adj.* **2.** *Scot.* capable of being defended or of making defence.

fencing (fĕn′sĭng), *n.* **1.** the act, practice, or art of using a sword, foil, etc., for defence and attack. **2.** a parrying of arguments; an evading of direct answers. **3.** an enclosure or railing. **4.** fences collectively. **5.** material for fences. **6.** *Slang.* the receiving of stolen goods.

fend (fĕnd), *v.t.* **1.** to ward off (often fol. by *off*): *to fend off blows.* **2.** *Archaic.* to defend. —*v.i.* **3.** to make defence; offer resistance. **4.** to parry. **5.** *Colloq.* to provide for: *to fend for oneself.* [aphetic var. of DEFEND]

fender (fĕn′də), *n.* **1.** one who or that which wards something off. **2.** a device on the front of a railway engine, or the like, for clearing the track of obstructions. **3.** *Now Chiefly U.S.* a bumper on a motor vehicle. **4.** *Naut.* a piece of timber, bundle of rope, or the like, hung over the side of a vessel to lessen shock or prevent chafing. **5.** a low metal guard before an open fireplace, to keep back falling coals. [aphetic var. of DEFENDER]

Fénelon (*Fr.* fĕn lôN′), *n.* **François de Salignac de La Mothe** (*Fr.* fräN swȧ də sȧ lē nyȧk də lȧ mŏt′), 1651–1715, French theologian and writer.

fenestella (fĕn′ĭs tĕl′ə), *n., pl.* **-tellae** (-tĕl′ē). *Archit.* **1.** a small window or window-like opening. **2.** a small window-like niche in the wall on the south side of an altar, containing the piscina, and frequently also the credence. [t. L, dim. of *fenestra* window]

fenestra (fĭ nĕs′trə), *n., pl.* **-trae** (-trē). **1.** *Anat., Zool.* a small opening or perforation, as in a bone. **2.** *Entomol.* a transparent spot in an otherwise opaque surface, as in the wings of certain butterflies and moths. **3.** *Archit.* a window-like opening. [t. L: window] —**fenes′tral,** *adj.*

fenestrated (fĭ nĕs′trā tĭd), *adj.* **1.** *Archit.* having windows; windowed; characterized by windows. **2.** pierced, perforated. Also, **fenes′trate.** [f. m. s. L *fenestrātus*, pp., furnished with windows + -ED[2]]

fenestration (fĕn′ĭs trā′shən), *n.* **1.** *Archit.* the arrangement of windows in a building. **2.** Also, **Lempert operation.** *Surg.* any operation which creates a small opening.

Fengtien (fĕng′tyĕn′), *n.* former name of **Liaoning.**

Fenian (fē′nyən), *n.* **1.** a member of an Irish revolutionary organization (Irish Republican Brotherhood) founded in New York in 1858, which had for its aim the establishment of an independent Irish republic. **2.** *Irish Legend.* a member of a roving band of warriors, the centre of numerous legends comparable to those of King Arthur and the Round Table. [appar. b. OIrish *fēn(e)* Irishman and OIrish *(f)iann* legendary band of warriors in service of Finn MacCool] —**Fe′nianism,** *n.*

fennec (fĕn′ĕk), *n.* a small North African fox, *Vulpes zerda*, of a pale fawn colour, and having large pointed ears. [t. Ar.: m. *fenek*]

fennel (fĕn′əl), *n.* **1.** an umbelliferous plant, *Foeniculum vulgare*, having yellow flowers, and bearing aromatic fruits used in cookery and medicine. **2.** the fruits (**fennel seed**) of this plant. **3.** any of various more or less similar plants, as *Ferula communis* (**giant fennel**), a tall ornamental apiaceous herb. [ME *fenel*, etc., OE *fenol, finol, finugl*, t. VL: m. s. *fēnuclum*, var. of L *faeniculum* fennel, dim. of *faenum* hay]

fennelflower (fĕn′əl flou′ə), *n.* **1.** any of the ranunculaceous herbs constituting the genus *Nigella*, esp. *N. sativa*, whose seeds are used in the East as a condiment and medicine. **2.** the flower of this plant.

fenny (fĕn′ĭ), *adj.* **1.** marshy; boggy. **2.** inhabiting, or growing in, fens. [ME; OE *fennig*, der. *fenn* fen]

Fenrir (fĕn′rĭə), *n. Scand. Myth.* a gigantic wolf-like water demon, son of Loki: slayer of Odin and slain by Vidar. Also, **Fenris** (fĕn′rĭs).

fenugreek (fĕn′yŏŏ grēk′), *n.* a plant, *Trigonella foenum-graecum*, indigenous to western Asia, but extensively cultivated elsewhere, chiefly for forage and for its mucilaginous seeds, which are used in medicine. [ME *fenegrek*, OE *fenogræcum*, t. L: m. *faenugraecum*, for *faenum graecum* Greek hay]

feod (fyŏŏd), *n.* feud[2]. See **fee** (defs 5, 6).

feoff (fĕf *for 1 and 2*; fĕf, fēf *for 3*), *n.* **1.** a fee or feud, or estate in land held of a feudal lord; a tenure of land subject to feudal obligations. **2.** a territory held in fee. —*v.t.* **3.** to invest with a fief or fee; enfeoff. [ME *feoff(en)*, t. AF: m. *feoffer*, var. of OF *fefier, fieffer*, der. *fieu* FEE] —**feoff′ment,** *n.* —**feof′for, feof′fer,** *n.*

feoffee (fĕf ē′, fēf ē′), *n.* a person invested with a fief.

-fer, a noun suffix with a corresponding adjective in *-ferous*, as *conifer* (a coniferous tree). [t. L: bearing, der. *ferre* bear]

feracious (fə rā′shəs), *adj.* *Obs.* fruitful; productive. [f. FERACI(TY) + -OUS]

feracity (fə răs′ĭ tĭ), *n.* *Obs.* fruitfulness. [t. L: m. s. *ferācitas*]

feral[1] (fĭə′rəl), *adj.* **1.** wild, or existing in a state of nature, as animals (or, sometimes, plants). **2.** having reverted to the wild state, as from domestication. **3.** of or characteristic of wild animals: *the feral state.* [f. s. L *fera* wild beast (prop. fem. of *ferus* wild) + -AL[1]]

feral[2] (fĭə′rəl), *adj.* *Archaic.* **1.** deadly, fatal. **2.** gloomy, funereal. [t. L: s. *fērālis*]

ferbam (fû′băm), *n.* *Chem.* a black insoluble powder, $[(CH_3)_2NCSS]_3Fe$, used as a fungicide; ferric dimethyldithiocarbonate.

Ferber (fû′bə), *n.* **Edna,** born 1887, U.S. novelist, short-story writer, and dramatist.

ferberite (fû′bə rīt′), *n.* a mineral of the wolframite group, theoretically pure ferrous tungstate, but frequently some of the iron is replaced by manganese.

fer-de-lance (fēə′də läns′), *n.* a large, very venomous snake, *Trimeresurus atrox*, of tropical America. [F: lit., iron (head) of a lance]

Ferdinand (*Ger.* fĕr′dē nȧnt), *n.* See **Franz Ferdinand.**

Ferdinand I (fû′dĭ nənd; *Ger.* fĕr′dē nȧnt). **1.** 1503–64, emperor of the Holy Roman Empire 1558–64, and king of Bohemia and Hungary 1526–64 (brother of Emperor Charles V). **2.** (*Prince of Saxe-Coburg-Gotha*), 1861–1948, ruling prince of Bulgaria 1887–1908, and tsar 1908 until he abdicated in 1918. **3.** (‘*Ferdinand the Great*’), died 1065, king of Castile 1037?–65, and Leon 1037–65; recognized as emperor of Spain 1056–65. **4.** 1793–1875, king of Hungary 1830–48, emperor of Austria 1835–48. **5.** 1751–1825, king of the Two Sicilies 1816–25. **6.** 1865–1927, king of Rumania 1914–27.

Ferdinand II, **1.** 1578–1637, emperor of the Holy Roman Empire 1619–37, king of Bohemia 1617–37, and king of Hungary 1618–37. **2.** 1452–1516, king of Aragon 1479–1516, and of Sicily 1468–1516. See **Ferdinand V.** **3.** 1810–59, king of the Two Sicilies 1830–59.

Ferdinand III, **1.** 1452–1516, king of Naples 1502–16. See **Ferdinand V.** **2.** 1608–57, king of Hungary 1625–57 and Holy Roman Emperor 1637–57.

Ferdinand V, (‘*the Catholic*’), 1452–1516, Spanish king who founded the Spanish monarchy. (As **Ferdinand II,** king of Aragon 1479–1516, and king of Sicily 1468–1516; as **Ferdinand III,** king of Naples 1502–16; as **Ferdinand V,** joint ruler of Castile with his wife Isabella I 1474–1504, and sole ruler of United Spain 1506–16.)

fere (fĭə), *n.* *Obs.* a companion; a mate. [ME; OE *gefēra*, der. *fōr* journey; akin to FARE]

feretory (fĕ′rĭ tə rĭ, -trĭ), *n., pl.* **-ries.** **1.** a shrine, usually portable, designed to hold the relics of saints. **2.** a room or chapel in which shrines were kept. [b. L *ferē(trum)* bier and (REPOSI)TORY; r. ME *fertre*, t. OF]

feria (fĭə′rĭ ə, fĕ′rĭ ə), *n.* *Rom. Cath. Ch.* a weekday not set apart for the observance of any specific feast.

ferial (fĭə′rĭ əl), *adj.* **1.** pertaining to a holiday. **2.** *Eccles.* pertaining to weekdays not set apart as festivals. [t. ML: s. *fēriālis*, der. L *fēria* holiday]

ferine (fĭə′rīn), *adj.* feral. [t. L: m. s. *ferinus*]

Feringi (fə rĭng′gĭ), *n.* (in India, usually in contemptuous use) **1.** a European or a person of European descent. **2.** a Portuguese born in India. Also, **Feringhee.** [ult. t. Pers.: m. *Farangī*, in Ar. *Faranjī*, lit., Frank]

ferity (fĕ′rĭ tĭ), *n.* **1.** a wild, untamed, or uncultivated state. **2.** savagery; ferocity. [t. L: m. s. *feritas* wildness]

Fermanagh (fə măn′ə), *n.* a county in Northern Ireland, in SW Ulster. 51,531 pop. (1961); 653 sq. mi. *Co. town:* Enniskillen.

fermata (fû mä′tə), *n., pl.* **-tas.** *Music.* a pause. [t. It.]

Fermat's principle (fû′mäz, fû mäz′), *Optics.* the principle which states that the path taken by a ray of light, or any other wave motion, in traversing the distance between any two points is such that the time taken is a minimum. [named after P. de *Fermat*, 1601–65, French mathematician]

ferment (*n.* fû′mĕnt; *v.* fə mĕnt′), *n.* **1.** any of various agents or substances which cause fermentation, esp.: **a.** any of various living organisms (**organized ferments**), as yeasts, moulds, certain bacteria, etc. **b.** any of certain complex substances derived from living cells (**unorganized ferments or enzymes**), as pepsin, etc. **2.** fermentation. **3.** agitation; excitement; tumult. —*v.t.* **4.** to act upon as a ferment. **5.** to cause to undergo fermentation. **6.** to inflame; foment. **7.** to agitate; excite. —*v.i.* **8.** to be fermented; undergo fermentation. **9.** to seethe with agitation or excitement. [t. L: s. *fermentum* leaven, agitation] —**ferment′able,** *adj.*

fermentation (fû′mĕn tā′shən), *n.* **1.** the act or process of fermenting. **2.** *Biochem.* a change brought about by a ferment, such as yeast enzymes which convert grape sugar into ethyl alcohol, etc. **3.** agitation; excitement.

fermentative (fə mĕn′tə tĭv), *adj.* **1.** tending to produce or undergo fermentation. **2.** pertaining to or of the nature of fermentation.

fermi (fû′mĭ; *It.* fĕr′mē), *n.* a unit of length, 10^{-13} cm.

Fermi (*It.* fĕr′mē), *n.* **Enrico** (*It.* ĕn rē′kō), 1901–54, Italian physicist, in the U.S. from 1939.

Fermi-Dirac statistics (fû′mĭ dĭ răk′, fēə′-), *Physics.* the branch of quantum statistics used with systems of identical particles whose wave function changes sign if any two particles are interchanged. [named after Enrico FERMI and Paul DIRAC]

fermion (fû′mĭ ən, fēə′-), *n.* *Physics.* any elementary particle which conforms to Fermi-Dirac statistics and has half integral spin, as a proton or neutron.

fermium (fû′myəm), *n.* *Chem.* a synthetic, radioactive element. *Symbol:* Fm; *at. no.:* 100. [f. FERM(I) + -IUM]

fern (fûn), *n.* *Bot.* any of the pteridophytes constituting the order *Filicales*, distinguished from other pteridophytes in having few leaves, large in proportion to the stems, and bearing sporangia on the undersurface or margin. [ME *ferne*, OE *fearn*, c. G *Farn*; akin to Skt *parna* feather] —**fern′like′,** *adj.*

Fernández (fû năn′dĕz; *Sp.* fĕr nȧn′dĕth), *n.* **Juan** (*Sp.* KHwȧn), *c.* 1536–1602, Spanish navigator and explorer of the western coast of South America and islands of the Pacific.

Fernando (*Sp.* fĕr nȧn′dō), *n.* Spanish for **Ferdinand.**

Fernando de Noronha (*Port.* fĕr nən′dōō dē nō rō′nyȧ), an island in the S Atlantic, ab. 125 mi. E of the easternmost tip of Brazil: a Brazilian penal colony. 581 pop. (1950); 10 sq. mi.

Fernando Po (fə năn′dō pō′), an island in the Bight of Biafra, near the W coast of Africa: an African province of Spain. 61,197 pop. (1961); ab. 800 sq. mi. *Cap.:* Santa Isabel. Also, **Fernando Poo.**

fernery (fû′nə rĭ), *n., pl.* **-ries.** a place or a glass case in which ferns are grown for ornament.

fern owl, **1.** the nightjar. **2.** the short-eared owl.

fern seed, the spores of ferns, formerly supposed to have the power to make persons invisible.

ferny (fû′nĭ), *adj.* **1.** pertaining to, consisting of, or like ferns. **2.** abounding in or overgrown with ferns.

ferocious (fə rō′shəs), *adj.* savagely fierce, as a wild beast, person, action, aspect, etc.; violently cruel. [f. FEROCI(TY) + -OUS] —**fero′ciously,** *adv.* —**fero′ciousness,** *n.* —**Syn.** See **fierce.**

ferocity (fə rŏs′ĭ tĭ), *n.* ferocious quality or state; savage fierceness. [t. L: m. s. *ferōcitas*]

-ferous, an adjective suffix meaning ‘bearing’, ‘producing’, ‘yielding’, ‘containing’, ‘conveying’, as in *auriferous, balsamiferous, coniferous, pestiferous.* [f. -FER producing, + -OUS]

Ferrara (fə rä′rə; *It.* fĕr rä′rä), *n.* a city in N Italy, near the Po: medieval university and cathedral. 157,931 (1966).

ferrate (fĕ′rāt), *n.* *Chem.* a salt of the hypothetical ferric acid. [f. s. L *ferrum* iron + -ATE[2]]

ferrel (fĕ′rəl), *n., v.t.,* **-relled, -relling** or (*U.S.*) **-reled, -reling.** ferrule.

Ferrel's law, the law that all bodies moving on the earth's surface are deflected to the right in the N hemisphere and to the left in the S hemisphere. [named after William *Ferrel*, 1817–91, U.S. meteorologist]

ferret[1] (fĕ′rĭt), *n.* **1.** a domesticated, albinistic, red-eyed form of the polecat, employed in Europe for hunting the burrows of rabbits and rats. **2.** a wild species, *Mustela nigripes* (**black-footed ferret**) yellowish brown with the tip of the tail and the legs black, inhabiting prairie regions of the U.S. as the plains of Nebraska and Kansas, and feeding largely on prairie dogs. —*v.t.* **3.** to drive out by, or as by, means of a ferret. **4.** to hunt with ferrets. **5.** to search out or bring to light: *to ferret out the facts.* —*v.i.* **6.** to search about. [ME *fyrette*, t. OF: m. *fuiret*, der. L *fūr* thief] —**fer′reter,** *n.* —**fer′rety,** *adj.*

Black-footed ferret, *Mustela nigripes* (Ab. 2 ft long)

ferret[2] (fĕ′rĭt), *n.* a narrow tape or ribbon, as of silk or cotton, used for binding, etc. [t. It.: m. *fioretto*, dim. of *fiore*, g. L *flōs* flower; conformed to FERRET[1]]

ferret badger, any of the small carnivores constituting the genus *Helictis*, of southern and eastern Asia.

ferri-, *Chem.* a word element meaning ‘iron’, implying esp. combination with ferric iron or ferrites. [var. of FERRO-]

ferriage (fĕ′rĭ ĭj), *n.* **1.** conveyance by a ferryboat or the like. **2.** the price charged for ferrying.

ferric (fĕ′rĭk), *adj.* *Chem.* of or containing iron, esp. in the trivalent state. [f. FERR(I)- + -IC]

ferric oxide, *Chem.* a dark red crystalline solid, Fe_2O_3, occurring naturally as haematite; used as a pigment, a mordant, and in polishing compounds.

Ferrier (fĕ′rĭ ə), *n.* **Kathleen,** 1912–53, English contralto.

ferriferous (fĕ rĭf′ə rəs), *adj.* producing or yielding iron.

ferrimagnetic (fĕ′rĭ măg nĕt′ĭk, fĕ′rĭ-), *adj.* *Physics.* pertaining to the type of magnetism, occurring in such materials as ferrites (def. 4), in which the magnetic moments of adjacent atoms are antiparallel and of unequal strength, or in which unequal numbers of magnetic moments are orientated in opposite directions. —**fer′rimag′netism,** *n.*

Ferris wheel (fĕ′rĭs), an amusement device at fairs, etc., consisting of a large upright wheel rotating about a fixed axis with seats suspended at intervals around its rim. [named after G. W. G. *Ferris,* 1859–96, U.S. engineer]

ferrite (fĕ′rīt), *n.* **1.** *Chem.* a compound formed when ferric oxide is combined with a more basic metallic oxide, as $NaFeO_2$. **2.** *Metall.* the pure alpha iron occurring in iron-carbon alloys, or any solid solution of which alpha iron is the solvent. **3.** *Geol.* any of certain indeterminable mineral substances (probably iron compounds) frequently observed in the microscopic examination of certain igneous rocks. **4.** one of a group of ceramic substances with the general formula $MO \cdot Fe_2O_3$ where M is a divalent metal; used, because of their ferrimagnetic (or, in some cases, ferromagnetic) properties, in computers and the electrical equipment of aircraft. **5.** *Elect.* ferrite core. See **core** (def. 3c).

ferritin (fĕ′rĭ tĭn), *n.* *Biochem.* a protein which contains iron; found in the liver and spleen and believed to act as a reservoir of iron for the whole body.

ferro-, a word element meaning 'iron'. In *Chem.*, *ferro-* implies esp. combination with ferrous iron as opposed to ferric iron. Also, **ferri-.** [comb. form repr. L *ferrum* iron]

ferrochromium (fĕ′rō krō′myəm), *n.* an alloy of iron and up to 70 per cent chromium. Also, **ferrochrome.**

ferroconcrete (fĕ′rō kŏng′krēt), *n.* reinforced concrete.

ferroelectric (fĕ′rō ĭ lĕk′trĭk), *Physics.* —*adj.* **1.** pertaining to a non-magnetic substance which possesses spontaneous electric polarization such that the polarization can be reversed by an electric field. —*n.* **2.** a ferroelectric substance.

Ferrol (*Sp.* fĕr rōl′), *n.* El Ferrol.

ferromagnesian (fĕ′rō măg nē′shən), *Geol.* —*adj.* **1.** (of minerals and rocks) containing iron and magnesium. —*n.* **2.** an iron-magnesium mineral.

ferromagnetic (fĕ′rō măg nĕt′ĭk), *adj.* *Physics.* pertaining to a substance, such as iron, which above the curie point possesses magnetic properties in the absence of an external magnetic field. —**ferromagnetism** (fĕ′rō măg′nĭ tĭz′əm), *n.*

ferromanganese (fĕ′rō măng′gə nēz′), *n.* an alloy of iron containing up to 90 per cent manganese.

ferromolybdenum (fĕ′rō mŏ lĭb′də nəm), *n.* an alloy of iron containing up to 65 per cent molybdenum.

ferrosilicon (fĕ′rō sĭl′ĭ kən), *n.* an alloy of iron containing up to 90 per cent silicon.

ferrotitanium (fĕ′rō tī tā′nyəm, -tĭ tā′-), *n.* an alloy of iron containing up to 45 per cent titanium.

ferrotungsten (fĕ′rō tŭng′stən), *n.* an alloy of iron containing up to 80 per cent tungsten.

ferrotype (fĕ′rō tīp′), *v.*, **-typed, -typing,** *n.* *Photog.* —*v.t.* **1.** to put a glossy surface on (a print) by pressing it while wet on a metal sheet (**ferrotype tin**). —*n.* **2.** a photograph taken on a sensitized sheet of enamelled iron or tin; a tintype. **3.** the process itself.

ferrous (fĕ′rəs), *adj.* *Chem.* of or containing iron, esp. in the divalent state.

ferrous sulphate, *Chem.* a green, soluble, crystalline solid, $FeSO_4.7H_2O$, used in dyeing, tanning, inks, pigments, photography, fertilizers, and medicine. Also, **green vitriol, iron sulphate, copperas.**

ferrovanadium (fĕ′rō və nā′dyəm), *n.* an alloy of iron containing up to 55 per cent vanadium.

ferrozirconium (fĕ′rō zû kō′nyəm), *n.* an alloy of iron containing up to 40 per cent zirconium.

ferruginous (fĕ ro͞o′jĭ nəs), *adj.* iron-bearing; containing iron. [t. L: m. *ferrūginus*, der. *ferrūgo* iron rust]

ferrule (fĕ′ro͞ol, -rəl), *n.*, *v.*, **-ruled, -ruling.** —*n.* **1.** a metal ring or cap put round the end of a post, stick, handle, etc., for strength or protection. **2.** (in steam boilers) a bush for expanding the end of a flue. —*v.i.* **3.** to furnish with a ferrule. Also, **ferrel.** [late ME *vyrell*, t. OF: m. *virelle*, g. L *viriola*, dim. of *viriae* bracelets]

ferry (fĕ′rĭ), *n.*, *pl.* **-ries,** *v.*, **-ried, -rying.** —*n.* **1.** a service with terminals and floating equipment, for transport from shore to shore across a body of water. **2.** a ferryboat. **3.** the legal right to ferry passengers, etc., and to charge toll for the service. —*v.t.* **4.** to carry or convey over water in a boat or plane. —*v.i.* **5.** to pass over water in a boat or by ferry. [ME *feri(en)*, OE *ferian*, akin to *faran* fare]

ferryboat (fĕ′rĭ bōt′), *n.* a boat used to convey passengers, vehicles, etc., across a river or the like.

ferryman (fĕ′rĭ mən), *n.*, *pl.* **-men.** one who owns or runs a ferry.

fertile (fû′tīl), *adj.* **1.** bearing or producing vegetation, crops, etc., abundantly, as land or soil. **2.** bearing offspring freely; prolific. **3.** abundantly productive or inventive: *a fertile imagination.* **4.** able to produce offspring. **5.** producing an abundance (fol. by *in*): *a land fertile in wheat.* **6.** conducive to productiveness: *fertile showers.* **7.** *Biol.* **a.** fertilized, as an egg or ovum; fecundated. **b.** capable of growth or development, as seeds or eggs. **8.** *Bot.* **a.** capable of producing sexual reproductive structures. **b.** capable of causing fertilization, as an anther with fully developed pollen. **c.** having spore-bearing organs, as a frond. **9.** *Physics.* (of an isotope, element, or substance) transformable into a fissile material. [ME, t. L: m. s. *fertilis* fruitful] —**fer′tilely,** *adv.* —**fer′tileness,** *n.* —**Syn. 1.** See **productive.**

Fertile Crescent, 1. an arc-shaped region favourable for agriculture extending from the Levant to Iraq. **2.** an area in the Middle and Near East, once fertile but now partly desert, in which it is believed that man first practised agriculture.

fertility (fû tĭl′ĭ tĭ), *n.* **1.** the state or quality of being fertile. **2.** *Biol.* the ability to produce offspring; power of reproduction. **3.** (of soil) the quality of supplying nutrients in proper amounts for plant growth when other factors are favourable. **4.** (*cap.*) **Sea of,** a plain, *Mare Fecunditas*, in the fourth and first quadrants of the face of the moon.

fertility cult, any of various primitive forms of worship in a settled agricultural community centred on the performance of magical rituals to ensure the continuance and abundance of crops, appropriate weather, and the perpetuity of the tribe.

fertility symbol, a symbol or object used in a fertility cult, esp. a phallic symbol.

fertilization (fû′tĭ lī zā′shən), *n.* **1.** the act or process of fertilizing. **2.** the state of being fertilized. **3.** *Biol.* **a.** the union of male and female gametic nuclei. **b.** fecundation or impregnation of animals or plants. **4.** the enrichment of soil for the production of crops, etc. Also, **fertilisation.**

fertilize (fû′tĭ līz′), *v.t.*, **-lized, -lizing. 1.** *Biol.* **a.** to render (an egg, ovum, or female cell) capable of development by union with the male element, or sperm. **b.** to fecundate or impregnate (an animal or plant). **2.** to make fertile; enrich (soil, etc.) for crops, etc. **3.** to make productive. Also, **fertilise.** —**fer′tiliz′able,** *adj.*

fertilizer (fû′tĭ lī′zə), *n.* **1.** any material used to fertilize the soil, esp. a commercial or chemical manure. **2.** one who or that which fertilizes an animal or plant. Also, **fertiliser.**

ferula (fĕ′ro͞o lə), *n.*, *pl.* **-lae** (-lē′). **1.** *Bot.* any plant of an umbelliferous genus, *Ferula*, chiefly of the Mediterranean region and central Asia, generally tall and coarse with dissected leaves, many of the Asian species yielding strongly scented, medicinal gum resins. **2.** a rod; a ferule. [t. L: rod, giant fennel]

ferulaceous (fĕ′ro͞o lā′shəs), *adj.* pertaining to reeds or canes; having a stalklike reed: *ferulaceous plants.* [t. L: m. *ferulāceus*, der. *ferula* giant fennel]

ferule (fĕ′ro͞ol, -rəl), *n.*, *v.*, **-ruled, -ruling.** —*n.* **1.** a rod, cane, or flat piece of wood for the punishment of children, by striking them, esp. on the hand. —*v.t.* **2.** to punish with a ferule. [OE *ferele* rod, t. L: m. *ferula*]

fervency (fû′vən sĭ), *n.* warmth or intensity of feeling; ardour.

fervent (fû′vənt), *adj.* **1.** having or showing great warmth and earnestness of feeling: *a fervent admirer, plea, etc.* **2.** hot; burning; glowing. [ME, t. L: s. *fervens*, ppr., boiling, glowing] —**fer′vently,** *adv.* —**fer′ventness,** *n.* —**Syn. 1.** fervid, fiery, ardent, eager, earnest, zealous, vehement, impassioned, passionate.

fervid (fû′vĭd), *adj.* **1.** heated or vehement in spirit, enthusiasm, etc.: *a fervid orator.* **2.** burning; glowing; hot. [t. L: s. *fervidus* burning] —**fer′vidly,** *adv.* —**fer′vidness,** *n.*

fervour (fû′və), *n.* **1.** great warmth and earnestness of feeling: *to speak with great fervour.* **2.** intense heat. Also, *U.S.*, **fervor.** [ME, t. OF, t. L: heat, passion] —**Syn. 1.** ardour, intensity, eagerness, enthusiasm.

Fescennine (fĕs′ĭ nīn′), *adj.* scurrilous; licentious; obscene: *Fescennine verse.* [t. L: m. s. *Fescenninus* pertaining to *Fescennia* in Etruria]

fescue (fĕs′kyōō), *n.* **1.** any grass of the genus *Festuca*, some species of which are cultivated for pasture or lawns. **2.** a small stick, twig, etc., used to point out the letters in teaching children to read. [ME *festue*, t. OF, g. L *festūca* stalk, straw]
fess (fĕs), *n. Her.* a wide horizontal band across the middle of an escutcheon. Also, **fesse.** [late ME *fesse*, t. AF, g. L *fascia* band]
fess point, *Her.* the central point of an escutcheon. Also, **fesse point.** See diag. under **escutcheon.**
fesswise (fĕs′wīz′), *adv. Her.* in the manner of a fess; across the shield. Also, **fessewise.**
festa (fĕs′tə), *n.* a feast, festival, or holiday. [It.]
festal (fĕs′tl), *adj.* pertaining to or befitting a feast, festival, or gala occasion. [late ME, t. OF, der. L *festum* a festival, feast] —**fes′tally,** *adv.*
fester (fĕs′tə), *v.i.* **1.** to generate purulent matter; suppurate. **2.** to cause ulceration, or rankle, as a foreign body in the flesh. **3.** to putrefy or rot. **4.** to rankle, as a feeling of resentment. —*v.t.* **5.** to cause to fester. —*n.* **6.** an ulcer; a rankling sore. **7.** a small, purulent, superficial sore. [ME *festre*, t. OF, g. L *fistula* ulcer]
festina lente (fĕs tē′nä lĕn′tā), *Latin.* make haste slowly; more haste less speed.
festination (fĕs′tĭ nā′shən), *n. Pathol.* a type of gait marked by an involuntary hurrying in walking, observed in certain nervous diseases. [t. L: s. *festīnātio* haste]
festival (fĕs′tĭ vəl), *n.* **1.** a periodic religious or other feast: *the festival of Christmas, a Roman festival.* **2.** any time of feasting; an anniversary for festive celebration. **3.** any course of festive activities. **4.** a series of musical, dramatic, or other performances. **5.** *Archaic.* merry-making; revelry. —*adj.* **6.** of, pertaining to, or befitting a feast or holiday; festal. [ME, t. ML: s. *festīvālis*, der. L *festīvus* FESTIVE]
festive (fĕs′tĭv), *adj.* **1.** pertaining to or suitable for a feast or festival. **2.** joyful; merry. Also, *Rare*, **festivous** (fĕs′tĭ vəs). [t. L: m. s. *festīvus* merry, lively] —**fes′tively,** *adv.* —**fes′tiveness,** *n.*
festivity (fĕs tĭv′ĭ tĭ), *n., pl.* **-ties. 1.** a festive celebration or occasion. **2.** (*pl.*) festive proceedings. **3.** festive character; festive gaiety or pleasure.
festoon (fĕs tōōn′), *n.* **1.** a string or chain of flowers, foliage, ribbon, etc., suspended in a curve between two points. **2.** a decorative representation of this, as in architectural work or on pottery. **3.** the curvature of the gum margin around the teeth. —*v.t.* **4.** to adorn with, or as with, festoons. **5.** to form into festoons. **6.** to connect by festoons. [t. F: m. *feston*, t. It.: m. *festone*, der. *festa* festival, FEAST]
festoonery (fĕs tōō′nə rĭ), *n.* **1.** a decoration of festoons. **2.** festoons collectively.
festschrift (fĕst′shrĭft′), *n., pl.* **-schriften** (-shrĭf′tən), **-schrifts.** a commemorative collection of articles, learned papers, etc., contributed by a number of authors, usually published in honour of a colleague. [G, lit., a festival writing]
fetal (fē′tl), *adj. Chiefly U.S.* foetal.
fetation (fē tā′shən), *n. Chiefly U.S.* foetation.
fetch (fĕch), *v.t.* **1.** to go and return with, or bring to or from a particular place: *to fetch a book from another room.* **2.** to cause to come to a particular place or condition; succeed in bringing: *to fetch a doctor.* **3.** to realize or bring in (a price, etc.). **4.** *Colloq.* to charm; captivate. **5.** to take (a breath). **6.** to utter (a sigh, groan, etc.). **7.** to deal or deliver (a stroke, blow, etc.). **8.** to perform or execute (a movement, step, leap, etc.). **9.** to start (a pump) by pouring water into the tap above the plunger; prime. **10.** *Chiefly Naut. or Dial.* to reach; arrive at. **11.** *Hunting.* (as a command to a dog) to retrieve (game). **12. fetch up,** *U.S. or Dial.* to bring up (a child, etc.). —*v.i.* **13.** to go and bring things. **14.** *Naut.* to move, go, or take a course: *to fetch about.* **15.** *Hunting.* to retrieve game. **16. fetch and carry,** to do minor menial jobs. **17. fetch up,** *Colloq.* **a.** to reach as a goal or final state; end up: *you'll fetch up in prison.* **b.** to vomit. **c.** *Naut.* to stop, as by running aground. —*n.* **18.** the act of fetching. **19.** the distance of fetching. **20.** the reach or stretch of a thing (specif. the uninterrupted distance travelled by a wave on the sea). **21.** a trick; dodge. **22.** the apparition of a living person; a wraith. **23.** *Archaic.* a stroke; effort: *a fetch of the imagination.* [ME *fecche(n)*, OE *feccan*, prob. var. of *fetian*] —**fetch′er,** *n.* —**Syn. 1.** See **bring.**
fetching (fĕch′ĭng), *adj. Colloq.* charming; captivating. —**fetch′ingly,** *adv.*
fete (fāt), *n., v.,* **feted, feting.** —*n.* **1.** a festive celebration or entertainment, esp. in aid of charity. **2.** a feast or festival. **3.** a festal day; a holiday. **4.** the festival of the saint after whom a child is named. —*v.t.* **5.** to entertain at or honour with a fete. Also, **fête.** [t. F. See FEAST]
fête champêtre (*Fr.* fĕt shäɴ pĕ′tr), *French.* an outdoor festival; a garden party.
fete day, a festival day.
fetial (fē′shəl), *adj.* **1.** pertaining to fetiales. **2.** concerned with declarations of war and treaties of peace: *fetial law.* **3.** heraldic. —*n.* **4.** one of the fetiales.
fetiales (fē′shĭ ā′lēz), *n.pl.* (in ancient Rome) a college of priests who acted as heralds and representatives of the people in disputes with foreign nations and in the declaration of war and the ratification of peace. [t. L]
fetichism (fē′tĭsh ĭz′əm, fĕt′ĭsh-), *n.* fetishism. —**fe′tichist,** *n.* —**fe′tichis′tic,** *adj.*
feticide (fē′tĭ sīd′), *n. Chiefly U.S.* foeticide.
fetid (fĕt′ĭd, fē′tĭd), *adj.* having a strong, offensive smell; stinking. Also, **foetid.** [t. L: s. *fētidus*, var. of *foetidus*] —**fet′idly,** *adv.* —**fet′idness, fetid′ity,** *n.*
fetish (fē′tĭsh, fĕt′ĭsh), *n.* **1.** a material, commonly an inanimate object, regarded with awe as being the embodiment or habitation of a potent spirit, or as having magical potency because of the materials and methods used in compounding it. **2.** any object of blind reverence. Also, **fetich.** [t. F: m. *fétich*, t. Pg.: m. *feitiço* orig. adj., artificial, g. L *factīcius* factitious] —**fe′tishlike′,** *adj.*
fetishism (fē′tĭsh ĭz′əm, fĕt′ĭsh-), *n.* **1.** belief in or use of fetishes. **2.** *Psychol.* the compulsive use of some inanimate object in attaining sexual gratification, such as a shoe, a lock of hair, stockings, underclothes, a neckpiece, etc. **3.** blind devotion. Also, **fetichism.** —**fe′tishis′tic,** *adj.*
fetishist (fē′tĭsh ĭst, fĕt′ĭsh-), *n.* a user of fetishes. Also, **fetichist.**
fetlock (fĕt′lŏk′), *n.* **1.** a part of a horse's leg situated behind the joint between the cannon bone and the great pastern bone, and bearing a tuft of hair. See illus. under **horse. 2.** this tuft of hair. **3.** the joint at this point (**fetlock joint**). [ME *fet(e)lok*, etc., c. d. G *Fissloch*; orig. obscure]
fetor (fē′tô, -tə), *n.* any strong offensive smell; a stench. Also, **foetor.** [t. L]
fetter (fĕt′ə), *n.* **1.** a chain or shackle placed on the feet. **2.** (*usually pl.*) anything that confines or restrains. —*v.t.* **3.** to put fetters upon. **4.** to confine; restrain. [ME and OE *feter*, c. OHG *fezzera*; akin to FOOT]
fetterless (fĕt′ə lĭs), *adj.* without fetters; unfettered.
fetterlock (fĕt′ə lŏk′), *n.* fetlock.
fettle (fĕt′l), *n.* **1.** state; condition: *in fine fettle.* —*v.t.* **2.** *Mech.* to remove the roughness from a casting and to verify that it is free from flaws, by hanging in chains and striking with a hammer. **3.** *Metall.* to line a furnace with loose material. **4.** *Archaic or Dial.* to put in order, put a finishing touch to. [ME *fetlen*, der. OE *fetel* belt]
fettling (fĕt′lĭng), *n. Metall.* the material with which the hearth of a puddling furnace or the like is lined, as a substance rich in oxides of iron.
fetus (fē′təs), *n. Chiefly U.S.* foetus. —**fe′tal,** *adj.*
feu (fyōō), *n., v.t. Scot. Law.* fee (defs. 5, 7). [ME *few*, t. OF: m. *fieu.* See FEE]
feuar (fyōō′ə), *n. Scot. Law.* one who holds land in fee.
Feuchtwanger (*Ger.* fŏYKHt′vȧng ər), *n.* **Lion** (*Ger.* lē′ŏn), 1884–1958, German novelist and dramatist.
feud[1] (fyōōd), *n.* **1.** a bitter, continuous hostility, esp. between two families, clans, etc. **2.** a quarrel or contention. [var. of *fead* (*a* being misread as *u*), ME *fede*, t. OF: m. *fe(i)de*, t. OHG: m. *fēhida* (G *Fehde*), c. OE *fǣhth* enmity. Cf. FOE] —**Syn. 2.** See **quarrel**[1].
feud[2] (fyōōd), *n. Law.* fee (def. 5). Also, **feod.** [t. ML: s. *feudum*, var. of *feodum.* See FEE]
feudal (fyōō′dl), *adj.* **1.** of, pertaining to, or of the nature of a feoff or fee: *a feudal estate.* **2.** of or pertaining to the holding of land in a feoff or fee. **3.** of or pertaining to the feudal system: *feudal law.* —**feu′dally,** *adv.*
feudal investiture, (in the feudal system) the public grant of the land by the lord to the tenant.
feudalism (fyōō′də lĭz′əm), *n.* the feudal organization, or its principles and practices. —**feu′dalist,** *n.* —**feu′dalis′tic,** *adj.*
feudality (fyōō dăl′ĭ tĭ), *n., pl.* **-ties. 1.** the state or quality of being feudal. **2.** the principles and practices of feudalism. **3.** a fief or fee.
feudalize (fyōō′də līz′), *v.t.,* **-lized, -lizing.** to make feudal; bring under the feudal system. Also, **feudalise.** —**feu′daliza′tion,** *n.*
feudal system, the organization in Europe during the Middle Ages, based on the holding of lands in fief or fee, and on the resulting relations between lord and vassal.
feudatory (fyōō′də tə rĭ, -trĭ), *n., pl.* **-ries.** *adj.* **1.** one who holds his lands by feudal tenure; a feudal vassal. **2.** a fief or fee. —*adj.* **3.** (of a person) owing feudal allegiance

to another. **4.** (of a kingdom) under the overlordship of an outside sovereign.

feudist[1] (fyo͞o′dĭst), *n. U.S.* a person who fights in a feud. [f. FEUD[1] + -IST]

feudist[2] (fyo͞o′dĭst), *n.* a writer or authority on feudal law. [f. FEUD[2] + -IST]

Feuerbach (*Ger.* fôʏ′ər bäKH), *n.* **Ludwig Andreas** (*Ger.* lo͞ot′ vĭKH än drā′äs), 1804–72, German philosopher.

Feuillant (*Fr.* fœ yäN′), *n.* a member of a club of constitutional royalists in the French Revolution, which disintegrated as the Revolution grew radical, violent, and antimonarchical. [t. F]

feuilleton (fŭ′ĭ tŏn′; *Fr.* fœy tôN′), *n. French.* **1.** a part of a newspaper (usually the bottom of one or more pages, marked off by a rule) devoted to light literature, fiction, criticism, etc. **2.** an item printed in the feuilleton.

fever (fē′və), *n.* **1.** a morbid condition of the body characterized by undue rise of temperature, quickening of the pulse, and disturbance of various bodily functions. **2.** any of a group of diseases in which high temperature is a prominent symptom: *scarlet fever.* **3.** intense nervous excitement. **4. fever pitch,** the height of excitement (of crowds). —*v.t.* **5.** to affect with or as with fever. [ME; OE *fefer,* t. L: m. s. *febris*] —**fe′vered,** *adj.* —**fe′verless,** *adj.*

feverfew (fē′və fyo͞o′), *n.* a perennial composite plant, *Chrysanthemum parthenium,* bearing small white flowers, formerly used as a febrifuge. [ME *fevyrfue,* OE *feferfug(i)e,* t. LL: m. *febrifugia* kind of plant, f. L: *febri(s)* fever + *-fugia.* See -FUGE]

fever heat, 1. the heat of fever; bodily heat exceeding 98·6 degrees F. **2.** feverish excitement.

feverish (fē′və rĭsh), *adj.* **1.** excited or restless, as if from fever. **2.** having fever, esp. a slight degree of fever. **3.** pertaining to, of the nature of, or resembling fever. **4.** infested with fever, as a region. **5.** having a tendency to produce fever, as food. —**fe′verishly,** *adv.* —**fe′verishness,** *n.*

feverous (fē′və rəs), *adj.* feverish. —**fe′verously,** *adv.*

fever-root (fē′və ro͞ot′), *n.* a North American caprifoliaceous herb, *Triosteum perfoliatum,* having a purgative and emetic root.

fever-tree (fē′və trē′), *n.* **1.** any of several trees which produce or are supposed to produce a febrifuge, as *Pinckneya pubens,* a small rubiaceous tree of the southeastern U.S., whose bark is used as a tonic and febrifuge. **2.** a tall, deciduous tree, *Acacia xanthophloea,* of S Africa, bearing yellow, scented flowers, and usually found in swampy places.

few (fyo͞o), *adj.* **1.** not many. —*n.* **2. the few,** the minority. **3. the Few,** fighter pilots who took part in the Battle of Britain. **4. a few,** a small number. **5. quite a few, a good few, some few,** *Colloq.* a fairly large number. [ME; OE *fēawe,* pl., c. OHG *fōhe*; akin to L *paucus,* Gk *paûros* little, in pl., few] —**few′ness,** *n.*

fewer (fyo͞o′ə), *adj., comp. of* **few.** a smaller number of.

—**Syn.** FEWER, LESS are sometimes confused because both imply a comparison with something larger (in number or in amount). FEWER applies only to number: *fewer trolleybuses are running now than ten years ago.* LESS is used in various ways. It is commonly applied to material in bulk, in reference to amount: *less petrol in the tank than we thought.* It is also used frequently with abstractions, esp. where the idea of amount is figuratively present: *less courage, less wealth.* LESS applies where such attributes as value, degree, etc. (but not size or number), are concerned: *a florin is less than a halfcrown* (in value); *a corporal is less than a sergeant* (in rank). —**Ant.** more.

fey (fā), *adj. Now Chiefly Scot.* **1.** fated to die. **2.** dying. **3.** in very high spirits, as formerly supposed to presage death. [ME; OE *fǣge* doomed to die, timid, c. G *feige* cowardly]

Feydeau (*Fr.* fē dō′), *n.* **Georges** (*Fr.* zhôrzh), 1862–1921, French dramatist.

fez (fĕz), *n., pl.* **fezzes.** a felt cap, usually of a red colour, having the shape of a truncated cone, and ornamented with a long black tassel, formerly the national headdress of the Turks. [t. Turk.; named after the town of FEZ]

Fez (fĕz), *n.* a town in N Morocco; the traditional northern capital of the former sultanate. 235,000 (est. 1965). See **Marrakech.**

Fez

Fezzan (fĕ zän′), *n.* a region in SW Libya: a portion of the Sahara with numerous oases. 54,438 pop. (1954); ab. 280,000 sq. mi. *Chief town:* Murzuq.

ff., 1. folios. **2.** and the following (pages, verses, etc.). **3.** *Music.* fortissimo.

F.F.A., Fellow of the Faculty of Actuaries (in Scotland).

f.f.a., 1. *Chem.* free fatty acid. **2.** free from alongside (ship).

Fg Off., Flying Officer.

F.G.S., Fellow of the Geological Society.

f-hole (ĕf′hōl′), *n.* either of a pair of holes in the table of a violin, shaped like an *f.*

F.I., Falkland Islands.

F.I.A., Fellow of the Institute of Actuaries.

fiacre (fĭ ä′krə; *Fr.* fyȧ′kr), *n.* a hackney coach. [t. F, named after the Hôtel de St *Fiacre* in Paris]

Fianarantsoa (*Fr.* fyȧ nȧ rȧNt sō ȧ′), *n.* a town in E central Malagasy Republic. 37,598 (1964).

fiancé (fĭ ŏn′sā; *Fr.* fyäN sė′), *n.* a man engaged to be married; a man to whom a woman is engaged. [t. F, pp. of *fiancer* betroth, ult. der. *fier* trust, g. L *fidere*] —**fian′cée,** *n. fem.*

Fianna (fē′ə nə), *n.* the Fenians (def. 2).

Fianna Fail (foil, fīl), an Irish nationalist party, organized in 1927 by Eamon De Valera, advocating establishment of an Irish Republic. [t. Irish: f. *Fianna* Fenians + *Fāil,* gen. sing. of *fāl* sod]

fiar (fē′ə), *n. Scot. Law.* the owner of land in fee simple.

fiasco (fĭ ăs′kō), *n., pl.* **-cos. 1.** an ignominious failure. **2.** a bottle or flask. [t. It.: lit., bottle; sense development obscure]

fiat (fī′ət, -ăt), *n.* **1.** an authoritative decree, sanction, or order. **2.** a formula containing the word *fiat,* by which a person in authority gave his sanction. [t. L: let it be done, or made]

fiat lux (fī ′ăt lo͝oks′), *Latin.* let there be light.

fib[1] (fĭb), *n., v.,* **fibbed, fibbing.** —*n.* **1.** a trivial falsehood. —*v.i.* **2.** to tell a fib. [short for *fibble-fable,* redupl. of FABLE] —**fib′ber,** *n.* —**Syn. 1.** See **falsehood.**

fib[2] (fĭb), *v.t.,* **fibbed, fibbing.** *Slang.* to strike; beat. [orig. unknown]

fibr-, a word element meaning 'fibre', as in *fibrin.* Also, **fibri-, fibro-.** [comb. form repr. L *fibra*]

fibre (fī′bə), *n.* **1.** a fine threadlike piece, as of cotton, jute, or asbestos. **2.** a slender filament. **3.** filaments collectively. **4.** matter composed of filaments. **5.** fibrous structure. **6.** character: *moral fibre.* **7.** *Bot.* **a.** filamentous matter from the bast tissue or other parts of plants, used for industrial purposes. **b.** a slender, threadlike root of a plant. **c.** a slender, threadlike bast cell. **8.** *Chem.* vulcanized fibre. Also, *U.S.,* **fiber.** [ME *fibre,* t. F, t. L: m. *fibra* fibre, filament] —**fi′bred,** *adj.* —**fi′breless,** *adj.*

fibreboard (fī′bə bôd′), *n.* **1.** a building material made of wood or other plant fibres compressed and cemented into rigid sheets. **2.** a sheet of fibreboard. Also, *U.S.,* **fiberboard.**

fibreglass (fī′bə gläs′), *n.* **1.** a material consisting of extremely fine filaments of glass which are combined in yarn and woven into fabrics, or are used in masses as an insulator or used embedded in plastic as a construction material for boat hulls, light car bodies, etc.; glass fibre. **2.** (*cap.*) a trademark for a range of these materials. Also, *U.S.,* **fiberglass, fiberglas.**

fibri-, var. of **fibro-.**

fibriform (fī′brĭ fôm′), *adj.* of the form of a fibre or fibres. [f. FIBRI- + -FORM]

fibril (fī′brĭl), *n.* a small or fine fibre. [t. NL: m. s. *fibrilla,* dim. of L *fibra* fibre]

fibrillar (fī′brĭ lə), *adj.* of, pertaining to, or of the nature of fibrils.

fibrillation (fī′brĭ lā′shən, fĭb′rĭ-), *n. Med.* a local contraction of single muscle fibres invisible under the skin.

fibrilliform (fī brĭl′ĭ fôm′), *adj.* of the form of a fibril.

fibrillose (fī′brĭ lōs′), *adj.* composed of or furnished with fibrils.

fibrin (fī′brĭn), *n.* **1.** *Biochem., Physiol.* a white, rough, fibrous protein, formed in the clotting of blood. **2.** *Bot.* a substance like fibrin found in some plants; gluten. [f. FIBR- + -IN[2]]

fibrino-, a word element representing **fibrin.**

fibrinogen (fī brĭn′ə jən), *n. Physiol.* a globulin occurring in blood and yielding fibrin in the coagulation of blood.

fibrinogenic (fī′brĭ nō jĕn′ĭk), *adj. Physiol.* producing fibrin. Also, **fibrinogenous** (fī′brĭ nŏj′ĭ nəs).

fibrinogenopoenia (fī′brĭ nō jĕn′ō pē′nyə, fī brĭn′ō-), *n. Physiol.* a state of decreased fibrinogen in the blood.

fibrinous (fī′brĭ nəs), *adj.* containing, composed of, or of the nature of fibrin.

fibro-, var. of **fibr-,** before consonants.

fibroid (fī′broid), *adj.* **1.** resembling fibre or fibrous tissue. **2.** composed of fibres, as a tumour. —*n.* **3.** *Pathol.* a tumour largely composed of smooth muscle and fibrous tissue.

fibroin (fī′brō ĭn), *n. Biochem.* an indigestible protein, a principal component of spiders' webs and silk.

fibrolite (fī′brə līt′), *n.* a mineral, aluminium silicate, Al_2SiO_5, occurring as aggregates of thin fibrous crystals in metamorphic rocks such as shales and mudstones; sillimanite.

fibroma (fī brō′mə), *n., pl.* **-mata** (-mə tə), **-mas.** *Pathol.*

a tumour consisting essentially of fibrous tissue. [NL: f. s. L *fibra* fibre + *-oma* -OMA]

fibroplasia (fī′brō plā′zyə), *n. Pathol.* the formation of fibrous tissue, as occurs in the healing of wounds.

fibrosis (fī brō′sĭs), *n. Pathol.* the development in an organ of excess fibrous connective tissue. [NL: f. s. L *fibra* fibre + *-osis* -OSIS]

fibrositis (fī′brə sī′tĭs), *n. Med.* an inflammatory change in fibrous tissue, as muscle sheaths, ligament tendons, fasciae, and the like, causing pain and difficulty in movement.

fibrous (fī′brəs), *adj.* containing, consisting of, or resembling fibres. —**fi′brously,** *adv.* —**fi′brousness,** *n.* [t. NL: m. s. *fibrōsus*, der. L *fibra* fibre]

fibrovascular (fī′brō văs′kyŏŏ lə), *adj.* (of a conducting strand in a leaf or stem) composed of phloem, xylem, and associated fibres which are frequently in the form of a complete or partial sheath.

fibster (fĭb′stə), *n. Colloq.* one who tells fibs.

fibula (fĭb′yŏŏ lə), *n., pl.* **-lae** (-lē′), **-las. 1.** *Anat.* the outer and thinner of the two bones of the lower leg, extending from the knee to the ankle. See diag. under **skeleton. 2.** *Zool.* a corresponding bone (often rudimentary, or ankylosed with the tibia) of the leg or hind limb of other animals. **3.** *Archaeol.* a clasp or brooch, usually more or less ornamented. [t. L: clasp, buckle, pin] —**fib′ular,** *adj.*

-fic, an adjective suffix meaning 'making', 'producing', 'causing', as in *colorific, frigorific, horrific, pacific, prolific, soporific.* [t. L: s. *-ficus* making. Cf. F. *-fique*]

-fication, a suffix of nouns of action or state corresponding to verbs ending in *-fy*, as in *deification, pacification.* [t. L: s. *-ficātio*, der. *-ficāre.* See -FY]

Fichte (*Ger.* fĭKH′tə), *n.* **Johann Gottlieb** (*Ger.* yō′hän gŏt′lēp), 1762–1814, German philosopher. —**Fichtean** (fĭKH′tĭ ən, fĭk′-), *adj.*

fichu (fē′shōō; *Fr.* fē shY′), *n.* a kind of scarf of muslin, lace, or the like, generally triangular in shape, worn about the neck by women, with the ends drawn together or crossed in front. [t. F, der. *ficher* to throw on in haste]

fickle (fĭk′l), *adj.* likely to change from caprice, irresolution, or instability. [ME *fikel*, OE *ficol* deceitful, treacherous, akin to *gefic* deceit, *befician* deceive, *ficung* fraud] —**fick′leness,** *n.* —**Syn.** unstable, unsteady, inconstant, changeable, variable, capricious, fitful.

fico (fē′kō), *n., pl.* **-coes.** *Archaic.* the merest trifle. [t. It., g. L *fīcus* fig]

fict., fiction.

fictile (fĭk′tĭl), *adj.* **1.** capable of being moulded; plastic. **2.** moulded into form by art. **3.** made of earth, clay, etc., by a potter. **4.** having to do with pottery. [t. L: m. s. *fictilis*, der. *fingere* form]

fiction (fĭk′shən), *n.* **1.** the branch of literature comprising works of imaginative narration, esp. in prose form. **2.** works of this class, as novels or short stories. **3.** something feigned, invented, or imagined; a made-up story. **4.** the act of feigning, inventing, or imagining. **5.** *Law.* a statement or supposition which is known to be untrue, made by authority of law to bring a case within the operation of a rule of law. [ME, t. L: s. *fictio* a making, fashioning, feigning]

—**Syn. 3.** FICTION, FABRICATION, FIGMENT suggest a story which is without basis in reality. FICTION suggests a story invented and fashioned either to entertain or to deceive: *clever fiction, pure fiction.* FABRICATION applies particularly to a false but carefully invented statement or series of statements, in which some truth is sometimes interwoven, the whole usually intended to deceive: *fabrications to lure speculators.* FIGMENT applies to a tale, idea, or statement often made up to explain, justify, or glorify oneself: *his rich uncle was a figment of his imagination.* —**Ant. 3.** fact.

fictional (fĭk′shən əl), *adj.* of, pertaining to, or of the nature of fiction. —**fic′tionally,** *adv.*

fictionist (fĭk′shə nĭst), *n.* a writer of fiction.

fictitious (fĭk tĭsh′əs), *adj.* **1.** counterfeit; false; not genuine: *fictitious names.* **2.** pertaining to or consisting of fiction; imaginatively produced or set forth; created by the imagination: *a fictitious hero.* [t. L: m. *fictīcius* artificial] —**ficti′tiously,** *adv.* —**ficti′tiousness,** *n.*

fictitious person, *Law.* a legal entity or artificial person, as a corporation.

fictive (fĭk′tĭv), *adj.* **1.** fictitious; imaginary. **2.** pertaining to the creation of fiction. —**fic′tively,** *adv.*

fid (fĭd), *n. Naut.* **1.** a stout piece of wood or metal passed through the heel of a topmast to keep the mast in position. **2.** a conical wooden pin used to open strands of rope in splicing. **3.** a bar or pin to support or steady something. [orig. obscure]

-fid, an adjective suffix meaning 'divided', 'lobed', as in *bifid, trifid, multifid, pinnatifid.* [t. L: s. *-fidus*, der. *findere* cleave]

Fid. Def., Fidei Defensor.

fiddle (fĭd′l), *n., v.,* **-dled, -dling.** —*n.* **1.** a stringed musical instrument of the viol class, esp. a violin (now only in familiar or contemptuous use, or to denote bowed instruments of the Orient and the Middle Ages). **2.** *Naut.* a device to prevent things from rolling off the table in bad weather. **3. fit as a fiddle,** in excellent health. **4. play second fiddle,** to take a minor part. **5.** *Colloq.* an illegal or underhand transaction or contrivance. —*v.i.* **6.** *Colloq.* to play on the fiddle. **7.** to make aimless movements, as with the hands. **8.** to trifle. **9. to have a face as long as a fiddle,** to look dismal. —*v.t.* **10.** *Colloq.* to play (a tune) on a fiddle. **11.** to trifle: *to fiddle time away.* **12.** to contrive by illegal or underhand means. [ME (and prob. OE) *fithele* (see FIDDLER), c. G *Fiedel*, Icel. *fidhla.* Cf. ML *vitula, vidula* VIOL]

fiddle-back (fĭd′l băk′), *n.* a chair-back shaped like a fiddle.

fiddle bow, a bow strung with horsehair with which the strings of the violin or a similar instrument are set in vibration.

fiddle-de-dee (fĭd′l dĭ dē′), *interj.* nonsense.

fiddle-faddle (fĭd′l făd′l), *n., v.,* **-dled, -dling.** *Colloq.* —*n.* **1.** nonsense; something trivial. —*v.i.* **2.** to fuss with trifles. [redupl. of FIDDLE, v.]

fiddlehead (fĭd′l hĕd′), *n.* an ornament at the bow of a ship, containing a scroll somewhat like that at the head of a violin.

fiddler (fĭd′lə), *n.* **1.** one who plays the fiddle. **2.** one who trifles, makes aimless movements, etc. **3.** *Colloq.* a cheat or rogue. [ME and OE *fithelere*, c. Icel. *fithlari*]

fiddler crab, any small Indo-Pacific burrowing crab of the genus *Uca*, the male of which has one greatly enlarged claw.

Fiddler crab, *Uca pugilator* (*Gelasmus annulipes*) (Shell width 1 in.)

fiddlestick (fĭd′l stĭk′), *n.* **1.** a fiddle bow. **2.** a mere nothing.

fiddlesticks (fĭd′l stĭks′), *interj.* nonsense.

fiddlewood (fĭd′l wŏŏd′), *n.* **1.** the heavy, hard, durable wood of various West Indian and other trees. **2.** any of the trees.

fiddling (fĭd′lĭng), *adj.* trifling; trivial.

fiddly (fĭd′lĭ), *adj. Colloq.* difficult or exacting, as something done with the hands.

F.I.D.E., (F *Fédération Internationale des Échecs*) International Chess Federation.

fideicommissary (fī′dĭ ī kŏm′ĭ sə rĭ), *n., pl.* **-ries,** *adj. Civil Law.* —*n.* **1.** the recipient of a fideicommissum. —*adj.* **2.** of, pertaining to, or resembling a fideicommissum. [t. L: m. s. *fideī commissārius.* See -ARY[1]]

fideicommissum (fī′dĭ ī kə mĭs′əm), *n., pl.* **-missa** (-mĭs′ə). *Civil Law.* a request by a testator that his heir convey a specified part of the estate to another person, or permit another person to enjoy such a part. [t. L, prop. neut. pp. of *fideī committere* entrust to faith]

Fidei Defensor (fī′dĭ ī′ dĭ fĕn′sô), *Latin.* Defender of the Faith, one of the titles of English sovereigns.

fidelity (fĭ dĕl′ĭ tĭ), *n., pl.* **-ties. 1.** the strict observance of promises, duties, etc. **2.** loyalty. **3.** conjugal faithfulness. **4.** strict adherence to truth or fact; (of persons) honesty, truthfulness; (of descriptions, copies, etc.) correspondence with the original. **5.** *Radio.* the ability of a transmitter or receiver to produce radio waves or sound which reproduce its input accurately (often in combination): *a high-fidelity receiver.* [t. L: m. s. *fidēlitas* faithfulness] —**Syn. 2.** See **loyalty.**

fidge (fĭj), *v.i.,* **fidged, fidging,** *n. Obs.* fidget. [var. of d. *fitch* v., c. Icel. *fīkja* move restlessly, be eager]

fidget (fĭj′ĭt), *v.i.* **1.** to move about restlessly or impatiently; be uneasy. —*v.t.* **2.** to cause to fidget; make uneasy. —*n.* **3.** (*often pl.*) condition of restlessness or uneasiness. **4.** one who fidgets. [der. FIDGE]

fidgety (fĭj′ĭ tĭ), *adj.* restless; uneasy. —**fidg′etiness,** *n.*

F.I.D.O., Fog Investigation Dispersal Operation.

fiducial (fĭ dyōō′shyəl), *adj.* **1.** *Physics, etc.* accepted as a fixed basis of reference or comparison: *a fiducial point.* **2.** based on or having truth: *fiducial dependence upon God.* [t. ML: s. *fīdūciālis*, der. L *fīdūcia* trust] —**fidu′cially,** *adv.*

fiduciary (fĭ dyōō′shyə rĭ), *adj., n., pl.* **-ries.** —*adj.* **1.** *Law.* of or pertaining to the relation between a fiduciary and his principal: *a fiduciary capacity, a fiduciary duty.* **2.** depending on public confidence for value or currency. **3.** *Obs.* like or based on truth or reliance. —*n.* **4.** *Law.* a person to whom property is entrusted to hold, control, or manage for another.

fiduciary note issue, that part of the note issue of the Bank of England, not covered by a holding of gold, and authorized by act of Parliament.

fidus Achates (fī′dəs ə kā′tēz), *Latin.* **1.** faithful Achates (the comrade of Aeneas). **2.** a devoted, trustworthy friend.

fie (fī), *interj.* an exclamation expressing: **1.** disgust, disapprobation, etc. **2.** humorous pretence of being shocked. [ME *fi*, t. OF, g. L *fī*, but cf. Icel. *fȳ*]

F.I.E., (F *Fédération Internationale d'Escrime*) International Fencing Federation.

fief (fēf), *n.* a feoff or fee. [t. F. See FEE]

field (fēld), *n.* **1.** a piece of open or cleared ground, esp. one suitable for pasture or tillage. **2.** a piece of ground devoted to sports or contests. **3.** *Horseracing.* all the contestants not individually favoured in betting: *to bet on the field.* **4.** *Hunting.* those following the hounds. **5.** *Cricket, etc.* that part of the ground on which the fielders play. **6.** *Cricket, etc.* the fielders collectively. **7.** *Mil.* **a.** the scene or area of active military operations. **b.** a battlefield. **c.** a battle. **8.** an expanse of anything: *a field of ice.* **9.** any region characterized by a particular feature or product: *a goldfield.* **10.** the surface of a canvas, shield, etc., on which something is portrayed. **11.** (in a flag) the ground of each division. **12.** a sphere, or range of activity, interest, opportunity, etc. **13.** a place of investigation, work, etc., away from one's office, laboratory, study, etc., esp. one where basic data and original material are gathered for later analysis. **14.** *Her.* the surface of a shield or escutcheon, or a single section of a quartered shield. **15.** *Physics.* a region of space influenced by some agent: *electric field, temperature field.* **16.** *Optics.* the entire area visible through or projected by an optical instrument at a given time. **17.** *Elect.* **a.** the main magnetic field of an electric motor or generator. **b.** the structure in a dynamo designed to establish magnetic lines of force in an armature. **18.** *Maths.* a number system which has the same properties relative to the operations of addition, subtraction, multiplication, and division as the number system of all real numbers: *the field of all rational numbers.* **19.** *Computers.* a group of columns on a punched card into which a unit of information is punched. **20.** *Obs.* open country: *beasts of the field.* —*v.t.* **21.** *Cricket, etc.* **a.** to stop, or catch, and throw (the ball) as a fielder. **b.** to place (a player or group of players) into the field to play. —*v.i.* **22.** *Cricket, etc.* **a.** to act as a fielder; field. **b.** to take the field. —*adj.* **23.** *Sport, etc.* of, or happening or competed on, a field rather than a track: *discus, pole vault and long jump, are field events.* **24.** *Mil.* of or pertaining to campaign and active combat service as distinguished from service in rear areas or at headquarters: *a field soldier.* **25.** of, pertaining to, or conducted in, the open air or close to primary sources of data or information. [ME and OE *feld*, c. G *Feld*]

Field (fēld), *n.* **John,** 1782–1837, Irish pianist and composer.

field allowance, *Mil.* extra pay for officers on active service.

field ambulance, a medical unit to give emergency treatment on the battlefield.

field artillery, *Mil.* artillery mobile enough to accompany troops in the field.

field battery, *Mil.* a battery of field-guns.

field book, 1. a surveyor's book for recording measurements. **2. a.** *Bot.* a book for preserving specimens while in the field. **b.** *Bot., Zool.* a notebook for recording observations in the field. **c.** a guide to the flora or fauna or one aspect of one.

field day, 1. a day devoted to outdoor activities or sports. **2.** a day on which a hunt meets. **3.** a day when explorations, investigations by a society, etc., are carried on in the field. **4.** *Mil.* **a.** a day on which operations in the field are practised. **b.** a day of display of manoeuvres, etc. **5.** an occasion of unrestricted enjoyment, amusement, etc. **6.** a day of brilliant or exciting events.

field emission, *Physics.* the emission of electrons from an unheated conductor as a result of an electric field.

fielder (fēl′də), *n.* **1.** *Cricket, etc.* a player who fields the ball. **2.** any member of the team which is fielding, as opposed to the one which is batting.

field event, an athletic event which does not take place on a track, as a jumping or throwing event.

fieldfare (fēld′fɛə′), *n.* a large European thrush, *Turdus pilaris*, of reddish brown colour, with a blackish tail and ashy head. [ME *feldefare* (with two *f's* by allit. assim.), late OE *feldeware* inhabitant of the fields]

field-glasses (fēld′glä′sĭz), *n.pl.* a compact binocular telescope for use out of doors. See **binoculars.**

field goal, *American Football.* a goal scored by kicking the ball over the crossbar of the opponent's goal.

field guidance, *Aeron.* guidance of a missile to a point within a natural (e.g. gravitational) or artificial (e.g. radio) field by means of the properties of that field.

field-gun (fēld′gŭn′), *n.* a cannon mounted on a carriage for service in the field.

field-gunnery (fēld′gŭn′ə rĭ), *n.* the act or practice of firing field-guns.

field hockey, hockey (as distinguished from *ice hockey*).

field hospital, a temporary hospital on or near a battlefield.

Fielding (fēl′dĭng), *n.* **Henry,** 1707–54, English novelist.

field lens, *Optics.* the lens in the eyepiece of an optical instrument which is farthest from the eye.

field madder (măd′ə), a small annual rubiaceous weed with pale mauve flowers, *Sherardia arvensis*, widespread in non-tropical regions.

field magnet, a magnet which is used to produce a magnetic field.

field marshal, an officer of the highest military rank in the British and certain other armies, and of the second highest rank in the French army.

fieldmouse (fēld′mous′), *n.* any of various short-tailed mice or voles inhabiting fields and meadows.

field officer, *Mil.* an officer of the rank of major, lieutenant colonel, or colonel.

field of force, *Physics.* field (def. 15).

field-piece (fēld′pēs′), *n.* *Mil.* a field-gun.

Fields (fēldz), *n.* **Gracie** (*Grace Stansfield*), born 1898, English popular singer.

fieldsman (fēldz′mən), *n., pl.* **-men.** a fielder in cricket.

field study, a planned study depending on first-hand observations and (in sociology) on inquiries and interviews. See **field work.**

field trial, a trial of animals, as hunting dogs, in actual performance in the field.

field trip, an investigation away from the classroom, laboratory, office, etc.

field winding, *Elect.* the electrically conducting circuit, usually a number of coils wound on individual poles and connected in series, which produces excitation in a motor or generator.

field work, work done in the field, as by a geologist, or a field study, as by a sociologist.

fieldwork (fēld′wûk′), *n.* *Fort.* a temporary fortification constructed in the field.

fiend (fēnd), *n.* **1.** Satan; the devil. **2.** any evil spirit. **3.** a diabolically cruel or wicked person. **4.** *Colloq.* a person or thing that causes mischief or annoyance. **5.** *Colloq.* one who is hopelessly addicted to some pernicious habit: *an opium fiend.* **6.** *Colloq.* one who is excessively interested in some game, sport, etc.: *a bridge fiend.* [ME *feend*, OE *fēond*, c. G *Feind*, all orig. ppr. of a verb meaning hate; cf. OE *fēo(ga)n*] —**fiend′like′,** *adj.*

fiendish (fēn′dĭsh), *adj.* **1.** resembling, or characteristic of, a fiend. **2.** diabolically cruel and wicked. —**fiend′ishly,** *adv.* —**fiend′ishness,** *n.*

fierce (fĭəs), *adj.* **fiercer, fiercest. 1.** wild or vehement in temper, appearance, or action: *fierce animals, fierce looks.* **2.** violent in force, intensity, etc.: *fierce winds.* **3.** furiously eager or intense: *fierce competition.* **4.** *Slang.* extremely bad, unpleasant, etc. [ME *fers, fiers*, t. OF, g. L *ferus* wild, fierce, cruel] —**fierce′ly,** *adv.* —**fierce′ness,** *n.*

—**Syn. 1.** savage, cruel, fell, brutal, barbarous, bloodthirsty, murderous. FIERCE, FEROCIOUS, TRUCULENT suggest vehemence and violence of manner and conduct. FIERCE suggests violence of temper, manner, or action: *fierce in repelling a foe.* FEROCIOUS implies fierceness or cruelty, esp. of a bloodthirsty kind, in disposition or action: *a ferocious glare, ferocious brutality towards helpless refugees.* TRUCULENT suggests an intimidating or bullying fierceness of manner or conduct: *his truculent attitude kept them terrified and submissive.* —**Ant. 1.** tame, mild.

fieri facias (fī′ə rī′ fā′shĭ əs), *Latin.* a writ commanding the sheriff to levy upon the goods, or the goods and lands, of a judgement debtor for the collection of the amount due. [L: lit., cause it to be done]

fiery (fī′ə rĭ), *adj.,* **fierier, fieriest. 1.** consisting of, attended with, characterized by, or containing fire: *a fiery discharge.* **2.** intensely hot, as winds, desert sands, etc. **3.** like or suggestive of fire: *a fiery heat, a fiery red.* **4.** flashing or glowing, as the eye. **5.** intensely ardent, impetuous, or passionate: *fiery courage, zeal, speech, etc.* **6.** easily angered; irritable. **7.** inflammable, as gas in a mine. **8.** containing inflammable gas, as a mine. **9.** inflamed, as a tumour or sore. **10.** causing a burning sensation, as liquors or condiments. —**fier′ily,** *adv.* —**fier′iness,** *n.* —**Syn. 3.** flaming, glowing, burning. **5.** fervent, vehement, spirited, impassioned.

fiery cross, 1. a wooden cross, charred or dipped in blood, formerly sent among Highlanders as a call to arms. **2.** a burning cross, the emblem of several organizations, notably the Ku Klux Klan.

Fiesole (*It.* fyĕ′zò lè), *n.* **1.** a hill town in central Italy, near Florence. 11,873 (1961). **2. Giovanni da** (*It.* jò vän′nē dä) (*Fra Angelico*), 1387–1455, Italian painter.

fiesta (fĭ ĕs′tə; *Sp.* fyĕs′tä), *n. Spanish.* **1.** a religious celebration; a saint's day. **2.** a holiday or festival.

fife (fīf), *n.*, *v.*, **fifed, fifing.** —*n.* **1.** a high-pitched flute much used in military music. —*v.i.*, *v.t.* **2.** to play on a fife. [t. G: m. *Pfeife* PIPE] —**fif′er,** *n.*

Fife (fīf), *n.* a county in E Scotland. 320,877 pop. (1965); 505 sq. mi. *Co. town:* Cupar. Also, **Fifeshire** (fīf′shĭə,-shə).

Fife

fife rail, *Naut.* a rail round the lower part of a mast, for securing belaying pins.

fifteen (fĭf′tēn′), *n.* **1.** a cardinal number, ten plus five. **2.** a symbol for this number, as 15 or XV. **3.** a set or group of fifteen, as a rugby union team. —*adj.* **4.** amounting to fifteen in number. [ME and OE *fiftene*, f. *fīf* FIVE + *-tēne* -TEEN]

fifteenth (fĭf′tēnth′), *adj.* **1.** next after the fourteenth. **2.** being one of fifteen equal parts. —*n.* **3.** a fifteenth part, esp. of one ($^1/_{15}$). **4.** the fifteenth member of a series.

fifth (fĭfth), *adj.* **1.** next after the fourth. **2.** being one of five equal parts. —*n.* **3.** a fifth part, esp. of one ($^1/_5$). **4.** the fifth member of a series. **5.** *Music.* **a.** a note on the fifth degree from another note (counted as the first). **b.** the interval between such notes. **c.** the harmonic combination of such notes. [earlier *fift*, ME *fifte*, OE *fīfta*; mod. *-th* from *fourth*, etc.] —**fifth′ly,** *adv.*

Fifth Amendment, the section of the Constitution of the U.S. concerning certain criminal proceedings, double jeopardy, etc. It is sometimes invoked by witnesses at legislative hearings to avoid giving self-incriminating testimony.

fifth column, **1.** a body of persons residing in a country who are in sympathy with its enemies, and who are serving enemy interests or are ready to assist an enemy attack. **2.** (originally) Franco sympathizers in Madrid during the civil war (in allusion to a statement in 1936 that the insurgents had four columns marching on Madrid and a fifth column of sympathizers in the city ready to rise and betray it). —**fifth columnist.**

fifth position, *Ballet.* a standing position similar to the first, but with the left foot in front, the heel and toe of the left foot adjacent to the toe and heel of the right foot.

Fifth Republic. See **Republic** (def. 4).

fifth wheel, **1.** a horizontal ring (or segment of a ring) consisting of two bands which slide on each other, placed above the front axle of a carriage and designed to support the forepart of the body while allowing it to turn freely in a horizontal plane. **2.** an extra wheel for a four-wheeled vehicle. **3.** any extra or superfluous thing or person.

fifty (fĭf′tĭ), *n.*, *pl.* **-ties,** *adj.* —*n.* **1.** a cardinal number, ten times five. **2.** a symbol for this number, as 50 or L. **3.** a set of fifty persons or things. **4.** (*pl.*) the numbers from 50 to 59 of a series, esp. with reference to years of age or the years of a century, esp. the 20th. —*adj.* **5.** amounting to fifty in number. [ME; OE *fīftig*, f. *fīf* FIVE + *-tig* -TY[1]] —**fif′tieth,** *adj.*, *n.*

fifty-fifty (fĭf′tĭ fĭf′tĭ), *adv.*, *adj. Colloq.* with equality of shares, as of profits.

fig[1] (fĭg), *n.* **1.** any tree or shrub of the moraceous genus *Ficus*, esp. a small tree, *F. carica*, native to south-western Asia, bearing a turbinate or pear-shaped fruit which is eaten fresh or preserved or dried. **2.** the fruit of such a tree or shrub, or of any related species. **3.** any of various plants having a fruit somewhat resembling the fig. **4.** the value of a fig; the merest trifle; the least bit. **5.** a gesture of contempt; a fico. [ME *fige*, t. OF, t. OPr.: m. *figa*, ult. der. L *ficus*]

fig[2] (fĭg), *v.*, **figged, figging,** *n. Colloq.* —*v.t.* **1.** to dress or array (fol by *out*). **2.** to furbish (fol. by *up*). —*n.* **3.** dress or array: *in full fig.* **4.** condition. [orig. uncert.]

fig., **1.** figurative. **2.** figuratively. **3.** figure; figures.

fight (fīt), *n.*, *v.*, **fought, fighting.** —*n.* **1.** a battle or combat. **2.** any quarrel, contest, or struggle. **3.** ability or inclination to fight: *there was no fight left in him, to show fight.* **4.** *Naval.* (formerly) a bulkhead or other screen for the protection of the men during a battle. —*v.i.* **5.** to engage in battle or in single combat; attempt to defeat, subdue, or destroy an adversary. **6.** to contend in any manner; strive vigorously for or against something. —*v.t.* **7.** to contend with in battle or combat; war against. **8.** to contend with or against in any manner. **9.** to carry on (a battle, duel, etc.). **10.** to maintain (a cause, quarrel, etc.) by fighting or contending. **11.** to make (one's way) by fighting or striving. **12.** to cause or set (a boxer, dog, etc.) to fight. **13.** to manage or manoeuvre (troops, ships, guns, planes, etc.) in battle. **14. fight down,** to repress or overcome. **15. fight it out,** to struggle till a decisive result is obtained. **16. fight off,** to struggle against; drive away. **17. fight shy of,** to keep carefully aloof from (a person, affair, etc.). [ME; OE *fe(o)htan*, c. G *fechten*] —**fight′able,** *adj.*

—**Syn. 1, 2.** encounter, engagement, affray, fray; melee, scuffle, tussle. FIGHT, COMBAT, CONFLICT, CONTEST denote a struggle of some kind. FIGHT connotes a hand-to-hand struggle for supremacy, literally or in a figurative sense. COMBAT suggests an armed encounter, to settle a dispute. CONFLICT implies a bodily, mental, or moral struggle caused by opposing views, beliefs, etc. CONTEST applies to either a friendly or a hostile struggle for a definite prize or aim.

fighter (fī′tə), *n.* **1.** one who fights. **2.** *Mil.* an aircraft designed to seek out and destroy enemy aircraft in the air, and to protect bomber aircraft.

fighter-bomber (fī′tə bŏm′ə), *n. Mil.* an aircraft that combines the functions of a fighter and a bomber.

fighting chance, a possibility of success following a struggle.

fighting cock, **1.** a gamecock. **2.** *Colloq.* a pugnacious person.

fighting fish, a small brilliantly coloured aquarium fish, a species of *Betta*, noted for the fighting habits of the males.

fighting fit, in very good physical condition.

Fighting French, (in World War II) those French who, under the leadership of General Charles de Gaulle, continued to resist the Nazis after the capitulation of France in 1940.

fighting top, (in sailing warships) the fore, main, and mizzen tops, which were platforms built round the lower masts, just above the lower yard. They were fighting stations manned by marksmen armed with muskets, who fired on those on the decks of enemy warships.

fig leaf, **1.** the leaf of a fig tree, esp. in allusion to the first covering of Adam and Eve, Gen. 3:7. **2.** something designed to conceal what is shameful or indecorous.

fig marigold, any of various herbs of the genus *Mesembryanthemum*, with showy white, yellow, or pink flowers.

figment (fĭg′mənt), *n.* **1.** a mere product of the imagination; a pure invention. **2.** a feigned, invented, or imagined story, theory, etc. [t. L: s. *figmentum* image, fiction, anything made] —**Syn. 2.** See **fiction.**

figural (fĭg′ə rəl, fĭg′yə rəl), *adj.* of, or pertaining to, figures.

figurant (fĭg′yŏŏ rənt; *Fr.* fē gʏ räɴ′), *n.* **1.** a ballet dancer who dances only with others in groups or figures. **2.** *Theat.* a minor character on the stage who has little or nothing to say. [t. F, ppr. of *figurer*, t. L: m. s. *figūrāre* form] —**figurante** (fĭg′yŏŏ rŏnt′; *Fr.* fē gʏ räɴt′), *n. fem.*

figurate (fĭg′yŏŏ rĭt), *adj.* **1.** of a certain determinate figure or shape. **2.** *Music.* characterized by the use of passing notes or other embellishments; florid. [t. L: m. s. *figūrātus*, pp., figured]

figuration (fĭg′yŏŏ rā′shən), *n.* **1.** the act of shaping into a particular figure. **2.** the resulting figure or shape. **3.** the act of representing figuratively. **4.** a figurative representation. **5.** the act of marking or adorning with designs. **6.** *Music.* **a.** the employment of passing notes or other embellishments. **b.** the figuring of a bass part.

figurative (fĭg′yŏŏ rə tĭv), *adj.* **1.** of the nature of or involving a figure of speech, esp. a metaphor; metaphorical; not literal: *a figurative expression.* **2.** metaphorically so called: *this remark was a figurative boomerang.* **3.** abounding in or addicted to figures of speech. **4.** representing by means of a figure or likeness, as in drawing or sculpture. **5.** representing by a figure or emblem; emblematic. —**fig′uratively,** *adv.* —**fig′urativeness,** *n.*

figure (fĭg′ə), *n.*, *v.*, **-ured, -uring.** —*n.* **1.** a written symbol other than a letter. **2.** a numerical symbol, esp. an Arabic numeral. **3.** an amount or value expressed in numbers. **4.** (*pl.*) the use of numbers in calculating: *poor at figures.* **5.** form or shape, as determined by outlines or exterior surfaces: *round, square, or cubical in figure.* **6.** the bodily form or frame: *a slender or graceful figure.* **7.** an individual bodily form, or a person with reference to form or appearance: *a tall figure stood in the doorway.* **8.** a person as he appears or as presented before the eyes of the world: *political figures.* **9.** a character or personage, esp. one of distinction: *a figure in society.* **10.** the appearance or impression made by a person, or sometimes a thing. **11.** a diagram or pictorial representation in a book, esp. a textbook. **12.** a representation, pictorial or sculptured, of something, esp. of the human form. **13.** an emblem or type: *the dove is a figure of peace.* **14.** *Rhet.* a figure of speech. **15.** a device or pattern, as in cloth. **16.** a movement, pattern, or series of movements in skating. **17.** a distinct movement or division of a dance. **18.** *Music.* a short succession of musical notes, either as melody or as a group of chords, which produces a single, complete and distinct impression. **19.** *Geom.* a combination of geometrical elements disposed in a particular form or shape: *the circle, square, and polygon are plane figures; the sphere, cube, and polyhedron are solid figures.* **20.** *Logic.* any of the forms of the syllogism with respect to the relative position of the middle term. **21.** *Optics.* the precise curve required on the surface of an optical element, esp. the mirror of a reflecting telescope. **22.** *Obs.* a phantasm or illusion. —*v.t.* **23.** to compute or calculate. **24.** to express in figures. **25.** to mark or adorn with figures, or with a pattern or design. **26.** to portray by speech or action. **27.** to represent or express by a figure of speech. **28.** to represent by a pictorial or sculptured figure, a diagram, or the like; picture or depict; trace (an outline, etc.). **29.** *U.S. Colloq.* to conclude, judge, reason, reflect. **30.** *Music.* **a.** to embellish with passing notes or other decorations. **b.** to write figures above or below (a bass part) to indicate accompanying chords. **31. figure out,** *Orig. U.S. Colloq.* **a.** to make a calculation of. **b.** to solve; understand; make out. —*v.i.* **32.** to compute or work with numerical figures. **33.** to make a figure or appearance; be conspicuous: *his name figures in the report.* **34.** *U.S. Colloq.* to be in accordance with expectations or reasonable likelihood. **35. figure on,** *U.S. Colloq.* **a.** to count or rely on. **b.** to take into consideration. [ME, t. F, t. L: m. s. *figūra* form, shape] —**fig′ureless,** *adj.* —**fig′urer,** *n.* —**Syn. 5.** See **form.**

figured (fĭg′əd), *adj.* **1.** formed or shaped. **2.** represented by a pictorial or sculptured figure. **3.** ornamented with a device or pattern: *figured silk, figured wallpaper.* **4.** *Music.* **a.** florid. **b.** having the accompanying chords indicated by figures. **5.** figurative, as language.

figured bass, *Music.* a bass part with numbers added under the notes to indicate the chords to be played.

figurehead (fĭg′ə hĕd′), *n.* **1.** a person who is nominally the head of a society, community, etc., but has no real authority or responsibility. **2.** *Naut.* an ornamental figure, as a statue or bust, placed over the cutwater of a ship.

figure of eight, 1. a kind of knot made in the shape of a figure 8. See illus. under **knot. 2.** a representation in outline of a figure 8 as traced in dancing, ice-skating, etc.

figure of speech, *Rhet.* a literary mode of expression, as a metaphor, simile, personification, antithesis, etc., in which words are used out of their literal sense, or out of ordinary locutions, to suggest a picture or image, or for other special effect; a trope.

figurine (fĭg′yŏŏ rēn′), *n.* a small ornamental figure of pottery, metalwork, etc.; statuette. [t. F, t. It.: m. *figurina,* dim. of *figura* FIGURE]

figwort (fĭg′wût′), *n.* **1.** any of numerous, usually coarse, herbs of the genus *Scrophularia.* **2.** any scrophulariaceous plant.

Fiji (fē jē′), *n.* a British colony in the S Pacific, N of New Zealand, comprising the **Fiji Islands** and a dependent group to the NW. 427,851 pop. (1962); 7040 sq. mi. *Cap.:* Suva. —**Fijian** (fē jē′ən), *adj., n.*

Fiji Islands

fikh (fĭk), *n.* Muslim jurisprudence; the legal foundations of Muslim religious, political, and civil life.

filagree (fĭl′ə grē′), *n., adj., v.t.* filigree.

filament (fĭl′ə mənt), *n.* **1.** a very fine thread or threadlike structure; a fibre or fibril. **2.** a single element of textile fibre (as silk), or mechanically produced fibre (as rayon or nylon). **3.** *Bot.* **a.** the stalklike portion of a stamen, supporting the anther. See diagram under **flower. b.** a long slender cell or series of attached cells, as in some algae, fungi, etc. **4.** *Ornith.* the barb of a down feather. **5.** *Elect.* (in an incandescent lamp) the threadlike conductor in the bulb which is raised to incandescence by the passage of current. **6.** *Electronics.* the heating element (sometimes also acting as a cathode) of a radio valve. It resembles an incandescent electric-lamp filament. **7.** *Pathol.* a threadlike substance sometimes contained in urine, or in fluids of inflammation. [t. LL: s. *filāmentum,* der. L *fīlum* thread]

filamentary (fĭl′ə mĕn′tə rĭ), *adj.* pertaining to or of the nature of a filament or filaments.

filamentous (fĭl′ə mĕn′təs), *adj.* **1.** composed of or containing filaments. **2.** resembling a filament. **3.** bearing filaments. **4.** pertaining to filaments.

filar (fī′lə), *adj.* **1.** of or pertaining to a thread or threads. **2.** having threads or the like. [f. s. L *fīlum* thread + -AR[1]]

filaria (fĭ lĕə′rĭ ə), *n., pl.* **-lariae** (-lĕə′rĭ ē′). any of the slender, threadlike nematode worms (family *Filariidae*), parasitic as adults in the blood or tissues of vertebrates, and developing as larvae in insects, etc., which become infected by sucking the embryos from the blood. [NL, der. L *fīlum* thread]

filarial (fĭ lĕə′rĭ əl), *adj.* **1.** belonging to the genus *Filaria* and allied genera of the family *Filariidae.* **2.** pertaining to infection by filariae: *filarial disease.*

filariasis (fĭl′ə rī′ə sĭs, fĭ lĕə′rĭ ā′sĭs), *n. Pathol.* the presence of filarial worms in the blood and lymph channels, in the lymph glands, and other tissues. [t. NL. See FILARIA, -ASIS]

filasse (fĭ lăs′), *n.* any of various vegetable fibres, other than cotton, processed for manufacture into yarn.

filature (fĭl′ə chə), *n.* **1.** the act of forming into threads. **2.** a reel for drawing off silk from cocoons. **3.** the reeling of silk from cocoons. **4.** an establishment for reeling silk. [t. F, der. LL *filāre* spin]

filbert (fĭl′bət), *n.* **1.** the thick-shelled, edible nut of certain cultivated varieties of hazel, esp. of *Corylus avellana.* **2.** a tree or shrub bearing such nuts. [ME; short for *filbert nut,* nut of (St) Philibert, so called because ripe about this saint's day, August 22nd]

filch (fĭlch), *v.t., v.i.* to steal (esp. something of small value); pilfer. [orig. unknown] —**filch′er,** *n.*

file[1] (fīl), *n., v.,* **filed, filing.** —*n.* **1.** any device, as a cabinet, in which papers, etc., are arranged or classified for convenient reference. **2.** a collection of papers so arranged or classified; any orderly collection of papers, etc. **3.** a string or wire on which papers are strung for preservation and reference. **4. on file,** on or in a file, or in orderly arrangement for convenient reference, as papers. **5.** a line of persons or things arranged one behind another esp. a group of soldiers moving in formation; Indian file; single file. **6.** one of the vertical lines of squares on a chessboard. **7.** a list or roll. —*v.t.* **8.** to place in a file. **9.** to arrange (papers, records, official documents, etc.) methodically for preservation and convenient reference. **10.** to place on record, register (a petition, etc.). **11.** *Law.* to bring (a suit) before a court of law. **12.** *Journalism.* to send (newspaper copy) to a newspaper or news agency. —*v.i.* **13.** to march in a file or line, one after another, as soldiers. **14.** *U.S.* to make application: *to file for a civil-service job.* [repr. F *fil* thread, string (g. L *fīlum*) and F *file* file, row, der. L *fīlum* thread] —**fil′er,** *n.*

file[2] (fīl), *n., v.,* **filed, filing.** —*n.* **1.** a metal (usually steel) tool of varying size and form, with numerous small cutting ridges or teeth on its surface, for smoothing or cutting metal and other substances. **2.** *Slang.* a cunning, shrewd, or artful person. —*v.t.* **3.** to reduce, smooth, cut, or remove with or as with a file. [ME; d. OE *fīl,* r. OE *fēol,* c. G *Feile*] —**fil′er,** *n.*

file[3] (fīl), *v.t.,* **filed, filing.** *Archaic or Dial.* to defile; pollute. [ME; OE *fȳlan* befoul, defile, der. *fūl* foul]

filefish (fīl′fĭsh′), *n., pl.* **-fishes,** (*esp. collectively*) **-fish. 1.** any of various fishes with rough, granular skin, as *Alutera schoepfi* of the Atlantic coast of the U.S. and southwards. **2.** triggerfish.

filet (fĭl′ĭt, fĭl′ā; *Fr.* fē lĕ′), *n., v.t.* fillet (defs 6, 10).

filet lace, a square mesh net or lace, originally knotted by hand but now copied by machine.

filet mignon (fĭl′ā mē′nyŏn; *Fr.* fē lĕ mē nyôɴ′), a small, tender fillet of beef.

filial (fĭl′yəl), *adj.* **1.** pertaining to or befitting a son or daughter: *filial obedience.* **2.** bearing the relation of a child to a parent. **3.** *Genetics.* indicating the sequence of generations from an original parent. First filial is shown as F_1, second filial as F_2, etc. [t. LL: s. *fīliālis,* f. s. L *fīlius* son, *fīlia* daughter + *-ālis* -AL[1]] —**fil′ially,** *adv.* —**fil′ialness,** *n.*

filiate (fĭl′ĭ āt′), *v.t.,* **-ated, -ating. 1.** to affiliate. **2.** *Law.* to determine judicially the paternity of, as a bastard child. [t. LL: m. s. *fīliātus,* pp. of *fīliāre* have a child, der. L *fīlius* son, *fīlia* daughter. Cf. AFFILIATE]

filiation (fĭl′ĭ ā′shən), *n.* **1.** the fact of being the child of a certain parent. **2.** descent as if from a parent; derivation. **3.** *Law.* the judicial determination of the paternity of a child, especially of an illegitimate one. **4.** the relation of one thing to another from which it is derived. **5.** the act of filiating. **6.** the state of being filiated. **7.** an affiliated branch, as of a society. [t. LL: s. *fīliātio,* der. *fīliāre* have a child]

filibeg (fĭl′ĭ bĕg′), *n.* the kilt or plaited skirt worn by Scottish Highlanders. Also, **fillibeg, philibeg.** [t. Gaelic: m. *feileadh-beag* small kilt (as distinguished from the large one formerly worn)]

filibuster (fĭl′ĭ bŭs′tə), *n.* **1.** *U.S.* **a.** the use of irregular or obstructive tactics by a minority in a legislative assembly to prevent the adoption of a measure generally favoured or to force a decision almost unanimously disliked. **b.** an exceptionally long speech or series of speeches to accomplish this purpose. **c.** a member of a minority in a legislature who makes such a speech. **2.** an irregular military adventurer; a freebooter or buccaneer. **3.** one who engages in an unlawful military expedition into a foreign country to inaugurate or to aid a revolution. —*v.i.* **4.** *U.S.* to impede legislation by irregular or obstructive tactics, esp. by making long speeches. **5.** to act as a freebooter, buccaneer, or irregular military adventurer. [t. Sp.: m. *filibustero,* t. D: m. *vrijbuiter* freebooter] —**fil′ibus′terer,** *n.* —**fil′ibust′erism,** *n.* —**fi′libust′erous,** *adj.*

filicide (fĭl′ĭ sīd′), *n.* **1.** one who kills his son or daughter. **2.** the act of killing one's son or daughter. [f. s. L *fīlius* son, *fīlia* daughter + -CIDE] —**fil′icid′al,** *adj.*

filiform (fĭl′ĭ fôm′, fī′lĭ-), *adj.* threadlike; filamentous. [f. s. L *fīlum* thread + -(I)FORM]

filigree (fĭl′ĭ grē′), *n., adj., v.,* **-greed, -greeing.** —*n.* **1.** ornamental work of fine wires, esp. lacy jewellers' work of scrolls and arabesques. **2.** anything very delicate or fanciful. —*adj.* **3.** composed of or resembling filigree. —*v.t.* **4.** to adorn with or form into filigree. Also, **filagree, fillagree.** [var. of *filigrane,* t. F, t. It.: m. *filigrana.* See FILE[1], GRAIN] —**fil′igreed′,** *adj.*

filigreed (fĭl′ĭ grēd′), *adj.* having filigree decorations.

filing clerk, an employee in an office who is chiefly concerned with the filing of letters, records, etc.

filings (fī′lĭngz), *n.pl.* particles removed by a file.

Filipine (fĭl′ĭ pēn′), *adj.* Philippine.

Filipino (fĭl′ĭ pē′nō; *Sp.* fē lē pē′nō), *n., pl.* **-nos** (-nōz; *Sp.* -nōs), *adj.* —*n.* **1.** a native of the Philippine Islands, esp. a member of a Christianized native tribe. —*adj.* **2.** Philippine. [t. Sp., der. *Felipe* Philip]

fill (fĭl), *v.t.* **1.** to make full; put as much as can be held into. **2.** to occupy to the full capacity: *water filled the basin, the crowd filled the hall.* **3.** to supply to fullness or plentifully: *to fill a house with furniture, to fill the heart with joy.* **4.** to satisfy, as food does. **5.** to put, as contents, into a receptacle. **6.** to be plentiful throughout: *fish filled the rivers.* **7.** to extend throughout; pervade completely: *the perfume filled the room.* **8.** to furnish (a vacancy or office) with an occupant or incumbent. **9.** to occupy and perform the duties of (a position, post, etc.). **10.** to execute (a business order). **11.** to supply (a blank space) with written matter, decorative work, etc. **12.** to meet (requirements, etc.) satisfactorily: *the book fills a long-felt want.* **13.** to make up or compound (a medical prescription). **14.** to stop up or close: *to fill a tooth or a crevice.* **15.** *Naut.* **a.** to distend (a sail) by pressure of the wind so as to impart headway to a vessel. **b.** to brace (a yard) so that the sail will catch the wind on its after side. **16.** to adulterate: *filled soaps.* **17.** *Civ. Eng.* to build up with fill (def. 24): *to fill low ground with gravel, sand, or earth.* —*v.i.* **18.** to become full: *the hall filled rapidly, her eyes filled with tears.* **19.** to become distended, as sails with the wind. **20.** to fill a cup or other receptacle; pour out drink, as into a cup. —*v.* **21.** Some special verb phrases are:

fill away, *Naut.* **1.** to fall off the wind and proceed on a board. **2.** to brace the yards, so that sails which have been aback will stand full.

fill in, 1. to fill (a hole, hollow, blank, etc.) with something put in. **2.** to complete (a document, design, etc.) by filling blank spaces. **3.** to put in or insert so as to fill: *to fill in omitted names.* **4.** to occupy, spend (time). **5.** to act as a substitute, replace.

fill out, 1. to distend (sails, etc.). **2.** to become larger, fuller, grow fat, expand, as the figure, etc. **3.** *U.S.* fill in (def. 2).

fill the bill, *Colloq.* to satisfy the requirements of the case: be or do what is wanted.

fill up, to fill completely.

—*n.* **22.** a full supply; enough to satisfy want or desire: *to eat one's fill.* **23.** an amount of something sufficient for filling; a charge. **24.** a mass of earth, stones, etc., used to fill a hollow, etc.

[ME *fille(n),* OE *fyllan,* c. G *füllen*; der. FULL[1]]

fillagree (fĭl′ə grē′), *n., adj., v.t.* filigree.

filled gold (fĭld), a gold plate mechanically welded to a backing of brass or other base metal and rolled, in which the gold is $^1/_{20}$ or more of the total weight.

filler (fĭl′ə), *n.* **1.** one who or that which fills. **2.** a thing or quantity of a material put in to fill something, or to fill in a gap. **3.** a liquid, paste, or paintlike substance used to fill in pores or cracks before painting or varnishing. **4.** a solid substance added to plastics, paints and elastomers either to modify their properties or reduce their cost; an extender. **5.** the tobacco forming the body of a cigar, as distinguished from the wrapper. **6.** *Journalism.* something used to fill a vacant space. **7.** *Bldg Trades, etc.* a sheet or plate inserted in a gap between two structural members. **8.** an implement used in filling, as a funnel. [f. FILL + -ER[1]]

fillér (*Hung.* fĕl′lĕr), *n., pl.* **-lér.** a Hungarian minor bronze coin formerly equal to a hundredth part of a pengö, and now equal to a hundredth part of a forint. [t. Hung.]

fillet (fĭl′ĭt), *n.* **1.** a narrow band of ribbon or the like bound round the head or hair. **2.** any narrow strip, as wood or metal. **3.** a strip of any material used for binding. **4.** *Bookbinding.* **a.** a decorative line impressed on a book's cover, usually at the top and bottom of the back. **b.** a rolling tool for impressing such lines. **5.** *Archit., etc.* **a.** a relatively narrow moulding with a plane face, as between other mouldings. **b.** the flat top of the ridge between two flutes of a column. **6.** *Cookery.* **a.** a strip or long (flat or thick) piece of meat or fish, esp. such as is easily detached from the bones or adjoining parts. **b.** a thick slice of meat, etc. **c.** a piece of veal or other meat boned, rolled, and tied, for roasting. **7.** *Anat.* a band of fibres, esp. of white nerve fibres in the brain. **8.** a raised rim or ridge, as a ring on the muzzle of a gun. —*v.t.* **9.** to bind or adorn with or as with a fillet. **10.** *Cookery.* **a.** to cut or prepare (meat or fish) as a fillet. **b.** to cut fillets from. Also, **filet** for 6, 10. [ME *filet,* t. F, dim. of *fil* thread, string, g. L *fīlum*]

fillibeg (fĭl′ĭ bĕg′), *n.* filibeg.

fill-in (fĭl′ĭn′), *n.* **1.** a substitute; stopgap. —*adj.* **2.** temporary: *a fill-in job during the summer vacation.*

filling (fĭl′ĭng), *n.* **1.** that which is put in to fill something: *the filling of a pie.* **2.** a substance in plastic form, as cement, amalgam, or gold foil, used to close a cavity in a tooth. **3.** the act of one who or that which fills; a making or becoming full.

filling station, a place where petrol and oil are sold for motor vehicles.

fillip (fĭl′ĭp), *v.t.* **1.** to strike with the nail of a finger snapped from the end of the thumb. **2.** to tap or strike smartly. **3.** to drive by or as by a fillip. —*v.i.* **4.** to make a fillip with the fingers. —*n.* **5.** the act or movement of filliping; a smart tap or stroke. **6.** anything that tends to rouse, excite, or revive; a stimulus. [appar. imit. Cf. FLIP]

fillister (fĭl′ĭs tə), *n.* *Carp.* a rabbet or groove, as one on a window sash to hold the glass and putty.

fillister plane, *Carp.* a plane for cutting rabbets or grooves.

Fillmore (fĭl′mô′), *n.* **Millard** (mĭl′əd), 1800–74, 13th president of the United States, 1850–53.

fill-up (fĭl′ŭp′), *n.* the act of filling up, charging, or replenishing, as the petrol tank of a motor car with petrol.

filly (fĭl′ĭ), *n., pl.* **-lies. 1.** a female colt or foal; a young mare. **2.** *Colloq.* a girl. [t. Scand.; cf. Icel. *fylja* female foal. See FOAL]

film (fĭlm), *n.* **1.** a thin layer or coating. **2.** a thin sheet of any material. **3.** *Photog.* **a.** the sensitive coating, as of gelatine and silver bromide, on a photographic plate. **b.** a strip or roll of cellulose nitrate or cellulose acetate composition coated with a sensitive emulsion, used instead of a photographic plate. **4.** *Films.* **a.** a film strip containing consecutive pictures or photographs of objects in motion presented to the eye, esp. by being thrown on to a screen by a projector so rapidly as to give the illusion that the objects or actors are moving. **b.** such a film strip representing an event, play, story, etc. **c.** (*pl.*) such film strips, or the stories, etc., contained on them, collectively. **5.** a thin skin or membrane. **6.** a delicate web of filaments or fine threads. —*v.t.* **7.** to cover with a film, or thin skin or pellicle. **8.** *Films.* **a.** to photograph with a film camera. **b.** to reproduce in the form of a film or films: *to film a novel.* —*v.i.* **9.** to become covered by a film. **10.** *Films.* **a.** to be reproduced in a film, esp. in a specific manner: *this story films easily.* **b.** to direct, make, or otherwise engage in the production of films. [ME *fylme,* OE *filmen*; akin to FELL[4]]

filmable (fĭl′mə bl), *adj.* (of a novel, play, etc.) suitable for filming.

film badge, a badge containing a masked photographic film, worn by workers who may come in contact with ionizing radiation, and used to indicate the extent of their exposure to these radiations.

filmic (fĭl′mĭk), *adj.* of, or like, a cinema film.

film library, an organized collection of films for private or public use, including reproductions of printed materials on film, slides, etc.

film pack, *U.S. Photog.* camera film so arranged in a stack that individual sheets can be brought successively into place.

filmset (fĭlm′sĕt′), *v.*, **-set, -setting,** *adj. Print.* —*v.t.* **1.** to set (type matter) photographically, without the use of hot metal. —*adj.* **2.** set photographically. —**film′set′ter,** *n.* —**film′set′ting,** *n.*, *adj.*

film star, a leading actor or actress who is or has been the star of many films.

film strip, a length of film containing a series of transparencies for projection on to a screen.

film theatre, a cinema.

filmy (fĭl′mĭ), *adj.*, **filmier, filmiest.** of the nature of, resembling, or covered with a film. —**film′ily,** *adv.* —**film′iness,** *n.*

filoplume (fĭl′ə plōōm′, fī′lə-), *n. Ornith.* a feather with a shaft but few or no barbs.

filose (fī′lōs), *adj.* **1.** threadlike. **2.** ending in a threadlike process. [f. s. L *fīlum* thread + -OSE[2]]

filter (fĭl′tə), *n.* **1.** any device in which cloth, paper, porous porcelain, or a layer of charcoal or sand, is held and through which liquid is passed to remove suspended impurities or to recover solids. **2.** any of various analogous devices, as for removing dust from air, impurities from tobacco smoke, or eliminating certain kinds of light rays. **3.** *Colloq.* a filter tip. **4.** *Photog.* a screen of dyed gelatine or glass used to control the rendering of colour or to diminish the intensity of light. **5.** *Physics.* a device for selecting waves or currents of certain frequencies only out of an aggregation including others. —*v.t.* **6.** to remove by the action of a filter. **7.** to act as a filter for. **8.** to pass through, or as through, a filter. —*v.i.* **9.** to percolate; pass through or as through a filter. **10.** (of a line of motor vehicles) to move in a certain direction independently of the general flow of traffic. [ME *filtre*, t. OF, t. ML: m. s. *feltrum* felt (used as a filter), ult. t. Gmc; cf. FELT[2]] —**fil′terer,** *n.*

filterable (fĭl′tə rə bl), *adj.* **1.** capable of being filtered. **2.** *Bacteriol.* capable of passing through bacteria-retaining filters: *a filterable virus.* Also, **filtrable** (fĭl′trə bl).

filter bed, a pond or tank having a false bottom covered with sand, and serving to filter river or pond waters.

filter cloth, a coarse heavy material used in filtering.

filter paper, pure cellulose paper used in filtering.

filter press, an apparatus used for filtering on an industrial scale, consisting of a series of metal or wooden frames covered with filter cloth between which the liquid to be filtered is pumped.

filter tip, **1.** a cigarette or cigar tip with a means of filtering the smoke. **2.** a cigarette or cigar provided with such a tip. —**fil′ter-tipped′,** *adj.*

filth (fĭlth), *n.* **1.** foul matter; offensive or disgusting dirt. **2.** foul condition. **3.** moral impurity, corruption, or obscenity. **4.** foul language. [ME; OE *fȳlth*, der. *fūl* foul]

filthy (fĭl′thĭ), *adj.*, **filthier, filthiest. 1.** foul with, characterized by, or having the nature of filth; disgustingly dirty. **2.** vile; obscene. **3.** (as a general epithet of strong condemnation) highly offensive or objectionable. **4.** *Colloq.* very unpleasant: *filthy weather.* —**filth′ily,** *adv.* —**filth′iness,** *n.* —**Syn. 1.** See **dirty.**

filtrate (fĭl′trāt), *v.*, **-trated, -trating,** *n.* —*v.t., v.i.* **1.** to filter. —*n.* **2.** liquid which has been passed through a filter. —**filtration** (fĭl trā′shən), *n.*

filum (fī′ləm), *n.*, *pl.* **-la** (-lə). *Latin.* a threadlike structure or part; a filament.

fimble (fĭm′bl), *n.* the male or staminate plant of hemp, which is harvested before the female or pistillate plant. [t. LG: m. *fimel*, t. F: m. (*chanvre*) *femelle*, lit., female hemp]

fimbria (fĭm′brĭ ə), *n.*, *pl.* **-briae** (-brĭ ē′). (*often pl.*) *Bot., Zool., Anat.* a fringe or fringed border. [t. L: thread, fringe] —**fim′brial,** *adj.*

fimbriate (fĭm′brĭ ĭt, -āt′), *adj. Bot., Zool.* fringed; bordered with hairs or with filiform processes. Also, **fim′briat′ed.**

fimbriation (fĭm′brĭ ā′shən), *n. Bot., Zool.* **1.** fimbriate or fringed condition. **2.** a fringe or fringelike part.

Fimbriate petals

fimbrillate (fĭm brĭl′ĭt, -āt), *adj. Bot., Zool.* bordered with, or having, a small or fine fringe. [f. s. NL *fimbrilla* (dim. of L *fimbria* FIMBRIA) + -ATE[1]]

fin (fĭn), *n.*, *v.*, **finned, finning.** —*n.* **1.** a membranous winglike or paddle-like organ attached to any of various parts of the body of fishes and certain other aquatic animals, used for propulsion, steering, or balancing. **2.** *Naut.* **a.** a fin-shaped plane on a submarine or boat. **b.** a fin keel. **3.** Also, *Chiefly U.S.*, **vertical stabilizer.** *Aeron.* any of certain small, subsidiary planes on an aircraft, in general placed parallel to the plane of symmetry. **4.** an external rib for cooling, used on radiators, the cylinders of air-cooled internal-combustion engines, etc. **5.** any part, as of a mechanism, resembling a fin. **6.** *Slang.* the arm or hand. —*v.t.* **7.** to cut off the fins from (a fish); carve or cut up, as a chub. —*v.i.* **8.** to move the fins; lash the water with the fins, as a whale when dying. [ME *finne*, OE *finn*, c. D *vin*, LG *finne*. Cf. L *pinna*] —**fin′less,** *adj.* —**fin′like′,** *adj.*

Fin., 1. Finland. **2.** Finnish.

fin., financial.

finable (fī′nə bl), *adj.* fineable.

finagle (fĭ nā′gl), *v.*, **-gled, -gling.** *Colloq.* —*v.i.* **1.** to practise deception or fraud. —*v.t.* **2.** to trick or cheat (a person); get (something) by guile or trickery. **3.** to wangle: *to finagle free tickets.* [var. of *fainaigue*; orig. uncert.] —**fina′gler,** *n.*

final (fī′nəl), *adj.* **1.** pertaining to or coming at the end; last in place, order, or time. **2.** ultimate: *the final goal.* **3.** conclusive or decisive. **4.** *Law.* **a.** precluding further controversy on the questions passed upon: *the decision of the House of Lords is final.* **b.** determining completely the rights of the parties, so that no further decision upon the merits of the issues is necessary: *a final judgement or decree.* **5.** constituting the end or purpose: *a final result.* **6.** pertaining to or expressing end or purpose: *a final clause.* **7.** *Phonet.* coming at the end of a word or syllable: *'t' is final in the word 'fit'.* —*n.* **8.** that which is last; that which forms an end or termination of a series. **9.** (*often pl.*) something final, as a decisive game or contest after preliminary ones. **10.** (*pl.*) a university degree examination. **11.** the last edition of a newspaper during the day. **12.** *Music.* the tonic note of a church mode. [ME, t. LL: s. *fīnālis*, der. L *fīnis* end] —**Syn. 1.** See **last**[1].

final causes, *Philos.* the doctrine that the course of events in the universe is explicable mainly by reference to ends or purposes by which all events are controlled.

finale (fĭ nä′lĭ; *It.* fē nä′lĕ), *n.* **1.** *Music.* the last piece, division, or movement of a concert, opera, or composition. **2.** the concluding part of any performance, course of proceedings, etc. [t. It., adj. used as n. See FINAL]

finalism (fī′nə lĭz′əm), *n. Philos.* the doctrine that nothing exists or was made except for a determinate end; the doctrine of final causes; teleology.

finalist (fī′nə lĭst), *n.* one who is entitled to take part in the final trial or round, as of an athletic contest.

finality (fī năl′ĭ tĭ), *n.*, *pl.* **-ties. 1.** the state, quality, or fact of being final; conclusiveness or decisiveness. **2.** something that is final; a final act, utterance, etc.

finalize (fī′nə līz′), *v.t.*, **-lized, -lizing.** to put into final form; conclude, settle. Also, **finalise.** —**fi′naliza′tion,** *n.*

finally (fī′nə lĭ), *adv.* **1.** at the final point or moment; in the end. **2.** in a final manner; conclusively or decisively.

finance (fĭ năns′, fī′năns), *n.*, *v.*, **-nanced, -nancing.** —*n.* **1.** the management of public revenues; the conduct or transaction of money matters generally, esp. such as affect the public, as in the fields of banking and investment. **2.** (*pl.*) pecuniary resources, as of a sovereign, state, company, or an individual; revenue. —*v.t.* **3.** to supply with means of payment; provide capital for; to obtain or furnish credit for. **4.** to manage financially. —*v.i.* **5.** to conduct financial operations; manage finances. [ME, t. OF: ending, payment, revenue, der. OF *finer* finish, settle, pay, der. *fin* end, settlement. See FINE[2]]

finance bill, *Govt.* a bill or act of a legislature to obtain public funds.

financial (fĭ năn′shəl, fī-), *adj.* **1.** pertaining to monetary receipts and expenditures; pertaining or relating to money matters; pecuniary: *financial operations.* **2.** of or pertaining to those commonly engaged in dealing with money and credit. —**finan′cially,** *adv.*

—**Syn. 1.** FINANCIAL, FISCAL, MONETARY, PECUNIARY refer to matters concerned with money. FINANCIAL usually refers to money matters or transactions of some size or importance: *a financial wizard.* FISCAL is used esp. in connection with government funds, or those of any organization: *the end of the fiscal year.* MONETARY relates especially to money as such: *a monetary system or standard.* PECUNIARY refers to money as used in making ordinary payments: *a pecuniary obligation or reward.*

Financial Times Ordinary Share Index, the Stock Exchange quotations for a fixed number of industrial ordinary shares selected by the *Financial Times* newspaper, used as an index to compare the fluctuations in share prices from day to day and year to year.

financial year, any twelve-monthly period at the end of which a government, company, etc., balances its accounts and determines its financial condition. Also, **fiscal year.**

financier (fĭ năn′sĭ ə, fī-), *n.* **1.** one skilled or engaged in financial operations, whether public, corporate, or individual. —*v.t.* **2.** to finance. [t. F, der. *finance* FINANCE]

finback (fĭn′băk′), *n.* any whalebone whale of the genus *Balaenoptera* having a prominent dorsal fin, as *B. musculus* of the northern Atlantic, or *B. physalus*, which attains a length of 60 or even 80 feet; a rorqual. Also, **finback whale, finner, finwhale.**

finch (fĭnch), *n.* **1.** any of numerous small passerine birds of the family *Fringillidae*, including the buntings, sparrows, crossbills, linnets, grosbeaks, etc., most of which have heavy, conical, seed-cracking bills. **2.** any of various non-fringilline birds. [ME; OE *finc*, c. D *vink*, G *Fink*]

Bullfinch, *Pyrrhula pyrrhula* (Length $5\frac{3}{4}$ in.)

Finchley (fĭnch′lĭ, fĭnsh′lĭ), *n.* a district in the NW outer London borough of Barnet.

find (fīnd), *v.*, **found, finding,** *n.* —*v.t.* **1.** to come upon by chance; meet. **2.** to learn, attain, or obtain by search or effort. **3.** to discover. **4.** to recover (something lost). **5.** to gain or regain the use of: *to find one's tongue.* **6.** to succeed in attaining; gain by effort: *find safety in flight, to find occasion for revenge.* **7.** to discover by experience or to perceive: *to find something to be true, find something new to be developing.* **8.** to ascertain by study or calculation: *to find the sum of several numbers.* **9.** *Law.* **a.** to determine after judicial inquiry: *find a person guilty.* **b.** to pronounce as an official act (an indictment, verdict, or judgement). **10.** to provide or furnish. **11. find fault,** to find cause of blame or complaint; express dissatisfaction. **12. find oneself,** to discover one's true vocation; learn one's abilities and how to use them. **13. find one's feet, a.** to be able to stand and walk. **b.** to be able to act independently without the help of others. **14. find out, a.** to discover in the course of time or experience; discover by search or inquiry; ascertain by study. **b.** to detect, as in an offence; discover the actions or character of; discover or detect (a fraud, imposture, etc.). **c.** to discover the identity of (a person). —*v.i.* **15.** to determine an issue after judicial inquiry: *the jury found for the plaintiff.* **16.** *Hunting.* to come upon game. —*n.* **17.** the act of finding; a discovery. **18.** something found; a discovery, esp. a valuable or gratifying discovery: *our cook was a real find.* [ME *finde(n)*, OE *findan*, c. G *finden*] —**find′able,** *adj.*

finder (fīn′də), *n.* **1.** one who or that which finds. **2.** *Photog.* a viewfinder. **3.** *Astron.* a small telescope attached to a larger for the purpose of finding an object more readily.

fin de siècle (*Fr.* făɴ də syĕ′kl), *French.* **1.** end of the century. **2.** a period comparatively free from social and moral traditions or conventions.

fin-de-siècle (*Fr.* făɴ də syĕ′kl), *adj.* **1.** of or pertaining to the period at the close of a century, esp. the end of the 19th century. **2.** decadent.

finding (fīn′dĭng), *n.* **1.** the act of one who or that which finds; discovery. **2.** that which is found or ascertained. **3.** *Law.* a decision or verdict after judicial inquiry. **4.** (*pl.*) tools, materials, etc., used by artisans.

fine[1] (fīn), *adj.*, **finer, finest,** *adv.*, *v.*, **fined, fining.** —*adj.* **1.** of the highest or of very high grade or quality. **2.** free from imperfections or impurities. **3.** choice, excellent, or admirable: *a fine sermon.* **4.** consisting of minute particles: *fine sand.* **5.** very thin or slender: *fine thread.* **6.** keen or sharp, as a tool. **7.** delicate in texture: *fine linen.* **8.** delicately fashioned. **9.** highly skilled or accomplished: *a fine musician.* **10.** trained down to the proper degree, as an athlete. **11.** characterized by or affecting refinement or elegance: *a fine lady.* **12.** polished or refined: *fine manners.* **13.** affectedly ornate or elegant: *fine writing.* **14.** delicate or subtle: *a fine distinction.* **15.** showy or smart; smartly dressed. **16.** good-looking or handsome. **17.** (of gold, silver, etc.) having a high proportion of pure metal, or having the proportion as specified. —*adv.* **18.** *Colloq.* in a fine manner; excellently or very well; elegantly; delicately; with nicety. **19.** *Billiards.* in such a way that the driven ball barely touches the object ball in passing. —*v.i.* **20.** to become fine or finer. —*v.t.* **21.** to make fine or finer. **22.** to clarify (wines or spirits) by filtration. —*n.* **23.** (*pl.*) the extremely small particles which may be present in a powder. [ME *fin*, t. OF, g. Common Rom. *fino*, back-formation from L *finire* FINISH]

—**Syn. 1.** superior; finished, consummate, perfect. FINE, CHOICE, ELEGANT, EXQUISITE are terms of praise with reference to quality. FINE is a general term: *a fine horse, person, book.* CHOICE implies a discriminating selection of the object in question: *a choice piece of steak.* ELEGANT suggests a refined and graceful superiority as is generally associated with luxury and a cultivated taste: *elegant furnishings.* EXQUISITE suggests an admirable delicacy, finish, or perfection: *an exquisite piece of lace.* **4.** powdered, pulverized. —**Ant. 1.** inferior.

fine[2] (fīn), *n.*, *v.*, **fined, fining.** —*n.* **1.** a sum of money exacted as a penalty for an offence or dereliction; a mulct. **2.** *Law.* **a.** a fee paid by a feudal tenant to the landlord, as on the renewal of tenure. **b.** a sum of money paid by a tenant on the commencement of his tenancy so that his rent may be small or nominal. **3.** *Law.* a conveyance of land through decree of a court, based upon a simulated lawsuit. **4.** *Archaic.* a penalty of any kind. **5. in fine,** finally; in short. —*v.t.* **6.** to subject to a fine, or pecuniary penalty; punish by a fine. [ME *fin*, t. OF, g. L *fīnis* boundary, end, ML settlement, fine]

fine[3] (fē′nā), *n. Music.* **1.** the end of a repeated section, whether *da capo* or *dal segno.* **2.** the end of a composition comprising several movements. [It.: end]

fineable (fī′nə bl), *adj.* subject or liable to a fine. Also, **finable.**

fine arts, those arts which seek expression through beautiful or significant modes; as architecture, sculpture, painting, music, and engraving.

fine boat, *Rowing.* a shell (def. 13).

fine-cut (fīn′ kŭt′), *adj.* (of tobacco) cut into very thin strips.

fine-draw (fīn′drô′), *v.t.*, **-drew, -drawn, -drawing.** **1.** *Sewing.* to sew together or up so finely or nicely that the joining is not noticeable. **2.** to draw out to extreme fineness, tenuity, or subtlety.

fine-drawn (fīn′drôn′), *adj.* drawn out to extreme fineness or thinness: *a fine-drawn wire* or *distinction.*

Fine Gael (fĭn′ə gāl′), a political party of the Republic of Ireland formed in 1933.

fine-grain (fīn′grān′), *adj. Photog.* **1.** (of an image) having an inconspicuous grain. **2.** (of a developer or film) permitting the grain of an image to be inconspicuous.

fine leg, *Cricket.* **1.** a leg-side fielding position almost directly behind the wicket. **2.** a fielder in this position.

finely (fīn′lĭ), *adv.* in a fine manner; excellently; elegantly; delicately; minutely; nicely; subtly.

fineness (fīn′nĭs), *n.* **1.** the state or quality of being fine. **2.** the proportion of pure metal (gold or silver) in an alloy, often expressed by the number of parts in 1000.

finery[1] (fī′nə rĭ), *n.*, *pl.* **-ries. 1.** fine or showy dress, ornaments, etc. **2.** *Rare.* smartness or elegance. [f. FINE[1], adj. + -ERY]

finery[2] (fī′nə rĭ), *n.*, *pl.* **-ries.** *Metall.* a hearth on which cast iron is converted into wrought iron. [t. F: m. *finerie*, der. *finer* FINE[1], v.]

fines herbes (*Fr.* fēn zĕrb′), *Cookery.* a combination of finely chopped herbs for flavouring soups, sauces, omelettes, etc. [F]

fine-spun (fīn′spŭn′), *adj.* **1.** spun or drawn out to a fine thread. **2.** highly or excessively refined or subtle.

finesse (fĭ nĕs′), *n.*, *v.*, **-nessed, -nessing.** —*n.* **1.** delicacy of execution; subtlety of discrimination. **2.** artful management; craft; strategy. **3.** an artifice or stratagem. **4.** *Cards.* an attempt to win a trick with a card while holding a higher card not in sequence with it, in the hope that the card or cards between will not be played. —*v.i.* **5.** to use finesse or artifice. **6.** to make a finesse at cards. —*v.t.* **7.** to bring by finesse or artifice. **8.** to make a finesse with (a card). [t. F, der. *fin* FINE[1], adj.]

finfoot (fĭn′fo͝ot′), *n.*, *pl.* **-foots.** any of certain pinnatiped or lobately webbed aquatic birds, family *Heliornithidae*, of South America, Asia, and Africa, related to the rails and coots.

fin-footed (fĭn′fo͝ot′ĭd), *adj. Ornith.* **1.** web-footed. **2.** having feet whose toes are separately furnished with flaps, as the finfoots and coots.

Fingal's Cave (fĭng′glz), an unusual cavern on the island of Staffa, in the Hebrides, Scotland. 227 ft long; 42 ft wide.

finger (fĭng′gə), *n.* **1.** any of the terminal members of the hand, esp. one other than the thumb. **2.** a part of a glove made to receive a finger. **3.** the breadth of a finger as a unit of length; digit. **4.** the length of a finger, $4\frac{1}{2}$ inches, or approximately that. **5.** something like or likened to a finger, or serving the purpose of a finger: *the finger of a clock.* **6.** any of various projecting parts of machines. **7.** Some special noun phrases are:

burn one's fingers, to get hurt or suffer loss from meddling with or engaging in anything.

have a finger in the pie, to have a share in the doing of something.

keep one's fingers crossed, to wish for good luck, or success in a particular enterprise.

lay or **put one's finger on,** to indicate exactly.

not lift a finger, to do nothing; make no attempt.

put the finger on, *Slang.* **1.** to inform against or identify (a criminal) to the police. **2.** to designate a victim, as of murder or other crime.

slip through one's fingers, to elude one, as a missed opportunity.

snap one's fingers at, to show disdain or contempt for.

twist round one's little finger, to dominate, influence easily.

—*v.t.* **8.** to touch with the fingers; handle; toy or meddle with. **9.** to pilfer; filch. **10.** *Music.* **a.** to play on (an instrument) with the fingers. **b.** to perform or mark (a passage of music) with a certain fingering (def. 2b). *—v.i.* **11.** to touch or handle something with the fingers. **12.** *Music.* **a.** to have its keys arranged for playing with the fingers, as a piano, clarinet, etc. **b.** to use the fingers in playing. [ME and OE; c. G *Finger*; akin to FIVE, FIST] —**fin′gerer,** *n.* —**fin′gerless,** *adj.*

fingerboard (fĭng′gə bôd′), *n.* **1.** (in a violin, guitar, etc.) the strip of wood on the neck against which the strings are stopped by the fingers. **2.** (in a piano, organ, etc.) the keyboard.

fingerbowl (fĭng′gə bōl′), *n.* a small bowl to hold water for rinsing the fingers at table.

fingerbreadth (fĭng′gə brĕtth′, -brĕdth′), *n.* the breadth of a finger: about ¾ of an inch. Also, **finger's breadth.**

fingergrass (fĭng′gə gräs′), *n.* a grass of southern Africa, *Digitaria eriantha,* of summer rainfall areas of the veld. Also, **krulgras.**

fingering[1] (fĭng′gə rĭng), *n.* **1.** the act of one who fingers. **2.** *Music.* **a.** the action or method of using the fingers in playing an instrument. **b.** the indication of the way the fingers are to be used in performing a piece of music.

fingering[2] (fĭng′gə rĭng), *n.* a kind of woollen yarn used in the manufacture of stockings.

fingerling (fĭng′gə lĭng), *n.* **1.** a young or small fish, esp. a very small salmon or a small trout. **2.** something very small. [f. FINGER + -LING[1]. Cf. G *Fingerling* thimble]

fingermark (fĭng′gə mäk′), *n.* a mark, esp. a smudge or stain, made by a finger.

fingernail (fĭng′gə nāl′), *n.* the nail at the end of a finger.

fingerplate (fĭng′gə plāt′), *n.* a plate fixed near the latch of a door to protect the surface from being soiled by fingermarks.

fingerpost (fĭng′gə pōst′), *n.* a signpost with an arm terminating in the shape of an index finger.

fingerprint (fĭng′gə prĭnt′), *n.* **1.** an impression of the markings of the inner surface of the last joint of the thumb or a finger. **2.** such an impression made with ink for purposes of identification. *—v.t.* **3.** to take the fingerprints of.

fingerstall (fĭng′gə stôl′), *n.* a covering used to protect a finger.

fingertip (fĭng′gə tĭp′), *n.* **1.** the tip of a finger. **2.** a covering used to protect the end of a finger. **3. at one's fingertips, a.** close at hand, within easy reach. **b.** readily at one's disposal, as a result of complete familiarity with the subject.

finger-wave (fĭng′gə wāv′), *n.* *Hairdressing.* a wave set by impressing the fingers into hair dampened with lotion.

finial (fī′nĭ əl), *n.* *Archit.* **1.** the ornamental termination of a pinnacle, gable, etc., usually foliated. **2.** a vertical termination; a cast, carved, or turned ornament capping another form. [ME, f. s. L *fīnis* end + -IAL]

finical (fĭn′ĭ kl), *adj.* **1.** excessively fastidious; too particular or fussy. **2.** (of things) overelaborate; containing too much unimportant detail. [f. FINE[1] + -ICAL] —**fin′ical′ity, fin′icalness,** *n.* —**fin′ically,** *adv.*

finicky (fĭn′ĭ kĭ), *adj.* finical. Also, **finikin** (fĭn′ĭ kĭn), **finicking** (fĭn′ĭ kĭng). [unexplained var. of FINICAL]

fining (fī′nĭng), *n.* **1.** the process by which fused glass becomes free from undissolved gases. **2.** the process of clarifying or filtering a wine or spirit to render it brilliant in appearance. [der. FINE[1], v.]

finis (fĭn′ĭs), *n.* *Latin.* end; conclusion (often used at the end of a book).

finish (fĭn′ĭsh), *v.t.* **1.** to bring (action, speech, work, affairs, etc.) to an end or to completion. **2.** to come to the end of (a course, period of time, etc.). **3.** to use up completely (often fol. by *up* or *off*): *to finish a plate of food.* **4.** to overcome completely; destroy or kill (often fol. by *off*). **5.** to complete and perfect in detail; put the final touches on. **6.** to put a finish on (wood, metal, etc.). **7.** to perfect (a person) in education, accomplishments, social graces, etc. *—v.i.* **8.** to come to an end. **9.** to complete a course, etc. **10.** *Obs.* to die. *—n.* **11.** the end or conclusion; the last stage. **12.** the end of a hunt, race, etc. **13.** a decisive ending: *a fight to the finish.* **14.** the quality of being finished or completed with smoothness, elegance, etc. **15.** educational or social polish. **16.** the manner in which a thing is finished in preparation, or an effect imparted in finishing: *a soft or dull finish.* **17.** the surface coating or texture of wood, metal, etc. **18.** something used or serving to finish, complete, or perfect a thing. **19.** woodwork, etc., esp. in the interior of a building, not essential to the structure but used for purposes of ornament, neatness, etc. **20.** a final coat of plaster or paint. **21.** a material for application in finishing. [ME *finisch(en),* t. F: m. *finiss-,* s. *finir,* g. L *fīnīre* bound, end] —**fin′isher,** *n.* **—Syn. 11.** See **end**[1].

finished (fĭn′ĭsht), *adj.* **1.** ended or completed. **2.** completed or perfected in all details, as a product. **3.** polished to the highest degree of excellence: *a finished poem.* **4.** highly accomplished, as a person. **—Syn. 4.** talented, skilled, gifted; trained.

finishing school, a school for completing the education of young women and preparing them for entrance into society.

Finistère (fĭn′ĭs tēə′; *Fr.* fē nēs tĕr′), *n.* a department in W France. 749,558 pop. (1962); 2714 sq. mi. *Cap.:* Quimper.

Finisterre (fĭn′ĭs tēə′; *Sp.* fē nēs tĕr′rĕ), *n.* **Cape,** a headland in NW Spain: the westernmost point of Spain.

finite (fī′nīt), *adj.* **1.** having bounds or limits; not too great or too small to be measurable. **2.** *Maths.* **a.** (of a class or integral number) capable of being completely counted. **b.** not infinite or infinitesimal. **3.** subject to limitations or conditions, as of space, time, circumstances, or the laws of nature: *finite existence.* *—n.* **4. the finite, a.** that which is finite. **b.** finite things collectively. [t. L: m. s. *fīnītus,* pp., bounded] —**fi′nitely,** *adv.* —**fi′niteness,** *n.*

finite verb, a verb limited by person, number, tense, mood, and aspect (opposed to the infinite forms: participle, infinitive, and gerund, which have only a few limitations).

finitude (fī′nĭ tyood′), *n.* the state of being finite.

fink (fĭngk), *n.* *Slang, Chiefly U.S.* **1.** a strike-breaker or blackleg. **2.** a policeman. **3.** a contemptible or undesirable person.

Finke (fĭngk), *n.* an intermittent river in Australia, flowing SE through Northern Territory and South Australia. In wet seasons it unites with the Macumba and reaches Lake Eyre. ab. 400 mi.

fin keel, *Naut.* a finlike projection extending downwards from the keel of a sailing boat, serving to prevent lateral motion and acting as additional ballast.

Finland (fĭn′lənd), *n.* **1.** Finnish, **Suomi.** a republic in N Europe: formerly a province of the Russian Empire. 4,446,222 pop. (1960); ab. 118,000 sq. mi. *Cap.:* Helsinki. **2. Gulf of,** an arm of the Baltic, S of Finland. See map under **Baltic.** —**Fin′lander,** *n.*

finlet (fĭn′lĭt), *n.* a small detached finlike appendage in certain fishes, as the mackerel.

Finn (fĭn), *n.* **1.** an inhabitant or native of Finland. **2.** any native speaker of Finnish, as in America or Russia. **3.** a speaker of any Finnic language.

finnan haddock (fĭn′ən), a name given to haddock when it is offered for sale in fishmongers' shops, either cured or fresh. Also, **finnan haddie** (hăd′ĭ). [lit., haddock of *Findhorn,* fishing port in Scotland]

finned (fĭnd), *adj.* having a fin or fins.

finner (fĭn′ə), *n.* finback.

Finnic (fĭn′ĭk), *adj.* **1.** designating Finnish and the languages most closely related to it, as Estonian, Lapp, and some minor languages of the north-western Soviet Union. **2.** designating all Finno-Ugric languages except the Ugric, or all except Ugric and Permian.

Finnish (fĭn′ĭsh), *n.* **1.** the principal language of Finland, a Finno-Ugric language, closely related to Estonian. *—adj.* **2.** of or pertaining to Finland or its inhabitants. **3.** Finnic.

Finnmark (fĭn′mäk; *Norw.* fĕn′märk), *n.* a district in N Norway. 73,929 pop. (est. 1964); 18,581 sq. mi.

Finno-Ugrian (fĭn′ō yoo′grĭ ən), *adj.* **1.** pertaining to the Finns and the Ugrians. *—n.* **2.** Finno-Ugric.

Finno-Ugric (fĭn′ō yoo′grĭk), *n.* a linguistic family of eastern Europe and western Siberia, including Finnish, Estonian, and Lapp, farther east the Zyrian and Votyak, and also the Ugric languages, such as Hungarian and Vogul. It is related to Samoyed.

finny (fĭn′ĭ), *adj.* **1.** pertaining to or abounding in fish. **2.** having fins; finned. **3.** finlike.

Finsbury (fĭnz′brĭ), *n.* a district of the N inner London borough of Islington.

Finsteraarhorn (fĭn′stə rä′hôn′), *n.* a mountain in S central Switzerland: the highest peak of the Bernese Alps. 14,026 ft.

finwhale (fĭn′wāl′), *n.* finback.

fiord (fyôd), *n.* a long, relatively narrow arm of the sea, bordered by steep cliffs, as on the coast of Norway. Also, **fjord.** [t. Norw. See FIRTH]

Fiordland (fyôd′lănd′), *n.* an area of scenic beauty in SW South Island, New Zealand. The **Fiordland National Park** (ab. 4723 sq. mi.) includes Lakes Manapouri and Te Anau.

fiorin (fī′ə rĭn), *n.* a perennial stoloniferous grass, *Agrostis stolonifera,* widespread throughout tropical regions.

fipple (fĭp′l), *n.* *Music.* a plug, stopping the upper end of a pipe.

fipple flute, *Music.* a flute equipped with a fipple.

fir (fû), *n.* **1.** any of the pyramidal coniferous trees constituting the genus *Abies*, as *A. balsamea*, the balsam fir. **2.** the wood of such a tree. [ME *firr(e)*, OE *fyrh*. Cf. OE *furh(wudu)* pine, Icel. *fura* fir; akin to L *quercus* oak]

Firbank (fûr′băngk′), *n.* **Ronald,** 1886–1926, English author.

Firdausi (*Pers.* fėr dow zē′), *n.* (*Abul Kasim Mansur*), A.D. *c.* 940–1020, Persian poet. Also, **Firdusi** (*Pers.* fėr do͞o zē′).

fire (fī′ə), *n.*, *v.*, **fired, firing.** —*n.* **1.** the active principle of burning or combustion, manifested by the evolution of light and heat. **2.** a burning mass of material, as on a hearth or in a furnace. **3.** the destructive burning of a building, town, forest, etc.; a conflagration. **4.** a composition or device for producing a conflagration or a fiery display: *Greek fire.* **5.** flashing light; luminous appearance. **6.** brilliance, as of a gem. **7.** burning passion; ardour; enthusiasm. **8.** liveliness of imagination. **9.** fever; inflammation. **10.** severe trial or trouble. **11.** exposure to fire by way of torture or ordeal. **12.** heating quality, as of strong drink. **13.** a spark or sparks. **14.** the discharge of firearms: *to open fire.* **15.** the effect of firing military weapons: *to place fire upon the enemy.* **16.** *Archaic.* lightning, or a thunderbolt. **17.** *Poetic.* a luminous object, as a star: *heavenly fires.* **18.** Some special noun phrases are:
between two fires, being attacked from both sides.
catch fire, to become ignited.
go through fire and water, to face any hardship or danger.
hang fire, 1. to be slow in exploding. **2.** to be irresolute, postponed or delayed.
lay a fire, to arrange fuel to be lit.
on fire, 1. ignited; burning. **2.** eager; ardent; zealous.
play with fire, to meddle carelessly or lightly with a dangerous matter.
set fire to or **set on fire, 1.** to cause to burn. **2.** to excite violently; inflame.
take fire, 1. to become ignited. **2.** to become filled with enthusiasm or zeal.
under fire, 1. exposed to enemy fire. **2.** under criticism or attack.
—*v.t.* **19.** to set on fire. **20.** to supply (a furnace, etc.) with fuel; attend to the fire of (a boiler, etc.). **21.** to expose to the action of fire; subject to heat. **22.** to apply heat in a kiln for baking or glazing; burn. **23.** to heat very slowly for the purpose of drying, as tea. **24.** to inflame, as with passion; fill with ardour. **25.** to inspire. **26.** to light or cause to glow as if on fire. **27.** to discharge, as a gun. **28.** to project (a missile) by discharging from a gun, etc. **29.** to subject to explosion or explosive force, as a mine. **30.** *Slang.* to dismiss from a job. **31.** *Vet. Sci.* to apply a heated iron to (the skin) in order to create a local inflammation of the superficial structures, thus favourably affecting deeper inflammatory processes. **32.** *Obs.* to drive out or away by, or as by, fire.
—*v.i.* **33.** to take fire; be kindled. **34.** to glow as if on fire. **35.** to become inflamed with passion; become excited. **36.** to go off, as a gun. **37.** to discharge a gun, etc.: *fire at a fleeing enemy.* **38.** to hurl a missile. **39.** (of an internal-combustion engine) to cause ignition of the air-fuel mixture in the cylinder or cylinders. **40. fire away,** *Colloq.* to begin speaking.
[ME; OE *fȳr*, c. D *vuur*, G *Feuer*; akin to Gk *pŷr*] —**fi′reable,** *adj.*

fire alarm, 1. a visible or audible notice that a fire has started. **2.** an apparatus for giving this notice.

firearm (fī′ər äm′), *n.* a small arms weapon from which a projectile is discharged by an explosion.

fireback (fī′ə băk′), *n.* **1.** the rear part of a fireplace. **2.** a decorated plate, esp. of cast iron, lining the rear of a fireplace.

fireball (fī′ə bôl′), *n.* **1.** a ball filled with explosive or combustible material, used as a projectile, to injure the enemy by explosion or to set fire to their works. **2.** a ball of fire, as the sun. **3.** a luminous meteor, sometimes exploding. **4.** lightning having the appearance of a globe of fire.

fire bay, *Fort.* that section of a fire trench occupied by riflemen, usually one squad to a bay.

firebird (fī′ə bûd′), *n.* the Baltimore oriole.

fire blight, a destructive bacterial disease of fruit trees, esp. apple and pear, caused by *Etwinia amylovora*.

fireboat (fī′ə bōt′), *n.* a powered vessel equipped for fighting fires.

fire bomb, an incendiary bomb.

fire boss, *U.S. Mining.* fireman (def. 4).

firebox (fī′ə bŏks′), *n.* **1.** the box or chamber in which the fire of a steam-boiler, etc., is placed. **2.** the furnace of a steam-engine, where coal, oil or other fuel is burned for the purpose of generating steam. **3.** *Obs.* a tinderbox.

firebrand (fī′ə brănd′), *n.* **1.** a piece of burning wood or other material. **2.** one who or that which kindles strife, inflames the passions, etc.

firebrat (fī′ə brăt′), *n.* a small insect, *Thermobia domestica*, found in warm places around furnaces, boilers, etc.

firebreak (fī′ə brāk′), *n.* a strip of ploughed or cleared land made to check the spread of fire.

firebrick (fī′ə brĭk′), *n.* a brick made of fireclay.

fire brigade, a body of firemen.

firebug (fī′ə bŭg′), *n.* *U.S. Colloq.* an incendiary.

fireclay (fī′ə klā′), *n.* a kind of clay capable of resisting high temperature, used for making crucibles, firebricks, etc.

fire-control (fī′ə kən trōl′), *n.* *Mil.* technical supervision of artillery fire or naval gunfire.

firecracker (fī′ə krăk′ə), *n.* cracker (def. 2).

firecrest (fī′ə krĕst′), *n.* a small bird, *Regulus ignicapillus*, distinguishable from the goldcrest by its black and white stripes about the eyes.

firedamp (fī′ə dămp′), *n.* **1.** a combustible gas, consisting chiefly of methane, formed esp. in coalmines, and dangerously explosive when mixed with certain proportions of atmospheric air. **2.** the explosive mixture itself.

fire department, *U.S.* the department of a local authority charged with the prevention and extinction of fires.

fire-direction (fī′ə dĭ rĕk′shən), *n.* *Mil.* tactical supervision of artillery fire.

firedog (fī′ə dŏg′), *n.* an andiron.

firedrake (fī′ə drāk′), *n.* a mythical dragon. [OE *fȳrdraca*, f. *fȳr* fire + *draca* dragon]

fire drill, 1. a practice drill for firemen, the passengers and crew of a ship, etc., to accustom them to their duties in case of fire. **2.** a drill for pupils in a school, employees in a factory, etc., to train them how to leave the building in case of fire.

fire-eater (fī′ər ē′tə), *n.* **1.** a juggler who pretends to eat fire. **2.** one who seeks occasion to fight or quarrel. —**fire′-eat′ing,** *adj.*

fire-engine (fī′ər ĕn′jĭn), *n.* a motor vehicle equipped for fire-fighting, now usually having a motor-driven pump for shooting water from fire hydrants, etc., or chemical solutions at high pressure.

fire-escape (fī′ə rĭ skāp′), *n.* an apparatus or structure used to escape from a burning building.

fire-extinguisher (fī′ə rĭk stĭng′gwĭsh ə), *n.* a portable device, usually containing water or chemicals under pressure, for putting out fires.

fire-fighter (fī′ə fī′tə), *n.* one whose activity or employment is to extinguish fires; a fireman. —**fire′-fight′ing,** *adj.*

fireflaught (fī′ə flôt′), *n.* *Chiefly Scot.* lightning. [f. FIRE, n. + *flaught* flash]

firefly (fī′ə flī′), *n.*, *pl.* **-flies.** any of the soft-bodied, nocturnal beetles of the family *Lampyridae*, which possess abdominal light-producing organs. The luminous larvae or wingless females are called **glow-worms.**

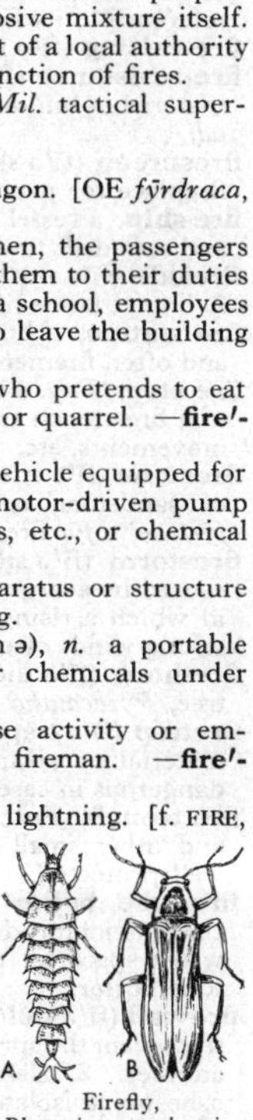

A B

Firefly, *Photuris pennsylvanica*
A, Larva; B, Adult
(Length 5½ in.)

fireguard (fī′ə gäd′), *n.* a framework of wire placed in front of a fireplace as a protection.

firehouse (fī′ə hous′), *n.* *U.S.* a fire station.

fire hydrant, a hydrant used as an emergency water supply for extinguishing fires.

fire insurance, insurance covering loss or damage through fire.

fire irons, implements used for tending a domestic fire, such as tongs, poker, etc.

fireless (fī′ə lĭs), *adj.* **1.** lacking fire; without a fire. **2.** without life or animation.

firelight (fī′ə līt′), *n.* the light from a fire, as on a hearth.

firelighter (fī′ə lī′tə), *n.* any highly inflammable material used for kindling fires.

firelock (fī′ə lŏk′), *n.* **1.** the flintlock musket, in whose lock the priming is ignited by sparks struck from flint and steel. **2.** (formerly) a soldier armed with such a gun.

fireman (fī′ə mən), *n.*, *pl.* **-men. 1.** a man employed to extinguish or prevent fires. **2.** a man employed to tend fires; a stoker. **3.** *Railways.* **a.** one who tends the fire of a steam locomotive and assists the driver. **b.** the assistant to the driver on a diesel or electric locomotive. **4.** *Mining.* a colliery official responsible for precautions against fire.

fire mark, a metal plate formerly attached to a building by insurance companies to indicate that it was insured.

fire-new (fī′ə nyo͞o′), *adj.* *Archaic.* brand-new.

Firenze (*It.* fē rĕn′tsė), *n.* Italian name of **Florence.**

fire office, the office of a fire-insurance company.

fire opal, a red Mexican opal, often with a colour play.

fireplace (fīʹə plās′), *n.* **1.** that part of a chimney which opens into a room and in which fuel is burnt. **2.** any open structure, usually of masonry, for containing fire, as at a camp site.
fireplug (fīʹə plŭg′), *n. U.S.* a fire hydrant.
fire point, the lowest temperature at which a substance ignites when a flame is put to it and continues to burn. Also, **firing point.**
fire policy, an insurance policy covering loss by fire.
firepot (fīʹə pŏt′), *n. Obs.* **1.** that part of a household furnace in which the fire is made. **2.** a pot containing explosives, etc., used as a missile.
fire power, *Mil.* **1.** the ability to deliver fire. **2.** the amount of fire delivered by a unit or weapon.
fireproof (fīʹə pro͞of′), *adj.* **1.** proof against fire; comparatively incombustible. *—v.t.* **2.** to make fireproof.
fireproofing (fīʹə pro͞oʹfĭng), *n.* **1.** the act or process of rendering fireproof. **2.** material for use in making anything fireproof.
firer (fīʹə rə), *n.* **1.** one who fires, sets on fire, treats with fire or heat, discharges a firearm, etc. **2.** a firearm with reference to its firing: *a single-firer, a rapid-firer.*
fire-raising (fīʹə rā′zĭng), *n.* arson. **—fire′-rais′er,** *n.*
fire-resistance (fīʹə rĭ zĭs′təns), *n.* the extent to which a material or building is resistant to fire. **—fire′-resis′tant,** *adj.*
firescreen (fīʹə skrēn′), *n.* a screen placed in front of a fireplace for protection or decoration.
fire ship, a vessel loaded with combustibles and explosives and set adrift to destroy an enemy's ships, etc.
fireside (fīʹə sīd′), *n.* **1.** the space about a fire or hearth. **2.** home; home life.
fire station, a building in which fire-fighting equipment and often firemen are housed.
fire step, *Fort.* a board or narrow ledge above the bottom of a fire trench from which men can fire, observe enemy movements, etc.
firestone (fīʹə stōn′), *n.* a fire-resisting stone, esp. a kind of sandstone used in fireplaces, furnaces, etc. [OE *fȳrstān,* f. *fȳr* fire + *stān* stone]
firestorm (fīʹə stôm′), *n.* an atmospheric phenomenon caused by a large fire, as after the mass bombing of a city, in which a rising column of air above the fire draws in strong winds often accompanied by rain.
firethorn (fīʹə thôn′), *n.* an evergreen bushy shrub or tree, *Pyracantha coccinea,* of S Europe and Asia Minor.
firetrap (fīʹə trăp′), *n.* a building which, because of the material or arrangement of the structure, is especially dangerous in case of fire.
fire trench, *Fort.* a trench from which men can fire rifles and other small arms and in which they are relatively well-protected.
fire-tube boiler (fīʹə tyo͞ob′), a boiler in which the combustion products pass through tubes immersed in the water space on their way to the chimney. See **water-tube boiler.**
firewall (fīʹə wôl′), *n.* **1.** a wall made of fireproof material to prevent the spread of a fire from one part of a building to another. **2.** *Aeron.* a wall made of stainless steel and asbestos to isolate the engine compartment from the rest of an aircraft.
firewarden (fīʹə wô′dn), *n. U.S.* a person having authority in the prevention or extinguishing of fires, as in towns or camps.
firewatcher (fīʹə wŏch′ə), *n.* one who watches for fires, esp. those caused by enemy bombing.
firewater (fīʹə wô′tə), *n.* strong alcoholic drink.
fireweed (fīʹə wēd′), *n.* any of various plants appearing in recently burnt clearings or districts, as the rosebay willowherb, *Chamaenerion angustifolium,* of Europe, or the composite weed, *Erechtites hieracifolia,* of North America.
firewood (fīʹə wo͝od′), *n.* wood for fuel.
firework (fīʹə wûk′), *n.* **1.** (*usually pl.*) a combustible or explosive device for producing a striking display of light or a loud noise, often also used in signalling at night, etc. **2.** (*pl.*) **a.** a pyrotechnic display. **b.** a display of anger or bad temper.
firing (fīʹə rĭng), *n.* **1.** the act of one who or that which fires. **2.** material for a fire; fuel. **3.** the act of baking ceramics or glass.
firing line, **1.** *Mil.* the positions at which troops are stationed to fire upon the enemy or targets. **2.** *Mil.* the troops firing from this line. **3.** the forefront of any activity.
firing order, the sequence in which the cylinders of an internal-combustion engine fires.
firing party, **1.** a military detachment assigned to fire a salute at the burial of a person being honoured. **2.** firing squad.
firing pin, *Ordn.* a plunger in the firing mechanism of a gun that strikes the primer and thus ignites the propelling charge of a projectile.
firing squad, a military detachment assigned to execute a condemned person by shooting.
firkin (fûʹkĭn), *n.* **1.** a unit of capacity equal to 9 gallons. **2.** a small wooden vessel for butter, etc. [ME *ferdekyn,* t. MD: m. *ferdelkijn,* dim. of *ferdel* firkin (lit., fourth part)]
firm[1] (fûm), *adj.* **1.** comparatively solid, hard, stiff, or rigid: *firm ground, flesh, texture.* **2.** securely fixed in place. **3.** steady; not shaking or trembling: *a firm hand or voice.* **4.** fixed, settled, or unalterable, as a belief or conviction, a decree, etc. **5.** steadfast or unwavering, as persons or principles. **6.** indicating firmness: *a firm countenance.* **7.** not fluctuating or falling, as prices or the market. *—v.t., v.i.* **8.** to make or become firm. *—adv.* **9.** firmly: *stand firm.* [t. L: s. *firmus*; r. ME *ferme,* t. OF] **—firm′ly,** *adv.* **—firm′ness,** *n.*
—Syn. 1. FIRM, HARD, SOLID, STIFF are applied to substances that tend to retain their form unaltered in spite of pressure or force. FIRM often implies that something has been brought from a more yielding state to a fixed or elastic one: *an increased amount of pectin makes jellies more firm.* HARD is applied to substances so resistant that it is difficult to make any impression upon their surface or to penetrate their interior: *as hard as a stone.* SOLID is applied to substances that without external support retain their form and resist pressure: *water in the form of ice is solid*; it sometimes denotes the opposite of hollow: *a solid block of marble.* STIFF implies rigidity that resists a bending force: *as stiff as a poker.* **5.** determined, immovable, resolute. **—Ant. 1.** yielding.
firm[2] (fûm), *n.* **1.** a business organization or partnership. **2.** the name or title under which associated parties transact business: *the firm of Jones & Co.* **3.** a team of medical officers in or attached to a hospital, headed by a physician or surgeon, specializing in one aspect or branch of medicine. [t. It., Sp.: m. *firma* signature, der. L *firmāre* confirm]
firmament (fûʹmə mənt), *n.* the vault of heaven; the sky. [ME, t. LL: s. *firmāmentum* firmament, L a support, prop] **—firmamental** (fû′mə mĕnʹtl), *adj.*
firman (fûʹmən, fə mänʹ), *n., pl.* **-mans.** an edict or administrative order issued by or in the name of an oriental sovereign (formerly by an Ottoman Turkish sultan). [t. Pers.: m. *fermān*]
firmer chisel (fûʹmə), a carpenter's chisel with a blade thin in proportion to its width, fixed to the handle by a tang, usually pushed by the hand and not driven with a mallet. [*firmer,* t. F: m. *fermoir,* b. *formoir* former (der. *former* form, t. L: m. *formāre*) and *fermer* make firm (g. L *firmāre*)]
firn (fĭən), *n.* névé. [t. G: (prop. adj.) of last year]
firry (fûʹrĭ), *adj.* **1.** of or pertaining to the fir. **2.** made of fir. **3.** abounding in firs.
first (fûst), *adj.* **1.** being before all others with respect to time, order, rank, importance, etc. (used as the ordinal number of *one*). **2.** *Music.* highest or chief among several voices or instruments of the same class: *first alto, first horn.* **3.** *Motor Vehicles.* of or pertaining to low transmission gear ratio. **4. at first blush,** at the first view; on first consideration. **5. at first hand,** from the first or original source. **6. first thing,** before anything else; at once; early. *—adv.* **7.** before all others or anything else in time, order, rank, etc. **8.** before some other thing, event, etc. **9.** for the first time. **10.** in preference to something else; rather; sooner. **11.** in the first place; firstly. **12. first and last,** altogether; in all. *—n.* **13.** that which is first in time, order, rank, etc. **14.** the beginning. **15.** the first part; the first member of a series. **16.** *Music.* **a.** the voice or instrument that takes the highest or chief part in its class, especially in an orchestra or chorus. **b.** a leader of a part or group of performers. **17.** *Motor Vehicles.* the lowest forward gear ratio; first gear. **18.** the first place in a race, etc. **19.** a first-class degree. **20.** (*pl.*) the best quality of certain articles of commerce. **21. at (the) first,** at the beginning or outset. **22. from the first,** from the beginning or outset. [ME; OE *fyrst,* c. OHG *furist,* G *Fürst* prince; a superl. form akin to FORE[1]]
first aid, emergency aid or treatment given to persons suffering from accident, etc., before the services of a doctor can be obtained. **—first′-aid′,** *adj.*
first base, **1.** *Baseball.* **a.** the first of the bases from the home plate. **b.** playing this position. **2. get to first base,** *Colloq., Chiefly U.S.* to make a slight amount of progress.
firstborn (fûstʹbôn′), *adj.* **1.** first in the order of birth; eldest. *—n.* **2.** a firstborn child. **3.** a first result or product.
first cause, **1.** a cause which does not depend upon another other: *God is the first cause.* **2.** any prime mover.
first class, the most luxurious class of accommodation for passengers on a ship, train, aircraft, etc.
first-class (fûstʹkläsʹ), *adj.* **1.** of the highest or best class of quality. **2.** best-equipped and most expensive: *a*

first-class carriage. **3.** given or entitled to preferential treatment: *first-class airmail.* **4.** denoting a degree bearing the highest class of honours in a university examination. *—adv.* **5.** by first-class conveyance: *to travel first-class.*

first cost, *Com.* cost not including profit.

First day, Sunday (used by the Quakers).

first-day cover (fûst′dā′), *Philately.* an envelope bearing a newly-issued stamp, posted and franked on the day of issue.

First Empire. See **Empire** (def. 5).

first fleet, *Austral.* the ships which took the first convict settlers to Australia in 1788. —**first′-fleet′er,** *adj.*

first floor, 1. the floor above the ground floor of a building. **2.** *U.S.* the ground floor of a building.

first-foot (fûst′fŏŏt′), *Scot.* —*n.* **1.** Also, **first′-foot′er.** the first person to enter a house on New Year's Day. —*v.t.* **2.** to enter (a house) first on New Year's Day. —*v.i.* **3.** to be the first to enter a house on New Year's Day; to go round making visits as a first-foot. —**first′-foot′ing,** *n.*

first fruit, (*usually pl.*) **1.** the earliest fruit of the season. **2.** the first product or result of anything.

first-generation (fûst′jĕn′ə rā′shən), *adj.* of or pertaining to a citizen of a country who is either foreign-born, and naturalized or born of foreign parents: *a first-generation American.*

first-hand (fûst′hănd′), *adv.* **1.** from the first or original source. *—adj.* **2.** of or pertaining to the first or original source. **3.** direct from the original source.

First International. See **international** (def. 5).

first lady, *U.S.* the wife of the president of the U.S., or of the governor of a state.

firstling (fûst′lĭng), *n.* **1.** the first of its kind to be produced or to appear. **2.** first offspring. **3.** the first product or result.

firstly (fûst′lĭ), *adv.* in the first place; first.

first mortgage, a mortgage having priority over all other mortgages on property.

first name, Christian name; forename.

first night, the first public performance of a play, etc. —**first-nighter** (fûst′nī′tə), *n.*

first offender, one convicted of an offence in law for the first time.

first person, *Gram.* the class of a pronoun or verb in which the speaker is the subject. See **person** (def. 13a).

first position, *Ballet.* a position of the feet in which the heels are back to back and the toes point out to the sides.

first principle, any law, axiom, or concept which represents the highest degree of generalization and which depends on fundamental principles.

first-rate (fûst′rāt′), *adj.* **1.** of the first rate or class. **2.** excellent; very good. *—adv.* **3.** *Colloq.* excellently.

First Reich. See **Reich** (def. 1).

First Republic. See **republic** (def. 4).

first speed, low gear.

first water, 1. the highest degree of fineness in a diamond or other precious stone. **2.** the highest rank.

firth (fûth), *n. Chiefly Scot.* a long, narrow indentation of the seacoast. Also, **frith.** [t. Scand.; cf. Icel. *firdh-*, s. *fjördhr* firth. Cf. FIORD]

fisc (fĭsk), *n.* a royal or state treasury; an exchequer. [t. L: s. *fiscus* basket, purse, treasury]

fiscal (fĭs′kl), *adj.* **1.** of or pertaining to the public treasury or revenues. **2.** pertaining to financial matters in general. *—n.* **3.** (in some countries) an official having the function of public prosecutor. [t. L: s. *fiscālis* belonging to the state treasury] —**fis′cally,** *adv.* —**Syn. 1.** See **financial.**

fiscal year, financial year.

Fischer (fĭsh′ə *for 1* ; *Ger.* fĭsh′ər *for 2*), *n.* **1. Annie,** born 1914, Hungarian pianist. **2. Emil Hermann** (*Ger.* ĕ mēl′ hĕr′män), 1852–1919, German chemist.

Fischer-Dieskau (*Ger.* fĭsh′ər dēs′kou), *n.* **Dietrich** (*Ger.* dē′trĭKH), born 1925, German baritone.

Fischer-Tropsch process (*Ger.* fĭsh′ər trŏpsh), *Chem.* any of several processes for the manufacture of hydrocarbons, or their derivatives, by the catalytic hydrogenation of carbon monoxide under high temperatures and pressures. [named after Franz *Fischer*, 1877–1947, and H. *Tropsch*, died 1935, German chemists]

Fischer von Erlach (*Ger.* fĭsh′ər fōn ĕr′läKH), **Johann Bernhard** (*Ger.* yō′hän bĕrn′härt), 1656–1723, Austrian baroque architect.

fish[1] (fĭsh), *n., pl.* **fishes,** (*esp. collectively*) **fish** (Note: in technical usage, *fishes* usually refers to several species, while *fish* refers to only one species.), *v.* *—n.* **1.** any of various cold-blooded, completely aquatic vertebrates, having gills, commonly fins, and typically an elongated body usually covered with scales. **2.** any of various other aquatic animals. **3.** the flesh of fishes used as food. **4. the Fishes,** *Astron., Astrol.* the zodiacal constellation or sign Pisces. **5.** *Colloq.* (with an adjective) a person: *a queer fish, a poor fish.* **6. cry stinking fish,** *Archaic.* to disparage oneself or one's efforts. **7. drink like a fish,** to drink alcoholic liquors to excess. **8. feed the fishes, a.** to be seasick. **b.** to drown. **9. fish out of water,** out of one's proper environment, ill at ease in unfamiliar surroundings. **10. neither fish nor fowl.** Also, **neither fish, flesh, fowl, nor good red herring.** neither one thing nor the other. **11. other fish to fry,** other matters requiring attention. **12. fine (pretty) kettle of fish,** trouble; confusion. *—v.t.* **13.** to catch or attempt to catch (fish or the like). **14.** to try to catch fish in (a stream, etc.). **15.** to draw as by fishing (fol. by *up, out,* etc.). **16.** to search through as by fishing. **17.** *Naut.* to hoist the flukes of (an anchor) up to the gunwale or rail by means of a tackle, to secure it to the deck. **18. fish out, a.** to exhaust of fish by fishing. **b.** to obtain by careful search or by artifice. *—v.i.* **19.** to catch or attempt to catch fish, as by angling or drawing a net. **20.** to search for or attempt to catch on to something under water, in mud, etc., by the use of a dredge, rake, hook, or the like. **21.** to seek to obtain something by artifice or indirectly: *to fish for compliments, information, etc.* **22. fish in troubled waters,** take advantage of uncertain conditions; profit from the difficulties of others. [ME; OE *fisc*, c. D *visch*, G *Fisch*; akin to L *piscis*] —**fish′able,** *adj.* —**fish′less,** *adj.* —**fish′like′,** *adj.*

fish[2] (fĭsh), *n.* **1.** *Naut.* a long strip of wood, iron, etc., used to strengthen a mast, joint, spar, etc. *—v.t.* **2.** *Naut.* to strengthen (a mast, joint, spar, etc.) by means of a fish. [t. OF: m. s. *ficher* to fix]

fish and chips, fish fillets coated with batter, and potato chips, both fried in deep fat or oil.

fishbolt (fĭsh′bōlt′), *n.* a bolt that secures a fishplate to the rail in a railway track.

fishbowl (fĭsh′bōl′), *n.* a glass bowl in which an ornamental fish is kept.

fishcake (fĭsh′kāk′), *n.* a fried ball or cake of shredded fish, esp. salt cod, and mashed potato. Also, **fish ball.**

fisher (fĭsh′ə), *n.* **1.** a fisherman. **2.** an animal that catches fish for food. **3.** a dark brown or blackish, somewhat foxlike marten, *Martes pennanti*, of northern North America. **4.** its fur.

Fisher (fĭsh′ə), *n.* **1. Geoffrey Francis, Baron of Lambeth,** born 1887, Archbishop of Canterbury 1945–61. **2. John Arbuthnot** (ä bŭth′nət), **1st Baron Fisher of Silverstone** (sĭl′ və stən), 1841–1920, British admiral.

fisherman (fĭsh′ə mən), *n., pl.* **-men. 1.** one engaged in fishing, whether for profit or pleasure. **2.** a vessel employed in fishing.

fisherman's bend, a knot consisting of two round turns and a half-hitch round them and the standing part, used commonly to bend a rope to an anchor or similar object.

fishery (fĭsh′ə rĭ), *n., pl.* **-ries. 1.** the occupation or industry of catching fish or taking other products of the sea or streams from the water. **2.** a place where such an industry is regularly carried on. **3.** a fishing establishment. **4.** *Law.* the right of fishing in certain waters.

fish glue, 1. any glue prepared from fish skins, bladders, or bones. **2.** isinglass.

fish-hawk (fĭsh′hôk′), *n.* the osprey.

fishhook (fĭsh′hŏŏk′), *n.* a barbed hook used in fishing.

fishing (fĭsh′ĭng), *n.* **1.** the art or practice of catching fish. **2.** a place or facilities for catching fish.

fishing line, a line used in fishing.

fishing rod, a long, flexible rod supporting a fishing line.

fishing smack, a sloop-rigged fishing vessel fitted with a well to keep the catch alive.

fishing tackle, the equipment used to catch fish.

fishjoint (fĭsh′joint′), *n.* a splice formed by fastening one or more fishplates to the sides of rails, beams, etc., which meet end to end; used esp. in connecting railway lines.

fish kettle, a deep oval container, usually having a perforated grid in the bottom, for poaching salmon, etc., sterilizing fruit, etc.

fish knife, a blunt, broad-bladed knife used for parting or cutting fish at table.

fish ladder, a series of ascending pools constructed so as to enable fish to swim upstream past a weir or dam.

fish-louse (fĭsh′lous′), *n., pl.* **-lice** (-līs′). *Zool.* any of numerous small crustaceans, esp. certain copepods, parasitic on fish.

fishmonger (fĭsh′mŭng′gə), *n.* a dealer in fish.

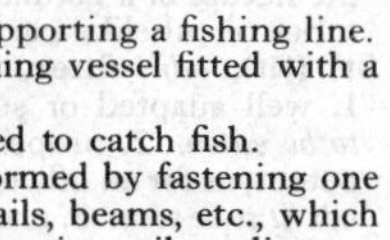

fishplate (fĭsh′plāt′), *n.* one of the splicing plates used in a fishjoint.

Rail fishplate

fishslice (fĭsh′slīs′), *n.* **1.** a broad-bladed kitchen implement with a long handle, for turning fish in frying. **2.** a broad-bladed implement for serving fish at table.

fish spear, a spear or lance, often with several tines, for spearing fish through ice or from a boat or shore.
fishtail (fĭsh′tāl′), *v.i.* **1.** to slow an aeroplane by causing its tail to move rapidly from side to side. —*n.* **2.** such a manoeuvre. **3.** a roughly triangular device attached to a Bunsen burner to give a flat, thin flame.
fishwife (fĭsh′wīf′), *n., pl.* **-wives. 1.** a woman who sells fish. **2.** a coarse-mannered woman who uses abusive language.
fishy (fĭsh′ĭ), *adj.,* **fishier, fishiest. 1.** fishlike in shape, smell, taste, etc. **2.** consisting of fish. **3.** abounding in fish. **4.** *Colloq.* improbable, as a story. **5.** *Colloq.* of questionable character. **6.** dull and expressionless: *fishy eyes.* —**fish′ily,** *adv.* —**fish′iness,** *n.*
fissi-, a word element meaning 'cleft'. [t. L, comb. form of *fissus,* pp.]
fissile (fĭs′ĭl), *adj.* **1.** capable of being split or divided; cleavable. **2.** *Physics.* (of an atom, isotope, or nucleus) capable of undergoing nuclear fission, esp. of an isotope which is capable of undergoing fission upon impact with a slow neutron. Also, *U.S.,* **fissionable** (fĭsh′ə nə bl). [t. L: m. s. *fissilis*]
fission (fĭsh′ən), *n.* **1.** the act of cleaving or splitting into parts. **2.** *Biol.* the division of an organism into new organisms as a process of reproduction. **3.** *Physics.* the splitting of the nucleus of a heavy atom, as uranium, to form the nuclei of lighter atoms. [t. L: s. *fissio* a cleaving]
fission bomb, an atomic weapon which depends on nuclear fission.
fissiparous (fĭ sĭp′ə rəs), *adj.* reproducing by fission.
fissirostral (fĭs′ĭ rŏs′trəl), *adj. Ornith.* **1.** having a broad, deeply cleft beak or bill, as the swallows and goatsuckers. **2.** (of the bill) deeply cleft.

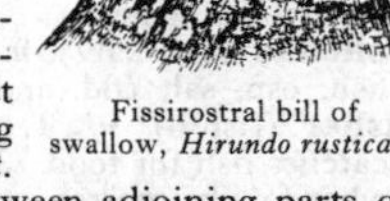
Fissirostral bill of swallow, *Hirundo rustica*

fissure (fĭsh′ə), *n., v.,* **-sured, -suring.** —*n.* **1.** a narrow opening produced by cleavage or separation of parts; a cleft. **2.** act of cleaving. **3.** the state of being cleft; cleavage. **4.** *Surg., Anat.* a natural division or groove between adjoining parts of like substance. —*v.t.* **5.** to make fissures in; cleave; split. —*v.i.* **6.** to open fissures; become split. [t. F, t. L: m. s. *fissūra* a cleft]
fist (fĭst), *n.* **1.** the hand closed tightly, with the fingers doubled into the palm. **2.** *Colloq.* the hand. **3.** *Colloq.* a person's handwriting. **4.** *Print.* the index sign (☛). —*v.t.* **5.** to strike with the fist. **6.** to grasp with the fist. [ME *fiste,* OE *fȳst,* c. G *Faust*]
fistful (fĭst′fo͝ol′), *n.* a handful.
fistic (fĭs′tĭk), *adj.* of boxing; pugilistic: *fistic heroes.*
fisticuff (fĭs′tĭ kŭf′), *n.* **1.** a cuff or blow with the fist. **2.** (*pl.*) combat with the fists. —*v.t., v.i.* **3.** to strike or fight with the fists. —**fist′icuff′er,** *n.*
fistula (fĭs′tyo͞o lə), *n., pl.* **-las, -lae** (-lē′). **1.** *Pathol.* a narrow passage or duct formed by disease or injury, as one leading from an abscess to a free surface, or from one cavity to another. **2.** *Vet. Sci.* any of various suppurative inflammations, as in the withers of a horse, characterized by the formation of passages or sinuses through the tissues and to the surface of the skin. **3.** *Obs.* a pipe, as a flute. [t. L: pipe, tube, reed, ulcer. Cf. FESTER]
fistulous (fĭs′tyo͞o ləs), *adj.* **1.** *Pathol.* pertaining to or of the nature of a fistula. **2.** tubelike; tubular. **3.** containing tubes or tubelike parts. Also, **fis′tular.**
fit[1] (fĭt), *adj.,* **fitter, fittest,** *v.,* **fitted, fitting,** *n.* —*adj.* **1.** well adapted or suited: *a fit choice or opportunity, fit to be eaten.* **2.** proper or becoming. **3.** qualified or competent, as for an office or function. **4.** worthy or deserving: *not fit to be seen.* **5.** prepared or ready: *crops fit for gathering.* **6.** in good physical condition, as an athlete, a racehorse, military troops, etc. **7.** in good health. —*v.t.* **8.** to be adapted to or suitable for (a purpose, object, occasion, etc.). **9.** to be proper or becoming for. **10.** to be of the right size or shape for. **11.** to conform or adjust to something: *to fit a ring to the finger.* **12.** to make qualified or competent: *qualities that fit one for leadership.* **13.** to prepare. **14.** to put with precise adjustment (fol. by *in, into, on, over, together,* etc.). **15.** to provide; furnish; equip: *fit a door with a new handle.* **16. fit out** or **up,** to furnish with clothing, equipment, furniture, fixtures, or other requisites. —*v.i.* **17.** to be suitable or proper. **18.** to be of the right size or shape, as a garment for the wearer, or any object or part for a thing to which it is applied. **19. fit in,** to be well adapted to. —*n.* **20.** the manner in which a thing fits: *a perfect fit.* **21.** something that fits: *that coat is a poor fit.* **22.** the process or a process of fitting. [late ME *fȳt*; orig. uncert.] —**fit′ness,** *n.*
fit[2] (fĭt), *n.* **1.** a sudden, acute attack or manifestation of a disease: *fit of epilepsy.* **2.** an access, spell, or period of emotion or feeling, inclination, activity, idleness, etc. **3.** convulsion. **4. by fits,** or **by fits and starts,** by irregular spells; fitfully; intermittently. **5. throw a fit,** to become very excited or angry. [ME; OE *fitt* fight, struggle]
fit[3] (fĭt), *n.* **1.** a song, ballad, or story. **2.** a division of a song, ballad, or story. [ME; OE *fitt*]
fitch (fĭch), *n.* **1.** the European polecat, *Mustela putorius.* **2.** its fur. Yellow fitch is often dyed to imitate other furs. **3.** a small brush made of this hair or of hog's hair. Also, **fitchet** (fĭch′ĭt), **fitchew** (fĭch′o͞o). [t. MD: m. *vitsche* polecat]
Fitch (fĭch), *n.* **John,** 1743–98, U.S. inventor of a steamboat in 1790.
fitful (fĭt′fəl), *adj.* coming, appearing, acting, etc., in fits or by spells; irregularly intermittent. [f. FIT[2] + -FUL] —**fit′fully,** *adv.* —**fit′fulness,** *n.*
fitly (fĭt′lĭ), *adv.* **1.** in a fit manner. **2.** at a fit time.
fitment (fĭt′mənt), *n.* **1.** equipment; furnishing, esp. that built to conform to the shape of a room. **2.** accessory; detachable part.
fitted (fĭt′ĭd), *adj.* **1.** made so as to conform to the shape of something else. **2.** (of carpets) extending from wall to wall. **3.** provided or equipped with accessories.
fitter (fĭt′ə), *n.* **1.** one who or that which fits. **2.** one who fits garments. **3.** one who fits together or adjusts the parts of machinery. **4.** one who supplies and fixes fittings or fixtures. **5.** one who furnishes or equips with whatever is necessary for some purpose.
fitting (fĭt′ĭng), *adj.* **1.** suitable or appropriate; proper or becoming. —*n.* **2.** the act of one who or that which fits. **3.** an act or instance of trying on clothes which are being made to determine proper fit. **4.** (of clothes) size. **5.** anything provided as equipment, parts, accessories, etc. **6.** (*pl.*) furnishings, fixtures, etc. —**fit′tingly,** *adv.* —**fit′tingness,** *n.*
fitting room, a room in a dress shop or a tailor's where customers can try on clothes.
FitzGerald (fĭts jĕ′rəld), *n.* **Edward,** 1809–83, English poet who translated some of the poems of Omar Khayyam.
Fitzgerald (fĭts jĕ′rəld), *n.* **1. Ella,** born 1918, U.S. jazz singer. **2. F(rancis) Scott (Key),** 1896–1940, U.S. novelist and short-story writer.
Fitzgerald-Lorentz contraction, *Physics.* an explanation of the negative result of the Michelson-Morley experiment put forward independently by Fitzgerald (1893) and Lorentz (1895). It assumes that bodies moving at a high velocity suffer a contraction in length. This contraction was later shown to be a consequence of the theory of relativity. [named after G. F. *Fitzgerald,* 1851–1901, Irish physicist, and H. A. LORENTZ]
Fitzroy (fĭts′roi), *n.* **1.** a river in N Western Australia flowing W then NW to the Indian Ocean. ab. 325 mi. **2.** a river in E Australia flowing E through Queensland to the Coral Sea. ab. 300 mi.
Fiume (*It.* fyo͞o′mĕ), *n.* former name for **Rijeka.**
Fiumicino (*It.* fyo͞o mē chē′nō), *n.* present name of the river **Rubicon.**
five (fīv), *n.* **1.** a cardinal number, four plus one. **2.** a symbol for this number, as 5 or V. **3.** a set of this many persons or things. **4.** a playing card, etc., with five pips. —*adj.* **5.** amounting to five in number. [ME; OE *fīf,* c. D *vijf,* G *fünf*; akin to L *quinque,* Gk *pénte*]
five-finger (fīv′fĭng′gə), *n.* **1.** any of certain species of potentilla with leaves of five leaflets, as *Potentilla canadensis.* **2.** bird's-foot trefoil. **3.** oxlip. **4.** Virginia creeper. —*adj.* **5.** for five fingers, as a piano exercise.
fivefold (fīv′fōld′), *adj.* **1.** comprising five parts or members. **2.** five times as great or as much. —*adv.* **3.** in fivefold measure.
five hundred, a form of euchre in which a joker and a widow are included and in which 500 points win.
Five Nations, a confederacy of Iroquoian Indians: the Mohawks, Oneidas, Onondagas, Cayugas, and Senecas.
fivepence (fĭf′pəns), *n.* five pennies.
fivepenny (fĭf′pə nĭ), *adj.* **1.** of the amount or value of fivepence. —*n.* **2.** something purchased for fivepence.
fivepins (fīv′pĭnz′), *n.pl.* **1.** (*construed as sing.*) a game played with five wooden pins at which a ball is bowled to knock them down. **2.** (*construed as pl.*) the pins used in this game. —**five′pin′,** *adj.*
fiver (fī′və), *n. Colloq.* **1.** a five-pound note or a five-dollar bill. **2.** anything that counts as five.
fives (fīvz), *n.* a ball game played with the hands or a bat in a walled court.
five-stones (fīv′stōnz′), *n.* a child's game played with a set of five small square pieces of stone, which are tossed on the palm of the hand and caught on the back of the hand.
fix (fĭks), *v.,* **fixed** or **fixt, fixing,** *n.* —*v.t.* **1.** to make fast, firm, or stable. **2.** to place definitely and more or

less permanently. **3.** to settle definitely; determine: *to fix a price.* **4.** to direct (the eyes, the attention, etc.) steadily. **5.** to attract and hold (the eye, the attention, etc.). **6.** to make set or rigid. **7.** to put into permanent form. **8.** to put or place (responsibility, blame, etc.) on a person. **9.** to assign or refer to a definite place, time, etc. **10.** to repair. **11.** to put in order or in good condition; adjust or arrange. **12.** to provide or supply with (something needed or wanted): *How are you fixed for money?* **13.** *Colloq.* to arrange matters with, or with respect to, esp. privately or dishonestly, so as to secure favourable action: *to fix a jury or a game.* **14.** *U.S.* to get (a meal); prepare (food). **15.** *Colloq.* to put in a condition or position to make no further trouble. **16.** *Colloq.* to get even with; get revenge upon. **17.** *Chem.* **a.** to make stable in consistency or condition; reduce from fluidity or volatility to a more permanent state. **b.** to convert atmospheric nitrogen into nitrates for use as fertilizers. **18.** *Photog.* to remove the light-sensitive silver halides from (a photographic image), rendering it permanent. **19.** *Microscopy.* to kill, make rigid, and preserve for microscopic study. **20. fix on.** Also, **fix upon.** to decide on, single out, choose. **21. fix up, a.** to arrange, organize, decide on. **b.** *U.S.* to put right, solve.
—*v.i.* **22.** to become fixed. **23.** to become set; assume a rigid or solid form. **24.** to become stable or permanent. **25.** to settle down.
—*n.* **26.** *Colloq.* a position from which it is difficult to escape; a predicament. **27.** *Colloq.* the determining of a position, as of an aeroplane, by mathematical, electronic, or other means. **28.** *Slang.* a shot of heroin or other drug. **29.** *Slang.* a bribe.
[late ME, t. ML: s. *fixāre*, freq. of L *fīgere* fix] —**fix′able,** *adj.* —**fix′er,** *n.*

—**Syn.** 1, 2. FIX, ESTABLISH imply making firm or permanent. TO FIX is to fasten in position securely or to make more or less permanent against change, esp. something already existing: *to fix a bayonet on a gun, fix a principle.* TO ESTABLISH is to make firm or permanent something (usually newly) originated, created, or ordained: *to establish a business, a claim to property.*

fixate (fĭk′sāt), *v.*, **-sated, -sating.** —*v.t.* **1.** to fix; make stable, as a sensation. —*v.i.* **2.** to become fixed. [appar. back-formation from FIXATION]

fixated (fĭk′sā tĭd, fĭk sā′tĭd), *adj. Psychol.* partially arrested in emotional and instinctual development.

fixation (fĭk sā′shən), *n.* **1.** the act of fixing. **2.** the state of being fixed. **3.** *Chem.* **a.** a reduction from a volatile or fluid to a stable or solid form. **b.** the process of converting atmospheric nitrogen into a useful compound, as a nitrate fertilizer. **4.** *Psychol.* a partial arrest of emotional and instinctual development at an early point in life, due to a severe traumatic experience or an overwhelming gratification. [ME, t. ML: s. *fixātio*, der. *fixāre*, freq. of L *fīgere* fix]

fixative (fĭk′sə tĭv), *adj.* **1.** serving to fix; making fixed or permanent. —*n.* **2.** a fixative substance, esp.: **a.** a gummy liquid sprayed on a drawing or pastel to prevent blurring. **b.** a solution for killing, hardening, and preserving material for microscopic study.

fixed (fĭkst), *adj.* **1.** made fast or firm; firmly implanted. **2.** rendered stable or permanent, as colour. **3.** set or intent upon something; steadily directed; set or rigid. **4.** definitely and permanently placed: *a fixed buoy.* **5.** definite; not fluctuating or varying: *fixed prices.* **6.** put in order. **7.** *Colloq.* arranged with, or arranged, privately or dishonestly. **8.** *Chem.* **a.** (of an element) taken into a compound from its free state. **b.** non-volatile, or not easily volatilized: *a fixed oil.* —**fixedly** (fĭk′sĭd lĭ), *adv.* —**fix′edness,** *n.*

fixed assets, any long-term assets which are held solely for use and not for conversion into cash, as land, buildings, machinery, etc. Also, **capital assets.**

fixed capital, capital which has been used to acquire property, execute permanent constructions, or erect plant and machinery intended for retention and employment with a view to making profits (as opposed to *circulating capital*).

fixed charge. 1. a legal charge on specific property, as contrasted with a floating charge, both of which are usually contained in a debenture. **2.** an expense which must be met. **3.** periodic obligation, as taxes, interest on shares, etc. **4.** (*pl.*) such charges as depreciation, rent, interest, etc., arising out of the maintenance of fixed assets.

fixed idea, 1. a persistent or obsessive idea, often delusional, from which a person cannot escape. **2.** *Psychol.* a delusional idea which dominates the mind in certain forms of insanity.

fixed liability, a long-term liability, as a mortgage, debenture.

fixed oil, *Chem.* a natural oil which is fixed (def. 8b), as lard oil, linseed oil, etc. Fixed oils occur in the cellular membranes, etc., of animals, and in the seeds, capsules, etc., of plants.

fixed satellite, *Aerospace.* an artificial earth satellite in a synchronous orbit.

fixed star, *Astron.* any of the stars which apparently always retain the same position with respect to one another.

fixed trust, a unit trust whose trust deed provides for a fixed portfolio of investments during the lifetime of the trust, save in exceptional circumstances (opposed to *flexible trust*).

fixing (fĭk′sĭng), *n.* **1.** the act of one who or that which fixes. **2.** (*pl.*) *U.S. Colloq.* appliances; trimmings.

fixity (fĭk′sĭ tĭ), *n.*, *pl.* **-ties. 1.** the state or quality of being fixed; stability; permanence. **2.** something fixed.

fixt (fĭkst), *v.* a pt. and pp. of **fix.**

fixture (fĭks′chə), *n.* **1.** something securely fixed in position; a permanently attached part or appendage of a house, etc.: *an electric-light fixture.* **2.** a person or thing long established in the same place or position. **3.** *Mach.* a device for holding the work in a machine tool, esp. where the machining is to be done in straight surfaces, as in a planer or a milling machine. **4.** *Law.* a moveable chattel (such as a machine, heating plant, etc.) which, by reason of annexation to real property and of adaptation to continuing use in connection with the realty, is considered a part of the realty. **5.** a sporting event to be held on a date arranged in advance, as a football match. **6.** an act of fixing. [var. of *fixure* (t. LL: m. s. *fixūra*) modelled on MIXTURE] —**fix′tureless,** *adj.*

Fizeau (*Fr.* fē zō′), *n.* **Armand Hippolyte Louis** (*Fr.* är mäɴ ē pō lēt lwē′), 1819–96, French physicist.

fizgig (fĭz′gĭg′), *n.* **1.** a frivolous, gadding girl or woman. **2.** a kind of hissing firework. **3.** a kind of whirling toy that makes a whizzing noise. **4.** a fish spear.

fizz (fĭz), *v.i.* **1.** to make a hissing or sputtering sound. —*n.* **2.** a hissing sound; effervescence. **3. a.** *Chiefly U.S.* soda-water or other effervescent water. **b.** *Orig. U.S.* an iced mixed drink made of alcohol, lemon juice, sugar, and soda-water. **4.** champagne. [back-formation from FIZZLE]

fizzle (fĭz′əl), *v.*, **-zled, -zling,** *n.* —*v.i.* **1.** to make a hissing or sputtering sound, esp. one that dies out weakly. **2.** *Colloq.* to fail ignominiously after a good start (often fol. by *out*). —*n.* **3.** a fizzling, hissing, or sputtering. **4.** *Colloq.* a fiasco; a failure. [f. obs. *fise* (t. Scand.; cf. Icel. *fīsa* break wind) + *-le*, freq. and dim. suffix]

fizzy (fĭz′ĭ), *adj.*, **-zier, -ziest. 1.** that fizzes; fizzing. **2.** (of a soft drink or beverage) carbonated.

fjeld (fyĕld), *n.* a high, bleak plateau on the Scandinavian peninsula. [t. Norw. See FELL[5]]

fjord (fyôd), *n.* fiord.

fl., 1. florin. **2.** (L *floruit*) flourished. **3.** fluid.

Fla, Florida.

flabbergast (flăb′ə gäst′), *v.t. Colloq.* to overcome with surprise and bewilderment; astound. [? f. FLABB(Y) + m. AGHAST]

flabby (flăb′ĭ), *adj.*, **-bier, -biest. 1.** hanging loosely or limply, as flesh, muscles, etc. **2.** having such flesh. **3.** lacking firmness, as character, persons, principles, utterances, etc.; feeble. [cf. earlier *flappy* (f. FLAP + -Y[1]) in same sense] —**flab′bily,** *adv.* —**flab′biness,** *n.*

flabellate (flə bĕl′ĭt, -āt), *adj. Bot., Zool.* fan-shaped. Also, **flabelliform** (flə bĕl′ĭ fôm′).

flabellum (flə bĕl′əm), *n.*, *pl.* **-bella** (-bĕl′ə). **1.** a fan, esp. one used in religious ceremonies. **2.** a fan-shaped part. [t. L: fan]

flaccid (flăk′sĭd), *adj.* soft and drooping; flabby; limp; not firm: *flaccid muscles.* [t. L: s. *flaccidus*] —**flaccid′ity, flac′cidness,** *n.* —**flac′cidly,** *adv.*

flacon (*Fr.* flȧ kôɴ′), *n. French.* a small bottle or flask with a stopper.

flag[1] (flăg), *n.*, *v.*, **flagged, flagging.** —*n.* **1.** a piece of cloth, commonly bunting, of varying size, shape, colour, and device, usually attached by one edge to a staff or cord, and used as an ensign, standard, symbol, signal, decoration, display, etc. **2.** *Naut.* a ship carrying an admiral's flag; a flagship. **3.** *Ornith.* the tuft of long feathers on the leg of falcons and most other hawks; the lengthened feathers on the crus or tibia. **4.** *Hunting.* the tail of a deer or of a setter dog. **5.** *Journalism.* masthead (def. 2). **6.** *Print.* a mark made by a proof corrector indicating an omission. **7.** a slip of paper used as a bookmark. **8.** an attachment to the meter of a taxi showing whether the taxi is engaged or not. **9. show the flag, a.** to assert one's claim or interest, esp. by the physical presence of troops, etc. **b.** *Colloq.* put in an appearance. **10. strike (lower) the flag, a.** to relinquish command, as of a ship. **b.** to submit or surrender. —*v.t.* **11.** to place a flag or flags over or on; decorate with flags. **12.** to signal or warn (a person, motor vehicle, etc.) with, or as with, a flag (sometimes fol. by *down*). **13.** to communicate (information) by, or as by, a flag. **14.** to decoy, as game, by waving a flag or the like to excite attention or curiosity. [appar. b. FLAP, n., and obs. *fag*, n., flap, flag; corresp. words in G, D, etc., t. E] —**flag′less,** *adj.*

flag[2] (flăg), *n.* **1.** any of various plants with long, sword-shaped leaves, as the sweet flag. **2.** the long, slender leaf of such a plant or of a cereal. [ME *flagge*; orig. uncert. Cf. D *vlag*]

flag[3] (flăg), *v.i.*, **flagged, flagging. 1.** to hang loosely or limply; droop. **2.** to fall off in vigour, energy, activity, interest, etc. [appar. b. FLAP, v., and FAG, v., in obs. sense of droop. See FLAG[1], n.]

flag[4] (flăg), *n., v.*, **flagged, flagging.** —*n.* **1.** a flat slab of stone used for paving, etc. **2.** (*pl.*) a walk paved with such slabs. —*v.t.* **3.** to pave with flags. [late ME *flagge* turf, prob. t. Scand.; cf. Icel. *flag, flaga*] —**flag′less,** *adj.*

flag captain, the commanding officer of a flagship.

flag day, 1. a day on which money is collected for charity by the sale of small flags. **2.** (*caps*) June 14th, the anniversary of the day (June 14th, 1777) when the U.S. Congress adopted the Stars and Stripes as the national emblem.

flagellant (flăj′ĭ lənt, flə jĕl′ənt), *n.* **1.** one who flagellates. **2.** one who flagellates or scourges himself for religious discipline or to obtain an emotional experience. **3.** (*often cap.*) one of a medieval European sect of fanatics that practised scourging in public. —*adj.* **4.** flagellating. [t. L: s. *flagellans*, ppr.]

flagellate (flăj′ĭ lāt′), *v.*, **-lated, -lating.** *adj., n.* —*v.t.* **1.** to whip; scourge; flog; lash. —*adj.* **2.** Also, **flag′ellat′ed.** *Biol.* having flagella. See **flagellum. 3.** *Bot.* producing filiform runners or runner-like branches, as the strawberry. —*n.* **4.** *Zool.* any of the *Flagellata*, a class of protozoans distinguished by having one or more long mobile filaments as locomotory organs. [t. L: m. s. *flagellātus*, pp., whipped] —**flag′ella′tion,** *n.* —**flag′ella′tor,** *n.*

flagelliform (flə jĕl′ĭ fôm′), *adj. Biol.* long, slender, and flexible, like the lash of a whip. [f. s. L *flagellum* a whip + -(I)FORM]

flagellum (flə jĕl′əm), *n., pl.* **-gella** (-jĕl′ə), **-gellums. 1.** *Biol.* a long, lashlike appendage serving as an organ of locomotion in certain reproductive bodies, bacteria, protozoans, etc. **2.** *Bot.* a runner. **3.** a whip or lash. [t. L: whip, scourge]

flageolet (flăj′ə lĕt′), *n.* a small end-blown flute with four fingerholes in front and two in the rear. [t. F, dim. of OF *flajol* flute, ult. der. L *flāre* blow]

Flageolet

flagging[1] (flăg′ĭng), *adj.* drooping; weakening; failing. —**flag′gingly,** *adv.* [f. FLAG[3] + -ING[2]]

flagging[2] (flăg′ĭng), *n.* **1.** flagstones collectively. **2.** a pavement of flagstones. [f. FLAG[4] + -ING[1]]

flaggy[1] (flăg′ĭ), *adj.* flagging; drooping; limp. [f. FLAG[3] + -Y[1]]

flaggy[2] (flăg′ĭ), *adj.* consisting of or resembling flags or flagstone; laminate. [f. FLAG[4] + -Y[1]]

flaggy[3] (flăg′ĭ), *adj.* abounding in, consisting of, or resembling the plants called flags. [f. FLAG[2] + -Y[1]]

flagitious (flə jĭsh′əs), *adj.* **1.** shamefully wicked, as persons, actions, times, etc. **2.** heinous or flagrant, as crime; infamous. [ME, t. L: m. s. *flāgitiōsus*] —**flagi′tiously,** *adv.* —**flagi′tiousness,** *n.*

flag lieutenant, an aide to a flag officer.

flagman (flăg′mən), *n., pl.* **-men.** one who signals with a flag.

flag of convenience, the flag of a country with which merchant ships owned by persons of other countries are registered in order to avoid taxes, etc.

flag of distress, a flag displayed as a signal of distress, generally at half-mast or upside down.

flag officer, a naval officer, as an admiral, vice-admiral, or rear admiral, entitled to display a flag showing his rank.

flag of truce, *Mil.* a white flag displayed as an invitation to the enemy to confer, or carried as a sign of peaceful intention by one sent to deal with the enemy.

flagon (flăg′ən), *n.* **1.** a large bottle for wine, etc. **2.** a vessel for holding liquids, as for use at table, esp. one with a handle, a spout, and usually a cover. [ME *flakon*, t. OF: m. *fla(s)con*; cf. ML *flasca* FLASK]

flagpole (flăg′pōl′), *n.* a staff or pole on which a flag is displayed. Also, **flagstaff** (flăg′stäf′).

flagrant (flā′grənt), *adj.* **1.** glaring; notorious; scandalous: *a flagrant crime, a flagrant offender.* **2.** *Rare.* blazing, burning, or glowing. [t. L: s. *flagrans*, ppr., blazing, burning] —**fla′grancy, fla′grance,** *n.* —**fla′grantly,** *adv.*

flagrante delicto (flə grăn′tĭ dĭ lĭk′tō), *Law.* while the crime is, or was, being committed. [L]

flagship (flăg′shĭp′), *n.* a ship which carries a flag officer of a fleet, squadron, or the like, and displays his flag.

Flagstad (flăg′stăt; *Norw.* flåk′stå), *n.* **Kirsten Marie** (*Norw.* KHĕr′stən mä′rē), 1895–1962, Norwegian operatic soprano.

flagstone (flăg′stōn′), *n.* **1.** a flat slab of stone used for paving, etc. **2.** (*pl.*) a walk paved with such slabs. **3.** rock, such as sandstone, shale, etc., which can be split up into slabs for paving.

flag-wagging (flăg′wăg′ĭng), *n.* **1.** *Naut.* signalling by the use of hand flags. **2.** excessive patriotic zeal; flag-waving. —*adj.* **3.** flag-waving.

flag-waving (flăg′wā′vĭng), *n.* **1.** an emotional, aggressive, or excessive display of patriotism. —*adj.* **2.** of, pertaining to, or denoting an excess of patriotism.

Flaherty (flĕə′tĭ), *n.* **Robert Joseph,** 1884–1951, U.S. pioneer in the making of documentary films.

flail (flāl), *n.* **1.** an instrument for threshing grain by hand, consisting of a staff or handle to one end of which is attached a freely swinging stick or bar. **2.** *Mil.* an implement derived from the threshing flail used as a weapon of war in the Middle Ages. —*v.t.* **3.** to strike with, or as if with, a flail. [ME *flegl*, OE *flygel*; akin to FLY]

flair (flĕə), *n.* **1.** talent; aptitude; keen perception. **2.** *Hunting.* scent; sense of smell. [t. F, der. *flairer* smell, g. L *frāgrāre*]

flak (flăk), *n.* anti-aircraft fire, esp. as experienced by the crews of military aircraft at which the fire is directed. [prop. *Fl.A.K.*, t. G, abbrev. of *Flieger-Abwehr-Kanone* anti-aircraft gun]

flake[1] (flāk), *n., v.*, **flaked, flaking.** —*n.* **1.** a small, flat, thin piece of anything. **2.** a small, detached piece or mass: *a flake of cloud.* **3.** a stratum or layer. —*v.i.* **4.** to peel off or separate in flakes. **5.** to fall in flakes, as snow. **6. flake out,** *Slang.* to collapse, faint, or fall asleep, esp. as a result of complete exhaustion. —*v.t.* **7.** to remove in flakes. **8.** to break flakes or chips from. **9.** to cover with or as with flakes. **10.** to form into flakes. [ME, appar. der. OE *flac-*, which occurs in *flacor* flying (said of arrows). Cf. also Icel. *flakka* be loose]

flake[2] (flāk), *n.* a frame, as for drying fish. [ME *flake*, *fleke*. Cf. Icel. *flaki, fleki* hurdle, wickerwork shield]

flake[3] (flāk), *n. Naut.* one fake of a cable or hawser laid in coils. [var. of FAKE[2]. Cf. G *Flechte*]

flake white, a pigment made from pure white lead.

flaky (flā′kĭ), *adj.*, **flakier, flakiest. 1.** of or like flakes. **2.** lying or cleaving off in flakes or layers. [f. FLAKE[1] + -Y[1]] —**flak′ily,** *adv.* —**flak′iness,** *n.*

flaky pastry, rough puff pastry.

flam (flăm), *n., v.*, **flammed, flamming.** *Dial or Colloq.* —*n.* **1.** a falsehood. **2.** a deception or trick. —*v.t., v.i.* **3.** to deceive; delude; cheat. [see FLIMFLAM]

flambé (flăm′bā; *Fr.* flän bė′), *adj. Cookery.* (of food) dressed or served in flaming spirits, esp. brandy. [t. F, pp. of *flamber* to flame]

flambeau (flăm′bō), *n., pl.* **-beaux** (-bōz), **-beaus. 1.** a flaming torch. **2.** a torch for use at night in illuminations, processions, etc. **3.** a large decorated candlestick, as of bronze. [t. F, der. OF *flambe* flame, earlier *flamble*, g. L *flammula*, dim. of *flamma* flame]

Flamborough Head (flăm′bə rə, -brə), *n.* a promontory on the E coast of England, in Yorkshire.

flamboyant (flăm boi′ənt), *adj.* **1.** flaming; gorgeous: *flamboyant colours.* **2.** florid; ornate; showy; *flamboyant rhetoric.* **3.** *Archit.* characterized by wavy, flamelike tracery, as in windows and openwork: applied to the highly ornate style of French Late Gothic architecture of the 15th century. —*n.* **4.** Also, **flamboyante.** a flowering tree bearing brilliant red flowers, *Poinciana regia*, of E Africa and Madagascar. [t. F, ppr. of *flamboyer* to flame, flare, der. OF *flambe*. See FLAMBEAU] —**flamboy′ance, flamboy′ancy,** *n.* —**flamboy′antly,** *adv.*

flame (flām), *n., v.*, **flamed, flaming.** —*n.* **1.** burning gas or vapour, as from wood, etc., undergoing combustion; a portion of ignited gas or vapour. **2.** (*often pl.*) state or condition of blazing combustion: *to burst into flames.* **3.** any flamelike condition; glow; inflamed condition. **4.** brilliant light; scintillating lustre. **5.** bright colouring; a streak or patch of colour. **6.** heat or ardour, as of zeal or passion. **7.** *Colloq.* an object of the passion of love; sweetheart. —*v.i.* **8.** to burn with a flame or flames; burst into flames; blaze. **9.** to glow like flame; shine brilliantly; flash. **10.** to burn as with flame, as passion; break into open anger, indignation, etc. (often fol. by *up*); blush violently. —*v.t.* **11.** to subject to the action of flame or fire. [ME, t. OF: m. *flamme*, g. L *flamma*] —**flame′less,** *adj.* —**flamelet** (flām′lĭt), *n.*

—**Syn. 1.** FLAME, BLAZE, CONFLAGRATION refer to the light and heat given off by combustion. FLAME is the common word, referring to a combustion of any size: *the light of a match flame.*

BLAZE usually denotes a quick, hot, bright, and comparatively large flame: *the fire burst into a blaze.* CONFLAGRATION refers to destructive flames which spread over a considerable area: *a conflagration destroyed Chicago.*

flame colour, bright reddish orange. —**flame′-col′-oured,** *adj.*

flame-hardening (flām′häd′nĭng), *n. Metall.* the rapid heating of the surface of iron or steel, by means of a flame, followed by quenching in order to harden the surface.

flame-holder (flām′hōl′də), *n. Aeron.* a device in certain jet engines that provides a sheltered zone for flame stabilization.

flame lily, a bulbous, liliaceous plant with deep orange perianth segments, *Gloriosa superba,* of tropical Asia and Africa.

flamen (flā′mĕn), *n., pl.* **flamens, flamines** (flăm′ĭ nēz′). *Rom. Antiq.* a priest devoted to the service of one particular deity. [t. L; r. ME *flamin(e)*]

flamenco (flə mĕng′kō), *n., pl.* **-cos.** a kind of Spanish music or dance, esp. of Andalusian gipsy style.

flame-out (flām′out′), *n. Aeron.* the failure of a jet engine as a result of an interruption in the fuel supply or imperfect combustion.

flameproof (flām′proof′), *adj.* **1.** not easily combustible. **2.** (of an electrical apparatus) designed so that an explosion within the apparatus will not ignite any inflammable gas outside it.

flame test, *Chem.* a qualitative test for detecting the presence of certain elements in substances by noting the coloration they impart to a flame.

flame-thrower (flām′thrō′ə), *n. Mil.* an apparatus, either mounted or portable, which throws a spray of oil that ignites in air.

flame-trap (flām′trăp′), *n.* any device in a fuel line, or the induction system of an engine, which prevents the flame from igniting the combustible mixture at the incorrect time or place.

flame-tree (flām′trē′), *n.* a sterculiaceous ornamental tree, *Brachychiton acerifolium,* of Australia, with scarlet, bell-shaped flowers.

flaming (flā′mĭng), *adj.* **1.** emitting flames; blazing; fiery. **2.** glowing; brilliant. **3.** violent; vehement; passionate. —**flam′ingly,** *adv.*

flamingo (flə mĭng′gō), *n., pl.* **-gos, -goes.** any of the aquatic birds constituting the family *Phoenicopteridae,* with very long neck and legs, webbed feet, bills bent downwards, and pinkish to scarlet plumage. [t. Pg., t. Sp.: m. *flamenco,* t. Pr.: m. *flamenc,* f. *flama* (g. L *flamma* FLAME) + suffix *-enc* (t. Gmc: m. *-ing*)]

Flamingo, *Phoenicopterus ruber* (Height 5 ft, length 4 ft)

Flaminian Way (flə mĭn′ĭ ən), an ancient Roman road extending from Rome N to Ariminum (Rimini) on the Adriatic coast. 215 mi.

Flaminius (flə mĭn′ĭ əs), *n.* **Gaius** (gī′əs), died 217 B.C., Roman general and statesman, defeated by Hannibal.

flammable (flăm′ə bl), *adj.* easily set on fire; combustible; inflammable. —**flam′mabil′ity,** *n.*

flamy (flā′mĭ), *adj.* of or like flame.

flan (flăn; *Fr.* flän), *n.* **1.** an open tart containing cheese, cream, or fruit. **2.** a piece of metal shaped ready to form a coin, but not yet stamped by the die. **3.** the metal of which a coin is made, as distinct from its design. [t. F]

flan-case (flăn′kās′), *n. Cookery.* a crust of pastry baked before a flan filling is added.

Flanders (flăn′dəz), *n.* a medieval country in W Europe, extending along the North Sea from the Strait of Dover to the mouth of the river Scheldt: the corresponding modern regions include the provinces of **East Flanders** and **West Flanders** in W Belgium, and the adjacent parts of N France and SW Netherlands.

Flanders

Flanders poppy, corn poppy.

flange (flănj), *n., v.,* **flanged, flanging.** —*n.* **1.** a projecting rim, collar, edge, ridge, or the like, on an object, for keeping it in place, attaching it to another object, strengthening it, etc. **2.** the horizontal portion or portions of steel shapes, such as the top and bottom flange of an I-beam. **3.** a device or tool for making flanges. —*v.i.* **4.** to project like, or take the form of, a flange.

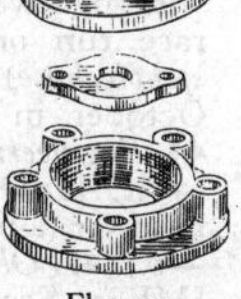
Flanges

[var. of *flanch,* n., from *flanch,* v., t. OF: s. *flanchir* bend, b. *flanc* FLANK and *flechier* (g. Rom. *flecticāre,* der. L *flectere*)] —**flange′less,** *adj.*

flank (flăngk), *n.* **1.** the side of an animal or a human being between the ribs and hip. **2.** the thin piece of flesh, constituting this part. **3.** a slice of meat from the flank. **4.** the side of anything, as of a building. **5.** *Mil., Naval.* the extreme right or left side of an army or fleet, or a subdivision of an army or fleet. **6.** *Fort.* **a.** the right or left side of a work or fortification. **b.** a part of a work that defends another work by a fire along the outside of its parapet. **c.** the part of a bastion which extends from the curtain to the face, etc. See diag. under **bastion. 7.** *Mach.* **a.** the part of the profile of a gearwheel which lies within the pitch circle or line. **b.** the working surface of a cam. —*v.t.* **8.** to stand or be placed or posted at the flank or side of. **9.** to defend or guard at the flank. **10.** to pass round or turn the flank of. —*v.i.* **11.** to occupy a position at the flank or side. **12.** to present the flank or side. [ME *flanke,* OE *flanc,* t. OF, t. Gmc; cf. OHG *hlancha*]

flanker (flăng′kə), *n.* **1.** one who or that which flanks. **2.** *Mil.* one of a body of soldiers employed on the flank of an army to guard a line of march. **3.** *Fort.* a fortification projecting so as to defend another work, or to command the flank of an assailing body.

flannel (flăn′əl), *n., v.,* **-elled, -elling** or (*U.S.*) **-eled, -eling.** —*n.* **1.** a warm, soft fabric of wool or blends of wool and cotton, wool and rayon, or cotton warp with wool filling. **2.** a face flannel. **3.** (*pl.*) an outer garment, esp. trousers, made of flannel. **4.** (*pl.*) *Obsolesc.* woollen undergarments. **5.** *Slang.* evasive or flattering talk. —*v.t.* **6.** to cover or clothe with flannel. **7.** to rub with flannel. **8.** *Slang.* to flatter or talk evasively to (often fol. by *up*). [orig. uncert.]

flannelette (flăn′ə lĕt′), *n.* a cotton fabric, plain or printed, napped on one side to imitate flannel.

flannelflower (flăn′əl flou′ə), *n.* an Australian plant, *Actinotus helianthi,* having white, flannel-like bracts below the flower.

flannelly (flăn′ə lĭ), *adj.* made of or resembling flannel.

flap (flăp), *v.,* **flapped, flapping,** *n.* —*v.i.* **1.** to swing or sway about loosely, esp. with noise: *a curtain or flag flaps in the wind.* **2.** to move up and down, as wings; flap the wings, or make similar movements. **3.** to strike a blow with something broad and flexible. **4.** *Colloq.* to panic, become flustered. —*v.t.* **5.** to move (arms, wings, etc.) up and down. **6.** to cause to swing or sway loosely, esp. with noise. **7.** to strike with something broad and flexible. **8.** *Colloq.* to toss, fold, shut, etc., smartly, roughly, or noisily. —*n.* **9.** a flapping motion. **10.** the noise produced by something that flaps. **11.** a blow given with something broad and flexible. **12.** something broad and flexible, or flat and thin, that hangs loosely, attached at one side only. **13.** *Surg.* a portion of skin or flesh partially separated from the body which may subsequently be transposed by grafting. **14.** *Aeron.* a wing surface that can be lifted in flight to modify lift and drag. **15.** *Colloq.* a state of panic or nervous excitement. [ME *flappe(n),* prob. of imit. orig.; cf. D *flappen* clap] —**flap′less,** *adj.*

flapdoodle (flăp′doo′dl), *n. Obs. Slang.* nonsense; bosh.

flapdragon (flăp′drăg′ən), *n.* **1.** a former pastime in which the players snatch raisins, plums, etc., out of burning brandy, and eat them. **2.** the object so caught and eaten.

flapjack (flăp′jăk′), *n.* a kind of pancake.

flapper (flăp′ə), *n.* **1.** something broad and flat for striking with, or for making a noise by striking. **2.** broad, flat, hinged or hanging piece; flap. **3.** a young bird just learning to fly. **4.** a young woman during the 1920s, esp. one freed from the traditional social and moral restraints. **5.** *Slang.* the hand.

flare (flĕə), *v.,* **flared, flaring,** *n.* —*v.i.* **1.** to burn with an unsteady, swaying flame, as a torch or candle in the wind. **2.** to blaze with a sudden burst of flame (often fol. by *up*). **3.** to start up or burst out in sudden fierce activity, passion, anger, etc. (sometimes fol. by *up* or *out*). **4.** to shine or glow. **5.** to spread gradually outwards as the end of a trumpet, or a ship's sides or bows. —*v.t.* **6.** to cause (a candle, etc.) to burn with a swaying flame. **7.** to display conspicuously or ostentatiously. **8.** to signal by flares of fire or light. **9.** to cause (something) to spread gradually outwards in form. **10.** *Metall.* to heat (a high-zinc brass) to such a high temperature that the zinc vapours begin to burn. —*n.* **11.** a flaring or swaying flame or light, as of torches in the wind. **12.** a sudden blaze or burst of flame. **13.** a sudden blaze of fire or light used as a signal or for illumination or guidance, etc. **14.** a device or substance used to produce such a blaze of fire or light. **15.** a sudden burst, as of zeal or of temper.

16. a gradual spread outwards in form; outward curvature: *the flare of a skirt.* 17. something that spreads out. 18. *Optics.* light reflected by the surfaces of an optical system. [orig. meaning spread out, display; b. FLY[1] and BARE[1], but cf. Norw. *flara* blaze]

flare-path (flĕə′päth′), *n.* an illuminated runway at an airport to enable aircraft to land or take off when normal visibility is insufficient.

flare-up (flĕər′ŭp′), *n.* 1. a sudden flaring up of flame or light. 2. *Colloq.* a sudden outburst of anger.

flaring (flĕə′rĭng), *adj.* 1. that flares; flaming; blazing. 2. glaringly bright or showy. 3. spreading gradually outwards in form. —**flar′ingly,** *adv.*

flash (flăsh), *n.* 1. a sudden, transitory outburst of flame or light: *a flash of lightning.* 2. a sudden, brief outburst or display of joy, wit, etc. 3. the time occupied by a flash of light; an instant: *to do something in a flash.* 4. ostentatious display. 5. a distinctive mark, an emblem, as on a soldier's uniform to identify his unit. 6. *Journalism.* a brief telegraphic dispatch, usually transmitting preliminary news of an important story or development. 7. *Photog.* **a.** flash photography. **b.** a flashgun. 8. *Obs.* the cant or jargon of thieves, vagabonds, etc. 9. *Naut., etc.* **a.** an extra volume or rush of water, as that produced by a dam or sluiceway, utilized to float a boat over shoals or for other purposes. **b.** the device, as a lock or sluice, used for this purpose. 10. **flash in the pan,** something which begins promisingly but has no lasting significance. —*v.i.* 11. to break forth into sudden flame or light, esp. transiently or intermittently: *he flashed crimson with rage.* 12. to speak or behave with sudden anger; to gleam. 13. to burst suddenly into view or perception: *the answer flashed into his mind.* 14. to move like a flash. 15. to break into sudden action. 16. *Colloq. or Slang.* to make a flash or sudden display. 17. *Obs.* to dash or splash, as the sea or waves.
—*v.t.* 18. to emit or send forth (fire or light) in sudden flashes. 19. to cause to flash, as powder by ignition or flashes. 20. to send forth like a flash. 21. to communicate instantaneously, as by telegraph. 22. *Colloq.* to make a sudden or ostentatious display of: *to flash one's diamonds.* 23. to increase the flow of water in (a river, etc.). 24. *Obs.* to dash or splash (water). 25. *Glassmaking.* **a.** to coat (plain glass or a glass object) with a film of coloured, opal, or white glass. **b.** to apply (such a coating). 26. *Bldg Trades.* to protect by flashing (def. 1).
—*adj.* 27. showy or ostentatious. 28. counterfeit or sham. 29. belonging or pertaining to sporting men. 30. *Obs.* belonging to or connected with thieves, vagabonds, etc., or their cant or jargon. [ME *flasche(n)* rise and dash (said of tidal waters); b. FLOW (or FLOOD) and WASH] —**flash′er,** *n.*
—**Syn.** 11. FLASH, GLANCE, GLINT, GLITTER mean to send forth a sudden gleam (or gleams) of bright light. To FLASH is to send forth light with a sudden, transient brilliancy: *a shooting star flashed briefly.* To GLANCE is to emit a brilliant flash of light as a reflection from a smooth surface: *sunlight glanced from the glass windscreen.* GLINT suggests a hard bright gleam of reflected light as from something polished or burnished: *light glints from silver or from burnished copper.* To GLITTER is to reflect (intermittently) from a hard surface flashes of light like bright coins: *ice glitters in moonlight.*

flashback (flăsh′băk′), *n.* a representation, during the course of a novel, film, etc., of some event or scene which occurred at a previous time.

flashboard (flăsh′bôd′), *n. Civ. Eng.* a board, or one of a series of boards, as on a milldam, used to increase the depth of the impounded water.

flashbulb (flăsh′bŭlb′), *n. Photog.* a glass bulb filled with oxygen and a thin sheet of magnesium or aluminium, giving a momentary bright light when fired, used as a light source.

flashcube (flăsh′kyo͞ob′), *n. Photog.* 1. a camera attachment consisting of four flashbulbs contained in a cube, which turns so that four photographs can be taken without reloading. 2. (*cap.*) a trademark for this.

flash flood, *Phys. Geog.* a sudden, destructive rush of water down a narrow gully or over a sloping surface in desert regions, due to heavy rains in the mountains or foothills. —**Syn.** See **flood.**

flashgun (flăsh′gŭn′), *n. Photog.* a device which discharges a flashbulb in synchronization with the camera shutter or which produces a flash by electronic means.

flashing (flăsh′ĭng), *n.* 1. *Bldg Trades.* a piece of sheet metal, etc., used to cover and protect certain joints and angles, as where a roof comes in contact with a wall or chimney. 2. *Bldg Trades.* a method of burning bricks to give them varied colours. 3. the act of creating an artificial flood in a conduit or stream, as in a sewer for cleansing it.

flashlight (flăsh′līt′), *n.* 1. any source of artificial light as used in flash photography. 2. a flash of light, or a light that flashes. 3. *Chiefly U.S.* an electric torch.

flashover (flăsh′ō′və), *Elect.* —*n.* 1. a disruptive discharge around or over the surface of a solid or liquid insulator. —*v.i.* 2. to establish a flashover.

flash photography, the use of a flashgun as a light source in photography. Also **flashlight photography.**

flash picture, a photograph taken by flash photography.

flashpoint (flăsh′point′), *n.* 1. the lowest temperature at which a volatile oil will give off explosive or ignitable vapours. 2. *Colloq.* the point or moment at which an explosion takes place or control is lost: *tempers reached flashpoint after the chairman's speech.*

flashy (flăsh′ĭ), *adj.,* **flashier, flashiest.** 1. sparkling or brilliant, esp. in a superficial way or for the moment. 2. pretentiously smart; showy; gaudy. 3. *Rare.* flashing with light. —**flash′ily,** *adv.* —**flash′iness,** *n.* —**Syn.** 2. See **gaudy**[1].

flask[1] (fläsk), *n.* 1. a bottle-shaped container made of glass, metal, etc.: *a flask of oil, a brandy flask.* 2. an iron container for shipping mercury, holding 76 lbs. 3. *Foundry.* a container into which sand is rammed to form a mould. [OE *flasce, flaxe.* Cf. FLAGON]

flask[2] (fläsk), *n. Ordn.* 1. the armoured plates making up the sides of a guncarriage trail. 2. *Obs.* the bed of a guncarriage. [t. d. F: m. *flasque* cheek of a guncarriage, g. LL *flasca* FLASK[1], t. Gmc. See FLAGON]

flasket (fläs′kĭt), *n.* 1. a small flask. 2. a long, shallow basket. [ME *flaskett,* t. OF: m. *flasquet* small flask, der. *flasque* FLASK[1]]

flat[1] (flăt), *adj.* **flatter, flattest,** *adv., n., v.,* **flatted, flatting.** —*adj.* 1. horizontally level: *a flat roof.* 2. level, even, or without inequalities of surface, as land, areas, surfaces, etc. 3. comparatively lacking in projection or depression of surface: *a broad flat face.* 4. lying at full length, as a person. 5. lying wholly on or against something: *a ladder flat against a wall.* 6. thrown down, laid low, or level with the ground, as fallen trees or buildings. 7. (of a race) run on a level course or track, without obstacles to be jumped. 8. having a generally level shape or appearance; not deep or thick: a flat plate. 9. (of the heel of a shoe) low and broad. 10. (of feet) having little or no arch. See **flatfoot.** 11. spread out, as an unrolled map, the open hand, etc. 12. collapsed; deflated: *a flat tyre.* 13. without qualification; unqualified, downright, or positive: *a flat denial, that's flat!* 14. without modification: *a flat rate, a flat price.* 15. uninteresting, dull, or tedious. 16. having lost its flavour, sharpness, or life, as wine, etc. 17. stale; tasteless or insipid, as food. 18. (of beer, etc.) having lost its effervescence. 19. pointless, as a remark, joke, etc. 20. commercially dull, as trade or the market. 21. lacking relief, contrast, or shading, as a painting. 22. not giving the effect of perspective: *the flat quality of medieval painting.* 23. *Painting.* without gloss; mat. 24. not clear, sharp, or ringing, as sound, a voice, etc. 25. *Music.* **a.** (of a note) lowered a semitone in pitch: *B flat.* **b.** below an intended pitch, as a note; too low (opposed to *sharp*). **c.** (of an interval) diminished. 26. *Gram.* derived without change in form, as English *to brush* from the noun *brush* and adverbs which do not add *-ly* to the adjective form, as *fast.* 27. *Naut.* (of a sail) **a.** cut with little or no fullness. **b.** trimmed as nearly fore-and-aft as possible, for sailing to windward.
—*adv.* 28. in a flat position; horizontally; levelly. 29. positively; absolutely. 30. exactly. 31. *Music.* below the true pitch. 32. *Finance.* without interest. 33. **brace a yard flat aback,** *Naut.* to set a yard so that the wind is nearly at right angles to the forward surface of the sail. 34. **fall flat,** to fall completely; fail to succeed in attracting interest, etc. 35. **flat out,** *Colloq.* **a.** as fast as possible. **b.** exhausted; unable to proceed.
—*n.* 36. something flat. 37. a flat surface, side or part of anything: *the flat of a blade, the flat of the hand.* 38. flat or level ground; a flat area. 39. a marsh. 40. a shallow. 41. *Music.* **a.** (in musical notation) the character ♭, which when attached to a note or a stave degree lowers its significance one chromatic semitone. **b.** a note one chromatic semitone below another. **c.** (on keyboard instruments, with reference to any given key) the key next below or to the left. 42. *Theat.* a piece of scenery consisting of a wooden frame, usually rectangular, covered with lightweight board or fabric. 43. *Horseracing.* **a.** a race run on a course without obstacles (opposed to *steeplechase*). **b.** (*often cap.*) the season, from March to October in Great Britain, when such races are run. 44. *Engineering.* an iron or steel bar of rectangular section.
—*v.t.* 45. *Obs. or U.S.* to make flat; flatten. 46. *Music.* to lower (a pitch) esp. one semitone.
—*v.i.* 47. *Obs. or U.S.* to become flat.
[ME, t. Scand.; cf. Icel. *flatr,* Sw. *flat*; akin to OE *flet*

floor. See FLAT[2]] —**flat′ly,** *adv.* —**flat′ness,** *n.* —**flat′-tish,** *adj.* —**Syn. 1.** See **level.**

flat[2] (flăt), *n.* **1.** a suite of rooms, usually on one floor only, forming a complete residence. **2.** *Obs.* a floor or storey of a building. [var. of obs. *flet,* OE *flet* floor, house, hall; akin to FLAT[1]]

flat-bed cylinder press (flăt′bĕd′). See **press**[1] (def. 32).

flatboat (flăt′bōt′), *n.* a large flat-bottomed boat for use in shallow water, esp. for floating down a river.

flatfish (flăt′fĭsh′), *n., pl.* **-fishes,** (*esp. collectively*) **-fish.** any of a group of fishes (often considered as constituting the suborder *Heterosomata*), including the halibut, flounder, sole, etc., having a greatly compressed body, and swimming on one side, and (in the adult) having both eyes on the upper side.

flatfoot (flăt′fŏŏt′), *n., pl.* **-feet. 1.** *Pathol.* **a.** a condition in which the arch of the foot is flattened so that the entire sole rests upon the ground. **b.** a foot with such an arch. **2.** *Slang.* a policeman.

flat-footed (flăt′fŏŏt′ĭd), *adj.* **1.** having flat feet. **2.** *Colloq.* clumsy and tactless. **3.** *Colloq.* taking or showing an uncompromising stand in a matter; firm and explicit. —**flat′-foot′edly,** *adv.* —**flat′-foot′edness,** *n.*

flat-head (flăt′hĕd′), *n.* any fish of the family *Platycephalidae,* of the Indian and Pacific Oceans, which are imported food fishes.

Flathead (flăt′hĕd′), *n.* **1.** one of a tribe of Salishan Indians of north-west Montana. **2.** a Chinook Indian.

flatiron (flăt′ī′ən), *n.* an iron with a flat face, heated for pressing clothes, etc.

flatlet (flăt′lĭt), *n.* **1.** a small flat. **2.** *Colloq.* a bed-sitter with cooking and washing facilities.

flatling (flăt′lĭng), *Archaic or Dial.* —*adv.* **1.** in a flat position; with the flat side, as of a sword. **2.** flatly or positively. —*adj.* **3.** dealt with the flat side.

flat-sawn (flăt′sôn′), *adj.* denoting a tree or timber that has been sawn up into flat slices, as distinct from being radially or tangentially sawn.

flat spin, 1. *Aeron.* the descent of an aircraft in a spiral, with the fuselage more or less horizontal; often becoming uncontrollable. **2.** *Colloq.* a state of great confusion.

flat spot, *Motor Vehicles.* an unresponsive point in acceleration, due to a weakening of the mixture in the carburettor at a certain throttle opening.

flatten (flăt′n), *v.t.* **1.** to make flat. **2.** *Slang.* to knock (someone) out. **3.** *Slang.* to crush or disconcert. —*v.i.* **4.** to become flat. **5.** *Aeron.* to fly into a horizontal position, as after a dive. —**flat′tener,** *n.*

flatter[1] (flăt′ə), *v.t.* **1.** to seek to please by complimentary speech or attentions; compliment or praise, esp. insincerely. **2.** to represent too favourably, as in portrayal. **3.** to show to advantage. **4.** to play upon the vanity or susceptibilities of; cajole, wheedle, or beguile. **5.** to gratify by compliments or attentions, or as a compliment does: *to feel flattered by an invitation.* **6.** to beguile with hopes; encourage (hopes); please (oneself) with the thought or belief (fol. by *that* and a clause): *he flattered himself (that) he might become the head of the school.* —*v.i.* **7.** to use flattery. [ME *flat(t)eren* float, flutter, fawn upon, OE *floterian* float, flutter; for sense development, cf. FLICKER[1], Icel. *fladhra* flatter; not directly connected with F *flatter* flatter] —**flat′terer,** *n.* —**flat′teringly,** *adv.*

flatter[2] (flăt′ə), *n.* **1.** one who or that which makes something flat. **2.** a hammer with a broad face, used by smiths. **3.** a drawplate with a flat orifice for drawing flat metal strips, as for watch springs, etc. [f. FLAT[1], v. + -ER[1]]

flattery (flăt′ə rĭ), *n., pl.* **-teries. 1.** the act of flattering. **2.** a flattering compliment or speech; excessive, insincere praise. [ME *flaterie,* t. OF, der. *flatere* a flatterer, der. *flater.* Cf. FLATTER[1]]

flattish (flăt′ĭsh), *adj.* somewhat flat.

flatulent (flăt′yŏŏ lənt), *adj.* **1.** generating gas in the alimentary canal. **2.** attended with or caused by, or suffering from, such an accumulation of gas. **3.** pretentious; empty. Also, *Now Obs.,* **flatuous** (flăt′yŏŏ əs). [t. F, der. L *flātus* a blowing] —**flat′ulence, flat′ulency,** *n.* —**flat′ulently,** *adv.*

flatus (flā′təs), *n.* an accumulation of gas in the stomach or intestines. [t. L: a blowing]

flatways (flăt′wāz′), *adv.* with the flat side (not the edge) foremost or in contact. Also, **flatwise** (flăt′wīz′).

flatworm (flăt′wûm′), *n.* any platyhelminth.

Flaubert (*Fr.* flō bĕr′), *n.* **Gustave** (*Fr.* gys tȧv′), 1821–1880, French novelist.

flaunch (flônch), *n.* **1.** a cement mortar fillet as in chimneys, manholes, or in drainage, to throw off water. **2.** the placing of this fillet. Also, **flaunching.** [var. of FLANGE]

flaunt (flônt), *v.i.* **1.** to parade or display oneself conspicuously or boldly. **2.** to wave conspicuously in the air. —*v.t.* **3.** to parade or display ostentatiously. —*n.* **4.** the act of flaunting. **5.** *Obs.* something flaunted. [t. Scand.; cf. Norw. *flanta* gad about, der. *flana* roam; akin to Gk *plánē* roaming (see PLANET)] —**flaunt′er,** *n.* —**flaunt′ingly,** *adv.* —**flaunt′y,** *adj.*

flautist (flô′tĭst), *n.* a flute player. Also, **flutist.** [t. It.: m. *flautista,* der. *flauto* flute]

flavescent (flə vĕs′ənt), *adj.* turning yellow; yellowish. [t. L: s. *flāvescens,* ppr.]

flavine (flā′vĭn), *n. Chem.* **1.** Also, **flavin.** a complex heterocyclic ketone which is common to the non-protein part of several important yellow enzymes, the flavoproteins. **2.** quercetin. [f. s. L *flāvus* yellow + -INE[2]]

-flavine, *Chem.* a word element indicating any of a number of natural derivatives of flavine, as *riboflavine.* Also, **-flavin.**

flavo-, a word element meaning 'yellow', as in *flavoprotein.* Also, before vowels, **flav-.** [comb. form repr. L *flāvus*]

flavone (flā′vōn), *n. Chem.* **1.** an organic compound, $C_{15}H_{10}O_2$, the parent substance of various yellow dyes. **2.** a derivative of this compound.

flavoprotein (flā′vō prō′tēn), *n. Biochem.* an enzyme, containing riboflavin and linked chemically with a protein, active in the oxidation of foods in animal cells.

flavopurpurin (flā′vō pû′pyŏŏ rĭn), *n. Chem.* a yellowish crystalline compound, $C_{14}H_8O_5$ (isomeric with purpurin), used in dyeing.

flavorous (flā′və rəs), *adj.* **1.** full of flavour. **2.** pleasant to the smell or taste.

flavour (flā′və), *n.* **1.** taste, esp. a characteristic taste, or a noticeable element in the taste, of a thing. **2.** a flavouring substance or extract. **3.** the characteristic quality of a thing: *a book which has the flavour of the sea.* **4.** a particular quality noticeable in a thing: *language with a strong nautical flavour.* **5.** *Obs.* smell, odour, or aroma. —*v.t.* **6.** to give flavour. Also, *U.S.,* **flavor.** [ME, t. OF: m. *flaur,* ult. der. L *frāgāre* emit an odour] —**fla′vourer,** *n.* —**fla′vourful,** *adj.* —**fla′vourless,** *adj.* —**Syn. 1.** See **taste.**

flavouring (flā′və rĭng), *n.* something that gives flavour; a substance or preparation used to give a particular flavour to food or drink. Also, *U.S.,* **flavoring.**

flavoursome (flā′və səm), *adj.* having a full, rich, pleasant flavour; tasty; flavourful.

flaw[1] (flô), *n.* **1.** a marring feature; a defect; a fault. **2.** a defect impairing legal soundness or validity: *flaw in a lease or a will.* **3.** a crack, break, breach, or rent. —*v.t.* **4.** to produce a flaw in. —*v.i.* **5.** to contract a flaw; become cracked or defective. [ME, t. Scand.; cf. Sw. *flaga* flake, flaw] —**flaw′less,** *adj.* —**flaw′lessly,** *adv.* —**flaw′lessness,** *n.* —**Syn. 1.** See **defect.**

flaw[2] (flô), *n.* **1.** a sudden gust or brief sharp storm of wind. **2.** a short spell of rough weather. **3.** *Obs.* a burst of feeling, fury, etc. [t. Scand.; cf. Sw. *flaga* gust]

flawy (flô′ĭ), *adj.* characterized by gusts, as wind.

flax (flăks), *n.* **1.** any plant of the genus *Linum,* esp. *L. usitatissimum,* a slender, erect annual plant with narrow, lance-shaped leaves and blue flowers, much cultivated for its fibre and seeds. **2.** the fibre of this plant, manufactured into linen yarn for thread or woven fabrics. **3.** any of various plants resembling flax. [ME; OE *fleax,* c. D and LG *vlas,* G *Flachs*]

flaxen (flăk′sən), *adj.* **1.** made of flax. **2.** resembling flax. **3.** pertaining to flax. **4.** of the pale yellowish colour of dressed flax. Also, **flax′y.**

Flaxman (flăks′mən), *n.* **John,** 1755–1826, English sculptor.

flaxseed (flăks′sēd′), *n.* the seed of flax, yielding linseed oil; linseed.

flay (flā), *v.t.* **1.** to strip off the skin or outer covering of. **2.** to criticize or reprove with scathing severity. **3.** to strip of money or property; fleece. [ME *flen,* etc., OE *flēan,* c. MD *vlaen,* Icel. *flā*] —**flay′er,** *n.*

flea (flē), *n.* **1.** any of numerous small, wingless, blood-sucking insects of the order *Siphonaptera,* parasitic upon mammals and birds, and noted for their powers of leaping. **2.** any of various small beetles and crustaceans which leap like a flea, or swim in a jumpy manner, as the water-flea and beach flea. **3. flea in one's ear,** *Slang.* **a.** a discomforting rebuke or rebuff; a sharp hint. **b.** a blow to the ear; a cuff. [ME *fle,* OE *flēah, flēa,* c. G *Floh;* akin to FLEE]

Dog flea, *Ctenocephalus canis* (Length ½ in.)

fleabag (flē′băg′), *n. Colloq.* **1.** a sleeping bag. **2.** a worthless creature ridden with fleas. **3.** an old hag.

fleabane (flē′bān′), *n.* any of various composite plants, as *Pulicaria dysenterica* of Europe, reputed to destroy or drive away fleas.

flea-beetle (flē′bē′tl), *n.* any of certain leaf beetles, noted for their ability to leap.

fleabite (flē′bīt′), *n.* **1.** the bite of a flea. **2.** the red spot caused by it. **3.** a trifling wound, annoyance, etc.

flea-bitten (flē′bĭt′n), *adj.* **1.** bitten by a flea or fleas. **2.** infested with fleas. **3.** (of a horse, etc.) having small reddish spots or streaks upon a lighter ground. **4.** *Colloq.* shabby; dirty.

fleam (flēm), *n.* **1.** the angle of rake between the cutting edge of a saw tooth and the plane of the blade. *—adj.* **2.** (of a saw tooth) having the shape of an isosceles triangle. [t. OF: m. *flieme*, ult. der. LL *phlebotomus* lancet, t. Gk: m. *phlebotómos* opening veins. Cf. PHLEBOTOMY]

flea market, an open-air market, esp. in S Europe, where second-hand, worthless, and sometimes stolen articles are sold.

fleapit (flē′pĭt′), *n. Slang.* a shabby, dirty room or building; specifically, a cinema.

fleawort (flē′wûrt′), *n.* **1.** a rough-leaved composite herb of Europe, *Inula conyza.* **2.** a European plantain, *Plantago psyllium*, whose seeds resemble fleas and are used in medicine.

flèche (flāsh; *Fr.* flĕsh), *n., pl.* **flèches** (flā′shĭz; *Fr.* flĕsh). **1.** *Archit.* **a.** a spire, esp. a small light spire decorating a roof. **b.** a slender spire rising from the junction of the nave and transepts of a church, or sometimes crowning the apse. **2.** *Fort.* a fieldwork consisting of two faces forming a salient angle, open at the gorge. **3.** *Fencing.* a method of running attack. [t. F: arrow, prob. t. Gmc; cf. FLY[1]]

fleck (flĕk), *n.* **1.** a spot or mark on the skin, as a freckle. **2.** any spot or patch of colour, light, etc. **3.** a speck; a small bit. [n. use of FLECK, v., or back-formation from *flecked*, ppl. adj., ME *flekked*; cf. G *Fleck* spot] *—v.t.* **4.** to mark with a fleck or flecks; spot; dapple. [t. Scand.; cf. Icel. *flekka*]

Flecker (flĕk′ə), *n.* **James Elroy,** 1884–1915, English poet.

fleckless (flĕk′lĭs), *adj.* without flecks or spots. **—fleck′-lessly,** *adv.*

flection (flĕk′shən), *n.* **1.** the act of bending. **2.** the state of being bent. **3.** a bend; a bent part. **4.** *Anat.* flexion. **5.** *Gram.* inflection. Also, **flexion** for 1–3. [t. L: m. s. *flexio* a bending] **—flec′tional,** *adj.* **—flec′tionless,** *adj.*

fled (flĕd), *n.* pt. and pp. of **flee.**

fledge (flĕj), *v.,* **fledged, fledging,** *adj.* *—v.t.* **1.** to bring up (a young bird) until it is able to fly. **2.** to furnish with or as with feathers or plumage; feather (an arrow). *—v.i.* **3.** (of a young bird) to acquire the feathers necessary for flight. *—adj.* **4.** *Archaic.* (of young birds) able to fly; having the wings developed for flight. [ME *flegge*, OE *-fligge*, in *unfligge* unfledged]

fledgling (flĕj′lĭng), *n.* **1.** a young bird just fledged. **2.** an inexperienced person. Also, **fledgeling.**

fledgy (flĕj′ĭ), *adj.,* **fledgier, fledgiest.** *Rare.* feathered or feathery.

flee (flē), *v.,* **fled, fleeing.** *—v.i.* **1.** to run away, as from danger, pursuers, etc.; take flight. **2.** to move swiftly; fly; speed. *—v.t.* **3.** to run away from (a place, person, etc.). [ME *flee(n)*, OE *flēon*, c. G *fliehen*]

fleece (flēs), *n., v.,* **fleeced, fleecing.** *—n.* **1.** the coat of wool that covers a sheep or some similar animal. **2.** the wool shorn from a sheep at one time. **3.** something resembling a fleece: *a fleece of hair.* **4.** a fabric with a soft, silky pile, used for warmth, as for lining garments. **5.** the soft nap or pile of such a fabric. *—v.t.* **6.** to deprive (a sheep) of the fleece. **7.** to strip of money or belongings; plunder; swindle. **8.** to overspread or line with or as with a fleece. [ME *flees*, OE *flēos*, c. G *Vliess*] **—fleece′able,** *adj.*

fleecy (flē′sĭ), *adj.,* **fleecier, fleeciest.** covered with, consisting of, or resembling a fleece or wool. **—fleec′-ily,** *adv.* **—fleec′iness,** *n.*

fleer[1] (fliə), *Dial.* *—v.i.* **1.** to grin or laugh coarsely or mockingly. *—v.t.* **2.** to fleer at; deride. *—n.* **3.** a fleering look; a jeer or gibe. [ME *flery(e)*, *flire.* Cf. Norw. *flire* grin] **—fleer′ingly,** *adv.*

fleer[2] (flē′ə), *n.* one who flees. [f. FLEE + -ER[1]]

fleet[1] (flēt), *n.* **1.** the largest organized unit of naval ships grouped for tactical or other purposes. **2.** the largest organization of warships under the command of a single officer. **3.** a number of naval vessels, or vessels carrying armed men. **4.** the vessels, aeroplanes, or vehicles collectively of a single transport company or undertaking. **5.** a number of aeroplanes, motor vehicles, etc., moving or operating in company. [ME *flete*, OE *flēot* ship, craft, der. *flēotan* float]

fleet[2] (flēt), *adj.* **1.** swift; rapid: *fleet of foot, a fleet horse.* *—v.i.* **2.** to move swiftly; fly. **3.** *Naut.* to change position; shift. **4.** *Archaic.* to glide away like a stream. **5.** *Archaic.* to fade, vanish. **6.** *Obs.* to float; drift. **7.** *Obs.* to swim; sail. *—v.t.* **8.** *Archaic.* to cause (time) to pass lightly or swiftly. **9.** *Naut.* to change the position of; shift. [ME *flete(n)*, v., OE *flēotan* float, c. G *fliessen* flow] **—fleet′ly,** *adv.* **—fleet′ness,** *n.*

fleet[3] (flēt), *n.* **1.** *Dial.* an arm of the sea; an inlet; a creek. **2. the Fleet,** a former London prison, long used for debtors. [ME *flete*, OE *flēot* flowing water, c. G *Fliess* brook]

Fleet (flēt), *n.* a town in England, in NE Hampshire. 13,672 (1961).

Fleet Admiral, the highest ranking officer in the U.S. Navy, ranking next above admiral.

Fleet Air Arm, the branch of the Royal Navy concerned with aviation; the naval airforce.

fleet-footed (flēt′fo͝ot′ĭd), *adj.* swift of foot.

fleeting (flē′tĭng), *adj.* gliding swiftly away; passing swiftly; transient; transitory. **—fleet′ingly,** *adv.* **—fleet′-ingness,** *n.*

Fleet Street, a street in central London, now the site of many newspaper offices: often used figuratively for the English newspaper world.

Fleetwood (flēt′wo͝od′), *n.* a seaport in England, in N Lancashire. 27,686 (1961).

Fleming (flĕm′ĭng), *n.* **1.** a native of Flanders. **2.** a Flemish-speaking Belgian.

Fleming (flĕm′ĭng), *n.* **1. Sir Alexander,** 1881–1955, Scottish bacteriologist; discoverer of penicillin, 1929. **2. Ian (Lancaster),** 1908–64, English thriller-writer; creator of James Bond. **3. Sir John Ambrose,** 1849–1945, English electrical engineer.

Fleming's rules, *Physics.* a set of rules relating the direction of motion, flux, and electromotive force in electrical machines. If the forefinger, second finger, and thumb of the right hand are extended at right angles to each other, the forefinger indicates the direction of the flux, the second finger the direction of the electromotive force, and the thumb the direction of motion in a generator. If the left hand is used the digits indicate directions in a motor.

Flemish (flĕm′ĭsh), *adj.* **1.** of or pertaining to Flanders, its people, or their language. **2.** of or denoting a school of painting developed in Flanders and N France in the 15th century, including Rubens, Van Dyke, and the brothers Van Eyck; characterized by cool, clear colours, sharply delineated forms, and accurate proportions and perspective. *—n.* **3.** the language of the Flemings, one of the official languages of Belgium, and a Germanic language closely related to Dutch. **4.** the people of Flanders collectively; the Flemings. [t. MFlem.: m. *Vlamisch* (D *Vlaamsch*)]

Flemish bond, a common arrangement in brickwork in which headers and stretchers alternate in every course.

flench (flĕnch), *v.t.,* **flenched, flenching. 1.** to strip the blubber or the skin from (a whale, seal, etc.). **2.** to strip off (blubber or skin). Also, **flense** (flĕns), **flinch.** [t. D: m. s. *flensen*]

Flensburg (*Ger.* flĕns′bo͝ork), *n.* a town in West Germany, in N Schleswig-Holstein. 96,500 (est. 1966). See map under **Schleswig-Holstein.**

flesh (flĕsh), *n.* **1.** the soft substance of an animal body, consisting of muscle and fat. **2.** muscular tissue. **3.** fatness; weight: *to put on flesh.* **4.** such substance of animals as an article of food, usually excluding fish and sometimes fowl; meat. **5.** the body, esp. as distinguished from the spirit or soul. **6.** man's physical or animal nature. **7.** mankind. **8.** living creatures generally. **9.** one's kindred or family, or a member of it. **10.** *Bot.* the soft pulpy portion of a fruit, vegetable, etc., as distinguished from the core, skin, shell, etc. **11.** the surface of the body, esp. with respect to colour. **12.** flesh colour; pinkish white with a tinge of yellow; pinkish cream. **13. in the flesh, a.** alive. **b.** in bodily form; in person. **14. pound of flesh,** a person's right or due, insisted on mercilessly with a total disregard for others. *—v.t.* **15.** to plunge (a weapon) into the flesh. **16.** *Hunting.* to feed (a hound or hawk) with flesh in order to make it more eager for the chase. **17.** *Archaic.* to incite and accustom (persons) to bloodshed or battle by an initial experience. **18.** *Archaic.* to inflame the ardour or passions or by a taste of indulgence. **19.** to feed full with flesh, and hence with fleshy enjoyments, spoil, etc. **20.** to clothe (a skeleton, etc.) with flesh; make fleshy. **21.** to remove adhering flesh from (hides), for leather and for manufacture. [ME; OE *flǣsc*, c. G *Fleisch*] **—flesh′less,** *adj.*

flesh and blood, 1. offspring or relatives: *one's own flesh and blood.* **2.** human nature: *more than flesh and blood can endure.*

flesh colour, a pinkish white colour with a tinge of yellow; a pinkish cream colour. **—flesh′-col′oured,** *adj.*

flesh-eater (flĕsh′ē′tə), *n.* a carnivore. **—flesh′-eat′ing,** *adj.*

flesher (flĕsh′ə), *n.* **1.** one who fleshes hides. **2.** a tool for fleshing hides. **3.** *Scot.* a butcher.

flesh-fly (flĕsh′flī′), *n.* any fly of the dipterous family *Sarcophagidae* which deposits its larvae in the flesh of living animals.

fleshhook (flĕsh′ho͝ok′), *n.* **1.** a hook for use in lifting meat, as from a pot. **2.** a hook to hang meat on.

fleshly (flĕsh′lĭ), *adj.*, **-lier, -liest. 1.** of or pertaining to the flesh or body; bodily, corporeal, or physical. **2.** carnal; sensual. **3.** worldly, rather than spiritual. **4.** *Obs.* having much flesh; fleshy. —**flesh′liness,** *n.*

fleshpot (flĕsh′pŏt′), *n.* **1.** *Obs.* a pot or vessel containing flesh or meat. **2.** (*pl.*) good or riotous living; luxury.

flesh wound, a wound which does not extend beyond the flesh; a slight wound.

fleshy (flĕsh′ĭ), *adj.*, **fleshier, fleshiest. 1.** having much flesh; plump; fat. **2.** consisting of or resembling flesh. **3.** *Bot.* consisting of fleshlike substance; pulpy, as a fruit; thick and tender, as a leaf. —**flesh′iness,** *n.*

fletch (flĕch), *v.t.* to provide (an arrow) with a feather.

fletcher (flĕch′ə), *n.* *Archaic.* one who makes or deals in arrows, or bows and arrows. [t. OF: m. *flechier*, der. *fleche* arrow]

Fletcher (flĕch′ə), *n.* **John,** 1579–1625, English dramatist who collaborated with Francis Beaumont.

fletton (flĕt′n), *adj.* **1.** denoting a yellowish kind of brick with two frogs, mass-produced in the Fens. —*n.* **2.** such a brick.

fleur-de-lis (flû′də-lē′), *n., pl.* **fleurs-de-lis** (flû′də lēz′). **1.** a heraldic device somewhat resembling three petals or floral segments of an iris tied by an encircling band. **2.** the distinctive bearing of the royal family of France. **3.** the iris (flower or plant). [t. F: lily flower; r. ME *flour-de-lys*, t. OF]

Fleurs-de-lis in three different forms

fleuron (flo͞oə′rŏn, -rən, flû′-), *n.* an ornamental flower-like design, used in printing, architecture, pastry-garnishing, etc.

fleury (flo͞oə′rĭ, flû′rĭ), *adj.* *Her.* **1.** bearing fleurs-de-lis. **2.** terminating in a fleur-de-lis: *a cross fleury.* Also, **flory.**

Fleury (*Fr.* flœ rē′), *n.* **1. André Hercule de** (äɴ drĕ′ ĕr kyl′ də), 1653–1743, French cardinal and statesman. **2. Claude** (klōd), 1640–1723, French ecclesiastical historian.

flew[1] (flo͞o), *v.* pt. of **fly**[1].

flew[2] (flo͞o), *n.* flue[3].

flews (flo͞oz), *n.pl.* the large pendulous upper lip of certain dogs, as bloodhounds.

flex (flĕks), *v.t., v.i.* **1.** to bend, as part of the body. —*n.* **2.** a small, flexible insulated electric cable or wire esp. for supplying power to movable domestic appliances. [t. L: s. *flexus*, pp.]

flexible (flĕk′sə bl), *adj.* **1.** capable of being bent; easily bent. **2.** susceptible of modification or adaptation; adaptable. **3.** willing or disposed to yield. [t. L: m. s. *flexibilis*] —**flex′ibil′ity, flex′ibleness,** *n.* —**flex′ibly,** *adv.*

—**Syn. 1.** FLEXIBLE, LIMBER, PLIANT refer to that which bends easily. FLEXIBLE refers to that which is capable of being bent and adds sometimes the idea of compressibility or expansibility: *a flexible piece of rubber hose.* LIMBER is esp. applied to the body to refer to ease of movement; it also resembles FLEXIBLE except that there is an idea of even greater ease in bending: *a young and limber body, a limber willow wand.* PLIANT stresses an inherent quality or tendency to bend which does not require force or pressure from the outside; it may mean merely adaptable or may have a derogatory sense: *a pliant mind, character.* —**Ant. 1.** stiff.

flexible trust, a unit trust whose trust deed provides for changes being made in the portfolio of investments at the discretion of the management company, usually after approval by the trustee company (opposed to *fixed trust*).

flexile (flĕk′sīl), *adj.* flexible; pliant; tractable; adaptable. [t. L: m. s. *flexilis*]

flexion (flĕk′shən), *n.* **1.** *Anat.* **a.** the motion of a joint which brings the connected parts continually nearer together; the action of any flexor muscle (opposed to *extension*). **b.** the state of a part so moved. **2.** flection (defs 1, 2, 3). [t. L: s. *flexio* a bending] —**flex′ional,** *adj.* —**flex′ionless,** *adj.*

flexor (flĕk′sə), *n.* *Anat.* a muscle which serves to flex or bend a part of the body. [NL. See FLEX, -OR[2]]

flexuosity (flĕk′syo͞o ŏs′ĭ tĭ), *n.* quality or condition of being flexuous.

flexuous (flĕk′syo͞o əs), *adj.* full of bends or curves; winding; sinuous. Also, **flexuose** (flĕk′syo͞o ōs′). [t. L: m. s. *flexuōsus*, der. *flexus* a bending] —**flex′uously,** *adv.*

flexure (flĕk′shə), *n.* **1.** the act of flexing or bending. **2.** the state of being flexed or bent. **3.** the part bent; a bend; a fold. [t. L: m. s. *flexūra* a bending] —**flex′ural,** *adj.*

fley (flā), *Scot. and N Dial.* —*v.t.* **1.** to put to flight; frighten away. **2.** to frighten. —*v.i.* **3.** to be afraid. Also, **flay.** [ME *fleyen*, OE *-flēgan*, causative of *fleōgan* fly]

flibbertigibbet (flĭb′ə tĭ jĭb′ĭt), *n.* **1.** a chattering or flighty person, usually a woman. **2.** (*cap.*) *Obs.* the name of a fiend.

flicflac (flĭk′flăk′), *n.* a step in dancing in which the feet strike rapidly together. [t. F; imit. of the sound]

flick (flĭk), *n.* **1.** a sudden light blow or stroke, as with a whip or the finger. **2.** the sound thus made. **3.** something thrown off with or as with a jerk: *a flick of spray.* **4.** (*usually pl.*) *Slang.* **a.** a cinema film. **b.** the cinema. —*v.t.* **5.** to strike lightly with a whip, the finger, etc. **6.** to remove with such a stroke: *to flick dust from one's coat, to flick away a crumb.* **7.** to move (something) with a sudden stroke or jerk. —*v.i.* **8.** to move with a jerk or jerks. **9.** to flutter. [late ME *flykke*; appar. imit.]

flicker[1] (flĭk′ə), *v.i.* **1.** to burn unsteadily; shine with a wavering light. **2.** to wave to and fro; vibrate; quiver. **3.** to flutter. —*v.t.* **4.** to cause to flicker. —*n.* **5.** an unsteady flame or light. **6.** a flickering; flickering movement. **7.** a brief spark: *a flicker of hope.* [ME *flickeren*, OE *flicorian* flutter] —**flick′eringly,** *adv.*

flicker[2] (flĭk′ə), *n.* any of several North American woodpeckers of the genus *Colaptes* with bright wing and tail linings, esp. *C. auratus*, of eastern parts of the continent. [imit. of the bird's note]

flick-knife (flĭk′nīf′), *n.* a knife the blade of which springs out at the press of a button on the handle; switch-blade.

flick-roll (flĭk′rōl′), *n.* *Aeron.* a snap-roll.

flier (flī′ə), *n.* **1.** something that flies, as a bird or insect. **2.** one who or that which moves with great speed. **3.** an aviator. **4.** some part of a machine having a rapid motion. **5.** *Colloq.* a flying jump or leap. **6.** *Archit.* a rectangular tread in a stair forming part of a straight flight of steps. **7.** *U.S.* a small leaflet. Also, **flyer.**

flight[1] (flīt), *n.* **1.** the act, manner, or power of flying. **2.** the distance covered or the course pursued by a flying object. **3.** a number of beings or things flying or passing through the air together: *a flight of swallows.* **4.** a journey by air, esp. by aeroplane. **5.** a scheduled trip on an airline. **6.** the basic tactical unit of military airforces, consisting of two or more aircraft. **7.** the act, principles, or art of flying an aeroplane. **8.** the progress of a spacecraft into space and, sometimes, back. **9.** swift movement in general. **10.** a soaring above or transcending ordinary bounds: *a flight of fancy.* **11.** *Horseracing.* a hurdle or fence. **12.** *Athletics.* a specific number, usually ten, of hurdles in a race. **13.** the real or artificial feathers at the back of an arrow, dart, etc., designed to make it fly straight. **14.** *Archit.* **a.** the series of steps or stairs between two adjacent landings. **b.** a series of steps, etc., ascending without change of direction. **15.** *Archery.* **a.** a light arrow for long-distance shooting. **b.** the distance covered by such an arrow. **16. in the first flight,** excellent; one of the best. —*v.i.* **17.** (of wild fowl) to fly in flights (def. 3). —*v.t.* **18.** to deliver (a cricket ball, dart, etc.) in a certain manner, esp. so that it flies comparatively slowly. **19.** to shoot (a bird) in flight. **20.** to attach feathers as flights to (arrows, darts, etc.). [ME; OE *flyht*, c. D *vlucht*; akin to FLY, v.]

flight[2] (flīt), *n.* **1.** the act of fleeing; hasty departure. **2. put to flight,** to force to flee; rout. **3. take (to) flight,** to flee. [ME; c. G *Flucht*; akin to FLEE]

flight arrow, *Archery.* **1.** an arrow having a conical or pyramidal head without barbs. **2.** a long and light arrow in general; a shaft or arrow for the longbow, as distinguished from the bolt.

flight deck, 1. the compartment of an aeroplane where the controls are situated. **2.** the upper deck of an aircraft-carrier, constructed and equipped for the landing and take-off of aircraft.

flight feather, *Ornith.* one of the large, stiff feathers which form most of the extent of a bird's wing, and which are essential to flight.

flight formation, two or more aeroplanes flying in some set arrangement.

flight indicator, an instrument, as an artificial horizon, which indicates the altitude of an aircraft.

flightless (flīt′lĭs), *adj.* incapable of flying.

flight lieutenant, 1. a commissioned rank in the Royal Air Force above that of flying officer and below that of squadron-leader, equivalent to captain in the army. **2.** a similar rank in any of various other airforces. **3.** an officer of this rank.

flight recorder, a box containing recording equipment which collects information about an aircraft's flight, used esp. to determine the cause of a crash.

flighty (flīʹtĭ), *adj.*, **-tier, -tiest. 1.** given to flights or sallies of fancy, caprice, etc.; volatile; frivolous. **2.** slightly delirious; light-headed; mildly crazy. **3.** emotionally unreliable; flirtatious. **4.** *Rare.* swift or fleet. [f. FLIGHT[1] + -Y[1]] —**flightʹily,** *adv.* —**flightʹiness,** *n.*

flimflam (flĭmʹflămʹ), *n.*, *v.*, **-flammed, -flamming.** *Colloq.* —*n.* **1.** a piece of nonsense; mere nonsense. **2.** a trick or deception; humbug. —*v.t.* **3.** to trick; delude; humbug; cheat. [cf. Icel. *flimska* mockery] —**flimʹflamʹmer,** *n.*

flimsy (flĭmʹzĭ), *adj.*, **-sier, -siest,** *n.*, *pl.* **-sies.** —*adj.* **1.** without material strength or solidity: *a flimsy material, a flimsy structure.* **2.** weak; inadequate; not carefully thought out: *a flimsy excuse or argument.* —*n.* **3.** a thin kind of paper, esp. for use in making several copies of a writing, telegraphic dispatch, etc., at once, as in newspaper work. **4.** a copy of a report or dispatch on such paper. **5.** *Obs.* a banknote. [f. FILM (by metathesis) + *-sy*, adj. suffix] —**flimʹsily,** *adv.* —**flimʹsiness,** *n.*

flinch[1] (flĭnch), *v.i.* **1.** to draw back or shrink from what is dangerous, difficult, or unpleasant. **2.** to shrink under pain; wince. —*v.t.* **3.** to draw back or withdraw from. —*n.* **4.** the act of flinching. [? nasalized var. of d. *flitch* flit, shift (one's) position] —**flinchʹer,** *n.* —**flinchʹingly,** *adv.*

flinch[2] (flĭnch), *v.t.* flench. [var. of FLENCH]

flinders (flĭnʹdəz), *n.pl.* splinters; small pieces or fragments. [cf. Norw. *flindra* splinter]

Flinders (flĭnʹdəz), *n.* **1. Matthew,** 1774–1814, English navigator and explorer. **2.** a river in Australia flowing N through Queensland to the Gulf of Carpentaria. Course ab. 520 mi.

Flinders bar, a cylindrically shaped bar of soft iron, placed vertically in brass holders on the fore and after sides of the binnacle to compensate the error to the compass caused by the magnetism in the ship. [named after Matthew FLINDERS]

Flinders Island, an island in Bass Strait, Australia. ab. 40 mi. long.

Flinders Range, a mountain range in E South Australia. Highest point, St Mary Peak, 3900 ft.

fling (flĭng), *v.*, **flung, flinging,** *n.* —*v.t.* **1.** to throw, cast, or hurl; throw with force or violence; throw with impatience disdain, etc. **2.** to put suddenly or violently: *to fling one into jail.* **3.** to send forth suddenly and rapidly: *to fling fresh troops into a battle.* **4.** to throw aside or off. **5.** to throw to the ground, as in wrestling or from horseback. —*v.i.* **6.** to move with haste or violence; rush; dash. **7.** to fly into violent and irregular motions, as a horse; throw the body about, as a person. **8.** to utter harsh or abusive language (usually fol. by *out*). —*n.* **9.** the act of flinging. **10.** a spell of unrestrained indulgence of one's impulses: *to have one's fling.* **11.** an attack upon or attempt at something, as in passing. **12.** a severe or contemptuous remark or gibe. **13.** a lively Scottish dance characterized by flinging movements of the legs and arms (commonly called **Highland fling**). **14. (at) full fling,** at full speed; with reckless abandon. [ME. Cf. Sw. *flänga* fly, race] —**flingʹer,** *n.*

flint (flĭnt), *n.* **1.** a hard kind of stone, a form of silica resembling chalcedony but more opaque, less pure, and less lustrous. **2.** a piece of this, esp. as used for striking fire. **3.** something very hard or obdurate. **4.** the source of the spark in an automatic cigarette lighter, usually an alloy of such metals as iron and cerium. —*v.t.* **5.** to furnish with a flint. [ME and OE, c. MD *vlint*, Dan. *flint.* Cf. PLINTH]

Flint (flĭnt), *n.* **1.** a city in the U.S., in SE Michigan. 196,940 (1960). **2.** a town in Wales, in N Flintshire. 13,707 (1961). **3.** Flintshire.

flint glass, 1. any colourless glass other than flat glass. **2.** glass of high dispersion made for optical purposes. Also, **optical flint glass.**

flintlock (flĭntʹlŏkʹ), *n.* **1.** a gunlock in which a piece of flint striking against steel produces sparks which ignite the priming. **2.** a firearm with such a lock.

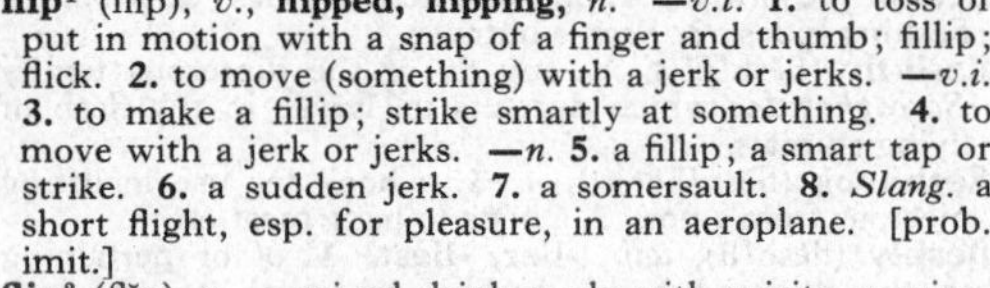

Flintlock fowling piece A, Steel struck by flint; B, Powder pan; C, Touchhole; D, Flint; E, Cock

Flints., Flintshire.

Flintshire (flĭntʹshĭə, -shə), *n.* a county in NE Wales. 149,888 pop. (1961); 256 sq. mi. *Co. town*: Mold. Also, **Flint.**

flinty (flĭnʹtĭ), *adj.*, **flintier, flintiest. 1.** composed of, containing, or resembling flint; hard as flint. **2.** obdurate; cruel; unmerciful: *a flinty heart.* —**flintʹily,** *adv.* —**flintʹiness,** *n.*

flip[1] (flĭp), *v.*, **flipped, flipping,** *n.* —*v.t.* **1.** to toss or put in motion with a snap of a finger and thumb; fillip; flick. **2.** to move (something) with a jerk or jerks. —*v.i.* **3.** to make a fillip; strike smartly at something. **4.** to move with a jerk or jerks. —*n.* **5.** a fillip; a smart tap or strike. **6.** a sudden jerk. **7.** a somersault. **8.** *Slang.* a short flight, esp. for pleasure, in an aeroplane. [prob. imit.]

flip[2] (flĭp), *n.* a mixed drink made with spirits or wine, sugar, and egg, sprinkled with powdered nutmeg. [? n. use of FLIP[1]]

flip[3] (flĭp), *adj.* **flipper, flippest.** *Colloq.* pert; flippant. [adj. use of FLIP[1]]

flip-flop (flĭpʹflŏpʹ), *n.* **1.** *Computers.* an electronic device used to store a binary digit. **2.** a banging to and fro. —*adv.* **3.** to and fro with banging; with repeated flapping.

flippant (flĭpʹənt), *adj.* **1.** clever or pert in speech. **2.** characterized by a shallow or disrespectful levity. **3.** *Obs.* voluble; talkative. **4.** *Obs. or Dial.* nimble, limber, or pliant. [orig. obscure, but cf. Icel. *fleipa* babble] —**flipʹpancy, flipʹpantness,** *n.* —**flipʹpantly,** *adv.*

flipper (flĭpʹə), *n.* **1.** a broad, flat limb, as of a seal, whale, etc., especially adapted for swimming. **2.** a device resembling in form an animal's flipper, usually made of rubber, used as an aid in swimming. **3.** *Slang.* the hand.

flip side, *Colloq.* the reverse of a gramophone record, usually carrying a song, etc., of less interest, or popularity.

flirt (flût), *v.i.* **1.** to trifle in love; play at love; coquet. **2.** to trifle or toy (with an idea, etc.). **3.** to move with a jerk or jerks; dart about. —*v.t.* **4.** to give a sudden or brisk motion to; wave smartly, as a fan. **5.** to throw or propel with a toss or jerk; fling suddenly. —*n.* **6.** a person (woman or man) given to flirting. **7.** a quick throw or toss; a sudden jerk; a darting motion. [imit.] —**flirtʹer,** *n.* —**flirtʹingly,** *adv.*

flirtation (flû tāʹshən), *n.* **1.** the act or practice of flirting; coquetry. **2.** a love affair which is not serious.

flirtatious (flû tāʹshəs), *adj.* **1.** given to flirtation. **2.** pertaining to flirtation. Also, **flirtʹy.** —**flirtaʹtiously,** *adv.* —**flirtaʹtiousness,** *n.*

flit (flĭt), *v.*, **flitted, flitting,** *n.* —*v.i.* **1.** to move lightly and swiftly; fly, dart, or skim along. **2.** to flutter, as a bird. **3.** to pass away quickly, as time. **4.** *Colloq.* to change one's residence, esp. quickly and surreptitiously. **5.** *Colloq.* to elope. **6.** *Obs. or Dial.* to depart or die. —*v.t.* **7.** *Archaic.* to remove; transfer; oust or dispossess. —*n.* **8.** a light, swift movement; a flutter. **9.** *Colloq.* a removal, esp. a surreptitious one. **10.** *Colloq.* an elopement. [ME *flitten*, t. Scand.; cf. Icel. *flytja* carry, convey] —**Syn. 1.** See **fly.**

flitch (flĭch), *n.* **1.** the side of a hog (or, formerly, some other animal) salted and cured: *a flitch of bacon.* **2.** a steak cut from a halibut. —*v.t.* **3.** to cut into flitches. [ME *flicche*, OE *flicce*, c. MLG *vlike*, Icel. *flikki*]

flitched beam, *Carp.* a beam formed by sandwiching a thin iron plate between two pieces of timber.

flite (flīt), *v.*, **flited, fliting,** *n.* *Now Scot. and N Dial.* —*v.i.* **1.** to dispute; wrangle; scold; jeer. —*n.* **2.** a dispute or wrangle; a scolding. Also, **flyte.** [ME *flite(n)*, OE *flītan* strive, contend]

fliting (flīʹtĭng), *n.* *Obs.* **1.** contention. **2.** war of words, in versified dialogue.

flitter[1] (flĭtʹə), *v.i.*, *v.t.* to flutter. [freq. of FLIT]

flitter[2] (flĭtʹə), *n.* one who or that which flits. [f. FLIT, v. + -ER[1]]

flittermouse (flĭtʹə mousʹ), *n.*, *pl.* **-mice.** *Obs.* a bat (animal). [f. FLITTER[1] + MOUSE. Cf. G *Fledermaus*]

flitting (flĭtʹĭng), *adj.* moving lightly and swiftly; passing quickly; fluttering. —**flitʹtingly,** *adv.*

flivver (flĭvʹə), *n.* *Orig. U.S. Slang.* something of unsatisfactory quality or inferior grade, as a motor car. [orig. meaning a failure; b. *flopper* (der. FLOP) and *fizzler* (der. FIZZLE)]

flixweed (flĭksʹwēdʹ), *n.* an annual cruciferous herb, *Descurainia sophia*, a native of temperate Europe and Asia, widely introduced elsewhere.

FLN, (F *Front de Libération Nationale*) a nationalist movement in any of several former French colonies, esp. Algeria.

float (flōt), *v.i.* **1.** to rest on the surface of a liquid; be buoyant. **2.** to move gently on the surface of a liquid; drift along. **3.** to rest or move in or as in a liquid, the air, etc. **4.** to move or hover before the eyes or in the mind. **5.** to pass from one to another, as a rumour. **6.** to move or drift about free from attachment. **7.** to be launched or floated, as a company, scheme, etc. **8.** *Com.* to be in circulation, as an acceptance; be awaiting maturity. —*v.t.* **9.** to cause to float. **10.** to cover with water; flood; irrigate. **11.** to launch (a company, scheme, etc.); set going. **12.** to sell on the market, as a stock or a bond.

13. to make smooth or level, as the surface of plaster. —*n.* 14. something that floats, as a raft. 15. something for buoying up. 16. an inflated bag to sustain a person in water; a life jacket. 17. *Plumbing, Mach., etc.* (in certain apparatus, cisterns, etc.) a device, as a hollow ball, which through its buoyancy automatically regulates the level, supply, or outlet of a liquid. 18. pontoon[1] (def. 2). 19. paddle (def. 2). 20. *Aeron.* a hollow, boatlike part under the wing or fuselage of an aeroplane enabling it to float on water. 21. *Angling.* a piece of cork for supporting a baited line in the water and showing by its movement when a fish bites. 22. *Zool.* an inflated organ that supports an animal in the water. 23. a platform on wheels, bearing a display, and drawn in a procession. 24. a low-bodied vehicle for transporting goods, esp. one powered by batteries: *a milk float.* 25. any of various tools for smoothing, levelling, or the like, as a kind of file, a plasterer's trowel, etc. 26. the loose yarn on the back of cloth due to a figure weave or brocading. 27. a quantity of money used by shopkeepers and others to provide change at the start of any transactions; the equivalent sum should remain at the finish of the proceedings. 28. (*pl.*) *Theat.* the footlights. [ME *flotie(n)*, OE *flotian*, c. Icel. *flota*, MD *vloten.* See FLEET[2], v.] —**float′er,** *n.*

floatable (flō′tə bl), *adj.* 1. capable of floating; that may be floated. 2. that can be floated on, as a river. —**float′abil′ity,** *n.*

floatage (flō′tĭj), *n.* flotage.

floatation (flō tā′shən), *n.* flotation.

floatboard (flōt′bôd′), *n.* a board of an undershot paddle-wheel.

float chamber, the petrol reservoir in a carburettor, in which the petrol level is kept constant by means of an induction valve operated by a float within the chamber.

float-feed (flōt′fēd′), *adj.* *Mach.* equipped with a float to control the feed, as in a carburettor.

floating (flō′tĭng), *adj.* 1. that floats. 2. free from attachment, or having but little attachment. 3. *Pathol.* **a.** freely movable. **b.** unduly movable, as certain organs, esp. the spleen or kidney. 4. not fixed or settled in a definite place or state: *floating population.* 5. *Finance.* **a.** in circulation or use, or not permanently invested, as capital. **b.** composed of sums due within a short time and not requiring frequent renewal or refinancing: *a floating debt.* 6. *Mach.* having a vibration-free suspension; working smoothly. —**float′ingly,** *adv.*

floating assets, assets which are continually changing, as cash, stock in trade, bills of exchange, etc.

floating bridge, 1. a bridge supported by boats, pontoons, etc. 2. a car ferry.

floating charge, *Com.* an equitable charge on the assets of a going concern, which does not become fixed and remains dormant until the company is wound up or breaks some condition, thus permitting the person(s) in whose favour the charge is created to intervene to protect his interests.

floating dock, a floating structure which may be lowered in the water to admit a ship and then raised to leave the ship dry for repairs, etc.; a floating dry dock.

floating heart, any of certain perennial aquatic herbs of the genus *Nymphoides*, esp. *N. lacunosum*, with floating, more or less heart-shaped leaves.

floating island, a floating island-like mass of earth and partly decayed vegetation held together by interlacing roots, sometimes built artificially on wooden platforms as in the Orient, or resulting naturally from the accumulation of plant litter on a water surface.

floating point number, *Computers.* a number represented by a fraction multiplied by a power of 10.

floating policy, a marine insurance policy which insures the goods stated in the policy in whatever ship they may travel.

floating ribs, *Anat.* the two lowest pairs of ribs in man, which are attached neither to the sternum nor to the cartilages of other ribs.

floating stock, stock not held for permanent investment and hence available for speculation; stock held by brokers and speculators rather than investors.

floating vote, floating voters collectively.

floating voter, a voter not committed to any political party, esp. one who votes for or against a government on the basis of its previous policies and performance.

floatstone (flōt′stōn′), *n.* an abrasive stone used by artisans for rubbing down masonry, concrete, etc.

floaty (flō′tĭ), *adj.* 1. able to float; buoyant. 2. (of a boat) drawing little water. 3. appearing to float: *a floaty chiffon dress.*

floc (flŏk), *n.* flock[2] (def. 4). [short for FLOCCULE]

floccillation (flŏk′sĭ lā′shən), *n.* *Pathol.* a picking of the bedclothes, etc., by the patient, usually a sign of great exhaustion. [f. s. **floccillus* (assumed dim. of L *floccus* flock of wool) + -ATION]

floccose (flŏk′ōs, flŏ kōs′), *adj.* 1. *Bot.* consisting of or bearing woolly tufts or long soft hairs. 2. flocculent. [t. LL: m. s. *floccōsus*, der. L *floccus* flock of wool]

flocculant (flŏk′yŏŏ lənt), *n.* *Chem.* a substance added to solutions to produce flocculation of suspended particles.

flocculate (flŏk′yŏŏ lāt′), *v.*, **-lated, -lating.** —*v.t.* 1. to form into flocculent masses. —*v.i.* 2. to form flocculent masses, as cloud, a chemical precipitate, etc.; form aggregated or compound masses of particles. —**floc′cula′tion,** *n.*

floccule (flŏk′yŏŏl), *n.* 1. something resembling a small flock or tuft of wool. 2. a bit of flocculent matter, as in a liquid. [t. NL: m. s. *flocculus.* See FLOCCULUS]

flocculent (flŏk′yŏŏ lənt), *adj.*, 1. like a flock or flocks of wool; covered with a soft woolly substance. 2. consisting of or containing loose woolly masses. 3. flaky. —**floc′culence,** *n.* —**floc′culently,** *adv.*

flocculent precipitate, *Chem.* a woolly-looking precipitate, like that of aluminium hydroxide, from the solution of an aluminium salt to which ammonia is added.

flocculus (flŏk′yŏŏ ləs), *n.*, *pl.* **-li** (-lī′). 1. floccule. 2. *Astron.* one of the bright or dark patches which mottle the sun's chromosphere, visible in spectroheliograms. 3. *Anat.* a small outgrowth on the anterior part of the undersurface of each cerebellar hemisphere. [NL, dim. of L *floccus* flock of wool]

floccus (flŏk′əs), *n.*, *pl.* **flocci** (flŏk′sī). 1. a small tuft of woolly hairs. 2. the covering or down of unfledged birds. [t. L]

flock[1] (flŏk), *n.* 1. a number of animals of one kind keeping, feeding, or herded together, now esp. of sheep or goats, or of birds. 2. a crowd; large number of people. 3. (in New Testament and ecclesiastical use) **a.** the Christian Church in relation to Christ. **b.** a single congregation in relation to its pastor. 4. *Now Rare.* a band or company of persons. —*v.i.* 5. to gather or go in a flock, company, or crowd. [ME; OE *floc*, c. Icel. *flokkr*] —**flock′less,** *adj.*

—**Syn.** 1, 2. bevy, covey, flight, gaggle; brood, hatch, litter; shoal, school, swarm. FLOCK, DROVE, HERD, PACK refer to a company of animals, often under the care or guidance of someone. FLOCK is the popular term, which applies to groups of animals, esp. of sheep or goats, and companies of birds: *this lamb is the choicest of the flock, a flock of wild geese flew overhead.* DROVE is esp. applied to a number of oxen, sheep, or swine when driven in a group: *a drove of oxen was taken to market, a large drove of swine filled the roadway.* HERD is usually applied to large animals such as cattle, originally under the charge of someone; but by extension, to other animals feeding or driven together: *a buffalo herd, a herd of elephants.* PACK applies to a number of animals kept together; or herding together for offensive or defensive purposes: *a pack of hounds kept for hunting, a pack of wolves.* As applied to crowds of people, HERD and PACK carry a contemptuous implication.

flock[2] (flŏk), *n.* 1. a lock or tuft of wool, hair, etc. 2. (*pl. or sing.*) wool refuse, shearings of cloth, old cloth torn to pieces, etc., used for stuffing mattresses, upholstering furniture, etc. 3. (*sing or pl.*) finely powdered wool, cloth, etc., used in making wallpaper. 4. a tuftlike mass, as in a chemical precipitate. —*v.t.* 5. to stuff with flock, as a mattress. 6. to cover or coat with flock, as wallpaper. [ME *flokke*, appar. t. OF: m. *floc*, g. L *floccus* flock of wool. Cf. OHG *floccho*]

flock dot, a pattern of dots or figures not woven but fastened to cloth with adhesive.

flock paper, wallpaper in which the embellishment consists of fine flock adhering to a previously prepared pattern.

flocky (flŏk′ĭ), *adj.*, **-kier, -kiest.** like flocks or tufts; flocculent.

Flodden (flŏd′n), *n.* a hill in Northumberland: the invading Scots were defeated here by the English, 1513. Also, **Flodden Field.**

floe (flō), *n.* 1. a field of floating ice formed on the surface of the sea, etc. 2. a detached floating portion of such a field. [? t. Norw.: m. *flo.* Cf. Icel. *flō*]

flog (flŏg), *v.t.* **flogged, flogging.** 1. to beat hard with a whip, stick, etc.; whip. 2. *Slang.* to sell or attempt to sell. 3. **flog a dead horse,** to make useless efforts. [? b. FLAY and *jog*, var. of JAG[1], v., prick, slash (but cf. FLAGELLATE)] —**flog′ger,** *n.*

flogging (flŏg′ĭng), *n.* punishment by beating or whipping.

flong (flŏng), *n.* *Print.* paper or other material from which a stereotype mould is made.

flood (flŭd), *n.* 1. a great flowing or overflowing of water, esp. over land not usually submerged. 2. **the Flood,** the universal deluge recorded as having occurred in the days of Noah. Gen. 7. 3. *Poetic.* the sea; a river; a lake; any large body of water in general. 4. any great outpouring or stream: *a flood of words, tears, light, lava, etc.* 5. the flowing in of the tide (opposed to *ebb*). —*v.t.*

6. to overflow in or cover with a flood; fill to overflowing. 7. to cover as with a flood. 8. to overwhelm with an abundance of something. —*v.i.* 9. to flow or pour in or as in a flood. 10. to rise in a flood; overflow. 11. *Med.* a. to suffer uterine haemorrhage. b. to have an excessive menstrual flow. [ME; OE *flōd*, c. G *Flut*] —**flood′able,** *adj.* —**flood′er,** *n.* —**flood′less,** *adj.*

—**Syn.** 1. FLOOD, DELUGE, FRESHET, INUNDATION refer to the overflowing of normally dry areas, usually after heavy rains. FLOOD is usually applied to the overflow of a great body of water, as for example a river, though it may refer to any water which overflows an area: *a flood along the river, a flood in a basement.* DELUGE suggests a great downpouring of water, usually with much destruction: *the rain came down in a deluge.* FRESHET suggests a small, quick overflow such as that caused by heavy rains: *a freshet in an abandoned watercourse.* INUNDATION, a literary word, suggests the covering of a great area of land by water: *the inundation of thousands of acres.*

flood control, *Civ. Eng.* the technique of controlling river flow with dams, dykes, artificial channels, etc., so as to minimize the occurrence of floods.

floodgate (flŭd′gāt′), *n.* 1. *Civ. Eng.* a gate designed to regulate the flow of water. 2. anything serving to control indiscriminate flow or passage.

floodlight (flŭd′līt′), *n.*, *v.*, **-lighted** or **-lit, -lighting.** —*n.* 1. an artificial light so directed or diffused as to give a comparatively uniform illumination over a given area. 2. a floodlight lamp or projector. —*v.t.* 3. to illuminate with or as with a floodlight.

floodlight projector, a powerful lamp having a reflector curved to produce a floodlight.

floodmark (flŭd′mäk′), *n.* a mark or line indicating the highest point of a flood, usually with a date beside it.

flood plain, *Phys. Geog.* a nearly flat plain along the course of a stream that is naturally subject to flooding at high water.

flood tide, the inflow of the tide; the rising tide.

floodwater (flŭd′wô′tə), *n.* the water that overflows in a flood; excess water.

floodway (flŭd′wā′), *n.* an artificial passage for floodwater. Also, **floodwater channel.**

floor (flô), *n.* 1. that part of a room or the like which forms its lower enclosing surface, and upon which one walks. 2. a storey of a building. Cf. **first floor.** 3. a level supporting surface in any structure: *the floor of a bridge.* 4. a platform or prepared level area for a particular use: *a threshing floor.* 5. the flat bottom of any more or less hollow place: *the floor of a cave.* 6. any more or less flat extent of surface. 7. *Colloq.* the ground. 8. the part of a legislative chamber, etc., where the members sit, and from which they speak. 9. the right of one member to speak from such a place in preference to other members: *to get or have the floor.* 10. the main part of a stock exchange or the like, as distinct from galleries, etc. 11. *Mining.* a. the bottom of a horizontal passageway. b. an underlying stratum, as of ore, usually flat. 12. *Naut.* that part of the bottom of a vessel on each side of the keelson which is most nearly horizontal. 13. the bottom, base, or minimum charged or paid: *a price or wage floor.* 14. **wipe the floor with,** *Colloq.* to overcome or vanquish totally. —*v.t.* 15. to cover or furnish with a floor. 16. to bring down to the floor or ground; knock down. 17. *Colloq.* to beat or defeat. 18. *Colloq.* to confound or nonplus: *to be floored by a problem.* [ME *flore*, OE *flōr*, c. G *Flur*] —**floor′less,** *adj.*

floorage (flô′rĭj), *n.* *Chiefly U.S.* floor space.

floorboard (flô′bôd′), *n.* a plank in a timber floor.

floorcloth (flô′klŏth′), *n.* 1. a cloth for washing or wiping floors. 2. a covering for floors esp. of linoleum or the like.

floorer (flô′rə), *n.* 1. one who lays floors. 2. a person or thing, as a blow, that knocks to the floor. 3. *Colloq.* something that beats, overwhelms, or confounds.

flooring (flô′rĭng), *n.* 1. a floor. 2. floors collectively. 3. materials for making or covering floors.

floor leader, *U.S. Govt.* the party member in either the Senate or the House who directs the activities of his party on the floor.

floor show, an entertainment given in a nightclub or cabaret, usually consisting of a series of singing, dancing, and/or comic episodes.

floor space, 1. space available on a floor. 2. selling space in a shop, as opposed to space for staff or storage purposes.

floorwalker (flô′wô′kə), *n.* a shopwalker.

floozy (flo͞o′zĭ), *n.*, *pl.* **-zies.** *Slang.* a worthless woman. Also, **floosy, floosie, floozie.**

flop (flŏp), *v.*, **flopped, flopping,** *n.* *Colloq.* —*v.i.* 1. to fall or plump down suddenly, esp. with noise; drop or turn with a sudden bump or thud. 2. to fall flat on the surface of water. 3. to yield or break down suddenly; fail. 4. to flap, as in the wind. 5. *U.S.* to change suddenly, as from one side or party to another (often fol. by *over*). —*v.t.* 6. to drop, throw, etc., with a sudden bump or thud. 7. to flap clumsily and heavily, as wings. —*n.* 8. the act of flopping. 9. the sound of flopping; a thud. 10. a failure. [var. of FLAP] —**flop′per,** *n.*

flophouse (flŏp′hous′), *n.* *U.S.* a dosshouse.

floppy (flŏp′ĭ), *adj.*, **-pier, -piest.** *Colloq.* tending to flop. —**flop′pily,** *adv.* —**flop′piness,** *n.*

flor., (L *floruit*) flourished.

flora (flô′rə), *n.*, *pl.* **floras, florae** (flô′rē). 1. the plants of a particular region or period, listed by species. 2. a work systematically describing such plants. 3. (*cap.*) the Roman goddess of flowers. [t. L, der. *flōs* flower]

floral (flô′rəl), *adj.* 1. pertaining to or consisting of flowers. 2. (*cap.*) of or pertaining to the goddess Flora. [t. L: s. *Flōrālis* (def. 2)] —**flo′rally,** *adv.*

floral envelope, *Bot.* the calyx and corolla of a flower.

Floréal (*Fr.* flō rĕ ăl′), *n.* (in the calendar of the first French republic) the eighth month of the year, extending from April 20th to May 19th.

floreated (flô′rĭ ā′tĭd), *adj.* floriated.

Florence (flŏ′rəns), *n.* a city in central Italy, in Tuscany, on the river Arno: capital of the former grand duchy of Tuscany. 454,401 (1966). Italian, **Firenze.**

Florence flask, a flat-bottomed, round flask with a long neck; used in laboratory experiments.

Florentine (flŏ′rən tīn′), *adj.* 1. of or pertaining to Florence: *the Florentine painters.* 2. *Cookery.* served with spinach. —*n.* 3. a native or inhabitant of Florence.

Flores (*Indon.* flō′rĕs *for 1*; *Port.* flō′rĭsh *for 2*), *n.* 1. one of the Lesser Sunda Islands in Indonesia, separated from Celebes by the **Flores Sea.** With adjacent islands, 194,203 pop. (1963); 7753 sq. mi. See map under **Bali.** 2. the westernmost island of the Azores, in the N Atlantic. 7832 pop. (1950); 55 sq. mi.

florescence (flô rĕs′əns), *n.* the act, state, or period of flowering; bloom. [t. NL: m. s. *flōrescentia*, der. L *flōrescens*, ppr., beginning to flower] —**flores′cent,** *adj.*

floret (flô′rĭt), *n.* 1. a small flower. 2. *Bot.* one of the closely clustered small flowers that make up the flower head of a composite flower, as the daisy. [cf. OF *florete*, dim. of *flor*, g. L *flōs* flower]

Florianópolis (flô′rĭ ə nŏp′ə lĭs; *Port.* flō ryə nŏp′o͞o lēs), *n.* a seaport on an island off the S coast of Brazil. 98,520 (1960). Formerly, **Desterro.**

floriated (flô′rĭ ā′tĭd), *adj.* decorated with floral ornamentation: *floriated columns.* Also, **floreated.**

floribunda (flô′rĭ bŭn′də) *n.*, *pl.* **-das.** a group of hybrid cultivated roses bearing flowers in large sprays.

floriculture (flô′rĭ kŭl′chə), *n.* the cultivation of flowers or flowering plants, esp. under glass. [f. L *flōri-* (comb. form of *flōs* flower) + CULTURE] —**flo′ricul′tural,** *adj.* —**flo′ricul′turist,** *n.*

florid (flŏ′rĭd), *adj.* 1. highly coloured or ruddy, as complexion, cheeks, etc. 2. flowery; excessively ornate; showy: *a florid prose style, florid music.* 3. *Archit.* abounding in decorative features, as in baroque or rococo styles. 4. *Archaic.* abounding in or consisting of flowers. [t. L: s. *flōridus* flowery] —**floridity** (flŏ rĭd′ĭ tĭ), **flor′idness,** *n.* —**flor′idly,** *adv.*

Florida (flŏ′rĭ də), *n.* a state in the SE United States between the Atlantic and the Gulf of Mexico. 4,951,560 pop. (1960); 58,560 sq. mi. *Cap.:* Tallahassee. *Abbrev.:* Fla. —**Floridian** (flŏ rĭd′ĭ ən), **Flor′idan,** *adj.*, *n.*

Florida Keys, a chain of small islands and reefs off S Florida. ab. 225 mi. long.

Florida Strait, a strait separating Florida from Cuba and the Bahama Islands and connecting the Gulf of Mexico with the Atlantic.

floriferous (flô rĭf′ə rəs), *adj.* flower-bearing. [f. L *flōrifer* bearing flowers + -OUS]

florin (flŏ′rĭn), *n.* 1. a silver coin of Britain and elsewhere worth 2 shillings or 10 new pence, first minted in 1849. 2. the gulden of the Netherlands. 3. a former gold coin weighing about 54 grains, first issued at Florence in 1252. 4. a former English gold coin of Edward III, worth 6 shillings. 5. a former gold coin of Austria, first issued in the 14th century. [ME, t. F, t. It.: m. *fiorino* a Florentine coin stamped with a lily, der. *fiore*, g. L *flōs* flower]

Florio (flô′rĭ ō′), *n.* **John,** 1553?–1625, English lexicographer and translator.

florist (flŏ′rĭst), *n.* a retailer of flowers, ornamental plants, etc.

floristic (flŏ rĭs′tĭk), *adj.* pertaining to a flora. —**florist′ically,** *adv.*

-florous, an adjectival suffix meaning 'flower', as in *uniflorous.* [t. L: m. *-flōrus* flowered]

flory (flô′rĭ), *adj.* fleury.

flos ferri (flŏs′fĕ′rĭ), *Mineral.* a coralloid variety of aragonite. [t. L: flower of iron]

floss (flŏs), *n.* **1.** the cottony fibre yielded by the silk-cotton trees. **2.** silk filaments with little or no twist, used in weaving as brocade or in embroidery. **3.** any silky filamentous matter, as the silk of maize. **4.** Also, **dental floss.** soft, waxed thread used for cleaning between the teeth. Also (for defs 1–3), **floss silk.** [t. Scand.; cf. Icel. *flos* shag of velvet]

flossy (flŏs′ĭ), *adj.* **flossier, flossiest.** made of or resembling floss.

flotage (flō′tĭj), *n.* **1.** the act of floating. **2.** the state of floating. **3.** floating power; buoyancy. **4.** *Colloq.* anything that floats; flotsam. **5.** the ships, etc., afloat on a river. **6.** the part of a ship above the water line. Also, **floatage.** [f. FLOAT, n. + -AGE. Cf. F *flottage*]

flotation (flō tā′shən), *n.* **1.** the act or state of floating. **2.** the floating or launching of a commercial venture, a loan, etc. **3.** *Metall.* a process for separating the different crystalline phases in a mass of powdered ore based on their ability to sink in, or float on, a given liquid. **4.** the science of floating bodies. Also, **floatation.** [var. of FLOATATION. Cf. F *flottaison* (see FLOTSAM)]

flote-grass (flōt′gräs′), *n.* a perennial grass, *Glyceria fluitans*, growing in shallow water throughout N temperate regions.

flotilla (flə tĭl′ə), *n.* **1.** number of small naval vessels; a subdivision of a fleet. **2.** a small fleet. [t. Sp., dim. of *flota* fleet, t. F: m. *flotte*, t. OE: m. *flota*]

Flotow (*Ger.* flō′tō), *n.* **Friedrich von** (*Ger.* frē′drĭKH fōn), 1812–83, German operatic composer.

flotsam (flŏt′səm), *n.* such part of the wreckage of a ship and its cargo as is found floating on the water. Cf. **jetsam.** [t. AF: m. *floteson*, der. *floter* float, t. OE: m. *flotian*]

flotsam and jetsam, 1. the wreckage of a ship and its cargo found either floating upon the sea or washed ashore. **2.** odds and ends.

flounce[1] (flouns), *v.*, **flounced, flouncing,** *n.* —*v.i.* **1.** to go with an impatient or angry fling of the body (fol. by *away, off, out*, etc.): *to flounce out of a room in a rage.* **2.** to throw the body about, as in floundering or struggling; twist; turn; jerk. —*n.* **3.** action of flouncing; a flouncing movement. [t. Scand.; cf. Norw. *flunsa* hurry]

flounce[2] (flouns), *n.*, *v.*, **flounced, flouncing.** —*n.* **1.** a strip of material, wider than a ruffle, gathered and attached at one edge and with the other edge left hanging: used for trimming, esp. on women's skirts. —*v.t.* **2.** to trim with a flounce or flounces. [var. of FROUNCE]

flouncing (floun′sĭng), *n.* **1.** material for flounces. **2.** trimming consisting of a flounce.

flounder[1] (floun′də), *v.i.* **1.** to struggle with stumbling or plunging movements (fol. by *along, on, through*, etc.). **2.** to struggle clumsily or helplessly in embarrassment or confusion. —*n.* **3.** the action of floundering; a floundering movement. [? b. FLOUNCE[1] and FOUNDER[2]]

flounder[2] (floun′də), *n.*, *pl.* **-ders,** (*esp. collectively*) **-der. 1.** a European marine flatfish, *Platichthys flesus*, widely caught for food. **2.** any of a number of similar or closely related non-European flatfishes. **3.** any flatfish other than soles. [ME, t. AF: m. *floundre*, t. Scand.; cf. Norw. *flundra*]

flour (flou′ə), *n.* **1.** the finely ground meal of wheat or other grain, esp. the finer meal separated by bolting. **2.** any fine, soft powder: *flour of emery.* —*v.t.* **3.** to make (grain, etc.) into flour; grind and bolt. **4.** to sprinkle or dredge with flour, as food or utensils in cookery. **5.** to break up (mercury, in amalgamation) into fine globules, which, owing to some impurity, do not unite with a precious metal. [ME; special use of FLOWER. Cf. F *fleur de farine* the flower or finest part of the meal] —**flour′less,** *adj.* —**flour′like′,** *adj.*

flourish (flŭ′rĭsh), *v.i.* **1.** to be in a vigorous state; thrive; prosper; be successful: *during this period art flourished.* **2.** to be in its or one's prime; be at the height of fame or excellence. **3.** to grow luxuriantly, or thrive in growth, as a plant. **4.** to make strokes or flourishes with a brandished weapon or the like. **5.** to make a parade or ostentatious display. **6.** to add embellishments or flourishes to writing, letters, etc. **7.** to speak or write in flowery or pretentious language. **8.** *Music.* **a.** to play a showy passage. **b.** to play in a showy manner. **c.** to sound a trumpet call or fanfare. —*v.t.* **9.** to brandish or wave (a sword, a stick, the limbs, etc.) about in the air. **10.** to parade, flaunt, or display ostentatiously: *to flourish one's wealth.* **11.** to embellish (writing, etc.) with sweeping or fanciful curves or lines. **12.** to adorn with decorative designs, colour, etc. —*n.* **13.** a brandishing or waving, as of a sword, a stick, or the like. **14.** a parade or ostentatious display. **15.** a decoration or embellishment in writing. **16.** *Rhet.* a parade of fine language; an expression used merely for effect. **17.** *Music.* **a.** an elaborate passage or addition largely for display. **b.** a trumpet call or fanfare. **18.** *Rare.* the condition of flourishing or thriving: *in full flourish.* **19.** *Obs.* the state of flowering. [ME *florish(en)*, t. OF: m. *floriss-*, s. *florir*, ult. der. L *flōrēre* bloom] —**flour′isher,** *n.* —**Syn. 2.** See **succeed.**

flourishing (flŭ′rĭ shĭng), *adj.* that flourishes; vigorous in growth; thriving; prosperous. —**flour′ishingly,** *adv.*

flour mill, a mill for making flour.

floury (flou′ə rĭ), *adj.* **1.** of, pertaining to, or resembling flour. **2.** covered or white with flour.

flout (flout), *v.t.* **1.** to mock; scoff at; treat with disdain or contempt. —*v.i.* **2.** to mock, gibe, or scoff (often fol. by *at*). —*n.* **3.** a flouting speech or action; a mocking insult; a gibe. [ME *floute(n)*, var. of FLUTE, v. Cf. D *fluiten* play the flute, mock, impose upon] —**flout′er,** *n.* —**flout′ingly,** *adv.*

flow (flō), *v.i.* **1.** to move along in a stream, as a liquid; circulate, as the blood. **2.** to stream or well forth; issue or proceed from a source; discharge a stream, as of blood. **3.** to come or go as in a stream, as persons or things. **4.** to proceed continuously and smoothly, like a stream, as thought, speech, or verse. **5.** to fall or hang loosely at full length, as hair. **6.** to overflow or abound with something: *a land flowing with milk and honey.* **7.** to rise and advance, as the tide (opposed to *ebb*). —*v.t.* **8.** to cause or permit to flow. **9.** to cover with water or other liquid; flood. —*n.* **10.** the act of flowing. **11.** movement in or as in a stream; any continuous movement, as of thought, speech, trade, etc., like that of a stream of water. **12.** the rate of flowing. **13.** the volume of fluid that flows through a passage of any given section in a unit of time. **14.** that which flows; a stream. **15.** an outpouring or discharge of something, as in a stream: *a flow of blood.* **16.** an overflowing. **17.** the rise of the tide; flood (opposed to *ebb*). **18.** *Scot.* an inlet of the sea. **19.** *Scot.* a flat, marshy tract of land. [ME *flowen*, OE *flōwan*, c. LG *flojen*, Icel. *flōa*]

—**Syn. 1.** FLOW, GUSH, SPOUT, SPURT refer to certain of the movements characteristic of fluids. FLOW is the general term: *water flows, a stream of blood flows.* To GUSH is to rush forth copiously from a cavity, in as large a volume as can issue therefrom, as the result of some strong impelling force: *the water will gush out if the main breaks.* SPOUT and SPURT both imply the ejecting of a liquid from a cavity by some internal impetus given to it. SPOUT implies a rather steady, possibly well-defined, jet or stream, not necessarily of long duration but always of considerable force: *a whale spouts.* SPURT implies a forcible, possibly sudden, spasmodic, or intermittent issue or jet: *the liquid spurted out suddenly when the bottle-top was opened.* SPOUT applies only to liquids; the other terms apply also to gases.

flowage (flō′ĭj), *n.* **1.** the act of flowing; flow; the state of being flooded. **2.** the flowing or overflowing liquid. **3.** *Mech.* gradual internal motion or deformation, without fracture, of a viscous solid such as asphalt.

flow chart, a diagram showing the step-by-step operation of a system. Also, **flow diagram, flow sheet.**

flower (flou′ə), *n.* **1.** the blossom of a plant. **2.** *Bot.* **a.** that part of a seed plant comprising the reproductive organs and their envelopes (if any), esp. when such envelopes are more or less conspicuous in form and colour. **b.** an analogous reproductive structure in other plants, as the mosses. **3.** a plant considered with reference to its blossom or cultivated for its floral beauty. **4.** the state of efflorescence or bloom: *plants in flower.* **5.** an ornament or decorative symbol representing a flower; fleuron. **6.** any ornament or adornment. **7.** a figure of speech. **8.** the finest or most flourishing state or period, as of life or beauty. **9.** the best or finest member or part of a number, body, or whole: *the flower of chivalry.* **10.** the finest or choicest product or example. **11.** (*pl.*) *Chem.* a substance in the form of a fine powder, esp. as obtained by sublimation: *flowers of sulphur.* —*v.i.* **12.** to produce flowers, or blossom, as a plant; to come to full bloom. **13.** to abound in flowers. **14.** to come out into full development. —*v.t.* **15.** to cover or deck with flowers. **16.** to decorate with a floral design. [ME *flour*, t. OF, g. L *flōs*] —**flow′er-like′,** *adj.*

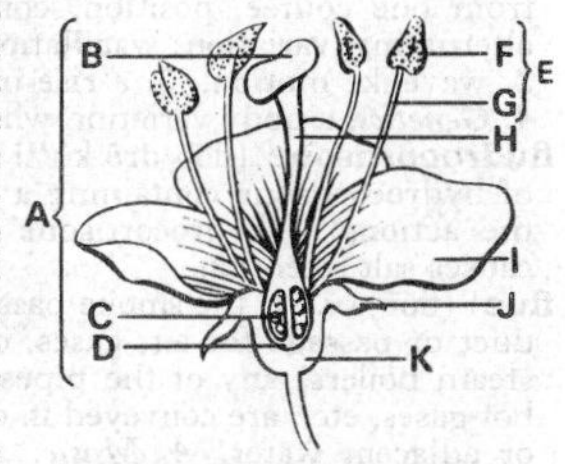

Stylized section of a flower
A, Pistil; B, Stigma; C, Ovule; D, Ovary; E, Stamen; F, Anther; G, Filament; H, Style; I, Petal; J, Sepal; K, Receptacle

flowerage (flou′ə rĭj), *n.* **1.** flowers collectively. **2.** floral ornament or decoration. **3.** *Rare.* the process or state of flowering.

flowerbed (flou′ə bĕd′), *n.* a plot of ground, esp. in a garden, where flowering plants are cultivated.

flower-de-luce (flou′ə də lōōs′), *n.* **1.** the iris (flower or plant). **2.** *Archaic.* the lily. [old var. of *fleur-de-lis* influenced by FLOWER]

flowered (flou′əd), *adj.* **1.** having flowers. **2.** decorated with flowers, or a floral pattern.

flowerer (flou′ə rə), *n.* a plant that flowers at a specific time, in a specific manner, etc.: *a late flowerer, an abundant flowerer.*

floweret (flou′ə rĭt), *n.* a small flower; a floret.

flower garden, a garden in which flowering plants, rather than vegetables or grass, are cultivated.

flower girl, a woman of any age selling flowers in the street.

flower head, *Bot.* an inflorescence consisting of a dense cluster of sessile florets; a capitulum.

flowering (flou′ə rĭng), *adj.* bearing flowers.

flowering dogwood, a deciduous cornaceous shrub, *Cornus florida,* native of the eastern U.S., widely planted for its pink and white flowers.

flowering rush, an aquatic herb of the family *Butomaceae,* with long narrow leaves and umbels of pink flowers, *Butomus umbellatus,* of Europe and temperate Asia.

flowerless (flou′ə lĭs), *adj.* **1.** without flowers. **2.** *Bot.* without a true seed; cryptogamic.

flower of Jove, a perennial herb of the family *Camyophyllaceae* from the central Alps, *Lychnis flos-Jovis,* often cultivated for its grey woolly foliage and bright red flowers.

flowerpot (flou′ə pŏt′), *n.* a pot to hold earth for a plant to grow in.

flowery (flou′ə rĭ), *adj.,* **-rier, -riest. 1.** abounding in or covered with flowers. **2.** containing highly ornate language: *a flowery style.* **3.** decorated with floral designs. —**flow′erily,** *adv.* —**flow′eriness,** *n.*

flowing (flō′ĭng), *adj.* **1.** that flows; moving in or as in a stream: *flowing water.* **2.** proceeding smoothly or easily: *flowing language.* **3.** smoothly and gracefully continuous throughout the length: *flowing lines or curves.* **4.** falling or hanging loosely at full length: *flowing hair, draperies, etc.* —**flow′ingly,** *adv.*

flown[1] (flōn), *v.* pp. of **fly**[1].

flown[2] (flōn), *adj.* **1.** decorated by means of colour freely blended or flowed, as a glaze. **2.** *Archaic.* filled to excess. [ME *flowen,* OE *flōwen,* pp. of *flōwan* flow]

flow sheet, a flow chart.

fl. oz., fluid ounce; fluid ounces.

Flt Lt, Flight Lieutenant.

flu (flōō), *n. Colloq.* influenza.

fluctuant (flŭk′tyōō ənt), *adj.* **1.** fluctuating; varying. **2.** *Med.* having a soft or liquid centre, as a boil, abscess, etc.

fluctuate (flŭk′tyōō āt′), *v.,* **-ated, -ating.** —*v.i.* **1.** to change continually, as by turns, from one course, position, condition, amount, etc., to another, as the mind, opinion, policy, prices, temperature, etc.; vary irregularly; be unstable. **2.** to move in waves or like waves. —*v.t. Rare.* **3.** to cause to fluctuate. [t. L: m. s. *fluctuātus,* pp., undulated] —**Syn. 1.** See **waver.**

fluctuation (flŭk′tyōō ā′shən), *n.* **1.** continual change from one course, position, condition, etc., to another; alternating variation; vacillation; wavering; instability. **2.** wavelike motion. **3.** a rise or fall in price, value, etc. **4.** *Genetics.* a body variation which is not inherited.

fludrocortisone (flōō′drō kô′tĭ zōn′), *n. Pharm.* a type of hydrocortisone containing a fluorine group which has the actions of hydrocortisone but is more potent and causes salt retention.

flue[1] (flōō), *n.* **1.** the smoke passage in a chimney. **2.** any duct or passage for air, gases, or the like. **3.** (in certain steam boilers) any of the pipes or tubes through which hot gases, etc., are conveyed in order to heat surrounding or adjacent water. **4.** *Music.* **a.** a fluepipe. **b.** the air passage in a fluepipe between the blowing end and the lateral hole. [earlier *flew,* ? repr. OE *flēwsa* a flowing, the form *flews* being taken for a plural]

flue[2] (flōō), *n.* downy matter; fluff. [? OE *flug-* in *flugol* swift, fleeting (akin to FLY[1], v.). Cf. LG *flug*] —**flue′y,** *adj.*

flue[3] (flōō), *n.* a kind of fishing net. Also, **flew.** [ME *flowe.* Cf. MD *vluwe* fishing net]

flue[4] (flōō), *n.* **1.** a barb of a feather. **2.** the fluke of an anchor. [orig. obscure. Cf. Sw. *fly*]

flue[5] (flōō), *v.i., v.t. Bldg Trades.* (at the sides of a fireplace, etc.) to splay. [ME, d. *flew* shallow]

flue gas, the gaseous combustion products from a boiler furnace consisting of a mixture of carbon dioxide, carbon monoxide, nitrogen, oxygen, and steam.

fluellen (flōō ĕl′ĭn), *n.* an annual scrophuluriaceous herb, with yellow and purple flowers, *Kickxia spuria,* found mostly in European cornfields. [t. Welsh: m. (*llysiau*) *Llewelyn* herbs of Llewelyn]

fluent (flōō′ənt), *adj.* **1.** flowing smoothly and easily: *to speak fluent French.* **2.** able to speak or write readily: *a fluent speaker.* **3.** easy; graceful: *fluent motion, curves, etc.* **4.** flowing, as a stream. **5.** *Rare.* capable of flowing, or fluid, as liquids or gases. **6.** *Rare.* not fixed or stable in form. [t. L: s. *fluens,* ppr., flowing] —**flu′ency, flu′entness,** *n.* —**flu′ently,** *adv.*

—**Syn. 1.** FLUENT, GLIB, VOLUBLE may refer to a flow of words. FLUENT suggests an easy and ready flow and is usually a term of commendation: *a fluent and interesting speech.* GLIB implies an excessive fluency divorced from sincerity or profundity; it often suggests talking smoothly and hurriedly to cover up or deceive, not giving the audience a chance to stop and think; it may also imply a plausible, prepared, and well-rehearsed lie: *he had a glib answer for everything.* VOLUBLE implies the overcopious, and often rapid flow of words, characteristic of a person who loves to talk and will spare his audience no details: *she overwhelmed him with her voluble answer.* —**Ant. 1.** hesitant.

fluepipe (flōō′pīp′), *n.* **1.** *Music.* an organ pipe in which a current of air striking a mouth or aperture produces the note. **2.** *Bldg Trades.* a pipe of some heat-resistant material leading smoke from a stove to a flue.

fluestop (flōō′stŏp′), *n. Music.* an organ stop whose sound is produced by fluepipes; any stop which is not a reedstop.

fluff (flŭf), *n.* **1.** light, downy particles, as of cotton. **2.** a downy mass; something downy or fluffy. **3.** *Colloq.* a blunder or error in execution, performance, etc. **4. bit of fluff,** *Slang.* a superficially attractive girl. —*v.t.* **5.** to make into fluff; shake or puff out (feathers, hair, etc.) into a fluffy mass. **6.** *Colloq.* to fail to perform properly: *to fluff a golf stroke, an examination, lines of a play.* —*v.i.* **7.** to become fluffy; move, float, or settle down like fluff. **8.** *Colloq.* to blunder; fail in performance or execution. [? b. FLUE[2] and PUFF]

fluffy (flŭf′ĭ), *adj.,* **fluffier, fluffiest.** of, like, or covered with fluff. —**fluff′ily,** *adv.* —**fluff′iness.** *n.*

flugelhorn (flōō′gl hôn′), *n.* a keyed brass instrument with cup mouthpiece and of conical bore, used mainly in brass bands. [t. G: m. *Flügelhorn,* lit. wing-horn]

fluid (flōō′ĭd), *n.* **1.** a substance which is capable of flowing and offers no permanent resistance to changes of shape; a liquid or a gas. —*adj.* **2.** capable of flowing; liquid or gaseous. **3.** consisting of or pertaining to fluids. **4.** changing readily; shifting; not fixed, stable, or rigid. [t. L: s. *fluidus,* der. *fluere* flow] —**flu′idal, fluid′ic,** *adj.* —**fluid′ity, flu′idness,** *n.* —**flu′idly,** *adv.* —**Syn. 1.** See **liquid.**

fluid drachm, a unit of capacity equal to one eighth of a British fluid ounce.

fluid dram, *U.S.* a unit of liquid measure equal to one eighth of a U.S. fluid ounce.

fluid drive, *Motor Vehicles.* a device for transmitting torque from one shaft to another, esp. for providing a smooth coupling between the engine of a motor vehicle and the transmission; consists of two vaned rotors in a sealed casing filled with oil. The driven rotor transmits its momentum to oil which in turn drives the second rotor. Also, **fluid flywheel, hydraulic torque convertor.**

fluid extract, *Pharm.* an alcoholic solution of a vegetable drug when 1 cc. of the preparation is equivalent, in activity, to one gram of the drug in powdered form.

fluidics (flōō ĭd′ĭks), *n.* the branch of computing which uses hydraulic systems to simulate problems and manipulate data. Fluidic systems are slow in operation compared with electronic circuits but are suitable for specialized applications. —**fluidic,** *adj.*

fluidize (flōō′ĭ dīz′), *v.t.* **1.** to handle solid particles as if they were liquids by transporting them in a stream of gas. **2.** to make fluid. Also, **fluidise.** —**flu′idiza′tion,** *n.* —**flu′idiz′er,** *n.*

fluid mechanics, an applied science embodying the basic principles of both gaseous and liquid flow.

fluid ounce, *n.* **1.** a unit of capacity equal to one-twentieth of a pint. **2.** *U.S.* a unit of liquid measure equal to one-sixteenth of a pint.

fluke[1] (flōōk), *n.* **1.** the flat triangular piece at the end of each arm of an anchor, which catches in the ground. **2.** a barb, or the barbed head, of a harpoon, etc. **3.** either half of the triangular tail of a whale. [? special use of FLUKE[3]]

fluke[2] (flōōk), *n., v.,* **fluked, fluking.** —*n.* **1.** any accidental advantage; a lucky chance. **2.** an accidentally successful stroke in billiards or other sports. —*v.t.* **3.** *Colloq.* to hit, make, or gain by a fluke. [orig. unknown. Cf. d. E *fluke* a guess]

fluke[3] (flōōk), *n.* **1.** the flounder, *Platichthys flesus.* **2.** any flounder. **3.** a trematode. [ME, var. of *flook,* OE *flōc*]

flukey (flōō′kĭ), *adj.,* **flukier, flukiest.** fluky.

fluky (flōō′kĭ), *adj.,* **flukier, flukiest. 1.** *Colloq.* obtained by chance rather than skill. **2.** uncertain, as a wind. [f. FLUKE[2] + -Y[1]] —**fluk′iness,** *n.*

flume (flōōm), *n.*, *v.*, **flumed, fluming.** *U.S.* —*n.* **1.** a deep narrow defile, esp. one containing a mountain torrent. **2.** an artificial channel or trough for conducting water, as one in which logs, etc., are transported. —*v.t.* **3.** to transport, as timber, in a flume. **4.** to divert (a river, etc.) by a flume. [ME, t. OF: m. *flum*, g. L *flūmen* stream]

flummery (flŭm′ə rĭ), *n.*, *pl.* **-ries. 1.** oatmeal or flour boiled with water until thick. **2.** any of various dishes made of flour, milk, eggs, sugar, etc. **3.** agreeable humbug; empty compliment. [t. Welsh: m. *llymru*]

flummox (flŭm′əks), *v.t.* *Slang.* to bewilder; confuse.

flump (flŭmp), *Colloq.* —*v.i.*, *v.t.* **1.** to plump down suddenly or heavily; flop. —*n.* **2.** act or sound of flumping. [b. FALL and PLUMP²]

flung (flŭng), *v.* pt. and pp. of **fling.**

flunk (flŭngk), *U.S. Colloq.* —*v.i.* **1.** to fail, as a student in a recitation or examination. **2.** to give up; back out (fol. by *out*). —*v.t.* **3.** to fail in (a recitation, etc.). **4.** to remove (a student) as unqualified from a school, course, etc. —*n.* **5.** a failure, as in a recitation or examination. [? akin to FLINCH¹, FUNK]

flunkey (flŭng′kĭ), *n.*, *pl.* **-keys. 1.** (esp. in contemptuous use) a male servant in livery; a lackey. **2.** a servile follower; a toady. [? alter. of FLANKER] —**flun′keydom, flun′keyism,** *n.* —**flun′keyish,** *adj.*

flunky (flŭng′kĭ), *n.*, *pl.* **-kies.** flunkey.

fluon (flōō′ŏn), *n.* *Chem.* **1.** a plastic with non-adhesive surface properties, polytetrafluorethylene; used as a coating on non-stick cooking utensils. **2.** (*cap.*) a trademark for this.

fluor (flōō′ô), *n.* fluorspar. [t. L: a flowing (so called from its use as a flux)]

fluor-¹, a word element indicating the presence of fluorine. [comb. form of FLUORINE]

fluor-², a word element indicating fluorescence. [comb. form of FLUORESCENCE]

fluorene (flōōə′rēn), *n.* *Chem.* a white crystalline aromatic hydrocarbon, $C_{13}H_{10}$, used in the manufacture of resins and dyes; ortho-diphenylene methane.

fluoresce (flōōə rĕs′), *v.i.*, **-resced, -rescing.** to exhibit the phenomena of fluorescence.

fluorescein (flōōə rĕs′ĭ ĭn), *n.* *Chem.* an orange-red water-insoluble compound, $C_{20}H_{12}O_5$, whose solutions in alkalis produce an orange colour and a green fluorescence. It is used as an indicator and in dyes. Also, **fluoresceine.**

fluorescence (flōōə rĕs′əns), *n.* *Physics, Chem.* **1.** the property possessed by certain substances of emitting light upon exposure to external radiation or bombardment by a stream of particles. **2.** the light or luminosity so produced.

fluorescent (flōōə rĕs′ənt), *adj.* possessing the property of fluorescence; exhibiting fluorescence.

fluorescent tube, an electric discharge tube in which light is produced by passage of electricity through a metallic vapour or gas enclosed in a tube or bulb.

fluoric (flōō ŏ′rĭk), *adj.* **1.** *Chem.* pertaining to or obtained from fluorine. **2.** *Mineral.* pertaining to or obtained from fluor. [t. F: m. *fluorique*, der. *fluor* fluid acid, t. L: a flowing]

fluoridation (flōōə′rĭ dā′shən), *n.* the addition of certain chemicals, such as sodium fluoride, to the public water supply to reduce tooth decay. —**fluor′idate′,** *v.t.*

fluoride (flōōə′rīd), *n.* *Chem.* **1.** a salt of hydrofluoric acid. **2.** an organic compound with one or more hydrogen atoms substituted by fluorine atoms, as methyl fluoride.

fluorinate (flōōə′rĭ nāt′), *v.t.*, **-nated, -nating.** *Chem.* to treat or combine with fluorine. —**fluo′rina′tion,** *n.*

fluorine (flōōə′rēn), *n.* *Chem.* a non-metallic element, a pale yellow corrosive gas, occurring combined, esp. in fluorspar, cryolite, phosphate rock, and other minerals. *Symbol:* F; *at. wt:* 18·9984; *at. no.:* 9.

fluorite (flōōə′rīt), *n.* *Chiefly U.S.* fluorspar.

fluoroborate (flōōə′rō bô′rāt), *n.* *Chem.* a salt of fluoroboric acid. Also, **fluoborate** (flōōə bô′rāt).

fluoroboric acid (flōōə′rō bŏ′rĭk), *Chem.* a colourless liquid HBF_4, used in the synthesis of fluoroborates. Also, **hydrofluoboric acid, fluoboric acid** (flōōə bŏ′rĭk).

fluorocarbon (flōōə′rō kä′bən), *n.* *Chem.* any of a class of compounds made by substituting fluorine for hydrogen in a hydrocarbon and characterized by great chemical stability. They are used as lubricants, fire-extinguishers, and in industrial applications in which resistance to heat, radioactivity, etc., is essential.

fluorophosphate (flōōə′rō fŏs′fāt), *n.* *Chem.* a salt or ester of fluorophosphoric acid. Also, **fluophosphate** (flōōə fŏs′fāt).

fluorophosphoric acid (flōōə′rō fŏs fŏ′rĭk), *Chem.* any of the three acids H_2PO_3F (*mono-*), HPO_2F_2 (*di-*), or HPF_6 (*hexa-*). Also, **fluophosphoric acid** (flōōə′fŏs fŏ′rĭk).

fluoroscope (flōōə′rə skōp′), *n.* a tube or box, fitted with a screen coated with a fluorescent substance, used for viewing objects exposed to X-rays or other radiation directed to, or focused upon, the screen. [f. FLUOR-² + -(O)SCOPE]

fluoroscopic (flōōə′rə skŏp′ĭk), *adj.* pertaining to the fluoroscope or to fluoroscopy. —**fluor′oscop′ically,** *adv.*

fluoroscopy (flōōə rŏs′kə pĭ), *n.* the act of using the fluoroscope, or of examining by means of a fluorescent screen, the shadows of bodies shown up by X-rays; screening.

fluorosilicate (flōōə′rō sĭl′ĭ kāt′, -kĭt), *n.* *Chem.* a salt of fluorosilicic acid. Also, **fluosilicate** (flōōə sĭl′ĭ kāt′, -kĭt).

fluorosilicic acid (flōōə′rō sĭ lĭs′ĭk), *Chem.* an unstable acid, H_2SiF_6, used in aqueous solution or in the form of its salts as a wood preservative, disinfectant, and hardening agent.

fluorspar (flōōə′spä′), *n.* a common mineral, calcium fluoride, CaF_2, occurring in colourless, green, blue, purple, and yellow crystals, usually in cubes: the principal source of fluorine. It is also used as a flux in metallurgy and for ornamental purposes. Also, **fluor;** *Chiefly U.S.*, **fluorite.**

Fluothane (flōōə′thān), *n.* *Trademark.* halothane, a general inhalant anaesthetic.

flurry (flŭ′rĭ), *n.*, *pl.* **-ries,** *v.*, **-ried, -rying.** —*n.* **1.** a sudden gust of wind. **2.** a light gusty shower or snowfall. **3.** commotion; sudden excitement or confusion; nervous hurry. **4.** *Stock Exchange.* a brief agitation in prices. —*v.t.* **5.** to put (a person) into a flurry; make nervous; confuse; fluster. [b. FLUTTER and HURRY]

flush¹ (flŭsh), *n.* **1.** a blush; a rosy glow. **2.** a rushing or overspreading flow, as of water. **3.** a rush of emotion; elation: *the first flush of success, of victory.* **4.** glowing freshness or vigour: *the flush of youth.* **5.** the hot stage of a fever. **6.** *Colloq.* an arrangement or mechanism for flushing drains, etc. —*v.t.* **7.** to redden; cause to blush or glow. **8.** to flood with water, as for cleansing purposes; wash out (a sewer, etc.). **9.** to animate or elate. —*v.i.* **10.** to blush; redden. **11.** to flow with a rush; flow and spread suddenly. [b. FLASH and GUSH; in some senses further blended with BLUSH] —**flush′er,** *n.*

flush² (flŭsh), *adj.* **1.** even or level, as with a surface; in one plane. **2.** well-supplied, as with money; affluent; prosperous. **3.** abundant or plentiful, as money. **4.** flushed with colour; blushing. **5.** full of vigour; lusty. **6.** quite full; full to overflowing. **7.** *Naut.* (of a deck) unbroken by deckhouses, etc., and having an even surface fore and aft or from stem to stern. **8.** *Print.* even or level with the right or left margins of the type page; without an indentation. —*adv.* **9.** so as to be flush or even. —*v.t.* **10.** to make flush or even. **11.** to fill or cover with mortar or cement. —*v.i.* **12.** to send out shoots, as plants in spring. —*n.* **13.** a fresh growth, as of shoots and leaves. [special use of FLUSH¹]

flush³ (flŭsh), *Hunting.* —*v.t.* **1.** to rouse and cause to start up or fly off: *to flush a woodcock.* —*v.i.* **2.** to fly out or start up suddenly. —*n.* **3.** a flushed bird, or flock of birds. [ME *flussh*, orig. uncert.]

flush⁴ (flŭsh), *Cards.* —*adj.* **1.** consisting entirely of cards of one suit: *a flush hand.* —*n.* **2.** a hand or set of cards all of one suit. See **royal flush, straight flush.** [cf. F (obs.) *flus*, var. of *flux* flow, flush (cf. E *run* of cards), t. L: s. *fluxus* FLUX]

Flushing (flŭsh′ing), *n.* a seaport in the SW Netherlands, on Walcheren Island. 28,856 (1964). Dutch, **Vlissingen.**

fluster (flŭs′tə), *v.t.* **1.** to confuse; make nervous. **2.** to excite and confuse with drink. —*v.i.* **3.** to become confused; become agitated or flurried. —*n.* **4.** confusion; flurry; nervous excitement. [cf. Icel. *flaustr* hurry, bustle and cf. BLUSTER]

flustrate (flŭs′trāt), *v.t.*, **-trated, -trating.** *Colloq.* to fluster. —**flustration** (flŭs trā′shən), *n.*

flute (flōōt), *n.*, *v.*, **fluted, fluting.** —*n.* **1.** a musical wind instrument consisting of a tube with a series of fingerholes or keys, in which the wind is directed against a sharp edge, either directly, as in the modern orchestral transverse flute, or through a flue, as in the recorder. **2.** an organ stop with wide flue pipes, having a flutelike tone. **3.** one who plays the flute; a flautist. **4.** *Archit.*, *etc.* a channel or furrow with a rounded section, as in a pillar. **5.** a groove in any material, as in a woman's ruffle. —*v.i.* **6.** to produce or utter flutelike sounds. **7.** to play a flute. —*v.t.* **8.** to utter in flutelike tones. **9.** to form longitudinal flutes or furrows in. [ME *flowte*, t. OF: m. *fleüte*, t. Pr.: m. *flauta*, ult. der. L *flātus*, pp., blown] —**flute′like′,** *adj.*

Flute

fluted (flōō′tĭd), *adj.* **1.** having flutes or grooves, as a pillar. **2.** fine, clear and mellow; flutelike: *fluted notes.*

fluter (flo͞o′tə), *n.* **1.** one who makes flutings. **2.** *Obs.* a flautist.

flutiness (flo͞o′tĭ nĭs), *n.* the quality of being fluty.

fluting (flo͞o′tĭng), *n.* **1.** fluted work; furrows up and down, as on a Corinthian column. **2.** a flute, groove, or furrow. **3.** the act of making flutes. **4.** the act of playing on the flute. **5.** the sound made by such playing; a flutelike sound.

fluting iron, a specially shaped iron for pressing ruffles, etc., into a fluted form.

flutist (flo͞o′tĭst), *n.* *Now Chiefly U.S.* flautist.

flutter (flŭt′ə), *v.i.* **1.** to flap or wave lightly in air, as a flag. **2.** (of birds, etc.) to flap or attempt to flap the wings, or fly with flapping movements. **3.** to move in quick, irregular motions. **4.** to beat fast and irregularly, as the heart. **5.** to be tremulous or agitated. **6.** to go with irregular motions or aimless course. **7.** *Swimming.* (of the feet) to move alternately up and down as a means of propulsion, as in the crawl and backstroke. —*v.t.* **8.** to cause to flutter; vibrate; agitate. **9.** to confuse; throw into a state of nervous excitement, mental agitation, or tremulous excitement. **10.** *Swimming.* to cause (the feet) to flutter. **11.** *Colloq.* to wager (a small amount). —*n.* **12.** a fluttering movement. **13.** a state of nervous excitement or mental agitation. **14.** sensation; stir: *to cause or make a flutter.* **15.** a rapid variation in pitch fidelity resulting from fluctuations in the speed of a recording. **16.** *Swimming.* flutter-kick. **17.** *Colloq.* a small wager or bet. [ME *floteren,* OE *floterian,* freq. of *flotian* float] —**flut′terer,** *n.* —**flut′teringly,** *adv.* —**Syn. 2.** See **fly**[1].

flutter-kick (flŭt′ə kĭk′), *n.* *Swimming.* the up-and-down movements of the legs in the crawl.

flutter-tongue (flŭt′ə tŭng′), *n.* a musical effect caused by trilling on wind instruments such as the flute and trumpet.

fluttery (flŭt′ə rĭ), *adj.* fluttering; apt to flutter.

fluty (flo͞o′tĭ), *adj.,* **-tier, -tiest.** flutelike, as in tone.

fluvial (flo͞o′vyəl), *adj.* of, pertaining to, or produced by a river. [t. L: s. *fluviālis,* der. *fluvius* river]

fluviatile (flo͞o′vĭ ə tĭl′, -tīl), *adj.* pertaining or peculiar to rivers; found in or near rivers. [t. L: m. s. *fluviātilis,* der. *fluvius* river]

flux (flŭks), *n.* **1.** a flowing or flow. **2.** the flowing in of the tide. **3.** continuous passage; continuous change: *to be in a state of flux.* **4.** *Pathol.* **a.** an abnormal or morbid discharge of blood or other matter from the body. **b.** dysentery (**bloody flux**). **5.** *Physics.* **a.** the rate of flow of a fluid, heat, or the like. **b.** luminous flux. **c.** magnetic flux. **d.** (in nuclear physics) the product of the number of particles per unit volume and their average velocity. **6.** *Chem., Metall., etc.* **a.** a substance, as borax or fluorspar, used to promote the fusion of metals or minerals. **b.** a non-metallic substance, as a salt or mixture of salts, used to protect the surface of molten metal from oxidation. **c.** (in the refining of scrap or other metal) a salt or mixture of salts which combines with non-metallic impurities, causing them to float or coagulate. **7.** fusion. —*v.t.* **8.** to melt; fuse; make fluid. **9.** *Obs.* to purge. —*v.i.* **10.** to flow. [ME, t. L: s. *fluxus* a flowing]

flux density, *Physics.* the magnetic or electric flux per unit of cross-sectional area.

fluxion (flŭk′shən), *n.* *Obs.* **1.** the act of flowing; a flow or flux. **2.** *Maths.* the derivative relative to the time, the rate of change of a varying quantity. —**flux′ional, fluxionary** (flŭk′shə nə rĭ), *adj.* —**flux′ionally,** *adv.*

fluxmeter (flŭks′mē′tə), *n.* *Physics.* an instrument for measuring magnetic flux.

fly[1] (flī), *v.,* **flew, flown, flying,** *n., pl.* **flies.** —*v.i.* **1.** to move through the air on wings, as a bird. **2.** to be borne through the air by the wind or any other force or agency. **3.** to float or flutter in the air, as a flag, the hair, etc. **4.** to travel through the air in an aircraft or as an aircraft does. **5.** to move or pass swiftly; move with a start or rush. **6.** to make an attack by flying, as a hawk does. **7.** to change rapidly and unexpectedly from one state to another: *to fly open.* **8.** to flee. **9. fly high,** to be ambitious. **10. fly in the face of,** to defy insultingly. **11. fly off the handle,** *Colloq.* to lose one's temper, esp. unexpectedly. **12. fly out,** *Colloq.* to lose one's temper; become suddenly violently angry. **13. let fly,** to make an attack, esp. verbal. —*v.t.* **14.** to cause to fly: *to fly a model aeroplane, a kite, a hawk.* **15.** to operate (an aircraft or spacecraft). **16.** to hoist aloft or bear aloft: *to fly a flag.* **17.** to travel over by flying. **18.** to transport by flying. **19.** to avoid; flee from. **20.** *Theat.* **a.** to raise (scenery) into the flies. **b.** to suspend (scenery) above a stage from the flies by means of wire rigging, etc. **21. fly a kite, a.** *Colloq.* to attempt to obtain reactions without disclosing one's true purpose. **b.** *U.S. Slang.* to undertake some other activity: *go fly a kite.* **22. fly at,** to attack. **23. let fly, a.** to throw or propel. **b.** to give free rein to, esp. in attacking: *he let fly his pent-up anger.* —*n.* **24.** a strip sewn along one edge of a garment, to aid in concealing the buttons or other fasteners. **25.** a flap forming the door of a tent. **26.** a piece of canvas extending over the ridgepole of a tent and forming an outer roof. **27.** the act of flying; a flight. **28.** *U.S.* the course of a flying object, as a ball. **29.** a light, single-horsed public carriage for passengers. **30.** *Mach.* a flywheel. **31.** *Horol.* a regulating device for chime and striking mechanisms, consisting of an arrangement of vanes on a revolving axis. **32.** *Print.* **a.** a contrivance for receiving and delivering separately printed sheets from a press. **b.** (formerly) one who removed printed matter from a press. **33.** the extent of a flag from the staff to the outer end, or the outer end itself. **34.** (*pl.*) *Theat.* the space and apparatus above the stage. **35. on the fly,** *U.S.* **a.** while still in flight; on the volley. **b.** hurriedly. [ME *flien,* OE *flēogan,* c. D *vliegen,* G *fliegen*]

—**Syn. 1.** FLY, FLIT, FLUTTER, HOVER, SOAR refer to moving through the air as on wings. FLY is the general term: *birds fly, aeroplanes fly.* To FLIT is to make short rapid flights from place to place: *a bird flits from tree to tree.* To FLUTTER is to agitate the wings tremulously, either without flying or in flying only short distances: *a young bird flutters out of a nest and in again.* To HOVER is to linger in the air, or to move over or about something within a narrow area or space: *hovering clouds, a hummingbird hovering over a blossom.* To SOAR is to (start to) fly upwards to a great height usually with little advance in any other direction, or else to (continue to) fly at a lofty height without visible movement of the wings: *above our heads great birds were soaring.*

fly[2] (flī), *n., pl.* **flies. 1.** any of the two-winged insects constituting the order *Diptera* (**true flies**), especially one of the family *Muscidae,* as the common housefly, *Musca domestica.* **2.** any of a number of other winged insects, as the mayfly or firefly. **3.** *Angling.* a fishhook dressed with silk, tinsel, etc., to resemble an insect. **4.** *S African.* a fly belt. **5. fly in the ointment,** a slight flaw that greatly diminishes the value or pleasure of something. **6. no flies on,** *Colloq.* **a.** not easily tricked; wary. **b.** *Obs.* honest. [ME *flye,* OE *flēoge, flȳge,* c. G *Fliege*] —**fly′less,** *adj.*

fly[3] (flī), *adj.* *Slang.* knowing; sharp. [? special use of FLY[1]]

flyable (flī′ə bl), *adj.* capable of being flown.

fly agaric, a very poisonous mushroom, *Amanita muscaria,* sometimes used for making a poison for flies.

fly-ash (flī′ăsh′), *n.* the fine ash produced from burning pulverized coal, found to have cement-like qualities in concrete and also sometimes used in brick-making.

fly-away (flī′ə wā′), *adj.* **1.** fluttering; streaming. **2.** flighty; volatile; frivolous.

flyback (flī′băk′), *n.* **1.** any instrument or device which resets itself rapidly, as a stopwatch. **2.** the act of resetting or returning to zero, as the return of the electron beam in a cathode-ray tube to its starting point after the completion of a line or trace.

fly ball, *Cricket, Baseball, etc.* a ball hit high into the air.

fly belt, (in southern Africa) an area infested with tsetse fly.

flyblow (flī′blō′), *v.t.* **1.** to deposit eggs or larvae on (meat). —*n.* **2.** the egg or young larva (maggot) of a blowfly, deposited on meat, etc.

flyblown (flī′blōn′), *adj.* **1.** tainted with flyblows. **2.** spoilt; corrupt.

flyboat (flī′bōt′), *n.* a fast vessel, esp. one designed for use on canals. [t. D: m. *vlieboot*]

flybook (flī′bo͝ok′), *n.* *Angling.* a booklike case for artificial flies.

fly-by-night (flī′bī nīt′), *Colloq.* —*adj.* **1.** irresponsible; unreliable. —*n.* **2.** a person who leaves secretly at night, as in order to avoid paying his debts. **3.** one who leads a gay night-life.

flycatcher (flī′kăch′ə), *n.* any of numerous small, insectivorous birds of the Old World family *Muscicapidae,* as the **spotted flycatcher,** *Muscicapa grisola,* of Europe.

flyer (flī′ə), *n.* flier.

fly-fish (flī′fĭsh′), *v.i.* *Angling.* to fish with artificial flies as bait. —**fly′-fish′er,** *n.* —**fly′-fish′ing,** *n.*

fly-floor (flī′flô′), *n.* *Theat.* a gallery running alongside the flies, where lines controlling the scenery, etc., are worked. Also, **fly-gallery** (flī′găl′ə rĭ).

fly half, *Rugby Football.* stand-off half.

fly honeysuckle, a deciduous caprifoliaceous shrub with yellowish paired flowers, *Lonicera xylosteum,* growing in woods and hedges throughout Europe, N and W Asia.

flying (flī′ĭng), *adj.* **1.** that flies; making flight or passing through the air: *a flying insect.* **2.** floating, fluttering or waving, or hanging or moving freely, in the air: *flying banners, flying hair.* **3.** extending through the air. **4.** moving swiftly. **5.** made while moving swiftly. **6.** hasty: *a flying trip.* **7.** designed for swiftness. **8.** fleeing, running away, or taking flight. 9. *Naut.* (of a sail) having none of its edges bent to spars or stays. —*n.* 10. the act of moving through the air on wings; flight.

flying boat, an aircraft, whose main body consists of a single hull or boat, that can take off and land on water.

flying bomb, a gyroscopically steered, winged bomb, powered by a pulse jet, used in World War II.

flying buttress, a segmental arch which carries the thrust of a wall over a space to a solid pier buttress. See illus. under **buttress.**

flying circus, *Colloq.* a group of aircraft operating together performing aerobatic manoeuvres.

flying column, *Mil.* (formerly) a force of troops equipped and organized to move swiftly and independently of a principal unit to which it is attached.

flying colours, 1. flags borne aloft. 2. triumphant success.

flying doctor, a medical practitioner operating an aerial service as one covering inland Australia.

flying dragon, flying lizard.

Flying Dutchman, 1. a legendary spectral Dutch ship supposed to be seen at sea, esp. near the Cape of Good Hope. 2. the captain of this ship, supposed to have been condemned to sail the sea, beating against the wind, till the Day of Judgement.

flying field, an airfield.

flying fish, 1. any of certain fishes with winglike pectoral fins which help them to glide for some distance through the air after leaping from the water, esp. of the family *Exocoetidae,* as *Exocoetus volitans.* 2. (*cap.*) *Astron.* the southern constellation Volans.

flying fox, 1. any large fruit-eating bat of the family *Pteropodidae,* esp. of the genus *Pteropus,* as *P. edulis,* of Old World tropical regions, having a foxlike head. 2. *Austral.* a cable-operated carrier over difficult country.

flying gurnard, any of several fishes of the family *Dactylopteridae,* esp. *Dactylopterus volitans,* having winglike pectoral fins, though apparently not able to fly.

flying jib, a triangular sail set outside of the jib. See illus. under **sail.**

flying kites, *Naut.* the lightest and highest sails on a sailing ship, set only in light or moderate winds.

flying lemur, a lemur-like mammal having a broad fold of skin on each side of the body to act as a wing in gliding from tree to tree. The species *Cynocephalus temminckii* is distributed over SE Asia and the East Indies, *Cynocephalus volans* in the Philippine area. They are the only representatives of the order *Dermoptera.*

flying lizard, any of the arboreal lizards of the genus *Draco* of south-eastern Asia and the East Indies, with extensible membranes along the sides by means of which they make long gliding leaps from tree to tree. Also, **flying dragon.**

flying machine, a contrivance which sustains itself in, and propels itself through, the air; an aeroplane or the like.

flying mare, *Wrestling.* a method of attack in which a wrestler grasps the wrist or head of his opponent, turns in the opposite direction, and throws him over his shoulder and down.

flying officer, a commissioned rank in the Royal Air Force above that of pilot officer and below flight lieutenant; equivalent to army lieutenant.

flying phalanger, any of a number of small phalangers of Australia and New Guinea having a parachute-like fold of skin at each side to give gliding assistance in leaping.

Flying phalanger, *Schoinobates volans* (Total length 3 ft, tail 1½ ft)

flying saucer, any of various disc-shaped objects allegedly seen flying at high speeds and altitudes.

flying shore, one of a set of horizontal supports of timber or metal, placed between two gable walls for support where a building in between has been demolished.

flying squad, 1. a detachment of police organized for special tasks, esp. in emergencies. 2. a special detachment of any other organization.

flying squirrel, a squirrel-like animal, esp. of the genus *Glaucomys,* as *G. volans* of the eastern U.S., with folds of skin connecting the fore and hind legs, enabling it to take long gliding leaps.

Flying squirrel, *Glaucomys volans* (Total length 10 in. to 1 ft, tail 4 in.)

flying start, 1. a start to a race by which competitors may approach the starting line at speed, but are disqualified or recalled if they cross it before the starting signal is given. 2. *Colloq.* a great advantage: *his first-hand knowledge of Italy gave him a flying start over other candidates.*

flying tackle, *Sport.* a dive at an opponent, usually at his legs, to unbalance him.

flying wing, an aircraft in which the fuselage forms an integral part of the wing structure.

flyleaf (flī′lēf′), *n., pl.* **-leaves** (-lēvz′). a blank leaf in the front or at the back of a book.

fly line, a line used in fly-fishing.

fly-loft (flī′lŏft′), *n.* the portion of a theatre building above the stage into which scenery may be raised.

flyman (flī′mən), *n., pl.* **-men.** *Theat.* a stagehand, esp. one who operates the apparatus in the flies.

fly-net (flī′nĕt′), *n.* a fringe or net to protect a horse from flies.

fly orchid, a European orchid with root-tubers and slender spikes of greenish brown flowers, *Ophrys insectifera.*

flyover (flī′ō′və), *n.* an intersection of two roads in which one is carried over the other on a bridge.

flypaper (flī′pā′pə), *n.* paper prepared to destroy flies by poisoning them or by catching them on its sticky surface.

fly-past (flī′päst′), *n.* a ceremonial flight of aircraft over a given point.

fly rail, a bracket that swings out to support the drop leaf of a table.

Fly River (flī), a river flowing from central New Guinea SE to the Gulf of Papua. ab. 650 mi.

fly rod, a light, flexible rod used in fly-fishing, usually made up in three pieces.

flyspeck (flī′spĕk′), *n.* 1. a speck or tiny stain from the excrement of a fly. 2. a minute spot. —*v.t.* 3. to mark with flyspecks.

flyte (flīt), *v.i.,* **flyted, flyting,** *n. Scot. and N Dial.* flite.

flytrap (flī′trăp′), *n.* 1. any of various plants which entrap insects, esp. Venus's flytrap. 2. a trap for flies.

flyweight (flī′wāt′), *n.* a boxer of 8 st. or less, lighter than a featherweight and a bantamweight.

flywheel (flī′wēl′), *n. Mach.* 1. a heavy wheel which by its momentum tends to equalize the speed of machinery with which it is connected. 2. a wheel used to carry the piston over dead centre.

FM, *Radio.* frequency modulation.

Fm, *Chem.* fermium.

fm, 1. fathom. 2. from.

F.M., field marshal.

f number, *Photog.* the ratio of the focal length of a lens system to its effective diameter: used to number aperture openings in a camera.

F.O., 1. field officer. 2. flying officer. 3. Foreign Office.

foal (fōl), *n.* 1. the young of the horse, ass, or any allied animal; a colt or filly. —*v.t., v.i.* 2. to bring forth (a foal). [ME *fole,* OE *fola,* c. OHG *folo*]

foam (fōm), *n.* 1. an aggregation of minute bubbles formed on the surface of a liquid by agitation, fermentation, etc. 2. the froth of perspiration formed on the skin of a horse or other animal from great exertion. 3. froth formed in the mouth, as in epilepsy and rabies. 4. a substance which on being discharged from a fire-extinguisher forms a layer of small stable bubbles. —*v.i.* 5. to form or gather foam; emit foam; froth. 6. **foam at the mouth,** to be speechless with some emotion, esp. with rage, etc. —*v.t.* 7. to cause to foam. [ME *fome,* OE *fām,* c. G *Feim*] —**foam′ingly,** *adv.* —**foam′less,** *adj.*

foamflower (fōm′flou′ə), *n.* a North American saxifragaceous herb, *Tiarella cordifolia,* which bears white flowers in the spring.

foam rubber, rubber so processed that it is light, firm, and spongy, used for mattresses, in furniture, for protective cushioning, etc.

foamy (fō′mĭ), *adj.,* **foamier, foamiest.** 1. covered with or full of foam. 2. consisting of foam. 3. resembling foam. 4. pertaining to foam. —**foam′ily,** *adv.* —**foam′iness,** *n.*

fob[1] (fŏb), *n.* 1. a small pocket just below the waistline in trousers or breeches (formerly in the waistband) to hold a watch, etc. 2. a short chain or ribbon with a seal or the like, attached to a watch and worn hanging from the pocket. [orig. unknown. Cf. d. HG *fuppe* pocket, *fuppen* to pocket stealthily]

fob[2] (fŏb), *v.t.,* **fobbed, fobbing.** 1. to palm off (fol. by *off*): *to fob off an inferior watch on a person.* 2. to put off (fol. by *off*): *to fob one off with promises.* 3. *Archaic.* to cheat; deceive. [akin to FOB[1]. Cf. G *foppen* deceive]

f.o.b., free on board.

focal (fō′kl), *adj.* of or pertaining to a focus. —**fo′cally,** *adv.*

focal infection, *Pathol., Dentistry.* an infection in which the bacteria are localized in some region, as the tissue round a tooth or a tonsil, from which they often spread to some other organ or structure of the body.

focalize (fōʹkə līzʹ), *v.t.*, **-lized, -lizing.** focus. Also, **focalise.** —foʹcalizaʹtion, *n.*

focal length, *Optics.* **1.** (of a mirror or lens) the distance from the optical centre to the focal point. **2.** (of a telescope) the distance between the object lens and its corresponding focal plane.

focal plane, *Optics.* **1.** the plane normal to the principal axis of a lens (or system of lenses) or a mirror, which passes through the focal point. **2.** the plane in which light rays from an external object are focused in a camera. **3.** the transverse plane in a telescope where the real image of a distant view is in focus.

focal plane shutter, *Photog.* a camera shutter, consisting of a roller blind with a slot in it, which is situated as close to the plate or film as possible.

focal point, 1. Also, **principal focus.** *Optics.* the focus for a beam of light rays parallel to the principal axis of a lens or mirror. **2.** *Colloq.* the main point of interest, agreement, disagreement, etc.

Foch (*Fr.* fŏsh), *n.* **Ferdinand** (*Fr.* fĕr dē näNʹ), 1851–1929, French marshal.

focsle (fōkʹsəl), *n.* forecastle. Also, **fo'c'sle.**

focus (fōʹkəs), *n.*, *pl.* **-ci** (-sī), **-cuses,** *v.*, **-cused, -cusing,** or **-cussed, -cussing.** —*n.* **1.** *Physics.* a point at which rays of light, heat, or other radiation, meet after being refracted or reflected. **2.** *Optics.* **a.** a point from which diverging rays appear to proceed, or a point at which converging rays would meet if they could be prolonged in the same direction (**virtual focus**). **b.** the focal length of a lens. **c.** clear and sharply defined condition of an image. **d.** the position of a viewed object, or the adjustment of an optical device, necessary to produce a clear image: *in focus, out of focus.* **3.** a central point, as of attraction, attention, or activity. **4.** *Geom.* one of the points from which the distances to any point of a given curve are in a linear relation. See diag. under **parabola. 5.** *Geol.* the point where an earthquake starts. **6.** *Pathol.* the primary centre from which a disease develops or in which it localizes. —*v.t.* **7.** to bring to a focus or into focus. **8.** to concentrate; to focus one's attention. —*v.i.* **9.** to become focused. [t. L: hearth, fireplace] —foʹcusable, *adj.* —foʹcuser, *n.*

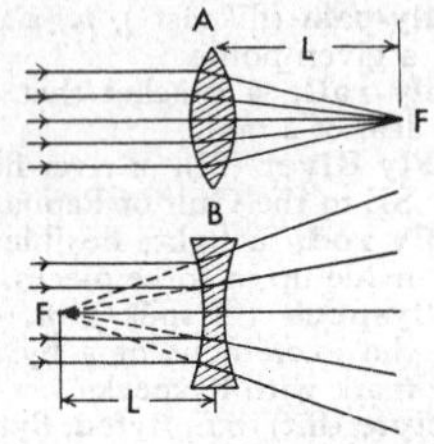

F, Focus; L, Focal length; A, Convex lens; B, Concave lens

fodder (fŏdʹə), *n.* **1.** food for livestock, esp. dried food, as hay, straw, etc. —*v.t.* **2.** to feed with or as with fodder. [ME; OE *fodder, fōdor,* c. G *Futter;* akin to FOOD] —**Syn. 1.** See **feed.**

fodgel (fŏjʹəl), *adj. Scot.* fat; stout; plump.

foe (fō), *n.* **1.** one who entertains enmity, hatred, or malice against another; an enemy. **2.** an enemy in war; hostile army. **3.** one belonging to a hostile army or nation. **4.** an opponent in a game, or contest. **5.** a person who is opposed in feeling, principle, etc., to something: *a foe to progress.* **6.** a thing that is opposed to or destructive of: *cleanliness is a foe to infection.* [ME *foo,* OE (*ge*)*fā*(*h*) enemy (absolute use of adj. meaning hostile). See FEUD[1]] —**Syn. 1.** See **enemy.**

foehn (fûn; *Ger.* fœn), *n. Meteorol.* föhn.

foeman (fōʹmən), *n.*, *pl.* **-men.** *Lit.* an enemy in war.

foetal (fēʹtl), *adj. Embryol.* of, pertaining to, or having the character of a foetus. Also, *Chiefly U.S.*, **fetal.**

foetation (fē tāʹshən), *n. Embryol.* pregnancy; gestation. Also, *Chiefly U.S.*, **fetation.**

foeticide (fēʹtĭ sīdʹ), *n.* the destruction of the life of a foetus. Also, *Chiefly U.S.*, **feticide.** [f. s. L *foetus* + -(I)CIDE] —foeʹticidʹal, *adj.*

foetid (fēʹtĭd), *adj.* fetid.

foetor (fēʹtə), *n.* fetor.

foetus (fēʹtəs), *n. Embryol.* the young of an animal in the womb or in the egg, esp. in its later stages. Also, *Chiefly U.S.*, **fetus.** [t. L: a bringing forth, offspring, young]

fog[1] (fŏg), *n.*, *v.*, **fogged, fogging.** —*n.* **1.** *Meteorol.* a cloudlike mass or layer of minute globules of water in the air near the earth's surface; thick mist. **2.** any darkened state of the atmosphere, or the diffused substance which causes it. **3.** a state of mental confusion or obscurity: *a fog of doubt.* **4.** *Photog.* a darkening of the whole or of parts of a developed plate or print from sources other than image-forming light in the camera. **5.** *Phys. Chem.* a colloidal system consisting of liquid particles dispersed in a gaseous medium. —*v.t.* **6.** to envelop with, or as with fog. **7.** *Photog.* to affect (a negative or print) by fog. **8.** to confuse; perplex; bewilder. —*v.i.* **9.** to become enveloped or obscured with, or as with, fog. **10.** *Photog.* to be affected by fog. [backformation from FOGGY. See FOG[2]] —**fogʹless,** *adj.* —**Syn. 3.** See **cloud.**

fog[2] (fŏg), *n.* **1.** a second growth of grass, as after mowing. **2.** long grass left standing in fields during the winter. [ME *fogge,* t. Scand.; cf. Norw. *fogg* long grass on damp ground, and obs. E *foggy* marshy]

fogbank (fŏgʹbăngkʹ), *n.* a stratum of fog as seen from a distance.

fogbound (fŏgʹboundʹ), *adj. Naut.* unable to navigate due to heavy fog.

fogey (fōʹgĭ), *n.*, *pl.* **-geys.** fogy.

foggage (fŏgʹĭj), *n. Chiefly Dial.* fog[2].

Foggia (*It.* fôdʹjä), *n.* a city in S Italy, in Apulia. 134,046 (1966).

foggy (fŏgʹĭ), *adj.*, **-gier, -giest. 1.** abounding in or thick with fog; misty. **2.** resembling fog; dim; obscure. **3.** *Photog.* affected by fog. [der. FOG[2]; orig. meaning marshy, thick, murky] —**fogʹgily,** *adv.* —**fogʹginess,** *n.*

foghorn (fŏgʹhônʹ), *n.* **1.** *Naut.* a horn for sounding warning signals, as to vessels, in foggy weather. **2.** *Colloq.* a deep, loud voice.

fog lamp, *Motor Vehicles.* a lamp designed to penetrate fog, light up the nearside kerb, etc.

fogram (fōʹgrəm), *adj.* **1.** old-fashioned; excessively conservative. —*n.* **2.** a fogy.

fog signal, any of various devices used as a warning by vehicles or vessels in fog.

fogy (fōʹgĭ), *n.*, *pl.* **-gies.** an old-fashioned or excessively conservative person (usually prec. by *old*). Also, **fogey.**

föhn (fûn; *Ger.* fœn), *n. Meteorol.* a hot, dry wind descending a mountain, in the valleys on the north side of the Alps. Also, **foehn.** [t. G, t. Romansh: m. *favugn,* g. L *Favōnius*]

foible (foiʹbl), *n.* **1.** a weak point or whimsy; a weakness or failing of character. **2.** the weaker part of a sword blade, between the middle and the point. [t. F, obs. form of *faible* FEEBLE] —**Syn. 1.** See **fault.**

foil[1] (foil), *v.t.* **1.** to frustrate (a person, an attempt, a purpose); baffle; balk. **2.** *Archaic.* to defeat; repulse; check. —*n.* **3.** *Archaic.* a defeat; check; repulse. [ME *foile(n),* t. OF: m. *fuler* trample, full (cloth). See FULL[2]]

foil[2] (foil), *n.* **1.** a metallic substance formed into very thin sheets by rolling and hammering: *gold, tin, aluminium, or lead foil.* **2.** the metallic backing applied to glass to form a mirror. **3.** a thin layer of metal placed under a gem in a closed setting, to improve its colour or brilliancy. **4.** anything that serves to set off another thing distinctly or to advantage by contrast. **5.** *Archit.* an arc or a rounded space between cusps, as in the tracery of a window or in other ornamentation. The number of foils varies, as in **trefoil** and **multifoil.** —*v.t.* **6.** to cover or back with foil. **7.** *Archit.* to ornament with foils. **8.** to set off by contrast. [ME *foile,* t. OF: m. *foil,* g. L *folium* leaf; akin to Gk *phýllon*]

Foils[2] (def. 5)
A, Trefoil; B, Quatrefoil

foil[3] (foil) *n.* **1.** a flexible, thin sword with a button at the point, for use in fencing. **2.** (*pl.*) the art of exercise or fencing with such swords. [orig. uncert.]

foilsman (foilzʹmən), *n.*, *pl.* **-men.** one who is expert at fencing with foils.

foin (foin), *Obs. or Archaic.* —*n.* **1.** a thrust with a weapon. —*v.i.* **2.** to thrust with a weapon; lunge. [appar. t. OF: m. *foine* fish spear, g. L *fuscina*]

foison (foiʹzən), *n. Archaic.* **1.** abundance; plenty. **2.** abundant harvest. [ME, t. OF, ult. der. L *fūsio* a pouring out]

foist (foist), *v.t.* **1.** to palm off or impose fraudulently or unwarrantably (fol. by *on* or *upon*): *to foist inferior goods on a customer.* **2.** to bring or put surreptitiously or fraudulently (fol. by *in* or *into*). [prob. t. D: m. *vuisten* to take in hand]

Foix (*Fr.* fwȧ), *n.* a town in S France, in Ariège department. 8900 (est. 1968).

Fokine (*Fr.* fō kēnʹ; *Russ.* fôʹkĭn), *n.* **Michel** (*Fr.* mē shĕlʹ), 1880–1942, Russian ballet-dancer and choreographer, in the U.S. from 1925.

Fokker (fŏkʹə; *Du.* fôkʹər), *n.* **Anthony Herman Gerard** (*Du.* ȧn tōʹnē hĕrʹmȧn KHēʹrōrt), 1890–1939, Dutch aeroplane designer and builder.

fol., 1. folio. **2.** followed. **3.** following.

fold[1] (fōld), *v.t.* **1.** to double or bend (cloth, paper, etc.) over upon itself. **2.** to bring into a compact form, or shut, by bending and laying parts together (often fol. by *up*): *to fold up a map.* **3.** to bring together (the arms, hands, legs, etc.) with one round another: *to fold one's arms on one's chest.* **4.** to bend or wind (fol. by *about, round,* etc.): *to fold one's arms about a person's neck.* **5.** to bring (the wings) close to the body, as a bird on alighting. **6.** to enclose; wrap: *to fold something in paper.* **7.** to clasp or embrace: *to fold someone in one's arms.* **8.** *Cookery.* to mix (*in*), as beaten eggwhites added to a batter or the like, by gently turning one part over another with a spoon, etc. *—v.i.* **9.** to be folded or be capable of folding: *the doors fold back.* **10.** to be closed or brought to an end, usually with financial loss, as a business enterprise or theatrical production. **11. fold up, a.** to collapse. **b.** to fail in business. *—n.* **12.** a part that is folded; pleat; layer: *to wrap something in folds of cloth.* **13.** a hollow made by folding: *to carry something in the fold of one's dress.* **14.** a crease made by folding. **15.** a hollow place in undulating ground: *a fold of the hills or mountains.* **16.** *Geol.* a portion of strata which is folded or bent (as an anticline or syncline), or which connects two horizontal or parallel portions of strata of different levels (as a monocline). **17.** a coil of a serpent, string, etc. **18.** an act of folding or doubling over. [ME *folde(n),* d. OE *faldan,* r. OE *fealdan,* c. G *falten*]

fold[2] (fōld), *n.* **1.** an enclosure for domestic animals, esp. sheep. **2.** the sheep contained in it. **3.** a flock of sheep. **4.** a church or congregation. **5. return to the fold,** to return, as to an accepted standard of behaviour. *—v.t.* **6.** to confine (sheep, etc.) in a fold. [ME *folde,* OE *fald, falod,* c. LG *falt* enclosure, yard]

-fold, a suffix attached to numerals and other quantitative words or stems to denote multiplication by or division into a certain number, as in *twofold, manifold.* [ME; d. OE *-fald,* r. OE *-feald,* c. G *-falt;* akin to Gk *-paltos,* as in *dipaltos* double]

foldboat (fōld′bōt′), *n.* faltboat.

folder (fōl′də), *n.* **1.** one who or that which folds. **2.** a folded printed sheet, as a circular or a timetable. **3.** an outer cover, usually a folded sheet of light cardboard, for papers.

folderol (fŏl′də rŏl′), *n.* falderal.

folding doors, a set of doors hinged together to fold flat against one another when opened.

fold mountains, mountains formed by massive folding and uplift as a result of compression in the earth's crust.

folia (fō′lĭ ə), *n.* pl. of **folium.**

foliaceous (fō′lĭ ā′shəs), *adj.* **1.** of the nature of a leaf; leaf-like. **2.** bearing leaves or leaf-like parts. **3.** pertaining to or consisting of leaves. **4.** consisting of leaf-like plates or laminae; foliated. [t. L: m. *foliāceus* leafy]

foliage (fō′lĭ ĭj), *n.* **1.** the leaves of a plant, collectively; leafage. **2.** leaves in general. **3.** the representation of leaves, flowers, and branches in architectural ornament, etc. [t. F: alter. (to conform to L *folium*) of *feuillage,* der. *feuille,* g. L *folium* leaf] **—fo′liaged,** *adj.*

foliar (fō′lĭ ə), *adj.* of, pertaining to, or having the nature of a leaf or leaves.

foliate (*adj.* fō′lĭ ĭt, -āt′; *v.* fō′lĭ āt′), *adj., v.,* **-ated, -ating.** *—adj.* **1.** having or covered with leaves. **2.** leaf-like. **3.** *Archit.* foliated (def. 3). *—v.i.* **4.** to put forth leaves. **5.** to split into thin leaf-like layers or laminae. *—v.t.* **6.** to shape like a leaf or leaves. **7.** to decorate with foils or foliage. **8.** to form into thin sheets. **9.** to spread over with a thin metallic backing. **10.** to number leaves (not pages) of (a book). [t. L: m. s. *foliātus* leafy]

foliated (fō′lĭ ā′tĭd), *adj.* **1.** shaped like a leaf or leaves. **2.** *Crystall.* consisting of thin and separable laminae. **3.** *Archit.* Also, **foliate. a.** ornamented with or composed of foils. **b.** ornamented with representations of foliage.

foliation (fō′lĭ ā′shən), *n.* **1.** the act of foliating or putting forth leaves. **2.** the state of being in leaf. **3.** *Bot.* the arrangement of leaves within the bud. **4.** leaves or foliage. **5.** the consecutive numbering of the leaves (not pages) of a book or manuscript. **6.** the total number of such leaves. **7.** *Geol.* the splitting up or the arrangement of certain rocks, or certain kinds of rocks, in leaf-like layers. **8.** ornamentation with foliage, or an arrangement of foliage. **9.** *Archit.* ornamentation with foils, or tracery so formed. **10.** formation into thin sheets. **11.** the application of foil to glass.

foliature (fō′lĭ ə chə), *n.* a cluster of leaves; foliage.

folic acid (fō′lĭk), *Biochem.* one of the B complex of vitamins that is used in the treatment of certain types of anaemia. [f. L FOL(IUM) leaf + -IC]

Foligno (*It.* fō lēn′nyō), *n.* a town in Italy, in Umbria. 50,051 (1966).

folio (fō′lĭ ō′), *n., pl.* **-lios,** *adj., v.,* **-lioed, -lioing.** *—n.* **1.** a sheet of paper folded once to make two leaves (four pages) of a book. **2.** a volume having pages of the largest size. **3.** a leaf of a manuscript or book numbered only on the front side. **4.** *Print.* the page number of a book. **5.** *Bookkeeping.* a page of an account book or a left-hand page and a right-hand page facing each other and having the same serial number. **6.** *Law.* a certain number of words (in Britain usually 72, or 90 for wills, in the U.S. generally 100) taken as a unit for computing the length of a document. *—adj.* **7.** pertaining to or having the format of a folio: a folio volume. *—v.t.* **8.** to number the leaves of (a book) on one side only. **9.** *Law.* to mark each folio in (a pleading, etc.) with the proper number. [t. L, abl. of *folium* leaf]

foliolate (fō′lĭ ə lāt′, fō lĭə′lĭt, -lāt′), *adj. Bot.* pertaining to or consisting of leaflets (often used in compounds, as *bifoliolate, trifoliolate,* etc.). [t. NL: m. s. *foliolātus,* der. *foliolum* a leaflet, dim. of L *folium* leaf]

foliose (fō′lĭ ōs′), *adj. Bot.* leafy. [t. L: m. s. *foliōsus*]

-folious, *Bot.* an adjective suffix meaning 'leafy'. [t. L: m. s. *foliōsus*]

folium (fō′lĭ əm), *n., pl.* **-lia** (-lĭ ə). **1.** a thin leaf-like stratum or layer; a lamella. **2.** *Geom.* a loop; part of a curve terminated at both ends by the same node. [t. L: leaf. See FOIL[2]]

folk (fōk), *n., pl.* **folk, folks,** *adj. —n.* **1.** people in general, esp. the common people. **2.** (*usually pl.*) people of a specified class or group: *poor folks.* **3.** (*pl.*) *Colloq.* the persons of one's own family; one's relatives. **4.** *Archaic.* a people or tribe. *—adj.* **5.** originating among the common people. **6.** of or pertaining to a folk song or folk singer. [ME; OE *folc,* c. D *volk,* G *Volk,* Sw. and Dan. *folk* people]

folk dance, **1.** a dance which originated among, and has been transmitted through, the common people. **2.** a piece of music for such a dance.

Folkestone (fōk′stən), *n.* a seaport and resort in SE England, in Kent, on the Straits of Dover. 44,154 (1961).

Folketing (fōl′kə tĭng; *Dan.* fōl′gə tĕng), *n.* the Danish parliament; formerly the lower house.

folk etymology, a type of pseudo-learned modification of linguistic forms according to a falsely assumed etymology, as in *Welsh rarebit* from *Welsh rabbit.*

folklore (fōk′lô′), *n.* **1.** the lore of the common people; the traditional beliefs, legends, customs, etc., of a people. **2.** the study of such lore. **—folk′lor′ist,** *n.* **—folk′loris′tic,** *adj.*

folkmoot (fōk′mo͞ot′), *n.* (formerly, in England) a general assembly of the people of a shire, town, etc. Also, **folkmote** (fōk′mōt′), **folk′mot′.** [ME; OE *folcmōt* folk meeting]

folk music, music, usually of simple character, originating and handed down among the common people.

folkright (fōk′rīt′), *n. Early Eng. Hist.* the right of the people under the customary law.

folk singer, one who sings folk songs.

folk song, **1.** a song, usually of simple or artless character, originating and handed down among the common people. **2.** a song in imitation of this type.

folksy (fōk′sĭ), *adj.* **1.** *Colloq.* rustic or imitative of the rustic. **2.** *U.S. Colloq.* sociable; friendly; unceremonious.

folktale (fōk′tāl′), *n.* a tale or legend originating and handed down among the common people. Also, **folk story.**

folkways (fōk′wāz′), *n.pl. Sociol.* the ways of living and acting in a human group, built up without conscious design but serving as compelling guides of conduct.

foll., following.

follicle (fŏl′ĭ kl), *n.* **1.** *Bot.* a dry one-celled seed vessel consisting of a single carpel, and dehiscent only by the ventral suture, as the fruit of larkspur. **2.** *Anat.* a small cavity, sac, or gland. [t. L: m. s. *folliculus,* dim. of *follis* bellows, bag]

Follicle of larkspur

follicular (fŏ lĭk′yo͞o lə), *adj.* **1.** pertaining to, consisting of, or resembling a follicle or follicles; provided with follicles. **2.** *Pathol.* pertaining to a follicle. Also, **folliculate** (fŏ lĭk′yo͞o lāt′), **follic′ulat′ed.**

folliculin (fŏ lĭk′yo͞o lĭn), *n.* oestrone.

follow (fŏl′ō), *v.t.* **1.** to come after in natural sequence, order of time, etc.; succeed. **2.** to go or come after; move behind in the same direction: *go on ahead and I'll follow you.* **3.** to accept as a guide or leader; accept the authority or example of, or adhere to, as a person. **4.** to conform to, comply with, or act in accordance with: *to follow a person's advice.* **5.** to imitate or copy. **6.** to move forward along (a path, etc.). **7.** to come after as a result or consequence; result from: *it follows from this that he must be innocent.* **8.** to go after or along with

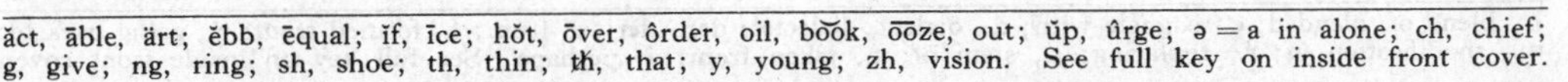

(a person, etc.) as a companion. **9.** to go in pursuit of: *to follow an enemy.* **10.** to endeavour to obtain or to attain to. **11.** to engage in or be concerned with as a pursuit: *to follow the sea.* **12.** to watch the movements, progress, or course of. **13.** to keep up to date with; observe the development of: *to follow the news.* **14.** to keep up with and understand (an argument, etc.): *do you follow me?* **15. follow out,** to execute; carry out to a conclusion. **16. follow through, a.** to carry out completely as a stroke in tennis or golf. **b.** to pursue an endeavour to its conclusion. **17. follow suit, a.** *Cards.* to play a card of the same suit as that first played. **b.** to follow the example of another. **18. follow up, a.** to pursue closely. **b.** to pursue to a conclusion. **c.** to take further action, investigation, etc., after the elapse of an interval of time; reopen. **d.** to increase the effect of by further action. *—v.i.* **19.** to come next after something else in natural sequence, order of time, etc. **20.** to happen or occur after something else; come next as an event. **21.** to attend. **22.** to go or come after a person or thing in motion: *go on ahead and I'll follow.* **23.** to result as an effect; occur as a consequence. *—n.* **24.** an act of following. **25.** *Billiards.* a stroke causing the player's ball to roll after the ball struck by it. [ME *folwe(n)*, OE *folgian*, c. G *folgen*] —**fol'lowable,** *adj.*

—**Syn. 9.** pursue, chase; trail, track, trace. **19.** FOLLOW, ENSUE, RESULT, SUCCEED imply coming after something else, in a natural sequence. FOLLOW is the general word: *we must wait to see what follows, a detailed account follows.* ENSUE implies a logical sequence, what might be expected normally to come after a given act, cause, etc., and indicates some duration: *when the power lines were cut, a crisis ensued.* RESULT emphasizes the connection between a cause or event and its effect, consequence, or outcome: *the accident resulted in injuries to those involved.* SUCCEED implies coming after in time, particularly coming into a title, office, etc.: *a son often succeeds to his father's title.* —**Ant. 1.** precede. **23.** cause.

follower (fŏl'ō ə), *n.* **1.** one who or that which follows. **2.** one who follows another in regard to his ideas or belief; disciple or adherent. **3.** a person who copies or imitates: *a dedicated follower of fashion.* **4.** an attendant or servant. **5.** *Obs.* a male admirer of a young woman. **6.** *Mach.* a part of a machine that receives motion from, or follows the motion of, another part.

—**Syn. 2.** FOLLOWER, ADHERENT, PARTISAN refer to one who demonstrates allegiance to a person, a doctrine, a cause, and the like. FOLLOWER often has an implication of personal relationship or of slavish acquiescence. ADHERENT, a more formal word, has also implications of more active championship of a person or a point of view. PARTISAN, ordinarily meaning a person prejudiced and unreasoning in adherence to a party, during World War II took on the meaning of a member of certain groups in occupied countries of Europe, who carried on underground resistance.

following (fŏl'ō ĭng), *n.* **1.** a body of followers, attendants, adherents, etc. **2. the following,** things, lines, pages, etc., that follow. *—adj.* **3.** that follows. **4.** that comes after or next in order or time: *the following day.* **5.** that is now to follow; now to be mentioned, described, related, or the like.

follow-my-leader (fŏl'ō mĭ lē'də), *n.* a children's game in which the players follow the actions and speech of the leader.

follow-on (fŏl'ō ŏn'), *n.* *Cricket.* an immediate second batting innings forced on a team which in the first innings scores less than half the runs scored by the opposing team.

follow-through (fŏl'ō thro͞o'), *n.* *Sport.* **1.** the completion of a motion, as in the stroke of a tennis racket or golf club. **2.** the portion of such a motion after the ball has been hit.

follow-up (fŏl'ō ŭp'), *n.* **1.** the act of following up. **2.** a letter or circular sent to a person to increase the effectiveness of a previous one, as in advertising. **3.** *Journalism.* a story providing further information on a news item already published. **4.** *Med.* an examination of a patient some time after initial treatment, in order to assess progress. *—adj.* **5.** (of business letters, etc.) sent to a prospective customer to obtain an additional order or offer.

folly (fŏl'ĭ), *n., pl.* **-lies. 1.** the state or quality of being foolish; lack of understanding or sense. **2.** a foolish action, practice, idea, etc.; an absurdity. **3.** *Archit.* a useless but costly structure, often in the form of a sham Gothic or classical ruin; especially popular in 18th-century England. **4.** (*pl.*) a theatrical revue. **5.** *Obs.* wickedness; wantonness. [ME *folie*, t. OF, der. *fol* mad. See FOOL[1]]

Folsom man (fŏl'səm), a member of a hypothetical New World prehistoric people which may have inhabited North America during the most recent (Pleistocene) glacial epoch. [so named from *Folsom*, New Mexico, where implements were discovered in 1925]

Fomalhaut (fō'mə lōt'), *n.* a star of the first magnitude in the constellation Southern Fish.

foment (fə mĕnt'), *v.t.* **1.** to promote the growth or development of; instigate or foster (discord, rebellion, etc.). **2.** to apply warm water or medicated liquid, cloths dipped in such liquid, or the like, to (the surface of the body). [t. LL: s. *fōmentāre*, der. L *fōmentum* a warm application] —**foment'er,** *n.*

fomentation (fō'mĕn tā'shən), *n.* **1.** instigation; encouragement of discord, rebellion, etc. **2.** the application of warm liquid, etc., to the surface of the body. **3.** the liquid, etc., so applied.

fomes (fō'mēz), *n., pl.* **fomites** (fō'mĭ tēz'), a substance, as bedding or clothing (but not food), capable of transmitting infection. [L: touchwood, tinder]

fond[1] (fŏnd), *adj.* **1.** liking (fol. by *of*): *fond of children, fond of drink.* **2.** loving: *give someone a fond look.* **3.** foolishly tender; over-affectionate; doting: *a fond parent.* **4.** cherished with strong or unreasoning affection: *nourish fond hopes.* **5.** *Archaic.* foolishly credulous or trusting. **6.** *Archaic or Dial.* foolish or silly. [ME *fonned*, pp. of *fonnen* be foolish; orig. uncert. Cf. FUN]

fond[2] (fŏnd; *Fr.* fôɴ), *n.* **1.** a background or groundwork, esp. of lace. **2.** *Obs.* fund; stock. [F. See FUND]

fondant (fŏn'dənt; *Fr.* fôɴ dăɴ'), *n.* **1.** a thick, creamy sugar paste, the basis of many sweets and icings. **2.** a sweet made of this paste. [t. F, prop. ppr. of *fondre* melt]

fondle (fŏn'dl), *v.,* **-dled, -dling.** *—v.t.* **1.** to handle or touch fondly; caress. **2.** *Obs.* to treat with fond indulgence. *—v.i.* **3.** to show fondness, as by manner, words, or caresses. [freq. of obs. *fond*, v.] —**fon'dler,** *n.*

fondly (fŏnd'lĭ), *adv.* **1.** in a fond manner; lovingly or affectionately. **2.** with complacent credulity.

fondness (fŏnd'nĭs), *n.* **1.** the state or quality of being fond. **2.** affectionateness or tenderness. **3.** doting affection. **4.** instinctive liking. **5.** *Archaic.* complacent credulity.

fondue (fŏn'dyo͞o; *Fr.* fôɴ dʏ'), *n.* a baked dish composed of grated cheese melted with butter, eggs, etc. [t. F, fem. pp. of *fondre* melt]

font[1] (fŏnt), *n.* **1.** a receptacle, usually of stone, as in a baptistery or church, for the water used in baptism. **2.** a receptacle for holy water; stoup. **3.** the reservoir for oil in a lamp. **4.** *Archaic.* a fountain. [ME and OE, t. L: s. *fons* baptismal font, spring, fountain]

Font[1] (def. 1)

font[2] (fŏnt), *n.* *U.S.* fount[2].

Fontainebleau (fŏn'tĭn blō'; *Fr.* fôɴ tĕn blȯ'), *n.* a town in N France, in Seine-et-Marne, SE of Paris: famous palace, long a favourite residence of French kings; extensive forest. 22,704 (1963).

Fontainebleau School, a group of painters, many of them Italian and Flemish, who worked on the decorations of the palace of Fontainebleau in the sixteenth century.

fontal (fŏn'tl), *adj.* **1.** pertaining to or issuing as from a fount or spring. **2.** pertaining to or being the source of something. **3.** of or pertaining to a font, as of baptism.

Fontana (fŏn tä'nə; *It.* fōn tä'nȧ), *n.* **Domenico** (*It.* dȯ mĕ'nē kȯ), 1543–1607, Italian architect.

Fontane (*Ger.* fŏn tä'nə), *n.* **Theodor** (*Ger.* tĕ'ȯ dōr), 1819–98, German poet, novelist, and essayist.

fontanelle (fŏn'tə nĕl'), *n.* *Anat.* one of the spaces, closed by membrane, between the bones of the foetal or young skull. Also, *Chiefly U.S.*, **fontanel.** [t. F: (fem.) dim. of *fontaine* FOUNTAIN]

Fontenelle (*Fr.* fôɴt nĕl'), *n.* **Bernard le Bovier de** (*Fr.* bĕr nȧr lə bȯ vyĕ' də), 1657–1757, French writer.

Fonteyn (fŏn tān'), *n.* **Dame Margot** (mä'gō) (*Margaret Hookham; Mrs Roberto Arias*), born 1919, English ballerina.

Foochow (fo͞o'chou'), *n.* a seaport in SE China: the capital of Fukien province. 623,000 (est. 1958).

food (fo͞od), *n.* **1.** what is eaten, or taken into the body, for nourishment. **2.** more or less solid nourishment (as opposed to *drink*). **3.** a particular kind of solid nourishment: *a breakfast food.* **4.** whatever supplies nourishment to organic bodies: *the food of plants.* **5.** anything serving as material for consumption or use: *food for thought.* [ME *fode*, OE *fōda*. Cf. FEED, FODDER, FOSTER] —**food'less,** *adj.*

—**Syn. 1.** FOOD, FARE, PROVISIONS, RATION(S) refer to nutriment for any organism, whether of man, animal, or plant. FOOD is the general word: *breakfast foods have become very popular, many animals prefer grass as food.* FARE refers to the whole range of foods which may nourish person, animal, or plant: *an extensive bill of fare, the fare of some animals is limited in range.* PROVISIONS is applied to a store or stock of necessary things, esp. food, prepared beforehand: *provisions for a journey.* RATION implies an allotment or allowance of provisions: *a daily ration for each man of a company.* RATIONS often mean food in general: *to be on short rations.*

Food and Agriculture Organization, the United Nations agency that administers development programmes for increase in food production, etc., in underdeveloped countries. *Abbrev.:* FAO.

food chain, *Ecol.* a series of organisms interrelated in their feeding habits, the smallest being fed upon by a larger one, which in turn feeds a still larger one, etc.

food poisoning (fo͞od′poi′zə nĭng, -poiz′nĭng), **1.** an acute illness caused by eating contaminated food, usually presenting gastrointestinal symptoms. It may be due to the ingestion of organisms, as salmonellae or toxins, formed by organisms as in staphylococcal food poisoning; or to organic insecticides present in the food. **2.** an illness caused by eating naturally poisonous substances such as poisonous mushrooms and berries.

foodstuff (fo͞od′stŭf′), *n.* a substance or material suitable for food.

food web, *Ecol.* a series of organisms related by predator–prey activities; a series of interrelated food chains.

fool[1] (fo͞ol), *n.* **1.** one who lacks sense; a silly or stupid person. **2.** a professional jester, formerly kept by a person of rank for amusement. **3.** one who is made to appear a fool; one who has been imposed on by others: *to make a fool of someone.* **4.** a weak-minded or idiotic person. *—v.t.* **5.** to make a fool of; impose on; trick; deceive. **6.** to spend foolishly, as time or money (fol. by *away*). *—v.i.* **7.** to act like a fool; joke; play. **8.** to potter, aimlessly; waste time: *to fool around with minor details.* **9.** to philander, or trifle with: *fooling around with a woman old enough to be his mother.* **10.** to play or meddle foolishly (fol. by *with*): *to fool with a loaded gun.* **11.** to jest; make believe: *I was only fooling.* [ME *fol*, t. OF (n. and adj.), ? g. L *follis* bellows, LL bag] **—Syn. 1.** simpleton, dolt, dunce, blockhead, numskull, ignoramus, dunderhead, ninny, nincompoop, booby, saphead, sap. **2.** buffoon, droll. **5.** delude, hoodwink, trick, cheat, gull, hoax, cozen. **8.** play, trifle, toy, dally, idle, dawdle, loiter, tarry.

fool[2] (fo͞ol), *n. Cookery.* a dish made of fruit stewed, made into a puree, and mixed with thick cream or custard: *gooseberry fool.* [prob. special use of FOOL[1]]

foolery (fo͞o′lə rĭ), *n., pl.* **-eries. 1.** foolish action or conduct. **2.** a foolish action, performance, or thing.

foolhardy (fo͞ol′hä′dĭ), *adj.*, **-dier, -diest.** bold without judgement; foolishly rash or venturesome. **—fool′har′dily,** *adv.* **—fool′har′diness,** *n.*

foolish (fo͞o′lĭsh), *adj.* **1.** silly; without sense: *a foolish person.* **2.** resulting from or evidencing folly; ill-considered; unwise: *a foolish action, speech, etc.* **3.** *Obs. or Archaic.* trifling, insignificant, or paltry. **—fool′ishly,** *adv.* **—fool′ishness,** *n.*

—Syn. 1, 2. FOOLISH, FATUOUS, SILLY, STUPID imply weakness of intellect and lack of judgement. FOOLISH implies lack of common sense or good judgement or, sometimes, weakness of mind: *a foolish decision, the child seems foolish.* FATUOUS implies being foolish, dull, and vacant in mind, but complacent and highly self-satisfied: *fatuous and self-important, fatuous answers.* SILLY denotes extreme and conspicuous foolishness; it may also refer to pointlessness of jokes, remarks, etc.: *silly and senseless behaviour, a perfectly silly statement.* STUPID implies natural slowness or dullness of intellect, or, sometimes, a benumbed or dazed state of mind; it is also used to mean foolish or silly: *well-meaning but stupid, rendered stupid by a blow, it is stupid to do such a thing.* **—Ant. 1.** wise, intelligent.

foolproof (fo͞ol′pro͞of′), *adj. Colloq.* **1.** involving no risk or harm, even when tampered with. **2.** never-failing: *a foolproof method.*

foolscap (fo͞olz′kăp′), *n.* **1.** a printing paper size, 13½ × 17 inches (so called from its former watermark, the outline of a fool's cap). **2.** *U.S.* writing paper, usually folded, varying in size from 12 × 15 to 12 × 16 inches. **3.** fool's cap.

fool's cap, 1. a kind of cap or hood, usually hung with bells, formerly worn by professional jesters. **2.** a conical paper cap sometimes worn by dunces at school as punishment.

fool's errand, an absurd or useless errand.

fool's gold, iron pyrites, sometimes mistaken for gold.

fool's paradise, a state of illusory happiness; enjoyment based on false beliefs or hopes.

fool's parsley, a fetid, poisonous umbelliferous herb, *Aethusa cynapium*, resembling parsley.

fool's watercress, an aquatic, perennial, umbelliferous herb, *Apium nodiflorum*, widely distributed in temperate regions and sometimes mistaken for the true watercress.

foot (fo͝ot), *n., pl.* **feet** or (*often for def. 20*) **foots,** *v.* *—n.* **1.** (in vertebrates) the terminal part of the leg, below the ankle joint, on which the body stands and moves. **2.** (in invertebrates) any part similar in position or function. **3.** such a part considered as the organ of locomotion. **4.** a unit or length derived from the length of the human foot: it is divided into 12 inches and equal to 30·48 centimetres. **5.** *Music.* **a.** a unit of measurement of a vibrating air column. **b.** the sound produced by such a length, as an eight-foot tone. **6.** infantry. **7.** walking or running motion. **8.** step; pace. **9.** any thing or part resembling a foot, as in function. **10.** (of furniture) a shaped or ornamented part terminating the leg. **11.** the flaring base or rim of a glass, teapot, etc. **12.** the part of a stocking, etc., covering the foot. **13.** the lowest part, or bottom, as of a hill, ladder, page, etc. **14.** the part of anything opposite the top or head. **15.** the end of a bed, grave, etc., towards which the feet are placed. **16.** *Print.* the part of the type body which forms the sides of the groove, at the base. **17.** the last, as of a series. **18.** *Obs.* that which is written at the bottom, as the total of an account. **19.** *Pros.* a group of syllables constituting a metrical unit of a verse. **20.** (*pl. often* **foots**) sediment or dregs. **21.** Some special noun phrases are:

at one's feet, 1. captive; at one's mercy. **2.** utterly devoted to one.

fall on one's feet, to be lucky.

feet first, dead.

get off on the right (or **wrong**) **foot,** to have a good (or bad) start.

have one foot in the grave, to be near death.

on foot, 1. on one's feet, rather than riding or sitting. **2.** in motion; astir. **3.** in active existence or operation.

put one's best foot forward, 1. to make as good an impression as possible. **2.** to do one's very best. **3.** to walk as fast as possible.

put one's foot down, to take a firm stand.

put one's foot in it, to make an embarrassing blunder.

put or **set someone on his feet, 1.** to enable someone to act without help from others; make someone financially independent. **2.** to restore someone to a former position or condition.

set foot in, to enter; go in.

set on foot, to start (something) going; originate.

stand on one's own feet, to be self-sufficient.

sweep off one's feet, 1. to cause someone to lose a footing, as a wave, etc. **2.** to impress or overwhelm.

—v.i. **22.** to walk; go on foot (often fol. by indefinite *it*). **23.** to move the feet to measure or music, or dance (often fol. by indefinite *it*). **24.** to total, as an account (fol. by *up*).

—v.t. **25.** to set foot on; walk or dance on. **26.** to traverse on foot. **27.** to make or attach a foot to: *to foot a stocking.* **28.** *Colloq. and Dial.* to add, as a column of figures, and set the sum at the foot (fol. by *up*). **29.** *Colloq.* to pay or settle, as a bill. **30.** to seize with talons, as a hawk. **31.** to establish. **32.** *Obs.* to kick. *—interj.* **33. my foot!** nonsense! (used as an exclamation of disbelief).

[ME; OE *fōt*, c. G *Fuss*; akin to L *pēs*, Gk *poús*]

footage (fo͝ot′ĭj), *n.* **1.** length or extent in feet: *the footage of timber.* **2.** *Mining.* **a.** payment by the running foot of work done. **b.** amount so paid. **3.** a length of film; the film used for a scene or scenes.

foot-and-mouth disease (fo͝ot′ən mouth′), *Vet. Sci.* a a contagious virus disease of cattle and other cloven-hoofed animals, characterized by a vesicular eruption about the hoofs and mouth. The disease very rarely affects man.

football (fo͝ot′bôl′), *n.* **1.** association football. **2.** Rugby football. **3.** American football. **4.** the ball itself used in these games. **—foot′bal′ler,** *n.*

Football Association, the body responsible for the organization and administration of association football in England.

Football League, 1. the governing body of all major professional association football clubs in England and Wales. **2.** the group of association football clubs governed by this body.

football pools, organized gambling on the results of football matches; the pools.

footbath (fo͝ot′bäth′), *n.* **1.** the act of bathing the feet. **2.** an apparatus for this purpose.

footboard (fo͝ot′bôd′), *n.* **1.** a board or small platform on which to support the foot or feet. **2.** an upright piece across the foot of a bedstead. **3.** a treadle.

footboy (fo͝ot′boi′), *n.* a boy in livery employed as a servant; page; lackey.

footbrake (fo͝ot′brāk′), *n.* a brake which is applied by pressure on a foot pedal.

footbridge (fo͝ot′brĭj′), *n.* a bridge intended for pedestrians only.

foot-candle (fo͝ot′kăn′dl), *n.* a unit of illumination equivalent to that produced by a standard candle at the distance of one foot: equivalent to one lumen per square foot.

footcloth (fo͝ot′klŏth′), *n.* **1.** *Archaic.* a carpet or rug. **2.** *Obs.* a richly ornamented caparison for a horse, hanging down to the ground.

footdrop (fo͝ot′drŏp′), *n. Pathol.* abnormal dropping of the foot, due to paralysis of the anterior leg muscles.

footed (fo͝ot′ĭd), *adj.* provided with a foot or feet: *a four-footed animal.*
footer (fo͝ot′ə), *n.* **1.** one who goes on foot; a walker. **2.** (with a numeral prefixed) a person or thing of the height or length in feet indicated: *a six-footer.* **3.** *Slang.* **a.** association football. **b.** Rugby football.
footfall (fo͝ot′fôl′), *n.* **1.** a footstep. **2.** the sound of footsteps.
foot-fault (fo͝ot′fôlt′), *Tennis.* —*n.* **1.** a service fault caused by the server failing to keep both feet behind the baseline before the ball is hit, or to keep at least one foot on the ground while serving. —*v.t.* **2.** to declare guilty of a foot-fault. —*v.i.* **3.** to commit a foot-fault.
footgear (fo͝ot′gīə′), *n.* covering for the feet, as shoes, boots, etc.
foothill (fo͝ot′hĭl′), *n.* a minor elevation at the base of a mountain or mountain range.
foothold (fo͝ot′hōld′), *n.* **1.** a hold or support for the feet; a place where one may stand or tread securely. **2.** firm footing; secure position.
footing (fo͝ot′ĭng), *n.* **1.** a secure position; foothold. **2.** the basis or foundation on which anything is established. **3.** a place or support for the feet; surface to stand on. **4.** the act of one that foots, or moves on foot, as in walking or dancing. **5.** a firm placing or stable position of the feet. **6.** the part of the foundation of wall, column, etc., that is in direct contact with the ground. **7.** position or status assigned to a person, etc., in estimation or treatment. **8.** mutual standing; reciprocal relation: *to be on a friendly footing with someone.* **9.** entrance into a new position or relationship. **10.** a fee demanded from a person upon his entrance into a trade, society, etc. **11.** the act of putting a foot to anything, as a stocking. **12.** that which is added as a foot. **13.** the act of adding up a column of figures. **14.** the amount of such a column as footed up.
footle (fo͞o′tl), *v.*, **-tled, -tling,** *n.* —*v.t.* **1.** to talk or act in a silly way. —*n.* **2.** nonsense; silliness. [orig. obscure. Cf. FOOTY, FOOZLE]
footless (fo͝ot′lĭs), *adj.* **1.** without a foot or feet. **2.** unsupported or unsubstantial. **3.** *U.S. Colloq.* awkward, helpless, or inefficient.
footlights (fo͝ot′līts′), *n.pl.* **1.** *Theat.* a row of lights at the front of the stage, nearly on a level with the feet of the performers. **2.** *Colloq.* the stage; acting profession.
footling (fo͝ot′lĭng), *adj. Colloq.* foolish; silly; trifling. [f. FOOTLE, V. + -ING[2]]
footloose (fo͝ot′lo͞os′), *adj.* free to go or travel about: not confined by responsibilities, etc.
footman (fo͝ot′mən), *n.*, *pl.* **-men. 1.** a male servant in livery who attends the door or the carriage, waits at table, etc. **2.** a metal stand before a fire, to keep something hot. **3.** *Obs.* a foot soldier.
footmark (fo͝ot′mäk′), *n.* a footprint.
footnote (fo͝ot′nōt′), *n.*, *v.*, **-noted, -noting.** —*n.* **1.** a note or comment at the foot of a page, referring to a specific part of the text on the page. **2.** an added comment, of less importance than the main text. —*v.t.* **3.** to add footnotes to a text.
footpace (fo͝ot′pās′), *n.* **1.** a walking pace. **2.** a raised portion of a floor. **3.** a landing or resting place at the end of a short flight of steps.
footpad (fo͝ot′păd′), *n.* a highwayman who robs on foot.
footpath (fo͝ot′päth′), *n.* a path for pedestrians only.
footplate (fo͝ot′plāt′), *n.* a platform in a locomotive on which the crew stand.
foot-plateman (fo͝ot′plāt′mən), *n.*, *pl.* **-men** (-mən). a driver or fireman of a railway locomotive.
foot-pound (fo͝ot′pound′), *n. Mech.* a unit of energy or work, the equivalent to that produced by a force of one pound moving through a distance of one foot.
foot-poundal (fo͝ot′poun′dl), *n. Mech.* a unit of energy equivalent to that produced by a force of one poundal moving through a distance of one foot.
foot-pound-second system (fo͝ot′pound sĕk′ənd), a system of units employed in science, based on the foot, pound, and second as the fundamental units of length, mass, and time.
footprint (fo͝ot′prĭnt′), *n.* a mark left by the foot.
footrest (fo͝ot′rĕst′), *n.* a low bench or stool used to support one's feet.
footrope (fo͝ot′rōp′), *n. Naut.* **1.** the portion of the boltrope to which the lower edge of a sail is sewn. **2.** a rope extended under a yard, for the men to stand on while reefing or furling.
footrot (fo͝ot′rŏt′), *n. Vet. Sci.* an infection of the feet of sheep, causing inflammatory changes of the toes and lameness.
foot rule, a ruler one foot in length.
foot-scraper (fo͝ot′skrā′pə), *n.* a metal grid set in a frame for cleaning mud off the bottoms of shoes before entering a house.
foot-slog (fo͝ot′slŏg′), *v.i. Colloq.* to march or tramp; slog on foot. —**foot′-slog′ger,** *n.*
foot soldier, an infantryman.
footsore (fo͝ot′sô′), *adj.* having sore or tender feet, as from much walking.
footstalk (fo͝ot′stôk′), *n. Bot., Zool.* a pedicel; peduncle.
footstall (fo͝ot′stôl′), *n.* **1.** the stirrup of a woman's side-saddle. **2.** *Archit.* the plinth or base of a pillar.
footstep (fo͝ot′stĕp′), *n.* **1.** a step or tread of the foot, or the sound produced by it; footfall. **2.** the distance traversed by the foot in stepping; a pace. **3.** a footprint. **4.** a step by which to ascend or descend. **5. follow in one's footsteps,** to succeed or imitate another.
footstock (fo͝ot′stŏk), *n.* tailstock.
footstool (fo͝ot′sto͞ol′), *n.* a low stool upon which to rest one's feet.
foot-ton (fo͝ot′tŭn′), *n. Mech.* a unit of work equivalent to the energy expended in raising a ton of 2240 lbs one foot.
foot-up (fo͝ot′ŭp′), *n. Rugby Football.* the illegal raising of the hooker's foot in a scrum before the ball has been put in.
footwall (fo͝ot′wôl′), *n. Mining.* the top of the rock stratum underlying a vein or bed of ore.
foot-warmer (fo͝ot′wô′mə), *n.* any of various contrivances for keeping the feet warm.
footway (fo͝ot′wā′), *n.* a way or path for pedestrians only.
footwear (fo͝ot′wĕə′), *n.* articles for wearing on the feet, esp. boots, shoes, slippers, etc.
footwork (fo͝ot′wûk′), *n.* **1.** the use of the feet, as in tennis, boxing, etc. **2.** skilful manoeuvring.
footworn (fo͝ot′wôn′), *adj.* **1.** worn by the feet: *a footworn pavement.* **2.** footsore.
footy (fo͞o′tĭ), *adj.*, **-tier, -tiest.** *Dial. or Colloq.* poor; worthless; paltry. [der. FOOT (def. 20)]
foozle (fo͞o′zəl), *v.*, **-zled, -zling,** *n.* —*v.t., v.i.* **1.** to bungle; play clumsily: *to foozle a stroke in golf.* —*n.* **2.** an act of foozling, esp. a bad stroke in golf. [cf. d. G *fuseln* work badly]
fop (fŏp), *n.* a man who is excessively concerned about his manners and appearance. [orig. uncert. Cf. FOB[2]]
foppery (fŏp′ə rĭ), *n.*, *pl.* **-peries. 1.** the manners, actions, dress, etc., of a fop. **2.** something foppish.
foppish (fŏp′ĭsh), *adj.* resembling or befitting a fop. —**fop′pishly,** *adv.* —**fop′pishness,** *n.*
for (fô; *unstressed* fə), *prep.* **1.** with the object or purpose of: *to go for a walk.* **2.** intended to belong to, suit the purposes or needs of, or be used in connection with: *a book for children, a box for gloves.* **3.** in order to obtain: *a suit for damages.* **4.** with inclination or tendency towards: *to long for a thing, to have an eye for beauty.* **5.** (as expressing a wish or desire for something to be obtained): *O for the wings of a dove.* **6.** in consideration of, or in return for: *three for a shilling, to be thanked for one's efforts.* **7.** appropriate or adapted to: *a subject for speculation.* **8.** with regard or respect to: *pressed for time, too warm for April.* **9.** during the continuance of: *for a long time.* **10.** in favour of, or on the side of: *to stand for honest government.* **11.** in place of, or instead of: *a substitute for butter.* **12.** in the interest of: *to act for a client.* **13.** as an offset to: *blow for blow.* **14.** in honour of: *to give a dinner for a person.* **15.** in punishment of: *fined for stealing.* **16.** with the purpose of reaching: *to start for London.* **17.** conducive to: *for the advantage of everybody.* **18.** in order to save: *to flee for one's life.* **19.** in order to become: *to go for a soldier.* **20.** in assignment or attribution to: *an engagement for this evening, it is for you to decide.* **21.** to allow of; to require: *too many for separate mention.* **22.** such as results in: *his reason for going.* **23.** as affecting the interests or circumstances of: *bad for one's health.* **24.** in proportion or with reference to: *tall for his age.* **25.** in the character of, or as being: *to know a thing for a fact.* **26.** by reason of, or because of: *to shout for joy, famed for its beauty.* **27.** in spite of: *for all that.* **28.** to the extent or amount of: *to walk for a mile.* **29.** (sometimes used to govern a noun or pronoun followed by an infinitive, in a construction equivalent to a clause with *that* and the auxiliary *should*, etc.): *it is time for him to go, or that he should go.* **30. for it,** *Slang.* about to suffer some punishment, injury, setback, or the like. **31. for to,** *Archaic.* in order to; to. —*conj.* **32.** seeing that; since. **33.** because. [ME and OE; c. OS *for*; akin to *fore*, adv. and prep.] —**Syn. 33.** See **because.**
for-, a prefix meaning 'away', 'off', 'to the uttermost', 'extremely', 'wrongly', or imparting a negative or privative force, occurring in words of Old or Middle English origin, many of which are now obsolete or archaic, as in *forswear, forbid.* [ME and OE. Cf. G *ver-*, Gk *peri-*, L *per-*]
for., **1.** foreign. **2.** forestry.

f.o.r., free on rail.

forage (fŏ′rĭj), *n.*, *v.*, **-raged, -raging.** —*n.* **1.** food for horses and cattle; fodder; provender. **2.** the seeking or obtaining such food. **3.** the act of searching for provisions of any kind. **4.** a raid. —*v.i.* **5.** to wander in search of supplies. **6.** to hunt or search about. **7.** to make a raid. —*v.t.* **8.** to collect forage from: strip of supplies; plunder. **9.** to supply with forage. **10.** to obtain by foraging. [ME, t. F: m. *fourrage*, der. OF *fuerre* fodder, t. Gmc (see FODDER)] —**for′ager,** *n.* —**Syn. 1.** See **feed.**

forage cap, an undress military cap.

foramen (fŏ rā′mĕn), *n.*, *pl.* **-ramina** (-răm′ĭ nə). an opening, orifice, or short passage, as in a bone or in the integument of the ovule of a plant. [t. L: hole]

foramen magnum (măg′nəm), *Latin.* the great hole in the occipital bone forming the passage from the cranial cavity to the spinal canal. [L: lit., great hole]

foraminate (fŏ răm′ĭ nĭt, -nāt′), *adj.* full of holes or foramina. Also, **foram′inous.**

foraminifer (fŏ′rə mĭn′ĭ fə), *n.* any of the *Foraminifera*, an extensive order of small, mostly marine rhizopods commonly having a calcareous shell perforated in many species by small holes or pores. [f. s. L *forāmen* hole + -(I)FER] —**foraminiferal** (fŏ răm′ĭ nĭf′ə rəl), **foram′inif′erous,** *adj.*

forasmuch (fə rəz mŭch′), *conj.* in view of the fact that; seeing that; since (fol. by *as*).

foray (fŏ′rā), *n.* **1.** a raid for the purpose of taking plunder. —*v.i.* **2.** to make a raid; forage; pillage. —*v.t.* **3.** to ravage in search of plunder. [ME *forrei(en)*, back-formation from *forreier* FORAYER]

forayer (fŏ′rā ə), *n.* a marauder. [ME *forreier*, t. OF: m. *forrier* forager]

forbade (fə băd′), *v.* pt. of **forbid.** Also, **forbad** (fə băd′).

forbear[1] (fô bĕə′), *v.*, **-bore, -borne, -bearing.** —*v.t.* **1.** to refrain from; desist from; cease. **2.** to refrain from using, etc.; keep back; withhold. **3.** *Archaic.* to endure. —*v.i.* **4.** to refrain; hold back. **5.** to be patient; show forbearance. [ME *forbere(n)*, OE *forberan.* See FOR-, BEAR[1]] —**forbear′er,** *n.* —**forbear′ingly,** *adv.*

forbear[2] (fô′bĕə′), *n.* forebear.

forbearance (fô bĕə′rəns), *n.* **1.** the act of forbearing; a refraining from something. **2.** forbearing conduct or quality; patient endurance; lenity. **3.** an abstaining from the enforcement of a right. **4.** *Obs.* a creditor's giving of indulgence after the day originally fixed for payment.

Forbes-Robertson (fôbz′rŏb′ət sən), *n.* **Sir Johnston,** 1853–1937, English actor and theatre manager.

forbid (fə bĭd′), *v.t.*, **-bade** or **-bad, -bidden** or **-bid, -bidding.** **1.** to command (a person, etc.) not to do, have, use, etc., something, or not to enter some place. **2.** to put an interdiction against (something); prohibit. **3.** to hinder or prevent; make impossible. **4.** to exclude; repel. [ME *forbede(n)*, OE *forbēodan*] —**forbid′der,** *n.*

—**Syn. 1.** FORBID, INHIBIT, PROHIBIT, TABOO indicate a command to refrain from some action. FORBID, a common and familiar word, usually denotes a direct or personal command of this sort: *I forbid you to go, to forbid children to play in the park.* INHIBIT implies a checking or hindering of impulses by the mind: *to inhibit one's desires.* PROHIBIT, a formal or legal word, means usually to forbid by official edict, enactment, or the like: *to prohibit the sale of drugs.* TABOO, primarily associated with primitive superstition, means to prohibit by common disapproval and by social custom: *to taboo a subject in polite conversation.* —**Ant. 1.** permit.

forbiddance (fə bĭd′ns), *n.* *Rare.* **1.** the act of forbidding. **2.** the state of being forbidden.

forbidden (fə bĭd′n), *v.* **1.** pp. of **forbid.** —*adj.* **2.** prohibited.

forbidden fruit, 1. the fruit of the tree of knowledge, eaten by Adam and Eve in defiance of God. Gen. 2:17, 3:3. **2.** unlawful pleasure, esp. illicit sexual pleasure.

forbidding (fə bĭd′ĭng), *adj.* **1.** causing dislike or fear: *a forbidding countenance.* **2.** repellent; dangerous-looking: *forbidding cliffs, clouds, etc.* —**forbid′dingly,** *adv.* —**forbid′dingness,** *n.*

forbore (fô bô′), *v.* pt. of **forbear**[1].

forborne (fô bôn′), *v.* pp. of **forbear**[1].

forby (fô bī′), *prep.*, *adv.* *Now Chiefly Scot. and Dial.* **1.** close by; near. **2.** besides. Also, **forbye.** [f. FOR- + BY]

force (fôs), *n.*, *v.*, **forced, forcing.** —*n.* **1.** strength; impetus; intensity of effect. **2.** might, as of a ruler or realm; strength for war. **3.** strength or power exerted upon an object; physical coercion; violence: *to use force in order to do something, to use force on a person.* **4.** *Law.* violence offered to persons or things, as the use of force in breaking into a house. **5.** power to influence, affect, or control; power to convince: *the force of an argument, the force of circumstances.* **6.** mental or moral strength; power of effective action or of overcoming resistance. **7.** (*often pl.*) a large body of armed men; an army. **8.** any body of persons combined for joint action: *an office force.* **9.** an organization of police, in England headed by a chief constable, and responsible for the policing of a county, county borough, or some other area. **10.** intensity or power of effect: *the force of her playing.* **11.** operation: *a law now in force.* **12.** *Physics.* **a.** an influence which produces or tends to produce motion or change of motion. **b.** the intensity of such an influence. **13.** any influence or agency analogous to physical force: *social forces.* **14.** binding power, as of an agreement. **15.** value; significance; meaning.

—*v.t.* **16.** to compel; constrain, or oblige (oneself or someone) to do something: *force someone to confess.* **17.** to drive or propel against resistance. **18.** to bring about or effect by force; bring about of necessity or as a necessary result: *force a passage, to force a smile, etc.* **19.** to put or impose (something) forcibly on or upon a person: *force something on someone's attention.* **20.** to compel by force; overcome the resistance of. **21.** to obtain or draw forth by or as by force; extort: *force a confession.* **22.** to overpower; enter or take by force. **23.** to break open (a door, lock, etc.). **24.** to cause (plants, fruits, etc.) to grow or mature at an increased rate by artificial means. **25.** to press, urge, or exert to violent effort or to the utmost. **26.** to use force upon. **27.** *Cards.* **a.** to compel (a player) to trump by leading a suit of which he has no cards. **b.** to compel a player to play (a particular card). **c.** to compel (a player) to play so as to make known the strength of his hand. **28.** *Obs.* to enforce (a law, etc.). **29.** *Obs.* to give force to; strengthen; reinforce.

—*v.i.* **30.** *Rare.* to make one's way by force.

[ME, t. F, g. VL *fortia*, der. L *fortis* strong] —**force′less,** *adj.* —**forc′er,** *n.* —**Syn. 1.** See **strength.**

forced (fôst), *adj.* **1.** enforced or compulsory: *forced labour.* **2.** strained, unnatural, or affected: *a forced smile.* **3.** subjected to force. **4.** emergency: *forced landing of an aeroplane.* **5.** *Maths.* denoting a change in a system caused by an outside agency. —**forcedly** (fô′sĭd lĭ), *adv.* —**for′cedness,** *n.*

forced march, *Mil.* any march longer than troops are usually expected to travel, and maintained with little time for resting or for servicing vehicles.

force-feed (fôs′fēd′), *n.*, *v.*, **-fed, -feeding.** —*n.* **1.** a means of lubrication used in most internal-combustion engines, characterized by the use of a pressure pump. —*v.t.* **2.** to compel to take food.

forceful (fôs′fəl), *adj.* **1.** full of force; powerful; vigorous; effective. **2.** acting or driven with force. —**force′fully,** *adv.* —**force′fulness,** *n.*

force majeure (*Fr.* fŏrs mȧ zhœr′), *French.* **1.** a superior force. **2.** *Law.* **a.** an unexpected and disruptive event operating to excuse a party from a contract. **b.** (of a clause) providing that a party to a contract shall be excused in case of war, strikes, etc.

forcemeat (fôs′mēt′), *n.* *Cookery.* meat chopped fine and seasoned, used as stuffing, etc. Also, **farcemeat.** [f. *force*, var. of obs. *farce* stuffing + MEAT]

forceps (fô′sĭps), *n.*, *pl.* **-ceps, -cipes** (-sĭ pēz′). **1.** an instrument, as pincers or tongs, for seizing and holding objects, as in surgical operations. **2.** *Zool.* a grasping organ resembling a forceps. [t. L] —**for′ceps-like′,** *adj.*

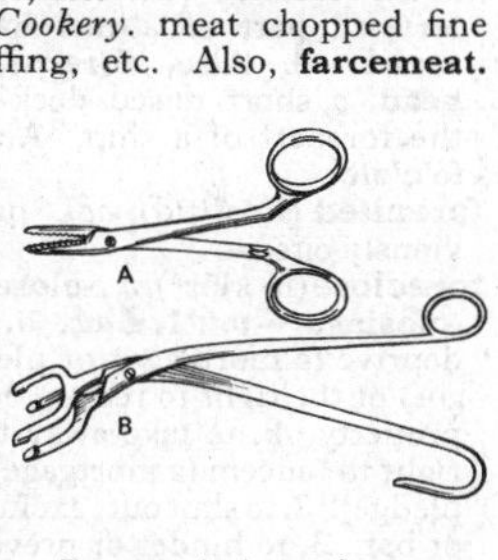

A

B

Forceps: A, Artery forceps; B, Sterilizer forceps

force-pump (fôs′pŭmp′), *n.* any pump which delivers a liquid under pressure, so as to eject it forcibly (opposed to *lift-pump*).

forcible (fô′sə bl), *adj.* **1.** effected by force. **2.** having force; producing a powerful effect; effective. **3.** convincing, as reasoning. **4.** characterized by the use of force or violence. —**for′cibleness, forc′ibil′ity,** *n.* —**for′cibly,** *adv.*

ford (fôd), *n.* **1.** a place where a river or other body of water may be crossed by wading. —*v.t.* **2.** to cross (a river, etc.) by a ford. [ME and OE, c. G *Furt*; akin to FARE, PORT] —**ford′able,** *adj.* —**ford′less,** *adj.*

Ford (fôd), *n.* **1. Ford Madox** (fôd′măd′əks), (*Ford Madox Hueffer*) 1873–1939, English author. **2. Henry,** 1863–1947, U.S. motor manufacturer. **3. John,** 1586–1640?, English dramatist.

fordo (fô dōō′), *v.t.*, **-did, -done, -doing.** *Archaic.* **1.** to do away with; kill; destroy. **2.** to ruin; undo. Also, **foredo.** [ME *fordon*, OE *fordon.* See FOR-, DO]

fordone (fô dŭn′), *adj. Archaic.* exhausted with fatigue.

fore[1] (fô), *adj.* **1.** situated at or towards the front, as compared with something else. **2.** first in place, time, order, rank, etc.; forward; earlier. *—adv.* **3.** *Naut.* at or towards the bow. See illus. under **aft. 4.** *Dial.* before. **5.** *Dial.* forward. *—n.* **6.** the forepart of anything; the front. **7.** *Naut.* the foremast. **8. to the fore, a.** to or at the front; to or in a conspicuous place or position. **b.** ready at hand. **c.** still alive. *—prep. and conj.* **9.** *Now Only Dial.* before. [special use of FORE-, detached from words like *forepart, forefather,* etc.]

fore[2] (fô), *interj. Golf.* a cry of warning to persons on a course who are liable to be struck by the ball. [prob. aphetic var. of BEFORE]

fore-, a prefix form of **before** meaning 'front' (*forehead, forecastle*), 'ahead of time' (*forecast, foretell*), 'superior' (*foreman*), etc. [ME and OE *for(e)*]

fore-and-aft (fô′rənd äft′), *adj. Naut.* **1.** in a line with the keel of a ship: *a fore-and-aft sail.* **2.** denoting a rig in which the principal sails are set on gaffs, stays, or masts, on the centre line of the vessel.

fore-and-after (fô′rənd äf′tə), *n. Naut.* a vessel with fore-and-aft sails, as a schooner.

fore-and-aft sail, *Naut.* any sail not set on a yard, usually bent to a gaff or set on a stay in the centre line. See **sail** (def. 1).

forearm[1] (fô′räm′), *n.* the part of the arm between the elbow and the wrist. [f. FORE- + ARM[1]]

forearm[2] (fôr äm′), *v.t.* to arm beforehand. [f. FORE- + ARM[2]]

forebear (fô′bĕə′), *n.* (*usually pl.*) an ancestor; forefather. Also, **forbear.** [ME (Scot.); f. FORE- + *bear* being (var. of *beer,* f. BE, v. + -ER[1])]

forebode (fô bōd′), *v.,* **-boded, -boding.** *—v.t.* **1.** to foretell or predict; portend; be an omen of; indicate beforehand: *clouds that forbode a storm.* **2.** to have a presentiment of (esp. evil). *—v.i.* **3.** to prophesy. **4.** to have a presentiment. **—forebod′er,** *n.*

foreboding (fô bō′dĭng), *n.* **1.** a prediction; portent. **2.** a presentiment. *—adj.* **3.** that forbodes, esp. evil. **—forebod′ingly,** *adv.*

forebrain (fô′brān′), *n. Anat.* **1.** that portion of the adult brain which develops from the prosencephalon. **2.** the prosencephalon.

forecast (fô′käst′), *v.,* **-cast** or **-casted, -casting,** *n.* *—v.t.* **1.** to conjecture beforehand; predict. **2.** to make a forecast of (the weather, etc.). **3.** to serve as a forecast of; foreshadow. **4.** to cast, contrive, or plan beforehand; prearrange. *—v.i.* **5.** to conjecture beforehand; make a forecast. **6.** to plan or arrange beforehand. *—n.* **7.** a conjecture as to something in the future. **8.** a prediction, esp. as to the weather. **9.** the act, practice, or faculty of forecasting. **10.** foresight in planning. **—fore′cast′er,** *n.* **—Syn. 1.** See **predict.**

forecastle (fōk′səl), *n. Naut.* **1.** the seamen's quarters in the forward part of a merchant vessel. **2.** Also, **forecastle head.** a short raised deck in the forepart of a ship. Also, **fo'c'sle.**

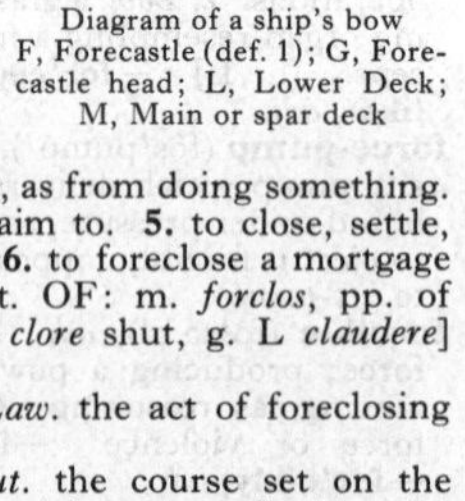

Diagram of a ship's bow
F, Forecastle (def. 1); G, Forecastle head; L, Lower Deck; M, Main or spar deck

forecited (fô′sī′tĭd), *adj.* previously cited.

foreclose (fô klōz′), *v.,* **-closed, -closing.** *—v.t.* **1.** *Law.* **a.** to deprive (a mortgagor or pledgor) of the right to redeem his property. **b.** to take away the right to redeem (a mortgage or pledge). **2.** to shut out; exclude or bar. **3.** to hinder or prevent, as from doing something. **4.** to establish an exclusive claim to. **5.** to close, settle, or answer beforehand. *—v.i.* **6.** to foreclose a mortgage or pledge. [ME *forclose(n),* t. OF: m. *forclos,* pp. of *forclore* exclude, f. *for-* out + *clore* shut, g. L *claudere*] **—foreclos′able,** *adj.*

foreclosure (fô klō′zhə), *n. Law.* the act of foreclosing a mortgage or pledge.

forecourse (fô′kôs′), *n. Naut.* the course set on the foremast (the foresail in a square-rigged vessel).

forecourt (fô′kôt′), *n.* a court in front of a building or a group of buildings.

foredate (fô′dāt′), *v.t.,* **-dated, -dating.** antedate.

foredeck (fô′dĕk′), *n. Naut.* the forward part of the spar deck.

foredo (fô do͞o′), *v.t.,* **-did, -done, -doing.** fordo.

foredoom (*v.* fô do͞om′; *n.* fô′do͞om′), *v.t.* **1.** to doom beforehand. *—n.* **2.** a doom ordained beforehand.

fore edge, the front outer edge of a book, opposite the bound edge.

forefather (fô′fä′thə), *n.* an ancestor.

forefeel (fô fēl′), *v.,* **-felt, -feeling,** *n.* *—v.t.* **1.** to feel or perceive beforehand; have a presentiment of. *—n.* **2.** a feeling beforehand.

forefend (fô fĕnd′), *v.t.* forfend.

forefinger (fô′fĭng′gə), *n.* the first finger, next to the thumb; the index finger.

forefoot (fô′fo͝ot′), *n., pl.* **-feet** (-fēt′). **1.** *Zool.* one of the front feet of a quadruped, or of an insect, etc. **2.** *Naut.* the forward end of the keel.

forefront (fô′frŭnt′), *n.* the foremost part or place.

foregather (fô găth′ə), *v.i.* forgather.

foregift (fô′gĭft′), *n. Law.* a premium sometimes paid in consideration of the granting of a lease.

forego[1] (fô gō′), *v.t., v.i.,* **-went, -gone, -going.** to go before; precede. [OE *foregān* go before, f. *fore-* FORE- + *gān* go] **—forego′er,** *n.*

forego[2] (fô gō′), *v.t.,* **-went, -gone, -going.** forgo. **—forego′er,** *n.*

foregoing (fô gō′ĭng), *adj.* going before; preceding: *the foregoing passage.*

foregone (fô gŏn′, fô′gŏn′), *adj.* that has gone before; previous; past. **—foregone′ness,** *n.*

foregone conclusion, 1. an inevitable conclusion or result. **2.** a conclusion, opinion, or decision formed in advance.

foreground (fô′ground′), *n.* the ground or parts situated, or represented as situated, in the front; the nearer portion of a scene (opposed to *background*).

foregut (fô′gŭt′), *n. Embryol., Zool.* the upper part of the embryonic digestive canal from which the pharynx, oesophagus, stomach, and part of the duodenum develop.

forehand (fô′hănd′), *adj.* **1.** made to the right side of the body (when the player is right-handed). **2.** being in front or ahead. **3.** foremost or leading. **4.** done beforehand; anticipative; given or made in advance, as a payment. *—n.* **5.** position in front or above; superior position; adventure. **6.** *Tennis, etc.* **a.** forehand stroke. **b.** that type of playing, or the stance taken when making such strokes. **7.** the part of a horse which is in front of the rider.

forehanded (fô′hăn′dĭd), *adj.* **1.** forehand, as a stroke in tennis, etc. **2.** *U.S.* providing for the future; prudent; thrifty. **3.** *U.S.* in easy circumstances; well-to-do. **—fore′hand′edness,** *n.*

forehead (fŏ′rĭd), *n.* **1.** the fore or front upper part of the head; the part of the face above the eyes; the brow. **2.** the fore or front part of anything. [ME *forehe(v)ed,* OE *forhēafod,* f. *for(e)-* FORE- + *hēafod* head]

foreign (fŏ′rĭn), *adj.* **1.** pertaining to, characteristic of, or derived from another country or nation; not native or domestic. **2.** pertaining to relations or dealings with other countries. **3.** external to one's own country or nation: *a foreign country.* **4.** carried on abroad, or with other countries: *foreign trade.* **5.** belonging to or coming from another district, province, society, etc. **6.** situated outside a district, province, etc. **7.** *Law.* outside the legal jurisdiction of the state; alien. **8.** belonging to or proceeding from other persons or things: *a statement supported by foreign testimony.* **9.** not belonging to the place or body where found: *a foreign substance in the eye.* **10.** not related to or connected with the thing under consideration: *foreign to our discussion.* **11.** alien in character; irrelevant or inappropriate; remote. **12.** strange or unfamiliar. [ME *forene,* t. OF: *forain,* ult. der. L *foras* out of doors, outside] **—for′eignness,** *n.*

foreign affairs, international relations; activities of a nation arising from its dealings with other nations.

foreign aid, financial and other aid given to underdeveloped countries by technologically more advanced ones.

foreign bill, any bill of exchange other than an inland bill.

foreign body, 1. a substance found in but not belonging to the human body. **2.** any unwanted object.

foreign correspondent, a correspondent, as of a newspaper, etc., sent abroad to write articles and news dispatches from a foreign country for publication in his own country.

foreigner (fŏ′rĭ nə), *n.* **1.** a person not native or naturalized in the country or jurisdiction under consideration; an alien. **2.** a thing produced in or coming from a foreign country. **—Syn. 1.** See **stranger.**

foreign exchange, 1. the buying and selling of the money of other countries. **2.** the money of other countries.

foreign exchange rate, the rate at which the money of one country is exchanged for that of another.

foreignism (fŏ′rĭ nĭz′əm), *n. U.S.* **1.** a foreign custom, etc. **2.** any trait or deviation from accepted speech standards that comes from the influence of a foreign language. **3.** imitation of anything foreign. **4.** foreign quality.

foreign legion, 1. a military body in the service of a state, including foreign volunteers. **2.** (*caps.*) a military body in the French Army, consisting of foreigners of all nationalities, and including Frenchmen, used mainly for military operations and duties outside France, formerly in northern Africa.

foreign minister, a government minister who conducts diplomatic relations with other countries.

foreign office, the department of a government concerned with the conduct of international relations.

foreign relations, 1. the relationship between nations arising out of their dealings with each other. **2.** the field of foreign affairs.

foreign secretary, the foreign minister in the British and some other governments.

forejudge[1] (fô jŭj′), *v.t.*, **-judged, -judging.** to judge beforehand; prejudge. [f. FORE- + JUDGE, V.]

forejudge[2] (fô jŭj′), *v.t.*, **-judged, -judging.** forjudge.

foreknow (fô nō′), *v.t.*, **-knew, -known, -knowing.** to know beforehand. **—foreknow′able,** *adj.* **—foreknow′ingly,** *adv.*

foreknowledge (fô nŏl′ĭj), *n.* knowledge of a thing before it exists or happens; prescience.

foreland (fô′lənd), *n.* **1.** a cape, headland, or promontory. **2.** land or territory lying in front. **3.** (*cap.*) either of two headlands on the SE coast of England, in Kent: the **North Foreland** on the Isle of Thanet, and the **South Foreland** 17 mi. S of this.

foreleg (fô′lĕg′), *n.* one of the front legs of a quadruped, or of an insect, etc.

forelimb (fô′lĭm′), *n.* a front limb of an animal.

forelock[1] (fô′lŏk′), *n.* **1.** the lock of hair that grows from the forepart of the head. **2.** a prominent or somewhat detached lock above the forehead. [f. FORE- + LOCK[2]]

forelock[2] (fô′lŏk′), *n.* **1.** a round or flat wedge of iron passed through a hole in the inner end of a bolt to prevent its withdrawal when a strain is placed on it. *—v.t.* **2.** to fasten by means of a forelock. [f. FORE- + LOCK[1]]

foreman (fô′mən), *n.*, *pl.* **-men. 1.** a man in charge of a group of workers. **2.** the spokesman of a jury. **—fore′manship′,** *n.*

foremast (fô′mäst′; *Naut.* -məst), *n.* *Naut.* the mast nearest the bow of a ship.

foremost (fô′mōst′), *adj., adv.* first in place, order, rank, etc. [f. FORE[1], adj. + -MOST, r. ME and OE *formest*, f. *forma* first (var. of *frum(a)*. Cf. L *primus*) + -EST]

forename (fô′nām′), *n.* a name that precedes the family name or surname; a first name.

forenamed (fô′nāmd′), *adj.* named before; mentioned before in the same writing or discourse.

forenoon (fô′no͞on′), *n.* **1.** the period of daylight before noon. **2.** the latter part of the morning, esp. the part ordinarily employed in transacting business. *—adj.* **3.** of or pertaining to the forenoon.

forensic (fə rĕn′sĭk), *adj.* **1.** pertaining to, connected with, or used in courts of law or public discussion and debate. **2.** adapted or suited to argumentation; argumentative. [f. L *forens(is)* of the forum + -IC] **—foren′sically,** *adv.*

forensic medicine, medical jurisprudence.

foreordain (fô′rô dān′), *v.t.* to ordain or appoint beforehand; predestinate. **—fore′ordain′ment,** *n.*

foreordination (fô rô′dĭ nā′shən), *n.* previous ordination or appointment; predestination.

forepart (fô′pät′), *n.* the fore, front, or early part.

forepeak (fô′pēk′), *n.* *Naut.* the part of the hold in the angle formed by the bow.

forequarter (fô′kwô′tə), *n.* (in cutting meat) the forward end of half of a carcass.

forereach (fô rēch′), *v.i.* **1.** to gain, as one ship on another. *—v.t.* **2.** to gain upon; overhaul and pass.

forerun (fô rŭn′), *v.t.*, **-ran, -run, -running. 1.** to run in front of; precede; be the precurser of. **2.** to anticipate or forestall. **3.** *Obs.* to outrun or outstrip.

forerunner (fô′rŭn′ə), *n.* **1.** a predecessor; ancestor. **2.** one who or that which foreruns; a herald or harbinger. **3.** a prognostic or portent. **4. the Forerunner,** John the Baptist.

foresaid (fô′sĕd′), *adj.* aforementioned; aforesaid.

foresail (fô′sāl′; *Naut.* -səl), *n.* *Naut.* **1.** the sail bent to the foreyard of a square-rigged vessel. See illus. under **sail. 2.** the principal sail on the foremast of a schooner. **3.** the forestay sail of a sloop, cutter, etc.

foresee (fô sē′), *v.*, **-saw, -seen, -seeing.** *—v.t.* **1.** to see beforehand; have prescience of; foreknow. *—v.i.* **2.** to exercise foresight. [ME; OE *foresēon*, f. *fore-* FORE- + *sēon* SEE[1]] **—foresee′able,** *adj.* **—forese′er,** *n.* **—Syn. 1.** See **predict.**

foreshadow (fô shăd′ō), *v.t.* to show or indicate beforehand; prefigure. **—foreshad′ower,** *n.*

foresheet (fô′shēt′), *n.* *Naut.* **1.** a sheet of a foresail. **2.** (*pl.*) the forward part of an open boat.

foreshore (fô′shô′), *n.* **1.** the forepart of the shore; the part of the shore between the ordinary high-water mark and low-water mark. **2.** the ground between the water's edge and the land cultivated or built upon.

foreshorten (fô shô′tn), *v.t.* to reduce the length of (a line, part, object, or the like, which lies in a plane not perpendicular to the line of sight) in order to give the proper impression to the eye by means of perspective. **—foreshort′ening,** *n.*

foreshow (fô shō′), *v.t.*, **-showed, -shown, -showing.** to show beforehand; foretell; foreshadow. [ME *forescewen*, OE *foresceāwian*, f. *fore-* FORE- + *sceāwian* show]

foreside (fô′sīd′), *n.* **1.** the front side or part. **2.** the upper side. **3.** *U.S.* a stretch of land fronting the sea.

foresight (fô′sīt′), *n.* **1.** care or provision for the future; provident care. **2.** the act or power of foreseeing; prevision; prescience. **3.** the act of looking forward. **4.** perception gained by or as by looking forward; prospect; a view into the future. **5.** *Survey.* **a.** a sight or reading taken on a forward point. **b.** (in levelling) a rod reading on a point the elevation of which is to be determined. **6.** a sight on the muzzle of a gun. **—fore′sight′ed,** *adj.* **—fore′sight′edness,** *n.* **—Syn. 1.** See **prudence.**

foreskin (fô′skĭn′), *n.* *Anat.* the prepuce.

forest (fŏ′rĭst), *n.* **1.** a large tract of land covered with trees; an extensive wood. **2.** the trees alone: *to cut down a forest.* **3.** *Law.* a tract of woody grounds and pastures, generally belonging to the sovereign, set apart for game. **4.** an area, once extensively wooded, now more or less cultivated: *Ashdown Forest.* **5.** a thick cluster of many things. *—v.t.* **6.** to cover with trees; convert into a forest. [ME, t. OF, g. VL *forestis* an unenclosed wood (as opposed to a park), der. L *foris* outside. See FOREIGN] **—for′ested,** *adj.* **—for′estless,** *adj.* **—for′est-like′,** *adj.*

—Syn. 1. FOREST, GROVE, WOOD refer to an area covered with trees. A FOREST is an extensive wooded area, preserving some of its primitive wildness and usually having game or wild animals in it: *Sherwood Forest, the Black Forest.* A GROVE is a group or cluster of trees, usually not very large in area and cleared of underbrush; it may consist of fruit or nut trees: *a shady grove, a grove of pines, an orange grove, a walnut grove.* A WOOD (WOODS) is a wooded tract smaller than a forest and resembling one, but less wild in character and nearer to civilization: *a wood covering several acres, lost in the woods.*

forestall (fô stôl′), *v.t.* **1.** to prevent, hinder, or thwart by action in advance; take measures concerning or deal with (a thing) in advance. **2.** to deal with, meet, or realize in advance of the natural or proper time; be beforehand with or get ahead of (a person, etc.) in action. **3.** to buy up (goods) in advance, in order to enhance the price. **4.** to prevent sales at (a fair, market etc.) by buying up or diverting goods. [ME *forstalle*, der. OE *foresteall* intervention (to defeat justice), waylaying. See FORE-, STALL[2]] **—forestall′er,** *n.* **—forestal′ment,** *n.*

forestation (fŏ′rĭs tā′shən), *n.* the planting of forests.

forestay (fô′stā′), *n.* *Naut.* a strong rope (now generally of wire) extending forward from the head of the foremast to the knightheads or stem to support the mast.

forestay sail (fô′stā′sāl′; *Naut.* -səl), *n.* *Naut.* a triangular sail set on the forestay, being the first sail in front of the forward (or single) mast.

forester (fŏ′rĭs tə), *n.* **1.** one who practises, or is versed in, forestry. **2.** an officer having charge of a forest. **3.** *Zool.* an animal of the forest. **4.** the great grey kangaroo, *Macropus canguru.* **5.** any of various moths of the family *Zygaenidae*, as *Procris statices*, a moth whose larva feeds on sorrel.

Forester (fŏ′rĭs tə), *n.* **C(ecil) S(cott),** 1899–1966, English novelist.

forestry (fŏ′rĭs trĭ), *n.* **1.** the science of planting and taking care of forests. **2.** the act of establishing and managing forests. **3.** forest land.

foretaste (*n.* fô′tāst′; *v.* fô tāst′), *n.*, *v.*, **-tasted, -tasting.** *—n.* **1.** a taste beforehand; anticipation. *—v.t.* **2.** to taste beforehand; enjoy by anticipation.

foretell (fô tĕl′), *v.*, **-told, -telling.** *—v.t.* **1.** to tell of beforehand; predict or prophesy. **2.** (of things) to foreshow. *—v.i.* **3.** to utter a prediction or a prophecy. **—foretell′er,** *n.*

forethought (fô′thôt′), *n.* **1.** provident care; prudence. **2.** a thinking of something beforehand; previous consideration; anticipation. **—Syn. 1.** See **prudence.**

forethoughtful (fô thôt′fəl), *adj.* full of or having forethought; provident. **—forethought′fully,** *adv.* **—forethought′fulness,** *n.*

foretime (fô′tīm′), *n.* former or past time; the past.

foretoken (*n.* fô′tō′kən; *v.* fô tō′kən), *n.* **1.** a premonitory token or sign. —*v.t.* **2.** to foreshadow. [ME *foretokne*, OE *foretācn*, f. *fore-* FORE- + *tācn* token]

foretop (fô′tŏp′; *for 1 also Naut.* -təp), *n.* **1.** *Naut.* a platform at the head of a foremast. **2.** the forelock of an animal, esp. a horse. **3.** *Obs.* a human forelock, or a lock of hair on the front of a wig.

fore-topgallant (fô′tŏp găl′ənt; *Naut.* -tə găl′-), *adj. Naut.* (of a mast, sail, yard, etc.) next above the fore-topmast. See illus. under **sail.**

fore-topgallant mast, *Naut.* the mast next above the fore-topmast.

fore-topmast (fô′tŏp′mäst′; *Naut.* -məst), *n. Naut.* the mast erected at the head of the foremast, above the foretop.

fore-topsail (fô′tŏp′săl′; *Naut.* -səl), *n. Naut.* the sail set on the fore-topmast. See illus. under **sail.**

for ever, 1. eternally; without ever ending: *to last for ever, go away for ever.* **2.** continually; incessantly: *he's for ever complaining.* Also, *U.S.*, **forever** (fô rev′ə, fə-).

forevermore (fə rĕv′ə mô′), *adv.* for ever hereafter. Also, **for ever more.**

forewarn (fô wôn′), *v.t.* to warn beforehand.

forewoman (fô′wo͝om′ən), *n., pl.* **-women.** a woman in charge of a group of workwomen.

foreword (fô′wûd′), *n.* a preface or introductory statement in a book, etc. **—Syn.** See **introduction.**

foreworn (fô wôn′), *adj. Archaic.* forworn.

foreyard (fô′yäd′), *n. Naut.* the lower yard on the foremast.

Forfar (fô′fə, -fä), *n.* **1.** a burgh in Scotland, the county town of Angus. 10,252 (1961). **2.** former name of **Angus.**

forfeit (fô′fĭt), *n.* **1.** a fine; a penalty. **2.** the act of forfeiting; forfeiture. **3.** something to which the right is lost by the commission of a crime or misdeed, the neglect of a duty, a breach of contract, etc. **4.** an article deposited in a game because of a mistake and redeemable by a fine or penalty. **5.** (*pl.*) a game so played. —*v.t.* **6.** to lose as a forfeit. **7.** to lose, or become liable to lose, in consequence of crime, fault, breach of engagement, etc. —*adj.* **8.** forfeited. [ME *forfet*, t. OF, pp. of *forfaire*, f. *for-* outside, wrongly + *faire* do] **—for′feitable,** *adj.* **—for′feiter,** *n.*

forfeiture (fô′fĭ chə), *n.* **1.** the act of forfeiting. **2.** that which is forfeited; a fine mulct.

forfend (fô fĕnd′), *v.t.* **1.** *U.S.* to defend, secure, or protect. **2.** *Archaic.* to fend off, avert, or prevent. Also, **forefend.** [ME; f. FOR- + FEND]

forficate (fô′fĭ kĭt, -kāt′), *adj.* deeply forked, as the tail of certain birds. [f. s. L *forfex* scissors + -ATE[1]]

forgat (fə găt′), *v. Archaic.* pt. of **forget.**

forgather (fô găŧħ′ə), *v.i.* **1.** to gather together; convene; assemble. **2.** to encounter or meet, esp. by accident. **3.** to associate or fraternize (fol. by *with*). Also, **foregather.**

forgave (fə gāv′), *v.* pt. of **forgive.**

forge[1] (fôj), *n., v.,* **forged, forging.** —*n.* **1.** the special fireplace, hearth, or furnace in which metal is heated before shaping. **2.** a smithy. —*v.t.* **3.** to form by heating and hammering; beat into shape. **4.** to form or make in any way. **5.** to invent (a fictitious story, a lie, etc.). **6.** to imitate (a signature, etc.) fraudulently; fabricate by false imitation. —*v.i.* **7.** to commit forgery. **8.** to work at a forge. [ME, t. OF, ult. g. L *fabrica* workshop] **—forge′able,** *adj.* **—forg′er,** *n.*

forge[2] (fôj), *v.i.,* **forged, forging.** to move ahead slowly, with difficulty, or by mere momentum (usually fol. by *ahead*). [orig. uncert.]

forgery (fô′jə rĭ), *n., pl.* **-geries. 1.** the making of a fraudulent imitation of a thing, or of something spurious which is put forth as genuine, as a coin, a work of art, a literary production, etc. **2.** something, as a coin, a work of art, a writing, etc., produced by forgery. **3.** *Law.* the false making or alteration of a writing by which the legal rights or obligations of another person are apparently affected; simulated signing of another person's name to any such writing (whether or not it is also the forger's name). **4.** the act of fabricating or producing falsely. **5.** *Archaic.* fictitious invention or deception.

forget (fə gĕt′), *v.,* **-got** or (*Archaic*) **-gat; -gotten** or **-got; -getting.** —*v.t.* **1.** to cease to remember; fail to remember; be unable to recall. **2.** to omit or neglect unintentionally (to do something). **3.** to omit to take; leave behind inadvertently: *to forget one's keys.* **4.** to omit to mention; leave unnoticed. **5.** to omit to think of; take no note of. **6.** to neglect wilfully; overlook, disregard, or slight. **7. forget oneself, a.** to say or do something improper. **b.** to fail to remember one's station, position, or character. **c.** to become absent-minded. **d.** to lose consciousness, as in sleep. —*v.i.* **8.** to cease or omit to think of something. [f. FOR- + GET; r. ME *foryete(n)*, OE *forg(i)etan*] **—forget′table,** *adj.* **—forget′ter,** *n.*

forgetful (fə gĕt′fəl), *adj.* **1.** apt to forget; that forgets: *a forgetful person.* **2.** heedless or neglectful (often fol. by *of*): *to be forgetful of others.* **3.** *Poetic.* causing to forget. **—forget′fully,** *adv.* **—forget′fulness,** *n.*

forgetive (fô′jĭ tĭv), *adj. Archaic.* inventive; creative. [? b. FORGE[1], v. and CREATIVE]

forget-me-not (fə gĕt′mĭ nŏt′), *n.* **1.** a small boraginaceous Old World plant, *Myosotis palustris*, bearing a light blue flower commonly regarded as an emblem of constancy and friendship. **2.** any of several other plants of the same genus. **3.** any of various similar plants.

forging (fô′jĭng), *n.* **1.** something forged; a piece of forged work in metal. **2.** (in horses) the act of striking and injuring the forelegs with the shoes of the hind legs while racing.

forgive (fə gĭv′), *v.,* **-gave, -given, -giving.** —*v.t.* **1.** to grant free pardon for or remission of (an offence, debt, etc.); pardon. **2.** to give up all claim on account of; remit (a debt, etc.). **3.** to grant free pardon to (a person). **4.** to cease to feel resentment against: *to forgive one's enemies.* —*v.i.* **5.** to pardon an offence or an offender. [f. FOR- + GIVE; r. ME *foryiven*, OE *forgiefan*] **—forgiv′able,** *adj.* **—forgiv′ably,** *adv.*

forgiveness (fə gĭv′nĭs), *n.* **1.** the act of forgiving. **2.** the state of being forgiven. **3.** disposition or willingness to forgive.

forgiving (fə gĭv′ĭng), *adj.* that forgives; disposed to forgive; indicating forgiveness. **—forgiv′ingly,** *adv.* **—forgiv′ingness,** *n.*

forgo (fô gō′), *v.t.,* **-went, -gone, -going. 1.** to abstain or refrain from; do without; give up, renounce, or resign. **2.** *Archaic.* to neglect or overlook. **3.** *Archaic.* to quit or leave. **4.** *Obs.* to go or pass by. Also, **forego.** [ME *forgon*, OE *forgān*. See FOR-, GO] **—forgo′er,** *n.*

forgot (fə gŏt′), *v.* pt. and pp. of **forget.**

forgotten (fə gŏt′n), *v.* pp. of **forget.**

forint (*Hung.* fô′rēnt), *n.* **1.** the monetary unit of Hungary, equal to 100 fillér, and equivalent to about £0·036 sterling. **2.** a coin of this value. [t. Hung.: FLORIN]

forjudge (fô jŭj′), *v.t.,* **-judged, -judging.** *Law.* to exclude, expel, dispossess, or deprive by a judgement. Also, **forejudge.** [ME *forjuge(n)*, t. OF: m. *forjugier*, f. *for-* out + *jugier* JUDGE, v.]

fork (fôk), *n.* **1.** an instrument having two or more prongs or tines, for holding, lifting, etc., as any of various agricultural tools, or an implement for handling food at table or in cooking. **2.** something resembling or suggesting this in form. **3.** a tuning fork. **4.** a forking, or dividing into branches. **5.** the point or part at which a thing, as a river or a road, divides into branches. **6.** each of the branches into which a thing forks. **7.** *Chiefly U.S.* a principal tributary of a river. **8.** *Obs.* the barbed head of an arrow. —*v.t.* **9.** to make fork-shaped. **10.** to pierce, raise, pitch, dig, etc., with a fork. **11.** *Chess.* to assail (two pieces) at the same time. **12.** *Slang.* to hand (fol. by *over* or *out*). —*v.i.* **13.** to form a fork; divide into branches. [ME *forke*, OE *forca*, t. L: m. *furca*] **—fork′ful,** *n.* **—fork′less,** *adj.* **—fork′like′,** *adj.*

forked (fôkt, fô′kĭd), *adj.* **1.** having a fork or forking branches. **2.** zigzag, as lightning. **—forkedly** (fô′kĭd lĭ), *adv.* **—fork′edness,** *n.*

forked lightning, lightning visible in wavy, zigzag, or broken lines.

fork-lift truck (fôk′lĭft′), an electric truck with two power-operated, parallel, horizontal arms for lifting and carrying goods, esp. in a warehouse or factory.

fork luncheon, a buffet luncheon spread on tables or sideboards from which the guests serve themselves. Also, **fork lunch.**

forky (fô′kĭ), *adj.* shaped like a fork; forked.

Forlì (*It.* fôr lē′), *n.* a town in N Italy, in Emilia. 100,562 (1966).

forlorn (fə lôn′), *adj.* **1.** abandoned, deserted, or forsaken (sometimes fol. by *of*). **2.** desolate or dreary; unhappy or miserable, as in feeling, condition, or appearance. **3.** desperate or hopeless. **4.** bereft (fol. by *of*). [var. of *forlore(n)*, pp. of (obs.) *forlese*, v., OE *forlēosan* lose, destroy. See FOR-, LORN] **—forlorn′ly,** *adv.* **—forlorn′ness,** *n.* **—Syn. 1.** See **desolate.**

forlorn hope, 1. a vain hope; an undertaking almost certain to fail. **2.** a perilous or desperate enterprise. **3.** a group of soldiers for some unusually perilous service. [t. D: alter. of *verloren hoop*, lit., lost troop]

form (fôm), *n.* **1.** definite shape; external shape or appearance considered apart from colour or material; configuration. **2.** the shape of a thing or person. **3.** a body, esp. that of a human being. **4.** something that gives or determines shape; a mould. **5.** a particular structural condition, character, or mode of being exhibited by a thing: *water in the form of ice.* **6.** the manner or style

of arranging and coordinating parts for a pleasing or effective result, as in literary or musical composition. **7.** the formal structure of a work of art; the organization and relationship of lines or colours in a painting or volumes and voids in a sculpture so as to create a coherent image. **8.** any assemblage of similar things constituting a component of a group, especially of a zoological group. **9.** *Crystall.* the combination of all the like faces possible on a crystal of given symmetry. **10.** due or proper shape; orderly arrangement of parts; good order. **11.** *Philos.* **a.** the structure, pattern, organization, or essential nature of anything. **b.** form or pattern considered in distinction from matter. **c.** (in Platonic use) an idea (def. 7c). **d.** (in Aristotelian use) that which gives to a thing its particular species or kind. **12.** *Logic.* the abstract relations of terms in a proposition, and of propositions to one another. **13.** a set, prescribed, or customary order or method of doing something. **14.** a set order of words, as for use in religious ritual or in a legal document. **15.** a document with blank spaces to be filled in with particulars before it is executed: *a tax form.* **16.** a typical document to be used as a guide in framing others for like cases: *a form for a deed.* **17.** a conventional method of procedure or behaviour. **18.** a formality or ceremony, often with implication of absence of real meaning. **19.** procedure, according to a set order or method. **20.** formality; ceremony; conformity to the usages of society. **21.** mere outward formality or ceremony; conventional observance of social usages. **22.** procedure or conduct, as judged by social standards. **23.** manner or method of performing something. **24.** condition, esp. good condition, with reference to fitness for performing. **25.** *Gram.* **a.** any word, part of a word, or group of words arranged in a construction, which recurs in various contexts in a language with relatively constant meaning. **b.** a particular shape of a form (def. 25a) when it occurs in several: *in 'I'm', ''m' is a form of 'am'.* **c.** a word with a particular inflectional ending or other modification, as *goes* is a form of *go.* **26. a.** a single division of a school containing pupils of about the same age or of the same level of scholastic progress. **b.** the pupils themselves in such a division. **27.** a bench or long seat. **28.** *U.S.* a forme. **29.** the bed, nest, or lair of a hare.
—*v.t.* **30.** to construct or frame. **31.** to make or produce. **32.** to serve to make up, or compose; serve for, or constitute. **33.** to place in order; arrange; organize. **34.** to frame (ideas, opinions, etc.) in the mind. **35.** to contract (habits, friendships, etc.). **36.** to give form or shape to; shape; fashion. **37.** to give a particular form to, or fashion in a particular manner. **38.** to mould by discipline or instruction. **39.** *Gram.* to stand in relation to (a particular derivative or other form) by virtue of the absence or presence of an affix or other grammatical element or change: *'man' forms its plural by the change of -a- to -e-.* **40.** *Mil.* to draw up in lines or in formation. —*v.i.* **41.** to take or assume form. **42.** to be formed or produced. **43.** to take a particular form or arrangement. [ME *forme,* t. OF, t. L: m. *forma* form, figure, model, mould, sort, ML seat]

—**Syn. 1.** FORM, FIGURE, OUTLINE, SHAPE refer to an appearance which can be recognized. FORM, FIGURE, and SHAPE are often used to mean recognizable lines as contrasted with colour and material; SHAPE is more colloquial than the others. OUTLINE refers to the line which delimits a form, figure, or shape: *the outline of a hill.* FIGURE usually refers to a concrete object, whereas FORM and SHAPE are often applied to abstractions: *the figure of a man, the shape of a cow, of the future.* FORM is the most widely applied to physical objects, mental images, methods of procedure, etc.: *the form of a cross, of a ceremony, of a poem.* —**Ant. 1.** substance.

-form, a suffix meaning 'having the form of', as in *cruciform.* [t. L: s. *-formis*]

formal (fô′məl), *adj.* **1.** being in accordance with conventional requirements; conventional. **2.** marked by form or ceremony: *a formal occasion.* **3.** observant of form, as persons; ceremonious. **4.** excessively ceremonious. **5.** being a matter of form only; perfunctory. **6.** made or done in accordance with forms ensuring validity: *a formal authorization.* **7.** being in accordance with prescribed or customary forms: *a formal siege.* **8.** *Fine Arts.* of or pertaining to the composition and the organization of the constituent elements in a work of art. **9.** academic; acquired in a recognized seat of learning. **10.** excessively regular or symmetrical. **11.** denoting language whose grammar and syntax are correct, and speech whose sounds are carefully formed without sounding stilted: *the language and speech of formal occasions.* See **informal** (def. 4). **12.** *Philos.* **a.** pertaining to form. **b.** (in Aristotelian use) not material; essential. **13.** pertaining to the form, shape, or mode of being of a thing, esp. as distinguished from the matter. **14.** being such in form, esp. in mere outward form. —**for′malness,** *n.*

—**Syn. 2.** FORMAL, ACADEMIC, CONVENTIONAL, CEREMONIAL, may have either favourable or unfavourable implications. FORMAL may mean in proper form, or may imply excessive emphasis on empty form. In the favourable sense, ACADEMIC applies to scholars or higher institutions of learning; it may, however, imply slavish conformance to mere rules, or to belief in impractical theories. CONVENTIONAL, in a favourable sense, applies to desirable conformity with accepted conventions or customs; but it may apply to arbitrary, forced, or superficial conformity. CEREMONIAL applies also to conformity, but with special reference to rites and rituals.

formaldehyde (fô măl′dĭ hīd′), *n. Chem.* a gas, H.CHO, used most often in the form of a 40 per cent aqueous solution, as a disinfectant and preservative, and in the manufacture of various resins and plastics. Also, **formaldehyd.** [f. FORM(IC) + ALDEHYDE]

formalin (fô′mə lĭn), *n.* an aqueous solution of formaldehyde used as a sterilizing solution for non-boilable material, and in the treatment of warts.

formalism (fô′mə lĭz′əm), *n.* **1.** strict adherence to, or observance of, prescribed or customary forms. **2.** (in religion) excessive attachment to external forms and observances. —**for′malist,** *n.* —**for′malis′tic,** *adj.*

formality (fô măl′ĭ tĭ), *n., pl.* **-ties. 1.** the condition or quality of being formal; accordance with prescribed, customary, or due forms; conventionality. **2.** rigorously methodical character. **3.** excessive regularity, or stiffness. **4.** observance of form or ceremony. **5.** marked or excessive ceremoniousness. **6.** an established order or mode of proceeding: *the formalities of judicial process.* **7.** a formal act or observance. **8.** something done merely for form's sake; a requirement of custom or etiquette.

formalize (fô′mə līz′), *v.,* **-lized, -lizing.** —*v.t.* **1.** to make formal. **2.** to give a definite form or shape to. —*v.i.* **3.** to be formal; act with formality. Also, **formalise.** —**for′maliza′tion,** *n.*

formal logic, the branch of logic concerned exclusively with the principles of deductive reasoning, and in consequence with the forms (as distinct from the content) of propositions.

formally (fô′mə lĭ), *adv.* **1.** in a formal manner. **2.** as regards form; in form.

format (fô′măt), *n.* **1.** the shape and size of a book or the like as determined by the number of times the original sheet has been folded to form the leaves. See **folio** (def. 2), **quarto, octavo, duodecimo,** etc. **2.** the general physical appearance of a book, newspaper, or magazine, etc., such as the typeface, binding, quality of paper, margins, etc. **3.** the plan or style of something: *the format of a television series.* [t. F, t. L: s. (*liber*) *formātus* (a book) formed (in a certain way)]

formate[1] (fô′māt), *n. Chem.* a salt or ester of formic acid. [f. FORM(IC) + -ATE[2]]

formate[2] (fô māt′), *v.i.,* **-mated, -mating.** *Aeron.* to fly in formation. [back-formation from FORMATION]

formation (fô mā′shən), *n.* **1.** the act or process of forming. **2.** the state of being formed. **3.** the manner in which a thing is formed; disposition of parts; formal structure or arrangement. **4.** *Mil.* a particular disposition of troops. **5.** a group of two or more aircraft flying as a unit according to a fixed plan. **6.** a team of ballroom dancers dancing according to a previously arranged sequence. **7.** something formed. **8.** *Geol.* **a.** a body of rocks classed as a unit for geologic mapping. **b.** the process of depositing material of a particular composition or origin.

formative (fô′mə tĭv), *adj.* **1.** giving form or shape; forming; shaping; fashioning; moulding. **2.** pertaining to formation or development: *the formative period of a nation.* **3.** *Biol.* **a.** capable of developing new cells or tissue by cell division and differentiation: *formative tissue.* **b.** concerned with the formation of an embryo, organ, or the like. **4.** *Gram.* pertaining to a formative. —*n.* **5.** *Gram.* a derivational affix, particularly one which determines the part of speech of the derived word, such as *-ness,* in *loudness, hardness,* etc. —**form′atively,** *adv.* —**form′ativeness,** *n.*

formative element, *Gram.* **1.** a morpheme which serves as an affix, not as a base (or root) in word formation. **2.** any non-inflectional morpheme, whether base or affix.

form class, *Gram.* a class of words or forms in a language with one or more grammatical features in common, as (in Latin) all masculine nouns in the nominative singular, or all masculine singular nouns, or all masculine nouns, or all singular nouns, or all nouns.

form drag, *Hydraulics, Aeron., etc.* that portion of the resisting force encountered by a body moving through a fluid or air which is due to irregularity of shape and hence can be reduced to a minimum by streamlining; pressure drag minus induced drag.

forme (fôm), *n. Print.* type arranged and secured in a chase to print from. Also, *U.S.,* **form.**

former[1] (fôʹmə), *adj.* **1.** preceding in time; prior or earlier. **2.** past, long past, or ancient. **3.** preceding in order; being the first of two. **4.** being the first mentioned of two. **5.** having held a particular office in the past: *a former president.* [ME, f. obs. *forme* (OE *forma* first) + -ER⁴. Cf. ME and OE *formest* foremost]

former[2] (fôʹmə), *n.* **1.** one who or that which forms or serves to form. **2.** *Elect.* a tool for giving a coil or winding a specified shape.

formerly (fôʹmə lĭ), *adv.* **1.** in time past; heretofore; of old. **2.** *Obs.* in time just past; just now.

Formica (fô mīʹkə), *n.* *Trademark.* a thermosetting plastic usually used in transparent or printed sheets as a chemical-proof and heat-resistant covering for furniture, wall panels, etc.

formic acid (fôʹmĭk), *Chem.* a colourless irritant liquid, HCOOH, once obtained from ants and other insects, but now manufactured synthetically. [*formic*, irreg. t. L: s. *formica* ant]

formicarium (fôʹmĭ kĕəʹrĭ əm), *n.*, *pl.* **-caria** (-kĕəʹrĭ ə). formicary. [t. ML, der. L *formīca* ant]

formicary (fôʹmĭ kə rĭ), *n.*, *pl.* **-caries.** an ants' nest.

formicate (fôʹmĭ kātʹ), *v.i.*, **-cated, -cating.** to swarm with moving beings, as ants. [t. L: m. s. *formīcātus*, pp. of *formīcāre* creep like ants]

formiciasis (fôʹmĭ sīʹ āʹsĭs), *n.* *Pathol.* a morbid condition caused by ant bites.

formidable (fôʹmĭ də bl), *adj.* **1.** that is to be feared or dreaded, esp. in encounters or dealings. **2.** of alarming strength, size, difficulty, etc. **3.** such as to inspire apprehension of defeat or failure. [t. F, t. L: m. s. *formīdābilis* causing fear] **—forʹmidableness, forʹmidabilʹity,** *n.* **—forʹmidably,** *adv.* **—Syn. 1.** dread, dreadful, appalling, threatening, menacing.

formless (fômʹlĭs), *adj.* wanting form or shape; shapeless; without a determinate or regular form. **—formʹlessly,** *adv.* **—formʹlessness,** *n.*

form letter, a letter, printed, duplicated, or typed, copies of which are sent to a number of people.

form master, a male teacher in charge of and responsible for the progress of a form.

form mistress, a female teacher in charge of a form.

Formosa (fô mōʹsə), *n.* Taiwan.

formroom (fômʹro͝omʹ, -ro͞omʹ), *n.* a classroom.

formula (fôʹmyo͝o lə), *n.*, *pl.* **-las, -lae** (-lēʹ). **1.** a set form of words, as for stating or declaring something definitely or authoritatively, for indicating procedure to be followed, or for prescribed use on some ceremonial occasion. **2.** *Maths.* a rule or principle frequently expressed in algebraic symbols. **3.** a fixed and successful method of doing something: *his book followed the usual formula of sex, sadism, and spying.* **4.** *Chem.* an expression of the constituents of a compound by symbols and figures, as an **empirical formula,** which merely indicates the number of each kind of atom in the molecule, as CH_2O, or a **structural formula,** which represents diagrammatically the linkage of each atom in the molecule, as H—O—H. **5.** a recipe or prescription. **6.** one of the classifications of racing cars, specifying dimensions and conditions with which cars in the class must comply. **7.** a formal statement of religious doctrine. [t. L, dim. of *forma* FORM, n.]

formularize (fôʹmyo͝o lə rīzʹ), *v.t.*, **-rized, -rizing.** formulate. Also, **formularise. —forʹmularizaʹtion,** *n.*

formulary (fôʹmyo͝o lə rĭ), *n.*, *pl.* **-ries,** *adj.* **—*n.* 1.** a collection or system of formulas. **2.** a set form of words; formula. **3.** (*cap.*) *Pharm.* Also, **National Formulary.** a book published at regular intervals in Great Britain under the supervision of the Joint Formulary Committee, representing the medical and pharmaceutical professions, providing a comprehensive guide to prescribing and drugs in medical usage. **—*adj.* 4.** of or pertaining to a formula or formulas. **5.** of the nature of a formula.

formulate (fôʹmyo͝o lātʹ), *v.t.*, **-lated, -lating. 1.** to express in precise form; state definitely or systematically. **2.** to reduce to or express in a formula. **—forʹmulaʹtion,** *n.* **—forʹmulaʹtor,** *n.*

formulism (fôʹmyo͝o lĭzʹəm), *n.* **1.** adherence to or systematic use of formulas. **2.** a system of formulas. **—forʹmulisʹtic,** *adj.*

formulize (fôʹmyo͝o līzʹ), *v.t.*, **-lized, -lizing.** formulate. Also, **formulise. —forʹmulizaʹtion,** *n.* **—forʹmulizʹer,** *n.*

formyl (fôʹmĭl), *n.* *Chem.* the radical, HCO, derived from formic acid. [f. FORM(IC) + -YL]

fornicate (fôʹnĭ kātʹ), *v.i.*, **-cated, -cating.** to commit fornication. [t. LL: m. s. *fornicātus*, pp. of *fornicārī*, der. L *fornix* (underground) brothel, arch, vault] **—forʹnicaʹtor,** *n.*

fornication (fôʹnĭ kāʹshən), *n.* **1.** voluntary sexual intercourse on the part of an unmarried person with a person of the opposite sex. **2.** *Bible.* **a.** adultery. **b.** idolatry.

fornix (fôʹnĭks), *n.*, *pl.* **-nices** (-nĭ sēzʹ). *Anat.* any of various arched or vaulted structures, as an arching fibrous formation in the brain. [t. L: arch, vault]

Forrest (fŏʹrĭst), *n.* **John, Baron,** 1847–1918, Australian explorer and statesman.

forsake (fə sākʹ), *v.t.*, **-sook, -saken, -saking. 1.** to desert or abandon: *forsake one's friends.* **2.** to give up or renounce (a habit, way of life, etc.). [ME *forsake(n)*, OE *forsacan* deny, give up, f. *for-* FOR- + *sacan* dispute] **—Syn. 1.** See **desert**[2].

forsaken (fə sāʹkən), *v.* **1.** pp. of **forsake. —*adj.* 2.** deserted; abandoned; forlorn. **—forsakʹenly,** *adv.* **—forsakʹenness,** *n.*

Forseti (fôʹsĭ tĭ), *n.* *Scand. Myth.* the god of justice, son of Balder.

forsook (fə so͝okʹ), *v.* pt. of **forsake.**

forsooth (fə so͞othʹ), *adv.* *Archaic.* in truth; in fact; indeed (now used ironically or derisively). [ME *forsooth(e)*, OE *forsōth* for sooth]

forspend (fô spĕndʹ), *v.t.*, **-spent, -spending.** to spend or use up completely, as strength; wear out or exhaust, as with exertion (occurs chiefly in pp.). [ME *forspend(en)*, OE *forspendan.* See FOR-, SPEND]

Forster (fôʹstə), *n.* **E(dward) M(organ),** 1879–1970, English novelist.

forsterite (fôʹstə rītʹ), *n.* a mineral of the olivine group, a silicate of magnesium, Mg_2SiO_4, occurring usually as white, greenish, or yellowish grains in basic igneous rocks. [named after J. R. *Forster*, 1729–98, German naturalist. See -ITE[1]]

forswear (fô swĕəʹ), *v.*, **-swore, -sworn, -swearing. —*v.t.* 1.** to reject or renounce upon oath or with protestations. **2.** to deny upon oath or with strong asseveration. **3.** to perjure (oneself). **—*v.i.* 4.** to swear falsely; commit perjury. [ME *forsweren*, OE *forswerian*; see FOR-, SWEAR] **—forswearʹer,** *n.*

forsworn (fô swônʹ), *v.* **1.** pp. of **forswear. —*adj.* 2.** perjured.

forsythia (fô sīʹthyə, -sīʹthĭ ə), *n.* any shrub of the oleaceous genus *Forsythia*, native to China and south-eastern Europe, species of which are much cultivated for their showy yellow flowers, appearing in early spring before the leaves. [NL, named after W. *Forsyth*, 1737–1804, English horticulturist]

fort (fôt), *n.* **1.** a strong or fortified place; any armed place surrounded by defensive works and occupied by troops; a fortification; a fortress. **2.** (in North America) a trading post. **3. hold the fort,** to maintain the existing position or state of affairs. [t. F, g. L *fortis* strong]

fort., **1.** fortification. **2.** fortified.

Fortaleza (*Port.* fòr tà lèʹzà), *n.* a seaport in E Brazil. 355,000 (1960). Also, **Ceará.**

fortalice (fôʹtə lĭs), *n.* **1.** a small fort; an outwork. **2.** *Obs.* a fortress. [ME, t. ML: m. s. *fortalitia, fortalitium*, der. L *fortis* strong]

Fort-de-France (*Fr.* fŏr də fräNsʹ), *n.* a seaport in and the capital of Martinique, in the French West Indies. 85,281 (1961).

forte[1] (fôt), *n.* **1.** a strong point, as of a person; that in which one excels. **2.** the stronger part of a sword blade between the middle and the hilt (opposed to *foible*). [t. F: m. *fort*, n. use of *fort*, adj. See FORT]

forte[2] (fôʹtĭ), *Music.* **—*adj.* 1.** loud; with force (opposed to *piano*). **—*adv.* 2.** loudly. **—*n.* 3.** a passage that is loud and forcible, or is intended to be so. [It., g. L *fortis* strong]

forte-piano (fôʹtĭ pyäʹnō), *adj.*, *adv.* *Music.* loud with immediate lapses into softness.

Fortescue (fôʹtĭ skyo͞oʹ), *n.* a river in Australia flowing NE then NW through Western Australia to the Indian Ocean. ab. 410 mi.

forth (fôth), *adv.* **1.** forwards; onwards or outwards in place or space. **2.** onwards in time, in order, or in a series: *from that day forth.* **3.** out, as from concealment or inaction; into view or consideration. **4.** away, as from a place or country; abroad. **5. and so forth,** and so on; and others; etcetera. **—*prep.* 6.** *Archaic.* out of; forth from. [ME and OE, c. G *fort*; akin to FURTHER]

Forth (fôth), *n.* **1.** a river of S Scotland flowing from SW Perthshire E to Firth of Forth. 65 mi. **2. Firth of,** an arm of the North Sea, in SE Scotland; the estuary of the river Forth, traversed by a railway bridge, 5330 ft long, and nearby road bridge. 50 mi.

forthcoming (fôthʹkŭmʹĭng), *adj.* **1.** coming forth, or about to come forth; about to appear; approaching in time. **2.** ready or available when required or expected. **—*n.* 3.** a coming forth; appearance.

forthright (*adj.*, *n.* fôthʹrītʹ; *adv.* fôthʹrītʹ, fôthʹrītʹ), *adj.* **1.** going straight to the point; outspoken. **2.** proceeding in a straight course; direct; straightforward. —*adv.* 3. straight or directly forward; in a direct manner. 4. straightaway; at once; immediately. —*n.* 5. *Archaic.* a straight course or path. —**forth′right′ness,** *n.*

forthwith (fôth′wĭth′, -wĭth′), *adv.* 1. immediately; at once; without delay. 2. as soon as can reasonably be expected.

fortieth (fô′tĭ ĭth), *adj.* 1. next after the thirty-ninth. 2. being one of forty equal parts. —*n.* 3. a fortieth part, esp. of one ($\frac{1}{40}$). 4. the fortieth member of a series.

fortification (fô′tĭ fĭ kā′shən), *n.* 1. the act of fortifying or strengthening. 2. that which fortifies or protects. 3. the art or science of constructing defensive military works. 4. (*often pl.*) a military work constructed for the purpose of strengthening a position; fortified place; fort; castle. —**Syn.** 4. fortress, citadel, stronghold.

fortify (fô′tĭ fī′), *v.*, **-fied, -fying.** —*v.t.* 1. to strengthen against attack; surround with defences; provide with defensive military works; protect with fortifications. 2. to furnish with a means of resisting force or standing strain, wear, etc. 3. to make strong; impart strength or vigour to, as the body. 4. to enrich and increase the effectiveness as of food, by adding further ingredients. 5. to strengthen mentally or morally. 6. to confirm or corroborate. 7. to add alcohol to (wines, etc.) —*v.i.* 8. to set up defensive works; erect fortifications. [ME *fortifie(n)*, t. F: m. *fortifier*, t. LL: m. *fortificāre*, f. *forti-* strong + *-ficāre* make] —**for′tifi′able,** *adj.* —**for′tifi′er,** *n.*

Fortin's barometer (fô′tĭnz), a type of mercury barometer for making accurate readings of the pressure of the atmosphere; contains an adjustable mercury cistern. [named after J. *Fortin*, 1750–1831, French physicist]

fortis (fô′tĭs), *adj.*, *n.*, *pl.* **-tes** (-tēz). *Phonet.* —*adj.* 1. pronounced with considerable muscular tension and breath pressure, resulting in a strong fricative or explosive sound: *f* and *p* are fortis, as compared to lenis *v* and *b*. —*n.* 2. a fortis consonant. [t. L: strong]

fortissimo (fô tĭs′ĭ mō′; *It.* fôr tēs′sē mô), *Music.* —*adj.* 1. very loud. —*adv.* 2. very loudly. [t. It., superl. of *forte*. See FORTE[2]]

fortitude (fô′tĭ tyo͞od′), *n.* patient courage under affliction, privation, or temptation; moral strength or endurance. [t. L: m. *fortitūdo*] —**Syn.** See **patience.**

fortitudinous (fô′tĭ tyo͞o′dĭ nəs), *adj.* having fortitude.

Fort Knox (nŏks), a militarily controlled area in N Kentucky; site of the storage place of the U.S. gold reserves since 1936.

Fort Lamy (fôt′ lä′mĭ; *Fr.* fôr là mē′), a city in and the capital of Chad, in the SW part. 45,000 (est. 1966).

fortnight (fôt′nīt′), *n.* the space of fourteen nights and days; two weeks. [ME *fourtenight*, contr. of OE *fēowertēne niht* fourteen nights]

fortnightly (fôt′nīt′lĭ), *adj.*, *adv.*, *n.*, *pl.* **-lies.** —*adj.* 1. occurring or appearing once a fortnight. —*adv.* 2. once a fortnight. —*n.* 3. a periodical issued every two weeks.

fortran (fô′trăn), *n.* *Computers.* an autocode for writing computer programs to perform scientific or engineering calculations. [short for *for(mula) tran(slation)*]

fortress (fô′trĭs), *n.* 1. a large fortified place; a fort or group of forts, often including a town. 2. any place of security. —*v.t.* 3. *Rare.* to furnish with or defend by a fortress: *the city is heavily fortressed.* [ME *forterresse*, t. OF, der. *fort* strong]

fortuitism (fô tyo͞o′ĭ tĭz′əm), *n.* *Philos.* the doctrine or belief that adaptations in nature come about by chance, and not by design. —**fortu′itist,** *n.*, *adj.*

fortuitous (fô tyo͞o′ĭ təs), *adj.* happening or produced by chance; accidental. [t. L: m. *fortuitus* casual] —**fortu′itously,** *adv.* —**fortu′itousness,** *n.* —**Syn.** See **accidental.**

fortuity (fô tyo͞o′ĭ tĭ), *n.*, *pl.* **-ties.** 1. fortuitous character; the fact of being accidental or casual. 2. accident or chance. 3. an accidental occurrence.

Fortuna (fô tyo͞o′nə), *n.* *Rom. Myth.* the goddess of fortune and chance, the counterpart of the Greek Tyche.

fortunate (fô′chə nĭt, fôch′nĭt), *adj.* 1. having good fortune; receiving good from uncertain or unexpected sources; lucky. 2. bringing or presaging good fortune; resulting favourably; auspicious. [ME, t. L: m. s. *fortūnātus*, pp., made prosperous or happy] —**for′tunately,** *adv.* —**for′tunateness,** *n.*

—**Syn.** 1, 2. FORTUNATE, HAPPY, LUCKY refer to persons who enjoy, or events which produce, good fortune. FORTUNATE implies that the success is obtained by the operation of favourable circumstances more than by direct effort; it is usually applied to grave or large matters (esp. those happening in the ordinary course of things): *fortunate in one's choice of a wife, a fortunate investment.* HAPPY emphasizes a pleasant ending or something which happens by chance at just the right moment: *by a happy accident I received the parcel on time.* LUCKY, a more colloquial word, is applied to situations of minor moment that turn out well by chance: *lucky at cards, my lucky day.*

fortune (fô′chən), *n.*, *v.*, **-tuned, -tuning.** —*n.* 1. position in life as determined by wealth: *to make one's fortune, a man of fortune.* 2. amount or stock of wealth. 3. great wealth; ample stock of wealth. 4. chance; luck. 5. (*often pl.*) that which falls or is to fall to one as his portion in life or in any particular proceeding. 6. lot; destiny. 7. (*often cap.*) chance personified, commonly regarded as a goddess distributing arbitrarily or capriciously the lots of life. 8. good luck; success; prosperity. 9. *Colloq.* a person of wealth, esp. a woman; an heiress. **10. tell someone's fortune,** to profess to foretell coming events in a person's life. —*v.t.* 11. *Archaic.* to endow with a fortune. —*v.i.* 12. *Rare.* to chance or happen; come by chance. [ME, t. F, t. L: m. s. *fortūna* chance, luck, fortune] —**for′tuneless,** *adj.*

fortune-hunter (fô′chən hŭn′tə), *n.* one who seeks to win a fortune, esp. through marriage. —**for′tune-hunt′ing,** *adj.*

fortune-teller (fô′chən tĕl′ə), *n.* one who professes to tell people what will happen in the future. —**for′tune-tell′ing,** *adj.*, *n.*

Fort Wayne (wān), a town in the U.S., in NE Indiana. 161,776 (1960).

Fort William, a town in Scotland, in Inverness-shire, at the SW end of the Caledonian Canal. 2715 (1961).

Fort Worth (wûth), a city in the U.S., in N Texas. 356,268 (1960).

forty (fô′tĭ), *n.*, *pl.* **-ties,** *adj.* —*n.* 1. a cardinal number, ten times four. 2. a symbol for this number, as 40 or XL or XXXX. 3. (*pl.*) the numbers from 40 to 49 of a series, usually with reference to the years of a person's age, or the years of a century, esp. the 20th. **4. roaring forties,** those parts of the oceans in the S hemisphere between latitudes 40° and 60° where north-westerly winds are constant throughout the year; noted for their gales. —*adj.* 5. amounting to forty in number. [ME *fourti*, OE *fēowertig*, f. *fēower* four + *-tig* -TY[1]]

Forty-Five (fô′tĭ fīv′), *n.* the Jacobite rebellion of 1745.

forty-niner (fô′tĭ nī′nə), *n.* (*sometimes cap.*) *U.S. Hist.* one of those who went to California in 1849, during the gold rush, in search of fortune.

forty winks, a short nap, esp. in the daytime.

forum (fô′rəm), *n.*, *pl.* **forums, fora** (fô′rə). 1. the marketplace or public square of an ancient Roman city, the centre of judicial and other business and a place of assembly for the people. 2. a court or tribunal: *the forum of public opinion.* 3. an assembly for the discussion of questions of public interest. **4. the Forum,** the forum in the ancient city of Rome. [t. L]

forward (fô′wəd; *also* fŏ′rəd *for def. 11*), *adj.* 1. directed towards a point in advance, moving ahead; onward: *a forward motion.* 2. being in a condition of advancement; well-advanced. 3. ready, prompt, or eager. 4. presumptuous, pert, or bold. 5. situated in the front or forepart. 6. lying in advance; fore. 7. of or pertaining to the future: *forward buying.* 8. radical or extreme, as persons or opinions. —*n.* 9. *Soccer, Hockey, etc.* a player stationed in advance of other members of his team; any player in the forward line. 10. **a.** *Rugby Union Football.* one of the eight players in a team who form the scrum, stand in line-outs, and act as a pack in rushing the ball forward and getting it to the three-quarters. **b.** *Rugby League Football.* one of six players with similar functions. —*adv.* 11. towards the bow or the front part of a ship or aeroplane. 12. forwards. —*v.t.* 13. to send forward; transmit, esp. to a new address: *to forward a letter.* 14. to advance or help onwards; hasten; promote. 15. *Bookbinding.* to prepare (a book) for the finisher. See **forwarding.** [ME and OE *for(e)ward.* See FORE[1], -WARD] —**for′wardly,** *adv.*

forward delivery, *Com.* delivery at a future date.

forwarder (fô′wə də), *n.* one who forwards or sends forward.

forward exchange, foreign currency bought or sold for future delivery.

forwarding (fô′wə dĭng), *n.* 1. *Bookbinding.* a stage which involves stitching, fitting the back, pasting, etc., just before the pages are placed in the completed book cover. 2. the act of one who forwards; the business of a forwarding agent.

forwarding agent, an agent who organizes the collection, forwarding and delivery of goods.

forward line, *Soccer, Hockey, etc.* the five attacking players of a team; outside left, outside right, centre-forward, inside left, and inside right.

forwardness (fô′wəd nĭs), *n.* 1. over-readiness to push oneself forward; presumption; boldness; lack of due modesty. 2. cheerful readiness; promptness; eagerness. 3. the condition of being forward or in advance.

forward pass, *Rugby Football.* a pass in which the ball is illegally thrown towards the opponent's goal.
forward quotation, *Com.* the price quoted on a forward delivery. Also, **forward price.**
forward rate, the price of forward exchange.
forwards (fô′wədz), *adv.* **1.** towards or at a place, point, or time in advance; onwards; ahead: *to move forwards, from this day forwards, to look forwards.* **2.** towards the front. **3.** out; forth; into view or consideration. Also (esp. in figurative senses), **forward.**

—**Syn. 1.** FORWARDS, ONWARDS, both indicate a direction towards the front or a movement in a frontward direction. FORWARDS applies to any movement towards what is or is conceived to be the front or a goal: *to face forwards, to move forwards in the aisles.* ONWARDS applies to any movement in continuance of a course: *to march onwards towards a goal.*

forwent (fô wĕnt′), *v.* pt. of **forgo.**
forwhy (fô wī′), *Archaic.* (sometimes in humorous use). —*adv.* **1.** why. —*conj.* **2.** because.
forworn (fô wôn′), *adj. Archaic.* worn-out; exhausted. Also, **foreworn.**
forzando (fôt săn′dō), *adv., adj. Music.* sforzando. [It., ger. of *forzare* force]
fossa (fŏs′ə), *n., pl.* **fossae** (fŏs′ē). **1.** *Anat.* a pit, cavity, or depression in a bone, etc. **2.** the most primitive member of the civet family, *Cryptoprocta ferox*, of Madagascar. [t. L: ditch, trench]
fosse (fŏs), *n.* **1.** a moat or defensive ditch in a fortification, usually filled with water. **2.** any ditch, trench, or canal. Also, **foss.** [ME, t. F, g. L *fossa* ditch]
fossette (fŏ sĕt′), *n.* a little hollow; a depression; a dimple. [t. F, dim. of *fosse* FOSSE]
fossick (fŏs′ĭk), *Austral.* —*v.i.* **1.** *Mining.* to undermine another's digging; search for waste gold in relinquished workings, washing places, etc. **2.** to search for any object by which to make gain: *to fossick for clients.* —*v.t.* **3.** to dig; hunt. [cf. d. *fossick* troublesome person, *fussick* bustle about, appar. f. FUSS + *-ick*, var. of -OCK] —**fos′sicker,** *n.*
fossil (fŏs′əl), *n.* **1.** any remains, impression, or trace of an animal or plant of a former geological age, as a skeleton or a footprint. **2.** *Colloq.* an outdated or old-fashioned person or thing. **3.** *Obs.* anything dug out of the earth. —*adj.* **4.** of the nature of a fossil: *fossil insects.* **5.** obtained from below the earth's surface: *fossil salt.* **6.** belonging to a past epoch or discarded system; antiquated. [t. L: s. *fossilis* dug up; r. earlier *fossile,* t. F] —**fos′sil-like′,** *adj.*
fossil fuel, the remains of organisms (or their products) embedded in the earth, with high carbon and/or hydrogen contents, which are used by man as fuels; esp. coal, oil, and natural gas.
fossiliferous (fŏs′ĭ lĭf′ə rəs), *adj.* bearing or containing fossils, as rocks or strata.
fossilize (fŏs′ĭ līz′), *v.,* **-lized, -lizing.** —*v.t.* **1.** *Geol.* to convert into a fossil; replace organic substances with mineral in the remains of an organism. **2.** to change as if into mere lifeless remains or traces of the past. **3.** to make rigidly antiquated, as persons, ideas, etc. —*v.i.* **4.** to become a fossil. Also, **fossilise.** —**fos′siliza′tion,** *n.*
fossorial (fŏ sô′rĭ əl), *adj. Zool.* **1.** digging or burrowing. **2.** adapted for digging, as the hands, feet, and skeleton of moles, armadillos, and aardvarks. [f. s. LL *fossōrius* (der. L *fossor* digger) + -AL[1]]
foster (fŏs′tə), *v.t.* **1.** to promote the growth or development of; further; encourage: *to foster foreign trade.* **2.** to bring up or rear, as a foster-child. **3.** to care for or cherish. **4.** to place (a child) in a foster home. **5.** *Obs.* to feed or nourish. —*n.* **6.** a foster-child. **7.** *Obs.* a cherisher. **8.** *Obs.* nourishment. [ME; OE *fōster* nourishment, *fōstrian* nourish; akin to FOOD] —**fos′terer,** *n.* —**Syn. 3.** See **cherish.**
Foster (fŏs′tə), *n.* **Stephen Collins,** 1826–64, U.S. songwriter.
fosterage (fŏs′tə rĭj), *n.* **1.** the act of fostering or rearing another's child as one's own. **2.** the condition of being a foster-child. **3.** the act of promoting or encouraging.
foster-brother (fŏs′tə brŭŧħ′ə), *n.* a boy brought up with another child of different parents.
foster care, the upbringing or the supervision of the upbringing of foster-children, in a private home or a public institution.
foster-child (fŏs′tə chīld′), *n., pl.* **-children.** a child brought up by someone not its own mother or father.
foster-daughter (fŏs′tə dô′tə), *n.* a girl brought up like one's own daughter, though not such by birth.
foster-father (fŏs′tə fä′ŧħə), *n.* one who takes the place of a father in raising a child.
foster home, a household in which a child is raised by a person or persons other than its natural father or mother.
fosterling (fŏs′tə lĭng), *n.* a foster-child. [ME; OE *fōstorling.* See FOSTER, n., -LING[1]]
foster-mother (fŏs′tə mŭŧħ′ə), *n.* **1.** a woman who takes the place of the mother in bringing up a child. **2.** a nurse.
foster-parent (fŏs′tə pĕə′rənt), *n.* a foster-father or foster-mother.
foster-sister (fŏs′tə sĭs′tə), *n.* a girl brought up with another child of different parents.
foster-son (fŏs′tə sŭn′), *n.* a boy brought up like one's own son, though not such by birth.
fostress (fŏs′trĭs), *n.* a woman who fosters.
fother (fŏŧħ′ə), *Naut.* —*v.i.* **1.** to stop a leak in a wooden hull by covering it with a sail or tarpaulin containing a thrumming of rope yarns and oakum. —*v.t.* **2.** to cover (a sail, etc.) with such a thrumming. [? t. D: m. s. *voederen* to line, or LG: m. s. *fodern* to line]
Fotheringhay (fŏŧħ′ə rĭng gā′), *n.* a village in E England, near Peterborough: Mary, Queen of Scots, was imprisoned and executed (1587) in the castle here. Also, **Fotheringay.**
Foucault (*Fr.* fo͞o kō′), *n.* **Jean Bernard Léon** (*Fr.* zhäɴ bĕr nȧr lĕ ôɴ′), 1819–68, French physicist.
Foucault current, *Elect.* an eddy current.
Foucault pendulum, *Astron.* a long thin pendulum which demonstrates the rotation of the earth by changing its plane of oscillation during the course of a day.
Fouché (fo͞o′shā), *n.* **Jacobs Johannes** (jā′kəbz jō hăn′ĭs), born 1899, South African statesman: president of the Republic of South Africa since 1968.
foudroyant (fo͞o droi′ənt; *Fr.* fo͞o drwȧ yäɴ′), *adj.* **1.** striking as with lightning; sudden and overwhelming in effect; stunning; dazzling. **2.** *Pathol.* (of disease) beginning in a sudden and severe form. [t. F, ppr. of *foudroyer* strike with lightning, der. *foudre* lightning, g. L *fulgur*]
fought (fôt), *v.* pt. and pp. of **fight.**
foughten (fô′tn), *adj. Archaic.* that has been the scene of fighting: *a foughten field.*
foul (foul), *adj.* **1.** grossly offensive to the senses; disgustingly loathsome; noisome: *a foul smell.* **2.** charged with or characterized by offensive or noisome matter: *foul air.* **3.** filthy or dirty, as places, vessels, or clothes. **4.** muddy, as a road. **5.** clogged or obstructed with foreign matter: *a foul chimney.* **6.** unfavourable or stormy, as weather. **7.** contrary, as the wind. **8.** grossly offensive in a moral sense. **9.** abominable, wicked, or vile, as deeds, crime, slander, etc. **10.** scurrilous, profane, or obscene, as language. **11.** contrary to the rules or established usages, as of a sport or game; unfair. **12.** *Sport.* pertaining to a foul ball; an infringement of a rule. **13.** in collision or obstructing contact: *a ship foul of a rock.* **14.** entangled, caught, or jammed: *a foul anchor.* **15.** abounding in errors or in marks of correction, as a printer's proof. **16.** *Dial.* not fair; ugly or unattractive. **17.** *Obs.* disfigured. —*adv.* **18.** in a foul manner; foully; unfairly. **19. fall foul of, a.** (of ships) to collide with. **b.** to quarrel with; come into conflict with.
—*n.* **20.** that which is foul. **21.** a collision or entanglement. **22.** a violation of the rules of a sport or game.
—*v.t.* **23.** to make foul; defile; soil. **24.** to clog or obstruct, as a chimney or the bore of a gun. **25.** to collide with. **26.** to cause to become entangled or caught, as a rope. **27.** to defile; dishonour; disgrace. **28.** *Naut.* to encumber (a ship's bottom) with seaweed, barnacles, etc. **29. foul up,** *Colloq.* to bungle or spoil; to cause confusion.
—*v.i.* **30.** to become foul. **31.** *Naut.* to come into collision, as two boats. **32.** to become entangled or clogged: *the rope fouled.* **33.** *Sport.* to make a foul play; give a foul blow. [ME; OE *fūl,* c. G *faul*; akin to L *pūs* pus, *pūtere* to stink] —**foul′ly,** *adv.* —**Syn. 3.** See **dirty.**
foulard (fo͞o läd′, fo͞o′lä), *n.* a soft lightweight silk or rayon of twill weave with printed design, for ties, trimmings, etc. [t. F, t. Swiss F: m. *foulat* fulled cloth, c. F *fouler* to full, g. L *fullāre*]
foul-minded (foul′mīn′dĭd), *adj.* having unclean thoughts. —**foul′-mind′edness,** *n.*
foul-mouthed (foul′mouŧħd′), *adj.* using scurrilous, profane, or obscene language; given to filthy or abusive speech.
foulness (foul′nĭs), *n.* **1.** the state or quality of being foul. **2.** that which is foul; foul matter; filth. **3.** wickedness. [ME; OE *fūlness.* See FOUL, adj., -NESS]
foul play, 1. any unfair or treacherous dealing, often such as involves murder. **2.** unfair conduct in a game.
fouls (foulz), *n. Vet. Sci.* an infection of the feet of cattle causing a foul-smelling inflammation between the toes and round the coronary band.
found[1] (found), *n.* **1.** pt. and pp. of **find. 2. all found,** inclusive of necessary provisions, etc.; with everything provided. [ME; OE *funde, fundon* pt., *funden* pp.]

found[2] (found), *v.t.* **1.** to set up or establish on a firm basis or for enduring existence: *to found a dynasty.* **2.** to lay the lowest part of, fix, or build (a structure) on a firm base or ground: *a house founded upon a rock.* **3.** to base or ground (fol. by *on* or *upon*): *a story founded on fact.* **4.** to afford a basis or ground for. *—v.i.* **5.** to be founded or based (fol. by *on* or *upon*). **6.** to base one's opinion (fol. by *on* or *upon*). [ME *founde(n)*, t. OF: m. *fonder*, g. L *fundāre* lay the bottom of, found]

found[3] (found), *v.t.* **1.** to melt and pour (metal, glass, etc.) into a mould. **2.** to form or make (an article) of molten material in a mould; cast. [ME *fond(en)*, t. OF: m. *fondre* melt, cast, g. L *fundere* pour, melt, cast]

foundation (foun dā′shən), *n.* **1.** that on which something is founded. **2.** the basis or ground of anything. **3.** the natural or prepared ground or base on which some structure rests. **4.** the lowest division of a building, wall, or the like, usually of masonry and partly or wholly below the surface of the ground. **5.** the act of founding, setting up, establishing, etc. **6.** the state of being founded. **7.** a donation or legacy for the support of an institution; an endowment. **8.** an endowed institution. **—Syn. 3.** See **base**[1].

foundation cream, a cosmetic cream or lotion used as a base for powder.

Foundation Day, a legal holiday in Australia, usually January 26th, to commemorate the British landings in 1788.

foundationer (foun dā′shə nə), *n.* a scholar (def. 3).

foundation garment, an undergarment, as a corset, corselet or girdle, worn by women to give support or contours to the figure.

foundation stone, 1. one of the stones forming the foundation of a building. **2.** a stone, set in a building near ground level, usually bearing the date of setting and some commemorative inscription.

founder[1] (foun′də), *n.* one who founds or establishes. [f. FOUND[2] + -ER[1]]

founder[2] (foun′də), *v.i.* **1.** to fill with water and sink, as a ship. **2.** to fall or sink down, as buildings, ground, etc. **3.** to suffer wreck, or fail utterly. **4.** to stumble, break down, or go lame, as a horse. **5.** *Vet. Sci.* (of a horse) to suffer from founder. *—v.t.* **6.** to cause to fill with water and sink, as a ship. **7.** *Vet. Sci.* to cause (a horse, etc.) to break down, go lame, or suffer from founder. *—n.* **8.** *Vet. Sci.* laminitis. [ME *foundren*, t. OF: m. *fondrer*, ult. der. L *fundus* bottom]

founder[3] (foun′də), *n.* one who founds or casts metal, etc. [f. FOUND[3] + -ER[1]]

founderous (foun′də rəs), *adj.* *Now Chiefly Dial.* miry; swampy.

founders' shares, *Finance.* shares created in order to remunerate the founder or promoter of a company; often receiving a large share of the net profit after certain fixed dividends have been paid on the ordinary and/or other classes of stock.

founders' type, *Print.* type cast in individual characters for setting by hand.

foundling (found′lĭng), *n.* an infant found abandoned; a child without a parent or guardian. [ME *found(e)ling*, f. *founde(n)*, pp. of FIND, v. + -LING[1]]

foundling hospital, (formerly) an institutional home for foundlings.

foundry (foun′drĭ), *n., pl.* **-dries. 1.** an establishment for the production of castings, in which molten metal is poured into moulds to shape the castings. **2.** the founding of metal, etc. **3.** things made by founding; castings. **4.** *Obs.* the casting of metals. [t. F: m. *fonderie*, der. *fondre* FOUND[3]]

foundry proof, *Print.* a proof pulled for a final checking before printing plates are made.

fount[1] (fount), *n.* **1.** a spring of water; fountain. **2.** a source or origin. [short for FOUNTAIN]

fount[2] (fount, fŏnt), *n. Print.* a complete assortment of type of one style and size. Also, *U.S.*, **font.** [t. F: m. *fonte*, der. *fondre* melt, cast. See FOUND[3]]

fountain (foun′tĭn), *n.* **1.** a spring or source of water; the source or head of a stream. **2.** the source or origin of anything. **3.** a jet or stream of water (or other liquid) made by mechanical means to spout or rise from an opening or structure, as to afford water for use, or to cool the air, or to serve for ornament. **4.** a structure for discharging such a jet or a number of jets, often an elaborate or artistic work with basins, sculptures, etc. **5.** a soda fountain. **6.** a reservoir for a liquid to be supplied gradually or continuously. [late ME *fontayne*, t. OF: m. *fontaine*, g. LL *fontāna*, prop. fem. of L *fontānus* of or from a spring] **—foun′tainless,** *adj.* **—foun′tain-like′,** *adj.*

fountainhead (foun′tĭn hĕd′), *n.* **1.** a fountain or spring from which a stream flows; the head or source of a stream. **2.** a primary source.

Fountain of Youth, a mythical spring, sought in the Bahama Islands and Florida by Ponce de León, Narváez, De Soto, and others. Indians of Central America believed that it was to the north, and that its waters would cure ills and renew youth.

fountain pen, a pen with a reservoir for supplying ink to the point of the nib.

Fouqué (*Ger.* fōō kĕ′), *n.* **Friedrich Heinrich Karl** (*Ger.* frē′drĭKH hīn′rĭKH kärl), (*Baron de La Motte-Fouqué*) 1777–1843, German novelist and poet.

Fouquet (*Fr.* fōō kĕ′), *n.* **Nicolas** (*Fr.* nē kŏ lȧ′), (*Marquis de Belle-Isle*), 1615–80, French minister under Louis XIV.

Fouquier-Tinville (*Fr.* fōō kyĕ tăN vēl′), *n.* **Antoine Quentin** (*Fr.* äN twȧn käN tăN′), 1747?–95, French revolutionary: prosecutor during the Reign of Terror.

four (fô), *n.* **1.** a cardinal number, three plus one. **2.** a symbol of this number, 4 or IV or IIII. **3.** a set of this many persons or things. **4.** a playing card, etc., with four pips. **5.** *Rowing.* **a.** a crew of four oarsmen. **b.** a racing boat for a crew of four and sometimes a cox. **6.** *Cricket.* a hit scoring four runs, when the ball is hit over the boundary, but first touches the ground inside the boundary. **7. on all fours,** on the hands and feet (or knees). *—adj.* **8.** amounting to four in number. [ME; OE *fēower*, c. D and G *vier* four; akin to L *quattuor*, Gk *téttares*]

fourchette (fōōə shĕt′), *n.* **1.** *Anat.* the fold of skin which forms the posterior margin of the vulva. **2.** *Ornith.* the furcula or united clavicles of a bird; the wishbone of a fowl. **3.** *Zool.* the frog of an animal's foot. **4.** a strip of leather or fabric joining front and back sections of a glove finger. [t. F, dim. of *fourche*, g. L *furca* fork]

four-cycle (fô′sī′kl), *n., adj.* *U.S.* four-stroke.

four-dimensional (fô′dĭ mĕn′shə nəl), *adj.* *Maths.* of a space having points, or a set having elements, which require four coordinates for their unique determination.

four-dimensional continuum. See **continuum** (def. 3).

Fourdrinier (fōōə drĭn′ĭ ə), *n.* **Henry,** 1766–1854, English inventor of paper-making machinery.

four-eyes (fôr′īz′), *n.* **1.** any of several species of fishes with eyes adapted for seeing above and below water, esp. the genus *Anableps.* **2.** *Slang.* a person who wears glasses.

four-flush (fô′flŭsh′), *n.* **1.** *Poker.* four cards of a possible flush, which, with one card of a different suit, make up a hand; an imperfect flush. **2.** *U.S. Colloq.* something full of pretensions; a bluff. *—v.i.* **3.** to act as a four-flusher.

four-flusher (fô′flŭsh′ə), *n.* *U.S. Colloq.* one who makes pretensions that he cannot or does not bear out.

fourfold (fô′fōld′), *adj.* **1.** comprising four parts or members. **2.** four times as great or as much. *—adv.* **3.** in fourfold measure.

four-footed (fô′fŏŏt′ĭd), *adj.* having four feet.

fourgon (*Fr.* fōōr gôN′), *n.* *French.* a long covered wagon for carrying luggage, goods, military supplies, etc.; a van or tumbrel. [F, ? identical with *fourgon* oven fork, der. OF *forgier* search, ult. der. L *forāre* bore]

four-handed (fô′hăn′dĭd), *adj.* **1.** involving four hands or players, as a game at cards. **2.** intended for four hands, as a piece of music for the piano. **3.** having four hands, or four feet adapted for use as hands; quadrumanous.

Four Horsemen of the Apocalypse, four riders symbolizing pestilence, war, famine, and death.

four hundred, the, *U.S.* the exclusive social set.

Fourier (fŏŏ′rĭ ā′; *Fr.* fōō ryĕ′), *n.* **1. François Marie Charles** (*Fr.* fräN swȧ mȧ rē shȧrl′), 1772–1837, French socialist, writer, and reformer. **2. Jean Baptiste Joseph** (*Fr.* zhäN bȧ tēst zhō zĕf′), 1768–1830, French mathematician and physicist.

Fourier analysis (fŏŏ′rĭ ā′, -rĭ ə), *Physics.* the decomposition of any periodic function such as a complex sound or electromagnetic wave-form into the sum of a number of sine and cosine functions. [named after J. B. J. FOURIER]

Fourierism (fŏŏ′rĭ ə rĭz′əm), *n.* the communal social system propounded by François Marie Charles Fourier, under which society was to be organized into phalanxes or associations, each large enough for all industrial and social requirements. **—Fou′rierist, Fourierite** (fŏŏ′rĭ ə rīt′), *n.* **—Fou′rieris′tic,** *adj.*

four-in-hand (fô′rĭn hănd′), *n.* **1.** a long scarf or tie to be tied in a flat slipknot with the ends left hanging. **2.** a vehicle drawn by four horses and driven by one person. **3.** a team of four horses. *—adj.* **4.** having to do with a four-in-hand.

four-leaf clover, 1. a cloverleaf having four leaflets instead of the usual three; it is said to bring good luck. **2.** a traffic junction arranged in this shape; cloverleaf (def. 2).

four-letter word, any of a number of short words, often

of four letters, held to be vulgar or offensive because of reference to sex or excrement.

four-masted (fô′mäs′tĭd), *adj. Naut.* carrying four masts.

Fournier (*Fr.* fo͝or nyē′), *n.* **Pierre (Léon Marie)** (*Fr.* pyĕr lē ôN mȧ rē′), born 1906, French cellist.

four-o'clock (fô′rə klŏk′), *n.* **1.** a common nyctaginaceous garden plant, *Mirabilis jalapa*, with red, white, yellow, or variegated flowers which open late in the afternoon. **2.** the Australian friarbird.

four of a kind, *Poker.* a set of four cards of the same denominations.

fourpence (fô′pəns), *n.* **1.** four pennies. **2.** a former silver coin of this value.

fourpenny (fô′pə nĭ), *n.* —*adj.* **1.** of the amount or value of fourpence. **2. fourpenny one,** *Slang.* a blow. —*n.* **3.** something purchased for fourpence.

four-poster (fô′pōs′tə), *n.* a bed with four posts supporting a canopy over the bed, and, sometimes, curtains.

four-pounder (fô′poun′də), *n.* a gun which fires a shell weighing four pounds.

fourragère (*Fr.* fo͞o rȧ zhĕr′), *n.* (in French and U.S. military use) **1.** an ornament of cord worn on the shoulder. **2.** such a cord awarded as an honorary decoration, as to members of a regiment or other unit that has received a requisite number of citations. [F]

fourscore (fô′skô′), *adj.* four times twenty; eighty.

four-seater (fô′sē′tə), *n.* a vehicle seating four people.

foursome (fô′səm), *n.* **1.** *Golf, etc.* a match played by four persons, two on each side. **2.** a company or set of four. —*adj.* **3.** consisting of four; performed by four persons together. See **eightsome.** [f. FOUR + -SOME[2]]

foursquare (fô′skwĕə′), *adj.* **1.** square. **2.** firm; steady. **3.** frank; blunt. —*adv.* **4.** without equivocation. —**four′-square′ly,** *adv.* —**four′square′ness,** *n.*

four-stroke (fô′strōk′), *adj.* **1.** denoting or pertaining to an internal-combustion engine cycle in which one piston stroke out of every four is a power stroke. **2.** powered by such an engine. —*n.* **3.** a four-stroke engine or vehicle.

fourteen (fô′tēn′), *n.* **1.** a cardinal number, ten plus four. **2.** a symbol for this number, as 14 or XIV or XIIII. —*adj.* **3.** amounting to fourteen in number. [ME *fourtene*, OE *fēowertēne.* See FOUR, -TEEN]

Fourteen Points, The, a statement of the war aims of the Allies, made by President Wilson on January 8th, 1918.

fourteenth (fô′tēnth′), *adj.* **1.** next after the thirteenth. **2.** being one of fourteen equal parts. —*n.* **3.** a fourteenth part, esp. of one ($\frac{1}{14}$). **4.** the fourteenth member of a series.

fourth (fôth), *adj.* **1.** next after the third. **2.** being one of four equal parts. —*n.* **3.** a fourth part, esp. of one ($\frac{1}{4}$). **4.** the fourth member of a series. **5.** *Music.* **a.** a note on the fourth degree from a given note (counted as the first). **b.** the interval between such notes. **c.** the harmonic combination of such notes. **6. the Fourth,** *U.S.* the Fourth of July. [ME; OE *fēo(we)rtha.* See FOUR, -TH[2]]

fourth dimension, the dimension of time, which is required in addition to the three dimensions of space, in order to locate a point in space-time. —**fourth′-dimen′-sional,** *adj.*

fourth estate, the public press, the newspapers, or the body of journalists.

Fourth International. See **international** (def. 10).

fourthly (fôth′lĭ), *adv.* in the fourth place.

Fourth of July, *U.S.* the date of the adoption of the Declaration of Independence, in 1776, observed as a public holiday.

fourth position, *Ballet.* a standing position in which the feet are at right angles to the direction of the body, the toes pointing out, with the left foot forward and the right foot back.

Fourth Republic. See **republic** (def. 4).

four-wheel (fô′wēl′), *adj.* **1.** having four wheels. **2.** functioning on or by four wheels: *four-wheel drive.*

four-wheeler (fô′wē′lə), *n.* a four-wheeled vehicle, esp. a horse-drawn carriage.

fouter (fo͞o′tə), *n.* (a word formerly used in expressions of contemptuous indifference): *a fouter for the world!* Also, **foutre.** [t. F: m. (*se*) *foutre* (*de*) care nothing for, g. L *futuere* have sexual intercourse with]

Fou Ts'ong (fo͞o′ tsŏng′), born 1934, Chinese pianist, in England since 1959.

fovea (fō′vyə), *n., pl.* **-veae** (-vĭ ē′). *Biol.* a small pit or depression in a bone or other structure. [t. L: small pit] —**fo′veal,** *adj.*

fovea centralis (sĕn trä′lĭs), *Anat.* a small pit or depression at the back of the retina forming the point of sharpest vision. [L]

foveate (fō′vĭ ĭt, -āt′), *adj. Biol.* having foveae; pitted.

Foveaux Strait (fō′vō), the sea channel between South Island and Stewart Island, New Zealand. ab. 18 mi. wide at its narrowest part.

foveola (fō vē′ə lə), *n., pl.* **-lae** (-lē′). *Biol.* a small fovea; a very small pit or depression. Also, **foveole.** [NL, dim. of L *fovea.* See FOVEA]

foveolate (fō′vĭ ə lāt′), *adj. Biol.* having foveolae, or very small pits. Also, **fo′veolat′ed.**

fowl (foul), *n., pl.* **fowls,** (*esp. collectively*) **fowl,** *v.* —*n.* **1.** the domestic or barnyard hen or cock (**domestic fowl**), a gallinaceous bird (often designated as *Gallus domesticus*) of the pheasant family, descended from wild species of *Gallus* (**jungle fowl**). **2.** any of various other gallinaceous or similar birds, as the turkey or duck. **3.** (in market and household use) a full-grown domestic fowl for food purposes (as distinguished from a chicken, or young fowl). **4.** the flesh or meat of a domestic fowl. **5.** any bird (now chiefly in combination): *waterfowl, wildfowl.* —*v.i.* **6.** to hunt or take wildfowl. [ME *foule*, OE *fugel*, c. G *Vogel*]

fowl cholera, a specific, acute, diarrhoeal disease of fowls, especially chickens, caused by a bacterium, *Pasteurella multocida.*

fowler (fou′lə), *n.* one who hunts, shoots, or snares birds, for sport or for a living.

Fowler (fou′lə), *n.* **Henry Watson,** 1858–1953, English grammarian and lexicographer.

fowling (fou′lĭng), *n.* the practice or sport of shooting or snaring birds.

fowling net, a net for catching birds.

fowling-piece (fou′lĭng pēs′), *n.* a shotgun for shooting wildfowl.

fowl pest, **1.** Also, **fowl plague.** an acute, highly fatal virus disease of all species of domestic fowls, characterized by weakness, lethargy, breathing trouble, and cyanosis. **2.** Newcastle disease.

fowl pox, a virus disease of chickens and other birds characterized by warty excrescences on the comb and wattles, and often by diphtheria-like changes in the mucous membranes of the head.

fox (fŏks), *n.* **1.** any of certain carnivores of the dog family (*Canidae*), esp. those constituting the genus *Vulpes*, smaller than the wolves, characterized by pointed muzzle, erect ears, and long, bushy tail. **2.** the fur of this animal. **3.** a cunning or crafty person. **4.** *Naut.* a seizing made by twisting several rope yarns together and rubbing them down. **5.** (*cap.*) **a.** a tribe of North American Algonquian Indians, formerly in Wisconsin, later merged with the Sac tribe. **b.** a member of this tribe. **6.** *Bible.* (sometimes) the jackal. —*v.t.* **7.** *Colloq.* to deceive or trick. **8.** *Obs.* to intoxicate or befuddle. **9.** *Obs.* to cause (papers, etc.) to discolour with reddish brown spots of mildew. **10.** *Obs.* to make sour, as beer. **11.** to repair or make (a shoe) with leather or other material applied so as to cover or form part of the upper front. —*v.i.* **12.** to act cunningly or craftily. **13.** *Obs.* (of papers, etc.) to become foxed. [ME and OE, c. G *Fuchs.* See VIXEN] —**fox′like′,** *adj.*

Red fox, *Vulpes fulva*
(Total length 3½ to 4 ft, tail 16 in.)

Fox (fŏks), *n.* **1. Charles James,** 1749–1806, English statesman and orator. **2. George,** 1624–91, English preacher and writer, founder of the Society of Friends. **3. John.** See **Foxe.**

fox-bat (fŏks′băt′), *n.* **1.** a flying fox. **2.** a fruit-bat.

foxberry (fŏks′bə rĭ, -brĭ), *n.* **1.** bearberry. **2.** cowberry.

fox brush, the bushy tail of a fox.

Foxe (fŏks), *n.* **John,** 1516–87, English clergyman and writer.

foxglove (fŏks′glŭv′), *n.* any plant of the scrophulariaceous genus *Digitalis*, esp. *D. purpurea* (the common foxglove), a native of Europe, bearing drooping, tubular, purple or white flowers, and leaves that are used as digitalis in medicine. [ME *foxes glove*, OE *foxes glōfa*]

foxgrape (fŏks′grāp′), *n.* either of two species of grape, *Vitis labrusca* of the northern U.S. or *V. rotundifolia* of the southern U.S., from which various cultivated varieties have been derived.

foxhole (fŏks′hōl′), *n.* a small pit, usually for one or two men, used for cover in a battle area.

foxhound (fŏks′hound′), *n.* one of a breed of fleet, keen-scented hounds trained to hunt foxes.

English foxhound
(23 in. high at the shoulder)

fox-hunting (fŏks′hŭn′tĭng), *n.* a sport in which the hunters follow a fox that is being pursued by a hound or hounds. —**fox′-hun′ter,** *n.*

foxtail (fŏks′tāl′), *n.* any of various grasses with soft, brushlike spikes of flowers.

fox-terrier (fŏks′tĕ′rĭ ə), *n.* one of a breed of small, active terriers, sometimes used for driving foxes from their holes, but kept chiefly as pets.

Smooth-haired fox-terrier (15 in. high at the shoulder)

foxtrot (fŏks′trŏt′), *n., v.,* **-trotted, -trotting.** —*n.* **1.** a ballroom dance, in 4/4 time, performed by couples, characterized by various combinations of short, quick steps. **2.** a pace, as of a horse, consisting of a series of short steps, as in slackening from a trot to a walk. —*v.i.* **3.** to dance a foxtrot.

foxy (fŏk′sĭ), *adj.,* **foxier, foxiest. 1.** foxlike; cunning or crafty. **2.** discoloured or foxed. **3.** yellowish or reddish brown; of the colour of the common red fox. **4.** impaired or defective in quality. **5.** (esp. of a painting) having an excessively reddish tone. **6.** (of wines) having the pronounced flavour natural to native American grape varieties, as that of foxgrape. —**fox′ily,** *adv.* —**fox′iness,** *n.*

foy (foi), *n. Dial.* **1.** a feast, gift, etc., given by or to a person about to start on a journey. **2.** a feast held on some special occasion, as at the end of the harvest. [t. MD: m. *foye,* prob. t. OF: m. *voie,* g. L *via* way]

foyer (foi′ə, foi′ā; *Fr.* fwȧ yĕ′), *n.* **1.** (in theatres and cinemas) the area between the outer lobby and the auditorium. **2.** a hall or anteroom, esp. in a hotel. [t. F: hearth, fireside (orig. a room to which theatre audiences went for warmth between the acts), g. Rom. *focārium,* der. L *focus* hearth]

fozy (fō′zĭ), *adj.,* **-zier, -ziest.** *Chiefly Scot.* **1.** spongy. **2.** (of a vegetable or fruit) not fresh; overripe. **3.** (of a person) fat; flabby. **4.** stupid; dull-witted. —**fo′ziness,** *n.*

f.p., 1. freezing point. **2.** Also, **F.P.** foot-pound.

f.p.s., 1. feet per second. **2.** frames per second.

f.p.s. system, foot-pound-second system.

Fr, 1. Father. **2.** *Chem.* francium.

Fr., 1. France. **2.** frater[1]. **3.** French. **4.** Friar. **5.** Friday.

fr., 1. fragment. **2.** (*pl.* **fr., frs**) franc. **3.** from.

Fra (frä), *n.* brother (a title of a friar): *Fra Giovanni.* [t. It., abbrev. of *frate* brother]

fracas (frăk′ä), *n.* a disorderly noise, disturbance, or fight; uproar. [t. F, t. It.: m. *fracasso,* der. *fracassare* smash, f. *fra-* (g. L *infrā* among) completely + *cassare* (ult. g. L *quassāre* to shake)]

fraction (frăk′shən), *n.* **1.** *Maths.* **a.** one or more aliquot parts of a unit or whole number; the ratio between any two numbers. **b.** a ratio of algebraic quantities analogous to the arithmetical vulgar fraction and similarly expressed. **2.** a part as distinct from the whole of anything: *only a fraction of the population is literate.* **3.** a piece broken off; fragment or bit. **4.** the act of breaking. **5.** *Eccles.* the breaking of bread in the Eucharistic service. —*v.t.* **6.** to divide into fractions. [ME, t. LL: s. *fractio,* der. L *frangere* break]

fractional (frăk′shə nəl), *adj.* **1.** pertaining to fractions; comprising a part or the parts of a unit; constituting a fraction: *fractional numbers.* **2.** partial, inconsiderable, or insignificant. **3.** *Chem.* of or denoting a process, as distillation, crystallization, or oxidation, by which the component substances of a mixture are separated according to differences in certain of their properties, as boiling point, critical temperature, solubility, etc. Also, **fractionary** (frăk′shə nə rĭ) for 1, 2. —**frac′tionally,** *adv.*

fractional currency, coins or paper money of a smaller denomination than the monetary unit.

fractionate (frăk′shə nāt′), *v.t.,* **-nated, -nating. 1.** to separate (a mixture) into its ingredients, or into portions having different properties, as by distillation or crystallization; subject to fractional distillation, crystallization, or the like. **2.** to obtain by such a process. —**frac′tiona′tion,** *n.* —**frac′tionat′or,** *n.*

fractionating column, a long vertical column forming part of a still, containing rings, plates or bubble caps, as used in fractional distillation.

fractionize (frăk′shə nīz′), *v.t., v.i.,* **-nized, -nizing.** to divide into fractions. Also, **fractionise.**

fractious (frăk′shəs), *adj.* **1.** cross, fretful, or peevish. **2.** refractory or unruly. [f. FRACTI(ON) (in obs. sense of discord) + -OUS, modelled on CAPTIOUS, etc.] —**frac′tiously,** *adv.* —**frac′tiousness,** *n.*

fracto-, a word element meaning 'broken'. [comb. form repr. L *fractus,* pp.]

fractocumulus (frăk′tō kyōō′myōō ləs), *n., pl.* **-li** (-lī′). *Meteorol.* very low, ragged clouds, slightly cumuliform, which often appear beneath nimbostratus clouds during active precipitation.

fractostratus (frăk′tō strā′təs), *n., pl.* **-ti** (-tī). *Meteorol.* very low, ragged clouds of stratiform appearance which often appear beneath nimbostratus clouds during active precipitation; scud clouds.

fracture (frăk′chə), *n., v.,* **-tured, -turing.** —*n.* **1.** the breaking of a bone, cartilage, etc., or the resulting condition (in a bone, called *simple* when the bone does not communicate with the exterior, and *compound* when there is also a laceration of the integuments permitting communication with the exterior). **2.** the characteristic manner of breaking. **3.** the characteristic appearance of a broken surface, as of a mineral. **4.** the act of breaking. **5.** the state of being broken. **6.** a break, breach, or split. —*v.t.* **7.** to break or crack. **8.** to cause or to suffer a fracture in (a bone, etc.). —*v.i.* **9.** to undergo fracture; break. [t. F, t. L: m. *fractūra* breach] —**frac′tural,** *adj.*

frae (frā), *prep., adv. Scot.* from.

fraenulum (frē′nyōō ləm, frĕn′-), *n., pl.* **-la. 1.** *Anat., Zool.* a small fraenum. **2.** *Entomol.* a strong spine or group of bristles on the hind wing of moths and butterflies projecting beneath the forewing and serving to hold the two wings together in flight. Also, **frenulum.** [NL, dim. of L *frænum* curb]

fraenum (frē′nəm), *n., pl.* **-na** (-nə). *Anat., Zool.* a little fold of membrane which checks or restrains the motion of a part, as the one which binds down the underside of the tongue. Also, **frenum.**

fragile (frăj′īl), *adj.* easily broken, shattered, or damaged; delicate; brittle; frail. [t. L: m. s. *fragilis*] —**frag′ilely,** *adv.* —**fragility** (frə jĭl′ĭ tĭ), **frag′ileness,** *n.* —**Syn.** See **frail**[1].

fragment (frăg′mənt), *n.* **1.** a part broken off or detached: *scattered fragments of rock.* **2.** a portion that is unfinished or incomplete: *fragments of a letter.* **3.** an odd piece, bit, or scrap. [t. L: s. *fragmentum*]

fragmental (frăg mĕn′tl), *adj.* **1.** fragmentary. **2.** *Geol.* clastic.

fragmentary (frăg′mən tə rĭ, -trĭ), *adj.* composed of fragments; broken; disconnected; incomplete: *fragmentary evidence, remains, etc.* —**frag′mentarily,** *adv.* —**frag′mentariness,** *n.*

fragmentation (frăg′mĕn tā′shən), *n.* **1.** the act or process of fragmenting. **2.** the disintegration or breakdown of norms of thought, behaviour, or social relationship. **3.** the fragments from an exploded bomb or hand grenade.

fragmentation bomb, a bomb which, when exploded, breaks into many small fragments which scatter at high speed.

fragmented (frăg mĕn′tĭd), *adj.* **1.** reduced to fragments. **2.** disorganized; broken down.

Fragonard (*Fr.* frȧ gō nȧr′), *n.* **Jean Honoré** (*Fr.* zhäɴ ō nō rĕ′), 1732–1806, French painter.

fragrance (frā′grəns), *n.* fragrant quality or odour; sweet scent. **—Syn.** See **perfume.**

fragrancy (frā′grən sĭ), *n., pl.* **-cies.** fragrance.

fragrant (frā′grənt), *adj.* **1.** having a pleasant odour; sweet-smelling; sweet-scented. **2.** delightful; pleasant: *fragrant memories.* [t. L: s. *frāgrans,* ppr., emitting an odour, smelling sweet] —**fra′grantly,** *adv.* **—Syn. 1.** perfumed, odorous, redolent.

fragrant orchid, an orchid, *Gymnadenia conopsea,* with dense spikes of strongly scented, reddish mauve flowers, found on non-acid soils in Europe, N and W Asia.

frail[1] (frāl), *adj.* **1.** weak; not robust; having delicate health. **2.** easily broken or destroyed; fragile. **3.** morally weak; not strong against temptation. [ME *frele,* t. OF, var. of *fraile,* g. L *fragilis* fragile] —**frail′ly,** *adv.* —**frail′ness,** *n.*

—**Syn. 1, 2.** FRAIL, BRITTLE, FRAGILE imply a delicacy or weakness of substance or construction. FRAIL applies particularly to health, and immaterial things: *a frail constitution, frail hopes.* BRITTLE implies a hard outside finish but delicate material which snaps or breaks to pieces easily: *brittle as glass.* FRAGILE implies that the object must be handled carefully to avoid breakage or damage: *fragile bric-a-brac.* —**Ant. 1.** sturdy.

frail[2] (frāl), *n.* **1.** a flexible basket made of rushes, used esp. for dried fruits, as dates, figs, or raisins. **2.** a certain quantity of raisins, about 75 lbs, contained in such a basket. [ME *frayel,* t. OF: m. *fraiel*]

frailty (frāl′tĭ), *n., pl.* **-ties. 1.** the quality or state of being frail. **2.** moral weakness; liability to yield to temptation. **3.** a fault proceeding from moral weakness.

fraise (frāz), *n.* **1.** *Fort.* a defence consisting of pointed stakes projecting from the ramparts in a horizontal or an inclined position. **2.** a ruff worn round the neck in the 16th century. [t. F, der. *fraiser* to frizzle, curl, t. Pr.: m. *frezar,* ult. der. a Gmc word; cf. OE *frīs* curled]

Fraktur (*Ger.* frȧk tōōr′), *n. Print.* a typeface, a style of black-letter or text, formerly much used in German typesetting.

F.R.A.M., Fellow of the Royal Academy of Music.

framboesia (frăm bē′zyə), *n.* yaws. Also, **frambesia.** [NL: Latinization of F *framboise* raspberry, g. Rom. *frambosia,* contr. of *frāga ambrosia* ambrosia strawberry]

frame (frām), *n.*, *v.*, **framed, framing.** —*n.* **1.** an enclosing border or case, as for a picture. **2.** anything composed of parts fitted and joined together; a structure. **3.** the sustaining parts of a structure fitted and joined together; framework or skeleton. **4.** the body, esp. the human body, with reference to its make or build. **5.** a structure for admitting or enclosing something. **6.** any of various machines operating on or within a framework. **7.** a machine or part of a machine used in textile production. **8.** the rigid part of a bicycle. **9.** a particular state, as of the mind: *an unhappy frame of mind.* **10.** form, constitution, or structure in general; system; order. **11.** *Shipbuilding.* **a.** one of the transverse structural members of a ship's hull, extending from the gunwale to the bilge or to the keel. **b. square frame,** a frame set perpendicularly to the vertical plane of the keel. **c. cant frame,** a frame set at an acute angle to the vertical plane of the keel. **12.** a structure placed in a beehive on which bees build a honeycomb. **13.** *Colloq.* (in baseball) an inning. **14.** *Snooker.* **a.** the triangular form used to set up the balls for a game. **b.** the balls as so set up. **c.** the period of play required to pocket them. **15.** one of the successive small pictures on a strip of film. **16.** *Electronics.* a quantity of information which is transmitted as a unit. —*v.t.* **17.** to form or make, as by fitting and uniting parts together; construct. **18.** to contrive, devise, or compose, as a plan, law, poem, etc. **19.** to conceive or imagine, as ideas, etc. **20.** to fashion or shape. **21.** to shape or to adapt to a particular purpose. **22.** *Colloq.* to contrive or prearrange fraudulently or falsely, as a plot, a race, etc. **23.** *Colloq.* to incriminate unjustly by a plot, as a person. **24.** to provide with or put into a frame, as a picture. **25.** *Obs.* to direct, as one's steps. —*v.i.* **26.** to betake oneself, or resort. **27.** to prepare, attempt, give promise, or manage to do something. [ME *frame(n)*, OE *framian* avail, profit, der. *fram* forward] —**frame′less,** *adj.* —**fram′er,** *n.*

framed building, a construction in which a framework (usually metal or wood) forms the supporting structure.

frame house, a sawn timber house sheathed outside with weatherboards or shingles.

frame of reference, **1.** *Sociol.* a set of standards to which individuals or groups refer, and which determine and sanction their behaviour and attitudes, esp. in norm-formation. **2.** *Maths.* a system of coordinates within which a particular set of conditions can be defined.

framesaw (frām′sô′), *n.* gangsaw.

frame-up (frām′ŭp′), *n.* *Colloq.* that which is framed, as a plot, or a contest whose result is fraudulently prearranged.

framework (frām′wŭk′), *n.* **1.** a structure composed of parts fitted and united together. **2.** one designed to support or enclose something; frame or skeleton. **3.** frames collectively. **4.** work done in, on, or with a frame.

framing (frā′mĭng), *n.* **1.** the act, process, or manner of constructing anything. **2.** the act of providing with a frame. **3.** framed work; a frame or a system of frames.

franc (frăngk; *Fr.* fräN), *n.* **1.** the monetary unit of France, equal to 100 centimes, and equivalent to about £0·0844 sterling. **2.** the monetary unit of Belgium, equivalent to about £0·0083 sterling. **3.** the monetary unit of Switzerland, equivalent to about £0·095 sterling. **4.** any of the monetary units of various other countries, as Algeria, Martinique, Senegal. **5.** a note or coin of the value of any of these. **6.** a former silver coin of France. *Abbrev.:* fr. [ME *frank*, t. OF: m. *franc*, so called from the ML legend *Francōrum rex* king of the Franks (or French), on the first coin]

France (*Fr.* fräNs), *n.* **Anatole** (*Fr.* à nà tōl′) (*Jacques Anatole Thibault*), 1844–1924, French novelist and essayist.

France (fräns), *n.* a republic in W Europe. 46,520,271 pop. (1962); 212,736 sq. mi. *Cap.:* Paris.

Francesca (*It.* fràn chĕs′kà), *n.* **Piero della** (*It.* pyĕ′rò dĕl là) (*Piero de' Franceschi*), *c.* 1420–92, Italian painter.

Francescatti (*Fr.* fräN sĕs kà tē′), *n.* **Zino** (*Fr.* zē nō′), born 1905, French violinist in the U.S.

Franche-Comté (*Fr.* fräNsh kōN tĕ′), *n.* **1.** a former province in E France: once a part of Burgundy. **2.** an administrative region in E France comprising the departments of Doubs, Haute-Saône, and Jura. 819,003 pop. (1961); 6058 sq. mi. *Cap.:* Besançon.

franchise (frăn′chīz), *n.* **1.** the rights of a citizen, esp. the right to vote. **2.** a privilege arising from the grant of a sovereign or government, or from prescription, which presupposes a grant. **3.** a privilege of a public nature conferred on an individual or body of individuals by a governmental grant. **4.** permission granted by a manufacturer to a distributor or retailer to sell his products. **5.** *Rare.* the district or jurisdiction to which the privilege of an individual or corporation extends. **6.** (orig.) a legal immunity or exemption from a particular burden, exaction, or the like. **7.** *Marine Insurance.* an amount or percentage specified in a policy, below which the insurer accepts no liability for any claim. [ME, t. OF, der. *franc* free, FRANK]

Francis (frän′sĭs), *n.* **Saint** (*Francis of Assisi*), 1181?–1226, Italian friar: founded Franciscan order.

Francis I, **1.** 1494–1547, king of France 1515–47. **2.** title of Francis II as emperor of Austria.

Francis II, 1768–1835, last emperor of the Holy Roman Empire, 1792–1806. As Francis I, he was the first emperor of Austria, 1804–35.

Franciscan (frăn sĭs′kən), *adj.* **1.** of or pertaining to St Francis of Assisi or the mendicant religious order founded by him (authorized by the pope in 1209; formally ratified in 1223). —*n.* **2.** a member of this order.

Francis Ferdinand, Franz Ferdinand.

Francis Joseph I, Franz Josef I.

Francis Joseph II, Franz Josef II.

Francis of Paula (*It.* pà′o͞o là), **Saint,** 1416–1507, Italian monk: founder of the order of Minims.

Francis of Sales (sālz; *Fr.* sàl), **Saint,** 1567–1622. French ecclesiastic and theologian: bishop of Geneva 1602–22.

Francis Xavier (zā′vĭ ə, zăv′ĭ-). See **Xavier.**

francium (frăn′sĭ əm), *n.* a radioactive element of the alkali metal group. *Symbol:* Fr; *at. no.:* 87. [f. FRANC(E), where first identified + -IUM]

Franck (*Fr.* fräNk), *n.* **César Auguste** (*Fr.* sĕ zär ō gYst′), 1822–90, French composer and organist, born in Belgium.

Franco (frăng′kō; *Sp.* fràn′kò), *n.* **Francisco** (*Sp.* fràn thēs′kò), born 1892, Spanish military leader and dictator: head of state since 1939.

Franco-, a word element meaning 'French' or 'France', as in *Franco-German.* [comb. form repr. ML *Francus* a Frank, a Frenchman]

francolin (frăng′kō lĭn), *n.* any of numerous Old World gallinaceous birds of the genus *Francolinus* and allied genera, esp. *F. vulgaris*, a species formerly common in southern Europe but now chiefly confined to Asia. [t. F, t. It.: m. *francolino*]

Franconia (frăng kō′nyə), *n.* a medieval duchy in Germany, largely in the valley of the river Main.

Franconian (frăng kō′nyən), *n.* **1.** the West Germanic language of the Franks, consisting of Frankish and related dialects. —*adj.* **2.** of or pertaining to Franconia. **3.** of or pertaining to Franconian.

Francophil (frăng′kō fĭl), *adj.* **1.** friendly to France or the French. —*n.* **2.** one who is friendly to France or the French. Also, **Francophile** (frăng′kō fīl′).

Francophobe (frăng′kō fōb′), *adj.* **1.** fearing or hating France. —*n.* **2.** one who fears or hates France.

Franco-Prussian War (frăng′kō prŭsh′ən), a war (1870–71) between France and Prussia, resulting in the ceding of Alsace and E Lorraine to Prussia.

franc-tireur (*Fr.* fräN tē rœr′), *n.*, *pl.* **francs-tireurs** (*Fr.* fräN tē rœr′). **1.** a sharpshooter; sniper. **2.** an irregular soldier; guerrilla fighter. [F: lit., free-shooter]

frangible (frăn′jĭ bl), *adj.* capable of being broken; breakable. [ME *frangebyll*, t. OF: m. *frangible*, der. L *frangere* break] —**fran′gibil′ity,** *n.*

frangipane (frăn′jĭ pān′), *n.* **1.** a kind of pastry cake, filled with cream, almonds, and sugar. **2.** frangipani. [t. F; said to be from *Frangipani*, the inventor]

frangipani (frăn′jĭ pä′nĭ), *n.*, *pl.* **-nies. 1.** a perfume prepared from, or imitating the scent of, the flower of the red jasmine, *Plumeria ruba*, an apocynaceous tree or shrub of tropical America. **2.** the tree or shrub itself. [said to be named after the inventor]

frank (frăngk), *adj.* **1.** open or unreserved in speech; candid or outspoken; sincere. **2.** undisguised; avowed; downright: *frank mutiny.* **3.** *Obs.* liberal or generous. **4.** *Obs.* free. —*n.* **5.** a signature or mark affixed by special privilege to a letter, parcel, or the like, to ensure its transmission free of charge, as by post. **6.** the privilege of franking letters, etc. **7.** a franked letter, parcel, etc. —*v.t.* **8.** to mark (a letter, parcel, etc.) for transmission free of the usual charge, by virtue of official or special privilege; send free of charge, as mail. **9.** to facilitate the coming of (a person). **10.** convey (a person) free of charge. **11.** to enable to pass or go freely. **12.** to secure exemption for. [ME, t. OF: m. *franc*, g. LL *francus* free, orig. Frank] —**frank′able,** *adj.* —**frank′er,** *n.*

—**Syn. 1.** FRANK, CANDID, OPEN, OUTSPOKEN imply a freedom and boldness in speaking. FRANK is applied to one unreserved in expressing the truth and his real opinions and sentiments: *a frank disagreement.* CANDID suggests one (sometimes unpleasantly) sincere and truthful or impartial and fair in judgement: *a candid expression of opinion.* OPEN implies a lack of reserve or of concealment: *open antagonism.* OUTSPOKEN applies to one who expresses himself freely, even when this is inappropriate: *outspoken disapproval.*

Frank (frăngk), *n.* **1.** a member of a group of ancient

Germanic peoples dwelling in the regions of the Rhine, one division of whom, the Salians, conquered Gaul about A.D. 500, founded an extensive kingdom, and gave origin to the name *France.* **2.** (in the Levant) any native or inhabitant of western Europe. [ME *Franke*, OE *Franca*, c. OHG *Franko*; usually said to be from the name of the national weapon. Cf. OE *franca* spear, javelin. See FRANK]

Frankenstein (frăng′kĭn stīn′), *n.* **1.** one who creates a monster or a destructive agency that he cannot control or that brings about his own ruin. **2.** the monster or destructive agency itself. [from the hero of Mary Shelley's novel, '*Frankenstein*', a student who created such a monster]

Frankfurt (frăngk′fət; *Ger.* frängk′fo͝ort), *n.* **1. Frankfurt am Main** (*Ger.* äm mīn′), a city in West Germany, in S Hesse, on the river Main. 684,800 (est. 1966). **2. Frankfurt an der Oder** (*Ger.* än dėr ō′dər), a town in East Germany, on the river Oder. 58,866 (1965). Also, *Now Obs.*, **Frankfort.**

frankfurter (frăngk′fû′tə), *n.* **1.** a reddish variety of sausage made of beef and pork, commonly cooked by steaming or boiling. **2.** (*cap.*) a native or inhabitant of Frankfurt. [t. G: Frankfurt (sausage)]

frankincense (frăng′kĭn sĕns′), *n.* an aromatic gum resin from various Asiatic and African trees of the genus *Boswellia*, esp. *B. carteri*: used chiefly for burning as incense or ceremonially. [ME *franke ensens*, t. OF: m. *franc encens* pure incense. See FRANK, INCENSE[1]]

Frankish (frăng′kĭsh), *adj.* **1.** of or pertaining to the Franks. —*n.* **2.** the language of the Franks (def. 1), a dialect of Franconian.

franklin (frăngk′lĭn), *n.* (in the late Middle Ages) a landowner of free but not noble birth. [ME *frankeleyn*, ult. der. ML *francus* free, FRANK]

Franklin (frăngk′lĭn), *n.* **1. Benjamin,** 1706–90, American statesman, diplomat, author, scientist, and inventor. **2. Sir John,** 1786–1847, English arctic explorer. **3.** a district in extreme N Canada, in the Northwest Territories, including Baffin Island, other arctic islands, and Boothia and Melville peninsulas. 549,253 sq. mi.

franklinite (frăngk′lĭ nīt′), *n.* a mineral of the spinel group, an oxide of zinc, manganese, and iron, occurring in black octahedral crystals or in masses: an ore of zinc. [named after *Franklin*, town in New Jersey, U.S.A., where it is found. See -ITE[1]]

frankly (frăngk′lĭ), *adv.* in a frank manner; freely; openly; unreservedly; candidly; plainly.

frankness (frăngk′nĭs), *n.* plainness of speech; candour; openness.

frankpledge (frăngk′plĕj′), *n.* *Early Eng. Law.* **1.** a system by which the inhabitants of a community were divided into groups of ten or more, whose members were responsible for one another's good behaviour. **2.** a member of such a group. **3.** the group itself. [t. AF: m. *franc plege*, mistranslation of OE *frithborg* peace-pledge]

frantic (frăn′tĭk), *adj.* **1.** wild with excitement, passion, fear, pain, etc.; frenzied; characterized by or pertaining to frenzy. **2.** *Archaic.* insane or mad. [ME *frentik*, t. OF: m. *frenetique*, t. L: m. *phrenēticus* delirious, t. Gk: m. *phrenētikós*] —**fran′tically, fran′ticly,** *adv.* —**fran′ticness,** *n.*

Franz Ferdinand (*Ger.* frănts′ fĕr′dē nänt), 1863–1914, Austrian archduke; his assassination precipitated the outbreak of World War I.

Franz Josef Land, an archipelago in the Arctic Ocean, E of Spitsbergen and N of Novaya Zemlya, belonging to the Soviet Union. Also, **Fridtjof Nansen Land.**

Franz Josef I (*Ger.* frănts′ yô′zĕf), 1830–1916, emperor of Austria 1848–1916; king of Hungary 1867–1916.

Franz Josef II, born 1906, prince of Liechtenstein since 1938.

frap (frăp), *v.t.*, **frapped, frapping.** *Naut.* to bind securely. [ME *frap*(*en*), t. OF: m. *fraper* strike]

frappé (frăp′ā; *Fr.* frȧ pė′), *n.* **1.** a fruit juice mixture frozen to a puree. **2.** a drink consisting of a liqueur poured over crushed ice. —*adj.* **3.** frozen; chilled; iced. [t. F, pp. of *frapper* ice (drinks), orig., beat, t. Gmc; cf. RAP]

F.R.A.S., Fellow of the Royal Astronomical Society.

Fraser (frā′zə), *n.* **1. Peter,** 1884–1950, New Zealand statesman, born in Scotland: prime minister 1940–49. **2.** a river in SW Canada, flowing S through British Columbia to the Pacific. 695 mi.

Fraserburgh (frā′zə bə rə, -brə), *n.* a burgh in Scotland, in NE Aberdeenshire. 10,642 (1961).

frat (frăt), *n.* *U.S. Slang.* a fraternity (def. 1).

fratch (frăch), *Dial.* —*v.t.* **1.** to quarrel; disagree. —*n.* **2.** a quarrel; dispute; argument.

frater[1] (frā′tə), *n.* a brother; comrade. [L: brother]

frater[2] (frā′tə), *n.* *Hist.* the refectory of a religious house. Also, **frat′ry.** [ME *freitur*, t. OF: m. *fraitur*, short for *refreitor*, repr. ML *refectōrium* REFECTORY]

fraternal (frə tû′nəl), *adj.* **1.** of or befitting a brother or brothers; brotherly. **2.** of or being a society of men associated in brotherly union, as for mutual aid or benefit: *a fraternal society.* [f. s. L *frāternus* brotherly + -AL[1]] —**frater′nalism,** *n.* —**frater′nally,** *adv.*

fraternity (frə tû′nĭ tĭ), *n.*, *pl.* **-ties. 1.** *U.S.* a student society organized for social and other purposes, and designated by two or more letters of the Greek alphabet. **2.** a body of persons associated as by ties of brotherhood. **3.** any body or class of persons having common purposes, interest, etc.: *the medical fraternity.* **4.** an organization of laymen for pious or charitable purposes. **5.** the relation of persons associated on the footing of brothers: *liberty, equality, and fraternity.* **6.** the relation of a brother or between brothers; brotherhood. [ME *fraternite*, t. L: m. s. *frāternitas* brotherhood]

fraternize (frăt′ə nīz′), *v.*, **-nized, -nizing.** —*v.i.* **1.** to associate in a fraternal or friendly way. **2.** to associate intimately with citizens of an enemy or conquered country. —*v.t.* **3.** *Rare.* to bring into fraternal association or sympathy. Also, **fraternise.** —**frat′erniza′tion,** *n.* —**frat′erniz′er,** *n.*

fratricide (frăt′rĭ sīd′, frā′trĭ-), *n.* **1.** one who kills his or her brother. **2.** the act of killing one's brother. [t. L: m. s. *frātricīda* (def. 1), *frātricīdium* (def. 2). See -CIDE] —**frat′ricid′al,** *adj.*

Frau (*Ger.* frou), *n.*, *pl.* **Frauen** (*Ger.* frou′ən). *German.* a married woman; a wife; a lady (as title, equivalent to *Mrs*).

fraud (frôd), *n.* **1.** deceit, trickery, sharp practice, or breach of confidence, by which it is sought to gain some unfair or dishonest advantage. **2.** a particular instance of such deceit or trickery: *election frauds.* **3.** any deception, artifice, or trick. **4.** one who makes deceitful pretences; impostor. [ME *fraude*, t. OF, t. L: m. s. *fraus* cheating, deceit] —**Syn. 1.** See **trick.**

fraudulent (frô′dyo͞o lənt), *adj.* **1.** given to or using fraud, as a person; cheating; dishonest. **2.** characterized by, involving, or proceeding from fraud, as actions, enterprise, methods, gains, etc. [ME, t. L: s. *fraudulentus* cheating] —**fraud′ulence, fraud′ulency,** *n.* —**fraud′ulently,** *adv.*

fraught (frôt), *adj.* **1.** involving; attended (with); full of): *an undertaking fraught with danger, a heart fraught with grief.* **2.** *Archaic or Poetic.* filled or laden (with): *ships fraught with precious wares.* —*n.* **3.** *Obs.* a load; cargo; freight (of a ship). [ME, t. MD or MLG: m. *vracht* freight money, FREIGHT. Cf. OHG *frēht* earnings]

Fräulein (frô′līn; *Ger.* frŏʏ′līn), *n.*, *pl.* **Fräulein.** *German.* an unmarried woman; a young lady (as a title, equivalent to *Miss*).

Fraunhofer (*Ger.* froun′hō fər), *n.* **Joseph von** (*Ger.* yō′zĕf fōn), 1787–1826, German optician and physicist.

Fraunhofer lines, the dark lines of the solar spectrum. [named after Joseph von FRAUNHOFER]

fraxinella (frăk′sĭ nĕl′ə), *n.* dittany (def. 3). [NL, dim. of L *fraxinus* ash tree]

fray[1] (frā), *n.* **1.** a noisy quarrel; contest; brawl; fight, skirmish, or battle. **2.** *Archaic.* fright. —*v.t.* **3.** *Archaic.* to frighten. —*v.i.* **4.** *Archaic.* to fight; brawl. [aphetic var. of AFFRAY]

fray[2] (frā), *v.t.* **1.** to wear (cloth, rope, etc.) to loose, ravelled threads or fibres at the edge or end; cause to ravel out. **2.** to wear by rubbing (sometimes fol. by *through*). **3.** to strain (a person's temper); exasperate; upset. —*v.i.* **4.** to become frayed, as cloth, etc.; ravel out. **5.** to rub against something. —*n.* **6.** a frayed part, as in cloth. [t. F: s. *frayer*, g. L *fricāre* rub]

Frazer (frā′zə), *n.* **Sir James George,** 1854–1941, Scottish anthropologist.

frazil (frā′zĭl), *n.* small spikes of ice which form in turbulent water.

frazzle (frăz′əl), *v.*, **-zled, -zling,** *n.* *U.S.* —*v.i.*, *v.t.* **1.** to fray; wear to threads or shreds. **2.** to weary; tire out. —*n.* **3.** a state of being frazzled or worn out. **4.** a remnant; shred. [b. FRAY[2] and *fazzle*, ME *faselin* unravel, c. G *faseln*]

F.R.C.M., Fellow of the Royal College of Music.

F.R.C.O., Fellow of the Royal College of Organists.

F.R.C.O.G., Fellow of the Royal College of Obstetricians and Gynaecologists.

F.R.C.P., Fellow of the Royal College of Physicians.

F.R.C.S., Fellow of the Royal College of Surgeons.

freak[1] (frēk), *n.* **1.** a sudden and apparently causeless change or turn of events, the mind, etc.; a capricious notion, occurrence, etc. **2.** any abnormal product or curiously unusual object; monstrosity. **3.** a person or animal on exhibition as an example of some strange deviation from nature. —*adj.* **4.** unusual; odd; irregular: *a freak copy of a book.* [? akin to OE *frīcian* dance]

freak² (frēk), *v.t.* **1.** to fleck, streak, or variegate. —*n.* **2.** a fleck or streak of colour. [? v. use of FREAK¹; appar. coined by Milton]

freakish (frē′kĭsh), *adj.* **1.** given to or full of freaks; whimsical; capricious. **2.** resembling a freak; queer; odd; grotesque. —**freak′ishly,** *adv.* —**freak′ishness,** *n.*

freaky (frē′kĭ), *adj.*, **-kier, -kiest.** freakish. —**freak′iness,** *n.*

freckle (frĕk′l), *n.*, *v.*, **-led, -ling.** —*n.* **1.** a small brownish yellow spot in the skin, esp. on the face, neck, or arms. **2.** any small spot or discoloration. —*v.t.* **3.** to cover with freckles or produce freckles on. —*v.i.* **4.** to become freckled. [b. obs. *frecken* freckle (t. Scand.; cf. Icel. *freknur*, pl.) and SPECKLE, n.] —**freck′led,** *adj.*

freckly (frĕk′lĭ), *adj.* covered with freckles.

Frederick I (frĕd′rĭk), **1.** Frederick Barbarossa. **2.** 1657–1713, first king of Prussia 1701–13.

Frederick II, 1. 1194–1250, German king, king of Sicily, and emperor of the Holy Roman Empire 1218–50. **2.** Frederick the Great.

Frederick III ('*the Wise*'), 1463–1525, elector of Saxony 1486–1525: protector of Martin Luther.

Frederick IX, born 1899, king of Denmark since 1947.

Frederick Barbarossa (bä′bə rōs′ə) (*Frederick I*), *c.* 1123–90, German king and emperor of the Holy Roman Empire 1152–90.

Fredericksburg (frĕd′rĭks bûg′), *n.* a town in the U.S., in NE Virginia: scene of a Confederate victory in the American Civil War, 1862. 12,158 (1950).

Frederick the Great (*Frederick II*), 1712–86, king of Prussia 1740–86.

Frederick William, 1. ('*the Great Elector*'), 1620–88, elector of Brandenburg who increased the power and importance of Prussia. **2.** 1882–1951, former crown prince of Germany 1888–1918; German general (son of William II of Germany).

Frederick William I, 1688–1740, king of Prussia 1713–40.

Frederick William II, 1744–97, king of Prussia 1786–97.

Frederick William III, 1770–1840, king of Prussia 1797–1840.

Frederick William IV, 1795–1861, king of Prussia 1840–61.

Fredericton (frĕd′rĭk tən), *n.* a town in SE Canada, on the river St John: the capital of New Brunswick: New Brunswick University founded 1785. 19,683 (1961).

free (frē), *adj.*, **freer, freest,** *adv.*, *v.*, **freed, freeing.** —*adj.* **1.** enjoying personal rights or liberty, as one not in slavery. **2.** pertaining to or reserved for those who enjoy personal liberty. **3.** possessed of, characterized by, or existing under civil liberty as opposed to arbitrary or despotic government, as a country or state, or its citizens, institutions, etc. **4.** enjoying political liberty or independence, as a people or country not under foreign rule. **5.** exempt from external authority, interference, restriction, etc., as a person, the will, thought, choice, action, etc.; independent; unfettered. **6.** at liberty, permitted, or able at will (to do something): *free to choose.* **7.** not subject to special regulation or restrictions, as trade: *free trade.* **8.** not literal, as a translation. **9.** not subject to rules, set forms, etc.: *the free song of a bird, free verse.* **10.** clear of obstructions or obstacles, as a corridor. **11.** available; unoccupied; not in use: *the managing director is now free.* **12.** exempt or released from something specified that controls, restrains, burdens, etc. (fol. by *from* or *of*): *free from matrimonial ties, free of taxes.* **13.** having immunity or being safe (usually fol. by *from*): *free from criticism.* **14.** uncombined chemically: *free oxygen.* **15.** that may be used by or open to all: *a free port, a free market.* **16.** general: *a free fight.* **17.** unimpeded, as motion or movements; easy, firm, or swift in movement: *a free step.* **18.** loose, or not held fast or attached: *to get one's arm free.* **19.** not joined to or in contact with something else: *a free surface.* **20.** acting without self-restraint or reserve: *too free with one's tongue.* **21.** frank and open; unconstrained, unceremonious, or familiar. **22.** unrestrained by decency; loose or licentious. **23.** ready in giving, liberal, or lavish: *to be free with one's advice.* **24.** given readily or in profusion, or unstinted. **25.** given without consideration of a return, as a gift. **26.** provided without, or not subject to, a charge or payment: *free milk.* **27.** admitted to entry and enjoyment at will (fol. by *of*): *to be free of a friend's house.* **28.** easily worked, as stone or land. **29.** *Naut.* (of a wind) blowing so that a boat can sail with sheets eased or yards squared; fair. **30.** *Phonet.* **a.** (of a vowel) situated in an open syllable. **b.** belonging to a class of vowels which need not be followed by a consonant: the vowel of *see* is one of the English free vowels. **31. free and easy,** informal, casual, without restraint. **32. make free with,** to treat or use too familiarly; take liberties with.
—*adv.* **33.** in a free manner; freely. **34.** without cost or charge. **35.** *Naut.* farther from the wind than when close-hauled: *to sail free.*
—*v.t.* **36.** make free; set at liberty; release from bondage, imprisonment, or restraint. **37.** to exempt or deliver (fol. by *from*). **38.** to relieve or rid (usually fol. by *of*). **39.** to disengage (fol. by *from* or *of*).
[ME; OE *frēo*, c. G *frei*, orig., dear, favoured. Cf. FRIEND] —**Syn. 36.** See **release.**

free agent, one who has the power to act freely and without constraint, and is not responsible to anyone for his actions.

free alongside ship, a term of sale meaning that the seller agrees to deliver the merchandise alongside ship without extra charge to buyer.

free association, *Psychoanal.* a technique based either on the first association called forth by each of a series of stimulus words or a train of thought elicited in response to a single word.

freeboard (frē′bôd′), *n.* *Naut.* the part of a ship's side between the waterline and the deck or gunwale.

freeboot (frē′bo͞ot′), *v.i.* to act as a freebooter.

freebooter (frē′bo͞o′tə), *n.* one who goes about in search of plunder; a pirate or buccaneer. [t. D: Anglicization of *vrijbuiter*, f. *vrij* free + *buit* booty + *-er* -ER¹]

freeborn (frē′bôn′), *adj.* **1.** born free, rather than in slavery, bondage, or vassalage. **2.** pertaining to or befitting persons born free.

Free Church, 1. the churches collectively which did not conform to the Church of England or accept the legislation passed to enforce uniformity in religion; the nonconformist churches. **2.** any such Protestant church in Great Britain or elsewhere. **3.** of or pertaining to such a church.

free city, a city having an independent government and forming a sovereign state by itself.

free companion, a member of a band of mercenary soldiers of the Middle Ages.

free company, a band of free companions.

freedman (frēd′măn′), *n.*, *pl.* **-men.** a man who has been freed from slavery. —**freed′wom′an,** *n. fem.*

freedom (frē′dəm), *n.* **1.** civil liberty, as opposed to subjection to an arbitrary or despotic government. **2.** political or national independence. **3.** a particular immunity or other privilege enjoyed, as by a city or corporation. **4.** personal liberty, as opposed to bondage or slavery. **5.** the state of being at liberty rather than in confinement or under physical restraint. **6.** exemption from external control, interference, regulation, etc. **7.** power of determining one's or its own action. **8.** *Philos.* the condition of the will as the volitional instigator of human actions; relative self-determination. **9.** absence of or release from ties, obligations, etc. **10.** exemption or immunity: *freedom from taxation.* **11.** exemption from the presence of anything specified (fol. by *from*): *freedom from fear.* **12.** ease or facility of movement or action. **13.** frankness of manner or speech. **14.** absence of ceremony or reserve; familiarity. **15.** a liberty taken. **16.** the right of enjoying all the privileges or peculiar rights of citizenship, membership, or the like: *the freedom of the city.* **17.** the right of frequenting, enjoying, or using at will: *to have the freedom of a friend's library.* [ME; OE *frēodōm.* See FREE, -DOM]
—**Syn. 1.** FREEDOM, INDEPENDENCE, LIBERTY refer to an absence of undue restrictions and an opportunity to exercise one's rights and powers. FREEDOM emphasizes the large opportunity given for the exercise of one's rights, powers, desires, or the like: *freedom of speech or conscience, freedom of movement.* INDEPENDENCE implies not only lack of restrictions but also the ability to stand alone, unsustained by anything else: *independence of thought promotes invention and discovery.* LIBERTY, though often interchanged with FREEDOM, is commonly used to refer to past or possible restriction, confinement, or subjection: *give me liberty or, give me death.* —**Ant. 1.** oppression.

freedom of the seas, *Internat. Law.* the doctrine that ships of neutral countries may sail anywhere on the high seas without interference by warring powers.

free energy, *Physics.* that portion of the energy of a system which is the maximum available for doing work.

free enterprise, the doctrine or practice of a minimum amount of government control of private business and industry.

free fall, *Aerospace.* **1.** the motion of any unpowered body travelling in a gravitational field. **2.** the part of a parachute descent before the parachute opens.

free-for-all (frē′fə rôl′), *n.* a fight, game, contest, etc., open to everyone. Also, **free fight.**

free form, a linguistic form which occurs sometimes or always by itself, not having the limitation of a bound form (which see), as *fire*.
Free French, earlier name of **Fighting French.**
free hand, unrestricted freedom, authority.
freehand (frē′hănd′), *adj., adv.* done by the hand without guiding instruments, measurements, or other aids.
free-handed (frē′hăn′dĭd), *adj.* **1.** open-handed; generous; liberal. **2.** having the hands free.
free-hearted (frē′hä′tĭd), *adj.* having a free heart; light-hearted; spontaneous; frank; generous.
freehold (frē′hōld′), *n. Law.* an estate in fee simple.
freeholder (frē′hōl′də), *n.* the owner of a freehold.
free house, a public house which is not bound to obtain all its supplies of beer, etc., from one brewing firm (distinguished from *tied house*).
free kick, *Soccer.* a kick (to be made without interference) awarded to one side after an infringement of the rules by the other.
freelance (frē′läns′), *n., v.,* **-lanced, -lancing,** *adj., adv.* —*n.* **1.** a journalist, commercial artist, etc., who does not work on a regular salaried basis for any one employer. **2.** a politician who is not attached to any particular political party. **3.** a mercenary soldier or military adventurer of the Middle Ages, often of knightly rank, who offered his services to any state, party, or cause. —*v.i.* **4.** to act or work as a freelance. —*adj.* **5.** of or pertaining to a freelance. —*adv.* **6.** in the manner of a freelance.
free-liver (frē′lĭv′ə), *n.* one who in his mode of life freely indulges his appetites. —**free′-liv′ing,** *adj., n.*
free love, the doctrine or practice of free choice in sexual relations, without restraint of legal marriage or of any continuing obligations independent of one's will.
freely (frē′lĭ), *adv.* in a free manner.
freeman (frē′mən), *n., pl.* **-men. 1.** a man who is free; a man who enjoys personal, civil, or political liberty. **2.** one who enjoys or is entitled to citizenship, franchise, or other peculiar privilege: *a freeman of the City of London.*
freemartin (frē′mä′tĭn), *n.* a generally sterile heifer calf twinborn with a bull. [orig. uncert.]
Freemason (frē′mā′sən), *n.* **1.** a member of a widely distributed secret order **(Free and Accepted Masons),** having for its object mutual assistance and the promotion of brotherly love among its members. **2.** (*l.c.*) *Hist.* **a.** one of a class of skilled stoneworkers of the Middle Ages, possessed of secret signs and passwords. **b.** a member of a society composed of such workers, with honorary members (known as *accepted masons*) who were not connected with the building trades. —**freemasonic** (frē′mə sŏn′ĭk), *adj.*
freemasonry (frē′mā′sən rĭ), *n.* **1.** secret or tacit brotherhood; instinctive sympathy. **2.** (*cap.*) the principles, practices, and institutions of Freemasons.
freeness (frē′nĭs), *n.* the state or quality of being free.
free on board, *Com.* a term of sale meaning that the seller agrees to deliver the merchandise aboard the carrier without extra charge to buyer.
free port, 1. a port open under equal conditions to all traders. **2.** a part or all of a port not included in customs territory so as to expedite transhipment of what is not to be imported.
free radical, *Chem.* a radical (def. 12) which exists independently for short periods during the course of a chemical reaction, or for larger periods under special conditions.
free-range (frē′rānj′), *adj.* **1.** of, pertaining to, or denoting chickens reared in an open or free environment rather than in a battery. **2.** of or denoting the eggs of such chickens.
free-rider (frē′rī′də), *n. Colloq.* a non-union worker who benefits from pay scales, etc., agreed by a trade union.
freesia (frē′zyə), *n.* any plant of the iridaceous genus *Freesia,* native in South Africa, cultivated for its fragrant white, yellow, or sometimes rose-coloured, tubular flowers. [NL; named after E. M. *Fries,* 1794–1878, Swedish botanist]
free silver, *Econ.* the free coinage of silver; esp. at a fixed ratio with gold.
free-soil (frē′soil′), *U.S. Hist.* —*adj.* **1.** opposing the extension of slavery into the territories of the U.S., or those parts of the country not yet elected into states. —*n.* **2.** (*cap.*) a political party supporting this principle, active 1848–56. —**free′-soil′er,** *n.*
free-spoken (frē′spō′kən), *adj.* given to speaking freely or without reserve. —**free′-spo′kenness,** *n.*
Free State, 1. Irish Free State. **2.** *U.S.* any non-slavery state prior to the Civil War. —**Free-Stater** (frē′stāt′ə), *n.*
freestone (frē′stōn′), *n.* **1.** any stone, as sandstone, which can be freely worked or quarried, esp. one which cuts well in all directions without splitting. **2.** a freestone fruit, esp. a peach or plum. —*adj.* **3.** made of freestone: *a freestone house.* **4.** having a stone from which the pulp is easily separated, as certain peaches and plums.
freestyle (frē′stīl′), *n.* **1.** *Swimming.* a race in which the competitors may use any stroke they choose, usually the crawl. **2.** *Wrestling.* a style of wrestling in which almost every kind of hold is permitted; all-in wrestling. —*adj.* **3.** of or pertaining to freestyle.
free-swimmer (frē′swĭm′ə), *n. Zool.* an animal, as a fish, that swims about freely.
free-swimming (frē′swĭm′ĭng), *adj. Zool.* (of aquatic animals) not fixed or attached; capable of swimming about freely.
freethinker (frē′thĭng′kə), *n.* one who forms his opinions independently of authority or tradition, esp. in matters of religion. —**free′think′ing,** *n., adj.*
free thought, thought unrestrained by deference to authority, esp. in matters of religion.
Freetown (frē′toun′), *n.* a seaport in W Africa, the capital of Sierra Leone. 128,000 (est. 1963). See map under **Sierra Leone.**
free trade, 1. trade between different countries, free from governmental restrictions or duties. **2.** international trade free from protective duties, etc., and subject only to such tariffs as are needed for revenue. **3.** the system, principles, or maintenance of such trade. **4.** *Obs.* smuggling.
free-trader (frē′trā′də), *n.* **1.** an advocate of free trade. **2.** *Obs.* a smuggler.
free verse, *Pros.* verse unhampered by fixed metrical forms, in extreme instances consisting of little more than rhythmic prose in lines of irregular length.
freeway (frē′wā′), *n. U.S.* a motorway.
freewheel (frē′wēl′), *n.* **1.** an overrunning clutch device in connection with the transmission gearbox of a motor vehicle which automatically disengages the drive shaft whenever it tends to rotate more rapidly than the shaft driving it. **2.** a form of rear bicycle wheel which has a device freeing it from the driving mechanism, as when the pedals are stopped in coasting. —*v.i.* **3.** to coast in a motor car, bicycle, etc., with the wheels disengaged from the driving mechanism.
free will, 1. free choice; voluntary decision. **2.** the doctrine that the conduct of human beings expresses personal choice and is not simply determined by physical or divine forces.
freewill (frē′wĭl′), *adj.* **1.** made or done freely or of one's own accord; voluntary: *a freewill offering.* **2.** of or pertaining to the metaphysical doctrine of the freedom of the will: *the freewill controversy.*
freeze (frēz), *v.,* **froze, frozen, freezing,** *n.* —*v.i.* **1.** to become hardened into ice or into a solid body; to change from the liquid to the solid state by loss of heat. **2.** to become hard or rigid because of loss of heat, as objects containing moisture. **3.** to become obstructed by the formation of ice, as pipes. **4.** to become fixed to something by or as by the action of frost. **5.** to be of the degree of cold at which water freezes: *it is freezing tonight.* **6.** to suffer the effects of intense cold; have the sensation of extreme cold. **7.** to die of frost or cold. **8.** to lose warmth of feeling; be chilled with fear, etc. **9. freeze over,** to become coated with ice. **10.** to stop suddenly; become immobilized, as through fear, shock, etc. —*v.t.* **11.** to congeal; harden into ice; change from a fluid to a solid state by loss of heat. **12.** to form ice on the surface of, as a river or pond. **13.** to obstruct or close by the formation of ice, as pipes (often fol. by *up*). **14.** to fix fast in ice. **15.** to harden or stiffen by cold, as objects containing moisture. **16.** to subject (something) to a freezing temperature, as in a refrigerator. **17.** to cause to suffer the effects of intense cold; produce the sensation of extreme cold in. **18.** to kill by frost or cold. **19.** to congeal as if by cold; chill with fear; dampen the enthusiasm of. **20.** to cause (someone) to become immobilized, as through fear, shock, etc. **21.** to exclude, or compel to withdraw, from society, business, etc., as by chilling behaviour, severe competition, etc. (fol. by *out*). **22.** *Finance.* to render impossible of liquidation or collection: *bank loans are frozen in business depressions.* **23.** to fix (wages, prices, etc.) at a specific level, usually by government order. **24.** to make insensitive (a part of the body) by artificial freezing, as for surgery. —*n.* **25.** the act of freezing. **26.** the state of being frozen. **27.** *Meteorol.* a period during which temperatures remain constantly below 32°F. **28.** a frost. **29.** legislative action by a government to fix wages, prices, etc., at a specific level. [ME *frese(n),* OE *frēosan,* c. G *frieren*] —**freez′able,** *adj.*
freeze-dry (frēz′drī′), *v.t.,* **-dried, -drying.** to dry (food, blood, serum, etc.) while frozen and under high vacuum, as for prolonged storage. —**freeze′-dry′ing,** *n.*

freezer (frē′zə), *n.* **1.** one who or that which freezes or chills. **2.** a machine containing cold brine, etc., for freezing ice-cream mixture or the like. **3.** a refrigerator or cabinet held at or below 0°C.

freeze-up (frēz′ŭp′), *n.* a spell of freezing weather.

freezing mixture, *Chem.* a mixture of two (or more) substances, esp. salt and ice, which produce a temperature below 0°C.

freezing point, the temperature at which a liquid freezes: *the freezing point of water is 32°F, 0°C.*

free zone, a free port area.

Frei (frā, frī), *n.* **Eduardo** (ĕd wä′dō), born 1911, Chilean statesman: president since 1964.

Freiburg (*Ger.* frī′bo͝ork), *n.* **1.** a town in West Germany, in SW Baden-Württemberg. 156,000 (est. 1966). **2.** German name of **Fribourg.**

freight (frāt), *n.* **1. a.** the cargo or lading, or any part of the cargo or lading, of a ship. **b.** merchandise transported by water or air. **2.** the transporting of goods by water. **3.** the charge made for transporting goods by water or air. **4.** *Chiefly U.S. and Can.* cargo or lading carried for pay either by land, water, or air. **5.** a goods train. —*v.t.* **6.** to load; burden. **7.** to load or lade with goods or merchandise for transport. **8.** *Chiefly U.S.* to transport as freight; send by freight. [ME *freyght*, t. MD or MLG: m. *vrecht*, var. of *vracht.* See FRAUGHT, n.] —**freight′less,** *adj.*

freightage (frā′tĭj), *n.* **1.** that which is freighted; cargo; lading. **2.** charge for the conveyance of freight.

freight car, *U.S.* a goods wagon; luggage van.

freight engine, *U.S.* a locomotive used for drawing goods trains.

freighter (frā′tə), *n.* **1.** one who charters and loads ships. **2.** one whose occupation it is to receive and forward freight. **3.** a cargo ship. **4.** an aircraft that carries merchandise.

freightliner (frāt′lī′nə), *n.* **1.** a fast railway goods service using containers. **2.** a train carrying such containers. **3.** (*cap.*) a trademark for this service.

freight terminal, a goods yard.

freight ton. See **ton**[1] (def. 3).

freight train, *Chiefly U.S.* a goods train.

Fremantle (frē′măn′tl), *n.* a seaport in SW Western Australia, near Perth. 21,980 (1961).

fremd (frĕmd, frāmd), *adj. Scot.* **1.** foreign; strange. **2.** unfriendly. Also, **frem, frem′it.** [ME and OE *fremde*, c. G *fremd*]

fremitus (frĕm′ĭ təs), *n., pl.* **-tus.** *Pathol.* a vibration, perceptible on palpation or auscultation. [t. L: a roaring, murmuring]

Frémont (frē′mŏnt), *n.* **John Charles,** 1813–90, U.S. explorer, general, and political leader; first presidential candidate of the Republican Party, in 1856.

French[1] (frĕnch), *n.* **Sir John Denton Pinkstone, 1st Earl of Ypres,** 1852–1925, British field marshal in World War I.

French[2] (frĕnch), *adj.* **1.** of, pertaining to, or characteristic of France, its inhabitants, or their language. —*n.* **2.** the people of France and their immediate descendants elsewhere, collectively. **3.** a Romance language, the language of France, official also in Belgium, Switzerland, and Canada. [ME; OE *Frencisc*, der. *Franca* FRANK]

French Academy, an association of forty scholars and men of letters, formally established in 1635 by Cardinal Richelieu and devoted chiefly to preserving the purity of the French language and establishing standards of correct usage. French, **Académie Française.**

French and Indian War, the war between France and England in America, 1754–60, in which the French were aided by Indian allies.

French bean, a small twining or bushy annual, leguminous herb, *Phaseolus vulgaris*, often cultivated for its slender green edible pods. Also, **kidney bean, haricot bean.**

French bread, white bread, usually in long, slender loaves with a crisp crust and tapering ends.

French Canada, that part of Canada, esp. Quebec, where people of French language and origin predominate. —**French′-Cana′dian,** *adj.*

French chalk, a talc for marking lines on cloth, etc.

French Community, an association of France and certain former overseas possessions: formed in 1958, it comprises the republics of France, Central Africa, Chad, Congo, Gabon, Senegal, and the Malagasy Republic.

French curve, a flat celluloid or wooden drawing instrument consisting of a number of different curves, used to guide the pen or pencil in drawing curves of varying radii; railway curve.

French doors, a pair of doors, often glazed, hinged to the doorjambs and opening in the middle.

French dressing, salad dressing prepared from oil, vinegar, salt, spices, etc.

French Equatorial Africa, a former federation of French territories, in central Africa: Chad, Gabon, Middle Congo, and Ubangi-Shari.

French fried potatoes, thin strips of potatoes fried in deep fat; chips.

French Guiana (gĭ ä′nə), an overseas department of France on the NE coast of South America; formerly a French colony. 33,698 pop. (1961); 7720 sq. mi. (with the dependent territory of Inini, 34,740 sq. mi.). *Cap.:* Cayenne. See map under **Guiana.**

French Guinea (gĭn′ĭ), a former overseas possession of France. See **Guinea** (def. 2).

French hales, a deciduous rosaceous tree, *Sorbus devoniensis*, confined to woods in SW England and SE Ireland.

French heel, a high, curved heel on a woman's shoe.

French horn, a mellow-toned brass wind instrument derived from the hunting horn and consisting of a long, coiled tube ending in a flaring bell. See illus. under **horn.**

Frenchify (frĕn′chĭ fī′), *v.t.,* **-fied, -fying.** (*sometimes l.c.*) to make French; imbue with French qualities.

French India, (formerly) the five small French provinces of Chandernagor, Karikal, Mahé, Pondicherry, and Yanaon, along or near the coast of India: now part of India.

French Indochina, the former French colonial federation of Cochin-China, the protectorates of Annam, Cambodia, Tonkin, and Laos, and the leased territory of Kwangchowan. Ultimately it consisted of the three independent states of Vietnam (divided into North Vietnam and South Vietnam), Cambodia, and Laos, Kwangchowan having reverted to the Chinese. See **Indochina.**

French knot, a type of embroidery stitch forming a decorative knot.

French leave, departure without ceremony, permission, or notice.

French letter, *Slang.* a sheath (def. 6).

French lilac, a perennial papilionaceous herb, *Galega officinalis*, occurring in Europe and W Asia.

Frenchman (frĕnch′mən), *n., pl.* **-men. 1.** a man belonging to the French nation. **2.** a French ship. —**Frenchwoman** (frĕnch′wo͝om′ən), *n. fem.*

French Morocco. See **Morocco.**

French mustard, a mild mustard made with vinegar.

French Oceania, former name of French Polynesia.

French pancake, a thin, light pancake, usually having a sweet or savoury filling.

French pastry, a short pastry, as used for piecrusts and filled with rich creams, fruit preparations, etc.

French polish, a solution of shellac in methylated spirits with or without the addition of some colouring material; used as a high-quality furniture finish.

French-polish (frĕnch′pŏl′ĭsh), *v.t.* to finish (a piece of furniture) with French polish. —**French′-pol′isher,** *n.* —**French′-pol′ishing,** *n.*

French Polynesia, a French overseas territory in the S Pacific, including the Society Islands, Marquesas Islands, and other widely scattered island groups. 84,550 pop. (1962); 1544 sq. mi. *Cap.:* Papeete. Formerly, **French Oceania.**

French Revolution, the movement that, beginning in 1789, overthrew the absolute monarchy of the Bourbons and the system of class privilege, and ended in the seizure of power by Napoleon in 1799.

French seam, *Sewing.* a seam in which the edges of the cloth are sewn first on the right side, then on the wrong, so as to be completely enclosed.

French Somaliland, an overseas territory of France in E Africa, on the Gulf of Aden. 81,000 (est. 1961); 8492 sq. mi. *Cap.:* Djibouti. See map under **Somali Republic.**

French Sudan, a former overseas territory in French West Africa. See **Mali.**

French Union, a former union of France and its overseas territories and departments and associated states as constituted in 1946: superseded by the French Community in 1958.

French West Africa, a former federation of eight French overseas territories in W Africa: Dahomey, French Guinea, French Sudan, Ivory Coast, Mauritania, Niger, Senegal, Dakar, and Upper Volta.

French West Indies, the French islands in the West Indies, comprising Guadeloupe and dependencies, and Martinique, administered as two overseas departments. 575,285 pop. (1961); 1114 sq. mi.

French window, a glazed folding door serving as a window and a door, and usually opening on to a garden or balcony.

Frenchy (frĕn′chĭ), *adj.,* **Frenchier, Frenchiest,** *n. Colloq.* —*adj.* **1.** characteristic or suggestive of the French. —*n.* **2.** a Frenchman.

frenetic (frĭ nĕt′ĭk), *adj.* frantic; frenzied. Also, **phrenetic.** [var. of PHRENETIC] —**frenet′ically,** *adv.*

frenulum (frĕn′yŏŏ ləm), *n.*, *pl.* **-la** (-lə). fraenulum.
frenum (frē′nəm), *n.*, *pl.* **-na** (-nə). *Anat.*, *Zool.* fraenum.
frenzied (frĕn′zĭd), *adj.* wildly excited or enthusiastic; frantic; mad. Also, **phrensied.**
frenzy (frĕn′zĭ), *n.*, *pl.* **-zies,** *v.*, **-zied, -zying.** —*n.* **1.** violent mental agitation; wild excitement or enthusiasm. **2.** the violent excitement of a paroxysm of mania; mental derangement; delirium. —*v.t.* **3.** to drive to frenzy; make frantic. Also, **phrensy.** [ME *frenesie*, t. OF, t. LL: m. *phrenēsis*, t. LGk, r. Gk *phrenîtis.* See PHRENITIS] —**Syn. 2.** madness, rage.
Freon (frē′ŏn), *n. Chem. Trademark.* any of a group of fluorinated hydrocarbons which are used as refrigerants and as dispersal fluids for insecticides.
freq., 1. frequent. **2.** frequentative. **3.** frequently.
frequency (frē′kwən sĭ), *n.*, *pl.* **-cies. 1.** Also, **fre′quence.** the state or fact of being frequent; frequent occurrence. **2.** rate or recurrence. **3.** *Physics.* **a.** the number of periods or regularly recurring events of any given kind in unit time, usually in one second; the reciprocal of the period. **b.** (of an alternating current) the number of cycles, or completed alternations, per second. **4.** *Maths.* the number of times an event occurs. **5.** *Statistics.* the number of items occurring in a given category. See **relative frequency.** [t. L: m. s. *frequentia*]
frequency distribution, *Statistics.* the set of frequencies associated with the different categories, intervals, or values to which items in a group belong.
frequency modulation, *Electronics.* a broadcasting system, relatively free from static, in which the frequency of the transmitted wave is modulated or varied in accordance with the amplitude and pitch of the signal (distinguished from *amplitude modulation*). *Abbrev.*: FM.
frequent (*adj.* frē′kwənt; *v.* frĭ kwĕnt′), *adj.* **1.** happening or occurring at short intervals: *to make frequent trips to a place.* **2.** constant, habitual, or regular: *a frequent guest.* **3.** at short distances apart: *a coast with frequent lighthouses.* —*v.t.* **4.** to visit often; go often to; be often in. [t. L: s. *frequens* crowded] —**frequent′er,** *n.*
frequentation (frē′kwĕn tā′shən), *n.* the practice of frequenting; habit of visiting often.
frequentative (frĭ kwĕn′tə tĭv), *Gram.* —*adj.* **1.** (of a derived verb, or of an aspect of verb inflection) expressing repetition of the action denoted by the underlying verb. —*n.* **2.** a frequentative or iterative verb. **3.** the frequentative or iterative aspect. **4.** a verb therein, as *wrestle* from *wrest.*
frequently (frē′kwənt lĭ), *adv.* often; many times; at short intervals. —**Syn.** See **often.**
frère (*Fr.* frĕr), *n.*, *pl.* **frères** (*Fr.* frĕr). *French.* **1.** brother; fellow member of an organization. **2.** friar; monk.
fresco (frĕs′kō), *n.*, *pl.* **-coes, -cos,** *v.*, **-coed, -coing.** —*n.* **1.** a method of painting on a wall, ceiling, or the like, made before the plaster is dry so that the colours become incorporated (**true fresco**), or, less properly, after the plaster has dried (**dry fresco**). **2.** a picture or design so painted. —*v.t.* **3.** to paint in fresco. [t. It.: cool, FRESH; t. Gmc] —**fres′coer,** *n.*
Frescobaldi (frĕs′kō băl′dĭ; *It.* frĕs kō bäl′dē), *n.* **Girolamo** (*It.* jē rō′lä mō), 1583–1643, Italian organist and composer.
fresh (frĕsh), *adj.* **1.** newly made or obtained, etc.: *fresh footprints.* **2.** newly arrived: *fresh from school.* **3.** new; not previously known, met with, etc.; novel. **4.** additional or further: *fresh supplies.* **5.** not salt: *fresh water.* **6.** retaining the original properties unimpaired; not deteriorated. **7.** not canned or frozen; not preserved by pickling, salting, drying, etc. **8.** not fatigued; brisk; vigorous. **9.** not faded, worn, obliterated, etc. **10.** looking youthful and healthy. **11.** pure, cool, or refreshing, as air. **12.** inexperienced. **13.** forward or presumptuous; cheeky. —*n.* **14.** the fresh part or time. **15.** a freshet. —*v.t.*, *v.i.* **16.** *Obs.* to make or become fresh. —*adv.* **17.** freshly. [ME; OE *fersc*, c. G *frisch*] —**fresh′ly,** *adv.* —**fresh′ness,** *n.* —**Syn. 1.** See **new. 12.** artless, untrained, raw, green. —**Ant. 1.** old. **12.** sophisticated.
fresh breeze, *Meteorol.* a wind of Beaufort scale force 5, about 21 m.p.h.
freshen (frĕsh′ən), *v.t.* **1.** to make fresh; refresh, revive, or renew. **2.** to remove saltiness from. **3.** *Naut.* to relieve, as a rope, by altering the position of a part exposed to friction. —*v.i.* **4.** to become or grow fresh. **5.** to make oneself fresh, as by washing, etc. (usually fol. by *up*). —**fresh′ener,** *n.*
freshet (frĕsh′ĭt), *n.* **1.** a sudden rise in the level of a stream, or a flood, due to heavy rains or the rapid melting of snow and ice. **2.** a freshwater stream flowing into the sea. [dim. of FRESH, used as n.] —**Syn. 1.** See **flood.**
fresh gale, *Meteorol.* a wind of Beaufort scale force 8, about 42 m.p.h.
freshman (frĕsh′mən), *n.*, *pl.* **-men. 1.** a student in the first year of the course at a university or college. **2.** a novice. Also, *Slang*, **fresh′er.**
freshwater (frĕsh′wô′tə), *adj.* **1.** of or living in water that is fresh, or not salt (opposed to *salt-water* or *marine*). **2.** accustomed to fresh water only, and not to the sea. **3.** having little experience. **4.** *U.S.* small or little known: *a freshwater college.*
freshwater herring, lake herring.
fresnel (frā′nĕl), *n.* *Physics.* a unit of frequency equal to 10^{12} cycles per second. [named after Augustin Jean *Fresnel*, 1788–1827, French physicist]
Fresno (frĕz′nō), *n.* a town in the U.S., in central California. 133,929 (1960).
fret[1] (frĕt), *v.*, **fretted, fretting,** *n.* —*v.i.* **1.** to give oneself up to feelings of irritation, resentful discontent, regret, worry, or the like. **2.** to cause corrosion; gnaw. **3.** to make a way by gnawing or corrosion. **4.** to become eaten, worn, or corroded. **5.** *Civ. Eng.* to scab. **6.** to move in agitation or commotion, as water. —*v.t.* **7.** to torment; irritate, annoy, or vex. **8.** to wear away or consume by gnawing, friction, rust, corrosives, etc. **9.** to form or make by wearing away a substance. **10.** to agitate (water). —*n.* **11.** an irritated state of mind; annoyance; vexation. **12.** erosion; corrosion; gnawing. **13.** a worn or eroded place. [ME *frete(n)*, OE *fretan*, c. G *fressen* eat] —**Syn. 7.** worry, harass. —**Ant. 7.** soothe.
fret[2] (frĕt), *n.*, *v.*, **fretted, fretting.** —*n.* **1.** an interlaced, angular design; fretwork. **2.** an angular design of bands within a border. —*v.t.* **3.** to ornament with a fret or fretwork. [ME *frette*, of uncert. orig.; cf. OF *frete* interlaced work, OE *frettewian*, var. of *fretwian*, *frætwian* adorn]

Fret[2] (def. 2)
Three Greek frets

fret[3] (frĕt), *n.*, *v.*, **fretted, fretting.** —*n.* **1.** any of the ridges of wood, metal, or string, set across the fingerboard of a lute or similar instrument which help the fingers to stop the strings at the correct points. —*v.t.* **2.** to provide with frets. [orig. uncert.]
fretful (frĕt′fəl), *adj.* disposed to fret; irritable or peevish. —**fret′fully,** *adv.* —**fret′fulness,** *n.* —**Syn.** petulant, querulous, impatient. —**Ant.** patient.
fretsaw (frĕt′sô′), *n.* a long, narrow-bladed saw used to cut ornamental work from thin wood.
fretted (frĕt′ĭd), *adj.* ornamented with frets.
fretwork (frĕt′wûk′), *n.* **1.** ornamental work consisting of interlacing parts, esp. work in which the design is formed by perforation. **2.** any pattern of dark and light, such as that of perforated fretwork.
Freud (froid; *Ger.* frŏYt), *n.* **Sigmund** (sĭg′mənd; *Ger.* zēk′mŏŏnt), 1856–1939, Austrian physician and psychoanalyst.
Freudian (froi′dyən), *adj.* **1.** of or pertaining to Sigmund Freud or his doctrines, esp. in respect to the causes and treatment of neurotic and psychopathic states, the interpretation of dreams, etc. —*n.* **2.** an adherent of the essential doctrines of Freud. —**Freud′ianism,** *n.*
Freudian slip, a slip of the tongue by which the speaker actually says something apposite or revealing, which was not primarily intended, but is taken to reveal the speaker's true or subconscious thoughts: *to say 'Nato is an organization for the prevention of peace' may have been a Freudian slip.*
Frey (frā), *n.* *Scand. Myth.* god of earth's fruitfulness and dispenser of wealth. [t. Icel.: m. *Freyr*]
Freya (frā′ə), *n.* *Scand. Myth.* goddess of fruitfulness and sexual love; the daughter of Njord and sister of Frey. [t. Icel.: m. *Freyja*]
Freyberg (frī′bûg), *n.* **Bernard, 1st Baron,** 1899–1963, New Zealand general.
Freytag (*Ger.* frī′tāk), *n.* **Gustav** (*Ger.* gŏŏs′tāf), 1816–95, German novelist and dramatist.
F.R.G.S., Fellow of the Royal Geographical Society.
Fri., Friday.
friable (frī′ə bl), *adj.* easily crumbled or reduced to powder; crumbly: *friable rock.* [t. L: m. s. *friābilis*] —**fri′abil′ity, fri′ableness,** *n.*
friar (frī′ə), *n.* *Rom. Cath. Ch.* a brother or member of one of certain religious orders, esp. the mendicant orders of Franciscans (**Grey Friars**), Dominicans (**Black Friars**), Carmelites (**hite Friars**), and Augustinians (**Austin Friars**). [ME *frere*, t. OF, g. L *frāter* brother] —**Syn.** See **monk.**
friarbird (frī′ə bûd′), *n.* any of various Australasian honey-eaters (*Meliphagidae*), esp. of the genus *Philemon.*
friar's balsam, *Med.* a tincture of benzoin.
friar's lantern, the ignis fatuus or will-o'-the-wisp.

Friar Tuck, the jolly friar of Robin Hood's band.
friary (frī′ə rĭ), *n.*, *pl.* **-ries. 1.** a convent of friars. **2.** a brotherhood of friars.
F.R.I.B.A., Fellow of the Royal Institute of British Architects.
fribble (frĭb′l), *v.*, **-bled, -bling,** *n.* —*v.i.* **1.** to act in a trifling or frivolous manner. —*v.t.* **2.** to waste foolishly. —*n.* **3.** a trifler. **4.** anything trifling or frivolous. **5.** frivolousness. [orig. uncert.]
Fribourg (*Fr.* frē bo͞or′), *n.* **1.** a canton in W Switzerland. 159,194 pop. (1960); 644 sq. mi. **2.** a town in and the capital of this canton. 32,583 (1960). German, **Freiburg.**
F.R.I.C., Fellow of the Royal Institute of Chemistry.
fricandeau (frĭk′ən dō′), *n.*, *pl.* **-deaus, -deaux** (-dōz′). a loin of veal, larded and braised, or roasted. [t. F]
fricassee (frĭk′ə sē′, frĭk′ə sē′), *n.*, *v.*, **-seed, -seeing.** —*n.* **1.** meat, esp. chicken or veal, stewed, and served in a white sauce made of its own stock. —*v.t.* **2.** to prepare as a fricassee. Also, *French,* **fricassée** (*Fr.* frē kȧ sė′). [t. F, der. *fricasser* to sauté and serve with sauce, t. Pr.: m. *fricassá,* der. *fricar* fry, g. Rom. *frīgicāre,* intensive of L *frīgere*]
fricative (frĭk′ə tĭv), *Phonet.* —*adj.* **1.** (of consonants) characterized by a noise produced by air being forced through an opening, as in *f, v, s,* etc. —*n.* **2.** a fricative consonant. [t. NL: m. s. *fricātīvus,* der. L *fricāre* rub]
F.R.I.C.S., Fellow of the Royal Institute of Chartered Surveyors.
friction (frĭk′shən), *n.* **1.** *Mech., Physics.* the resistance to the relative motion (sliding or rolling) of surfaces of bodies in contact. **2.** the rubbing of the surface of one body against that of another. **3.** clashing or conflict, as of opinions, etc. [t. L: s. *frictio* a rubbing] —**fric′tionless,** *adj.*
frictional (frĭk′ shə nəl), *adj.* **1.** of, pertaining to, or of the nature of friction. **2.** moved, worked, or produced by friction. —**fric′tionally,** *adv.*
friction clutch, *Mach.* a clutch in which one rotating member turns another by the friction between them.
Friday (frī′dĭ), *n.* **1.** the sixth day of the week, following Thursday. **2.** the native companion of Defoe's Robinson Crusoe. **3.** a devoted or servile follower. [ME; OE *Frīgedæg* Freo's day, f. *Frige,* gen. sing. of *Frēo* (OE goddess identified with Venus) + *dæg* day; *Frēo* is identical with OE adj. *frēo* free]
fridge (frĭj), *n.* a refrigerator.
Fridtjof Nansen Land (*Dan.* frĕd′yŏf nȧn′sən), Franz Josef Land.
fried (frīd), *adj.* **1.** cooked in fat. —*v.* **2.** pt. and pp. of **fry**[1].
Friedel-Crafts reaction (frē′dl krȧfts′), *Chem.* a reaction for the synthesis of aromatic hydrocarbons depending on the action of alkyl halides on benzene derivatives in the presence of such catalysts as anhydrous aluminium chloride. [named after C. *Friedel,* 1832–99, French chemist, and J. M. *Cràfts,* 1839–1917, American chemist]
Friedrich (*Ger.* frē′drĭKH), *n.* See **Frederick.**
friend (frĕnd), *n.* **1.** one attached to another by feelings of affection or personal regard. **2.** a well-wisher, patron, or supporter. **3.** one who is on good terms with another; one not hostile. **4.** a member of the same nation, party, etc. **5.** (*cap.*) a member of the Society of Friends; Quaker. [ME; OE *frēond,* c. D *vriend,* G *Freund,* Goth. *frijonds,* all orig. ppr. of a verb meaning love (in OE, *frēogan*). Cf. FRIDAY, FREE] —**friend′less,** *adj.* —**friend′lessness,** *n.* —**Syn. 1.** companion, comrade, chum, crony. See **acquaintance.**
friendly (frĕnd′lĭ), *adj.*, **-lier, -liest,** *adv.* —*adj.* **1.** characteristic of or befitting a friend; showing friendship: *a friendly greeting.* **2.** like a friend; kind. **3.** favourably disposed; inclined to approve, help, or support. **4.** not hostile or at variance; amicable. —*adv.* **5.** in a friendly manner; like a friend. [ME *frendly,* OE *frēondlīc*] —**friend′lily,** *adv.* —**friend′liness,** *n.* —**Syn. 3.** amiable, cordial, genial, kindly.
Friendly Islands, Tonga.
friendly society, a society which by voluntary subscriptions provides for the relief or maintenance of its members and their families in sickness, old age, etc.
friendship (frĕnd′shĭp), *n.* **1.** friendly feeling or disposition. **2.** the state of being a friend; association as friends. **3.** a friendly relation or intimacy.
frier (frī′ə), *n.* fryer.
Friesian (frē′zyən), *n.* **1.** one of a breed of dairy cattle, usually black and white in colouring. **2.** Frisian. —*adj.* **3.** of or pertaining to this breed of cattle. **4.** Frisian.
Friesland (frēz′lənd; *Du.* frēs′lŏnt), *n.* a province in N Netherlands. 490,976 pop. (est. 1963); 1431 sq. mi. *Cap.:* Leeuwarden.
frieze[1] (frēz), *n.* **1.** that part of an entablature between the architrave and the cornice, commonly ornamented with sculpture. See diag. under **column. 2.** any similar decorative band or feature, as on a wall. [t. F: m. *frise,* ult. orig. uncert.]
frieze[2] (frēz), *n.* heavy, napped woollen cloth for coats. [t. MD: m. *frise* coarse, hairy cloth. Cf. FRAISE, FRIZZ]
frig (frĭg), *v.i.*, **frigged, frigging.** *Taboo.* **1.** to masturbate. **2.** to fuck. **3.** to behave in a stupid manner (often fol. by *around*). [t. L: m. s. *fricāre* rub]
frigate (frĭg′ĭt), *n.* **1.** (formerly) a naval vessel next in size to a ship of the line. **2.** a small destroyer used as an escort vessel. [t. F: m. *frégate,* t. It.: m. *fregata*]
frigate-bird (frĭg′ĭt bûd′), *n.* either of two species of rapacious totipalmate marine birds, *Fregata aquila* and *F. minor,* noted for their powers of flight; man-o'-war bird.
Frigg (frĭg), *n.* *Scand. Myth.* wife of Odin and queen of the gods (often confused with Freya). Also, **Frigga** (frĭg′ə). [t. Icel.]
fright (frīt), *n.* **1.** sudden and extreme fear; a sudden terror. **2.** a person or thing of shocking, grotesque, or ridiculous appearance. —*v.t.* **3.** *Poetic.* to frighten. [ME *frighte,* OE *fryhto,* metathetic var. of *fyrhto*; akin to G *Furcht*] —**Syn. 1.** dismay, consternation. See **terror.**
frighten (frī′tn), *v.t.* **1.** to throw into a fright; terrify; scare. **2.** to drive (fol. by *away, off,* etc.) by scaring. —**fright′ener,** *n.* —**fright′eningly,** *adv.*
—**Syn. 1.** FRIGHTEN, ALARM, SCARE, TERRIFY, APPAL mean to arouse fear in a person or animal. To FRIGHTEN is to shock with sudden, startling, but usually short-lived fear, especially that arising from the apprehension of physical harm: *to frighten someone by a sudden noise.* To ALARM is to arouse the feelings through the realization of some imminent or unexpected danger: *to alarm someone by a scream.* To SCARE is to frighten into a loss of poise or dignity, often in fun: *a sudden noise may scare anyone.* To TERRIFY is to strike with violent, overwhelming, or paralysing fear: *to terrify a city by lawless acts.* To APPAL is to overcome or confound by dread, dismay, or horror: *the suffering caused by the earthquake appalled him.*
frightened (frī′tnd), *adj.* **1.** thrown into a fright. **2.** afraid (fol. by *of*). —**Syn. 2.** See **afraid.**
frightful (frīt′fəl), *adj.* **1.** such as to cause fright; dreadful, terrible, or alarming. **2.** horrible, shocking, or revolting. **3.** *Colloq.* unpleasant; disagreeable: *we had a frightful time.* **4.** *Colloq.* very great. —**fright′fully,** *adv.* —**fright′fulness,** *n.* —**Syn. 1.** fearful, awful. **2.** hideous. —**Ant. 1.** reassuring.
frigid (frĭj′ĭd), *adj.* **1.** very cold in temperature: *a frigid climate.* **2.** without warmth of feeling; without ardour or enthusiasm. **3.** stiff or formal. **4.** (of a woman) **a.** abnormally averse to sexual intercourse. **b.** sexually unresponsive. [t. L: s. *frigidus*] —**frigid′ity, frig′idness,** *n.* —**frig′idly,** *adv.*
Frigid Zone, the regions between the poles and the polar circles.
frigorific (frĭg′ə rĭf′ĭk), *adj.* causing or producing cold. [t. L: s. *frīgorificus* cooling]
frijol (frē′hōl; *Sp.* frēKH ōl′), *n.*, *pl.* **frijoles** (frē′hōlz; *Sp.* frēKH ō′lĕs). a cultivated bean of the genus *Phaseolus,* much used for food in Mexico, etc. Also, **frihole** (frē hō′lĭ; *Sp.* frēKH ō′lė). [t. Sp.]
frill (frĭl), *n.* **1.** a trimming consisting of a strip of material or lace, gathered at one edge and left loose at the other; a ruffle. **2.** something resembling such a trimming, as the fringe of hair on the chest of some dogs. **3.** *Colloq.* affectation of manner, style, etc. **4.** something superfluous or useless. **5.** *Photog.* a wrinkling or loosening of an emulsion at the edges, usually the result of high temperature in developing, fixing, etc. —*v.t.* **6.** to trim or ornament with a frill or frills. **7.** to form into a frill. —*v.i.* **8.** *Photog.* (of an emulsion) to become wrinkled or loose. [? t. Flem.: m. *frul* frill (of a collar), *frullen* have frills] —**frill′y,** *adj.*
frilling (frĭl′ĭng), *n.*, frilled edging.
Frimaire (*Fr.* frē mĕr′), *n.* (in the calendar of the first French republic) the third month of the year, from November 21st to December 20th. [t. F, der. *frimas* hoarfrost, der. OF *frim,* t. Gmc. See RIME[2]]
fringe (frĭnj), *n.*, *v.*, **fringed, fringing,** *adj.* —*n.* **1.** an ornamental bordering having projecting lengths of thread, cord, etc., either loose or variously arranged or combined. **2.** anything resembling or suggesting this: *a fringe of trees about a field.* **3.** hair falling over the brow. **4.** border; margin; outer part or extremity. **5.** *Optics.* one of the alternate light and dark bands produced by diffraction or interference. —*v.t.* **6.** to furnish with or as with a fringe. **7.** to serve as a fringe for. —*adj.* **8.** accessory; supplementary: *fringe benefits.* [ME *frenge,* t. OF, g. LL *fimbria* border, fringe] —**fringe′less,** *adj.* —**fringe′like′,** *adj.* —**fring′y,** *adj.*
fringe benefit, any remuneration received in addition to one's wage, as a pension, travel allowance, etc.

fringed waterlily, an aquatic perennial, *Nymphoides peltata*, of the family *Menyanthaceae*, with floating leaves and small groups of yellow flowers, widespread in ponds and slow-flowing rivers of N temperate regions.

fringe tree, an oleaceous shrub or small tree, *Chionanthus virginicus*, of the southern U.S., bearing panicles of white flowers with long, narrow petals.

fringilline (frĭn jĭl′ĭn, -īn), *adj.* belonging or pertaining to the *Fringillidae*, the finch family, which includes the sparrows, canaries, linnets, etc., as well as various finches. [f. s. L *fringilla* kind of bird + -INE[1]]

frippery (frĭp′ə rĭ), *n., pl.* **-ries. 1.** finery in dress, esp. when tawdry. **2.** empty display; ostentation. **3.** trifles. [t. F: m. *friperie*, OF *freperie*, der. *frepe* rag]

Fris., Frisian.

Frisch (*Ger.* frĭsh), *n.* **Max** (*Ger.* mȧks), born 1911, Swiss dramatist.

Frisches Haff (*Ger.* frĭsh′əs hȧf′), a lagoon on the Baltic coast of Poland. 52 mi. long; 4–12 mi. wide.

Frisco (frĭs′kō), *n. Colloq.* San Francisco.

frisé (frē′zā), *n.* a rug or upholstery fabric made with pile in uncut loops or in a combination of cut and uncut.

frisette (frĭ zĕt′), *n.* a fringe of curled or frizzed hair, esp. artificial, worn on the forehead by women. [t. F: little curl, frizz, der. *friser* to curl]

friseur (*Fr.* frē zœr′), *n. French.* a hairdresser.

Frisian (frĭz′ĭ ən), *adj.* **1.** of or pertaining to Friesland, its inhabitants, or their language. *—n.* **2.** one of the people of Friesland. **3.** the Germanic language most closely related to English, spoken in Friesland and nearby islands. Also, **Friesian.**

Frisian Islands, a chain of islands in the North Sea stretching along the coasts of the Netherlands, Denmark, and West Germany: includes groups belonging to the Netherlands (**West Frisians**) and to West Germany (**East Frisians**), and a group divided between West Germany and Denmark (**North Frisians**).

frisk (frĭsk), *v.i.* **1.** to dance, leap, skip, or gambol, as in frolic. *—v.t.* **2.** *Slang.* to search (a person) for concealed weapons, etc., by feeling his clothing. **3.** *Slang.* to steal something from (someone) in this way. *—n.* **4.** a leap, skip, or caper. **5.** a frolic. [orig. adj., t. OF: m. *frisque*, t. Gmc; cf. G *frisch* lively] —**frisk′er,** *n.*

frisket (frĭs′kĭt), *n. Print.* an iron frame to hold in place a sheet of paper to be printed.

frisky (frĭs′kĭ), *adj.,* **friskier, friskiest.** lively; frolicsome; playful. —**frisk′ily,** *adv.* —**frisk′iness,** *n.*

frit (frĭt), *n., v.,* **fritted, fritting.** *—n.* **1.** *Ceramics.* **a.** a fused or partially fused material used as a basis for glazes or enamels. **b.** the composition from which artificial soft porcelain is made. **2.** *Dentistry.* the material from which the glazed portion of artificial teeth is made. **3.** (in medieval glass-making) fused or calcined material, ready to serve as part of the batch for glass-making. *—v.t.* **4.** to fuse (materials) in making a frit. [t. F: m. *fritte*, t. It.: m. *fritta*, der. *friggere* (g. L *frīgere*) roast, fry]

frit fly, a minute fly, *Oscinosoma frit*, whose larva is an injurious pest to wheat and other cereals.

frith[1] (frĭth), *n. Chiefly Scot.* a firth. [metathetic var. of FIRTH]

frith[2] (frĭth), *n. Archaic or Dial.* a tract of wooded land; brushwood. [ME *fryht*; OE *(ge)fyrhthe*]

Frith (frĭth), *n.* **William Powell,** 1819–1909, English painter.

fritillary (frĭ tĭl′ə rĭ), *n., pl.* **-ries. 1.** any of several orange-brown butterflies which are silver-spotted beneath, of the genus *Argynnis* and allies. **2.** any plant of the liliaceous genus *Fritillaria*, esp. *F. meleagris*, with solitary, nodding chequered purple or white flowers, occurring in damp pastures in Europe but frequently cultivated. [t. NL: m. s. *fritillāria*, der. L *fritillus* dicebox]

fritter[1] (frĭt′ə), *v.t.* **1.** to disperse or squander piecemeal, or waste little by little (usually fol. by *away*): *to fritter away one's money.* **2.** to break or tear into small pieces or shreds. *—n.* **3.** a small piece, fragment, or shred. [earlier *fitter*, der. *fit* part] —**frit′terer,** *n.*

fritter[2] (frĭt′ə), *n.* a small cake of batter, sometimes containing fruit, clams, or some other ingredient, fried in deep fat or sautéed in a frying pan. [ME *frytour*, t. OF: m. *friture*, der. *frire* FRY]

Fritz (frĭts), *n. Slang.* **1.** a German, esp. a German soldier. **2.** Germans or a German army collectively.

Friulian (frĭ o͞o′lyən), *n.* a Rhaeto-Romanic language spoken by about half a million people in NE Italy.

Friuli-Venezia Giulia (*It.* frē o͞o′lē vė nĕt′tsyȧ jo͞o′lyȧ), an autonomous region in NE Italy, formerly part of Venezia Giulia, most of which was ceded to Yugoslavia. 1,205,222 pop. (1961); 2947 sq. mi.

frivol (frĭv′əl), *v.,* **-olled, -olling.** *Colloq. —v.i.* **1.** to behave frivolously; trifle. *—v.t.* **2.** to spend frivolously (fol. by *away*). [back-formation from FRIVOLOUS] —**friv′oller,** *n.*

frivolity (frĭ vŏl′ĭ tĭ), *n., pl.* **-ties. 1.** the quality or state of being frivolous. **2.** a frivolous act or thing.

frivolous (frĭv′ə ləs), *adj.* **1.** of little or no weight, worth, or importance; not worthy of serious notice: *a frivolous objection.* **2.** characterized by lack of seriousness or sense: *frivolous conduct.* **3.** given to trifling or levity, as persons. [t. L: m. *frīvolus* silly, trifling, paltry] —**friv′olously,** *adv.* —**friv′olousness,** *n.* —**Syn. 1.** trifling, petty, paltry, trivial. **3.** idle, silly, foolish. —**Ant. 1.** weighty. **3.** serious.

frizz (frĭz), *v.,* **frizzed, frizzing,** *n., pl.* **frizzes.** *—v.t., v.i.* **1.** to form into small, crisp curls or little tufts. *—n.* **2.** the state of being frizzed. **3.** something frizzed; frizzed hair. Also, **friz.** [back-formation from FRIZZLE[1]]

frizzle[1] (frĭz′əl), *v.,* **-zled, -zling,** *n. —v.t.* **1.** to frizz. *—n.* **2.** a short, crisp curl. [orig. obscure. Cf. OE *fris* curled] —**friz′zler,** *n.*

frizzle[2] (frĭz′əl), *v.,* **-zled, -zling.** *—v.i.* **1.** to make a sizzling or sputtering noise in frying or the like. *—v.t.* **2.** to crisp (meat, etc.) by frying. [b. FRY and FIZZLE]

frizzy (frĭz′ĭ), *adj.* curly: *frizzy hair.* Also, *U.S.,* **frizzly** (frĭz′lĭ).

fro (frō), *adv.* **1.** from; back. **2. to and fro, a.** back and forth. **b.** hither and thither. [ME, earlier *frā*, t. Scand.; cf. Icel. *frā*, c. OE *fram* from]

Frobisher (frō′bĭ shə), *n.* **Sir Martin,** 1535?–94, English navigator and explorer.

frock (frŏk), *n.* **1.** a dress, esp. for a small girl. **2.** a loose outer garment worn by peasants and workmen; smock. **3.** a coarse outer garment with large sleeves, worn by monks. **4.** a frockcoat. *—v.t.* **5.** to provide with or clothe in a frock. **6.** to invest with priestly or clerical office. [ME *froke*, t. OF: m. *froc*; ult. orig. uncert.] —**frock′less,** *adj.*

frockcoat (frŏk′kōt′), *n.* a man's close-fitting coat, usually double-breasted, extending to about the knees.

Froebel (frû′bl; *Ger.* frœ′bəl), *n.* **Friedrich** (*Ger.* frē′drĭkh), 1782–1852, German educational reformer; founder of the kindergarten system.

frog[1] (frŏg), *n., v.,* **frogged, frogging.** *—n.* **1.** any of various tailless amphibians (order *Salientia*), esp. of the web-footed aquatic species constituting the genus *Rana* and allied genera. **2.** any of various froglike amphibians. **3.** a slight hoarseness due to mucus on the vocal cords: *a frog in the throat.* **4.** (*cap.*) (contemptuous) Frenchman. **5.** a small, heavy holder placed in a bowl or vase to hold flower stems in position. **6.** an indentation on a brick. **7.** an attachment suspended from a belt for supporting a sword. *—v.i.* **8.** to catch, or search for, frogs. [ME *frogge*, OE *frogga*; akin to G *Frosch*] —**frog′like′,** *adj.*

Frog,[1] *Rana catesbeiana* (Length up to 8 in.)

frog[2] (frŏg), *n.* **1.** an ornamental fastening for the front of a coat, consisting of a button and a loop through which it passes. **2.** a device at the intersection of two railway tracks, to permit the wheels and flanges on one track to cross or branch from the other, or a similar device on a system of overhead wires as on a tramway or electric railway. [? t. Pg.: m. *froco*, g. L *floccus* FLOCK[2]]

Frog[2] (def. 1)

frog[3] (frŏg), *n.* a triangular mass of elastic, horny substance in the middle of the sole of the foot of a horse or related animal. [special use of FROG[1]]

frogbit (frŏg′bĭt′), *n.* a floating aquatic herb, *Hydrocharis morsus-ranae*, of the family *Hydrocharitaceae*, with white unisexual flowers, found in ponds and ditches throughout Europe and Asia.

frogfish (frŏg′fĭsh′), *n., pl.* **-fishes,** (*esp. collectively*) **-fish. 1.** any of the anglers (def. 3) constituting the family *Antennariidae*, characterized by a wide froglike mouth and broad limblike fins. **2.** an angler (def. 2).

froghopper (frŏg′hŏp′ə), *n.* any of various small, leaping, homopterous insects (family *Cercopidae*) whose young live in a spittle-like secretion on plants; spittle insect; cuckoo-spit.

frog kick, *Swimming.* a type of kick in which the legs are bent at the knees, extended outwards, and then brought together forcefully.

frogman (frŏg′mən), *n., pl.* **-men.** a swimmer specially equipped for underwater demolition, salvage, scientific exploration, etc.

frogmarch (frŏg′mäch′), *n.* **1.** a method of carrying a resisting prisoner, face downwards with four men each holding a limb. *—v.t.* **2.** to carry (a prisoner) in this way.

frogmouth (frŏg′mouth′), *n.* mopoke (def. 2).

frog orchid, an orchid, *Coeloglossum viride*, with loose spikes of small greenish flowers, found in Europe, W Asia and N America, esp. on non-acid grassland.

frogspawn (frŏg′spôn′), *n.* **1.** frogs' eggs; the spawn of frogs or a frog. **2.** any member of the genus of red algae *Batrachospermum.*

frogspit (frŏg′spĭt′), *n.* any of several filamentous fresh-water green algae forming floating masses. Also, **frog-spittle** (frŏg′spĭt′l).

Froissart (*Fr.* frwȧ sȧr′), *n.* **Jean** (*Fr.* zhäN), *c.* 1337–*c.* 1410, French chronicler.

frolic (frŏl′ĭk), *n.*, *v.*, **-icked, -icking,** *adj.* —*n.* **1.** merry play; gay prank; gaiety; fun. **2.** a merrymaking. —*v.i.* **3.** to play merrily; have fun; play merry pranks. —*adj.* **4.** gay; merry; full of mirth or pranks; full of fun. [t. D: m. *vrolijk* joyful (c. G *fröhlich*), f. *vro* glad + *lijk* like] —**frol′icker,** *n.*

frolicsome (frŏl′ĭk səm), *adj.* merrily playful; full of fun. —**frol′icsomely,** *adv.* —**frol′icsomeness,** *n.*

from (frŏm; *unstressed* frəm), *prep.* a particle specifying a starting point, and hence used to express removal or separation in space, time, order, etc., discrimination or distinction, source or origin, instrumentality, and cause or reason: *a train running west from London, from that time onwards, to wander from one's purpose, to refrain from laughing, sketches drawn from nature.* [ME and OE, var. of *fram*, prep., from, as adv., forwards, forth, c. OHG and Goth. *fram*, prep. and adv., Icel. *frā*, prep. (cf. FRO), *fram*, adv.]

Frome (frōm, frōōm), *n.* **Lake,** a saline flat in the E of South Australia. ab. 1800 sq. mi.

Fromentin (*Fr.* frŏ mäN tăN′), *n.* **Eugène** (*Fr.* œ zhĕn′), 1820–76, French painter and writer.

fromenty (frō′mən tĭ), *n.* frumenty.

Fromm (frŏm; *Ger.* frŏm), *n.* **Erich** (ĕ′rĭk; *Ger.* ė′rĭKH), born 1900, U.S. writer on psychology, born in Germany.

frond (frŏnd), *n. Bot.* **1.** a finely divided leaf, often large (properly applied to the ferns and some of the palms). **2.** a leaf-like expansion not differentiated into stem and foliage, as in lichens. [t. L: s. *frons* leafy branch] —**frond′-ed,** *adj.* —**frond′less,** *adj.*

Fronde (*Fr.* frôNd), *n. French.* **1.** a parliamentary and aristocratic rebellion against the court party and Cardinal Mazarin during the minority of Louis XIV of France. **2.** the groups which waged this rebellion.

frondescence (frŏn dĕs′əns), *n.* **1.** the process or period of coming into leaf. **2.** foliage. [t. NL: m. s. *frondescentia*, der. s. L *frondescens*, ppr. of *frondescere*, freq. of *frondēre* put forth leaves] —**frondes′cent,** *adj.*

Frondizi (frŏn dē′zĭ), *n.* **Arturo** (ä tōōə′rō), born 1908, Argentinian statesman: president of Argentina 1958–62.

frons (frŏnz), *n.* the facial area of an insect's head above or behind the clypeus.

front (frŭnt), *n.* **1.** the foremost part or surface of anything. **2.** the part or side of anything, as a house, which seems to look out or be directed forwards. **3.** any side or face, as of a house. **4.** a place or position directly before anything. **5.** *Mil.* **a.** the foremost line or part of an army, etc. **b.** a line of battle. **c.** the place where active operations are carried on. **6.** land facing a road, river, etc. **7.** a seaside promenade. **8.** *Colloq.* someone or something which serves as a cover for another activity, esp. an illegal or disreputable one. **9.** *Colloq.* outward impression of rank, position, or wealth. **10.** bearing or demeanour in confronting anything: *a calm front.* **11.** cool assurance, or impudence. **12.** the forehead, or the entire face. **13.** a coalition or movement to achieve a particular end, usually political: *people's front.* **14.** something attached or worn at the forepart, as a shirt-front, a dicky, etc. **15.** *Meteorol.* a surface of discontinuity separating two dissimilar air-masses.

—*adj.* **16.** of or pertaining to the front. **17.** situated in or at the front. **18.** *Phonet.* pronounced with the tongue relatively far forward in the mouth: *the vowels of 'beet' and 'gait' are front vowels.*

—*v.t.* **19.** to have the front towards; face: *our house fronts the lake.* **20.** to meet face to face; confront. **21.** to face in opposition, hostility, or defiance. **22.** to furnish or supply with a front. **23.** to serve as a front to.

—*v.i.* **24.** to have or turn the front in some specified direction: *our house fronts on to the lake.*

[ME, t. L: s. *frons* forehead, front] —**front′less,** *adj.*

frontage (frŭn′tĭj), *n.* **1.** the front of a building or plot of land. **2.** the lineal extent of this front. **3.** the direction it faces. **4.** land abutting on a river, street, etc. **5.** the space lying between a building and the street, etc.

frontager (frŭn′tĭ jə), *n.* one owning or occupying land which abuts on to a highway, river, or seashore.

frontal (frŭn′tl), *adj.* **1.** of, in, or at the front: *a frontal attack.* **2.** *Anat.* denoting or pertaining to the bone (or pair of bones) forming the forehead, or to the forehead in general. **3.** *Meteorol.* of or pertaining to the division between dissimilar air-masses. —*n.* **4.** *Eccles.* a movable cover or hanging for the front of an altar. **5.** *Anat.* a bone of the forehead; frontal bone. See diag. under **cranium.** [t. LL: s. *frontālis*, der. L *frons* front; r. ME *frountel*, t. OF: m. *frontel*] —**front′ally,** *adv.*

frontbencher (frŭnt′bĕn′chə), *n.* a member of the British House of Commons who is a government minister or Opposition spokesman. —**front′bench′,** *adj.*

Frontenac (*Fr.* frôNt nȧk′), *n.* **Louis de Buade de** (*Fr.* lwē de bY ȧd′ də), *c.* 1620–98, French governor of Canada.

frontier (frŭn′tĭ ə, -tyə), *n.* **1.** that part of a country which borders another country; boundary; border; extreme limit. **2.** *U.S.* that part of a country which forms the border of its settled or inhabited regions. **3.** (often *pl.*) the incompletely developed region of a field of knowledge, etc.: *frontiers of philosophy.* —*adj.* **4.** of or on the frontier: *a frontier town.* [ME *frountere*, t. OF: m. *frontiere*, der. *front* in sense of opposite side]

frontiersman (frŭn′tyəz mən), *n.*, *pl.* **-men.** a man who lives on the frontier.

frontispiece (frŭn′tĭs pēs′), *n.* **1.** an illustrated leaf preceding the titlepage of a book. **2.** *Archit.* **a.** the most richly decorated and usually central portion of the principal face of a building. **b.** the pediment over a door, gate, etc. [alter. (conformed to *piece*) of earlier *frontispice*, t. F, t. ML: m. s. *frontispicium*, f. L. *fronti-* front + *-spicium* look]

frontlet (frŭnt′lĭt), *n.* **1.** the forehead of an animal. **2.** *Ornith.* the forehead when marked by a different colour or texture of the plumage. **3.** something worn on the head. **4.** *Judaism.* a phylactery worn on the head. **5.** a cloth hanging over the upper part of an altar frontal. [ME *frontlette*, t. OF: m. *frontelet*, dim. of *frontel* FRONTAL, n.]

frontogenesis (frŭn′tō jĕn′ĭ sĭs), *n. Meteorol.* the development, or marked intensification, of a front (def. 15).

frontolysis (frŭn tŏl′ĭ sĭs), *n. Meteorol.* the disappearance, or marked weakening of a front (def. 15).

front-page (frŭnt′pāj′), *adj.* of consequence; worth putting on the first page of a newspaper.

Front Range, a mountain range in the U.S., the easternmost range of the Rocky Mountains, extending from central Colorado to S Wyoming. Highest peak, Grays Peak, 14,274 ft.

frontwards (frŭnt′wədz), *adv.* towards the front. Also, **front′ward.**

frore (frô), *adj. Archaic.* **1.** frozen. **2.** frosty; intensely cold. [old pp. of FREEZE]

frost (frŏst), *n.* **1.** a state of the temperature which causes the freezing of water. **2. degrees of frost,** degrees below freezing point: *we had ten degrees of frost* (i.e., 22°F). **3.** a covering of minute ice needles, formed from the atmosphere at night upon the ground and exposed objects when these have cooled by radiation below the dewpoint, and when the dewpoint is below freezing point (**white frost** or **hoarfrost**). **4.** the act or process of freezing. **5.** coldness of manner or temperature. **6.** crushed glass of paper thickness, used for decorative purposes. **7.** *Colloq.* a coolness between persons. **8.** *Slang.* a failure. —*v.t.* **9.** to cover with frost. **10.** to give a frostlike surface to (glass, etc.). **11.** *U.S.* to ice (a cake, etc.). **12.** to kill or injure by frost. —*v.i.* **13.** to freeze or become covered with frost (often fol. by *up* or *over*). [ME and OE *frost*, *forst*, c. D *vorst*, G *Frost*, Icel. *frost*, akin to FREEZE] —**frost′less,** *adj.* —**frost′like′.** *adj.*

Frost (frŏst), *n.* **Robert (Lee),** 1874–1963, U.S. poet.

frostbite (frŏst′bīt′), *n.*, *v.*, **-bit, -bitten, -biting.** —*n.* **1.** the inflamed, sometimes gangrenous effect on a part of the body, especially the extremities, due to excessive exposure to extreme cold. —*v.t.* **2.** to injure by frost or extreme cold.

frostbitten (frŏst′bĭt′n), *adj.* injured by frost or extreme cold.

frosted (frŏs′tĭd), *adj.* **1.** covered with frost. **2.** (of glass) made opaque by etching or sandblasting.

frosting (frŏs′tĭng), *n.* **1.** a preparation of loaf sugar, water, eggwhites, and cream of tartar; a fluffy icing used to cover and decorate cakes. **2.** *U.S.* icing. **3.** a lustreless finish, as of metal or glass. **4.** a material used for decorative work, as signs, etc., made from coarse, powdered glass flakes.

frost point, *Meteorol.* hoarfrost point.

frostwork (frŏst′wûk′), *n.* **1.** the delicate tracery formed by frost, esp. on glass. **2.** similar ornamentation, as on metal.

frosty (frŏs′tĭ), *adj.*, **-tier, -tiest.** **1.** attended with or producing frost; freezing; very cold: *frosty weather.* **2.** consisting of or covered with a frost. **3.** lacking warmth of feeling. **4.** resembling frost; white or grey, as hair.

5. of or characteristic of old age. —**frost′ily,** *adv.* —**frost′iness,** *n.* —**frost′less,** *adj.*

froth (frŏth), *n.* **1.** an aggregation of bubbles, as on a fermented liquid or at the mouth of a hard-driven horse; foam. **2.** a foam of saliva or fluid resulting from disease. **3.** something unsubstantial or evanescent, as idle talk; trivial ideas. —*v.t.* **4.** to cover with froth. **5.** to cause to foam. **6.** to emit like froth. —*v.i.* **7.** to give out froth; foam. [ME *frothe*, ? t. Scand.; cf. Icel. *frodha.* Cf. also OE *āfrēothan* form froth]

froth flotation, a process for separating a mixture of finely divided minerals by agitating them in a froth of water and oil, so that some float and others sink.

frothy (frŏth′ĭ), *adj.*, **-ier, -iest. 1.** of, like, or having froth; foamy. **2.** unsubstantial; trifling; shallow. —**froth′ily,** *adv.* —**froth′iness,** *n.*

Froude (frōōd), *n.* **James Anthony,** 1818–94, English historian.

froufrou (frōō′frōō′), *n.* a rustling, particularly the rustling of silk, as in a woman's dress. [t. F]

frounce (frouns), *n.*, *v.*, **frounced, frouncing.** —*n.* **1.** *Archaic.* affectation; empty show. —*v.t.* **2.** to curl the hair of. **3.** *Obs.* to pleat. —*v.i.* **4.** *Obs.* to frown. [ME *fronce(n)*, t. OF: m. *froncier*, der. *fronce* a wrinkle, fold, t. Gmc; cf. Icel. *hrukka*, G *Runzel* wrinkle]

froward (frō′əd), *adj.* perverse; wilfully contrary; refractory; not easily managed. [ME. See FRO, -WARD] —**fro′wardly,** *adv.* —**fro′wardness,** *n.* —**Syn.** obstinate, wilful, disobedient. —**Ant.** docile.

frown (froun), *v.i.* **1.** to contract the brow as in displeasure or deep thought; scowl. **2.** to look displeased; have an angry look. **3.** to look disapprovingly (fol. by *on* or *upon*): *to frown upon a scheme.* —*v.t.* **4.** to express by a frown. —*n.* **5.** a frowning look; scowl. **6.** any expression or show of disapproval. [ME *froune(n)*, t. OF: m. *froignier*, der. *froigne* surly expression; of Celtic orig.] —**frown′er,** *n.* —**frown′ingly,** *adv.*

frowst (froust), *n.* **1.** a hot stuffy atmosphere. —*v.t.* **2.** to lounge about in such an atmosphere. [orig. unknown]

frowsty (frous′tĭ), *adj.* ill-smelling; musty; close-smelling.

frowzy (frou′zĭ), *adj.*, **-zier, -ziest. 1.** dirty and untidy; slovenly. **2.** ill-smelling; musty. Also, **frows′y, frouzy.** [akin to FROWSTY] —**frowz′ily,** *adv.* —**frowz′iness,** *n.*

froze (frōz), *v.* pt. of **freeze.**

frozen (frō′zən), *v.* **1.** pp. of **freeze.** —*adj.* **2.** congealed by cold; covered with ice, as a stream. **3.** frigid; very cold. **4.** injured or killed by frost or cold. **5.** obstructed by ice, as pipes. **6.** (of food) preserved by refrigeration. **7.** chilly or cold in manner; unfeeling: *a frozen stare.* **8.** *Finance.* rendered impossible of liquidation, as by business conditions: *frozen loans.* [pp. of FREEZE] —**fro′zenly,** *adv.* —**fro′zenness,** *n.*

F.R.S., Fellow of the Royal Society.

frt, freight.

Fructidor (*Fr.* frʏk tē dôr′), *n.* (in the calendar of the first French republic) the twelfth month of the year, extending from August 18th to September 16th. [t. F, f. L *fructi-* fruit + s. Gk *dôron* gift]

fructiferous (frŭk tĭf′ə rəs), *adj.* fruit-bearing; producing fruit. [f. L *fructifer* fruit-bearing + -OUS]

fructification (frŭk′tĭ fĭ kā′shən), *n.* **1.** the act of fructifying; the fruiting of a plant. **2.** the fruit of a plant. **3.** the organs of fruiting.

fructify (frŭk′tĭ fī′), *v.*, **-fied, -fying.** —*v.i.* **1.** to bear fruit. —*v.t.* **2.** to make fruitful or productive; fertilize. [ME *fructifie(n)*, t. F: m. *fructifier*, t. L: m. *fructificāre* bear fruit]

fructose (frŭk′tōs), *n.* *Chem.* a laevorotatory ketose sugar, $C_6H_{12}O_6$, known also as laevulose. It is an intensely sweet carbohydrate occurring in honey and invert sugar. [f. s. L *fructus* fruit + -OSE[2]]

fructuous (frŭk′tyŏŏ əs), *adj.* fruitful; profitable. —**fruc′tuously,** *adv.* —**fruc′tuousness,** *n.*

frug (frŭg), *n.*, *v.*, **frugged, frugging.** —*n.* **1.** a dance derived from the twist. —*v.i.* **2.** to dance the frug.

frugal (frōō′gl), *adj.* **1.** economical in use or expenditure; prudently saving or sparing. **2.** entailing little expense; costing little; scanty; meagre. [t. L: s. *frūgālis* economical] —**frugality** (frōō găl′ĭ tĭ), **fru′galness,** *n.* —**fru′gally,** *adv.* —**Syn. 1.** self-denying, thrifty, chary, provident. See **economical.** —**Ant. 1.** extravagant.

fruit (frōōt), *n.* **1.** any product of vegetable growth useful to men or animals. **2.** *Bot.* **a.** the developed ovary of a seed plant with its contents and accessory parts, as the peapod, nut, tomato, pineapple, etc. **b.** the edible part of a plant developed from a flower, with any accessory tissues, as the peach, mulberry, banana, etc. **c.** the spores and accessory organs of a cryptogam. **3.** anything produced or accruing; product, result, or effect; return or profit. **4.** *Slang.* a girl. **5.** *U.S. Slang.* a homosexual. —*v.i.* **6.** to bear or bring to bear fruit. [ME, t. OF, g. L *fructus* enjoyment, proceeds, fruit] —**fruit′like′,** *adj.*

fruitage (frōō′tĭj), *n.* **1.** the bearing of fruit. **2.** fruits collectively. **3.** product or result.

fruitarian (frōō tĕə′rĭ ən), *n.* one whose diet consists mainly of fruit. [f. FRUIT + -ARIAN, modelled on *vegetarian*]

fruit-bat (frōōt′băt′), *n.* any large bat of the suborder *Megacheiroptera*, of the Old World.

fruit cake, a rich cake containing currants, nuts, lemon peel, etc.

fruit cup, an assortment of fruits served in a glass or a cup as an appetizer or dessert.

fruiter (frōō′tə), *n.* **1.** a ship employed in transporting fruit. **2.** a fruit-grower.

fruiterer (frōō′tə rə), *n.* a dealer in fruit.

fruit-fly (frōōt′flī′), *n.* **1.** any small fly of the dipterous family *Trypetidae*, which includes many seriously destructive pests, as the Mediterranean fruit-fly. **2.** any member of the genus *Drosophila*, the vinegar flies.

fruitful (frōōt′fəl), *adj.* **1.** abounding in fruit, as trees or other plants; bearing fruit abundantly. **2.** producing an abundant growth, as of fruit. **3.** productive of results; profitable: *fruitful investigations.* —**fruit′fully,** *adv.* —**fruit′fulness,** *n.* —**Syn. 2, 3.** prolific, fertile. See **productive.** —**Ant. 3.** barren.

fruition (frōō ĭsh′ən), *n.* **1.** attainment of anything desired; attainment of maturity; realization of results: *the fruition of one's labours.* **2.** enjoyment, as of something attained or realized. **3.** the state of bearing fruit. [ME, t. LL: s. *fruitio* enjoyment]

fruit jar, a large-mouthed bottle, usually with an airtight cover, for preserving fruit.

fruit knife, a small knife used for cutting and paring fruit at table.

fruitless (frōōt′lĭs), *adj.* **1.** useless; unproductive; vain; without results. **2.** without fruit; barren. —**fruit′lessly,** *adv.* —**fruit′lessness,** *n.* —**Syn. 1.** ineffective, abortive, unprofitable, bootless, futile.

fruit machine, a coin-operated gambling machine.

fruit salad, a salad composed of various kinds of fruit cut up and mixed together.

fruit sugar, *Chem.* fructose.

fruit tree, a tree bearing edible fruit.

fruity (frōō′tĭ), *adj.*, **-tier, -tiest. 1.** resembling fruit; having the taste or flavour of fruit. **2.** (of a voice) mellow, florid. **3.** sexually suggestive; salacious.

frumentaceous (frōō′mĕn tā′shəs), *adj.* of the nature of or resembling wheat or other grain. [t. LL: m. *frūmentāceus* of grain]

frumenty (frōō′mən tĭ), *n.* hulled wheat boiled in milk and seasoned with sugar, etc. Also, **fromenty, furmenty, furmety.** [ME *frumentee*, t. OF, der. *frument*, g. L *frūmentum* grain]

frump (frŭmp), *n.* a dowdy, drably dressed woman. [orig. unknown]

frumpish (frŭm′pĭsh), *adj.* dowdy and unattractive. —**frump′ishly,** *adv.* —**frump′ishness,** *n.*

frumpy (frŭm′pĭ), *adj.*, **-pier, -piest.** frumpish. —**frump′ily,** *adv.* —**frump′iness,** *n.*

Frunze (*Russ.* frōōn′zĭ), *n.* a city in the SW Soviet Union in Asia: capital of Kirghiz Republic. 360,000 (est. 1965).

frustrate (frŭs trāt′), *v.*, **-trated, -trating,** *adj.* —*v.t.* **1.** to make (plans, efforts, etc.) of no avail; defeat; baffle; nullify. **2.** to disappoint or thwart (a person). —*adj.* **3.** *Archaic.* frustrated. [t. L: m. s. *frustrātus*, pp., having disappointed or deceived] —**Syn. 1.** balk, foil, circumvent. See **thwart.** —**Ant. 1.** assist.

frustration (frŭs trā′shən), *n.* **1.** the state or quality of being frustrated. **2.** *Psychol.* the feeling aroused by the prevention of sought gratifications and satisfactions, often by sources outside oneself.

frustule (frŭs′tyŏŏl), *n.* *Bot.* the siliceous cell wall of a diatom. [t. LL: m. s. *frustulum*, dim. of *frustum* piece, bit]

frustum (frŭs′təm), *n.*, *pl.* **-ta** (-tə), **-tums.** *Geom.* **1.** the part of a conical solid left after cutting off a top portion by a plane parallel to the base. **2.** the part of a conical solid between two cutting planes. [t. L: piece, bit]

F, Frustum of a cone

frutescent (frōō tĕs′ənt), *adj.* *Bot.* tending to be shrublike; shrubby. [irreg. f. L *frut(ex)* shrub, bush + -ESCENT] —**frutes′cence,** *n.*

fruticose (frōō′tĭ kōs′), *adj.* *Bot.* having the form of a shrub; shrublike. [t. L: m. s. *fruticōsus* bushy]

fry[1] (frī), *v.*, **fried, frying,** *n.*, *pl.* **fries.** —*v.t.* **1.** to cook in fat, oil, etc., usually over direct heat. —*v.i.* **2.** to undergo cooking in fat, oil, etc. —*n.* **3.** a dish of something fried. **4.** *U.S.* an occasion at which the chief food is fried, frequently outdoors: *a fish fry.* [ME *frye(n)*, t. F: m. *frire*, g. L *frīgere*]

fry[2] (frī), *n., pl.* **fry. 1.** the young of fishes, or of some other animals, as frogs. **2.** young or small fishes or other young creatures, as children, collectively. **3. small fry,** unimportant or insignificant people; young children. [ME; cf. Icel. *frjō*, Sw. *frö*, Goth. *fraiw* seed]

Fry (frī), *n.* **1. Christopher,** born 1907, English dramatist. **2. Elizabeth,** 1780–1845, English Quaker and prison reformer. **3. Maxwell,** born 1899, English architect. **4. Roger Eliot,** 1866–1934, English painter and art critic.

fryer (frī′ə), *n.* one who or that which fries. Also, **frier.**

frying pan, a shallow pan with a long handle, in which food is fried.

f.s., foot-second.

F.S.A., 1. Fellow of the Society of Antiquaries. **2.** Fellow of the Society of Arts.

F.S.E., Fellow of the Society of Engineers.

ft, 1. feet. **2.** foot. **3.** fort.

fth., fathom. Also, **fthm**

ft-lb., foot-pound.

ft-pdl, foot-poundal.

Fuad I (fo͞o′äd), (*Ahmed Fuad*), 1868–1936, king of Egypt, 1922–36.

fubsy (fŭb′zĭ), *adj. Colloq.* short and fat; stumpy. [orig. unknown]

Fuchs (fo͝oks, fo͞oks), *n.* **Sir Vivian Ernest,** born 1908, English Antarctic explorer and scientist.

fuchsia (fyo͞o′shə), *n.* **1.** any plant of the onagraceous genus *Fuchsia*, which includes many varieties cultivated for their handsome drooping flowers. **2.** a herbaceous shrub, *Zaushneria californica*, with large crimson flowers. **3.** bright purplish red. [NL, named after Leonhard *Fuchs*, 1501–66, German botanist. See -IA]

fuchsine (fo͞ok′sēn), *n.* a germicidal, coal-tar dye obtained by oxidizing a mixture of aniline and the toluidines; magenta. The dye is a greenish solid which forms deep red solutions. Also, **fuchsin** (fo͞ok′sĭn). [f. FUCHS(IA) + -INE[2]; so named from its likeness to the flower in colour]

fuchsite (fo͞ok′sīt), *n.* a green variety of muscovite in which some of the aluminium is replaced by chromium. [named after J. N. von *Fuchs*, 19th-century German geologist]

Fuchu (fo͞o′cho͞o), *n.* a town in Japan, in SE central Honshu island. 126,519 (1966).

fuck (fŭk), *Taboo.* —*v.t.* **1.** (of males) to have sexual intercourse with. **2.** *Slang.* to treat unfairly, deceive, or cause inconvenience, distress, etc., to (often fol. by *about*, *around*, etc.). **3. fuck up,** *Slang.* to make a mess of; ruin. —*v.i.* **4.** to have sexual intercourse. **5.** *Slang.* to behave stupidly or inanely (often fol. by *about*, *around*, etc.). **6. fuck off, a.** to masturbate. **b.** (often used offensively) to go away; depart. —*n.* **7.** the act of sexual intercourse. —*interj.* **8.** (an offensive exclamation of disgust or annoyance, often used as a mere intensive.) [ME, ?OE; c. G *ficken*]

fuckable (fŭk′ə bl), *adj. Taboo.* sexually desirable.

fucked-out (fŭkt′out′), *adj. Taboo Slang.* **1.** exhausted. **2.** broken-down, esp. through age.

fucker (fŭk′ə), *n. Taboo.* **1.** one who fucks. **2.** (offensively) a contemptible person. **3.** (not necessarily offensive) any person.

fucking (fŭk′ĭng), *adj., adv. Taboo.* (a widely used, sometimes offensive intensive.)

fucoid (fyo͞o′koid), *adj.* **1.** resembling, or allied to, seaweeds of the genus *Fucus.* See **fucus.** —*n.* **2.** a fucoid seaweed. [f. FUC(US) + -OID]

fucus (fyo͞o′kəs), *n., pl.* **-ci** (-sī), **-cuses.** any seaweed of the genus *Fucus*, olive brown algae with branching fronds and often air-bladders. [t. L: rock lichen]

fuddle (fŭd′l), *v.*, **-dled, -dling.** —*v.t.* **1.** to intoxicate. **2.** to muddle or confuse. —*v.i.* **3.** to tipple. —*n.* **4.** an intoxicated or confused state.

fuddy-duddy (fŭd′ĭ dŭd′ĭ), *n. Colloq.* a fussy, stuffy, or old-fashioned person.

fudge[1] (fŭj), *n.* a kind of soft sweet composed of sugar, butter, milk, chocolate, or the like. [orig. uncert.]

fudge[2] (fŭj), *n., v.*, **fudged, fudging.** —*n.* **1.** nonsense or bosh (sometimes used as a contemptuous interjection). —*v.i.* **2.** to talk nonsense. [orig. unknown]

fudge[3] (fŭj), *n., v.*, **fudged, fudging.** —*n.* **1.** a small stereotype or a few lines of specially prepared type which may replace a detachable part of the page plate of a newspaper in order to admit a late bulletin without replating the whole page. **2.** the bulletin thus printed, often in colour. **3.** a machine or attachment for printing such a bulletin. —*v.t.* **4.** to put together in a makeshift, clumsy, or dishonest way; fake. [var. of FADGE]

Fuegian (fyo͞o ē′jĭ ən, fwā′jĭ ən), *adj.* **1.** of or belonging to Tierra del Fuego or its indigenous Indians. —*n.* **2.** a native or inhabitant of Tierra del Fuego.

Fuehrer (fyo͞oə′rə; *Ger.* fʏ′rər), *n.* Führer.

fuel (fyo͞oəl), *n., v.*, **-elled, -elling,** or (*U.S.*) **-eled, -eling.** —*n.* **1.** combustible matter used to maintain fire, as coal, wood, oil etc. **2.** a fissile material used in a nuclear reactor to produce energy. **3.** the means of sustaining or increasing passion, ardour, etc. **4. add fuel to the flames,** to aggravate. —*v.t.* **5.** to supply with fuel. —*v.i.* **6.** to procure or take in fuel. [ME *fuelle*, t. OF: m. *feuaile*, ult. der. L *focus* hearth, fireplace]

fuel cell, 1. a continuously fed battery in which a chemical reaction is used directly to produce electricity. **2.** one of a number of fuel tanks.

fuel element, an element of nuclear fuel for use in a nuclear reactor, esp. uranium encased in a canister.

fuel-injection (fyo͞oəl′ĭn jĕk′shən), *n.* a method of spraying liquid fuel directly into the cylinders of an internal-combustion engine instead of using a carburettor. —**fuel′-injec′tor,** *n.*

fuel oil, an oil used for fuel, esp. one used as a substitute for coal, as crude petroleum.

fug (fŭg), *n. Colloq.* a stuffy or smoky atmosphere. —**fug′gy,** *adj.*

Fuga (*It.* fo͞o′gȧ), *n.* **Fernandino** (*It.* fĕr nȧn dē′nō), 1699–1782, Italian architect.

fugacious (fyo͞o gā′shəs), *adj.* **1.** *Bot.* falling or fading early. **2.** fleeting; transitory. [f. obs. *fugacy* flight (der. L *fugāx* apt to flee) + -OUS] —**fuga′ciously,** *adv.* —**fugacity** (fyo͞o găs′ĭ tĭ), *n.*

fugal (fyo͞o′gl), *adj. Music.* of or pertaining to a fugue, or composed in the style of a fugue. —**fu′gally,** *adv.*

fugato (*It.* fo͞o gȧ′tō), *adv. Music.* **1.** in fugue style, but not according to strict rules. —*n.* **2.** music in this style. [It.]

-fuge, a word element referring to 'flight', as in *refuge.* [comb. form repr. L *-fugia*, der. *fugāre* put to flight]

Fugger (*Ger.* fo͝og′ər), *n.* a German family of bankers and merchants of the 14th to 17th centuries.

fugitive (fyo͞o′jĭ tĭv), *n.* **1.** a person who is fleeing; a runaway. —*adj.* **2.** having taken flight, or run away: *a fugitive slave.* **3.** fleeting; transitory. **4.** dealing with subjects of passing interest, as writings; ephemeral. **5.** wandering, roving, or vagabond. [t. L: m. s. *fugitīvus* fleeing; r. ME *fugitif*, t. F] —**fu′gitively,** *adv.* —**fu′gitiveness,** *n.*

fugleman (fyo͞o′gl măn′), *n., pl.* **-men. 1.** a well-drilled soldier placed in front of a military company as a model for others. **2.** anyone serving as an example. [t. G: m. *Flügelmann*, lit., wing man]

fugue (fyo͞og), *n.* **1.** *Music.* a polyphonic composition based upon one, two, or even more themes, which are enunciated by the several voices or parts in turn, subjected to contrapuntal treatment, and gradually built up into a complex form having somewhat distinct divisions or stages of development and a marked climax at the end. **2.** *Psychol.* a period of loss of memory, when the individual disappears from his usual haunts. [t. F, t. It.: m. *fuga*, g. L *fuga* flight] —**fugue′like′,** *adj.*

Führer (fyo͞oə′rə; *Ger.* fʏ′rər), *n. German.* **1.** leader. **2. der** (*Ger.* dĕr) **Führer,** the leader (applied esp. to Adolf Hitler). Also, **Fuehrer.**

Fujairah (fo͞o jĕə′rə), *n.* See **Trucial States.**

Fuji (fo͞o′jĭ), *n.* an extinct volcano in central Japan, on Honshu island: it is the highest mountain in Japan and is renowned for its beautiful symmetry. 12,395 ft. Also, **Fujiyama** (fo͞o′jĭ yä′mə) or **Fujisan** (fo͞o′jĭ săn′).

Fujisawa (fo͞o′jĭ sä wä′, -sä′wä), *n.* a town in Japan, in SE central Honshu island. 175,183 (1966).

Fukien (fo͞o′kyĕn′), *n.* a maritime province in SE China. 14,650,000 pop. (est. 1957); 45,845 sq. mi. *Cap.:* Foochow.

Fukui (fo͞o ko͞o′ĭ), *n.* a town in Japan, in W central Honshu island. 169,636 (1966).

Fukuoka (fo͞o′ko͞o ō′kə), *n.* a city in SW Japan, on Kyushu island. 749,808 (1966).

Fukushima (fo͞o′ko͞o shĭ mä′, -shē′mə), *n.* a town in Japan, in NE central Hokkaido island. 173,678 (1965).

Fukuyama (fo͞o ko͞o′yä mä′), *n.* a town in Japan, in SW Honshu island. 170,158 (1966).

-ful, a suffix meaning: **1.** full or of characterized by: *shameful, beautiful, careful, thoughtful.* **2.** tending or able to: *wakeful, harmful.* **3.** as much as will fill: *spoonful, handful.* [ME and OE *-full, -ful*, repr. *full, ful* FULL[1]]

Fula (fo͞o′lä), *n.* Fulani (def. 3).

Fulah (fo͞o′lä), *n., pl.* **-lah.** Fulani (defs 1, 2). Also, **Fula.**

Fulani (fo͞o lä′nĭ, fo͞o′lə nĭ), *n.* **1.** Also, **Fulah.** a people of mixed Mediterranean and Negro origin, scattered through Sudan from Senegal eastwards. **2.** Also, **Fulah.** a member of such people. **3.** Also, **Fula.** the language of this people. **4.** a trade language used by other tribes in areas of W Africa. **5.** a W African breed of large, humped cattle.

Fulbright (fo͝ol′brīt′), *n.* **1. James William,** born 1905, U.S. politician. **2.** Also, **Fulbright scholarship.** a grant awarded to U.S. citizens for research or study abroad, or to citizens of other countries for research or study in the U.S.

fulcrum (fŭl′krəm), *n., pl.* **-crums, -cra** (-krə). **1.** the support, or point of rest, on which a lever turns in moving a body. **2.** a prop. [t. L: bedpost]

F, Fulcrum; L, Lever

fulfil (fo͝ol fĭl′), *v.t.,* **-filled, -filling. 1.** to carry out, or bring to consummation, as a prophecy, promise, etc. **2.** to perform or do, as duty; obey or follow, as commands. **3.** to satisfy (requirements, etc.). **4.** to bring to an end, finish, or complete, as a period of time. Also, *U.S.,* **fulfill.** [ME *fulfill(en),* OE *fullfyllan,* f. *full,* adj., full + *fyllan,* v., fill] **—fulfil′ler,** *n.* **—Syn. 2.** execute, discharge.

fulfilment (fo͝ol fĭl′mənt), *n.* a fulfilling or carrying out; performance; completion; realization; satisfaction. Also, *U.S.,* **fulfillment.**

fulgent (fŭl′jənt), *adj.* shining brightly; resplendent. [ME, t. L: s. *fulgens,* ppr.] **—ful′gently,** *adv.*

fulgid (fŭl′jĭd), *adj. Archaic.* flashing; glittering; shining.

fulgor (fŭl′gô, -gə), *n. Archaic.* a brilliant, flashing light; brightness, splendour. Also, **fulgour. —ful′gorous,** *adj.*

fulgurant (fŭl′gyo͞o rənt), *adj.* flashing like lightning. [t. L: s. *fulgurans,* ppr.]

fulgurate (fŭl′gyo͞o rāt′), *v.,* **-rated, -rating.** *—v.i.* **1.** to flash or dart like lightning. *—v.t.* **2.** *Med.* to destroy (esp. an abnormal growth) by electricity. [t. L: m. s. *fulgurātus,* pp.] **—ful′gura′tion,** *n.*

fulgurating (fŭl′gyo͞o rā′tĭng), *adj. Med.* (of pains) sharp and intermittent, like flashes of lightning.

fulgurite (fŭl′gyo͞o rīt′), *n.* a tube formed in sand or rock by lightning. [f. L *fulgur* lightning + -ITE[1]]

fulgurous (fŭl′gyo͞o rəs), *adj.* resembling lightning.

Fulham (fo͝ol′əm), *n.* a district of the SW inner London borough of Hammersmith.

fuliginous (fyo͞o lĭj′ĭ nəs), *adj.* **1.** sooty; smoky. **2.** dull or brownish dark grey. [t. LL: m. s. *fūlīginōsus* full of soot]

full[1] (fo͝ol), *adj.* **1.** filled; containing all that can be held; filled to utmost capacity: *a full cup.* **2.** complete; entire; maximum: *a full supply.* **3.** of the maximum size, amount, extent, volume, etc.: *a full mile, full pay, the full moon.* **4.** (of garments, etc.) wide, ample, or having ample folds. **5.** abundant; well-supplied: *a pocket full of money.* **6.** filled or rounded out, as in form. **7.** *Music.* ample and complete in volume or richness of sound. **8.** (of wines) having considerable body. **9.** (of a horse) still ungelded. **10.** being fully or entirely such: *a full brother.* **11. full and by,** *Naut.* with the sails full and sailing close to the wind. **12. full of,** engrossed with or absorbed in. **13. full of oneself,** conceited; egoistic. **14. full up, a.** filled to capacity. **b.** *Colloq.* (of a person) replete; having eaten enough. **15. in full cry,** in hot pursuit, as dogs in the chase. **16. in full force,** with no-one missing. *—adv.* **17.** completely or entirely. **18.** exactly or directly: *the blow struck him full in the face.* **19.** *Archaic.* very: *full well.* *—v.t.* **20.** *Sewing.* to ease one side of a seam into the other, by gathers or tucks. *—v.i.* **21.** to become full. *—n.* **22. in full, a.** without reduction; to or for the full amount: *a receipt in full.* **b.** without abbreviation or contraction. **23. to the full,** in full measure; to the utmost extent. **24.** (of the moon) the stage of complete illumination. See diag. under **moon.** [ME and OE *full, ful,* c. G *voll;* akin to L *plēnus,* Gk *plḗrēs*] **—ful′ly,** *adv.*

full[2] (fo͝ol), *v.t.* **1.** to cleanse and thicken (cloth, etc.) by special processes in manufacture. *—v.i.* **2.** (of cloth, etc.) to become compacted or felted. [ME *fulle(n),* back-formation from FULLER[1]]

full age, adulthood, after one's minority; the age of 21.

full-back (fo͝ol′băk′), *n. Football, etc.* a player whose main purpose is to defend his own goal.

full binding, a complete binding of a volume in any one material, generally leather.

full blood, 1. an individual of unmixed ancestry; a purebred. **2.** relationship through both parents.

full-blooded (fo͝ol′blŭd′ĭd), *adj.* **1.** of unmixed ancestry; thoroughbred. **2.** vigorous; virile; hearty.

full-blown (fo͝ol′blōn′), *adj.* **1.** in full bloom: *a full-blown rose.* **2.** completely developed.

full board, (in a hotel or the like) the provision of sleeping accommodation and all main meals.

full-bodied (fo͝ol′bŏd′ĭd), *adj.* with all the flavour and strength possible.

full brother, a brother both of whose parents are the same as one's own. Also, **whole brother.**

full dress, ceremonial or formal evening attire.

full-dress (fo͝ol′drĕs′), *adj.* **1.** denoting, pertaining to, or requiring full dress. **2.** formal and of some importance.

fuller[1] (fo͝ol′ə), *n.* one who fulls cloth. [ME; OE *fullere,* f. L *full(o)* fuller + *-ere* -ER[1]]

fuller[2] (fo͝ol′ə), *n.* a half-round set hammer used for grooving and spreading iron. [appar. f. FULL[1], v., to make full + -ER[1]]

Fuller (fo͝ol′ə), **1. Richard Buckminster** (rĭch′əd bŭk′-mĭn′stə), born 1895, U.S. architect. **2. Thomas,** 1608–61, English clergyman and historian.

fuller's earth, an absorbent clay, used for removing grease from cloth, etc., in fulling, as a filter, medically, as a dusting powder, and in paints as an extender.

fuller's teasel, a teasel, *Dipsacus fullonum,* of which the dried heads were used for raising the nap on cloth.

full-faced (fo͝ol′fāst′), *adj.* **1.** having a plump or round face. **2.** facing squarely towards the spectator or in a given direction. **3.** *Printing.* (of type) bold-faced.

full-grown (fo͝ol′grōn′), *adj.* fully grown; mature.

full house, 1. *Poker.* a hand consisting of three of a kind and a pair, as three queens and two tens. **2.** a theatre or cinema filled to capacity. **3.** (in bingo) a fully covered card.

full-length (fo͝ol′lĕngth′), *adj.* **1.** fully stretched. **2.** (of a portrait) showing the whole figure. **3.** unabridged. **4.** of standard length.

full moon, the moon when the whole of its disc is illuminated. See **moon** (def. 2c).

full nelson, *Wrestling.* a hold, illegal under most rules, in which both arms pass from behind under the opponent's armpits and the hands are joined behind his neck.

fullness (fo͝ol′nĭs), *n.* **1.** the state of being full. **2. the fullness of time,** the proper or destined time. Also, *Chiefly U.S.,* **fulness.**

full out, 1. written out in full. **2.** *Print.* not indented.

full pitch, *Cricket.* a ball bowled which travels the whole way between the two wickets without touching the ground. Also, **full toss.**

full radiator, *Physics.* a light source emitting radiation, the spectral distribution of which depends only on its temperature and not on the nature of the source. Also, **black-body radiator.**

full-rigged (fo͝ol′rĭgd′), *adj.* **1.** *Naut.* having three or more masts and with all square sails set on all masts. **2.** having all equipment.

full-scale (fo͝ol′skāl′), *adj.* **1.** (of a drawing, etc.) identical in size to the original. **2.** large; important; thorough: *a full-scale attack.*

full sister, a sister both of whose parents are the same as one's own. Also, **whole sister.**

full stop, the point or character (.) used to mark the end of a complete declarative sentence, indicate an abbreviation, etc.; a period.

full tilt, *Colloq.* at top speed: *the bus was going full tilt for the station.*

full time, all normal working hours.

full-time (fo͝ol′tīm′), *adj.* **1.** of, or pertaining to, or taking all the normal working hours. **2.** of, or pertaining to, something which occupies a person all the time. *—adv.* **3.** during all normal working hours.

full toss, *Cricket.* (a ball bowled) full pitch.

fully fashioned, (of knitted garments and esp. of stockings) shaped to fit closely.

fully fledged, 1. able to fly. **2.** fully developed. **3.** of full rank or standing. **4.** fully qualified or established: *a fully fledged professor.*

fulmar (fo͝ol′mə), *n.* any of certain oceanic birds of the petrel family, esp. *Fulmarus glacialis,* a gull-like arctic species. [? lit., foul gull (with allusion to its stench), t. Scand; cf. Icel. *fūll* foul, *mār* gull]

fulminant (fŭl′mĭ nənt), *adj.* **1.** fulminating. **2.** *Pathol.* developing or progressing suddenly: *fulminant plague.* [t. L: s. *fulminans,* ppr., lightening]

fulminate (fŭl′mĭ nāt′), *v.,* **-nated, -nating,** *n.* *—v.i.* **1.** to explode with a loud noise; detonate. **2.** to issue denunciations or the like (often fol. by *against*). *—v.t.* **3.** to cause to explode. *—n.* **4.** *Chem.* one of a group of unstable, explosive compounds derived from fulminic acid; esp. the mercury salt of fulminic acid which is a powerful detonating agent. [t. L: m. s. *fulminātus,* pp., lightened] **—ful′mina′tor,** *n.* **—ful′mina′tory,** *adj.*

fulminating compound, *Chem.* a fulminate.

fulminating gold, *Chem.* the explosive, yellow precipitate formed when ammonia is added to a solution of gold chloride.

fulminating powder, *Chem.* **1.** powder which explodes by percussion. **2.** a fulminate.

fulmination (fŭl′mĭ nā′shən), *n.* **1.** a violent denunciation or censure. **2.** violent explosion.

fulminic acid (fŭl mĭn′ĭk), *Chem.* an acid, HONC, an isomer of cyanic acid, found only in its salts, the fulminates.

fulminous (fŭl′mĭ nəs), *adj.* connected with, or resembling, thunder and lightning.

fulness (fo͝ol′nĭs), *n. Chiefly U.S.* fullness.

fulsome (fo͝ol′səm), *adj.* **1.** offensive to good taste, esp. as being excessive; gross; insincere: *fulsome praise.* **2.** disgusting, nauseating. [ME *fulsum*: f. FULL[1] + -SOME[1]; evidence of assoc. with FOUL] —**ful′somely,** *adv.* —**ful′someness,** *n.*

Fulton (fo͝ol′tən), *n.* **Robert,** 1765–1815, American engineer and nautical inventor.

fulvous (fŭl′vəs), *adj.* tawny; dull yellowish grey or brown. [t. L: m. *fulvus* deep yellow]

fumaric acid (fyo͞o măr′ĭk), *Chem.* a dibasic acid, $COOH.(CH)_2.COOH$, isomeric with maleic acid, occurring in small amounts in almost all living cells as a component of the citric acid cycle and in greater amounts in several plants.

fumarole (fyo͞o′mə rōl′), *n.* a hole in or near a volcano, from which vapour issues. [t. F: m. *fumerolle*, g. LL *fūmāriolum*, dim. of L *fūmārium* smoke chamber]

fumble (fŭm′bl), *v.*, **-bled, -bling,** *n.* —*v.i.* **1.** to feel or grope about clumsily (fol. by *at, with, after, for*). **2.** to hesitate in speaking; to speak indistinctly. **3.** *Sport.* to fumble the ball. —*v.t.* **4.** to handle clumsily. **5.** *Sport.* to fail to catch and hold (a ball) or to catch and hold (it) clumsily. —*n.* **6.** the act of fumbling. **7.** a bungling attempt at something. [t. LG: m. *fummeln*; cf. Sw. *fumla* grope] —**fum′bler,** *n.* —**fum′bling,** *adj., n.* —**fum′blingly,** *adv.*

fume (fyo͞om), *n., v.,* **fumed, fuming.** —*n.* **1.** (*often pl.*) any smokelike or vaporous exhalation from matter or substances. **2.** an odorous exhalation, as from flowers. **3.** an irritable or angry mood: *to be in a fume.* —*v.t.* **4.** to send forth as fumes. **5.** to disperse or drive away in vapours; send up as vapour. **6.** to treat with fumes, to fumigate. —*v.i.* **7.** (of smoke, a vapour, etc.) to rise or pass off. **8.** to emit fumes. **9.** to show irritation or anger. [ME, t. OF: m. *fum*, g. L *fūmus* smoke, steam, fume] —**fume′less,** *adj.* —**fume′like′,** *adj.* —**fum′ingly,** *adv.* —**Syn. 9.** chafe, fret, rage.

fumed (fyo͞omd), *adj.* darkened or coloured by exposure to ammonia fumes, as oak and other wood.

fumigate (fyo͞o′mĭ gāt′), *v.t.*, **-gated, -gating.** to expose to smoke or fumes, as in disinfecting. [t. L: m. s. *fūmigātus*, pp., smoked] —**fu′miga′tion,** *n.*

fumigator (fyo͞o′mĭ gā′tə), *n.* **1.** one who or that which fumigates. **2.** a structure in which plants are fumigated to destroy insects.

fuming sulphuric acid, *Chem.* a solution of sulphur trioxide in concentrated sulphuric acid; oleum. Also, **Nordhausen acid, pyrosulphuric acid.**

fumitory (fyo͞o′mĭ tə rĭ), *n., pl.* **-ries.** any plant of the genus *Fumaria*, of the family *Fumariaceae*, esp. a delicate herb, *F. officinalis*, with finely dissected leaves and racemes of purplish flowers, formerly used medicinally. [ME *fumeter*, t. OF: m. *fumeterre*, t. ML: m. *fūmus terrae* smoke of the earth]

fumy (fyo͞o′mĭ), *adj.*, **-mier, -miest.** composed of or full of fumes; fumelike.

fun (fŭn), *n., v.,* **funned, funning.** —*n.* **1.** mirthful sport or diversion; merry amusement; joking; playfulness. **2. for** or **in fun,** as a joke; playfully; not seriously. **3. like fun,** *Colloq.* not at all. **4. make fun of, poke fun at,** to ridicule. —*v.i.* **5.** *Colloq.* to make fun; joke. —*adj.* **6.** *Colloq.* of, or pertaining to fun; amusing. [? d. var. of obs. *fon*, v., befool. See FOND[1]]

Funabashi (fo͞o nä′bä shĭ), *n.* a seaport in Japan, in SE Hokkaido island. 10 mi. E of Tokyo. 223,989 (1965).

funambulist (fyo͞o năm′byo͝o lĭst), *n.* a tightrope walker. [f. s. L *fūnambulus* rope-dancer + -IST] —**funam′bulism,** *n.*

Funchal (*Port.* fo͞oɴ shäl′), *n.* a seaport in and the capital of the Madeira islands: winter resort. 95,765 (1960).

function (fŭngk′shən), *n.* **1.** the kind of action or activity proper to a person, thing, or institution. **2.** any ceremonious public or social gathering or occasion. **3.** *Maths.* a mathematical quantity whose value depends upon the values of other quantities, called the arguments or independent variables of the function. **4.** *Gram.* **a.** the grammatical role which a linguistic form plays, or the position which it occupies in a particular construction. **b.** the grammatical roles or the positions of a linguistic form or form class collectively. —*v.i.* **5.** to perform a function, or one's or its functions; act; serve; operate; carry out normal work, activity, or processes. **6.** *Gram.* to have or exercise a function: *in earlier English the present tense often functioned as the future.* [t. L: s. *functio* performance] —**func′tionless,** *adj.*

functional (fŭngk′shə nəl), *adj.* **1.** of or pertaining to a function or functions. **2.** designed or adapted primarily to perform some operation or duty: *a functional building.* **3.** capable of operating or functioning. **4.** pertaining to an algebraic operation: *a functional symbol.* —**func′tionally,** *adv.*

functional disease, *Pathol.* a disease in which there is a morbid change in the function of an organ, but no structural alteration in the tissues involved (opposed to *organic disease*).

functionalism (fŭngk′shə nə lĭz′əm), *n.* the doctrine or practice in furniture design, architecture, etc., under which such factors as material and form are determined primarily by functional considerations.

functionality (fŭngk′shə năl′ĭ tĭ), *n.* **1.** the functional character of someone or something. **2.** *Maths.* the condition of being a function.

functionalize (fŭngk′shə nə līz′), *v.t.* **1.** to make functional or more functional. **2.** to place or assign to some function or office. Also, **functionalise.**

functionary (fŭngk′shə nə rĭ), *n., pl.* **-ries.** an official.

fund (fŭnd), *n.* **1.** a stock of money or pecuniary resources. **2.** a store or stock of something, now often of something immaterial: *a fund of knowledge.* **3.** (*pl.*) money in hand; pecuniary resources. **4.** (*pl.*) various stocks of the national debt in which the general public may invest. **5.** (*pl., usually cap.*) consols and other government securities. —*v.t.* **6.** to put into a fund or store. **7.** to convert (a floating debt or debts) into a more or less permanent debt or loan, represented by interest-bearing bonds. **8.** to arrange for (a debt or debts) to be on a long-term basis. **9.** to invest (money) in a fund or funds. **10.** to provide a fund to pay the interest or principle of (a debt). [t. L: s. *fundus* bottom, estate; r. FOND[2] in most of its meanings]

fundament (fŭn′də mənt), *n.* the buttocks. [t. L: s. *fundāmentum* foundation; r. ME *fondement*, t. OF]

fundamental (fŭn′də mĕn′tl), *adj.* **1.** serving as, or being a component part of, a foundation or basis; basic; underlying: fundamental principles. **2.** of or affecting the foundation or basis: *a fundamental change.* **3.** essential; primary; original. **4.** *Music.* (of a chord) having its root as its lowest note. —*n.* **5.** a leading or primary principle, rule, law, or the like, which serves as the groundwork of a system; essential part. **6.** Also, **fundamental note** or **tone.** *Music.* **a.** the root of a chord. **b.** the primary note of the harmonic series. **7.** *Physics.* the component of lowest frequency in a composite wave. [t. NL: s. *fundāmentālis*, der. L *fundāmentum* foundation] —**fun′damental′ity,** *n.* —**fun′damen′tally,** *adv.*

fundamental bass, *Music.* a bass consisting of the roots of the chords employed.

fundamentalism (fŭn′də mĕn′tə lĭz′əm), *n.* **1.** a movement in American Protestantism which stresses the inerrancy of the Bible not only in matters of faith and morals but also as literal historical record and prophecy, e.g., of creation, the virgin birth of Christ, his second advent, etc. (opposed to *modernism*). **2.** the faith in the Bible so stressed. —**fun′damen′talist,** *n., adj.*

fundamental particle, *Physics.* elementary particle.

fundamental unit, *Physics.* one of the units (esp. those of mass, length, and time) taken as a basis for a system of units.

funded debt, a government debt, not repayable at any specific time, for the interest on which certain funds are appropriated.

fundus (fŭn′dəs), *n. Anat.* the base of an organ, or the part opposite to or remote from an aperture. [t. L: bottom]

Fundy (fŭn′dĭ), *n.* **Bay of,** a deep inlet of the Atlantic in SE Canada between New Brunswick and Nova Scotia: noted for its swift tidal currents, sometimes rising 70 ft.

Fünen (*Ger.* fʏ′nən), *n.* German name of **Fyn.**

funeral (fyo͞o′nə rəl, fyo͞on′rəl), *n.* **1.** the ceremonies connected with the disposition of the body of a dead person; obsequies. **2.** a funeral procession. **3.** *Slang.* business; worry; concern: *that's his funeral.* —*adj.* **4.** of or pertaining to a funeral. [ME, t. ML: s. *fūnerālis*, der. L *fūnus* funeral, death]

funeral director, an undertaker.

funerary (fyo͞o′nə rə rĭ), *adj.* of or pertaining to a funeral or burial: *a funerary urn.*

funereal (fyo͞o nĭə′rĭ əl), *adj.* **1.** of or pertaining to a funeral. **2.** mournful; gloomy; dismal. [f. s. L *fūnereus* of a funeral + -AL[1]] —**fune′really,** *adv.*

funfair (fŭn′fēə′), *n.* an outdoor entertainment with sideshows, mechanical amusements, etc.; a fair.

Fünfkirchen (*Ger.* fʏnf kĭrʹKHən), *n.* German name of **Pécs.**

fungal (fŭngʹgl), *adj.* **1.** fungous. —*n.* **2.** a fungus.

fungate (fŭngʹgāt), *v.i. Pathol.* to grow in fungus-like masses.

fungi (fŭnʹjī, fŭngʹgī), *n.* pl. of **fungus.**

fungible (fŭnʹjĭ bl), *Law.* —*adj.* **1.** of such a nature that one instance or portion may be replaced by another in respect of function, office, or use: usually confined to goods. —*n.* **2.** a fungible thing, as money or grain. [t. ML: m. s. *fungibilis,* der. L *fungī* fulfil the office of]

fungicide (fŭnʹjĭ sīdʹ), *n.* an agent, such as a spray or dust, used for destroying fungi. [f. *fungi-* (comb. form of FUNGUS) + -CIDE] —**funʹgicidʹal,** *adj.*

fungiform (fŭnʹjĭ fômʹ), *adj.* having the form of a fungus or mushroom. [f. *fungi-* (comb. form of FUNGUS) + -FORM]

fungoid (fŭngʹgoid), *adj.* **1.** resembling a fungus; of the nature of a fungus. **2.** *Pathol.* characterized by fungus-like morbid growths.

fungous (fŭngʹgəs), *adj.* **1.** of, pertaining to, or caused by fungi; fungal. **2.** of the nature of or resembling a fungus. [ME, t. L: m. s. *fungōsus,* der. *fungus* sponge, mushroom, fungus]

fungus (fŭngʹgəs), *n., pl.* **fungi** (fŭnʹjī, fŭngʹgī), **funguses,** *adj.* —*n.* **1.** any of the *Fungi,* a group of thallophytes including the mushrooms, moulds, mildews, rusts, smuts, etc., characterized chiefly by absence of chlorophyll and by subsisting upon dead or living organic matter. **2.** *Pathol.* a spongy morbid growth, as proud flesh formed in a wound. —*adj.* **3.** fungous. [t. L: mushroom, fungus] —**funʹgus-likeʹ,** *adj.*

funicle (fyo͞oʹnĭ kl), *n. Bot.* the stalk of an ovule or seed. [t. L: m. s. *fūniculus,* dim. of *fūnis* rope]

funicular (fyo͞o nĭkʹyo͞o lə), *adj.* **1.** of or pertaining to a rope or cord, or its tension. **2.** worked by a rope or the like. —*n.* **3.** a funicular railway. [f. s. L *fūniculus* little rope + -AR[1]]

funicular railway, a railway system of short length operating up steep gradients, in which cable-linked trains move up and down simultaneously, thus minimizing the pull of gravity.

funiculate (fyo͞o nĭkʹyo͞o lĭt, -lātʹ), *adj. Bot.* having a funicle.

funiculus (fyo͞o nĭkʹyo͞o ləs), *n., pl.* **-li** (-līʹ). **1.** *Anat.* a cordlike structure, esp. one of the three main nerve tracts of each half of the spinal cord. **2.** *Bot.* a funicle. [t. L, dim. of *fūnis* rope]

funk (fŭngk), *Colloq.* —*n.* **1.** cowering fear; state of fright or terror. **2.** one who funks; a coward. —*v.t.* **3.** to be afraid of. **4.** to frighten. **5.** to shrink from; try to shirk. —*v.i.* **6.** to shrink or quail in fear. [cf. OF *funicle* terrible, g. L *phrenēticus.* See FRANTIC]

funnel (fŭnʹəl), *n., v.,* **-nelled, -nelling** or (*U.S.*) **-neled, -neling.** —*n.* **1.** a cone-shaped utensil with a tube at the apex, for conducting liquid, etc., through a small opening, as into a bottle. **2.** a metal chimney, esp. of a ship or a steam-engine. **3.** a flue, tube, or shaft, as for ventilation. —*v.t.* **4.** to converge or concentrate: *to funnel all one's energies into a job.* [ME *fonel,* t. OF, ult. g. LL *fundibulum,* L *infundibulum*] —**funʹnel-likeʹ,** *adj.*

funnel cloud, a funnel-shaped cloud formed from the core of a waterspout or tornado.

funnies (fŭnʹĭz), *n.pl. U.S. Colloq.* **1.** comic strips. **2.** the section of a newspaper containing them.

funny (fŭnʹĭ), *adj.,* **-nier, -niest. 1.** affording fun; amusing; comical. **2.** curious; strange; queer; odd. **3.** *Colloq.* insolent. —*n.* **4.** *Colloq.* a joke. [f. FUN, n. + -Y[1]] —**funʹnily,** *adv.* —**funʹniness,** *n.*

—**Syn. 1.** comic, farcial, absurd, ridiculous, droll, witty, facetious, humorous. FUNNY, LAUGHABLE, LUDICROUS refer to that which excites laughter. FUNNY and LAUGHABLE are both applied to that which provokes laughter or deserves to be laughed at; FUNNY is a colloquial term loosely applied and in popular use is commonly interchangeable with the other terms: *a funny story, scene, joke, a laughable incident, mistake.* That which is LUDICROUS excites laughter by its incongruity and foolish absurdity: *the monkey's attempts to imitate the woman were ludicrous.* —**Ant. 1.** solemn, serious.

funny bone, the part of the elbow where the ulnar nerve passes by the internal condyle of the humerus, which when struck causes a peculiar tingling sensation in the arm and hand. Also, *U.S.,* **crazy bone.**

funny business, *Colloq.* **1.** foolish behaviour. **2.** underhand, dubious, or dishonest dealings.

fur (fû), *n., v.,* **furred, furring.** —*n.* **1.** the skin of certain animals (as the sable, ermine, beaver, etc.), covered with a fine, soft, thick, hairy coating. **2.** the cured and treated skin of certain of these animals used for lining or trimming garments or for entire garments. **3.** (*usually pl.*) an article of dress made of or with such material, as a fur coat or stole. **4.** any coating resembling or suggesting fur, as one of morbid matter on the tongue. **5.** the gritty insoluble deposit formed on the inside of boilers, kettles, etc., when hard water is boiled, consisting of calcium, magnesium, and iron carbonates. **6.** *Her.* any of several patterns that are classified as tinctures. **7. make the fur fly,** *Colloq.* to quarrel noisily; make a scene or disturbance. —*v.t.* **8.** to line, face, or trim (a garment, etc.) with fur. **9.** to clothe (a person) with fur. **10.** to coat with foul or deposited matter. **11.** *Bldg Trades.* to apply furring to (a wall, etc.) —*adj.* **12.** of or pertaining to fur. [ME *furre,* t. OF: m. *forrer* line with fur, orig. encase, der. *forre* sheath, t. Gmc; cf. G *Futter* sheath] —**furʹless,** *adj.*

furan (fyo͞oəʹrăn, fyo͞o rănʹ), *n. Chem.* a colourless liquid, C_4H_4O, an unsaturated five-membered ring compound derived from furfural. Also, **furfuran.** [var. of FURFURAN, t. G, f. L *furfur* bran + *-an* -ANE]

furbelow (fûʹbĭ lōʹ), *n.* **1.** a pleated or gathered trimming on a woman's gown or the like; flounce. **2.** any bit of showy trimming or finery. —*v.t.* **3.** to ornament with or as with furbelows. [var. of FALBALA]

furbish (fûʹbĭsh), *v.t.* **1.** to restore to freshness of appearance or condition (often fol. by *up*). **2.** to remove rust from (armour, weapons, etc.); polish; burnish. [ME *furbish(en),* t. OF: m. *forbiss-,* s. *forbir* polish, clean, t. Gmc; cf. OHG *furban*] —**furʹbisher,** *n.*

furcate (*adj.* fûʹkāt, -kĭt; *v.* fûʹkāt), *adj., v.,* **-cated, -cating.** —*adj.* **1.** forked. —*v.i.* **2.** to form a fork; divide into branches. [t. ML: m. s. *furcātus* cloven, der. L *furca* fork] —**furcation** (fû kāʹshən), *n.*

furcula (fûʹkyo͞o lə), *n., pl.* **-lae** (-lēʹ). the forked clavicular bone of a bird; wishbone. [t. L, dim. of *furca* fork] —**furʹcular,** *adj.*

furculum (fûʹkyo͞o ləm), *n., pl.* **-la** (-lə). furcula. [NL, incorrectly formed dim. of L *furca* fork]

furfur (fûʹfə), *n., pl.* **-fures** (-fyo͞o rēzʹ, -fə rēzʹ). **1.** dandruff; scurf. **2.** *Physiol.* any epidermal scale. **3.** the bran of grain. [t. L]

furfuraceous (fûʹfyo͞o rāʹshəs), *adj.* **1.** branlike. **2.** scaly; scurfy. [t. LL: m. *furfurāceus*]

furfural (fûʹfə rălʹ), *n. Chem.* an oily liquid aldehyde, $C_4H_3O.CHO$, with an aromatic odour, obtained by distilling bran, sugar, wood, etc., with dilute sulphuric acid: used in the manufacture of plastics and in refining lubricating oils. [f. L *furfur* bran + AL(DEHYDE)]

furfuran (fûʹfə rănʹ), *n. Chem.* furan.

Furies (fyo͞oəʹrĭz), *n.pl. Class. Myth.* See **fury** (def. 3).

furious (fyo͞oəʹrĭ əs), *adj.* **1.** full of fury, violent passion, or rage. **2.** intensely violent, as wind, storms, etc. **3.** of unrestrained energy, speed, etc.: *furious activity.* [ME, t. L: m. s. *furiōsus* raging] —**fuʹriously,** *adv.* —**fuʹriousness,** *n.*

furl (fûl), *v.t.* **1.** to draw into a compact roll, as a sail against a spar or a flag against its staff. —*v.i.* **2.** to become furled. —*n.* **3.** the act of furling or state of being furled. **4.** a roll resulting from being furled. [cf. F *ferler,* OF *ferlier,* f. *fer* firm (g. L *firmus*) + *lier* to bind (g. L *ligāre*)]

furlong (fûʹlŏngʹ), *n.* a unit of distance, equal to 220 yards or $\frac{1}{8}$ mi. [ME; OE *furlang,* f. *furh* furrow + *lang* long]

furlough (fûʹlō), *n.* **1.** *Chiefly U.S.* leave of absence, esp. a period of holiday leave. —*v.t.* **2.** *U.S.* to grant a furlough to. [var. of *furloff,* t. D: m. *verlof* leave, furlough. Cf. G *Verlaub* leave, permission; current pronunciation due to assoc. with *dough, though*]

furmenty (fûʹmən tĭ), *n.* frumenty. Also, **furmety** (fûʹmĭ tĭ).

furnace (fûʹnĭs), *n.* **1.** a structure or apparatus in which to generate heat, as for heating buildings, smelting ores, producing steam, etc. **2.** a place of burning heat. [ME *furneise,* t. OF: m. *fornais, fornaise,* g. s. L *fornax* oven] —**furʹnace-likeʹ,** *adj.*

furnish (fûʹnĭsh), *v.t.* **1.** to provide or supply. **2.** to fit up (a house, room, etc.) with necessary appliances, esp. furniture. [ME *furnisshe(n),* t. OF: m. *furniss-,* s. *furnir* accomplish, furnish, t. Gmc; cf. OHG *frumjan* provide] —**furʹnisher,** *n.*

—**Syn. 1, 2.** FURNISH, APPOINT, EQUIP all refer to providing something necessary. FURNISH emphasizes the idea of providing necessary or customary services or appliances in living quarters: *to furnish board, a room.* APPOINT (now found only in WELL-APPOINTED) means to furnish completely with all requisites or accessories or in an elegant style: *a well-appointed house.* EQUIP means to supply with necessary materials or apparatus for some service, action, or undertaking; it emphasizes preparation: *to equip a vessel, a soldier.*

furnishing (fûʹnĭ shĭng), *n.* **1.** that with which anything is furnished. **2.** (*pl.*) fittings, appliances, articles of furniture, etc., for a house or room. **3.** (*pl.*) *U.S.* accessories of dress: *men's furnishings.*

furniture (fûʹnĭ chə), *n.* **1.** the movable articles, as tables, chairs, bedsteads, desks, cabinets, etc., required for use or ornament in a house, office, or the like. **2.** fittings, apparatus, or necessary accessories for something. **3.** *Print.* pieces of wood or metal, less than type-high, set in and about pages of type to fill them out and hold the type in place. [t. F: m. *fourniture*, der. *fournir* FURNISH]

Furnivall (fûˈnĭ vəl), *n.* **Frederick James,** 1825–1910, English philologist and editor.

furore (fyo͝o rôˈrĭ), *n.* **1.** a general outburst of enthusiasm or excitement. **2.** a prevailing mania or craze. **3.** fury; rage; madness. Also, *Chiefly U.S.*, **furor** (fyo͝oˈrô). [t. L: a raging; r. late ME *fureur*, t. F]

furphy (fûˈfĭ), *n. Austral.* a rumour; canard.

furred (fûd), *adj.* **1.** having fur. **2.** made with or of fur, as garments. **3.** clad in fur or furs, as persons. **4.** coated with morbid matter, as the tongue.

furrier (fŭˈrĭ ə), *n.* a dealer in or dresser of furs.

furriery (fŭˈrĭ ə rĭ), *n., pl.* **-eries.** *Archaic.* **1.** furs in general. **2.** the business or trade of a furrier.

furring (fûˈrĭng), *n.* **1.** the act of lining, trimming, or clothing with fur. **2.** the fur used. **3.** the formation of a coating of matter on something, as on the tongue. **4.** *Bldg Trades.* **a.** the nailing on of thin strips of board, as to furnish a level surface for lathing or plastering, to provide airspace between a wall and plastering, etc. **b.** materials so used.

furrow (fŭˈrō), *n.* **1.** a narrow trench made in the ground, esp. by a plough. **2.** a narrow, trenchlike depression in any surface: *the furrows of a wrinkled face.* **3.** *Anat.* a groove. —*v.t.* **4.** to make a furrow or furrows in; plough (land, etc.). **5.** to make wrinkles in (the face, etc.). [ME *forwe, furgh(e)*, OE *furh*, c. G *Furche*; akin to L *porca* ridge between furrows] —**furˈrower,** *n.* —**furˈrowless,** *adj.* —**furˈrow-like′, furˈrowy,** *adj.*

furry (fûˈrĭ), *adj.*, **-rier, -riest.** **1.** made of or with fur. **2.** covered with fur; wearing fur. **3.** consisting of or resembling fur. —**furˈriness,** *n.*

fur seal, any of various species of eared seal, as *Callorhinus alascanus*, which have under the outer hair a thick coat of fur of great commercial value (distinguished from *hair seal*).

Fur seal, *Callorhinus alascanus* (Male 7 ft long, female about 4 ft)

Fürth (*Ger.* fʏrt), *n.* a town in West Germany, in central Bavaria, near Nuremberg.

further (fûˈthə), *compar. adv. and adj., superl.* **furthest,** *v.* —*adv.* **1.** at or to a greater distance; farther. **2.** at or to a more advanced point; to a greater extent; farther. **3.** in addition; moreover. —*adj.* **4.** more distant or remote; farther. **5.** more extended. **6.** additional; more. —*v.t.* **7.** to help forward (a work, undertaking, cause, etc.); promote; advance; forward. [ME *further(e), furthra*, OE *furthor* (orig. compar. of *forth FORTH); c. G *vordere* more advanced] —**furˈtherer,** *n.*

furtherance (fûˈthə rəns), *n.* the act of furthering; promotion; advancement.

further education, full-time or part-time post-secondary education (other than university education) for persons beyond the compulsory school-leaving age.

furthermore (fûˈthə mô′), *adv.* moreover; in addition.

furthermost (fûˈthə mōst′), *adj.* most distant.

furthest (fûˈthĭst), *adj., adv.* superl. of **further.** [ME, coined as a superl. of FURTHER. Cf. FARTHEST]

furtive (fûˈtĭv), *adj.* **1.** taken, done, used, etc., by stealth; secret: *a furtive glance.* **2.** sly; shifty: *a furtive manner.* [t. L: m. s. *furtīvus* stolen] —**furˈtively,** *adv.* —**furˈtiveness,** *n.*

Furtwängler (*Ger.* fo͝ortˈvĕng lər), *n.* **Wilhelm** (*Ger.* vĭlˈhĕlm), 1886–1954, German conductor.

furuncle (fyo͝oəˈ rŭng′kl), *n. Pathol.* a boil or inflammatory sore. [t. L: m. s. *fūrunculus* a petty thief, a boil] —**furunˈcular,** *adj.* —**furunˈculous,** *adj.*

furunculosis (fyo͝o rŭng′kyo͝o lōˈsĭs), *n. Pathol.* the morbid state characterized by the presence of furuncles.

fury (fyo͝oəˈrĭ), *n., pl.* **-ries.** **1.** frenzied or unrestrained violent passion, esp. anger. **2.** violence; vehemence; fierceness. **3.** (*cap.*) one of the avenging deities of classical mythology (in female form, with serpents twined in their hair), in later accounts three in number and called Alecto, Megaera, and Tisiphone. **4.** a fierce and violent person, esp. a woman. **5. like fury,** *Colloq.* furiously; violently. [ME, t. L: m. s. *furia* rage, madness] —**Syn.** **1.** furore, frenzy, rage, ire, wrath. See **anger.**

furze (fûz), *n.* gorse. [ME *furse, firse*, OE *fyrs*]

furzy (fûˈzĭ), *adj.* **1.** of or pertaining to furze. **2.** overgrown with furze.

fusain (fyo͞o zănˈ; *Fr.* fʏ zăNˈ), *n.* **1.** a fine charcoal used in drawing, made from the wood of the spindle tree. **2.** a drawing made with it. **3.** a charcoal-like constituent of coal consisting of plant remains from which the volatile matter has been eliminated. [t. F: spindle tree, charcoal made from its wood, der. L *fūsus* spindle]

Fusan (fo͞oˈsănˈ), *n.* former name of **Pusan.**

fuscous (fŭsˈkəs), *adj.* dark brownish grey; dark; dusky. [t. L: m. *fuscus* dark]

fuse[1] (fyo͞oz), *n., v.,* **fused, fusing.** —*n.* **1.** *Elect.* a device for preventing an excessive current from passing through a circuit, consisting of a piece of wire of low melting point, which breaks the circuit by melting if the current exceeds a specified value. **2.** a tube, ribbon, or the like, filled or saturated with combustible matter, for igniting an explosive. **3.** a mechanical or electronic device to detonate an explosive charge. —*v.i.* **4.** to blow a fuse. Also, *Chiefly U.S.*, **fuze.** [t. It.: m. *fuso*, g. L *fūsus* spindle] —**fuseˈless,** *adj.* —**fuseˈlike′,** *adj.*

fuse[2] (fyo͞oz), *v.,* **fused, fusing.** —*v.t.* **1.** to combine or blend by melting together; melt. **2.** to unite or blend into a whole, as if by melting together. —*v.i.* **3.** to become liquid under the action of heat; melt. **4.** to become united or blended, as if by melting together. [t. L: m. s. *fūsus*, pp., poured, melted, cast] —**Syn.** **1.** See **melt.** **2.** amalgamate, merge, liquefy, dissolve, smelt.

Fuse (fo͞oˈsā), *n.* a town in Japan, in S Honshu island. 271,704 (1966).

fuse box, a box containing fuses.

fused silica, silica glass.

fusee (fyo͞o zēˈ), *n.* **1.** a kind of match with a large head, for outdoor use. **2.** *Horol.* a spirally grooved, conical pulley and chain arrangement for counteracting the diminishing power of the uncoiling mainspring. **3.** a tumour on the bone of a horse's leg. **4.** a fuse. [t. F: spindleful, der. OF *fus* spindle, g. L *fūsus*]

fuselage (fyo͞oˈzĭ läzh′), *n.* the framework of the body of an aeroplane. [t. F, der. *fuselé* spindle-shaped, der. *fuseau* spindle, der. L *fūsus*]

fuse link, *Elect.* an element, made of fusible wire or cast from fusible metal, inserted in a fuse (def. 1).

fusel oil (fyo͞oˈzəl), a mixture of amyl alcohols obtained as a by-product in the fermentation of grains. [*fusel*, t. G: inferior liquor or spirits]

fuse wire, wire used as a fuse. See **fuse**[1] (def. 1).

Fushun (fo͞oˈshŭnˈ, fyo͞oˈ-), *n.* a city in Liaoning province, NE China. 1,019,000 (est. 1958).

fusibility (fyo͞oˈzə bĭlˈĭ tĭ), *n.* **1.** the quality of being fusible, or convertible from a solid to a fluid state by heat. **2.** the degree to which a substance is fusible.

fusible (fyo͞oˈzə bl), *adj.* capable of being fused or melted. —**fuˈsibleness,** *n.*

fusible metal, *Metall.* any of various alloys, as one of bismuth, lead, and tin, which melt at comparatively low temperatures, and hence can be used for making various safety devices. Also, **fusible alloy.**

fusible plug, a safety device consisting of a low-melting alloy which is designed to release pressure, in a piece of industrial or domestic equipment, at a predetermined temperature.

fusiform (fyo͞oˈzĭ fôm′), *adj.* spindle-shaped; rounded and tapering from the middle towards each end, as some roots. [f. s. L *fūsus* spindle + -(I)FORM]

fusil[1] (fyo͞oˈzĭl), *n.* a light musket or firelock. [t. F, in OF *foisil* steel for striking fire, ult. der. L *focus* hearth]

fusil[2] (fyo͞oˈzĭl), *n. Her.* a bearing in the form of an elongated lozenge. [t. MF: m. *fusel*, ult. der. L *fūsus* spindle. Cf. FUSE[1]]

fusilier (fyo͞oˈzĭ lĭəˈ), *n.* **1.** a term used in the names of certain British regiments. **2.** formerly a soldier armed with a fusil. Also, **fusileer.** [t. F, der. *fusil* musket]

fusillade (fyo͞oˈzĭ lādˈ), *n., v.,* **-laded, -lading.** —*n.* **1.** a simultaneous or continuous discharge of firearms. **2.** an execution carried out by this means. **3.** a general discharge or outpouring of anything: *a fusillade of questions.* —*v.t.* **4.** to attack (a plane) or shoot down (persons) by a fusillade. [t. F, der. *fusiller* shoot, der. *fusil* musket, FUSIL[1]]

fusion (fyo͞oˈzhən), *n.* **1.** the act or process of fusing. **2.** the state of being fused. **3.** that which is fused. **4.** *Politics.* **a.** the coalition of parties or factions. **b.** the body resulting from such coalition. **5.** *Physics.* a thermonuclear reaction in which nuclei of light atoms join to form nuclei of heavier atoms, as the combination of deuterium atoms to form helium atoms. **6.** *Psychol.* the combination of two or more stimuli into an unanalysed, and sometimes unanalysable impression. [t. L: s. *fūsio* a pouring out]

fusion bomb, a hydrogen bomb.

fusionism (fyo͞oˈzhə nĭz′əm), *n. Politics.* the principle, policy, or practice of fusion. —**fuˈsionist,** *n., adj.*

fuss (fŭs), *n.* **1.** an excessive display of anxious activity; needless or useless bustle. **2.** a commotion, argument, or dispute. **3.** a person given to fussing. **4. make a fuss of,** to treat with special care and affection. —*v.i.* **5.** to make a fuss; make much ado about trifles; to move fussily about. —*v.t.* **6.** to put into a fuss; disturb with trifles; bother. **7. fuss over,** to pay excessive attention to. [orig. unknown] —**fuss′er,** *n.* —**Syn. 1.** pother, to-do, stir, commotion.

fusspot (fŭs′pŏt′), *n. Colloq.* a fussy person. Also, *U.S.*, **fuss-budget** (fŭs′bŭj′ĭt).

fussy (fŭs′ĭ), *adj.*, **-sier, -siest. 1.** excessively busy with trifles; anxious or particular about petty details. **2.** (of clothes, etc.) elaborately made or trimmed. **3.** full of excessive detail. —**fuss′ily,** *adv.* —**fuss′iness,** *n.*

fustanella (fŭs′tə nĕl′ə), *n.* a short stiff white skirt worn by men in Albania and some parts of Greece. [t. It., t. Mod. Gk: m. *phoustánella*]

fustian (fŭs′tĭ ən), *n.* **1.** a stout fabric of cotton and flax. **2.** a stout twilled cotton fabric with a short nap or pile. **3.** inflated or turgid language in writing or speaking; bombast; rant; claptrap. —*adj.* **4.** made of fustian. **5.** pompous or bombastic, as language. **6.** worthless; cheap. [ME, t. OF: m. *fustaigne*, g. LL *fustāneum* (der. L *fustis* cudgel), translation of Gk *xýlinon*, der. *xýlon* wood]

fustic (fŭs′tĭk), *n.* **1.** the wood of a large moraceous tree (**old fustic**), *Chlorophora tinctoria*, of tropical America, yielding a light yellow dye. **2.** the tree itself. **3.** a small anacardiaceous European shrub (**young fustic**), *Rhus cotinus*, from which a yellow dye is extracted. **4.** the dye of either. **5.** any of several other dyewoods. [t. F: m. *fustoc*, t. Sp., t. Ar.: m. *fustuq*; akin to Gk *pistákē* pistachio tree; from Pers.]

fustigate (fŭs′tĭ gāt′), *v.t.*, **-gated, -gating.** *Archaic.* to cudgel; beat; punish. [t. L: m. s. *fustīgātus*, pp., cudgelled to death] —**fus′tiga′tion,** *n.* —**fus′tiga′tor,** *n.*

fusty (fŭs′tĭ), *adj.*, **-tier, -tiest. 1.** mouldy; musty; having a stale smell; stuffy. **2.** old-fashioned; fogyish. **3.** stubbornly old-fashioned and out-of-date. [der. *fust*, n., t. OF: wine cask, log, g. L *fustis* cudgel] —**fust′ily,** *adv.* —**fust′iness,** *n.*

fut (fŭt), *adv.*, *interj.* phut.

fut., future.

futhorc (fo͞o′thôk), *n.* the runic alphabet. Also, **futhork, futharc** (fo͞o′thäk), **futhark.** [name consisting of its first six letters]

futile (fyo͞o′tīl), *adj.* **1.** incapable of producing any result; ineffective; useless; not successful. **2.** *Obs.* trifling; not important. [t. L: m. s. *fut(t)ilis* untrustworthy, vain, lit., that easily pours out] —**fu′tilely,** *adv.* —**fu′tileness,** *n.* —**Syn. 1.** ineffectual, unavailing, vain, idle, profitless, unprofitable, bootless. See **useless. 2.** trivial, frivolous. —**Ant. 1.** effectual.

futilitarian (fyo͞o tĭl′ĭ tẽə′rĭ ən), *adj.* **1.** believing that human hopes are vain and human strivings unjustified. —*n.* **2.** one who holds this belief. **3.** one who devotes himself to profitless pursuits. [der. FUTILITY, modelled on UTILITARIAN]

futility (fyo͞o tĭl′ĭ tĭ), *n., pl.* **-ties. 1.** the quality of being futile; ineffectiveness; uselessness. **2.** unimportance. **3.** a futile act or event.

futtock (fŭt′ək), *n. Naut.* one of the curved timbers in a frame or rib of a wooden ship. [orig. unknown]

futtock band, *Naut.* an iron band fitted round the lower mast, abreast of the lower yard, to which the truss of the yard is anchored. It also serves to secure the lower ends of the futtock shrouds. Also, **futtock hoop.**

futtock plank, *Naut.* the plank of the ceiling of a ship (the wooden surface at the bottom of the hold) next to the keelson.

futtock plate, *Naut.* an iron plate, fitted round the edge of the lower top, to which the lower ends of the topmast rigging and the upper ends of the futtock shrouds are secured.

futtock shrouds, *Naut.* short lengths of iron or steel rods, or wire, extending from the futtock band to the futtock plate and fitted with eyes at either end.

future (fyo͞o′chə), *n.* **1.** time that is to be or come hereafter. **2.** what will exist or happen in future time. **3.** a future condition, esp. of success or prosperity. **4.** *Gram.* **a.** the future tense. **b.** another future formation or construction. **c.** a form therein, as *he will come.* **5.** (*usually pl.*) a speculative purchase or sale of commodities for future receipt or delivery. —*adj.* **6.** that is to be or come hereafter: *future events, at some future day.* **7.** pertaining to or connected with time to come: *one's future prospects, future hopes.* **8.** *Gram.* designating a tense, or other verb formation or construction, which refers to events or states in time to come. [ME *futur*, t. L: s. *futūrus*, future participle of *esse* be]

futureless (fyo͞o′chə lĭs), *adj.* without a future; having no prospect of future betterment or prosperity.

future life, a form of life which is believed to follow mortal death; afterlife.

future perfect, *Gram.* **1.** perfect with respect to a temporal point of reference in the future. **2.** designating a tense, or other verb formation or construction, with such meaning. **3. a.** the future perfect tense. **b.** another verb formation or construction with future perfect meaning. **c.** a form therein, as *he will have come.*

futurism (fyo͞o′chə rĭz′əm), *n.* an artistic and literary doctrine or movement evolved in Italy about 1910, requiring complete abandonment of traditional usage and reconstruction of art and life on the basis of the dynamic, revolutionary, mechanical present and the future.

futurist (fyo͞o′chə rĭst), *adj.* **1.** of or pertaining to work of futurism. —*n.* **2.** a futurist artist or writer. **3.** *Theol.* one who believes in the fulfilment of the prophecies in the Bible.

futuristic (fyo͞o′chə rĭs′tĭk) *adj.* **1.** of or pertaining to futurism. **2.** *Colloq.* (of a work of art or the like) in a modern style; without reference to traditional forms, etc. **3.** *Colloq.* bizarre; unusual.

futurity (fyo͞o tyo͞oə′rĭ tĭ), *n., pl.* **-ties. 1.** future time. **2.** a future state or condition; a future event. **3.** the quality of being future. **4.** a futurity race.

futurity race, *U.S. Horseracing.* a race for which the entries are nominated long before the running.

fuze (fyo͞oz), *n. Chiefly U.S.* fuse[1].

fuzz (fŭz), *n.* **1.** loose, light, fibrous, or fluffy matter. **2.** a mass or coating of such matter. **3.** *Colloq.* a blur. **4.** *Colloq.* frizzy hair. **5.** *Slang.* the police force or a policeman. [cf. D *voos* spongy]

fuzzy (fŭz′ĭ), *adj.*, **-zier, -ziest. 1.** of the nature of or resembling fuzz. **2.** covered with fuzz. **3.** indistinct; blurred. —**fuzz′ily,** *adv.* —**fuzz′iness,** *n.*

fuzzy-wuzzy (fŭz′ĭ wŭz′ĭ), *n. Slang.* (used offensively) any coloured native, esp. of Africa. [used orig. of Sudanese tribesmen]

f.v., (L *folio verso*) on the back of the page.

fwd, forward.

-fy, a suffix meaning: **1.** to make; cause to be; render: *simplify, beautify.* **2.** to become; be made: *liquefy.* Also, **-ify.** [t. F: m. s. *-fier*, g. L *-ficāre* do, make]

fyke (fīk), *n. U.S.* a bag-shaped fish trap. [t. D: m. *fuik*]

fylfot (fĭl′fŏt), *n.* swastika. [? var. of *fill-foot* foot-filler]

Fyn (*Dan.* fʏn), *n.* an island in S Denmark. 376,872 pop. (1960); 1149 sq. mi. *Cap.:* Odense. German, **Fünen.**

Fyzabad (fī′zə băd′), *n.* a town in N India, in Uttar Pradesh. 88,296 (1961).

F.Z.S., Fellow of the Zoological Society.

G

G, g (jē), *n., pl.* **G's** or **Gs, g's** or **gs. 1.** the seventh letter of the English alphabet. **2.** the seventh in order of a series. **3.** *Music.* **a.** the fifth degree in the scale of C major or the seventh in the relative minor scale of A minor. **b.** a written or printed note representing this tone. **c.** a key, string, or pipe tuned to this note. **d.** (in solmization) the fifth note of the scale, called **sol.**

G, 1. German. **2.** *Physics.* the constant of gravitation. **3.** *U.S. Slang.* (grand) a thousand dollars.

g, *Physics.* **1.** the acceleration due to gravity. It varies slightly according to latitude and altitude: accepted value at Greenwich 32·19 feet per second. **2.** a unit of acceleration equal to 32 feet per second per second.

G., 1. German. **2.** (specific) gravity. **3.** Gulf.

g., 1. *Elect.* conductance. **2.** gauge. **3.** gender. **4.** genitive. **5.** going back to. **6.** gram. **7.** guinea.

Ga, 1. *Chem.* gallium. **2.** Georgia.

G.A., General Assembly.

g.a., general average.

gab (găb), *v.*, **gabbed, gabbing,** *n. Colloq.* —*v.i.* **1.** to talk idly; chatter. —*n.* **2.** idle talk; chatter. **3.** glib speech: *the gift of the gab.* **4.** *Mach.* a hook or prong engaging with some other part to give motion to a process. [var. of GOB² mouth, t. Gaelic or Irish] —**gab'ber,** *n.*

Gabar (gä'bə), *n.* a member of an Iranian sect of Zoroastrians.

gabble (găb'l), *v.*, **-bled, -bling,** *n.* —*v.i.* **1.** to talk rapidly and unintelligibly; jabber. **2.** (of geese, etc.) to cackle. —*v.t.* **3.** to utter rapidly and unintelligibly. —*n.* **4.** rapid, unintelligible talk. [freq. of GAB] —**gab'bler,** *n.*

gabbro (găb'rō), *n.*, *pl.* **-bros.** *Geol.* a granular igneous rock, a mixture of labradorite, augite, etc. [t. It.]

gabby (găb'ĭ), *adj.*, **-bier, -biest.** loquacious.

gabelle (gă bĕl'), *n.* **1.** a tax; an excise. **2.** (in France before 1790) a tax on salt. [t. F, t. Pr.: m. *gabela*, t. It.: m. *gabella* tax, t. Ar.: m. (*al*) *qabāla* the impost]

gaberdine (găb'ə dēn', găb'ə dēn'), *n.* **1.** a closely woven twill fabric of worsted, cotton, or spun rayon. **2.** a man's long, loose cloak or frock, worn in the Middle Ages. Also (*esp. def. 1*), **gabardine.** [t. Sp.: m. *gabardina*, ult. der. MHG *wallevart* pilgrimage]

gaberlunzie (găb'ə lŭn'zĭ), *n.* *Scot.* a beggar.

Gaberones (găb'ə rōnz'), *n.* a town in and the capital of Botswana, in the SE part. 12,000 (est. 1965).

Gabès (gä'bĕs), *n.* **Gulf of,** a gulf of the Mediterranean on the E coast of Tunisia.

gabion (gā'byən), *n.* **1.** a cylinder of wickerwork filled with earth, used as a military defence. **2.** a cylinder filled with stones and sunk in water, used in laying the foundations of a dam or jetty. [t. F, t. It.: m. *gabbione*, aug. of *gabbia*, g. L *cavea* cage]

gabionade (gā'byə nād'), *n.* **1.** a work formed of or with gabions. **2.** a row of gabions sunk in a stream to control the current. [t. F: m. *gabionnade*. See GABION]

gable (gā'bl), *n.*, *v.*, **-bled, -bling.** *Archit.* —*n.* **1.** the triangular wall enclosed by the two slopes of a roof and a horizontal line across the eaves. **2.** anything resembling a gable in shape. —*v.t.* **3.** to build with a gable or gables; form as a gable (chiefly in **gabled,** pp). [ME, prob. t. Scand.; cf. Icel. *gafl*. Cf. also OHG *gabala*, G *Gabel* fork] —**ga'ble-like',** *adj.*

Gable (def. 1)

gable end, the end wall of a building where it is surmounted by a gable.

gable roof, a ridged roof terminating at one or both ends in a gable.

gablet (gāb'lĭt), *n.* a little gable.

gable window, **1.** a window in or under a gable. **2.** a window having its upper part shaped like a gable.

Gabon (*Fr.* gȧ bôɴ'), *n.* **1.** a republic in SW equatorial Africa: independent member of the French Community: formerly part of French Equatorial Africa. 450,000 pop. (est. 1961); 102,290 sq. mi. *Cap.:* Libreville. **2.** an estuary in this republic. Also, **Gabun** (gə bōōn').

Gabonese (găb'ə nēz'), *adj.*, *n.*, *pl.* **-nese.** —*adj.* **1.** of or pertaining to Gabon or the Gabonese. —*n.* **2.** an inhabitant of Gabon.

Gaboriau (*Fr.* gȧ bŏ ryō'), *n.* **Émile** (*Fr.* ĕ mēl'), 1835–73, French novelist.

Gabriel (gā'brĭ əl), *n.* one of the archangels, appearing usually as a divine messenger. Dan. 8:16, 9:21. Luke, 1:19, 26. [t. Heb.: m. *Gabrī'ēl* the man of God]

Gabriel (*Fr.* gȧ brē ĕl'), *n.* **Jacques-Ange** (*Fr.* zhȧk äɴzh'), 1698–1782, French architect.

gaby (gā'bĭ), *n.*, *pl.* **-bies.** *Colloq.* a fool. [orig. uncert.]

gad¹ (găd), *v.*, **gadded, gadding,** *n.* —*v.i.* **1.** to move restlessly or idly about (usually fol. by *about*). —*n.* **2.** the act of gadding. [? special use of GAD²] —**gad'der,** *n.*

gad² (găd), *n.*, *v.*, **gadded, gadding.** —*n.* **1.** a goad for driving cattle. **2.** a pointed mining tool for breaking up rock, coal, etc. —*v.t.* **3.** to break up with a mining gad. [ME, t. Scand.; cf. Icel. *gaddr* spike]

Gad (găd), *n.*, *interj.* *Archaic.* a euphemistic form of *God* used as a mild oath. Also, **gad.**

Gad (găd), *n.* **1.** son of Jacob by Zilpah. Gen. 30:11, etc. **2.** a Hebrew prophet of the court of David. 2 Sam. 24:11–19. **3.** one of the twelve tribes of Israel.

gadabout (găd'ə bout'), *n.* *Colloq.* one who gads; a restless person, esp. one who leads an active social life.

gadfly (găd'flī'), *n.*, *pl.* **-flies.** **1.** any fly that goads or stings domestic animals, as many voracious, bloodsucking flies of the dipterous family *Tabanidae*. **2.** *Colloq.* an irritating person. [f. GAD² + FLY]

Gadfly, *Tabanus ruficornis* (Ab. 1 in. long)

gadget (găj'ĭt), *n.* a mechanical contrivance or device; any ingenious article. [orig. uncert. Cf. F *gâchette*]

gadgetry (găj'ĭ trĭ), *n.* gadgets collectively.

Gadhelic (gă dĕl'ĭk), *adj.*, *n.* Goidelic.

gadid (gā'dĭd), *n.* a fish of the cod family, *Gadidae*. [f. s. NL *gadus* cod + -ID²]

gadoid (gā'doid), *adj.* **1.** belonging to or resembling the *Anacanthini*, an order of soft-finned fishes including the cod, haddock, etc. —*n.* **2.** a gadoid fish. [f. s. NL *gadus* cod (t. Gk: m. *gádos* kind of fish) + -OID]

gadolinite (găd'ə lĭ nīt'), *n.* a silicate ore from which the rare-earth metals gadolinium, holmium, and rhenium are extracted. [named after J. *Gadolin*, 1760–1852, Finnish chemist. See -ITE¹]

gadolinium (găd'ə lĭn'yəm), *n.* *Chem.* a rare-earth metallic element. *Symbol:* Gd; *at. wt:* 157 25; *at. no.:* 64. [f. GADOLIN(ITE) + -IUM]

gadroon (gə drōōn'), *n.* **1.** *Archit.* an elaborately carved or indented convex moulding. **2.** a decorative series of curved inverted flutings, or of convex and concave flutings, as on silversmith's work. [t. F: m. *godron*, der. *goder* crease, pucker] —**gadrooned',** *adj.*

Gadsden (gădz'dən), *n.* **James,** 1788–1858, U.S. railway promoter and diplomat.

Gadsden Purchase, The, a tract of 45,535 sq. mi., now contained in New Mexico and Arizona, purchased from Mexico for $10,000,000 in 1853, the treaty being negotiated by James Gadsden.

gadwall (găd'wôl'), *n.*, *pl.* **-walls,** (*esp. collectively*) **-wall.** a wild duck, *Anas strepera*, found in temperate parts of the Northern Hemisphere.

gadzooks (găd zōōks'), *interj.* *Archaic.* (a mild oath). [appar. var. of *God's hooks* the nails of Christ]

Gaea (jē'ə), *n.* *Gk Myth.* the earth goddess, who bore Oceanus, Cronus, and the Titans. [t. Gk: m. *Gaîa*]

Gaekwar (gīk'wä), *n.* title of the ruler of Baroda. Also, **Gaikwar.** [t. Marathi: lit., cowherd]

Gael (gāl), *n.* **1.** a Scottish Celt or Highlander. **2.** *Rare.* an Irish Celt. [t. Scot. Gaelic: m. *Gaidheal*, O Irish *Gaidel*]

Gael., Gaelic.

Gaelic (gā'lĭk), *n.* **1.** the Celtic language of ancient Ireland and any of the languages that developed from it (Irish, Scottish, Gaelic, and Manx). **2.** Goidelic. —*adj.* **3.** of or pertaining to the Gaels or their language.

gaff¹ (găf), *n.* **1.** a strong hook with a handle, used for landing large fish. **2.** a metal spur for a gamecock. **3.** *Naut.* the spar extending the upper edge of a fore-and-aft sail. —*v.t.* **4.** to hook or land with a gaff. [ME *gaffe*, t. OF: boathook, prob. of Celtic orig.]

G, Gaff (def. 3)

gaff² (găf), *Slang.* —*n.* **1.** cheap place of amusement. —*v.i.* **2.** to gamble. [? orig., a place of outcry or humbug, special use of d. *gaff* loud, rude talk (OE *gaf* in *gafspræc* foolish speech, scurrility)]

gaff³ (găf), *n.* *Slang.* **1.** *Rare.* humbug; nonsense. **2. blow the gaff,** to disclose a secret. [orig. obscure]

gaffe (găf; *Fr.* gȧf), *n.* a social blunder. [t. F]

gaffer (găf'ə), *n.* **1.** a rustic title or term for an old man. **2.** an overseer or foreman. **3.** *Colloq.* an owner, senior partner, or the like. **4.** *Slang.* father. [var. of late ME *godfar* (contracted form of GODFATHER)]

gaff-topsail (găf'tŏp'sāl'; *Naut.* -səl), *n.* *Naut.* a light triangular sail above a gaff, which extends its foot.

gag¹ (găg), *v.*, **gagged, gagging,** *n.* —*v.t.* **1.** to stop up the mouth so as to prevent sound or speech. **2.** to restrain by force or authority from freedom of speech. **3.** to fasten open the jaws of, as in surgical operations. **4.** *U.S. or Dial.* to cause to heave with nausea. —*v.i.* **5.** *U.S. or Dial.* to heave with nausea. —*n.* **6.** something thrust into the mouth to prevent speech. **7.** any violent or authoritative suppression of freedom of speech. **8.** *Parl. Proc.* closure. **9.** a surgical instrument for holding the jaws open. [prob. imit. of the sound made in choking] —**gag'ger,** *n.*

gag² (găg), *v.*, **gagged, gagging,** *n.* *Slang.* —*v.t.* **1.** to introduce interpolations into (an actor's part) (fol. by *up*). **2.** to deceive; hoax. —*v.i.* **3.** to introduce interpolations or gags in acting. **4.** to play on one's credulity by false stories, etc. **5.** to make jokes. —*n.* **6.** a joke. **7.** an interpolation introduced by an actor into his part. **8.** any contrived piece of word play or horseplay. [cf. Icel. *gagg* yelp] —**gag'ger,** *n.*

gaga (gä'gä), *adj.* *Slang.* **1.** senile. **2.** fatuous; dotty. [imit.]

Gagarin (gä gä'rĭn; *Russ.* gȧ gȧ'rĭn), *n.* **Major Yuri Alekseyevitch** (*Russ.* yōō'rĭ ə lĭk syĕ'yĭ vĭch), 1934–68, Soviet cosmonaut; made first flight in space, in the spacecraft Vostok I, on April 12th, 1961.

gage¹ (gāj), *n.*, *v.*, **gaged, gaging.** —*n.* **1.** something, as a glove, thrown down in token of challenge to combat. **2.** a challenge. **3.** a pledge or pawn; security. —*v.t.* **4.** *Archaic.* to pledge, stake, or wager. [ME, t. OF: pledge, security; of Gmc orig. Cf. WAGE]

gage² (gāj), *n.*, *v.t.*, **gaged, gaging.** gauge. —**gag'er,** *n.*

gage³ (gāj), *n.* any of several plums, varieties of *Prunus domestica.* [short for GREENGAGE]

Gage (gāj), *n.* **Thomas,** 1721–87, British general in America, 1763–76.

gaggle (găg'l), *v.*, **-gled, -gling,** *n.* —*v.i.* **1.** to cackle. —*n.* **2.** a flock of geese. **3.** a cackle. [imit.]

gagroot (găg'rōōt'), *n.* a plant, *Lobelia inflata,* with emetic properties; Indian tobacco.

gahnite (gä'nīt), *n.* a dark green to black mineral of the spinel group, zinc aluminate, $ZnAl_2O_4$; zinc-spinel. [named after J. G. *Gahn,* 1745–1818, Swedish chemist. See -ITE¹]

gaiety (gā'ə tĭ), *n.*, *pl.* **-ties. 1.** the state of being gay or cheerful; gay spirits. **2.** (*often pl.*) merrymaking or festivity: *the gaieties of the New Year season.* **3.** showiness; finery: *gaiety of dress.* [t. F: m. *gaieté, gaité,* der. *gai* GAY]
—**Syn. 1.** merriment, mirth, glee, jollity, joyousness, liveliness, sportiveness, hilarity, vivacity. —**Ant. 1.** sadness.

Gaikwar (gīk'wä), *n.* Gaekwar.

Gaillard Cut (gĭl yäd', gā'läd), an artificial defile excavated for the Panama Canal, 10 mi. NW of the city of Panama. ab. 8 mi. long.

gaillardia (gā lä'dĭ ə), *n.* any plant of the American composite genus *Gaillardia,* several species of which are cultivated for their showy flowers. [NL: named after M. *Gaillard* de Marentonneau, 18th-century French botanist]

gaily (gā'lĭ), *adv.* **1.** merrily. **2.** showily.

gain¹ (gān), *v.t.* **1.** to obtain; secure (something desired); acquire: *gain time.* **2.** to win; get in competition: *gain the prize.* **3.** to acquire as an increase or addition: *to gain weight, speed, etc.* **4.** to obtain as a profit: *he gained ten pounds by that transaction.* **5.** to reach by effort; get to; arrive at: *to gain a good harbour.* —*v.i.* **6.** to improve; make progress; advance. **7.** to get nearer, as in pursuit (fol. by *on* or *upon*). **8.** to get farther away (from pursuers). **9. gain ground, a.** to make an advance, as in the face of opposition. **b.** to obtain an advantage. **10. gain time,** to delay; achieve a postponement. —*n.* **11.** profit; advantage. **12.** (*pl.*) profits; winnings. **13.** an increase or advance. **14.** the act of gaining; acquisition. **15.** *Radio.* the ratio of the output of an amplifier to the input. [t. F: m. *gagner,* of Gmc orig.] —**gain'able,** *adj.*
—**Syn. 1.** GAIN, ATTAIN, EARN, WIN imply obtaining a reward or something advantageous. GAIN carries the least suggestion of method or of effort expended. ATTAIN emphasizes the reaching of a goal. EARN emphasizes the exertions and labour expended which deserve reward. WIN emphasizes attainment in spite of competition or opposition. **13.** addition, increment, acquisition. —**Ant. 1.** lose.

gain² (gān), *n.* **1.** a notch or dado cut across the edge of a board, usually made to support a cross board. —*v.t.* **2.** to make a gain or gains in. [? akin to obs. *gane,* OE *ganian,* c. Icel. *gana* gape]

gainer (gā'nə), *n.* **1.** one who or that which gains. **2.** a type of dive in which the diver takes off facing forwards, and jumps upwards and backwards to enter the water facing the board.

gainful (gān'fəl), *adj.* profitable; lucrative. —**gain'fully,** *adv.* —**gain'fulness,** *n.*

gainly (gān'lĭ), *adj. Obs. or Dial.* agile; handsome. [der. *gain,* obs. adj., t. Scand.; cf. Icel. *gegn* straight, favourable, c. OE *gegn-,* in *gegnum,* adv., straight on, *gegnunga,* adv., directly] —**gain'liness,** *n.*

gainsay (gān'sā'), *v.t.*, **-said, -saying. 1.** to deny. **2.** to speak or act against. [f. *gain-* against + SAY] —**gain'-say'er,** *n.*

Gainsborough (gānz'bə rə, -brə), *n.* **1. Thomas,** 1727–88, English painter, esp. of portraits and landscapes. **2.** a town in England, in NW Lincolnshire. 17,276 (1961).

'gainst (gĕnst *or* gānst), *prep.*, *conj.* against. Also, **gainst.**

Gairdner (gĕəd'nə, gäd'-), *n.* **Lake,** a salt lake in S South Australia. ab. 100 mi. long.

gait (gāt), *n.* **1.** the manner of walking or stepping, esp. of a horse, as the walk, trot, canter, gallop, single-foot, etc. —*v.t.* **2.** to teach a uniform gait to. [Scot. and N Eng. sp. of GATE in various senses, incl. those above]

gaited (gā'tĭd), *adj.* having a specified gait: *slow-gaited, heavy-gaited oxen.*

gaiter (gā'tə), *n.* a covering of cloth, leather, etc., for the ankle and instep, and sometimes also the lower leg, worn over the shoe, etc. [t. F: m. *guêtre*]

Gaitskell (gāt'skĭl), *n.* **Hugh Todd Naylor,** 1906–63, English politician: leader of the Labour Party 1955–63.

Gaius (gī'əs), *n.* A.D. *c.* 110–*c.* 180, Roman jurist.

gal (găl), *n. Slang.* girl.

Gal., Galatians.

gal., gallon; gallons.

gala (gä'lə), *adj.* **1.** festive; festal; showy: *his visits were always gala occasions.* —*n.* **2.** a celebration; festive occasion. **3.** festal pomp or dress. [t. F, t. It.: festal pomp, finery, t. OF: m. *gale* joy, pleasure, t. MD: m. *wale* riches]

galactagogue (gə lăk'tə gŏg'), *adj.* **1.** increasing the amount of milk collected, either with or without increasing the amount secreted. —*n.* **2.** a galactagogue agent or medicine. [f. Gk: m. *galakt-* milk (s. *gála*) + m. s. *-agōgós* bringing]

galactan (gə lăk'tən), *n. Biochem.* any of the anhydrides of galactose, composing several gums, agar, and fruit pectins.

galactic (gə lăk'tĭk), *adj.* **1.** *Astron.* pertaining to any galaxy, esp. the Milky Way. **2.** *Physiol.* pertaining to or stimulating the secretion of milk. [t. Gk: m. s. *galaktikós* milky]

galactic circle, *Astron.* that great circle which most nearly coincides with the middle of the Milky Way. Also, **galactic equator.**

galactic coordinates, *Astron.* a system of coordinates for defining the position of a celestial body with reference to the Milky Way, based on galactic latitude and longitude.

galactic latitude. See **latitude** (def. 3).

galactic longitude. See **longitude** (def. 2b).

galactic plane, *Astron.* the plane of the galactic circle.

galactic poles, *Astron.* the two opposite points on the celestial sphere that are farthest north and south of the Milky Way.

galactopoietic (gə lăk'tō poi ĕt'ĭk), *adj.* **1.** increasing the secretion of milk, though not necessarily the amount collected. —*n.* **2.** a galactopoietic agent or medicine. [f. Gk: m. *galakto-* milk (comb. form of *gála*) + m. s. *poiētikós* making]

galactose (gə lăk'tōs), *n. Chem.* a hexose sugar, $C_6H_{12}O_6$, either laevorotatory or dextrorotatory, the latter being derived from milk sugar by hydrolysis. [f. m. s. Gk *gála* milk + -OSE²]

galago (gə lā'gō), *n.* a bushbaby or African lemuroid. [NL, ? t. Wolof: m. *golokh* monkey]

galah (gə lä'), *n. Austral.* **1.** a pink and grey cockatoo, *Kakatoe roseicapilla.* **2.** *Colloq.* a fool; simpleton. [t. native Australian]

Galahad (găl'ə hăd'), *n.* **Sir, 1.** *Arthurian Legend.* the noblest and purest knight of the Round Table, son of Lancelot and Elaine and fated to retrieve the Holy Grail. **2.** a man of ideal purity of heart and life.

galangal (gə lăng'gl), *n.* the aromatic, medicinal rhizome of certain plants of the ginger family, esp. *Alpinia officinarum,* of China and the East Indies. [var. of GALINGALE]

galantine (găl'ən tēn'), *n.* a dish of meat or poultry, boned, spiced, jellied and served cold.

galanty show (gə lăn'tĭ), *Obs.* a shadow pantomime.

Galápagos Islands (gə lăp'ə gəs; *Sp.* gä lä'pä gōs), an archipelago on the equator in the Pacific, ab. 600 mi. W of and belonging to Ecuador: many unique species of animal life. 2412 pop. (1962); 3029 sq. mi. Spanish, **Archipiélago de Colón.**

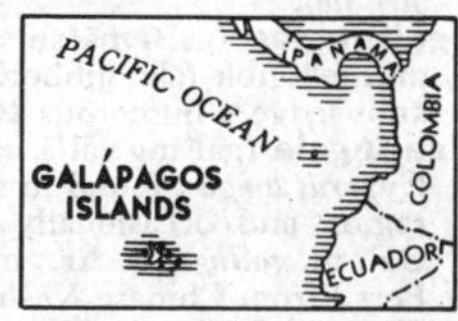

Galápagos Islands

Galashiels (găl'ə shēlz'), *n.* a burgh in Scotland, in Selkirkshire. 12,374 (1961).

galatea (găl'ə tĭə'), *n.* a strong, striped cotton fabric used for clothing, esp. for sailor suits. [from the name of a British man-of-war (*c.* 1867)]

Galatea (găl'ə tĭə'), *n. Gk Legend.* an ivory statue of a maiden, brought to life by Aphrodite in response to the prayers of the sculptor, Pygmalion, who had fallen in love with his work.

Galaţi (*Rum.* gä lätsy'), *n.* a city in E Rumania: a port on the Danube. 112,465 (est. 1964). Also, **Galatz** (*Ger.* gä läts').

Galatia (gə lā'shyə), *n.* an ancient country in central Asia Minor: later a Roman province. —**Ga la'tian,** *adj.*, *n.*

Galatians (gə lā'shyənz), *n.pl.* the book of the New Testament called in full 'The Epistle of Paul the Apostle to the Galatians'.

galavant (găl'ə vănt'), *v.i.* gallivant.

galaxy (găl'ək sĭ), *n.*, *pl.* **-axies. 1.** *Astron.* **a.** (*usually cap.*) the Milky Way. **b.** any large system of stars held together by mutual gravitation and separated from any other similar system by vast regions of space. **2.** any brilliant or splendid assemblage. [ME *galaxye,* t. ML: m. *galaxia,* var. of *galaxias,* t. Gk, der. *gála* milk]

Galba (găl′bə), *n.* **Servius Sulpicius** (sû′vĭ əs sŭl pĭsh′əs), 5? B.C.–A.D. 69, Roman emperor A.D. 68–69.

galbanum (găl′bə nəm), *n.* a gum resin with a peculiar disagreeable odour, obtained from certain Asiatic plants of the apiaceous genus *Ferula*: used in medicine and the arts. [t. L (Vulgate); answering to Gk *chalbánē* (Septuagint), rendering Heb. *ḥelbĕnāh*]

gale[1] (gāl), *n.* **1.** a strong wind. **2.** *Meteorol.* a wind with a velocity between about 30 and about 65 miles per hour. **3.** *Colloq.* a noisy outburst: *a gale of laughter.* **4.** *Archaic.* a gentle breeze. [orig. uncert.]

gale[2] (gāl), *n.* bog myrtle. [ME *gayl*, OE *gagel*, c. D *gagel*, G *Gagel*]

gale[3] (gāl), *n.* a periodic payment, as of rent. [? contraction of GAVEL]

galea (gā′lĭ ə), *n.*, *pl.* **-leae** (-lĭ ē′). *Bot.* any part of the calyx or corolla in the form of a helmet, as the upper lip of the corolla of the monkshood. [t. L: helmet]

galeate (gā′lĭ āt′), *adj.* *Bot.* having a galea. Also, **ga′leat′ed.**

galeiform (gā′lĭ ĭ fôm′), *adj.* helmet-shaped; resembling a galea. [f. s. L *galea* helmet + -(I)FORM]

Galen (gā′lĭn), *n.* **1. Claudius** (klô′dyəs), A.D. *c.* 130–*c.* 200, Greek physician and writer on medicine. **2.** *Archaic.* a physician.

galena (gə lē′nə), *n.* a very common heavy (sp. gr. 7·6) mineral, lead sulphide, PbS, occurring in lead-grey crystals, usually cubes, and cleavable masses: the principal ore of lead. Also, **galenite** (gə lē′nīt). [t. L: lead ore]

Galenic (gə lĕn′ĭk), *adj.* of or pertaining to Galen, or his principles, or his methods.

Galenism (gā′lĭ nĭz′əm), *n.* the medical system or principles of Galen. **—Ga′lenist,** *n.*

Galicia (gə lĭsh′ĭ ə), *n.* **1.** a former crownland of Austria, included in S Poland after World War I, and now partly in the Soviet Union. ab. 30,500 sq. mi. **2.** a maritime region in NW Spain: a former kingdom, and later a province. 11,256 sq. mi. **—Gali′cian,** *adj.*, *n.*

Galilean (găl′ĭ lē′ən), *adj.* **1.** of or pertaining to Galilee. *—n.* **2.** a native or inhabitant of Galilee. **3.** *Hist. Rare.* a Christian. **4. the Galilean,** Jesus. [f. GALILE(E) + -AN]

galilee (găl′ĭ lē′), *n.* a porch or vestibule, often on the ground floor of a tower, at the entrance of some English churches. [t. MF, t. ML: m. s. *galilaea*, a galilee, orig. (L) the province of Galilee; said to refer to the 'Galilee of the Gentiles' in Matt. 4:15]

Galilee (găl′ĭ lē′), *n.* **1.** an ancient Roman province in what is now N Israel. **2. Sea of.** Also, **Sea of Tiberias.** a lake in NE Israel through which the river Jordan flows. 14 mi. long; 682 ft below sea-level.

Sea of Galilee

Galileo (găl′ĭ lā′ō), *n.* (*Galileo Galilei*), 1564–1642, Italian physicist and astronomer. **—Galilean** (găl′ĭ lā′ən), *adj.*

galimatias (găl′ĭ mā′shĭ əs, -măt′ĭ əs), *n.* confused or unintelligible talk; gibberish. [t. F: f. ? + m. Gk *-matheia* knowledge, a humorous 16th-cent. formation]

galingale (găl′ĭng gāl′), *n.* a tall cyperaceous perennial, *Cyperus longus*, found in wet places in the Mediterranean region and occasionally in southern Britain. [ME, t. OF: m. *galingal*, t. Ar.: m. *khalanjān*, said to be (through Pers.) from Chinese *Ko-liang-kiang*, lit., wild ginger from Ko, a prefecture in Canton province]

galiot (găl′ĭ ət), *n.* galliot.

galipot (găl′ĭ pŏt′), *n.* a kind of turpentine exuded on the stems of certain species of pine. Also, **gallipot.** [t. F, earlier *garipot* resin, prob. t. D: m. *harpuis*, c. MLG *harpois* boiled and skimmed resin]

gall[1] (gôl), *n.* **1.** something very bitter or severe. **2.** bitterness of spirit; rancour. **3.** bile. **4.** *U.S. Slang.* impudence; effrontery. [ME; d. OE *galla*, r. OE *gealla*, c. G *Galle*; akin to L *fel*, Gk *cholḗ* gall, bile]

gall[2] (gôl), *v.t.* **1.** to make sore by rubbing; chafe severely. **2.** to vex; irritate: *galled by sarcasm.* *—v.i.* **3.** to be or become chafed. *—n.* **4.** a sore on the skin, esp. of a horse, due to rubbing; excoriation. **5.** something irritating. **6.** a state of irritation. [special use of GALL[1]]

gall[3] (gôl), *n.* any abnormal vegetable growth or excrescence on plants, caused by various agents, including insects, nematodes, fungi, bacteria, viruses, chemicals, and mechanical injuries. [ME *galle*, t. F, g. L *galla* the oak apple]

Galla (găl′ə), *n.*, *pl.* **-las, -la. 1.** a people of S Ethiopia and E Africa. **2.** a member of this people. **3.** the Cushitic language of this people.

gallant (*adj.* găl′ənt *for 1–3, 6*; gə lănt′, găl′ənt *for 4, 5*; *n.* găl′ənt, gə lănt′; *v.* gə lănt′, găl′ənt), *adj.* **1.** brave, high-spirited, or chivalrous. **2.** stately: *a gallant sight.* **3.** gay or showy, as in dress. **4.** polite and attentive to women; courtly. **5.** amorous. **6.** *Brit. Parl. Proc.* belonging to the armed services: *the honourable and gallant member.* *—n.* **7.** a man of spirit or mettle. **8.** a gay and dashing man. **9.** a man particularly attentive to women. **10.** a suitor or lover. **11.** a paramour. *—v.i., v.t.* **12.** to play the gallant (with); flirt (with). [ME *galaunt*, t. OF: m. *galant*, der. *gale* GALA] **—gal′lantly,** *adv.* **—gal′lantness,** *n.* **—Syn. 1.** valiant, courageous, heroic. See **brave. —Ant. 1.** cowardly, craven.

gallantry (găl′ən trĭ), *n.*, *pl.* **-tries. 1.** dashing courage; heroic bravery. **2.** gallant or courtly attention to women. **3.** a gallant action or speech. **—Syn. 1.** bravery, valour, heroism. **2.** chivalry, courtliness.

gallant soldier, a small composite annual herb, *Galinsoga parviflora*, a native of S America, but now a widespread weed in Europe and elsewhere.

gall bladder, *Anat.* a vesicle attached to the liver which receives bile from the hepatic ducts, concentrates it, and discharges it after meals. See diag. under **stomach.**

Galle (*Sinh.* găl′lə), *n.* a seaport in SW Ceylon. 64,942 (1963).

galleass (găl′ĭ ăs′), *n.* a large war galley formerly used in the Mediterranean, generally with three masts and rowed by slaves. Also, **galliass.** [t. MF: m. *galeace*, t. It.: m. *galeaza*, aug. of *galea* GALLEY]

Gallegos (*Sp.* gä lyĕ′gôs), *n.* **Rómulo** (*Sp.* rô′mo͞o lô), 1884–1969, Venezuelan writer and politician.

galleon (găl′ĭ ən), *n.* a kind of large sailing vessel formerly used by the Spaniards and others. [t. Sp.: m. *galeón*, aug. of *galea* GALLEY]

gallery (găl′ə rĭ), *n.*, *pl.* **-leries. 1.** a long, narrow, covered walk, open at one or both sides. **2.** a corridor, usually large and with ornate walls and ceiling. **3.** a raised platform or passageway along the outside or inside of the wall of a building; balcony. **4.** a platform projecting from the interior walls of a church, theatre, etc., to provide seats or room for a part of the audience. **5.** the highest of such platforms in a theatre, usually containing the cheapest seats. **6.** the occupants of such a platform in a theatre. **7.** any body of spectators or auditors. **8. play to the gallery,** to seek applause by playing to popular taste rather than considered judgement. **9.** a room, series of rooms, or building devoted to the exhibition of works of art. **10.** a collection of art for exhibition. **11.** a room or building in which to take pictures, practise shooting, etc. **12.** *Naut.* a balcony-like structure or platform at the stern or quarter of old ships. **13.** a passageway made by an animal. **14.** any of various tunnels or passages, as an underground passage in a fortification, a tunnel within the body of a dam, etc. **15.** *Mining.* a level or drift. [t. It.: m. s. *galleria*, t. ML: m. *galilaea* GALILEE] **—gal′leried,** *adj.*

galley (găl′ĭ), *n.*, *pl.* **-leys. 1.** an early seagoing vessel propelled by oars or by oars and sails. **2.** a large rowing boat. **3.** the kitchen of a ship. **4.** *Print.* **a.** a long, narrow tray, usually of metal, for holding type which has been set. **b.** galley proof. [ME *galeie*, t. ML: m. *galeia*, t. LGk: m. *galaía*]

galley proof, *Print.* proof from type on a galley.

galley slave, 1. a person condemned to work at the oar on a galley. **2.** an overworked person; drudge.

gallfly (gôl′flī′), *n.*, *pl.* **-flies.** a gall wasp.

galliard (găl′yəd), *n.* **1.** a spirited dance for two dancers in triple rhythm, common in the 16th and 17th centuries. *—adj.* **2.** *Archaic.* lively or gay. [ME, t. OF, prob. der. Celtic **galli-* might, ability]

galliass (găl′ĭ ăs′), *n.* galleass.

gallic[1] (găl′ĭk), *adj.* *Chem.* of or containing gallium, esp. in the trivalent state. [f. GALL(IUM) + -IC]

gallic[2] (găl′ĭk), *adj.* pertaining to or derived from plant galls: *gallic acid.* [f. GALL[3] + -IC]

Gallic (găl′ĭk), *adj.* **1.** pertaining to the Gauls or Gaul. **2.** pertaining to the French or France. [t. L: s. *Gallicus*, der. *Gallus* a Gaul]

gallic acid, *Chem.* an acid, $C_6H_2(OH)_3CO_2H$, a white or yellowish crystalline powder found in nut-galls, mangoes, and other plants.

Gallican (găl′ĭ kən), *adj.* **1.** pertaining to the Roman Catholic Church in France. **2.** pertaining to a section of the Roman Catholic Church in France before 1870, which wished to restrict papal authority and widen the authority of general councils, the bishops, and temporal rulers.

Gallicanism (găl′ĭ kə nĭz′əm), *n.* *Eccles.* a religious opinion peculiar to France that wished to curtail the papal authority in favour of that of the bishops and the temporal order.

Gallice (găl′ĭ sĭ), *adv.* in French. [ML]

Gallicism (găl′ĭ sĭz′əm), *n.* (*sometimes l.c.*) **1.** a French linguistic peculiarity. **2.** a French idiom or expression used in another language.

Gallicize (găl′ĭ sīz′), *v.t.*, *v.i.*, **-cized, -cizing.** (*sometimes l.c.*) to make or become French in language, character, etc. Also, **Gallicise.**

Galli-Curci (găl′ĭ ko͞oə′chĭ; *It.* gäl lē ko͞or′chē), *n.* **Amelita** (*It.* ä mė lē′tä), 1889–1964, Italian soprano.

galligaskins (găl′ĭ găs′kĭnz), *n.pl.* **1.** a kind of loose hose or breeches worn in the 16th and 17th centuries. **2.** loose breeches in general. **3.** leggings or gaiters of leather. [appar. alter. of F *garguesque*, metathetic var. of *greguesque*, t. It.: m. *grechesa*, from *alla grechesa* in the Greek manner]

gallimaufry (găl′ĭ mô′frĭ), *n.*, *pl.* **-fries. 1.** a hotchpotch; jumble; confused medley. **2.** *Now Chiefly U.S.* a ragout or hash. [t. F: m. *galimafrée*, orig. unknown]

gallinacean (găl′ĭ nā′shən), *n.* **1.** a gallinaceous bird. —*adj.* **2.** gallinaceous.

gallinaceous (găl′ĭ nā′shəs), *adj.* **1.** pertaining to or resembling the domestic fowls. **2.** belonging to the group or order *Galliformes*, which includes the domestic fowls, pheasants, grouse, partridges, etc. [t. L: m. *gallīnāceus* pertaining to poultry]

Gallinas (*Sp.* gäl lyē′näs), *n.* **Punta** (*Sp.* po͞on′tä), a cape in NE Colombia: northernmost point of South America.

galling (gô′lĭng), *adj.* that galls; chafing; irritating; exasperating. —**gall′ingly,** *adv.*

gallinule (găl′ĭ nyo͞ol′), *n.* any of certain long-toed aquatic birds of the rail family, as the **Florida gallinule,** *Gallinula chloropus cachinnans*, and the European moorhen, *G. c. chloropus.* [t. NL: m. s. *Gallīnula*, the typical genus (LL: chicken), dim. of L *gallīna* hen]

galliot (găl′ĭ ət), *n.* a small galley propelled by both sails and oars. Also, **galiot.** [ME *galiote*, t. OF, dim. of *galie* GALLEY]

Gallipoli Peninsula (gə lĭp′əlĭ), a peninsula in European Turkey between the Dardanelles and the Aegean: the scene of a disastrous British naval and land campaign, 1915–16. ab. 60 mi. long.

Gallipoli Peninsula

gallipot[1] (găl′ĭ pŏt′), *n.* a small glazed pot used by pharmacists for medicines, etc. [? f. GALLEY + POT[1] (as if brought or imported in galleys)]

gallipot[2] (găl′ĭ pŏt′), *n.* galipot.

gallium (găl′ĭ əm), *n.* *Chem.* a rare, bluish white, easily fusible trivalent metallic element, used in high-temperature thermometers on account of its high boiling point (1700°C) and low melting point (30°C). *Symbol:* Ga; *at. wt:* 69·72; *at. no.:* 31; *sp. gr.:* 5·91 at 20°C. [NL, said to be der. L *gallus* cock, trans. of F *coq*, from the name of the discoverer, *Lecoq* de Boisbaudran]

gallivant (găl′ĭ vănt′), *v.i.* to gad gaily or frivolously. Also, **galavant.** [? humorous alter. of GALLANT]

gall midge, any small fly of the family *Cecidomyidae* which makes galls on plants.

gallnut (gôl′nŭt′), *n.* a nutlike gall on plants.

Gallo-, a word element meaning 'Gallic'. [t. L, comb. form of *Gallus* a Gaul]

galloglass (găl′ō gläs′), *n.* *Irish Hist.* one of a class of soldiers or retainers maintained by a chieftain. Also, **gallowglass.** [t. Irish: m. *gallóglach*, f. *gall* foreigner + *óglach* servant, warrior]

gallon (găl′ən), *n.* **1.** a fundamental British unit of capacity, also used in Commonwealth and other countries, for the measurement of liquids and dry goods, defined as the volume occupied by 10 lbs of distilled water under specified conditions; equal to 4·546 litres; imperial gallon. **2.** a U.S. measure of liquid commodities only, defined in the U.S. as 231 cubic inches; equal to 3·785 litres. One imperial gallon equals 1·20094 U.S. gallons. [ME *galun*, t. ONF, ult. der. *Gallic galla* vessel, bowl]

galloon (gə lo͞on′), *n.* a braid or trimming of worsted, silk or rayon tinsel, gold or silver, etc. [t. F: m. *galon*, der. *galonner* trim with GALLOON, orig. adorn (the head or hair) with bands or ribbons, der. OF *gale* GALA]

galloot (gə lo͞ot′), *n.* *U.S. Slang.* galoot.

gallop (găl′əp), *v.i.* **1.** to ride a horse at a gallop; ride at full speed. **2.** to run rapidly by leaps, as a horse; go at a gallop. **3.** to go fast, race, or hurry, as a person, the tongue, time, etc. —*v.t.* **4.** to cause (a horse, etc.) to gallop. —*n.* **5.** a fast gait of the horse (or other quadruped) in which in the course of each stride all four feet are off the ground at once. **6.** a run or ride at this gait. **7.** a rapid rate of going, or a course of going at this rate. **8.** (*often pl.*) a tract of open countryside, as of downland, where racehorses are exercised. [t. F: m. s. *galoper*, t. OLG: m. *wala hlōpan* run well] —**gal′loper,** *n.*

gallopade (găl′ə pād′), *n.* **1.** a sprightly kind of dance, originally Hungarian. **2.** the music for it. [t. F: m. *galopade*, der. *galoper* GALLOP]

galloping (găl′ə pĭng), *adj.* **1.** moving at a gallop or quickly. **2.** advancing or encroaching rapidly: *galloping consumption.*

Gallo-Rom., Gallo-Romance.

Gallo-Romance (găl′ō rō măns′), *n.* the vernacular language, a development from Latin, spoken in France about A.D. 600–900. Also, **Gallo-Roman** (găl′ō rō′mən).

gallous (găl′əs), *adj.* *Chem.* containing divalent gallium.

Galloway (găl′ə wā′), *n.* **1.** a region in SW Scotland comprising the counties of Wigtown and SW Kirkcudbright W of the Dee. The **Mull of Galloway** is the southernmost point of Scotland. **2.** one of a breed of beef cattle originating in this region, with a coat of curly black hair. **3.** one of a breed of small strong horses first raised in Galloway.

gallowglass (găl′ō gläs′), *n.* galloglass.

gallows (găl′ōz), *n.*, *pl.* **-lows, -lowses. 1.** a wooden frame, consisting of a crossbeam on two uprights, on which condemned persons were, and in certain countries still are, executed by hanging. **2.** a similar structure, as for suspending something or for gymnastic exercise. **3.** execution by hanging. **4.** (*often pl.*) *Dial.* galluses. [ME *galwes*, OE *galgan*, pl. of *g(e)alga* gallows, c. G *Galgen*]

gallows bird, *Colloq.* one who deserves to be hanged.

gallows bitts, *Naut.* vertical frames on the deck of a ship for supporting spare spars.

gallows top, *Naut.* timbers placed across the top of the gallows bitts to secure spare spars.

gallows tree, *Archaic.* gallows.

gallstone (gôl′stōn′), *n.* *Pathol.* a calculus or stone formed in the bile or gall passages.

Gallup (găl′əp), *n.* **George Horace,** born 1901, U.S. statistician.

Gallup Poll, *Trademark.* the questioning of a representative cross-section of the population in order to assess public opinion, as of voting intentions.

galluses (găl′ə sĭz), *n.pl.* *Chiefly Dial., esp. U.S. Dial.* braces for trousers. [var. of GALLOWSES]

gall wasp, an insect of the hymenopterous family *Cynipidae*, whose larvae cause galls on plants.

galoot (gə lo͞ot′), *n.* *U.S. Slang.* an awkward, silly fellow. Also, **galloot.**

galop (găl′əp), *n.* **1.** a lively round dance in duple time. **2.** music for, or in the rhythm of, this dance. [t. F]

galore (gə lô′), *adv.* **1.** in abundance. —*n.* **2.** *Obs.* abundance. [t. Irish: m. *go leōr* (Gaelic *gu leōir*) to sufficiency]

galosh (gə lŏsh′), *n.*, *pl.* **-loshes. 1.** (*usually pl.*) an overshoe of rubber or other waterproof substance for protection against wet, cold, etc. **2.** a piece of leather running round the lower part of boot or shoe uppers. **3.** *Obs.* a rustic shoe, clog or sandal. Also, **galoche, golosh.** [ME *galoche*, t. F, prob. g. L *gallicula* Gallic (sandal), b. *gallica* Gallic and *caligula* soldier's boot]

gals, gallons.

Galsworthy (gôlz′wûr′thĭ, gălz′-), *n.* **John,** 1867–1933, English novelist, dramatist, and short-story writer.

Galton (gôl′tən), *n.* **Sir Francis,** 1822–1911, British scientist and writer. —**Galtonian** (gôl tō′nyən), *adj.*

Galty Mountains (gôl′tĭ, găl′tĭ), a range of low mountains in counties Limerick and Tipperary, Ireland. Highest point, Galtymore Mountain, 3018 ft. Also, **Galtee Mountains.**

galumph (gə lŭmpf′, -lŭmf′), *v.i.* to bound exultantly. [b. GALLOP + TRIUMPH: coined by Lewis Carroll]

Galvani (găl vä′nĭ; *It.* gäl vä′nē), *n.* **Luigi** (*It.* lwē′jē), 1737–98, an Italian physiologist whose experiments led to the discovery that electricity may result from chemical action.

galvanic (găl văn′ĭk), *adj.* **1.** pertaining to or produced by galvanism; producing or caused by an electric current. **2.** affecting or affected as if by galvanism. [f. GALVAN(I) + -IC] —**galvan′ically,** *adv.*

galvanic battery, a voltaic battery.

galvanic cell, *Elect.* an electrolytic cell capable of producing electric energy by electrochemical action.

galvanism (găl′və nĭz′əm), *n.* **1.** *Elect.* electricity, esp. as produced by chemical action. **2.** *Med.* the therapeutic application of electricity to the body.

galvanize (găl′və nīz′), *v.t.*, **-nized, -nizing. 1.** to stimulate by or as by a galvanic current. **2.** to startle into sudden activity. **3.** to coat (metal, esp. iron or steel) with zinc. Also, **galvanise.** —**gal′vaniza′tion,** *n.* —**gal′vaniz′er,** *n.*

galvanized iron, iron coated with zinc to prevent rust.

galvano-, a combining form representing **galvanic, galvanism,** as in *galvanocautery.*

galvanocautery (găl′və nō kô′tə rĭ, găl văn′ō-), *n., pl.* **-ries.** *Med.* **1.** a cautery heated by a galvanic current. **2.** cauterization by such means.

galvanometer (găl′və nŏm′ĭ tə), *n.* an instrument for detecting the existence and determining the strength and direction of an electric current.

galvanometry (găl′və nŏm′ĭ trĭ), *n.* the art or process of determining the strength of electric currents. —**galvanometric** (găl′və nō mĕt′rĭk, găl văn′ō-), *adj.*

galvanoscope (găl′və nə skōp′, găl văn′ə-), *n.* an instrument for detecting the existence, and determining the direction of an electric current. —**galvanoscopic** (găl′və nə skŏp′ĭk, găl văn′ə-), *adj.*

galvanotropism (găl′və nŏt′rə pĭz′əm), *n. Bot.* the movements in growing organs induced by the passage of electric currents.

Galway (gôl′wā′), *n.* **1.** a county in W Republic of Ireland, in Connaught. 149,887 pop. (1961); 2293 sq. mi. **2.** its county town: a seaport. 22,028 (1961).

Galway Bay, a bay between counties Clare and Galway in W Ireland. 30 mi. long.

galyak (găl′yăk, găl yăk′), *n.* a fur from the pelt of lambs or kids. [t. Uzbek]

gam[1] (găm), *n., v.,* **gammed, gamming.** —*n.* **1.** a herd or school of whales. **2.** *Naut. and U.S. Dial.* a social meeting, visit, or the like, as between vessels at sea. —*v.i.* **3.** (of whales) to congregate in a school. **4.** *Naut. and U.S. Dial.* to have a gam; meet socially. —*v.t.* **5.** *Naut. and U.S. Dial.* to have a gam with. [var. of GAME[1]]

gam[2] (găm), *n. Slang.* a leg. [var. of obs. *gamb*, t. ONF: m. *gambe.* Cf. OF *jambe* leg]

Gama (gä′mə; *Port.* gə′mə), *n.* **Vasco da** (văs′kō də; *Port.* vàsh′ko͞o də), *c.* 1469–1524, Portuguese navigator and discoverer of the sea route from Portugal around the continent of Africa to India.

gamba (găm′bə), *n. Music.* **1.** an organ stop intended to have a stringlike tone. **2.** viola da gamba.

gambado[1] (găm bā′dō), *n., pl.* **-dos, -does. 1.** one of a pair of large protective boots or gaiters fixed to a saddle instead of stirrups. **2.** any long gaiter or legging. [f. It. *gamba* leg + suffix *-ado*]

gambado[2] (găm bā′dō), *n.* **1.** a bound or leap by a horse. **2.** an escapade. Also, **gambade** (găm bād′). [t. F: m. *gambade,* influenced by GAMBADO[1]. Cf. GAMBOL]

gambeson (găm′bĭ sən), *n.* a medieval military garment of leather or quilted cloth, padded, and worn under mail, but also worn as the principal garment of defence. [ME *gambisoune,* t. OF: m. *gambison,* of Gmc orig.]

Gambetta (găm bĕt′ə; *Fr.* gäɴ bĕ tȧ′), *n.* **Léon** (*Fr.* lĕ ôɴ′), 1838–82, French statesman.

Gambia (găm′bĭ ə), *n.* **1.** a large river in W Africa, flowing W to the Atlantic. ab. 500 mi. **2.** Also, **The Gambia.** an independent state extending inland along both sides of this river; member of the Commonwealth. 315,486 pop. (1963); 4003 sq. mi. *Cap.:* Bathurst. See map under **Senegal.** —**Gam′bian,** *adj., n.*

gambier (găm′bĭ ə), *n.* an astringent extract similar to catechu, obtained from the leaves and young shoots of *Uncaria gambir,* a tropical Asiatic rubiaceous shrub: used in medicine, dyeing, tanning, etc. Also, **gambir.** [t. Malay: m. *gambir*]

gambit (găm′bĭt), *n.* **1.** *Chess.* an opening in which the player seeks by sacrificing a pawn or other piece to obtain some advantage. **2.** any act or course of action by which one seeks to obtain some advantage. [t. F, t. It.: m. *gambetto* a tripping-up, der. *gamba* leg]

gamble (găm′bl), *v.,* **-bled, -bling,** *n.* —*v.i.* **1.** to play at any game of chance for stakes. **2.** to stake or risk money, or anything of value, on the outcome of something involving chance. **3.** to act on favourable hopes or assessment: *in calling the general election, the prime minister is gambling on public acceptance of his policies to date.* —*v.t.* **4.** to lose or squander by betting (usually fol. by *away*). **5.** to risk or venture. —*n.* **6.** *Colloq.* any matter or thing involving risk or uncertainty. **7.** *Colloq.* a venture in or as in gambling. [? d. var. of ME *gamenen,* OE *gamenian* to sport, play] —**gam′bler,** *n.* —**gam′bling,** *n.*

gamboge (găm bōj′, -bo͞ozh′), *n.* **1.** Also, **cambogia.** a gum resin from various trees of the genus *Garcinia,* esp. *G. hanburyi,* of Cambodia, Thailand, etc.: used as a yellow pigment and as a cathartic. **2.** yellow or yellow-orange. [t. NL: m. s. *gambogium,* der. *Camboja* CAMBODIA]

gambol (găm′bl), *v.,* **-bolled, -bolling** or (*U.S.*) **-boled, -boling,** *n.* —*v.i.* **1.** to skip about, as in dancing or playing; frolic. —*n.* **2.** a skipping or frisking about; frolic. [earlier *gambald,* t. F: m. *gambade* a leap, t. It.: m. *gambata* a kick, der. *gamba* leg] —**Syn. 1.** spring, caper, frisk, romp.

gambrel (găm′brəl), *n.* **1.** the hock of an animal, esp. of a horse. **2.** cambrel. [t. ONF: m. **gamberel* butcher's cambrel, der. *gambe,* g. LL *gamba* hoof, leg]

gambrel roof, 1. a roof having a small gablet at the summit of a hipped end. **2.** *U.S.* a mansard roof. —**gam′brel-roofed′,** *adj.*

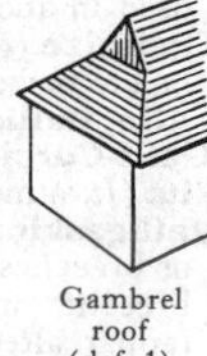

Gambrel roof (def. 1)

Gambrinus (găm brī′nəs), *n.* mythical Flemish king, reputed inventor of beer.

game[1] (gām), *n., adj.,* **gamer, gamest,** *v.,* **gamed, gaming.** —*n.* **1.** an amusement or pastime: *children's games.* **2.** the apparatus employed in playing any of certain games: *a shop selling toys and games.* **3.** a contest for amusement in the form of a trial of chance, skill, or endurance, according to set rules; a match: *games of football, golf, etc.* **4.** a single contest at play, or a definite portion of play in a particular game: *a rubber of three games in bridge.* **5.** the number of points required to win a game. **6.** a particular manner or style of playing a game. **7.** a proceeding carried on like a game: *the game of diplomacy.* **8.** *Colloq.* business or profession. **9.** *Slang.* prostitution. **10.** a trick; strategy: *to see through someone's game.* **11.** sport of any kind; joke: *to make game of a person.* **12.** wild animals, including birds and fishes, such as are hunted or taken for sport or profit. **13.** the flesh of wild animals or game, used for food. **14.** any object of pursuit or attack; prey. **15.** fighting spirit; pluck. **16. play the game,** to act fairly or justly, or in accordance with recognized rules. —*adj.* **17.** pertaining to animals hunted or taken as game. **18.** having the fighting spirit of a gamecock; plucky: *a game sportsman.* **19.** *Colloq.* willing; having the spirit or will (often fol. by *for* or an infinitive). —*v.i.* **20.** to play games of chance for stakes; gamble. —*v.t.* **21.** to squander in gaming (fol. by *away*). [ME; OE *gamen,* c. OHG *gaman* glee] —**game′ly,** *adv.* —**game′ness,** *n.* —**Syn. 1.** sport, contest; diversion. See **play. 10.** scheme, artifice, stratagem. **12.** prey, quarry.

game[2] (gām), *adj. Colloq.* lame: *a game leg.* [orig. uncert.]

gamebag (gām′băg′), *n.* a strong bag of canvas, leather, or the like, for holding game birds or other game.

game bird, a bird hunted for sport or profit, or protected by law.

gamecock (gām′kŏk′), *n.* a cock bred and trained for fighting, or one of a fighting breed.

game fish, an edible fish capable of affording sport to the angler in its capture.

game fowl, 1. a fowl of any species regarded as game or the object of hunting. **2.** a domestic fowl of a breed much used for fighting.

gamekeeper (gām′kē′pə), *n.* a person employed, as on an estate, to take care of game, prevent poaching, etc.

gamelan (găm′ĭ lăn′), *n.* a type of South-East Asian orchestral ensemble, characterized by the complex rhythms of its music. [t. Malay: name of a rhythm instrument]

game laws, the body of laws enacted for the preservation of game, as by restricting open seasons and the manner of taking.

game point, *Tennis, etc.* a point that could decide the game if scored by the leading player.

game reserve, an area of land set aside for the preservation of wild animals.

gamesmanship (gāmz′mən shĭp′), *n. Colloq.* the art or practice of winning games without actually cheating, by disconcerting the opponent.

gamesome (gām′səm), *adj.* full of play; frolicsome. —**game′somely,** *adv.* —**game′someness,** *n.*

gamester (gām′stə), *n.* a person who gambles habitually; gambler. [f. GAME[1] + -STER]

gametangium (găm′ĭ tăn′jĭ əm), *n., pl.* **-gia** (-jĭ ə). *Bot.* an organ or body producing gametes. [NL, f. Gk: s. *gametē* wife, *gamétēs* husband + m. *angeîon* vessel]

gamete (găm′ēt, gă mēt′), *n. Biol.* either of the two germ cells which unite to form a new organism; a mature reproductive cell. [t. NL: m. s. *gameta,* t. Gk: m. *gametē* wife or m. *gamétēs* husband] —**gametal** (gə mē′tl), **gametic** (gə mĕt′ĭk), *adj.*

gametocyte (gə mē′tō sīt′), *n. Biol.* a cell that produces gametes.

gametogenesis (găm′ĭ tō jĕn′ĭ sĭs), *n. Biol.* the development of gametes.

gametophore (gə mē′tō fô′), *n. Bot.* a part or structure producing gametes.

gametophyte (gə mē′tō fīt′), *n. Bot.* the sexual form of a plant in the alternation of generations (opposed to *sporophyte*).

game warden, an official who enforces game laws.

gamey (gā′mĭ), *adj.* gamy.

gamic (găm′ĭk), *adj. Biol.* sexual (opposed to *agamic*). [t. Gk: m. s. *gamikós* of or for marriage]

gamin (găm′ĭn; *Fr.* gȧ măɴ′), *n.* **1.** a neglected boy left to run about the streets; street Arab. **2.** a mischievous boy. [t. F; orig. uncert.]

gamine (găm′ēn), *n.* **1.** a female street Arab. **2.** a mischievous, boylike girl or woman, esp. one of small stature. [t. F: fem. of GAMIN]
gaming (gā′mĭng), *n.* gambling.
gamma (găm′ə), *n.* **1.** the third letter (Γ, γ, = English G, g) of the Greek alphabet. **2.** the third of any series (used esp. in scientific classification). **3.** a unit of weight equal to one microgram. **4.** the third highest examination mark, usually the lowest mark awarded.
gammadion (gă mā′dyən), *n., pl.* **-dia** (-dyə). an ornamental figure consisting of combinations of the Greek capital gamma, esp. in the form of a swastika or fylfot, or of a voided Greek cross. [t. MGk, var. of *gammátion*, dim. of Gk *gámma* gamma]
gamma globulin, a protein component of blood plasma containing antibodies effective against certain microorganisms, as in measles, infectious hepatitis, and poliomyelitis.
gamma iron, *Metall.* a form of iron which is nonmagnetic and which, when pure, exists between approx. 900°C and 1400°C; consists of face-centred cubic crystals.
gamma rays, *Physics.* rays similar to X-rays, but of higher frequency and penetrating power, forming part of the radiation of radioactive substance.
gammer (găm′ə), *n. Obs. or Dial.* an old woman. [var. of late ME *godmor* (contr. of GODMOTHER)]
Gammexane (gə mĕk′sān, găm′ĭk sān′), *n. Trademark.* a powerful synthetic stomach and contact insecticide; gamma isomer of benzene hexachloride.
gammon[1] (găm′ən), *n.* **1.** the game of backgammon. **2.** *Backgammon.* a victory in which the winner throws off all his men before his opponent throws off any. —*v.t.* **3.** *Backgammon.* to win a gammon over. [? special use of ME and OE *gamen.* See GAME[1]]
gammon[2] (găm′ən), *n.* **1.** a smoked or cured ham. **2.** the lower end of a side of bacon. [ME *gambon*, t. ONF: ham, der. *gambe* hoof, leg, g. LL *gamba*]
gammon[3] (găm′ən), *Colloq.* —*n.* **1.** deceitful nonsense; bosh. —*v.i.* **2.** to talk gammon. **3.** to make pretence. —*v.t.* **4.** to deceive with nonsense. [see GAMMON[1]]
gammon[4] (găm′ən), *v.t. Naut.* to fasten (a bowsprit) to the stem of a ship. [? akin to GAMMON[2]]
gammy (găm′ĭ), *adj. Colloq.* game[2]; lame.
gamo-, *Biol.* a word element meaning 'sexual union'. [comb. form repr. Gk *gámos* marriage]
gamogenesis (găm′ō jĕn′ĭ sĭs), *n. Biol.* sexual reproduction. —**gamogenetic** (găm′ō jĭ nĕt′ĭk), *adj.* —**gam′ogenet′ically,** *adv.*
gamopetalous (găm′ō pĕt′ə ləs), *adj. Bot.* having the petals united.
gamophyllous (găm′ō fĭl′əs), *adj. Bot.* having leaves united by their edges.
gamosepalous (găm′ō sĕp′ə ləs), *adj. Bot.* having the sepals united. See illus. under **calyx.**

Gamopetalous flower

-gamous, an adjectival word element corresponding to the noun element **-gamy,** as in *polygamous.* [t. Gk: m. *-gamos* marrying]
gamp (gămp), *n. Slang.* an umbrella. [said to be from the umbrella of Mrs Sarah *Gamp* in Dickens's '*Martin Chuzzlewit*']
gamut (găm′ət), *n.* **1.** the whole scale or range. **2.** *Music.* **a.** the whole series of recognized musical notes. **b.** the major scale. [t. ML: contr. of *gamma ut*, f. *gamma*, used to represent the first or lowest tone (G) in the medieval scale + *ut* (later *do*); the notes of the scale being named from a L hymn to St John: *Ut* queant laxis *re*sonare fibris, *Mi*ra gestorum *fa*muli tuorum, *Sol*ve polluti *la*bi reatum, *S*ancte *I*ohannes. See GUIDO D'AREZZO]
gamy (gā′mĭ), *adj.*, **gamier, gamiest.** **1.** having the flavour of game, esp. game kept uncooked until slightly high, as preferred by connoisseurs: *the meat had a gamy flavour.* **2.** plucky. Also, **gamey.** —**gam′ily,** *adv.* —**gam′iness,** *n.*
-gamy, **1.** a word element meaning 'marriage', as in *polygamy.* **2.** *Biol.* a word element meaning 'sexual union', as in *allogamy.* [t. Gk: m. s. *-gamia*, der. *-gamos* marrying, married]
gan (găn), *v. Archaic.* began.
ganch (gănch), *Hist.* —*v.t.* **1.** to impale on hooks or stakes as a means of execution. —*n.* **2.** the apparatus of hooks or stakes for ganching people. **3.** punishment by ganching. Also, **gaunch.** [t. F: s. *gancher*, t. It.: m. *ganciare*, der. *gancio* hook]
Gand (*Fr.* gäɴ), *n.* French name of **Ghent.**
Ganda (găn′də), *n.* **1.** a people of Uganda. **2.** a member of this people. **3.** the form of Bantu spoken by this people.
gander (găn′də), *n.* **1.** the male of the goose. **2.** *Slang.* a stupid or foolish man. **3.** *Slang.* a look at something. [ME; OE *gan(d)ra*, c. MLG *ganre*, D *gander*, g. Vernerian var. of Gmc *gans-* goose]
Gander (găn′də), *n.* an airport in NE Newfoundland: formerly much used by transatlantic aircraft as a fuel stop.
Gandhi (găn′dĭ), *n.* **1. Mrs Indira** (ĭn′də rə), born 1917, Indian politician (daughter of Jawaharlal Nehru); prime minister of India since 1966. **2. Mohandas Karamchand** (mō′hən dŭs′ kŭ′rəm chŭnd′), (*Mahatma Gandhi*), 1869–1948, Hindu religious and political leader and social reformer.
Gandhian (găn′dĭ ən), *adj.* of or pertaining to M. K. Gandhi, his beliefs, or his practices.
Gandhi-ism (găn′dĭ ĭz′əm), *n.* the beliefs and practices of M. K. Gandhi, esp. civil disobedience, satyagraha, etc.
Gandzha (*Russ.* gȧnd′zhə), *n.* former name of **Kirovabad.**
gang[1] (găng), *n.* **1.** a band or group: *a gang of boys.* **2.** a group of persons working together; squad; shift: *a gang of labourers.* **3.** a group of persons associated for a particular purpose (used esp. in a contemptuous sense or of disreputable and/or violent persons): *a gang of thieves.* **4.** a set of tools, etc., arranged to work together or simultaneously. [ME and OE; orig. 'a going'; sense of 'group' from OE *gang* in *gangdæg* processional day]
—*v.t.* **5.** to arrange in gangs; form into a gang.
—*v.i.* **6.** *Colloq.* to form or act as a gang. **7.** *Scot.* to walk; go. **8. gang up on,** to attack in a gang; combine against. [ME *gong(e)*, *gang(en)*, OE *gongan*, *gangan*, c. OHG *gangan*] —**Syn. 1.** company, crowd, crew.
gang[2] (găng), *n.* gangue.
gangboard (găng′bôd′), *n. Naut.* a raised narrow walk connecting the forecastle directly with the quarter deck.
gang cultivator, a cultivator having several tines mounted to be operated as a gang.
ganger (găng′ə), *n.* the foreman of a gang of labourers.
Ganges (găn′jēz), *n.* a river flowing from the Himalayas in N India SE to the Bay of Bengal: sacred to the Hindus. ab. 1500 mi.

CHINA
WEST PAKISTAN
HIMALAYAS
East Pakistan
RIVER GANGES
INDIA
Calcutta
BURMA
Bay of Bengal

River Ganges

gang-gang (găng′găng′), *n.* an Australian cockatoo, *Callocephalon fimbriatum.* [t. native Australian]
ganghook (găng′ho͝ok′), *n. Angling.* a hook made by joining back-to-back the shanks of two or three hooks.
ganglia (găng′glĭ ə), *n.* pl. of **ganglion.**
gangliated (găng′glĭ ā′tĭd), *adj.* having ganglia. Also, **gangliate** (găng′glĭ ĭt, -āt′).
gangling (găng′glĭng), *adj.* awkwardly tall and spindly; lank and loosely built. Also, **gan′gly** (găng′glĭ). [akin to obs. *gangrel* gangling person, der. GANG[1]]
ganglion (găng′glĭ ən), *n., pl.* **-glia** (-glĭ ə), **-glions.** **1.** *Anat.* grey matter outside the brain and spinal cord. **2.** *Pathol.* a cyst or enlargement in connection with the sheath of a tendon, usually at the wrist. **3.** a centre of intellectual or industrial force, activity, etc. [t. LL: kind of swelling, t. Gk: tumour under the skin, on or near a tendon] —**ganglionic** (găng′glĭ ŏn′ĭk), *adj.*
ganglionectomy (găng′glĭ ə nĕk′tə mĭ), *n., pl.* **-mies.** *Surg.* the excision of a ganglion.
gangmill (găng′mĭl′), *n.* a sawmill in which several saws fitted in a reciprocating frame cut simultaneously.
gangplank (găng′plăngk′), *n.* a plank, often with cleats, or a long, narrow, flat structure, used as a temporary bridge in passing into and out of a ship, etc.
gang plough, **1.** a plough with several bottoms. **2.** a combination of ploughs in one frame.
gangrene (găng′grēn), *n., v.,* **-grened, -grening.** *Pathol.* —*n.* **1.** the dying of tissue, as from interruption of circulation; mortification. —*v.t., v.i.* **2.** to affect or become affected with gangrene. [t. L: m. s. *gangraena*, t. Gk: m. *gángraina* an eating sore] —**gangrenous** (găng′grĭ nəs), *adj.*
gangsaw (găng′sô′), *n.* one of the several blades fitted in a frame forming part of a gangmill. Also, **framesaw.**
gangster (găng′stə), *n.* a member of a gang of criminals.
gangue (găng), *n.* the stony or earthy minerals occurring with the metallic ore in a vein or deposit. Also, **gang.** [t. F, t. G: m. *Gang* mineral vein, lode]
gangway (găng′wā′), *n.* **1.** a passageway. **2.** *Naut.* **a.** any of various passageways on a ship, as that between the rail and the cabins or houses on the deck. **b.** an opening or removable section of a ship's rail for the gangplank. **c.** a gangplank. **d.** a platform and ladder or stairway slung over the side of a ship. **3.** an aisle in a theatre. **4.** (in the British House of Commons) an aisle separating the seats of the more influential from those of the less influential members of each party. **5.** a temporary path of planks, as at a building site. **6.** *Mining.* a main

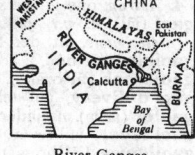

passage or level. **7.** the ramp up which logs are moved into a sawmill; logway. —*interj.* **8.** clear the way! [OE *gangweg*]
Ganis (găn′ĭs), *n.* **Bors de.** See **Bors** (def. 1).
ganister (găn′ĭs tə), *n.* a highly refractory, siliceous rock, used to line furnaces, sometimes artificially made by mixing ground quartz with a bonding material. [orig. uncert.]
ganna (gä′nə), *n. S African.* a chenopodiaceous plant, *Salsola aphylla,* of salt soils of temperate regions; a source of impure carbonate of soda, formerly used by Boers for soap. Also, **kanna.** [t. Afrikaans]
gannet (găn′ĭt), *n.* any of several large pelagic birds of the family *Sulidae,* esp. the common gannet, *Sula bassana,* of the Atlantic coasts of Europe and North America. [ME and OE *ganet,* akin to D *gent* gander]
ganoid (găn′oid), *adj.* **1.** belonging or pertaining to the *Ganoidei,* a group of fishes, many of which have hard, smooth scales, as the sturgeons, etc. **2.** (of fish scales) having a smooth, shining surface. —*n.* **3.** a ganoid fish. [f. s. Gk *gános* brightness + -OID]
gantlet[1] (gănt′lĭt, gônt′-), *n. Now Chiefly U.S.* gauntlet[1].
gantlet[2] (gănt′lĭt, gônt′-), *n., v.t. U.S.* gauntlet[2].
gantline (gănt′līn′, -lĭn), *n. Naut.* a rope temporarily made fast or rove through a block, as for hoisting rigging, raising a man to the rigging, etc. [alter. of *girtline*]
gantry (găn′trĭ), *n., pl.* **-tries. 1.** a spanning framework, as a bridgelike portion of certain cranes, a structure holding railway signals above the tracks, etc. **2.** a frame supporting something, as a missile standing vertical before blast-off. **3.** a simple frame holding a barrel or cask. Also, **gauntry.** [f. *gaun* (contr. of GALLON) + m. *-tree* supporting frame]
Ganymede (găn′ĭ mēd′), *n.* **1.** *Class. Myth.* a Trojan youth carried off (according to one legend, by an eagle) to become cupbearer to Zeus. **2.** *Colloq.* (in humorous use) a young waiter. **3.** *Colloq.* a young male homosexual. **4.** *Astron.* one of the satellites of Jupiter.
gaol (jāl), *n., v.t.* jail. [ME *gay(h)ole, gaile,* t. ONF: m. *gaiole, gaole,* ult. der. L *cavea* cavity, cage]
gaolbird (jāl′bûd′), *n.* jailbird.
gaolbreak (jāl′brāk′), *n.* jailbreak.
gaol delivery, jail delivery.
gaoler (jā′lə), *n.* jailer.
gaol fever, jail fever.
gaolhouse (jāl′hous′), *n., pl.* **-houses** (-hou′zĭz). *U.S.* jail.
gap (găp), *n., v.,* **gapped, gapping.** —*n.* **1.** a break or opening, as in a fence, wall, or the like; breach. **2.** a vacant space or interval. **3.** a wide divergence. **4.** a deep, sloping ravine or cleft cutting a mountain ridge. **5.** *Aeron.* the distance between one supporting plane of an aeroplane and another above or below it. —*v.t.* **6.** to make a gap, opening, or breach in. [ME, t. Scand.; cf. Sw. *gap* opening, chasm, *gapa* GAPE] —**gap′less,** *adj.*
gape (gāp), *v.,* **gaped, gaping,** *n.* —*v.i.* **1.** to open the mouth involuntarily or as the result of hunger, sleepiness, or absorbed attention. **2.** to stare with open mouth, as in wonder. **3.** to open as a gap; split or become open wide. —*n.* **4.** a breach or rent; wide opening. **5.** the act of gaping. **6.** a stare, as with open mouth. **7.** astonishment. **8.** *Zool.* the width of the open mouth. [ME *gapen,* t. Scand.; cf. Icel. and Sw. *gapa* open the mouth, c. G *gaffen*] —**gap′-ingly,** *adv.* —**Syn. 2.** See **gaze.**
gaper (gā′pə), *n.* **1.** one who or that which gapes. **2.** comber.
gapes (gāps), *n.pl.* (*construed as sing.*) **1.** *Vet. Sci.* a disease of poultry and other birds, attended with frequent gaping, due to infestation of the trachea and bronchi with gape-worms. **2.** a fit of yawning.
gapeseed (gāp′sēd′), *n. Now Chiefly Dial.* **1.** the act of staring. **2. seek, buy,** or **sow gapeseed,** to stare open-mouthed.
gapeworm (gāp′wûm′), *n.* a nematode worm, *Syngamus trachea,* which causes gapes.
gap-toothed (găp′tōōtht′), *adj.* having a gap between the teeth, esp. the two incisors of either jaw. Also, **gat-toothed.**
gar[1] (gä), *n., pl.* **gars,** (esp. collectively) **gar. 1.** a sea-water fish, *Rhamphistoma belone,* of the N Atlantic, having both jaws prolonged into a beak. **2.** a predacious fish of the genus *Lepisosteus* (including several species, all of North American fresh waters), covered with very hard diamond-shaped ganoid scales and having a beak armed with large teeth. **3.** needlefish (def. 1). Also, **garfish, garpike.** [short for GARFISH]
gar[2] (gä), *v.t.,* **garred, garring.** *Scot. and N Dial.* to cause; compel; make (someone or something): *ye gar folk look foolish.* [ME (N d.) *gere(n),* t. Scand.; cf. Icel. *gerva,* c. OE *gierwan* prepare]
garage (gă′räzh, gă′rĭj), *n., v.,* **-raged, -raging.** —*n.* **1.** a building for sheltering a motor vehicle or vehicles. **2.** an establishment where motor vehicles are repaired, petrol is sold, etc. —*v.t.* **3.** to put or keep in a garage. [t. F, der. *garer* put in shelter, t. Pr.: m. *garar* keep, heed, t. Gmc; cf. OHG *warōn* heed]
Garamond (gă′rə mŏnd′), *n.* a kind of type designed in 1540 by Claude Garamond, French typefounder.
garb[1] (gäb), *n.* **1.** fashion or mode of dress, esp. of a distinctive kind. **2.** clothes. **3.** covering, semblance, or form. —*v.t.* **4.** to dress; clothe. [t. F: m. *garbe,* t. It.: m. *garbo* grace, t. Gmc; cf. MHG *garwe* GEAR] —**Syn. 2.** dress, costume, attire, apparel, habiliments, garments.
garb[2] (gäb), *n. Her.* a wheatsheaf.
garbage (gä′bĭj), *n.* **1.** refuse animal and vegetable matter. **2.** *Chiefly U.S.* household, esp. kitchen, waste; rubbish; refuse. **3.** anything worthless, undesirable, or unnecessary.
garble (gä′bl), *v.,* **-bled, -bling,** *n.* —*v.t.* **1.** to make unfair or misleading selections from (facts, statements, writings, etc.); corrupt. **2.** to make incomprehensible. **3.** *Obs.* to take out the best of. —*n.* **4.** the process of garbling. [t. It.: m. *garbellare,* t. Ar.: m. *gharbala* sift, ? t. LL: m. *crēbellāre,* der. *cērbellum* little sieve] —**gar′bler,** *n.*
Garbo (gä′bō), *n.* **Greta** (*Greta Louisa Gustafsson*), born 1905, Swedish film actress.
garboard (gä′bôd′), *n. Naut.* the strake of planks laid next to the keel. Also, **garboard strake.** [t. D: m. *gaarboord*]
García Lorca (*Sp.* gȧr thē′ȧ lôr′kȧ), **Federico** (*Sp.* fĕ dĕ rē′kô), 1899–1936, Spanish poet, dramatist, essayist, and theatrical director.
garçon (*Fr.* gȧr sôɴ′), *n., pl.* **-çons** (*Fr.* -sôɴ′). *French.* **1.** a male employee or servant. **2.** a waiter. [F: boy]
Gard (*Fr.* gȧr), *n.* a department in S France. 435,482 pop. (1962); 2271 sq. mi. *Cap.:* Nîmes.
Garda (*It.* gȧr′dȧ), *n.* **Lago di** (*It.* lȧ′gô dē), a lake in N Italy: largest of the Italian lakes. 35 mi. long; 143 sq. mi.
gardant (gä′dənt), *adj. Her.* guardant.
garden (gä′dn), *n.* **1.** a plot of ground devoted to the cultivation of useful or ornamental plants. **2.** a piece of ground, or other space, commonly with ornamental plants, trees, etc., used as a place of recreation: *a botanical garden, a roof garden.* **3.** a fertile and delightful spot or region. —*adj.* **4.** pertaining to or produced in a garden. **5.** (of recent urban developments) deliberately planned so as to have many garden-like open spaces: *a garden city.* **6. lead up the garden path,** *Colloq.* to mislead, hoax, or delude. —*v.i.* **7.** to lay out or cultivate a garden. —*v.t.* **8.** to cultivate as a garden. [ME *gardin,* t. ONF, of Gmc orig.; cf. G *Garten*] —**gar′denless,** *adj.* —**gar′den-like′,** *adj.*
gardener (gäd′nə), *n.* **1.** a person employed to take care of a garden. **2.** one who gardens.
gardenia (gä dē′nyə), *n.* any of the evergreen trees and shrubs of the rubiaceous genus *Gardenia,* native in the warmer parts of the Eastern Hemisphere, including species, as *G. jasminoides,* the Cape jasmine, cultivated for their fragrant, waxlike, white flowers. [NL; named after Dr Alexander *Garden,* 1730–91]
gardening (gäd′nĭng), *n.* **1.** the act of cultivating a garden. **2.** the work or art of a gardener.
Garden of Eden, Eden.
garden party, an afternoon party held on a lawn.
garden warbler, any of various small birds esteemed in Italy as a table delicacy, as the warblers of the family *Sylvidae,* esp. *Sylvia hortensis.*
garderobe (gäd′rōb′), *n. Hist.* **1.** a wardrobe. **2.** a private bedroom. **3.** a latrine; privy. **4.** an armoury.
Gardez (gä′dĕz), *n.* a town in E Afghanistan. 46,000 (est. 1962).
Gardiner (gäd′nə), *n.* **1. Samuel Rawson,** 1829–1902, English historian. **2. Stephen,** 1483–1555, English bishop and statesman.
garefowl (gĕə′foul′), *n.* the great auk. [t. Scand.; cf. Icel. *geir-fugl*]
Gareth (gă′rĕth), *n. Arthurian Legend.* nephew of King Arthur.
Garfield (gä′fēld′), *n.* **James Abram** (ā′brəm), 1831–81, twentieth president of the United States, in 1881.
garfish (gä′fĭsh′), *n., pl.* **-fishes,** (*esp. collectively*) **-fish.** gar[1]. [ME *garfysshe,* f. *gar* (OE *gār* spear) + *fysshe* FISH]
garganey (gä′gə nĭ), *n.* a small Old World species of duck, *Anas querquedula.* [erroneous var. of It. *garganello,* der. Rom. root *garg-* throat]
Gargantua (gä găn′tyōō ə), *n.* the amiable giant and king, of enormous capacity for eating and drinking, in Rabelais' *Gargantua and Pantagruel.*
Gargantuan (gä găn′tyōō ən), *adj.* gigantic; enormous; prodigious.

garget (gäʹgĭt), *n.* *Vet. Sci.* inflammation of the udder of cows, etc., caused by bacteria; mastitis. [ME, t. OF: m. *gargate* throat, perh. orig. a disease of the throat]

gargle (gäʹgl), *v.*, **-gled, -gling,** *n.* **—***v.t.* **1.** to wash or rinse (the throat or mouth) with a liquid held in the throat and kept in motion by a stream of air from the lungs. **—***v.i.* **2.** to gargle the throat or mouth. **—***n.* **3.** any liquid used for gargling. [t. F: m. *gargouiller*, der. *gargouille* throat. Cf. L *gurgulio* gullet]

gargoyle (gäʹgoil), *n.* a spout, often terminating in a grotesque head (animal or human) with open mouth, projecting from the gutter of a building for carrying off rainwater. [ME *gargulye*, t. OF: m. *gargouille*, *gargoule*, appar. the same word as *gargouille* throat. See GARGLE]

Gargoyle

garial (gäʹrĭ əl), *n.* gavial.

garibaldi (găʹrĭ bôlʹdĭ), *n.* **1.** a loose blouse worn by women and children in mid-19th century, made in imitation of the red shirts worn by the soldiers of Garibaldi. **2.** a type of biscuit with dried fruit sandwiched between two thin layers of sweet pastry.

Garibaldi (găʹrĭ bôlʹdĭ; *It.* gȧ rē bälʹdē), *n.*, **Giuseppe** (*It.* jōō zĕpʹ pė), 1807–82, Italian patriot and general. **—Gaʹribalʹdian,** *adj.*, *n.*

garish (gěəʹrĭsh), *adj.* **1.** glaring, or excessively bright. **2.** crudely gay or showy, as dress, etc. **3.** excessively ornate, as structures, writings, etc. [earlier *gaurish*, der. obs. *gaure* stare, freq. of ME *gawe* stare] **—gaʹrishly,** *adv.* **—gaʹrishness,** *n.* **—Syn. 2.** See **gaudy**[1].

garland (gäʹlənd), *n.* **1.** a wreath or string of flowers, leaves, or other material, worn for ornament or as an honour, or hung on something as a decoration. **2.** a representation of such a wreath or festoon. **3.** a collection of short literary pieces, usually poems and ballads; a miscellany. **4.** *Naut.* a band, collar, or grummet, as of rope, for various purposes. **—***v.t.* **5.** to crown with a garland; deck with garlands. [ME *garlande*, t. OF] **—garʹlandless,** *adj.* **—garʹland-likeʹ,** *adj.*

garlic (gäʹlĭk), *n.* **1.** a hardy liliaceous plant, *Allium sativum*, whose strong-scented pungent bulb is used in cookery and medicine. **2.** any of various other species of the same genus. **3.** the bulb of any such plant. **—***adj.* **4.** seasoned with or containing garlic. [ME *garlec*, OE *gārlēac*, f. *gār* spear + *lēac* leek]

garlicky (gäʹlĭ kĭ), *adj.* like or containing garlic.

garlic mustard, a biennial cruciferous herb, *Alliaria petiolata*, with a strong-smelling root and small white flowers, widespread in shady places throughout N temperate regions.

Garm (gäm), *n.* *Scand. Myth.* the dog that guards the entrance to Niflheim.

garment (gäʹmənt), *n.* **1.** any article of clothing. **2.** outer covering; outward appearance. **—***v.t.* **3.** to clothe. [ME, t. OF: m. *garnement*, der. *garnir* equip. See GARNISH] **—garʹmentless,** *adj.*

garner (gäʹnə), *v.t.* **1.** to collect or deposit in or as in a garner; hoard. **—***n.* **2.** a granary. **3.** a store of anything. [ME, t. OF: m. *gernier*, *grenier*, g. L *grānārium* GRANARY]

garnet[1] (gäʹnĭt), *n.* **1.** any of a group of hard, vitreous minerals, silicates of calcium, magnesium, iron, or manganese with aluminium or iron, varying in colour. A deep red transparent variety is used as a gem and as an abrasive (**garnet paper**). **2.** deep red, as of a garnet. [ME *gernet*, t. OF: m. *grenat*, t. ML: m. s. *grānātum* garnet, also pomegranate, prop. neut. of *grānātus* having grains or seeds] **—garʹnet-likeʹ,** *adj.*

garnet[2] (gäʹnĭt), *n.* *Naut.* a form of hoisting tackle. [orig. uncert. Cf. D *granaat*]

Garnett (gäʹnĭt), *n.* **Constance,** 1862–1946, English translator from Russian.

Garnier (*Fr.* gȧr nyėʹ), *n.* **1. Charles,** 1825–98, French architect. **2.** his son, **Tony,** 1869–1948, French architect.

garnierite (gäʹnĭ ə rītʹ), *n.* a mineral, hydrous nickel magnesium silicate, occurring in earthy, green masses: an important ore of nickel. [named after Jules *Garnier*, French geologist. See -ITE[1]]

garnish (gäʹnĭsh), *v.t.* **1.** to fit out with something that adorns or decorates. **2.** to decorate (a dish) for the table. **3.** *Law.* **a.** to warn; give notice. **b.** *Obs.* to summon as party to litigation already pending between others. **c.** to attach, as money due or property belonging to a debtor, while it is in the hands of a third person, by warning the latter not to pay it over or surrender it. **4.** *Slang.* to exact money from. **—***n.* **5.** something placed round or added to a dish for decorative effect or relish. **6.** adornment or decoration. **7.** *Slang.* money extracted from a prisoner or worker by his fellow prisoners, boss, etc . [ME *garnisshe(n)*, t. OF: m. *garniss-*, s. *garnir* prepare, WARN; of Gmc orig.] **—garʹnisher,** *n.* **—Syn. 1.** embellish, ornament, beautify, trim.

garnishee (gäʹnĭ shēʹ), *v.*, **-sheed, -sheeing,** *n.* *Law.* **—***v.t.* **1.** to attach (money or property) by garnishment. **2.** to make (a person) a garnishee. **—***n.* **3.** a person served with a garnishment.

garnishment (gäʹnĭsh mənt), *n.* **1.** adornment; decoration. **2.** *Law.* **a.** a warning or notice. **b.** a summons to appear in litigation pending between others. **c.** a warning served on a person, at the suit of a creditor plaintiff, to hold, subject to the court's direction, money or property of the defendant in his possession.

garniture (gäʹnĭ chə), *n.* anything that garnishes; decoration; adornment. [t. F, der. *garnir*. See GARNISH]

Garonne (*Fr.* gȧ rŏnʹ), *n.* a river in SW France, flowing from the Pyrenees NW to the Gironde. ab. 350 mi.

garotte (gə rŏtʹ), *n.*, *v.t.*, **-rotted, -rotting.** garrotte.

garpike (gäʹpīkʹ), *n.* gar[1].

garret (găʹrĭt), *n.* attic (def. 1). [ME *garite*, t. OF: watchtower, der. *garix* defend. See GARRISON]

garreteer (găʹrĭ tĭəʹ), *n.* a person living in a garret, esp. a literary hack.

Garrick (găʹrĭk), *n.* **David,** 1717–79, English actor and theatrical manager.

garrison (găʹrĭ sən), *n.* **1.** a body of troops stationed in a fortified place. **2.** the place where they are stationed. **—***v.t.* **3.** to provide (a fort, town, etc.) with a garrison. **4.** to occupy (a fort, post, station, etc.). **5.** to put on duty in a fort, post, station, etc. [ME *garison*, t. OF: defence, der. *garir* defend, of Gmc orig.]

Garrison (găʹrĭ sən), *n.* **William Lloyd,** 1805–79, U.S. leader in the abolition movement.

garrison town, a town in which a garrison is stationed.

garron (găʹrən), *n.* a small and inferior kind of horse, bred and used chiefly in Ireland and Scotland. [t. Gaelic: m. *gearran*]

garrot (găʹrət), *n.* the goldeneye (duck). [t. F]

garrotte (gə rŏtʹ), *n.*, *v.*, **-rotted, -rotting.** **—***n.* **1.** a Spanish mode of capital punishment, orig. by means of an instrument causing death by strangulation, later by one injuring the spinal column at the base of the brain. **2.** the instrument used. **3.** strangulation or throttling, esp. for the purpose of robbery. **—***v.t.* **4.** to execute by the garrotte. **5.** to throttle, esp. for the purpose of robbery. Also, **garotte, garrote.** [t. Sp.: orig. a stick (formerly used in drawing a cord tight), t. Pr.: m. *garrot* cudgel, stick for twisting a cord tight, der. Celtic *garra* leg] **—garrottʹer,** *n.*

garrulity (gă rōōʹlĭ tĭ), *n.* the quality of being garrulous; talkativeness; loquacity.

garrulous (găʹrōō ləs), *adj.* **1.** given to much talking, esp. about trifles. **2.** wordy or diffuse, as speech. [t. L: m. *garrulus* talkative] **—garʹrulously,** *adv.* **—garʹrulousness,** *n.* **—Syn. 1.** See **talkative.**

garter (gäʹtə), *n.* **1.** a fastening, often in the form of a band passing round the leg, to keep up the stocking. **2.** the badge of the **Order of the Garter,** the highest English order of knighthood, founded in 1348. **3.** membership of the order. **4.** (*cap.*) the order itself. **—***v.t.* **5.** to fasten with a garter. [ME, t. ONF: m. *gartier*, der. *garet* the bend of the knee, der. Celtic *garra* leg]

garter belt, *U.S.* a suspender belt.

garter snake, *U.S.* any of various harmless snakes of the genus *Thamnophis*, usually with three light stripes on body and tail.

garter stitch, 1. a plain stitch in knitting. **2.** the pattern produced by this.

garth (gäth), *n.* **1.** the open court enclosed by a cloister (in full, **cloister-garth**). **2.** *Archaic or Dial.* a yard or garden. [ME, t. Scand.; cf. Icel. *gardhr*, c. YARD[2]]

Gary (gěəʹrĭ, găʹrĭ), *n.* a town in the U.S., in NW Indiana: a port on Lake Michigan. 178,320 (1960).

gas[1] (găs), *n.*, *pl.* **gases,** *v.*, **gassed, gassing.** **—***n.* **1.** *Physics.* a substance consisting of atoms or molecules which are sufficiently mobile for it to occupy the whole of the space in which it is contained. **2.** any such fluid substance or mixture of substances, other than air. **3.** any such fluid substance used as a fuel for heating or lighting, esp. coal gas or natural gas. **4.** any such fluid substance or mixture of substances used as an anaesthetic. **5.** *Coal-Mining.* an explosive mixture of firedamp with air. **6.** an aeriform fluid, or a mistlike assemblage of fine particles suspended in air, used in warfare to asphyxiate, poison, or stupefy the enemy. **7.** *Slang.* empty talk. **—***v.t.* **8.** to supply with gas. **9.** to affect, overcome, or asphyxiate with gas or fumes. **10.** to singe (yarns or fabrics) with a gas flame to remove superfluous fibres. **11.** to treat or impregnate with gas. **12.** *Slang.* to talk nonsense or speak boastfully to. **—***v.i.* **13.** to give off gas, as a storage battery being charged. **14.** *Slang.* to indulge in empty talk idly. [coined by J. B.

van Helmont, 1577–1644, Flemish chemist; suggested by Gk *cháos* chaos] —**gas′less,** *adj.*

gas² (găs), *n. Chiefly U.S. Colloq.* **1.** petrol. **2.** the accelerator pedal in a motor vehicle. **3. step on the gas,** to hurry. [shortened form of GASOLINE]

gas attack, an attack in which asphyxiating or poisonous gases are employed, as by liberating the gases, and allowing the wind to carry the fumes, or by gas shells.

gasbag (găs′băg′), *n.* **1.** a bag for holding gas, as in a balloon or dirigible. **2.** *Slang.* an empty, voluble talker; a windbag.

gas barrel, wrought-iron tubes or pipes, originally used exclusively for distributing gas from the mains, now used for a variety of purposes.

gas black, the soot of a natural gas flame, used in paints; fine carbon.

gas bracket, a gas pipe with burners projecting from a wall.

gas burner, the tip, jet, or end piece of a gas fixture, from which the gas issues to be ignited.

gas carbon, a hard deposit of almost pure carbon which forms inside coal-gas retorts: used for making carbon electrodes.

gas chamber, an airtight room in which animals or human beings are killed by means of a poisonous gas. Also, **gas oven.**

gas chromatography, *Chem.* a very sensitive method of analysing a complex mixture of volatile substances, which depends on the relative speeds with which the various components of the mixture pass through a long, narrow tube packed with an inert material which can be coated with a non-volatile liquid.

gas coal, a soft coal suitable for making gas.

Gascoigne (găs′koin), *n.* **George,** *c.* 1525–77, English poet and dramatist.

Gascon (găs′kən), *n.* **1.** a native of Gascony, the inhabitants of which were noted for their boastfulness. **2.** (*l.c.*) a boaster or braggart. —*adj.* **3.** pertaining to Gascony and its people. [t. F, g. s. L *Vasco* Basque]

gasconade (găs′kə nād′), *n.*, *v.*, **-naded, -nading.** —*n.* **1.** extravagant boasting; boastful talk. —*v.i.* **2.** to boast extravagantly; bluster. [t. F: m. *gasconnade*, der. *gascon* GASCON]

gas constant, *Physics.* the constant, R, in the gas laws; its value is 1·987 calories per degree centigrade per gram molecule.

Gascony (găs′kə nĭ), *n.* a former province in SW France. French, **Gascogne** (*Fr.* gȧs kōny′).

Gascony

gas cooker, a stove for cooking by gas.

Gascoyne (găs′koin), *n.* a river in Australia flowing W through Western Australia to the Indian Ocean. Course ab. 510 mi.

gas engine, an internal-combustion engine which is driven by a mixture of gas and air.

gaseous (găs′ĭ əs), *adj.* having the nature of, in the form of, or pertaining to gas. —**gas′eousness,** *n.*

gas field, a region in which natural gas occurs.

gas fire, a fire in which heat is supplied by gas.

gas-fired (găs′fī′əd), *adj.* fuelled or heated by gas.

gas fitter, a person who installs gas pipes and gas-operated equipment.

gas fitting, **1.** the work or business of a gas fitter. **2.** (*pl.*) fittings for the employment of gas for illuminating and heating purposes.

gas fixture, a permanent fixture attached to a gas pipe in the ceiling or wall of a room, as a more or less ornamental pipe (without or with branches) bearing a burner (or burners) and regulating devices.

gas gangrene, a gangrenous infection developing in wounds, esp. deep wounds with closed spaces, due to bacteria which form gases in the subcutaneous tissues.

gash (găsh), *n.* **1.** a long, deep wound or cut, esp. in the flesh; a slash. —*v.t.* **2.** to make a long, deep cut in; slash. [earlier *garsh*, t. ONF: m. s. *garser* scarify]

gas helmet, *Mil.* a type of gasmask.

gas-holder (găs′hōl′də), *n.* a gasometer.

gasiform (găs′ĭ fôm′), *adj.* gaseous.

gasify (găs′ĭ fī′), *v.t.*, *v.i.*, **-fied, -fying.** to convert into or become a gas. —**gas′ifica′tion,** *n.*

gas jet, gas burner.

Gaskell (găs′kl), *n.* **Mrs** (*Elizabeth Cleghorn Stevenson Gaskell*), 1810–65, English novelist.

gasket (găs′kĭt), *n.* **1.** anything used as a packing or jointing material for making joints fluid-tight. **2.** a suitably punched asbestos sheet, usually sandwiched between thin sheets of copper, for making a gastight joint, esp. between the cylinder block and the cylinder head of an internal-combustion engine. **3.** *Naut.* one of several bands or lines used to bind a furled sail to a yard, etc. [orig. uncert. Cf. It. *gassetta* gasket]

gaskin (găs′kĭn), *n.* that part of a horse's hind leg from knee to hip joint; the second thigh. See illus. under **horse.**

gas lamp, a lamp in which the illumination is provided by the burning of gas.

gas laws, *Physics*, *Chem.* laws, esp. Boyle's law and Charles's law, which relate the pressure, volume, and temperature of a gas. The combined ideal gas law states that for 1 gram molecule of an ideal gas the product of the pressure and the volume is equal to the product of the absolute temperature and a universal constant known as the **gas constant** (which has the value 1·987 calories per degree centigrade).

gaslight (găs′līt′), *n.* **1.** light produced by the combustion of illuminating gas. **2.** a gas burner.

gas main, a large pipe for distributing gas from the gasworks to industrial or domestic consumers.

gasman (găs′măn′), *n.* **1.** a man who works for a gas undertaking, esp. one who reads household gas meters. **2.** a gas fitter.

gas mantle, a chemically prepared, incombustible network hood for a gas jet which, when the jet is lit, becomes incandescent and gives a brilliant light.

gas maser, *Physics.* a maser in which microwave radiation interacts with gas molecules.

gasmask (găs′mäsk′), *n.* a masklike device worn to protect against noxious gases, fumes, etc., as in warfare or in certain industries, the air inhaled by the wearer being filtered through charcoal and chemicals.

gas meter, an apparatus for measuring and recording the amount of gas produced or consumed.

gas oil, the oil which remains after petrol and paraffin have been distilled from crude petroleum; used as a fuel for diesel engines and for carburetting water gas. Also, **diesel oil.**

gasolier (găs′ə lĭə′), *n.* a chandelier for gas lamps. [f. GAS + -O- + *-lier* in CHANDELIER]

gasoline (găs′ə lēn′), *n. U.S.* petrol. Also, **gas′olene′.** [f. GAS + -OL² + -INE²]

gasometer (gă sŏm′ĭ tə), *n.* **1.** a large tank or reservoir for storing gas, esp. at a gasworks. **2.** a laboratory apparatus for measuring or storing gas. Also, **gas-holder.** —**gas′omet′ric, gas′omet′rical,** *adj.* [t. F: m. *gazomètre*. See GAS METER]

gas oven, **1.** a gas cooker. **2.** a gas chamber.

gasp (gäsp), *n.* **1.** a sudden, short breath; convulsive effort to breathe. **2.** a short, convulsive utterance, esp. as a result of fear or surprise. —*v.i.* **3.** to catch the breath, or struggle for breath, with open mouth, as from exhaustion; breathe convulsively. **4.** to long with breathless eagerness; desire; crave (fol. by *for* or *after*). —*v.t.* **5.** to utter with gasps (often fol. by *out*, *forth*, *away*, etc.). **6.** to breathe or emit with gasps (often fol. by *away*). [ME *gaspe(n)*, *gayspe(n)*, t. Scand.; cf. Icel. *geispa*, metathetic var. of *geipsa* yawn; akin to OE *gipian* yawn, *gipung* open mouth] —**Syn. 3.** See **pant.**

Gaspé Peninsula (găs′pā; *Fr.* gȧs pē′), a peninsula in SE Canada, in Quebec province, between New Brunswick and the St Lawrence.

gasper (găs′pə), *n.* **1.** *Slang.* a cigarette. **2.** one who or that which gasps.

gas pipe, a pipe for conveying gas.

gas range, *U.S.* a gas cooker.

gas ring, a hollow iron ring with perforations or jets supplied with gas under pressure, used for cooking.

Gassendi (*Fr.* gȧ säɴ dē′), *n.* **Pierre** (*Fr.* pyĕr), 1592–1655, French philosopher and scientist.

gasser (găs′ə), *n.* **1.** one who or that which gasses. **2.** a well or boring yielding natural gas.

gas shell, *Mil.* an explosive shell containing a liquid or other material which, when the shell bursts, is converted into an asphyxiating or poisonous gas or vapour.

gassing (găs′ĭng), *n.* **1.** the act of one who or that which gasses. **2.** an affecting or overcoming with gas or fumes, as in battle. **3.** the evolution of gases during electrolysis. **4.** a process by which a material is gassed.

gas stove, a gas cooker.

gassy (găs′ĭ), *adj.*, **-sier, -siest.** **1.** full of or containing gas. **2.** like gas. **3.** *Slang.* characterized by gas or empty talk; given to gassing. —**gas′siness,** *n.*

gastero-, var. of **gastro-.**

gasteropod (găs′tə rə pŏd′, -trə pŏd′), *n.* gastropod.

gas thermometer, a device for measuring temperature by observing the change in either pressure or volume of an enclosed gas.

gastight (găs′tīt′), *adj.* **1.** not penetrable by a gas. **2.** not admitting a given gas under a given pressure.

gastr-, var. of **gastro-,** before vowels, as in *gastralgia.*

gastralgia (găs trăl′jĭ ə), *n. Pathol.* **1.** neuralgia of the stomach. **2.** any stomach pain. [f. GASTR- + -ALGIA]

gastrectomy (găs trĕk′tə mĭ), *n., pl.* **-mies.** *Surg.* the excision of the stomach.

gastric (găs′trĭk), *adj.* pertaining to the stomach.

gastric juice, *Biochem.* the digestive fluid secreted by the glands of the stomach, and containing pepsin and other enzymes.

gastric ulcer, *Pathol.* an erosion of the stomach's inner wall.

gastrin (găs′trĭn), *n. Biochem.* a hormone found in extracts of the pyloric mucosa which stimulates secretion by the gastric glands.

gastritis (găs trī′tĭs), *n. Pathol.* inflammation of the stomach, esp. of its mucous membrane. [f. GASTR- + -ITIS] —**gastritic** (găs trĭt′ĭk), *adj.*

gastro-, a word element meaning 'stomach', as in *gastropod, gastrology*. Also, **gastero-, gastr-.** [t. Gk, comb. form of *gastḗr*]

gastroenteritis (găs′trō ĕn′tə rī′tĭs), *n. Pathol.* inflammation of the stomach and intestines. [f. GASTRO- + ENTER(O)- + -ITIS]

gastroentero-, a combining form meaning 'gastric and enteric', as in *gastroenterology*. [f. GASTRO- + ENTERO-]

gastroenterology (găs′trō ĕn′tə rŏl′ə jĭ), *n.* the study of the structure and diseases of digestive organs.

gastroenterostomy (găs′trō ĕn′tə rŏs′tə mĭ), *n., pl.* **-mies.** *Surg.* the making of a new opening between the stomach and the small intestine.

gastrolith (găs′trə lĭth), *n. Pathol.* a calculus or stony concretion in the stomach.

gastrology (găs trŏl′ə jĭ), *n.* **1.** the study of the structure, functions, and diseases of the stomach. **2.** cookery or good eating. —**gastrol′oger,** *n.* —**gastrological** (găs′trə lŏj′ĭ kl), *adj.*

gastronome (găs′trə nōm′), *n.* a gourmet; epicure. Also, **gastronomer** (găs trŏn′ə mə). [t. F, der. *gastronomie* GASTRONOMY]

gastronomy (găs trŏn′ə mĭ), *n.* the art or science of good eating. [t. F: m. *gastronomie,* t. Gk: m. s. *gastronomía*] —**gastronomic** (găs′trə nŏm′ĭk), **gas′tronom′ical,** *adj.* —**gas′tronom′ically,** *adv.* —**gastron′omist,** *n.*

gastropod (găs′trə pŏd′), *n.* any of the *Gastropoda,* a class of molluscs comprising the snails, having a shell of a single valve, usually spirally coiled, and a ventral muscular foot on which they glide about. Also, **gasteropod.** [t. NL: s. *Gastropoda,* pl. See GASTRO-, -POD]

gastroscope (găs′trə skōp′), *n. Med.* an instrument for direct visual inspection of the interior of the stomach. —**gastroscopic** (găs′trə skŏp′ĭk), *adj.*

gastroscopy (găs trŏs′kə pĭ), *n. Med.* examination with a gastroscope to detect disease.

gastrostomy (găs trŏs′tə mĭ), *n., pl.* **-mies.** *Surg.* the operation of cutting into the stomach and leaving a more or less permanent opening for feeding or drainage.

gastrotomy (găs trŏt′ə mĭ), *n., pl.* **-mies.** *Surg.* the operation of cutting into the stomach.

gastrotrich (găs′trə trĭk′), *n.* one of the microscopic multicellular worms belonging to the *Gastrotricha,* having bands of cilia on the ventral side of the body.

gastrovascular (găs′trō văs′kyŏŏ lə), *adj. Zool.* serving for digestion and circulation, as a cavity.

gastrula (găs′trŏŏ lə), *n., pl.* **-lae** (-lē′). *Embryol.* the developing embryo when it consists of the three germ layers, occupying their characteristic positions. [NL, dim. of Gk *gastḗr* belly, stomach] —**gas′trular,** *adj.*

gastrulate (găs′trŏŏ lāt′), *v.i.,* **-lated, -lating.** *Embryol.* to undergo gastrulation.

gastrulation (găs′trŏŏ lā′shən), *n. Embryol.* **1.** the formation of a gastrula. **2.** any process (as that of invagination) by which a blastula or other form of embryo is converted into a gastrula.

gas turbine. See **turbine** (def. 2).

gas well, a well which yields natural gas rather than oil.

gasworks (găs′wûks′), *n.* an industrial plant which produces coal gas or any other type of heating or illuminating gas, as well as the other by-products of coal gasification.

gat[1] (găt), *v. Archaic.* pt. of **get.**

gat[2] (găt), *n.* an opening between sandbanks; a strait.

gat[3] (găt), *n. Slang.* a gun, pistol, or revolver. [shortened form of GATLING GUN]

gate[1] (gāt), *n., v.,* **gated, gating.** —*n.* **1.** the movable barrier, as a swinging frame, often of openwork, in a fence or wall, or to close any passageway. **2.** an opening for passage into an enclosure such as a fenced yard or walled city. **3.** a structure built about such an opening and containing the barrier. **4.** any narrow means of access or entrance. **5.** a mountain pass or gap, esp. one on a political boundary. **6.** a device for regulating the passage of water, steam, or the like, as in a dam, pipe, etc.; valve. **7.** a starting gate. **8.** the number of persons who pay for admission to an athletic contest or other exhibition. **9.** gate money. **10.** payment at a tollgate. **11.** *Motor Vehicles.* the H-shaped arrangement of slots controlling the movement of a gearlever. **12.** a sash or frame for a saw or gang of saws. **13.** *Elect.* an electronic circuit which controls the passage of information signals according to the state of one or more control signals. **14.** *Foundry.* a channel or opening in a mould through which molten metal enters the mould cavity to form a casting. —*v.t.* **15.** to punish by restricting (a student) within the college or school gates. [ME *gat, gate,* OE *gatu* gates, pl. of *geat* opening in a wall, c. LG and D *gat* hole, breach] —**gate′less,** *adj.* —**gate′like′,** *adj.* —**gate′man,** *n.*

gate[2] (gāt), *n. Archaic.* a way, road, or path.

gateau (găt′ō), *n., pl.* **-teaux** (-tōz, -tō). an elaborate cake or dessert having a base of sponge, biscuit, or pastry, on top of which fruit, jelly, cream, etc., are added as garnish. Also, *French,* **gâteau** (*Fr.* gȧ tō′). [t. F: *gâteau* cake]

gatecrash (gāt′krăsh′), *v.t. Colloq.* to attend (a party) uninvited, or to attend (a public entertainment, etc.) without a ticket. —**gate′crash′er,** *n.*

gatehouse (gāt′hous′), *n.* **1.** a house at or over a gate, used as the keeper's quarters, a fortification, etc. **2.** valve house.

gatekeeper (gāt′kē′pə), *n.* one in charge of a gate.

gate-leg table (gāt′lĕg′), a table having drop leaves which are supported when open by legs which swing out and are usually connected by crosspieces. Also, **gate-legged table.**

gate money, the receipts taken for admission to an athletic contest or other exhibition.

gatepost (gāt′pōst′), *n.* the post on which a gate is hung, or the one against which it is closed.

Gateshead (gāts′hĕd′), *n.* a seaport in England, in N Durham, on the Tyne opposite Newcastle. 101,760 (est. 1964).

gateway (gāt′wā′), *n.* **1.** a passage or entrance which is closed or may be closed by a gate. **2.** a frame or arch in which a gate is hung; structure built at or over a gate. **3.** any means of entering or leaving a place.

gather (găth′ə), *v.t.* **1.** to bring (persons, animals, or things) together into one company or aggregate. **2.** to get together from various places or sources; collect gradually. **3.** to learn or infer from observation: *I gather that he'll be leaving.* **4.** to pick (any crop or natural yield) from its place of growth or formation: *to gather grain, fruit, or flowers.* **5.** to wrap or draw around or close to someone or something: *to gather a person into one's arms.* **6.** to pick up piece by piece. **7.** to attract: *to gather a crowd.* **8.** to take by selection from among other things; sort out; cull. **9.** to assemble or collect (one's energies or oneself) as for an effort (often fol. by *up*). **10.** to contract (the brow) into wrinkles. **11.** to draw up (cloth) on a thread in fine folds or puckers by running a thread through. **12.** *Bookbinding.* to assemble (the printed sheets of a book) in their proper sequence to be bound. **13.** to increase (speed, etc.) as a moving vehicle. **14.** *Naut.* to gain (way) from a dead stop or extremely slow speed. —*v.i.* **15.** to come together or assemble: *to gather round a fire, to gather in crowds.* **16.** to collect or accumulate. **17.** to grow as by accretion; increase. **18.** to come to a head, as a sore in suppurating. **19. to be gathered to one's fathers,** to die. —*n.* **20.** a drawing together; contraction. **21.** (*usually pl.*) a fold or pucker in gathered cloth, etc. [ME *gader(en),* OE *gaderian,* der. *geador* together, akin to *gæd* fellowship. Cf. TOGETHER, GOOD] —**gath′erable,** *adj.* —**gath′erer,** *n.*

—**Syn. 2.** GATHER, ASSEMBLE, COLLECT, MUSTER, MARSHAL imply bringing or drawing together. GATHER expresses the general idea usually with no implication of arrangement: *to gather seashells.* ASSEMBLE is used of objects or facts brought together preparatory to arranging them: *to assemble data for a report.* COLLECT implies purposeful accumulation to form an ordered whole: *to collect evidence.* MUSTER, primarily a military term, suggests thoroughness in the process of collection: *to muster all his resources.* MARSHAL, another term primarily military, suggests rigorously ordered, purposeful arrangement: *to marshal facts for effective presentation.* **3.** deduce, conclude, assume. **4.** pluck, crop, reap, glean, garner, harvest. —**Ant. 1.** disperse.

gathering (găth′ə rĭng), *n.* **1.** the act of one who or that which gathers. **2.** that which is gathered together. **3.** an assembly or meeting; a crowd. **4.** a collection or assemblage of anything. **5.** an inflamed and suppurating swelling. **6.** a gather or series of gathers in cloth. **7.** *Bookbinding.* a section in a book, usually a sheet cut into several leaves. —**Syn. 3.** assemblage, assembly, convocation, congregation, concourse, company, throng. **5.** boil, abscess.

gating signal, a signal which controls the passage of other signals by means of an electronic gate.

Gatling gun (găt′lĭng), an early type of machine gun consisting of a revolving cluster of barrels round a central axis, each barrel being automatically loaded and fired during every revolution of the cluster. [named after R. J. *Gatling*, 1818–1903, American inventor]

G.A.T.T., General Agreement on Tariffs and Trade.

gat-toothed (găt′tōōtht′), *adj.* gap-toothed.

Gatún (*Sp.* gä tōōn′), *n.* **1.** a town in the N Panama Canal Zone. 2477 (1950). **2.** a dam near this town. 1½ mi. long.

Gatún Lake, an artificial lake in the Canal Zone, part of the Panama Canal, created by Gatún dam. 164 sq. mi. See map under **Panama.**

Gatwick Airport (găt′wĭk′), an airport in Surrey, serving London.

gauche (gōsh), *adj.* awkward; clumsy; tactless: *her apology was as gauche as if she had been a schoolgirl.* [t. F. See GAUCHERIE]

gaucherie (gō′shə rĭ; *Fr.* gōsh rē′), *n.* **1.** awkwardness; clumsiness; tactlessness. **2.** an awkward or tactless movement, act, etc. [t. F, der. *gauche* awkward, lit., left (hand)]

gaucho (gou′chō; *Sp.* gäw′chō), *n., pl.* **-chos** (-chōz; *Sp.* -chōs), a native cowboy of the South American pampas, of mixed Spanish and Indian descent. [t. Sp.]

gaud (gôd), *n.* a showy ornament. [ME *gaude,* ? t. AF, der. *gaudir* rejoice, jest, t. L: m. *gaudēre*]

gaudery (gô′də rĭ), *n., pl.* **-ries. 1.** ostentatious show. **2.** finery; fine or showy things: *she stood in the doorway resplendent in her gaudery.*

Gaudí (*Sp.* gäw dē′), *n.* **Antonio,** 1852–1926, Spanish architect.

gaudy[1] (gô′dĭ), *adj.*, **-dier, -diest. 1.** brilliant; excessively showy. **2.** showy without taste; vulgarly showy; flashy. [orig. attributive use of GAUDY[2] large bead of rosary, feast; later taken as der. GAUD, n.] **—gaud′ily,** *adv.* **—gaud′iness,** *n.*

—Syn. 2. tawdry. GAUDY, FLASHY, GARISH, SHOWY agree in the idea of conspicuousness and, often, bad taste. That which is GAUDY challenges the eye, as by brilliant colours or evident cost, and is not in good taste: *a gaudy hat.* FLASHY suggests insistent and vulgar display, in rather a sporty manner: *a flashy tie.* GARISH suggests a glaring brightness, or crude vividness of colour, and too much ornamentation: *garish decorations.* SHOWY applies to that which is strikingly conspicuous, but not necessarily offensive to good taste: *a garden of showy flowers, a showy dress.* **—Ant. 2.** modest, sober.

gaudy[2] (gô′dĭ), *n., pl.* **-dies.** a festival or merrymaking, esp. an annual college feast. [ME, t. L: m. s. *gaudium* joy]

gauffer (gō′fə), *n., v.t.* goffer.

gauge (gāj), *v.*, **gauged, gauging,** *n.* **—*v.t.* 1.** to appraise, estimate, or judge. **2.** to determine the dimensions, capacity, quantity, or force of; measure, as with a gauge. **3.** to make conformable to a standard. **4.** *Plastering.* to prepare (plaster) in a certain gauge, as for hardness. **5.** to cut or rub (bricks or stones) to a uniform size or shape. **6.** to mark off or set out (a measurement, or measured distance). **7.** to gather (cloth). **—*n.* 8.** a standard of measure; standard dimension or quantity. **9.** a means of estimating or judging; criterion; test. **10.** extent; scope; capacity. **11.** any instrument for measuring pressure, volume, or dimensions, as a pressure gauge, micrometer gauge, etc. **12.** *Ordn.* the internal diameter of a gun bore. **13.** the thickness or diameter of various (usually thin) objects. **14.** the distance between the rails in a railway system. In most countries the **standard gauge** is 4 feet 8½ inches; **broad gauge** is wider, and **narrow gauge** narrower, than this. **15.** the position of one ship with reference to another and to the wind. **16.** *Plastering.* the quantity of plaster of Paris mixed with common plaster to accelerate its setting. Also, **gage.** [late ME, t. ONF: m. s. *gauger,* ult. der. *gal-* measuring rod; of Celtic orig.] **—gauge′able,** *adj.*

gauge pressure, the pressure as indicated by a pressure gauge; i.e., the extent to which the pressure being measured exceeds the pressure of the atmosphere (opposed to *absolute pressure.* See **absolute** (def. 8c).

gauger (gā′jə), *n.* **1.** one who or that which gauges. **2.** an exciseman. Also, **gager.**

Gauguin (*Fr.* gō găɴ′), *n.* **Paul** (*Fr.* pōl), 1848–1903, French painter.

Gauhati (gou hä′tĭ), *n.* a town in India, in NW Assam. 100,707 (1961).

Gaul (gôl), *n.* **1.** a vast ancient region in W Europe, including what is now N Italy, France, Belgium, and parts of the Netherlands, Germany, and Switzerland: divided by the Alps into **Cisalpine Gaul** (N Italy) and **Transalpine Gaul. 2.** an inhabitant of this country. **3.** a Frenchman. [t. F: m. *Gaule,* t. Gmc (cf. OHG *walh* foreigner, esp. Gaul), b. with L *Gallus, Gallia* Gaul]

Gauleiter (*Ger.* gou′lī tər), *n.* a Nazi official, head of one of the former political districts of Germany.

Gaulish (gô′lĭsh), *n.* **1.** the extinct language of ancient Gaul, a Celtic language. **—*adj.* 2.** of or pertaining to Gaul, its inhabitants, or their language.

Gaullism (gō′lĭz′əm, gô′-), *n.* **1.** a French political movement led by Charles de Gaulle. **2.** the principles and policies of this movement.

Gaullist (gō′lĭst, gô′lĭst), *n.* **1.** a supporter of Gaullism. **2.** a Frenchman who, during World War II, supported de Gaulle in his opposition to the German occupation of France.

gaultheria (gôl thĭə′rĭ ə), *n.* any of the aromatic evergreen shrubs constituting the ericaceous genus *Gaultheria,* as *G. procumbens,* the American wintergreen. [NL; named after J. F. *Gaultier,* d. 1756, Canadian botanist]

gaunch (gônch), *v.t., n. Hist.* ganch.

gaunt (gônt), *adj.* **1.** abnormally thin; emaciated; haggard. **2.** bleak, desolate, or grim, as places or things. [ME, t. d. F: m. *gaunet* yellowish] **—gaunt′ly,** *adv.* **—gaunt′ness,** *n.* **—Syn. 1.** lean, spare, scraggy, lank; angular, bony, raw-boned. See **thin. —Ant. 1.** stout.

Gaunt (gônt), *n.* **John of** (*Duke of Lancaster*), 1340–99, English soldier and statesman; fourth son of Edward III and founder of the royal house of Lancaster (his son became Henry IV).

gauntlet[1] (gônt′lĭt), *n.* **1.** a medieval glove, as of mail or plate, to protect the hand. See illus. under **armour. 2.** a glove with a cuff-like extension for the wrist. **3.** the cuff itself. **4. take up the gauntlet,** to accept a challenge, orig. to a duel. **5. throw down the gauntlet,** to extend a challenge, orig. to a duel. Also, **gantlet.** [ME, t. OF: m. *gantelet,* dim. of *gant* glove, t. Gmc; cf. OSw. *wante*]

gauntlet[2] (gônt′lĭt), *n.* **1. run the gauntlet, a.** to be forced to run between two rows of men who strike at one with switches or other weapons as one passes (formerly a common military punishment). **b.** to undertake an extremely hazardous operation. **2.** a section of interlaced railway or tramway tracks. **—*v.t.* 3.** to lay down as a gauntlet: *to gauntlet tracks.* Also, *U.S.*, **gantlet.** [alter. by assoc. with GAUNTLET[1] of earlier *gantlope,* t. Sw.: m. *gatlopp,* lit., lane run, f. *gata* way, lane + *lopp* a running course]

gauntry (gôn′trĭ), *n., pl.* **-tries.** gantry.

gaur (gou′ə), *n.* the largest of all wild cattle, *Bos gaurus,* living in forest areas of India, Burma, and Malaya.

gauss (gous), *n. Physics.* **1.** a unit of magnetic induction such that an induction of one gauss will result in one volt per centimetre of length in a linear conductor moved perpendicularly across the induction at a speed of one centimetre per second. **2.** *Obs.* oersted (def. 1). [named after K. F. GAUSS]

Gauss (*Ger.* gous), *n.* **Karl Friedrich** (*Ger.* kärl frē′drĭkh), 1777–1855, German mathematician. **—Gaussian** (gou′sĭ ən), *adj.*

Gautama (gou′tə mə), *n.* 563?–483? B.C., Buddha; Siddhartha. Also, **Gotama.**

Gautier (*Fr.* gō tyē′), *n.* **Théophile** (*Fr.* tē ō fēl′), 1811–72, French poet, novelist, and critic of art and literature.

gauze (gôz), *n.* **1.** any thin transparent fabric made from any fibre in a plain or leno weave. **2.** some similar open material, as of wire. **3.** a thin haze. [t. F: m. *gaze,* named after GAZA] **—gauze′like′,** *adj.*

gauzy (gô′zĭ), *adj.*, **-zier, -ziest.** like gauze; thin as gauze. **—gauz′iness,** *n.*

gavage (găv′äzh, găv′ĭj; *Fr.* gä väzh′), *n.* forced feeding, as of poultry or human beings, as by a flexible tube. [t. F, der. *gaver* to gorge]

gave (gāv), *v.* pt. of **give.**

gavel (găv′əl), *n.* a small mallet used by a presiding officer to signal for attention or order. [back-formation from *gavelock,* OE *gafeluc* spear]

gavelkind (găv′əl kīnd′), *n. Law, Obs.* **1.** a customary system of land tenure, whose chief feature was equal division of inherited land among the heirs. **2.** a tenure of land in which the tenant was liable for money rent rather than labour or military service. **3.** the land so held. [ME *gavelkynde, gavelikind,* f. OE *gafol* tax, tribute + *gecynd* KIND[2]]

gavial (gā′vyəl), *n.* a large Indian crocodile, *Gavialis gangeticus,* with elongated jaws. Also, **garial.** [t. F, t. Hind.: m. *ghariyāl*]

Head of gavial, *Gavialis gangeticus* (Total length ab. 20 ft)

Gävle (*Sw.* yĕv′lə), *n.* a seaport in E Sweden. 59,670 (1964).

gavotte (gə vŏt′), *n.* **1.** an old French dance in moderately quick 4/4 time. **2.** a piece of music for, or in the rhythm of, this dance, often forming one of the movements in the classical suite, usually following the saraband. Also,

gavot. [t. F, t. Pr.: m. *gavoto* dance of the Gavots (Alpine mountaineers), der. pre-Rom. *gav-* mountain stream]

Gawain (gä′wān), *n. Arthurian Legend.* one of the knights of the Round Table.

Gawain and the Green Knight, Sir, a 14th-century alliterative poem.

gawk (gôk), *n.* **1.** an awkward, foolish person. —*v.i.* **2.** *Colloq.* to act like a gawk; stare stupidly. [appar. repr. OE word meaning fool, f. *gagol* foolish + *-oc* -OCK; used attributively in *gawk hand, gallock hand* left hand]

gawky (gô′kĭ), *adj.*, **-kier, -kiest.** awkward; ungainly; clumsy. —**gawk′ily,** *adv.* —**gawk′iness,** *n.*

gay (gā), *adj.*, **gayer, gayest. 1.** having or showing a joyous mood: *gay spirits, music, scenes, etc.* **2.** bright or showy: *gay colours, flowers, ornaments, etc.* **3.** given to or abounding in social or other pleasures: *a gay social season.* **4.** dissipated; licentious. **5.** *Colloq.* camp; homosexual. [ME, t. OF: m. *gai*; orig. uncert.] —**gay′ness,** *n.*

—**Syn. 1.** gleeful, jovial, glad, joyous, light-hearted; lively, vivacious, frolicsome, sportive, hilarious. GAY, JOLLY, JOYFUL, MERRY describe a happy or light-hearted mood. GAY suggests a lightness of heart or liveliness of mood that is openly manifested: *when hearts were young and gay.* JOLLY indicates a good-humoured, natural, expansive gaiety of mood or disposition: *a jolly crowd at a party.* JOYFUL suggests gladness, happiness, rejoicing: *joyful over the good news.* MERRY is often interchangeable with GAY: *a merry disposition, a merry party*; it suggests, even more than the latter, convivial animated enjoyment. —**Ant. 1.** solemn. **2.** sedate, sober.

Gay (gā), *n.* **John,** 1685–1732, English poet and dramatist.

Gaya (gä′yə, gī′ə), *n.* a city in NE India: a famous place of Hindu pilgrimage. 151,105 (1961).

Gay-Lussac (*Fr.* gĕ lʏ săk′), *n.* **Joseph Louis** (*Fr.* zhô zef lwē′), 1778–1850, French chemist and physicist.

Gay-Lussac's law, *Physics.* the law which states that when gases combine they do so in a simple ratio by volume to each other and to the gaseous product.

gaz., 1. gazette. 2. gazetteer.

Gaza (gä′zə), *n.* a seaport adjacent to SW Israel: ancient trade route centre. 37,820 (est. 1952).

Gaza Strip, a coastal area formerly in the Palestine mandate; administered by Israel since 1967.

gaze (gāz), *v.*, **gazed, gazing,** *n.* —*v.i.* **1.** to look steadily or intently; look with curiosity, wonder, etc. —*n.* **2.** a steady or intent look. [ME, t. Scand.; cf. d. Sw. *gasa* gape, stare] —**gaz′er,** *n.*

—**Syn. 1.** GAZE, STARE, GAPE suggest looking fixedly at something. To GAZE is to look steadily and intently at something; esp. at that which excites admiration, curiosity, or interest: *to gaze at scenery, at a scientific experiment.* To STARE is to gaze with eyes wide open, as from surprise, wonder, alarm, stupidity, or impertinence: *to stare unbelievingly or rudely.* GAPE is a word with uncomplimentary connotations; it suggests open-mouthed, often ignorant or rustic wonderment or curiosity: *to gape at a high building.*

gazebo (gə zē′bō), *n.*, *pl.* **-bos, -boes.** a structure commanding an extensive prospect, esp. a turret, pavilion, or summerhouse. [? f. GAZE, v. + L (*vid*)*ēbō* I shall see]

gazehound (gāz′hound′), *n.* a hound that hunts by sight rather than scent.

gazelle (gə zĕl′), *n.* any of various small antelopes of the genus *Gazella* and allied genera, noted for their graceful movements and lustrous eyes. [t. F, t. Ar.: m. *ghazāl*] —**gazelle′-like′,** *adj.*

Thomson's gazelle, *Gazella thomsoni* (Ab. 26 in. high at the shoulder)

gazette (gə zĕt′), *n.*, *v.*, **-zetted, -zetting.** —*n.* **1.** a newspaper (now common only in newspaper titles). **2.** an official government journal, containing lists of government appointments and promotions, bankruptcies, etc. —*v.t.* **3.** to publish, announce, or list in a gazette. [t. F, t. It.: m. *gazzetta*, var. of Venetian *gazeta*, orig. a Venetian coin (the price of the gazette), dim. of *gaza* magpie]

gazetteer (găz′ĭ tĭə′), *n.* **1.** a geographical dictionary. **2.** a journalist, esp. one appointed and paid by the government. [t. F (obs.): m. *gazettier*]

Gaziantep (*Turk.* gä zē′än tĕp), *n.* a city in S Turkey. 124,097 (1960). Also, **Aintab.**

G.B., Great Britain.

G.B.E., Knight (or Dame) Grand Cross of (the Order of) the British Empire.

G.C., George Cross.

G.C.B., Knight Grand Cross of (the Order of) the Bath.

G.C.D., greatest common divisor. Also, **g.c.d.**

G.C.E., General Certificate of Education.

G.C.F., greatest common factor. Also, **g.c.f.**

G clef, *Music.* a sign indicating the position of G above middle C; treble clef. See illus. under **clef.**

G.C.M., greatest common measure. Also, **g.c.m.**

G.C.M.G., Knight Grand Cross of (the Order of) St Michael and St George.

G.C.V.O., Knight (or Dame) Grand Cross of the (Royal) Victorian Order.

Gd, *Chem.* gadolinium.

Gdańsk (*Pol.* gdȧɪɴsk), *n.* Polish name of **Danzig.**

gds, goods.

Gdynia (*Pol.* gdĭ′nyȧ), *n.* a seaport in N Poland, on the Bay of Danzig. 161,000 (est. 1964).

Ge, *Chem.* germanium.

gean (gēn), *n.* a deciduous rosaceous tree, *Prunus avium*, a native of Europe and W Asia, from which many varieties of cultivated sweet cherries have been derived.

geanticline (jē ăn′tĭ klīn′), *n. Geol.* an anticline extending over a relatively large part of the earth's surface. [f. Gk *gê* earth + ANTICLINE]

gear (gĭə), *n.* **1.** *Mach.* **a.** a mechanism for transmitting or changing motion, as by toothed wheels. **b.** a toothed wheel which engages with another wheel or part. **c.** the connection or engagement of toothed wheels with each other: *in gear, out of gear, in high gear, in low gear.* **d.** a group of parts in a complex machine that operates for a single purpose. See also illus. under **differential. 2.** implements, tools, or apparatus, esp. as used for a particular operation; harness; tackle. **3.** *Naut.* **a.** the ropes, blocks, etc., belonging to a particular sail or spar. **b.** the tools and equipment used on a ship. **4.** movable property; goods, clothes; personal possessions. **5.** *Slang.* fashionable clothes. **6.** *Archaic.* armour or arms. —*adj.* **7.** *Slang.* fashionable, delightful, or excellent. —*v.t.* **8.** to provide with gearing; connect by gearing; put (machinery) into gear. **9.** to provide with gear; supply; fit; harness. **10.** to prepare, adjust, orientate (someone or something) to a particular situation. **11.** *Stock Exchange.* to borrow money on debentures in order to increase the amount of total capital in relation to the equity capital of (a utility, etc.) (usually fol. by *up*). —*v.i.* **12.** to fit exactly, as one part of gearing into another; come into or be in gear. [ME *gere*, t. Scand.; cf. Icel. *gervi*, *görvi* gear, apparel; akin to OE *gearwe*, pl., equipment, *gearu* ready] —**gear′less,** *adj.*

A B C
Gears
A, Bevel gears; B, Herringbone or double helical gears; C, Spur gears

gearbox (gĭə′bŏks′), *n.* the casing in which gears are enclosed, esp. in a motor vehicle.

gearing (gĭə′rĭng), *n.* **1.** the parts collectively by which motion is transmitted in machinery, esp. a train of toothed wheels. **2.** the act of equipping with gears. **3.** the method of installation of such gears. **4.** *Stock Exchange.* the relationship of total invested capital to equity capital.

gearlever (gĭə′lē′və), *n.* a device for selecting or connecting gears for transmitting power, esp. in a motor vehicle. Also, *esp. U.S.*, **gearshift** (gĭə′shĭft′).

gearwheel (gĭə′wēl′), *n.* a wheel having teeth or cogs which engage with those of another wheel or part; cogwheel.

geb., (G *geboren*) born.

gecko (gĕk′ō), *n.*, *pl.* **-os, -oes.** a small, harmless lizard of the family *Geckonidae*, mostly nocturnal, many with adhesive pads on the toes. [t. Malay: m. *gēkoq*; imit.]

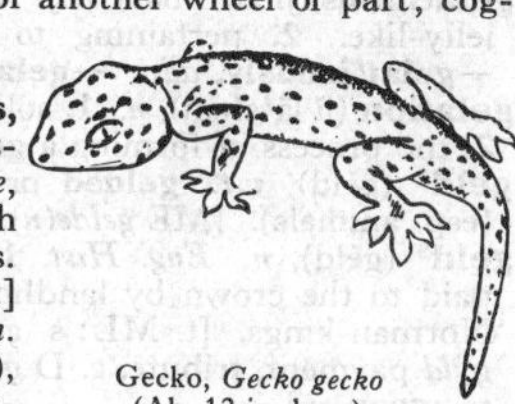
Gecko, *Gecko gecko* (Ab. 12 in. long)

Gedda (*Sw.* jĕd′dȧ), *n.* **Nicolai** (*Sw.* nē′kô lȧy), born 1925, Swedish operatic tenor.

gee[1] (jē), *interj.*, *n.* (a word of command to horses, etc., directing them to go faster (fol. by *up*).)

gee[2] (jē), *interj. U.S.* (a mild exclamation of surprise or delight.) [a euphemistic var. of JESUS]

geebung (jē′bŭng), *n. Austral.* **1.** any tree of the genus *Persoonia.* **2.** the fruit of this tree. [t. native Australian]

gee-gee (jē′jē), *n. Childish.* a horse.

geelbek (gēl′bĕk), *n.* **1.** a duck of Africa, *Anas undulata*; yellowbill. **2.** a food fish of S African waters, *Atractoscion aequidens*; Cape salmon. [t. Afrikaans: yellow beak, mouth]

Geelong (jē′lŏng′), *n.* a seaport in SE Australia, in Victoria. 99,000 (1965).

geelslang (gēl′slăng), *n. S African.* the Cape cobra. [t. Afrikaans: yellow snake]

Geelvink Bay (*Du.* KHĕl′vĭngk), a large bay on the NW coast of New Guinea.

geese (gēs), *n.* pl. of **goose.**

geest (gēst), *n. Geol.* old deposits produced by flowing water. [t. LG: dry or sandy soil]

geezer (gē′zə), *n. Slang.* an odd character. [var. of *guiser* (f. GUISE (def. 6) + -ER[1]), repr. d. pronunciation]

gegenschein (gā′gən shīn′), *n. Astron.* a faint illumination of the sky at night which is sometimes seen opposite the sun; caused by sunlight being reflected by meteoric dust in space. [G: counterglow]

Gehenna (gĭ hĕn′ə), *n.* **1.** *Old Test.* the valley of Hinnom, near Jerusalem, regarded as a place of abomination (II Kings 23:10), and used as a place to cast refuse, with fires kept burning to prevent pestilence. **2.** *New Test. and Rabbinical Literature.* hell. **3.** any place of extreme torment or suffering. [t. LL, t. Gk: m. *Géenna*, t. Heb.: m. *Gē-Hinnōm* hell, short for *gē ben Hinnōm*, lit., valley of the son of Hinnom. See Jer. 19:5]

gehlenite (gā′lə nīt′), *n.* a mineral silicate of aluminium and calcium, $Ca_2Al_2SiO_7$, occurring in green or brown prismatic crystals. [named after A.F. *Gehlen*, 1775–1815, German chemist. See -ITE[1]]

Geiger counter (gī′gə), an instrument for detecting and counting ionizing particles, consisting of a tube which conducts electricity when the gas within is ionized by such a particle. It is used in measuring the degree of radioactivity in an area left by the explosion of an atom bomb, in investigations of cosmic rays, etc. Also, **Geiger-Müller counter.** [named after Hans *Geiger*, 1882–1947, German physicist]

Geikie (gē′kĭ), *n.* **Sir Archibald,** 1835–1924, Scottish geologist.

geisha (gā′shə), *n., pl.* **-sha, -shas.** a Japanese singing and dancing girl. [t. Jap.]

Geissler tube (gīs′lə), a sealed glass tube with platinum connections at the ends, containing rarefied gas made luminous by an electrical discharge. [named after H. *Geissler*, 1814–79, the (German) inventor]

gel (jĕl), *n., v.,* **gelled, gelling.** *Phys. Chem.* —*n.* **1.** a semirigid colloidal dispersion of a solid with a liquid or gas, as jelly, glue, or silica gel. —*v.i.* **2.** to form or become a gel. [short for GELATINE]

Gela (*It.* jĕ′lȧ), *n.* a town in S Sicily. 62,041 (1966).

gelada (jĕl′ə də, jĭ lä′də, gĕl′-, gĭ-), *n.* a hairy baboon, *Theropithecus gelada*, of NE Africa.

gelatine (jĕl′ə tēn′), *n.* **1.** a brittle, nearly transparent, faintly yellow, odourless, and almost tasteless organic substance, obtained by boiling in water the ligaments, bones, skin, etc., of animals, and forming the basis of jellies, glues, and the like. **2.** any of various similar substances, as vegetable gelatine. **3.** a preparation or product in which gelatine (defs. 1 or 2) is the essential constituent. Also, **gelatin** (jĕl′ə tĭn). [t. F: (m.) *gélatine*, t. It.: m. *gelatina*, der. *gelata* jelly, g. L *gelāta*, pp. fem. frozen, congealed]

gelatinize (jĭ lăt′ĭ nīz′), *v.,* **-nized, -nizing.** —*v.t.* **1.** to make gelatinous. **2.** to coat with gelatine, as paper. —*v.i.* **3.** to become gelatinous. Also, **gelatinise.** —**gelat′iniza′tion,** *n.*

gelatinoid (jĭ lăt′ĭ noid′), *adj.* **1.** resembling gelatine; gelatinous. —*n.* **2.** a gelatinoid substance.

gelatinous (jĭ lăt′ĭ nəs), *adj.* **1.** having the nature of jelly; jelly-like. **2.** pertaining to or consisting of gelatine. —**gelat′inously,** *adv.* —**gelat′inousness,** *n.*

gelation (jĭ lā′shən), *n.* **1.** solidification by cold; freezing. **2.** the process of forming a gel. [t. L: s. *gelātio* freezing]

geld[1] (gĕld), *v.t.,* **gelded** or **gelt, gelding.** to castrate (esp. animals). [ME *gelde(n)*, t. Scand.; cf. Icel. *gelda*]

geld[2] (gĕld), *n. Eng. Hist.* **1.** a payment; tax. **2.** a tax paid to the crown by landholders under the Saxon and Norman kings. [t. ML: s. *geldum*, t. OE: m. *geld*, *gield*, *gyld* payment, tribute, c. D *geld* and G *Geld* money; akin to YIELD, V.]

Gelderland (gĕl′də lănd′; *Du.* KHĕl′dər lŏnt), *n.* a province in the E Netherlands. 1,359,527 pop. (est. 1963); 1965 sq. mi. *Cap.:* Arnhem. Also, **Guelders.**

gelding (gĕl′dĭng), *n.* a castrated animal, esp. a horse. [ME, t. Scand.; cf. Icel. *geldingr*]

Gelée (*Fr.* zhə lĕ′), *n.* **Claude** (*Fr.* klōd). See **Lorrain.**

gelid (jĕl′ĭd), *adj.* very cold; icy. [t. L: s. *gelidus* icy cold] —**gelid′ity, gel′idness,** *n.* —**gel′idly,** *adv.*

gelignite (jĕl′ĭg nīt′), *n.* an explosive consisting of nitroglycerine, nitrocellulose, potassium nitrate, and wood pulp: used for blasting.

Gelsenkirchen (*Ger.* gĕl zən kĭr′KHən), *n.* a city in W West Germany, in W central North Rhine-Westphalia, in the Ruhr. 367,000 (est. 1966).

gelt (gĕlt), *v.* a pt. and pp. of **geld.**

gem (jĕm), *n., v.,* **gemmed, gemming.** —*n.* **1.** a stone used in jewellery, fashioned to bring out its beauty. **2.** something likened to, or prized as, a gem because of its beauty or worth, esp. something small: *the gem of the collection.* **3.** a printing type (4 point) between brilliant and diamond. —*v.t.* **4.** to adorn with or as with gems. [ME, t. F: m. *gemme*, g. L *gemma* bud, jewel; r. OE *gim* (c. OHG *gimma*), ult. t. L] —**gem′like′,** *adj.* —**gem′my,** *adj.*

Gemara (gĕ mä′rə), *n. Jewish Lit.* the later of the two sections of the Talmud, consisting of a commentary on the Mishnah; the Talmud. [t. Aram.: completion]

geminate (*adj.* jĕm′ĭ nĭt, -nāt′; *v.* jĕm′ĭ nāt′), *v.,* **-nated, -nating,** *adj.* —*v.t., v.i.* **1.** to make or become double or paired. —*adj.* **2.** twin; combined in pairs; coupled. [t. L: m. s. *gemĭnātus*, pp., doubled] —**gem′inately,** *adv.*

gemination (jĕm′ĭ nā′shən), *n.* **1.** a doubling; duplication; repetition. **2.** *Phonetics.* the doubling of a single consonant. **3.** *Rhet. Obs.* the immediate repetition of a word, phrase, etc., for rhetorical effect.

Gemini (jĕm′ĭ nī′), *n.pl., gen.* **Geminorum** (jĕm′ĭ nô′rəm). **1.** *Astron.* the Twins, a zodiacal constellation containing the bright stars Castor and Pollux. **2.** the third sign of the zodiac. See diag. under **zodiac.** [t. L, pl. of *geminus* twin]

gemma (jĕm′ə), *n., pl.* **gemmae** (jĕm′ē). **1.** *Bot.* a cell or cluster of cells, or a leaf- or budlike body, which separates from the parent plant and forms a new plant, as in mosses, liverworts, etc. **2.** a bud, esp. a leaf bud. **3.** *Zool.* a bud of tissues from which a new individual may develop; gemmule. [t. L: bud, germ. Cf. GEM]

gemmate (jĕm′āt), *adj., v.,* **-mated, -mating.** *Bot.* —*adj.* **1.** having buds; increasing by budding. —*v.i.* **2.** to put forth buds; increase by budding. [t. L: m. s. *gemmātus*, pp., increased by budding, set with gems]

gemmation (jĕ mā′shən), *n. Bot.* the process of reproduction by gemmae.

gemmule (jĕm′yo͞ol), *n.* **1.** *Bot.* gemma. **2.** *Zool.* an asexually produced mass of cells that will develop into an animal. **3.** *Biol.* one of the hypothetical living units conceived by Darwin as the bearers of the hereditary attributes. [t. L: m. *gemmula*, dim. of *gemma* bud]

gemot (gĭ mōt′), *n. Early Eng. Hist.* a meeting or an assembly, as for judicial or legislative purposes. Also, **gemote.** [OE *gemōt*, f. *ge-* together + *mōt* meeting. Cf. MOOT]

gemsbok (gĕmz′bŏk′), *n.* a large antelope, *Oryx beisa*, of southern Africa, having long, straight horns and a long, tufted tail. [t. Afrikaans: chamois buck]

gemstone (jĕm′stōn′), *n.* a precious stone; gem; jewel.

-gen, a suffix meaning: **1.** something produced, or growing: *acrogen, endogen, exogen.* **2.** something that produces: *hydrogen, oxygen.* [t. F: m. *-gène*, ult. t. Gk: m. *-genēs* born, produced, der. *gen-* bear, produce]

Gen., **1.** *Mil.* General. **2.** Genesis. **3.** Geneva.

gen., **1.** gender. **2.** general. **3.** genitive. **4.** genus.

gen (jĕn), *n., v.,* **genned, genning.** —*n.* **1.** *Colloq.* general information. **2.** all the necessary information about a subject. —*v.i.* **3.** *Colloq.* to become informed (about), to learn or read up (about) (fol. by *up*). [shortened form of *general information*]

gendarme (zhŏn′däm; *Fr.* zhäɴ dȧrm′), *n., pl.* **-darmes** (-dämz; *Fr.* -dȧrm′). **1.** one of a corps of military police, esp. in France. **2.** *Phys. Geog.* a rock tower or pinnacle on an arête. [t. F, formed as sing. from *gens d'armes* men of arms]

gendarmerie (*Fr.* zhäɴ dȧr mə rē′), *n.* gendarmes collectively. Also, **gendarmery** (zhŏn dä′mə rĭ).

gender (jĕn′də), *n.* **1.** *Gram.* **a.** (in many languages) a set of classes which together include all nouns, membership in a particular class being shown by the form of the noun itself or by the form or choice of words that modify, replace, or otherwise refer to the noun; e.g., in Eng., the choice of *he* to replace *the man,* of *she* to replace *the woman,* of *it* to replace *the table,* of *it* or *she* to replace *the ship.* The number of genders in different languages varies from two to more than twenty; often the classification correlates in part with sex or animateness. The most familiar sets of genders are of three classes (e.g. Latin and German, *masculine, feminine, neuter*) or of two (e.g. French and Spanish, *masculine* and *feminine*; Dutch, *common* and *neuter*). **b.** one class of such a set. **c.** such classes or sets collectively or in general. **2.** *Colloq.* sex. **3.** *Obs.* kind, sort, or class. [ME *gendre*, t. OF, t. L: m. s. *genus* race, kind, sort, gender. Cf. GENUS, GENRE] —**gen′derless,** *adj.*

gene (jēn), *n. Biol.* the unit of inheritance, associated with deoxyribonucleic acid, which is situated on and transmitted by the chromosome, and which develops into a hereditary character as it reacts with the environment and with the other genes. [t. Gk: s. *geneá* breed, kind]

genealogical tree, family tree.

genealogy (jē′nĭ ăl′ə jĭ), *n., pl.* **-gies.** **1.** an account of the descent of a person or family through an ancestral line. **2.** the investigation of pedigrees as a department of knowledge. [ME, t. LL: m. s. *geneālogia*, t. Gk: tracing of descent] —**genealogical** (jē′nĭ ə lŏj′ĭ kl), **ge′nealog′ic,** *adj.* —**ge′nealog′ically,** *adv.* —**genealogist** (jē′nĭ ăl′ə jĭst), *n.* —**Syn. 2.** See **pedigree.**

genera (jĕn′ə rə), *n.* pl. of **genus.**

generable (jĕn′ə rə bl), *adj.* that may be created or produced. [t. L: m. *generābilis*]

general (jĕn′ə rəl, jĕn′rəl), *adj.* **1.** pertaining to, affecting, including, or participated in by all members of a class or group; not partial or particular: *a general election.* **2.** common to many or most of a community; prevalent; usual: *the general practice.* **3.** not restricted to one class or field; miscellaneous: *the general public, general knowledge.* **4.** not limited to a detail of application; not specific or special: *general instructions.* **5.** indefinite or vague: *to refer to a matter in a general way.* **6.** having extended command, or superior or chief rank (often follows noun): *a general officer, governor-general.* —*n.* **7.** *Mil.* **a.** an officer next in rank above a lieutenant general and below a field marshal. **b.** a general officer. **c.** one who fulfils the function of a general officer; a military commander: *Julius Caesar was a great general.* **8.** *Eccles.* the chief of certain religious orders. **9.** a general statement or principle. **10.** *Archaic.* the general public. **11.** *Obs.* a servant, esp. a maid doing general housework. **12. in general, a.** with respect to the whole class referred to. **b.** as a general rule; commonly. [ME, t. L: s. *generālis*, of or belonging to a (whole) race, kind, the opposite of *speciālis* special, particular. See GENUS] —**gen′eralness,** *n.*

—**Syn. 1, 2.** customary, regular, ordinary. GENERAL, COMMON, POPULAR, UNIVERSAL agree in the idea of being non-exclusive and widespread. GENERAL means belonging to, or prevailing throughout, a whole class or body collectively, irrespective of individuals: *a general belief.* COMMON means shared by all, and belonging to one as much as another: *a common fund, interests.* POPULAR means belonging to, or adapted for, or favoured by the people or the public generally, rather than by a particular (esp. a superior) class: *the popular conception, a popular candidate.* UNIVERSAL means found everywhere, and with no exceptions: *a universal longing.* —**Ant. 1.** special, limited.

General Agreement on Tariffs and Trade, an international trade agreement made in 1948 to safeguard tariffs against other forms of economic protection. *Abbrev.:* G.A.T.T.

General American Speech, the standard pronunciation of American English, without any regional accent.

General Assembly, 1. the highest court or synod of the Presbyterian Church in Scotland, Ireland, and the U.S. **2.** one of the principal bodies within the United Nations, and the only one in which all members are represented.

General Certificate of Education, a secondary school examination in England and Wales on three levels (Ordinary, Advanced, and Scholarship), conducted by university boards and taken within a range of individual subjects. *Abbrev.:* G.C.E.

general degree, a non-specialized university degree usually involving the study of two or three different subjects.

general election, a major governmental election, in Britain held at least every five years, when each constituency elects a representative for the House of Commons.

generalissimo (jĕn′ə rə lĭs′ĭ mō′, jĕn′rə-), *n., pl.* **-mos. 1.** the supreme commander of several armies acting together. **2.** the supreme commander of all the forces of a country. [t. It., superl. of *generale* general, der. L *generālis.* See GENERAL]

generality (jĕn′ə răl′ĭ tĭ), *n., pl.* **-ties. 1.** a general or vague statement: *to speak in vague generalities.* **2.** general principle; general rule or law. **3.** *Archaic.* the greater part or majority: *the generality of people.* **4.** state or quality of being general.

generalization (jĕn′rə lī zā′shən), *n.* **1.** the act or process of generalizing. **2.** a result of this process; general statement, idea, or principle. **3.** *Logic.* **a.** a proposition asserting something to be true either of all members of a certain class or of an indefinite part of that class. **b.** the process of obtaining such propositions. Also, **generalisation.**

generalize (jĕn′rə līz′), *v.,* **-lized, -lizing.** —*v.t.* **1.** to give a general (rather than specific or special) character to. **2.** to infer (a general principle, etc.) from facts, etc. **3.** to make general; bring into general use or knowledge. —*v.i.* **4.** to form general notions. **5.** to deal in generalities. **6.** to make general inferences. Also, **generalise.**

generally (jĕn′rə̆ lĭ), *adv.* **1.** with respect to the larger part, or for the most part: *a claim generally recognized.* **2.** usually; commonly; ordinarily: *he generally comes at noon.* **3.** without reference to particular persons or things: *generally speaking.* —**Syn. 2.** See **often.**

general officer, *Mil.* an officer above the rank of brigadier, holding the rank of either major general, lieutenant general, or general, having command of military formations larger than a brigade or having the duties of a staff officer at a higher headquarters, as the Ministry of Defence.

general paralysis of the insane, *Pathol.* a syphilitic brain disorder characterized by chronic inflammation and degeneration of cerebral tissue, resulting in mental and physical deterioration. *Abbrev.:* G.P.I. Also, **general paresis.**

General Post Office, the government department headed by a postmaster general, which controls postal and telephone services. *Abbrev.:* G.P.O.

general practice, medical practice involving responsibility for the general health of a number of people in a district.

general practitioner, a doctor who does not specialize in any particular branch of medicine; a doctor in general practice. *Abbrev.:* G.P.

general-purpose (jĕn′rəl pû′pəs), *adj.* of broad usage; not restricted in function.

generalship (jĕn′rəl shĭp′), *n.* **1.** skill as commander of a large military force or unit. **2.** management or tactics. **3.** the rank or functions of a general.

general staff, *Mil.* a group of officers without command, whose duties are to assist high commanders in planning and carrying out orders in peace and war.

general strike, 1. a mass strike in all or many trades and industries in a section or in all parts of a country. **2.** (*caps.*) the strike of 1926, involving about one-quarter of Great Britain's organized workers.

general theory of relativity, *Physics.* See **relativity.**

general warrant, *Hist.* a warrant for the arrest of persons not named individually, issued by the Secretary of State.

generate (jĕn′ə rāt′), *v.t.,* **-rated, -rating. 1.** to bring into existence; give rise to; produce; cause to be: *to generate electricity.* **2.** *Obs.* to beget, to procreate. **3.** *Maths.* to trace out (a figure) by the motion of another figure. [t. L: m. s. *generātus*, pp., begotten]

generating station, an industrial building in which electricity is generated.

generation (jĕn′ə rā′shən), *n.* **1.** the whole body of individuals born about the same time: *the rising generation.* **2.** the age or average lifetime of a generation; term of years (commonly 30) accepted as the average difference of age between one generation of a family and the next. **3.** a single step in natural descent, as of human beings, animals, or plants. **4.** the act or process of generating; procreation. **5.** the fact of being generated. **6.** production by natural or artificial processes; evolution, as of heat or sound. **7.** the offspring of a given parent or parents, considered as a single step in descent. **8.** *Biol.* a form or phase of a plant or animal, with reference to the manner of its reproduction. **9.** *Maths.* the production of a geometrical figure by the motion of another figure. **10.** a period of technological development marked by features non-existent in the previous period. [ME, t. L: s. *generātio*]

generation time, *Physics.* the average time between the creation of a neutron by nuclear fission and a subsequent fission produced by that neutron.

generative (jĕn′ə rə tĭv), *adj.* **1.** pertaining to the production of offspring. **2.** capable of producing.

generator (jĕn′ə rā′tə), *n.* **1.** a machine which converts mechanical energy into electrical energy; dynamo. **2.** *Chem.* an apparatus for producing a gas or vapour. **3.** one who or that which generates. [t. L]

generatrix (jĕn′ə rā′trĭks), *n., pl.* **generatrices** (jĕn′ə rā′trī sēz′). *Maths.* an element generating a figure. [t. L, fem. of *generator*]

generic (jĭ nĕ′rĭk), *adj.* **1.** pertaining to a genus. **2.** applicable or referring to all the members of a genus or class. Also, **gener′ical.** [f. s. L *genus* kind + -IC. Cf. F *générique*] —**gener′ically,** *adv.*

generosity (jĕn′ə rŏs′ĭ tĭ), *n., pl.* **-ties. 1.** readiness or liberality in giving. **2.** freedom from meanness or smallness of mind or character. **3.** a generous act. —**Syn. 1.** munificence. **2.** nobleness. —**Ant. 1.** stinginess; meanness.

generous (jĕn′ə rəs, jĕn′rəs), *adj.* **1.** munificent or bountiful; unselfish: *a generous giver or gift.* **2.** free from meanness or smallness of mind or character. **3.** furnished liberally; abundant: *a generous portion.* **4.** rich or strong, as wine. **5.** fertile, as soil. [t. L: m. s. *generōsus* of noble birth] —**gen′erously,** *adv.* —**gen′erousness,** *n.* —**Syn. 1.** liberal, open-handed, free. **2.** high-minded, noble. **3.** ample, plentiful. —**Ant. 1.** selfish. **2.** mean. **3.** meagre.

genesis (jĕn′ĭ sĭs), *n., pl.* **-ses** (-sēz′). origin; production; creation. [ME, t. L, t. Gk: origin, creation]

Genesis (jĕn′ĭ sĭs), *n.* the first book of the Old Testament, telling of the beginnings of the world and of man. [special use of Gk *génesis* origin, creation]

genet[1] (jĕn′ĭt), *n.* **1.** any of the small Old World carnivores constituting the genus *Genetta*, esp. *G. vulgaris*, allied to the civets but without a scent pouch, yielding a soft fur. **2.** the fur of such an animal. Also, **genette.** [ME *genete*, t. OF, t. Sp.: m. *gineta*, t. Ar.: m. *jarnait*]

genet[2] (jĕn′ĭt), *n. Obs.* jennet.

Genet (*Fr.* zhə nĕ′), *n.* **Jean** (*Fr.* zhäN), born 1910, French dramatist and novelist.

genetic (jĭ nĕt′ĭk), *adj.* **1.** *Biol.* pertaining or according to genetics. **2.** pertaining to genesis or origin. Also, **genet′ical.** [t. Gk: m. s. *genetikós* generative] —**genet′ically,** *adv.*

geneticist (jĭ nĕt′ĭ sĭst), *n.* one versed in genetics or a student of genetics.

genetics (jĭ nĕt′ĭks), *n. Biol.* the science of heredity, dealing with resemblances and differences of related organisms flowing from the interaction of their genes and the environment. [pl. of GENETIC (def. 2). See -ICS]

geneva (jĭ nē′və), *n.* Hollands gin. [t. D: m. *genever*, t. OF: m. *genevre*, g. L *jūniperus* juniper]

Geneva (jĭ nē′və), *n.* **1.** a city in SW Switzerland, on Lake Geneva: seat of the League of Nations, 1920–46. 176,183 (1960). **2.** a canton in SW Switzerland consisting mainly of the city of Geneva and suburbs. 259,234 pop. (1960). 109 sq. mi. **3. Lake Geneva.** Also, **Lake Leman.** a lake between SW Switzerland and France. 45 mi. long; 225 sq. mi. French, **Genève** (zhə nĕv′); German, **Genf** (gĕnf).

Geneva bands, two bands, or pendant strips, worn at the throat as part of a clerical garb: worn orig. by the Swiss Calvinist clergy.

Geneva Convention, *Mil.* an international agreement establishing rules for the treatment during war of the sick, the wounded, and prisoners of war.

Geneva cross, a red Greek cross on a white ground, displayed in war, etc., to distinguish ambulances, hospitals, and persons serving them; Red Cross.

Geneva gown, a loose, large-sleeved, black preaching gown worn by Protestant clergymen: so-named from its use by the Genevan Calvinist clergy.

Genevan (jĭ nē′vən), *adj.* **1.** of or pertaining to Geneva. **2.** Calvinistic. —*n.* **3.** a native or inhabitant of Geneva. **4.** a Calvinist.

Genevieve (zhĕn′vĭ āv′; *Fr.* zhən vyĕv′), *n.* **Saint,** A.D. *c.* 422–512, French nun, patron saint of Paris.

Genf (*Ger.* gĕnf), *n.* German name of **Geneva.**

Genghis Khan (gĕng′gĭs kän′), 1162–1227, Mongol conqueror of most of Asia and of E Europe to the river Dnieper. Also, **Jenghis Khan, Jenghiz Khan.**

genial[1] (jē′nyəl), *adj.* **1.** sympathetically cheerful; cordial: *a genial disposition, a genial host.* **2.** enlivening; supporting life; pleasantly warm, or mild. **3.** *Rare.* characterized by genius. [t. L: s. *geniālis* festive, jovial, pleasant, lit., pertaining to generation or to marriage] —**gen′ially,** *adv.* —**gen′ialness,** *n.* —**Syn. 1.** friendly, hearty, pleasant, agreeable. —**Ant. 1.** sullen.

genial[2] (jĭ nī′əl), *adj. Anat., Zool.* of or pertaining to the chin. [f. m. s. Gk *géneion* chin + -AL[1]]

geniality (jē′nĭ ăl′ĭ tĭ), *n.* genial quality; sympathetic cheerfulness or kindliness.

genic (jĕn′ĭk), *adj. Biol.* of, relating to, resembling, or arising from a gene or genes.

geniculate (jĭ nĭk′yŏŏ lĭt, -lāt′), *adj. Anat., Biol.* **1.** having kneelike joints or bends. **2.** bent at a joint like a knee. [t. L: m. s. *geniculātus* knotted]

geniculation (jĭ nĭk′yŏŏ lā′shən), *n.* **1.** geniculate state. **2.** a geniculate formation. [t. LL: s. *geniculātio* a bending of the knee]

genie (jē′nĭ), *n.* a jinnee or spirit of Arabian mythology. [t. F, t. L: m. *genius.* See GENIUS]

genii (jē′nĭ ī′), *n.* pl. of **genius** (defs. 5, 6, 8).

genipap (jĕn′ĭ păp′), *n.* **1.** the edible fruit of a tropical American rubiaceous tree, *Genipa americana*, about the size of an orange. **2.** the plant. [t. Pg.: m. *genipapo*; of Tupi orig.]

genista (jĭ nĭs′tə), *n.* any shrub or small tree belonging to the papilionaceous genus *Genista.*

genital (jĕn′ĭ tl), *adj.* pertaining to generation or the organs of generation. [t. L: s. *genitālis*]

genitalia (jĕn′ĭ tā′lyə), *n.pl.* the genitals. [t. L]

genitals (jĕn′ĭ tlz), *n.pl.* the reproductive organs, esp. the external organs.

genitive (jĕn′ĭ tĭv), *Gram.* —*adj.* **1.** (in some inflected languages) denoting the case of nouns generally used to modify other nouns, often indicating possession, but used also in expressions of measure, origin, characteristic: *Examples: John's* hat, *man's* fate, *week's* holiday, *duty's* call. **2.** denoting the affix or other element characteristic of this case, or a word containing such an element. **3.** similar to such a case form in function or meaning. —*n.* **4.** the genitive case. **5.** a word in that case. **6.** a construction of similar meaning. [ME, t. L: m. s. *genitīvus*, lit., pertaining to generation] —**genitival** (jĕn′ĭ tī′vəl), *adj.* —**gen′iti′vally,** *adv.*

genito-urinary (jĕn′ĭ tō yŏŏ′rĭ nə rĭ), *adj. Anat., Physiol.* denoting or pertaining to the genital and urinary organs; urogenital. [f. *genito-* (comb. form of GENITAL) + URINARY]

genius (jē′nyəs), *n., pl.* **geniuses** for 1–4, 7, **genii** (jē′nĭ ī′) for 5, 6, 8. **1.** exceptional natural capacity for creative and original conceptions; the highest level of mental ability. **2.** a person having such capacity. **3.** natural ability or capacity: *a task suited to one's genius.* **4.** distinctive character or spirit, as of a nation, period, language, etc. **5.** the guardian spirit of a place, institution, etc. **6.** either of two mutually opposed spirits, one good and the other evil, supposed to attend a person throughout his life. **7.** a person who strongly influences the character, conduct, or destiny of another: *an evil genius.* **8.** (*now chiefly or only in pl.*) any demon or spirit, esp. a genie or jinnee. [t. L: tutelary spirit, any spiritual being, disposition, orig. a male generative or creative principle. Cf. GENIAL[1], GENITAL, GENUS, GENESIS, KIN] —**Syn. 3.** gift, talent, aptitude, faculty.

genius loci (jē′nĭ əs lō′sī), *Latin.* **1.** guardian of a place. **2.** the peculiar character of a place with reference to the impression that it makes on the mind.

Genk (*Fl.* KHĕngk), *n.* a town in NE Belgium. 54,924 (est. 1964).

gennet (jĕn′ĭt), *n. Obs.* jennet.

genoa (jĕn′ə wə), *n. Naut.* a large balloon jib set in a yacht in light winds.

Genoa (jĕn′ō ə), *n.* a seaport in NW Italy. 846,893 (1966). Italian, **Genova** (*It.* jĕ′nō vä). See map under **Monaco.**

Genoa cake, a rich fruit cake, generally decorated with almonds.

genocide (jĕn′ō sīd′), *n.* extermination of a national or racial group as a planned move. [f. Gk *géno(s)* race + -CIDE; coined by Dr Raphael Lemkin, 1944] —**gen′ocid′al,** *adj.*

Genoese (jĕn′ō ēz′), *adj., n., pl.* **-ese.** —*adj.* **1.** of Genoa. —*n.* **2.** a native or inhabitant of Genoa.

genotype (jĕn′ō tīp′), *n. Genetics.* **1.** the fundamental hereditary constitution of an organism. **2.** its breeding formula of genes. **3.** a group of organisms with a common heredity. [f. Gk *géno(s)* origin, race + -TYPE] —**genotypic** (jĕn′ō tĭp′ĭk), *adj.* —**gen′otyp′ically,** *adv.*

-genous, an adjective suffix derived from nouns in **-gen** and **-geny.** [f. -GEN + -OUS]

genre (*Fr.* zhäN′r), *n.* **1.** genus; kind; sort; style. **2.** *Painting, etc.* the category in which scenes from ordinary life are represented (as distinguished from landscapes, etc.). —*adj.* **3.** of or pertaining to genre (def. 2). [t. F: kind. See GENDER]

genro (gĕn′rō′), *n.pl.* elder statesmen (def. 2). [t. Jap.: old men]

gens (jĕnz), *n., pl.* **gentes** (jĕn′tēz). **1.** a group of families in ancient Rome claiming descent from a common ancestor and united by a common name and common religious rites. **2.** *Anthropol.* a group tracing descent in the male line. [t. L; also race, people]

Gensan (gĕn′săn′), *n.* Japanese name of **Wŏnsan.**

Genseric (gĕn′sə rĭk), *n.* A.D. *c.* 390–477, king of the Vandals, conqueror in northern Africa and Italy.

gent (jĕnt), *n.* (often in humorous use) gentleman.

Gent (*Flem.* KHĕnt), *n.* Flemish name of **Ghent.**

genteel (jĕn tēl′), *adj.* **1.** belonging or suited to polite society. **2.** well-bred or refined; polite; elegant; stylish. **3.** affectedly proper in manners and speech. [t. F: m. *gentil.* See GENTLE] —**genteel′ly,** *adv.* —**genteel′ness,** *n.*

gentian (jĕn′shən), *n.* **1.** any plant of the large genus *Gentiana*, comprising herbs having commonly blue flowers, less frequently yellow, white, or red; esp. *G. crinita* (one of the **fringed gentians**), of eastern North America, with blue, delicately fringed corolla, and *G. lutea*, a yellow-flowered European species. **2.** any of various plants resembling the gentian. **3.** the root of *G. lutea*, or a preparation of it, used as a tonic. [ME *gencian*, t. L: m. s. *gentiana*; said to be named after *Gentius*, an Illyrian king]

gentianaceous (jĕn′shĭ ə nā′shəs), *adj.* belonging to the *Gentianaceae*, or gentian family of plants.

gentian violet, crystal violet.

gentile (jĕn′tīl), *adj.* **1.** of or pertaining to any people not Jewish. **2.** Christian as distinguished from Jewish. **3.** (among Mormons) of or pertaining to any people not Mormon. **4.** *Obs.* heathen or pagan. **5.** (of a linguistic expression) expressing nationality or local extractions. —*n.* **6.** a person who is not Jewish, esp. a Christian.

7. (among Mormons) one not a Mormon. **8.** *Rare.* a heathen or pagan. Also, **Gentile.** [ME *gentil,* t. L: s. *gentīlis* belonging to a people, national, LL foreign]

gentility (jĕn tĭl′ĭ tĭ), *n., pl.* **-ties. 1.** superior refinement or elegance, possessed or affected. **2.** gentle birth.

gentle (jĕn′tl), *adj.,* **-tler, -tlest,** *v.,* **-tled, -tling.** —*adj.* **1.** mild, kindly, or amiable: *gentle words.* **2.** not severe, rough, or violent: *a gentle wind, a gentle lap.* **3.** moderate; gradual: *gentle heat, a gentle slope.* **4.** of good birth or family; well-born. **5.** characteristic of good birth; honourable; respectable. **6.** easily handled or managed: *a gentle animal.* **7.** soft or low: *a gentle sound.* **8.** *Archaic.* polite; refined. **9.** *Archaic.* noble; chivalrous: *a gentle knight.* —*v.t.* **10.** to tame; render tractable. **11.** *Rare.* to mollify (a person). **12.** *Obs.* to ennoble; dignify. [ME *gentil,* t. OF: of good family, noble, excellent, g. L *gentīlis.* See GENTILE] **—gen′tleness,** *n.* **—gen′tly,** *adv.*

—Syn. 1. soft, bland, peaceful, pacific, soothing; kind, tender, humane, lenient, merciful. GENTLE, MEEK, MILD, refer to an absence of bad temper or belligerence. GENTLE has reference esp. to disposition and behaviour, and often suggests a deliberate or voluntary kindness or forbearance in dealing with others: *a gentle pat, gentle with children.* MEEK implies a submissive spirit, and may even indicate undue submission in the face of insult or injustice: *meek and even servile or weak.* MILD suggests absence of harshness or severity, rather because of natural character or temperament than conscious choice: *a mild rebuke, a mild manner.* **—Ant. 1.** arrogant.

gentle breeze, *Meteorol.* a wind of Beaufort scale force 3, i.e. one about 10 miles per hour.

gentlefolk (jĕn′tl fōk′), *n.pl.* persons of good family and breeding. Also, **gen′tlefolks′.**

gentleman (jĕn′tl mən), *n., pl.* **-men. 1.** a man of good breeding, education, and manners. **2.** (as a polite form of speech) any man. **3.** a male personal servant, or valet, esp. of a man of social position. **4.** a man of good social standing by birth, esp. one who does not work for a living. **5.** *Hist.* a man above the rank of yeoman. **—gen′tleman-like′,** *adj.*

gentleman-at-arms (jĕn′tl mən ət ämz′), *n., pl.* **gentlemen-at-arms.** one of a guard of forty gentlemen with their officers who attend the sovereign on state occasions.

gentleman-commoner (jĕn′tl mən kŏm′ə nə), *n., pl.* **gentlemen-commoners.** (formerly) a member of a class of commoners enjoying special privileges, in the Universities of Oxford and Cambridge.

gentlemanly (jĕn′tl mən lĭ), *adj.* like or befitting a gentleman; well-bred. **—gen′tlemanliness,** *n.*

gentlemen's (jĕn′tl mənz), *n. Colloq.* a public lavatory for men. Also, **gents, gents′.**

gentlemen's agreement, an agreement binding as a matter of honour alone, not enforceable at law.

gentle sex, women.

gentlewoman (jĕn′tl wo͝om′ən), *n., pl.* **-women. 1.** a woman of good family or breeding; a lady. **2.** *Hist.* a woman who attends upon a lady of rank. **—gen′tlewom′anly,** *adj.* **—gen′tlewom′anliness,** *n.*

gentry (jĕn′trĭ), *n.* **1.** well-born and well-bred people. **2.** the class below the nobility. [ME, f. *gent* noble + -RY]

genu (jĕn′yo͞o), *n., pl.* **genua** (jĕn′yo͞o ə). *Anat., Zool.* **1.** the knee. **2.** a kneelike part or bend. [L]

genuflect (jĕn′yo͞o flĕkt′), *v.i.* to bend the knee or knees, esp. in reverence. [t. ML: s. *genūflectere,* f. L *genū* knee + *flectere* bend] **—gen′uflec′tor,** *n.*

genuflection (jĕn′yo͞o flĕk′shən), *n.* the act of bending the knee or knees, esp. in worship. Also, **gen′uflex′ion.** [t. ML: m. s. *genūflexio,* der. ML *genūflectere* bend the knee]

genuine (jĕn′yo͞o ĭn), *adj.* **1.** being truly such; real; authentic: *genuine regret, genuine worth.* **2.** properly so called: *genuine leprosy.* **3.** sincere; free from pretence or affectation: *a genuine person.* **4.** proceeding from the original stock; pure in breed: *a genuine Celtic people.* [t. L: m. s. *genuīnus* native, natural, authentic, genuine] **—gen′uinely,** *adv.* **—gen′uineness,** *n.*

genus (jē′nəs), *n., pl.* **genera** (jĕn′ə rə). **1.** a kind; sort; class. **2.** *Biol.* the usual major subdivision of a family or subfamily, usually consisting of more than one species, essentially very similar to one another and regarded as phylogenetically very closely related. The genus designation is the first part of the scientific name of a species, as in *Lynx canadensis,* the Canadian lynx. **3.** *Logic.* a class or group of individuals including subordinate groups called *species.* [t. L: race, stock, kind, sort, gender (c. Gk *génos*)]

-geny, a suffix meaning 'origin', as in *phylogeny.* [t. Gk: m. s. *-geneia,* der. *-genēs* born, produced. See -GEN]

geo-, a word element meaning 'the earth', as in *geocentric.* [t. Gk, comb. form of *gê*]

Geo., George.

geocentric (jē′ō sĕn′trĭk), *adj.* **1.** *Astron.* as viewed or measured from the centre of the earth: *the geocentric altitude of a star.* **2.** having or representing the earth as a centre: *a geocentric theory of the universe.* Also, **ge′ocen′trical. —ge′ocen′trically,** *adv.*

geocentric parallax. See **parallax** (def. 2).

geochemistry (jē′ō kĕm′ĭs trĭ), *n.* the science dealing with the chemical changes in, and the composition of, the earth's crust. **—geochemical** (jē′ō kĕm′ĭ kl), *adj.* **—ge′ochem′ist,** *n.*

geochronology (jē′ō krə nŏl′ə jĭ), *n.* the study of the earth's chronology based on geological information. **—geochronological** (jē′ō krŏn′ə lŏj′ĭ kl), *adj.*

geod., 1. geodesy. **2.** geodetic.

geode (jē′ōd), *n. Geol.* **1.** a rounded hollow in a rock coated with crystals which have grown freely inwards. **2.** a hollow concretion so formed. [t. F, t. L: m. s. *geōdēs* jewel, t. Gk: adj., earthlike] **—geodic** (jĭ ŏd′ĭk), *adj.*

geodesic (jē′ō dĕs′ĭk, -dē′sĭk), *adj.* **1.** Also, **ge′odes′ical.** pertaining to the geometry of curved surfaces, in which geodesic lines take the place of the straight lines of plane geometry. —*n.* **2.** a geodesic line.

geodesic line, *Maths.* the shortest line lying on a given surface and connecting two given points.

geodesy (jĭ ŏd′ĭ sĭ), *n.* that branch of applied mathematics which determines the shape and area of large tracts of country, the exact position of geographical points, and the curvature, shape, and dimensions of the earth. Also, **geodetics** (jē′ō dĕt′ĭks). [t. NL: m. s. *geōdaesia,* t. Gk: m. *geōdaisía* art of mensuration] **—geod′esist,** *n.*

geodetic (jē′ō dĕt′ĭk), *adj.* **1.** pertaining to geodesy. **2.** geodesic. Also, **ge′odet′ical. —ge′odet′ically,** *adv.*

geodynamics (jē′ō dī năm′ĭks), *n.* the study of the dynamics of the forces inside the earth. **—ge′odynam′ic, ge′odynam′ical,** *adj.* **—ge′odynam′icist,** *n.*

Geoffrey of Monmouth (jĕf′rĭ), 1100?–54, English chronicler.

geog., 1. geographer. **2.** geographic; geographical. **3.** geography.

geognosy (jĭ ŏg′nə sĭ), *n.* that branch of geology which treats of the constituent parts of the earth, its envelope of air and water, its crust, and the condition of its interior. [f. GEO- + m. s. Gk *-gnōsia* knowledge]

geographer (jĭ ŏg′rə fə), *n.* one who specializes in the study and writing of geography.

geographical (jĭə grăf′ĭ kl), *adj.* **1.** of or pertaining to geography. **2.** referring to or characteristic of a certain locality, esp. in reference to its location in relation to other places. Also, **geograph′ic. —geograph′ically,** *adv.*

geographical mile. See **mile** (def. 1b).

geographic determinism, *Sociol.* the doctrine which regards geographical conditions as the determining or moulding agency of group life.

geographic environment, *Sociol.* the entire natural surroundings of man, independent of his activity but underlying and conditioning it.

geography (jĭ ŏg′rə fĭ), *n., pl.* **-phies. 1.** the study of the areal differentiation of the earth's surface, as shown in the character, arrangement, and interrelations over the world of elements such as climate, relief, soil, vegetation, population, land use, industries, or states, and of the unit areas formed by the complex of these individual elements. **2.** the topographical features of a region, usually of the earth, but sometimes of Mars, the moon, etc. **3.** a book, esp. a textbook, on this subject. [t. L: m. s. *geōgraphia,* t. Gk]

geoid (jē′oid), *n.* **1.** an imaginary surface which coincides with the mean sea-level over the ocean and its extension under the continents. **2.** the geometrical figure formed by this surface, an ellipsoid flattened at the poles. [t. Gk: m. s. *geoeidēs* earthlike]

geol., 1. geologic; geological. **2.** geologist. **3.** geology.

geological (jĭə lŏj′ĭ kl), *adj.* of or pertaining to geology. Also, **geolog′ic. —geolog′ically,** *adv.*

geological time, the portion of time in earth history from the formation of the earth to the beginning of the historical period; it extends 4500–5000 million years and is divided into four eras.

geologize (jĭ ŏl′ə jīz′), *v.,* **-gized, -gizing.** —*v.i.* **1.** to study geology. —*v.t.* **2.** to examine geologically. Also, **geologise.**

geology (jĭ ŏl′ə jĭ), *n., pl.* **-gies. 1.** the science which treats of the earth, the rocks of which it is composed, and the changes which it has undergone or is undergoing. **2.** the geological features of a locality. [t. NL: m. s. *geōlogia.* See GEO-, -LOGY] **—geol′ogist,** *n.*

geom., 1. geometric. **2.** geometrical. **3.** geometry.

geomagnetic (jē′ō măg nĕt′ĭk), *adj.* of or pertaining to terrestrial magnetism.

geomancer (jē′ō măn′sə), *n.* one versed in or practising geomancy.

geomancy (jē′ō măn′sĭ), *n.* divination by means of the figure made by a handful of earth thrown down at random, or, by figures or lines formed by a number of dots made at random. [ME *geomancie,* t. ML: m. *geōmantia,* f. Gk (see GEO-, -MANCY)]

geometer (jĭ ŏm′ĭ tə), *n.* geometrician. [t. L: m. s. *geōmetra, geōmetrēs,* t. Gk: (m.) *geōmétrēs* land-measurer, geometer]

geometric (jĭə mĕt′rĭk), *adj.* **1.** of or pertaining to geometry; according to the principles of geometry. **2.** resembling or employing the lines or figures in geometry. **3.** of or pertaining to painting, sculpture, or ornamentation of predominantly geometrical characteristics or figures. Also, **geomet′rical.** —**geomet′rically,** *adv.*

geometrical optics, the study of optical problems in terms of light rays and their geometry.

geometrician (jĭ ŏm′ĭ trĭsh′ən, jĭ′ŏm ĭ-), *n.* an expert in geometry.

geometric mean, *Maths.* the means of n positive numbers obtained by taking the nth root of the product of the numbers: *the geometric mean of 6 and 24 is 12.*

geometric progression, *Maths.* a sequence of terms in which the ratio of any term to its predecessor is a constant; e.g., 1, 3, 9, 27, 81 and 243; 144, 12, 1, $\frac{1}{12}$

geometric ratio, *Maths.* the ratio of consecutive terms in a geometric progression.

geometric series, *Maths.* an infinite series of the form $c + cx + cx^2 + cx^3 \ldots$ where both c and x are real numbers.

geometrid (jĭ ŏm′ĭ trĭd), *adj.* **1.** of or relating to the moths of the family *Geometridae,* the larvae of which are called measuring worms or loopers. —*n.* **2.** a geometrid moth. [t. NL: s. *Geōmetridae,* der. L *geōmetra* GEOMETER]

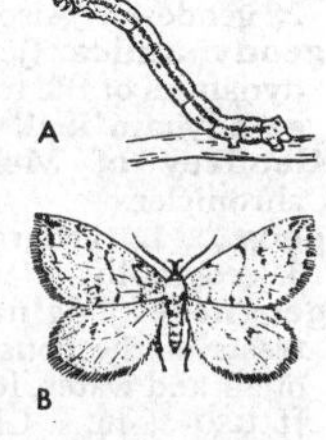

Geometrid moth, *Alsophila pometaria* A, Larva; B, Moth

geometrize (jĭ ŏm′ĭ trīz′), *v.*, **-trized, -trizing.** —*v.i.* **1.** to work by geometrical methods. —*v.t.* **2.** to put into geometric form. Also, **geometrise.**

geometry (jĭ ŏm′ĭ trĭ), *n.* **1.** that branch of mathematics which deduces the properties of figures in space. **2.** the shape of a surface or solid. [ME *geometrie,* t. L: m. *geōmetria,* t. Gk]

geometry set, a set of instruments for use in geometry.

geomorphic (jē′ō mô′fĭk), *adj.* **1.** of or pertaining to the figure of the earth, or the forms of its surface. **2.** resembling the earth in form.

geomorphology (jē′ō mô fŏl′ə jĭ), *n.* the study of the characteristics, origin, and development of land forms.

geophagy (jĭ ŏf′ə jĭ), *n.* the practice of eating earthy matter, esp. clay or chalk. [f. GEO- + -PHAGY]

geophilous (jĭ ŏf′ĭ ləs), *adj. Bot., Zool.* terrestrial, as certain snails, or any plant fruiting underground.

geophysics (jē′ō fĭz′ĭks), *n.* the physics of the earth, dealing esp. with the study of inaccessible portions of the earth by instruments and apparatus such as the torsion balance, seismograph, and magnetometer. —**ge′ophys′ical,** *adj.* —**ge′ophys′icist,** *n.*

geophyte (jē′ō fīt′), *n. Bot.* a plant with underground buds.

geopolitics (jē′ō pŏl′ĭ tĭks), *n.* the application of political and economic geography to the external political problems of states, notably problems of national power, frontiers, and possibilities for expansion.

geoponic (jē′ō pŏn′ĭk), *adj.* of or pertaining to tillage or agriculture; agricultural. [t. Gk: m. s. *geōponikós*]

geoponics (jē′ō pŏn′ĭks), *n.* the art or science of agriculture.

georama (jē′ō rä′mə), *n.* a large hollow globe on the inside of which is depicted a map of the earth's surface, to be viewed by a spectator within the globe. [t. F, f. Gk: *gê* earth + *(h)órama* view]

Geordie[1] (jô′dĭ), *n. Colloq.* **1.** a miner, esp. one from the region around the river Tyne, in Northumberland. **2.** a collier vessel, esp. one based on the river Tyne. **3.** a person who works or lives near the river Tyne. **4.** (formerly) a George; a guinea. [dim. of *George,* proper name]

Geordie[2] (jô′dĭ), *n. Scot. and N Dial.* a miner's safety lamp. [named after *George* Stephenson. See GEORDIE[1]]

George (jôj), *n.* **1. David Lloyd.** See **Lloyd George. 2. Saint,** died A.D. 303?, Christian martyr, patron saint of England. **3. Lake,** a lake in E New York State. 36 mi. long. **4. Lake,** a lake in Australia, in SE New South Wales. 17 mi. long. **5.** a jewel worn as part of the Order of the Garter. **6.** (formerly) a coin, esp. a guinea, showing the image of St George. —*interj.* **7. by George!** (an exclamation or mild oath.)

George (*Ger.* gē ŏr′gə), *n.* **Stefan** (*Ger.* shtĕ′fän), 1868–1933, German poet.

George I, 1. 1660–1727, king of England 1714–27; first king of the House of Hanover. **2.** 1845–1913, king of Greece 1863–1913.

George II, 1. 1683–1760, king of England 1727–60 (son of George I). **2.** 1890–1947, king of Greece 1922–23 and 1935–47.

George III, 1738–1820, king of England 1760–1820 (grandson of George II).

George IV, 1762–1830, king of England 1820–30 (son of George III).

George V, 1865–1936, king of England 1910–36 (son of Edward VII).

George VI, 1895–1952, king of England 1936–52 (second son of George V; brother of Edward VIII).

George Cross, a medal for outstanding heroism, awarded mainly to civilians.

George Medal, a medal for heroism, awarded mainly to civilians.

George Town, a former name of **Penang.**

Georgetown (jôj′toun′), *n.* a seaport in and the capital of Guyana. 162,000 (1964).

georgette (jô jĕt′), *n.* sheer silk or rayon crepe of dull texture. Also, **georgette crepe.**

Georgia (jô′jyə), *n.* **1.** a state in the SE United States. 4,342,000 (1963); 58,876 sq. mi. *Cap.:* Atlanta. *Abbrev.:* Ga. **2.** Official name, **Georgian Soviet Socialist Republic.** a constituent republic of the Soviet Union in Caucasia, bordering on the Black Sea: it was an independent kingdom for ab. 2000 years. 4,410,000 pop. (1964); ab. 26,900 sq. mi. *Cap.:* Tiflis. **3. Strait of,** an inlet of the Pacific in SW Canada between Vancouver Island and the mainland of British Columbia.

Georgia (def. 2)

Georgian (jô′jyən), *adj., n.* **1.** pertaining to the four Georges, kings of England (1714–1830), or the period of their reigns. **2.** pertaining to George V, 1910–36, or the period of his reign. **3.** of or pertaining to the state of Georgia in the U.S. **4.** pertaining to Georgia in the Soviet Union. —*n.* **5.** a person, esp. a writer, of either of the Georgian periods in England. **6.** the styles or character of a Georgian period. **7.** a native or inhabitant of the state of Georgia. **8.** a native or inhabitant of Georgia in the Soviet Union. **9.** the most important South Caucasian language.

Georgian Bay, the NE part of Lake Huron, in Ontario, Canada. ab. 6000 sq. mi.

Georgian glass, a common type of opaque glass, often used in roof lights, and frequently wired to prevent accidents when broken.

georgic (jô′jĭk), *adj.* **1.** agricultural. —*n.* **2.** a poem on agricultural matters. [t. L: s. *geōrgicus* agricultural, t. Gk: m. *geōrgikós*]

Georgina (jô jē′nə), *n.* a river in Australia flowing SE through Northern Territory and Queensland, joining with the Hamilton from Eyre Creek. ab. 800 mi.

geostatic (jē′ō stăt′ĭk), *adj.* of or pertaining to the pressure exerted by a mass of earth or other similar substance.

geostationary orbit (jē′ō stā′shə nə rĭ, -stăsh′nə rĭ), *Astron.* synchronous orbit.

geostrophic wind speed (jē′ō strŏf′ĭk), *Meteorol.* the speed of the wind calculated from the pressure gradient, the air density, the rotational velocity of the earth, and the latitude, but neglecting the curvature of the path of the air.

geosynclinal (jē′ō sĭn klī′nəl), *adj. Geol.* **1.** pertaining to a synclinal fold which involves a relatively large part of the earth's surface. —*n.* **2.** a geosyncline.

geosyncline (jē′ō sĭn′klīn), *n. Geol.* a portion of the earth's crust subjected to downward warping during a large fraction of geological time; a geosynclinal fold.

geotaxis (jē′ō tăk′sis), *n. Biol.* a movement of an organism towards or away from a gravitational force. —**ge′otac′tic,** *adj.*

geotectonic (jē′ō tĕk tŏn′ĭk), *adj.* pertaining to the structure of the earth's crust or to the arrangement and form of its constituents.

geothermal (jē′ō thû′məl), *adj.* of or pertaining to the internal heat of the earth.

geotropic (jē′ō trŏp′ĭk), *adj. Biol.* taking a particular direction with reference to the earth: **a. positively geotropic,** directed downwards. **b. negatively geotropic,** directed upwards. **c. transversely geotropic,** directed horizontally. —**ge′otrop′ically,** *adv.*

geotropism (jĭ ŏt′rə pĭz′əm), *n. Biol.* a tropism orientated with respect to gravitation, as the direction of growth of plants or the ability of some animals to avoid an upside-down position in the air.

Ger., 1. German. 2. Germany.

ger., 1. gerund. 2. gerundive.

Gera (*Ger.* gĕ′rȧ), *n.* a town in S East Germany. 106,841 (1964).

gerah (gĭə′rə), *n.* a Hebrew weight and coin, equal to $\frac{1}{20}$ of a shekel. [t. Heb.: m. *gērāh*, t. Akkadian: m. *girū*]

Geraldton waxflower (jĕ′rəl tən), an evergreen myrtaceous shrub of W Australia, *Chamaelaucium uncinatum.*

geraniaceous (jĭ rā′nĭ ā′shəs), *adj.* belonging to the *Geraniaceae*, or geranium family of plants.

geranial (jĭ rā′nyəl), *n. Chem.* citral.

geranium (jĭ rā′nyəm), *n.* **1.** any of the plants of the genus *Geranium*, most of which have pink or purple flowers, and some of which, as *G. maculatum*, have an astringent root used in medicine; cranesbill. **2.** a plant of the allied genus *Pelargonium*, of which many species are well known in cultivation for their showy flowers (as the **scarlet geraniums**) or their fragrant leaves (as the **rose geraniums**). [t. L, t. Gk: m. *geránion* crane's-bill]

geratology (jĕ′rə tŏl′ə jĭ), *n.* the study of the decline of life, as in old age or in animals approaching extinction. [f. s. Gk *géras* old age + -(o)logy]

gerbil (jû′bĭl), *n.* any of numerous jerboa-like rodents (genus *Gerbillus*, etc.) of Asia, Africa, and southern Russia, belonging to the mouse family, and forming the subfamily *Gerbillinae.* Also, **gerbille.** [t. F: m. *gerbille*, t. NL: m. s. *gerbillus*, dim. of *gerbo* jerboa]

gerent (jĕ′rənt), *n.* a ruling power; manager. [t. L: s. *gerens*, ppr., bearing, conducting, managing]

gerenuk (gĕ′rĭ no͝ok′), *n.* a giraffe antelope, *Litocranius walleri*, a rare antelope from eastern Africa. [t. Somali: m. *garanug*]

gerfalcon (jû′fôl′kən, -fô′-), *n.* gyrfalcon.

geriatrics (jĕ′rĭ ăt′rĭks), *n.* the science of the medical and hygienic care of, or the diseases of, aged persons. **—geriatrician** (jĕ′rĭ ə trĭsh′ən), **ge′riat′rist,** *n.* **—ge′riat′ric,** *adj.*

Géricault (*Fr.* zhĕ rē kō′), *n.* **Théodore** (*Fr.* tĕ ō dôr′), 1791–1824, French painter.

Gerlachovka (*Cz.* gĕr′lȧ KHŏf kȧ), *n.* the highest peak of the Tatra Mountains, in Czechoslovakia. 8737 ft.

germ (jûm), *n.* **1.** a micro-organism, esp. when disease-producing; microbe. **2.** that from which anything springs as if from a seed. **3.** *Embryol.* **a.** a bud, offshoot, or seed. **b.** the rudiment of a living organism; an embryo in its early stages. **4.** *Biol.* the initial stage in development or evolution, as a germ cell or ancestral form. [t. F: m. *germe.* See germen] **—germ′less,** *adj.*

german (jû′mən), *adj.* **1.** sprung from the same father and mother (always placed after the noun): *a brother-german.* **2.** sprung from the brother or sister of one's father or mother, or from brothers or sisters: *a cousin-german.* **3.** *Obs.* germane. [t. L: s. *germānus* having the same father (and mother); r. ME *germain*, t. OF]

German (jû′mən), *adj.* **1.** of or pertaining to Germany, its inhabitants, or their language. *—n.* **2.** a native or inhabitant of Germany. **3.** a Germanic language, the language of Germany and Austria and an official language of Switzerland. **4.** High German. **5.** (*l.c.*) *Chiefly U.S.* an elaborate kind of dance; cotillion. **6.** (*l.c.*) *Chiefly U.S.* a party at which only or chiefly the german is danced. [t. L: s. *Germānus*; orig. uncert.]

German (jû′mən), *n.* **Sir Edward,** 1862–1936, English composer.

German Baptist Brethren. See **Dunker.**

German Democratic Republic, official name of **East Germany.**

germander (jû măn′də), *n.* **1.** any of the herbs or shrubs constituting the labiate genus *Teucrium*, as *T. chamaedrys*, a purple-flowered European species, and *T. canadense*, an American species. **2.** a species of speedwell (**germander speedwell**). See **speedwell.** [t. ML: m. s. *germandra*, t. LGk: m. *chamándra*, alter. of Gk *chamaídrys*, lit., ground oak]

germane (jû mān′), *adj.* closely related; pertinent: *a remark germane to the question.* [var. of german]

German East Africa, a former German territory in E Africa: now comprised of Tanzania, Rwanda, and Burundi.

germanic (jû măn′ĭk), *adj. Chem.* of or containing germanium, esp. in the tetravalent state. [f. german(ium) + -ic]

Germanic (jû măn′ĭk), *adj.* **1.** of the Teutonic race, the peoples belonging to it, or the group of languages spoken by these peoples; Teutonic. **2.** of the Germans; German. *—n.* **3.** a group of Indo-European languages, including English, German, Dutch, Gothic, and the Scandinavian languages. [t. L: s. *Germānicus*]

Germanicus Caesar (jû măn′ĭ kəs), 15 B.C. – A.D. 19, Roman general.

Germanism (jû′mə nĭz′əm), *n.* **1.** a characteristic German usage, or idiom. **2.** German modes of thought, action, etc. **3.** attachment to what is German.

germanium (jû mā′nyəm), *n. Chem.* a rare metallic element, normally tetravalent, with a greyish white colour. *Symbol:* Ge; *at. wt:* 72·59; *at. no.:* 32; *sp. gr.:* 5·36 at 20°C. [NL, der. L *Germānia* country of the Germans]

Germanize (jû′mə nīz′), *v.t., v.i.,* **-nized, -nizing. 1.** to make or become German in character, sentiment, etc. **2.** to translate into German. Also, **Germanise. —Ger′maniza′tion,** *n.*

German measles, *Pathol.* a contagious disease, usually mild, accompanied by fever, often some sore throat, and a rash resembling that of scarlet fever, teratogenic in the first trimester of pregnancy; rubella.

German Ocean, the North Sea.

germanous (jû măn′əs), *adj. Chem.* containing divalent germanium.

German shepherd dog, *U.S.* alsatian.

German silver, a white alloy of copper, zinc, and nickel, used for making utensils, drawing instruments, etc.

German South-West Africa, a former German protectorate, now administered by the Republic of South Africa. See **South-West Africa.**

Germany (jû′mə nĭ), *n.* a country in central Europe; traditional capital: Berlin; German name, **Deutschland.** After World War II, N East Prussia was transferred to the Soviet Union and the rest of the territory E of the Oder–Neisse line to Poland. The remainder was divided into four zones of occupation: British, French, U.S., and Russian. It is now divided into **West Germany** and **East Germany** (which see).

germ cell, *Biol.* the sexual reproductive cell at any stage from the primordial cell to the mature gamete.

germen (jû′mən), *n.* any of the cells found in the early stages of the embryonic development of an animal, from which gametes are ultimately formed. [t. L: sprout]

germicide (jû′mĭ sīd′), *n.* an agent that kills germs or micro-organisms. [f. germ + -(i)cide] **—ger′micid′al,** *adj.*

germinal (jû′mĭ nəl), *adj.* **1.** pertaining to a germ or germs. **2.** of the nature of a germ or germ cell. **3.** in the earliest stage of development: *germinal ideas.*

Germinal (jû′mĭ nəl; *Fr.* zhĕr mē nȧl′), *n.* (in the calendar of the first French Republic) the seventh month of the year, extending from March 21st to April 19th. [F, t. NL: m. *germinālis*, der. L *germen, germinis* sprout]

germinal disc, *Embryol.* blastoderm.

germinal vesicle, *Embryol.* the large, vesicular nucleus of an ovum before the polar bodies are formed.

germinant (jû′mĭ nənt), *adj.* germinating.

germinate (jû′mĭ nāt′), *v.,* **-nated, -nating.** *—v.i.* **1.** to begin to grow or develop. **2.** *Bot.* **a.** to develop into a plant or individual, as a seed, or as a spore, bulb, or the like. **b.** to sprout; put forth shoots. *—v.t.* **3.** to cause to develop; produce. [t. L: m. s. *germinātus*, pp.] **—ger′mina′tion,** *n.* **—ger′mina′tor,** *n.*

germinative (jû′mĭ nā′tĭv), *adj.* capable of germinating or developing; pertaining to germination.

Germiston (jû′mĭs tən), *n.* a city in the NE Republic of South Africa, in the Transvaal. 214,393 (1960).

germ layer, one of the three primary embryonic cell layers, i.e., ectoderm, endoderm, and mesoderm.

germ plasm, the protoplasm of the germ cells containing the units of heredity (chromosomes and genes).

germ theory, 1. *Biol.* the theory that living matter cannot be produced by evolution or development from non-living matter, but is necessarily produced from germs or seeds; the doctrine of biogenesis. **2.** *Pathol.* the theory that infectious diseases, etc., are due to the agency of germs or micro-organisms.

germ warfare, biological warfare.

Gérôme (*Fr.* zhĕ rōm′), *n.* **Jean Léon** (*Fr.* zhäɴ lĕ ôɴ′), 1824–1904, French painter and sculptor.

Geronimo (jĭ rŏn′ĭ mō′), *n. c.* 1834–1909, Apache Indian chief.

gerontocracy (jĕ′rŏn tŏk′rə sĭ), *n., pl.* **-cies. 1.** government by old men. **2.** a governing body consisting of old men. [f. s. Gk *gérōn* old man + -(o)cracy]

gerontology (jĕ′rŏn tŏl′ə jĭ), *n.* the study of old age, its diseases and phenomena. **—ger′ontol′ogist,** *n.*

-gerous, a combining form meaning 'bearing' or 'producing', as in *setigerous.* [f. L *-ger* bearing + -ous]

gerrymander (jĕ′rĭ măn′də), *v.t.* **1.** *Politics.* to subject (a constituency, etc.) to a gerrymander. **2.** to manipulate unfairly. *—n.* **3.** *Politics.* an arbitrary arrangement of the political divisions of a constituency, etc., made so as to give one party an unfair advantage in elections. [f. *Gerry* (governor of Massachusetts, whose party in 1812 redistricted Massachusetts) + (SALA)MANDER (from a fancied resemblance to this animal of the gerrymandered map of Massachusetts)]

Gers (*Fr.* zhĕr, zhĕrs), *n.* a department in SW France. 182,264 pop. (1962); 2429 sq. mi. *Cap.:* Auch.

Gershwin (gûsh′wĭn), *n.* **George,** 1898–1937, U.S. composer.

gerund (jĕ′rənd), *n.* *Gram.* **1.** (in Latin and some other languages) a derived noun form of verbs, having (in Latin) all case forms but the nominative. *Example:* Latin *dicendī* gen., *dicendō*, dat., abl., *dicendum*, acc., 'saying'. No nominative form occurs. **2.** *Gram.* (sometimes, from similarity of meaning) the English *-ing* form of a verb (*loving*) when in nominal function. *Hunting* and *writing* are gerunds in the sentences 'Hunting is good exercise' and 'writing is easy'. **3.** (sometimes, in other languages) a form similar to the Latin gerund in meaning or function. [t. LL: m. s. *gerundium*, der. L *gerundum*, var. of *gerendum*, ger. of L *gerere* bear, conduct] —**gerundial** (jĭ rŭn′dyəl), *adj.*

gerundive (jĭ rŭn′dĭv), *n.* **1.** (in Latin) the future passive particle, similar to the gerund in formation. *Example: Haec dicendum est* 'This must be said'. —*adj.* **2.** resembling a gerund. [t. LL: m. s. *gerundīvus*, der. *gerundium* GERUND] —**gerundival** (jĕ′rən dī′vəl), *adj.* —**gerun′dively,** *adv.*

Geryon (gē′rĭ ən), *n.* *Class. Legend.* a monster whose cattle Hercules carried off.

gesso (jĕs′ō), *n.* **1.** gypsum, or plaster of Paris, prepared with glue for use as a surface for painting. **2.** any plaster-like preparation to fit a surface for painting, gilding, etc. **3.** a prepared surface of plaster or plaster-like material for painting, etc. [t. It., g. L *gypsum* GYPSUM]

gest (jĕst), *n.* *Archaic.* **1.** a metrical romance or history. **2.** a story or tale. **3.** a deed or exploit. Also, **geste.** [ME *geste*, t. OF, t. L: m. *gesta* deeds, prop. pp. neut. pl.]

Gestalt (gə shtält′), *n., pl.* **-stalten** (-shtăl′tən). *Psychol.* an organized configuration or pattern of experiences or of acts: *the Gestalt of a melody is distinct from the separate notes.* [t. G: form]

Gestalt psychology, a school of psychology which believes that experiences and conduct do not occur through the summation of reflexes or other individual elements but through configurations called *Gestalten*, which operate individually or interact mutually.

Gestapo (gĕs tä′pō), *n.* the Secret State Police of Nazi Germany. [G *ge(heime) Sta(ats)po(lizei)*]

Gesta Romanorum (jĕs′tə rō′mə nô′rəm), a popular collection of stories in Latin, compiled late in the 13th century.

gestate (jĕs′tāt), *v.t.*, **-tated, -tating.** to carry in the womb during the period from conception to delivery. [t. L: m. s. *gestātus*, pp., carried]

gestation (jĕs tā′shən), *n.* the act or period of gestating. [t. L: s. *gestātio* a carrying]

gestic (jĕs′tĭk), *adj.* *Obs.* pertaining to bodily motions, esp. dancing. Also, **ges′tical.** [f. s. L *gestus* gesture + -IC]

gesticulate (jĕs tĭk′yŏŏ lāt′), *v.i.*, **-lated, -lating. 1.** to make or use gestures, esp. in an animated or excited manner with or instead of speech. —*v.t.* **2.** to express by gesturing. [t. L: m. s. *gesticulātus*, pp., having made mimic gestures] —**gestic′ula′tor,** *n.*

gesticulation (jĕs tĭk′yŏŏ lā′shən), *n.* **1.** the act of gesticulating. **2.** an animated or excited gesture.

gesticulatory (jĕs tĭk′yŏŏ lə tə rĭ, -trĭ), *adj.* characterized by or making gesticulations. Also, **gestic′ulative.**

gesture (jĕs′chə), *n.*, *v.*, **-tured, -turing.** —*n.* **1.** movement of the body, head, arms, hands, or face expressive of an idea or an emotion: *the gestures of an orator, a gesture of impatience.* **2.** any action or proceeding intended for effect or as a formality; demonstration: *a gesture of friendship.* —*v.i.* **3.** to make or use gestures. —*v.t.* **4.** to express by gestures. [ME, t. ML: m. *gestūra*, der. L *gerere* bear, conduct] —**ges′turer,** *n.*

Gesundheit (*Ger.* gə zŏŏnt′hīt), *n.* *German.* soundness; health (used after a person has sneezed or as a toast).

get (gĕt), *v.*, **got** or (*Archaic*) **gat; got; getting;** *n.* —*v.t.* **1.** to obtain, gain, or acquire by any means: *to get favour by service, get a good price.* **2.** to fetch or bring: *I will go and get it.* **3.** to receive or be awarded: *I got a present, he got five years for theft.* **4.** to obtain by labour; earn: *to get one's living.* **5.** to acquire a mental grasp or command of; learn: *get a lesson by heart.* **6.** to hear or understand: *I didn't get the last word.* **7.** to be afflicted with (an illness, etc.): *have you got a cold?* **8.** to reach or communicate with (someone): *get him on the phone.* **9.** to cause to be or do: *to get a friend appointed, get one's hair cut, get the fire to burn.* **10.** *Obs.* to capture; seize upon. **11.** *Colloq.* to be under an obligation to; be obliged to: *you have got to go.* **12.** to prevail on: *get him to speak.* **13.** to prepare; make ready: *to get dinner.* **14.** to beget (now usually of animals). **15.** *Slang.* to hit: *the bullet got him in the leg.* **16.** *Slang.* to make a physical assault on, esp. in vengeance: *I'll get you for that.* **17.** *Colloq.* to grasp or understand the meaning or intention of (a person). **18.** *Colloq.* to have an unspecified effect upon, as irritation, anger, amusement. **19.** *Colloq.* to kill. —*v.i.* **20.** to come to or arrive: *to get home.* **21.** to become; grow: *to get tired.* **22.** to succeed in coming or going (fol. by *away, in, into, out, over, through,* etc.). —*v.* **23.** Some special verb phrases are:

get about, 1. to move about. **2.** (of rumours, etc.) to become known.

get across, 1. to make understood. **2.** *Colloq.* to irritate or annoy; hinder. **3.** *Theat.* to communicate successfully (to an audience).

get ahead, to be successful; make progress.

get along, 1. to go; go off. **2.** nonsense! (an exclamation of disbelief). **3.** See **get on.**

get around, 1. to move about. **2.** (of rumours, etc.) to become known.

get at, 1. to reach; make contact with: *I can't get at it.* **2.** *Colloq.* to hint at or imply: *what's she getting at?* **3.** *Colloq.* to tamper with, as by corruption or bribery.

get away, *Colloq.* to escape.

get away with, to avoid punishment or blame for.

get back, 1. to return. **2.** to recover or make as a profit on. **3.** to take vengeance on (fol. by *at*).

get by, to manage; carry on in spite of difficulties.

get cracking, *Colloq.* to begin vigorously; hurry.

get down, 1. to bring or come down. **2.** to concentrate or attend to (fol. by *to*).

get even with, to square accounts with.

get going, to begin; act; make haste.

get off, 1. to escape; evade consequences. **2.** to start a journey; leave. **3.** to dismount from (a horse or train). **4.** *Colloq.* to cease to interfere: *I told him where to get off.* **5.** *Colloq.* to begin a flirtation (fol. by *with*).

get on or **along, 1.** to make progress; proceed; advance. **2.** to succeed; manage. **3.** to agree or be friendly (with).

get one's own back, to be revenged.

get out, to become publicly known.

get over, 1. to overcome (a difficulty, etc.). **2.** to recover from: *to get over a shock or illness.*

get round, 1. to outwit. **2.** to cajole or ingratiate oneself with (someone). **3.** to overcome (difficulties, etc.).

get round to, to come at length to (doing something).

get (someone) down, to depress, discourage (someone).

get through to, 1. to make a telephone connection with. **2.** *Colloq.* to make understand.

get up, 1. to arise; sit up or stand. **2.** to rise from bed. **3.** to ascend or mount. **4.** to increase in force or violence (of wind, sea, etc.). **5.** to dress elaborately. **6.** to prepare, arrange, or organize. **7.** to acquire a knowledge of: *to get up a subject.* **8.** to produce in a specified style, as a book. **9.** to work up (a feeling, etc.). **10.** to be involved in (esp. mischief, etc.) (fol. by *to*).

—*n.* **24.** (in tennis, etc.) a return of a stroke which would normally be a point for the opponent. **25.** an offspring, now only of animals. **26.** *Slang.* a brat; a contemptible little person.

[ME *geten*, t. Scand.; cf. Icel. *geta*, c. OE *gietan* (G *-gessen* in *vergessen* forget): akin to L *-hendere* in *prehendere* seize, take, and to Gk *chandánein* hold, contain] —**get′table,** *adj.*

—**Syn.** 1–5. GET, OBTAIN, ACQUIRE, PROCURE, SECURE imply gaining possession of something. GET may apply to coming into possession in any manner, and either voluntarily or not. OBTAIN suggests putting forth effort to gain possession, and ACQUIRE stresses the possessing after an (often prolonged) effort. PROCURE suggests the method of obtaining as that of search or choice. SECURE, considered in bad taste as a would-be-elegant substitute for GET, is, however, when used with discrimination, a perfectly proper word. It suggests making possession sure and safe, after obtaining something by competition or the like.

get-at-able (gĕt ăt′ə bl), *adj.* *Colloq.* that may be reached or attained; accessible.

get-away (gĕt′ə wā′), *Colloq.* —*n.* **1.** a getting away; an escape. **2.** the start of a race. —*adj.* **3.** pertaining to a get-away: *the get-away car was found.*

Gethsemane (gĕth sĕm′ə nĭ), *n.* **1.** a garden east of Jerusalem, near the brook Kedron: the scene of Christ's agony and betrayal. Matt. 26:36, etc. **2.** (*l.c.*) a scene or occasion of suffering.

getter (gĕt′ə), *n.* **1.** a substance used for removing the last traces of gas from such devices as radio valves; if the gas is air, magnesium is often used because, when vaporized, it combines chemically with both oxygen and nitrogen. **2.** one who or that which gets.

get-together (gĕt′tə gĕth′ə), *n. Colloq.* **1.** a meeting. **2.** a small and informal social gathering.

Gettysburg (gĕt′ĭz bûg′), *n.* a borough in the U.S., in S Pennsylvania, site of an important defeat of Confederate forces, 1863, during the American Civil War; national cemetery and military park. 7960 (1960).

Gettysburg Address, President Lincoln's address at the dedication of the national cemetery at Gettysburg, in 1863.

get-up (gĕt′ŭp′), *n. Colloq.* **1.** style of production; appearance: *get-up of a book.* **2.** style of dress; costume.

geum (jē′əm), *n.* any plant of the genus *Geum*, of the rose family; avens.

GeV, *Physics.* giga-electron volt.

gewgaw (gyōō′gô), *n.* **1.** a bit of gaudy or useless finery. —*adj.* **2.** showy, but paltry.

geyser (gī′zə *for 1*; gē′zə *for 2*), *n.* **1.** a hot spring which intermittently sends up fountain-like jets of water and steam into the air. **2.** a hot-water heater. [t. Icel.: m. *Geysir*, i.e. gusher, name of a hot spring in Iceland, der. *geysa* rush furiously, gush]

geyserite (gī′zə rīt′), *n.* a variety of opaline silica deposited about the orifices of geysers and hot springs; sinter.

G.G., Girl Guides.

g.gr., great gross.

Ghana (gä′nə), *n.* a republic in West Africa comprising the former colonies of the Gold Coast and Ashanti, the protectorate of the Northern Territories, and the U.N. trusteeship of British Togoland: member of the Commonwealth of Nations. 6,726,000 pop. (1960); 92,100 sq. mi. *Cap.:* Accra. —**Ghanaian** (gä nā′ən), *adj., n.*

gharry (găr′ĭ), *n.* (in India) a horse-drawn cart or carriage. [t. Hind.: m. *gari*]

ghastly (gäst′lĭ), *adj.*, **-lier, -liest,** *adv.* —*adj.* **1.** frightful; dreadful; horrible: *a ghastly murder.* **2.** deathly pale: *a ghastly look.* **3.** *Colloq.* bad; unpleasant; shocking: *a ghastly failure.* —*adv.* **4.** *Archaic.* in a ghastly manner; horribly. **5.** *Archaic.* with a deathlike aspect: *ghastly pale.* [ME *gastly*, OE *gāstlic* spectral, f. *gāst* spirit + *-lic* -LY] —**ghast′liness,** *n.* —**Syn. 1.** hideous, grisly.

ghat (gôt), *n.* (in India) **1.** a passage or stairway descending to a river. **2.** a mountain pass. **3.** (*pl.*) a range of mountains. Also, **ghaut.** [t. Hind.]

Ghats (gôts), *n.pl.* two low mountain ranges in S India, along the E and W margins of the Deccan plateau: the **Eastern Ghats,** parallel to the coast of the Bay of Bengal, and the **Western Ghats,** bordering on the Arabian Sea.

ghazi (gä′zĭ), *n., pl.* **-zis. 1.** a Muslim warrior fighting against non-Muslims. **2.** (*cap.*) a title given in Turkey to a victorious high-ranking warrior, sultan, etc. [t. Ar., ppr. of *ghazā* fight]

ghee (gē), *n.* (in the East Indies) a kind of liquid butter, clarified by boiling, made from the milk of cows and buffaloes. [t. Hind.: m. *ghī*]

Ghent (gĕnt), *n.* a city in NW Belgium: a port at the confluence of the Scheldt and Lys rivers, connected with the sea by a ship canal, 21½ mi. long, to the Scheldt estuary at Terheuzen in the Netherlands: treaty, 1814. 155,951 (est. 1963). French, **Gand.** Flemish, **Gent.**

gherkin (gûr′kĭn), *n.* **1.** the small, immature fruit of some common varieties of cucumber, used in pickling. **2.** the small, spiny fruit of a cucurbitaceous vine, *Cucumis anguria*, of the West Indies, the southern U.S., etc., used in pickling. **3.** the plant yielding it. [var. of *gurchen* (t. G), with substitution of -KIN for G dim. *-chen*. Cf. D *gurkje*, Pol. *ogurek*, etc., ult. der. LGk *angoúrion* watermelon]

ghetto (gĕt′ō), *n., pl.* **ghettos, ghettoes. 1.** any quarter inhabited chiefly by Jews. **2.** a quarter in a city in which Jews were formerly required to live. **3.** a quarter in a city in which any minority group lives. [t. It. (Venetian): b. Heb. *ghēt* separation and It. *ge(t)to* foundry (der. *getar* cast, ult. der. L *jacere* throw), as name of Jewish quarter in Venice in the 16th cent.]

Ghibelline (gĭb′ĭ lĭn′), *n.* **1.** a member of the imperial and aristocratic party of medieval Italy, opposed to the Guelphs. —*adj.* **2.** of or pertaining to the Ghibellines. [t. It.: m. *Ghibellino*, t. G: m. *Waiblingen*, name of an estate belonging to the imperial family]

Ghiberti (*It.* gē bĕr′tē), *n.* **Lorenzo** (*It.* lō rĕn′tsō), 1378?–1455, Florentine sculptor.

ghilgai (gĭl′gī, -gē), *n. Austral.* a saucer-shaped depression in the ground; a natural waterhole. [t. native Australian]

Ghirlandaio (*It.* gēr län dä′yō), *n.* (*Domenico di Tommaso Curradi di Doffo Bigordi*) 1449–94, Italian painter.

ghost (gōst), *n.* **1.** the soul of a dead person, a disembodied spirit imagined as wandering among or haunting living persons. **2.** a mere shadow or semblance: *ghost of a chance.* **3.** (*cap*) a spiritual being: *Holy Ghost.* **4.** *Obs.* spirit; principle of life. **5. give up the ghost,** to die. **6.** *Colloq.* ghost writer. **7.** *Optics, Television.* a bright spot or secondary image, from a defect of the instrument. **8.** a red blood corpuscle with no haemoglobin, rendering it colourless. —*v.t.* **9.** to write for someone else who is publicly known as the author. **10.** to haunt. [ME *goost*, OE *gāst*, c. G *Geist* spirit. Cf. GHASTLY] —**ghost′like′,** *adj.*

—**Syn. 1.** apparition, phantom, phantasm, wraith, revenant; shade, spook. GHOST, SPECTRE, SPIRIT all refer to the disembodied soul of a person. A GHOST is the soul or spirit of a deceased person, which appears or otherwise makes its presence known to man: *the ghost of a drowned child.* A SPECTRE is a ghost or apparition of more or less weird, unearthly, or terrifying aspect: *a frightening spectre.* SPIRIT is often interchangeable with GHOST but may mean a supernatural being, usually with an indication of good or malign intent towards man: *the spirit of a friend, an evil spirit.*

ghost dance, 1. a religious movement of western North American Indian tribes in the late 19th century, prophesying the coming of a liberator to restore the Indian race, both dead and alive, to a regenerated earth. **2.** a ritual dance, part of this religion, conveying the message of salvation.

ghostly (gōst′lĭ), *adj.*, **-lier, -liest. 1.** of or pertaining to a ghost; spectral. **2.** *Archaic or Literary.* spiritual. —**ghost′liness,** *n.*

ghost word, a word with no etymological basis, created through the misunderstanding of an editor, or the mistake of a scribe or printer.

ghost writer, one who does literary work for someone else who takes the credit.

ghoul (gōōl), *n.* **1.** an evil demon of oriental legend, supposed to feed on human beings, and esp. to rob graves, prey on corpses, etc. **2.** grave robber. **3.** one who revels in what is revolting. [t. Ar.: m. *ghūl*] —**ghoul′ish,** *adj.* —**ghoul′ishly,** *adv.* —**ghoul′ishness,** *n.*

G.H.Q., *Mil.* General Headquarters.

ghyll (gĭl), *n.* gill³. [var. sp. of GILL³ introduced by Wordsworth]

G.I., *U.S. Colloq.* **1.** a soldier, usually other than an officer, in any of the U.S. armed forces. **2.** *U.S. Army.* government issue. —*attributive.* **3.** of or standardized by the army: *G.I. shoes.*

Giacometti (*It.* jä kō mĕt′tē), *n.* **Alberto** (*It.* äl bĕr′tō), 1901–66, Swiss sculptor and painter.

giant (jī′ənt), *n.* **1.** one of a race of beings in Greek mythology, of more than human size and strength, who were subdued by the Olympian gods. **2.** an imaginary being of human form but superhuman size, strength, etc. **3.** a person or thing of unusually great size, endowments, importance, etc.: *an intellectual giant.* **4.** monitor (def. 6). —*adj.* **5.** gigantic; huge: *the giant cactus.* **6.** great or eminent above others. [ME *geant*, t. OF; r. OE *gigant*, t. L: s. *gigās*, t. Gk] —**giantess** (jī′ən tĭs), *n. fem.*

giantism (jī′ən tĭz′əm), *n.* **1.** the quality or character of a giant. **2.** *Pathol.* gigantism.

giant panda, panda (def. 2).

Giant's Causeway, a promontory composed of hexagonal besalt columns in N county Antrim, Northern Ireland.

giant star, *Astron.* a star of great luminosity and mass, such as Arcturus or Betelgeuse.

giaour (jou′ə), *n.* infidel (a Turkish word for a non-Muslim, esp. a Christian). [t. Turk.: m. *giaur*, t. Pers.: m. *gaur*, var. of *gabr*]

Gib., Gibraltar.

gibber¹ (jĭb′ə), *v.i.* **1.** to speak inarticulately; chatter. —*n.* **2.** gibbering utterance. [? freq. of obs. *gib*, v., caterwaul, behave like a cat; sense devel. and pronunciation influenced by assoc. with *jabber*]

gibber² (gĭb′ə), *n. Austral.* a stone; boulder. [t. native Australian]

gibberellic acid (jĭb′ə rĕl′ĭk), *Biochem.* a metabolic product of the fungus *Gibberella fujikuroa*, $C_{18}H_{21}O_4$-COOH; stimulates plant growth.

gibberish (jĭb′ə rĭsh), *n.* rapid, unintelligible talk. [f. GIBBER + -ISH¹ (modelled on *English*)]

gibbet (jĭb′ĭt), *n., v.,* **-beted, -beting.** —*n.* **1.** gallows with a projecting arm at the top, from which formerly the bodies of criminals were hung in chains and left suspended after execution. —*v.t.* **2.** to hang on a gibbet. **3.** to put to death by hanging on a gibbet. **4.** to hold up to public scorn. [ME *gibet*, t. OF, appar. dim. of *gibe* staff]

Gibbon, *Hylobates lar* (2½ ft long)

gibbon (gĭb′ən), *n.* any of the small, slender, long-armed anthropoid apes, genus *Hylobates*, of arboreal habits, found in the East Indies and southern Asia. [t. F, appar. from a dialect of India]

Gibbon (gĭb′ən), *n.* **Edward,** 1737–94, English historian.

Gibbons (gĭb′ənz), *n.* **1. Grinling** (grĭn′lĭng), 1648–1721, English sculptor and wood carver. **2. Orlando** (ô lăn′dō), 1583–1625, English composer and organist.

gibbosity (gĭ bŏs′ĭ tĭ), *n., pl.* **-ties. 1.** the state of being gibbous. **2.** a protuberance or swelling.

gibbous (gĭb′əs), *adj.* **1.** humpbacked. **2.** (of a heavenly body) so viewed as to appear convex on both margins, as the moon when more than half-full but less than full. See diag. under **moon.** Also, **gibbose** (gĭb′ōs). [t. L: m. s. *gibbōsus* humped] —**gib′bously,** *adv.* —**gib′bousness,** *n.*

Gibbs (gĭbz), *n.* **1. Sir Humphrey Vicary** (vĭk′ə rĭ), born 1902, governor of Rhodesia 1960–69. **2. James,** 1682–1754, Scottish architect.

gibbsite (gĭb′zīt), *n.* a mineral, hydrated aluminium oxide, $AL_2O_3.3H_2O$, occurring in whitish or greyish crystals and masses, an important constituent of bauxite ore. [named after G. *Gibbs,* died 1833, U.S. mineralogist. See -ITE[1]]

gibe (jīb), *v.,* **gibed, gibing,** *n.* —*v.i.* **1.** to utter mocking words; scoff; jeer. —*v.t.* **2.** to taunt; deride; flout. —*n.* **3.** a taunting or sarcastic remark. Also, **jibe.** [? t. OF: m. s. *giber* handle roughly, shake, der. *gibe* staff, billhook] —**gib′er,** *n.* —**gib′ingly,** *adj.*

Gibeon (gĭb′ĭ ən), *n.* an ancient town in Palestine (now in Jordan), near Jerusalem. Josh. 9:3, etc.

Gibeonite (gĭb′ĭ ə nīt′), *n. Bible.* one of the inhabitants of Gibeon, who were condemned by Joshua to be hewers of wood and drawers of water for the Israelites. Josh. 9.

giblet (jĭb′lĭt), *n.* (*usually pl.*) the heart, liver, or gizzard from a fowl, often cooked separately. [ME *gibelet,* t. OF: dish of game]

Gibraltar (jĭ brôl′tə), *n.* **1.** a British crown colony comprising a fortress and seaport situated on a narrow promontory near the S tip of Spain. 24,075 pop. (1961); 2½ sq. mi. **2. Rock of,** a long, precipitous mountain nearly coextensive with this colony: one of the Pillars of Hercules. 1396 ft. high; 2½ mi. long. **3. Strait of,** a strait between Europe and Africa at the Atlantic entrance to the Mediterranean. 8½–23 mi. wide.

Gibraltar

Gibraltarian (jĭb′rôl tēə′rĭ ən), *adj., n.*

Gibson (gĭb′sən), *n.* **Charles Dana** (dā′nə), 1867–1944, U.S. artist and illustrator who created the portrait of the idealized American girl of the 1890s.

Gibson Desert, a sandy waste in the interior of Western Australia, between the Great Sandy and Great Victoria Deserts.

gid (gĭd), *n. Vet. Sci.* a disease in sheep, etc., due to infestation of the brain with larvae of the tapeworm, *Multiceps multiceps*; sturdy. [back-formation from GIDDY, adj.]

giddy (gĭd′ĭ), *adj.,* **-dier, -diest,** *v.,* **-died, -dying.** —*adj.* **1.** frivolously light; impulsive; flighty: *a giddy mind, a giddy girl.* **2.** affected with vertigo; dizzy. **3.** attended with or causing dizziness: *a giddy climb.* —*v.t., v.i.,* **4.** to make or become giddy. [ME *gidy,* OE *gydig* mad, der. *god*; orig. sense presumably god-possessed, in a state of divine frenzy] —**gid′dily,** *adv.* —**gid′diness,** *n.* —**Syn. 1.** unstable, volatile. **2.** light-headed, vertiginous. —**Ant. 1.** steady, stable.

Gide (*Fr.* zhēd), *n.* **André** (*Fr.* äɴ drē′), 1869–1951, French novelist, essayist, and critic.

Gideon (gĭd′ĭ ən), *n. Bible.* Hebrew liberator and religious leader, conqueror of the Midianites and judge in Israel for forty years. Judges 6–8. [var. of *Gedeon* (Septuagint), t. Heb.: m. *Gid'ōn*]

Gideon Bible, a Bible left in hotel rooms and elsewhere, financed by an interdenominational society (the **Gideon Society** or **Gideons**) founded in the U.S. in 1899.

gidgee (gĭj′ĭ), *n.* a small Australian tree with narrow phyllodes, *Acacia homalophylla.* [t. native Australian]

Gielgud (gĭl′go͝od, gēl′-), *n.* **Sir John,** born 1904, English actor and producer.

Gieseking (*Ger.* gē′zə kĭng), *n.* **Walter** (*Ger.* väl′tər), 1895–1956, German pianist and composer.

Giessen (*Ger.* gē′sən), *n.* a town in West Germany, in central Hesse. 72,500 (est. 1966).

gifblaar (gĭf′blä), *n.* a perennial shrub, *Dichapetalum cymosum,* of southern Africa, deadly poisonous to livestock. [t. Afrikaans: poison leaf]

gifbol (gĭf′bŏl), *n.* an amaryllidaceous plant, *Boophone disticha,* of southern Africa, the bulbs of which yield latex formerly used for poison arrows. [t. Afrikaans: poison bulb]

gift (gĭft), *n.* **1.** something given; a present. **2.** the act of giving. **3.** the power or right of giving. **4.** a quality, or special ability; natural endowment; talent. **5.** *Colloq.* anything very easily obtained or understood. —*v.t.* **6.** to present with as a gift; bestow gifts upon; endow with. [ME, t. Scand.; cf. Icel. *gift,* c. OE *gift* husband's gift to wife at marriage, G *Gift* poison, etc.; akin to GIVE v.] —**Syn. 1.** donation, contribution, offering, boon, alms, gratuity. See **present[2].**

gifted (gĭf′tĭd), *adj.* endowed with natural gifts; talented: *a gifted artist.*

gift-horse (gĭft′hôs′), *n.* **look a gift-horse in the mouth,** to criticize a gift; accept a gift ungratefully.

gift token, a voucher given as a present allowing the recipient to choose goods worth a specified amount, usually from a specified shop. Also, **gift voucher.**

gift-wrap (gĭft′răp′), *v.t.,* **-wrapped, -wrapping.** to wrap (an article) with ornate paper, ribbon, etc., as for a gift. —**gift′wrap′ping,** *n.*

Gifu (gē′fo͞o′), *n.* a city in central Japan, in SW central Honshu island. 358,190 (1965).

gig[1] (gĭg), *n., v.,* **gigged, gigging.** —*n.* **1.** *Naut.* **a.** a long, fast-pulling boat used esp. for racing. **b.** the boat reserved for a ship's captain. **2.** a light, two-wheeled one-horse carriage. —*v.i.* **3.** to ride in a gig. [orig. uncert.]

Gig[1] (def. 2)

gig[2] (gĭg), *n., v.,* **gigged, gigging.** —*n.* **1.** a spear used in fishing. **2.** a device, commonly four hooks secured back to back, for dragging through a school of fish to hook them through the body. —*v.t., v.i.* **3.** to catch (fish) with a gig. [short for *fizgig,* t. Sp.: m. *fisga* harpoon]

gig[3] (gĭg), *v.t.,* **gigged, gigging.** *Austral., Brit. Dial.* to taunt; provoke. [orig. unknown]

gig[4] (gĭg), *n. Slang.* **1.** the booking for a jazzman or pop star to perform at a concert. **2.** a concert of jazz or pop music. **3.** any job or occupation. [orig. unknown]

giga-, a prefix denoting one thousand million (10^9). [f. Gk: irreg. comb. form of *gígās* giant]

giga-electron volt, *Physics.* 10 electron volts. *Abbrev.*: GeV. *U.S. equivalent*: BeV.

gigantean (jī′găn tē′ən), *adj.* gigantic. [f. s. L *gigantēus* + -AN. See GIANT]

gigantesque (jī′găn tĕsk′), *adj.* of a gigantic kind; suited to a giant. [t. F, t. It.: m. *gigantesco,* der. *gigante,* t. L: m. s. *gigās* GIANT]

gigantic (jī găn′tĭk), *adj.* **1.** of, like, or befitting a giant. **2.** very large; huge. [f. s. L *gigās* GIANT + -IC] —**gigan′tically,** *adv.* —**gigan′ticness,** *n.*
—**Syn. 2.** enormous, immense, prodigious, herculean, cyclopean, titanic. GIGANTIC, COLOSSAL, MAMMOTH, MONSTROUS are used of whatever is physically or metaphorically of great magnitude. GIGANTIC refers to the size of a giant: *a gigantic stalk of wheat.* COLOSSAL to that of a colossus: *a colossal skeleton of a brontosaurus.* MAMMOTH to that of the animal of that name: *a mammoth jaw of a prehistoric animal.* MONSTROUS means unusual or out of the normal in some striking way, as in size: *a monstrous blunder.* —**Ant. 2.** tiny.

gigantism (jī′găn tĭz′əm, jī găn′tĭz-), *n. Pathol.* abnormally great development in size or stature of the whole body, or of parts of the body, most often due to dysfunction of the pituitary gland. Also, **giantism.**

gigantomachia (jī găn′tō mā′kĭ ə), *n.* **1.** a war of giants, esp. the war of the giants of Greek mythology against the Olympian gods. **2.** a representation of this, as in sculpture. Also, **gigantomachy** (jī′găn tŏm′ə kĭ). [t. LL, t. Gk: the battle of the giants]

giggle (gĭg′l), *v.,* **-gled, -gling,** *n.* —*v.i.* **1.** to laugh in a silly, undignified way, as from youthful spirits or ill-controlled amusement; titter. —*n.* **2.** a silly, spasmodic laugh; a titter. [appar. back-formation from obs. *giglet* giddy, laughing girl, der. obs. *gig* flighty, giddy girl. Cf. D *gigelen,* G *gickeln* giggle] —**gig′gler,** *n.*

giggly (gĭg′lĭ), *adj.,* **-glier, -gliest.** inclined to giggle.

Gigli (*It.* jēl′lyē), *n.* **Beniamino** (*It.* bĕ nyä mē′nō), 1890–1957, Italian operatic tenor.

gigolo (zhĭg′ə lō′), *n., pl.* **-los. 1.** a man supported by a woman, esp. a young man supported by an older woman in return for companionship. **2.** a male professional dancing partner. [t. F]

gigot (jĭg′ət), *n.* **1.** a leg-of-mutton sleeve. **2.** a leg of mutton. [t. F, dim. of d. F *gigue* leg, der. *giguer* hop, dance, der. OF *gigue* fiddle, t. Gmc; cf. G *Geige*]

gigue (zhēg), *n.* **1.** *Dancing.* jig[2] (def. 1). **2.** *Music.* lively music for this dance. **3.** *Music.* a jig[2] (def. 2), often forming the concluding movement in the classical suite. [t. F. See JIG]

Gijón (*Sp.* KHē KHōn′), *n.* a town in N Spain; seaport. 134,011 (1965).

Gila (hē′lə), *n.* a river in the U.S., flowing from SW New Mexico W across S Arizona to the Colorado river. 630 mi.

Gila monster, a large, venomous lizard, *Heloderma suspectum*, of the south-western U.S., having the skin studded with yellow or orange and black headlike tubercles. [named after the GILA river, in Arizona]

gilbert (gĭl′bət), *n. Elect.* the c.g.s. unit of magnetomotive force, equal to 0·7958 ampere turns. [named after W. *Gilbert*, 1540–1603, English scientist]

Gilbert (gĭl′bət), *n.* **1. Sir Humphrey,** 1539?–83, English soldier, navigator, and colonizer of America. **2. Sir William Schwenck** (shwĕngk), 1836–1911, English dramatist, humorist, and poet; collaborator with Sullivan.

Gilbert and Ellice Islands (ĕl′ĭs), a British colony in the central Pacific, comprising the Gilbert and Ellice groups and other widely scattered islands. 48,364 pop. (1963); 203 sq. mi.

Gilbertian (gĭl bû′tĭ ən), *adj.* whimsically or paradoxically humorous in the style of Sir W. S. Gilbert.

gild[1] (gĭld), *v.t.*, **gilded** or **gilt, gilding. 1.** to coat with gold, gold leaf, or gold-coloured substance. **2.** to give a bright, pleasing, or specious aspect to. **3. gild the lily,** to spoil beauty by overembellishment. **4.** *Obs.* to make red, as with blood. [ME *gilden*, OE *gyldan*, der. GOLD. def. 3 is a misquotation from Shakespeare's *King John*, IV ii 11, 'To gild refined gold, to paint the lily.']

gild[2] (gĭld), *n.* guild. **—gildsman** (gĭldz′mən), *n.*

gilded (gĭl′dĭd), *adj.* **1.** covered or enhanced with gold, or something coloured gold. **2.** having a superficially showy and attractive exterior, covering something of little worth. **3. gilded youth,** a young man of wealth and fashion, usually idle.

gilder[1] (gĭl′də), *n.* one who or that which gilds. [f. GILD[1] + -ER[1]]

gilder[2] (gĭl′də), *n.* guilder.

gildhall (gĭld′hôl′), *n.* guildhall.

gilding (gĭl′dĭng), *n.* **1.** the application of gilt. **2.** the gold leaf or other material with which anything is gilded. **3.** the golden surface produced. **4.** any deceptive coating or aspect used to give a fine appearance.

Gilead (gĭl′ĭ ăd′), *n.* **1.** an ancient district of Palestine, E of the river Jordan, in present Jordan. **2. Mount,** a mountain in NW Jordan. 3596 ft.

Gilgamesh (gĭl′gə mĕsh′), *n.* a mythical Sumerian king, the hero of a Sumerian epic.

gill[1] (gĭl), *n.* **1.** an aquatic respiratory organ, either external or internal, usually feathery, platelike, or filamentous. **2.** one of the radiating vertical plates on the underside of the cap of an agaric. **3.** the ground ivy. *—v.t.* **4.** to catch (fish) by the gills in a gill net. **5.** to gut or clean (fish). [ME *gile*, t. Scand.; cf. Sw. *gäl*, Dan. *gælle*] **—gilled,** *adj.* **—gill′-like′,** *adj.*

gill[2] (jĭl), *n.* a unit of liquid measure equal to ¼ pint. [ME *gille*, t. OF: wine measure. Cf. GALLON]

gill[3] (gĭl), *n. Dial.* **1.** a deep rocky ravine, often wooded, forming the course of a stream. **2.** a stream; rivulet; brook. Also, **ghyll.** [ME, t. Scand.; cf. Icel. *gil*]

Gill (gĭl), *n.* **Eric,** 1882–1940, English carver, engraver, and author.

gill fungus (gĭl), an agaricaceous fungus.

gillie (gĭl′ĭ), *n.*, *v.*, **-lied, -lying.** *Scot. —n.* **1.** a sportsman's attendant, esp. a guide for hunting or fishing. **2.** a male attendant or personal servant of a Highland chieftain. *—v.t.* **3.** to act as a gillie. Also, **gilly.** [t. Gaelic: m. *gille* lad, servant]

Gillingham (jĭl′ĭng əm), *n.* a town in England, in N Kent. 77,070 (est. 1964).

gill net (gĭl), a curtain-like net, suspended vertically in the water, with meshes of such a size as to catch by the gills a fish that has thrust its head through.

Gill sans, *Print.* the first sans-serif type, designed by Eric Gill; cut in 1928.

gilly (gĭl′ĭ), *n.*, *pl.* **-lies.** *Scot.* gillie.

Gilly (*Ger.* zhĭl′ē), **Friedrich** (*Ger.* frē′drĭKH), 1772–1800, German architect.

gillyflower (jĭl′ĭ flou′ə), *n.* **1.** the name for various flowers, as for example, the wallflower, *Cheiranthus cheiri*, the common stock gillyflower, *Matthiola incana*, etc. **2.** *Archaic or Dial.* the clove pink. Also, **gilliflower.** [alter. of ME *gilofre*, t. OF: clove, g. L *caryophyllon*, t. Gk: m. *karyóphyllon* clove tree]

gilsonite (gĭl′sə nīt′), *n.* an extremely pure asphalt particularly valuable for the manufacture of paints and varnishes, chiefly found in the U.S., in Utah; uintaite. [named after S. H. *Gilson* of Salt Lake City. See -ITE[1]]

gilt[1] (gĭlt), *v.* **1.** a pt. and pp. of **gild**[1]. *—adj.* **2.** gilded; golden in colour. *—n.* **3.** the gold or other material applied in gilding; gilding.

gilt[2] (gĭlt), *n.* a sow that has not produced piglets and that has not reached an evident stage of pregnancy. [ME *gilte*, t. Scand.; cf. Icel. *gylta*]

gilt-edged (gĭlt′ĕjd′), *adj.* **1.** having the edges gilded: *gilt-edged paper.* **2.** of the highest order or quality: *gilt-edged securities.*

gilthead (gĭlt′hĕd′), *n.* any of several sea-breams, having a crescent-shaped golden band across the eyes, esp. *Sparus auratus.*

gimbals (jĭm′blz), *n.*, *pl.* a contrivance for keeping a suspended object, as a ship's compass, horizontal. [pl. of *gimbal* (now used only attributively and in composition), var. of *gimmal*, ME *gemel*, t. OF: twin]

gimcrack (jĭm′krăk′), *n.* **1.** a showy, useless trifle; gewgaw. *—adj.* **2.** showy but useless. [orig. uncert.]

gimlet (gĭm′lĭt), *n.* **1.** a small tool for boring holes, consisting of a shaft with a pointed screw at one end and a handle at the other. *—v.t.* **2.** to pierce with or as with a gimlet. *—adj.* **3.** able to bore through, or penetrate. **4.** deeply penetrating, or thought to be deeply penetrating: *gimlet eyes.* [ME *gymlet*, t. OF: m. *guimbelet*, dim. of **guimbel* WIMBLE]

Gimlet

gimmick (gĭm′ĭk), *n.* **1.** *Colloq.* a pronounced eccentricity of dress, manner, voice, etc., or an eccentric action or device, esp. one exploited to gain publicity. **2.** any tricky device or means. **3.** *U.S. Slang.* a device by which a magician works a trick. [? b. *gimmer* trick finger-ring and MAGIC]

gimmickry (gĭm′ĭk rĭ), *n.* gimmicks collectively.

gimp (gĭmp), *n.* a flat trimming of silk, wool, or other cord, sometimes stiffened with wire, for garments, curtains, etc. [appar. t. D; ult. orig. unknown]

gin[1] (jĭn), *n.* an alcoholic beverage obtained by redistilling spirits with flavouring agents, esp. juniper berries, orange peel, angelica root, etc. [short for GENEVA]

gin[2] (jĭn), *n.*, *v.*, **ginned, ginning.** *—n.* **1.** a machine for separating cotton from its seeds, as a cotton gin. **2.** a trap or snare for game, etc. *—v.t.* **3.** to clear (cotton) of seeds with a gin. **4.** to catch (game, etc.) in a gin. [ME; aphetic var. of OF *engin* ENGINE] **—gin′ner,** *n.*

gin[3] (gĭn), *v.i.*, *v.t.*, **gan, gun, ginning.** *Archaic or Poetic.* begin. [ME *ginnen*, OE *ginnan*, aphetic var. of *onginnan*. Cf. OE *beginnan* BEGIN]

gin[4] (jĭn), *n. Cards.* a rummy game in which a player with a total of 10 unmatched points or less may end the game. Also, **gin rummy.** [? a pun: *gin* = *rum*]

gin[5] (jĭn), *n. Austral.* an Aborigine woman. [t. native Australian]

gingal (jĭn′gôl), *n.* jingal. Also, **gingall.**

gingeli (jĭn′jĭ lĭ), *n.* gingili. Also, **gingelly.**

ginger (jĭn′jə), *n.* **1.** the pungent, spicy rhizome of any of the reedlike plants of the genus *Zingiber*, esp. of *Z. officinale*, variously used in cookery and medicine. **2.** any of these plants, native in the East Indies, but now cultivated in most tropical countries. **3.** a reddish brown or tawny colour. **4.** (of hair) red. **5.** *Colloq.* piquancy; animation. *—v.t.* **6.** to treat or flavour with ginger. **7.** *Colloq.* to impart spiciness or piquancy to; make lively. [ME *gingivere*, OE *gingifere*, t. LL: m. *gingiber*, L *zingiberi*, t. Gk: m. *zingíberis* ginger, appar. t. Prakrit: m. *singabēra*]

ginger ale, a soft drink, flavoured with ginger, used for mixing with spirits, esp. whisky.

ginger beer, a non-alcoholic carbonated drink of water, sugar, yeast, etc., flavoured with ginger.

ginger biscuit, a small, flat, often round biscuit flavoured with ginger.

gingerbread (jĭn′jə brĕd′), *n.* **1.** a kind of cake flavoured with ginger and treacle or golden syrup. **2.** something showy but unsubstantial and inartistic. *—adj.* **3.** showy but unsubstantial and inartistic. [alter. of ME *gingimbrat* preserved ginger, t. ML: s. **gingimbratum*, der. *gingiber* GINGER]

gingerbread tree, a rosaceous tree, *Parinarium macrophyllum*, of western Africa, with a large, edible, farinaceous fruit (**gingerbread plum**).

ginger group, a splinter group of members of an association, who join together to modernize, activate, or enliven their association and its other members.

gingerly (jĭn′jə lĭ), *adv.* **1.** with extreme care or caution; warily. **2.** *Obs.* mincingly; daintily. *—adj.* **3.** cautious or wary. **—gin′gerliness,** *n.*

ginger nut, a ginger biscuit.

gingersnap (jĭn′jə snăp′), *n.* a brittle, wafer-like biscuit flavoured with ginger.

gingery (jĭn′jə rĭ), *adj.* **1.** ginger-like; pungent; spicy. **2.** of the colour of ginger.

gingham (gĭng′əm), *n.* yarn-dyed, plain-weave cotton fabric, usually striped or checked. [t. F: m. *guingan*, ult. t. Malay: m. *ginggang*, lit., striped]

gingili (jĭn′jĭ lĭ), *n.*, *pl.* **-lis. 1.** the sesame (plant). **2.** its oil. Also, **gingeli, gingelly.** [t. Hind.: m. *jinjalī*, ult. t. Ar.: m. *juljulān*]

gingiva (jĭn jī′və), *n. Med.* gum[2]. [t. L]

gingival (jĭn jī′ vəl), jĭn′jĭ vəl), *adj.* **1.** of or pertaining to the gums. **2.** *Phonet.* made at the gums; alveolar. [f. s. L *gingiva* gum + -AL[1]]

gingivitis (jĭn′jĭ vī′tĭs), *n. Pathol.* inflammation of the gums.

ginglymus (gĭng′glĭ məs, jĭng′-), *n. Anat.* a joint that permits movement in one plane only, i.e. like a hinge. [t. NL, t. Gk: m. *gínglymos* hinge] —**ging′lymoid′,** *adj.*

ginkgo (gĭngk′gō), *n., pl.* **-goes.** a large, ornamental, gymnospermous tree, *Ginkgo biloba*, native to China, with fan-shaped leaves, fleshy fruit, and edible nuts; maidenhair tree. Also, **ging′ko.** [t. Jap.]

ginnery (jĭn′ə rĭ), *n., pl.* **-neries.** a mill for ginning cotton.

gin rummy, gin[4].

Ginsberg (gĭnz′bûg), *n.* **Allen,** born 1926, U.S. poet.

ginseng (jĭn′sĕng), *n.* **1.** either of two araliaceous plants, *Panax schinseng* of China, Korea, etc., and *P. quinquefolium* of North America, yielding an aromatic root which is extensively used in medicine by the Chinese. **2.** the root itself. **3.** a preparation made from it. [t. Chinese (Mandarin): m. *jên shên*, f. *jên* man + *shên*, of obscure meaning]

Giono (*Fr.* zhyŏ nō′), *n.* **Jean** (*Fr.* zhäɴ), born 1895, French novelist.

Giorgio Martini (*It.* jôr′jō mär tē′nē), **Francesco di** (*It.* frän chĕs′kō dē), 1439–1501, Italian early Renaissance architect.

Giorgione (*It.* jôr jō′nĕ), *n.* (*Giorgione da Castelfranco, Giorgio Barbarelli*), 1478?–1511, Italian painter.

Giotto (jŏt′ō; *It.* jŏt′tō), *n. c.*1266–1337, Florentine painter and architect.

gip[1] (jĭp), *v.t.*, **gipped, gipping,** *n.* gyp[1]. —**gip′per,** *n.*

gip[2] (jĭp), *n. Slang.* gyp[3].

Gippsland (gĭps′lănd′), *n.* a district in Australia along the SE coast of Victoria. ab. 12,000 sq. mi.

gipsy (jĭp′sĭ), *n., pl.* **-sies. 1.** (*often cap.*) one of a nomadic Caucasian minority race of Hindu origin. **2.** (*often cap.*) Romany; the language of the gipsies. **3.** a person who resembles or lives like a gipsy. **4.** a gipsy winch. —*adj.* **5.** of or pertaining to the gipsies. Also, **gypsy.** [backformation from *gipcyan*, aphetic var. of EGYPTIAN] —**gip′sy-like′,** *adj.*

gipsy moth, a moth, *Lymantria dispar*, whose caterpillar is destructive to trees.

gipsy winch, *Naut.* a small winch or crab.

gipsywort (jĭp′sĭ wûrt′), *n.* an erect perennial herb with small white flowers, *Lycopus europaeus*, family *Labiatae*, common on the banks of rivers and lakes in Europe and W Asia.

giraffe (jĭ răf′), *n.* **1.** a tall, long-necked, spotted ruminant, *Giraffa camelopardalis*, of Africa, the tallest of existing quadrupeds. **2.** (*cap.*) *Astron.* the northern constellation Camelopard. [t. F (now *girafe*), t. Ar.: m. *zarāfah*, prob. of African orig.]

Giraffe, *Giraffa camelopardalis* (Ab. 18 ft high)

girandole (jĭ′rən dōl′), *n.* **1.** a rotating and radiating firework. **2.** *Fort.* a group of connected mines. **3.** an ornate branched support for candles or other lights. **4.** a pendant jewel surrounded by smaller jewels. Also, **girandola** (jĭ răn′də lə). [t. F, t. It.: m. *girandola*, der. *girare* turn, g. L *gȳrāre.* See GYRATE]

girasol (jĭ′rə sōl′, -sŏl′), *n.* a variety of opal which reflects a floating luminous glow. Also, **girasole, girosol.** [t. F, t. It.: m. *girasole*, f. *gira(re)* turn + *sol(e)* sun, in imitation of Gk *hēliotrópion*]

Giraud (*Fr.* zhē rō′), *n.* **Henri Honoré** (*Fr.* äɴ rē ō nō rĕ′), 1879–1949, French general.

Giraudoux (*Fr.* zhē rō do͞o′), *n.* **Jean,** 1882–1944, French novelist and dramatist.

gird[1] (gûd), *v.t.*, **girt** or **girded, girding. 1.** to encircle with a belt or girdle **2.** to surround; hem in. **3.** to prepare (oneself) mentally for action (often fol. by *up*). **4.** to endue. [ME *girde(n)*, OE *gyrdan*, c. G *gürten*]

gird[2] (gûd), *v.i.* **1.** to gibe; jeer (fol. by *at*). —*v.t.* **2.** *Obs.* to gibe or jeer at; taunt. —*n.* **3.** *Archaic.* a gibe. [ME; orig. obscure]

girder (gû′də), *n.* **1.** (in structural work) any main horizontal supporting member or beam, as of steel, reinforced concrete or wood. **2.** one of the principal horizontal timbers which support the joists in certain floors. [f. GIRD[1] + -ER[1]]

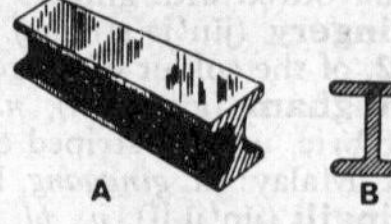

Girder
A, Steel girder; B, Cross-section of a steel girder

girdle[1] (gû′dl), *n., v.,* **-dled, -dling.** —*n.* **1.** a belt, cord, or the like, worn about the waist. **2.** a lightweight undergarment which supports the abdominal region of the body. **3.** any encircling band; compass; limit. **4.** *Gems.* the edge about a brilliant or other cut stone at the junction of the upper and lower faces. **5.** *Anat.* the bony framework which unites the upper or lower extremities to the axial skeleton. **6.** a ring made about a tree trunk, etc., by cutting the bark. —*v.t.* **7.** to encircle with a belt; gird. **8.** to encompass; enclose; encircle. **9.** to cut away the bark in a ring about (a tree, branch, etc.), thus causing death. [ME; OE *gyrdel*, der. *gyrdan* gird[1]] —**gir′dle-like′,** *adj.* —**gir′dler,** *n.*

girdle[2] (gû′dl), *n.* griddle.

girdlecake (gû′dl kāk′), *n.* griddlecake.

Girgenti (*It.* jēr jĕn′tē), *n.* former name of **Agrigento.**

Giri (gĭə′rĭ), *n.* **Varahgiri Venkata** (vŭ′rə gĭə′rĭ vĕng′kə tə), born 1894, president of India from 1969.

girl (gûl), *n.* **1.** a female child or young person. **2.** a young unmarried woman. **3.** a female servant, esp. (in India, Africa, and elsewhere) a native female servant. **4.** *Colloq.* a sweetheart. **5.** *Colloq.* a woman. **6.** see **old girl.** [ME *gurle, girle* child, young person, OE *gyrl-* in *gyrlgyden* virgin goddess. Cf. LG *gör(e)* young person]

girl Friday, *Slang.* a female secretary and general assistant in an office.

girlfriend (gûl′frĕnd′), *n.* **1.** a female friend. **2.** a young woman for whom a man or boy has a special interest in or is attracted to; a sweetheart.

girl guide, a member of an organization of girls (**Girl Guides**) founded in England in 1910 by Lady Agnes Baden-Powell, to develop health, citizenship, character, and home-making ability.

girlhood (gûl′ho͝od′), *n.* **1.** the state or time of being a girl. **2.** girls collectively.

girlie (gû′lĭ), *n.* **1.** *Colloq.* a girl. —*adj.* **2.** illustrating or featuring nude or nearly nude women: *a girlie magazine.*

girlish (gû′lĭsh), *adj.* of, like, or befitting a girl: *girlish laughter.* —**girl′ishly,** *adv.* —**girl′ishness,** *n.*

girl scout, a member of any of several sister organizations of the Girl Guides, in the U.S. and elsewhere.

Giro (jī′ə rō′), *n.* a system of settling accounts, as between debtors and creditors, without the transfer of actual cash, by dealing directly through the banks or post office. [t. Gk: m. s. *gýros* circuit]

Gironde (*Fr.* zhē rōɴd′), *n.* **1.** an estuary in SW France, formed by the junction of the rivers Garonne and Dordogne. ab. 45 mi. long. **2.** a department in SW France. 935,448 pop. (1962); 4141 sq. mi. *Cap.:* Bordeaux. **3. the Gironde,** the party of the Girondists.

Girondist (jĭ rŏn′dĭst), *n.* **1.** a member of a French political party of moderate republicans (1791–93), whose leaders were deputies from the department of Gironde. —*adj.* **2.** of or pertaining to the Girondists. —**Giron′dism,** *n.*

girt (gût), *v.* **1.** a pt. and pp. of **gird**[1]. —*adj.* **2.** *Naut.* (of a vessel) moored so tightly as to prevent swinging.

girth (gûth), *n.* **1.** the measure around anything; circumference. **2.** a band passed under the belly of a horse, etc., to secure a saddle or pack on its back. **3.** a band or girdle. —*v.t.* **4.** to bind or fasten with a girth. **5.** to girdle; encircle. [ME *girth, gerth*, t. Scand.; cf. Icel. *gjördh* girdle, hoop; akin to GIRD[1]]

girtline (gût′līn′), *n. Naut.* a gantline.

gisarme (gĭ zäm′), *n.* a medieval shafted weapon with a scythelike cutting blade from the back edge of which emerges a long slender blade with a sharp point. [ME *gisharme(e)*, t. OF: m. *g(u)isarme*; orig. uncert.]

Gisborne (gĭz′bən). *n.* a seaport in New Zealand, in NE North Island. 24,100 (est. 1964).

Gissing (gĭs′ĭng), *n.* **George Robert,** 1857–1903, English novelist.

gist (jĭst), *n.* **1.** the substance or pith of a matter; essential part: *the gist of an argument.* **2.** the ground on which a legal action rests. [t. OF, 3rd pers. sing. pres. ind. of *gesir* lie, rest, g. L *jacēre*]

gittern (gĭt′ûn), *n.* cittern. [ME *gitern(e)*, t. OF: m. *guiterne.* Cf. GUITAR]

Giulini (*It.* jo͞o lē′nē), *n.* **Carlo Maria** (*It.* kär′lō mä rē′ä), born 1914, Italian conductor.

Giulio Romano (*It.* jo͞o′lyō rō mä′nō), (*Giulio Pippi*), 1492?–1546, Italian painter and architect.

give (gĭv), *v.*, **gave, given, giving,** *n.* —*v.t.* **1.** to deliver freely; bestow; hand over: *give someone a present.* **2.** to deliver to another in exchange for something; pay. **3.** to grant permission or opportunity to; enable; assign; award. **4.** to set forth or show; present; offer. **5.** to present to, or as to an audience: *My Lords, Ladies, and Gentlemen, I give you the Lord Mayor of London.* **6.** to propose as the subject of a toast: *I give you the Queen.*

7. to assign as a basis of calculation or reasoning; suppose; assume: *given these facts.* **8.** to assign to someone as his right, lot, etc.: *to give a child a name, to give him the benefit of the doubt.* **9.** to be prepared to assign: *I don't give twopence for your views.* **10.** to set aside for a specified purpose: *he gives great attention to detail.* **11.** to furnish or provide: *give aid, evidence, etc.* **12.** to afford or yield; produce: *give satisfaction, good results, etc.* **13.** to make, do, or perform: *give a start, a lurch, etc.* **14.** to issue; put forth, emit, or utter: *to give a cry, a command, etc.* **15.** to cause: *I was given to understand.* **16.** to impart or communicate: *give advice, give someone a cold.* **17.** to deal or administer: *give one a blow, a medicine, the sacrament, etc.* **18.** to relinquish or surrender: *to give ground, place, etc.* **19.** to put forth; emit (fol. by *off* or *out*). **20.** to produce; present: *to give a play.* **21.** to act as host at (a social function, etc.): *to give a party.* **22.** to pledge: *to give one's word of honour.* —*v.i.* **23.** to make a gift or gifts. **24.** to yield, as to pressure or strain; draw back; relax. **25.** to break down; fail. **26.** to be situated facing a specified direction: *the house gives on to the seafront.* —*v.* **27.** Some special verb phrases are:

give away, **1.** to give as a present. **2.** to hand over (the bride) to the bridegroom at a wedding. **3.** *Slang.* to let (a secret) be known. **4.** to betray (a person).

give birth to, **1.** to bear. **2.** to be the origin of.

give in, **1.** to yield; acknowledge defeat. **2.** to hand in.

give of, to devote or contribute largely of.

give out, **1.** to become worn out or used up. **2.** to send out, emit. **3.** to distribute; issue. **4.** to announce publicly.

give over, **1.** to transfer. **2.** to assign for a specific purpose: *the evening was given over to feasting.* **3.** *Colloq.* to desist.

give rise to, to be the origin of; cause; result in.

give up, **1.** to lose all hope. **2.** to abandon as hopeless. **3.** to desist from; forsake: *give up a task.* **4.** to surrender. **5.** to devote entirely.

—*n.* **28.** the act or fact of yielding to pressure; elasticity. [ME, t. Scand. (cf. Dan. *give*); r. ME *yeve(n)*, *yive(n)*, OE *gefan*, *gi(e)fan*, c. D *geven*, G *geben*, Goth. *giban*. Cf. GIFT] —**giv′able,** *adj.* —**giv′er,** *n.*

—**Syn. 1.** offer, vouchsafe, impart, accord, furnish, provide, supply, donate, contribute. GIVE, CONFER, GRANT, PRESENT may mean that something concrete or abstract is bestowed on one person by another. GIVE is the general word: *to give someone a book, permission, etc.* CONFER usually means to give an honour or a favour; it implies courteous and gracious giving: *to confer a degree.* GRANT is limited to the idea of acceding to a request; it may apply to the bestowal of privileges, or the fulfilment of an expressed wish: *to grant a charter, a prayer, permission, etc.* PRESENT, a more formal word than GIVE, usually implies a certain ceremony in the giving: *to present a citation to a regiment.*

give-and-take (gĭv′ən tāk′), *n.* **1.** a method of dealing by compromise or mutual concession; cooperation. **2.** good-humoured exchange of talk, ideas, etc.

give-away (gĭv′ə wā′), *Colloq.* —*n.* **1.** a betrayal, usually unintentional. **2.** a premium given with various articles to promote sales, etc. —*adj.* **3.** (of a television programme, etc.) characterized by the awarding of prizes, money, etc., to recipients chosen, usually, through a question-and-answer contest.

given (gĭv′ən), *v.* **1.** pp. of give. —*adj.* **2.** stated, fixed, or specified: *at a given time.* **3.** addicted or disposed (often fol. by *to*): *given to drink.* **4.** bestowed as a gift; conferred. **5.** assigned as a basis of calculation, reasoning, etc.: *given A and B, C follows.* **6.** *Maths.* known or determined: *a given magnitude.* **7.** (on official documents) executed and delivered as of the date specified.

given name, *U.S.* Christian name.

Giza (gē′zə), *n.* El Giza. Also, **Gizeh.**

gizzard (gĭz′əd), *n.* the grinding or muscular stomach of birds, the organ in which food is triturated after leaving the glandular stomach; ventriculus. [ME *giser*, t. OF, ult. g. L *gigēria* cooked entrails of poultry]

Gk, Greek.

Gl, *Chem.* glucinum.

glabella (glə bĕl′ə), *n.*, *pl.* **-bellae** (-bĕl′ē). *Anat.* the flat area of bone between the eyebrows, used as a craniometric point. [NL, prop. fem. of L *glabellus* smooth, hairless, dim. of *glaber.* See GLABROUS]

glabellum (glə bĕl′əm), *n.*, *pl.* **-bella.** glabella.

glabrate (glā′brāt, -brĭt), *adj.* **1.** *Zool.* smooth; glabrous. **2.** *Bot.* becoming glabrous; somewhat glabrous.

glabrous (glā′brəs), *adj. Zool., Bot.* smooth; having a surface devoid of hair or pubescence. [f. s. L *glaber* smooth, hairless + -OUS]

glacé (glăs′ĭ; *Fr.* glȧ sĕ′), *adj.* **1.** iced or sugared, as cake. **2.** crystallized, as fruits. **3.** finished with a gloss, as kid or silk. **4.** *U.S.* frozen. [F, pp. of *glacer*, der. *glace* ice, ult. g. L *glacies*]

glacial (glā′syəl), *adj.* **1.** characterized by the presence of ice in extensive masses or glaciers. **2.** due to or associated with the action of ice or glaciers. **3.** of or pertaining to glaciers or ice sheets. **4.** cold as ice; icy. **5.** *Chem.* of or tending to assume an icelike form, as certain acids. [t. L: s. *glaciālis* icy] —**gla′cially,** *adv.*

glacial acetic acid, a 99·5 per cent concentration of acetic acid.

glacial epoch, **1.** the geologically recent Pleistocene epoch, during which much of the Northern Hemisphere was covered by great ice sheets; ice age. **2.** any one of the Eocene, Permian, Carboniferous, Cambrian, and Pre-Cambrian glaciations or ice ages. Also, **glacial episode.**

glacial meal, rock-flour.

glaciate (glăs′ĭ āt′), *v.t.*, **-ated, -ating.** **1.** to cover with ice or glaciers. **2.** to affect by glacial action. —**glaciation** (glăs′ĭ ā′shən), *n.*

glacier (glăs′ĭ ə), *n.* an extended mass of ice formed from snow falling and accumulating over the years and moving very slowly, either descending from high mountains, as in valley glaciers, or moving outwards from centres of accumulation, as in continental glaciers. [t. F, der. *glace* ice, ult. g. L *glacies*] —**gla′ciered,** *adj.*

glaciology (glăs′ĭ ŏl′ə jĭ, glā′sĭ-), *n.* the study of ice and geological phenomena involving the action of ice. —**glac′iol′ogist,** *n.*

glacis (glăs′ĭs, glăs′ĭ), *n.* **1.** a gentle slope. **2.** *Fort.* a bank of earth in front of the counterscarp or covered way of a fort, having an easy slope towards the field or open country. [t. F: orig., icy or slippery place, der. OF *glacier* slip. See GLACÉ]

glad (glăd), *adj.*, **gladder, gladdest.** **1.** delighted or pleased (fol. by *of, at*, etc., or an infinitive or clause): *to be glad at the news, glad to go, glad that one has come.* **2.** characterized by or showing cheerfulness, joy, or pleasure, as looks, utterances, etc. **3.** attended with or causing joy or pleasure: *a glad occasion, glad tidings.* **4.** willing. —*v.t.* **5.** *Archaic.* to make glad. [ME; OE *glæd*, c. Icel. *gladhr* bright, glad, D *glad* and G *glatt* smooth; akin to L *glaber* smooth] —**glad′ly,** *adv.* —**glad′ness,** *n.* —**Syn. 1.** elated, delighted, gratified. —**Ant. 1.** sad.

Gladbeck (*Ger.* glȧt′bĕk), *n.* a town in West Germany, in NW central North Rhine-Westphalia. 82,700 (est. 1966).

gladden (glăd′n), *v.t.* **1.** to make glad. —*v.i.* **2.** *Obs.* to be glad. —**glad′dener,** *n.* —**Syn. 1.** See **cheer.**

gladdon (glăd′n), *n.* a dark green iridaceous perennial herb, *Iris foetidissima*, widespread in W Europe and N Africa, usually on calcareous soils; stinking iris.

glade (glād), *n.* an open space in a forest. [akin to GLAD (in obs. sense 'bright')]

gladiate (glăd′ĭ ĭt, -āt′, glā′dĭ-), *adj. Bot.* sword-shaped. [f. s. L *gladius* sword + -ATE[1]]

gladiator (glăd′ĭ ā′tə), *n.* **1.** *Rom. Hist.* a person, often a slave or captive, who fought in public with a sword or other weapon to entertain the people. **2.** one who takes up a cause or right; a controversialist. [t. L]

gladiatorial (glăd′ĭ ə tô′rĭ əl), *adj.* pertaining to gladiators or to their combats.

gladiola (glăd′ĭ ō′lə), *n.* gladiolus. [t. L, neut. pl. treated as if fem. sing. See GLADIOLUS]

gladiolus (glăd′ĭ ō′ləs), *n.*, *pl.* **-lus, -li** (-lī), **-luses.** any plant of the iridaceous genus *Gladiolus*, native esp. in South Africa, with erect, gladiate leaves, and spikes of variously coloured flowers. [t. L, dim. of *gladius* sword]

gladsome (glăd′səm), *adj.* **1.** making joyful; delightful. **2.** glad. —**glad′somely,** *adv.* —**glad′someness,** *n.*

Gladstone (glăd′stən), *n.* **1. William Ewart** (yōō′ət), 1809–98, British statesman: prime minister 1868–74, 1880–85, 1886, 1892–94. **2.** a Gladstone bag. **3.** a four-wheeled horse-drawn carriage with a calash top, two inside seats, and driver and dicky seats.

Gladstone bag, a light travelling bag or small portmanteau hinged to open into two compartments. [named after W. E. GLADSTONE]

glair (glĕə), *n.* **1.** the white of an egg. **2.** a glaze or size made of it. **3.** any viscous substance like eggwhite. —*v.t.* **4.** to coat with glair. [ME *glaire*, t. OF, ult. der. L *clārus* clear]

glairy (glĕə′rĭ), *adj.* **1.** of the nature of glair; viscous. **2.** covered with glair. Also, **glaireous** (glĕə′rĭ əs). —**glair′iness,** *n.*

glaive (glāv), *n. Archaic.* a sword or broadsword. [ME *gleyve*, t. OF: m. *glaive* lance, sword, g. L *gladius* sword]

Glam., Glamorganshire.

Glamorganshire (glə mô′gən shiə′, -shə), *n.* a county in SE Wales. 1,229,728 pop. (1961); 816 sq. mi. *Co. town:* Cardiff. Also, **Glamor′gan.** *Abbrev.:* Glam.

glamorize (glăm′ə rīz′), *v.t.*, **-rized, -rizing.** to make glamorous or give an appearance of glamour to. Also, **glamorise.**

glamorous (glăm′ə rəs), *adj.* full of glamour or charm. Also, **glamourous.** —**glam′orously,** *adv.*

glamour (glăm′ə), *n.* **1.** alluring and often illusory charm; fascination. **2.** magic or enchantment; spell; witchery. Also, *U.S.*, **glamor.** [earlier *glammar*, dissimilated var. of GRAMMAR in sense of 'occult learning', 'magic']

glance[1] (gläns), *v.*, **glanced, glancing,** *n.* —*v.i.* **1.** to look quickly or briefly. **2.** to gleam or flash. **3.** to go off in an oblique direction from an object struck: *a missile glances away.* **4.** to allude briefly in passing. —*v.t.* **5.** *Obs.* to cast a glance or brief look at; catch a glimpse of. **6.** to cast or reflect, as a gleam. —*n.* **7.** a quick or brief look. **8.** a gleam or flash of light. **9.** a glancing off, as of a missile after striking. **10.** a reference in passing. **11.** *Cricket.* a stroke in which the ball is allowed to glance off the bat. [late ME; nasalized var. of ME *glacen* strike a glancing blow, t. OF: m. *glacer* slip] —**Syn. 2.** See **flash.**

glance[2] (gläns), *n.* *Mining, Mineral.* any of various minerals having a lustre which indicates their metallic nature. [t. G: m. *Glanz*, lit., brightness, lustre]

gland[1] (glănd), *n.* **1.** *Anat.* **a.** an organ by which certain constituents are separated from the blood for use in the body or for ejection from it, or by which certain changes are produced in the blood or lymph. **b.** any of various organs or structures likened to true glands. **2.** *Bot.* a secreting organ or structure, esp. one on or near a surface. [t. F: m. *glande*, m. OF *glandre*, g. L *glandula*, dim. of *glans* acorn] —**gland′less,** *adj.* —**gland′like′,** *adj.*

gland[2] (glănd), *n.* a device for preventing a fluid from leaking from any container or vessel where a rotating or reciprocating shaft emerges from it. [? special use of GLAND[1]]

glandered (glăn′dəd), *adj.* affected with glanders.

glanders (glăn′dez), *n.* *Vet. Sci.* a contagious disease. of horses, mules, etc., communicable to man, due to a micro-organism (*Bacillus mallei*), and characterized by swellings beneath the jaw and a profuse mucous discharge from the nostrils. [late ME, t. OF: m. *glandres*, g. L *glandulae* (swollen) glands] —**glan′derous,** *adj.*

glandular (glăn′dyŏŏ lə), *adj.* **1.** consisting of, containing, or bearing glands. **2.** of, pertaining to, or resembling a gland.

glandular fever, *Pathol.* an acute infectious disease characterized by sudden fever, a benign swelling of lymph nodes, and increase in leucocytes having only one nucleus in the bloodstream; infectious mononucleosis.

glandulous (glăn′dyŏŏ ləs), *adj.* *Obs.* glandular. [t. L: m. s. *glandulōsus*]

glans (glănz), *n.*, *pl.* **glandes** (glăn′dēz). *Anat.* the head of the penis (**glans penis**) or of the clitoris (**glans clitoridis**). [t. L: lit., acorn]

glare[1] (glĕə), *n.*, *v.*, **glared, glaring.** —*n.* **1.** a strong, dazzling light; brilliant lustre. **2.** dazzling or showy appearance; showiness. **3.** a fierce or piercing look. —*v.i.* **4.** to shine with a strong, dazzling light. **5.** to be too brilliantly ornamented. **6.** to be intensely bright in colour. **7.** to be conspicuous. **8.** to look with a fierce or piercing stare. —*v.t.* **9.** to express with a glare. [ME *glaren*, c. MD and MLG *glaren*; akin to GLASS (cf. OE *glæren* glassy)]

—**Syn. 4.** See **shine. 8.** GLARE, GLOWER, GLOAT all have connotations of emotion which accompany an intense gaze. To GLARE is to look piercingly or angrily: *a tiger glares at its victims.* To GLOWER is to look fiercely and threateningly, as from wrath; it suggests a scowl together with a glare: *to glower at a persistently mischievous child.* To GLOAT meant originally to look with exultation, avaricious or malignant, on something or someone: *a tyrant gloating over the helplessness of his victim.* Today, however, it may simply imply inner exultation.

glare[2] (glĕə), *n.* **1.** a bright, smooth surface, as of ice. —*adj.* **2.** bright and smooth; glassy: *glare ice.* [special uses of GLARE[1]]

glaring (glĕə′rĭng), *adj.* **1.** that glares; brilliant; dazzling. **2.** excessively bright; garish. **3.** very conspicuous: *glaring defects.* **4.** staring fiercely. —**glar′ingly,** *adv.* —**glar′ingness,** *n.*

Glarus (*Ger.* glä′rōōs), *n.* **1.** a canton in E Switzerland. 40,148 pop. (1960); 264 sq. mi. **2.** a town in and the capital of this canton. 5724 (1957).

glary[1] (glĕə′rĭ), *adj.* brilliant; glaring. [f. GLARE[1] + -Y[1]]

glary[2] (glĕə′rĭ), *adj.* *U.S.* smooth and slippery, as ice. [early mod. E *glarie* icy. Cf. OE *glæren* glassy]

Glasgow (gläs′gō, gläz′gō), *n.* a seaport in SW Scotland, in N Lanarkshire on the Clyde; university, founded 1451; shipyards. 1,019,582 (est. 1964).

glass (gläs), *n.* **1.** a hard, brittle, more or less transparent substance produced by fusion, usually consisting of mutually dissolved silica and silicates (the ordinary variety used for windows, bottles, and the like, containing silica, soda, and lime). See **crown glass** and **flint glass. 2.** any artificial or natural substance having similar properties and composition, as fused borax, obsidian, etc. **3.** something made of glass, as a window, mirror, lens, barometer, etc. **4.** (*pl.*) a device to aid defective vision, consisting usually of two glass lenses set in a frame which rests on the nose and is held in place by pieces passing over the ears. **5.** things made of glass collectively; glassware. **6.** a glass container for drinking water, etc. **7.** quantity or contents of a drinking glass; glassful. **8.** volcanic glass. —*adj.* **9.** made of glass. **10.** furnished or fitted with panes of glass; glazed. —*v.t.* **11.** to fit with panes of glass; cover with or encase in glass. **12.** *Poetic.* to reflect: *trees glass themselves in the lake.* [ME *glas*, OE *glæs*, c. D *glas* and G *Glas*] —**glass′less,** *adj.* —**glass′like′,** *adj.*

glass-blowing (gläs′blō′ĭng), *n.* **1.** the art or process of forming glass into ware by blowing by mouth or mechanically. **2.** the operation of working glass in a flame, starting with tubing, rod, or cane, and forming laboratory apparatus, ornaments, or knick-knacks. —**glass′-blow′er,** *n.*

glass brick, a hollow block of translucent glass, usually with one surface patterned, used in constructing partitions, etc.

glasscloth (gläs′klŏth′), *n.* a cloth, often of linen, used for drying and polishing drinking glasses, etc.; a teacloth.

glass-cutter (gläs′kŭt′ə), *n.* **1.** a person who cuts or etches the surface of glass. **2.** a tool for cutting glass.

glass fibre, a bulk material composed of fibres of glass, having special heat insulating values; fibreglass.

glassful (gläs′fŏŏl′), *n.*, *pl.* **-fuls.** as much as a glass holds.

glass harmonica, an instrument consisting of a series of glass bowls graduated in size which can be played by the friction of the moistened finger.

glasshouse (gläs′hous′), *n.* **1.** a greenhouse. **2.** *Mil. Slang.* a military prison.

glassine (glă sēn′), *n.* a glazed, semitransparent paper, used for book jackets, etc.

glass-making (gläs′mā′kĭng), *n.* the art of making glass or glassware. —**glass′-mak′er,** *n.*

glassman (gläs′mən), *n.*, *pl.* **-men. 1.** one who makes or sells glass. **2.** a glazier.

glasspaper (gläs′pā′pə), *n.* **1.** a strong paper coated with a layer of glass particles, resembling sandpaper. —*v.t.* **2.** to smooth or polish with glasspaper.

glass snake, 1. a limbless, snakelike lizard, *Ophisaurus ventralis*, of the southern U.S., having an extremely fragile tail. **2.** any of certain similar lizards of Europe and Asia.

glass tank, a reverberatory furnace in which glass is melted directly under the flames.

glassware (gläs′wĕə′), *n.* articles of glass.

glass wool, glass spun into very fine threads so that it resembles cottonwool; used in filtering corrosive liquids, for insulation, etc.

glasswork (gläs′wûk′), *n.* **1.** the manufacture of glass and glassware. **2.** the fitting of glass; glazing. **3.** articles of glass collectively; glassware.

glass-worker (gläs′wû′kə), *n.* one who works in glass.

glassworks (gläs′wûks′), *n.pl. or sing.* a factory in which glass is manufactured.

glasswort (gläs′wût′), *n.* **1.** any of the herbs with succulent leafless stems constituting the chenopodiaceous genus *Salicornia*, and formerly much used (when burnt to ashes) as a source of soda for glass-making. **2.** the saltwort, *Salsola kali* (**prickly glasswort**).

glassy (gläs′ĭ), *adj.*, **glassier, glassiest. 1.** resembling glass, as in transparency, smoothness, etc. **2.** having a fixed, unintelligent stare. **3.** of the nature of glass; vitreous. —**glass′ily,** *adv.* —**glass′iness,** *n.*

Glaswegian (glăs wē′jĭ ən, -jən), *adj.* **1.** of or pertaining to Glasgow or its inhabitants. —*n.* **2.** a native or inhabitant of Glasgow.

glauberite (glou′bə rīt′, glô′-), *n.* a mineral sulphate of calcium and sodium, $Na_2Ca(SO_4)_2$, usually occurring with rock salt in saline deposits. [named after J. R. *Glauber*. See GLAUBER SALT]

Glauber salt (glou′bə), sodium sulphate, used as a cathartic, etc. Also, **Glauber's salt.** [named after J. R. *Glauber*, 1604–68, German chemist]

Glauce (glô′sĭ), *n.* *Class. Myth.* Creüsa (def. 1).

glaucoma (glô kō′mə), *n.* *Pathol.* a disease of the eye, characterized by increased pressure within the eyeball with progressive loss of vision. [t. Gk: m. *glaúkōma* opacity of the crystalline lens. See GLAUCOUS] —**glaucomatous** (glô kō′mə təs, -kŏm′ə-), *adj.*

glauconite (glô′kə nīt′), *n.* a greenish micaceous mineral, essentially of a hydrous silicate of potassium, aluminium, and iron, and occurring in greensand, clays, etc. —**glauconitic** (glô′kə nĭt′ĭk), *adj.* [f. m. Gk *glaukón*, neut. adj., bluish green + -ITE[1]]

glaucous (glô′kəs), *adj.* **1.** light bluish green or greenish blue. **2.** *Bot.* covered with a whitish bloom, as a plum. [t. L: m. *glaucus*, t. Gk: m. *glaukós* gleaming, silvery, grey, bluish green]

glaucous gull, a large white and pale grey gull, *Latus hyperboreus*, of arctic regions.

glaze (glāz), *v.*, **glazed, glazing,** *n.* —*v.t.* **1.** to furnish or fit with glass; cover with glass. **2.** to produce a vitreous or glossy surface on (pottery, pastry, etc.). **3.** to cover with glaze. **4.** *Painting.* to cover (a painted surface or parts of it) with a thin layer of transparent colour in order to modify the tone. **5.** to cover with a smooth lustrous coating; give a glassy surface to, as by polishing. —*v.i.* **6.** to become glazed or glassy. —*n.* **7.** a smooth, glossy surface or coating. **8.** the substance for producing it. **9.** *Ceramics.* **a.** the vitreous or glossy surface or coating on glazed pottery. **b.** the substance or material used to produce such a surface. **10.** *Painting.* a thin layer of transparent colour, spread over a painted surface. **11.** a smooth glossy surface on certain fabrics, produced by means of a friction calender. **12.** *Cookery.* **a.** something used to coat a food, esp. sugar or the white of egg. **b.** stock cooked down to a thin paste, for applying to the surface of meats. **13.** *U.S.* glaze ice. [ME *glasen*, der. *glas* GLASS] —**glaz′er,** *n.* —**glaz′y,** *adj.*

glaze ice, *Meteorol.* a smooth layer of ice which is sometimes formed on terrestrial objects or aircraft when rain is falling and the ground or air temperatures are below freezing point; silver frost. Also, **glazed frost.**

glazier (glā′zyə), *n.* one who fits windows, etc., with glass. [ME *glasier*, f. *glas* GLASS + -IER] —**gla′ziery,** *n.*

glazing (glā′zĭng), *n.* **1.** the act of furnishing or fitting with glass; business of a glazier. **2.** glass set, or to be set, in frames, etc. **3.** the act of applying a glaze. **4.** the glassy surface of anything glazed.

Glazounov (glăz′ə nŏf′; *Russ.* glə zo͞o nôf′), *n.* **Alexander,** 1865–1936, Russian composer.

G.L.C., Greater London Council.

gleam (glēm), *n.* **1.** a flash or beam of light. **2.** dim or subdued light. **3.** a brief or slight manifestation: *a gleam of hope.* —*v.i.* **4.** to send forth a gleam or gleams. **5.** to appear suddenly and clearly, like a flash of light. —*v.t.* **6.** *Rare.* to send forth in gleams. [ME *glem(e)*, OE *glǣm*, c. OHG *gleimo* glow-worm; akin to OS *glīmo* brightness, etc. See GLIMMER, GLIMPSE]

—**Syn. 1.** GLEAM, RAY, GLIMMER are terms for a stream of light. GLEAM denotes a not very brilliant, and often intermittent, stream of light: *the distant gleam from a lighted window.* RAY usually implies a smaller amount of light than a beam; a single line of light: *a ray through a pinprick in a window shade.* GLIMMER indicates a feeble, unsteady light: *a faint glimmer of moonlight.*

glean (glēn), *v.t.* **1.** to gather slowly and laboriously in bits. **2.** to gather (grain, etc.) after the reapers or regular gatherers. **3.** to discover or find out. —*v.i.* **4.** to collect or gather anything little by little or slowly. **5.** to gather what is left by reapers. [ME *glene(n)*, t. OF: m. *glener*, g. LL *glenāre*, of Celtic orig.] —**glean′er,** *n.*

gleaning (glē′nĭng), *n.* **1.** the act of one who gleans. **2.** (*usually pl.*) that which is gleaned.

glebe (glēb), *n.* **1.** glebe land. **2.** *Poetic.* soil; field. [ME, t. L: m. s. *glēba*, *glaeba* clod, soil, land]

glebe house, a dwelling whose rental is available to augment the stipend of the incumbent of the parish or cure specified.

glebe land, land bequeathed to a specified parish or benefice so that its rental or crops may be employed to augment the income of their incumbent.

glede (glēd), *n.* the common European kite, *Milvus ictinus.* Also, **gled** (glĕd). [ME; OE *glida*, c. Icel. *gledha*; akin to GLIDE]

glee (glē), *n.* **1.** demonstrative joy; exultation. **2.** a kind of unaccompanied part-song, grave or gay, for three or more voices. [ME; OE *glēo*, c. Icel. *glȳ*] —**Syn. 1.** merriment, jollity, hilarity. See **mirth.**

glee club, *Chiefly U.S.* a club or group for singing choral music.

gleeful (glē′fəl), *adj.* full of glee; merry; exultant. —**glee′fully,** *adv.* —**glee′fulness,** *n.*

gleeman (glē′mən), *n.*, *pl.* **-men.** *Archaic.* a strolling professional singer or minstrel. [OE *glēomann*]

gleesome (glē′səm), *adj.* gleeful. —**glee′somely,** *adv.* —**glee′someness,** *n.*

gleet (glēt), *n.* *Pathol.* **1.** a thin, morbid discharge, as from a wound. **2.** a persistent or chronic gonorrhoea. [ME *glette*, t. OF: slime, mucus, pus, foul matter]

gleisoil (glā′soil′), *n.* a greyish soil of poor quality, the result of impeded drainage. Also, **gley soil.**

Gleiwitz (*Ger.* glī′vĭts), *n.* German name of **Gliwice.**

glen (glĕn), *n.* a small, narrow, secluded valley. [ME, t. Gaelic: m. *gle(a)nn*, c. Welsh *glyn*] —**glen′like′,** *adj.*

Glencoe (glĕn′kō′), *n.* a narrow valley in Argyllshire, Scotland: site of the massacre of the Macdonald clan by the Campbells, 1692.

Glendale (glĕn′dāl′), *n.* a city in the U.S., in SW California, near Los Angeles. 199,422 (1960).

Glendower (glĕn dou′ə), *n.* **Owen,** 1359?–1416?, Welsh rebel against Henry IV of England.

glengarry (glĕn gă′rĭ), *n.*, *pl.* **-ries.** a Scottish Highlander's cap, with straight sides, a crease along the top, and sometimes short ribbon streamers at the back, worn by Highlanders as part of military dress. [named after *Glengarry*, valley in Inverness-shire, Scotland]

glenoid (glē′noid), *adj.* *Anat.* **1.** shallow or slightly cupped, as the articular cavities of the scapula. **2.** pertaining to such a cavity. [t. Gk: m. s. *glēnoeidḗs* like a shallow joint socket. See -OID]

Glenrothes (glĕn rŏth′ĭs), *n.* a new town in Scotland, in Fife. 12,746 (1961).

gliadin (glī′ə dĭn), *n.* *Biochem.* a prolamine obtained from wheat and rye. Also, **gliadine** (glī′ ə dēn′, -dĭn).

glib (glĭb), *adj.*, **glibber, glibbest. 1.** ready and fluent, often thoughtlessly or insincerely so: *glib speakers, a glib tongue.* **2.** easy, as action or manner. [back-formation from obs. *glibbery* slippery, t. D: m. *glibberig*] —**glib′ly,** *adv.* —**glib′ness,** *n.* —**Syn. 1.** See **fluent.**

glide (glīd), *v.*, **glided, gliding,** *n.* —*v.i.* **1.** to move smoothly along, as if without effort or difficulty, as a flying bird, a boat, a skater, etc. **2.** to pass by gradual or insensible change (often fol. by *along*, *away*, *by*, etc.). **3.** to go quietly or unperceived; slip (fol. by *in*, *out*, etc.). **4.** *Aeron.* to move in the air, esp. at an easy angle downwards, by the action of gravity or by virtue of momentum already acquired. **5.** *Music.* to pass from note to note without a break; slur. —*v.t.* **6.** to cause to glide. —*n.* **7.** a gliding movement, as in dancing. **8.** a dance in which such movements are employed. **9.** *Music.* a slur (def. 8a). **10.** *Phonet.* **a.** a transitional sound produced while passing from the articulation required by one speech sound to that required by the next, such as the 'y' sound often heard between the *i* and *e* of *quiet.* **b.** a semivowel. **11.** *Cricket.* the deflection of a ball by the batsman to the leg side. [ME *glide(n)*, OE *glīdan*, c. G *gleiten*] —**glid′ingly,** *adv.* —**Syn. 1.** See **slide.**

glider (glī′də), *n.* **1.** one who or that which glides. **2.** *Aeron.* a motorless aeroplane for gliding from a higher to a lower level by the action of gravity, or from a lower to a higher level by the action of air currents.

glimmer (glĭm′ə), *n.* **1.** a faint or unsteady light; gleam. **2.** a dim perception; inkling. —*v.i.* **3.** to shine faintly or unsteadily; twinkle; flicker. **4.** to appear faintly or dimly. [ME *glemer(en)* gleam, c. G *glimmern.* Cf. OE *gleomu* splendour] —**Syn. 1.** See **gleam.**

glimmering (glĭm′ə rĭng), *n.* **1.** a faint or unsteady light; a glimmer. **2.** a faint glimpse; inkling. —*adj.* **3.** that glimmers. —**glim′meringly,** *adv.*

glimpse (glĭmps), *n.*, *v.*, **glimpsed, glimpsing.** —*n.* **1.** a momentary sight or view. **2.** a momentary or slight appearance. **3.** a vague idea; inkling. **4.** *Archaic.* a gleam, as of light. —*v.t.* **5.** to catch a glimpse of. —*v.i.* **6.** to look briefly, or glance (fol. by *at*). **7.** *Poetic.* to come into view; appear faintly. [ME *glymsen*, c. MHG *glimsen* glow; akin to GLIMMER] —**glimps′er,** *n.*

Glinka (glĭng′kə; *Russ.* glēn′kə), *n.* **Mikhail Ivanovich** (*Russ.* mĭKH ä ēl′), 1803?–57, Russian composer.

glint (glĭnt), *n.* **1.** a gleam or glimmer; flash. **2.** glinting brightness; lustre. —*v.i.* **3.** to gleam or flash. **4.** to move suddenly; dart. —*v.t.* **5.** to cause to glint; reflect. [ME *glynt*, var. of obs. *glent*, t. Scand.; cf. d. Sw. *glänta*, *glinta* slip, shine] —**Syn. 3.** See **flash.**

glioma (glī ō′mə), *n.*, *pl.* **-mata** (-mə tə), **-mas.** *Pathol.* a tumour arising from and consisting of neuroglia. [NL, f. s. Gk *glía* glue + *-ōma* -OMA] —**gliomatous** (glī ō′mə təs), *adj.*

glissade (glĭ säd′, -sād′), *n.*, *v.*, **-saded, -sading.** —*n.* **1.** a skilful glide over snow or ice in descending a mountain. **2.** *Dancing.* a sliding or gliding step. —*v.i.* **3.** to perform a glissade. [t. F, der. *glisser* slip, slide, b. OF *glacier* slip and *glier* slide (t. Gmc; cf. GLIDE)]

glissando (glĭ săn′dō), *adj.*, *n.*, *pl.* **-di** (-dē). *Music.* —*adj.* **1.** performed with a gliding effect by sliding one finger rapidly over the keys of a piano or strings of a harp. —*n.* **2.** a glissando passage. **3.** (in string playing) a slide. [pseudo-It., t. F: m. *glissant*, ppr. of *glisser* slide]

glisten (glĭs′ən), *v.i.* **1.** to shine with a sparkling light or a faint intermittent glow. —*n.* **2.** a glistening; sparkle. [ME *glis(t)nen*, OE *glisnian*, der. *glisian* glitter. See -EN[1]] —**glis′teningly,** *adv.*

—**Syn.** **1.** GLISTEN, SHIMMER, SPARKLE refer to different ways in which light is reflected from surfaces. GLISTEN refers to a lustrous light as from something sleek or wet, or it may refer to myriads of tiny gleams reflected from small surfaces: *wet fur glistens, snow glistens in the sunlight.* SHIMMER refers to the changing play of light on a (generally moving) surface, as of water or silk: *moonbeams shimmer on water, silk shimmers in a high light.* To SPARKLE is to give off sparks or small ignited particles, or to send forth small but brilliant gleams: *a diamond sparkles as with numerous points of light.*

glister (glĭs′tə), *v.i.* **1.** *Archaic.* to glisten; glitter. —*n.* **2.** *Archaic or Dial.* a glistening; glitter. [ME; freq. of obs. v. *glist* glitter, var. of GLISTEN (? back-formation)]

glitter (glĭt′ə), *v.i.* **1.** to shine with a brilliant, sparkling light or lustre. **2.** to make a brilliant show: *glittering scenes of a court.* —*n.* **3.** glittering light or lustre; splendour. [ME, t. Scand.; cf. Icel. *glitra*, freq. of *glita* shine; cf. OE *glitenian*, G *gleissen* shine, glitter] —**glit′teringly,** *adv.* —**Syn. 1.** See **flash.**

glittery (glĭt′ə rĭ), *adj.* glittering; sparkling.

Gliwice (*Pol.* glē vē′tsĕ), *n.* a town in SW Poland. 147,000 (est. 1964). German, **Gleiwitz.**

gloaming (glō′mĭng), *n. Poetic.* twilight; dusk. [ME *gloming*, OE *glōmung*, der. *glōm* twilight; mod. *-oa-* (instead of *-oo-*) presumably by assoc. with GLOW]

gloat (glōt), *v.i.* **1.** to gaze with exultation; dwell mentally upon something with intense (and often evil) satisfaction: *to gloat over another's misfortunes.* —*n.* **2.** the act of gloating. [cf. Icel. *glotta* grin, smile scornfully, d. Sw. *glotta* peep, G *glotzen* stare] —**gloat′er,** *n.* —**gloat′ingly,** *adv.* —**Syn.** See **glare**[1].

glob (glŏb), *n. Colloq.* a rounded lump of some soft but pliable substance: *a glob of cream.* [? b. GLOBE and BLOB]

global (glō′bl), *adj.* **1.** spherical; globe-shaped. **2.** pertaining to or covering the whole world. **3.** all-embracing; comprehensive. —**glob′ally,** *adv.*

globate (glō′bāt), *adj.* shaped like a globe. Also, **glo′bated.** [t. L: m. s. *globātus*, pp., formed into a ball]

globe (glōb), *n., v.,* **globed, globing.** —*n.* **1.** the earth (usually prec. by *the*). **2.** a planet or other celestial body. **3.** a sphere on which is depicted a map of the earth (**terrestrial globe**) or of the heavens (**celestial globe**). **4.** a spherical body; sphere. **5.** anything more or less spherical, as a lampshade or a glass fishbowl. **6.** *Hist.* a golden ball borne as an emblem of sovereignty. —*v.t.* **7.** to form into a globe. —*v.i.* **8.** to take the form of a globe. [t. F, t. L: m. *globus* round body or mass, ball, globe] —**globe′like′,** *adj.* —**Syn. 1.** See **earth. 4.** See **ball**[1].

globe artichoke, a type of artichoke, *Cynara scolymus*, widely cultivated for food.

globefish (glōb′fĭsh′), *n., pl.* **-fishes,** (*esp. collectively*) **-fish.** a puffer (def. 2).

globeflower (glōb′flou′ə), *n.* a ranunculaceous plant, *Trollius europaeus*, of Europe, having pale yellow globelike flowers.

globe thistle, a coarse perennial herb, *Echinops sphaerocephalus*, family *Compositae*, with spherical heads of blue, one-flowered capitula; a native of central and S Europe and W Asia, frequently grown in gardens.

globetrotter (glōb′trŏt′ə), *n. Colloq.* one who travels widely, esp. for sightseeing. —**globe′trot′ting,** *n., adj.*

globigerina (glō bĭj′ə rī′nə), *n., pl.* **-nae** (-nē). a marine protozoan belonging to the *Foraminifera*, the shell of which, falling to the ocean floor upon death, forms a mud known as the **globigerina ooze.**

globin (glō′bĭn), *n. Biochem.* a protein contained in haemoglobin. [f. s. L *globus* GLOBE + -IN[2]]

globoid (glō′boid), *adj.* **1.** approximately globular. —*n.* **2.** a globoid figure or body.

globose (glō′bōs, glō bōs′), *adj.* globelike; globe-shaped, or nearly so. Also, **globous** (glō′bəs). [t. L: m. s. *globōsus* round as a ball] —**glo′bosely,** *adv.* —**globosity** (glō bŏs′ĭ tĭ), *n.*

globular (glŏb′yŏŏ lə), *adj.* **1.** global. **2.** composed of globules. —**glob′ular′ity,** *n.* —**glob′ularly,** *adv.*

globular cluster, *Astron.* one of many self-contained, approximately spherical clusters of about a hundred thousand stars which are gravitationally associated with the Milky Way although they appear to be outside it.

globule (glŏb′yōōl), *n.* a small spherical body. [t. F, t. L: m. *globulus*, dim. of *globus* GLOBE]

globulin (glŏb′yŏŏ lĭn), *n. Biochem.* any of a group of water-insoluble proteins which are soluble in dilute solutions of mineral salts. [f. GLOBULE + -IN[2]]

glockenspiel (glŏk′ən spēl′; *Ger.* glŏk′ən shpēl), *n. Music.* **1.** a set of steel bars mounted in a frame and struck with hammers, used by military bands. **2.** a small keyboard instrument, imitating the sound of bells. **3.** a set of bells; carillon. [t. G: f. *glocken-*, comb. form of *Glocke* bell + *Spiel* play]

glomerate (glŏm′ə rĭt), *adj.* compactly clustered. [t. L: m. s. *glomerātus*, pp., wound or formed into a ball]

glomeration (glŏm′ə rā′shən), *n.* **1.** glomerate condition; conglomeration. **2.** a glomerate mass.

glomerule (glŏm′ə rōōl′), *n. Bot.* a cyme condensed into a headlike cluster. [t. F, t. NL: m. s. *glomerulus*, dim. of L *glomus* ball (of yarn, thread, etc.)]

glomerulus (glō mĕ′rōō ləs), *n., pl.* **-li** (-lī′). *Anat.* a compact cluster of capillaries, esp. a cluster of vascular tufts in the kidney. [NL. See GLOMERULE] —**glome′rular,** *adj.*

Glomma (*Nor.* glō′mȧ), *n.* a river in Norway flowing S into the Skagerrak. 375 mi.

glonoine (glŏn′ō ĭn -ēn′), *n. Chem., Pharm.* nitroglycerine: esp. so called in medicine. Also, **glonoin** (glŏn′ō ĭn). [said to be f. GL(YCERINE) + chemical symbols *O* (oxygen) and NO_3 (nitric anhydride) + -INE[2]]

gloom[1] (glōōm), *n.* **1.** darkness; dimness. —*v.i.* **2.** to appear or become dark or gloomy. —*v.t.* **3.** to make dark or sombre. [OE *glōm* twilight. See GLOAMING, GLOW] —**Syn. 1.** shadow, shade. —**Ant. 1.** brightness.

gloom[2] (glōōm), *n.* **1.** a state of melancholy or depression; low spirits. **2.** a despondent look or expression. —*v.i.* **3.** to look dismal or dejected; frown. —*v.t.* **4.** to fill with gloom; make gloomy or sad. [ME *gloum(b)e*, *glomme* frown, lower. See GLUM] —**Syn. 1.** dejection, despondency. —**Ant. 1.** cheerfulness.

gloomy[1] (glōō′mĭ), *adj.,* **gloomier, gloomiest.** dark; deeply shaded. [f. GLOOM[1] + -Y[1]] —**Syn.** See **dark.**

gloomy[2] (glōō′mĭ), *adj.,* **gloomier, gloomiest. 1.** causing gloom; depressing: *a gloomy prospect.* **2.** affected with or expressive of gloom; melancholy. [f. GLOOM[2] + -Y[1]] —**gloom′ily,** *adv.* —**gloom′iness,** *n.* —**Syn. 2.** dejected, downcast, downhearted, sad, despondent.

gloria (glô′rĭ ə), *n.* a closely-woven, half-silk fabric, usually in plain weave; orig. used for dusters, but now made for umbrella cloths.

Gloria (glô′rĭ ä′), *n.* **1.** (in Christian liturgical worship) the great, or greater, doxology beginning 'Gloria in excelsis Deo' (Glory be to God on high), the lesser doxology beginning 'Gloria Patri' (Glory be to the Father), or the response 'Gloria tibi, Domine' (Glory be to thee, O Lord). **2.** (*l.c.*) a repetition of one of these. **3.** (*l.c.*) a musical setting for one of these, esp. the first. **4.** (*l.c.*) a halo, nimbus, or aureole, or an ornament in imitation of one. [t. L: glory]

Gloria in Excelsis Deo (glô′rĭ ä′ ĭn ĕk sĕl′sĭs dā′ō), the hymn beginning, in Latin, 'Gloria in Excelsis Deo' (Glory in the highest to God), and, in the English version, 'Glory be to God on high'.

Gloria Patri (glô′rĭ ə păt′rĭ), the short hymn 'Glory be to the Father, and to the Son, and to the Holy Ghost. As it was in the beginning, is now, and ever shall be, world without end. Amen.'

glorification (glô′rĭ fĭ kā′shən), *n.* **1.** the act of glorifying; exaltation to the glory of heaven. **2.** the state of being glorified. **3.** *Colloq.* a celebration or jubilation. **4.** *Colloq.* a glorified or more splendid form of something.

glorify (glô′rĭ fī′), *v.t.,* **-fied, -fying. 1.** to magnify with praise; extol. **2.** to transform into something more splendid. **3.** to make glorious; invest with glory. **4.** to promote the glory of (God); ascribe glory and praise in adoration to (God). [ME *glorify(en)*, t. OF: m. *glorifier*, t. LL: m. *glōrificāre.* See GLORY, -FY] —**glo′rifi′able,** *adj.* —**glo′rifi′er,** *n.*

gloriole (glô′rĭ ōl′), *n.* a halo, nimbus, or aureole. [t. F, t. L: m. s. *glōriola*, dim. of *glōria* GLORY, n.]

glorious (glô′rĭ əs), *adj.* **1.** admirable; delightful: *to have a glorious time.* **2.** conferring glory: *a glorious victory.* **3.** full of glory; entitled to great renown: *England is glorious in her poetry.* **4.** brilliantly beautiful: *the glorious heavens.* [ME, t. AF, t. L: m. s. *glōriōsus* full of glory] —**glo′riously,** *adv.* —**glo′riousness,** *n.* —**Syn. 3.** famous, renowned; illustrious.

Glorious Revolution, The, *Eng. Hist.* the political events of 1688–89 as a result of which James II was expelled and the sovereignty conferred on William and Mary. Also, **The Bloodless Revolution.**

glory (glô′rĭ), *n., pl.* **glories,** *v.,* **gloried, glorying.** —*n.* **1.** exalted praise, honour, or distinction, accorded by common consent: *paths of glory.* **2.** something that makes honoured or illustrious; a distinguished ornament; an object of pride. **3.** adoring praise or thanksgiving: *give glory to God.* **4.** resplendent beauty or magnificence: *the glory of God.* **5.** a state of splendour, magnificence, or greatest prosperity. **6.** a state of contentment, as one resulting from a triumphant achievement. **7.** the splendour and bliss of heaven; heaven. **8.** a ring, circle, or surrounding radiance of light represented about the head or the whole figure of a sacred person, as Christ, a saint, etc.; a halo, nimbus, or aureole. —*v.i.* **9.** to exult with triumph; rejoice proudly. **10.** to be boastful;

exult arrogantly (fol. by *in*). —*interj.* **11.** (*cap.*) Also, **Glory be!** (a mild expression of surprise, elation, or exultation.) [ME, t. OF: m. *glorie*, t. L: m. *glōria* glory, fame, vainglory, boasting] —**Syn. 1.** fame, eminence. **5.** grandeur, pomp. —**Ant. 1.** disgrace.

glory hole, 1. a cupboard, small room, etc., where odds and ends can be stored with no regard to order. **2.** *Naut.* the accommodation for stewards in the old passenger liners; usually well down in the bow where a large number slept in bunks in one compartment.

glory-of-the-snow (glô′rĭ əv thə snō′), *n.* a cultivated lilaceous plant with blue flowers, *Chionodoya luciliae.*

glory pea, kaka beak.

Glos., Gloucestershire.

gloss[1] (glŏs), *n.* **1.** a superficial lustre: *gloss of satin.* **2.** an external show; specious appearance. —*v.t.* **3.** to put a gloss upon. **4.** to give a specious appearance to (often fol. by *over*). [t. Scand.; cf. Icel. *glossi* spark] —**gloss′er,** *n.* —**gloss′less,** *adj.* —**Syn. 1.** sheen, polish, glaze. See **polish.**

gloss[2] (glŏs), *n.* **1.** an explanation by means of a marginal or interlinear note, of a technical or unusual expression in a manuscript text. **2.** a series of verbal interpretations of a text. **3.** a glossary. **4.** an artfully misleading interpretation. —*v.t.* **5.** to insert glosses on; annotate. **6.** to give a specious interpretation of; explain away (often fol. by *over*): *to gloss over a mistake.* —*v.i.* **7.** to make glosses. [t. L: s. *glossa* (explanation of) hard word, t. Gk: lit., tongue. Cf. GLOZE] —**gloss′er,** *n.*

gloss., glossary.

glossa (glŏs′ə), *n. Anat.* the tongue. —**gloss′al,** *adj.*

Glossa (glŏs′ə), *n.* **Cape,** a promontory in SW Albania.

glossary (glŏs′ə rĭ), *n., pl.* **-ries.** a list of basic technical, dialectal, and difficult terms in a subject or field, with definitions. [t. L: m. s. *glossārium*, der. *glossa* GLOSS[2]] —**glossarial** (glŏ sâ′rĭ əl), *adj.* —**glos′sarist,** *n.*

glossator (glŏ sā′tə), *n.* **1.** a writer of glosses. **2.** one of the early medieval interpreters (not later than 1250) of the Roman and canon laws. [t. ML, ult. der. L *glossa* GLOSS[2]]

glossectomy (glŏ sĕk′tə mĭ), *n., pl.* **-mies.** *Surg.* the removal of the tongue.

glossitis (glŏ sī′tĭs), *n. Pathol.* inflammation of the tongue. [f. *glosso-* (see GLOSSOLOGY) + -ITIS]

glossology (glŏ sŏl′ə jĭ), *n. Obs.* linguistics. [f. *glosso-* (t. Gk, comb. form of *glôssa* tongue) + -LOGY]

Glossop (glŏs′əp), *n.* a town in England, in N Derbyshire. 17,500 (1961).

glossopteris (glŏ sŏp′tə rĭs), *n.* a genus of extinct plants the fossil remains of which are found widely in Permo-Carboniferous rocks of the Southern Hemisphere. They constituted an important element of the vegetation of the ancient continent of Gondwana.

glossy (glŏs′ĭ), *adj.,* **glossier, glossiest. 1.** having a gloss; lustrous. **2.** having a specious appearance; plausible. —*n.* **3.** a photograph printed on glossy paper. **4.** an expensively produced magazine, printed on glossy paper, and stylish and sophisticated in content. [f. GLOSS[1], n. + -Y[1]] —**gloss′ily,** *adv.* —**gloss′iness,** *n.* —**Syn. 1.** shining, polished, glazed; smooth, sleek. —**Ant. 1.** dull.

glost (glŏst), *n. Ceramics.* glaze.

-glot, a suffix indicating proficiency in language, as in *polyglot.* [t. Gk: m. s. *glôtta* tongue]

glottal (glŏt′l), *adj.* **1.** pertaining to the glottis or tongue. **2.** *Phonet.* articulated in the glottis.

glottal stop, *Phonet.* a stop consonant made by closing the glottis so tightly that no breath can pass through, as in *yep* yes, *nope* no.

glottic (glŏt′ĭk), *adj.* **1.** pertaining to the glottis and tongue; glottal. **2.** *Obs.* linguistic.

glottis (glŏt′ĭs), *n.* the opening at the upper part of the larynx, between the vocal cords. [t. NL, t. Gk: the mouth of the windpipe]

glottology (glŏ tŏl′ə jĭ), *n. Obs.* linguistics. [f. *glotto-* (t. Gk, comb. form of *glôtta* tongue) + -LOGY] —**glottologic** (glŏt′ə lŏj′ĭk), **glot′tolog′ical,** *adj.* —**glottol′ogist,** *n.*

Gloucester (glŏs′tə), *n.* **Duke of, 1.** See **Humphrey** (def. 1.). **2.** See **Richard III. 3.** See **Thomas of Woodstock. 4.** a city in SW England: port on the Severn; the county town of Gloucestershire. 71,650 (est. 1964). **5.** Gloucestershire.

Gloucestershire (glŏs′tə shĭə′, -shə), *n.* a county in SW England. 1,001,706 pop. (est. 1961); 1255 sq. mi. *Co. town:* Gloucester. Also, **Gloucester.**

glove (glŭv), *n., v.,* **gloved, gloving.** —*n.* **1.** a covering for the hand, now made with a separate sheath for each finger and for the thumb. **2.** a boxing glove. **3. take up** or **throw down the glove.** See **gauntlet**[1] (defs 4 and 5). **4.** See **kidgloves.** —*v.t.* **5.** to cover with or as with a glove; provide with gloves. **6.** to serve as a glove for. [ME; OE *glōf*, c. Icel. *glōfi*] —**glove′less,** *adj.* —**glove′like′,** *adj.*

glove box, a metal box used by workers who have to manipulate radioactive materials, or materials requiring a dust-free, sterile, or inert atmosphere; manipulation is carried out by means of gloves attached to ports in the walls of the box.

glove compartment, a small compartment, set into the dashboard of a motor car, for the storage of small articles.

glover (glŭv′ə), *n.* one who makes or sells gloves.

glow (glō), *n.* **1.** light emitted by a substance heated to luminosity; incandescence. **2.** brightness of colour. **3.** a state of bodily heat. **4.** warmth of emotion or passion; ardour. —*v.i.* **5.** to emit bright light and heat without flame; be incandescent. **6.** to shine like something intensely heated. **7.** to exhibit a strong, bright colour; be lustrously red or brilliant. **8.** to be excessively hot. **9.** to be animated with emotion. [ME *glowe(n)*, OE *glōwan*, akin to G *glühen*, Icel. *glōa*]

glow discharge, *Physics.* a discharge of electricity through a low-pressure gas which is usually luminous.

glower (glou′ə), *v.i.* **1.** to look angrily; stare with sullen dislike or discontent. —*n.* **2.** a glowering look; frown. [freq. of obs. *glow* stare, of uncert. orig.] —**glow′eringly,** *adv.* —**Syn. 1.** See **glare**[1].

glowing (glō′ĭng), *adj.* **1.** incandescent. **2.** rich and warm in colouring: *glowing colours.* **3.** exhibiting the glow of health, excitement, etc. **4.** ardent or impassioned: *a glowing account.* —**glow′ingly,** *adv.*

glow lamp, *Electronics.* a lamp which produces light by means of a flow of electricity through a gas.

glow-worm (glō′wûm′), *n.* **1.** a European beetle, *Lampyris noctiluca*, the wingless female of which emits a greenish light from the end of the abdomen. **2.** any of the fireflies of the family *Lampyridae* or their larvae.

gloxinia (glŏk sĭn′yə), *n.* the garden name of tuberous-rooted plants of the genus *Sinningia*, esp. a widely cultivated species, *S. speciosa*, having large white, red, or purple bell-shaped flowers. [NL; named after B. P. *Gloxin*, 18th-cent. German botanist]

gloze (glōz), *v.,* **glozed, glozing,** *n.* —*v.t.* **1.** to explain away; extenuate; gloss over (usually fol. by *over*). **2.** to palliate with specious talk. —*v.i.* **3.** *Obs.* to make glosses; comment. —*n.* **4.** *Rare.* flattery or deceit. **5.** *Obs.* a specious show. [ME *glose*, t. OF. See GLOSS[2]]

Glubb (glŭb), *n.* **Sir John Bagot** (băg′ət) (*Glubb Pasha*), born 1897, British soldier; commander of the Arab Legion 1939–56.

glucagon (glo͞o′kə gŏn′, -gən), *n. Biochem.* a hormone produced by the pancreas that increases the blood's sugar concentration.

glucinum (glo͞o sī′nəm), *n. Chem.* beryllium. *Symbol:* Gl. Also, **glucinium** (glo͞o sĭn′ĭ əm). [NL, der. Gk *glykýs* sweet (some of the salts having a sweet taste)]

Gluck (*Ger.* glo͝ok), *n.* **Christoph Willibald von** (*Ger.* krĭs′tŏf vĭl′ē balt fŏn), 1714–87, German operatic composer.

gluconeogenesis (glo͞o′kō nē′ō jĕn′ĭ sĭs), *n.* the formation of sugar by the liver from non-carbohydrate molecules.

glucoprotein (glo͞o′kō prō′tēn), *n.* glycoprotein.

glucose (glo͞o′kōs), *n.* **1.** *Chem.* a sugar, $C_6H_{12}O_6$, having several optically different forms, the common or dextrorotatory form (d-glucose) occurring in many fruits, animal tissues and fluids, etc., and having a sweetness about one half that of ordinary sugar. The laevorotatory form (l-glucose) is rare and not naturally occurring. **2.** a syrup containing dextrose, maltose, and dextrine, obtained by the incomplete hydrolysis of starch. [t. F, f. m. s. Gk *glykýs* sweet + *-ose* -OSE[2]]

glucoside (glo͞o′kō sīd′), *n. Chem.* one of an extensive group of compounds which yield glucose and some other substance or substances when treated with a dilute acid or when decomposed by a ferment or enzyme. [f. GLUCOS(E) + -IDE] —**glu′cosid′al,** *adj.*

glucosuria (glo͞o′kō syo͝o′rĭ ə), *n. Pathol.* glycosuria.

glue (glo͞o), *n., v.,* **glued, gluing.** —*n.* **1.** an impure gelatine obtained by boiling skins, hoofs, and other animal substances in water, and used for various purposes in the arts, esp. as an adhesive medium in uniting substances. **2.** any of various preparations of this substance. **3.** any adhesive substance made from any natural or synthetic resin or material. —*v.t.* **4.** to join or fasten with glue. **5.** to fix or attach firmly, as if with glue; make adhere closely. [ME, t. OF: m. *glu*, g. LL *glus.* Cf. GLUTEN] —**glue′like′,** *adj.* —**glu′er,** *n.*

gluepot (glo͞o′pŏt′), *n.* **1.** a vessel in which glue is melted. **2.** a container for glue.

gluey (glo͞o′ĭ), *adj.,* **gluier, gluiest. 1.** like glue; viscid; sticky. **2.** full of or smeared with glue. —**glu′eyness,** *n.*

glum (glŭm), *adj.*, **glummer, glummest.** gloomily sullen or silent; dejected. [cf. LG *glum* turbid, muddy; akin to GLOOM[2]] —**glum′ly,** *adv.* —**glum′ness,** *n.*
glumaceous (glo͞o mā′shəs), *adj.* **1.** glumelike. **2.** consisting of or having glumes.
glume (glo͞om), *n. Bot.* one of the characteristic bracts of the inflorescence of grasses, sedges, etc., esp. one of the pair of bracts at the base of a spikelet. [t. L: m. s. *glūma* hull or husk (of grain)] —**glume′like′,** *adj.*
glut (glŭt), *v.*, **glutted, glutting,** *n.* —*v.t.* **1.** to feed or fill to satiety; sate: *to glut the appetite.* **2.** to feed or fill to excess; cloy. **3. glut the market,** to overstock the market; furnish a supply of any article largely in excess of the demand, so that the price is unusually low. **4.** to choke up: *glut a channel.* —*v.i.* **5.** to eat to satiety. —*n.* **6.** a full supply. **7.** a surfeit. **8.** the act of glutting. **9.** the state of being glutted. [ME *glotye(n)*, appar. der. obs. *glut*, n., glutton, t. OF: adj., greedy. See GLUTTON[1]]
glutamic acid (glo͞o tăm′ĭk), *Chem., Biochem.* an amino acid, $HOOCCH_2CH_2CH(NH_2)COOH$, occurring in proteins of seeds and beet; used in the form of its sodium salt as a food flavouring.
glutamine (glo͞o′tə mēn′, -mĭn), *n. Chem., Biochem.* an amino acid, $NH_2COCH_2CH_2CH(NH_2)COOH$, occurring in proteins. [f. GLUT(EN) + -AMINE]
glutathione (glo͞o′tə thī′ōn, -thī ōn′), *n. Biochem.* a peptide found in blood and animal tissues, in embryos and germinating seedlings: important in metabolic actions and as a carrier of oxygen.
gluteal (glo͞o tē′əl, glo͞o′tĭ əl), *adj. Anat.* pertaining to buttock muscles or the buttocks. Also, **glutae′al.** [f. GLUTE(US) + -AL[1]]
glutelin (glo͞o′tĭ lĭn), *n. Biochem.* any of a group of simple proteins of vegetable origin, esp. from wheat.
gluten (glo͞o′tən), *n.* **1.** the tough, viscid nitrogenous substance remaining when the flour of wheat or other grain is washed to remove the starch. **2.** glue, or some gluey substance. [t. L: glue, akin to LL *glus* GLUE]
gluten bread, bread made from gluten flour.
gluten flour, wheat flour from which a large part of the starch has been removed, thus increasing the proportion of gluten.
glutenous (glo͞o′tə nəs), *adj.* **1.** like gluten. **2.** containing gluten, esp. in large amounts.
gluteus (glo͞o tē′əs), *n., pl.* **-tei** (-tē′ī). *Anat.* any one of three specific muscles of the buttocks. Also, **glutae′us.** [NL, der. Gk *gloutós* rump, pl. buttocks]
glutinous (glo͞o′tĭ nəs), *adj.* of the nature of glue; gluey; viscid; sticky. [t. L: m. s. *glūtinōsus* gluey, viscous] —**glu′tinously,** *adv.* —**glu′tinousness, glutinosity** (glo͞o′tĭ nŏs′ĭ tĭ), *n.*
glutose (glo͞o′tōs), *n.* an ingredient of the syrupy mixture obtained by the action of alkali on laevulose, or in the unfermentable reducing portion of cane molasses.
glutton[1] (glŭt′n), *n.* **1.** one who eats to excess; a gormandizer. **2.** one who indulges in something excessively. [ME *glutun*, t. OF: m. *glouton*, g. L *glūto, glutto*]
glutton[2] (glŭt′n), *n. Zool.* a thickset, voracious mammal, *Gulo gulo*, of the weasel family, measuring from 2 to 3 feet in length, and inhabiting northern regions. The kind found in America is usually called the **wolverine,** and is practically identical with that of Europe and Asia. [ult. t. Sw.: trans. of *fjällfräs* (through G *Vielfrass*), whence also NL name of animal, *gulo*]
gluttonize (glŭt′ə nīz′), *v.*, **-nized, -nizing.** —*v.i.* **1.** to eat like a glutton. —*v.t.* **2.** to feast gluttonously on. Also, **gluttonise.**
gluttonous (glŭt′ə nəs), *adj.* **1.** given to excessive eating; voracious. **2.** greedy; insatiable. —**glut′tonously,** *adv.* —**glut′tonousness,** *n.*
gluttony (glŭt′ə nĭ), *n., pl.* **-tonies.** excess in eating.
glycaemia (glī sē′myə), *n. Pathol.* an abnormal amount of sugar in the blood. Also, *U.S.*, **glycemia.**
glyceric (glĭ sĕ′rĭk), *adj. Chem.* pertaining to or derived from glycerol.
glyceric acid, *Chem.* a colourless, syrupy fluid, $CH_2OHCHOHCOOH$, produced during the fermentation of alcohol.
glyceride (glĭs′ə rīd′), *n., Chem.* one of a group of esters obtained from glycerol in combination with acids. [f. GLYCER(INE) + -IDE]
glycerine (glĭs′ə rĭn, -ə rēn′), *n. Chem.* glycerol. Also, **glycerin** (glĭs′ə rĭn). [t. F: m. *glycérine*, f. m. s. Gk *glykerós* sweet + -INE[2]]
glycerol (glĭs′ə rŏl′), *n. Chem.* a colourless, odourless, liquid alcohol, $HOCH_2CHOHCH_2OH$, of syrupy consistency and sweet taste, obtained by the saponification of natural fats and oils, and used in the arts, in medicine, in icing for cakes, etc.
glyceryl (glĭs′ə rĭl), *adj. Chem.* denoting or pertaining to the trivalent radical ($-CH_2(CH-)CH_2-$) derived from glycerine. [f. GLYCER(INE) + -YL]
glycine (glī′sēn, glī sēn′), *n. Chem.* a sweet-tasting, colourless, crystalline compound, H_2NCH_2COOH, the simplest amino acid, obtained by hydrolysis of proteins. [f. m. Gk *glyk(ýs)* sweet + -INE[2]]
glycocholic acid (glī′kō kŏl′ĭk, -kō′lĭk), *Biochem.* an acid, $C_{26}H_{43}NO_6$, occurring as a sodium salt in bile, which on hydrolysis yields glycine and cholic acid.
glycogen (glī′kō jĕn′), *n. Biochem.* a white, tasteless, polysaccharide $(C_6H_{10}O_5)_x$, usually stored in the liver, and easily hydrolysed into glucose. [f. m. s. Gk *glykýs* sweet + -GEN] —**gly′cogen′ic,** *adj.*
glycol (glī′kŏl), *n. Chem.* **1.** a colourless, sweet-tasting liquid, CH_2OHCH_2OH, used as an antifreeze in motor vehicles. **2.** any of a group of alcohols containing two hydroxyl groups. [b. GLYC(ERINE) and (ALCOH)OL]
glycolic (glī kŏl′ĭk), *adj. Chem.* pertaining to or derived from glycol, as **glycolic acid,** $HOCH_2COOH$.
glycolysis (glī kŏl′ĭ sĭs), *n. Biochem.* the catabolism of sugars and starch by enzymes accompanied by the release of energy and the production of lactic or pyruvic acid.
glycoprotein (glī′kō prō′tēn), *n. Biochem.* any of a group of complex proteins containing a carbohydrate combined with a simple protein, as mucin, etc. Also, **glucoprotein, glycopeptide** (glī′kō pĕp′tīd). [f. m. s. Gk *glykýs* sweet + PROTEIN]
glycoside (glī′kō sīd′), *n. Chem.* any monosaccharide in which one hydrogen atom is replaced by an organic radical.
glycosuria (glī′kō syo͝oə′rĭ ə), *n. Pathol.* excretion of glucose in the urine, as in diabetes. Also, **glucosuria.** [NL, f. F *glycose* GLUCOSE + *-uria* -URIA] —**gly′cosu′ric,** *adj.*
Glyndebourne (glīn′bôn′), *n.* a private opera house in Sussex, founded by John Christie in 1934.
glyoxalin (glī ŏk′sə lĭn), *n. Chem.* imidazole.
glyph (glĭf), *n.* **1.** *Archit.* an ornamental channel or groove, usually vertical, as in a Doric frieze. **2.** a sculptured figure. **3.** *Archaeol.* a pictograph or hieroglyph. [t. Gk: s. *glyphḗ* carving] —**glyph′ic,** *adj.*
glyptal resin (glĭp′tl), *Chem.* any of a group of adhesive resins formed by reacting polyhydric alcohols (esp. glycerol) with polybasic acids or their anhydrides (as phthalic anhydride).
glyptic (glĭp′tĭk), *adj.* of or pertaining to carving or engraving, esp. on precious stones. [t. Gk: m. s. *glyptikós* of engraving]
glyptodont (glĭp′tə dŏnt′), *n.* any mammal of the genus *Glyptodon*, having the body covered with a horny armour.
glyptography (glĭp tŏg′rə fĭ), *n.* **1.** the description or study of engraved gems, etc. **2.** the art or process of engraving on gems or the like. [f. Gk *glyptó(s)* carved + -GRAPHY]
gm, gram; grams.
G.M., **1.** General Manager. **2.** George Medal. **3.** Grand Marshal. **4.** Grand Master.
G-man (jē′măn′), *n. U.S.* an agent for the FBI.
GmbH, (G *Gesellschaft mit beschränkter Haftung*) company with limited liability.
G.M.C., General Medical Council.
Gmc, Germanic.
G.M.T., Greenwich Mean Time.
gn., guinea.
gnar (nä), *v.i.*, **gnarred, gnarring.** to snarl; growl.
gnarl (näl), *n.* **1.** a knotty protuberance on a tree; knot. —*v.t.* **2.** to twist. [back-formation from GNARLED]
gnarled (näld), *adj.* **1.** (of trees) full of or covered with gnarls. **2.** (of persons) **a.** having a rugged, weather-beaten appearance. **b.** cross-grained; perverse; cantankerous. Also, **gnarl′y.** [var. of KNURLED]
gnash (năsh), *v.t.* **1.** to grind (the teeth) together, esp. in rage or pain. **2.** to bite with grinding teeth. —*v.i.* **3.** to gnash the teeth. —*n.* **4.** the act of gnashing. [unexplained var. of obs. *gnast*, t. Scand.; cf. Icel. *gnastan* gnashing]
gnat (năt), *n.* any of certain small dipterous insects (mosquitoes) of the family *Culicidae*, esp. *Culex pipiens.* [ME; OE *gnæt(t)*, c. d. G *Gnatze*] —**gnat′like′,** *adj.*

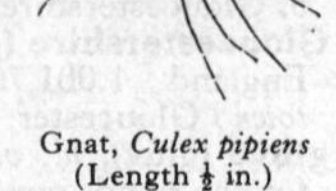
Gnat, *Culex pipiens* (Length ½ in.)

gnathion (nā′thĭ ŏn′, năth′ĭ-), *n. Anat.* the lowest point on the anterior margin of the lower jaw in the mid-sagittal plane. [NL, dim. of Gk *gnáthos* jaw] —**gna′thic,** *adj.*
-gnathous, an adjectival word element referring to the jaw, as in *prognathous.* [f. s. Gk *gnáthos* jaw + -OUS]
gnaw (nô), *v.*, **gnawed, gnawed** or **gnawn, gnawing.** —*v.t.* **1.** to wear away or remove by persistent biting.

2. to make by gnawing. 3. to corrode; consume. 4. to consume with passion; torment. —*v.i.* 5. to bite persistently. 6. to cause corrosion. 7. to act as if by corrosion. [ME *gnawe(n)*, OE *gnagan*, c. G *nagen*] —**gnaw′er,** *n.*

gnawing (nô′ĭng), *n.* 1. the act of one who or that which gnaws. 2. a persistent pain suggesting gnawing: *the gnawings of hunger.* —**gnaw′ingly,** *adv.*

G.N.C., General Nursing Council.

gneiss (nīs), *n.* a metamorphic rock, generally made up of bands which differ in colour and composition, some bands being rich in felspar and quartz, others rich in hornblende or mica. [t. G] —**gneiss′ic,** *adj.*

gneissoid (nī′soid), *adj.* resembling gneiss.

gnocchi (nŏk′ĭ, gə nŏk′ĭ, gnŏk′ĭ; *It.* nyŏk′kē), *n. Cookery.* an Italian dish of square or round shapes of semolina paste, used to garnish soup and the like, or served as a savoury dish with cheese sauce. [It.]

gnome[1] (nōm), *n.* one of a species of diminutive beings fabled to inhabit the interior of the earth and to act as guardians of its treasures, usually thought of as shrivelled little old men; a troll. [t. F, t. NL (Paracelsus): m. s. *gnomus*] —**gnom′ish,** *adj.* —**Syn.** See **goblin, sylph.**

gnome[2] (nōm), *n.* a short, pithy expression of a general truth; aphorism. [t. Gk: judgement, opinion, maxim]

gnomic (nō′mĭk, nŏm′ĭk), *adj.* 1. like or containing gnomes or aphorisms. 2. of, pertaining to, or denoting a writer of aphorisms, esp. certain Greek poets. Also, **gno′mical.** [t. Gk: m. s. *gnōmikós*] —**gno′mically,** *adv.*

gnomist (nō′mĭst), *n.* a writer of aphorisms.

gnomon (nō′mŏn), *n.* 1. a vertical shaft, column, obelisk, or the like, used (esp. by the ancients) as an astronomical instrument for determining the altitude of the sun, the position of a place, etc., by noting the length of the shadow cast at noon. 2. the vertical triangular plate of a sundial. 3. *Geom.* the part of a parallelogram which remains after a similar parallelogram has been taken away from one of its corners. [t. L, t. Gk: one who knows, an indicator] —**gnomon′ic, gnomon′ical,** *adj.* —**gnomon′ically,** *adv.*

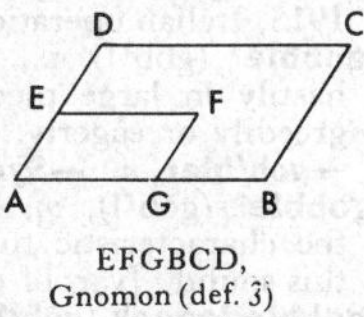

EFGBCD, Gnomon (def. 3)

gnosis (nō′sĭs), *n.* a knowledge of spiritual things; mystical knowledge. [NL, t. Gk: knowledge]

-gnosis, a suffix referring to recognition, esp. of a morbid condition, as in *prognosis.* [t. Gk: knowledge]

gnostic (nŏs′tĭk), *adj.* Also, **gnos′tical.** 1. pertaining to knowledge. 2. possessing knowledge, esp. esoteric knowledge of spiritual things. 3. (*cap.*) pertaining to or characteristic of the Gnostics. —*n.* 4. (*cap.*) a member of any of certain sects among the early Christians who claimed to have superior knowledge of spiritual things, and explained the world as created by powers or agencies arising as emanations from the Godhead. [t. LL: s. *Gnosticus*, t. Gk: m. *gnōstikós* pertaining to knowledge] —**Gnos′ticism,** *n.*

Gnosticize (nŏs′tĭ sīz′), *v.*, **-cized, -cizing.** —*v.i.* 1. to adopt or maintain Gnostic views. —*v.t.* 2. to explain on Gnostic principles; give a Gnostic colouring to. Also, **Gnosticise.**

G.N.P., *Econ.* gross national product.

gns, guineas.

gnu (noo͞), *n.*, *pl.* **gnus,** (*esp. collectively*) **gnu.** any of several African antelopes constituting the genus *Connochaetes*, characterized by an oxlike head, curved horns, and a long, flowing tail; a wildebeest. [t. Xhosa: m. *nqu*]

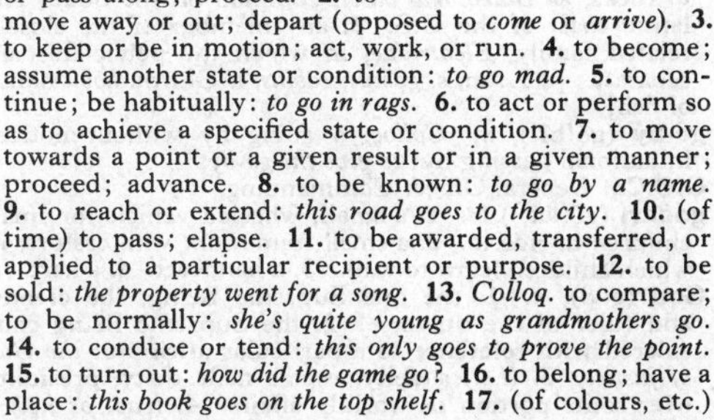
Gnu, *Connochaetes taurinus* (4½ ft high at the shoulder)

go (gō), *v.*, **went, gone, going,** *n.*, *pl.* **goes..** —*v.i.* 1. to move or pass along; proceed. 2. to move away or out; depart (opposed to *come* or *arrive*). 3. to keep or be in motion; act, work, or run. 4. to become; assume another state or condition: *to go mad.* 5. to continue; be habitually: *to go in rags.* 6. to act or perform so as to achieve a specified state or condition. 7. to move towards a point or a given result or in a given manner; proceed; advance. 8. to be known: *to go by a name.* 9. to reach or extend: *this road goes to the city.* 10. (of time) to pass; elapse. 11. to be awarded, transferred, or applied to a particular recipient or purpose. 12. to be sold: *the property went for a song.* 13. *Colloq.* to compare; to be normally: *she's quite young as grandmothers go.* 14. to conduce or tend: *this only goes to prove the point.* 15. to turn out: *how did the game go?* 16. to belong; have a place: *this book goes on the top shelf.* 17. (of colours, etc.) to harmonize; be compatible; be suited. 18. to fit into, round, etc. 19. to be used up, finished or consumed. 20. to develop, especially with reference to success or failure. 21. to be phrased: *how do the words go?* 22. to resort; have recourse: *to go to court.* 23. to be given up; be worn out; be lost or ended. 24. to die. 25. to fail; give way. 26. to begin; come into action: *here goes!* 27. to be acceptable: *anything goes.* 28. to carry final authority: *what I say goes.* 29. to be contained (fol. by *into*: *4 goes into 12.* 30. to contribute in amount or quantity; be requisite: *16 ounces go to the pound.* 31. to contribute to a result: *the items which go to make up a total.* 32. to be about, intending, or destined (used in the pres. part. fol. by an infinitive): *he is going to write.* —*v.t.* 33. to proceed on: *he went his way.* 34. to share equally (fol. by a complementary substantive): *to go halves.* 35. to make (a sound, effect, etc.) when operated (fol. by a complementary substantive): *the gun went bang.* 36. to weigh: *he went 14 stone exactly at the weigh-in.* 37. *Cards.* to bid. 38. *U.S. Colloq.* to risk or wager. —*v.* 39. Some special verb phrases are:

be going places, to be likely to achieve notable success.

go about, *Naut.* to change course.

go ahead, 1. to proceed with permission. 2. to take the lead; to be in the forefront: *the big horse went ahead in the first four seconds.*

go along, 1. to agree: *I can't go along with that.* 2. nonsense! (an exclamation of disbelief).

go around, 1. to move about; circulate. 2. to be enough for all.

go at, 1. to undertake with vigour. 2. to attack.

go back on, *Colloq.* 1. to fail (someone); let (someone) down. 2. to fail to keep (one's word, promise, etc.).

go by, 1. to pass. 2. to be guided by.

go down, 1. to descend; slope down. 2. to be defeated. 3. to be remembered by posterity. 4. to fall ill: *he has gone down with mumps.* 5. *Slang.* to be sent to prison. 6. to leave university at the end of the term or permanently (according to context). 7. *Bridge.* to fail to make one's contract.

go for, 1. to attack; set upon. 2. to be attracted to. 3. to aim for: *he's going for the chairmanship.*

go in for, to make (a thing) one's particular interest.

go into, to investigate or study thoroughly.

go in with, to enter a partnership or other agreement with.

go it alone, to act alone.

go off, 1. to be discharged; explode. 2. (of food, etc.) to become bad; deteriorate: *the meat's gone off.* 3. to take place in a specified manner: *the rehearsal went off well.* 4. *Colloq.* to come to dislike.

go on, 1. to go ahead; proceed. 2. to manage; do. 3. to behave; act. 4. to take place. 5. to chatter continually. 6. nonsense! (an exclamation of disbelief).

go out, 1. to come to a stop; end: *the light went out.* 2. to attend social functions, etc. 3. *Cards.* to dispose of the last card in one's hand.

go out with, to frequent the society of; date regularly.

go over, 1. to read or reread. 2. to repeat. 3. to examine. 4. to have an effect as specified: *my proposal went over very badly.* 5. *Rugby Football.* to score a try.

go slow, to restrict output deliberately as an industrial sanction.

go through, 1. to undergo; endure. 2. to examine in order. 3. to be accepted.

go through with, to complete; bring to a finish.

go under, to be overwhelmed; be ruined.

go up, 1. to rise or ascend; advance. 2. to go to university at the beginning of term.

go with, *Colloq.* 1. to harmonize with. 2. to frequent the society of.

go without saying, to be self-evident.

let go, 1. to release. 2. to give free reign to (one's emotion, etc.), esp. in making an attack.

let oneself go, 1. to cease to care for one's appearance. 2. to become uninhibited.

—*n.* 40. the act of going: *the come and go of the seasons.* 41. *Colloq.* energy, spirit, or animation: *to be full of go.* 42. *Colloq.* a try at something; attempt: *to have a go at something.* 43. **little go,** the first or preliminary examination at Cambridge University for the degree of B.A. 44. one's turn to play. 45. *Colloq.* something that goes well; a success: *to make a go of something.* 46. *U.S. Colloq.* a bargain: *it's a go!* 47. **from the word go,** from the beginning. 48. **on the go,** *Colloq.* constantly going; very active. —*adj.* 49. *U.S.* ready; functioning properly: *all instruments are go.* [ME *go(n)*, OE *gān*; akin to D *gaan*, MLG *gān*, OHG *gān*, *gēn*, G *gehen.* Cf. GANG[2], v.] —**go′er,** *n.* —**Syn.** 1. walk, run, ride, travel, advance. —**Ant.** 1. stay.

G.O., 1. general office. 2. general order.

goa (gō′ə), *n.* the black-tailed gazelle, *Procapra picticaudata*, of the Tibetan plateau. [t. Tibetan: m. *dgoba*]

Goa (gō′ə), *n.* a former district of Portuguese India, on the Arabian Sea, ab. 250 mi. S of Bombay: annexed by India in 1961. *Cap.:* Panjam.

goad (gōd), *n.* **1.** a stick with a pointed end, for driving cattle, etc. **2.** anything that pricks or wounds like such a stick; a stimulus. *—v.t.* **3.** to prick or drive with or as with a goad; incite. [ME *gode*, OE *gād*, c. Langobardic *gaida* arrowhead] **—goad′like′,** *adj.* **—Syn. 3.** spur.

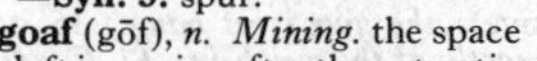
Goa, *Procapra picticaudata* (2 ft high at the shoulder)

goaf (gōf), *n. Mining.* the space left in a mine after the extraction of coal; sometimes packed with waste; gob.

go-ahead (gō′ə hĕd′), *adj.* **1.** going forward; advancing. **2.** progressive; active; enterprising. *—n.* **3.** permission to proceed.

goal (gōl), *n.* **1.** that towards which effort is directed; aim or end. **2.** the terminal point in a race. **3.** a pole or other object by which this is marked. **4.** an area, basket, cage or object or structure towards which the players strive to advance the ball, etc. **5.** the act of throwing or kicking the ball through or over the goal. **6.** the score made by accomplishing this. [ME *gol* boundary, limit. Cf. OE *gælan* hinder, impede] **—goal′-less,** *adj.*

goal area, 1. *Football.* a rectangular space, on a full-sized pitch 20 yards wide and 6 yards deep, in front of each goal. **2.** *Hockey.* a semicircular space in front of each goal. A goal is discounted unless the shot is made within the goal area.

goalie (gō′lĭ), *n. Colloq.* a goalkeeper.

goalkeeper (gōl′kē′pə), *n. Soccer, Hockey, etc.* a player whose special duty it is to prevent the ball from going through, into, or over the goal.

goal kick, *Soccer.* a free kick from a corner of the pitch taken by the defending side if the ball has crossed the goal line after last being touched by a member of the attacking side.

goal line, *Sport.* a line, on which the goal stands, marking each end of the field of play.

goal mouth, *Soccer.* the area immediately in front of the goal.

goalpost (gōl′pōst′), *n.* either of the two posts which support a bar across them, and form the goal in football, etc.

goanna (gō ăn′ə), *n. Austral.* any of several monitor lizards of the family *Varanidae.* [m. IGUANA]

goat (gōt), *n.* **1.** any animal of the genus *Capra* (family *Bovidae*), comprising various agile hollow-horned ruminants closely related to the sheep, found native in rocky and mountainous regions of the Old World, and including domesticated forms common throughout the world. **2.** any of various allied animals, as *Oreamnos montanus* (**Rocky Mountain goat**), a ruminant of western North America. **3.** (*cap.*) *Astron.* the zodiacal constellation or sign Capricorn. **4.** *Slang.* a scapegoat; one who is the butt of a joke. **5.** *Colloq.* a lecher; a licentious man. **6.** (*pl.*) (in collocations with *sheep*) evil, bad, or inferior people or things. **7. get one's goat,** *Slang.* to annoy; enrage; infuriate. [ME *gote, goot*, OE *gāt*, c. G *Geiss*; akin to L *haedus* kid] **—goat′like′,** *adj.*

Goat, *Capra hireus* (2½ ft high)

goat antelope, 1. a goatlike antelope of the genus *Naemorhedus*, as the goral, *N. goral*, or *N. crispus* of Japan. **2.** any antelope of the tribe *Rupicaprini*, a subdivision of the sheep and goat family, and including the chamois, goral serow, and Rocky Mountain goat.

goatee (gō tē′), *n.* a man's beard trimmed to a tuft or a point on the chin.

goatfish (gōt′fĭsh′), *n., pl.* **-fishes,** (*esp. collectively*) **-fish.** any fish of the tropical and subtropical marine family *Mullidae*, having a pair of long barbels below the mouth, and including species highly esteemed as a delicacy by the ancient Romans; surmullet; red mullet.

goat god, any deity with the legs and feet of a goat, as Pan or the satyrs.

goatherd (gōt′hûd′), *n.* one who tends goats.

goatish (gō′tĭsh), *adj.* like a goat; lustful. **—goat′ishly,** *adv.* **—goat′ishness,** *n.*

goatsbeard (gōts′bĭəd′), *n.* **1.** a composite plant, *Tragopogon pratensis*, a perennial herb of N temperate regions producing spherical heads of fruits, each bearing a stalked, feathery pappus. **2.** an American rosaceous herb, *Aruncus sylvester*, with long, slender spikes of small flowers.

goatskin (gōt′skĭn′), *n.* **1.** the skin or hide of a goat. **2.** leather made from it.

goat's-rue (gōts′rōō′), *n.* **1.** a European leguminous herb, *Galega officinalis*, formerly used in medicine. **2.** an American leguminous herb, *Telphrosia virginiana.*

goatsucker (gōt′sŭk′ə), *n.* **1.** a non-passerine nocturnal bird, *Caprimulgus europaeus*, of Europe, with flat head and wide mouth, formerly supposed to suck the milk of goats. **2.** any of the group of chiefly nocturnal or crepuscular birds to which this species belongs, usually regarded as including two families, the *Caprimulgidae* (**true goatsuckers**) and the *Podargidae* (**frogmouths**).

go-away bird (gō′ə wā bûd′), *S African.* the grey lourie, family *Musophagidae.* [imit.]

gob[1] (gŏb), *n.* a mass or lump. [ME *gobbe* lump, mass, appar. t. OF: m. *go(u)be*, ult. of Gallic derivation]

gob[2] (gŏb), *Slang. —n.* **1.** the mouth. *—v.i.* **2.** to spit or expectorate. [t. Gaelic or Irish. Cf. GAB]

gob[3] (gŏb), *n.* goaf.

gobbet (gŏb′ĭt), *n.* **1.** a fragment or hunk, esp. of raw flesh. **2.** *Archaic or Dial.* a lump or mass. [ME *gobet*, t. OF, dim of *gobe* GOB[1]]

Gobbi (gŏb′ĭ; *It.* gŏb′bē), *n.* **Tito** (tē′tō; *It.* tĕ′tō), born 1915, Italian operatic baritone.

gobble[1] (gŏb′l), *v.,* **-bled, -bling.** *—v.t.* **1.** to swallow hastily in large pieces; gulp. **2.** *Slang.* to seize upon greedily or eagerly. *—v.i.* **3.** to eat hastily. [der. GOB[1]] **—gob′bler,** *n.* **—Syn. 1.** bolt, devour.

gobble[2] (gŏb′l), *v.,* **-bled, -bling,** *n. —v.i.* **1.** to make the characteristic throaty cry of a turkey cock. *—n.* **2.** this sound. [var. of GABBLE taken as imit. of the cry]

gobbledegook (gŏb′l dĭ gōōk′), *n. Colloq.* language characterized by circumlocution and jargon: *the gobbledegook of government reports.* Also, **gobbledy-gook.** [grotesque coinage modelled on HOBBLEDEHOY. Final element *gook* may be slang word for tramp, var. of GOWK. Cf. GOBBLE, GOO]

gobbler (gŏb′lə), *n.* a turkey cock.

Gobelin (gō′bə lĭn; *Fr.* gŏ blăN′), *adj.* **1.** made at the tapestry factory of the Gobelins in Paris. **2.** resembling the tapestry made at the Gobelins. *—n.* **3.** a tapestry made at the Gobelins factory in Paris.

go-between (gō′bĭ twēn′), *n.* one who acts as agent between persons or parties.

Gobi (gō′bĭ), *n.* a desert in E Asia, mostly in Mongolia. ab. 500,000 sq. mi. Chinese, **Shamo.**

gobioid (gō′bĭ oid′), *adj.* **1.** of or resembling a goby. *—n.* **2.** a gobioid fish.

goblet (gŏb′lĭt), *n.* **1.** a drinking glass with a foot and stem. **2.** *Archaic.* a bowl-shaped drinking vessel. [ME *gobelet*, t. OF, dim. of *gobel* cup; ult. of Celtic orig.]

goblin (gŏb′lĭn), *n.* a grotesque mischievous sprite or elf. [ME *gobelin*, t. F (obs.), t. MHG: m. *kobold* goblin] **—Syn.** GOBLIN, GNOME, GREMLIN refer to imaginary beings, thought to be malevolent to man. GOBLINS are demons of any size, usually in human or animal forms, which are supposed to assail, afflict, and even torture human beings: '*Be thou a spirit of health or goblin damn'd, . . .*' (Shak. Hamlet I, iv). GNOMES are small beings, like ugly little old men, who live in the earth, guarding mines, treasures, etc. They are mysteriously malevolent and terrify human beings by causing dreadful mishaps to occur. GREMLINS are invisible beings who were said by pilots in World War II to cause all sorts of things to go wrong with aeroplanes.

gobstopper (gŏb′stŏp′ə), *n.* a large, round, hard sweet of layers of different colours.

goby (gō′bĭ), *n., pl.* **-bies,** (*esp. collectively*) **-by. 1.** any member of the *Gobiidae*, a family of marine and freshwater fishes, mostly small and having the pelvic fins united to form a suctorial disc that enables them to cling to rocks, as *Baleosoma basci*, common on the South Atlantic coast of the U.S. **2.** any member of the closely related family, *Eleotridae*, in which the pelvic fins are separate. [t. L: m. s. *gōbius, cōbius*, t. Gk: m. *kōbiós* kind of fish]

go-by (gō′bī′), *n. Colloq.* a going by without notice; intentional passing by: *to give the go-by.*

G.O.C., General Officer Commanding.

gocart (gō′kät′), *n.* **1.** a small, wheeled vehicle for small children to ride in. **2.** a small framework with castors, in which children learn to walk. **3.** a handcart. **4.** a kart.

God (gŏd), *n.* **1.** the one Supreme Being, the creator and ruler of the universe. **2.** the Supreme Being considered with reference to a particular attribute: *the God of justice.* **3.** (*l.c.*) a deity, esp. a male deity, presiding over some portion of worldly affairs. **4.** (*cap. or l.c.*) a supreme being according to some particular conception: *the God of pantheism.* **5.** (*l.c.*) an image of a deity; an idol. **6.** (*l.c.*) any deified person or object. **7.** (*l.c., pl.*) the highest gallery in a theatre. *—interj.* **8.** (an oath or exclamation used to express weariness, annoyance, disappointment, etc.) [ME and OE, c. D *god*, G *Gott*, Icel. *godh*, Goth. *guth*]

Godalming (gŏd′l mĭng), *n.* a town in England, in W central Surrey. 15,780 (1961).

Godard (*Fr.* gō dȧr′), *n.* **Jean-Luc** (*Fr.* zhäɴ lʏk′), born 1930, French film director.

Godavari (*Hind.* gō dä′vē rē), *n.* a river flowing from W India SE to the Bay of Bengal. ab. 900 mi.

godchild (gŏd′chīld′), *n., pl.* **-children.** one for whom a person (godparent) stands sponsor at baptism.

goddamn (gŏd′dăm′), *interj.* **1.** (an oath expressing irritation, fury, etc.) *—adj., adv.* **2.** Also, **goddamned,** damned.

Goddard (gŏd′əd, gŏd′äd), *n.* **Robert Hutchings** (rŏb′-ət hŭch′ĭngz), 1882–1945, U.S. rocket pioneer.

goddaughter (gŏd′dô′tə), *n.* a female godchild.

goddess (gŏd′ĭs), *n.* **1.** a female god or deity. **2.** a woman of extraordinary beauty. **3.** an adored woman. **—god′-dess-hood′, god′dess-ship′,** *n.*

Godefroy de Bouillon (*Fr.* gŏd frwȧ də bo͞o yôɴ′), *c.* 1060–1100, French crusader.

Goderich (gō′drĭch), *n.* **Frederick John Robinson, Viscount** (*1st Earl of Ripon*), 1782–1859, English statesman: prime minister 1827–28.

Godesberg (*Ger.* gō′dəs bĕrk), *n.* **Bad.** See **Bad Godesberg.**

godetia (gə dē′shə), *n.* any of the commonly cultivated annuals with colourful flowers, of N America, belonging to the onagraceous genus *Oenothera.* [named after C. H. *Godet*, 1797–1879, Swiss botanist]

godfather (gŏd′fä′ᵺə), *n.* **1.** a man who stands sponsor for a child at baptism or confirmation. *—v.t.* **2.** to act as godfather to; be sponsor for.

god-fearing (gŏd′fĭə′rĭng), *adj.* pious; deeply religious.

godforsaken (gŏd′fə sā′kən), *adj., Colloq.* desolate; remote.

Godhead (gŏd′hĕd′), *n.* **1.** the essential being of God; the Supreme Being. **2.** (*l.c.*) godhood or godship. **3.** (*l.c.*) a deity; god or goddess.

godhood (gŏd′ho͝od′), *n.* divine character; godship.

Godiva (gə dī′və), *n.* (*Lady Godiva*) wife of Leofric, Earl of Mercia (11th century). According to legend. she rode naked through the streets of Coventry to win relief for the people from a burdensome tax.

godless (gŏd′lĭs), *adj.* **1.** having or acknowledging no God. **2.** wicked. **—god′lessly,** *adv.* **—god′lessness,** *n.*

godlike (gŏd′līk′), *adj.* like or befitting a god, or God. **—god′like′ness,** *n.*

godly (gŏd′lĭ), *adj.,* **-lier, -liest. 1.** conforming to God's laws; pious. **2.** *Archaic.* coming from God; divine. **—god′lily,** *adv.* **—god′liness,** *n.* **—Syn. 1.** devout, religious; saintly. **—Ant. 1.** wicked, ungodly.

godmother (gŏd′mŭᵺ′ə), *n.* **1.** a woman who sponsors a child at baptism. **2.** a female sponsor. *—v.t.* **3.** to act as godmother to; sponsor.

Godolphin (gə dŏl′fĭn), *n.* **Sidney, 1st Earl of,** 1645–1712, English statesman and financier.

godown (gō′doun′), *n.* (in India and eastern Asia) a warehouse. [t. Malay: m. *godong*]

godparent (gŏd′pĕə′rənt), *n.* a godfather or godmother.

godroon (gə dro͞on′), *n.* gadroon.

God's acre, a burial ground; cemetery.

God save the Queen, the British national anthem. Author and composer unknown. Also, when the reigning monarch is a man, **God save the King.**

godsend (gŏd′sĕnd′), *n.* something unexpected but particularly welcome and timely, as if sent by God. [earlier *God's send*, var. (under influence of *send*, v.) of *God's sond* or *sand*, OE *sond, sand* message, service]

godship (gŏd′shĭp′), *n.* the rank or character of a god.

godson (gŏd′sŭn′), *n.* a male godchild.

godspeed (gŏd′spēd′), *n., interj.* God speed you: a wish of success to one setting out on a journey or undertaking.

Godthaab (*Dan.* gŏd′hŏb), *n.* the capital of Greenland, in the SW part. 5500 (est. 1967).

Godunov (*Russ.* gə do͝o nôf′), *n.* **Boris Feodorovich** (*Russ.* bȧ rĕs′fyô′də rə vĭch), 1552–1605, Russian regent and tsar, 1598–1605.

Godward (gŏd′wəd), *adv.* **1.** Also, **Godwards.** towards God. *—adj.* **2.** directed towards God.

Godwin (gŏd′wĭn), *n.* **1.** (*Earl of Wessex*) died 1053, English statesman. **2. Mrs,** (*Mary Wollstonecraft*) 1759–1797, English writer (wife of William). **3. William,** 1756–1836, British political philosopher and writer.

Godwin Austen (gŏd′wĭn ôs′tĭn). See **K2.**

godwit (gŏd′wĭt′), *n.* any of several large shorebirds of the genus *Limosa*, all with long, slightly up-curved bills, as the **black-tailed godwit,** *Limosa limosa*, of Europe.

Goebbels (*Ger.* gœb′əls), *n.* **Paul Joseph** (*Ger.* poul yō′zĕf), 1897–1945, German Nazi leader and propagandist.

goer (gō′ə), *n.* **1.** a person who attends regularly (usually used in combination): *a cinemagoer.* **2.** *Slang.* one who or that which moves fast.

Goering (*Ger.* gœ′rĭng), *n.* **Hermann** (*Ger.* hĕr′män), 1893–1946, German field marshal and Nazi party leader.

goes (gōz), *v.* **1.** 3rd pers. sing. pres. of **go.** *—n.* **2.** pl. of **go.**

Goethals (gō′thəlz), *n.* **George Washington,** 1858–1928, U.S. army engineer, in charge of building the Panama Canal.

Goethe (*Ger.* gœ′tə), *n.* **Johann Wolfgang von** (*Ger.* yō′hän vŏlf′gäng fŏn), 1749–1832, German poet, dramatist, novelist, and philosopher.

goethite (gō′thīt, gû′tīt), *n.* a very common mineral, iron hydroxide, FeO(OH), occurring in crystals, but more commonly in yellow or brown earthy masses, an ore of iron. Also, **göthite.** [named after the poet GOETHE. See -ITE[1]]

goffer (gō′fə), *n.* **1.** an ornamental plaiting used for the frills and borders of women's caps, etc. *—v.t.* **2.** to flute (a frill, etc.), as with a heated iron. **3.** to impress (book edges, etc.) with an ornamental pattern. Also, **gauffer.** [t. F: m. *gauffer* stamp cloth, paper, etc., der. *gaufre* honeycomb, waffle, t. D: m. *wafel.* See WAFER]

go-getter (gō′gĕt′ə), *n. Colloq.* an enterprising, aggressive person.

goggle (gŏg′l), *n., v.,* **-gled, -gling.** *—n.* **1.** (*pl.*) spectacles often with special rims so devised as to protect the eyes from injury. **2.** a goggling look. *—v.i.* **3.** to stare with bulging eyes. **4.** (of the eyes) to roll; bulge and stare. **5.** to roll the eyes. *—v.t.* **6.** to roll (the eyes). [ME *gogelen* look aside; orig. uncert.]

goggle-box (gŏg′l bŏks′), *n. Slang.* television.

goggle-eyed (gŏg′l īd′), *adj., adv.* with prominent, rolling eyes, esp. as a mark of astonishment: *she stared goggle-eyed at the apparition.*

Gogh (gŏk, gŏf, gŏKH; *Du.* KHôKH), *n.* **Vincent van** (*Du.* vĭn sĕnt′ vŏn), 1853–90, Dutch painter.

goglet (gŏg′lĭt), *n.* (in India, etc.) a long-necked vessel, usually of porous earthenware to permit evaporation, used as a water-cooler. [earlier *gurglet*, t. Pg.: m. *gorgoleta*, ult. der. L *gurga* abyss, throat]

Gogol (gō′gŏl; *Russ.* gô′gəly), *n.* **Nikolai Vasilievich** (*Russ.* nĭ kȧ lāy′ vȧ sē′lyĭ vĭch), 1809–52, Russian novelist, short-story writer, and dramatist.

Goiânia (*Port.* gō yə′nyȧ), *n.* a town in SE central Brazil. 153,505 (1960).

Goidelic (goi dĕl′ĭk), *adj.* **1.** of or pertaining to the Gaels or their language. *—n.* **2.** *Ling.* the Gaelic subgroup of Celtic. Also, **Gadhelic.** [f. m. OIrish *Goideal* a Gael + -IC]

going (gō′ĭng), *n.* **1.** a going away; departure: *a safe going and return.* **2.** the condition of something, as of the ground on a racecourse: *the going was bad.* **3.** (*usually pl.*) way; deportment. *—adj.* **4.** moving or working, as machinery. **5.** that goes; in existence. **6.** flourishing in business: *a going concern.* **7.** having to do with a going business: *the going value of a company.* **8.** departing. **9. going on,** nearly: *it is going on four o'clock.*

going-over (gō′ĭng ō′və), *n., pl.* **goings-over. 1.** *Colloq.* a thorough examination. **2.** *Slang.* a severe beating or thrashing.

goings-on (gō′ĭngz ŏn′), *n., pl. Colloq.* **1.** actions; conduct; behaviour (used chiefly with depreciative force): *we were shocked by the goings-on at the office party.* **2.** current events: *she only kept in touch with the goings-on at home through newspapers.*

goitre (goi′tə), *n. Pathol.* an enlargement of the thyroid gland, on the front and sides of the neck. Also, *U.S.,* **goiter.** [t. F: ult. der. L *guttur* throat]

goitrous (goi′trəs), *adj.* pertaining to or affected with goitre.

Go-kart (gō′kät′), *n. Trademark.* a kart.

Golborne (gŏl′bən), *n.* a town in England, in S Lancashire. 21,277 (1961).

Golconda (gŏl kŏn′də), *n.* **1.** an ancient city of India, the ruins of which are near the capital city of Hyderabad state: once the capital of a powerful Muslim kingdom, it was renowned for its wealth and diamond cutting. **2.** (*often l.c.*) a mine or source of wealth.

gold (gōld), *n.* **1.** a precious yellow metal, highly malleable and ductile, and free from liability to rust. *Symbol.:* Au; *at. wt:* 16·967; *at. no.:* 79; *sp. gr.:* 19·3 at 20°C. **2.** coin made of it. **3.** money; wealth. **4.** something likened to this metal in brightness, preciousness, etc.: *a heart of gold.*

5. bright metallic yellow, sometimes tending towards brown. **6.** *Archery.* the centre or bull's-eye of a target. *—adj.* **7.** consisting of gold. **8.** pertaining to gold. **9.** like gold. **10.** of the colour of gold. [ME and OE, c. G *Gold*; akin to Russ. *zoloto*]

gold basis, adaptation of prices to a gold standard.

gold-beater's skin, the prepared outside membrane of the large intestine of the ox, used by gold-beaters to lay between the leaves of the metal while they beat it.

gold-beating (gōld′bē′tĭng), *n.* the art or process of beating out gold into gold leaf. **—gold′-beat′er,** *n.*

gold bullion standard, a monetary system permitting the movement of gold bullion into and out of the country for international payments, in which the central authority buys and sells gold at the current market rate, and token money (not gold coins) forms the money in circulation.

Gold Coast, a former British territory in W Africa; became independent within the Commonwealth of Nations in 1957. See **Ghana.**

goldcrest (gōld′krĕst′), *n.* a tiny bird, *Regulus regulus*, with a bright yellow patch on the crown of its head and black bands above the eyes.

gold-digger (gōld′dĭg′ə), *n.* **1.** one who digs or seeks for gold in a goldfield. **2.** *Colloq.* a woman who uses her feminine arts to extract profit from men.

gold-digging (gōld′dĭg′ĭng), *n.* **1.** the work of digging for gold. **2.** (*pl.*) a region where digging or seeking for gold, esp. by placer mining, is carried on.

gold dust, gold in fine particles.

golden (gōl′dən), *adj.* **1.** of the colour of gold; yellow; bright, metallic, or lustrous like gold. **2.** made or consisting of gold: *golden keys.* **3.** resembling gold in value; most excellent: *a golden opportunity.* **4.** flourishing; joyous: *the golden hours.* **5.** gifted; fortunate and destined for success. **6.** indicating the 50th event of a series, as a wedding anniversary. **—gold′enly,** *adv.* **—gold′enness,** *n.*

golden age, 1. (in Greek and Roman mythology) the first and best age of the world, when mankind lived in innocence and happiness. **2.** the most flourishing period in the history of a nation, literature, etc.

golden aster, any plant of a North American genus, *Chrysopsis*, of aster-like composites with bright golden-yellow flowers, esp. a wild flower species, *C. mariana*, abundant in the eastern U.S.

golden calf, 1. *Bible.* a golden idol set up by Aaron. Ex. 32. **2.** *Bible.* either of the two similar idols set up by Jeroboam. I Kings, 12:28, 29. **3.** *Colloq.* wealth and material possessions.

golden cat, either of two medium-sized felines with golden-brown fur, *Felis aurata* of W Africa, and *F. temininck*i of SE Asia.

golden chain, laburnum.

Golden Delicious, *Hort.* a variety of yellow apple.

golden eagle, a large eagle, *Aquila chrysaëtos*, of both the eastern and western hemispheres (so called because of the golden-brown feathers on the back of the neck).

goldeneye (gōl′dən ī′), *n., pl.* **-eyes,** (*esp. collectively*) **-eye.** a diving duck of the subfamily *Aythyinae* and genus *Glaucionetta*, with bright yellow eyes, as *G. clangula*, of Europe and America; whistler; garrot.

Golden Fleece, *Gk Legend.* the fleece of gold taken from the ram on which Phrixus was carried to Colchis, recovered from King Aeëtes by the Argonautic expedition under Jason. See **Medea.**

Golden Gate, a strait in W California between San Francisco Bay and the Pacific: spanned by the **Golden Gate Bridge,** whose channel span of 4200 ft is one of the longest single spans in the world.

golden goose, *Gk Legend.* a goose which laid one golden egg a day and was killed by its impatient owner who wanted all the gold immediately.

golden hamster, a short-tailed burrowing rodent, *Mesocricetus auratus*, with a golden coat, widely kept as a pet. The only known wild species are those which have escaped captivity.

Golden Horde, the army of Mongol Tartars that overran Eastern Europe in the 13th century.

Golden Horn, an inlet of the Bosporus in European Turkey, which forms the inner port of Istanbul.

golden mantella, a small gold-coloured frog, *Mantella aurantiaca*, from Madagascar, a member of the *Rariidae* family.

golden mean, the happy medium between extremes; moderate course of action. [trans. of L *aurea mediocritas* (Horace)]

golden pheasant, an Asiatic pheasant, *Chrysolophus pictus*, with rich yellow and orange tones in the head and neck plumage of the male.

golden plover, either of two plovers with yellow spotting above; the European species is *Pluvialis apricaria*; the American, *P. dominica.*

golden rain, laburnum.

golden retriever, one of a breed of retrievers with thick, wavy, golden coat.

golden robin, Baltimore oriole.

goldenrod (gōl′dən rŏd′), *n.* **1.** any plant of the composite genus *Solidago*, most species of which bear numerous small yellow flowers. **2.** any of various related composite plants, as *Brachychaeta sphacelata* (**false goldenrod**).

golden rule, 1. the rule of conduct, *Whatsoever ye would that men should do to you, do ye even so to them.* Matt. 7:12. **2.** rule of three. **3.** any very important rule, esp. of conduct.

golden samphire, a perennial herb with narrow fleshy leaves and yellow capitula, *Inula crithmoides*, family *Compositae*, which grows in coastal regions of Europe and W Asia.

Dwarf goldenrod, *Solidago nemoralis* (Height 2 ft)

golden saxifrage, any of several small perennial saxifragaceous herbs of wet places, as *Chrysosplenium oppositifolium*, the **opposite-leaved golden saxifrage** of W and central Europe.

goldenseal (gōl′dən.sēl′), *n.* **1.** a ranunculaceous herb, *Hydrastis canadensis*, with a thick yellow rootstock. **2.** the rhizomes and roots of this plant, formerly much used in medicine.

golden section, the division of a line so that the shorter segment is to the longer as the longer is to the whole; regarded as an ideal division.

golden syrup, a supersaturated solution of sucrose and invert sugars, derived from sugar processing; used in cooking and as a sauce for porridge, desserts, etc.

golden wattle, 1. a broad-leafed Australian acacia, *Acacia pycnantha*, yielding useful gum and tanbark. **2.** any similar acacia, esp. *A. longifolia*, of Australia and Tasmania.

golden wedding, the fiftieth anniversary of a wedding.

gold-exchange standard (gōld′ĭks chānj′), a monetary system whose monetary unit is kept at a fixed relation with that of a country on the gold standard by dealings in foreign exchange by the central authority, the money in circulation being token money.

goldeye (gōld′ī′), *n., pl.* **-eyes,** (*esp. collectively*) **-eye.** a silvery, herring-like, fish, *Amphiodon alosoides*, of the fresh waters of central N America, noted as a game fish.

goldfield (gōld′fēld′), *n.* a district in which gold is mined.

gold-filled (gōld′fĭld′), *adj.* containing a filling of cheaper metal within a layer of gold.

goldfinch (gōld′fĭnch′), *n.* **1.** a European fringilline songbird, *Carduelis carduelis*, having a crimson face and wings marked with yellow. **2.** any of certain small American finches, esp. *Spinus tristis*, the male of which has yellow body plumage in summer. [ME; OE *goldfinc.* See GOLD, FINCH]

goldfish (gōld′fĭsh′), *n., pl.* **-fishes,** (*esp. collectively*) **-fish. 1.** a small fish, *Carassius auratus*, of the carp family and orig. native in China, prized for aquariums and pools because of its golden colouring and odd form (produced by artificial selection). **2.** (*cap.*) *Astron.* the southern constellation Dorado or Swordfish.

goldfish-bowl (gōld′fĭsh bōl′), *n.* **1.** a fishbowl. **2.** *Colloq.* a state of helpless exposure to public curiosity; lack of privacy.

gold foil, gold beaten into thin sheets (many times thicker than gold leaf).

goldilocks (gōl′dĭ lŏks′), *n., construed as sing. or pl.* (*sometimes cap.*) **1.** a person with golden hair. **2.** a perennial ranunculaceous herb, *Ranunculus auricomus*, common in woods of Europe and N Asia. **3.** a perennial herbaceous composite, *Aster linosyris*, found mostly on limestone in central and S Europe.

Golding (gōl′dĭng), *n.* **William (Gerald),** born 1911, English novelist.

gold leaf, gold beaten into a very thin sheet, used for gilding, etc.

goldmine (gōld′mīn′), *n.* **1.** a mine yielding gold. **2.** a source of great wealth. **3.** a source of anything required: *a goldmine of information.*

gold note, *U.S.* a banknote payable in gold coin.

gold-of-pleasure (gōld′əv plĕzh′ə), *n.* a brassicaceous herb, *Camelina sativa*, with small yellowish flowers.

Goldoni (*It.* gôl dô′nē), *n.* **Carlo** (*It.* kär′lô), 1707–93, Italian dramatist.

gold plate, 1. a plating, esp. electroplating, of gold. **2.** articles and utensils collectively, esp. tableware, of gold plate or, orig., solid gold.

gold point, the point at which it is equally expensive to buy (or sell), exchange, or export (or import) gold in adjustment of foreign claims (or counterclaims).

gold reserve, the total gold coin and bullion held by a central authority either national or international. It is used to make international payments, and nationally to maintain the value of the token notes and coinage issued on behalf of the government.

gold rush, a large-scale emigration of people to a region where gold has been discovered, as that to California in 1849.

gold-sinny (gōld′sĭn′ĭ), *n.* a wrasse, *Ctenolabrus niprestris,* found along the south coasts of the British Isles.

goldsmith (gōld′smĭth′), *n.* one who makes or sells articles of gold (down to the 18th cent., often acting also as a banker). [ME and OE]

Goldsmith (gōld′smĭth′), *n.* **Oliver,** 1728–74, English poet, novelist, and dramatist.

goldsmith beetle, a brilliant golden scarabaeid beetle of Europe, *Cetonia aurata.*

gold standard, a monetary system in which there is a free mintage of gold into standard legal coins, free movement of gold into and out of the country, and in which the currency unit is based on gold of a fixed weight and fineness.

goldstick (gōld′stĭk′), *n.* **1.** a gilded rod carried on state occasions by the colonel of the Life Guards or the captain of the gentlemen-at-arms. **2.** the bearer of it.

goldstone (gōld′stōn′), *n.* aventurine (def. 1).

goldthread (gōld′thrĕd′), *n.* **1.** a white-flowered ranunculaceous herb, *Coptis groenlandica,* with a slender yellow root. **2.** the root itself, used in medicine.

golem (gō′lĕm), *n.* **1.** *Jewish Legend.* a figure constructed to represent a human being, and endowed with life, by human agency. **2.** an automaton. [t. Heb.]

golf (gŏlf), *n.* **1.** an outdoor game, in which a small resilient ball is driven with special clubs into a series of holes, distributed at various distances over a course having natural or artificial obstacles, the object being to get the ball into each hole in as few strokes as possible. —*v.i.* **2.** to play golf. [ME (Scot.); orig. uncert.] —**golf′er,** *n.*

golf bag, a bag, often made of canvas, used for carrying golf clubs, balls, etc.

golf club, 1. any of the various implements for striking the ball in golf. **2.** an organization of golf players. **3.** a club with grounds for members to play golf on, often combined with various social amenities.

golf links, (*pl. sometimes construed as sing.*) the ground or course over which golf is played. Also, **golf course.**

Golgotha (gŏl′gə thə), *n.* **1.** Calvary. **2.** a place of suffering or sacrifice. [t. L (Vulgate), t. Gk (N.T.), t. Aram.: m. *goghaltā,* Heb. *gulgolĕth* skull; see John 19:17]

goliard (gō′lyəd), *n.* one of a number of wandering scholars, clerics, or students in Germany, France, and England, chiefly in the 12th and 13th centuries, noted for their rioting and intemperance, and as the authors of satirical Latin verse. [late ME, t. OF: lit., glutton, der. *gole,* g. L *gula* throat, palate, gluttony] —**goliardic** (gō lyä′dĭk), *adj.*

goliardery (gō lyä′də rĭ), *n.* the poems of the goliards.

Goliath (gə lī′əth), *n.* the giant champion of the Philistines whom David is reputed to have killed with a stone from a sling. I Sam. 17:4. Cf. II Sam. 21:19 and I Chron. 20:5. [t. L (Vulgate), t. Gk (Septuagint), repr. Heb. *Golyath*]

goliath frog, the largest known frog, *Rana goliath,* almost 12 in. long, native of the Congo region of Africa.

golliwog (gŏl′ĭ wŏg′), *n.* a soft, black-faced doll. Also, **gollywog.** [var. of *Golliwogg,* name of a doll coined *c.* 1910 by Florence and Bertha Upton, U.S. writers for children]

golly[1] (gŏl′ĭ), *interj. Colloq.* (a mild expletive expressing surprise, etc.) [a euphemistic var. of *God!*]

golly[2] (gŏl′ĭ), *n.* a golliwog.

golosh (gə lŏsh′), *n.* galosh.

Goltz (*Ger.* gōlts), *n.* **Baron Colmar von der** (*Ger.* kōl′mär fōn dĕr), 1843–1916, German field marshal in Turkey.

G.O.M., grand old man (originally applied to W. E. Gladstone).

gombo (gŭm′bō), *n.* gumbo.

gombroon (gŏm bro͞on′), *n.* a type of Persian pottery ware. [named after a town on the Persian Gulf]

Gomel (*Russ.* gô′mĭly), *n.* a city in the W Soviet Union in Europe, on a tributary of the Dnieper. 216,000 (est. 1965).

gomerel (gŏm′ə rĭl), *n. Scot. and N Dial.* a fool. Also, **gomeral, gomeril** (gŏm′ə rĭl). [f. obs. *gome* man (OE *guma,* c. L *homo*) + -REL]

Gomorrah (gə mŏ′rə), *n.* **1.** an ancient city destroyed (with Sodom) for the wickedness of its inhabitants. Gen. 18–19. **2.** any very wicked place. Also, **Gomorrha.**

Gompers (gŏm′pəz), *n.* **Samuel,** 1850–1924, U.S. trade-union leader; one of the founders of the American Federation of Labor and its president, 1886–94, 1896–1924.

gomphosis (gŏm fō′sĭs), *n. Anat.* an immovable articulation in which one bone or part is received in a cavity in another, as a tooth in its socket. [NL, t. Gk: a bolting together]

gom pou (gŏm′pō′), the largest bustard of southern Africa, *Choriotis kori.* [t. Afrikaans: gum peacock]

Gomulka (gō mo͞ol′kə; *Pol.* gō mo͞o′kȧ), *n.* **Wladyslaw** (*Pol.* vwȧ dĭs′wȧf), born 1905, Polish statesman, First Secretary of the Central Committee of the Politburo of the United Workers' Party, from 1956.

gomuti (gə mo͞o′tĭ), *n., pl.* **-tis. 1.** Also, **gomuti palm.** a sago palm, *Arenga pinnata,* of the East Indies: source of palm sugar. **2.** a black, horsehair-like fibre obtained from it, used for making rope, etc. [t. Malay]

-gon, a suffix denoting geometrical figures having a certain number or kind of angles, as in *polygon, pentagon.* [t. Gk: m. *-gōnos* (neut. *-gōnon*) -angled, -angular]

gonad (gŏn′ăd), *n. Anat.* the sex gland, male or female, in which germ cells develop and appropriate sex hormones are produced. [t. Gk: s. *gonár* womb] —**gon′adal, gonadial** (gŏ nā′dyəl), **gonadic** (gŏ năd′ĭk), *adj.*

gonadotropic (gŏn′ə dō trŏp′ĭk, gə năd′ō-), *adj. Biochem.* pertaining to hormones (gonadotropins) formed in the hypophysis or the placenta which affect the activity of the ovary or testis. Also, **gonadotrophic** (gŏn′ə dō trŏf′ĭk, gə năd′ō-).

gonadotropin (gŏn′ə dŏt′rə pĭn, gŏ năd′ō trō′pĭn), *n. Biochem.* a hormone having affinity for or a stimulating effect on the gonads.

Goncharov (*Russ.* gən chȧ rôf′), *n.* **Ivan Aleksandrovich** (*Russ.* ĭ vȧn′ ə lĭk sȧn′drə vĭch), 1812–91, Russian novelist.

Goncourt (*Fr.* gôɴ ko͞or′), *n.* **1. Edmond Louis Antoine Huot de** (*Fr.* ĕd môɴ lwē äɴ twȧn ʏó′də), 1822–96, and his brother, **Jules Alfred Huot de** (*Fr.* zhʏl ȧl frĕd′), 1830–70, French art critics, historians, and novelists, who collaborated in writing novels until the death of Jules. **2. Prix,** an award of money, made by a French literary society for the best prose work of each year.

Gond (gŏnd), *n.* a member of an aboriginal race of Dravidian stock in central India and the Deccan.

Gondar (gŏn′dä), *n.* a city in NW Ethiopia, N of Lake Tana: a former capital. 25,000 (est. 1962).

gondola (gŏn′də lə), *n.* **1.** a long, narrow boat with a high peak at each end and often a small cabin near the middle, used on the Venetian canals and usually propelled at the stern by a single oar or pole. **2.** the car of a dirigible. **3.** the basket suspended beneath a balloon, for carrying passengers, instruments, etc. **4.** *U.S.* lighter[2] (def. 1). [t. It. (Venetian), der. *gondolar, gongolarsi,* ult. der. Rom. root *dond-* to rock]

Gondola (def. 1)

gondolier (gŏn′də lĭə′), *n.* a man who rows or poles a gondola. [t. F, t. It.: m. *gondoliere,* der. *gondola*]

Gondomar (*Sp.* gòn dò mär′), *n.* **Diego Sarmiento de Acuña** (*Sp.* dyĕ′gò sȧr myĕn′tò dĕ ȧ ko͞o′nyȧ), **Count of,** 1567–1626, Spanish diplomat.

Gondwana (gŏnd wä′nə), *n. Geol.* a great land mass in the Southern Hemisphere thought to have joined America, Africa, southern Asia, and Australia in Palaeozoic and part of Mesozoic time. Also, **Gondwa′naland′.**

gone (gŏn), *v.* **1.** pp. of **go.** —*adj.* **2.** departed; left. **3.** lost or hopeless. **4.** used up. **5.** that has departed or passed away; dead. **6.** weak and faint: *a gone feeling.* **7.** pregnant. **8.** *Colloq.* exhilarated; in a state of excitement (as by the influence of drugs, jazz, etc.). **9. far gone,** *Colloq.* **a.** much advanced; deeply involved. **b.** extremely mad. **c.** extremely drunk. **d.** almost exhausted. **e.** dying. **10. gone on,** *Slang.* infatuated with.

goneness (gŏn′nĭs), *n.* sinking sensation; faintness.

goner (gŏn′ə), *n. Slang.* a person or thing that is dead, lost, or past recovery.

gonfalon (gŏn′fə lən), *n.* **1.** a banner suspended from a crossbar, often with several streamers or tails. **2.** the standard used esp. by the medieval Italian republics. [t. It.: m. *gonfalone,* t. OHG: m. *gundfano,* lit., war flag]

gonfalonier (gŏn′fə lə nĭə′), *n.* **1.** the bearer of a gonfalon. **2.** the chief magistrate or some other elected official in any of several medieval Italian republics. [t. It.: m. *gonfaloniere*]

gong (gŏng), *n.* **1.** *Music.* an oriental bronze disc with the rim turned up, to be struck with a soft-headed stick.

2. any saucer-shaped bell, esp. one sounded by a hammer. 3. *Slang.* a medal. —*v.t.* 4. to warn or summon with the striking of a gong. [t. Malay] —**gong′like′,** *adj.*

Gongora (*Sp.* gôn′gô rä), **Luis de** (*Sp.* lwēs′ dĕ), 1561–1627, Spanish poet.

Gongorism (gŏng′gə rĭz′əm), *n.* affected elegance of style introduced into Spanish literature in imitation of the Spanish poet, Gongora.

gonidium (gə nĭd′ĭ əm), *n.*, *pl.* **-nidia** (-nĭd′ĭ ə). *Bot.* (among algae): 1. any one-celled asexual reproductive body, as a tetraspore or zoospore. 2. an algal cell, or a filament of an alga, growing within the thallus of a lichen. [NL, f. Gk: s. *gónos* offspring, seed + m. *-idion* -IDION] —**gonid′ial,** *adj.*

goniometer (gō′nĭ ŏm′ĭ tə), *n.* an instrument for measuring solid angles, as of crystals. [t. F: m. *goniomètre*, f. Gk *gōnio-* angle + *-mètre* -METER[1]] —**goniometric** (gō′-nĭ ə mĕt′rĭk), **go′niomet′rical,** *adj.* —**go′niom′etry,** *n.*

gonion (gō′nĭ ən), *n.*, *pl.* **-nia** (-nĭ ə). *Anat.* the tip of the angle of the lower jaw. [NL, der. Gk *gōnía* angle]

gonium (gō′nĭ əm), *n.*, *pl.* **-nia** (-nĭ ə). *Biol.* the germ cell during the phase marked by mitosis. [NL]

-gonium, *Bot., Biol.* a word element referring to reproductive cells. [t. NL, t. Gk: m. *-gonia*, comb. form repr. *goneía* generation]

gono-, a word element meaning 'sexual' or 'reproductive', as in *gonococcus*. [t. Gk, comb. form of *gónos, gonḗ* seed, generation, etc.]

gonococcus (gŏn′ō kŏk′əs), *n.*, *pl.* **-cocci** (-kŏk′sī). the causative organism of gonorrhoea. [NL. See GONO-, -COCCUS] —**gon′ococ′cal,** *adj.*

gonocyte (gŏn′ō sīt′), *n.* *Biol.* a germ cell, esp. during the maturation phase; oocyte; spermatocyte.

gonophore (gŏn′ō fô′), *n.* 1. *Zool.* an asexually produced bud in hydrozoans that gives rise to a medusa or its equivalent. 2. *Bot.* a prolongation of the axis of a flower above the perianth, bearing the stamens and pistil.

gonorrhoea (gŏn′ə rĭə′), *n.* *Pathol.* a contagious, purulent inflammation of the urethra or the vagina, due to the gonococcus. Also, *Chiefly U.S.*, **gonorrhea.** [t. LL, t. Gk: m. *gonórrhoia*, f. *gono-* GONO- + *rhoia* a flow] —**gon′-orrhoeal′,** *adj.*

-gony, a word element meaning 'production', 'genesis', 'origination', as in *cosmogony, theogony*. [t. L: m. s. *-gonia*, t. Gk. See -GONIUM and cf. -GENY]

goo (go͞o), *n.* *Slang.* sticky matter. [short for BURGOO]

goober (go͞o′bə), *n.* *U.S.* the peanut. Also, **goober pea.** [t. Angolan: m. *nguba*]

Gooch crucible (go͞och), a laboratory filter consisting of a shallow porcelain cup the flat bottom of which contains small holes over which a layer of asbestos fibres are placed.

good (go͝od), *adj.*, **better, best,** *n.*, *interj.*, *adv.* —*adj.* 1. morally excellent; righteous; pious: *a good man.* 2. satisfactory in quality, quantity, or degree; excellent: *good food, good health.* 3. right; proper; qualified; fit: *do whatever seems good to you, his credit is good.* 4. well-behaved: *a good child.* 5. kind, beneficent, or friendly: *to do a good turn.* 6. wholesome; beneficial. 7. fresh and palatable; not tainted. 8. honourable or worthy; in good standing: *a good name, Mr Hood and his good lady.* 9. refined; well-bred; educated. 10. reliable; safe: *good securities.* 11. genuine; sound or valid: *good judgement, good reasons.* 12. loyal; close: *a good friend.* 13. attractive; fine; beautiful: *she has a good figure.* 14. (of the complexion) without blemish or flaw. 15. agreeable; pleasant; genial: *have a good time.* 16. pleasurable; exciting. 17. satisfactory for the purpose; advantageous: *a good day for fishing.* 18. sufficient or ample: *a good supply.* 19. (of clothes) best or newest. 20. full: *a good day's journey.* 21. competent or skilful; clever: *a good manager, good at arithmetic.* 22. fairly great: *a good deal.* 23. **as good as,** in effect; practically: *he as good as said it.* —*n.* 24. profit; worth; advantage; benefit: *what good will that do?, to work for the common good.* 25. excellence or merit; righteousness; kindness; virtue: *to be a power for good, do good.* 26. (*sometimes cap.*) the force which governs and brings about righteousness and virtue. 27. a good, commendable, or desirable thing. 28. (*pl.*) possessions, esp. movable effects or personal chattels. 29. (*pl.*) articles of trade; wares; merchandise, esp. that which is transported by land. 30. (*pl.*) *Colloq.* what has been promised or is expected: *to deliver the goods.* 31. *Colloq.* the genuine article. 32. (*pl.*) *U.S. Colloq.* evidence of guilt, as stolen articles: *to catch with the goods.* 33. **for good** or **for good and all,** finally and permanently; for ever: *to leave a place for good (and all).* 34. **make good, a.** to make recompense for; pay for. **b.** to keep to an agreement; fulfil. **c.** to be successful. **d.** to prove the truth of; substantiate. —*interj.* 35. (an expression of approval or satisfaction.) [ME; OE *gōd*, c. D *goed*, G *gut*, Icel. *gōdhr*, Goth. *gōths* good; ? orig. meaning fitting, suitable, and akin to GATHER] —**Syn.** 1. pure, moral, virtuous; conscientious, meritorious, worthy, exemplary. 2. commendable, admirable. 17. favourable, auspicious, propitious, fortunate; profitable, useful. 18. full, adequate. 21. efficient, proficient, capable, dexterous, adroit, apt. 28. See **property.** —**Ant.** 1. bad, evil.

good afternoon, (a conventional expression used at a meeting or parting in the afternoon.)

Good Book, the Bible.

goodbye (go͝od′bī′), *interj.* *n.*, *pl.* **-byes.** —*interj.* 1. farewell (a conventional expression used at parting). —*n.* 2. a farewell. Also, *esp. U.S.*, **goodby.** [contr. of *God be with you (ye)*]

good cheer, 1. cheerful spirits: courage: *to be of good cheer.* 2. feasting and merrymaking: *to make good cheer.* 3. good fare or food; feasting: *to be fond of good cheer.*

good conduct, orderly behaviour, esp. in conformity with the law.

good day, (a conventional expression used at a meeting or a parting during the day.)

good egg, *Slang.* 1. a pleasant, agreeable, trustworthy person. 2. (an exclamation of pleasurable surprise.)

good evening, (a conventional expression used at a meeting or a parting during the evening.)

good faith, 1. honesty of purpose or sincerity of declaration: *to act in good faith.* 2. expectation of such qualities in others: *to take a job in good faith.*

good fellowship, a pleasant or genial spirit; conviviality.

good form, conduct that satisfies current commonly accepted standards.

good-for-nothing (go͝od′fə nŭth′ĭng), *adj.* 1. worthless. —*n.* 2. a worthless person.

Good Friday, the Friday before Easter, a holy day of the Christian Church, observed as the anniversary of the crucifixion of Jesus.

good-hearted (go͝od′hä′tĭd), *adj.* kind; considerate. —**good′-heart′edly,** *adv.* —**good′-heart′edness,** *n.*

Good Hope, Cape of. See **Cape of Good Hope.**

good humour, a cheerful or amiable mood.

good-humoured (go͝od′hyo͞o′məd), *adj.* having or showing a pleasant, amiable mood: *good-humoured man, a good-humoured remark.* —**good′-hu′mouredly,** *adv.* —**good′-hu′mouredness,** *n.*

goodish (go͝od′ĭsh), *adj.* rather good; fairly good.

Good-King-Henry (go͝od′kĭng′hĕn′rĭ), *n.* an erect, perennial chenopodiaceous herb, *Chenopodium bonus-henricus*, a widespread northern European weed.

good life, 1. a life led according to religious laws and moral conventions. 2. a life filled with material luxuries and comfort.

good-looking (go͝od′lo͝ok′ĭng), *adj.* of good appearance; handsome.

good looks, handsome personal appearance.

goodly (go͝od′lĭ), *adj.*, **-lier, -liest.** 1. of a good quality: *a goodly gift.* 2. of good or fine appearance. 3. of good size or amount: *a goodly sum.* —**good′liness,** *n.*

goodman (go͝od′mən), *n.*, *pl.* **-men.** *Archaic or Dial.* 1. title of respect used for those below the rank of gentleman, esp. a farmer or yeoman. 2. the master of a household; husband.

good morning, (a conventional expression used at a meeting or a parting during the morning.)

good nature, pleasant disposition; cheerful nature.

good-natured (go͝od′nā′chəd), *adj.* having or showing good nature or a pleasant or complaisant disposition or mood; good-humoured. —**good′-na′turedly,** *adv.* —**good′-na′turedness,** *n.*

goodness (go͝od′nĭs), *n.* 1. moral excellence; virtue. 2. kindly feeling; kindness; generosity. 3. excellence of quality: *goodness of workmanship.* 4. the best part of anything; essence; strength. 5. (used in various exclamatory or emphatic expressions): *thank goodness!* —*interj.* 6. (an exclamation expressing mild surprise.)

—**Syn.** 1. GOODNESS, MORALITY, VIRTUE refer to qualities of character or conduct which entitle the possessor to approval and esteem. GOODNESS is the simple word for the general quality recognized in character or conduct: *many could tell of her goodness and kindness.* MORALITY implies conformity to the recognized standards of right conduct: *a citizen of the highest morality.* VIRTUE is a rather formal word, and suggests usually GOODNESS that is consciously or steadily maintained, often in spite of temptations or evil influences: *of unassailable virtue, firm and of unwavering virtue.* —**Ant.** 1. badness, evil, vice.

good night, (a conventional expression used at a meeting or, more usually, a parting during the evening or night.)

goodnight (go͝od′nīt′), *n.* 1. a farewell; a leave-taking. —*adj.* 2. of or pertaining to a parting, esp. final or at night: *a goodnight kiss.*

good offices, **1.** mediating services in a dispute. **2.** influence esp. with someone in power.
good-oh (gŏŏd′ō′), *interj.* (an exclamation of approval or satisfaction.)
good Samaritan, a person who is compassionate and helpful to one in distress. See Luke 10:30–37.
Good Shepherd, Jesus Christ.
good-sized (gŏŏd′sīzd′), *adj.* of ample size; largish.
goods lift, a lift for the carriage of goods (as against people), as in a block of flats or offices; service lift.
good speed, good fortune, or success: *to wish a person good speed.*
goods train, a train of goods wagons.
goods truck, a railway wagon for carrying goods, merchandise, etc. Also, **goods wagon.**
goods yard, a railway yard where goods are delivered and collected. Also, **freight terminal.**
good-tempered (gŏŏd′tĕm′pəd), *adj.* good-natured; amiable. —**good′-tem′peredly,** *adv.*
good use, (in a language) standard use or usage.
goodwife (gŏŏd′wīf′), *n., pl.* **-wives** (-wīvz′). *Archaic* **1.** the mistress of a household. **2.** a title of respect for a woman.
goodwill (gŏŏd′wĭl′), *n.* **1.** friendly disposition; benevolence; favour. **2.** cheerful acquiescence. **3.** *Com.* an intangible, saleable asset arising from the reputation of a business and its relations with its customers, distinct from the value of its stock, etc. Also, **good will.** —**Syn. 1.** See **favour.**
Goodwin Sands (gŏŏd′wĭn), a dangerous line of shoals at the N entrance to the Strait of Dover, ab. 6 mi. off the SE coast of England. ab. 10 mi. long.
goody[1] (gŏŏd′ĭ), *n., pl.,* **goodies,** *adj., interj. Colloq.* —*n.* **1.** (*pl.*) sweets or cakes. —*adj.* **2.** sickly or sentimentally good; affecting goodness. —*interj.* **3.** wonderful! how nice! [f. GOOD, adj. + -Y[1]]
goody[2] (gŏŏd′ĭ), *n., pl.* **goodies.** a polite term formerly applied to a woman in humble life. [var. of GOODWIFE]
Goodyear (gŏŏd′yĭə′), *n.* **Charles,** 1800–60, U.S. inventor (of vulcanized rubber).
goody-goody (gŏŏd′ĭ gŏŏd′ĭ), *n., pl.* **-goodies,** *adj. Colloq.* **1.** a sentimentally or priggishly good person. —*adj.* **2.** affecting goodness.
gooey (gōō′ĭ), *adj.,* **gooier, gooiest.** *Slang.* **1.** like goo; sticky; viscoid. **2.** overemotional; sentimental.
goof (gōōf), *Slang.* —*n.* **1.** a foolish or stupid person. —*v.i.* **2.** to blunder; slip up. —*v.t.* **3.** to bungle (something); botch (often fol. by *up*). [appar. var. of obs. *goff* dolt, t. F: m. *goffe*] —**goof′y,** *adj.* —**goof′ily,** *adv.* —**goof′iness,** *n.*
goog (gŏŏg), *n. Austral. Slang.* an egg. [Brit. English dial.]
googly (gōō′glĭ), *n., pl.* **-glies.** *Cricket.* a ball bowled as if to break one way which then breaks in the other.
Goole (gōōl), *n.* a river port in England, in the West Riding of Yorkshire. 18,891 (1961).
goon (gōōn), *n. Slang.* **1.** a stupid person. **2.** *U.S.* a hired thug used by one side or the other in a labour dispute. **3.** a hooligan or tough.
goop (gōōp), *n. U.S. Slang.* a bad-mannered person.
goosander (gōō săn′də), *n.* **1.** a saw-billed fish-eating duck, *Mergus merganser,* of Europe and North America. **2.** any merganser.
goose (gōōs), *n., pl.* **geese** for 1–4, 6; **gooses** for 5. **1.** any of numerous wild or domesticated web-footed birds of the family *Anatidae,* most of them larger and with a longer neck than the ducks: the principal genera are *Anser, Branta,* and *Chen.* **2.** the female of this bird, as distinguished from the male (or gander). **3.** the flesh of the goose. **4.** a silly or foolish person; simpleton. **5.** a tailors' smoothing-iron with a curved handle. **6.** *Obs.* a game played with counters. **7. cook one's goose,** *Colloq.* **a.** to frustrate or ruin a person's hopes or plans. **b.** to spoil one's chances irrevocably. [ME *gos(e), goos,* OE *gós* (pl. *gēs*), c. D and G *Gans,* Icel. *gās* goose; akin to L *anser,* Gk *chēn*] —**goose′like′,** *adj.*
gooseberry (gŏŏz′bə rĭ, -brĭ), *n., pl.* **-ries.** **1.** the small, edible, acid, globular fruit or berry of certain prevailingly prickly shrubs of the genus *Ribes,* esp. *R. grossularia.* **2.** the shrub itself. **3. play gooseberry,** to act as chaperon.
gooseflesh (gōōs′flĕsh′), *n.* a rough condition of the skin, resembling that of a plucked goose, as induced by cold or fear.
goosefoot (gōōs′fŏŏt′), *n., pl.* **-foots.** **1.** any plant of the genus *Chenopodium,* containing many widely distributed herbs and shrubs with minute green flowers. **2.** any chenopodiaceous plant.
goosegog (gŏŏz′gŏg), *n. Slang.* a gooseberry.
goosegrass (gōōs′gräs′), *n.* cleavers.
goose grease, the melted fat of the goose, used in domestic medicine as an ointment.
gooseherd (gōōs′hûd′), *n.* one who tends geese.
gooseneck (gōōs′nĕk′), *n.* something curved like the neck of a goose, as an iron hook for attaching a boom to a mast, or a flexible stand for a desk lamp.
Goosens (gōō′sənz), *n.* **Léon Jean** (lā′ŏn jēn′), born 1897, English oboist.
goose pimples, gooseflesh. —**goose′-pim′ply,** *adj.*
goosestep (gōōs′stĕp′), *n., v.* **-stepped, -stepping.** —*n.* **1.** a military exercise in which the body is balanced on one foot (without advancing) while the other foot is swung forwards and back. **2.** an exaggerated marching step in which the legs are swung high with straight, stiff knees. —*v.i.* **3.** to walk or march in a goosestep.
goosewinged (gōōs′wĭngd′), *adj. Naut.* (of a square sail, usually a lower topsail) having the leeside hauled up and made fast and the weather side set, as in strong winds.
gopher (gō′fə), *n.* **1.** any of various ground squirrels of western North America, as *Citellus* (or *Spermophilus*) *tridecemlineatus.* **2.** any of various burrowing rodents of the genera *Geomys, Thomomys,* etc. (family *Geomyidae*), of western and southern North America and Central America, with large external fur-lined cheek pouches (also called **pocket gopher** and *pouched rat*). **3.** an edible, burrowing land tortoise, *Gopherus* (or *Testudo*) *polyphemus,* of the south-eastern U.S. **4.** Also, **gopher snake.** a burrowing snake, *Compsosoma corais,* of the southern U.S. [? t. F: m. *gaufre* honeycomb. See GOFFER]

Gopher, *Geomys bursarius* (Total length 13 in.)

gopherwood (gō′fə wŏŏd′), *n.* **1.** *U.S.* yellowwood. **2.** an unidentified wood used in building Noah's ark. See Gen. 6:14. [f. *gopher,* a tree (t. Heb.) + WOOD[1]]
gora (gō′rə, gô′-), *n.* a musical instrument of the Hottentots of South Africa, consisting of a length of sinew with a small piece of shaped quill at one end, stretched along a wooden stave. It is sounded by blowing against the quill, different harmonics being resonated by varying the mouth cavity. [t. Hottentot: *'gora*]
Gorakhpur (gô′rək pŏŏə′), *n.* a town in India, in SE Uttar Pradesh. 180,255 (1961).
goral (gô′rəl), *n.* a goat antelope, *Naemorhedus goral,* of mountainous south-eastern Asia, having small horns shorter than the distance apart at their bases.
gorblimey (gô blī′mĭ), *Slang.* —*interj.* **1.** (an expression of surprise or amazement.) —*adj.* **2.** vulgar; of or pertaining to the poor or working classes: *he wears gorblimey trousers.* Also, **gorblimy.** [alter of GOD BLIND ME]
gorcock (gô′kŏk′), *n.* the moorcock, or male red grouse, *Lagopus scoticus,* of Great Britain. [orig. obscure]
Gordian (gô′dyən), *adj.* **1.** pertaining to Gordius, ancient king of Phrygia, who tied a knot (the **Gordian knot**) which was to be undone only by one who should rule Asia, and which was summarily cut by Alexander the Great. **2.** resembling the Gordian knot; intricate. **3. cut the Gordian knot,** to devise and use instantly a drastic solution to a problem.
Gordon (gô′dn), *n.* **1. Charles George,** 1833–85, British general and administrator in China and Egypt. **2. Lord George,** 1751–93, English politician. **3. George Hamilton.** See **Aberdeen, 4th Earl of.**
Gordon setter, a black, long-haired variety of setter dog with red or tan marks on the muzzle, neck, and legs.
gore[1] (gô), *n.* blood that is shed, esp. when clotted. [ME; OE *gor* dung, dirt, c. D *goor,* OHG *gor* filth]
gore[2] (gô), *v.t.,* **gored, goring.** (of an animal) to pierce with the horns or tusks. [ME *goren.* Cf. GORE[3]]
gore[3] (gô), *n., v.,* **gored, goring.** —*n.* **1.** a triangular piece of cloth, etc., inserted in a garment, a sail, etc., to give greater width or secure the desired shape or adjustment. **2.** one of the breadths (mostly tapering, or shaped) of a woman's skirt. —*v.t.* **3.** to make or furnish with a gore or gores. [ME; OE *gāra* corner (c. G *Gehre* gusset), der. *gār* spear]
gorge (gôj), *n., v.,* **gorged, gorging.** —*n.* **1.** a narrow cleft with steep, rocky walls, esp. one through which a stream runs. **2.** a gorging or gluttonous meal. **3.** that which is swallowed; contents of the stomach. **4.** strong disgust; repulsion: *one's gorge rises in resentment.* **5.** a choking mass. **6.** *Fort.* the rear entrance or part of a bastion or similar outwork. See diag. under **bastion.** **7.** *Archaic.* the throat; gullet. —*v.t.* **8.** to stuff with food (mainly reflexive and passive): *gorged with food, he gorged himself.* **9.** to swallow, esp. greedily. **10.** to choke up (mainly passive). —*v.i.* **11.** to eat greedily. [ME, t. OF: throat, g. LL *gurga,* b. L *gurges* stream, abyss and *gula* throat] —**gorg′er,** *n.* —**Syn. 8.** glut, stuff. **9.** bolt, gulp, gobble.

gorgeous (gô′jəs), *adj.* **1.** sumptuous; magnificent; splendid in appearance or colouring: *she was wearing a gorgeous necklace.* **2.** *Colloq.* very good, pleasing, or enjoyable: *I had a gorgeous weekend.* [late ME, t. OF: m. *gorgias* fashionable, gay; orig. uncert.] **—gor′geously,** *adv.* **—gor′geousness,** *n.* **—Syn. 1.** rich, superb, grand; brilliant, resplendent. See **magnificent.**

gorgerin (gô′jə rĭn), *n. Archit.* the necklike portion of a capital of a column, or a feature forming the junction between a shaft and its capital. [t. F, der. *gorge* throat]

gorget (gô′jĭt), *n.* **1.** a piece of armour for the throat. See illus. under **armour. 2.** a form of wimple, or neck and chest covering, worn by women in the Middle Ages. **3.** a crescent-shaped badge, worn round the neck by officers in the 17th and 18th centuries as a sign of rank. **4.** a patch on the throat of a bird or other animal, distinguished by its colour or otherwise. [late ME, t. OF: m. *gorgete*, dim. of *gorge* throat]

Gorgias (gô′jĭ əs), *n.* ?485 B.C.–380 B.C. Greek philosopher.

Gorgon (gô′gən), *n.* **1.** *Gk Legend.* any of three sisters, Stheno, Euryale, and Medusa, whose heads were covered with snakes instead of hair, and whose glance turned the beholder to stone. **2.** (*l.c.*) a terrible or repulsive woman. **—Gorgonian** (gô gō′nyən), *adj.*

gorgoneion (gô′gə nē′ŏn), *n., pl.* **-neia** (-nē′ə). a representation of the head of a Gorgon, esp. that of Medusa. [t. Gk]

gorgonian (gô gō′nyən), *n.* **1.** any of various alcyonarian corals of the order *Gorgonacea*, having branching or horny skeletons. *—adj.* **2.** belonging or pertaining to the order *Gorgonacea.*

Gorgonzola (gô′gən zō′lə), *n.* a strongly flavoured, Italian, semi-hard variety of milk cheese veined with mould. [named after *Gorgonzola*, town in N Italy]

gorhen (gô′hĕn′), *n.* the female red grouse. [cf. GORCOCK]

gorilla (gə rĭl′ə), *n.* **1.** the largest of the anthropoid apes, *Gorilla gorilla*, ground-living and vegetarian, of western equatorial Africa. **2.** an ugly, brutal fellow. [t. NL, t. Gk; said to be of African orig.] **—goril′la-like′,** *adj.*

Gorilla, *Gorilla gorilla* (Standing height 6 ft)

Göring (*Ger.* gœ′rĭng), *n.* Goering.

Gorizia (*It.* gō rēt′tsyä), *n.* a town in NE Italy, on the river Isonzo, N of Trieste. 40,627 (1961). German, **Görz** (*Ger.* gœrts).

Gorki (gô′kĭ; *Russ.* gôry′kĭy), *n.* **1. Maxim** (măk′sĭm; *Russ.* mäk sēm′) (*Aleksey Maksimovich Pyeshkov*), 1868–1936, Russian novelist, short-story writer, and dramatist. **2.** Formerly, **Nizhni Novgorod.** a city in the central Soviet Union in Europe, on the Volga. 1,085,000 (est. 1965).

Görlitz (*Ger.* gœr′lĭts), *n.* a town in SE East Germany on the river Neisse (the Polish boundary). 89,578 (1963).

Gorlovka (*Russ.* gôr′ləf kə), *n.* a city in the SW Soviet Union in Europe. 337,000 (est. 1965).

gormand (gô′mənd), *n.* gourmand.

gormandize (gô′mən dīz′), *v.,* **-dized, -dizing,** *n.* *—v.i., v.t.* **1.** to eat like a glutton. *—n.* **2.** *Rare.* the habits of a glutton. Also, **gormandise.** [t. F: m. *gourmandise* gluttony] **—gor′mandiz′er,** *n.*

gormless (gôm′lĭs), *adj. Slang.* (of a person) dull; stupid; senseless. [var. of d. *gaumless*, f. *gaum* attention, heed (t. Scand.; cf. Icel. *gaumr*) + -LESS]

gorse (gôs), *n.* any plant of the leguminous genus *Ulex*, esp. *U. europaeus*, a low, much-branched, spiny shrub with yellow flowers, common on waste lands in Europe; furze. [ME *gorst*, OE *gors(t)*; akin to G *Gerste*, L *hordeum* barley] **—gors′y,** *adj.*

Gorse, *Ulex europaeus*

Gorton (gô′tn), *n.* **John (Grey),** born 1911, Australian statesman: prime minister since 1968.

gory (gō′rĭ), *adj.,* **gorier, goriest. 1.** covered or stained with gore; bloody. **2.** resembling gore. **3.** *Colloq.* distasteful or unpleasant: *he read the gory details of the accident.* **—gor′ily,** *adv.* **—gor′iness,** *n.*

gosh (gŏsh), *interj.* (an exclamation or mild oath.) [a euphemistic var. of *God!*]

goshawk (gŏs′hôk′), *n.* any of various powerful, short-winged hawks formerly much used in falconry, as *Accipiter gentilis* of Europe and America. [ME *goshawke*, OE *gōshafoc* goosehawk]

Goshawk, Accipiter gentilis (length up to 26 in.)

Goshen (gō′shən), *n.* **1.** a pastoral region in Lower Egypt, colonized by the Israelites before the Exodus. Gen. 45:10, etc. **2.** a land or place of plenty and comfort.

Goshen

gosling (gŏz′lĭng), *n.* **1.** a young goose. **2.** a foolish, inexperienced person. [ME *goselyng*, var. (by assoc. with GOOSE) of *geslyng*, t. Scand.; cf. Icel. *gæslingr*, f. *gās* goose + *-lingr*, dim. suffix (see -LING[1])]

go-slow (gō′slō′), *Colloq.* *—n.* **1.** a deliberate curtailment of output by workers as an industrial sanction; ca′-canny; work-to-rule. *—adj.* **2.** of or pertaining to a go-slow.

gospel (gŏs′pl), *n.* **1.** the body of doctrine taught by Christ and the apostles; Christian revelation. **2.** glad tidings, esp. concerning salvation and the kingdom of God as announced to the world by Christ. **3.** the story of Christ's life and teachings, esp. as contained in the first four books of the New Testament. **4.** (*usually cap.*) one of these books. **5.** (*often cap.*) *Eccles.* an extract from one of the four Gospels, forming part of the Eucharist service in certain Churches. **6.** something regarded as true and implicitly believed: *to take for gospel.* **7.** a doctrine regarded as of prime importance: *political gospel.* *—adj.* **8.** pertaining to the gospel. **9.** in accordance with the gospel; evangelical. [ME *go(d)spel*, OE *gōdspel*, f. *gōd* GOOD + *spell* tidings (SPELL[2]), trans. of L *ēvangelium.* See EVANGEL]

gospeller (gŏs′pə lə), *n.* **1.** *Eccles.* a Wyclifite, Protestant or Puritan. **2.** see **hot gospeller.** Also, *U.S.*, **gospeler.**

gospel side, the left-hand side of a church facing the alter. Cf. **epistle side.**

Gosplan (gŏs′plăn′), *n.* the official planning organization of the U.S.S.R., which draws up plans embracing trade and industry, agriculture, education, and popular health. [f. *gos(udar)* national + *plan* PLAN]

Gosport (gŏs′pôt′), *n.* a seaport in England, in Hampshire, near Portsmouth; naval depot. 62,457 (1961).

Gossaert (*Du.* KHô′särt), *n.* **Jan** (*Du.* yŏn), real name of **Mabuse.**

gossamer (gŏs′ə mə), *n.* **1.** a fine filmy cobweb, seen on grass and bushes, or floating in the air in calm weather, esp. in autumn. **2.** a thread or a web of this substance. **3.** an extremely delicate variety of gauze. **4.** any finely spun, silken fabric. *—adj.* **5.** Also, **gossamery** (gŏs′ə mə rĭ), of or like gossamer; thin and light. [ME *gos(e)-somer.* See GOOSE, SUMMER; possibly first used as name for late mild autumn (Indian summer), time when goose was a favourite dish (cf. G *Gänsemonat* November), then transferred to the filmy matter also found in that season]

Gosse (gŏs), *n.* **Sir Edmund William,** 1849–1928. English critic and poet.

gossip (gŏs′ĭp), *n., v.,* **-siped** or **-sipped, -siping** or **-sipping.** *—n.* **1.** idle talk, esp. about the affairs of others. **2.** light, familiar talk or writing. **3.** a person, esp. a woman, given to tattling or idle talk. **4.** *Archaic.* a friend, esp. a woman. **5.** *Archaic or Dial.* a godparent. *—v.i.* **6.** to talk idly, esp. about the affairs of others; go about tattling. *—v.t.* **7.** to repeat like a gossip. **8.** *Archaic.* to stand godparent to. [ME *gossib*, OE *godsibb*, orig., godparent, f. *god* GOD + *sibb* related (see SIB[1], adj.)] **—gos′siper,** *n.* **—gos′siping,** *n.* **—gos′sipingly,** *adv.*

—Syn. 1. GOSSIP, SCANDAL apply to idle talk and news-mongering about the affairs of others. GOSSIP is light chat or talk: *gossip about the neighbours.* SCANDAL is rumour or general talk that is damaging to reputation; it is usually more or less malicious: *a scandal involving bribes.*

gossipmonger (gŏs′ĭp mŭng′gə), *n.* one especially addicted to gossiping.

gossipy (gŏs′ĭ pĭ), *adj.* **1.** given to or fond of gossip. **2.** full of gossip.

gossoon (gŏ so͞on′), *n. Anglo-Irish.* **1.** a boy. **2.** a male servant. [alter. of GARÇON]

got (gŏt), *v.* pt. and pp. of **get.**

Gotama (gō′tə mə), *n.* Buddha. See **Gautama.**

Göteborg (*Swed.* yœ tə bŏry′), *n.* a seaport in SW Sweden, on the Kattegat. 416,220 (1965). Also, **Gothenburg** (gŏth′ən bûg′; *Ger.* gō′tən bo͝ork).

Goth (gŏth), *n.* **1.** one of a Teutonic people who, in the 3rd to 5th century A.D., invaded and settled in parts of the Roman Empire. **2.** a barbarian; rude person. [ME *Gothe*, t. LL: m. s. *Gothī*, pl.; r. OE *Gotan*, pl. (*Gota*, sing.), c. Goth. *Gut-* in *Gut-thiuda* Goth people]

Goth., Gothic.

Gotha (gō′thə; *Ger.* gō′tä), *n.* a town in SW East Germany, in Thuringia. 57,692 (1965).

Gotham (gō′təm for 1; gŏth′əm, gō′thəm for 2), *n.* **1.** an English village, proverbial for the foolishness of its inhabitants. **2.** the city of New York.

Gothic (gŏth′ĭk), *adj.* **1.** *Archit.* denoting or pertaining to a style originating in France and spreading over western Europe from the 12th to the 16th century, characterized by a design emphasizing skeleton construction, the elimination of wall planes, the comparatively great height of the buildings, the pointed arch, rib vaulting, and the flying buttress. **2.** of or pertaining to the Gothic Revival. **3.** (orig. in derogatory use) denoting all European art of the 12th to the 16th century. **4.** (sometimes in disparagement) pertaining to the Middle Ages; barbarous; rude. **5.** (esp. in literature) stressing irregularity and details, usually of a grotesque or horrible nature: *a Gothic novel.* **6.** *Print.* having elaborate pointed characters, as Fraktur. —*n.* **7.** Gothic architecture, sculpture, or decoration **8.** an extinct Germanic language, preserved especially in Ulfilas's Bible (4th cent.). **9.** blackletter. **10.** Fraktur. [t. LL: s. *Gothicus*] —**Goth′ically,** *adv.*

Gothicism (gŏth′ĭ sĭz′əm), *n.* **1.** conformity or devotion to the Gothic style of architecture. **2.** a mixture of the elevated and the bizarre, often with many details, as distinct from the unity and simplicity of classicism. **3.** adherence to aspects of Gothic culture. **4.** (*also l.c.*) barbarism; rudeness. **5.** a Gothic idiom.

Gothicize (gŏth′ĭ sīz′), *v.t.*, **-cized, -cizing. 1.** to make Gothic, as in style. **2.** to make pseudo-medieval. Also, **Gothicise.**

Gothic Revival, an 18th and 19th century style of art, architecture, etc., in imitation of medieval models.

göthite (gû′tīt), *n.* goethite.

Gotland (gŏt′lənd; *Swed.* gŏt′lȧnt), *n.* an island in the Baltic, forming a province of Sweden. 53,662 pop. (est. 1963); 1212 sq. mi. *Cap.:* Visby. Also, **Gottland.**

gotten (gŏt′n), *v. U.S.* a pp. of **get.**

Götterdammerung (gŏt′ə dĕm′ə ro͝ong′), *n. German Myth.* the twilight of the gods; the final destruction of the world by the forces of evil.

Göttingen (*Ger.* gœt′ĭng ən), *n.* a town in West Germany, in SE Lower Saxony. 111,800 (est. 1966).

Gott mit uns (*Ger.* gŏt′mĭt o͞ons′), *German.* God [is (or be)] with us.

Gottwald (*Cz.* gŏt′vȧlt), *n.* **Klement** (*Cz.* klĕ′mĕnt), 1896–1953, Czech statesman: prime minister of Czechoslovakia 1946–48; president 1948–53.

Gottwaldov (*Cz.* gŏt′vȧl dŏf), *n.* a town in central Czechoslovakia. 62,000 (est. 1965).

gouache (go͞o äsh′; *Fr.* gwȧsh), *n.* **1.** a method of painting with opaque watercolours prepared with gum. **2.** an opaque colour used in painting a gouache. **3.** a work executed in this medium. [F, t. It.: m. *guazzo* puddle, spray of water, g. L *aquātio* a watering, der. *aqua* water]

Gouda (gou′də; *Du.* ᴋʜôw′dȧ), *n.* **1.** a town in W Netherlands, NE of Rotterdam. 43,779 (1963). **2.** a cheese made from whole milk or partly skimmed milk, coloured with saffron, and marketed in bladders or in coloured wax skins.

gouge (gouj), *n., v.,* **gouged, gouging.** —*n.* **1.** a chisel whose blade has a concavo-convex cross-section, the bevel being ground on either the inside or the outside of the cutting end of the tool. **2.** a groove or hole made by gouging. —*v.t.* **3.** to scoop out or turn with or as with a gouge: *gouge a channel, gouge holes.* **4.** to dig or force out with or as with a gouge: *to gouge out an eye.* [t. F, g. LL *gu(l)bia*; of Celtic orig.] —**goug′er,** *n.*

Gouges

goulash (go͞o′lăsh), *n.* **1.** a stew of beef, veal, vegetables, etc., with paprika or other seasoning. **2.** *Bridge.* a deal of unshuffled cards distributed in rounds of five, five, and three, with very unusual results.

Goulburn (gōl′bûn′), *n.* **1.** a river in Australia, flowing W through New South Wales to the river Murray. 345 mi. **2.** a town in Australia, in New South Wales. 20,610 (est. 1965).

Gould (go͞old), *n.* **Jay,** 1836–92, U.S. financier and capitalist.

Gounod (go͞o′nō; *Fr.* go͞o nō′), *n.* **Charles François** (*Fr.* shȧrl fräɴ swȧ′), 1818–93, French composer.

gouramy (go͝oə′rə mĭ), *n., pl.* **-mis. 1.** a large, air-breathing, nest-building, freshwater, Asiatic fish, *Osphronemus goramy,* highly prized for food. **2.** any of a number of smaller, air-breathing, nest-building, Asiatic fishes (genera *Trichogaster, Colisa,* and *Trichopsis*) widely cultivated in home aquariums, as the **dwarf gouramy,** *Colisa lalia.* Also, **gourami.** [t. Malay]

gourd (go͝oəd), *n.* **1.** the fruit of any of various cucurbitaceous plants, esp. that of *Lagenaria siceraria* (**bottle gourd**), whose dried shell is used for bottles, bowls, etc., or that of certain forms of *Cucurbita pepo* sometimes cultivated for ornament. **2.** a plant bearing such a fruit. **3.** a dried and excavated gourd shell used as a bottle, ladle, flask, etc. **4.** a gourd-shaped, small-necked bottle or flask. [ME, t. F: m. *gourde,* g. L *cucurbita*] —**gourd′-like′,** *adj.* —**gourd-shaped** (go͝oəd′shāpt′), *adj.*

gourde (go͝oəd), *n.* **1.** the monetary unit of Haiti, equal to 100 centimes, and equivalent to about £0·084 sterling. **2.** a note of this value. [t. F, fem. of *gourd* numb, slow, heavy, g. L *gurdus* dull, obtuse]

gourmand (go͝oə′mənd; *Fr.* go͞or mäɴ′), *n.* one fond of good eating. Also, **gormand.** [late ME, t. F: gluttonous, der. *gourmet* GOURMET]

gourmet (go͝oə′mā; *Fr.* go͞or mĕ′), *n.* a connoisseur in the delicacies of the table; an epicure. [t. F, in OF also *groumet* wine-taster, wine merchant's man. Cf. GROOM]

Gourmont (*Fr.* go͞or mōɴ′), *n.* **Remy de** (*Fr.* rə mē′də), 1858–1915, French critic and novelist.

gout (gout), *n.* **1.** a constitutional disease characterized by painful inflammation of the joints (chiefly those in the feet and hands, and esp. in the big toe), and by excess of uric acid in the blood. **2.** *Archaic.* a drop, splash, or spot, esp. of blood. [ME *goute,* t. OF, g. L *gutta* a drop, ML gout]

goût (*Fr.* go͞o), *n. French.* taste; perception. [F, g. L *gustus* taste]

goutweed (gout′wēd′), *n.* bishop's weed, *Aegopodium podagraria.*

gouty (gou′tĭ), *adj.,* **goutier, goutiest. 1.** pertaining to or having the nature of gout. **2.** causing gout. **3.** diseased with or subject to gout. **4.** swollen as if from gout. —**gout′ily,** *adv.* —**gout′iness,** *n.*

gouvernante (*Fr.* go͞o vĕr näɴt′), *n. French.* **1.** a chaperon. **2.** a governess.

Gov., governor.

gov., 1. governor. **2.** government.

govern (gŭv′ən), *v.t.* **1.** to rule by right of authority, as a sovereign does: *to govern a state.* **2.** to exercise a directing or restraining influence over; guide: *the motives governing a decision.* **3.** to hold in check: *to govern one's temper.* **4.** to serve as or constitute a law for: *the principles governing a case.* **5.** *Gram.* to be accompanied by (a particular form) as in '*they helped us*', not '*they helped we*'; the verb '*helped*' is said to govern the objective case of the pronoun. **6.** to regulate (an engine speed) with a governor. —*v.i.* **7.** to exercise the function of government. **8.** to have predominating influence. [ME *governe(n),* t. OF: m. *governer,* g. L *gubernāre,* t. Gk: m. *kybernân* steer, guide, govern] —**gov′ernable,** *adj.* —**Syn. 1.** See **rule.**

governance (gŭv′ə nəns), *n.* **1.** government; exercise of authority; control. **2.** method or system of government or management.

governess (gŭv′ə nĭs), *n.* a woman who directs the education of children, generally in their own homes.

government (gŭv′ən mənt), *n.* **1.** the authoritative direction and restraint exercised over the actions of men in communities, societies, and states; direction of the affairs of a state, etc.; political rule and administration: *government is necessary to the existence of society.* **2.** the form or system of rule by which a state, community, etc., is governed: *monarchical government, episcopal government.* **3.** (*sometimes construed as pl.*) the governing body of persons in a state, community, etc.; the executive power; the administration: *the government was defeated in the last election.* **4.** direction; control; rule: *the government of one's conduct.* **5.** the district governed; a province. **6.** *Gram.* the established usage which requires that one word in a sentence should cause another to be of a particular form. —**governmental** (gŭv′ən mĕn′tl), *adj.* —**gov′ernmen′tally,** *adv.*

governor (gŭv′ə nə), *n.* **1.** one charged with the direction or control of an institution, society, etc.: *governors of a bank, governor of a prison.* **2.** the representative of the sovereign with statutory powers, in a British dependent territory. **3.** a ruler or chief magistrate appointed to govern a province, town, fort, or the like. **4.** the executive head of a state in the U.S. **5.** *Mach.* a device for regulating a supply of fuel in an engine for ensuring uniform speed regardless of the load. **6.** *Colloq.* **a.** one's employer. **b.** any person of superior status. [ME *governour,* t. OF: m. *governeor,* g. L *gubernātor* steersman, director]

governor-general (gŭv′ə nə jĕn′rəl, gŭv′nə-), *n., pl.* **governor-generals, governors-general.** the representative of the sovereign, without statutory powers, in certain independent Commonwealth countries.

governorship (gŭv′ə nə shĭp′), *n.* a governor's duties, term in office, etc.

Govt, government. Also, **govt.**

gowan (gou′ən), *n. Scot. and N Dial.* any of various yellow or white field flowers, esp. the English daisy. [? var. of obs. *gollan,* t. Scand.; cf. Icel. *gullinn* golden]

Gower (gou′ə, gô), *n.* **1. John,** *c* 1325–1408, English poet. **2.** Welsh, **Gwyr.** a peninsula in Glamorganshire, Wales. ab. 75 sq. mi.

gowk (gouk), *n.* *Chiefly Dial.* **1.** the cuckoo. **2.** a fool or simpleton. [ME *goke*, t. Scand.; cf. Icel. *gaukr*, c. OE *gēac* cuckoo, G *Gauch* cuckoo, fool]

gown (goun), *n.* **1.** a woman's dress, usually formal, comprising bodice and skirt, usually joined. **2.** a loose, flowing, outer garment in various forms, worn by men or women as distinctive of office, profession, or status: *a judge's gown, an academic gown.* **3.** members collectively of the university at Oxford and Cambridge. *—v.t., v.i.* **4.** to dress in, or put on, a gown. [ME *goune*, t. OF, g. LL *gunna*; of uncert. orig.] **—Syn. 1.** See **dress.**

gownsman (gounz′mən), *n., pl.* **-men.** a man who wears a gown indicating his office, profession, or status.

Gowon (gou′ŏn), *n.* **Major General Yakubu** (yä′ko͞o bo͞o′), born 1934, head of state of Nigeria since 1966.

Goya (goi′ə; *Sp.* gô′yä), **Francisco de** (*Sp.* frän thēs′kô dĕ) (*Francisco José de Goya y Lucientes*), 1746–1828, Spanish painter and etcher.

G.P., 1. graduated pension. 2. Grand Prix. 3. *Music.* general pause. 4. general practitioner.

G.P.I., general paralysis of the insane.

G.P.O., General Post Office.

G.P.U. (jē′pē yo͞o′; *Russ.* gĕ pĕ o͞o′), the secret service of the U.S.S.R. from 1922, when Cheka was reorganized, until 1935, when the N.K.V.D., the official state police, was formed. Also, **Ogpu.** Cf. **K.G.B.** [Russ. *G(osudarstvennoe) P(oliticheskoe) U(pravlenie)*]

Gr., 1. Grecian. 2. Greece. 3. Greek.

gr., 1. grade. 2. grain; grains. 3. gram; grams. 4. gross.

G.R., (L *Georgius Rex*) King George.

Graaff (gräf; *Afrik.* KHräf), *n.* **Sir de Villiers** (də vĭl′yəz), born 1913, South African politician.

Graafian follicle (grä′fĭ ən), *Anat.* one of many small vesicles within the ovary which, at the time of ovulation, discharge an ovum. Also, **Graafian vesicle.** [named after R. de *Graaf*, 1641–73, Dutch anatomist]

grab (grăb), *v.,* **grabbed, grabbing,** *n.* *—v.t.* **1.** to seize suddenly and eagerly; snatch. **2.** to take illegal possession of; seize forcibly or unscrupulously: *to grab land.* *—n.* **3.** a sudden, eager grasp or snatch. **4.** seizure or acquisition by violent or unscrupulous means. **5.** that which is grabbed. **6.** a mechanical device for gripping objects. [c. MD and MLG *grabben*, Sw. *grabba*] **—grab′ber,** *n.*

grab bag, *U.S.* lucky dip.

grabble (grăb′l), *v.i.,* **-bled, -bling. 1.** to feel or search with the hands; grope. **2.** to sprawl; scramble. [freq. of GRAB. Cf. D *grabbelen*]

graben (grä′bən), *n.* rift valley. [t. G: ditch]

grabrope (grăb′rōp′), *n.* *Naut.* any of certain lines or ropes on a ship for boatmen to take hold of when coming alongside. Also, **grab′line′.**

Gracchi (grăk′ē), *n., pl.* Gaius and Tiberius Gracchus.

Gracchus (grăk′əs), *n.* **1. Gaius Sempronius** (gī′əs sĕm prō′nĭ əs), 153?–121 B.C. Roman political reformer and orator. **2.** his brother, **Tiberius Sempronius** (tī-bĭə′rĭ əs), 163?–133 B.C. Roman reformer and orator.

grace (grās), *n., v.,* **graced, gracing.** *—n.* **1.** elegance or beauty of form, manner, motion, or act. **2.** a pleasing or attractive quality or endowment. **3.** favour or goodwill. **4.** manifestation of favour, esp. as by a superior. **5.** mercy; clemency; pardon. **6.** favour shown in granting a delay or temporary immunity: *an act of grace.* **7.** (*pl.*) affected manner; manifestation of pride or vanity: *to put on airs and graces.* **8.** *Law.* an allowance of time to a debtor before suit can be brought against him after his debt has by its terms become payable: *days of grace.* **9.** *Theol.* **a.** the free, unmerited favour and love of God. **b.** the influence or spirit of God operating in man to regenerate or strengthen. **c.** a virtue or excellence of divine origin: *the Christian graces.* **10. fall from grace, a.** *Theol.* to descend into sin or disfavour with God. **b.** to lose favour, esp. with someone in authority. **11. state of grace,** *Theol.* **a.** condition of being in God's favour. **b.** condition of being one of the elect. **12.** spiritual strength: *the grace to perform a duty.* **13.** a short prayer before or after a meal, in which a blessing is asked and thanks are given. **14.** *Music.* an embellishment consisting of a note or notes not essential to the harmony or melody, as an appoggiatura, an inverted mordent, etc. **15.** (*usually cap.*) a formal title used in addressing or mentioning a duke, duchess, or archbishop, and formerly also a sovereign (prec. by *your, his,* etc.). **16.** (*cap.*) *Class. Myth.* one of three sister goddesses, commonly given as **Aglaia** (brilliance), **Euphrosyne** (joy), and **halia** (bloom), presiding over all beauty and charm in nature and humanity. **17. have the grace to,** to be so kind as to (do something). **18. with (a) bad grace,** unwillingly; reluctantly: *he conceded defeat with bad grace.* **19. with (a) good grace,** willingly; ungrudgingly: *the team lost the match with good grace.* *—v.t.* **20.** to lend or add grace to; adorn. **21.** to favour or honour: *to grace an occasion with one's presence.* **22.** *Music.* to add grace-notes, cadenzas, etc., to. [ME, t. OF, t. L: m. s. *grātia* favour, gratitude, agreeableness] **—Syn. 1.** attractiveness, charm, gracefulness. **4.** kindness. **5.** lenity. **20.** embellish, beautify; honour, enhance.

Grace (grās), *n.* **W(illiam) G(ilbert),** 1848–1915, English cricketer.

grace-cup (grās′kŭp′), *n.* **1.** a cup, as of wine, passed round at the end of the meal for the final health or toast. **2.** the drink.

graceful (grās′fəl), *adj.* characterized by grace of form, manner, movement, or speech; elegant; easy or effective. **—grace′fully,** *adv.* **—grace′fulness,** *n.*

graceless (grās′lĭs), *adj.* **1.** wanting grace, pleasing elegance, or charm. **2.** without any sense of right or propriety. **—grace′lessly,** *adv.* **—grace′lessness,** *n.*

grace-note (grās′nōt′), *n.* *Music.* a note not essential to the harmony or melody, added as an embellishment, esp. an appoggiatura.

gracile (grăs′ĭl), *adj.* **1.** gracefully slender. **2.** slender; thin. [t. L: m. s. *gracilis* slender] **—gracil′ity** (gră sĭl′ĭ tĭ), *n.*

gracing[1] (grā′sĭng), *n.* the act or fact of a person or thing that graces.

gracing[2] (grā′sĭng), *n.* greycing.

gracioso (grăs′ĭ ō′sō; *Sp.* grä thyô′sô), *n., pl.* **-sos. 1.** a character in Spanish comedy, resembling the English clown. **2.** a low comic character. **3.** *Obs.* a favourite. [Sp., der. *gracia* wit, grace, t. L: m. *grātia*]

gracious (grā′shəs), *adj.* **1.** disposed to show grace or favour; kind; benevolent; courteous. **2.** indulgent or beneficent in a condescending or patronizing way, esp. to inferiors. **3.** merciful or compassionate. **4.** *Obs.* fortunate or happy. *—interj.* **5.** (an exclamation of surprise, etc.) [ME, t. OF, t. L: m. s. *grātiōsus* enjoying or showing favour] **—gra′ciously,** *adv.* **—gra′ciousness, graciosity** (grā′shĭ ŏs′ĭ tĭ), *n.* **—Syn. 1.** kindly, benign. See **kind. —Ant. 1.** churlish, surly.

grackle (grăk′l), *n.* **1.** any of various birds of the Old World family *Sturnidae* (starlings), or of the American family *Icteridae* (American starlings, blackbirds, etc.), as the crow blackbird or **purple grackle** (*Guiscalus quiscula*). **2.** the green woodpecker. [t. L: m. s. *grāculus* jackdaw]

grad., 1. graduate. 2. graduated.

gradate (grə dāt′), *v.,* **-dated, -dating.** *—v.i.* **1.** to pass by insensible degrees, as one colour into another. *—v.t.* **2.** to cause to gradate. **3.** to arrange in grades.

gradation (grə dā′shən), *n.* **1.** any process or change taking place through a series of stages, by degrees, or gradually. **2.** (*usually pl.*) a stage, degree, or grade in such a series. **3.** the passing of one tint or shade of colour to another, or one surface to another, by very small degrees, as in painting, sculpture, etc. **4.** the act of grading. **5.** ablaut (def. 2). **—grada′tional,** *adj.* **—grada′tionally,** *adv.*

grade (grād), *n., v.,* **graded, grading.** *—n.* **1.** a degree in a scale, as of rank, advancement, quality, value, intensity, etc. **2.** a class of persons or things of the same relative rank, quality, etc. **3.** a step or stage in a course or process. **4.** *U.S.* form (def. 26). **5.** (*pl.*) *U.S.* the divisions of a school or the school itself. **6.** *U.S.* a number, letter, etc., indicating the relative quality of a student's work in a course, examination, or special subject. **7.** inclination with the horizontal of a road, railway, etc., usually expressed by stating the vertical rise or fall as a percentage of the horizontal distance. **8.** *Bldg Trades.* the ground level around a building. **9.** an animal resulting from a cross between a parent of common stock and one of a pure breed. **10. make the grade,** to reach a desired minimum level of achievement, qualification. *—v.t.* **11.** to arrange in a series of grades; class; sort. **12.** to determine the grade of. **13.** to cause to pass by degrees, as from one colour or shade to another. **14.** to reduce to a level or to practicable degrees of inclination: *to grade a road.* **15.** to cross (a nondescript animal or a low-grade one) with one of a pure breed. *—v.i.* **16.** to be graded. **17.** to be of a particular grade or quality. [t. F, t. L: m. s. *gradus* step, stage, degree] **—gra′der,** *n.*

-grade, a word element meaning 'walking', 'moving', 'going', as in *retrograde.* [comb. form repr. L *gradus* step, or *gradī*, v., walk. See GRADE, GRADIENT]

grade crossing, *U.S.* a crossing of a railway line and a road or another line at the same level. Cf. **level crossing.**

gradely (grād′lĭ), *Dial.* *—adj.* **1.** fine; excellent. **2.** real;

proper. —*adv.* **3.** carefully; well. **4.** exactly. [ME *graithly*, t. Scand.; cf. Icel. *greithliga*]

grade school, *U.S.* a primary school.

grade separation, the separation of the levels at which roads, railways, paths, etc., intersect in order to prevent traffic conflicts or accidents.

gradient (grā′dyənt), *n.* **1.** the degree of inclination, or the rate of ascent or descent, in a railway, etc. **2.** an inclined surface; grade; ramp. **3.** *Physics.* **a.** change in a variable quantity, as temperature or pressure, per unit distance. **b.** a curve representing such a rate of change. —*adj.* **4.** rising or descending by regular degrees of inclination. **5.** progressing by walking as an animal; gressorial. **6.** of a type suitable for walking, as some birds' feet. [t. L: s. *gradiens*, ppr., walking, going]

gradient post, a short post beside a railway track indicating a change of gradient.

gradient wind speed, *Meteorol.* the speed of the wind calculated as for geostrophic wind speed, but taking into account the curvature of the path of the air.

gradin (grā′dĭn; *Fr.* grȧ dăN′), *n.* **1.** one of a series of steps or seats raised one above another. **2.** *Eccles.* a shelf or one of a series of shelves behind and above an altar. Also, **gradine** (grə dēn′). [t. F, t. It.: m. *gradino*, der. *grado* GRADE]

gradiograph (grā′dĭ ə grăf′, -gräf′), *n. Survey.* a straightedge with a horizontal upper edge and a lower edge sloping at a required gradient, used for measuring slope, laying pipes, etc.

gradiometer (grā′dĭ ŏm′ĭ tə), *n. Survey.* a telescopic instrument for setting out gradients.

gradual (grăj′o͝o əl), *adj.* **1.** taking place, changing, moving, etc., by degrees or little by little: *gradual improvement in health.* **2.** rising or descending at an even, moderate inclination: *a gradual slope.* —*n.* **3.** *Eccles.* **a.** an antiphon sung between the epistle and the gospel in the Eucharistic service. **b.** a book containing the words and music of the parts of the liturgy which are sung by the choir. [t. ML: s. *graduālis* (as n., *graduāle*), der. L *gradus* step, grade] —**grad′ually,** *adv.* —**grad′ualness,** *n.* —**Syn. 1.** See **slow.**

gradualism (grăj′o͝o ə lĭz′əm), *n.* the principle of achieving an end step by step instead of in one movement or action. [f. GRADUAL + -ISM] —**grad′ualist,** *n., adj.*

graduate (*adj., n.* grăd′yo͞o ĭt; *v.* grăd′yo͞o āt′), *n., adj., v.,* **-ated, -ating.** —*n.* **1.** one who has received a degree on completing a course of study, as at a university or college. **2.** a student who holds the first or bachelor's degree and is studying for an advanced degree. **3.** *Rare.* a cylindrical or tapering graduated vessel of glass, for measuring. —*adj.* **4.** that has graduated: *a graduate student.* **5.** of or pertaining to graduates: *a graduate course.* —*v.i.* **6.** to receive a degree or diploma on completing a course of study. **7.** to pass by degrees; change gradually. —*v.t.* **8.** to arrange in grades or gradations; establish gradation in. **9.** to divide into or mark with degrees or other divisions, as the scale of a thermometer. **10.** *Chiefly U.S.* to confer a university degree or diploma upon. [t. ML: m. s. *graduātus*, pp. of *graduāre* admit to an academic degree, der. L *gradus* step, grade] —**grad′ua′tor,** *n.*

graduated pension, that part of a worker's retirement pension over and above the basic pension, paid by the state in proportion to deductions previously made from his wages.

graduation (grăd′yo͞o ā′shən), *n.* **1.** the act of graduating. **2.** the state of having graduated. **3.** the ceremony of conferring a university degree.

gradus (grā′dəs), *n.* **1.** *Music.* a work consisting wholly or in part, of exercises of increasing difficulty. **2.** a simple dictionary of Latin prosody. [t. L: short for *gradus ad Parnassum* step to Parnassus]

Graeae (grē′ē), *n.pl. Gk Myth.* three ancient sea deities, who had only one eye and one tooth among them and were the protectresses of the Gorgons, their sisters. Also, **Graiae.**

Graecia Magna (grē′syə măg′nə), Magna Graecia.

Graecism (grē′sĭz′əm), *n.* **1.** the spirit of Greek thought, etc. **2.** adoption or imitation of this. **3.** an idiom or peculiarity of Greek. Also, *Chiefly U.S.*, **Grecism.**

Graecize (grē′sīz), *v.t., v.i.,* **-cized, -cizing.** —*v.t.* **1.** to impart Greek characteristics to. **2.** to translate into Greek. —*v.i.* **3.** to conform to what is Greek; adopt Greek speech, customs, etc. Also, **Graecise,** *Chiefly U.S.*, **Grecize.** [t. L: m. s. *Graecizare*, der. *Graecus* Greek. See -IZE]

Graeco-, a word element meaning 'Greek'. Also, *Chiefly U.S.*, **Greco-.** [t. L: comb. form of *Graecus*]

Graf (gräf), *n., pl.* **Grafen** (grä′fən). a count; a title of nobility in Germany, Austria, and Sweden, which corresponds to English earl and French comte. [cf. BURGRAVE, LANDGRAVE, MARGRAVE]

graffito (gră fē′tō), *n., pl.* **-ti** (-tē). **1.** *Archaeol.* an ancient drawing or writing scratched on a wall or other surface. **2.** (*pl.*) drawings or words, usually obscene, written on the walls of public lavatories and elsewhere. [t. It., der. *graffio* a scratch, ult. der. Gk *gráphein* mark, draw, write]

graft[1] (gräft), *n.* **1.** *Hort.* **a.** a shoot or part of a plant (the scion) inserted in a groove, slit, or the like in another plant or tree (the stock) so as to become nourished by and united with it. **b.** the plant or tree (the united stock and scion) resulting from such an operation. **c.** the place where the scion is inserted. **2.** *Surg.* a portion of living tissue surgically transplanted from one part of an individual to another, or from one individual to another, with a view to its adhesion and growth. **3.** the act of grafting. —*v.t.* **4.** to insert (a graft) into a plant or tree; insert a scion of (one plant) into another plant. **5.** to cause (a plant) to reproduce through grafting. **6.** *Surg.* to transplant (a portion of living tissue) as a graft. **7.** to insert as if by grafting: *to graft a pagan custom upon Christian institutions.* **8.** *Naut.* **a.** to finish off (an eye splice) by tapering the ends of the strands of rope in a decorative way. **b.** to taper (a rope's end) and wrap it round with yarns, usually marline, to give a fancy effect. —*v.t.* **9.** to insert scions from one tree, or kind of tree, into another. **10.** to become grafted. [earlier *graff*, ME *grafe*, t. OF: orig., stylus, pencil, t. LL: m. s. *graphium*, t. Gk: m. *grapheîon* stylus] —**graft′er,** *n.* —**graft′ing,** *n.*

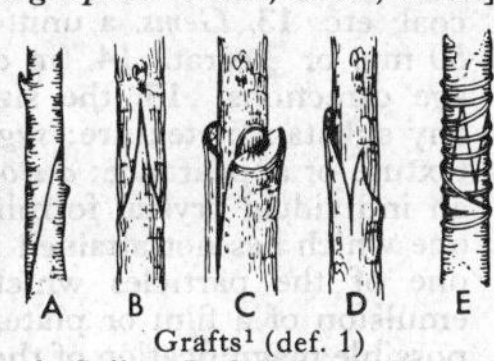

Grafts[1] (def. 1)
A, Splice; B, Saddle; C, Notch; D, E, Whip or tongue

graft[2] (gräft), *Colloq. or Dial.* —*n.* **1.** work, esp. hard work. **2.** the acquisition of gain or advantage by dishonest, unfair, or shady means, esp. through the abuse of one's position or influence in politics, business, etc. **3.** a particular instance, method, or means of thus acquiring gain. **4.** the gain or advantage acquired. —*v.t.* **5.** to obtain by graft. —*v.i.* **6.** to practise graft. [? identical with GRAFT[1] in expression *spade(s) graft* var. of *spade(s)-graff*, lit., spade's digging (depth of earth thrown up at a single spading), OE *græf* trench. See GRAVE[1]] —**graft′er,** *n.*

graft hybrid, a plant chimera produced as a result of natural or artificial grafting.

Grafton (gräf′tən), *n.* **Augustus Henry Fitzroy, 3rd Duke,** 1735–1811, English statesman: prime minister 1766–70.

graham (grā′əm), *adj. U.S.* made of graham flour.

Graham (grā′əm), *n.* **1. Martha,** born ?1890, U.S. dancer. **2. William Franklin** (*Billy*), born 1918, U.S. evangelist.

Grahame (grā′əm), *n.* **Kenneth,** 1859–1932, Scottish writer, esp. of children's stories.

graham flour, *U.S.* unbolted wheat flour containing all the wheat grain; wholemeal flour. [named after S. *Graham*, 1794–1851, U.S. reformer of dietetics]

Graham Land (grā′əm), a large peninsula of Antarctica, S of South America: one of the Falkland Island Dependencies.

Graham's law, *Physics.* (of gaseous diffusion) the principle that at a given temperature and pressure, the rate of diffusion of a gas is inversely proportional to the square root of its density. [named after Thomas *Graham*, 1805–69, Scottish chemist]

Graiae (grā′ē, grī′ē), *n.pl.* Graeae.

grail (grāl), *n.* a cup (also taken as a chalice) which according to medieval legend was used by Jesus at the Last Supper, and in which Joseph of Arimathaea received the last drops of Jesus's blood at the cross: used often as a symbol for a lost, pure kind of Christianity; Holy Grail. [ME *grayle*, t. OF: m. *graal*, t. ML: m. s. *gradāle* plate, or der. L *crātēr* bowl, t. Gk: m. *krātēr*]

grain (grān), *n.* **1.** a small hard seed, esp. a seed of one of the cereal plants: wheat, rye, oats, barley, maize, or millet. **2.** the gathered seeds of cereal plants in the mass. **3.** the plants themselves, whether standing or gathered. **4.** any small, hard particle, as of sand, gold, pepper, gunpowder, etc. **5.** the smallest unit of weight in most systems, originally determined by the weight of a plump grain of wheat. In the British and U.S. systems —avoirdupois, troy, and apothecaries' — the grain is identical. In an avoirdupois ounce there are 437·5 grains; in the troy and apothecaries' ounces there are 480 grains. **6.** the smallest possible amount of anything: *a grain of truth.* **7. with a grain of salt,** with some reserve; without wholly believing. **8.** the arrangement or direction

of fibres in wood, or the resulting appearance or markings. **9.** the side of leather from which the hair has been removed. **10.** a stamped pattern to imitate natural grain of leather: used on leather, plastic or cloth to simulate a different type of natural leather. **11.** the fibres or yarn in a piece of fabric as differentiated from the fabric itself. **12.** lamination or cleavage of stone, coal, etc. **13.** *Gems.* a unit of weight for pearls equal to 50 mg. or ¼ carat. **14.** (in diamond polishing) the cleavage directions. **15.** the size of constituent particles of any substance; texture: *sugar of fine grain.* **16.** granular texture or appearance: *a stone of coarse grain.* **17.** *Metall.* an individual crystal forming part of a pure metal, esp. one which has not attained its regular shape. **18.** *Photog.* one of the particles which constitute a photographic emulsion of a film or plate, the size of which limits the possible magnification of the projected image. **19.** temper or natural character: *to go against the grain.* **20.** *Aerospace.* the solid propellant in a rocket, specially shaped to give the required combustion characteristics. **21.** *Obs.* colour or hue.
—*v.t.* **22.** to form into grains, granulate. **23.** to give a granular appearance to. **24.** to paint in imitation of the grain of wood, stone, etc. **25.** *Tanning.* to remove the hair from (skins); soften and raise the grain of (leather). [coalescence of two ME words: ME *greyn*, t. OF: m. *grain*, g. L *grānum* grain, seed; and ME *grayne* red dye, t. OF: m. *graine*, g. L *grāna*, pl. of *grānum* grain] —**grain′er,** *n.* —**grain′less,** *adj.*

grain alcohol, alcohol made from grain; ethyl alcohol.

grain elevator, a lift or machine which raises grain to another floor.

Grainger (grān′jə), *n.* **Percy Aldridge** (ôl′drĭj), 1882–1961, Australian pianist and composer.

grain growth, *Metall.* a coarsening of crystal structure under certain conditions of heating, due to some crystals absorbing adjacent ones.

grains[1] (grānz), *n.pl.* (*often construed as sing.*) an iron instrument with barbed prongs, for spearing or harpooning fish. [earlier also *grainse*, t. Icel.: m. *grein* division, branch; cf. Sw. *gren*]

grains[2] (grānz), *n.pl. Brewing.* the refuse malt and other insoluble residue left after the wort has been run off.

grains of paradise, the pungent, peppery seeds of either of two zingiberaceous plants, *Aframomum melegueta* and *A. granum-paradisi*, of Africa: used to strengthen cordials, etc., and in veterinary medicine.

grainy (grā′nĭ), *adj.*, **grainier, grainiest. 1.** grainlike or granular. **2.** full of grains or grain. **3.** resembling the grain of wood, etc. —**grain′iness,** *n.*

grallatorial (grăl′ə tô′rĭ əl), *adj.* belonging or pertaining to the wading birds, as the snipe, cranes, storks, herons, etc., many species of which have very long legs. [f. L *grallātor* one who goes on stilts + -IAL]

gram[1] (grăm), *n.* a metric unit of mass, equal to 15·432 grains; one thousandth of a kilogram. Also, **gramme.** [t. F: m. *gramme*, t. LL: m. *gramma*, t. Gk: a small weight, orig. something drawn]

gram[2] (grăm), *n.* **1.** (in the Orient) the chickpea, there used as a food for man and cattle. **2.** any of various other plants, as *Phaseolus aureus* (**green gram**) and *P. mungo* (**black gram**), beans cultivated in India as a food crop. [t. Pg.: m. *grão*, g. L *grānum* GRAIN[1]]

-gram[1], a word element meaning something drawn or written, as in *diagram, epigram, telegram, monogram.* [t. Gk: m. *-gramma* something drawn or written, or m. *-grammon* pertaining to a stroke or line]

-gram[2], a word element meaning grams; of or pertaining to a gram, as in *kilogram.* [t. Gk: m. *grámma* small weight]

gram., 1, grammar. **2.** grammatical.

grama grass (grä′mə), any range grass of the western and south-western U.S. of the genus *Bouteloua*, as *B. gracilis*, the commonest species. [*grama*, t. Sp.: kind of grass, g. L *grāmen* grass]

gramarye (grăm′ə rĭ), *n. Archaic.* occult learning; magic. Also **gramary.** [ME *grammarie, gramarye*, t. OF: GRAMMAR, magic]

gram atom, *Chem.* that quantity of an element whose weight in grams is numerically equal to the atomic weight of the element. Also, **gram atomic weight.**

gram calorie. See **calorie** (def. 1a).

gram equivalent, *Chem.* the equivalent weight of a substance or radical expressed in grams.

gramercy (grə mû′sĭ), *interj. Archaic.* **1.** many thanks. **2.** (an exclamation of surprise or sudden feeling.) [ME, t. OF: m. *grant merci.* See GRAND, MERCY]

gramicidin (grăm′ĭ sī′dĭn), *n. Pharm.* an antibiotic which destroys Gram-positive bacteria. See **Gram's method.** [*Gram-(positive)* + -I- + -CIDE + -IN[2]]

gramineous (grā mĭn′ĭ əs), *adj.* **1.** grasslike. **2.** pertaining or belonging to the *Gramineae* (or *Poaceae*) family, the grass family of plants. [t. L: m. *grāmineus* pertaining to grass]

graminivorous (grăm′ĭ nĭv′ə-rəs), *adj.* **1.** feeding on seeds or like food. **2.** adapted for feeding on grain, as the jaws, teeth, etc., of squirrels and other rodents.

grammalogue (grăm′ə lŏg′), *n.* a word represented by a single letter sign.

grammar (grăm′ə), *n.* **1.** the features of a language (sounds, words, formation and arrangement of words, etc.) considered systematically as a whole, especially with reference to their mutual contrasts and relations: *English grammar.* **2.** an account of the preceding. **3.** a similar account comparing two or more languages, or different stages of the same language. **4.** speech or writing in accordance with standard usage: *he knows his grammar.* **5.** the elements of any science, art, or subject. **6.** a book treating them. [ME *grammer*, t. OF: m. *grammaire*, t. L: m. *grammatica*, t. Gk: m. *grammatikḗ* grammar, prop. fem. of *grammatikós* pertaining to letters or literature] —**gram′marless,** *adj.*

grammarian (grə mĕə′rĭ ən), *n.* **1.** a specialist in the study of grammar. **2.** a person who claims, or is reputed to establish, standards of usage in a language.

grammar school, 1. a secondary school providing academic education for children who pass the eleven-plus examination, or who are selected as suitable for this type of education. **2.** (formerly) a school in which Latin and Greek grammar were the principal subjects taught. **3.** *U.S.* a school intermediate between a primary school and a high school.

grammatical (grə măt′ĭ kl), *adj.* **1.** of or pertaining to grammar: *grammatical analysis.* **2.** conforming to standard usage: *grammatical speech.* —**grammat′ically,** *adv.* —**grammat′icalness,** *n.*

grammaticism (grə măt′ĭ sĭz′əm), *n.* a point of grammar.

gramme (grăm), *n.* gram[1].

gram molecule, *Chem.* that quantity of a substance whose weight in grams is numerically equal to the number which expresses the molecular weight of the substance. Also, **gram′-molec′ular weight.**

Gramont (*Fr.* grȧ môɴ′), *n.* **Philibert de** (*Fr.* fē lē bĕr′ də), 1621–1707, French courtier, soldier, and adventurer.

gramophone (grăm′ə fōn′), *n.* a machine for reproducing the sounds recorded on a flat circular shellac or plastic record; a record-player. Also, *esp. U.S.*, **phonograph.** [*gramo-*, repr. -GRAM[1], + -PHONE; r. earlier Brit. and modern U.S. PHONOGRAPH]

gramophone record, record (def. 17).

Grampian Mountains (grăm′pyən), the SE Highlands of Scotland. Highest peak, Ben Nevis, 4406 ft. Also, **Grampians, Grampian Highlands.**

grampus (grăm′pəs), *n.* **1.** a cetacean, *Grampus griseus*, of the dolphin family, widely distributed in northern seas. **2.** any of various related cetaceans, as the killer, *Orca orca.* [earlier *graundepose*, alter. of *grapays*, t. OF: m. *graspeis*, g. ML *crassus piscis* fat fish]

Gram's method (grămz), a method of bacterial staining in which the film is first stained with crystal violet and then with Gram's iodine solution. It permits the classification of bacteria, **Gram-positive** species keeping the violet dye, and **Gram-negative** species being decolorized. [named after H. C. J. *Gram*, 1853–1938, Danish physician]

Granada (grə nä′də; *Sp.* grȧ nȧ′dȧ), *n.* **1.** a medieval kingdom along the Mediterranean coast of S Spain. See map under **Castile. 2.** a city in S Spain: the capital of this former kingdom and last stronghold of the Moors in Spain; site of the Alhambra. 161,851 (1965).

granadilla (grăn′ə dĭl′ə), *n.* **1.** the edible fruit of certain species of passionflower, esp. *Passiflora edulis* (**purple granadilla**) and *P. quadrangularis* (**giant granadilla**). **2.** any of the plants yielding these fruits. [t. Sp., dim. of *granada* pomegranate. See GRENADE]

Granados (*Sp.* grȧ nȧ′dōs), *n.* **Enrique** (*Sp.* ĕn rē′kĕ) (*Enrique Granados Campina*), 1867–1916, Spanish composer and pianist.

granary (grăn′ə rĭ), *n.*, *pl.* **-ries. 1.** a storehouse or repository for grain, esp. after it has been threshed or husked. **2.** a region abounding in grain. [t. L: m. s. *grānārium*]

Gran Canaria (*Sp.* grȧn′kȧ nȧ′ryȧ), one of the Canary Islands. 650 sq. mi. *Cap.:* Las Palmas. Also, **Grand Canary.**

Gran Chaco (*Sp.* grȧn chȧ′kō), an extensive subtropical region in Argentina, Bolivia, and Paraguay. ab. 300,000 sq. mi. See **Chaco.**

grand (grănd), *adj.* **1.** imposing in size or appearance or general effect: *grand mountain scenery.* **2.** stately, majestic, or dignified. **3.** lofty: *grand ideas.* **4.** magnificent or splendid: *a grand palace, display, etc.* **5.** noble or fine: *a grand old man.* **6.** highest, or very high, in rank or official dignity: *a grand potentate.* **7.** main or principal; chief: *the grand staircase.* **8.** of great importance, distinction, or pretension: *grand personages.* **9.** complete or comprehensive: *a grand total.* **10.** *Colloq.* first-rate; very good; splendid: *to have a grand time, grand weather.* **11.** *Music.* **a.** written on a large scale or for a large ensemble: *a grand fugue.* **b.** applied to compositions which contain all the regular parts or movements in a complete form. **12.** *Genealogy.* one degree more remote in ascent or descent (used in compounds), as in *grand-aunt, grandchild, etc.* —*n.* **13.** a grand piano. **14.** *U.S. Slang.* a thousand dollars. [ME *graunt*, t. OF, g. L *grandis* large, full-grown, great, grand] —**grand'ly,** *adv.* —**grand'ness,** *n.* —**Syn. 4.** great, large, palatial. —**Ant. 1.** insignificant.

grandad (grăn'dăd'), *n.* *Colloq.* grandfather. Also, **grand-dad.**

grand-aunt (grănd'änt'), *n.* a great-aunt.

Grand Banks, an extensive shoal SE of Newfoundland: one of the world's greatest fishing grounds. ab. 300 mi. long; ab. 40,000 sq. mi. Also, **Grand Bank.**

Grand Canal, 1. a canal in E China, extending from Peking S to Hangchow; the longest canal in the world. ab. 1060 mi. **2.** a large canal in Venice, Italy, forming the main thoroughfare.

Grand Canary, Gran Canaria.

Grand Canyon, a gorge of the Colorado river in N Arizona. Over 200 mi. long; 2000 to 6000 ft deep.

grandchild (grăn'chīld'), *n., pl.* **-children.** a child of one's son or daughter.

Grand Coulee (ko͞o'lĭ), **1.** a dry canyon in central Washington, cut by the Columbia river in the Pleistocene Glaciation. 52 mi. long; over 400 ft deep. **2.** a dam on the Columbia river at the N end of this canyon. 550 ft high.

grand-daughter (grăn'dô'tə), *n.* a daughter of one's son or daughter.

grand duchess, 1. the wife or widow of a grand duke. **2.** a woman who rules a grand duchy in her own right. **3.** a daughter of a tsar or of a tsar's son.

grand duchy, a territory ruled by a grand duke or grand duchess.

grand duke, 1. the sovereign of a territory called a grand duchy, ranking next below a king. **2.** a son of a tsar or of a tsar's son.

Grande (grăn'dĭ, grănd; *Port.* grən'dē), *n.* **Rio.** See **Rio Grande.**

grande dame (*Fr.* gräNd dȧm'), *French.* a great lady.

grandee (grăn dē'), *n.* a Spanish nobleman of the highest rank. [t. Sp., Pg.: m. *grande* great (person). See GRAND]

grandeur (grăn'jə), *n.* the state or quality of being grand; imposing greatness; exalted rank, dignity, or importance. [t. F, der. *grand* GRAND] —**Syn.** stateliness, majesty, sublimity; pomp, splendour, state.

grandfather (grăn'fä'thə), *n.* the father of one's father or mother.

grandfather clause, *U.S. Hist.* a state constitutional clause disfranchising Negroes, held void in 1915.

grandfather clock, a clock with a pendulum, in a tall wooden case.

grandfatherly (grăn'fä'thə lĭ), *adj.* **1.** of, or in the manner of, a grandfather. **2.** indulgent; kindly.

Grand Guignol (grŏn' gē nyŏl'; *Fr.* gräN gē nyŏl'), **1.** a short horrific drama. **2.** of or pertaining to dramas of this kind. [name of a theatre in Paris]

grandiloquence (grăn dĭl'ə kwəns), *n.* lofty speech; bombast. [f. s. L *grandiloquus* speaking loftily + -ENCE]

grandiloquent (grăn dĭl'ə kwənt), *adj.* speaking or expressed in a lofty or pompous style; bombastic. —**grandil'oquently,** *adv.* —**Ant.** simple.

grandiose (grăn'dĭ ōs'), *adj.* **1.** grand in an imposing or impressive way. **2.** affectedly grand or stately; pompous. [t. F, t. It.: m. GRANDIOSO. See -OSE[1]] —**gran'diose'ly,** *adv.* —**grandiosity** (grăn'dĭ ŏs'ĭ tĭ), *n.*

grandioso (grăn'dĭ ō'sō; *It.* grȧn dyŏ'sŏ), *adj.* *Music.* majestic; broad. [t. It.: der. L *grandis* GRAND]

grand jury, *U.S. Law.* a jury of (usually) 12 to 23 persons designated to inquire into alleged violations of the law in order to ascertain whether the evidence is sufficient to warrant trial by a petty jury.

Grand Lama. See **Dalai Lama.**

grand larceny. See **larceny.**

grandma (grăn'mä'), *n.* *Colloq.* grandmother.

grand mal (grŏn'măl'; *Fr.* gräN mȧl'), a major epileptic attack with a loss of consciousness. [F: great illness, epilepsy]

grandmamma (grăn'mə mä'), *n.* *Obs.* grandmother.

Grand Master, 1. the head of a lodge of freemasons, a friendly society, a religious order of knighthood, or the like. **2.** *Chess, Bridge, etc.* an outstandingly expert player, and winner of numerous competitions, tournaments, etc.

grand monde (*Fr.* gräN mōNd'), *French.* the fashionable world; high society. [F: lit., the great world]

grandmother (grăn'mŭth'ə), *n.* the mother of one's father or mother.

grandmotherly (grăn'mŭth'ə lĭ), *adj.* **1.** of or in the manner of a grandmother. **2.** like a grandmother.

Grand Mufti, the head of the Muslim Arab community in Jerusalem, long chosen from the Husseini family.

Grand National, an annual steeplechase, founded in 1839 and run at Aintree, Liverpool.

grand-nephew (grăn'nĕv'yo͞o, -nĕf'yo͞o), *n.* great-nephew.

grand-niece (grăn'nēs'), *n.* great-niece.

grand opera, a drama interpreted by music, the text being sung throughout.

grandpa (grăn'pä'), *n.* *Colloq.* grandfather.

grandpapa (grăn'pə pä'), *n.* *Obs.* grandfather.

grandparent (grăn'pēə'rənt), *n.* a parent of a parent.

grand piano. See **piano** (def. 2).

Grand Prix (grŏn' prē', grŏm'-; *Fr.* gräN prē'), *Motor Racing, Cycling, Horseracing, etc.* any of various major races held annually. [F: a great prize]

Grand Rapids, a town in the U.S., in S Michigan. 177,313 (1960).

Grand Remonstrance, *Eng. Hist.* a list of grievances against the rule of Charles I drawn up by the Long Parliament (1640).

grandsire (grăn'sī'ə), *n.* *Archaic.* **1.** a grandfather. **2.** a forefather. **3.** an old man.

grand slam. See **slam**[2] (def. 1).

grandson (grăn'sŭn'), *n.* a son of one's son or daughter.

grandstand (grănd'stănd'), *n.* **1.** the principal stand for spectators at a racecourse, athletic field, etc. **2.** the people sitting in the grandstand. —*adj.* **3.** of or pertaining to a grandstand or the spectators in it. **4.** clearly visible or perceived: *a grandstand view of a road accident.*

grandstand finish, a closely contested finish to a race.

grand tour, (formerly) an extended tour on the continent of Europe, esp. as the finishing course in the education of young Englishmen of good family.

grand-uncle (grănd'ŭng'kl), *n.* great-uncle.

grand vizier, *Hist.* the chief officer of state of various Muslim countries, as in the former Ottoman Empire.

grange (grānj), *n.* **1.** a farm. **2.** a country dwelling house with its various farm buildings; dwelling of a yeoman or gentleman farmer. **3.** (formerly) an outlying farmhouse with barns, etc., belonging to a feudal manor or a religious establishment, where crops and tithes in kind were stored. [ME *graunge*, t. AF, var. of OF *grange*, g. LL *grānica*, der. L *grānum* grain]

Grangemouth (grānj'məth), *n.* a burgh in Scotland, in Stirlingshire: shipbuilding. 18,860 (1961).

granger (grān'jə), *n.* *U.S.* a farmer.

grangerize (grān'jə rīz'), *v.t.*, **-rized, -rizing. 1.** to augment the illustrative content of (a book) by inserting additional prints, drawings, engravings, etc., not included in the original volume. **2.** to mutilate (books) in order to get illustrative material for such a purpose. Also, **grangerise.** [after J. *Granger*, whose 'Biographical History of England' (1769) was arranged for such illustration]

granite (grăn'ĭt), *n.* **1.** a granular igneous rock composed chiefly of felspar (orthoclase) and quartz, usually with one or more other minerals, as mica, hornblende, etc.: much used in building, and for monuments, etc. **2.** great hardness or firmness. [t. It.: m. *granito*, orig. pp., grained, of *granire*, der. *grano*, g. L *grānum* grain] —**gran'itelike',** *adj.* —**granit'ic,** *adj.*

graniteware (grăn'ĭt wēə'), *n.* **1.** a kind of ironware with a grey, stonelike enamel. **2.** pottery with a speckled appearance like granite. **3.** a semivitreous white pottery somewhat harder than earthenware.

granitite (grăn'ĭ tīt'), *n.* a granite rich in biotite.

granivorous (gră nĭv'ə rəs), *adj.* feeding on grain and seeds.

Granjon (grăn'jən), *n.* *Print.* a style of type originally cut by the French designer Robert Granjon.

granny (grăn'ĭ), *n., pl.* **-nies.** *Colloq.* **1.** a grandmother. **2.** an old woman. **3.** a fussy person. **4.** granny knot. Also, **grannie.**

granny knot, *Naut.* a reef or square knot in which the second part is crossed the wrong way, making it liable to slip or jam. See illus. under **knot.**

granophyre (grăn'ō fī'ə), *n.* a fine-grained or porphyritic granitic rock with a micrographic intergrowth of the minerals of the groundmass. [t. G: m. *Granophyr*, f. *grano-* (comb. form of *Granit* GRANITE) + (*Por*)*phyr* porphyry] —**granophyric** (grăn'ō fĭ'rĭk), *adj.*

grant (gränt), *v.t.* **1.** to bestow or confer, esp. by a formal act: *to grant a right* **2.** to give or accord: *to grant permission.* **3.** to agree or accede to: *to grant a request.* **4.** to admit or concede; accept for the sake of argument: *I grant that point.* **5.** to transfer or convey, esp. by deed or writing: *to grant property.* **6. take for granted,** to accept without appreciation. **—*n.*** **7.** that which is granted, as a privilege or right, a sum of money, as for a student's maintenance, or a tract of land. **8.** the act of granting. **9.** *Law.* an instrument which conveys property. [ME *grant(en)*, t. AF: m. *granter* promise, authorize, confirm, approve, ult. der L *crēdens*, ppr. of *crēdere* trust, believe] **—grant′able,** *adj.* **—grant′er,** *n.* **—Syn. 2.** See **give.**

Grant (gränt), *n.* **Ulysses S(impson),** 1822–85, Union general in the American Civil War and 18th president of the U.S., 1869–77.

Granta (grän′tə), *n.* the river Cam at Cambridge.

grantee (grän tē′), *n. Law.* one to whom a grant is made.

Granth (grŭnt), *n.* the sacred scripture of the Sikhs.

Grantham (grăn′thəm), *n.* a town in England, in SW Lincolnshire. 25,048 (1961).

grant-in-aid (gränt′ĭn ād′), *n.* a government grant made to a colony or dependency.

grant of probate, *Law.* an instrument issued by a court or public official authorizing an executor to take control of and dispose of the estate of a deceased person, where the deceased made a will.

grantor (grän tô′, grän′tə), *n. Law.* one who makes a grant.

granular (grăn′yo͞o lə), *adj.* **1.** of the nature of granules. **2.** composed of or bearing granules or grains. **3.** showing a granulated structure. **—gran′ular′ity,** *n.* **—gran′ularly,** *adv.*

granulate (grăn′yo͞o lāt′), *v.*, **-lated, -lating. —*v.t.*** **1.** to form into granules or grains. **2.** to raise in granules; make rough on the surface. **—*v.i.*** **3.** to become granular. **4.** *Pathol.* to form granulation tissue. [f. GRANUL(E) + -ATE[1]] **—gran′ula′tor,** *n.*

granulated sugar, a coarsely ground, white sugar, used for sweetening.

granulation (grăn′yo͞o lā′shən), *n.* **1.** the act or process of granulating. **2.** granulated condition. **3.** one of the grains of a granulated surface. **4.** *Pathol.* **a.** the formation of granulation tissue, esp. in healing. **b.** granulation tissue. **5.** *Astron.* one of the small short-lived features of the solar surface which in the aggregate give it a mottled appearance when viewed with a telescope.

granulation tissue, tissue formed in ulcers and in early wound healing and repair, composed largely of newly growing capillaries and so called from its irregular surface in open wounds; proud flesh.

granule (grăn′yo͞ol), *n.* **1.** a little grain. **2.** a small dry mass able to move independently of its fellows. [t. LL: m. s. *grānulum*, dim. of L *grānum* GRAIN]

granulite (grăn′yo͞o līt′), *n. Geol.* a metamorphic rock composed of granular minerals of uniform size, such as quartz, felspar, or pyroxene, and showing a definite banding. **—granulitic** (grăn′yo͞o lĭt′ĭk), *adj.*

granulocyte (grăn′yo͞o lə sīt′), *n. Anat.* any blood cell containing specific granules.

granuloma (grăn′yo͞o lō′mə), *n. Pathol.* a tumour of granulation tissue. [m. L GRANUL(UM) small grain + -OMA]

Granville (grăn′vĭl), *n.* **John Carteret, Earl of,** 1690–1763, English statesman.

Granville-Barker (grăn′vĭl bä′kə), *n.* **Harley,** 1877–1946, English dramatist, actor, and critic.

grape (grāp), *n.* **1.** the edible, pulpy, smooth-skinned berry or fruit which grows in clusters on vines of the genus *Vitis*, and from which wine is made. **2.** any vine bearing this fruit. **3.** *Colloq.* wine. **4.** dull, dark purplish red. **5.** (*pl.*) *Vet. Sci.* a morbid growth on the fetlock of a horse, resembling a bunch of grapes. **6.** *Archaic.* grapeshot. [ME, t. OF, var. of *crape* cluster of fruit or flowers, orig. hook; of Gmc orig. (cf. G. *Krapf* hook). Cf. GRAPNEL, GRAPPLE] **—grape′less,** *adj.* **—grape′like′,** *adj.*

grapefruit (grāp′fro͞ot′), *n.* **1.** a large roundish, yellow-skinned edible citrus fruit with a juicy, acid pulp. **2.** the tropical or semitropical rutaceous tree, *Citrus paradisi*, yielding it.

grape hyacinth, any plant of the liliaceous genus *Muscari*, as *M. botryoides*, a species whose globular blue flowers resemble tiny grapes.

grapery (grā′pə rĭ), *n.*, *pl.* **-ries. 1.** a building where grapes are grown. **2.** a plantation of grapevines.

grapeshot (grāp′shŏt′), *n. Archaic.* a cluster of small cast-iron balls used as a charge for a cannon.

grape sugar, dextrose.

grapevine (grāp′vīn′), *n.* **1.** a vine that bears grapes. **2.** *Colloq.* the means by which any form of information is passed, esp. word of mouth. **3.** *Wrestling.* a hold in which a wrestler twists his own leg round his opponent's leg.

graph (grăf, gräf), *n.* **1.** a diagram representing a system of connections or interrelations among two or more things by a number of distinctive dots, lines, bars, etc. **2.** *Maths.* a curve as representing a given function. **—*v.t.*** **3.** to draw (a curve) as representing a given function. [short for *graphic formula.* See GRAPHIC] **—Syn. 1.** See **map.**

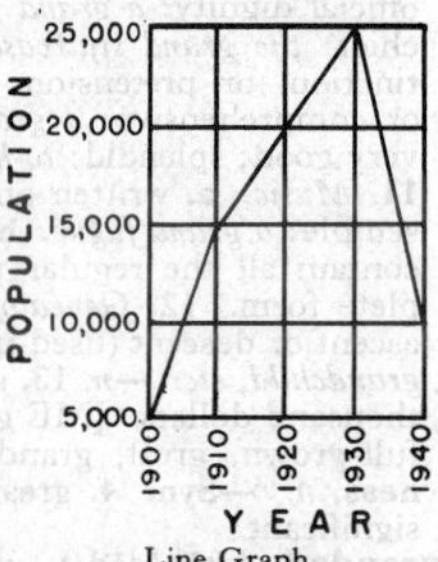

Line Graph

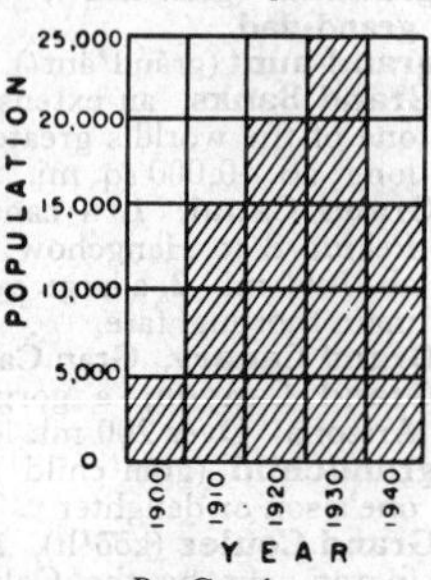

Bar Graph

graph-, var. of **grapho-** before vowels.

-graph, a word element meaning: **1.** drawn or written, as in *autograph.* **2.** something drawn or written, as in *lithograph, monograph.* **3.** an apparatus for drawing, writing, recording, etc., as in *barograph.* [t. Gk: s. *-graphos* (something) drawn or written, also one who draws or writes. See GRAPHIC]

grapheme (grăf′ēm), *n. Linguistics.* the smallest unit of writing or printing that distinguishes one meaning from another, as in English any of the letters of the alphabet.

graphic (grăf′ĭk), *adj.* **1.** lifelike; vivid: *a graphic description of a scene.* **2.** pertaining to the use of diagrams, graphs, mathematical curves, or the like; diagrammatic. **3.** pertaining to writing: *graphic symbols.* **4.** *Geol.* possessing that kind of texture produced in a rock when certain constituents crystallize in such a way as to appear like written characters on the surfaces or sections of the rock. **5.** *Maths.* pertaining to the determination of values, solving of problems, etc., by direct measurement on diagrams instead of by ordinary calculations. **6.** of the graphic arts. Also, **graph′ical.** [t. L: s. *graphicus*, t. Gk: m. *graphikós*, der. *graphḗ* drawing, writing] **—graph′ically,** *adv.* **—graph′icalness,** *n.* **—Syn. 1.** See **picturesque.**

graphic arts, drawing, engraving, etching, painting, and other arts involving the use of lines and strokes to express or convey ideas in terms of forms.

graphics (grăf′ĭks), *n.* **1.** the art of drawing, esp. as concerned with mathematics, engineering, etc. **2.** the science of calculating by diagrams. [f. GRAPH + -ICS]

graphite (grăf′īt), *n.* a very common mineral, soft native carbon, occurring in black to dark grey foliated masses with metallic lustre and greasy feel: used in so-called lead pencils, as a lubricant, for making crucibles and other refractories, etc.; plumbago; black lead. [t. G: m. *Graphit*, f. s. Gk *gráphein* mark, draw, write + *-it* -ITE[1]] **—graphitic** (grə fĭt′ĭk), *adj.*

graphitize (grăf′ĭ tīz′), *v.t.*, **-tized, -tizing. 1.** to convert into graphite. **2.** to cover (the surface of an object) with graphite. Also, **graphitise. —graph′itiza′tion,** *n.*

grapho-, a word element meaning 'writing', as in *graphology.* Also, **graph-.** [t. Gk, comb. form of *graphḗ*]

graphology (gră fŏl′ə jĭ), *n.* the study of handwriting, esp. as regarded as an expression of the writer's character. **—graphol′ogist,** *n.*

graphospasm (grăf′ō spăz′əm), *n.* writer's cramp.

graph paper, paper on which lines or squares have been printed in order to make it suitable for plotting graphs.

-graphy, a combining form denoting some process or form of drawing, representing, writing, recording, describing, etc., or an art or science concerned with some such thing, as in *biography, choreography, geography, orthography, photography.* [t. Gk: m. s. *graphía*, der. *gráphos.* See -GRAPH, -Y[3]]

grapnel (grăp′nəl), *n.* **1.** a device consisting essentially of one or more hooks or clamps, for grasping or holding something; a grapple; grappling iron. **2.** a small anchor with three or more flukes. Also, *Naut.*, **grappling iron.** [ME *grapenel*, dim. of OF *grapin* kind of hook, dim. of *grape* hook. See GRAPE]

Grapnel (def. 2)

grapple (grăp′l), *n.*, *v.*, **-pled, -pling. —*n.*** **1.** a hook or an iron instrument by which one thing, as a ship, fastens on another; a grapnel. **2.** a seizing or gripping.

3. a grip or close hold in wrestling or hand-to-hand fighting. —*v.t.* 4. to seize, hold, or fasten with or as with a grapple. 5. to engage in a struggle or close encounter with. —*v.i.* 6. to hold or make fast to something as with a grapple. 7. to use a grapple. 8. to seize another, or each other, in a firm grip, as in wrestling; clinch. 9. to try to overcome or deal (fol. by *with*): *to grapple with a problem.* [appar. a freq. of OE *gegræppian* seize, assoc. with GRAPNEL] —**grap′pler,** *n.*

grapple-plant (grăp′l plänt′), *n.* a southern African plant of the family *Pedaliaceae, Harpagophytum procumbens,* with woody hooked fruits widely dispersed on the fur of animals.

grappling (grăp′lĭng), *n.* 1. that by which anything is seized and held. 2. a grapnel.

grappling iron, a grapnel. Also, **grappling hook.**

graptolite (grăp′tə līt′), *n.* any of the *Graptolithina,* an order of extinct coelenterates commonly found as fossils. —**graptolitic** (grăp′tə lĭt′ĭk), *adj.*

grapy (grā′pĭ), *adj.* of, like, or composed of grapes.

Grasmere (gräs′mĭə′), *n.* 1. a lake in NW England, in Westmorland. 1 mi. long. 2. a village on this lake: Wordsworth's home, 1799–1808.

grasp (gräsp), *v.t.* 1. to seize and hold by or as by clasping with the fingers. 2. to seize upon; hold firmly. 3. to lay hold of with the mind; comprehend; understand. —*v.i.* 4. to make the motion of seizing; seize something firmly or eagerly. 5. to catch at; try to seize (fol. by *at*): *a drowning man grasps at a straw.* —*n.* 6. a grasping or gripping; grip of the hand. 7. power of seizing and holding; reach: *to have a thing within one's grasp.* 8. hold, possession, or mastery: *to wrest power from the grasp of a usurper.* 9. mental hold or comprehension: *a subject beyond one's grasp.* 10. broad or thorough comprehension: *a good grasp of a subject.* [ME *graspen, grapsen,* c. LG *grapsen*; akin to OE *gegræppian* seize] —**grasp′able,** *adj.* —**grasp′er,** *n.*

—**Syn.** 1. grip, clutch; grab. See **catch.** 6, 9. GRASP, REACH refer to the power of seizing, either concretely or figuratively. GRASP suggests actually seizing and closing the hand upon something (or figuratively thoroughly comprehending something) and therefore refers to something within one's possession or immediate possibility of possession: *a good grasp of a problem, immense mental grasp.* REACH suggests a stretching out of (usually) the hand to touch, strike, or if possible, seize something; it therefore refers to a potentiality of possession which requires an effort. Figuratively, it implies perhaps a faint conception of something still too far beyond one to be completely understood. —**Ant.** 1. release.

grasping (gräs′pĭng), *adj.* 1. that grasps. 2. greedy. —**grasp′ingly,** *adv.*—**grasp′ingness,** *n.*

grass (gräs), *n.* 1. any plant of the family *Gramineae* (or *Poaceae*), characterized by jointed stems, sheathing leaves, flower spikelets, and fruit consisting of a seedlike grain or caryopsis (**true grasses**). 2. herbage in general, or the plants on which grazing animals pasture or which are cut and dried as hay. 3. the grass-covered ground. 4. pasture: *half of the farm is grass, to put animals to grass.* 5. (*pl.*) stalks or sprays of grass: *filled with dried grasses.* 6. the season of the new growth of grass. 7. *Slang.* an informer. 8. **put out to grass, a.** to withdraw (a racehorse) from racing, etc., due to old age. **b.** *Colloq.* to retire (a person). 9. **let the grass grow under one's feet,** to be lax in one's efforts; miss an opportunity. —*v.t.* 10. to cover with grass or turf. 11. to feed with growing grass; pasture. 12. to lay on the grass, as for the purpose of bleaching. —*v.i.* 13. to feed on growing grass; graze. 14. to produce grass; become covered with grass. 15. *Slang.* to inform the authorities, esp. the police of criminal activities or the like. [ME *gras,* OE *græs,* c. D, G, Icel. and Goth. *gras*; akin to GROW and GREEN] —**grass′less,** *adj.* —**grass′like′,** *adj.*

Grass (*Ger.* gräs), *n.* **Günter** (*Ger.* gʏn′tər), born 1927, German novelist.

Grasse (*Fr.* gräs), *n.* 1. **François Joseph Paul, Comte de** (*Fr.* fräɴ swä zhō zĕf pōl′), (*Marquis de Grasse-Tilly*), 1722–88, French admiral. 2. a town in S France, in Alpes-Maritimes department, near the coast; tourist centre; perfume industry. 27,226 (1963).

grassfinch (gräs′fĭnch′), *n.* any of various Australian weaverbirds, esp. of the genus *Poephila.*

grass-green (gräs′grēn′), *adj.* yellowish green.

grasshopper (gräs′hŏp′ə), *n.* any of numerous orthopterous insects which are terrestrial, herbivorous and have hind legs for leaping. Many are very destructive to vegetation, as the locusts, certain katydids, etc.

Grasshopper, *Melanoplus fermurrubrum* (Length 1⅜ in.)

grassland (gräs′lănd′), *n.* an area in which the natural vegetation consists largely of perennial grasses, where trees are either limited to stream valleys or are widely scattered, characteristic of subhumid and semi-arid climates.

grass of Parnassus, any of the genus *Parnassia* (family *Saxifragaceae* or *Parnassiaceae*) of perennials of marshy areas, having broad, smooth leaves and single pale flowers.

grass parakeet, any of several Australian parakeets, esp. the budgerigar.

grass poly (pŏl′ĭ), a small lythraceous annual herb with pale pink flowers, *Lythrum hyssopifolia.*

grassquit (gräs′kwĭt′), *n.* any of several small fringilline birds, esp. of the genus *Tiaris,* as the **melodious grassquit,** *Tiaris canora,* of Cuba.

grassroots (gräs′rōōts′), *Orig. U.S. Colloq.* —*n.* 1. the basic essentials or foundation. —*adj.* 2. pertaining to, close to, or emerging spontaneously from the people.

grass snake, a non-venomous, dark green snake, *Natrix natrix,* having two yellow patches behind the head: the largest British snake.

grasstree (gräs′trē′), *n.* 1. any member of the Australian liliaceous genus *Xanthorrhoea,* comprising plants with a stout woody stem bearing a tuft of long grasslike leaves and a dense flower spike. 2. any of various similar plants of Australasia.

grass widow, 1. a woman whose husband is temporarily absent. 2. *U.S.* a woman who is separated, divorced, or lives apart from her husband.

grass widower, 1. a man whose wife is temporarily absent. 2. *U.S.* a man who is separated, divorced, or lives apart from his wife.

grass-wrack (gräs′răk′), *n.* the eelgrass, *Zostera marina.*

grassy (grä′sĭ), *adj.,* **-sier, -siest.** 1. covered with grass. 2. pertaining to or consisting of grass; grasslike. —**grass′iness,** *n.*

grate[1] (grāt), *n., v.,* **grated, grating.** —*n.* 1. a frame of metal bars for holding fuel when burning, as in a fireplace or furnace. 2. a framework of parallel or crossed bars used as a partition, guard, cover, or the like. 3. a fireplace. —*v.t.* 4. to furnish with a grate or grates. [ME, ult. t. It., g. L *crātis* wickerwork, hurdle. Cf. CRATE] —**grate′less,** *adj.* —**grate′like′,** *adj.*

grate[2] (grāt), *v.,* **grated, grating.** —*v.i.* 1. to have an irritating or unpleasant effect on the feelings. 2. to make a sound as of rough scraping. 3. to sound harshly; jar: *to grate on the ear.* 4. to scrape or rub with rough or noisy friction, as one thing on or against another. —*v.t.* 5. to rub together with a harsh, jarring sound: *to grate the teeth.* 6. to reduce to small particles by rubbing against a rough surface or a surface with many sharp-edged openings: *to grate a nutmeg.* 7. *Archaic.* to wear down or away by rough friction. [ME, t. OF: m. *grater*; of Gmc orig. (cf. G *kratzen* scratch)] —**grat′er,** *n.* —**grat′ing,** *adj.* —**grat′ingly,** *adv.*

grateful (grāt′fəl), *adj.* 1. warmly or deeply appreciative of kindness or benefits received; thankful: *I am grateful to you for your kindness.* 2. actuated by or expressing gratitude: *a grateful letter.* 3. pleasing to the mind or senses; agreeable or welcome; refreshing: *grateful slumber.* [f. obs. *grate* pleasing, thankful (t. L: m. s. *grātus*) + -FUL] —**grate′fully,** *adv.* —**grate′fulness,** *n.*

—**Syn.** 1. GRATEFUL, THANKFUL describe an appreciative attitude for what one has received. GRATEFUL indicates a warm or deep appreciation of personal kindness as shown to one: *grateful for favours, grateful to one's neighbours for help in time of trouble.* THANKFUL indicates a disposition to express gratitude by giving thanks, as to a benefactor or to a merciful Providence; there is often a sense of deliverance as well as of appreciation: *thankful that one's life was spared in an accident, thankful for the comfort of one's general situation.*

Gratian (grā′shyən), *n.* (*Flavius Gratianus*), A.D. 359–383, Roman Emperor A.D. 375–383.

graticule (grăt′ĭ kyōōl′), *n.* 1. a grid of meridians of longitude and parallels of latitude drawn on a particular map projection; the basis on which a map or chart is plotted. 2. *Physics.* a reticle.

gratification (grăt′ĭ fĭ kā′shən), *n.* 1. the state of being gratified; great satisfaction. 2. something that gratifies; source of pleasure or satisfaction. 3. the act of gratifying. 4. *Archaic.* a reward, recompense, or gratuity.

gratify (grăt′ĭ fī′), *v.t.,* **-fied, -fying.** 1. to give pleasure to (persons) by satisfying desires or humouring inclinations or feelings. 2. to satisfy; indulge; humour: *to gratify desires or appetites.* 3. *Obs.* to reward; remunerate. [t. F: m. s. *gratifier,* t. L: m. *grātificāri* do a favour to, oblige, gratify] —**grat′ifi′er,** *n.* —**Syn.** 1. See **humour.**

gratifying (grăt′ĭ fī′ĭng), *adj.* that gratifies; pleasing; satisfying. —**grat′ify′ingly,** *adv.* —**Syn.** See **interesting.**

gratin (grăt′ĭn; *Fr.* grä tăɴ′), *n.* See **au gratin.** [F, der. *gratter,* earlier *grater* scrape. See GRATE[2]]

grating (grā′tĭng), *n.* 1. a partition or frame of parallel or crossing bars; open latticework of wood or metal serving as a cover or guard, but admitting light, air, etc. 2. *Physics.* a diffraction grating.

gratis (grā′tĭs, grăt′ĭs), *adv.* **1.** for nothing; gratuitously. *—adj.* **2.** free of cost; gratuitous. [t. L]

gratitude (grăt′ĭ tyōōd′), *n.* the quality or feeling of being grateful or thankful. [t. LL: m. *grātitūdo*, der. L *grātus* pleasing, thankful]

Grattan (grăt′n), *n.* **Henry,** 1746–1820, Irish statesman and orator.

grattoir (grăt′wä; *Fr.* grȧ twȧr′), *n. Archaeol.* a chipped stone implement used for working wood or leather; scraper. [t. F, der. *gratter* scrape]

gratuitous (grə tyōō′ĭ təs), *adj.* **1.** freely bestowed or obtained; free. **2.** being without reason, cause, or justification: *a gratuitous insult.* **3.** *Law.* given without receiving any return value. [t. L: m. *grātuitus* free, spontaneous] **—gratu′itously,** *adv.* **—gratu′itousness,** *n.*

gratuity (grə tyōō′ĭ tĭ), *n., pl.* **-ties. 1.** a gift, usually of money, over and above payment due for service; tip. **2.** that which is given without claim or demand. **3.** a bounty given to soldiers.

gratulate (grăt′yōō lāt′), *v.,* **-lated, -lating.** *Archaic.* *—v.t.* **1.** to hail with joy; express joy at. **2.** to congratulate. *—v.i.* **3.** to express joy. [t. L: m. s. *grātulātus*, pp., having expressed joy, congratulated, or thanked] **—gratulatory** (grăt′yōō lə tə rĭ, -trĭ), *adj.*

gratulation (grăt′yōō lā′shən), *n. Archaic.* **1.** a feeling of joy. **2.** the expression of joy.

Graubünden (*Ger.* grou bʏn′dən), *n.* German name of **Grisons.**

graupel (grou′pl), *n. Meterol.* soft hail. [t. G, dim. of *Graupe* hulled grain]

gravamen (grə vā′mĕn), *n., pl.* **-vamina** (-văm′ĭ nə, -vā′mĭ nə). *Law.* **1.** that part of an accusation which weighs most heavily against the accused; the burden or substantial part of a charge or complaint. **2.** a grievance. [t. LL, der. L *gravāre* load, weigh down. Cf. GRIEVE]

grave[1] (grāv), *n.* **1.** an excavation made in the earth to receive a dead body in burial. **2.** any place of interment; a tomb or sepulchre. **3.** any place that becomes the receptacle of what is dead, lost or past: *the grave of dead reputations.* **4.** death: *O grave, where is thy victory?* **5. have one foot in the grave,** to be infirm, old, or near death. **6. to turn in one's grave,** (of a dead person), to be thought likely to have been offended or horrified by a modern event or events. [ME; OE *græf*, c. G *Grab.* See GRAVE[3]]

grave[2] (gräv *for 4 and 6; otherwise* grāv), *adj.,* **graver, gravest,** *n. —adj.* **1.** dignified; sedate; serious; earnest; solemn: *a grave person, grave thoughts, grave ceremonies.* **2.** weighty, momentous, or important: *grave responsibilities.* **3.** important or critical; involving serious issues: *a grave situation.* **4.** *Phonet.* **a.** spoken on a low pitch or falling pitch because of musical accent. **b.** denoting or having a particular accent (`) indicating orig. a comparatively low pitch (as in ancient Greek); later, quality of sound (as in the French *père*), distinct syllabic value (as in *belovèd*), etc. **5.** *Rare.* (of colours) dull; sombre. *—n.* **6.** the grave accent. [t. F, t. L: m. s. *gravis* heavy] **—grave′ly,** *adv.* **—grave′ness,** *n.*

—Syn. 1. GRAVE, SOBER, SOLEMN refer to the condition of being serious in demeanour or appearance. GRAVE indicates a weighty dignity, or the character, aspect, demeanour, speech, etc., of one conscious of heavy responsibilities or cares, or of threatening possibilities: *the jury looked grave while studying the evidence.* SOBER (from its original sense of freedom from intoxication, and hence temperate, staid, sedate) has come to indicate absence of levity, gaiety, or mirth, and thus to be akin to serious and grave: *as sober as a judge, a sober expression on one's face.* SOLEMN implies an impressive seriousness and deep earnestness: *the minister's voice was solemn as he announced the text.* **—Ant. 1.** gay, frivolous.

grave[3] (grāv), *v.t.,* **graved, graved** or **graven, graving.** *Archaic.* **1.** to incise or engrave. **2.** to impress deeply: *graven on the mind.* [ME *grave(n)*, OE *grafan*, c. G *graben.* Cf. GRAVE[1], GROOVE, and GRAVURE]

grave[4] (grāv), *v.t.,* **graved, graving.** *Naut.* to clean (a ship's bottom or a ship) by burning or scraping off accretions and paving it over with pitch. [orig. obscure]

grave[5] (grä′vĭ), *Music. —adj.* **1.** slow; solemn. *—adv.* **2.** slowly; solemnly. [It., g. L *gravis* GRAVE[2]]

graveclothes (grāv′klōz′, -klōthz′), *n.pl.* the clothes in which a dead body is interred; cerements.

gravel (grăv′əl), *n., v.,* **-elled, -elling** or (*U.S.*) **-eled, -eling.** *—n.* **1.** small stones and pebbles, or a mixture of these with sand. **2.** *Pathol.* **a.** a collection of small calculi formed in the kidneys. **b.** the disease characterized by such concretions. *—v.t.* **3.** to cover with gravel. **4.** to bring to a standstill from perplexity; puzzle. [ME, t. OF: m. *gravele*, dim. of *grave* sandy shore; of Celtic orig.]

gravel-blind (grăv′əl blīnd′), *adj.* more blind or dim-sighted than sand-blind and less than stone-blind.

gravelly (grăv′ə lĭ), *adj.* **1.** abounding in gravel. **2.** consisting of or resembling gravel. **3.** (of a voice) harsh.

gravemente (*It.* grȧ vĕ mĕn′tĕ), *adv. Italian.* gravely.

graven (grā′vən), *v.* **1.** pp. of **grave**[3]. *—adj.* **2.** deeply impressed; firmly fixed. **3.** *Archaic.* carved; engraved.

Gravenhage, 's (sKHrȧ vən hä′KHə), *n.* Dutch name of **The Hague.**

graven image, an idol.

graver (grā′və), *n.* **1.** any of various tools for chasing, engraving, etc., as a burin. **2.** *Archaic.* an engraver.

Graves (grāvz), *n.* **Robert (Ranke** (rang′kə)), born 1895, English poet, novelist, and critic, born in Wales.

Graves (*Fr.* gräv), *n.pl.* a class of red and white Bordeaux wines, esp. the white.

Graves' disease (grāvz), *Pathol.* a disease characterized by an enlarged thyroid, rapid pulse, and increased basal metabolism due to excessive thyroid secretion. [named after R. J. *Graves*, 1796–1853, Irish physician]

Gravesend (grāvz′ĕnd′), *n.* a seaport in SE England, in Kent, on the Thames. 51,950 (est. 1964).

gravestone (grāv′stōn′), *n.* a stone marking a grave.

Gravettian (grə vĕt′ĭ ən), *adj.* of, pertaining to, or characteristic of an Upper Palaeolithic culture of Europe. [after *La Gravette* on the Dordogne, France; see -IAN]

graveyard (grāv′yäd′), *n.* cemetery; burial ground.

gravid (grăv′ĭd), *adj.* pregnant. [t. L: s. *gravidus*] **—gravidity** (grə vĭd′ĭ tĭ), *n.*

gravimetric (grăv′ĭ mĕt′rĭk), *adj.* **1.** of or pertaining to measurement by weight. **2.** *Chem.* denoting a method of analysing compound bodies by finding the weight of their elements (opposed to *volumetric*). Also, **grav′imet′rical.** **—grav′imet′rically,** *adv.*

gravimetry (grə vĭm′ĭ trĭ), *n.* the measurement of weight or density. [f. L *gravi(s)* heavy + -METRY]

graving dock (grā′vĭng), a dry dock.

gravitate (grăv′ĭ tāt′), *v.i.,* **-tated, -tating. 1.** to move or tend to move under the influence of gravitational force. **2.** to tend towards the lowest level; sink; fall. **3.** to have a natural tendency or be strongly attracted (fol. by *to* or *towards*). [t. NL: s. *gravitātus*, pp., der. L *gravis* heavy]

gravitation (grăv′ĭ tā′shən), *n.* **1.** *Physics.* **a.** that force of attraction between all particles or bodies, or that acceleration of one towards another, of which the fall of bodies to the earth is an instance. **b.** an act or process caused by this force. **2.** a sinking or falling. **3.** natural tendency towards some point or object of influence: *the gravitation of people towards suburbs.* **—grav′ita′tional,** *adj.* **—grav′ita′tionally,** *adv.*

gravitational constant, *Physics.* the constant appearing in Newton's law of gravitation, equal to $6{\cdot}670 \times 10^{-8}$ in the c.g.s. system.

gravitational field, *Physics.* the region in which a body with a finite mass exerts an appreciable force of attraction on another body of finite mass.

gravitative (grăv′ĭ tā′tĭv), *adj.* **1.** of or pertaining to gravitation. **2.** tending or causing to gravitate.

gravity (grăv′ĭ tĭ), *n., pl.* **-ties. 1.** the force of attraction by which terrestrial bodies tend to fall towards the centre of the earth. **2.** heaviness or weight: *the centre of gravity, specific gravity.* **3.** gravitation in general. **4.** seriousness; dignity; solemnity: *to preserve one's gravity.* **5.** serious or critical character: *the gravity of the situation.* **6.** lowness in pitch, as of sounds. [t. L: m. s. *gravitas* heaviness]

gravity cell, *Elect.* a cell with horizontal electrodes in which the two electrolytes lie in separate layers as a result of their difference in specific gravity.

gravity feed, 1. the supplying of materials, fuels, etc., by the force of gravity alone. **2.** any system designed for this purpose.

gravure (grə vyōōə′), *n.* **1.** a process of photomechanical printing, such as photogravure or rotogravure. **2.** a plate or print produced by gravure. **3.** the metal or wooden plate used in photogravure. [t. F: engraving, der. *graver* engrave, t. Gmc; cf. GRAVE[3]]

gravy (grā′vĭ), *n., pl.* **-vies.** the fat and juices that drip from cooking meat, often made into a dressing for meat, etc. [ME *grave*, t. OF: kind of dressing]

gravy boat, a small boat-shaped (or other) vessel for serving gravy or sauce.

gray (grā), *adj., n., v. U.S.* grey.

Gray (grā), *n.* **Thomas,** 1716–71, English poet.

grayling (grā′lĭng), *n.* **1.** any of the freshwater fishes constituting the genus *Thymallus*, allied to the trout, but having a longer and higher dorsal fin of resplendent colour. **2.** any of certain sombre grey moths of the family *Satyridae.*

Gray's Inn (grāz). See **Inns of Court.**

Graz (*Ger.* grâts), *n.* a city in SE Austria. 237,080 (1961).

graze[1] (grāz), *v.,* **grazed, grazing.** *—v.i.* **1.** to feed on growing herbage, as cattle, sheep, etc. *—v.t.* **2.** to feed on (growing grass). **3.** to put cattle, sheep, etc., to feed on (grass, pasture, etc.). **4.** to tend (cattle, sheep, etc.) while at pasture. [ME *grase(n)*, OE *grasian*, der. *græs* GRASS] **—graz′er,** *n.*

graze² (grāz), *v.*, **grazed, grazing,** *n.* **—***v.t.* **1.** to touch or rub lightly in passing. **2.** to scrape the skin from; abrade. **—***v.i.* **3.** to touch or rub something lightly, or so as to produce slight abrasion, in passing. **—***n.* **4.** a grazing; a touching or rubbing lightly in passing. **5.** a slight scratch in passing; abrasion. [orig. uncert.]

grazier (grā′zyə), *n.* one who grazes or feeds cattle for the market.

grazing (grā′zĭng), *n.* pastureland; a pasture.

grease (*n.* grēs; *v.* grēs, grēz), *n.*, *v.*, **greased, greasing.** **—***n.* **1.** the melted or rendered fat of animals, esp. when in a soft state. **2.** fatty or oily matter in general: lubricant. **3.** Also, **grease wool.** wool, as shorn, before being cleansed of the oily matter. **4.** *Vet. Sci.* inflammation of a horse's skin in the fetlock region, attended with an oily secretion. **—***v.t.* **5.** to put grease on; lubricate: *he greased the axle but it did no good.* **6.** to smear with grease. **7.** to cause to run easily. **8. grease (someone's) palm,** *Slang.* to bribe (a person). [ME *grese*, t. OF: m. *graisse*, g. L *crassus* fat] **—grease′less,** *adj.* **—greas′er,** *n.*

grease gun, a hand-operated device for forcing grease into bearings under pressure.

greasepaint (grēs′pānt′), *n.* **1.** a mixture of tallow or hard grease and a pigment, used by actors for painting their faces. **2.** any theatrical make-up.

greaseproof (grēs′pro͞of′), *adj.* impervious to grease: *greaseproof paper.*

greasewood (grēs′wo͝od′), *n.* a chenopodiaceous shrub, *Sarcobatus vermiculatus*, of the alkaline regions of the western U.S., containing a small amount of oil and used for fuel. Also, **greasebush** (grēs′bo͝osh′).

greasy (grē′sĭ, -zĭ), *adj.*, **-sier, -siest.** **1.** smeared or soiled with grease. **2.** composed of or containing grease; oily: *greasy food.* **3.** greaselike in appearance or to the touch; slippery. **4.** *Vet. Sci.* affected with grease. **—greas′ily,** *adv.* **—greas′iness,** *n.*

great (grāt), *adj.* **1.** unusually or comparatively large in size or dimensions: *a great house, lake, or fire.* **2.** large in number; numerous: *a great many, in great detail.* **3.** unusual or considerable in degree: *great pain.* **4.** notable or remarkable: *a great occasion.* **5.** distinguished; famous: *Alexander the Great.* **6.** of much consequence; important: *great issues.* **7.** chief or principal: *the great seal.* **8.** of high rank, official position, or social standing: *a great noble.* **9.** of noble or lofty character: *great thoughts.* **10.** much in use or favour: *'humour' was a great word with the old physiologists.* **11.** being such in an extreme degree: *great friends, a great talker.* **12.** of extraordinary powers; having unusual merit; very admirable: *a great statesman.* **13.** *U.S. Colloq.* much addicted (usually fol. by *on* or *at*). **14.** *U.S. Colloq.* skilful or expert (usually fol. by *on* or *at*). **15.** *Colloq.* first-rate; very good; fine: *we had a great time.* **16.** one degree more remote in direct ascent or descent than a specified relationship: *great-grandfather.* **17.** *Archaic.* pregnant. **—***n.* **18.** *Colloq.* a great person; a person who has accomplished great achievements. **19.** great organ. **20.** See **Greats.** [ME *greet*, OE *grēat*, c. D *groot*, G *gross*] **—great′ness,** *n.*

—Syn. 1. immense, enormous, gigantic. GREAT, BIG, LARGE refer to size, extent, and degree. In reference to the size and extent of concrete objects, BIG is the most general and most colloquial word, LARGE is somewhat more formal, and GREAT is highly formal and even poetic, suggesting also that the object is notable or imposing: *a big tree, a large tree, a great oak; a big field, a large field, great plains.* When the reference is to degree or a quality, GREAT is the usual word: *great beauty, great mistake, great surprise,* though BIG sometimes alternates with it in colloquial style: *a big mistake, a big surprise;* LARGE is not used in reference to degree, but may be used with a quantitative reference: *a large number* (*great number*). 5. eminent, renowned, illustrious. 6. weighty, serious, momentous. **—Ant.** 1. little, small.

great auk, a large flightless seabird, *Plautus impennis*, of the North Atlantic, now extinct.

great-aunt (grāt′änt′), *n.* a father's or mother's aunt.

Great Australian Bight, a wide, open bay in S Australia.

Great Barrier Island, an island off NE North Island, New Zealand. ab. 20 mi. long and 10 mi. wide.

Great Barrier Reef, a coral reef parallel to the coast of Queensland, in NE Australia. ab. 1250 mi. long.

Great Basin, a region without drainage to the sea, in the W United States, including most of Nevada and parts of Utah, California, Oregon, and Idaho. ab. 210,000 sq. mi.

Great Bear, *Astron.* Ursa Major, the most prominent constellation in the northern heavens, containing the seven stars that form the Plough.

Great Bear Lake, a large lake in NW Canada, in the Northwest Territories. ab. 11,800 sq. mi.

Great Britain, an island of NW Europe, separated from the mainland by the English Channel and the North Sea: since 1707 the name has applied politically to England, Scotland, and Wales. 51,402,623 pop. (1961); 88,139 sq. mi. See **United Kingdom.**

great circle, **1.** a circle on a sphere the plane of which passes through the centre of the sphere. Cf. **small circle.** **2.** the line of shortest distance between two points on the surface of the earth.

greatcoat (grāt′kōt′), *n. Now Chiefly Mil.* a heavy overcoat.

great council, *Eng. Hist.* an assembly, composed of the tenants in chief of Norman kings.

Great Dane, one of a breed of large, powerful, short-haired dogs, somewhat resembling the mastiff.

Great Dane (30 in. high or more at the shoulder)

Great Divide, **1.** the continental divide of North America: the Rocky Mountains. **2.** any similar continental divide. **3.** separation between life and death: *across the Great Divide.* **4.** a crucial stage; crisis.

Great Dividing Range, a series of dissected plateaus forming mountain ranges in the E of Australia, extending from Cape York in N Queensland to Wilson's Promontory in S Victoria.

Great Dog, *Astron.* the constellation, Canis Major.

Great Eastern, a large steamship, propelled both by screw and paddles, designed by I. K. Brunel and launched in 1858.

greaten (grā′tn), *Archaic.* **—***v.t.* **1.** to make greater; enlarge; increase. **—***v.i.* **2.** to become greater.

Greater Antilles. See **Antilles.**

Greater London. See **London** (def. 3).

Great Escarpment, a series of mountain ranges in SE Republic of South Africa, formed by the edge of the South African plateau, and including the Drakensberg, Stormberg and Nuveld Range.

greatest common factor. See **common factor.**

Great Fish River, **1.** a river in southern Africa flowing S then SE through E Cape Province to the Indian Ocean. 400 mi. **2.** a river in the Republic of South Africa flowing N through W Cape Province to the river Zak. 230 mi.

Great Glen, a valley of Inverness-shire, Scotland, with a series of lochs linked by the Caledonian Canal.

great-grandchild (grāt′grăn′chīld′), *n.*, *pl.* **-children.** a grandchild of one's son or daughter.

great-granddaughter (grāt′grăn′dô′tə), *n.* a granddaughter of one's son or daughter.

great-grandfather (grāt′grăn′fä′thə), *n.* a parent's grandfather.

great-grandmother (grāt′grăn′mŭth′ə), *n.* a parent's grandmother.

great-grandparent (grāt′grăn′pēə′rənt), *n.* a grandfather or grandmother of one's father or mother.

great-grandson (grāt′grăn′sŭn′), *n.* a son's or daughter's grandson.

great gross, a unit of quantity equal to 12 gross. *Abbrev.:* g.gr.

great-hearted (grāt′hä′tĭd), *adj.* **1.** having or showing a generous heart; magnanimous. **2.** high-spirited; courageous; fearless. **—great′-heart′edness,** *n.*

Great Indian Desert, Thar.

Great Lake, a lake in Tasmania. 3380 ft above sea-level. 55 sq. mi.

Great Lakes, a series of five large lakes between the United States and Canada, connected with the Atlantic by the St Lawrence: Lakes Erie, Huron, Michigan, Ontario, and Superior.

greatly (grāt′lĭ), *adv.* **1.** in or to a great degree; much. **2.** in a great manner.

Great Mogul, **1.** an emperor of the Mogul empire of India, which flourished from 1526 to 1761 and continued nominally until 1857. **2.** (*l.c.*) an important or distinguished person.

great-nephew (grāt′nĕv′yo͞o, -nĕf′yo͞o), *n.* a son of one's nephew or niece.

great-niece (grāt′nēs′), *n.* a daughter of one's nephew or niece.

great organ, *Music.* **1.** the main section of an organ. **2.** the manual controlling this.

Great Ouse. See **Ouse** (def. 2).

Great Paternoster Point, a promontory in the Republic of South Africa, on the W coast of Cape Province.

Great Plains, a semi-arid region E of the Rocky Mountains of the United States and Canada.

great primer, *Print., Obs.* a size of type equivalent to 18 point.

Great Russian, a member of the main stock of the Russian people, dwelling chiefly in the northern and central parts of the Soviet Union in Europe.

Greats (grāts), *n.pl.* **1.** the course in classics or *Literae Humaniores* at Oxford University. **2.** the final examination for the B.A. in this subject.

Great Salt Lake, a shallow salt lake in the U.S., in NW Utah. ab. 2300 sq. mi.; ab. 80 mi. long; maximum depth, 60 ft.

Great Sandy Desert, a vast area of sandy waste in N Western Australia. 500 mi. wide; ab. 160,000 sq. mi.

Great Schism, a period of controversy in the Roman Catholic Church (1378–1417) during which there were two rival popes, one at Rome and one at Avignon.

Great Scott, (a euphemistic var. of *Great God.*) Also, **Great Scot.**

great seal, 1. the principal seal of a government or state. **2.** (*caps.*) the keeper of the great seal of England, the Lord Chancellor.

Great Slave Lake, a large lake in NW Canada, in the Northwest Territories. ab. 10,700 sq. mi.

Great Smoky Mountains, a mountain range in the U.S., in North Carolina and Tennessee: a part of the Appalachian system. Highest peak, Clingman's Dome, 6642 ft. Also, **Smoky Mountains** or **Great Smokies.**

Great Trek, *S African Hist.* a mass emigration of settlers of Dutch origin from the Cape of Good Hope to the N and E, about 1835–46.

great-uncle (grāt′ŭng′kl), *n.* an uncle of one's father or mother.

Great Victoria Desert, a vast area of sand hills and sandy plains in S Western Australia and South Australia. 125,000 sq. mi.

Great Wall of China, a system of walls constructed as a defence for China, against the nomads of the regions that are now Mongolia and Manchuria: completed in the third century B.C., but later repeatedly modified and rebuilt. ab. 1400 mi. long.

Great War, World War I.

Great Week, *Eastern Church.* Holy Week.

great white heron, a large white egret, *Casmerodius albus*, of south-eastern Europe, tropical Africa, Asia, New Zealand, and America.

great willowherb, the willowherb.

Great Yarmouth (yär′məth), a fishing port in England, in SE Norfolk. 52,720 (est. 1964).

greave (grēv), *n.* armour for the leg from knee to ankle, usually of front and back plates. See illus. under **armour.** [ME *greves* (pl.), t. OF; orig. obscure]

greaves (grēvz), *n.pl.* the sediment of melted tallow or animal fat, used as dog food, fish bait, etc. [t. LG: m. *greven*]

grebe (grēb), *n.* any of several diving birds of the order *Colymbiformes*, related to the loons, but having lobate rather than webbed toes and a rudimentary tail, as the **great crested grebe,** *Colymbus cristatus*, of Europe, and the **pied-billed grebe,** *Podilymbus podiceps*, of America. [t. F, orig. uncert.]

Great crested grebe, *Colymbus cristatus* (14 in. long)

Grecian (grē′shən), *adj.* **1.** Greek. —*n.* **2.** a Greek. **3.** an expert in, or student of the Greek language or literature.

Grecian nose, a straight nose continuing the line of the forehead without a dip.

Grecism (grē′sĭz′əm), *n.* *Chiefly U.S.* Graecism.

Grecize (grē′sīz), *v.t., v.i.,* **-cized, -cizing.** *Chiefly U.S.* Graecize. Also, **Grecise.**

Greco (grĕk′ō), *n.* **El.** See **El Greco.**

Greco-, var. of **Graeco-.**

gree[1] (grē), *n.* *Archaic and Scot.* **1.** superiority, mastery, or victory. **2.** the prize for victory. [ME *gre*, t. OF, g. L *gradus* step]

gree[2] (grē), *n.* *Obs. or Archaic.* **1.** favour; goodwill. **2.** satisfaction, as for an injury. [ME *gre*, t. OF, g. L *grātum*, adj. neut., pleasing, grateful]

gree[3] (grē), *v.t., v.i.,* **greed, greeing.** *Scot. and N Dial.* to bring or come into accord. [aphetic var. of AGREE. Cf. F *gréer*]

Greece (grēs), *n.* a kingdom in S Europe at the S end of the Balkan Peninsula. 8,388,553 pop. (1961); 50,147 sq. mi. *Cap.:* Athens. Ancient Greek, **Hellas.** See map under **Macedonia.**

greed (grēd), *n.* inordinate or rapacious desire, esp. for food or wealth. [OE *grǣd* (only in dat. pl.), c. Icel. *grādhr* hunger, greed, Goth. *grēdus* hunger] —**greed′less,** *adj.*
—**Syn.** avidity, avarice, cupidity, covetousness. GREED, GREEDINESS denote an excessive, extreme desire for something, often more than one's proper share. GREED means avid desire for food or wealth (unless some other application is indicated) and is mostly uncomplimentary in implications: *his greed drove him to exploit his workers.* GREEDINESS, when unqualified, suggests a craving for food; it may, however, be applied to all avid desires, and need not be always uncomplimentary: *greediness for knowledge, fame, praise.*

greedy (grē′dĭ), *adj.,* **-dier, -diest. 1.** very eager for wealth; avaricious. **2.** greatly desiring food or drink. **3.** keenly desirous; eager (often fol. by *of*): *greedy of praise.* [ME *gredy*, d. OE *grēdig*, r. OE *grǣdig*. See GREED] —**greed′ily,** *adv.* —**greed′iness,** *n.* —**Syn. 1.** grasping, rapacious. **2.** ravenous, voracious, gluttonous.

greegree (grē′grē), *n.* grigri.

Greek (grēk), *adj.* **1.** of or pertaining to Greece, the Greeks, or their language. **2.** pertaining to the Greek Church. —*n.* **3.** a native or inhabitant of Greece. **4.** the language of the ancient Greeks and any of the languages which have developed from it, such as Hellenistic Greek, Biblical Greek, the Koine, and Modern Greek. **5.** anything unintelligible, as speech, etc.: *it's Greek to me.* **6.** a member of the Greek Orthodox Church. **7.** the group of Indo-European languages to which Greek belongs; Hellenic. [ME *Grekes* (pl.), OE *Grēcas*, learned var. of *Crēcas* (pl.), ult. t. L: m. *Graecī*, pl. of *Graecus* a Greek, t. Gk: m. *Graikós*, orig. adj.]

Greek Catholic, 1. a communicant of any Greek Orthodox Church. **2.** a Greek or Byzantine acknowledging allegiance to the pope and to the faith of the Western Church but disagreeing in forms of liturgy and ritual: a Uniat.

Greek cross, a cross consisting of an upright crossed in the middle by a horizontal piece of the same length. See illus. under **cross.**

Greek fire, an inflammable mixture used by the Byzantine Greeks to set fire to enemy ships, etc.

Greek Orthodox Church, 1. the Orthodox Church. **2.** Also, **Greek Church.** that part of the Orthodox Church which constitutes the established Church in Greece.

Greeley (grē′lĭ), *n.* **Horace,** 1811–72, U.S. politician.

green (grēn), *adj.* **1.** of the colour of growing foliage, between yellow and blue in the spectrum. **2.** covered with herbage or foliage; verdant: *green fields.* **3.** characterized by the presence of verdure. **4.** consisting of green vegetables: *a green salad.* **5.** full of life and vigour. **6.** unseasoned; not dried or cured: *green timber.* **7.** not fully developed or perfected in growth or condition; unripe; not properly aged. **8.** immature in age or judgement; untrained; inexperienced: *a green hand.* **9.** simple; gullible; easily fooled. **10.** fresh, recent, or new: *a green wound.* **11.** pale; sickly; wan: *green with fear.* **12.** freshly killed; *green meat.* **13.** not fired, as bricks or pottery. **14.** *Metall.* (in moulding) the moist condition of the sand used in founding. **15.** (of concrete, cement or mortar) freshly poured and not completely set. —*n.* **16.** green colour. **17.** green colouring matter, paint, etc. **18.** green material or clothing. **19.** grassy land; a plot of grassy ground. **20.** *Golf.* **a.** the whole course or links on which golf is played. **b.** a putting green alone. **21.** a piece of grassy ground constituting a town or village common. **22.** (*pl.*) **a.** the leaves and stems of plants, as cabbage, used for food. **b.** fresh leaves or branches of trees, shrubs, etc., used for decoration. —*v.i., v.t.* **23.** to become or make green. [ME and OE *grēne*, c. G *grün*; akin to GROW]

Green (grēn), *n.* **John Richard,** 1837–83, English historian.

green acid, *Chem.* one of a number of mixtures of sulphonic acids used in the manufacture of detergents.

green algae, *Bot.* algae belonging to the class *Chlorophyceae*, grass-green in colour.

greenback (grēn′băk′), *n.* *U.S. Colloq.* a U.S. legal-tender note, usually printed in green on the back, originally issued against the credit of the country and not against gold or silver on deposit.

Green Bay, an arm of Lake Michigan, in NE Wisconsin. ab. 90 mi. long.

green bean, the narrow, green, edible seedpod of any of various varieties of bean (plant), as the young pod of the French bean, *Phaseolus vulgaris*, or the runner bean, *P. multiflorus*.

green belt, an area of parks and unoccupied ground surrounding a town, on which building is not permitted.

greenbrier (grēn′brī′ə), *n.* **1.** a climbing liliaceous plant, *Smilax rotundifolia*, of the eastern U.S., with prickly stem and thick leaves. **2.** any plant of this genus.

green corn, sweet corn (def. 2).

green dragon, an American araceous herb, *Arisaema dracontium*, with a greenish or whitish spathe.

Greene (grēn), *n.* **1. Graham,** born 1904, English novelist. **2. Nathanael,** 1742–86, American general in the War of Independence. **3. Robert,** *c.* 1560–92, English dramatic poet and pamphleteer.

green earth, *Painting.* a green pigment consisting of ferrous hydroxide and silicic acid.

greenery (grē′nə rĭ), *n., pl.* **-eries. 1.** green foliage or vegetation; verdure. **2.** a place where green plants are reared or kept.

greenery-yallery (grē′nə rĭ yăl′ə rĭ), *adj.* pertaining or appropriate to Art Nouveau or the aesthetic movement associated with it.

green-eyed (grēn′īd′), *adj.* jealous.

greenfinch (grēn′fĭnch′), *n.* a European finch, *Chloris chloris,* with green and yellow plumage.

green fingers, skill in gardening and plant-growing.

green flash, a phenomenon sometimes observed in a clear atmosphere at sunset when the very last part of the sun to remain above the horizon appears as a bright green light.

greenfly (grēn′flī′), *n.* any of the small hemipterous insects of the family *Aphididae,* coloured green, which feed by sucking the juices of plants; aphid.

greengage (grēn′gāj′), *n.* one of several varieties of light green plums. [f. GREEN + *Gage,* named after Sir William *Gage,* who introduced it into England *c.* 1725]

green gland, *Zool.* one of the pair of excretory organs in the head region of decapod crustaceans.

greengrocer (grēn′grō′sə), *n.* a retailer of fresh vegetables and fruit. **—green′gro′cery,** *n.*

greenhead (grēn′hĕd′), *n.* a male mallard.

greenheart (grēn′hät′), *n.* **1.** a South American lauraceous tree, *Ocotea* (or *nectandra*) *Rodiaei,* whose hard, durable wood is often used for wharves, bridges, and in shipbuilding, and whose bark yields bebeerine; bebeeru. **2.** any of certain other timber trees of tropical America. **3.** their valuable greenish wood.

green heron, a small American heron, *Butorides virescens,* with glossy green wings.

greenhide (grēn′hīd′), *n. Austral., N.Z.* rawhide.

greenhorn (grēn′hôn′), *n. Colloq.* **1.** a raw, inexperienced person. **2.** a person easily imposed upon. [orig. applied to an ox with green or young horns]

greenhouse (grēn′hous′), *n.* a building, chiefly of glass, for the cultivation or protection of plants.

greening (grē′nĭng), *n.* any variety of apple the skin of which is green when ripe. [f. GREEN, adj. + -ING[1]]

greenish (grē′nĭsh), *adj.* somewhat green; having a tinge of green.

Greenland (grēn′lənd), *n.* an overseas territory of Denmark NE of North America: the largest island in the world. 33,140 pop. (1960); ab. 840,000 sq. mi. (over 700,000 sq. mi. ice-capped). See map under **Spitsbergen.** **—Green′lander,** *n.*

Greenland Sea, a part of the Arctic Ocean lying NE of Greenland and N of Iceland.

Greenland spar, cryolite.

greenlet (grēn′lĭt), *n.* vireo.

green light, 1. a green lamp, used as a signal to mean 'go'. **2.** *Colloq.* permission; authorization.

greenling (grēn′lĭng), *n.* any of the spiny-finned fishes constituting the genus *Hexagrammos,* found about rocks and kelp in the N Pacific Ocean.

green manure, *Agric.* **1.** a green crop, esp. clover and other nitrogen-fixing plants, ploughed into the soil for fertilizer. **2.** manure which has not undergone decay.

green monkey, a monkey, *Cercopithecus aethiops sabaeus,* of West Africa, with a greenish grey back and yellow tail.

Green Mountains, a mountain range in the U.S., in Vermont: a part of the Appalachian system. Highest peak, Mt Mansfield, 4393 ft.

greenness (grēn′nĭs), *n.* **1.** the state or quality of being green. **2.** verdure; green vegetation. **3.** lack of experience; immaturity. **4.** naivety; gullibility; innocence.

Greenock (grē′nək, grēn′ək), *n.* a seaport in SW Scotland, in Renfrewshire, on the Firth of Clyde: shipbuilding. 74,578 (1961).

green pepper, 1. the fruit of the bell or sweet pepper, *Capsicum frutescens* var. *grossum.* **2.** the mild, unripe fruit of any of the garden peppers, *Capsicum frutescens,* used as a green vegetable.

green plover, lapwing.

Green River, a river in the U.S., flowing from W Wyoming S through E Utah to the Colorado. 730 mi.

greenroom (grēn′ro͞om′, -ro͝om′), *n.* a retiring room in a theatre, for the use of the actors and actresses when not required on the stage.

greensand (grēn′sănd′), *n.* **1.** a sandstone containing much glauconite, which gives it a greenish hue. **2.** moulding sand, rich in organic matter, as used in a foundry.

Greensboro (grēnz′bə rə, -brə), *n.* a town in the U.S., in N North Carolina. 119,574 (1960).

greenshank (grēn′shăngk′), *n.* a common European shorebird, *Glottis nebularia,* with green legs.

green soap, a soap made chiefly from potassium hydroxide and linseed oil, used in treating skin diseases.

greenstick fracture (grēn′stĭk′), *Med.* a partial fracture in which only one side of a bone is broken.

greenstone[1] (grēn′stōn′), *n.* any of various altered basaltic rocks having a dark green colour caused by the presence of chlorite, epidote, etc.

greenstone[2] (grēn′stōn′), *n.* a dark green gem found on the W coast of New Zealand and highly prized by the Maori.

greenstuff (grēn′stŭf′), *n.* green vegetables, as cabbage, etc.

greensward (grēn′swôd′), *n.* turf green with grass.

green tea, a tea subjected to a heating process without previous special withering and fermenting.

green thumb, *U.S.* green fingers.

green turtle, a sea turtle, *Chelonia mydas,* common in tropical waters, occasionally found around the southern coast of the British Isles; its flesh is used for turtle soup.

green vegetables, vegetables useful for the part grown above the ground; leafy vegetables.

green vitriol, ferrous sulphate, $FeSO_4.7H_2O$, in the form of bluish green crystals; copperas.

Greenwich (grĭn′ĭj), *n.* a SE inner borough of London: the prime meridian passes through here. 230,100 (est. 1965).

Greenwich Mean Time, a standard time based on the meridian through Greenwich. Formerly the standard time for the British Isles and elsewhere. *Abbrev.*: G.M.T. See **British Standard Time.**

Greenwich Village (grĕn′ĭch), a section of New York City in Manhattan: artists' and writers' centre.

green-winged teal, a small freshwater duck of America, *Anas carolinensis,* or *A. crecca* of Europe, having a shining green speculum in the wing.

greenwood (grēn′wo͝od′), *n.* a wood or forest when green, as in summer.

green woodpecker, a woodpecker, *Picus viridis,* of Europe, Asia, and N Africa, with dull green upper parts and a yellowish rump.

greet[1] (grēt), *v.t.* **1.** to address with some form of salutation; welcome. **2.** to receive with demonstrations of feeling. **3.** to manifest itself to: *music greets the ear.* **—*v.i.*** **4.** to give salutations on meeting. [ME *grete(n),* OE *grētan,* c. G *grüssen*] **—greet′er,** *n.* **—Syn. 1.** hail, accost.

greet[2] (grēt), *Archaic, Scot. and N Dial.* **—*v.i.* 1.** to weep; lament; grieve. **—*v.t.* 2.** to lament; bewail. [ME *grete,* OE *grētan,* north. var. of *grǣtan,* c. Icel. *grāta*]

greeting (grē′tĭng), *n.* **1.** the act or words of one who greets. **2.** (*usually pl.*) a friendly message: *send greetings.*

gregale (grĭ gā′lĭ), *n.* a north-eastern wind in the Mediterranean area. [t. It., t. LL: m. s. *Grecāl(is)* Greek]

gregarine (grĕg′ə rīn′, -rĭn), *n.* **1.** a type of sporozoan parasite that inhabits the digestive and other cavities of various invertebrates and produces cysts filled with spores. **—*adj.* 2.** having the characteristics of or pertaining to a gregarine or gregarines. [t. NL: m. s. *Gregarina,* der. L *gregārius* GREGARIOUS]

gregarious (grĭ gēə′rĭ əs), *adj.* **1.** living in flocks or herds, as animals. **2.** *Bot.* growing in open clusters; not matted together. **3.** fond of company; sociable. **4.** pertaining to a flock or crowd. [t. L: m. *gregārius*] **—gregar′iously,** *adv.* **—gregar′iousness,** *n.*

Gregg (grĕg), *n.* **John Robert,** 1867–1948, U.S. inventor of a shorthand system.

grego (grē′gō, grā′-), *n., pl.* **-gos.** a short coarse jacket or cloak with a hood, worn by the Greeks and the Levantines. [? t. Pg., g. L *Graecus* Greek, adj.]

Gregorian (grĭ gô′rĭ ən), *adj.* of or pertaining to any of the popes named Gregory.

Gregorian calendar, the reformed Julian calendar now in use, according to which the ordinary year consists of 365 days, and a leap year of 366 days occurs in every year whose number is exactly divisible by 4 except centenary years whose numbers are not exactly divisible by 400, as 1700, 1800, and 1900.

Gregorian chant, plainsong.

Gregorian telescope, a telescope similar to the Cassegrainian telescope, but less common.

Gregorian tones, tone (def. 8b).

Gregory (grĕg′ə rĭ), *n.* **Lady Augusta** (*Augusta Persse*), 1852–1932, Irish dramatist, poet, and writer.

Gregory I (grĕg′ə rĭ), **Saint** (*'Gregory the Great'*), A.D. *c.* 540–604, Italian cleric; pope A.D. 590–604.

Gregory VII, Saint (*Hildebrand*), *c.* 1020–1085, Italian ecclesiastic; pope 1073–85.

Gregory XIII, (*Ugo Buoncompagni*), 1502–85, Italian ecclesiastic; pope 1572–85: devised modern calendar.

Gregory of Nyssa (nĭs′ə), **Saint,** A.D. *c.* 335–*c.* 395, Christian bishop and theologian of Asia Minor.

Gregory of Tours, Saint, A.D. 538?–594, Frankish bishop and historian.

greisen (grī′zən), *n.* an altered rock of granitic texture composed chiefly of quartz and mica, common in the tin mines of Saxony. [t. G]

gremial (grē′mĭ əl), *n.* a cloth placed on a bishop's lap when he sits in celebrating mass or in conferring orders. [t. LL: s. *gremiālis* (as n., ML *gremiāle*), der. L *gremium* lap, bosom]

gremlin (grĕm′lĭn), *n.* a mischievous invisible being, said by airmen in World War II to cause engine trouble and mechanical difficulties. **—Syn.** See **goblin.**

Grenada (grĕ nā′də), *n.* a British colony in the Windward Islands, in the West Indies, consisting of the island of Grenada and the S part of the Grenadines. 88,677 pop. (1960); 133 sq. mi. *Cap.:* St George's.

grenade (grĭ nād′), *n.* **1.** a small explosive shell thrown by hand or fired from a rifle. **2.** a glass missile for scattering chemicals in order to put out fires, spread tear gas, etc. [t. F, t. Sp.: m. *granada* pomegranate, der. *granado* having grains, g. L *grānātus*]

grenadier (grĕn′ə dĭə′), *n.* **1.** (in the British Army) a member of the first regiment of household infantry (**Grenadier Guards**). **2.** (formerly) a soldier in an elite unit of men specially chosen for their height and strength. **3.** (formerly) a soldier who threw grenades. **4.** any of several fish of the family *Macuoridae*, deep-sea fish with sharp, pointed tails. [t. F, der. *grenade* GRENADE]

grenadin (grĕn′ə dĭn), *n.* a small slice of fillet of veal, larded, braised, and served with a vegetable garnish.

grenadine[1] (grĕn′ə dēn′), *n.* a thin dress fabric of leno weave in silk, nylon, rayon, or wool. [t. F, ? named after *Granada*, in Spain]

grenadine[2] (grĕn′ə dēn′, grĕn′ə dēn′), *n.* a syrup made from pomegranate juice, used as a sweetening and colouring agent. [t. F, dim. of *grenade* pomegranate. See GRENADE]

Grenadines (grĕn′ə dēnz′, grĕn′ə dēnz′), *n.pl.* a chain of ab. 600 islands in the West Indies belonging partly to Grenada and partly to St Vincent.

Grenfell (grĕn′fĕl), *n.* **Sir Wilfred Thomason,** 1865–1940, English physician and missionary in Labrador and Newfoundland.

Grenoble (grə nō′bl; *Fr.* grə nō′bl), *n.* a town in France, in Isère department, on the river Isère. 156,707 (1962).

Grenville (grĕn′vĭl), *n.* **1. George,** 1712–70, British statesman: prime minister 1763–65. **2. Sir Richard,** *c.* 1541–91, English naval commander. **3. William Wyndham (Baron Grenville),** 1759–1834, British statesman: prime minister 1806–07 (son of George Grenville).

Gresham (grĕsh′əm), *n.* **Sir Thomas,** 1519?–1579, English merchant and financier.

Gresham's law, *Econ.* the tendency of the inferior of two forms of currency to circulate more freely than, or to the exclusion of, the superior, because of the hoarding of the latter. [named after Sir Thomas GRESHAM]

gressorial (grĕ sô′rĭ əl), *adj. Zool.* adapted for walking, as the feet of some birds. [f. s. NL *gressōrius* + -AL[1]]

Gretna Green (grĕt′nə), a village in S Scotland, near the English border, to which couples used to elope to get married to avoid the need for parental consent.

Greuze (grûz; *Fr.* grœz), *n.* **Jean Baptiste** (*Fr.* zhäɴ bȧ tēst′), 1725–1805, French painter.

Greville (grĕv′ĭl), *n.* **Fulke, 1st Baron Brooke,** 1554–1628, English poet and statesman.

grew (groo͞), *v.* pt. of **grow.**

grewsome (groo͞′səm), *adj.* gruesome.

grey (grā), *adj.* **1.** of a colour between white and black, having no definite hue; ash-coloured; technically of an achromatic colour. **2.** dark, overcast, dismal, gloomy. **3.** grey-haired. **4.** pertaining to old age. **5.** old or ancient. **—*n.* 6.** any achromatic colour; any colour with zero chroma from white to black. **7.** something of this colour. **8.** grey material or clothing: *to dress in grey.* **9.** an unbleached and undyed condition. **10.** a grey horse. **—*v.t., v.i.* 11.** to make or become grey. Also, *Chiefly U.S.*, **gray.** [ME; OE *grǣg*, c. G *grau*] **—grey′ly,** *adv.* **—grey′ness,** *n.*

Grey (grā), *n.* **1. Charles, 2nd Earl Grey,** 1764–1845, British statesman; prime minister 1830–34. **2. Sir Edward, Viscount Fallodon,** 1862–1933, British statesman. **3. Sir George,** 1812–98, English statesman and colonial administrator: prime minister of New Zealand 1877–79. **4. Lady Jane** (*Lady Jane Dudley*), 1537–54, descendant of Henry VII; executed as usurper of the Crown.

greyback (grā′băk′), *n.* **1.** any of various animals, as a bird, the knot, *Tringa canutus*, and a whale, *Rhachianectes glaucus*, of the northern Pacific. **2.** *U.S. Colloq.* a Confederate soldier.

greybeard (grā′bĭəd′), *n.* **1.** a man whose beard is grey; old man; sage. **2.** a kind of earthenware or stoneware jug.

grey cast iron, *Metall.* a form of cast iron in which the carbon is present as graphite. Also, **grey iron.** See **white cast iron.**

greycing (grā′sĭng), *n. Colloq.* greyhound racing. Also, **gracing.**

grey duck, any of several ducks in which certain immature or female plumages are predominantly grey, as the gadwall, *Anas strepera*, and the pintail, *A. acuta.*

grey eminence, one who exercises power through another while keeping in the background. [trans. of F ÉMINENCE GRISE]

Grey Friar, a Franciscan friar.

grey-headed (grā′hĕd′ĭd), *adj.* **1.** having grey hair. **2.** of or pertaining to old men. **3.** of long duration; timeworn.

greyhen (grā′hĕn′), *n.* the female of the black cock.

greyhound (grā′hound′), *n.* **1.** one of a breed of tall, slender dogs, notable for keen sight and for fleetness. **2.** *Colloq.* a swift ship, esp. a fast ocean liner. [ME *gre(i)hound*, appar. t. Scand.; cf. Icel. *greyhundr*, f. *grey* dog, bitch + *hundr* HOUND[1]; r. OE *grighund*]

Greyhound
(28 in. high at shoulder)

greyish (grā′ĭsh), *adj.* having a tinge of grey; similar to grey.

greylag (grā′lăg′), *n.* the common grey wild goose, *Anser anser*, of Europe. Also, **grey goose.**

grey lourie, a bird, *Corythaixoides concolon* (family *Musophagidae*), grey in colour, the size of a large pigeon and with a crested head, inhabiting central and S Africa; go-away bird.

grey matter, 1. *Anat.* nervous tissue, esp. of the brain and spinal cord, containing both fibres and nerve cells, and of a dark reddish grey colour. **2.** *Colloq.* brains or intellect.

grey mould, 1. a plant disease, caused by any of several fungi, characterized by a grey, furry growth on the diseased parts. **2.** any of several fungi causing this, as *Botrytis cinerca.*

Greynville (grĕn′vĭl), *n.* **Sir Richard.** See **Grenville.**

grey parrot, an excellent talking bird, *Psittacus erithacus*, of Africa, very commonly kept as a pet.

grey plover, a large plover, *Squatarola squatarola*, of both the New and the Old World, called 'grey plover' in Europe because it is grey in winter plumage, 'black-bellied plover' in America because of the strikingly black underparts of the breeding plumage.

grey squirrel, a greyish-coloured American squirrel, *Sciurus carolinensis*, of eastern North America; now common in S England.

greywacke (grā′wăk′ə), *n. Geol.* a dark-coloured sandstone or grit, containing fragments of various rocks, such as slate or schist. [half trans., half adoption of G *Grauwache.* See WACKE]

grey wolf, the timber wolf.

gribble (grĭb′l), *n.* a small marine isopod crustacean, *Limnoria*, which destroys submerged timber by boring into it. [? akin to GRUB]

grid (grĭd), *n.* **1.** a grating of crossed bars; gridiron. **2.** *Elect.* a metallic framework employed in a storage cell or battery for conducting the electric current and supporting the active material. **3.** a network of cables, pipes, etc., for the distribution and supply of electricity, gas, water, etc. **4.** *Electronics.* the electrode in a radio valve, usually made of parallel wires, a helix or coil of wire, or a screen, and controlling the electron flow between the other electrodes. **5.** a network of horizontal and vertical lines superimposed on a map in order to give a basis for referring to points on the map. **6.** *Motor Racing.* starting grid. [back-formation from GRIDIRON]

grid bias, *Electronics.* a fixed voltage applied between the cathode and the grid of a radio valve.

grid circuit, *Electronics.* that part of a circuit which contains the cathode and the grid of a radio valve.

grid condenser, *Electronics.* a condenser arranged in series with the grid circuit.

grid current, *Electronics.* the current which moves within a radio valve from the grid to the cathode.

griddle (grĭd′l), *n., v.,* **-dled, -dling.** **—*n.* 1.** a flat, heated surface on top of a stove for cooking oatcakes, biscuits, etc. **—*v.t.* 2.** to cook on a griddle. Also, **girdle.** [ME *gredil*, t. OF: gridiron. See GRILL[1]]

griddlecake (grĭd′l kāk′), *n.* a thin cake of batter cooked on a griddle. Also, **girdlecake.**

gride (grīd), *v.,* **grided, griding,** *n.* **—*v.i.* 1.** to grate; grind; scrape harshly; make a grating sound. **—*v.t.* 2.** to pierce or cut. —*n.* **3.** a griding or grating sound. [metathetic var. of GIRD²]

gridiron (grĭd′ī′ən), *n.* **1.** a utensil consisting of parallel metal bars on which to grill meat, etc. **2.** any framework or network resembling a gridiron. **3.** *American Football.* the field of play, so called on account of the transverse white lines crossing it every five yards. **4.** a structure above the stage of a theatre, from which hung scenery, etc., is manipulated. [ME *gredirne*, etc., r. ME *gredire*, assimilated var. of *gredile* GRIDDLE; variants in *-irne*, *-iron* show pop. etymological assoc. with ME *iren*, *irne* iron]

grid leak, *Electronics.* a high-resistance device which permits excessive charges on the grid to leak off or escape.

grief (grēf), *n.* **1.** keen mental suffering or distress over affliction or loss; sharp sorrow; painful regret. **2.** a cause or occasion of keen distress or sorrow. **3. come to grief,** to come to a bad end; turn out badly. [ME, t. OF, der. *grever* GRIEVE] —**grief′less,** *adj.* —**Syn. 1.** anguish, heartache, woe; sadness. See **sorrow.**

grief-stricken (grēf′strĭk′ən), *adj.* stricken or smitten with grief or sorrow; afflicted.

Grieg (*Nor.* grēg), *n.* **Edvard** (*Nor.* ĕd′vȧrd), 1843–1907, Norwegian composer.

grievance (grē′vəns), *n.* **1.** a wrong, real or fancied, considered as grounds for complaint: *a popular grievance.* **2.** resentment or complaint, or the grounds for complaint, against an unjust act: *to have a grievance against someone.* —**Syn. 1.** injustice, injury.

grieve (grēv), *v.*, **grieved, grieving.** —*v.i.* **1.** to feel grief; sorrow. —*v.t.* **2.** to distress mentally; cause to feel grief or sorrow. **3.** *Obs.* to oppress or wrong. [ME *greve(n)*, t. OF: m. *grever*, ult. g. L *gravāre* weigh down] —**griev′er,** *n.* —**griev′ingly,** *adv.*

—**Syn. 1.** lament, weep. GRIEVE, MOURN imply showing suffering caused by sorrow. GRIEVE is the stronger word, implying deep mental suffering often endured alone and in silence, but revealed by one's aspect: *to grieve over the loss (or death) of a friend.* MOURN usually refers to manifesting sorrow outwardly, either with or without sincerity: *to mourn publicly and wear black.*

Grieve (grēv), *n.* **Christopher Murray.** See **McDiarmid, Hugh.**

grievous (grē′vəs), *adj.* **1.** causing grief or sorrow: *grievous news.* **2.** flagrant; atrocious: *a grievous fault.* **3.** full of or expressing grief; sorrowful: *a grievous cry.* **4.** *Archaic.* burdensome or oppressive. [ME *grevous*, t. OF, der. *grever* GRIEVE] —**griev′ously,** *adv.* —**griev′ousness,** *n.* —**Syn. 2.** deplorable, lamentable, calamitous, heinous.

Griff

griff (grĭf), *n.* *Archit.* an ornament at the base of a column, projecting from the torus towards a corner of the plinth. Also, **griffe.** [t. F: claw; of Gmc orig.]

griffin¹ (grĭf′ĭn), *n.* *Gk Myth.* a mythical monster, usually having the head and wings of an eagle and the body of a lion. Also, **griffon, gryphon.** [ME *griffon*, t. OF: m. *grifon*, der. L *grȳphus*, var. of *grýps*, t. Gk]

Griffin¹

griffin² (grĭf′ĭn), *n.* (in India and the East) a newcomer. [orig. uncert.]

Griffith (grĭf′ĭth), *n.* **D(avid) L(ewelyn) W(ark),** 1880–1948, U.S. film director.

griffon¹ (grĭf′ən), *n.* a vulture of the genus *Gyps*, esp. *G. fulvus* of southern Europe. [t. F. See GRIFFIN¹]

griffon² (grĭf′ən), *n.* **1.** a small, wiry-haired pet dog of Belgian origin. **2.** one of a breed of coarse-haired hunting dogs combining the qualities of the pointer and the setter. [t. F; akin to GRIFFIN¹]

griffon³ (grĭf′ən), *n.* griffin¹.

grig (grĭg), *n.* *Dial.* **1.** a cricket or grasshopper. **2.** a small or young eel. **3.** a lively person. [orig. uncert.]

Grignard reagent (grē′nyä, grē nyä′), *Chem.* any of a group of alkyl magnesium halides which are used in organic synthesis. [named after F. A. V. *Grignard*, 1871–1935, French organic chemist]

grigri (grē′grē), *n.*, *pl.* **-gris.** an African charm, amulet, or fetish. Also, **greegree.** [? t. Wolof]

grike (grīk), *n.* a furrow developed in a horizontal limestone surface by solution, usually along the line of a joint. Also, **gryke.**

grill¹ (grĭl), *n.* **1.** a grated utensil for broiling meat, etc., over a fire; gridiron. **2.** a dish of grilled meat, etc. **3.** grillroom. **4.** *Philately.* a series of small pyramidal impressions in parallel rows impressed or embossed on a stamp. —*v.t.* **5.** to broil on a gridiron or other apparatus over or before a fire. **6.** to torment with heat. **7.** to mark with a series of parallel bars like those of a grill. **8.** *Colloq.* to subject to severe and persistent cross-examination or questioning. —*v.i.* **9.** to undergo broiling. [t. F: m. *gril* gridiron, ult. g. L *crāticulum*, dim. of *crātis* wickerwork, hurdle. Cf. GRILLE] —**grill′er,** *n.*

grill² (grĭl), *n.* grille.

grillage (grĭl′ĭj), *n.* a framework of crossbeams used as a foundation on treacherous ground. [t. F, der. *grille.* See GRILL¹]

grille (grĭl), *n.* **1.** a lattice or openwork screen, as a window or gate, usually of metal and often of decorative design. **2.** a grating or screen in a ventilation system. **3.** an ornamental metal screen at the front of a motor car. **4.** *Real Tennis.* a square-shaped opening in the far corner of the court, on the side of the hazard. [t. F: grating. See GRILL¹] —**grilled,** *adj.*

Grillparzer (*Ger.* grĭl′pȧr tsər), *n.* **Franz** (*Ger.* frȧnts), 1791–1872, Austrian poet and dramatist.

grillroom (grĭl′ro͞om′), *n.* a room in a hotel or restaurant where meats, etc., are grilled and served.

grilse (grĭls), *n.*, *pl.* **grilse.** a salmon returning from the sea to the river for the first time. [ME; orig. unknown]

grim (grĭm), *adj.*, **grimmer, grimmest. 1.** stern; unrelenting; uncompromising: *grim necessity.* **2.** of a sinister or ghastly character; repellent: *a grim joke.* **3.** of a fierce or forbidding aspect: *a grim countenance.* **4.** fierce, savage, or cruel: *grim warrior.* **5.** *Colloq.* disagreeable; unpleasant. [ME and OE, c. OS, OHG *grim*, Icel. *grimmr*] —**grim′ly,** *adv.* —**grim′ness,** *n.* —**Syn. 1.** harsh, unyielding. **3.** severe, stern, harsh, hard. —**Ant. 3.** gentle.

grimace (grĭ mās′), *n.*, *v.*, **-maced, -macing.** —*n.* **1.** a wry face; facial contortion; ugly facial expression. —*v.i.* **2.** to make grimaces. [t. F, t. Sp.: m. *grimazo* panic, fear, der. *grima* fright, t. Goth.] —**grimac′er,** *n.*

Grimaldi (grĭ môl′dĭ), *n.* **Joseph,** 1779–1837, English comic actor, mime, and clown.

grimalkin (grĭ măl′kĭn), *n.* **1.** a cat. **2.** an old cat. **3.** an ill-tempered old woman. [appar. f. m. GREY + *malkin*, dim. of *Maud*, proper name]

grime (grīm), *n.*, *v.*, **grimed, griming.** —*n.* **1.** dirt or foul matter, esp. on or ingrained in a surface. —*v.t.* **2.** to cover with dirt; soil; make very dirty. [appar. special use of OE *grīma* mask, to denote layer of dust, etc., that forms on the face and elsewhere. Cf. Flem. *grym*]

Grimm (*Ger.* grĭm), *n.* **Jakob Ludwig Karl** (*Ger.* yä′kŏp lo͞ot′vĭKH kȧrl), 1785–1863, and his brother, **Wilhelm Karl** (*Ger.* vĭl′hĕlm kȧrl), 1786–1859, German philologists and collectors of fairytales.

Grimmelshausen (*Ger.* grĭm′əls hou zən), *n.* **Hans Jakob Christoffel von** (*Ger.* hȧns yä′kŏp krĭs′tŏf əl fŏn), *c.* 1620–76, German author.

Grimm's law (grĭmz), *Linguistics.* the statement of a system of consonant changes from primitive Indo-European into the Germanic languages, especially as differently reflected in Low and High German, formulated by Jakob Grimm during 1820–22 and independently recognized by Rasmus Rask (1818).

Grimond (grĭm′ənd), *n.* **Joseph** ('*Jo*'), born 1913, British politician: Liberal party leader 1957–67.

Grimsby (grĭmz′bĭ), *n.* a seaport in England, in N Lincolnshire, at the mouth of the Humber. 96,665 (1961).

grimy (grī′mĭ), *adj.*, **grimier, grimiest.** covered with grime; dirty. —**grim′ily,** *adv.* —**grim′iness,** *n.*

grin (grĭn), *v.*, **grinned, grinning,** *n.* —*v.i.* **1.** to smile broadly, or with a wide distension of the mouth. **2.** to draw back the lips so as to show the teeth, as a snarling dog or a person in pain. —*v.t.* **3.** to express or produce by grinning. —*n.* **4.** the act of grinning; a broad smile. **5.** the act of withdrawing the lips and showing the teeth. [ME *grinn(en)*, OE *grennian*] —**grin′ner,** *n.* —**grin′ningly,** *adv.* —**Syn. 1.** See **laugh.**

grind (grīnd), *v.*, **ground** or (*Rare*) **grinded, grinding,** *n.* —*v.t.* **1.** to wear, smooth, or sharpen by friction; whet: *to grind a lens, an axe, etc.* **2.** to reduce to fine particles, as by pounding or crushing; bray, triturate, or pulverize. **3.** to oppress or torment. **4.** to rub harshly or gratingly; grate together; grit: *to grind one's teeth.* **5.** to operate by turning a crank: *to grind a barrel organ.* **6.** to produce by pulverizing, turning a crank, etc.: *to grind flour.* —*v.i.* **7.** to perform the operation of reducing to fine particles. **8.** to rub harshly; grate. **9.** to be or become ground. **10.** to be polished or sharpened by friction. **11.** *Colloq.* to work or study laboriously. **12.** *Slang.* to rotate the pelvis, during or as during sexual intercourse or erotic dancing. —*n.* **13.** the act of grinding. **14.** a grinding sound. **15.** *Colloq.* laborious or monotonous work; close or laborious study. **16.** *Colloq.* a diligent or laborious student. [ME *grind(en)*, OE *grindan.* Cf. L *frendere* gnash the teeth, grind to pieces] —**grind′ingly,** *adv.* —**Syn. 2.** crush, powder, comminute. **3.** harass, persecute.

grindelia (grĭn dē′lĭ ə), *n.* **1.** any of the coarse, yellow-flowered asteraceous herbs constituting the genus *Grindelia.* **2.** the dried leaves and tops of certain species of this plant, used in medicine. [NL; named after D. H. *Grindel,* 1777–1836, Russian scientist]

grinder (grīn′də), *n.* **1.** one who or that which grinds. **2.** a sharpener of tools. **3.** a molar tooth.

grindery (grīn′də rĭ), *n.* **1.** materials and tools used by shoemakers. **2.** a place where tools, knives, etc., are ground.

grinding wheel, an abrasive wheel used for cutting and finishing metal.

grindstone (grīnd′stōn′), *n.* **1.** a rotating solid stone wheel used for sharpening, shaping, etc. **2.** a millstone.

gringo (grĭng′gō), *n., pl.* **-gos.** (among Spanish Americans) a foreigner, esp. an Anglo-Saxon. [Mex. Sp. use of Sp. *gringo* gibberish]

grip (grĭp), *n., v.,* **gripped** or **gript, gripping.** —*n.* **1.** the act of grasping; a seizing and holding fast; firm grasp: *the grip of a vice.* **2.** the power of gripping. **3.** a grasp, hold or control. **4.** a travelling bag; holdall. **5.** mental or intellectual hold; competence. **6.** a special mode of clasping hands. **7.** something which seizes and holds, as a clutching device on a cable car. **8.** a handle or hilt. **9.** a sudden, sharp pain; spasm of pain. **10.** grippe. **11. come (get) to grips with,** to deal with, tackle (an enemy, a problem, etc.) —*v.t.* **12.** to grasp or seize firmly; hold fast. **13.** to take hold on; hold the interest of: *to grip the mind.* **14.** to attach by a grip or clutch. —*v.i.* **15.** to take firm hold; hold fast. **16.** to take hold on the mind. [ME and OE *gripe* grasp, c. G *Griff,* OE *gripa* handful, sheaf. See GRIPE, v.] —**grip′per,** *n.* —**grip′pingly,** *adv.*

gripe (grīp), *v.,* **griped, griping,** *n.* —*v.t.* **1.** to seize and hold firmly; grip; grasp; clutch. **2.** to distress or oppress. **3.** to produce pain in (the bowels) as if by constriction. **4.** *Naut.* to secure (a ship's boat) on the deck or on the davits in order to prevent movement at sea. —*v.i.* **5.** to grasp or clutch, as a miser at gain. **6.** to suffer pain in the bowels. **7.** *Colloq.* to complain constantly; grumble. **8.** *Naut.* to tend to come up into the wind. —*n.* **9.** the act of griping, grasping, or clutching. **10.** a firm hold; clutch. **11.** a grasp; hold; control. **12.** that which grips or clutches; a claw or grip. **13.** *Naut.* **a.** cutwater (def. 1). **b.** (*pl.*) lashing by which a bbat is secured on the deck or on the davits of a ship. **14.** a handle, hilt, etc. **15.** (*usually pl.*) *Pathol.* an intermittent spasmodic pain in the bowels. [ME *gripe(n),* OE *grīpan,* c. D *grijpen,* G *greifen* gripe, seize. Cf. GRIP, GROPE] —**grip′er,** *n.*

grippe (grĭp), *n.* influenza. [t. F, der. *gripper* seize, b. with Russ. *khrip* hoarseness] —**grippe′like′,** *adj.*

gripsack (grĭp′săk′), *n. U.S.* a travelling bag; grip.

gript (grĭpt), *v. Poetic.* pt. and pp. of **grip.**

Griqua (grē′kwə, grĭk′wə), *n.* a person of mixed descent in the Republic of South Africa, esp. in Griqualand.

Griqualand (grĭk′wə lănd′), *n.* the name given to two districts in the Republic of South Africa: **1. Griqualand West,** in northern part of Cape Province. **2. Griqualand East,** part of the Transkei native reserve in eastern Cape Province.

Gris (*Sp.* grēs), *n.* **Juan** (*Sp.* KHwän), 1887–1927, Spanish painter.

grisaille (grĭ zāl′, *Fr.* grē zȧy′), *n.* **1.** monochromatic painting in shades of grey, usually representing objects in relief. **2.** a painting, a stained-glass window, etc., in this style. [t. F, der. *gris* grey. See GRIZZLE]

Griselda (grĭ zĕl′də), *n.* a woman of exemplary meekness and patience. [a character in Boccaccio, Chaucer, and elsewhere]

griseous (grĭs′ĭ əs, grĭz′-), *adj.* bluish or pearl grey. [t. ML: m. *griseus*]

grisette (grĭ zĕt′), *n.* a French working girl or shop-girl. [t. F: orig., a common grey fabric worn by working girls, der. *gris* grey. See GRIZZLE]

grisly (grĭz′lĭ), *adj.,* **-lier, -liest. 1.** such as to cause a shuddering horror; gruesome: *a grisly monster.* **2.** formidable; grim: *a grisly countenance.* [ME; late OE *grislic* horrible. Cf. OE *āgrīsan* shudder] —**gris′liness,** *n.*

grison (grī′sən, grĭz′ən), *n.* a musteline carnivore, *Grison vittata,* of South and Central America, having the upper surface of the body greyish white and the lower dark brown. [t. F, der. *gris* grey]

Grisons (grē′zŏn; *Fr.* grē zôɴ′), *n.* a canton in E Switzerland. 147,458 pop. (1960); 2747 sq. mi. *Cap.:* Chur. German, **Graubünden.**

grist (grĭst), *n.* **1.** corn to be ground. **2.** ground corn; meal produced from grinding. **3.** a quantity of malt for one brewing; the amount of meal from one grinding. **4.** *U.S. Colloq.* a quantity or lot. [ME; OE *grīst,* der. *grindan* GRIND]

gristle (grĭs′əl), *n.* cartilage. [ME and OE; c. OFris. and MLG *gristel.* Cf. OE *grost* cartilage]

gristly (grĭs′lĭ), *adj.* of the nature of, containing, or pertaining to gristle; cartilaginous.

gristmill (grĭst′mĭl′), *n.* a mill for grinding grain.

grit (grĭt), *n., v.,* **gritted, gritting.** —*n.* **1.** fine, stony, or hard particles such as are deposited like dust from the air or occur as impurities in food, etc. **2.** a coarse-grained siliceous rock, usually with sharp, angular grains. **3.** firmness of character; indomitable spirit; pluck. —*v.t.* **4.** to grate or grind: *to grit the teeth.* —*v.i.* **5.** to give forth a grating sound, as of sand under the feet; grate. [ME *gre(e)t,* OE *grēot,* c. G *Griess.* Cf. GRITS] —**grit′less,** *adj.*
—**Syn. 2.** sand, gravel. **3.** resolution, fortitude, courage.

grits (grĭts), *n.pl.* **1.** a grain, esp. oats, hulled and often coarsely ground. **2.** *U.S.* coarsely ground hominy. [ME *gryttes,* OE *gryttan* (pl.), c. G *Grütze*]

gritty (grĭt′ĭ), *adj.,* **-tier, -tiest. 1.** consisting of, containing, or resembling grit; sandy. **2.** resolute and courageous; plucky. —**grit′tily,** *adv.* —**grit′tiness,** *n.*

Grivas (grē′văs), *n.* **Georgios** (jô′jĭ əs), born 1898, Greek guerrilla leader in Cyprus.

grivet (grĭv′ĭt), *n.* a small Abyssinian monkey, *Cercopithecus aethiops,* with a greyish back, grey tail, black face, and dark extremities. [orig. unknown]

grizzle[1] (grĭz′əl), *v.,* **-zled, -zling,** *adj., n.* —*v.i., v.t.* **1.** to become or make grey. —*adj.* **2.** grey; devoid of hue. —*n.* **3.** grey hair. **4.** a grey wig. [ME *grisel,* t. OF, der. *gris* grey; of Gmc orig. (cf. G *greis* grey, hoary)]

grizzle[2] (grĭz′əl), *v.i.,* **-zled, -zling.** to whimper; whine; complain fretfully.

grizzled (grĭz′əld), *adj.* **1.** grey-haired, or partly grey-haired. **2.** grey.

grizzly (grĭz′lĭ), *adj.,* **-zlier, -zliest,** *n., pl.* **-zlies.** —*adj.* **1.** somewhat grey; greyish. **2.** grey-haired. —*n.* **3.** a grizzly bear.

grizzly bear, a large, ferocious bear, *Ursus horribilis,* of western North America, varying in colour from greyish to brownish.

Grizzly bear, *Ursus horribilis* (6 to 8½ ft long, 3 to 3½ ft high at the shoulder)

gro., gross; 144 articles.

groan (grōn), *n.* **1.** a low, mournful sound uttered in pain or grief. **2.** a deep murmur uttered in derision, disapproval, etc. **3.** a deep grating or creaking noise, as of wood, etc. —*v.i.* **4.** to utter a deep inarticulate sound expressive of grief or pain; moan. **5.** to make a sound similar to a groan; creak; resound harshly. **6.** to be overburdened or overloaded. **7.** to suffer lamentably (fol. by *beneath, under, with*) —*v.t.* **8.** to utter or salute with groans. [ME *grone(n),* OE *grānian,* akin to G *greinen* whine] —**groan′er,** *n.* —**groan′ing,** *n., adj.* —**groan′ingly,** *adv.*

—**Syn. 1.** GROAN, MOAN refer to sounds indicating suffering. A GROAN is a brief, strong, deep-throated sound emitted involuntarily under pressure of pain or suffering: *the wounded man groaned when they lifted him.* A MOAN is a prolonged, more or less continuous, low, inarticulate sound indicative of suffering, either physical or mental: *she was moaning after the operation.*

groat (grōt), *n.* an English silver coin, issued 1351–1662, worth fourpence. [ME *groot,* t. MD: lit., thick (coin)]

groats (grōts), *n.pl.* **1.** hulled and crushed (or whole) grain, as oats. **2.** the parts of oat kernels used as food. [ME *grotes,* OE *grotan* coarse meal. Cf. OE *grot* particle]

grocer (grō′sə), *n.* a dealer in general supplies for the table, as flour, sugar, coffee, etc., and in other articles of household use. [ME *grosser,* t. OF: m. *grossier,* ult. der. LL *grossus* gross]

grocery (grō′sə rĭ), *n., pl.* **-ceries. 1.** a grocer's store. **2.** (*usually pl.*) a commodity sold by grocers. **3.** the business of a grocer.

Grock (grŏk), *n.* (*Adrien Wettich*), 1880–1959, Swiss clown.

Grodno (*Russ.* grôd′nə), *n.* a town in the W Soviet Union, on the river Niemen: formerly Polish. 72,000 (1959).

grog (grŏg), *n.* **1.** a mixture of alcoholic drink, esp. rum, and water. **2.** strong drink. [said to be from 'Old *Grog*', nickname of Admiral Vernon (with allusion to his *grogram* cloak), who in 1740 ordered the mixture to be served instead of pure spirits to sailors]

groggery (grŏg′ə rĭ), *n., pl.* **-geries.** *U.S. Slang.* a saloon.

groggy (grŏg′ĭ), *adj.,* **-gier, -giest.** *Colloq.* **1.** staggering, as from exhaustion or blows. **2.** drunk; intoxicated. —**grog′gily,** *adv.* —**grog′giness,** *n.*

grogram (grŏg′rəm), *n.* a coarse fabric of silk, of silk and mohair or wool, or of wool, formerly in use. [t. F: m. *gros grain.* See GROSGRAIN]

grogshop (grŏg′shŏp′), *n.* (formerly) a cheap tavern.

groin (groin), *n.* **1.** *Anat.* the fold or hollow on either side of the body where the thigh joins the abdomen. **2.** *Archit.* the curved line or edge formed by the intersection of two vaults. **3.** groyne. —*v.t.* **4.** *Archit.* to form with groins. [earlier *gryne*, ME *grynde*. Cf. OE *grynde* abyss, akin to *grund* bottom, GROUND]

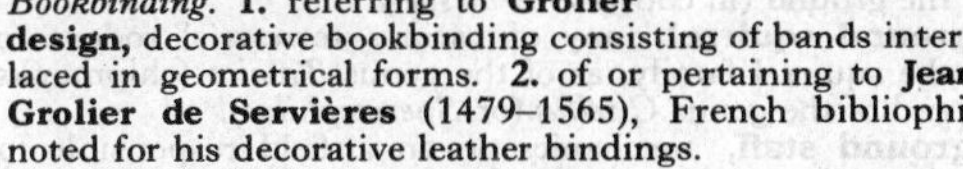

A, A, Groins (def. 2)

Grolier (grō′lĭ ə; *Fr.* grŏ lyĕ′), *adj. Bookbinding.* **1.** referring to **Grolier design,** decorative bookbinding consisting of bands interlaced in geometrical forms. **2.** of or pertaining to **Jean Grolier de Servières** (1479–1565), French bibliophil noted for his decorative leather bindings.

grommet (grŏm′ĭt), *n.* grummet.

gromwell (grŏm′wəl), *n.* any plant of the boraginaceous genus *Lithospermum*, comprising hairy herbs with varicoloured flowers and smooth, stony nutlets. [ME *gromyl*, t. OF: m. *gromil*, g. L *gruīnum milium* crane millet]

Gromyko (grŏ mē′kō; *Russ.* grà mĭ′kə), *n.* **Andrei Andreievich** (*Russ.* ăn dryĕy′ ăn dryĕ′yĭ vĭch), born 1909, Soviet statesman and diplomat.

Gronchi (grŏng′kĭ; *It.* grôn′kē), *n.* **Giovanni** (*It.* jō vän′nē), born 1887, Italian statesman: president 1955–62.

Groningen (grō′nĭng ən; *Du.* KHrō′nĭng ə), *n.* **1.** a province in the NE Netherlands. 508,173 pop. (1966); 923 sq. mi. **2.** its capital, in the central part. 152,513 (1965).

groom (grōōm, grŏŏm), *n.* **1.** a man or boy in charge of horses or the stable. **2.** a man newly married, or about to be married; bridegroom. **3.** any of several officers of a royal household. **4.** *Archaic.* a manservant. —*v.t.* **5.** to tend carefully as to person and dress: make neat or tidy. **6.** to tend (horses). **7.** to prepare for a position, election, etc.: *groom a political candidate.* [ME *grom(e)* boy, groom; cf. D *grom* offspring; appar. akin to GROW]

groom's cake, a fruit cake in layers of graduated sizes, served at a wedding.

groomsman (grōōmz′mən, grŏŏmz′-), *n., pl.* **-men.** a man who attends the bridegroom at a wedding.

Groote (grōōt; *Du.* KHrōt), *n.* **Gerhard** (gĕə′hät; *Du.* KHĕ′rōrt) (*Gerhardus Magnus*), 1340–84, Dutch religious reformer and founder of a monastic order ('Brothers of the Common Life'). Also, **Groot, Grœte.**

groove (grōōv), *n., v.,* **grooved, grooving.** —*n.* **1.** a furrow or channel cut by a tool. **2.** a rut, furrow, or channel formed by any agency. **3.** a fixed routine: *to get into a groove.* **4.** *Print.* the furrow at the bottom of a piece of type. See diag. under **type. 5.** the track of a gramophone record in which the needle or stylus rides. **6. in the groove,** *Slang.* in an excited or satisfied emotional state, as through listening to jazz. —*v.t.* **7.** to cut a groove in; furrow. **8.** to fix in a groove. [ME *grofe*, *groof* mining shaft, OE *grōf* ditch, sewer, c. G *Grube* ditch, pit; akin to GRAVE[1], GRAVE[3]] —**groove′less,** *adj.* —**groove′like′,** *adj.*

groovy (grōō′vĭ), *adj. Slang.* **1.** exciting, satisfying, or pleasurable, as jazz. **2.** appreciative: *a groovy audience.*

grope (grōp), *v.,* **groped, groping.** —*v.i.* **1.** to feel about with the hands; feel one's way. **2.** to search blindly or uncertainly. —*v.t.* **3.** to seek by or as by feeling. [ME *grop(i)en*, OE *grāpian*, der. *grāp*, n., grasp; akin to GRIPE, v.] —**grop′er,** *n.* —**grop′ingly,** *adv.*

groper (grō′pə), *n. Austral.* any fish of the genus *Oligoros.* [var. of GROUPER]

Gropius (grō′pĭ əs; *Ger.* grô′pē ōōs), *n.* **Walter** (wôl′tə; *Ger.* väl′tər), 1883–1969, German architect in the U.S.

Gros (*Fr.* grō), *n.* **Antoine Jean** (*Fr.* äN twän zhäN′), **Baron,** 1771–1835, French painter.

grosbeak (grōs′bēk′), *n.* any of various finches having a large, stout conical bill, as the pine grosbeak, *Pinicola enucleator.* [t. F: m. *grosbec* large beak]

groschen (grō′shən), *n., pl.* **-schen. 1.** an Austrian bronze coin valued at one hundredth of a schilling. **2.** *Colloq.* the 10-pfennig German nickel coin. **3.** a former small German silver coin. [t. G, f. MHG *grosse*, lit., thick (coin) + *-chen* dim. suffix. See GROSS]

gros de Londres (*Fr.* grō də lôN′dr), *French.* a cross-ribbed, silk dress fabric with ribs alternating in colour or in coarse and fine yarn.

gros de Naples (grō′də nā′plz), a silk fabric in plain weave, with more threads in the warp than the weft.

gros de Tours (grō′də tōōə′), a silk dress fabric with two- or three-fold warp in plain weave, and tram weft.

grosgrain (grō′grān′), *n.* heavy, corded, silk or rayon ribbon or fabric. [t. F: m. *gros grain* large grain. Cf. GROGRAM]

gros point (grō′point′), *pl.* **gros points.** a stitch in embroidery worked over a double-thread canvas; tent stitch. [t. F: large point]

gross (grōs), *adj., n., pl.* **grosses** for *6*, **gross** for 7; *v.* —*adj.* **1.** whole, entire, or total, esp. without having been subjected to deduction, as for charges, loss, etc.: *gross profits.* **2.** glaring or flagrant: *gross injustice.* **3.** morally coarse; lacking refinement; indelicate, or indecent: *gross tastes.* **4.** large, big, or bulky. **5.** thick; dense; heavy: *gross vegetation.* —*n.* **6.** the main body, bulk or mass. **7.** a unit consisting of twelve dozen, or 144. —*v.t.* **8.** to make a gross profit of; earn a total of. [ME, t. OF: m. *gros* large (as n., *grosse* twelve dozen), g. LL *grossus* thick] —**gross′ly,** *adv.* —**gross′ness,** *n.* —**Syn. 2.** shameful, outrageous, heinous. **3.** low, animal, sensual.

Grosseto (*It.* grōs sĕ′tō), *n.* a town in Italy, in SW Tuscany. 57,798 (1966).

gross ton, 2,240 lbs.

grossularite (grŏs′yōō lə rīt′), *n.* a mineral, calcium aluminium garnet, $Ca_3Al_2Si_3O_{12}$, occurring in crystals. [f. s. NL *grossulāria* gooseberry + -ITE[1]]

Grosswardein (*Ger.* grōs vär dīn′), *n.* German name of **Oradea.**

gross weight, total weight without deduction for tare, tret, or waste.

Grosz (grōs), *n.* **George,** 1893–1959, German painter, in the U.S. from 1932.

grot (grŏt), *n. Poetic.* a grotto. [t. F: m. *grotte*, t. It.: m. *grotta.* See GROTTO]

Grote (grōt), *n.* **George,** 1794–1871, English historian.

grotesque (grō tĕsk′), *adj.* **1.** fantastic in the shaping and combination of forms, as in decorative work combining incongruous human and animal figures with scrolls, foliage, etc. **2.** odd or unnatural in shape, appearance, or character; fantastically ugly or absurd; bizarre. —*n.* **3.** any grotesque object or thing. [t. F, t. It.: m. *grottesco* (as n., *grottesca* grotesque decoration, such appar. as was found in ancient excavated dwellings), der. *grotta.* See GROTTO] —**grotesque′ly,** *adv.* —**grotesque′ness,** *n.*

16th century grotesque work

grotesquerie (grō tĕs′kə rĭ), *n., pl.* **-queries. 1.** grotesque character. **2.** something grotesque. **3.** grotesque work. Also, **grotesquery.**

Grotius (grō′tĭ əs), *n.* **Hugo** (*Huig De Groot*), 1583–1645, Dutch jurist and statesman.

grotto (grŏt′ō), *n., pl.* **-toes, -tos. 1.** a cave or cavern. **2.** an artificial cavern-like recess or structure. [t. It.: m. *grotta*, g. VL *crupta*, in L *crypta* subterranean passage or chamber, crypt, t. Gk: m. *krýptē* vault]

grotty (grot′ĭ), *adj. Slang.* **1.** dirty; filthy. **2.** useless; rubbishy. [alter. of GROTESQUE]

grouch (grouch), *Colloq.* —*v.i.* **1.** to be sulky or morose; show discontent; complain. —*n.* **2.** a sulky or morose person. **3.** a sulky or morose mood. [var. of obs. *grutch*, t. OF: m. *groucher* grumble]

grouchy (grou′chĭ), *adj.,* **-chier, -chiest.** *Colloq.* sullenly discontented; sulky; morose; ill-tempered. —**grouch′ily,** *adv.* —**grouch′iness,** *n.*

Grouchy (*Fr.* grōō shē′), **Emmanuel** (*Fr.* ĕ mȧ nY ĕl′), **Marquis de,** 1766–1847, French general.

ground[1] (ground), *n.* **1.** the earth's solid surface; firm or dry land: *fall to the ground.* **2.** earth or soil: *stony ground.* **3.** land having a special character: *rising ground.* **4.** (*often pl.*) a tract of land occupied, or appropriated to a special use: *hospital grounds.* **5.** (*often pl.*) the foundation or basis on which a theory or action rests; motive; reason: *grounds for a statement.* **6.** a field of study; topic for discussion; subject of a discourse: *the inquiry covered a great deal of ground; the conversation touched on delicate ground.* **7.** the underlying or main surface or background, in painting, decorative work, lace, etc. **8.** (*pl.*) dregs or sediment: *coffee grounds.* **9.** *Elect.* earth (def. 11). **10.** *Music.* a ground bass. **11.** *Naut.* the solid bottom under water. **12.** *Com.* groundage. **13.** Some special noun phrases are:

break new ground, to begin a fresh operation.

common ground, matters on which agreement exists.

cut the ground from under one's feet, cut the ground from under someone, to anticipate the arguments, plans, etc., of another to his disconcertion.

down to the ground, *Colloq.* completely, entirely.

gain ground, to advance; make progress.

give ground, to give way.

hold or stand one's ground, to maintain one's position.

lose ground, 1. to lose what one has gained; retreat; give way. **2.** to become less well known or accepted.

run to ground, 1. to hunt down; track down. 2. *Hunting.* to pursue (an animal) to its burrow or hole.
shift one's ground, to take another position or defence in an argument or situation.
—*adj.* **14.** situated on or at, or adjacent to, the surface of the earth: *the ground floor.* **15.** pertaining to the ground. **16.** *Mil.* operating on land: ground forces. —*v.t.* **17.** to lay or set on the ground. **18.** to place on a foundation; found; fix firmly; settle or establish. **19.** to instruct in elements or first principles. **20.** to furnish with a ground or background on decorative work, etc. **21.** *U.S. Elect.* to establish an earth for (a circuit, device, etc.). **22.** *Naut.* to run aground. **23.** to prevent (an aircraft or a pilot) from flying. —*v.i.* **24.** to come to or strike the ground. [ME and OE *grund,* c. D *grond,* G *Grund* bottom, ground] —**Syn. 2.** land, mould, loam, earth. **5.** premise.
ground² (ground), *v.* **1.** pt. and pp. of **grind.** —*adj.* **2.** reduced to fine particles or dust by grinding. **3.** having the surface abraded or roughened by or as by grinding: *ground glass.* [see GRIND]
groundage (groun′dĭj), *n.* a tax levied on vessels stopping at a port.
ground bait, bait dropped to the bottom of the water.
ground bass (bās), *Music.* a short passage in bass continually repeated.
ground beetle, any of the numerous beetles of the family *Carabidae,* most of which are terrestrial.
ground cherry, a North American solanaceous herb, *Physalis pubescens,* cultivated for its yellow edible berry.
ground colour, 1. a primary coat of paint. **2.** the background or main colour of a painting, etc.
ground control, *Aeron.* a system in which information from ground radar installations about his position is continuously transmitted to a pilot to aid him in landing his aircraft.
ground crew, ground staff.
ground elder, bishop's weed, *Aegopodium podagraria.*
grounder (groun′də), *n.* *Baseball, etc.* a ball knocked or thrown along the ground and not rising into the air.
ground floor, 1. the floor at or near ground level. Cf. **first floor. 2.** *U.S. Colloq.* the most advantageous position or relationship in a business matter or deal.
ground glass, 1. glass whose polished surface has been removed by grinding, to diffuse light. **2.** glass ground into fine particles for use as an abrasive, etc.
ground hog, *U.S.* woodchuck.
ground ice, ice which forms below the surface of a body of water, as a lake, etc., and attaches itself to the bottom or to submerged objects. Also, **anchor-ice.**
grounding (groun′dĭng), *n.* fundamental knowledge of a subject: *a good grounding in mathematics.*
ground ivy, a trailing labiate herb, *Nepeta hederacea,* bearing blue flowers.
groundless (ground′lĭs), *adj.* without basis or reason: *groundless fears.* —**ground′lessly,** *adv.* —**ground′lessness,** *n.*
groundling (ground′lĭng), *n.* **1.** a plant or animal that lives on or close to the ground. **2.** any of various fishes that live at the bottom of the water. **3.** a spectator, reader, or other person of inferior tastes; an uncritical or uncultured person. **4.** *Obs.* a spectator in the pit of a theatre which formerly was literally on the ground.
ground loop, *Aeron.* a sharp horizontal loop performed, usually involuntarily, while touching the ground.
groundmass (ground′măs′), *n.* the crystalline, granular, or glassy base or matrix of a porphyry, in which the more prominent crystals are embedded.
groundnut (ground′nŭt′), *n.* **1.** a small papilionaceous herb from Brazil, *Arachis hypogaea,* widely grown for its valuable seed pods which are pushed underground by elongating stalks as they mature. **2.** its edible tuber pod, or the like.
ground owl, burrowing owl.
ground pine, 1. a European labiate herb, *Ajuga chamaepitys,* having a resinous odour. **2.** any of several species of club moss, particularly *Lycopodium obscurum* and *L. complanatum.*
ground plan, 1. the plan of a ground floor of a building. **2.** first or fundamental plan.
ground plate, 1. *Elect.* a metal plate used for making a ground connection to earth. **2.** a groundsel².
ground plum, 1. a leguminous plant, *Astragalus caryocarpus,* of the American prairie regions. **2.** its plum-shaped fruit.
ground rent, the rent at which land is leased to a tenant for a specified term, usually ninety-nine years.
groundsel¹ (groun′səl), *n.* any plant of the genus *Senecio* of the aster family, as *S. vulgaris,* a weed bearing small yellow flowers. [ME *grundeswilie,* etc., OE *g(r)undeswelge,* etc., appar. f. *gund* pus + *swelgan* swallow (from its use in medicine); or f. *grund* ground + *swelgan* (from its speed in spreading)]
groundsel² (ground′səl), *n.* the lowest horizontal timber of a frame or building lying next to the ground. Also, **groundsill, groundsell.**
groundsheet (ground′shēt′), *n.* a waterproof sheet spread on the ground to give protection against dampness.
groundsman (groundz′mən), *n., pl.* **-men.** a man responsible for the care and maintenance of a cricket ground, sports field, etc.
ground speed, the speed of an aircraft in reference to the ground (in contrast to *airspeed*).
ground squirrel, any of various terrestrial rodents of the squirrel family, as of the genus *Tamias* (chipmunks) and of the genus *Citellus* (or *Spermophilus*).
ground staff, mechanics on an airfield responsible for the maintenance of aircraft; non-flying personnel on an airfield.
ground state, *Physics.* the most stable energy state of a particle, nucleus, atom, or molecule.
ground swell, a broad, deep swell or rolling of the sea, due to a distant storm or gale.
ground water, the water beneath the surface of the ground, consisting largely of surface water that has seeped down; the source of water in springs and wells.
ground wave, *Radio.* a radio wave which travels close to the surface of the ground (opposed to *sky wave*). Also, **direct wave, ground ray.**
groundwork (ground′wûk′), *n.* the foundation, base, or basis of anything.
ground zero, the point on the surface of the earth directly below the point at which a nuclear weapon explodes, or the centre of the crater if the weapon is exploded on the ground.
group (groo͞p), *n.* **1.** any assemblage of persons or things; cluster; aggregation. **2.** a number of persons or things ranged or considered together as being related in some way. **3.** *Ethnol.* a classification more limited than a branch. **4.** a number of businesses, companies, etc., administratively and financially connected. **5.** *Chem.* **a.** a number of atoms in a molecule connected or arranged together in some manner; a radical: the hydroxyl group, = OH. **b.** a vertical column of the periodic table containing elements with similar properties. **6.** *Linguistics.* **a.** a subdivision of a family, usually the greatest. **b.** any grouping of languages, whether geographically, on the basis of relationship, or otherwise. **7.** *Geol.* a division of stratified rocks comprising two or more formations. **8.** *Mil.* **a.** a force, composed of units or sub-units of different arms, e.g. battalion group or brigade group. **b.** (in the Royal Air Force) an operational and administrative subdivision of a command. **9.** *Music.* a section of an orchestra, comprising the instruments of the same class. **10.** *Art.* a number of figures or objects arranged together. **11.** blood group. —*v.t.* **12.** to place in a group, as with others. **13.** to arrange in or form into a group or groups. —*v.i.* **14.** to form a group. **15.** to be part of a group. [t. F: m. *groupe,* t. It.: m. *gruppo;* ult. of Gmc orig.]
group captain, a commissioned rank in the Royal Air Force above that of wing-commander and below air commodore; equivalent to colonel.
grouper (groo͞′pə), *n., pl.* **-pers,** (*esp. collectively*) **-per.** any of various serranoid fishes, esp. of the genus *Epinephelus,* as *E. morio* (**red grouper**), an important food fish of the southern Atlantic coast of the U.S., West Indies, etc. [t. Pg.: m. *garupa,* appar. repr. some S Amer. name]
grouping (groo͞′pĭng), *n.* **1.** the act of forming a group. **2.** an arrangement in a group.
group marriage, a form of marriage in which a group of males are united with a group of females to form a single conjugal unit.
grouse¹ (grous), *n., pl.* **grouse.** any of numerous gallinaceous birds of the family *Tetraonidae,* including such important game species as the **red grouse** (*Lagopus scoticus*) of Great Britain, **black grouse** (*Lyrurus tetrix*) and capercailzie or **woodgrouse** (*Tetrao urogallus*) of Europe, and **spruce grouse** (*Canachites canadensis*) and **ruffed grouse** (*Bonasa umbellus*) of North America. [orig. uncert.] —**grouse′like′,** *adj.*

Ruffed grouse, *Bonasa umbellus* (18 in. long)

grouse² (grous), *v.,* **groused, grousing,** *n., Colloq.* —*v.i.* **1.** to grumble; complain. —*n.* **2.** a complaint. [orig. unknown. Cf. GROUCH] —**grous′er,** *n.*
grout (grout), *n.* **1.** a thin coarse mortar poured into the

joints of masonry and brickwork. **2.** a fine finishing plaster for walls and ceilings. **3.** (*usually pl.*) lees or grounds. **4.** coarse meal or porridge. **5.** (*pl.*) groats. —*v.t.* **6.** to fill up, form, or finish the spaces between (stones, etc.) with grout. **7.** to use as grout. [OE *grūt*; akin to GRITS, GROATS, and GRIT]

grove (grōv), *n.* a small wood or plantation of trees. [ME; OE *grāf*] —**Syn.** See **forest.**

Grove (grōv), *n.* **Sir George,** 1820–1900, English musicologist.

grovel (grŏv′əl), *v.i.*, **-elled, -elling** or (*U.S.*) **-eled, -eling. 1.** to humble oneself or act in an abject manner, as in fear or in mean servility. **2.** to lie or move with the face downwards and the body prostrate, esp. in abject humility, fear, etc. [back-formation from *grovelling*, adv. (f. obs. *grufe* face down (t. Scand.) + -LING²), taken for ppr.]

grow (grō), *v.*, **grew, grown, growing.** —*v.i.* **1.** to increase by natural development, as any living organism or part by assimilation of nutriment; increase in size or substance. **2.** to arise or issue as from a germ, stock, or originating source. **3.** to increase gradually; become greater. **4.** to become gradually attached or united by or as by growth. **5.** to come to be, or become, by degrees: *to grow old.* **6. grow up, a.** to increase in growth; attain maturity. **b.** to spring up; arise. —*v.t.* **7.** to cause to grow: *he grows corn.* **8.** to allow to grow: *to grow a beard.* **9.** to cover with a growth (used in the passive): *a field grown with corn.* **10. grow on, a.** to obtain an increasing influence, effect, etc. **b.** to win the affection or admiration of by degrees. **11. grow out of, a.** to become too big or too mature for; outgrow. **b.** to develop from; originate in. [ME *growe(n)*, OE *grōwan*, akin to D *groeien*, OHG *gruwan*, Icel. *grōa*. Cf. GRASS, GREEN]

grower (grō′ə), *n.* **1.** one who grows anything. **2.** a plant that grows in a certain way: *a quick grower.*

growing pains, 1. dull, indefinite pains in the limbs during childhood and adolescence, often popularly associated with the process of growing. **2.** difficulties attending any new project.

growl (groul), *v.i.* **1.** to utter a deep guttural sound of anger or hostility: *a dog growls.* **2.** to murmur or complain angrily; grumble. **3.** to rumble. —*v.t.* **4.** to express by growling. —*n.* **5.** the act or sound of growling. [ME *groule* rumble (said of the bowels), c. G *grollen* rumble] —**growl′ingly,** *adv.* —**Syn. 2.** See **complain.**

growler (grou′lə), *n.* **1.** one who or that which growls. **2.** *Slang.* a four-wheeled hansom cab. **3.** *U.S. Slang.* a pitcher, pail, or other vessel brought by a customer for beer.

grown (grōn), *adj.* **1.** advanced in growth: *a grown boy.* **2.** arrived at full growth or maturity; adult: *a grown man.* —*v.* **3.** pp. of **grow.**

grown-up (grōn′ŭp′), *adj.* **1.** having reached the age of maturity. **2.** characteristic of or suitable for adults. —*n.* **3.** a grown-up person; an adult.

growth (grōth), *n.* **1.** the act, process, or manner of growing; development; gradual increase. **2.** stage of development. **3.** something that has grown or developed by or as by a natural process; a product: *a growth of weeds.* **4.** *Pathol.* a morbid mass of tissue, as a tumour. **5.** a source; origin: *vegetables of English growth.* —**Syn. 1.** augmentation, expansion.

groyne (groin), *n.* a small jetty built out into the sea or a river in order to prevent erosion of the beach or bank. Also, **groin.**

Grozny (*Russ.* grôz′nĭy), *n.* a city in the S Soviet Union in Europe, in Caucasia. 314,000 (est. 1965).

grub (grŭb), *n.*, *v.*, **grubbed, grubbing.** —*n.* **1.** the bulky larva of certain insects, esp. of scarabaeid and other beetles. **2.** a dull, plodding person; drudge. **3.** *Slang.* food or victuals. —*v.t.* **4.** to dig; clear of roots, etc. **5.** to dig up by the roots; uproot (often fol. by *up* or *out*). **6.** *Slang.* to supply with food. —*v.i.* **7.** to dig; search by or as by digging. **8.** to lead a laborious or grovelling life; drudge. **9.** to make laborious research; study closely. **10.** *Slang.* to take 'grub' or food. [ME *grubbe(n)* dig. Cf. G *grübeln* grub, rake, rack (the brains), Icel. *gryfja* hole, pit; prob. akin to GRAVE¹] —**grub′ber,** *n.*

grubby (grŭb′ĭ), *adj.*, **-bier, -biest. 1.** dirty; slovenly. **2.** infested with or affected by grubs or larvae. [f. GRUB, n. + -Y¹] —**grub′bily,** *adv.* —**grub′biness,** *n.*

grub hoe, a heavy hoe for grubbing up roots, etc.

grubsaw (grŭb′sô′), *n.* a saw for cutting stone by hand.

grubscrew (grŭb′skrōō′), *n.* setscrew.

grubstake (grŭb′stāk′), *n.*, *v.*, **-staked, -staking.** *U.S.* —*n.* **1.** provisions, outfit, etc., furnished to a prospector or the like, on condition of participating in the profits of his discoveries. —*v.t.* **2.** to furnish with a grubstake.

Grub Street, a London street (now Milton Street) once much inhabited by needy authors and literary hacks.

grubstreet (grŭb′strēt′), *adj.* produced by a hack; of poor quality: *grubstreet books.*

grudge (grŭj), *n.*, *v.*, **grudged, grudging.** —*n.* **1.** a feeling of ill will or resentment excited by some special cause, as a personal injury or insult, etc. —*v.t.* **2.** to give or permit with reluctance; submit to unwillingly. **3.** to be dissatisfied at seeing the good fortune of (another). —*v.i.* **4.** to feel dissatisfaction or ill will. [earlier *grutch*, ME *gruche(n)*, t. OF: m. *gruchier*, *groucier* murmur, grumble; orig. uncert. Cf. GROUCH] —**grudge′less,** *adj.* —**grudg′er,** *n.* —**grudg′ingly,** *adv.*

—**Syn. 1.** GRUDGE, MALICE, SPITE refer to ill will held against another or others. A GRUDGE is a feeling of resentment harboured because of some real or fancied wrong: *to hold a grudge because of jealousy, she has a grudge against him.* MALICE is the state of mind which delights in doing harm, or seeing harm done, to others, whether expressing itself in an attempt seriously to injure or merely in sardonic humour: *malice in watching someone's embarrassment, to tell lies about someone out of malice.* SPITE is petty, and often sudden, resentment that manifests itself usually in trifling retaliations: *to reveal a secret out of spite, to build a high fence between properties out of spite.* **3.** begrudge, envy.

gruel (grōō′əl), *n.*, *v.*, **-elled, -elling** or (*U.S.*) **-eled, -eling.** —*n.* **1.** a light, usually thin, cooked cereal made by boiling meal, esp. oatmeal, in water or milk. **2.** any similar substance. —*v.t.* **3.** to punish or use severely; exhaust; disable. [ME, t. OF: meal, g. dim. of ML *grūtum*, t. Gmc. Cf. GROUT]

gruelling (grōō′ə lĭng), *adj.* **1.** exhausting; very tiring; severe. —*n.* **2.** any trying or exhausting procedure or experience. Also, *U.S.*, **grueling.**

gruesome (grōō′səm), *adj.* such as to make one shudder; inspiring horror; revolting. Also, **grewsome.** [f. *grue*, v., shudder (c. G *grauen*, Dan. *grue*) + -SOME¹. Cf. G *grausam* horrible] —**grue′somely,** *adv.* —**grue′someness,** *n.*

gruff (grŭf), *adj.* **1.** low and harsh; hoarse: *a gruff voice.* **2.** rough; surly: *a gruff manner.* [earlier *grof*, t. D, f. *ge-* prefix (c. OE *ge-*) + *rof*, akin to OE *hrēof* rough] —**gruff′ly,** *adv.* —**gruff′ness,** *n.* —**Syn. 1.** harsh. **2.** grumpy, brusque. —**Ant. 1.** pleasant. **2.** courteous.

grugru (grōō′grōō), *n.* any of several spiny palms of tropical America, esp. *Acrocomia sclerocarpa.*

grumble (grŭm′bl), *v.*, **-bled, -bling,** *n.* —*v.i.* **1.** to murmur in discontent; complain ill-humouredly. **2.** to utter low, indistinct sounds; growl. **3.** to rumble: *the thunder grumbled.* —*v.t.* **4.** to express or utter with murmuring or complaining. —*n.* **5.** an ill-humoured complaining; murmur; growl. **6.** (*pl.*) a grumbling, discontented mood. **7.** a rumble. [? freq. of OE *grymman* wail, mourn. Cf. OE *grymettan* grunt, roar, rage, G *grummeln* rumble, F *grommeter* mutter] —**grum′bler,** *n.* —**grum′blingly,** *adv.* —**Syn. 1.** See **complain.**

grume (grōōm), *n.* **1.** a thick, viscous fluid. **2.** *Med.* a clot of blood. [t. LL: m. s. *grūmus* little heap]

grummet (grŭm′ĭt), *n.* **1.** *Mach.* a ring or eyelet of metal, rubber, etc. **2.** *Naut.* an eyelet of rope, metal, or the like, as on the edge of a sail. Also, **grommet.** [t. F: m. *grommette* (obs.) curb of bridle, ult. der. LL *grumus* throat]

grumous (grōō′məs), *adj.* *Bot.* formed of clustered grains, granules, etc., as certain roots. Also, **grumose** (grōō′mōs). [f. *grume* (t. L: m. s. *grūmus* little heap, hillock) + -OUS]

grumpy (grŭm′pĭ), *adj.*, **-pier, -piest.** surly; ill-tempered. [f. *grump* the sulks (b. GRUNT and DUMP) + -Y¹] —**grump′ily,** *adj.* —**grump′iness,** *n.*

Grundyism (grŭn′dĭ ĭz′əm), *n.* prudery; narrow-mindedness; excessive attachment to conventional behaviour. [after Mrs *Grundy*, a person mentioned in Thomas Morton's play *Speed the Plough* (1798)]

Grünewald (*Ger.* grʏ′nə vȧlt), *n.* **Matthias** (*Ger.* mȧ tē′ȧs), *c.* 1470–1528, German painter.

Grunitsky (grōō nĭt′skĭ), *n.* **Nicolas,** 1913–69, Togolese statesman: president of the Republic of Togo 1963–67.

grunt (grŭnt), *v.i.* **1.** to utter the deep guttural sound characteristic of a pig. **2.** to utter a similar sound. **3.** to grumble, as in discontent. —*v.t.* **4.** to express with a grunt. —*n.* **5.** the sound of grunting. **6.** any of various marine fishes of the family *Pomadasyidae* which can emit a grunting sound, as *Pomadasys operculare* of S African waters. [ME *grunten*, OE *grunnettan*, freq. of *grunian* grunt. Cf. G *grunzen*, L *grunnire*] —**grunt′ingly,** *adv.*

grunter (grŭn′tə), *n.* **1.** a pig. **2.** any animal or person that grunts. **3.** grunt (def. 6).

Gruyère (grōō′yĕə; *Fr.* grʏ yĕr′), *n.* a firm, pale yellow variety of French and Swiss cheese with many holes. [named after *Gruyère*, district in Switzerland]

gryke (grīk), *n.* grike.

gryphon (grĭf′ən), *n.* griffin.

grysbok (grās′bŏk, grĭs′-), *n.* a small hardy antelope of southern Africa, *Nototragus melanotis.* [t. Afrikaans: grey buck]

G-string (jē′strĭng′), *n.* **1.** a loincloth or breechcloth. **2.** a similar covering, usually decorated, worn by women entertainers for striptease dancing, etc. [orig. uncert.]

G-suit (jē′syōōt′), *n.* a garment which under high positive acceleration exerts pressure on the abdomen and lower parts of the body to retard the flow of blood away from the upper part.

gt, great

Gt Br., Great Britain. Also, **Gt Brit.**

gtd, guaranteed.

G.U., genito-urinary.

guacharo (gwä′chə rō′), *n.*, *pl.* **-ros.** a nocturnal fruit-eating South American bird, *Steatornis caripensis*, valued by the natives for the oil produced from the fat of the young. [t. Sp., t. Araucanian: m. *uachar* cave]

guaco (gwä′kō), *n.*, *pl.* **-cos. 1.** a climbing asteraceous plant, *Mikania guaco*, of tropical America. **2.** its medicinal leaves, or a substance obtained from them, used as an antidote for snakebites. **3.** a tropical American plant, *Aristolochia maxima*, also used for snakebites. [t. Sp.; from native name]

Guadalajara (*Sp.* gwä dä lä KHä′rä), *n.* a city in W Mexico. 1,048,351 (est. 1965).

Guadalcanal (gwŏd′l kə năl′; *Sp.* gwä däl kä näl′), *n.* one of the Solomon Islands in the S Pacific: U.S. victory over the Japanese, 1942–43. 14,000 pop. (est. 1951); ab. 2500 sq. mi.

Guadalquivir (gwŏd′l kwĭ vĭə′; *Sp.* gwä däl kē bēr′), *n.* a river in S Spain, flowing W to the Gulf of Cadiz. 374 mi.

Guadalupe Hidalgo (*Sp.* gwä dä lōō′pē ē däl′gō), a city in the Federal District of Mexico: famous shrine; peace treaty, 1848. 60,239 (1950). Official name, **Gustavo A. Madero.**

Guadeloupe (gwä′də lōōp′), *n.* two islands separated by a narrow channel in the Leeward Islands of the West Indies: together with five dependencies they form a department of France. 283,223 pop. (1961); 687 sq. mi. *Cap.:* Basse-Terre.

Guadiana (*Sp.* gwä dyä′nä), *n.* a river flowing from central Spain S through SE Portugal to the Gulf of Cadiz. 515 mi.

guaiacol (gwī′ə kŏl′), *n.* *Chem.* a colourless liquid, $CH_3OC_6H_4OH$, resembling creosote, obtained by distillation from guaiacum resin, and in other ways: used to treat phthisis, bronchitis, etc. [f. GUAIAC(UM) + -OL[2]]

guaiacum (gwī′ə kəm), *n.* **1.** any of the hard-wooded tropical American trees and shrubs constituting the zygophyllaceous genus *Guaiacum*, esp. *G. officinale* of the West Indies and South America, and *G. sanctum* of the West Indies and Florida. **2.** the hard, heavy wood of such a tree. See **lignum vitae** (def. 1). **3.** a greenish brown resin obtained from such a tree, used as a remedy for rheumatism, cutaneous eruptions, etc. Also, **guaiac** (gwī′ăk). [NL, der. Sp. *guayaco*; from Haitian]

Guaira (*Sp.* gwäy′rä), *n.* **La.** See **La Guaira.**

Guam (gwäm), *n.* an island belonging to the U.S. in the N Pacific, E of the Philippine Islands: the largest of the Marianas group; U.S. naval base. 67,044 pop. (1960); 206 sq. mi. *Cap.:* Agaña.

guan (gwän), *n.* any of various large gallinaceous birds constituting the subfamily *Penelopinae* (family *Cracidae*), chiefly of Central and South America, allied to the curassows. [? of W Ind. orig.]

guanaco (gwä nä′kō), *n.*, *pl.* **-cos.** a wild South American ruminant, *Lama guanicoe*, of which the llama and alpaca are thought to be domesticated varieties, related to the camels. [t. Sp., t. Quechua: m. *huanacu*]

Guanaco, *Lama guanicoe* (3 ft high at the shoulder)

guanase (gwä′nās), *n.* *Biochem.* an enzyme found in thymus, adrenals, and pancreas which converts guanine into xanthine. [f. GUAN(INE) + -ASE]

guanidine (gwä′nĭ dĭn, -dēn′), *n.* a strongly caustic substance, $HN{:}C(NH_2)_2$, forming crystalline salts and a wide variety of organic derivatives: used in the manufacture of plastics, resins, rubber accelerators, explosives, etc. Also, **guanidin** (gwăn′ĭ dĭn, gwä′nĭ-). [der. GUANINE with infixed -ID[3]]

guanine (gwä′nēn, gōō′ə nēn′), *n.* *Biochem.* a purine base, $C_5H_5N_5O$, present in all living cells, mainly in combined form, as in nucleic acids; it is also found in guano. [f. GUANO + -INE[2]]

guano (gwä′nō), *n.*, *pl.* **-nos. 1.** a natural manure composed chiefly of the excrement of seabirds, found esp. on islands near the Peruvian coast. **2.** any similar substance, as an artificial fertilizer made from fish. [t. Sp., t. Quechua: m. *huanu* dung]

guanosine (gwä′nə sĭn, -sēn′), *n.* *Biochem.* a compound of guanine and ribose, present in all living cells, mainly in combined form, as in ribonucleic acids.

Guantánamo (*Sp.* gwän tä′nä mō), *n.* a town in SE Cuba. 124,685 (1960).

Guantánamo Bay, a bay on the SE coast of Cuba: U.S. naval station.

guanylic acid (gwä′nĭ lĭk, gwə nĭl′ĭk), *Biochem.* the monophosphate of guanosine, present in all living cells, mainly in combined form, as in ribonucleic acids.

Guaporé (*Sp.* gwä pō rē′), *n.* a river forming part of the boundary between Brazil and Bolivia, flowing NW to the Mamoré river. ab. 900 mi.

guarana (gwə rä′nə), *n.* **1.** a dried paste made from the seeds of a Brazilian shrub, *Paullinia cupana.* **2.** a drink made from this. [t. Sp. or Pg., t. Tupi]

guarani (gwä′rə nĭ), *n.*, *pl.* **-ni, -nis.** the monetary unit of Paraguay, equal to 100 céntimos, and equivalent to about ⅜d. sterling (£0·003).

Guaraní (gwä′rə nē′), *n.*, *pl.* **-nís, -níes,** (*esp. collectively*) **-ni. 1.** an important central South American tribe of Tupian family and affiliation. **2.** a member of this tribe. **3.** the Tupian language of the Guaraní tribe.

guarantee (găr′ən tē′), *n.*, *v.*, **-teed, -teeing.** —*n.* **1.** guaranty (def. 1). **2.** a promise or assurance, esp. one given in writing by a manufacturer, that something is of a specified quality, and generally including an undertaking to make good any defects under certain conditions. **3.** one who gives a guarantee or guaranty; guarantor. **4.** one to whom a guarantee is made. **5.** guaranty (def. 2). **6.** something that has the force or effect of a guaranty: *wealth is no guarantee of happiness.* —*v.t.* **7.** to secure, as by giving or taking security. **8.** to make oneself answerable for on behalf of one primarily responsible: *to guarantee the carrying out of a contract.* **9.** to undertake to secure to another, as rights or possessions. **10.** to serve as a warrant or guarantee for. **11.** to engage (to do something). **12.** to engage to protect or indemnify (fol. by *from*, *against*, or *in*): *to guarantee one against loss.* **13.** to promise. [appar. for GUARANTY]

guarantor (găr′ən tô′), *n.* one who makes or gives a guarantee or guaranty.

guaranty (găr′ən tĭ), *n.*, *pl.* **-ties,** *v.*, **-tied, -tying.** —*n.* **1.** a warrant, pledge, or promise accepting responsibility for the discharging of another's liabilities, as the payment of a debt. **2.** that which is taken or presented as security. **3.** the act of giving security. **4.** one who acts as a guarantor. —*v.t.* **5.** to guarantee. [t. AF: m. *guarantie*, der. *guarant*, *warant* WARRANT]

guard (gäd), *v.t.* **1.** to keep safe from harm; protect; watch over. **2.** to keep under close watch in order to prevent escape, outbreaks, etc.: *to guard a prisoner.* **3.** to keep in check, from caution or prudence: *to guard the tongue.* **4.** to provide with some safeguard or protective appliance, etc. —*v.i.* **5.** to take precautions (fol. by *against*): *to guard against errors.* **6.** to give protection; keep watch; be watchful. —*n.* **7.** one who guards, protects, or keeps a protecting or restraining watch. **8.** one who keeps watch over prisoners or others under restraint. **9.** a body of men, esp. soldiers, charged with guarding a place from disturbance, theft, fire, etc. **10.** restraining watch, as over a prisoner or other person under restraint: *to be kept under close guard.* **11.** a contrivance, appliance, or attachment designed for guarding against injury, loss, etc. **12.** something intended or serving to guard or protect; a safeguard. **13.** a posture of defence or readiness, as in fencing, boxing, bayonet drill, etc. **14.** (*cap., pl.*) Life Guards, Horse Guards, etc. **15.** *American Football.* either of two players holding a position of defence at the right and left of the centre, in the forward line. **16.** *Basketball.* one of the defensive players in a team. **17.** an official in general charge of a railway train. **18. off one's guard.** Also, **off guard.** unprepared to meet a sudden attack; unwary. **19. on one's guard.** Also, **on guard.** watchful or vigilant against attack; cautious; wary. [ME *garde*, t. F, of Gmc orig.; see WARD] —**guard′able,** *adj.* —**guard′er,** *n.* —**Syn. 1.** shield, safeguard; preserve, save. See **defend. 7.** defender, protector; watchman; sentry, sentinel, patrol. **12.** defence, protection; bulwark, shield.

Guardafui (gwä′də fōō′ĭ), *n.* **Cape,** a cape at the E extremity of Africa in NE Somalia.

guardant (gä′dnt), *adj.* *Her.* (of an animal) shown full face, with the body seen from the side. Also, **gardant.** [t. F: m. *gardant*, ppr. of *garder*]

guard cell, *Bot.* either of two specialized epidermal cells which flank the pore of a stoma and usually cause it to open and close.

guard commander, *Mil.* a non-commissioned officer in charge of a guard.

guarded (gä′dĭd), *adj.* **1.** cautious; careful: *to be guarded in one's speech.* **2.** protected or watched, as by a guard. —**guard′edly,** *adv.* —**guard′edness,** *n.*

Guardi (*It.* gwär′dē), *n.* **Francesco** (*It.* frän chĕs′kō), 1712–93, Italian painter.

guardian (gä′dyən), *n.* **1.** one who guards, protects, or preserves. **2.** *Law.* one who is entrusted by law with the care of the person or property, or both, of another, as of a minor or of some other person legally incapable of managing his own affairs. —*adj.* **3.** guarding; protecting: *a guardian angel.* [ME *gardein*, t. AF, der. *g(u)arde* GUARD, n.] —**guard′ianship′,** *n.* —**Syn. 1.** protector, defender. **2.** trustee, warden, keeper.

guardrail (gäd′rāl′), *n.* **1.** a protective railing; banister; handrail. **2.** *Railways.* checkrail.

guard ring, a ring placed on a finger to prevent another ring from slipping off.

guardroom (gäd′ro͞om′), *n.* a room or building used for accommodating military personnel performing guard duties and also for the detention of defaulters. Also, **guardhouse.**

guardsman (gädz′mən), *n., pl.* **-men. 1.** a man who acts as a guard. **2.** a soldier in a Guards regiment. **3.** *U.S.* a member of the National Guard.

guard's van, a railway wagon for the guard, usually attached to the rear of a train; brake van.

Guarini (gwä rē′nĭ), *n.* **Guarino** (gwä rē′nō), 1624–1683, Italian architect.

Guarneri (*It.* gwär nĕ′rē), *n.* **1. Giuseppe Antonio** (*It.* jo͞o zĕp′pĕ än tŏ′nyō), (*Joseph Guarnerius*), 1683–1745, Italian violin-maker. **2.** a violin made by him or by a member of his family. Also, **Guarnerius** (gwä nîə′rĭ əs), **Guarnieri** (*It.* gwär nyĕ′rē).

Guat., Guatemala.

Guatemala (gwăt′ĭ mä′lə; *Sp.* gwä tĕ mä′lä), *n.* **1.** a republic in Central America. 4,016,624 pop. (est. 1962); 42,042 sq. mi. **2.** Also, **Guatemala City.** the capital of this republic. 572,937 (est. 1964). —**Gua′tema′lan,** *adj., n.*

guava (gwä′və), *n.* **1.** any of various trees or shrubs of the myrtaceous genus *Psidium*, esp. *P. Guajava*, natives of tropical or subtropical America, with a fruit used for jelly, etc. **2.** the fruit, used for making jam, jelly, etc. [t. Sp.: m. *guayaba*; from S Amer. name]

Guayaquil (*Sp.* gwä yä kēl′), *n.* a seaport in W Ecuador, on the **Gulf of Guayaquil,** an arm of the Pacific. 506,037 (1962).

guayule (gwə yo͞o′lĭ), *n.* **1.** a rubber-yielding bushlike composite plant, *Parthenium argentatum*, of northern Mexico, etc. **2.** the rubber obtained from this plant. [t. Mex. Sp., t. Nahuatl: m. *cuauhuli*]

gubernaculum (gyo͞o′bə năk′yo͞o ləm), *n. Anat.* a guiding structure, esp. **gubernaculum dentis,** a connective tissue band joining the sac of an unerupted tooth with the gum, and **gubernaculum testis.** a cord in the foetus between the epididymis and the bottom of the scrotum. [L: helm]

gubernatorial (gyo͞o′bə nə tô′rĭ əl), *adj.* of or pertaining to a governor. [f. L *gubernātor* steersman, governor + -IAL]

guberniya (*Russ.* go͞o bĕr′nĭ yə), *n.* **1.** (in the Soviet Union) an administrative division of the volosts, smaller than a district. **2.** (in Russia before 1917) an administrative division equivalent to the province.

guddle (gŭd′l), *v.,* **-dled, -dling.** *Scot.* —*v.t.* **1.** to fish with the hands by groping under rocks or stones on the banks of a river, etc. —*v.i.* **2.** to catch fish in this manner.

gude (gʏd), *adj., adv., n. Scot. and N Dial.* good.

Gude (gʏd), *n. Scot. and N Dial.* God.

gudgeon[1] (gŭj′ən), *n.* **1.** a small European freshwater fish, *Gobio gobio*, of the minnow family, with a threadlike barbel at the corner of the mouth: easily caught, and much used for bait. **2.** any of certain related fish. **3.** one who is easily duped or cheated. **4.** a bait or allurement. —*v.t.* **5.** to dupe; cheat. [ME *gogen*, t. OF: m. *goujon*, g. s. L *gōbio*, var. of *gōbius* GOBY]

gudgeon[2] (gŭj′ən), *n.* the ring portion of a hinge which fits on to and turns on a pin or hook. [ME *gudyon*, t. OF: m. *goujon*, ? g. LL *gubia* chisel]

gudgeon pin, the pin which connects the piston of an internal-combustion engine to the little end bearing of the connecting rod. Also, **gudgeon wrist pin.**

Gudrun (go͝od′ro͞on), *n.* **1.** (in the Volsunga saga) daughter of the king of the Nibelungs; wife of Sigurd and later of Atli. **2.** the heroine of the Middle High German epic poem called by her name. Also, **Kudrun.**

guelder-rose (gĕl′də rōz′), *n.* the European snowball, *Viburnum opulus* var. *roseum.* [named after *Geldern*, German town, or *Gelder(land)*, Dutch province of which Geldern was formerly capital]

Guelders (gĕl′dəz), *n.* Gelderland.

Guelph (gwĕlf), *n.* **1.** a member of the papal and popular party in medieval Italy, opposed to the Ghibellines. **2.** a member of a secret society in Italy in the early 19th century, opposed to foreign rulers and reactionary ideas. **3.** former name of the British royal house of **Windsor.** Also, **Guelf.** [t. It.: m. *Guelfo*, t. G: m. *Welf*, name of the founder of a princely German family] —**Guelph′ic,** *adj.*

guenon (*Fr.* gə nôɴ′), *n.* any of the agile, long-tailed African monkeys, of the genus *Cercopithecus*, with their hairs many-banded, giving a speckled coloration. [t. F]

guerdon (gû′dn), *Poetic.* —*n.* **1.** a reward, recompense, or requital. —*v.t.* **2.** to give a guerdon to; reward. [ME, t. OF, var. of *werdoun*, t. ML: m. s. *widerdonum*, alter. (prob. by assoc. with L *dōnum* gift), of OHG *widarlōn*, f. *widar* again, back + *lōn* reward, c. OE *witherlēan*]

guereza (gĕ′rĭ zə), *n.* any of several African monkeys of the genus *Colubus*, having a coat of silky hair, usually black and white. [Ethiopian native name]

Guericke (*Ger.* gė′rĭ kə), *n.* **Otto von** (*Ger.* ŏ′tō fŏn), 1602–86, German physicist.

Guernica (gû nĕ′kə; *Sp.* gĕr nĕ′kä), *n.* a town in N Spain destroyed in 1937 by German bombers serving the nationalist forces in the Spanish Civil War: subject of a painting by Pablo Picasso.

Guernsey (gûn′zĭ), *n., pl.* **-seys. 1. Isle of,** one of the Channel Islands, in the English Channel. 45,150 pop. (1961); 24½ sq. mi. **2.** one of a breed of dairy cattle originating in Guernsey, giving a rich golden-coloured milk. **3.** (*l.c.*) a close-fitting knitted woollen sweater, much worn by seamen.

guerrilla (gə rĭl′ə), *n.* **1.** a member of a small, independent band of soldiers which harasses the enemy by surprise raids, attacks on communication and supply lines, etc. —*adj.* **2.** pertaining to such fighters or their method of warfare. Also, **guerilla.** [t. Sp., dim. of *guerra* WAR]

Guesde (*Fr.* gĕd), *n.* **Jules** (*Fr.* zhʏl) (*Mathieu Basile*), 1845–1922, French socialist leader, editor, and writer.

guess (gĕs), *v.t.* **1.** to form an opinion of at random or from evidence admittedly uncertain: *to guess the age of a woman.* **2.** to estimate or conjecture correctly: *to guess a riddle.* **3.** to think, believe, or suppose: *I guess I can get there in time.* —*v.i.* **4.** to form an estimate or conjecture (often fol. by *at*): *to guess at the height of a building.* **5.** to estimate or conjecture correctly. —*n.* **6.** a notion, judgement, or conclusion gathered from mere probability or imperfect information; conjecture; surmise. **7.** the act of forming an opinion in this manner. [ME *gessen*, prob. t. Scand.: cf. MDan. *getze, gitse* (Dan. *gisse*) f. *get-* guess + *-s* suffix, c. MD *gessen*, MLG *gissen*] —**guess′able,** *adj.* —**guess′er,** *n.* —**guess′ingly,** *adv.*

—**Syn. 1, 2, 4.** suppose. GUESS, GUESS AT, CONJECTURE, SURMISE imply attempting to form an opinion as to the probable. To GUESS is to risk an opinion regarding something one does not know about; or, wholly or partly by chance, to arrive at the correct answer to a question: *to guess the outcome of a game.* GUESS AT implies more haphazard or random guessing: *to guess at the solution of a crime.* To CONJECTURE is to make inferences in the absence of sufficient evidence to establish certainty: *to conjecture the circumstances of the crime.* SURMISE implies making an intuitive conjecture which may or may not be correct: *to surmise the motives which led to it.* —**Ant.** 3. know.

guesswork (gĕs′wûk′), *n.* work or procedure based on guessing; conjecture.

guest (gĕst), *n.* **1.** a person entertained at the house or table of another. **2.** one who receives the hospitality of a club, a city, or the like. **3.** a person who pays for lodging, and sometimes food, at a hotel, etc. **4.** *Zool.* a commensal (chiefly of insects living in other insects' nests). —*v.t.* **5.** *Rare.* to entertain as a guest. —*v.i.* **6.** *Rare.* to be a guest. [ME *gest(e)*, t. Scand. (cf. Icel. *gestr*); r. OE *g(i)est*, c. D *gast*, G *Gast*; akin to L *hostis* stranger, enemy] —**guest′less,** *adj.* —**Syn. 1, 3.** See **visitor.**

guesthouse (gĕst′hous′), *n., pl.* **-houses** (-hou′zĭz). a house for the accommodation of paying guests; boarding house; hotel.

guest night, an evening on which members of a society, club, etc., entertain guests to dinner.

guestroom (gĕst′ro͞om′, -ro͝om′), *n.* a room for the accommodation of guests.

guestrope (gĕst′rōp′), *n.* **1.** a line along a ship's side or from a boom for boats to make fast alongside. **2.** a line, in addition to the towrope, to steady a boat in tow.

guff (gŭf), *n. Colloq.* empty or foolish talk; humbug; nonsense.

guffaw (gŭ fô′), *n.* **1.** a loud, coarse burst of laughter. —*v.i.* **2.** to laugh loudly and boisterously.

Gui (*It.* go͞o′ē), *n.* **Vittorio** (*It.* vĕt tŏ′ryō), born 1885, Italian conductor and composer.

Gui., Guiana.

Guiana (gī ăn′ə), *n.* **1.** a vast tropical region in NE South America, bounded by the Orinoco, Río Negro, Amazon, and the Atlantic. ab. 690,000 sq. mi. **2.** a coastal portion of this region, including Guyana, French Guiana, and Surinam. 969,298 pop. (est. 1962); 175,275 sq. mi.

Guiana (def. 2)

Guianese (gī′ə nēz′), *adj., n., pl.* **-nese.** —*adj.* **1.** of or pertaining to Guiana, its inhabitants, or their language. —*n.* **2.** an inhabitant of Guiana. Also, **Guianan** (gī ăn′ən).

guidance (gī′dns), *n.* **1.** the act of guiding; leadership; direction. **2.** that which guides. **3.** advice; instruction.

guide (gīd), *v.,* **guided, guiding,** *n.* —*v.t.* **1.** to lead or conduct on the way, as to a place or through a region; show the way to. **2.** to direct the movement or course of: *to guide a horse.* **3.** to lead, direct or advise in any course or action. —*n.* **4.** one who guides, esp. one employed to guide travellers, tourists, mountaineers, etc. **5.** a mark or the like to direct the eye. **6.** guidebook. **7.** guidepost. **8.** a contrivance for regulating progressive motion or action: *a sewing-machine guide.* **9.** a spirit believed to direct the utterances of a medium. **10.** a Girl Guide. [ME *guide(n),* t. OF: m. *guider,* t. Gmc; cf. OE *witan* look after] —**guid′able,** *adj.* —**guide′less,** *adj.* —**guid′er,** *n.*
—**Syn. 1.** pilot, steer. GUIDE, CONDUCT, DIRECT, LEAD imply showing the way or pointing out or determining the course to be taken. GUIDE implies continuous presence or agency in showing or indicating a course: *to guide a traveller.* To CONDUCT is to precede or escort to a place, sometimes with a degree of ceremony: *to conduct a guest to his room.* To DIRECT is to give information for guidance, or instructions or orders for a course of procedure: *to direct someone to the station.* To LEAD is to bring onwards in a course, guiding by contact or by going in advance; hence, fig., to influence or induce to some course of conduct: *to lead a procession, to lead astray.* —**Ant. 3.** follow.

guide bars, bars which guide the crosshead of a steam engine to avoid lateral thrust on the piston rod. Also, **slide bars.**

guidebook (gīd′bo͝ok′), *n.* a book of directions and information for travellers, tourists, etc.

guided missile, *Aeron.* a missile whose flight path can be controlled throughout its flight either by radio signals from an external source or by internal homing devices.

guide-dog (gīd′dŏg′), *n.* a dog specially trained to lead or guide a blind person.

guided wave, *Physics.* electromagnetic radiation which is guided along a conductor or an insulating surface as opposed to travelling through space.

guidepost (gīd′pōst′), *n.* signpost.

guider (gī′də), *n.* **1.** one who guides. **2.** an officer in a company of Girl Guides or Brownies.

guide rope, 1. *Aeron.* a long rope trailing along the ground from a balloon and used to regulate altitude and act as a brake. **2.** a rope fastened to a hoisting or towing line, to guide the object being moved.

Guido d'Arezzo (*It.* gwē′dō dä rĕt′tsō), A.D. *c.* 990–*c.* 1050, Italian or French monk, reformer of musical notation.

guidon (gī′dn), *n. Mil.* **1.** a flag or pennant used as a standard by dragoon regiments. **2.** the officer carrying it. [t. F, t. It.: m. *guidone,* b. *guidare* GUIDE and *gonfalone* GONFALON]

Guienne (*Fr.* gē ĕn′), *n.* a former province in SW France. Also, **Guyenne.**

Guignet's green (gē′nyāz), chrome green. [named after A. *Guignet,* 19th-century French artist]

guild (gĭld), *n.* **1.** an organization of persons with common professional or cultural interests formed for mutual aid and protection. **2.** *Hist.* one of the associations, numerous in the Middle Ages, formed for mutual aid and protection or for a common purpose, most frequently by persons associated in trade or industry. **3.** *Bot.* a group of plants, such as parasites, having a similar habit of growth and nutrition. Also, **gild.** [ME *gild(e),* t. Scand. (cf. Icel. *gildi* guild, payment); r. OE *gegyld* guild; akin to G *Geld* money, Goth. *gild* tribute]

guilder (gĭl′də), *n.* gulden. Also, **gilder.** [early mod. E *gildren,* var. of ME *guldren,* both t. D: m. (with intrusive *-r-*) *gulden*]

Guildford (gĭl′fəd), *n.* a cathedral town in England, the county town of Surrey. 53,976 (1961).

guildhall (gĭld′hôl′), *n.* **1.** the hall of a guild or corporation; town hall. **2.** *Hist.* a guild assembly hall. Also, **gildhall.**

guildsman (gĭldz′mən), *n., pl.* **-men.** a member of a guild. Also, **gildsman.**

guild socialism, a form of socialism by which workers' guilds manage and control government-owned industry.

guile (gīl), *n.* insidious cunning; deceitfulness; treachery. [ME, t. OF; of Gmc orig., and akin to WILE] —**Syn.** See **deceit.**

guileful (gīl′fəl), *adj.* full of guile; wily; deceitful; treacherous. —**guile′fully,** *adv.* —**guile′fulness,** *n.*

guileless (gīl′lĭs), *adj.* free from guile; sincere; honest; frank. —**guile′lessly,** *adv.* —**guile′lessness,** *n.*

guillemot (gĭl′ĭ mŏt′), *n.* any of several relatively narrow-billed northern oceanic birds of the genera *Cepphus* and *Uria,* as the **black guillemot,** *Cepphus grylle,* and **common guillemot,** *Uria aalge.* [t. F, appar. dim. of *Guillaume* William]

guilloche (gĭ lŏsh′), *n.* an ornamental band or field with paired ribbons or lines flowing in interlaced curves. [t. F: graining tool, der. MF *goie* a kind of sickle, d. var. of F *gouge* GOUGE, n.]

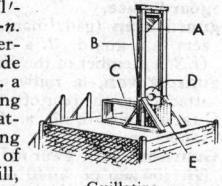

Guilloche

guillotine (*n.* gĭl′ə tēn′; *v.* gĭl′ə tēn′), *n., v.,* **-tined, -tining.** —*n.* **1.** a machine for beheading persons by means of a heavy blade falling in two grooved posts. **2.** a surgical instrument for cutting the tonsils. **3.** a device incorporating a long blade for trimming paper. **4.** *Parl. Proc.* a method of cutting short discussion of a bill, etc. —*v.t.* **5.** *Parl. Proc.* to cut short discussion of (a bill, etc.). **6.** to behead by the guillotine. [t. F; named after J. I. *Guillotin,* 1738–1814, French physician, who urged its use] —**guil′lotin′er,** *n.*

Guillotine
A, Knife; B, Cord which releases knife; C, Board to which victim is tied; D, Hole for head of victim; E, Basket

guilt (gĭlt), *n.* **1.** the fact or state of having committed an offence or crime; grave culpability, as for some conscious violation of moral or penal law. **2.** a feeling of responsibility or remorse for some crime, wrong, etc., either real or imagined. [ME *gilt,* OE *gylt* offence] —**Syn. 1.** guiltiness. **2.** criminality. —**Ant. 1.** innocence.

guiltless (gĭlt′lĭs), *adj.* **1.** free from guilt; innocent. **2.** having no knowledge or experience (fol. by *of*). **3.** destitute or devoid (fol. by *of*). —**guilt′lessly,** *adv.* —**guilt′lessness,** *n.* —**Syn.** See **innocent.**

guilty (gĭl′tĭ), *adj.,* **-tier, -tiest. 1.** having incurred guilt or grave culpability, as by committing an offence or crime; justly chargeable with guilt (often fol. by *of*): *guilty of murder.* **2.** characterized by, connected with, or involving guilt: *guilty intent.* **3.** affected with or showing a sense of guilt: *a guilty conscience.* [ME *gilti,* OE *gyltig*] —**guilt′ily,** *adv.* —**guilt′iness,** *n.*

Guimard (*Fr.* gē mȧr′), *n.* **Hector** (*Fr.* ĕk tŏr′), 1867–1942, French Art Nouveau architect.

guimpe (gĭmp), *n.* a kind of chemisette or yoke of lace, embroidery, or other material, worn with a dress cut low at the neck. [earlier *gimp,* c. D *gimp*]

Guin., Guinea.

Guinea (gĭn′ĭ), *n.* **1.** a coastal region in W Africa, extending from the river Gambia to the Gabon estuary. **2.** an independent republic in W Africa, on the Atlantic coast. 2,726,868 pop. (est. 1960); ab. 96,900 sq. mi. *Cap.:* Conakry. Formerly, **French Guinea. 3. Gulf of,** a large open bay in the angle of W Africa. **4.** (*l.c.*) a British gold coin issued from 1663 to 1813, at first of a nominal value of 20 shillings, but having since 1717 a fixed value of 21 shillings. **5.** (until 1971) the sum of 21 shillings. **6.** (*l.c.*) *Colloq.* guineafowl.

Guinea corn, durra.

guineafowl (gĭn′ĭ foul′), *n.* any member of an African gallinaceous bird family, the *Numididae,* which has (usually) dark grey plumage with small white spots, one species of which is now domesticated throughout the world and valued for its flesh and eggs.

Guineafowl, *Numida meleagris* (25 in. long)

guinea hen, 1. the female of the guineafowl. **2.** any guineafowl.

Guinea pepper, pepper pods, esp. of *Capsicum frutescens* var. *longum,* from which cayenne is ground.

guineapig (gĭn′ĭ pĭg′), *n.* **1.** a short-eared, short-tailed rodent of the genus *Cavia,* usually white, black, and tawny, much used in scientific experiments, commonly regarded as the domesticated form of one of the South American wild

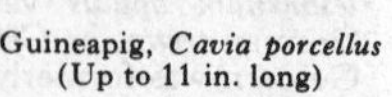
Guineapig, *Cavia porcellus* (Up to 11 in. long)

b., blend of, blended; c., cognate with; d., dialect, dialectal; der., derived from; f., formed from; g., going back to; m., modification of; r., replacing; s., stem of; t., taken from; ?, perhaps. See full key on inside front cover.

species of cavy. **2.** *Colloq.* a person used as the subject of any sort of experiment. [f. GUINEA + PIG; reason for associating animal with Guinea unknown]

Guinea worm, a long, slender, nematode worm, *Dracunculus medinensis*, parasitic under the skin of man and other animals, common in parts of India and Africa.

Guinevere (gwĭn′ĭ vĭə′), *n. Arthurian Legend.* wife of King Arthur, and mistress of Lancelot. Also, **Guinever** (gwĭn′ĭ və).

Guinness (gĭn′ĭs), *n. Trademark.* a bitter stout.

guipure (gĭ pyŏŏə′; *Fr.* gē pʏr′), *n.* **1.** any of various laces, often heavy, made of linen, silk, etc., with the pattern connected by brides (rather than by a net ground). **2.** any of various laces or trimmings formerly in use, made with cords or heavy threads, metal, etc. [t. F, der. *guiper* cover or whip with silk, etc., t. Gmc; cf. WIPE, WHIP]

Guiscard (*Fr.* gēs kȧr′), *n.* **Robert** (*Fr.* rō bĕr′) (*Robert de Hauteville*), *c.* 1015–85, Norman conqueror in Italy.

guise (gīz), *n., v.,* **guised, guising.** —*n.* **1.** external appearance in general; aspect or semblance: *an old principle in a new guise.* **2.** assumed appearance or mere semblance: *under the guise of friendship.* **3.** style of dress: *in the guise of a shepherdess.* **4.** *Obs.* manner; mode. —*v.t.* **5.** *Archaic.* to dress; attire. —*v.i.* **6.** *Scot. and N Dial.* to go in disguise. [ME, t. OF, t. Gmc; cf. WISE[2]] —**Syn. 1.** See **appearance.**

Guise (*Fr.* gēz), *n.* **1. François de Lorraine** (*Fr.* fräɴ swȧ də lō rĕn′), **Duc de,** 1519–63, French general and statesman. **2. Henri I de Lorraine** (*Fr.* äɴ rē′), **Duc de,** 1550–88, French general and leader of opposition to the Huguenots.

guitar (gĭ tä′), *n.* a musical stringed instrument with a long fretted neck and a flat, somewhat violin-like body. The strings, usually six in number, are plucked or twanged with the fingers or a plectrum. [t. Sp.: m. *guitarra*, t. Gk: m. *kithára* cithara] —**guitar′ist,** *n.* —**guitar′-like′,** *adj.*

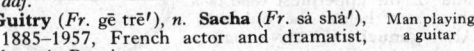

Man playing a guitar

Guitry (*Fr.* gē trē′), *n.* **Sacha** (*Fr.* sȧ shȧ′), 1885–1957, French actor and dramatist, born in Russia.

Guizot (*Fr.* gē zō′), *n.* **François Pierre Guillaume** (*Fr.* fräɴ swȧ pyĕr gē yōm′), 1787–1874, French historian and statesman.

Gujarat (gōō′jə rät′), *n.* **1.** a region in W India, N of the Narbada river. **2.** a state in W India: 20,633,350 pop. (1961), 72,138 sq. mi. *Cap.:* Ahmedabad. Also, **Gujerat.**

Gujarati (gōō′jə rä′tĭ), *n.* **1.** an Indic language of western India. **2.** a native or inhabitant of Gujarat.

Gujranwala (gōōj rän′wŭl′ə), *n.* a city in NE West Pakistan, in W Punjab. 196,154 (1961).

gulch (gŭlch), *n. U.S.* a deep, narrow ravine, esp. one marking the course of a stream or torrent. [orig. uncert]

gulden (gŏŏl′dən), *n.* **1.** the monetary unit of the Netherlands, equal to 100 cents, and equivalent to about £0·115 sterling. *Abbrev.:* Fl. **2.** a note or silver coin of this value. **3.** the monetary unit of the Netherlands Antilles, equal to 100 cents, and equivalent to about £0·223 sterling. **4.** a note or silver coin of this value. **5.** the monetary unit of Surinam, equal to 100 cents, and equivalent to about £0·221 sterling. **6.** a note or silver coin of this value. **7.** any of several silver or gold coins formerly current in Germany, Austria, and the Low Countries. Also, **guilder, gilder.** [t. D: lit., golden]

Gülek Bogaz (gyōō lĕk′ bō gäz′), Turkish name of the **Cilician Gates.**

gules (gyōōlz), *n. Her.* red. [ME *goules*, t. OF: m. *gueules* red fur neckpiece, ult. der. *gole* throat, g. L *gula*]

gulf (gŭlf), *n.* **1.** a portion of an ocean or sea partly enclosed by land. **2.** a deep hollow; chasm or abyss. **3.** any wide separation, as in station, education, etc. **4.** something that engulfs or swallows up. —*v.t.* **5.** to swallow like a gulf, or as in a gulf; engulf. [ME *goulf*, t. OF: m. *golfe*, t. It.: m. *golfo*, t. LGk: m. *kólphos*, Gk *kólpos* bosom, gulf] —**gulf′-like′,** *adj.*

gulf rupee, 1. the monetary unit of Muscat and Oman, and of the Trucial States other than Dubai, equivalent to £0·075 sterling. **2.** a banknote or coin of this value. **3.** a former monetary unit of Bahrain, Qatar, and the Trucial States, based on the Indian rupee.

Gulf States, those states of the U.S. bordering on the Gulf of Mexico: Florida, Alabama, Mississippi, Louisiana, and Texas.

Gulf Stream, a warm oceanic current issuing from the Gulf of Mexico, flowing N along the U.S. coast.

Gulf Stream Drift, a continuation of the Gulf Stream north-easterly across the Atlantic Ocean towards the British Isles; North Atlantic Drift.

gulfweed (gŭlf′wēd′), *n.* **1.** a coarse, olive brown seaweed, *Sargassum bacciferum*, found in the Gulf Stream and elsewhere, characterized by numerous berry-like air vesicles. **2.** any seaweed related to it.

gull[1] (gŭl), *n.* any of numerous long-winged, web-footed, aquatic birds constituting the subfamily *Larinae* (family *Laridae*), esp. of the genus *Larus*, usually white with grey back and wings. [ME *gull(e)*, ? repr. OE word (unrecorded) akin to OE *giellan* yell]

Herring gull, *Larus argentatus* (Up to 26 in. long)

gull[2] (gŭl), *v.t.* **1.** to deceive; trick; cheat. —*n.* **2.** one easily deceived or cheated; a dupe. [? akin to obs. *gull*, v., swallow]

Gullah (gŭl′ə), *n.* **1.** a member of a Negro people settled as slaves on the sea islands and coastal region of Georgia and South Carolina. **2.** their English dialect.

gullet (gŭl′ĭt), *n.* **1.** the oesophagus, or tube by which food and drink swallowed pass to the stomach. **2.** the throat or pharynx. **3.** something like the oesophagus. **4.** a channel for water. **5.** a gully or ravine. **6.** a preparatory cut in excavations. [ME *golet*, t. OF: m. *goulet*, ult. der. L *gula* throat]

gullible (gŭl′ə bl), *adj.* easily deceived or cheated. —**gul′libil′ity,** *n.* —**gul′libly,** *adv.*

gully (gŭl′ĭ), *n., pl.* **-lies,** *v.,* **-lied, -lying.** —*n.* **1.** a small valley or canyon cut by running water. **2.** a ditch or gutter. **3.** *Cricket.* **a.** a fielding position between the slips and point. **b.** the fielder in this position. —*v.t.* **4.** to make gullies in. **5.** to form (channels) by the action of water. Also, **gulley.** [appar. var. of GULLET, with substitution of -Y[3] for F *-et*]

gulp (gŭlp), *v.i.* **1.** to gasp or choke as when taking large draughts of liquids. —*v.t.* **2.** to swallow eagerly, or in large draughts or pieces (usually fol. by *down*). **3.** to take in, as by swallowing eagerly; choke back: *to gulp down a sob.* —*n.* **4.** the act of gulping. **5.** the amount swallowed at one time; mouthful. [ME *gulpe(n)*. Cf. D *gulpen* gulp, Norw. *glupa* swallow] —**gulp′er,** *n.*

gum[1] (gŭm), *n., v.,* **gummed, gumming.** —*n.* **1.** any of various viscid, amorphous exudations from plants, hardening on exposure to air, and soluble in, or forming a viscid mass with, water. **2.** any of various similar exudations, as resin or the like. **3.** a preparation of such a substance, as for use in the arts, etc. **4.** chewing gum. **5.** a hard, gelatinous sweet. **6.** mucilage; glue. **7.** rubber. **8.** a gum tree. **9.** *Philately.* See **original gum. 10.** *Chiefly U.S. Dial.* a rubber overshoe. —*v.t.* **11.** to smear, stiffen, or stick together with gum. **12.** to clog with or as with some gummy substance (often fol. by *up*). —*v.i.* **13.** to exude or form gum. **14.** to become gummy; become clogged with some gummy substance. [ME *gomme*, t. OF. g. var. of L *gummi*, t. Gk: m. *kómmi*] —**gum′like′,** *adj.*

gum[2] (gŭm), *n.* (*often pl.*) the firm, fleshy tissue covering the alveolar parts of either jaw and enveloping the bases of the teeth. [ME *gome*, OE *gōma* palate, inside of the mouth; akin to Icel. *gōmr*, G *Gaumen* palate]

gum[3] (gŭm), *interj.* (a mild oath; a euphemism for *God*): *by gum.*

gum ammoniac, a medicinal gum resin from the umbelliferous plant, *Dorema ammoniacum*, of Persia, etc.

gum arabic, a gum obtained from *Acacia senegal* and other species of acacia: used in calico printing in making mucilage, ink, and the like, in medicine, etc.

gum benzoin, benzoin (def. 1). Also, **gum benjamin.**

gumbo (gŭm′bō), *n., pl.* **-bos.** *U.S.* **1.** the okra plant. **2.** its mucilaginous pods. **3.** soup or stew, usually containing chicken, thickened with okra pods. **4.** a silty soil, chiefly in the southern and western U.S., becoming very sticky when wet. Also, **gombo.** [from Angolan name]

gumboil (gŭm′boil′), *n.* a small abscess on the gum.

gumboot (gŭm′bōōt′), *n.* a rubber boot reaching to the knee or thigh.

gumbotil (gŭm′bə tĭl), *n. Geol.* a sticky clay formed by the thorough weathering of glacial drift, the thickness of the clay furnishing means for comparing relative lengths of interglacial ages. [f. GUMBO + *-til*, form of TILL[4]]

gumdrop (gŭm′drŏp′), *n. U.S.* gum[1] (def. 5).

gumma (gŭm′ə), *n., pl.* **gummas, gummata** (gŭm′ə tə). *Pathol.* the rubbery, tumour-like lesion of tertiary syphilis. [NL, der. L *gummi* GUM[1]]

gummatous (gŭm′ə təs), *adj.* **1.** of the nature of or resembling a gumma. **2.** pertaining to a gumma.

gummite (gŭm′ĭt), *n.* a yellow to red alteration product of pitchblende, having a greasy lustre, and occurring in gumlike masses; a minor ore of uranium.

gummosis (gŭ mō′sĭs), *n. Bot.* an abnormal condition of certain plants such as the cherry, plum, sugar cane, cotton, etc., which causes the excessive formation of gum. [NL, f. L *gumm(i)* + -OSIS. See GUM[1]]

gummous (gŭm′əs), *adj.* consisting of or resembling gum; gummy.

gummy (gŭm′ĭ), *adj.*, **-mier, -miest. 1.** of the nature of gum; viscid. **2.** covered with or clogged by gum or sticky matter. **3.** exuding gum. **—gum′miness,** *n.*

gum plant, a plant of the composite genus *Grindelia*, of the western U.S., covered with a viscid secretion.

gumption (gŭmp′shən), *n. Colloq.* **1.** initiative; resourcefulness. **2.** shrewd, practical common sense. [orig. Scot.]

gum resin, a plant exudation consisting of a mixture of gums and resins, as bdellium, gamboge, etc.

gumshoe (gŭm′sho͞o′), *n.*, *v.*, **-shoed, -shoeing.** *—n.* **1.** galosh, rubber overshoe. **2.** *U.S. Slang.* **a.** one who goes about softly, as if wearing rubber shoes. **b.** a policeman or detective. *—v.i.* **3.** *U.S. Slang.* to go softly as if wearing rubber shoes; move or act stealthily.

gum tree, 1. any tree that exudes gum, as a eucalyptus, the sour gum, the sweet gum, etc. **2.** any of various other gum-yielding trees, as the sapodilla. **3. up a gum tree,** *Slang.* in difficulties; in a predicament.

gumwood (gŭm′wo͝od′), *n.* the wood of a gum tree, esp. the wood of the eucalyptus of Australia, or a gum tree of the western U.S.

gun[1] (gŭn), *n.*, *v.*, **gunned, gunning.** *—n.* **1.** a metallic tube, with its stock or carriage and attachments, from which heavy missiles are thrown by the force of an explosive; a piece of ordnance. **2.** any portable firearm, as a rifle, revolver, etc. **3.** a long-barrelled cannon, having a flat trajectory. **4.** any similar device for projecting something: *an airgun, cement gun.* **5.** a member of a shooting party. **6. blow great guns,** (of a wind) to blow violently. **7. stick to one's guns,** to maintain one's position in an argument, etc., against opposition. *—v.i.* **8.** to hunt with a gun. **9.** to shoot with a gun. *—v.t.* **10.** to shoot with a gun, (often fol. by *down*). **11.** *Aeron. Slang.* to cause to increase in speed very quickly. **12.** to feed fuel to, suddenly and quickly: *to gun an engine.* **13. gun for,** *Slang.* to seek (a person) with the intention to harm or kill. [ME *gunne, gonne,* appar. short for *Gunilda* (L), *gonnyld* (ME), name for engine of war, ult. t. Scand.; cf. Icel. *Gunna*, short for *Gunnhildr*, woman's name] **—gun′less,** *adj.*

gun[2] (gŭn), *v. Archaic.* pp. of **gin**[3].

gunboat (gŭn′bōt′), *n.* a small vessel of light draught, carrying mounted guns.

guncarriage (gŭn′kăr′ĭj), *n.* the carriage or structure on which a gun is mounted, and from which it is fired.

guncotton (gŭn′kŏt′n), *n.* a highly explosive cellulose nitrate, made by digesting clean cotton in a mixture of 1 part nitric acid and 3 parts sulphuric acid.

gun dog, a trained dog which accompanies hunters when they shoot game, esp. game birds.

gunfire (gŭn′fī′ə), *n.* the firing of a gun or guns.

gunflint (gŭn′flĭnt′), *n.* the flint in a flintlock.

Gunite (gŭn′īt), *n. Trademark.* a specially strong kind of concrete, made of a mixture of cement, sand, and mortar, thrown on to a surface or framework by a compressed-air ejector.

gunlock (gŭn′lŏk′), *n.* the mechanism of a firearm by which the charge is exploded.

gunman (gŭn′mən), *n.*, *pl.* **-men. 1.** a man armed with, or expert with, a gun, esp. one ready to use a gun unlawfully. **2.** one who makes guns.

gunmetal (gŭn′mĕt′l), *n.* **1.** any of various alloys or metallic substances with a dark grey or blackish colour or finish, used for chains, belt buckles, etc. **2.** a dark grey with bluish or purplish tinge. **3.** a bronze formerly much employed for cannon.

Gunnar (go͝on′ä), *n.* brother of Gudrun and husband of Brunhild in the *Völsunga Saga.* [Icel.]

gunnel[1] (gŭn′əl), *n.* any of certain elongate blennies (fishes), esp. the butterfish, *Pholis gunnellus*, which is found in the northern Atlantic. [orig. uncert.]

gunnel[2] (gŭn′əl), *n.* gunwale.

gunner (gŭn′ə), *n.* **1.** one who works a gun or cannon. **2.** *Mil.* **a.** a private in the artillery. **b.** any artilleryman. **3.** *Naut.* a warrant officer in charge of a battery of guns.

gunnery (gŭn′ə rĭ), *n.* **1.** the art and science of constructing and managing guns, esp. large guns. **2.** the firing of guns. **3.** guns collectively.

gunning (gŭn′ĭng), *n.* **1.** the act, practice, or art of shooting with guns. **2.** hunting of game with guns.

gunny (gŭn′ĭ), *n.* **1.** a strong, coarse material made commonly from jute, used for sacking, etc. **2.** Also, **gunnybag** (gŭn′ĭ băg′), **gunnysack** (gŭn′ĭ săk′). a bag or sack made of this material. [t. Hind.: m. *gōnī*]

gunpaper (gŭn′pā′pə), *n. Mil.* a type of paper treated with nitric acid so that it has a composition similar to that of guncotton.

gunport (gŭn′pôt′), *n.* an aperture in a ship, aircraft, armoured vehicle, fortification, etc., through which a gun can be fired.

gunpowder (gŭn′pou′də), *n.* **1.** an explosive mixture of saltpetre (potassium nitrate), sulphur, and charcoal, used esp. in gunnery. **2.** a fine variety of green China tea, each leaf of which is rolled into a little ball.

Gunpowder Plot, *Hist.* an unsuccessful plot or supposed plot led by Guy Fawkes to kill King James I, the Lords, and the Commons assembled in Parliament on November 5th, 1605, by an explosion of gunpowder, in revenge for the laws against Roman Catholics.

gunroom (gŭn′ro͝om′, -ro͞om′), *n.* **1.** a room in which guns are kept. **2.** *Naut.* a mess, for the use of junior naval officers.

gun-running (gŭn′rŭn′ĭng), *n.* the smuggling of guns, etc., into a country. **—gun′-run′ner,** *n.*

gunshot (gŭn′shŏt′), *n.* **1.** a shot fired from a gun. **2.** the range of a gun: *out of gunshot.* **3.** the shooting of a gun. *—adj.* **4.** made by a gunshot.

gun-shy (gŭn′shī′), *adj.* frightened by the use of guns.

gunsmith (gŭn′smĭth′), *n.* one who makes or repairs firearms.

gunstock (gŭn′stŏk′), *n.* the stock or support in which the barrel of a shoulder weapon is fixed.

Gunter (gŭn′tə), *n.* **Edmund,** 1581–1626, English mathematician and inventor of various measuring instruments and scales.

Gunter's chain (gŭn′təz). See **chain** (def. 9).

Gunther (go͝on′tə), *n.* (in the Nibelungen epic) a Burgundian king, brother of Kriemhild and husband of Brunhild.

Guntur (go͝on to͝oə′), *n.* a city in India, in central Andhra Pradesh. 187,122 (1961).

gunwale (gŭn′əl), *n. Naut.* **1.** the upper edge of a vessel's or boat's side. **2.** the uppermost wale of a ship, next below the bulwarks. Also, **gunnel.** [f. GUN + *wale* a plank; so called because guns were set upon it]

G, Gunwale; K, Keel; T, Thwart

gunya (gŭn′yə), *n. Austral.* an Aborigine's hut. [t. native Australian]

gunyang (gŭn′yăng), *n.* an edible fruit of Australia, *Solanum laciniatum* or *S. rescum.* Also, **kangaroo apple.** [t. native Australian]

guppy (gŭp′ĭ), *n.*, *pl.* **-pies.** a live-bearing top minnow, *Lebistes reticulatus*, of the family *Poeciliidae*, common in home aquariums.

gurgitation (gû′jĭ tā′shən), *n.* surging rise and fall; ebullient motion, as of water. [f. s. LL *gurgitātus*, pp., engulfed + -ION]

gurgle (gû′gl), *v.*, **-gled, -gling,** *n.* *—v.i.* **1.** to flow in a broken, irregular, noisy current: *water gurgles from a bottle.* **2.** to make a sound as of water doing this (often used of birds or of human beings). *—v.t.* **3.** to utter with a gurgling sound. *—n.* **4.** the act or noise of gurgling. [? imit. Cf. G *gurgeln* GARGLE] **—gur′glingly,** *adv.*

Gurkha (go͝oə′kə, gû′kə), *n.* a member of a warlike Rajput people, Hindu in religion, living in Nepal.

gurnard (gû′nəd), *n.*, *pl.* **-nards,** (*esp. collectively*) **-nard. 1.** any of various marine acanthopterygian fishes, esp. of the genus *Trigla* of Europe and the genus *Prionotus* of America, having a spiny head with mailed cheeks, and three pairs of free, finger-like pectoral rays. **2.** any of various similar fishes. See **flying gurnard.** [ME, t. OF: m. *gornard*, prob. lit., grunter, der. Pr. *gourgna* grunt, ult. der. L *grunnire* grunt]

Gürsel (*Turk.* gyr sĕl′), *n.* **Cemal** (*Turk.* jĕ mäl′), 1895–1966, Turkish general and statesman; president of the Republic of Turkey 1961–66.

guru (go͞o′ro͞o, go͞o′ro͞o), *n.* **1.** (in Hinduism) a preceptor and spiritual guide. **2.** *Colloq.* any spiritual leader or teacher. [t. Hindi]

gush (gŭsh), *v.i.* **1.** to issue with force, as a fluid escaping from confinement; flow suddenly and copiously. **2.** *Colloq.* to express oneself extravagantly or emotionally; talk effusively. **3.** to have a copious flow of something, as of blood, tears, etc. *—v.t.* **4.** to emit suddenly, forcibly, or copiously. *—n.* **5.** a sudden and copious emission of a fluid. **6.** the fluid emitted. **7.** gushing or effusive language. [ME *gusche*, ? ult. f. *gus-* (see GUST) + *-k* suffix. Cf. Icel. *gusa*] **—gush′ingly,** *adv.* **—Syn. 1.** pour, stream, spurt, spout. See **flow.**

gusher (gŭsh′ə), *n.* **1.** *Colloq.* a person who gushes. **2.** a flowing oilwell, usually of large capacity.

gushy (gŭsh′ĭ), *adj.*, **gushier, gushiest.** *Colloq.* given to or marked by gush or effusiveness. —**gush′iness,** *n.*

gusset (gŭs′ĭt), *n.* **1.** an angular piece of material inserted in a garment to strengthen, enlarge or give freedom of movement to some part of it. **2.** a metal bracket for strengthening a structure at a joint or angle. **3.** *Armour.* **a.** a mail strip in the armpit region sewn to cloth sleeves. **b.** a narrow articulated plate of the breastplate adjacent to the arm. —*v.t.* **4.** to provide with a gusset. [ME, t. OF: m. *gousset*, der. *gousse* pod, husk]

gust (gŭst), *n.* **1.** a sudden, strong blast of wind. **2.** a sudden rush or burst of water, fire, smoke, sound, etc. **3.** an outburst of passionate feeling. [t. Scand.; cf. Icel. *gustr* a gust, blast, f. *gus-* (akin to *gjōsa, gusa* gush) + *-t* suffix] —**Syn. 1.** See **wind**[1].

gustation (gŭs tā′shən), *n.* **1.** the act of tasting. **2.** the faculty of taste.

gustative (gŭs′tə tĭv), *adj.* of or pertaining to taste or tasting. Also, **gustatory** (gŭs′tə tə rĭ, gŭs′tə trĭ).

Gustavo A. Madero (*Sp.* gōōs tä′bō mä dĕ′rō), official name of **Guadalupe Hidalgo.**

Gustavus I (gōōs tä′vəs) (*Gustavus Vasa*), 1496–1560, king of Sweden 1523–60.

Gustavus V, 1858–1950, king of Sweden 1907–50.

Gustavus VI (*Gustav Adolf*), born 1882, king of Sweden since 1950.

Gustavus Adolphus (ə dŏl′fəs), 1594–1632, king of Sweden 1611–32. Also, **Gustavus II.**

gusto (gŭs′tō), *n.* **1.** keen relish or hearty enjoyment, as in eating, drinking, or in action or speech generally: *to tell a story with gusto.* **2.** individual taste or liking. [t. It., g. L *gustus* taste, relish]

gusty (gŭs′tĭ), *adj.*, **gustier, gustiest. 1.** blowing or coming in gusts, as wind, rain, storms, etc. **2.** affected or marked by gusts of wind, etc.: *gusty day.* **3.** occurring or characterized by sudden bursts or outbursts, as sound, laughter, etc. —**gust′ily,** *adv.* —**gust′iness,** *n.*

gut (gŭt), *n.*, *v.*, **gutted, gutting.** —*n.* **1.** the alimentary canal between the pylorus and the anus, or some portion of it. **2.** (*pl.*) the bowels or entrails. **3.** (*pl.*) *Slang.* courage; stamina; endurance: *to have guts.* **4.** the substance forming the case of the intestine; intestinal tissue or fibre: *sheep's gut.* **5.** a preparation of the intestines of an animal used for various purposes, as for violin strings, tennis rackets, fishing lines, etc. **6.** the silken substance taken from a silkworm killed when about to spin its cocoon, used in making snells for fishhooks. **7.** a narrow passage, as a channel of water or a defile between hills. —*v.t.* **8.** to take out the guts or entrails of; disembowel. **9.** to plunder of contents. **10.** to destroy the interior of: *fire gutted the building.* [ME; OE *guttas*, pl., akin to *gēotan* pour] —**Syn. 3.** pluck.

gutbucket (gŭt′bŭk′ĭt), *adj.* *Jazz.* in a low-down, primitive style.

Gutenberg (gōō′tən bûg′; *Ger.* -bĕrk), *n.* **Johannes** (*Ger.* yō hä′nəs) (*Johann Gensfleisch*), *c.* 1398–1468, German printer.

Gutenberg Bible, an edition of the Vulgate printed at Mainz before 1456, ascribed to Gutenberg and others: prob. the first large book printed with movable type.

Gütersloh (*Ger.* gʏ′tər slō), *n.* a town in West Germany, in N North Rhine-Westphalia. 55,200 (est. 1966).

Guthrie (gŭth′rĭ), *n.* **Sir (William) Tyrone** (tĭ rōn′, tī′rōn), born 1900, British theatrical producer.

guti (gōō′tĭ), *n.* *Rhodesian and S African.* a period of overcast weather and light rain associated with south-westerly winds from the sea. [t. Shona: m. *makute*]

gutta (gŭt′ə), *n.*, *pl.* **guttae** (gŭt′ē). **1.** a drop, or something resembling one. **2.** *Archit.* one of a series of pendent ornaments, generally in the form of a frustum of a cone, attached to the underside of the mutules, etc., of the Doric entablature. [t. L: a drop]

gutta-percha (gŭt′ə pû′chə), *n.* the coagulated milky juice, nearly white when pure, of various Malaysian sapotaceous trees, esp. *Palaquium gutta*, variously used in the arts, medicine, and manufactures, as for insulating electric wires. [f. Malay: m. *getah* gum, balsam + *percha* kind of tree producing the substance]

gutter (gŭt′ə), *n.* **1.** a channel at the side (or in the middle) of a road or street, for leading off surface water. **2.** any channel, trough, or the like for carrying off fluid. **3.** a channel at the eaves or on the roof of a building, for carrying off rainwater. **4.** a furrow or channel made by running water. **5.** the abode or resort of the lowest class of persons in the community: *the language of the gutter.* **6.** *Print.* the inner margin of a page. —*v.i.* **7.** to flow in streams. **8.** to form gutters, as water does. **9.** (of a lighted candle) to melt away rapidly and irregularly. —*v.t.* **10.** to make gutters in; channel. **11.** to furnish with a gutter or gutters: *to gutter a house or shed.* [ME *goter*, t. OF: m. *goutiere*, ult. der. L *gutta* a drop] —**gut′terlike′,** *adj.* —**gut′tery,** *adj.*

guttersnipe (gŭt′ə snīp′), *n.* a street child of the lowest class; urchin; gamin.

guttural (gŭt′ə rəl), *adj.* **1.** pertaining to the throat. **2.** harsh; throaty. **3.** *Phonet.* pertaining to sounds articulated in the back of the mouth, esp. the velars. —*n.* **4.** a guttural sound. [t. NL: s. *gutturālis*, der. L *guttur* throat] —**gut′turally,** *adv.* —**gut′turalness,** *n.*

guy[1] (gī), *n.*, *v.*, **guyed, guying.** —*n.* **1.** a person of grotesque appearance; a person wearing ridiculous clothes. **2.** a grotesque effigy of Guy Fawkes, the leader of the Gunpowder Plot, carried about and burnt on Guy Fawkes Day. **3.** *U.S. Slang.* a fellow or person. —*v.t.* **4.** *Slang.* to jeer at or make fun of; ridicule. [from *Guy* Fawkes]

guy[2] (gī), *n.*, *v.*, **guyed, guying.** —*n.* **1.** a rope or appliance used to guide and steady a thing being hoisted or lowered, or to secure anything liable to shift its position. —*v.t.* **2.** to guide, steady, or secure with a guy or guys. [ME *gye*, t. OF: m. *guie* a guide, der. *guier* GUIDE]

Guyana (gī ăn′ə), *n.* a country on the NE coast of South America; a member of the Commonwealth of Nations. 650,000 pop. (est. 1965); 82,978 sq. mi. *Cap.:* Georgetown. Formerly a colony, **British Guiana.** See map under **Guiana.**

Guyenne (*Fr.* gē ĕn′), *n.* Guienne.

Guy Fawkes Day (gī′fôks′), November 5th, the anniversary of the Gunpowder Plot, celebrated by fireworks, etc.

guyver (gī′və), *n.* *Austral. Slang.* plausible talk; ingratiating behaviour.

guzzle (gŭz′əl), *v.i.*, *v.t.*, **-zled, -zling.** to drink frequently and greedily: *they sat there all evening guzzling their beer.* —**guz′zler,** *n.*

Gwalior (gwä′lĭ ô′), *n.* **1.** a former state in central India, now part of Madhya Pradesh. **2.** a town in N Madhya Pradesh. 300,587 (1961).

G.W.R., Great Western Railway.

Gwydir (gwī′də), *n.* a river in E Australia, flowing W through New South Wales to the Barwon river. ab. 415 mi.

Gwyn (gwĭn), *n.* **Nell,** 1650–87, English actress and mistress of Charles II.

gwyniad (gwĭn′ĭ ăd′), *n.* a rare fish, *Coregonus pennantii*, found in Bala Lake, N Wales. [t. Welsh]

Gwyr (*Welsh.* gwĭr), *n.* Welsh name of **Gower.**

gybe (jīb), *v.*, **gybed, gybing,** *n.* *Naut.* —*v.i.* **1.** to shift from one side to the other when running before the wind, as a fore-and-aft sail or its boom. **2.** to alter the course so that the sail shifts in this manner. —*v.t.* **3.** to cause (a sail, etc.) to gybe. —*n.* **4.** the act of gybing. Also, **jibe.** [t. D: m. *gijben*]

gym (jĭm), *n.* **1.** gymnasium. **2.** gymnastics.

gymkhana (jĭm kä′nə), *n.* **1.** a display of athletic sports, esp. equestrian events. **2.** the place where this is held. [t. Hind.: m. *gendkhāna*, lit., ball house]

gymnasia (jĭm nā′ zyə), *n.* a pl. of **gymnasium.**

gymnasiarch (jĭm nā′zĭ äk′), *n.* a magistrate who superintended the gymnasia and certain public games in ancient Athens. [t. L: s. *gymnasiarchus*, t. Gk: m. *gymnasíarchos*]

gymnasium (jĭm nā′zyəm), *n.*, *pl.*, **-siums, -sia** (-zyə). **1.** a building or room designed and equipped for physical education activities. **2.** a place where Greek youths met for exercise and discussion. [t. L, t. Gk: m. *gymnásion* (see def. 2)]

Gymnasium (jĭm nā′zyəm; *Ger.* gʏm nä′zē ōōm), *n.* (in N continental Europe, etc.) a boys' secondary school emphasizing classical studies. [G, t. L. See GYMNASIUM]

gymnast (jĭm′năst), *n.* one trained and skilled in, or a teacher of, gymnastics. [t. Gk: s. *gymnastḗs* trainer of athletes]

gymnastic (jĭm năs′tĭk), *adj.* pertaining to exercises which develop flexibility, strength, and agility. —**gymnas′tically,** *adv.*

gymnastics (jĭm năs′tĭks), *n.* **1.** (*construed as pl.*) gymnastic exercises. **2.** (*construed as sing.*) the practice or art of gymnastic exercises.

gymnosperm (jĭm′nō spûm′), *n.* *Bot.* a plant having its seeds exposed or naked, not enclosed in an ovary (opposed to *angiosperm*). [t. NL: s. *gymnospermus*, t. Gk: m. *gymnóspermos*]

gymnospermous (jĭm′nō spû′məs), *adj.* *Bot.* of the gymnosperm class; having naked seeds.

gyn-, var. of **gyno-,** occurring before vowels, as in *gynarchy.*

gynaeceum (jī′nĭ sē′əm), *n.*, *pl.* **-cea** (-sē′ə). **1.** *Bot.* gynoecium. **2.** (among the Greeks) that part of a dwelling used by women. Also, **gynaecium** (jī′nĭ sī′əm). [t. L, t. Gk: m. *gynaikeîon*, neut. sing. of adj. *gynaikeîos* of or pertaining to women]

gynaecocracy (jī′nĭ kŏk′rə sĭ), *n.*, *pl.* **-cies.** government by a woman or women. Also, *U.S.*, **gynecocracy.** [t. Gk: m. s. *gynaikokratía*]

gynaecologist (gī′nĭ kŏl′ə jĭst), *n.* a doctor who specializes in women's diseases. Also, *U.S.*, **gynecologist.**

gynaecology (gī′nĭ kŏl′ə jĭ), *n.* that department of medical science which deals with the functions and diseases peculiar to women. Also, *U.S.*, **gynecology.** [f. m. Gk *gynaiko-* (comb. form of *gynḗ* woman) + -LOGY] —**gynaecological** (gī′nĭ kə lŏj′ĭ kl), *adj.*

gynaecomorphous (jī′nĭ kō mô′fəs), *adj. Biol.* having the form, appearance, or attributes of a female. Also, *U.S.*, **gynecomorphous.** [t. Gk: m. *gynaikómorphos* in the shape of a woman]

gynandromorph (jī năn′drō môf′), *n. Biol.* an organism with characteristics of both sexes. [f. m. s. Gk *gýnandros* of doubtful sex + -MORPH] —**gynan′dromorph′ic, gynan′dromorph′ous,** *adj.* —**gynan′dromorph′ism, gynan′dromor′phy,** *n.*

gynandrous (jī năn′drəs, jĭ-), *adj. Bot.* having the stamens borne on the pistil and united in a column, as in orchids. [t. Gk: m. *gýnandros* of doubtful sex]

gynarchy (jī′nä′kĭ), *n.*, *pl.* **-chies.** government by a woman or women.

gynecium (jī nē′sĭ əm), *n.*, *pl.* **-cia** (-sĭ ə). *Chiefly U.S.* gynoeceum.

gyniatrics (jī′nĭ ăt′rĭks), *n.* the treatment of diseases peculiar to women. [f. Gk *gyn(ḗ)* woman + -IATRIC(S)]

gyno-, a word element meaning 'woman', 'female', as in *gynogenic.* Also, **gyn-.** [t. Gk, comb. form of *gynḗ* woman]

gynoecium (jī nē′sĭ əm), *n.*, *pl.* **-cia** (-sĭ ə). *Bot.* the pistil, or the pistils collectively, of a flower. Also, **gynaeceum, gynaecium, gynecium.** [t. NL, f. *gyn-* GYN- + m. Gk *oikíon* house]

gynogenic (jī′nō jĕn′ĭk), *adj. Embryol.* female-producing or feminizing (opposed to *androgenic*).

gynophore (jī′nō fô′), *n. Bot.* the elongated pedicel or stalk bearing the pistil in some flowers.

-gynous, **1.** an adjective combining form referring to the female sex, as in *androgynous.* **2.** a suffix meaning 'woman'. [t. Gk: m. *-gynos*, der. *gynḗ* woman]

Györ (*Hung.* dyœr), *n.* a town in NW Hungary. 72,319 (1962).

gyp[1] (jĭp), *v.*, **gypped, gypping,** *n. U.S. Slang.* —*v.t.* **1.** to swindle; cheat; defraud or rob by some sharp practice. **2.** to obtain by swindling or cheating; steal. —*n.* **3.** a swindle. **4.** a swindler or cheat. Also, **gip.** [orig. uncert.] —**gyp′per,** *n.*

gyp[2] (jĭp), *n. Colloq.* a male college servant, as at Cambridge and Durham universities. [short for GYPSY]

gyp[3] (jĭp), *n. Slang.* pain; severe punishment; torture. Also, **gip.**

gypsophila (jĭp sŏf′ĭ lə), *n.* any of the genus *Gypsophila* of slender, graceful herbs, chiefly Mediterranean, allied to the pinks and having small panicled flowers. [NL, f. Gk: *gýpso(s)* chalk + *phíla*, neut. pl. of *phílos*, adj., fond of]

gypsum (jĭp′səm), *n.* a very common mineral, hydrated calcium sulphate, $CaSO_4 . 2H_2O$, occurring in crystals and in masses, soft enough to be scratched by the fingernail: used to make plaster of Paris, as an ornamental material, as a fertilizer, etc. [t. L, t. Gk: m. *gýpsos* chalk, gypsum]

gypsy (jĭp′sĭ), *n.*, *pl.* **-sies,** *adj.* gipsy.

gypsy moth, gipsy moth.

gypsy winch, gipsy winch.

gypsywort (jĭp′sĭ wût′), *n.* gipsywort.

gyrate (*adj.* jī′ə rĭt; *v.* jī rāt′), *v.*, **-rated, -rating,** *adj.* —*v.i.* **1.** to move in a circle or spiral, or round a fixed point; whirl. —*adj.* **2.** *Zool.* having convolutions. [t. L: m. s. *gyrātus*, pp., wheeled round, turned]

gyration (jī rā′shən), *n.* the act of gyrating; circular or spiral motion; revolution; rotation; whirling.

gyratory (jī′ə rə tə rĭ, -trĭ), *adj.* moving in a circle or spiral; gyrating.

gyre (jī′ə), *n. Poetic.* **1.** a ring or circle. **2.** a circular course or motion.

gyrfalcon (jû′fôl′kən, -fô′kən), *n.* any of various large arctic and subarctic falcons, as the **white gyrfalcon,** *Falco rusticolus.* Also, **gerfalcon.** [ME, t. OF: m. *gerfaucon*; of Gmc orig.]

White gyrfalcon, *Falco rusticolus* (Length 2 ft)

gyro (jī′ə rō), *n.*, *pl.* **-ros. 1.** gyrocompass. **2.** gyroscope. [short for GYROCOMPASS, GYROSCOPE]

gyro-, a word element meaning: **1.** 'ring'; 'circle'. **2.** 'spiral'. [t. Gk, comb. form of *gŷros* ring, circle]

gyrocompass (jī′ə rō kŭm′pəs), *n.* a device used like the ordinary compass for determining directions, but employing a continuously driven gyroscope instead of a magnetized needle or bar, the gyroscope being so mounted that its axis constantly maintains its position with reference to the geographical north, thus dealing with true geographical meridians used in navigation instead of magnetic meridians. Also, **gyroscopic compass.**

gyromagnetic ratio, (jī′ə rō măg nĕt′ĭk), *Physics.* the ratio of the magnetic moment of an atom, nucleus, or particle to its angular momentum.

gyroplane (jī′ə rə plān′), *n.* an autogyro.

gyroscope (jī′ə rə skōp′), *n.* an apparatus consisting of a rotating wheel so mounted that its axis can turn freely in certain or all directions, and capable of maintaining the same absolute direction in space in spite of movements of the mountings and surrounding parts. It is based on the principle that a body rotating steadily about an axis will tend to resist changes in the direction of the axis, and is used to maintain equilibrium, as in an aeroplane or ship, to determine direction, etc. [t. F. See GYRO-, -SCOPE] —**gyroscopic** (jī′ə rə skŏp′ĭk), *adj.*

Gyroscope

gyroscopic compass, gyrocompass. Also, **gyrostatic compass.**

gyrose (jī′ə rōz′), *adj.* marked with wavy lines.

gyrostabilizer (jī′ə rō stā′bĭ lī′zə), *n.* a device for stabilizing a seagoing vessel by counteracting its rolling motion from side to side, consisting essentially of a rotating gyroscope weighing about 1 per cent of the displacement of the vessel. Also, **gyrostabiliser.**

gyrostat (jī′ə rō stăt′), *n.* a modification of the gyroscope, consisting of a rotating wheel pivoted within a rigid case.

gyrostatic (jī′ə rō stăt′ĭk), *adj.* pertaining to the gyrostat or to gyrostatics. —**gy′rostat′ically,** *adv.*

gyrostatics (jī′ə rō stăt′ĭks), *n. Mech.* the science which deals with the laws of rotating bodies.

gyrus (jī′ə rəs), *n.*, *pl.* **gyri** (jī′ə rī′). *Anat.* a convolution, esp. of the brain. [t. L, t. Gk: m. *gŷros* ring, circle]

gyve (jīv), *n.*, *v.*, **gyved, gyving.** —*n.* **1.** (*usually pl.*) a shackle, esp. for the leg; fetter. —*v.t.* **2.** to shackle. [ME *gives, gyves* (pl.); orig. uncert.]

H, h (āch), *n.*, *pl.* **H's** or **Hs, h's** or **hs. 1.** a consonant, the 8th letter of the English alphabet. **2.** (as a symbol) the eighth in a series.

H, 1. (of pencils) hard. **2.** *Elect.* henry. **3.** hydrant. **4.** *Chem.* hydrogen. **5.** *Physics.* **a.** intensity of magnetic field. **b.** enthalpy.

h, *Physics.* Planck's constant.

h., 1. harbour. **2.** hard. **3.** hardness. **4.** height. **5.** high. **6.** hour. **7.** hundred. **8.** husband.

ha (hä), *interj.* (an exclamation of surprise, interrogation, suspicion, triumph, etc.) Also, **hah.**

ha., hectare.

h. a., (L *hoc anno*) in this year.

haaf (häf), *n.* a deep-sea fishing ground off the Orkney and Shetland Islands. [t. Scand.; cf. Icel. *haf* sea]

Haakon VII (hô′kŏn), 1872–1957, king of Norway 1905–1957; exiled in England 1940–45.

haar (hä), *n.* a sea-fog on the east coast of England and Scotland. [d. var. of HOAR]

Haarlem (hä′ləm; *Du.* här′lĕm), *n.* a city in W Netherlands, in S North Holland, W of Amsterdam. 172,017 (1965).

Hab., Habakkuk.

Habakkuk (hăb′ə kək), *n.* **1.** a Hebrew prophet and poet. **2.** his book of prophecies, the eighth of the minor prophets of the Old Testament.

Habana (*Sp.* ȧ bȧ′nȧ), *n.* Spanish name of **Havana.**

habanera (hăb′ə nyĕə′rə), *n.* **1.** a dance of Cuban origin. **2.** the music for this dance, in two-four time.

habeas corpus (hā′byəs kô′pəs), *Law.* a writ requiring the body of a person to be brought before a judge or court, esp. for investigation of a restraint of the person's liberty, used as a protection against illegal imprisonment. [L: you may have the body, the first words of the writ]

haberdasher (hăb′ə dăsh′ə), *n.* **1.** a seller of small wares, as buttons, needles, ribbons, etc. **2.** *U.S.* a men's outfitters. [orig. obscure. Cf. AF *hapertas* kind of fabric]

haberdashery (hăb′ə dăsh′ə rĭ), *n., pl.* **-ries. 1.** a haberdasher's shop, counter, or section of a department store. **2.** the goods sold there.

habergeon (hăb′ə jən), *n.* **1.** a short hauberk. **2.** any hauberk. Also, **haubergeon.** [ME *haubergeon,* t. OF, dim. of *hauberc* HAUBERK]

Haber process (hä′bə), *Chem.* an industrial process for preparing ammonia from atmospheric nitrogen, whereby nitrogen is heated with hydrogen under high pressure in the presence of a catalyst; gaseous ammonia being formed according to the equation $N_2 + 3H_2 = 2NH_3$. [named after Fritz *Haber*, 1868–1934, German chemist]

habile (hăb′ēl), *adj.* skilful; dexterous. [t. F, t. L: m. *habilis* fit, apt]

habiliment (hə bĭl′ĭ mənt), *n.* **1.** (*pl.*) clothes or garments, esp. those suited to a particular occasion. **2.** dress; attire. [ME *habylement,* t. OF: m. *habillement,* der. *habiller* dress, der. *habile* (see HABILE)] **—habil′imented,** *adj.*

habilitate (hə bĭl′ĭ tāt′), *v.t.,* **-tated, -tating. 1.** *Western U.S.* to furnish money or means to work (a mine). **2.** *Archaic.* to clothe or dress. [t. ML: m. s. *habilitātus,* pp. of *habilitāre,* der. L *habilitas* ability] **—habil′ita′tion,** *n.* **—habil′ita′tor,** *n.*

habit (hăb′ĭt), *n.* **1.** a disposition or tendency, constantly shown, to act in a certain way. **2.** such a disposition acquired by frequent repetition of an act. **3.** a particular practice, custom, or usage. **4.** an addiction to, or compulsive need of, esp. narcotics. **5.** customary practice or use: *to act from force of habit.* **6.** mental character or disposition: *habit of mind.* **7.** characteristic bodily or physical condition: *habit of body.* **8.** the characteristic form, aspect, mode of growth, etc., of an animal or plant: *a twining habit.* **9.** *Chem.* the characteristic crystalline form of a mineral. **10.** garb of a particular rank, profession, religious order, etc.: *monk's habit.* **11.** a woman's riding dress. *—v.t.* **12.** to clothe; array. **13.** *Obs.* to dwell in. *—v.i.* **14.** *Obs.* to dwell. [t. L: s. *habitus* condition, appearance, dress; r. ME *abit,* t. OF] **—Syn. 3.** See **custom.**

habitable (hăb′ĭ tə bl), *adj.* capable of being inhabited. **—hab′itabil′ity, hab′itableness,** *n.* **—hab′itably,** *adv.*

habitant (hăb′ĭ tənt; *for 2 also Fr.* ȧ bē täɴ′), *n.* **1.** an inhabitant. **2.** a French settler in Canada or Louisiana, or a descendant of one, esp. one of the farming class. [late ME, t. F, t. L: s. *habitans,* ppr., dwelling]

habitat (hăb′ĭ tăt′), *n.* **1.** the native environment or kind of place where a given animal or plant naturally lives or grows, as warm seas, mountain tops, fresh waters, etc. **2.** place of abode; habitation. [t. L: it inhabits]

habitation (hăb′ĭ tā′shən), *n.* **1.** a place of abode; dwelling. **2.** the act of inhabiting; occupancy by inhabitants. **—Syn. 1.** residence, domicile, quarters.

habitual (hə bĭt′yŏŏ əl), *adj.* **1.** of the nature of a habit, or fixed by or resulting from habit: *habitual courtesy.* **2.** being such by habit: *a habitual drunkard.* **3.** commonly used (by a given person): *she took her habitual place at the table.* [t. LL: s. *habituālis*] **—habit′ually,** *adv.* **—habit′ualness,** *n.* **—Syn. 2.** confirmed, inveterate. **3.** See **usual. —Ant. 2.** occasional. **3.** unaccustomed.

habituate (hə bĭt′yŏŏ āt′), *v.t.,* **-ated, -ating. 1.** to accustom (a person, the mind, etc.), as to something; make used (*to*). **2.** *U.S. Colloq.* to frequent. [t. LL: m. s. *habituātus,* pp. of *habituāre* bring into a condition, der. L *habitus* HABIT] **—habit′ua′tion,** *n.* **—Syn. 1.** familiarize; inure, harden, acclimatize, acclimate.

habitude (hăb′ĭ tyōōd′), *n.* **1.** customary condition, character, or habit. **2.** a habit or custom. **3.** *Obs.* relationship. [t. F, t. L: m. *habitūdo* condition]

habitué (hə bĭt′yŏŏ ā′; *Fr.* ȧ bē twė′), *n.* a habitual frequenter of a place. [t. F, pp. of *habituer* HABITUATE]

haboob (hə bōōb′), *n.* a sandstorm or dust storm of North Africa. [t. Ar.: strong wind]

Habsburg (hăps′bûg; *Ger.* hȧps′bŏŏrk), *n.* a German princely family, prominent since the 11th century, which has furnished sovereigns to the Holy Roman Empire, Austria, Spain, etc. Also, **Hapsburg.** [shortening of *Habichtsburg* (hawk's castle), a castle in Switzerland]

H.A.C., Honourable Artillery Company.

Hachinohe (hăch′ĭ nō′hĭ, -nō′ĭ), *n.* a town in Japan, in N Honshu island. 189,387 (1965).

Hachioji (hăch′ĭ ō′jĭ), *n.* a town in Japan, in SE Honshu island, W of Tokyo. 207,753 (1965).

hachure (hă shyŏŏə′), *n., v.,* **-chured, -churing.** *—n.* **1.** (in drawing, engraving, etc.) hatching. **2.** (on a map) shading used to indicate relief features, consisting of lines drawn parallel to the slopes and varying in width with the degree of slope. *—v.t.* **3.** to mark or shade with, or indicate by, hachures. [t. F, der. *hacher* HATCH[3]]

hacienda (hăs′ĭ ĕn′də; *Sp.* ȧ thyĕn′dȧ), *n. Spanish American.* **1.** a landed estate, ranch, or farm. **2.** the main house on such an estate; a country house. **3.** a stock-raising, mining, or manufacturing establishment in the country. [t. Sp.: landed property, estate, g. L *facienda* things to be done, neut. pl. ger. of *facere* do]

hack[1] (hăk), *v.t.* **1.** to cut, notch, or chop irregularly, as with heavy blows. **2.** to break up the surface of (the ground). **3.** to clear (a path, etc.) by cutting down brush, etc. **4.** to damage by cutting harshly or ruthlessly: *the subeditor hacked the article to bits.* **5.** to kick the shins of intentionally, as in Rugby football. *—v.i.* **6.** to make rough cuts or notches; deal cutting blows. **7.** to kick an opponent's shins intentionally, as in Rugby football. *—n.* **8.** a cut, gash, or notch. **9.** a tool, as an axe, hoe, pick, etc., for hacking. **10.** an act of hacking; a cutting blow. **11.** a short, broken cough. **12.** a gash in the skin produced by a kick, as in Rugby football. **13.** a kick. [ME *hacke(n),* OE (*tō*)*haccian* hack to pieces, c. D *hakken,* G *hacken*] **—hack′er,** *n.* **—Syn. 1.** See **cut.**

hack[2] (hăk), *n.* **1.** a horse kept for common hire, or adapted for general work, esp. ordinary riding. **2.** a saddle-horse for the road. **3.** an old or worn-out horse; a jade. **4.** a person who for a living undertakes literary or other work of little or no originality and permanent value; one who does hackwork. **5.** *U.S.* a coach or carriage kept for hire; a hackney. **6.** *U.S. Colloq.* a taxi. *—v.t.* **7.** to make a hack of; let out for hire. **8.** to make trite or stale by frequent use; hackney. *—v.i.* **9.** to ride on the road at an ordinary pace, as distinguished from cross-country or military riding. **10.** *U.S. Colloq.* to drive a taxi. *—adj.* **11.** hired; of a hired sort: *hack work.* **12.** hackneyed; trite. [short for HACKNEY]

hack[3] (hăk), *n.* **1.** a rack for holding cattle fodder. **2.** a solid foundation or low platform on which newly formed bricks are stacked to dry before burning. *—v.t.* **3.** to place (bricks) on a hack, as for drying.

hackamore (hăk′ə mô′), *n. U.S.* **1.** a coil of rope which passes through the horse's mouth and about his neck, used to break a horse. **2.** *Western U.S.* any of several forms of halter used esp. for breaking horses.

hackberry (hăk′bĕ′rĭ), *n., pl.* **-ries. 1.** the small, edible, cherry-like fruit of American trees of the ulmaceous genus *Celtis.* **2.** a tree bearing this fruit. **3.** its wood. [var. of *hagberry,* t. Scand.; cf. Dan. *haeggebrær*]

hackbut (hăk′bŭt), *n. Archaic.* arquebus. [t. MF: m. *haquebute,* b. *buter* to butt and MF *haquebusche* (t. MD: m. *hakebus,* lit., a hook gun)]

hack hammer, an adzelike tool for dressing stone.

hacking cough, a deep, harsh, frequently repeated cough.

hacking jacket, 1. a riding jacket, with tight waist, slanted pockets with flaps, and vents at the sides or back. **2.** a man's sports jacket with vents at the sides or back.

hackle[1] (hăk′l), *n., v.,* **-led, -ling.** *—n.* **1.** one of the long, slender feathers on the neck or saddle of certain birds, as the domestic cock, much used in making artificial flies for anglers. **2.** the whole neck plumage of the domestic cock, etc. **3.** (*pl.*) the hair on a dog's neck. **4. with one's hackles up,** very angry; on the point of fighting. **5.** *Angling.* **a.** an artificial fly's legs made with hackles (def. 1). **b.** a hackle fly. **6.** a comb for dressing flax or hemp. *—v.t.* **7.** *Angling.* to supply with a hackle. **8.** to comb, as flax or hemp. [ME *hakell.* See HECKLE] **—hack′ler,** *n.*

hackle[2] (hăk′l), *v.t.,* **-led, -ling.** to cut roughly; hack; mangle. [freq. of HACK[1], c. MD *hakkelen*]

hackle fly, an artificial fly made with hackles.

hackly (hăk′lĭ), *adj.* rough or jagged. [f. HACKLE[2] + -Y[1]]

hackney (hăk′nĭ), *n., pl.* **-neys,** *adj., v.,* **-neyed, -neying.** *—n.* **1.** a horse for ordinary riding or driving. **2.** *Obs.* a horse kept for hire. **3.** a carriage kept for hire. *—adj.* **4.** let out, employed, or done for hire. *—v.t.* **5.** to make common, stale, or trite by frequent use. **6.** to use as a hackney. [ME *hakeney*; orig. uncert.]

Hackney (hăk′nĭ), *n.* a NE inner London borough. 254,300 (1965).

hackney-carriage (hăk′nĭ kă′rĭj), *n.* any carriage or vehicle which plies for hire, orig. horse-drawn.

hackney-coach (hăk′nĭ kōch′), *n.* a four-wheeled carriage, drawn by two horses, having six seats and kept for hire.

hackneyed (hăk′nĭd), *adj.* **1.** made commonplace or trite; stale. **2.** habituated. **—Syn. 1.** See **commonplace.**

hacksaw (hăk′sô′), *n.* a saw used for cutting metal, consisting typically of a narrow, fine-toothed blade fixed in a frame.

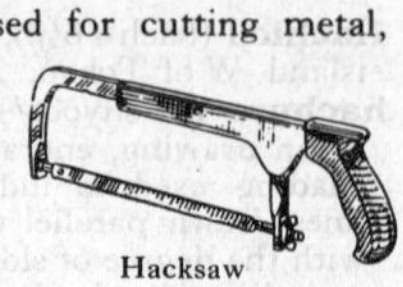

Hacksaw

hackwork (hăk′wûk′), *n.* literary or other drudgery, as for publishers.

had (hăd), *v.* pt. and pp. of **have.**

Haddington (hăd′ĭng tən), *n.* **1.** a burgh in Scotland, the county town of East Lothian. 5506 (1961). **2.** former name of **East Lothian.**

haddock (hăd′ək), *n., pl.* **-docks,** (*esp. collectively*) **-dock.** a food fish, *Melanogrammus aeglefinus*, of the northern Atlantic, related to but smaller than the cod. [ME *haddoc*; orig. unknown]

hade (hād), *n., v.,* **haded, hading.** *Geol.* **—***n.* **1.** the angle between a fault plane and a vertical plane striking parallel to the fault. **—***v.i.* **2.** to incline from a vertical position. [orig. uncert.]

Hades (hā′dēz), *n.* **1.** *Gk Myth.* **a.** the gloomy subterranean abode of departed spirits or shades over which Pluto ruled. **b.** Pluto; the lord of the underworld. **2.** (in the Revised Version of the New Testament) the abode or state of the dead. **3.** (*l.c.*) *Colloq.* hell. [t. Gk: m. *Haídēs* (orig. *aídēs*)] **—Hadean** (hā dē′ən, hā′dĭ ən), *adj.*

Hadfield (hăd′fēld′), *n.* **Sir Robert Abbott,** 1858–1940, English scientist and metallurgist.

Hadhramaut (hä′drə môt′), *n.* a region along the S coast of the Arabian peninsula, in South Yemen. Also, **Hadramaut.**

hadj (hăj), *n.* hajj.

hadji (hăj′ĭ), *n., pl.* **hadjis.** hajji.

hadn't (hăd′nt), a contraction of *had not.*

Hadrian (hā′drĭ ən), *n.* A.D. 76–138, Roman emperor A.D. 117–138. Also, **Adrian.**

Hadrian's Wall, a wall of defence for the Roman province of Britain, constructed by Hadrian between Solway Firth and the mouth of the Tyne.

Hadrian's Wall

hae (hā), *v.t. Scot.* have.

Haeckel (*Ger.* hĕk′əl), *n.* **Ernst Heinrich** (*Ger.* ĕrnst hīn′rĭkh), 1834–1919, German biologist and philosopher.

haem (hēm), *n. Biochem.* a complex organic pigment containing iron, carbon, hydrogen, nitrogen and oxygen, and present, linked chemically to protein, in haemoglobin. Also, *Chiefly U.S.*, **heme.**

haem-, var. of **haemo-,** before vowels, as in *haemal.* Also, *Chiefly U.S.*, **hem-.** Cf. **haemat-.**

haema-, var. of **haemo-.** Also, *Chiefly U.S.*, **hema-.**

haemachrome (hē′mə krōm′, hĕm′ə-), *n.* the red colouring matter of the blood.

haemal (hē′məl), *adj.* **1.** of or pertaining to the blood or blood vessels. **2.** *Zool.* denoting, pertaining to, or on the side of the body ventral to the spinal axis, containing the heart and great blood vessels.

haemat-, a prefix equivalent to **haemo-,** as in *haematin.* Also, **haemato-;** *Chiefly U.S.*, **hemat-, hemato-.**

haematic (hē măt′ĭk), *adj.* **1.** of or pertaining to blood; haemic. **2.** acting on the blood, as a medicine. **—***n.* **3.** a haematic medicine. [t. Gk: m. s. *haimatikós* of the blood]

haematin (hĕm′ə tĭn, hē′mə-), *n. Biochem.* a pigment containing iron, produced in the decomposition of haemoglobin as the result of oxidization of the haem component.

haematinic (hĕm′ə tĭn′ĭk, hē′mə-), *n.* **1.** a medicine, as a compound of iron, which tends to increase the amount of haematin or haemoglobin in the blood. **—***adj.* **2.** of or obtained from haematin.

haematite (hĕm′ə tīt′), *n.* a very common mineral, iron oxide, Fe_2O_3, occurring in steel-grey to black crystals and in red earthy masses; the principal ore of iron. [t. L: m. s. *haematites* haematite, t. Gk: m. *haimatítēs* bloodlike] **—haematitic** (hĕm′ə tĭt′ĭk), *adj.*

haemato-, a prefix equivalent to **haemo-,** as in *haematogenesis.* Also, *Chiefly U.S.*, **hemato-.**

haematocele (hĕm′ə tō sēl′, hē′mə-), *n. Pathol.* (usually) a haemorrhage imprisoned in membranous tissue.

haematocryal (hĕm′ə tō krī′əl, hē′mə-), *adj.* cold-blooded.

haematogenesis (hĕm′ə tō jĕn′ĭ sĭs), *n.* formation of blood.

haematogenous (hĕm′ə tŏj′ĭ nəs, hē′mə-), *adj.* **1.** originating in the blood. **2.** blood-producing.

haematoid (hē′mə toid′, hĕm′ə-), *adj.* bloodlike. [t. Gk: m. s. *haimatoeidḗs* bloodlike]

haematology (hē′mə tŏl′ə jĭ), *n. Med.* the study of the nature, function, and diseases of the blood. [f. HAEMATO- + -LOGY] **—haem′atolog′ical,** *adj.* **—haem′atolog′ically,** *adv.* **—haem′atol′ogist,** *n.*

haematoma (hē′mə tō′mə, hĕm′ə-), *n., pl.* **-mata** (-mə tə), **-mas.** *Pathol.* a bruise or collection of blood in a tissue.

haematopoiesis (hĕm′ə tō poi ē′sĭs, hē′mə-), *n.* the formation of blood. [t. NL, f. Gk: m. *haimato-* HAEMATO- + *poíēsis* a making] **—haematopoietic** (hĕm′ə tō poi ĕt′ĭk, hē′mə-), *adj.*

haematosis (hĕm′ə tō′sĭs, hĕm′ə-), *n.* **1.** the formation of blood. **2.** *Physiol.* the conversion of venous into arterial blood; oxygenation in the lungs. [t. Gk: m. *haimátōsis*, der. *haimatoûn* make into blood]

haematothermal (hĕm′ə tō thû′məl, hē′mə-), *adj.* warm-blooded.

haematoxylin (hē′mə tŏk′sĭ lĭn), *n.* **1.** a leguminous plant of a genus *Haematoxylon*, of which only one species, *H. campechianum*, the logwood tree, is known. **2.** the wood of the logwood. **3.** *Chem.* a colourless or pale yellow crystalline compound, $C_{16}H_{14}O_6.3H_2O$, the colouring matter of logwood, used as a mordant dye and as an indicator. [f. s. NL *haematoxylum* logwood (f. Gk *haimato-* HAEMATO- + m. *xýlon* wood) + -IN[2]]

-haemia, var. of **-aemia.** Also, *Chiefly U.S.*, **-hemia.**

haemic (hē′mĭk, hĕm′ĭk), *adj.* haematic.

haemin (hē′mĭn), *n.* the microscopic reddish brown crystals, resulting when a sodium chloride crystal, a drop of glacial acetic acid, and some blood are heated on a slide; used to show the presence of blood. [f. HAEM- + -IN[2]]

haemo-, a word element meaning 'blood' as in *haemolysis.* Also, **haem-;** *Chiefly U.S.*, **hemo-.** Cf. **haema-, haemat-, haemato-.** [t. Gk: m. *haimo-*, comb. form of *haîma*]

haemocyte (hē′mō sīt′), *n.* **1.** a red blood corpuscle. **2.** any blood cell.

haemocytometer (hē′mō sī tŏm′ĭ tə), *n.* an instrument for counting blood cells. Also, **haemacytometer.**

haemoglobin (hē′mō glō′bĭn, hĕm′ō-), *n. Biochem., Physiol.* the protein colouring matter of the red blood corpuscles, which serves to convey oxygen to the tissues; occurring in reduced form **(reduced haemoglobin)** in venous blood, and in combination with oxygen **(oxyhaemoglobin)** in arterial blood. [short for *haematoglobulin*, f. *haemato-* (for HAEMATIN) + GLOBULIN]

haemoid (hē′moid), *adj.* bloodlike.

haemoleucocyte (hē′mō lo͞o′kə sīt′, hĕm′ō-), *n. Anat.* any white blood cell that circulates in the blood. Also, **haemoleukocyte.**

haemolysin (hē′mō lī′sĭn, hĕm′ō-, hĭ mŏl′ĭ-), *n. Med.* an antibody which, in cooperation with a material in fresh blood, causes dissolution of the red blood corpuscles.

haemolysis (hĭ mŏl′ĭ sĭs), *n. Med.* the breaking down of the red blood cells with liberation of haemoglobin. **—haemolytic** (hē′mō lĭt′ĭk, hĕm′ō-), *adj.*

haemophilia (hē′mō fĭl′ĭ ə), *n. Pathol.* a morbid condition, usually congenital, characterized by a tendency to bleed immoderately, as from an insignificant wound, caused by improper coagulation of the blood. [NL, t. Gk: m. *haimo-* HAEMO- + *philía* affection, fondness]

haemophiliac (hē′mō fĭl′ĭ ăk′), *n.* a person or organism which has haemophilia.

haemophilic (hē′mō fĭl′ĭk, hĕm′ō-), *adj.* **1.** affected by haemophilia. **2.** *Biol.* (of bacteria) developing best in a culture containing blood, or in blood itself.

haemoptysis (hĭ mŏp′tĭ sĭs), *n. Pathol.* the expectoration of blood or bloody mucus. [t. NL, f. Gk: m. *haimo-* HAEMO- + *ptýsis* spitting]

haemorrhage (hĕm′ə rĭj), *n.* a discharge of blood, as from a ruptured blood vessel. [t. L: m. s. *haemorrhagia*, t. Gk: m. *haimorrhagía* a violent bleeding] **—haemorrhagic** (hĕm′ə răj′ĭk), *adj.*

haemorrhagic septicaemia, *Vet. Sci.* an acute infectious disease of animals, marked by fever, catarrhal symptoms, pneumonia, and general blood infection.

haemorrhoid (hĕm′ə roid′), *n. Pathol.* a dilatation of the veins under the skin of the anus; a pile. [t. L: m. s. *haemorrhoida* piles, t. Gk: m. s. *haemorrhoís*] **—haem′orrhoi′dal,** *adj.*

haemorrhoidectomy (hĕm′ə roi dĕk′tə mĭ), *n., pl.* **-mies.** *Surg.* the operation for removal of haemorrhoids.

haemostasis (hē′mō stā′sĭs, hĕm′ō-), *n. Med.* the arrest of haemorrhage.

haemostat (hē′mō stăt′, hĕm′ō-), *n.* an instrument or agent used to compress or treat bleeding vessels in order to arrest haemorrhage.

haemostatic (hē′mō stăt′ĭk, hĕm′o-), *adj.* **1.** arresting haemorrhage, as a drug, styptic. **2.** pertaining to stagnation of the blood. **—***n.* **3.** a haemostatic agent or substance.

haeremai (hĕ′rə mī′, hī′rə mī′), *interj. N.Z.* (an expression of welcome.) [t. Maori]

haeres (hĭə′rēz), *n.*, *pl.* **haeredes** (hĭ rē′dēz). heres.

hafiz (hăf′ĭz), *n.* a title of a Muslim who knows the Koran by heart. [t. Ar.: *hāfiz* a guard, one who keeps (in memory)]

Hafiz (hăf′ĭz), *n.* died *c.* 1389, Persian poet.

hafnium (hăf′nyəm), *n. Chem.* a metallic element with a valency of four, found in zirconium ores. *Symbol:* Hf; *at. wt:* 178·49; *at. no.:* 72; *sp. gr.:* 12·1. [f. *Hafn(ia)*, L name of Copenhagen + -IUM]

haft (häft), *n.* **1.** a handle, esp. of a knife, sword, dagger, etc. —*v.t.* **2.** to furnish with a haft or handle; set in a haft. [ME; OE *hæft*, c. D and G *Heft*]

haftarah (hăf′tə rä′, hăf tä′rə), *n.* haphtarah.

hag[1] (hăg), *n.* **1.** a repulsive, often vicious or malicious, old woman. **2.** a witch. **3.** a hagfish. [ME *hagge*, *hegge*; appar. a familiar short form (with hypocoristic gemination) of OE *hægtesse* fury, witch; akin to G *Hexe* witch] —**hag′like′,** *adj.*

hag[2] (hăg, häg), *n. Scot. and Dial.* **1.** a soft spot in boggy land. **2.** a firm spot in a bog. [ME *hag* chasm, t. Scand.; cf. Icel. *högg* a cut, ravine]

Hag., Haggai.

Hagar (hā′gä, -gə), *n. Bible.* Egyptian concubine of Abraham, mother of Ishmael. Gen. 16.

hagbut (hăg′bŭt), *n. Archaic.* arquebus.

Hagen (hä′gən), *n.* (in the *Nibelungenlied*) the slayer of Siegfried. [G, c. OE *Hagena*]

Hagen (*Ger.* hȧ′gən), *n.* a town in Germany, in central North Rhine-Westphalia. 203,000 (est. 1966).

hagfish (hăg′fĭsh′), *n.*, *pl.* **-fishes,** (*esp. collectively*) **-fish.** any of the eel-like marine cyclostomes constituting the group or order *Hyperotreta*, notable esp. for their circular suctorial mouth and their habit of boring into the bodies of fishes.

Hagfish, *Myxine glutinosa* (Length 1½ ft)

Haggadah (hə gä′də), *n.*, *pl.* **-doth** (-dōth), *Jewish Lit.* **1.** that part of Jewish traditional literature not concerned with the Law. **2.** the free exposition or homiletic illustration of the Scripture. **3.** the ritual used on the first two nights of Passover. **4.** a book containing it. Also, **Haggada.** [t. Heb.: (m.) *haggādāh* narrative, der. *higgīd* tell] —**haggadic** (hə găd′ĭk, -gä′dĭk), **haggad′ical,** *adj.*

haggadist (hə gä′dĭst), *n.* **1.** a writer of Haggadoth. **2.** a student of the Haggadah. —**haggadistic** (hăg′ə dĭs′tĭk), *adj.*

Haggai (hăg′ā ī′), *n.* **1.** fl. 520 B.C., the tenth of the minor prophets of Israel. **2.** his book in the Old Testament.

haggard (hăg′əd), *adj.* **1.** wild-looking, as from prolonged suffering, anxiety, exertion, want, etc.; careworn; gaunt. **2.** *Falconry.* wild or untamed, esp. of a hawk caught after it has assumed adult plumage. [orig. uncert. Cf. F *hagard* (? t. E)] —**hag′gardly,** *adv.* —**hag′gardness,** *n.* —**Syn. 1.** emaciated, drawn; hollow-eyed. —**Ant. 1.** unstrained.

Haggard (hăg′əd), *n.* **(Sir) H(enry) Rider,** 1856–1925, English novelist.

hagged (hăgd, hăg′ĭd), *adj. Dial.* **1.** haglike. **2.** haggard (def. 1).

haggis (hăg′ĭs), *n. Chiefly Scot.* a dish made of the heart, liver, etc., of a sheep, etc., minced with suet and oatmeal, seasoned, and boiled in the stomach of the animal. [? f. *hag* chop + *es*, OE *æs* food, meat]

haggish (hăg′ĭsh), *adj.* of or like a hag; old and ugly. —**hag′gishly,** *adv.* —**hag′gishness,** *n.*

haggle (hăg′l), *v.*, **-gled, -gling,** *n.* —*v.i.* **1.** to bargain in a petty and tedious manner. **2.** to wrangle, dispute, or cavil. —*v.t.* **3.** *Archaic.* to harass with wrangling or haggling. **4.** to mangle in cutting; hack. —*n.* **5.** the act of haggling; wrangle or dispute over terms. [freq. of d. *hag*, v., cut, hew, hack, t. Scand.; cf. Icel. *höggva* strike, hack, c. OE *hēawan* hew] —**hag′gler,** *n.* —**Syn. 1.** chaffer, higgle; negotiate.

hagiarchy (hăg′ĭ ä′kĭ), *n.*, *pl.* **-chies.** hagiocracy.

hagio-, a word element meaning 'saint'. Also, **hagi-.** [t. Gk, comb. form of *hágios* sacred, holy]

hagiocracy (hăg′ĭ ŏk′rə sĭ), *n.*, *pl.* **-cies.** government by a body of persons esteemed as holy.

Hagiographa (hăg′ĭ ŏg′rə fə), *n.pl.* the third of the three Jewish divisions of the Old Testament, variously arranged, but usually comprising the Psalms, Proverbs, Job, Canticles, Ruth, Lamentations, Ecclesiastes, Esther, Daniel, Ezra, Nehemiah, and Chronicles. [t. LL, f. Gk: *hagio-* HAGIO- + *grapha* (for *gráphia*) writings]

hagiographer (hăg′ĭ ŏg′rə fə), *n.* **1.** one of the writers of the Hagiographa. **2.** a writer of lives of the saints; a hagiologist. Also, **hag′iog′raphist.**

hagiography (hăg′ĭ ŏg′rə fĭ), *n.*, *pl.* **-phies.** the writing and critical study of the lives of the saints; hagiology. —**hagiographic** (hăg′ĭ ə grăf′ĭk), **hag′iograph′ical,** *adj.*

hagiolatry (hăg′ĭ ŏl′ə trĭ), *n.* the veneration of saints. [f. HAGIO- + *-latry* (see LATRIA)] —**hag′iol′ater,** *n.* —**hag′iol′atrous,** *adj.*

hagiology (hăg′ĭ ŏl′ə jĭ), *n.*, *pl.* **-gies. 1.** that branch of literature which deals with the lives and legends of the saints. **2.** a work on these. **3.** a collection of such lives or legends. —**hagiologic** (hăg′ĭ ə lŏj′ĭk), **hag′iolog′ical,** *adj.* —**hagiologist,** *n.*

hagioscope (hăg′ĭ ə skōp′), *n.* a small opening in a church wall, giving worshippers a view of the high altar; a squint. —**hagioscopic** (hăg′ĭ ə skŏp′ĭk), *adj.*

hag-ridden (hăg′rĭd′n), *adj.* worried or tormented, as by a witch.

Hague (hāg), *n.* **The,** a city in W Netherlands, near the North Sea: seat of the government, royal residence, and Permanent Court of International Justice. 598,709 (1965). Dutch, **Den Haag,** or **'s Gravenhage.**

The Hague

Hague Tribunal, The, the permanent court of arbitration for the peaceful settlement of international disputes, established at The Hague by the international peace conference of 1899, whose panel of jurists nominates a list of persons from which the United Nations International Court of Justice is elected.

hah (hä), *interj.* ha.

ha-ha[1] (hä′hä′), *interj.* (an imitation of the sound of laughter used as an exclamation of amusement, surprise, derision, etc.)

ha-ha[2] (hä′hä′), *n.* a wall or other barrier, set in a ditch or depression to divide land without marring the landscape; a sunk fence. [t. F: m. *haha*]

Hahn (*Ger.* hȧn), *n.* **Otto** (*Ger.* ŏt′ō), 1879–1968, German physicist.

Hahnemann (hä′nə mən; *Ger.* hȧ′nə mȧn), *n.* **Samuel** (săm′yo͞o əl; *Ger.* zȧ′mo͞o ĕl) (*Christian Friedrich Samuel*), 1755–1843, German physician: founder of homoeopathy. —**Hahnemannian** (hä′nə măn′ĭ ən), *adj.* —**Hah′nemannism,** *n.*

Haida (hī′də), *n.* **1.** an American Indian language of south-eastern Alaska. **2.** a linguistic stock of the Na-Dene phylum, including Haida (def. 1).

Haidar Ali (hī′dər ä′lĭ), Hyder Ali.

Haiduk (hī′do͝ok), *n.* **1.** one of a class of mercenary soldiers in 16th-century Hungary. **2.** a patriotic brigand in the Slav portions of the Balkan Peninsula. **3.** a male servant or attendant dressed in Hungarian semi-military costume. Also, **Heyduck, Heyduke, Heyduc, Heiduc, Heiduk.** [repr. Hung. *hajduk* (pl. of *hajdu*) kind of foot soldiers, and Polish *hajduk* retainers, ult. t. Turk.: m. *haidud* marauder, brigand]

Haifa (hī′fə), *n.* a seaport in NW Israel. 201,000 (est. 1964). See map under **Israel.**

Haig (hāg), *n.* **Douglas, 1st Earl,** 1861–1928, British field marshal: commander-in-chief of the British forces in France from 1915–18.

haik (hīk, hāk), *n.* an oblong cloth used as an outer garment by the Arabs. Also, **haick.** [t. Ar.: m. *hayk*, der. *hāk* weave]

Haikou (hī′kou′), *n.* a port in China, on Hainan island, in Kwangtung province. 402,000 (est. 1958).

hail[1] (hāl), *v.t.* **1.** to salute or greet; welcome. **2.** to salute or name as: *to hail one victor.* **3.** to acclaim; to approve with enthusiasm. **4.** to call out to, in order to attract attention: *to hail a person.* —*v.i.* **5.** to call out in order to greet, attract attention, etc. **6. hail from,** to belong to as the place of residence, point of departure, etc. —*n.* **7.** a shout or call to attract attention. **8.** the act of hailing. **9.** a salutation or greeting. **10. within hail,** within reach of the voice. —*interj.* **11.** *Poetic and Literary.* (an exclamation of salutation or greeting.) [ME *haile(n)*, der. obs. *hail*, n. and adj., health(y), t. Scand.; cf. Icel. *heill* health, healthy, c. OE *hǣl* (n.), *hāl* (adj.). Cf. WASSAIL] —**hail′er,** *n.*

hail[2] (hāl), *n.* **1.** pellets or small, usually rounded, balls of ice falling from the clouds in a shower. **2.** a shower or storm of such pellets. **3.** a shower of anything: *a hail of bullets.* —*v.i.* **4.** to pour down hail. **5.** to fall as hail. —*v.t.* **6.** to pour down as or like hail. [ME *hail(e)*, OE *hægl*, c. D and G *Hagel*]

Haile Selassie (hī′lĭ sĭ läs′ĭ), born 1890, emperor of Ethiopia 1930–36 and since 1941; exiled in England 1936–41.

hail-fellow (hāl′fĕl′ō), *adj. Colloq.* **1.** on familiar terms. **2.** sociable; genial. Also, **hail-fellow-well-met.**

Hail Mary, Ave Maria.

hailstone (hāl′stōn′), *n.* a pellet of hail. [ME, f. HAIL[2] + STONE; r. ME *hawelstone*, OE *hagolstān*]

hailstorm (hāl′stôm′), *n.* a storm with hail.

Hainan (hī′năn′), *n.* an island in the South China Sea, separated from the mainland of S China by **Hainan Strait** (15 mi. wide): a part of Kwangtung province. 2,700,000 pop. (est. 1956); ab. 13,200 sq. mi.

Hainaut (*Fr.* ĕ nō′), *n.* **1.** a medieval county in territory now in SW Belgium and N France. **2.** a province in SE Belgium. 1,321,714 pop. (est. 1963); 1436 sq. mi. *Cap.:* Mons.

Haiphong (hī′fŏng′), *n.* a seaport in North Vietnam, near the Gulf of Tonkin. 369,248 (1963).

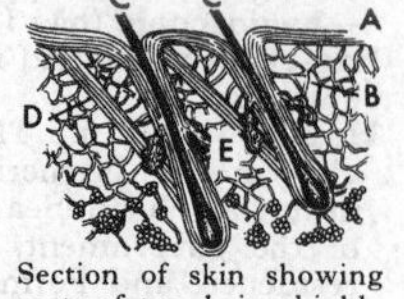

Section of skin showing roots of two hairs, highly magnified: A, Cuticle; B, Deeper root parts of skin; C, Single hair; D, Erecting muscle; E, Sebaceous glands

hair (hĕə), *n.* **1.** the natural covering of the human head. **2.** the aggregate of hairs which grow on an animal. **3.** one of the numerous fine, usually cylindrical filaments growing from the skin and forming the coat of most mammals. **4.** a similar fine, filamentous outgrowth from the body of insects, etc. **5.** *Bot.* a filamentous outgrowth of the epidermis. **6.** cloth made of hair from such animals as camel and alpaca. **7.** a very small magnitude, measure, degree, etc.: *he lost the race by a hair.* **8. get in someone's hair,** *Slang.* to irritate or annoy someone. **9. keep your hair on,** *Slang.* keep calm; do not get angry. **10. let one's hair down,** to behave informally or relaxedly. **11. make one's hair stand on end,** to fill with terror; terrify. **12. split hairs,** to make fine or unnecessary distinctions. **13. tear one's hair out,** to show extreme emotion, as anger, anxiety, etc. **14. without turning a hair,** showing no emotion; keeping placid and unmoved. [ME *ha(i)re*, t. Scand. (cf. Icel. *hār*); r. ME *her(e)*, OE *hær*, c. D *haar*, G *Haar*] —**hair′like′,** *adj.*

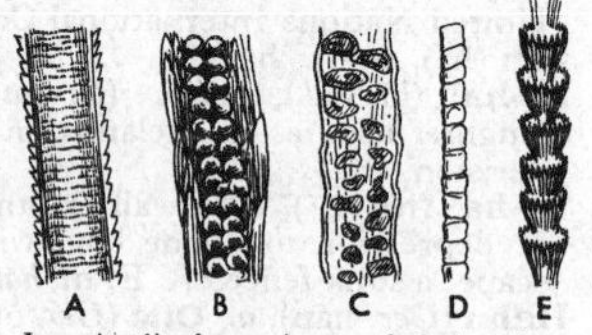

Longitudinal sections of hairs (enlarged): A, Man; B, Sable; C, Mouse. External view: D, Mouse; E, Indian bat

hairball (hĕə′bôl′), *n.* a ball of hair in the stomach of a cat, etc., formed as a result of the animal's licking its coat.

hairbreadth (hĕə′brĕtth′, -brĕdth′), *n., adj.* hair's-breadth.

hairbrush (hĕə′brŭsh′), *n.* a brush for grooming the hair.

haircloth (hĕə′klŏth′), *n.* cloth woven of hair from horses' tails and manes with cotton warp, for interlinings of clothes, etc.

haircut (hĕə′kŭt′), *n.* **1.** the act or instance of cutting the hair. **2.** the style in which the hair is cut and worn.

hairdo (hĕə′do͞o′), *n., pl.* **-dos. 1.** the style in which a woman's hair is arranged, cut, tinted, etc. **2.** the hair so arranged.

hairdresser (hĕə′drĕs′ə), *n.* one who arranges or cuts hair, esp. women's hair.

hairdressing (hĕə′drĕs′ĭng), *n.* **1.** the cutting, styling, tinting, and arranging of hair, esp. women's hair. **2.** the occupation of a hairdresser. **3.** a tonic or preparation for the hair.

hair follicle, *Anat.* a small cavity from which a hair develops.

hairgrass (hĕə′gräs′), *n.* any of several species of grasses belonging to the genus *Deschampsia*, as the **wavy hairgrass,** *D. flexuosa*, widespread on acid soils in N temperate regions.

hairgrip (hĕə′grĭp′), *n.* a metal hairpin with two slender prongs which clamp together in order to hold the hair. Also, **hairclip.**

hairless (hĕə′lĭs), *adj.* without hair; bald. —**hair′lessness,** *n.*

hairline (hĕə′līn′), *n.* **1.** the line formed at the junction of the hair with the forehead. **2.** a very slender line. **3.** worsted fabric woven with very fine lines or stripes. **4.** *Print.* **a.** a very thin line on the face of a type. **b.** a style of type consisting entirely of such lines. **c.** a thin rule used for printing fine lines. **d.** unwanted lines between letters, caused by worn matrices. See diag. under **type.**

hairnet (hĕə′nĕt′), *n.* a loosely woven net of hair, nylon, silk, etc., used to cover the hair and hold it in place.

hairpiece (hĕə′pēs′), *n.* false or substitute hair, usually mounted on a canvas and wire frame attached to the real hair to enhance or glamorize a style.

hairpin (hĕə′pĭn′), *n.* **1.** a slender U-shaped piece of wire, shell, etc., used by women to fasten up the hair or hold a headdress. —*adj.* **2.** (of a road, track, etc.) doubling back in a U-shape.

hair-raiser (hĕə′rā′zə), *n.* anything, as a story, that arouses fear or terror.

hair-raising (hĕə′rā′zĭng), *adj.* terrifying.

hair salt, natural aluminium sulphate.

hair's-breadth (hĕəz′brĕtth′, -brĕdth′), *n.* **1.** a very small space or distance. —*adj.* **2.** extremely narrow or close. Also, **hairsbreadth, hairbreadth.**

hair seal, any of various seals with coarse hair and no soft underlying fur (distinguished from *fur seal*).

hairshirt (hĕə′shût′), *n.* a garment of coarse haircloth, worn next to the skin by ascetics and penitents.

hair slide, slide (def. 14).

hairspace (hĕə′spās′), *n. Print.* the thinnest metal space used to separate words, etc.

hairsplitter (hĕə′splĭt′ə), *n.* one who makes fine or unnecessary distinctions. —**hair′split′ting,** *n., adj.*

hairspring (hĕə′sprĭng′), *n.* a fine, spiralled spring in a watch or clock for regulating the balance wheel.

hairstreak (hĕə′strēk′), *n.* any of certain small dark butterflies of the family *Lycaenidae*, distinguished by one or two thin tails on each of the hind wings.

hairstroke (hĕə′strōk′), *n.* a fine line in writing or printing.

hairstyle (hĕə′stīl′), *n.* the style in which hair is arranged. —**hair′styl′ist,** *n.*

hair-trigger (hĕə′trĭg′ə), *n.* a trigger that allows the firing mechanism of a firearm to be operated by very slight pressure.

hairworm (hĕə′wûm′), *n.* any of a number of small, slender worms of the family *Trichostrongylidae*, parasitic in the alimentary canals of various animals.

hairy (hĕə′rĭ), *adj.*, **-rier, -riest. 1.** covered with hair; having much hair. **2.** consisting of or resembling hair. —**hair′iness,** *n.*

hairy frog, a frog of W Africa, *Astylosternus robustus*, having glandular hairlike filaments covering part of its back and sides, believed to function as accessory breathing organs.

Haiti (hā′tĭ), *n.* **1.** a republic in the West Indies, occupying the W part of the island of Hispaniola. 4,000,000 pop. (est. 1961); 10,714 sq. mi. *Cap.:* Port-au-Prince. **2.** former name of **Hispaniola.** —**Haitian** (hā′shyən), *adj., n.*

Haiti (def. 1)

hajj (hăj), *n.* the pilgrimage to Mecca, which every good Muslim is supposed to make at least once in his lifetime. Also, **hadj.** [t. Ar.: pilgrimage]

hajji (hăj′ĭ), *n., pl.* **-jis. 1.** a Muslim who has performed his hajj to Mecca. **2.** a Greek or Armenian who has visited the Holy Sepulchre at Jerusalem. Also, **hadji.** [t. Turk., t. Ar.: m. *hājji* pilgrim]

haka (hä′kä), *n. N.Z.* the ceremonial war dance of the Maori. [t. Maori]

hake (hāk), *n., pl.* **hakes,** (*esp. collectively*) **hake. 1.** any of several marine gadoid fishes of the genus *Merluccius*, related to the cod, as *M. merluccius* of European coasts. **2.** any of various related marine fishes, esp. of the genus *Urophycis*, or allied genera, as *U. tenius* (**white hake**) of the New England coast. [ME, special use of OE *haca* hook. Cf. MLG *haken* kipper salmon]

hakim[1] (hă kēm′), *n.* (in Muslim countries) **1.** a wise or learned man. **2.** a physician. Also, **hakeem** (hă kēm′). [t. Ar.: m. *hakīm* wise, wise man]

hakim[2] (hăk′ēm), *n.* (in Muslim countries) a ruler; governor; judge. [t. Ar.: m. *hākim* governor]

Hakluyt (hăk′lo͞ot), *n.* **Richard,** 1552?–1616, English geographer and editor of explorers' narratives.

Hakodate (hăk′ō dä′tĭ), *n.* a seaport in N Japan at the S end of Hokkaido island. 243,418 (1965).

hal-, var. of **halo-** before vowels, as in *halite*.

Halafian (hə lä′fĭ ən), *adj.* of or belonging to the Neolithic culture widespread from Iran to the Mediterranean, characterized by decorated pottery and an abundance of figurines. [named after *Tell Halaf*, a site in N Syria]

Halakah (hä′lə KHä′, hə lä′kə), *n.* that part of Jewish traditional literature concerned with the Law. Also, **Halacha** (hä′lə KHä′, hə lä′kə). [t. Heb.: m. *halākāh* rule to go by]

halation (hə lā′shən), *n. Photog.* the blurring in a negative or print of very light areas (as a window in an interior view) caused by the reflection of light from the back of the support on which the emulsion is coated. [f. HAL(o) + -ATION]

halberd (hăl′bəd), *n.* a shafted weapon with an axelike cutting blade, beak, and apical spike, used esp. in the

15th and 16th centuries. Also, **halbert** (hăl′bət), **haubert** (hô′bət). [late ME *haubert*, t. MF: m. *hallebarde*, t. MHG: m. *helmbarde*]

halberdier (hăl′bə dĭə′), *n.* a soldier, guard, or attendant armed with a halberd.

Head of halberd

halcyon (hăl′sĭ ən), *n.* **1.** a bird, usually identified with the kingfisher, fabled by the ancients to breed about the time of the winter solstice in a nest floating on the sea, and to have the power of charming winds and waves into calmness. **2.** any of various kingfishers, esp. of the genus *Halcyon.* —*adj.* **3.** calm, tranquil, or peaceful. **4.** carefree; joyous. **5.** of or pertaining to the halcyon or kingfisher. [t. L, pseudo-etymological var. of *alcyon*, t. Gk: m. *alkyṓn* kingfisher]

halcyon days, 1. days of fine and calm weather about the winter solstice, when the halcyon was anciently believed to brood; esp. the seven days before and as many after the winter solstice. **2.** days of peace and tranquillity.

Haldane (hôl′dān), *n.* **1. John Burdon Sanderson,** 1892–1964, Scottish biochemist, geneticist, and writer. **2.** his father, **John Scott,** 1860–1936, Scottish physiologist and writer on science. **3. Richard Burdon** (*Viscount Haldane of Cloan*), 1856–1928, British statesman and jurist (brother of John Scott Haldane).

hale[1] (hāl), *adj.*, **haler, halest. 1.** free from disease or infirmity; robust; vigorous. **2.** *Scot. and N Dial.* free from injury or defect. [ME; OE *hāl*, c. Icel. *heill* hale, whole] —**hale′ness,** *n.* —**Syn. 1.** sound, healthy, hearty. See **strong.** —**Ant. 1.** sickly.

hale[2] (hāl), *v.t.*, **haled, haling. 1.** to haul, pull, or draw with force. **2.** to drag, or bring as by dragging: *to hale a man into court.* [ME *hale(n)*, t. OF: m. *haler* hale, haul, t. Gmc; cf. OHG *halōn*, G *holen* fetch] —**hal′er,** *n.*

Hale (hāl), *n.* **Sir Matthew,** 1609–76, English jurist: Lord Chief Justice 1671–76.

Haleakala (hä′lä ä′kä lä′), *n.* an extinct volcano in the Hawaiian Islands, on the island of Maui. Crater, 19 sq. mi.; ab. 2000 ft deep; 10,032 ft high.

Halesowen (hālz′ō′ĭn), *n.* a town in England, in N Worcestershire. 44,445 (1961).

Halévy (*Fr.* à lė vē′), *n.* **Jacques François Fromental Elie** (*Fr.* zhȧk fräɴ swȧ frō mäɴ tȧl ė lē′), 1799–1862, French composer and teacher of music.

half (häf), *n., pl.* **halves** (hävz), *adj., adv.* —*n.* **1.** one of the two equal (or approximately equal) parts into which anything is or may be divided. **2.** *Sport.* either of the two periods of a game. **3.** *Football.* a half-back. **4.** *Golf.* an equal score (with the opponent) either on a hole or a round. **5.** one of a pair. **6.** *Colloq.* a half-pint, esp. of beer. **7. go halves,** to share equally. —*adj.* **8.** being one of the two eq̈ual (or approximately equal) parts into which anything is or may be divided. **9.** being equal to only about half of the full measure: *half speed.* **10.** partial or incomplete. —*adv.* **11.** to the extent or measure of half: *a bucket half full of water.* **12.** in part; partly. **13.** to some extent. **14. by half,** by a great deal; by too much: *too clever by half.* **15. not half,** *Slang.* **a.** not really; not at all: *his first poems were not half bad.* **b.** very; surprisingly: *his paintings are not half good.* —*interj.* **16. not half,** *Slang.* very much. [ME and OE, c. MD and MLG *halve* side, half]

half-a-crown (häf′ə kroun′), *n.* a halfcrown.

half-a-dozen (häf′ə dŭz′ən), *n., adj.* half-dozen.

half-adder (häf′ăd′ə), *n. Computers, etc.* a circuit which performs part of the function of adding two numbers.

half-and-half (häf′ən häf′), *adj.* **1.** half one thing and half another. —*adv.* **2.** in two equal portions. —*n.* **3.** a mixture of two things. **4.** a mixture of two beers, esp. mild and bitter.

half-back (häf′băk′), *n.* **1.** *Soccer.* one of three players in the next line behind the forward line. **2.** *Rugby Football.* one of two players, either scrum half or stand-off half. **3.** a position in which such a player plays.

half-baked (häf′bākt′), *adj.* **1.** insufficiently cooked. **2.** *Colloq.* not completed: *a half-baked scheme.* **3.** *Colloq.* lacking mature judgement or experience: *half-baked theorists.*

halfbeak (häf′bēk′), *n.* any of certain marine fishes constituting the genus *Hemirhamphus* and allied genera, having a long protruding lower jaw.

half-binding (häf′bīn′dĭng), *n.* a book having a leather binding on the back and corners, and paper or cloth sides.

half-blood (häf′blŭd′), *n.* **1.** the relation between persons having only one of their parents in common. **2.** a half-breed.

half-blooded (häf′blŭd′ĭd), *adj.* having parents of different breeds, races, or the like.

half-boot (häf′bo͞ot′), *n.* a boot reaching about halfway to the knee.

half-bound (häf′bound′), *adj.* bound in half-binding.

half-breed (häf′brēd′), *n.* **1.** the offspring of parents of different races; one who is half-blooded. **2.** the offspring of a white person and an American Indian. —*adj.* **3.** Also, **half-bred.** of or pertaining to the offspring of parents of different races.

half-brother (häf′brŭth′ə), *n.* a brother by one parent only.

half-cadence (häf′kā′dns), *n. Music.* a cadence ending with dominant harmony.

half-caste (häf′käst′), *n.* **1.** a person of mixed race. **2.** one of mixed European and Hindu or Muslim parentage. —*adj.* **3.** of or pertaining to such a person.

half-cock (häf′kŏk′), *n.* **1.** the position of the hammer of a firearm when held halfway by mechanism so that it will not operate. **2. go off at half-cock,** to act prematurely.

halfcrown (häf′kroun′), *n.* **1.** (until 1970) a cupronickel or silver coin of the United Kingdom worth 2*s.* 6*d.* **2.** any similar coin of certain other countries. —*adj.* **3.** of the price or value of a halfcrown.

half-day (häf′dā′), *n.* a half-holiday.

half-dollar (häf′dŏl′ə), *n.* **1.** a silver coin of the U.S. worth 50 cents. **2.** *Slang.* a halfcrown.

half-dozen (häf′dŭz′ən), *n., adj.* six. Also, **half-a-dozen.**

half-face (häf′fās′), *n.* **1.** a profile. —*adj., adv.* **2.** in profile.

half-hardy (häf′hä′dĭ), *adj.* (of plants) growing out of doors, except during winter.

half-hearted (häf′hä′tĭd), *adj.* having or showing little enthusiasm. —**half′-heart′edly,** *adv.* —**half′-heart′edness,** *n.* —**Syn.** indifferent, perfunctory. —**Ant.** enthusiastic.

half-hitch (häf′hĭch′), *n.* a hitch formed by passing the end of a rope round its standing part and bringing it up through the bight. See illus. under **knot.**

half-holiday (häf′hŏl′ĭ dĭ), *n.* part, usually the afternoon, of a working day given for recreation.

half-hour (häf′ou′ə), *n.* **1.** a period of thirty minutes. **2.** the midpoint between the hours. —*adj.* **3.** of or pertaining to a period of thirty minutes.

half-hourly (häf′ou′ə lĭ), *adj.* **1.** of or lasting a half-hour. **2.** occurring once every half-hour. —*adv.* **3.** during a half-hour.

half-leather (häf′lĕth′ə), *n. Bookbinding.* half-binding.

half-length (häf′lĕngth′), *n.* **1.** a portrait showing only the upper part of the body, including the hands. —*adj.* **2.** of or denoting such a portrait.

half-life (häf′līf′), *n. Physics, etc.* the time required for one half of a sample of unstable material to undergo chemical change, as the disintegration of radioactive material, the chemical change of free radicals, etc.

half-light (häf′līt′), *n.* light of much less than normal intensity; twilight.

half-mast (häf′mäst′), *n.* **1.** a position approximately halfway below the top of a mast, staff, etc. —*v.t.* **2.** to place (a flag) at half-mast (as a mark of respect for the dead, or as a signal of distress).

half-measure (häf′mĕzh′ə), *n.* an inadequate measure, esp. one taken as a compromise.

halfmens (hălf′mĕns), *n.* a southern African plant, *Adenium namaquanum*, of the family *Apocynaceae*, having a thick upright stem surmounted by a crown of leaves, supposed to resemble a human being. [t. Afrikaans: half person]

half-moon (häf′mo͞on′), *n.* **1.** See **moon** (def. 2b). **2.** something of the shape of a half-moon or crescent.

half-mourning (häf′mô′nĭng), *n.* **1.** a mourning garb less sombre than full mourning. **2.** the period during which it is worn.

half-nelson (häf′nĕl′sən), *n. Wrestling.* a hold, usually from behind, in which the wrestler pushes one arm under his opponent's arm and places his hand on the nape of his opponent's neck.

half-note (häf′nōt′), *n. U.S. Music.* a minim.

half-pay (häf′pā′), *n.* **1.** half the full wages or salary. **2.** a reduced allowance paid to a British army or naval officer when not in actual service after retirement. —*adj.* **3.** of or pertaining to a person on half-pay.

halfpenny (hāp′nĭ), *n., pl.* **halfpennies** (hāp′nĭz) *for 1, 2*; **halfpence** (hā′pəns) for *3*; *adj.* —*n.* **1.** a bronze coin of the United Kingdom of half the value of a penny. **2.** any similar coin of certain other countries. **3.** the sum of half a penny. —*adj.* **4.** of the price or value of a halfpenny. **5.** of trifling value.

halfpennyworth (hā′pəth), *n.* **1.** as much as may be bought for a halfpenny. **2.** a trifling amount.

half-pint (häf′pīnt′), *n.* **1.** half of one pint. **2.** a small person, esp. a small woman. —*adj.* **3.** of or containing a half-pint. **4.** of or pertaining to a small person.

half-sister (häf′sĭs′tə), *n.* a sister by one parent only.

half-size (häf′sīz′), *n.* any size, esp. of clothing or the like, which is halfway between two sizes.

half-slip (häf′slĭp′), *n.* a petticoat or slip that hangs from the waist.

half-sole (häf′sōl′), *n.* **1.** that part of the sole of a boot or shoe which extends from the shank to the end of the toe. —*v.t.* **2.** to repair by putting on a new half-sole.

half-sovereign (häf′sŏv′rĭn), *n.* a British gold coin discontinued in 1917, which was worth 10 shillings and weighed about 61·6372 grains troy.

half-step (häf′stĕp′), *n.* *U.S. Music.* a semitone.

half-term (häf′tûm′), *n.* **1.** a short holiday of two or three days in the middle of a school term. —*adj.* **2.** of or pertaining to such a holiday.

half-thickness (häf′thĭk′nĭs), *n.* *Physics.* the thickness of a specified material which when introduced into the path of a beam of radiation, reduces its intensity to half its original value. Also, **half-value layer.**

half-tide (häf′tīd′), *n.* the state of the tide when halfway between high water and low water.

half-timbered (häf′tĭm′bəd), *adj.* (of a house or building) having the frame and principal supports of timber, but with the interstices filled in with masonry, plaster, or the like. —**half′-tim′bering,** *n.*

half-time (häf′tīm′), *n.* *Sport.* a rest period or interval between the two halves of a game, match, etc.

half-title (häf′tī′tl), *n.* **1.** the short title of a book printed on the page preceding the titlepage. **2.** the title of any subdivision of a book when printed on a separate page. **3.** the page on which the half-title is printed.

halftone (häf′tōn′), *n.* **1.** *Painting, Photog., etc.* a value intermediate between high light and deep shade. **2.** *Photoengraving.* **a.** a process in which gradation of tone is obtained by a system of minute dots produced by a screen, placed in the camera a short distance in front of the sensitized plate. **b.** the metal plate made by photoengraving for reproduction by letterpress printing. **c.** a print from it. —*adj.* **3.** pertaining to, using, or used in, the halftone process.

half-tone (häf′tōn′), *n.* *U.S. Music.* a semitone.

halftrack (häf′trăk′), *n.* a motor vehicle with its driving wheels on caterpillar tracks.

half-truth (häf′trōōth′), *n.* a proposition or statement only partly true, esp. a statement intended to mislead or deceive.

half-volley (häf′vŏl′ĭ), *n.*, *v.*, **-leyed, -leying.** *Sport.* —*n.* **1.** a delivered ball or its return, hit or kicked the moment after it bounces from the ground. —*v.t.*, *v.i.* **2.** to hit or play (a half-volley).

half-wave rectifier (häf′wāv′), *Elect.* a rectifier which allows current to flow only during half of a cycle of an alternating current.

halfway (häf′wā′), *adv.* **1.** half over the way: *to go halfway to a place.* **2.** to or at half the distance: *the rope reaches only halfway.* **3. meet halfway,** to compromise. —*adj.* **4.** midway, as between two places or points. **5.** going to or covering only half the full extent; partial: *halfway measures.*

halfwit (häf′wĭt′), *n.* one who is feeble-minded.

half-witted (häf′wĭt′ĭd), *adj.* feeble-minded. —**half′-wit′tedly,** *adv.* —**half′-wit′tedness,** *n.*

half-year (häf′yĭə′), *n.* six months. —**half′-year′ly,** *adj.*, *adv.*

halibut (hăl′ĭ bət), *n.*, *pl.* **-buts,** (*esp. collectively*) **-but.** **1.** either of two species of large flatfishes, *Hippoglossus hippoglossus* of the North Atlantic and *H. stenolepis* of the North Pacific; the largest of the flatfishes and widely used for food. **2.** any of various other similar flatfishes. Also, **holibut.** [ME *halybutte,* appar. f. *haly* (OE *hālig* holy) + *butte* kind of fish; so called because eaten on holy days. Cf. G. *Heilbutt*]

Halicarnassus (hăl′ĭ kä năs′əs), *n.* an ancient city of Caria, in SW Asia Minor: site of the Mausoleum, one of the seven wonders of the ancient world.

halide (hăl′īd), *Chem.* —*n.* **1.** a compound, usually of two elements only, one of which is a halogen. —*adj.* **2.** of the nature of, or pertaining to, a halide; haloid. Also, **halid** (hăl′ĭd). [f. HAL(OGEN) + -IDE]

Halifax (hăl′ĭ făks′), *n.* **1. 1st Earl of** (*Charles Montagu*), 1661–1715, English statesman. **2. Earl of** (*Edward Frederick Lindley Wood*), 1881–1959, British statesman and diplomat. **3. 1st Marquess of** (*George Savile 'The Trimmer'*), 1633–95, English statesman. **4.** a county borough in England in the West Riding of Yorkshire. 95,450 (est. 1964). **5.** a seaport in SE Canada: the capital of Nova Scotia. 92,511 (1961).

halite (hăl′īt), *n.* rock-salt. [f. HAL- + -ITE[1]]

halitosis (hăl′ĭ tō′sĭs), *n.* bad or offensive breath. [NL: f. s. L *hālitus* breath + *-ōsis* -OSIS]

halitus (hăl′ĭ təs), *n.* an expired breath.

hall (hôl), *n.* **1.** the entrance room or vestibule of a house or building. **2.** a corridor or passageway in a building. **3.** a large and impressive room of public nature. **4.** a large building for residence, instruction, or other purposes, as in a university or college. **5.** the occupants of such a building. **6.** (in English colleges) **a.** a large room in which the members and students dine. **b.** dinner in such a room. **7.** a self-governing association of scholars, not incorporated as a college but now having identical functions, at a university, as at Oxford and Cambridge. **8.** the proprietor's residence on a large landed estate. **9.** the chief room in a medieval castle or similar structure, used for eating, sleeping, and entertaining. **10.** the house of a medieval chieftain or noble. **11.** (*often pl.*) music hall. [ME and OE, c. OHG *halla,* akin to OE *helan* cover, hide, L *cēlāre* hide, Gk *kalýptein* cover]

Hall (hôl), *n.* **Charles Francis,** 1821–71, U.S. arctic explorer.

Hallam (hăl′əm), *n.* **1. Arthur Henry,** 1811–33, English poet and essayist: subject of Tennyson's *In Memoriam.* **2.** his father, **Henry,** 1777–1859, English historian.

Hallé (hăl′ĭ), *n.* **Sir Charles,** 1819–95, British pianist born in Germany; founder of an orchestra bearing his name.

Halle (*Ger.* hä′lə), *n.* a city in S East Germany. 276,421 (1965).

Hall effect, *Physics.* the potential difference which develops across a strip of metal which is longitudinally conducting an electric current and which is subjected to a transverse magnetic field. The potential difference is in a plane at right angles to both the current and the magnetic field.

hallel (hə lāl′, hăl′ĕl), *n.* *Judaism.* a hymn of praise, usually Psalm 136, or formed from Psalms 113–118. [t. Heb.: m. *hallēl* praise]

hallelujah (hăl′ĭ lōō′yə), *interj.* **1.** Praise ye the Lord! —*n.* **2.** an exclamation of 'hallelujah!'. **3.** a musical composition wholly or principally based upon the word *hallelujah.* Also, **halleluiah, alleluia.** [t. Heb.: m. *hallelūyah* praise ye Jehovah]

Halley (hăl′ĭ), *n.* **Edmund,** 1656–1742, English astronomer.

Halley's comet, *Astron.* a comet which appears every 75 or 76 years; last appearance, 1910. [named after Edmund HALLEY, who first predicted its return]

halliard (hăl′yəd), *n.* halyard.

hallmark (hôl′mäk′), *n.* **1.** an official mark or stamp indicating a standard of purity, used in marking gold and silver articles assayed by the Goldsmiths' Company. **2.** any mark or special indication of genuineness, good quality, etc. **3.** any outstanding feature or characteristic. —*v.t.* **4.** to stamp with such a mark. Also, **plate-mark.** [from Goldsmiths' *Hall,* the seat of the Goldsmiths' Company]

hallo (hə lō′), *interj.*, *n.*, *v.* hello. Also, **halloa** (hə lō′).

hall of fame, (*often cap.*) **1.** *Chiefly U.S.* a building containing statues, busts, etc., commemorating or honouring famous or worthy people. **2.** a group of famous people considered worthy of acclaim.

halloo (hə lōō′), *interj.*, *n.*, *pl.* **-loos,** *v.* —*interj.* **1.** (an exclamation used to attract attention, to incite the dogs to the chase, etc.) —*n.* **2.** the cry 'halloo!'. —*v.i.* **3.** to call with a loud voice; shout; cry, as after dogs. —*v.t.* **4.** to incite or chase with shouts and cries of 'halloo!'. **5.** to cry aloud to. **6.** to hunt with shouts. [var. of HOLLO]

hallow[1] (hăl′ō), *v.t.* **1.** to make holy; sanctify; consecrate. **2.** to honour as holy. [ME *hal(o)we(n),* OE *hālgian,* der. *hālig* HOLY]

hallow[2] (hə lō′), *interj.*, *n.*, *v.* halloo. [var. of HALLOO]

hallowed (hăl′ōd; *in liturgical use often* hăl′ō ĭd), *adj.* **1.** made holy; sacred; consecrated. **2.** honoured or observed as holy. —**hal′lowedness,** *n.* —**Syn. 1.** See **holy.**

Halloween (hăl′ō ēn′), *n.* the evening of Oct. 31st; the eve of All Saints' Day. Also, **Hallowe'en.** [f. *hallow* saint + *een,* var. of *even* EVE]

Hallowmas (hăl′ō măs′), *n.* *Archaic.* the feast of Allhallows or All Saints' Day, on Nov. 1st.

hallstand (hôl′stănd′), *n.* a piece of furniture, usually placed in an entrance hall, and designed to hold hats, coats and umbrellas, etc.

Hallstattian (hăl stăt′ĭ ən), *adj.* pertaining to a variously dated pre-Christian stage of culture in central Europe, characterized by the use of bronze, the introduction of iron, artistic work in pottery, jewellery, etc. [named after *Hallstatt,* a village in central Austria, near which a burial ground of the period was found]

hallucal (hăl′yŏŏ kl), *adj.* *Anat.* referring to the big toe. [f. s. NL *hallux* (see HALLUX) + -AL[1]]

hallucinate (hə lōō′sĭ nāt′), *v.*, **-nated, -nating.** —*v.t.*

1. to affect with hallucinations. —*v.i.* 2. to experience hallucinations. [t. L: m. s. *hallūcinātus*, pp. of *(h)allūcinārī* wander in mind, dream]

hallucination (hə lo͞o′sĭ nā′shən), *n.* 1. an apparent perception, as by sight or hearing, for which there is no real external cause. 2. a suffering from illusion or false notions. —**Syn.** 1. See **illusion.**

hallucinatory (hə lo͞o′sĭ nə tə rĭ, -trĭ), *adj.* pertaining to or characterized by hallucination.

hallucinosis (hə lo͞o′sĭ nō′sĭs), *n.* *Psychol.* a psychosis or state characterized and produced by hallucinations. [f. HALLUCIN(ATION) + -OSIS]

hallux (hăl′əks), *n., pl.* **-luces** (-lyo͞o sēz′). *Anat., Zool.* the innermost of the five digits normally present in the hind foot of air-breathing vertebrates, as: **a.** (in man) the big toe. **b.** (in birds) the hind toe. [NL, m. L *(h)allex* big toe, with *-u-* by assoc. with *(h)allus* thumb]

hallway (hôl′wā′), *n.* 1. *U.S.* a corridor, as in a building. 2. an entrance hall.

halm (hôm), *n.* haulm.

halma (hăl′mə), *n.* a game played on a chequered board by two, three, or four players; the object being to move one's pieces from one corner of the board to the opposite corner by leaping over other pieces. [t. Gk: leap]

Halmahera (*Indon.* häl mä hĕ′rä), *n.* an island in Indonesia: the largest of the Moluccas. 100,000 pop. (est. 1961); 6928 sq. mi. Also, **Jilolo.**

halo (hā′lō), *n., pl.* **-loes, -los,** *v.,* **-loed, -loing.** —*n.* 1. a radiance surrounding the head in the representation of a sacred personage. 2. an ideal glory investing an object viewed with feeling or sentiment: *the halo around Shakespeare's plays.* 3. *Meteorol.* a circle of light, appearing round the sun or moon, caused by the refraction of light in suspended ice crystals. —*v.t.* 4. to surround with a halo. —*v.i.* 5. *Rare.* to form a halo. [t. L: m. *halōs*, t. Gk: disc, halo, threshing floor (on which the oxen trod out a circular path)] —**ha′lo-like′,** *adj.*

halo-, a word element meaning 'salt', as in *halogen.* [t. Gk, comb. form of *háls*]

halogen (hăl′ə jĕn′), *n.* *Chem.* any of the electronegative elements fluorine, chlorine, iodine, bromine, and astatine, which form binary salts by direct union with metals.

halogenation (hăl′ə jĭ nā′shən), *n.* the introduction of a halogen into an organic compound.

haloid (hăl′oid), *adj.* 1. denoting any halogen derivative. —*n.* 2. a haloid salt or derivative.

halophilous (hə lŏf′ĭ ləs), *adj.* (of an animal or plant) capable of living in salt water.

halophyte (hăl′ə fīt′), *n.* a plant which grows in salty or alkaline soil. —**halophytic** (hăl′ə fĭt′ĭk), *adj.*

halothane (hăl′ō thān′), *n.* *Pharm.* a volatile, sweetish liquid, $CF_3CHBrCl$, used as an anaesthetic inhalant.

halotrichite (hə lŏt′rĭ kīt′), *n.* a mineral consisting of yellowish fibrous crystals of hydrated iron and aluminium sulphate, $FeAl_2(SO_4)_4.24H_2O$.

Hals (häls; *Du.* hŏls), *n.* **Frans** (fräns; *Du.* frŏns), 1580?–1666, Dutch portrait painter.

Hälsingborg (*Swed.* hĕl sĕng bŏry′), *n.* a seaport in SW Sweden, opposite Helsingör. 78,474 (1964).

halt[1] (hôlt), *v.i.* 1. to make a temporary stop, as in marching, etc. —*v.t.* 2. to cause to halt. —*n.* 3. a temporary stop. 4. a stopping-place on a railway line, smaller than a station, where a train stops only briefly. —*interj.* 5. (a command to stop and stand motionless, esp. as to troops.) [t. G: stoppage] —**Syn.** 2. See **stop.**

halt[2] (hôlt), *v.i.* 1. to falter as in speech, reasoning, etc. 2. to be in doubt; waver; hesitate. 3. *Archaic.* to be lame; walk lamely; limp. —*adj.* 4. *Archaic.* lame; limping. —*n.* 5. *Archaic.* lameness; a limp. [ME; OE *h(e)alt*, c. OHG *halz*] —**halt′ing,** *adj.* —**halt′ingly,** *adv.* —**halt′ingness,** *n.*

halter[1] (hôl′tə), *n.* 1. a rope or strap with a noose or headstall, for leading or fastening horses or cattle. 2. a rope with a noose for hanging criminals. 3. death by hanging. 4. a halter-neck. —*v.t.* 5. to put a halter on; restrain as by a halter. 6. to hang (a person). [ME; OE *hælftre*, c. G *Halfter*] —**hal′ter-like′,** *adj.*

halter[2] (hôl′tə), *n.* one who halts or hesitates. [f. HALT[2] + -ER[1]]

halter[3] (hôl′tə), *n.* one who halts or stops. [f. HALT[1] + -ER[1]]

haltere (hăl′tĭə), *n., pl.* **halteres** (hăl tĭə′rēz). one of a pair of modified hind wings of a fly (order *Diptera*) reduced to slender, club-shaped appendages, used for balancing in flight; balancer. Also, *Chiefly U.S.,* **halter.** [t. L, t. Gk: usually pl. (*haltêres*) leaping weights]

halter-neck (hôl′tə nĕk′), *n.* 1. a neckline of a woman's dress, blouse, etc., which, fastened by thin straps behind the neck, leaves the back and arms bare. —*adj.* 2. of or pertaining to a garment with such a neckline.

halvah (hăl′vä), *n.* a sweet confection of Middle Eastern origin, containing honey and sesame seeds. [t. Yiddish, ult. t. Ar.: m. *halwa* sweetmeat]

halve (häv), *v.t.,* **halved, halving.** 1. to divide in halves; share equally. 2. to reduce to half. 3. *Golf.* to play (a hole, match, etc.) in the same number of strokes, as two opponents. [ME *halven*, der. HALF]

halves (hävz), *n.* 1. pl. of **half.** 2. **by halves, a.** incompletely. **b.** half-heartedly. 3. **go halves,** divide equally; share.

halyard (hăl′yəd), *n.* a rope or tackle used to hoist or lower a sail, yard, flag, etc. Also, **halliard.** [ME *halier*, *hallyer* that which hales or hauls (f. HALE[2] + -IER); influenced by YARD[1]]

ham (hăm), *n., v.,* **hammed, hamming.** —*n.* 1. one of the rear quarters of a pig, esp. the heavy-muscled part, between hip and hock. 2. the meat of this part. 3. the part of the leg behind the knee. 4. (*often pl.*) the back of the thigh, or the thigh and the buttock together. 5. *Theat. Slang.* **a.** an actor who overacts. **b.** overacting. 6. *Slang.* an amateur: *a radio ham.* —*v.i.* 7. *Theat. Slang.* to act with exaggerated expression of emotion; overact. [ME *hamme*, OE *hamm*, c. OHG *hamma* angle of the knee. Cf. LL *camba* bend of leg]

Ham (hăm), *n.* *Bible.* second son of Noah. Gen. 10:1.

Hama (hä′mä), *n.* a city in W Upper Syria. 228,124 (est. 1964).

hamada (hə mä′də), *n.* a tract of upland stony desert, stripped of sand and dust, in the Sahara. Also, **hammada.**

Hamadan (hăm′ə dăn′; *Persian* hăm ă dän′), *n.* a city in W Iran. 114,610 (est. 1964). See **Ecbatana.**

hamadryad (hăm′ə drī′əd, -ăd), *n., pl.* **-ads, -ades** (-ə dēz′). 1. *Class. Myth.* one of a class of wood nymphs fabled to live and die with the tree which she inhabited. 2. Also, **king cobra.** a snake, *Naja hannah*, of India and SE Asia, up to 17 ft long; the longest of all poisonous snakes. [t. L: s. *Hamādryas*, t. Gk: f. *háma* together + *dryás* wood nymph]

Hamamatsu (häm′ə mät′so͞o), *n.* a city in central Japan, on S central Honshu island. 392,632 (1965).

hamamelidaceous (hăm′ə mē′lĭ dā′shəs, -mĕl′ĭ-), *adj.* belonging to the *Hamamelidaceae*, a family of shrubs and trees including the witch-hazel, etc. [f. s. NL *hamamēlis* (t. Gk: a kind of medlar) + -ACEOUS]

Haman (hā′măn), *n.* *Bible.* (in the Book of Esther) an enemy of the Jews who was hanged when his plot for their destruction was exposed.

hamate (hā′māt), *adj.* *Anat.* 1. hook-shaped. 2. having a hooklike process. —*n.* 3. the medial of the four bones of the distal row of the carpus. [t. L: m. s. *hāmātus*]

Hamborn (*Ger.* häm′bŏrn), *n.* See **Duisburg.**

Hamburg (hăm′bûg; *Ger.* häm′bo͝ork), *n.* a city and Land in N West Germany, on the Elbe: the largest seaport in continental Europe, formerly a member of the Hanseatic League. 1,851,300 (est. 1966). See map under **Hanseatic League.**

hamburger (hăm′bû′gə), *n.* 1. a flat round cake of minced beef, seasoned and fried. 2. a bread roll, or soft bun containing such meat, cooked and served often with onion, etc.

hame (hām), *n.* either of two curved pieces lying upon the collar in the harness of an animal, to which the traces are fastened. See illus. under **harness.** [ME, t. MD; akin to G *Hamen* fishhook, dragnet, OE *hamele* rowlock]

hamel (hăm′əl), *n.* *S African.* a castrated ram; wether. [t. Afrikaans, c. G *Hammel* mutton]

Hameln (*Ger.* hä′məln), *n.* a town in N West Germany, on the river Weser: scene of the legend of the Pied Piper of Hamelin. 50,300 (est. 1959). Also, **Hamelin** (hăm′ĭ lĭn).

hamerkop (hā′mə kŏp′, hăm′ə-), *n.* a heron-like bird, *Scopus umbretta*, the sole member of the family *Scopidae*, of Africa, Madagascar, and Arabia, coloured brown and having a broad, flat bill and a crest projecting backwards from its head. Also, **hammerhead.** [t. Afrikaans: hammerhead]

Hamersley Range (hăm′əz lĭ), a mountain range in NW Western Australia. Highest point, Mt Bruce, 4027 ft.

ham-fisted (hăm′fĭs′tĭd), *adj.* ham-handed.

ham-handed (hăm′hăn′dĭd), *adj.* clumsy. Also, **ham-fisted.**

Hamilcar Barca (hă mĭl′kä bä′kə, hăm′ĭl kä′), died 228? B.C., Carthaginian general: Hannibal's father.

Hamilton (hăm′ĭl tən), *n.* 1. **Alexander,** 1757–1804, American statesman and writer on government. 2. **Lady Emma** (*Amy*, or *Emily, Lyon*), 1765?–1815, mistress of Viscount Nelson. 3. **Sir Ian Standish Monteith** (ĭən′ mŏn tēth′), 1853–1947, British general. 4. **Sir William,** 1788–1856, Scottish philosopher. 5. **Sir William Rowan,**

1805–65, Irish mathematician and astronomer. **6.** a city in SE Canada: a port near the W end of Lake Ontario. 275,670 (est. 1964). **7.** a town in central North Island, New Zealand. 59,500 (est. 1965). **8.** a burgh in S Scotland, in Lanarkshire, SE of Glasgow. 41,928 (1961). **9.** the capital of Bermuda. 2800 (est. 1964). **10.** a river in N Australia flowing SW through Queensland, joining the Georgina to form Eyre Creek. **11. Mount,** a mountain of the Coast Range in California, near San Francisco: site of Lick Observatory. 4209 ft.

Hamite (hăm′īt), *n.* **1.** a descendant of Ham. Gen. 10:1, 6–20. **2.** a member of any of various nations of Africa, as the ancient Egyptians and modern Berbers.

Hamitic (hă mĭt′ĭk, hə-), *adj.* **1.** of or pertaining to the Hamites or their speech. *—n.* **2.** a family of languages related to the Semitic, spoken in North Africa, including ancient Egyptian and modern Berber.

hamlet (hăm′lĭt), *n.* **1.** a small village. **2.** a little cluster of houses in the country. **3.** a village without a church of its own, but belonging to the parish of another village or a town. [ME *hamelet*, t. OF, dim. of *hamel* hamlet, dim. of *ham*, t. Gmc; cf. OE *hamm* enclosed land]

Hamm (*Ger.* häm), *n.* a town in West Germany, in N North Rhine-Westphalia. 72,500 (est. 1966).

hammada (hə mä′də), *n.* hamada.

Hammarskjöld (hăm′ə shûld′; *Swed.* hä′mär shœld), *n.* **Dag (Hjalmar Agne Carl)** (*Swed.* däg yäl′mär äng′nĕ kärl), 1905–61, Swedish statesman; secretary-general of United Nations 1953–61.

hammer (hăm′ə), *n.* **1.** an instrument consisting of a solid head, usually of metal, set crosswise on a handle, used for beating metals, driving in nails, etc. **2.** any of various instruments or devices resembling a hammer in form, action, or use. **3.** *Firearms.* that part of the lock which by its fall or action causes the discharge, as by exploding the percussion cap; the cock. **4.** one of the padded levers by which the strings of a piano are struck. **5.** *Athletics.* a metal ball attached to a long, flexible handle, used in certain throwing contests. **6.** *Anat.* the malleus. **7. come** or **go under the hammer,** to be sold by auction. *—v.t.* **8.** to beat or drive with or as with a hammer. **9.** to form with a hammer (often fol. by *out*). **10.** to fasten by or as by using a hammer. **11.** to put together or build with a hammer and nails. **12.** to hit with some force; pound. **13.** to contrive or work out laboriously (often fol. by *out*). **14.** to state forcefully; present (facts, etc.) aggressively. **15.** to interrogate or criticize relentlessly: *the Prime Minister was hammered in the House at question time.* **16.** *Stock Exchange.* **a.** to announce a defaulter on the Stock Exchange. **b.** to depress or beat down (the price of a stock). *—v.i.* **17.** to strike blows with or as with a hammer. **18.** to make persistent or laborious attempts. [ME *hamer*, OE *hamor*, c. G *Hammer*] **—ham′merer,** *n.* **—ham′merless,** *adj.* **—ham′mer-like′,** *adj.*

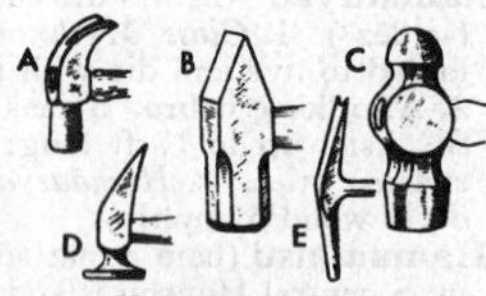

Hammers (def. 1)
A, Nail hammer (claw type); B, Engineer's hammer; C, Machinist's hammer (ball peen type); D, Shoemaker's hammer; E, Carpetlayer's hammer

hammer and sickle, **1.** the emblem of the Soviet Union, adopted in 1923. **2.** any similar emblem of communism outside the Soviet Union.

hammer and tongs, *Colloq.* with great noise, vigour, or violence.

hammerbeam (hăm′ə bēm′), *n.* a horizontal timber beam, which supports a wooden arch in a roof truss.

hammered work, metalwork formed by the hammers, anvils, punches, etc., of craftsmen.

Hammerfest (hăm′ə fĕst′), *n.* a seaport in N Norway: the northernmost town in Europe. 5604 (1961).

hammerhead (hăm′ə hĕd′), *n.* **1.** the head of a hammer. **2.** any of the sharks constituting the genus *Sphyrna*, characterized by a head expanded laterally so as to resemble a double-headed hammer, esp. *S. zygaena*, a widely distributed species. **3.** hamerkop.

Hammerhead, *Sphyrna zygaena* (Length 15 ft)

hammer lock, *Wrestling.* a hold, banned in amateur wrestling, whereby the opponent's arm is twisted and pushed behind his back.

hammer sedge, a small cyperaceous perennial, *Carex hirta*, widespread in damp woods and meadows throughout Europe and temperate Asia.

Hammersmith (hăm′ə smĭth′), *n.* a SW inner borough of London. 217,400 (1964).

Hammerstein (hăm′ə stīn′), *n.* **1. Oscar,** 1847?–1919, U.S. theatrical manager, born in Germany. **2.** his grandson, **Oscar** (*Oscar Hammerstein II*), 1895–1960, U.S. lyricist and librettist.

hammertoe (hăm′ə tō′), *n.* *Pathol.* a clawlike deformity of the toe.

hammock (hăm′ək), *n.* a kind of hanging bed or couch made of canvas, netting, or the like. [t. Sp.: m. *hamaca*; of W Ind. orig.] **—ham′mock-like′,** *adj.*

Hammond (hăm′ənd), *n.* a town in the U.S., in N Indiana. 111,698 (1960).

Hammurabi (hăm′o͝o rä′bĭ), *n.* fl. *c.* 2100 B.C., king of Babylonia: famous code of laws made in his reign.

Hampden (hămp′dən, hăm′dən), *n.* **John,** 1594–1643, English statesman who defended the rights of the House of Commons against Charles I.

hamper[1] (hăm′pə), *v.t.* **1.** to impede; hinder; hold back. *—n.* **2.** *Naut.* articles which, while necessary to a ship's equipment, are often in the way. [ME *hampren*, orig. uncert.] **—Syn. 1.** obstruct, encumber, trammel. See **prevent. —Ant. 1.** assist.

hamper[2] (hăm′pə), *n.* a large basket or wickerwork receptacle, usually with a cover. [ME *hampere*; syncopated var. of HANAPER]

Hampshire (hămp′shĭə, -shə), *n.* a county in S England, including the administrative counties of Southampton and Isle of Wight. 1,366,084 pop. (1961); 1650 sq. mi. *Co. town:* Winchester. *Abbrev.:* Hants.

Hampstead (hămp′stĭd), *n.* a district of the NW inner London borough of Camden.

Hampton Court, a royal palace on the river Thames, built by Cardinal Wolsey.

hamster (hăm′stə), *n.* **1.** any of a number of short-tailed, stout-bodied, burrowing rodents, having large cheek pouches, and inhabiting parts of Europe and Asia, as *Cricetus cricetus*. **2.** the fur of such an animal. [t. G]

Hamster, *Cricetus cricetus* (Ab. 10 in. long)

hamstring (hăm′strĭng′), *n.*, *v.*, **-strung** or (*Rare*) **-stringed, -stringing.** *—n.* **1.** (in man) any of the tendons which bound the ham, or hollow of the knee. **2.** (in quadrupeds) the great tendon at the back of the hock. *—v.t.* **3.** to cut the hamstring or hamstrings of and thus disable. **4.** to cripple; render useless; thwart.

Hamsun (*Norw.* häm′so͝on), *n.* **Knut** (*Norw.* kno͞ot), 1859–1952, Norwegian novelist.

hamulus (hăm′yo͝o ləs), *n.*, *pl.* **-li** (-lī′). *Anat., Zool., Bot., etc.* a small hook or hooklike process. [t. L, dim. of *hāmus* a hook]

Han (hăn), *n.* **1.** a Chinese dynasty, 206 B.C. – A.D. 220, with an interregnum, A.D. 9–25, known as the **Earlier** or **Western Han** before the interregnum and as the **Later** or **Eastern Han** afterwards. The Han was distinguished for the revival of letters and the beginnings of Buddhism; its bureaucracy became a model for later dynasties. **2.** a river flowing from central China into the Yangtze at Hankow. ab. 900 mi.

hanaper (hăn′ə pə), *n.* a wicker receptacle for documents. [ME *hanypere*, t. OF: m. *hanapier* case for holding a cup, der. *hanap* cup, t. Gmc; cf. OS *hnapp* cup]

Hanau (*Ger.* hä′nou), *n.* a town in West Germany, in S Hesse. 52,800 (est. 1966).

hance (häns), *n.* **1.** *Naut.* a curved rise to a higher part, as of the bulwarks from the waist to the quarterdeck. **2.** *Archit.* **a.** the sharply curving portion nearest the impost at either side of an elliptical or similar arch. **b.** the haunch of an arch. [n. use of *hance*, v., raise (now obs.), aphetic var. of ENHANCE]

Hancock (hăn′kŏk′), *n.* **John,** 1737–93, American statesman: first signatory of the Declaration of Independence.

hand (hănd), *n.* **1.** (in man) the terminal, prehensile part of the arm, consisting of the palm and five digits. **2.** the corresponding part of the forelimb in any of the higher vertebrates. **3.** the terminal part of any limb when prehensile, as the hind foot of a monkey, the chela of a crustacean, or (in falconry) the foot of a hawk. **4.** something resembling a hand in shape or function: *the hands of a clock.* **5.** a symbol used in writing or printing to draw attention to something. **6.** a person employed in manual labour; worker; labourer: *a factory hand.* **7.** a person who does a specified thing: *a book by several hands.* **8.** the persons of any company or number: *all hands gave assistance, all hands on deck.* **9.** (*often pl.*) possession or power; control, custody, or care: *to have someone's fate in one's hands.* **10.** agency; active cooperation in doing something: *a helping hand.* **11.** side: *on every hand.* **12.** a side of a subject, question, etc.: *on the other hand.* **13.** a source, as of information or of

supply: *at first hand.* **14.** style of handwriting. **15.** a person's signature. **16.** skill; execution; touch: *a painting that shows a master's hand.* **17.** a person, with reference to action, ability, or skill: *a poor hand at writing letters.* **18.** a pledge of marriage. **19.** a linear measure used in giving the height of horses, etc., equal to four inches. **20.** *Cards.* **a.** the cards dealt to or held by each player at one time. **b.** the person holding the cards. **c.** a single part of a game, in which all the cards dealt at one time are played. **21.** *Rom. Law.* the husband's control over the wife. **22.** skill or knack at manipulating the reins. **23.** a bundle or bunch of various fruit, leaves, etc., as a cluster of bananas or tobacco leaves tied together. **24.** a round or outburst of applause for a performer: *to get a hand.* **25.** Some special noun phrases are:
a heavy hand, severity or oppression.
a high hand, dictatorial manner or arbitrary conduct.
at hand, **1.** within reach; nearby. **2.** near in time. **3.** ready for use.
at the hand or **hands of,** from the action or agency of.
by hand, by the use of the hands (as opposed to any other means): *to make pottery by hand.*
change hands, to pass from one owner to another.
come to hand, to be received; come within one's reach.
eat out of one's hand, to be entirely subservient to.
force someone's hand, to compel someone to act prematurely or against his better judgement.
free hand, freedom to act as desired.
from hand to hand, from one person to another.
from hand to mouth, **1.** by eating at once whatever one gets. **2.** with attention to immediate wants only.
give one's hand on, to vouch for.
hand and glove or **hand in glove,** on very intimate terms; in league with.
hand in hand, **1.** with hands mutually clasped. **2.** conjointly or concurrently.
hand over fist, **1.** easily. **2.** in large quantities: *to make money hand over fist.*
hands down, totally; completely; easily.
hands off, keep off; refrain from blows or touching.
hands up!, raise the hands (as a sign of surrender).
hand to hand, in close combat; at close quarters.
have a hand in, to have a part or concern in doing.
have one's hands full, to be fully occupied.
in good hands, in the care of someone trustworthy.
in hand, **1.** under control. **2.** in immediate possession: *cash in hand.* **3.** in process: *keep to the matter in hand.*
keep one's hand in, keep in practice.
lay hands on, to assault; to beat up.
lay one's hands on, *Colloq.* to obtain.
off one's hands, out of one's responsible charge or care.
old hand, an experienced person; veteran.
on hand, **1.** in immediate possession: *cash on hand.* **2.** before one for attention. **3.** present.
on or **upon one's hands,** under one's care, management, or responsibility.
out of hand, **1.** beyond control: *to let one's temper get out of hand.* **2.** at once; without delay. **3.** no longer in process; over and done with.
play into the hands of, to act, without full realization, against one's best interest and in the interest of (an enemy or potential opponent).
shake hands, to clasp another's right hand as a salutation, in closing a bargain, etc.
show of hands, a voting procedure by which a motion is passed or lost on the basis of an estimate of the number of hands raised.
take a hand in, to have a part or concern in doing.
take in hand, **1.** to assume responsibility for. **2.** to subject to vigorous discipline.
throw in one's hand, to give up; stop doing something; surrender.
to hand, **1.** within reach; at hand. **2.** into one's immediate possession.
try one's hand, to attempt, esp. for the first time.
turn one's hand to, to turn one's energies to; set to work at.
upper hand, a position of marked superiority; whip hand.
wash one's hands of, to have nothing more to do with.
—*v.t.* **26.** to deliver or pass with the hand. **27.** to help or conduct with the hand. **28.** *Naut.* to furl, as a sail. **29.** to pass on; transmit (fol. by *on*). **30. hand down,** **a.** to deliver the decision of a court. **b.** to transmit from the higher to the lower, in space or time: *to hand down to posterity.* **31. hand in,** to present for acceptance. **32. hand it to,** to give due credit to. **33. hand out,** to distribute. **34. hand off,** *Rugby Football.* to thrust off an opponent who is tackling. **35. hand over,** **a.** to deliver into another's keeping. **b.** to give up or yield control of. —*adj.* **36.** of or belonging to the hand. **37.** done or made by hand. **38.** that may be carried in, or worn on, the hand. **39.** operated by hand.
[ME and OE, c. G *Hand*] —**hand′less,** *adj.* —**hand′like′,** *adj.*

handbag (hănd′băg′), *n.* a woman's small pouch or bag for carrying in the hand, to contain money and make-up, etc.

handball (hănd′bôl′), *n.* **1.** a game in which a small ball is batted against a wall with the (usually gloved) hand. **2.** the kind of ball used in this game.

handbarrow (hănd′bă′rō), *n.* **1.** a frame with handles at each end by which it is carried. **2.** a handcart.

handbell (hănd′bĕl′), *n.* a bell rung by hand, esp. one that is part of a set for musical performance.

handbill (hănd′bĭl′), *n.* a small printed bill or announcement, usually for distribution by hand.

handbook (hănd′bŏŏk′), *n.* **1.** a small book or treatise serving for guidance, as in an occupation or study: *handbook of car maintenance.* **2.** a guidebook for travellers.

handbrake (hănd′brāk′), *n.* a brake operated by a hand lever.

handbreadth (hănd′brĕth′, -brĕdth′), *n.* a unit of linear measure from $2\frac{1}{2}$ to 4 inches. Also, **hand's-breadth.**

h. & c., hot and cold (water).

handcart (hănd′kät′), *n.* a small cart drawn or pushed by hand.

handclap (hănd′klăp′), *n.* the striking of one palm against the other, usually repeatedly to indicate appreciation.

handcuff (hănd′kŭf′), *n.* **1.** a ring-shaped shackle for the wrist, usually one of a pair connected by a short chain or linked bar. —*v.t.* **2.** to put handcuffs on.

handed (hăn′dĭd), *adj.* **1.** having a hand or hands. **2.** having a hand characterized in some specified manner: *right-handed.* **3.** done by a specified number of hands: *a double-handed game.*

Handel (hăn′dl), *n.* **George Frederick** (*Georg Friedrich Händel*), 1685–1759, British composer born in Germany.

handfeed (hănd′fēd′), *v.t.*, **-fed, -feeding.** to raise animals, etc., by feeding by hand.

handful (hănd′fŏŏl′), *n.*, *pl.* **-fuls. 1.** as much or as many as the hand can grasp or contain. **2.** a small quantity or number: *a handful of men.* **3.** *Colloq.* a thing or a person that is as much as one can manage.

hand glass, **1.** a small mirror with a handle. **2.** a magnifying glass for holding in the hand.

hand grenade, a grenade or explosive shell which is thrown by hand and exploded either by impact or by means of a fuse.

handgrip (hănd′grĭp′), *n.* **1.** a grasping with the hand; a grip, as in greeting. **2.** (*pl.*) hand-to-hand combat. **3.** a handle. [ME; OE *handgripe*]

hand-held (hănd′hĕld′), *adj.* held in the hand; supported only by the unaided hand.

handhold (hănd′hōld′), *n.* **1.** a grip with the hand. **2.** a thing that can be taken hold of by the hand, as for support.

hand-horn (hănd′hôn′), *n.* the natural horn, producing only the harmonic series; changing this is effected by inserting crooks of different lengths.

handicap (hăn′dĭ kăp′), *n.*, *v.*, **-capped, -capping.** —*n.* **1.** a race or other contest in which certain disadvantages or advantages of weight, distance, time, past records, etc., are placed upon competitors to equalize their chances of winning. **2.** the disadvantage or advantage itself. **3.** any encumbrance or disadvantage that makes success more difficult. **4.** a physical disability. —*v.t.* **5.** to serve as a handicap or disadvantage to: *his age handicaps him.* **6.** to subject to a disadvantageous handicap, as a competitor of recognized superiority. **7.** to assign handicaps to (competitors). [orig. *hand i' cap* (with *i'* for *in* before a consonant); reason for this name uncert.] —**hand′icap′per,** *n.*

handicapped (hăn′dĭ kăpt′), *adj.* **1.** disabled; crippled. **2.** mentally retarded. **3.** (of a player, competitor, etc.) having a handicap.

handicraft (hăn′dĭ kräft′), *n.* **1.** manual skill. **2.** a manual art or occupation. [alter. of earlier *handcraft*, OE *handcræft*, modelled on HANDIWORK]

handicraftsman (hăn′dĭ kräfts′mən), *n.*, *pl.* **-men.** a person skilled in a handicraft; craftsman.

handily (hăn′dĭ lĭ), *adv.* **1.** dexterously; expertly. **2.** conveniently.

handiness (hăn′dĭ nĭs), *n.* **1.** the state or character of being handy or expert. **2.** the quality of being easily handled; convenience.

hand-in-glove (hănd′ĭn glŭv′), *adj.*, *adv.* in close collaboration (with).

handiwork (hăn′dĭ wûk′), *n.* **1.** work done or a thing or things made by the hands. **2.** the labour or action of a particular doer or maker: *the handiwork of man.*

3. the result of one's action or agency. [ME *handiwerk*, OE *handgeweorc*]
handkerchief (hăng′kə chĭf, -chēf′), *n.* **1.** a small piece of linen, silk, soft paper, or other fabric, usually square, carried about the person for wiping the face, nose, etc. **2.** a neckerchief or a kerchief. [f. HAND + KERCHIEF]
handle (hăn′dl), *n., v.,* **-dled, -dling.** —*n.* **1.** a part of a thing which is intended to be grasped by the hand in using or moving it. **2.** that by which anything may be held. **3.** something that may be taken advantage of in effecting a purpose. **4.** the feel or touch, as of textiles. **5.** *Slang.* a title in front of a name. —*v.t.* **6.** to touch or feel with the hand; use the hands on, as in picking up. **7.** to manage in use with the hands; manipulate. **8.** to wield, employ, or use: *to handle one's fists well in a fight.* **9.** to manage, direct, or control: *to handle troops.* **10.** to deal with or treat, as a matter or subject. **11.** to deal with or treat in a particular way: *to handle a person with tact.* **12.** to deal or trade in (goods, etc.). —*v.i.* **13.** to respond to handling. [ME *handlen*, OE *handlian* (c. G *handeln*), der. *hand* HAND] —**han′dled,** *adj.* —**han′dleless,** *adj.*
handlebar (hăn′dl bä′), *n.* (*usually pl.*) the curved steering bar of a bicycle, motorcycle, etc., in front of the rider.
handlebar moustache, a moustache with curved ends.
handler (hăn′dlə), *n.* **1.** a person or thing that handles. **2.** *Boxing.* a person who assists in the training of a fighter or is his second during the fight. **3.** the individual who manages and arouses a dog, etc., in a contest.
Handley Page (hănd′lĭ pāj′), **Sir Frederick.** See **Page.**
handling (hăn′dlĭng), *n.* **1.** a touching, grasping, or using with the hands. **2.** management; treatment. **3.** the process of packing, moving, carrying or transporting something. —*adj.* **4.** of or pertaining to this process.
handmade (hănd′mād′), *adj.* made by hand, not machine.
handmaid (hănd′mād′), *n.* a female servant or personal attendant. Also, **hand′maid′en.**
hand-me-down (hănd′mĭ doun′, hăn′-), *n. U.S. Colloq.* reach-me-down.
hand-off (hănd′ŏf′), *n. Rugby Football.* a thrust with the hand open, made by a player carrying the ball, to foil the tackle of an opponent.
hand organ, a portable barrel organ played by means of a crank turned by hand.
hand-out (hănd′out′), *n.* **1.** a prepared statement issued to the press. **2.** a free sample given as for advertisement. **3.** *U.S.* a portion of food or the like given to a beggar.
hand-pick (hănd′pĭk′), *v.t.* **1.** to pick by hand. **2.** to select carefully. —**hand′-picked′,** *adj.*
handrail (hănd′rāl′), *n.* a rail serving as a support or guard at the side of a stairway, platform, etc.
handsaw (hănd′sô′), *n.* a saw used with one hand.
hand's-breadth (hăndz′brĕtth′, -brĕdth′), *n.* handbreadth.
handsel (hăn′səl), *n., v.,* **-selled, -selling** or (*U.S.*) **-seled, -seling.** —*n.* **1.** a gift or token for good luck or as an expression of good wishes, as at the beginning of the new year, or at entering upon a new state, situation, or enterprise. **2.** a first instalment of payment. **3.** the first use or experience of anything; foretaste. —*v.t.* **4.** to give a handsel to. **5.** to inaugurate auspiciously. **6.** to use, try, or experience for the first time. Also, **hansel.** [ME *handselne*, OE *handselen*, lit., hand gift; akin to Icel. *handsal* the binding of a bargain by joining hands]
handset (hănd′sĕt′), *n., v.,* **-set, -setting,** *adj.* —*n.* **1.** a part of a telephone combining both the receiver and the transmitter, one at each end of a handle. —*v.t.* **2.** *Print.* to set (type) by hand. —*adj.* **3.** *Print.* (of type) set by hand.
handshake (hănd′shāk′), *n.* **1.** a clasping of another's right hand as in salutation, congratulation, agreement, etc. **2. golden handshake,** a sum of money given to an executive or the like on loss of employment or retirement.
handsome (hăn′səm), *adj.,* **-somer, -somest. 1.** of fine or admirable appearance; comely; tastefully or elegantly fine: *a handsome person.* **2.** considerable, ample, or liberal in amount: *a handsome fortune.* **3.** gracious; generous: *a handsome gift.* **4.** *U.S. Colloq.* dexterous; graceful: *a handsome speech.* [ME *handsom*, f. HAND + -SOME[1]; orig., easy to handle] —**hand′somely,** *adv.* —**hand′someness,** *n.* —**Syn. 1.** See **beautiful.**
handspike (hănd′spīk′), *n.* a bar used as a lever. [t. D: m. *handspeck* hand bar, assimilated to *spike*]
handspring (hănd′sprĭng′), *n.* a kind of somersault in which the body is supported upon one or both hands while turning in the air.
handstand (hănd′stănd′), *n.* the act, or an instance of balancing upside down on one's hands.
hand-to-hand (hănd′tə hănd′), *adj.* in close combat; at close quarters.
hand-to-mouth (hănd′tə mouth′), *adj.* precarious; unsettled.
handwork (hănd′wûk′), *n.* work done by hand, as distinguished from that done by machine.
handwriting (hănd′rī′tĭng), *n.* **1.** writing done with the hand. **2.** a kind or style of writing.
handwritten (hănd′rĭt′n), *adj.* written by hand.
handy (hăn′dĭ), *adj.,* **-dier, -diest. 1.** ready to hand; conveniently accessible: *to have aspirins handy.* **2.** ready or skilful with the hands; deft; dexterous. **3.** convenient to handle; easily manipulated or manoeuvred: *a handy ship.* **4.** convenient or useful: *a handy tool.*
Handy (hăn′dĭ), *n.* **W(illiam) C(hristopher),** 1873–1958, U.S. jazz composer, esp. of blues.
handyman (hăn′dĭ măn′), *n.* a man hired to do odd jobs.
hanepoot (hăn′ĭ po͝ot′), *n.* a full-flavoured South African variety of grape, orig. from the Mediterranean area. [t. Afrikaans: lit., cock foot]
hang (hăng), *v.,* **hung** or (esp. for capital punishment and suicide) **hanged, hanging,** *n.* —*v.t.* **1.** to fasten or attach (a thing) so that it is supported only from above; suspend. **2.** to suspend so as to allow free movement, as on a hinge. **3.** to fasten or suspend (a person) on a gallows or the like, esp. as a method of capital punishment. **4.** to suspend by the neck until dead. **5.** *Archaic.* to crucify. **6.** to let droop or bend downwards: *to hang one's head in shame.* **7.** to furnish or decorate with something suspended: *to hang a room with tapestries.* **8.** to fasten into position; fix at a proper angle: *to hang a scythe.* **9.** to attach (paper, etc.) to walls. **10.** to suspend (game) by the feet until it becomes high. **11.** *Arts.* **a.** to exhibit (a picture or pictures). **b.** to exhibit the work of (a painter or the like). **12.** to hinge (a door, window, etc.) to its frame. **13.** (used in maledictions and emphatic expressions): *I'll be hanged if I do.* **14.** to keep (a jury) from rendering a verdict, as one juror by refusing to agree with the others. —*v.i.* **15.** to be suspended; dangle. **16.** to swing freely, as on a hinge. **17.** to be suspended from a cross or gallows; suffer death in this way as punishment. **18.** to bend forwards or downwards; lean over; incline downwards. **19.** to be conditioned or contingent; be dependent. **20.** to hold fast, cling, or adhere; rest for support (fol. by *on* or *upon*). **21.** to be doubtful or undecided; waver or hesitate; remain unfinished. **22.** to loiter or linger: *to hang about a place.* **23.** to rest, float, or hover in the air. **24.** to impend; be imminent. **25.** to remain in attention or consideration: *to hang upon a person's words.* **26.** *Arts.* **a.** to be exhibited, as in an art gallery. **b.** to have one's works exhibited. **27.** to fail to agree, as a jury. —*v.* **28.** Some special verb phrases are:
hang about or **around, 1.** to spend time (in one's company). **2.** to loiter.
hang back, to resist advance; be reluctant to proceed.
hang in the balance, to be in doubt or suspense.
hang on, 1. to persevere; to maintain existing conditions with effort. **2.** to linger.
hang out, 1. to lean through an opening. **2.** *Slang.* to live at or frequent a particular place. **3.** to suspend in open view; display: *to hang out a banner.*
hang together, 1. to hold together; remain united. **2.** to be consistent: *his statements do not hang together.*
hang up, 1. to suspend on a hook or peg. **2.** *U.S.* to hold up. **3.** to break off telephonic communication.
—*n.* **29.** the way in which a thing hangs: *the hang of a curtain.* **30.** *Colloq.* the precise manner of doing, using, etc., something: *to get the hang of a tool.* **31.** *Colloq.* meaning or force: *to get the hang of a subject.* **32.** the least degree of care, concern, etc. (in mild expletives): *not to give a hang.* [fusion of three verbs: (1) ME and OE *hōn* (orig., v.t.), now obs.; (2) ME *hang(i)en*, OE *hangian* (orig., v.i.); (3) ME *heng(e)*, *hing*, t. Scand. (cf. Icel. *hengja* cause to hang)]
—**Syn. 3.** HANG, LYNCH through a widespread misconception have been thought of as synonyms. They do have in common the meaning of 'to put to death', but lynching is not always by hanging. HANG, in the sense of 'execute', is in accordance with a legal sentence, the method of execution being to suspend by the neck until dead. To LYNCH, however, implies the summary putting to death, by any method, of someone charged with a flagrant offence (though guilt may not have been proved). Lynching is done by private persons, usually a mob, without legal authority.
hangar (hăng′ə), *n.* **1.** a shed or shelter. **2.** a shed for aeroplanes or airships. [t. F, ? t. Gmc]
hangbird (hăng′bûd′), *n.* a bird that builds a hanging nest, esp. the Baltimore oriole.
Hangchow (hăng′chou′), *n.* a seaport in and the capital of Chekiang province, in E China. 794,000 (est. 1958).
hangdog (hăng′dŏg′), *adj.* **1.** (of persons) having a mean or sneaking appearance. **2.** mean; sneaking: *a hangdog look.* —*n.* **3.** a degraded, contemptible person.
hanger (hăng′ə), *n.* **1.** one who hangs. **2.** that on which anything is hung. **3.** a shaped support for a coat or other garment. **4.** something by which a thing is hung, as a loop

on a garment. **5.** *Motor Vehicles, etc.* a double-hinged device linking the chassis with each spring. **6.** a light sabre of the 17th and 18th centuries, often worn at sea.

hanger-on (hăng′ər ŏn′), *n., pl.* **hangers-on.** one who clings to a service, place, or connection; follower.

hanging (hăng′ĭng), *n.* **1.** capital punishment by suspension with strangulation on a gallows. **2.** (*often pl.*) something that hangs or is hung on the walls of a room, as a drapery, tapestry, etc. **3.** the act of one who or that which hangs; suspension. *—adj.* **4.** deserving punishment by hanging. **5.** inclined to inflict death by hanging: *a hanging judge.* **6.** that hangs; pendent; overhanging. **7.** situated on a steep slope or at a height: *a hanging garden.* **8.** directed downwards: *a hanging look.* **9.** made for hanging an object on.

hanging buttress, *Archit.* a decorative buttress usually supported by a corbel.

Hanging Gardens of Babylon, one of the seven wonders of the ancient world, believed to be the ornamental gardens on the terraced ziggurats of ancient Babylon.

hanging indentation, *Print., etc.* an indentation of uniform amount at the beginning of each line except the first, which is of full width. Also, **hanging indent.**

hanging valley, *Geog.* a tributary valley in a mountainous area, which joins the main valley by a sudden sharp descent, as a result of glacial erosion.

hangman (hăng′mən), *n., pl.* **-men.** one who hangs persons condemned to death; public executioner.

hangnail (hăng′nāl′), *n.* a small piece of partly detached skin at the side or base of the fingernail. Also, **agnail.** [aspirated var. of *angnail,* OE *angnægl*; the aspirated form became standard by popular etymology (assoc. with HANG)]

hang-out (hăng′out′), *n. Slang.* a place where one lives or frequently visits.

hangover (hăng′ō′və), *n. Colloq.* **1.** something remaining behind from a former period or state of affairs. **2.** the after-effects of excessive indulgence in alcoholic drink.

hank (hăngk), *n.* **1.** a skein, as of thread or yarn. **2.** a definite length of thread or yarn: *a hank of cotton yarn measures 840 yards, of worsted 560 yards.* **3.** a coil, knot, or loop: *a hank of hair.* **4.** *Naut.* a ring, as of iron or wood, round a stay, to which a sail is attached. [ME, t. Scand.; cf. Icel. *hönk* hank, coil, skein]

hanker (hăng′kə), *v.i.* to have a restless or incessant longing (often fol. by *after, for,* or an infinitive). [cf. d. D *hankeren*] *—***han′kerer,** *n.*

hankering (hăng′kə rĭng), *n.* a longing; craving.

hanky (hăng′kĭ), *n. Colloq.* a handkerchief. Also, **hankie.**

hanky-panky (hăng′kĭ păng′kĭ), *n. Slang.* **1.** trickery; subterfuge or the like. **2.** jugglery or legerdemain.

Hannibal (hăn′ĭ bl), *n.* 247–183? B.C., Carthaginian general who crossed the Alps and invaded Italy.

Hannover (*Ger.* hȧ nō′fər), *n.* German name of **Hanover.**

Hanoi (hă noi′), *n.* the capital of North Vietnam, in the N part. 643,576 (1963). See map under **Vietnam.**

Hanover (hăn′ə və), *n.* **1.** German, **Hannover.** a former province in N West Germany; now a district in Lower Saxony. 14,944 sq. mi. **2.** German, **Hannover.** a city in West Germany, capital of Lower Saxony, in the central part. 547,800 (est. 1966). **3.** the name of the English royal family from 1714 to 1901.

Hanoverian (hăn′ə vĭə′rĭ ən), *adj.* **1.** of or pertaining to the former ruling house of Hanover. *—n.* **2.** a supporter of the house of Hanover.

Hansard (hăn′säd), *n.* the official printed reports of British parliamentary debates, so called after a family of former compilers.

Hanse (hăns), *n.* **1.** a company or guild of merchants. **2.** a fee paid to a medieval trading guild. **3.** Also, **Hanse Towns.** Hanseatic League. Also, **Hansa** (hăn′sə). [ME, t. OF, t. MHG: company (of merchants)]

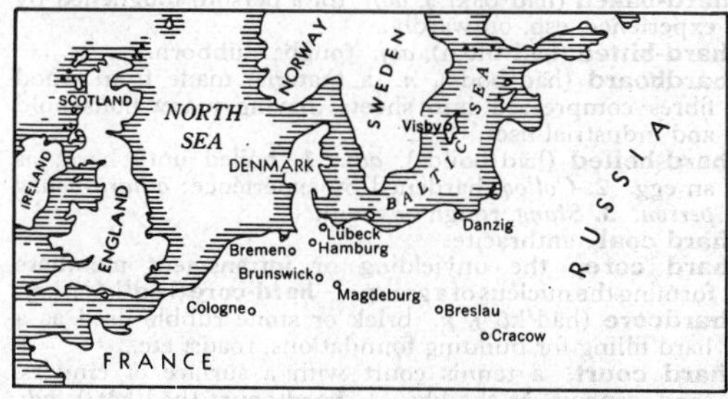

Centres of the Hanseatic League

Hanseatic League (hăn′sĭ ăt′ĭk), a medieval league of towns of northern Germany and adjacent countries for the promotion and protection of commerce.

hansel (hăn′səl), *n., v.t.,* **-selled, -selling.** handsel.

Hansen's disease (hăn′sənz), *Pathol.* leprosy. [named after Gerhard Henrik Armauer *Hansen,* 1841–1912, Norwegian physician who discovered leprosy-causing *Mycobacterium leprae*]

hansom (hăn′səm), *n.* a low-hung, two-wheeled, covered vehicle drawn by one horse, for two passengers, the driver being mounted on an elevated seat behind, and the reins running over the roof. [named after J. A. *Hansom,* English patentee (1834)]

Hansom

Hantan (hăn′tăn′), *n.* a city in NE China, in Hopeh province. 380,000 (est. 1958).

Hants (hănts), *n.* Hampshire.

Hanukkah (hä′nŏŏ kä′; *Heb.* -KHä′), *n.* the Feast of the Dedication, a Jewish festival in commemoration of the victory of the Maccabees, lasting eight days (mostly in December). [t. Heb.: m. *ḥanukkāh* dedication]

hanuman (hŭn′ŏŏ män′), *n., pl.* **-mans** *for 1.* **1.** a long-tailed monkey, *Presbytis entellus,* of S Asia, considered sacred in India. **2.** (*cap.*) *Hindu Myth.* a monkey chief who is a conspicuous figure in the Ramayana. [t. Hind.: lit., the one with a jaw, the jawed one]

hap (hăp), *n., v.,* **happed, happing.** *Archaic. —n.* **1.** one's luck or lot. **2.** an occurrence, happening, or accident. *—v.i.* **3.** to happen: *if it so hap.* [ME, t. Scand.; cf. Icel. *happ* hap, chance, good luck. Cf. OE *gehæp,* adj., fit, convenient]

ha'pence (hā′pəns), *n.* halfpence.

ha'penny (hāp′nĭ), *n., pl.* **-nies.** halfpenny.

haphazard (hăp′hăz′əd), *adj.* **1.** determined by or dependent on mere chance: *a haphazard remark. —adv.* **2.** in a haphazard manner; at random; by chance. *—n.* **3.** mere chance; accident: *to proceed at haphazard.* [f. HAP + HAZARD] *—***hap′haz′ardly,** *adv. —***hap′haz′ardness,** *n.*

haphtarah (hăf′tə rä′, hăf tä′rə), *n., pl.* **-roth** (-rōth′). a portion of the Prophets read immediately after a portion of the Pentateuch in the Jewish synagogue on sabbaths and festivals. Also, **haftarah.** [t. Heb.: conclusion]

hapless (hăp′lĭs), *adj.* luckless; unfortunate; unlucky. *—***hap′lessly,** *adv. —***hap′lessness,** *n.*

haplite (hăp′līt), *n. Geol.* aplite.

haplo-, a word element meaning 'single', 'simple'. [t. Gk, comb. form of *haplóos*]

haplography (hăp lŏg′rə fĭ), *n.* the omission of a word, syllable, or letter in writing, where it occurs twice in succession, as in *hippotamus* for *hippopotamus.*

haploid (hăp′loid), *adj.* Also, **haploi′dic. 1.** single; simple. **2.** *Biol.* pertaining to a single set of chromosomes. *—n.* **3.** *Biol.* an organism or cell having only one complete set of chromosomes, ordinarily half the normal diploid number.

haplology (hăp lŏl′ə jĭ), *n. Gram.* the syncope of a syllable within a word, as *syllabi(fi)cation.* [f. HAPLO- + -LOGY]

haplosis (hăp lō′sĭs), *n. Biol.* the production of haploid chromosome groups during meiosis.

haply (hăp′lĭ), *adv. Archaic.* perhaps; by chance.

ha'p'orth (hā′pəth), *n.* halfpennyworth.

happen (hăp′ən), *v.i.* **1.** to come to pass, take place, or occur. **2.** to come to pass by chance; occur without apparent reason or design; chance. **3.** to have the fortune or lot (to do or be as specified): *I happened to see him.* **4.** to befall, as to a person or thing. **5.** to come by chance (fol. by *on* or *upon*). **6.** *U.S.* to be, come, or go (as specified) by chance: *to happen in to see a friend. —adv.* **7.** *Dial.* perhaps. [ME *happene(n), hapnen*; f. HAP, n. + -EN[1]]

—Syn. 1. HAPPEN, CHANCE, OCCUR refer to the taking place of an event. HAPPEN, which originally denoted the taking place by hap or chance, is now the most general word for coming to pass: *an accident has happened.* CHANCE suggests the fortuitousness of an event: *it chanced to rain that day.* OCCUR is often interchangeable with HAPPEN, but is more formal, and is usually more specific as to time and event: *his death occurred the following year.*

happening (hăp′ə nĭng, hăp′nĭng), *n.* **1.** an occurrence: event. **2.** a dramatic or similar performance consisting chiefly of a series of discontinuous events, often involving audience participation.

happily (hăp′ĭ lĭ), *adv.* **1.** in a happy manner; with pleasure. **2.** luckily. **3.** with skill; aptly; appropriately.

happiness (hăp′ĭ nĭs), *n.* **1.** the quality or state of being happy. **2.** good fortune; pleasure, content, or gladness. **3.** aptness or felicity, as of expression.

—Syn. 1. beatitude, blessedness, contentedness. HAPPINESS, BLISS, CONTENTMENT, FELICITY imply an active or passive state of pleasure or pleasurable satisfaction. HAPPINESS results from the possession or attainment of what one considers good: *the happiness of visiting one's family.* BLISS is unalloyed happiness or supreme delight: *the bliss of perfect companionship.* CONTENTMENT is a peaceful kind of HAPPINESS in which one rests without desires, even though every wish may not have been gratified: *contentment in one's surroundings.* FELICITY is a formal word for happiness of an especially fortunate kind: *to wish a young couple felicity in life.* —Ant. 1. wretchedness.

happy (hăp′ĭ), *adj.*, **-pier, -piest.** **1.** characterized by or indicative of pleasure, content, or gladness: *a happy mood.* **2.** delighted, pleased, or glad, as over a particular thing: *to be happy to see a person.* **3.** favoured by fortune; fortunate or lucky: *a happy event.* **4.** apt or felicitous, as actions, utterances, ideas, etc. **5.** *Colloq.* showing an excessive liking for, or quick to use an item indicated (used in combination): *trigger-happy.* [ME; f. HAP, n. + -Y[1]] **—Syn. 1.** joyous, joyful, glad, blithe, cheerful. **3.** favourable, propitious. See **fortunate. 4.** appropriate, fitting. **—Ant. 1.** depressed. **3.** unlucky.

happy-go-lucky (hăp′ĭ gō lŭk′ĭ), *adj.* **1.** trusting cheerfully to luck. *—adv.* **2.** haphazard; by mere chance.

Happy Hunting Grounds, 1. (in North American Indian mythology) the world inhabited by souls after death; the afterlife. **2.** (*usually sing., l.c.*) *Colloq.* a suitable place for an activity: *village churches are a happy hunting ground for brass-rubbers.*

Hapsburg (hăps′bûg; *Ger.* häps′bŏŏrk), *n.* Habsburg.

hapten (hăp′tən), *n.* an incomplete antigen.

hapuka (hä′pōō kä′), *n.* the grouper, *Polyprion prognathus*, a large fish of the family *Serranidae*, which inhabits the Indian and Pacific oceans. [t. Maori]

harakiri (hă′rə kĭ′rĭ), *n.* suicide by ripping open the abdomen with a dagger or knife: national form of honourable suicide in Japan, formerly practised among the higher classes when disgraced or sentenced to death. Also, **harakari** (hă′rə kä′rĭ), **harikari.** [t. Jap.: belly cut]

Harald I (hă′rəld), ('*Harold Fairhair*'), 850?–933, king of Norway 860–930.

harangue (hə răng′), *n.*, *v.*, **-rangued, -ranguing.** *—n.* **1.** a passionate, vehement speech; noisy and intemperate address. **2.** any long, declamatory or pompous speech. *—v.t.* **3.** to address in a harangue. *—v.i.* **4.** to deliver a harangue. [t. F, t. Gmc; cf. OE and OHG *hring* RING[1]] **—harangu′er,** *n.* **—Syn. 1.** See **speech.**

Harar (hä′rə), *n.* a city in Ethiopia. 38,000 (est. 1962).

harass (hă′rəs), *v.t.* **1.** to trouble by repeated attacks, incursions, etc., as in war or hostilities; harry; raid. **2.** to disturb persistently; torment, as with troubles, cares, etc. [t. F: s. *harasser*, der. OF *harer* set a dog on] **—har′asser,** *n.* **—har′assingly,** *adv.* **—harassment** (hă′rəs mənt), *n.* **—Syn. 2.** badger, vex, pester, plague. See **worry.**

Harbin (hä′bēn′, -bĭn′), *n.* a city in NE China, the capital of Heilungkiang province. 1,595,000 (est. 1958). See map under **Lake Baikal.**

harbinger (hä′bĭn jə), *n.* **1.** one who goes before and makes known the approach of another. **2.** that which foreshadows a future event; an omen. **3.** *Obs.* one sent in advance of troops, a royal train, etc., to provide or secure lodgings and other accommodations. *—v.t.* **4.** to act as harbinger to; herald the coming of. [ME *herbergere*, t. OF: m. *herbergeor*, der. *herbergier* provide lodging for, der. *herberge* lodging, t. Gmc. See HARBOUR]

harbour (hä′bə), *n.* **1.** a portion of a body of water along the shore deep enough for ships, and so situated with respect to coastal features, whether natural or artificial, as to provide protection from winds, waves, and currents. **2.** any place of shelter or refuge. *—v.t.* **3.** to give shelter to: *to harbour refugees.* **4.** to conceal; give a place to hide: *to harbour smuggled goods.* **5.** to entertain in the mind; indulge (usually unfavourable or evil feelings): *to harbour suspicion.* **6.** to shelter (a ship) in a harbour or haven. *—v.i.* **7.** (of a ship, etc.) to take shelter in a harbour. Also, *U.S.*, **harbor.** [ME *herber(we)*, *hereberge*, OE *herebeorg* lodgings, quarters, f. *here* army + *(ge)beorg* refuge; c. G *Herberge*] **—har′bourer,** *n.* **—har′bourless,** *adj.*

—Syn. 1. HARBOUR, HAVEN, PORT indicate a shelter for ships. A HARBOUR may be natural or artificially constructed or improved: *a fine harbour on the east coast.* A HAVEN is usually a natural harbour which can be utilized by ships as a place of safety; the word is common in poetic use: *a haven in time of storm, a haven of refuge.* A PORT is a HARBOUR viewed esp. in its commercial relations, though it is also frequently applied in the meaning of HARBOUR or HAVEN: *a thriving port, any old port in a storm.* **5.** See **cherish.**

harbourage (hä′bə rĭj), *n.* **1.** shelter for ships, as in a harbour. **2.** shelter or lodging. **3.** a place of shelter.

harbourmaster (hä′bə mäs′tə), *n.* an officer in charge of harbour regulations, such as the mooring of vessels.

harbour of refuge, a harbour on an inhospitable coast, used for shelter in bad weather, but having none of the facilities of a port.

harbour seal. See **seal**[2] (def. 1).

hard (häd), *adj.* **1.** solid and firm to the touch; not soft. **2.** firmly formed; tight: *a hard knot.* **3.** difficult to do or accomplish; fatiguing; troublesome: *a hard task.* **4.** difficult or troublesome with respect to an action specified: *hard to please.* **5.** difficult to deal with, manage, control, overcome, or understand: *a hard problem.* **6.** involving or performed with great exertion, energy, or persistence: *hard work.* **7.** carrying on work in this manner: *a hard worker.* **8.** vigorous or violent; severe: *a hard rain.* **9.** oppressive; harsh; rough: *hard treatment.* **10.** unpleasant; unfair; bad: *hard luck.* **11.** austere; uncomfortable; causing pain, poverty, etc.: *hard times.* **12.** unfeeling; callous: *a hard heart.* **13.** harsh or severe in dealing with others: *a hard master.* **14.** incapable of being denied or explained away: *hard facts.* **15.** harsh or unfriendly; not easily moved: *hard feelings.* **16.** harsh or unpleasant to the eye, ear, or aesthetic sense. **17.** severe or rigorous in terms: *a hard bargain.* **18.** not swayed by sentiment or sophistry; shrewd: *to have a hard head.* **19.** *Colloq.* incorrigible; disreputable: *a hard case.* **20.** *Now Chiefly Dial.* niggardly; stingy. **21.** in coin rather than in paper currency, or as distinguished from other property: *hard cash.* **22.** *Chiefly U.S.* strong; alcoholic or intoxicating: *hard liquor.* **23.** (of water) containing mineral salts which interfere with the action of the soap. **24.** *Physics.* (of radiation) of short wavelength and high penetrating power. **25.** *Agric.* denoting wheats with high gluten content, milled for a bread flour as contrasted with pastry flour. **26.** *Phonet.* **a.** (of consonants) fortis. **b.** (of *c* and *g*) pronounced as in *come* and *go.* **c.** (of consonants in Slavic languages) not palatalized. **27. hard of hearing,** partly deaf. **28. hard up,** *Colloq.* urgently in need of something, esp. money. **29. put the hard word on,** *Austral. Slang.* to ask a favour of.
—adv. **30.** with great exertion; with vigour or violence: *to work hard.* **31.** earnestly or intently: *to look hard at a thing.* **32.** harshly or severely; badly; gallingly: *it goes hard.* **33.** so as to be solid or firm: *frozen hard.* **34. hard by,** close or nearby. **35. hard put to it,** in great difficulties. **36.** *Naut.* closely, fully, or to the extreme limit: *hard aport.* [ME; OE *heard*, c. G *hart*]

—Syn. 1. inflexible, rigid, unyielding, resisting, adamantine, flinty, impenetrable. See **firm**[1]. **3.** toilsome, burdensome, wearisome, exhausting. HARD, DIFFICULT both describe something resistant to one's efforts or one's endurance. HARD is the general word: *hard times, it was hard to endure the severe weather.* DIFFICULT means not easy, and particularly denotes that which requires special effort or skill: *a difficult task.* **5.** perplexing, puzzling, intricate, knotty, tough. **6.** arduous, onerous, laborious. **9.** severe, rigorous, grinding, cruel, merciless, unsparing. **13.** stern, austere, strict, exacting. HARD, CALLOUS, UNFEELING, UNSYMPATHETIC imply a lack of interest in, feeling for, or sympathy with others. HARD implies insensibility, either natural or acquired, so that the plight of others makes no impression on one: *a hard taskmaster.* CALLOUS may mean the same, or that one himself becomes insensitive to hurt, as the result of continued repression and indifference: *a callous answer, callous to criticism.* UNFEELING implies natural inability to feel with and for others: *an unfeeling and thoughtless remark.* UNSYMPATHETIC implies an indifference which makes no attempt to pity, etc.: *unsympathetic towards distress.*

hard and fast, 1. strongly binding; not to be set aside or violated: *hard and fast rules.* **2.** firmly and securely: *bound hard and fast.*

Hardanger (*Norw.* här dång′ər), *n.* a fiord in SW Norway. 114 mi. long.

hardback (häd′băk′), *n.* **1.** a book bound in stiff covers, usually of boards covered with cloth, etc. *—adj.* **2.** of, denoting, or pertaining to such books or the publishing of such books; casebound. Cf. **paperback.**

hard-baked (häd′bākt′), *adj.* (of a person) toughened by experience, esp. outwardly.

hard-bitten (häd′bĭt′n), *adj.* tough; stubborn.

hardboard (häd′bôd′), *n.* a material made from wood fibres compressed into sheets, having many household and industrial uses.

hard-boiled (häd′boild′), *adj.* **1.** boiled until hard, as an egg. **2.** *Colloq.* hardened by experience: *a hard-boiled person.* **3.** *Slang.* rough or tough.

hard coal, anthracite.

hard core, the unyielding or intransigent members forming the nucleus of a group. **—hard-core** (häd′kô′), *adj.*

hardcore (häd′kô′), *n.* brick or stone rubble used as a hard filling for building foundations, roads, etc.

hard court, a tennis court with a surface of cinders, sand, asphalt, or the like. **—hard-court** (häd′kôt′), *adj.*

hard drinker, one who drinks alcohol persistently and to excess.

hard-edge (häd′ĕj′), *adj. Art.* of or pertaining to a modern school of painting originating in the U.S. which defines abstract areas of colour with clean edges.

harden[1] (hä′dn), *v.t.* **1.** to make hard or harder. **2.** to make obdurate or unyielding; make unfeeling or pitiless: *to harden one's heart.* **3.** to strengthen or confirm with respect to any element of character; toughen. **4.** to make hardy, robust, or capable of endurance. *—v.i.* **5.** to become hard or harder. **6.** to become obdurate, unfeeling, or pitiless. **7.** to become inured or toughened. **8.** *Com.* (of prices, the market, etc.) **a.** to become higher; rise. **b.** to cease to fluctuate. [f. HARD + -EN[1]] **—Syn. 1.** solidify, indurate; petrify, ossify. **3.** fortify, steel, brace, nerve. **—Ant. 1.** soften. **3.** weaken. **4.** debilitate.

harden[2] (hä′dn), *n.* a coarse fabric made from hards.

Hardenberg (*Ger.* här′dən bĕrk), *n.* **Friedrich von** (*Ger.* frē′drĭkh fōn) (*Novalis*), 1772–1801, German poet.

hardened (hä′dnd), *adj.* **1.** made hard; indurated; inured. **2.** obdurate; unfeeling.

hardener (hä′də nə), *n.* **1.** a person or thing that hardens. **2.** one who hardens a specified thing. **3.** a substance mixed with paint or other protective covering to make the finish harder or more durable.

hardening (hä′də nĭng), *n.* **1.** a material which hardens another, as an alloy added to iron to make steel. **2.** the process of becoming hard or rigid.

harder (hä′də), *n.* a sea fish, *Mugil cephalus*, a large, striped, edible member of the mullet family (*Mugilidae*) of warm seas. Also, **springer.**

hard-favoured (häd′fā′vəd), *adj.* having a hard, unpleasant countenance.

hard-featured (häd′fē′chəd), *adj.* having hard and forbidding features.

hard fern, a small fern, *Blechnum spicant*, with separate sterile and fertile leaves, widespread in N temperate regions on non-alkaline soils.

hard-fisted (häd′fĭs′tĭd), *adj.* **1.** niggardly; stingy. **2.** having hard or strong hands, as a labourer.

hardhack (häd′hăk′), *n.* a woolly-leaved rosaceous shrub, *Spiraea tomentosa*, of North America, having terminal panicles of rose-coloured or white flowers.

hard-handed (häd′hăn′dĭd), *adj.* **1.** having hands hardened by toil. **2.** ruling with a strong or cruel hand.

hard-headed (häd′hĕd′ĭd), *adj.* not easily moved or deceived; practical; shrewd. **—hard′-head′edly,** *adv.* **—hard′-head′edness,** *n.*

hardheads (häd′hĕdz′), *n.* a perennial herbaceous composite, *Centaurea nigra*, with reddish purple capitula, a native of W Europe introduced in New Zealand and N America; knapweed.

hard-hearted (häd′hä′tĭd), *adj.* unfeeling; unmerciful; pitiless. **—hard′-heart′edly,** *adv.* **—hard′-heart′edness,** *n.*

Hardicanute (hä′dĭ kə nyōōt′), *n. c.* 1019–42, king of Denmark 1035–42, and king of England 1040–42. Also, **Hardicnut.**

Hardie (hä′dĭ), *n.* **(James) Keir** (kĭə), 1856–1915, Scottish Labour leader.

hardihood (hä′dĭ hŏŏd′), *n.* hardy spirit or character; boldness or daring.

hardily (hä′dĭ lĭ), *adv.* in a hardy manner.

hardiness (hä′dĭ nĭs), *n.* **1.** robustness; capability of endurance; strength. **2.** hardihood; audacity.

Harding (hä′dĭng), *n.* **Warren Gamaliel** (gə mā′lĭ əl), 1865–1923, 29th president of the U.S., 1921–23.

hard labour, (in Britain before 1948) labour imposed on prisoners as a punishment, often as part of the sentence.

hard lines, *Colloq.* bad luck; unfair treatment.

hardly (häd′lĭ), *adv.* **1.** barely; almost not at all: *hardly any, hardly ever.* **2.** not quite: *that is hardly true.* **3.** with little likelihood: *he will hardly come now.* **4.** with trouble or difficulty. **5.** harshly or severely.

—Syn. 1. HARDLY, BARELY, SCARCELY imply a narrow margin by which performance was, is, or will be achieved. HARDLY, though often interchangeable with SCARCELY and BARELY, usually emphasizes the idea of the difficulty involved: *we could hardly endure the winter.* BARELY emphasizes the narrowness of the margin of safety, 'only just and no more': *we barely succeeded.* SCARCELY implies a very narrow margin, below satisfactory performance: *we can scarcely read.*

hard-mouthed (häd′mouŧħd′), *adj.* **1.** (of horses) difficult to control with a bit. **2.** (of a person) given to swearing and coarse language.

hardness (häd′nĭs), *n.* **1.** the state or quality of being hard. **2.** an instance of this quality. **3.** that quality in impure water which is imparted by the presence of dissolved salts, especially calcium sulphate. **4.** *Mineral.* the comparative capacity of a substance to scratch another or be scratched by another. See **Mohs scale.**

hardpad (häd′păd′), *n. Vet. Sci.* an infectious disease of dogs, caused by a filterable virus.

hardpan (häd′păn′), *n.* **1.** any layer of firm detrital matter, as of clay, underlying soft soil. **2.** hard, unbroken ground. **3.** solid foundation; hard underlying reality.

hard rubber, rubber vulcanized with a large amount of sulphur, usually 25–35 per cent, to render it stiff and comparatively inflexible.

hard-rush (häd′rŭsh′), *n.* a glaucous, tufted, juncaceous perennial, *Juncus inflexus*, widespread in damp places in temperate regions.

hards (hädz), *n.pl.* the refuse or coarser parts of flax or hemp, separated in hackling. Also, **hurds.** [ME *herdes*, OE *heordan*]

hard sauce, a sauce made by creaming butter and brown sugar, flavoured with brandy or rum, served with Christmas and other rich puddings.

hard sell, a method of advertising or selling which is direct, forceful, and insistent; high-pressure salesmanship. See **soft sell.**

hard-set (häd′sĕt′), *adj.* **1.** in a difficult position. **2.** firmly or rigidly set. **3.** determined; obstinate.

hard-shell (häd′shĕl′), *adj.* **1.** having a firm, hard shell, as a crab in its normal state, not having recently moulted. **2.** *U.S. Colloq.* rigid or uncompromising.

hardship (häd′shĭp), *n.* **1.** a condition that bears hard upon one; severe toil, trial, oppression, or need. **2.** an instance of this; something hard to bear.

—Syn. 1. HARDSHIP, PRIVATION, AUSTERITY are terms for something hard to endure. HARDSHIP applies to a circumstance in which excessive and painful effort of some kind is required, as enduring acute discomfort from cold, battling over rough terrain, and the like. PRIVATION has particular reference to lack of food, clothing, and other necessities or comforts. AUSTERITY not only includes the ideas of privation and hardship but also implies deliberate control of emotional reactions to these. **—Ant. 1.** ease.

hard shoulder, a verge with a firm surface to the side of a motorway where emergency stops can be made.

hard-spun (häd′spŭn′), *adj.* (of yarn) compactly twisted in spinning.

hardtack (häd′tăk′), *n.* a kind of hard biscuit used esp. by sailors. [f. HARD + *tack* taste]

hardtop (häd′tŏp′), *n.* a motor car, esp. a sports car, which is not convertible.

hardware (häd′wĕə′), *n.* **1.** metal goods, as tools, locks, hinges, cutlery, etc; ironmongery. **2.** the mechanical equipment necessary for conducting an activity, usually distinguished from the theory and design which make the activity possible. **3.** *Mil.* arms and the machinery of war generally. **4.** *Computers.* the metal, glass, and other durable parts in a computer system (opposed to *software*).

hardwood (häd′wŏŏd′), *n.* **1.** the hard, compact wood or timber of various trees, as the oak, cherry, maple, mahogany, etc. **2.** a tree yielding such wood.

hardy[1] (hä′dĭ), *adj.*, **-dier, -diest. 1.** capable of enduring fatigue, hardship, exposure, etc.: *hardy animals.* **2.** (of plants) able to withstand the cold of winter in the open air. **3.** requiring great physical endurance: *the hardiest sports.* **4.** bold or daring; courageous, as persons, actions, etc. **5.** unduly bold; presumptuous; foolhardy. [ME *hardi*, t. OF, pp. of *hardir* harden, t. Gmc; akin to HARD] **—Syn. 1.** vigorous, sturdy, robust, hale.

hardy[2] (hä′dĭ), *n., pl.* **-dies.** a chisel or fuller with a square shank for insertion into a square hole (**hardy-hole**) in a blacksmith's anvil. [appar. der. HARD]

Hardy (hä′dĭ), *n.* **1. Oliver.** See **Laurel and Hardy. 2. Thomas,** 1840–1928, English novelist and poet.

hare (hĕə), *n., pl.* **hares,** (*esp. collectively*) **hare,** *v.*, **hared, haring.** *—n.* **1.** any rodent-like mammal of the genus *Lepus* (family *Leporidae*), with long ears, divided upper lip, short tail, and lengthened hind limbs adapted for leaping. **2.** any of the larger species of this genus, as distinguished from certain of the smaller ones known as rabbits. **3.** any of various similar animals of the same family. **4.** the person chased or pursued in the game of hare and hounds. **5. start a hare,** to bring an irrelevant point into an argument. *—v.i.* **6.** to run fast. [ME; OE *hara*, c. Dan. *hare*; akin to G *Hase.* Cf. OE *hasu* grey] **—hare′like′,** *adj.*

hare and hounds, an outdoor game in which certain players (**hares**) start off in advance on a long run, leaving a trail, as by scattering small pieces of paper (**scent**), the other players (**hounds**) following the trail so marked in an effort to catch the hares before they reach home; a paperchase.

harebell (hĕə′bĕl′), *n.* a low campanulaceous herb, the bluebell of Scotland, *Campanula rotundifolia*, with blue, bell-shaped flowers.

harebrained (hĕə′brānd′), *adj.* irrational; reckless.

harelip (hĕə′lĭp′), *n.* **1.** a congenitally deformed lip, usually the upper one, in which there is a vertical fissure causing it to resemble the cleft lip of a hare. **2.** the deformity itself. **—hare′-lipped′,** *adj.*

harem (hĕə′rəm, hä rēm′), *n.* **1.** that part of an oriental palace or house reserved for the residence of women. **2.** the women in an oriental household: mother, sisters, wives, concubines, daughters, entertainers, servants, etc. [t. Ar.: m. *ḥarīm*, lit., (something) forbidden]

hare's-ear (hĕəz′ĭə′), *n.* a small umbelliferous annual with yellow flowers, *Bupleurum rotundifolium*, a weed of cultivated land, native in Europe and W Asia but introduced into other temperate regions.

hare's-foot (hĕəz′fo͝ot′), *n.* a small papilionaceous annual, *Trifolium arvense*, with hairy cylindrical heads of pink flowers, widespread in temperate regions on sandy soils.

hare's-tail (hĕəz′tāl′), *n.* **1.** a small annual grass, *Lagurus ovatus*, with soft, woolly, ovoid flowering heads, occurring in sandy places in SW Europe and Mediterranean regions. **2.** the cotton grass, *Eriophorum vaginatum*.

Hargreaves (hä′grēvz), *n.* **James,** died 1778, English inventor (of the spinning jenny).

haricot (hăr′ĭ kō′), *n.* **1.** the French bean, *Phaseolus vulgaris*. **2.** its pod, **haricot vert** (green bean). **3.** its seed, when pale, **haricot blanc** (white bean), and when dark, **haricot rouge** (red bean). See **kidney bean.** [t. F, identical with *haricot* ragout]

harikari (hä′rĭ kä′rĭ), *n.* harakiri.

Haringey (hă′rĭng gā′), *n.* a N outer borough of London. 258,400 (1961).

hark (häk), *v.i.* **1.** to listen; hearken (used chiefly in the imperative). **2. hark back, a.** to return to a previous point or subject, as in discourse or thought; revert. **b.** (of hounds) to return along the course in order to regain a lost scent. —*v.t.* **3.** *Archaic.* to listen to; hear. —*n.* **4.** a hunter's cry to hounds. [ME *herk(i)en*, c. OFris. *herkia*. Cf. HEARKEN]

harken (hä′kən), *v.i., v.t. Chiefly U.S.* hearken.

harl (häl), *n.* herl.

Harlem (hä′ləm), *n.* the chief Negro section of New York City, in the NE part of Manhattan.

Harlequin (hä′lĭ kwĭn), *n.* **1.** (*sometimes l.c.*) a droll character in comedy (orig. the early Italian) and pantomime, usually masked, dressed in particoloured spangled tights, and bearing a wooden sword or magic wand. **2.** (*l.c.*) a buffoon. **3.** (*l.c.*) any one of various small, handsomely marked snakes. —*adj.* **4.** (*l.c.*) fancifully varied in colour, decoration, etc. [t. F; OF *Harlequin*, *Herlequin*, t. ME: m. *Herle King* King Herla (mythical figure); modern meaning from It. *arlecchino*, t. F: m. *Harlequin*]

harlequinade (hä′lĭ kwĭ nād′), *n.* **1.** a pantomime or similar play in which the harlequin plays the principal part. **2.** buffoonery. See **commedia dell'arte.** [t. F: m. *arlequinade*]

harlequin duck, a small North American diving duck, *Histrionicus histrionicus*, in which the male is bluish grey, marked with black, white, and chestnut.

harlequinesque (hä′lĭ kwĭ nĕsk′), *adj.* in the style or manner of a harlequin.

Harley (hä′lĭ), *n.* **Robert.** See **Oxford** (def. 1).

Harley Street, a street in London, noted for the doctors who have consulting rooms there.

harlot (hä′lət), *n.* **1.** a promiscuous woman; prostitute. —*adj.* **2.** pertaining to or like a harlot; low. [ME, t. OF: rogue, knave; orig. uncert.]

harlotry (hä′lə trĭ), *n., pl.* **-ries. 1.** the practice or trade of prostitution. **2.** harlots collectively.

Harlow (hä′lō), *n.* a new town in England, in Essex. 68,736 (1965).

harm (häm), *n.* **1.** injury; damage; hurt: *to do him bodily harm.* **2.** moral injury; evil; wrong. —*v.t.* **3.** to do harm to; injure; damage; hurt. [ME; OE *hearm*, c. G *Harm*. Cf. Russ. *sram* shame] —**harm′er,** *n.* —**Syn. 1, 2.** See **damage.**

harmattan (hä măt′ən), *n.* a dry, parching land wind, charged with dust, from the desert in West Africa. [t. W African (Fanti or Tshi)]

harmful (häm′fəl), *adj.* fraught with or doing harm. —**harm′fully,** *adv.* —**harm′fulness,** *n.* —**Syn.** injurious, hurtful, detrimental. —**Ant.** beneficial.

harmless (häm′lĭs), *adj.* **1.** without power or tendency to harm: *harmless play.* **2.** *Rare.* unharmed. —**harm′lessly,** *adv.* —**harm′lessness,** *n.*

harmonic (hä mŏn′ĭk), *adj.* **1.** pertaining to harmony, as distinguished from melody and rhythm. **2.** marked by harmony; in harmony; concordant; consonant. **3.** *Physics.* denoting an integral multiple of a given frequency, thus 256, 512, 768, cycles per second are the *first, second,* and *third harmonics* of 256 cycles per second. **4.** *Maths.* having relations resembling those of musical concords: *a harmonic progression is a series of numbers the reciprocals of which are in arithmetic progression.* —*n.* **5.** an overtone. [t. L: s. *harmonicus*, t. Gk: m. *harmonikós* skilled in music] —**harmon′ically,** *adv.*

harmonica (hä mŏn′ĭ kə), *n.* **1.** a musical instrument having a set of small metallic reeds mounted in a case and played by the breath; a mouth organ. **2.** any of various percussion instruments which use graduated bars of metal or other hard material as sounding elements. [t. L, n. use of fem. of *harmonicus* HARMONIC]

harmonic mean, *Statistics.* the mean of *n* positive numbers obtained by taking the reciprocal of the average of the reciprocals of the numbers.

harmonic minor, *Music.* the minor scale from which chords are formed, having the sixth degree a semitone above the dominant and the seventh degree a semitone below the tonic.

harmonic motion, *Physics.* See **simple harmonic motion.**

harmonicon (hä mŏn′ĭ kən), *n.* any of various musical instruments, as a harmonica or an orchestrion. [t. Gk: m. *harmonikón* (neut.) harmonic]

harmonics (hä mŏn′ĭks), *n. Music.* **1.** the science of musical sounds. **2.** (*construed as pl.*) the partials or overtones of a fundamental note. Cf. **harmonic** (def. 2). **3.** (*construed as pl.*) the flageolet-like notes of a string (as a violin string) made to vibrate by touching lightly at a given point and bowing or plucking, so as to bring out an overtone, while suppressing the fundamental. [pl. of HARMONIC. See -ICS]

harmonic series, 1. *Maths.* any series in which the reciprocals of the terms form an arithmetic progression. **2.** *Music.* the complete range of upper partials produced from and by a fundamental note.

harmonious (hä mō′nyəs), *adj.* **1.** marked by agreement in feeling or action: *a harmonious group.* **2.** forming a pleasingly consistent whole; congruous. **3.** agreeable to the ear; tuneful; melodious. —**harmo′niously,** *adv.* —**harmo′niousness,** *n.* —**Syn. 1.** amicable, congenial; sympathetic. **2.** concordant, congruent, consonant, consistent. —**Ant. 1, 3.** discordant.

harmonist (hä′mə nĭst), *n.* **1.** one skilled in harmony. **2.** one who makes a harmony, as of the Gospels.

harmonistic (hä′mə nĭs′tĭk), *adj.* **1.** pertaining to a harmonist or harmony. **2.** pertaining to the collation and harmonizing of parallel passages, as of the Gospels. —**har′monis′tically,** *adv.*

harmonium (hä mō′nyəm), *n.* a reed organ, esp. one in which the air is forced outwards through the reeds. [t. F, der. *harmonie*, t. L: m. *harmonia* HARMONY]

harmonize (hä′mə nīz′), *v.,* **-nized, -nizing.** —*v.t.* **1.** to bring into harmony, accord, or agreement: *to harmonize the views.* **2.** *Music.* to accompany with appropriate harmony. —*v.i.* **3.** to be in agreement in action, sense, or feeling. **4.** to sing in harmony. Also, **harmonise.** —**har′moniza′tion,** *n.*

harmony (hä′mə nĭ), *n., pl.* **-nies. 1.** agreement; accord; harmonious relations. **2.** a consistent, orderly, or pleasing arrangement of parts; congruity. **3.** *Music.* **a.** any simultaneous combination of notes. **b.** the simultaneous combination of notes; chordal structure, as distinguished from melody and rhythm. **c.** the science of the structure, relations, and practical combination of chords. **4.** an arrangement of the contents of the Gospels (either of all four or of the first three) designed to show their parallelism, mutual relations, and differences. [ME *harmonie*, t. F, t. L: m. *harmonia*, t. Gk: a joining, concord, music]

—**Syn. 1.** concord, unity, peace, amity, friendship. **2.** consonance, conformity, correspondence, consistency. **3.** HARMONY, MELODY in music suggest a combination of sounds from voices or musical instruments. HARMONY is the blending of simultaneous sounds of different pitch or quality, making chords: *harmony in part-singing, harmony between violins and horns.* MELODY is the rhythmical combination of successive sounds of various pitch, making up the tune or air: *a tuneful melody to accompany cheerful words.* —**Ant. 1.** discord. **3.** dissonance.

harmotome (hä′mə tōm′), *n.* a mineral of the zeolite group, consisting of a hydrated silicate of barium and aluminium, which occurs in twinned crystals. [t. F, f. Gk: s. *harmós* joint + -(*o*)*tomē* section]

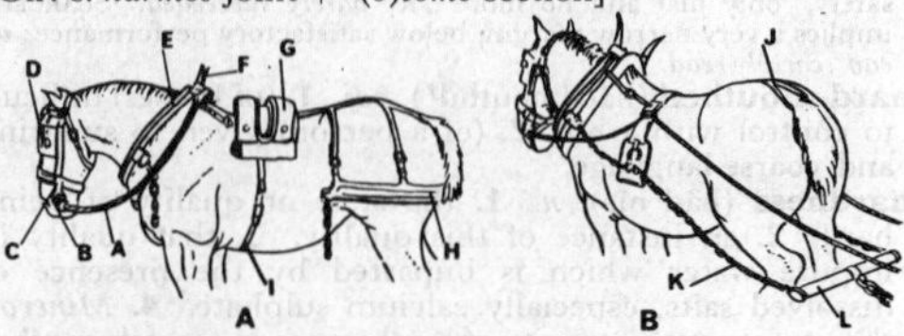

Harness: **A,** Cart gear; **B,** Plough gear

A, Reins; B, Bit; C, Bridle; D, Blinkers; E, Collar; F, Hames; G, Saddle; H, Breeching; I, Girth; J, Crupper; K, Trace; L, Whippletree

harness (hä′nĭs), *n.* **1.** the combination of straps, bands, and other parts forming the working gear of a horse or other draught animal (except the ox). 2. routine of work: *to die in harness.* 3. *Archaic.* armour for men or horses (or other animals), or a suit of armour. —*v.t.* 4. to put harness on (a horse, etc.); attach by a harness, as to a vehicle. 5. to bring under conditions for working: *to harness water-power.* 6. *Archaic.* to array in armour or equipments of war. [ME, t. OF: m. *harnies,* ? t. OHG; cf. Icel. *herr* army (c. OE *here*) + *nest* provisions] —**har′nesser,** *n.* —**har′nessless,** *adj.* —**har′ness-like′,** *adj.*

Harold I (hă′rəld) (surnamed *Harefoot*), died 1040, king of England 1035–40 (son of Canute).

Harold II, *c.* 1022–1066, king of England in 1066 (successor of Edward the Confessor and son of Earl Godwin); defeated by William the Conqueror in Battle of Hastings.

harp (häp), *n.* 1. a musical instrument consisting of a triangular frame (comprising a sounding-board, a pillar, and a curved neck) and strings stretched between sounding-board and neck and plucked with the fingers. —*v.i.* 2. to play on a harp. 3. to dwell persistently or tediously in speaking or writing (fol. by *on* or *upon*). —*v.t.* 4. *Poetic.* to bring, put, etc., by playing on a harp. 5. *Archaic.* to give voice or utterance to. [ME *harp(e),* OE *hearpe,* c. D *harp,* G *Harfe,* Icel. *harpa*] —**harp′er,** *n.*

Harp
A, Pedestal; B, Pedals; C, Back; D, Sounding-board; E, Neck; F, Pillar

Harpenden (hä′pən dən), *n.* a town in England, in central Hertfordshire. 18,307 (1961).

Harpers Ferry (hä′pəz), a town in NE West Virginia at the confluence of the Shenandoah and Potomac rivers: John Brown's raid, 1859. Also, **Harper's Ferry.**

harpings (hä′pĭngz), *n.pl. Naut.* the stout wales about the bow of a ship. Also, **harpins** (hä′pĭnz).

harpist (hä′pĭst), *n.* one who plays on the harp, esp. professionally.

harpoon (hä po͞on′), *n.* 1. a barbed, spearlike missile attached to a rope, and thrown by hand or shot from a gun, used in catching whales and large fish. —*v.t.* 2. to strike, catch, or kill with or as with a harpoon. [t. D: m. *harpoen,* t. F: m. *harpon,* der. *harper* grapple, of Gmc orig.] —**harpoon′er,** *n.* —**harpoon′-like′,** *adj.*

harpsichord (häp′sĭ kôd′), *n.* a keyboard instrument, precursor of the piano, in common use from the 16th to the 18th century, and revived in the 20th, in which the strings are plucked by leather or quill points connected with the keys. [t. F (obs.): m. *harpechorde,* f. *harpe* (of Gmc orig.) harp + *chorde* string (see CHORD[1])] —**harp′sichord′ist,** *n.*

harpuisbossie (hä pois′bŏs′ĭ), *n.* a composite evergreen shrub, *Eurypos multifidus,* of southern Africa, yielding a resin formerly used medicinally. [t. Afrikaans: resin bush]

Harpy (hä′pĭ), *n., pl.* **-pies.** 1. *Gk Myth.* a rapacious and filthy monster having a woman's head and a bird's body. 2. (*l.c.*) a rapacious person. [t. L: m. s. *harpȳia,* t. Gk: lit., snatcher]

harpy eagle, a large, powerful, crested bird of prey, *Thrasaetus harpyia,* of tropical America.

harquebus (hä′kwĭ bəs), *n.* arquebus.

harquebusier (hä′kwĭ bə sĭə′), *n.* a soldier armed with a harquebus.

harridan (hă′rĭ dən), *n.* a disreputable violent woman; vicious old hag. [cf. F *haridelle* sorry horse, jade]

harrier[1] (hă′rĭ ə), *n.* 1. one who or that which harries. 2. any of several hawks of the genus *Circus* (family *Falconidae*), all of which course back and forth over pasture-lands searching for the small birds and mammals on which they feed. [f. HARRY, v., + -ER[1]]

harrier[2] (hă′rĭ ə), *n.* 1. a breed of small hounds employed in hunting the hare. 2. a cross-country runner. [special use of HARRIER[1], by assoc. with HARE]

Harriman (hă′rĭ mən), *n.* **William Averell,** born 1891, U.S. diplomat.

Harringay (hă′rĭng gā′), *n.* a district in the N London borough of Haringey: site of a former sports arena.

Harris (hă′rĭs), *n.* 1. **Joel Chandler** (jō′əl), 1848–1908, U.S. author: creator of Uncle Remus. 2. an island of the Outer Hebrides, Inverness-shire, Scotland. 3285 pop. (1961); 193 sq. mi.

Harrisburg (hă′rĭs bûg′), *n.* a town in the U.S., the capital of Pennsylvania, in the S part, on the Susquehanna river. 79,697 (1960).

Harrison (hă′rĭ sən), *n.* 1. **Benjamin,** 1833–1901, 23rd president of the U.S. 1889–93. 2. **George.** See **Beatles.** 3. Benjamin's grandfather, **William Henry,** 1773–1841, U.S. general: 9th president of the U.S. in 1841.

Harris tweed, *Trademark.* a loosely woven tweed made and finished by hand in the Outer Hebrides, esp. in the islands of Lewis and Harris.

Harrogate (hă′rə gĭt), *n.* a spa town in England, in the West Riding of Yorkshire. 56,345 (1961).

Harrovian (hə rō′vyən), *adj.* 1. of or pertaining to Harrow. —*n.* 2. a pupil, past or present, of Harrow School.

harrow (hă′rō), *n.* 1. a wheelless agricultural implement set with teeth, upright discs, etc., usually of iron, drawn over ploughed land to level it, break clods, etc. —*v.t.* 2. to draw a harrow over (land, etc.); break or tear with a harrow. 3. to disturb keenly or painfully; distress the mind, feelings, etc. —*v.i.* 4. to be broken up by harrowing, as soil, etc. [ME *haru, harwe.* Cf. Icel. *herfi* harrow, MLG *harke* rake] —**har′rower,** *n.* —**har′rowingly,** *adv.*

Harrow (hă′rō), *n.* 1. a NW outer London borough. 209,500 (1961). 2. a boy's public school situated here (founded 1571). Also, **Harrow-on-the-Hill** (hă′rō ŏn ᵺə hĭl′).

harrowing (hă′rō ĭng), *adj.* disturbing or distressing to the mind, feelings, etc.

harry (hă′rĭ), *v.,* **-ried, -rying.** —*v.t.* 1. to harass by forced exactions, rapacious demands, etc.; torment; worry. 2. to ravage, as in war; devastate. —*v.i.* 3. to make harassing incursions. [ME *herien,* OE *her(g)ian* ravage (der. *here* army), c. G (*ver*)*heeren* harry, lay waste] —**Syn. 2.** plunder, strip, rob.

harsh (häsh), *adj.* 1. ungentle and unpleasant in action or effect: *harsh treatment.* 2. rough to the touch or to any of the senses: *a harsh surface, a harsh voice.* 3. jarring upon the aesthetic senses; inartistic: *his painting was full of harsh lines and clashing colours.* [unexplained doublet of ME *harsk.* Cf. Dan. *harsk* rancid, G *harsch* harsh, rough, hard] —**harsh′ly,** *adv.* —**harsh′ness,** *n.* —**Syn. 1.** severe, austere; brusque, rough; hard, unfeeling, unkind, brutal. See **stern**[1]. 3. discordant, dissonant, inharmonious. —**Ant. 1.** mild. 3. pleasing.

harslet (häz′lĭt, häs′-), *n.* haslet.

hart (hät), *n., pl.* **harts,** (*esp. collectively*) **hart.** a male of the deer, commonly the red deer, *Cervus elaphus,* esp. after its fifth year. [ME *hert,* OE *heort,* c. G *Hirsch;* akin to L *cervus* stag]

hartal (hä′täl), *n.* (in India) a day of mourning: a form of passive resistance including the closing of shops. [t. Hind.: m. *hathtal* market stoppage]

Hartbees (hät′bēz′), *n.* an intermittent river in the Republic of South Africa flowing NW through Cape Province to the Orange river. Course ab. 70 mi.

Harte (hät), *n.* **(Francis) Bret,** 1839–1902, U.S. author, esp. of short stories.

hartebeest (hä′tĭ bēst′), *n.* 1. a large antelope of southern Africa of the genus *Alcephalus,* as *A. caama,* of a red colour, having a long face with naked muzzle. 2. any of various allied African antelopes, as some species of the genus *Demaliscus.* [t. Afrikaans: hart beast]

Hartebeest, *Alcephalus buselaphus* (4½ ft high at the shoulder)

Hartford (hät′fəd), *n.* a town in the U.S., the capital of Connecticut, in the central part: a port on the Connecticut river. 162,178 (1960).

Hartlepool (hät′lĭ po͞ol′), *n.* a seaport in England, in Durham. 17,675 (1961).

Hartley (hät′lĭ), *n.* **David,** 1705–57, English physician and philosopher.

Hartnell (hät′nəl), *n.* **Norman,** born 1901, English couturier.

Harts (häts), *n.* a river in the Republic of South Africa flowing SW through Transvaal and to the Vaal in Cape Province. 270 mi.

hartshorn (häts′hôn′), *n.* 1. the antler of the hart, formerly much used as a source of ammonia. 2. *Old Chem., Pharm.* ammonium carbonate; sal volatile. [var. of *hart's horn*]

hart's-tongue (häts′tŭng′), *n.* a fern, *Phyllitis scolopendrium,* which has long simple fronds.

Harty (hä′tĭ), *n.* **Sir Herbert Hamilton,** 1880–1941, Irish conductor, composer, and pianist.

harum-scarum (hĕə′rəm skĕə′rəm), *adj.* 1. reckless; rash. —*adv.* 2. recklessly; wildly. —*n.* 3. a reckless person. 4. reckless conduct. [? var. of *hare 'em scare 'em* (with obs. *hare* harry, scare)]

Harun al-Rashid (hă ro͞o′năl ră shēd′), A.D. 763?–809, caliph of Baghdad A.D. 786–809. One of the greatest

Abbasids, he was made almost a legendary hero in the *Arabian Nights.*

haruspex (hə rŭs′pĕks), *n.*, *pl.* **haruspices** (hə rŭs′pĭ sēz′). (in ancient Rome) one of a class of minor priests who practised divination, esp. from the entrails of animals killed in sacrifice. [t. L]

Harvard (hä′vəd), *n.* **1. John,** 1607–38, English nonconformist minister who settled in America and was a principal benefactor of Harvard College, now Harvard University. **2.** the university founded by John Harvard in 1636, in the U.S., at Cambridge, Mass.

harvest (hä′vĭst), *n.* **1.** the gathering of crops. **2.** the season of gathering ripened crops, esp. of grain. **3.** a crop or yield, as of grain. **4.** a supply of anything gathered at maturity and stored up: *a harvest of nuts.* **5.** the product or result of any labour or process. —*v.t.* **6.** to gather, as a crop. **7.** to gather the crop from: *to harvest the fields.* —*v.i.* **8.** to gather a crop; reap. [ME; OE *hærfest*, c. G *Herbst* autumn] —**har′vesting,** *n.* —**har′vestless,** *adj.* —**Syn. 3.** See **crop.**

harvester (hä′vĭs tə), *n.* **1.** one who harvests; a reaper. **2.** any of various machines for harvesting field crops, such as grain, flax, potatoes, etc. **3.** harvestman (def. 2).

harvest festival, a thanksgiving service for harvest.

harvest home, 1. the bringing home of the harvest. **2.** the time of doing it. **3.** a festival celebrated at the close of the harvest.

harvestman (hä′vĭst mən), *n.*, *pl.* **-men. 1.** a man engaged in harvesting. **2.** any of the arachnids of the order *Opiliones* (or *Phalangida*), comprising spider-like creatures with small rounded body and usually very long legs; daddy-long-legs.

harvest mite, an adult chigger.

harvest moon, the moon at and about the period of fullness which is nearest to the autumnal equinox.

harvest mouse, a small rodent, *Micromys minutus*, of the family *Muridae*, inhabiting cornfields and hedgerows of Europe and Asia; 4½ in. long, half of this length consisting of the prehensile tail.

harvest tick, any of various acarids in an immature stage, common in late summer and autumn, which attach themselves to the skin of man and animals; harvest mite.

A B
Harvest ticks (magnified) A, *Leptus irritans*; B, *Trombidium americanum*

Harvey (hä′vĭ), *n.* **William,** 1578–1657, English physician, discoverer of the circulation of the blood.

Harwell (hä′wəl), *n.* a village near Didcot, Berkshire; site of the Atomic Energy Research Establishment.

Harwich (hă′rĭj), *n.* a seaport in England, in NE Essex. 13,699 (1961).

Harz Mountains (häts), a range of low mountains in central Germany between the rivers Elbe and Weser. Highest peak, Brocken, 3745 ft.

has (hăz), *v.* 3rd pers. sing. pres. indic. of **have.**

Hasa (hä′sə), *n.* a region in E Saudi Arabia, on the Persian Gulf. Also, **El Hasa.**

Hasan (hă sän′, hăs′ən), *n.* a son of Ali by Fatima, daughter of Mohammed.

has-been (hăz′bĭn′), *n.* *Colloq.* a person or thing that is no longer effective, successful, popular, etc.

Hasdrubal (hăz′dro͞o bl), *n.* **1.** died 207 B.C., Carthaginian general (brother of Hannibal). **2.** died 221 B.C., Carthaginian general (brother-in-law of Hannibal).

Hašek (*Cz.* hä′shĕk), *n.* **Jaroslav** (*Cz.* yä′rô släf), 1883–1923, Czech novelist and short-story writer.

hash (hăsh), *n.* **1.** a dish of chopped, cooked meat, reheated in a highly seasoned sauce. **2.** a mess, jumble, or muddle. **3.** any preparation of old material worked over. **4. make a hash of,** to spoil or make a mess of something. —*v.t.* **5.** to chop into small pieces; mince; make into a hash. [t. F: m. s. *hacher*, der. *hache* axe. See HATCHET, and cf. HATCH[3]]

Hashemite Kingdom of Jordan (hăsh′ĭ mīt′), official name of **Jordan.**

hashish (hăsh′ēsh, -ĭsh), *n.* **1.** the flowering tops, leaves, etc., of Indian hemp, smoked, chewed, or otherwise used in the Orient as a narcotic and intoxicant. **2.** any of certain preparations made from this plant.

Haskovo (*Bulg.* KHäs′kô vô), *n.* a town in S central Bulgaria. 56,460 (1964).

haslet (hāz′lĭt), *n.* the edible entrails of a pig or other animal, as used for food. Also, **harslet.** [ME *hastelet*, t. OF: roasted bit of meat, der. *haste* spit, g. L *hasta* spear]

Haslingden (hăz′lĭng dən), *n.* a town in England, in E Lancashire. 14,370 (1961).

hasn't (hăz′nt), contraction of *has not.*

hasp (häsp), *n.* **1.** a clasp for a door, lid, etc., esp. one passing over a staple and fastened by a pin or a padlock. —*v.t.* **2.** to fasten with or as with a hasp. [ME *hasp(e)*, OE *hæsp*, *hæpse*, c. G *Haspe*; akin to Icel. *hespa*]

Hassan II (hə sän′), born 1930, king of Morocco since 1961.

Hasselt (*Fr.* à sĕlt′; *Flem.* hŏs′əlt), *n.* a town in Belgium, the capital of Limbourg province. 38,773 (1966).

hassle (hăs′əl), *n.* *U.S. Colloq.* quarrel; squabble.

hassock (hăs′ək), *n.* **1.** a thick, firm cushion used as a footstool or for kneeling. **2.** a rank tuft of coarse grass or sedge, as in a bog. **3.** in Kent, soft calcareous sandstone. [ME; OE *hassuc* coarse grass]

hast (hăst), *v.* *Archaic.* 2nd pers. sing. pres. indic. of **have.**

hastate (hăs′tāt), *adj.* *Bot.* (of a leaf) triangular or shaped like a halberd, with two spreading lobes at the base. [t. L: m. s. *hastātus* armed with a spear]

Hastate leaf

haste (hāst), *n.*, *v.*, **hasted, hasting.** —*n.* **1.** energetic speed in motion or action. **2.** speed as a result of urgency. **3.** quickness without due reflection; thoughtless or rash speed: *haste makes waste.* **4. in haste,** with speed, quickly. **5. make haste, a.** to exert oneself to do something quickly. **b.** (with adjunct) to go with haste. —*v.t.*, *v.i.* **6.** *Archaic.* to hasten. [ME, t. OF, t. Gmc; cf. OE *hæst* violence] —**Syn. 1.** swiftness, celerity, quickness; rapidity. **2.** hurry, flurry, bustle.

hasten (hā′sən), *v.i.* **1.** to move or act with haste; proceed with haste; hurry: *to hasten to a place.* —*v.t.* **2.** to cause to hasten; accelerate. —**has′tener,** *n.* —**Syn. 2.** urge, press; expedite, quicken, precipitate. —**Ant. 1.** lag. **2.** delay.

Hastings (hās′tĭngz), *n.* **1. Warren,** 1732–1818, British statesman: first governor-general of India 1773–85. **2.** a seaport in SE England, in East Sussex: William the Conqueror defeated the Anglo-Saxons near here (on Senlac Hill), 1066. 66,690 (est. 1964). **3.** a town in New Zealand, in E North Island. 26,900 (est. 1965).

Hastings

hasty (hās′tĭ), *adj.*, **hastier, hastiest. 1.** moving or acting with haste; speedy; quick; hurried. **2.** made or done with haste or speed: *a hasty visit.* **3.** unduly quick in movement or action; precipitate; rash: *hasty reply.* **4.** done with or characterized by thoughtless or angry haste: *hasty words.* **5.** easily excited to anger; quick-tempered; irascible. [ME, t. OF: m. *hastif*, der. *haste* HASTE] —**hast′ily,** *adv.* —**hast′iness,** *n.* —**Syn. 1.** swift; rapid, fast. **3.** foolhardy, reckless. —**Ant. 1.** slow. **3.** deliberate.

hasty pudding, *U.S.* cornmeal mush.

hat (hăt), *n.*, *v.*, **hatted, hatting.** —*n.* **1.** a shaped covering for the head, usually with a crown and a brim, worn outdoors. **2.** *Rom. Cath. Ch.* **a.** the distinctive red head covering of a cardinal. **b.** the office or dignity of cardinal. **3. at the drop of a hat,** on the spur of the moment; without preliminaries. **4. bad hat,** *Colloq.* a bad or immoral person. **5. eat one's hat,** *Colloq.* to be very surprised if a certain event happens: *if he wins this game I'll eat my hat.* **6. my hat!,** (an exclamation of surprise and disbelief.) **7. old hat,** *Colloq.* (of ideas, etc.) old-fashioned; out of date. **8. talk through one's hat,** *Colloq.* to talk nonsense; speak without knowledge of the true facts. **9. under one's hat,** *Colloq.* secret, confidential: *keep this information under your hat.* —*v.t.* **10.** to provide with a hat; put a hat on. [ME; OE *hætt* head covering, c. Icel. *höttr* hood; akin to HOOD] —**hat′less,** *adj.* —**hat′like′,** *adj.*

hatable (hā′tə bl), *adj.* hateable.

hatband (hăt′bănd′), *n.* **1.** a band or ribbon placed about the crown of a hat, just above the brim. **2.** a black band similarly worn as a sign of mourning.

hatbox (hăt′bŏks′), *n.* a case or box for a hat.

hatch[1] (hăch), *v.t.* **1.** to bring forth (young) from the egg. **2.** to cause young to emerge from (the egg). **3.** to contrive; devise; concoct: *to hatch a plot.* —*v.i.* **4.** to be hatched. —*n.* **5.** the act of hatching. **6.** that which is hatched, as a brood. [ME *hacche*, akin to G *hecken*] —**hatch′er,** *n.* —**Syn. 1.** incubate, brood.

hatch[2] (hăch), *n.* **1.** a cover for an opening in a ship's deck, a floor, a roof, or the like. **2.** the opening itself. **3.** (*often pl.*) a hatchway. **4.** a ship's deck: *under hatches.* **5.** an opening in the floor or roof of a building. **6.** the cover over such an opening. **7.** the lower half of a divided door. **8.** a wicket. **9.** an opening in the wall between a kitchen and dining room, through which food is served. [ME *hacche*, OE *hæcc* grating, hatch]

hatch³ (hăch), *v.t.* **1.** to mark with lines, esp. closely set parallel lines, as for shading in drawing or engraving. —*n.* **2.** a shading line in drawing or engraving. [t. F: m. *hacher* chop, hash, hatch. See HASH]

hatchel (hăch′əl), *n.*, *v.*, **-elled, -elling.** —*n.* **1.** an instrument for cleaning flax; heckle. —*v.t.* **2.** to heckle. [phonetic doublet of HACKLE¹. Cf. HECKLE] —**hatch′eller,** *n.*

hatchery (hăch′ə rĭ), *n.*, *pl.* **-eries.** a place for hatching eggs of hens, fish, etc.

hatchet (hăch′ĭt), *n.* **1.** a small, short-handled axe for use with one hand. **2.** a tomahawk. **3. bury the hatchet,** to make peace. **4. dig up** (or **take up) the hatchet,** to prepare for war. [ME, t. F: m. *hachette*, dim. of *hache* axe, t. Gmc; cf. HACK¹] —**hatch′et-like′,** *adj.*

hatchet face, a sharp, narrow face. —**hatch′et-faced′,** *adj.*

hatching (hăch′ĭng), *n.* a series of lines, generally parallel, used in shading or modelling. [f. HATCH³ + -ING¹]

hatchment (hăch′mənt), *n. Her.* a square tablet, set diagonally, bearing the arms of a deceased person. [aspirated var. of *atch(e)ment*, syncopated form of ACHIEVEMENT]

Hatchment

hatchway (hăch′wā′), *n.* **1.** an opening (covered by a hatch) in a ship's deck, for passage to parts below, esp. the hold; hatch. **2.** the opening of any trapdoor, as in a floor, ceiling, or roof.

hate (hāt), *v.*, **hated, hating,** *n.* —*v.t.* **1.** to regard with a strong or passionate dislike; detest. **2.** to dislike; be unwilling: *I hate to do it.* —*v.i.* **3.** to feel hatred. —*n.* **4.** hatred; strong dislike. **5.** the object of hatred. [ME *hat(i)en*, OE *hatian*, c. G *hassen*] —**hat′er,** *n.*

—**Syn. 1.** loathe, execrate; despise. HATE, ABHOR, DETEST, ABOMINATE imply feeling intense dislike or aversion towards something. HATE, the simple and general word, suggests extreme dislike and a feeling of enmity: *to hate autocracy.* ABHOR expresses a deep-rooted horror, and a sense of repugnance: *to abhor cruelty.* DETEST implies intense, even vehement, dislike and antipathy, besides a sense of disdain: *to detest a combination of ignorance and arrogance.* ABOMINATE expresses a strong feeling of disgust and repulsion towards something thought of as unworthy, unlucky, and the like: *to abominate treachery.*

hateable (hā′tə bl), *adj.* deserving to be hated. Also, **hatable.**

hateful (hāt′fəl), *adj.* **1.** exciting hate; detestable; odious. **2.** *Archaic.* full of hate; malignant; malevolent. —**hate′fully,** *adv.* —**hate′fulness,** *n.*

—**Syn. 1.** abominable, execrable, abhorrent, repugnant; invidious, loathsome. HATEFUL, OBNOXIOUS, ODIOUS, OFFENSIVE refer to that which causes strong dislike or annoyance. HATEFUL implies actually causing hatred or extremely strong dislike: *the sight of him is hateful to me.* OBNOXIOUS emphasizes causing annoyance or discomfort by objectionable qualities: *his rude manner made him seem obnoxious, his greedy ways made him obnoxious to his companions.* ODIOUS emphasizes the disagreeable or displeasing: *an odious little man, odious servility.* OFFENSIVE emphasizes the distaste and resentment caused by something which may be either displeasing or insulting: *an offensive odour, remark.* —**Ant. 1.** likeable, pleasant, agreeable.

Hatfield (hăt′fēld′), *n.* a new town in England, in Hertfordshire. 20,516 (1961).

hath (hăth), *v. Archaic.* 3rd pers. sing. pres. indic. of **have.**

Hathaway (hăth′ə wā′), *n.* **Anne,** 1557–1623, the wife of William Shakespeare.

Hathor (hăth′ô), *n. Egypt. Myth.* the goddess of love and joy, often represented with the head, horns, or ears of a cow. [t. Egyptian: the castle of Hor]

Hathoric (hă thô′rĭk, -thŏ′-), *adj.* **1.** of or pertaining to Hathor. **2.** *Archit.* decorated with a face or head assumed to represent this goddess, as the capital of a column.

hatpin (hăt′pĭn′), *n.* a long, often decorated pin, used by women to secure a hat to the hair.

hatred (hā′trĭd), *n.* the feeling of one who hates; intense dislike; detestation. [ME *hatered(en)*, f. *hate* hate + *-reden*, OE *-rǣden* suffix making abstract nouns]

hatstand (hăt′stănd′), *n.* a tall stand with spreading arms or pegs on which hats, coats, etc., are hung.

hatter (hăt′ə), *n.* **1.** a maker or seller of hats. **2.** *Austral. Colloq.* **a.** a miner who works alone. **b.** an eccentric. **3. mad as a hatter,** very eccentric; crazy.

Hatteras (hăt′ə rəs), *n.* **Cape,** a promontory on an island off the E coast of North Carolina: dangerous to shipping.

hat-trick (hăt′trĭk′), *n.* **1.** *Cricket.* the act by a bowler of taking three wickets with three successive balls. **2.** any similar feat in other sports involving a set of three items.

haubergeon (hô′bə jən), *n.* habergeon.

hauberk (hô′bûk), *n.* a piece of armour originally intended for the protection of the neck and shoulders, but early developed into a long coat of mail reaching below the knees. [ME, t. OF: m. *hauberc*, t. Gmc; cf. OHG *halsberg* neck protection]

Hauberk

hauerite (hou′ə rīt′), *n.* a rare mineral consisting of manganese sulphide which occurs as small dark crystals in clay, etc.

Haugesund (*Norw.* hœy′gə sōōn), *n.* a seaport in S Norway. 20,000 (est. 1960).

haughty (hô′tĭ), *adj.*, **-tier, -tiest. 1.** disdainfully proud; arrogant; supercilious. **2.** *Archaic.* exalted; lofty, or noble. [extended form of *haught*, orig. *haut*, t. F: high, in OF *halt*, g. L *altus*, b. with OG *hauh* (later *hōh*) high] —**haugh′tily,** *adv.* —**haugh′tiness,** *n.* —**Syn. 1.** lordly, disdainful, contemptuous. See **proud.** —**Ant. 1.** humble, unpretentious, unassuming.

haul (hôl), *v.t.* **1.** to pull or draw with force; move or transport by drawing. **2. haul over the coals,** *Colloq.* to rebuke; scold. **3. haul up,** *Colloq.* **a.** to bring up, as before a superior, for reprimand; call to account. **b.** to change the course of (a ship), esp. so as to sail closer to the wind. —*v.i.* **4.** to pull or tug. **5.** to change one's course of procedure or action; go in a given direction. **6.** *Naut.* to sail, as in a particular direction. **7.** (of the wind) to change direction, shift, or veer (often fol. by *round* or *to*). **8. haul off, a.** *Naut.* to change the course of a ship so as to get farther off from an object. **b.** to draw off or away. —*n.* **9.** the act of hauling; a strong pull or tug. **10.** that which is hauled. **11.** the distance over which anything is hauled. **12.** *Fishing.* **a.** the quantity of fish taken at one draught of the net. **b.** the draught of a fishing net. **13.** *Colloq.* the taking or acquisition of anything, or that which is taken. [earlier *hall*, phonetic var. of HALE²] —**haul′er,** *n.* —**Syn. 1.** See **draw.**

haulage (hô′lĭj), *n.* **1.** the act or labour of hauling. **2.** transport, esp. heavy road transport. **3.** charge for hauling.

haulier (hô′lĭ ə), *n.* **1.** a person or company engaged in haulage (def. 2). **2.** *Obs.* a workman in a coalmine who hauls coal tubs.

haulm (hôm), *n.* **1.** stems or stalks collectively, as of grain or of peas, beans, hops, etc., esp. as used for litter or thatching. **2.** a single stem or stalk. Also, **halm.** [ME *halm*, OE *healm*, c. D *halm* and G *Halm*]

haunch (hônch), *n.* **1.** the hip. **2.** the fleshy part of the body about the hip. **3.** a hindquarter of an animal. See illus. under **horse. 4.** the leg and loin of an animal, as used for food. **5.** *Archit.* **a.** either side of an arch, extending from the vertex or crown to the impost. **b.** the part of a beam projecting below a floor or roof slab. [ME *hanche*, t. OF, t. Gmc; cf. MD *hancke*]

haunchbone (hônch′bōn′), *n.* the ilium or hipbone.

haunt (hônt), *v.t.* **1.** to reappear frequently to after death; visit habitually as a supposed spirit or ghost. **2.** to intrude upon continually; recur persistently: *memories that haunt one.* **3.** to worry or disturb: *his guilt haunted him.* **4.** to resort to much; visit frequently. **5.** to frequent the company of; be often with. —*v.i.* **6.** to reappear continually, as a disembodied spirit. **7.** to resort habitually. **8.** to associate, as with a person. —*n.* **9.** (*often pl.*) a place of frequent resort: *to revisit one's old haunts.* **10.** *Dial.* a ghost. [ME *haunten*, t. OF: m. *hanter* haunt, dwell, t. OE: m. *hāmettan* shelter, der. *hām* home] —**haunt′er,** *n.* —**haunt′ingly,** *adv.*

haunted (hôn′tĭd), *adj.* **1.** frequented or visited by ghosts: *a haunted house.* **2.** preoccupied or worried by something: *haunted by fear.*

haunting (hôn′tĭng), *adj.* **1.** (of music) fascinating, evoking memories. **2.** (of a memory, etc.) recurring persistently.

Hauptmann (*Ger.* houpt′män), *n.* **Gerhart** (*Ger.* gĕr′härt), 1862–1946, German dramatist, novelist, and poet.

Hauraki Gulf (hou′răk′ĭ), a wide indentation on the NE coast of North Island, New Zealand, into which the Firth of Thames opens and on which the city of Auckland stands.

Hausa (hou′sə), *n.* **1.** a prominent Negro stock in northern Nigeria, and in parts of Niger and Cameroun. **2.** their language, used widely in western Africa as a language of commerce.

Haussmann (*Fr.* ōs män′), *n.* **Baron Georges Eugène** (*Fr.* zhôrzh œ zhĕn′), 1809–91, French architect.

haustellum (hô stĕl′əm), *n.*, *pl.* **haustella** (hô stĕl′ə). (in certain crustaceans and insects) an organ or part of the proboscis adapted for sucking blood or plant juices. [NL, dim. of L *haustrum* machine for drawing water] —**haustel′late,** *adj.*

haustorium (hô stô′rĭ əm), *n., pl.* **haustoria** (hô stôr′ĭ ə). *Bot.* an intracellular feeding organ of a parasite which does not kill the host cells but lives with them. [NL, der. *haustor* drinker]

hautboy (ō′boi), *n.* **1.** oboe. **2.** a large kind of strawberry, *Fragaria elatior.* [t. F: m. *hautbois,* f. *haut* high + *bois* wood; named with reference to its high notes]

haute couture (ōt′ko͞o tyo͞oə′; *Fr.* ôt ko͞o tʏr′), *French.* high fashion; the clothes designed and made by the most famous couturiers.

haute cuisine (ōt′kwĭ zēn′; *Fr.* ôt kʏē zēn′), *French.* cooking to a high standard.

haute école (*Fr.* ôt ė kôl′), *French.* an elaborate method of training horses for exhibition.

Haute-Garonne (*Fr.* ôt gȧ rôn′), *n.* a department in S France. 594,633 pop. (1962); 2458 sq. mi. *Cap.:* Toulouse.

Haute-Loire (*Fr.* ôt lwȧr′), *n.* a department in central France. 211,036 pop. (1962); 1931 sq. mi. *Cap.:* Le Puy.

Haute-Marne (*Fr.* ôt mȧrn′), *n.* a department in E France. 208,466 pop. (1962); 2416 sq. mi. *Cap.:* Chaumont.

Haute-Normandie (*Fr.* ôt nôr mäɴ dē′), *n.* an administrative region in N France comprising the departments of Eure and Seine-Maritime. 1,397,748 pop. (1962); 4778 sq. mi. *Cap.:* Rouen.

Hautes-Alpes (*Fr.* ôts ȧlp′), *n.* a department in SE France. 87,436 pop. (1962); 2179 sq. mi. *Cap.:* Gap.

Haute-Saône (*Fr.* ôt sôn′), *n.* a department in E France. 208,440 pop. (1962); 2075 sq. mi. *Cap.:* Vesoul.

Haute-Savoie (*Fr.* ôt sȧ vwȧ′), *n.* a department in E France. 329,230 pop. (1962); 1775 sq. mi. *Cap.:* Annecy.

Hautes-Pyrénées (*Fr.* ôt pē rė nė′), *n.* a department in SW France. 211,433 pop. (1962); 1751 sq. mi. *Cap.:* Tarbes.

hauteur (ō tû′; *Fr.* ō tœr′), *n.* haughty manner or spirit; haughtiness. [t. F, der. *haut* high. See HAUGHTY]

Haute-Vienne (*Fr.* ôt vyĕn′), *n.* a department in central France. 332,514 pop. (1962); 2145 sq. mi. *Cap.:* Limoges.

haut monde (*Fr.* ôt môɴd′), *French.* high society.

Haut-Rhin (*Fr.* ō răɴ′), *n.* a department in NE France. 547,920 pop. (1962); 1354 sq. mi. *Cap.:* Colmar.

Hauts-de-Seine (*Fr.* ō də sĕn′), *n.* a department in N central France. 1,393,000 pop. (est. 1962); 68 sq. mi. *Cap.:* Nanterre.

Havana (hə văn′ə), *n.* **1.** Spanish, **Habana.** a seaport in and the capital of Cuba, on the NW coast. 787,765 (1960). See map under **Haiti.** **2.** a cigar made in Cuba or of Cuban tobacco.

have (hăv), *v., pres.* 1 **have,** 2 **have** or **hast,** 3 **has** or **hath,** *pl.* **have** *pt. and past part.* **had** pres. part. **having.** —*v.t.* **1.** to possess; own; to hold for use; contain: *to have property, the work has an index.* **2.** to hold or possess in some other relation, as of kindred, relative position, etc.: *to have one's opponent down.* **3.** to get, receive, or take: *to have no news.* **4.** to be required, compelled, or under obligation (fol. by an infinitive): *I have to stop now.* **5.** to experience, enjoy, or suffer: *to have a pleasant time.* **6.** to eat, drink, or partake of: *he had a meal.* **7.** to hold in mind, sight, etc.: *to have doubts.* **8.** to require or cause (to do something, be done, or as specified): *have it ready at five.* **9.** to engage in or perform: *to have a talk.* **10.** to show or exhibit in action: *to have a care.* **11.** to permit or allow: *I will not have it.* **12.** to assert or maintain: *rumour has it so.* **13.** to know or understand: *to have neither Latin nor Greek.* **14.** to give birth to: *to have a baby.* **15.** to wear (fol. by *on*). **16.** *Colloq.* to hold at a disadvantage: *he has you there.* **17.** *Slang.* to outwit, deceive, or cheat: *a person not easily had.* —*v.* **18.** Some special verb phrases are:

had better, ought to: *you had better do as you are told.*

had rather, to consider as preferable: *I had rather you came early.* Also, **had sooner.**

have at, *Archaic.* to attack.

have done, to cease or finish (often fol. by *with*).

have had it, *Colloq.* **1.** to be fated beyond hope of recovery, to die, be defeated, etc. **2.** to have failed to take advantage of a last chance. **3.** to become out of fashion or no longer popular.

have it away, *Taboo Slang.* to have sexual intercourse.

have it coming to one, *Colloq.* to deserve an unpleasant fate.

have it in for, *Colloq.* to hold a grudge against.

have it off, *Taboo Slang.* to have sexual intercourse.

have it out, to come to a final understanding by discussion.

have on, 1. to be wearing. **2.** to have arranged or planned.

have someone in (or **over**), to invite or entertain someone at home.

have someone on, *Colloq.* to tease or deceive a person.

have to do with, 1. to have dealings with: *she will have nothing to do with him.* **2.** to concern: *that has nothing to do with you.*

have up, *Colloq.* to bring before the authorities, esp. in court: *he was had up for theft.*

not having any, *Slang.* **1.** refusing to accept something. **2.** refusing to join in some activity.

—*v.i.* **19.** to possess money, etc.; be well off. —*aux. v.* **20.** (used with the past participle of a verb to form a compound or perfect tense): *they have gone.* [ME *have(n),* OE *habban,* c. D *hebben,* G *haben,* Icel. *hafa,* Goth. *haban;* akin to L *capere* take]

—**Syn. 1.** HAVE, HOLD, OCCUPY, OWN mean to be, in varying degrees, in the possession of something. HAVE, being the most general word, admits of the widest range of application: *to have money, rights, discretion, a disease, a glimpse, an idea; to have a friend's umbrella.* To HOLD is to have in one's grasp or one's control, but not necessarily as one's own: *to hold stakes.* To OCCUPY is to hold and use, but not necessarily by any right of ownership: *to occupy a chair, a house, a position.* To OWN is to have the full rights of property in a thing, which, however, another may be holding or enjoying: *to own a house which is rented.* To ENJOY is to own and take pleasure in so doing. —**Ant. 1.** lack.

havelock (hăv′lŏk′), *n.* a military cap cover with a flap hanging over the back of the neck, for protection from the sun. [named after H. *Havelock,* 1795–1857, British general]

haven (hā′vən), *n.* **1.** a harbour or port. **2.** an inlet of a sea or river mouth where ships can obtain good anchorage. **3.** any place of shelter and safety. —*v.t.* **4.** to shelter as in a haven. [ME; OE *hæfen,* c. G *Hafen*] —**ha′venless,** *adj.* —**Syn.** See **harbour.**

haven't (hăv′nt), contraction of *have not.*

Havering (hā′və rĭng), *n.* an E outer London borough. 249,300 (1961).

haversack (hăv′ə săk′), *n.* **1.** a soldier's bag for rations. **2.** any bag carried on the back or shoulders, used for provisions and the like. [t. F: m. *havresac,* t. LG: m. *habersack,* lit., oat sack]

Haversian canal (hă vû′shən), a microscopic channel in bone, through which a blood vessel runs. [named after C. *Havers,* 1650–1702, English anatomist]

Havířov (*Cz.* hȧ′vē rzhŏf), *n.* a town in N central Czechoslovakia near Ostrava. 68,000 (est. 1965).

havoc (hăv′ək), *n., v.,* **-ocked, -ocking.** —*n.* **1.** devastation; ruinous damage. **2. play havoc with,** to ruin; destroy. **3.** *Archaic.* a word used as the signal for pillage in warfare: *to cry havoc.* —*v.t.* **4.** to work havoc upon. —*v.i.* **5.** to work havoc. [ME *havok,* t. AF, var. of OF *havot,* used esp. in phrase *crier havot* cry havoc, give the call for pillaging; prob. from Gmc] —**hav′ocker,** *n.* —**Syn. 1.** See **ruin.**

Havre (hä′vrə; *Fr.* ȧ′vr), *n.* See **Le Havre.**

haw[1] (hô), *n.* the fruit of the Old World hawthorn, *Crataegus oxyacantha,* or of other species of the same genus. [ME; OE *haga.* Cf. HAWTHORN]

haw[2] (hô), *n. Obs. or Dial.* a yard or enclosure. [ME; OE *haga* hedge, c. D *haag* hedge, enclosure]

haw[3] (hô), *interj.* **1.** (an utterance marking hesitation in speech.) —*n.* **2.** the utterance 'haw'. —*v.i.* **3.** to use 'haw', as in hesitation. [imit.]

haw[4] (hô), *n.* the nictitating membrane of a horse, dog, etc., formerly only when inflamed. [orig. uncert.]

Hawaii (hə wī′ē), *n.* **1.** Hawaiian Islands. **2.** the largest of the Hawaiian Islands. 61,332 pop. (1960); 4021 sq. mi.

Hawaiian (hə wī′yən), *adj.* **1.** of or pertaining to Hawaii. —*n.* **2.** a native or inhabitant of Hawaii. **3.** the aboriginal language of Hawaii, a Polynesian language.

Hawaiian Islands, a group of islands in the N Pacific, 2090 mi. SW of San Francisco, forming a state of the United States. 632,772 pop. (1960); 6454 sq. mi. *Cap.:* Honolulu. Also, **Hawaii.** Formerly, **Territory of Hawaii, Sandwich Islands.**

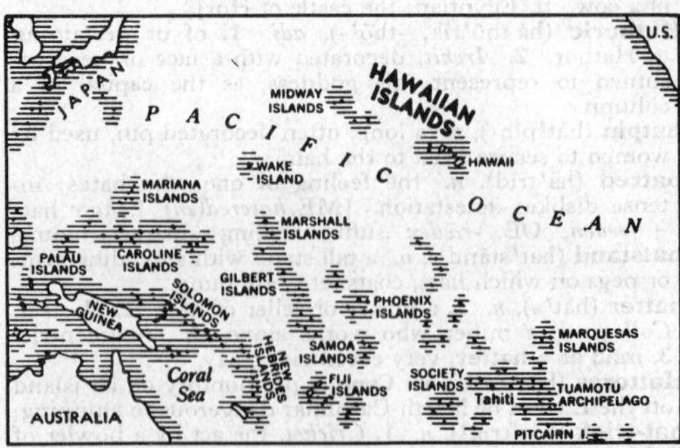

Hawaiian Islands

hawfinch (hô′fĭnch′), *n.* a European grosbeak, *Coccothraustes coccothraustes.*

haw-haw (hô′hô′), *interj.* **1.** (an affected utterance marking hesitation in speech.) —*n.* **2.** the utterance 'haw-haw'. **3.** loud vulgar laughter; a guffaw. —*v.i.* **4.** to guffaw; laugh loudly. —*adj.* **5.** affectedly superior in enunciation.

Haw-Haw (hô′hô′), *n.* **Lord.** See **Joyce, William.**

Hawick (hô′ĭk), *n.* a burgh in Scotland, in Roxburgh. 16,204 (1961).

hawk[1] (hôk), *n.* **1.** any of numerous diurnal birds of prey of the family *Falconidae,* as the falcons, buzzards, kites, harriers, etc., esp. the short-winged, long-tailed accipiters, as the goshawk. **2.** any of certain non-falconiform birds, as the nighthawk. **3.** a person who preys on others, as a sharper. **4.** a politician or political adviser who favours aggressive or intransigent military policies (opposed to *dove*). —*v.i.* **5.** to fly, or hunt on the wing, like a hawk. **6.** to hunt with hawks trained to pursue game. —*v.t.* **7. hawk about,** to spread, esp. news and the like. [ME *hauk(e)*, OE *hafoc,* c. G *Habicht*] —**hawk′ish,** *adj.* —**hawk′like′,** *adj.*

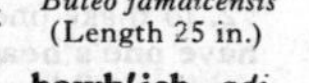

Red-tailed hawk, *Buteo jamaicensis* (Length 25 in.)

hawk[2] (hôk), *v.t.* **1.** to offer for sale by outcry in a street or from door to door. —*v.i.* **2.** to carry wares about; peddle. [back-formation from HAWKER[2]]

hawk[3] (hôk), *v.i.* **1.** to make an effort to raise phlegm from the throat; clear the throat noisily. —*v.t.* **2.** to raise by hawking: *to hawk up phlegm.* —*n.* **3.** a noisy effort to clear the throat. [imit.]

hawk[4] (hôk), *n.* a small square board with a handle underneath, used by plasterers to hold small quantities of mortar. [orig. uncert.]

hawkbill (hôk′bĭl′), *n.* hawk's-bill.

hawkbit (hôk′bĭt′), *n.* any of the perennial composite herbs belonging to the genus *Leontodon,* as *L. autumnalis,* the **autumnal hawkbit,** a common plant of grassy places throughout Europe and N and W Asia.

Hawke Bay, a wide indentation of the Pacific Ocean on the E coast of North Island, New Zealand.

hawker[1] (hô′kə), *n.* a falconer. [f. HAWK[1], v. + -ER[1]]

hawker[2] (hô′kə), *n.* one who travels from place to place or house to house selling goods. [appar. t. MLG: m. *hoker.* Cf. G *Höker,* D *heuker* retail dealer. See HUCKSTER]

hawk-eyed (hôk′īd′), *adj.* having very keen eyes.

hawking (hô′kĭng), *n.* falconry.

Hawkins (hô′kĭnz), *n.* **Sir John,** 1532–95, English naval commander and slave-trader. Also, **Hawkyns.**

hawkmoth (hôk′mŏth′), *n.* any of certain moths of the family *Sphingidae,* noted for their very swift flight and ability to hover while sipping nectar from flowers.

hawknose (hôk′nōz′), *n.* a nose curved like the beak of a hawk. —**hawk′-nosed′,** *adj.*

hawk-owl (hôk′oul′), *n.* a strikingly barred grey and white owl, *Surnia ulula,* of northern parts of the Northern Hemisphere, so named because it is diurnal.

hawk's-beard (hôks′bĭəd′), *n.* any herb of the composite genus *Crepis,* having yellow or orange flowers.

hawk's-bill (hôks′bĭl′), *n.* a turtle, *Eretmochelys imbricata,* yielding tortoiseshell and having a mouth shaped like the bill of a hawk. Also, **hawkbill, hawk's-bill turtle.**

hawk's-eye (hôks′ī′), *n.* a dark blue chatoyant stone used for ornament; a silicified crocidolite.

Hawksmoor (hôks′mô′, -mo͝oə′), *n.* **Nicholas,** 1661–1736, English baroque architect.

hawkweed (hôk′wēd′), *n.* **1.** any herb of the composite genus *Hieracium,* with yellow, orange, or red flowers. **2.** any of various related plants.

Hawkyns (hô′kĭnz), *n.* Hawkins.

hawse (hôz), *n.* **1.** the part of a ship's bow having holes for the cables to pass through. **2.** a hawsehole. **3.** the space between the stem of a ship at anchor and the anchors. **4.** the situation of a ship's cables when she is moored with both bow anchors: *a clear hawse.* [ME *halse,* prob. t. Scand.; cf. Icel. *hāls* part of ship's bow, front sheet of sail, lit., neck, c. OE *hals* neck]

hawsehole (hôz′hōl′), *n.* a hole in the bow of a ship, through which a cable is passed.

hawser (hô′zə), *n. Naut.* a small cable or large rope used in warping, mooring, towing, etc. [ME *haucer,* der. OF *haucier* raise, ult. der. L *altus* high]

hawser bend, a knot uniting the ends of two hawsers.

hawser-laid (hô′zə lād′), *adj.* **1.** (of a rope) having its yarns spun right-handed and laid up left-handed into strands; the strands are then laid up right-handed to complete the rope. **2.** cable-laid.

hawthorn (hô′thôn′), *n.* **1.** any species of the rosaceous genus *Crataegus,* usually small trees with stiff thorns, cultivated in hedges for their white or pink blossoms and bright-coloured fruits; may. **2.** a thorny shrub, *Crataegus oxyacantha,* native in the Old World. [ME; OE *haguthorn,* c. D *haagdoorn.* See HAW[1]]

Hawthorne (hô′thôn′), *n.* **Nathaniel,** 1804–64, U.S. novelist and short-story writer.

hay[1] (hā), *n.* **1.** grass cut and dried for use as fodder. **2.** grass mowed or intended for mowing. **3. hit the hay,** to go to bed. **4. make hay, a.** to cut grass for fodder. **b.** to scatter everything in disorder. —*v.t.* **5.** to convert (grass) into hay. **6.** to furnish (horses, etc.) with hay. [ME; OE *hēg, hieg,* c. G *Heu*]

hay[2] (hā), *n.* a kind of old country dance with winding movements. Also, **hey.** [t. F (15th cent.): m. *haye* kind of dance]

hay[3] (hā), *n. Archaic.* hedge. [ME; OE *hege*]

haycock (hā′kŏk′), *n.* a small conical pile of hay thrown up in a hayfield, while the hay is awaiting removal to a barn.

Haydn (*Ger.* hī′dən), *n.* **(Franz) Joseph** (*Ger.* fränts yō′sĕf), 1732–1809, Austrian composer.

Haydon (hā′dn), *n.* **Benjamin Robert,** 1786–1846, English historical painter.

Hayes (hāz), *n.* **Rutherford Birchard** (bû′chəd), 1822–93, 19th president of the U.S. 1877–81.

hay fever, a catarrhal affection of the mucous membranes of the eyes and respiratory tract, attacking susceptible persons (usually) during the summer, and due to the action of the pollen of certain plants.

hayfield (hā′fēld′), *n.* a field in which grass is grown for making into hay, or where haymaking is in progress.

hayfork (hā′fôk′), *n.* a fork used for turning or lifting hay, operated either by hand or machine.

hayloft (hā′lŏft′), *n.* a loft in a stable or barn, for the storage of hay.

haymaker (hā′mā′kə), *n.* **1.** one who makes hay. **2.** one who tosses and spreads hay to dry after it has been mowed. **3.** *Boxing Slang.* a swinging, knock-out blow. —**hay′mak′ing,** *n.*

Haymarket (hā′mä′kĭt), *n.* the site of a famous London market (1664–1830), now well known for the theatres situated there.

haymow (hā′mou′), *n.* **1.** a mow or mass of hay stored in a barn. **2.** the place in a barn where hay is stored. **3.** a rick or stack of hay.

hayrack (hā′răk′), *n.* **1.** a rack for holding hay for feeding horses or cattle. **2.** *U.S.* a rack or framework mounted on a wagon, for use in carrying hay, straw, etc. **3.** *U.S.* the wagon and rack together.

hayrick (hā′rĭk′), *n.* a haystack.

hayseed (hā′sēd′), *n.* **1.** grass seed, esp. that shaken out of hay. **2.** small bits of the chaff, etc., of hay. **3.** *U.S. Slang.* a countryman or rustic.

haystack (hā′stăk′), *n.* a stack of hay with a conical or ridged top, built up in the open air for preservation, and sometimes thatched or covered. Also, **hayrick.**

hayward (hā′wôd′), *n. Obs.* an officer having charge of hedges and fences, esp. to keep cattle from breaking through, and to impound strays. [ME *heiward.* See HAY[3], WARD]

haywire (hā′wī′ə), *n.* **1.** wire used to bind hay. —*adj.* **2.** *Slang.* in disorder; out of order. **3.** *Slang.* out of control; crazy: *to go haywire.*

hazard (hăz′əd), *n.* **1.** a risk; exposure to danger or harm. **2.** the cause of such a risk; a potential source of harm, injury, difficulty, etc.: *the motor car has become a major hazard in modern life.* **3.** chance; uncertainty. **4.** the uncertainty of the result in throwing a die. **5.** a game for any number of players played with two dice, complicated by various arbitrary rules, formerly much played. **6.** *Golf.* an obstacle, as a bunker, road, bush, water, or the like, on the course. **7.** *Real Tennis.* **a.** any of certain openings in the walls of the court, the striking of a ball into which scores the striker a point. **b.** that side of the court into which the ball is served (**hazard side**). **8.** *Billiards.* a stroke made when a ball, other than the striker's ball, is pocketed after contact with another ball (**winning hazard**), or when the striker's ball is pocketed after contact with another ball (**losing hazard**). **9.** *Show-jumping.* a fence or other obstacle on a show-jumping course. **10. at hazard, a.** at risk; staked. **b.** by chance: *we met at hazard.* —*v.t.* **11.** to venture to offer (a statement, conjecture, etc.). **12.** to put to the risk of being lost; to expose to risk. **13.** to take or run the risk of (a misfortune, penalty, etc.). **14.** to venture upon (anything of doubtful issue). [ME *hasard,* t. OF, t. Ar.: m. *az-zahr* the die] —**haz′ardable,** *adj.* —**haz′arder,** *n.* —**haz′ardless,** *adj.* —**Syn. 1.** See **danger.** —**Ant. 1.** safety.

hazardous (hăz′ə dəs), *adj.* **1.** full of risk; perilous;

risky. 2. dependent on chance: *a hazardous contract.* —**haz′ardously,** *adv.* —**haz′ardousness,** *n.*

haze[1] (hāz), *n.* **1.** an aggregation of minute suspended particles of vapour, dust, etc., near the surface of the earth, causing an appearance of thin mist in the atmosphere. **2.** obscurity or vagueness of the mind, perception, feelings, etc. [orig. obscure] —**Syn. 2.** See **cloud.**

haze[2] (hāz), *v.t.*, **hazed, hazing. 1.** *U.S.* to subject (freshmen or newcomers) to abusive or ridiculous tricks. **2.** *Chiefly Naut.* to harass with unnecessary or disagreeable tasks. [cf. MF *haser* irritate, annoy] —**haz′er,** *n.*

hazel (hā′zəl), *n.* **1.** any shrub or small tree of the betulaceous genus *Corylus*, which bears edible nuts, as *C. avellana* of Europe or *C. americana* and *C. cornuta* of America. **2.** any of certain other shrubs or trees (as *Pomaderris apetala*, a rhamnaceous shrub of Australia, etc.), or their wood. **3.** the hazelnut or filbert. **4.** the wood of a hazel. **5.** light reddish brown of a hazelnut. —*adj.* **6.** of or pertaining to the hazel. **7.** made of the wood of the hazel. **8.** having a hazel colour. [ME *hazel(l)*, OE *hæs(e)l*, c. G *Hasel*; akin to L *corylus* hazel shrub]

hazelnut (hā′zəl nŭt′), *n.* the nut of the hazel.

hazing (hā′zĭng), *n.* the act or practice of one who hazes.

Hazlitt (hăz′lĭt), *n.* **William,** 1778–1830, English critic and essayist.

hazy (hā′zĭ), *adj.*, **-zier, -ziest. 1.** characterized by the presence of haze; misty: *hazy weather.* **2.** lacking distinctness; vague; confused: *a hazy proposition.* —**ha′zily,** *adv.* —**ha′ziness,** *n.*

hazzan (hə zän′, hä′zən), *n.* chazzan.

HB, (of pencils) hard and black.

H.B.M., His (or Her) Britannic Majesty.

H-bomb, hydrogen bomb.

H.C., House of Commons.

H.C.F., highest common factor. Also, **h.c.f.**

hd, 1. hand. 2. head.

hdqrs, headquarters.

he (hē; *unstressed* hĭ, ē, ĭ), *pron., poss.* **his,** *obj.* **him,** *pl.* **they;** *n., pl.* **hes. 1.** the male being in question or last mentioned. **2.** anyone; that person: *he who hesitates is lost.* —*n.* **3.** a man or any male person or animal (correlative to *she*). —*adj.* **4.** male or masculine, esp. of animals. [ME *he*, OE *hē* (gen. *his*, dat. *him*, acc. *hine*), c. OS *he*, *hi*, OFris. *hi*, *he*. Cf. SHE, HER, IT, HENCE, HERE, HITHER]

He, *Chem.* helium.

H.E., 1. His Eminence. 2. His Excellency. 3. (*sometimes l.c.*) high explosive.

head (hĕd), *n.* **1.** the upper part of the human body, joined to the trunk by the neck. **2.** the corresponding part of an animal's body. **3.** the head considered as the seat of thought, memory, understanding, etc.: *to have a head for mathematics.* **4.** the position of leadership; chief command; greatest authority. **5.** one to whom others are subordinate; a leader or chief. **6.** that part of anything which forms or is regarded as forming the top, summit, or upper end: *head of a pin, head of a page.* **7.** the foremost part or end of anything; a projecting part: *head of a procession, head of a rock.* **8.** a person considered with reference to his mind, disposition, attributes, etc.: *wise heads, crowned heads.* **9.** a person or animal considered merely as one of a number (often with *pl.* **head**): *ten head of cattle, to charge so much a head.* **10.** a measurement to show the difference in height between two people, or the distance between two horses in a race. **11.** culmination or crisis; conclusion: *to bring matters to a head.* **12.** the hair covering the head: *to comb someone's head.* **13.** something resembling a head in form: *a head of lettuce.* **14.** a rounded or compact part of a plant, usually at the top of the stem, as of leaves (as in the cabbage or lettuce), leafstalks (as in the celery), flower buds (as in the cauliflower), sessile florets, etc. **15.** the striking part of an instrument, tool, weapon, or the like, as opposed to the gripping part. **16.** the maturated part of an abscess, boil, etc. **17.** a projecting point of a coast, esp. when high, as a cape, headland, or promontory. **18.** the obverse of a coin, as bearing a head or other principal figure (opposed to *tail*). **19.** one of the chief points or divisions of a discourse; topic. **20.** *Archaic.* strength or force gradually attained; progress. **21.** the source of a river or stream. **22.** froth or foam, as that formed on pouring beer. **23.** the headline or group of headlines at the top of a newspaper article. **24.** *Naut.* **a.** the forepart of a ship, etc. **b.** the upper edge (or corner) of a sail. **c.** the upper end of any spar, derrick, etc. **d.** a shaped vertical timber. **25.** *Gram.* **a.** that member of an endocentric construction which belongs to the same form class and may play the same grammatical role as the construction itself. **b.** the member upon which another depends and to which it is subordinate; e.g., in *the first prize*, *first prize* is head and *the* is attribute, and in *first prize*, the head is *prize* and the attribute is *first.* **26.** the stretched membrane covering the end of a drum or similar instrument. **27.** *Mining.* a level or road driven into the solid coal for proving or working a mine. **28.** the height of the free surface of a liquid above a given level. **29.** *Mach.* a device on turning and boring machines, esp. lathes, holding one or more cutting tools to the work. **30.** the pressure of a confined body of steam, etc., per unit of area. **31.** the height of a column of fluid required for a certain pressure. **32.** the part or parts of a tape-recorder which come into direct contact with the tape and serve to record, reproduce, or erase electromagnetic impulses on it. **33.** Some special noun phrases are:

bite someone's head off, to speak angrily to, esp. in an unexpected rebuke.

by (or **down by**) **the head,** *Naut.* so loaded as to draw more water forward than aft.

come to a head, to reach a crisis.

give someone (or **something**) **his head, 1.** to allow a person greater freedom. **2.** to allow a horse greater freedom in running.

go to one's head, 1. to make one confused or dizzy. **2.** to make one conceited.

have one's head on one's shoulders, to have a balanced and sensible outlook.

head and shoulders (above), by far superior to.

head over heels, 1. upside-down, headlong, as after a somersault. **2.** completely, utterly.

keep one's head above water, to remain in control of a difficult situation, esp. a financial one.

lay (or **put**) **heads together,** to come together to scheme.

lose one's head, to panic, become flustered, esp. in an emergency.

make head or tail of, to understand; work out: *I can't make head or tail of this question.*

off one's head, mad, very excited, delirious.

one's head off, to an extreme, excessively.

on one's own head, as one's own responsibility.

out of one's head, from one's mind, memory, imagination, etc.: *that story has come completely out of my head.*

out of one's mind, demented, delirious.

over one's head, 1. passing over one having a prior claim or a superior position. **2.** beyond one's comprehension.

take (it) into one's head, to conceive an idea, plan, or the like.

turn someone's head, to make someone vain or conceited.

—*adj.* **34.** situated at the top or front: *the head division of a parade.* **35.** being in the position of leadership or superiority. **36.** coming from in front: *a headwind.* —*v.t.* **37.** to go at the head of or in front of; lead, precede: *to head a list.* **38.** to outdo or excel. **39.** to be the head or chief of. **40.** to turn the head or front of in a specified direction: *to head one's boat for the shore.* **41.** to go round the head of (a stream, etc.). **42.** to furnish or fit with a head. **43.** to take the head of (an animal) off. **44.** to poll (a tree). **45.** *Football.* to propel (the ball) by action of the head. **46. head off,** to intercept (something) and force (it) to change course. —*v.i.* **47.** to move forwards towards a point specified; direct one's course; go in a certain direction (often fol. by *for*). **48.** to come or grow to a head; form a head. [ME *he(v)ed*, OE *hēafod*, c. D *hoofd*, G *Haupt*, Icel. *höfudh*, Goth. *haubith*] —**head′like′,** *adj.* —**Syn. 5.** commander, director. **35.** cardinal, foremost, first. —**Ant. 35.** subordinate.

-head, a suffix denoting state, condition, character, etc.: *godhead*, and other words, now mostly archaic or obsolete, many being superseded by forms in **-hood.** [ME *-hede, -hed*, der. *hede* rank, condition, character; akin to OE *hād*, whence the suffix -HOOD]

headache (hĕd′āk′), *n.* **1.** a pain situated in the head. **2.** *Colloq.* a troublesome or worrying problem. —**head′a′chy,** *adj.*

headband (hĕd′bănd′), *n.* **1.** a band worn round the head; a fillet. **2.** a band sewn to the head and tail of the back of a book, sometimes as decoration but usually to protect and strengthen the binding.

headboard (hĕd′bôd′), *n.* a board forming the head of anything, esp. of a bed.

head boy, a senior boy in a school, appointed or elected to lead and represent the other pupils, help maintain discipline, etc. —**head girl,** *fem.*

headcheese (hĕd′chēz′), *n. U.S.* brawn.

headdress (hĕd′drĕs′), *n.* **1.** a covering or decoration for the head. **2.** *Obs.* an arrangement of the hair.

headed (hĕd′ĭd), *adj.* **1.** having a heading. **2.** shaped or grown into a head.

-headed, a suffix meaning: **1.** having a specified kind of head: *long-headed, wrong-headed.* **2.** having a specified number of heads: *two-headed.*

header (hĕd′ə), *n.* **1.** one who or an apparatus which removes or puts a head on something. **2.** a form of reaping machine which cuts off and gathers only the heads of the grain. **3.** a chamber to which the ends of a number of tubes are connected so that water or steam may pass freely from one tube to the other. **4.** *Building.* a brick or stone laid with its length across the thickness of a wall. Cf. **Flemish bond. 5.** *Football.* a shot made with the head. **6.** *Colloq.* a plunge or dive headfirst, as into water.

headfirst (hĕd′fûst′), *adv.* **1.** with the head in front or bent forwards; headlong. **2.** rashly; precipitately. Also, **headforemost,** (hĕd′fô′mōst′).

headgate (hĕd′gāt′), *n.* **1.** a control gate at the upstream end of a canal or lock. **2.** a floodgate of a race, sluice, etc.

headgear (hĕd′gĭə′), *n.* **1.** any covering for the head. **2.** the parts of a harness about an animal's head. **3.** *Mining.* the framework spanning a pit shaft and used for raising and lowering the cages.

head-hunting (hĕd′hŭn′tĭng), *n.* (among certain savage tribes) the practice of making incursions for procuring human heads as trophies or for use in religious ceremonies. —**head′-hunt′er,** *n.*

heading (hĕd′ĭng), *n.* **1.** something that serves as a head, top, or front. **2.** a title or caption of a page, chapter, etc. **3.** a section of a subject of discourse; a topic. **4.** a horizontal passage in the earth, as for an intended tunnel, for working a mine, for ventilation or drainage, etc.; a drift. **5.** the end of such a passage. **6.** *Aeron.* the angle made by the longitudinal axis of an aircraft in flight with a given meridian. **7.** *Naut.* the pocket in a flag, containing the rope.

headlamp (hĕd′lămp′), *n.* a headlight.

headland (hĕd′lənd *for 1*; hĕd′lănd′ *for 2*), *n.* **1.** a promontory extending into a large body of water, such as a sea or lake. **2.** a strip of unploughed land at the ends of furrows or near a fence or border.

headless (hĕd′lĭs), *adj.* **1.** having no head; deprived of the head. **2.** without a leader or chief. **3.** foolish; stupid. [ME *he(ve)dles,* OE *hēafodlēas.* See -LESS]

headlight (hĕd′līt′), *n.* a lamp equipped with a reflector, on the front of any vehicle.

headline (hĕd′līn′), *n., v.,* **-lined, -lining.** —*n.* **1.** a display line over an article, etc., as in a newspaper. **2.** the line at the top of a page, containing the title, pagination, etc. —*v.t.* **3.** to furnish with a headline.

headlock (hĕd′lŏk′), *n.* *Wrestling.* a hold in which a wrestler locks his arm around his opponent's head.

headlong (hĕd′lŏng′), *adv.* **1.** headfirst: *to plunge headlong.* **2.** rashly; without deliberation. **3.** precipitately; with great speed. —*adj.* **4.** done or going with the head foremost. **5.** characterized by haste; precipitate. **6.** rash; impetuous. **7.** *Archaic.* steep; precipitous. [late ME *hedlong,* f. *hed* HEAD + *long,* adv. suffix; r. *headling,* ME *hedlyng.* See -LING[2]]

headman (hĕd′mən), *n., pl.* **-men.** a chief man; a chief or leader. [ME *hevedmon,* OE *hēafodman*]

headmaster (hĕd′mäs′tə), *n.* the principal master of a school. —**head′mas′tership′,** *n.* —**headmistress** (hĕd′mĭs′trĭs), *n. fem.*

head money, 1. a tax of so much per head or person. **2.** a reward paid for each person captured or brought in. **3.** a reward for the head of an outlaw or enemy.

headmost (hĕd′mōst′), *adj.* foremost; most advanced.

head note, *Music.* a vocal note so produced as to bring the cavities of the nose and head into sympathetic vibration. Also, **head voice;** *Chiefly U.S.,* **head tone.**

head-on (hĕd′ŏn′), *adj., adv.* with the head foremost: *a head-on collision.*

headphone (hĕd′fōn′), *n.* *Radio., Teleph.* (*often pl.*) a device consisting of one or two earphones with attachments for holding them over the ears.

headpiece (hĕd′pēs′), *n.* **1.** armour for the head; a helmet. **2.** any covering for the head. **3.** headphones. **4.** the head as the seat of the intellect; judgement. **5.** the top piece or part of any of various things. **6.** *Print.* a decorative piece at the head of a page, chapter, etc.

headpin (hĕd′pĭn′), *n.* **1.** *Tenpin Bowling.* the number one pin situated at the apex of the tenpin triangle. **2.** kingpin.

headquarters (hĕd′kwô′təz), *n.pl. or sing.* **1.** any centre from which official orders are issued: *police headquarters.* **2.** any centre of operations. **3.** the offices of a military commander; the place where a commander customarily issues his orders. **4.** a military unit consisting of the commander, his staff, and other assistants. **5.** the building occupied by a headquarters.

headrace (hĕd′rās′), *n.* the race, flume, or channel leading to a waterwheel or the like.

head resistance, *Aeron.* profile drag.

headrest (hĕd′rĕst′), *n.* a rest or support of any kind for the head.

headroom (hĕd′ro͝om′, -ro͞om′), *n.* the clear height from floor to ceiling; the clearance of a bridge, between the decks of a ship, etc.

headsails (hĕd′sālz′; *Naut.* -səlz), *n.pl.* *Naut.* sails set forward of the foremast.

headscarf (hĕd′skäf′), *n.* a square piece of material worn by women as a covering for the head. Also, **headsquare** (hĕd′skwĕə′).

head sea, *Naut.* a sea in which the waves approach the vessel from the direction steered.

headset (hĕd′sĕt′), *n.* *Chiefly U.S.* headphones.

headship (hĕd′shĭp), *n.* the position of head or chief; chief authority; leadership; supremacy.

headsman (hĕdz′mən), *n., pl.* **-men.** one who beheads condemned persons; a public executioner.

headspring (hĕd′sprĭng′), *n.* **1.** the fountainhead or source of a stream. **2.** the source of anything.

headstall (hĕd′stôl′), *n.* that part of a bridle or halter which encompasses the head.

headstock (hĕd′stŏk′), *n.* the part of a machine containing the working members, as the assembly supporting and driving the live spindle in a lathe.

headstone (hĕd′stōn′), *n.* a stone set at the head of a grave.

headstream (hĕd′strēm′), *n.* a stream that forms the source, or one of the sources, of a river.

headstrong (hĕd′strŏng′), *adj.* **1.** bent on having one's own way; wilful. **2.** proceeding from wilfulness: *a headstrong course.* —**head′strong′ness,** *n.* —**Syn. 1.** stubborn, obstinate. See **wilful.**

head tone, *Chiefly U.S.* head note.

head voice, head note.

headwaters (hĕd′wô′təz), *n.pl.* the upper tributaries of a river.

headway (hĕd′wā′), *n.* **1.** motion forwards or ahead; advance. **2.** progress in general. **3.** rate of progress. **4.** the interval between two trains, etc., travelling in the same direction over the same route. **5.** *Archaic.* clear space in height, as in a doorway or under an arch.

headwind (hĕd′wĭnd′), *n.* a wind that blows directly against the course of a ship or the like.

headword (hĕd′wûd′), *n.* a word heading or beginning a chapter, paragraph, or the like.

headwork (hĕd′wûk′), *n.* mental labour; thought. —**head′work′er,** *n.*

heady (hĕd′ĭ), *adj.,* **-ier, -iest. 1.** rashly impetuous. **2.** intoxicating. [ME *he(ve)di.* See HEAD, n., -Y[1]] —**head′ily,** *adv.* —**head′iness,** *n.*

heal (hēl), *v.t.* **1.** to make whole or sound; restore to health; free from ailment. **2.** to free from anything evil or distressing; amend: *to heal a quarrel.* **3.** to cleanse or purify. —*v.i.* **4.** to effect a cure. **5.** to become whole or sound; get well (often fol. by *up* or *over*). [ME *hele(n),* OE *hǣlan,* der. *hāl* hale, WHOLE] —**heal′er,** *n.* —**heal′ing,** *n.* —**heal′ingly,** *adv.* —**Syn. 1.** See **cure.**

healing (hē′lĭng), *adj.* **1.** that heals; curing; curative. **2.** growing sound; getting well.

health (hĕlth), *n.* **1.** soundness of body; freedom from disease or ailment. **2.** the general condition of the body or mind with reference to soundness and vigour: *good health.* **3.** a polite or complimentary wish for a person's health, happiness, etc., esp. as a toast. [ME *helthe,* OE *hǣlth,* der. *hāl* hale, whole. See WHOLE, -TH[1]]

health centre, a welfare centre set up by a local authority with a National Health Service staff, for the care of the general health of the residents in that area, esp. mothers and babies.

healthful (hĕlth′fəl), *adj.* **1.** conducive to health; wholesome, or salutary: *healthful diet.* **2.** healthy. —**health′fully,** *adv.* —**health′fulness,** *n.* —**Syn. 2.** See **healthy.**

health physics, the branch of physics dealing with the effects of ionizing radiation on living organisms, esp. with the protection of human beings from those effects.

health visitor, a state-registered nurse appointed to visit and look after the health of people in a certain area, esp. mothers and babies, the old and sick.

healthy (hĕl′thĭ), *adj.,* **-thier, -thiest. 1.** possessing or enjoying health: *healthy body or mind.* **2.** pertaining to or characteristic of health: *a healthy appearance.* **3.** conducive to health, or healthful: *healthy recreations.* —**health′ily,** *adv.* —**health′iness,** *n.*

—**Syn. 1.** hale, hearty, robust, vigorous, strong; sound, well. **3.** nutritious, nourishing; hygienic, salubrious; invigorating, bracing. HEALTHY, HEALTHFUL, SALUTARY, WHOLESOME refer to that which promotes health. HEALTHY, while applied esp. to what possesses health, is also used of what is conducive to health: *a healthy climate, not a healthy place to be.* HEALTHFUL is applied chiefly to what is conducive to health: *healthful diet or exercise.* SALUTARY is applied to that which is conducive to well-being generally, as well as beneficial in preserving or in restoring health: *salutary effects, to take salutary measures.* It is used also of what is morally beneficial: *to have a salutary fear of consequences.* WHOLESOME has connotations of attractive freshness and purity; it applies to what is good for one, physically, morally, or both: *wholesome food or air, wholesome influences or advice.* **—Ant.** 1. sick, ill. 3. injurious.

Heanor (hē′nə), *n.* a town in England, in SE Derbyshire. 23,867 (1961).

heap (hēp), *n.* **1.** an assemblage of things lying one on another; a pile: *a heap of stones.* **2.** *Colloq.* a great quantity or number; a multitude. **3.** *Colloq.* something very old and dilapidated, esp. a motor car. **4. strike all of a heap,** *Colloq.* to dumbfound, amaze, overwhelm. **—*v.t.*** **5.** to gather, put, or cast in a heap; pile (often fol. by *up, on, together,* etc.). **6.** to accumulate or amass (often fol. by *up*): *to heap up riches.* **7.** to cast or bestow in great quantity: *to heap blessings or insults upon a person.* **8.** to load or supply abundantly with something: *to heap a person with favours.* **—*v.i.*** **9.** to become heaped or piled, as sand, snow, etc.; rise in a heap or heaps. [ME *heep,* OE *hēap* heap, multitude, troop, c. LG *hōp*: akin to G *Haufen*] **—heap′er,** *n.* **—Syn. 1.** mass, stack; accumulation.

hear (hĭə), *v.,* **heard** (hûd), **hearing.** **—*v.t.*** **1.** to perceive by the ear. **2.** to listen to: *to refuse to hear a person.* **3.** to learn by the ear or by being told; be informed of: *to hear news.* **4.** to be among the audience at or of: *to hear an opera.* **5.** to give a formal, official, or judicial hearing to, as a sovereign, a teacher, an assembly, or a judge does. **6.** to listen to with favour, assent, or compliance. **7. hear out,** to listen to (someone or something) until the end. **—*v.i.*** **8.** to have perception of sound by the ear; have the sense of hearing. **9.** to listen or take heed (in imperative, 'hear! hear!', used to applaud or show approval of a speaker's words). **10.** to receive information by the ear or otherwise: *to hear from a friend.* **11.** to listen with favour or assent: *he would not hear of it.* [ME *here(n),* OE *hēran,* c. G *hören*] **—hear′er,** *n.*

—Syn. 1, 2. HEAR, LISTEN apply to the perception of sound. To HEAR is to have such perception by means of the auditory sense: *to hear distant bells.* To LISTEN is to give attention in order to hear and understand the meaning of a sound or sounds: *to listen to what is being said, to listen for a well-known footstep.* **—Ant.** 6. disregard.

hearing (hĭə′rĭng), *n.* **1.** the faculty or sense by which sound is perceived. **2.** the act of perceiving sound. **3.** opportunity to be heard: *to grant a hearing.* **4.** *Law.* the trial of an action. **5.** earshot: *out of hearing.*

hearing aid, a compact, inconspicuous amplifier worn to improve one's hearing.

hearken (hä′kən), *Archaic.* **—*v.i.*** **1.** to listen; to give heed or attend to what is said. **—*v.t.*** **2.** to listen to; hear. Also, **harken.** [ME *herken,* OE *he(o)rcnian*; akin to HARK] **—heark′ener,** *n.*

hearsay (hĭə′sā′), *n.* gossip; rumour.

hearsay rule, *Law.* the rule that a statement made by a person not called as a witness is inadmissible evidence.

hearse (hûs), *n.* **1.** a funeral vehicle for conveying a dead person to the place of burial. **2.** a triangular frame for holding candles, used at the service of Tenebrae in Holy Week. [ME *herse,* t. OF: m. *herce* harrow, frame, ult. g. L *hirpex, irpex* large rake used as harrow]

Hearst (hûst), *n.* **William Randolph,** 1863–1951, U.S. editor and publisher.

heart (hät), *n.* **1.** a hollow muscular organ which by rhythmic contraction and dilatation keeps the blood in circulation throughout the body. **2.** this organ considered as the seat of life, or vital powers, or of thought, feeling, or emotion: *to die of a broken heart.* **3.** the seat of emotions and affections (often in contrast to the *head* as the seat of the intellect): *to win a person's heart.* **4.** feeling; sensibility; capacity for sympathy: *to have no heart.* **5.** spirit, courage, or enthusiasm: *to take heart.* **6.** the innermost or middle part of anything. **7.** the vital or essential part; core: *the very heart of the matter.* **8.** the breast or bosom: *to clasp a person to one's heart.* **9.** a person, esp. in expressions of praise or affection: *dear heart.* **10.** a figure or object with rounded sides meeting in an obtuse point at the bottom and curving inwards to a cusp at the top. **11.** *Cards.* **a.** a playing card of a suit marked with heart-shaped figures in red. **b.** (*pl.*) the suit of cards bearing this symbol. **c.** (*pl. construed as sing.*) a game in which the players try to avoid taking tricks containing hearts. **12.** *Bot.* the core of a tree; the solid central part without sap or albumen. **13.** good condition for production, growth, etc., as of land or crops. **14.** Some special noun phrases are:

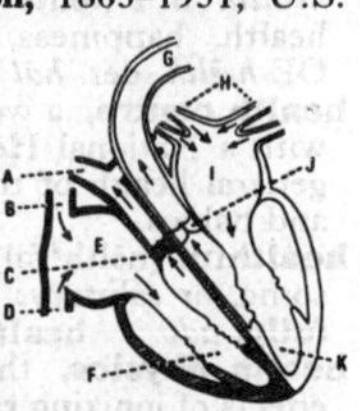

Heart (def. 1)
A, Pulmonary artery; B, Superior vena cava; C, Pulmonary valve; D, Inferior vena cava; E, Right auricle; F, Right ventricle; G, Aorta; H, Pulmonary veins; I, Left auricle; J, Aortic valve; K, Left ventricle

Heart (def. 10)

after one's own heart, appealing to one's taste or affection.
at heart, in one's heart, thoughts, or feelings; in reality.
break the heart of, **1.** to disappoint grievously in love. **2.** to crush with sorrow or grief.
by heart, from memory; committing to memory.
close to one's heart, deeply affecting one's interests and affections.
cry one's heart out, to cry bitterly or violently.
from (the bottom of) one's heart, sincerely.
have a change of heart, to reverse a decision or opinion.
have a heart, to show mercy.
have at heart, to cherish as an object, aim, etc.
have one's heart in one's mouth, to be very frightened.
have the heart, **1.** to have enough courage. **2.** (in negative sentences) to be unfeeling enough.
heart and soul, completely; wholly.
heart of hearts, at the depth of one's feelings: *he knew in his heart of hearts that he was wrong.*
heart of oak, a courageous and long-suffering spirit.
lose one's heart, to fall in love.
set one's heart at rest, to ease one's anxieties: *the doctor was able to set her heart at rest.*
set one's heart on, to desire greatly; to resolve to obtain (something).
take to heart, **1.** to think seriously about. **2.** to be deeply affected by; grieve over.
to one's heart's content, as much as one wishes.
wear one's heart upon one's sleeve, to reveal openly one's feelings, intentions, etc.
with all one's heart, with all willingness; heartily.
—*v.t.* *Archaic.* **15.** to encourage. **16.** to fix in the heart. [ME *herte,* OE *heorte,* c. G *Herz*]

heartache (hät′āk′), *n.* mental anguish; painful sorrow.

heart attack, **1.** myocardial infarction. **2.** coronary thrombosis.

heartbeat (hät′bēt′), *n.* *Physiol.* a pulsation of the heart, including one complete systole and diastole.

heartbreak (hät′brāk′), *n.* crushing sorrow or grief.

heartbreaking (hät′brā′kĭng), *adj.* causing heartbreak. **—heart′break′er,** *n.*

heartbroken (hät′brō′kən), *adj.* crushed with sorrow or grief. **—heart′bro′kenly,** *adv.* **—heart′bro′kenness,** *n.*

heartburn (hät′bûn′), *n.* **1.** a burning sensation in the epigastrium. **2.** envy; bitter jealousy.

heartburning (hät′bû′nĭng), *n.* rankling discontent, esp. from envy or jealousy; a grudge.

heart disease, any condition of the heart which impairs its functioning.

hearted (hä′tĭd), *adj.* having a specified kind of heart: *hard-hearted, tender-hearted.*

hearten (hä′tn), *v.t.* to give courage to; cheer.

heart failure, inability of the heart to pump adequate blood for maintenance of the circulation.

heartfelt (hät′fĕlt′), *adj.* deeply or sincerely felt; earnest; sincere: *heartfelt joy or words.*

heart-free (hät′frē′), *adj.* not in love.

hearth (häth), *n.* **1.** that part of the floor of a room on which the fire is made or above which is a stove, fireplace, furnace, etc. **2.** the fireside; home. **3.** *Metall.* **a.** the lower part of a blast furnace, cupola, etc., in which the molten metal collects and from which it is tapped out. **b.** the part of an open hearth, reverberatory furnace, etc., upon which the charge is placed and melted down or refined. **c.** a brazier, chafing dish, or box for charcoal. [ME *herth(e),* OE *he(o)rth,* c. G *Herd*; akin to L *carbo* charcoal]

hearthrug (häth′rŭg′), *n.* a rug laid in front of the fireplace.

hearthstone (häth′stōn′), *n.* **1.** a stone forming a hearth. **2.** the fireside; home. **3.** a soft stone, or a preparation of powdered stone and clay, used to whiten or scour hearths, steps, floors, etc.

heartily (hä′tĭ lĭ), *adv.* **1.** in a hearty manner; sincerely; cordially. **2.** eagerly; enthusiastically. **3.** with a hearty appetite. **4.** thoroughly; completely.

heartland (hät′lănd), *n.* the central area of a continent or land mass, farthest removed from the sea.

heartless (hät′lĭs), *adj.* **1.** without heart or feeling; unfeeling; cruel: *heartless words.* **2.** *Archaic.* without courage. **—heart′lessly,** *adv.* **—heart′lessness,** *n.*

heart-lung machine (hät′lŭng′), *Med.* a machine used at operations to take over the action of the heart and lungs to allow surgery to be performed on them.

heart murmur, a sound caused by turbulent blood flow through the heart.

heart-rending (hät′rĕn′dĭng), *adj.* causing acute mental anguish. —**heart′-rend′ingly,** *adv.*
hearts (häts), *n.* See **heart** (def. 11c).
heart-searching (hät′sû′chĭng), *adj.* involving a close examination of one's deepest feelings.
heart's-ease (häts′ēz′), *n.* **1.** peace of mind. **2.** the pansy, or some other plant of the genus *Viola.* [ME *hertes ese.* See HEART, EASE]
heartseed (hät′sēd′), *n.* balloon vine.
heart-shaped (hät′shāpt′), *adj.* having the shape of a heart; cordate.
heartsick (hät′sĭk′), *adj.* **1.** sick at heart; grievously depressed or unhappy. **2.** characterized by or showing grievous depression. —**heart′sick′ness,** *n.*
heartsore (hät′sô′), *adj.* **1.** sore at heart; grieved. **2.** showing grief.
heart-stricken (hät′strĭk′ən), *adj.* deeply affected with grief, etc. Also, **heart-struck** (hät′strŭk′).
heartstrings (hät′strĭngz′), *n.pl.* the deepest feelings; the strongest affections: *to pull at one's heartstrings.*
heart-throb (hät′thrŏb′), *n.* the object of an infatuation, usually a member of the opposite sex, as a pop singer, film star, or the like.
heart-to-heart (hät′tə hät′), *adj.* frank; sincere.
heart-whole (hät′hōl′), *adj.* **1.** having the heart untouched by love. **2.** wholehearted; sincere.
heartwood (hät′wŏŏd′), *n.* the hard central wood of the trunk of an exogenous tree; the duramen.
heartworm (hät′wûm′), *n.* a filarial worm living in the heart and pulmonary arteries of dogs.
hearty (hä′tĭ), *adj.*, **-tier, -tiest,** *n., pl.* **-ties.** —*adj.* **1.** warm-hearted; affectionate; cordial; friendly: *a hearty welcome.* **2.** heartfelt; genuine; sincere: *hearty approval or disiike.* **3.** enthusiastic or zealous; vigorous: *a hearty laugh.* **4.** physically vigorous; strong and well: *hale and hearty.* **5.** substantial or satisfying: *a hearty meal.* **6.** enjoying or requiring abundant food: *a hearty appetite.* **7.** (of soil) fertile. —*n.* **8.** *Colloq.* a brave or good fellow. **9.** a sailor. —**heart′iness,** *n.* —**Syn. 1.** warm, genial. **4.** healthy, hale.
heat (hēt), *n.* **1.** the quality or condition of being hot. **2.** the sensation of hotness or warmth; heated bodily condition. **3.** *Psychol.* a blended sensation, caused by stimulating the warmth and cold receptors on the skin. **4.** a form of energy resident in the random motion of molecules, which will raise the temperature of the body to which it is added. **5.** hot condition of the atmosphere or physical environment; hot season or weather. **6.** warmth or intensity of feeling: *the heat of an argument.* **7.** a fit of passion. **8.** the height of greatest intensity of any action: *to do a thing at white heat.* **9.** a single intense effort. **10.** a single course in or division of a race or other contest. **11.** a single operation of heating, as of metal in a furnace, in the heat-treating and melting of metals. **12.** *Zool.* **a.** sexual excitement in animals, esp. females. **b.** the period or duration of such excitement. —*v.t.* **13.** to make hot or warm. **14.** to excite in mind or feeling; inflame with passion. —*v.i.* **15.** to become hot or warm. **16.** to become excited in mind or feeling. [ME *hete,* OE *hǣtu;* akin to G *Hitze*] —**heat′less,** *adj.* —**Syn. 1.** hotness, warmth, caloric. **5.** caloricity. **6.** ardour, fervour; vehemence, rage. —**Ant. 1.** cold. **6.** indifference.
heat balance, an evaluation of the efficiency of a furnace, steam-engine, or other equipment, by drawing up a balance sheet of the heat input and heat output.
heat barrier, thermal barrier.
heat capacity, *Physics.* the heat required to raise the temperature of a unit mass of a substance one degree C; water equivalent. Also, **thermal capacity.**
heat content, *Physics.* enthalpy.
heat death, *Thermodynamics.* (of the universe) the proposition that the universe will come to an end when all its components are at the same temperature: the entropy of the universe will then be at a maximum and its available energy nil. This follows from the second law of thermodynamics if the universe is considered a closed system.
heated (hē′tĭd), *adj.* **1.** warmed; having the temperature raised. **2.** inflamed; vehement; angry.
heat engine, an engine which transforms heat energy into mechanical energy.
heater (hē′tə), *n.* **1.** an apparatus for heating, as a furnace. **2.** *Electronics.* that element of a radio valve which carries the current for heating a cathode.
heat exchanger, any device for transferring the heat of one fluid to another, without allowing them to mix.
heath (hēth), *n.* **1.** a tract of open and uncultivated land; waste land overgrown with shrubs. **2.** any of various low evergreen ericaceous shrubs common on waste land, as *Calluna vulgaris,* the common heather of England and Scotland with small pinkish purple flowers. **3.** any plant of the genus *Erica,* or of the family *Ericaceae.* See **ericaceous. 4.** any of several heathlike but not ericaceous shrubs, as *Frankenia lævis* (**sea heath**) of European coasts. [ME; OE *hǣth,* c. D *heide* and G *Heide*] —**heath′like′,** *adj.*
Heath (hēth), *n.* **Edward (Richard George),** born 1916, British statesman, leader of the Conservative Party since 1965; prime minister since 1970.
heathberry (hēth′bĕ′rĭ), *n., pl.* **-ries. 1.** crowberry. **2.** any berry found on heaths, esp. the bilberry.
heathbird (hēth′bûd′), *n.* the black grouse.
heathcock (hēth′kŏk′), *n.* the male black grouse.
heathen (hē′tħən), *n., pl.* **-thens, -then,** *adj.* —*n.* **1.** an unconverted individual of a people which does not acknowledge the God of the Bible; one who is neither Christian, Jewish, nor Muslim; pagan. **2.** an irreligious or unenlightened person. —*adj.* **3.** pagan; pertaining to the heathen. **4.** irreligious or unenlightened. [ME *hethen,* OE *hǣthen,* n., adj., c. D *heiden,* n., G *Heide,* n., Icel. *heidhinn,* adj.; commonly explained as meaning orig. heath-dweller. See HEATH[1], and cf. PAGAN] —**hea′thenness,** *n.*
—**Syn. 4.** HEATHEN, PAGAN are both applied to peoples who are not Christian, Jewish, or Muslim. HEATHEN is often distinctively applied to unenlightened or barbaric idolaters, such as certain primitive tribes: *heathen rites, idols.* PAGAN, though applying to any of the more civilized peoples not worshipping according to the three religions mentioned above, is almost exclusively used in speaking of the ancient Greeks and Romans: *a pagan poem, a pagan civilization.*
heathendom (hē′tħən dəm), *n.* **1.** heathenism; heathen worship or customs. **2.** heathen lands or people.
heathenish (hē′tħə nĭsh), *adj.* **1.** pertaining to the heathen. **2.** like or befitting the heathen; barbarous. —**hea′thenishly,** *adv.* —**hea′thenishness,** *n.*
heathenism (hē′tħə nĭz′əm), *n.* **1.** the condition, belief, or practice of a heathen. **2.** pagan worship; irreligion. **3.** barbaric morals or behaviour; barbarism.
heathenize (hē′tħə nīz′), *v.,* **-nized, -nizing.** —*v.t.* **1.** to make heathen or heathenish. —*v.i.* **2.** to become heathen or heathenish. **3.** to practise heathenism. Also, **heathenise.**
heathenry (hē′tħən rĭ), *n.* **1.** heathenism. **2.** heathen people; the heathen.
heather (hĕtħ′ə), *n.* any of various heaths, esp. *Calluna vulgaris* (**Scotch heather**). See **heath** (def. 2). [b. HEATH and obs. *hadder* heather (orig. uncert.)]
heather-mixture (hĕtħ′ə mĭks′chə), *adj.* having the colour and appearance of heather, esp. as certain fabrics or wools of a mixed or speckled hue.
heathery (hĕtħ′ə rĭ), *adj.* **1.** of or like heather. **2.** abounding in heather. Also, **heathy** (hē′thĭ).
heath grass, a European grass, *Sieglingia decumbens,* growing in spongy, wet, cold soils. Also, **heather grass.**
heath-hen (hēth′hĕn′), *n.* the female black grouse.
Heath Robinson, 1. having a ridiculously complicated, impractical appearance. **2.** impractical and absurdly complex, as a scheme. [after the drawings of William *Heath Robinson,* 1872–1944, English cartoonist]
Heathrow Airport (hēth′rō′), the main airport serving London, situated W of London. Also, **London Airport.**
heat lightning, flashes of light near the horizon on summer evenings, reflections of more distant lightning.
heat of combustion, *Phys. Chem.* the quantity of heat evolved when one gram molecule of a substance burns in oxygen.
heat of formation, *Phys. Chem.* the quantity of heat evolved or absorbed when one gram molecule of a compound is formed from its element in the normal state. The heat of formations of the elements is taken as zero.
heat of fusion, *Physics.* See **latent heat** (def. 1).
heat of reaction, *Phys. Chem.* the quantity of heat evolved, or absorbed during a chemical reaction, usually per unit weight of reactant, at constant temperature and pressure.
heat of solution, *Phys. Chem.* the quantity of heat evolved or absorbed when one gram molecule of a substance is dissolved in a large volume of water.
heat of vaporization, *Physics.* See **latent heat** (def. 2).
heat pump, a device which, by means of a compressible refrigerant, transfers heat from a body (the atmosphere, the earth, a lake, etc.) and then either pumps it back into the body (for heating) or elsewhere (for cooling).
heat reservoir, storage heater.
heat-resisting steel, *Metall.* steel which contains a high percentage of chromium and possibly nickel and/or tungsten; used when high resistance to oxidization or good mechanical properties are required at high temperatures.
heat shield, a device which protects men or equipment from heat; esp. a shield in front of a spacecraft to protect it from excessive heat on re-entry into the earth's atmosphere.

heatstroke (hēt′strōk′), *n.* collapse or fever caused by exposure to excessive heat.
heat-treat (hēt′trēt′), *v.t. Metall.* to subject (a metal) to heat treatment.
heat treatment, *Metall.* any process in which a metal is subjected to one or more temperature cycles in the solid state, to confer desirable properties on it.
heatwave (hēt′wāv′), *n.* **1.** an air mass of high temperature, covering an extended area and moving relatively slowly. **2.** a prolonged period of excessively warm weather.
heaume (hōm), *n.* a large supplemental medieval headpiece reaching to the shoulders and worn over an inner helmet. [t. F. See HELMET]
heave (hēv), *v.,* **heaved** or (*esp. Naut.*) **hove, heaving,** *n.* —*v.t.* **1.** to raise or lift with effort or force; hoist. **2.** to lift and throw, often with effort or force: *to heave an anchor overboard.* **3.** *Naut.* **a.** to haul, draw, or pull, as by a cable. **b.** to cause (a ship) to move in a certain direction. **4.** to utter laboriously or painfully: *to heave a sigh.* **5.** to cause to rise and fall with or as with a swelling motion. **6.** to raise or force up in a swelling movement; force to bulge. **7.** *Geol.* to cause a horizontal displacement in (a stratum, vein, etc.). See **heave** (def. 19). **8. heave to,** to stop the headway of (a vessel), esp. by bringing the head to the wind and trimming the sails so that they act against one another; to stop (a vessel). —*v.i.* **9.** to rise and fall with or as with a swelling motion. **10.** to breathe with effort; pant. **11.** to vomit; retch. **12.** to rise as if thrust up, as a hill; swell or bulge. **13.** *Naut.* **a.** to haul or pull, as at a cable; to push, as at the bar of a capstan. **b.** to move a ship, or move as a ship does, by such action. **c.** to move or go (fol. by *about, ahead,* etc.). **14. heave in sight,** to rise into view as from below the horizon, as a ship. **15. heave to,** *Naut.* to heave a vessel to. —*interj.* **16. heave ho!,** (an exclamation used by sailors when heaving the anchor up, etc.) —*n.* **17.** the act of heaving. **18.** (of the sea) the force exerted by the swell. **19.** *Geol.* the horizontal component of the apparent displacement resulting from a fault, measured in a vertical plane perpendicular to its strike. **20.** (*pl. construed as sing.*) *Vet. Sci.* a disease of horses, similar to asthma in man, characterized by difficult breathing; broken wind. [ME *heve(n),* OE *hebban* (pret. *hōf, hefde,* pp. *hafen*), c. G *heben;* akin to L *capere* take] —**Syn. 1.** See **raise.**
heaven (hĕv′ən), *n.* **1.** the abode of God, the angels, and the spirits of the righteous after death; the place or state of existence of the blessed after the mortal life. **2.** (*cap., often pl.*) the celestial powers; God. **3.** a euphemistic term for God in various emphatic expressions: *for heaven's sake.* **4.** (*chiefly pl.*) the sky or firmament, or expanse of space surrounding the earth. **5.** a place or state of supreme bliss: *a heaven on earth.* **6. heavens!,** (an interjection to express surprise.) **7. move heaven and earth,** to do all that is possible. **8.** See **seventh heaven.** [ME *heven,* OE *hefen, heofon* (c. MLG *heven*), appar. akin to Goth. *himins,* Icel. *himinn*]
heaven-born (hĕv′ən bôn′), *adj.* **1.** very talented; born with a special aptitude. **2.** of heavenly birth.
heavenly (hĕv′ən lĭ), *adj.* **1.** resembling or befitting heaven; blissful; beautiful: *a heavenly spot.* **2.** of or in the heavens: *the heavenly bodies.* **3.** of, belonging to, or coming from the heaven of God, the angels, etc. **4.** celestial or divine: *heavenly peace.* —**heav′enliness,** *n.* —**Syn. 4.** blessed, beatific. —**Ant. 4.** infernal, hellish.
heaven-sent (hĕv′ən sĕnt′), *adj.* sent by heaven; providential.
heavenward (hĕv′ən wəd), *adj.* **1.** directed towards heaven. —*adv.* **2.** heavenwards.
heavenwards (hĕv′ən wədz), *adv.* towards heaven. Also, **heavenward.**
heaver (hē′və), *n.* **1.** one who or that which heaves. **2.** *Naut.* a staff, generally from two to three feet long, used for twisting or heaving a tight rope or strap.
heaves (hēvz), *n.* See **heave** (def. 20).
heavier-than-air (hĕv′ĭ ə t͟hən ĕə′), *adj. Aeron.* **1.** of greater specific gravity than the air, as aeroplanes. **2.** of or pertaining to such aircraft.
heavily (hĕv′ĭ lĭ), *adv.* **1.** with great weight or burden: *a heavily loaded wagon.* **2.** in an oppressive manner: *cares weigh heavily upon him.* **3.** with great force; violently. **4.** severely; intensely: *to suffer heavily.* **5.** to a large amount; densely; thickly: *heavily wooded.* **6.** laboriously; sluggishly: *he walked heavily across the room.*
heaviness (hĕv′ĭ nĭs), *n.* the state or quality of being heavy; weight; burden; gravity.
Heaviside (hĕv′ĭ sīd′), *n.* **Oliver,** 1850–1925, English physicist.
Heaviside layer, the lower region, or regions, of the ionosphere chiefly responsible for the reflection of radio waves of certain frequencies, thus making long-distance short-wave radio communication possible; Kennelly-Heaviside layer. [named after Oliver HEAVISIDE]
heavy (hĕv′ĭ), *adj.,* **-ier, -iest,** *n., pl.* **-ies,** *adv.* —*adj.* **1.** of great weight; hard to lift or carry: *a heavy load.* **2.** of great amount, force, intensity, etc.: *a heavy vote.* **3.** bearing hard upon; burdensome; harsh; distressing: *heavy taxes.* **4.** having much weight in proportion to bulk; being of high specific gravity: *a heavy metal.* **5.** broad, thick, or coarse; not delicate: *heavy lines.* **6.** of more than the usual, average, or specified weight: *heavy cargo.* **7.** connected or concerned with the manufacture of goods of more than the usual weight: *heavy industry.* **8.** *Mil.* **a.** heavily armed or equipped. **b.** of the larger sizes: *heavy weapons.* **9.** serious; intense: *a heavy offence.* **10.** hard to deal with; trying; difficult: *a heavy task.* **11.** being such in an unusual degree: *a heavy smoker.* **12.** weighted or laden: *air heavy with moisture.* **13.** depressed with trouble or sorrow; showing sorrow: *a heavy heart.* **14.** overcast or cloudy: *heavy sky.* **15.** clumsy; slow in movement or action. **16.** without vivacity or interest; ponderous; dull: *a heavy style.* **17.** loud and deep: *a heavy sound.* **18.** exceptionally dense in substance; insufficiently raised or leavened; thick: *heavy bread.* **19.** not easily digested: *heavy food.* **20.** pregnant. **21.** *Theat.* sober, serious, or sombre: *a heavy part.* **22.** *Chem.* referring to an isotope of greater atomic weight: *heavy hydrogen.* —*n.* **23.** *Theat.* **a.** a villainous part or character. **b.** an actor who plays villainous parts or characters. **24.** *Mil.* a gun of great weight or heavy calibre. —*adv.* **25.** heavily. [ME *hevi,* OE *hefig,* der. *hefe* weight; akin to HEAVE, v.]
—**Syn. 1.** ponderous, massive. **9.** HEAVY, MOMENTOUS, WEIGHTY refer to anything having a considerable amount of figurative weight. HEAVY suggests the carrying of a figurative burden: *words heavy with menace.* MOMENTOUS emphasizes the idea of great and usually serious consequences: *a momentous occasion, statement.* WEIGHTY refers to something heavy with importance, often concerned with public affairs, which may require deliberation and careful judgement: *a weighty matter, problem.* **13.** serious, grave; gloomy, sad. —**Ant. 1.** light. **13.** cheerful.
heavy-armed (hĕv′ĭ ämd′), *adj.* (formerly) equipped with heavy arms or armour, as troops.
heavy-duty (hĕv′ĭ dyo͞o′tĭ), *adj.* **1.** sturdy; durable. **2.** having a high import or export tax rate.
heavy earth, baryta.
heavy-handed (hĕv′ĭ hăn′dĭd), *adj.* **1.** oppressive; harsh. **2.** clumsy. —**heav′y-hand′edness,** *n.*
heavy-hearted (hĕv′ĭ hä′tĭd), *adj.* sorrowful; melancholy; dejected. —**heav′y-heart′edness,** *n.*
heavy hydrogen, *Chem.* **1.** any of the heavy isotopes of hydrogen. **2.** deuterium.
heavy-laden (hĕv′ĭ lā′dn), *adj.* **1.** laden with a heavy burden. **2.** very weary or troubled.
heavy spar, barytes.
heavy water, water in which hydrogen atoms have been replaced by deuterium, used mainly as a source of deuterons for experiments in nuclear physics. *Symbol:* D_2O; *sp. gr.:* 1·1056 at 25°C.
heavyweight (hĕv′ĭ wāt′), *n.* **1.** one of more than average weight. **2.** a boxer or other contestant in the heaviest group; an amateur fighter exceeding 12 st. 10 lbs in weight or a professional fighter exceeding 12 st. 7 lbs in weight. **3.** *Colloq.* a person of considerable power, influence, or forcefulness in a certain field, as a writer, philosopher, or statesman.
Heb., **1.** Hebrew. **2.** Hebrews.
Hebbel (*Ger.* hĕb′əl), *n.* **Friedrich** (*Ger.* frē′drĭKH), 1813–63, German poet and dramatist.
Hebburn (hĕb′ən), *n.* a town in England, in Durham, on the river Tyne: shipbuilding. 25,042 (1961).
hebdomad (hĕb′də măd′), *n.* **1.** the number seven. **2.** seven days; a week. [t. L: s. *hebdomas,* t. Gk]
hebdomadal (hĕb dŏm′ə dl), *adj.* weekly. Also, **hebdomadary** (hĕb dŏm′ə də rĭ, -drĭ). [t. LL: s. *hebdomadālis*] —**hebdom′adally,** *adv.*
Hebdomadal Council, (at Oxford University) a representative board of professors and teachers meeting weekly.
Hebe (hē′bĭ), *n. Gk Myth.* the goddess of youth and spring, cupbearer (before Ganymede) of Olympus, and wife of Hercules. [t. L, t. Gk: youth, youthful prime]
hebephrenia (hē′bĭ frē′nyə), *n. Psychol.* a form of dementia praecox incident to the age of puberty, characterized by childish behaviour, hallucinations, and emotional deterioration. [f. Gk: *hḗbē* youth + *phrḗn* mind + *-ia* -IA]
Heber (hē′bə), *n.* **Reginald,** 1783–1826, English bishop and hymn-writer.
Hébert (*Fr.* ė bĕr′), *n.* **Jacques René** (*Fr.* zhäk rə nĕ′), 1755–94, French journalist and revolutionary leader.
hebetate (hĕb′ĭ tāt′), *v.,* **-tated, -tating,** *adj.* —*v.t., v.i.*

1. to make or become dull or blunt. —*adj.* 2. *Bot.* having a blunt, soft point, as awns. [t. L: m. s. *hebetātus*, pp., blunted, dulled] —**heb′eta′tion,** *n.*

hebetic (hĭ bĕt′ĭk), *adj. Physiol.* pertaining to or occurring in puberty. [t. Gk: m. s. *hēbētikós* youthful]

hebetude (hĕb′ĭ tyo͞od′), *n.* the state of being dull; lethargy; mental dullness. [t. LL: m. *hebetūdo*, der. L *hebes* dull]

Hebraic (hĭ brā′ĭk), *adj.* Hebrew. [t. LL: s. *Hebraicus*, t. Gk: m. *Hebraikós*; r. OE *Ebrēisc*] —**Hebra′ically,** *adv.*

Hebraism (hē′brā ĭz′əm), *n.* **1.** a Hebrew idiom. **2.** Hebrew character, spirit, thought, or practice.

Hebraist (hē′brā ĭst), *n.* **1.** one versed in Hebrew language and learning. **2.** one imbued with the Hebrew spirit.

Hebraistic (hē′brā ĭs′tĭk), *adj.* pertaining to Hebraists or Hebraism. Also, **He′brais′tical.**

Hebraize (hē′brā īz′), *v.*, **-ized, -izing.** —*v.t.* **1.** to make Hebrew. —*v.i.* **2.** to become Hebrew. **3.** to conform to the Hebrew usage or type. **4.** to use a Hebrew idiom or manner of speech. Also, **Hebraise.** [t. Gk: s. *hebraízein* speak Hebrew]

Hebrew (hē′bro͞o), *n.* **1.** a member of that branch of the Semitic race descended from the line of Abraham; an Israelite; a Jew. **2.** a Semitic language, the language of the ancient Hebrews, which although not a vernacular after 100 B.C. was retained as the scholarly and liturgical language of Jews and now is used as the language of Israeli Jews. —*adj.* **3.** of or pertaining to the Hebrews or their language. [ME *Ebreu*, t. OF, t. ML: m. s. *Ebreus*, L *Hebraeus*, t. Gk: m. *Hebraîos*, t. Aram.: m. *'Ebhrāyā*, t. Heb.: m. *'Ibhrī*, said to mean 'one from beyond'; r. OE *Ebrēas* (pl.), t. ML: m. *Ebrēī*]

Hebrews (hē′bro͞oz), *n.* a New Testament epistle, preserved among the Epistles of Paul.

Hebrides (hĕb′rĭ dēz′), *n.pl.* a group of islands off the W coast of and belonging to Scotland; divided into the **Outer Hebrides** (Lewis, Harris, etc.) and **Inner Hebrides** (Skye, Mull, etc.). 61,795 pop. (1951); ab. 2900 sq. mi. Also, **Western Islands.** —**Heb′ride′an,** *adj.*

Hebron (hĕb′rŏn, hē′brŏn), *n.* a town in Jordan. 37,911 (1961).

Hecate (hĕk′ə tĭ), *n. Gk Myth.* a goddess, often represented in triple form, associated with sorcery and witchcraft, having power on earth, sea, and in the heavens; sometimes identified with Artemis as a moon-goddess. Also, **Hekate.** [t. L, t. Gk: m. *Hekátē*, prop. fem. of *hékatos* far darting (epithet of Apollo)]

hecatomb (hĕk′ə tōm′, -to͞om′), *n.* **1.** a great public sacrifice, orig. of a hundred oxen, as to the Greek gods. **2.** any great slaughter. [t. L: m. *hecatombē*, t. Gk: m. *hekatómbē*]

Hecht (hĕkt), *n.* **Ben,** 1894–1964, U.S. writer.

heck (hĕk), *n.*, *interj.* (a euphemism for hell.)

heckelphone (hĕk′l fōn′), *n.* a bass oboe, sounding an octave lower in pitch than the oboe. [named after Wilhelm *Heckel*, 20th-century German instrument-maker, the inventor. See -PHONE]

heckle (hĕk′l), *v.*, **-led, -ling,** *n.* —*v.t.* **1.** Also, **hatchel.** to badger or torment; harass, esp. a public speaker, with questions and gibes. **2.** to cut (flax or hemp) with a hatchel. [der. HECKLE, n.] —*n.* **3.** hatchel. [late ME *hekele*, n., phonetic var. of ME *hechele*; akin to HACKLE[1], HATCHEL] —**heck′ler,** *n.* —**heck′ling,** *n.*

hectare (hĕk′tä), *n.* a surface measure, the common unit of land measure in the metric system, equal to 100 ares, or 10,000 square metres, equivalent to 2·471 acres. [t. F. See HECTO-, ARE[2]]

hectic (hĕk′tĭk), *adj.* **1.** characterized by great excitement, passions, etc.: *hectic pleasures.* **2.** marking a particular habit or condition of body, as the fever of phthisis (**hectic fever**) when this is attended by flushed cheeks (**hectic flush**), hot skin, and emaciation. **3.** pertaining to or affected with such fever; consumptive. —*n.* **4.** a hectic fever. **5.** a hectic flush. **6.** a consumptive person. [t. LL: s. *hecticus*, t. Gk: m. *hektikós* habitual, hectic] —**hec′tically,** *adv.*

hecto-, a word element meaning 'hundred', used in the metric system to indicate the multiplication of the unit by 100. [comb. form representing Greek *hekatón*]

hectocotylus (hĕk′tō kŏt′ĭ ləs), *n.*, *pl.* **-li** (lī′). *Zool.* a modified arm of the male of certain cephalopods which is used to transfer sperm into the female. [NL, f. *hecto-* HECTO- + m. Gk *kotýlē* cup]

hectogram (hĕk′tō grăm′), *n. Metric System.* a unit of 100 grams, equivalent to 3·527 ounces avoirdupois. Also, **hektogram; hectogramme.**

hectograph (hĕk′tō grăf′, -gräf′), *n.* **1.** a process for making copies of a writing, etc., from a prepared gelatine surface to which the original has been transferred. **2.** the apparatus used. —*v.t.* **3.** to copy with the hectograph.

hectolitre (hĕk′tō lē′tə), *n. Metric System.* a unit of capacity of 100 litres, equivalent to 21·998 imperial gallons. Also, **hektolitre;** *Chiefly U.S.*, **hectoliter.**

hectometre (hĕk′tō mē′tə), *n. Metric System.* a measure of length equal to 100 metres, or 328·08 ft. Also, *Chiefly U.S.*, **hectometer.**

Hector (hĕk′tə), *n.* **1.** the eldest son of Priam and husband of Andromache: a prominent warrior in the Trojan wars, slain by Achilles. **2.** (*l.c.*) a blustering, domineering fellow; a swashbuckler; a bully. —*v.t.* **3.** (*l.c.*) to treat with insolence; bully; torment. —*v.i.* **4.** (*l.c.*) to act in a blustering, domineering way; be a bully.

Hecuba (hĕk′yo͞o bə), *n. Gk Legend.* the wife of Priam.

he'd (hēd; *unstressed* hĭd, ēd, ĭd), contraction of: **1.** he had. **2.** he would.

heddle (hĕd′l), *n.* (in a loom) one of the sets of vertical cords or wires, forming the principal part of the harness which guides the warp threads. [metathetic var. of *heald*, OE *hefeld* thread (for weaving)]

hedenbergite (hĕd′n bûr′gīt, -bə gīt′), *n.* a mineral of the pyroxene group, $CaFe(SiO_3)_2$; occurs in limestones in the form of black crystals. [named after L. *Hedenberg*, 19th-century Swedish chemist]

hedge (hĕj), *n.*, *v.*, **hedged, hedging.** —*n.* **1.** a row of bushes or small trees planted close together, esp. when forming a fence or boundary. **2.** any barrier or boundary. **3.** an act or a means of hedging a bet or the like. —*v.t.* **4.** to enclose with or separate by a hedge (often fol. by *in*, *off*, *about*, etc.): *to hedge a garden.* **5.** to surround, as with a hedge; hem in (often fol. by *in*). **6.** to surround so as to prevent escape or hinder free movement; obstruct (often fol. by *in* or *up*): *to be hedged by difficulties.* **7.** to protect (a bet, etc.) by taking some offsetting risk. —*v.i.* **8.** to avoid taking an open or decisive course. **9.** to protect a bet, speculation, etc., by taking some offsetting risk. **10.** *Finance.* to enter transactions that will protect against loss through a compensatory price movement. [ME *hegge*, OE *hegge* (oblique case), c. G *Hecke.* Cf. HAW[1], HAY[1]]

hedgehog (hĕj′hŏg′), *n.* **1.** an insectivorous mammal frequenting hedges and gardens, having spiny hairs on the back and sides, and found esp. in Europe. **2.** *U.S.* the porcupine. Also, **hedgepig** (hĕj′pĭg′).

Hedgehog, *Erinaceus europaeus* (10 to 11 in. long)

hedgehop (hĕj′hŏp′), *v.i.* to fly an aeroplane at a very low altitude, as for spraying crops, bombing in warfare, etc. —**hedge′hop′per,** *n.* —**hedge′hop′ping,** *n.*, *adj.*

hedge-hyssop (hĕj′hĭs′əp), *n.* **1.** any of the low herbs constituting the scrophulariaceous genus *Gratiola*, as *G. officinalis*, a medicinal species of Europe. **2.** any of certain similar plants, as *Scutellaria minor*, an English skullcap.

hedge-mustard (hĕj′mŭs′təd), *n.* a cruciferous annual, *Sisymbrium officinale*, with stiff erect stems and yellow flowers, widespread as a weed of cultivation in temperate regions.

hedge-parsley (hĕj′päs′lĭ), *n.* any of several species of annual umbelliferous plants belonging to the genus *Torilis*, as *T. japonica*, the **upright hedge-parsley,** widespread in temperate regions.

hedger (hĕj′ə), *n.* **1.** one who makes or repairs hedges. **2.** one who hedges in betting, etc.

hedgerow (hĕj′rō′), *n.* a row of bushes or trees forming a hedge.

hedge-sparrow (hĕj′spă′rō), *n.* a small European passerine bird, *Prunella modularis*, which frequents hedges and which is an accentor rather than a true sparrow.

hedgy (hĕj′ĭ), *adj.* abounding in hedges.

Hedin (*Swed.* hĕ dēn′), *n.* **Sven Anders** (*Swed.* svĕn än′dərs), 1865–1952, Swedish explorer in Asia.

Hedjaz (hē jăz′), *n.* Hejaz.

hedonic (hē dŏn′ĭk), *adj.* **1.** pertaining to or consisting in pleasure. **2.** pertaining to hedonism or hedonics. [t. Gk: m. s. *hēdonikós* pleasurable] —**hedon′ically,** *adv.*

hedonics (hē dŏn′ĭks), *n. Psychol.* the study of pleasurable and painful states of consciousness.

hedonism (hē′də nĭz′əm), *n.* **1.** the doctrine that pleasure or happiness is the highest good. **2.** devotion to pleasure. —**he′donist,** *n.*, *adj.* —**he′donis′tic,** *adj.* —**he′donis′tically,** *adv.*

-hedron, a combining form denoting geometrical solid figures having a certain number of faces, as in *polyhedron.* [t. Gk: etymological m. *-edron*, neut. of *-edros*, adj., having bases, -sided, der. *hédra* seat, base]

heebie-jeebies (hē′bĭ jē′bĭz), *n.pl. Slang.* a condition of nervousness. [coined by W. DeBeck, 1890–1942, U.S. cartoonist]

heed (hēd), *v.t.* **1.** to give attention to; regard; notice.

—*v.i.* **2.** to give attention; have regard. —*n.* **3.** careful attention; notice; observation (usually with *give* or *take*). [ME *hede(n)*, OE *hēdan*, c. G *hüten* attend to, mind; akin to HOOD, n.] —**heed′er,** *n.* —**Syn. 1.** note, observe, consider. **3.** consideration, care.

heedful (hēd′fəl), *adj.* attentive; mindful: *heedful of others.* —**heed′fully,** *adv.* —**heed′fulness,** *n.*

heedless (hēd′lĭs), *adj.* careless; thoughtless; unmindful. —**heed′lessly,** *adv.* —**heed′lessness,** *n.*

heehaw (hē′hô′), *n.* **1.** the braying sound made by an ass. **2.** rude laughter. —*v.i.* **3.** to bray. [imit.]

heel[1] (hēl), *n.* **1.** (in man) the back part of the foot, below and behind the ankle. **2.** an analogous part in other vertebrates. **3.** either hind foot or hoof of some animals, as the horse. **4.** the foot as a whole: *small fauns with cloven heel.* **5.** the part of a stocking, shoe, or the like, covering the heel. **6.** a solid part of wood, rubber, etc., attached to the sole of a shoe, under the heel. **7.** the part of the palm of a hand or glove nearest the wrist. **8.** something resembling the human heel in position, shape, etc.: *heel of bread.* **9.** the latter or concluding part of anything: *heel of a session.* **10.** *Bot.* the older basal part of a shoot removed from a plant which usually produces roots readily when planted. **11.** *Naut.* **a.** the after end of a ship's keel. **b.** the lower part of a mast, a boom, a sternpost, a rafter, etc. **12.** the crook in the head of a golf club. **13.** *Slang.* a contemptible person. **14.** Some special noun phrases are:

at one's heels, close behind one.

cool (or kick) one's heels, *Colloq.* to be kept waiting, esp. as deliberate policy.

down at heel, **1.** having the shoe heels worn down. **2.** shabby. **3.** slipshod or slovenly.

kick up one's heels, to enjoy oneself.

lay by the heels, to capture; seize.

on the heels of, closely following.

show a clean pair of heels, to escape by outdistancing pursuers.

take to one's heels, to run off or away.

to heel, **1.** (of a dog) following a person with the nose close to his left heel. **2.** under control.

—*v.t.* **15.** to furnish with heels, as shoes. **16.** to perform (a dance) with the heels. **17.** *Golf.* to strike the (ball) with the heel of the club. **18.** *Rugby Football.* to kick the (ball) through or out of the scrum with the heel. **19.** to follow at the heels of. **20.** to arm (a gamecock) with spurs. **21. heel in,** to plant cuttings or plants temporarily before putting them in their permanent growing site.

—*v.i.* **22.** to follow at one's heels. **23.** to use the heels, as in dancing. **24.** *Rugby Football.* to heel the ball.

[ME; OE *hēl(a)*, appar. der. *hōh* HOCK. Cf. D *hiel*, Icel. *hæll*] —**heel′er,** *n.* —**heel′-less,** *adj.*

heel[2] (hēl), *v.i.* **1.** (of a ship, etc.) to lean to one side; cant; tilt. —*v.t.* **2.** to cause to lean or cant. —*n.* **3.** a heeling movement; a cant. [earlier *heeld*, ME *helde(n)*, OE *h(i)eldan* bend, incline, der. *heald*, adj., sloping]

heel[3] (hēl), *n.* *Colloq.* a cad; a despicable character. [special use of HEEL[1]]

heel-and-toe (hēl′ən tō′), *adj.* denoting a pace, as in walking contests, in which the heel of the front foot touches ground before the toes of the rear one leave it.

heelpiece (hēl′pēs′), *n.* **1.** a piece serving as or fitted to a heel of a shoe or stocking. **2.** a terminal part of anything.

heelpost (hēl′pōst′), *n.* a post made to withstand strain, forming or fitted to the heel or end of something, as the post on which a gate or door is hinged.

heeltap (hēl′tăp′), *n.* **1.** a layer of leather or the like in a shoe heel; a lift. **2.** a small quantity of a drink left in a glass after drinking. **3.** dregs; residue.

Heenan (hē′nən), *n.* **Cardinal John,** born 1905, Roman Catholic Archbishop of Westminster since 1963.

Heerlen (*Du.* hėr′lə), *n.* a town in the Netherlands, in S Limburg. 75,877 (1965).

heft (hĕft), *n.* **1.** *Obs. or Dial.* weight; heaviness. —*v.t.* **2.** to try the weight of by lifting. **3.** *U.S. Colloq. and Brit. Dial.* to heave or lift. [der. HEAVE]

hefty (hĕf′tĭ), *adj.*, **-tier, -tiest.** *Colloq.* **1.** heavy; weighty. **2.** big and strong; powerful; muscular. —**hef′tily,** *adv.* —**hef′tiness,** *n.*

Hegel (hā′gl; *Ger.* hė′gəl), *n.* **Georg Wilhelm Friedrich** (*Ger.* gė ōrk′ vĭl′hĕlm frē′drĭKH), 1770–1831, German philosopher.

Hegelian (hā gē′lyən), *adj.* **1.** of or pertaining to Hegel or to Hegelianism. —*n.* **2.** one who accepts the philosophical opinions of Hegel.

Hegelian dialectic, (in Hegelianism) the pattern or mechanism of development by inner conflict, the scheme of which is *thesis, antithesis*, and *synthesis* (i.e., an original tendency, its opposing tendency, and their unification in a new movement).

Hegelianism (hā gē′lyə nĭz′əm), *n.* the philosophical system of Hegel, which during the second quarter of the 19th century was the leading system of metaphysical thought in Germany.

hegemony (hĭ gĕm′ə nĭ), *n.*, *pl.* **-nies.** **1.** leadership or predominant influence exercised by one state over others, as in a confederation. **2.** leadership; predominance. [t. Gk: m. s. *hēgemonía*] —**hegemonic** (hĕg′ĭ mŏn′ ĭk), *adj.*

Hegira (hĕj′ĭ rə), *n.* **1.** the flight of Mohammed from persecutions in Mecca to his successes in Medina. The date, A.D. 622, is the starting point in the Muslim calendar. **2.** the Muslim era itself. **3.** (*l.c.*) a flight similar to Mohammed's. Also, **Hejira.** [t. ML, t. Ar.: m. *hijra* departure, migration]

hegumen (hĭ gyo͞o′mĕn), *n.* *Gk Orth. Ch.* the head of a monastery. Also, **hegumenos** (hĭ gyo͞o′mĭ nŏs′). [t. ML: s. *hēgūmenus*, t. Gk: m. *hēgoúmenos*, prop. ppr. of *hēgeîsthai* lead]

Heidegger (hī′dĭ gə; *Ger.* hī′dĕ gər), *n.* **Martin,** born 1889, German philosopher.

Heidelberg (hī′dl bûg′; *Ger.* hī′dəl bĕrk), *n.* a city in West Germany, in N Baden-Württemberg: university, founded 1385. 124,400 (est. 1966).

Heidelberg jaw, *Anthropol.* a lower jaw supposed to belong to a very early human species, found in 1907 near Heidelberg, Germany.

Heidelberg man, the primitive man reconstructed from the Heidelberg jaw.

Heidenheim (*Ger.* hī′dən hīm), *n.* a town in Germany, in E Baden-Württemberg. 50,600 (est. 1966).

Heiduc (hī′do͝ok), *n.* Haiduk. Also, **Heiduk.**

heifer (hĕf′ə), *n.* a cow that has not produced a calf and is under three years of age. [ME *hayfre*, OE *hēa(h)-f(o)re, hēahfru*, f. *hēah* HIGH (i.e. grown) + *-fore*, fem. equivalent of *fearr* bull. Cf. Gk *póris* young cow]

Heifetz (hī′fĭts), *n.* **Jascha** (yăsh′ə), born 1901, Russian-born violinist in the U.S.

heigh (hā), *interj.* (an exclamation used to call attention, give encouragement, etc.) Also, **hey, ha.**

heigh-ho (hā′hō′), *interj.* (an exclamation of melancholy, weariness, surprise, or exultation.)

height (hīt), *n.* **1.** the state of being high. **2.** extent upwards; altitude; stature; distance upwards; elevation: *height of an object above the ground.* **3.** considerable or great altitude or elevation. **4.** a high place or level; a hill or mountain. **5.** the highest part; the top; apex. **6.** the highest or culminating point; utmost degree: *the height of the season.* **7.** high degree, as of a quality. [ME; OE *hiehtho, hē(a)hthu.* See HIGH, -TH[1]]

—**Syn. 2.** HEIGHT, ALTITUDE, ELEVATION refer to distance above a level. HEIGHT denotes extent upwards (as from foot to head) as well as any measurable distance above a given level: *the tree has a height of ten feet; they climbed to a great height.* ALTITUDE usually refers to the distance, determined by instruments, above a given level: *altitude of an aeroplane.* ELEVATION implies a distance to which something has been raised or uplifted above a level: *a hill's elevation above sea-level.* **5.** summit. **6.** zenith, culmination. —**Ant. 2.** depth.

heighten (hī′tn), *v.t.* **1.** to increase the height of; make higher. **2.** to increase the intensity of, as in a drawing: *to heighten a picture with Chinese white.* —*v.i.* **3.** to become higher. **4.** to increase; augment. —**height′ener,** *n.* —**Syn. 1.** See **elevate.**

height-to-paper (hīt′tə pā′pə), *n.* *Print.* the standard length of type from foot to face ($\frac{11}{12}$ inch in Great Britain).

heil (hīl), *interj.* *German.* hail! (a greeting).

Heilbronn (*Ger.* hīl′bRŏn), *n.* a town in West Germany, in N Baden-Württemberg. 96,000 (est. 1966).

Heilungkiang (hā′lo͝ong′kyăng′), *n.* a province in NE China. 14,860,000 pop. (1957). *Cap.:* Harbin.

Heimdall (hām′däl), *n.* *Scand. Myth.* the god of light, the guardian against the giants of the bridge of the gods; the slayer of Loki. [t. Icel.: s. *Heimdallr*]

Heine (*Ger.* hī′nə), *n.* **Heinrich** (*Ger.* hīn′rĭKH), 1797–1856, German lyric and satiric poet, journalist, and critic.

Heinemann (*Ger.* hī′nə mán), *n.* **Gustav** (*Ger.* go͝os′táf), born 1899, German statesman: president of West Germany since 1969.

heinous (hā′nəs, hē′nəs), *adj.* hateful; odious; gravely reprehensible: *a heinous offence.* [ME *heynous*, t. OF: m. *hainos*, der. *haine* hatred, der. *haïr* hate; of Gmc orig. and akin to HATE] —**hei′nously,** *adv.* —**hei′nousness,** *n.* —**Syn.** wicked, infamous. —**Ant.** trivial.

heir (ĕə), *n.* **1.** *Law.* one who inherits, or has a right of inheritance in, the (real) property of an intestate person. **2.** *Civil Law.* one who inherits the property of a deceased person, testate or intestate, and is liable for the payments of the debts of the deceased and of the legacies. **3.** one to whom something falls or is due. **4.** a person, society, etc., considered as the continuer of a tradition, policy, or the like previously established. —*v.t.* **5.** to inherit; succeed to. [ME, t. OF, g. L *hēres*] —**heir′less,** *adj.*

heir apparent, *pl.* **heirs apparent.** an heir whose right is indefeasible, provided he survives the ancestor.

heir-at-law (ĕə′rət lô′), *n.*, *pl.* **heirs-at-law.** an heir by legal right.

heir by custom, one whose right as an heir is determined by customary modes of descent, as gavelkind, and the like.

heirdom (ĕə′dəm), *n.* heirship; inheritance.

heiress (ĕə′rĭs), *n.* **1.** a female heir. **2.** a woman inheriting or expected to inherit considerable wealth.

heirloom (ĕə′lo͞om′), *n.* **1.** any family possession transmitted from generation to generation. **2.** *Law.* a chattel that descends to the heir, as a portrait of an ancestor, etc. [f. HEIR + LOOM[1], orig. tool or implement]

heir presumptive, an heir whose expectation may be defeated by the birth of a nearer heir.

heirship (ĕə′shĭp), *n.* the position or rights of an heir; right of inheritance; inheritance.

Heisenberg (*Ger.* hī′zən bĕrk), *n.* **Werner Karl** (*Ger.* vĕr′nər kȧrl), born 1901, German physicist.

Heisenberg's uncertainty principle, *Physics.* uncertainty principle.

Hejaz (hē jăz′), *n.* a former independent kingdom in W Arabia, bordering on the Red Sea, now forming a part of Saudi Arabia: the holy cities of Islam, Mecca and Medina, are in Hejaz. ab. 2,000,000 pop.; ab. 150,000 sq. mi. *Cap.:* Mecca. Also, **Hedjaz.**

Hejira (hĕj′ĭ rə), *n.* Hegira.

Hekate (hĕk′ə tĭ), *n.* Hecate.

hektare (hĕk′tä), *n.* hectare.

hekto-, var. of **hecto-.**

hektogram (hĕk′tō grăm′), *n.* hectogram.

hektolitre (hĕk′tō lē′tə), *n.* hectolitre.

Hel (hĕl), *n.* *Scand. Myth.* the goddess of Niflheim, the realm of the dead: the daughter of Loki. [t. Icel.]

Helanca (hĭ lăng′kə), *n.* *Trademark.* a crimped thermoplastic yarn.

held (hĕld), *v.* pt. and pp. of **hold.**

Helen (hĕl′ĭn), *n.* *Gk Legend.* the beautiful daughter of Zeus and Leda, and the wife of Menelaus of Sparta. Her abduction by Paris caused the Trojan war. See **apple of discord.**

Helena (hĕl′ĭ nə), *n.* a town in the U.S., the capital of Montana, in the W part. 20,227 (1960).

Helgoland (hĕl′gō lănd′; *Ger.* hĕl′gō lȧnt), *n.* Heligoland.

heli-, var. of **helio-,** before vowels, as in *helianthus.*

heliacal (hĭ lī′ə kl), *adj.* *Astron.* pertaining to or occurring near the sun, esp. applied to such risings and settings of a star as are most nearly coincident with those of the sun while yet being visible. Also, **heliac** (hē′lĭ ăk′). [f. s. LL *hēliacus* (t. Gk: m. *hēliakós* of the sun) + -AL[1]] —**heli′acally,** *adv.*

helianthus (hē′lĭ ăn′thəs), *n.* a sunflower. [NL, f. Gk: s. *hḗlios* sun + m. *ánthos* flower]

helical (hĕl′ĭ kl), *adj.* pertaining to or having the form of a helix. [f. s. L *helix* HELIX + -AL[1]] —**hel′ically,** *adv.*

helical gear, a gearwheel in which the teeth are at an angle to the wheel axis and form part of a helix described on the face of the wheel.

helices (hĕl′ĭ sēz′), *n.* pl. of **helix.**

helicoid (hĕl′ĭ koid′), *adj.* **1.** coiled or curving like a helix; spiral. —*n.* **2.** *Geom.* a warped surface generated by a straight line so moving as always to cut or touch a fixed helix. [t. Gk: m. s. *helikoeidḗs* of spiral form] —**hel′icoi′dal,** *adj.* —**hel′icoi′dally,** *adv.*

Helicon (hĕl′ĭ kən), *n.* **1.** a mountain in S Greece, in Boeotia, regarded in ancient Greece as the source of poetry and poetic inspiration. From it flowed the fountains of Aganippe and Hippocrene, associated with the Muses. 5738 ft. **2.** (*l.c.*) a tuba in coiled form to be carried over the shoulder in cavalry bands. —**Heliconian** (hĕl′ĭ kō′nyən), *adj.*

helicopter (hĕl′ĭ kŏp′tə), *n.* any of a class of heavier-than-air craft which are lifted and sustained in the air by helicoid surfaces or propellers turning on vertical axes by virtue of power supplied from an engine. [t. F: m. *hélicoptère*, f. *hélico-* (comb. form. See HELIX) + m. s. Gk *pterón* wing]

Heligoland (hĕl′ĭ gō lănd′), *n.* a German island in the North Sea: its heavy fortifications were destroyed, 1947; British naval victory in nearby **Heligoland Bight,** 1914. 1492 (1962); ¼ sq. mi. Also, **Helgoland**

helio-, a word element meaning 'sun', as in *heliocentric.* Also, **heli-.** [t. Gk, comb. form of *hḗlios*]

heliocentric (hē′lĭ ō sĕn′trĭk), *adj.* *Astron.* **1.** as viewed or measured from the centre of the sun. **2.** having or representing the sun as a centre. —**he′liocen′trically,** *adv.*

heliocentric parallax. See **parallax** (def. 3).

heliodor (hĕl′ĭ ə dô′), *n.* a variety of clear yellow beryl, which occurs in SW Africa: used in jewellery.

Heliogabalus (hē′lĭ ō găb′ə ləs), *n.* Elagabalus.

heliogram (hē′lĭ ō grăm′), *n.* a heliographic message. [f. HELIO(GRAPH) + (TELE)GRAM]

heliograph (hē′lĭ ō grăf′, -gräf′), *n.* **1.** a device for signalling by means of a movable mirror which flashes beams of light to a distance. **2.** an apparatus for photographing the sun. —*v.t.*, *v.i.* **3.** to communicate by heliograph. —**heliographer** (hē′lĭ ŏg′rə fə), *n.* —**heliographic** (hē′lĭ ō grăf′ĭk), *adj.* —**he′liog′raphy,** *n.*

heliolatry (hē′lĭ ŏl′ə trĭ), *n.* worship of the sun. —**he′liol′ater,** *n.* —**hel′iol′atrous,** *adj.*

heliometer (hē′lĭ ŏm′ĭ tə), *n.* *Astron.* an instrument for measuring the diameter of the sun and the angular distance between two celestial bodies.

Heliopolis (hē′lĭ ŏp′ə lĭs), *n.* **1.** Biblical, **On.** an ancient ruined city in N Egypt, on the Nile delta. **2.** ancient Greek name of **Baalbek.**

Helios (hē′lĭ ŏs′), *n.* *Gk Myth.* the sun-god, son of Hyperion and father of Phaëthon, represented as driving a chariot across the sky. [t. Gk: the sun, the sun-god]

heliostat (hē′lĭ ō stăt′), *n.* an instrument consisting of a mirror moved by clockwork, for reflecting the sun's rays in a fixed direction.

heliotaxis (hē′lĭ ō tăk′sĭs), *n.* *Biol.* a phototaxis in response to sunlight. —**heliotactic** (hē′lĭ ō tăk′tĭk), *adj.*

heliotherapy (hē′lĭ ō thĕ′rə pĭ), *n.* treatment of disease by means of sunlight.

heliotrope (hĕl′yə trōp′, hē′lyə-), *n.* **1.** *Bot.* any plant that turns towards the sun. **2.** any herb or shrub of the boraginaceous genus *Heliotropium*, esp. *H. arborescens* (*peruvianum*), a garden plant with small, fragrant purple flowers. **3.** the medicinal valerian (*Valeriana officinalis*). **4.** light tint of purple; reddish lavender. **5.** bloodstone. **6.** a form of heliograph used in surveying in which a mirror is used to reflect the sun's rays and a line of sight enables the operator to transmit the reflected beam in the direction of the observer. [t. F, t. L: m. s. *hēliotropium*, t. Gk: m. *hēliotrópion* sundial, plant, bloodstone]

heliotropic (hē′lĭ ō trŏp′ĭk), *adj.* *Bot.* growing towards the light. —**he′liotrop′ically,** *adv.*

heliotropism (hē′lĭ ŏt′rə pĭz′əm), *n.* heliotropic habit of growth.

heliotype (hē′lĭ ō tīp′), *n.*, *v.*, **-typed, -typing.** —*n.* **1.** a picture or print produced by a photomechanical process in which the impression in ink is taken directly from a prepared gelatine film which has been exposed under a negative. **2.** Also, **heliotypy** (hē′lĭ ō tī′pĭ). the process itself. —*v.t.* **3.** to make a heliotype of. —**heliotypic** (hē′lĭ ō tĭp′ĭk), *adj.*

heliozoan (hē′lĭ ō zō′ən), *n.* **1.** one of the *Heliozoa*, an order of protozoans, distinguished by a spherical body and radiating pseudopodia. —*adj.* **2.** belonging or pertaining to the *Heliozoa.*

heliport (hĕl′ĭ pôt′), *n.* a landing place for helicopters, often the roof of a building.

helium (hē′lyəm), *n.* *Chem.* an inert gaseous element present in the sun's atmosphere, certain minerals, natural gas, etc., and also occurring as a radioactive decomposition product. *Symbol:* He; *at. wt:* 4·0026; *at. no.:* 2; *density:* 0·1785 at 0°C and 760 mm. pressure. [NL, der. Gk *hḗlios* sun]

helix (hē′lĭks), *n.*, *pl.* **helices** (hĕl′ĭ sēz′), **helixes. 1.** a spiral. **2.** *Archit.* **a.** a spiral ornament. **b.** a volute under the abacus of the Corinthian capital. **3.** *Geom.* the curve assumed by a straight line drawn on a plane when that plane is wrapped round a cylindrical surface of any kind, especially a right circular cylinder, as the curve of a screw thread. **4.** *Anat.* the curved fold forming most of the rim of the external ear. See diag. under **ear.** [t. L, t. Gk: anything of spiral shape]

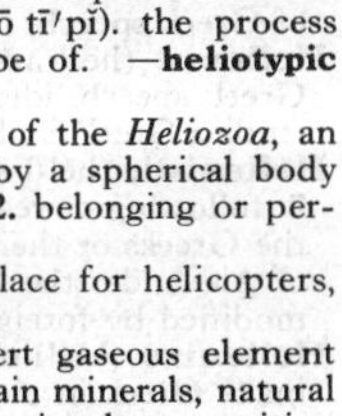

Helix in a Corinthian capital (def. 2b)

hell (hĕl), *n.* **1.** the place or state of punishment of the wicked after death; the abode of evil and condemned spirits; Gehenna or Tartarus. **2.** any place or state of torment or misery: *a hell on earth.* **3.** the powers of evil. **4.** anything that causes torment; any severe or extremely unpleasant experience, either mental or physical. **5.** the abode of the dead; Sheol or Hades. **6.** a gambling house. **7.** a receptacle into which a tailor throws his shreds or a printer his type. **8.** Some special noun phrases are:
for the hell of it, for no specific reason; for its own sake.
hell for leather, at top speed; recklessly fast.
hell of a, 1. appallingly difficult, unpleasant, etc. **2.** notable; remarkable.

like hell, 1. very much (used as general intensive). 2. not at all; definitely not.
play hell with, 1. to cause considerable damage, injury, or harm to. 2. *Colloq.* to reprimand severely; scold.
—*interj.* 9. (an exclamation of annoyance, disgust, etc.) [ME *helle*, OE *hel(l)*, c. G *Hölle*. Cf. HALL] —**Syn.** 2. inferno, Abaddon, pandemonium, Avernus. —**Ant.** 2. paradise.

he'll (hēl; *unstressed* hĭl, ēl, ĭl), contraction of: 1. he will. 2. he shall.

Helladic (hĕ lăd'ĭk), *adj.* of or pertaining to the Bronze Age culture on the mainland of ancient Greece, *c* 2900–1100 B.C. [t. L: s. *Helladicus*, t. Gk: m. *Helladikós* of or from Greece]

Hellas (hĕl'ăs), *n.* ancient and modern Greek name of **Greece.**

hellbender (hĕl'bĕn'də), *n.* a large aquatic salamander, *Cryptobranchus alleganiensis*, of the Ohio and certain other American rivers.

Hellbender, *Cryptobranchus alleganiensis* (Length 18 in.)

hell-bent (hĕl'bĕnt'), *adj.* stubbornly or recklessly determined.

hellbox (hĕl'bŏks'), *n.* a printer's hell (def. 7).

hellbroth (hĕl'brŏth'), *n.* a magical broth prepared for an infernal purpose.

hellcat (hĕl'kăt'), *n.* 1. an evil-tempered, unmanageable woman. 2. a hag or witch.

hellebore (hĕl'ĭ bô'), *n.* 1. any plant of the ranunculaceous genus *Helleborus*, esp. *H. niger* (**black hellebore**), a European herb with showy flowers; Christmas rose. 2. any of the coarse herbs constituting the melanthaceous genus *Veratrum*, as *V. album* (**European white hellebore**). 3. the powdered root of American white hellebore, used to kill lice and caterpillars. [t. Gk: m. s. *helléboros*; r. earlier *ellebor(e)*, ME *el(l)bre*, etc., t. L: m. *elleborus*]

Hellen (hĕl'ĭn), *n. Gk Legend.* a king of Phthia (in Thessaly), eponymous ancestor of the Hellenes.

Hellene (hĕl'ēn), *n.* a Greek. [t. Gk: m. *Héllēn*]

Hellenic (hĕ lĕn'ĭk, -lē'nĭk), *adj.* 1. pertaining to the modern Greeks. 2. pertaining to the ancient Greeks, or their language, culture, etc., before the time of Alexander the Great (contrasted with *Hellenistic*). —*n.* 3. a group of Indo-European languages, including Greek. 4. Greek, especially Modern Greek.

Hellenism (hĕl'ĭ nĭz'əm), *n.* 1. ancient Greek culture or ideals. 2. the character or spirit of the Greeks. 3. adoption of Greek speech, ideas, or customs.

Hellenist (hĕl'ĭ nĭst), *n.* 1. one who adopts or adopted Greek speech, ideas, or customs. 2. one who admires or studies Greek civilization. [t. Gk: s. *Hellēnistḗs*]

Hellenistic (hĕl'ĭ nĭs'tĭk), *adj.* 1. pertaining to Hellenists. 2. following or resembling Greek usage. 3. pertaining to the Greeks or their language, culture, etc., after the time of Alexander the Great when Greek characteristics were modified by foreign elements. —**Hel'lenist'ically,** *adv.*

Hellenize (hĕl'ĭ nīz'), *v.*, **-nized, -nizing.** —*v.t.* 1. to make Greek in character. —*v.i.* 2. to adopt Greek ideas or customs. Also, **Hellenise.** [t. Gk: m. s. *Hellēnízein*] —**Hel'leniza'tion,** *n.* —**Hel'leniz'er,** *n.*

heller (hĕl'ə), *n.*, *pl.* **heller.** 1. a small German coin formerly current, generally worth half a pfennig. 2. a copper Austrian coin equal to one hundredth of a krone. 3. Czechoslovakian money of account equal to one hundredth of a koruna. [G]

Helles (hĕl'ĭs), *n.* **Cape,** a cape in European Turkey at the S end of Gallipoli Peninsula.

Hellespont (hĕl'ĭ spŏnt'), *n.* ancient name of the **Dardanelles.** [t. Gk: m. *Hellḗspontos*]

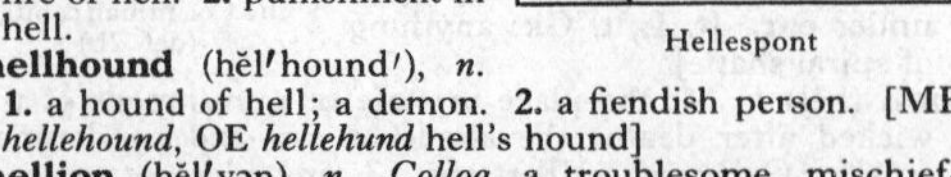

Hellespont

hellfire (hĕl'fī'ə), *n.* 1. the fire of hell. 2. punishment in hell.

hellhound (hĕl'hound'), *n.* 1. a hound of hell; a demon. 2. a fiendish person. [ME *hellehound*, OE *hellehund* hell's hound]

hellion (hĕl'yən), *n. Colloq.* a troublesome, mischief-making person. [HELL + *-ion* as in *scullion*]

hellish (hĕl'ĭsh), *adj.* 1. of, like, or befitting hell; infernal; wicked. 2. *Colloq.* extremely difficult, unpleasant, etc. —**hell'ishly,** *adv.* —**hell'ishness,** *n.*

hello (hĕ lō', hə-, hĕl'ō), *interj.*, *n.*, *pl.* **-los,** *v.*, **-loed, -loing.** —*interj.* 1. (an exclamation to attract attention, answer a telephone, or express greeting.) 2. (an exclamation of surprise, etc.) —*n.* 3. the call 'hello'. —*v.i.* 4. to call 'hello'. Also, **hallo, hullo.** [var. of HALLO]

helm[1] (hĕlm), *n.* 1. the tiller or wheel by which the rudder of a vessel is controlled. 2. the entire steering apparatus. 3. a moving of the helm. 4. the place or post of control: *the helm of affairs.* —*v.t.* 5. to steer; direct. [ME *helme*, OE *helma*; akin to MHG *helm* handle, Icel. *hjālm* rudder] —**helm'less,** *adj.*

helm[2] (hĕlm), *n.* 1. *Archaic.* a helmet. —*v.t.* 2. to furnish or cover with a helmet. [ME and OE, c. D *helm* and G *Helm.* See HELMET]

Helmand (hĕl'mənd), *n.* a river flowing from E Afghanistan SW to a lake in E Iran. ab. 650 mi.

helmet (hĕl'mĭt), *n.* 1. a defensive covering for the head: **a.** any of various forms of protective head covering worn by soldiers, firemen, divers, etc. **b.** medieval armour for the head. **c.** *Fencing, Singlestick, etc.* a protective device for the head and face consisting of reinforced wire mesh. 2. anything resembling a helmet in form or position. [ME, t. OF, dim. of *helme* helm, helmet, t. Gmc. See HELM[2]] —**hel'meted,** *adj.*

Helmets
A, Medieval; B, Modern

Helmholtz (*Ger.* hĕlm'hōlts), *n.* **Hermann Ludwig Ferdinand von** (*Ger.* hĕr'män lo͞ot'vĭKH fĕr'dĭ nänt fŏn), 1821–94, German physiologist and physicist.

helminth (hĕl'mĭnth), *n.* a worm, especially a parasitic worm. [t. Gk: s. *hélmins*] —**helminthoid** (hĕl'mĭn thoid', hĕl mĭn'thoid), *adj.*

helminthiasis (hĕl'mĭn thī'ə sĭs), *n. Pathol.* a condition characterized by worms in the body. [NL, f. s. Gk *helminthiân* suffer from worms + -(*i*)*āsis* -(I)ASIS]

helminthic (hĕl mĭn'thĭk), *adj.* 1. pertaining to worms. 2. expelling intestinal worms. Also, **helmin'thous.**

helminthoid (hĕl mĭn'thoid, hĕl'mĭn thoid'), *adj.* resembling or shaped like a helminth; vermiform.

helminthology (hĕl'mĭn thŏl'ə jĭ), *n.* the science of worms, especially of parasitic worms. —**helminthological** (hĕl'mĭn thə lŏj'ĭ kl), *adj.* —**hel'mintholog'ically,** *adv.*

helmsman (hĕlmz'mən), *n.*, *pl.* **-men.** the man at the helm who steers a ship; a steersman.

Héloïse (*Fr.* ĕ lō ēz'), *n. c.* 1100–64, pupil, mistress, and wife of Abelard, later an abbess. See **Abelard.**

helophyte (hĕl'ə fīt'), *n.* a plant growing in mud or marsh. —**helophytic** (hĕl'ə fĭt'ĭk), *adj.*

helot (hĕl'ət), *n.* 1. (*often cap.*) one of the serfs in ancient Sparta, owned by the state and under allotment to landowners. 2. a serf or slave; a bondman.

helotism (hĕl'ə tĭz'əm), *n.* serfdom. Also, **hel'otage.**

helotry (hĕl'ə trĭ), *n.* 1. serfdom; slavery. 2. helots collectively.

Helou (*Fr.* ĕ lo͞o'), *n.* **Charles** (*Fr.* shȧrl), born 1911, president of Lebanon since 1964.

help (hĕlp), *v.*, **helped** or (*Archaic*) **holp; helped** or (*Archaic*) **holpen; helping;** *n.* —*v.t.* 1. to cooperate effectively with a person; aid; assist: *to help a man in his work.* 2. to furnish aid to; contribute strength or means to; assist in doing: *remedies that help digestion.* 3. to succour; save; rescue. 4. to relieve (someone) in need, sickness, pain, or distress. 5. to refrain from; avoid (with *can* or *cannot*): *he can't help doing it.* 6. to remedy, stop, or prevent: *nothing will help now.* 7. to contribute an improvement to: *the use of a little make-up would help her appearance.* 8. to serve food to at table (fol. by *to*): *help her to salad.* 9. **help oneself (to),** to take or appropriate at will. —*v.i.* 10. to give aid; be of service or advantage: *every little helps.* 11. **help out,** to be of assistance; assist one in or as in a crisis or difficulty. —*n.* 12. the act of helping; aid or assistance; relief or succour. 13. a person or thing that helps. 14. a hired helper. 15. a body of such helpers. 16. a domestic servant or a farm labourer. 17. means of remedying, stopping, or preventing: *the thing is done, and there is no help for it now.* 18. *Rare or Dial.* a helping (def. 2). —*interj.* 19. (a call for assistance.) [ME *helpe(n)*, OE *helpen*, c. G *helfen*] —**help'able,** *adj.*

—**Syn.** 1. encourage, befriend; support, second, uphold, back, abet. HELP, AID, ASSIST, SUCCOUR agree in the idea of furnishing another with something needed, especially when the need comes at a particular time. HELP implies furnishing anything that furthers his efforts or relieves his wants or necessities. AID and ASSIST, somewhat more formal, imply especially a furthering or seconding of another's efforts. AID implies a more active helping; ASSIST implies less need and less help. To SUCCOUR is to give timely help and relief in difficulty or distress. 2. facilitate, further, promote, foster. 4. ameliorate, alleviate, remedy, cure, heal. 12. support, backing. —**Ant.** 1. hinder. 4. afflict.

helper (hĕl'pə), *n.* a person or thing that helps. —**Syn.** aid, assistant; supporter, backer, auxiliary, ally.

helpful (hĕlp′fəl), *adj.* giving or affording help; useful. —**help′fully,** *adv.* —**help′fulness,** *n.* —**Syn.** useful, convenient; beneficial, advantageous.

helping (hĕl′pĭng), *n.* **1.** the act of one who or that which helps. **2.** a portion served to a person at one time. —*adj.* **3.** giving assistance, support, etc.: *a helping hand.* —**help′ingly,** *adv.*

helpless (hĕlp′lĭs), *adj.* **1.** unable to help oneself; weak or dependent: *a helpless invalid.* **2.** without help, aid, or succour. **3.** incapable, inefficient, or shiftless. **4.** *Rare.* affording no help. —**help′lessly,** *adv.* —**help′lessness,** *n.*

Helpmann (hĕlp′mən), *n.* **Robert,** born 1909, Australian dancer, actor, and choreographer.

helpmate (hĕlp′māt′), *n.* **1.** a companion and helper. **2.** a wife or husband. [f. HELP + MATE. Cf. HELPMEET]

helpmeet (hĕlp′mēt′), *n. Archaic.* helpmate. [erroneously from Gen. 2:18, 20, 'an help meet for him']

Helsingör (*Dan.* hĕl sèng œr′), *n.* a seaport in NE Denmark, on Zealand island: the scene of Shakespeare's *Hamlet.* 29,218 (est. 1965). Also, **Elsinore.**

Helsinki (hĕl′sĭng′kĭ), *n.* a seaport in and the capital of Finland, on the S coast. 496,193 (1965). Swedish, **Helsingfors** (hĕl′sĭng fôz′).

helter-skelter (hĕl′tə skĕl′tə), *adv.* **1.** in headlong, disorderly haste: *to run helter-skelter.* —*n.* **2.** tumultuous haste or disorder. **3.** a helter-skelter flight, course, or performance. **4.** a tower with an external spiral slide, as at a fairground. —*adj.* **5.** confused; disorderly; carelessly hurried. [imit.]

helve (hĕlv), *n., v.,* **helved, helving.** —*n.* **1.** the handle of an axe, hatchet, hammer, or the like. —*v.t.* **2.** to furnish with a helve. [ME; OE *h(i)elfe*]

Helvellyn (hĕl vĕl′ĭn), *n.* a mountain in NW England, in the Lake District. 3118 ft.

Helvetia (hĕl vē′shyə), *n.* **1.** an Alpine region in Roman times, corresponding to the W and N parts of modern Switzerland. **2.** *Poetic.* Switzerland.

Helvetian (hĕl vē′shyən), *adj.* **1.** of or pertaining to Helvetia or the Helvetii. **2.** Swiss. —*n.* **3.** one of the Helvetii. **4.** a Swiss. [f. s. L *Helvētius* + -AN]

Helvetic (hĕl vĕt′ĭk), *n.* **1.** a Swiss Protestant; a Zwinglian. —*adj.* **2.** Helvetian.

Helvetii (hĕl vē′shĭ ī′), *n.pl.* the ancient inhabitants of Helvetia in the time of Julius Caesar. [L]

Helvétius (hĕl vē′shyəs; *Fr.* ĕl vė syʏs′), *n.* **Claude Adrien** (*Fr.* klōd ȧ drē ăɴ′), 1715–71, French philosopher.

hem[1] (hĕm), *v.,* **hemmed, hemming,** *n.* —*v.t.* **1.** to enclose or confine (fol. by *in, round,* or *about*): *hemmed in by enemies.* **2.** to fold back and sew down the edge of (cloth, a garment, etc.). **3.** to form an edge or border to or about. —*n.* **4.** the edge made by folding back the margin of cloth and sewing it down. **5.** the edge or border of a garment, etc., esp. at the bottom. **6.** the edge, border, or margin of anything. [ME *hemm(e),* OE *hem,* prob. akin to *hamm* enclosure]

hem[2] (hĕm), *interj., n., v.,* **hemmed, hemming.** —*interj.* **1.** (an utterance resembling a slight clearing of the throat, used to attract attention, express doubt, etc.) —*n.* **2.** the utterance or sound of 'hem'. —*v.i.* **3.** to utter the sound 'hem'. **4.** to hesitate in speaking. **5. hem and haw,** to avoid giving a direct answer. [imit.]

hem-, *Chiefly U.S.* var. of **haem-.** For words beginning in **hem-, hema-, hemo-,** see preferred spelling under **haem-, haema-, haemo-.**

he-man (hē′măn′), *n. Colloq.* a tough or aggressively masculine man.

Hemans (hĕm′ənz), *n.* **Mrs** (*Felicia Dorothea Browne*), 1793–1835, English poet.

heme (hēm), *n. Chiefly U.S.* haem.

Hemel Hempstead (hĕm′əl hĕm′stĭd), a new town in England, in Hertfordshire. 54,954 (1961).

hemelytron (hĕ mĕl′ĭ trŏn′), *n., pl.* **-tra** (-trə). *Entomol.* one of the fore wings of hemipterous and especially heteropterous insects, leathery at the base and membranous at the tip. Also, **hemielytron.** [var. of *hemielytron,* f. HEMI- + ELYTRON] —**hemel′ytral,** *adj.*

hemeralopia (hĕm′ə rə lō′pyə), *n.* day blindness.

hemi-, a prefix meaning 'half', as in *hemialgia.* Cf. **semi-.** [t. Gk]

hemialgia (hĕm′ĭ ăl′jĭ ə), *n. Pathol.* pain or neuralgia involving only one side of the body or head.

hemicellulose (hĕm′ĭ sĕl′yŏŏ lōs′), *n. Chem.* any of a group of gummy polysaccharides, intermediate in complexity between sugar and cellulose, which hydrolyse to monosaccharides more readily than cellulose.

hemichordate (hĕm′ĭ kô′dāt), *adj.* **1.** denoting or pertaining to the *Hemichordata,* a chordate subphylum that comprises a large number of small, widely distributed marine animals. —*n.* **2.** a hemichordate animal.

hemicrania (hĕm′ĭ krā′nyə), *n. Pathol. Obs.* pain in one side of the head; migraine. [t. LL, t. Gk: m. *hēmikrānia* a pain on one side of the head]

hemicycle (hĕm′ĭ sī′kl), *n.* **1.** a semicircle. **2.** a semicircular structure. [t. F, t. L: m. s. *hēmicyclium,* t. Gk: m. *hēmikýklion*] —**hem′icy′clic,** *adj.*

hemidemisemiquaver (hĕm′ĭ dĕm′ĭ sĕm′ĭ kwā′və), *n. Music.* a note having one sixty-fourth of the time value of a semibreve.

hemielytron (hĕm′ĭ ĕl′ĭ trŏn′), *n., pl.* **-tra** (-trə). hemelytron.

hemihedral (hĕm′ĭ hē′drəl), *adj.* (of a crystal) having only half the planes or faces required by the maximum symmetry of the system to which it belongs. [f. HEMI- + s. Gk *hédra* seat, base + -AL[1]] —**hem′ihe′drally,** *adv.* —**hem′ihe′drism, hem′ihe′dry,** *n.*

hemihydrate (hĕm′ĭ hī′drāt), *n. Chem.* a hydrate in which there are two molecules of the compound for each molecule of water.

hemimorphic (hĕm′ĭ mô′fĭk), *adj.* (of a crystal) having the two ends of an axis unlike in their planes or modifications; lacking a centre of symmetry. —**hem′imor′phism, hem′imor′phy,** *n.*

hemimorphite (hĕm′ĭ mô′fīt), *n.* a mineral, hydrous zinc silicate, $Zn_4Si_2O_7(OH)_2H_2O$, an ore of zinc. Also, *U.S.,* **calamine.**

Hemingway (hĕm′ĭng wā′), *n.* **Ernest,** 1898–1961, U.S. novelist and short-story writer.

hemiplegia (hĕm′ĭ plē′jĭ ə), *n. Pathol.* paralysis of one side of the body, resulting from a disease of the brain or of the spinal cord. —**hem′iple′gic,** *adj.*

hemipterous (hĭ mĭp′tə rəs), *adj.* belonging or pertaining to insects of the order *Hemiptera,* including the true bugs (*Heteroptera*), whose forewings are in part thickened and leathery, and the cicadas, leaf-hoppers, aphids, etc. (*Homoptera*) whose wings are entirely membranous. [f. HEMI- + s. Gk *pterón* wing + -OUS]

hemisphere (hĕm′ĭ sfĭə′), *n.* **1.** half of the terrestrial globe or celestial sphere. **2.** a map or projection of either of these. **3.** the half of a sphere. **4.** *Anat.* either of the lateral halves of the cerebrum. [t. L: m. s. *hēmisphaerium,* t. Gk: m. *hēmisphaírion*; r. ME *emysperie,* t. OF: m. *emispere*]

hemispherical (hĕm′ĭ sfĕ′rĭ kl), *adj.* **1.** of or pertaining to a hemisphere. **2.** in the form of a hemisphere. Also, **hem′ispher′ic.** —**hem′ispher′ically,** *adv.*

hemispheroid (hĕm′ĭ sfĭə′roid), *n.* half of a spheroid. —**hem′ispheroi′dal,** *adj.*

hemistich (hĕm′ĭ stĭk′), *n. Pros.* **1.** the exact or approximate half of a stich, or poetic verse or line, esp. as divided by a caesura or the like. **2.** an incomplete line, or a line of less than the usual length. [t. L: m. s. *hēmistichium,* t. Gk: m. *hēmistíchion*] —**hemistichal** (hĕm′ĭ stĭk′l, hĕm′ĭ stĭk′l), *adj.*

hemiterpene (hĕm′ĭ tû′pēn), *n. Chem.* one of a group of hydrocarbon isomers of the general formula C_5H_8, related to, and half the molecular weight of, the terpenes.

hemitrope (hĕm′ĭ trōp′), *adj., n. Crystall.* twin. [t. F. See HEMI-, -TROPE] —**hemitropic** (hĕm′ĭ trŏp′ĭk), *adj.*

hemline (hĕm′līn′), *n.* the bottom edge of a dress, skirt, etc.

hemlock (hĕm′lŏk′), *n.* **1.** a poisonous umbelliferous herb, *Conium maculatum,* with spotted stems, finely divided leaves, and small white flowers, used medicinally as a powerful sedative. **2.** a poisonous drink made from this herb. **3. a.** the hemlock spruce. **b.** its wood. [ME *hemeluc,* OE *hemlic, hym(e)lic(e),* ? f. *hymele* hop plant + *-k* suffix (see -OCK). Note that hemlock and hops agree in having a sedative effect]

hemlock spruce, any of the trees of the coniferous genus *Tsuga,* esp. a tree of eastern North America, *T. canadensis,* whose bark is used in tanning.

hemlock water-dropwort, a perennial umbelliferous herb, *Oenanthe crocata,* found in wet places in SW Europe, including the British Isles.

hemmer (hĕm′ə), *n.* **1.** one who or that which hems. **2.** a sewing-machine attachment for hemming edges.

hemo-, *Chiefly U.S.* var. of **haemo-.** Also, **hem-.** For words beginning in **heme-,** see preferred spelling under **haemo-.**

hemp (hĕmp), *n.* **1.** a tall, annual moraceous herb, *Cannabis sativa,* native in Asia, but cultivated in many parts of the world. **2.** the tough fibre of this plant, used for making coarse fabrics, ropes, etc. **3.** an East Indian variety, *Cannabis sativa indica* (or *Cannabis indica*), of common hemp, yielding hashish, bhang, cannabin, etc. **4.** any of various plants resembling hemp. **5.** any of various fibres similar to hemp. **6.** a narcotic drug obtained from Indian hemp. [ME; OE *henep, hænep,* c. G *Hanf,* Gk *kánnabis* CANNABIS]

hemp agrimony, a European composite herb, *Eupatorium cannabinum*, with dull purplish flowers.
hempen (hĕm′pən), *adj.* **1.** made of hemp. **2.** of or pertaining to hemp. **3.** resembling hemp.
hemp nettle, 1. a coarse labiate weed, *Galeopsis tetrahit*, likened to the hemp from its general appearance, and to the nettle from its bristly hairs. **2.** any plant of the genus *Galeopsis*.
hempseed (hĕmp′sēd′), *n.* the seed of hemp, used as a food for cagebirds.
hempy (hĕm′pĭ), *adj. Scot. and N Dial.* mischievous; roguish. [HEMP + -Y[1]; from the hempen rope by which a person was said to deserve to be hanged]
hemstitch (hĕm′stĭch′), *v.t.* **1.** to hem along a line from which threads have been drawn out, stitching the cross-threads into a series of little groups. —*n.* **2.** the stitch used or the needlework done in hemstitching. [f. HEM[1], n. + STITCH[1], v.]
hen (hĕn), *n.* **1.** the female of the domestic fowl. **2.** the female of any bird, esp. of a gallinaceous bird. **3.** *Colloq.* a woman, esp. a fussy or foolish woman. [ME and OE *hen(n)* (der. OE *hana* cock), c. G *Henne*]
hen-and-chickens (hĕn′ən chĭk′ĭnz), *n.* **1.** any of several herbs, esp. those having offshoot or runner plants growing around the parent. **2.** a species of houseleek, *Sempervivum globiferum*, native of Europe. **3.** the ground ivy, *Glecoma hederacea*.
henbane (hĕn′bān′), *n.* a solanaceous Old World herb, *Hyoscyamus niger*, bearing sticky, hairy foliage with a disagreeable smell, and yellowish brown flowers, and possessing narcotic and poisonous properties: esp. destructive to domestic fowls. [ME. See HEN, BANE]
henbit (hĕn′bĭt′), *n.* a labiate weed, *Lamium amplexicaule*, with small purplish flowers.
hence (hĕns), *adv.* **1.** as an inference from this fact; for this reason; therefore: *of the best quality and hence satisfactory.* **2.** *Archaic.* from this time onwards; henceforth. **3.** *Archaic.* at the end of a given period: *a month hence.* **4.** *Archaic.* from this source or origin. **5.** *Archaic.* from this place; away from here. —*interj.* **6.** *Archaic.* depart! [ME *hen(ne)s*, f. *hen* hence (OE *heona*, *heonan*) + -(*e*)*s*, adv. suffix]
henceforth (hĕns′fôth′), *adv.* from this time forth; from now on. Also, **henceforwards** (hĕns′fô′wədz), **henceforward.**
henchman (hĕnch′mən), *n., pl.* **-men. 1.** a trusty attendant or follower. **2.** a ruthless and unscrupulous follower. **3.** *Obs.* a squire or page. [ME *henchemanne*, *henxtman*, prob. orig. meaning groom, and appar. f. OE *hengest* stallion + *mann* man]
hendecagon (hĕn dĕk′ə gən), *n.* a polygon having eleven angles and eleven sides. [f. m. Gk *héndeka* eleven + -GON] —**hendecagonal** (hĕn′dĭ kăg′ə nəl), *adj.*
hendecahedron (hĕn′dĭ kə hĕd′rən, -hē′drən), *n.* a solid figure with eleven faces.
hendecasyllable (hĕn′dĕk ə sĭl′ə bl), *n. Pros.* a metrical line of eleven syllables. [t. L: m. *hendecasyllabus* (conformed to SYLLABLE), t. Gk: m. *hendekasýllabos*] —**hendecasyllabic** (hĕn′dek ə sĭ lăb′ĭk), *adj., n.*
Henderson (hĕn′də sən), *n.* **Arthur,** 1863–1935, British socialist and statesman.
hendiadys (hĕn dĭ′ə dĭs), *n. Rhet.* a figure in which a complex idea is expressed by two words connected by a copulative conjunction: 'to look with eyes and envy' instead of 'with envious eyes'. [t. LL, der. Gk phrase *hèn dià dyoîn* one through two]
Hendon (hĕn′dən), *n.* a district in the NW outer London borough of Barnet.
henequen (hĕn′ĭ kĭn), *n.* the fibre of an agave, *Agave fourcroydes*, of Yucatan, used for making ropes, coarse fabrics, etc. Also, **henequin.** [t. Sp.: m. *jeniquén*; from native name]
henfish (hĕn′fĭsh′), *n.* the lumpsucker.
Hengelo (*Du.* hĕng′ə lō), *n.* a town in E Netherlands, in Overijssel. 65,932 (1965).
Hengist (hĕng′gĭst), *n.* died A.D. 488, chief of the Jutes; joint founder with Horsa of the English kingdom of Kent.
henhouse (hĕn′hous′), *n.* a coop for hens or other fowl.
Henley (hĕn′lĭ), *n.* **William Ernest,** 1849–1903, English poet, critic, and editor.
Henley-on-Thames (hĕn′lĭ ŏn tĕmz′), *n.* a municipal borough in SE Oxfordshire, on the Thames: annual regatta. 9131 (1961).
henna (hĕn′ə), *n.* **1.** a shrub or small tree, *Lawsonia inermis*, of Asia and the Levant. **2.** a reddish orange dye or cosmetic made from the leaves of this plant. **3.** reddish or orange-brown. —*v.t.* **4.** to tint or dye with henna. [t. Ar.: m. *ḥinnā'*]
hennery (hĕn′ə rĭ), *n., pl.* **-neries.** a place where domestic fowls are kept.
henotheism (hĕn′ō thē ĭz′əm), *n.* **1.** the worship of one particular divinity among others existent, in contrast with *monotheism*, which teaches that there exists only one God. **2.** ascription of supreme divine attributes to whichever one of several gods is at the time addressed. [f. *heno-* (comb. form repr. Gk neut. *hén* one) + THEISM] —**hen′otheist,** *n.* —**hen′otheis′tic,** *adj.*
hen party, a party exclusively for women (opposed to *stag party*).
henpeck (hĕn′pĕk′), *v.t.* (of a wife) to domineer over (her husband). —**hen′pecked′,** *adj.*
henrun (hĕn′rŭn′), *n.* an enclosure for domestic fowls.
henry (hĕn′rĭ), *n., pl.* **-rys.** *Elect.* the derived SI unit of inductance, equivalent to the inductance of a circuit in which an electromotive force of one volt is produced by a current in the circuit which varies at the rate of one ampere per second. *Symbol:* H [named after Joseph HENRY]
Henry (hĕn′rĭ), *n.* **1. Joseph,** 1797–1878, U.S. physicist. **2. O.** (*William Sidney Porter*), 1862–1910, U.S. short-story writer. **3. Patrick,** 1736–99, American patriot, orator, and statesman.
Henry I, 1. 1068–1135, king of England 1100–35 (brother of William II). **2.** 1008?–1060, king of France 1031–60.
Henry II, 1. (*of Anjou*) 1133–89, king of England 1154–89 (successor of Stephen and 1st king of Plantagenet line). **2.** 1519–59, king of France 1547–59.
Henry III, 1. (*of Winchester*) 1207–72, king of England 1216–72 (son of John). **2.** 1551–89, king of France 1574–89.
Henry IV, 1. 1050–1106, emperor of Holy Roman Empire 1056–1106. **2.** (*Bolingbroke*), 1367–1413, king of England 1399–1413 (successor of Richard II, son of John of Gaunt, and 1st king of house of Lancaster). **3.** (*of Navarre*) 1553–1610, king of France 1589–1610.
Henry V, (*of Monmouth*), 1387–1422, king of England 1413–22 (son of Henry IV).
Henry VI, 1421–71, king of England 1422–61 and 1470–71 (son of Henry V).
Henry VII, 1457–1509, king of England 1485–1509 (successor of Richard III and 1st king of house of Tudor).
Henry VIII, 1491–1547, king of England 1509–47, and of Ireland 1541–47 (son of Henry VII).
Henry of Portugal ('*the Navigator*'), 1394–1460, prince of Portugal, promoter of geographic exploration.
Henry's law, *Physics.* the principle that the weight of a gas dissolved by a given volume of liquid at constant temperature is directly proportional to the pressure of the gas. [named after William *Henry*, 1774–1836, English chemist]
Henslowe (hĕnz′lō), *n.* **Philip,** died 1616, English theatre manager.
Henty (hĕn′tĭ), *n.* **George Alfred,** 1832–1902, English author of boys' stories.
Henze (*Ger.* hĕnt′sə), *n.* **Hans Werner** (*Ger.* häns vĕr′nər), born 1926, German composer.
hep (hĕp), *adj. U.S. Slang.* having inside knowledge, or being informed of current styles, esp. in jazz (often fol. by *to*): *to be hep to swing music.*
heparin (hĕp′ə rĭn), *n. Biochem., Med.* a polysaccharide containing sulphate groups produced in the liver which prevents the coagulation of the blood, and is used in the treatment of thrombosis. [f. Gk *hêpar* + -IN[2]]
hepatic (hĭ păt′ĭk), *adj.* **1.** of or pertaining to the liver. **2.** acting on the liver, as a medicine. **3.** liver-coloured; dark reddish brown. **4.** *Bot.* belonging or pertaining to the liverworts. —*n.* **5.** a medicine acting on the liver. **6.** a liverwort. [t. L: s. *hēpaticus*, t. Gk: m. *hēpatikós* of the liver]
hepatica (hĭ păt′ĭ kə), *n., pl.* **-ces, -cae** (-sē′). any of the ranunculaceous herbs, with three-lobed leaves and delicate purplish, pink, or white flowers constituting the genus *Hepatica*. [NL, prop. fem. of L *hēpaticus* HEPATIC]
hepatitis (hĕp′ə tī′tĭs), *n. Pathol.* inflammation of the liver. [NL, f. s. Gk *hêpar* liver + *-ītis* -ITIS]
hepatize (hĕp′ə tīz′), *v.t.,* **-tized, -tizing.** *Pathol.* to convert (a lung, etc.) into liver-like tissue by engorgement. Also, **hepatise.** —**hep′atiza′tion,** *n.*
hepcat (hĕp′kăt′), *n. Jazz Slang.* an expert performer, or a knowing admirer, of jazz.
Hephaestus (hĭ fēs′təs), *n. Gk Myth.* the god of fire and metalworking. [t. Gk: m. *Hḗphaistos*]
Hepplewhite (hĕp′l wīt′), *n.* **1. George,** died 1786, English furniture designer and cabinet-maker. —*adj.* **2.** in the style of Hepplewhite.
hepta-, a prefix meaning 'seven'. Also, before vowels, **hept-.** [t. Gk, comb. form of *heptá*]
heptad (hĕp′tăd), *n.* **1.** the number seven. **2.** a group of seven. **3.** *Chem.* an element, atom, or radical having a valency of seven. [t. LL: s. *heptas*, t. Gk: seven]

heptagon (hĕp′tə gən), *n.* a polygon having seven angles and seven sides. [t. Gk: s. *heptágōnos* seven-cornered] —**heptagonal** (hĕp tăg′ə nəl), *adj.*

heptahedron (hĕp′tə hē′drən), *n., pl.* **-drons, -dra** (-drə). a solid figure having seven faces. —**hep′tahe′dral,** *adj.*

Regular Irregular
Heptagons

heptamerous (hĕp tăm′ə rəs), *adj.* **1.** consisting of or divided into seven parts. **2.** *Bot.* (of flowers) having seven members in each whorl.

heptameter (hĕp tăm′ĭ tə), *n. Pros.* a verse of seven metrical feet. [t. LL: m. *heptametrum,* t. Gk: m. *heptámetron*] —**heptametrical** (hĕp′tə mĕt′rĭ kl), *adj.*

heptane (hĕp′tān), *n. Chem.* any of nine isomeric hydrocarbons, C_7H_{16}, of the methane series, some of which are obtained from petroleum: used in fuels, as solvents, and as chemical intermediates.

heptangular (hĕp tăng′gyo͝o lə), *adj.* having seven angles.

heptarchy (hăp′tä′kĭ), *n., pl.* **-chies. 1.** a government by seven persons. **2.** a group of seven states or kingdoms, each under its own ruler. **3.** (*often cap.*) the seven principal concurrent early English kingdoms. [f. HEPT- + -ARCHY] —**hep′tarch,** *n.* —**heptar′chic,** *adj.*

heptastich (hĕp′tə stĭk′), *n. Pros.* a strophe, stanza, or poem consisting of seven lines or verses. [f. HEPTA- + s. Gk *stichos* row, line]

Heptateuch (hĕp′tə tyo͞ok′), *n.* the first seven books of the Old Testament. [t. LL: s. *Heptateuchos,* t. Gk: seven-volume (work)]

heptavalent (hĕp tăv′ə lənt, hĕp′tə vā′lənt), *adj. Chem.* having a valency of seven; septivalent.

heptose (hĕp′tōs, -tōz), *n. Chem.* any of a group of monosaccharides which contain seven oxygen atoms.

Hepworth (hĕp′wəth), *n.* **Barbara,** born 1903, English abstract sculptor.

her (hû; *unstressed* hə, ə), *pron.* **1.** the objective case of *she.* —*adj.* **2.** the possessive form of *she,* used before a noun (cf. **hers**). **3.** of, belonging to, or having to do with a female person or personified thing. [ME *her(e),* OE *hire,* gen. and dat. of *hēo* she (fem. of *hē* he)]

her., 1. heraldic. **2.** heraldry.

Hera (hĭə′rə), *n. Gk Myth.* a goddess, wife and sister of Zeus and queen of heaven. Also, **Here.** [t. L, t. Gk]

Heraclea (hĕ′rə klē′ə), *n.* an ancient city in S Italy, near the Gulf of Taranto: Roman defeat, 280 B.C.

Heracles (hĕ′rə klēz′), *n.* Greek name of **Hercules.** Also, **Herakles.** —**Her′acle′an,** *adj.*

Heraclid (hĕ′rə klĭd), *n., pl.* **Heraclidae** (hĕ′rə klī′dē). a descendant of Hercules, esp. one of the Dorian aristocracy of Sparta, who claimed descent from him. Also, **Heraklid.** —**Heraclidan** (hĕ′rə klī′dn), *adj.*

Heraclitean (hĕ′rə klī′tĭ ən), *adj.* **1.** of or pertaining to the philosophy of Heraclitus (**Heracliteanism**), holding that all things are perpetually changing, according to an established and unchanging principle, the logos. —*n.* **2.** an adherent of Heraclitean philosophy.

Heraclitus (hĕ′rə klī′təs), *n.* (*'the Weeping Philosopher'*), *c.* 535–*c.* 475 B.C., Greek philosopher.

Heraclius (hĕ′rə klī′əs), *n.* A.D. *c.* 575–641, Byzantine emperor A.D. 610–641.

Herakleion (hĭ răk′lĭ ŏn′), *n.* Greek name of **Candia.**

herald (hĕ′rəld), *n.* **1.** a messenger; forerunner or harbinger. **2.** one who proclaims or announces (often used as the name of a newspaper). **3.** a royal or official proclaimer or messenger. **4.** an officer who arranged tournaments and other medieval functions, announced challenges, marshalled combatants, etc., later employed also to arrange tourneys, processions, funerals, etc., and to regulate the use of armorial bearings. —*v.t.* **5.** to give tidings of; proclaim. **6.** to usher in. [t. ML: s. *heraldus* (of Gmc orig.): r. ME *heraud,* t. OF: m. *herau(l)t*]

heraldic (hĕ răl′dĭk), *adj.* of or pertaining to heralds or heraldry. —**heral′dically,** *adv.*

heraldry (hĕ′rəl drĭ), *n., pl.* **-dries. 1.** the science of armorial bearings. **2.** the art of blazoning armorial bearings, of settling the right of persons to bear arms or to use certain bearings, of tracing and recording genealogies, of recording honours, and of deciding questions of precedence. **3.** the office or duty of a herald. **4.** a heraldic device, or a collection of such devices. **5.** a coat of arms; armorial bearings. **6.** heraldic symbolism. **7.** heraldic pomp or ceremony.

Heralds' College, College of Arms.

herald snake, a nocturnal African snake, *Leptodira hotanbaeia,* of the family *Colubridae,* olive-brown in colour, with a bright red upper lip.

Herat (hĕ răt′), *n.* a city in NW Afghanistan. 62,000 (1964).

Hérault (*Fr.* ė rō′), *n.* a department in S France. 516,658 pop. (1962); 2403 sq. mi. *Cap.:* Montpellier.

herb (hûb), *n.* **1.** a flowering plant whose stem above ground does not become woody and persistent. **2.** such a plant when valued for its medicinal properties, flavour, scent, or the like. **3.** *Rare.* herbage. [ME *(h)erbe,* t. F, g. L *herba* vegetation, grass, herb] —**herb′less,** *adj.* —**herb′like′,** *adj.*

herbaceous (hû bā′shəs), *adj.* **1.** of, pertaining to, or of the nature of a herb; herblike. **2.** (of plants or plant parts) not woody. **3.** (of flowers, sepals, etc.) having the texture, colour, etc., of an ordinary foliage leaf.

herbage (hû′bĭj), *n.* **1.** non-woody vegetation. **2.** the succulent parts (leaves and stems) of herbaceous plants. **3.** vegetation grazed by animals; pasturage. [ME, t. F, der. *herbe* grass. See HERB]

herbal (hû′bl), *adj.* **1.** of, pertaining to, or consisting of herbs. —*n.* **2.** a treatise on herbs or plants. **3.** a herbarium.

herbalist (hû′bə lĭst), *n.* **1.** one who collects or deals in herbs, esp. medicinal herbs. **2.** one who heals by the use of medicinal herbs. **3.** (formerly) an expert in herbs or plants.

herbarium (hû bĕə′rĭ əm), *n., pl.* **-bariums, -baria** (-bĕə′rĭ ə). **1.** a collection of dried plants systematically arranged. **2.** a room or building in which a herbarium is kept. Also, **herb′ary.** [t. LL, der. L *herba* HERB. Cf. ARBOUR]

Herbart (*Ger.* hĕr′bärt), *n.* **Johann Friedrich** (*Ger.* yō′hän frē′drĭKH), 1776–1841, German philosopher.

Herbartian (hû bä′tĭ ən), *adj.* **1.** of or pertaining to Herbart's system of philosophy. —*n.* **2.** one who accepts the doctrines of Herbart. —**Herbar′tianism,** *n.*

herb bennet, 1. a European perennial rosaceous herb, *Geum urbanum,* having yellow flowers and an aromatic, tonic, and astringent root. **2.** any avens. [ME *herbe beneit,* prob. t. OF: m. *herbe beneite,* trans. of ML *herba benedicta* blessed herb]

herb Christopher, the baneberry, *Actaea spicata.*

Herbert (hû′bət), *n.* **George,** 1593–1633, English poet.

herb Gerard, the bishop's weed, *Aegopodium podagraria.*

herbivore (hû′bĭ vô′), *n.* a herbivorous animal.

herbivorous (hû bĭv′ə rəs), *adj.* feeding on plants. [t. NL: m. *herbivorus* herb-eating. See HERB, -VOROUS]

herb Paris, a European liliaceous herb, *Paris quadrifolia,* formerly used in medicine.

herb Peter, the cowslip.

herb Robert, a species of geranium, *Geranium robertianum,* with reddish purple flowers.

herby (hû′bĭ), *adj.* **1.** abounding in herbs or grass. **2.** pertaining to or like herbs.

Hercegovina (*Serb.* hĕr′tsĕ gôv ē nä), *n.* Serbo-Croat name of **Herzegovina.**

Herculaneum (hû′kyo͝o lā′nyəm), *n.* a buried city at the foot of Mt Vesuvius, in SW Italy: destroyed together with Pompeii by an eruption, A.D. 79.

herculean (hû′kyo͝o lē′ən), *adj.* **1.** requiring the strength of a Hercules; very hard to perform: *a herculean task.* **2.** prodigious in strength, courage, or size. **3.** (*cap.*) of or relating to Hercules.

Hercules (hû′kyo͝o lēz′), *n.* Also, **Alcides. 1.** Also, *Greek,* **Heracles, Herakles.** *Class. Myth.* a celebrated hero of great strength and courage who performed twelve extraordinary tasks. **2.** a northern constellation, between Lyra and Corona Borealis. [t. L, t. Gk: m. *Hēraklês,* lit., having the glory of Hera]

Hercules'-club (hû′kyo͝o lēz klŭb′), *n.* **1.** a prickly rutaceous tree of N America, *Zanthoxylum clava-herculis,* with a medicinal bark and berries. **2.** a prickly araliaceous shrub of N America, *Aralia spinosa,* with medicinal bark and root.

Hercules' Pillars. See **Pillars of Hercules.**

Hercynian (hû sĭn′ĭ ən), *n.* Armorican.

herd¹ (hûd), *n.* **1.** a number of animals, esp. cattle, kept, feeding, or travelling together; drove; flock. **2.** a large company of people (now in a disparaging sense). **3. the herd,** the common people; the rabble. —*v.i.* **4.** to unite or go in a herd; to assemble or associate as a herd. —*v.t.* **5.** to form into or as if into a herd. [ME; OE *heord,* c. G *Herde*] —**Syn. 1.** See **flock¹**.

herd² (hûd), *n.* **1.** a herdsman (usually in combination): *cowherd.* —*v.t.* **2.** to tend, drive, or lead a herd of cattle, sheep, etc. [ME; OE *hierde,* c. G *Hirte*; der. Gmc stem represented by HERD¹]

herder (hû′də), *n. U.S.* a herdsman.

Herder (*Ger.* hĕr′dər), *n.* **Johann Gottfried von** (*Ger.* yō′hän gŏt′frēt fŏn), 1744–1803, German philosopher and poet.

herdic (hû′dĭk), *n. U.S.* a low-hung carriage with two or four wheels, having the entrance at the back and the seats at the side. [named after P. *Herdic,* the inventor]

herd instinct, the instinct which urges men or animals to cluster or act in a group, to conform, or follow the herd.

herdsman (hûdz′mən), *n., pl.* **-men. 1.** the keeper of a herd. **2.** (*cap.*) *Astron.* the northern constellation Boötes.

Herdwick (häd′wĭk), *n.* one of a hardy breed of mountain sheep, originating in the English Lake District, the lambs of which are born black.

here (hĭə), *adv.* **1.** in this place; in this spot or locality (opposed to *there*): *put it here.* **2.** to or towards this place; hither: *come here.* **3.** at this point; at this juncture: *here the speaker paused.* **4.** (often used in pointing out or emphasizing some person or thing present): *my friend here knows the circumstances.* **5.** present (used in answer to rollcall, etc.). **6.** in the present life or state. **7.** Some special adverb phrases are:
here and now, at this very moment; immediately.
here and there, 1. in this place and in that; in various places; at intervals. **2.** hither and thither; to and fro.
here goes!, (an exclamation to show one's resolution on beginning some bold or unpleasant act.)
here's to, a formula in offering a toast: *here's to you!*
here we (or **you**) **are,** *Colloq.* here is what we (or you) want, or are looking for.
neither here nor there, irrelevant; unimportant.
—*n.* **8.** this place. **9.** this world; this life. **10. here and now, a.** the immediate present. **b.** this world; this life. [ME; OE *hēr*, c. D and G *hier*, Icel. and Goth. *hēr*; from the demonstrative stem represented by HE]

Here (hĭə′rĭ), *n.* Hera.

here-, a word element meaning 'this (place)', 'this (time)', etc., used in combination with certain adverbs and prepositions. [special use of HERE]

hereabout (hĭə′rə bout′), *adv.* about this place; in this neighbourhood. Also, **hereabouts.**

hereafter (hĭər äf′tə), *adv.* **1.** after this in time or order; at some future time. **2.** in the world to come. —*n.* **3.** a future life; the world to come. **4.** time to come; the future. [ME *hereafter*, OE *hērӕfter*, f. *hēr* HERE + *ӕfter* AFTER]

hereat (hĭər ăt′), *adv.* **1.** at this time; when this happened. **2.** by reason of this; because of this.

hereby (hĭə bī′), *adv.* **1.** by this; by means of this; as a result of this. **2.** *Archaic.* nearby.

hereditable (hĭ rĕd′ĭ tə bl), *adj.* heritable. [t. F (obs.), der. LL *hērēditāre* inherit, der. L *hēres* heir] —**hered′itabil′ity,** *n.* —**hered′itably,** *adv.*

hereditament (hĕ′rĭ dĭt′ə mənt), *n. Law.* any inheritable estate or interest in property. [t. ML: s. *hērēditāmentum*, der. LL *hērēditāre.* See HEREDITABLE]

hereditary (hĭ rĕd′ĭ tə rĭ, -trĭ), *adj.* **1.** passing, or capable of passing, naturally from parents to offspring: *hereditary traits.* **2.** pertaining to inheritance or heredity: *hereditary descent.* **3.** being such through feelings, etc., derived from predecessors: *a hereditary enemy.* **4.** *Law.* **a.** descending by inheritance. **b.** transmitted or transmissible in the line of descent by force of law. **c.** holding a title, etc., by inheritance: *a hereditary proprietor.* [t. L: m. s. *hērēditārius* of an inheritance] —**hered′itarily,** *adv.* —**hered′itariness,** *n.*

heredity (hĭ rĕd′ĭ tĭ), *n., pl.* **-ties. 1.** *Biol.* the transmission of genetic characteristics from parents to progeny; the factor which determines the extent to which an individual resembles his or its progenitors, dependent upon the separation and regrouping of genes during meiosis and fertilization. **2.** the genetic characteristics transmitted to an individual by its parents. [t. L: m. s. *hērēditas* heirship, inheritance]

Hereford (hĕ′rĭ fəd), *n.* **1.** one of a highly productive, hardy, early maturing breed of beef cattle originating in Herefordshire, characterized by a red body, white face, and other white markings. **2.** a cathedral city in W England, county town of Herefordshire. 41,300 (est. 1962). **3.** Herefordshire.

Herefordshire (hĕ′rĭ fəd shĭə′, -shə), *n.* a county in W England. 130,919 pop. (1961); 842 sq. mi. *Co. town:* Hereford. Also, **Hereford.**

Herefs., Herefordshire.

herein (hĭər ĭn′), *adv.* **1.** in or into this place. **2.** in this fact, circumstance, etc.; in view of this. [ME and OE *hērinne*, f. *hēr* HERE + *inne* IN, adv.]

hereinafter (hĭə′rĭn äf′tə), *adv.* afterwards in this document, statement, etc.

hereinbefore (hĭə′rĭn bĭ fô′), *adv.* before in this document, statement, etc.

hereinto (hĭər ĭn′too͞), *adv.* **1.** into this place. **2.** into this matter or affair.

hereof (hĭər ŏv′), *adv.* **1.** of this: *upon the receipt hereof.* **2.** concerning this: more hereof later.

hereon (hĭər ŏn′), *adv.* hereupon.

Herero (hĭə′rə rō′, hə rĭə′rō), *n., pl.* **-ros,** (*esp. collectively*) **-ro. 1.** a member of a people of South-West Africa of no certainly known affinity. **2.** their language. —*adj.* **3.** of or pertaining to this people or their language.

heres (hĭə′rēz), *n., pl.* **heredes** (hĭ rē′dēz). *Civil Law.* an heir. Also, **haeres.** [L]

heresiarch (hĭ rē′zĭ äk′), *n.* a leader in heresy; the chief of a heretical sect. [t. LL: m. s. *haeresiarcha*, t. Gk: m. *hairesiárchēs* leader of a school]

heresy (hĕ′rə sĭ), *n., pl.* **-sies. 1.** doctrine contrary to the orthodox or accepted doctrine of a church or religious system. **2.** the maintaining of such an opinion or doctrine. [ME (*h*)*eresie*, t. OF, der. L *haeresis*, t. Gk: m. *haíresis* a taking, choice]

heretic (hĕ′rə tĭk), *n.* **1.** a professed believer who maintains religious opinions contrary to those accepted by his church or rejects doctrines prescribed by his church. —*adj.* **2.** heretical. [ME *heretyke*, t. F: m. *hérétique*, t. LL: m. s. *haereticus*, adj., n., t. Gk: m. *hairetikós* heretical, able to choose]

heretical (hĭ rĕt′ĭ kl), *adj.* of, pertaining to, or like heretics or heresy. —**heret′ically,** *adv.*

hereto (hĭə too͞′), *adv.* to this place, thing, document, circumstance, proposition, etc.: *attached hereto.*

heretofore (hĭə′too͞ fô′), *adv.* before this time.

hereunder (hĭər ŭn′də), *adv.* **1.** under this; subsequently set down. **2.** under authority of this.

hereunto (hĭə′rŭn too͞′), *adv.* hereto.

hereupon (hĭə′rə pŏn′), *adv.* upon this; following immediately upon this.

Hereward (hĕ′rĭ wəd), *n.* ('*the Wake*') Anglo-Saxon defender of the Isle of Ely and Fens against William the Conqueror, 1070–71: an English folk hero.

herewith (hĭə wĭth′, -wĭth′), *adv.* **1.** together with this. **2.** by means of this.

Herford (*Ger.* hĕr′fôrt), *n.* a town in West Germany, in NE North Rhine-Westphalia. 55,400 (est. 1966).

Hering (*Ger.* hė′rĭng), *n.* **Ewald** (*Ger.* ė′vält), 1834–1918, German physiologist and psychologist.

heriot (hĕ′rĭ ət), *n. Eng. Hist., Law.* a feudal service or tribute, orig. of military equipment, etc., due to the lord of a manor on a tenant's death. [ME; OE *heregeatwa* war gear, f. *here* army + *geatwa*, pl., equipment]

heritable (hĕ′rĭ tə bl), *adj.* **1.** capable of being inherited; inheritable; hereditary. **2.** capable of inheriting. [ME, t. OF, der. *heriter.* See HERITAGE] —**her′itabil′ity,** *n.* —**her′itably,** *adv.*

heritage (hĕ′rĭ tĭj), *n.* **1.** that which comes or belongs to one by reason of birth; an inherited lot or portion. **2.** something reserved for one: *the heritage of the righteous.* **3.** *Law.* **a.** that which has been or may be inherited by legal descent or succession. **b.** any property, esp. land, that devolves by right of inheritance. **4.** *Bible.* God's chosen people; the Israelites. [ME (*h*)*eritage*, t. OF, der. *heriter* inherit, g. LL *hērēditāre*] —**Syn. 1.** See **inheritance.**

heritance (hĕ′rĭ təns), *n. Archaic.* inheritance.

heritor (hĕ′rĭ tə), *n.* **1.** *Scot.* a landholder in a parish. **2.** *Archaic.* inheritor. [ME *heriter*, t. AF, g. L *hērēditārius* HEREDITARY] —**heritress** (hĕ′rĭ trĭs), *n. fem.*

herl (hûl), *n.* **1.** a barb, or the barbs, of a feather, much used in dressing anglers' flies. **2.** a fly so dressed. Also, **harl.** [ME *herle, harle*, t. MLG: fibre]

herm (hûm), *n.* a kind of monument or statue, common in ancient Athens, consisting of a head, usually that of the god Hermes, supported on a quadrangular pillar corresponding roughly in mass to the absent body. Also, **herma, hermes.**

Herm (Upper part of a double herm)

herma (hû′mə), *n., pl.* **-mae** (-mē), **-mai** (-mī). herm. [t. L, also *Hermēs*, t. Gk]

hermaphrodite (hû măf′rə dīt′), *n.* **1.** an animal or a flower having normally both the male and the female organs of generation. **2.** a person or thing in which two opposite qualities are combined. —*adj.* **3.** of or like a hermaphrodite. **4.** combining two opposite qualities. **5.** *Bot.* monoclinous. [ME, t. L: m. s. *hermaphrodītus*, t. Gk: m. *hermaphróditos.* As proper name, son of Hermes and Aphrodite, who became united in body with the nymph Salmacis while bathing in her fountain] —**hermaphroditic** (hû măf′rə dĭt′ĭk), **hermaph′rodit′ical,** *adj.* —**hermaph′rodit′ically,** *adv.*

hermaphrodite brig, (formerly) a brigantine.

hermaphroditism (hû măf′rə dī tĭz′əm), *n.* the condition of a hermaphrodite.

hermeneutic (hû′mĭ nyoo͞′tĭk), *adj.* interpretative; explanatory. Also, **her′meneu′tical.** [t. Gk: m. s. *hermēneutikós* of interpreting] —**her′meneu′tically,** *adv.* —**her′meneu′tist,** *n.*

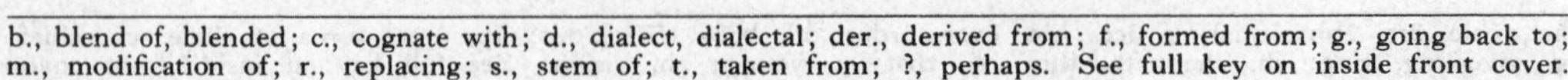

hermeneutics (hûʹmĭ nyo͞oʹtĭks), *n.* **1.** the science of interpretation, esp. of the Scriptures. **2.** that branch of theology which treats of the principles of biblical exegesis.

Hermes (hûʹmēz), *n., pl.* (def. 2) **-mae** (-mē), **-mai** (-mī). **1.** *Gk Myth.* a deity, herald and messenger of the gods, and god of roads, commerce, invention, cunning, and theft. **2.** (*l.c.*) *Gk Antiq.* herm.

Hermes Trismegistus (trĭsʹmə jĭsʹtəs), a name given by neoplatonists and others to the Egyptian god Thoth, who was to some extent identified with the Grecian Hermes, and to whom were attributed various works embodying mystical, theosophical, astrological, and alchemical doctrines. [t. Gk: m. *Hermês trismégistos* thrice greatest Hermes]

hermetic (hû mĕtʹĭk), *adj.* **1.** made airtight by fusion or sealing. **2.** pertaining to occult science, esp. alchemy. **3.** (*cap.*) of Hermes Trismegistus or the writings, etc., ascribed to him. Also, **hermetʹical.** [t. ML: s. *hermēticus*, der. L *Hermēs*, t. Gk]

hermetically (hû mĕtʹĭ kə lĭ), *adv.* so as to be airtight: *hermetically sealed.*

Hermione (hû mīʹə nĭ), *n. Class. Legend.* the daughter of Menelaus and Helen: wife of Orestes.

hermit (hûʹmĭt), *n.* **1.** one who has retired to a solitary place for a life of religious seclusion. **2.** any person living in seclusion. **3.** *Zool.* an animal of solitary habits. **4.** *Obs.* a beadsman. [ME (*h*)*ermite*, t. OF, t. LL: m. *erēmita*, t. Gk: m. *erēmítēs* a hermit, prop. adj., of the desert] **—hermitʹic, hermitʹical,** *adj.* **—hermitʹically,** *adv.* **—herʹmit-likeʹ,** *adj.*

hermitage (hûʹmĭ tĭj), *n.* **1.** the abode of a hermit. **2.** any secluded habitation. **3.** (*cap.*) a full-bodied wine produced in SE France. **4.** (*cap.*) an art museum in Leningrad; orig. a palace, built by Catherine the Great.

hermit crab, any of numerous decapod crustaceans of the genera *Pagurus, Eupagurus*, etc., which protect their exposed soft parts by occupying the cast-off shell of a univalve mollusc.

hermit sheep, *N.Z.* a sheep that leaves the flock and wanders in inaccessible mountain country.

Hermon (hûʹmən), *n.* **Mount,** a mountain in SW Syria, in the Anti-Lebanon range. ab. 9200 ft.

Hermosillo (*Sp.* ĕr mȯ sēʹlyȧ), *n.* a town in NW Mexico. 143,215 (est. 1965).

hern[1] (hûn), *n. Archaic or Dial.* heron.

hern[2] (hûn), *pron. Dial.* hers. [ME *hiren.* Cf. *my, mine; thy, thine*]

Herne (*Ger.* hĕrʹnə), *n.* a town in West Germany, in central North Rhine-Westphalia. 107,100 (est. 1966).

Herne Bay (hûn), a town in England, in NE Kent: seaside resort. 21,273 (1961).

hernia (hûʹnyə), *n., pl.* **-nias.** *Pathol.* the protrusion of an organ or tissue through an opening in its surrounding tissues, esp. in the abdominal region; a rupture. [ME, t. L] **—herʹnial,** *adj.*

herniorrhaphy (hûʹnĭ ŏʹrə fĭ), *n., pl.* **-phies.** *Surg.* the operation for repair of a hernia.

hernshaw (hûnʹshô), *n. Dial.* a heron, esp. a young heron.

hero (hĭəʹrō), *n., pl.* **-roes.** **1.** a man of distinguished courage or performance, admired for his noble qualities. **2.** one invested with heroic qualities in the opinion of others. **3.** the principal male character in a story, play, etc. **4.** (in early mythological antiquity) a being of godlike prowess and beneficence, esp. one who came to be honoured as a divinity. **5.** (in the Homeric period) a warrior chieftain of special strength, courage, or ability. **6.** (in later periods of antiquity) an immortal being intermediate in nature between gods and men. [back-formation from ME *heroës*, pl., t. L, t. Gk]

Hero (hĭəʹrō), *n.* fl. 1st cent. A.D. or earlier, Greek mathematician and scientist, of Alexandria. Also, **Heron.**

Hero and Leander (lĭ ănʹdə), *Gk Legend.* two lovers in a late Greek poem. Leander, a youth of Abydos, swam the Hellespont nightly to visit Hero. On a stormy night the guiding lamp in her tower at Sestos was extinguished and he was drowned. Hero, finding his body, hurled herself to the rocks beside it.

Herod (hĕʹrəd), *n.* (*the Great*) died 4 B.C., king of the Jews from 37 to 4 B.C.

Herod Agrippa (ə grĭpʹə), 10 B.C.–A.D. 44, king of Judea A.D. 41–44.

Herod Antipas (ănʹtĭ păsʹ), died after A.D. 39, ruler of Galilee A.D. 4–39; executed John the Baptist and presided at the trial of Jesus.

Herodian (hĕ rōʹdyən), *adj.* **1.** pertaining to Herod the Great, his family, or its partisans. **—***n.* **2.** a partisan of Herod the Great.

Herodias (hĕ rōʹdĭ ăsʹ), *n. Bible.* the wife of Herod Antipas and mother of Salome. She was responsible for the death of John the Baptist. See **Salome.**

Herodotus (hĕ rŏdʹə təs), *n.* 484?–425? B.C., Greek historian.

heroic (hĭ rōʹĭk), *adj.* Also, **heroʹical.** **1.** of or pertaining to heroes. **2.** suitable to the character of a hero; daring; noble. **3.** having or displaying the character or attributes of a hero; intrepid; determined: *a heroic explorer.* **4.** having or involving recourse to bold, daring, or extreme measures. **5.** dealing with or applicable to heroes, as in literature. **6.** of or pertaining to the heroes of antiquity: *the heroic age.* **7.** used in heroic poetry. See **heroic verse.** **8.** resembling heroic poetry in language or style; magniloquent; grand. **9.** (of style or language) high-flown; heightened; extravagant. **10.** *Arts.* of a size larger than life and (usually) less than colossal. **—***n.* **11.** (*usually pl.*) heroic verse. **12.** (*pl.*) extravagant language or sentiment. **—heroʹically,** *adv.* **—heroʹicalness, heroʹicness,** *n.* **—Syn.** **1.** intrepid, valiant, dauntless, gallant. **—Ant.** **1.** cowardly.

heroic age, the time when the heroes of Greek antiquity are supposed to have lived.

heroic couplet, *Eng. Pros.* a pair of rhyming iambic lines of ten syllables, used in heroic verse.

heroic verse, a form of verse adapted to the treatment of heroic or exalted themes: in classical poetry, the hexameter; in English, German, and Italian, the iambic of ten syllables; and in French, the Alexandrine (which see). The following is an example of English heroic verse:

Achilles' wrath, to Greece the direful spring
Of woes unnumbered, heavenly goddess, sing!

heroin (hĕʹrō ĭn), *n. Pharm.* **1.** a derivative of morphine, $C_{21}H_{23}NO_5$, formerly used as a sedative, etc., and constituting a dangerous addictive drug; diamorphine. **2.** (*cap.*) a trademark for this drug. [t. G, f. Gk *hḗrō*(*s*) HERO + *-in* -IN[2]]

heroine (hĕʹrō ĭn), *n.* **1.** a woman of heroic character; a female hero. **2.** the principal female character in a story, play, etc. [t. L, t. Gk, der. *hḗrōs* hero]

heroism (hĕʹrō ĭzʹəm), *n.* **1.** the qualities of a hero or heroine. **2.** heroic conduct; valour. **—Syn.** **1.** intrepidity, valour, prowess, gallantry. **—Ant.** **2.** timidity.

heron (hĕʹrən), *n.* any of the long-legged, long-necked, long-billed wading birds constituting the family *Ardeidae*, including the true herons, bitterns, egrets, etc. [ME *heiroun*, t. OF: m. *hairon*, ult. t. Gmc; cf. OHG *heiger*]

Great blue heron, *Ardea herodias* (Height 4 to 5 ft)

Heron (hĭəʹrŏn), *n.* Hero.

heronry (hĕʹrən rĭ), *n., pl.* **-ries.** a place where a colony of herons breeds.

hero-worship (hĭəʹrō wûʹshĭp), *n., v.,* **-shipped, -shipping** or (*U.S.*) **-shiped, -shiping.** **—***n.* **1.** profound reverence for great men or their memory. **2.** the worship of deified heroes, as practised by the ancients. **3.** admiration or adulation for another person. **—***v.t.* **4.** to feel reverence or adulation for. **—heʹro-worʹshipper,** *n.*

herp., herpetology. Also, **herpet.**

herpes (hûʹpēz), *n. Pathol.* any of certain inflammatory infections of the skin or mucous membrane, characterized by clusters of vesicles which tend to spread. [t. L, t. Gk: lit., a creeping] **—herpetic** (hû pĕtʹĭk), *adj.*

herpes facialis (fāʹshĭ āʹlĭs), *Pathol.* cold sore, esp. on the lips. Also, **herpes labialis** (lāʹbĭ āʹlĭs). [L]

herpes simplex (sĭmʹplĕks), *n. Pathol.* cold sore.

herpes zoster (zŏsʹtə), *Pathol.* shingles.

herpetology (hûʹpĭ tŏlʹə jĭ), *n.* the branch of zoology that treats of reptiles and amphibians. [f. s. Gk *herpetón* reptile + -(O)LOGY] **—herpetological** (hûʹpĭ tə lŏjʹĭ kl), *adj.* **—herʹpetologʹically,** *adv.* **—herʹpetolʹogist,** *n.*

Herr (*Ger.* hĕr), *n., pl.* **Herren** (*Ger.* hĕʹrən). *German.* Mr; sir.

Herrenvolk (*Ger.* hĕʹrən fōlk), *n. German.* the master race.

Herrera (*Sp.* ĕr rĕʹrȧ), *n.* **Francisco de** (*Sp.* frȧn thĕsʹkȯ dĕ), 1576–1656, Spanish painter.

Herrick (hĕʹrĭk), *n.* **Robert,** 1591–1674, English poet.

herring (hĕʹrĭng), *n., pl.* **-rings,** (*esp. collectively*) **-ring.** any fish of the marine family *Clupeidae*, including *Clupea harengus*, an important food fish which occurs in enormous shoals in the North Sea and the north Atlantic. See **red herring.** [ME *hering*, OE *hǣring*, c. G *Häring*]

Herringbone

herringbone (hĕʹrĭng bōnʹ), *n., adj., v.* **-boned, -boning.** **—***n.* **1.** a pattern consisting of adjoining rows of parallel lines so arranged that any two rows have the form of a V or inverted V; used in masonry, textiles, embroidery, etc. 2. an embroidery stitch resembling cross-stitch. —*adj.* 3. having or resembling herringbone. —*v.t.* 4. to make or pattern in herringbone.

herringbone bond, a distinctive form of masonry peculiar to Anglo-Saxon architecture. An ornamental form of brickwork used to fill panels of half-timbering.

herringbone gear, a helical gear with V-shaped teeth, one half of each tooth forming part of a right-handed helix and the other half forming part of a left-handed helix. Also, **double helical gear.** See illus. under **gear.**

herring gull, a common large gull, *Larus argentatus.*

Herriot (*Fr.* ĕ ryō′), *n.* **Edouard** (*Fr.* ĕ dwär′), 1872–1957, French statesman and writer.

Herrnhuter (hĕən′hōō′tə, hĕə′rən-), *n.* a member of the Moravians or United Brethren. [named after *Herrnhut*, in Saxony, where a Moravian sect settled in 1722]

hers (hûz), *pron.* 1. (form of the possessive *her*, used predicatively or without a noun following): *the fault was hers.* 2. the person(s) or thing(s) belonging to her: *herself and hers, a friend of hers.*

Herschel (hû′shəl), *n.* 1. **Sir John Frederick William,** 1792–1871, English astronomer. 2. his father, **Sir William** (*Friedrich Wilhelm Herschel*), 1738–1822, German-born British astronomer.

herself (hə sĕlf′; *medially often* ə-), *pron.* 1. a reflexive form of *her*: *she cut herself.* 2. an emphatic form of *her* or *she* used: **a.** as object: *she used it for herself.* **b.** in apposition to a subject or object: *she herself did it.* 3. her proper or normal self; her normal state of mind (used after *be*, *become*, or *come to*): *she is herself again.*

Herten (*Ger.* hĕr′tən), *n.* a town in West Germany, in central North Rhine-Westphalia. 52,600 (est. 1966).

Hertford (hä′fəd), *n.* 1. a town in England, the county town of Hertfordshire. 15,737 (1961). 2. Hertfordshire.

Hertfordshire (hä′fəd shiə′, -shə), *n.* a county in SE England. 832,901 pop. (1961); 632 sq. mi. *Co. town:* Hertford. Also, **Hert′ford.**

Hertogenbosch, 's (*Du.* sĕr tō KHən bôs′), *n.* See **'s Hertogenbosch.**

Herts., Hertfordshire.

hertz (hûts), *n. Physics.* the derived SI unit of frequency, defined as the frequency of a periodic phenomenon of which the periodic time is one second; one cycle per second. *Symbol:* Hz [named after H. R. HERTZ]

Hertz (hûts; *Ger.* hĕrts), *n.* **Heinrich Rudolph** (*Ger.* hīn′rĭKH rōō′dôlf), 1857–94, German physicist. —**Hertzian** (hût′sĭ ən), *adj.*

Hertzian wave, an electromagnetic wave, artificially produced as a means of transmission in radiotelegraphy: first fully investigated by Hertz.

Hertzog (hût′sŏg), *n.* **James Harry Munnik** (mŭn′ĭk), 1866–1942, South African statesman and general: prime minister 1924–39.

Hertzsprung-Russell diagram (hût′sprŭng rŭs′əl), *Astron.* a graph in which the absolute luminosity of a star is plotted against its spectral type (an indication of its temperature). The theory of stellar evolution has been derived from these diagrams. *Abbrev.:* H-R diagram. [named after Ejnar *Hertzsprung*, 1873–1969, Danish astronomer, and Henry Norris *Russell*, 1873–1957, American astronomer]

Herzegovina (hĕə′tsĭ gō vē′nə), *n.* a former Turkish province in S Europe: a part of Austria-Hungary, 1878–1914; now a part of Bosnia and Herzegovina. Serbo-Croat, **Hercegovina.** —**Her′zegovi′nian,** *adj., n.*

Herzl (*Ger.* hĕr′tsəl), *n.* **Theodor** (*Ger.* tĕ′ō dōr), 1860–1904, Hungarian-born leader of modern Zionism.

he's (hēz; *unstressed* hĭz, ēz, ĭz), contraction of *he is* or *he has.*

Heshvan (hĕsh′văn), *n.* (in the Jewish calendar) the second month of the civil year and eighth of the ecclesiastical year. Also, **Heshwan, Hesvan, Marcheshvan, Cheshvan.**

Hesiod (hĕs′ĭ ŏd′), *n.* fl. 8th century B.C., Greek poet. —**Hesiodic** (hĕs′ĭ ŏd′ĭk), *adj.*

Hesione (hĭ sī′ə nĭ), *n. Gk Legend.* daughter of Laomedon, King of Troy, rescued from a sea-monster by Hercules.

hesitancy (hĕz′ĭ tən sĭ), *n., pl.* **-cies.** hesitation; indecision. Also, **hes′itance.** [t. L: m. s. *haesitantia* stammering]

hesitant (hĕz′ĭ tənt), *adj.* 1. hesitating; undecided. 2. lacking readiness of speech. —**hes′itantly,** *adv.*

hesitate (hĕz′ĭ tāt′), *v.i.*, **-tated, -tating.** 1. to hold back in doubt or indecision: *to hesitate to believe.* 2. to have scrupulous doubts; be unwilling. 3. to pause. 4. to falter in speech; stammer. [t. L: m. s. *haesitātus*, pp., stuck fast] —**hes′ita′tor,** *n.* —**hes′itat′ingly,** *adv.* —**Syn.** 1. waver, vacillate, falter. 3. demur, delay. —**Ant.** 1. decide. 3. hasten.

hesitation (hĕz′ĭ tā′shən), *n.* 1. the act of hesitating; a delay from uncertainty of mind: *to be lost by hesitation.* 2. a state of doubt. 3. a halting or faltering in speech. —**Syn.** 1. hesitancy, indecision, irresolution, vacillation.

hesitative (hĕz′ĭ tā′tĭv), *adj.* characterized by hesitation; hesitating. —**hes′ita′tively,** *adv.*

Hesper (hĕs′pə), *n.* Hesperus.

Hesperian (hĕs pĭə′rĭ ən), *adj.* 1. western, applied to Italy in ancient Greek contexts, and to Spain in Roman contexts. 2. of or pertaining to the Hesperides. [f. s. L *Hesperius* (t. Gk: m. *hespérios* at evening, western) + -AN]

Hesperides (hĕs pĕ′rĭ dēz′), *n.pl. Gk Myth.* certain nymphs, variously given as from three to seven, fabled to guard, with the aid of a serpent, a garden at the western end of the world in which grew golden apples, the wedding gift of Gaea to Hera. [t. L, t. Gk, prop. pl. of *hesperis* western] —**Hesperidian** (hĕs′pə rĭd′ĭ ən), *adj.*

hesperidin (hĕs pĕ′rĭ dĭn), *n.* a crystallizable glucoside found in the spongy envelope of oranges and lemons. [f. s. Gk *Hesperides*, a class of plants including the orange + -IN[2]]

hesperidium (hĕs′pə rĭd′ĭ əm), *n., pl.* **-peridia** (-pərĭd′ĭ ə). *Bot.* the fruit of a citrus plant, as an orange.

Hesperus (hĕs′pə rəs), *n.* the evening star, esp. Venus. Also, **Hesper.** [t. L, t. Gk: m. *Hésperos* the evening star, orig. adj., of or at evening, western]

Hess (hĕs), *n.* 1. **Dame Myra,** 1890–1965, English pianist. 2. **(Walther Richard) Rudolf,** born 1894, German Nazi leader.

Hesse (hĕs′ĭ *for 1;* hĕs′ə *for 2*), *n.* 1. **Hermann,** 1877–1962, German novelist and poet: Nobel Prize, 1946. 2. a Land in West Germany. 5,239,700 pop. (est. 1966); 8150 sq. mi. *Cap.:* Wiesbaden. German, **Hessen** (*Ger.* hĕs′ən).

Hesse-Nassau (hĕs′ĭ năs′ô), *n.* a former state in W Germany; now a part of Hesse. German, **Hessen-Nassau** (*Ger.* hĕs′ən näs′ou).

hessian (hĕs′ĭ ən), *n.* a strong fabric made from jute, used for sacks, carpet backing, etc. Also, *U.S.*, **burlap.**

Hessian (hĕs′ĭ ən), *adj.* 1. of or pertaining to Hesse or its inhabitants. —*n.* 2. a native or inhabitant of Hesse. 3. *U.S.* a Hessian mercenary used by England during the War of Independence. 4. *U.S.* a hireling or ruffian.

Hessian boots, high tasselled boots fashionable in England during the early 19th century.

Hessian fly, a small dipterous insect, *Mayetiola destructor*, whose larva is one of the most destructive pests of wheat.

A B C

Hessian fly, *Mayetiola destructor* A, Larva; B, Pupa; C, Adult (male)

hessite (hĕs′īt), *n.* a grey mineral of silver telluride, Ag_2Te, which occurs in cubic crystals.

hessonite (hĕs′ə nīt′), *n.* a yellowish or brownish variety of garnet, sometimes used in jewellery. Also, **essonite.** [f. Gk *hḗssōn* less, inferior + -ITE[1]]

Hess's law (hĕs′ĭz), *Chem.* the law which states that if a chemical reaction occurs in stages, the sum of the heat evolved in each state is equal to the total heat evolved when the reaction occurs directly. [named after G. H. *Hess*, 1806–50, Russian chemist]

hest (hĕst), *n. Archaic.* behest. [ME *hest(e)*, OE *hǣs*, akin to *hātan* bid]

Hestia (hĕs′tĭ ə), *n. Gk Myth.* goddess of the hearth and hearth fire.

Hesvan (hĕs′văn), *n.* Heshvan.

Hesychast (hĕs′ĭ kăst′), *n.* one of a sect of mystics which originated in the 14th century among the monks on Mt Athos, Greece. [t. Gk: s. *hēsychastḗs* a recluse] —**Hes′ychast′ic,** *adj.*

hetaera (hĭ tē′ə rə), *n., pl.* **-taerae** (-tē′ə rē′). a female paramour, or concubine, esp. in ancient Greece. [t. Gk: m. *hetaîra*, fem. of *hetaîros* companion]

hetaerism (hĭ tĭə′rĭz′əm), *n.* female companionship outside marriage, of both a sexual and intellectual or artistic nature. Also, **hetairism.** —**hetae′rist,** *n.* —**hetaeristic** (hĕt′ĭə rĭs′tĭk), *adj.* —**het′aeris′tically,** *adv.*

hetaira (hĭ tī′ə rə), *n., pl.* **-tairai** (-tī′ə rī′). hetaera.

hetero (hĕt′ə rō′), *adj., n. Slang.* heterosexual.

hetero-, a word element meaning 'other' or 'different', as in *heterocercal.* Also, before vowels, **heter-.** [t. Gk, comb. form of *héteros*]

heterocercal (hĕt′ə rō sû′kl), *adj. Ichthyol.* 1. having an unequally divided tail or caudal fin, the backbone running into a much larger upper lobe. 2. denoting such a tail or caudal fin (cf. *homocercal*). [f. HETERO- + m. s. Gk *kérkos* tail + -AL[1]]

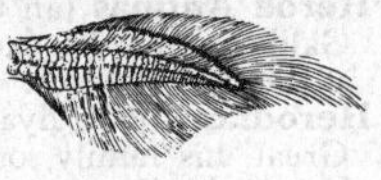

Heterocercal tail

heterochromatic (hĕt′ə rō krō măt′ĭk), *adj.* **1.** of, having, or pertaining to more than one colour. **2.** having a pattern of mixed colours.

heterochromatin (hĕt′ə rō krō′mə tĭn), *n. Biol.* chromatin which remains compact during mitosis. Sex chromosomes may consist entirely of heterochromatin.

heterochromous (hĕt′ə rō krō′məs), *adj.* of different colours. [t. Gk: m. *heteróchrōmos*]

heteroclite (hĕt′ə rō klīt′), *adj.* **1.** exceptional or anomalous. **2.** *Gram.* irregular in inflection. *—n.* **3.** a person or thing that deviates from the ordinary rule or form. **4.** *Gram.* a heteroclite word. [t. F, t. LL: m. s. *heteroclitus,* t. Gk: m. *heteróklitos* irregularly inflected]

heterocyclic (hĕt′ə rō sī′klĭk, -sĭk′lĭk), *adj.* **1.** *Chem.* referring to organic chemistry as dealing with ring compounds with both carbon atoms and atoms of other elements in the ring. **2.** *Chem.* denoting such compounds. **3.** *Bot.* having different numbers of parts in different whorls.

heterodox (hĕt′ə rə dŏks′, hĕt′rə-), *adj.*. **1.** not in accordance with established or accepted doctrines or opinions, esp. in theology. **2.** holding unorthodox doctrines or opinions. [t. Gk: s. *heteródoxos* of another opinion]

heterodoxy (hĕt′ə rə dŏk′sĭ, hĕt′rə-), *n., pl.* **-doxies. 1.** heterodox state or quality. **2.** a heterodox opinion, etc.

heterodyne (hĕt′ə rə dīn′), *adj., n., v.,* **-dyned, -dyning.** *Radio. —adj.* **1.** denoting or pertaining to a method of receiving continuous-wave radiotelegraph signals by impressing upon the continuous radiofrequency oscillations another set of radiofrequency oscillations of a slightly different frequency, the interference resulting in fluctuations or beats of audio frequency. *—n.* **2.** a heterodyne method. *—v.i.* **3.** to produce a heterodyne effect.

heteroecious (hĕt′ə rē′shəs), *adj. Biol.* pertaining to or characterized by heteroecism. [f. HETER- + m. s. Gk *oikía* house + -OUS]

heteroecism (hĕt′ə rē′sĭz′əm), *n. Biol.* the development of different stages of a parasitic species on different host plants, as in fungi.

heterogamete (hĕt′ə rō gă mēt′), *n. Biol.* a gamete of different character from one of the opposite sex (opposed to *isogamete*).

heterogamous (hĕt′ə rŏg′ə məs), *adj.* **1.** *Biol.* having unlike gametes, or reproducing by the union of such gametes (opposed to *isogamous*). **2.** *Bot.* having flowers or florets of two sexually different kinds (opposed to *homogamous*).

heterogamy (hĕt′ə rŏg′ə mĭ), *n.* heterogamous state.

heterogeneity (hĕt′ə rō jĭ nē′ĭ tĭ), *n., pl.* **-ties.** the character or state of being heterogeneous; composition from dissimilar parts; disparateness.

heterogeneous (hĕt′ə rō jē′nyəs), *adj.* **1.** different in kind; unlike; incongruous. **2.** composed of parts of different kinds; having widely unlike elements or constituents; not homogeneous. [t. ML: m. *heterogeneus,* t. Gk: m. *heterogenḗs* of different kinds] **—het′eroge′neously,** *adv.* **—het′eroge′neousness,** *n.*

heterogenous (hĕt′ə rŏj′ĭ nəs), *adj. Biol., Pathol.* having its source outside the organism; having a foreign origin.

heterogonous (hĕt′ə rŏg′ə nəs), *adj.* **1.** *Bot.* noting or pertaining to monoclinous flowers of two or more kinds occurring on different individuals of the same species, the kinds differing in the relative length of stamens and pistils (opposed to *homogonous*). **2.** *Zool.* heterogynous.

heterogony (hĕt′ə rŏg′ə nĭ), *n. Biol.* **a.** the alteration of dioecious and hermaphrodite individuals in successive generations, as in certain nematodes. **b.** (in more recent usage) the alternation of parthenogenetic and sexual generations.

heterogynous (hĕt′ə rŏj′ĭ nəs), *adj. Zool.* having females of two different kinds, one sexual and the other abortive or neuter, as ants.

heterologous (hĕt′ə rŏl′ə gəs), *adj.* **1.** having a different relation; not corresponding. **2.** *Pathol.* consisting of tissue unlike the normal tissue, as a tumour.

heterology (hĕt′ə rŏl′ə jĭ), *n.* **1.** *Biol.* the lack of correspondence of organic structures as the result of unlike origins of constituent parts. **2.** *Pathol.* abnormality; structural difference from a type or normal standard.

heterolysis (hĕt′ə rŏl′ĭ sĭs), *n. Biochem.* dissolution of the cells of one organism by the lysins of another.

heteromerous (hĕt′ə rŏm′ə rəs), *adj.* having or consisting of parts which differ in quality, number of elements, or the like: *a heteromerous flower.*

heteromorphic (hĕt′ə rō mô′fĭk), *adj.* **1.** *Biol.* dissimilar in shape, structure, or magnitude. **2.** *Entomol.* undergoing complete metamorphosis; possessing varying forms. Also, **het′eromor′phous. —het′eromor′phism, het′eromor′phy,** *n.*

heteronomous (hĕt′ə rŏn′ə məs), *adj.* **1.** subject to or involving different laws. **2.** pertaining to, or characterized by, heteronomy. **3.** *Biol.* characterizing an organism which is metameric, or segmented, most or all of whose segments are specialized in different ways. [f. HETERO- + s. Gk *nómos* law + -OUS]

heteronomy (hĕt′ə rŏn′ə mĭ), *n.* condition of being under the rule of another (opposed to *autonomy*).

heteronym (hĕt′ə rō nĭm′), *n.* a word having a different sound and meaning from another, but the same spelling, as *lead* (to conduct) and *lead* (a metal).

heteronymous (hĕt′ə rŏn′ĭ məs), *adj.* **1.** pertaining to or of the nature of a heteronym. **2.** having different names, as a pair of correlatives. **3.** *Optics.* denoting or pertaining to the images formed in a kind of double vision in which the image seen by the right eye is on the left side, and vice versa. [t. Gk: m. *heterónymos* having a different name]

Heteroousian (hĕt′ə rō o͞o′sĭ ən, -ou′sĭ ən), *n.* **1.** *Eccles.* one who believes the Father and Son to be unlike in substance or essence; an Arian (opposed to *Homoousian*). *—adj.* **2.** of or pertaining to the Heteroousians or their doctrine. [f. s. LGk *heterooúsios* of different nature + -AN]

heterophyllous (hĕt′ə rō fĭl′əs), *adj. Bot.* having different kinds of leaves on the same plant. [f. HETERO- + s. Gk *phýllon* leaf + -OUS] **—het′erophyl′ly,** *n.*

heteroplasty (hĕt′ə rō plăs′tĭ), *n. Surg.* the repair of lesions with tissue from another individual. **—het′eroplas′tic,** *adj.*

heteropterous (hĕt′ə rŏp′tə rəs), *adj.* pertaining to the true bugs, *Heteroptera,* which constitute a suborder of the order *Hemiptera.* [f. s. NL *Heteroptera,* class name (f. *hetero-* HETERO- + Gk *pterá* wings) + -OUS]

heterosexual (hĕt′ə rō sĕk′syo͞o əl), *adj.* **1.** *Biol.* pertaining to the other sex or to both sexes. **2.** exhibiting or pertaining to heterosexuality. *—n.* **3.** a heterosexual person.

heterosexuality (hĕt′ə rō sĕk′syo͞o ăl′ĭ tĭ), *n.* sexual feeling for a person (or persons) of opposite sex.

heterosis (hĕt′ə rō′sĭs), *n. Genetics.* the increase in growth, size, fecundity, function, yield, or other characters in hybrids over those of the parents. [t. LGk: alteration]

heterosporous (hĕt′ə rŏs′pə rəs, -rō spô′rəs), *adj. Bot.* having more than one kind of spore.

heterospory (hĕt′ə rŏs′pə rĭ), *n. Bot.* the production of both microspores and megaspores.

heterotaxis (hĕt′ə rō tăk′sĭs), *n.* abnormal or irregular arrangement, as of parts of the body, geological strata, etc. (opposed to *homotaxis*). Also, **het′erotax′y. —het′erotax′ic, het′erotac′tic,** *adj.*

heterothallic (hĕt′ə rō thăl′ĭk), *adj. Bot.* having mycelia of two unlike types both of which must participate in the sexual process (opposed to *homothallic*). [f. HETERO- + s. Gk *thallós* shoot, sprout + -IC] **—het′erothal′lism,** *n.*

heterotopia (hĕt′ə rō tō′pyə), *n. Pathol.* **1.** misplacement or displacement, as of an organ. **2.** the formation of tissue in a part where it is abnormal. Also, **heterotopy** (hĕt′ə rŏt′ə pĭ). [NL, f. Gk: *hetero-* HETERO- + *-topia* (der. *tópos* place)] **—heterotopic** (hĕt′ə rō tŏp′ĭk), **heterotopous** (hĕt′ə rŏt′ə pəs), *adj.*

heterotrophic (hĕt′ə rō trŏf′ĭk), *adj. Biol.* incapable of synthesizing proteins and carbohydrates, as animals and dependent plants (opposed to *autotrophic*).

heterotypic (hĕt′ə rō tĭp′ĭk), *adj. Biol.* applying meiotic division which reduces the chromosome number during the development of the reproductive cells. Also, **het′erotyp′ical.**

heterozygote (hĕt′ə rō zī′gōt, -zĭg′ōt), *n. Genetics.* a hybrid containing genes for two unlike characteristics; an organism which will not breed true to type. **—heterozygous** (hĕt′ə rō zī′gəs), *adj.*

hetman (hĕt′mən), *n., pl.* **-mans.** a Cossack chief; ataman. [t. Pol., t. G: m. *Hauptmann* captain]

Hetton (hĕt′n), *n.* a town in England, in E Durham. 17,463 (1961).

het-up (hĕt′ŭp′), *adj. Colloq.* anxious; worried. Also in predicative use, **het up.** [alter. of HEATED-UP]

heugh (hyo͝oKH), *n. Scot. and N Dial.* **1.** a precipice or cliff. **2.** a ravine with steep, overhanging sides. Also, **heuch.** [ME *hōgh,* OE *hōh*; akin to HANG. Cf. G *Höhe* height]

heulandite (hyo͞o′lən dīt′), *n.* a mineral of the zeolite group, hydrous calcium aluminium silicate, $CaAl_2$-$Si_7O_{18}.6H_2O$, which occurs as monoclinic crystals in igneous rocks. [named after Henry *Heuland,* 19th-century English mineralogist; see -ITE[1]]

heurism (hyo͝oə′rĭz′əm), *n.* the heuristic method or principle in teaching.

heuristic (hyo͝oə rĭs′tĭk), *adj.* **1.** serving to find out;

furthering investigation. **2.** (of a teaching method) encouraging the student to discover for himself. **3.** *Maths.* (of a method of solving problems) one for which no algorithm exists and which therefore depends on inductive reasoning from past experience of similar problems. [appar. b. Gk *heurís(kein)* find + obs. *(heure)tic* inventive (t. Gk: m. s. *heuretikós*)] **—heuris′tically,** *adv.*

Heusler alloy (hyo͞os′lə; *Ger.* hoʏs′lər), any of various manganese and other non-ferromagnetic metals which exhibit ferromagnetism. [named after Conrad *Heusler,* 19th-century German mining engineer]

hew (hyo͞o), *v.*, **hewed, hewed** or **hewn, hewing.** *—v.t.* **1.** to strike forcibly with an axe, sword, or the like; chop; hack. **2.** to make or shape with cutting blows: *to hew a passage.* **3.** to sever (a part) from a whole by means of cutting leaves (fol. by *away, off, out, from,* etc.). **4.** to cut down; fell: *to hew down trees.* *—v.i.* **5.** to deal cutting blows; to cut. [ME *hewe(n),* OE *hēawan,* c. G *hauen*] **—hew′er,** *n.* **—Syn. 1.** See **cut.**

hewers of wood and drawers of water, menial workers. Joshua 9:21.

hex (hĕks), *v.t., n. U.S. Colloq. or Dial.* *—n.* **1.** to bewitch; practise witchcraft on. *—n.* **2.** a witch. **3.** a spell. [t. G: m. *Hexe* witch. See HAG[1]]

hexa-, a prefix meaning 'six', as in *hexagon.* Also, before vowels **hex-.** [t. Gk, comb. form of *héx*]

hexachord (hĕk′sə kôd′), *n. Music.* a diatonic series of six degrees, having (in medieval music) a semitone between the third and fourth notes and whole tones between the others. [t. LGk: s. *hexáchordos*]

hexad (hĕk′săd), *n.* **1.** the number six. **2.** a group or series of six. [t. LL: s. *hexas,* t. Gk: six] **—hexad′ic,** *adj.*

hexadecane (hĕk′sə dĭ kān′, hĕk′sə dĕk′ān), *n. Chem.* cetane.

hexagon (hĕk′sə gən), *n.* a polygon having six angles and six sides.

hexagonal (hĕk săg′ə nəl), *adj.* **1.** of, pertaining to, or having the form of a hexagon. **2.** having a hexagon as a base or cross-section. **3.** divided into hexagons, as a surface. **4.** *Crystall.* denoting or pertaining to the hexagonal system. **—hexag′onally,** *adv.*

Hexagon

hexagonal system, *Crystall.* a system of crystallization characterized by three equal lateral axes intersecting at angles of 60° and a vertical axis of hexagonal symmetry and of different length at right angles to them.

hexagram (hĕk′sə grăm′), *n.* **1.** a six-pointed starlike figure formed of two equilateral triangles placed concentrically with their sides parallel, and on opposite sides of the centre. **2.** *Geom.* a figure of six lines.

Hexagram

hexahedron (hĕk′sə hē′drən), *n., pl.* **-drons, -dra** (-drə). a solid figure having six faces. **—hex′ahe′dral,** *adj.*

hexamerous (hĕk săm′ə rəs), *adj.* **1.** consisting of or divided into six parts. **2.** *Zool.* having a radially symmetrical arrangement of organs in six groups. **3.** *Bot.* having six members in each whorl.

hexameter (hĕk săm′ĭ tə), *n.* **1.** *Pros.* the dactylic verse of six feet, of Greek and Latin epic and other poetry (**dactylic hexameter**), in which the first four feet are dactyls or spondees, the fifth is ordinarily a dactyl, and the last is a trochee or spondee with a caesura usually following the long syllable in the third foot. **2.** any hexameter verse. *—adj.* **3.** consisting of six metrical feet. [t. L, t. Gk: m. *hexámetros* of six measures] **—hexametric** (hĕk′sə mĕt′rĭk), **hex′amet′rical,** *adj.*

hexamethylene-tetramine (hĕk′sə mĕth′ĭ lēn tĕt′rəmēn′), *n. Chem.* a colourless crystalline compound, $C_6H_{12}N_4$, used as a urinary antiseptic, an accelerator, an absorbent in gasmasks, and in the manufacture of synthetic resins. Also, **hex′ameth′ylene-tet′ramin** (-tĕt′rəmĭn).

hexamine (hĕk′sə mēn′, hĕk săm′ēn), *n. Chem., Trademark.* hexamethylene-tetramine.

hexane (hĕk′sān), *n. Chem.* any of the five isomeric saturated hydrocarbons, C_6H_{14}, derived from the fractional distillation of petroleum. [f. Gk *héx* six (with reference to the atoms of carbon) + -ANE]

hexangular (hĕk săng′gyo͝o lə), *adj.* having six angles.

hexapla (hĕk′sə plə), *n.* an edition of the Old Testament containing six versions in parallel columns, as one compiled by Origen. [t. Gk, prop. neut. pl. of *hexaplóos* sixfold] **—hex′aplar,** *adj.*

hexapod (hĕk′sə pŏd′), *n.* **1.** one of the *Hexapoda*; insect. *—adj.* **2.** having six feet. [t. Gk: s. *hexápous* six-footed] **—hexapodous** (hĕk săp′ə dəs), *adj.*

hexapody (hĕk săp′ə dĭ), *n., pl.* **-dies.** *Pros.* a line or verse consisting of six metrical feet.

hexarchy (hĕk′sä′kĭ), *n., pl.* **-chies.** a group of six states or kingdoms, each under its own ruler.

hexastich (hĕk′sə stĭk′), *n. Pros.* a strophe, stanza, or poem consisting of six lines or verses. Also, **hexastichon** (hĕks ăs′tĭ kŏn′). [t. Gk: s. *hexástichos* of six rows or lines]

Hexateuch (hĕk′sə tyo͞ok′), *n.* the first six books of the Old Testament. [f. HEXA- + s. Gk *teûchos* book] **—Hex′ateuch′al,** *adj.*

hexavalent (hĕk săv′ə lənt, hĕk′sə vā′lənt), *adj. Chem.* having a valency of six; sexivalent, sexavalent.

hexogen (hĕk′sə jən), *n. Chem.* cyclonite.

hexone (hĕk′sōn), *n. Chem.* any of various organic ketones which contain six atoms of carbon in the molecule. [f. Gk *héx* six + -ONE, after G *Hexon*]

hexosan (hĕk′sə săn′), *n.* any of a group of hemicelluloses which hydrolyse to hexoses. [f. HEXOS(E) + -AN]

hexose (hĕk′sōs), *n. Chem.* any of a class of sugars containing six atoms of carbon, as glucose and fructose.

hexyl (hĕk′sĭl), *n. Chem.* the univalent radical, C_6H_{13}, derived from hexane.

hexyl-resorcinol (hĕk′sĭl rĭ zô′sĭ nŏl′), *n.* a colourless, crystalline antiseptic, $C_{12}H_{18}O_2$, which is less toxic and more powerful than phenol.

hey[1] (hā), *interj.* (an exclamation to express pleasure, surprise, bewilderment, etc., or to call attention.)

hey[2] (hā), *n.* hay[2].

heyday (hā′dā′), *n.* **1.** the stage or period of highest vigour or fullest strength. **2.** high spirits. *—interj.* **3.** *Archaic.* (an exclamation of cheerfulness, surprise, wonder, etc.) [alter. of HIGH DAY]

Heyduck (hī′do͝ok), *n.* Haiduk. Also, **Hey′duke.**

Heyerdahl (*Norw.* hĕ′yər dȧl), *n.* **Thor** (*Norw.* tòr), born 1914, Norwegian anthropologist: leader of the Kon-Tiki expedition.

hey-presto (hā′prĕs′tō), *interj.* (an exclamation of triumph, etc., on the completion of a conjuring trick, feat, etc.)

Heyse (*Ger.* hī′zə), *n.* **Paul Johann Ludwig von** (*Ger.* poul yō′hȧn lo͞ot′vĭKH fōn), 1830–1914, German writer.

Heywood (hā′wo͝od′), *n.* **1. John,** 1497?–1580?, English dramatist and epigrammatist. **2. Thomas,** died 1641, English dramatist, actor, and poet. **3.** a town in England, in SE Lancashire. 24,090 (1961).

Hezekiah (hĕz′ĭ kī′ə), *n.* a king of Judah of the 8th–7th centuries B.C. II Kings 18, etc.

Hf, *Chem.* hafnium.

h.f., **1.** (*sometimes cap.*) *Elect.* high frequency. **2.** high fidelity.

HG, High German.

Hg, (L *hydrargyrum*) *Chem.* mercury.

hg., hectogram.

H.G., **1.** His, or Her, Grace. **2.** High German. **3.** Home Guard.

H.H., **1.** His, or Her, Highness. **2.** His Holiness.

hhd, hogshead.

hi (hī), *interj.* (an exclamation, esp. of greeting.)

H.I., Hawaiian Islands.

hiatus (hī ā′təs), *n., pl.* **-tuses, -tus. 1.** a break, with a part missing; an interruption; lacuna: *a hiatus in a manuscript.* **2.** a gap or opening. **3.** *Gram. and Pros.* a break or slight pause due to the coming together without contraction of two vowels in successive words or syllables. **4.** *Anat.* a natural fissure, cleft, or foramen in a bone or other structure. [t. L: gap]

Hiawatha (hī′ə wŏth′ə), *n.* the central figure of *The Song of Hiawatha* (1855), a poem by Longfellow.

hibachi (hĭ bä′chĭ), *n.* a portable brazier on which foods are barbecued, consisting of a heavy wire grill over a pot-shaped container for burning charcoal. [t. Jap.]

hibernaculum (hī′bə năk′yo͝o ləm), *n., pl.* **-la** (-lə). **1.** a protective case or covering for winter, as of an animal or a plant bud. **2.** Also, **hibernacle** (hī′bə năk′l). winter quarters, as of a hibernating animal. [t. L: winter residence]

hibernal (hī bû′nəl), *adj.* of or pertaining to winter; wintry. [t. LL: s. *hībernālis* wintry]

hibernate (hī′bə nāt′), *v.i.*, **-nated, -nating. 1.** to spend the winter in close quarters in a dormant condition, as certain animals. **2.** to withdraw into or remain in seclusion. [t. L: m. s. *hībernātus,* pp., wintered] **—hi′berna′tion,** *n.*

Hibernia (hī bû′nyə), *n.* Latin or literary name of **Ireland.**

Hibernian (hī bû′nyən), *adj.* **1.** Irish. *—n.* **2.** a native of Ireland. [f. s. L *Hibernia* Ireland + -AN]

Hibernicism (hī bû′nĭ sĭz′əm), *n.* **1.** an idiom peculiar to Irish English. **2.** an Irish characteristic. Also, **Hibernianism** (hī bû′nĭ ə nĭz′əm).

Hibernicize (hī bû′nĭ sīz′), *v.t.* to make Irish in form or character. Also, **Hibernicise.**

hibiscus (hĭ bĭs′kəs), *n.* any of the herbs, shrubs, or trees of the malvaceous genus *Hibiscus*, many of which, as the shrub althaea, *H. syriacus*, have large showy flowers. [t. L, t. Gk: m. *hibiskos* mallow]

hiccup (hĭk′ŭp), *n.* **1.** a quick, involuntary inspiration suddenly checked by closure of the glottis, producing a characteristic sound. **2.** (*usually pl.*) the condition of having such spasms: *to have the hiccups.* —*v.i.* **3.** to make the sound of a hiccup. **4.** to have the hiccups. Also, **hiccough** (hĭk′ŭp). [earlier *hickock*, f. *hick* (imit.) + -OCK. Cf. LG *hick* hiccup]

hic et ubique (hĭk′ĕt o͞o′bĭ kwā′), *Latin.* here and everywhere.

hic jacet (hĭk′yăk′ĕt), *Latin.* here lies (often used to begin epitaphs on tombstones).

hick (hĭk), *Slang.* —*n.* **1.** an unsophisticated person. **2.** a farmer. —*adj.* **3.** pertaining to or characteristic of hicks. [familiar form of *Richard*, man's name]

hickey (hĭk′ĭ), *n., pl.* **-eys.** *Slang.* **1.** any device. **2.** a hick.

Hickok (hĭk′ŏk), *n.* **James Butler** (*'Wild Bill'*), 1837–76, U.S. frontiersman.

hickory (hĭk′ə rĭ), *n., pl.* **-ries.** **1.** any of the North American trees constituting the juglandaceous genus *Carya*, certain of which, as the pecan, *C. illinoensis* (*C. Pecan*), bear sweet, edible nuts **(hickory nuts),** and others, as the shagbark, *C. ovata*, yield valuable hard wood and edible nuts. **2.** the wood of such a tree. **3.** a switch, stick, etc., of this wood. [t. Amer. Ind. (Va.). Cf. Algonquian *pawcohiccoro* walnut kernel mush]

hid (hĭd), *v.* pt. and pp. of **hide.**

hidage (hī′dĭj), *n. Old Eng. Law.* a tax assessed on every hide of land.

hidalgo (hĭ dăl′gō; *Sp.* ē dȧl′gō), *n., pl.* **-gos** (-gōz; *Sp.* -gōs). (in Spain) a man of the lower nobility. [t. Sp., contr. of *hijo de algo* son of (man of) property]

Hidatsa (hē dät′sə), *n.* **1.** a member of a Siouan tribe dwelling on the Missouri river. **2.** their language.

hidden (hĭd′n), *adj.* **1.** concealed; obscure; latent. —*v.* **2.** pp. of **hide.** —**Syn.** secret, covert; occult.

hiddenite (hĭd′ə nīt′), *n.* a rare, transparent emerald green or yellowish green variety of spodumene, a valuable gem. [named after W. E. *Hidden*, who discovered it (1879). See -ITE[1]]

hide[1] (hīd), *v.*, **hid, hidden** or **hid, hiding.** —*v.t.* **1.** to conceal from sight; prevent from being seen or discovered. **2.** to obstruct the view of; cover up: *the sun was hidden by clouds.* **3.** to conceal from knowledge; keep secret: *to hide one's feelings.* **4. hide one's head,** *Colloq.* to be ashamed. —*v.i.* **5.** to conceal oneself; lie concealed. —*n.* **6.** a covered place to hide in while shooting or observing wildlife. [ME *hide(n)*, OE *hȳdan*, c. MLG *hüden*] —**hid′er,** *n.*

—**Syn. 1.** screen, mask, cloak, veil, shroud, disguise. HIDE, CONCEAL, SECRETE mean to put out of sight or in a secret place. HIDE is the general word: *to hide or conceal one's money or purpose, a dog hides a bone.* CONCEAL, somewhat more formal, is to cover from sight: *a rock hid or concealed them from view.* SECRETE means to hide carefully, in order to keep secret: *the banker secretes important papers.* **3.** dissemble, suppress. —**Ant. 1.** reveal, display.

hide[2] (hīd), *n., v.*, **hided, hiding.** —*n.* **1.** the skin of an animal, esp. one of the larger animals, raw or dressed: *the hide of a calf.* **2.** *Slang.* the human skin. **3. a thick hide,** *Colloq.* insensitivity to criticism. **4. hide nor hair,** not a vestige; no clue. —*v.t.* **5.** *Colloq.* to flog or thrash. [ME; OE *hȳd*, c. G *Haut*] —**Syn. 1.** See **skin.**

hide[3] (hīd), *n.* an old English measure of land, usually 120 acres, considered adequate for one free family and its dependants. [ME; OE *hīd(e)*, *hīg(i)d*, f. *hīg(an)* family, household + *-id*, suffix of appurtenance]

hide-and-seek (hīd′n sēk′), *n.* a children's game in which some hide and others seek them.

hideaway (hīd′ə wā′), *n. Colloq.* a place of concealment; a refuge.

hidebound (hīd′bound′), *adj.* **1.** narrow and rigid in opinion: *a hidebound pedant.* **2.** (of a horse, etc.) having the back and ribs bound tightly by the hide. [f. HIDE[2] + BOUND]

hideous (hĭd′ĭ əs), *adj.* **1.** horrible or frightful to the senses; very ugly: *a hideous monster.* **2.** shocking or revolting to the moral sense: *a hideous crime.* [ME *hidous*, t. AF, der. *hi(s)de* horror, fear; orig. uncert.] —**hid′eously,** *adv.* —**hid′eousness, hideosity** (hĭd′ĭ ŏs′ĭ tĭ), *n.* —**Syn. 1, 2.** grisly, grim; repulsive, detestable, odious. —**Ant. 1.** attractive, pleasing.

hide-out (hīd′out′), *n.* a hiding-place; refuge.

hiding[1] (hī′dĭng), *n.* **1.** the act of concealing; concealment: *to remain in hiding.* **2.** a place or means of concealment. [f. HIDE[1] + -ING[1]]

hiding[2] (hī′dĭng), *n. Colloq.* a flogging or thrashing. [f. HIDE[2] + -ING[1]]

hidrosis (hĭ drō′sĭs), *n. Pathol.* **1.** excessive perspiration due to drugs, disease, or the like. **2.** any of certain diseases characterized by sweating. [NL, special use of Gk *hídrōsis* perspiration] —**hidrotic** (hĭ drŏt′ĭk), *adj.*

hie (hī), *v.i.*, **hied, hieing.** to hasten; speed; go in haste. [ME; OE *hīgian* strive. Cf. D *hijgen* pant]

hielamon (hē′lə mən), *n. Austral.* a shield made of bark or wood. [t. native Australian]

hier-, var. of **hiero-** before a vowel, as in *hierarchy.*

hierarch (hī′ə räk′), *n.* **1.** one who rules or has authority in sacred things. **2.** a chief priest. **3.** one of a body of officials or minor priests in some ancient Greek temples. [t. ML: s. *hierarcha*, t. Gk: m. *hierárchēs* steward of sacred rites] —**hi′erar′chal,** *adj.*

hierarchical (hī′ə rä′kĭ kl), *adj.* of or belonging to a hierarchy. Also, **hi′erar′chic.** —**hi′erar′chically,** *adv.*

hierarchism (hī′ə rä kĭz′əm), *n.* hierarchical principles, rule, or influence.

hierarchy (hī′ə rä′kĭ), *n., pl.* **-chies.** **1.** any system of persons or things in a graded order, etc. **2.** *Science.* a series of successive terms of different rank. The terms *phylum, class, order, family, genus,* and *species* constitute a hierarchy in zoology. **3.** government by ecclesiastical rulers. **4.** the power or dominion of a hierarch. **5.** an organized body of ecclesiastical officials in successive ranks or orders: *the Roman Catholic hierarchy.* **6.** one of the three divisions of the angels, each made up of three orders, conceived as constituting a graded body. **7.** the collective body of angels **(celestial hierarchy).**

hieratic (hī′ə răt′ĭk), *adj.* **1.** pertaining to priests or to the priesthood; priestly. **2.** denoting or pertaining to a form of ancient Egyptian writing consisting of abridged forms of hieroglyphics, used by the priests in their records. **3.** denoting or pertaining to certain styles in art whose types or methods are fixed by or as by religious tradition. —*n.* **4.** ancient Egyptian hieratic writing. Also, **hi′erat′ical.** [t. L: s. *hierāticus*, t. Gk: m. *hierātikós* priestly, sacerdotal] —**hi′erat′ically,** *adv.*

hiero-, a word element meaning 'sacred', as in *hierocracy.* Also, before a vowel, **hier-.** [t. Gk, comb. form of *hierós* holy]

hierocracy (hī′ə rŏk′rə sĭ), *n., pl.* **-cies.** rule or government by priests or ecclesiastics. —**hierocrat** (hī′ə rə krăt′), *n.* —**hierocratic** (hī′ə rə krăt′ĭk), *adj.*

hierodule (hī′ə rə dyo͞ol′), *n.* a slave in an ancient Greek temple, dedicated to the service of a deity. —**hie′rodu′lic,** *adj.* [t. Gk: m. s. *hieródoulos* temple slave]

hieroglyphic (hī′ə rə glĭf′ĭk), *adj.* Also, **hi′eroglyph′ical.** **1.** designating or pertaining to a writing system, particularly that of the ancient Egyptians, in which many of the symbols are conventionalized pictures of the thing named by the words for which the symbols stand. **2.** inscribed with hieroglyphic symbols. **3.** hard to decipher; hard to read. —*n.* **4.** Also, **hi′eroglyph′.** a hieroglyphic symbol. **5.** (*usually pl.*) hieroglyphic writing. **6.** a figure or symbol with a hidden meaning. **7.** (*pl.*) writing difficult to decipher. [t. LL: s. *hieroglyphicus*, t. Gk: m. *hieroglyphikós*] —**hi′eroglyph′ically,** *adv.*

Hieroglyphics

hieroglyphist (hī′ə rə glĭf′ĭst, hī′ə rŏg′lĭ fĭst), *n.* **1.** a student of hieroglyphics. **2.** a writer of hieroglyphics.

hierogram (hī′ə rə grăm′), *n.* a sacred, esp. hieroglyphic, symbol.

hierogrammat (hī′ə rə grăm′ət), *n.* a writer of sacred records, esp. in hieroglyphics. Also, **hierogrammate** (hī′ə rə grăm′ăt, -ĭt). —**hi′erogrammat′ic, hi′erogrammat′ical,** *adj.* —**hi′erogram′matist,** *n.*

hierolatry (hī′ə rŏl′ə trĭ), *n.* hagiolatry. —**hi′erol′ater,** *n.* —**hi′erol′atrous,** *adj.*

hierology (hī′ə rŏl′ə jĭ), *n.* literature or learning regarding sacred things. —**hi′erolog′ic, hi′erolog′ical,** *adj.* —**hi′erolog′ically,** *adv.* —**hi′erol′ogist,** *n.*

Hieronymite (hī′ə rŏn′ĭ mīt′), *n.* a member of the Congregation of Hermits of St Jerome.

Hieronymus (hī′ə rŏn′ĭ məs), *n.* (Saint) Jerome. —**Hieronymic** (hī′ə rə nĭm′ĭk), —**Hieronymian** (hī′ə rə nĭm′ĭ ən), *adj.*

hierophant (hī′ə rə fănt′), *n.* **1.** (in ancient Greece, etc.) an official expounder of rites of worship and sacrifice. **2.** any interpreter of sacred mysteries or esoteric principles. [t. LL: s. *hierophantēs*, t. Gk] —**hierophantic** (hī′ə rə făn′tĭk), *adj.* —**hi′erophan′tically,** *adv.*

hifalutin (hī′fə lo͞o′tĭn), *adj. Colloq.* highfalutin.

hi-fi (hī′fī′), *adj.* **1.** high-fidelity. —*n.* **2.** a high-fidelity gramophone, etc.

higgle (hĭg′l), *v.i.*, **-gled, -gling.** to bargain, esp. in a petty way; haggle. [appar. var. of HAGGLE]

higgledy-piggledy (hĭg′l dĭ pĭg′l dĭ), *Colloq.* —*adv.* **1.** in a jumbled confusion. —*adj.* **2.** confused; jumbled.

higgler (hĭg′lə), *n.* a huckster or pedlar.

high (hī), *adj.* **1.** having a great or considerable reach or extent upwards; lofty; tall. **2.** having a specified extent upwards. **3.** situated above the ground or some base; elevated. **4.** far above the horizon, as a heavenly body. **5.** lying or being above the general level: *high ground.* **6.** of more than average or normal height or depth: *the river was high after the rain.* **7.** intensified; exceeding the common degree or measure; strong; intense, energetic: *high speed.* **8.** assigning or attributing a great amount, value, or excellence: *high estimate.* **9.** expensive, costly, or dear. **10.** exalted in rank, station, estimation, etc.; of exalted character or quality: *a high official.* **11.** *Music.* **a.** acute in pitch. **b.** a little sharp, or above the desired pitch. **12.** produced by relatively rapid vibrations; shrill: *high sounds.* **13.** extending to or from an elevation: *a high dive.* **14.** of great amount, degree, force, etc.: *a high temperature.* **15.** chief; principal; main: *the high altar of a church.* **16.** of great consequence; important; grave; serious: *high treason.* **17.** lofty; haughty; arrogant: *he spoke in a high and mighty manner.* **18.** advanced to the utmost extent, or to the culmination: *high tide.* **19.** elated; merry or hilarious: *high spirits.* **20.** *Colloq.* intoxicated or elated with alcohol or drugs. **21.** luxurious; extravagant: *high living.* **22.** remote: *high latitude, high antiquity.* **23.** extreme in opinion or doctrine, esp. religious or political. **24.** designating or pertaining to highland or inland regions. **25.** *Biol.* having a relatively complex structure: *the higher mammals.* **26.** *Phonet.* pronounced with the tongue relatively close to the roof of the mouth: *'feed' and 'food' have high vowels.* **27.** (of meat, esp. game) tending towards a desirable amount of decomposition; slightly tainted. **28.** having a comparatively large amount of a particular constituent: *high-protein food.* **29.** *Cards.* **a.** having greater value than another card. **b.** capable of taking a trick; being a winning card. **30. high relief.** See **relief** (defs 9, 10) and **alto-rilievo.** —*adv.* **31.** at or to a high point, place, or level, or a high rank or estimate, a high amount or price, or a high degree. **32.** *Naut.* close to the wind (said of a ship when sailing by the wind, with reference to the smallest angle with the wind at which the sails will remain full and the ship make headway). **33. high and dry, a.** (of a ship) wholly above water-level at low tide. **b.** *Colloq.* abandoned; stranded; deserted. **34. high and low,** everywhere. **35.** that which is high; a high level: *share prices reached a new high.* —*n.* **36.** *U.S.* top gear. **37.** *Meteorol.* a pressure system characterized by relatively high pressure at its centre; an anticyclone. **38.** *U.S. Colloq.* high school. **39.** *Cards.* the ace or highest trump out. **40. on high, a.** at or to a height; above. **b.** in heaven. [ME *heigh*, etc., OE *hēah*, c. G *hoch*]

—**Syn. 1.** HIGH, LOFTY, TALL, TOWERING refer to that which has considerable height. HIGH is a general term, and denotes either extension upwards or position at a considerable height: *six feet high, a high shelf.* LOFTY denotes imposing or even inspiring height: *lofty crags.* TALL is applied either to that which is high in proportion to its breadth, or to anything higher than the average of its kind: *a tall tree, building.* TOWERING is applied to that which rises to a great or conspicuous height as compared with something else: *a towering mountain, cliff.* **10.** elevated, eminent. —**Ant. 1.** low.

highball (hī′bôl′), *n. U.S.* whisky or other liquor diluted with water, soda, or ginger ale, and served with ice in a tall glass.

highbinder (hī′bīn′də), *n. U.S. Slang.* **1.** a member of a secret Chinese band or society employed for blackmail, assassination, etc. **2.** a ruffian or rowdy. **3.** a confidence man; swindler. **4.** a corrupt or dishonest politician or official.

highborn (hī′bôn′), *adj.* of high rank by birth.

highboy (hī′boi′), *n. U.S.* a tallboy.

highbred (hī′brĕd′), *adj.* **1.** of superior breed. **2.** characteristic of superior breeding: *highbred manners.*

highbrow (hī′brou′), *Colloq.* —*n.* **1.** a person of intellectual tastes. Cf. **lowbrow.** —*adj.* **2.** of or pertaining to highbrows. **3.** being a highbrow.

highchair (hī′chĕə′), *n.* a tall chair for use by a young child at mealtimes.

High Church, a party in the Anglican Church which lays great stress on church authority and jurisdiction, ritual, etc. (opposed to *Low Church* and *Broad Church*). —**High′-Church′,** *adj.* —**High′-Church′man,** *n.*

high-class (hī′kläs′), *adj.* of superior quality.

high-coloured (hī′kŭl′əd), *adj.* **1.** strong or glaring in colour. **2.** florid or red: *a high-coloured complexion.*

high comedy, comedy dealing with polite society, depending largely on witty dialogue. Cf. **low comedy.**

high commissioner, the chief representative of a sovereign member of the Commonwealth of Nations in the country of another sovereign member, usually equivalent in rank to an ambassador.

high court, a supreme court of justice.

High Court of Justice, (in Great Britain) the lower branch of the Supreme Court of Judicature, consisting of the Queen's Bench division, Chancery division, and Probate, Divorce, and Admiralty division.

high day, 1. a holy or festal day. **2.** heyday.

higher criticism, the study of literature, esp. the Bible, by scientific and historical techniques.

higher education, education beyond secondary education.

higher mathematics, the more scientifically treated and advanced portions of mathematics customarily embracing all beyond ordinary arithmetic, geometry, algebra, and trigonometry.

Higher National Certificate, an advanced technical qualification obtained after a two-year part-time course. *Abbrev.:* H.N.C. See **Ordinary National Certificate.**

Higher National Diploma, an advanced technical qualification obtained after a full-time or three-year sandwich course. *Abbrev.:* H.N.D. See **Ordinary National Diploma.**

higher-up (hī′ər ŭp′), *n. Colloq.* one occupying a superior position.

high explosive, a class of explosive, as TNT, in which the reaction is so rapid as to be practically instantaneous, used for bursting charges in shells and bombs.

highfalutin (hī′fə lōō′tĭn), *adj. Colloq.* pompous; haughty; pretentious. Also, **hifalutin, highfaluting.**

high-fidelity (hī′fĭ dĕl′ĭ tĭ), *adj. Electronics.* (of an amplifier, radio receiver, etc.) reproducing the full audio range of the original signal of sounds with relatively little distortion. Also, **hi-fi.**

high-flier (hī′flī′ə), *n.* **1.** one who or that which flies high. **2.** one who is extravagant or goes to extremes in aims, pretensions, opinions, etc. Also, **high-flyer.**

high-flown (hī′flōn′), *adj.* **1.** extravagant in aims, pretensions, etc. **2.** pretentiously lofty; bombastic.

high-flying (hī′flī′ĭng), *adj.* **1.** that flies high, as a bird. **2.** extravagant or extreme in aims, opinions, etc.

high frequency, a radio frequency in the range 3 to 30 megacycles per second. *Abbrev.:* h.f. —**high′-fre′quency,** *adj.*

high-frequency welding, radiofrequency welding.

High German, 1. any form of the German of central and southern Germany, Switzerland, and Austria, including Old High German and Middle High German. **2.** standard German.

high-grade (hī′grād′), *adj.* **1.** of superior quality. **2.** (of ore) with a relatively high yield of the metal for which it is mined.

high-handed (hī′hăn′dĭd), *adj.* overbearing; arbitrary: *a high-handed manner.* —**high′-hand′edly,** *adv.* —**high′-hand′edness,** *n.*

high hat, a top hat.

high-hat (*v.* hī′hăt′; *adj.* hī′hăt′), *v.*, **-hatted, -hatting,** *adj. Slang, Chiefly U.S.* —*v.t.* **1.** to snub or treat condescendingly. —*adj.* **2.** snobbish; affectedly superior.

high-heeled (hī′hēld′), *adj.* (of a shoe) having a long, slender, raised, tapering heel. Also, **high-heel.**

highhole (hī′hōl′), *n. U.S. Dial.* flicker². Also **highholder** (hī′hōl′də).

highjack (hī′jăk′), *v.t., v.i. Orig. U.S. Slang.* hijack.

high jinks (hī′jĭngks′), *Slang.* boisterous, unrestrained merrymaking.

high jump, 1. *Athletics.* a vertical jump in which one attempts to go as high as possible. **2.** *Athletics.* a contest for the highest such jump. **3. for the high jump,** *Slang.* (to be) about to face an unpleasant experience, esp. a punishment or reprimand.

highland (hī′lənd), *n.* **1.** an elevated region; a plateau: *a jutting highland.* **2.** (*pl.*) a mountainous region or elevated part of a country. —*adj.* **3.** of, pertaining to, or characteristic of highlands.

Highlander (hī′lən də), *n.* **1.** a member of the Gaelic race of the Highlands. **2.** a soldier of a Highland regiment. **3.** (*l.c.*) an inhabitant of high land.

Highland fling, a vigorous Scottish country dance, a form of the reel.

Highlands (hī′ləndz), *n.pl.* **1.** a mountainous region of Scotland N of the Lowlands, divided into the **North-west** or **Western Highlands** NW of the Caledonian Canal, and the **Grampian Highlands** or **Grampian Mountains** to the SW; highest point, Ben Nevis 4406 ft. **2.** the NW Highlands, excluding the Grampian Highlands.

high-level (hī′lĕv′əl), *adj.* **1.** carried out at or from a high altitude. **2.** involving or engaged in by persons holding a high position or rank.

highlight (hī′līt′), *v.*, **-lighted, -lighting,** *n.* —*v.t.* **1.** to emphasize or make prominent. **2.** (in photography, painting, etc.) to emphasize (the areas of greatest brightness) with paint or by exposing lighter areas. —*n.* 3. a conspicuous or striking part: *the highlight of his talk.* 4. *Art.* the point of most intense light in a picture or form.

highly (hī′lĭ), *adv.* 1. in or to a high degree: *highly amusing.* 2. with high appreciation or praise: *to speak highly of a person.* 3. at or to a high price.

highly strung, tense; in a state of (esp. nervous) tension: *highly strung nerves, highly strung people.* Also, **high′-strung′,** *adj.*

High Mass, *Rom. Cath. Ch.* a mass celebrated according to the complete rite by a priest or prelate attended by a deacon and subdeacon, parts of the mass being chanted or sung by the ministers and parts by the choir. During a High Mass incense is burnt before the oblations, the altar, the ministers, and the people.

high-minded (hī′mīn′dĭd), *adj.* 1. having or showing high, exalted principles or feelings: *a high-minded ruler.* 2. proud or arrogant. —**high′-mind′edly,** *adv.* —**high′-mind′edness,** *n.* —**Syn.** 1. See **noble.**

high-necked (hī′nĕkt′), *adj.* (of a garment) high at the neck.

highness (hī′nĭs), *n.* 1. the state of being high; loftiness; dignity. 2. (*cap.*) a title of honour given to royal or princely personages (prec. by *His, Your,* etc.).

high-octane (hī′ŏk′tān), *adj.* (of a petrol) having a relatively high octane number, characterized by high efficiency and good antiknock properties. See **octane number.**

High Peak. See **Peak District.**

high-pitched (hī′pĭcht′), *adj.* 1. *Music.* played or sung at a high pitch. 2. (of a discussion, argument, etc.) marked by strong feeling; emotionally intense. 3. (of a roof) nearly perpendicular; steep. 4. aspiring; lofty; lofty in tone.

high place, (in Semitic religions) a place of worship, usually on a hilltop.

high-powered (hī′pou′əd), *adj.* 1. (of an optical instrument) capable of giving a high magnification. 2. energetic; vigorous; forceful: *a high-powered sales campaign.*

high-pressure (hī′prĕsh′ə), *adj.* 1. having or involving a pressure above the normal: *high-pressure steam.* 2. vigorous; persistent: *high-pressure salesmanship.*

high-priced (hī′prīst′), *adj.* expensive. —**Syn.** See **expensive.**

high priest, 1. a chief priest. 2. an influential or powerful person in a high position. 3. *Judaism.* in the priestly hierarchy, the highest-ranking priest who alone may enter the holy of holies.

high-proof (hī′prōōf′), *adj.* containing a high percentage of alcohol: *high-proof spirits.*

high-rise (hī′rīz′), *adj.* multistorey.

highroad (hī′rōd′), *n.* 1. a main road; a highway. 2. an easy or certain course: *the highroad to success.*

high school, 1. *U.S.* a secondary school corresponding to a British grammar school. 2. *Brit. Obsolesc.* a grammar school.

high sea, 1. sea or ocean beyond a country's territorial waters. 2. (*usually pl.*) the open, unenclosed waters of any sea or ocean; common highway. 3. (*usually pl.*) the area within which transactions are subject to court of admiralty jurisdiction.

high-sounding (hī′soun′dĭng), *adj.* having an imposing or pretentious sound: *high-sounding titles.*

high-speed (hī′spēd′), *adj.* 1. operating, or capable of operating at a high speed. 2. *Photog.* (of film) useable with low illumination and short exposures. 3. (of steel) especially hard and capable of retaining its hardness even at red heat, so that it can be used for lathe tools.

high-spirited (hī′spĭ′rĭ tĭd), *adj.* having a high, proud, or bold spirit; mettlesome.

high spot, an outstanding feature, esp. of a programme of entertainment.

high-stepping (hī′stĕp′ĭng), *adj.* 1. (of a horse) moving with the leg raised high off the ground. 2. (of a person) fashionably dressed; having fashionable pretensions. 3. *U.S.* dedicated to the pursuit of pleasure; leading a hectic life. —**high′-step′per,** *n.*

high-strung (hī′strŭng′), *adj.* highly strung.

hight (hīt), *adj. Archaic.* called or named: *Childe Harold was he hight.* [ME; OE *heht,* reduplicated preterite of *hātan* name, call, promise, command, c. G *heissen*; current meaning taken from OE *hātte,* passive of *hātan*]

high table, a table, especially one on a dais, at which the senior members of a college take their meals.

high tea, a main evening meal with meat, fish, etc., (usually taking the place of dinner), at which tea is served.

high-tension (hī′tĕn′shən), *adj. Elect.* (of a device, circuit, circuit component, etc.) subjected to, or capable of operating under, a relatively high voltage, usually 1000 volts or more. *Abbrev.:* H.T.

high tide, 1. the tide at high water. 2. the time of high water. 3. the culminating point.

high time, 1. the right time; the time just before it is too late: *it's high time that was done.* 2. *Slang.* an enjoyable and gay time: *a high old time at the party.*

high-toned (hī′tōnd′), *adj.* 1. high in tone or pitch. 2. having high principles; dignified. 3. *U.S. Colloq.* of, or with pretensions to, superior social status.

high treason, treason against the sovereign or state.

highty-tighty (hī′tĭ tī′tĭ), *interj., adj.* hoity-toity.

high-up (hī′ŭp′), *adj., n., pl.* **-ups.** —*adj.* 1. holding an important position or rank. —*n.* 2. a person of great importance or high rank.

high water, 1. high tide. 2. water at its greatest elevation, as in a river.

high-water mark (hī′wô′tə), 1. a mark showing the highest level reached by a body of water. 2. the highest point of anything.

highway (hī′wā′), *n.* 1. a main road, as one between towns. 2. any public passage, either a road or waterway. 3. any main or ordinary route, track, or course.

Highway Code, a code compiled by the Ministry of Transport for the guidance of drivers of motor vehicles, etc., using the public roads.

highwayman (hī′wā mən), *n., pl.* **-men.** a robber on the highway, esp. one on horseback.

high-wrought (hī′rôt′), *adj.* 1. wrought with a high degree of skill; ornate. 2. highly agitated.

High Wycombe (hī′wĭk′əm), *n.* a town in England, in S Buckinghamshire. 49,981 (1961).

H.I.H., His, or Her, Imperial Highness.

Hiiumaa (hē′ōō mä′), *n.* an island in the Baltic, E of and belonging to the Estonian Republic of the Soviet Union. 373 sq. mi. Danish, **Dagö.**

hijack (hī′jăk′), *v.t.* 1. to steal (something) in transit, as a lorry and the goods it carries. —*v.i.* 2. to engage in such stealing. Also, **highjack.** [back-formation from HIJACKER]

hijacker (hī′jăk′ə), *n.* one who hijacks. [f. HIGH(WAYMAN) + *jacker,* appar. der. *jack,* v., hunt by night with aid of a jacklight]

hike (hīk), *v.,* **hiked, hiking,** *n.* —*v.i.* 1. to walk a long distance, esp. through country districts, for pleasure. —*n.* 2. a long walk in the country. [? akin to HITCH] —**hik′er,** *n.*

hilarious (hĭ lĕə′rĭ əs), *adj.* 1. boisterously gay. 2. cheerful. 3. funny; provoking mirth. [f. HILARI(TY) + -OUS] —**hilar′iously,** *adv.* —**hilar′iousness,** *n.*

hilarity (hĭ lă′rĭ tĭ), *n.* 1. boisterous gaiety. 2. cheerfulness. [t. L: m. s. *hilaritas*] —**Syn.** 1. See **mirth.**

Hilary of Poitiers (hĭl′ə rĭ), **Saint,** A.D. *c.* 300–368, French bishop and theologian. French, **Hilaire** (*Fr.* ē lĕr′).

Hilary term, an English law sitting and (at some universities, etc.) university term, between variable dates, but usually beginning in January and ending in March or April.

Hildebrand (hĭl′də brănd′). *n.* See **Gregory VII.**

Hildebrandt (*Ger.* hĭl′də brȧnt), *n.* **Johann Lukas von** (*Ger.* yō′hȧn lōō′kȧs fōn), 1668–1745, Austrian baroque architect.

Hildesheim (*Ger.* hĭl′dəs hīm), *n.* a town in West Germany, in SE Lower Saxony. 98,500 (est. 1966).

Hildesheimer (*Ger.* hĭl′dəs hī mər), *n.* **Wolfgang** (*Ger.* vŏlf′gȧng), born 1916, German writer and dramatist.

hill (hĭl), *n.* 1. a conspicuous natural elevation of the earth's surface, smaller than a mountain. 2. an artificial heap or pile: *anthill.* 3. a little heap of earth raised about a cultivated plant or a cluster of such plants. —*v.t.* 4. to form into a hill or heap. 5. to bank up (a plant, etc.) with earth. [ME; OE *hyll,* c. MD *hille*; akin to L *collis* hill, *columen* top, *columna* COLUMN] —**hill′er,** *n.* —**Syn.** 1. eminence; mound, knoll, hillock; foothill.

Hill (hĭl), *n.* 1. **James Jerome,** 1838–1916, U.S. railway builder and financier, born in Canada. 2. **Octavia,** 1838–1911, English social reformer. 3. **Sir Rowland,** 1795–1879, originator of the penny postage.

Hillary (hĭl′ə rĭ), *n.* **Sir Edmund,** born 1919, New Zealand explorer and mountaineer: climbed Mt Everest 1953.

hillbilly (hĭl′bĭl′ĭ), *n., pl.* a rustic or yokel living in the backwoods or mountains of the Southern U.S. [f. HILL + *Billy,* pet var. of *William,* man's name]

Hilliard (hĭl′ĭ əd), *n.* **Nicholas,** *c.* 1547–1619, English miniaturist. Also, **Hillyarde.**

Hillingdon (hĭl′ĭng dən), *n.* a W outer London borough. 232,000 (est. 1965).

hillock (hĭl′ək), *n.* a little hill. —**hill′ocky,** *adj.*

hillside (hĭl′sīd′), *n.* the side or slope of a hill.

hill site, situation on a hill; an elevated site.

hill station, any town or resort in S Asia at a high altitude where relief may be found from the tropical heat.

hilltop (hĭl′tŏp′), *n.* the top or summit of a hill.

hilly (hĭl′ĭ), *adj.*, **hillier, hilliest. 1.** abounding in hills: *hilly country.* **2.** elevated; steep. **—hill′iness,** *n.*

hilt (hĭlt), *n.* **1.** the handle of a sword or dagger. **2.** the handle of any weapon or tool. **3. to the hilt,** fully; completely: *armed to the hilt.* *—v.t.* **4.** to furnish with a hilt. [ME *hylt*, OE *hilt, hilte*, c. MD *hilt, hilte*; of obscure orig.] —**hilt′ed,** *adj.*

hilum (hī′ləm), *n., pl.* **-la** (-lə). **1.** *Bot.* **a.** the mark or scar on a seed produced by separation from its funicle or placenta. See diag. under **seed. b.** the nucleus of a granule of starch. **2.** *Anat.* the region at which the vessels, nerves, etc., enter or emerge from a part. [t. L: little thing, trifle]

Hilversum (hĭl′və so͝om′; *Du.* hĭl′vər sʏm), *n.* a town in the Netherlands, in E North Holland. 102,992 (1965).

him (hĭm), *pron.* objective case of *he.* [ME and OE: dat. of *hē* HE]

H.I.M., His, or Her, Imperial Majesty.

Himachal Pradesh (hĭ mä′chəl prä dĕsh′), a centrally administered territory in N India. 1,351,144 pop. (1961); 10,904 sq. mi. *Cap.:* Simla.

Himalayas (hĭm′ə lā′əz, hĭ mä′lyəz), *n.pl.* **The,** a lofty mountain system extending ab. 1500 mi. along the border between India and Tibet. Highest peak (in the world), Mt Everest, 29,028 ft. Also, **The Himalaya** or **Himalaya Mountains.** See map under **Punjab.** [t. Skt: lit., snow dwelling] —**Himalayan** (hĭm′ə lā′ən), *adj.*

himation (hĭ măt′ĭ ŏn′), *n., pl.* **-matia** (-măt′ĭ ə). *Gk Antiq.* a garment consisting of a rectangular piece of cloth thrown over the left shoulder and wrapped about the body. [t. Gk]

Himeji (hē′mĭ jē′), *n.* a city in S Japan, on Honshu island, W of Kobe. 367,807 (1965).

Himmler (*Ger.* hĭm′lər), *n.* **Heinrich** (*Ger.* hĭn′rĭkh), 1900–45, Nazi leader in Germany; chief of police and head of the Gestapo and the SS from 1936.

himself (hĭm sĕlf′; *medially often* ĭm-), *pron.* **1.** a reflexive form of *him*: *he cut himself.* **2.** an emphatic form of *him* or *he used*: **a.** as object: *he used it for himself.* **b.** in apposition to a subject or object: *he himself did it.* **3.** his proper or normal self; his usual state of mind (used after *be, become,* or *come to*): *he is himself again.*

Himyarite (hĭm′yə rīt′), *n.* **1.** one of an ancient people of southern Arabia, of an advanced civilization, speaking an Arabic dialect closely akin to Ethiopic. **2.** a descendant of these people. *—adj.* **3.** Himyaritic. [f. Ar. *Himyar* (name of a tribe and an old dynasty of Yemen) + -ITE[1]]

Himyaritic (hĭm′yə rĭt′ĭk), *adj.* **1.** pertaining to the Himyarites and to the remains of their civilization. *—n.* **2.** a Semitic language anciently spoken in southern Arabia.

hinau (hē′nou), *n.* an evergreen tree, *Elaeocarpus dentatus*, of New Zealand, with straw-coloured flowers. [t. Maori]

Hinckley (hĭngk′lĭ), *n.* a town in England, on the Leicestershire-Warwickshire border. 41,573 (1961).

hind[1] (hīnd), *adj.*, **hinder, hindmost** or **hindermost.** situated behind or at the back; posterior: *the hind legs of an animal.* [? short for BEHIND, but cf. OE *hindan*, adv., from behind, G *hinten*, adv.] **—Syn.** See **back[1].**

hind[2] (hīnd), *n.* *Zool.* the female of the deer, chiefly the red deer, esp. in and after the third year. [ME and OE; c. Icel. *hind.* Cf. D *hinde* and G *Hinde*]

hind[3] (hīnd), *n.* *Archaic.* **1.** a peasant or rustic. **2.** a farm worker, esp. a skilled one. **3.** a bailiff; steward. [ME *hine*, sing., earlier ME and OE *hīne*, pl., der. *hī(g)na*, gen. pl. of *hīgan* members of a household, domestics. See HIDE[3]]

Hind., 1. Hindustan. 2. Hindustani.

hindbrain (hīnd′brān′), *n.* *Anat.* **1.** the cerebellum, pons, and medulla oblongata or the embryonic nervous tissue from which they develop; the entire rhombencephalon or some part of it. **2.** the metencephalon.

Hindemith (*Ger.* hĭn′də mĭt), *n.* **Paul** (*Ger.* poul), 1895–1963, German composer.

Hindenburg (hĭn′dən bûg′; *Ger.* -bo͝ork), *n.* **1. Paul von** (*Ger.* poul fŏn) (*Paul von Beneckendorff und von Hindenburg*), 1847–1934, German field marshal; 2nd president of Germany 1925–34. **2.** German name of **Zabrze.**

Hindenburg line, a line of elaborate fortification established by the German army in World War I, near the French-Belgian border, from Lille SE to Metz.

hinder[1] (hĭn′də), *v.t.* **1.** to interrupt; check; retard: *to be hindered by storms.* **2.** to prevent from acting or taking place; stop: *to hinder a man from committing a crime.* *—v.i.* 3. to be an obstacle or impediment. [ME *hindre(n)*, OE *hindrian* (c. G *hindern*, etc.) der. *hinder* behind, back] **—hin′derer,** *n.* **—hin′deringly,** *adv.* **—Syn. 1.** impede, encumber, delay, hamper, obstruct, trammel. **2.** block, thwart. See **prevent. —Ant. 1.** expedite. **2.** aid.

hinder[2] (hīn′də), *adj.* situated at the rear or back; posterior: *the hinder part of the ship.* [ME, appar. repr. OE *hinder*, adv., behind, c. G *hinter*, prep.]

hindgut (hīnd′gŭt′), *n.* *Embryol., Zool.* the lower portion of the embryonic digestive canal from which the colon and rectum develop.

Hindi (hĭn′dĭ), *n.* **1.** one of the modern Indic languages of northern India, usually divided into Eastern and Western Hindi. **2.** a literary language derived from Hindustani, used by Hindus. [t. Hind., der. *Hind* India]

Hindley (hīnd′lĭ), *n.* a town in England, in central S Lancashire. 19,395 (1961).

hindmost (hīnd′mōst′), *adj.* farthest behind; nearest the rear; last. Also, **hindermost** (hīn′də mōst′).

Hindoo (hĭn do͞o′), *n., pl.* **-doos,** *adj.* Hindu.

Hindooism (hĭn′do͞o ĭz′əm), *n.* Hinduism.

Hindoostani (hĭn′do͞o stä′nĭ), *adj., n.* Hindustani.

hindquarter (hīnd′kwô′tə), *n.* **1.** the posterior end of a halved carcass of beef, lamb, etc., sectioned usually between the twelfth and thirteenth ribs. **2.** rear part.

hindrance (hĭn′drəns), *n.* **1.** an impeding, stopping, or preventing. **2.** a means or cause of hindering. **—Syn. 2.** impediment, encumbrance, obstruction, check; restraint. See **obstacle. —Ant. 2.** aid.

hindsight (hīnd′sīt′), *n.* perception of the nature and exigencies of a case after the event: *hindsight is easier than foresight.*

Hindu (hĭn do͞o′), *n.* **1.** a native of India who adheres to Hinduism. **2.** any person who adheres to Hinduism. *—adj.* **3.** of or pertaining to Hindus or Hinduism. Also, **Hindoo.** [t. Hind., Pers., der. *Hind* India]

Hinduism (hĭn′do͞o ĭz′əm), *n.* the dominant religion of India, evolved from the teaching of the Vedas, comprising a complex body of religious, social, cultural, and philosophical beliefs, and characterized by a system of divinely ordained caste. Although it has a general tendency towards pantheism, in its popular form it is polytheistic and is marked by an absence of creed or dogma, an elaborate ritual, and a belief in reincarnation. Also, **Hindooism.**

Hindu Kush (hĭn′do͞o ko͞osh′), a lofty mountain system largely in NE Afghanistan, extending W from the Himalayas. Highest peak, Tirach Mir, 25,420 ft. Also, **Hindu Kush Mountains.**

Hindustan (hĭn′do͞o stän′), *n.* **1.** Persian name of India, esp. the part N of the Deccan. **2.** the predominantly Hindu areas of India as contrasted with the predominantly Muslim areas of Pakistan. See **India.**

Hindustani (hĭn′do͞o stä′nĭ), *n.* **1.** a standard language or lingua franca of northern India based on a dialect of Western Hindi spoken around Delhi. *—adj.* **2.** of or pertaining to Hindustan, its people, or their languages. Also, **Hindoostani.** [t. Hind., Pers., der. HINDUSTAN]

hindward (hīnd′wəd), *adj.* backward. **—hindwards,** *adv.*

hinge (hĭnj), *n., v.,* **hinged, hinging. —***n.* **1.** the movable joint or device on which a door, gate, shutter, lid, or the like, turns or moves. **2.** a natural anatomical joint at which motion occurs about a transverse axis, as that of the knee or a bivalve shell. **3.** that on which something turns or depends; principle; central rule. *—v.i.* **4.** to depend or turn on, or as if on, a hinge: *everything hinges on his decision.* *—v.t.* **5.** to furnish with or attach by a a hinge or hinges. **6.** to attach as by a hinge. **7.** to cause to depend: *to hinge action upon future sales.* [ME *heng, hing*, OE *hencg.* See HANG, v.] **—hinged,** *adj.*

hinny (hĭn′ĭ), *n., pl.* **-nies.** the offspring of a stallion and she-donkey. See **mule[1]** (defs 1, 2). [t. L: m. s. *hinnus*]

Hinshelwood (hĭn′shəl wo͝od′), *n.* **Sir Cyril Norman,** born 1897, English chemist.

hint (hĭnt), *n.* **1.** an indirect or covert suggestion or implication; an intimation. **2.** a brief, helpful suggestion; a piece of advice. **3.** a very small or barely perceptible amount. **4.** *Obs.* an occasion or opportunity. *—v.t.* **5.** to give a hint of. *—v.i.* **6.** to make indirect suggestion or allusion (usually fol. by *at*). [var. of *hent*, n., der. HENT, v., seize] **—hint′er,** *n.*

—Syn. 1. allusion, insinuation, innuendo; memorandum, reminder; inkling. **5.** imply. HINT, INTIMATE, INSINUATE, SUGGEST denote the conveying of an idea to the mind indirectly or without full or explicit statement. To HINT is to convey an idea covertly or indirectly, but intelligibly: *to hint that one would like a certain present, to hint that bits of gossip might be true.* To INTIMATE is to give a barely perceptible hint, often with the purpose of influencing action: *to intimate that something may be possible.* To INSINUATE is to hint artfully, often at what one would not dare to say directly: *to insinuate something against someone's reputation.* SUGGEST denotes particularly recalling something to the mind or starting a new train of thought by means of association of ideas: *the name doesn't suggest anything to me.* **—Ant. 5.** express, declare.

hinterland (hĭn′tə lănd′), *n.* **1.** an inland area supplying goods to a port. **2.** the land lying behind a coast district.

3. an area or sphere of influence in the unoccupied interior claimed by the state possessing the coast. **4.** the remote or less developed parts of a country. [t. G: lit., hinder land, i.e. land behind]

hip[1] (hĭp), *n.*, *v.*, **hipped, hipping.** —*n.* **1.** the projecting part of each side of the body formed by the side of the pelvis and the upper part of the femur, with the flesh covering them; the haunch. **2.** the hip joint. **3. have someone on** (or **upon**) **the hip,** to have someone at a disadvantage. **4.** *Archit.* the inclined projecting angle formed by the junction of a sloping side and a sloping end, or of two adjacent sloping sides, of a roof. See illus. under **hip roof.** —*v.t.* **5.** to injure or dislocate the hip of. **6.** *Archit.* to form (a roof) with a hip or hips. [ME; OE *hype*, c. G. *Hüfte*] —**hip′less,** *adj.* —**hip′like′,** *adj.*

hip[2] (hĭp), *n.* the ripe fruit of a rose, esp. of a wild rose. [ME *hepe*, OE *hēope* hip, brier, c. OHG *hiufo* bramble]

hip[3] (hĭp), *interj.* (an exclamation used in cheers or in signalling for cheers): *hip, hip, hurrah!* [orig. unknown]

hip[4] (hĭp), *adj. U.S. Slang.* hep.

hipbath (hĭp′bäth′), *n.* a bath in which one can sit, but not lie down.

hipbone (hĭp′bōn′), *n.* the innominate bone.

hipflask (hĭp′fläsk′), *n.* a flask, usually containing alcoholic liquor, carried in a hip pocket.

hip joint, the joint between the hip and the thigh.

hipparch (hĭp′äk), *n.* (in ancient Greece) a commander of cavalry. [t. Gk: s. *hípparchos*]

Hipparchus (hĭ pä′kəs), *n.* **1.** died 514 B.C., tyrant of Athens. **2.** fl. 146–126 B.C., Greek astronomer, mathematician, and geographer.

hipped[1] (hĭpt), *adj.* **1.** having hips. **2.** *Archit.* formed with a hip or hips, as a roof. [f. HIP[1] + -ED[3]]

hipped[2] (hĭpt), *adj.* **1.** *U.S. Slang.* greatly interested in; having an obsession (usually fol. by *on*): *he's hipped on playing a tuba.* **2.** Also, **hip′pish.** melancholy; depressed; bored. [earlier *hypped*, der. *hyp*, n., short form of HYPOCHONDRIA]

hippie (hĭp′ĭ), *n.* one who rejects conventional social values in favour of new standards of awareness, sometimes drug-induced, universal love or union with nature, etc. [? f. HIP[4] + -IE]

hippo (hĭp′ō), *n.*, *pl.* **-pos.** *Colloq.* hippopotamus.

Hippo (hĭp′ō), *n.* Hippo Regius.

hippocampus (hĭp′ō kăm′pəs), *n.*, *pl.* **-pi** (-pī). **1.** *Class. Myth.* a seahorse with two forefeet, and a body ending in the tail of a dolphin or fish. **2.** *Anat.* an enfolding of cerebral cortex into the cavity of a cerebral hemisphere having the shape in cross-section of a seahorse. [t. L: a sea-monster, t. Gk: m. *hippokámpos*]

hippocras (hĭp′ō krăs′), *n.* an old cordial made of wine mixed with spices, etc. [ME *ypocras*, t. OF; from the name of HIPPOCRATES]

Hippocrates (hĭ pŏk′rə tēz′), *n.* 460?–357 B.C., Greek physician, known as the father of medicine. —**Hippocratic** (hĭp′ō krăt′ĭk), *adj.*

Hippocratic oath, an oath embodying the duties and obligations of physicians, sometimes taken by those about to enter upon the practice of medicine.

Hippocrene (hĭp′ō krēn′, hĭp′ō krē′nĭ), *n.* a spring on Mount Helicon, sacred to the Muses and regarded as a source of poetic inspiration. [t. L, t. Gk: m. *Hippokrēnē*, for *Hippou krēnē* horse's fountain]

hippodrome (hĭp′ə drōm′), *n.* **1.** an arena or structure for equestrian and other spectacles. **2.** (in ancient Greece and Rome) a course or circus for horseraces and chariot races. **3.** a variety theatre; music hall. [t. L: m. s. *hippodromos* a racecourse, t. Gk]

hippogriff (hĭp′ō grĭf′), *n.* a fabulous creature resembling a griffin but having the body and hind parts of a horse. Also, **hippogryph.** [t. F: m. *hippogriffe*, t. It.: m. *ippogrifo*, f. *ippo-* (t. Gk: m. *hippos* horse) + *grifo* GRIFFIN[1]]

Hippolyte (hĭ pŏl′ĭ tē′), *n. Gk Legend.* a queen of the Amazons, married to Theseus. Also, **Hippol′yta.**

Hippolytus (hĭ pŏl′ĭ təs), *n. Gk Legend.* the son of Theseus by Hippolyte, who was falsely accused by his stepmother Phaedra of raping her. Theseus called upon Poseidon for vengeance, and the god sent a sea-monster which caused Hippolytus's horses to drag him to death.

Hippomenes (hĭ pŏm′ĭ nēz′), *n.* (in some stories) the successful suitor of Atalanta.

hippopotamus (hĭp′ə pŏt′ə məs), *n.*, *pl.* **-muses, -mi** (-mī′). a large herbivorous mammal, *Hippopotamus amphibius*, having a thick hairless body, short legs, and large head and muzzle, found in and near the rivers, lakes, etc., of Africa, and able to remain under water for a considerable time. [t. L, t. Gk: lit., river-horse; r. ME *ypotame*, t. OF, t. ML: m. *ypotamus*]

Hippopotamus, *Hippototamus amphibius* (4½ ft high at shoulder, length 13 ft)

Hippo Regius (hĭp′ō rē′jĭ əs), a seaport of ancient Numidia: St Augustine was bishop here; the site of modern Annaba, Algeria. Also, **Hippo.**

Hippo Zarytus (hĭp′ō zə rī′təs), an ancient city in N Africa: the site of modern Bizerte.

hippy[1] (hĭp′ĭ), *adj. Colloq.* having large hips.

hippy[2] (hĭp′ĭ), *n.* hippie.

hip roof, *Archit.* a roof with sloping ends and sides; a hipped roof.

H, Hip roof

hipshot (hĭp′shŏt′), *adj.* **1.** having the hip dislocated. **2.** lame; awkward. [f. HIP[1], n. + SHOT[2], pp.]

hipster (hĭp′stə), *adj.* **1.** (of trousers or skirt) hanging from the hips, not from the waist. —*n.* **2.** (*pl.*) a pair of trousers or a skirt hanging thus. **3.** *Slang.* a hippie.

Hirakata (hĭ rä′kə tə, hĭ′rə kä′tə), *n.* a town in Japan, in S Honshu island. 127,520 (1965).

Hiram (hī′ə rəm), *n.* 10th-century B.C. king of Tyre. I Kings 5.

Hiratsuka (hĭ răt′so͝o kə, hĭ′rət so͞o′kə), *n.* a town in Japan, in SE central Honshu island. 134,931 (1965).

hircine (hû′sīn), *adj.* **1.** of, pertaining to, or resembling a goat. **2.** having a goatish smell. **3.** lustful. [t. L: m. s. *hircīnus* of a goat]

hire (hī′ə), *v.*, **hired, hiring,** *n.* —*v.t.* **1.** to engage the services of for payment: *to hire a clerk.* **2.** to engage the temporary use of for payment: *to hire a car.* **3.** to grant the temporary use of, or the services of, for a payment. (often fol. by *out*). —*n.* **4.** the price or compensation paid, or contracted to be paid, for the temporary use of something or for personal services or labour; pay. **5.** the act of hiring. [ME; OE *hȳr*, c. G *Heuer*] —**hir′eable,** *adj.* —**hir′er,** *n.*

—**Syn. 1, 2.** let, lease. HIRE, CHARTER, RENT refer to paying money for the use of something. HIRE is a general word, most commonly applied to paying money for labour or services, but is also used in reference to paying for the temporary use of transport, halls, etc. CHARTER formerly meant to pay for the use of a vessel, but is now applied with increasing frequency to hiring any conveyance for the use of a group: *to charter a boat, a bus.* RENT is used in the latter sense, also, but is usually applied to paying a set sum once or at regular intervals for the use of a dwelling, room, personal effects, etc.: *to rent business premises.*

hireling (hī′ə lĭng), *n.* **1.** one working only for payment (now usually in contempt). **2.** a mercenary. —*adj.* **3.** serving for hire (now usually in contempt). **4.** venal; mercenary.

hire-purchase (hī′ə pû′chĭs), *n.* **1.** a system whereby a person pays for a commodity by regular instalments, while having full use of it after the first payment. —*adj.* **2.** pertaining to or bought with the aid of such a system.

Hirohito (hĭ′rō hē′tō), *n.* born 1901, emperor of Japan since 1926.

Hirosaki (hĭ rō′sə kĭ, hĭ′rə sä′kĭ), *n.* a town in Japan, in N Honshu island. 151,624 (1965).

Hiroshima (hĭ′rŏ shē′mə, hĭ rŏsh′ĭ mə), *n.* a seaport in SW Japan, on Honshu island: the first military use of the atomic bomb, Aug. 6th, 1945. 343,968 (1940); 171,902 (1946); 504,245 (1965).

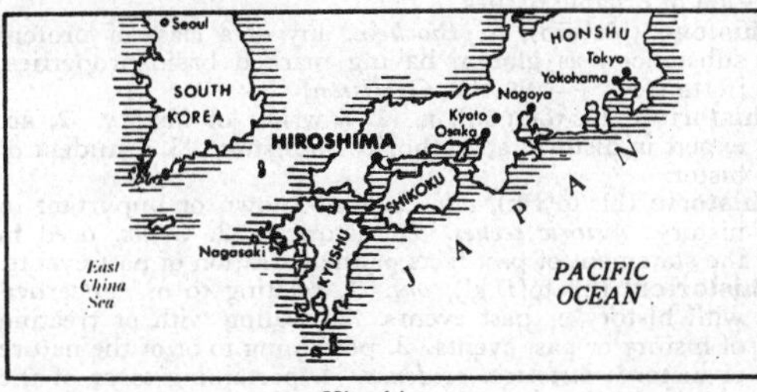

Hiroshima

hirsute (hû′syo͞ot), *adj.* **1.** hairy. **2.** *Bot., Zool.* covered with long, rather stiff hairs. **3.** of, pertaining to, or of the nature of hair. [t. L: m. s. *hirsūtus* rough, hairy] —**hir′suteness,** *n.*

Hirudinea (hĭ′ro͞o dĭn′ĭ ə), *n.pl.* a class of annelid worms comprising the leeches. [NL, der. L *hirūdo* leech]

hirundine (hĭ rŭn′dīn), *adj.* of, pertaining to, or resembling the swallow. [t. LL: s. *hirundineus*]

his (hĭz), *pron.* **1.** the possessive form of *he*: *this book is his.* **2.** the person(s) or thing(s) belonging to him: *himself and his, a friend of his.* —*adj.* **3.** belonging to, pertaining to, or owned by him; made, done, experienced etc., by him. [ME and OE; gen. of masc. *hē* HE, also of neut. *hit* IT]

Hispania (hĭs păn′ĭ ə), *n. Poetic.* Spain. [t. L: the Spanish peninsula (with Portugal)]

Hispanic (hĭs păn′ĭk), *adj.* **1.** Spanish. **2.** Latin American.

Hispanicism (hĭs păn′ĭ sĭz′əm), *n.* a Spanish idiom.

Hispanicize (hĭs păn′ĭ sīz′), *v.t.*, **-cized, -cizing.** to make Spanish, as in culture or custom; bring under Spanish influence or control. Also, **Hispanicise.**

Hispaniola (hĭs′păn ĭ ō′lə; *Sp.* ēs pä nyō′lä), *n.* an island in the West Indies, comprising the republic of Haiti and the Dominican Republic. 7,000,000 pop. (est. 1960); 29,843 sq. mi. Formerly, **Haiti.**

hispid (hĭs′pĭd), *adj. Bot., Zool.* rough with stiff hairs, bristles, or minute spines. [t. L: s. *hispidus*] **—hispid′ity,** *n.*

hiss (hĭs), *v.i.* **1.** to make or emit a sharp sound like that of the letter *s* prolonged, as a goose or a snake does, or as steam does rushing through a small opening. **2.** to express disapproval or contempt by making this sound. *—v.t.* **3.** to express disapproval of by hissing. **4.** to force or drive by hissing (fol. by *away, down,* etc.). **5.** to utter with a hiss. *—n.* **6.** a hissing sound, esp. in disapproval. [unexplained var. of d. E *hish*, ME *hisshe(n)* hiss, OE *hyscan* jeer at, rail] **—hiss′er,** *n.*

hissing (hĭs′ĭng), *n.* **1.** the act of hissing. **2.** the sound of a hiss. **3.** *Archaic.* an occasion or object of scorn.

hist (hĭst), *interj.* **1.** (a sibilant exclamation used to attract attention, command silence, etc.) *—v.t.* **2.** to use the exclamation 'hist' to. [var. of WHIST[1]. Cf. HUSH]

hist., 1. histology. **2.** historical. **3.** history.

histaminase (hĭs tăm′ĭ nās′), *n. Biochem.* an enzyme capable of making histamine inactive, used in treating allergies.

histamine (hĭs′tə mēn′, -mĭn), *n. Biochem.* an amine, $C_5H_9N_3$, obtained from histidine and found in ergot. It is released by the tissues in allergic reactions, is a powerful uterine stimulant, and lowers the blood pressure. [f. HIST(IDINE) + AMINE] **—histaminic** (hĭs′tə mĭn′ĭk), *adj.*

histidine (hĭs′tĭ dēn′, -dĭn), *n. Chem., Biochem.* an amino acid, $C_6H_9N_3O_2$, occurring in proteins, and converted by putrefactive organisms into histamine. [f. HIST(O)- + -ID[3] + -INE[2]. Cf. G. *Histidin*]

histo-, a word element meaning 'tissue', as in *histogen.* Also, before vowels, **hist-.** [t. Gk, comb. form of *histós* web, tissue]

histogen (hĭs′tə jĕn′), *n. Bot.* the regions in a plant in which tissues undergo differentiation.

histogenesis (hĭs′tō jĕn′ĭ sĭs), *n. Biol.* the formation and differentiation of a tissue.

histogram (hĭs′tə grăm′), *n. Statistics.* a graph of a frequency distribution in which equal intervals of values are marked on a horizontal axis and the frequency corresponding to each interval is indicated by the height of a rectangle having the interval as its base.

histoid (hĭs′toid), *adj. Pathol.* denoting a tumour composed of connective tissue or its equivalent.

histology (hĭs tŏl′ə jĭ), *n.* **1.** the science that treats of organic tissues. **2.** the study of the structure, esp. the microscopic structure, of organic tissues. **—histological** (hĭs′tə lŏj′ĭ kl), **his′tolog′ic,** *adj.* **—histol′ogist,** *n.*

histolysis (hĭs tŏl′ĭ sĭs), *n. Biol.* disintegration or dissolution of organic tissues.

histone (hĭs′tōn), *n. Biochem.* any of a class of protein substances, as globin, having marked basic properties. [f. HIST(O)- + -ONE. Cf. G *Histon*]

historian (hĭs tô′rĭ ən), *n.* **1.** a writer of history. **2.** an expert in history; an authority on history. **3.** a student of history.

historic (hĭs tŏ′rĭk), *adj.* **1.** well-known or important in history: *historic scenes.* **2.** historical. **3.** *Gram.* used in the statement of past facts or the narration of past events.

historical (hĭs tŏ′rĭ kl), *adj.* **1.** relating to or concerned with history or past events. **2.** dealing with or treating of history or past events. **3.** pertaining to or of the nature of history: *historical evidence.* **4.** pertaining to or of the nature of history as opposed to legend or fiction: *the historical King Arthur.* **5.** narrated or mentioned in history; belonging to the past. **6.** historic (def. 1). **7.** *Gram.* historic (def. 3). [f. s. L *historicus* (t. Gk: m. *historikós*) + -AL[1]] **—histor′ically,** *adv.* **—histor′icalness,** *n.*

historical geography, 1. the study of the geography of a past period or periods. **2.** geographic history.

historical materialism, that part of Marxist theory which maintains that ideas and institutions develop as a superstructure upon an economic base, that they are altered as a result of class struggles, and that each ruling class produces another which will destroy it, the final stage being the emergence of a classless society.

historical method, the development of general principles by the study of the historical facts.

historical present, historic present.

historical school, 1. a group of 19th-century German economists who maintained that a country's economic life is a product of its past and could be understood only by a study of its institutions. **2.** *Law.* the school of jurists who maintain that law is not to be regarded as made by commands of the sovereign, but is the result of its historical and social circumstances.

historicism (hĭs tŏ′rĭ sĭz′əm), *n.* the belief that all social and cultural facts are historically determined, that the standards of one age are inapplicable to any other, and that periods in history should only be studied in terms of their own values. **—histor′icist,** *n., adj.*

historicity (hĭs′tə rĭs′ĭ tĭ), *n.* historical authenticity.

historiographer (hĭs′tô rĭ ŏg′rə fə), *n.* **1.** a historian. **2.** an official historian, as of a court, an institution, etc. [f. s. LL *historiographus* (t. Gk: m. *historiográphos*) + -ER[1]]

historiography (hĭs′tô rĭ ŏg′rə fĭ), *n.* the writing of history, esp. as based on the critical examination and evaluation of material taken from primary sources.

history (hĭs′tə rĭ, hĭs′trĭ), *n., pl.* **-ries. 1.** the branch of knowledge dealing with past events. **2.** the record of past events, esp. in connection with the human race. **3.** a continuous, systematic written narrative, in order of time, of past events as relating to a particular people, country, period, person, etc. **4.** the aggregate of past events. **5.** a past worthy of record or out of the ordinary: *a ship with a history.* **6.** a systematic account of any set of natural phenomena, without reference to time. **7.** a drama representing historical events. [ME, t. L: m. s. *historia*, t. Gk: a learning or knowing by inquiry, information, narrative, history] **—Syn. 2.** account, record, chronicle; annals. See **narrative.**

histrionic (hĭs′trĭ ŏn′ĭk), *adj.* **1.** of or pertaining to actors or acting. **2.** artificial; theatrical. Also, **his′trion′ical.** [t. LL: s. *histriōnicus*] **—his′trion′ically,** *adv.*

histrionics (hĭs′trĭ ŏn′ĭks), *n.pl.* **1.** dramatic representation; theatricals; acting. **2.** artificial or melodramatic behaviour, speech, etc., for effect.

hit (hĭt), *v.,* **hit, hitting,** *n. —v.t.* **1.** to deal a blow or stroke; bring forcibly into collision: *to hit a child.* **2.** to come against with an impact or collision, as a missile, a flying fragment, a falling body, or the like does. **3.** to reach with a missile, a weapon, a blow, or the like (intentionally or otherwise), as one throwing, shooting, or striking. **4.** to succeed in striking: *to hit the mark.* **5.** to drive or propel by a stroke. **6.** to have a marked effect on; affect severely. **7.** to assail effectively and sharply. **8.** to reach (a specified level or figure). **9.** to be published in or appear in (a newspaper). **10.** to come or light upon; meet; find: *to hit the right road.* **11.** to guess correctly. **12.** to succeed in representing or producing exactly: *to hit a likeness in a portrait.* **13.** *U.S. Colloq.* to arrive at: *to hit town.* **14.** *U.S. Colloq.* to begin to travel on: *to hit the trail.* **15. hit it off,** *Colloq.* to get on well together; agree. **16. hit off,** to represent, reproduce, or describe briefly and aptly; imitate. **17. hit on** or **upon,** to come upon unexpectedly; find by chance. *—v.i.* **18.** to strike with a missile, a weapon, or the like; deal a blow or blows (often fol. by *out*). *—n.* **19.** an impact or collision, as of one thing against another. **20.** a stroke that reaches an object; blow. **21.** *Backgammon.* **a.** a game won by a player after his opponent has thrown off one or more men from the board. **b.** any winning game. **22.** a successful stroke, performance, or production; success: *the play is a hit.* **23.** an effective or telling expression or saying; gibe; taunt. [ME *hitte(n)*, OE *hittan*, t. Scand.; cf. Icel. *hitta* come upon (by chance), meet] **—hit′table,** *adj.* **—hit′ter,** *n.* **—Syn. 1.** See **strike, beat.**

Hitachi (hĭ tä′chĭ), *n.* a town in Japan, in E central Hokkaido island. 179,703 (1965).

hit-and-run (hĭt′n rŭn′), *adj.* **1.** denoting or pertaining to the driver of a motor vehicle who leaves the scene of an accident in which he was involved without stopping to give assistance or fulfil any legal obligations. **2.** (of an air-raid) lasting only a short time and marked by a rapid withdrawal from the area of attack.

hitch (hĭch), *v.t.* **1.** to make fast, esp. temporarily, by means of a hook, rope, strap, etc.; tether. **2.** to harness (an animal) to a vehicle (often fol. by *up*). **3.** to raise with jerks (usually fol. by *up*): *to hitch up one's trousers.* **4.** to move or draw (something) with a jerk. **5.** *Colloq.* to obtain or seek to obtain (a ride) from a passing vehicle. *—v.i.* **6.** to harness an animal to a vehicle (fol. by *up*). **7.** to become fastened or caught, as on something. **8.** to stick, as when caught. **9.** to fasten oneself or itself to something (often fol. by *on*). **10.** *Colloq.* to seek to obtain a ride from passing vehicles. *—n.* **11.** a making fast, as to something, esp. temporarily. **12.** *Naut., etc.* any of various forms of knot or fastening made with rope or the like. See illus. under **knot.** **13.** a halt; an obstruction: *a hitch in the proceedings.* **14.** a hitching movement; a jerk or pull. **15.** a fastening that joins a movable tool to the mechanism that pulls it. **16.** *U.S. Colloq.* a period of military service. **17.** *Colloq.* a ride from a passing vehicle. [ME *hytche(n)*; orig. uncert.] **—hitch′er,** *n.* **—Syn. 1.** fasten, attach, tie, tether. **2.** yoke. **—Ant. 1.** loosen.

Hitchcock (hĭch′kŏk′), *n.* **Alfred Joseph,** born 1899, English film director in the U.S. after 1939.

hitched (hĭcht), *adj. Slang.* married.

hitchhike (hĭch′hīk′), *v.i.*, **-hiked, -hiking.** *Colloq.* to travel by obtaining rides in passing vehicles. **—hitch′-hik′er,** *n.*

Hitchin (hĭch′ĭn), *n.* a town in England, in N Hertfordshire. 24,243 (1961).

hitching post, a post to which horses, etc., are tied.

hither (hĭth′ə), *adv.* **1.** to or towards this place; here: *to come hither.* **2. hither and thither,** this way and that; in various directions. **—*adj.* 3.** on or towards this side; nearer: *the hither side of the hill.* **4.** earlier; more remote. [ME and OE *hider*, c. Icel. *hedhra*; der. demonstrative stem represented by HE]

hithermost (hĭth′ə mōst′), *adj.* nearest in this direction.

hitherto (hĭth′ə to͞o′), *adv.* **1.** up to this time; until now: *a fact hitherto unknown.* **2.** *Archaic.* to here.

hitherwards (hĭth′ə wədz), *adv. Archaic.* hither. Also, **hitherward.**

Hitler (hĭt′lə), *n.* **Adolf** (ăd′ŏlf; *Ger.* ȧ′dŏlf) (*'der Führer'*), 1889–1945, Nazi dictator of Germany, born in Austria: chancellor 1933–45; dictator 1934–45.

Hitlerism (hĭt′lə rĭz′əm), *n.* the principles, policies, and methods of the Nazi party as expounded and developed by Adolf Hitler.

Hitlerite (hĭt′lə rīt′), *n.* **1.** an advocate of Hitlerism; a follower of Adolf Hitler. **—*adj.* 2.** of or pertaining to Hitler or Hitlerism.

hit-or-miss (hĭt′ô mĭs′), *adj.* haphazard; random.

Hittite (hĭt′īt), *n.* **1.** one of a powerful, civilized ancient people who flourished in Asia Minor and adjoining regions (1900–1200 B.C.). **2.** an extinct language of the Indo-European family, preserved in cuneiform inscriptions. **3.** inscriptions, in hieroglyphics, of a language related to the preceding. **—*adj.* 4.** having to do with the Hittites or their language. [f. Heb. *Hitt(īm)*, (cf. Hittite *Khatti*) + -ITE[1], r. earlier *Hethite* (cf. Vulgate *Hethaeī*)]

hive (hīv), *n.*, *v.*, **hived, hiving.** **—*n.* 1.** an artificial shelter for honeybees; a beehive. **2.** the bees inhabiting a hive. **3.** something resembling a beehive in structure or use. **4.** a place swarming with busy occupants: *a hive of industry.* **5.** a swarming or teeming multitude. **—*v.t.* 6.** to gather into or cause to enter a hive. **7.** to shelter as in a hive. **8.** to store up in a hive. **9.** to lay up for future use or enjoyment. **10. hive off,** *Com. Colloq.* to assign production (of goods, etc.) to a subsidiary company. **—*v.i.* 11.** to enter a hive. **12.** to live together in a hive. [ME; OE *hȳf.* Cf. Icel. *hūfr* ship's hull] **—hive′less,** *adj.* **—hive′like′,** *adj.*

hives (hīvz), *n.* any of various eruptive diseases of the skin, as the weals of urticaria. [orig. Scot.]

H.J., (L *hic jacet*) here lies.

H.J.S., (L *hic jacet sepultus*) here lies buried.

hl., hectolitre.

H.L., House of Lords.

hm., hectometre.

H.M., His (or Her) Majesty.

H.M.S., **1.** His, or Her, Majesty's Service. **2.** His, or Her, Majesty's Ship.

H.M.S.O., His, or Her, Majesty's Stationery Office.

H.N.C., Higher National Certificate.

H.N.D., Higher National Diploma.

Ho, *Chem.* holmium.

ho (hō), *interj.* **1.** (an exclamation of surprise, exultation.) **2.** (a call to attract attention (sometimes specially used after a word denoting a destination)): *westward ho!* [ME; c. Icel. *hō*]

H.O., Head Office; Home Office.

hoactzin (hō ăk′tsĭn), *n.* hoatzin.

Hoangho (wăng′hō′), *n.* Hwang Ho.

hoar (hô), *adj.* **1.** covered with hoarfrost. **2.** *Archaic.* grey-haired with age; hoary; old. **—*n.* 3.** a hoary coating or appearance. **4.** hoarfrost. [ME *hor*, OE *hār*, c. G *hehr* august, sublime]

hoard (hôd), *n.* **1.** an accumulation of something for preservation or future use: *a hoard of gold.* **—*v.t.* 2.** to accumulate for preservation or future use, esp. in a secluded place. **—*v.i.* 3.** to accumulate money, food, or the like, esp. in a secluded place. [ME *hord(e)*, OE *hord*, c. OHG *hort* treasure] **—hoard′er,** *n.*

hoarding[1] (hô′dĭng), *n.* **1.** the act of one who hoards. **2.** (*pl.*) that which is hoarded. [f. HOARD + -ING[1]]

hoarding[2] (hô′dĭng), *n.* **1.** a temporary fence enclosing a building during erection. **2.** a billboard. [der. obs. *hoard*, n., appar. t. MD: m. *horde* hurdle. Cf. obs. F *hourd* scaffolding]

Hoare (hô), *n.* **Sir Samuel John Gurney** (gû′nĭ). See **Templewood.**

hoarfrost (hô′frŏst′), *n.* frost (def. 3).

hoarfrost point, *Meteorol.* the temperature to which humid air must be cooled, without change of pressure or humidity, for it to become saturated in the presence of ice. Also, **frost point.**

hoarhound (hô′hound′), *n.* horehound.

hoarse (hôs), *adj.*, **hoarser, hoarsest.** **1.** having a vocal tone characterized by weakness of intensity and excessive breathiness; husky. **2.** having a raucous voice. **3.** making a harsh, low sound. [ME *hoors*, appar. t. Scand.; cf. Icel. *hāss*; r. ME *hoos*, OE *hās*, c. LG *hēs*] **—hoarse′ly,** *adv.* **—hoarse′ness,** *n.* **—Syn. 1.** gruff, harsh, grating.

hoarsen (hô′sən), *v.t.*, *v.i.* to make or become hoarse.

hoary (hô′rĭ), *adj.*, **hoarier, hoariest.** **1.** grey or white with age. **2.** ancient or venerable. **3.** grey or white. **—hoar′iness,** *n.*

hoary cress, a cruciferous perennial herb, *Cardaria draba*, a vigorous weed of cultivated land in temperate regions, spreading by means of underground stolons and root buds. Also, **hoary pepperwort** (pĕp′ə wût′).

hoatzin (hō ăt′sĭn), *n.* a South American crested bird, *Opisthocomus hoazin*, remarkable for claws on its wings. Also, **hoactzin.** [t. Amer. Sp., t. Nahuatl *uatzin* pheasant]

hoax (hōks), *n.* **1.** a humorous or mischievous deception, esp. a practical joke. **—*v.t.* 2.** to deceive by a hoax. [appar. contr. of HOCUS] **—hoax′er,** *n.*

hob[1] (hŏb), *n.* **1.** a projection or shelf around a fireplace, for kettles, saucepans, etc. **2.** a rounded peg or pin used as a target in certain games, as quoits. **3.** any of these games. **4.** the hardened-steel master tool used in hobbing. [var. of obs. *hub* hob (in a fireplace); ? same as HUB]

hob[2] (hŏb), *n.* **1.** a hobgoblin or elf. **2.** *Colloq.* mischief: *to play hob.* [ME *Hob*, for *Robert*, or *Robin*, man's name]

Hobart (hō′bät), *n.* a seaport in and the capital of Tasmania, in the S part. 121,275 (1963). See map under **Tasmania.**

Hobbema (hŏb′ĭ mə; *Du.* hôb′ə mȧ), *n.* **Meindert** (*Du.* māyn′dərt), *c.* 1638–1709, Dutch landscape painter.

Hobbes (hŏbz), *n.* **Thomas,** 1588–1679, English philosopher.

hobbing (hŏb′ĭng), *n.* a process of forming a mould cavity by forcing a hardened-steel master into a softer cavity blank to form a mould.

Hobbism (hŏb′ĭz′əm), *n.* the doctrines of Hobbes, who advocated unreserved submission on the part of the subject to the will of the sovereign in all things.

hobble (hŏb′l), *v.*, **-bled, -bling,** *n.* **—*v.i.* 1.** to walk lamely; limp. **2.** to proceed irregularly and haltingly: *hobbling verse.* **—*v.t.* 3.** to cause to limp. **4.** to fasten together the legs of (a horse, etc.) so as to prevent free motion. **5.** to embarrass; impede; perplex. **—*n.* 6.** the act of hobbling; an uneven, halting gait; a limp. **7.** a rope, strap, etc., used to hobble an animal. **8.** *Dial or Colloq.* an awkward or difficult situation. [ME *hobelen*; appar. akin to *hob* protuberance, uneven ground. Cf. d. HG *hoppeln* jolt] **—hob′bler,** *n.* **—hob′bling,** *adj.* **—hob′-blingly,** *adv.*

hobbledehoy (hŏb′l dĭ hoi′), *n.* **1.** an adolescent boy. **2.** an awkward, clumsy boy. [orig. uncert.]

hobble skirt, a woman's ankle-length skirt which is so narrow at the bottom that it restricts her ability to walk.

Hobbs (hŏbz), *n.* **Sir John Berry** (*Jack*), 1882–1963, English cricketer.

hobby[1] (hŏb′ĭ), *n.*, *pl.* **-bies.** **1.** a spare-time activity or pastime, etc., pursued for pleasure or recreation **2.** *Archaic.* a small horse. **3.** a child's hobbyhorse. [ME *hoby*, *hobyn*, prob. for *Robin*, or *Robert*, man's name. Cf. DOBBIN, HOB[2]. Def. 2 was original meaning, whence def. 3 and *hobbyhorse.* Def. 1 is short for *hobbyhorse*] **—hob′byist,** *n.*

hobby[2] (hŏb′ĭ), *n.*, *pl.* **-bies.** a small Old World falcon, *Falco subbuteo*, formerly flown at such small game as larks. [ME, t. OF: m. *hobet*, dim. of *hobe* hobby (falcon), prob. ult. der. L *albus* white (as applied to a special kind of falcon), ? also b. with OF *hober* hop]

hobbyhorse (hŏb′ĭ hôs′), *n.* **1.** a stick with a horse's head, or a rocking horse, ridden by children. **2.** a figure of a horse, attached at the waist of a performer in a morris dance, pantomime, etc. **3.** a favourite topic; obsessive notion.

hobgoblin (hŏb′gŏb′lĭn), *n.* **1.** anything causing superstitious fear; a bogy. **2.** a mischievous goblin. **3.** (*cap.*) Puck; Robin Goodfellow. [f. HOB[2] + GOBLIN]

hobnail (hŏb′nāl′), *n.* a large-headed nail for protecting the soles of heavy boots and shoes. [f. HOB[1] + NAIL]

hobnailed (hŏb′nāld′), *adj.* **1.** furnished with hobnails. **2.** *Chiefly U.S.* rustic or uncouth.

hobnob (hŏb′nŏb′), *v.i.*, **-nobbed, -nobbing. 1.** to associate on very friendly terms: *hobnobbing with the management got him his golden handshake.* **2.** to drink together. [earlier *hab or nab* alternately, lit., have or have not]

hobo (hō′bō), *n., pl.* **-bos, -boes.** *U.S.* **1.** a tramp or vagrant. **2.** a migratory worker. [rhyming formation, ? based on *beau* fop, used as (sarcastic) word of greeting, e.g. in *hey, bo!*] —**ho′boism,** *n.*

hobson-jobson (hŏb′sən jŏb′sən), *n.* the assimilation of a word or words from a foreign language to the sound of a familiar word or words in the mother tongue. [Anglo-Indian m. Ar. *yā Hasan! yā Husain!* O Hasan! O Husain! (a cry repeated at the Muharram festival as an expression of mourning for Hasan and Husain, the grandsons of the prophet Mohammed): *hobson-jobson* itself an example of this]

Hobson's choice (hŏb′sənz), the choice of taking either the thing offered or nothing; the absence of real choice. [after Thomas *Hobson*, about 1544–1631, of Cambridge, who hired out horses, and obliged each customer to take the horse nearest the stable door or none at all]

Hochheimer (hŏk′hī′mə; *Ger.* hōKH′hī mər), *n.* a Rhine wine produced at Hochheim, near Mainz, West Germany.

Ho Chi Minh (hō′chē′mĭn′), 1892–1969, Vietnamese statesman: president of North Vietnam 1945–69.

hock[1] (hŏk), *n* **1.** the joint in the hind leg of the horse, etc., above the fetlock joint, corresponding to the ankle in man but raised from the ground and protruding backwards when bent. See illus. under **horse. 2.** a corresponding joint in a fowl —*v.t.* **3.** to hamstring. [ME *hoch, hogh, howh,* OE *hōh* hock, heel. Cf. HEEL[1]]

hock[2] (hŏk), *n.* any white Rhine wine. [short for *Hockamore* HOCHHEIMER]

hock[3] (hŏk), *v.t., n. Orig. U.S. Slang.* pawn. [t. D: m. *hok* hovel, prison, debt]

hocket (hŏk′ĭt), *n. Music.* the arbitrary insertion of rests into a vocal phrase by medieval contrapuntists. [ME, t. OF: m. *hocquet* interruption, hiccup]

hockey (hŏk′ĭ), *n.* a game in which opposing sides seek with sticks curved at one end to drive a ball (in **field hockey**) or puck (in **ice hockey**) into their opponents' goal. [der. *hock* stick with hook at one end, var. of HOOK]

hockey stick, *n.* a long stick curved at the base for hitting the ball in hockey.

hockshop (hŏk′shŏp′), *n. U.S. Slang.* pawnshop.

hocus (hō′kəs), *v.t.*, **-cused, -cusing,** or **-cussed, -cussing. 1.** to play a trick on; hoax; cheat. **2.** to stupefy with a drug or a drugged drink. **3.** to drug (drink).

hocus-pocus (hō′kəs pō′kəs), *n., v.*, **-cused, -cusing,** or **-cussed, -cussing.** —*n.* **1.** a formula used in conjuring or incantations. **2.** a juggler's trick; sleight of hand. **3.** trickery or deception. **4.** unnecessary mystification or elaboration extended to cover deception or something basically simple. —*v.t.* **5.** to play tricks on or with. —*v.i.* **6.** to perform tricks; practise deception. [orig. jugglers' jargon, simulating Latin]

hod (hŏd), *n.* **1.** a portable trough for carrying mortar, bricks, etc., fixed crosswise on top of a pole and carried on the shoulder. **2.** a coalscuttle. [cf. MD *hodde* basket, c. HG *hotte*, OF *hotte* (t. G), d. E *hot* (t. OF) pannier]

Hodeida (hō dā′də), *n.* the chief seaport of Yemen, in the W part, on the Red Sea. 45,000 (est. 1965).

hodgepodge (hŏj′pŏj′), *n. Chiefly U.S.* hotchpotch.

Hodgkin's disease (hŏj′kĭnz), *Pathol.* a malignant disease of lymphatic tissue. [named after Thomas *Hodgkin*, 1798–1866, English physician]

hodman (hŏd′mən), *n., pl.* **-men.** a bricklayer's assistant.

Hódmezövásárhely (*Hung.* hōd′mĕ zœ vāsh ăr hĕy), *n.* a town in SE Hungary. 53,200 (est. 1962).

hodograph (hŏd′ə grăf′, -gräf′), *n. Mech.* the curve drawn through the ends of the vectors which represent the velocities of a particle at successive instants; used to determine the acceleration of a particle moving along a curved path. [f. Gk *hodó(s)* way + -GRAPH]

hodometer (hŏ dŏm′ĭ tə), *n.* odometer.

hodoscope (hŏd′ə skōp′), *n. Physics.* an apparatus for tracing the path of a charged particle, esp. a cosmic-ray particle.

hoe (hō), *n., v.*, **hoed, hoeing.** —*n.* **1.** a long-handled implement with a thin, flat blade usually set transversely, used to break up the surface of the ground, destroy weeds, etc. —*v.t.* **2.** to dig, scrape, weed, cultivate, etc., with a hoe. —*v.i.* **3.** to use a hoe. [ME *howe*, t. OF: m. *houe*, t. Gmc; cf. G *Haue*] —**ho′er,** *n.* —**hoe′-like′,** *adj.*

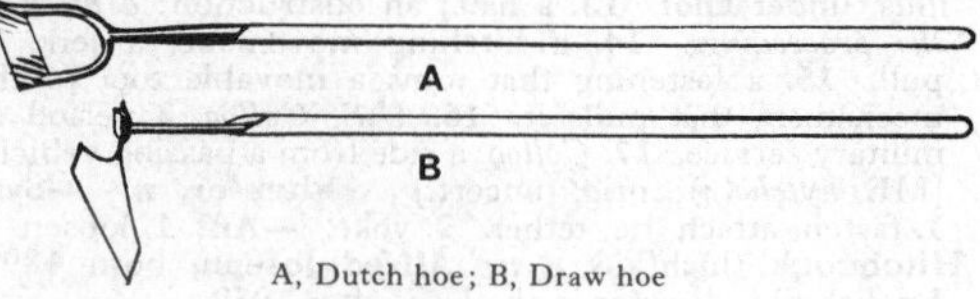

A, Dutch hoe; B, Draw hoe

hoecake (hō′kāk′), *n. Southern U.S.* a cake made with Indian meal, originally baked on a hoe.

Hoek van Holland (*Du.* hōōk′ vŏn hô′lŏnt), Dutch name of **Hook of Holland.**

Hof (*Ger.* hōf), *n.* a town in West Germany, in NE Bavaria. 55,700 (est. 1966).

Hofer (*Ger.* hō′fər), *n.* **Andreas** (*Ger.* ăn drē′ăs), 1767–1810, Tyrolese patriot.

Hoffmann (*Ger.* hŏf′măn), *n.* **Ernst Theodor Wilhelm** (*Ger.* ĕrnst tē′ō dōr vĭl′hĕlm), 1776–1822, German writer, musician, painter, and jurist.

Hofmannsthal (*Ger.* hōf′măns tăl), *n.* **Hugo von** (*Ger.* hōō′gō fōn), 1874–1929, Austrian poet and playwright.

hog (hŏg), *n., v.*, **hogged, hogging.** —*n.* **1.** a mammal of the family *Suidae*; a pig (in the U.S., the general word). **2.** a domesticated swine, esp. a castrated boar, bred for slaughter. **3.** Also, **hogg, hogget** (hŏg′ĭt). a sheep up to the age of about one year, which has not yet been shorn. **4.** *Colloq.* a selfish, gluttonous, or filthy person. **5.** *Naut.* a broom for cleaning the underwater parts of a ship. **6. go the whole hog,** *Colloq.* to do completely and thoroughly; to commit oneself unreservedly to a course of action. —*v.t.* **7.** *Slang.* to appropriate selfishly; take more than one's share of. **8.** to arch (the back) upwards like that of a hog. **9.** to cut (a horse's mane) short. —*v.i.* **10.** (of a ship's hull) to droop at both ends because of a structural defect; sag. [ME; OE *hogg*, t. OBritish; cf. Welsh *hwch* sow] —**hog′like′**

hogan (hō′gən), *n.* a Navaho Indian dwelling, a structure of posts and branches covered with earth.

Hogarth (hō′gäth), *n.* **William,** 1697–1764, English painter and engraver. —**Hogarth′ian,** *adj.*

hogback (hŏg′băk′), *n. Chiefly U.S.* hogsback.

hog cholera, *Chiefly U.S.* swine fever.

hogfish (hŏg′fĭsh′), *n., pl.* **-fishes,** (*esp. collectively*) **-fish.** any of various fishes, as *Lachnolaemus maximus*, a labroid food fish of the Florida coast and the West Indies, or *Percina caprodes*, found in American lakes and streams, or *Orthopristis chrysopterus*, one of the grunts of the southern coasts of the U.S.

Hogg (hŏg), *n.* **James** (*'the Ettrick Shepherd'*), 1770–1835, Scottish poet.

hoggin (hŏg′ĭn), *n.* gravel containing clay, used for making roads.

hoggish (hŏg′ĭsh), *adj.* **1.** like or befitting a hog. **2.** selfish; gluttonous; filthy. —**hog′gishly,** *adv.* —**hog′gishness,** *n.*

hogmanay (hŏg′mə nā′, hŏg′mə nā′), *n. Scot.* (*often cap.*) **1.** New Year's Eve. **2.** the celebrations held on this occasion. [t. ONF: m. *hoguinané*, OF *aguillanneuf* New Year's Eve; ult. orig. unknown]

hognose snake (hŏg′nōz′), any of the harmless American snakes constituting the genus *Heterodon*, notable for their hoglike snouts and their curious actions and contortions when disturbed.

hognut (hŏg′nŭt′), *n.* **1.** the nut of the brown hickory, *Carya glabra.* **2.** the tree itself. **3.** the pignut. **4.** the earthnut of Europe, *Conopodium denudatum.*

hog peanut, a twining fabaceous plant, *Amphicarpa bracteata*, with pods which ripen in or on the ground.

hogsback (hŏgz′băk′), *n. Geol.* a long, sharply crested ridge, generally formed of steeply inclined strata that are especially resistant to erosion. Also, *Chiefly U.S.*, **hogback.**

hog's-fennel (hŏgz′fĕn′əl), *n.* any of several species of umbelliferous plants of the genus *Peucedanum*, as *P. palustre*, a biennial occurring in wet places in Europe and W Asia; sulphur-weed.

hogshead (hŏgz′hĕd′), *n.* **1.** a large cask of varying capacity (depending on locality and use). **2.** one of various liquid measures, esp. 52½ imperial gallons generally, or 54 imperial gallons in the case of beer or cider. [ME *hoggeshed*, lit., hog's head; unexplained]

hogtie (hŏg′tī′), *v.t.*, **-tied, -tying.** *Chiefly U.S.* **1.** to tie as a hog is tied, with all four feet together. **2.** to hamper.

Hogue (*Fr.* ŏg), *n.* **La** (*Fr.* lă). See **La Hogue.**

hogwash (hŏg′wŏsh′), *n.* **1.** refuse given to hogs; swill. **2.** any worthless stuff. **3.** meaningless or insincere talk, etc.

hogweed (hŏg′wēd′), *n.* cow-parsnip; keck[2].

Hohenlinden (hō′ən lĭn′dən), *n.* a village in S West Germany, in Bavaria, near Munich: French victory over the Austrians, 1800.

Hohenlohe (hō′ən lō′ə), *n.* a German princely family, fl. 12th–19th centuries.

Hohenstaufen (hō′ən shtou′fən; *Ger.* hō ən-), *n.* a German princely family, founded in the 11th century, which ruled Germany 1138–1208 and 1215–54, and Sicily 1194–1266.

Hohenzollern (hō′ən zŏl′ən; *Ger.* hō ən tsŏl′ərn), *n.* a German princely family which attained prominence after 1415 as rulers of Brandenburg, Prussia, which became the kingdom of Prussia in 1701: rulers of the German Empire 1871–1918, and of Rumania 1866–1947.

hoick (hoik), *v.i., v.t.* to rise or to cause to rise sharply or abruptly.

hoicks (hoiks), *interj.* (a cry used to incite hounds in hunting.) Also, **hoick** (hoik).

hoiden (hoi′dn), *n., adj.* hoyden.

hoi polloi (hoi′ pə loi′), the common people; the masses (sometimes preceded pleonastically by *the*). [Gk: the many]

hoist (hoist), *v.t.* **1.** to raise or lift, esp. by some mechanical appliance: *to hoist sail.* **—***n.* **2.** an apparatus for hoisting, as a lift. **3.** a lift for heavy goods; goods lift. **4.** the act of hoisting; a lift. **5.** *Naut.* **a.** the vertical length of any sail other than a course. **b.** the perpendicular height of a sail or flag. **c.** a string of flags raised as a signal. [later form of *hoise*; cf. G *hissen*] **—hoist′er,** *n.* **—Syn. 1.** See **raise.**

hoity-toity (hoi′tĭ toi′tĭ), *interj.* **1.** (an exclamation denoting surprise or disapproval.) **2.** giddy; flighty. **3.** assuming; haughty. Also, **highty-tighty.** [redupl. deriv. of obs. *hoit,* v., to romp, riot]

hokey-pokey (hō′kĭ pō′kĭ), *n.* **1.** hocus-pocus; trickery. **2.** ice-cream sold in the street.

Hokkaido (hŏ kī′dō), *n.* a large island in N Japan. 5,000,000 pop. (est. 1962); 30,303 sq. mi. Formerly, **Yezo.** See map under **Kurile Islands.**

Hokonui (hō′kə nōō′ĭ), *adj.* *Geol.* **1.** pertaining to a geological period or system of rocks in New Zealand which correspond with the Triassic and Jurassic periods or systems. **2.** of or denoting the major mountain-building episode at the close of the Hokonui period and which preceded the Cretaceous period in New Zealand.

hokum (hō′kəm), *n.* *U.S. Slang.* **1.** nonsense; bunk. **2.** elements of low comedy or farce introduced into a play or the like for the laughs they may bring. **3.** sentimental or pathetic matter of an elementary or stereotyped kind introduced into a play or the like. [b. HOCUS-POCUS and BUNKUM]

Hokusai (hŏk′ ōō sī′), *n.* **Katsushika** (kăt′sōō shē′kə), 1760–1849, Japanese painter and illustrator.

Holarctic (hŏ läk′tĭk), *adj.* of or pertaining to a biogeographical region comprising the Palaearctic and the Nearctic regions.

Holbein (hŏl′bīn), *n.* **1. Hans** (hănz; *Ger.* häns) (*'the elder'*), *c.* 1460–1524, German painter. **2.** his son, **Hans** (*'the younger'*), 1497?–1543, German painter.

Holborn (hō′bən), *n.* **1.** a district in central London. **2.** an east-west thoroughfare in this district.

hold[1] (hōld), *v.,* **held; held** or (*Archaic*) **holden; holding;** *n.* **—***v.t.* **1.** to have or keep in the hand; keep fast; grasp. **2.** to reserve; retain; set aside. **3.** to bear, sustain, or support with the hand, arms, etc., or by any means. **4.** to keep in a specified state, relation, etc.: *to hold the enemy in check.* **5.** to keep in custody; detain. **6.** to engage in; preside over; carry on; pursue; observe or celebrate: *to hold a meeting.* **7.** to have the ownership or use of; keep as one's own; occupy: *to hold office.* **8.** to contain or be capable of containing: *this basket holds two bushels.* **9.** to have or keep in the mind; think or believe; entertain: *to hold a belief.* **10.** to regard or consider: *to hold a person responsible.* **11.** to decide legally. **12.** to regard with affection: *to hold one dear.* **13.** to keep forcibly, as against an adversary. **—***v.i.* **14.** to remain or continue in a specified state, relation, etc.: *to hold still.* **15.** to remain fast; adhere; cling: *the anchor holds.* **16.** to keep or maintain a grasp on something. **17.** to maintain one's position against opposition; continue in resistance. **18.** to hold property by some tenure; derive title (fol. by *from* or *of*). **19.** to remain attached, faithful, or steadfast: *to hold to one's purpose.* **20.** to remain valid; be in force: *the rule does not hold.* **21.** to refrain or forbear (usually in the imperative). **—***v.* **22.** Some special verb phrases are:

hold back, 1. to restrain or check. **2.** to retain possession of; keep back; withhold.

hold down, to continue to hold (a position, job, etc.), esp. in spite of difficulties.

hold forth, 1. to put forward; propose. **2.** to harangue.

hold good, to be true; be valid.

hold in, 1. to restrain, check, or curb. **2.** to restrain or contain oneself.

hold it, stop!; don't move!

hold off, 1. to keep aloof or at a distance. **2.** to refrain from action.

hold on, 1. to keep fast hold on something. **2.** to continue; persist. **3.** *Colloq.* to stop or halt (chiefly in the imperative).

hold one's own, to maintain one's position or condition.

hold one's tongue or **one's peace,** to keep silent; cease or refrain from speaking.

hold out, 1. to offer or present. **2.** to extend or stretch forth. **3.** to continue to exist; last. **4.** to refuse to yield or submit. **5.** *Orig. U.S. Slang.* to keep back something expected or due.

hold over, 1. to keep for future consideration or action; postpone. **2.** *Music.* to prolong (a note) from one to the next.

hold to, to abide by; keep to.

hold up, 1. to keep in an erect position. **2.** to present to notice; exhibit; display. **3.** to hinder; delay. **4.** to stop by force in order to rob.

hold water, 1. to retain water; not let water run through. **2.** to prove sound, tenable, or valid: *Mr Black's claims will not hold water.*

hold with, to agree with; approve of.

—*n.* **23.** the act of holding fast by a grasp of the hand or by some other physical means; grasp; grip: *take hold.* **24.** something to hold a thing by, as a handle; something to grasp for support. **25.** a thing that holds fast or supports something else. **26.** a controlling force, or dominating influence: *to have a hold on a person.* **27.** *Archaic.* a fortified place, or stronghold.

[ME *holden,* OE *h(e)aldan,* c. G *halten*] **—Syn. 7.** possess, own. See **have. 8.** See **contain. 10.** deem, esteem.

hold[2] (hōld), *n.* *Naut.* the interior of a ship below the deck, esp. where the cargo is stowed. [var. of HOLE, c. D *hol* hole, hold]

holdall (hōld′ôl′), *n.* a portable case or bag.

holdback (hōld′băk′), *n.* **1.** the iron or strap on the shaft of a vehicle to which the breeching of the harness is attached, enabling the horse to hold back or to back the vehicle. **2.** a restraint; check.

holder (hōl′də), *n.* **1.** something to hold a thing with. **2.** one who has the ownership, possession, or use of something; an owner; a tenant. **3.** *Law.* one who has the legal right to enforce a negotiable instrument.

Hölderlin (*Ger.* hœl′ dər lēn), *n.* **Friedrich** (*Ger.* frē′-drĭKH), 1770–1843, German poet.

holdfast (hōld′făst′), *n.* **1.** something used to hold or secure a thing in place; a catch, hook, or clamp. **2.** *Bot.* any of several sucker-like organs serving to attach a plant to something.

holding (hōl′dĭng), *n.* **1.** the act of one who or that which holds. **2.** land, or a piece of land, held, esp. of a superior. **3.** (*often pl.*) property owned, esp. stocks, shares, and land.

holding company, *Finance.* **1.** a company controlling, or able to control, other companies by virtue of share ownership in these companies. **2.** a company which owns stocks or securities of other companies, deriving income from them.

holdover (hōld′ō′və), *n.* *U.S. Colloq.* something which remains behind from a former period.

hold-up (hōld′ŭp′), *n.* *Colloq.* **1.** a forcible stopping and robbing of a person. **2.** a delay; stoppage.

hole (hōl), *n., v.,* **holed, holing. —***n.* **1.** an opening through anything; an aperture. **2.** a hollow place in a solid body or mass; a cavity: *a hole in the ground.* **3.** the excavated habitation of an animal; a burrow. **4.** a small, dingy, or mean abode. **5.** a dungeon; place of confinement. **6.** *Colloq.* an embarrassing position or predicament: *to find oneself in a hole.* **7.** *U.S.* a cove or small harbour. **8.** *Colloq.* a fault or flaw: *to pick holes in a plan.* **9.** *Sport.* **a.** a small cavity, into which a marble, ball, or the like is to be played. **b.** a score made by so playing. **10.** *Golf.* **a.** the small cavity into which the ball is to be placed. **b.** the distance between the tee and the hole. **c.** the score made by playing the ball from the tee to its corresponding hole. **11.** *Electronics.* the absence of an electron in the valency structure of a semiconductor; acts as a mobile vacancy with positive charge and mass. **—***v.t.* **12.** to make a hole or holes in. **13.** to put or drive into a hole. **14.** *Golf.* to drive the ball into (a hole). **15.** to bore (a tunnel, etc.) **—***v.i.* **16.** to make a hole or holes. **17.** *Golf.* to drive the ball into a hole (often fol. by *out*). **18.** *U.S.* to go into a hole; retire for the winter, as a hibernating animal (usually fol. by *up*). [ME; OE *hol* hole, cave, den, orig. neut. of *hol,* adj., c. G *hohl* hollow] **—hole′less,** *adj.* **—hole′y,** *adj.*

—**Syn.** 1, 2. HOLE, CAVITY, EXCAVATION refer to a hollow place in anything. HOLE is the common word for this idea: *a hole in turf.* CAVITY is a more formal or scientific term for a hollow within the body or in a substance, whether with or without a passage outwards: *a cavity in a tooth, the cranial cavity.* An EXCAVATION is an extended hole made by digging out or removing material: *an excavation before the construction of a building.*

hole-and-corner (hōl′ən kô′nə), *adj.* furtive; secretive; underhand.

Holguín (*Sp.* ōl gēn′), *n.* a town in E Cuba. 226,779 (1960).

holibut (hŏl′ĭ bət), *n., pl.* **-buts,** (esp. collectively) **-but.** halibut.

holiday (hŏl′ĭ dĭ), *n.* **1.** a day fixed by law or custom on which ordinary business is suspended in commemoration of some event or in honour of some person, etc. **2.** any day of exemption from labour. **3.** a religious feast; holy day. **4.** (*often pl.*) a period of cessation from work, or of recreation; a vacation. —*adj.* **5.** pertaining to a festival; joyous: *a holiday mood.* **6.** suited only to a holiday. —*v.i.* **7.** to take a holiday: *to holiday at the seaside.* [ME; OE *hāligdæg* holy day]

holiday camp, a holiday centre, usually at the seaside, in which a wide variety of sports facilities, holiday activities, etc., are provided, many of them being organized on a communal basis.

holiday-maker (hŏl′ĭ dĭ mā′kə), *n.* a person on holiday, esp. at a resort.

holier-than-thou (hō′lĭ ə thən thou′), *adj.* sanctimonious; smug; self-righteous.

holily (hō′lĭ lĭ), *adv.* **1.** piously or devoutly. **2.** in a sacred manner. [ME; OE *hāliglīce,* f. *hālig* HOLY + *-līce* -LY]

holiness (hō′lĭ nĭs), *n.* **1.** the state or character of being holy; sanctity. **2.** (*cap.*) a title of the pope, and formerly also of other high ecclesiastical dignitaries, etc. (prec. by *his* or *your*). [ME *holynesse,* OE *hālignes*]

Holinshed (hŏl′ĭn shĕd′), *n.* **Raphael,** died *c.* 1580, English chronicler.

holism (hō′lĭz′əm), *n. Philos.* the theory that wholes (which are more than the mere sums of their parts) are fundamental aspects of the real. [f. HOL(O)- + -ISM] —**ho′list,** *n.* —**holis′tic,** *adj.*

holland (hŏl′ənd), *n.* a kind of coarse linen fabric.

Holland (hŏl′ənd), *n.* **1.** the Netherlands. **2.** a medieval county and province on the North Sea, now in North and South Holland provinces of Netherlands **3.** official name, **The Parts of Holland.** an administrative division of Lincolnshire. 103,327 pop. (1961); 419 sq. mi. *Chief town:* Boston.

hollandaise sauce (hŏl′ən dāz′), a yellow sauce of eggs, lemon juice or vinegar, butter, and seasonings.

Hollander (hŏl′ən də), *n.* a native of the Netherlands; a Dutchman.

Hollands (hŏl′əndz), *n.* a gin originally made in Holland, distinguished from other gins by the addition of juniper.

holler (hŏl′ə), *Dial.* —*v.i.* **1.** to cry aloud; shout. —*v.t.* **2.** to shout (something). —*n.* **3.** a loud cry of pain, surprise, to attract attention, etc. [var. of HOLLO]

hollo (hŏl′ō), *interj., n., v.* **1.** hello. **2.** halloo.

hollow (hŏl′ō), *adj.* **1.** having a hole or cavity within; not solid; empty: *a hollow ball.* **2.** having a depression or concavity: *a hollow surface.* **3.** sunken, as the cheeks or eyes. **4.** (of sound) not resonant; dull, muffled, or deep: *a hollow voice.* **5.** without substantial or real worth; vain: *a hollow victory.* **6.** insincere or false: *hollow compliments.* **7.** hungry. —*n.* **8.** an empty space within anything; a hole; a depression or cavity. **9.** a valley: *the hollow of a hill.* —*v.t.* **10.** to make hollow. **11.** form by making hollow (often fol. by *out*). —*v.i.* **12.** to become hollow. —*adv.* **13.** in a hollow manner. **14.** *Colloq.* utterly: *to beat someone hollow.* [ME *hol(o)u, holw(e),* n., adj., OE *holh* hollow (place)] —**hol′lowly,** *adv.* —**hol′lowness,** *n.*

hollow-eyed (hŏl′ō īd′), *adj.* having sunken eyes.

hollowware (hŏl′ō wĕə′), *n.* hollow utensils, such as pots and pans, made of metal. Also, **holloware.**

holly (hŏl′ĭ), *n., pl.* **-lies.** **1.** any of the trees or shrubs of the genus *Ilex,* esp. those species having glossy, spiny-edged leaves and small, whitish flowers succeeded by bright red berries. **2.** the foliage and berries, much used for decoration, esp. during the Christmas season. [ME *holig, holi,* OE *holegn* (with loss of *-n*); akin to D *hulst.,* G *Hulst,* F *houx,* Welsh *celyn*]

holly fern, a rhizomatous fern with toothed pinnae, *Polystichum lonchitis,* found on non-acid mountain rocks of the N temperate zone.

hollyhock (hŏl′ĭ hŏk′), *n.* **1.** a tall malvaceous plant, *Althea rosea,* common in cultivation, having showy flowers of various colours. **2.** the flower itself. [ME *holihoc,* f. *holi* HOLY + *hoc* mallow, OE *hocc*]

holly oak, the holm oak.

Hollywood (hŏl′ĭ wo͝od′), *n.* the NW part of Los Angeles, California: centre of American film industry.

holm[1] (hōm), *n. Dial. and Scot.* **1.** a low, flat tract of land beside a river or stream. **2.** a small island, esp. one in a river or lake. [ME and OE, t. Scand.; cf. Icel. *holmr* islet]

holm[2] (hōm), *n.* **1.** the holm oak. **2.** *Dial.* the holly. [ME; dissimilated var. of *holn,* OE *holen* holly (dental + dental became dental + labial)]

Holman Hunt (hōl′mən hŭnt′), **William.** See **Hunt, William Holman.**

Holmes (hōmz), *n.* **1. Oliver Wendell,** 1809–94, U.S. author and physician. **2.** his son, **Oliver Wendell,** 1841–1935, associate justice of the U.S. Supreme Court 1902–32. **3. Sherlock,** a detective in many mystery stories by Sir Arthur Conan Doyle.

Holmfirth (hōm′fûth′), *n.* a town in England, in the West Riding of Yorkshire. 18,391 (1961).

holmic (hŏl′mĭk), *adj. Chem.* of or containing holmium in the trivalent state.

holmium (hŏl′mĭ əm), *n. Chem.* a rare-earth element found in gadolinite. *Symbol:* Ho; *at. wt:* 164·94; *at. no.:* 67. [NL; named after *Stockholm,* in Sweden]

holm oak, an evergreen oak, *Quercus ilex,* of southern Europe, with foliage resembling that of the holly.

holo-, a word element meaning 'whole' or 'entire', as in *holocaust.* [t. Gk, comb. form of *hólos*]

holoblastic (hŏl′ə blăs′tĭk), *adj. Embryol.* (of eggs which undergo total cleavage) wholly germinal (opposed to *meroblastic*).

holocaine (hŏl′ə kān′), *n.* **1.** *Chem.* a colourless crystalline basic compound, $C_{18}H_{22}N_2O_2$, used as a local anaesthetic. **2.** *Pharm.* a local anaesthetic resembling cocaine in its action, used chiefly for the eye.

holocaust (hŏl′ə kôst′), *n.* **1.** great or wholesale destruction of life, esp. by fire. **2.** an offering devoted wholly to burning; a burnt offering. [t. LL: s. *holocaustum,* t. Gk: m. *holókauston* a burnt offering, prop. neut. of *holókaustos* burnt whole] —**hol′ocaus′tic,** *adj.*

Holocene (hŏl′ə sēn′), *adj. Geol.* designating or pertaining to the Recent era. [f. HOLO- + -CENE]

Holofernes (hŏl′ə fû′nēz), *n. Bible.* a general of Nebuchadnezzar killed by Judith, in the apocryphal Book of Judith.

hologram (hŏl′ə grăm′), *n.* a negative produced by holography.

holograph (hŏl′ə grăf′, -grāf′), *adj.* **1.** wholly written by the person in whose name it appears: *a holograph letter.* —*n.* **2.** a holograph writing. [t. LL: s. *holographus,* t. Gk: m. *hológraphos*]

holographic (hŏl′ə grăf′ĭk), *adj. Law.* (of wills) totally in the handwriting of the testator.

holography (hŏ lŏg′rə fĭ), *n.* a form of photography in which no lens is used and in which a photographic plate records the interference pattern between two portions of a laser beam.

holohedral (hŏl′ə hē′drəl), *adj.* (of a crystal) having all the planes or faces required by the maximum symmetry of the system to which it belongs. [f. HOLO- + s. Gk *hédra* seat, base + -AL[1]] —**hol′ohed′rism,** *n.*

Holon (hŏl′ŏn, KHŏl′ŏn), *n.* a town in W Israel, near Tel-Aviv. 65,000 (est. 1964).

holophote (hŏl′ə fōt′), *n.* an apparatus by which practically all the light from a lighthouse lamp, etc., is thrown in the desired direction. [f. HOLO- + m. s. Gk *phôs* light] —**hol′opho′tal,** *adj.*

holophrastic (hŏl′ə frăs′tĭk), *adj.* expressing a whole phrase or sentence in a single word. [f. HOLO- + m. s. Gk *phrastikós* suited for expressing]

holophytic (hŏl′ō fĭt′ĭk), *adj.* obtaining nutriment by the synthesization of inorganic substances, in the manner of green plants.

holothurian (hŏl′ə thyo͞oə′rĭ ən), *n.* any of the *Holothuroidea,* a class of echinoderms known as sea-cucumbers, having a long leathery body and tentacles round the anterior end. [f. s. NL *Holothuria* genus name (t. L, t. Gk: m. *holothoúria*) + -AN]

holozoic (hŏl′ō zō′ĭk), *adj. Biol.* feeding on organisms or on solid matter derived from them, in the manner of most animals.

holp (hōlp), *v. Archaic.* pt. of **help.**

holpen (hōl′pən), *v. Archaic.* pp. of **help.**

hols (hŏlz), *n.pl. Colloq.* holidays (def. 4).

Holst (hōlst), *n.* **Gustav Theodore** (go͞os′täv thĭə′dô), 1874–1934, English composer.

Holstein (hŏl′stīn; *Ger.* hōl′shtīn), *n.* **1.** Also, **Holstein-Friesian** (hŏl′stīn frē′zyən). one of a breed of large, black-and-white dairy cattle, originating in North Holland and Friesland. **2.** a district in N Germany at the base of the peninsula of Jutland: a former duchy. See **Schleswig-Holstein.**

Holstein, *Bos taurus* (4 ft high at the shoulder)

holster (hōl′stə), *n.* a leather case for a pistol, attached to a belt or a saddle. [var. of *hulster*, t. Sw.: m. *hölster*, whence also D *holster*; akin to OE *heolstor* cover] —**hol′stered,** *adj.*

holt (hōlt), *n. Chiefly Poetic.* **1.** a wood or grove. **2.** a wooded hill. [ME *holte*, OE *holt*, c. G *Holz* wood]

Holt (hōlt), *n.* **Harold Edward,** 1908–68, Australian statesman: prime minister 1966–68.

holus-bolus (hō′ləs bō′ləs), *adv. Colloq.* all at once.

holy (hō′lĭ), *adj.*, **-lier, -liest,** *n., pl.* **-lies.** —*adj.* **1.** specially recognized as or declared sacred by religious use or authority; consecrated: *a holy day.* **2.** dedicated or devoted to the service of God, the Church, or religion: *a holy man.* **3.** saintly or godly; pious or devout. **4.** of religious purity, exaltation, solemnity, etc.: *a holy love.* **5.** entitled to worship or profound religious reverence because of divine character or origin, or connection with God or divinity: *holy Bible.* **6.** religious: *holy rites.* **7. holy terror,** *Colloq.* a person difficult to deal with; an alarming or frightening person. —*n.* **8.** a place of worship; a sacred place. **9.** that which is holy. [ME *holi*, OE *hālig, hāleg*, c. D and G *heilig*, akin to HALE[1] and HEAL]

—**Syn. 1.** blessed. HOLY, SACRED, CONSECRATED, HALLOWED imply possession of a sanctity which is the object of religious veneration. HOLY refers to the divine, that which has its sanctity directly from God or is connected with Him: *Remember the Sabbath day to keep it holy.* That which is SACRED, while sometimes accepted as entitled to religious veneration, may have its sanctity from human authority: *a sacred oath.* That which is CONSECRATED is specially or formally dedicated to some religious use: *a life consecrated to service.* That which is HALLOWED has been made holy by being worshipped: *a hallowed shrine.*

Holy Alliance, a league formed by the principal sovereigns of Europe (without the pope and the rulers of Britain and Turkey) in 1815 after the fall of Napoleon, with the professed object of Christian brotherhood, but the practical object of repressing revolution.

Holy Bible, Bible (def. 1).

Holy City, a city regarded as particularly sacred by the adherents of a religious faith, as Jerusalem by Jews and Christians, Mecca and Medina by Muslims, and Varanasi by Hindus.

Holy Communion. See **communion** (def. 5b).

holy day, a consecrated day or religious festival, esp. one other than Sunday.

Holy Father, a title of the pope.

Holy Ghost, the third person of the Trinity.

Holy Grail, grail.

holy-grass (hō′lĭ gräs′), *n.* a tufted perennial grass, *Hierochloë odorata*, occurring in wet places throughout the northern part of the N temperate zone.

Holyhead (hŏl′ĭ hĕd′), *n.* a town in Wales, the county town of Anglesey. 10,412 (1961).

Holy Innocents' Day, Dec. 28th, a day of religious observance commemorating the slaughter of the children of Bethlehem by Herod's order; Childermas. Matt. 2:16.

Holy Island, Lindisfarne.

Holy Land, Palestine, now divided between Israel and Jordan.

Holyoake (hō′lĭ ōk′), *n.* **Keith Jacka** (jăk′ə), born 1904, New Zealand statesman: prime minister since 1960.

Holy Office, a congregation of the Roman Catholic Church entrusted with matters pertaining to faith and morals. Cf. **inquisition** (def. 6).

holy of holies, **1.** a place of special sacredness. **2.** the inner and smaller chamber of the Jewish tabernacle and temple entered only by the high priest and but once a year.

holy orders, **1.** the rite or sacrament of ordination. **2.** the rank or status of an ordained Christian minister. **3.** the major degrees or grades of the Christian ministry.

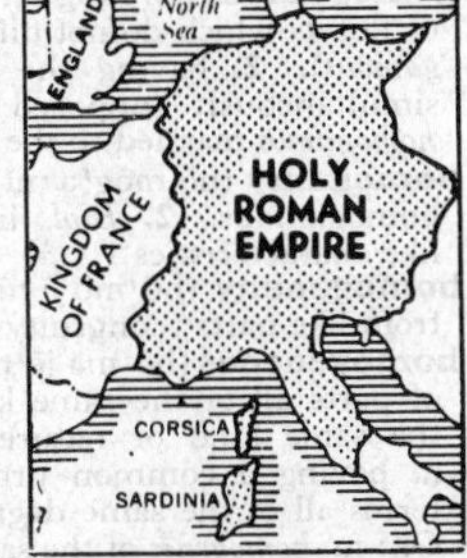

Holy Roman Empire

Holy Roman Empire, the empire in western and central Europe which began with the coronation of Otto the Great, king of Germany, as Roman emperor A.D. 962, and ended with the renunciation of the Roman imperial title by Francis II in 1806, regarded theoretically as the continuation of the Western Empire and as the temporal form of a universal dominion whose spiritual head was the pope. It is sometimes regarded as originating with Charlemagne, who was crowned Roman emperor A.D. 800.

Holy Rood, **1.** the cross on which Jesus died. **2.** (*l.c.*) a crucifix, esp. one above a rood screen.

Holy Saturday, the Saturday in Holy Week.

Holy Scripture, scripture (def. 1).

Holy See, *Rom. Cath. Ch.* **1.** the see of Rome; the office or jurisdiction of the pope. **2.** the papal court.

Holy Sepulchre, the sepulchre in which the body of Jesus lay between His burial and His resurrection.

Holy Spirit, the Holy Ghost.

holystone (hōl′lĭ stōn′), *n., v.,* **-stoned, -stoning.** —*n.* **1.** a soft sandstone used for scrubbing the decks of a ship. —*v.t.* **2.** to scrub with a holystone.

Holy Thursday, **1.** Ascension Day. **2.** *Rom. Cath. Ch.* Thursday in Holy Week; Maundy Thursday.

holytide (hō′lĭ tīd′), *n. Archaic.* a holy season.

Holytown (hŏl′ĭ toun′), *n.* a town in Scotland, in Lanarkshire, near Glasgow. 20,669 (1961).

holy war, a war waged for an allegedly holy purpose; a crusade.

holy water, water blessed by a priest.

Holy Week, the week preceding Easter Sunday.

Holy Writ, the Scriptures.

homage (hŏm′ĭj), *n.* **1.** respect or reverence paid or rendered. **2.** the formal acknowledgement by which a feudal tenant or vassal declared himself to be the man of his lord, owing him faith and service. **3.** the relation thus established of a vassal to his lord. **4.** something done or given in acknowledgement or consideration of vassalage. [ME, t. OF, ult. der. LL *homo* vassal, L man] —**Syn. 1.** deference, obeisance; honour, tribute.

homburg (hŏm′bûg), *n.* a felt hat with a soft crown dented lengthways and a narrow brim.

home (hōm), *n., adj., adv., v.,* **homed, homing.** —*n.* **1.** a house, or other shelter that is the fixed residence of a person, a family, or a household. **2.** a place of one's domestic affections. **3.** an institution for the homeless, sick, etc. **4.** the dwelling place or retreat of an animal. **5.** the place or region where something is native or most common. **6.** any place of existence or refuge: *a heavenly home.* **7.** one's native place or own country. **8.** (in games) the goal; finishing post; base. **9.** *Baseball.* the plate at which the batter stands and which he must return to and touch after running round the bases, in order to score a run. **10. at home, a.** in one's own house or country. **b.** in a situation familiar to one; at ease. **c.** prepared to receive social visits. **d.** familiar with; accustomed to; well-informed. **e.** (of a football team, etc.) in one's own town or one's own grounds. —*adj.* **11.** of, pertaining to, or connected with one's home, town, centre of operations, or country; domestic. **12.** that strikes home, or to the mark aimed at; to the point: *a home thrust.* —*adv.* **13.** to, towards, or at home: *to go home.* **14.** deep; to the heart; effectively and completely. **15.** to the mark or point aimed at: *to strike home.* **16.** *Naut.* all the way; as far as possible: *to heave the hawser home.* **17. bring home to,** to cause (someone) to realize fully. **18. nothing to write home about,** not remarkable; unexciting; inferior. —*v.i.* **19.** to go or return home. **20.** (of guided missiles, aircraft, etc.) to proceed, esp. under control of an automatic aiming mechanism towards an airport, fixed or moving target, etc., (often fol. by *in, on* or *on to*). **21.** to have the home where specified. —*v.t.* **22.** to bring or send home. **23.** to provide with a home. **24.** to direct, esp. under control of an automatic aiming device, towards an airport, target, etc. [ME; OE *hām* home, dwelling, c. G *Heim*] —**Syn. 1.** abode; dwelling, habitation; domicile, residence. See **house.**

Home, Sir Alec Douglas-. See **Douglas-Home, Sir Alec.**

home-bred (hōm′brĕd′), *adj.* **1.** bred at home; native; indigenous; domestic. **2.** unpolished; unsophisticated.

home-brewed (hōm′bro͞od′), *adj.* (of beer or other beverage) brewed at home, as for home consumption.

homecoming (hōm′kŭm′ĭng), *n.* a return to a home.

home counties, the counties which border on London.

home economics, *Chiefly U.S.* the art and science of home-making, including the purchase, preparation, and service of food, the selection and making of clothing, the choice of furnishings, the care of children, etc.

home-grown (hōm′grōn′), *adj.* (esp. of fruit and vegetables) produced in one's own country, region, estate, garden, etc.

Home Guard, a territorial force of part-time volunteers organized for the defence of Britain during World War II.

home help, an employee of a local authority who helps families with routine domestic tasks, which sickness, old age, etc., have made difficult to perform.

homeland (hōm′lănd′), *n.* one's native land.

homeless (hōm′lĭs), *adj.* **1.** having no home. **2.** *Rare.* affording no home: *the homeless sea.* —**home′lessly,** *adv.* —**home′lessness,** *n.*

homelike (hōm′līk′), *adj.* like or suggestive of home; familiar; comfortable.

homely (hōm′lĭ), *adj.*, **-lier, -liest. 1.** proper or suited to the home or to ordinary domestic life; plain; unpretentious: *homely fare.* **2.** *U.S.* not good-looking; unattractive: *a homely girl.* [ME] —**home′liness,** *n.* —**Syn. 1.** See **simple.**

home-made (hōm′mād′), *adj.* made at home.

homeo-, var. of **homoeo-.**

Home Office, the government department in Britain dealing with domestic affairs.

homeomorphism (hō′myə mô′fĭz′əm), *n.* homoeomorphism. —**ho′meomor′phous,** *adj.*

homeopathy (hō′mĭ ŏp′ə thĭ), *n.* homoeopathy. —**homeopathic** (hō′myə păth′ĭk), *adj.* —**ho′meopath′ically,** *adv.* —**homeopathist** (hō′mĭ ŏp′ə thĭst), **homeopath** (hō′myə păth′), *n.*

homer[1] (hō′mə), *n.* *Colloq.* **1.** *Baseball.* a home run. **2.** a homing pigeon. [f. HOME + -ER[1]]

homer[2] (hō′mə), *n.* a Hebrew unit of capacity equal to 10 baths in liquid measure or 10 ephahs in dry measure; kor. [t. Heb.: m. *khomer*, lit., heap]

Homer (hō′mə), *n.* *c.* 10th cent. B.C., Greek epic poet, reputed author of the *Iliad* and *Odyssey.*

Homeric (hō mĕ′rĭk), *adj.* **1.** of, pertaining to, or suggestive of Homer or his poetry. **2.** heroic, imposing. **3.** epic (def. 7). —**Homer′ically,** *adv.*

Homeric laughter, loud, hearty laughter.

home rule, self-government in internal affairs by the inhabitants of a dependent country.

home-ruler (hōm′ro͞o′lə), *n.* an advocate of home rule.

home run, *Baseball.* a run made on a hit which enables the batter, without aid from fielding errors of the opponents, to make a non-stop circuit of the bases.

Home Secretary, the secretary of state for the Home Office.

homesick (hōm′sĭk′), *adj.* ill or depressed from a longing for home. —**home′sick′ness,** *n.*

home signal, *Railways.* a signal for controlling train movements into or through a section or block. Cf. **distant signal.**

homespun (hōm′spŭn′), *adj.* **1.** spun or made at home: *homespun cloth.* **2.** made of such cloth. **3.** plain; unpolished; simple. —*n.* **4.** cloth made at home, or of homespun yarn. **5.** cloth of similar appearance to that hand-spun and hand-woven. **6.** *Obs.* a rustic person.

homestead (hōm′stĕd′, -stĭd), *n.* **1.** *U.S.* a dwelling with its land and buildings, occupied by the owner as a home, and exempted by law from seizure or sale for debt. **2.** any dwelling with its land and buildings. [OE *hāmstede*, f. *hām* HOME + *stede* place]

Homestead Act, a special act (1862) of the U.S. Congress which made lands in the West available to settlers without payments.

homesteader (hōm′stĕd′ə), *n.* **1.** one who holds a homestead. **2.** *U.S.* a settler under the Homestead Act.

home straight, *Athletics.* the straight part of a circuit track where the finishing line is placed. Cf. **back straight.**

home stretch, the straight part of a racetrack leading to the finish line, after the last turn.

home thrust, 1. a deep thrust with a weapon. **2.** an effective, cutting remark.

home town, the town in which a person lives or was born.

home truth, a disagreeable statement of fact that hurts the sensibilities.

homeward (hōm′wəd), *adj.* **1.** directed towards home. —*adv.* **2.** homewards.

homewards (hōm′wədz), *adv.* towards home. Also, **homeward.**

homework (hōm′wûk′), *n.* the part of a lesson or lessons prepared outside school hours.

homey (hō′mĭ), *adj.* homy.

homicidal (hŏm′ĭ sī′dl), *adj.* **1.** pertaining to homicide. **2.** having a tendency to homicide. —**hom′icid′ally,** *adv.*

homicide (hŏm′ĭ sīd′), *n.* **1.** the killing of one human being by another. **2.** a murderer. [ME, t. OF, t. L: m. s. *homicīdium* (def. 1), *homicīda* (def. 2). See -CIDE]

homiletic (hŏm′ĭ lĕt′ĭk), *adj.* **1.** pertaining to preaching or to homilies. **2.** of the nature of a homily. **3.** of homiletics. Also, **hom′ilet′ical.** [t. Gk: m. s. *homilētikós* affable] —**hom′ilet′ically,** *adv.*

homiletics (hŏm′ĭ lĕt′ĭks), *n.* the art of preaching; the branch of practical theology that treats of homilies or sermons. [pl. of HOMILETIC. See -ICS]

homilist (hŏm′ĭ lĭst), *n.* one who writes or delivers homilies.

homily (hŏm′ĭ lĭ), *n.*, *pl.* **-lies. 1.** a religious discourse addressed to a congregation; a sermon. **2.** an admonitory or moralizing discourse. [t. ML: m. s. *homilia*, t. Gk: discourse; r. ME *omelie*, t. OF]

homing (hō′mĭng), *adj.* **1.** directing or guiding towards home; returning home. **2.** having the ability to return home, esp. from a long distance.

homing device, a mechanism incorporated into a guided missile, aeroplane, etc., which aims it towards its objective.

homing pigeon, a pigeon trained to fly home from a distance, employed to carry messages.

hominid (hŏm′ĭ nĭd), *n.* *Zool.* a member of the *Hominidae*, a family comprising man and manlike fossils.

hominy (hŏm′ĭ nĭ), *n.* maize hulled and crushed or coarsely ground: prepared for use as food by boiling in water or milk. [t. Algonquian (New England or Va.); cf. *tackhummin* grind corn (der. *ahām* he beats, he pounds + *min* berry, fruit)]

homo (hō′mō), *n.*, *adj.* *Slang.* homosexual.

Homo (hō′mō), *n.*, *pl.* **Homines** (hŏm′ĭ nēz′). the primate genus that includes modern man, *Homo sapiens*, and a number of closely related extinct species, as the Neanderthal man. [L: man]

homo-, a combining form meaning 'the same' (opposed to *hetero-*), as in *homocercal.* [t. Gk, comb. form of *homós* same]

homocentric (hō′mō sĕn′trĭk), *adj.* **1.** having the same centre; concentric. **2.** diverging from, or converging to, the same centre.

homocercal (hō′mō sû′kl, hŏm′ō-), *adj.* *Ichthyol.* **1.** having the tail or the caudal fin symmetrical as to its upper and under halves. **2.** denoting such a tail or caudal fin. [f. HOMO- + m. s. Gk *kérkos* tail + -AL[1]]

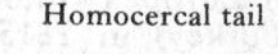
Homocercal tail

homochromatic (hō′mō krō măt′ĭk, hŏm′ō-), *adj.* of or pertaining to one hue only: monochromatic. —**homochromatism** (hō′mō krō′mə tĭz′əm, hŏm′ō-), *n.*

homochromous (hō′mə krō′məs, hŏm′ə-), *adj.* *Bot., Zool.* being all of one colour, as a composite flower or flower head. [t. Gk: m. *homóchrōmos*]

homocyclic (hō′mō sī′klĭk), *adj.* *Chem.* (of organic compounds) containing a ring structure of atoms of the same element, esp. carbon.

homodont (hō′mə dŏnt′), *adj.* having teeth all of the same kind, as most vertebrates other than mammals.

homoeo-, a word element meaning 'similar' or 'like', as in *homoeomorphism.* Also, **homeo-, homoio-.** [t. Gk: m. *homoio-*, comb. form of *hómoios* like]

homoeomorphism (hō′myə mô′fĭz′əm), *n.* similarity in crystalline form, but not necessarily in chemical composition. Also, **homeomorphism.** [f. m. s. Gk *homoiómorphos* of like form + -ISM] —**ho′moeomor′phous,** *adj.*

homoeopathic (hō′myə păth′ĭk), *adj.* **1.** of, pertaining to, or according to the principles of homoeopathy. **2.** practising or advocating homoeopathy. Also, **homeopathic.** —**ho′moeopath′ically,** *adv.*

homoeopathist (hō′mĭ ŏp′ə thĭst), *n.* one who practises or favours homoeopathy. Also, **homeopathist, homoeopath** (hō′myə păth′).

homoeopathy (hō′mĭ ŏp′ə thĭ), *n.* a method of treating disease by drugs, given in minute doses, which produce in a healthy person symptoms similar to those of the disease (opposed to *allopathy*). Also, **homeopathy.**

homoeostasis (hō′mĭ ō stā′sĭs), *n.* a tendency towards the maintenance of internal stability of a system, as by co-ordinated functioning of brain, heart, liver, etc. [f. HOMOEO- + STASIS] —**homoeostatic** (hō′mĭ ō stăt′ĭk), *adj.*

homoeotransplant (hō′mĭ ō trănz′plänt′, -träns′-), *n.* a piece of tissue taken from one individual and transplanted to another individual of the same species.

homogamous (hŏ mŏg′ə məs), *adj.* *Bot.* **1.** having flowers or florets which do not differ sexually (opposed to *heterogamous*). **2.** having the stamens and pistils maturing simultaneously (opposed to *dichogamous*). [t. Gk: m. *homógamos* married to the same wife]

homogamy (hŏ mŏg′ə mĭ), *n.* **1.** *Bot.* the state of being homogamous. **2.** *Biol.* interbreeding of individuals of like characteristics.

homogeneity (hō′mō jĭ nē′ĭ tĭ, hŏm′ō-), *n.* composition from like parts; congruity of constitution.

homogeneous (hō′mə jē′nyəs, hŏm′ə-), *adj.* **1.** composed of parts all of the same kind; not heterogeneous. **2.** of the same kind or nature; essentially alike. **3.** *Maths.* **a.** having a common property. **b.** denoting a sum of terms all of the same degree. [t. ML: m. *homogeneus*, t. Gk: m. *homogenḗs* of the same kind] —**ho′moge′neously,** *adv.* —**ho′moge′neousness,** *n.*

homogenize (hŏ mŏj′ĭ nīz′), *v.t.*, **-nized, -nizing.** to make homogeneous; form by mixing and emulsifying: *homogenized milk.* Also, **homogenise.** —**homogenization** (hŏ mŏj′ĭ nī zā′shən), *n.* —**homogenizer** (hŏ mŏj′ĭ nī′zə), *n.*

homogenous (hŏ mŏj′ĭ nəs), *adj. Biol.* corresponding in structure because of a common origin.

homogeny (hŏ mŏj′ĭ nĭ), *n. Biol.* correspondence of structure and embryological development. [t. Gk: m. *homogéneia* community of origin]

homogonous (hŏ mŏg′ə nəs), *adj. Bot.* pertaining to monoclinous flowers which do not differ in the relative length of stamens and pistils. —**homog′onously,** *adv.*

homogony (hŏ mŏg′ə nĭ), *n. Bot.* the state of being homogonous. [f. HOMO- + s. Gk *gónos* offspring + -Y[3]]

homograph (hŏm′ō grăf′, -gräf′), *n.* a word of the same written form as another, but of different origin and meaning, as *fair*[1] and *fair*[2]. —**hom′ograph′ic,** *adj.*

homoio-, var. of **homoeo-.**

homoiothermic (hə moi′ō thû′mĭk), *adj. Zool.* warm-blooded; having a constant body temperature, as most birds and mammals. Also, **homoi′other′mal, homoi′other′mous.**

Homoiousian (hō′moi o͞o′sĭ ən, -ou′sĭ ən), *n.* **1.** one of a 4th-century church party which maintained that the essence of the Son is similar to, but not the same as, that of the Father (distinguished from *Homoousian*). —*adj.* **2.** relating to the Homoiousians or their belief. [f. s. LGk *homoioúsios* of like substance + -AN]

homologate (hŏ mŏl′ə gāt′), *v.t.*, **-gated, -gating.** to approve; ratify. [t. ML: m. s. *homologātus*, pp. of *homologāre*, t. Gk: m. *homologein* agree to, allow] —**homol′oga′tion,** *n.*

homological (hŏm′ə lŏj′ĭ kl), *adj.* homologous. Also, **hom′olog′ic.** —**hom′olog′ically,** *adv.*

homologize (hŏ mŏl′ə jīz′), *v.*, **-gized, -gizing.** —*v.t.* **1.** to make or show to be homologous. —*v.i.* **2.** to be homologous; correspond. Also, **homologise.**

homologous (hŏ mŏl′ə gəs), *adj.* **1.** having the same or a similar relation; corresponding, as in relative position, structure, etc. **2.** *Biol.* corresponding in type of structure and in origin, but not necessarily in function: *the wing of a bird and the foreleg of a horse are homologous.* **3.** *Chem.* of the same chemical type, but differing by a fixed increment in certain constituents. **4.** *Med., etc.* pertaining to the relation between bacteria and the immune serum prepared from them. [t. ML: m. *homologus*, or t. Gk: m. *homólogos* agreeing, of one mind]

homologous chromosomes, *Biol.* pairs of similar chromosomes, one of maternal, the other of paternal origin, which carry the Mendelian pairs of alleles or genes.

homologue (hŏm′ə lŏg′), *n.* **1.** something homologous. **2.** *Biol.* a homologous organ or part. **3.** *Chem.* any member of a homologous series of compounds.

homology (hŏ mŏl′ə jĭ), *n.*, *pl.* **-gies.** **1.** the state of being homologous; homologous relation or correspondence. **2.** *Biol.* **a.** a fundamental similarity due to community of descent. **b.** a structural similarity of two segments of one animal based on a common developmental origin. **3.** *Chem.* the similarity of organic compounds of a series in which each member differs from its adjacent compounds by a single group. [t. LL: m. s. *homologia*, t. Gk: agreement, assent, conformity]

homomorphism (hō′mō mô′fĭz′əm, hŏm′-), *n.* **1.** *Biol.* correspondence in form or external appearance but not in type of structure and in origin. **2.** *Bot.* possession of perfect flowers of only one kind. **3.** *Zool.* resemblance between the young and the adult. Also, **ho′momor′phy.** —**ho′momor′phic, ho′momor′phous,** *adj.*

homonym (hŏm′ə nĭm), *n.* **1.** a word like another in sound and perhaps in spelling, but different in meaning, as *meat* and *meet.* **2.** a homophone. **3.** a homograph. **4.** a namesake. **5.** *Biol.* a name given to a species or genus, which has been used at an earlier date for a different species or genus, and which is therefore rejected. [t. L: s. *homōnymus* having the same name, t. Gk: m. *homṓnymos*] —**hom′onym′ic,** *adj.*

homonymous (hŏ mŏn′ĭ məs), *adj.* **1.** of the nature of homonyms; having the same name. **2.** *Optics.* denoting or pertaining to the images formed in a kind of double vision in which the image seen by the right eye is on the right side and vice versa.

homonymy (hŏ mŏn′ĭ mĭ), *n.* homonymous state.

Homoousian (hō′mō o͞o′sĭ ən, -ou′sĭ ən, hŏm′ō-), *n.* **1.** one of a 4th-century church party which maintained that the essence or substance of the Father and the Son is the same (distinguished from *Homoiousian*). —*adj.* **2.** (*l.c.*) pertaining to the Homoousians or their doctrines. [f. s. LGk *homooúsios* of the same substance + -AN]

homophone (hŏm′ə fōn′), *n.* **1.** *Phonet.* a word pronounced the same as another, whether spelled the same or not: *heir* and *air* are homophones. **2.** (in writing) an element which represents the same spoken unit as another, as (usually) English *ks* and *x.*

homophonic (hŏm′ə fŏn′ĭk), *adj.* **1.** having the same sound. **2.** having one part or melody predominating (opposed to *polyphonic*). [f. s. Gk *homóphōnos* of the same sound + -IC]

homophonous (hŏ mŏf′ə nəs), *adj.* identical in pronunciation.

homophony (hŏ mŏf′ə nĭ), *n.* **1.** the quality of being homophonic. **2.** homophonic music.

homopolar (hō′mō pō′lə), *adj. Chem.* of uniform polarity; not ionized.

homopolar bond, *Chem.* a covalent bond.

homopterous (hŏ mŏp′tə rəs), *adj.* pertaining or belonging to the *Homoptera*, a suborder of hemipterous insects having wings of the same texture throughout, comprising the aphids, cicadas, etc. [t. Gk: m. *homópteros* with the same plumage]

Homo sapiens (hō′mō săp′ĭ ĕnz′), modern man, the single surviving species of the genus *Homo* and of the primate family, *Hominidae*, to which it belongs. [L]

homosexual (hō′mō sĕk′syo͞o əl, hŏm′ə-), *adj.* **1.** pertaining to or exhibiting homosexuality. —*n.* **2.** a homosexual person.

homosexuality (hō′mō sĕk′syo͞o ăl′ĭ tĭ, hŏm′ə-), *n.* sexual feeling for a person of the same sex.

homosporous (hŏ mŏs′pə rəs, hō′mō spô′rəs), *adj. Bot.* having spores of one kind only.

homospory (hŏ mŏs′pə rĭ), *n.* the production of a single kind of spore, neither microspore nor megaspore.

homotaxis (hō′mō tăk′sĭs, hŏm′ō-), *n.* similarity of arrangement, as of geological strata, which, though not necessarily contemporaneous, have the same relative position. —**ho′motax′ic,** *adj.*

homothalic (hō′mō thăl′ĭk, hŏm′ō-), *adj. Bot.* having all mycelia alike, the opposite sexual functions being performed by different cells of single mycelium. [f. HOMO- + s. Gk *thallós* sprout + -IC]

homothetic (hō′mō thĕt′ĭk), *adj. Geom.* similarly placed; similar.

homozygosis (hō′mō zī gō′sĭs, -zĭ-, hŏm′ō-), *n. Biol.* the union of like gametes, resulting in a homozygote. [f. HOMO- + Gk *zýgōsis* joining]

homozygote (hō′mō zī′gōt, -zĭg′ōt, hŏm′ə-), *n. Biol.* an organism with identical pairs of genes with respect to any given pair of hereditary characters, and hence breeding true for those characteristics. —**homozygous** (hō′mə zī′gəs, hŏm′ə-), *adj.*

Homs (hŏms), *n.* a town in W Syria. 186,000 (est. 1965).

homunculus (hŏ mŭng′kyo͞o ləs), *n.*, *pl.* **-li** (-lī′). **1.** a diminutive human; dwarf. **2.** a fully formed miniature human being, once believed, according to certain medical theories, to be found in the spermatozoon. Also, **homun′cule.** [t. L, dim. of *homo* man]

homy (hō′mĭ), *adj.*, **-mier, -miest.** *Colloq.* homelike; comfortable; friendly. Also, **homey.** —**Syn.** See **simple.**

Hon., Honourable.

hon., **1.** honourably. **2.** honorary.

Honan (hō′năn′), *n.* a province in E China. 48,670,000 pop. (est. 1957); 59,459 sq. mi. *Cap.:* Chengchow.

Hond., Honduras.

Hondo (hŏn′dō), *n.* Honshu.

Honduras (hŏn dyo͞oə′rəs), *n.* **1.** a republic in Central America. 1,884,765 pop. (1961); 43,278 sq. mi. *Cap.:* Tegucigalpa. **2.** See **British Honduras.** —**Hondu′ran,** *adj.*, *n.*

hone[1] (hōn), *n.*, *v.*, —*n.* **1.** a whetstone of fine, compact texture, esp. one for sharpening razors. —*v.t.* **2.** to sharpen on or as on a hone: *to hone a razor.* [ME; OE *hān* stone, rock, c. Icel. *hein* hone]

hone[2] (hōn), *Dial.* —*v.i.* **1.** to moan; grieve. —*v.t.* **2.** to hanker after; long for. [t. OF: m. *hogner* growl, ult. t. Gmc]

Honegger (hŏn′ĭ gə; *Ger.* hô′nĕ gər), *n.* **Arthur** (ä′thə; *Ger.* är′to͝or), 1892–1955, Swiss composer.

honest (ŏn′ĭst), *adj.* **1.** honourable in principles, intentions, and actions; upright: *an honest person.* **2.** showing uprightness and fairness: *honest methods.* **3.** acquired fairly: *honest money.* **4.** open; sincere: *an honest face.* **5.** genuine or unadulterated: *honest commodities.* **6.** truthful; creditable; candid. **7.** chaste or virtuous; respectable. [ME *honeste*, t. OF, t. L: m. *honestus* honourable, worthy, virtuous] —**hon′estly,** *adv.* —**Syn.** **1.** fair, just, incorruptible, trusty, trustworthy; truthful. **4.** straightforward, frank, candid. —**Ant.** **1.** corrupt.

honesty (ŏn′ĭs tĭ), *n.* **1.** the quality or fact of being honest; uprightness, probity, or integrity. **2.** truthfulness, sincerity, or frankness. **3.** freedom from deceit or fraud. 4. *Bot.* a cruciferous herb, *Lunaria annua*, with purple flowers and semitransparent satiny pods. 5. *Archaic.* chastity. **—Syn. 1.** fairness, justice; rectitude. 2. candour. See **honour. —Ant. 1.** crookedness.

honewort (hōn′wûrt′), *n.* any of several umbelliferous plants, esp. a kind of parsley.

honey (hŭn′ĭ), *n., pl.* **honeys,** *adj., v.,* **honeyed, honeying.** *—n.* **1.** a sweet, viscid fluid produced by bees from the nectar collected from flowers, and stored in their nests or hives as food. **2.** the nectar of flowers. **3.** any of various similar products produced by insects or in other ways. **4.** something sweet, delicious, or delightful: *the honey of flattery.* **5.** sweet one; darling (a term of endearment). *—adj.* **6.** of or like honey; sweet; dear. *—v.i.* **7.** *Archaic or U.S.* to talk sweetly; use endearments. [ME *huny*, OE *hunig*, c. D *honig*, G *Honig*] **—hon′ey-like′,** *adj.*

honeybee (hŭn′ĭ bē′), *n.* a bee that collects and stores honey, specif. *Apis mellifera.*

honeycomb (hŭn′ĭ kōm′), *n.* **1.** a structure of wax containing rows of hexagonal cells, formed by bees for the reception of honey and pollen and of their eggs. **2.** any substance, as a casting of iron, etc., having cells like those of a honeycomb. **3.** the reticulum of a ruminant. *—adj.* **4.** having the structure or appearance of a honeycomb: *honeycomb weave.* *—v.t.* **5.** to reduce to a honeycomb; pierce with many holes or cavities: *a rock honeycombed with passages.* [ME *hunycomb*, OE *hunigcamb*]

honeydew (hŭn′ĭ dyōō′), *n.* **1.** the sweet material which exudes from the leaves of certain plants in hot weather. **2.** a sugary material secreted by aphids, leaf-hoppers, etc.

honeydew melon, a sweet-flavoured, white-fleshed muskmelon with a smooth, pale green rind.

honey-eater (hŭn′ĭ ē′tə), *n.* any of numerous oscine birds constituting the family *Meliphagidae*, chiefly of Australasia, with a bill and tongue adapted for extracting the nectar from flowers.

honeyed (hŭn′ĭd), *adj.* **1.** dulcet or mellifluous; ingratiating: *honeyed words.* **2.** containing, consisting of, or resembling honey: *honeyed drinks.*

honey-guide (hŭn′ĭ gīd′), *n.* any of various small, dull-coloured non-passerine birds (genus *Indicator*, *Prodotiscus*, *Melichneutes*, etc.), of Africa, Asia, and the East Indies, some of which are said to guide men or animals to places where honey may be found.

honey-locust (hŭn′ĭ lō′kəst), *n.* a thorny North American tree, *Gleditsia triacanthos*, bearing small compound leaves and pods with a sweet pulp.

honeymoon (hŭn′ĭ mōōn′), *n.* **1.** a holiday spent by a newly married couple before settling down. **2.** the first weeks immediately after marriage. **3.** any period of happy or harmonious relationship. *—v.i.* **4.** to spend one's honeymoon (usually fol. by *in* or *at*). **—hon′eymoon′er,** *n.*

honey mouse, a small, insectiverous, marsupial mammal, *Tarsipes rostratus*, of western Australia.

honey plant, any plant especially useful in furnishing nectar to bees, as the cleome or figwort.

honey-sucker (hŭn′ĭ sŭk′ə), *n.* **1.** a bird that eats the nectar of flowers. **2.** a honey-eater.

honeysuckle (hŭn′ĭ sŭk′l), *n.* **1.** any of the upright or climbing shrubs constituting the caprifoliaceous genus *Lonicera*, some species of which are cultivated for their fragrant white, yellow, or red tubular flowers. **2.** any of various other fragrant or ornamental plants. **3.** any of several Australian trees or shrubs of the genus *Banksia.* [ME *honiesoukel*, f. *honisouke* (OE *hunisūce*) lit., honeysuck + *-el*, dim. suffix] **—hon′eysuck′led,** *adj.*

honeysweet (hŭn′ĭ swēt′), *adj.* sweet as honey.

hong (hŏng), *n.* **1.** (in China) a group of rooms or buildings forming a warehouse, factory, etc. **2.** one of the foreign factories formerly maintained at Canton. [t. Chinese (Cantonese): row, rank (Mandarin *hang*)]

hongi (hŏng′ĭ), *n.* *N.Z.* a Maori greeting, expressed by touching noses. [t. Maori]

Hong Kong (hŏng′kŏng′), **1.** a British crown colony in SE China, comprising the island of Hong Kong (32 sq. mi.) and the adjacent mainland. 3,642,500 (est. 1963); 398 sq. mi. *Cap.:* Victoria. See map under **Taiwan. 2.** Victoria (def. 4). Also, **Hongkong.**

honi soit qui mal y pense (*Fr.* ō nē swȧ′ kē mȧl ē päNs′), *French.* shamed be he who thinks evil of it (motto of the Order of the Garter).

honk (hŏngk), *n.* **1.** the cry of the wild goose. **2.** any similar sound, as a motor-car horn. *—v.i.* **3.** to emit a honk. [imit.] **—honk′er,** *n.*

honky-tonk (hŏng′kĭ tŏngk′), *—n.* **1.** *U.S. Slang.* a cheap, sordid nightclub, dance hall, etc. *—adj.* **2.** *U.S. Slang.* of or pertaining to a honky-tonk. **3.** *Music.* of or pertaining to a style of ragtime piano-playing. [orig. uncert.]

Honolulu (hŏn′ə lōō′lōō), *n.* a seaport in the Hawaiian Islands, on the island of Oahu: capital of Hawaii. 294,179 (1960).

honor (ŏn′ə), *n., v.t. U.S.* honour. **—hon′orable,** *adj.*

honorarium (ŏn′ə rēə′rĭ əm), *n., pl.* **-rariums, -raria** (-rēə′rĭ ə). **1.** an honorary reward, as in recognition of professional services on which no price may be set. **2.** a fee for services rendered by a professional person. [t. L, prop. neut. of *honōrārius* HONORARY]

honorary (ŏn′ə rə rĭ, ŏn′rə rĭ), *adj.* **1.** given for honour only, without the usual duties, privileges, emoluments, etc.: *an honorary title.* **2.** holding a title or position conferred for honour only: *an honorary president.* **3.** (of an obligation) depending on one's honour for fulfilment. **4.** given, made, or serving as a token of honour: *an honorary gift.* **5.** conferring an honour. [t. L: m. s. *honōrārius* relating to honour]

honorific (ŏn′ə rĭf′ĭk), *adj.* Also, **hon′orif′ical. 1.** doing or conferring honour. **2.** having the quality of an honorific. *—n.* **3.** (in certain languages, as Chinese and Japanese) a class of forms used to show respect, especially in direct address. **4.** a title or term of respect. *Examples: Doctor, Professor, Rt Hon.* [t. L: s. *honōrificus.* See HONOUR, n., -(I)FIC] **—hon′orif′ically,** *adv.*

Honorius (hō nô′rĭ əs), *n.* **1. Flavius** (flā′vyəs), A.D. 384–423, Roman emperor of the Western Empire A.D. 395–423. **2.** the name of four popes.

honour (ŏn′ə), *n.* **1.** high public esteem; fame; glory: *a roll of honour.* **2.** credit or reputation for behaviour that is becoming or worthy. **3.** a source of credit or distinction: *to be an honour to one's family.* **4.** high respect, as for worth, merit, or rank: *to be held in honour.* **5.** such respect manifested: *to be received with honour.* **6.** a special privilege or favour: *I have the honour to acknowledge your letter.* **7.** (*usually pl.*) high rank, dignity, or distinction: *political honours.* **8.** a deferential title, esp. of certain judges (prec. by *his, your,* etc.). **9.** high-minded character or principles; fine sense of one's obligations: *a man of honour.* **10.** (*pl.*) (in universities) **a.** scholastic or academic achievement in a degree examination higher than that required for a pass degree. **b.** the grade of scholarship achieved: *first-class honours.* **c.** the course of study. **11.** chastity or purity in a woman. **12.** *Bridge.* any one of the five highest ranking cards in each suit; for scoring purposes, any one of the highest cards of the trump suit or any one of the four aces at no trump. **13.** *Whist.* any of the four highest trump cards. **14.** *Golf.* the preference of teeing off before the other players or side, given after the first hole to the player or players who won the previous hole. **15. do honour to, a.** to show respect to. **b.** to be a credit to. **16. do the honours,** to act or preside as host. **17. on** or **upon one's honour, a.** acknowledging personal responsibility for one's actions. **b.** pledging one's reputation as to the truthfulness of a statement, etc. **c.** promising obedience or good behaviour. *—v.t.* **18.** to hold in honour or high respect; revere. **19.** to treat with honour. **20.** to confer honour or distinction upon. **21.** to worship (the Supreme Being). **22.** to show a courteous regard for: *to honour an invitation.* **23.** *Com.* to accept and pay (a cheque, etc.) when due. **24.** to accept the validity of (a document, etc.). Also, *U.S.,* **honor.** [ME *onor, honour, honor*, t. OF: m. *onur*, g. L *honor* honour, repute] **—hon′ourer,** *n.* **—hon′ourless,** *adj.*

—Syn. 4. respect, deference, homage; reverence, veneration. HONOUR, CONSIDERATION, DISTINCTION refer to the regard in which a man is held by his fellows. HONOUR suggests a combination of liking and respect: *his townsmen held him in great honour.* CONSIDERATION suggests honour because of proved worth: *a man worthy of the highest consideration.* DISTINCTION suggests particular honour because of qualities or accomplishments: *he achieved distinction at an early age as a violinist.* **9.** probity, uprightness. HONOUR, HONESTY, INTEGRITY, SINCERITY refer to one who is characterized by possession of the highest moral principles and the absence of deceit or fraud. HONOUR denotes a fine sense of, and a strict conformity to, what is considered morally right or due: *a high sense of honour, on one's honour.* HONESTY denotes the presence of probity and particularly the absence of deceit or fraud, esp. in business dealings: *uncompromising honesty and trustworthiness.* INTEGRITY indicates a soundness of moral principle which no power or influence can impair: *a man of unquestioned integrity and dependability.* SINCERITY implies absence of dissimulation or deceit, and a strong adherence to truth: *his sincerity was evident in every word.* **18.** esteem, venerate. **—Ant. 9.** dishonesty.

honourable (ŏn′ə rə bl, ŏn′rə bl), *adj.* **1.** in accordance with principles of honour; upright: *an honourable man.* **2.** of high rank, dignity, or distinction; noble, illustrious, or distinguished. **3.** entitling to honour or distinction: prefixed to the Christian names of younger sons of earls and all children of viscounts and barons, to the names of all justices of the High Court who are not Lords Justices or Lords of Appeal, to the names of certain other officials, and (within the House of Commons) to 'member' or 'gentleman' when one M.P. is referring to another.

Abbrev.: Hon. **4.** (of persons or things) worthy of honour and high respect. **5.** bringing honour or credit; consistent with honour: *an honourable peace.* Also, *U.S.*, **honorable.** —**hon′ourableness,** *n.* —**hon′ourably,** *adv.* —**Syn. 1.** honest, noble, high-minded. **4.** estimable. —**Ant. 1.** untrustworthy.

honour point, *Her.* a point midway between the fess point and top of an escutcheon. See diag. under **escutcheon.**

honours list, the British civil awards of honours and ranks, approved by the Sovereign and published on January 1st and June 10th of each year.

honours of war, *Mil.* privileges granted to a capitulating force, as of marching out of their camp or entrenchments with all their arms and with colours flying.

Honshu (hŏn′sho͞o), *n.* the chief island of Japan. 71,343,511 (1960); 88,851 sq. mi. Also, **Hondo.**

Honthorst (*Du.* hônt′hôrst), *n.* **Gerard van** (*Du.* KHè′-rŏrt vŏn), 1590–1656, Dutch painter.

hooch (ho͞och), *n. U.S. Slang.* **1.** alcoholic beverages. **2.** alcoholic liquor illicitly distilled and distributed. [short for *hoochinoo*, alter. of *Hutanuwu*, name of Alaskan Indian tribe which made alcoholic liquor]

Hooch (*Du.* hōKH), *n.* **Pieter de** (*Du.* pē′tər də), 1629–after 84, Dutch painter. Also, **Hoogh.**

hood (ho͝od), *n.* **1.** a soft or flexible covering for the head and neck, either separate or attached to a cloak or the like. **2.** something resembling or suggesting this, as a hood-shaped petal or sepal, etc. **3.** a piece of hood-shaped material, attached to an academic gown, the colour and material of the lining depending on the degree held and the university by which the degree was awarded. **4.** the top of a motor car. **5.** *U.S.* a motor-car bonnet. **6.** *Falconry.* a cover for the entire head of a hawk, used when it is not in pursuit of game. **7.** *U.S. Slang.* a hoodlum. —*v.t.* **8.** to furnish with a hood. **9.** to cover with, or as with, a hood. [ME *hode*, OE *hōd*, c. G *Hut* hat] —**hood′less,** *adj.* —**hood′like′,** *adj.*

Hood (ho͝od), *n.* **1. Thomas,** 1799–1845, English poet and humorist. **2. Robin.** See **Robin Hood. 3. Mount,** a volcanic peak in N Oregon, in the Cascade Range. 11,253 ft.

-hood, a suffix denoting state, condition, character, nature, etc., or a body of persons of a particular character or class: *childhood, likelihood, priesthood, sisterhood.* [ME *-hode, -hod*, OE *-hād*, c. G *-heit*; orig. separate word, OE *hād* condition, state, etc.]

hooded (ho͝od′ĭd), *adj.* **1.** having, or covered with, a hood. **2.** hood-shaped. **3.** *Zool.* having on the head a hoodlike formation, crest, arrangement of colours, or the like. **4.** *Bot.* cucullate.

hooded seal, *Zool.* bladdernose.

hoodie (ho͝od′ĭ; *Scot.* ho͞o′dĭ), *n. Scot.* the hooded crow, *Corvus cornix.* Also, **hoodie crow.**

hoodlum (ho͝od′ləm), *n.* **1.** a petty gangster; ruffian. **2.** a destructive, noisy, or rough child or young person. [orig. uncert.] —**hood′lumism,** *n.*

hoodman-blind (ho͝od′mən blīnd′), *n. Archaic.* blindman's buff.

hood mould, (in Gothic and Elizabethan architecture) a projecting moulding over the headstone or arch to a door or window. Also, **label mould.**

hoodoo (ho͞o′do͞o), *n., pl.* **-doos,** *v.,* **-dooed, -dooing.** —*n.* **1.** voodoo. **2.** *Colloq.* a person or thing that brings bad luck. **3.** *Colloq.* bad luck. **4.** an earth pillar. —*v.t.* **5.** *Colloq.* to bring or cause bad luck to. [appar. var. of VOODOO]

hoodwink (ho͝od′wĭngk′), *v.t.* **1.** to deceive; humbug. **2.** to blindfold. **3.** to cover or hide. —**hood′wink′er,** *n.*

hooey (ho͞o′ĭ), *U.S. Slang.* —*interj.* **1.** (an exclamation of disapproval.) —*n.* **2.** silly or worthless stuff; nonsense.

hoof (ho͞of), *n., pl.* **hoofs, hooves,** *v.* —*n.* **1.** the horny covering protecting the ends of the digits or encasing the foot in certain animals, as the ox, horse, etc. **2.** the entire foot of a horse, donkey, etc. **3.** a hoofed animal; one of a herd. **4.** (in humorous use) the human foot. **5. on the hoof,** (of livestock) alive, not butchered. —*v.i.* **6. hoof it,** *Slang.* to walk. **7.** *Colloq.* to dance. [ME; OE *hōf*, c. G *Huf*] —**hoof′like′,** *adj.*

hoofbound (ho͞of′bound′), *adj.* (of horses) having the heels of the hoofs dry and contracted, causing lameness.

hoofed (ho͞oft), *adj.* having hoofs; ungulate.

hoofer (ho͞o′fə), *n. U.S. Slang.* one who makes dancing an occupation, as a chorus girl.

Hooghly (ho͞o′glĭ), *n.* a river in NE India, in W Bengal: the westernmost channel by which the Ganges enters the Bay of Bengal. ab. 120 mi. Also, **Hugli.**

hook (ho͝ok), *n.* **1.** a curved or angular piece of metal or other firm substance catching, pulling, or sustaining something. **2.** a fishhook. **3.** that which catches; a snare; a trap. **4.** something curved or bent like a hook, as a mark or symbol, etc. **5.** a sharp curve or angle in the length or course of anything. **6.** a curved spit of land. **7.** a recurved and pointed organ or appendage of an animal or plant. **8.** *Golf.* a drive or other stroke which curves to the left of the player striking the ball. **9.** *Cricket.* a curving stroke of the bat, whereby the ball is driven to the on side of the field. **10.** *Boxing.* a curving blow made with the arm bent, and coming in to the opponent from the side: *right hook.* **11.** *Music.* a stroke or line attached to the stem of a quaver, semiquaver, etc. **12.** (*pl.*) *Slang.* fingers. **13. by hook or by crook,** by any means, fair or foul. **14. hook, line, and sinker,** completely. **15. off the hook,** *Slang.* out of a serious predicament. **16. on one's own hook,** *Slang.* on one's own responsibility. **17. on the hook, a.** waiting; being delayed. **b.** in a difficult predicament. —*v.t.* **18.** to seize, fasten, or catch hold of and draw with or as with a hook. **19.** to catch (fish) with a fishhook. **20.** *Slang.* to seize by stealth, pilfer, or steal. **21.** to catch by artifice. **22.** to catch on the horns, or attack with the horns. **23.** to catch hold of and draw (loops of yarn) through cloth with or as with a hook. **24.** to make hook-shaped; crook. **25.** *Rugby Football.* to use the foot to obtain the ball in the scrum and kick it backwards to a team member. **26.** *Hockey.* to hook another player's stick. **27.** *Boxing.* to deliver a hook. **28.** *Cricket, Golf.* to hit (the ball) with a hook. **29.** *Slang.* to marry: *she's managed to hook a rich man.* **30. hook up, a.** to fasten with a hook or hooks. **b.** to put together (mechanical apparatus) and connect it to the source of power. **31. hook it,** *Slang.* to depart; clear off. —*v.i.* **32.** to become attached or fastened by or as by a hook; join on. **33.** to curve or bend like a hook. **34.** *Rugby Football.* to act as hooker. **35.** *Boxing.* to deliver a hook. **36.** *Cricket, Golf.* **a.** (of the player) to make a hooking stroke. **b.** (of the ball) to describe a course to the left or on side of the player after being hooked. **37.** *Slang.* to depart; clear off. [ME *hoke*, OE *hōc*, c. D *hoek* hook, angle, corner, point of land] —**hook′less,** *adj.* —**hook′like′,** *adj.*

hookah (ho͝ok′ə), *n.* a tobacco pipe with a long, flexible tube by which the smoke is drawn through a vessel of water and thus cooled. Also, **hooka.** [t. Ar.: m. *ḥuqqa* box, vase, pipe for smoking]

Hookah

hook and eye, a fastening arrangement consisting of a hook on one part, which catches on to a bar or loop on the other part.

Hooke (ho͝ok), *n.* **Robert,** 1635–1703, English physicist.

hooked (ho͝okt), *adj.* **1.** bent like a hook; hook-shaped. **2.** having a hook or hooks. **3.** made with a hook. **4.** caught, as a fish. **5.** *Slang.* addicted; obsessed. **6.** *Slang.* married. —**hookedness** (ho͝ok′ĭd nĭs), *n.*

hooked rug, *U.S.* a rug made by drawing loops of yarn or cloth through a foundation of gunny, or the like, to form a pattern.

hooker (ho͝ok′ə), *n.* **1.** *Colloq.* a kind of small fishing smack. **2.** any old-fashioned or clumsy vessel. **3.** *Rugby Football.* **a.** the central forward in the front row of the scrum, whose job it is to pull back the ball with his foot. **b.** the position played by such a forward. [t. D: m. *hoeker*, der. *hoek* HOOK]

Hooker (ho͝ok′ə), *n.* **Richard,** 1554?–1600, English author and clergyman.

Hooke's law, *Physics.* the principle that, within the elastic limit, the strain on a body is proportional to the stress producing it. [named after R. HOOKE]

hooknose (ho͝ok′nōz′), *n.* an aquiline or beaklike nose.

hook-nosed (ho͝ok′nōzd′), *adj.* having a hooknose.

Hook of Holland (ho͝ok), a cape and harbour in SW Netherlands. Dutch, **Hoek van Holland.**

hook-up (ho͝ok′ŭp′), *n. Chiefly U.S.* **1.** *Radio.* **a.** a diagram of radio apparatus, showing the connection of the different elements. **b.** the elements as set up for operation. **2.** combination; connection. **3.** *Radio, Television.* a link-up, often temporary, of different stations for a special broadcast.

hookworm (ho͝ok′wûm′), *n.* **1.** any of certain blood-sucking nematode worms, as *Ancylostoma duodenale* and *Necator americanus*, parasitic in the intestine of man and other animals. **2.** hookworm disease.

hookworm disease, a disease characterized by severe anaemia, caused by hookworms.

hooky[1] (ho͝ok′ĭ), *adj.* **1.** full of hooks. **2.** hook-shaped. [f. HOOK + -Y[1]]

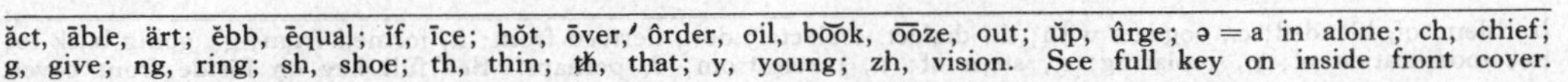

hooky[2] (ho͝ok′ĭ), *n. Colloq.* unjustifiable absence from school (used in the phrase *play hooky*). Also, **hookey.** [f. HOOK (def. 37) + -Y³]

hooligan (ho͞o′lĭ gən), *Slang.* —*n.* **1.** a hoodlum; young street rough. —*adj.* **2.** of or like hooligans. [var. of *Houlihan*, Irish surname which came to be assoc. with rowdies] —**hoo′liganism,** *n.*

hoop (ho͞op), *n.* **1.** a circular band or ring of metal, wood, or other stiff material. **2.** such a band to hold together the staves of a cask, barrel, etc. **3.** a large ring of iron or wood or plastic for a child to roll along the ground. **4.** something resembling a hoop. **5.** that part of a finger ring which surrounds the finger. **6.** one of the iron arches used in croquet. **7.** a circular band of stiff material used to expand a woman's skirt. **8.** a hoop skirt. **9.** a large ring, with paper stretched over it through which circus animals, etc., jump. **10. go through the hoop,** go through a bad time; undergo an ordeal. —*v.t.* **11.** to bind or fasten with a hoop or hoops. **12.** to encircle; embrace. [ME *hop(e)*, late OE *hōp*, c. D *hope*] —**hooped,** *adj.* —**hoop′like′,** *adj.*

hoopla (ho͞op′lä′), *n.* a game in which hoops are thrown in an attempt to encircle objects offered as prizes.

hoopoe (ho͞o′po͞o), *n.* any of the Old World non-passerine birds constituting the family *Upupidae*, esp. *Upupa epops*, a European species with an erectile fanlike crest. [var. of obs. *hoopoop*, c. LG *huppup* (imit. of its cry); cf. L *upupa*]

hoop skirt, 1. a woman's skirt, made to stand out from the waist by an undergarment of flexible hoops connected by tapes. **2.** the framework for such a skirt.

hoop snake, a harmless snake, *Abastor erythrogrammus*, formerly believed to take its tail in its mouth and roll along like a hoop.

hooray (ho͞o rā′), *interj., v.i., n.* hurrah. Also, **hoorah.**

hooroo (ho͞o′ro͞o, ho͞o′ro͞o′, ho͞o ro͞o′), *interj. Austral.* goodbye.

hoosegow (ho͞os′gou), *n. U.S. Slang.* a jail. Also, **hoosgow.** [t. Sp.: m. *juzga(d)o*, court of justice; (in Mex. Sp.) jail]

hoot[1] (ho͞ot), *v.i.* **1.** to cry out or shout, esp. in disapproval or derision. **2.** (of an owl) to utter its cry. **3.** to utter a similar sound. **4.** to blow a horn or factory hooter; honk. —*v.t.* **5.** to assail with shouts of disapproval or derision. **6.** to drive (*out, away, off*, etc.) by hooting. **7.** to express in hoots. —*n.* **8.** the cry of an owl. **9.** any similar sound, as an inarticulate shout. **10.** a cry or shout, esp. of disapproval or derision. **11.** *Colloq.* a thing of no value: *I don't give a hoot.* **12.** an amusing or funny thing. [ME *huten*; prob. imit.] —**hoot′er,** *n.*

hoot[2] (ho͞ot), *n. N.Z. Slang.* money. [t. Maori]

hootch (ho͞och), *n.* hooch.

hooter (ho͞o′tə), *n.* **1.** one who hoots. **2.** a factory siren. **3.** a horn on a motor vehicle. **4.** *Slang.* a nose.

hoot owl, an owl that hoots (distinguished from *screech owl*).

hoots (ho͞ots), *interj. Scot.* (an exclamation expressing dissatisfaction or impatience.)

Hoover (ho͞o′və), *n. Trademark.* a vacuum cleaner.

Hoover (ho͞o′və), *n.* **Herbert Clark,** 1874–1964, 31st president of the U.S. 1929–33.

Hoover Dam, official name of **Boulder Dam.**

Hooverville (ho͞o′və vĭl), *n. U.S.* a collection of huts and shacks, as at the edge of a city, housing the unemployed during the 1930s. [named after Herbert HOOVER]

hooves (ho͞ovz), *n.* a pl. of **hoof.**

hop[1] (hŏp), *v.,* **hopped, hopping,** *n.* —*v.i.* **1.** to leap; move by leaping with all feet off the ground. **2.** to spring or leap on one foot. **3.** to make a flight or trip. **4.** *U.S. Colloq.* (of an aeroplane, etc.) to leave the ground in beginning a flight (often fol. by *off*). **5.** *Colloq.* to dance. **6.** to limp. **7. hop off.** Also, **hop it.** *Colloq.* to go away; leave. —*v.t.* **8.** *Colloq.* to jump off (something elevated), or over (a fence, ditch, etc.). **9.** *Colloq.* to board or alight from a train, etc. (fol. by *on* or *off*). **10.** *Colloq.* (of an aeroplane, etc.) to cross by a flight. —*n.* **11.** an act of hopping; short leap. **12.** a leap on one foot. **13.** *Colloq.* a flight of an aeroplane. **14.** *Colloq.* a dance, or dancing party. **15.** *Slang.* opium. **16. on the hop, a.** unprepared. **b.** busy, moving. [ME *hoppen*, OE *hoppian*, c. G *hopfen*]

hop[2] (hŏp), *n., v.,* **hopped, hopping.** —*n.* **1.** one of the twining plants of three species of the genus *Humulus*, the male flowers of which grow in panicled racemes and the female in conelike forms. **2.** (*pl.*) the dried ripe cones of the female flowers of the hop plant, used in brewing, medicine, etc. —*v.t.* **3.** to treat or flavour with hops. [ME *hoppe*, t. MD, c. G *Hopfen*]

hop-clover (hŏp′klō′və), *n.* a trefoil, *Trifolium procumbens*, whose withered yellow flowers resemble the strobiluses of hop.

hope (hōp), *n., v.,* **hoped, hoping.** —*n.* **1.** expectation of something desired; desire accompanied by expectation. **2.** a particular instance of such expectation or desire: *a hope of success.* **3.** confidence in a future event; ground for expecting something: *there is no hope of his recovery.* **4.** a person or thing that expectations are centred in: *the hope of the family.* —*v.t.* **5.** to look forward to with desire and more or less confidence. **6.** to trust in the truth of a matter (with a clause): *I hope that you are satisfied.* —*v.i.* **7.** to have an expectation of something desired: *we hope to see you, to hope for his pardon.* **8.** *Archaic.* to trust or rely. **9. hope against hope,** to continue to hope, although there are not apparent grounds for such hope. [ME; OE *hopa*, c. G *Hoffe*] —**Syn. 7.** See **expect.** —**ho′pingly,** *adv.*

Hope (hōp), *n.* **Anthony** (*Sir Anthony Hope Hawkins*), 1863–1933, English novelist.

hope chest, *U.S.* a bottom drawer.

hopeful (hōp′fəl), *adj.* **1.** full of hope; expressing hope: *hopeful words.* **2.** exciting hope; promising advantage or success: *a hopeful prospect.* —*n.* **3.** a promising young person. —**hope′fully,** *adv.* —**hope′fulness,** *n.* —**Syn. 1.** expectant, sanguine; optimistic, confident.

Hopeh (hō′pā′), *n.* a province in NE China. 44,720,000 (1958). *Cap.:* Tientsin. Also, **Hopei.**

hopeless (hōp′lĭs), *adj.* **1.** affording no hope; desperate: *a hopeless case.* **2.** without hope; despairing: *hopeless grief.* **3.** not possible to resolve or solve: *a hopeless problem.* **4.** not able to learn, perform, act, etc., incompetent: *a hopeless pupil.* —**hope′lessly,** *adv.* —**hope′lessness,** *n.* —**Syn. 1, 2.** HOPELESS, DESPAIRING, DESPONDENT, DESPERATE all describe an absence of hope. HOPELESS is used of a feeling of futility and passive abandonment of oneself to fate: *hopeless and grim, he still clung to the cliff.* DESPAIRING refers to the loss of hope in regard to a particular situation whether important or trivial; it suggests an intellectual judgement concerning probabilities: *despairing of victory, despairing of finding his gloves.* DESPONDENT always suggests melancholy and depression; it refers to an emotional state rather than to an intellectual judgement: *despondent over ill-health; she became more and more despondent and suspicious.* DESPERATE conveys a suggestion of recklessness resulting from loss of hope: *as the time grew shorter, he became desperate.* DESPERATE may apply either to feelings or to situations: *the case seems hopeless but is not yet desperate; a desperate remedy.* DESPAIRING and DESPONDENT may apply only to feelings.

hop-garden (hŏp′gä′dn), *n.* a field of hops.

Hopi (hō′pĭ), *n., pl.* **-pis. 1.** a Pueblo tribe of Shoshonean speech affiliation inhabiting (now) nine stone-built towns in northern Arizona. **2.** their language.

Hopkins (hŏp′kĭnz), *n.* **1. Sir Frederick Gowland,** 1861–1947, English biochemist. **2. Gerard Manley,** 1844–89, English poet. **3. Harry Lloyd,** 1890–1946, U.S. administrator: special assistant to President Roosevelt 1942.

hoplite (hŏp′līt), *n.* a heavily armed foot soldier of ancient Greece. [t. Gk: m. s. *hoplītēs*]

hop-o'-my-thumb (hŏp′ə mĭ thŭm′), *n.* a tiny person.

hopped-up (hŏpt′ŭp′), *adj. U.S. Slang.* very roused; excited. Also, in predicative use, **hopped up.**

hopper (hŏp′ə), *n.* **1.** one who or that which hops. **2.** any one of various jumping insects, as grasshoppers, leafhoppers, cheese maggots, etc. **3.** a funnel-shaped chamber in which materials are stored temporarily and later discharged through the bottom. **4.** a hop-picker.

hopper car, *Railways.* a wagon for coal, sand, etc., with devices by which the contents can be speedily dumped.

hop-picker (hŏp′pĭk′ə), *n.* one who or a machine which picks hops.

hopping (hŏp′ĭng), *adj.* **1.** moving rapidly. **2. hopping mad,** very annoyed; furious. —*n.* **3.** the act of gathering hops.

hopple (hŏp′l), *v.t.,* **-pled, -pling.** to hobble; tether.

Hoppner (hŏp′nə), *n.* **John,** 1758–1810, English painter.

hopsack (hŏp′săk′), *n.* **1.** a coarse, jute sacking material. **2.** a fabric with coarse surface, used to make clothing. Also, **hop′sack′ing.**

hopscotch (hŏp′skŏch′), *n.* a children's game in which the player hops from one compartment to another of a diagram traced on the ground, without touching a line. [f. HOP¹ + SCOTCH (def. 2)]

hop, step, and jump, triple jump.

hopvine (hŏp′vīn′), *n.* **1.** the stem of a hop plant. **2.** the plant itself.

hor., 1. horizon. **2.** horizontal. **3.** horology.

Horace (hŏ′rĭs), *n.* (*Quintus Horatius Flaccus*), 65–8 B.C., Roman lyric poet and satirist.

Horae (hô′rē), *n.pl. Gk Myth.* goddesses of the seasons and of the hours, and hence of regularity and orderliness.

horal (hô′rəl), *adj.* pertaining to an hour or hours; hourly. [t. LL: s. *hōrālis*, der. L *hōra* HOUR]

horary (hô′rə rĭ), *adj.* **1.** pertaining to an hour; indicating the hours: *the horary circle.* **2.** occurring every hour; hourly. **3.** lasting an hour. [t. ML: m. s. *hōrārius*, der. L *hōra* HOUR]

Horatian (hŏ rā′shyən), *adj.* **1.** of or pertaining to Horace. **2.** resembling the poetry or style of Horace.

Horatian ode. See **ode** (def. 5).

Horatius (hŏ rā′shyəs), *n. Rom. Legend.* a hero celebrated for his defence of the bridge over the Tiber against the Etruscans.

horde (hôd), *n., v.,* **horded, hording.** —*n.* **1.** a great company or multitude (often in disparagement). **2.** a tribe or troop of Asiatic nomads. **3.** any nomadic group. **4.** a moving pack of animals, insects, etc. —*v.i.* **5.** to gather in a horde. [t. F, ult. t. Turk.: m. *urdū* camp. See URDU]

Horeb (hô′rĕb), *n. Bible.* (apparently) Mount Sinai.

horehound (hô′hound′), *n.* **1.** a perennial herb, *Marrubium vulgare*, a native in the Old World, with downy leaves and small whitish flowers and containing a bitter medicinal juice. **2.** any of various plants of the mint family. Also, **hoarhound.** [ME *horehune*, OE *hārhūne*, f. *hār* grey + *hūne* horehound]

horizon (hə rī′zən), *n.* **1.** the line or circle which forms the apparent boundary between earth and sky (**apparent** or **visible horizon**). **2.** *Astron.* **a.** the plane which is tangent to the earth at the place of the observer and extends to the celestial sphere (**sensible horizon**). **b.** the great circle of the celestial sphere whose plane is parallel to the sensible horizon of a particular place and passes through the centre of the earth, or the plane itself (**astronomical** or **celestial horizon**). **3.** the limit or range of perception, knowledge, or the like. **4.** *Geol.* a plane in rock strata characterized by particular features, as occurrence of distinctive fossil species. **5.** one of the series of distinctive layers found in a vertical cross-section of any well-developed soil. [t. L, t. Gk: bounding circle, horizon, prop. ppr., bounding; r. ME *orizonte*, t. OF] —**hori′zonless,** *adj.*

horizontal (hŏ′rĭ zŏn′tl), *adj.* **1.** at right-angles to the vertical: *a horizontal position.* **2.** reclining. **3.** near, on, or parallel to the horizon. **4.** of or pertaining to the horizon. **5.** measured or contained in a plane parallel to the horizon: *a horizontal distance.* —*n.* **6.** a horizontal line, plane, position, etc. —**hor′izontal′ity, hor′izon′talness,** *n.* —**hor′izon′tally,** *adv.*

horizontal bar, *Gymnastics.* a bar for swinging, chinning, and other gymnastic exercises.

horizontal intensity, the component of the earth's magnetic field which acts in a horizontal direction; equal to the product of the total intensity and the cosine of the angle of dip.

horizontal mobility, *Sociol.* the movement of individuals or groups from one position to another without lowering or raising their occupational or social status.

horizontal stabilizer, *Chiefly U.S. Aeron.* tailplane.

hormone (hô′mōn), *n. Physiol.* any of various substances which are formed in endocrine organs and which activate specifically receptive organs when transported to them by the body fluids. The internal secretions of the thyroid gland, pancreas, etc., are hormones. [t. Gk: m. *hormôn*, ppr., setting in motion] —**hormo′nal,** *adj.*

Hormuz (hô′mŭz), *n.* **Strait of,** a strait between Iran and the Trucial States, connecting the Persian Gulf and the Gulf of Oman. Also, **Ormuz.**

horn (hôn), *n.* **1.** a hard, projected, often curved and pointed, hollow and permanent growth (usually one of a pair, a right and a left) on the head of certain mammals, as cattle, sheep, goats, antelopes, etc. (**true horn**). **2.** each of the pair of solid, deciduous, usually branched bony growths, or antlers, on the head of a deer. **3.** some similar growth, as the tusk of a narwhal. **4.** a process projecting from the head of an animal and suggestive of a horn, as a feeler, tentacle, crest, etc. **5.** the substance of which true horns are composed. **6.** any similar substance, as that of hoofs, nails, corns, etc. **7.** an article made of horn, as a thimble, a spoon, or a shoehorn. **8.** any hornlike projection or extremity. **9.** something formed from or resembling the hollow horn of an animal: *a drinking horn.* **10.** a part like a horn of an animal attributed to deities, demons, etc.: *the devil's horn.* **11.** *Obs.* the imaginary projection on a cuckold's brow. **12.** *Music.* a wind instrument, orig. formed from the hollow horn of an animal but now usually made of brass or other metal or material. **13.** *Slang.* a trumpet. **14.** an instrument for sounding a warning signal: *a klaxon horn.* **15.** *Aeron.* a local projecting balance on the control surfaces of an aircraft. **16.** *Radio.* a tube of varying cross-section used in some loudspeakers to couple the diaphragm to the sound transmitting space. **17.** the high protuberant part at the front and top of a saddle; the pommel. **18.** one of the extremities of the crescent moon. **19.** a symbol of power, as in the Bible: *a horn of salvation.* **20.** *Logic.* each of the alternatives of a dilemma. **21. draw in one's horns,** to economize; reduce one's activities; retreat. —*v.t.* **22.** to butt or gore with the horns. **23.** to furnish with horns. —*v.i.* **24. horn in,** *Slang.* to thrust oneself forward obtrusively. —*adj.* **25.** made of horn. [ME *horn(e)*, OE *horn*, c. G *Horn*; akin to L *cornu*, Gk *kéras* horn] —**horned,** *adj.* —**horn′less,** *adj.* —**horn′like′,** *adj.*

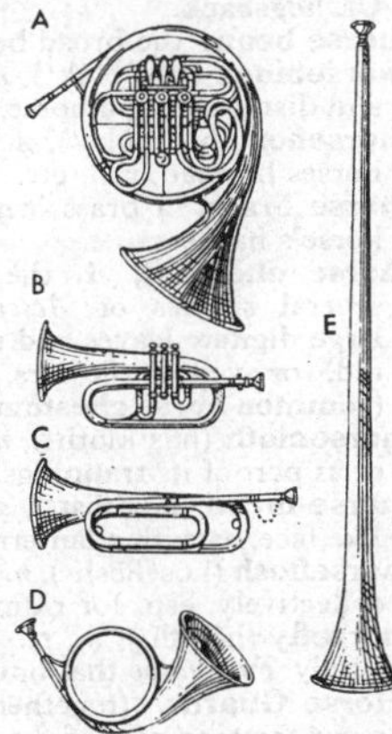

Horns
A, French horn; B and C, Military bugles with and without keys; D, Continental hunting horn; E, Coaching horn

Horn (hôn), *n.* **Cape,** a headland on a small island at the S extremity of South America.

hornbeam (hôn′bēm′), *n.* any of the shrubs or small trees constituting the betulaceous genus *Carpinus*, with a heavy, hard wood, as *C. betulus*, a native of Europe and N Asia, also found in heavy soils of SE England.

hornbill (hôn′bĭl′), *n.* any of the large non-passerine, tropical Old World birds constituting the family *Bucerotidae*, characterized by a very large bill surmounted by a horny protuberance, sometimes of enormous size.

hornblende (hôn′blĕnd′), *n.* any of the common black or dark-coloured aluminous varieties of amphibole. [t. G] —**horn′blen′dic,** *adj.*

hornblende schist, *Geol.* a variety of schist containing needles of hornblende which lie in parallel planes in the rock.

hornbook (hôn′bo͝ok′), *n.* **1.** a leaf or page containing the alphabet, religious materials, etc., covered with a sheet of transparent horn and fixed in a frame with a handle, formerly used in teaching children to read. **2.** a primer, or book of rudiments.

Hornchurch (hôn′chûch′), *n.* a town in the NE outer London borough of Havering.

horned pondweed, a slender, submerged, perennial, *Zanichellia palustris*, belonging to the *Zanichelliaceae*, widespread in fresh or brackish water.

horned poppy, any of several species of papaveraceous herbs of Europe and W Asia, belonging to the genus *Glaucium*, esp. the **yellow horned poppy,** *G. flavum*, with large flowers and long curved capsules.

horned pout, a large-headed freshwater catfish, *Ameiurus nebulosus*, with conspicuous barbels.

horned toad, any of various small, harmless lizards, genus *Phrynosoma*, of western North America, with flattened body and hornlike spines on the head and body.

horned viper. See **viper** (def. 3).

hornet (hô′nĭt), *n.* any large, strong, social wasp of the family *Vespidae* having an exceptionally severe sting, as the **giant hornet** of Europe, *Vespa crabo*, and the **bald-faced hornet,** *Vespula maculata*, of North America. [ME *harnete*, OE *hyrnet(u)*, c. G *Hornisse*]

Bald-faced hornet, *Vespula maculata* (drone) (Length 7 in.)

hornet's nest, a great deal of trouble, hostility.

hornito (hô nē′tō; *Sp.* ȯr nē′tȯ), *n., pl.* **-tos** (-tōz; *Sp.* -tȯs). *Geol.* a low oven-shaped mound, common in the volcanic districts of South America, etc., usually emitting hot smoke and vapours from its sides and summit. [t. Sp., dim. of *horno*, g. L *furnus* oven]

horn-mad (hôn′măd′), *adj.* **1.** enraged enough to gore with the horns, as a bull. **2.** raging mad; furious.

horn of plenty, the cornucopia.

hornpipe (hôn′pīp′), *n.* **1.** an English folk clarinet with an ox horn to conceal the reed and another one to form the bell. **2.** a lively dance (orig. to hornpipe music) usually by a single person, popular among sailors. **3.** a piece of music for or in the style of such a dance.

horn-rimmed (hôn′rĭmd′), *adj.* (of spectacles) with frames or rims made of horn, tortoiseshell, or a plastic in imitation of horn.

Hornsey (hôn′zĭ), *n.* a district of the N outer London borough of Haringey.

horn silver, cerargyrite.

hornstone (hôn′stōn′), *n.* **1.** a variety of quartz resembling flint. **2.** an argillaceous rock baked and partly recrystallized by the heat of an igneous intrusion.

horntail (hôn′tāl′), *n.* any of various wasplike insects of the family *Siricidae*, the females of which have a hornlike spine at the end of the abdomen.

hornworm (hôn′wûm′), *n.* any of various caterpillars of hawkmoths, characterized by a hornlike caudal projection.

hornwort (hôn′wût′), *n.* any plant of the genus *Ceratophyllum*, comprising aquatic herbs common in ponds and slow streams.

horny (hô′nĭ), *adj.*, **-nier, -niest. 1.** hornlike through hardening; callous: *horny hands.* **2.** consisting of a horn or a hornlike substance; corneous. **3.** more or less translucent, like horn. **4.** having a horn or horns or hornlike projections. **—horn′iness,** *n.*

horol., horology.

horologe (hŏ′rə lŏj′), *n.* any instrument for indicating the time. [t. L: m. s. *hōrologium*, t. Gk: m. *hōrológion* an instrument for telling the hour; r. ME *orloge*, t. OF]

horologic (hŏ′rə lŏj′ĭk), *adj.* pertaining to a horologe or to horology. Also, **hor′olog′ical.**

horologist (hŏ rŏl′ə jĭst), *n.* an expert in horology. Also, **horol′oger.**

horology (hŏ rŏl′ə jĭ), *n.* the art or science of making timepieces or of measuring time.

horoscope (hŏ′rə skōp′), *n.* **1.** a diagram of the heavens for use in calculating nativities, etc. **2.** the art or practice of foretelling future events by observation of the stars and planets. [ME and OE *horoscopus*, t. L, t. Gk: m. *hōroskópos* nativity, horoscope]

horoscopy (hŏ rŏs′kə pĭ), *n.* **1.** the casting or taking of horoscopes. **2.** the aspects of the heavens at a given moment, esp. that of a person's birth.

Horowitz (hŏ′rə vĭts), *n.* **Vladimir** (vlăd′ĭ mĭə′), born 1904, Russian pianist in the U.S.

horrendous (hŏ rĕn′dəs), *adj.* dreadful; horrible. [t. L: m. *horrendus*, ger. of *horrēre* bristle, shudder] **—horren′dously,** *adv.*

horrent (hŏ′rənt), *adj.* bristling; standing erect like bristles. [t. L: s. *horrens*, ppr., standing on end. Cf. HORRID]

horrible (hŏ′rə bl), *adj.* **1.** causing or tending to cause horror; dreadful: *a horrible sight.* **2.** extremely unpleasant; deplorable; excessive: *horrible conditions.* [ME, t. OF, t. L: m. *horribilis* terrible, fearful] **—hor′ribleness,** *n.* **—hor′ribly,** *adv.* **—Syn. 1.** terrible, awful, appalling, frightful; hideous, grim, ghastly, shocking, revolting, repulsive, horrid. **—Ant. 1.** attractive.

horrid (hŏ′rĭd), *adj.* **1.** such as to cause horror; dreadful; abominable. **2.** *Colloq.* extremely unpleasant or disagreeable: *horrid weather.* [t. L: s. *horridus* bristling, rough] **—hor′ridly,** *adv.* **—hor′ridness,** *n.*

horrific (hŏ rĭf′ĭk), *adj.* causing horror. [t. L: s. *horrificus*]

horrify (hŏ′rĭ fī′), *v.t.*, **-fied, -fying.** to cause to feel horror; strike with horror; shock intensely. [t. L: m. *horrificāre* cause horror] **—hor′rifica′tion,** *n.*

horripilation (hŏ rĭp′ĭ lā′shən), *n.* a bristling of the hair on the skin from cold, fear, etc.; gooseflesh. [t. LL: s. *horripilātio*, der. L *horripilāre* bristle with hairs]

horror (hŏ′rə), *n.* **1.** a shuddering fear or abhorrence; a painful emotion excited by something frightful or shocking: *to shrink back in horror.* **2.** anything that excites such a feeling: *the horrors of war.* **3.** a character, look, appearance, etc., such as to excite a shuddering fear: *a scene of horror.* **4.** *Colloq.* something considered atrocious or bad: *that hat is a horror.* **5.** a painful or intense aversion or repugnance: *a horror of publicity.* **6.** (*pl.*) *Slang.* **a.** extreme depression. **b.** delirium tremens. **7.** *Obs.* a bristling. [t. L; r. ME *orrour*, t. OF] **—Syn. 1.** See **terror.**

horror comic, a magazine in comic-strip form exploiting horrific themes.

horror film, a film which treats supernatural or horrific subjects in a sensational way.

horror-struck (hŏ′rə strŭk′), *adj.* filled with horror; shocked. Also, **hor′ror-strick′en.**

Horsa (hô′sə), *n.* died A.D. 455, chief of the Jutes; brother of Hengist. Cf. **Hengist.**

hors de combat (*Fr.* ŏr də kôɴ bá′), *French.* **1.** out of the fight; disabled; no longer able to fight. **2.** unable to act, participate, etc., because of illness; laid low.

hors d'oeuvre (ô dû′vr), *pl.* **d'oeuvres** (dû′vr). **1.** any dish served as the first course of a meal. **2.** a dish consisting of a selection of hot or cold garnished ingredients, including cold meats, fish, salads, and the like. [t. F: aside from (the main body of the) work]

horse (hôs), *n.*, *pl.* **horses,** (*esp. collectively*) **horse,** *v.*, **horsed, horsing,** *adj.* **—***n.* **1.** a large, solid-hoofed quadruped, *Equus caballus*, domesticated since prehistoric times, and employed as a beast of draught and burden and for carrying a rider. **2.** the male horse, in distinction from the female or mare; a stallion or gelding. **3.** any animal of the family *Equidae* (**horse family**), which includes the ass, zebra, etc. **4.** soldiers serving on horseback; cavalry: *a thousand horse.* **5.** something on which a person rides, sits, or exercises, as if on a horse's back: *rocking horse.* **6.** a leather-covered block, adjustable in height, used for vaulting and other gymnastic exercises. **7.** a frame, block, etc., with legs on which something is mounted or supported. **8.** *Naut.* a metal rod or the like fitted to the deck of a sailing ship, to which is attached a traveller which retains the main sheet while allowing it to run from side to side. See illus. under **traveller. 9.** *Mining.* a mass of rock enclosed within a lode or vein. **10.** Some special noun phrases are:

a dark horse, a person of unknown potential.

back the wrong horse, to support the wrong or losing contender.

from the horse's mouth, *Colloq.* from an authoritative source.

hold one's horses, to restrain one's impulses; hold back.

horse of another colour, a different thing altogether.

look a gift-horse in the mouth. See **gift-horse.**

get on one's high horse, to stand on one's dignity.

white horse, the foamy crest of a wave.

willing horse, a willing worker.

—*v.t.* **11.** to provide with a horse or horses. **12.** to set on horseback. **13.** to set or carry on a peron's back or on one's own back. **14.** *Obs.* **a.** to place on a person's back or on a wooden horse or the like to be flogged. **b.** to flog. **15.** *Colloq.* to drive or urge (a person) at work, esp. unfairly or tyrannically. **—***v.i.* **16.** to mount or go on a horse. **17. horse about** or **around,** to act or play roughly or boisterously. **—***adj.* **18.** unusually large for one of its kind. **19.** of or pertaining to a horse or horses. **20.** mounted on horses. [ME and OE *hors*, c. OS and OHG *hros*, G *Ross*, Icel. *hross*]

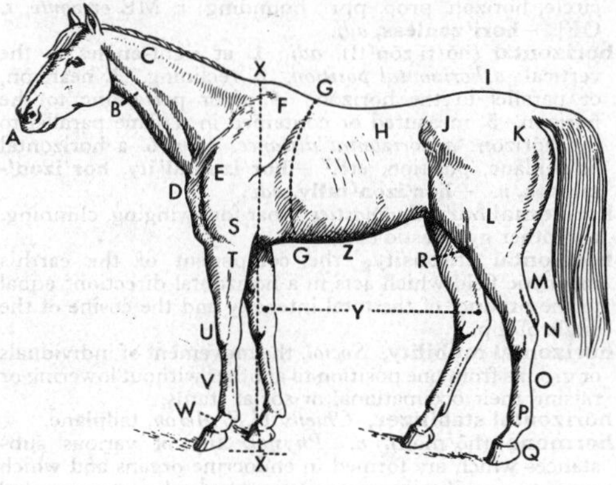

Horse
A, Muzzle; B, Jugular groove; C, Crest; D, Chest; E, Shoulder; F, Withers; G–G, Girth; H, Loin; I, Croup; J, Hip; K, Hindquarters; L, Thigh; M, Gaskin; N, Hock; O, Cannon bone; P, Fetlock; Q, Hoof; R, Stifle; S, Elbow; T, Forearm; U, Knee; V, Shank; W, Pastern; X–X Height; Y, Chestnut; Z, Belly

horseback (hôs′băk′), *n.* **1.** the back of a horse: *on horseback.* **2.** *U.S.* a low ridge of sand, gravel, or rock. Cf. **hogsback.**

horse bean, the broad bean, *Vicia faba.*

horseblock (hôs′blŏk′), *n.* a step or block for mounting and dismounting a horse.

horsebox (hôs′bŏks′), *n.* a van or trailer for conveying horses by road, rail, etc.

horse brass, a brass ornament, originally as worn on a horse's harness.

horse chestnut, 1. the shiny, brown nutlike seed of several species of *Aesculus*, ornamental trees bearing large digitate leaves and upright clusters of showy white, red, or yellow flowers, principally *A. hippocastanum* (**common horse chestnut**). **2.** the tree itself.

horsecloth (hôs′klŏth′), *n.* a cloth used to cover a horse, or as part of its trappings.

horse-faced (hôs′fāst′), *adj.* having a supposedly horse-like face, as with a lantern jaw, and prominent teeth.

horseflesh (hôs′flĕsh′), *n.* **1.** the flesh of a horse. **2.** horses collectively, esp. for riding, racing, etc.

horsefly (hôs′flī′), *n.*, *pl.* **-flies.** any of certain flies of the family *Tabanidae* that bite horses; gadfly.

Horse Guards, (together with the Life Guards) a regiment forming part of the sovereign's Household Brigade.

horsehair (hôs′hĕə′), *n.* **1.** a hair, or the hair, of a horse, esp. from the mane or tail. **2.** a sturdy, glossy fabric woven of horsehair. **—***adj.* **3.** made of or pertaining to horsehair. **4.** (of upholstered furniture) stuffed or padded with horsehair.

horsehide (hôs′hīd′), *n.* **1.** the hide of a horse. **2.** leather made from the hide of a horse.

horse latitudes, *Naut.* belts of northern and southern latitudes lying between the region of westerly winds and the region of the trade winds, marked by light baffling winds and occasional calms.

horse laugh, a loud, coarse laugh.

horseleech (hôs′lēch′), *n.* a large leech, as *Haemopsis sanguisorba,* said to attack the mouths of horses while they are drinking.

horseless (hôs′lĭs), *adj.* **1.** without a horse. **2.** self-propelled: *a horseless carriage.*

horse-mackerel (hôs′măk′rəl), *n.* **1.** a surface-living sea fish, *Caranx trachurus,* occasionally found in British coastal waters. **2.** the common tunny, *Thunnus thynnus.* **3.** a carangoid fish, *Trachurus symmetricus,* of the Pacific coast of the U.S. **4.** any of various similar or related fishes, as *T. trachurus* of South African coastal waters.

horseman (hôs′mən), *n., pl.* **-men. 1.** a rider on horseback. **2.** one who attends to horses or is skilled in managing them.

horsemanship (hôs′mən shĭp′), *n.* **1.** the management of horses. **2.** equestrian skill.

horse marine, *U.S.* **1.** a member of an imaginary corps of mounted marines. **2.** (formerly) a marine mounted on horseback, or a cavalryman doing duty on board ship. **3.** a person out of his element.

horsemeat (hôs′mēt′), *n.* the flesh of a horse used as animal food, etc.

horsemint (hôs′mĭnt′), *n.* **1.** a wild mint, *Mentha longifolia,* orig. a native of Europe. **2.** any of various other menthaceous plants, as *Monarda punctata,* an erect odorous herb of America.

horse mushroom, a large, platelike, coarse mushroom.

horse nettle, a prickly North American solanaceous weed, *Solanum carolinense.*

horse opera, a television, radio, or film drama about the Wild West, as one featuring cowboys and Indians, gold prospectors, or the like.

horse pick, a metal hook used for removing stones, etc., lodged in a horse's hoof.

horse pistol, a kind of large pistol formerly carried by horsemen.

horseplay (hôs′plā′), *n.* rough or boisterous play.

horsepower (hôs′pou′ə), *n.* a unit for measuring power, or rate of work, equivalent to 550 foot-pounds per second.

horserace (hôs′rās′), *n.* a race between horses with jockeys.

horseracing (hôs′rā′sĭng), *n.* the practice or sport of racing with horses.

horseradish (hôs′răd′ĭsh), *n.* **1.** a cultivated cruciferous plant, *Armoracia rusticana.* **2.** its pungent root, ground and used as a condiment and in medicine.

horserake (hôs′rāk′), *n.* a large, wheeled rake drawn by a horse.

horse sense, *Colloq.* plain, practical, common sense.

horseshit (hôs′shĭt′), *n. Chiefly U.S. Taboo Slang.* nonsense; rubbish; bullshit.

T / H

Horseshoe T, Toe calk; H, Heel calk

horseshoe (hôs′shōō′), *n., v.,* **-shoed, -shoeing.** —*n.* **1.** a U-shaped iron plate nailed to a horse's hoof to protect it. **2.** something shaped like a horseshoe. **3.** *U.S.* (*pl. construed as sing.*) a game using horseshoes or similar pieces, the object being to throw the piece so as to encircle an iron stake 30 or 40 feet away. —*v.t.* **4.** to put horseshoes on; to shoe. —*adj.* **5.** with the shape of a horseshoe.

horseshoe crab, any of various marine arthropods, esp. of the genus *Limulus,* with a carapace shaped somewhat like a horseshoe; king crab.

horseshoe vetch, a small, spreading papilionaceous perennial, *Hippocrepis comosa* with heads of few, long-stalked yellow flowers, found on calcareous soils of W and S Europe.

horseshow (hôs′shō′), *n.* a competitive display of the qualities and capabilities of horses and their riders.

horse tail, a ponytail.

horsetail (hôs′tāl′), *n.* **1.** any of the perennial, herbaceous, pteridophytic plants constituting the widely distributed genus *Equisetum,* characterized by hollow, jointed stems. **2.** a horse's tail formerly used as a Turkish military standard or as an ensign of a pasha, the number of tails increasing with rise in rank.

Horseshoe crab, *Limulus polyphemus* (Ab. 2 ft long)

horse-trading (hôs′trā′dĭng), *n.* shrewd and close bargaining. —**horse′-tra′der,** *n.*

horsewhip (hôs′wĭp′), *n., v.,* **-whipped, -whipping.** —*n.* **1.** a whip for controlling horses. —*v.t.* **2.** to beat with a horsewhip.

horsewoman (hôs′wōōm′ən), *n., pl.* **-women. 1.** a woman who rides on horseback. **2.** a woman who is skilful in managing or riding horses.

Horsforth (hôs′fəth), *n.* a town in England, in the West Riding of Yorkshire. 15,351 (1961).

Horsham (hô′shəm), *n.* a town in England, in East Sussex. 21,255 (1961).

horst (hôst), *n.* a portion of the earth's crust, bounded on at least two sides by faults, that has been moved upwards in relation to adjacent portions. [t. G: eyrie]

horsy (hô′sĭ), *adj.,* **-sier, -siest. 1.** pertaining to, characteristic of, or of the nature of a horse or horses: *horsy talk.* **2.** dealing with, interested in, or devoted to horses, horseracing, etc. **3.** *Slang.* large and supposedly horselike in appearance or manner. —**hors′iness,** *n.*

hort., 1. horticultural. **2.** horticulture.

Horta (hô′tə), *n.* **Baron Victor,** 1861–1947, Belgian architect.

hortative (hô′tə tĭv), *adj.* hortatory. [t. L: m. s. *hortātīvus*] —**hor′tatively,** *adv.*

hortatory (hô′tə tə rĭ, -trĭ), *adj.* encouraging; inciting, exhorting; urging to some course of conduct or action: *a hortatory address.* [t. LL: m. s. *hortātōrius* encouraging]

Hortense (*Fr.* ŏr täNs′), *n.* (*Eugénie Hortense de Beauharnais*), 1783–1837, queen of Holland (mother of Louis Napoleon).

Horthy (*Hung.* hór′tē), *n.* **Miklos von** (*Hung.* mē′klōsh fôn), 1868–1957, Hungarian admiral; regent of Hungary 1920–45.

horticulture (hô′tĭ kŭl′chə), *n.* **1.** the cultivation of a garden. **2.** the art and science of cultivating garden plants. [f. *horti-* (comb. form of L *hortus* garden) + CULTURE] —**hor′ticul′tural,** *adj.* —**hor′ticul′turist,** *n.*

hortus siccus (hô′təs sĭk′əs), a collection of dried plants; a herbarium. [t. L: dry garden]

Horus (hô′rəs), *n. Egyptian Myth.* a solar deity, the son of Osiris and Isis. [t. LL, t. Gk: m. *Hôros,* t. Egyptian: m. *Hur,* lit., hawk]

Horwich (hŏ′rĭj), *n.* a town in England, in S Lancashire, near Bolton. 16,067 (1961).

Hos., Hosea.

hosanna (hō zăn′ə), *interj.* **1.** (an exclamation, orig. an appeal to God for deliverance, used in praise of God or Christ.) —*n.* **2.** a cry of 'hosanna'. **3.** a shout of praise or adoration; an acclamation. [t. LL, t. Gk, t. Heb.: m. *hōsh(i)'āhnnā* save, pray!]

hose (hōz), *n., pl.* **hose,** (*Archaic*) **hosen,** *v.,* **hosed, hosing.** —*n.* **1.** an article of clothing for the foot and lower part of the leg; a stocking. **2.** a garment for the legs and thighs, as tights or breeches, formerly worn by men. **3.** a flexible tube for conveying water, etc., to a desired point: *a garden hose.* **4.** a sheath, or sheathing part, as that enclosing the kernel of grain. —*v.t.* **5.** to water, wash, or drench by means of a hose. [ME and OE, c. D *hoos,* G *Hose,* Icel. *hosa*]

Hosea (hō zĭə′), *n.* **1.** a Hebrew prophet of the 8th century B.C. **2.** the first of the books of the minor prophets in the Old Testament. [t. Heb.: m. *Hōshēa',* with *s* from *Osēe* (Vulgate and Septuagint)]

hosepipe (hōz′pīp′), *n.* a hose (def. 3).

hosier (hō′zyə), *n.* one who makes or deals in hose or stockings, or goods knitted or woven like hose.

hosiery (hō′zyə rĭ), *n.* **1.** hose or stockings of any kind. **2.** the business of a hosier.

hosp., hospital.

hospice (hŏs′pĭs), *n.* a house of shelter or rest for pilgrims, strangers, etc., esp. one kept by a religious order. [t. F, t. L: m. s. *hospitium* hospitality]

hospitable (hŏs′pĭ tə bl, hŏs pĭt′ə bl), *adj.* **1.** affording a generous welcome to guests or strangers: *a hospitable city.* **2.** inclined to or characterized by hospitality: *a hospitable reception.* **3.** favourably receptive or open (fol. by *to*): *hospitable to new ideas.* [t. F (obs.), f. s. LL *hospitāre* receive as a guest + *-able* -ABLE] —**hos′pitableness,** *n.* —**hos′pitably,** *adv.*

hospital (hŏs′pĭ tl), *n.* **1.** an institution in which sick or injured persons are given medical or surgical treatment. **2.** a similar establishment for the care of animals. **3.** *Archaic.* an old people's home. **4.** a shop for repairing specific things: *a dolls' hospital.* [ME, t. OF, t. LL: s. *hospitāle* inn, prop. neut. of L *hospitālis* pertaining to guests, hospitable]

—**Syn. 1.** retreat. HOSPITAL, ASYLUM, SANATORIUM are names of institutions for persons needing some kind of care. A HOSPITAL is an institution in which sick or injured persons are given medical or surgical treatment, ray therapy, etc.: *the woman was in the hospital awaiting an operation.* An ASYLUM is an institution (usually

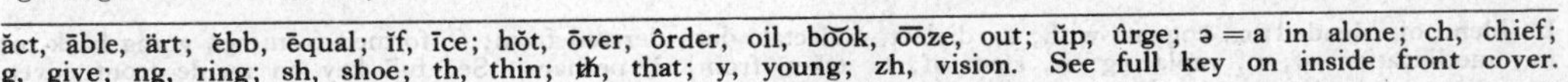

owned by the state) for the care of particularly afflicted or dependent persons; though it originally meant a place of refuge, the word has acquired unpleasant connotations, so that HOSPITAL is now the preferred term for that type of institution also: *a mental asylum.* SANATORIUM usually means an institution for persons needing mainly rest or special treatment: *a sanatorium for tubercular patients.*

hospital corner, 1. a method of folding corners of bedclothes when bed-making, in order to give them a mitred appearance. 2. the corner so made.

Hospitalet (*Sp.* ȯs pē tä lėt′), *n.* a town in NE Spain. 175,482 (1965).

hospitality (hŏs′pĭ tăl′ĭ tĭ), *n.*, *pl.* **-ties.** the reception and entertainment of guests or strangers with liberality and kindness.

hospitalize (hŏs′pĭ tə līz′), *v.t.*, **-lized, -lizing.** to place for care in a hospital. Also, **hospitalise.** —**hos′pitaliza′tion,** *n.*

Hospitaller (hŏs′pĭ tə lə), *n.* **1.** a member of a religious and military order (**Knights Hospitallers**) taking its origin about the time of the first Crusade (1096–99) from a hospital at Jerusalem. **2.** (*l.c.*) a person, esp. a member of a religious order, devoted to the care of the sick or needy in hospitals. Also, *U.S.*, **Hospitaler.** [ME, t. OF: m. *hospitalier*, der. *hospital* HOSPITAL]

hospital orderly, *Mil.* a serviceman of any of the three services carrying out medical duties in hospital wards.

hospital ship, a ship built or specially converted for use as transport for sick and wounded in wartime.

hospitium (hŏs pĭt′ĭ əm), *n.*, *pl.* **-pitia** (-pĭt′ĭ ə). a hospice.

hospodar (hŏs′pə dä′), *n.* a former title of governors or princes of Walachia and Moldavia. [Rumanian]

host[1] (hōst), *n.* **1.** one who entertains guests in his own home or elsewhere: *the host at a theatre party.* **2.** the landlord of an inn. **3.** an animal or plant from which a parasite obtains nutrition. [ME *(h)oste*, t. OF, g. L *hospes* host, guest, stranger. Cf. GUEST, HOST[2]]

host[2] (hōst), *n.* **1.** a multitude or great number of persons or things: *a host of details.* **2.** *Archaic.* an army. [ME, t. OF, g. L *hostis* stranger, enemy, ML army. Cf. GUEST, HOST[1]]

Host (hōst), *n.* *Eccles.* the bread consecrated in the celebration of the Eucharist; a consecrated wafer. [ME *hoste*, t. ML: m. s. *hostia*, in L animal sacrificed]

hostage (hŏs′tĭj), *n.* **1.** a person given or held as a security for the performance of certain actions. **2.** *Obs.* the condition of a hostage. **3.** a security or pledge. [ME *(h)ostage*, t. OF, der. *oste* guest, g. s. L *hospes* and ? b. with s. L *obses* hostage] —**hos′tageship′,** *n.*

hostel (hŏs′tl), *n.* **1.** a supervised place of accommodation, usually supplying board and lodging, provided at a comparatively low cost, as one for students, nurses, or the like. **2.** a youth hostel. **3.** *Archaic.* an inn. [ME *(h)ostel*, t. OF, der. *oste* guest]

hostelry (hŏs′tl rĭ), *n.*, *pl.* **-ries.** *Archaic.* a hostel or inn. [ME *(h)ostelerie*, t. OF, der. *hostel.* See HOSTEL]

hostess (hōs′tĭs), *n.* **1.** a female host; a woman who entertains guests. **2.** an air-hostess. **3.** a paid dancing partner. **4.** a female innkeeper.

hostess gown, a full-length semi-formal dress, esp. worn when entertaining at home; an informal evening dress.

hostile (hŏs′tīl), *adj.* **1.** opposed in feeling, action, or character; unfriendly; antagonistic: *hostile criticism.* **2.** of or characteristic of an enemy: *hostile ground.* [late ME, t. L: m. s. *hostīlis*, der. *hostis* enemy. See HOST[2]] —**hos′tilely,** *adv.*

—**Syn.** 1. warlike; adverse, averse, opposed. HOSTILE, INIMICAL indicate that which characterizes an enemy or something injurious to one's interests. HOSTILE applies to the spirit, attitude, or action of an enemy: *they showed a hostile and menacing attitude.* INIMICAL applies to an antagonistic or injurious tendency or influence: *their remarks were inimical to his reputation.* —**Ant.** 2. amicable.

hostile witness, a witness who is biased against the party examining him.

hostility (hŏs tĭl′ĭ tĭ), *n.*, *pl.* **-ties.** **1.** hostile state; enmity; antagonism. **2.** a hostile act. **3.** (*pl.*) acts of warfare. —**Syn.** 1. animosity, ill-will, unfriendliness; opposition. 3. war, warfare, fighting.

hostler (ŏs′lə), *n.* *Archaic.* an ostler.

hot (hŏt), *adj.*, **hotter, hottest,** *adv.*, *v.*, **hotted, hotting.** —*adj.* **1.** having or communicating heat; having a high temperature: *a hot stove.* **2.** having a sensation of great bodily heat; attended with or producing such a sensation. **3.** having an effect as of burning on the tongue, skin, etc., as pepper, mustard, a blister, etc. **4.** having or showing intense feeling; ardent or fervent; vehement; excited: *hot temper.* **5.** lustful. **6.** violent, furious, or intense: *the hottest battle.* **7.** strong or fresh, as a scent or trail. **8.** new: *hot from the press.* **9.** following very closely; close: *to be hot on one's heels.* **10.** (of colours) startlingly brilliant. **11.** *Games.* close to the sought-for object or answer. **12.** *Slang.* fashionable and exciting. **13.** *Jazz.* **a.** arousing, or capable of arousing, enthusiasm and admiration; intense; compulsive. **b.** (of a musician) playing such music. **14.** *Slang.* recently stolen or otherwise illegally obtained. **15.** radioactive, esp. to a degree injurious to health. **16. blow hot and cold,** change attitudes frequently; vacillate. **17. in hot water,** *Colloq.* in trouble. **18. make (it, etc.) hot for,** *Colloq.* to make (a place or a situation) unpleasant for. **19. not so hot,** *Colloq.* not very good; disappointing. **20. sell** or **go like hot cakes,** to sell or be removed quickly, esp. in large quantities. —*adv.* **21.** in a hot manner; hotly. —*v.t.* **22.** to heat (usually fol. by *up*). [ME *ho(o)t*, OE *hāt*, c. G *heiss*] —**hot′ly,** *adv.* —**hot′ness,** *n.* —**Syn.** 1. heated; torrid, sultry. 3. pungent, biting, peppery. 4. angry. —**Ant.** 1. cold.

hot air, *Slang.* empty, pretentious talk or writing.

hotbed (hŏt′bĕd′), *n.* **1.** a bed of earth, heated by fermenting manure, etc., and usually covered with glass, for growing plants out of season. **2.** a place favouring rapid growth, esp. of something bad: *a hotbed of vice.*

hot-blooded (hŏt′blŭd′ĭd), *adj.* virile; adventurous; excitable; impetuous.

hotbox (hŏt′bŏks′), *n.* an overheated journal box, on a railway carriage or locomotive, caused by the friction of a rapidly revolving axle.

hotchpot (hŏch′pŏt′), *n.* *Law.* the bringing together of shares or properties in order to divide them equally, esp. when they are to be divided among the children of a parent dying intestate. [ME *hochepot*, t. OF: ragout, f. *hocher* shake + *pot* pot]

hotchpotch (hŏch′pŏch′), *n.* **1.** a heterogeneous mixture; a jumble. **2.** *Law.* hotchpot. **3.** a thick soup or stew made from meat and vegetables. Also, *Chiefly U.S.*, **hodgepodge.** [rhyming var. of HOTCHPOT]

hot cockles, a children's game in which someone covers his eyes and attempts to guess who has hit him.

hot cross bun, a bun with a cross on it, eaten chiefly on Good Friday.

hot dog, *Colloq.* a hot frankfurter or sausage, esp. as served in a split roll.

hotel (hō tĕl′; ō tĕl′), *n.* a commercial establishment offering lodging, food, etc., for travellers, etc. [t. F: (earlier *hostel*) HOSTEL]

—**Syn.** HOTEL, HOUSE, INN, TAVERN refer to establishments for the lodging or entertainment of travellers and others. HOTEL is the common word, suggesting a more or less commodious establishment with up-to-date appointments though this is not necessarily true: *Grand Hotel, the best hotel in the city.* The word HOUSE is often used in the name of a particular hotel, the connotation being wealth and luxury: *the Parker House, the Palmer House.* INN suggests a place of homelike comfort and old-time appearance or ways: *The George Inn, The Wayside Inn.* A TAVERN is a house where alcoholic beverages are sold for drinking on the premises.

Hôtel des Invalides (*Fr.* ȯ tĕl dė zăɴ vȧ lēd′), the site in Paris of Napoleon's tomb: orig. a hospital for invalided veterans.

hôtel de ville (*Fr.* ȯ tĕl də vēl′), *French.* a town hall.

hôtel Dieu (*Fr.* ȯ tĕl dyœ′), *French.* a hospital.

hotfoot (hŏt′fo͝ot′), *adv.* with great speed in going; in hot haste.

hot-galvanize (hŏt′găl′və nīz′), *v.t.*, **-nized, -nizing.** *Metall.* to coat another metal with zinc by immersing it in a bath of molten zinc. Also, **hot-galvanise.**

hot-gospeller (hŏt′gŏs′pə lə), *n.* *Colloq.* a revivalist preacher. Also, *U.S.*, **hot-gospeler.**

hothead (hŏt′hĕd′), *n.* a hot-headed person.

hot-headed (hŏt′hĕd′ĭd), *adj.* hot or fiery in spirit or temper; impetuous; rash. —**hot′-head′edly,** *adv.* —**hot′-head′edness,** *n.*

hothouse (hŏt′hous′), *n.* **1.** an artificially heated greenhouse for the cultivation of tender plants. —*adj.* **2.** of or pertaining to a delicate plant grown in a hothouse. **3.** *Colloq.* delicate; over-protected.

hot line, a direct telephone connection open to immediate communication in an emergency, as between the heads of state of the Soviet Union and the U.S.

hot pack, a hot compress.

hotplate (hŏt′plāt′), *n.* **1.** a portable appliance for cooking or keeping food warm. **2.** a solid, electrically heated metal plate, usually on top of an electric cooker, upon which food, etc., may be heated or cooked.

hotpot (hŏt′pŏt′), *n.* mutton or beef cooked with potatoes, etc., in a covered pot.

hot potato, *Colloq.* a risky situation, difficult person, or any other thing which needs careful handling.

hot-press (hŏt′prĕs′), *n.* **1.** a machine applying heat in conjunction with mechanical pressure, as for producing a smooth surface on paper, for expressing oil, etc. —*v.t.* **2.** to subject to treatment in a hot-press.

hot rod, *Slang.* a car (usually an old one) whose engine has been altered for increased speed.

hot seat, *Colloq.* a position involving difficulties or danger.
hot spot, a place where a dangerous political situation exists or may develop into revolution, war, etc.
hot spring, a naturally heated spring with water warmer than 98°F, often containing mineral substances in solution.
hotspur (hŏtʹspû/), *n.* an impetuous person; a hothead. [first applied to Sir Henry PERCY]
hot stuff, *Colloq.* **1.** a woman or girl who is sexually exciting. **2.** something of great excellence or interest.
hot-tempered (hŏtʹtĕmʹpəd), *adj.* short-tempered; having a quick temper.
Hottentot (hŏtʹən tŏt/), *n.* **1.** a member of a native African race of yellowish brown colour and low stature, sometimes said to be of mixed Bushman and Bantu origin. **2.** the language of the Hottentots, having no certain affinity. [t. D (Afrikaans), imit. of the language]
Hottentot fig, sour fig.
Hotter (*Ger.* hŏtʹər), *n.* **Hans,** born 1909, German Wagnerian baritone.
hot-tin (hŏtʹtĭnʹ), *v.t. Metall.* to coat another metal with tin by immersing it in a bath of molten tin.
hot-water bottle (hŏtʹwôʹtə), a container, usually of rubber, of a flat oblong shape, which is filled with hot water and used to warm parts of the body, or a bed. Also, *U.S.*, **hot-water bag.**
hot-wire (hŏtʹwīʹə), *adj. Elect.* (of an ammeter or voltmeter) depending upon the expansion, or change in resistance, of a wire when it is heated by the passage of a current.
hot-work (hŏtʹwûk/), *v.t. Metall.* to shape a metal by rolling, forging, etc., at a temperature high enough to permit recrystallization.
Houdan (hōōʹdăn), *n.* a breed of the domestic fowl of French origin, having a heavy, globular crest and evenly mottled black-and-white plumage. [named after *Houdan*, town in France, near Paris]
Houdini (hōō dēʹnĭ), *n.* **Harry** (*Erich Weiss*), 1874–1926, U.S. magician.
Houdon (*Fr.* ōō dôNʹ), *n.* **Jean Antoine** (*Fr.* zhäN näN-twänʹ), 1741–1828, French sculptor.
Houghton-le-Spring (hōʹtn lə sprĭngʹ), *n.* a town in England, in NE Durham. 31,049 (1961).
Houmayun (hōō mäʹyōōn), *n.* Humayun.
hound[1] (hound), *n.* **1.** a dog of any of various breeds used in the chase and commonly hunting by scent. **2.** any dog. **3.** *Slang.* a mean, despicable fellow. **4.** *U.S. Slang.* an addict. **5.** a player in hare and hounds. **6. follow the hounds,** to follow a hunt, esp. on foot. **7. ride to hounds,** to foxhunt. —*v.t.* **8.** to hunt or track with hounds, or as a hound does; pursue. **9.** to harass unceasingly. **10.** to incite (a hound, etc.) to pursuit or attack; urge on. [ME; OE *hund*, c. G *Hund*. Cf. L *canis*, Gk *kýōn* dog]
hound[2] (hound), *n.* **1.** *Naut.* a projection at a masthead, serving to support rigging or trestletrees. **2.** *Chiefly U.S.* a bar, usually used in pairs, to strengthen various portions of the running gear of a vehicle. [ME *hūn*, t. Scand.; cf. Icel. *hūnn* knob at the masthead]
hound's-tongue (houndzʹtŭngʹ), *n.* **1.** a troublesome boraginaceous weed, *Cynoglossum officinale*, with prickly nutlets and tonguelike leaves. **2.** any other plant of the genus *Cynoglossum*. [ME and OE *hundestunge*, trans. of L *cynoglōssum*, t. Gk: m. *kynóglōsson* dog-tongued]
hound's-tooth (houndzʹtōōth/), *adj.* **1.** printed, decorated, or woven with a pattern of broken checks. —*n.* **2.** a pattern of contrasting jagged checks.
Hounslow (hounzʹlō), *n.* a SW outer London borough. 209,100 (1964).
Houphouet-Boigny (*Fr.* ōō fwĕ bwȧ nyēʹ), *n.* **Félix** (*Fr.* fĕ lēksʹ), born 1905, president of the Republic of the Ivory Coast since 1960.
hour (ouʹə), *n.* **1.** a space of time equal to one 24th part of a mean solar day or civil day; 60 minutes. **2.** a short or limited period of time. **3.** a particular or appointed time: *his hour of triumph.* **4.** the present time: *the man of the hour.* **5.** any definite time of day, or the time indicated by a timepiece: *what is the hour?* **6.** (*pl.*) time spent in work, study, etc.: *after hours, office hours.* **7.** (*pl.*) customary time of going to bed and getting up: *to keep late hours.* **8.** distance normally covered in an hour's travelling. **9.** *Astron.* **a.** a unit of measure of right ascension, etc., representing 15 degrees, or the 24th part of a great circle. **b.** See **sidereal hour. 10.** a single period of class instruction. **11.** (*pl.*) *Eccles.* **a.** the seven stated times of the day for prayer and devotion. **b.** the offices or services prescribed for these times. **c.** a book containing them. **12. the Hours,** *Class. Myth.* the Horae. **13. one's hour, a.** death; the time to die. **b.** a crucial moment. [ME *ure, ore, hore*, t. OF, g. L *hōra* time, season, hour, t. Gk; akin to YEAR]
hour circle, *Astron.* any great circle in the celestial sphere passing through the celestial poles.
hourglass (ouʹə gläs/), *n.* **1.** an instrument for measuring time, consisting of two bulbs of glass joined by a narrow passage through which a quantity of sand (or mercury) runs in just an hour. —*adj.* **2.** having a narrow waist.

Hourglass

hour hand, the hand that indicates the hours on a clock or watch.
houri (hōōəʹrĭ), *n., pl.* **-ris. 1.** one of the beautiful virgins provided in paradise to all faithful Muslims. **2.** any alluring woman, esp. of oriental origin. [t. F, t. Pers.: m. *hūrī*, der. Ar. *ḥūr*, pl. of *haurā'* having black eyes like a gazelle]
hourly (ouʹə lĭ), *adj.* **1.** of, pertaining to, occurring, or done each successive hour. **2.** frequent; continual. —*adv.* **3.** every hour; hour by hour. **4.** frequently.
house (*n.* and *adj.* hous; *v.* houz), *n. pl.* **houses** (houʹzĭz), *v.*, **housed, housing.** —*n.* **1.** a building for human habitation. **2.** a place of lodgement, rest, etc., as of an animal. **3.** a household. **4.** a building for any purpose: *a house of worship.* **5.** a place of entertainment: *a theatre.* **6.** the audience of a theatre, etc. **7.** an inn; a public house. **8.** a family regarded as consisting of ancestors and descendants: *the house of Habsburg.* **9.** the building in which a legislative or deliberative body meets. **10.** the body itself: *the House of Commons.* **11.** a quorum of such a body. **12.** the Stock Exchange in London. **13.** a firm or commercial establishment: *the house of Rothschild.* **14.** an advisory or deliberative group, esp. in Church or university affairs. **15.** a residential hall for students as in some universities. **16.** a subdivision of a school, comprising children of all ages and classes. **17.** a boarding-house attached to and forming part of a school. **18.** the members of such a subdivision, or boarding house. **19.** the management of a gambling casino or commercial establishment. **20.** *Astrol.* **a.** one of the twelve divisions of the heavens. **b.** a sign of the zodiac in which a planet exerts its greatest influence. **21. keep house,** to manage a house; look after a home. **22. keep open house,** to be very hospitable. **23. like a house on fire,** very well; with great rapidity. **24. put** or **set one's house in order,** to put one's affairs into good condition. **25. bring down the house,** to be extraordinarily well received or applauded. **26. on the house,** free; as a gift from the management. **27. safe as houses,** completely safe. —*v.t.* **28.** to put or receive into a house; provide with a house. **29.** to give shelter to; harbour; lodge. **30.** to remove from exposure; put in a safe place. **31.** *Naut.* to place in a secure or protected position. **32.** *Carp.* to fix in a socket or the like. —*v.i.* **33.** to take shelter; dwell. —*adj.* **34.** for, or suitable for a house. **35.** of or pertaining to a house. [ME *hous*, OE *hūs*, c. D *huis*, G *Haus*, Icel. and Goth. *hūs*] —**houseʹless,** *adj.*
—**Syn. 1.** domicile. HOUSE, DWELLING, RESIDENCE, HOME are terms applied to a place to live in. DWELLING is now chiefly poetic, or in legal use, as in a lease. RESIDENCE implies size and elegance of structure and surroundings. These two terms and HOUSE have always had reference to the structure to be lived in. HOME has recently taken on this meaning and become practically equivalent to HOUSE, the new meaning tending to crowd out the older connotations of family ties and domestic comfort. See **hotel.**
house agent, estate agent.
house arrest, confinement to one's place of residence (by an authority).
houseboat (housʹbōt/), *n.* a boat fitted up for use as a floating dwelling but not suited to rough water.
housebound (housʹbound/), *adj.* restricted or confined to the house, as through ill-health.
houseboy (housʹboi/), *n.* a male servant, esp. in a British colonial possession, who helps in the house.
housebreaker (housʹbrāʹkə), *n.* **1.** one who breaks into and enters a house with felonious intent. **2.** one who demolishes houses. —**houseʹ breakʹing,** *n.*
housecarl (housʹkäl/), *n.* a member of the household troops or bodyguard of a Danish or early English king or noble. [modernization of OE *hūscarl*, t. Scand.; cf. Icel. *hūskarl* houseman]
housecoat (housʹkōt/), *n.* a dresslike garment of one piece, fastening down the front, and often long, worn about the house.
housedog (housʹdŏg/), *n.* a dog trained to guard the house; a watchdog.
housefather (housʹfäʹthə), *n.* a man who is in charge of a group, esp. of children in the care of a local authority, who live together.
house flag, a flag flown by a ship, denoting which company or owner it belongs to.
housefly (housʹflī/), *n., pl.* **-flies. 1.** a common dipterous insect, *Musca domestica*, found in nearly all parts of the

world. 2. any of several other dipterous insects resembling this.

houseful (hous′fo͝ol′), *n.* as much as a house can hold or comfortably accommodate.

household (hous′hōld′, -ōld′), *n.* **1.** the people of a house collectively; a family, including servants, etc.; a domestic establishment. **—*adj.*** **2.** of or pertaining to a household; domestic: *household furniture.* **3.** used for maintaining and keeping a house. **4.** of or pertaining to the royal or imperial household. **5.** very common.

Housefly, *Musca domestica* (Length ¼ in.)

Household Brigade, the regiments of cavalry and foot guards which provide escorts and guards for the sovereign and the royal family.

householder (hous′hōl′də), *n.* **1.** one who holds or occupies a house. **2.** the head of a family.

household word, a byword; a well-known phrase or word.

house journal, an internal journal of a company, presenting its news to its employees. Also, **house magazine.**

housekeeper (hous′kē′pə), *n.* **1.** a paid employee who is hired to run a house; direct the domestic work, catering, etc. **2.** a female employee of a hotel responsible for the cleaning staff.

housekeeping (hous′kē′pĭng), *n.* **1.** the maintaining of a house or domestic establishment. **2.** the management of household affairs. **3.** the money used for this purpose.

housel (hou′zəl), *n. Archaic.* the Eucharist. [ME; OE *hūsl*, c. Goth. *hūnsl* sacrifice]

houseleek (hous′lēk′), *n.* **1.** a crassulaceous herb, *Sempervivum tectorum*, with pink flowers and thick, succulent leaves, found growing on the roofs and walls of houses. **2.** any plant of the genus *Sempervivum.*

houselights (hous′līts′), *n.* the auditorium lights of a theatre, cinema, etc., which are lowered during a performance.

houseline (hous′līn′), *n. Naut.* a small line of three strands, used for seizings, etc.

housemaid (hous′mād′), *n.* a female servant employed in general work in a household.

housemaid's knee, *Pathol.* inflammation of the bursa over the anterior region of the knee.

houseman (hous′mən), *n., pl.* **-men.** a member of the medical staff of a hospital, commonly a recent medical graduate acting as assistant to a physician or surgeon.

house martin, a bird, *Delichon urbica*, of the family *Hirundinidae* (swallow family), about 5 inches long, of Europe and Asia, which nests on cliffs and the walls of houses.

housemaster (hous′mäs′tə), *n.* (in some boys' schools) a teacher who is in charge of a house. **—housemistress** (hous′mĭs′trĭs), *n. fem.*

housemother (hous′mŭth′ə), *n.* a woman who is in charge of a group, esp. of children in the care of a local authority, who live together.

house mouse, a rodent, *Mus musculus*, of the family *Muridae* which originally lived wild on the steppes of Asia, but which has come to live commensally with man in all parts of the world.

House of Burgesses, the assembly of representatives in colonial Virginia.

house of cards, a flimsy structure or plan, liable to collapse at any minute.

House of Commons, the elective house of the British parliament.

house of correction, a place for the confinement and reform of persons convicted of minor offences and not regarded as confirmed criminals.

House of Councillors, the upper house of the Japanese Diet.

House of Delegates, the lower house of the General Assembly in Virginia, West Virginia, and Maryland.

House of God, a building devoted to religious observances; a church; chapel, etc.

house of ill repute, a brothel. Also, **house of evil repute, house of ill fame.**

House of Keys, the elective or lower house of the legislature of the Isle of Man.

House of Lords, the non-elective house of the parliament of Great Britain and Northern Ireland, also functioning as the highest branch of the supreme judicature, to which appeals may lie from the Court of Appeal.

House of Representatives, the lower legislative branch in national and state governing bodies, as in the United States, Australia, Mexico, Japan, etc.

house organ, a periodical issued by a business house, etc., presenting news of its activities, etc.

houseparent (hous′pĕə′rənt), *n.* a housemother or a housefather, who looks after children who are in the care of a local authority.

house party, **1.** an entertainment of guests for some days at a host's house, esp. in the country. **2.** the guests.

house physician, a resident physician in a hospital, or other public institution.

houseproud (hous′proud′), *adj.* overcareful about the cleaning of a house and the appearance of its contents.

houseroom (hous′ro͞om′, hous′ro͝om′), *n.* space or accommodation in a house.

house sparrow, a grey and brown bird, *Passer domesticus*, of the family *Ploceidae*, about 5⅞ in. long, from Europe, Asia and N Africa, and, by introduction, Australia and America.

house surgeon, a resident surgeon in a hospital.

house-to-house (hous′tə hous′), *adj.* carried out systematically through all the buildings in a neighbourhood, etc.: *a house-to-house search by the police.*

housetop (hous′tŏp′), *n.* **1.** the top or roof of a house. **2. from the housetops,** *Colloq.* publicly.

house-trained (hous′trānd′), *adj.* (of a pet) trained to excrete outside the house.

house-warming (hous′wô′mĭng), *n.* a party to celebrate beginning one's occupancy of a new house.

housewife (hous′wīf′; *or usually* hŭz′ĭf *for 2*), *n., pl.* **-wives** (-wīvz′). **1.** the woman in charge of a household, esp. a wife who does no other job. **2.** a small case for needles, thread, etc.

housewifely (hous′wīf′lĭ), *adj.* of, like, or befitting a housewife. **—house′wife′liness,** *n.*

housewifery (hous′wĭf′ə rĭ, -wīf′rĭ), *n.* the function or work of a housewife; housekeeping.

housework (hous′wûk′), *n.* the work of cleaning, cooking, etc., to be done in housekeeping.

housey-housey (hou′zĭ hou′zĭ), *n.* a variety of lotto or bingo, played as a gambling game.

housing[1] (hou′zĭng), *n.* **1.** something serving as a shelter, covering, or the like; a shelter; lodging. **2.** houses collectively. **3.** the act of one who houses or puts under shelter. **4.** the providing of houses for the community: *the housing of immigrants.* **5.** *Mach.* a frame, plate or the like, that supports a part of a machine, etc. **6.** *Carp.* the space made in one piece of wood, or the like, for the insertion of another. **7.** *Naut.* **a.** the inboard end of a bowsprit. **b.** the part of a mast which is below deck. [f. HOUSE, v. + -ING[1]]

housing[2] (hou′zĭng), *n.* **1.** a covering of cloth for the back and flanks of a horse or other animal, for protection or ornament. **2.** a covering of cloth or the like. **3.** (*often pl.*) a caparison or trapping. [f. *house* (ME, t. OF: m. *houce*) covering of cloth + -ING[1]]

housing association, a non-profitmaking society or body for constructing, improving or managing houses.

Housman (hous′mən), *n.* **A(lfred) E(dward),** 1859–1936, English poet and classical scholar.

Houston (hyo͞o′stən), *n.* a city in the U.S., in SE Texas: a port on a ship canal, ab. 50 mi. from the Gulf of Mexico. 938,219 (1960).

houting (hou′tĭng), *n.* a seafish, *Coregonus oxyrhynchus*, that spawns in fresh waters; a popular food fish of European waters.

Houyhnhnm (ho͞o ĭn′əm), *n.* (in Swift's *Gulliver's Travels*) one of a race of horses endowed with reason, who rule the Yahoos, a race of degraded, brutish creatures having the form of man.

hove (hōv), *v.* pt. and pp. of **heave.**

Hove (hōv), *n.* a seaside resort in England, in East Sussex, near Brighton. 72,973 (1961).

hovel (hŭv′əl, hŏv′-), *n., v.,* **-elled, -elling,** or (*U.S.*) **-eled, -eling.** **—*n.*** **1.** a small, mean dwelling house; a wretched hut. **2.** an open shed, as for sheltering cattle, tools, etc. **—*v.t.*** **3.** *Obs.* to shelter or lodge as in a hovel. [ME *hovel, hovyl*; orig. uncert.]

hover (hŏv′ə), *v.i.* **1.** to hang fluttering or suspended in the air: *a hovering bird.* **2.** to keep lingering about; wait near at hand. **3.** to remain in an uncertain or irresolute state; waver: *hovering between life and death.* **—*n.*** **4.** the act of hovering. **5.** the state of hovering. [ME *hoveren*, freq. of *hoven* hover; orig. uncert.] **—hov′erer,** *n.* **—hov′eringly,** *adv.* **—Syn. 1.** See **fly**[1].

hovercraft (hŏv′ə kräft′), *n.* **1.** a vehicle able to travel in close proximity to the ground or water, on a cushion of air created by and contained within a curtain of air formed by one or more streams of air ejected downwards from the periphery of the vehicle. **2.** (*cap.*) a trademark for this vehicle.

hoverfly (hŏv′ə flī′), *n.* a name given to several of the larger flies of the family *Syrphidae* which have wasp-like markings, and the habit of hovering during flight.

how (hou), *adv.* **1.** in what way or manner; by what means: *how did it happen?* **2.** to what extent, degree, etc.: *how much?* **3.** at what price: *how do you sell these* *apples?* **4.** in what state or condition: *how are you?* **5.** for what reason; why. **6.** to what effect or with what meaning: *how do you mean?* **7.** what? **8.** (used to add intensity): *how well I remember.* **9. and how,** *Slang.* very much indeed; certainly. **10. how come?** *Colloq.* how did this happen; why? **11. how's that? a.** what is the explanation of that? **b.** *Cricket.* Also, **howzat?** an appeal by the fielding side to the umpire to declare a batsman out. —*conj.* **12.** concerning the condition or state in which: *she wondered how she appeared to a stranger.* **13.** concerning the extent or degree to which: *I don't mind how long you take.* **14.** concerning the means or way in which: *it worried him how she got to work.* **15.** in whatever manner: *come how you like.* —*n.* **16.** a question beginning with 'how'. **17.** *Colloq.* way or manner of doing: *to consider the hows of a problem.* [ME *hou, how,* OE *hū*, c. D *hoe*; akin to WHO]

Howard (hou′əd), *n.* **1. Catherine,** *c.* 1520–42, fifth wife of Henry VIII. **2. Charles, Lord Howard of Effingham,** 1536–1624, High Admiral at the time of the Armada. **3. Sir Ebenezer,** 1850–1928, English architectural theorist. **4. Henry.** See **Surrey,** Earl of. **5. John,** 1726–90, English prison reformer.

howbeit (hou bē′ĭt), *adv.* **1.** nevertheless. —*conj.* **2.** *Obs.* although. [ME *how be hit* however it may be. Cf. ALBEIT]

howdah (hou′də), *n.* (in the East Indies) a seat, commonly with a railing and a canopy, placed on the back of an elephant. [t. Hind.: m. *haudah*, t. Ar.: m. *haudaj*]

Howe (hou), *n.* **1. Elias,** 1819–67, U.S. inventor (of the sewing machine). **2. Julia Ward,** 1819–1910, U.S. author. **3. Richard,** 1725–99, British admiral. **4. William,** (*5th Viscount Howe*) 1729–1814, British general: commander-in-chief of the British forces 1775–78, in the War of American Independence. **5. Cape,** a headland at the SE tip of Australia, on the border of New South Wales and Victoria.

howe'er (hou ĕə′), *conj., adv.* however.

however (hou ĕv′ə), *conj.* **1.** nevertheless; yet; in spite of that. —*adv.* **2.** to whatever extent or degree; no matter how (far, much, etc.). **3.** in whatever manner. **4.** Also, **how ever.** (interrogatively) how in any circumstances: *however did you manage?* —*conj.* **5.** nevertheless: *today, however, she decided to travel.* **6.** in whatever condition, state, or manner: *go there however you like.* [ME] —**Syn. 1.** See BUT[1].

howitzer (hou′ĭt sə), *n.* a comparatively short-barrelled cannon, used esp. for shelling at a steep angle, as in reaching troops behind cover. [earlier *hauwitzer*, appar. t. D: m. *houwitser*, der. *houwits(e)* catapult. Cf. G *Haubitze*, earlier *haufnitz*, t. Czech: m. *houfnice* catapult]

howl (houl), *v.i.* **1.** to utter a loud, prolonged, mournful cry, as that of a dog or wolf. **2.** to utter a similar cry in distress, pain, rage, etc.; wail. **3.** to make a sound like an animal howling: *the wind is howling.* —*v.t.* **4.** to utter with howls. **5.** to drive or force by howls (often fol. by *down*). —*n.* **6.** the cry of a dog, wolf, etc. **7.** a cry or wail, as of pain or rage. **8.** a sound like wailing: *the howl of the wind.* **9.** a loud scornful laugh or yell. [ME *houle.* Cf. G *heulen*; imit.]

howler (hou′lə), *n.* **1.** one who or that which howls. **2.** Also, **howling monkey.** any of the large, prehensile-tailed tropical American monkeys of the genus *Alouatta*, the males of which make a howling noise. **3.** *Colloq.* an especially glaring and ludicrous blunder. **4.** *Elect.* a device for testing telephone apparatus which provides a suitable current by using acoustic feedback between the telephone transmitter and receiver.

howling (hou′lĭng), *adj.* **1.** producing or uttering a howl. **2.** *Colloq.* enormous; very great: *his play was a howling success.*

Howrah (hou′rə), *n.* a city in NE India, in W Bengal, on the Hooghly river opposite Calcutta. 512,598 (1961).

howsoever (hou′sō ĕv′ə), *adv.* **1.** to whatsoever extent or degree. **2.** in whatsoever manner.

Howth Head (hōth), a promontory in the E of Co. Dublin, Ireland.

howzat (hou zăt′), *interj.* *Cricket, Colloq.* how's that; an appeal by the fielding side to the umpire to declare a batsman out.

Hoxha (*Alb.* hò′jà), *n.* **Enver** (*Alb.* èm′vèr), born 1908, Albanian political leader: Secretary-General of the Albanian Communist Party since 1943; First Secretary of the Central Committee since 1954.

hoy[1] (hoi), *n.* **1.** a sloop-rigged boat, single-decked and used for fishing. **2.** a small boat used in harbour, as a ferry between a ship and the shore.

hoy[2] (hoi), *interj.* (an exclamation to attract attention.)

Hoy (hoi), *n.* the second largest of the Orkney Islands, Scotland. ab. 78 sq. mi. 995 pop. (est. 1963).

hoyden (hoi′dn), *n.* **1.** a rude or ill-bred girl; tomboy. —*adj.* **2.** hoydenish; boisterous. Also, **hoiden.** [orig. uncert.] —**hoy′denish,** *adj.* —**hoy′denishness,** *n.*

Hoylake (hoi′lāk′), *n.* a town in England, in NW Cheshire. 32,268 (1961).

Hoyle (hoil), *n.* **1. Edmund** or **Edmond,** 1672–1769, English writer on card games. **2. Fred,** born 1915, English astronomer.

HP, **1.** *Elect.* high power. **2.** high pressure. **3.** horsepower.

H.P., **1.** *Elect.* high power. **2.** high pressure. **3.** hire purchase. **4.** horsepower. **5.** house physician. **6.** Houses of Parliament.

h.p., horsepower. Also, **hp.**

H.Q., headquarters. Also, **h.q.**

Hr, (*Ger. Herr*) equivalent of **Mr.**

hr, *pl.* **hrs.** hour; hours.

H.R., House of Representatives.

Hradec Králové (*Cz.* hrä′děts krä′lō vě), *n.* a town in N central Czechoslovakia. 60,000 (est. 1965).

H-R diagram, Hertzsprung-Russell diagram.

H.R.E., Holy Roman Empire.

H.R.H., His, or Her, Royal Highness.

H.R.I.P., (L *hic requiescit in pace*) here rests in peace.

Hrolf (hrŏlf), *n.* See **Rollo.**

H.S., **1.** Home Secretary. **2.** house surgeon.

h.s., (L *hoc sensu*) in this sense.

H.S.H., His, or Her, Serene Highness.

Hsinking (shĭn′kĭng′), *n.* Changchun.

H.S.M., His, or Her, Serene Majesty.

H.S.S., (L *historicae societatis socius*) Fellow of the Historical Society.

Hsuan Chiao (shwän′ chou′), Taoism.

ht, height.

H.T., high tension.

Huáscar (*Sp.* wäs′kär), *n.* *c.* 1495–1533, Inca ruler of Peru.

Huascarán (*Sp.* wäs kä rän′), *n.* a mountain in W Peru, in the Andes. 22,205 ft.

hub (hŭb), *n.* **1.** the central part of a wheel, as that part into which the spokes are inserted. See diag. under **felloe.** **2.** the part in central position around which all else revolves: *the hub of the universe.* **3. the Hub,** *U.S. Colloq.* Boston, U.S.A. **4.** the peg or hob used as a target in quoits, etc. **5.** *Coining.* a design of hardened steel in relief used as a punch in making a die. [cf. HOB[1]]

hubble-bubble (hŭb′l bŭb′l), *n.* **1.** a crude type of hookah. **2.** a bubbling sound. **3.** confusion; turmoil.

Hubble's constant (hŭb′lz), *Astron.* the ratio of the distance between the local group of galaxies and a receding cluster of galaxies, to the rate at which the distant cluster recedes. [named after Edwin Powell *Hubble*, 1889–1953, U.S. astronomer]

hubbub (hŭb′ŭb), *n.* **1.** a loud, confused noise, as of many voices. **2.** tumult; uproar. —**Syn. 1.** See **noise.**

hubby (hŭb′ĭ), *Slang.* husband.

Hubli (hōō′blĭ), *n.* a town in India, in W Mysore. 171,326 (1961).

hubris (hyōō′brĭs), *n.* insolence or wanton violence stemming from excessive pride. Also, **hybris.** [Gk] —**hubristic** (hyōō brĭs′tĭk), *adj.* —**hubris′tically,** *adv.*

huckaback (hŭk′ə băk′), *n.* towelling of linen or cotton, of a distinctive weave. Also, **huck.**

huckleberry (hŭk′l bĕ′rĭ), *n., pl.* **-ries. 1.** the dark blue or black edible berry of any of various shrubs of the American ericaceous genus *Gaylussacia.* **2.** a shrub yielding such a berry. **3.** blueberry (def. 1). [var. of *hurtleberry* WHORTLEBERRY]

hucklebone (hŭk′l bōn′), *n.* *Anat.* **1.** the anklebone, astragalus, or talus. **2.** *Obs.* the hipbone.

huckster (hŭk′stə), *n.* Also, **huck′sterer. 1.** a retailer of small articles; a hawker. **2.** a street pedlar of fruit and vegetables. **3.** a cheaply mercenary person. —*v.i.* **4.** to deal in small articles or make petty bargains. [ME *huccster, hokester.* Cf. G *höken* to retail goods]

Huddersfield (hŭd′əz fēld′), *n.* a county borough in the West Riding of Yorkshire: manufacturing. 130,302 (1961).

huddle (hŭd′l), *v.,* **-dled, -dling,** *n.* —*v.t.* **1.** to heap or crowd together confusedly. **2.** to draw (oneself) closely together; nestle (often fol. by *up*). **3.** to do hastily and carelessly (often fol. by *up, over,* or *together*). **4.** to put on (clothes) with careless haste (often fol. by *on*). —*v.i.* **5.** to gather or crowd together in a confused mass. —*n.* **6.** a confused heap, mass, or crowd; a jumble. **7.** confusion or disorder. **8.** *Colloq.* a conference held in secret. [orig. uncert.; cf. ME *hodre*, c. LG *hudren*] —**hud′dler,** *n.*

Hudibrastic (hyōō′dĭ brăs′tĭk), *adj.* **1.** of or pertaining to, or resembling the style of, Samuel Butler's *Hudibras* (published 1663–78), a mock-heroic satirical poem written in tetrameter couplets. **2.** of a playful burlesque style.

Hudson (hŭd′sən), *n.* **1. Henry,** died 1611?, English navigator and explorer in North America. **2. William Henry,** 1841–1922, English naturalist and author. **3.** a river in E New York State, flowing S to New York Bay. 306 mi.

Hudson Bay, a large inland sea in N Canada. ab. 850 mi. long; ab. 600 mi. wide; ab. 400,000 sq. mi.

Hudson's Bay Company, a company chartered in 1670 to trade in furs with the North American Indians.

Hudson seal, muskrat fur which has been plucked and dyed to give the appearance of seal.

Hudson Strait, a strait connecting Hudson Bay and the Atlantic. ab. 450 mi. long; ab. 100 mi. wide. See map under **Baffin Bay.**

hue[1] (hyo͞o), *n.* **1.** that property of colour by which the various regions of the spectrum are distinguished, as red, blue, etc. **2.** variety of a colour; a tint: *pale hues.* **3.** colour: *all the hues of the rainbow.* **4.** *Obs.* form or appearance. **5.** *Obs.* complexion. [ME *hewe,* OE *hīw* form, appearance, colour]

hue[2] (hyo͞o), *n.* outcry, as of pursuers; clamour. [ME *hu,* t. OF, der. *heur* cry out, shout; prob. imit.]

Hué (*Fr.* wė), *n.* a seaport in N South Vietnam: former capital of Annam. 103,500 (est. 1962).

hue and cry, 1. *Law.* the pursuit of a felon or an offender with loud outcries or clamour to give an alarm. **2.** a proclamation for the capture of a criminal. **3.** any public clamour against or over something.

hued (hyo͞od), *adj.* having a hue or colour: *golden-hued.*

Huelva (*Sp.* wĕl′bä), *n.* a seaport in SW Spain, near the Gulf of Cadiz. 82,400 (1965).

huff (hŭf), *n.* **1.** a sudden swell of anger; a fit of resentment: *to leave in a huff.* —*v.t.* **2.** to give offence to; make angry. **3.** to treat with arrogance or contempt; bluster at; hector or bully. **4.** *Draughts.* to remove (a piece) from the board as a penalty for failing to make a compulsory capture. —*v.i.* **5.** to take offence. **6.** *Archaic.* to swell with pride or arrogance; swagger or bluster. **7.** *Dial.* to puff or blow. [imit.]

huffish (hŭf′ĭsh), *adj.* **1.** petulant. **2.** swaggering; hectoring. —**huff′ishly,** *adv.* —**huff′ishness,** *n.*

huffy (hŭf′ĭ), *adj.,* **-fier, -fiest. 1.** easily offended or touchy. **2.** offended; sulky: *a huffy mood.* —**huff′ily,** *adv.* —**huff′iness,** *n.*

Hufuf (hə fo͞of′), *n.* a town and oasis in E Saudi Arabia. 85,000 (est. 1962).

hug (hŭg), *v.,* **hugged, hugging,** *n.* —*v.t.* **1.** to clasp tightly in the arms, esp. with affection; embrace. **2.** to cling firmly or fondly to: *to hug an opinion.* **3.** to keep close to, as in sailing or going along: *to hug the shore.* **4. hug oneself,** congratulate oneself; be self-satisfied. —*v.i.* **5.** *Archaic.* to cling together; lie close. —*n.* **6.** a tight clasp with the arms; a warm embrace. [cf. Icel. *hugga* console]

huge (hyo͞oj), *adj.,* **huger, hugest. 1.** extraordinarily large in bulk, quantity, or extent: *a huge mountain.* **2.** large in scope, character, extent. [ME *huge, hoge;* ? aphetic var. of OF *ahuge* great, large, high; orig. uncert.] —**huge′ly,** *adv.* —**huge′ness,** *n.*

—**Syn.** mammoth, gigantic, colossal; vast; stupendous; bulky. HUGE, ENORMOUS, IMMENSE, TREMENDOUS imply great magnitude. HUGE, when used of concrete objects, usually adds the idea of massiveness, bulkiness: *a huge mass of rock, a huge collection of antiques.* ENORMOUS, lit. out of the norm, applies to what exceeds in extent, magnitude, or degree, a norm or standard: *an enormous iceberg, enormous curiosity.* TREMENDOUS applies to anything so huge as to be astonishing or to inspire awe: *a tremendous amount of equipment.* IMMENSE, lit. not measurable, is particularly applicable to what is exceedingly great, without reference to a standard: *immense buildings.* All are used figuratively: *a huge success, enormous curiosity, tremendous effort, immense joy.* —**Ant.** small, tiny, diminutive.

hugger-mugger (hŭg′ə mŭg′ə), *n.* **1.** disorder or confusion; a muddle. **2.** *Archaic.* secrecy or concealment: *in hugger-mugger.* —*adj.* **3.** secret or clandestine. **4.** disorderly or confused. —*v.t.* **5.** to keep secret or concealed. —*v.i.* **6.** to act secretly; take secret counsel.

Hugh Capet (hyo͞o′ kā′pĭt, kăp′ĭt; *Fr.* kȧ pĕ′). See **Capet.**

Hughes (hyo͞oz), *n.* **1. Thomas,** 1822–96, English author. **2. William Morris,** 1864–1952, Australian statesman; prime minister 1915–23.

Hugli (ho͞o′glĭ), *n.* Hooghly.

hug-me-tight (hŭg′mē tīt′), *n.* *Chiefly U.S.* a tight, sometimes sleeveless, knitted garment.

Hugo (hyo͞o′gō; *Fr.* y gō′), *n.* **Victor Marie** (*Fr.* vēk tôr mȧ rē′), **(Viscount),** 1802–85, French poet, novelist, and dramatist.

Huguenot (hyo͞o′gə nō′, -nŏt′), *n.* a member of the Reformed or Calvinistic communion of France in the 16th and 17th centuries; a French Protestant. [t. F, earlier *eiguenot,* t. Swiss G: m. *Eidgenosse* confederate, f. *Eid* oath + *Genoss* companion, associate, influenced by name *Hugues* Hugh]

Huhehot (ho͞o′hĭ hŏt′, ho͞o′ĭ-), *n.* a city in and capital of the Inner Mongolian Autonomous Region of North China. 320,000 (est. 1958). Formerly, **Kweisui.**

huia (ho͞o′yə), *n.* a New Zealand bird, *Heteralocha acutirostris,* having feathers prized by the Maori. [t. Maori]

huilbos (hoil′bŏs), *n.* a tall caesalpiniaceous ornamental tree, *Peltophorum africanum,* with yellow flowers and acacia-like leaves, the bark of which has medicinal uses; African wattle; kajatehout. [t. Afrikaans: lit., howling bush]

hula-hula (ho͞o′lə ho͞o′lə), *n.* a kind of native Hawaiian dance with intricate arm movements which tell a story in pantomime. Also, **hu′la.** [t. Hawaiian]

hula skirt, 1. a skirt made of grass blades bound to a waistband and worn by a hula dancer. **2.** any similar skirt made in plastic, etc.

hulk (hŭlk), *n.* **1.** the body of an old or dismantled ship. **2.** a vessel specially built to serve as a storehouse, prison, etc., and not for sea service. **3.** a bulky or unwieldy person or mass of anything. **4.** a burnt-out or stripped vehicle, building, or the like. **5.** *Archaic.* a heavy unwieldy vessel. —*v.i.* **6.** *U.S.* to loom in bulky form; be bulky (often fol. by *up*). [ME *hulke,* OE *hulc,* prob. t. ML: s. *hulcus,* t. Gk: m. *holkás* trading vessel]

hulking (hŭl′kĭng), *adj.* bulky; heavy and clumsy. Also, **hulk′y.**

hull[1] (hŭl), *n.* **1.** the husk, shell, or outer covering of a seed or fruit. **2.** the calyx of certain fruits, as the strawberry and raspberry. **3.** any covering or envelope. —*v.t.* **4.** to remove the hull of. [ME; OE *hulu* husk, pod; akin to *helan* cover, hide. Cf. HALL, HELL, HOLE] —**hull′er,** *n.*

hull[2] (hŭl), *n.* **1.** the frame or body of a ship, exclusive of masts, yards, sails, and rigging. **2.** *Aeron.* the boatlike fuselage of a flying boat on which the plane lands or takes off. —*v.t.* **3.** to strike or pierce the hull of (a ship), as with a torpedo. [orig. uncert. Cf. HULL[1], HOLD[2], HOLE]

Hull (hŭl), *n.* **1. Cordell,** 1871–1955, U.S. statesman: Secretary of State 1933–44. **2.** Official name, **Kingston upon Hull.** a seaport in the East Riding of Yorkshire on the Humber estuary. 303,268 (1961). **3.** a town in Canada, in Quebec. 56,929 (1961).

hullabaloo (hŭl′ə bə lo͞o′), *n.* a clamorous noise or disturbance; an uproar.

hullo (hŭ lō′), *interj., n., v.* hello.

hulloo (hŭl′lō′, hŭ lō′), *interj., n., v.* halloo.

hum (hŭm), *v.,* **hummed, humming,** *n., interj.* —*v.i.* **1.** to make a low, continuous, droning sound. **2.** to give forth an indistinct sound of mingled voices or noises. **3.** to utter an indistinct sound in hesitation, embarrassment, dissatisfaction, etc.; hem. **4.** to sing with closed lips, without articulating words. **5.** *Colloq.* to be in a state of busy activity: *to make things hum.* **6.** *Colloq.* to smell strongly, esp. disagreeably. —*v.t.* **7.** to sound, sing, or utter by humming. **8.** to bring, put, etc., by humming: *to hum a child to sleep.* —*n.* **9.** the act or sound of humming; an inarticulate or indistinct murmur; a hem. —*interj.* **10.** (an inarticulate sound uttered in hesitation, dissatisfaction, etc.) [ME *humme,* c. G *hummen* hum; imit. Cf. HUMBLEBEE] —**hum′mer,** *n.*

human (hyo͞o′mən), *adj.* **1.** of, pertaining to, or characteristic of man: *human nature.* **2.** having the nature of man; being a man: *the human race.* **3.** of or pertaining to mankind generally: *human affairs.* —*n.* **4** a human being. [t. L: s. *hūmānus* of a man; r. ME *humain,* t. OF] —**hu′manness,** *n.*

—**Syn. 1.** HUMAN, HUMANE may refer to that which is, or should be, characteristic of human beings. In thus describing characteristics, HUMAN may refer to good and bad traits of mankind alike (*human kindness, human weakness*), with, perhaps, more emphasis upon the latter, HUMAN being seen then in contrast to DIVINE: *to err is human, to forgive divine; he was only human.* HUMANE (the original spelling of HUMAN, and since 1700 restricted in meaning) takes into account only the nobler aspects of man: a HUMANE person is, specifically, one actuated by benevolence in his treatment of his fellows, or of helpless animals; the word once had also connotations of courtesy and refinement (hence, the application of HUMANE to those branches of learning intended to refine the mind).

human being, a member of the human race, *Homo sapiens.*

humane (hyo͞o mān′), *adj.* **1.** characterized by tenderness and compassion for the suffering or distressed: *humane feelings.* **2.** (of branches of learning or literature) tending to refine; polite: *humane studies.* [var. of HUMAN. Cf. GERMANE, GERMAN] —**humane′ly,** *adv.* —**humane′ness,** *n.* —**Syn. 1.** merciful, kind, kindhearted, tender. See **human.** —**Ant. 1.** brutal.

humane society, (*often cap.*) an organization devoted to humane principles, esp. with regard to animals.

humanism (hyo͞o′mə nĭz′əm), *n.* **1.** any system or mode of thought or action in which human interests predominate. **2.** devotion to or study of the humanities;

polite learning; literary culture. **3.** (*sometimes cap.*) the studies, principles or culture of the Humanists (def. 4).

humanist (hyoo͞/mə nĭst), *n.* **1.** a student of human nature or affairs. **2.** one devoted to or versed in the humanities. **3.** a classical scholar. **4.** (*sometimes cap.*) one of the scholars of the Renaissance who pursued and disseminated the study and understanding of the cultures of ancient Rome and Greece. **5.** (*sometimes cap.*) one who favours the thought and practice of a humanist philosophy. —**hu/manis/tic,** *adj.*

humanitarian (hyoo͞ măn/ĭ târ/rĭ ən), *adj.* **1.** having regard to the interests of all mankind; broadly philanthropic. **2.** pertaining to ethical or theological humanitarianism. —*n.* **3.** one who professes ethical or theological humanitarianism. **4.** a philanthropist.

humanitarianism (hyoo͞ măn/ĭ târ/rĭ ə nĭz/əm), *n.* **1.** humanitarian principles or practices; comprehensive philanthropy. **2.** *Ethics.* **a.** the doctrine that man's obligations are concerned wholly with the welfare of the human race. **b.** the doctrine that mankind may become perfect without divine aid. **3.** *Theol.* the doctrine that Jesus Christ possessed a human nature only.

humanity (hyoo͞ măn/ĭ tĭ), *n., pl.* **-ties. 1.** the human race; mankind. **2.** the condition or quality of being human; human nature. **3.** the quality of being humane; kindness; benevolence. **4. the humanities, a.** the study of the Latin and Greek classics. **b.** the study of literature, philosophy, art, etc., as distinguished from the social and physical sciences. [ME *humanitee*, t. F: *humanité*, t. L: m. s. *hūmānitas*]

humanize (hyoo͞/mə nīz/), *v.,* **-nized, -nizing.** —*v.t.* **1.** to make humane, kind, or gentle. **2.** to make human. —*v.i.* **3.** to become human or humane. Also, **humanise.** —**hu/maniza/tion,** *n.* —**hu/maniz/er,** *n.*

humankind (hyoo͞/mən kīnd/), *n.* the human race.

humanly (hyoo͞/mən lĭ), *adv.* **1.** in a human manner; by human means. **2.** according to human knowledge, or capability. **3.** from a human point of view.

human nature, 1. the quality inherent in all persons by virtue of their common humanity. **2.** *Sociol.* the make-up or conduct of human beings that distinguishes them from other animal forms, generally regarded as produced by living in primary groups.

humanum est errare (hoo͞ mä/noo͞m ĕst ĕ rä/rĭ), *Latin.* to err is human.

Humayun (hoo͞ mä/yoo͞n), *n.* 1508–56, Mogul emperor of Hindustan. Also, **Houmayun.**

Humber (hŭm/bə), *n.* the estuary of the rivers Ouse and Trent in E England. 37 mi. long.

Humbert I (hŭm/bət), Umberto I.

humble (hŭm/bl), *adj.,* **-bler, -blest,** *v.,* **-bled, -bling.** —*adj.* **1.** low in station, grade of importance, etc.; lowly: *humble origin.* **2.** modest; meek; without pride. **3.** courteously respectful: *in my humble opinion.* **4.** low in height, level, etc. —*v.t.* **5.** to lower in condition, importance, or dignity; abase. **6.** to make meek: *to humble one's heart.* [ME, t. OF, g. L *humilis* low, humble] —**hum/bleness,** *n.* —**hum/bler,** *n.* —**hum/bling,** *adj.* —**hum/bly,** *adv.*

—**Syn. 1.** unassuming, plain, common, poor. **2.** submissive. **5.** HUMBLE, DEGRADE, HUMILIATE suggest lowering or causing to seem lower. To HUMBLE is to bring down the pride of another (often righteously) or to reduce him to a state of abasement: *to humble an arrogant enemy.* To DEGRADE is to demote in rank or standing, or to reduce to a low level in condition, manners, or morals: *to degrade an officer, one's dependants.* To HUMILIATE is to make others feel or appear inadequate or unworthy, esp. in some public setting: *to humiliate a sensitive person.* —**Ant. 1.** noble, illustrious. **2.** self-assertive. **3.** insolent; proud. **5.** elevate. **6.** exalt.

humblebee (hŭm/bl bē/), *n.* bumblebee.

humble pie, 1. *Obs.* a pie made of the umbles (innards; less delectable parts) of deer, etc. **2. eat humble pie,** to be humiliated; be forced to apologize humbly.

Humboldt (hŭm/bōlt; *Ger.* hoo͝m/bōlt), *n.* **1. Friedrich Heinrich Alexander** (*Ger.* frē/drĭKH hĭn/rĭKH á lĕk sán/-dər), **Baron von,** 1769–1859, German scientist and writer. **2. Karl Wilhelm** (*Ger.* kärl vĭl/hĕlm), **Baron von,** 1767–1835, German philologist and statesman.

humbug (hŭm/bŭg/), *n., v.,* **-bugged, -bugging.** —*n.* **1.** *Obs.* a deluding trick; a hoax; a fraud. **2.** *Colloq.* a quality of falseness or deception. **3.** *Colloq.* one who seeks to impose deceitfully upon others; a cheat; an imposter. **4.** a kind of hard, peppermint sweet, usually having a striped pattern. —*v.t.* **5.** to impose upon by humbug or false pretence; delude. —*v.i.* **6.** to practise humbug. [orig. unknown] —**hum/bug/ger,** *n.* —**Syn. 1.** imposture, deception. **2.** pretence, sham. **3.** pretender, deceiver, charlatan.

humbuggery (hŭm/bŭg/ə rĭ), *n.* pretence; sham.

humdinger (hŭm/dĭng/ə), *n. Slang.* a person or thing remarkable of its kind.

humdrum (hŭm/drŭm/), *adj.* **1.** lacking variety; dull: *a humdrum existence.* —*n.* **2.** humdrum character or routine; monotony. **3.** monotonous or tedious talk. **4.** a dull boring fellow. [varied redupl. of HUM]

Hume (hyoo͞m), *n.* **1. David,** 1711–76, Scottish philosopher and historian. **2.** See **Murray** (def. 4).

humeral (hyoo͞/mə rəl), *adj.* **1.** of the shoulder. **2.** *Anat., Zool.* of or related to the humerus or brachium. [f. s. L *humerus* shoulder + -AL[1]]

humerus (hyoo͞/mə rəs), *n., pl.* **-meri** (-mə rī/). *Anat., Zool.* **1.** (in man) the single long bone in the arm which extends from the shoulder to the elbow. See diag. under **shoulder. 2.** the brachium. **3.** a corresponding bone in the forelimb of other animals or in the wings of birds. [t. L, var. of *umerus* shoulder]

humic (hyoo͞/mĭk), *adj. Chem.* of or denoting something (as an acid) derived from humus. [f. s. L *humus* ground, mould + -IC]

humid (hyoo͞/mĭd), *adj.* moist or damp, with liquid or vapour: *humid air.* [t. L: s. *(h)ūmidus* moist] —**hu/-midly,** *adv.* —**hu/midness,** *n.* —**Syn.** See **damp.**

humidifier (hyoo͞ mĭd/ĭ fī/ə), *n.* a device for regulating air moisture content and temperature in an air-conditioned room or building.

humidify (hyoo͞ mĭd/ĭ fī/), *v.t.,* **-fied, -fying.** to make humid. —**humid/ifica/tion,** *n.* —**humid/ifi/er,** *n.*

humidistat (hyoo͞ mĭd/ĭ stăt/), *n.* a hygrostat.

humidity (hyoo͞ mĭd/ĭ tĭ), *n.* **1.** humid condition; dampness. **2.** *Meteorol.* **a.** the condition of the atmosphere with regard to its water-vapour content. **b.** the ratio, expressed as a percentage, of the water-vapour present in the atmosphere to the amount required to saturate it at the same temperature (the **relative humidity**). **c.** the mass of water-vapour present in unit volume of air, esp. per cubic metre (the **absolute humidity,** or **vapour concentration**).

humidor (hyoo͞/mĭ dô/), *n.* a container or storage room for cigars or other preparations of tobacco, fitted with means for keeping the tobacco suitably moist.

humiliate (hyoo͞ mĭl/ĭ āt/), *v.t.,* **-ated, -ating.** to lower the pride or self-respect of; cause a painful loss of dignity to; mortify. [t. LL: m. s. *humiliātus*, pp., humbled] —**Syn.** degrade, abase, debase; dishonour, disgrace, shame. See **humble.** See also **ashamed.** —**humiliative** (hyoo͞-mĭl/yə tĭv), *adj.* —**humil/ia/tor,** *n.* —**humil/iatory,** *adj.*

humiliation (hyoo͞ mĭl/ĭ ā/shən), *n.* **1.** the act of humiliating. **2.** the state or feeling of being humiliated; mortification. —**Syn. 2.** See **shame.**

humility (hyoo͞ mĭl/ĭ tĭ), *n., pl.* **-ties.** the quality of being humble; modest sense of one's own significance. [ME *humilite*, t. F, t. L: m. s. *humilitas*] —**Syn.** lowliness, meekness. —**Ant.** pride.

humming (hŭm/ĭng), *adj.* **1.** that hums; buzzing. **2.** *Colloq.* extraordinarily active, intense, great, or big. **3.** *Colloq.* foaming, strong, or heady: *humming ale.*

hummingbird (hŭm/ĭng bûd/), *n.* any of numerous very small American birds constituting the family *Trochilidae*, characterized by narrow wings whose rapid vibration produces a hum, by slender bill, and usually by brilliant plumage.

Ruby-throated hummingbird, *Archilochus colubris* (Ab. 3½ in. long)

hummingbird moth, any of the hawkmoths.

hummock (hŭm/ək), *n.* **1.** an elevated tract rising above the general level of a marshy region. **2.** a knoll or hillock. **3.** a ridge in an icefield.

hummocky (hŭm/ə kĭ), *adj.* **1.** abounding in hummocks. **2.** like a hummock.

humor (hyoo͞/mə), *n., v.t. U.S.* humour.

humoresque (hyoo͞/mə rĕsk/), *n.* a musical composition of humorous or capricious character. [t. G: m. *Humoreske*, f. L *hūmor* HUMOUR + *-eske* -ESQUE]

humorist (hyoo͞/mə rĭst), *n.* **1.** one who exercises the faculty of humour. **2.** a professional writer, actor, etc., whose work is humorous. —**hu/moris/tic,** *adj.*

humorous (hyoo͞/mə rəs), *adj.* **1.** characterized by humour; amusing; funny: *the humorous side of things.* **2.** having or showing the faculty of humour; droll; facetious: *a humorous person.* **3.** *Obs.* pertaining or due to the bodily humours. **4.** *Obs.* moist. —**hu/morously,** *adv.* —**hu/-morousness,** *n.*

—**Syn. 1.** jocose, jocular, comic, comical. HUMOROUS, WITTY, FACETIOUS, WAGGISH imply that which arises from cleverness or a sense of fun. HUMOROUS implies a genuine sense of fun and the comic, impersonal or gently personal: *a humorous account, a humorous view of life.* WITTY implies quickness to perceive the amusing, striking, or unusual and to express it cleverly and entertainingly; it sometimes becomes rather sharp and unkind, particularly in quick repartee of a personal nature: *a witty and interesting companion, witty at someone else's expense.* FACETIOUS suggests a desire or attempt to be jocular or witty, usually unsuccessful or inappropriate or trifling: *a facetious treatment of a serious subject.* WAGGISH suggests the spirit of sly mischief and roguery of the constant joker (making jokes, not playing them), with no harm intended: *a waggish good humour.* —**Ant. 1.** solemn, sober, serious.

humour (hyo͞o′mə), *n.* **1.** the quality of being funny: *the humour of a situation.* **2.** the faculty of perceiving what is amusing or comical: *sense of humour.* **3.** the faculty of expressing the amusing or comical. **4.** speech or writing showing this faculty. **5.** mental disposition or tendency; frame of mind. **6.** capricious or freakish inclination; whim or caprice; odd traits. **7.** *Obs. Physiol.* one of the four chief bodily fluids, blood, choler or yellow bile, phlegm, and melancholy or black bile (**cardinal humours**), regarded as determining, by their relative proportions in the system, a person's physical and mental constitution. **8.** *Biol.* any animal or plant fluid, whether natural or morbid, such as the blood or lymph. **9. out of humour,** displeased or dissatisfied; cross. —*v.t.* **10.** to comply with the humour of; indulge: *to humour a child.* **11.** to accommodate oneself to. Also, *U.S.*, **humor.** [ME *humour*, t. AF, g. L *(h)ūmor* moisture, liquid] —**hu′mourless,** *adj.*

—**Syn. 3.** HUMOUR, WIT are contrasting terms which agree in referring to an ability to express a sense of the clever or amusing. HUMOUR consists in the bringing together of certain incongruities which arise naturally from situation or character, frequently so as to illustrate some fundamental absurdity in human nature or conduct; it is a more kindly trait than wit: *a genial and mellow type of humour.* WIT is a purely intellectual, often spontaneous, manifestation of cleverness and quickness of apprehension in discovering analogies between things really unlike, and expressing them in brief, diverting, and sometimes sharp observations or remarks: *humour produces a smile, but wit produces sudden laughter.* **5.** temperament, mood. **10.** HUMOUR, GRATIFY, INDULGE imply attempting to satisfy the wishes or whims of (oneself or) others. To HUMOUR is to comply with the mood, fancy, or caprice of another, as in order to satisfy, soothe, or manage: *to humour an invalid, a child.* To GRATIFY is to please by satisfying the likings or desires: *to gratify someone by praising him.* INDULGE suggests a yielding to wishes by way of favour or complaisance, and may imply a habitual or excessive yielding to whims: *to indulge an unreasonable demand, to indulge an irresponsible son.* —**Ant. 10.** discipline, restrain.

hump (hŭmp), *n.* **1.** a rounded protuberance, esp. on the back, as that due to abnormal curvature of the spine in man, or that normally present in certain animals such as the camel and bison. **2.** a low, rounded rise of ground; hummock. **3. the hump, a.** *Slang.* a fit of bad humour: *to get the hump.* **b.** (*cap.*) *U.S. Slang.* (in World War II) the Himalayas. **4. over the hump,** over the worst part or period of a difficult, dangerous, etc., time. —*v.t.* **5.** to raise (the back, etc.) in a hump. **6.** *U.S. Slang.* to exert (oneself) in a great effort. **7.** *Austral. Slang.* **a.** to place or bear on the back or shoulder. **b.** to carry. —*v.i.* **8.** to rise in a hump. **9.** *U.S. Slang.* to exert oneself. [back-formation from HUMPBACKED] —**humped,** *adj.* —**hump′-less,** *adj.* —**hump′like,** *adj.*

humpback (hŭmp′băk′), *n.* **1.** a back with a hump. **2.** one who has such a back; hunchback. **3.** a whale of the genus *Megaptera*, with a humplike back.

humpback bridge, an abrupt, steep road bridge, often narrow.

humpbacked (hŭmp′băkt′), *adj.* having a hump on the back. [b. *crumpbacked* and *huckbacked* (or *hunchbacked*)]

Humperdinck (*Ger.* ho͝om′pər dĭngk), *n.* **Engelbert** (*Ger.* ĕng′əl bĕrt), 1854–1921, German composer.

humph (hŭmf), *interj.* (an expression indicating disbelief, dissatisfaction, contempt, etc.)

Humphrey (hŭm′frĭ), *n.* **1. Duke of Gloucester,** 1391–1447, English soldier and statesman (youngest son of Henry IV). **2. Hubert Horatio,** born 1911, vice-president of the U.S. 1965–69.

Humpty Dumpty (hŭmp′tĭ dŭmp′tĭ), the subject of a nursery rhyme; he (an egg) fell from a wall and could not be put together again.

humpy[1] (hŭm′pĭ), *adj.*, **-pier, -piest. 1.** full of humps. **2.** humplike.

humpy[2] (hŭm′pĭ), *n.* *Austral.* **1.** an Aborigine's hut. **2.** any rude or temporary dwelling. [t. native Australian]

humus (hyo͞o′məs), *n.* the dark organic material in soils, produced by the decomposition of vegetable or animal matter, essential to fertility and favourable moisture supply. [t. L: earth, ground]

Hun (hŭn), *n.* **1.** a member of a warlike Asiatic people who devastated Europe in the 4th and 5th centuries. **2.** a barbarous, destructive person. **3.** *Slang.* **a.** a German soldier, unit, aircraft, or the like, in World Wars I and II. **b.** any German. [sing. of *Huns*, OE *Hūnas*, Icel. *Hūnar*. Cf. LL *Hunnī*, Chinese *Han*; all from native name]

Hunan (ho͞o′nän′), *n.* a province in S China. ab. 36,220,000 (est. 1957). *Cap.*: Changsha.

hunch (hŭnch), *v.t.* **1.** to thrust out or up in a hump: *to hunch one's back.* —*v.i.* **2.** to walk, sit, or stand in a bent position (usually fol. by *up*). —*n.* **3.** a hump. **4.** *Colloq.* a premonition or suspicion. **5.** a lump or thick piece. [appar. back-formation from HUNCHBACKED]

hunchback (hŭnch′băk′), *n.* humpback (def. 2).

hunchbacked (hŭnch′băkt′), *adj.* humpbacked. [b. *huckbacked* and *bunchbacked*]

hundred (hŭn′drəd), *n.*, *pl.* **-dreds,** (*as after a numeral*) **-dred. 1.** a cardinal number, ten times ten. **2.** a symbol for this number, as 100 or C. **3.** a set of a hundred persons or things: *a hundred of the men.* **4.** *Colloq.* one hundred pounds. **5.** a historical administrative division of an English county. **6.** *U.S.* a similar division in colonial Pennsylvania, Delaware, and Virginia, and still surviving in Delaware. —*adj.* **7.** amounting to one hundred in number. [ME *hondred*, OE *hundred*, c. G *hundert*]

hundred days, the period between March 20th, 1815, when Napoleon entered Paris after escaping from Elba, to June 29th, 1815, when he abdicated after the battle of Waterloo.

hundredfold (hŭn′drəd fōld′), *adj.* **1.** comprising a hundred parts or members. **2.** a hundred times as great or as much. —*adv.* **3.** in a hundredfold measure.

hundred-per-cent (hŭn′drəd pə sĕnt′), *adj.* completely; entirely.

hundred-percenter (hŭn′drəd pə sĕn′tə), *n.* *U.S.* a patriotic, or sometimes jingoistic, person.

hundreds and thousands, grains of brightly coloured sugar, used in decorating cakes, sweets, etc.

hundredth (hŭn′drədth), *adj.* **1.** next after the ninety-ninth. **2.** being one of a hundred equal parts. —*n.* **3.** a hundredth part, esp. of one ($\frac{1}{100}$). **4.** the hundredth member of a series.

hundredweight (hŭn′drəd wāt′), *n.*, *pl.* **-weights,** (*as after a numeral*) **-weight.** a unit of avoirdupois weight commonly equivalent to 112 lbs in England and 100 lbs in the U.S. *Abbrev.*: cwt.

Hundred Years War, the series of wars between France and England from 1338 to 1453.

hung (hŭng), *v.* pt. and pp. of **hang.**

Hung., 1. Hungarian. **2.** Hungary.

Hungarian (hŭng gâr′ĭ ən), *adj.* **1.** of or pertaining to Hungary or its people. —*n.* **2.** a native or inhabitant of Hungary; a Magyar. **3.** the language of Hungary, of the Ugric group; Magyar. [f. HUNGARY + -AN]

Hungary (hŭng′gə rĭ), *n.* a republic in central Europe. 9,977,870 pop. (1960); 35,926 sq. mi. *Cap.*: Budapest. Hungarian, **Magyarország.**

hunger (hŭng′gə), *n.* **1.** the painful sensation or state of exhaustion caused by need of food: *to collapse from hunger.* **2.** a craving appetite; need for food. **3.** strong or eager desire: *hunger for praise.* —*v.i.* **4.** to feel hunger; be hungry. **5.** to have a strong desire. —*v.t.* **6.** *Obs.* to subject to hunger; starve. [ME; OE *hungor*, c. G *Hunger*]

hunger-march (hŭng′gə mäch′), *n.* a march undertaken by unemployed or hungry workers to draw attention to their troubles. —**hung′er-march′er,** *n.*

hunger-strike (hŭng′gə strīk′), *n.* a persistent refusal to eat, as a protest against imprisonment, restraint, compulsion, etc.

Hung Hsiu-chüan (ho͝ong′ syo͞o′chwän′), 1812–64, Chinese popular leader: leader of the Taiping rebellion 1859–64.

Hungnam (ho͝ong′näm′), *n.* a seaport in E central North Korea. 150,000 (est. 1963).

hungry (hŭng′grĭ), *adj.*, **-grier, -griest. 1.** craving food; having a keen appetite. **2.** indicating, characteristic of, or characterized by hunger: *a lean and hungry look.* **3.** strongly or eagerly desirous. **4.** lacking needful or desirable elements; not fertile; poor: *hungry land.* **5.** marked by scarcity of food. [ME; OE *hungrig*. See -Y[1]] —**hung′rily,** *adv.* —**hung′riness,** *n.*

—**Syn. 1.** ravenous, famishing. HUNGRY, FAMISHED, STARVED describe a condition resulting from a lack of food. HUNGRY is a general word, expressing various degrees of eagerness or craving for food: *hungry between meals, desperately hungry after a long fast, hungry as a bear.* FAMISHED denotes the condition of one reduced to actual suffering from want of food but sometimes is used lightly or in an exaggerated statement: *famished after being lost in a wilderness, simply famished* (hungry). STARVED denotes a condition resulting from long-continued lack or insufficiency of food, and implies enfeeblement, emaciation, or death (originally death from any cause, but now death from lack of food): *to look thin and starved; by the end of the terrible winter, thousands had starved* (*to death*). It is also used humorously: *I'm simply starved* (hungry). —**Ant. 1.** satiated, surfeited, full.

hunk (hŭngk), *n.* *Colloq.* a large piece or lump; a chunk.

hunks (hŭngks), *n. sing. and pl.* **1.** a crabbed, disagreeable person. **2.** a covetous, sordid man; a miser.

hunky[1] (hŭng′kĭ), *adj. U.S. Slang.* **1.** Also, **hunky-dory** (hŭng′kĭ dô′rĭ). satisfactory; well; right. **2.** even; leaving no balance. [orig. unknown]

hunky[2] (hŭng′kĭ), *n., pl.* **-kies. 1.** *U.S. Slang and Derogatory.* an unskilled or semiskilled workman of foreign birth, esp. a Hungarian; bohunk. *—adj.* **2.** *Slang.* (of men) large and, usually, attractive to women. [? der. HUNGARIAN]

hunt (hŭnt), *v.t.* **1.** to chase (game or other wild animals) for the purpose of catching or killing. **2.** to scour (a region) in pursuit of game. **3.** to use or manage (a horse, etc.) in the chase. **4.** to pursue with force, hostility, etc.: *he was hunted from the village.* **5.** to search for; seek; endeavour to obtain or find. **6.** to search (a place) thoroughly. **7.** *Bellringing.* to alter the place of (a bell) in a hunt. *—v.i.* **8.** to engage in the chase. **9.** to make a search or quest (often fol. by *for* or *after*). **10.** *Bellringing.* to alter the place of a bell in its set according to certain rules. **11.** *Mach.* to oscillate periodically as the speed of an engine or the position of a needle of a measuring instrument. *—n.* **12.** the act of hunting game or other wild animals; the chase. **13.** a body of persons associated for the purpose of hunting; an association of huntsmen. **14.** a pack of hounds engaged in the chase. **15.** a district hunted with hounds. **16.** pursuit. **17.** a search. **18.** *Bellringing.* a regularly varying order of permutations in the ringing of a group of from five to twelve bells. [ME *hunte(n)*, OE *huntian*, der. *hunta* hunter. Cf. OE *hentan* pursue] **—Syn. 1.** pursue, track.

Hunt (hŭnt), *n.* **1. (James Henry) Leigh** (lē), 1784–1859, English essayist and poet. **2. (William) Holman,** 1827–1910, English painter.

hunt ball, a ball given by members of a hunt.

hunter (hŭn′tə), *n.* **1.** a huntsman. **2.** one who searches or seeks for something: *a fortune-hunter.* **3.** a horse used, or trained for use in hunting. **4.** an animal that hunts game or prey, esp. a dog. **5.** (*cap.*) the northern constellation Orion. **6.** a watch with a hinged cover to protect its face.

Hunter (hŭn′tə), *n.* **John,** 1728–93, Scottish surgeon.

hunter's moon, the first full moon following the harvest moon, in October.

hunting (hŭn′tĭng), *n.* **1.** the act of one who or that which hunts. **2.** *Elect.* the periodic oscillating of a rotating electromechanical system about a mean space position, as in a synchronous motor. **3.** any periodic variation in the speed of an engine, or in the position of the needle of a measuring instrument. *—adj.* **4.** of, for, or engaged in hunting: *a hunting cap.*

hunting box, a lodge or house, in or near a hunting or shooting area, rented or occupied during the season. Also, **hunting lodge.**

hunting case, a watchcase with a hinged cover to protect the crystal, orig. against accidents in hunting.

Huntingdon (hŭn′tĭng dən), *n.* **1.** a town in England, the county town of Huntingdonshire. 8812 (1961). **2.** Huntingdonshire.

Huntingdonshire (hŭn′tĭng dən shĭə′, -shə), *n.* a county in E England. 78,879 pop. (1961); 366 sq. mi. *Co. town:* Huntingdon. *Abbrev.:* Hunts. Also, **Huntingdon.**

hunting horn, 1. a cylindrical instrument, about 9 in. long, used in foxhunting to give signals. **2.** an early form of orchestral horn, consisting of a conical tube coiled in a circle, used in hunting in some countries for giving the signals. See illus. under **horn.**

hunting knife, a knife sometimes used to kill game, but more commonly to skin and cut it up.

hunting watch, a hunter (def. 6).

huntress (hŭn′trĭs), *n.* **1.** a huntswoman. **2.** a mare employed in hunting.

Hunts., Huntingdonshire.

huntsman (hŭnts′mən), *n., pl.* **-men. 1.** the man in charge of hounds during a hunt. **2.** one who hunts game, etc.

huntsman's-cup (hŭnts′mənz kŭp′), *n.* a plant of the genus *Sarracentia,* particularly *S. purpurea,* the pitcher plant of bogs.

huntsman spider, *Austral.* a large non-venomous spider, *Isopoda immanis.*

huntswoman (hŭnts′wŏŏm′ən), *n.* a woman who hunts.

Hunyadi (hōōn′yä′dĭ; *Hung.* hōō′nyŏ dē), *n.* **János** (*Hung.* yä′nōsh) (*Johannes Corvinus Huniades*), *c.* 1387–1456, Hungarian patriot.

Huon pine (hyōō′ŏn), a large taxaceous tree, *Dacrydium franklinii,* of Tasmania. [named after the river *Huon,* in Tasmania]

Hupa (hōō′pə), *n.* an Athabascan language of north-western California.

Hupeh (hōō′pā′), *n.* a province in central China. 30,790,000 (est. 1957). *Cap.:* Wuhan.

hurdle (hû′dl), *n., v.,* **-dled, -dling.** *—n.* **1.** a barrier in a racetrack, to be leapt by the contestants. **2. the hurdles,** a race in which such barriers are leapt. **3.** a difficult problem to be overcome; obstacle. **4.** a movable rectangular frame of interlaced twigs, crossed bars, or the like, as for a temporary fence. **5.** any of various obstacles, as a hedge, low wall, fence, over which horses must jump in steeplechasing, etc. **6.** a frame or sledge on which criminals were formerly drawn to the place of execution. *—v.t.* **7.** to leap over (a hurdle, etc.) as in a race. **8.** to master (a difficulty, problem, etc.). **9.** to construct with hurdles; enclose with hurdles. *—v.i.* **10.** to leap over a hurdle or other barrier. [ME *hirdel, hurdel,* OE *hyrdel,* f. *hyrd-* (c. G *Hürde* hurdle) + *-l* suffix; akin to L *crātis* wickerwork, Gk *kýrtos* basket, cage] **—hur′dler,** *n.*

hurds (hûdz), *n.pl.* hards.

hurdy-gurdy (hû′dĭ gû′dĭ), *n., pl.* **-dies. 1.** a barrel organ or similar instrument played by turning a crank. **2.** a lute or guitar-shaped stringed musical instrument sounded by the revolution, against the strings, of a rosined wheel turned by a crank. [appar. imit.]

hurl (hûl), *v.t.* **1.** to drive or throw with great force. **2.** to throw down; overthrow. **3.** to utter with vehemence. *—v.i.* **4.** to throw a missile. *—n.* **5.** a forcible or violent throw; a fling. [ME *hurlen*; early assoc. with HURTLE, but prop. freq. of obs. *hurr* (imit.) make a vibrating sound. Cf. obs. *hurling,* n., roll of thunder, d. G *hurlen* roll, rumble (said of thunder)] **—hurl′er,** *n.*

hurly (hû′lĭ), *n., pl.* **-lies.** commotion; hurly-burly.

hurly-burly (hû′lĭ bû′lĭ), *n., pl.* **-burlies,** *adj. —n.* **1.** commotion; tumult. *—adj.* **2.** full of commotion; tumultuous. [m. *hurling and burling*]

Huron (hyŏŏə′rən), *n.* **1. Lake,** a lake between Lakes Michigan and Erie: second in area of the Great Lakes. ab. 23,000 sq. mi. **2.** one of an Indian tribe, the north-western member of the Iroquoian family, living west of Lake Huron. [t. F: unkempt person, bristly savage; applied to Indians about 1600]

hurrah (hōō rä′), *interj.* **1.** (an exclamation of joy, exultation, applause, or the like.) *—v.i.* **2.** to shout 'hurrah'. *—n.* **3.** the exclamation 'hurrah'. Also, **hurray** (hōō rā′), **hooray.**

hurricane (hŭ′rĭ kən), *n.* **1.** a violent tropical cyclonic storm. **2.** a storm of the most intense severity. **3.** *Meteorol.* a wind of Beaufort scale force 12, i.e. one more than 78 miles per hour. **4.** anything suggesting a violent storm. [t. Sp.: m. *huracán,* t. Carib]

hurricane deck, a light upper deck on passenger steamers, etc.

hurricane lamp, 1. an oil lamp the flame of which is protected by a glass chimney or other similar device. **2.** a candlestick with a chimney.

hurried (hŭ′rĭd), *adj.* **1.** driven or impelled to hurry, as a person. **2.** characterized by or done with hurry; hasty. **—hur′riedly,** *adj.* **—hur′riedness,** *n.*

hurry (hŭ′rĭ), *v.,* **-ried, -rying,** *n., pl.* **-ries.** *—v.i.* **1.** to move, proceed, or act with haste, often undue haste. *—v.t.* **2.** to drive or move (someone or something) with speed, often with confused haste. **3.** to hasten; urge forwards (often fol. by *up*). **4.** to impel with undue haste to thoughtless action: *to be hurried into a decision. —n.* **5.** need or desire for haste: *to be in a hurry to begin.* **6.** hurried movement or action; haste. [orig. obscure; ? imit.] **—hur′ryingly,** *adv.* **—Syn. 1.** See **rush**[1]. **3.** accelerate, quicken; expediate; hustle. **6.** bustle; celerity; expedition, dispatch. **—Ant. 3.** delay.

hurry-scurry (hŭ′rĭ skŭ′rĭ), *n., pl.* **-ries,** *adv., adj., v.,* **-ried, -rying.** *—n.* **1.** headlong, disorderly haste; hurry and confusion. *—adv.* **2.** with hurrying and scurrying. **3.** confusedly; in a bustle. *—adj.* **4.** characterized by headlong, disorderly flight or haste. *—v.i.* **5.** to rush or go hurry-scurry. Also, **hurry-skurry.** [var. reduplication of HURRY]

hurst (hûst), *n.* **1.** a copse or wood. **2.** a wooded hill. [ME, OE *hyrst*; c. LG *horst*]

hurt (hût), *v.,* **hurt, hurting,** *n. —v.t.* **1.** to cause bodily injury to (with or without consequent pain). **2.** to cause bodily pain to or in: *the wound still hurts him.* **3.** to damage (a material object, etc.) by striking, rough use, or otherwise: *to hurt furniture.* **4.** to affect adversely; harm: *to hurt one's reputation.* **5.** to cause mental pain to; grieve: *to hurt one's feelings. —v.i.* **6.** to cause pain (bodily or mental): *my finger still hurts.* **7.** to cause injury, damage, or harm. *—n.* **8.** a blow that inflicts a wound; bodily injury. **9.** injury; damage or harm. **10.** an injury that gives mental pain, as an insult. [ME *hurte(n),* prob. t. OF: m. *hurter* strike against, der. *hurt* a blow] **—Syn. 8.** See **injury.**

hurter (hû′tə), *n.* **1.** a supporting or strengthening part. **2.** (in a vehicle) a butting piece on the shoulder of an axle against which the hub strikes. [ME *hurtour,* f. HURT, v. + *-our* -OR[2]. Cf. F *hurtoir* a knocker]

hurtful (hûrt′fəl), *adj.* such as to cause hurt or injury; injurious; harmful. —**hurt′fully,** *adv.* —**hurt′fulness,** *n.* —**Syn.** destructive, pernicious; noxious.

Hürth (*Ger.* hʏrt), *n.* a town in West Germany in SW North Rhine-Westphalia. 50,000 (est. 1966).

hurtle (hûr′tl), *v.,* **-tled, -tling,** *n.* —*v.i.* **1.** to rush violently and noisily. **2.** to resound, as in collision or rapid motion. **3.** *Rare.* to strike together or against something. —*v.t.* **4.** to drive violently; fling; dash. **5.** to dash against; collide with. —*n.* **6.** *Poet.* clash; collision; shock; clatter. [ME; freq. of HURT]

Hurunui (hoo′roo noo′ĭ), *n.* a river in N South Island, New Zealand, flowing E to the Pacific Ocean. 90 mi.

Hus (hŭs; *Ger., Czech.* hoos), *n.* **Jan** (*Czech.* yän). See **Huss, John.**

Husain (hoo sän′, -sīn′), *n.* **Zakir** (zä kĭə′), 1897–1969, Indian statesman: president 1967–69.

Husák (*Slov.* hoo′säk), *n.* **Gustav** (*Slov.* goo′ståf), born 1913, Czechoslovak statesman: first secretary of the Communist Party since 1969.

husband (hŭz′bənd), *n.* **1.** the man of a married pair (correlative of *wife*). —*v.t.* **2.** to manage, esp. with prudent economy; economize: *to husband one's resources.* **3.** *Rare.* to provide with a husband. **4.** *Rare.* to act as a husband; marry. **5.** *Obs.* to till; cultivate. [ME *husbond(e),* OE *hūsbōnda,* f. *hūs* house + *bōnda* householder (t. Scand.; cf. Icel *bōndi*)] —**hus′bandless,** *adj.*

husbandman (hŭz′bənd mən), *n., pl.* **-men.** a farmer.

husbandry (hŭz′bən drĭ), *n.* **1.** the business of a farmer; agriculture; farming. **2.** careful or thrifty management; frugality; thrift. **3.** the management of domestic affairs, or of resources generally.

Husein ibn-Ali (hoo sīn′ ĭb′ən ä′lĭ; hoo sän′), 1856–1931, king of Hejaz 1916–24.

hush[1] (hŭsh), *interj.* **1.** (a command to be silent or quiet.) —*v.i.* **2.** to become or be silent or quiet. —*v.t.* **3.** to make silent; silence. **4.** to suppress mention of; keep concealed. **5.** to calm or allay: *to hush someone's fears.* —*n.* **6.** silence or quiet, esp. after noise. —*adj.* **7.** *Archaic.* silent; quiet. [appar. back-formation from ME *hussht,* also *hust, huyst,* adj. (orig. interj.), taken as pp. Cf. WHIST[1]]

hush[2] (hŭsh), *v.t.* **1.** to wash away (surface soil) to expose the underlying rock formation for prospecting. **2.** to wash (an ore) in a strong cascade of water so that the earth is carried away. —*n.* **3.** *Dial.* a flow or gush of water, esp. an artificial flow. [imit.]

hushaby (hŭsh′ə bī′), *v.i.* (used imperatively) go to sleep; be still.

hush-hush (hŭsh′hŭsh′), *adj. Colloq.* highly confidential.

hush money, a bribe to keep silent about something.

husk (hŭsk), *n.* **1.** the dry external covering of certain fruits or seeds, esp. of an ear of maize. **2.** the enveloping or outer part of anything, esp. when dry or worthless. —*v.t.* **3.** to remove the husk from. [ME *huske;* f. *hus-* (cf. OE *hosu* pod, husk) + *-k* suffix. See -OCK] —**husk′er,** *n.* —**husk′like′,** *adj.*

husking (hŭs′kĭng), *n.* the act of removing husks, esp. those of maize.

Huskisson (hŭs′kĭ sən), *n.* **William,** 1770–1830, English statesman and pioneer free-trader.

husky[1] (hŭs′kĭ), *adj.,* **-kier, -kiest,** *n., pl.* **-kies.** —*adj.* **1.** *Colloq.* burly; big and strong. **2.** having a semi-whispered vocal tone; somewhat hoarse. **3.** abounding in husks. **4.** like husks. —*n.* **5.** *U.S. Colloq.* a big and strong person. [f. HUSK, n. + -Y[1]] —**husk′ily,** *adv.* —**husk′iness,** *n.*

husky[2] (hŭs′kĭ), *n., pl.* **-kies.** (*also cap.*) an Eskimo dog. [? a shortened var. of ESKIMO]

Huss (hŭs; *Ger., Czech.* hoos), *n.* **John,** 1369?–1415, Bohemian religious reformer and martyr. Also, **Hus.**

hussar (hoo zä′), *n.* **1.** (orig.) one of a body of light Hungarian cavalry formed during the 15th century. **2.** one of a class of similar troops, usually with striking or showy uniforms, in European armies. [t. Hung.: m. *huszár,* orig. freebooter, t. OSerbian: m. *husar,* var. of *kursar,* t. It.: m. *corsaro* CORSAIR]

Hussein (hoo sän′), *n.* born 1935, king of Jordan since 1952.

Husserl (*Ger.* hoos′ərl), *n.* **Edmund** (*Ger.* ĕt′moont), 1859–1938, German philosopher.

Hussite (hŭs′īt), *n.* **1.** a follower of John Huss. —*adj.* **2.** of or pertaining to John Huss or the Hussites.

hussy (hŭs′ĭ, hŭz′ĭ), *n., pl.* **-sies.** **1.** an ill-behaved girl. **2.** a worthless, lewd woman. [familiar var. of HOUSEWIFE (ME *huswif*)]

hustings (hŭs′tĭngz), *n.pl. or sing.* **1.** (*sing., cap.*) a court of record in the City of London, formerly the principal court in the City. **2.** the temporary platform from which candidates for Parliament were (before 1872) nominated and addressed the electors. **3.** any electioneering platform. **4.** election proceedings. [ME *husting,* t. Scand.; cf. Icel. *hūsthing* house assembly, council summoned by king or leader]

hustle (hŭs′əl), *v.,* **-tled, -tling,** *n.* —*v.i.* **1.** to proceed or work rapidly or energetically. **2.** to push or force one's way. —*v.t.* **3.** to force roughly or hurriedly: *they hustled him out of the city.* **4.** to shake, push, or shove roughly. —*n.* **5.** energetic activity, as in work. **6.** discourteous shoving, pushing, or jostling. [var. sp. of *hussell, hus(s)le,* t. D: s. *husselen,* assimilated var. of *hutselen,* freq. of *hutsen* shake, jog] —**hus′tler,** *n.*

Huston (hyoo′stən), *n.* **John,** born 1906, *U.S.* film director.

hut (hŭt), *n., v.,* **hutted, hutting.** —*n.* **1.** a small, rude, or humble dwelling. **2.** *Mil.* a wooden or metal structure for the temporary housing of troops. —*v.t.* **3.** to place in or furnish with a hut. —*v.i.* **4.** to lodge or take shelter in a hut. [t. F: m. *hutte,* t. G: m. *Hütte;* prob. akin to HIDE[1]] —**hut′like′,** *adj.*

hutch (hŭch), *n.* **1.** a coop for confining small animals: *rabbit hutch.* **2.** a hut or cabin. **3.** a shack or shanty. **4.** a chest, box, or trough: *a grain hutch.* **5.** a baker's kneading trough. —*v.t.* **6.** to put away in or as in a hutch; hoard. [ME *huche,* t. OF, t. ML: m. s. *hūtica* chest; ? of Gmc orig.]

Hutchinson (hŭch′ĭn sən), *n.* **1. Mrs Anne Marbury,** 1590?–1643, British religious enthusiast in New England. **2. Thomas,** 1711–80, British colonial governor of Massachusetts 1769–74.

hutment (hŭt′mənt), *n.* an encampment of huts.

Huxley (hŭks′lĭ), *n.* **1. Aldous Leonard** (ôl′dəs), 1894–1964, English novelist and essayist. **2.** his brother, **Sir Julian Sorrell,** born 1887, English biologist and writer. **3.** their grandfather, **Thomas Henry,** 1825–95, English biologist and writer.

Huygens (hī′gənz; *Du.* hœy′KHəns), *n.* **Christian** (*Du.* krĭs′tĭ än), 1629–95, Dutch mathematician, physicist, and astronomer. Also, **Huyghens.**

Huygens' eyepiece, *Optics.* an eyepiece which is often used in microscopes, consisting of two plano-convex lenses with their plane sides towards the observer. The lenses are separated by a distance of half the sum of the focal lengths, which are in the ratio 3 to 1 (the lens of shorter focal length being nearer the observer).

Huysmans (*Du.* hœys′mŏns; *Fr.* wēs mäNs′), *n.* **Joris Karl** (*Du.* yō′rĭs kärl), 1848–1907, French novelist.

huzza (hoo zä′), *interj., n., pl.* **-zas,** *v.,* **-zaed, -zaing.** —*interj.* **1.** (an exclamation of exultation, applause, or the like.) —*n.* **2.** the exclamation 'huzza'. —*v.i.* **3.** to shout 'huzza'. —*v.t.* **4.** to salute with huzzas: *crowds huzzaed the triumphant hero.*

Hwang Ho (wăng′ hō′), a river flowing from W China into the Gulf of Pohai. ab. 2700 mi. Also, **Hoangho, Yellow River.** See map under **Yangtze.**

hyacinth (hī′ə sĭnth), *n.* **1.** any of the bulbous liliaceous plants constituting the genus *Hyacinthus,* esp. *H. orientalis,* widely cultivated for its spikes of fragrant, white or coloured, bell-shaped flowers. **2.** a hyacinth bulb or flower. **3.** (among the ancients) a plant supposed to spring from the blood of Hyacinthus and variously identified as iris, gladiolus, larkspur, etc. **4.** a reddish orange zircon; the jacinth. **5.** (among the ancients) an uncertain gem, possibly our amethyst or sapphire. [t. L: s. *hyacinthus,* t. Gk: m. *hyákinthos* kind of flower, also a gem. Cf. JACINTH]

hyacinthine (hī′ə sĭn′thĭn), *adj.* **1.** of or like the hyacinth. **2.** adorned with hyacinths.

Hyacinthus (hī′ə sĭn′thəs), *n. Gk Myth.* a beautiful youth (loved by Apollo but killed out of jealousy by Zephyrus) from whose blood sprang a flower marked with the letters of an exclamation of grief, 'AI AI'.

Hyades (hī′ə dēz′), *n.pl.* **1.** *Astron.* a group of stars comprising a moving cluster in the constellation Taurus, supposed by the ancients to indicate the approach of rain when they rose with the sun. **2.** *Gk Myth.* a group of nymphs, sisters of the Pleiades.

hyaena (hī ē′nə), *n.* hyena.

hyaline (hī′ə lĭn), *n.* **1.** something glassy or transparent. —*adj.* **2.** glassy; crystalline; transparent. [t. LL: m. s. *hyalinus,* t. Gk: m. *hyálinos* of glass]

hyaline cartilage, *Anat.* the typical translucent form of cartilage, containing little fibrous tissue.

hyalite (hī′ə līt′), *n.* a colourless variety of opal, sometimes transparent like glass, and sometimes whitish and translucent. [f. HYAL(O)- + -ITE[1]]

hyalo-, a word element meaning 'glass'. Also, before vowels, **hyal-.** [t. Gk, comb. form of *hýalos*]

hyaloid (hī′ə loid′), *n.* **1.** *Anat.* the hyaloid membrane of the eye. —*adj.* **2.** glassy; hyaline. [t. Gk: m. s. *hyaloeidḗs* like glass. See HYALO-, -OID]

hyaloid membrane, *Anat.* the capsule of the vitreous humour of the eye, a delicate, pellucid, and nearly structureless membrane.

hyalophane (hī ăl′ə fān′), *n.* a rare form of felspar containing some barium; occurs in colourless crystals in dolomite.

hyaloplasm (hī′ə lō plăz′əm), *n. Biol.* the pellucid portion of the protoplasm of a cell, as distinguished from the granular and reticular portions.

hyaluronic acid (hī′ə lyo͞o rŏn′ĭk), *Biochem.* any of a group of complex polysaccharides found in the vitreous humour of the eye, umbilical cord, synovial fluid, and other animal tissues.

hybrid (hī′brĭd), *n.* **1.** the offspring of two animals or plants of different races, breeds, varieties, species, or genera. **2.** a half-breed; a mongrel. **3.** anything derived from heterogeneous sources, or composed of elements of different or incongruous kinds. **4.** a word derived from elements of different languages. —*adj.* **5.** bred from two distinct races, breeds, varieties, species, or genera. **6.** composed of elements of different or incongruous kinds. **7.** (of a word) composed of elements originally drawn from different languages. [t. L: s. *hybrida*, var. of *hibrida* offspring of a tame sow and wild boar, a mongrel]

—**Syn. 5.** HYBRID, MONGREL refer to animals or plants of mixed origin. HYBRID is the scientific term: *hybrid corn, a hybrid variety of sheep.* MONGREL, used originally of dogs to denote especially the offspring of repeated crossings of different breeds, is now extended to other animals and to plants; it is usually depreciatory, as denoting mixed, nondescript, or degenerate breed or character: *a mongrel pup.* —**Ant. 5.** purebred, thoroughbred.

hybridism (hī′brĭ dĭz′əm), *n.* **1.** Also, **hybridity** (hī brĭd′ĭ tĭ). hybrid character. **2.** the production of hybrids.

hybridize (hī′brĭ dīz′), *v.*, **-dized, -dizing.** —*v.t.* **1.** to cause to produce hybrids; cross. **2.** to form in a hybrid manner. —*v.i.* **3.** to cause the production of hybrids by crossing different species, etc. Also, **hybridise.** —**hy′bridiz′able,** *adj.* —**hy′bridiza′tion,** *n.* —**hy′bridiz′er,** *n.*

hybris (hī′brĭs), *n.* hubris.

hydantoin (hī dăn′tō ĭn), *n.* a colourless, needle-like, crystalline compound, $C_3H_4N_2O_2$, used in the synthesis of pharmaceutical substances and resins. [irreg. f. Gk *hýd(ōr)* water + *(all)antoin* (f. ALLANTO(IS) + -IN[2])]

hydatid (hī′də tĭd), *n.* **1.** a cyst with watery contents, produced in man and animals by a tapeworm in the larval state. **2.** the encysted larva of a tapeworm; a cysticercus. [t. Gk: s. *hydatís* watery vesicle]

Hyde (hīd), *n.* **1. Douglas,** 1860–1949, Irish author and statesman: president of Eire 1938–45. **2. Edward.** See **Clarendon,** 1st Earl of. **3. Mr,** the criminal side of the leading character in Stevenson's *Dr Jekyll and Mr Hyde.* See **Jekyll and Hyde. 4.** a town in England, in NE Cheshire. 31,741 (1961).

Hyde Park, a park in London.

Hyderabad (hī′də rə băd′, -băd′, hī′drə-), *n.* **1.** a former state in S India: now a part of Andhra Pradesh. **2.** a city in India, the capital of Andhra Pradesh, in the western part. 1,251,119 (1961). **3.** a city in Pakistan, in the province of West Pakistan, on the Indus. 454,500 (1961).

Hyder Ali (hī′dər ä′lĭ), 1722–1782, a Muslim ruler of Mysore from 1761, and military leader against the British in India. Also, **Haidar Ali.**

hydnocarpate (hĭd′nō kä′pāt), *n. Chem.* a salt or ester of hydnocarpic acid. [f. s. NL *hydnocarpus* (f. Gk: *hýdno(n)* truffle + m. *karpós* fruit) + -ATE[2]]

hydnocarpic acid (hĭd′nō kä′pĭk), *Chem.* a white crystalline acid, $C_5H_7(CH_2)_{10}COOH$, obtained from chaulmoogra oil, used to treat leprosy.

hydr-¹, var. of **hydro-¹,** before vowels, as in *hydrangea.*

hydr-², var. of **hydro-²,** before vowels, as in *hydrazine.*

hydra (hī′drə), *n., pl.* **-dras, -drae** (-drē). **1.** (*cap. or l.c.*) *Gk Myth.* a monstrous serpent, slain by Hercules, represented as having nine heads, each of which was replaced by two after being cut off, unless the wound was cauterized. **2.** *Zool.* any of the freshwater polyps constituting the genus *Hydra.* **3.** any persistent evil arising from many sources or difficult to overcome. **4.** (*cap.*) *Astron.* a southern constellation, representing a sea-serpent. [t. L, t. Gk: water-serpent; r. ME *ydre*, t. OF]

hydracid (hī drăs′ĭd), *n. Chem.* an acid which contains no oxygen.

hydrangea (hī drān′jə), *n.* any shrub of the genus *Hydrangea*, species of which are cultivated for their large showy white, pink, or blue flower clusters. [t. NL, f. *hydr-* HYDR-¹ + m. Gk *angeîa*, pl. of *angeîon* vessel; so called from cup-shaped seed capsule]

hydrant (hī′drənt), *n.* an upright pipe with a spout, nozzle, or other outlet, usually in the street, for drawing water from a main or service pipe.

hydranth (hī′drănth), *n.* the terminal part of a hydroid polyp that bears the mouth and tentacles and contains the stomach region. [f. HYDR(A) (def. 2) + s. Gk *ánthos* flower]

hydrargyriasis (hī′drä jĭ rī′ə sĭs), *n. Pathol.* mercurial poisoning; mercurialism.

hydrargyrum (hī drä′jĭ rəm), *n. Chem.* mercury. [NL, der. L *hydrargyrus*, t. Gk: m. *hydrárgyros*]

hydrastine (hī drăs′tēn, -tĭn), *n.* an alkaloid found in the root of goldenseal. [f. HYDRASTIS + -INE[2]]

hydrastinine (hī drăs′tĭ nēn′), *n.* a substance used as a uterine stimulant.

hydrastis (hī drăs′tĭs), *n.* goldenseal (def. 2).

hydrate (hī′drāt), *n., v.,* **-drated, -drating.** *Chem.* —*n.* **1.** any of a class of compounds containing chemically combined water, esp. salts containing water of crystallization. —*v.t.* **2.** to combine chemically with water. —**hydra′tion,** *n.* —**hy′drator,** *n.*

hydrated (hī′drā tĭd), *adj.* chemically combined with water in its molecular form.

hydraul., hydraulics.

hydraulic (hī drô′lĭk), *adj.* **1.** operated by or employing water or other liquid. **2.** pertaining to water or other liquid, or to hydraulics. **3.** hardening under water, as a cement. [t. L: s. *hydraulicus*, t. Gk: m. *hydraulikós* pertaining to the water organ, an ancient musical instrument] —**hydrau′lically,** *adv.*

hydraulic accumulator, 1. a device, consisting of a hydraulic ram loaded with a heavy weight, for storing water under pressure in order to equalize the load on a pump supply machinery when the demand is intermittent. **2.** any apparatus for absorbing shock or storing energy in a hydraulic system.

hydraulic brake, a brake operated by fluid pressures in cylinders and connecting tubular lines.

hydraulic machinery, mechanical devices such as pumps, turbines, couplings, etc., in which the flow of a liquid either produces or is produced by their operation.

hydraulic press, a machine permitting a small force applied to a small piston to produce through fluid pressure a large force on a large piston.

hydraulic ram, a device by which the energy of descending water is utilized to raise a part of the water to a height greater than that of the source.

hydraulics (hī drô′lĭks), *n.* the science treating of the laws governing water or other liquids in motion and their applications in engineering; practical or applied hydrodynamics. [pl. of HYDRAULIC. See -ICS]

hydraulic torque converter, fluid drive.

hydrazine (hī′drə zēn′, -zĭn), *n. Chem.* **1.** a compound, N_2H_4, which is a weak base in solution and forms a large number of salts resembling ammonium salts, used as a reducing agent and as a jet-propulsion fuel. **2.** a class of substances derived by replacing one or more hydrogen atoms in hydrazine by an organic radical. [f. HYDR-² + AZ(O)- + -INE[2]]

hydrazo group, *Chem.* the bivalent group -HN.NH-. Also, **hydrazo radical.**

hydrazoic (hī′drə zō′ĭk), *adj. Chem.* denoting or pertaining to hydrazoic acid; triazoic.

hydrazoic acid, *Chem.* an acid composed of hydrogen and nitrogen, HN_3, occurring as a very explosive, colourless liquid with a penetrating smell.

hydrazone (hī′drə zōn′), *n. Chem.* any of a class of compounds formed from the condensation of an aldehyde or ketone with hydrazine.

hydria (hī′drĭ ə), *n. Archaeol.* (in ancient Greece) a large jar or pitcher with two or three handles, for carrying water. [t. Gk]

hydric (hī′drĭk), *adj. Chem.* pertaining to, or containing, hydrogen.

hydride (hī′drīd), *n. Chem.* **1.** a compound of hydrogen with another element or a radical. **2.** (formerly) a hydroxide.

hydriodic acid (hī′drĭ ŏd′ĭk), *Chem.* **1.** a colourless gas, HI, with a suffocating smell. **2.** an aqueous solution of this gas. [f. HYDR-² + IOD(INE) + -IC]

hydro (hī′drō), *n.* a hotel or resort having facilities for people undergoing hydropathic treatment. [short for HYDROPATHIC]

hydro-¹, a word element meaning 'water', as in *hydrogen.* Also, **hydr-.** [t. Gk, comb. form of *hýdōr* water]

hydro-², *Chem.* a word element often indicating combination of hydrogen with a negative element or radical: *hydrobromic.* Also, **hydr-.** [comb. form of HYDROGEN]

hydro-airplane (hī′drō ĕə′plān′), *n. U.S.* a hydroplane.

hydrobromic acid (hī′drō brō′mĭk), *Chem.* **1.** a colourless gas, HBr, with a pungent smell. **2.** an aqueous solution of this gas.

hydrocarbon (hī′drō kä′bən), *n. Chem.* any of a class of compounds containing only hydrogen and carbon, such as methane, CH_4, ethylene, C_2H_4, acetylene, C_2H_2, and benzene, C_6H_6 [f. HYDRO-[2] + CARBON]

hydrocele (hī′drō sēl′), *n. Pathol.* an accumulation of serous fluid, usually about the testis. [t. L, t. Gk: m. *hydrokḗlē*]

hydrocellulose (hī′drō sĕl′yōō lōs′), *n. Chem.* a gelatinous substance obtained by partially hydrolysing cellulose; used in the manufacture of paper and certain textiles.

hydrocephalus (hī′drō sĕf′ə ləs), *n. Pathol.* an accumulation of serous fluid within the cranium, esp. in infancy, often causing great enlargement of the head. Also, **hydrocephaly** (hī′drō sĕf′ə lĭ). [NL, t. Gk: m. *hydroképhalon* water in the head] —**hydrocephalic** (hī′drō sĕ făl′ĭk), **hy′droceph′alous,** *adj.*

hydrochloric acid (hī′drə klŏ′rĭk), *Chem.* a colourless gas, HCl, or an aqueous solution of it, which is extensively used in chemical and industrial processes; muriatic acid. [f. HYDRO-[1] + CHLORIC]

hydrochloride (hī′drə klô′rīd), *n. Chem.* a salt formed by the direct union of hydrochloric acid with an organic base, rendering the latter more soluble.

hydrocortisone (hī′drō kô′tĭ zōn′), *n. Pharm.* a compound secreted from the adrenal gland, used esp. as an anti-inflammatory agent.

hydrocyanic acid (hī′drō sī ăn′ĭk), *Chem.* a colourless, poisonous liquid, HCN, with a smell like that of bitter almonds; prussic acid. [f. HYDRO-[2] + CYANIC]

hydrodynamic (hī′drō dī năm′ĭk, -dĭ-), *adj.* **1.** pertaining to forces in or motions of fluids. **2.** pertaining to hydrodynamics.

hydrodynamics (hī′drō dī năm′ĭks, -dĭ-), *n.* the science of the mechanics of fluids, generally liquids, including hydrostatics and hydrokinetics.

hydro-electric (hī′drō ĭ lĕk′trĭk), *adj.* pertaining to the generation and distribution of electric energy derived from the energy of falling water or other hydraulic source. —**hydro-electricity** (hī′drō ĭ lĕk′trĭs′ĭ tĭ), *n.*

hydrofluoboric acid (hī′drō flōōə bō′rĭk), *Chem.* fluoroboric acid.

hydrofluoric acid (hī′drō flōō ŏ′rĭk), *Chem.* a colourless, corrosive, volatile liquid, HF, used for etching glass and as a condensing agent in chemical syntheses, such as alkylation. [f. HYDRO-[2] + FLOURIC]

hydrofoil (hī′drə foil′), *n.* **1.** one of two or more ski-like members, mounted at the ends of struts beneath a boat, supporting the hull above the surface of the water when a certain speed has been attained. **2.** a boat equipped with such members.

hydrogen (hī′drĭ jən), *n. Chem.* a colourless, odourless, inflammable gas, which combines chemically with oxygen to form water: the lightest of the known elements. *Symbol:* H; *at. wt:* 1·00797; *at. no.:* 1; *weight of one litre at 760 mm. pressure and 0° C:* 0·08987 g. [t. F: m. *hydrogène*, f. *hydro-* HYDRO-[1] + *-gène* -GEN]

hydrogenate (hī drŏj′ĭ nāt′), *v.t.*, **-nated, -nating.** to combine or treat with hydrogen. —**hydro′gena′tion,** *n.*

hydrogen bomb, a bomb whose potency is based on the release of nuclear energy resulting from the fusion of hydrogen isotopes in the formation of helium. It is many times more powerful than the atom bomb.

hydrogen bond, *Chem.* a weak chemical bond of considerable importance which occurs between a hydrogen atom attached to a strongly electronegative atom and a second strongly electronegative atom with a lone pair of electrons, as fluorine, oxygen, nitrogen.

hydrogen ion, *Chem.* ionized hydrogen of the form H^+.

hydrogen ion concentration, *Chem.* the number of grams of hydrogen ions in a litre of solution; a measure of the acidity or alkalinity of a solution. See ***p*H.**

hydrogenize (hī drŏj′ĭ nīz′), *v.t.*, **-nized, -nizing.** hydrogenate. Also, **hydrogenise.**

hydrogenous (hī drŏj′ĭ nəs), *adj.* **1.** of or containing hydrogen. **2.** formed or produced by water.

hydrogen peroxide, *Chem.* a colourless, unstable, oily liquid, H_2O_2, the aqueous solution of which is used as an antiseptic and a bleaching agent.

hydrogen sulphide, *Chem.* a colourless, inflammable, cumulatively poisonous gas, H_2S, smelling like rotten eggs; sulphuretted hydrogen.

hydrograph (hī′drə grăf′, -grāf′), *n.* a graph showing the seasonal change in the level, flow, or velocity of water in a channel, reservoir, or the like.

hydrography (hī drŏg′rə fĭ), *n.* **1.** the science of the measurement, description, and mapping of the surface waters of the earth, with special reference to their use for navigation. **2.** those parts of a map, collectively, that represent surface waters. —**hydrog′rapher,** *n.* —**hydrographic** (hī′drə grăf′ĭk), **hy′drograph′ical,** *adj.* —**hy′drograph′ically,** *adv.*

hydroid (hī′droid), *adj.* **1.** denoting or pertaining to that form of hydrozoan which is asexual and grows into branching colonies by budding. —*n.* **2.** that phase of a hydrozoan coelenterate that consists of polyp forms usually growing as an attached colony. [f. HYDR(A) (def. 2) + -OID]

hydrokinetic (hī′drō kĭ nĕt′ĭk, -kī-), *adj.* **1.** pertaining to the motion of fluids. **2.** pertaining to hydrokinetics. Also, **hy′drokinet′ical.**

hydrokinetics (hī′drō kĭ nĕt′ĭks, -kī-), *n.* the branch of hydrodynamics that treats of the laws governing liquids or gases in motion.

hydrolase (hī′drə lāz′), *n. Biochem.* any enzyme that catalyses a hydrolytic reaction.

hydrolith (hī′drə lĭth), *n. Chem.* calcium hydride, CaH_2.

hydrology (hī drŏl′ə jĭ), *n.* the science dealing with water on the land, or under the earth's surface, its properties, laws, geographical distribution, etc. —**hydrologic** (hī′drə lŏj′ĭk), **hy′drolog′ical,** *adj.* —**hydrol′ogist,** *n.*

hydrolysate (hī drŏl′ĭ sāt′), *n. Chem.* any compound formed by hydrolysis.

hydrolyse (hī′drə līz′), *v.t., v.i.*, **-lysed, -lysing.** to subject or be subjected to hydrolysis. Also, *U.S.*, **hydrolyze.** —**hy′drolys′able,** *adj.*

hydrolysis (hī drŏl′ĭ sĭs), *n., pl.* **-ses** (-sēz′). chemical decomposition by which a compound is resolved into other compounds by taking up the elements of water.

hydrolyte (hī′drə līt′), *n. Chem.* a substance subjected to hydrolysis.

hydrolytic (hī′drə lĭt′ĭk), *adj.* producing hydrolysis, or related to the process or results of hydrolysis.

hydromancy (hī′drō măn′sĭ), *n.* divination by means of water. [t. F: m. *hydromancie*, t. LL: m. s. *hydromantia*, f. Gk: *hydro-* HYDRO-[1] + m. *manteía* divination] —**hy′droman′tic,** *adj.*

hydromechanics (hī′drō mĭ kăn′ĭks), *n.* hydrodynamics. —**hy′dromechan′ical,** *adj.*

hydromedusa (hī′drō mĭ dyōō′sə), *n., pl.* **-sas, -sae** (-sē). the medusa form of a hydrozoan coelenterate. [NL. See HYDRO-[1], MEDUSA] —**hy′dromedu′san,** *adj.*

hydromel (hī′drō mĕl′), *n.* a liquid consisting of honey and water: when fermented, known also as mead. [t. L: m. *hydromeli*, t. Gk: honey water]

hydrometallurgy (hī′drō mĕt′ə lû′jĭ), *n.* the practice of extracting metals from ores by leaching with solutions such as mercury, cyanides, acids, brines, etc. —**hy′dromet′allur′gical,** *adj.*

hydrometeor (hī′drō mē′tĭ ə), *n. Meteorol.* the state or effect of water, water-vapour, or ice in the atmosphere, as rain, ice crystals, hail, fog, and clouds. —**hy′drome′teorol′ogy,** *n.*

hydrometer (hī drŏm′ĭ tə), *n.* a sealed cylinder with weighted bulb and graduated stem for determining the specific gravity of liquids by reading the level of the liquid on the emerging stem. —**hydrometric** (hī′drō mĕt′rĭk), **hy′dromet′rical,** *adj.* —**hydrom′etry,** *n.*

hydronium (hī drō′nyəm), *adj. Chem.* (of a hydrogen ion) hydrated with a water molecule, forming the unstable group, H_3O^+.

hydropathy (hī drŏp′ə thĭ), *n.* the treatment of disease by the use of water; hydrotherapy. [f. HYDRO-[1] + -PATHY] —**hydropathic** (hī′drō păth′ĭk), **hy′dropath′ical,** *adj.* —**hydrop′athist, hy′dropath′,** *n.*

hydrophane (hī′drō fān′), *n.* a partly translucent variety of opal, which becomes more translucent when immersed in water. —**hydrophanous** (hī drŏf′ə nəs), *adj.*

hydrophilic (hī′drō fĭl′ĭk), *adj. Chem.* having an affinity for water.

hydrophilous (hī drŏf′ĭ ləs), *adj.* (of flowers) pollinated by the agency of water currents.

hydrophobia (hī′drə fō′byə), *n. Pathol.* **1.** rabies. **2.** a morbid dread of water, as in rabies; any morbid or unnatural dread of water. [t. LL, t. Gk: horror of water]

hydrophobic (hī′drə fō′bĭk), *adj.* **1.** *Pathol.* of or pertaining to hydrophobia. **2.** *Chem.* having little or no affinity for water.

hydrophone (hī′drə fōn′), *n.* **1.** an instrument employing the principles of the microphone, used to detect the flow of water through a pipe. **2.** a device for locating sources of sound under water, as for detecting submarines by the noise of their engines, etc. **3.** *Med.* an instrument used in auscultation, whereby sounds are intensified through a column of water.

hydrophyllaceous (hī′drō fĭ lā′shəs), *adj.* of or belonging to the small but widespread angiosperm family *Hydrophyllaceae*, consisting mainly of herbaceous plants.

hydrophyte (hī′drō fīt′), *n.* a plant growing in water or very moist ground. —**hydrophytic** (hī′drō fĭt′ĭk), *adj.*

hydropic (hī drŏp′ĭk), *adj.* dropsical. Also, **hydrop′ical.** [t. L: s. *hydrōpicus*, t. Gk: m. *hydrōpikós*; r. ME *ydropik*, t. OF]

hydroplane (hī′drō plān′), *n.*, *v.*, **-planed, -planing.** —*n.* **1.** an aeroplane provided with floats, or with a boatlike underpart, enabling it to light upon or ascend from water. **2.** an attachment to an aeroplane enabling it to glide on the water. **3.** a light, high-powered boat, usually with one or more steps in the bottom, designed to plane along the surface of the water at very high speeds. **4.** a horizontal rudder for submerging or elevating a submarine boat. —*v.i.* **5.** to skim over water in the manner of a hydroplane. **6.** to travel in a hydroplane (boat).

hydroponics (hī′drō pŏn′ĭks), *n.* the cultivation of plants by placing the roots in liquid nutrient solutions rather than in soil; soilless growth of plants. [f. HYDRO-¹ + s. L *ponere* place + -ICS] —**hy′dropon′ic,** *adj.*

hydroquinone (hī′drō kwĭ nōn′), *n.* **1.** *Chem.* a white, crystalline compound, $C_6H_4(OH)_2$, formed by the reduction of quinone, used to inhibit autoxidation reactions. **2.** *Pharm.* an antipyretic. Also, **hydroquinol** (hī′drō kwĭn′ōl).

hydros., hydrostatics.

hydroscope (hī′drə skōp′), *n.* an optical apparatus which enables the observer to view objects below the surface of the sea. —**hydroscopic** (hī′drə skŏp′ĭk), *adj.*

hydrosol (hī′drə sŏl′), *n.* *Phys. Chem.* a colloidal suspension in water. [f. HYDRO- + SOL(UTION)]

hydrosome (hī′drə sōm′), *n.* *Zool.* the entire body of a compound hydrozoan. Also, **hydrosoma** (hī′drə sō′mə).

hydrosphere (hī′drə sfĭə′), *n.* the water on the surface of the globe; the water of the oceans.

hydrostat (hī′drō stăt′), *n.* **1.** an electrical device for detecting the presence of water, as from overflow or leakage. **2.** any of various devices for preventing injury to a steam-boiler from a low water level.

hydrostatic (hī′drō stăt′ĭk), *adj.* of or pertaining to hydrostatics. Also, **hy′drostat′ical.** —**hy′drostat′ically,** *adv.*

hydrostatics (hī′drō stăt′ĭks), *n.* the statics of fluids, a branch of science usually confined to the equilibrium and pressure of liquids.

hydrosulphate (hī′drō sŭl′fāt), *n.* *Chem.* a compound between sulphuric acid and an organic base, esp. with alkaloids.

hydrosulphide (hī′drō sŭl′fīd), *n.* *Chem.* **1.** a compound containing the univalent radical –HS. **2.** (loosely) a sulphide.

hydrosulphite (hī′drō sŭl′fīt), *n.* sodium hyposulphite, $Na_2S_2O_4$, used as a bleach.

hydrosulphuric acid (hī′drō sŭl fyŏŏ′rĭk), *Chem.* an aqueous solution of hydrogen sulphide.

hydrosulphurous (hī′drō sŭl′fə rəs), *adj.* hyposulphurous (acid).

hydrotaxis (hī′drō tăk′sĭs), *n.* a movement of organisms towards or away from water.

hydrotherapeutics (hī′drō thĕ′rə pyŏŏ′tĭks), *n.* that branch of therapeutics which deals with the curative use of water. —**hy′drother′apeu′tic,** *adj.*

hydrotherapy (hī′drō thĕ′rə pĭ), *n.* treatment of disease by means of water. —**hydrotherapic** (hī′drō thĭ răp′ĭk), *adj.*

hydrothermal (hī′drō thû′məl), *adj.* *Geol.* **1.** denoting or pertaining to the action of hot, aqueous solutions or gases within or on the surface of the earth. **2.** designating the results of such action.

hydrothorax (hī′drō thō′răks), *n.* *Pathol.* the presence of serous fluid in one or both pleural cavities. —**hydrothoracic** (hī′drō thō răs′ĭk), *adj.*

hydrotropic (hī′drō trŏp′ĭk), *adj.* *Bot.* **1.** turning or tending towards moisture, as growing organs. **2.** taking a particular direction with reference to moisture.

hydrotropism (hī drŏt′rə pĭz′əm), *n.* *Bot., Zool.* **1.** a tropism in response to water. **2.** hydrotropic tendency or growth.

hydrous (hī′drəs), *adj.* **1.** containing water. **2.** *Chem.* containing water or its elements in some kind of union, as in hydrates or in hydroxides.

hydroxide (hī drŏk′sīd), *n.* *Chem.* a compound containing the hydroxyl (OH) group.

hydroxy acid (hī drŏk′sĭ), **1.** organic acid containing both a carboxyl and a hydroxyl group. **2.** one of a class of organic acids containing a hydroxyl group and showing properties of both an alcohol and acid.

hydroxylamine (hī drŏk′sĭl ə mēn′, -ăm′ĭn), *n.* *Chem.* an unstable, weakly basic, crystalline compound, NH_2OH, used as a reducing agent, analytical reagent, and chemical intermediate.

hydroxyl radical or **group** (hī drŏk′sĭl), *Chem.* a univalent radical or group, OH, containing hydrogen and oxygen. Also, **hydroxy group, hydrox′yl.**

hydrozoan (hī′drō zō′ən), *adj.* **1.** pertaining to the *Hydrozoa*, a class of coelenterates that comprises solitary or colonial polyps and free-swimming medusas. —*n.* **2.** a member of the *Hydrozoa*. [f. s. NL *Hydrozōōn* (f. *hydro-*, comb. form of *hydra* (def. 2) + m. Gk *zôion* animal) + -AN]

Hydrus (hī′drəs), *n.* *Astron.* the southern constellation Sea-Serpent.

hyena (hī ē′nə), *n.* any of the nocturnal carnivores of the family *Hyaenidae*, feeding chiefly on carrion, as *Hyaena hyaena*, the **striped laughing hyena,** an African and Asiatic species about the size of a large dog. *H. brunnea*, the **brown hyena** of southern Africa, and *Crocuta crocuta*, the **spotted hyena** of Africa S of the Sahara. Also, **hyaena.** [t. L: m. *hyaena*, t. Gk: m. *hýaina*, der. *hýs* hog; r. ME *hiene*, t. OF]

Striped hyena, *Hyaena hyaena* (Length 3½ ft)

hyeto-, a word element meaning 'rain'. [comb. form of Gk *hyetós*]

hyetograph (hī′ĭ tə grăf′, -gräf′), *n.* *Meteorol.* **1.** an instrument for collecting, measuring, and recording rainfall. **2.** a map or chart showing average rainfall in a particular locality.

Hygeia (hī jē′ə), *n.* *Class. Myth.* the goddess of health, daughter of Aesculapius. [t. Gk, late var. of *Hygíeia*, personification of *hygíeia* health]

hygiene (hī′jēn), *n.* the science which deals with the preservation of health. Also, **hygienics** (hī jē′nĭks). [t. F, t. Gk: m. s. *hygieinós* healthful, sanitary]

hygienic (hī jē′nĭk), *adj.* **1.** sanitary. **2.** pertaining to hygiene. —**hygie′nically,** *adv.* —**Syn. 1.** See **sanitary.**

hygienist (hī′jē nĭst), *n.* an expert in hygiene. Also, **hygeist** (hī′jē ĭst), **hy′geist.**

hygro-, a word element meaning 'wet', 'moist'. Also, before vowels, **hygr-.** [t. Gk, comb. form of *hygrós*]

hygrogram (hī′grə grăm′), *n.* a record of the relative humidity of the atmosphere, as measured by a hygrograph.

hygrograph (hī′grə grăf′, -gräf′), *n.* a self-recording hygrometer.

hygrometer (hī grŏm′ĭ tə), *n.* an instrument for determing the humidity of the atmosphere.

hygrometric (hī′grə mĕt′rĭk), *adj.* pertaining to the hygrometer or hygrometry.

hygrometry (hī grŏm′ĭ trĭ), *n.* the branch of physics that examines the humidity of air and gases.

hygroscope (hī′grə skōp′), *n.* an instrument which indicates the approximate humidity of the air.

hygroscopic (hī′grə skŏp′ĭk), *adj.* absorbing or attracting moisture from the air.

hygrostat (hī′grə stăt′), *n.* an apparatus for keeping the humidity constant; a humidistat.

Hyksos (hĭk′sŏs), *n.pl.* a succession of foreign rulers of Egypt between the 13th and 18th dynasties, *c.* 1680–1580 B.C.

hyla (hī′lə), *n.* a tree toad. [NL, t. Gk: m. *hýlē* wood]

hylo-, a word element meaning 'wood', 'matter'. [t. Gk, comb. form of *hýlē*]

hylozoism (hī′lə zō′ĭz′əm), *n.* the doctrine that matter is inseparable from life, which is a property of matter. [f. HYLO- + s. Gk *zōḗ* life + -ISM] —**hy′lozo′ist,** *n.* —**hy′lozois′tic,** *adj.* —**hy′lozois′tically,** *adv.*

hymen (hī′mĕn), *n.* *Anat.* a fold of mucous membrane partially closing the external orifice of the vagina. [t. Gk: thin skin, membrane]

Hymen (hī′mĕn), *n.* *Gk Myth.* the god of marriage, represented as a young man bearing a bridal torch.

hymeneal (hī′mĕ nē′əl), *adj.* **1.** pertaining to marriage. —*n.* **2.** marriage song.

hymenium (hī mē′nĭ əm), *n.*, *pl.* **-nia** (-nĭ ə). *Bot.* the spore-producing layer in most ascomycete or basidiomycete fungi.

hymenopter (hī′mĭ nŏp′tə), *n.* hymenopteron. —**hy′menop′teran,** *adj.*, *n.*

hymenopteron (hī′mĭ nŏp′tə rən), *n.*, *pl.* **-tera** (-tə rə). a hymenopterous insect.

hymenopterous (hī′mĭ nŏp′tə rəs), *adj.* belonging or pertaining to the *Hymenoptera*, an order of insects having (when winged) four membranous wings, and including the wasps, bees, ants, ichneumon flies, sawflies, etc. [t. Gk: m. *hymenópteros* membrane-winged]

Hymettus (hī mĕt′əs), *n.* a mountain in SE Greece, near Athens: famous for honey produced there. 3370 ft.

hymn (hĭm), *n.* **1.** a song or ode in praise or honour of God, a deity, a nation, etc. —*v.t.* **2.** to praise or celebrate in a hymn; express in a hymn. —*v.i.* **3.** to sing hymns. [t. LL: s. *hymnus*, t. Gk: m. *hýmnos*; r. ME *ymne* (t. OF) and ME *ymyn*, OE *ym(e)n*, t. LL (Eccl.): (m.) s. *ymnus*] —**hymn′like′,** *adj.*

hymnal (hĭm′nəl), *n.* **1.** Also, **hymn′book′.** a book of hymns for use in divine worship. —*adj.* **2.** of or pertaining to hymns.

hymnist (hĭm′nĭst), *n.* a composer of hymns.

hymnody (hĭm′nə dĭ), *n.* **1.** the singing or the composition of hymns or sacred songs. **2.** hymns collectively. [t. ML: m. s. *hymnōdia*, t. Gk: m. *hymnōidía* the singing of a hymn] —**hym′nodist,** *n.*

hymnology (hĭm nŏl′ə jĭ), *n.* **1.** the study of hymns, their history, classification, etc. **2.** the composition of hymns. **3.** hymns collectively. —**hymnologic** (hĭm′-nə lŏj′ĭk), **hym′nolog′ical,** *adj.* —**hymnol′ogist,** *n.*

hyoid (hī′oid), *Anat.* —*adj.* **1.** denoting or pertaining to a U-shaped bone at the root of the tongue in man, or a corresponding bone or collection of bones in animals. See diag. under **mouth.** —*n.* **2.** the hyoid bone, cartilage, arch, ligament, etc. [t. NL: m. s. *hyoïdēs*, t. Gk: m. *hyoeidḗs* shaped like the letter upsilon]

hyoscine (hī′ə sēn′), *n.* **1.** *Chem.* an alkaloid chemically identical with scopolamine, used as a mydriatic, etc. **2.** (*cap.*) a trademark for this substance. [syncopated var. of HYOSCYAMINE]

hyoscyamine (hī′ə sī′ə mēn′, -mĭn), *n. Chem.* a poisonous alkaloid, $C_{17}H_{23}NO_3$, obtained from henbane and other solanaceous plants, used as a sedative, mydriatic, etc. [f. s. L *hyoscyamus* (t. Gk: m. *hyoskýamos* henbane, lit., hog's bean) + -INE[2]]

hyp., **1.** hypotenuse. **2.** hypothesis. **3.** hypothetical.

hyp-, var. of **hypo-,** before most vowels, as in *hypaesthesia.*

hypabyssal (hĭp′ə bĭs′əl), *adj. Geol.* intermediate in texture, as some igneous rocks, between coarse-grained forms and extrusive lava.

hypaesthesia (hĭp′ēs thē′zyə), *n. Pathol.* diminished sense of pain, heat, cold, or touch. Also, *Chiefly U.S.*, **hypesthesia.** —**hypaesthesic** (hĭp′ēs thē′sĭk), *adj.*

hypaethral (hĭ pē′thrəl, hī-), *adj.* open to the sky or having no roof, as a building (used esp. of classical architecture). [f. s. L *hypaethrus* (t. Gk: m. *hýpaithros* under the sky) + -AL[1]]

hypallage (hĭ păl′ə jĭ), *n. Rhet.* a figure of speech in which two elements are reversed.

hypanthium (hĭ păn′thĭ əm), *n., pl.* **-thia** (-thĭ ə). *Bot.* a fleshy, cup-shaped part of some flowers situated above or below the ovary and bearing the sepals, petals, and stamens on its rim.

Hypatia (hī pā′shyə), *n.* died A.D. 415, a wise and beautiful woman of Alexandria, Egypt.

hyper-, **1.** a prefix meaning 'over', and usually implying excess or exaggeration. **2.** *Chem.* the same as **super-,** indicating the highest of a series of compounds: *hyperchloric acid.* The prefix *per-* is now generally used for *hyper-*: *perchloric, permanganic,* etc. [t. Gk, repr. *hypér*, prep., over, above, beyond, as adv. overmuch, beyond measure; akin to SUPER, OVER]

hyperacidity (hī′pə rə sĭd′ĭ tĭ), *n.* excessive acidity as of the gastric juice. —**hyperacid** (hī′pər ăs′ĭd), *adj.*

hyperacusis (hī′pə rə kyōō′sĭs), *n. Pathol.* excessive acuteness of the sense of hearing. [NL, f. Gk: *hyper-* HYPER- + m. *ákousis* hearing]

hyperaemia (hī′pə rē′myə), *n. Pathol.* an increase in the blood in any part of the body. Also, *Chiefly U.S.*, **hyperemia.** [NL. See HYPER-, -EMIA] —**hy′perae′mic,** *adj.*

hyperaesthesia (hī′pə rēs thē′zyə), *n. Pathol.* increased sense of pain, heat, cold, or touch. Also, *Chiefly U.S.*, **hyperesthesia.** —**hyperaesthetic** (hī′pə rēs thĕt′ĭk), *adj.*

hyperalgesia (hī′pə răl jē′zyə), *n. Pathol.* an exaggerated feeling or sense of pain. [NL, f. Gk: *hyper-* HYPER- + s. *álgēsis* sense of pain + *-ia* -IA] —**hy′peralge′sic,** *adj.*

hyperbola (hī pû′bə lə), *n., pl.* **-las.** *Geom.* a curve consisting of two distinct and similar branches, formed by the intersection of a plane with a right circular cone when the plane makes a greater angle with the base than does the generator of the cone. [NL, t. Gk: m. *hyperbolḗ*, lit., a throwing beyond. See HYPERBOLE]

Hyperbola
DBE, GAH, Opposite branches of a hyperbola; F, F, Foci; C, Centre; AB, Transverse axis; A′B′, Conjugate axis; NCP, a diameter

hyperbole (hī pû′bə lĭ), *n. Rhet.* obvious exaggeration, for effect; an extravagant statement not intended to be taken literally. [t. L, t. Gk: a throwing beyond, excess, hyperbole, also a hyperbola]

hyperbolic (hī′pə bŏl′ĭk), *adj.* **1.** having the nature of hyperbole; exaggerated. **2.** using hyperbole, or exaggerating. **3.** of or pertaining to the hyperbola. Also, **hy′perbol′ical.** —**hy′perbol′ically,** *adv.*

hyperbolic functions, *Maths.* six functions which express angles in terms of distances between points on a hyperbola; analogous to the trigonometrical ratios, they are written sinh, cosh, tanh, cosech sech, cotanh. Sinh x is defined as $(e^x - e^{-x})$ and cosh x as $(e^x + e^{-x})$. The remaining four functions are derived from sinh and cosh on the same basis as the trigonometrical ratios.

hyperbolic paraboloid roof, a shell roof of double curvature, generated by straight lines, with all horizontal sections hyperbolas and all diagonal sections parabolas.

hyperbolism (hī pû′bə lĭz′əm), *n.* the use of hyperbole.

hyperbolize (hī pû′bə līz′), *v.,* **-lized, -lizing.** —*v.i.* **1.** to use hyperbole; exaggerate. —*v.t.* **2.** to represent or express with hyperbole or exaggeration. Also, **hyperbolise.**

hyperboloid (hī pû′bə loid′), *n. Maths.* a quadric surface having a finite centre and some of its plane sections hyperbolas.

Hyperborean (hī′pə bô′rĭ ən), *n.* **1.** *Gk Legend.* one of a people supposed to live in a land of perpetual sunshine and plenty beyond the north wind. —*adj.* **2.** of the Hyperboreans. **3.** (*sometimes l.c.*) arctic; frigid. [t. LL: s. *Hyperboreānus*, in L *Hyperboreus*, t. Gk: m. *Hyperbóreos* beyond the north wind. See BOREAS]

hypercritic (hī′pə krĭt′ĭk), *n.* one who is excessively or captiously critical.

hypercritical (hī′pə krĭt′ĭ kl), *adj.* excessively critical; overcritical. —**hy′percrit′ically,** *adv.*

hyperdulia (hī′pə dyōō lī′ə), *n. Rom. Cath. Theol.* the veneration offered to the Virgin Mary as the most exalted of mere creatures. [t. ML. See HYPER-, DULIA]

hyperemesis (hī′pər ĕm′ĭ sĭs), *n. Med.* excessive vomiting, esp. **hyperemesis gravidarum,** excessive vomiting occurring during pregnancy.

hyperemia (hī′pə rē′myə), *n. Chiefly U.S.* hyperaemia. —**hy′pere′mic,** *adj.*

hyperesthesia (hī′pə rēs thē′zyə), *n. Chiefly U.S.* hyperaesthesia. —**hyperesthetic** (hī′pə rēs thĕt′ĭk), *adj.*

hypereutectoid (hī′pə yōō tĕk′toid), *adj. Metall.* **1.** (of steel) containing more carbon than eutectoid steel, i.e. more than 0·9 per cent. **2.** (of any alloy) containing more of the alloying element than the eutectoid element.

hyperextension (hī′pə rĭk stĕn′shən), *n. Physiol.* **1.** the extension of a part beyond the plane of the body, as when the arm is drawn back to its maximum extent. **2.** the state of being so drawn.

hyperfine structure (hī′pə fīn′), *Physics.* **1.** the occurrence of very closely spaced energy levels in an atom, due to coupling between the momentum of the orbital electrons and the spin of the nucleus. **2.** the splitting of certain spectral lines due either to the effect described in def. 1 or to the presence of different isotopes.

hyperfocal distance (hī′pə fō′kl), *Photog.* the distance in front of a camera lens beyond which all objects are in focus, for a given f number.

hyperglycaemia (hī′pə glī sē′myə), *n. Pathol.* an excessive amount of sugar in the blood. Also, *U.S.*, **hyperglycemia.**

hypergolic (hī′pə gŏl′ĭk), *adj.* (of a rocket fuel) igniting spontaneously when mixed with an oxidant.

Hyperion (hī pĭə′rĭ ən), *n. Gk Myth.* **1.** a Titan, a son of Uranus and Gaea: the father of Helios, Selene, and Eos. **2.** (later) Apollo. [t. L, t. Gk]

hyperirritability (hī′pə rĭ′rĭ tə bĭl′ĭ tĭ), *n. Med.* increased irritability.

hyperkinesia (hī′pə kĭ nē′zyə, -kī-), *n. Pathol.* abnormal amount of muscular action; spasm. [NL, f. Gk: *hyper-* HYPER- + s. *kī́nēsis* movement + *-ia* -IA] —**hyperkinetic** (hī′pə kĭ nĕt′ĭk, -kī-), *adj.*

hypermeter (hī pû′mĭ tə), *n. Pros.* a verse or line having one or more syllables at the end in addition to those proper to the metre. —**hypermetric** (hī′pə mĕt′rĭk), **hy′permet′rical,** *adj.*

hypermetropia (hī′pə mĭ trō′pyə), *n. Pathol.* a condition of the eye in which parallel rays are focused behind the retina, distant objects being seen more distinctly than near ones; long-sightedness. [NL, f. Gk: s. *hypérmetros* beyond measure + *-opia* -OPIA]

hypermetropic (hī′pə mĭ trŏp′ĭk), *adj.* pertaining to or affected with hypermetropia; long-sighted.

Hypermnestra (hī′pûm nĕs′trə), *n. Gk Legend.* the one daughter of Danaüs who refused to kill her husband as commanded by her father.

hyperon (hī′pə rŏn′), *n. Physics.* any of a group of elementary particles which have short lives and greater mass than a neutron.

hyperopia (hī′pə rō′pyə), *n.* hypermetropia. —**hyperopic** (hī′pə rŏp′ĭk), *adj.*

hyperosmia (hī′pə rŏz′mĭ ə), *n. Med.* increased acuteness in the sense of smell.

hyperostosis (hī′pə rŏs tō′sĭs), *n., pl.* **-ses** (-sēz). *Anat., Pathol.* **1.** an increase or outgrowth of bony tissue. **2.** an overgrowth of bone.

hyperparasite (hī′pə păr′ə sīt′), *n. Biol.* an organism which lives parasitically in or on another parasite.

hyperphysical (hī′pə fĭz′ĭ kl), *adj.* above or beyond the physical; immaterial; supernatural.

hyperpiesia (hī′pə pī ē′zyə), *n. Pathol.* unusually high blood pressure. [NL, f. Gk: *hyper-* HYPER- + s. *píesis* pressure + *-ia* -IA]

hyperpituitarism (hī′pə pĭ tyo͞o′ĭ tə rĭz′əm), *n. Pathol.* **1.** overactivity of the pituitary gland. **2.** the resultant condition, i.e., gigantism or acromegaly.

hyperplasia (hī′pə plăz′yə), *n.* **1.** *Pathol., Bot.* abnormal multiplication of cells. **2.** *Pathol.* enlargement of a part due to numerical increase of its cells. —**hyperplasic** (hī′pə plăs′ĭk), **hy′perplas′tic,** *adj.*

hyperploid (hī′pə ploid′), *adj. Biol.* pertaining to a chromosome number in excess of the diploid but not a multiple of it. [f. HYPER- + (DI)PLOID]

hyperpnoea (hī′pəp nē′ə, hī′pə nē′ə), *n. Pathol.* increased intake and depth of respiration. Also, *Chiefly U.S.,* **hyperpnea.** [NL, f. Gk: *hyper-* HYPER- + m. *pnoiē* breathing]

hyperpyrexia (hī′pə pī rĕk′syə), *n. Pathol.* an abnormally high fever. —**hyperpyretic** (hī′pə pī rĕt′ĭk), **hy′perpyrex′ial,** *adj.*

hypersensitive (hī′pə sĕn′sĭ tĭv), *adj.* **1.** excessively sensitive. **2.** *Pathol.* allergic to a substance to which a normal individual does not react. —**hy′persen′sitiveness, hy′persen′sitiv′ity,** *n.*

hypersonic (hī′pə sŏn′ĭk), *adj.* describing a velocity in excess of mach 5. See **mach number.**

hyperspace (hī′pə spās′), *n. Maths.* a Euclidean space of more than three dimensions.

hypersthene (hī′pə sthēn′), *n.* a common mineral of the pyroxene group, iron magnesium silicate, occurring in green to black masses as an important constituent of basic igneous rocks. [f. HYPER- + m. s. Gk *sthénos* strength (with reference to frangibility)] —**hypersthenic** (hī′pə sthĕn′ĭk), *adj.*

hypertension (hī′pə tĕn′shən), *n. Pathol.* **1.** elevation of the blood pressure, especially the diastolic pressure. **2.** an arterial disease of which this is the outstanding sign.

hyperthyroidism (hī′pə thī′roi dĭz′əm), *n. Pathol.* **1.** overactivity of the thyroid gland. **2.** a pathological condition, consisting of a complex of symptoms, produced by this. —**hy′perthy′roid,** *n.*

hypertonic (hī′pə tŏn′ĭk), *adj.* **1.** *Physiol.* possessing too much tone. **2.** *Chem.* denoting a solution of higher osmotic pressure than another solution with which it is compared.

hypertrophy (hī pû′trə fĭ), *n., pl.* **-phies,** *v.,* **-phied, -phying.** —*n.* **1.** *Pathol., Bot.* enlargement of a part or organ; excessive growth. **2.** excessive growth or accumulation of any kind. —*v.t., v.i.* **3.** to affect with or undergo hypertrophy. —**hypertrophic** (hī′pə trŏf′ĭk), *adj.*

hyperventilation (hī′pə vĕn′tĭ lā′shən), *n. Med.* abnormally increased respiration.

hypesthesia (hĭp′ēs thē′zyə), *n. Chiefly U.S.* hypaesthesia. —**hypesthesic** (hĭp′ēs thē′sĭk), *adj.*

hypethral (hĭ pē′thrəl, hī-), *adj. Chiefly U.S.* hypaethral.

hypha (hī′fə), *n., pl.* **-phae** (-fē). *Bot.* (in fungi) one of the threadlike elements of the mycelium. [NL, t. Gk: m. *hyphḗ* web] —**hy′phal,** *adj.*

hyphen (hī′fən), *n.* **1.** a short stroke (-) used to connect the parts of a compound word or the parts of a word divided for any purpose. —*v.t.* **2.** hyphenate. [t. LL, t. Gk: name of sign, special use of *hyphén,* adv., prop. phrase *hyph' hén* under one, together]

hyphenate (hī′fə nāt′), *v.,* **-nated, -nating,** *adj.* —*v.t.* **1.** to join by a hyphen. **2.** to write with a hyphen. —*adj.* **3.** hyphenated. —**hy′phena′tion,** *n.*

hyphenize (hī′fə nīz′), *v.t.,* **-nized, -nizing.** hyphenate. Also, **hyphenise.**

hypno-, a word element meaning 'sleep' or 'hypnosis', as in *hypnology.* Also, before vowels (usually), **hypn-.** [t. Gk, comb. form of *hýpnos* sleep]

hypnoanalysis (hĭp′nō ə năl′ĭ sĭs), *n. Psychoanal.* a method employed by some psychoanalysts who attempt to secure analytic data, free associations, and early emotional reactions while the patient is under hypnosis.

hypnogenesis (hĭp′nō jĕn′ĭ sĭs), *n. Med.* the inducing of a hypnotic state.

hypnoidal (hĭp noi′dl), *adj. Psychol.* in a state which resembles that of mild hypnosis but is (usually) not induced hypnotically. Also, **hyp′noid.**

hypnology (hĭp nŏl′ə jĭ), *n.* the science dealing with the phenomena of sleep or hypnosis. —**hypnologic** (hĭp′nə lŏj′ĭk), **hyp′nolog′ical,** *adj.* —**hypnol′ogist,** *n.*

hypnosis (hĭp nō′sĭs), *n., pl.* **-ses** (-sēz). **1.** *Psychol.* a condition or state, allied to normal sleep, which can be artificially produced and is characterized by marked susceptibility to suggestions, more or less loss of sensation, etc. **2.** the production of sleep. **3.** a sleepy condition. **4.** hypnotism. [NL, der. Gk *hypnoûn* put to sleep]

hypnotherapy (hĭp′nō thĕ′rə pĭ), *n.* treatment of disease by means of hypnotism. —**hypnotherapeutic** (hĭp′nō thĕ′rə pyo͞o′tĭk), *adj.*

hypnotic (hĭp nŏt′ĭk), *adj.* **1.** pertaining to hypnosis or hypnotism. **2.** susceptible to hypnotism, as a person. **3.** hypnotized. **4.** inducing sleep. —*n.* **5.** an agent or drug that produces sleep; a sedative. **6.** one subject to hypnotic influence. **7.** a person under the influence of hypnotism. [t. LL: s. *hypnōticus,* t. Gk: m. *hypnōtikós* inclined to sleep] —**hypnot′ically,** *adv.*

hypnotism (hĭp′nə tĭz′əm), *n.* **1.** the science dealing with the induction of hypnosis. **2.** the induction of hypnosis. **3.** hypnosis.

hypnotist (hĭp′nə tĭst), *n.* one who hypnotizes.

hypnotize (hĭp′nə tīz′), *v.t.,* **-tized, -tizing.** to put in the hypnotic state. Also, **hyp′notise′.** —**hyp′notiz′able,** *adj.* —**hyp′notiza′tion,** *n.* —**hyp′notiz′er,** *n.*

hypo[1] (hī′pō), *n. Chem.* sodium thiosulphate, $Na_2S_2O_3 \cdot 5H_2O$, a photographic fixing agent. [short for HYPOSULPHITE]

hypo[2] (hī′pō), *n. Slang.* a hypodermic needle or injection. [short for HYPODERMIC]

hypo-, **1.** a prefix meaning 'under', either in place or in degree ('less', 'less than'). **2.** *Chem.* a prefix applied to the inorganic acids (as *hypochlorous acid*) and to their salts (as *potassium hypochlorite*) to indicate a low valency state for the designated element. Also, **hyp-.** [t. Gk, repr. *hypó,* prep. and adv., under; akin to SUB-]

hypoacidity (hī′pō ə sĭd′ĭ tĭ), *n.* acidity in a lesser degree than is usual or normal, as of the gastric juice.

hypoblast (hī′pə blăst′), *n. Embryol.* the inner layer of a gastrula, consisting of endoblast, or endoblast and mesoblast. —**hy′poblas′tic,** *adj.*

hypocaust (hī′pə kôst′), *n.* a hollow space or system of flues in the floor or walls of a Roman building or room, which received and distributed the heat from a furnace. [t. L: s. *hypocaustum,* t. Gk: m. *hypókauston* room heated from below]

hypochlorite (hī′pə klô′rīt), *n. Chem.* a salt or ester of hypochlorous acid.

hypochlorous acid (hī′pə klô′rəs), *Chem.* an acid, $HClO$, whose solutions have strong bleaching properties.

hypochondria (hī′pə kŏn′drĭ ə), *n.* **1.** Also, **hypochondriasis** (hī′pō kŏn drī′ə sĭs). *Psychol.* a morbid condition characterized by depressed spirits and fancies of ill health, referable to the physical condition of the body or one of its parts. **2.** (*orig. as pl.*) the parts of the body under the cartilage of the breastbone and above the navel. [t. LL: pl., the abdomen, t. Gk: m. *hypochóndria* (neut. pl.) def. 2; orig. thought to be the seat of melancholy]

hypochondriac (hī′pə kŏn′drĭ ăk′), *adj.* Also, **hypochondriacal** (hī′pō kŏn drī′ə kl). **1.** pertaining to or suffering from hypochondria or morbid depression. **2.** of or pertaining to the hypochondria (def. 2): *the hypochondriac regions.* —*n.* **3.** a person suffering from or subject to hypochondria. —**hy′pochondri′acally,** *adv.*

hypochondrium (hī′pə kŏn′drĭ əm), *n., pl.* **-dria** (-drĭ ə). *Anat., Zool.* **1.** either of two regions of the human abdomen, situated on opposite sides (left and right) of the epigastrium, above the lumbar regions. **2.** a corresponding region in lower animals. [NL]

hypocoristic (hī′pə kô rĭs′tĭk), *adj.* endearing, as a pet name; diminutive; euphemistic. [t. Gk: m. s. *hypokoristikós*] —**hy′pocoris′tically,** *adv.* —**hypocorism** (hĭ pŏk′ə rĭz′əm), *n.*

hypocotyl (hī′pə kŏt′ĭl), *n. Bot.* (in the embryo of a plant) that part of the stem below cotyledons. [f. HYPO- + COTYL(EDON)] —**hy′pocot′ylous,** *adj.*

P
C
H
R

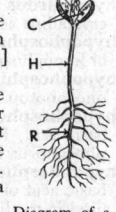

Diagram of a seedling of a bean
H, Hypocotyl; C, Cotyledons; P, Plumule; R, Roots

hypocrisy (hĭ pŏk′rə sĭ), *n., pl.* **-sies.** **1.** the act of pretending to have a character or beliefs, principles, etc., that one does not possess. **2.** pretence of virtue or piety; false goodness. [ME *ypocrisie,* t. OF, t. LL: m. s. *hypocrisis,* t. Gk: m. *hypókrisis* acting of a part, pretence] —**Syn. 1.** See **deceit.**

hypocrite (hĭp′ə krĭt), *n.* one given to hypocrisy; one who feigns virtue or piety; a pretender. [ME *ypocrite,* t. OF, t. LL: m. s. *hypocrita,* t. Gk: m. *hypokritḗs* actor, pretender, hypocrite] —**hyp′ocrit′ical,** *adj.* —**hyp′ocrit′ically,** *adv.*

hypocycloid (hī′pə sī′kloid), *n. Geom.* a curve generated by the motion of a point on the circumference of a circle which rolls internally, without slipping, on a given circle. —**hy′pocycloi′dal,** *adj.*

hypoderm (hī′pə dûm′), *n.* **1.** *Zool.* the epidermis of an arthropod, situated beneath the cuticle. **2.** *Bot.* hypodermis. —**hy′poder′mal,** *adj.*

H, Hypocycloid traced by a point P; C′, Centre of moving circle; C, Centre of fixed circle

hypodermic (hī′pə dû′mĭk), *adj.* **1.** characterized by the introduction of medical remedies under the skin: *hypodermic injection.* **2.** introduced under the skin: *a hypodermic needle.* **3.** pertaining to parts under the skin. **4.** lying under the skin, as tissue. —*n.* **5.** a hypodermic remedy. **6.** a hypodermic injection. **7.** the administration of drugs into subcutaneous body tissues. **8.** a hypodermic syringe. —**hy′poder′mically,** *adv.*

hypodermic needle, a hollow needle used to inject solutions subcutaneously.

hypodermic syringe, a small glass piston or barrel syringe having a detachable hollow needle used to inject solutions subcutaneously; now also made of other materials, as plastics.

hypodermis (hī′pə dû′mĭs), *n.* **1.** *Zool.* the surface epithelium of an invertebrate when covered over by the non-cellular secretion that it produces. **2.** *Bot.* a tissue or layer of cells beneath the epidermis. [NL]

hypo-eutectoid (hī′pō yōō tĕk′toid), *adj.* *Metall.* (of steel) containing less carbon than eutectoid steel, i.e. less than 0·9 per cent.

hypogastric (hī′pə găs′trĭk), *adj.* *Anat.* **1.** situated below the stomach. **2.** of or pertaining to the hypogastrium.

hypogastrium (hī′pə găs′trĭ əm), *n.*, *pl.* **-tria** (-trĭ ə). *Anat.* **1.** the lower part of the abdomen. **2.** the region between the right and left iliac regions. [NL, t. Gk: m. *hypogástrion,* prop. neut. of *hypogástrios* abdominal]

hypogeal (hī′pə jē′əl), *adj.* underground; subterranean. [f. s. L *hypogēus* (t. Gk: m. *hypógeios* underground) + -AL[1]]

hypogene (hī′pə jēn′), *adj.* *Geol.* formed beneath the earth's surface, as granite (opposed to *epigene*). [f. HYPO- + *-gene* (var. of -GEN)]

hypogenous (hī pŏj′ĭ nəs), *adj.* *Bot.* growing beneath, or on the undersurface, as fungi on leaves.

hypogeous (hī′pə jē′əs, hĭp′ə-), *adj.* **1.** underground; subterranean. **2.** *Bot.* growing or remaining underground. [t. L: m. *hypogēus,* t. Gk: m. *hypógeios*]

hypogeum (hī′pə jē′əm), *n.*, *pl.* **-gea** (-jē′ə). *Anc. Archit.* **1.** the underground part of a building. **2.** an underground structure or burial chamber; an artificial cave. [t. L, t. Gk: m. *hypógeion,* neut. of *hypógeios* underground]

hypoglossal (hī′pə glŏs′əl), *Anat., Zool.* —*adj.* situated under the tongue wholly or in part. [f. HYPO- + s. Gk *glôssa* tongue + -AL[1]]

hypoglossal nerve, either of the last pair of cranial nerves which gives rise to the movements of the tongue; twelfth cranial nerve.

hypoglycaemia (hī′pō glī sē′myə), *n.* *Med.* a decreased sugar level in the blood. Also, *U.S.*, **hypoglycemia.**

hypognathous (hī pŏg′nə thəs), *adj.* *Zool.* **1.** having a protruding lower jaw. **2.** having downwardly directed mouthparts.

hypogynous (hī pŏj′ĭ nəs), *adj.* *Bot.* **1.** situated on the receptacle beneath the pistil, as stamens, etc. **2.** having stamens, etc., so arranged. —**hypog′yny,** *n.*

hyponasty (hī′pə năs′tĭ), *n.* *Bot.* increased growth along the lower surface of an organ or part, causing it to bend upwards. [f. HYPO- + s. Gk *nastós* pressed close, compact + -Y[3]] —**hy′ponas′tic,** *adj.*

hyponitrite (hī′pə nī′trīt), *n.* *Chem.* a salt or ester of hyponitrous acid.

hyponitrous acid (hī′pə nī′trəs), *Chem.* an unstable crystalline acid, $H_2N_2O_2$.

hypophosphate (hī′pə fŏs′fāt), *n.* *Chem.* a salt or ester of hypophosphoric acid.

hypophosphite (hī′pə fŏs′fīt), *n.* *Chem.* a salt of hypophosphorous acid.

hypophosphoric acid (hī′pə fŏs fŏ′rĭk), *Chem.* a tetrabasic acid, $H_4P_2O_6$, produced by the slow oxidation of phosphorus in moist air.

hypophosphorous acid (hī′pə fŏs′fə rəs), *Chem.* a monobasic acid of phosphorus, H_3PO_2, having salts which are used in medicine.

hypophysis (hī pŏf′ĭ sĭs), *n.*, *pl.* **-ses** (-sēz′). *Anat.* the pituitary gland of the brain. [NL, t. Gk: undergrowth, process]

hypopituitarism (hī′pə pĭ tyōō′ĭ tə rĭz′əm), *n.* *Pathol.* **1.** abnormally diminished activity of the pituitary gland. **2.** the pathological condition produced by this, resulting in obesity, retention of adolescent traits, and, in extreme cases, dwarfism.

hypoplasia (hī′pō plăz′yə), *n.* **1.** *Pathol., Bot.* abnormal deficiency of cells or structural elements. **2.** *Pathol.* an underdeveloped condition in which an organ or structure remains immature or subnormal in size. [f. HYPO- + -PLASIA]

hypopyon (hī pō′pĭ ŏn′), *n.* *Pathol.* an effusion of pus into the anterior chamber of the eye, or that cavity which contains the aqueous humour. [NL, t. Gk: ulcer, prop. neut. of *hypópyos* tending to suppuration]

hypostasis (hī pŏs′tə sĭs), *n.*, *pl.* **-ses** (-sēz′). **1.** *Metaphys.* **a.** that which stands under and supports; foundation. **b.** the underlying or essential part of anything as distinguished from attributes; substance, essence, or essential principle. **2.** *Theol.* **a.** one of the three real and distinct subsistences in the one undivided substance or essence of God. **b.** a person of the Trinity. **c.** the one personality of Christ in which His two natures, human and divine, are united. **3.** *Med.* the accumulation of blood or solids of a fluid by gravity due to poor circulation or standing. [t. LL, t. Gk: substance, nature, essence, also sediment]

hypostasize (hī pŏs′tə sīz′), *v.t.*, **-sized, -sizing.** hypostatize. Also, **hypostasise.**

hypostatic (hī′pə stăt′ĭk), *adj.* **1.** of or pertaining to a hypostasis; elementary. **2.** *Theol.* pertaining to or constituting a distinct personal being or subsistence. **3.** *Med.* arising from downward pressure. **4.** *Genetics.* (of nonallelic genes) recessive. Also, **hy′postat′ical.** [t. Gk: m. s. *hypostatikós* pertaining to substance] —**hy′postat′ically,** *adv.*

hypostatize (hī pŏs′tə tīz′), *v.t.*, **-tized, -tizing.** to treat or regard as a distinct substance or reality. Also, **hypostatise.** —**hypos′tatiza′tion,** *n.*

hypostyle (hī′pō stīl′), *Archit.* —*adj.* **1.** having many columns carrying the roof or ceiling: *a hypostyle hall.* —*n.* **2.** a hypostyle structure. [t. Gk: m. s. *hypóstȳlos* resting on pillars]

hyposulphite (hī′pə sŭl′fīt), *n.* *Chem.* **1.** a salt of hyposulphurous acid. **2.** sodium thiosulphate, antichlor, or hypo ($Na_2S_2O_3.5H_2O$), a bleach and photographic fixing agent.

hyposulphurous acid (hī′pə sŭl′fə rəs), an acid, $H_2S_2O_4$ next in a series below sulphurous acid.

hypotaxis (hī′pō tăk′sĭs), *n.* *Gram.* dependent relation or construction, as of clauses. [NL, t. Gk: subjection] —**hy′potac′tic,** *adj.*

hypotension (hī′pō tĕn′shən), *n.* *Pathol.* abnormally low blood pressure.

hypotenuse (hī pŏt′ĭ nyōōz′), *n.* *Geom.* the side of a right-angled triangle opposite the right angle. Also, *Obs.*, **hypothenuse.** [t. LL: m. s. *hypotēnūsa,* t. Gk: m. *hypoteínousa,* ppr. fem., subtending]

Hypotenuse of a right-angled triangle

hypothalamus (hī′pə thăl′ə məs), *n.* *Anat.* the portion of the diencephalon concerned with emotional expression and visceral responses.

hypothec (hī pŏth′ĭk), *n.* *Rom. and Scot. Law.* a security in favour of a creditor over the property of his debtor without possession of it. It may be created by agreement or by operation of law. [t. LL: s. *hypothēca,* t. Gk: m. *hypothḗkē* deposit, pledge]

hypothecary (hī pŏth′ĭ kə rĭ), *adj.* **1.** of or pertaining to a hypothec. **2.** created or secured by a hypothec.

hypothecate (hī pŏth′ĭ kāt′), *v.t.*, **-cated, -cating.** **1.** to pledge to a creditor as security without delivering over; mortgage. **2.** to put in pledge by delivery, as stocks given as security for a loan. [t. ML: m. s. *hypothēcātus,* pp., of *hypothēcāre,* der. LL *hypothēca* HYPOTHEC] —**hypoth′eca′tion,** *n.* —**hypoth′eca′tor,** *n.*

hypothenuse (hī pŏth′ĭ nyōōz′), *n.* *Obs.* hypotenuse.

hypothermia (hī′pō thû′myə), *n.* **1.** subnormal body temperature. **2.** the artificial reduction of body temperature to slow metabolic processes: usually to facilitate heart surgery. [f. HYPO- + Gk *thérm(ē)* heat + -IA] —**hy′pother′mal,** *adj.*

hypothesis (hī pŏth′ĭ sĭs), *n.*, *pl.* **-ses** (-sēz′). **1.** a proposition (or set of propositions) proposed as an explanation for the occurrence of some specified group of phenomena, either asserted merely as a provisional conjecture to guide investigation (a **working hypothesis**), or accepted as highly probable in the light of established facts. **2.** a proposition assumed as a premise in an argument. **3.** the antecedent of a conditional proposition. **4.** a mere assumption or guess. [NL, t. Gk: supposition, basis] —**Syn. 1.** See **theory.**

hypothesize (hī pŏth′ĭ sīz′), *v.*, **-sized, -sizing.** —*v.i.* **1.** to form a hypothesis. —*v.t.* **2.** to assume by hypothesis. Also, **hypothesise.**

hypothetical (hī′pə thĕt′ĭ kl), *adj.* **1.** assumed by hypothesis; supposed: *a hypothetical case.* **2.** pertaining to, involving, or of the nature of hypothesis: *hypothetical reasoning.* **3.** given to making hypotheses: *a hypothetical person.* **4.** *Logic.* **a.** conditional; characterizing propositions having the form *if A, then B.* **b.** (of a syllogism) having a premise which is a hypothetical proposition. **c.** (of a proposition) not well supported by evidence, whose status is therefore highly conjectural. Also, **hy'pothet'ic.** [f. *hypothetic* (t. Gk: m. s. *hypothetikós* supposed) + -AL[1]] —**hy'pothet'ically,** *adv.*

hypothyroidism (hī'pō thī'roi dĭz'əm), *n. Pathol.* **1.** abnormally diminished activity of the thyroid gland. **2.** the condition produced by a deficiency of thyroid secretion, resulting in goitre, myxoedema, and, in children, cretinism.

hypotonic (hī'pə tŏn'ĭk), *adj.* **1.** *Physiol.* under the normal tone. **2.** *Chem.* denoting a solution of lower osmotic pressure than one with which it is compared.

hypoxanthine (hī'pə zăn'thēn, -thĭn), *n. Chem.* a crystalline compound, $C_5H_4N_4O$, related to xanthine and found in animal and vegetable tissues. —**hy'poxan'thic,** *adj.*

hypoxia (hī pŏk'sĭ ə), *n. Pathol.* sickness due to acute lack of oxygen in the blood and tissues of the body.

hypsography (hĭp sŏg'rə fĭ), *n.* a branch of geography which deals with the measurement and mapping of areas of the earth's surface with reference to sea-level. —**hypsographic** (hĭp'sə grăf'ĭk), **hyp'sograph'ical,** *adj.*

hypsometer (hĭp sŏm'ĭ tə), *n.* **1.** an instrument for measuring altitude by determining the boiling point of a liquid at the given height. **2.** (sometimes) the boiler of a hypsometer. [f. Gk *hýpso(s)* height + -METER[1]]

hypsometry (hip sŏm'ĭ trĭ), *n.* vertical control in mapping; the establishment of elevations or altitudes. —**hypsometric** (hĭp'sə mĕt'rĭk), **hyp'somet'rical,** *adj.* —**hyp'somet'rically,** *adv.*

hyracoid (hī'rə koid'), *adj.* belonging or pertaining to the order *Hyracoidea*, that comprises the hyraxes. [f. s. NL *hyrax* HYRAX + -OID] —**hyracoidean** (hī'rə koi'dĭ ən), *adj., n.*

hyrax (hī'răks), *n., pl.* **hyraxes, hyraces** (hī'rə sēz'). any of a number of small, timid mammals of SW Asia and Africa, superficially resembling rodents but having tiny hoofs and other distinctive characteristics. They constitute a separate order, the *Hyracoidea*, the **rock hyrax,** genus *Procavia* (or *Hyrax*), living mostly in rocky places, the closely similar **tree hyrax** of Africa, genus *Dendrohyrax*, being arboreal. [NL, t. Gk: shrewmouse]

Hyrcania (hû kā'nyə), *n.* an ancient province of the Persian empire, SE of the Caspian Sea. —**Hyrca'nian,** *adj.*

hyson (hī'sən), *n.* a Chinese green tea, the early crop and the inferior leaves being called **young hyson** and **hyson skin** respectively. [t. Chinese (Cantonese): m. *hei-ch'un*, lit., blooming spring (Mandarin *hsi-ch'un*)]

hyssop (hĭs'əp), *n.* **1.** an aromatic labiate herb, *Hyssopus officinalis*, with blue flowers. **2.** (in the Bible and derived use) a plant, perhaps the caper, whose twigs were used in ceremonial sprinkling. [t. L: s. *hyssōpus*, t. Gk: m. *hýssōpos* kind of plant; r. OE *ysope*]

hyster-, var. of **hystero-,** before vowels, as in *hysterectomy.*

hysterectomy (hĭs'tə rĕk'tə mĭ), *n., pl.* **-mies.** *Surg.* the excision of the uterus.

hysteresis (hĭs'tə rē'sĭs), *n. Physics.* the extent to which the strain in a material reflects the stress to which it has been subjected in the past as well as its present stress; the time-lag exhibited by a material in reacting to the stress to which it is subjected, esp. with reference to magnetic forces applied to a ferromagnetic material. [NL, t. Gk: deficiency] —**hysteretic** (hĭs'tə rĕt'ĭk), *adj.*

hysteresis loop, loop[1] (def. 7b).

hysteresis loss, *Physics.* the loss of energy, as heat, by a system exhibiting hysteresis.

hysteria (hĭs tĭə'rĭ ə), *n.* **1.** morbid or senseless emotionalism; emotional frenzy. **2.** a psychoneurotic disorder characterized by violent emotional outbreaks, perversion of sensory and motor functions, and various morbid effects due to autosuggestion. [f. HYSTER(IC)- + -IA]

hysteric (hĭs tĕ'rĭk), *n.* **1.** (*usually pl.*) a fit of hysteria; hysteria. **2.** a person subject to hysteria. —*adj.* **3.** hysterical.

hysterical (hĭs tĕ'rĭ kl), *adj.* **1.** resembling or suggesting hysteria; emotionally disordered. **2.** of, pertaining to, or characteristic of hysteria: *Her hysterical behaviour at the funeral revealed how much she really loved him.* **3.** suffering from or subject to hysteria. [f. s. L *hystericus* (t. Gk: m. *hysterikós* suffering in the uterus) + -AL[1]] —**hyster'ically,** *adv.*

hysterical fever, an increase in temperature without obvious cause other than hysteria.

hystero-, a word element meaning 'uterus', as in *hysterotomy.* Also, **hyster-.** [t. Gk, comb. form of *hystéra*]

hysteroid (hĭs'tə roid'), *adj.* resembling hysteria. Also, **hys'teroi'dal.** [f. HYSTER- + -OID]

hysteron proteron (hĭs'tə rŏn' prŏt'ə rŏn'), **1.** *Logic.* an attempted proof of a proposition which is based on premises that can be established only with the help of that proposition. This involves a fallacy, since it inverts the true order of logical dependence. **2.** *Rhet.* a figure of speech in which the logical order of two elements in discourse is reversed. [t. LL, t. Gk: *hýsteron* (neut. of *hýsteros* latter), *próteron* (neut. of *próteros* being before, sooner)]

hysterotomy (hĭs'tə rŏt'ə mĭ), *n., pl.* **-mies.** *Surg.* the operation of cutting into the uterus, as used in Caesarean section.

hystricomorphic (hĭs'trĭ kō môr'fĭk), *adj.* belonging or pertaining to the *Hystricomorpha*, the suborder of rodents that includes the porcupines, chinchilla, agouti, coypu, guineapig, etc. [f. *hystrico-* (comb. form of L *hystrix* porcupine, t. Gk) + -MORPHIC]

hyzone (hī'zon), *n. Chem.* triatomic hydrogen, H_3.

Hz, *Physics.* hertz.

I

I[1], i (ī), *n., pl.* **I's** or **Is, i's** or **is.** **1.** the ninth letter and third vowel of the English alphabet. **2.** the ninth in any series. **3.** any sound represented by the letter I. **4.** an I-shaped object. **5.** Roman numeral for one. See **Roman numerals.**

I[2] (ī), *pron., nom.* **I,** *poss.* **my** or **mine,** *obj.* **me;** *pl. nom.* **we,** *poss.* **ours** or **our,** *obj.* **us;** *n., pl.* **I's.** —*pron.* **1.** the subject form of the singular pronoun of the first person, used by a speaker of himself. —*n.* **2.** the pronoun *I* used as a noun: *the 'I' in this novel is John.* **3.** *Metaphys.* the ego. [ME *ik, ich, i*, OE *ic, ih*, c. G *ich*; akin to L *ego*, Gk *egō*]

I, **1.** *Chem.* iodine. **2.** *Elect.* current.

I., **1.** Independent. **2.** Island; Islands. **3.** Isle; Isles.

i, *Maths.* the imaginary number $\sqrt{-1}$; the square root of minus one.

i., **1.** intransitive. **2.** island.

-i-, an ending for the first element of many compounds, originally found in the combining form of many Latin words, but often used in English as a connective irrespective of etymology, as in *cuneiform, Frenchify*, etc.

-ia, a suffix of nouns, esp. having restricted application in various fields, thus, in medicine (disease: *malaria*), in geography (countries: *Rumania*), in botany (genera: *Wisteria*), in names of Roman feasts (*Lupercalia*), in Latin or Latinizing plurals (*Reptilia, bacteria*), and in collectives (*insignia, militia*). [t. L or Gk, both f. *-i-* orig. or connective vowel + *-a* (fem. sing. nom. ending) or *-a* (neut. pl. nom. ending)]

Ia, Iowa.

IAA, International Academy of Astronautics.

IAEA, International Atomic Energy Agency.

IAF, International Astronautical Federation.

-ial, var. of **-al[1],** as in *judicial, imperial.* [t. L: s. *-iālis, -iāle*, adj. suffix, f. *-i-*, orig. or connective vowel + *ālis, -āle* -AL]

iamb (ī'ăm, ī'ămb), *n. Pros.* a metrical foot of two syllables, a short followed by a long, or an unaccented by an accented (˘ ¯), as in *Come live with me and be my love.* [t. L: s. *iambus* an iambic verse or poem, t. Gk: m. *iambos*]

iambic (ī ăm'bĭk), *adj.* **1.** *Pros.* **a.** pertaining to the iamb. **b.** consisting of or employing an iamb or iambs. **2.** *Gk Lit.* of a kind of satirical poetry written in iambs. —*n.* **3.** *Pros.* **a.** an iamb. **b.** (*usually pl.*) a verse or poem consisting of iambs. **4.** a satirical poem in this metre. —**iam'bically,** *adv.*

iambus (ī ăm'bəs), *n., pl.* **-bi** (-bī), **-buses.** iamb.

-ian, var. of **-an,** as in *amphibian, Grecian.* [t. L: s. *-iānus*, f. *-i-* orig. or connective vowel + *-ānus* -AN]

-iana. See **-ian, -ana.**

Iaşi (*Rum.* yȧshy), *n.* Rumanian name of **Jassy.**

-iasis, a suffix of nouns denoting state or condition, esp. a morbid condition or a form of disease, as in *ankylostomiasis.* [NL, t. Gk: f. *-i-* orig. or connective vowel (see -I-) + *-āsis* -ASIS]

iatric (ī ăt′rĭk), *adj.* pertaining to a physician or to medicine. Also, **iat′rical.** [t. Gk: s. *iātrikós*]

iatrochemistry (ī ăt′rō kĕm′ĭs trĭ), *n.* medieval medical chemistry.

iatrogenic (ī ăt′rō jĕn′ĭk), *adj.* (of an illness, real or imagined) caused or produced by diagnosis or treatment by a physician.

-iatry, a combining form meaning 'medical care', as in *psychiatry.* [t. Gk: m. s. *iātreía* healing]

ib., ibidem.

Ibadan (ĭ băd′ən), *n.* the capital of Western Nigeria, in the central part. 600,000 (est. 1963).

Ibagué (*Sp.* ē bȧ gĕ′), *n.* a town in W central Colombia. 163,661 (1964).

Ibáñez (*Sp.* ē bȧ′nyĕth), *n.* See **Blasco Ibáñez.**

Ibaraki (ē′bə rä′kĭ), *n.* a town in Japan, in S Honshu island. 115,136 (1965).

I-beam (ī′bēm′), *n.* a beam in the shape of the capital I.

Iberia (ī bĭə′rĭ ə), *n.* **1.** Also, **Iberian Peninsula.** a peninsula in SW Europe, comprising Spain and Portugal. **2.** an ancient region S of the Caucasus: modern Georgia. [t. L, t. Gk, ancient Greek name of Spain]

Iberian (ī bĭə′rĭ ən), *adj.* **1.** of or pertaining to Iberia in Europe or its inhabitants. **2.** *Ethnol.* denoting or pertaining to a dark dolichocephalic race inhabiting parts of southern Europe and northern Africa, comprising the ancient Iberians, some of the ancient Britons, and other peoples, and their descendants. **3.** of or pertaining to ancient Iberia in Asia or its inhabitants. *—n.* **4.** one of the ancient inhabitants of Iberia in Europe, from whom the Basques are supposed to be descended. **5.** the language of the ancient Iberians of Europe, from which Basque developed. **6.** one of the ancient inhabitants of Iberia in Asia.

Iberville, d' (*Fr.* dē bĕr vēl′), *n.* **Pierre le Moyne** (*Fr.* pyĕr lə mwȧn′), **Sieur,** 1661–1706, French naval officer, born in Canada: founder of first Louisiana settlement (1699).

ibex (ī′bĕks), *n., pl.* **ibexes, ibices** (ī′bĭ sēz′), (*esp. collectively*) **ibex.** any of various Old World wild goats with large recurved horns, esp. *Capra ibex*, of the Alps and Apennines. [t. L]

Ibex, *Capra ibex sibirica* (About 3 ft 4 in. high at the shoulder, 5 ft long, horns 4 ft 8 in.)

ibid., ibidem.

ibidem (ĭ bī′dĕm), *adv. Latin.* in the same book, chapter, page, etc.

ibis (ī′bĭs), *n., pl.* **ibises** (ī′bĭ sĭz), (*esp. collectively*) **ibis. 1.** any of various large wading birds of warm regions, allied to the herons and storks, forming the family *Threskiornithidae.* **2.** the **sacred ibis,** *Threskiornis aethiopica* of Egypt and other parts of Africa, with white and black plumage, venerated by the ancient Egyptians. [t. L, t. Gk; of Egyptian orig.]

Ibiza (*Sp.* ē bē′thȧ), *n.* Spanish name of **Iviza.**

-ible, var. of **-able,** occurring in words taken from the Latin, as in *credible, horrible, legible, visible,* or modelled on the Latin type as *addible* (for *addable*), *reducible.* [ME *-ible,* t. OF, t. L: m. s. *-ibilis,* var. of *-bilis* after consonant stems. See -BLE]

Sacred ibis, *Threskiornis aethiopica* (Length 2½ ft)

ibn-Ali (ĭb′ən ä′lĭ), *n.* See **Husein ibn-Ali.**

ibn-Rushd (ĭb′ən ro͞osht′), *n.* Arabic name of **Averroës.**

ibn-Saud (ĭb′ən soud′), *n.* **1. Abdul-Aziz** (ăb′do͞ol ă zēz′), 1880–1953, ruler of Nejd 1901–32, king of Saudi Arabia 1932–53. **2.** his son, **Abdul-Aziz al Faisal** (ăl fī′səl), 1901–69, king 1953–64.

ibn-Sina (ĭb′ən sē′nə), *n.* Arabic name of **Avicenna.**

Ibo (ē′bō), *n.* **1.** a Negro people living in the area of the lower Niger river. **2.** a member of this people. **3.** the language of this people, used esp. for trade and education in SE Nigeria.

Ibrahim Pasha (ĭb′rə hēm′ pä′shə), 1789–1848, Egyptian general, governor of Syria.

IBRD, International Bank for Reconstruction and Development.

Ibsen (ĭb′sən; *Nor.* ĕp′sən), *n.* **Henrik** (*Nor.* hĕn′rĕk), 1828–1906, Norwegian dramatist and poet.

-ic, 1. a suffix forming adjectives from nouns or stems not used as words themselves, meaning 'pertaining or belonging to' (*poetic, metallic, Homeric*), found extensively in adjective nouns of a similar type (*public, magic*), and in nouns the adjectives of which end in *-ical,* (*music, critic*). **2.** *Chem.* a suffix showing that an element is present in a compound at a high valency; at least higher than when the suffix *-ous* is used. [repr. in part s. Gk *-ikos*; often s. L *-icus*; sometimes F *-ique*]

Içа (*Port.* ē sȧ′), *n.* Brazilian name of **Putumayo.**

-ical, a compound suffix forming adjectives from nouns (*rhetorical*), providing synonyms to words ending in *-ic* (*poetical*), and providing an adjective with additional meanings to those in the *-ic* form (*economical*). [f. -IC + -AL[1]; in some cases repr. LL *-icālis,* f. adj. endings *-ic(us)* -IC + *-ālis* -AL[1]]

ICAO, International Civil Aviation Organization.

Icarian (ĭ kēə′rĭ ən, ī kēə′-), *adj.* of or like Icarus.

Icarus (ĭk′ə rəs, ī′kə-), *n. Gk Legend.* the son of Daedalus. Together they escaped from Crete using wings made of wax and feathers, but Icarus, flying so high that the sun melted his wings, drowned in the Aegean.

ICBM, intercontinental ballistic missile. Also, **I.C.B.M.**

ice (īs), *n., v.,* **iced, icing,** *adj. —n.* **1.** the solid form of water, produced by freezing; frozen water. **2.** the frozen surface of a body of water. **3.** any substance resembling this: *camphor ice.* **4.** ice-cream. **5.** *U.S.* a frozen dessert made of sweetened water and fruit juice. **6.** *U.S.* icing. **7.** reserve; formality: *to break the ice.* **8.** *U.S. Slang.* a diamond or diamonds. **9. cut no ice,** *Colloq.* to have no importance. **10. on ice,** waiting or in readiness: *he kept the project on ice for some time.* **11. on thin ice,** in a risky or delicate situation. *—v.t.* **12.** to cover with ice. **13.** to change into ice; freeze. **14.** to cool with ice, as a drink. **15.** to refrigerate with ice. **16.** to make cold as if with ice. **17.** to cover (cakes, etc.) with icing. *—v.i.* **18.** to freeze. **19.** to become covered with ice (often fol. by *up*). *—adj.* **20.** of ice. [ME *is(e),* OE *īs,* c. G *Eis*] **—ice′less,** *adj.* **—ice′like′,** *adj.*

-ice, a suffix used in many nouns to indicate state or quality, as in *service, justice.* [ME *-is(e), -ys(e),* etc., t. OF: m. *-ice, -ise,* g. L *-itius, -itia, -itium*]

ice age, (*sometimes caps*) *Geol.* the glacial epoch.

ice-axe (īs′ăks′), *n.* an axe used by mountaineers, etc., to cut footholds in ice.

icebag (īs′băg′), *n.* a bag containing ice, applied to the head.

iceberg (īs′bûg′), *n.* a large floating mass of ice, detached from a glacier and carried out to sea. [half Anglicization, half adoption of D *ijsberg* ice mountain, c. G *Eisberg,* Sw. *isberg*]

iceblink (īs′blĭngk′), *n.* a luminous appearance near the horizon, due to the reflection of light from ice.

iceboat (īs′bōt′), *n.* **1.** ice-yacht. **2.** icebreaker (def. 1).

icebound (īs′bound′), *adj.* **1.** held fast or hemmed in by ice; frozen in: *an icebound ship.* **2.** obstructed or shut off by ice: *an icebound harbour.*

icebox (īs′bŏks′), *n.* **1.** a box or chest to hold ice for keeping food, etc., cool. **2.** a compartment in a refrigerator for keeping ice. **3.** *U.S.* a refrigerator.

icebreaker (īs′brā′kə), *n.* **1.** a strong ship for breaking channels through ice. **2.** a tool or machine for chopping ice into small pieces. **3.** a structure of masonry or timber for protection against moving ice.

ice bucket, a small bucket containing cubes of ice for adding to drinks, or crushed ice in which a bottle of wine or the like is immersed to cool.

icecap (īs′kăp′), *n.* a cap of ice over an area (sometimes vast), sloping in all directions from the centre.

ice-cold (īs′kōld′), *adj.* cold as ice.

ice-cream (īs′krēm′), *n.* **1.** a frozen food made of cream, rich milk, or evaporated milk, sweetened and variously flavoured. **2.** (in commercial use) a food made in imitation of this, and containing milk, egg whites, custard powder, cornflower, etc.

ice-cream soda, ice-cream with combinations of syrups, fruit, jam, or milk, served in a tall glass topped up with ginger beer.

ice-cube (īs′kyo͞ob′), *n.* a small cube of ice, made by freezing water in an icetray in a refrigerator.

iced (īst), *adj.* **1.** covered with ice. **2.** cooled by means of ice. **3.** *Cooking.* covered with icing.

icefall (īs′fôl′), *n.* a sudden steepening in a glacier marked by deep crevasses and perched ice blocks.

icefield (īs′fēld′), *n.* a very large icefloe.

ice fish, the Maori chief (fish).

icefloe (īs′flō′), *n.* a sheet of floating ice.

icefoot (īs′fo͝ot′), *n.* a belt of ice along the shore in polar regions, formed where snow on the shore meets the sea water.

ice-free (īs′frē′), *adj.* (of a port, river, or the like) free from ice, and therefore navigable, all the year round.
icefront (īs′frŭnt′), *n.* the cliff-like edge of a floating icesheet or the end of a glacier which discharges to the sea.
ice hockey, a game resembling hockey, played on an icerink by two teams of six players each, with a puck in place of a ball.
icehouse (īs′hous′), *n.* a building for storing ice.
Icel., 1. Iceland. 2. Icelandic.
Iceland (īs′lənd), *n.* a large island in the N Atlantic between Greenland and Denmark: formerly Danish, it has been an independent republic since 1944. 190,230 pop. (1964); 39,698 sq. mi. *Cap.*: Reykjavik. See map under **Spitsbergen.** —**Icelander** (īs′lăn′də, -lən də), *n.*
Icelandic (īs lăn′dĭk), *adj.* **1.** pertaining to Iceland, its inhabitants, or their language. —*n.* **2.** the language of Iceland, a Scandinavian language.
Iceland moss, an edible lichen, *Cetraria islandica*, of arctic regions, used to some extent in medicine.
Iceland poppy, a poppy, esp. *Papaver nudicaule*, of arctic regions, having white or yellow flowers.
Iceland spar, a transparent variety of calcite that is double-refracting and is used for polarizing light.
ice lolly, a flavoured frozen confection on a stick.
iceman (īs′măn′), *n. U.S.* one who makes, delivers, or sells ice.
ice needles, *Meteorol.* a form of precipitation consisting of very small ice crystals that seem to float in the air.
IC engine, internal-combustion engine.
Iceni (ī sē′nī), *n.pl.* an ancient Celtic tribe of eastern England, whose queen, Boadicea, headed the insurrection of A.D. 61 against the Romans. [t. L]
icepack (īs′păk′), *n.* **1.** a large area of floating ice, as in arctic seas. **2.** a cold compress consisting of a bag filled with crushed ice.
icepick (īs′pĭk′), *n.* a pick or other tool for breaking ice.
ice plant, a low succulent plant, *Mesembryanthemum crystallinum*, orig. of the Old World, with leaves covered by glistening vesicles.
ice point, the temperature of equilibrium between ice and water under normal atmospheric pressure; the melting point of ice.
icerink (īs′rĭngk′), *n.* See **rink** (defs 1, 3, and 4).
ice-sailing (īs′sā′lĭng), *n.* the sport of racing ice-yachts across ice.
ice-scoured area (īs′skou′əd), *Phys. Geog.* an area having surface features resulting from scouring by an advancing icesheet during glaciation.
icesheet (īs′shēt′), *n.* **1.** a broad, thick sheet of ice covering an extensive area for a long period of time. **2.** a glacier covering a large part of a continent.
iceshelf (īs′shĕlf′), *n.* a floating icesheet which covers an extensive area of ocean.
ice show, an entertainment, often a pantomime, performed on ice.
ice skate, (*usually pl.*) **1.** a thin metal runner attached to the shoe, for skating on ice. **2.** a shoe fitted with such a runner.
ice-skate (īs′skāt′), *v.i.*, **-skated, -skating.** to skate on ice.
icetray (īs′trā′), *n.* a metal tray for icing water into cubes in the icebox of a refrigerator.
ice-yacht (īs′yŏt′), *n.* a triangular wooden frame fitted with steel runners and sails, for ice-sailing.
ich dien (*Ger.* ĭKH dēn′), *German.* I serve (motto of the Prince of Wales).
Ichinomiya (ē′chĭ nō′mĭ yə), *n.* a town in Japan, in SW central Honshu island. 203,743 (1965).
ichneumon (ĭk nyo͞o′mən), *n.* **1.** a slender carnivorous mammal, *Herpestes ichneumon*, of Egypt, resembling the weasel in form and habits, but the size of a cat: said to devour crocodiles' eggs. **2.** an ichneumon fly. [t. L, t. Gk: lit., tracker]
ichneumon fly, any insect belonging to the large hymenopterous family *Ichneumonidae*, whose larvae are parasites and destroy caterpillars and other larvae.
ichnite (ĭk′nīt), *n. Palaeontol.* a fossil footprint. [f. s. Gk *íchnos* track + -ITE¹]
ichnography (ĭk nŏg′rə fĭ), *n.*, *pl.* **-phies. 1.** the drawing of ground plans. **2.** a ground plan. [t. L: m. s. *ichnographia*, t. Gk: a tracing out. See -GRAPHY] —**ichnographic** (ĭk′nə grăf′ĭk), **ich′nograph′ical,** *adj.* —**ich′nograph′ically,** *adv.*
ichor¹ (ī′kô), *n. Class. Myth.* an ethereal fluid supposed to flow in the veins of the gods. [t. Gk]
ichor² (ī′kô), *n. Pathol.* an acrid watery discharge, as from an ulcer or wound. [NL, t. Gk, special use of *ichṓr* ICHOR¹] —**ichorous** (ī′kə rəs), *adj.*
ichth., ichthyology. Also, **ichthyol.**
ichthyic (ĭk′thĭ ĭk), *adj.* piscine. [t. Gk: m. s. *ichthyïkós* fishy]
ichthyo-, a word element meaning 'fish', as in *ichthyology*. Also, before vowels, **ichthy-.** [t. Gk, comb. form of *ichthýs*]
ichthyoid (ĭk′thĭ oid′), *adj.* **1.** Also, **ich′thyoi′dal.** fishlike. —*n.* **2.** any fishlike vertebrate. [t. Gk: m. s. *ichthyoeidḗs* fishlike. See -OID]
ichthyol (ĭk′thĭ ŏl′), *n. Pharm.* **1.** Also, **ichthammol.** a dark brown to black syrupy compound, $C_{28}H_{36}O_6S_3(NH_3)_2 \cdot 2H_2O$, used as an astringent, antiseptic, and alternative, esp. for skin diseases. **2.** (*cap.*) a trademark for this drug. [f. ICHTHY- + -OL²; so called because obtained from rocks containing fossilized fishes]
ichthyology (ĭk′thĭ ŏl′ə jĭ), *n.* the branch of zoology that treats of fishes. —**ichthyologic** (ĭk′thĭ ə lŏj′ĭk), **ich′thyolog′ical,** *adj.* —**ich′thyol′ogist,** *n.*
ichthyornis (ĭk′thĭ ô′nĭs), *n.* any of an extinct genus of toothed birds, *Ichthyornis*, with vertebrae resembling those of fishes. [NL, f. Gk: *ichthy-* ICHTHY- + *órnis* bird]
ichthyosaur (ĭk′thĭ ə sô′), *n.* any of an extinct order, *Ichthyosauria*, of marine reptiles, fishlike in form, ranging from 4 to 40 feet in length, with a round tapering body, a large head, four paddle-like flippers, and a vertical caudal fin. [t. NL: s. *ichthyosaurus*, f. Gk: *ichthyo-* ICHTHYO- + m. *saûros* lizard]

Ichthyosaur, *Stenopterygius quadriscissus* (Length 4 ft)

ichthyosaurus (ĭk′thĭ ə sô′rəs), *n.*, *pl.* **-sauri** (-sô′rī). ichthyosaur.
ichthyosis (ĭk′thĭ ō′sĭs), *n. Pathol.* a congenital disease in which the epidermis continually flakes off in large scales or plates. —**ichthyotic** (ĭk′thĭ ŏt′ĭk), *adj.*
-ician, a compound suffix especially applied to an expert in a field, as in *geometrician*. [f. -IC + -IAN; r. ME *-icien*, t. OF]
icicle (ī′sĭ kl), *n.* a pendent tapering mass of ice formed by the freezing of dripping water. [ME *isykle*, OE *īsgicel*, f. *īs* ice + *gicel* icicle. Cf. Icel. *jökull* mass of ice, glacier] —**i′cicled,** *adj.*
icily (ī′sĭ lĭ), *adv.* in an icy manner.
iciness (ī′sĭ nĭs), *n.* the state of being icy or very cold.
icing (ī′sĭng), *n.* **1.** a preparation of sugar, often made with egg whites, for covering cakes, etc. **2.** frosting.
icing index, *Meteorol.* an estimate of the probability of ice formation at a particular place and time.
icing sugar, a finely ground powdered sugar.
ici on parle français (*Fr.* ē sē′ ôN pȧrl fräN sĕ′), *French.* French spoken here.
ICJ, International Court of Justice.
icker (ĭk′ə), *n. Scot.* an ear of corn. [d. var. of EAR², OE (Northumbrian) *eher*, *æhher*]
icon (ī′kŏn), *n.*, *pl.* **icons. 1.** a picture, image, or other representation. **2.** *Eastern Ch.* a representation in painting, enamel, etc., of some sacred personage, as Christ or a saint or angel, itself venerated as sacred. **3.** a sign or representation which stands for its object by virtue of a resemblance or analogy to it. Also, **eikon, ikon.** [t. L, t. Gk: m. *eikṓn* likeness, image] —**Syn. 2.** See **image.**
iconic (ī kŏn′ĭk), *adj.* **1.** pertaining to or of the nature of an icon, portrait, or image. **2.** *Art.* (of statues, portraits, etc.) executed according to a convention or tradition. Also, **icon′ical.** [t. L: s. *iconicus*, t. Gk: m. *eikonikós* representing a figure, copied]
Iconium (ī kō′nyəm), *n.* ancient name of **Konya.**
icono-, a word element meaning 'likeness' or 'image', as in *iconography*. [t. Gk, comb. form of *eikṓn*]
iconoclasm (ī kŏn′ə klăz′əm), *n.* the action or spirit of iconoclasts.
iconoclast (ī kŏn′ə klăst′), *n.* **1.** a breaker or destroyer of images, esp. those set up for religious veneration. **2.** one who attacks cherished beliefs as based on error or superstition. [t. LL: s. *iconoclastēs*, t. LGk: m. *eikonoklástēs*, f. *eikono-* ICONO- + *klástēs* breaker] —**icon′oclas′tic,** *adj.* —**icon′oclas′tically,** *adv.*
iconographic (ī kŏn′ə grăf′ĭk), *adj.* of or pertaining to icons or iconography. Also, **icon′ograph′ical.**
iconography (ī′kō nŏg′rə fĭ), *n.*, *pl.* **-phies. 1.** the making of an icon; representation by means of drawing, painting, or carving figures, etc. **2.** the subject matter of an icon, image, or representation, or of groups of them. **3.** the description or analysis of icons. [t. ML: m. s. *iconographia*, t. Gk: m. *eikonographía*. See ICONO-, -GRAPHY]
iconolatry (ī′kō nŏl′ə trĭ), *n.* the worship or adoration of icons. —**i′conol′ater,** *n.*
iconology (ī′kō nŏl′ə jĭ), *n.* **1.** the branch of knowledge concerned with pictorial or sculptural representations. **2.** such representations collectively. **3.** a description or

interpretation of statues, pictures, etc. **4.** symbolical representation. **—iconological** (ī kŏn′ə lŏj′ĭ kl), *adj.* **—i′conol′ogist,** *n.*

iconoscope (ī kŏn′ə skōp′), *n. Television.* **1.** the cathode-ray tube which focuses the optical image which the cathode-ray beam scans. **2.** (*cap.*) a trademark for this tube.

iconostasis (ī′kŏ nŏs′tə sĭs), *n., pl.* **-ses** (-sēz′). *Eastern Ch.* a partition or screen on which icons are placed, separating the sanctuary from the main part of the church. Also, **iconostas** (ī kŏn′ə stăs′). [NL, t. NGk: m. *eikonóstasis*, f. Gk: *eikono-* ICONO- + *stásis* a standing, station]

icosahedron (ī′kə sə hē′drən), *n., pl.* **-drons, -dra** (-drə). a solid figure having twenty faces. [t. Gk: m. *eikosáedron*] **—i′cosahe′dral,** *adj.*

Icosahedron (regular)

-ics, a suffix of nouns, originally plural as denoting things pertaining to a particular subject, but now mostly used as singular as denoting the body of matters, facts, knowledge, principles, etc., pertaining to a subject, and hence a science or art, as in *ethics, physics, politics, tactics.* [pl. of -IC; orig. repr. Gk *-iká* (in L *-ica*), neut. pl. adj., suffix meaning (things) pertaining to]

I.C.S., Indian Civil Service.

icteric (ĭk tĕ′rĭk), *adj. Pathol.* pertaining to or affected with icterus; jaundiced. Also, **icter′ical.** [t. L: s. *ictericus*, t. Gk: m. *ikterikós*]

icterus (ĭk′tə rəs), *n. Pathol.* jaundice. [NL, t. Gk: m. *íkteros*]

Ictinus (ĭk tī′nəs), *n.* fl. *c.* 440 B.C., Athenian architect; designer of the Parthenon.

ictus (ĭk′təs), *n., pl.* **-tuses, -tus. 1.** *Pros.* rhythmical or metrical stress. **2.** *Pathol.* **a.** a fit. **b.** a stroke, as sunstroke. [t. L: blow, stroke]

icy (ī′sĭ), *adj.,* **icier, iciest. 1.** made of or covered with ice. **2.** resembling ice. **3.** cold: *icy wind.* **4.** slippery: *icy road.* **5.** without warmth of feeling; frigid: *an icy stare.* [late ME *isy*, OE *īsig*. See ICE, -Y[1]]

id (ĭd), *n. Psychoanal.* the part of the psyche residing in the unconscious which is the source of instinctive energy. Its impulses, which seek satisfaction in accordance with the pleasure principle, are modified by the ego and the superego before they are given overt expression. [special use of L *id* it, as trans. of G *Es*]

I'd (īd), contradiction of *I would, I should,* or *I had.*

-id[1], **1.** a noun suffix meaning 'daughter of', as in *Nereid*, and used also (*Astron.*) to form names of meteors appearing to radiate in showers from particular constellations, etc., as in *Andromedid.* **2.** a suffix used in naming epics, as in *Aeneid.* [t. L: *-id-* (nom. *-is*), fem. patronymic suffix, t. Gk]

-id[2], a suffix of nouns and adjectives indicating members of a zoological family, as in *cichlid*, or of some other group or division, as in *acarid, arachnid.* [t. NL: s. *-idae*, in zoological family names pl. of L *-idēs* (masc. patronymic suffix), t. Gk; sometimes, t. NL: s. *-ida*, in group names, taken as neut. pl. of L *-idēs.* Cf. F *-ide*]

-id[3], var. of **-ide,** as in *parotid.*

-id[4], a quasi-suffix common in adjectives, esp. of states which appeal to the senses, as in *torrid, acid.* [t. L: s. *-idus*]

id., idem.

Ida (ī′də), *n.* **Mount, 1.** a peak in NW Asia Minor, overlooking the site of ancient Troy and the Aegean. 5810 ft. **2.** modern name, **Mount Psiloriti.** the highest mountain of Crete. 8058 ft.

Ida., Idaho. Also, **Id.**

-idae, *Zool.* a suffix of the names of families, as in *Canidae.* [(N)L, t. Gk: m. *-idai*, pl. of *-idēs*, patronymic suffix]

Idaho (ī′də hō′), *n.* a state in the NW United States. 667,191 pop. (1960); 83,557 sq. mi. *Cap.:* Boise. *Abbrev.:* Ida., Id. **—I′daho′an,** *n., adj.*

I.D.B., *Chiefly S African.* illicit diamond buying.

-ide, a noun suffix in names of chemical compounds, as in *bromide.* Also, **-id**[3]. [abstracted from OXIDE]

idea (ī dĭə′), *n.* **1.** any conception existing in the mind as the result of mental apprehension or activity. **2.** a thought, conception, or notion: *what an idea!* **3.** an impression: *a general idea of what it's like.* **4.** an opinion, view, or belief. **5.** a plan of action; an intention: *the idea of becoming an engineer.* **6.** a fantasy. **7.** *Philos.* **a.** a concept developed by the mind (if empirical, in close connection with sense perception). **b.** a conception of what is desirable, or what ought to be; a governing conception or principle; ideal. **c.** (in Platonic philosophy) an archetype or pattern of which the individual objects in any natural class are imperfect copies and from which they derive their being. **d.** (in Kantian philosophy) a concept formed from notions and transcending the possibility of experience. **8.** *Music.* a theme, phrase, or figure. **9.** *Obs.* a likeness. **10.** *Obs.* a mental image. [t. L, t. Gk, der. *ideîn* see; orig. in def. 7c] **—idea′less,** *adj.*

ideal (ī dĭəl′), *n.* **1.** a conception of something in its highest perfection. **2.** a standard of perfection or excellence. **3.** a person or thing regarded as realizing such a conception or conforming to such a standard, and taken as a model for imitation. **4.** an ultimate object or aim of endeavour, esp. one of high or noble character. **5.** that which exists only in idea. **—***adj.* **6.** conceived as constituting a standard of perfection or excellence: *ideal beauty.* **7.** regarded as perfect of its kind; best: *an ideal spot for a home.* **8.** existing only in idea. **9.** not real or practical; visionary. **10.** based upon an ideal or ideals: *the ideal school in art.* **11.** *Philos.* **a.** existing as an archetype or Platonic idea. **b.** pertaining to a possible state of affairs considered as highly desirable. **c.** pertaining to or of the nature of idealism. [t. LL: s. *ideālis*, der. L *idea* IDEA] **—ideal′ness,** *n.*

—Syn. 1, 2. IDEAL, EXAMPLE, MODEL refer to something considered as a standard to strive towards or something considered worthy of imitation. An IDEAL is a concept or standard of perfection, existing merely as an image in the mind, or based upon a person or upon conduct: *the high ideals of a religious person; Sir Philip Sidney was considered the ideal of gentlemanly conduct.* An EXAMPLE is a person or his conduct or achievements regarded as worthy of being followed or imitated in a general way; or sometimes, as properly to be avoided: *an example of courage; a bad example to one's children.* A MODEL is primarily a physical shape to be closely copied, but is also a pattern for exact imitation in conduct or character: *they took their leader as a model.*

ideal gas, *Physics.* the theoretical concept of a gas consisting of perfectly elastic molecules between which no forces of attraction exist; a gas which obeys the ideal gas law; perfect gas.

ideal gas law, *Physics.* See **gas laws.**

idealism (ī dĭə′lĭz′əm), *n.* **1.** the cherishing or pursuit of ideals, as for attainment. **2.** the practice of idealizing. **3.** something idealized; an ideal representation. **4.** the imaginative treatment of subjects in art or literature, usually on a high ethical plane and devoid of accidental details (opposed to *realism*). **5.** *Philos.* **a.** any system or theory which maintains that the real is of the nature of thought, or that the object of external perception consists of ideas. **b.** the tendency to represent things in an ideal form, or as they ought to be rather than as they are, with emphasis on values.

idealist (ī dĭə′lĭst), *n.* **1.** one who cherishes or pursues ideals, as for attainment. **2.** a visionary or unpractical person. **3.** one who represents things as they might be rather than as they are. **4.** a writer or artist who treats subjects imaginatively. **5.** one who accepts the doctrines of idealism. **—***adj.* **6.** idealistic.

idealistic (ī dĭə′lĭs′tĭk), *adj.* pertaining to idealism or to idealists. **—ideal′is′tically,** *adv.*

ideality (ī′dĭ ăl′ĭ tĭ), *n., pl.* **-ties. 1.** ideal quality or character. **2.** capacity to idealize. **3.** *Philos.* the state of existing only in idea and not in actuality.

idealize (ī dĭə′līz), *v.,* **-lized, -lizing. —***v.t.* **1.** to make ideal; represent in an ideal form or character; exalt to an ideal perfection or excellence. **—***v.i.* **2.** to represent something in an ideal form; imagine or form an ideal or ideals. Also, **idealise. —ideal′iza′tion,** *n.* **—ideal′iz′er,** *n.*

ideally (ī dĭə′lĭ), *adv.* **1.** in accordance with an ideal; perfectly. **2.** in idea, thought, or imagination.

ideal type, *Sociol.* an imaginary construction of what an object would be if it were allowed to develop without any interference from accidental or irrelevant factors.

ideate (*v.* ī dē′āt; *n.* ī dē′ĭt, -āt), *v.,* **-ated, -ating,** *n.* **—***v.t.* **1.** to form in idea, thought, or imagination. **—***v.i.* **2.** to form ideas; think. **—***n.* **3.** *Philos.* the object of which an idea is formed. **—i′dea′tion,** *n.* **—i′dea′tional,** *adj.* **—i′dea′tionally,** *adv.*

idée fixe (*Fr.* ē dĕ fēks′), *French.* a fixed idea; obsession.

idem (ī′dĕm, ĭd′ĕm), *pron., adj. Latin.* the same as previously given or mentioned.

identic (ī dĕn′tĭk), *adj.* **1.** *Obs.* identical. **2.** *Diplomacy.* (of action, notes, etc.) identical in form, as when two or more governments deal simultaneously with another government. [t. ML: s. *identicus*]

identical (ī dĕn′tĭ kl), *adj.* **1.** agreeing exactly. **2.** same, or being the same one. [f. IDENTIC + -AL[1]. See IDENTITY] **—iden′tically,** *adv.* **—iden′ticalness,** *n.*

identical classes, *Logic.* classes denoted by two terms whose extensions contain the same individuals as members.

identical proposition, a proposition expressed by a sentence in which the subject and predicate have the same meaning.

identical twin, one of a pair of twins of the same sex which develop from one fertilized ovum.

identification (ī dĕn′tĭ fĭ kā′shən), *n.* **1.** the act of identifying. **2.** the state of being identified. **3.** something that identifies one: *have you any identification?*

identify (ī dĕn′tĭ fī′), *v.*, **-fied, -fying.** —*v.t.* **1.** to recognize or establish as being a particular person or thing; attest or prove to be as purported or asserted: *to identify handwriting, identify the bearer of a cheque.* **2.** to make, represent to be, or regard or treat as the same or identical. **3.** to associate in feeling, interest, action, etc. (fol. by *with*). **4.** *Biol.* to determine to what group (a given specimen) belongs. **5.** *Psychol.* to make (oneself) one with another person by putting oneself in his place. **6.** to serve as a means of identification for. —*v.i.* **7.** to make oneself one with another or others. —**iden′tifi′able,** *adj.* —**iden′tifi′er,** *n.*

Identikit (ī dĕn′tĭ kĭt′), *n. Trademark.* a number of alternative, typical facial characteristics which can be superimposed upon a frame to form a likeness; used by police as a system of criminal identification.

identity (ī dĕn′tĭ tĭ), *n.*, *pl.* **-ties. 1.** the state or fact of remaining the same one, as under varying aspects or conditions. **2.** the condition of being oneself or itself, and not another: *he doubted his own identity.* **3.** condition or character as to who a person or what a thing is: *a case of mistaken identity.* **4.** the state or fact of being the same one. **5.** exact likeness in nature or qualities. **6.** an instance or point of sameness or likeness. **7.** *Maths.* an equation which is true for all values of its variables. —*adj.* **8.** effective as a means of identification: *an identity bracelet.* [t. LL: m. s. *identitas*, appar. f. L *identi-* (as in *identidem* repeatedly), for *īdem* the same + *-tas* -TY²]

ideo-, a word element meaning 'idea', as in *ideograph.* [t. Gk, comb. form of *idéa* idea]

ideograph (ĭd′ĭ ō grăf′, -gräf′), *n.* a written symbol representing the idea of something directly, and not its name or sound. Also, **ideogram** (ĭd′ĭ ō grăm′). —**ideographic** (ĭd′ĭ ō grăf′ ĭk), **id′eograph′ical,** *adj.* —**id′eograph′ically,** *adv.*

ideography (ĭd′ĭ ŏg′rə fĭ), *n.* the use of ideographs.

ideological (ī′dĭ ə lŏj′ĭ kl), *adj.* **1.** pertaining to ideology. **2.** speculative; visionary. Also, **i′deolog′ic.** —**i′deolog′ically,** *adv.*

ideologist (ī′dĭ ŏl′ə jĭst), *n.* **1.** an expert in ideology. **2.** one who deals with systems of ideas. **3.** one who advocates or is preoccupied by a specific ideology. **4.** a visionary.

ideology (ī′dĭ ŏl′ə jĭ), *n.*, *pl.* **-gies. 1.** the body of doctrine, myth, and symbols of a social movement, institution, class, or large group. **2.** such a body of doctrine, etc., with reference to some political and cultural plan, as that of fascism, together with the devices for putting it into operation. **3.** *Philos.* **a.** the science of ideas. **b.** a system which derives ideas exclusively from sensation. **4.** theorizing of a visionary or unpractical nature.

ides (īdz), *n.pl.* (in the ancient Roman calendar) the 15th day of March, May, July, or October, and the 13th day of the other months. [t. F, t. L: m. *īdūs*, pl.]

id est (ĭd ĕst′), *Latin.* that is.

idio-, a word element meaning 'peculiar' or 'proper to one', as in *idiosyncrasy.* [t. Gk, comb. form of *ídios* own, private, peculiar]

idioblast (ĭd′ĭ ō blăst′), *n. Bot.* a cell which differs greatly from the surrounding cells or tissue.

idiocy (ĭd′ĭ ə sĭ), *n.*, *pl.* **-cies. 1.** the condition of being an idiot; extreme degree of mental deficiency. **2.** senseless folly. [? t. Gk: m. s. *idiōteía* uncouthness, defenceless condition; or der. IDIOT, on model of *prophecy* from *prophet*]

idiographic (ĭd′ĭ ō grăf′ĭk), *adj. Psychol.* pertaining to the intensive study of an individual case, as a personality or social situation (opposed to *nomothetic*).

idiom (ĭd′ĭ əm), *n.* **1.** a form of expression peculiar to a language, esp. one having a significance other than its literal one. **2.** a variety or form of a language; a dialect. **3.** the language peculiar to a people. **4.** the peculiar character or genius of a language. **5.** a distinct style or character, as in music, art, etc.: *the idiom of Bach.* [t. LL: m. *idiōma*, t. Gk: a peculiarity]

idiomatic (ĭd′ĭ ə măt′ĭk), *adj.* **1.** peculiar to or characteristic of a particular language. **2.** exhibiting the characteristic modes of expression of a speaker, group, dialect, etc. Also, **id′iomat′ical.** [t. Gk: m. s. *idiōmatikós*] —**id′iomat′ically,** *adv.* —**id′iomat′icalness,** *n.*

idiomorphic (ĭd′ĭ ō môr′fĭk), *adj.* **1.** denoting or pertaining to a mineral constituent of a rock, which has its own characteristic outward crystalline form, and not one forced upon it by the other constituents of the rock. **2.** having its own form. —**id′iomor′phically,** *adv.*

idiopathic (ĭd′ĭ ō păth′ĭk), *adj. Pathol.* of unknown cause, as a disease.

idiopathy (ĭd′ĭ ŏp′ə thĭ), *n.*, *pl.* **-thies.** *Pathol.* a disease not preceded or occasioned by any other. [t. Gk: m. s. *idiopátheia.* See IDIO-, -PATHY]

idiophone (ĭd′ĭ ə fōn′), *n. Music.* an instrument made of some solid, naturally sonorous material, as cymbals, xylophones, glass harmonicas, etc.

idioplasm (ĭd′ĭ ō plăz′əm), *n. Biol.* germ plasm. —**id′ioplas′mic, idioplasmatic** (ĭd′ĭ ō plăz măt′ĭk), *adj.*

idiosyncrasy (ĭd′ĭ ə sĭng′krə sĭ), *n.*, *pl.* **-sies. 1.** any tendency, characteristic, mode of expression, or the like, peculiar to an individual. **2.** the physical constitution peculiar to an individual. **3.** a peculiarity of the physical or the mental constitution, esp. susceptibility towards drugs, food, etc. See **allergy** (def. 1). [t. Gk: m. s. *idiosynkrāsía*] —**idiosyncratic** (ĭd′ĭ ə sĭng krăt′ĭk), *adj.* —**id′iosyncrat′ically,** *adv.*

idiot (ĭd′ĭ ət), *n.* **1.** an utterly foolish or senseless person. **2.** one hopelessly deficient, esp. from birth, in the ordinary mental powers; one lacking the capacity to develop beyond the mental level of three or four years. **3.** one whose intelligence quotient is below 55 and who is therefore considered ineducable. [ME, t. L: s. *idiōta*, t. Gk: m. *idiṓtēs* a private, non-professional, or ignorant person]

idiotic (ĭd′ĭ ŏt′ĭk), *adj.* of or like an idiot; senselessly foolish. Also, **id′iot′ical.** [t. LL: s. *idiōticus*, t. Gk: m. *idiōtikós* private, unskilful] —**id′iot′ically,** *adv.* —**Syn.** half-witted, stupid. —**Ant.** intelligent.

idiotism (ĭd′ĭ ə tĭz′əm), *n.* **1.** idiotic conduct or action. **2.** *Rare.* idiocy. **3.** *Obs.* an idiom. [f. IDIOT + -ISM; in def. 3, t. F: m. *idiotisme*, t. LL: m. s. *idiōtismus* a common way of speaking, t. Gk: m. *idiōtismós* common manners]

idiot tape, *Print.* the computer input tape for automatic typesetting.

-idium, a diminutive suffix (Latinization of Greek *-idion*) used in zoological, biological, botanical, anatomical, and chemical terms.

idle (ī′dl), *adj.*, **idler, idlest,** *v.* **idled, idling.** —*adj.* **1.** unemployed, or doing nothing: *idle workmen.* **2.** unoccupied, as time: *idle hours.* **3.** not kept busy or in use or operation: *idle machinery.* **4.** habitually doing nothing or avoiding work. **5.** of no real worth, importance, or significance: *idle talk.* **6.** baseless or groundless: *idle fears.* **7.** frivolous or vain: *idle pleasures.* **8.** futile or ineffective: *idle threats.* **9.** useless: *idle rage.* —*v.i.* **10.** to pass time in idleness. **11.** to move, loiter, or saunter idly. **12.** *Mach.* to operate, usually at minimum speed, while the transmission is disengaged. —*v.t.* **13.** to pass (time) in idleness. **14.** to cause (a person) to be idle. [ME and OE *īdel*, c. G *eitel*] —**i′dleness,** *n.* —**i′dly,** *adv.*

—**Syn. 1.** IDLE, INDOLENT, LAZY, SLOTHFUL apply to one who is not active. To be IDLE is to be inactive or not working at a job. The word may be derogatory, but not necessarily so, since one may be relaxing temporarily or may be idle through necessity: *pleasantly idle on holiday, to be idle because one is unemployed or because necessary supplies are lacking.* The INDOLENT person is naturally disposed to avoid exertion: *indolent and slow in movement, an indolent and contented fisherman.* The LAZY person is averse to exertion or work, and esp. to continued application; the word is usually derogatory: *too lazy to earn a living; incurably lazy.* SLOTHFUL denotes a reprehensible unwillingness to do such work as is demanded of man: *so slothful as to be a burden on others.* **11.** See **loiter.** —**Ant. 1.** busy, industrious.

idle pulley, *Mach.* a loose pulley made to press or rest on a belt in order to tighten or guide it.

idler (ī′dlə), *n.* **1.** one who idles. **2.** *Mach.* an idle pulley or wheel.

idlesse (ī′dlĕs), *n. Poetic.* idleness.

idle wheel, *Mach.* **1.** a cogwheel placed between two other cogwheels in order to transfer the motion of one to the other without changing the direction of rotation. **2.** an idle pulley.

I, Idle wheel; C, Cogwheel

Idlewild (ī′dl wīld′), *n.* former name of **John F. Kennedy International Airport.**

Ido (ē′dō), *n.* a revised and simplified form of Esperanto, introduced in 1907.

idocrase (ī′də krās′, ĭd′ə-), *n.* the mineral vesuvianite. [t. F, f. Gk: m. *eîdos* form + m. *krâsis* mixture]

idol (ī′dl), *n.* **1.** an image or other material object representing a deity to which religious worship is addressed. **2.** *Bible.* a false god, as of a heathen people. **3.** any person or thing blindly adored or revered. **4.** a mere image or semblance of something, visible but without substance, as a phantom. **5.** a figment of the mind. **6.** a false conception or notion; fallacy. [ME, t. OF: m. *idole*, t. L: m. *idōlum*, t. Gk: m. *eídōlon* image, phantom, idol] —**Syn. 1.** See **image.**

idolater (ī dŏl′ə tə), *n.* **1.** a worshipper of idols. **2.** an adorer or devotee. Also, **idolist** (ī′də lĭst). [ME *idolatrer*, t. OF: m. *idolatre*, g. LL *īdōlolatrēs*, t. Gk: m. *eidōlolátrēs* idol worshipper] —**idolatress** (ī dŏl′ə trĭs), *n. fem.*

idolatrize (ī dŏl′ə trīz′), *v.*, **-trized, -trizing.** —*v.t.* 1. to idolize. —*v.i.* 2. to worship idols. Also, **idolatrise.**

idolatrous (ī dŏl′ə trəs), *adj.* **1.** pertaining to or of the nature of idolatry. **2.** worshipping idols. **3.** blindly adoring. **4.** *Obs.* used in or designed for idolatry. —**idol′atrously,** *adv.* —**idol′atrousness,** *n.*

idolatry (ī dŏl′ə trĭ), *n.*, *pl.* **-tries. 1.** the worship of idols. **2.** blind adoration, reverence, or devotion. [ME *idolatrie*, t. OF, g. LL *īdōlolatrīa*, t. Gk: m. *eidōlolatreía*]

idolism (ī′də lĭz′əm), *n.* **1.** idolatry. **2.** idolizing.

idolize (ī′də līz′), *v.t.*, **-lized, -lizing.** to regard with blind adoration or devotion. Also, **idolise.** —**i′doliza′tion,** *n.* —**i′doliz′er,** *n.*

Idomeneus (ī dŏm′ĭ nyōōs′), *n. Gk Legend.* a Cretan king and important chief of the Greek army in the Trojan War.

idoneous (ī dō′nyəs), *adj.* apt or suitable. [t. L: m. *idōneus*]

Idris (ĭd′rĭs), *n.* (*Sayyid Mohammed Idris as-Sanusi*), born 1890, king of Libya 1950–69.

Idumaea (ī′dyōō mē′ə), *n.* Greek name of **Edom.** Also, **Idumea.** —**I′dumae′an,** *adj.*, *n.*

Idun (ē′dōōn), *n. Scand. Myth.* Ithunn.

idyll (ĭd′ĭl), *n.* **1.** a poem or prose composition consisting of a 'little picture', usually describing pastoral scenes or events or any charmingly simple episode, appealing incident, or the like. **2.** a simple descriptive or narrative piece in verse or prose. **3.** material suitable for an idyll. **4.** an episode or scene of idyllic charm. **5.** *Music.* a composition, usually instrumental, of a pastoral or sentimental character. Also, *U.S.*, **idyl.** [t. L: m. s. *īdyllium*, t. Gk: m. *eidýllion*, dim. of *eidos* form]

idyllic (ī dĭl′ĭk), *adj.* **1.** suitable for or suggestive of an idyll; charmingly simple or poetic. **2.** of, pertaining to, or of the nature of an idyll. —**idyl′lically,** *adv.*

idyllist (ī′dĭ lĭst), *n.* a writer of idylls. Also, *U.S.*, **i′dylist.**

-ie, a hypocoristic suffix of nouns, same as **-y²**, as in *dearie, laddie, Willie.*

IE, Indo-European.

i.e., id est.

Ieper (*Flem.* ē′pər), *n.* Flemish name of **Ypres.**

-ier, var. of **-eer,** as in *brigadier, halberdier,* etc. [t. F, g. L *-ārius*]

-ies, a word element representing the plural formation of nouns and third person singular of verbs for words ending in *-y*, *-ie*, and sometimes *-ey*. See **-s²** and **-s³**; **-es.**

if (ĭf), *conj.* **1.** in case that; granting or supposing that; on condition that. **2.** even though. **3.** whether. **4. if only,** (used to introduce a phrase expressing a wish, esp. one that cannot now be fulfilled or is thought unlikely to be fulfilled): *If only I had known! If only he would come!* —*n.* **5.** a condition; a supposition. [ME; OE *gif*, c. Icel. *if*, later *ef* if (also used as n., *ef* doubt)]

—**Syn. 1, 2.** IF, PROVIDED, PROVIDING imply a condition on which something depends. IF is general. It may be used to indicate suppositions or hypothetical conditions (often involving doubt or uncertainty): *if you like, we can go straight home*; *if I had known, I wouldn't have gone.* IF may mean 'even though': *if I am wrong, you are not right.* It may mean 'whenever': *if I do not understand, I ask questions.* PROVIDED always indicates some stipulation: *I will subscribe ten shillings provided that you do, too; provided he goes, we can go along.* PROVIDING means condition only: *providing he comes, we shall be able to go out.*

i.f., *Radio.* intermediate frequency. Also, **I.F.**

IFC, International Finance Corporation.

Ife (ē′fĭ), *n.* a town in central Western Nigeria. 111,000 (est. 1963).

Ifni (*Sp.* ēf′nē), *n.* a Spanish province on the NW coast of Africa. 51,517 pop. (1964); 580 sq. mi.

I.F.R., *Aeron.* instrument flight rules.

-ify, var. of **-fy,** used when the preceding stem or word element ends in a consonant, as in *intensify.* [f. -I- + -FY]

IG, Indo-Germanic.

I.G., Inspector General.

Igdrasil (ĭg′drə sĭl), *n. Scand. Myth.* Yggdrasil.

igloo (ĭg′lōō), *n.*, *pl.* **-loos. 1.** a dome-shaped Eskimo hut, built of blocks of hard snow. **2.** an excavation made by a seal in the snow over its breathing hole in the ice. [t. Eskimo: house]

Ignatius (ĭg nā′shyəs), *n.* **Saint** (*Ignatius Theophorus*), died A.D. 107?, bishop of Antioch: Christian martyr.

Ignatius of Loyola (loi ō′lə), **Saint** (*Iñigo López de Recalde*), 1491–1556, Spanish soldier and priest: founder of the Jesuit order.

igneous (ĭg′nĭ əs), *adj.* pertaining to or of the nature of fire. [t. L: m. *igneus* of fire]

igneous rock, *Geol.* rock formed from magma which has cooled and solidified either at the earth's surface (volcanic rock) or deep within the earth's crust (plutonic rock).

ignescent (ĭg nĕs′ənt), *adj.* **1.** emitting sparks of fire, as certain stones when struck with steel. **2.** bursting into flame. —*n.* **3.** an ignescent substance. [t. L: s. *ignescens*, ppr., taking fire]

ignis fatuus (ĭg′nĭs făt′yōō əs), *pl.* **ignes fatui** (ĭg′nēz făt′yōō ī′). **1.** a flitting phosphorescent light seen at night, chiefly over marshy ground, and supposed to be due to spontaneous combustion of gas from decomposed organic matter; a will-o'-the-wisp. **2.** something deluding or misleading. [L: foolish fire]

ignite (ĭg nīt′), *v.*, **-nited, -niting.** —*v.t.* **1.** to set on fire; kindle. **2.** *Chem.* to heat intensely; roast. —*v.i.* **3.** to take fire; begin to burn. [t. L: m. s. *ignītus*, pp.] —**ignit′able, ignit′ible,** *adj.* —**ignit′abil′ity, ignit′ibil′ity,** *n.* —**Syn. 1.** See **kindle.**

igniter (ĭg nī′tə), *n.* **1.** one who or that which ignites. **2.** *Electronics.* the carborundum rod used to initiate the discharge in an ignitron tube.

ignition (ĭg nĭsh′ən), *n.* **1.** the act of igniting. **2.** the state of being ignited. **3.** (in an internal-combustion engine) the process which ignites the fuel in the cylinder. **4.** a means or device for igniting.

ignition coil, an induction coil used in an internal-combustion engine for converting the battery voltage to the high tension required by the sparking plugs.

ignitron (ĭg nī′trŏn, ĭg′nĭ trŏn′), *n. Electronics.* a mercury-pool cathode-arc rectifier with a carborundum rod projecting into the mercury pool. The tube conducts current when the anode is positive. [f. IGNI(TION) + (ELEC)TRON]

ignoble (ĭg nō′bl), *adj.* **1.** of low character, aims, etc.; mean; base. **2.** of low grade or quality; inferior. **3.** not noble; of humble birth or station. **4.** *Falconry.* denoting short-winged hawks which chase or rake after the quarry (opposite to *noble*). [t. L: m. s. *ignōbilis* unknown, low-born] —**ig′nobil′ity, igno′bleness,** *n.* —**igno′bly,** *adv.* —**Syn. 1.** degraded, dishonourable, contemptible, vulgar. **3.** lowly, obscure, plebeian.

ignominious (ĭg′nə mĭn′ĭ əs), *adj.* **1.** marked by or attended with ignominy; discreditable; humiliating: *an ignominious retreat.* **2.** covered with or deserving ignominy; contemptible. [t. L: m. s. *ignōminiōsus*] —**ig′nomin′iously,** *adv.* —**ig′nomin′iousness,** *n.*

ignominy (ĭg′nə mĭ nĭ), *n.*, *pl.* **-minies. 1.** disgrace; dishonour; public contempt. **2.** base quality or conduct; a cause of disgrace. [t. L: m. s. *ignōminia* disgrace, dishonour] —**Syn. 1.** See **disgrace.**

ignoramus (ĭg′nə rā′məs), *n.*, *pl.* **-muses.** an ignorant person. [t. L: we do not know, we disregard]

ignorance (ĭg′nə rəns), *n.* the state or fact of being ignorant; lack of knowledge, learning, or information.

ignorant (ĭg′nə rənt), *adj.* **1.** destitute of knowledge; unlearned. **2.** lacking knowledge or information as to a particular subject or fact. **3.** uninformed; unaware. **4.** due to or showing lack of knowledge: *an ignorant statement.* [ME, t. L: s. *ignōrans*, ppr., not knowing] —**ig′norantly,** *adv.*

—**Syn. 1, 2.** IGNORANT, ILLITERATE, UNLETTERED, UNEDUCATED mean lacking in knowledge or in training. IGNORANT may mean knowing little or nothing, or it may mean uninformed about a particular subject: *an ignorant person can be dangerous*; *to be ignorant of mathematics.* ILLITERATE originally meant lacking a knowledge of literature or similar learning, but is specifically applied to one unable to read or write: *the illiterate voter; necessary training for illiterate soldiers.* UNLETTERED is a translation of the word ILLITERATE, but emphasizes the idea of being without knowledge of or love of literature: *unlettered though highly trained in science.* UNEDUCATED refers especially to lack of schooling or to lack of access to knowledge similarly acquired: *uneducated but intelligent.*

ignore (ĭg nô′), *v.t.*, **-nored, -noring. 1.** to refrain from noticing or recognizing: *ignore his remarks.* **2.** *U.S. Law.* (of the grand jury) to reject (a bill of indictment) as without sufficient evidence. [t. L: m. s. *ignōrāre* not to know, disregard] —**ignor′able,** *adj.* —**ignor′er,** *n.* —**Syn. 1.** overlook; slight, disregard.

Igorot (ĭg′ə rōt′, ē′gə-), *n.*, *pl.* **-rot, -rots.** a member of a people of the Malay stock in northern Luzon in the Philippines, comprising various tribes, some noted as head-hunters. Also, **Igorrote** (ē′gə rō′tĭ). [t. Sp.: m. *igorrote*, from native name]

Igraine (ĭ grān′), *n. Arthurian Legend.* the mother of King Arthur. Also, **Ygerne.**

iguana (ĭ gwā′nə), *n.* **1.** any lizard of the genus *Iguana* of tropical America, esp. *I. iguana*, a large, arboreal, herbivorous species 5 feet or more in length, esteemed as food. **2.** a lizard of a related genus. [t. Sp.,

Iguana, *Iguana iguana* (Length up to 6 ft)

t. Arawak: m. *iwana*] —**iguanian** (ĭ gwä′nĭ ən), *adj.*, *n.*

iguanid (ĭ gwä′nĭd), *n.* any lizard of the family *Iguanidae*, having widespread distribution among tropical islands of the Southern Hemisphere, most of which are arboreal to a certain extent, a few species being semi-aquatic.

iguanodon (ĭ gwä′nə dŏn′), *n.* any member of the extinct bipedal dinosaurian genus *Iguanodon*, found as a fossil in Europe, comprising reptiles from 15 to 30 feet long, with denticulate teeth like those of the iguana. [f. IGUAN(A) + m. s. Gk *odoús* tooth]

Iguassú (*Port.* ē gwȧ sōō′), *n.* a river in S Brazil, flowing W to the Paraná river. 380 mi.

Iguassú Falls, falls of great volume on the river Iguassú, on the boundary between Brazil and Argentina. 210 ft high. Also, **Victoria Falls.**

I.G.Y., International Geophysical Year.

I.H.B., International Hockey Board.

I.H.D., International Hydrological Decade.

ihram (ĭ räm′), *n.* the dress worn by Muslim pilgrims to Mecca, consisting of two white cotton cloths, one round the waist, the other over the left shoulder. [t. Ar., der. *ḥarama* forbid]

IHS, shortening of Greek ΙΗΣΟΥΣ Jesus, sometimes taken as representing: **1.** (L *Iesus Hominum Salvator*) Jesus, Saviour of Men. **2.** (L *In Hoc Signo Vinces*) in this sign (the cross) shalt thou conquer. **3.** (L *In Hoc Salus*) in this (cross) is salvation.

IJssel (*Du.* ĕy′səl), *n.* a branch of the Rhine in central Netherlands, flowing N to IJssel Lake. 70 mi.

IJssel Lake, a lake in NW Netherlands: created by dyking the Zuider Zee. 465 sq. mi. Dutch, **IJsselmeer.**

Ikhnaton (ĭk nä′tən), *n.* See **Amenhotep IV.**

ikon (ī′kŏn), *n.* icon.

il-[1], var. of **in-**[2], (by assimilation) before *l*, as in *illation*.

il-[2], var. of **in-**[3], (by assimilation) before *l*, as in *illogical*.

-il, var. of **-ile,** as in *civil*.

ilang-ilang (ē′lăng ē′lăng), *n.* ylang-ylang.

-ile, a suffix of adjectives expressing capability, susceptibility, liability, aptitude, etc., as in *agile, docile, ductile, fragile, prehensile, tensile, volatile*. Also, **-il.** [t. L: m. s. *-ilis*; also used to repr. L *-īlis*]

ileac (ĭl′ĭ ăk′), *adj.* of or pertaining to the ileum.

Île de France (*Fr.* ēl də fräNs′), **1.** a former province in N France, including Paris and the region around it. **2.** former name of **Mauritius.**

Île du Diable (*Fr.* ēl dʏ dyȧ′bl), French name of **Devil's Island.**

ileitis (ĭl′ĭ ī′tĭs), *n.* inflammation of the ileum.

ileo-, a word element meaning 'ileum', as in *ileostomy*. [t. L, comb. form of *ileum* groin, flank]

ileostomy (ĭl′ĭ ŏs′tə mĭ), *n.*, *pl.* **-mies.** *Surg.* the formation of an artificial opening into the ileum.

Ilesha (ĭ lā′shə), *n.* a town in W Nigeria. 72,000 (est. 1963).

ileum (ĭl′ĭ əm), *n.* **1.** *Anat.* the third and lowest division of the small intestine, continuous with the jejunum and ending at the caecum. See diag. under **intestine. 2.** *Entomol.* a narrower part of the intestine of an insect, following the stomach. [NL, in LL groin, flank, in L (usually pl.) *īlia* flanks, entrails]

ileus (ĭl′ĭ əs), *n.* *Pathol.* intestinal obstruction. [t. L, t. Gk: m. *ileós*, var. of *eileós* colic]

ilex (ī′lĕks), *n.* **1.** the holm oak. **2.** any tree or shrub of the genus *Ilex*. **3.** holly. [NL: the holly genus, L the holm oak]

Ilford (ĭl′fəd), *n.* a town in SE England, in the NE outer London borough of Redbridge. 178,024 (1961).

iliac (ĭl′ĭ ăk′), *adj.* of or pertaining to the ilium. [t. LL: s. *īliacus* pertaining to the flank, der. L *īlium*]

Iliad (ĭl′ĭ əd), *n.* **1.** a Greek epic poem describing the siege of Troy, ascribed to Homer. **2.** any similar poem; a long narrative. **3.** a long series of woes, etc. [t. L: s. *Ilias*, t. Gk, der. *Ilion* Ilium, Troy] —**Iliadic** (ĭl′ĭ ăd′ĭk), *adj.*

Ilion (ĭl′ĭ ən), *n.* Greek name of ancient **Troy.**

-ility, a compound suffix making abstract nouns from adjectives by replacing the adj. suffixes: *-il(e), -le*, as in *civility, sterility, ability*. [t. F: m. *-ilité*, t. L: m. *-ilitas*]

ilium (ĭl′ĭ əm), *n.*, *pl.* **ilia** (ĭl′ĭ ə). *Anat.* the broad upper portion of either innominate bone. See diag. under **pelvis.** [NL, special use of L *īlium* flank]

Ilium (ĭl′ĭ əm), *n.* Latin name of ancient **Troy.**

ilk (ĭlk), *adj.* **1.** same. **2.** *Scot. and N Dial.* each; every. —*n.* **3.** family, class, or kind: *he and all his ilk*. [ME *ilk*, OE *elc, ylc*, var. of *ælc* EACH]

ilka (ĭl′kə), *adj.* *Scot. and N Dial.* ilk. [f. ILK + A[1] (indef. art.)]

Ilkeston (ĭl′kĭs tən), *n.* a town in England, in Derbyshire. 34,672 (1961).

Ilkley (ĭlk′lĭ), *n.* a town in England, in the West Riding of Yorkshire. 18,519 (1961).

ill (ĭl), *adj.*, **worse, worst,** *n.*, *adv.* —*adj.* **1.** physically disordered, as the health; unwell, sick, or indisposed. **2.** evil, wicked, or bad: *ill repute*. **3.** objectionable, unsatisfactory, poor, or faulty: *ill manners*. **4.** hostile or unkindly: *ill feeling*. **5.** unfavourable or adverse: *ill luck*. **6.** unskilful; inexpert. —*n.* **7.** evil. **8.** harm or injury. **9.** a disease or ailment. **10.** trouble or misfortune. **11.** *Archaic.* wickedness or sin. —*adv.* **12.** in an ill manner; wickedly. **13.** unsatisfactorily or poorly: *ill at ease*. **14.** in a hostile or unfriendly manner. **15.** unfavourably or unfortunately. **16.** with displeasure or offence. **17.** faultily or improperly. **18.** with trouble, difficulty, or inconvenience: *buying a new car is an expense we can ill afford*. [ME *ill*, t. Scand.; cf. Icel. *illr* ill, bad]

—**Syn. 1.** ILL, SICK mean being in bad health, not being well. ILL is the more formal word. SICK usually has connotations of nausea; it is, however, used before nouns, in the collective and in set phrases: *he is ill, she felt ill, he looks ill; a sick man, to care for the sick*, and the like. **2.** See **bad.** —**Ant. 1.** well, healthy.

I'll (īl), contraction of *I will* or *I shall*.

Ill., Illinois.

ill., **1.** illustrated. **2.** illustration.

ill-advised (ĭl′əd vīzd′), *adj.* acting or done without due consideration; imprudent. —**ill-advisedly** (ĭl′əd vī′zĭd lĭ), *adv.*

Illampu (*Sp.* ē lyäm′pōō), *n.* See **Sorata, Mount.**

ill-at-ease (ĭl′ət ēz′), *adj.* uncomfortable; uneasy. Also, in predicative use, **ill at ease.**

illation (ĭ lā′shən), *n.* **1.** the act of inferring. **2.** an inference or conclusion. [t. LL: s. *illātio* a carrying in]

illative (ĭ lā′tĭv), *adj.* pertaining to or expressing illation; inferential: *an illative word such as 'therefore'*. [t. L: m. s. *illātīvus*] —**illa′tively,** *adv.*

illaudable (ĭ lô′də bl), *adj.* not laudable. —**illaud′ably,** *adv.*

ill-boding (ĭl′bō′dĭng), *adj.* foreboding evil; inauspicious; unlucky: *ill-boding stars*.

ill-bred (ĭl′brĕd′), *adj.* showing or due to lack of proper breeding; unmannerly; rude: *he remained serene in a houseful of ill-bred children*. —**ill-breeding** (ĭl′brē′dĭng), *n.*

ill-conditioned (ĭl′kən dĭsh′ənd), *adj.* churlish; surly.

ill-disposed (ĭl′dĭs pōzd′), *adj.* unsympathetic; unfriendly.

Ille-et-Vilaine (*Fr.* ēl ė vē lĕn′), *n.* a department in W France. 614,268 pop. (1962); 2700 sq. mi. *Cap.*: Rennes.

illegal (ĭ lē′gl), *adj.* not legal; unauthorized. [t. ML: s. *illēgālis*, f. L: *il-* IL- + *lēgālis* LEGAL] —**ille′gally,** *adv.* —**ille′galness,** *n.* —**Syn.** unlawful; illegitimate; illicit; unlicensed.

illegality (ĭl′ĭ găl′ĭ tĭ), *n.*, *pl.* **-ties. 1.** illegal condition or quality; unlawfulness. **2.** an illegal act.

illegalize (ĭ lē′gə līz′), *v.t.* to make illegal: *they even wanted to illegalize smoking*. Also, **illegalise.**

illegible (ĭ lĕj′ə bl), *adj.* not legible; impossible or hard to read or decipher: *this letter is completely illegible*. —**illeg′ibil′ity, illeg′ibleness,** *n.* —**illeg′ibly,** *adv.*

illegitimacy (ĭl′ĭ jĭt′ĭ mə sĭ), *n.*, *pl.* **-cies.** the state or quality of being illegitimate.

illegitimate (ĭl′ĭ jĭt′ĭ mĭt), *adj.*, *v.*, **-mated, -mating,** *n.* **1.** not legitimate; unlawful: *an illegitimate act*. **2.** born out of wedlock: *an illegitimate child*. **3.** irregular; not in good usage. **4.** *Logic.* not in accordance with the principle of inference. —*v.t.* **5.** to pronounce illegitimate. —*n.* **6.** a bastard; an illegitimate person. —**il′legit′imately,** *adv.*

ill fame, bad repute or name. —**ill′-famed′,** *adj.*

ill-fated (ĭl′fā′tĭd), *adj.* **1.** destined to an unhappy fate: *an ill-fated person*. **2.** bringing bad fortune.

ill-favoured (ĭl′fā′vəd), *adj.* **1.** not pleasant in appearance; ugly: *an ill-favoured child*. **2.** offensive; unpleasant; objectionable. —**ill′-fa′vouredly,** *adv.* —**ill′-fa′vouredness,** *n.*

ill feeling, enmity or resentment.

ill-founded (ĭl′foun′dĭd), *adj.* on a weak or illogical basis: *an ill-founded plea for mercy*.

ill-gotten (ĭl′gŏt′n), *adj.* acquired by evil means.

ill humour, a disagreeable mood. —**ill′-hu′moured** (ĭl′hyōō′məd), *adj.* —**ill′-hu′mouredly,** *adv.*

illiberal (ĭ lĭb′ə rəl, ĭ lĭb′rəl), *adj.* **1.** narrow-minded; bigoted. **2.** without culture; unscholarly; vulgar. **3.** *Rare.* not generous in giving; niggardly. [t. L: s. *illīberālis* mean, sordid] —**illib′eral′ity, illib′eralness,** *n.* —**illib′erally,** *adv.*

illicit (ĭ lĭs′ĭt), *adj.* not permitted or authorized; unlicensed; unlawful. [t. L: s. *illicitus* forbidden] —**illic′itly,** *adv.* —**illic′itness,** *n.*

illicit diamond buying, (in South Africa) the practice of trading in precious stones without an official licence. *Abbrev.*: I.D.B.

Illimani (*Sp.* ē lyē mä′nē), *n.* a mountain in W Bolivia, in the Andes, near La Paz. 21,188 ft.

illimitable (ĭ lĭm′ĭ tə bl), *adj.* not limitable; limitless; boundless. —**illim′itabil′ity, illim′itableness,** *n.* —**illim′itably,** *adv.*

illinium (ĭ lĭn′ĭ əm), *n. Chem.* a former name for **promethium.** [f. ILLIN(OIS) + -IUM]

Illinois (ĭl′ĭ noi′), *n.* **1.** a state in the central United States: a part of the Midwest. 10,081,158 pop. (1960); 56,400 sq. mi. *Cap.:* Springfield. *Abbrev.:* Ill. **2.** a river flowing from NE Illinois SW to the Mississippi, connected by a canal with Lake Michigan. 273 mi. [t. F, t. Illinois Indian, c. Shawnee *hileni,* Fox *ineniwa* man, g. Proto-Algonquian *elenyiwa*] —**Illinoisan** (ĭl′ĭ noi′zən), *n., adj.*

Illinois (ĭl′ĭ noi′), *n., pl.* **-nois** (-noi′, -noiz′). **1.** (*pl.*) a confederacy of North American Indians of Algonquian stock, formerly occupying Illinois and adjoining regions westward. **2.** an Indian of this confederacy.

illiteracy (ĭ lĭt′ə rə sĭ), *n., pl.* **-cies. 1.** lack of ability to read and write. **2.** the state of being illiterate; lack of education. **3.** *Rare.* a literal or a literary error.

illiterate (ĭ lĭt′ə rĭt), *adj.* **1.** unable to read and write: *an illiterate tribe.* **2.** lacking education. **3.** showing lack of culture. —*n.* **4.** an illiterate person. [t. L: m. s. *illiterātus* unlettered] —**illit′erately,** *adv.* —**illit′erateness,** *n.* —**Syn. 1.** See **ignorant.**

ill-judged (ĭl′jŭjd′), *adj.* injudicious; unwise.

ill-looking (ĭl′lo͝ok′ĭng), *adj.* **1.** ugly. **2.** sinister.

ill-mannered (ĭl′măn′əd), *adj.* having bad manners; impolite; rude. —**ill′-man′neredly,** *adv.*

ill nature, unkindly or unpleasant disposition.

ill-natured (ĭl′nā′chəd), *adj.* **1.** having or showing an unkindly or unpleasant disposition. **2.** cross; peevish. —**ill′-na′turedly,** *adv.* —**ill′-na′turedness,** *n.* —**Syn.** See **cross.**

illness (ĭl′nĭs), *n.* **1.** a state of bad health; sickness. **2.** an attack of sickness. **3.** *Obs.* wickedness.

illogical (ĭ lŏj′ĭ kl), *adj.* not logical; contrary to or disregardful of the rules of logic; unreasonable. —**illog′ical′ity, illog′icalness,** *n.* —**illog′ically,** *adv.*

ill-omened (ĭl′ō′mĭnd), *adj.* having or attended by bad omens; ill-starred.

ill-starred (ĭl′städ′), *adj.* **1.** under the influence of an evil star; ill-fated; unlucky. **2.** disastrous.

ill temper, bad disposition.

ill-tempered (ĭl′tĕm′pəd), *adj.* irritable; morose; bad-tempered. —**ill′-tem′peredly,** *adv.* —**ill′-tem′peredness,** *n.*

ill-timed (ĭl′tīmd′), *adj.* badly timed; inopportune.

ill-treat (ĭl′trēt′), *v.t.* to treat badly; maltreat. —**ill′-treat′ment,** *n.*

ill turn, an unkind and vicious act.

illume (ĭ lyo͞om′), *v.t.,* **-lumed, -luming.** *Poetic.* to illuminate.

illuminant (ĭ lyo͞o′mĭ nənt), *n.* an illuminating agent or material.

illuminate (*v.* ĭ lyo͞o′mĭ nāt′; *adj., n.* ĭ lyo͞o′mĭ nĭt, -nāt′), *v.,* **-nated, -nating,** *adj., n.* —*v.t.* **1.** to supply with light; light up. **2.** to throw light on (a subject); make lucid or clear. **3.** to decorate with lights, as in celebration. **4.** to enlighten, as with knowledge. **5.** to make resplendent or illustrious. **6.** to decorate (a letter, a page, a manuscript, etc.) with colour, gold, or the like. —*v.i.* **7.** to display lights, as in celebration. **8.** to become illuminated. —*adj.* **9.** *Archaic.* illuminated. **10.** *Obs.* enlightened. —*n.* **11.** *Archaic.* one who is or affects to be specially enlightened. [t. L: m. s. *illūminātus,* pp.] —**illu′minat′ing,** *adj.* —**illu′minat′ingly,** *adv.*

illuminati (ĭ lo͞o′mĭ nä′tē), *n.pl., sing.* **-to** (-tō). **1.** persons possessing or claiming to possess superior enlightenment. **2.** (*cap.*) a name given to different religious societies or sects because of their claim to enlightenment. [t. L, pl. of *illūminātus* enlightened]

illumination (ĭ lyo͞o′mĭ nā′shən), *n.* **1.** the act of illuminating. **2.** the fact or condition of being illuminated. **3.** a decoration consisting of lights. **4.** intellectual or spiritual enlightenment. **5.** the intensity of light falling at a given place on a lighted surface; the luminus flux per unit area at a given point on an intercepting surface. **6.** a supply of light. **7.** decoration, as of a letter, page, or manuscript, with a painted design in colour, gold, etc.

illuminative (ĭ lyo͞o′mĭ nə tĭv), *adj.* illuminating.

illuminator (ĭ lyo͞o′mĭ nā′tə), *n.* **1.** one who or that which illuminates. **2.** a device for illuminating, such as a light source with lens or a mirror for concentrating light. **3.** one who paints manuscripts, books, etc., with designs in colour, gold, or the like.

illumine (ĭ lyo͞o′mĭn), *v.t., v.i.,* **-mined, -mining.** to illuminate or be illuminated. [ME *illumyne(n),* t. F: m. *illuminer,* t. L: m. *illūmināre* light up] —**illu′minable,** *adj.*

illuminism (ĭ lyo͞o′mĭ nĭz′əm), *n.* **1.** the doctrines or claims of illuminati. **2.** a doctrine advocating enlightenment. —**illu′minist,** *n.*

illuminometer (ĭ lyo͞o′mĭ nŏm′ĭ tə), *n.* a type of photometer.

illus., 1. illustrated. **2.** illustration.

ill use (yo͞os), bad, unjust, or cruel treatment. Also, **ill usage.**

ill-use (ĭl′yo͞oz′), *v.t.,* **-used, -using.** to treat badly, unjustly, or cruelly.

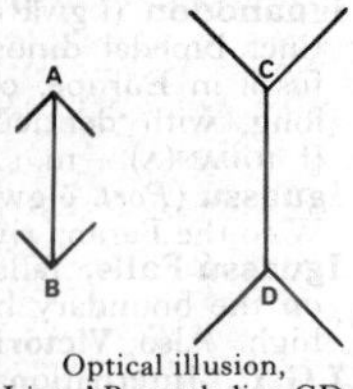

illusion (ĭ lo͞o′zhən), *n.* **1.** something that deceives by producing a false impression. **2.** the act of deceiving; deception; delusion; mockery. **3.** the state of being deceived, or an instance of this; a false impression or belief. **4.** *Psychol.* a perception of a thing which misrepresents it, or gives it qualities not present in reality. **5.** a very thin, delicate kind of tulle. [ME, t. L: s. *illūsio* mocking, illusion]

Optical illusion, Line AB equals line CD

—**Syn. 1.** ILLUSION, DELUSION, HALLUCINATION refer to mental deceptions which arise from various causes. An ILLUSION is a false mental image or conception which may be a misinterpretation of a real appearance or may be something imagined. It may be pleasing, harmless, or even useful: *a mirage is an illusion, he had an illusion that the doorman was a general.* A DELUSION is a fixed mistaken conception of something which really exists, and is not capable of correction or removal by examination or reasoning. DELUSIONS are often mischievous or harmful, as those of a fanatic or a lunatic: *the delusion that all food is poisoned.* A HALLUCINATION is a completely groundless false conception, belief, or opinion, caused by a disordered imagination; it is particularly frequent today in the pathological sense, according to which it denotes hearing or seeing something that does not exist: *hallucinations caused by nervous disorders.* —**Ant. 1.** reality.

illusionary (ĭ lo͞o′zhə nə rĭ), *adj.* pertaining to or characterized by illusions. Also, **illusional** (ĭ lo͞o′zhə nəl).

illusionism (ĭ lo͞o′zhə nĭz′əm), *n.* **1.** a theory or doctrine that the material world is an illusion. **2.** (in painting) the effect of deceiving the eye into believing that a painted surface represents an actual scene. Cf. **trompe l'oeil.**

illusionist (ĭ lo͞o′zhə nĭst), *n.* **1.** one subject to illusions. **2.** a conjurer or magician. **3.** an adherent of illusionism.

illusive (ĭ lo͞o′sĭv), *adj.* illusory. —**illu′sively,** *adv.* —**illu′siveness,** *n.*

illusory (ĭ lo͞o′sə rĭ), *adj.* **1.** causing illusion; deceptive. **2.** of the nature of an illusion; unreal. —**illu′sorily,** *adv.* —**illu′soriness,** *n.*

illust., 1. illustrated. **2.** illustration.

illustrate (ĭl′ə strāt′), *v.t.,* **-strated, -strating. 1.** to make clear or intelligible, as by examples; exemplify. **2.** to furnish (a book, etc.) with drawings or pictorial representations intended for elucidation or adornment. **3.** *Archaic.* to enlighten. [t. L: m. s. *illustrātus,* pp., illuminated]

illustrated (ĭl′ə strā′tĭd), *adj.* **1.** bearing illustrations; pictorially decorated. —*n.* **2.** an illustrated magazine.

illustration (ĭl′ə strā′shən), *n.* **1.** that which illustrates, as a picture in a book, etc. **2.** a comparison or an example intended for explanation or corroboration. **3.** the act of rendering clear; explanation; elucidation. **4.** *Rare.* illustriousness; distinction. —**il′lustra′tional,** *adj.* —**Syn. 2.** See **case**[1]

illustrative (ĭl′ə strā′tĭv), *adj.* serving to illustrate. —**il′lustra′tively,** *adv.*

illustrator (ĭl′ə strā′tə), *n.* **1.** an artist who makes illustrations. **2.** one who or that which illustrates.

illustrious (ĭ lŭs′trĭ əs), *adj.* **1.** highly distinguished; renowned; famous. **2.** glorious, as deeds, etc. **3.** *Obs.* luminous; bright. [f. L *illustri(s)* lit up, bright + -OUS] —**illus′triously,** *adv.* —**illus′triousness,** *n.*

ill will, hostile or unfriendly feeling. —**ill-willed** (ĭl′wĭld′), *adj.*

ill-wisher (ĭl′wĭsh′ə, ĭl′wĭsh′ə), *n.* one who wishes ill fortune to another.

illy (ĭl′ĭ, ĭl′lĭ), *adv. Dial.* ill.

Illyria (ĭ lĭ′rĭ ə), *n.* an ancient country along the E coast of the Adriatic.

Illyrian (ĭ lĭ′rĭ ən), *adj.* **1.** pertaining to Illyria. —*n.* **2.** a native or inhabitant of Illyria. **3.** an extinct Indo-European language probably allied with Albanian. **4.** a group of Indo-European languages including Albanian.

ilmenite (ĭl′mĭ nīt′), *n.* a very common black mineral, iron titanate, $FeTiO_3$, occurring in crystals but more commonly massive. [f. *Ilmen* (name of mountain range in the Urals) + -ITE[1]]

I.L.O., 1. International Labour Organization. **2.** International Labour Office.

Iloilo (ē′lō ē′lō), *n.* a seaport in the Philippines, capital of Panay, in the SE part. 151,266 (1960).

Ilokano (ē′lō kä′nō), *n., pl.* **-nos** (-nōz). **1.** an Indonesian language of Luzon. **2.** (in the Philippines) a Christian Malay. [t. Sp.: m. *Ilocano*, der. *Ilocos* the name of two provinces, lit., river run, from Tagalog *ilog* river]

I.L.P., Independent Labour Party.

i.l.s., *Aeron.* instrument landing system.

I'm (īm), contraction of *I am.*

im-[1], var. of **in-**[2] used before *b*, *m*, and *p*, as in *imbrute, immingle.*

im-[2], var. of **in-**[3] used before *b*, *m*, and *p*, as in *immoral, imparity, imperishable.*

im-[3], var. of **in-**[1], before *b*, *m*, and *p*, as in *imbed, impearl.* Also, **em-**[1].

Imabari (ĭ mä′bə rĭ, ē′mə bä′rĭ), *n.* a town in Japan, in W Shikoku. 104,470 (1965).

image (ĭm′ĭj), *n., v.,* **-aged, -aging.** —*n.* **1.** a likeness or similitude of a person, animal, or thing. **2.** an optical counterpart or appearance of an object, such as is produced by reflection from a mirror, refraction by a lens, or the passage of luminous rays through a small aperture. **3.** a mental picture or representation; an idea or conception. **4.** *Psychol.* the reliving of a sensation in the absence of the original stimulus. **5.** form, appearance, or semblance. **6.** a counterpart or copy: *the child is the image of its mother.* **7.** a symbol or emblem. **8.** a type or embodiment. **9.** a description of something in speech or writing. **10.** *Rhet.* a figure of speech, esp. a metaphor or a simile. **11.** *Archaic.* an illusion or apparition. —*v.t.* **12.** to picture or represent in the mind; imagine; conceive. **13.** to make an image of. **14.** to set forth in speech or writing; describe. **15.** to reflect the likeness of; mirror. **16.** to symbolize or typify. **17.** *Rare.* to resemble. [ME, t. F, t. L: m. *imāgo* copy, image]

—**Syn. 1.** IMAGE, ICON, IDOL refer to material representations of persons or things. An IMAGE is a representation as in a statue or effigy, and is sometimes regarded as an object of worship: *to set up an image of Apollo, an image of a saint, graven images.* An ICON, in the Greek or Orthodox Eastern Church, is a representation of Christ, an angel, or a saint, in painting, relief, mosaic, or the like: *at least two icons are found in each church.* Small icons are also carried by the peasants; these are folded tablets of wood or metal, with representations of sacred subjects in enamel or in designs of black and white or silver: *an icon is honoured by offerings of incense and lights.* An IDOL is an image, statue, or the like, representing a deity and worshipped as such: *wooden idols,* fig., *the idol of wealth.*

imagery (ĭm′ĭj rĭ, ĭm′ĭj ə rĭ), *n., pl.* **-ries. 1.** the formation of images, figures, or likenesses of things, or such images collectively: *a dream's dim imagery.* **2.** *Psychol.* a person's tendencies to form images. **3.** images or statues. **4.** the use of rhetorical images. **5.** figurative description or illustration; rhetorical images collectively.

imaginable (ĭ măj′ĭ nə bl), *adj.* capable of being imagined or conceived. —**imag′inableness,** *n.* —**imag′inably,** *adv.*

imaginal (ĭ măj′ĭ nəl), *adj. Entomol.* **1.** of or pertaining to an imago. **2.** in the form of an imago.

imaginary (ĭ măj′ĭ nə rĭ, -ĭn rĭ), *adj., n., pl.* **-ries.** —*adj.* **1.** existing only in the imagination or fancy; not real; fancied: *an imaginary illness.* **2.** *Maths.* denoting or pertaining to a quantity or expression involving the square root of a negative quantity. —*n.* **3.** *Maths.* an imaginary expression or quantity. —**imag′inarily,** *adv.* —**imag′inariness,** *n.* —**Syn. 1.** visionary, shadowy, chimerical; baseless, unreal.

imagination (ĭ măj′ĭ nā′shən), *n.* **1.** the action of imagining, or of forming mental images or concepts of what is not actually present to the senses. **2.** the faculty of forming such images or concepts. **3.** the power of reproducing images stored in the memory under the suggestion of associated images (**reproductive imagination**), or of recombining former experiences in the creation of new images different from any known by experience (**productive** or **creative imagination**). **4.** the faculty of producing ideal creations consistent with reality, as in literature (distinguished from *fancy*). **5.** the product of imagining; a conception or mental creation, often a baseless or fanciful one. **6.** *Archaic.* a plan, scheme, or plot. [ME, t. L: s. *imāginātio*] —**imag′ina′tional,** *adj.* —**Syn. 4.** See **fancy.**

imaginative (ĭ măj′ĭ nə tĭv), *adj.* **1.** characterized by or bearing evidence of imagination: *an imaginative tale.* **2.** pertaining to or concerned with imagination: *the imaginative faculty.* **3.** given to imagining, as persons. **4.** having exceptional powers of imagination. **5.** fanciful. —**imag′inatively,** *adv.* —**imag′inativeness,** *n.*

imagine (ĭ măj′ĭn), *v.,* **-ined, -ining.** —*v.t.* **1.** to form a mental image of (something not actually present to the senses). **2.** to think, believe, or fancy. **3.** to assume or suppose. **4.** to conjecture or guess: *I cannot imagine what you mean.* **5.** *Archaic.* to plan, scheme, or plot. —*v.i.* **6.** to form mental images of things not present to the senses; use the imagination. **7.** to suppose; think; conjecture. [ME *imagine(n)*, t. F: m. *imaginer*, t. L: m. *imāginārī* picture to oneself, fancy] —**imag′iner,** *n.*

—**Syn. 1.** IMAGINE, CONCEIVE OF, REALIZE refer to bringing something before the mind. To IMAGINE is, literally, to form a mental image of something: *imagine yourself in London.* To CONCEIVE is to relate ideas or feelings to one another in a pattern: *how has the author conceived the first act of his play?* To CONCEIVE OF is to comprehend through the intellect something not perceived through the senses: *he conceived of a world free from pain.* To REALIZE is to make an imagined thing real or concrete to oneself, to grasp fully its implications: *to realize the extent of one's folly.*

imagism (ĭm′ĭ jĭz′əm), *n.* a method or movement in poetic composition, originating about 1912, which aimed particularly at 'images' or clear pictures of what the poet has in mind, and used rhythm or cadence rather than the conventional metrical forms. See **free verse.** —**im′agist,** *n., adj.* —**im′agis′tic,** *adj.*

imago (ĭ mā′gō), *n., pl.* **imagos, imagines** (ĭ mā′jĭ nēz′). **1.** *Entomol.* an adult insect. **2.** *Psychol.* an idealized concept of a loved one, formed in childhood and retained uncorrected in adult life. [NL, special use of L *imāgo* image]

imam (ĭ mäm′), *n.* **1.** the officiating priest of a mosque. **2.** the title for a Muslim religious leader or chief. **3.** one of a succession of seven or twelve religious leaders, believed to be divinely inspired, of the Shiites. Also, **imaum** (ĭ mäm′, ĭ môm′). [t. Ar.: m. *imām* leader, guide]

imamate (ĭ mä′māt), *n.* **1.** the office of an imam. **2.** the region or territory governed by an imam.

imaret (ĭ mä′rĕt), *n.* (among the Turks) a hospice for pilgrims, etc. [Turk., t. Ar.: m. *'imāra(t)* building, dwelling place]

Imbaba (ĭm bä′bä), *n.* a town in N Egypt, in the Nile delta. 136,000 (1960).

imbalance (ĭm băl′əns), *n.* **1.** the state or condition of lacking balance. **2.** faulty muscular or glandular coordination.

imbecile (ĭm′bĭ sēl′, -sīl′), *n.* **1.** a person of defective mentality above the grade of idiocy. **2.** *Colloq.* a silly person; fool. —*adj.* **3.** mentally feeble. **4.** showing mental feebleness or incapacity. **5.** silly; absurd. **6.** *Rare.* weak or feeble. [t. F, t. L: m. s. *imbēcillus* weak, feeble] —**im′becile′ly,** *adv.*

imbecility (ĭm′bĭ sĭl′ĭ tĭ), *n., pl.* **-ties. 1.** feebleness of mind; mental weakness that falls short of absolute idiocy. **2.** an instance or point of weakness or feebleness. **3.** silliness or absurdity. **4.** an instance of this.

imbed (ĭm bĕd′), *v.t.,* **-bedded, -bedding.** embed.

imbibe (ĭm bīb′), *v.,* **-bibed, -bibing.** —*v.t.* **1.** to drink in, or drink. **2.** to absorb or take in as if by drinking. **3.** to take or receive into the mind, as knowledge, ideas, etc. —*v.i.* **4.** to drink; absorb liquid or moisture. **5.** *Obs.* to soak or saturate; imbue. [ME, t. L: m. *imbibere* drink in] —**imbib′er,** *n.* —**Syn. 1.** See **drink.**

imbibition (ĭm′bĭ bĭsh′ən), *n.* **1.** the act of imbibing. **2.** *Chem.* the absorption or adsorption of a liquid by a solid or gel causing swelling. **3.** *Photog.* the absorption of a dye by gelatine in colour printing.

A, Imbricate flower; B, Imbricate scale of cone

imbricate (*adj.* ĭm′brĭ kĭt, -kāt′; *v.* ĭm′brĭ kāt′), *adj., v.,* **-cated, -cating.** —*adj.* Also, **im′bricat′ed. 1.** bent and hollowed like a roof tile. **2.** of, like, or decorated with lines or curves resembling overlapping tiles. **3.** *Biol.* overlapping like tiles, as scales, leaves, etc. **4.** characterized by, or as by, overlapping scales. —*v.t., v.i.* **5.** to overlap like tiles or shingles. [t. L: m. s. *imbricātus*, pp., covered with tiles] —**im′bricately,** *adv.* —**im′brica′tive,** *adj.*

imbrication (ĭm′brĭ kā′shən), *n.* **1.** an overlapping, as of tiles or shingles. **2.** a decorative pattern imitating this.

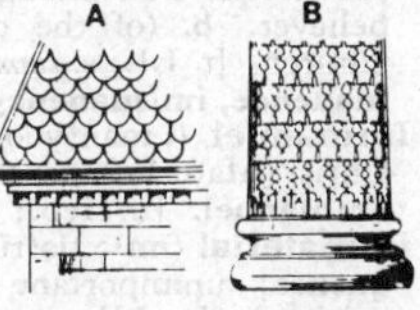

A, Imbrication on roof tiles; B, Ornamental imbrication on a column

imbroglio (ĭm brō′lĭ ō′), *n., pl.* **-os. 1.** an intricate and perplexing state of affairs; a complicated or difficult situation. **2.** a misunderstanding or disagreement of a complicated nature, as between persons or nations. **3.** a confused heap. [t. It.: confusion, der. *imbrogliare* confuse, embroil]

imbrue (ĭm broo′), *v.t.,* **-brued, -bruing. 1.** to wet in or with something that stains, now esp. blood; stain with blood. **2.** to permeate; impregnate (usually fol. by *with*). [ME *enbrewe(n)*, t. OF: m. *embreuver* give to drink, ult. der. L *bibere* drink] —**imbrue′ment,** *n.*

imbrute (ĭm broot′), *v.t., v.i.,* **-bruted, -bruting.** to degrade or sink to the level of a brute. Also, **embrute.** [f. IM-[1] + BRUTE, n.] —**imbrute′ment,** *n.*

imbue (ĭm byōō′), *v.t.*, **-bued, -buing. 1.** to impregnate or inspire, as with feelings, opinions, etc. **2.** to saturate with moisture, impregnate with colour, etc. **3.** to imbrue. [t. L: m. s. *imbuere*] **—imbue′ment,** *n.*

I.M.F., International Monetary Fund.

imidazole (ĭm′ĭ dăz′ōl, -ĭ də zōl′), *n. Chem.* an organic heterocyclic compound, $C_3H_4N_2$; glyoxalin. [f. IMID(E) + AZ(O)- + -OLE]

imide (ĭm′ĭd), *n. Chem.* a compound derived from ammonia by replacement of two hydrogen atoms by acidic radicals, characterized by the NH group. Also, **imid** (ĭm′ĭd). [arbitrary alter. of AMIDE]

imido-, *Chem.* a combining form indicating an imide.

imine (ĭ mēn′, ĭm′ēn), *n. Chem.* a compound containing the NH group united with a non-acid radical. [alter. of AMINE modelled on IMIDE]

imino-, a combining form indicating an imine.

imit., 1. imitation. **2.** imitative.

imitable (ĭm′ĭ tə bl), *adj.* that may be imitated. **—im′itabil′ity,** *n.*

imitate (ĭm′ĭ tāt′), *v.t.*, **-tated, -tating. 1.** to follow or endeavour to follow in action or manner. **2.** to mimic or counterfeit. **3.** to make a copy of; reproduce closely. **4.** to have or assume the appearance of; simulate. [t. L: m. s. *imitātus*, pp., having copied] **—im′ita′tor,** *n.*

—Syn. 3. IMITATE, COPY, DUPLICATE, REPRODUCE all mean to follow or try to follow an example or pattern. IMITATE is the general word for the idea: *to imitate someone's handwriting, behaviour.* To COPY is to make a fairly exact imitation of an original creation: *to copy a sentence, a dress, a picture.* To DUPLICATE is to produce something which exactly resembles or corresponds to something else; both may be originals: *to duplicate the terms of two contracts.* To REPRODUCE is to make a likeness or reconstruction of an original: *to reproduce a 16th-century theatre.*

imitation (ĭm′ĭ tā′shən), *n.* **1.** a result or product of imitating. **2.** the act of imitating. **3.** *Sociol.* the copying of patterns of activity and thought of other groups or individuals. **4.** *Biol.* close external resemblance of an organism to some other organism or to objects in its environment. **5.** *Psychol.* a response or state of mind brought about by observation and copying in some respects the act of another. **6.** a counterfeit. **7.** a literary composition that imitates the manner or subject of another author or work. **8.** mimesis. **9.** *Music.* the repetition of a melodic phrase at a different pitch or key from the original, or in a different voice part. **—*adj.* 10.** made to imitate a genuine or superior article or thing: *imitation pearls.* [t. L: s. *imitātio*] **—im′ita′tional,** *adj.*

imitative (ĭm′ĭ tə tĭv), *adj.* **1.** imitating or copying, or given to imitating. **2.** characterized by or involving imitation or copying. **3.** *Biol.* mimetic. **4.** made in imitation of something. **5.** onomatopoeic. **—im′itatively,** *adv.* **—im′itativeness,** *n.*

immaculate (ĭ măk′yōō lĭt), *adj.* **1.** free from spot or stain; spotlessly clean, as linen. **2.** free from moral blemish or impurity; pure, or undefiled. **3.** free from fault or flaw; free from errors, as a text. **4.** *Zool., Bot.* without spots or coloured marks; unicolour. [late ME, t. L: m. s. *immaculātus* unspotted] **—immac′ulacy, immac′ulateness,** *n.* **—immac′ulately,** *adv.*

Immaculate Conception, *Rom. Cath. Ch.* the unique privilege by which the Virgin Mary was conceived in her mother's womb without the stain of original sin, through the anticipated merits of Jesus Christ.

immanent (ĭm′ə nənt), *adj.* **1.** remaining within; indwelling; inherent. **2.** (of a mental act) taking place within the mind of the subject, and having no effect outside it. **3.** *Theol.* **a.** of or pertaining to the continuing presence of God among His people and in each individual believer. **b.** (of the deity) seen as indwelling in the Church. [t. LL: s. *immanens*, ppr., remaining in] **—im′manence, im′manency,** *n.* **—im′manently,** *adv.*

Immanuel (ĭ măn′yōō əl), *n.* a name to be given to Christ (Matt. 1:23) as the son of a virgin (Isa. 7:14). Also, **Emmanuel.** [t. Heb.: m. *'Immānū'ēl*, lit., God with us]

immaterial (ĭm′ə tĭə′rĭ əl), *adj.* **1.** of no essential consequence; unimportant. **2.** not material; incorporeal; spiritual. [t. ML: s. *immāteriālis*, f. LL: *im-* IM-[2] + *māteriālis* MATERIAL; r. ME *immaterielle*, t. F] **—im′mate′rially,** *adv.* **—im′mate′rialness,** *n.*

immaterialism (ĭm′ə tĭə′rĭ ə lĭz′əm), *n.* the doctrine that there is no material world, but that only immaterial substances or spiritual beings exist (opposed to *materialism*). **—im′mate′rialist,** *n.*

immateriality (ĭm′ə tĭə′rĭ ăl′ĭ tĭ), *n., pl.* **-ties. 1.** the state or character of being immaterial. **2.** something immaterial.

immaterialize (ĭm′ə tĭə′rĭ ə līz′), *v.t.*, **-lized, -lizing.** to make immaterial. Also, **immaterialise.**

immature (ĭm′ə tyōōə′), *adj.* **1.** not mature, ripe, developed, or perfected. **2.** *Phys. Geog.* youthful. **3.** *Archaic.* premature. [t. L: m. s. *immātūrus* unripe] **—im′mature′ly,** *adv.* **—im′matu′rity, im′mature′ness,** *n.*

immeasurable (ĭ mĕzh′ə rə bl), *adj.* incapable of being measured; limitless. **—immeas′urabil′ity, immeas′urableness,** *n.* **—immeas′urably,** *adv.*

immediacy (ĭ mē′dyə sĭ), *n.* **1.** the character of being immediate. **2.** *Philos.* **a.** that nature of a thing in virtue of which it exists, acts, or appears, directly and not through any intervening object, operation, or representation. **b.** that which the mind experiences when anything exists, acts, or appears thus.

immediate (ĭ mē′dyət), *adj.* **1.** occurring or accomplished without delay; instant: *an immediate reply.* **2.** pertaining to the present time or moment: *our immediate plans.* **3.** having no time intervening; present or next adjacent: *the immediate future.* **4.** having no object or space intervening; nearest or next: *in the immediate vicinity.* **5.** without intervening medium or agent; direct: *an immediate cause.* **6.** having a direct bearing: *immediate consideration.* **7.** *Metaphys.* indemonstrable; intuitive. [t. ML: m. s. *immediātus* not mediate] **—imme′diateness,** *n.* **—Syn. 5.** See **direct.**

immediately (ĭ mē′dyət lĭ), *adv.* **1.** without lapse of time, or without delay; instantly; at once. **2.** without intervening medium or agent; concerning or affecting directly. **3.** with no object or space intervening. **4.** closely: *immediately in the vicinity.* **—*conj.* 5.** immediately that; the moment that; as soon as.

—Syn. 1. IMMEDIATELY, DIRECTLY, INSTANTLY, PRESENTLY, were originally close synonyms denoting complete absence of delay or of any lapse of time. INSTANTLY is the only one retaining the meaning of action or occurrence on the instant: *he replied instantly to the accusation.* IMMEDIATELY may have the same force: *he immediately got up*; more often, a slight delay: *the game will begin immediately.* DIRECTLY and PRESENTLY have weakened greatly in meaning and at present imply an appreciable lapse of time, so that they are equivalent to *soon,* or *in a little while*: *You go ahead; we'll be there presently (directly).* DIRECTLY is more immediate than PRESENTLY. Expressions which have supplanted them in the original sense are *right away* and *at once*: *he will come right away, I want to see him at once.*

immedicable (ĭ mĕd′ĭ kə bl), *adj.* incurable.

Immelmann turn (ĭm′əl män′, -mən), a manoeuvre in which an aeroplane makes a half-loop, then resumes its normal level position by making a half-roll: used to gain altitude while changing to the opposite direction. [named after Max *Immelmann*, 1890–1916, German pilot in World War I]

immemorial (ĭm′ĭ mô′rĭ əl), *adj.* extending back beyond memory, record, or knowledge: *from time immemorial.* [t. ML: s. *immemoriālis*, f. L: *im-* IM-[2] + *memoriālis* MEMORIAL] **—im′memo′rially,** *adv.*

immense (ĭ mĕns′), *adj.* **1.** vast; huge; very great: *an immense territory.* **2.** immeasurable; boundless. **3.** *Slang.* very good or fine. [t. L: m. s. *immensus* boundless, unmeasured] **—immense′ly,** *adv.* **—immense′ness,** *n.* **—Syn. 1.** See **huge.**

immensity (ĭ mĕn′sĭ tĭ), *n., pl.* **-ties. 1.** vastness; hugeness; enormous extent: *the immensity of the Roman empire.* **2.** the state of being immense; boundless extent; infinity. **3.** a vast expanse; an immense quantity.

immensurable (ĭ mĕn′shə rə bl, -shrə bl), *adj.* immeasurable. [t. LL: m. s. *immensurābilis*] **—immen′surabil′ity,** *n.*

immerge (ĭ mûj′), *v.*, **-merged, -merging.** *Rare.* **—*v.t.* 1.** to immerse. **—*v.i.* 2.** to plunge, as into a fluid. **3.** to disappear as by plunging. [t. L: m. s. *immergere*] **—immer′gence,** *n.*

immerse (ĭ mûs′), *v.t.*, **-mersed, -mersing. 1.** to plunge into or place under a liquid; dip; sink. **2.** to baptize by immersion. **3.** to embed; bury. **4.** to involve deeply; absorb. [t. L: m. s. *immersus*, pp., dipped] **—Syn. 1.** See **dip.**

immersed (ĭ mûst′), *adj.* **1.** plunged or sunk in or as in a liquid. **2.** *Biol.* somewhat or wholly sunk in the surrounding parts, as an organ. **3.** *Rare.* baptized.

immersion (ĭ mû′shən), *n.* **1.** the act of immersing. **2.** the state of being immersed. **3.** baptism by plunging the whole person into water. **4.** the state of being deeply engaged; absorption. **5.** *Colloq.* an immersion heater. **6.** *Astron.* the disappearance of a celestial body by passing either behind another or into its shadow. Cf. **emersion.**

immersion heater, an electrical heater, usually thermostatically controlled, immersed in a liquid to heat it.

immersionism (ĭ mû′shə nĭz′əm), *n.* **1.** the doctrine that immersion is essential to Christian baptism. **2.** the practice of baptism by immersion. **—immer′sionist,** *n.*

immersion objective, *Optics.* a type of lens used in microscopes in which the lowest lens of the objective system is immersed in a drop of cedar-wood oil placed on the slide to be examined.

immesh (ĭm mĕsh′), *v.t.* enmesh.

immethodical (ĭm′mĭ thŏd′ĭ kl), *adj.* not methodical; without method. —**im′method′ically,** *adv.*

immigrant (ĭm′ĭ grənt), *n.* **1.** one who or that which immigrates. **2.** a person who migrates into a country for permanent residence. —*adj.* **3.** immigrating.

immigrate (ĭm′ĭ grāt′), *v.*, **-grated, -grating.** —*v.i.* **1.** to pass or come into a new habitat or place of residence. **2.** to come into a country of which one is not a native for the purpose of permanent residence. —*v.t.* **3.** to introduce as settlers. [t. L: m. s. *immigrātus*, pp.] —**Syn. 1.** See **migrate.**

immigration (ĭm′ĭ grā′shən), *n.* **1.** the act of immigrating. **2.** immigrants collectively.

imminence (ĭm′ĭ nəns), *n.* **1.** the state or fact of being imminent or impending: *imminence of war.* **2.** that which is imminent; impending evil or danger.

imminent (ĭm′ĭ nənt), *adj.* **1.** likely to occur at any moment; impending: *war is imminent.* **2.** projecting or leaning forward; overhanging. [t. L: s. *imminens*, ppr., projecting over] —**im′minently,** *adv.*

—**Syn. 1.** IMMINENT, IMPENDING, THREATENING apply to that which menaces or portends misfortune or disaster. IMMINENT is applied to danger or evil that hangs, as it were, over one's head, ready to fall at any moment: *because of recent heavy rains, a flood was imminent.* IMPENDING is similarly used, but with less suggestion of immediateness: *a reform has been impending for some time.* THREATENING is applied loosely to that which indicates coming evil, or conveys some ominous or unfavourable suggestion: *threatening weather, sky, a threatening frown.* —**Ant. 1.** distant, remote.

immingle (ĭm mĭng′gl), *v.t., v.i.*, **-gled, -gling.** to mingle in; intermingle.

immiscible (ĭ mĭs′ə bl), *adj.* not miscible; incapable of being mixed. —**immis′cibil′ity,** *n.* —**immis′cibly,** *adv.*

immitigable (ĭ mĭt′ĭ gə bl), *adj.* not mitigable; not to be mitigated. [t. LL: m. s. *immītigābilis*] —**immit′igabil′ity,** *n.* —**immit′igably,** *adv.*

immix (ĭm mĭks′), *v.t.* to mix in; mingle. [back-formation from ME *immixt*, pp. (t. L: s. *immixtus*, pp., intermingled), appar. taken as pp. of E formation]

immixture (ĭm mĭks′chə), *n.* **1.** the act of immixing. **2.** the state of being immixed; involvement.

immobile (ĭ mō′bĭl), *adj.* **1.** not mobile; immovable. **2.** that does not move; motionless. [t. L: m. s. *immōbilis*; r. ME *inmobill*, f. IN-³ + MOBIL(E)]

immobility (ĭm′ō bĭl′ĭ tĭ), *n.* the character or condition of being immobile or irremovable.

immobilize (ĭ mō′bĭ līz′), *v.t.*, **-lized, -lizing.** **1.** to make immobile; fix so as to be or become immovable. **2.** *Finance.* to establish a monetary reserve by withdrawing (specie) from circulation; create fixed capital in place of (circulating capital). **3.** to deprive of the capacity for mobilization. Also, **immobilise.** —**immo′biliza′tion,** *n.*

immoderate (ĭ mŏd′ə rĭt, ĭ mŏd′rĭt), *adj.* **1.** not moderate; exceeding just or reasonable limits; excessive; extreme. **2.** *Obs.* intemperate. **3.** *Obs.* without bounds. [t. L: m. s. *immoderātus* without measure] —**immod′erately,** *adv.* —**immod′erateness,** *n.* —**Syn. 1.** exorbitant, unreasonable; inordinate; extravagant.

immoderation (ĭ mŏd′ə rā′shən), *n.* lack of moderation.

immodest (ĭ mŏd′ĭst), *adj.* **1.** not modest in conduct, utterance, etc.; indecent; shameless. **2.** not modest in assertion or pretension; forward; impudent. —**immod′estly,** *adv.* —**immod′esty,** *n.*

immolate (ĭm′ō lāt′), *v.t.*, **-lated, -lating.** **1.** to sacrifice. **2.** to kill as a sacrificial victim; offer in sacrifice. [t. L: m. s. *immolātus*, pp., sacrificed, orig., sprinkled with sacrificial meal] —**im′mola′tor,** *n.*

immolation (ĭm′ō lā′shən), *n.* **1.** the act of immolating. **2.** the state of being immolated. **3.** a sacrifice.

immoral (ĭ mŏ′rəl), *adj.* not moral; not conforming to the moral law; not conforming to accepted patterns of conduct. —**immor′ally,** *adv.*

—**Syn.** IMMORAL, SINFUL, ABANDONED, DEPRAVED describe one who indulges in loose living. IMMORAL (the weakest of these words), referring to conduct, applies to one who does not obey or conform to standards of morality, but is licentious and perhaps dissipated. SINFUL, also referring to conduct, applies to one who offends against a religious (as opposed to a more general moral) code. ABANDONED, referring to condition, applies to one hopelessly, and usually passively, sunk in wickedness and unrestrained appetites. DEPRAVED, referring to character, applies to one who voluntarily seeks evil and viciousness. See **amoral.**

immorality (ĭm′ə răl′ĭ tĭ), *n.*, *pl.* **-ties.** **1.** immoral quality, character, or conduct; wickedness; vice. **2.** sexual impurity; unchastity. **3.** an immoral act.

immortal (ĭ mô′tl), *adj.* **1.** not mortal; not liable or subject to death; undying. **2.** remembered or celebrated through all time. **3.** not liable to perish or decay; imperishable; everlasting. **4.** perpetual, lasting, or constant: *an immortal enemy.* **5.** pertaining to immortal beings or immortality. —*n.* **6.** an immortal being. **7.** a person, esp. an author, of enduring fame. **8.** (*usually pl.*) one of the gods of classical mythology. [ME, t. L: s. *immortālis* undying] —**immor′tally,** *adv.*

immortality (ĭm′ô tăl′ĭ tĭ), *n.* **1.** immortal condition or quality; unending life. **2.** enduring fame.

immortalize (ĭ mô′tə līz′), *v.t.*, **-lized, -lizing.** **1.** to make immortal; endow with immortality. **2.** to bestow unending fame upon; perpetuate. Also, **immortalise.** —**immor′taliza′tion,** *n.* —**immor′taliz′er,** *n.*

immortelle (ĭm′ô tĕl′), *n.* an everlasting plant or flower, esp. *Xeranthemum annuum.* [t. F, prop. fem. of *immortel*, t. L: m. s. *immortālia* IMMORTAL]

immotile (ĭ mō′tĭl), *adj.* not motile.

immovable (ĭ mōō′və bl), *adj.* **1.** incapable of being moved; fixed; stationary. **2.** not moving; motionless. **3.** not subject to change; unalterable. **4.** incapable of being affected with feeling; emotionless: *an immovable heart or face.* **5.** incapable of being moved from one's purpose, opinion, etc.; steadfast; unyielding. **6.** not changing from one date to another in different years: *an immovable feast.* **7.** *Law.* **a.** not liable to be removed, or permanent in place. **b.** (of property) real, as distinguished from personal. —*n.* **8.** something immovable. **9.** (*pl.*) *Law.* lands and the appurtenances thereof, as trees, buildings, etc. Also (esp. defs 7 and 9), **immoveable.** —**immov′abil′ity, immov′ableness,** *n.* —**immov′ably,** *adv.*

immune (ĭ myōōn′), *adj.* **1.** protected from a disease or the like, as by inoculation. **2.** exempt. —*n.* **3.** one who is immune. [ME, t. L: m. s. *immūnis* exempt]

immunity (ĭ myōō′nĭ tĭ), *n.*, *pl.* **-ties.** **1.** the state of being immune from, or insusceptible to, a particular disease or the like. **2.** exemption from any natural or usual liability. **3.** exemption from obligation, service, duty, or liability to taxation, jurisdiction, etc. **4.** special privilege. **5.** *Eccles.* **a.** the exemption of ecclesiastical persons and things from secular or civil liabilities, duties, and burdens. **b.** a particular exemption of this kind. [ME, t. L: m. s. *immūnitas* exemption, ML sanctuary] —**Syn. 1.** See **exemption.**

immunize (ĭm′yōō nīz′), *v.t.*, **-nized, -nizing.** to make immune. Also, **immunise.** —**im′muniza′tion,** *n.*

immunology (ĭm′yōō nŏl′ə jĭ), *n.* that branch of medical science which deals with immunity from disease and the production of such immunity. —**immunologic** (ĭ myōō′nə lŏj′ĭk), **immu′nolog′ical,** *adj.* —**im′munol′ogist,** *n.*

immure (ĭ myŏŏə′), *v.t.*, **-mured, -muring.** **1.** to enclose within walls. **2.** to shut in; confine. **3.** to imprison. **4.** to build into or entomb in a wall. **5.** *Obs.* to surround with walls; fortify. [t. ML: m. s. *immūrāre*, der. L *im-* IM-¹ + *mūrus* wall] —**immure′ment,** *n.*

immusical (ĭ myōō′zĭ kl), *adj.* *Rare.* unmusical.

immutable (ĭ myōō′tə bl), *adj.* not mutable; unchangeable; unalterable; changeless. —**immu′tabil′ity, immu′tableness,** *n.* —**immu′tably,** *adv.*

Imola (*It.* ē′mō lä), *n.* a town in N Italy, in Emilia. 54,598 (1966).

imp (ĭmp), *n.* **1.** a little devil or demon; an evil spirit. **2.** a mischievous child. **3.** *Archaic.* a scion or offshoot. **4.** *Archaic.* an offspring. —*v.t.* **5.** *Falconry.* **a.** to graft (feathers) into a wing. **b.** to furnish (a wing, etc.) with feathers, as to make good losses or deficiencies and improve powers of flight. **6.** *Rare.* to add a piece to; mend or repair. [ME and OE *impe* a shoot, a graft]

Imp., **1.** (L *Imperator*) Emperor. **2.** (L *Imperatrix*) Empress.

imp., **1.** imperative. **2.** imperfect. **3.** imperial. **4.** impersonal. **5.** import. **6.** important. **7.** importer. **8.** imprimatur.

impact (*n.* ĭm′păkt; *v.* ĭm păkt′), *n.* **1.** the striking of one body against another. **2.** an impinging: *the impact of light on the eye.* **3.** forcible contact or impinging: *the tremendous impact of the shot.* **4.** influence or effect exerted by a new idea, concept, ideology, etc. —*v.t.* **5.** to drive or press closely or firmly into something; pack in. [t. L: s. *impactus*, pp., driven in]

impacted (ĭm păk′tĭd), *adj.* **1.** wedged in. **2.** *Dentistry.* denoting a tooth incapable of growing out or erupting and remaining within the jawbone. **3.** driven together; tightly packed.

impaction (ĭm păk′shən), *n.* **1.** the act of impacting. **2.** the state of being impacted; close fixation. **3.** *Dentistry.* a tooth which has not erupted that is embedded in the jawbone.

impact test, a test applied to a metal, or other material, to determine its resistance to a suddenly applied stress.

impair (ĭm pĕə′), *v.t., v.i.* **1.** to make or become worse; diminish in value, excellence, etc. —*n.* **2.** *Archaic.*

impairment. [ME *empeire(n)*, t. OF: m. *empeirer*, ult. der. L *im-* IM-[1] + *pējor* worse] —**impair′er,** *n.* —**impair′ment,** *n.* —**Syn. 1.** See **injure.**

impala (ĭm pä′lə), *n.* an antelope, *Aepyceros melampus*, from S and E Africa, which can leap up to 30 ft. [t. Zulu]

impale (ĭm pāl′), *v.t.*, **-paled, -paling. 1.** to fix upon a sharpened stake or the like. **2.** to pierce with a sharpened stake thrust up through the body, as for torture or punishment. **3.** to fix upon, or pierce through with, anything pointed. **4.** to make helpless as if pierced through. **5.** *Rare.* to enclose with or as with pales or stakes; fence in; hem in. **6.** to combine (two coats of arms) on one shield by putting them side by side with a vertical line between. Also, **empale.** [t. ML: m. s. *impālāre*, der. L *im-* IM-[1] + *pālus* stake] —**impale′ment,** *n.*

impalpable (ĭm păl′pə bl), *adj.* **1.** not palpable; incapable of being perceived by the sense of touch; intangible. **2.** incapable of being readily grasped by the mind: *impalpable distinctions.* **3.** (of powder) so fine that when rubbed between the fingers no grit is felt. —**impal′pabil′ity,** *n.* —**impal′pably,** *adv.*

impanation (ĭm′pă nā′shən), *n. Theol.* the doctrine that the body and blood of Christ are in the bread and wine after consecration. [t. ML: s. *impānātio*, der. *impānāre* embody in bread, der. L *im-* IM-[1] + *pānis* bread]

impanel (ĭm păn′əl), *v.t.*, **-elled, -elling** or (*U.S.*) **-eled, -eling.** empanel.

imparadise (ĭm pă′rə dīs′), *v.t.*, **-dised, -dising. 1.** to put in or as in paradise; make supremely happy. **2.** to make a paradise of.

imparipinnate (ĭm′pă rĭ pĭn′āt, -pĭn′ĭt), *adj. Bot.* pinnate with a terminal leaflet.

imparity (ĭm pă′rĭ tĭ), *n., pl.* **-ties.** lack of parity or equality; disparity; an inequality.

impark (ĭm päk′), *v.t.* **1.** to shut up as in a park. **2.** to enclose as a park. [t. AF: m. s. *enparker.* See IM-[1], PARK] —**im′parka′tion,** *n.*

impart (ĭm pät′), *v.t.* **1.** to make known, tell, or relate: *to impart a secret.* **2.** to give, bestow, or communicate. **3.** to grant a part or share of. —*v.i.* **4.** *Archaic.* to grant a part or share; give. [ME, t. L: m. *impartire* share] —**im′parta′tion, impart′ment,** *n.* —**impart′er,** *n.* —**Syn. 1.** See **communicate.**

impartial (ĭm pä′shəl), *adj.* not partial; unbiased; just. —**impartiality** (ĭm′pä shĭ ăl′ĭ tĭ), **impar′tialness,** *n.* —**impar′tially,** *adv.* —**Syn.** See **fair**[1].

impartible (ĭm pä′tə bl), *adj.* not partible; indivisible. [t. LL: m. s. *impartībilis*] —**impart′ibil′ity,** *n.* —**impart′ibly,** *adv.*

impassable (ĭm päs′ə bl), *adj.* not passable; that cannot be passed over, through, or along: *muddy, impassable roads.* —**impass′abil′ity, impass′ableness,** *n.* —**impass′ably,** *adv.*

impasse (ăm päs′; *Fr.* ăɴ pàs′), *n.* **1.** a position from which there is no escape. **2.** a road or way that has no outlet. [t. F]

impassible (ĭm păs′ə bl), *adj.* **1.** incapable of suffering pain. **2.** incapable of suffering harm. **3.** incapable of emotion; impassive. [t. LL: m. s. *impassibilis.* See IM-[2], PASSIBLE] —**impas′sibil′ity, impas′sibleness,** *n.* —**impas′sibly,** *adv.*

impassion (ĭm păsh′ən), *v.t.* to fill, or affect strongly, with passion. [t. It.: s. *impassionare*, der. *im-* IM-[1] + *passione* PASSION]

impassionate (ĭm păsh′ə nĭt), *adj. Now Rare.* **1.** free from passion; dispassionate. **2.** impassioned. [t. It.: m. *impassionato*, pp., der. *im-* IM-[2] + *passione* PASSION]

impassioned (ĭm păsh′ənd), *adj.* filled with passion; passionate; ardent. —**impas′sionedly,** *adv.* —**impas′sionedness,** *n.*

impassive (ĭm păs′ĭv), *adj.* **1.** without emotion; apathetic; unmoved. **2.** calm; serene. **3.** unconscious. **4.** not subject to suffering. —**impas′sively,** *adv.* —**impas′siveness, impassivity** (ĭm′pă sĭv′ĭ tĭ), *n.*

impaste (ĭm pāst′), *v.t.*, **-pasted, -pasting. 1.** to cover with or enclose in a paste. **2.** to form into a paste. **3.** to lay on thickly, as paste. [t. It.: m. s. *impastare*, der. *im-* IM-[1] + *pasta* (g. LL *pasta* PASTE)] —**impastation** (ĭm′păs tā′shən), *n.*

impasto (ĭm păs′tō), *n. Painting.* **1.** the laying on of colours thickly. **2.** colour so laid on. [t. It., der. *impastare.* See IMPASTE]

impatience (ĭm pā′shəns), *n.* **1.** lack of patience. **2.** eager desire for relief or change; restlessness. **3.** intolerance of anything that thwarts or hinders.

impatiens (ĭm pā′shĭ ĕnz′), *n.* any of a genus, *Impatiens*, of annual balsaminaceous plants having irregular flowers, in which the calyx and corolla are not clearly distinguishable. [NL, n. use of L ppr. See IMPATIENT]

impatient (ĭm pā′shənt), *adj.* **1.** not patient; not bearing pain, opposition, etc., with composure. **2.** indicating lack of patience: *an impatient answer.* **3.** intolerant (fol. by *of*): *impatient of any interruptions.* **4.** restless in desire or expectation; eagerly desirous (to do something). [ME *impacient*, t. L: m. s. *impatiens* not bearing or enduring] —**impa′tiently,** *adv.*

impavid (ĭm păv′ĭd), *adj. Rare.* fearless. [t. L: s. *impavidus*] —**impav′idly,** *adv.*

impawn (ĭm pôn′), *v.t.* to put in pawn; pledge.

impeach (ĭm pēch′), *v.t.* **1.** to challenge the credibility of: *to impeach a witness.* **2.** to bring an accusation against a person in respect of treason or some other grave criminal offence. **3.** to call in question; cast an imputation upon: *to impeach one's motives.* **4.** *Chiefly U.S.* to accuse (usually a public official) before a competent tribunal of misconduct in office. —*n.* **5.** *Obs.* impeachment. [ME *empeche(n)*, t. OF: m. *empechier* hinder, g. LL *impedicāre* catch, entangle, der. L *in-* IN-[2] + *pedica* fetter] —**impeach′er,** *n.*

impeachable (ĭm pē′chə bl), *adj.* **1.** liable to be impeached. **2.** making one liable to impeachment, as an offence. —**impeach′abil′ity,** *n.*

impeachment (ĭm pēch′mənt), *n.* **1.** the act of impeaching. **2.** *U.S.* (in Congress or a state legislature) the presentation of formal charges against a public official by the lower house, trial to be before the upper house. **3.** *Obs.* (in England) a criminal accusation brought by the House of Commons against a person for any grave public offence, as treason, to be tried by the House of Lords.

impearl (ĭm pûl′), *v.t.* **1.** to form into pearl-like drops. **2.** to make pearl-like or pearly. **3.** *Poetic.* to adorn with pearls or pearl-like drops.

impeccable (ĭm pĕk′ə bl), *adj.* **1.** faultless or irreproachable: *impeccable manners.* **2.** not liable to sin; exempt from the possibility of doing wrong. —*n.* **3.** an impeccable person. [t. LL: m. s. *impeccābilis.* Cf. PECCABLE] —**impec′cabil′ity,** *n.* —**impec′cably,** *adv.*

impeccant (ĭm pĕk′ənt), *adj.* not sinning; sinless. —**impec′cancy,** *n.*

impecunious (ĭm′pĭ kyōō′nyəs), *adj.* having no money; penniless; poor. —**im′pecu′niously,** *adv.* —**im′pecu′niousness, impecuniosity** (ĭm′pĭ kyōō′nĭ ŏs′ĭ tĭ), *n.* —**Syn.** See **poor.**

impedance (ĭm pē′dns), *n.* **1.** *Elect.* the apparent resistance, or total opposition to current of an alternating current circuit, consisting of two components, reactance and true or ohmic resistance. **2.** *Physics.* the ratio of pressure to particle velocity at a given point in a soundwave. [f. IMPEDE + -ANCE]

impede (ĭm pēd′), *v.t.*, **-peded, -peding.** to retard in movement or progress by means of obstacles or hindrances; obstruct; hinder. [t. L: m. s. *impedire* entangle, hamper (orig., as to the feet)] —**imped′er,** *n.* —**imped′ingly,** *adv.* —**Syn.** See **prevent.**

impedient (ĭm pē′dyənt), *adj.* **1.** impeding. —*n.* **2.** that which impedes. [t. L: s. *impediens*, ppr.]

impediment (ĭm pĕd′ĭ mənt), *n.* **1.** some physical defect, esp. a speech disorder: *an impediment in speech.* **2.** obstruction or hindrance; obstacle. **3.** (*usually pl.*) impedimenta. **4.** *Law.* (esp. *Eccles.*) **a.** a bar, usually of blood or affinity, to marriage: *a diriment impediment.* **b.** a restraint on marriage, preventing a completely lawful union: *a minor impediment.* [ME, t. L: s. *impedimentum* hindrance] —**imped′imen′tal, impedimentary** (ĭm pĕd′ĭ mĕn′tə rĭ), *adj.* —**Syn. 2.** See **obstacle.**

impedimenta (ĭm pĕd′ĭ mĕn′tə), *n.pl.* **1.** baggage, etc., which impedes progress, as supplies carried with an army. **2.** *Law.* impediments. [t. L]

impeditive (ĭm pĕd′ĭ tĭv), *adj.* tending to impede.

impel (ĭm pĕl′), *v.t.*, **-pelled, -pelling. 1.** to drive or urge forward; press on; incite or constrain to action in any way. **2.** to drive, or cause to move, onwards; propel; impart motion to. [t. L: m. s. *impellere*] —**Syn. 1.** See **compel.**

impellent (ĭm pĕl′ənt), *adj.* **1.** impelling. —*n.* **2.** an impelling agency or force.

impeller (ĭm pĕl′ə), *n.* **1.** one who or that which impels. **2.** the rotating member of a centrifugal pump, turbine, fluid coupling, etc.

impend (ĭm pĕnd′), *v.i.* **1.** to be imminent; be near at hand. **2.** to threaten. **3.** to hang or be suspended; overhang (fol. by *over*). [t. L: s. *impendēre* hang over]

impendent (ĭm pĕn′dənt), *adj.* impending. —**impend′ence, impend′ency,** *n.*

impending (ĭm pĕn′dĭng), *adj.* **1.** about to happen; imminent. **2.** overhanging. —**Syn. 1.** See **imminent.**

impenetrability (ĭm pĕn′ĭ trə bĭl′ĭ tĭ), *n.* **1.** impenetrable quality. **2.** *Physics.* that property of matter in virtue of which two bodies cannot occupy the same space simultaneously.

impenetrable (ĭm pĕn′ĭ trə bl), *adj.* **1.** not penetrable;

that cannot be penetrated, pierced, or entered. **2.** inaccessible to ideas, influences, etc. **3.** incapable of being comprehended; unfathomable: *an impenetrable mystery.* **4.** *Physics.* excluding all other bodies from the space occupied. **—impen′etrableness,** *n.* **—impen′etrably,** *adv.*

impenitent (ĭm pĕn′ĭ tənt), *adj.* not penitent; obdurate. **—impen′itence, impen′itency, impen′itentness,** *n.* **—impen′itently,** *adv.*

impennate (ĭm pĕn′āt), *adj.* featherless or wingless.

imper., imperative.

imperative (ĭm pĕ′rə tĭv), *adj.* **1.** not to be avoided or evaded: *an imperative duty.* **2.** of the nature of or expressing a command; commanding. **3.** *Gram.* designating or pertaining to the verb mode specialized for use in command, requests, and the like, or a verb inflected for this mode, as *listen! go! run!* etc. **—***n.* **4.** a command. **5.** *Gram.* **a.** the imperative mode. **b.** a verb therein. [t. L: m. s. *imperātīvus* of a command] **—imperatival** (ĭm pĕ′rə tī′vəl), *adj.* **—imper′atively,** *adv.* **—imper′ativeness,** *n.*

imperator (ĭm′pə rä′tô), *n.* **1.** an absolute or supreme ruler. **2.** a title of the Roman emperors. **3.** a temporary title accorded a victorious Roman general. [t. L. Cf. EMPEROR] **—imperatorial** (ĭm pĕ′rə tô′rĭ əl), *adj.* **—imper′ato′rially,** *adv.*

imperceptible (ĭm′pə sĕp′tə bl), *adj.* **1.** very slight, gradual, or subtle: *imperceptible gradations.* **2.** not perceptible; not affecting the perceptive faculties. **—***n.* **3.** that which is imperceptible. **—im′percep′tibil′ity, im′percep′tibleness,** *n.* **—im′percep′tibly,** *adv.*

imperception (ĭm′pə sĕp′shən), *n.* lack of perception.

imperceptive (ĭm′pə sĕp′tĭv), *adj.* not perceptive; lacking perception. **—imperceptivity** (ĭm′pə sĕp tĭv′ĭ tĭ), **im′percep′tiveness,** *n.*

imperf., imperfect.

imperfect (ĭm pû′fĭkt), *adj.* **1.** characterized by or subject to defects. **2.** not perfect; lacking completeness: *imperfect vision.* **3.** *Bot.* (of a flower) lacking certain parts; esp., diclinous. **4.** *Gram.* denoting action or state still in process at some temporal point of reference, particularly in the past. In English, action in process is expressed in six tense forms of the verb called the progressive tenses: present progressive, *he is carrying*; past progressive, *he was carrying*; past perfect progressive, *he had been carrying.* **5.** *Law.* without legal effect or support; unenforceable. **6.** *Music.* denoting the consonances of third and sixth. Cf. **perfect** (def. 13a). **—***n.* **7.** *Gram.* **a.** the imperfect tense. **b.** another verb formation or construction with imperfect meaning. **c.** a form therein. For example: Latin *portabam,* 'I was carrying' or English *was doing* in *he was doing it when I came.* [t. L: s. *imperfectus* unfinished; r. ME *imparfit,* t. F: m. *imparfait*] **—imper′fectly,** *adv.* **—imper′fectness,** *n.*

—Syn. 2. IMPERFECT, RUDIMENTARY, UNDEVELOPED mean not complete or fully developed. That which is IMPERFECT is not complete or is defective in some respect; it may have met with some mishap while it was still developing: *an imperfect specimen of butterfly, imperfect knowledge of a subject.* That which is RUDIMENTARY is still in an early stage of development or in an embryonic stage; or it may be a vestige of something the development of which has been arrested: *rudimentary buds, the rudimentary facts, rudimentary organs.* That which is UNDEVELOPED is not fully grown, or not grown to normal size or extent: *an undeveloped adolescent, an undeveloped talent.* **—Ant.** 1, 2. complete, perfect, developed.

imperfect cadence, *Music.* a cadence in which there is a progression from a tonic chord, or a chord other than dominant or tonic, to the dominant chord.

imperfection (ĭm′pə fĕk′shən), *n.* **1.** an imperfect detail: *a law full of imperfections.* **2.** the character or condition of being imperfect.

imperfective (ĭm′pə fĕk′tĭv), *Gram.* **—***adj.* **1.** denoting an aspect of the verb, as in Russian, which indicates incompleteness of the action or state at a temporal point of reference. **—***n.* **2.** the imperfective aspect. **3.** a verb in this aspect.

imperforate (ĭm pû′fə rĭt, -rāt′), *adj.* **1.** Also, **imper′forat′ed.** not perforate; having no perforation. **2.** *Philately.* having no perforations or cuts to separate the individual stamps readily. **—***n.* **3.** an imperforate stamp. **—imper′fora′tion,** *n.*

imperial (ĭm pĭə′rĭ əl), *adj.* **1.** of or pertaining to an empire. **2.** of or pertaining to an emperor or empress. **3.** characterizing the rule or authority of a sovereign state over its dependencies. **4.** of the nature or rank of an emperor or supreme ruler. **5.** of a commanding quality, manner, or aspect. **6.** domineering; imperious. **7.** befitting an emperor or empress; very fine or grand; magnificent. **8.** of special size or quality, as various products, commodities, etc. **9.** (of weights and measures) conforming to the standards legally established in Great Britain. **10.** (*often cap.*) of or pertaining to the British Empire. **—***n.* **11.** a small pointed beard growing beneath the lower lip. **12.** a size of paper, 22 × 30 inches in Great Britain, 23 × 31 inches in America. **13.** a Russian gold coin originally worth 10 roubles, and from 1897 to 1917 worth 15 roubles. **14.** the top of a carriage, esp. of a diligence. **15.** a case for luggage carried there. **16.** a member of an imperial party or of imperial troops. **17.** an emperor or empress. **18.** any of various articles of special size or quality. [ME, t. L: s. *imperiālis* of the empire or emperor] **—impe′rially,** *adv.* **—impe′rialness,** *n.*

imperial bushel, bushel (def. 1).

imperial gallon, gallon (def. 1).

imperialism (ĭm pĭə′rĭ ə lĭz′əm), *n.* **1.** the policy of extending the rule or authority of an empire or nation over foreign countries, or of acquiring and holding colonies and dependencies. **2.** advocacy of imperial interests. **3.** the policy of so uniting the separate parts of an empire with separate governments as to secure for certain purposes a single state. **4.** imperial government. **5.** an imperial system of government. **—impe′rialist,** *n., adj.* **—impe′rialis′tic,** *adj.* **—impe′rialis′tically,** *adv.*

imperialize (ĭm pĭə′rĭ ə līz′), *v.t.,* **-lized, -lizing. 1.** to cause to belong to an empire; rule according to imperial government. **2.** to render imperial. Also, **imperialise.**

imperil (ĭm pĕ′rĭl), *v.t.,* **-rilled, -rilling,** or (*U.S.*) **-riled, -riling.** to put in peril; endanger. **—imper′ilment,** *n.*

imperious (ĭm pĭə′rĭ əs), *adj.* **1.** domineering, dictatorial, or overbearing: *an imperious tyrant, imperious temper.* **2.** urgent; imperative: *imperious need.* [t. L: m. s. *imperiōsus* commanding] **—impe′riously,** *adv.* **—impe′riousness,** *n.*

imperishable (ĭm pĕ′rĭ shə bl), *adj.* not perishable; indestructible; enduring. **—imper′ishabil′ity, imper′ishableness,** *n.* **—imper′ishably,** *adv.*

imperium (ĭm pĭə′rĭ əm), *n., pl.* **-peria** (-pĭə′rĭ ə). command; supreme power. [t. L. Cf. EMPIRE]

impermanent (ĭm pû′mə nənt), *adj.* not permanent. **—imper′manence, imper′manency,** *n.*

impermeable (ĭm pû′myə bl), *adj.* **1.** not permeable; impassable. **2.** (of substances) not permitting the passage of a fluid through the pores, interstices, etc. **—imper′meabil′ity, imper′meableness,** *n.* **—imper′meably,** *adv.*

impers., impersonal.

impersonal (ĭm pû′sə nəl), *adj.* **1.** not personal; without personal reference or connection: *an impersonal remark.* **2.** having no personality: *an impersonal deity.* **3.** *Gram.* **a.** (of a verb) having only third person singular forms, rarely if ever accompanied by an expressed subject, as Latin *pluit* (it is raining), or accompanied regularly by a non-significant subject word, as English *it is raining.* **b.** (of a pronoun) indefinite, as French *on* (one). **—***n.* **4.** *Gram.* an impersonal verb or pronoun. **—imper′sonally,** *adv.*

impersonality (ĭm pû′sə năl′ĭ tĭ), *n.* the quality of being impersonal.

impersonalize (ĭm pû′sə nə līz′), *v.t.,* **-lized, -lizing.** to make impersonal. Also, **impersonalise.**

impersonate (ĭm pû′sə nāt′), *v.,* **-nated, -nating,** *adj.* **—***v.t.* **1.** to assume the character of; pretend to be. **2.** to represent in personal or bodily form; personify; typify. **3.** to personate, esp. on the stage. **—***adj.* **4.** embodied in a person; invested with personality. **—imper′sona′tion,** *n.* **—imper′sona′tor,** *n.*

impertinence (ĭm pû′tĭ nəns), *n.* **1.** unmannerly intrusion or presumption; insolence. **2.** impertinent quality or action; irrelevance. **3.** inappropriateness or incongruity. **4.** triviality or absurdity. **5.** something impertinent.

impertinency (ĭm pû′tĭ nən sĭ), *n., pl.* **-cies.** impertinence.

impertinent (ĭm pû′tĭ nənt), *adj.* **1.** intrusive or presumptuous, as persons or their actions: *an impertinent boy.* **2.** not pertinent or relevant; irrelevant: *any impertinent detail.* **3.** inappropriate or incongruous. **4.** trivial, silly, or absurd. [ME, t. LL: s. *impertinens* not belonging] **—imper′tinently,** *adv.*

—Syn. 1. IMPERTINENT, IMPUDENT, INSOLENT refer to bold, rude, and arrogant behaviour. IMPERTINENT, from its primary meaning of not pertinent and hence inappropriate or out of place, has come to imply often an unseemly intrusion into what does not concern one, or a presumptuous rudeness towards one entitled to deference or respect: *an impertinent interruption, question, manner towards a teacher.* IMPUDENT suggests a bold and shameless impertinence: *an impudent speech, young rascal.* INSOLENT suggests insulting or arrogantly contemptuous behaviour: *unbearably insolent towards those in authority.* **—Ant.** 1. polite, civil, deferential.

imperturbable (ĭm′pə tû′bə bl), *adj.* incapable of being perturbed or agitated; not easily excited; calm: *imperturbable composure.* —**im′perturb′abil′ity, im′perturb′ableness,** *n.* —**im′perturb′ably,** *adv.*

imperturbation (ĭm′pû tû bā′shən), *n.* freedom from perturbation; tranquillity; calmness.

impervious (ĭm pû′vyəs), *adj.* **1.** not pervious; impermeable: *impervious to water.* **2.** impenetrable: *impervious to reason.* Also, **imper′viable.** —**imper′viously,** *adv.* —**imper′viousness,** *n.*

impetigo (ĭm′pĭ tī′gō), *n. Pathol.* a contagious skin disease, esp. of children, marked by a superficial pustular eruption, particularly on the face. [t. L, der. *impetere* attack] —**impetiginous** (ĭm′pĭ tĭj′ĭ nəs), *adj.*

impetrate (ĭm′pĭ trāt′), *v.t.*, **-trated, -trating. 1.** to obtain by entreaty. **2.** *Rare.* to entreat, or ask urgently for. [t. L: m. s. *impetrātus*, pp., obtained by request] —**im′petra′tion,** *n.* —**im′petra′tive,** *adj.* —**im′petra′tor,** *n.*

impetuosity (ĭm pĕt′yōō ŏs′ĭ tĭ), *n., pl.* **-ties. 1.** impetuous quality. **2.** an impetuous action.

impetuous (ĭm pĕt′yōō əs), *adj.* **1.** acting with or characterized by a sudden or rash energy: *an impetuous girl.* **2.** having great impetus; moving with great force; violent: *the impetuous winds.* [ME, t. LL: m. s. *impetuōsus*, der. L *impetus* an attack] —**impet′uously,** *adv.* —**impet′uousness,** *n.*

—**Syn. 1.** IMPETUOUS, IMPULSIVE both refer to persons who are hasty and precipitate in action, or to actions not preceded by thought. IMPETUOUS suggests eagerness, violence, rashness: *impetuous vivacity, impetuous desire, impetuous words.* IMPULSIVE emphasizes spontaneity and lack of reflection: *an impulsive act of generosity.* —**Ant.** 1. cautious, deliberate.

impetus (ĭm′pĭ təs), *n., pl.* **-tuses. 1.** moving force; impulse; stimulus: *a fresh impetus.* **2.** the force with which a moving body tends to maintain its velocity and overcome resistance; energy of motion. [t. L: onset]

impf., imperfect.

Imphal (ĭm fäl′, ĭm′fəl), *n.* a town in and the capital of Manipur territory, in NE India. 67,717 (1961).

impi (ĭm′pĭ), *n., pl.* **-pies.** a band of Bantu warriors. [Zulu]

impiety (ĭm pī′ə tĭ), *n., pl.* **-ties. 1.** lack of piety; lack of reverence for God; ungodliness. **2.** lack of dutifulness or respect. **3.** an impious act, practice, etc.

impinge (ĭm pĭnj′), *v.*, **-pinged, -pinging.** —*v.i.* **1.** to strike or dash; collide (fol. by *on, upon,* or *against*): *rays of light impinging on the eye.* **2.** to encroach or infringe (fol. by *on* or *upon*). **3.** to make an impression (*on*). —*v.t.* **4.** *Obs.* to come into violent contact with. [t. L: m. s. *impingere* drive in or at, strike against] —**impin′gent,** *adj.* —**impinge′ment,** *n.*

impious (ĭm′pĭ əs), *adj.* **1.** not pious; lacking reverence for God; ungodly. **2.** *Rare.* not reverent towards parents. [t. L: m. *impius*] —**im′piously,** *adv.* —**im′piousness,** *n.*

impish (ĭmp′ĭsh), *adj.* of or like an imp; mischievous. —**imp′ishly,** *adv.* —**imp′ishness,** *n.*

implacable (ĭm plăk′ə bl), *adj.* not placable; not to be appeased or pacified; inexorable: *an implacable enemy.* —**implac′abil′ity, implac′ableness,** *n.* —**implac′ably,** *adv.* —**Syn.** See **inflexible.**

implacental (ĭm′plə sĕn′tl), *adj. Zool.* having no placenta, as a monotreme or marsupial.

implant (*v.* ĭm plänt′; *n.* ĭm′plänt′), *v.t.* **1.** to instil or inculcate: *implant sound principles.* **2.** to plant in something; infix: *implant living tissue.* **3.** to plant: *implant the seeds.* —*n.* **4.** *Med.* **a.** tissue implanted into the body by grafting. **b.** a small tube containing a radioactive substance, as radium, surgically implanted in tissue for the treatment of tumours, cancer, etc. [f. IM-[1] + PLANT, v.] —**implant′er,** *n.*

implantation (ĭm′plän tā′shən), *n.* **1.** the act of implanting. **2.** the state of being implanted. **3.** *Pathol.* **a.** the movement of cells to a new region. **b.** metastasis, when spontaneous. **4.** *Med.* the application of solid medicine underneath the skin.

implausible (ĭm plô′zə bl), *adj.* not plausible; not having the appearance of truth or credibility. —**implau′sibil′ity,** *n.* —**implau′sibly,** *adv.*

implead (ĭm plēd′), *v.t.* **1.** to sue in a court of justice. **2.** *Obs.* to accuse; impeach. **3.** *Rare.* to plead (a suit, etc.). [ME *emplede(n)*, t. AF: m. *empleder*, var. of OF *emplaidier*, f. *em-* IM-[1] + *plaidier* PLEAD]

implement (*n.* ĭm′plĭ mənt; *v.* -mĕnt′), *n.* **1.** an instrument, tool, or utensil: *agricultural implements.* **2.** an article of equipment or outfit, as household furniture or utensils, ecclesiastical vessels or vestments, etc. **3.** a means; agent. —*v.t.* **4.** to provide with implements. **5.** to execute, as a piece of work. **6.** to satisfy, as requirements or conditions. **7.** to fill up or supplement. [late ME, t. LL: s. *implementum* a filling up (hence, prob., a thing that completes a want), der. L *implēre* fill up] —**im′plemen′tal,** *adj.* —**im′plementa′tion,** *n.* —**Syn. 1.** See **tool.**

impletion (ĭm plē′shən), *n.* **1.** the act of filling. **2.** the state of being filled. **3.** that which fills up; a filling. [t. LL: s. *implētio*, der. L *implēre* fill up]

implicate (ĭm′plĭ kāt′), *v.t.*, **-cated, -cating. 1.** to involve as being concerned in a matter, affair, condition, etc.: *to be implicated in a crime.* **2.** to imply as a necessary circumstance, or as something to be inferred or understood. **3.** to affect, or cause to be affected. **4.** to fold or twist together; intertwine; interlace: *implicated leaves.* [t. L: m. s. *implicātus*, pp., entangled, involved] —**Syn. 1.** See **involve.**

implication (ĭm′plĭ kā′shən), *n.* **1.** the act of implying. **2.** the state of being implied. **3.** something implied or suggested as naturally to be inferred without being expressly stated. **4.** *Logic.* the relation which holds between two propositions (or classes of propositions) in virtue of which one is logically deducible from the other. **5.** the act of involving. **6.** the state of being involved in some matter: *implication in a conspiracy.* **7.** the act of intertwining or entangling. **8.** the resulting condition.

implicative (ĭm′plĭ kā′tĭv, ĭm plĭk′ə tĭv), *adj.* tending to implicate or imply; characterized by or involving implication. —**im′plica′tively,** *adv.*

implicit (ĭm plĭs′ĭt), *adj.* **1.** (of belief, confidence, obedience, etc.) unquestioning, unreserved, or absolute. **2.** implied, rather than expressly stated: *an implicit consent.* **3.** virtually contained (fol. by *in*). **4.** *Maths.* (of a fraction) having the dependent variable not explicitly expressed in terms of the independent variables. **5.** *Obs.* entangled. [t. L: s. *implicitus*, var. of *implicātus*, pp., entangled, involved] —**implic′itly,** *adv.* —**implic′itness,** *n.*

implied (ĭm plīd′), *adj.* involved, indicated, or suggested by implying: tacitly understood: *an implied rebuke.*

impliedly (ĭm plī′ĭd lĭ), *adv.* by implication.

implode (ĭm plōd′), *v.*, **-ploded, -ploding.** —*v.i.* **1.** to burst inwards (opposed to *explode*). —*v.t.* **2.** *Phonet.* to pronounce by implosion. [f. IM-[1] + *-plode*, modelled on EXPLODE]

implore (ĭm plôr′), *v.*, **-plored, -ploring.** —*v.t.* **1.** to call upon in urgent or piteous supplication, as for aid or mercy; beseech; entreat: *they implored him to go.* **2.** to make urgent supplication for (aid, mercy, pardon, etc.): *implore forgiveness.* —*v.i.* **3.** to make urgent or piteous supplication. [t. L: m. s. *implōrāre* invoke with tears] —**im′plora′tion,** *n.* —**imploratory** (ĭm plôr′ə tə rĭ, -trĭ), *adj.* —**implor′er,** *n.* —**implor′ingly,** *adv.* —**implor′ingness,** *n.* —**Syn. 2.** crave, beg. —**Ant. 2.** spurn, reject.

implosion (ĭm plō′zhən), *n.* **1.** a bursting inwards (opposed to *explosion*). **2.** *Phonet.* (of stops) **a.** a beginning marked by abrupt interruption of the breath stream, as for *p, t, k.* **b.** an ending marked by abrupt intake of air. [f. IM-[1] + *-plosion*, modelled on EXPLOSION]

implosive (ĭm plō′sĭv), *Phonet.* —*adj.* **1.** characterized by a partial vacuum behind the point of closure. —*n.* **2.** an implosive stop.

imply (ĭm plī′), *v.t.*, **-plied, -plying. 1.** to involve as a necessary circumstance: *speech implies a speaker.* **2.** (of words) to signify or mean. **3.** to indicate or suggest, as something naturally to be inferred, without express statement. **4.** *Obs.* to enfold. [ME *implie(n)*, t. OF: m. *emplier*, g. L *implicāre* enfold, entangle, involve]

impolicy (ĭm pŏl′ĭ sĭ), *n.* bad policy; inexpediency.

impolite (ĭm′pə līt′), *adj.* not polite or courteous; uncivil; rude. —**im′polite′ly,** *adv.* —**im′polite′ness,** *n.* —**Syn.** discourteous, disrespectful; insolent.

impolitic (ĭm pŏl′ĭ tĭk), *adj.* inexpedient; injudicious. —**impol′iticly,** *adv.* —**impol′iticness,** *n.*

imponderable (ĭm pŏn′də rə bl, -drə bl), *adj.* **1.** not ponderable; that cannot be weighed. —*n.* **2.** an imponderable thing, force, or agency. —**impon′derabil′ity, impon′derableness,** *n.* —**impon′derably,** *adv.*

import (*v.* ĭm pôt′, ĭm′pôt′; *n.* ĭm′pôt′), *v.t.* **1.** to bring in from a foreign country, as merchandise or commodities, for sale, use, processing, or re-export. **2.** to bring or introduce from one use, connection, or relation into another. **3.** to convey as a meaning or implication, as words, statements, actions, etc., do; to make known or express. **4.** to be of consequence or importance to; concern. **5.** to be incumbent on; be the duty of. —*v.i.* **6.** to be of consequence or importance; matter. —*n.* **7.** that which is imported from abroad; an imported commodity or article. **8.** the act of importing or bringing in; importation, as of goods from abroad. **9.** meaning; implication; purport. **10.** consequence or importance. [ME, t. L: s. *importāre* bring in, bring about] —**import′able,** *adj.* —**import′abil′ity,** *n.* —**import′er,** *n.*

importance (ĭm pô′tns), *n.* **1.** the quality or fact of being important. **2.** important position or standing; personal or social consequence. **3.** consequential air or manner. **4.** *Obs.* an important matter. **5.** *Obs.* importunity. **6.** *Obs.* import or meaning.

—**Syn. 1.** IMPORTANCE, CONSEQUENCE refer to a quality, character, or standing such as to entitle to attention or consideration. IMPORTANCE, referring originally to the bringing or involving of noteworthy results, is the general term. CONSEQUENCE, though of the same general sense, is a weaker word, less suggestive of seriousness, dignity, or extensiveness: *fair weather is a matter of consequence to the tourist, but of real importance to the farmer.*

important (ĭm pô′tnt), *adj.* **1.** of much significance or consequence: *an important event.* **2.** mattering much (fol. by *to*): *details important to a fair decision.* **3.** of more than ordinary title to consideration or notice: *an important example.* **4.** prominent: *an important part.* **5.** of considerable influence or authority, as a person, position, etc. **6.** of social consequence or distinction, as a person, family, etc. **7.** pompous. **8.** *Obs.* importunate. [t. F, t. ML: s. *importans*, ppr. of *importāre* be of consequence, L bring in, cause] —**impor′tantly,** *adv.*

importation (ĭm′pô tā′shən), *n.* **1.** the bringing in of merchandise from foreign countries, for sale, use, processing, or re-export. **2.** something imported; an import.

importee (ĭm′pô tē′), *n.* a person imported from abroad.

importunacy (ĭm pô′tyo͝o nə sĭ), *n.* the quality of being importunate.

importunate (ĭm pô′tyo͝o nĭt), *adj.* **1.** urgent or persistent in solicitation. **2.** pertinacious, as solicitations or demands. **3.** troublesome. —**impor′tunately,** *adv.* —**impor′tunateness,** *n.*

importune (ĭm pô′tyo͞on), *v.*, **-tuned, -tuning,** *adj.* —*v.t.* **1.** to beset with solicitations; beg urgently or persistently. **2.** to beg for (something) urgently or persistently. **3.** *Obs.* to annoy. **4.** *Obs.* to press; impel. —*v.i.* **5.** to make urgent or persistent solicitations. —*adj.* **6.** importunate. [ME, t. MF: m. *importun*, t. L: s. *importūnus* unfit, inconvenient, troublesome] —**impor′tunely,** *adv.* —**impor′tuner,** *n.*

importunity (ĭm′pô tyo͞o′nĭ tĭ), *n.*, *pl.* **-ties. 1.** the state of being importunate; persistence in solicitation. **2.** (*pl.*) importunate solicitations or demands.

impose (ĭm pōz′), *v.*, **-posed, -posing.** —*v.t.* **1.** to lay on or set as something to be borne, endured, obeyed, fulfilled, etc.: *to impose taxes.* **2.** to put or set by, or as by, authority: *to impose an arbitrary meaning upon words.* **3.** to obtrude or thrust (oneself, one's company, etc.) upon others. **4.** to pass or palm off fraudulently or deceptively. **5.** to lay (the hands) ceremonially on the head of a candidate for confirmation or ordination, or on the sick or those in distress. **6.** *Print.* to lay (type pages, etc.) in proper order on an imposing stone or the like and secure in a chase for printing. **7.** to subject to some penalty, etc. **8.** *Archaic.* to put or place on something, or in a particular place. —*v.i.* **9.** to make an impression on the mind; impose one's or its authority or influence. **10.** to obtrude oneself or one's requirements, as upon others. **11.** to presume, as upon patience, good nature, etc. **12.** (of something fraudulent) to produce a false impression or act with a delusive effect (fol. by *upon* or *on*). [t. F: m. s. *imposer*, f. *im-* IM-[1] + *poser* put (see POSE[1])] —**impos′able,** *adj.* —**impos′er,** *n.*

imposing (ĭm pō′zĭng), *adj.* making an impression on the mind, as by great size, stately appearance, etc. —**impos′ingly,** *adv.* —**impos′ingness,** *n.*

imposing stone, *Print.* a slab resting upon a frame, on which pages of type or plates are imposed and corrected.

imposition (ĭm′pə zĭsh′ən), *n.* **1.** the laying on of something as a burden, obligation, etc. **2.** something imposed, as a burden, levy, tax, etc.; an unusual or extraordinarily burdensome requirement or task. **3.** a literary exercise imposed as at school as a punishment. **4.** the act of imposing by or as by authority. **5.** an imposing upon a person as by taking undue advantage of his good nature, or something that has the effect of doing this. **6.** the act of imposing fraudulently or deceptively on others; imposture. **7.** the ceremonial laying on of hands, as in confirmation. **8.** *Print.* the arrangement of pages in proper order in a chase for printing. **9.** *Rare.* the act of putting, placing, or laying on.

impossibility (ĭm pŏs′ə bĭl′ĭ tĭ, ĭm′pŏs-), *n.*, *pl.* **-ties. 1.** the quality of being impossible. **2.** something impossible.

impossible (ĭm pŏs′ə bl), *adj.* **1.** not possible; that cannot be, exist, or happen. **2.** that cannot be done or effected. **3.** that cannot be true, as a rumour. **4.** not to be done, endured, etc., with any degree of reason or propriety: *an impossible situation.* **5.** utterly impracticable. **6.** hopelessly unsuitable, undesirable, or objectionable: *an impossible person.* [ME, t. L: m. s. *impossibilis*] —**impos′sibly,** *adv.*

impost[1] (ĭm′pōst′), *n.* **1.** a tax, tribute, or duty. **2.** a customs duty. **3.** *Horseracing.* the weight (including that of the jockey) assigned to a horse in a race. [t. ML: s. *impostus* a tax, L *impositus* laid on]

impost[2] (ĭm′pōst′), *n.* *Archit.* **1.** the point where an arch rests on a wall or column. See diag. under **arch. 2.** a horizontal block supported by upright stones. [t. F: m. *imposte*, t. It.: m. *imposta* architectural impost, der. *impostare* set upon, der. L *positus*, pp., placed]

impostor (ĭm pŏs′tə), *n.* **1.** one who imposes fraudulently upon others. **2.** one who practises deception under an assumed character or name. [t. LL, der. L *impōnere* impose] —**Syn. 1.** pretender, deceiver, cheat.

impostume (ĭm pŏs′tyo͞om), *n.* *Archaic.* an abscess. Also, **imposthume.** [ME *empostume*, t. OF, var. of *apostume*, t. LL: m. *apostūma*, var. of *apostēma*, t. Gk: lit., separation (of pus)]

imposture (ĭm pŏs′chə), *n.* **1.** the action or practice of imposing fraudulently upon others. **2.** deception practised under an assumed character or name, as by an impostor. **3.** an instance or piece of fraudulent imposition. [t. LL: m. s. *impostūra*, der. L *impōnere* impose] —**impos′turous,** *adj.*

imposure (ĭm pō′zhə), *n.* *Rare.* imposition.

impotence (ĭm′pə təns), *n.* **1.** the condition or quality of being impotent; weakness. **2.** complete failure of sexual power, esp. in the male. **3.** *Obs.* lack of self-restraint. Also, **im′potency.**

impotent (ĭm′pə tənt), *adj.* **1.** not potent; lacking power or ability. **2.** utterly unable (to do something). **3.** without force or effectiveness. **4.** lacking bodily strength, or physically helpless, as an aged person or a cripple. **5.** wholly lacking in sexual power. **6.** *Obs.* without restraint. —**im′potently,** *adv.*

impound (ĭm pound′), *v.t.* **1.** to shut up in a pound, as a stray animal. **2.** to confine within an enclosure or within limits: *water impounded in a reservoir.* **3.** to seize, take, or appropriate summarily. **4.** to seize and retain in custody of the law, as a document for evidence. —**impound′able,** *adj.* —**impound′ment, impoundage** (ĭm poun′dĭj), *n.* —**impound′er,** *n.*

impoverish (ĭm pŏv′ə rĭsh, -pŏv′rĭsh), *v.t.* **1.** to reduce to poverty: *a country impoverished by war.* **2.** to make poor in quality, productiveness, etc.; exhaust the strength or richness of: *to impoverish the soil.* Also, *Obs.*, **empoverish.** [ME *empoveris(en)*, t. OF: m. *empoveriss-*, s. *empoverir*, der. *em-* EM-[1] + *povre* POOR] —**impov′erisher,** *n.* —**impov′erishment,** *n.*

impoverished (ĭm pŏv′ə rĭsht, -pŏv′rĭsht), *adj.* **1.** reduced to poverty. **2.** poor in quality. —**Syn.** See **poor.**

impracticable (ĭm prăk′tĭ kə bl), *adj.* **1.** not practicable; that cannot be put into practice with the available means: *an impracticable plan.* **2.** unsuitable for practical use or purposes, as a device, material, etc. **3.** (of ground, places, etc.) impassable. **4.** (of persons, etc.) hard to deal with because of stubbornness, stupidity, etc. —**imprac′ticabil′ity, imprac′ticableness,** *n.* —**imprac′ticably,** *adv.*

impractical (ĭm prăk′tĭ kl), *adj.* not practical. —**imprac′tical′ity, imprac′ticalness,** *n.*

imprecate (ĭm′prĭ kāt′), *v.t.*, **-cated, -cating.** to call down or invoke (esp. evil or curses), as upon a person. [t. L: m. s. *imprecātus*, pp., having invoked] —**im′preca′tor,** *n.* —**imprecatory** (ĭm′prĭ kā′tə rĭ), *adj.*

imprecation (ĭm′prĭ kā′shən), *n.* **1.** the act of imprecating; cursing. **2.** a curse or malediction.

imprecise (ĭm′prĭ sīs′), *adj.* not precise; ill-defined. —**im′precise′ly,** *adv.* —**im′precise′ness,** *n.*

imprecision (ĭm′prĭ sĭzh′ən), *n.* lack of precision; inexactness.

impregnable (ĭm prĕg′nə bl), *adj.* **1.** strong enough to resist attack; not to be taken by force: *an impregnable fort.* **2.** not to be overcome or overthrown: *an impregnable argument.* [ME *imprenable*, t. F: f. *im-* IM-[1] + *prenable* PREGNABLE] —**impreg′nabil′ity,** *n.* —**impreg′nably,** *adv.* —**Syn. 1.** See **invincible.**

impregnate (*v.* ĭm′prĕg nāt′; *adj.* ĭm prĕg′nĭt, -nāt), *v.*, **-nated, -nating,** *adj.* —*v.t.* Also, *Obs. or Poetic,* **impregn** (ĭm prēn′). **1.** to make pregnant; get with child or young. **2.** to fertilize. **3.** to charge with something infused or permeating throughout; saturate. **4.** to fill interstices with a substance. **5.** to furnish with some actuating or modifying element infused or introduced; imbue, infect, or tincture. —*adj.* **6.** impregnated. [t. LL: m. s. *impraegnātus*, pp., made pregnant] —**im′pregna′tion,** *n.* —**im′pregna′tor,** *n.*

impresa (ĭm prā′zə), *n.*, *pl.* **-sas.** *Obs.* **1.** a device or emblem. **2.** a motto. Also, **imprese** (ĭm prēz′). [t. It.: enterprise]

impresario (ĭm′prə sä′rĭ ō′), *n.*, *pl.* **-os,** *It.* **-sari** (-sä′rē).

1. the organizer or manager of an opera, ballet, or theatre company or orchestra. 2. a personal manager, teacher, or trainer of concert artists. [t. It., der. *impresa* enterprise]

imprescriptible (ĭm′prĭ skrĭp′tə bl), *adj. Law.* not subject to prescription. —**im′prescrip′tibly,** *adv.*

impress[1] (*v.* ĭm prĕs′; *n.* ĭm′prĕs′), *v.*, **-pressed** or (*Archaic*) **-prest; -pressing;** *n.* —*v.t.* 1. to affect deeply or strongly in mind or feelings; influence in opinion. 2. to fix deeply or firmly in the mind or memory, as ideas, facts, etc. 3. to urge, as something to be remembered or done. 4. to press (a thing) into or on something. 5. to produce (a mark, figure, etc.) by pressure; stamp; imprint. 6. to apply with pressure, so as to leave a mark. 7. to subject to, or mark by, pressure with something. 8. to furnish with a mark, figure, etc., by or as by stamping. —*n.* 9. the act of impressing. 10. a mark made by or as by pressure; stamp; imprint. 11. a distinctive character or effect imparted. [ME *impresse(n)*, t. L: m. s. *impressus*, pp., pressed upon] —**impress′er,** *n.*

impress[2] (*v.* ĭm prĕs′; *n.* ĭm′prĕs′), *v.*, **-pressed** or (*Archaic*) **-prest; -pressing;** *n.* —*v.t.* 1. to press or force into public service, as seamen. 2. to seize or take for public use. 3. to enlist or persuade (to aid). —*n.* 4. *Obs.* impressment. [f. IM-[1] + PRESS[2]]

impressible (ĭm prĕs′ə bl), *adj.* capable of being impressed; impressionable. —**impress′ibil′ity,** *n.*

impression (ĭm prĕsh′ən), *n.* 1. a strong effect produced on the intellect, feelings, or conscience. 2. the first and immediate effect upon the mind in outward or inward perception; sensation. 3. the effect produced by an agency or influence. 4. a notion, remembrance, or belief, often one that is vague or indistinct. 5. a mark, indentation, figure, etc., produced by pressure. 6. *Print., etc.* **a.** the process or result of printing from type, plates, etc. **b.** a printed copy from type, a plate, an engraved block, etc. **c.** one of a number of printings made at different times from the same set of type, without alteration (as distinguished from an *edition*). **d.** the total number of copies of a book, etc., printed at one time from the one setting of type. 7. *Dentistry.* a mould taken in plastic materials or plaster of Paris of teeth and the surrounding tissues. 8. an image in the mind caused by something external to it. 9. the act of impressing. 10. the state of being impressed. 11. an imitation, esp. one given for entertainment, of the idiosyncrasies of some well-known person or type. [ME, t. L: s. *impressio*. See IMPRESS[1]]

impressionable (ĭm prĕsh′ə nə bl, -prĕsh′nə-), *adj.* 1. easily impressed or influenced; susceptible. 2. capable of being impressed. —**impres′sionabil′ity, impres′sionableness,** *n.*

impressionism (ĭm prĕsh′ə nĭz′əm), *n.* 1. a way of painting (developed 1865–75) with informal subject matter and effects of light noted directly as they impress the artist, and developed as a method of expressing luminosity with juxtaposed touches of pure colour. 2. a musical or literary style intended to convey an effect or overall impression of a subject. —**impres′sionist,** *n., adj.* —**impres′sionis′tic,** *adj.*

impressive (ĭm prĕs′ĭv), *adj.* such as to impress the mind; arousing solemn feelings: *an impressive ceremony.* —**impres′sively,** *adv.* —**impres′siveness,** *n.*

impressment (ĭm prĕs′mənt), *n.* the impressing of men, property, etc., as for public service or use. [f. IMPRESS[2] + -MENT]

impressure (ĭm prĕsh′ə), *n. Archaic.* impression.

imprest[1] (ĭm′prĕst), *n.* 1. an advance of money, esp. for some public business. 2. (formerly) an advance payment made to a soldier or sailor at enlistment. [f. IM-[1] + *prest* (t. OF: s. *prester* lend, g. L *praestāre* stand for). Cf. It. *imprestare* lend]

imprest[2] (ĭm prĕst′), *v. Archaic.* pt. and pp. of **impress.**

imprimatur (ĭm′prĭ mā′tə, -mä′tə), *n.* 1. an official licence to print or publish a book, etc. 2. licence; sanction; approval. [NL: let it be printed]

imprimis (ĭm prī′mĭs), *adv. Latin.* in the first place.

imprint (*n.* ĭm′prĭnt′; *v.* ĭm prĭnt′), *n.* 1. a mark made by pressure; a figure impressed or printed on something. 2. any impression or impressed effect. 3. *Bibliog.* information printed at the foot or back of the titlepage of a book indicating the name of the publisher, usually supplemented with the place and date of publication. 4. the printer's name and address as indicated on any printed matter. —*v.t.* 5. to impress (a quality, character, or distinguishing mark). 6. to produce (a mark, etc.) on something by pressure. 7. to bestow (a kiss). 8. to fix firmly on the mind, memory, etc. 9. to make an imprint upon. [ME *empreynte(n)*, t. OF: m. *empreinter*, der. *empreinte* a stamp, ult. der. L *imprimere* impress, imprint] —**imprint′er,** *n.*

imprison (ĭm prĭz′ən), *v.t.* 1. to put into or confine in a prison; detain in custody. 2. to shut up as if in a prison; hold in restraint. —**impris′onment,** *n.*

improbability (ĭm prŏb′ə bĭl′ĭ tĭ, ĭm′prŏb-), *n., pl.* **-ties.** 1. the quality or fact of being improbable; unlikelihood. 2. something improbable or unlikely.

improbable (ĭm prŏb′ə bl), *adj.* not probable; unlikely to be true or to happen. —**improb′ably,** *adv.*

improbity (ĭm prō′bĭ tĭ), *n.* the reverse of probity; dishonesty; wickedness. [ME *improbite*, t. L: m. s. *improbitas* wickedness]

impromptu (ĭm prŏmp′tyōō), *adj.* 1. made or done without previous preparation: *an impromptu address.* 2. suddenly or hastily prepared, made, etc.: *an impromptu dinner.* 3. improvised, or having the character of an improvisation, as music. —*adv.* 4. without preparation: *verses written impromptu.* —*n.* 5. something impromptu; an impromptu speech, musical composition, performance, etc. 6. a short musical composition suggesting improvisation. [t. L: m. *in promptū* in readiness] —**Syn.** 1. See **extemporaneous.**

improper (ĭm prŏp′ə), *adj.* 1. not proper; not strictly belonging, applicable, or right: *an improper use for a thing.* 2. not in accordance with propriety of behaviour, manners, etc.: *improper conduct.* 3. unsuitable or inappropriate, as for the purpose or occasion: *improper tools.* 4. abnormal or irregular. —**improp′erly,** *adv.* —**improp′erness,** *n.*

—**Syn.** 1–3. IMPROPER, INDECENT, UNBECOMING, UNSEEMLY are applied to that which is unfitting or not in accordance with propriety. IMPROPER has a wide range, being applied to whatever is not suitable or fitting, and often specifically to what does not conform to the standards of conventional morality: *improper diet, improper behaviour in church, improper language.* INDECENT, a strong word, is applied to what is offensively contrary to standards of propriety and esp. of modesty: *indecent behaviour, language.* UNBECOMING is applied to what is especially unfitting in the person concerned: *conduct unbecoming a minister.* UNSEEMLY is applied to whatever is unfitting or improper under the circumstances: *unseemly mirth.* —**Ant.** 1. fitting. 2. modest. 3. suitable.

improper fraction, a fraction having the numerator greater than the denominator.

impropriate (*adj.* ĭm prō′prĭ ĭt, -āt′; *v.* ĭm prō′prĭ āt′), *adj., v.,* **-ated, -ating.** —*adj.* 1. *Eccles. Law.* devolved into the hands of a layman. 2. *Obs.* appropriated to private use. —*v.t.* 3. *Eccles. Law.* to place (ecclesiastical property) in lay hands. 4. *Obs.* to appropriate. [t. ML: m. s. *impropriātus*, pp. of *impropriāre*, der. L *im-* IM-[1] + *proprius* one's own, PROPER] —**impro′pria′tion,** *n.*

impropriator (ĭm prō′prĭ ā′tə), *n.* a layman in possession of church property or revenues.

impropriety (ĭm′prə prī′ə tĭ), *n., pl.* **-ties.** 1. the quality of being improper; incorrectness. 2. inappropriateness. 3. unseemliness. 4. an erroneous or unsuitable expression, act, etc. 5. an improper use of a word.

improve (ĭm prōōv′), *v.,* **-proved, -proving.** —*v.t.* 1. to bring into a more desirable or excellent condition: *to improve one's health.* 2. to make (land) more profitable or valuable by enclosure, cultivation, etc.; increase the value of (property) by betterments, as buildings. 3. to turn to account; make good use of: *to improve an opportunity.* —*v.i.* 4. to increase in value, excellence, etc.; become better: *the situation is improving.* 5. to make improvements (fol. by *on* or *upon*): *to improve on one's earlier work.* [t. AF: m. *emprower*, der. OF *em-* IM-[1] + *prou* profit] —**improv′able,** *adj.* —**improv′abil′ity, improv′ableness,** *n.* —**improv′ably,** *adv.* —**improv′er,** *n.* —**improv′ingly,** *adv.*

—**Syn.** 1. IMPROVE, AMELIORATE, BETTER imply bringing to a more desirable state. IMPROVE usually implies remedying a lack or a felt need: *to improve a process, oneself (gain additional knowledge, etc.).* AMELIORATE, a formal word, implies improving oppressive, unjust, or difficult conditions: *to ameliorate working conditions.* TO BETTER is to improve conditions which, though not bad, are unsatisfying: *to better an attempt, oneself (gain a higher salary or position).* —**Ant.** 1. worsen.

improvement (ĭm prōōv′mənt), *n.* 1. the act of improving. 2. the state of being improved. 3. a change or addition whereby a thing is improved. 4. some thing or person that represents an advance on another in excellence or achievement. 5. a bringing into a more valuable or desirable condition, as of land; a making or becoming better; a betterment. 6. something done or added to land which increases its value. 7. profitable use: *the improvement of one's time.*

improvident (ĭm prŏv′ĭ dənt), *adj.* 1. not provident; lacking foresight; incautious or unwary. 2. neglecting to provide for future needs. —**improv′idence,** *n.* —**improv′idently,** *adv.* —**Syn.** 1. thoughtless, careless, heedless. 2. shiftless, thriftless, unthrifty; wasteful, prodigal. —**Ant.** 1. prudent. 2. economical.

improvisation (ĭm′prə vī zā′shən), *n.* 1. the act of improvising. 2. something improvised.

improvisator (ĭm prŏv′ĭ zā′tə, ĭm′prə vī-), *n.* one who improvises.

improvisatory (ĭm′prə vī zā′tə rĭ), *adj.* of or pertaining to an improvisator or improvisation. **—improvisatorial** (ĭm prŏv′ĭ zə tô′rĭ əl), *adj.* **—improv′isato′rially,** *adv.*

improvise (ĭm′prə vīz′), *v.*, **-vised, -vising.** *—v.t.* **1.** to prepare or provide offhand or hastily; extemporize. **2.** to compose (verse, music, etc.) on the spur of the moment. **3.** to recite, sing, etc., extemporaneously. *—v.i.* **4.** to compose, utter, or execute anything extemporaneously: *he improvised in rhyme.* [t. F: m. s. *improviser*, t. It.: m. *improvvisare*, der. *improvviso* extempore, g. L *imprōvisus* unforeseen, unexpected] **—im′provis′er,** *n.*

improvised (ĭm′prə vīzd′), *adj.* made or said without previous preparation. **—Syn.** See **extemporaneous.**

improvvisatore (*It.* ēm prŏv vē zä tô′rĕ), *n.*, *pl.* **-ri** (*It.* -rē). *Italian.* an improvisator.

imprudent (ĭm proo′dnt), *adj.* not prudent; lacking prudence or discretion. [t. L: s. *imprūdens*] **—impru′dence,** *n.* **—impru′dently,** *adv.*

impudence (ĭm′pyŏŏ dəns), *n.* **1.** the quality or fact of being impudent; effrontery; insolence. **2.** impudent conduct or language. **3.** *Obs.* lack of modesty; shamelessness. Also, **im′pudency.** **—Syn. 1.** impertinence, rudeness; brazenness, face. **—Ant. 1.** courtesy.

impudent (ĭm′pyŏŏ dənt), *adj.* **1.** characterized by a shameless boldness, assurance, or effrontery: *impudent behaviour.* **2.** *Obs.* shameless or brazenly immodest. [t. L: s. *impudens* shameless] **—im′pudently,** *adv.* **—Syn. 1.** insolent, rude; saucy, pert; brazen. See **impertinent.** **—Ant. 1.** polite.

impudicity (ĭm′pyŏŏ dĭs′ĭ tĭ), *n.* immodesty.

impugn (ĭm pyoon′), *v.t.* **1.** to assail by words or arguments, as statements, motives, veracity, etc.; call in question; challenge as false. **2.** *Rare.* to assail a person for his statements or actions. [ME *impugne(n)*, t. OF: m. *impugner*, t. L: m. *impugnāre* attack] **—impugn′able,** *adj.* **—impugnation** (ĭm′pŭg nā′shən), **impugnment** (ĭm pyoon′mənt), *n.* **—impugn′er,** *n.*

impuissant (ĭm pyoo′ĭ sənt), *adj.* impotent; feeble; weak. [t. F. See IM-², PUISSANT] **—impu′issance,** *n.*

impulse (ĭm′pŭls), *n.* **1.** the inciting influence of a particular feeling, mental state, etc.: *to act under the impulse of pity.* **2.** sudden, involuntary inclination prompting to action, or a particular instance of it: *to be swayed by impulse.* **3.** an impelling action or force, driving onwards or inducing motion. **4.** the effect of an impelling force; motion induced; impetus given. **5.** *Physiol.* a stimulus conveyed by the nervous system, muscle fibres, etc., either exciting or limiting organic functioning. **6.** *Mech.* the product of a force and the time during which it acts (sometimes restricted to cases in which the force is great and the time short, as in the blows of a hammer). **7.** *Elect.* a single, usually sudden, flow of current in one direction. [t. L: m. s. *impulsus* a push against]

impulse turbine. See **turbine.**

impulsion (ĭm pŭl′shən), *n.* **1.** the act of impelling, driving onwards, or pushing. **2.** the resulting state or effect; impulse; impetus. **3.** the inciting influence of some feeling or motive; mental impulse. **4.** constraining or inciting action on the mind or conduct: *divine impulsion.* [ME, t. L: s. *impulsio* influence, instigation]

impulsive (ĭm pŭl′sĭv), *adj.* **1.** actuated or swayed by emotional or involuntary impulses: *an impulsive child.* **2.** having the power or effect of impelling; characterized by impulsion: *impulsive forces.* **3.** inciting to action: *an impulsive influence on humanity.* **4.** *Mech.* (of forces) acting momentarily; not continuous. **—impul′sively,** *adv.* **—impul′siveness,** *n.* **—Syn. 1.** See **impetuous.**

impunity (ĭm pyoo′nĭ tĭ), *n.* exemption from punishment or ill consequences. [t. L: m. s. *impūnitas* omission of punishment] **—Syn.** See **exemption.**

impure (ĭm pyŏŏə′), *adj.* **1.** not pure; mixed with extraneous matter, esp. of an inferior or contaminating kind: *impure water.* **2.** modified by admixture, as colour. **3.** mixed or combined with something else: *an impure style of architecture.* **4.** ceremonially unclean, as things, animals, etc. **5.** not morally pure; unchaste: *impure language.* **6.** marked by foreign and unsuitable or objectionable elements or characteristics, as a style of art or of literary expression. [t. L: m. s. *impūrus* not pure] **—impure′ly,** *adv.* **—impure′ness,** *n.*

impurity (ĭm pyŏŏə′rĭ tĭ), *n.*, *pl.* **-ties.** **1.** the quality or state of being impure. **2.** (*often pl.*) that which is or makes impure: *impurities in drinking water.*

imputable (ĭm pyoo′tə bl), *adj.* that may be imputed; attributable. **—imput′abil′ity, imput′ableness,** *n.* **—imput′ably,** *adv.*

imputation (ĭm′pyŏŏ tā′shən), *n.* **1.** the act of imputing. **2.** an attribution, esp. of fault, crime, etc.

impute (ĭm pyoot′), *v.t.*, **-puted, -puting.** **1.** to attribute (something discreditable) to a person. **2.** to attribute or ascribe. **3.** *Law.* to charge. **4.** *Theol.* to attribute (righteousness, guilt, etc.) vicariously; ascribe as derived from another. **5.** *Obs.* to charge (a person) with fault. [ME, t. L: m. s. *imputāre* bring into the reckoning] **—imputative** (ĭm pyoo′tə tĭv), *adj.* **—imput′atively,** *adv.* **—imput′ativeness,** *n.* **—imput′er,** *n.* **—Syn. 2.** See **attribute.**

impv., imperative.

in (ĭn), *prep.* a particle expressing: **1.** inclusion within space or limits, a whole, material or immaterial surroundings, etc.: *in the city, in the army, dressed in white, in politics.* **2.** inclusion within, or occurrence during the course of or at the expiry of, a period or limit of time: *in ancient times, to do a task in an hour, return in ten minutes.* **3.** situation, condition, occupation, action, manner, relation, means, etc.: *in darkness, in sickness, in service, in crossing the street, in confidence, in French.* **4.** object or purpose: *in honour of the event.* **5.** motion or direction from without to a point within (now usually into), or transition from one state to another: *to put in operation, break in two.* **6.** pregnancy with: *the mare's in foal again.* **7. in for, a.** about to undergo, esp. something boring or disagreeable. **b.** entered for. **c.** involved to the limit of. **8. in that,** for the reason that. **9. in on,** having a share or a part of. *—adv.* **10.** in or into some place, position, state, relation, etc. **11.** on the inside, or within. **12.** in one's house or office. **13.** in office or power. **14.** in possession or occupancy. **15.** having the turn to play, in a game. *—adj.* **16.** that is or gets in; internal; inward; incoming; inbound. **17.** in favour; on friendly terms: *he's in with the managing director.* **18.** in fashion: *Mexican jewellery is in this year.* **19.** in season: *strawberries are in now.* **20.** alight: *leave the fire in overnight.* *—n.* **21.** (*pl.*) those who are in, as the political party in power. **22.** influence; pull; connection: *she has an in with the management—she married a director.* **23. ins and outs, a.** nooks or recesses; windings and turnings. **b.** intricacies. [ME and OE, c. D and G *in*, Icel. *i*, Goth. *in*; akin to L *in*, Gk *en*]

in-¹, a prefix representing English *in*, as in *income, indwelling, inland*, but used also as a verb-formative with transitive, intensive, or sometimes little apparent force, as in *intrust, inweave*, etc. It often assumes the same phases as **in-²**, as **en-, em-**, and **im-³**. [ME and OE; repr. IN, adv.]

in-², a prefix of Latin origin meaning primarily 'in', but used also as a verb-formative with the same force as **in-¹**, as in *incarcerate, incantation.* Also, **-il¹, im-¹, ir-².** Cf. **em-, en-.** [t. L, repr. *in*, prep. (in F *en*), c. IN, prep.]

in-³, a prefix of Latin origin corresponding to English *un-*, having a negative or privative force, freely used as an English formative, esp. of adjectives and their derivatives and of nouns, as in *inattention, indefensible, inexpensive, inorganic, invariable.* This prefix assumes the same phonetic phases as **in-²**, as in *impartial, immeasurable, illiterate, irregular*, etc. In French it became *en-* and thus occurs unfelt in such words as *enemy* (French *ennemi*, Latin *inimicus*, lit., not friendly). Also, **il-², im-², ir-².** [t. L; akin to Gk *an-*, *a-* A-⁶, and UN-¹]

—Syn. The prefixes IN- and UN- may both have, among other uses, a negative force. IN- is the form from the classical languages (Greek and Latin) and is therefore used most in learned words or in words derived from those languages: *inaccessible, inaccuracy, inadequate*, etc. UN- is the native form going back to Old English, used in words of native origin, and sometimes used in combination with words of other origins, if these words are in common use: *unloving, unmanly, unfeeling, unnecessary, unsafe.* Occasionally the prefix UN- is used with a frequently used word in a common meaning, as in *unsanitary* (not clean), and IN- with the same word in a more technical sense, as *insanitary* (likely to cause disease).

-in¹, a suffix used in adjectives of Greek or Latin origin meaning 'pertaining to' and (in nouns thence derived) also imitated in English, as in *coffin, cousin, lupin*, etc.; and occurring unfelt in abstract nouns formed as nouns in Latin, as *ruin.* [ME *-in, -ine*, t. OF, t. L: m. *-inus, -ina, -inum*, t. Gk: m. *-inos, -inē, -inon*]

-in², a noun suffix used in chemical and mineralogical nomenclature without any formal significance, though it is usually restricted to certain neutral compounds, glycerides, glucosides, and proteids as *albumin, butyrin.* In some compounds, as *glycerine*, the spelling *-ine* is also used, although an attempt is made to restrict *-ine* to basic compounds. [t. NL: s. *-ina.* See -INE²]

In, *Chem.* indium.

in., inch; inches.

inability (ĭn′ə bĭl′ĭ tĭ), *n.* lack of ability; lack of power, capacity, or means. **—Syn.** See **disability.**

in absentia (ĭn′ăb sĕn′tĭ ä′), *Latin.* in or during (one's) absence.

inaccessible (ĭn′ăk sĕs′ə bl), *adj.* not accessible; unapproachable. —**in′acces′sibil′ity, in′acces′sibleness,** *n.* —**in′acces′sibly,** *adv.*

inaccuracy (ĭn ăk′yŏŏ rə sĭ), *n., pl.* **-cies. 1.** the quality of being inaccurate. **2.** that which is inaccurate. —**Syn. 2.** error, mistake, blunder, slip.

inaccurate (ĭn ăk′yŏŏ rĭt), *adj.* not accurate. —**inac′curately,** *adv.* —**inac′curateness,** *n.* —**Syn.** inexact, loose; incorrect, erroneous, wrong, faulty.

Inachus (ĭn′ə kəs), *n. Gk Myth.* a river god who became the first king of Argos; father of Io.

inaction (ĭn ăk′shən), *n.* absence of action; idleness.

inactivate (ĭn ăk′tĭ vāt′), *v.t.,* **-vated, -vating. 1.** to make inactive. **2.** *Med.* to stop the activity of (certain biological substances).

inactive (ĭn ăk′tĭv), *adj.* **1.** not active; inert. **2.** indolent; sluggish; passive. **3.** *Chiefly U.S. Mil.* not on active duty or status. **4.** *Phys. Chem.* denoting a compound which does not rotate the plane of vibration of polarized light. —**inactivation** (ĭn′ăk tĭ vā′shən, ĭn ăk′-), *n.* —**inac′tively,** *adv.* —**in′activ′ity, inac′tiveness,** *n.*

—**Syn. 1, 2.** INACTIVE, DORMANT, INERT, SLUGGISH, TORPID suggest lack of activity. INACTIVE indicates absence of action, indisposition to activity, or cessation of activity: *an inactive compound, life, file of papers.* DORMANT suggests the quiescence or inactivity of that which sleeps but may be roused to action: *a dormant volcano.* INERT suggests the condition of dead matter, with no inherent power of motion or action; it may also mean unable to move, or heavy and hard to move: *an inert mass, inert from hunger.* SLUGGISH expresses slowness of natural activity or of that which does not move readily or vigorously: *a sluggish stream, brain.* TORPID suggests a state of suspended physical powers, a condition particularly of animals which hibernate: *snakes are torpid in cold weather.* —**Ant. 1.** lively.

inadaptable (ĭn′ə dăp′tə bl), *adj.* not adaptable; incapable of being adapted. —**in′adapt′abil′ity,** *n.*

inadequate (ĭn ăd′ĭ kwĭt), *adj.* not adequate. —**inad′equacy, inad′equateness,** *n.* —**inad′equately,** *adv.* —**Syn.** inapt, incompetent; insufficient, incommensurate; defective, imperfect, incomplete.

inadmissible (ĭn′əd mĭs′ə bl), *adj.* not admissible: *inadmissible evidence.* —**in′admis′sibil′ity,** *n.* —**in′admis′sibly,** *adv.*

inadvertence (ĭn′əd vûr′tns), *n.* **1.** the quality of being inadvertent; heedlessness. **2.** an act or effect of inattention; an oversight. [t. ML: m. s. *inadvertentia*]

inadvertency (ĭn′əd vûr′tn sĭ), *n., pl.* **-cies.** inadvertence.

inadvertent (ĭn′əd vûr′tnt), *adj.* **1.** not attentive; heedless. **2.** characterized by lack of attention, as actions, etc. **3.** unintentional: *an inadvertent insult.* —**in′advert′ently,** *adv.*

inadvisable (ĭn′əd vī′zə bl), *adj.* not advisable; inexpedient. —**in′advis′abil′ity,** *n.* —**in′advis′ably,** *adv.*

-inae, *Zool.* a suffix of the names of subfamilies. [t. L, fem. pl. of adjectives ending in *-inus.* See -INE[1]]

in aeternum (ĭn′ē tûr′nəm), *Latin.* for ever.

inalienable (ĭn ā′lyə nə bl), *adj.* not alienable; that cannot be transferred to another: *inalienable rights.* —**ina′lienabil′ity,** *n.* —**ina′lienably,** *adv.*

inalterable (ĭn ôl′tə rə bl, -trə bl), *adj.* not alterable. —**inal′terabil′ity,** *n.* —**inal′terably,** *adv.*

inamorata (ĭn ăm′ə rä′tə, ĭn′ăm-), *n., pl.* **-tas.** a female lover; a woman who loves or is loved. [t. It.: m. *innamorata* sweetheart (fem.), der. *amore* love, g. L *amor*]

inamorato (ĭn ăm′ə rä′tō, ĭn′ăm-), *n.* a male lover. [see INAMORATA]

in-and-in (ĭn′ənd ĭn′), *adv.* repeatedly within the same family, strain, etc.: *to breed stock in-and-in.*

inane (ĭ nān′), *adj.* **1.** lacking sense or ideas; silly: *inane questions.* **2.** empty; void. —*n.* **3.** that which is inane or void; the void of infinite space. [t. L: m. s. *inānis* empty, vain] —**inane′ly,** *adv.*

inanimate (ĭn ăn′ĭ mĭt), *adj.* **1.** not animate; lifeless. **2.** spiritless; sluggish; dull. —**inan′imately,** *adv.* —**inan′imateness,** *n.*

inanition (ĭn′ə nĭsh′ən), *n.* **1.** exhaustion from lack of nourishment; starvation. **2.** emptiness. [ME, t. LL: s. *inānītio*, der. L *inānīre* make empty]

inanity (ĭ năn′ ĭ tĭ), *n., pl.* **-ties. 1.** lack of sense or ideas; silliness. **2.** an inane remark, etc. **3.** emptiness.

inappeasable (ĭn′ə pē′zə bl), *adj.* not appeasable; not to be appeased: *inappeasable anger.*

inappetence (ĭn ăp′ ĭ təns), *n.* lack of appetence or appetite. Also, **inap′petency.**

inapplicable (ĭn ăp′lĭ kə bl), *adj.* not applicable; unsuitable. —**inap′plicabil′ity, inap′plicableness,** *n.* —**inap′plicably,** *adv.*

inapposite (ĭn ăp′ə zĭt), *adj.* not apposite; not pertinent. —**inap′positely,** *adv.* —**inap′positeness,** *n.*

inappreciable (ĭn′ə prē′shə bl), *adj.* imperceptible; insignificant: *an inappreciable difference.* —**in′appre′ciably,** *adv.*

inappreciative (ĭn′ə prē′shə tĭv), *adj.* unappreciative. —**in′appre′ciatively,** *adv.* —**in′appre′ciativeness,** *n.*

inapprehensible (ĭn′ăp rĭ hĕn′ sə bl), *adj.* not to be grasped by the senses or intellect.

inapprehension (ĭn′ăp rĭ hĕn′shən), *n.* lack of apprehension.

inapprehensive (ĭn′ăp rĭ hĕn′sĭv), *adj.* **1.** not apprehensive (often fol. by *of*). **2.** without apprehension.

inapproachable (ĭn′ə prō′chə bl), *adj.* **1.** not approachable. **2.** without rival. —**in′approach′abil′ity,** *n.* —**in′approach′ably,** *adv.*

inappropriate (ĭn′ə prō′prĭ ĭt), *adj.* not appropriate. —**in′appro′priately,** *adv.* —**in′appro′priateness,** *n.*

inapt (ĭn ăpt′), *adj.* **1.** not apt or fitted. **2.** without aptitude or capacity. —**inapt′ly,** *adv.* —**inapt′ness,** *n.* —**Syn. 1.** unsuited, unsuitable, inappropriate.

inaptitude (ĭn ăp′ tĭ tyōōd′), *n.* **1.** lack of aptitude; unfitness. **2.** unskilfulness.

inarch (ĭn ärch′), *v.t. Hort.* to graft by uniting a growing branch to a stock without separating the branch from its parent stock. [f. IN-[2] + ARCH[1]]

Inarching

inarm (ĭn ärm′), *v.t.* to hold in, or as in, the arms.

inarticulate (ĭn′är tĭk′ yŏŏ lĭt), *adj.* **1.** not articulate; not uttered or emitted with expressive or intelligible modulations: *inarticulate sounds.* **2.** unable to use articulate speech: *inarticulate with rage.* **3.** unable to express oneself clearly and fluently in speech. **4.** *Anat., Zool.* not jointed; having no articulation or joint. [t. LL: m. s. *inarticulātus* not distinct. See IN-[3], ARTICULATE] —**in′artic′ulately,** *adv.* —**in′artic′ulateness,** *n.*

inartificial (ĭn är′tĭ fĭsh′ əl), *adj.* **1.** not artificial; natural; artless; plain or simple. **2.** inartistic. —**inar′tifi′cial′ity,** *n.* —**inar′tifi′cially,** *adv.*

inartistic (ĭn′ä tĭs′tĭk), *adj.* **1.** not artistic; aesthetically poor. **2.** lacking in artistic sense. Also, **in′artis′tical.** —**in′artis′tically,** *adv.*

inasmuch as (ĭn′əz mŭch′), **1.** in view of the fact that; seeing that; since. **2.** in so far as; to such a degree as. —**Syn. 1.** See **because.**

inattention (ĭn′ə tĕn′shən), *n.* **1.** lack of attention; negligence. **2.** an act of neglect.

inattentive (ĭn′ə tĕn′tĭv), *adj.* not attentive. —**in′atten′tively,** *adv.* —**in′atten′tiveness,** *n.*

inaudible (ĭn ô′ də bl), *adj.* incapable of being heard. —**inau′dibil′ity,** *n.* —**inau′dibly,** *adv.*

inaugural (ĭn ô′ gyŏŏ rəl), *adj.* **1.** of or pertaining to an inauguration. —*n.* **2.** an address, as by a president, at the beginning of a term of office. [t. F, der. *inaugurer,* t. L: m. *inaugurāre* INAUGURATE]

inaugurate (ĭn ô′ gyŏŏ rāt′), *v.t.,* **-rated, -rating. 1.** to make a formal beginning of; initiate; commence; begin. **2.** to induct into office with formal ceremonies; install. **3.** to introduce into public use by some formal ceremony. [t. L: m. s. *inaugurātus*, pp., consecrated or installed with augural ceremonies] —**inau′gura′tion,** *n.* —**inau′gurator,** *n.*

inauspicious (ĭn′ô spĭsh′ əs), *adj.* not auspicious; ill-omened; unfavourable; unlucky. —**in′auspi′ciously,** *adv.* —**in′auspi′ciousness,** *n.*

inbeing (ĭn′bē′ĭng), *n.* **1.** the condition of existing in something else; immanence. **2.** inward nature.

inboard (ĭn′bôd′), *adv., adj. Naut.* within the hull or interior, or towards the centre, of a ship.

inborn (ĭn′bôn′), *adj.* implanted by nature; innate. —**Syn.** inbred, inherent, natural, native. —**Ant.** acquired.

inbound (ĭn′bound′), *adj.* inward bound: *inbound ships.*

inbreathe (ĭn brēth′), *v.t.,* **-breathed, -breathing. 1.** to breathe in; infuse. **2.** to inspire.

inbred (ĭn′brĕd′), *adj.* **1.** bred within; innate; native. **2.** resulting from or involved in inbreeding.

inbreed (ĭn′brēd′), *v.t.,* **-bred, -breeding. 1.** to breed (animals) in-and-in. **2.** to breed within; engender.

inbreeding (ĭn′brē′dĭng), *n. Biol.* the mating of related individuals such as cousins, sire-daughter, brother-sister, or self-fertilized plants. Inbreeding automatically fixes the genes, making them homozygous.

inburst (ĭn′bûst′), *n. Rare.* a bursting in; irruption.

inc., 1. included. **2.** including. **3.** inclusive. **4.** (*also cap.*) incorporated. **5.** increase.

Inca (ĭng′kə), *n.* **1.** one of the dominant groups of South American Indians who occupied Peru prior to the Spanish conquest. **2.** the chief ruler of the race. [t. Sp., Pg., t. Quechua] —**In′can,** *n., adj.*

incalculable (ĭn kăl′kyŏŏ lə bl), *adj.* **1.** that cannot be calculated; beyond calculation. **2.** that cannot be forecast. **3.** uncertain. —**incal′culabil′ity, incal′culableness,** *n.* —**incal′culably,** *adv.*

incalescent (ĭn′kə lĕs′ənt), *adj.* increasing in heat. [t. L: s. *incalescens*, ppr.] —**in′cales′cence,** *n.*

incandesce (ĭn′kăn dĕs′), *v.i., v.t.,* **-desced, -descing.** to glow or cause to glow with heat. [t. L: m. s. *incandescere* grow hot, glow]

incandescence (ĭn′kăn dĕs′əns), *n.* the state of a body caused by approximately white heat, when it may be used as a source of artificial light.

incandescent (ĭn′kăn dĕs′ənt), *adj.* **1.** (of light, etc.) produced by incandescence. **2.** glowing or white with heat. **3.** intensely bright; brilliant. [t. L: s. *incandescens*, ppr., growing hot] —**in′candes′cently,** *adv.*

incandescent lamp, a lamp whose light is due to the glowing of some material, as the common electric lamp which contains a filament rendered luminous by the passage of current through it.

incantation (ĭn′kăn tā′shən), *n.* **1.** the chanting or uttering of words purporting to have magical power. **2.** the formula employed; a spell or charm. **3.** magical ceremonies. **4.** magic; sorcery. [ME *incantacion*, t. LL: m. s. *incantātio* enchantment]

incapable (ĭn kā′pə bl), *adj.* **1.** not capable. **2.** not having the capacity or power for a specified act or function (fol. by *of*). **3.** not open to the influence; not susceptible or admitting (fol. by *of*): *incapable of exact measurement.* **4.** without ordinary capability or ability; incompetent: *incapable workers.* **5.** without qualification, esp. legal qualification (often fol. by *of*): *incapable of holding public office.* —*n.* **6.** a thoroughly incompetent person. [t. LL: m. s. *incapābilis.* See IN-³, CAPABLE] —**inca′pabil′ity, inca′pableness,** *n.* —**inca′pably,** *adv.*

—**Syn. 1.** INCAPABLE, INCOMPETENT, INEFFICIENT, UNABLE are applied to one who or that which is lacking in ability, preparation, or power for whatever is to be done. INCAPABLE usually means inherently lacking in ability or power: *incapable of appreciating music; a bridge incapable of carrying heavy loads.* INCOMPETENT, generally used only of persons, means unfit or unqualified for a particular task: *incompetent as an administrator.* INEFFICIENT means wasteful in the use of effort or power: *an inefficient manager, inefficient methods.* UNABLE usually refers to a temporary condition of inability to do some specific thing: *unable to relax, to go to a concert.*

incapacious (ĭn′kə pā′shəs), *adj.* **1.** *Obs.* not capacious; lacking capacity; narrow; limited. **2.** *Rare.* mentally incapable. [f. INCAPACI(TY) + -OUS] —**in′capa′ciousness,** *n.*

incapacitate (ĭn′kə păs′ĭ tāt′), *v.t.,* **-tated, -tating. 1.** to deprive of capacity; make incapable or unfit; disqualify. **2.** *Law.* to deprive of power to perform acts with legal consequences. —**in′capac′ita′tion,** *n.*

incapacity (ĭn′kə păs′ĭ tĭ), *n., pl.* **-ties. 1.** lack of capacity; incapability. **2.** legal disqualification. [t. ML: m. *incapācitas*]

incarcerate (*v.* ĭn kä′sə rāt′; *adj.* ĭn kä′sə rĭt, -sə rāt′), *v.,* **-rated, -rating,** *adj.* —*v.t.* **1.** to imprison; confine. **2.** to enclose; constrict closely. —*adj.* **3.** imprisoned. [t. ML: m. s. *incarcerātus*, pp. of *incarcerāre*, der. L *in-* IN-² + *carcer* prison] —**incar′cera′tion,** *n.* —**incar′cera′tor,** *n.*

incardinate (ĭn kä′dĭ nāt′), *v.t.,* **-nated, -nating. 1.** to institute as a cardinal. **2.** to institute as chief presbyter, priest, etc., in a particular church or place. [t. ML: m. s. *incardinātus*, pp. See CARDINAL] —**incar′dina′tion,** *n.*

incarnadine (ĭn kä′ nə dīn′), *adj., n., v.,* **-dined, -dining.** —*adj.* **1.** flesh-coloured; pale red. **2.** crimson. —*n.* **3.** an incarnadine colour. —*v.t.* **4.** to make incarnadine. [t. F: m. *incarnadin*, t. d. It.: m. *incarnadino*, ult. der. LL *incarnātus.* See INCARNATE]

incarnate (*adj.* ĭn kä′nĭt, -nāt; *v.* ĭn′kä nāt′) *adj., v.,* **-nated, -nating.** —*adj.* **1.** embodied in flesh; invested with a bodily, esp. a human, form: *a devil incarnate.* **2.** personified or typified, as a quality or idea: *chivalry incarnate.* **3.** flesh-coloured or crimson. —*v.t.* **4.** to put into or represent in a concrete form, as an idea. **5.** to be the embodiment or type of. **6.** to embody in flesh; invest with a bodily, esp. a human, form. [ME, t. LL: m. s. *incarnātus*, pp., made flesh]

incarnation (ĭn′kä nā′shən), *n.* **1.** an incarnate being or form. **2.** a living being embodying a deity or spirit. **3.** assumption of human form or nature, as by a divine being: *the incarnation of God in Christ.* **4.** a person or thing representing or exhibiting some quality, idea, etc., in typical form. **5.** the act of incarnating. **6.** the state of being incarnated. [ME, t. LL: s. *incarnātio*]

incase (ĭn kās′), *v.t.,* **-cased, -casing.** encase.

incaution (ĭn kô′shən), *n.* lack of caution; heedlessness; carelessness. [f. IN-³ + CAUTION]

incautious (ĭn kô′shəs), *adj.* not cautious; careless; rash; heedless. —**incau′tiously,** *adv.* —**incau′tiousness,** *n.*

incendiarism (ĭn sĕn′dyə rĭz′əm), *n.* **1.** the act or practice of an incendiary; malicious burning. **2.** inflammatory agitation; the arousing of passions or violence.

incendiary (ĭn sĕn′ dyə rĭ), *adj., n., pl.* **-aries.** —*adj.* **1.** used or adapted for setting property on fire: *incendiary bombs.* **2.** of or pertaining to the criminal setting on fire of property. **3.** tending to arouse strife, sedition, etc.; inflammatory: *incendiary speeches.* —*n.* **4.** one who maliciously sets fire to buildings or other property. **5.** *Mil.* a shell, bomb, etc., containing phosphorus or similar material producing great heat. **6.** one who stirs up strife, sedition, etc.; an agitator. [t. L: m. s. *incendiārius* causing fire]

incense[1] (ĭn′sĕns), *n., v.,* **-censed, -censing.** —*n.* **1.** an aromatic gum or other substance producing a sweet smell when burnt, used esp. in religious ceremonies. **2.** the perfume or smoke arising from such a substance when burnt. **3.** any pleasant perfume or fragrance. **4.** homage or adulation. —*v.t.* **5.** to perfume with incense. **6.** to burn incense for. —*v.i.* **7.** to burn or offer incense. [t. LL: m. s. *incensum* incense, prop. pp. neut. of L *incendere* set on fire; r. ME *encens*, t. OF]

incense[2] (ĭn sĕns′), *v.t.,* **-censed, -censing.** to inflame with wrath; make angry; enrage. [ME *incence(n)*, t. L: m. s. *incensus*, pp., set on fire, kindled] —**incense′ment,** *n.* —**Syn.** See **enrage.**

incensory (ĭn′sĕn′sə rĭ), *n.* a vessel for burning incense.

incentive (ĭn sĕn′tĭv), *n.* **1.** that which incites to action, etc. —*adj.* **2.** inciting, as to action; stimulating; provocative. [ME, t. L: m. s. *incentīvus* inciting, setting the tune] —**incen′tively,** *adv.* —**Syn. 1.** See **motive.**

incept (ĭn sĕpt′), *v.i.* **1.** to complete the taking of a degree of master or doctor in a university, esp. Cambridge. —*v.t.* **2.** to take in; intussuscept. [t. L: s. *inceptus*, pp. begun, commenced] —**incep′tor,** *n.*

inception (ĭn sĕp′shən), *n.* **1.** beginning; start. **2.** the act of incepting in a university.

inceptive (ĭn sĕp′tĭv), *adj.* **1.** *Gram.* (of a derived verb, or of an aspect in verb inflection) expressing the beginning of the action indicated by the underlying verb. For example: Latin verbs in *-sco* generally have inceptive force, as *calescō* 'become or begin to be hot' from *caleō* 'be hot'. **2.** beginning; initial. —*n.* **3.** *Gram.* **a.** the inceptive aspect. **b.** a verb in the inceptive aspect. —**incep′tively,** *adv.*

incertitude (ĭn sû′tĭ tyōōd′), *n.* **1.** uncertainty; doubtfulness. **2.** insecurity. [f. IN-³ + CERTITUDE]

incessant (ĭn sĕs′ənt), *adj.* continuing without interruption: *an incessant noise.* [t. LL: s. *incessans* unceasing] —**inces′sancy, inces′santness,** *n.* —**inces′santly,** *adv.* —**Syn.** ceaseless, unceasing, continual, continuous, constant. —**Ant.** intermittent.

incest (ĭn′sĕst), *n.* **1.** sexual intercourse between persons closely related by blood. **2.** the crime of sexual intercourse between persons within the degrees of consanguinity in which marriage is forbidden. [ME, t. L: s. *incestus* or *incestum* (neut.) unchaste]

incestuous (ĭn sĕs′tyōō əs), *adj.* **1.** guilty of incest. **2.** involving incest. —**inces′tuously,** *adv.* —**inces′tuousness,** *n.*

inch[1] (ĭnch), *n.* **1.** a unit of length, $\frac{1}{12}$ foot, equivalent to 2·54 centimetres. **2.** a very small amount of anything. **3. by inches, a.** by a narrow margin: *he escaped death by inches.* **b.** Also, **inch by inch,** by degrees; very gradually. **4. every inch,** in every respect: *every inch a king.* **5. within an inch of,** almost; very near: *she came within an inch of being knocked down by a car.* —*v.t., v.i.* **6.** to move by inches or small degrees. [ME; OE *ynce*, t. L: m. s. *uncia* twelfth part, inch, ounce. Cf. OUNCE[1]]

inch[2] (ĭnch), *n. Scot.* a small island. [ME, t. Gaelic: m. *innse*, gen. of *innis* island]

inchmeal (ĭnch′mēl′), *adv.* by inches; inch by inch; little by little (often prec. by *by*).

inchoate (ĭn′kō āt′), *adj.* **1.** just begun; incipient. **2.** rudimentary. **3.** lacking organization; unformed. [t. L: m. s. *inchoātus, incohātus*, pp., begun] —**in′choate′ly,** *adv.* —**in′choate′ness,** *n.*

inchoation (ĭn′kō ā′shən), *n.* beginning; origin.

inchoative (ĭn kō′ə tĭv), *adj.* **1.** *Gram.* inceptive. **2.** *Rare.* inchoate. —*n.* **3.** *Gram.* an inceptive.

Inchon (ĭn′chŏn′), *n.* a seaport in W South Korea. 430,054 (1963). Also **Chemulpo.** Japanese, **Jinsen.**

inchworm (ĭnch′wûm′), *n.* measuring worm.

incidence (ĭn′sĭ dəns), *n.* **1.** the range of occurrence or influence of a thing, or the extent of its effects: *the incidence of a disease.* **2.** the falling, or direction or manner of falling, of a ray of light, etc., on a surface. **3.** a falling upon, affecting, or befalling. **4.** the fact or the manner of being incident. **5.** *Geom.* partial coincidence of two figures, as of a line and a plane containing it.

incident (ĭn′sĭ dənt), *n.* **1.** an occurrence or event. **2.** a distinct piece of action, or an episode, as in a story or play. **3.** something that occurs casually in connection with something else. **4.** something appertaining or attaching to something else. **5. a.** an occurrence, such as a clash between troops of countries whose relations are already strained, which is liable to have grave consequences. **b.** a disturbance, esp. one of a serious nature such as a riot or rebellion, about which precise information is lacking. *—adj.* **6.** likely or apt to happen (fol. by *to*). **7.** naturally appertaining: *hardships incident to the life of an explorer.* **8.** conjoined or attaching, esp. as subordinate to a principal thing. **9.** falling or striking on something. [ME, t. L: s. *incidens*, ppr., befalling] **—Syn. 1.** See **event.**

incidental (ĭn′sĭ dĕn′tl), *adj.* **1.** happening or likely to happen in fortuitous or subordinate conjunction with something else. **2.** liable to happen or naturally appertaining (fol. by *to*). **3.** incurred casually and in addition to the regular or main amount: *incidental expenses.* *—n.* **4.** something incidental, as a circumstance. **5.** (*pl.*) minor expenses. **—Syn. 1.** casual, chance, fortuitous; contingent. **—Ant. 1.** fundamental.

incidentally (ĭn′sĭ dĕn′tə lĭ), *adv.* **1.** in an incidental manner. **2.** by the way.

incidental music, music played during the action of a film, play, etc., but not forming an essential part of the performance.

incinerate (ĭn sĭn′ə rāt′), *v.t., v.i.*, **-rated, -rating.** to burn or reduce to ashes; cremate. [t. ML: m. s. *incinerātus*, pp. of *incinerāre*, der. L *in-* IN-² + *cinis* ashes] **—incin′era′tion,** *n.*

incinerator (ĭn sĭn′ə rā′tə), *n.* a furnace or apparatus for incinerating.

incipient (ĭn sĭp′ĭ ənt), *adj.* beginning to exist or appear; in an initial stage. [t. L: s. *incipiens*, ppr.] **—incip′ience, incip′iency,** *n.* **—incip′iently,** *adv.*

incipit (ĭn′kĭ pĭt), *Latin.* (here) begins.

incise (ĭn sīz′), *v.t.*, **-cised, -cising. 1.** to cut into; cut marks, etc. upon. **2.** to make (marks, etc.) by cutting; engrave; carve. [t. F: m. s. *inciser*, ult. der. L *incīsus*, pp., cut into]

incised (ĭn sīzd′), *adj.* **1.** cut into: *the incised gums.* **2.** made by cutting: *an incised wound.*

incision (ĭn sĭzh′ən), *n.* **1.** a cut, gash, or notch. **2.** the act of incising. **3.** a cutting into, esp. for surgical purposes. **4.** incisiveness; keenness. [ME, t. L: s. *incīsio*]

incisive (ĭn sī′sĭv), *adj.* **1.** penetrating, trenchant, or biting: *an incisive tone of voice.* **2.** sharp; keen; acute. **3.** adapted for cutting: *the incisive teeth.* **—inci′sively,** *adv.* **—inci′siveness,** *n.*

incisor (ĭn sī′zə), *n.* a tooth in the anterior part of the jaw adapted for cutting. [t. NL]

incisory (ĭn sī′sə rĭ), *adj.* adapted for cutting, as the incisor teeth.

incisure (ĭn sĭzh′ə), *n.* *Anat.* a notch, as in a bone or other structure. **—incis′ural,** *adj.*

incite (ĭn sīt′), *v.t.*, **-cited, -citing.** to urge on; stimulate or prompt to action. [late ME, t. L: m. s. *incitāre* set in motion] **—incitation** (ĭn′sī tā′shən), *n.* **—incit′er,** *n.* **—incit′ingly,** *adv.* **—Syn.** encourage; instigate, provoke, goad, spur, arouse, fire; induce.

incitement (ĭn sīt′mənt), *n.* **1.** the act of inciting. **2.** the state of being incited. **3.** that which incites; motive; incentive.

incivility (ĭn′sĭ vĭl′ĭ tĭ), *n., pl.* **-ties. 1.** the quality or fact of being uncivil; uncivil behaviour or treatment. **2.** an uncivil act.

incivism (ĭn′sĭv′ĭz əm), *n.* neglect of one's duty as a citizen; lack of patriotism.

incl., 1. including. **2.** inclusive.

in-clearing (ĭn′klĭə′rĭng), *n.* *Banking.* the total of cheques, etc., drawn on a member bank of a clearing house, and received by that bank for settlement from the clearing house.

inclement (ĭn klĕm′ənt), *adj.* (of the weather, etc.) not clement; severe or harsh. [t. L: s. *inclēmens* harsh] **—inclem′ency,** *n.* **—inclem′ently,** *adv.*

inclinable (ĭn klī′nə bl), *adj.* **1.** having a mental bent or tendency in a certain direction; inclined. **2.** favourable. **3.** capable of being inclined.

inclination (ĭn′klĭ nā′shən), *n.* **1.** a set or bent (esp. of the mind or will); a liking or preference: *much against his inclination.* **2.** that to which one is inclined. **3.** the act of inclining. **4.** the state of being inclined. **5.** deviation or amount of deviation from a normal, esp. horizontal or vertical, direction or position. **6.** an inclined surface. **7.** *Maths.* the difference in direction of two lines or two planes as measured by the angle. **8.** *Astron.* **a.** one of the elements of an orbit of a planet, etc. **b.** the angle between the orbital plane and the ecliptic or other suitably chosen plane. **9.** dip (def. 26). [late ME, t. L: s. *inclīnātio* a leaning] **—in′clina′tional,** *adj.* **—Syn. 1.** tendency; propensity. **—Ant. 1.** distaste.

inclinatory (ĭn klī′nə tə rĭ, -trĭ), *adj.* related to or characterized by inclination.

incline (*v.* ĭn klīn′; *n.* ĭn′klīn, ĭn klīn′), *v.*, **-clined, -clining,** *n.* *—v.i.* **1.** to have a mental tendency; be disposed. **2.** to deviate from the vertical or horizontal; slant. **3.** to tend, in a physical sense; approximate: *the leaves incline to a blue.* **4.** to tend in course or character. **5.** to lean; bend. *—v.t.* **6.** to dispose (a person) in mind, habit, etc. (fol. by *to*). **7.** to bow (the head, etc.) **8.** to cause to lean or bend in a particular direction. **9.** to turn towards (to listen favourably): *incline one's ear.* *—n.* **10.** an inclined surface; a slope. [t. L: m. s. *inclīnāre* incline; r. ME *enclyne*, t. OF: m. *encliner*] **—inclin′er,** *n.*

inclined (ĭn klīnd′), *adj.* **1.** disposed, esp. favourably (fol. by *to*): *inclined to stay.* **2.** having a (physical) tendency. **3.** deviating in direction from the horizontal or vertical; sloping. **4.** in a direction making an angle with anything else.

inclined plane, a plane surface inclined to the horizon, or forming with a horizontal plane any angle but a right angle.

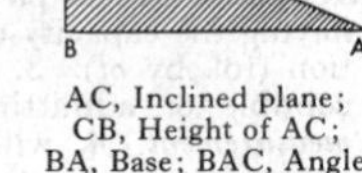

AC, Inclined plane; CB, Height of AC; BA, Base; BAC, Angle of inclination

inclinometer (ĭn′klĭ nŏm′ĭ tə), *n.* **1.** *Aeron.* an instrument for measuring the angle an aircraft makes with the horizontal. **2.** an instrument for determining the inclination or dip of the earth's magnetic force using a magnetic needle. [f. INCLINE + -O- + METER¹]

inclose (ĭn klōz′), *v.t.*, **-closed, -closing.** *Law or Archaic.* enclose. **—inclos′er,** *n.*

inclosure (ĭn klō′zhə), *n.* enclosure.

include (ĭn klo͞od′), *v.t.*, **-cluded, -cluding. 1.** to contain, embrace, or comprise, as a whole does parts or any part or element. **2.** to place in an aggregate, class, category, or the like. **3.** to contain as a subordinate element; involve as a factor. [ME *include(n)*, t. L: m. *inclūdere* shut in] **—includ′ible, includ′able,** *adj.*

—Syn. 1. INCLUDE, COMPREHEND, COMPRISE, EMBRACE imply containing parts of a whole. To INCLUDE is to contain as a part or member, or among the parts and members, of a whole: *the list includes many new names.* To COMPREHEND is to have within the limits, scope, or range of references, as either a part or the whole number of items concerned: *the plan comprehends several projects.* To COMPRISE is to consist of, as the various parts serving to make up the whole: *this genus comprises fifty species.* EMBRACE emphasizes the extent or assortment of that which is included: *the report embraces a great variety of subjects.* **—Ant. 1.** exclude.

included (ĭn klo͞o′dĭd), *adj.* **1.** enclosed; embraced; comprised. **2.** *Bot.* not projecting beyond the mouth of the corolla, as stamens or a style.

incluse (ĭn klo͞os′), *n.* recluse (def. 2).

inclusion (ĭn klo͞o′zhən), *n.* **1.** the act of including. **2.** the state of being included. **3.** that which is included. **4.** *Biol.* a body suspended in the cytoplasm, as a granule, etc. **5.** *Mineral.* a solid body or a body of gas or liquid enclosed within the mass of a mineral. [t. L: s. *inclūsio*]

inclusion body, *Pathol.* a particle which takes a characteristic stain, found in a virus-infected cell.

inclusive (ĭn klo͞o′sĭv), *adj.* **1.** including in consideration or account, as the stated limit or extremes: *from six to ten inclusive.* **2.** including a great deal, or including everything concerned; comprehensive. **3.** that includes; enclosing; embracing. **4. inclusive of,** including. **—inclu′sively,** *adv.* **—inclu′siveness,** *n.*

incoercible (ĭn′kō û′sə bl), *adj.* **1.** not coercible. **2.** *Physics.* incapable of being reduced to a liquid form by any amount of pressure.

incog (ĭn kŏg′), *adj., adv., n.* *Colloq.* incognita or incognito.

incogitable (ĭn kŏj′ĭ tə bl), *adj.* unthinkable. [t. LL: m. s. *incogitābilis*] **—incog′itabil′ity,** *n.*

incogitant (ĭn kŏj′ĭ tənt), *adj.* **1.** thoughtless; inconsiderate. **2.** not having the faculty of thinking.

incognita (ĭn kŏg′nĭ tə), *adj., n., pl.* **-tas, -te** (-tā). *—adj.* **1.** (of a woman or girl) having the real name or identity concealed. *—n.* **2.** a woman or girl who is incognita. [fem. of INCOGNITO]

incognito (ĭn kŏg′nĭ tō′), *adj., adv., n., pl.* **-tos, -ti** (-tē). *—adj.* **1.** having one's identity concealed, as under an assumed name (esp. to avoid notice or formal attentions). *—adv.* **2.** with the real identity concealed: *to travel incognito.* *—n.* **3.** one who is incognito. **4.** the state of being incognito. **5.** the character or disguise assumed by an incognito or incognita. [t. It., t. L: m. *incognitus* unknown]

incognizant (ĭn kŏg′nĭ zənt), *adj.* not cognizant; without knowledge; unaware (fol. by *of.*) **—incog′nizance,** *n.*

incoherence (ĭn′kō hĭə′rəns), *n.* **1.** the state of being incoherent. **2.** something incoherent; an incoherent statement, etc.

incoherency (ĭn′kō hĭə′rən sĭ), *n.*, *pl.* **-cies.** incoherence.
incoherent (ĭn′kō hĭə′rənt), *adj.* **1.** without logical connection; disjointed; rambling: *an incoherent sentence.* **2.** characterized by such thought or language, as a person: *incoherent with rage.* **3.** not coherent or cohering: *an incoherent mixture.* **4.** without physical cohesion; loose: *incoherent dust.* **5.** without unity or harmony of elements: *an incoherent public.* **6.** without congruity of parts; uncoordinated. **7.** naturally different, or incompatible, as things. —**in′coher′ently,** *adv.*
incombustible (ĭn′kəm bŭs′tə bl), *adj.* **1.** not combustible; incapable of being burnt. —*n.* **2.** an incombustible substance. —**in′combus′tibil′ity, in′combus′tibleness,** *n.* —**in′combus′tibly,** *adv.*
income (ĭn′kəm), *n.* **1.** the returns that come in periodically, esp. annually, from one's work, property, business, etc.; revenue; receipts. **2.** something that comes in. **3.** *Rare.* a coming in. —**Syn. 1.** interest, salary, wages, annuity, gain, return, earnings. —**Ant. 1.** outgo, expenditure.
incomer (ĭn′kŭm′ə), *n.* **1.** one who comes in. **2.** an immigrant. **3.** an intruder. **4.** a successor.
income tax, a tax levied on incomes; an annual government tax on personal incomes, usually graduated and with certain deductions and exemptions.
incoming (ĭn′kŭm′ĭng), *adj.* **1.** coming in: *the incoming tide.* **2.** succeeding, as an office-holder. **3.** accruing as profit. **4.** entering; beginning. —*n.* **5.** a coming in; arrival: *the incoming of spring.* **6.** (*usually pl.*) that which comes in, esp. revenue.
incommensurable (ĭn′kə mĕn′shə rə bl, -shrə bl), *adj.* **1.** not commensurable; having no common measure or standard or comparison. **2.** utterly disproportionate. **3.** *Maths.* (of two or more quantities) having no common measure. —*n.* **4.** that which is incommensurable. **5.** *Maths.* one of two or more incommensurable quantities. —**in′commen′surabil′ity, in′commen′surableness,** *n.* —**in′commen′surably,** *adv.*
incommensurate (ĭn′kə mĕn′shə rĭt, -shrĭt), *adj.* **1.** not commensurate; disproportionate; inadequate: *means incommensurate to our wants.* **2.** incommensurable. —**in′commen′surately,** *adv.* —**in′commen′surateness,** *n.*
incommode (ĭn′kə mōd′), *v.t.*, **-moded, -moding. 1.** to inconvenience or discomfort. **2.** to impede; hinder. [t. L: m. s. *incommodāre*]
incommodious (ĭn′kə mō′dyəs), *adj.* **1.** not affording sufficient room. **2.** inconvenient. —**in′commo′diously,** *adv.* —**in′commo′diousness,** *n.*
incommodity (ĭn′kə mŏd′ĭ tĭ), *n.*, *pl.* **-ties, 1.** inconvenience. **2.** something inconvenient.
incommunicable (ĭn′kə myōō′nĭ kə bl), *adj.* **1.** incapable of being communicated, imparted, or told to others. **2.** incommunicative. —**in′commu′nicabil′ity, in′commu′nicableness,** *n.* —**in′commu′nicably,** *adv.*
incommunicado (ĭn′kə myōō′nĭ kä′dō), *adj.* (esp. of a prisoner) deprived of communication with others. [t. Sp.: m. *incomunicado,* der. *comunicar* COMMUNICATE]
incommunicative (ĭn′kə myōō′ nĭ kə tĭv), *adj.* not communicative; reserved. —**in′commu′nicatively,** *adv.* —**in′commu′nicativeness,** *n.*
incommutable (ĭn′kə myōō′tə bl), *adj.* **1.** not exchangeable. **2.** unchangeable. —**in′commut′abil′ity, in′commut′ableness,** *n.* —**in′commut′ably,** *adv.*
incompact (ĭn′kəm păkt′), *adj.* not compact; loose. —**in′compact′ly,** *adv.* —**in′compact′ness,** *n.*
incomparable (ĭn kŏm′pə rə bl, -prə bl), *adj.* **1.** matchless or unequalled: *incomparable beauty.* **2.** not comparable. —**incom′parabil′ity, incom′parableness,** *n.* —**incom′parably,** *adv.*
incompatible (ĭn′kəm păt′ə bl), *adj.* **1.** not compatible; incapable of existing together in harmony. **2.** contrary or opposed in character; discordant. **3.** that cannot coexist or be conjoined. **4.** *Logic.* (of two or more propositions) that cannot be true simultaneously. **5.** (of positions, ranks, etc.) unable to be held simultaneously by one person. **6.** *Pharm., Med.* pertaining to drugs or the like which interfere with one another chemically or physiologically and therefore cannot be prescribed together. —*n.* **7.** (*usually pl.*) an incompatible person or thing. **8.** an incompatible drug or the like. **9.** (*pl.*) *Logic.* **a.** two or more propositions which cannot be true simultaneously. **b.** two or more attributes which cannot simultaneously belong to the same object. —**in′compat′ibil′ity, in′compat′ibleness,** *n.* —**in′compat′ibly,** *adv.* —**Syn. 1.** See **inconsistent.**
incompetence (ĭn kŏm′pĭ təns), *n.* **1.** the character or condition of being incompetent; inability. **2.** *Law.* the condition of lacking the power to act with legal effectiveness. Also, **incom′petency.**
incompetent (ĭn kŏm′pĭ tənt), *adj.* **1.** not competent; lacking qualification or ability: *an incompetent candidate.* **2.** characterized by or showing incompetence. **3.** *Law.* not legally qualified; inadmissible, as evidence. —*n.* **4.** an incompetent person. **5.** *Law.* a person lacking power to act with legal effectiveness. [t. LL: s. *incompetens* insufficient] —**incom′petently,** *adv.* —**Syn. 1.** See **incapable.**
incomplete (ĭn′kəm plēt′), *adj.* not complete; lacking some part. [ME, t. LL: m. s. *incomplētus*] —**in′complete′ly,** *adv.* —**in′complete′ness, in′comple′tion,** *n.*
incompliant (ĭn′kəm plī′ənt), *adj.* **1.** not compliant; unyielding. **2.** not pliant. —**in′compli′ance, in′compli′ancy,** *n.* —**in′compli′antly,** *adv.*
incomprehensible (ĭn′kŏm prĭ hĕn′sə bl, ĭn kŏm′-), *adj.* not comprehensible; not understandable; unintelligible. —**in′comprehen′sibil′ity, in′comprehen′sibleness,** *n.* —**in′comprehen′sibly,** *adv.*
incomprehension (ĭn′kŏm prĭ hĕn′shən), *n.* failure to understand; lack of comprehension: *he greeted my explanation with a blank look of incomprehension.*
incomprehensive (ĭn′kŏm prĭ hĕn′sĭv, ĭn kŏm′-), *adj.* not comprehensive. —**in′comprehen′sively,** *adv.* —**in′comprehen′siveness,** *n.*
incompressible (ĭn′kəm prĕs′ə bl), *adj.* not compressible. —**in′compress′ibil′ity,** *n.*
incomputable (ĭn′kəm pyōō′tə bl), *adj.* incalculable.
inconceivable (ĭn′kən sē′və bl), *adj.* not conceivable; unimaginable; unthinkable; incredible. —**in′conceiv′abil′ity, in′conceiv′ableness,** *n.* —**in′conceiv′ably,** *adv.*
inconclusive (ĭn′kən klōō′sĭv), *adj.* **1.** not conclusive; not such as to settle a question: *inconclusive evidence.* **2.** without final results: *inconclusive experiments.* —**in′conclu′sively,** *adv.* —**in′conclu′siveness,** *n.*
incondensable (ĭn′kən dĕn′sə bl), *adj.* not condensable; incapable of being condensed. —**in′conden′sabil′ity,** *n.*
incondite (ĭn kŏn′dĭt), *adj.* **1.** ill-constructed. **2.** crude; rough. [t. L: m. s. *inconditus* disordered]
inconformity (ĭn′kən fô′mĭ tĭ), *n.* lack of conformity; failure or refusal to conform.
incongruent (ĭn kŏng′grōō ənt), *adj.* not congruent; incongruous. —**incon′gruence,** *n.* —**incon′gruently,** *adv.*
incongruity (ĭn′kŏng grōō′ĭ tĭ), *n.*, *pl.* **-ties. 1.** the quality of being incongruous. **2.** something incongruous.
incongruous (ĭn kŏng′grōō əs), *adj.* **1.** out of keeping or place; inappropriate; unbecoming; absurd: *an incongruous effect.* **2.** not harmonious in character; inconsonant; lacking harmony of parts: *incongruous mixtures.* **3.** inconsistent: *acts incongruous with their principles.* [t. L: m. *incongruus*] —**incon′gruously,** *adv.* —**incon′gruousness,** *n.* —**Syn. 3.** See **inconsistent.**
inconsecutive (ĭn′kən sĕk′yōō tĭv), *adj.* not consecutive. —**in′consec′utively,** *adj.* —**in′consec′utiveness,** *n.*
inconsequent (ĭn kŏn′sĭ kwənt), *adj.* **1.** characterized by lack of sequence in thought, speech, or action. **2.** not following from the premises: *an inconsequent deduction.* **3.** characterized by lack of logical sequence: *inconsequent reasoning.* **4.** irrelevant: *an inconsequent remark.* **5.** not in keeping with the general character or design: *inconsequent ornamentation.* [t. L: s. *inconsequens* without connection] —**incon′sequence,** *n.* —**incon′sequently,** *adv.*
inconsequential (ĭn′kŏn sĭ kwĕn′shəl, ĭn kŏn′-), *adj.* **1.** of no consequence; trivial. **2.** inconsequent; illogical; irrelevant. —**in′consequen′tial′ity,** *n.* —**in′consequen′tially,** *adv.*
inconsiderable (ĭn′kən sĭd′ə rə bl, -sĭd′rə bl), *adj.* **1.** small as in value, amount, size, etc. **2.** not worthy of consideration or notice; trivial. —**in′consid′erableness,** *n.* —**in′consid′erably,** *adv.*
inconsiderate (ĭn′kən sĭd′ə rĭt, -sĭd′rĭt), *adj.* **1.** without due regard for the rights or feelings of others: *it was inconsiderate of him to forget.* **2.** done or acting without consideration; thoughtless. —**in′consid′erately,** *adv.* —**in′consid′erateness, in′consid′era′tion,** *n.*
inconsistency (ĭn′kən sĭs′tən sĭ), *n.*, *pl.* **-cies. 1.** the quality of being inconsistent. **2.** something inconsistent. Also, **in′consist′ence.**
inconsistent (ĭn′kən sĭs′tənt), *adj.* **1.** lacking in harmony between the different parts or elements; self-contradictory. **2.** lacking agreement, as one thing with another, or two or more things in relation to each other; at variance. **3.** not consistent in principles, conduct, etc. **4.** acting at variance with professed principles. **5.** *Logic.* incompatible. —**in′consist′ently,** *adv.*

—**Syn.** 2. INCONSISTENT, INCOMPATIBLE, INCONGRUOUS refer to things which are out of keeping with each other. That which is INCONSISTENT involves variance, discrepancy, or even contradiction, esp. from the point of view of truth, reason, or logic: *his actions are inconsistent with his statements.* INCOMPATIBLE implies incapability of close association or harmonious relationship, as from differences of nature, character, temperament, and the like:

actions incompatible with honesty of purpose, qualities which make two people incompatible. That which is INCONGRUOUS is inappropriate or out of keeping, often to the point of being ridiculous or absurd: *incongruous characters or situations frequently provide a basis for comedy.* —**Ant.** 1. harmonious.

inconsolable (ĭn′kən sō′lə bl), *adj.* not consolable: *inconsolable grief.* —**in′consol′abil′ity, in′consol′ableness,** *n.* —**in′consol′ably,** *adv.*

inconsonant (ĭn kŏn′sə nənt), *adj.* not consonant or in accord. —**incon′sonance,** *n.* —**incon′sonantly,** *adv.*

inconspicuous (ĭn′kən spĭk′yo͝o əs), *adj.* not conspicuous, noticeable, or prominent. —**in′conspic′uously,** *adv.* —**in′conspic′uousness,** *n.*

inconstant (ĭn kŏn′stənt), *adj.* not constant; changeable; fickle; variable: *inconstant winds.* —**incon′stancy,** *n.* —**incon′stantly,** *adv.*

inconsumable (ĭn′kən syo͞o′mə bl), *adj.* not consumable; incapable of being consumed.

incontestable (ĭn′kən tĕs′tə bl), *adj.* not contestable; not admitting of dispute; incontrovertible: *incontestable proof.* —**in′contest′abil′ity, in′contest′ableness,** *n.* —**in′contest′ably,** *adv.*

incontinent[1] (ĭn kŏn′tĭ nənt), *adj.* **1.** not continent; not holding or held in; unceasing or unrestrained: *an incontinent flow of talk.* **2.** lacking in restraint, esp. over the sexual appetite. **3.** unable to contain or retain (usually fol. by *of*). **4.** *Pathol.* unable to restrain natural discharges or evacuations. [ME, t. L: s. *incontinens* not holding back] —**incon′tinence, incon′tinency,** *n.* —**incon′tinently,** *adv.*

incontinent[2] (ĭn kŏn′tĭ nənt), *adv. Archaic.* immediately; at once; straightway. Also, **incon′tinently.** [ME, t. F, t. LL: m. *in continenti* (*tempore*) in continuous (time), without pause]

incontrollable (ĭn′kən trō′lə bl), *adj.* not controllable; uncontrollable: *an incontrollable desire.*

incontrovertible (ĭn′kŏn trə vû′tə bl, ĭn kŏn′-), *adj.* not controvertible; indisputable. —**in′controvert′ibil′ity, in′controvert′ibleness,** *n.* —**in′controvert′ibly,** *adv.*

inconvenience (ĭn′kən vē′nyəns), *n., v.,* **-ienced, -iencing.** —*n.* **1.** the quality or state of being inconvenient. **2.** an inconvenient circumstance or thing; something that causes discomfort, trouble, etc. —*v.t.* **3.** to put to inconvenience; incommode.

inconveniency (ĭn′kən vē′nyən sĭ), *n., pl.* **-cies.** inconvenience.

inconvenient (ĭn′kən ve′nyənt), *adj.* arranged or happening in such a way as to be awkward, inopportune, disadvantageous, or troublesome: *an inconvenient time for a visit.* [ME, t. L: s. *inconveniens* not consonant] —**in′conven′iently,** *adv.* —**Syn.** untimely; annoying.

inconvertible (ĭn′kən vû′tə bl), *adj.* **1.** (of paper money) not capable of being converted into specie. **2.** not interchangeable. —**in′convert′ibil′ity, in′convert′ibleness,** *n.* —**in′convert′ibly,** *adv.*

inconvincible (ĭn′kən vĭn′sə bl), *adj.* not convincible; incapable of being convinced. —**in′convin′cibil′ity,** *n.* —**in′convin′cibly,** *adv.*

incoordinate (ĭn′kō ô′dĭ nĭt), *adj.* not coordinate; not coordinated.

incoordination (ĭn′kō ô′dĭ nā′shən), *n.* lack of coordination.

incor., **1.** Also, **incorp.** incorporated. **2.** incorrect.

incorporate[1] (*v.* ĭn kô′pə rāt′; *adj.* ĭn kô′pə rĭt, -prĭt), *v.,* **-rated, -rating,** *adj.* —*v.t.* **1.** to create or form a legal corporation. **2.** to form into a society or organization. **3.** to put or introduce into a body or mass as an integral part or parts. **4.** to take in or include as a part or parts, as the body or mass does. **5.** to form or combine into one body or uniform substance, as ingredients. **6.** to embody. —*v.i.* **7.** to unite or combine so as to form one body. **8.** to form a corporation. —*adj.* **9.** incorporated, as a company. **10.** combined into one body, mass, or substance. **11.** *Obs.* embodied. [ME, t. LL: m. s. *incorporātus*, pp., embodied. See IN-[2]] —**incorporative** (ĭn kô′pə rə tĭv), *adj.*

incorporate[2] (ĭn kô′pə rĭt, -prĭt), *adj.* not embodied; incorporeal. [t. LL: m. s. *incorporātus.* See IN-[3]]

incorporated (ĭn kô′pə rā′tĭd), *adj.* **1.** formed or constituted as a legal corporation. **2.** combined in one body; made part of.

incorporation (ĭn kô′pə rā′shən), *n.* **1.** the act of incorporating. **2.** the state of being incorporated.

incorporator (ĭn kô′pə rā′tə), *n.* **1.** *U.S.* one of the signers of the articles or certificate of incorporation. **2.** *U.S.* one of the persons to whom the charter is granted in a corporation created by special act of the legislature. **3.** one who incorporates.

incorporeal (ĭn′kô pô′rĭ əl), *adj.* **1.** not corporeal or material; spiritual. **2.** pertaining to non-material beings. **3.** *Law.* without material existence, but existing in contemplation of law, as a franchise. —**in′corpo′really,** *adv.*

incorporeity (ĭn kô′pə rē′ĭ tĭ, ĭn′kô-), *n., pl.* **-ties.** the quality of being incorporeal; disembodied existence or entity. Also, **in′corpo′real′ity.**

incorrect (ĭn′kə rĕkt′), *adj.* **1.** not correct as to fact: *an incorrect statement.* **2.** improper: *incorrect behaviour.* **3.** not correct in form or manner: *an incorrect copy.* —**in′correct′ly,** *adv.* —**in′correct′ness,** *n.* —**Syn.** **1.** erroneous, inaccurate, inexact; untrue, wrong. **2.** faulty, improper.

incorrigible (ĭn kŏ′rĭ jə bl), *adj.* **1.** not corrigible; bad beyond correction or reform: *an incorrigible liar.* **2.** impervious to punishment; wilful; uncontrollable: *an incorrigible child.* **3.** firmly fixed; not easily changed: *an incorrigible habit.* —*n.* **4.** one who is incorrigible. —**incor′rigibil′ity, incor′rigibleness,** *n.* —**incor′rigibly,** *adv.*

incorrupt (ĭn′kə rŭpt′), *adj.* **1.** not corrupt; not debased or perverted; morally upright. **2.** not to be bribed. **3.** *Obs.* free from decomposition or putrefaction. **4.** not vitiated by errors or alterations. Also, **in′corrupt′ed.** —**in′corrupt′ly,** *adv.* —**in′corrupt′ness,** *n.*

incorruptible (ĭn′kə rŭp′tə bl), *adj.* **1.** incapable of physical corruption; everlasting; eternal. **2.** that cannot be perverted or bribed: *incorruptible by money.* —**in′corrupt′ibil′ity, in′corrupt′ibleness,** *n.* —**in′corrupt′ibly,** *adv.*

incorruption (ĭn′kə rŭp′shən), *n. Archaic.* incorrupt condition.

incr., **1.** increased. **2.** increasing.

incrassate (*v.* ĭn krăs′āt; *adj.* ĭn krăs′ĭt, -āt), *v.,* **-sated, -sating,** *adj.* —*v.t.* **1.** *Obs.* to thicken. **2.** *Pharm.* to make (a liquid) thicker by addition of another substance or by evaporation. —*v.i.* **3.** *Obs.* to become thick or thicker. —*adj.* **4.** Also, **incras′sated.** *Bot., Entomol.* thickened or swollen. [t. LL: m. s. *incrassātus*, pp.] —**in′crassa′tion,** *n.*

increase (*v.* ĭn krēs′; *n.* ĭn′krēs), *v.,* **-creased, -creasing,** *n.* —*v.t.* **1.** to make greater in any respect; augment; add to. **2.** to make more numerous. —*v.i.* **3.** to become greater or more numerous: *sales increased.* **4.** to multiply by propagation. **5.** *Poetic.* to wax, as the moon. —*n.* **6.** growth or augmentation in numbers: *the increase of crime.* **7.** multiplication by propagation; production of offspring. **8.** offspring or progeny. **9.** the act or process of increasing. **10.** that by which something is increased. **11.** the result of increasing. **12.** produce of the earth. **13.** product; profit; interest. [ME *encrese(n)*, t. AF: m. *encres(s)-*, var. of OF *encreis(s)-*, s. *encreistre*, g. L *increscere*] —**increas′able,** *adj.* —**increas′er,** *n.* —**increas′ingly,** *adv.*

—**Syn.** **1.** INCREASE, AUGMENT, ENLARGE may all mean to make larger. To INCREASE means to make greater, as in quantity, extent, degree: *to increase someone's salary, to increase the velocity, increase the* (*degree of*) *concentration.* ENLARGE means to increase in size, extent, or range: *to enlarge a building, a business, one's conceptions.* AUGMENT, a more formal word, means to increase or enlarge especially by addition from the outside: *to augment one's income* (*by doing extra work*).

increate (ɪn′krĭ āt′, ĭn′krĭ āt′), *adj.* **1.** not created; uncreated. **2.** existing without having been created.

incredible (ĭn krĕd′ə bl), *adj.* **1.** seeming too extraordinary to be possible: *an incredible act of heroism.* **2.** not credible; that cannot be believed. —**incred′ibil′ity, incred′ibleness,** *n.* —**incred′ibly,** *adv.*

incredulity (ĭn′krĭ dyo͞o′lĭ tĭ), *n.* the quality of being incredulous; a refusal of belief.

incredulous (ĭn krĕd′yo͝o ləs), *adj.* **1.** not credulous; indisposed to believe; sceptical. **2.** indicating unbelief: *an incredulous smile.* —**incred′ulously,** *adv.* —**incred′ulousness,** *n.* —**Syn.** **1.** See **doubtful.**

increment (ĭn′krĭ mənt, ĭng′-), *n.* **1.** something added or gained; an addition or increase. **2.** profit. **3.** the act or process of increasing; growth. **4.** *Maths.* **a.** the difference between two values of a variable; an increase (positive, negative, or zero) in an independent variable. **b.** the increase of a function due to this. [ME, t. L: s. *incrēmentum* an increase] —**incremental** (ĭn′krĭ mĕn′tl), *adj.*

increscent (ĭn krĕs′ənt), *adj.* increasing or waxing, as the moon. [t. L: s. *increscens*, ppr.]

incretion (ĭn krē′shən), *n.* **1.** a substance, as an autacoid, secreted internally. **2.** the process of such secretion. [back-formation from *incretionary*, f. IN-[2] + *-cretionary*, modelled on CONCRETIONARY]

incriminate (ĭn krĭm′ĭ nāt′), *v.t.,* **-nated, -nating.** **1.** to charge with a crime or fault. **2.** to involve in an accusation. [t. ML: m. s. *incrīminātus*, pp. accused of a crime. See IN-[2], CRIMINATE] —**incrim′ina′tion,** *n.* —**incrim′ina′tor,** *n.* —**incriminatory** (ĭn krĭm′ĭ nə tə rĭ, -trĭ), *adj.*

incrust (ĭn krŭst′), *v.t.* encrust.

incrustation (ĭn′krŭs tā′shən), *n.* encrustation.

incubate (ĭn′kyŏŏ bāt′, ĭng′-), *v.*, **-bated, -bating.** —*v.t.* **1.** to sit upon (eggs) for the purpose of hatching. **2.** to hatch (eggs), as by sitting upon them or by artificial heat. **3.** to maintain (bacterial cultures, etc.) at the most favourable temperature for development. **4.** to keep at even temperature, as prematurely born infants. **5.** to produce as if by hatching; formulate; develop; give shape to. —*v.i.* **6.** to sit upon eggs. **7.** to undergo incubation. **8.** to grow; take shape. [t. L: m. s. *incubātus*, pp., hatched, sat on] —**in′cuba′tive, in′cuba′tory,** *adj.*

incubation (ĭn′kyŏŏ bā′shən, ĭng′-), *n.* **1.** the act or process of incubating. **2.** the condition or quality of being incubated. —**in′cuba′tional,** *adj.*

incubation period, *Pathol.* the period between infection and the appearance of signs of a disease.

incubator (ĭn′kyŏŏ bā′tə, ĭng′-), *n.* **1.** an apparatus for hatching eggs artificially, consisting essentially of a case heated by a lamp or the like. **2.** a boxlike apparatus in which prematurely born infants are kept at a constant and suitable temperature. **3.** a device in which bacterial cultures, etc., are developed at a constant suitable temperature. **4.** one who or that which incubates. [t. L]

incubus (ĭn′kyŏŏ bəs, ĭng′-), *n.*, *pl.* **-bi** (-bī′), **-buses.** **1.** an imaginary demon or evil spirit supposed to descend upon sleeping persons, esp. one reputed to have sexual intercourse with sleeping women. **2.** something that weighs upon or oppresses one like a nightmare. **3.** a nightmare. [ME, t. LL: nightmare, ML a demon, der. L *incubāre* lie on]

incudes (ĭn kyōō′dēz), *n.* pl. of **incus.**

inculcate (ĭn′kŭl kāt′), *v.t.*, **-cated, -cating.** to impress by repeated statement or admonition; teach persistently and earnestly; instil (usually fol. by *upon* or *in*). [t. L: m. s. *inculcātus*, pp., stamped in, impressed upon] —**in′culca′tion,** *n.* —**in′culca′tor,** *n.*

inculpable (ĭn kŭl′pə bl), *adj.* not culpable; blameless. —**incul′pably,** *adv.*

inculpate (ĭn′kŭl pāt′), *v.t.*, **-pated, -pating.** **1.** to charge with fault; blame; accuse. **2.** to involve in a charge; incriminate. [t. ML: m. s. *inculpātus*, pp. of *inculpāre*, f. *in-* IN-[2] + *culpāre* blame] —**in′culpa′tion,** *n.*

inculpatory (ĭn kŭl′pə tə rĭ, -trĭ), *adj.* tending to inculpate; imputing blame; incriminating.

incult (ĭn kŭlt′), *adj. Archaic.* **1.** uncultivated; untilled. **2.** wild; rude; unrefined. [t. L: s. *incultus*]

incumbency (ĭn kŭm′bən sĭ), *n.*, *pl.* **-cies.** **1.** that which is incumbent. **2.** an incumbent weight or mass. **3.** the position or office of the holder of an ecclesiastical benefice. **4.** *Rare.* the state of being incumbent. **5.** *Rare.* a duty or obligation.

incumbent (ĭn kŭm′bənt), *adj.* **1.** resting on one; obligatory: *a duty incumbent upon me.* **2.** lying, leaning, or pressing on something: *incumbent posture.* —*n.* **3.** the holder of an office. **4.** one who holds an ecclesiastical benefice. [ME, t. L: s. *incumbens*, ppr., leaning upon] —**incum′bently,** *adv.*

incumber (ĭn kŭm′bə), *v.t.* encumber.

incumbrance (ĭn kŭm′brəns), *n.* encumbrance.

incunabula (ĭn′kyŏŏ năb′yŏŏ lə), *n.pl.*, *sing.* **-lum** (-ləm). **1.** books produced in the infancy of printing (before 1500) from movable type. **2.** the earliest stages or first traces of anything. [t. L: cradle, beginning, swaddling clothes] —**in′cunab′ular,** *adj.*

incur (ĭn kû′), *v.t.*, **-curred, -curring.** **1.** to run or fall into (some consequence, usually undesirable or injurious). **2.** to become liable or subject to through one's own action; bring upon oneself: *to incur his displeasure.* [ME, t. L: m. s. *incurrere* run into, or against] —**incur′rable,** *adj.*

incurable (ĭn kyŏŏə′rə bl), *adj.* **1.** not curable. —*n.* **2.** one suffering from an incurable disease. —**incur′abil′ity, incur′ableness,** *n.* —**incur′ably,** *adv.*

incurious (ĭn kyŏŏə′rĭ əs), *adj.* **1.** not curious; inattentive or unobservant. **2.** indifferent. **3.** deficient in interest or novelty. —**incuriosity** (ĭn′kyŏŏə rĭ ŏs′ĭ tĭ), **incu′riousness,** *n.* —**incu′riously,** *adv.*

incurrence (ĭn kŭ′rəns), *n.* the act of incurring, bringing on, or subjecting oneself to something.

incurrent (ĭn kŭ′rənt), *adj.* carrying, or relating to, an inward current. [t. L: s. *incurrens*, ppr., running into]

incursion (ĭn kû′shən), *n.* **1.** a hostile entrance into or invasion of a place or territory, esp. one of sudden character; raid; attack. **2.** a harmful inroad. **3.** a running in: *the incursion of sea-water.* [ME, t. L: s. *incursio* onset]

incursive (ĭn kû′sĭv), *adj.* making incursions.

incurvate (*adj.* ĭn kû′vĭt, -vāt; *v.* ĭn′kû vāt′), *adj.*, *v.*, **-vated, -vating.** —*adj.* **1.** curved, esp. inwards. —*v.t.* **2.** to make curved; turn from a straight line or course; curve, esp. inwards. [t. L: m. s. *incurvātus*, pp., bent in] —**in′curva′tion, incur′vature,** *n.*

incurve (*v.* ĭn kûv′; *n.* ĭn′kûv′), *v.*, *n.*, **-curved, -curving,** —*v.t.* **1.** to curve inwards. —*n.* **2.** *Baseball.* an inward-curving ball, i.e. towards the batter. [t. L: m. s. *incurvāre* bend in]

incus (ĭng′kəs), *n.*, *pl.* **incudes** (ĭn kyōō′dēz). *Anat.* the middle one of a chain of three small bones in the middle ear of man and other mammals. See **malleus** and **stapes.** See diag. under **ear.** [t. L: anvil]

incuse (ĭn kyōōz′), *adj.*, *n.*, *v.*, **-cused, -cusing.** —*adj.* **1.** hammered or stamped in, as a figure on a coin. —*n.* **2.** an incuse figure or impression. —*v.t.* **3.** to hammer or stamp, as a figure on a coin. [t. L: m. s. *incūsus*, pp., forged with a hammer]

Ind (ĭnd), *n.* **1.** *Now Poetic.* India. **2.** *Obs.* the Indies.

ind-, var. of **indo-** before vowels, as in *indene.*

Ind., **1.** India. **2.** Indian. **3.** Indiana. **4.** Indies.

ind., **1.** independent. **2.** index. **3.** indicative.

indaba (ĭn dä′bə), *n. S African.* **1.** a meeting with or between natives, esp. native councillors; a conference or consultation. **2.** *Colloq.* concern; affair. [t. Zulu: affair, business, topic]

indamine (ĭn′də mēn′), *n. Chem.* any of a certain series of basic organic compounds which form bluish and greenish salts: used in the manufacture of dyes. [f. IND(IGO) + AMINE]

Indanthrene (ĭn dăn′thrēn), *n. Chem. Trademark.* a blue, insoluble, anthraquinone dyestuff, $C_{28}H_{14}O_4N_2$.

indebt (ĭn dĕt′), *v.t.* to place under obligation for benefits, favours, assistance, etc., received [first used in pp., ME *endetted*, after OF *endetter*, der. *en-* EN-[1] + *dette* DEBT]

indebted (ĭn dĕt′ĭd), *adj.* **1.** owing money. **2.** being under an obligation for benefits, favours, assistance etc., received.

indebtedness (ĭn dĕt′ĭd nĭs), *n.* **1.** the state of being indebted. **2.** an amount owed. **3.** debts collectively.

indecency (ĭn dē′sən sĭ), *n.*, *pl.* **-cies.** **1.** the quality of being indecent. **2.** impropriety; indelicacy or immodesty. **3.** obscenity. **4.** an indecent act, remark, etc.

indecent (ĭn dē′sənt), *adj.* **1.** offending against recognized standards of propriety or good taste; vulgar: *indecent language.* **2.** not decent; unbecoming or unseemly: *indecent conduct.* —**inde′cently,** *adv.* —**Syn. 2.** See **improper.**

indecent assault, *Law.* an assault in which an individual is subjected to some form of sexual activity, esp. against his or her will.

indeciduate (ĭn′dĭ sĭd′yŏŏ ĭt, -āt′) *adj.* **1.** *Zool.* not deciduate. **2.** *Bot.* having permanent leaves.

indeciduous (ĭn′dĭ sĭd′yŏŏ əs), *adj. Bot.* **1.** not deciduous, as leaves. **2.** (of trees) evergreen.

indecipherable (ĭn′dĭ sī′fə rə bl, -frə bl), *adj.* not decipherable. —**in′deci′pherabil′ity,** *n.*

indecision (ĭn′dĭ sĭzh′ən), *n.* inability to decide.

indecisive (ĭn′dĭ sī′sĭv), *adj.* **1.** not decisive or conclusive: *a severe but indecisive battle.* **2.** characterized by indecision, as persons; irresolute; undecided. —**in′deci′sively,** *adv.* —**in′deci′siveness,** *n.*

indecl., indeclinable.

indeclinable (ĭn′dĭ klī′nə bl), *adj. Gram.* not declined, especially of a word belonging to a form class most of whose members are declined, as the Latin adjective *decem* (ten). —**in′declin′ably,** *adv.*

indecomposable (ĭn′dē kəm pō′zə bl), *adj.* not decomposable.

indecorous (ĭn dĕk′ə rəs), *adj.* not decorous; violating propriety; unseemly. [t. L: m. *indecōrus*] —**indec′orously,** *adv.* —**indec′orousness,** *n.*

indecorum (ĭn′dĭ kô′rəm), *n.* **1.** indecorous behaviour or character. **2.** something indecorous. [t. L, prop. neut. of *indecōrus* indecorous]

indeed (ĭn dēd′), *adv.* **1.** in fact; in reality; in truth; truly (used for emphasis, to confirm and amplify a previous statement, to intensify, to indicate a concession or admission, or, interrogatively, to obtain confirmation). —*interj.* **2.** (an expression of surprise, incredulity, irony, etc.) [ME *in dede.* See IN, prep., DEED, n.]

indef., indefinite.

indefatigable (ĭn′dĭ făt′ĭ gə bl), *adj.* incapable of being tired out; not yielding to fatigue. [t. L: m. s. *indēfatīgābilis*] —**in′defat′igabil′ity, in′defat′igableness,** *n.* —**in′defat′igably,** *adv.*

indefeasible (ĭn′dĭ fē′zə bl), *adj.* not defeasible; not to be annulled or made void; not forfeitable. —**in′defea′sibil′ity,** *n.* —**in′defea′sibly,** *adv.*

indefectible (ĭn′dĭ fĕk′tə bl), *adj.* **1.** not defectible; not liable to defect or failure; unfailing. **2.** not liable to fault or imperfection; faultless. —**in′defect′ibil′ity,** *n.* —**in′defect′ibly,** *adv.*

indefective (ĭn′dĭ fĕk′tĭv), *adj. Obs.* not defective.

indefensible (ĭn′dĭ fĕn′sə bl), *adj.* **1.** that cannot be justified; inexcusable: *an indefensible remark.* **2.** that cannot be defended by force of arms: *an indefensible frontier.* —**in′defen′sibil′ity, in′defen′sibleness,** *n.* —**in′defen′sibly,** *adv.*

indefinable (ĭn′dĭ fī′nə bl), *adj.* not definable; indescribable. —**in′defin′ableness,** *n.* —**in′defin′ably,** *adv.*

indefinite (ĭn dĕf′ĭ nĭt), *adj.* **1.** not definite; without fixed or specified limit; unlimited: *an indefinite number.* **2.** not clearly defined or determined; not precise. **3.** *Gram.* not specifying precisely, as the indefinite pronoun *some.* **4.** *Bot.* **a.** very numerous or not easily counted, as stamens. **b.** (of an inflorescence) indeterminate. [t. L: m. s. *indēfīnītus*] —**indef′initely,** *adv.* —**indef′initeness,** *n.* —**Syn. 2.** vague, obscure.

indefinite article, *Gram.* the article (as *a, an*) which classes as 'single and unidentified' the noun it modifies.

indehiscent (ĭn′dĭ hĭs′ənt), *adj. Bot.* not dehiscent; not opening at maturity. —**in′dehis′cence,** *n.*

indelible (ĭn dĕl′ĭ bl), *adj.* **1.** incapable of being deleted or obliterated: *an indelible impression.* **2.** making indelible marks: *an indelible pencil.* [t. L: m. s. *indēlēbilis* that cannot be destroyed] —**indel′ibil′ity, indel′ibleness,** *n.* —**indel′ibly,** *adv.*

indelicacy (ĭn dĕl′ĭ kə sĭ), *n., pl.* **-cies. 1.** the quality of being indelicate. **2.** something indelicate.

indelicate (ĭn dĕl′ĭ kĭt), *adj.* **1.** not delicate; lacking delicacy. **2.** offensive to a sense of propriety, or modesty; unrefined. —**indel′icately,** *adv.*

indemnification (ĭn dĕm′nĭ fĭ kā′shən), *n.* **1.** the act of indemnifying. **2.** the state of being indemnified. **3.** that which serves to indemnify; compensation.

indemnify (ĭn dĕm′nĭ fī′), *v.t.,* **-fied, -fying. 1.** to compensate for damage or loss sustained, expense incurred, etc. **2.** to engage to make good or secure against anticipated loss; give security against (future damage or liability). —**indem′nifi′er,** *n.*

indemnitee (ĭn dĕm′nĭ tē′), *n. U.S.* one who receives indemnity.

indemnitor (ĭn dĕm′nĭ tə), *n. U.S.* one who gives indemnity.

indemnity (ĭn dĕm′nĭ tĭ), *n., pl.* **-ties. 1.** protection or security against damage or loss. **2.** compensation for damage or loss sustained. **3.** something paid by way of such compensation. **4.** legal protection, as by insurance from liabilities or penalties incurred by one's actions. **5.** legal exemption from penalties attaching to unconstitutional or illegal actions, granted to public officers and other persons. [late ME, t. LL: m. s. *indemnitas,* der. L *indemnis* unharmed]

indemonstrable (ĭn′dĭ mŏn′strə bl, ĭn dĕm′ən-), *adj.* not demonstrable; incapable of being demonstrated or proved. —**in′demon′strabil′ity,** *n.* —**in′demon′strably,** *adv.*

indene (ĭn′dēn), *n. Chem.* a colourless liquid hydrocarbon, C_9H_8, obtained from coal tar by fractional distillation. [f. IND- + -ENE]

indent[1] (*v.* ĭn dĕnt′; *n.* ĭn′dĕnt′), *v.t.* **1.** to form deep recesses in: *the sea indents the coast.* **2.** to set in or back from the margin, as the first line of a paragraph. **3.** to sever (a document drawn up in duplicate) along an irregular line as a means of identification. **4.** to cut or tear the edge of (copies of a document) in an irregular way. **5.** to make toothlike notches in; notch. **6.** to indenture, as an apprentice. **7.** to draw an order upon. **8.** to order, as commodities. —*v.i.* **9.** to form a recess. **10.** to enter into an agreement by indenture; make a compact. **11.** to make out an order or requisition in duplicate. **12.** *Mil.* to make a requisition. **13.** *Obs.* to draw upon a person or thing for something. —*n.* **14.** a toothlike notch or deep recess; an indentation. **15.** an indention. **16.** an official requisition for stores. **17.** an order for goods. **18.** an indenture. **19.** a certificate issued by the U.S. government at the close of the War of Independence for the principal or interest due on the public debt. [ME *endente(n),* t. OF: m. *endenter,* der. *en-* EN-[1] + *dent* tooth] —**indent′er,** *n.*

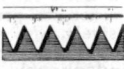

Indented moulding

indent[2] (*v.* ĭn dĕnt′; *n.* ĭn′dĕnt′), *v.t.* **1.** to dent or press in so as to form a dent. **2.** to make a dent in. —*n.* **3.** a dent. [ME, f. IN-[2] + DENT[1]]

indentation (ĭn′dĕn tā′shən), *n.* **1.** a cut, notch, or deep recess: *various bays and indentations.* **2.** a series of incisions or notches. **3.** a notching or being notched. **4.** an indention. [f. INDENT[1] + -ATION]

indention (ĭn dĕn′shən), *n.* **1.** an indenting. **2.** an indentation. **3.** an indenting of a line or lines, and leaving of blank space. **4.** the blank space so left.

indenture (ĭn dĕn′chə), *n., v.,* **-tured, -turing.** —*n.* **1.** a deed or agreement executed in two or more copies with edges correspondingly indented as a means of identification. **2.** any deed, contract, or sealed agreement between two or more parties. **3.** a contract by which a person, as an apprentice, is bound to service. **4.** any official or formal list, certificate, etc., authenticated for use as a voucher or the like. **5.** the formal agreement between a group of bondholders and the debtor as to the terms of the debt. **6.** indentation. —*v.t.* **7.** to bind by indenture, as an apprentice. **8.** *Obs.* to indent; wrinkle; furrow. [ME *endenture,* t. OF: m. *endenteure* indentation]

independence (ĭn′dĭ pĕn′dəns), *n.* **1.** the state or quality of being independent. **2.** freedom from subjection, or from the influence of others. **3.** exemption from external control or support. **4.** a competency. —**Syn. 1.** See **freedom.**

Independence (ĭn′dĭ pĕn′dəns), *n.* a city in W Missouri: starting point of the Santa Fe and Oregon trails. 62,328 (1960).

Independence Day, *U.S.* July 4th, a holiday commemorating the adoption of the Declaration of Independence on July 4th, 1776.

independency (ĭn′dĭ pĕn′dən sĭ), *n., pl.* **-cies. 1.** independence. **2.** a territory not under the control of any other power. **3.** (*cap.*) *Eccles.* **a.** the principle that the individual congregation or church is an autonomous and equalitarian society free from any external ecclesiastical control. **b.** the polity based on this principle.

independent (ĭn′dĭ pĕn′dənt), *adj.* **1.** not influenced by others in matters of opinion, conduct, etc.; thinking or acting for oneself: *an independent person.* **2.** not subject to another's authority or jurisdiction; autonomous; free. **3.** not influenced by the thought or action of others: *independent research.* **4.** not dependent; not depending or contingent on something else for existence, operation, etc. **5.** not relying on another or others for aid or support. **6.** declining others' aid or support; refusing to be under obligation to others. **7.** possessing a competency. **8.** sufficient to support a person so that he does not have to look for a living. **9.** expressive of a spirit of independence; self-confident; unconstrained. **10.** free from party commitments in voting. **11.** *Maths.* (of a quantity or function) not depending upon another for value. **12.** (*cap.*) *Eccles.* of or pertaining to the Independents. —*n.* **13.** an independent person or thing. **14.** *Pol.* one who votes without blind loyalty to any organized party. **15.** (*cap.*) *Eccles.* an adherent of an Independency. **16.** a Congregationalist. —**in′depend′ently,** *adv.*

independent front suspension, *Motor Vehicles.* a method of suspending the front wheels of a motor vehicle to the chassis by individual spindle and coil-spring mountings for each wheel.

independent means, private means.

independent school, any school providing full-time education for children of school age, without support from the government or local authorities and including most public schools.

Independent Television Authority, a public corporation created in 1954, providing an alternative television service to that of the B.B.C. The Authority owns and operates transmitting stations and exercises wide powers over the choice of programmes, which are provided under contract by commercial companies, which also arrange for the inclusion of advertising matter. *Abbrev.:* I.T.A.

indescribable (ĭn′dĭ skrī′bə bl), *adj.* not describable. —**in′describ′abil′ity,** *n.* —**in′describ′ably,** *adv.*

indestructible (ĭn′dĭ strŭk′tə bl), *adj.* not destructible. —**in′destruct′ibil′ity, in′destruct′ibleness,** *n.* —**in′destruct′ibly,** *adv.*

indeterminable (ĭn′dĭ tû′mĭ nə bl), *adj.* **1.** not determinable; incapable of being ascertained. **2.** incapable of being decided or settled. —**in′deter′minably,** *adv.*

indeterminacy principle, *Physics.* uncertainty principle.

indeterminate (ĭn′dĭ tû′mĭ nĭt), *adj.* **1.** not determinate; not fixed in extent; indefinite; uncertain. **2.** not clear; vague: *a cloudy and indeterminate meaning.* **3.** not established. **4.** not settled or decided. **5.** *Maths.* (of a quantity) having no fixed value. **6.** *Bot.* (of an inflorescence) having the axis or axes not ending in a flower or bud, thus allowing further elongation. **7.** *Engineering.* (of a framework, etc.) such that its forces cannot be determined by simple vector analysis. —**in′deter′minately,** *adv.* —**in′deter′minacy, in′deter′minateness,** *n.*

indeterminate sentence, *Law.* a penalty imposed by a court which has relatively wide limits or no limits, as imprisonment for one to ten years.

indetermination (ĭn′dĭ tû′mĭ nā′shən), *n.* **1.** the condition or quality of being indeterminate. **2.** an unsettled state, as of the mind.

indeterminism (ĭn′dĭ tû′mĭ nĭz′əm), *n. Philos.* **1.** the doctrine that human actions, though somewhat influenced by pre-existing psychological and other conditions, are not entirely governed by them, but contain a certain freedom and spontaneity. **2.** the theory that the will is to some extent independent of the strength of motives, or may itself modify their strength in choice. —**in/-deter/minist,** *n., adj.*

index (ĭn/dĕks), *n., pl.* **-dexes, -dices** (-dĭ sēz/), *v.* —*n.* **1.** a detailed alphabetical key to names, places, and topics in a book with reference to their page number, etc. in the book. **2.** something used or serving to point out; a sign, token, or indication: *a true index of his character.* **3.** something that serves to direct attention to some fact, condition, etc.; a guiding principle. **4.** a pointer or indicator in a scientific instrument. **5.** a piece of wood, metal, or the like, serving as a pointer or indicator. **6.** *Print., etc.* a sign (☛) used to point out a particular note, paragraph, etc. **7.** the index finger; the forefinger. **8.** *Science.* a number or formula expressing some property, ratio, etc., of a thing indicated. **9.** *Alg.* **a.** an exponent. **b.** the integer n in a radical $\sqrt[n]{\ }$ defining the n-th root: $\sqrt[3]{7}$ *is a radical having index three.* **10.** (*cap.*) a list of books which Roman Catholics are forbidden by Church authority to read without special permission, or which are not to be read unless expurgated or corrected (L *Index Librorum Prohibitorum,* **Index of Prohibited Books**), or a list of books of the latter class only, with specification of objectionable passages (L *Index Expurgatorius,* **Expurgatory Index**). **11.** *Obs.* a table of contents. **12.** *Obs.* a preface. —*v.t.* **13.** to provide with an index, as a book. **14.** to enter in an index, as a word. **15.** to serve to indicate. [ME, t. L: index, forefinger, sign] —**in/dexer,** *n.* —**indexical** (ĭn dĕk/sĭ kl), *adj.* —**in/dexless,** *adj.*

index finger, the forefinger.

index number, *Statistics.* a series of numbers which shows relative changes in prices, immigration, etc.

index of retail prices, official name of the **cost-of-living index.**

India (ĭn/dyə), *n.* a country in S Asia, a member of the Commonwealth of Nations, comprising most of former British India and the majority of the former British-protected Indian states ruled by native princes. India became a dominion in 1947 and an independent republic in 1950. 439,235,082 pop. (1961); 1,246,880 sq. mi. *Cap.:* New Delhi. [OE, t. L, t. Gk, der. *Indós* river Indus (t. Pers.: m. *Hind,* c. Skt *Sindhu* river Indus, orig. river)]

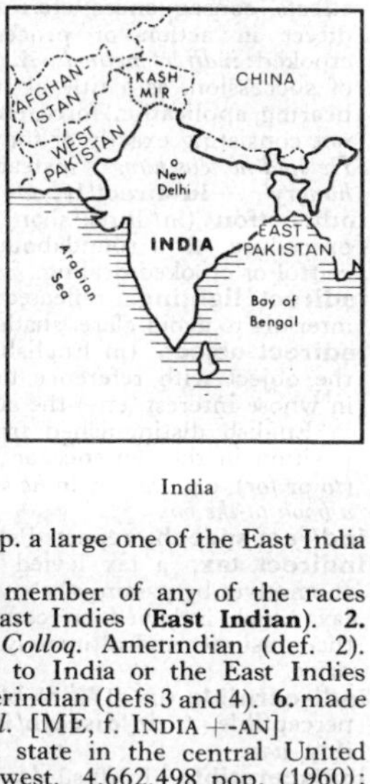

India

Indiaman (ĭn/dyə mən), *n., pl.* **-men.** (formerly) a ship in the India trade, esp. a large one of the East India Company.

Indian (ĭn/dyən), *n.* **1.** a member of any of the races native to India or the East Indies (**East Indian**). **2.** Amerindian (def. 1). **3.** *Colloq.* Amerindian (def. 2). —*adj.* **4.** of or pertaining to India or the East Indies (often **East Indian**). **5.** Amerindian (defs 3 and 4). **6.** made of Indian corn: *Indian meal.* [ME, f. INDIA + -AN]

Indiana (ĭn/dĭ ăn/ə), *n.* a state in the central United States: a part of the Midwest. 4,662,498 pop. (1960); 36,291 sq. mi. *Cap.:* Indianapolis. *Abbrev.:* Ind. —**Indianian** (ĭn/dĭ ăn/ĭ ən), *adj. n.*

Indian agency, headquarters of an Indian agent.

Indian agent, an official representing the United States in dealing with a Red Indian tribe or tribes.

Indianapolis (ĭn/dĭ ə năp/ə lĭs), *n.* a city in the U.S., the capital of Indiana, in the central part. 476,258 (1960).

Indian club, a bottle-shaped wooden club, one of a pair swung by the hands in gymnastics.

Indian corn, maize.

Indian Desert, Thar.

Indian Empire, British India, and the Indian states ruled by native princes but under indirect British control: in 1947 divided between India and Pakistan.

Indian file, single file, as of persons walking.

Indian hemp, **1.** a plant, genus *Apocynum,* native to America, whose root has laxative and emetic properties. **2.** an East Indian variety of hemp, *Cannabis sativa* or *indica.* Cf. **cannabis.**

Indian ink, **1.** a black pigment consisting of lampblack mixed with glue. **2.** a liquid ink from this. Also, *U.S.,* **India ink.**

indianite (ĭn/dĭ ə nīt/), *n.* anorthite.

Indian liquorice, a fabaceous woody shrub, *Abrus precatorius,* of India, etc., whose seeds are used for beads, and whose root is employed as a substitute for liquorice.

Indian meal, cornmeal (def. 2).

Indian millet, durra.

Indian Mutiny, a revolt of native Indian regiments in British India, 1857–59, resulting in the transfer of the administration of India from the East India Company to the Crown.

Indian Ocean, an ocean S of Asia, E of Africa, and W of Australia, ab. 28,350,000 sq. mi.

Indian pipe, a leafless saprophytic plant, *Monotropa uniflora,* of North America and Asia, having a solitary flower, and resembling a tobacco pipe.

Indian red, **1.** earth of a yellowish-red colour, found esp. in the Persian Gulf, which serves as a pigment and as a polish for gold and silver objects. **2.** a pigment of that colour prepared by oxidizing the salts of iron.

Indian rice, a gramineous plant of marshes of the central and south-eastern U.S., *Zizania aquatica.*

Indian summer, **1.** a period of mild, dry, calm weather, usually accompanied by a hazy atmosphere, occurring in late summer or autumn. **2.** a peaceful and quiet old age.

Indian Territory, a former territory of the United States: now in E Oklahoma. ab. 31,000 sq. mi.

Indian tobacco, a common American herb, *Lobelia inflata,* with small blue flowers and inflated capsules.

India paper, **1.** a thin, soft, absorbent paper made in the Orient, used for impressions of engravings. **2.** a thin, tough, opaque paper used in printing Bibles, prayer-books, large reference works, etc.

India print, a cotton fabric block-printed in India.

indiarubber (ĭn/dyə rŭb/ə), *n.* **1.** a highly elastic substance obtained from the milky juice of numerous tropical plants, used for rubbing out pencil marks, and variously in the arts and manufactures; caoutchouc; gum elastic; rubber. **2.** *U.S. Obs.* a rubber overshoe. —*adj.* **3.** of, made of, or pertaining to indiarubber. Also, **india rubber.**

Indic (ĭn/dĭk), *adj.* **1.** of or pertaining to India; Indian. **2.** of or pertaining to a subgroup of the Indo-Iranian languages including Sanskrit and many modern languages of India, Pakistan, and Ceylon. [t. L: s. *Indicus,* t. Gk: m. *Indikós*]

indic., **1.** indicating. **2.** Also, **ind.** indicative.

indican (ĭn/dĭ kən), *n.* **1.** *Chem.* a glucoside, $C_{14}H_{17}NO_6$, which occurs in plants yielding indigo, and from which indigo is obtained. **2.** *Biochem.* a component of urine, indoxyl potassium sulphate, $C_8H_6NO_4SK$. [f. s. L *indicum* indigo + -AN]

indicant (ĭn/dĭ kənt), *adj.* **1.** indicating; indicative. —*n.* **2.** that which indicates.

indicate (ĭn/dĭ kāt/), *v.t.,* **-cated, -cating.** **1.** to be a sign of; betoken; imply: *his hesitation indicates unwillingness.* **2.** to point out or point to; direct attention to: *to indicate a place on a map.* **3.** to show, or make known: *the thermometer indicates temperature.* **4.** to state or express, esp. briefly or in a general way: *to indicate one's intentions.* **5.** *Med.* **a.** (of symptoms, etc.) to point out (a particular remedy, treatment, etc.) as suitable or necessary. **b.** to show the presence of (a disease, etc.). [t. L: m. s. *indicātus,* pp.]

indicated airspeed, *Aeron.* the reading of an airspeed indicator which, at high altitudes, will be lower than the true airspeed owing to the lower air density.

indicated horsepower, the horsepower developed by a reciprocating engine as calculated from the indicator diagram: it exceeds the brake horsepower by the power lost in the engine by friction, pumping etc.

indication (ĭn/dĭ kā/shən), *n.* **1.** anything serving to indicate or point out, as a sign, token, etc. **2.** *Med.* a special symptom or the like which points out a suitable remedy or treatment or shows the presence of a disease. **3.** the act of indicating. **4.** the degree marked by an instrument.

indicative (ĭn dĭk/ə tĭv), *adj.* **1.** that indicates; pointing out; suggestive (fol. by *of*). **2.** *Gram.* designating or pertaining to the mood of the verb used in ordinary statements, questions, etc., in contrast to hypothetical statements or those made without reference to a specific actor or time of action. For example: in the sentence *John plays football,* the verb *plays* is in the indicative mood. —*n.* **3.** *Gram.* **a.** the indicative mood. **b.** a verb in the indicative. [late ME, t. L: m. s. *indicātīvus*] —**indic/-atively,** *adv.*

indicator (ĭn/dĭ kā/tə), *n.* **1.** one who or that which indicates. **2.** a pointing or directing device, as a pointer on an instrument or a flashing light on a motor car. **3.** an instrument which indicates the condition of a machine, etc. **4.** a pressure gauge; an apparatus for recording the variations of pressure or vacuum in the cylinder of an engine. **5.** *Chem.* a substance used (esp. in volumetric analysis) to indicate (as by a change in colour) the condition of a solution, the point at which a certain reaction ends and another begins, etc.

indicator diagram, a graphical representation of the pressure and volume changes of the working fluid within the cylinder of a reciprocating engine or pump as obtained with an indicator.

indicatory (ĭn dĭk′ə tə rĭ, -trĭ), *adj.* serving to indicate.

indices (ĭn′dĭ sēz′), *n.* pl. of **index.**

indicia (ĭn dĭsh′yə), *n. pl., sing.* **-dicium** (-dĭsh′yəm). signs; markings; indications. [t. L, pl. of *indicium* sign, mark] —**indicial** (ĭn dĭsh′yəl), *adj.*

indict (ĭn dīt′), *v.t.* **1.** to charge with an offence or crime; accuse. **2.** *U.S.* (of a grand jury) to bring a formal accusation against, as a means of bringing to trial. [ME *endite(n)*, t. AF: m. *enditer* accuse, indict. Cf. OF *enditer* INDITE] —**indict′er,** *n.*

indictable (ĭn dī′tə bl), *adj.* **1.** liable to be indicted, as a person. **2.** making one liable to be indicted, as an offence.

indiction (ĭn dĭk′shən), *n.* **1.** a proclamation made every 15 years in the later Roman Empire, fixing the valuation of property to be used as a basis for taxation. **2.** a tax based on such valuation. **3.** the recurring fiscal period of 15 years in the Roman Empire, long used for dating ordinary events. **4.** a specified year in this period. **5.** the number indicating it. **6.** *Rare.* authoritative proclamation. [ME, t. L: s. *indictio*]

indictment (ĭn dīt′mənt), *n.* **1.** the act of indicting. **2.** *Law.* a formal written accusation (formerly presented by a grand jury) for the purpose of trial by jury. **3.** an accusation. **4.** the state of being indicted.

Indies (ĭn′dĭz), *n.pl.* **1.** the West Indies. **2.** a region in and near S and SE Asia: India, Indochina, and the East Indies. **3.** the East Indies.

indifference (ĭn dĭf′rəns), *n.* **1.** lack of interest or concern. **2.** unimportance. **3.** the quality or fact of being indifferent. **4.** mediocre quality.

—**Syn. 1.** INDIFFERENCE, UNCONCERN, LISTLESSNESS, APATHY, INSENSIBILITY all imply lack of feeling. INDIFFERENCE denotes an absence of feeling or interest; UNCONCERN, an absence of concern or solicitude, a calm or cool indifference in the face of what might be expected to cause uneasiness or apprehension; LISTLESSNESS, an absence of inclination or interest, a languid indifference to what is going on about one; APATHY, profound indifference suggestive of mental faculties either naturally sluggish or dulled by sickness or grief. INSENSIBILITY denotes an absence of capacity for feeling, or of susceptibility to emotional influence. —**Ant. 1.** eagerness, responsiveness.

indifferent (ĭn dĭf′rənt), *adj.* **1.** without interest or concern; not caring: apathetic. **2.** having neither favourable nor unfavourable feelings towards some thing or person; impartial. **3.** neutral in character or quality; neither good nor bad: *an indifferent specimen.* **4.** falling short of any standard of excellence; not very good: *an indifferent play*; *indifferent health.* **5.** of only moderate amount, extent, etc. **6.** not making a difference, or mattering, either way, as to a person. **7.** immaterial or unimportant. **8.** not essential or obligatory, as an observance. **9.** making no difference or distinction, as between persons or things: *indifferent justice.* **10.** neutral in chemical, electrical, or magnetic quality. **11.** *Biol.* not differentiated or specialized, as cells or tissues. [ME, t. L: s. *indifferens* (def. 3)] —**indif′ferently,** *adv.*

indifferentism (ĭn dĭf′rən tĭz′əm), *n.* **1.** systematic indifference. **2.** adiaphorism. **3.** the principle that differences of religious belief are essentially unimportant. —**indif′ferentist,** *n.*

indigence (ĭn′dĭ jəns), *n.* indigent state; poverty.

indigene (ĭn′dĭ jēn′), *n.* one who or that which is indigenous or native; a native; an autochthon. [t. F, t. L: m. *indigena*]

indigenous (ĭn dĭj′ĭ nəs), *adj.* **1.** originating in and characterizing a particular region or country; native (usually fol. by *to*): *the plants indigenous to Canada.* **2.** innate; inherent; natural (usually fol. by *to*). [t. LL: m. *indigenus*, der. L *indigena* native] —**indig′enously,** *adv.* —**indig′enousness,** *n.*

indigent (ĭn′dĭ jənt), *adj.* lacking the necessities of life; needy; poor. [ME, t. L: s. *indigens*, ppr.] —**in′digently,** *adv.*

indigested (ĭn′dĭ jĕs′tĭd), *adj.* **1.** without arrangement or order. **2.** unformed or shapeless. **3.** not digested; undigested. **4.** not duly considered.

indigestible (ĭn′dĭ jĕs′tə bl), *adj.* not digestible; not easily digested. —**in′digest′ibil′ity, in′digest′ibleness,** *n.* —**in′digest′ibly,** *adv.*

indigestion (ĭn′dĭ jĕs′chən), *n.* incapability of, or difficulty in, digesting food; dyspepsia.

indigestive (ĭn′dĭ jĕs′tĭv), *adj.* attended with or suffering from indigestion; dyspeptic.

indign (ĭn dīn′), *adj.* **1.** *Archaic.* unworthy. **2.** *Archaic.* unbecoming or disgraceful. **3.** *Now Poetic.* undeserved. [ME *indigne*, t. F, t. L: m. s. *indignus*]

indignant (ĭn dĭg′nənt), *adj.* affected with or characterized by indignation. [t. L: s. *indignans*, ppr., deeming unworthy] —**indig′nantly,** *adv.*

indignation (ĭn′dĭg nā′shən), *n.* strong displeasure at something deemed unworthy, unjust, or base; righteous anger. —**Syn.** See **anger.**

indignity (ĭn dĭg′nĭ tĭ), *n., pl.* **-ties. 1.** injury to dignity; slighting or contemptuous treatment; a humiliating affront, insult, or injury. **2.** *Obs.* unworthiness. **3.** *Obs.* disgrace or disgraceful action. [t. L: m. s. *indignitas* unworthiness] —**Syn. 1.** See **insult.**

indigo (ĭn′dĭ gō′), *n., pl.* **-gos,** *adj.* —*n.* **1.** a blue dye obtained from various plants, esp. of the genus *Indigofera.* **2.** indigo blue or indigotin, the colouring principle of this dye. **3.** a plant of the leguminous genus *Indigofera.* **4.** a deep violet blue between violet and blue in the spectrum. —*adj.* **5.** of the colour indigo. [t. Sp. or Pg., t. L: m. s. *indicum* indigo, lit., Indian (dye), t. Gk: m. *indikón*] —**indigotic** (ĭn′dĭ gŏt′ĭk), *adj.*

indigo blue, 1. the colour indigo. **2.** the essential colouring principle (a chemical compound, $C_{16}H_{10}N_2O_2$), which is contained, together with other substances, in the dye indigo, and which can also be prepared artificially.

indigo bunting, a North American fringilline songbird, *Passerina evania*, the male of which is indigo blue. Also, **indigo bird, indigo finch.**

indigoid (ĭn′dĭ goid′), *adj.* **1.** of or pertaining to that group of vat dyes which have a molecular structure like that of indigo. —*n.* **2.** an indigoid substance. [f. INDIG(O) + -OID]

indigotin (ĭn dĭg′ə tĭn, ĭn′dĭ gō′tĭn), *n.* indigo blue.

indirect (ĭn′dĭ rĕkt′), *adj.* **1.** not direct in space; deviating from a straight line: *an indirect course in sailing.* **2.** coming or resulting otherwise than directly or immediately, as effects, consequences, etc.: *an indirect advantage.* **3.** not direct in action or procedure; not straightforward; crooked: *indirect methods.* **4.** not descending in a direct line of succession, as a title or inheritance. **5.** not direct in bearing, application, force, etc.: *indirect evidence.* **6.** *Gram.* not consisting exactly of the words originally used, as in *He said he was hungry* instead of the direct *He said, 'I am hungry'.* —**in′direct′ly,** *adv.* —**in′direct′ness,** *n.*

indirection (ĭn′dĭ rĕk′shən), *n.* **1.** indirect action or procedure. **2.** a roundabout course or method. **3.** deceitful or crooked dealing.

indirect lighting, reflected or diffused light, used in interiors to avoid glare, shadows, etc.

indirect object, (in English and some other languages) the object with reference to which (for whose benefit, in whose interest, etc.) the action of a verb is performed, in English distinguished from the direct object by its position in the sentence or by the use of a preposition (*to* or *for*), e.g. *the boy* in *he gave the boy a book* or *he gave a book to the boy.*

indirect speech, reported speech.

indirect tax, a tax levied on persons who reimburse themselves by passing the cost on to others, e.g. purchase tax which is levied on commodities before they reach the consumer and ultimately paid as part of their market price.

indiscernible (ĭn′dĭ sû′nə bl), *adj.* not discernible; imperceptible. —**in′discern′ibleness,** *n.* —**in′discern′ibly,** *adv.*

indiscerptible (ĭn′dĭ sûp′tə bl), *adj.* not discerptible; indivisible. —**in′discerp′tibil′ity,** *n.*

indiscipline (ĭn dĭs′ĭ plĭn), *n.* lack of discipline.

indiscoverable (ĭn′dĭs kŭv′ə rə bl), *adj.* not discoverable; undiscoverable.

indiscreet (ĭn′dĭs krēt′), *adj.* not discreet; lacking prudence; lacking sound judgement: *indiscreet praise.* —**in′discreet′ly,** *adv.* —**in′discreet′ness,** *n.*

indiscrete (ĭn′dĭs krēt′), *adj.* not discrete. [t. L: m. s. *indiscrētus* not separated]

indiscretion (ĭn′dĭs krĕsh′ən), *n.* **1.** lack of discretion; imprudence. **2.** an indiscreet act or step.

indiscriminate (ĭn′dĭs krĭm′ĭ nĭt), *adj.* **1.** not discriminating; making no distinction: *indiscriminate in one's friendships.* **2.** not discriminate; confused: *indiscriminate slaughter.* —**in′discrim′inately,** *adv.* —**in′discrim′inateness,** *n.* —**Syn. 1.** See **miscellaneous.**

indiscriminating (ĭn′dĭs krĭm′ĭ nā′tĭng), *adj.* not discriminating. —**in′discrim′inat′ingly,** *adv.*

indiscrimination (ĭn′dĭs krĭm′ĭ nā′shən), *n.* **1.** the fact of not discriminating. **2.** the condition of not being discriminated. **3.** lack of discrimination. —**indiscriminative** (ĭn′dĭs krĭm′ĭ nə tĭv), *adj.*

indispensable (ĭn′dĭs pĕn′sə bl), *adj.* **1.** not dispensable; absolutely necessary or requisite: *an indispensable man.*

2. that cannot be disregarded or neglected: *an indispensable obligation.* —*n.* 3. one who or that which is indispensable. —**in/dispen/sabil/ity, in/dispen/sableness,** *n.* —**in/-dispen/sably,** *adv.* —**Syn.** 1. See **necessary.**

indispose (ĭn/dĭs pōz/), *v.t.*, **-posed, -posing.** 1. to put out of the proper condition (for something); make unfit; disqualify. 2. to make ill, esp. slightly. 3. to disincline; render averse or unwilling.

indisposed (ĭn/dĭs pōzd/), *adj.* 1. sick or ill, esp. slightly: *indisposed with a cold.* 2. disinclined or unwilling. —**Syn.** 1. See **sick.**

indisposition (ĭn/dĭs pə zĭsh/ən), *n.* 1. the state of being indisposed; a slight illness. 2. disinclination; unwillingness.

indisputable (ĭn/dĭs pyōō/tə bl), *adj.* not disputable; not open to question. —**in/disput/abil/ity, in/disput/-ableness,** *n.* —**in/disput/ably,** *adv.*

indissoluble (ĭn/dĭ sŏl/yŏŏ bl), *adj.* 1. not dissoluble; incapable of being dissolved, decomposed, undone, or destroyed. 2. firm or stable. 3. perpetually binding or obligatory. —**in/dissol/ubil/ity, in/dissol/ubleness,** *n.* —**in/dissol/ubly,** *adv.*

indistinct (ĭn/dĭs tĭngkt/), *adj.* 1. not distinct; not clearly marked off or defined. 2. not clearly distinguishable or perceptible, as to the eye, ear, or mind. 3. not distinguishing clearly. [t. L: s. *indistinctus*] —**in/-distinct/ly,** *adv.* —**in/distinct/ness,** *n.*

indistinctive (ĭn/dĭs tĭngk/tĭv), *adj.* 1. without distinctive characteristics. 2. not capable of making distinction. —**in/distinc/tively,** *adv.* —**in/distinc/tiveness,** *n.*

indistinguishable (ĭn/dĭs tĭng/gwĭ shə bl), *adj.* 1. not distinguishable. 2. indiscernible. —**in/distin/guishable-ness,** *n.* —**in/distin/guishably,** *adv.*

indite (ĭn dīt/), *v.t.*, **-dited, -diting.** 1. to compose or write, as a speech, poem, etc. 2. *Archaic.* to treat in a literary composition. 3. *Obs.* to dictate. [ME *endite(n)*, t. OF: m. *enditer* dictate, write, g. L *in-*[2] IN-[2] + *dictāre* pronounce. Cf. INDICT] —**indite/ment,** *n.* —**indit/er,** *n.*

indium (ĭn/dĭ əm), *n.* *Chem.* a rare metallic element, soft, white, malleable and easily fusible, found combined in various ores, esp. sphalerite: so called from the two indigo-blue lines in its spectrum. *Symbol:* In; *at. wt:* 114·82; *at. no.:* 49; *sp. gr.:* 7·3 at 20°C. [f. IND(O)- + -IUM]

indivertible (ĭn/dĭ vû/tə bl), *adj.* not divertible; not to be turned aside. —**in/divert/ibly,** *adv.*

individual (ĭn/dĭ vĭd/yŏŏ əl), *adj.* 1. single; particular; separate. 2. existing as a distinct, indivisible entity, or considered as such: *individual members.* 3. pertaining or peculiar to a single person or thing: *individual tastes.* 4. intended for the use of one person only: *individual portions.* 5. distinguished by peculiar and marked characteristics; exhibiting individuality: *a highly individual style.* 6. of which each is different or of a different design from the others: *a set of individual coffee cups.* —*n.* 7. a single human being, as distinguished from a group. 8. a person: *a strange individual.* 9. a distinct, indivisible entity; a single thing, being, instance, or item. 10. a group considered as a unit. 11. *Biol.* **a.** a single or simple organism capable of independent existence. **b.** a member of a compound organism or colony, as one of the distinct elements or zooids which make up a compound hydrozoan, or sometimes (when a whole plant or tree is regarded as a colony or compound organism) a single shoot or bud. [ME, t. ML: m. s. *indīviduālis*, der. L *indīviduus* indivisible] —**Syn.** 7. See **person.**

individualism (ĭn/dĭ vĭd/yŏŏ ə lĭz/əm), *n.* 1. a social theory advocating the liberty, rights, or independent action of the individual. 2. the principle or habit of independent thought or action. 3. the pursuit of individual rather than common or collective interests; egoism. 4. individual character; individuality. 5. an individual peculiarity. 6. *Philos.* **a.** the doctrine of pure egoism, or that nothing exists but the individual self. **b.** the doctrine that nothing is real but individual things. **c.** the principle that all actions are determined by, or at least exist for, the benefit of the individual.

individualist (ĭn/dĭ vĭd/yŏŏ ə lĭst), *n.* 1. one characterized by individualism in thought or action. 2. an advocate of individualism. —**in/divid/ualis/tic,** *adj.*

individuality (ĭn/dĭ vĭd/yŏŏ ăl/ĭ tĭ), *n.*, *pl.* **-ties.** 1. the particular character, or aggregate of qualities, which distinguishes one person or thing from others: *a person of marked individuality.* 2. (*pl.*) individual characteristics. 3. a person or thing of individual or distinctive character. 4. the state or quality of being individual; existence as a distinct individual. 5. the interests of the individual as distinguished from the interests of the community. 6. *Archaic.* the state or quality of being indivisible or inseparable. —**Syn.** 1. See **character.**

individualize (ĭn/dĭ vĭd/yŏŏ ə līz/), *v.t.*, **-lized, -lizing.** 1. to make individual; give an individual or distinctive character to. 2. to mention, indicate, or consider individually; specify; particularize. Also, **individualise.** —**in/divid/ualiza/tion,** *n.* —**in/divid/ualiz/er,** *n.*

individually (ĭn/dĭ vĭd/yŏŏ ə lĭ), *adv.* 1. in an individual manner. 2. separately. 3. personally.

individuate (ĭn/dĭ vĭd/yŏŏ āt/), *v.t.*, **-ated, -ating.** 1. to form an individual or distinct entity. 2. to give an individual or distinctive character to; individualize. [t. ML: m. s. *indīviduātus*, pp. of *indīviduāre*, der. L *indīviduus.* See INDIVIDUAL]

individuation (ĭn/dĭ vĭd/yŏŏ ā/shən), *n.* 1. the act of individuating. 2. the state of being individuated; individual existence; individuality. 3. *Philos.* the determination or contraction of a general nature to an individual mode of existence; development of the individual from the general.

indivisible (ĭn/dĭ vĭz/ə bl), *adj.* 1. not divisible; incapable of being divided: *one nation indivisible.* —*n.* 2. something indivisible. —**in/divis/ibil/ity, in/divis/ibleness,** *n.* —**in/divis/ibly,** *adv.*

Indo-, a word element meaning 'of or in India' as in *Indo-African* (of India and Africa), or 'Indian' as in *Indo-British* (British in India). [t. L, t. Gk, comb. form of L *Indus*, Gk *Indós*]

indo-, a combining form of **indigo.** Also, **ind-.**

Indo-Aryan (ĭn/dō ĕə/rĭ ən), *n.* 1. a member of one of the peoples of India and Pakistan who are Indo-European in speech and Caucasian in physical characteristics. —*adj.* 2. Indic (def. 2). 3. of or pertaining to the Indo-Aryans.

Indochina (ĭn/dō chī/nə), *n.* 1. Also, **Farther India.** a peninsula in SE Asia between the Bay of Bengal and the South China Sea, comprising South Vietnam, North Vietnam, Cambodia, Laos, Thailand, Malaya, and Burma. 2. See **French Indochina.**

Indochina

Indochinese (ĭn/dō chī nēz/), *adj.*, *n.*, *pl.* **-nese.** —*adj.* 1. of or pertaining to Indochina. 2. of or pertaining to the Mongoloid peoples of Indochina or their languages. —*n.* 3. Sino-Tibetan.

indocile (ĭn dō/sĭl), *adj.* not docile; not amenable to teaching. —**indocility** (ĭn/dō sĭl/ĭ tĭ) *n.*

indoctrinate (ĭn dŏk/trĭ nāt/), *v.t.*, **-nated, -nating.** 1. to instruct (in a doctrine, etc.). 2. to teach or inculcate. 3. to imbue (a person, etc.) with learning. [f. IN-[2] + s. L *doctrīna* teaching, DOCTRINE + -ATE[1]] —**indoc/trina/-tion,** *n.* —**indoc/trina/tor,** *n.*

Indo-European (ĭn/dō yŏŏə/rə pē/ən), *n.* 1. a major family of languages that includes most of the languages of Europe (now spread to other parts of the world), many of those of Asia, and a few scattered others. 2. the prehistoric parent language of this family. 3. a member of any of the peoples speaking an Indo-European language. —*adj.* 4. of or pertaining to Indo-European. 5. speaking an Indo-European language.

Indo-Germanic (ĭn/dō jə măn/ĭk), *n.*, *adj.* (formerly in use) Indo-European.

Indo-Hittite (ĭn/dō hĭt/īt), *n.* a linguistic stock comprising Indo-European and the Anatolian languages.

Indo-Iranian (ĭn/dō ī rā/nyən), *n.* one of the principal groups within the Indo-European family of languages, including Persian and the Indo-European languages of India and Pakistan.

indole (ĭn/dōl), *n.* *Chem.* a colourless, low-melting solid, C_8H_7N, with a faecal smell, found in the oil of jasmine and clove and as a putrefaction product from animals' intestines, used in perfumery and as a reagent. Also, **indol** (ĭn/dōl, -dŏl). [f. IND- + -OLE]

indolence (ĭn/də ləns), *n.* the state of being indolent. [t. L: m. s. *indolentia* freedom from pain]

indolent (ĭn/də lənt), *adj.* 1. having or showing a disposition to avoid exertion: *an indolent person.* 2. *Pathol.* sluggish. [t. LL: s. *indolens* not suffering] —**in/dolently,** *adv.* —**Syn.** 1. See **idle.**

indomitable (ĭn dŏm/ĭ tə bl), *adj.* that cannot be subdued or overcome, as persons, pride, courage, etc. [t. LL: m. s. *indomitābilis*, der. L *in-* IN-[3] + s. *domitāre* (freq. of *domāre* tame)] —**indom/itableness,** *n.* —**indom/itably,** *adv.* —**Syn.** See **invincible.**

Indonesia (ĭn/dō nē/zyə), *n.* 1. the Malay Archipelago; the East Indies. 2. **Republic of,** a republic in the Malay Archipelago, including Sumatra, Java, Celebes, parts of Borneo, New Guinea, and Timor, the Moluccas, and associated islands. 97,085,348 pop. (1961); ab. 580,000 sq. mi. *Cap.:* Djakarta. Formerly, **Dutch East Indies.**

Indonesian (ĭn′dō nē′zyən), *n.* **1.** a member of the ethnic group consisting of the native peoples of Indonesia, the Filipinos, and the Malays of Malaya. **2.** a member of a light-coloured race supposed to have been dominant in the Malay Archipelago before the Malays, and believed to constitute one element of the present mixed population of Malaysia and perhaps Polynesia. **3.** the official language of the Republic of Indonesia, based mainly on Malay. **4.** a group of Austronesian languages, including those of the Philippines, the Malagasy Republic, Taiwan, and Indonesia, as well as Malay. —*adj.* **5.** of or pertaining to the Malay Archipelago. **6.** of or pertaining to Indonesia, the Indonesians, or their languages. [f. INDO- + s. Gk *nêsos* island + -IAN]

indoor (ĭn′dôr′), *adj.* occurring, used, etc., in a house or building, rather than out of doors: *indoor games.*

indoors (ĭn′dôz′), *adv.* in or into a house or building.

indophenol (ĭn′dō fē′nōl), *n.* **1.** a coal-tar dye resembling indigo and giving indigo-blue shades. **2.** any of various related dyes. [f. INDO- + PHENOL]

Indore (ĭn dô′), *n.* **1.** a former state in central India; now part of Madhya Pradesh. **2.** a city in India, in W Madhya Pradesh. 394,941 (1961).

indorse (ĭn dôs′), *v.t.*, **-dorsed, -dorsing.** *Chiefly U.S.* endorse. [var. of ENDORSE, conformed to ML *indorsāre* put on the back. See IN-², DORSUM] —**indors′able,** *adj.* —**indorsee** (ĭn′dô sē′, ĭn dô′sē), *n.* —**indorse′ment,** *n.* —**indors′er,** *n.*

indoxyl (ĭn dŏk′sĭl), *n. Chem.* a crystalline compound, C_8H_7NO, which is formed by the hydrolysis of indican and is readily oxidized to furnish indigo.

Indra (ĭn′drə), *n. Hinduism.* the greatest of the Vedic gods, the god of rain and thunder.

in-draught (ĭn′dräft′), *n.* **1.** a draught or drawing inward. **2.** an inward flow or current.

indrawn (ĭn′drôn′), *adj.* drawn in; introspective.

Indre (*Fr.* ăɴ′dr), *n.* a department in central France. 251,432 pop. (1962); 2667 sq. mi. *Cap.:* Châteauroux.

Indre-et-Loire (*Fr.* ăɴ drė lwȧr′), *n.* a department in W central France. 395,210 pop. (1962); 2378 sq. mi. *Cap.:* Tours.

indri (ĭn′drĭ), *n.*, *pl.* **-dris.** a short-tailed lemur, *Indri indri*, of Madagascar, about two feet in length. [t. Malagasy, said to be an exclamation, 'lo! see!', erroneously taken as the name of the animal]

indubitable (ĭn dyōō′bĭ tə bl), *adj.* that cannot be doubted; unquestionable; certain. —**indu′bitableness,** *n.* —**indu′bitably,** *adv.*

induce (ĭn dyōōs′), *v.t.*, **-duced, -ducing. 1.** to lead or move by persuasion or influence, as to some action, state of mind, etc.: *to induce a person to go.* **2.** to bring about, produce, or cause: *opium induces sleep,* **3.** *Physics.* to produce (an electric current, etc.) by induction. **4.** *Logic.* to assert or establish (a proposition about a class of phenomena) on the basis of observations on a number of particular facts. [ME *induce(n)*, t. L: m. *indūcere* lead in, bring in, persuade] —**induc′er,** *n.* —**induc′ible,** *adj.* —**Syn. 1.** See **persuade.**

induced drag, *Aeron.* that part of drag which is caused by lift.

induced radioactivity, *Physics.* radioactivity which has been induced in stable elements by bombarding them with high-energy particles (e.g. neutrons). Also, **artificial radioactivity.**

inducement (ĭn dyōōs′mənt), *n.* **1.** the act of inducing. **2.** something that induces or persuades; an incentive. —**Syn. 2.** See **motive.**

induct (ĭn dŭkt′), *v.t.* **1.** to lead or bring in; introduce, esp. formally, as into a place, office, etc. **2.** to introduce in knowledge or experience (fol. by *to*). **3.** *U.S.* to call up for military service. [ME, t. L: s. *inductus*, pp.]

inductance (ĭn dŭk′təns), *n. Elect.* **1.** that property of a circuit by virtue of which electromagnetic induction takes place. See **mutual inductance** and **self-inductance. 2.** a piece of equipment providing inductance in a circuit or other system; inductor.

inductee (ĭn′dŭk tē′), *n. U.S.* a person called up for military service.

inductile (ĭn dŭk′tĭl), *adj.* not ductile; not pliable. —**inductility** (ĭn′dŭk tĭl′ĭ tĭ), *n.*

induction (ĭn dŭk′shən), *n.* **1.** *Elect., Magnetism.* **a.** the process by which a body having electrical or magnetic properties calls forth similar properties in a neighbouring body without direct contact, as (1) the process by which the relative motion of a wire and magnetic field produces an e.m.f. in the wire; (2) the process by which a changing current in a circuit produces an e.m.f. in the same or a neighbouring circuit. **b.** a tendency of electric currents to resist change. **2.** *Logic.* **a.** the process of discovering explanations for a set of particular facts, by estimating the weight of observational evidence in favour of a proposition which (usually) asserts something about that entire class of facts. **b.** a conclusion reached by this process. **3.** a bringing forward or adducing, as of facts, evidence, etc. **4.** the act of inducing, bringing about, or causing: *induction by the hypnotic state.* **5.** *Physiol.* the process whereby a tissue stimulates or alters other adjacent tissues. **6.** the act of inducing; introduction or initiation. **7.** formal introduction into an office or benefice; installation. **8.** an introductory unit in a literary work; a prelude or scene, independent of the main performance but related to it. **9.** *Archaic.* a preface. [ME, t. L: s. *inductio*]

induction coil, *Elect.* a transformer designed as two concentric coils with a common soft iron core, with the inner coil (primary) of few turns and the outer coil (secondary) of a great number of turns. When the primary is excited by rapidly interrupted or variable current, high voltage is induced in the secondary.

induction heating, *Elect.* a form of heating of electrically conducting materials by the currents induced in them by an alternating magnetic field. Also, **eddy current heating.**

induction motor, *Elect.* a type of electric motor in which an alternating current fed to the primary winding causes an induced current to flow through the secondary winding of the rotor; the interaction between these currents causes the rotation of the rotor.

induction stroke, the downward movement of the piston in a reciprocating engine which draws the explosive charge into the cylinder.

induction valve, the valve through which the explosive charge is drawn into the cylinder of a reciprocating engine. Also, **induction port, inlet valve.**

inductive (ĭn dŭk′tĭv), *adj.* **1.** pertaining to or involving electrical or magnetic induction. **2.** operating by induction: *an inductive machine.* **3.** pertaining to or employing logical induction. **4.** *Physiol.* eliciting some reaction within an organism. **5.** serving to induce; leading or influencing (fol. by *to*). **6.** introductory. —**induc′tively,** *adv.* —**induc′tiveness,** *n.* —**Syn. 3.** See **deductive.**

inductivity (ĭn′dŭk tĭv′ĭ tĭ), *n.*, *pl.* **-ties. 1.** an inductive property. **2.** capacity of producing induction. **3.** inductance.

inductor (ĭn dŭk′tə), *n.* **1.** *Elect.* a device, the primary purpose of which is to introduce inductance into an electric circuit. **2.** one who inducts, as into office.

indue (ĭn dyōō′), *v.t.*, **-dued, -duing.** endue.

indulge (ĭn dŭlj′), *v.*, **-dulged, -dulging.** —*v.i.* **1.** to indulge oneself; yield to an inclination (often fol. by *in*): *to indulge in apple pie.* **2.** *Colloq.* to drink alcohol in excessive amounts. —*v.t.* **3.** to yield to, satisfy, or gratify (desires, feelings, etc.). **4.** to yield to the wishes or whims of: *to indulge a child.* **5.** to allow (oneself) to follow one's own will (fol. by *in*). **6.** *Com.* to grant an extension of time, for payment or performance, to (a person, etc.) or on (a bill, etc.). **7.** *Now Rare.* to grant (something) by favour. [t. L: m. s. *indulgēre* be kind, yield, grant] —**indul′ger,** *n.* —**indul′gingly,** *adv.* —**Syn. 3.** See **humour.**

indulgence (ĭn dŭl′jəns), *n.*, *v.*, **-genced, -gencing.** —*n.* **1.** the act or practice of indulging; gratification of desire. **2.** indulgent allowance or tolerance. **3.** humouring. **4.** something granted or taken in gratification of desire. **5.** *Rom. Cath. Ch.* a remission of the temporal punishment still due to sin after it has been forgiven. **6.** *Eng. and Scot. Hist.* (in the reigns of Charles II and James II) a grant by the king to Protestant Dissenters and Roman Catholics freeing them from certain penalties imposed upon them by legislation on account of their religion. **7.** *Com.* an extension, through favour, of time for payment or performance. —*v.t.* **8.** *Rom. Cath. Ch.* to furnish with an indulgence.

indulgency (ĭn dŭl′jən sĭ), *n.*, *pl.* **-cies.** indulgence.

indulgent (ĭn dŭl′jənt), *adj.* characterized by or showing indulgence: *an indulgent parent.* [t. L: s. *indulgens*, ppr.] —**indul′gently,** *adv.*

induline (ĭn′dyōō lĭn′, -lĭn), *n.*, any of a large class of dyes yielding colours similar to indigo. [f. IND- + *ul-* (t. L: s. *-ulum*, dim. suffix) + -INE²]

indult (ĭn dŭlt′), *n. Rom. Cath. Ch.* a general faculty granted for a specific time or a specific number of cases by the Holy See to bishops and others, of doing something not permitted by the common law of the Church; a grant, privilege, favour. [t. LL: s. *indultum* indulgence, prop. pp. neut.]

indumentum (ĭn′dyōō mĕn′təm), *n. Bot., Zool.,* a thick covering of hair, feathers, or the like.

induna (ĭn dyo͞o′nə), *n.* a chief or councillor among the Zulus in southern Africa. [Zulu]

induplicate (ĭn dyo͞o′plĭ kĭt, -kāt′), *adj. Bot.* folded or rolled inwards (said of the parts of the calyx or corolla in aestivation when the edges are bent abruptly towards the axis, or of leaves in vernation when the edges are rolled inwards and then arranged about the axis without overlapping). Also, **indu′plicative.** [f. IN-² + DUPLICATE (def. 2)] —**indu′plica′tion,** *n.*

indurate (*v.* ĭn′dyo͝oə rāt′; *adj.* ĭn′dyo͝oə rĭt), *v.*, **-rated, -rating,** *adj.* —*v.t., v.i.* **1.** to make or become hard; harden; inure. —*adj.* **2.** hardened; callous; inured. [ME, t. L: m. s. *indūrātus*, pp.] —**in′dura′tion,** *n.* —**in′dura′tive,** *adj.*

Indus (ĭn′dəs), *n.* a river flowing from W Tibet through Kashmir and SW through West Pakistan to the Arabian Sea. ab. 2000 mi.

indusium (ĭn dyo͞o′zyəm), *n., pl.* **-sia** (-zyə). **1.** *Bot.* a membranous outgrowth covering the sori in ferns. **2.** *Anat., Zool.* an enveloping layer or membrane. **3.** *Embryol.* the amnion. [t. L: tunic] —**indu′sial,** *adj.*

industrial (ĭn dŭs′trĭ əl), *adj.* **1.** of or pertaining to, of the nature of, or resulting from industry or productive labour: *the industrial arts.* **2.** having highly developed industries: *an industrial nation.* **3.** engaged in an industry or industries: *industrial workers.* **4.** pertaining to the workers in industries: *industrial training.* **5.** designed for use in industry: *industrial diamonds.* —*n.* **6.** a worker in some industry, esp. a manufacturing industry. **7.** one who conducts or owns an industrial enterprise. **8.** (*pl.*) stocks and shares in industrial enterprises. [f. m. INDUSTRY + -AL¹. Cf. F *industriel*] —**indus′trially,** *adv.*

industrial estate, a tract of land specially allocated for the building of factories, etc.

industrialism (ĭn dŭs′trĭ ə lĭz′əm), *n.* an economic organization of society built largely on mechanized industry rather than agriculture, craftsmanship, or commerce.

industrialist (ĭn dŭs′trĭ ə lĭst), *n.* one who conducts or owns an industrial enterprise.

industrialize (ĭn dŭs′trĭ ə līz′), *v.t.*, **-lized, -lizing.** to introduce industry into (an area) on a large scale. Also, **industrialise.** —**indus′trializa′tion,** *n.*

Industrial Revolution, the term applied to the social and economic changes in England from the mid 18th to the mid 19th centuries during the beginnings and growth of modern industrialism.

Industrial Workers of the World, an international industrial union, organized in Chicago in 1905. It disintegrated after World War I. *Abbrev.:* I.W.W.

industrious (ĭn dŭs′trĭ əs), *adj.* **1.** hard-working; diligent: *an industrious person.* **2.** *Obs.* skilful. [t. L: m. s. *industriōsus* diligent] —**indus′triously,** *adv.* —**indus′triousness,** *n.* —**Syn. 1.** See **busy.**

industry (ĭn′dəs trĭ), *n., pl.* **-tries. 1.** a particular branch of trade or manufacture: *the steel industry.* **2.** any large-scale business activity: *the tourist industry.* **3.** manufacture or trade as a whole: *the growth of industry in underdeveloped countries.* **4.** the ownership and management of companies, factories, etc.: *friction between labour and industry.* **5.** systematic work or labour. **6.** assiduous activity at any work or task. [ME *industrie*, t. L: m. *industria* diligence]

indwell (ĭn′dwĕl′), *v.*, **-dwelt, -dwelling.** —*v.t.* **1.** to inhabit. —*v.i.* **2.** to dwell (fol. by *in*). —**in′dwell′er,** *n.*

Indy, d′ (*Fr.* dăɴ dē′), *n.* **Vincent** (*Fr.* văɴ sāɴ′), 1851–1931, French composer.

-ine¹, an adjective suffix meaning 'of or pertaining to', 'of the nature of', 'made of', 'like', as in *asinine, crystalline, equine, marine.* [t. L: m. *-īnus*; also m. *-inus*, t. Gk: m. *-inos*]

-ine², **1.** a noun suffix denoting some action, procedure, art, place, etc., as in *discipline, doctrine, medicine, latrine.* **2.** a suffix occurring in many nouns of later formation and various meanings, as in *famine, routine, grenadine, vaseline.* **3.** a noun suffix used particularly in chemical terms, as *bromine, chlorine,* and esp. names of basic substances, as *amine, aniline, caffeine, quinine, quinoline.* Cf. **-in**². [t. F, g. L *-ina*, orig. fem. of *-inus*; also used to repr. Gk *-inē*, fem. n. suffix, as in *heroine*]

inearth (ĭn ûrth′), *v.t. Chiefly Poetic.* to bury; inter.

inebriant (ĭ nē′brĭ ənt), *adj.* **1.** inebriating; intoxicating. —*n.* **2.** an intoxicant. [t. L: s. *inēbrians*, ppr.]

inebriate (*v.* ĭ nē′brĭ āt′; *n., adj.* ĭ nē′brĭ ĭt), *v.*, **-ated, -ating,** *n., adj.* —*v.t.* **1.** to make drunk; intoxicate. **2.** to intoxicate mentally or emotionally; exhilarate. —*n.* **3.** an intoxicated person. **4.** a habitual drunkard. —*adj.* **5.** Also, **ine′briat′ed.** drunk; intoxicated. [t. L: m. s. *inēbriātus*, pp.] —**ine′bria′tion,** *n.* —**Syn. 4.** See **drunkard.**

inebriety (ĭn′ĭ brī′ə tĭ), *n.* drunkenness.

inedible (ĭn ĕd′ ĭ bl), *adj.* not edible; unfit to be eaten. —**ined′ibil′ity,** *n.*

inedited (ĭn ĕd′ĭ tĭd), *adj.* **1.** unpublished. **2.** not edited.

ineducable (ĭn ĕd′yo͝o kə bl), *adj.* incapable of being educated, esp. as a result of mental retardation.

ineffable (ĭn ĕf′ə bl), *adj.* **1.** that cannot be uttered or expressed; inexpressible; unspeakable: *ineffable joy.* **2.** that must not be uttered: *the ineffable name.* [ME, t. L: m. s. *ineffābilis*] —**inef′fabil′ity, inef′fableness,** *n.* —**inef′fably,** *adv.*

ineffaceable (ĭn′ĭ fā′sə bl), *adj.* not effaceable; indelible: an ineffaceable impression. —**in′efface′abil′ity,** *n.* —**in′efface′ably,** *adv.*

ineffective (ĭn′ĭ fĕk′tĭv), *adj.* **1.** not effective; ineffectual, as efforts. **2.** inefficient, as a person. **3.** lacking in artistic effect, as a design or work. —**in′effec′tively,** *adv.* —**in′effec′tiveness,** *n.*

ineffectual (ĭn′ĭ fĕk′tyo͞o əl), *adj.* **1.** not effectual; without satisfactory or decisive effect: *an ineffectual remedy.* **2.** unavailing; futile: *his efforts were ineffectual.* **3.** powerless or impotent. —**in′effec′tual′ity, in′effec′tualness,** *n.* —**in′effec′tually,** *adv.* —**Syn. 2.** See **useless.**

inefficacious (ĭn′ĕf ĭ kā′shəs), *adj.* not able to produce the desired effect. —**in′effica′ciously,** *adv.* —**in′effica′ciousness, inefficacity** (ĭn′ĕf ĭ kăs′ĭ tĭ), *n.*

inefficacy (ĭn ĕf′ĭ kə sĭ), *n.* lack of efficacy or power to produce the desired effect.

inefficiency (ĭn′ĭ fĭsh′ən sĭ), *n.* the condition or quality of being inefficient; lack of efficiency.

inefficient (ĭn′ĭ fĭsh′ənt), *adj.* not efficient; unable to effect or accomplish in a capable, economical way. —**in′effi′ciently,** *adv.* —**Syn.** See **incapable.**

inelastic (ĭn′ĭ lăs′tĭk), *adj.* not elastic; lacking elasticity; unyielding. —**inelasticity** (ĭn′ĭ lăs tĭs′ĭ tĭ), *n.*

inelegance (ĭn ĕl′ĭ gəns), *n.* **1.** the state or character of being inelegant; lack of elegance. **2.** that which is inelegant or ungraceful.

inelegancy (ĭn ĕl′ĭ gən sĭ), *n., pl.* **-cies.** inelegance.

inelegant (ĭn ĕl′ĭ gənt), *adj.* not elegant; not nice or refined; vulgar. —**inel′egantly,** *adv.*

ineligible (ĭn ĕl′ĭ jə bl), *adj.* **1.** not eligible; not proper or suitable for choice. **2.** legally disqualified to hold an office. **3.** legally disqualified to function as a juror, voter, witness, or to become the recipient of a privilege. —*n.* **4.** one who is ineligible, esp. as a suitor, husband, or member of an athletic team. —**inel′igibil′ity,** *n.* —**inel′igibly,** *adv.*

ineloquent (ĭn ĕl′ə kwənt), *adj.* not eloquent. —**inel′oquence,** *n.* —**inel′oquently,** *adv.*

ineluctable (ĭn′ĭ lŭk′tə bl), *adj.* that cannot be escaped from, as a fate. [t. L: m. s. *inēluctābilis*] —**in′eluc′tabil′ity,** *n.* —**in′eluc′tably,** *adv.*

ineludible (ĭn′ĭ lo͞o′də bl), *adj.* not eludible; inescapable. —**in′elud′ibly,** *adv.*

inept (ĭn ĕpt′), *adj.* **1.** not apt, fitted, or suitable; unsuitable. **2.** inappropriate; out of place. **3.** absurd or foolish, as a proceeding, remark, etc. [t. L: s. *ineptus*] —**inept′ly,** *adv.* —**inept′ness,** *n.*

ineptitude (ĭn ĕp′tĭ tyo͞od′), *n.* **1.** the quality of being inept. **2.** an inept act or remark.

inequality (ĭn′ĭ kwŏl′ĭ tĭ), *n., pl.* **-ties. 1.** the condition of being unequal; lack of equality; disparity: *inequality of treatment.* **2.** social disparity: *the inequality between the rich and the poor.* **3.** inadequacy. **4.** injustice; partiality. **5.** unevenness, as of surface. **6.** an instance of unevenness. **7.** variableness, as of climate. **8.** *Astron.* **a.** any component part of the departure from uniformity in astronomical phenomena, esp. in orbital motion. **b.** the amount of such a departure. **9.** *Maths.* an expression of two unequal quantities connected by the sign $>$ or $<$, as, $a > b$, '*a* is greater than *b*'; $a < b$, '*a* is less than *b*'. [late ME, t. ML: m. s. *inaequālitas* unevenness]

inequi-, a word element meaning 'unequal' or 'unequally', as in *inequidistant.* [f. IN-³ + EQUI-]

inequilateral (ĭn′ē kwĭ lăt′ə rəl), *adj.* not equilateral. —**in′equilat′erally,** *adv.*

inequitable (ĭn ĕk′wĭ tə bl), *adj.* not equitable; unfair. —**ineq′uitably,** *adv.*

inequity (ĭn ĕk′wĭ tĭ), *n., pl.* **-ties. 1.** lack of equity; unfairness. **2.** an unfair circumstance or proceeding.

ineradicable (ĭn′ĭ răd′ĭ kə bl), *adj.* not eradicable; that cannot be eradicated, rooted out, or removed utterly. —**in′erad′icably,** *adv.*

inerasable (ĭn′ĭ rā′zə bl), *adj.* not erasable; not to be erased or effaced. —**in′eras′ably,** *adv.*

inerrable (ĭ nĕ′rə bl), *adj.* incapable of erring; infallible. [t. LL: m. s. *inerrābilis*] —**iner′rabil′ity, iner′rableness,** *n.* —**iner′rably,** *adv.*

inerrant (ĭ nĕ′rənt), *adj.* free from error. [t. L: s. *inerrans*, ppr., not wandering] —**iner′rancy,** *n.*

inerratic (ĭn/ĭ răt/ĭk), *adj.* not erratic or wandering; fixed, as a so-called 'fixed' star.

inert (ĭ nût/), *adj.* **1.** having no inherent power of action, motion, or resistance: *inert matter.* **2.** without active properties, as a drug. **3.** of an inactive or sluggish habit or nature. [t. L: s. *iners* unskilled, idle] —**inert/ly,** *adv.* —**inert/ness,** *n.* —**Syn. 3.** See **inactive.**

inert gas, *Chem.* See **rare gas.**

inertia (ĭ nû/shyə), *n.* **1.** inert condition; inactivity; sluggishness. **2.** *Physics.* **a.** that property of matter by which it retains its state of rest or of uniform rectilinear motion so long as it is not acted upon by an external force. **b.** an analogous property of a force: *electric inertia.* [t. L: lack of skill, inactivity] —**iner/tial,** *adj.*

inertial guidance, *Aeron.* a system of missile guidance in which velocities or distances, deduced from accelerations measured within the missile, are compared with data stored before launching.

inertial system, *Physics.* a frame of reference in which a body only changes velocity if acted upon by a force; a frame of reference in which Newtonian mechanics apply.

inescapable (ĭn/ĭs kā/pə bl), *adj.* that cannot be escaped or ignored.

inescutcheon (ĭn/ĭ skŭch/ən), *n. Her.* an escutcheon borne as a charge.

I'ness., Inverness-shire.

in esse (ĭn ĕs/ĭ), *Latin.* in being; in actuality; actually existing (contrasted with *in posse*).

inessential (ĭn/ĭ sĕn/shəl), *adj.* **1.** not essential; not necessary. **2.** without essence; insubstantial. —*n.* **3.** that which is not essential. —**in/essen/tial/ity,** *n.*

inestimable (ĭn ĕs/tĭ mə bl), *adj.* **1.** that cannot be estimated, or too great to be estimated. **2.** of incalculable value. [ME, t. F, t. L: m. s. *inaestimābilis.* See IN-[3], ESTIMABLE] —**ines/timably,** *adv.*

inevitable (ĭn ĕv/ĭ tə bl), *adj.* **1.** that cannot be avoided, evaded, or escaped; certain or necessary: *an inevitable conclusion.* **2.** sure to befall, happen, or come, by the very nature of things. —*n.* **3.** that which is unavoidable. [ME, t. L: m. s. *inēvitābilis.* See IN-[3], EVITABLE] —**inev/itabil/ity, inev/itableness,** *n.* —**inev/itably,** *adv.*

inexact (ĭn/ĭg zăkt/), *adj.* not exact; not strictly accurate. —**in/exact/ly,** *adv.* —**in/exact/ness,** *n.*

inexactitude (ĭn/ĭg zăk/tĭ tyo͞od/), *n.* the state or character of being inexact or inaccurate; inexactness. [f. IN-[3] + EXACTITUDE]

inexcusable (ĭn/ĭk skyo͞o/zə bl), *adj.* not excusable; incapable of being justified. —**in/excus/abil/ity, in/excus/ableness,** *n.* —**in/excus/ably,** *adv.*

inexecution (ĭn ĕk/sĭ kyo͞o/shən), *n.* lack or neglect of execution.

inexertion (ĭn/ĭg zû/shən), *n.* lack of exertion.

inexhaustible (ĭn/ĭg zôs/tə bl), *adj.* **1.** not exhaustible; incapable of being exhausted: *an inexhaustible supply.* **2.** unfailing; tireless. —**in/exhaust/ibil/ity, in/exhaust/ibleness,** *n.* —**in/exhaust/ibly,** *adv.*

inexistent[1] (ĭn/ĭg zĭs/tənt), *adj.* not existent; having no existence. —**in/exist/ence, in/exist/ency,** *n.*

inexistent[2] (ĭn/ĭg zĭs/tənt), *adj.* existing within; inherent.

inexorable (ĭn ĕk/sə rə bl), *adj.* **1.** unyielding or unalterable: *inexorable facts.* **2.** not to be persuaded, moved, or affected by prayers or entreaties. [t. L: m. s. *inexōrābilis.* See IN-[3], EXORABLE] —**inex/orabil/ity, inex/orableness,** *n.* —**inex/orably,** *adv.* —**Syn. 2.** relentless, unrelenting, implacable. See **inflexible.**

inexpedient (ĭn/ĭk spē/dyənt), *adj.* not expedient; not suitable, judicious, or advisable. —**in/expe/dience, in/expe/diency,** *n.* —**in/expe/diently,** *adv.*

inexpensive (ĭn/ĭk spĕn/sĭv), *adj.* not expensive; costing little. —**in/expen/sively,** *adv.* —**in/expen/siveness,** *n.* —**Syn.** See **cheap.**

inexperience (ĭn/ĭk spĭə/rĭ əns), *n.* lack of experience, or of knowledge or skill gained from experience.

inexperienced (ĭn/ĭk spĭə/rĭ ənst), *adj.* not experienced; without knowledge or skill gained from experience. —**Syn.** untrained, unskilled, inexpert; raw, green.

inexpert (ĭn ĕk/spût), *adj.* not expert; unskilled. —**inex/pertly,** *adv.* —**inex/pertness,** *n.*

inexpiable (ĭn ĕk/spĭ ə bl), *adj.* **1.** not to be expiated; admitting of no expiation or atonement: *an inexpiable crime.* **2.** not to be appeased by expiation; implacable: *inexpiable hate.* [t. L: m. s. *inexpiābilis*] —**inex/piableness,** *n.* —**inex/piably,** *adv.*

inexplicable (ĭn ĕk/splĭ kə bl, ĭn/ĭk splĭk/ə bl), *adj.* not explicable; incapable of being explained. [late ME, t. L: m. s. *inexplicābilis* that cannot be unfolded] —**inex/plicabil/ity, inex/plicableness,** *n.* —**inex/plicably,** *adv.*

inexplicit (ĭn/ĭk splĭs/ĭt), *adj.* not explicit or clear; not clearly stated. [t. L: s. *inexplicitus*] —**in/explic/itly,** *adv.* —**in/explic/itness,** *n.*

inexpressible (ĭn/ĭk sprĕs/ə bl), *adj.* not expressible; that cannot be uttered or represented in words: *inexpressible grief.* —**in/express/ibil/ity, in/express/ibleness,** *n.* —**in/express/ibly,** *adv.*

inexpressive (ĭn/ĭk sprĕs/ĭv), *adj.* **1.** not expressive; lacking in expression. **2.** *Archaic.* inexpressible. —**in/express/ively,** *adv.* —**in/express/iveness,** *n.*

inexpugnable (ĭn/ĭks pŭg/nə bl), *adj.* that cannot be taken by force; impregnable; unconquerable: *an inexpugnable fort.* [t. L: m. s. *inexpugnābilis*] —**in/expug/nabil/ity, in/expug/nableness,** *n.* —**in/expug/nably,** *adv.*

inextensible (ĭn/ĭk stĕn/sə bl), *adj.* not extensible. —**in/exten/sibil/ity,** *n.*

in extenso (ĭn/ĭk stĕn/sō), *Latin.* at full length.

inextinguishable (ĭn/ĭk stĭng/gwĭ shə bl), *adj.* not extinguishable; not to be extinguished, quenched, suppressed, or brought to an end: *inextinguishable fire, inextinguishable rage.* —**in/extin/guishably,** *adv.*

inextirpable (ĭn/ĭk stû/pə bl), *adj.* incapable of being extirpated: *an inextirpable disease.*

in extremis (ĭn/ĭk strē/mĭs), *Latin.* **1.** in extremity. **2.** near death.

inextricable (ĭn ĕk/strĭ kə bl), *adj.* **1.** from which one cannot extricate oneself: *an inextricable maze.* **2.** that cannot be disentangled, undone, or loosed, as a tangle, knot, grasp, etc. **3.** hopelessly intricate, involved, or perplexing: *inextricable confusion.* [late ME, t. L: m. s. *inextricābilis*] —**inex/tricabil/ity, inex/tricableness,** *n.* —**inex/tricably,** *adv.*

inf., **1.** (*also cap.*) infantry. **2.** infinitive. **3.** infinity. **4.** information. **5.** (L *infra*) below; after.

infallible (ĭn făl/ə bl), *adj.* **1.** not fallible; exempt from liability to error, as persons, their judgement, pronouncements, etc. **2.** absolutely trustworthy or sure: *an infallible rule.* **3.** unfailing in operation; certain: *an infallible remedy.* **4.** *Rom. Cath. Ch.* immune from fallacy or liability to error in expounding matters of faith or morals in virtue of the promise made by Christ to the Church. —*n.* **5.** an infallible person or thing. [late ME, t. ML: m. s. *infallibilis.* See IN-[3], FALLIBLE] —**infal/libil/ity, infal/libleness,** *n.* —**infal/libly,** *adv.* —**Syn. 2, 3.** See **reliable.**

infamous (ĭn/fə məs), *adj.* **1.** of ill fame; having an extremely bad reputation: *an infamous city.* **2.** such as to deserve or to cause evil repute; detestable; shamefully bad: *infamous conduct.* **3.** *Law.* **a.** deprived of credit and of certain rights as a citizen, in consequence of conviction of certain offences. **b.** (of offences, etc.) involving such deprivation. [ME, t. ML: m. s. *infāmōsus* (in L *infāmis*)] —**in/famously,** *adv.* —**in/famousness,** *n.* —**Syn. 1.** disreputable, notorious. **2.** disgraceful, scandalous; nefarious, wicked. —**Ant. 1.** honoured. **2.** praiseworthy.

infamy (ĭn/fə mĭ), *n., pl.* **-mies. 1.** ill fame, shameful notoriety, or public reproach. **2.** infamous character or conduct. **3.** an infamous act or circumstance. **4.** *Law.* the loss of credit incurred by conviction of an infamous offence, affecting a witness's credibility but not his right to give evidence. [late ME, t. L: m. s. *infāmia*] —**Syn. 1.** See **disgrace.**

infancy (ĭn/fən sĭ), *n., pl.* **-cies. 1.** the state or period of being an infant; babyhood; early childhood. **2.** the corresponding period in the existence of anything: *the infancy of the world.* **3.** infants collectively. **4.** *Law.* the period of life to the age of majority (in the common law, to the end of the twenty-first year); minority; nonage. [t. L: m. s. *infantia,* lit., inability to speak]

infant (ĭn/fənt), *n.* **1.** a child during the earliest period of its life, or a baby. **2.** *Law.* a person who is not of full age, esp. one who has not attained the age of twenty-one years. **3.** a beginner, as in learning. **4.** anything in the first period of existence or the first stage of progress. —*adj.* **5.** of or pertaining to infants or infancy: *infant years.* **6.** being in infancy: *an infant child.* **7.** being in the earliest stage: *an infant industry.* **8.** of or pertaining to the legal state of infancy; minor. [t. L: s. *infans* young child, prop. adj., not speaking; r. ME *enfaunt,* t. OF] —**in/fanthood/,** *n.*

infanta (ĭn făn/tə), *n.* **1.** a daughter of the king of Spain or of Portugal. **2.** an infante's wife. [t. Sp. and Pg. See INFANTE]

infante (ĭn făn/tĭ), *n.* a son of the king of Spain or of Portugal, not heir to the throne. [t. Sp. and Pg., g. L *infans* INFANT]

infanticide (ĭn făn/tĭ sīd/), *n.* **1.** the killing of an infant. **2.** the practice of killing newborn children. **3.** one who kills an infant. [t. LL: m. s. *infanticidium* (defs 1 and 2), *infanticīda* (def. 3). See -CIDE]

infantile (ĭn/fən tīl/), *adj.* **1.** characteristic of or befitting an infant; babyish; childish: *infantile behaviour.*

2. of or pertaining to infants: *infantile disease.* **3.** being in the earliest stage. [t. LL: m. s. *infantilis*] **—Syn. 1.** See **childish.**
infantile paralysis, poliomyelitis.
infantilism (ĭn făn′tĭ lĭz′əm), *n.* **1.** a pattern of speech characterized by those deviations from normal articulation or voice that are typical of very young children. **2.** *Psychol.* the persistence in an adult of markedly childish anatomical, physiological, or psychological characteristics.
infantine (ĭn′fən tīn′), *adj.* infantile.
infantry (ĭn′fən trĭ), *n.* soldiers or military units that fight on foot, with bayonets, rifles, machine guns, grenades, mortars, etc. [t. F: m. *infanterie*, t. It.: m. *infanteria*, der. *infante* youth, foot soldier. See INFANT]
infantryman (ĭn′fən trĭ mən), *n.*, *pl.* **-men.** a soldier of the infantry.
infants' school, (in Britain) a primary school for children from about five to seven years of age. Also, **infant school.**
infarct (ĭn făkt′), *n. Pathol.* a circumscribed portion of tissue which has been suddenly deprived of its blood supply by embolism or thrombosis and which, as a result, is undergoing death (necrosis), to be replaced by scar tissue. [t. L: s. *infar(c)tus*, pp., stuffed in]
infarction (ĭn făk′shən), *n. Pathol.* **1.** the formation of an infarct. **2.** an infarct.
infare (ĭn′fēə′), *n. Dial.* a reception given on entering a new house, esp. for a newly married couple.
infatuate (*v.* ĭn făt′yo͞o āt′; *adj.*, *n.* ĭn făt′yo͞o ĭt, -āt′), *v.*, **-ated, -ating,** *adj.* **—***v.t.* **1.** to affect with folly; make fatuous. **2.** to inspire or possess with a foolish or unreasoning passion, as of love. **—***adj.* **3.** infatuated. **—***n.* **4.** a person who is infatuated. [t. L: m. s. *infatuātus*, pp., made foolish]
infatuated (ĭn făt′yo͞o ā′tĭd), *adj.* made foolish by love; blindly in love. **—infat′uat′edly,** *adv.*
infatuation (ĭn făt′yo͞o ā′shən), *n.* **1.** the act of infatuating. **2.** the state of being infatuated. **3.** foolish or all-absorbing passion. **4.** the object of one's infatuation.
infeasible (ĭn fē′zə bl), *adj.* not feasible; impracticable. **—infea′sibil′ity,** *n.*
infect (ĭn fĕkt′), *v.t.* **1.** to impregnate (a person, organ, wound, etc.) with disease-producing germs. **2.** to affect with disease. **3.** to impregnate with something that affects quality, character, or condition, esp. unfavourably: *to infect the air with poison gas.* **4.** to taint, contaminate, or affect morally: *infected with greed.* **5.** to imbue with some pernicious belief, opinion, etc. **6.** to affect so as to influence feeling or action: *his courage infected the others.* **7.** *Law.* to taint with illegality, or expose to penalty, forfeiture, etc. **—***adj.* **8.** *Archaic.* infected. [ME *infect(en)*, t. L: (m.) s. *infectus*, pp., put in, dyed, imbued, infected] **—infec′tor,** *n.*
infection (ĭn fĕk′shən), *n.* **1.** the action of infecting. **2.** an infecting with germs of disease, as through the medium of infected insects, air, water, clothing, etc. **3.** an infecting agency or influence. **4.** the state of being infected. **5.** an infectious disease. **6.** the condition of suffering an infection. **7.** an influence or impulse passing from one to another and affecting feeling or action.
infectious (ĭn fĕk′shəs), *adj.* **1.** communicable by infection, as diseases. **2.** causing or communicating infection. **3.** tending to spread from one to another: *laughter is infectious.* **4.** *Law.* capable of contaminating with illegality; exposing to seizure or forfeiture. **5.** *Obs.* diseased. **—infec′tiously,** *adv.* **—infec′tiousness,** *n.* **—Syn. 3.** See **contagious.**
infectious disease, 1. a disease caused by germs, as bacteria or filterable viruses. **2.** any disease, produced by the action of a micro-organism in the body, which may or may not be contagious.
infective (ĭn fĕk′tĭv), *adj.* infectious. **—infec′tively,** *adv.* **—infec′tiveness, in′fectiv′ity,** *n.*
infecund (ĭn fē′kənd), *adj.* not fecund; unfruitful; barren. **—infecundity** (ĭn′fĭ kŭn′dĭ tĭ), *n.*
infelicitous (ĭn′fĭ lĭs′ĭ təs), *adj.* **1.** not felicitous, happy, or fortunate; unhappy. **2.** inapt or inappropriate: *an infelicitous remark.* **—in′felic′itously,** *adv.*
infelicity (ĭn′fĭ lĭs′ĭ tĭ), *n.*, *pl.* **-ties. 1.** the state of being unhappy; unhappiness. **2.** ill fortune. **3.** an unfortunate circumstance; a misfortune. **4.** inaptness or inappropriateness as of action or expression. **5.** something inapt or infelicitous: *infelicities of style.* **6.** a tactless remark or act.
infelt (ĭn′fĕlt′), *adj.* felt within; heartfelt.
infer (ĭn fû′), *v.*, **-ferred, -ferring. —***v.t.* **1.** to derive by reasoning; conclude or judge from premises or evidence. **2.** *Colloq.* (of facts, circumstances, statements, etc.) to indicate or involve as a conclusion; imply. **3.** *Colloq.* to imply or hint. **—***v.i.* **4.** to draw a conclusion, as by reasoning. [t. L: s. *inferre* bring in or on, infer] **—inferable** (ĭn fû′rə bl), *adj.* **—infer′ably,** *adv.*
inference (ĭn′fə rəns, -frəns), *n.* **1.** the act or process of inferring. **2.** that which is inferred. **3.** *Colloq.* implication. **4.** *Logic.* **a.** the process of deriving the strict logical consequences of assumed premises. **b.** the process of arriving at some conclusion which, though it is not logically derivable from the assumed premises, possesses some degree of probability relative to the premises. **c.** a proposition reached by a process of inference.
inferential (ĭn′fə rĕn′shəl), *adj.* pertaining to or depending on inference. **—in′feren′tially,** *adv.*
inferior (ĭn fĭə′rĭ ə), *adj.* **1.** lower in station, rank, or degree (fol. by *to*). **2.** of comparatively low grade; poor in quality: *an inferior brand.* **3.** less important, valuable, or excellent: *an inferior workman.* **4.** lower in place or position (now chiefly in scientific or technical use). **5.** *Bot.* **a.** situated below some other organ. **b.** (of a calyx) inserted below the ovary. **c.** (of an ovary) having a superior calyx. **6.** *Astron.* **a.** (of a planet) having an orbit within that of the earth: applied to the planets Mercury and Venus. **b.** (of a conjunction of an inferior planet) taking place between the sun and the earth. **c.** lying below the horizon: *the inferior part of a meridian.* **7.** *Print.* lower than the main line of type, as the figures in chemical formulae; subscript. **—***n.* **8.** one inferior to another or others, as in rank or merit. **9.** *Print.* an inferior letter or figure; a subscript. [ME, t. L, compar. of *inferus* being below, under, nether. Cf. UNDER] **—inferiority** (ĭn fĭə′rĭ ŏ′rĭ tĭ), *n.* **—infe′riorly,** *adv.*
inferiority complex, 1. *Psychiatry.* a complex arising from intense feelings of inferiority, and resulting in either extreme reticence or aggressiveness due to overcompensation. **2.** *Colloq.* a feeling of inferiority or inadequacy.
inferior court, *Law.* (in England) a county court and any court with jurisdiction to hear civil cases, other than the High Court of Justice.
infernal (ĭn fû′nəl), *adj.* **1.** of or pertaining to the lower world of classical mythology: *the infernal regions.* **2.** of, inhabiting, or befitting hell. **3.** hellish; fiendish; diabolical: *an infernal plot.* **4.** *Colloq.* abominable; confounded: *an infernal nuisance.* [ME, t. LL: s. *infernālis* of the lower regions] **—infernality** (ĭn′fû năl′ĭ tĭ), *n.* **—infer′nally,** *adv.*
infernal machine, an explosive mechanical apparatus intended to destroy life or property, esp. one disguised as something harmless.
inferno (ĭn fû′nō), *n.*, *pl.* **-nos. 1.** hell; the infernal regions. **2.** an infernal or hell-like region. [t. It.: hell, g. L *infernus* underground]
infertile (ĭn fû′tīl), *adj.* not fertile; unfruitful; unproductive; barren: *infertile soil.* **—infertility** (ĭn′fû tĭl′ĭ tĭ), *n.*
infest (ĭn fĕst′), *v.t.* **1.** to haunt or overrun in a troublesome manner, as predatory bands, destructive animals, vermin, etc., do. **2.** to be numerous in, as anything troublesome: *the cares that infest the day.* **3.** *Archaic.* to harass. [late ME, t. L: s. *infestāre* assail, molest] **—infest′er,** *n.*
infestation (ĭn′fĕs tā′shən), *n.* **1.** the act of infesting. **2.** the state of being infested. **3.** a harassing or troublesome invasion.
infeudation (ĭn′fyo͞o dā′shən), *n. Old Eng. Law.* **1.** the grant of an estate in fee. **2.** the relation of lord and vassal established by the grant and acceptance of such an estate. [t. ML: s. *infeudātio*, der. *infeudāre* enfeoff]
infidel (ĭn′fĭ dl), *n.* **1.** an unbeliever. **2.** one who does not accept a particular faith, esp. Christianity (formerly applied by Christians esp. to a Muslim). **3.** (in Muslim use) one who does not accept the Muslim faith. **—***adj.* **4.** without religious faith. **5.** due to or manifesting unbelief. **6.** not accepting a particular faith, esp. Christianity or Islam; heathen. **7.** rejecting the Christian religion while accepting no other; not believing in the Bible or any divine revelation (used especially of persons belonging to Christian communities). **8.** of or pertaining to unbelievers or infidels. [late ME, t. L: s. *infidēlis* unfaithful, LL unbelieving] **—Syn. 2, 3.** See **atheist.**
infidelity (ĭn′fĭ dĕl′ĭ tĭ), *n.*, *pl.* **-ties. 1.** unfaithfulness. **2.** adultery. **3.** lack of religious faith, esp. Christian. **4.** a breach of trust.
infield (ĭn′fēld′), *n.* **1.** *Cricket.* the part of the field near the wickets. **2.** *Baseball.* the diamond. **3.** that part of farmlands nearest to the main farm buildings.
infielder (ĭn′fēl′də), *n. Cricket, Baseball.* a player stationed in the infield.
infighter (ĭn′fī′tə), *n.* one who practises or is adept at infighting.
infighting (ĭn′fī′tĭng), *n.* **1.** *Boxing.* fighting at close quarters, so that blows using the full reach of the arm cannot be delivered. **2.** the secret and often ruthless struggle that takes place between members of the same

organization competing for the same position, between rival firms competing for a contract, or the like.

infilling (ĭn′fĭl′ĭng), *n. Bldg Trades.* brickwork fitted inside a timber frame as in half-timbered buildings, for fire or thermal insulation.

infiltrate (ĭn′fĭl trāt′), *v.*, **-trated, -trating,** *n.* —*v.t.* **1.** to filter into or through; permeate. **2.** to cause to pass in by, or as by, filtering: *the troops infiltrated the enemy lines.* —*v.i.* **3.** to pass in or through a substance, etc., by or as by filtering. —*n.* **4.** that which infiltrates. **5.** *Pathol.* cells or a substance which pass into the tissues and form a morbid accumulation. —**in′filtra′tive,** *adj.* —**in′filtra′tor,** *n.*

infiltration (ĭn′fĭl trā′shən), *n.* **1.** the act or process of infiltrating. **2.** the state of being infiltrated. **3.** that which infiltrates; an infiltrate. **4.** *Mil.* a method of attack in which small bodies of soldiers or individual soldiers penetrate into the enemy's line at weak or unguarded points, in order to bring fire eventually upon the enemy's flanks or rear.

infin., infinitive.

infinite (ĭn′fĭ nĭt), *adj.* **1.** immeasurably great: *a truth of infinite importance.* **2.** indefinitely or exceedingly great: *infinite sums of money.* **3.** unbounded or unlimited; perfect: *the infinite wisdom of God.* **4.** endless or innumerable; inexhaustible. **5.** *Maths.* **a.** not finite. **b.** (of an assemblage) having the same number of elements as some proper part of itself. —*n.* **6.** that which is infinite. **7. the Infinite** or **the Infinite Being,** God. **8.** *Maths.* an infinite quantity or magnitude. **9.** the boundless regions of space. [ME, t. L: m. s. *infīnītus*] —**in′finitely,** *adv.* —**in′finiteness,** *n.*

infinitesimal (ĭn′fĭn ĭ tĕs′ĭ məl), *adj.* **1.** indefinitely or exceedingly small: *the infinitesimal vessels of the nervous system.* **2.** immeasurably small; less than an assignable quantity: *to an infinitesimal degree.* **3.** pertaining to or involving infinitesimals. —*n.* **4.** an infinitesimal quantity. **5.** *Maths.* a variable having zero as a limit. —**in′finites′imally,** *adv.*

infinitesimal calculus, the differential calculus and the integral calculus, considered together.

infinitival (ĭn fĭn′ĭ tī′vəl), *adj. Gram.* of or pertaining to the infinitive mode. —**infin′iti′vally,** *adv.*

infinitive (ĭn fĭn′ĭ tĭv), *Gram.* —*n.* **1.** (in many languages) a noun form derived from verbs, which names the action or state without specifying the subject, as Latin *esse* to be, *fuisse* to have been. **2.** (in English) the simple form of the verb (*come, take, eat*) used after certain other verbs (I didn't *come*), or this simple form preceded by *to* (the **marked infinitive,** I wanted *to come*). —*adj.* **3.** of or pertaining to the infinitive or its meaning. [late ME, t. LL: m. s. *infīnītīvus* unlimited, indefinite] —**infin′itively,** *adv.*

infinitude (ĭn fĭn′ĭ tyo͞od′), *n.* **1.** infinity: *divine infinitude.* **2.** an infinite extent, amount, or number.

infinity (ĭn fĭn′ĭ tĭ), *n.*, *pl.* **-ties. 1.** the state of being infinite: *the infinity of God.* **2.** that which is infinite. **3.** infinite space, time, or quantity: *any time short of infinity.* **4.** an infinite extent, amount, or number. **5.** an indefinitely great amount or number. **6.** *Maths.* **a.** the concept of increasing without bound. **b.** infinite distance, or an infinitely distant part of space. **7.** *Photog.* a distance between the subject and the camera lens sufficiently large for all the light rays reflected by the subject to be regarded as parallel. [ME *infinite*, t. L: m. s. *infīnitās*]

infirm (ĭn fûm′), *adj.* **1.** feeble in body or health. **2.** not steadfast, unfaltering, or resolute, as persons, the mind, etc.: *infirm of purpose.* **3.** not firm, solid, or strong: *an infirm support.* **4.** unsound or invalid, as an argument, a title, etc. —*v.t.* **5.** *Archaic.* to invalidate. [ME, t. L: s. *infirmus*] —**infirm′ly,** *adv.* —**infirm′ness,** *n.*

infirmary (ĭn fû′mə rĭ), *n.*, *pl.* **-ries.** a place for the care of the infirm, sick, or injured; a hospital. [t. ML: m. s. *infirmāria*, der. L *infirmus* infirm]

infirmity (ĭn fû′mĭ tĭ), *n.*, *pl.* **-ties. 1.** a physical weakness or ailment: *the infirmities of age.* **2.** the state of being infirm; lack of strength. **3.** a moral weakness or failing. [ME *infirmyte*, t. L: m. s. *infirmitas*]

infix (*v.* ĭn fĭks′; *n.* ĭn′fĭks′), *v.t.* **1.** to fix, fasten, or drive in: *he infixed the fatal spear.* **2.** to implant: *the habits they infixed.* **3.** to fix in the mind or memory, as a fact or idea; impress. **4.** *Gram.* to add as an infix. —*v.i.* **5.** *Gram.* (of a linguistic form) to admit an infix. —*n.* **6.** *Gram.* an affix which is inserted within the body of the element to which it is added, as Latin *m* in *accumbō* I lie down, as compared with *accubuī* I lay down. [t. L: s. *infixus*, pp., fastened in] —**infix′ion,** *n.*

in flagrante delicto (ĭn′flə grăn′tĭ dĭ lĭk′tō), *Latin.* in the very act of committing the offence.

inflame (ĭn flām′), *v.*, **-flamed, -flaming.** —*v.t.* **1.** to set aflame or afire. **2.** to light or redden with or as with flames: *the setting sun inflames the sky.* **3.** to kindle or excite (passions, desires, etc.). **4.** to arouse to a high degree of passion or feeling. **5.** to cause to redden through anger, rage, or some other emotion. **6.** to make more violent. **7.** to excite inflammation in: *her eyes were inflamed with crying.* **8.** to raise (the blood, bodily tissue, etc.) to a morbid or feverish heat. —*v.i.* **9.** to burst into flame; take fire. **10.** to be kindled, as passion. **11.** to become hot with passion, as the heart. **12.** to become morbidly affected with inflammation. [ME *enflame(n)*, t. OF: m. *enflamer*, g. L *inflammāre* set on fire] —**inflam′er,** *n.* —**inflam′ingly,** *adv.* —**Syn. 1.** See **kindle.**

inflammable (ĭn flăm′ə bl), *adj.* **1.** capable of being set on fire; combustible. **2.** easily roused to passion; excitable. —*n.* **3.** something inflammable. —**inflam′mabil′ity, inflam′mableness,** *n.* —**inflam′mably,** *adv.*

inflammation (ĭn′flə mā′shən), *n.* **1.** the act of inflaming. **2.** the state of being inflamed. **3.** *Pathol.* a reaction of the body to injurious agents, commonly characterized by heat, redness, swelling, pain, etc., and disturbed function.

inflammatory (ĭn flăm′ə tə rĭ, -trĭ), *adj.* **1.** tending to inflame; kindling passion, anger, etc.: *inflammatory speeches.* **2.** *Pathol.* pertaining to or attended with inflammation. —**inflam′matorily,** *adv.*

inflate (ĭn flāt′), *v.*, **-flated, -flating.** —*v.t.* **1.** to distend; swell or puff out; dilate. **2.** to distend with gas: *inflate a balloon.* **3.** to puff up with pride, satisfaction, etc. **4.** to elate. **5.** to expand (currency, prices, etc.) unduly; raise above the previous or proper amount or value. —*v.i.* **6.** to cause inflation. **7.** to become inflated. [t. L: m. s. *inflātus*, pp., puffed up] —**infla′table,** *adj.* —**infla′tor,** *n.* —**Syn. 1.** See **expand.**

inflated (ĭn flā′tĭd), *adj.* **1.** distended with air or gas; swollen. **2.** puffed up, as with pride. **3.** turgid or bombastic, as language. **4.** resulting from inflation: *inflated values of land.* **5.** unduly expanded, as currency. **6.** *Bot.* hollow or swelled out with air: *inflated perianth.* —**infla′tedness,** *n.*

inflation (ĭn flā′shən), *n.* **1.** undue expansion or increase of the currency of a country, esp. by the issuing of paper money not redeemable in specie. **2.** a substantial rise of prices caused by an undue expansion in paper money or bank credit. **3.** the act of inflating. **4.** the state of being inflated.

inflationary (ĭn flā′shə nə rĭ), *adj.* of or causing inflation: *inflationary legislation.*

inflationism (ĭn flā′shə nĭz′əm), *n.* the policy or practice of inflation through expansion of currency or bank deposits.

inflationist (ĭn flā′shə nĭst), *n.* an advocate of inflation through expansion of currency or bank deposits.

inflect (ĭn flĕkt′), *v.t.* **1.** to bend; turn from a direct line or course. **2.** to modulate (the voice). **3.** *Gram.* **a.** to apply inflection to (a word). **b.** to recite or display all, or a distinct set of, the inflections of (a word), in a fixed order: *to inflect Latin* '*amō*' as '*amō, amās, amat*', *etc., or* '*nauta*' *as* '*nauta, nautae, nautae, nautam, nautā*', etc. **4.** *Bot.* to bend in. —*v.i.* **5.** *Gram.* to be characterized by inflection. [ME *inflecte(n)*, t. L: m. *inflectere* bend] —**inflec′tive,** *adj.* —**inflec′tor,** *n.*

inflection (ĭn flĕk′shən), *n.* **1.** modulation of the voice; change in pitch or tone of voice. **2.** *Gram.* **a.** the existence in a language of sets of forms built normally on a single stem, having different syntactic functions and meanings, but all those of a single stem being members of the same fundamental part of speech and constituting forms of the same 'word'. **b.** the set of forms of a single word, or a recital or display thereof in a fixed order. **c.** a single pattern of formation of such sets, as *noun inflection, verb inflection.* **d.** a change in the form of a word, generally by affixation, by means of which a change of meaning or relationship to some other word or group of words is indicated. **e.** the affix added to the stem to produce this change. For example: the *-s* in *dogs* and *-ed* in *played* are inflections. **3.** a bend or angle. **4.** *Maths.* a change of curvature from convex to concave or vice versa. Also, **inflexion.** —**inflec′tional,** *adj.* —**inflec′tionally,** *adv.* —**inflec′tionless,** *adj.*

inflection point, *Maths.* a point of inflection on a curve.

inflexed (ĭn flĕkst′), *adj. Bot., Zool.* inflected; bent or folded downwards or inwards: *an inflexed leaf.*

inflexible (ĭn flĕk′sə bl), *adj.* **1.** not flexible; rigid: *an inflexible rod.* **2.** unyielding in temper or purpose: *inflexible to threats.* **3.** unalterable; not permitting variation. [ME, t. L: m. s. *inflexibilis.* See IN-³, FLEXIBLE] —**inflex′ibil′ity, inflex′ibleness,** *n.* —**inflex′ibly,** *adv.*

—**Syn. 2.** INFLEXIBLE, RELENTLESS, IMPLACABLE, INEXORABLE imply having the quality of not being turned from a purpose.

INFLEXIBLE means unbending, adhering undeviatingly to a set plan, purpose, or the like: *inflexible to interpretation of rules, an inflexible will.* RELENTLESS suggests such a pitiless and unremitting following of purpose as to convey a sense of inevitableness: *as relentless as the passing of time.* IMPLACABLE means incapable of being placated or appeased: *implacable in wrath.* INEXORABLE means stern, rigorous, and unmoved by prayer or entreaty: *inexorable in demanding payment.* **—Ant.** 2. pliant.

inflexion (ĭn flĕk′shən), *n.* inflection. **—inflex′ional,** *adj.* **—inflex′ionally,** *adv.* **—inflex′ionless,** *adj.*

inflict (ĭn flĭkt′), *v.t.* **1.** to lay on: *to inflict a dozen lashes.* **2.** to impose as something that must be borne or suffered: *to inflict punishment.* **3.** to impose (anything unwelcome). [t. L: s. *inflictus*, pp., struck against] **—inflic′tor,** *n.* **—inflic′tive,** *adj.*

infliction (ĭn flĭk′shən), *n.* **1.** the act of inflicting. **2.** something inflicted, as punishment, suffering, etc.

inflorescence (ĭn′flô rĕs′əns), *n.* **1.** a flowering or blossoming. **2.** *Bot.* **a.** the arrangement of flowers on the axis. **b.** the flowering part of a plant. **c.** a flower cluster. **d.** flowers collectively. **e.** a single flower. [t. NL: m. s. *inflōrescentia*, der. LL *inflōrescens*, ppr., coming into flower] **—in′flores′cent,** *adj.*

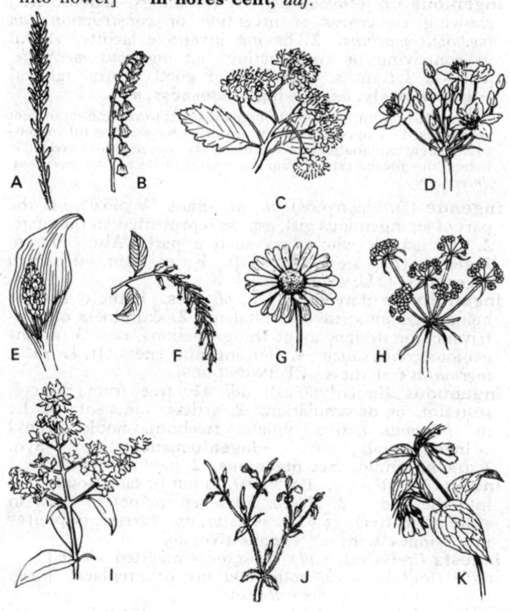

Forms of inflorescence

A, Spike of plantain, genus *Plantago*; B, Raceme of lily-of-the-valley, genus *Convallaria*; C. Corymb of white beam, *Sorbus aria*; D, Umbel of flowering rush, genus *Butonus*; E, Spadix within the spathe of calla, *Calla palustris*; F, Female catkin of willow, genus *Salix*; G, Capitulum of moon daisy, *Chrysanthemum leucanthemum*; H, Compound umbel of water-parsnip, *Sium latifolium*; I, Panicle of privet, genus *Ligustrum*; J, Dichasial cyme of chickweed, genus *Stellaria*; K, Cincinnus of comphrey, genus *Symphytum*

inflow (ĭn′flō′), *n.* that which flows in; influx.

influence (ĭn′flōō əns), *n., v.,* **-enced, -encing.** **—***n.* **1.** invisible or insensible action exerted by one thing or person on another. **2.** power of producing effects by invisible or insensible means: *spheres of influence.* **3.** a thing or person that exerts action by invisible or insensible means: *beneficial influences.* **4.** *Astrol.* **a.** the supposed radiation of an ethereal fluid from the stars, regarded in astrology as affecting human actions and destinies, etc. **b.** the exercise of occult power by the stars, or such power as exercised. **5.** *Poetic.* the exercise of similar power by human beings. **6.** *Obs.* electrostatic induction. **7.** *Obs.* influx. **—***v.t.* **8.** to exercise influence on; modify, affect, or sway: *to influence a person by bribery.* **9.** to move or impel to, or to do, something. [ME, t. ML: m. s. *influentia*, lit., a flowing in, der. L *influens* influent] **—in′fluencer,** *n.* **—Syn.** **2.** sway, rule. See **authority.**

influent (ĭn′flōō ənt), *adj.* **1.** flowing in. **—***n.* **2.** a tributary. [ME, t. L: s. *influens*, ppr., flowing in]

influential (ĭn′flōō ĕn′shəl), *adj.* having or exerting influence, esp. great influence. [f. s. ML *influentia* INFLUENCE + -AL[1]] **—in′fluen′tially,** *adv.*

influenza (ĭn′flōō ĕn′zə), *n.* **1.** *Pathol.* an acute, extremely contagious, commonly epidemic disease characterized by general prostration, and occurring in several forms with varying symptoms, usually with nasal catarrh and bronchial inflammation, and due to a specific virus; grippe. **2.** *Vet. Sci.* an acute, contagious disease occurring in horses and swine, manifested by fever, depression, and catarrhal inflammations of the eyes, nasal passages, and bronchi. [t. It.: influx of disease, epidemic, influenza. See INFLUENCE] **—in′fluen′zal,** *adj.* **—in′fluen′za-like′,** *adj.*

influx (ĭn′flŭks′), *n.* **1.** the act of flowing in; an inflow. **2.** the place or point at which one stream flows into another or into the sea. **3.** the mouth of a stream. **4.** the arrival of people or things in large numbers or great quantity. [t. LL: s. *influxus*, der. L *influere* flow in]

infold (ĭn fōld′), *v.t.* *Chiefly U.S.* **1.** to enfold. **2.** to fold in. **—infold′er,** *n.* **—infold′ment,** *n.*

inform[1] (ĭn fôm′), *v.t.* **1.** to impart knowledge of a fact or circumstance to: *I informed him of my arrival.* **2.** to supply (oneself) with knowledge of a matter or subject: *he informed himself of all the pertinent facts.* **3.** to give character to; pervade with determining effect on the character. **4.** to animate or inspire. **5.** *Obs.* to train or instruct. **6.** *Obs.* to make known; disclose. **7.** *Obs.* to impart form to. **—***v.i.* **8.** to give information, esp. to furnish incriminating evidence to a prosecuting officer. [t. L: s. *infōrmāre*; r. ME *enforme*, t. OF] **—inform′ingly,** *adv.* **—Syn.** **1.** apprise; notify, advise, tell. **2.** acquaint.

inform[2] (ĭn fôm′), *adj.* without form; formless. [t. L: s. *informis* shapeless. See IN-[3]]

informal (ĭn fô′məl), *adj.* **1.** not according to prescribed or customary forms; irregular: *informal proceedings.* **2.** without formality; unceremonious: *an informal visit.* **3.** not requiring formal dress: *an informal dinner.* **4.** denoting speech characterized by colloquial usage, having the flexibility of grammar, syntax, and pronunciation allowable in conversation. **5.** characterizing the second singular pronominal or verbal form, or its use, in certain languages: *the informal 'tu' in French.* **—infor′mally,** *adv.* **—Syn.** **4.** See **colloquial.**

informality (ĭn′fô măl′ĭ tĭ), *n., pl.* **-ties.** **1.** the state of being informal; absence of formality. **2.** an informal act.

informant (ĭn fô′mənt), *n.* one who informs or gives information.

information (ĭn′fə mā′shən), *n.* **1.** knowledge communicated or received concerning some fact or circumstance; news. **2.** knowledge on various subjects, however acquired. **3.** the act of informing. **4.** the state of being informed. **5.** *Law.* **a.** an official criminal charge presented, usually by the prosecuting officers of the state. **b.** a criminal charge made under oath, before a justice of the peace, of an offence punishable summarily. **6.** (in communication theory) a quantitative measure of the contents of a message. [t. L: s. *infōrmātio*; r. ME *enformacion*, t. OF] **—in′forma′tional,** *adj.*

—Syn. **2.** INFORMATION, KNOWLEDGE, WISDOM are terms for human acquirements through reading, study, and practical experience. INFORMATION applies to facts told, read, communicated, which may be unorganized and even unrelated: *to pick up useful information.* KNOWLEDGE is an organized body of information, or the comprehension and understanding consequent on having acquired and organized a body of facts: *a knowledge of chemistry.* WISDOM is a knowledge of people, life, and conduct, with the facts so thoroughly assimilated as to have produced sagacity, judgement, and insight: *to use wisdom in handling people.* **—Ant.** **2.** ignorance.

information theory, *Telecom.* the theory of coding and transmitting messages over channels subject to interference.

informative (ĭn fô′mə tĭv), *adj.* affording information; instructive: *an informative book.* Also, **informatory** (ĭn fô′mə tə rĭ, -trĭ).

informer (ĭn fô′mə), *n.* **1.** one who furnishes incriminating evidence to a prosecuting officer. **2.** an informant.

infortune (ĭn fô′chən), *n.* **1.** *Astrol.* a planet or aspect of evil influence, esp. Saturn or Mars. **2.** *Obs.* misfortune. [ME, t. F. See IN-[3], FORTUNE]

infra (ĭn′frə), *adv.* *Latin.* below (in a text). Cf. **supra.**

infra-, a prefix meaning 'below' or 'beneath', as in *infraaxillary* (below the axilla). [t. L, repr. *infrā*, adv. and prep., below, beneath]

infracostal (ĭn′frə kŏs′tl), *adj.* below the ribs.

infract (ĭn frăkt′), *v.t.* to break; violate or infringe. [t. L: s. *infractus*, pp., broken off] **—infrac′tor,** *n.*

infraction (ĭn frăk′shən), *n.* breach; violation; infringement: *an infraction of a treaty or law.*

infra dig (ĭn′frə dĭg′), *Colloq.* beneath one's dignity. [abbrev. L *infra dignitatem*]

infralapsarian (ĭn′frə lăp sēə′rĭ ən), *n.* **1.** one who believes in infralapsarianism. **—***adj.* **2.** pertaining to infralapsarianism or those who hold it. [f. INFRA- + s. L *lapsus* a fall + -ARIAN]

infralapsarianism (ĭn′frə lăp sēə′rĭ ə nĭz′əm), *n.* *Theol.* the primitive doctrine adopted by the Calvinists from

St Augustine's writings, that God planned the creation, permitted the fall, elected a chosen number, planned their redemption, and suffered the remainder to be eternally punished as a preconceived overall plan for the universe.

infrangible (ĭn frăn′jĭ bl), *adj.* **1.** unbreakable. **2.** inviolable. —**infran′gibil′ity, infran′gibleness,** *n.* —**infran′gibly,** *adv.*

infra-red (ĭn′frə rĕd′), *n.* **1.** the part of the invisible spectrum contiguous to the red end of the visible spectrum, comprising radiation of greater wavelength than that of red light. —*adj.* **2.** denoting or pertaining to the infra-red or its component rays: *infra-red radiation.*

infrasonic (ĭn′frə sŏn′ĭk), *adj.* of velocities, approximately equal to the velocity of sound in the medium.

infrequency (ĭn frē′kwən sĭ), *n.* the state of being infrequent. Also, **infre′quence.**

infrequent (ĭn frē′kwənt), *adj.* **1.** happening or occurring at long intervals or not often: *infrequent visits.* **2.** not constant, habitual, or regular: *an infrequent visitor.* **3.** not plentiful. —**infre′quently,** *adv.*

infringe (ĭn frĭnj′), *v.*, **-fringed, -fringing.** —*v.t.* **1.** to commit a breach or infraction of; violate or transgress. —*v.i.* **2.** to encroach or trespass (fol. by *on* or *upon*): *don't infringe on his privacy.* [t. L: m. s. *infringere* break off] —**infring′er,** *n.* —**Syn. 2.** See **trespass.**

infringement (ĭn frĭnj′mənt), *n.* **1.** a breach or infraction, as of a law, right, or obligation; violation; transgression. **2.** the act of infringing.

infundibuliform (ĭn′fŭn dĭb′yo͝o lĭ fôm′), *adj. Bot.* funnel-shaped.

infundibulum (ĭn′fŭn dĭb′yo͝o ləm), *n., pl.* **-la** (-lə). **1.** a funnel-shaped organ or part. **2.** *Anat.* **a.** a funnel-shaped extension of the cerebrum connecting the pituitary body to the base of the brain. **b.** a space in the right auricle at the root of the pulmonary artery. [t. L: funnel] —**infundibular** (ĭn′fŭn dĭb′yo͝o lə), **infundibulate** (ĭn′fŭn-dĭb′yo͝o lĭt, -lāt′), *adj.*

Infundibuliform corolla of morning-glory, *Ipomoea purpurea*

infuriate (*v.* ĭn fyo͝oə′rĭ āt′; *adj.* ĭn fyo͝oə′rĭ ĭt), *v.*, **-ated, -ating,** *adj.* —*v.t.* **1.** to make furious; enrage. —*adj.* **2.** *Archaic.* infuriated. [t. ML: m. s. *infuriātus*, pp., enraged] —**infu′riately,** *adv.* —**infu′riat′ingly,** *adv.* —**infu′ria′tion,** *n.* —**Syn. 1.** See **enrage.**

infuscate (ĭn fŭs′kāt), *adj. Entomol.* darkened with a fuscous or brownish shade. Also, **infus′cated.** [t. L: m. s. *infuscātus*, pp., darkened]

infuse (ĭn fyo͞oz′), *v.t.*, **-fused, -fusing. 1.** to introduce as by pouring; cause to penetrate; instil (fol. by *into*). **2.** to imbue or inspire (*with*). **3.** to pour in. **4.** to steep or soak (a plant, etc.) in a liquid so as to extract its soluble properties or ingredients. **5.** *Cookery.* to boil slowly in a solution. [ME, t. L: m. s. *infūsus*, pp., poured in or on] —**infus′er,** *n.*

infusible[1] (ĭn fyo͞o′zə bl), *adj.* not fusible; incapable of being fused or melted. [f. IN-[3] + FUSIBLE] —**infu′sibil′ity, infu′sibleness,** *n.*

infusible[2] (ĭn fyo͞o′zə bl), *adj.* capable of being infused. [f. INFUSE, v. + -IBLE]

infusion (ĭn fyo͞o′zhən), *n.* **1.** the act of infusing. **2.** that which is infused. **3.** a liquid extract obtained from a substance by steeping or soaking it in water. **4.** *Med.* **a.** the introduction of a saline or other solution into a vein, artery, or tissue. **b.** the solution used.

infusionism (ĭn fyo͞o′zhə nĭz′əm), *n. Theol.* the doctrine that at birth a pre-existent soul is planted in the human body for its earthly lifetime. —**infu′sionist,** *n.*

infusive (ĭn fyo͞o′sĭv), *adj.* infusing.

infusorial (ĭn′fyo͞o zô′rĭ əl), *adj.* containing or consisting of infusorians: *infusorial earth.*

infusorian (ĭn′fyo͞o zô′rĭ ən), *n. Biol.* **1.** any protozoan of the class *Infusoria*, mostly microscopic and aquatic, having vibratile cilia. **2.** *Obs.* any of a miscellaneous variety of minute or microscopic animal and vegetable organisms (constituting the old group *Infusoria*) frequently developed in infusions of decaying organic matter. —*adj.* **3.** of, denoting, or pertaining to the *Infusoria.* [f. NL *Infusori(a)* (der. L *infusus*, pp., poured in) + -AN]

in futuro (ĭn′fyo͞o tyo͝oə′rō), *Latin.* in the future.

-ing[1], a suffix of nouns formed from verbs, expressing the action of the verb or its result, product, material, etc., as in *the art of building, a new building, cotton wadding.* It is also used to form nouns from words other than verbs, as in *offing, shirting.* Verbal nouns ending in *-ing* are often used attributively, as in *the printing trade*, and in composition, as in *drinking song.* In some compounds, as *sewing machine*, the first element might reasonably be regarded as the participial adjective (see **-ing**[2]), the compound thus meaning 'a machine that sews': but it is commonly taken as a verbal noun, the compound being explained as 'a machine for sewing'. [ME *-ing*, OE *-ing, -ung*]

-ing[2], a suffix forming the present participle of verbs, such participles often being used as adjectives (participial adjectives), as in *warring factions.* Cf. **-ing**[1]. [ME *-ing, -inge*; r. ME *-inde, -ende*, OE *-ende*]

ingather (ĭn găth′ə), *v.t.* to gather in; collect; bring in, as a harvest. —**ingath′erer,** *n.*

Inge (ĭng), *n.* **William Ralph,** 1860–1954, English writer; dean of St Paul's Cathedral 1911–34.

ingeminate (ĭn jĕm′ĭ nāt′), *v.t.*, **-nated, -nating.** to repeat; reiterate. [t. L: m. s. *ingemĭnātus*, pp., redoubled] —**ingem′ina′tion,** *n.*

ingenerate[1] (ĭn jĕn′ə rĭt), *adj.* not generated; self-existent. [t. LL: m. s. *ingenerātus.* See IN-[3]]

ingenerate[2] (*v.* ĭn jĕn′ə rāt′; *adj.* ĭn jĕn′ə rĭt), *v.*, **-rated, -rating,** *adj. Archaic.* —*v.t.* **1.** to engender. —*adj.* **2.** inborn; innate. [t. L: m. s. *ingenerātus*, pp., generated within. See IN-[2]] —**ingen′era′tion,** *n.*

ingenious (ĭn jē′nyəs), *adj.* **1.** (of things, actions, etc.) showing cleverness of invention or construction: *an ingenious machine.* **2.** having inventive faculty; skilful in contriving or constructing: *an ingenious mechanic.* [ME, t. L: m. s. *ingeniōsus* of good natural talents] —**inge′niously,** *adv.* —**inge′niousness,** *n.*

—**Syn. 2.** INGENIOUS, INGENUOUS are distinct words and should not be confused. INGENIOUS means inventive or resourceful in contriving new explanations or methods, etc.: *an ingenious executive.* INGENUOUS means candid, free from guile or deceit: *an ingenuous, sincere reply.*

ingenue (ăn′zhā nyo͞o′), *n., pl.* **-nues** (-nyo͞oz′). **1.** the part of an ingenuous girl, esp. as represented on the stage. **2.** the actress who plays such a part. Also, *French,* **ingénue** (*Fr.* ăɴ zhĕ nʏ′). [t. F: m. fem. of *ingénu* ingenuous, t. L: s. *ingenuus*]

ingenuity (ĭn′jĭ nyo͞o′ĭ tĭ), *n., pl.* **-ties. 1.** the quality of being ingenious; inventive talent. **2.** skilfulness of contrivance or design, as of things, actions, etc. **3.** an ingenious contrivance. **4.** *Obs.* ingenuousness. [t. L: m. s. *ingenuitas* frankness. Cf. INGENUOUS]

ingenuous (ĭn jĕn′yo͝o əs), *adj.* **1.** free from reserve, restraint, or dissimulation. **2.** artless; innocent. [t. L: m. *ingenuus* native, innate, freeborn, noble, frank] —**ingen′uously,** *adv.* —**ingen′uousness,** *n.* —**Syn. 1.** frank, candid. See **ingenious. 2.** naive, guileless.

ingest (ĭn jĕst′), *v.t.* **1.** *Physiol.* to put or take (food, etc.) into the body. **2.** *Aeron.* (of a jet engine) to draw in (foreign matter). [t. L: s. *ingestus*, pp., carried, or poured in] —**inges′tion,** *n.* —**inges′tive,** *adj.*

ingesta (ĭn jĕs′tə), *n.pl.* substances ingested. [t. L]

ingle (ĭng′gl), *n.* a household fire or fireplace. [orig. uncert. Cf. Gaelic *aingeal* fire]

inglenook (ĭng′gl no͝ok′), *n.* a corner by the fire.

ingleside (ĭng′gl sīd′), *n. Dial.* a fireside.

inglorious (ĭn glô′rĭ əs), *adj.* **1.** shameful; disgraceful: *inglorious flight.* **2.** *Archaic.* not famous. —**inglo′riously,** *adv.* —**inglo′riousness,** *n.*

ingoing (ĭn′gō′ĭng), *adj.* **1.** going in; entering. —*n.* **2.** *Law.* expense incurred in the purchase of fixtures, etc., left by a previous tenant.

Ingolstadt (*Ger.* ĭng′gŏl shtȧt), *n.* a town in West Germany, in central Bavaria. 69,200 (est. 1966).

ingot (ĭng′gət), *n.* **1.** the casting obtained when melted metal is poured into a mould (**ingot mould**) with the expectation that it be further processed. **2.** a cast metal mass, formed by rolling, etc., or by smelting and casting to shape. —*v.t.* **3.** to make ingots of; shape into ingots. [ME: mould for metal. Cf. OE *ingyte* pouring in]

ingot iron, *Metall.* a very low carbon steel, usually made in an open hearth furnace, containing only very small quantities of other elements.

ingrain (*v.* ĭn grān′; *adj., n.* ĭn′grān′), *v.t.* **1.** to fix deeply and firmly, as in the nature or mind. —*adj.* **2.** ingrained. **3.** (of carpets) made of yarn dyed before weaving, and so woven as to show the pattern on both sides. **4.** dyed in grain, or through the fibre. **5.** dyed in the yarn, or in a raw state, before manufacture. —*n.* **6.** yarn, wool, etc., dyed before manufacture. **7.** an ingrain carpet. Also, **engrain** for 1, 2.

ingrained (ĭn grānd′, ĭn′grānd′), *adj.* **1.** fixed firmly; deep-rooted: *ingrained habits.* **2.** inveterate; thorough.

ingrate (ĭn grāt′), *Archaic.* —*n.* **1.** an ungrateful person. —*adj.* **2.** ungrateful. [ME, t. L: m. s. *ingrātus* unpleasing, not grateful]

ingratiate (ĭn grā′shĭ āt′), *v.t.*, **-ated, -ating.** to establish (oneself) in the favour or good graces of others. [f. IN-[2] + s. L *grātia* favour, grace + -ATE[1]] —**ingra′tiat′ingly,** *adv.* —**ingra′tia′tion,** *n.*

ingratiatory (ĭn grā′shyə tə rĭ, -trĭ), *adj.* serving or intended to ingratiate.

ingratitude (ĭn grăt′ĭ tyōōd′), *n.* the state of being ungrateful; unthankfulness.

ingravescent (ĭn′grə vĕs′ənt), *adj. Pathol.* increasing in severity, as a disease. [t. L: s. *ingravescens*, ppr., growing heavier] —**in′graves′cence,** *n.*

ingredient (ĭn grē′dyənt), *n.* **1.** something that enters as an element into a mixture: *the ingredients of a cake.* **2.** a constituent element of anything. [late ME, t. L: s. *ingrediens*, ppr., entering] —**Syn. 1.** See **element.**

Ingres (*Fr.* ăɴ′gr), *n.* **Jean Auguste Dominique** (*Fr.* zhäɴ ȯ gʏst dŏ mē nĕk′), 1780–1867, French painter.

ingress (ĭn′grĕs), *n.* **1.** the act of going in or entering. **2.** the right of going in. **3.** a means or place of going in; an entrance. [ME, t. L: s. *ingressus* entrance] —**ingres′sion,** *n.* —**ingres′sive,** *adj.* —**ingres′siveness,** *n.*

in-group (ĭn′grōōp′), *n. Sociol.* a group reserving favourable treatment and acceptance to its own members and denying them to members of other groups.

ingrowing (ĭn′grō′ĭng), *adj.* **1.** growing into the flesh: *an ingrowing toenail.* **2.** growing within or inwards.

ingrown (ĭn′grōn′), *adj.* **1.** having grown into the flesh. **2.** grown within or inwards.

ingrowth (ĭn′grōth′), *n.* **1.** growth inwards. **2.** something formed by growth inwards.

inguinal (ĭng′gwĭ nəl), *adj.* of, pertaining to, or situated in the groin. [t. L: s. *inguinālis*]

ingulf (ĭn gŭlf′), *v.t.* engulf.

ingurgitate (ĭn gû′jĭ tāt′), *v.*, **-tated, -tating.** —*v.t.* **1.** to swallow greedily or in great quantity, as food. **2.** to engulf. —*v.i.* **3.** to drink largely; swill. [t. L: m. s. *ingurgitātus*, pp., poured in] —**ingur′gita′tion,** *n.*

inhabit (ĭn hăb′ĭt), *v.t.* **1.** to live or dwell in (a place), as persons or animals. **2.** to have its seat, or exist, in. —*v.i.* **3.** *Archaic.* to live or dwell, as in a place. [t. L: s. *inhabitāre*; r. ME *enhabite*, t. F] —**inhab′itable,** *adj.* —**inhab′itabil′ity,** *n.* —**inhab′ita′tion,** *n.*

inhabitancy (ĭn hăb′ĭ tən sĭ), *n.*, *pl.* **-cies.** residence as an inhabitant. Also, **inhab′itance.**

inhabitant (ĭn hăb′ĭ tənt), *n.* a person or an animal that inhabits a place; a permanent resident. Also, *Obs.*, **inhab′iter.** [late ME, t. L: s. *inhabitans*, ppr., dwelling in]

inhalant (ĭn hā′lənt), *adj.* **1.** serving for inhalation. —*n.* **2.** an apparatus or medicine used for inhaling.

inhalation (ĭn′hə lā′shən), *n.* **1.** the act of inhaling. **2.** a medicinal preparation to be inhaled.

inhalator (ĭn′hə lā′tə), *n.* an apparatus to help one inhale air, anaesthetic, medicinal vapours, etc.

inhale (ĭn hāl′), *v.*, **-haled, -haling.** —*v.t.* **1.** to breathe in; draw in by, or as by, breathing: *to inhale air.* —*v.i.* **2.** to draw into the lungs, esp. smoke of cigarettes, cigars, etc.: *do you inhale?* [t. L: m. s. *inhālāre*]

inhaler (ĭn hā′lə), *n.* **1.** an apparatus used in inhaling medicinal vapours, anaesthetics, etc. **2.** one who inhales.

Inhambane (*Port.* ē nyəm bə′nə), *n.* a seaport in SE Mozambique. 67,265 (1960).

inharmonic (ĭn′hä mŏn′ĭk), *adj.* not harmonic.

inharmonious (ĭn′hä mō′nyəs), *adj.* **1.** not harmonious; discordant. **2.** not congenial; disagreeable. [f. IN-[3] + HARMONIOUS] —**in′harmo′niously,** *adv.* —**in′harmo′niousness,** *n.*

inhaul (ĭn′hôl′), *n. Naut.* a rope for hauling in a sail or spar. Also, **in′haul′er.**

inhere (ĭn hĭə′), *v.i.*, **-hered, -hering.** to exist permanently and inseparably (in), as a quality, attribute, or element; belong intrinsically; be inherent. [t. L: m. s. *inhaerēre* stick in or to]

inherence (ĭn hĭə′rəns), *n.* **1.** the state or fact of inhering or being inherent. **2.** *Philos.* the relation of an attribute to its subject.

inherency (ĭn hĭə′rən sĭ), *n.*, *pl.* **-cies. 1.** inherence. **2.** something inherent.

inherent (ĭn hĭə′rənt), *adj.* **1.** existing in something as a permanent and inseparable element, quality, or attribute. **2.** *Gram.* standing before a noun. **3.** *Obs.* inhering; infixed. [t. L: m. s. *inhaerens*, ppr., sticking in or to] —**inher′ently,** *adv.* —**Syn. 1.** See **essential.**

inherit (ĭn hĕ′rĭt), *v.t.* **1.** to take or receive (property, a right, a title, etc.) as the heir of the former owner. **2.** to succeed (a person) as heir. **3.** to receive (anything) as by succession from predecessors. **4.** to possess as a hereditary characteristic. **5.** to receive as one's portion. **6.** *Obs.* to make (one) heir (fol. by *of*). —*v.i.* **7.** to take or receive property, etc., as being heir to it. **8.** to have succession as heir. **9.** to receive qualities, powers, duties, etc., as by inheritance (fol. by *from*). [ME *enherite(n)*, t. OF: m. *enheriter*, f. *en-* EN-[1] + *heriter* (g. L *hērēditāre* inherit)]

inheritable (ĭn hĕ′rĭ tə bl), *adj.* **1.** capable of being inherited. **2.** capable of inheriting; qualified to inherit. —**inher′itabil′ity, inher′itableness,** *n.* —**inher′itably,** *adv.*

inheritance (ĭn hĕ′rĭ təns), *n.* **1.** that which is or may be inherited; any property passing at the owner's death to the heir or those entitled to succeed. **2.** a hereditary characteristic or characteristics collectively. **3.** anything received from progenitors or predecessors as if by succession: *an inheritance of family pride.* **4.** portion, peculiar possession, or heritage: *the inheritance of the saints.* **5.** the act or fact of inheriting: *to receive property by inheritance.* **6.** *Obs.* the right of inheriting.

—**Syn. 1.** INHERITANCE, HERITAGE denote something inherited. INHERITANCE is the common term for property or any possession that comes to an heir: *an inheritance from one's parents, a farm came to him by inheritance.* HERITAGE, a dignified or literary word, indicates whatever is bequeathed to a subsequent generation by an individual or by society: *our heritage from Greece and Rome.*

inherited (ĭn hĕ′rĭ tĭd), *adj.* **1.** received by inheritance. **2.** *Gram.* found also in an earlier stage of the same language, esp. in the earliest reconstructed stage.

inheritor (ĭn hĕ′rĭ tə), *n.* one who inherits; heir. —**inheritress** (ĭn hĕ′rĭ trĭs), *n. fem.*

inheritrix (ĭn hĕ′rĭ trĭks), *n.*, *pl.* **inheritrices** (ĭn hĕ′rĭ trī′sēz), a female inheritor.

inhesion (ĭn hē′zhən), *n.* the state or fact of inhering; inherence. [t. LL: m. s. *inhaesio*]

inhibit (ĭn hĭb′ĭt), *v.t.* **1.** to restrain, hinder, arrest, or check (an action, impulse, etc.). **2.** to prohibit; forbid. **3.** *Chem.* to decrease the rate of a chemical reaction or to stop it completely. [late ME, t. L: s. *inhibitus*, pp., held back, restrained] —**inhib′iter,** *n.* —**Syn. 2.** See **forbid.**

inhibition (ĭn′ĭ bĭsh′ən, ĭn′hĭ-), *n.* **1.** the act of inhibiting. **2.** the state of being inhibited. **3.** *Psychol.* the blocking of any psychological process by another psychological process. **4.** *Physiol.* a restraining, arresting, or checking, as of action: **a.** the reduction of a reflex or other activity as the result of an antagonistic stimulation. **b.** a state created at synapses making them less excitable to other sources of stimulation. **5.** *Eccles. Law.* the order by a bishop that a clergyman should cease from performing any duty.

inhibitor (ĭn hĭb′ĭ tə), *n.* **1.** *Chem.* a substance that retards or prevents a chemical reaction. **2.** an inhibiter.

inhibitory (ĭn hĭb′ĭ tə rĭ, -trĭ), *adj.* serving or tending to inhibit. Also, **inhib′itive.**

in hoc signo vinces (ĭn hŏk sĭg′nō vĭng′kēz), *Latin.* in this sign shalt thou conquer (motto used by Constantine the Great, from his vision of a cross with these words before battle).

inhospitable (ĭn hŏs′pĭ tə bl; *less often* ĭn′hŏs pĭt′ə bl), *adj.* **1.** not inclined to or characterized by hospitality, as persons, actions, etc. **2.** (of a region, climate, etc.) not offering shelter, favourable conditions, etc. —**inhos′pitableness,** *n.* —**inhos′pitably,** *adv.*

inhospitality (ĭn′hŏs pĭ tăl′ĭ tĭ, ĭn hŏs′-), *n.* lack of hospitality; inhospitable attitude towards visitors, etc.

inhuman (ĭn hyōō′mən), *adj.* **1.** lacking natural human feeling or sympathy for others; brutal. **2.** not human. [late ME *unhumayn*, t. L: m. s. *inhūmānus.* See IN-[3]] —**inhu′manly,** *adv.* —**inhu′manness,** *n.*

inhumane (ĭn′hyōō mān′), *adj.* not humane; lacking humanity or kindness. —**in′humane′ly,** *adv.*

inhumanity (ĭn′hyōō măn′ĭ tĭ), *n.*, *pl.* **-ties. 1.** the state or quality of being inhuman or inhumane; cruelty: *man's inhumanity to man.* **2.** an inhuman or inhumane act.

inhumation (ĭn′hyōō mā′shən), *n.* the act of inhuming, especially as opposed to cremation; burial.

inhume (ĭn hyōōm′), *v.t.*, **-humed, -huming.** to bury; inter. [t. L: m. s. *inhumāre* bury in the ground]

Inini (*Fr.* ē nē nē′), *n.* a dependent territory of S French Guiana, very little explored. 5000 pop. (est. 1965); 30,000 sq. mi.

inimical (ĭ nĭm′ĭ kl), *adj.* **1.** adverse in tendency or effect: *a climate inimical to health.* **2.** unfriendly or hostile. [t. LL: s. *inimīcālis*, der. L *inimīcus* unfriendly, an enemy] —**inim′ical′ity,** *n.* —**inim′ically,** *adv.* —**Syn. 1.** See **hostile.**

inimitable (ĭ nĭm′ĭ tə bl), *adj.* incapable of being imitated; surpassing imitation. —**inim′itabil′ity, inim′itableness,** *n.* —**inim′itably,** *adv.*

inion (ĭn′ĭ ən), *n. Anat.* a point at the external occipital protuberance of the skull. [t. NL, t. Gk: back of the head]

iniquitous (ĭ nĭk′wĭ təs), *adj.* characterized by iniquity. —**iniq′uitously,** *adv.* —**iniq′uitousness,** *n.*

iniquity (ĭ nĭk′wĭ tĭ), *n.*, *pl.* **-ties. 1.** gross injustice; wickedness. **2.** a violation of right or duty; wicked action; sin. [ME *iniquite*, t. L: m. s. *inīquitas* injustice]

init., initial.

initial (ĭ nĭsh′əl), *adj.*, *n.*, *v.*, **-ialled, -ialling** or (*U.S.*)

-ialed, -ialing. —*adj.* 1. of or pertaining to the beginning; incipient: *the initial step in a process.* 2. at the beginning of a word or syllable. —*n.* 3. an initial letter, as of a word. 4. the first letter of a proper name. 5. a letter of extra size or ornamental character used at the beginning of a chapter or other division of a book, etc. —*v.t.* 6. to mark or sign with an initial or initials, esp. as an indication of responsibility for or approval of the contents. [t. L: s. *initiālis* of the beginning] —**ini′tially,** *adv.*

initiate (*v.* ĭ nĭsh′ĭ āt′; *adj., n.* ĭ nĭsh′ĭ ĭt, -āt′), *v.*, **-ated, -ating,** *adj., n.* —*v.t.* 1. to begin, set going, or originate: *to initiate reforms.* 2. to introduce into the knowledge of some art or subject. 3. to admit with formal rites into secret knowledge, a society, etc. 4. to propose (a measure) by initiative procedure: *to initiate a constitutional amendment.* —*adj. Obsolesc.* 5. initiated; begun. 6. admitted into a society, etc., or into the knowledge of a subject. —*n.* 7. one who has been initiated. [t. L: m. s. *initiātus*, pp., begun, initiated] —**ini′tia′tor,** *n.* —**initiatress** (ĭ nĭsh′ĭ ā′trĭs), **initiatrix** (ĭ nĭsh′ĭ ā′trĭks), *n. fem.* —**Syn.** 1. commence; introduce, inaugurate. See **begin.** —**Ant.** 1. discontinue.

initiation (ĭ nĭsh′ĭ ā′shən), *n.* 1. formal admission into a society, etc. 2. the ceremony of admission. 3. the act of initiating. 4. the fact of being initiated.

initiative (ĭ nĭsh′ĭ ə tĭv), *n.* 1. an introductory act or step; leading action: *to take the initiative.* 2. readiness and ability in initiating action; enterprise: *to lack initiative.* 3. *Govt.* (in certain countries) **a.** a procedure by which a specified number of voters may propose a statute, constitutional amendment, or ordinance, and compel a popular vote on its adoption. **b.** the general right or ability to present a new bill or measure, as in a legislature. —*adj.* 4. serving to initiate; pertaining to initiation. —**ini′tiatively,** *adv.*

initiatory (ĭ nĭsh′ĭ ə tə rĭ, -trĭ), *adj.* 1. introductory; initial: *an initiatory step.* 2. serving to initiate or admit into a society, etc. —**ini′tiatorily,** *adv.*

inject (ĭn jĕkt′), *v.t.* 1. to force (a fluid) into a passage, cavity, or tissue. 2. to force a fluid into (a person, tissue, etc.) esp. for medical purposes. 3. to introduce (something new or different) into a thing: *to inject comedy into a situation.* 4. to introduce arbitrarily or inappropriately. 5. to interject (a remark, suggestion, etc.), as into conversation. [t. L: s. *injectus*, pp., thrown or put in]

injected (ĭn jĕk′tĭd), *adj. Med.* inflamed; reddened; hyperaemic; bloodshot.

injection (ĭn jĕk′shən), *n.* 1. the act of injecting. 2. that which is injected. 3. a liquid injected into the body, esp. for medical purposes, as a hypodermic or an enema. 4. the state of being hyperaemic or bloodshot. 5. fuel-injection.

injection moulding, a process for moulding thermoplastic materials by heating them and then injecting them under pressure into a cool closed mould.

injector (ĭn jĕk′tə), *n.* 1. one who or that which injects. 2. a device for forcing water into a steam boiler. 3. a device for spraying fuel into the cylinders of a compression-ignition engine.

injudicious (ĭn′jo͞o dĭsh′əs), *adj.* not judicious; showing lack of judgement; unwise; imprudent. —**in′judi′ciously,** *adv.* —**in′judi′ciousness,** *n.*

Injun (ĭn′jən), *n. Slang.* a North American Indian.

injunction (ĭn jŭngk′shən), *n.* 1. *Law.* a judicial process or order requiring the person or persons to whom it is directed to do or (more commonly) not to do a particular thing. 2. the act of enjoining. 3. that which is enjoined; a command, order or admonition. [t. LL: s. *injunctio* command] —**injunc′tive,** *adj.*

injure (ĭn′jə), *v.t.*, **-jured, -juring.** 1. to do or cause harm of any kind to; damage; hurt; impair: *to injure the hand.* 2. to do wrong or injustice to. [back-formation from INJURY, n., r. earlier *injury*, v.] —**in′jurer,** *n.*

—**Syn.** 1. INJURE, IMPAIR mean to harm or damage something. INJURE is a general term referring to any kind or degree of damage: *to injure one's spine, to injure one's reputation.* To IMPAIR is to make imperfect in any way, often with a suggestion of progressive deterioration and of permanency in the result: *one's health is impaired by addiction to drugs.* —**Ant.** 1. benefit.

injured (ĭn′jəd), *adj.* 1. harmed, damaged, or hurt. 2. offended; wronged: *an injured look.*

injurious (ĭn jo͝oə′rĭ əs), *adj.* 1. harmful, hurtful, or detrimental, as in effect: *injurious habits.* 2. doing or involving injury or wrong, as to another. 3. insulting or abusive. [late ME, t. L: m. s. *injūriōsus*, wrongful] —**inju′riously,** *adv.* —**inju′riousness,** *n.* —**Syn.** 1. deleterious, pernicious; baneful, destructive, ruinous. 2. unjust, wrongful, prejudicial. 3. offensive; derogatory, defamatory, slanderous. —**Ant.** 1. beneficial.

injury (ĭn′jə rĭ), *n., pl.* **-ries.** 1. harm of any kind done or sustained: *to escape without injury.* 2. a particular form or instance of harm: *severe bodily injuries.* 3. wrong or injustice done or suffered. 4. *Law.* a wrong or detriment caused by the deliberate or negligent act of another and actionable in a court of law. 5. *Obs.* injurious speech; calumny. [ME *injurie*, t. L: m. *injūria* wrong, harm, insult]

—**Syn.** 1-3. INJURY, HURT, WOUND refer to material or moral impairments or wrongs. INJURY, originally denoting a wrong done or suffered, is hence used for any kind of evil, impairment, or loss, caused or sustained: *physical injury, injury to one's reputation.* HURT suggests esp. physical injury, often bodily injury attended with pain: *a bad hurt from a fall.* A WOUND is usually a physical hurt caused by cutting, shooting, etc., or an emotional hurt: *a serious wound in the shoulder, to inflict a wound by betraying some-one's trust.* —**Ant.** 1. benefit.

injury time, *Sport.* extension of the playing time of a match to compensate for any time lost through injury.

injustice (ĭn jŭs′tĭs), *n.* 1. the quality or fact of being unjust. 2. unjust action or treatment; violation of another's rights. 3. an unjust act or circumstance. [ME, t. F, t. L: m. s. *injustitia*]

ink (ĭngk), *n.* 1. a fluid or viscous substance used for writing or printing. 2. a dark, protective fluid ejected by the cuttlefish and other cephalopods. —*v.t.* 3. to mark, stain, cover, or smear with ink. [ME *inke, enke*, t. OF: m. *enque*, g. LL *encaustum*, t. Gk: m. *énkauston* kind of ink] —**ink′er,** *n.* —**ink′less,** *adj.* —**ink′like′,** *adj.*

inkberry (ĭngk′bĕ′rĭ), *n., pl.* **-ries.** 1. a shrub, *Ilex glabra*, with leathery evergreen leaves and black berries. 2. its berry.

ink-cap (ĭngk′kăp′), *n.* any of various mushrooms of the genus *Coprinus*, whose gills disintegrate into blackish liquid after the spores mature, esp. *C. atramentarius.* Also, **inky cap.**

Inkerman (ĭng′kə mən; *Russ.* ĭn kĭr män′), *n.* a village in the SW Soviet Union, in the Crimea: Russian defeat, 1854.

inkhorn (ĭngk′hôn′), *n.* a small container of horn or other material, formerly used to hold writing ink.

inkhorn term, a pedantic or affectedly erudite term taken from another language, esp. Latin or Greek; common in the 16th century in English.

inkle (ĭng′kl), *n.* 1. a kind of linen tape. 2. the linen thread or yarn from which this tape is made.

inkling (ĭng′klĭng), *n.* 1. a hint, intimation, or slight suggestion. 2. a vague idea or notion. [f. *inkle*, v., hint (ME *incle*) + -ING[1]. Cf. OE *inca* suspicion]

inkpot (ĭngk′pŏt′), *n.* a cuplike container for ink.

inkstand (ĭngk′stănd′), *n.* a stand for holding ink, pens, etc.

ink table, *Print.* a flat metal surface over which the ink is distributed at a desired consistency. Also, **ink slab, inking table, inking slab.**

inkwell (ĭngk′wĕl′), *n.* a container for ink, esp. one let into the surface of a desk.

inky (ĭng′kĭ), *adj.*, **-ier, -iest.** 1. black as ink: *inky shadows.* 2. resembling ink. 3. stained with ink: *inky fingers.* 4. of or pertaining to ink. 5. consisting of or containing ink. 6. written with ink. —**ink′iness,** *n.*

inlaid (ĭn′lād′, ĭn lād′), *adj.* 1. set in the surface of a thing: *an inlaid design in wood.* 2. decorated or made with a design set in the surface: *an inlaid table.*

inland (*adj.* ĭn′lənd; *adv., n.* ĭn′lănd′), *adj.* 1. pertaining to or situated in the interior part of a country or region: *inland cities.* 2. carried on within a country; domestic; not foreign: *inland trade.* 3. confined to a country. —*adv.* 4. in or towards the interior of a country. —*n.* 5. the interior part of a country, away from the border. [ME and OE; f. IN-[1] + LAND]

inland bill, a bill of exchange either both drawn and payable within the British Isles or drawn within the British Isles upon some person resident therein.

inlander (ĭn′lən də), *n.* a person living inland.

inland revenue, 1. revenue from taxes, stamp duties, and excise duties levied within a country. 2. (*caps.*) the authority responsible for the collection of such revenue.

Inland Sea, a sea in SW Japan, enclosed by the islands of Honshu, Shikoku, and Kyushu. ab. 240 mi. long.

in-law (ĭn′lô′), *n.* a relative by marriage.

inlay (*v.* ĭn lā′; *n.* ĭn′lā′), *v.*, **-laid, -laying,** *n.* —*v.t.* 1. to decorate (an object) with veneers of fine materials set in its surface. 2. to insert, or apply (layers of fine materials) in a surface of an object. 3. *Hort.* to place (a fitted scion) into a prepared stock, as in an inlay graft. —*n.* 4. inlaid work. 5. veneer of fine material inserted in something else, esp. for ornament. 6. a design or decoration made by inlaying. 7. *Dentistry.* a filling of metal, porcelain, or plastic which is fitted and fastened into a tooth as a solid mass. 8. *Hort.* an inlay graft. 9. the act or process of inlaying. —**in′lay′er,** *n.*

inlay graft, *Hort.* a graft in which the scion is matched into a place in the stock from which a piece of corresponding bark has been removed.

inlet (*n.* ĭn′lĕt′; *v.* ĭn lĕt′), *n., v.,* **-let, -letting.** —*n.* **1.** an indentation of a shore line, usually long and narrow, or a narrow passage between islands. **2.** a place of admission; an entrance. **3.** something put in or inserted. —*v.t.* **4.** to put in; insert.

inlet valve, induction valve.

inlier (ĭn′lī′ə), *n. Geol.* an outcrop of a formation completely surrounded by another of later date.

in loc. cit., (L *in loco citato*) in the place cited.

in loco (ĭn lō′kō), *Latin.* in place; in the proper place.

in loco parentis (ĭn lō′kō pə rĕn′tĭs), *Latin.* in the place of a parent; replacing a parent.

inly (ĭn′lĭ), *adv. Archaic.* **1.** inwardly. **2.** intimately; deeply; sincerely. —*adj.* **3.** *Obs.* inward. [ME *inliche,* OE *inlice,* der. *inlic* inward]

inmate (ĭn′māt′), *n.* **1.** one of those confined in a hospital, prison, etc. **2.** *Archaic.* one who dwells with another or others in the same house. [f. IN-¹ + MATE¹]

in medias res (ĭn mē′dĭ ăs rās′), *Latin.* in the middle of things: *Homer began his story in medias res.*

in mem., in memoriam.

in memoriam (ĭn′mĭ mô′rĭ ăm′), in memory (of); to the memory (of); as a memorial (to). [t. L]

inmesh (ĭn mĕsh′), *v.t.* enmesh.

inmost (ĭn′mōst′), *adj.* **1.** situated farthest within: *the inmost recesses of the forest.* **2.** most intimate: *one's inmost thoughts.* [ME; OE *innemest,* a double superl., f. *inne* within + *-m-* + *-est* (superl. suffix). See IN-¹, -MOST]

inn (ĭn), *n.* **1.** a public house that provides lodging, food, etc., for travellers and others; a small hotel: *a wayside inn.* **2.** a tavern. **3. a.** a house or place of residence for students (now only in names of buildings derived from such use): *the Inns of Court.* **b.** a legal society occupying such a house. [ME *inne,* OE *inn* house] —**inn′less,** *adj.* —**Syn. 1.** See **hotel.**

Inn (ĭn), *n.* a river flowing from E Switzerland through Austria and Germany into the Danube. 320 mi.

innards (ĭn′ədz), *n.* the inward parts of the body; entrails; viscera. [alter. of INWARDS¹]

innate (ĭ nāt′, ĭn′āt), *adj.* **1.** inborn; existing or as if existing in one from birth: *innate modesty.* **2.** inherent in the essential character of something. **3.** arising from the constitution of the mind, rather than acquired from experience: *innate ideas.* [late ME *innat,* t. L: s. *innātus,* pp., inborn] —**innate′ly,** *adv.* —**innate′ness,** *n.*

inner (ĭn′ə), *adj.* **1.** situated farther within; interior: *an inner door.* **2.** more intimate, private, or secret: *the inner circle of his friends.* **3.** mental or spiritual: *the inner life.* **4.** not obvious; esoteric: *an inner meaning.* —*n.* **5.** the ring next surrounding the bull's-eye of a target. **6.** a shot that strikes this; the second highest score. [ME; OE *innera,* compar. of *inne* within. Cf. INMOST] —**in′nerness,** *n.*

inner bar, *Law.* Queen's Counsel collectively.

inner-directed (ĭn′ə dĭ rĕk′tĭd), *adj.* guided by one's own set of values rather than external pressures. —**in′ner-direc′tion,** *n.*

Inner Light, (as used by the Society of Friends) the light of Christ in the soul.

inner man, 1. the soul; spiritual and intellectual aspect of a person. **2.** *Colloq.* the stomach or appetite.

Inner Mongolia. See **Mongolia** (def. 2).

innermost (ĭn′ə mōst′), *adj.* **1.** farthest inwards; inmost. —*n.* **2.** innermost part. [ME, f. INNER + -MOST]

Inner Temple. See **Inns of Court.**

inner tube, an inflatable, airtight rubber tube which fits inside the outer cover of a pneumatic tyre.

innervate (ĭn′û vāt′), *v.t.,* **-vated, -vating. 1.** to communicate nervous energy to; stimulate through nerves. **2.** to grow nerves into. [f. IN-² + NERVE + -ATE¹]

innervation (ĭn′û vā′shən), *n.* **1.** the act of innervating. **2.** the state of being innervated. **3.** *Anat.* the disposition of nerves in a body or some part of it.

innerve (ĭ nûv′), *v.t.,* **-nerved, -nerving.** to supply with nervous energy; invigorate; animate.

Inness (ĭn′ĭs), *n.* **1. George,** 1825–94, U.S. painter. **2.** his son **George,** 1854–1926, U.S. painter.

inning (ĭn′ĭng), *n.* **1.** reclaiming, as of marsh or flooded land. **2.** (*usually pl.*) land reclaimed from the sea, etc. **3.** enclosure, as of waste land. **4.** harvesting, as of crops. **5.** *Baseball.* a round in which both teams bat, with each side getting three outs. **6.** *U.S.* innings (defs 2 and 3). [ME *inninge,* OE *innung* a putting in]

innings (ĭn′ĭngz), *n.pl.* (*construed as sing.*) **1.** *Cricket.* **a.** the turn of any one member of the batting team to bat. **b.** one of the major divisions of a match, consisting of the turns at batting of all the members of one team until they are all out or until the team declares. **c.** the runs scored during such a turn or such a division. **2.** a similar opportunity to score in certain other games. **3.** any opportunity for some activity; a turn. **4.** land reclaimed from the sea, etc.; inning.

innkeeper (ĭn′kē′pə), *n.* the keeper of an inn. Also, *Now Rare,* **innholder** (ĭn′hōl′də).

innocence (ĭn′ə səns), *n.* **1.** the state or fact of being innocent; freedom from sin or moral wrong. **2.** freedom from legal or specific wrong; guiltlessness: *the prisoner proved his innocence.* **3.** simplicity or guilelessness. **4.** chastity. **5.** lack of knowledge or sense. **6.** harmlessness or innocuousness. **7.** an innocent person or thing. Also, *Obs.,* **in′nocency.**

innocent (ĭn′ə sənt), *adj.* **1.** free from any moral wrong; not tainted with sin; pure: *innocent children.* **2.** free from legal or specific wrong; guiltless: *to be innocent of crime.* **3.** not involving evil intent or motive: *an innocent misrepresentation.* **4.** free from any quality that can cause physical or moral injury; harmless: *innocent fun.* **5.** devoid (fol. by *of*): *a law innocent of merit.* **6.** having or showing the simplicity or naivety of an unworldly person: *she looks so innocent.* —*n.* **7.** an innocent person. **8.** a young child. **9.** a guileless person. **10.** a simpleton or idiot. [ME, t. L: s. *innocens* harmless] —**in′nocently,** *adv.*

—**Syn. 1.** sinless, virtuous; faultless, impeccable. **2.** INNOCENT, BLAMELESS, GUILTLESS imply freedom from the responsibility of having done wrong. INNOCENT may imply having done no wrong at any time, and having not even a knowledge of evil: *an innocent victim.* BLAMELESS denotes freedom from blame, esp. moral blame: *a blameless life.* GUILTLESS denotes freedom from guilt or responsibility for wrongdoing, usually in a particular instance: *guiltless of a crime.* **6.** simple, naive, unsophisticated, artless, guileless, ingenuous. —**Ant. 1.** guilty.

Innocent (ĭn′ə sənt), *n.* the name adopted by thirteen popes, esp.: **1. Innocent II** (*Gregorio Papareschi*), died 1143, pope 1130–43. **2. Innocent III** (*Giovanni Lotario de' Conti*), 1161?–1216, pope 1198–1216. **3. Innocent IV** (*Sinibaldo de Fieschi*), died 1254, pope 1243–54. **4. Innocent XI** (*Bendetto Odescalchi*), 1611–89, pope 1676–89.

Innocents' Day. See **Holy Innocents' Day.**

innocuous (ĭ nŏk′yo͞o əs), *adj.* not harmful or injurious; harmless. [t. L: m. *innocuus*] —**innoc′uously,** *adv.* —**innoc′uousness,** *n.*

innominate (ĭ nŏm′ĭ nĭt), *adj.* having no name; anonymous. [t. LL: m. s. *innominātus* unnamed]

innominate bone, *Anat.* either of the two bones forming the sides of the pelvis, each consisting of three consolidated bones, known as ilium, ischium, and pubis. See diag. under **pelvis.**

innovate (ĭn′ə vāt′), *v.,* **-vated, -vating.** —*v.i.* **1.** to bring in something new; make changes in anything established (fol. by *on* or *in*). —*v.t.* **2.** to bring in (something new) for the first time. **3.** *Obs.* to alter. [t. L: m. s. *innovātus,* pp., renewed, altered] —**in′nova′tive, in′nova′tory,** *adj.* —**in′nova′tor,** *n.*

innovation (ĭn′ə vā′shən), *n.* **1.** something new or different introduced. **2.** the act of innovating; introduction of new things or methods. —**in′nova′tional,** *adj.* —**in′nova′tionist,** *n.*

innoxious (ĭ nŏk′shəs), *adj.* harmless; innocuous. —**innox′iously,** *adv.* —**innox′iousness,** *n.*

Innsbruck (ĭnz′bro͝ok; *Ger.* ĭns′bro͝ok), *n.* a city in W Austria, on the river Inn. 100,695 (1961).

Inns of Court, 1. the four voluntary legal societies in England (**Lincoln's Inn,** the **Inner Temple,** the **Middle Temple,** and **Gray's Inn**), which have the exclusive privilege of calling candidates to the English bar, after they have received such instruction and taken such examinations as the Inns provide. **2.** the buildings owned and used by the Inns.

innuendo (ĭn′yo͞o ĕn′dō), *n., pl.* **-dos, -does. 1.** an indirect intimation about a person or thing, esp. of a derogatory nature. **2.** *Law.* **a.** a parenthetic explanation or specification in a pleading. **b.** (in an action for slander or libel) the explanation and elucidation of the words alleged to be defamatory. **c.** the word or expression thus explained. [t. L: intimation, abl. gerund of *innuere* give a nod, intimate]

innumerable (ĭ nyo͞o′mə rə bl, -nyo͞om′rə bl), *adj.* **1.** very numerous. **2.** incapable of being numbered or counted. Also, **innu′merous.** —**innu′merableness, innu′merabil′ity,** *n.* —**innu′merably,** *adv.* —**Syn. 1.** See **many.**

innutrition (ĭn′yo͞o trĭsh′ən), *n.* lack of nutrition. —**in′nutri′tious,** *adj.*

inobservance (ĭn′əb zû′vəns), *n.* **1.** lack of observance or noticing; inattention: *drowsy inobservance.* **2.** non-observance. —**in′observ′ant,** *adj.*

inoccupation (ĭn′ŏk yo͞o pā′shən), *n.* lack of occupation.

inoculable (ĭ nŏk′yo͞o lə bl), *adj.* capable of being inoculated. —**inoc′ulabil′ity,** *n.*

inoculant (ĭ nŏk′yŏŏ lənt), *n.* an inoculating substance.

inoculate (ĭ nŏk′yŏŏ lāt′), *v.*, **-lated, -lating,** *n.* —*v.t.* **1.** to implant (a disease) in a person or animal by the introduction of germs or virus, as through a puncture, in order to produce a mild form of the disease and thus secure immunity. **2.** to impregnate (a person or animal) thus. **3.** to introduce (micro-organisms) into surroundings suited to their growth, esp. into the body. **4.** to imbue (a person, etc.), as with ideas. —*v.i.* **5.** to perform inoculation. —*n.* **6.** a substance to be inoculated. [late ME, t. L: m. s. *inoculātus*, pp., grafted, implanted] —**inoculative** (ĭ nŏk′yŏŏ lə tĭv), *adj.* —**inoc′ula′tor,** *n.*

inoculation (ĭ nŏk′yŏŏ lā′shən), *n.* **1.** the act of inoculating. **2.** the substance inoculated.

inoculum (ĭ nŏk′yŏŏ ləm), *n.* the substance used to make an inoculation. [NL]

inodorous (ĭn ō′də rəs), *adj.* not odorous; odourless; having no smell. —**ino′dorously,** *adv.* —**ino′dorousness,** *n.*

inoffensive (ĭn′ə fĕn′sĭv), *adj.* **1.** doing no harm; harmless; unoffending: *a mild, inoffensive man.* **2.** not objectionable, or not being a cause of offence. —**in′offen′sively,** *adv.* —**in′offen′siveness,** *n.*

inofficious (ĭn′ə fĭsh′əs), *adj.* **1.** *Law.* not in accordance with moral duty: *an inofficious testament or will* (one disposing of property contrary to the dictates of natural affection or to just expectations). **2.** *Obs.* disobliging. [t. L: m. s. *inofficiōsus.* See IN-³, OFFICIOUS] —**in′offic′iously,** *adv.* —**in′offic′iousness,** *n.*

Inönü (*Turk.* ē′nœ nʏ), *n.* **Ismet** (*Turk.* ĕs′mĕt), born 1884, president of Turkey 1938–50, prime minister 1923–24, 1925–37, and 1961–65.

inoperable (ĭn ŏp′ə rə bl, -ŏp′rə-), *adj.* **1.** not operable. **2.** not admitting of a surgical operation without risk.

inoperative (ĭn ŏp′ə rə tĭv, -ŏp′rə-), *adj.* **1.** not operative; not in operation. **2.** without effect: *inoperative remedies.* —**inop′erativeness,** *n.*

inopportune (ĭn ŏp′ə tyŏŏn′), *adj.* not opportune; inappropriate; (with regard to time) unseasonable: *an inopportune visit.* —**inop′portune′ly,** *adv.* —**inop′portune′ness, inop′portun′ity,** *n.*

inordinate (ĭn ô′dĭ nĭt), *adj.* **1.** not within proper limits; excessive: *inordinate demands.* **2.** disorderly. **3.** unrestrained in conduct, etc. **4.** irregular: *inordinate hours.* [ME *inordinat,* t. L: s. *inordinātus* disordered] —**inordinacy** (ĭn ô′dĭ nə sĭ), **inor′dinateness,** *n.* —**inor′dinately,** *adv.*

inorg., inorganic.

inorganic (ĭn′ô găn′ĭk), *adj.* **1.** not having the organization which characterizes living bodies. **2.** not characterized by vital processes. **3.** *Chem.* denoting or pertaining to compounds not containing carbon, excepting cyanides and carbonates. Cf. **organic** (def. 1). **4.** not fundamental; extraneous. —**in′organ′ically,** *adv.*

inorganic chemistry, the branch of chemistry which treats of inorganic substances.

inosculate (ĭn ŏs′kyŏŏ lāt′), *v.i., v.t.,* **-lated, -lating.** **1.** to unite by openings, as arteries in anastomosis. **2.** to connect or join so as to become or make continuous, as fibres. **3.** to unite intimately. [f. IN-² + m. s. LL *osculātus,* pp., supplied with a mouth or outlet] —**inos′cula′tion,** *n.*

inositol (ĭ nō′sĭ tŏl′), *n. Chem.* a sweet crystalline substance, $C_6H_6(OH)_6$, first found in heart muscle, but widely distributed in plants and seeds as phytin, and also occurring in animal tissue and in urine. [f. *inosit(e)* (f. *in-,* comb. form repr. Gk *ís* fibre, + -OS(E)² + -ITE¹) + -OL¹]

in-patient (ĭn′pā′shənt), *n.* a patient who is lodged and fed as well as treated in a hospital.

in perpetuum (ĭn′pû pĕt′yŏŏ əm), *Latin.* for ever.

in personam (ĭn′pû sō′năm), *Latin.* against a person, as a legal proceeding (contrasted with *in rem*).

in petto (ĭn pĕt′ō; *It.* ēn pĕt′tò), *Italian.* not disclosed (of cardinals whom the Pope appoints but does not name in consistory). [lit., in the breast]

in posse (ĭn pŏs′ĭ), *Latin.* in possibility, rather than in actual existence (distinguished from *in esse*).

input (ĭn′pŏŏt′), *n.* **1.** that which is put in. **2.** the current or voltage fed to an electrical machine, circuit, or device. **3.** *Computers.* information which is fed into a computer before it performs a computation. **4.** *Scot.* a contribution.

inquest (ĭn′kwĕst′), *n.* **1.** a legal or judicial inquiry, esp. before a jury. **2.** one made by a coroner (**coroner's inquest**). **3.** the body of men appointed to hold such an inquiry, esp. a coroner's jury. **4.** their decision or finding. **5.** *Colloq.* an inquiry into the reasons for the failure of a project, etc. [ME *enqueste,* t. OF, g. L *inquisita* (*rēs*) (a thing) inquired into, prop. pp. fem.]

inquietude (ĭn kwī′ĭ tyŏŏd′), *n.* **1.** restlessness; uneasiness. **2.** (*pl.*) disquieting thoughts.

inquiline (ĭn′kwĭ lĭn′), *n.* **1.** *Zool.* an animal that lives in an abode properly belonging to another; a guest. —*adj.* **2.** of the nature of an inquiline. [t. L: m. s. *inquilīnus*] —**inquilinity** (ĭn′kwĭ lĭn′ĭ tĭ), *n.* —**inquilinous** (ĭn′kwĭ lī′nəs), *adj.*

inquire (ĭn kwī′ə), *v.*, **-quired, -quiring.** —*v.i.* **1.** to make investigation (fol. by *into*). **2.** *Chiefly U.S.* enquire. —*v.t.* **3.** *Chiefly U.S.* enquire. [t. L: m. s. *inquīrere,* r. ME *enquere,* t. OF] —**inquir′er,** *n.*

inquiring (ĭn kwī′ə rĭng), *adj.* **1.** given to inquiry or research; seeking information or knowledge: *an inquiring mind.* **2.** questioning; curious: *an inquiring look.*

inquiry (ĭn kwī′ə rĭ), *n., pl.* **-ries.** **1.** an investigation, as into a matter. **2.** the act of inquiring, or seeking information by questioning; interrogation. **3.** *Chiefly U.S.* enquiry (def. 2). Also, **enquiry.** —**Syn. 2.** See **investigation.**

inquisition (ĭn′kwĭ zĭsh′ən), *n.* **1.** the act of inquiring; inquiry; research. **2.** an investigation, or process of inquiry. **3.** an inquiry conducted by judicial officers or such non-judicial officers as coroners. **4.** the finding of such an inquiry. **5.** the document embodying the result of such inquiry. **6.** (*cap.*) *Rom. Cath. Ch.* a special tribunal for the defence of Catholic teaching in faith and morals, the judgement of heresy, the application of canonical punishment, and the judgement of mixed marriages and the Pauline privileges. [ME *inquisicion,* t. L: m. s. *inquīsītio* a searching into] —**in′quisi′tional,** *adj.*

inquisitionist (ĭn kwĭ zĭsh′ə nĭst), *n.* an inquisitor.

inquisitive (ĭn kwĭz′ĭ tĭv), *adj.* **1.** unduly curious; prying. **2.** inquiring; desirous of or eager for knowledge. —*n.* **3.** an inquisitive person. —**inquis′itively,** *adv.* —**inquis′itiveness,** *n.* —**Syn. 1.** See **curious.**

inquisitor (ĭn kwĭz′ĭ tə), *n.* **1.** one who makes inquisition. **2.** a questioner, esp. an inquisitive one. **3.** one who investigates by virtue of his office. **4.** a member of the Inquisition. —**inquisitress** (ĭn kwĭz′ĭ trĭs), *n. fem.*

inquisitorial (ĭn kwĭz′ĭ tô′rĭ əl), *adj.* **1.** pertaining to an inquisitor or inquisitors, or to inquisition. **2.** exercising the office of an inquisitor. **3.** *Law.* pertaining to a trial with one person or group acting as prosecutor and judge, or to secret criminal prosecutions. **4.** resembling an inquisitor. **5.** inquisitive. —**inquis′ito′rially,** *adv.* —**inquis′ito′rialness,** *n.*

in re (ĭn rā′), *Latin.* in the matter of.

in rem (ĭn rĕm′), *Latin.* against a thing, as a legal proceeding for its recovery (contrasted with *in personam*).

in rerum natura (ĭn rēə′rŏŏm nă tŏŏ′rä), *Latin.* in the nature of things.

I.N.R.I., (L *Iesus Nazarenus, Rex Iudaeorum*) Jesus of Nazareth, King of the Jews.

inroad (ĭn′rōd′), *n.* **1.** forcible or serious encroachment: *inroads on our savings.* **2.** a hostile or predatory incursion; a raid; a foray.

inrush (ĭn′rŭsh′), *n.* a rushing in; an influx. —**in′rush′ing,** *n., adj.*

ins, inches.

ins., **1.** inches. **2.** inspector. **3.** insulated. **4.** insurance.

insalivate (ĭn săl′ĭ vāt′), *v.t.,* **-vated, -vating.** to mix with saliva, as food. —**insal′iva′tion,** *n.*

insalubrious (ĭn′sə lŏŏ′brĭ əs), *adj.* unfavourable to health. —**in′salu′briously,** *adv.* —**insalubrity** (ĭn′sə lŏŏ′brĭ tĭ), *n.*

insane (ĭn sān′), *adj.* **1.** not sane; not of sound mind; mentally deranged. **2.** characteristic of one mentally deranged. **3.** *Chiefly U.S.* set apart for the care and confinement of mentally deranged persons: *an insane asylum.* **4.** utterly senseless: *an insane attempt.* —**insane′ly,** *adv.* —**insane′ness,** *n.* —**Syn. 1.** demented; lunatic, crazed, crazy; maniacal. See **mad. 2.** foolish, senseless.

insanitary (ĭn săn′ĭ tə rĭ, -trĭ), *adj.* not sanitary; unclean and likely to carry infection: *insanitary houses.* —**insan′itariness,** *n.*

insanitation (ĭn săn′ĭ tā′shən), *n.* lack of sanitation or sanitary regulation; insanitary condition.

insanity (ĭn săn′ĭ tĭ), *n., pl.* **-ties.** **1.** the condition of being insane; more or less permanent derangement of one or more psychical functions, due to disease of the mind. **2.** *Law.* such unsoundness of mind as affects legal responsibility or capacity. **3.** extreme folly. —**Syn. 1.** derangement, dementia; lunacy, craziness, madness.

insatiable (ĭn sā′shyə bl), *adj.* not satiable; incapable of being satisfied: *insatiable desire.* —**insa′tiabil′ity, insa′tiableness,** *n.* —**insa′tiably,** *adv.*

insatiate (ĭn sā′shĭ ĭt), *adj.* insatiable: *insatiate greed.* —**insa′tiately,** *adv.* —**insa′tiateness,** *n.*

inscape (ĭn′skāp′), *n.* the essential inner nature of a thing, person, emotion, etc. [f. IN-¹+(LAND)SCAPE, coined by Gerard Manley Hopkins]

inscribe (ĭn skrīb′), *v.t.,* **-scribed, -scribing.** **1.** to write or engrave (words, characters, etc.). **2.** to mark (a surface) with words, characters, etc., esp. in a durable or conspicuous way. **3.** to address or dedicate (a book, photograph, etc.) informally, esp. by a handwritten note. **4.** to enrol, as on an official list. **5.** *Obs.* **a.** to record or register the names of purchasers of (stocks, etc.). **b.** to issue (stock) without certificates, the names of the stockholders being written in a register. **6.** *Geom.* to draw or delineate (one figure) within another figure so that the inner lies in the boundary of the outer at as many points as possible. [t. L: m. s. *inscrībere* write in or upon] —**inscrib′able,** *adj.* —**inscrib′er,** *n.*

inscription (ĭn skrĭp′shən), *n.* **1.** something inscribed. **2.** a brief, more or less informal dedication, as of a book or a work of art. **3.** a note inscribed in a book, usually signed. **4.** *Archaeol.* a historical, religious, or other record cut, impressed, painted, or written on stone, brick, metal, or other hard surface. **5.** the act of inscribing. **6.** *Obs.* an inscribing of issued securities. [ME, t. L: s. *inscriptio*] —**inscrip′tional,** *adj.* —**inscrip′tionless,** *adj.*

inscriptive (ĭn skrĭp′tĭv), *adj.* pertaining to or of the nature of an inscription. —**inscrip′tively,** *adv.*

inscroll (ĭn skrōl′), *v.t.* to write on a scroll.

inscrutable (ĭn skrōō′tə bl), *adj.* **1.** incapable of being searched into or scrutinized; impenetrable to investigation. **2.** not easily understood; mysterious; enigmatic. **3.** impenetrable or unfathomable physically. [late ME, t. LL: m. s. *inscrūtābilis*] —**inscru′tabil′ity, inscru′tableness,** *n.* —**inscru′tably,** *adv.* —**Syn. 1.** See **mysterious.**

insculp (ĭn skŭlp′), *v.t.* *Now Rare.* to carve in or on something; engrave. [t. L: s. *insculpere*]

insect (ĭn′sĕkt), *n.* **1.** *Zool.* any animal of the subphylum or class *Insecta*, a group of small, air-breathing arthropods characterized by a body clearly divided into three parts, head, thorax, and abdomen, and by having only three pairs of legs, and usually having two pairs of wings. **2.** any small, air-breathing arthropod, such as a spider, tick, or centipede, having superficial, general similarity to the *Insecta.* **3.** *Colloq.* a contemptible person. —*adj.* **4.** of, pertaining to, or like an insect. **5.** *Colloq.* contemptible. [t. L: s. *insectum* (so-called from the segmented form), prop. neut. of *insectus*, pp., cut in or up] —**in′sect-like′,** *adj.*

Insect (grasshopper)
A, Head; B, Thorax; C, Abdomen; D, Wings; E, Antenna; F, Simple eye; G, Compound eye; H, Palpus; I, Leg; J, Ear; K, Spiracle; L, Ovipositor

insectarium (ĭn′sĕk tēə′rĭ əm), *n., pl.* **-tariums, -taria** (-tēə′rĭ ə). a place in which a collection of living insects is kept, as in a zoo. [NL]

insectary (ĭn sĕk′tə rĭ), *n., pl.* **-ries.** a laboratory for the study of live insects, their life histories, effects on plants, reaction to insecticides, etc.

insecticide (ĭn sĕk′tĭ sīd′), *n.* **1.** a substance or preparation used for killing insects. **2.** the killing of insects. [f. s. L *insectum* + -(I)CIDE] —**insec′ticid′al,** *adj.*

insectivore (ĭn sĕk′tĭ vô′), *n.* **1.** an insectivorous animal or plant. **2.** any of the *Insectivora*, the mammalian order that includes the moles, the shrews, and the hedgehogs. [t. NL: m. s. *insectivorus*, f. L: s. *insectum* insect + *-i-* + *-vorus* devouring]

insectivorous (ĭn′sĕk tĭv′ə rəs), *adj.* adapted to feeding on insects, as shrews, moles, hedgehogs, etc.

insecure (ĭn′sĭ kyŏŏə′), *adj.* **1.** exposed to danger; unsafe. **2.** not firm or safe: *insecure foundations.* **3.** not free from fear, doubt, etc. —**in′secure′ly,** *adv.* —**Syn. 2.** See **uncertain.**

insecurity (ĭn′sĭ kyŏŏə′rĭ tĭ), *n., pl.* **-ties. 1.** unsafe condition; lack of assurance or sureness; uncertainty; instability. **2.** something insecure.

inseminate (ĭn sĕm′ĭ nāt′), *v.t.,* **-nated, -nating. 1.** to sow; inject seed into. **2.** to introduce semen into (a female) to cause fertilization; impregnate. **3.** to sow as seed in something; implant. [t. L: m. s. *insēminātus*, pp., sown, planted in] —**insem′ina′tion,** *n.*

insensate (ĭn sĕn′sāt, -sĭt), *adj.* **1.** not endowed with sensation: *insensate stone.* **2.** without feeling; unfeeling. **3.** without sense, understanding, or judgement. —**insen′sately,** *adv.* —**insen′sateness,** *n.*

insensibility (ĭn sĕn′sə bĭl′ĭ tĭ), *n., pl.* **-ties. 1.** lack of physical sensibility; absence of feeling or sensation. **2.** lack of moral sensibility or susceptibility of emotion. —**Syn. 2.** See **indifference.**

insensible (ĭn sĕn′sə bl), *adj.* **1.** incapable of feeling or perceiving; deprived of sensation; unconscious, as a person after a violent blow. **2.** without, or not subject to, a particular feeling: *insensible to shame.* **3.** unconscious, unaware, or unappreciative: *we are not insensible of your kindness.* **4.** not perceptible by the senses: *insensible transitions.* **5.** unresponsive in feeling. **6.** not susceptible of emotion or passion; void of any feeling. **7.** *Now Rare.* not endowed with feeling or sensation, as matter. —**insen′sibly,** *adv.*

insensitive (ĭn sĕn′sĭ tĭv), *adj.* **1.** not sensitive: *an insensitive skin.* **2.** not susceptible to agencies or influences: *insensitive to light.* **3.** deficient in sensibility or acuteness of feeling: *an insensitive nature.* —**insen′sitiveness, insen′sitiv′ity,** *n.*

insentient (ĭn sĕn′shyənt), *adj.* without sensation or feeling; inanimate. —**insen′tience,** *n.*

inseparable (ĭn sĕp′ə rə bl, -sĕp′rə-), *adj.* **1.** incapable of being separated, parted, or disjoined: *inseparable companions.* —*n.* (*usually pl.*) **2.** something inseparable. **3.** an inseparable companion or friend. —**insep′arabil′ity, insep′arableness,** *n.* —**insep′arably,** *adv.*

insert (*v.* ĭn sût′; *n.* ĭn′sût), *v.t.* **1.** to put or set in: *to insert a key in a lock.* **2.** to introduce into the body of something: *to insert an advertisement in a newspaper.* —*n.* **3.** something inserted, or to be inserted. **4.** an extra leaf printed independently of the sheets comprising a book but included when the book is bound. [t. L: s. *insertus*, pp., put in] —**insert′er,** *n.*

inserted (ĭn sû′tĭd), *adj.* **1.** *Bot.* (esp. of the parts of a flower) attached to or growing out of some part. **2.** *Anat.* having an insertion, as a muscle, tendon, or ligament; attached, as the more movable end of a muscle.

insertion (ĭn sû′shən), *n.* **1.** the act of inserting: *each insertion of an advertisement.* **2.** something inserted: *an insertion into a text.* **3.** *Bot., Zool., etc.* **a.** the manner or place of attachment, as of an organ. **b.** attachment of a part or organ, with special reference to the site or manner of such attachment. **4.** lace, embroidery, or the like, to be sewn at each edge between parts of other material.

insessorial (ĭn′sĕ sô′rĭ əl), *adj.* **1.** adapted for perching, as a bird's foot. **2.** habitually perching, as a bird. **3.** of or pertaining to birds that perch. [f. s. NL *Insessorēs* the perching birds (considered as an order), pl. of *insessor* (f. *in* on + *sessor* sitter) + -IAL]

inset (*n.* ĭn′sĕt′; *v.* ĭn sĕt′), *n., v.,* **-set, -setting.** —*n.* **1.** something inserted; an insert. **2.** a smaller picture, map, etc., inserted within the border of a larger one. **3.** *Theat.* a small scene played within another for rapid scene-shifting. **4.** influx. **5.** the act of setting in. —*v.t.* **6.** to set in; insert. **7.** to insert as an inset. **8.** to insert an inset in.

insheathe (ĭn shēth′), *v.t.,* **-sheathed, -sheathing.** to enclose in or as in a sheath; sheathe.

inshore (ĭn′shô′), *adj.* **1.** close to the shore: *the ship lay inshore.* **2.** lying near the shore; operating close to the shore: *inshore fishing.* —*adv.* **3.** towards the shore: *they went closer inshore.*

inshrine (ĭn shrīn′), *v.t.,* **-shrined, -shrining.** enshrine.

inside (ĭn sīd′), *prep.* **1.** on the inner side of; within: *inside the circle.* **2.** before the elapse of: *inside an hour.* —*adv.* **3.** in or into the inner part: *to go inside.* **4.** indoors: *he is working inside.* **5.** by nature; fundamentally: *inside, he's very kind.* **6.** *Colloq.* to or in prison. —*n.* **7.** the inner part; interior: *the inside of the house.* **8.** the inner side or surface: *the inside of the hand.* **9.** (*often pl.*) *Colloq.* the inward parts of the body, esp. the stomach and intestines. **10.** the inward nature. **11.** an inside passenger or place in a coach, etc. **12.** (*pl.*) internal thoughts or feelings, etc. **13.** the part of a curved track or course nearer to the centre of the curves; the inside lane: *a horse coming up fast on the inside; the inside of the bend.* **14.** an inner group of persons having private knowledge about a circumstance or case. **15.** *Soccer, etc.* Also, **inside forward.** an inside left or inside right. **16. inside out, a.** with the inner side reversed to face outwards. **b.** thoroughly; completely: *he knows his job inside out.* —*adj.* **17.** situated or being on or in the inside; interior. **18.** acting, employed, done, or originating within a building or place: *the robbery was an inside job.* **19.** derived from the inner circle of those concerned in and having private knowledge of a case: *inside information.* **20.** running nearer to the centre and therefore shorter: *the inside lane of a track.*

—**Syn. 7.** INSIDE, INTERIOR both refer to the inner part or space within something. INSIDE is a common word, and is used with reference to things of any size, small or large: *the inside of a pocket.* INTERIOR, somewhat more formal, denotes the inner part or the space or the regions within; it usually suggests considerable size or extent, and sometimes a richness of decoration: *the interior of a country; interior of a cathedral.* —**Ant. 7.** outside, exterior.

inside left, *Soccer, etc.* a player in the forward line between centre-forward and outside left.

insider (ĭn sī′də), *n.* **1.** one who is inside some place, society, etc. **2.** *Colloq.* one who is within a limited circle of persons who understand the actual facts of a case. **3.** *Colloq.* one who has some special advantage.

inside right, *Soccer, etc.* a player in the forward line between centre-forward and outside right.

insidious (ĭn sĭd′ĭ əs), *adj.* **1.** intended to entrap or beguile: *an insidious design.* **2.** stealthily treacherous or deceitful: *an insidious enemy.* **3.** operating or proceeding inconspicuously but with grave effect: *an insidious disease.* [t. L: m. s. *insidiōsus* cunning, artful] —**insid′iously,** *adv.* —**insid′iousness,** *n.*

insight (ĭn′sīt′), *n.* **1.** an understanding gained or given of something: *this little insight into the life of the village.* **2.** penetrating mental vision or discernment; faculty of seeing into inner character or underlying truth: *a man of great insight.* **3.** *Psychol.* **a.** the sudden grasping of a solution; configurational learning. **b.** the ability to see oneself as others see one; self-knowledge. **c.** (in psychiatry) the capacity of a mental patient to know that he is suffering from mental disorder. [ME; f. IN-[1] + SIGHT]

insignia (ĭn sĭg′nĭ ə), *n.pl., sing.* **insigne** (-nē). **1.** badges or distinguishing marks of office or honour: *military insignia.* **2.** distinguishing marks or signs of anything: *insignia of mourning.* [t. L, pl. of *insigne* mark, badge, prop. neut. of *insignis* distinguished by a mark]

insignificance (ĭn′sĭg nĭf′ĭ kəns), *n.* the quality or condition of being insignificant; lack of significance.

insignificancy (ĭn′sĭg nĭf′ĭ kən sĭ), *n., pl.* **-cies. 1.** insignificance. **2.** an insignificant person or thing.

insignificant (ĭn′sĭg nĭf′ĭ kənt), *adj.* **1.** unimportant, trifling, or petty, as things, matters, details, etc. **2.** too small to be important: *an insignificant sum.* **3.** of no consequence, influence, or distinction, as persons. **4.** without weight of character; contemptible: *an insignificant fellow.* **5.** without meaning; meaningless, as terms. —*n.* **6.** a word, thing, or person without significance. —**in′signif′icantly,** *adv.*

insincere (ĭn′sĭn sĭə′), *adj.* not sincere; not honest in the expression of actual feeling. —**in′sincere′ly,** *adv.*

insincerity (ĭn′sĭn sĕ′rĭ tĭ), *n., pl.* **-ties.** the quality of being insincere; lack of sincerity; deceitfulness.

insinuate (ĭn sĭn′yōō āt′), *v.,* **-ated, -ating.** —*v.t.* **1.** to suggest or hint slyly. **2.** instil or infuse subtly or artfully into the mind: *to insinuate doubt.* **3.** to bring or introduce into a position or relation by indirect or artful methods: *to insinuate oneself into the favour of another.* —*v.i.* **4.** to make insinuations. [t. L: m. s. *insinuātus,* pp., brought in by windings or turnings] —**insin′uat′ingly,** *adv.* —**insinuative** (ĭn sĭn′yōō ə tĭv), *adj.* —**insin′ua′tor,** *n.* —**Syn. 1.** See **hint.**

insinuation (ĭn sĭn′yōō ā′shən), *n.* **1.** covert or artful suggestion or hinting, as of something not plainly stated. **2.** a suggestion or hint of this kind. **3.** subtle or artful instilment into the mind. **4.** the act of insinuating. **5.** ingratiation: *he made his way by flattery and insinuation.* **6.** the art or power of stealing into the affections and pleasing. **7.** an ingratiating act or speech.

insipid (ĭn sĭp′ĭd), *adj.* **1.** without distinctive, interesting, or attractive qualities: *an insipid tale.* **2.** without sufficient taste to be pleasing, as food or drink: *a rather insipid fruit.* [t. LL: s. *insipidus* tasteless] —**in′sipid′ity, insip′idness,** *n.* —**insip′idly,** *adv.*

insipience (ĭn sĭp′ĭ əns), *n.* lack of wisdom; folly. [late ME, t. L: m. s. *insipientia*] —**insip′ient,** *adj.* —**insip′iently,** *adv.*

insist (ĭn sĭst′), *v.i.* **1.** to be emphatic, firm, or pertinacious on some matter of desire, demand, intention, etc.: *he insisted on that privilege.* **2.** to lay emphasis in assertion: *to insist on the justice of a claim.* **3.** to assert or maintain positively. **4.** to dwell with earnestness or emphasis (fol. by *on* or *upon*): *to insist on a point in a discourse.* [t. L: s. *insistere* insist, stand or press upon] —**insist′er,** *n.*

insistence (ĭn sĭs′təns), *n.* **1.** the act or fact of insisting. **2.** the quality of being insistent.

insistency (ĭn sĭs′tən sĭ), *n., pl.* **-cies. 1.** the quality of being insistent; insistence. **2.** that which is insistent.

insistent (ĭn sĭs′tənt), *adj.* **1.** insisting; earnest or emphatic in dwelling upon, maintaining, or demanding something; persistent. **2.** compelling attention or notice: *an insistent tone.* —**insist′ently,** *adv.*

in situ (ĭn sĭt′yōō), *Latin.* in its original place.

insnare (ĭn snĕə′), *v.t.,* **-snared, -snaring.** ensnare.

insobriety (ĭn′sō brī′ə tĭ), *n.* lack of sobriety.

insociable (ĭn sō′shə bl), *adj.* unsociable. —**inso′ciabil′ity,** *n.* —**inso′ciably,** *adv.*

in so far, to such an extent (usually fol. by *as*). Also, *Chiefly U.S.,* **insofar** (ĭn′sə fä′), *adv.*

insolate (ĭn′sō lāt′), *v.t.,* **-lated, -lating.** to expose to the sun's rays; treat by exposure to the sun's rays. [t. L: m. s. *insōlātus,* pp., placed in the sun]

insolation (ĭn′sō lā′shən), *n.* **1.** exposure to the sun's rays, specif. as a process of treatment. **2.** *Pathol.* sunstroke. **3.** *Meteorol.* solar radiation received on a given body or over a given area. [t. LL: s. *insōlātio*]

insole (ĭn′sōl′), *n.* **1.** the inner sole of a shoe or boot. **2.** a thickness of warm or waterproof material laid as an inner sole within a shoe.

insolence (ĭn′sə ləns), *n.* **1.** insolent behaviour or speech. **2.** the quality of being insolent.

insolent (ĭn′sə lənt), *adj.* **1.** boldly rude or disrespectful; contemptuously impertinent; insulting: *an insolent reply.* —*n.* **2.** an insolent person. [ME, t. L: s. *insolens* unaccustomed, unusual, excessive, arrogant] —**in′solently,** *adv.* —**Syn. 1.** See **impertinent.**

insoluble (ĭn sŏl′yōō bl), *adj.* **1.** incapable of being dissolved: *insoluble salts.* **2.** that cannot be solved: *an insoluble problem.* [ME, t. L: s. *insolūbilis*] —**insol′ubil′ity, insol′ubleness,** *n.* —**insol′ubly,** *adv.*

insolvable (ĭn sŏl′və bl), *adj.* incapable of being solved or explained: *an insolvable problem.* —**insol′vabil′ity,** *n.* —**insol′vably,** *adv.*

insolvency (ĭn sŏl′vən sĭ), *n.* the condition of being insolvent; bankruptcy.

insolvent (ĭn sŏl′vənt), *Law.* —*adj.* **1.** not solvent; unable to satisfy creditors or discharge liabilities, either because liabilities exceed assets or because of inability to pay debts as they mature. **2.** pertaining to bankrupt persons or bankruptcy. —*n.* **3.** one who is insolvent.

insomnia (ĭn sŏm′nĭ ə), *n.* inability to sleep, esp. when chronic; sleeplessness. [t. L] —**insom′nious,** *adj.*

insomniac (ĭn sŏm′nĭ ăk′), *n.* **1.** one who suffers from insomnia. —*adj.* **2.** suffering from insomnia. **3.** of, pertaining to, or causing insomnia.

in so much, 1. to such an extent or degree (*that*); so (*that*). **2.** inasmuch (*as*). Also, *Chiefly U.S.,* **insomuch** (ĭn′sō mŭch′), *adv.*

insouciance (ĭn sōō′syəns; *Fr.* ăN sōō syäNs′), *n.* the quality of being insouciant. [t. F, der. *insouciant* INSOUCIANT]

insouciant (ĭn sōō′syənt; *Fr.* ăN sōō syäN′), *adj.* free from concern; without anxiety; carefree. [t. F, der. *soucier* care, g. L *sollicitāre*] —**insou′ciantly,** *adv.*

insoul (ĭn sōl′), *v.t.* ensoul.

inspan (ĭn spăn′), *v.t.,* **-spanned, -spanning.** *S African.* to yoke or harness. [t. Afrikaans: m. s. *inspannen*]

inspect (ĭn spĕkt′), *v.t.* **1.** to look carefully at or over; view closely and critically: *to inspect every part.* **2.** to view or examine formally or officially: *to inspect troops.* [t. L: s. *inspectus,* pp.]

inspection (ĭn spĕk′shən), *n.* **1.** inspecting, esp. careful or critical inspecting or viewing. **2.** formal or official viewing or examination: *an inspection of the troops.* [ME, t. L: s. *inspectio*] —**inspec′tional,** *adj.* —**Syn. 2.** See **examination.**

inspective (ĭn spĕk′tĭv), *adj.* **1.** given to making inspection. **2.** pertaining to inspection.

inspector (ĭn spĕk′tə), *n.* **1.** one who inspects. **2.** an officer appointed to inspect. **3.** one who makes assessments for taxation purposes: *an inspector of taxes.* **4.** a police officer ranking above sergeant and below chief inspector. **5.** the rank of any of these. [t. L] —**inspec′toral, inspectorial** (ĭn′spĕk tô′rĭ əl), *adj.* —**inspec′torship′,** *n.*

inspectorate (ĭn spĕk′tə rĭt), *n.* **1.** the office or function of an inspector. **2.** a body of inspectors. **3.** a district under an inspector.

insphere (ĭn sfĭə′), *v.t.,* **-sphered, -sphering.** ensphere.

inspirable (ĭn spī′ə rə bl), *adj.* capable of being inspired.

inspiration (ĭn′spĭ rā′shən), *n.* **1.** an inspiring or animating action or influence: *I cannot write without inspiration.* **2.** something inspired, as a thought. **3.** a result of inspired activity. **4.** a thing or person that inspires. **5.** *Theol.* **a.** a divine influence directly and immediately exerted upon the mind or soul of a man. **b.** the divine quality of the writings or words of men so influenced. **6.** the drawing of air into the lungs; inhalation. **7.** the act of inspiring. **8.** the state of being inspired.

inspirational (ĭn′spĭ rā′shə nəl), *adj.* **1.** imparting inspiration. **2.** under the influence of inspiration; inspired. **3.** of or pertaining to inspiration. —**in′spira′tionally,** *adv.*

inspiratory (ĭn spī′ə rə tə rĭ, -trĭ), *adj.* pertaining to inspiration or inhalation.

inspire (ĭn spī′ə), *v.,* **-spired, -spiring.** —*v.t.* **1.** to infuse an animating, quickening, or exalting influence into: *his courage inspired his followers.* **2.** to produce or arouse (a feeling, thought, etc.): *to inspire confidence in others.* **3.** to affect with a specified feeling, thought, etc.:

inspire a person with distrust. **4.** to influence or impel: *opposition inspired him to a greater effort.* **5.** to animate, as an influence, feeling, thought, or the like does: *inspired by a belief in a better future.* **6.** to communicate or suggest by a divine or supernatural influence: *writings inspired by God.* **7.** to guide or control by divine influence. **8.** to prompt or instigate (utterances, etc.) by influence without avowal of responsibility. **9.** to give rise to, occasion, or cause. **10.** to take (air, gases, etc.) into the lungs in breathing; inhale. **11.** *Archaic.* to infuse (breath, life, etc. *into*) by breathing. **12.** *Archaic.* to breathe into or upon. —*v.i.* **13.** to give inspiration. **14.** to inhale. [ME *inspire(n)*, t. L: m. *inspīrāre* breathe into] —**inspir′er,** *n.* —**inspir′ingly,** *adv.*

inspirit (ĭn spĭr′ĭt), *v.t.* to infuse (new) spirit or life into. —**inspir′itingly,** *adv.*

inspissate (ĭn spĭs′āt), *v.t., v.i.,* **-sated, -sating.** to thicken, as by evaporation; make or become dense. [t. LL: m. s. *inspissātus*, pp.] —**in′spissa′tion,** *n.*

inst., **1.** instant (def. 5). **2.** (*also cap.*) institute. **3.** (*also cap.*) institution. **4.** instrumental.

instability (ĭn′stə bĭl′ĭ tĭ), *n.* the state of being instable; lack of stability or firmness.

instable (ĭn stā′bl), *adj.* not stable; unstable.

install (ĭn stôl′), *v.t.* **1.** to place in position for service or use, as a system of electric lighting, etc. **2.** to establish in any office, position, or place. **3.** to induct into an office, etc., with ceremonies or formalities, as by seating in a stall or official seat. [t. ML: s. *installāre.* See IN-², STALL¹] —**install′er,** *n.*

installation (ĭn′stə lā′shən), *n.* **1.** something installed. **2.** a system of machinery or apparatus placed in position for use. **3.** the act of installing. **4.** the fact of being installed. **5.** *Mil.* a military facility comprising an area or a number of buildings, containing soldiers or equipment. [t. ML: s. *installātio*]

instalment¹ (ĭn stôl′mənt), *n.* **1.** any of several parts into which a debt or other sum payable is divided for payment at successive fixed times: *to pay for furniture by instalments.* **2.** a single portion of something furnished or issued by parts at successive times: *a serial in six instalments.* Also, *U.S.*, **installment.** [f. IN-² + obs. *stalment* instalment (der. STALL¹, v., arrange payment)]

instalment² (ĭn stôl′mənt), *n.* **1.** the act of installing. **2.** the fact of being installed; installation. Also, *U.S.*, **installment.** [f. INSTALL, v. + -MENT]

instance (ĭn′stəns), *n., v.,* **-stanced, -stancing.** —*n.* **1.** a case of anything: *fresh instances of oppression.* **2.** an example put forth in proof or illustration: *an instance of carelessness.* **3.** legal process (now chiefly in certain expressions): *a court of first instance.* **4.** *Archaic.* urgency. **5.** *Obs.* an impelling motive. **6. at the instance of,** at the urgency, solicitation, instigation, or suggestion of. **7. for instance,** for example; as an example. —*v.t.* **8.** to cite as an instance or example. **9.** *Now Rare.* to exemplify by an instance. —*v.i.* **10.** *Now Rare.* to cite an instance. [ME *instaunce*, t. AF, t. L: m. s. *instantia* presence, urgency] —**Syn. 2.** See **case¹.**

instancy (ĭn′stən sĭ), *n.* **1.** the quality of being instant; urgency; pressing nature. **2.** *Rare.* immediateness.

instant (ĭn′stənt), *n.* **1.** an infinitesimal or very short space of time; a moment: *not an instant too soon.* **2.** the point of time now present, or present with reference to some action or event. **3.** a particular moment: *at the instant of contact.* —*adj.* **4.** succeeding without any interval of time; immediate: *instant relief.* **5.** present; current (now used elliptically): *the 10th instant* (the tenth day of the present month). **6.** pressing or urgent: *instant need.* **7.** (of a foodstuff) ready for immediate and simple preparation, as by adding water: *instant coffee.* —*adv.* **8.** *Archaic.* instantly. [late ME, t. L: s. *instans*, ppr., standing upon, insisting, being at hand] —**Syn. 1.** See **minute¹.**

instantaneity (ĭn′stăn tə nē′ĭ tĭ), *n.* the quality or fact of being instantaneous; instantaneousness.

instantaneous (ĭn′stən tā′nyəs), *adj.* **1.** occurring, done, or completed in an instant: *an instantaneous explosion.* **2.** existing at or pertaining to a particular instant: *the instantaneous position of something.* —**in′stanta′neously,** *adv.* —**in′stanta′neousness,** *n.*

instantaneous frequency, *Elect.* the rate of change of phase of an oscillation, expressed in radians per second divided by 2π.

instanter (ĭn stăn′tə), *adv.* instantly. [t. L: urgently]

instantly (ĭn′stənt lĭ), *adv.* **1.** immediately; at once. **2.** *Archaic.* urgently. —**Syn. 1.** See **immediately.**

instar¹ (ĭn′stä), *n.* an insect in any one of its periods of post-embryonic growth between moults. [t. L: form, likeness]

instar² (ĭn stä′), *v.t.,* **-starred, -starring.** **1.** to place as a star. **2.** to make a star of. **3.** to set with or as with stars. [f. IN-¹ + STAR]

instate (ĭn stāt′), *v.t.,* **-stated, -stating.** **1.** to put into a certain state, condition, or position; install. **2.** *Obs.* to endow with something. —**instate′ment,** *n.*

in statu quo (ĭn stăt′yōō kwō′), *Latin.* in the state in which (anything was or is).

instauration (ĭn′stô rā′shən), *n.* renewal; restoration; renovation; repair. [t. L: s. *instaurātio*]

instead (ĭn stĕd′), *adv.* **1.** in the stead or place; in lieu (fol. by *of*): *come by plane instead of by train.* **2.** in one's (its, their, etc.) stead: *she sent the boy instead.* [orig. two words, *in stead* in place]

instep (ĭn′stĕp′), *n.* **1.** the arched upper surface of the human foot between the toes and the ankle. **2.** the part of a shoe, stocking, etc., over the instep. **3.** the front of the hind leg of a horse, etc., between the hock and the pastern joint; cannon. [appar. f. IN-¹ + STEP]

instigate (ĭn′stĭ gāt′), *v.t.,* **-gated, -gating.** **1.** to spur on, set on, or incite to some action or course: *to instigate someone to commit a crime.* **2.** to bring about by incitement; foment: *to instigate a quarrel.* [t. L: m. s. *instigātus*, pp.] —**in′stiga′tive,** *adj.* —**in′stiga′tor,** *n.*

instigation (ĭn′stĭ gā′shən), *n.* **1.** the act of instigating. **2.** an incentive. [late ME, t. L: s. *instigātio*]

instil (ĭn stĭl′), *v.t.,* **-stilled, -stilling.** **1.** to infuse slowly or by degrees into the mind or feelings; insinuate; inject: *courtesy must be instilled in childhood.* **2.** to put in drop by drop. Also, *Chiefly U.S.,* **instill.** [t. L: s. *instillāre* pour in by drops] —**instill′er,** *n.* —**instil′ment,** *n.*

instillation (ĭn′stĭ lā′shən), *n.* **1.** the act of instilling. **2.** something instilled.

instinct¹ (ĭn′stĭngkt), *n.* **1.** *Sociol., Psychol., etc.* an inborn pattern of activity and response common to a given biological stock. **2.** innate impulse or natural inclination, or a particular natural inclination or tendency. **3.** a natural aptitude or gift for something: *an instinct for art.* **4.** natural intuitive power. [late ME, t. L: s. *instinctus*, n., instigation, impulse]

instinct² (ĭn stĭngkt′), *adj.* urged or animated from within; infused or filled with some active principle (fol. by *with*). [t. L: s. *instinctus*, pp., instigated, impelled]

instinctive (ĭn stĭngk′tĭv), *adj.* **1.** pertaining to or of the nature of instinct. **2.** prompted by or resulting from instinct. Also, **instinctual** (ĭn stĭngk′tyōō əl). —**instinc′tively,** *adv.*

institute (ĭn′stĭ tyōōt′), *v.,* **-tuted, -tuting,** *n.* —*v.t.* **1.** to set up or establish: *institute a government.* **2.** to set on foot; inaugurate; initiate: *institute a new course.* **3.** to set in operation: *institute a suit.* **4.** to bring into use or practice: *to institute laws.* **5.** to establish in an office or position. **6.** *Eccles.* to assign to or invest with a spiritual charge. —*n.* **7.** a society or organization for carrying on a particular work, as of literary, scientific, or educational character. **8.** the building occupied by such a society. **9.** *Educ.* **a.** an institution, generally beyond the secondary school level, devoted to instruction in technical subjects, usually separate but sometimes organized as a part of a university. **b.** a unit within a university organized for advanced instruction and research in a relatively narrow field of subject matter. **c.** a short instructional programme set up for a particular group interested in some specialized type of activity. **10.** an established principle, law, custom, or organization. **11.** (*pl.*) **a.** an elementary textbook of law designed for beginners. **b.** (*cap.*) Also, **Institutes of Justinian.** an elementary treatise on Roman law, in four books, part of the Corpus Juris Civilis. **12.** something instituted. [ME *institut*, pp., set up, established, t. L: s. *institūtus*]

instituter (ĭn′stĭ tyōō′tə), *n.* institutor.

institution (ĭn′stĭ tyōō′shən), *n.* **1.** an organization or establishment for the promotion of a particular object, usually one for some public, educational, charitable, or similar purpose. **2.** a building used for such work, as a college, school, hospital, mental hospital, or the like. **3.** a concern engaged in some activity, as an insurance company. **4.** *Sociol.* an organized pattern of group behaviour, well-established and accepted as a fundamental part of a culture, such as slavery. **5.** any established law, custom, etc. **6.** any familiar practice or object. **7.** the act of instituting or setting up; establishment: *the institution of laws.* **8.** *Eccles.* **a.** the origination of the Eucharist, and enactment of its observance, by Christ. **b.** the investment of a clergyman with a spiritual charge.

institutional (ĭn′stĭ tyōō′shə nəl), *adj.* **1.** of, pertaining to, or established by institution. **2.** pertaining to organized societies or to the buildings used for their work. **3.** of the nature of an institution. **4.** characterized by uniformity and dullness. **5.** pertaining to institutes or principles, esp. of jurisprudence. —**in′stitu′tionally,** *adv.*

institutionalism (ĭn′stĭ tyo͞o′shə nə lĭz′əm), *n.* **1.** the system of institutions or organized societies for public, charitable, or similar purposes. **2.** strong attachment to established institutions, as of religion.

institutionalize (ĭn′stĭ tyo͞o′shə nə līz′), *v.t.*, **-lized, -lizing.** **1.** to make institutional. **2.** to make into or treat as an institution. **3.** to put (a person) into an institution. Also, **institutionalise.**

institutionary (ĭn′stĭ tyo͞o′shə nə rĭ), *adj.* **1.** of or relating to an institution or to institutions; institutional. **2.** of or pertaining to institution, esp. ecclesiastical institution.

institutive (ĭn′stĭ tyo͞o′tĭv), *adj.* tending or intended to institute or establish. **—in′stitu′tively,** *adv.*

institutor (ĭn′stĭ tyo͞o′tə), *n.* one who institutes or founds. Also, **instituter.**

instr., **1.** instructor. **2.** instrument. **3.** instrumental.

instruct (ĭn strŭkt′), *v.t.* **1.** to direct or command; furnish with orders or directions: *the doctor instructed me to diet.* **2.** to furnish with knowledge, esp. by a systematic method; teach; train; educate. **3.** to furnish with information; inform or apprise. **4.** *Law.* **a.** to give instructions, as a client to a solicitor, or a solicitor to a barrister. **b.** (of a judge) to outline or explain the legal principles involved in a case, for the guidance of (the jury). [late ME *instructe*, t. L: m. s. *instructus*, pp., built, prepared, furnished, instructed] **—Syn. 2.** tutor, coach; drill, discipline; indoctrinate; school.

instruction (ĭn strŭk′shən), *n.* **1.** the act or practice of instructing or teaching; education. **2.** knowledge or information imparted. **3.** an item of such knowledge or information. **4.** (*usually pl.*) an order or direction. **5.** the act of furnishing with authoritative directions. **6.** *Computers.* a number or symbol which causes a computer to perform some specified action. **7.** (*pl.*) *Law.* the factual information and directives given by a client to a solicitor, or by a solicitor to a barrister. [late ME *instruccion*, t. L: m. s. *instructio*] **—instruc′tional,** *adj.* **—Syn. 1.** tutoring, coaching; training, drill; indoctrination; schooling. **5.** command, mandate.

instructive (ĭn strŭk′tĭv), *adj.* serving to instruct or inform; conveying instruction, knowledge, or information. **—instruc′tively,** *adv.* **—instruc′tiveness,** *n.*

instructor (ĭn strŭk′tə), *n.* **1.** one who instructs; a teacher. **2.** the academic rank given in American colleges to a teacher inferior in grade to the lowest grade of professor. [late ME, t. ML: teacher, L preparer] **—instruc′torless,** *adj.* **—instruc′torship′,** *n.* **—instructress** (ĭn strŭk′trĭs), *n. fem.* **—Syn. 1.** tutor, schoolmaster, preceptor, pedagogue.

instrument (ĭn′strə mənt), *n.* **1.** a mechanical device or contrivance; a tool; an implement: *a surgeon's instruments.* **2.** a contrivance for producing musical sounds: *a stringed instrument.* **3.** a thing with or by which something is effected; a means; an agency: *an instrument of government.* **4.** a formal legal document, as a contract, promissory note, deed, grant, etc. **5.** one who is used by another. **6.** a device for measuring the present value of a quantity under observation. **7.** *Elect.* an electrical device which displays information about the state of some part of an aircraft, motor car, etc. **—***v.t.* **8.** *Music.* to arrange (a piece of music) for instruments, esp. for an orchestra. [ME, t. L: m. s. *instrūmentum*] **—Syn. 1.** See **tool.**

instrumental (ĭn′strə mĕn′tl), *adj.* **1.** serving as an instrument or means. **2.** of or pertaining to an instrument. **3.** performed on or written for a musical instrument or musical instruments: *instrumental music.* **4.** *Gram.* **a.** (in some inflected languages) denoting a case having as its chief function the indication of means or agency. For example: Old English *beseah blīthe andwlitan* 'looked with a happy countenance'. **b.** denoting the affix or other element characteristic of this case, or a word containing such an element. **c.** similar to such a case form in function or meaning, as the Latin *instrumental ablative, gladiō* 'by means of a sword'. **—***n.* **5.** a piece of music, usually pop, performed without vocal accompaniment. **6.** *Gram.* **a.** the instrumental case. **b.** a word in that case. **c.** a construction of similar meaning. [ME, t. ML: s. *instrūmentālis*]

instrumentalism (ĭn′strə mĕn′tə lĭz′əm), *n.* *Philos.* a form of pragmatism which maintains that the function of thought is to be instrumental to control of the environment and that ideas have value according to their function in human experience or progress.

instrumentalist (ĭn′strə mĕn′tə lĭst), *n.* **1.** one who performs on a musical instrument. **2.** an advocate of instrumentalism. **—***adj.* **3.** of or pertaining to instrumentalism.

instrumentality (ĭn′strə mĕn tăl′ĭ tĭ), *n.*, *pl.* **-ties.** **1.** the quality of being instrumental. **2.** the fact or function of serving some purpose. **3.** a means or agency.

instrumentally (ĭn′strə mĕn′tə lĭ), *adv.* **1.** by the use of an instrument. **2.** with or on an instrument.

instrumentation (ĭn′strə mĕn tā′shən), *n.* **1.** the arranging of music for instruments, esp. for an orchestra. **2.** the use of, or work done by, instruments. **3.** instrumental agency; instrumentality.

instrument flight rules, *Aeron.* the aviation code of regulations for flying using instruments for navigation, etc.

instrument landing system, *Aeron.* a radio-navigation landing aid which provides an approaching aircraft with lateral and vertical guidance and with marker-beacon indications at specified points.

insubordinate (ĭn′sə bô′də nĭt), *adj.* **1.** not submitting to authority; disobedient: *insubordinate crew.* **2.** not lower. **—***n.* **3.** one who is insubordinate. **—in′subor′dinately,** *adv.* **—in′subor′dina′tion,** *n.*

insubstantial (ĭn′səb stăn′shəl), *adj.* **1.** not substantial; slight. **2.** without reality; unreal: *the insubstantial stuff of dreams.* **—in′substan′tial′ity,** *n.*

insufferable (ĭn sŭf′ə rə bl, -sŭf′rə-), *adj.* not to be endured; intolerable; unbearable: *insufferable insolence.* **—insuf′ferableness,** *n.* **—insuf′ferably,** *adv.*

insufficiency (ĭn′sə fĭsh′ən sĭ), *n.* deficiency in amount, force, or fitness; inadequateness. Also, **in′suffi′cience.**

insufficient (ĭn′sə fĭsh′ənt), *adj.* **1.** not sufficient; lacking in what is necessary or required: *an insufficient answer.* **2.** deficient in force, quality, or amount; inadequate: *insufficient protection.* **—in′suffi′ciently,** *adv.*

insufflate (ĭn′sŭ flāt′), *v.t.*, **-flated, -flating.** **1.** to blow or breathe (something) in. **2.** *Med.* to blow (air or a medicinal substance) into some opening or upon some part of the body. **3.** *Eccles.* to breathe upon, especially upon one being baptized or the water of baptism. [t. LL: m. s. *insufflātus*, pp., breathed into] **—in′suffla′tion,** *n.* **—insufflator** (ĭn′sŭ flā′tə), *n.*

insular (ĭn′syo͞o lə), *adj.* **1.** of or pertaining to an island or islands: *insular possessions.* **2.** dwelling or situated on an island. **3.** forming an island: *insular rocks.* **4.** detached; standing alone. **5.** characteristic or suggestive of inhabitants of an island. **6.** narrow or illiberal: *insular prejudices.* **7.** *Pathol.* occurring in or characterized by one or more isolated spots, patches, or the like. **8.** *Anat.* pertaining to existing tissue, as an island (def. 6), esp. to the islets of Langerhans. **—***n.* **9.** an inhabitant of an island. [t. LL: s. *insulāris* of an island] **—insularity** (ĭn′syo͞o lăr′ĭ tĭ), *n.* **—in′sularism,** *n.* **—in′sularly,** *adv.*

insular climate, a type of climate characterized by little seasonal temperature change and associated with coastal areas and islands in temperate latitudes.

insulate (ĭn′syo͞o lāt′), *v.t.*, **-lated, -lating.** **1.** to cover or surround (an electric wire, etc.) with non-conducting material. **2.** *Physics, etc.* to separate by the interposition of a non-conductor, in order to prevent or reduce the transfer of electricity, heat, or sound. **3.** to place in an isolated situation or condition; segregate. [t. L: m. s. *insulātus* made into an island]

insulating tape, *Elect.* tape which has been impregnated with an adhesive insulating compound; used for covering joints in wires, etc.

insulation (ĭn′syo͞o lā′shən), *n.* **1.** material used for insulating. **2.** the act of insulating. **3.** the resulting state.

insulator (ĭn′syo͞o lā′tə), *n.* **1.** *Elect.* **a.** a material of such low conductivity that the flow of current through it is usually negligible. **b.** insulating material, often glass or porcelain, in a unit form so designed as to support a charged conductor and electrically isolate it. **2.** one who or that which insulates.

insulin (ĭn′syo͞o lĭn), *n.* **1.** *Med.* an extract obtained from the pancreas of animals (which contains the hormone of this organ, furnished by its islands), used in the treatment of diabetes, and causing a reduction of sugar in the blood and urine. **2.** (*cap.*) a trademark for this extract. [f. s.·L *insula* island (with reference to the islands of the pancreas) + -IN[2]]

insult (*v.* ĭn sŭlt′; *n.* ĭn′sŭlt), *v.t.* **1.** to treat insolently or with contemptuous rudeness; affront. **2.** *Archaic.* to attack; assault. **—***v.i.* **3.** *Archaic.* to behave with insolent triumph; exult contemptuously (fol. by *on*, *upon*, or *over*). **—***n.* **4.** an insolent or contemptuously rude action or speech; affront. **5.** something having the effect of an affront. **6.** *Archaic.* an attack or assault. [t. L: s. *insultāre* leap on or at, insult] **—insult′er,** *n.* **—insult′ing,** *adj.* **—insult′ingly,** *adv.*

—Syn. 4. INSULT, INDIGNITY, AFFRONT, SLIGHT imply an act which injures another's honour, self-respect, etc. INSULT implies such insolence of speech or manner as deeply humiliates or wounds one's feelings and arouses to anger. INDIGNITY is especially used of inconsiderate, contemptuous treatment towards one entitled to respect. AFFRONT implies open disrespect or offence shown, as it were, to the face; SLIGHT, perhaps only inadvertent, indifference or disregard, but may indicate ill-concealed contempt.

insuperable (ĭn syo͞o′pə rə bl, -prə bl), *adj.* incapable of being passed over, overcome, or surmounted: *an insuperable barrier.* —**insu′perabil′ity, insu′perableness,** *n.* —**insu′perably,** *adv.*

insupportable (ĭn′sə pô′tə bl), *adj.* not endurable; insufferable. —**in′support′ableness,** *n.* —**in′support′ably,** *adv.*

insuppressible (ĭn′sə prĕs′ə bl), *adj.* that cannot be suppressed. —**in′suppress′ibly,** *adv.*

insurable (ĭn sho͝oə′rə bl, -shô′-), *adj.* **1.** capable of being insured, as against risk of loss or harm. **2.** proper to be insured. —**insur′abil′ity,** *n.*

insurance (ĭn sho͝oə′rəns, -shô′-), *n.* **1.** the act, system, or business of insuring property, life, the person, etc., against loss or harm arising in specified contingencies, as fire, accident, death, disablement, or the like, in consideration of a payment proportionate to the risk involved. **2.** the contract thus made, set forth in a written or printed agreement (policy). **3.** the amount for which anything is insured. **4.** the premium paid for insuring a thing.

insurant (ĭn sho͝oə′rənt, -shô′-), *n.* the person who takes out an insurance policy.

insure (ĭn sho͝oə′, ĭn shô′), *v.*, **-sured, -suring.** —*v.t.* **1.** to guarantee against risk of loss or harm. **2.** to secure indemnity to or on, in case of loss, damage, or death. **3.** to issue or procure an insurance policy on. **4.** *Chiefly U.S.* to ensure. —*v.i.* **5.** to issue or procure an insurance policy. [var. of ENSURE]

insured (ĭn sho͝oəd′, ĭn shôd′), *n.* a person covered by an insurance policy.

insurer (ĭn sho͝oə′rə, -shô′-), *n.* **1.** one who contracts to indemnify against losses, etc. **2.** one who insures.

insurgence (ĭn sû′jəns), *n.* an act of insurgency.

insurgency (ĭn sû′jən sĭ), *n.* **1.** the state of being insurgent. **2.** a condition of insurrection against an existing government by a group not recognized as a belligerent.

insurgent (ĭn sû′jənt), *n.* **1.** one who rises in forcible opposition to lawful authority; one who engages in armed resistance to a government or to the execution of laws. —*adj.* **2.** rising in revolt; rebellious. **3.** (of the sea, etc.) rising or surging up. [t. L: s. *insurgens*, ppr., rising on or up]

insurmountable (ĭn′sə moun′tə bl), *adj.* incapable of being surmounted, passed over, or overcome: *an insurmountable obstacle.* —**in′surmount′ably,** *adv.*

insurrection (ĭn′sə rĕk′shən), *n.* **1.** the act of rising in arms or open resistance against civil or established authority. **2.** a revolt. [late ME, t. LL: s. *insurrectio*, der. L *insurgere* rise up] —**in′surrec′tional,** *adj.* —**in′surrec′tionally,** *adv.* —**in′surrec′tionism,** *n.* —**in′surrec′tionist,** *n.* —**Syn. 2.** See **revolt.**

insurrectionary (ĭn′sə rĕk′shə nə rĭ), *adj.*, *n.*, *pl.* **-ries.** —*adj.* **1.** pertaining to or of the nature of insurrection. **2.** given to insurrection. —*n.* **3.** one who engages in insurrection; an insurgent.

insusceptible (ĭn′sə sĕp′tə bl), *adj.* **1.** not liable to be affected or influenced by (fol. by *of*): *insusceptible of flattery.* **2.** not accessible or sensitive (fol. by *to*): *insusceptible to infection.* —**in′suscep′tibil′ity,** *n.*

inswathe (ĭn swāŧħ′), *v.t.*, **-swathed, -swathing.** to enswathe.

inswept (ĭn′swĕpt′), *adj.* tapering at the front or tip, as an aeroplane wing.

inswinger (ĭn′swĭng′ə), *n.* *Cricket.* a ball bowled so as to swerve from off to leg.

int., 1. interest. **2.** interior. **3.** interjection. **4.** internal. **5.** international. **6.** interpreter. **7.** intransitive.

intact (ĭn tăkt′), *adj.* remaining uninjured, unaltered, sound, or whole; unimpaired. [late ME, t. L: s. *intactus*] —**intact′ness,** *n.* —**Syn.** See **complete.**

intaglio (ĭn tä′lĭ ō′; *It.* ēn tȧ′lyō), *n.*, *pl.* **intaglios, intagli** (*It.* ēn tȧ′lyē). **1.** a gem, seal, piece of jewellery, or the like, cut with an incised or sunken design. **2.** incised carving, as opposed to carving in relief. **3.** ornamentation with a figure or design sunk below the surface. **4.** an incised or countersunk die. **5.** a figure or design so produced. **6.** a print-making process by which the printing ink is transferred to paper, etc., from areas sunk below the surface. [t. It., der. *intagliare* cut in, engrave] —**intagliated** (ĭn tä′lĭ ā′tĭd), *adj.*

intake (ĭn′tāk′), *n.* **1.** the point at which a fluid is taken into a channel, pipe, etc. **2.** the act of taking in. **3.** that which is taken in. **4.** the quantity taken in: *the intake of oxygen.* **5.** a narrowing or contraction.

intangible (ĭn tăn′jĭ bl), *adj.* **1.** incapable of being perceived by the sense of touch, as incorporeal or immaterial things. **2.** not definite or clear to the mind: *intangible arguments.* **3.** (of an asset) existing only in connection with something else, as the goodwill of a business. —*n.* **4.** something intangible. —**intan′gibil′ity, intan′gibleness,** *n.* —**intan′gibly,** *adv.*

intarsia (ĭn tä′sĭ ə), *n.* a highly developed form of inlay or marquetry in wood, originally as produced in Italy during the Renaissance. [t. It., der. *intarsiare* inlay]

integer (ĭn′tĭ jə), *n.* **1.** one of the numbers 0, 1, 2, 3, 4, etc.; a whole number, as distinguished from a fraction or a mixed number. **2.** a complete entity. [t. L: untouched, whole, entire]

integer vitae (ĭn′tĭ jə vī′tē), *Latin.* blameless in life; innocent. (Horace, *Odes*, I)

integrable (ĭn′tĭ grə bl), *adj.* *Maths.* capable of being integrated, as a mathematical function or differential equation.

integral (ĭn′tĭ grəl), *adj.* **1.** of or pertaining to a whole; belonging as a part of the whole; constituent or component: *the integral parts of the human body.* **2.** necessary to the completeness of the whole. **3.** made up of parts which together constitute a whole. **4.** *Rare.* entire or complete: *his integral love.* **5.** *Arith.* pertaining to or being an integer; not fractional. **6.** *Maths.* pertaining to or involving integrals. —*n.* **7.** an integral whole. **8.** *Maths.* the result of the operation inverse to differentiation (see **integration,** def. 4); an expression from which a given function, equation, or system of equations is derived by differentiation. [t. LL: s. *integrālis*] —**integrality** (ĭn′tĭ grăl′ĭ tĭ), *n.* —**in′tegrally,** *adv.*

integral calculus, the branch of mathematics dealing with the finding and properties of integrals.

integrand (ĭn′tĭ grănd′), *n.* *Maths.* the expression to be integrated. [t. L: s. *integrandus*, ger. of *integrāre* make whole]

integrant (ĭn′tĭ grənt), *adj.* **1.** making up, or belonging as a part to, a whole; constituent. —*n.* **2.** an integrant part. [t. L: s. *integrans*, ppr., making whole]

integrate (ĭn′tĭ grāt′), *v.*, **-grated, -grating.** —*v.t.* **1.** to bring together (parts) into a whole. **2.** to make up or complete as a whole, as parts do. **3.** to indicate the total amount or the mean value of. **4.** *Maths.* to find the integral of. **5.** to combine (educational facilities, student bodies, and other systems, previously segregated by race), into one unified system. **6.** to amalgamate (a racial or religious minority group) with the rest of the community. —*v.i.* **7.** *Chiefly U.S.* (of educational and other public systems) to become unified. [t. L: m. s. *integrātus*, pp., made whole] —**in′tegra′tive,** *adj.*

integrated circuit, *Electronics.* an electronic circuit formed on a single block of material by etching.

integration (ĭn′tĭ grā′shən), *n.* **1.** the act of integrating; combination into an integral whole. **2.** behaviour, as of the individual, in harmony with the environment. **3.** *Psychol.* the organization of personality traits into a hierarchy of functions. **4.** *Maths.* the operation of finding the integral of a function or equation (the inverse of *differentiation*). **5.** the combination of educational and other public facilities, previously segregated by race, into one unified system. **6.** the amalgamation of a racial or religious minority group with the rest of the community. [t. L: s. *integrātio* renewal, restoration]

integrationist (ĭn′tĭ grā′shə nĭst), *n.* *Chiefly U.S.* one who favours integration (def. 5).

integrator (ĭn′tĭ grā′tə), *n.* **1.** one who or that which integrates. **2.** an instrument for performing numerical integrations.

integrity (ĭn tĕg′rĭ tĭ), *n.* **1.** soundness of moral principle and character; uprightness; honesty. **2.** the state of being whole, entire, or undiminished: *to preserve the integrity of the empire.* **3.** sound, unimpaired, or perfect condition: *the integrity of the text.* [late ME, t. L: m. s. *integritas*] —**Syn. 1.** See **honour.**

integument (ĭn tĕg′yo͝o mənt), *n.* **1.** a skin, shell, rind, or the like. **2.** a covering. [t. L: s. *integumentum*]

integumentary (ĭn tĕg′yo͝o mĕn′tə rĭ), *adj.* of, pertaining to, or like an integument.

intellect (ĭn′tĭ lĕkt′), *n.* **1.** the power or faculty of the mind by which one knows, understands, or reasons, as distinct from that by which one feels and that by which one wills; the understanding. **2.** understanding or mental capacity, esp. of a high order. **3.** a particular mind or intelligence, esp. of a high order. **4.** the person possessing it. **5.** minds collectively, as of a number of persons, or the persons themselves. [ME, t. L: s. *intellectus* a discerning, perceiving] —**Syn. 1.** See **mind.**

intellection (ĭn′tĭ lĕk′shən), *n.* **1.** the action or process of understanding; the exercise of the intellect. **2.** a particular act of the intellect. **3.** a conception or idea as the result of such an act.

intellective (ĭn′tĭ lĕk′tĭv), *adj.* **1.** having power to understand; intelligent. **2.** of or pertaining to the intellect. —**in′tellec′tively,** *adv.*

intellectual (ĭn′tĭ lĕk′tyo͞o əl), *adj.* **1.** appealing to or engaging the intellect: *intellectual pursuits.* **2.** of or pertaining to the intellect: *intellectual powers.* **3.** directed or inclined towards things that involve the intellect: *intellectual tastes.* **4.** possessing or showing intellect or mental capacity, esp. to a high degree: *an intellectual writer.* **5.** characterized by or suggesting a predominance of intellect: *an intellectual face.* —*n.* **6.** an intellectual being or person. **7.** a member of a class or group professing, or supposed to possess, enlightened judgement and opinions with respect to public or political questions. **8.** (*pl.*) *Rare.* things pertaining to the intellect. **9.** (*pl.*) *Archaic.* the mental faculties. [ME, t. L: s. *intellectuālis*] —**in′tellec′tually,** *adv.* —**in′tellec′tualness,** *n.* —**Syn. 4.** See **intelligent.**

intellectualism (ĭn′tĭ lĕk′tyo͞o ə lĭz′əm), *n.* **1.** the exercise of the intellect; devotion to intellectual pursuits. **2.** *Philos.* **a.** the doctrine that knowledge is wholly or chiefly derived from pure reason. **b.** the belief that reason is the ultimate principle of reality. —**in′tellec′tualist,** *n.* —**in′tellec′tualis′tic,** *adj.*

intellectuality (ĭn′tĭ lĕk′tyo͞o ăl′ĭ tĭ), *n., pl.* **-ties. 1.** the quality of being intellectual. **2.** intellectual character or power.

intellectualize (ĭn′tĭ lĕk′tyo͞o ə līz′), *v.t., v.i.,* **-lized, -lizing.** to make or become intellectual; consider or treat in intellectual terms. Also, **intellectualise.** —**in′tellec′tualiza′tion,** *n.*

intelligence (ĭn tĕl′ĭ jəns), *n.* **1.** capacity for understanding and for other forms of adaptive behaviour; aptitude in grasping truths, facts, meaning, etc. **2.** good mental capacity: *a task requiring intelligence.* **3.** the faculty of understanding. **4.** (*often cap.*) an intelligent being, esp. an incorporeal one. **5.** knowledge of an event, circumstance, etc., received or imparted; news; information. **6.** the gathering or distribution of information, esp. secret information which might prove detrimental to an enemy. **7.** a staff of persons engaged in obtaining such information; secret service. **8.** *Obs.* interchange of information, thoughts, etc., or communication. —**Syn. 1.** See **mind.**

intelligence quotient, the mental age divided by the actual age. A child with a mental age of 12 years and an actual age of 10 years has an intelligence quotient, or IQ, of 1·2 (usually expressed as 120). In the computation of the IQ, age above 15 or 16 is commonly ignored.

intelligencer (ĭn tĕl′ĭ jən sə), *n.* **1.** an informer; a spy. **2.** *Archaic.* one who or that which conveys information.

intelligence test, any of several psychological tests, either verbal or non-verbal, which attempt to measure the mental development, as opposed to the educational achievement, of an individual.

intelligent (ĭn tĕl′ĭ jənt), *adj.* **1.** having a good understanding or mental capacity; quick to understand, as persons or animals: *intelligent pupils.* **2.** showing quickness of understanding, as actions, utterances, etc.: *an intelligent answer.* **3.** having the faculty of understanding: *an intelligent being.* **4.** *Rare.* having understanding or knowledge (fol. by *of*). [t. L: s. *intelligens,* var. of *intellegens,* ppr.] —**intel′ligently,** *adv.*

—**Syn. 1.** INTELLIGENT, INTELLECTUAL describe distinctive mental capacity. INTELLIGENT often suggests a natural quickness of understanding: *an intelligent reader.* INTELLECTUAL implies not only having a high degree of understanding, but also a capacity and taste for the higher forms of knowledge. **2.** See **sharp.**

intelligential (ĭn tĕl′ĭ jĕn′shəl), *adj.* **1.** of or pertaining to the intelligence or understanding. **2.** endowed with intelligence. **3.** conveying information.

intelligentsia (ĭn tĕl′ĭ jĕnt′sĭ ə), *n.pl.* a class or group of persons having or claiming special enlightenment in views or principles; the intellectuals. [t. Russ., t. L: m. *intelligentia* intelligence]

intelligibility (ĭn tĕl′ĭ jə bĭl′ĭ tĭ), *n., pl.* **-ties. 1.** the quality or character of being intelligible; capability of being understood. **2.** something intelligible.

intelligible (ĭn tĕl′ĭ jə bl), *adj.* **1.** capable of being understood; comprehensible. **2.** *Philos.* apprehensible by the mind. [ME, t. L: m. s. *intelligibilis,* var. of *intellegibilis*] —**intel′ligibleness,** *n.* —**intel′ligibly,** *adv.*

intemerate (ĭn tĕm′ə rĭt), *adj.* *Now Rare.* inviolate; undefiled; unsullied; pure. [t. L: m. s. *intemerātus*]

intemperance (ĭn tĕm′pə rəns, -prəns), *n.* **1.** immoderate indulgence in alcoholic drink. **2.** excessive indulgence of a natural appetite or passion. **3.** lack of moderation or due restraint, as in action or speech.

intemperate (ĭn tĕm′pə rĭt, -prĭt), *adj.* **1.** given to or characterized by immoderate indulgence in intoxicating drink. **2.** immoderate as regards indulgence of appetite or passion. **3.** not temperate; unrestrained or unbridled. **4.** extreme in temperature, as climate, etc. —**intem′perately,** *adv.* —**intem′perateness,** *n.*

intend (ĭn tĕnd′), *v.t.* **1.** to have in mind as something to be done or brought about: *he intends to enlist.* **2.** to design or mean for a particular purpose, use, recipient, etc.: *a book intended for reference.* **3.** to design to express or indicate. **4.** *Obs.* (of words, etc.) to signify. **5.** *Obs.* to direct (the eyes, mind, etc.). —*v.i.* **6.** to have a purpose or design: *he may intend otherwise.* **7.** *Obs.* to set out on one's course. [ME *intende(n),* t. L: m. *intendere* extend, intend; r. ME *entenden,* t. OF: m. *entendre*] —**intend′er,** *n.*

—**Syn. 1.** INTEND, MEAN, DESIGN, PROPOSE imply knowing what one wishes to do and setting this as a goal. To INTEND is to have in mind something willed to be done or brought about: *no offence was intended.* MEAN is a simpler word for the same idea as INTEND, but suggests perhaps less definite thought or conscious choice: *he means to go away.* DESIGN implies planning to effect a particular result; the things to be done have a definite relationship to one another: *to design a plan for Christmas decorations.* PROPOSE suggests setting up a programme before oneself for accomplishment, or offering it for consideration: *we propose to beautify our city.*

intendance (ĭn tĕn′dəns), *n.* **1.** *Chiefly French Hist.* a department of the public service, as in France, or the officials in charge of it. **2.** the function of an intendant; superintendence; intendancy.

intendancy (ĭn tĕn′dən sĭ), *n., pl.* **-cies. 1.** the office or function of an intendant. **2.** a body of intendants. **3.** *Hist.* a district under the charge of an intendant.

intendant (ĭn tĕn′dənt), *n.* **1.** one who has the direction or management of some public business, the affairs of an establishment, etc.; a superintendent. **2.** *Hist.* the title of various public officials in France and elsewhere. [t. F, t. L: m. s. *intendens,* ppr., extending, attending]

intended (ĭn tĕn′dĭd), *adj.* **1.** purposed or designed: *to produce the intended effect.* **2.** prospective: *one's intended wife.* —*n.* **3.** *Colloq.* an intended husband or wife.

intendment (ĭn tĕnd′mənt), *n.* **1.** *Law.* the manner of understanding, construing, or viewing something; the true meaning as fixed by law. **2.** *Obs.* a presumption. **3.** *Obs.* intention; design; purpose.

intenerate (ĭn tĕn′ə rāt′), *v.t.,* **-rated, -rating.** *Now Rare.* to make soft or tender; soften. [f. IN-[2] + L *tener* TENDER[1] + -ATE[1]] —**inten′era′tion,** *n.*

intens., intensive.

intense (ĭn tĕns′), *adj.* **1.** existing or occurring in a high or extreme degree: *intense heat.* **2.** acute, strong, or vehement, as sensations, feelings, or emotions: *intense anxiety.* **3.** of an extreme kind; very great, strong, keen, severe, etc.: *an intense gale.* **4.** *Photog.* **a.** strong: *intense light.* **b.** dense (def. 4). **5.** having or exhibiting some characteristic quality in a high degree. **6.** strenuous or earnest, as activity, exertion, diligence, thought, etc.: *an intense life.* **7.** having or showing great strength or vehemence of feeling, as a person, the face, language, etc. **8.** susceptible to strong emotion; emotional: *an intense person.* [ME, t. L: m. s. *intensus,* pp., stretched tight, intense] —**intense′ly,** *adv.* —**intense′ness,** *n.*

intensify (ĭn tĕn′sĭ fī′), *v.,* **-fied, -fying.** —*v.t.* **1.** to make intense or more intense. **2.** *Photog.* to increase the contrast or density of (an image) on a negative or print. —*v.i.* **3.** to become intense or more intense. —**inten′sifica′tion,** *n.* —**inten′sifi′er,** *n.* —**Syn. 1.** See **aggravate.**

intension (ĭn tĕn′shən), *n.* **1.** intensification; increase in degree. **2.** intensity; high degree. **3.** relative intensity; degree. **4.** exertion of the mind; determination. **5.** *Logic.* the sum of the attributes contained in a concept or connoted by a term. Cf. **extension** (def. 10). [t. L: s. *intensio*]

intensitometer (ĭn tĕn′sĭ tŏm′ĭ tə), *n.* a device for measuring the intensity of X-rays during an exposure in radiography.

intensity (ĭn tĕn′sĭ tĭ), *n., pl.* **-ties. 1.** the quality or condition of being intense. **2.** great energy, strength, vehemence, etc., as of activity, thought, or feeling. **3.** high or extreme degree, as of cold. **4.** the degree or extent to which something is intense. **5. a.** loudness or softness of vocal tone. **b.** carrying power of voice. **6.** the strength or sharpness of a colour due especially to its degree of freedom from admixture with its complementary colour. **7.** *Photog.* **a.** strength, as of light. **b.** density (def. 5). **8.** *Physics.* **a.** the strength of an electric current in amperes. **b.** potential difference; voltage. **c.** the strength of an electrical or magnetic field. **d.** the magnitude, as of a force, per unit of area, volume, etc.

intensive (ĭn tĕn′sĭv), *adj.* **1.** of, pertaining to, or characterized by intensity: *intensive fire from machine guns.* **2.** intensifying. **3.** *Med.* **a.** increasing in intensity or degree. **b.** instituting treatment to the limit of safety. **4.** *Econ.* of or denoting methods designed to increase effectiveness, as, in agriculture, a more thorough tillage, the application of fertilizers, etc., to secure the most from each acre (opposed to *extensive*). **5.** *Gram.* indicating increased emphasis or force. For example: *certainly, tremendously* are intensive adverbs. *—n.* **6.** something that intensifies. **7.** *Gram.* an intensive element or formation, as *-self* in *himself*, or Latin *-tō* in *iac-tō*, 'I hurl' compared with *iacio*, 'I throw'. [t. ML: m. s. *intensīvus*] —**inten'sively,** *adv.* —**inten'siveness,** *n.*

intent¹ (ĭn tĕnt'), *n.* **1.** an intending or purposing, as to commit some act: *criminal intent.* **2.** that which is intended; purpose; aim; design; intention: *my intent was to buy.* **3.** *Law.* the state of a person's mind which directs his actions towards a specific object. **4. to all intents and purposes, a.** for all practical purposes; practically. **b.** for all the ends and purposes in view. **5.** the end or object intended. **6.** *Obs.* meaning. [partly ME *intent*, var. of *entent*, t. OF: intention, g. L *intentus* a stretching out; partly ME *intente*, var. of *entente*, t. OF: purpose, ult. der. L *intendere* stretch out] **—Syn. 2.** See **intention.**

intent² (ĭn tĕnt'), *adj.* **1.** firmly or steadfastly fixed or directed (upon something): *an intent gaze.* **2.** having the gaze or thoughts earnestly fixed on something: *intent on one's job.* **3.** bent, as on some purpose: *intent on revenge.* **4.** earnest: *an intent person.* [t. L: s. *intentus*, pp., stretched, intent] —**intent'ly,** *adv.* —**intent'ness,** *n.*

intention (ĭn tĕn'shən), *n.* **1.** the act of determining mentally upon some action or result; a purpose or design. **2.** the end or object intended. **3.** (*pl.*) *Colloq.* purposes with respect to a proposal of marriage. **4.** the act or fact of intending or purposing. **5.** *Logic.* **a.** the mental act of initially directing attention to something. **b. first intention,** direct cognition of an object viewed or thought through its general concept rather than subsumed under it. **c. second intention,** cognition of an object viewed or thought as an embodiment of one or more general concepts, the attention being directed to the concepts as well as to the object. **6.** *Surg., Med.* a manner or process of healing, as in the healing of a lesion or fracture without granulation (**healing by first intention**) or the healing of a wound by granulation after suppuration (**healing by second intention**). **7.** meaning. **8.** *Obs.* intentness. [t. L: s. *intentio*; r. ME *entencion*, t. OF]

—Syn. 2. INTENTION, INTENT, PURPOSE all refer to a wish which one means to carry out. INTENTION is the general word: *his intentions are good.* INTENT is chiefly legal or poetic: *intent to kill.* PURPOSE implies having a goal or a settled determination to achieve something: *there was no purpose in his actions.*

intentional (ĭn tĕn'shə nəl), *adj.* **1.** done with intention or on purpose: *an intentional insult.* **2.** of or pertaining to intention or purpose. **3.** *Metaphys.* **a.** pertaining to an appearance, phenomenon, or representation in the mind; phenomenal; representational. **b.** pertaining to the capacity of mind to refer to objects of all sorts. —**inten'tionally,** *adv.* **—Syn. 1.** See **deliberate.**

inter (ĭn tû'), *v.t.*, **-terred, -terring. 1.** to deposit (a dead body, etc.) in a grave or tomb; bury, esp. with ceremonies. **2.** *Obs.* to put into the earth. [ME *entere(n)*, t. OF: m. *enterrer*, der. *en-* EN-¹ + *terre* earth (g. L *terra*)]

inter-, a prefix meaning 'between', 'among', 'mutually', 'reciprocally', 'together', as in *intercellular, intercity, intermarry, interweave.* [t. L, comb. form of *inter*, adv. and prep., between, among, during]

interact (ĭn'tər ăkt'), *v.i.* to act on each other. —**in'terac'tive,** *adj.*

interaction (ĭn'tər ăk'shən), *n.* action on each other; reciprocal action.

inter alia (ĭn'tər ā'lĭ ə), *Latin.* among other things.

inter alios (ĭn'tər ā'lĭ ōs'), *Latin.* among others.

inter-Allied (ĭn'tər ə līd', -ăl'īd), *adj.* between or among allied nations, esp. the Allies of World War I.

interatomic (ĭn'tə rə tŏm'ĭk), *adj.* between atoms.

interblend (ĭn'tə blĕnd'), *v.t., v.i.*, **-blended** or **-blent, -blending.** to blend, one with another.

interborough (ĭn'tə bŭ'rə), *adj.* between boroughs.

interbrain (ĭn'tə brān'), *n. Anat.* the diencephalon.

interbreed (ĭn'tə brēd'), *v.t., v.i.*, **-bred, -breeding.** to breed by the crossing of different animal or plant species, breeds, varieties, or individuals.

intercalary (ĭn tû'kə lə rĭ), *adj.* **1.** interpolated; interposed; intervening. **2.** inserted or interpolated in the calendar, as an extra day, month, etc., to make the calendar year equal to the solar year. **3.** having such an inserted day, month, etc., as a year. [t. L: m. s. *intercalārius*]

intercalate (ĭn tû'kə lāt'), *v.t.*, **-lated, -lating. 1.** to interpolate; interpose. **2.** to insert (an extra day, month, etc.) in the calendar, to make the calendar year equal to the solar year. [t. L: m. s. *intercalātus*, pp.] —**intercalative** (ĭn tû'kə lə tĭv), *adj.*

intercalation (ĭn tû'kə lā'shən), *n.* **1.** the act of intercalating; insertion or interpolation, as in a series. **2.** that which is intercalated; an interpolation.

intercede (ĭn'tə sēd'), *v.i.*, **-ceded, -ceding. 1.** to interpose on behalf of one in difficulty or trouble, as by pleading or petition: *to intercede with the governor for a condemned man.* **2.** *Rom. Hist.* (of a tribune or other magistrate) to interpose a veto. [t. L: m. s. *intercēdere* intervene] —**in'terced'er,** *n.*

intercellular (ĭn'tə sĕl'yŏŏ lə), *adj.* situated between or among cells or cellules.

intercept (*v.* ĭn'tə sĕpt'; *n.* ĭn'tə sĕpt'), *v.t.* **1.** to take or seize on the way from one place to another; cut off from the intended destination: *to intercept a messenger.* **2.** to stop the natural course of (light, water, etc.). **3.** to stop or check (passage, etc.). **4.** to prevent or cut off the operation or effect of: *to intercept the view.* **5.** to cut off from access, sight, etc. **6.** *Chiefly Maths.* to mark off or include, as between two points or lines. *—n.* **7.** an interception. **8.** *Maths.* an intercepted part of a line. [t. L: s. *interceptus*, pp.] —**in'tercep'tive,** *adj.*

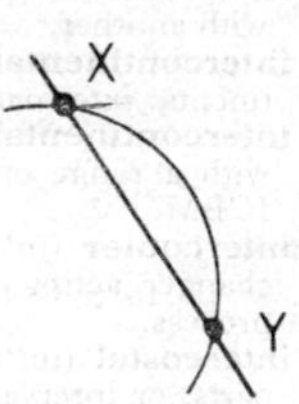

Arc of circle intercepted by line between points X and Y

interception (ĭn'tə sĕp'shən), *n.* **1.** the act of intercepting. **2.** the state or fact of being intercepted. **3.** *Mil.* the engaging of an enemy force in an attempt to hinder or prevent it from carrying out its mission.

interceptor (ĭn'tə sĕp'tə), *n.* **1.** one who or that which intercepts. **2.** *Mil.* a type of fighter aircraft with a high rate of climb and speed, used chiefly for the interception of enemy aircraft. Also, **in'tercept'er.**

intercession (ĭn'tə sĕsh'ən), *n.* **1.** the act of interceding. **2.** an interposing or pleading on behalf of one in difficulty or trouble. **3.** *Eccles.* **a.** an interposing or pleading with God on behalf of another or others, as that of Christ (see Heb. 7:25) or that of the saints on behalf of men. **b.** a pleading against others (see Rom. 11:2). **4.** *Rom. Hist.* the interposing of a veto, as by a tribune. [t. L: s. *intercessio*] —**in'terces'sional,** *adj.*

intercessor (ĭn'tə sĕs'ə, ĭn'tə sĕs'ə), *n.* one who intercedes.

intercessory (ĭn'tə sĕs'ə rĭ), *adj.* making intercession: *the Lord's Prayer has an intercessory petition.*

interchange (*v.* ĭn'tə chānj'; *n.* ĭn'tə chānj'), *v.* **-changed, -changing,** *n.* *—v.t.* **1.** to put each of (two things) in the place of the other. **2.** to cause (one thing) to change places with another; transpose. **3.** to give and receive (things) reciprocally; exchange: *they interchanged gifts.* **4.** to cause to follow one another alternately: *to interchange cares with pleasures.* *—v.i.* **5.** to occur by turns or in succession; alternate. **6.** to change places, as two persons or things, or as one with another. *—n.* **7.** the act of interchanging; reciprocal exchange: *the interchange of commodities.* **8.** a changing of places, as between two persons or things, or of one with another. **9.** alternation; alternate succession. **10.** any major road junction, esp. where motorways converge. [f. INTER- + CHANGE; r. ME *enterchaunge*, t. OF: m. *entrechangier* (v.), *entrechange* (n.)] —**in'terchang'er,** *n.*

interchangeable (ĭn'tə chān'jə bl), *adj.* **1.** capable of being put or used in the place of each other, as two things: *interchangeable words.* **2.** (of one thing) that may be put in the place of, or may change places with, something else. —**in'terchange'abil'ity, in'terchange'ableness,** *n.* —**in'terchange'ably,** *adv.* **—Syn. 2.** See **exchangeable.**

interchange station, a railway station where two or more lines converge or cross, and passengers may change from one to another.

intercity (ĭn'tə sĭt'ĭ), *adj.* between cities.

interclavicle (ĭn'tə klăv'ĭ kl), *n. Zool., Anat.* a median membrane bone developed between the collarbones, or in front of the breastbone, in many vertebrates. —**interclavicular** (ĭn'tə klə vĭk'yŏŏ lə), *adj.*

intercollegiate (ĭn'tə kə lē'jĭ ĭt), *adj.* between colleges, or representative of different colleges.

intercolonial (ĭn'tə kə lō'nyəl), *adj.* between colonies, as of one country. —**in'tercolo'nially,** *adv.*

intercolumniation (ĭn'tə kə lŭm'nĭ ā'shən), *n. Archit.* **1.** the space between two adjacent columns, usually the clear space between the lower parts of the shafts. **2.** the system of spacing between columns. [f. s. L *intercolumnium* space between columns + -ATION]

intercom (ĭn'tə kŏm'), *n. Colloq.* an intercommunication system, as of an aeroplane or a tank.

intercommon (ĭn'tə kŏm'ən), *v.i. Eng. Law.* to share in the use of a common. [ME *entercomen*, t. AF: m. *entrecomuner*, f. *entre-* INTER- + *comuner* share]

intercommunicate (ĭn'tə kə myōō'nĭ kāt'), *v.t., v.i.,*

-cated, -cating. to communicate mutually, as people or rooms. —**in'tercommu'nica'tion,** *n.* —**intercommunicative** (ĭn'tə kə myo͞o'nĭ kə tĭv), *adj.*
intercommunion (ĭn'tə kə myo͞o'nyən), *n.* mutual communion, association, or relations.
intercommunity (ĭn'tə kə myo͞o'nĭ tĭ), *n., pl.* **-ties.** common ownership, use, participation, etc.
interconnect (ĭn'tə kə nĕkt'), *v.t., v.i.* to connect, one with another. —**in'terconnec'tion,** *n.*
intercontinental (ĭn'tə kŏn'tĭ nĕn'tl), *adj.* between continents: *intercontinental trade.*
intercontinental ballistic missile, a ballistic missile with a range of at least 3500 nautical miles. *Abbrev.:* ICBM.
intercooler (ĭn'tə ko͞o'lə), *n.* an intermediate heat exchanger, acting between two stages of a heating or cooling process.
intercostal (ĭn'tə kŏs'tl), *adj.* **1.** pertaining to muscles, parts, or intervals between the ribs. **2.** situated between the ribs. —*n.* **3.** an intercostal muscle, part, or space. [t. NL: s. *intercostālis.* See INTER-, COSTA, -AL[1]] —**in'tercos'tally,** *adv.*
intercourse (ĭn'tə kôs'), *n.* **1.** dealings or communication between individuals. **2.** interchange of thoughts, feelings, etc. **3.** sexual intercourse. [f. INTER- + COURSE; r. late ME *entercourse,* t. OF: m. *entrecors,* g. L *intercursus* a running between]
intercrop (ĭn'tə krŏp'), *v.t., v.i.,* **-cropped, -cropping.** *Agric.* to use (the space) between the rows of an orchard, vineyard, or field for the simultaneous production of a different cultivated crop.
intercross (ĭn'tə krŏs'), *v.t.* **1.** to cross (things), one with another. **2.** to cross (each other), as streets do. **3.** to cross in interbreeding. —*v.i.* **4.** to cross each other. **5.** to interbreed. —*n.* **6.** an instance of cross-fertilization.
intercrystalline fracture (ĭn'tə krĭs'tə lĭn'), *Metall.* the fracture of a metal in which the line of failure passes round the boundaries of the crystals rather than through the crystals themselves. Cf. **transcrystalline fracture.**
intercurrent (ĭn'tə kŭ'rənt), *adj.* **1.** intervening, as of time or events. **2.** *Pathol.* (of a disease) occurring while another disease is in progress. [t. L: s. *intercurrens,* ppr., running between, intervening] —**in'tercur'rence,** *n.*
interdenominational (ĭn'tə dĭ nŏm'ĭ nā'shə nəl), *adj.* between or involving two or more (religious) denominations.
interdental (ĭn'tə dĕn'tl), *adj.* **1.** between teeth. **2.** *Phonet.* with the tip of the tongue between the upper and lower front teeth.
interdepartmental (ĭn'tə dē'pät mĕn'tl), *adj.* between or involving two or more departments.
interdependent (ĭn'tə dĭ pĕn'dənt), *adj.* mutually dependent; dependent on each other. —**in'terdepend'ence, in'terdepend'ency,** *n.* —**in'terdepend'ently,** *adv.*
interdict (*n.* ĭn'tə dĭkt', ĭn'tə dĭt'; *v.* ĭn'tə dĭkt', ĭn'tə dĭt'), *n.* **1.** *Rom. Law.* a general or special order of the Roman praetor forbidding or commanding an act; the procedure by which an interdict was sought. **2.** *Civil Law.* any prohibitory act or decree of a court or an administrative officer. **3.** *Scots Law.* an injunction. **4.** *Rom. Cath. Ch.* a punishment by which the faithful, remaining in communion with the Church, are prohibited from participation in certain sacred acts. —*v.t.* **5.** *Eccles.* to prohibit the exercise of (stated privileges and functions within the Church). **6.** to forbid; prohibit. [t. L: s. *interdictus,* pp.; r. ME *entredite(n),* t. OF: m. *entredit,* pp. of *entredire*] —**in'terdic'tive,** *adj.* —**in'terdic'tor,** *n.*
interdiction (ĭn'tə dĭk'shən), *n.* **1.** the act of interdicting. **2.** the state of being interdicted. **3.** an interdict.
interdictory (ĭn'tə dĭk'tə rĭ), *adj.* interdicting.
interest (ĭn'trĭst), *n.* **1.** the feeling of one whose attention or curiosity is particularly engaged by something: *to have great interest in a subject.* **2.** a particular feeling of this kind: *a man of varied intellectual interests.* **3.** the power of exciting such feeling; interesting quality: *questions of great interest.* **4.** concernment, importance, or moment: *a matter of primary interest.* **5.** a business, cause, or the like, in which a number of persons are interested. **6.** a share in the ownership of property, in a commercial or financial undertaking, or the like. **7.** any right of ownership in property, commercial undertakings, etc. **8.** a number or group of persons, or a party, having a common interest: *the banking interest.* **9.** something in which one has an interest, as of ownership, advantage, attention, etc. **10.** the relation of being affected by something in respect of advantage or detriment: *an arbitrator having no interest in the outcome.* **11.** benefit or advantage: *to have one's own interest in mind.* **12.** regard for one's own advantage or profit; self-interest: *rival interests.* **13.** *Com.* **a.** payment, or a sum paid, for the use of money borrowed (the principal), or for the forbearance of a debt. **b.** the rate per cent per unit of time represented by such payment. **14.** something added or thrown in above an exact equivalent. **15.** *Obs.* influence from personal importance or capability; power of influencing the action of others. **16. in the interest** (or **interests) of,** on the side of what is advantageous to; on behalf of: *in the interest of good government.* —*v.t.* **17.** to engage or excite the attention or curiosity of: *a story which interested him greatly.* **18.** to concern (a person, etc.) in something; involve: *every citizen is interested in this law.* **19.** to cause to take a personal concern or share; induce to participate: *to interest a person in an enterprise.* **20.** *Rare.* to concern, relate to, or affect. [late ME, n. use of L *interest* it concerns; r. ME *interesse,* t. ML: compensation for loss, n. use of L inf.]
interested (ĭn'trĭs tĭd), *adj.* **1.** having an interest in something; concerned: *those interested should apply in person.* **2.** participating; having an interest or share; having money involved: *one interested in the funds.* **3.** having the attention or curiosity engaged: *an interested spectator.* **4.** characterized by a feeling of interest. **5.** influenced by personal or selfish motives: *an interested witness.* —**in'terestedly,** *adv.* —**in'terestedness,** *n.*
interesting (ĭn'trĭs tĭng), *adj.* **1.** arousing a feeling of interest: *an interesting face.* **2.** engaging or exciting and holding the attention or curiosity: *an interesting book.* —**in'terestingly,** *adv.* —**in'terestingness,** *n.*

—**Syn. 2.** INTERESTING, PLEASING, GRATIFYING mean satisfying to the mind. That which is INTERESTING occupies the mind with no connotation of pleasure or displeasure: *an interesting account of a battle.* That which is PLEASING engages the mind favourably: *a pleasing account of the wedding.* That which is GRATIFYING fulfils expectations, requirements, etc.: *a gratifying account of his whereabouts, a book gratifying in its detail.*

interface (ĭn'tə fās'), *n.* **1.** a surface regarded as the common boundary of two bodies or spaces. **2.** *Chem.* the surface which separates two phases. **3.** the point or area at which any two systems or disciplines interact: *the interface between a computer and a typesetting machine.*
interfacial (ĭn'tə fā'shəl), *adj.* **1.** included between two faces. **2.** pertaining to an interface.
interfacial surface tension, *Phys. Chem.* the surface tension at the interface between two immiscible liquids. Also, **interfacial tension.**
interfere (ĭn'tə fĭə'), *v.i.,* **-fered, -fering. 1.** to clash; come into collision; be in opposition: *the claims of two nations may interfere.* **2.** to come into opposition, as one thing with another, esp. with the effect of hampering action or procedure: *these interruptions interfere with the work.* **3.** to interpose or intervene for a particular purpose. **4.** to take a part in the affairs of others; meddle: *to interfere in others' disputes.* **5.** (of things) to strike against each other, or one against another, so as to hamper or hinder action; come into physical collision. **6.** to strike one foot or leg against the opposite foot or leg in going, as a horse. **7.** *Physics.* to cause interference. [t. OF: m. *entreferir* strike each other, f. *entre-* INTER- + *ferir* (g. L *ferīre* strike)] —**in'terfer'er,** *n.* —**in'terfer'ingly,** *adv.*
interference (ĭn'tə fĭə'rəns), *n.* **1.** the act or fact of interfering. **2.** *Physics.* the reciprocal action of waves (as of light, sound, etc.), when meeting, by which they reinforce or cancel each other. **3.** *Radio.* **a.** the jumbling of radio signals by receiving signals other than the desired ones. **b.** the signals which produce the incoherence.
interference drag, *Aeron.* additional drag due to interaction of two aerodynamic bodies.
interference pattern, *Physics.* the alternating dark and light bands produced by interference. Also, **interference fringes.**
interferential (ĭn'tə fə rĕn'shəl), *adj.* of or pertaining to interference.
interferometer (ĭn'tə fə rŏm'ĭ tə), *n.* *Physics.* an instrument for measuring small lengths or distances by means of the interference of two rays of light.
interferon (ĭn'tə fĭə'rŏn), *n.* *Biochem.* protein substance, produced by animal cells in response to virus infection, that inhibits replication of virus particles.
interfile (ĭn'tə fīl'), *v.t.,* **-filed, -filing.** to combine into a single arrangement (two or more similarly arranged sets of items, as cards, documents, etc.).
interflow (*v.* ĭn'tə flō'; *n.* ĭn'tə flō'), *v.i.* **1.** to flow into each other; intermingle. —*n.* **2.** an interflowing.
interfluent (ĭn'tə flo͞o'ənt), *adj.* interflowing.
interfluve (ĭn'tə flo͞ov'), *n.* *Phys. Geog.* the higher land separating adjacent stream valleys.
interfold (ĭn'tə fōld'), *v.t.* to fold, one within another; fold together.
interfuse (ĭn'tə fyo͞oz'), *v.,* **-fused, -fusing.** —*v.t.* **1.** to

pour (something) between or through; diffuse throughout. **2.** to intersperse, intermingle, or permeate with something. **3.** to blend or fuse, one with another. *—v.i.* **4.** to become blended or fused, one with another. [t. L: m. s. *interfūsus*, pp.] **—in′terfu′sion,** *n.*

intergalactic (ĭn′tə gə lăk′tĭk), *adj.* existing or occurring between galaxies.

interglacial (ĭn′tə glā′syəl), *adj. Geol.* occurring or formed between times of glacial action.

intergrade (*n.* ĭn′tə grād′; *v.* ĭn′tə grād′), *n., v.,* **-graded, -grading.** *—n.* **1.** an intermediate grade. *—v.i.* **2.** to pass gradually, one into another, as different species. **—in′tergrada′tion,** *n.* **—intergradient** (ĭn′tə grā′dyənt), *adj.*

intergrowth (ĭn′tə grōth′), *n.* growth or growing together, as of one thing with another.

interim (ĭn′tə rĭm), *n.* **1.** an intervening time; the meantime: *in the interim.* **2.** a temporary or provisional arrangement. **3.** (*cap.*) *Eccles. Hist.* any of three provisional arrangements for the settlement of religious differences between German Protestants and Roman Catholics during the Reformation. *—adj.* **4.** belonging to or connected with an intervening period of time: *an interim dividend.* **5.** temporary; provisional: *an interim order.* *—adv.* **6.** *Now Rare.* meantime. [t. L: in the meantime]

interior (ĭn tĭə′rĭ ə), *adj.* **1.** being within; inside of anything; internal; farther towards a centre: *the interior parts of a house.* **2.** of or pertaining to that which is within; inside: *an interior view.* **3.** situated inside of and at a distance from the coast or border: *the interior parts of a country.* **4.** pertaining to the inland. **5.** domestic: *the interior trade.* **6.** inner, private, or secret: *an interior cabinet.* **7.** mental or spiritual. **8.** *Geom.* (of an angle) inner, as an angle formed between two parallel lines when cut by a third line, or an angle formed by two adjacent sides of a closed polygon. *—n.* **9.** the internal part; the inside. **10.** *Art.* **a.** the inside part of a building, considered as a whole from the point of view of artistic design or general effect, convenience, etc., or a single room or apartment so considered. **b.** a pictorial representation of the inside of a building, room, etc. **11.** the inland parts of a region, country, etc.: *the interior of Africa.* **12.** the domestic affairs of a country as distinguished from its foreign affairs: *the Department of the Interior.* **13.** the inner or inward nature or character of anything. [t. L: inner] **—interiority** (ĭn tĭə′rĭ ŏ′rĭ tĭ), *n.* **—inte′riorly,** *adv.* **—Syn.** **9.** See **inside.**

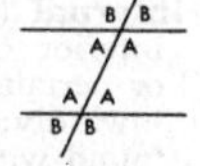

A, Interior angle; B, Exterior angle

interior decorator, a person whose occupation is planning the decoration, furnishings, draperies, etc., of homes, rooms, or offices.

interior drainage, a drainage system whose waters do not flow to the sea either above or below ground, but evaporate within the land area. Also, **internal drainage.**

interj., interjection.

interjacent (ĭn′tə jā′sənt), *adj.* lying between; intervening; intermediate.

interject (ĭn′tə jĕkt′), *v.t.* **1.** to throw in abruptly between other things. **2.** to interpolate; interpose: *to interject a careless remark.* **3.** *Rare.* to come between. [t. L: s. *interjectus*, pp.] **—in′terjec′tor,** *n.*

interjection (ĭn′tə jĕk′shən), *n.* **1.** the act of throwing between; an interjecting. **2.** the utterance of ejaculations expressive of emotion; an ejaculation or exclamation. **3.** something, as a remark, interjected. **4.** *Gram.* **a.** (in many languages) a form class, or 'part of speech', comprising words which constitute utterances or clauses in themselves, without grammatical connection. **b.** such a word, as English *tut-tut!* Such words often include speech sounds not otherwise found in the language. **c.** any word or construction similarly used, as English *goodness me!* **—in′terjec′tional,** *adj.* **—in′terjec′tionally,** *adv.*

interjectory (ĭn′tə jĕk′tə rĭ), *adj.* **1.** interjectional. **2.** interjected. **—in′terjec′torily,** *adv.*

interknit (ĭn′tə nĭt′), *v.t.,* **-knitted** or **-knit, -knitting.** to knit together, one with another; intertwine.

interlace (ĭn′tə lās′), *v.,* **-laced, -lacing.** *—v.i.* **1.** to cross one another as if woven together; intertwine; blend intricately: *interlacing boughs.* *—v.t.* **2.** to dispose (threads, strips, parts, branches, etc.) so as to intercross one another, passing alternately over and under. **3.** to mingle; blend. **4.** to diversify as with threads woven in. **5.** to intersperse or intermingle. **6.** *Railways, etc.* to lay (two railway tracks) so that the inner rails overlap, as in a section passing through a tunnel or over a bridge, in order to narrow the roadbed without switching to a single track. **—in′terlace′ment,** *n.*

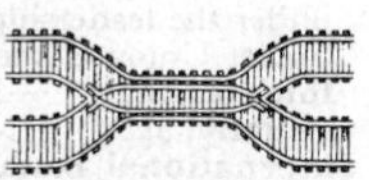
Interlaced track (See interlace def. 6)

Interlaken (ĭn′tə lä′kən), *n.* a town in central Switzerland between the lakes of Brienz and Thun: tourist centre. 4900 (1965).

interlaminate (ĭn′tə lăm′ĭ nāt′), *v.t.,* **-nated, -nating.** to interlay or lay between laminae; interstratify. **—in′terlam′ina′tion,** *n.*

interlard (ĭn′tə läd′), *v.t.* **1.** to diversify with something intermixed or interjected; intersperse (fol. by *with*): *to interlard one's speech with oaths.* **2.** (of things) to be intermixed in. **3.** *Obs.* to mix, as fat with lean. [t. F: m. s. *entrelarder*, f. *entre-* INTER- + *larder* LARD, v.]

interlay (ĭn′tə lā′), *v.t.,* **-laid, -laying. 1.** to lay between; interpose. **2.** to diversify with something laid between or inserted: *silver interlaid with gold.*

interleaf (*n.* ĭn′tə lēf′; *v.* ĭn′tə lēf′), *n., pl.* **-leaves** (-lēvz′), *v.* *—n.* **1.** an additional leaf, usually blank, inserted between or bound with the regular printed leaves of a book; slipsheet. *—v.t., v.i.* **2.** to interleave.

interleave (ĭn′tə lēv′), *v.* **-leaved, -leaving.** *—v.t.* **1.** to provide blank leaves in (a book) for notes or written comments. **2.** to insert blank leaves between (the regular printed leaves), as to protect the illustrations, etc. **3.** to insert (blank leaves) between printed leaves. *—v.i.* **4.** to insert blank leaves or sheets between printed leaves or sheets after printing or during binding. Also, **interleaf.**

interlibrary loan (ĭn′tə lī′brə rĭ), **1.** a system by which one library borrows a publication from another library. **2.** a loan made in this way.

interline¹ (ĭn′tə līn′), *v.t.,* **-lined, -lining. 1.** to write or insert (words, etc.) between the lines of writing or print. **2.** to mark or inscribe (a document, book, etc.) between the lines. [late ME, t. ML: s. *interlineāre*]

interline² (ĭn′tə līn′), *v.t.,* **-lined, -lining.** to provide (a garment) with an inner lining, between the ordinary lining and the outer fabric. [f. INTER- + LINE²]

interlineal (ĭn′tə lĭn′ĭ əl), *adj.* **1.** interlinear. **2.** *Rare.* alternating in lines. **—in′terlin′eally,** *adv.*

interlinear (ĭn′tə lĭn′ĭ ə), *adj.* **1.** situated between the lines; inserted between lines. **2.** having interpolated lines; interlined: *an interlinear translation.* **3.** *Obs.* having the same text in various languages set in alternate lines: *the interlinear Bible.*

interlineate (ĭn′tə lĭn′ĭ āt′), *v.t.,* **-ated, -ating.** to interline¹. **—in′terlin′ea′tion,** *n.*

Interlingua (ĭn′tə lĭng′gwə), *n.* an auxiliary international language developed between 1924 and 1951, based primarily upon the principal languages of the Western world. It was devised mainly to facilitate scientific communication.

interlining¹ (ĭn′tə lī′nĭng), *n.* **1.** an inner lining placed between the ordinary lining and the outer fabric of a garment. **2.** material used for this purpose. [f. INTERLINE² + -ING¹]

interlining² (ĭn′tə lī′nĭng), *n.* interlineation.

interlink (ĭn′tə lĭngk′), *v.t., v.i.* **1.** to link, one with another. *—n.* **2.** a connecting link.

interlock (ĭn′tə lŏk′), *v.i.* **1.** to engage with each other: *interlocking branches.* **2.** to fit into each other, as parts of machinery, so that all action is simultaneous. **3.** (of railway points, signals, etc.) to arrange and operate in an interlocking system. *—v.t.* **4.** to lock one with another. **5.** to fit the parts of (something) together so that all must move together, or in the same way. **6.** *Railways.* to arrange (points, etc.) so that their positions are not independent of one another and their movements succeed each other in prearranged order. *—n.* **7.** *Textiles.* a smooth knitted fabric, esp. one made of cotton yarn. **—in′terlock′er,** *n.*

interlocution (ĭn′tə lō kyōō′shən), *n.* conversation; dialogue. [t. L: s. *interlocūtio* a speaking between]

interlocutor (ĭn′tə lŏk′yōō tə), *n.* **1.** one who takes part in a conversation or dialogue. **2.** one who enters into conversation with another. **3.** the man in the middle of the line of performers of a minstrel troupe, who carries on a conversation with the end men. **—interlocutress** (ĭn′tə lŏk′yōō trĭs), **in′terloc′utrice, interlocutrix** (ĭn′tə lŏk′yōō trĭks), *n. fem.*

interlocutory (ĭn′tə lŏk′yōō tə rĭ, -trĭ), *adj.* **1.** of the nature of, pertaining to, or occurring in conversation: *interlocutory instruction.* **2.** interjected into the main course of speech. **3.** *Law.* **a.** incidental to the final judgement in an action; not finally decisive of a case. **b.** pertaining to a provisional decision.

interlope (ĭn′tə lōp′), *v.i.,* **-loped, -loping. 1.** to intrude into some region or field of trade without a proper licence. **2.** to thrust oneself into the affairs of others. [f. INTER- + LOPE, v.] **—in′terlop′er,** *n.*

interlude (ĭn′tə lo͞od′), *n.* **1.** an intervening episode, period, space, etc. **2.** a form of short dramatic piece, esp. of a light or farcical character, formerly introduced between the parts of miracle plays and moralities or given as part of other entertainments. **3.** one of the early English farces or comedies (such as those by John Heywood) which grew out of such pieces. **4.** an intermediate performance or entertainment, as between the acts of a play. **5.** an instrumental passage or a piece of music rendered between the parts of a song, church service, drama, etc. [ME, t. ML: m. s. *interlūdium*, f. *inter-* INTER- + *-lūdium*, der. L *lūdus* play]

interlunar (ĭn′tə lo͞o′nə), *adj.* pertaining to the moon's monthly period of invisibility between the old moon and the new.

interlunation (ĭn′tə lo͞o nā′shən), *n.* the interlunar period.

intermarry (ĭn′tə mă′rĭ), *v.i.*, **-ried, -rying. 1.** to become connected by marriage, as two families, tribes, or castes. **2.** to marry within the limits of the family or of near relationship. **3.** to marry, one with another. **—in′termar′riage,** *n.*

intermaxillary (ĭn′tə măk sĭl′ə rĭ), *adj.* **1.** situated between the maxillary or upper jawbones. **2.** of or pertaining to the back and middle of the upper jaw: *intermaxillary teeth.* **3.** (in *Crustacea*) situated between those somites of the head which bear the maxillae.

intermeddle (ĭn′tə mĕd′l), *v.i.*, **-dled, -dling.** to take part in a matter, esp. officiously; interfere; meddle. **—in′termed′dler,** *n.*

intermediacy (ĭn′tə mē′dyə sĭ), *n.* the state of being intermediate, or of acting intermediately.

intermediary (ĭn′tə mē′dyə rĭ), *adj., n., pl.* **-aries.** *—adj.* **1.** being between; intermediate. **2.** acting between persons, parties, etc.; serving as an intermediate agent or agency: *an intermediary power.* *—n.* **3.** an intermediate agent or agency; a go-between. **4.** a medium or means. **5.** an intermediate form or stage.

intermediate[1] (ĭn′tə mē′dyət), *adj.* **1.** being, situated, or acting between two points, stages, things, persons, etc.: *the intermediate links.* **2.** *Geol.* (of igneous rocks) having between 52 and 65 per cent silica. *—n.* **3.** something intermediate. **4.** *Chem.* a derivative of the initial material formed before the desired product of a chemical process. **5.** Also, **intermediate examination.** the first examination in certain university degree courses or in courses leading to a professional qualification. **6.** *Rare.* an intermediary. [t. ML: m. s. *intermediātus*, der. L *intermedius* between] **—in′terme′diately,** *adv.* **—in′terme′diateness,** *n.*

intermediate[2] (ĭn′tə mē′dĭ āt′), *v.i.*, **-ated, -ating.** to act as an intermediary; intervene; mediate. [f. INTER- + MEDIATE, v.] **—in′terme′dia′tion,** *n.* **—in′terme′dia′tor,** *n.*

intermediate frequency, *Radio.* the middle frequency in a superheterodyne receiver, at which most of the amplification takes place.

intermediate range ballistic missile, a ballistic missile with a range of 800 to 1500 nautical miles. *Abbrev.:* IRBM.

interment (ĭn tû′mənt), *n.* the act of interring; burial.

intermezzo (ĭn′tə mĕt′sō; *It.* ēn tėr mĕd′dzō), *n., pl.* **-zos, -zi** (-sē; *It.* -dzē). **1.** a short dramatic, musical, or other entertainment of light character introduced between the acts of a drama or opera. **2.** a short musical composition between main divisions of an extended musical work. **3.** an independent musical composition of similar character. [t. It., g. L *intermedius* between]

intermigration (ĭn′tə mī grā′shən), *n.* reciprocal migration; interchange of habitat by migrating bodies.

interminable (ĭn tû′mĭ nə bl), *adj.* **1.** that cannot be terminated; unending: *interminable talk.* **2.** endless; having no limits: *interminable sufferings.* [ME, t. LL: m. s. *interminābilis*] **—inter′minably,** *adv.*

intermingle (ĭn′tə mĭng′gl), *v.t., v.i.*, **-gled, -gling.** to mingle, one with another. **—in′termin′glement,** *n.*

intermission (ĭn′tə mĭsh′ən), *n.* **1.** *Orig. U.S.* an interval, esp. in the cinema. **2.** the act of intermitting. **3.** the state of being intermitted. [t. L: s. *intermissio*]

intermissive (ĭn′tə mĭs′ĭv), *adj.* **1.** characterized by intermission. **2.** intermittent.

intermit (ĭn′tə mĭt′), *v.*, **-mitted, -mitting.** *—v.t.* **1.** to discontinue temporarily; suspend. *—v.i.* **2.** to stop or pause at intervals, or be intermittent. **3.** to cease, stop, or break off operations for a time. [t. L: m. s. *intermittere* leave off, omit, leave an interval] **—in′termit′tingly,** *adv.*

intermittent (ĭn′tə mĭt′nt), *adj.* **1.** that intermits, or ceases for a time: *an intermittent process.* **2.** alternately ceasing and beginning again: *an intermittent fever.* **3.** (of streams, lakes, or springs) recurrent; showing water only part of the time. **—in′termit′tence, in′termit′tency,** *n.* **—in′termit′tently,** *adv.*

intermittent fever, a fever in which feverish periods lasting a few hours alternate with periods in which the temperature is normal.

intermix (ĭn′tə mĭks′), *v.t., v.i.* to intermingle.

intermixture (ĭn′tə mĭks′chə), *n.* **1.** the act of intermixing. **2.** a mass of ingredients mixed together. **3.** something added by intermixing.

intermolecular (ĭn′tə mə lĕk′yo͝o lə), *adj.* between molecules.

intermundane (ĭn′tə mŭn′dān), *adj.* between worlds.

intern[1] (*v.* ĭn tûn′; *n.* ĭn′tûn), *v.t.* **1.** to oblige to reside within prescribed limits under prohibition to leave them, as prisoners of war or enemy aliens, or as combatant troops who take refuge in a neutral country. **2.** to hold within a country until the termination of a war, as a vessel of a belligerent which has put into a neutral port and remained beyond a limited period allowed. *—n.* **3.** *Chiefly U.S.* an internee. [t. F: s. *interner*, ult. der. L *internus* internal]

intern[2] (ĭn′tûn), *U.S.* *—n.* **1.** Also, **interne.** a resident member of the medical staff of a hospital, approximately equivalent to a British houseman. *—v.i.* **2.** to be or perform the duties of an intern. [t. F: m. *interne*, t. L: m. *internus* internal] **—in′ternship′,** *n.*

intern[3] (ĭn tûn′), *adj., n. Archaic.* internal. [t. L: s. *internus*]

internal (ĭn tû′nəl), *adj.* **1.** situated or existing in the interior of something; interior: *internal organs.* **2.** of or pertaining to the inside or inner part. **3.** to be taken inwardly: *internal stimulants.* **4.** existing, occurring, or found within the limits or scope of something. **5.** existing or occurring within a country; domestic: *internal affairs.* **6.** pertaining to the domestic affairs of a country. **7.** studying or studied within the confines of a university or similar institution, and subject to its discipline, etc. **8.** of the mind or soul; mental or spiritual; subjective. **9.** *Anat., Zool.* inner; not superficial; away from the surface or next to the axis of the body or of a part: *the internal carotid artery.* *—n.* **10.** (*pl.*) entrails. **11.** (*pl.*) inner or intrinsic attributes. [t. ML: s. *internālis*, der. L *internus* inward] **—in′ternal′ity,** *n.* **—inter′nally,** *adv.*

internal-combustion (ĭn tû′nəl kəm bŭs′chən), *adj.* of or pertaining to an internal-combustion engine.

internal-combustion engine, an engine of one or more working cylinders in which the process of combustion takes place within the cylinder.

internal drainage, interior drainage.

internal medicine, the branch of medicine concerned with the diagnosis and cure of internal disorders.

internat., international.

international (ĭn′tə năsh′ə nəl), *adj.* **1.** between or among nations: *an international armament race.* **2.** of or pertaining to different nations or their citizens: *a matter of international concern.* **3.** pertaining to the relations between nations: *international law.* **4.** (*cap.*) of or pertaining to any association known as an International. *—n.* **5.** (*cap.*) a socialist association (in full, **International Workingmen's Association**) intended to unite the working classes of all countries in promoting their own interests and social and industrial reforms, by political means, formed in London in 1864, and dissolved in Philadelphia in 1876 (**First International**). **6.** (*cap.*) an international socialist association formed in 1889, uniting socialist groups or political parties of various countries, and holding international congresses from time to time (**Second International**). **7.** (*cap.*) an ultraradical and communist association formed in Moscow, under Bolshevist auspices, in 1919 (dissolved, 1943), uniting communist groups of various countries and advocating the attainment of its ends by revolutionary or violent measures (**Third** or **Communist International**). **8.** (*cap.*) the socialist organization formed in 1921 (**Vienna International,** often called the **Two-and-a-half International**). **9.** (*cap.*) the socialist association formed in 1923 by the uniting of the Second International and the Vienna International at Hamburg and called in full the **Labour and Socialist International.** **10.** a loose federation of small ultraradical groups formed in 1936 (orig. under the leadership of Leon Trotsky), and hostile to the Soviet Union (sometimes called the **Fourth** or **Trotskyist International**). **—in′terna′tional′ity,** *n.* **—in′terna′tionally,** *adv.*

International Bank for Reconstruction and Development, official name of the **World Bank.**

international candle. See **candle** (def. 3c).

International Court of Justice, a court established in 1945 by the United Nations, to decide disputes between nations.

international date line, date line (def. 2).

Internationale (*Fr.* ăɴ tĕr nȧ syŏ nȧl′), *n.* a revolutionary song, first sung in France in 1871 and since popular as a song of workers and Communists.

International Geophysical Year, the 18-month period from July 1st, 1957 to Dec. 31st, 1958, designated as a time of intensive geophysical exploration and sharing of knowledge by scientists of all countries.

International Hydrological Decade, the ten-year period from 1965 designated as a period of cooperative research in hydrology among a group of nations.

internationalism (ĭn′tə năsh′ə nə lĭz′əm), *n.* **1.** the principle of cooperation among nations, to promote their common good, sometimes as contrasted with nationalism, or devotion to the interests of a particular nation. **2.** international character, relations, cooperation, or control. **3.** (*cap.*) the principles or methods advocated by any association known as an International.

internationalist (ĭn′tə năsh′ə nə lĭst), *n.* **1.** an advocate of internationalism. **2.** one versed in international law and relations. **3.** (*cap.*) a member or adherent of an International.

internationalize (ĭn′tə năsh′ə nə līz′), *v.t.*, **-lized, -lizing.** to make international; bring under international control. Also, **internationalise.** —**in′terna′tionaliza′tion,** *n.*

International Labour Organization, an organization formed in 1919, devoted to standardizing international labour practices and including representatives of government, management, and labour.

international law, the body of rules which civilized nations recognize as binding them in their conduct towards one another.

International Monetary Fund, an international organization set up by the United Nations and the International Bank for Reconstruction and Development, to stabilize relations between currencies of the subscribing countries, maintaining a monetary fund from which they may draw to correct deficits in their balance of payments.

international nautical mile. See **mile** (def. 1c). Also, **international air mile.**

International Phonetic Alphabet, an alphabet designed to provide a consistent and universally understood system of letters and other symbols for writing the speech sounds of all languages.

international sea and swell scale, a combined scale for recording the sea from calm to confused, by figures 0 to 90 read horizontally, and the swell from low to heavy, by figures 00 to 99 read vertically. Also, **Douglas scale.**

international standard atmosphere, *Aeron.* a standard scale of atmosphere agreed between countries for use in comparing the performance of aircraft and missiles.

international temperature scale, *Physics.* an internationally agreed scale of temperature which is defined to conform as closely as possible to the thermodynamic centigrade scale: based on the ice point, steam point, and melting points of various elements.

International Year of the Quiet Sun, the year 1964, in which a group of nations agreed to take the opportunity of relative solar inactivity to intensify their solar research.

interne (ĭn′tûn), *n.* intern².

internecine (ĭn′tə nē′sīn), *adj.* **1.** mutually destructive. **2.** characterized by great slaughter. [t. L: m. s. *internecīnus*, der. *internecium* slaughter]

internee (ĭn′tû nē′), *n.* one interned as a prisoner of war.

internment (ĭn tûn′mənt), *n.* **1.** the act of interning. **2.** the state or condition of being interned; confinement.

internment camp, (during wartime) a military camp for the confinement of enemy aliens, prisoners of war, etc.

internode (ĭn′tə nōd′), *n.* a part or space between two nodes, knots, or joints, as the portion of a plant stem between two nodes. —**in′ternod′al,** *adj.*

inter nos (ĭn′tə nōs′), *Latin.* between or among us.

internuncial (ĭn′tə nŭn′shəl), *adj. Anat.* (of a nerve cell or a chain of nerve cells) linking the incoming and outgoing nerve fibres of the nervous system.

internuncio (ĭn′tə nŭn′shĭ ō′), *n., pl.* **-cios.** a papal ambassador ranking next below a nuncio. [t. It., t. L: m. *internuntius*]

interoceanic (ĭn′tər ō′shĭ ăn′ĭk), *adj.* between oceans.

interoceptive (ĭn′tə rō sĕp′tĭv), *adj. Physiol.* pertaining to interoceptors, the stimuli impinging upon them, and the nerve impulses initiated by them.

interoceptor (ĭn′tə rō sĕp′tə), *n.* a nerve ending or sense organ responding to stimuli originating from within the body. [f. *intero-* inside (NL comb. form modelled on *extero-* outside) + *-ceptor.* See RECEPTOR]

interosculate (ĭn′tər ŏs′kyo͝o lāt′), *v.i., v.t.*, **-lated, -lating.** **1.** to interpenetrate; inosculate. **2.** to form a connecting link. —**in′teros′cula′tion,** *n.*

interpellant (ĭn′tə pĕl′ənt), *n.* one who interpellates. [t. F, ppr. of *interpeller*, t. L: m. *interpellāre* interrupt in speaking]

interpellate (ĭn tû′pĕ lāt′), *v.t.*, **-lated, -lating.** to call formally upon (a minister or member of the government) in interpellation. [t. L: m. s. *interpellātus*, pp., interrupted in speaking] —**interpellator** (ĭn tû′pĕ lā′tə), *n.*

interpellation (ĭn tû′pĕ lā′shən), *n.* a procedure in some legislative bodies of asking a government official to explain an act or policy, usually leading in parliamentary government to a vote of confidence. [t. L: s. *interpellātio* interruption]

interpenetrate (ĭn′tə pĕn′ĭ trāt′), *v.*, **-trated, -trating.** —*v.t.* **1.** to penetrate thoroughly; permeate. **2.** to penetrate reciprocally. —*v.i.* **3.** to penetrate between things or parts. **4.** to penetrate each other. —**in′terpen′etra′tion,** *n.* —**interpenetrative** (ĭn′tə pĕn′ĭ trə tĭv), *adj.*

interphone (ĭn′tə fōn′), *n.* a telephone connecting offices, stations, etc., as in a building or ship; an intercom.

interplanetary (ĭn′tə plăn′ĭ tə rĭ, -trĭ), *adj. Astron.* situated within the solar system, but not within the atmosphere of the sun or any planet.

interplay (*n.* ĭn′tə plā′; *v.* ĭn′tə plā′), *n.* **1.** reciprocal play, action, or influence: *the interplay of plot and character.* —*v.i.* **2.** to exert influence on each other.

interplead (ĭn′tə plēd′), *v.i. Law.* to litigate with each other in order to determine which is the rightful claimant against a third party.

interpleader (ĭn′tə plē′də), *n. Law.* **1.** a proceeding by which two parties making the same claim against a third party determine judicially which is the rightful claimant. **2.** a party who interpleads.

Interpol (ĭn′tə pŏl′), *n.* the International Criminal Police Commission.

interpolate (ĭn tû′pə lāt′), *v.*, **-lated, -lating.** —*v.t.* **1.** to alter (a text, etc.) by the insertion of new matter, esp. deceptively or without authorization. **2.** to insert (new or spurious matter) thus. **3.** to introduce (something additional or extraneous) between other things or parts; interject; interpose; intercalate. **4.** *Maths.* to insert or find intermediate terms in (a sequence). —*v.i.* **5.** to make interpolations. [t. L: m. s. *interpolātus*, pp., furbished, altered, falsified] —**inter′pola′tor,** *n.* —**interpolative** (ĭn tû′pə lə tĭv), *adj.*

interpolation (ĭn tû′pə lā′shən), *n.* **1.** the act of interpolating. **2.** the fact of being interpolated. **3.** something interpolated, as a passage introduced into a text.

interpose (ĭn′tə pōz′), *v.*, **-posed, -posing.** —*v.t.* **1.** to place between; cause to intervene: *to interpose an opaque body between a light and the eye.* **2.** to put (a barrier, obstacle, etc.) between, or in the way. **3.** to bring (influence, action, etc.) to bear between parties, or on behalf of a party or person. **4.** to put in (a remark, etc.) in the midst of a conversation, discourse, or the like. —*v.i.* **5.** to come between other things; assume an intervening position or relation. **6.** to step in between parties at variance; mediate. **7.** to put in or make a remark by way of interruption. [t. F: m. s. *interposer.* See INTER-, POSE¹] —**in′terpos′al,** *n.* —**in′terpos′er,** *n.* —**in′terpos′ingly,** *adv.*

interposition (ĭn′tə pə zĭsh′ən), *n.* **1.** the act or fact of interposing or of being interposed. **2.** something interposed.

interpret (ĭn tû′prĭt), *v.t.* **1.** to set forth the meaning of; explain or elucidate: *to interpret omens.* **2.** to explain, construe, or understand in a particular way: *to interpret a reply as favourable.* **3.** to bring out the meaning of (a dramatic work, music, etc.) by performance or execution. **4.** to translate. —*v.i.* **5.** to translate what is said in a foreign language. **6.** to give an explanation. [ME *interprete(n)*, t. L: m. *interpretārī* explain] —**inter′pretable,** *adj.* —**inter′pretabil′ity,** *n.* —**inter′pretive,** *adj.* —**inter′pretively,** *adv.* —**Syn. 1.** See **explain.**

interpretation (ĭn tû′prĭ tā′shən), *n.* **1.** the act of interpreting; elucidation: *the interpretation of nature.* **2.** an explanation given: *to put a wrong interpretation on a passage.* **3.** a construction placed upon something: *a charitable interpretation.* **4.** a way of interpreting. **5.** the rendering of a dramatic part, music, etc., so as to bring out the meaning, or to indicate one's particular conception of it. **6.** translation. [ME, t. L: s. *interpretātio*] —**inter′preta′tional,** *adj.*

interpretative (ĭn tû′prĭ tə tĭv), *adj.* **1.** serving to interpret; explanatory. **2.** deduced by interpretation. —**inter′pretatively,** *adv.*

interpreter (ĭn tû′prĭ tə), *n.* **1.** one who interprets. **2.** *Computers.* **a.** a program which causes a computer to obey instructions in some code different from the basic code of the computer. **b.** a machine which interprets the holes on a punched card.

interracial (ĭn′tə rā′shəl), *adj.* **1.** existing between races, or members of different races. **2.** of or for persons of different races: *interracial camps for children.*

interradial (ĭn′tə rā′dyəl), *adj.* situated between the radii or rays: *the interradial petals in an echinoderm.*
interregnum (ĭn′tə rĕg′nəm), *n., pl.* **-nums, -na** (-nə). **1.** an interval of time between the close of a sovereign's reign and the accession of his normal or legitimate successor. **2.** any period during which a state has no ruler or only a temporary executive. **3.** any pause or interruption in continuity. [t. L, f. *inter-* INTER- + *regnum* REIGN] —**in′terreg′nal,** *adj.*
interrelate (ĭn′tə rĭ lāt′), *v.t.,* **-lated, -lating.** to bring into reciprocal relation.
interrelated (ĭn′tə rĭ lā′tĭd), *adj.* reciprocally related.
interrelation (ĭn′tə rĭ lā′shən), *n.* reciprocal relation. —**in′terrela′tionship′,** *n.*
interrex (ĭn′tə rĕks′), *n., pl.* **interreges** (ĭn′tə rē′jēz). a person holding supreme authority in a state during an interregnum. [t. L, f. *inter-* INTER- + *rex* king]
interrog., **1.** interrogation. **2.** interrogative.
interrogate (ĭn tĕ′rə gāt′), *v.,* **-gated, -gating.** —*v.t.* **1.** to ask a question or a series of questions of (a person), esp. closely or formally. **2.** to examine by questions; question: *they were interrogated by the police.* —*v.i.* **3.** to ask questions. **4.** *Elect.* to send a signal to a transponder. [late ME, t. L: m. s. *interrogātus,* pp.] —**inter′rogat′ingly,** *adv.* —**inter′roga′tor,** *n.*
interrogation (ĭn tĕ′rə gā′shən), *n.* **1.** the act of interrogating; questioning. **2.** an instance of being interrogated or questioned. **3.** a question. **4.** an interrogation mark. —**inter′roga′tional,** *adj.*
interrogation mark, question mark.
interrogative (ĭn′tə rŏg′ə tĭv), *adj.* **1.** pertaining to or conveying a question. **2.** *Gram.* (of an element or construction) forming or constituting a question: *an interrogative pronoun, an interrogative sentence.* —*n.* **3.** *Gram.* an interrogative word, element, or construction, as '*who?*' and '*what?*' —**in′terrog′atively,** *adv.*
interrogatory (ĭn′tə rŏg′ə tə rĭ, -trĭ), *adj., n., pl.* **-tories.** —*adj.* **1.** interrogative; questioning. —*n.* **2.** a question or inquiry. **3.** *Law.* a formal or written question. —**in′terrog′atorily,** *adv.*
in terrorem clause (ĭn′tĕ rô′rĕm), *Law.* a clause in a will which makes a gift of personalty subject to a condition.
interrupt (ĭn′tə rŭpt′), *v.t.* **1.** to make a break in (an otherwise continuous extent, course, process, condition, etc.). **2.** to break off or cause to cease, as in the midst or course: *he interrupted his work to answer the bell.* **3.** to stop (a person) in the midst of doing or saying something, esp. as by an interjected remark: *I don't want to be interrupted.* —*v.i.* **4.** to cause a break or discontinuance; interrupt action or speech: *please don't interrupt.* [ME *interrupte(n),* t. L: m. s. *interruptus,* pp., broken apart] —**in′terrup′tive,** *adj.*

—**Syn.** **1, 3.** INTERRUPT, DISCONTINUE, SUSPEND imply breaking off something temporarily or permanently. INTERRUPT may have either meaning: *to interrupt a meeting.* To DISCONTINUE is to stop or leave off, often permanently: *to discontinue a building programme.* To SUSPEND is to break off relations, operations, proceedings, privileges, etc., for a longer or shorter period, usually intending to resume at a stated time: *to suspend operation during a strike.*

interrupted cadence, *Music.* a cadence in which there is a progression from a dominant chord to a submediant one or to one other than dominant or tonic, which implies by its partial completeness an expected tonic chord.
interrupted screw, a screw with a discontinuous helix, as in a cannon breech, formed by cutting away part or parts of the thread, sometimes with part of the shaft beneath, used with a corresponding locknut.
interrupter (ĭn′tə rŭp′tə), *n.* **1.** one who or that which interrupts. **2.** *Elect.* a device for interrupting or periodically making and breaking a circuit. Also, **in′terrup′tor.**
interruption (ĭn′tə rŭp′shən), *n.* **1.** the act of interrupting. **2.** the state of being interrupted. **3.** something that interrupts. **4.** cessation; intermission.
interscapular (ĭn′tə skăp′yo͝o lə), *adj.* *Anat., Zool.* between the scapulae or shoulder blades.
inter se (ĭn′tə sā′), *Latin.* **1.** among or between themselves. **2.** (in livestock breeding) the mating of animals similarly bred to each other.
intersect (ĭn′tə sĕkt′), *v.t.* **1.** to cut or divide by passing through or lying across: *one road intersects another.* —*v.i.* **2.** to cross, as lines. **3.** *Geom.* to have, as two geometrical loci, one or more points in common: *intersecting lines.* [t. L: s. *intersectus,* pp., cut off]
intersection (ĭn′tə sĕk′shən), *n.* the act, fact, or place of intersecting. —**in′tersec′tional,** *adj.*
interseptal (ĭn′tə sĕp′tl), *adj.* between septa.
intersex (ĭn′tə sĕks′), *n.* *Biol.* an individual displaying characteristics of both the male and female sexes of the species.
intersexual (ĭn′tə sĕk′ syo͞o əl), *adj.* **1.** *Biol.* of or pertaining to an intersex. **2.** existing between the sexes.
intersidereal (ĭn′tə sī dĭə′rĭ əl), *adj.* interstellar.
interspace (*n.* ĭn′tə spās′; *v.* ĭn′tə spās′), *n., v.,* **-spaced, -spacing.** —*n.* **1.** a space between things. **2.** an intervening interval of time. —*v.t.* **3.** to put a space between. **4.** to occupy or fill the space between. —**in′terspa′tial,** *adj.*
intersperse (ĭn′tə spûs′), *v.t.,* **-spersed, -spersing.** **1.** to scatter here and there among other things: *to intersperse flowers among shrubs.* **2.** to diversify with something scattered or introduced here and there: *his speech was interspersed with long and boring quotations from the poets.* [t. L: m. s. *interspersus* strewn] —**interspersion** (ĭn′tə spû′shən), *n.*
interstate (ĭn′tə stāt′), *adj.* between or jointly involving states: *interstate commerce.* Cf. **intrastate.**
interstellar (ĭn′tə stĕl′ə), *adj.* between the stars; intersidereal: *interstellar matter.*
interstice (ĭn tû′stĭs), *n.* **1.** an intervening space. **2.** a small or narrow space between things or parts; small chink, crevice, or opening. [t. L: m. s. *interstitium* space between]
interstitial (ĭn′tə stĭsh′əl), *adj.* **1.** pertaining to, situated in, or forming interstices. **2.** *Anat.* situated between the cellular elements of a structure or part: *interstitial tissue.* —*n.* **3.** *Crystall.* a defect in a crystal caused by an extra atom or ion between normal sites in the lattice. —**in′tersti′tially,** *adv.*
interstitial compound, *Chem.* a compound of a metal and certain metalloids in which the metalloid atoms occupy interstices between the atoms of the metal lattice.
interstratify (ĭn′tə străt′ĭ fī′), *v.,* **-fied, -fying.** —*v.i.* **1.** to lie in interposed or alternate strata. —*v.t.* **2.** to interlay with or interpose between other strata. **3.** to arrange in alternate strata. —**in′terstrat′ifica′tion,** *n.*
intertexture (ĭn′tə tĕks′chə), *n.* **1.** the act of interweaving. **2.** the condition of being interwoven. **3.** something formed by interweaving.
intertribal (ĭn′tə trī′bl), *adj.* between tribes: *intertribal warfare.*
intertropical (ĭn′tə trŏp′ĭ kl), *adj.* *Geog.* between the tropics (of Cancer and Capricorn).
intertwine (ĭn′tə twīn′), *v.t., v.i.,* **-twined, -twining.** to twine together. —**in′tertwine′ment,** *n.* —**in′tertwin′ingly,** *adv.*
intertwist (ĭn′tə twĭst′), *v.t., v.i.* to twist together. —**in′tertwist′ingly,** *adv.*
interurban (ĭn′tər û′bən), *adj.* between cities or towns.
interval (ĭn′tə vəl), *n.* **1.** an intervening period of time: *an interval of fifty years.* **2.** a period of cessation; a pause: *intervals between attacks.* **3.** a period during which action temporarily ceases; a break, as between acts of a play in the theatre. **4.** a space intervening between things, points, limits, qualities, etc.: *an interval of ten feet between columns.* **5. at intervals,** at particular times or places with gaps in between. **6.** the space between soldiers or units in military formation. **7.** *Music.* the difference in pitch between two notes as, **a. harmonic interval,** an interval between two notes sounded simultaneously. **b. melodic interval,** an interval between two notes sounded successively. [ME *intervall,* t. L: s. *intervallum*]
intervale (ĭn′tə vāl′), *n.* *U.S. and Canada.* a low-lying tract of land, as along a river, between hills, etc. [var. of INTERVAL, assoc. with VALE[1]]
intervene (ĭn′tə vēn′), *v.i.,* **-vened, -vening.** **1.** to come between in action; intercede: *to intervene in a dispute.* **2.** to come or be between, as in place, time, or a series. **3.** to fall or happen between other events or periods: *nothing interesting has intervened.* **4.** (of things) to occur incidentally so as to modify a result. **5.** to come in, as something not belonging. **6.** *Law.* to interpose and become a party to a suit pending between other parties. [t. L: m. s. *intervenire* come between] —**in′terven′er,** *n.*
intervenient (ĭn′tə vē′nyənt), *adj.* **1.** intervening, as in place, time, order, or action. **2.** incidental.
intervention (ĭn′tə vĕn′shən), *n.* **1.** the act or fact of intervening. **2.** the interposition or interference of one state in the affairs of another: *intervention in the domestic policies of smaller nations.* —**in′terven′tional,** *adj.*
interventionist (ĭn′tə vĕn′shə nĭst), *n.* one who favours intervention, as in the affairs of another state.
interview (ĭn′tə vyo͞o′), *n.* **1.** a meeting of persons face to face, esp. for formal conference in business, etc., or for radio and television entertainment, etc. **2.** the conversation of a writer or reporter with a person or persons from whom material for a news or feature story or other writing is sought. **3.** the report of such conversation. —*v.t.* **4.** to have an interview with: *to interview the presi-*

dent. [t. F: m. *entrevue*, der. *entrevoir*, refl., see (each other), f. *entre-* INTER- + *voir* (g. L *vidēre*) see] **—in′terview′er,** *n.*

Intervision (ĭn′tə vĭzh′ən), *n.* a system for exchanging programmes and programme materials between eight television organizations of Eastern Europe.

intervolve (ĭn′tə vŏlv′), *v.t., v.i.,* **-volved, -volving.** to roll, wind, or involve, one within another. [f. INTER- + m. s. L *volvere* roll]

interweave (ĭn′tə wēv′), *v.,* **-wove** or **-weaved; -woven** or **-wove** or **-weaved; -weaving.** *—v.t.* **1.** to weave together, one with another, as threads, strands, branches, roots, etc. **2.** to intermingle or combine as if by weaving: *to interweave truth with fiction.* *—v.i.* **3.** to become woven together, interlaced, or intermingled. **—in′terweave′ment,** *n.* **—in′terweav′er,** *n.*

intestacy (ĭn tĕs′tə sĭ), *n.* the state or fact of being intestate at death.

intestate (ĭn tĕs′tāt, -tĭt), *adj.* **1.** (of a person) dying without having made a will. **2.** (of things) not disposed of by will; not legally devised or bequeathed. *—n.* **3.** one who dies intestate. [ME, t. L: m. s. *intestātus* having made no will]

intestinal (ĭn tĕs′tĭ nəl, ĭn′tĕs tī′nəl), *adj.* **1.** of or pertaining to the intestine. **2.** occurring or found in the intestine. [t. ML: s. *intestīnālis*] **—intes′tinally,** *adv.*

intestine (ĭn tĕs′tĭn), *n. Anat.* **1.** (*often pl.*) the lower part of the alimentary canal, extending from the pylorus to the anus. **2.** a definite portion of this part. The **small intestine** comprises the duodenum, jejunum, and ileum; the **large intestine** comprises the caecum, colon, and rectum. *—adj.* **3.** internal; domestic; civil: *intestine strife.* [t. L: m. s. *intestīna*, pl., entrails]

Human intestines
A, End of oesophagus; B, Cardiac end of stomach; C, Stomach; D, Duodenum; E, Jejunum; F, Small intestine; G, Ileum; H, Vermiform appendix; I, Caecum; J, Large intestine; K, Ascending colon; L, Transverse colon; M, Descending colon; N, Rectum; O, Anus

inthrall (ĭn thrôl′), *v.t.* enthrall. Also, *U.S.*, **inthral.**

inthrone (ĭn thrōn′), *v.t.,* **-throned, -throning.** enthrone.

intima (ĭn′tĭ mə), *n., pl.* **-mae** (-mē′). *Anat.* the innermost membrane or lining of some organ or part, esp. that of an artery, vein, or lymphatic. [t. NL, prop. fem. of L *intimus* inmost]

intimacy (ĭn′tĭ mə sĭ), *n., pl.* **-cies. 1.** the state of being intimate; intimate association or friendship. **2.** an instance of this. **3.** sexual intercourse.

intimate[1] (ĭn′tĭ mĭt), *adj.* **1.** associated in close personal relations: *an intimate friend.* **2.** characterized by or involving personally close or familiar association: *an intimate gathering.* **3.** private; closely personal: *one's intimate affairs.* **4.** maintaining sexual relations. **5.** (of acquaintance, knowledge, etc.) arising from close personal connection or familiar experience. **6.** detailed; deep: *a more intimate analysis.* **7.** close union or combination of particles or elements: *an intimate mixture.* **8.** inmost; deep within. **9.** pertaining to the inmost or essential nature; intrinsic: *the intimate structure of an organism.* **10.** pertaining to or existing in the inmost mind: *intimate beliefs.* *—n.* **11.** an intimate friend or associate. [in form t. LL: m. s. *intimātus*, pp., put or pressed into, but with sense of L *intimus* inmost] **—in′timately,** *adv.* **—in′timateness,** *n.* **—Syn. 1.** See **familiar.**

intimate[2] (ĭn′tĭ māt′), *v.t.,* **-mated, -mating. 1.** to make known indirectly; hint; suggest. **2.** *Rare.* to make known, esp. formally; announce. [t. LL: m. s. *intimātus*, pp., put or pressed into, announced] **—in′tima′tion,** *n.* **—Syn. 1.** See **hint.**

intimidate (ĭn tĭm′ĭ dāt′), *v.t.,* **-dated, -dating. 1.** to make timid, or inspire with fear; overawe; cow. **2.** to force into or deter from some action by inducing fear: *to intimidate a voter.* [t. ML: m. s. *intimidātus*, pp., made afraid. See TIMID] **—intim′ida′tion,** *n.* **—intim′ida′tor,** *n.* **—Syn. 2.** See **discourage.**

intimism (ĭn′tĭ mĭz′əm), *n.* a style of painting, as that of Bonnard and Vuillard, showing everyday life in domestic interiors. **—in′timist,** *n.*

intinction (ĭn tĭngk′shən), *n.* (in the Eucharistic service) the act of steeping the bread in the wine, to enable the communicants to receive the two conjointly. [t. LL: s. *intinctio*, der. L *intingere* dip in]

intitule (ĭn tĭt′yo͞ol), *v.t.,* **-uled, -uling.** *Archaic.* to give a title to; entitle. [t. LL: m. s. *intitulāre*, der. L *in-* IN-[2] + *titulus* TITLE] **—intit′ula′tion,** *n.*

into (*before consonants* ĭn′tə; *otherwise* ĭn′to͞o), *prep.* **1.** in to; in and to (expressing motion or direction towards the inner part of a place or thing, and hence entrance or inclusion within limits, or change to new circumstances, relations, condition, form, etc.). **2.** *Maths.* being the divisor of: *2 into 10 equals 5.* [ME *in to*]

intoed (ĭn′tōd′), *adj.* having inwardly turned toes.

intolerable (ĭn tŏl′ə rə bl, -tŏl′rə-), *adj.* **1.** not tolerable; unendurable; insufferable: *intolerable agony.* *—adv.* **2.** *Obs.* exceedingly. **—intol′erabil′ity, intol′erableness,** *n.* **—intol′erably,** *adv.* **—Syn. 1.** unbearable.

intolerance (ĭn tŏl′ə rəns), *n.* **1.** lack of toleration; indisposition to tolerate contrary opinions or beliefs. **2.** incapacity or indisposition to bear or endure: *intolerance of heat.* **3.** an intolerant act.

intolerant (ĭn tŏl′ə rənt), *adj.* **1.** not tolerating contrary opinions, esp. in religious matters; bigoted: *an intolerant zealot.* **2.** unable or indisposed to tolerate or endure (fol. by *of*): *intolerant of excesses.* *—n.* **3.** an intolerant person. **—intol′erantly,** *adv.*

—Syn. 1. INTOLERANT, FANATICAL, BIGOTED refer to strongly illiberal attitudes. INTOLERANT implies active (often violent) refusal to allow others to have or put into practice beliefs different from one's own: *intolerant in politics.* To be BIGOTED is to be so strongly attached to one's own belief as to be hostile to all others: *a bigoted person.* FANATICAL applies to unreasonable, often violent, action in maintaining one's beliefs and (often religious) practices: *a fanatical religious sect.* **—Ant.** liberal.

intomb (ĭn to͞om′), *v.t.* entomb. **—intomb′ment,** *n.*

intonate (ĭn′tō nāt′), *v.t.,* **-nated, -nating. 1.** to utter with a particular tone or modulation of voice. **2.** to intone or chant. [t. ML: m. s. *intonātus*, pp.]

intonation (ĭn′tō nā′shən), *n.* **1.** the pattern or melody of pitch changes revealed in connected speech; esp. the pitch pattern of a sentence, which distinguishes kinds of sentences and speakers of different nationalities. **2.** the act of intonating. **3.** the manner of producing musical notes, specifically the relation in pitch of notes to their key or harmony. **4.** the opening phrase in a Gregorian chant, usually sung by only one or two voices.

intone (ĭn tōn′), *v.,* **-toned, -toning.** *—v.t.* **1.** to utter with a particular tone; intonate. **2.** to give tone or variety of tone to; vocalize. **3.** to utter in a singing voice (the first notes of a section in a liturgical service). **4.** to recite in monotone. *—v.i.* **5.** to speak or recite in a singing voice, esp. in monotone. **6.** *Music.* to produce a note, or a particular series of notes, like a scale, esp. with the voice; sing or chant. [late ME, t. ML: m. s. *intonāre*. Cf. INTONATE] **—inton′er,** *n.*

intorsion (ĭn tô′shən), *n.* a twisting or winding, as of the stem of a plant.

intort (ĭn tôt′), *v.t.* to twist inwards, curl, or wind: *intorted horns.* [t. L: s. *intortus*, pp.]

in toto (ĭn tō′tō), *Latin.* in all; in the whole; wholly.

intoxicant (ĭn tŏk′sĭ kənt), *adj.* **1.** intoxicating. *—n.* **2.** an intoxicating agent, as liquor or certain drugs.

intoxicate (*v.* ĭn tŏk′sĭ kāt′; *adj.* ĭn tŏk′sĭ kĭt, -kāt′), *v.,* **-cated, -cating,** *adj.* *—v.t.* **1.** to affect temporarily with loss of control over the physical and mental powers, by means of alcoholic liquor, a drug, or other substance. **2.** to excite mentally beyond self-control or reason. **3.** *Obs.* to poison. *—v.i.* **4.** to cause or produce intoxication: *an intoxicating liquor.* *—adj.* **5.** *Archaic.* intoxicated. [ME, t. ML: m. s. *intoxicātus*, pp., poisoned. See TOXIC] **—intox′icat′ingly,** *adv.* **—intox′ica′tive,** *adj.*

intoxicated (ĭn tŏk′sĭ kā′tĭd), *adj.* **1.** drunk. **2.** excited mentally beyond reason or self-control.

intoxication (ĭn tŏk′sĭ kā′shən), *n.* **1.** inebriation; drunkenness. **2.** *Pathol.* poisoning. **3.** the act of intoxicating. **4.** overpowering action or effect upon the mind.

intr., intransitive.

intra-, a prefix meaning 'within', freely used as an English formative, esp. in scientific terms, sometimes in opposition to *extra-.* Cf. **intro-.** [t. L, repr. *intrā*, adv. and prep., within, akin to *interior* inner, and *inter* between]

intra-atomic (ĭn′trə ə tŏm′ĭk), *adj.* within an atom or atoms.

intracardiac (ĭn′trə kä′dĭ ăk′), *adj.* within the heart.

intracellular (ĭn′trə sĕl′yo͝o lə), *adj.* within a cell or cells.

intracranial (ĭn′trə krā′nyəl), *adj.* within the cranium or skull.

intractable (ĭn trăk′tə bl), *adj.* **1.** not docile; stubborn: *an intractable disposition.* **2.** (of things) hard to deal with; unmanageable. **—intrac′tabil′ity, intrac′tableness,** *n.* **intrac′tably,** *adv.*

intrados (ĭn trā′dŏs), *n. Archit.* the interior curve or surface of an arch or vault; soffit. Cf. **extrados.** See diag. under **arch.** [t. F, f. L *intra-* INTRA- + F *dos* (g. L *dorsum* back)]

intramolecular (ĭn′trə mə lĕk′yŏŏ lə), *adj.* within the molecule or molecules.

intramural (ĭn′trə myŏŏə′rəl), *adj.* **1.** within the walls or enclosing limits, as of a city or a building. **2.** *Anat.* within the substance of a wall, as of an organ. **3.** *Chiefly U.S.* engaged in or pertaining to a single college, or its students.

intra muros (ĭn′trə myŏŏə′rōs), *Latin.* within the walls, as of a city.

intramuscular (ĭn′trə mŭs′kyŏŏ lə), *adj.* situated or occurring within a muscle.

intrans., intransitive.

intransigent (ĭn trăn′sĭ jənt), *adj.* **1.** uncompromising, esp. in politics; irreconcilable. **—*n.*** **2.** one who is irreconcilable, esp. in politics. Also, *French,* **intransigeant** (*Fr.* ăN trăN zē zhăN′). [t. F: m. *intransigeant,* t. Sp., der. (*los*) *intransigentes* revolutionary party refusing compromise, f. L: *in-* IN-³ + *transigentēs,* ppr. pl., coming to an agreement] **—intran′sigence, intran′sigency,** *n.* **—intran′sigently,** *adv.*

intransitive (ĭn trăn′sĭ tĭv), *adj.* **1.** having the quality of an intransitive verb. **—*n.*** **2.** an intransitive verb. **—intran′sitively,** *adv.*

intransitive verb, a verb that is never accompanied by a direct object, as *come, sit, lie,* etc.

in transitu (ĭn trăn′sĭ tyŏŏ′), *Latin.* in transit; on the way.

intrant (ĭn′trənt), *n.* one who enters (esp. a college, association, etc.); entrant. [t. L: s. *intrans,* ppr., entering]

intranuclear (ĭn′trə nyŏŏ′klĭ ə), *adj.* within a nucleus or nuclei.

intra-ocular (ĭn′trə ŏk′yŏŏ lə), *adj.* situated or occurring within the eyeball.

intrastate (ĭn′trə stāt′), *adj.* within a state, esp. one of the United States: *instrastate commerce.*

intratelluric (ĭn′trə tĕ lyŏŏə′rĭk), *adj.* *Geol.* **1.** situated in, taking place in, or resulting from action, within the earth itself, usually within the earth's crust. **2.** designating the period of crystallization of an eruptive rock which precedes its extrusion on the surface or the crystals in a porphyritic lava formed prior to its extrusion.

intra-uterine (ĭn′trə yŏŏ′tə rīn′), *adj.* *Med.* within the uterus.

intravenous (ĭn′trə vē′nəs), *adj.* **1.** within a vein or the veins. **2.** denoting or pertaining to an injection into a vein. **—in′trave′nously,** *adv.*

intrazonal soil (ĭn′trə zō′nəl), *Geol.* one of a group of mature soils which have been more affected by some local factor or relief or rock type than by climate and vegetation.

intreat (ĭn trēt′), *v.t., v.i.* *Archaic.* entreat.

intrench (ĭn trĕnch′), *v.t., v.i.* entrench. **—intrench′er,** *n.* **—intrench′ment,** *n.*

intrepid (ĭn trĕp′ĭd), *adj.* fearless; dauntless: *intrepid courage.* [t. L: s. *intrepidus* not alarmed] **—in′trepid′ity,** *n.* **—intrep′idly,** *adv.*

intricacy (ĭn′trĭ kə sĭ), *n., pl.* **-cies.** **1.** intricate character or state. **2.** an intricate part, action, etc.

intricate (ĭn′trĭ kĭt), *adj.* **1.** perplexingly entangled or involved: *a maze of intricate paths.* **2.** confusingly complex; complicated; hard to understand: *an intricate machine.* [late ME, t. L: m. s. *intricātus,* pp., entangled] **—in′tricately,** *adv.* **—in′tricateness,** *n.*

intrigant (ĭn′trĭ gənt; *Fr.* ăN trē găN′), *n., pl.* **-gants** (-gənts; *Fr.* -găN′). one who carries on intrigue. Also, **in′triguant.** [t. F, t. It.: m. *intrigante,* ppr. of *intrigare.* See INTRIGUE, v.]

intrigante (ĭn′trĭ gŏnt′; *Fr.* ăN trē găNt′), *n., pl.* **-gantes** (-gŏnts′; *Fr.* -găNt′). a woman intrigant. Also, **in′triguante′.**

intrigue (*v.* ĭn trēg′; *n.* ĭn trēg′, ĭn′trēg), *v.,* **-trigued, -triguing,** *n.* **—*v.t.*** **1.** to excite the curiosity or interest of by puzzling, novel, or otherwise arresting qualities. **2.** to take the fancy of: *her hat intrigued me.* **3.** to beguile by appeal to the curiosity, interest, or fancy (fol. by *into*). **4.** to puzzle: *I am intrigued by this event.* **5.** to bring or force by underhand machinations. **6.** *Now Rare.* to entangle. **7.** *Obs.* to trick or cheat. **8.** *Obs.* to plot for. **—*v.i.*** **9.** to use underhand machinations; plot craftily. **10.** to carry on a clandestine or illicit love affair. **—*n.*** **11.** the use of underhand machinations to accomplish designs. **12.** a plot or crafty dealing: *political intrigues.* **13.** a clandestine or illicit love affair. **14.** the series of complications forming the plot of a play. [t. F: s. *intriguer,* t. It.: m. *intrigare,* g. L *intricāre* entangle, perplex] **—intri′guer,** *n.* **—intri′guingly,** *adv.*

intrinsic (ĭn trĭn′sĭk), *adj.* **1.** belonging to a thing by its very nature: *intrinsic merit.* **2.** *Anat.* (of certain muscles, nerves, etc.) belonging to or lying within a given part. Also, **intrin′sical.** [t. ML: m. s. *intrinsecus* inward (L inwardly)] **—intrin′sically,** *adv.* **—Syn. 1.** See **essential. —Ant. 1.** accidental.

intrinsic energy, *Thermodynamics.* the total energy stored within a material system: the absolute value is usually unimportant but changes in intrinsic energy are important in thermodynamic calculations.

intro (ĭn′trō), *n., pl.* **-tros.** *Colloq.* an introduction.

intro-, a prefix meaning 'inwardly', 'within', occasionally used as an English formative. Cf. **intra-.** [t. L, repr. *intro,* adv., inwardly, within]

intro., 1. introduction. 2. introductory. Also, **introd.**

introduce (ĭn′trə dyŏŏs′), *v.t.,* **-duced, -ducing. 1.** to bring into notice, knowledge, use, vogue, etc.: *to introduce a fashion.* **2.** to bring forward for consideration, as a proposed bill in Parliament, etc. **3.** to bring forward with preliminary or preparatory matter: *to introduce a subject with a long preface.* **4.** to bring (a person) to the knowledge or experience of something (fol. by *to*): *to introduce a person to chess.* **5.** to lead, bring, or put into a place, position, surroundings, relations, etc.: *to introduce a figure into a design.* **6.** to bring (a person) into the acquaintance of another: *he introduced his sister to us.* **7.** to present formally, as to a person, an audience, or society. [late ME, t. L: m. s. *intrōdūcere* lead in] **—in′troduc′er,** *n.* **—in′troduc′ible,** *adj.*

—Syn. 6, 7. INTRODUCE, PRESENT mean to bring persons into personal acquaintance with each other, as by announcement of names, and the like. INTRODUCE is the ordinary term, referring to making persons acquainted who are ostensibly equals: *to introduce a friend to one's sister.* PRESENT, a more formal term, suggests a degree of ceremony in the process, and implies (if only as a matter of compliment) superior dignity, rank, or importance in the person to whom another is presented: *to present a diplomat to the Queen.*

introduction (ĭn′trə dŭk′shən), *n.* **1.** the act of introducing. **2.** a formal presentation of one person to another or others. **3.** something introduced. **4.** a preliminary part, as of a book, musical composition, or the like, leading up to the main part. **5.** an elementary treatise: *an introduction to botany.* [ME, t. L: s. *intrōductio*]

—Syn. 4. INTRODUCTION, FOREWORD, PREFACE refer to material given at the front of a book to explain or introduce it to the reader. An INTRODUCTION is a formal preliminary statement or guide to the book: *his purpose is stated in the introduction.* A FOREWORD is often an informal statement made to the reader. It is the same as PREFACE, but FOREWORD was substituted for it during the vogue for restoring native terms: *an unusual foreword, a short preface.*

introductory (ĭn′trə dŭk′tə rĭ), *adj.* serving to introduce; preliminary; prefatory. Also, **in′troduc′tive. —in′troduc′torily,** *adv.* **—Syn.** See **preliminary.**

introit (ĭn′troit), *n.* **1.** *Rom. Cath. Ch.* a shortened psalm, preceded and followed by an antiphon, spoken in English at the beginning of mass, or sung in Latin at a solemn celebration. **2.** *Anglican Ch.* a psalm or anthem sung as the celebrant of the holy communion is entering the sanctuary. [late ME, t. L: s. *introitus* entrance]

introitus (ĭn trō′ĭ təs), *n.* *Anat.* the entrance to a cavity or space, esp. the vagina. [L]

introjection (ĭn′trə jĕk′shən), *n.* *Psychoanal.* a primitive and early unconscious psychic process by which an external object or individual is represented by an image which in turn is incorporated into the psychic apparatus of someone else. [f. INTRO- + s. L *-jectio* a throwing]

intromit (ĭn′trə mĭt′), *v.t.,* **-mitted, -mitting.** *Now Rare.* to send, put, or let in; introduce; admit. [ME *intromitte(n),* t. L: m. *intrōmittere* send in] **—intromission** (ĭn′trə mĭsh′ən), *n.* **—in′tromit′tent,** *adj.*

introrse (ĭn trôs′), *adj.* *Bot.* turned or facing inwards, as anthers which open towards the gynoecium. [t. L: m. s. *introrsus*] **—introrse′ly,** *adv.*

introspect (ĭn′trə spĕkt′), *v.i.* **1.** to practise introspection; consider one's own internal state or feelings. **—*v.t.*** **2.** to look into; examine. [t. L: s. *intrōspectus,* pp., looked into] **—in′trospec′tive,** *adj.* **—in′trospec′tively,** *adv.* **—in′trospec′tiveness,** *n.*

introspection (ĭn′trə spĕk′shən), *n.* observation or examination of one's own mental states or processes.

introversion (ĭn′trə vû′shən), *n.* **1.** the act of introverting. **2.** introverted state. **3.** *Psychol.* interest directed inwards or upon the self. Cf. **extroversion. —introversive** (ĭn′trə vû′sĭv), *adj.*

introvert (*n., adj.* ĭn′trə vût′; *v.* ĭn′trə vût′), *n.* **1.** *Psychol.* one characterized by introversion; a person concerned chiefly with his own thoughts. Cf. **extrovert. 2.** *Zool., etc.* a part that is or can be introverted. **—*adj.*** **3.** marked by introversion. **—*v.t.*** **4.** to turn inwards. **5.** to direct (the mind, etc.) inwards or upon the self. **6.** *Zool., etc.* to sheathe a part of, within another part; invaginate. [f. INTRO- + s. L *vertere* turn]

intrude (ĭn trŏŏd′), *v.,* **-truded, -truding. —*v.t.*** **1.** to thrust or bring in without reason, permission, or welcome. **2.** *Geol.* to thrust or force in. **—*v.i.*** **3.** to thrust oneself in; come uninvited: *to intrude upon his privacy.*

[t. L: m. s. *intrūdere* thrust in] —**intrud′er,** *n.* —**intrud′ingly,** *adv.* —**Syn.** 3. See **trespass.**

intrusion (ĭn trōō′zhən), *n.* **1.** the act of intruding: *an unwarranted intrusion.* **2.** *Law.* a wrongful entry after the determination of a particular estate, made before the remainderman or reversioner has entered. **3.** *Geol.* **a.** the forcing of extraneous matter, as molten rock, into some other formation. **b.** the matter forced in.

intrusive (ĭn trōō′sĭv), *adj.* **1.** intruding. **2.** characterized by or involving intrusion. **3.** apt to intrude; coming unbidden or without welcome. **4.** *Geol.* **a.** (of rocks) having been forced, while molten or plastic, into fissures or other openings or between layers of other rocks. **b.** denoting or pertaining to plutonic rocks. **5.** *Phonet.* inserted without grammatical or historical justification. —**intru′sively,** *adv.* —**intru′siveness,** *n.*

intrust (ĭn trŭst′), *v.t.* entrust.

intubate (ĭn′tyōō bāt′), *v.t.*, **-bated, -bating.** *Med.* **1.** to insert a tube into. **2.** to treat by inserting a tube, as into the larynx. —**in′tuba′tion,** *n.*

intuit (ĭn tyōō′ĭt), *v.t., v.i.*, **-ited, -iting.** to know, or receive knowledge, by intuition. [t. L: s. *intuitus*, pp.]

intuition (ĭn′tyōō ĭsh′ən), *n.* **1.** direct perception of truths, facts, etc., independently of any reasoning process. **2.** a truth or fact thus perceived. **3.** the ability to perceive in this way. **4.** *Philos.* **a.** an immediate cognition of an object not inferred or determined by a previous cognition of the same object. **b.** any object or truth so discerned. **c.** pure, untaught, non-inferential knowledge. [t. ML: s. *intuitio*, der. L *intuērī* look at, consider]

intuitional (ĭn′tyōō ĭsh′ə nəl), *adj.* **1.** pertaining to or of the nature of intuition. **2.** characterized by intuition; having intuition. **3.** based on intuition as a principle. —**in′tui′tionally,** *adv.*

intuitionalism (ĭn′tyōō ĭsh′ə nə lĭz′əm), *n.* intuitionism. —**in′tui′tionalist,** *n.*

intuitionism (ĭn′tyōō ĭsh′ə nĭz′əm), *n.* **1.** *Ethics.* the doctrine that moral values and duties can be discerned directly. **2.** *Metaphys.* **a.** the doctrine that in perception external objects are given immediately, without the intervention of a representative idea. **b.** the doctrine that knowledge rests upon axiomatic truths discerned directly. —**in′tui′tionist,** *n., adj.*

intuitive (ĭn tyōō′ĭ tĭv), *adj.* **1.** perceiving by intuition, as a person, the mind, etc. **2.** perceived by, resulting from, or involving intuition: *intuitive knowledge.* **3.** of the nature of intuition. —**intu′itively,** *adv.* —**intu′itiveness,** *n.*

intuitivism (ĭn tyōō′ĭ tĭ vĭz′əm), *n.* **1.** ethical intuitionism. **2.** intuitive perception; insight. —**intu′itivist,** *n.*

intumesce (ĭn′tyōō mĕs′), *v.i.*, **-mesced, -mescing. 1.** to swell up, as with heat; become tumid. **2.** to bubble up. [t. L: s. *intumescere* swell up]

intumescence (ĭn′tyōō mĕs′əns), *n.* **1.** a swelling up as with congestion. **2.** swollen state. **3.** a swollen mass. —**in′tumes′cent,** *adj.*

inturn (ĭn′tûn′), *n.* an inward turn, as of the toes.

intussuscept (ĭn′təs sə sĕpt′), *v.t.* to take within, as one part of the intestine into an adjacent part; invaginate. [back-formation from INTUSSUSCEPTION] —**in′tussuscep′tive,** *adj.*

intussusception (ĭn′təs sə sĕp′shən), *n.* **1.** a taking within. **2.** *Pathol.* the slipping of one part within another; invagination. [f. L: *intus* within + s. *susceptio* a taking up]

intwine (ĭn twīn′), *v.t., v.i.*, **-twined, -twining.** entwine.

intwist (ĭn twĭst′), *v.t.* entwist.

inulin (ĭn′yōō lĭn), *n.* *Chem.* a polysaccharide obtained from the roots of certain plants, esp. elecampane, dahlia, and Jerusalem artichoke, which undergoes hydrolysis. [f. s. L *inula* elecampane + -IN [2]]

inunction (ĭn ŭngk′shən), *n.* **1.** the act of anointing. **2.** *Med.* the rubbing in of an oil or ointment. **3.** *Archaic.* an unguent. [late ME, t. L: s. *inunctio* an anointing]

inundant (ĭn ŭn′dənt), *adj.* *Poetic.* inundating.

inundate (ĭn′ŭn dāt′), *v.t.*, **-dated, -dating. 1.** to overspread with a flood; overflow; flood; deluge. **2.** to overspread as with or in a flood; overwhelm. [t. L: m. s. *inundātus*, pp., overflowed] —**in′unda′tion,** *n.* —**in′unda′tor,** *n.*

inurbane (ĭn′û bān′), *adj.* not urbane; lacking in courtesy or suavity. —**inurbanity** (ĭn′û băn′ĭ tĭ), *n.* —**in′urbane′ly,** *adv.*

inure (ĭ nyōōə′), *v.*, **inured, inuring.** —*v.t.* **1.** to toughen or harden by exercise; accustom; habituate (fol. by *to*): *to inure a person to danger.* —*v.i.* **2.** to come into use; take or have effect. Also, **enure.** [late ME, v. use of obs. phrase *in ure* in use, f. IN, prep., + obs. *ure* use, work (t. AF, g. L *opera*)] —**inure′ment,** *n.*

inurn (ĭn ûn′), *v.t.* **1.** to put into an urn, esp. a funeral urn. **2.** to bury; inter. —**inurn′ment,** *n.*

inutile (ĭn yōō′tĭl), *adj.* useless; of no use or service; unprofitable. [late ME, t. L: m. s. *inūtilis*]

inutility (ĭn′yōō tĭl′ĭ tĭ), *n.*, *pl.* **-ties. 1.** uselessness. **2.** a useless thing or person.

inv., 1. invented. **2.** inventor. **3.** invoice.

in vacuo (ĭn văk′yōō ō′), *Latin.* in a vacuum.

invade (ĭn vād′). *v.*, **-vaded, -vading.** —*v.t.* **1.** to enter as an enemy; go into with hostile intent: *Caesar invaded Britain.* **2.** to enter like an enemy: *locusts invaded the fields.* **3.** (of a disease, etc.) to enter, as to cause disease, injury, etc.: *the poison invaded his system.* **4.** to enter as if to take possession: *to invade a friend's quarters.* **5.** to intrude upon: *to invade the privacy of a family.* **6.** to encroach or infringe upon: *to invade the rights of citizens.* **7.** to penetrate: *the smell of cooking invaded the bedrooms.* —*v.i.* **8.** to make an invasion. [late ME, t. L: m. s. *invādere* go into, attack] —**invad′er,** *n.*

invaginable (ĭn văj′ĭ nə bl), *adj.* *Rare.* capable of being invaginated; susceptible of invagination.

invaginate (*v.* ĭn văj′ĭ nāt′; *adj.* ĭn văj′ĭ nĭt, -nāt′), *v.*, **-nated, -nating,** *adj.* —*v.t.* **1.** to insert or receive as into a sheath; sheathe. **2.** to fold or draw (a tubular organ, etc.) back within itself; introvert; intussuscept. —*v.i.* **3.** to become invaginated; undergo invagination. **4.** to form a pocket by turning in. —*adj.* **5.** invaginated. [f. IN-[2] + s. L *vāgina* sheath + -ATE[1]]

invagination (ĭn văj′ĭ nā′shən), *n.* **1.** the act or process of invaginating. **2.** *Embryol.* the inward movement of a portion of the wall of a blastula in the formation of a gastrula. **3.** *Pathol.* intussusception.

invalid[1] (ĭn′və lēd′, -lĭd), *n.* **1.** an infirm or sickly person: *a hopeless invalid.* **2.** a serviceman disabled for active service. —*adj.* **3.** deficient in health; weak; sick: *his invalid sister.* **4.** of or for invalids: *invalid diets.* —*v.t.* **5.** to affect with disease; make an invalid: *invalided for life.* **6.** to class, or remove from active service, as an invalid. —*v.i.* **7.** to become an invalid. **8.** (of a serviceman) to retire from active service because of illness or injury. [t. L: s. *invalidus* infirm, not strong]

invalid[2] (ĭn văl′ĭd), *adj.* **1.** not valid; of no force, weight, or cogency; weak: *invalid arguments.* **2.** without legal force, or void, as a contract. [f. IN-[3] + VALID] —**inval′idly,** *adv.*

invalidate (ĭn văl′ĭ dāt′), *v.t.* **-dated, -dating. 1.** to render invalid. **2.** to deprive of legal force or efficacy. —**inval′ida′tion,** *n.* —**inval′ida′tor,** *n.*

invalid chair, a chair, usually collapsible, and always mobile, used for the transport of invalids unable to walk.

invalidism (ĭn′və lĭ dĭz′əm), *n.* prolonged ill health.

invalidity (ĭn′və lĭd′ĭ tĭ), *n.* lack of validity.

invaluable (ĭn văl′yōō ə bl), *adj.* that cannot be valued or appraised; of inestimable value. —**inval′uableness,** *n.* —**inval′uably,** *adv.* —**Syn.** priceless, precious. —**Ant.** worthless.

invar (ĭn vä′), *n.* **1.** an iron alloy, containing 35·5 per cent nickel, having a very low coefficient of expansion at atmospheric temperatures. **2.** (*cap.*) a trademark for this alloy. [short for INVARIABLE]

invariable (ĭn vĕə′rĭ ə bl), *adj.* **1.** not variable or not capable of being varied; not changing or not capable of being changed; always the same. —*n.* **2.** *Maths.* an invariable quantity; a constant. —**invar′iabil′ity, invar′iableness,** *n.* —**invar′iably,** *adv.* —**Syn.** unalterable, unchanging, uniform, constant.

invariant (ĭn vĕə′rĭ ənt), *adj.* **1.** unvarying; invariable; constant. —*n.* **2.** *Maths.* an invariable.

invasion (ĭn vā′zhən), *n.* **1.** the act of invading or entering as an enemy. **2.** the entrance or advent of anything troublesome or harmful, as disease. **3.** entrance as if to take possession or overrun. **4.** infringement by intrusion. [t. LL: s. *invāsio* an attack]

invasive (ĭn vā′sĭv), *adj.* **1.** characterized by or involving invasion; offensive: *invasive war.* **2.** invading, or tending to invade; intrusive.

invective (ĭn vĕk′tĭv), *n.* **1.** vehement denunciation; an utterance of violent censure or reproach. **2.** a railing accusation; vituperation. —*adj.* **3.** censoriously abusive; vituperative; denunciatory. [ME, t. LL: m. s. *invectivus* abusive] —**invec′tively,** *adv.* —**invec′tiveness,** *n.* —**Syn. 1.** See **abuse.**

inveigh (ĭn vā′), *v.i.* to attack vehemently in words; rail: *to inveigh against democracy.* [ME *inveh*, t. L: s. *invehere* carry or bear into, assail] —**inveigh′er,** *n.*

inveigle (ĭn vē′gl), *v.t.*, **-gled, -gling. 1.** to draw by beguiling or artful inducements (fol. by *into*, sometimes *from, away*, etc.): *to inveigle a person into playing bridge.* **2.** to allure, win, or seduce by beguiling. [late ME *enve(u)gle*, t. F: m. s. *aveugler* blind, delude] —**invei′glement,** *n.* —**invei′gler,** *n.*

invent (ĭn vĕnt′), *v.t.* **1.** to originate as a product of one's own contrivance: *to invent a machine.* **2.** to produce or create with the imagination: *to invent a story.* **3.** to make up or fabricate as something merely fictitious or false: *to invent excuses.* **4.** *Obs.* to come upon; find. —*v.i.* **5.** to devise something new, as by ingenuity. [late ME, t. L: s. *inventus*, pp., discovered, found out] —**in·vent′ible,** *adj.* —**Syn. 1.** See **discover.**

inventer (ĭn vĕn′tə), *n.* inventor.

invention (ĭn vĕn′shən), *n.* **1.** the act of inventing. **2.** *Patent Law.* the conception of an idea and the means or apparatus by which the result is obtained. **3.** anything invented or devised. **4.** the exercise of imaginative or creative power in literature or art. **5.** the act of producing or creating by exercise of the imagination. **6.** the power or faculty of inventing, devising, or originating. **7.** something fabricated, as a false statement. **8.** *Sociol.* the creation of a new culture trait, pattern, etc. **9.** *Music.* a short piece, contrapuntal in nature, generally based on one subject. **10.** *Speech.* (classically) one of the five steps in speech preparation, the process of choosing ideas appropriate to the subject, audience, and occasion. **11.** *Archaic.* the act of finding. [ME, t. L: s. *inventio*]

inventive (ĭn vĕn′tĭv), *adj.* **1.** apt at inventing, devising, or contriving. **2.** having the function of inventing. **3.** pertaining to, involving, or showing invention. —**inven′tively,** *adv.* —**inven′tiveness,** *n.*

inventor (ĭn vĕn′tə), *n.* one who invents, esp. one who devises some new process, appliance, machine, or article; one who makes inventions. Also, **inventer.**

inventory (ĭn′vən trĭ), *n.*, *pl.* **-tories,** *v.*, **-toried, -torying.** —*n.* **1.** a detailed descriptive list of articles, with number, quantity, and value of each. **2.** a formal list of movables, as of a merchant's stock of goods. **3.** a complete listing of work in progress, raw materials, finished goods on hand, etc., made each year by a business concern. **4.** items in such a list. **5.** the value of a stock of goods. —*v.t.* **6.** to make an inventory of; enter in an inventory. [late ME, t. ML: m. s. *inventōrium*, L *inventārium* list] —**inventorial** (ĭn′vən tô′rĭ əl), *adj.* —**in′vento′rially,** *adv.* —**Syn. 1.** See **list**[1].

inveracity (ĭn′və răs′ĭ tĭ), *n.*, *pl.* **-ties. 1.** untruthfulness. **2.** an untruth.

Invercargill (ĭn′və kä′gĭl), *n.* a town in New Zealand, in S South Island. 41,088 (1961).

Inverness (ĭn′və nĕs′), *n.* **1.** a burgh in Scotland, the county town of Inverness-shire. 29,774 (1961). **2.** Inverness-shire. **3.** an overcoat with a long removable cape (**Inverness cape**).

Inverness-shire (ĭn′və nĕs′shĭə, -shə), *n.* a county in NW Scotland. 83,425 pop. (1961); 4211 sq. mi. *Co. town:* Inverness. *Abbrev.:* I'ness. Also, **Inverness.**

inverse (*adj.*, *n.* ĭn vûs′, ĭn′vûs; *v.* ĭn vûs′), *adj.*, *n.*, *v.*, **-versed, -versing.** —*adj.* **1.** reversed in position, direction, or tendency: *inverse order.* **2.** opposite to in nature or effect, as a mathematical relation or operation: *subtraction is the inverse operation to addition.* **3.** inverted, or turned upside down. —*n.* **4.** an inverted state or condition. **5.** that which is inverse; the direct opposite. —*v.t.* **6.** *Now Rare.* to invert. [t. L: m. s. *inversus*, pp., turned about] —**inverse′ly,** *adv.*

inverse function, *Maths.* the function which replaces another function when the dependent and independent variables of the first function are interchanged, as log x is the inverse function of e^x. If y is a trigonometrical ratio of the angle x, as $y = \sin x$, then x is the inverse function of y, i.e. $x = \arcsin y$ or $\sin^{-1}y$.

inverse square law, any law which states that the intensity of an effect at a point B, due to a source A, varies inversely as the square of the distance AB.

inversion (ĭn vû′shən), *n.* **1.** the act of inverting. **2.** an inverted state. **3.** anything inverted. **4.** any change from the normal word order or syntactic construction of a language, esp. for literary effect, as 'came the dawn'. **5.** *Anat.* the turning inwards of a part, as the foot (opposed to *eversion*). **6.** *Chem.* a hydrolysis of certain carbohydrates, as cane sugar, which results in a reversal of direction of the rotary power of the carbohydrate solution, the plane of polarized light being bent from right to left or vice versa. **7.** *Music.* **a.** the process, or result, of transposing the notes of an interval or chord so that the original bass becomes an upper voice. **b.** (in counterpoint) the transposition of the upper voice part below the lower, and vice versa. **c.** presentation of a melody in contrary motion to its original form. **8.** *Psychiatry.* assumption of the sexual role of the opposite sex; homosexuality. **9.** *Phonet.* retroflexion. **10.** *Meteorol.* a reversal in the normal temperature lapse rate, in which the temperature rises with increased elevation, instead of falling. **11.** something inverted. **12.** *Rhet.* reversal of the usual or natural order of words; anastrophe. [t. L: s. *inversio*]

inversive (ĭn vû′sĭv), *adj.* characterized by inversion.

invert (*v.* ĭn vût′; *adj.*, *n.* ĭn′vût), *v.t.* **1.** to turn upside down, inside out, or inwards. **2.** to reverse in position, direction, or order. **3.** to turn or change to the opposite or contrary, as in nature, bearing, or effect: *to invert a process.* **4.** *Chem.* to subject to inversion. See **inversion** (def. 6). **5.** *Phonet.* to articulate, as a retroflex vowel. —*adj.* **6.** *Chem.* inverted. —*n.* **7.** one who or that which is inverted. **8.** a homosexual. **9.** the lowest visible surface; the floor of a culvert, drain, or sewer. [t. L: s. *invertere* turn about, upset] —**invert′ible,** *adj.* —**Syn. 2.** See **reverse.**

invertase (ĭn vû′tās), *n.* *Biochem.* an enzyme which causes the inversion of cane sugar, thus changing it into invert sugar. It is found in yeast and in the digestive juices of animals; sucrase. [INVERT + -ASE]

invertebrate (ĭn vû′tĭ brĭt, -brāt′), *adj.* **1.** *Zool.* not vertebrate; without a backbone. **2.** of or pertaining to animals without backbones. **3.** without strength of character. —*n.* **4.** an invertebrate animal. **5.** one who lacks strength of character. —**invertebracy** (ĭn vû′tĭ brə sĭ), **inver′tebrateness,** *n.*

inverted commas, quotation marks.

inverted mordent, *Music.* a melodic embellishment consisting of a rapid alternation of a principal note with a note one degree above it. Also, **pralltriller.**

inverter (ĭn vû′tə), *n.* **1.** one who or that which inverts. **2.** *Elect.* a converter. **3.** *Electronics.* an amplifier which inverts its input signal. Also, **invertor.**

invert soap, an emulsifiable salt whose action is responsible for soapy qualities.

invert sugar, a mixture of glucose and fructose formed naturally in fruits and produced artificially in syrups or fondants by treating cane sugar with acids.

invest (ĭn vĕst′), *v.t.* **1.** to put (money) to use, by purchase or expenditure, in something offering profitable returns, esp. interest or income. **2.** to spend: *to invest large sums in books.* **3.** to clothe. **4.** to cover or adorn as an article of attire does. **5.** *Rare.* to put on (a garment, etc.). **6.** to cover or surround as if with a garment, or like a garment: *spring invests the trees with leaves.* **7.** to surround (a place) with military forces or works so as to prevent approach or escape; besiege. **8.** to endue or endow: *to invest a friend with every virtue.* **9.** to belong to, as a quality or character does. **10.** to settle or vest (a power, right, etc.), as in a person. **11.** to clothe in or with the insignia of office. **12.** to install in an office or position; furnish with power, authority, rank, etc. —*v.i.* **13.** to invest money; make an investment. **14. invest in,** *Colloq.* to buy; spend money on. [late ME, t. L: s. *investīre* clothe] —**inves′tor,** *n.*

investigable (ĭn vĕs′tĭ gə bl), *adj.* capable of being investigated.

investigate (ĭn vĕs′tĭ gāt′), *v.*, **-gated, -gating.** —*v.t.* **1.** to search or inquire into; search or examine into the particulars of; examine in detail. **2.** to examine in order to obtain the true facts: *to investigate a murder.* —*v.i.* **3.** to make inquiry, examination, or investigation. [t. L: m. s. *investīgātus*, pp., tracked, traced out] —**inves′tiga′tive, investigatory** (ĭn vĕs′tĭ gā′tə rĭ), *adj.* —**inves′tiga′tor,** *n.*

investigation (ĭn vĕs′tĭ gā′shən), *n.* the act or process of investigating; a searching inquiry in order to ascertain facts; a detailed or careful examination.

—**Syn.** INVESTIGATION, EXAMINATION, INQUIRY, RESEARCH express the idea of an active effort to find out something. An INVESTIGATION is a systematic, minute, and thorough attempt to learn the facts about something complex or hidden; it is often formal and official: *an investigation of a bank robbery.* An EXAMINATION is an orderly attempt to obtain information about or to make a test of something, often something open to observation: *a physical examination.* An INQUIRY is an investigation made by asking questions rather than by inspection, or fig., by study of available evidence: *an inquiry into a proposed share issue.* RESEARCH is careful and sustained investigation usually into a subject covering a wide range, or into remote recesses of knowledge: *chemical research.*

investitive (ĭn vĕs′tĭ tĭv), *adj.* **1.** serving to invest: *an investitive act.* **2.** pertaining to investiture.

investiture (ĭn vĕs′tĭ chə), *n.* **1.** the act of investing. **2.** the formal bestowal or presentation of a possessory or prescriptive right, as to a fief, usually involving the giving of insignia. **3.** the state of being invested, as with a garment, quality, etc. **4.** *Archaic.* that which invests. [ME, t. ML: m. *investītūra*]

investment (ĭn vĕst′mənt), *n.* **1.** the investing of money or capital in order to secure profitable returns, esp. interest or income. **2.** a particular instance or mode of investing. **3.** a thing invested in. **4.** that which is invested. **5.** the act of investing or state of being invested, as with a garment. **6.** *Biol.* any covering, coating, outer layer, or integument, as of an animal or vegetable body. **7.** *Archaic.* a garment or vestment. **8.** an investing with a quality, attribute, etc. **9.** the investiture with an office, dignity, or right. **10.** the surrounding of a place with military forces or works, as in besieging.

investment trust, a trust whose function is the judicious buying and selling of shares of companies at the discretion of its board of management.

inveteracy (ĭn vĕt′ə rə sĭ), *n.* the state of being inveterate: *the inveteracy of people's prejudices.*

inveterate (ĭn vĕt′ə rĭt), *adj.* **1.** confirmed in a habit, practice, feeling, or the like: *an inveterate gambler.* **2.** firmly established by long continuance, as a disease or sore, a habit or practice (often bad), or a feeling (often hostile); chronic. [ME *inveterat,* t. L: s. *inveterātus,* pp., rendered old] —**invet′erately,** *adv.* —**invet′erateness,** *n.*

invidious (ĭn vĭd′ĭ əs), *adj.* **1.** such as to bring odium, unpopularity, or envious dislike: *an invidious honour.* **2.** calculated to excite ill will or resentment or give offence: *invidious remarks.* **3.** offensively or unfairly discriminating: *invidious comparisons.* **4.** *Obs.* envious. [t. L: m. s. *invidiōsus* envious] —**invid′iously,** *adv.* —**invid′iousness,** *n.*

invigilate (ĭn vĭj′ĭ lāt′), *v.i.,* **-lated, -lating. 1.** to keep watch over students at an examination. **2.** *Obs.* to keep watch. [t. L: m. s. *invigilātus,* pp., watched over] —**invig′ila′tion,** *n.* —**invig′ila′tor,** *n.*

invigorant (ĭn vĭg′ə rənt), *n.* a tonic.

invigorate (ĭn vĭg′ə rāt′), *v.t.,* **-rated, -rating.** to give vigour to; fill with life and energy: *to invigorate the body.* [f. IN-[2] + VIGO(U)R + -ATE[1]] —**invig′orat′ingly,** *adv.* —**invig′ora′tion,** *n.* —**invigorative** (ĭn vĭg′ə rə tĭv), *adj.* —**invig′oratively,** *adv.* —**invig′ora′tor,** *n.* —**Syn.** See **animate.**

invincible (ĭn vĭn′sə bl), *adj.* **1.** that cannot be conquered or vanquished: *an invincible force.* **2.** insuperable; insurmountable: *invincible difficulties.* [ME, t. L: m. s. *invincibilis.* See IN-[3], VINCIBLE] —**invin′cibil′ity, invin′cibleness,** *n.* —**invin′cibly,** *adv.*

—**Syn. 1.** INVINCIBLE, IMPREGNABLE, INDOMITABLE suggest that which cannot be overcome or mastered. INVINCIBLE is applied to that which cannot be conquered in combat or war, or overcome or subdued in any manner: ***an invincible army, invincible courage.*** IMPREGNABLE is applied to a place or position that cannot be taken by assault or siege, and hence to whatever is proof against attack: ***an impregnable fortress, impregnable virtue.*** INDOMITABLE implies having an unyielding spirit, or stubborn persistence in the face of opposition or difficulty: ***indomitable will.*** —**Ant. 1.** conquerable.

Invincible Armada, Armada (def. 1).

inviolable (ĭn vī′ə lə bl), *adj.* **1.** that must not be violated; that is to be kept free from violence or violation of any kind, or treated as if sacred: *an inviolable sanctuary.* **2.** that cannot be violated, subjected to violence, or injured. —**invi′olabil′ity, invi′olableness,** *n.* —**invi′olably,** *adv.*

inviolate (ĭn vī′ə lĭt, -lāt′), *adj.* **1.** free from violation, injury, desecration, or outrage. **2.** undisturbed. **3.** unbroken. **4.** not infringed. —**inviolacy** (ĭn vī′ə lə sĭ), **invi′olateness,** *n.* —**invi′olately,** *adv.*

invisible (ĭn vĭz′ə bl), *adj.* **1.** not visible; not perceptible by the eye: *invisible agents of the Devil.* **2.** withdrawn from or out of sight. **3.** not perceptible or discernible by the mind: *invisible differences.* **4.** (of colours) of a very deep shade, or a scarcely distinguishable hue: *invisible green.* **5.** not ordinarily found in financial statements: *goodwill is an invisible asset.* **6.** concealed from public knowledge. —*n.* **7.** an invisible thing or being. **8.** (prec. by *the*) **a.** the unseen or spiritual world. **b.** (*cap.*) God. —**invis′ibil′ity, invis′ibleness,** *n.* —**invis′ibly,** *adv.*

invisible exports, services, as banking commissions, insurance premiums, freight charges, etc., which earn foreign currency for the country providing them.

invisible imports, activities, services incurred, etc., as holidays abroad, which spend currency in foreign countries.

invisible ink, a fluid used for writing or drawing that is invisible until the surface is processed in some way, as by heating or chemical treatment.

invisible mending, a process of mending in which the torn threads are joined individually, so that the mend is almost invisible.

invitation (ĭn′vĭ tā′shən), *n.* **1.** the act of inviting. **2.** the written or spoken form with which a person is invited. **3.** attraction or allurement. —*adj.* **4.** restricted to invited individuals or teams: *an invitation golf match.* [t. L: s. *invitātio*]

invitatory (ĭn vī′tə tə rĭ, -trĭ), *adj.* serving to invite; conveying an invitation.

invite (*v.* ĭn vīt′; *n.* ĭn′vīt), *v.,* **-vited, -viting,** *n.* —*v.t.* **1.** to ask in a kindly, courteous, or complimentary way, to come or go to some place, gathering, entertainment, etc., or to do something: *to invite friends to dinner.* **2.** to request politely or formally: *to invite donations.* **3.** to act so as to bring on or render probable: *to invite danger.* **4.** to give occasion for. **5.** to attract, allure, or tempt. —*n.* **6.** *Slang.* an invitation. [t. L: m. s. *invītāre*] —**invit′er,** *n.* —**Syn. 1.** See **call.**

invitee (ĭn′vī tē′), *n.* a person entering another's premises by invitation.

inviting (ĭn vī′tĭng), *adj.* that invites; esp., attractive, alluring, or tempting: *an inviting offer.* —**invit′ingly,** *adv.* —**invit′ingness,** *n.*

in vitro (ĭn vē′trō), *Biol.* in an artificial environment, as a test tube. [t. L: lit., in a glass]

in vivo (ĭn vē′vō), *Biol.* within a living organism. [t. L: lit., within the living body]

invocate (ĭn′və kāt′), *v.t.,* **-cated, -cating.** *Now Rare.* invoke. [t. L: m. s. *invocātus,* pp.] —**invocative** (ĭn vŏk′ə tĭv), *adj.* —**in′voca′tor,** *n.*

invocation (ĭn′və kā′shən), *n.* **1.** the act of invoking; calling upon a deity, etc., for aid, protection, inspiration, etc. **2.** a form of words used in invoking, esp. as part of a public religious service. **3.** an entreaty for aid and guidance from a Muse, deity, etc., at the beginning of an epic or epic-like poem. **4.** a calling upon a spirit by incantation, or the incantation or magical formula used.

invocatory (ĭn vŏk′ə tə rĭ, -trĭ), *adj.* pertaining to or of the nature of invocation.

invoice (ĭn′vois), *n., v.,* **-voiced, -voicing.** —*n.* **1.** a written list of merchandise, with prices, delivered or sent to a buyer. **2.** an itemized bill containing the prices which comprise the total charge. **3.** *Rare.* the merchandise or shipment itself. —*v.t.* **4.** to present an invoice to (a customer, or the like). **5.** to make an invoice of. **6.** to enter in an invoice. [m. *invoyes,* pl. of (obs.) *invoy* invoice, t. F: m. *envoy* sending, thing sent. See ENVOY[1]]

invoke (ĭn vōk′), *v.t.,* **-voked, -voking. 1.** to call for with earnest desire; make supplication or prayer for: *to invoke God's mercy.* **2.** to call on (a divine being, etc.), as in prayer. **3.** to appeal to, as for confirmation. **4.** to call on to come or to do something. **5.** to call forth or upon (a spirit) by incantation; conjure. [late ME, t. L: m. *invocāre*] —**invok′er,** *n.*

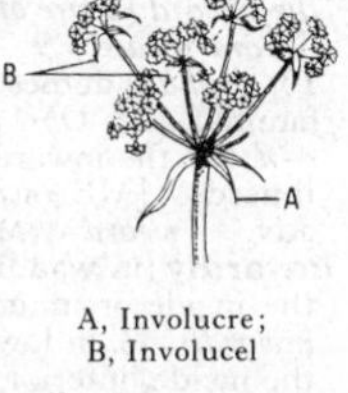

A, Involucre; B, Involucel

involucel (ĭn vŏl′yŏŏ sĕl′), *n. Bot.* a secondary involucre, as in a compound cluster of flowers. [t. NL: m. s. *involucellum,* dim. of L *involūcrum* cover] —**invol′ucel′late,** *adj.*

involucrate (ĭn′və lōō′krĭt, -krāt), *adj.* having an involucre.

involucre (ĭn′və lōō′kə), *n.* **1.** *Bot.* a collection or rosette of bracts subtending a flower cluster, umbel, or the like. **2.** a covering, esp. a membranous one. [t. F, t. L: m. *involūcrum* wrapper, covering] —**in′volu′cral,** *adj.*

involucrum (ĭn′və lōō′krəm), *n., pl.* **-cra** (-krə). involucre.

involuntary (ĭn vŏl′ən tə rĭ, -trĭ), *adj.* **1.** not voluntary; acting, or done or made without one's own volition, or otherwise than by one's own will or choice: *an involuntary listener.* **2.** unintentional. **3.** *Physiol.* acting independently of, or done or occurring without, conscious control: *involuntary muscles.* —**invol′untarily,** *adv.* —**invol′untariness,** *n.* —**Syn. 1, 3.** See **automatic.**

Involute leaves of poplar

involute (ĭn′və lōōt′), *adj.* **1.** involved or intricate. **2.** *Bot.* rolled inwards from the edge, as a leaf. **3.** *Zool.* (of shells) having the whorls closely wound. —*n.* **4.** *Geom.* any curve of which a given curve is the evolute. [t. L: m. s. *involutus,* pp., rolled up] —**in′volut′edly,** *adv.*

involute gear teeth, gear teeth in which the profile is the involute of a circle.

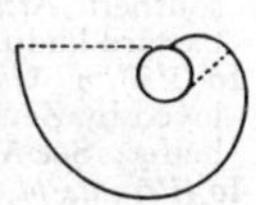
Involute of a circle

involution (ĭn′və lōō′shən), *n.* **1.** the act of involving. **2.** the state of being involved. **3.** something complicated. **4.** *Bot., etc.* **a.** a rolling up or folding in on itself. **b.** a part so formed. **5.** *Biol.* retrograde development; degeneration. **6.** *Physiol.* bodily changes involving a lessening of activity, esp. of the sex organs, occurring in late middle age. **7.** *Gram.* complicated construction; the separation of the subject from its predicate by the interjection of matter that should follow the verb or be placed in another sentence. **8.** *Maths.* **a.** the raising of a quantity or expression to any given power. **b.** a function that is its own inverse. [t. LL: s. *involūtio* a rolling up] —**in′volu′tional,** *adj.*

involve (ĭn vŏlv′), *v.t.,* **-volved, -volving. 1.** to include as a necessary circumstance, condition, or consequence; imply; entail. **2.** to affect, as something within the scope of operation. **3.** to include, contain, or comprehend within itself or its scope. **4.** to bring into an intricate or complicated form or condition. **5.** to bring into difficulties (fol. by *with*): *a plot to involve one government with another.* **6.** to cause to be inextricably associated or concerned, as in something embarrassing or unfavourable. **7.** to combine inextricably (fol. by *with*). **8.** to implicate, as in guilt or crime, or in any matter or affair. **9.** to be highly or excessively interested in. **10.** to roll, wrap, or shroud, as in something that surrounds. **11.** to envelop or enfold, as the surrounding thing does. **12.** to swallow up, engulf, or overwhelm. **13.** to roll up on itself; wind spirally, coil, or wreathe. **14.** *Maths. Obs.* to raise to a given power. [ME, t. L: m. s. *involvere* roll in or on, enwrap, involve] —**involve′ment,** *n.* —**involv′er,** *n.*

—**Syn. 6.** INVOLVE, ENTANGLE, IMPLICATE imply getting a person connected or bound up with something from which it is difficult for him to extricate himself. To INVOLVE is to bring more or less deeply into something, esp. of a complicated, embarrassing, or troublesome nature: *to involve someone in debt.* To ENTANGLE (usually pass. or reflex.) is to involve so deeply in a tangle as to confuse and make helpless: *to entangle oneself in a mass of contradictory statements.* To IMPLICATE is to connect a person with something discreditable or wrong: *implicated in a plot.* —**Ant. 6.** extricate.

invulnerable (ĭn vŭl′nə rə bl, -nrə bl), *adj.* **1.** incapable of being wounded, hurt, or damaged. **2.** proof against attack: *invulnerable arguments.* —**invul′nerabil′ity, invul′nerableness,** *n.* —**invul′nerably,** *adv.*

inwale (ĭn′wāl′), *n. Naut.* a wale in a boat running along the inside of the top of the upper fore and aft plating.

inwall (ĭn wôl′), *v.t.* to enwall.

inward (ĭn′wəd), *adj.* **1.** proceeding or directed towards the inside or interior. **2.** situated within; interior, internal: *an inward room.* **3.** pertaining to the inside or inner part. **4.** situated within the body: *the inward parts.* **5.** pertaining to the inside of the body: *inward convulsions.* **6.** inland: *inward passage.* **7.** intrinsic; inherent; essential: *the inward nature of a thing.* **8.** inner, mental, or spiritual: *inward peace.* **9.** muffled or indistinct, as the voice. **10.** *Archaic.* domestic. **11.** *Obs.* closely personal; intimate; familiar. **12.** *Obs.* private or secret. —*adv.* **13.** inwards. —*n.* **14.** the inward or internal part; the inside. **15.** (*pl.*) innards. [ME *in(ne)ward,* OE *in(ne)weard,* f. *in(ne)* IN, adv. + *-weard* -WARD]

inwardly (ĭn′wəd lĭ), *adv.* **1.** in or on, or with reference to, the inside or inner part. **2.** privately; secretly: *laughing inwardly.* **3.** in low tones; not aloud. **4.** *Archaic.* towards the inside, interior, or centre.

inwardness (ĭn′wəd nĭs), *n.* **1.** the state of being inward or internal. **2.** depth of thought or feeling; earnestness. **3.** occupation with what concerns man's inner nature; spirituality. **4.** the inward or intrinsic character of a thing. **5.** inward meaning. **6.** *Obs.* intimacy.

inwards[1] (ĭn′ədz), *n.pl.* innards.

inwards[2] (ĭn′wədz), *adv.* **1.** towards the inside or interior, as of a place, a space, or a body. **2.** into the mind or soul. **3.** in the mind or soul, or mentally or spiritually; inwardly. **4.** *Rare.* in the inside or interior. Also, **inward.** [f. INWARD + adv. genitive *-s*]

inweave (ĭn wēv′), *v.t.,* **-wove** or **-weaved; -woven** or **-weaved; -weaving.** enweave.

inwind (ĭn wīnd′), *v.t.,* **-wound, -winding.** enwind.

inwrap (ĭn răp′), *v.t.,* **-wrapped, -wrapping.** enwrap.

inwreathe (ĭn rēth′), *v.t.,* **-wreathed, -wreathing.** enwreathe.

inwrought (ĭn′rôt′), *adj.* **1.** wrought or worked with something by way of decoration. **2.** wrought or worked in, as a decorative pattern. **3.** worked in or closely combined with something.

inyala (ĭn yä′lə), *n.* a small antelope, *Tragelaphus angasi,* of southern Africa, having a white stripe down the back; bastard kudu. Also, **nyala.** [t. Zulu]

Io (ī′ō), *n. Gk Legend.* the daughter of Inachus of Argos, loved by Zeus and changed by jealous Hera into a white heifer. See **Argus** (def. 1).

Io (ī′ō), *n., pl.* **Ios.** Io moth.

Io, *Chem.* ionium.

Ioannina (*Gk* yô ä′nē nä), *n.* a town in NW Greece. 34,997 (1961). Serbo-Croat, **Janina** or **Yanina.**

iod-, var. of **iodo-,** usually before vowels, as in *iodic.*

iodate (ī′ə dāt′), *n., v.,* **-dated, -dating.** —*n.* **1.** *Chem.* a salt of iodic acid, as *sodium iodate,* $NaIO_3$. —*v.t.* **2.** to iodize. —**i′oda′tion,** *n.*

iodic (ī ŏd′ĭk), *adj. Chem.* containing iodine, esp. in the pentavalent state. [f. IOD- + -IC]

iodic acid, *Chem.* a white crystalline water-soluble solid, HIO_3, which forms iodates.

iodide (ī′ə dīd′), *n. Chem.* a compound, usually of two elements only, one of which is iodine; a salt of hydriodic acid. Also, **iodid** (ī′ə dĭd).

iodimetry (ī′ə dĭm′ĭ trĭ), *n. Chem.* iodometry.

iodine (ī′ə dēn′), *n. Chem.* a non-metallic element occurring, at ordinary temperatures, as a greyish black crystalline solid, which sublimes to a dense violet vapour when heated: used in medicine as an antiseptic; the radioactive isotope, iodine-131, is used in the diagnosis and treatment of disorders of the thyroid gland. *Symbol:* I; *at. wt:* 126·9044; *at. no.:* 53; *sp. gr.:* (solid) 4·93 at 20°C. Also, **iodin** (ī′ə dĭn). [f. F *iode* iodine (t. Gk: m. *iṓdēs,* prop., rust-coloured, but taken to mean violet-like) + -INE[2]]

iodine value, *Chem.* a measure of the amount of unsaturated fatty acid present in a fat, oil, resin or other natural product: the weight of iodine absorbed by 100 grams of the substance.

iodism (ī′ə dĭz′əm), *n. Pathol.* a morbid condition due to the use of iodine or its compounds.

iodize (ī′ə dīz′), *v.t.,* **-dized, -dizing.** to treat, impregnate, or affect with iodine. Also, **iodise.** —**i′odiz′er,** *n.*

iodo-, a word element meaning 'iodine', as in *iodometry.* Also, **iod-.** [comb. form repr. NL *iōdum*]

iodoform (ī ŏd′ə fôm′), *n. Chem.* a yellowish crystalline compound, CHI_3, analogous to chloroform: used as an antiseptic. [f. IODO- + FORM(YL)]

iodol (ī′ə dŏl′), *n. Chem.* a crystalline compound, C_4HI_4N: used as a substitute for iodoform.

iodometry (ī′ə dŏm′ĭ trĭ), *n. Chem.* a volumetric analytical procedure for determining iodine, or materials which will liberate iodine or react with iodine. Also, **iodimetry.** —**iodometric** (ī′ə dō mĕt′rĭk), *adj.*

iodous (ī ŏd′əs), *adj.* **1.** *Chem.* containing iodine, esp. in the divalent state. **2.** like iodine.

I.O.F., Independent Order of Foresters.

iolite (ī′ə līt′), *n.* cordierite. [f. Gk *ío(n)* violet + -LITE]

I.O.M., Isle of Man.

Io moth (ī′ō), a showy and beautiful moth of North America, *Automeris io,* of yellow coloration, with prominent pink and bluish eyespots on the hind wings.

ion (ī′ən), *n. Physics, Chem.* **1.** an electrically charged atom, radical, or molecule, formed by the loss or gain of one or more electrons. **Positive ions,** created by electron loss, are called *cations* and are attracted to the cathode in electrolysis. **Negative ions,** created by electron gain, are called *anions* and are attracted to the anode. The valency of an ion is equal to the number of electrons lost or gained and is indicated by a plus sign for cations and minus for anions, thus: Na^+, Cl^-, Ca^{++}, $S^=$. **2.** one of the electrically charged particles formed in a gas by the action of an electric discharge, etc. [t. Gk, ppr. neut. of *iénai* go] —**ionic** (ī ŏn′ĭk), *adj.*

-ion, a suffix of nouns denoting action or process, state or condition, or sometimes things or persons, as in *allusion, communion, flexion, fusion, legion, opinion, suspicion, union.* Also, **-tion** and **-ation.** Cf. **-cion, -xion.** [t. L: s. *-io,* suffix forming nouns, esp. from verbs]

Iona (ī ō′nə), *n.* a small island in the Hebrides, off the W coast of Scotland: centre of early Celtic Christianity.

ion engine, a rocket engine, the thrust of which is obtained by the electrostatic acceleration of ionized particles. Also, *Chiefly U.S.,* **ion jet.**

Ionesco (*Fr.* yŏ nĕs kō′), *n.* **Eugène** (*Fr.* œ zhĕn′), born 1912, French dramatist, born in Rumania.

ion exchange, the process of reciprocal transfer of ions between a solution and a resin.

Ionia (ī ō′nyə), *n.* an ancient region on the W coast of Asia Minor and adjacent islands: colonized by the ancient Greeks.

Ionian (ī ō′nyən), *adj.* **1.** pertaining to Ionia. **2.** pertaining to a branch of the Greek race named after Ion, the legendary founder. —*n.* **3.** an Ionian Greek.

Ionian Islands, the islands along the W coast of Greece, including Corfu, Levkas, Ithaca, Cephalonia, and Zante, and Cerigo off the S coast.

Ionian mode, *Music.* a scale, represented by the white keys of a keyboard instrument, beginning on C.

Ionian Sea, an arm of the Mediterranean between S Italy, E Sicily, and Greece.

Ionic (ī ŏn′ĭk), *adj.* **1.** *Archit.* denoting or pertaining to one of the three Greek orders, distinguished by its slender proportions, the volutes on the capitals, and the continuous (often figured) frieze. See illus. under **order.** **2.** *Pros.* denoting or employing one of two feet consisting of two long and two short syllables: **the greater Ionic,** two long and two short syllables, ¯ ¯ ˘ ˘; **the lesser Ionic,** two short and two long syllables, ˘ ˘ ¯ ¯. **3.** pertaining to the Ionians. **4.** (*l.c.*) *Chem.* of, or pertaining to, ions. —*n.* **5.** *Pros.* an Ionic foot, verse, or metre. **6.** (*also l.c.*) *Print.* a style of typeface without strong distinction between thick and thin strokes, often used as a newspaper typeface. **7.** a dialect of ancient Greek, including Attic and the language of Homer. [t. L: s. *Iōnicus*, t. Gk: m. *Iōnikós*]

ionic bond, *Chem.* an electrovalency (def. 2).

ionic hypothesis, *Chem.* the hypothesis that those compounds which, when dissolved in water, render it conductive do so by splitting up into charged atoms, or groups of atoms, called ions; the passage of these ions through the solution constitutes an electric current.

ionic mobility, *Chem.* the velocity of an ion in an electric field of one volt per centimetre.

ionium (ī ōʹnĭ əm), *n.* *Chem.* a naturally occurring radioactive isotope of thorium. *Symbol:* Io; *at. wt:* 230; *at. no.:* 90.

ionization chamber, *Physics.* a device for measuring the strength of ionizing radiation; consisting of a gas-filled chamber containing two electrodes between which a potential difference is maintained. The radiation ionizes the gas and the current flowing between the electrodes is a measure of its strength.

ionization potential, *Physics.* the energy in electron-volts required to remove an electron from an atom.

ionize (īʹə nīzʹ), *v.*, **-nized, -nizing.** —*v.t.* **1.** to separate or change into ions. **2.** to produce ions in. —*v.i.* **3.** to become changed into ions, as by dissolving. Also, **ionise.** —**ionization** (īʹə nī zāʹshən), *n.* —**iʹonizʹer,** *n.*

ionizing radiation, *Physics.* any radiation (either electromagnetic or corpuscular) which causes ionization in the matter through which it passes.

ionone (īʹə nōnʹ), *n.* either one or a mixture of two unsaturated ketones, $C_{13}H_{20}O$, used in perfumery.

ionosphere (ī ŏnʹə sfĭəʹ), *n.* **1.** the succession of ionized layers that constitute the outer regions of the earth's atmosphere beyond the stratosphere, considered as beginning with the Heaviside layer at about 60 miles, and extending several hundred miles up. **2.** *Obsolesc.* the Heaviside layer.

I.O.O.F., Independent Order of Odd Fellows.

iota (ī ōʹtə), *n.* **1.** the ninth letter (Ι, ι, = English I, i) of the Greek alphabet (the smallest letter). **2.** a very small quantity; a tittle; a jot.

iotacism (ī ōʹtə sĭzʹəm), *n.* conversion of other vowel sounds into that of iota (English ē). [t. L: s. *iōtacismus*, t. Gk: m. *iōtakismós*]

IOU (īʹōʹyōōʹ), a written acknowledgement of a debt, containing the expression *I O U* (I owe you). Also, **I.O.U.**

-ious, a termination consisting of the suffix **-ous** with a preceding original or euphonic vowel **i.** Cf. **-eous.**

I.O.W., Isle of Wight.

Iowa (īʹō ə; *locally* īʹə wāʹ), *n.* **1.** a state in the central United States: a part of the Midwest. 2,757,537 pop. (1960); 56,280 sq. mi. *Cap.:* Des Moines. *Abbrev.:* Ia. **2.** a river flowing from N Iowa SE to the Mississippi. 291 mi. **3.** a Siouan language. —**Iowan** (īʹō ən), *adj., n.*

IPA, International Phonetic Alphabet.

ipecacuanha (ĭpʹĭ kăkʹyōō ănʹə), *n.* **1.** the dried root of two small shrubby South American rubiaceous plants, *Cephaelis ipecacuanha*, and *C. acuminata*, used as an emetic, purgative, etc. **2.** a drug consisting of the roots of these plants. **3.** the plants themselves. Also, *Chiefly U.S.*, **ipecac** (ĭpʹĭ kăkʹ). [t. Pg., t. Tupi: m. *ipe-kaa-guéne*, f. *ipeh* low + *kaâ* leaves + *guéne* vomit]

Iphigenia (ĭfʹĭ jĭ nīʹə), *n.* *Gk Legend.* the daughter of Agamemnon and Clytemnestra. She became a priestess of Artemis after the goddess saved her from sacrifice by Agamemnon. She saved her brother Orestes' life. According to one version she was sacrificed by her father.

Ipoh (ēʹpō), *n.* a town in Malaysia, in central Perak. 125,770 (1957).

ipomoea (ĭpʹə mēʹə, īʹpə-), *n.* **1.** any plant of the genus *Ipomoea*, of the morning-glory family, containing many species with ornamental flowers. **2.** the dried root of the convolvulaceous plant, *Ipomoea orizabensis*, yielding a resin which is a cathartic. [t. NL, f. Gk: s. *ips* kind of worm + m. *hómoios* like]

ipse dixit (ĭpʹsā dĭkʹsĭt), *Latin.* **1.** he himself said it. **2.** an assertion without proof.

ipso facto (ĭpʹsō făkʹtō), *Latin.* by the fact itself; by that very fact: *it is condemned ipso facto.*

Ipsus (ĭpʹsəs), *n.* an ancient village in central Asia Minor, in Phrygia: the scene of a battle between the successors of Alexander the Great, 301 B.C.

Ipswich (ĭpsʹwĭch), *n.* **1.** a town in England, the county town of Suffolk. 117,395 (1961). **2.** a town in Australia, in SE Queensland. 52,000 (est. 1964).

IQ, intelligence quotient. Also, **I.Q.**

i.q., (L *idem quod*) the same as.

I.Q.S.Y., International Year of the Quiet Sun.

Iquique (*Sp.* ē kēʹkē), *n.* a seaport in N Chile. 51,468 (1960).

Iquitos (*Sp.* ē kēʹtôs), *n.* a river port in NE Peru, on the upper Amazon. 55,695 (1961).

Ir, *Chem.* iridium.

ir-[1], var. of **in-**[2], before *r*, as in *irradiate.*

ir-[2], var. of **in-**[3], before *r*, as in *irreducible.*

Ir., **1.** Ireland. **2.** Irish.

I.R., Inland Revenue.

I.R.A., Irish Republican Army.

iracund (īʹə rə kŭndʹ), *adj.* prone to anger; irascible. [t. L: s. *īrācundus* angry] —**iʹracunʹdity,** *n.*

irade (ĭ räʹdĭ), *n.* a decree of a Muslim ruler, as (formerly) the Sultan of Turkey. [Turk., t. Ar.: m. *irāda* will, desire]

Irak (ĭ räkʹ; *Ar.* ē räkʹ), *n.* Iraq.

Iran (ĭ ränʹ; *Pers.* ē ränʹ), *n.* a kingdom in SW Asia; former official name (until 1935), **Persia.** 20,849,000 pop. (est. 1960); ab. 635,000 sq. mi. *Cap.:* Teheran.

Iranian (ĭ rāʹnyən), *adj.* **1.** pertaining to Iran (or Persia). **2.** pertaining to Iranian (def. 3). —*n.* **3.** a subgroup of Indo-European languages including Persian and Pushtu. **4.** Persian (the language). **5.** an inhabitant of Iran; a Persian.

Iraq (ĭ räkʹ; *Ar.* ē räkʹ), *n.* a republic in SW Asia, N of Saudi Arabia and W of Iran, centring in the Tigris-Euphrates basin of Mesopotamia. 6,803,153 pop. (1962); 172,000 sq. mi. *Cap.:* Baghdad. Also, **Irak.**

Iraq

Iraqi (ĭ räʹkĭ; *Ar.* ē räʹkē), *n., pl.* **-qis,** *adj.* —*n.* **1.** a native of Iraq. **2.** Also, **Iraqi Arabic.** the dialect of Arabic spoken in Iraq. —*adj.* **3.** of or pertaining to Iraq or its inhabitants.

irascible (ĭ răsʹĭ bl), *adj.* **1.** easily provoked to anger: *an irascible old man.* **2.** characterized by, excited by, or arising from anger: *an irascible nature.* [ME, t. LL: m. s. *irascibilis*] —**irasʹcibilʹity, irasʹcibleness,** *n.* —**irasʹcibly,** *adv.*

irate (ī rātʹ), *adj.* angry; enraged: *the irate colonel.* [t. L: m. s. *īrātus*, pp.] —**irateʹly,** *adv.*

Irbid (ĭəʹbĭd), *n.* a town in N Jordan. 60,000 (est. 1965).

IRBM, intermediate range ballistic missile.

ire (īʹə), *n.* anger; wrath. [ME, t. OF, t. L: m. *ira*] —**ireʹless,** *adj.*

Ire., Ireland.

ireful (īʹə fəl), *adj.* **1.** full of ire; wrathful: *an ireful look.* **2.** irascible. —**ireʹfully,** *adv.* —**ireʹfulness,** *n.*

Ireland (ī ʹə lənd), *n.* **1.** a large western island of the British Isles, comprising Northern Ireland and the Republic of Ireland. 32,375 sq. mi. Latin, **Hibernia.** **2.** See **Northern Ireland.** **3.** **Republic of,** a republic occupying most of the S part of the island of Ireland. 2,818,341 pop. (1961); 27,137 sq. mi. *Cap.:* Dublin. Formerly, (1922–37) **Irish Free State;** (1937–49) **Eire.** Gaelic, **Eire.**

Ireland (īʹə lənd), *n.* **John,** 1879–1962, English composer.

Irene (ī rēʹnĭ), *n.* *Gk Myth.* the daughter of Themis by Zeus. She became the goddess of peace.

irenic (ī rēʹnĭk), *adj.* peaceful; tending to promote or encourage peace or peaceful arts. Also, **ireʹnical.** [t. Gk: m. s. *eirēnikós*]

irenics (ī rēʹnĭks), *n.* irenic theology.

iridaceous (ĭʹrĭ dāʹshəs), *adj.* **1.** belonging to the *Iridaceae*, or iris family of plants, which includes, besides various flags, the crocus, gladiolus, and freesia. **2.** resembling or pertaining to plants of the genus *Iris.* [f. s. NL *Iris* the iris genus (see IRIS) + -ACEOUS]

iridescence (ĭʹrĭ dĕsʹəns), *n.* iridescent quality; a play of lustrous, changing colours.

iridescent (ĭʹrĭ dĕsʹənt), *adj.* displaying colours like those of the rainbow. [f. s. L *īris* rainbow + -ESCENT] —**irʹidesʹcently,** *adv.*

iridic (ī rĭdʹĭk, ĭ rĭdʹ-), *adj.* *Chem.* of or containing iridium, esp. in the tetravalent state.

iridium (ī rĭdʹĭ əm, ĭ rĭdʹ-), *n.* *Chem.* a precious metallic element resembling platinum: used in platinum alloys and for the points of gold pens. *Symbol:* Ir; *at. wt:* 192·2; *at. no.:* 77; *sp. gr.:* 22·4 at 20°C. [t. NL, der. L *iris* rainbow; named from its iridescence in solution]

iridize (ĭʹrĭ dīzʹ, īʹrĭ-), *v.t.*, **-dized, -dizing.** to cover with iridium. Also, **iridise.** —**irʹidizaʹtion,** *n.*

iridosmine (ĭʹrĭ dŏsʹmĭn, īʹrĭ-), *n.* a native alloy of iridium and osmium, usually containing some rhodium, ruthenium, platinum, etc., used esp. for the points of gold pens. Also, **iridosmium** (ĭʹrĭ dŏsʹmĭ əm, īʹrĭ-), **osmiridium.** [f. IRID(IUM) + OSM(IUM) + -INE[3]]

iridous (ĭʹrĭ dəs, īʹrĭ-), *adj.* *Chem.* containing trivalent iridium.

iris (ī′ə rĭs), *n., pl.* **irises, irides** (ī′ə rĭ dēz′). **1.** *Anat.* the contractile circular diaphragm forming the coloured portion of the eye and containing a circular opening (the pupil) in its centre. See diag. under **eye. 2.** *Bot.* **a.** a family of plants, *Iridaceae.* **b.** any plant of the genus *Iris,* including various perennial herbs with handsome flowers and sword-shaped leaves; the fleur-de-lis or flag. **c.** the flower of any such plant. **d.** orrisroot. **3.** (*cap.*) *Gk Myth.* a messenger of the gods, regarded as the goddess of the rainbow. **4.** a rainbow. **5.** any appearance like a rainbow. **6.** an iris diaphragm. [ME, t. L, t. Gk]

iris diaphragm, *Optics, Photog.* a composite diaphragm with a central aperture readily adjustable for size, used to regulate the amount of light admitted to a lens or optical system.

Irish (ī′ə rĭsh), *adj., n., pl.* **Irish.** —*adj.* **1.** of or characteristic of Ireland or its people. —*n.* **2.** the inhabitants of Ireland and their descendants elsewhere. **3.** the aboriginal Celtic-speaking people of Ireland. **4.** the Celtic language of Ireland in its historical (Old Irish, Middle Irish) or modern form. **5.** Irish English. [ME *Irisc, Iris(c)h,* der. OE *Iras,* pl., people of Ireland (c. Icel. *Irar*)]

Irish bull, bull².

Irish coffee, a mixture of hot coffee and whisky served with a whipped cream topping.

Irish English, 1. the English dialects spoken in Ireland. **2.** the standard English of Ireland.

Irish Free State, former name of the **Republic of Ireland** (1922–37).

Irishism (ī′ə rĭ shĭz′əm), *n.* an Irish idiom, custom, etc.

Irishman (ī′ə rĭsh mən), *n., pl.* **-men.** a man born in Ireland or of Irish ancestry. —**I′rishwom′an,** *n. fem.*

Irish moss, 1. a purplish brown, cartilaginous seaweed, *Chondrus crispus,* of the Atlantic coasts of Europe and North America; carrageen. **2.** this seaweed, dried and bleached, used as a substitute for gelatine, and commercially as a thickening agent.

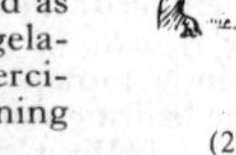

Irish setter
(27 in. high at shoulder)

Irish Pale. See **pale²** (def. 6).

Irish Republican Army, a secret Irish nationalist organization, formed to promote guerrilla activities against the British and later against Northern Ireland; voluntarily disbanded in 1962. *Abbrev.:* I.R.A.

Irish Sea, a part of the Atlantic between Ireland and England. See map under **Hadrian's Wall.**

Irish setter, a rich chestnut-coloured variety of setter.

Irish stew, a stew usually made of mutton, lamb, or beef, with potatoes, onions, etc.

Irish terrier
(18 in. high at shoulder)

Irish terrier, one of a breed of small, active, intelligent dogs with wiry hair, usually of a reddish tinge.

Irish water-spaniel, one of an ancient breed of spaniels, notable for its coat of dense crisp ringlets, usually liver-coloured.

Irish wolfhound, a shaggy-coated breed of wolfhound, the tallest known dog, developed in Ireland as early as the 3rd century A.D.

Irish yew, a widely cultivated columnar form of the common yew, *Taxus baccata* var. *fastigiata.*

Irish wolfhound
(31 in. high at shoulder)

iritis (ī rī′tĭs), *n. Pathol.* inflammation of the iris of the eye. [t. NL; f. IR(IS) + -ITIS] —**iritic** (ī rĭt′ĭk), *adj.*

irk (ûk), *v.t.* to weary, annoy, or trouble: *it irked him to wait.* [ME *irke, yrk(e)* tire, t. Scand.; cf. Icel. *yrkja* work, c. OE *wyrcan;* see WORK]

irksome (ûk′səm), *adj.* **1.** causing weariness, disgust, or annoyance: *irksome restrictions.* **2.** *Obs.* distressing. —**irk′somely,** *adv.* —**irk′someness,** *n.* —**Syn. 1.** See **tedious.**

Irkutsk (û ko͝otsk′; *Russ.* ĭr ko͝otsk′), *n.* a city in the S Soviet Union in Asia, W of Lake Baikal. 401,000 (est. 1965).

I.R.O., Inland Revenue Office.

iron (ī′ən), *n.* **1.** *Chem.* a ductile, malleable, silver-white metallic element, scarcely known in a pure condition, but abundantly used in its crude or impure forms containing carbon (**pig-iron, cast iron, steel,** and **wrought iron**: see these entries) for making tools, implements, machinery, etc. *Symbol:* Fe (L *ferrum*); *at. wt:* 55·847; *at. no.:* 26; *sp. gr.:* 7·86 at 20°C. **2.** something hard, strong, rigid, unyielding, or the like: *hearts of iron.* **3.** an instrument, utensil, weapon, etc., made of iron. **4.** an iron or steel implement used heated for smoothing or pressing cloth, etc. **5.** an iron-headed golf club intermediate between a cleek and a mashie: *a driving iron.* **6.** a branding iron. **7.** *Slang.* a pistol. **8.** *Archaic.* a sword. **9.** a harpoon. **10.** *Med.* a preparation of iron, or containing iron, used as a tonic, etc. **11.** (*pl.*) an iron shackle or fetter. **12. in irons,** *Naut.* lying head to the wind and having no headway, unable to fall off on either tack. **13. strike while the iron is hot,** to take immediate action, while the opportunity is still available. **14. too many irons in the fire,** too many undertakings. —*adj.* **15.** made of iron. **16.** resembling iron in colour, firmness, etc.: *an iron will.* **17.** stern, harsh, or cruel. **18.** not to be broken. **19.** degenerate, debased, or wicked. **20.** pertaining to the Iron Age. —*adj.* **21.** capable of great endurance; extremely robust or hardy. **22.** firmly binding or clasping. —*v.t.* **23.** to smooth or press with a heated iron, as clothes, etc. **24.** to furnish, mount, or arm with iron. **25.** to shackle or fetter with irons. **26. iron out, a.** to press (a garment, etc.). **b.** to smooth and remove (problems and difficulties, etc.). —*v.i.* **27.** to press clothes, etc., with a heated iron. [ME *iren, ysen,* OE *iren, īsen, īsern,* c. G *Eisen*] —**i′ronless,** *adj.* —**i′ron-like′,** *adj.*

Iron Age, 1. *Archaeol.* the time during which early man lived and made implements of iron, and which followed the Stone and Bronze Ages. **2.** (*l.c.*) *Class. Myth.* the last and worst age of the world. **3.** (*l.c.*) any age or period of degeneracy or wickedness.

ironbark (ī′ən bäk′), *n.* any of the various Australian eucalyptuses with a hard, solid bark, as *Eucalyptus resinifera,* a tall tree yielding a valuable timber, and a gum.

ironbound (ī′ən bound′), *adj.* **1.** bound with iron. **2.** rock-bound; rugged. **3.** hard, rigid, or unyielding.

ironclad (ī′ən klăd′ *for 1 and 2*; ī′ən klăd′ *for 3*), *adj.* **1.** covered or cased with iron plates, as a vessel for naval warfare; armour-plated. **2.** very rigid or strict: *an ironclad agreement.* —*n.* **3.** a warship of the middle and late 19th century fitted with armour plating.

Iron Cross, a German Order founded in 1813, medals of which are awarded for outstanding bravery.

Iron Curtain, 1. a rigid division of Europe, formed by ideological differences between those European countries partly or wholly within the Soviet sphere of influence and those partly or wholly within the American sphere of influence; physically formed by the frontiers between West Germany, Austria, and Italy on the one side, and East Germany, Czechoslovakia, Hungary, and Yugoslavia on the other. **2.** the state of censorship, control of movement, etc., pertaining in the countries of Eastern Europe.

Iron Duke, The, nickname of the first Duke of Wellington.

irone (ī rōn′, ī′ə rōn), *n. Chem.* a colourless liquid, $C_{13}H_{20}O$, obtained from the orrisroot, and used in perfumery.

ironer (ī′ə nə), *n.* one who or that which irons.

iron-fisted (ī′ən fĭs′tĭd), *adj.* **1.** ruthless. **2.** close-fisted; niggardly.

Iron Gate, a gorge cut by the Danube through the Carpathian Mountains, between Yugoslavia and SW Rumania. 2 mi. long. Also, **Iron Gates.**

The Iron Gate

iron glance, haematite.

iron-grey (ī′ən grā′), *adj.* of a grey like that of freshly broken iron.

Iron Guard, a Rumanian anti-Semitic fascist party, eliminated after World War II.

iron hand, severe control; strictness.

iron-handed (ī′ən hăn′dĭd), *adj.* controlling with severity or strictness; iron-fisted.

iron horse, *Archaic.* **1.** a locomotive. **2.** a bicycle or tricycle.

ironic (ī rŏn′ĭk), *adj.* **1.** pertaining to, of the nature of, or characterized by irony: *an ironic compliment.* **2.** using, or addicted to irony: *an ironic speaker.* **3.** of the nature of or containing irony. Also, **ironical** (ī rŏn′ĭ kl). [t. L: s. *īrōnicus,* t. Gk: m. *eirōnikós* dissembling, feigning ignorance] —**iron′ically,** *adv.* —**iron′icalness,** *n.*

ironing (ī′ə nĭng), *n.* **1.** the act or process of pressing clothes, sheets, etc., with a heated iron. **2.** clothes, linen, etc., that have been ironed, or are to be ironed.

ironing-board (ī′ə nĭng bôd′), *n.* a flat narrow board, usually cloth-covered, often mounted on legs which can be folded to lie flat, and used for pressing clothes, linen, etc.

iron lung, a chamber in which alternate pulsations of high and low pressure can be used to force normal lung movements, used esp. in some cases of poliomyelitis.

ironmaster (ī′ən mäs′tə), *n.* a manufacturer of iron; the master of ironworks.

ironmonger (ī′ən mŭng′gə), *n.* metal ware, tools, cutlery, locks, etc.

ironmongery (ī′ən mŭng′gə rĭ), *n., pl.* **-ries.** the goods, shop, or business of an ironmonger.

iron mould, **1.** a stain on cloth, etc., made by rusty iron or ink. **2.** damp mould developing in clothing waiting to be ironed.

iron olivine, fayalite.

iron pyrites, **1.** pyrite, or ordinary pyrites; fool's gold. **2.** marcasite. **3.** pyrrhotite.

iron rations, emergency reserve rations, esp. those of troops in wartime.

ironroot (ī′ən ro͞ot′), *n.* a variable chenopodiaceous annual, *Atriplex patula*, with a long tough root, widespread as a weed of cultivated land in Europe and W Asia.

ironside (ī′ən sīd′), *n.* **1.** a person with great power of endurance or resistance. **2.** (*cap., usually pl.*) **a.** Edmund II of England. **b.** Oliver Cromwell. **c.** one of Cromwell's troopers. **3.** (*pl.*) an ironclad.

ironsmith (ī′ən smĭth′), *n.* a worker in iron; a blacksmith.

ironstone (ī′ən stōn′), *n.* any ore of iron (commonly a carbonate of iron) with clayey or siliceous impurities.

iron sulphate, ferrous sulphate.

ironware (ī′ən wĕə′), *n.* articles of iron, as pots, kettles, tools, etc.; hardware.

ironwood (ī′ən wo͝od′), *n.* **1.** any of various trees with hard, heavy wood, as *Carpinus caroliniana*, an American species of hornbeam, or *Lyonothamnus floribundus*, found on the islands off the coast of southern California. **2.** the wood.

ironwork (ī′ən wûk′), *n.* **1.** work in iron. **2.** parts or articles made of iron: *ornamental ironwork.*

ironworker (ī′ən wû′kə), *n.* a worker in iron.

ironworks (ī′ən wûks′), *n. pl. or sing.* an establishment where iron is smelted or where it is cast or wrought.

irony[1] (ī′ə rə nĭ), *n., pl.* **-nies.** **1.** a figure of speech or literary device in which the literal meaning is the opposite of that intended, esp., as in the Greek sense, when the locution understates the effect intended: employed in ridicule or merely playfully. **2.** an ironical utterance or expression. **3.** simulated ignorance in discussion (**Socratic irony**). **4.** the quality or effect, or implication of a speech or situation in a play or the like understood by the audience but not grasped by the characters of the piece (**dramatic irony**). **5.** an outcome of events contrary to what was, or might have been, expected. **6.** an ironical quality. [t. L: m. s. *irōnia*, t. Gk: m. *eirōneía* dissimulation, understatement]

—**Syn.** **1.** IRONY, SARCASM, SATIRE agree in indicating derision of something or someone. In IRONY the essential feature is the contradiction between the literal and the intended meaning, since one thing is said and another is implied; it attacks or derides, or, often, is merely playful: '*Beautiful weather, isn't it?*' (the weather is perfectly detestable). '*If you try hard, you may be able to do worse*' (what you have done is quite bad enough). In SARCASM the characteristic feature is the harsh or cutting quality; it may be ironical or may state directly what is meant: '*A fine musician you've turned out to be! You couldn't play one piece correctly if you had two assistants.*' SATIRE, originally applied to a literary composition which attacks by means of irony or sarcasm, denotes also the use of such means formally in writing or speaking, for some serious purpose (as the exposing or denouncing of abuses) or in a malicious or merely playful spirit: *Swift's satires*; *a speech of satire against the wasteful government administration.*

irony[2] (ī′ə nĭ), *adj.* consisting of, containing, or resembling iron. [ME *yrony*; f. IRON + -Y[1]]

Iroquoian (ĭ′rə kwoi′ən), *adj.* belonging to or constituting a linguistic family of the Iroquoian-Caddoan stock of North American Indians, of Canada and the eastern U.S., including the Iroquois confederacy, the Cherokees, Wyandots or Hurons, Erie, and others.

Iroquoian-Caddoan (ĭ′rə kwoi′ən kăd′ō ən), *n.* an American Indian linguistic stock combining the Iroquoian and Caddoan families and perhaps related to the Siouan-Muskogean stock.

Iroquois (ĭ′rə kwoi′, -kwoiz′), *n. sing. and pl.* **1.** a member of the Indian confederacy, the Five Nations, comprising the Mohawks, Oneidas, Onondagas, Cayugas, and Senecas, with, later, the Tuscaroras. —*adj.* **2.** belonging or relating to the Iroquois or their tribes. [t. F, f. m. Algonquian *irinakhoiw* real adders + F suffix *-ois*]

irradiant (ĭ rā′dyənt), *adj.* irradiating; radiant; shining. —**irra′diance, irra′diancy,** *n.*

irradiate (*v.* ĭ rā′dĭ āt′; *adj.* ĭ rā′dĭ ĭt, -āt′), *v.,* **-ated, -ating,** *adj.* —*v.t.* **1.** to shed rays of light upon; illuminate. **2.** to illumine intellectually or spiritually. **3.** to brighten as if with light. **4.** to radiate (light, etc.). **5.** to heat with radiant energy. **6.** to cure or treat by exposure to radiation, as of ultraviolet light. **7.** to expose to radiation. —*v.i.* **8.** to emit rays; shine. **9.** to become radiant. —*adj.* **10.** irradiated; bright. [t. L: m. s. *irradiātus*, pp., illumined] —**irradiative** (ĭ rā′dĭ ə tĭv), *adj.* —**irra′dia′tor,** *n.*

irradiation (ĭ rā′dĭ ā′shən), *n.* **1.** the act of irradiating. **2.** the state of being irradiated. **3.** intellectual or spiritual enlightenment. **4.** a ray of light; a beam. **5.** *Optics.* the apparent enlargement of a bright object when seen against a dark ground. **6.** the use of X-rays or other radiations for the treatment of disease, etc. **7.** the process of exposure to radiation. **8.** the intensity of radiation falling on a given point; radiant energy received per unit of time per unit area of irradiated surface.

irrational (ĭ răsh′ə nəl), *adj.* **1.** without the faculty of, or not endowed with, reason: *irrational animals.* **2.** without, or deprived of, sound judgement. **3.** not in accordance with reason; utterly illogical: *irrational fear.* **4.** *Arith.* not capable of being exactly expressed by a ratio of two integers. **5.** *Maths.* (of functions) not expressible as the ratio of two polynomials. **6.** *Gk and Lat. Pros.* **a.** of or pertaining to a substitution in the normal metrical pattern, esp. a long syllable for a short syllable. **b.** denoting a foot containing such a substitution. —*n.* **7.** an irrational number or quantity. [late ME, t. L: s. *irratiōnālis*] —**irra′tionally,** *adv.* —**irra′tionalness,** *n.*

irrationalism (ĭ răsh′ə nə lĭz′əm), *n.* irrationality.

irrationality (ĭ răsh′ə năl′ĭ tĭ), *n., pl.* **-ties.** **1.** the quality of being irrational. **2.** an irrational, illogical, or absurd action, thought, etc.

irrationalize (ĭ răsh′ə nə līz′, -răsh′nə-), *v.t.,* **-lized, -lizing.** to render irrational. Also, **irrationalise.**

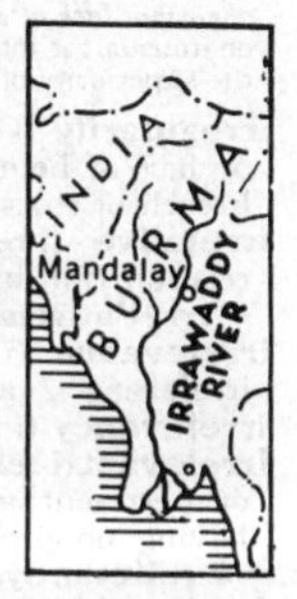

Irrawaddy

Irrawaddy (ĭ′rə wŏd′ĭ), *n.* a river flowing S through Burma to the Bay of Bengal. ab. 1250 mi.

irreclaimable (ĭ′rĭ klā′mə bl), *adj.* not reclaimable; incapable of being reclaimed. —**ir′reclaim′abil′ity, ir′reclaim′ableness,** *n.* —**ir′reclaim′ably,** *adv.*

irreconcilable (ĭ rĕk′ən sī′lə bl, *for emphasis often* ĭ rĕk′ən sī′-), *adj.* **1.** that cannot be harmonized or adjusted; incompatible: *two irreconcilable statements.* **2.** that cannot be brought to acquiescence or content; implacably opposed: *irreconcilable enemies.* —*n.* **3.** one who or that which is irreconcilable. **4.** one who remains opposed to agreement or compromise. —**irrec′oncil′abil′ity, irrec′oncil′ableness,** *n.* —**irrec′oncil′ably,** *adv.*

irrecoverable (ĭ′rĭ kŭv′ə rə bl, -kŭv′rə-), *adj.* **1.** that cannot be regained: *an irrecoverable debt.* **2.** that cannot be remedied or rectified: *irrecoverable sorrow.* —**ir′recov′erableness,** *n.* —**ir′recov′erably,** *adv.*

irrecusable (ĭ′rĭ kyo͞o′zə bl), *adj.* not to be objected to or rejected. [t. LL: m. s. *irrecūsābilis* not to be refused] —**ir′recu′sably,** *adv.*

irredeemable (ĭ′rĭ dē′mə bl), *adj.* **1.** not redeemable; incapable of being bought back or paid off. **2.** not convertible into specie, as paper money. **3.** beyond redemption; irreclaimable. **4.** irremediable, irreparable, or hopeless. —**ir′redeem′ableness,** *n.* —**ir′redeem′ably,** *adv.*

irredentist (ĭ′rĭ dĕn′tĭst), *n.* **1.** (*usually cap.*) a member of an Italian association which became prominent in 1878, advocating the redemption, or the incorporation into Italy, of certain neighbouring regions (**Italia irredenta**) having a primarily Italian population. **2.** a member of a party in any country advocating the acquiring of some region, actually included in another country, but claimed as properly belonging to the former country by reason of racial, cultural, ethnic, historical or other ties. —*adj.* **3.** pertaining to or advocating irredentism. [t. It.: s. *irredentista*, der. (*Italia*) *irredenta* (Italy) unredeemed, fem. of *irredento*, f. L: *in-* IN-[3] + m. *redemptus*, pp., redeemed] —**ir′reden′tism,** *n.*

irreducible (ĭ′rĭ dyo͞o′sə bl), *adj.* **1.** not reducible; incapable of being reduced or diminished: *the irreducible minimum.* **2.** incapable of being brought into a different condition or form. —**ir′reduc′ibil′ity, ir′reduc′ibleness,** *n.* —**ir′reduc′ibly,** *adv.*

irrefragable (ĭ rĕf′rə gə bl), *adj.* not to be refuted; undeniable. [t. LL: m. s. *irrefragābilis*] —**irref′ragabil′ity, irref′ragableness,** *n.* —**irref′ragably,** *adv.*

irrefrangible (ĭ′rĭ frăn′jə bl), *adj.* **1.** not to be broken or violated; inviolable: *an irrefrangible rule of etiquette.* **2.** incapable of being refracted: *X-rays are irrefrangible.* —**ir′refran′gibly,** *adv.*

irrefutable (ĭ rĕf′yŏŏ tə bl, ĭ′rĭ fyōō′tə bl), *adj.* not refutable; incontrovertible: *irrefutable logic.* —**irref′utabil′ity,** *n.* —**irref′utably,** *adv.*

irreg., **1.** irregular. **2.** irregularly.

irregardless (ĭ′rĭ gäd′lĭs), *adj. Colloq.* regardless (not generally regarded as good usage).

irregular (ĭ rĕg′yŏŏ lə), *adj.* **1.** without symmetry, even shape, formal arrangement, etc.: *an irregular pattern.* **2.** not characterized by any fixed principle, method, or rate: *irregular intervals.* **3.** not according to rule, or to the accepted principle, method, course, order, etc. **4.** not conformed or conforming to rules of justice or morality, as conduct, transactions, mode of life, etc., or persons. **5.** *Bot.* not uniform; (of a flower) having the members of some or all of its floral circles or whorls differing from one another in size or shape, or extent of union. **6.** *Gram.* not conforming to the most prevalent pattern of formation, inflection, construction, etc.: *the verbs 'keep' and 'see' are irregular in their inflection.* **7.** *Mil.* (formerly, of troops) not belonging to the established forces. —*n.* **8.** one who or that which is irregular. **9.** *Mil.* a soldier not of a regular military force. [t. ML: s. *irregulāris*; r. ME *irreguler*, t. OF. See IR-², REGULAR] —**irreg′ularly,** *adv.*

—**Syn.** **1.** unsymmetrical, uneven. **2.** unmethodical, unsystematic; disorderly, capricious, erratic, eccentric, lawless. **3.** anomalous, unusual. IRREGULAR, ABNORMAL, EXCEPTIONAL imply a deviation from the regular, the normal, the ordinary, or the usual. IRREGULAR, not according to rule, refers to any deviation, as in form, arrangement, action, and the like; it may imply such deviation as a mere fact, or as regrettable, or even censurable. ABNORMAL implies a deviation from the common rule, resulting in a nontypical form or nature of a thing: *a two-headed calf is abnormal, abnormal lack of emotion.* EXCEPTIONAL means out of the ordinary or unusual; it may refer merely to the rarity of occurrence, or to the superiority of quality: *an exceptional case, an exceptional mind.*

irregularity (ĭ rĕg′yŏŏ lă′rĭ tĭ), *n., pl.* **-ties.** **1.** the state or fact of being irregular. **2.** something irregular. **3.** a breach of rules, etiquette, or principle.

irrelative (ĭ rĕl′ə tĭv), *adj.* **1.** not relative; without relation (fol. by *to*). **2.** irrelevant. —**irrel′atively,** *adv.* —**irrel′ativeness,** *n.*

irrelevance (ĭ rĕl′ĭ vəns), *n.* **1.** the quality of being irrelevant. **2.** an irrelevant thing, act, etc.

irrelevancy (ĭ rĕl′ĭ vən sĭ), *n., pl.* **-cies.** irrelevance.

irrelevant (ĭ rĕl′ĭ vənt), *adj.* **1.** not relevant; not applicable or pertinent: *irrelevant remarks.* **2.** *Law.* (of evidence) having no probative value upon any issue in the case. —**irrel′evantly,** *adv.*

irrelievable (ĭ′rĭ lē′və bl), *adj.* not relievable.

irreligion (ĭ′rĭ lĭj′ən), *n.* **1.** lack of religion. **2.** hostility to or disregard of religion; impiety. —**ir′reli′gionist,** *n.*

irreligious (ĭ′rĭ lĭj′əs), *adj.* **1.** not religious; impious; ungodly. **2.** showing disregard for or hostility to religion. [t. LL: m. s. *irreligiōsus*] —**ir′reli′giously,** *adv.* —**ir′reli′giousness,** *n.*

irremeable (ĭ rĕm′ĭ ə bl, ĭ rē′mĭ-), *adj.* from which one cannot return. [t. L: m. s. *irremeābilis*] —**irrem′eably,** *adv.*

irremediable (ĭ′rĭ mē′dyə bl), *adj.* not remediable; irreparable: *irremediable disease.* —**ir′reme′diableness,** *n.* —**ir′reme′diably,** *adv.*

irremissible (ĭ′rĭ mĭs′ə bl), *adj.* **1.** not remissible; unpardonable, as a sin. **2.** that cannot be remitted, as a duty. —**ir′remis′sibil′ity, ir′remis′sibleness,** *n.* —**ir′remis′sibly,** *adv.*

irremovable (ĭ′rĭ mōō′və bl), *adj.* not removable. —**ir′remov′abil′ity,** *n.* —**ir′remov′ably,** *adv.*

irreparable (ĭ rĕp′ə rə bl, ĭ rĕp′rə bl), *adj.* not reparable; incapable of being rectified, remedied, or made good: *an irreparable loss.* —**irrep′arabil′ity, irrep′arableness,** *n.* —**irrep′arably,** *adv.*

irrepealable (ĭ′rĭ pē′lə bl), *adj.* not repealable. —**ir′repea′lably,** *adv.*

irreplaceable (ĭ′rĭ plā′sə bl), *adj.* that cannot be replaced: *an irreplaceable souvenir.*

irreplevisable (ĭ′rĭ plĕv′ĭ sə bl), *adj. Law.* not replevisable or repleviable: that cannot be replevied. Also, **irrepleviable** (ĭ′rĭ plĕv′yə bl).

irrepressible (ĭ′rĭ prĕs′ə bl), *adj.* not repressible. —**ir′repress′ibil′ity, ir′repress′ibleness,** *n.* —**ir′repress′ibly,** *adv.*

irreproachable (ĭ′rĭ prō′chə bl), *adj.* not reproachable; free from blame. —**ir′reproach′abil′ity, ir′reproach′ableness,** *n.* —**ir′reproach′ably,** *adv.*

irresistible (ĭ′rĭ zĭs′tə bl), *adj.* not resistible; that cannot be resisted or withstood; tempting: *an irresistible impulse.* —**ir′resist′ibil′ity, ir′resist′ibleness,** *n.* —**ir′resist′ibly,** *adv.*

irresolute (ĭ rĕz′ə lōōt′), *adj.* not resolute; doubtful or undecided; infirm of purpose; vacillating. —**irres′olute′ly,** *adv.* —**irres′olute′ness,** *n.*

irresolution (ĭ rĕz′ə lōō′shən), *n.* lack of resolution; lack of decision or purpose; vacillation.

irresolvable (ĭ′rĭ zŏl′və bl), *adj.* not resolvable; incapable of being resolved; not analysable; not solvable.

irrespective (ĭ′rĭ spĕk′tĭv), *adj.* without regard to something else, esp. something specified; independent (fol. by *of*): *irrespective of all rights.* —**ir′respec′tively,** *adv.*

irrespirable (ĭ rĕs′pĭ rə bl, ĭ′rĭ spī′ə rə bl), *adj.* not respirable; unfit for respiration.

irresponsible (ĭ′rĭ spŏn′sə bl), *adj.* **1.** not responsible; not answerable or accountable: *an irresponsible ruler.* **2.** not capable of responsibility; done without a sense of responsibility: *mentally irresponsible.* —*n.* **3.** an irresponsible person. —**ir′respon′sibil′ity, ir′respon′sibleness,** *n.* —**ir′respon′sibly,** *adv.*

irresponsive (ĭ′rĭ spŏn′sĭv), *adj.* not responsive; not responding, or not responding readily, as in speech, action, or feeling. —**ir′respon′siveness,** *n.*

irretentive (ĭ′rĭ tĕn′tĭv), *adj.* not retentive; lacking power to retain, esp. mentally. —**ir′reten′tiveness,** *n.*

irretraceable (ĭ′rĭ trā′sə bl), *adj.* not retraceable; that cannot be retraced: *an irretraceable step.*

irretrievable (ĭ′rĭ trē′və bl), *adj.* not retrievable; irrecoverable; irreparable. —**ir′retriev′abil′ity, ir′retriev′ableness,** *n.* —**ir′retriev′ably,** *adv.*

irreverence (ĭ rĕv′ə rəns, ĭ rĕv′rəns), *n.* **1.** the quality of being irreverent; lack of reverence or respect. **2.** the condition of not being reverenced: *to be held in irreverence.*

irreverent (ĭ rĕv′ə rənt, ĭ rĕv′rənt), *adj.* not reverent; manifesting or characterized by irreverence; deficient in veneration or respect: *an irreverent reply.* [t. L: s. *irreverens*] —**irrev′erently,** *adv.*

irreversible (ĭ′rĭ vû′sə bl), *adj.* not reversible; that cannot be reversed. —**ir′revers′ibil′ity, ir′revers′ibleness,** *n.* —**ir′revers′ibly,** *adv.*

irrevocable (ĭ rĕv′ə kə bl), *adj.* not to be revoked or recalled; that cannot be repealed or annulled: *an irrevocable decree.* —**irrev′ocabil′ity, irrev′ocableness,** *n.* —**irrev′ocably,** *adv.*

irrigable (ĭ′rĭ gə bl), *adj.* that may be irrigated.

irrigate (ĭ′rĭ gāt′), *v.t.,* **-gated, -gating.** **1.** to supply (land) with water by means of streams passing through it, esp. artificial streams provided to promote vegetation. **2.** *Med.* to supply (a wound, etc.) with a constant flow of some liquid. **3.** *Now Rare.* to moisten; wet. [t. L: m. s. *irrigātus*, pp.] —**ir′riga′tor,** *n.*

irrigation (ĭ′rĭ gā′shən), *n.* **1.** the supplying of land with water from artificial channels to promote vegetation. **2.** *Med.* the covering or washing out of anything with water or other liquid for the purpose of making or keeping it moist, as in local medical treatment. **3.** the state of being irrigated. —**ir′riga′tional,** *adj.*

irrigative (ĭ′rĭ gā′tĭv), *adj.* serving for or pertaining to irrigation.

irriguous (ĭ rĭg′yŏŏ əs), *adj. Now Rare.* well-watered, as land. [t. L: m. *irriguus*]

irritability (ĭ′rĭ tə bĭl′ĭ tĭ), *n., pl.* **-ties.** **1.** the quality of being irritable. **2.** an irritable state or condition. **3.** *Physiol., Biol.* the ability to be excited to a characteristic action or function by the application of some stimulus, as heat, etc. [t. L: m. s. *irrītābilitas*]

irritable (ĭ′rĭ tə bl), *adj.* **1.** easily irritated; readily excited to impatience or anger. **2.** *Physiol., Biol.* displaying irritability (def. 3). **3.** *Pathol.* susceptible to physical irritation; liable to shrink, become inflamed, etc., when stimulated: *an irritable wound.* [t. L: m. s. *irrītābilis*] —**ir′ritableness,** *n.* —**ir′ritably,** *adv.*

irritant (ĭ′rĭ tənt), *adj.* **1.** irritating. —*n.* **2.** anything that irritates. **3.** *Pathol., Med.* something, as a poison or a therapeutic agent, producing irritation. [t. L: s. *irrītans*, ppr.] —**ir′ritancy,** *n.*

irritate (ĭ′rĭ tāt′), *v.t.,* **-tated, -tating.** **1.** to excite to impatience or anger. **2.** *Physiol., Biol.* to excite (a living system) to some characteristic action or function. **3.** *Pathol.* to bring (a bodily part, etc.) to an abnormally excited or sensitive condition. [t. L: m. s. *irrītātus*, pp.] —**ir′rita′tor,** *n.*

—**Syn.** **1.** vex, chafe, fret, gall, nettle, ruffle, pique; incense, anger, enrage, infuriate. IRRITATE, EXASPERATE, PROVOKE mean to annoy or stir to anger. To IRRITATE is to excite to impatience or angry feeling, often of no great depth or duration: *to irritate by refusing to explain an action.* To EXASPERATE is to irritate to a point where self-control is threatened or lost: *to exasperate by continual delays and excuses.* To PROVOKE is to stir to a sudden, strong feeling of resentful anger as by unwarrantable acts or wanton annoyance: *to tease and provoke an animal until it attacks one.*

irritating (ĭr′rĭ tā′tĭng), *adj.* causing irritation; provoking: *an irritating reply.* —**ir′ritat′ingly,** *adv.*
irritation (ĭr′rĭ tā′shən), *n.* **1.** the act of irritating. **2.** the state of being irritated. **3.** *Physiol., Pathol.* **a.** the bringing of a bodily part or organ to an abnormally excited or sensitive condition. **b.** the condition itself.
irritative (ĭr′rĭ tā′tĭv), *adj.* **1.** serving or tending to irritate. **2.** *Pathol.* characterized or produced by irritation of some bodily part, etc.: *an irritative fever.*
irrupt (ĭ rŭpt′), *v.i.* to burst or intrude suddenly.
irruption (ĭ rŭp′shən), *n.* a breaking or bursting in; a violent incursion or invasion. [t. L: s. *irruptio*]
irruptive (ĭ rŭp′tĭv), *adj.* **1.** characterized by or pertaining to irruption. **2.** *Geol.* intrusive.
Irtish (*Russ.* ĭr tĭsh′), *n.* a river flowing from the Altai Mountains NW through the W Soviet Union in Asia to the river Ob. ab. 2300 mi. Also, **Irtysh.**
Irvine (û′vĭn), *n.* a seaport in Scotland, in Ayrshire. 16,910 (1961).
Irving (û′vĭng), *n.* **1. Sir Henry** (*John Henry Brodribb*), 1838–1905, English actor. **2. Washington,** 1783–1859, U.S. essayist, story writer, and historian.
is (ĭz), *v.* 3rd pers. sing. pres. indic. of **be.** [OE *is*, c. Icel. *es*; *er*; akin to G *ist*, Goth. *ist*, L *est*, Gk *estī*, Skt *asti.* See BE]
is-, var. of **iso-,** before some vowels, as in *isallobar.*
Is., 1. Also, **Isa.** Isaiah. **2.** Also, **is.** Island. **3.** Isle.
I.S.A., International Standard Atmosphere.
Isaac (ī′zək), *n.* a patriarch, son of Abraham and Sarah, and father of Jacob. Gen. 17:19. [t. L (Vulgate), t. Gk (Septuagint), t. Heb.: m. *Yitshāq*, lit., laughs]
Isaacs (ī′zəks), *n.* **Sir Isaac Alfred,** 1855–1948, Australian jurist: governor-general of Australia 1931–36.
isabel (ĭz′ə bĕl′), *n.* **1.** a dingy yellowish grey colour. —*adj.* **2.** of the colour of isabel. Also, **isabella** (ĭz′ə bĕl′ə), **isabelline** (ĭz′ə bĕl′ĭn, -ĭn).
Isabella I (ĭz′ə bĕl′ə) (*the Catholic*), 1451–1504, joint ruler, 1474–1504, of Castile and León, with her husband Ferdinand V, and patron of Columbus. Also, *Spanish,* **Isabel** (*Sp.* ē sä bĕl′).
isagogic (ī′sə gŏj′ĭk), *adj.* **1.** introductory, esp. to the interpretation of the Bible. —*n.* **2.** (*usually pl.*) **a.** introductory studies. **b.** the department of theology which is introductory to exegesis and the literary history of the Bible. [t. L: s. *īsagōgicus* introductory, t. Gk: m. *eisagōgikós*, lit., leading into]
Isaiah (ī zī′ə), *n.* **1.** a major Hebrew prophet of the 8th century B.C. **2.** a long book of the Old Testament, belonging to the second division of the Hebrew canon and the first book of the major prophets. [ult. t. Heb.: m. *Yeshaʻyāh*, lit., Jehovah's salvation]
isallobar (ī săl′ə bä′), *n.* *Meteorol.* a line on a weather map connecting places having equal pressure changes. [f. IS- + ALLO- + -BAR. See ISOBAR]
isallotherm (ī săl′ə thûm′), *n.* *Meteorol.* a line on a weather map connecting points having equal temperature variations over a given period.
Isandhlwana (ē′sănd lwä′nə), *n.* a mountain in the Republic of South Africa, in NE Natal: defeat of British by Zulus under Cetywayo, 1879.
Isar (*Ger.* ē′zär), *n.* a river flowing from W Austria NE through S West Germany to the Danube. 215 mi.
isarithm (ī′sə rĭth′əm), *n.* isopleth.
Iscariot (ĭs kă′rĭ ət), *n.* **1.** the surname of Judas, the betrayer of Jesus. Mark 3:19, 14:10–11. **2.** one who betrays another; a traitor. [t. L: s. *Iscariōta*, t. Gk: m. *Iskariṓtēs*, t. Heb.: m. *īsh-qerīyōth* man of *Kerioth* (a place in Palestine)]
ischaemia (ĭs kē′mĭ ə), *n.* *Pathol.* local anaemia produced by local obstacles to the arterial flow. Also, **ischemia.** [t. NL, f. s. Gk *íschein* check + *-aemia* -AEMIA] —**ischaemic** (ĭs kē′mĭk), *adj.*
Ischia (ĭs′kĭ ə; *It.* ē′skyä), *n.* **1.** an island off the SW coast of Italy, near Naples: earthquake, 1883. 10,385 (1951); 18 sq. mi. See map under **Salerno. 2.** a seaport on this island. 3188 (1951).
ischiadic (ĭs′kĭ ăd′ĭk), *adj.* pertaining to the ischium; sciatic. Also, **ischiatic** (ĭs′kĭ ăt′ĭk).
ischium (ĭs′kĭ əm), *n., pl.* **-chia** (-kĭ ə). *Anat.* **1.** the lowermost of the three parts composing either innominate bone. See diag. under **pelvis. 2.** either of the bones on which the body rests when sitting. [t. NL, t. Gk: m. *ischíon* hip joint, haunch, ischium] —**is′chial,** *adj.*
Ise (ē′sā), *n.* a town in Japan, in S central Honshu island. 102,395 (1965).
-ise[1], var. of **-ize,** as in *realise.*
-ise[2], a noun suffix indicating quality, condition, or function, as in *merchandise, franchise.*
isenthalpic (ī′sĕn thăl′pĭk), *adj.* *Thermodynamics.* of equal or constant enthalpy.
isentropic (ī′sĕn trŏp′ĭk), *adj.* *Thermodynamics.* of equal or constant entropy.
Isère (*Fr.* ē zĕr′), *n.* **1.** a river in SE France, flowing from the Alps to the river Rhone. ab. 150 mi. **2.** a department in SE France. 729,789 pop. (1962); 3180 sq. mi. *Cap.*: Grenoble.
Iserlohn (*Ger.* ē zər lōn′), *n.* a town in West Germany, in central North Rhine-Westphalia. 57,400 (est. 1966).
Iseult (ē zōōlt′), *n.* *Arthurian Legend.* **1.** the daughter of Angush, king of Ireland, and wife of Mark, king of Cornwall, loved by Tristram. **2.** the daughter of the king of Brittany, and wife of Tristram. Also, **Isolde, Isolt.**
Isfahan (ĭs′fə hän′: *Pers.* ĕs fä hän′), *n.* a city in central Iran: the capital of Persia from the 16th to the 18th centuries. 339,909 (est. 1964). Also, **Ispahan.**
-ish[1], **1.** a suffix used to form adjectives from nouns, with the sense of: **a.** 'belonging to' (a people, country, etc.), as in *British, Danish, English, Spanish.* **b.** 'after the manner of', 'having the characteristics of', 'like', as in *babyish, girlish, mulish* (such words being now often depreciatory). **c.** 'addicted to', 'inclined or tending to', as in *bookish, freakish.* **2.** a suffix used to form adjectives from other adjectives, with the sense of 'somewhat', 'rather', as in *oldish, reddish, sweetish.* [ME; OE *-isc*, c. G *-isch*, Gk *-iskos*; akin to -ESQUE]
—**Syn. 1.** The suffixes -ISH, -LIKE, -LY, agree in indicating that something resembles something else. One of the common meanings of -ISH is derogatory; that is, it indicates that something has the bad qualities of something else, or that it has qualities similar which are not suitable to it: *childish, mannish* (of a woman). The suffix -LIKE, in the formation of adjectives, is usually complimentary: *childlike innocence, godlike serenity.* In an adverbial function, it may be slightly disparaging: *manlike, he wanted to run the show.* The suffix -LY, when it means having the nature or character of, is distinctly complimentary: *kingly, manly, motherly.*
-ish[2], a suffix forming simple verbs. [t. F: m. *-iss-*, extended stem of verbs in *-ir*, g. L *-isc-*, in inceptive verbs]
Isherwood (ĭsh′ə wŏŏd′), *n.* **Christopher,** born 1904, English novelist and dramatist living in the U.S.
Ishmael (ĭsh′mā əl), *n.* **1.** the outcast son of Abraham and Hagar. See Gen. 16:11, 12. **2.** any outcast. [t. Heb.: m. *Yishmāʻēl*, lit., God will hear]
Ishmaelite (ĭsh′mĭ ə līt′), *n.* **1.** a descendant of Ishmael (from whom the Arabs claim descent). **2.** a wanderer; an outcast. —**Ish′maelit′ish,** *adj.*
Ishtar (ĭsh′tä), *n.* the chief goddess of the Babylonians and Assyrians. Cf. **Astarte.** [t. Akkadian]
Isidore of Seville (ĭz′ĭ dô′), (*Isidorus Hispalensis*), A.D. *c.* 560–636, Spanish archbishop and Latin encyclopedist.
isinglass (ī′zĭng gläs′), *n.* a pure, transparent or translucent form of gelatine, esp. that derived from the air bladders of certain fishes. [t. MD: pop. m. (by assoc. with GLASS) of *hysenblas*, c. G *Hausenblase* isinglass, lit., sturgeon bladder]
Isis (ī′sĭs), *n.* **1.** an Egyptian goddess, sister and wife of Osiris, usually distinguished by the solar disc and cow's horns on her head. **2.** the river Thames at Oxford. [t. L, t. Gk, t. Egyptian: m. *Ese*]
Iskander Bey (ĭs kăn′də bā′), Scanderbeg.
Iskenderun (*Turk.* ēs kĕn′dĕ rōōn), *n.* a seaport in S Turkey, on the **Gulf of Iskenderun,** an inlet of the Mediterranean. 62,061 (1960). Also, **Alexandretta.**
isl., 1. (*pl.* **isls.**) island. **2.** isle.
Islam (ĭz′läm), *n.* **1.** the religion of the Muslims, based on the teachings of the prophet Mohammed as set down in the Koran: its fundamental principle is absolute submission to a unique and personal god, Allah. **2.** the whole body of Muslim believers, their civilization, and their lands. [t. Ar.: submission (to the will of God)] —**Islamic** (ĭz lăm′ĭk), **Islamitic** (ĭz′lă mĭt′ĭk), *adj.*
Islamic Republic of Mauritania, official name of Mauritania (def. 1).
Islamism (ĭz′lə mĭz′əm), *n.* the religion of Islam.
Islamite (ĭz′lə mīt′), *n.* a Muslim.
Islamize (ĭz′lə mīz′), *v.i., v.t.,* **-mized, -mizing.** to convert to or bring under the influence or control of Islam. Also, **Islamise.**
island (ī′lənd), *n.* **1.** a tract of land completely surrounded by water, and not large enough to be called a continent. **2.** a clump of woodland in a prairie. **3.** an isolated hill. **4.** something resembling an island. **5.** a platform in the middle of a street, at a crossing, for the safety of pedestrians. **6.** *Physiol., Anat.* an isolated portion of tissue or aggregation of cells. —*v.t.* **7.** to make into an island. **8.** to dot with islands. **9.** to place on an island; isolate. [ME *iland, yland,* OE *iland, igland,* f. *īg, īeg* island + *land* land; *-s-* inserted through erroneous assoc. with ISLE] —**is′land-like′,** *adj.*
islander (ī′lən də), *n.* a native or inhabitant of an island.
Islands of the Blessed, *Gk Myth.* the imaginary lands

said to lie in the remote western part of the ocean whither after death the souls of heroes and good men were supposed to be transported.
island universe, *Astron.* a galaxy.
Islay (ī′lā), *n.* an island of the Inner Hebrides, Argyllshire, Scotland. ab. 25 mi. long, 19 mi. wide. 3866 (1961).
isle (īl), *n., v.,* **isled, isling.** —*n.* **1.** a small island: *the Scilly Isles.* **2.** *Now Chiefly Poetic.* an island. —*v.t.* **3.** to make into or as into an isle. **4.** to place on or as on an isle. —*v.t.* **5.** to dwell or remain on an isle. [ME *isle, ile,* t. OF, g. L *insula*]
Isle of Man. See **Man, Isle of.**
Isle of Pines. See **Pines, Isle of.**
Isle of Wight. See **Wight, Isle of.**
islet (ī′lĭt), *n.* a small island. [t. F: m. *islette* (now *îlette*), dim. of *isle* ISLE]
Islington (ĭz′lĭng tən), *n.* a N inner borough of London. 259,600 (est. 1965).
isls., islands.
ism (ĭz′əm), *n.* a distinctive doctrine, theory, system, or practice: *this is the age of isms.* [n. use of -ISM]
-ism, a suffix of nouns denoting action or practice, state or condition, principles, doctrines, a usage or characteristic, etc., as in *baptism, barbarism, criticism, Darwinism, plagiarism, realism.* Cf. **-ist** and **-ize.** [ult. (often directly) t. Gk: s. *-ismos, -isma,* noun suffix. See -IZE]
Ismailia (ĭz′mī lĭə′), *n.* a town in NE Egypt, at the midpoint of the Suez Canal. 111,000 (1962).
Ismailian (ĭz′mä ē′lyən), *n.* a member of a sect of Shiite Muslims whose doctrines vary widely from those of orthodox Muslims.
Ismail Pasha (ĭz′mä ēl′ pä′shə), 1830–95, viceroy and khedive of Egypt 1863–79.
isn't (ĭz′nt), contraction of *is not.*
iso-, **1.** a prefix meaning 'equal'. **2.** *Chem.* a prefix added to the name of one compound to denote another isomeric with it. Also, **is-.** [t. Gk, comb. form of *ísos* equal]
isoagglutination (ī′sō ə glo͞o′tə nā′shən), *n. Med.* the clumping of the red blood cells of an animal by a transfusion from another animal of the same species.
isoagglutinin (ī′sō ə glo͞o′tĭ nĭn), *n.* an agglutinin which can effect isoagglutination.
isobar (ī′sō bär′), *n.* **1.** *Meteorol., etc.* a line drawn on a weather map, etc., connecting all points having the same barometric pressure (reduced to sea-level), measured in millibars or in inches of mercury, at a specified time or over a certain period. **2.** *Physics, Chem.* Also, **isobare** (ī′sō bêə′). one of two or more atoms of different atomic number, but having the same atomic weight. [t. Gk: s. *isobarḗs* of equal weight]

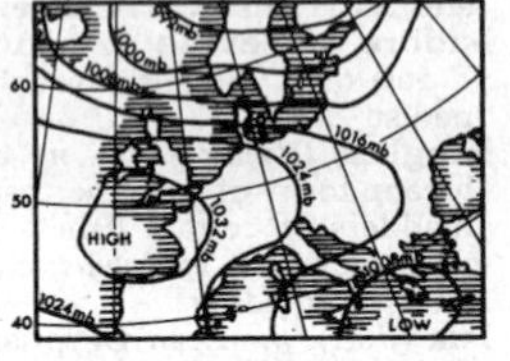
Isobars (def. 1). mb, Millibars

isobaric (ī′sō băr′ĭk), *adj.* **1.** having or showing equal barometric pressure. **2.** of or pertaining to isobars.
isobath (ī′sō băth′), *n. Geog.* a line drawn on a chart of the oceans, connecting all points having the same depth. —**i′sobath′ic,** *adj.*
isobilateral (ī′sō bī lăt′ə rəl), *adj.* of or pertaining to leaves which are more or less vertical and with both sides having the same structure, as those of the genus *Iris.*
isobutane (ī′sō byo͞o′tān), *n. Chem.* an isomeric form of butane, $(CH_3)_2.CH.CH_3$, used as a fuel and refrigerant.
isobutylene (ī′sō byo͞o′tĭ lēn′), *n. Chem.* a colourless inflammable gas, $(CH_3)_2.C=CH_2$, used in the manufacture of butyl rubber. Also, **isobutene** (ī′sō byo͞o′tēn).
isocarpic (ī′so kä′pĭk), *adj. Bot.* having carpels equal in number to the other floral parts.
isocheim (ī′sō kīm′), *n. Meteorol.* a line on a map connecting places which have the same mean winter temperature. Also, **isochime.** [f. ISO- + m. s. Gk *cheîma* winter] —**i′sochei′mal,** *adj.*
isochor (ī′sō kô′), *n. Physics.* a line representing the variation in pressure with temperature, under a constant volume. Also, **isochore.** [f. ISO- + s. Gk *chṓra* place] —**isochoric** (ī′sō kŏ′rĭk), *adj.*
isochromatic (ī′sō krō măt′ĭk), *adj.* **1.** *Optics.* having the same colour or tint. **2.** *Physics.* involving radiation of constant wavelength or frequency. **3.** orthochromatic.
isochronal (ī sŏk′rə nəl), *adj.* **1.** equal or uniform in time. **2.** performed in equal intervals of time. **3.** characterized by motions or vibrations of equal duration. [f. s. Gk *isóchronos* equal in age or time + -AL[1]] —**isoch′ronally,** *adv.*
isochronism (ī sŏk′rə nĭz′əm), *n.* isochronal character or action.
isochronize (ī sŏk′rə nīz′), *v.t.,* **-nized, -nizing.** to make isochronal. Also, **isochronise.**
isochronous (ī sŏk′rə nəs), *adj.* isochronal. —**isoch′ronously,** *adv.*
isochroous (ī sŏk′rō əs), *adj.* having the same colour throughout.
isoclinal (ī′sō klī′nəl), *adj.* **1.** of or pertaining to equal inclination; inclining or dipping in the same direction. **2.** denoting or pertaining to a line on the earth's surface connecting points of equal dip or inclination of the earth's magnetic field. **3.** *Geol.* denoting or pertaining to a fold of strata which is of the nature of an isocline. —*n.* **4.** an isoclinal line. Also, **isoclinic** (ī′sō klĭn′ĭk). [f. s. Gk *isoklinḗs* equally balanced + -AL[1]]

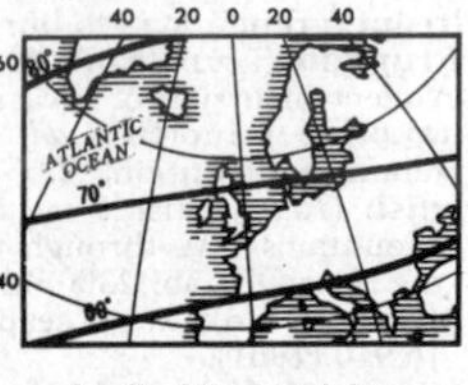

Isoclinal lines (def. 2)

isocline (ī′sō klīn′), *n. Geol.* a fold of strata so tightly compressed that the parts on each side dip in the same direction. [t. Gk: m. s. *isoklinḗs* equally balanced]
isocracy (ī sŏk′rə sĭ), *n., pl.* **-cies.** a government in which all have equal political power. [t. Gk: m. s. *isokratía.* See ISO-, -CRACY] —**isocratic** (ī′sō krăt′ĭk), *adj.*
Isocrates (ī sŏk′rə tēz′), *n.* 436–338 B.C., an Athenian orator and teacher of oratory.
isocyanide (ī′sō sī′ə nīd′), *n. Chem.* a compound containing the group —NC; carbylamine.
isocyanine (ī′sō sī′ə nēn′, -nĭn), *n. Chem.* a member of the cyanines. See **cyanine.**
isodiametric (ī′sō dī′ə mĕt′rĭk), *adj.* **1.** having equal diameters or axes. **2.** *Bot.* having the diameter similar throughout, as a cell. **3.** (of crystals) having two, or three, equal horizontal axes and a third, or fourth, unequal axis at right angles thereto.
isodiaphere (ī′sō dī′ə fĭə′), *n. Physics.* one of two or more nuclides in which the difference between the number of neutrons and protons is the same; as a nuclide and its decay product after it has emitted an alpha particle. [f. ISO- + m. s. Gk *diaphérein* differ]
isodimorphism (ī′sō dī mô′fĭz′əm), *n. Crystall.* isomorphism between the forms of two dimorphous substances. —**i′sodimor′phous,** *adj.*
isodynamic (ī′sō dī năm′ĭk, -dĭ-), *adj.* **1.** pertaining to or characterized by equality of force, intensity, or the like. **2.** denoting or pertaining to a line on the earth's surface connecting points of equal horizontal intensity of the earth's magnetic field. Also, **i′sodynam′ical.**
isoelectric point (ī′sō ĭ lĕk′trĭk), *Chem.* the *p*H at which a substance is electrically neutral or least ionized.
isoelectronic (ī′sō ĭ lĕk trŏn′ĭk), *adj. Physics, Chem.* signifying a set of elements having similar chemical properties by virtue of their atomic structure.
isoenzyme (ī′sō ĕn′zīm), *n. Biochem.* any of two or more forms of an enzyme.
isogamete (ī′sō gă mēt′), *n. Biol.* one of a pair of conjugating gametes, exhibiting no sexual or morphological differentiation.
isogamous (ī sŏg′ə məs), *adj. Biol.* having two similar gametes in which no differentiation can be distinguished, or reproducing by the union of such gametes (opposed to *heterogamous*).
isogamy (ī sŏg′ə mĭ), *n. Biol.* the fusion of two gametes of similar form, as in certain algae.
isogenous (ī sŏj′ĭ nəs), *adj. Biol.* of the same or similar origin, as parts derived from the same or corresponding tissues of the embryo. [f. ISO- + -GENOUS] —**isog′eny,** *n.*
isogeotherm (ī′sō jē′ō thûm′), *n. Phys. Geog.* an imaginary line or surface passing through points in the interior of the earth which have the same mean temperature. [f. ISO- + GEO- + s. Gk *thérmē* heat] —**i′soge′other′mal, i′soge′other′mic,** *adj.*
isogloss (ī′sō glŏs′), *n.* an imaginary line separating two localities which differ in some feature of their speech. [f. ISO- + s. Gk *glôssa* word, speech, tongue]
isogon (ī′sə gŏn′), *n.* **1.** a line on a map of the earth's surface connecting points of equal declination of the earth's magnetic field; an isogonic or isogonal line. **2.** *Geom.* an equiangular polygon. [t. Gk: m. s. *isogṓnios* having equal angles]
isogonic (ī′sə gŏn′ĭk), *adj.* **1.** having or pertaining to equal angles. **2.** denoting or pertaining to an isogon. —*n.* **3.** an isogon. Also, **isogonal** (ī sŏg′ə nəl).
isogram (ī′sō grăm′), *n. Meteorol., Geog.* an isopleth.
isograph (ī′sō grăf′, -gräf′), *n.* a line drawn on a map to indicate areas having common linguistic characteristics. —**isographic** (ī′sō grăf′ĭk), *adj.*

isohaline (ī′sō hā′lēn, -līn), *n.* a line drawn on a map of the sea or ocean, connecting points where salinity is equal.
isohel (ī′sō hĕl′), *n.* a line drawn on a map, etc., connecting places which receive equal amounts of sunshine.
isohyet (ī′sō hī′ət), *n.* a line drawn on a map connecting points having equal rainfall at a certain time or for a stated period. [f. ISO- + s. Gk *hyetós* rain]
isolable (ī′sə lə bl), *adj.* that can be isolated.
isolate (ī′sə lāt′), *v.t.*, **-lated, -lating. 1.** to set or place apart; detach or separate so as to be alone. **2.** *Med.* to keep (an infected person) from contact with non-infected ones. **3.** *Chem.* to obtain (a substance) in an uncombined or pure state. **4.** *Elect.* to insulate. [back-formation from *isolated*, ppl. adj., f. s. It. *isolato* (g. L *insulātus*; see INSULATE) + -ED²] —**i′sola′tor,** *n.*
isolating language, a language which uses few or no bound forms.
isolation (ī′sə lā′shən), *n.* **1.** the act of isolating. **2.** the state of being isolated. **3.** the complete separation from others of a person suffering from a contagious or infectious disease. **4.** the separation of a nation from other nations by a policy of non-participation in international affairs. **5.** *Sociol.* See **social isolation.** —**Syn. 2.** See **solitude.**
isolationist (ī′sə lā′shə nĭst), *n.* one who favours a policy of non-participation in international affairs. —**i′sola′tionism,** *n.*
Isolde (ĭ zōl′də; *Ger.* ē zōl′də), *n.* Iseult. Also, **Isolt** (ĭ zōlt′).
isoleucine (ī′sō lōō′sēn, -sĭn), *n. Chem., Biochem.* an amino acid, $C_2H_5CH(CH_3)CH(NH_2)COOH$, occurring in proteins.
isologue (ī′sə lŏg′), *n. Chem.* one of two or more compounds with a similar molecular structure but which contain different numbers of atoms of the same valency.
isomagnetic (ī′sō măg nĕt′ĭk), *adj.* **1.** denoting or pertaining to an imaginary line on the earth's surface, or a corresponding line on a map or the like, connecting places which have the same magnetic elements. —*n.* **2.** an isomagnetic line.
isomer (ī′sə mə), *n. Chem.* **1.** a compound which is isomeric with one or more other compounds. **2.** *Physics.* a nuclide which is isomeric with one or more other nuclides.
isomerase (ī sŏm′ə rās′), *n. Biochem.* any enzyme that catalyses the conversion of one chemical isomer into another.
isomeric (ī′sō mĕ′rĭk), *adj.* **1.** *Chem.* (of compounds) composed of the same kinds and numbers of atoms which differ from each other in the arrangement of the atoms and, therefore, in one or more properties. **2.** *Physics.* (of nuclides) having the same atomic number and mass but a different energy state. [f. s. Gk *isomerḗs* having equal parts + -IC]
isomerism (ī sŏm′ə rĭz′əm), *n.* the state or condition of being isomeric.
isomerize (ī sŏm′ə rīz′), *v.t., v.i.*, **-rized, -rizing.** *Chem.* to convert from isomeric form to another. Also, **isomerise.**
isomerous (ī sŏm′ə rəs), *adj.* **1.** having an equal number of parts, markings, etc. **2.** *Bot.* (of a flower) having the same number of members in each whorl.
isometric (ī′sō mĕt′rĭk), *adj.* **1.** pertaining to or having equality of measure. **2.** *Crystall.* denoting or pertaining to that system of crystallization which is characterized by three equal axes at right angles to one another. **3.** *Pros.* of equal measure; made up of regular feet. **4.** (of a projection, drawing, etc., representing a solid object), having three mutually perpendicular axes represented as being equally inclined to the plane of projection, all lines being drawn to scale. Also, **i′somet′rical.** [f. s. Gk *isómetros* of equal measure + -IC] —**i′somet′rically,** *adv.*
isometropia (ī′sō mĭ trō′pyə), *n. Ophthalm.* a condition in which the refraction is the same in the two eyes. [f. ISO- + s. Gk *métron* measure + -OPIA]
isometry (ī sŏm′ĭ trĭ), *n.* **1.** equality of measure. **2.** *Geog.* equality with respect to height above sea-level.
isomorph (ī′sō môf′), *n.* **1.** an organism which is isomorphic with another or others. **2.** an isomorphous substance.
isomorphic (ī′sō mô′fĭk), *adj.* **1.** *Biol.* being of the same or of like form; different in ancestry, but alike in appearance. **2.** *Crystall.* isomorphous.
isomorphism (ī′sō mô′fĭz′əm), *n.* the state or property of being isomorphous or isomorphic.
isomorphous (ī′sō mô′fəs), *adj. Chem., Crystall.* (of a substance) undergoing a more or less extended, continuous variation in chemical composition, with accompanying variations in physical and chemical properties, but maintaining the same crystal structure.
isoneph (ī′sō nĕf′), *n.* a line on a map, etc., connecting places which have the same amounts of cloud cover.
isoniazid (ī′sō nī′ə zĭd), *n. Chem.* isonicotinic acid hydrazide, $C_6H_7N_3O$, used in the treatment of tuberculosis.
isonomy (ī sŏn′ə mĭ), *n.* equality of political rights. [t. Gk: m. s. *isonomía*] —**isonomic** (ī′sō nŏm′ĭk), *adj.*
Isonzo (*It.* ē zón′tsó), *n.* a river forming a part of the boundary between Italy and Yugoslavia, flowing from the Julian Alps S to the Gulf of Trieste. 75 mi.
iso-octane (ī′sō ŏk′tān), *n.* an isomer of octane used to determine the knocking qualities of a fuel.
isopiestic (ī′sō pī ĕs′tĭk), *adj.* **1.** isobaric; denoting equal pressure. —*n.* **2.** an isobar (def. 1). [f. ISO- + s. Gk *piestós*, vbl. adj. of *piézein* press + -IC]
isopleth (ī′sō plĕth′), *n. Meteorol., Geog., etc.* a line drawn on a map or chart through all points having the same numerical value of any element, or of the ratio of values of two elements. Also, **isogram.** [t. Gk: s. *isoplēthḗs* equal in number]
isopod (ī′sō pŏd′), *n.* **1.** any of the *Isopoda*, an order or suborder of crustaceans (freshwater, marine, and terrestrial) with seven pairs of legs, and body flattened dorsoventrally. —*adj.* **2.** pertaining to the *Isopoda.* **3.** having the feet all alike, or similar in character. [t. NL: s. *Isopoda*, pl., genus type. See ISO-, -POD] —**isopodan** (ī sŏp′ə dən), *adj., n.* —**isop′odous,** *adj.*
isoprene (ī′sō prēn′), *n. Chem.* a colourless liquid hydrocarbon, C_5H_8, of the terpene class, produced from rubber or from oil of turpentine by pyrolysis and convertible into rubber by polymerization. [? f. ISO- + PR(OPYL) + -ENE]
isopropyl (ī′sō prō′pĭl), *n. Chem.* the univalent radical, $(CH_3)_2CH$.
isopropyl alcohol, *Chem* a colourless liquid, $CH_3CHOH\ CH_3$, used in the manufacture of antifreeze and as a solvent.
isopropyl ether, a colourless liquid, $(C_3H_7)_2O$, used as a solvent for waxes, fats, etc.
isopteran (ī sŏp′tə rən), *adj.* **1.** belonging to the insect order *Isoptera*, which contains the termites or white ants. —*n.* **2.** an isopteran insect.
isosceles (ī sŏs′ĭ lēz′), *adj.* (of a triangle) having two sides equal. See illus. under **triangle.** [t. LL, t. Gk: m. *isoskelḗs* with equal legs]
isoseismic (ī′sō sīz′mĭk), *adj.* **1.** pertaining to equal intensity of earthquake shock. **2.** denoting or pertaining to an imaginary line on the earth's surface connecting points characterized by such intensity. —*n.* **3.** an isoseismic line. Also, **i′soseis′mal.**
isostasy (ī sŏs′tə sĭ), *n.* **1.** *Geol.* the equilibrium of the earth's crust, a condition in which the forces tending to elevate balance those tending to depress. **2.** equilibrium when there is pressure from all sides; hydrostatic equilibrium. [f. ISO- + m. Gk *stásis* a standing]
isostatic (ī′sō stăt′ĭk), *adj.* pertaining to or characterized by isostasy. —**i′sostat′ically,** *adv.*
isosteric (ī′sō stĕ′rĭk), *adj. Chem.* pertaining to compounds which have similar physical properties owing to a similarity in the molecular configuration of the atoms, even though the atom may be of different elements.
isosterism (ī sŏs′tə rĭz′əm), *n. Chem.* the quality or state of being isosteric.
isothere (ī′sō thĭə′), *n. Meteorol.* a line connecting places on the earth's surface which have the same mean summer temperature. [f. ISO- + m. s. Gk *théros* summer] —**isotheral** (ī sŏth′ə rəl), *adj.*
isotherm (ī′sō thûm′), *n.* **1.** *Meteorol.* a line connecting points on the earth's surface having the same (mean) temperature. **2.** *Physics, Chem.* an isothermal line. [f. ISO- + s. Gk *thérmē* heat]
isothermal (ī′sō thû′məl), *adj.* **1.** *Physics, Chem.* pertaining to or indicating equality of temperature. **2.** *Meteorol.* of or pertaining to an isotherm. —*n.* **3.** *Meteorol.* an isotherm. —**i′sother′mally,** *adv.*
isothermal line, *Physics, Chem.* a line or graph showing relations of variables under conditions of uniform temperature.
isothermal process, a process which takes place without change in temperature.
isotone (ī′sə tōn′), *n. Physics.* one of two or more atoms whose nuclei contain the same number of neutrons although they have different atomic numbers.
isotonic (ī′sō tŏn′ĭk), *adj.* **1.** pertaining to solutions characterized by equal osmotic pressure. **2.** *Physiol.* **a.** denoting or pertaining to a solution containing just enough salt to prevent the destruction of the red blood corpuscles when added to the blood. **b.** denoting or pertaining to a contraction of a muscle when under a constant tension. **3.** *Music.* of or characterized by equal tones. [f. s. Gk *isótonos* having equal accent or tone + -IC]
isotope (ī′sə tōp′), *n. Chem.* any of two or more forms of a chemical element, having the same number of protons in the nucleus and, hence, the same atomic number, but having different numbers of neutrons in the

nucleus and, hence, different atomic weights. There are 275 isotopes of the 81 stable elements in addition to over 800 radioactive isotopes, so that isotopic forms of every element are known. Isotopes of a single element possess almost identical properties. [f. ISO- + m. s. Gk *tópos* place] —**isotopic** (ī′sə tŏp′ĭk), *adj.*

isotopic number, *Physics.* the difference between the number of neutrons and the number of protons in an isotope; neutron excess.

isotopic spin, *Physics.* a quantum number used to work out the properties of groups of elementary particles when the members of the group are identical except in respect of charge: no rotation is implied but the concept bears a formal resemblance to angular momentum.

isotopy (ī sŏt′ə pĭ), *n.* isotopic character.

isotropic (ī′sō trŏp′ĭk), *adj.* **1.** *Physics.* having one or more properties that are the same in all directions. **2.** *Zool.* lacking axes which are predetermined, as in some eggs. Also, **isotropous** (ī sŏt′rə pəs). [f. ISO- + s. Gk *trópos* turn, way + -IC]

isotropy (ī sŏt′rə pĭ), *n.* the state or property of being isotropic.

Ispahan (ĭs′pə hän′), *n.* Isfahan.

Israel (ĭz′rā əl), *n.* **1.** a name given to Jacob after he had wrestled with the angel. Gen. 32:28. **2.** the people traditionally descended from Israel or Jacob; the Hebrew or Jewish people. **3.** God's chosen people; the elect. **4.** a republic in SW Asia, on the Mediterranean: formed as a Jewish state May, 1948. 2,430,100. pop. (1964); 7984 sq. mi. *Cap.:* Jerusalem. **5.** the northern kingdom of the Hebrews, including the ten tribes, sometimes called by the name of the chief tribe, Ephraim. *Cap.:* Samaria. **6.** the northern and southern kingdoms of the Hebrews. **7.** the Christian Church. Gal. 6:16. [ult. t. Heb.: m. *Yisrā'ēl* (appar.) he who striveth with God]

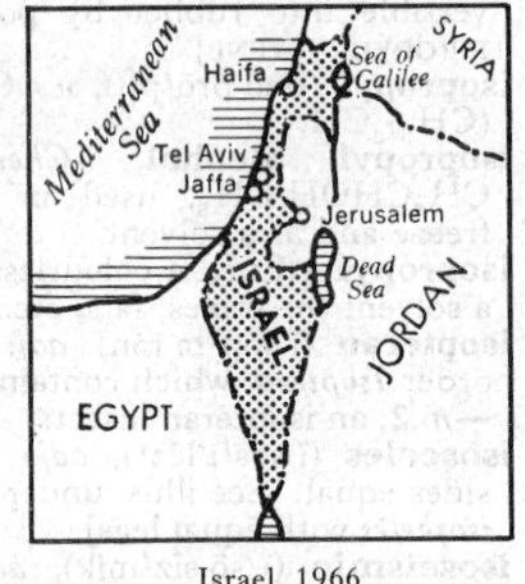

Israel, 1966

Israeli (ĭz rā′lĭ), *n., pl.* **-lis,** *adj.* —*n.* **1.** a native or inhabitant of Israel (def. 4). —*adj.* **2.** of Israel (def. 4).

Israelite (ĭz′rĭ ə līt′), *n.* **1.** a descendant of Israel or Jacob; a Hebrew; a Jew. **2.** one of God's chosen people. —*adj.* **3.** pertaining to Israel; Jewish.

Israelitish (ĭz′rĭ ə lī′tĭsh), *adj.* of the Israelites; Hebrew. Also, **Israelitic** (ĭz′rĭ ə lĭt′ĭk).

Israfil (ĭz′rə fēl′), *n.* (in the Koran) the angel of music, destined to announce the end of the world. Also, **Israfel.**

issuable (ĭsh′yōō ə bl), *adj.* **1.** that may be issued or may issue. **2.** forthcoming. **3.** *Law.* that admits of issue being taken. [f. ISSU(E) + -ABLE] —**is′suably,** *adv.*

issuance (ĭsh′yōō əns), *n.* **1.** the act of issuing. **2.** issue.

issuant (ĭsh′yōō ənt), *adj.* **1.** *Rare.* emerging. **2.** *Her.* (of a beast) having only the upper half seen.

issue (ĭsh′yōō), *n., v.,* **issued, issuing.** —*n.* **1.** the act of sending, or promulgation; delivery; emission. **2.** that which is issued. **3.** a quantity issued at one time: *the latest issue of a periodical.* **4.** *Bibliog.* the printing of copies of a work from the original setting of type, but with some slight changes in the preliminary or appended matter. **5.** a point in question or dispute, as between contending parties in an action at law. **6.** a point or matter the decision of which is of special or public importance: *the political issues.* **7.** a point the decision of which determines a matter: *the real issue.* **8.** a point at which a matter is ready for decision: *to bring a case to an issue.* **9.** something proceeding from any source, as a product, effect, result, or consequence. **10.** the ultimate result, event, or outcome of a proceeding, affair, etc.: *the issue of a contest.* **11.** a distribution of food (rations), clothing, equipment, or ammunition to a number of officers or servicemen, or to a military unit. **12.** offspring or progeny: *to die without issue.* **13.** a going, coming, passing, or flowing out: *free issue and entry.* **14.** a place or means of egress; an outlet or vent. **15.** that which comes out, as an outflowing stream. **16.** *Pathol.* **a.** a discharge of blood, pus, or the like. **b.** an incision, ulcer, or the like emitting such a discharge. **17.** *Chiefly Law.* the yield or profit from land or other property. **18.** *Obs.* a proceeding or action. **19. at issue, a.** in controversy: *a point at issue.* **b.** in disagreement. **c.** inconsistent; inharmonious (fol. by *with*). **20. join issue, a.** to join in controversy. **b.** to submit an issue jointly for legal decision. **21. take issue,** to disagree. —*v.t.* **22.** to put out; deliver for use, sale, etc.; put into circulation. **23.** to print (a publication) for sale or distribution. **24.** to distribute (food, clothing, etc.) to one or more officers or servicemen or to a military unit. **25.** to send out; discharge; emit. —*v.i.* **26.** to go, pass, or flow out; come forth; emerge: *to issue forth to battle.* **27.** to be sent or put forth authoritatively or publicly, as a writ, money, etc. **28.** to be published, as a book. **29.** to come or proceed from any source. **30.** to arise as a result or consequence; result. **31.** *Now Chiefly Law.* to proceed as offspring, or be born or descended. **32.** *Chiefly Law.* to come as a yield or profit, as from land. **33.** to have the specified outcome. **34.** to result (often fol. by *in*). **35.** to end. [ME, t. OF, der. pp. of *issir, eissir,* g. L *exīre* go out] —**is′sueless,** *adj.* —**is′suer,** *n.* —**Syn. 26.** See **emerge.**

Issus (ĭs′əs), *n.* an ancient town of Cilicia, in Asia Minor, near modern Iskenderun: victory of Alexander over Darius III, 333 B.C.

Issyk-Kul (*Russ.* ĭs sĭk′kōōly′), *n.* a large mountain lake in the SW Soviet Union in Asia. ab. 2240 sq. mi.

-ist, a suffix of nouns, often accompanying verbs ending in *-ize* or nouns ending in *-ism,* denoting one who does, practises, or is concerned with something, or holds certain principles, doctrines, etc., as in *apologist, dramatist, machinist, plagiarist, realist, socialist, theorist.* [ult. (often directly) t. Gk: s. *-istēs* noun suffix. See -IZE, -ISM]

Issy-les-Moulineaux (*Fr.* ē sē lĕ mōō lē nō′), *n.* a town in N France, in Seine department. 51,776 (1962).

Istanbul (ĭs′tăn bōōl′: *Turk.* ĕs tän′bōōl), *n.* a city in European Turkey, on the Bosporus. 1,466,535 (1960). Formerly, **Constantinople.** Ancient, **Byzantium.** [Turk. alter of MGk *eis tēn pólin* in (to) the city]

Isth., isthmus. Also, **isth.**

isthmian (ĭsth′mĭ ən), *adj.* **1.** of or pertaining to an isthmus. **2.** (*cap.*) of the Isthmus of Corinth or of Panama. —*n.* **3.** a native or inhabitant of an isthmus.

Isthmian games, one of the great national festivals of ancient Greece, held every two years on the Isthmus of Corinth.

isthmus (ĭs′məs), *n., pl.* **-muses. 1.** a narrow strip of land, bordered on both sides by water, connecting two larger bodies of land. **2.** *Anat., etc.* a connecting part, organ, or passage, esp. when narrow or joining structures or cavities larger than itself. [t. L, t. Gk: m. *isthmós* narrow passage, neck, isthmus]

-istic, a suffix of adjectives (and in the plural of nouns from adjectives) formed from nouns in *-ist,* and having reference to such nouns, or to associated nouns in *-ism,* as in *deistic, euphuistic, puristic,* etc. In nouns it has usually a plural form, as in *linguistics.* [f. -IST + -IC]

-istical. See **-istic, -al**[1].

-istics. See **-istic, -ics.**

istle (ĭst′lĭ), *n.* a fibre from various tropical American trees of the species *Agave* or *Yucca,* used in making carpets, etc. Also, **ixtle.** [t. Amer. Sp., t. Nahuatl: m. *ixtli*]

Istria (ĭs′trĭ ə; *It.* ē′stryȧ), *n.* a peninsula at the N end of the Adriatic, in NE Italy and NW Yugoslavia. —**Is′trian,** *adj., n.*

it (ĭt), *pron., poss.* **its** or (*Obs.* or *Dial.*) **it,** *obj.* **it,** *pl.* **they;** *n.* —*pron.* a personal pronoun of the third person and neuter gender, corresponding to *he* and *she,* used: **1.** as a substitute for a neuter noun or a noun representing something possessing sex when sex is not particularized or considered: *the baby lost its rattle.* **2.** to refer to some matter expressed or understood, or some thing or notion not definitely conceived: *how goes it?* **3.** to refer to the subject of inquiry or attention, whether impersonal or personal, in sentences asking or stating what or who this is: *who is it? it is I.* **4.** as the grammatical subject of a clause of which the logical subject is a phrase or clause, generally following, regarded as in apposition to it: *it is hard to believe that.* **5.** in impersonal constructions: *it snows.* **6.** without definite force after an intransitive verb: *to foot it* (go on foot). —*n.* **7.** (in children's games) the player called upon to perform some task, as in tag the one who must catch the other players. **8.** *Colloq.* sex appeal. **9. with it, a.** in accordance with current trends and fashions; fashionable. **b.** well-informed and quick-witted. [ME and OE *hit* (gen. *his,* dat. *him,* acc. *hit*), neut. of *he* HE]

I.T.A., Independent Television Authority.

i.t.a., initial teaching alphabet.

itacolumite (ĭt′ə kŏl′yōō mīt′), *n.* a sandstone consisting of interlocking quartz grains and mica scales, found in Brazil, North Carolina, etc., and remarkable for its flexibility when in thin slabs. [f. *Itacolumi,* mountain in Brazil + -ITE[1]]

Ital., 1. Italian. **2.** Italy. Also, **It.**

ital., italic (type).

Italia (*It.* ē tä′lyä), *n.* Italian name of **Italy.**

Italia irredenta (*It.* ĕr rĕ dĕn′tä). See **irredentist.**

Italian (ĭ tăl′yən), *adj.* **1.** of or pertaining to Italy, its people, or their language. —*n.* **2.** a native or inhabitant of Italy. **3.** a Romance language, the language of Italy, official also in Switzerland. [ME, t. L: s. *Italiānus*]

Italianate (ĭ tăl′yə nāt′), *adj., v.,* **-nated, -nating.** —*adj.* **1.** Italianized; conforming to the Italian type or style. —*v.t.* **2.** to Italianize.

Italianism (ĭ tăl′yə nĭz′əm), *n.* **1.** an Italian practice, trait, or idiom. **2.** Italian quality or spirit.

Italianize (ĭ tăl′yə nīz′), *v.,* **-nized, -nizing.** —*v.i.* **1.** to become Italian in manner, etc.; speak Italian. —*v.t.* **2.** to make Italian. Also, **Italianise.** —**Ital′ianiza′tion,** *n.*

Italian rye grass, a widely cultivated and naturalized annual or biennial grass from W and S Europe, *Lolium multiflorum.*

italic (ĭ tăl′ĭk), *adj.* **1.** designating or pertaining to a style of printing types in which the letters usually slope to the right (thus, *italic*), patterned upon a compact manuscript hand, and used for emphasis, etc. **2.** (*cap.*) of or pertaining to Italy, esp. ancient Italy or its tribes. —*n.* **3.** (*often pl.*) italic type. **4.** (*cap.*) a principal group of Indo-European languages, including Latin and other languages of ancient Italy, notably Oscan and Umbrian, and closely related to Celtic. [t. L: s. *Italicus*]

Italicism (ĭ tăl′ĭ sĭz′əm), *n.* Italianism.

italicize (ĭ tăl′ĭ sīz′), *v.,* **-cized, -cizing.** —*v.t.* **1.** to print in italic type. **2.** to underscore with a single line, as in indicating italics. —*v.i.* **3.** to use italics. Also, **italicise.**

Italy (ĭt′ə lĭ), *n.* a republic in S Europe, comprising a peninsula S of the Alps, and the islands of Sicily, Sardinia, Elba, etc.: a kingdom 1870–1946. 50,463,762 pop. (1961); 119,772 sq. mi. *Cap.:* Rome. Italian, **Italia.**

Itami (ē′tə mĭ), *n.* a town in Japan, in W Honshu island. 121,380 (1965).

itch (ĭch), *v.i.* **1.** to have or feel a peculiar irritation of the skin which causes a desire to scratch the part affected. **2.** to have a desire to do or to get something: *itch after fame.* **3. an itching palm,** a grasping disposition; greed. —*n.* **4.** the sensation of itching. **5. the itch,** a contagious disease caused by the itch mite which burrows into the skin; scabies. **6.** an uneasy or restless desire or longing: *an itch for authorship.* [ME (*y*)*icchen,* OE *gicc*(*e*)*an,* c. D *jeuken,* G *jucken*]

itch mite, a parasitic mite, *Sarcoptes scabiei,* causing itch or scabies in man and a form of mange in animals.

itchy (ĭch′ĭ), *adj.,* **-ier, -iest.** **1.** having an itching sensation. **2.** of the nature of itching. —**itch′iness,** *n.*

-ite[1], a suffix of nouns denoting esp. **1.** persons associated with a place, tribe, leader, doctrine, system, etc., as in *Campbellite, Israelite, labourite.* **2.** minerals and fossils, as in *ammonite, anthracite.* **3.** explosives, as in *cordite, dynamite.* **4.** chemical compounds, esp. salts of acids whose names end in *-ous,* as in *phosphite, sulphites.* **5.** pharmaceutical and commercial products, as in *vulcanite.* **6.** a member or component of a part of the body, as in *somite.* [ult. (often directly) t. Gk: m. *-ītēs* (fem. *-itis*), noun and adj. suffix. Cf. -ITIS]

-ite[2], a suffix forming adjectives and nouns from adjectives, and some verbs, as in *composite, opposite, requisite, erudite,* etc. [t. L: m. *-itus, -ītus,* pp. ending]

item (*n., v.* ī′təm; *adv.* ī′tĕm), *n.* **1.** a separate article or particular: *fifty items on the list.* **2.** a separate piece of information or news, as in a newspaper. **3.** *Obs.* an admonition or warning. **4.** *Obs.* an intimation or hint. —*v.t.* **5.** to set down or enter as an item, or by or in items. **6.** to make a note or memorandum of. —*adv.* **7.** *Obs. or Archaic.* likewise. [ME, t. L: (adv.) just so, likewise]

itemize (ī′tə mīz′), *v.t.,* **-mized, -mizing.** to state by items; give the particulars of: *to itemize an account.* Also, **itemise.** —**i′temiza′tion,** *n.* —**i′temiz′er,** *n.*

iterance (ĭt′ə rəns), *n.* iteration.

iterant (ĭt′ə rənt), *adj.* repeating. [t. L: s. *iterans,* ppr.]

iterate (ĭt′ə rāt′), *v.t.,* **-rated, -rating.** **1.** to utter again or repeatedly. **2.** to do (something) over again or repeatedly. [t. L: m. s. *iterātus,* pp.] —**it′era′tion,** *n.*

iterative (ĭt′ə rə tĭv), *adj.* **1.** repeating; making repetition; repetitious. **2.** *Gram.* frequentative.

Ithaca (ĭth′ə kə), *n.* one of the Ionian islands, off the W coast of Greece: the legendary home of Ulysses. 2662 pop. (1961); 37 sq. mi.

Ithunn (ē′thōōn), *n.* *Scand. Myth.* the goddess, wife of Bragi, who guarded in Asgard the apples eaten by the gods to preserve their youth. Also, **Ithun, Idun.**

ithyphallic (ĭth′ĭ făl′ĭk), *adj.* **1.** pertaining to the phallus, as carried in ancient festivals of Bacchus. **2.** grossly indecent; obscene. **3.** *Anc. Pros.* denoting or pertaining to any of several metres employed in hymns sung in Bacchic processions. —*n.* **4.** a poem in ithyphallic metre. **5.** an indecent poem. [t. L: s. *ithyphallicus,* t. Gk: m. *ithyphallikós,* der. *īthýphallos* erect phallus]

itinerancy (ī tĭn′ə rən sĭ, ĭ tĭn′-) *n.* **1.** the act of travelling from place to place. **2.** a going about from place to place in the discharge of duty or the prosecution of business. **3.** a body of itinerants. **4.** the state of being itinerant. **5.** the system of rotation governing the ministry of the Methodist Church. Also, **itin′eracy.**

itinerant (ī tĭn′ə rənt, ĭ tĭn′-), *adj.* **1.** itinerating; journeying; travelling from place to place, or on a circuit, as a preacher, judge, or pedlar. —*n.* **2.** one who travels from place to place, esp. for duty or business. [t. LL: s. *itinerans,* ppr.] —**itin′erantly,** *adv.*

itinerary (ī tĭn′ə rə rĭ, ĭ tĭn′-), *n., pl.* **-ries,** *adj.* —*n.* **1.** a line of travel; a route. **2.** an account of a journey; a record of travel. **3.** a book describing a route or routes of travel, with information for travellers. **4.** a plan of travel. —*adj.* **5.** pertaining to travelling or travel routes. **6.** *Rare.* itinerant.

itinerate (ī tĭn′ə rāt′, ĭ tĭn′-), *v.i.,* **-rated, -rating.** to go from place to place, esp. in a regular circuit, as to preach. [t. LL: m. s. *itinerātus,* pp.] —**itin′era′tion,** *n.*

-ition, a noun suffix, as in *expedition, extradition,* etc., being *-tion* with a preceding original or formative vowel, or, in other words, **-ite**[1] + **-ion.** [t. L: s. *-itio, -ītio.* Cf. F *-ition,* G *-ition*]

-itious, an adjective suffix occurring in adjectives associated with nouns in *-ition,* as *expeditious,* etc. [t. L: m. *-icius, -īcius*]

-itis, a noun suffix used in pathological terms denoting inflammation of some part or organ, as in *bronchitis, gastritis, neuritis.* [t. Gk. See -ITE[1]]

-itive, a suffix of adjectives and nouns of adjectival origin, as in *definitive, fugitive.* [t. L: m. s. *-itīvus, -ītīvus*]

it'll (ĭt l), **1.** a contraction of *it will.* **2.** a contraction of *it shall.*

Ito (ē′tō), *n.* **Prince Ito Hirobumi** (hē′rō bōō′mĭ), 1841–1909, Japanese statesman.

ITO, International Trade Organization.

-itol, *Chem.* a suffix used in names of alcohols containing more than one hydroxyl group. [f. -ITE[1] + -OL[1]]

its (ĭts), *adj., possessive pron.* possessive form of *it.* [poss. case of IT, formerly written *it's*]

it's (ĭts), contraction of *it is.*

itself (ĭt sĕlf′), *pron.* **1.** the reflexive form of *it*: *a thermostatically controlled electric fire switches itself off.* **2.** an emphatic form of *it* used: **a.** as object: *the earth gathers its fruits to itself.* **b.** in opposition to a subject or object: *the moon itself is dead.* **3.** in its normal or usual state: *the child is itself again.*

ITU, International Telecommunication Union.

Ituraea (ĭ tŏŏə′rĭ ə), *n.* the NE part of ancient Palestine. See map under **Jericho.** Also, **Iturea.**

I.T.V., Independent Television.

-ity, a suffix forming abstract nouns of condition, characteristics, etc., as in *jollity, civility, Latinity.* [ME *-ite,* t. F: m. *-ité,* g. L *-itāt-,* s. *-itas*]

I.U.D., intra-uterine device.

-ium, a suffix representing Latin neuter suffix, used esp. to form names of metallic elements.

Ivan III (ī′vən; *Russ.* ĭ vän′) (*the Great*), 1440–1505, grand duke of Muscovy 1462–1505.

Ivan IV (*the Terrible*), 1530–84, grand duke of Muscovy 1533–47, and first tsar of Russia, 1547–84.

Ivanovo (*Russ.* ĭ vä′nə və), *n.* a city in the central Soviet Union in Europe. 389,000 (est. 1965). Formerly, **Ivanovo-Voznesensk** (*Russ.* ĭ vä′nə və vəz nĭ syĕnsk′).

I've (īv), contraction of *I have.*

-ive, a suffix of adjectives (and nouns of adjectival origin) expressing tendency, disposition, function, connection, etc., as in *active, corrective, destructive, detective, passive, sportive.* Cf. **-ative.** [t. L: m. s. *-īvus;* also repr. F *-if* (masc.), *-ive* (fem.), g. L]

Ives (īvz), *n.* **Frederick Eugene,** 1856–1937, U.S. inventor.

ivied (ī′vĭd), *adj.* covered or overgrown with ivy.

Iviza (ĭ vē′zə), *n.* a Spanish island in the Balearic Islands, in the W Mediterranean. Spanish, **Ibiza.**

ivory (ī′və rĭ, ī′vrĭ), *n., pl.* **-ries,** *adj.* —*n.* **1.** the hard white substance, a variety of dentine, composing the main part of the tusks of the elephant, walrus, etc., used for carvings, billiard balls, etc. **2.** a tusk, as of an elephant. **3.** dentine of any kind. **4.** some substance resembling ivory. **5.** *Slang.* a tooth, or the teeth. **6.** an article made of ivory, as a carving or a billiard ball. **7.** (*pl.*) *Slang.* **a.** the keys of a piano, accordion, etc. **b.** dice. **8.** the hard endosperm (**vegetable ivory**) of the ivory nut, used for ornamental purposes, buttons, etc. **9.** creamy white. *—adj.* **10.** consisting or made of ivory. **11.** of the colour ivory. [ME *yvory*, etc., t. OF: m. *yvoire*, g. L *eboreus* made of ivory] —**i′vory-like′,** *adj.*

ivory black, a fine black pigment made by calcining ivory.

Ivory Coast, a republic in W Africa: independent member of the French Community; formerly part of French West Africa. 3,600,000 pop. (1962); 127,520 sq. mi. *Cap.:* Abidjan. See map under **Timbuktu.**

ivory gull, a white arctic gull, *Pagophila eburnea.*

ivory nut, 1. the seed of a low-growing South American palm, *Phytelephas macrocarpa,* forming the source of vegetable ivory. **2.** a similar seed from other palms.

ivory palm, the palm yielding the common ivory nut.

ivory tower, 1. a place withdrawn from the world and worldly acts and attitudes. **2.** an attitude of aloofness from or contempt for worldly matters or behaviour. [trans. of F *tour d'ivoire,* first used by Sainte-Beuve]

Ivry-sur-Seine (*Fr.* ē vrē sʏr sĕn′), *n.* a river port in N France, in Seine department. 53,406 (1962).

ivy (ī′vĭ), *n., pl.* **ivies. 1.** a climbing vine, *Hedera helix,* with smooth, shiny, evergreen leaves, yellowish inconspicuous flowers, and black berries, widely grown as an ornamental. **2.** any of various other climbing or trailing plants, as *Parthenocissus tricuspidata* (**Japanese ivy**), *Glechoma hederacea* (**ground ivy**), etc. [ME; OE *īfig*; akin to G *Efeu*] —**i′vy-like′,** *adj.*

Ivy, *Hedera helix*

Ivy League, *U.S.* **1.** a group of highly regarded universities and colleges; esp. Yale, Harvard, Princeton, Columbia, Dartmouth, Cornell, Pennsylvania, and Brown, with high social and scholastic reputations. **2.** of, or pertaining to these universities, colleges, their students or graduates.

Iwakuni (ĭ wä′ko͞o nĭ, ē′wə ko͞o′nĭ), *n.* a town in Japan, in S central Honshu island. 105,931 (1965).

iwis (ĭ wĭs′), *adv. Obs.* certainly. Also, **ywis.** [ME adv. use of neut. of OE adj. *gewis* certain, c. D *gewis,* G *gewiss* certain, certainly; akin to WIT, v., know]

Iwo (ē′wō), *n.* a town in W Western Nigeria. 100,000 (est. 1963).

Iwo Jima (ē′wō jē′mə), one of the Volcano Islands, in the N Pacific, S of Japan: taken by U.S. forces, 1945.

I.W.W., Industrial Workers of the World.

Ixelles (*Fr.* ēk sĕl′), *n.* a town in central Belgium, now part of Brussels. 94,007 (1965).

ixia (ĭk′sĭ ə), *n.* any plant of the iridaceous genus *Ixia,* comprising southern African plants with sword-shaped leaves and showy ornamental flowers. [t. NL (named with ref. to the juice), t. Gk: birdlime]

Ixion (ĭk sī′ən), *n. Gk Legend.* a king of the Lapithae, who was punished by Zeus for his love for Hera by being bound on an eternally revolving wheel in Tartarus.

Ixtaccihuatl (*Sp.* ēs tȧk thē′wȧ tl), *n.* an extinct volcano in S central Mexico. 17,342 ft. Also, **Iztaccihuatl.**

ixtle (ĭks′tlĭ, ĭs′-), *n.* istle.

Iyeyasu (ē′yĭ yä′so͞o), *n.* **Tokugawa** (tŏk′o͞o gä′wə), 1542–1616, Japanese general and statesman.

Iyyar (ē′yä), *n.* (in the Jewish calendar) the eighth month of the civil year; the second month of the ecclesiastical year. Also, **Iyar.** [t. Heb., ult. from Akkadian]

izard (ĭz′əd), *n.* the chamois which inhabits the Pyrenees. [t. F: m. *isard*]

-ization, a noun suffix, combination of **-ize** with **-ation.**

-ize, a suffix of verbs having the sense (**a**) intransitively, of following some line of action, practice, policy, etc., as in *Atticize, apologize, economize, theorize, tyrannize,* or of becoming (as indicated), as *crystallize* and *oxidize* (intr.), and (**b**) transitively, of acting towards or upon, treating, or affecting in a particular way, as in *baptize, colonize,* or of making or rendering (as indicated), as in *civilize, legalize.* Also, **-ise**[1]. Cf. **-ism** and **-ist.** [ult. (often directly) t. Gk: m. s. *-izein.* Cf. F *-iser,* G *-isieren,* etc.]

Izhevsk (*Russ.* ĭ zhĕfsk′), *n.* a city in the E Soviet Union in Europe. 351,000 (est. 1965).

Izmir (*Turk.* ēz′mēr), *n.* a seaport in W Turkey on the **Gulf of Izmir,** an arm of the Aegean: important city of Asia Minor since ancient times. 360,829 (1960). Formerly, **Smyrna.**

Izmit (*Turk.* ēz′mēt), *n.* a town in NW Turkey. 73,488 (1960).

Iztaccihuatl (*Sp.* ēs tȧk thē′wȧ tl), *n.* Ixtaccihuatl.

izzard (ĭz′əd), *n. Archaic.* the letter Z. [unexplained var. of ZED]

J

J, j (jā), *n., pl.* **J's** or **Js, j's** or **js. 1.** a consonant, the 10th letter of the English alphabet. **2.** Roman numeral for 1.

J, *Physics.* joule.

J., 1. journal. **2.** Judge. **3.** Justice.

j, the imaginary number, $\sqrt{-1}$.

Ja., January.

J.A., Judge Advocate.

jab (jăb), *v.,* **jabbed, jabbing,** *n.* —*v.t., v.i.* **1.** to poke, or thrust smartly or sharply, as with the end or point of something. —*n.* **2.** a poke with the end or point of something; a smart or sharp thrust. Also, **job.** [var. (orig. Scot.) of JOB[2]]

Jabalpur (jŭb′l po͝o ə′), *n.* a town in India, in central Madhya Pradesh. 295,375 (1961). Also, **Jubbulpore.**

jabber (jăb′ə), *v.i., v.t.* **1.** to talk or utter rapidly, indistinctly, imperfectly, or nonsensically; chatter. —*n.* **2.** rapid or nonsensical talk or utterance; gibberish. [appar. imit.] —**jab′berer,** *n.* —**jab′beringly,** *adv.*

jabiru (jăb′ĭ ro͞o′), *n.* a large wading bird, *Jabiru mycteria,* of the stork family, inhabiting the warmer parts of America. [t. Tupi-Guarani]

jaborandi (jăb′ə răn′dĭ), *n., pl.* **-dis. 1.** any of certain South American shrubs of the rutaceous genus *Pilocarpus.* **2.** the dried leaflets of *Pilocarpus jaborandi* and other species containing the alkaloid pilocarpine, used as a sudorific and sialagogue and in ophthalmology. [t. Tupi-Guarani]

jabot (zhăb′ō), *n.* a falling ruffle, cascade, or other arrangement of lace, embroidery, or the like, worn at the neck or the front of a dress by women and formerly by men. [t. F: lit., bird's crop]

jacamar (jăk′ə mä′), *n.* any bird of the tropical American family *Galbulidae,* usually bright green above, with long bills. [t. Tupi: m. *jacamáciri*]

jaçana (jăs′ə nä′), *n.* lily-trotter. [t. Pg., t. Tupi: m. *jasanā*]

jacaranda (jăk′ə răn′də), *n.* **1.** any of the tall tropical American trees constituting the bignoniaceous genus *Jacaranda.* **2.** their fragrant ornamental wood. **3.** any of various related or similar trees. **4.** their wood. [t. Tupi-Guarani]

Jacarta (jə kä′tə), *n.* Djakarta.

jacinth (jăs′ĭnth), *n.* hyacinth (def. 4). [ME *iacynt,* t. OF: m. *jacinte,* g. L *hyacinthus* HYACINTH]

jack[1] (jăk), *n.* **1.** a man or fellow. **2.** (*cap. or l.c.*) a sailor. **3.** any of various mechanical contrivances or devices, as a contrivance for raising heavy weights short distances. **4.** a device for turning a spit, etc. **5.** any of the four knaves in playing cards. **6. a.** (*pl.*) a children's game in which pebbles or small metal objects are tossed and caught. **b.** any of the objects used in this game. **7.** a small bowl used as a mark for the players to aim at, in the game of bowls. **8.** a small union or ensign used by a ship or vessel as a signal, etc., and flown from the jackstaff as an indication of nationality. **9.** jackass. **10.** jack rabbit. **11.** *Elect.* a connecting device to which the wires of a circuit may be attached and which is arranged for the insertion of a plug. **12.** *Naut.* a horizontal bar or crosstree of iron at the topgallant masthead. **13.** *Music.* the moving part of the mechanism of early keyboard instruments that holds the quill or plectrum. **14.** any of several carangoid fishes, esp. of the genus *Caranx.* **15. every man jack,** everyone without exception. —*v.t.* **16.** to lift or move with or as with a jack, or contrivance for raising (usually fol. by *up*). **17.** *Colloq.* to raise (prices, wages, etc.) (usually fol. by *up*). **18.** *U.S.* to seek (game or fish) with a cresset or jacklight. [orig. proper name *Jack,* earlier *Jacken,* dissimilated var. of *Jankin,* f. *Jan* John + -KIN]

A B

Jack (def. 3) A, Lifting foot; B, Handle

jack[2] (jăk), *n.* **1.** a Polynesian moraceous tree, *Artocarpus leterophyllus,* with a fruit resembling breadfruit. **2.** the fruit itself, one of the largest known (up to more than 60 lbs). [t. Pg.: m. *jaca,* t. Malayalam: m. *chakka*]

jack[3] (jăk), *n.* **1.** a defensive coat, usually of leather, formerly worn by foot soldiers and others. **2.** *Archaic.* a container for alcoholic drink, orig. of waxed leather coated with tar. [ME *iacke*, t. OF: m. *jaque, jaques*, t. Sp.: m. *jaco*, ? t. Ar.: m. *shakk*]

jack-a-dandy (jăk′ə dăn′dĭ), *n.*, *pl.* **-dies.** dandy[1] (def. 1).

jackal (jăk′ôl), *n.* **1.** any of several races of wild dog of the genus *Canis*, esp. *Canis aureus*, of Asia and Africa, which hunt in packs at night and which were formerly supposed to hunt prey for the lion. **2.** one who does drudgery for another, or who meanly serves the purpose of another. [t. Turk.: m. *chakāl*, t. Pers.: m. *shag(h)āl*]

Black-backed jackal, *Canis mesomelas* (Total length 3 ft, tail 1 ft)

jackanapes (jăk′ə nāps′), *n.* **1.** a pert, presuming young man; whippersnapper. **2.** a mischievous child. **3.** a conceited person; coxcomb. **4.** *Archaic.* an ape or monkey. [var. of ME *Jack Napes*, nickname of William, Duke of Suffolk, 1396–1450, whose badge was an ape's clog and chain; prob. orig. used as name for tame ape or monkey]

jackass (jăk′ăs′), *n.* **1.** a male donkey. **2.** a very stupid or foolish person. **3.** *Naut.* a bag or plug for stopping a hawse pipe to prevent water from entering. **4.** laughing jackass; kookaburra.

jackblock (jăk′blŏk′), *n. Bldg Trades, Trademark.* liftslab.

jackboot (jăk′bo͞ot′), *n.* a large leather boot reaching up to and sometimes over the knee, orig. one serving as armour. **—jack′boot′ed,** *adj.*

jack crosstree, jack (def. 12).

jackdaw (jăk′dô′), *n.* **1.** a glossy black European bird, *Corvus monedula.* of the crow family, frequenting steeples, ruins, etc. **2.** the great-tailed grackle, *Cassidix mexicanus*, a large glossy blackbird of the southern U.S. and Mexico. [f. JACK[1] + DAW, n.]

jackeroo (jăk′ə ro͞o′), *n. Austral.* an apprentice station hand on a sheep or cattle station. Also, **jackaroo.** [b. JACK[1] Christian name + KANGAROO]

jacket (jăk′ĭt), *n.* **1.** a short coat, in various forms, worn by both men and women. **2.** something designed to be fastened about the body for other purpose than clothing: *a straitjacket.* **3.** Also, **dust jacket, dust cover.** a detachable paper cover, usually illustrated in colour, for protecting the binding of a book. **4.** the skin of a potato when it has been baked. **5.** the outer casing or covering of a boiler, pipe, tank, etc. **6.** the natural coat of certain animals. **7.** *U.S.* a folded paper or open envelope containing an official document. **—*v.t.* 8.** to cover with a jacket. [ME *iaquet*, t. OF: m. *jaquete*, dim. of *jaque* JACK[3]] **—jack′eted,** *adj.* **—jack′etless,** *adj.* **—jack′etlike′,** *adj.*

jackfish (jăk′fĭsh′), *n.* the pike.

Jack Frost, frost or freezing cold personified.

jackhammer (jăk′hăm′ə), *n.* a hand-held hammer-drill operated by compressed air; used for drilling rocks.

jack-in-office (jăk′ĭn ŏf′ĭs), *n.* a self-important petty official.

jack-in-the-box (jăk′ĭn thə bŏks′), *n.* a toy consisting of a figure, enclosed in a box, which springs out when the lid is unfastened. Also, **jack-in-a-box.**

Jack Ketch (kĕch), a public executioner or hangman. [from the English executioner, *Jack* (or John) *Ketch*, died 1686]

jackknife (jăk′nīf′), *n.*, *pl.* **-knives,** *v.*, **-knifed, -knifing.** **—*n.* 1.** a large knife with a blade that folds into the handle. **2.** a type of dive in which the diver assumes a folded position of the body while moving through the air, and straightens out before entering the water. **—*v.i.* 3.** (of an articulated lorry) to go out of control in such a way that the trailer swings round towards the driver's cab.

jack ladder, *Naut.* Jacob's ladder (def. 2).

jacklight (jăk′līt′), *n. U.S.* a portable cresset, oil-burning lantern, or electric light used in hunting or fishing at night.

jack-of-all-trades (jăk′əv ôl′trādz′), *n.* one who can turn his hand to anything but who has no one special skill.

jack-o'-lantern (jăk′ə lăn′tən), *n.* **1.** a lantern made from a hollowed-out pumpkin, with holes cut to represent human eyes, nose, mouth, etc. **2.** ignis fatuus.

jack pine, a slender pine, *Pinus banksiana*, covering tracts of barren land in Canada and the northern U.S.

jack plane, (in carpentry) a plane used for rough work.

jackpot (jăk′pŏt′), *n.* **1.** *Poker.* a pool that accumulates until a player opens the betting with a pair of jacks or better. **2.** the chief prize in a lottery, or a game or contest such as bingo, a quiz, etc. **3. hit the jackpot,** to achieve great success; be very lucky.

jack rabbit, any of various large hares of western North America, having very long limbs and ears.

Black-tailed jack rabbit, *Lepus alleni* (2 ft long)

jackscrew (jăk′skro͞o′), *n.* screw-jack.

jackshaft (jăk′shăft′), *n. Mach.* a short shaft, usually intermediate between the motor or engine and the machine to be driven.

jacksnipe (jăk′snīp′), *n.* **1.** a small, relatively short-billed snipe, *Limnocryptes minima*, of Europe and Asia. **2.** any of several related snipes. [f. JACK[1] + SNIPE]

Jackson (jăk′sən), *n.* **1. Andrew,** 1767–1845, U.S. general, 7th president of the U.S., 1829–37. **2. Thomas Jonathan** ('*Stonewall Jackson*'), 1824–63, Confederate general in the American Civil War. **3.** a town in the U.S., the capital of Mississippi, in the central part. 167,000 (est. 1965).

Jacksonville (jăk′sən vĭl′), *n.* a seaport in the U.S., in NE Florida. 201,030 (1960).

jackstaff (jăk′stăf′), *n.* a flagstaff at the bow of a vessel on which the jack is flown.

jackstay (jăk′stā′), *n. Naut.* a rope, rod, or the like, on a yard, used for tying the head of a square sail to the yard, and as a handrail.

jackstone (jăk′stōn′), *n.* jack (def. 6).

jackstraw (jăk′strô′), *n.* **1.** a straw-stuffed figure of a man. **2.** an insignificant person. **3.** one of a number of straws, or strips of wood, bone, etc., used in a game in which they are thrown on a table in confusion and are to be picked up singly without disturbing the others. **4.** (*pl. construed as sing.*) the game itself.

Jack Tar, a sailor. Also, **jack tar.**

Jack the Ripper, the nickname of the unknown murderer of a number of prostitutes in East London, 1888–89.

jackyard (jăk′yäd′), *n. Naut.* a small boom used to extend a topsail in a yacht.

Jacob (jā′kəb), *n.* a son of Isaac, the younger twin brother of Esau, and father of the 12 patriarchs. Gen. 25:24–34. [t. LL: s. *Jacōbus*, t. Gk: m. *Iákōbos* Jacob, James, t. Heb.: m. *Ya'aqōb* Jacob, explained as one who takes by the heel, a supplanter. See Gen. 25:26, 27:36]

Jacobean (jăk′ə bē′ən), *adj.* **1.** of or pertaining to James I of England or his times. **2.** of or pertaining to the late English Gothic style of architecture and furnishings, showing Italian influence, which flourished in the first half of the 17th century. **—*n.* 3.** a Jacobean writer, personage, etc. [f. m. s. NL *Jacōbaeus*, der. LL *Jacōbus* James (see JACOB) + -AN]

Jacobin (jăk′ə bĭn), *n.* **1.** a member of a famous club or society of French revolutionaries organized in 1789, so called from the Dominican convent in Paris in which they met. They developed clubs throughout France and worked for the success of the Mountain (def. 4) and the Reign of Terror. **2.** an extreme radical, esp. in politics. **3.** a Dominican friar. **4.** (*l.c.*) an artificial variety of the domestic pigeon, whose neck feathers form a hood. [ME, t. ML: s. *Jacōbinus*, der. LL *Jacōbus* James (see JACOB)] **—Jac′obin′ic, Jac′obin′ical,** *adj.* **—Jac′obin′ically,** *adv.*

Jacobinism (jăk′ə bĭ nĭz′əm), *n.* **1.** the principles of the Jacobins. **2.** extreme radicalism, esp. in politics.

Jacobinize (jăk′ə bĭ nīz′), *v.t.*, **-nized, -nizing.** to imbue with Jacobinism. Also, **Jacobinise.**

Jacobite (jăk′ə bīt′), *n.* **1.** a partisan or adherent of James II of England after his overthrow (1688), or of his descendants. **2.** a member of the Syrian Monophysitic Church, founded in the 6th century A.D. [t. ML: m. *Jacōbīta*, der. LL *Jacōbus* James (see JACOB)] **—Jacobitic** (jăk′ə bĭt′ĭk), **Jac′obit′ical,** *adj.*

Jacobitism (jăk′ə bī tĭz′əm), *n.* the principles of the Jacobites.

Jacobs (jā′kəbz), *n.* **W(illiam) W(ymark)** (wī′mäk′), 1863–1943, English short-story writer.

Jacobsen (*Dan.* yä′kŏb sən), *n.* **Arne** (*Dan.* är′nə), born 1902, Danish architect.

jacobsite (jā′kəb zīt′), *n.* a rare magnetic mineral consisting of oxides of magnesium, manganese, and iron. [named after *Jacobsberg*, area in Sweden. See -ITE[1]]

Jacob's ladder, **1.** *Bible.* a ladder leading up to heaven which Jacob saw in his dream. Gen. 28:12. **2.** *Naut.* a rope or wire ladder with wooden rungs.

Jacob's-ladder (jā′kəbz lăd′ə), *n.* **1.** a garden plant, *Polemonium caeruleum*, whose leaves have a ladder-like arrangement. **2.** any of certain related species.

jacobus (jə kō′bəs), *n.* an English gold coin struck in the reign of James I. [t. LL. See JACOB]

jaconet (jăk′ə nĭt), *n.* a lightweight cotton fabric, used in the manufacture of surgical dressings. [t. Urdu: m. *jagannāthī*, after *Jagannāthpūrī* in Orissa, India, where this fabric was originally made]

Jacquard loom (jăk′äd; *Fr.* zhȧ kȧr′), a pattern loom for weaving elaborate designs. [named after J. M. *Jacquard*, 1752–1834, French inventor]

Jacquard weave, a fabric woven on a Jacquard loom.

Jacquerie (*Fr.* zhȧk rē′), *n.* **1.** the revolt of the peasants of northern France against the nobles in 1358. **2.** (*l.c.*) any revolt of peasants. [F: (in OF *Jaquerie*) peasants; der. *Jaques* (see JACK[1]) taken as a name for a peasant]

jactation (jăk tā′shən), *n.* **1.** boasting. **2.** *Pathol.* a restless tossing of the body. [t. L: s. *jactātio* a throwing]

jactitation (jăk′tĭ tā′shən), *n.* **1.** *Law.* the assertion of a false claim, to the injury of another. **2.** *Pathol.* jactation (def. 2). [t. ML: s. *jactitātio*, der. L *jactitāre* bring forward in public, utter]

jade[1] (jād), *n.* **1.** either of two minerals, jadeite or nephrite, sometimes green, highly esteemed as an ornamental stone for carvings, jewellery, etc. **2.** Also, **jade green.** green, varying from bluish green to yellowish green. [t. F, t. Sp.: m. (*piedra de*) *ijada*, lit., (stone of) colic (Sp. *ijada* pain in the side, colic, der. L *ilia* flanks. See ILIUM)] —**jade′like′,** *adj.*

jade[2] (jād), *n.*, *v.*, **jaded, jading.** —*n.* **1.** a horse, esp. one of inferior breed, or worn out, or vicious. **2.** (in opprobrious use) a woman. —*v.t.*, *v.i.* **3.** to make or become exhausted by working hard; to weary or fatigue; tire. [ME, orig. uncert. Cf. Icel. *jalda* mare] —**jad′ish,** *adj.* —**jad′ishly,** *adv.* —**jad′ishness,** *n.*

jaded (jā′dĭd), *adj.* **1.** worn out. **2.** sated: *a jaded appetite.* —**jad′edly,** *adv.* —**jad′edness,** *n.*

jade green, the colour of jade.

jadeite (jā′dīt), *n.* a mineral, essentially sodium aluminium silicate, $NaAlSi_2O_6$, occurring in tough masses, whitish to dark green. See **jade**[1] (def. 1).

jaeger (yā′gə), *n.* **1.** any of the rapacious seabirds constituting the family *Stercorariidae* which pursue weaker birds in order to make them disgorge their prey; a skua. **2.** a hunter. **3.** a member of any of certain groups of sharpshooters in the German or Austrian army. Also, **jäger, yager.** [t. G: hunter, der. *jagen* hunt]

Jaén (*Sp.* KHȧ ĕn′), *n.* a town in S Spain. 72,337 (1965).

Jaffa (jăf′ə), *n.* **1.** a seaport in W Israel forming part of Tel-Aviv. Ancient, **Joppa. 2.** a variety of orange grown in Israel.

Jaffna (jăf′nə), *n.* a seaport in N Ceylon. 94,248 (1963).

jag[1] (jăg), *n.*, *v.*, **jagged, jagging.** —*n.* **1.** a sharp projection on an edge or surface. —*v.t.* **2.** to cut or slash, esp. in points or pendants along the edge; form notches, teeth, or ragged points in. [ME *jaggen*; ? imit.]

jag[2] (jăg), *n.* **1.** *Dial.* a load, as of hay or wood. **2.** *Slang.* a drinking bout. **3.** *Slang.* a state of intoxication. [? orig. a load of broom or furze. Cf. OE *ceacga* broom, furze]

J.A.G., Judge Advocate General.

Jagan (jā′gən), *n.* **Cheddi** (chĕd′ĭ), born 1918, Guyanese politician, prime minister 1961–64.

Jagannath (jŭg′ə nät′, -nôt′), *n.* Juggernaut. Also, **Jagannatha** (jŭg′ə nät′hə).

jäger (yā′gə), *n.* jaeger.

jagged (jăg′ĭd), *adj.* having notches, teeth, or ragged edges. —**jag′gedly,** *adv.* —**jag′gedness,** *n.*

jaggy (jăg′ĭ), *adj.*, **-gier, -giest.** jagged; notched.

jaguar (jăg′yŏŏ ə), *n.* a large, ferocious, spotted feline, *Panthera onca,* of tropical America. [t. Tupi-Guarani: m. *jaguara*]

Jaguar, *Panthera onca* (Total length ab. 7 ft, tail 2 ft)

jaguarondi (jăg′wə rŏn′dĭ), *n.*, *pl.* **-dis.** a short-legged long-bodied South American cat, *Felis eyra.* Also, **jaguarundi** (jăg′wə rŭn′dĭ). [t. Tupi-Guarani]

Jahveh (yä′vā), *n.* Yahweh. Also, **Jahve, Jah** (yä).

jai alai (*Sp.* KHáy ȧ lȧy′), a game resembling handball, esp. popular in Cuba, played on an indoor court with basket-like rackets. [t. Sp., t. Basque: merry game]

jail (jāl), *n.* **1.** a prison. —*v.t.* **2.** to take into or hold in custody; imprison. Also, **gaol.** [ME *jaiole*, t. OF: prison, cage; ult. der. L *cavea* cavity, enclosure, cage. See GAOL] —**jail′less,** *adj.* —**jail′-like′,** *adj.*

jailbird (jāl′bûd′), *n.* one who is or has been confined in jail; a criminal. Also, **gaolbird.**

jailbreak (jāl′brāk′), *n.* an escape from prison by means of force. Also, **gaolbreak.**

jail delivery, 1. a deliverance of imprisoned persons, esp. by force. **2.** the act of clearing a jail of prisoners by bringing them to trial, as at the assizes. Also, **gaol delivery.**

jailer (jā′lə), *n.* one in charge of a jail; prison warder. Also, **gaoler, jailor.**

jail fever, typhus. Also, **gaol fever.**

jailhouse (jāl′hous′), *n.*, *pl.* **-houses** (-hou′zĭz). *U.S.* jail. Also, **gaolhouse.**

Jain (jīn), *n.* **1.** an adherent of Jainism. —*adj.* **2.** of or pertaining to the Jains or their religion. [t. Hind.: m. *jaina*, g. Skt *jaina*, der. *jina*, lit., conqueror]

Jainism (jī′nĭz′əm), *n.* a dualistic, ascetic religion founded in the 6th century B.C. by a Hindu reformer as a revolt against the caste system and the vague world spirit of Hinduism. —**Jain′ist,** *n.*

Jaipur (jī pŏŏə′), *n.* **1.** a former state in N India, now part of Rajasthan. **2.** a city in India, the capital of Rajasthan, in the E part; known as the 'pink city' because of its buildings of that colour. 403,444 (1961).

Jakarta (jə kä′tə), *n.* Djakarta.

jakes (jāks), *n. Archaic.* lavatory.

Jalalabad (jə lä′lə bäd′), *n.* a town in E Afghanistan. 44,000 (est. 1962).

jalap (jăl′əp), *n.* **1.** a purgative drug from the tuberous root of a plant, *Ipomoea purga* (*Exogonium jalapa*), of Mexico, or of some other convolvulaceous plants. **2.** any of these plants. [t. Sp.: m. *jalapa*; named after the city. See JALAPA] —**jalapic** (jă lăp′ĭk), *adj.*

Jalapa (*Sp.* KHä lȧ′pȧ), *n.* a city in E Mexico. 66,509 (1960).

jalapin (jăl′ə pĭn), *n.* a resin which is one of the purgative principles of jalap. [f. JALAP + -IN[2]]

jalopy (jə lŏp′ĭ), *n.*, *pl.* **-lopies.** *Colloq.* an old, decrepit, or unpretentious motor car.

jalousie (zhăl′ŏŏ zē′), *n.* a kind of blind or shutter made with slats fixed at an angle. [t. F: lit., jealousy]

jam[1] (jăm), *v.*, **jammed, jamming,** *n.* —*v.t.* **1.** to press or squeeze tightly between bodies or surfaces, so that motion or extrication is made difficult or impossible. **2.** to bruise or crush by squeezing. **3.** to press, push, or thrust violently, as into a confined space or against some object. **4.** to fill or block up by crowding: *crowds jam the doors.* **5.** to cause to become wedged, caught, or displaced, so that it cannot work, as a machine, part, etc. **6.** *Radio.* **a.** to interfere with (signals, etc.) by sending out others of approximately the same frequency. **b.** (of signals, etc.) to interfere with (other signals, etc.). —*v.i.* **7.** to become wedged or fixed; stick fast. **8.** to press or push violently, as into a confined space or against one another. **9.** (of a machine, etc.) to become unworkable as through the wedging or displacement of a part. **10.** *Jazz.* to take part in a jam session. —*n.* **11.** the act of jamming. **12.** the state of being jammed. **13.** a mass of vehicles, people, or objects jammed together: *a traffic jam.* **14.** *Colloq.* a difficult or awkward situation; a fix. [appar. imit. Cf. CHAMP[1]] —**Syn. 1.** wedge, pack, crowd; ram, force.

jam[2] (jăm), *n.* a preserve of whole fruit, slightly crushed, boiled with sugar. [? same as JAM[1]] —**jam′like′,** *adj.*

Jamaica

Jam., Jamaica.

Jamaica (jə mā′kə), *n.* an island in the West Indies, S of Cuba: formerly a British colony; became independent on August 6th, 1962; member of the Commonwealth of Nations. 1,613,148 (1960); 4413 sq. mi. *Cap.:* Kingston.

Jamaican (jə mā′kən), *adj.* **1.** of, pertaining to, or obtained from the island of Jamaica. —*n.* **2.** a native or an inhabitant of Jamaica.

jamb (jăm), *n.* **1.** the side of an opening; a vertical piece forming the side of a doorway, window, or the like. **2.** jambeau. Also, **jambe.** [ME *jambe*, t. F: leg, jamb, g. LL *gamba* hoof]

J, Jamb

jambeau (jăm′bō), *n.*, *pl.* **-beaux** (-bōz). armour for the leg; a greave. See illustration under **armour.**

jamboree (jăm′bə rē′), *n.* **1.** a large gathering or rally of boy scouts, usually national or international. **2.** *Colloq.* a carousal; any noisy merrymaking. [appar. b. JABBER and F *soirée*, with *-m-* from JAM[1] crowd]

James (jāmz), *n.* **1.** an apostle, son of Zebedee and brother of the apostle John. (Matt. 4:21). **2.** ('*James the Lord's brother*') the reputed author of the Epistle of James. Gal. 1:19, Mark, 6:3. **3.** Also, **James the Less.**

('*James the son of Alphaeus*') an apostle. Matt. 10:3. **4.** the General Epistle of James, in the New Testament. **5.** the name of six kings of Scotland. **6. Henry,** 1843–1916, U.S. novelist in England (brother of William James). **7. Jesse (Woodson)** (wo͝od′sən), 1847–82, U.S. outlaw and bandit. **8. William,** 1842–1910, U.S. psychologist and philosopher (brother of Henry James). **—James′-ian,** *adj.*

James I, 1566–1625, king of England 1603–25; as **James VI,** king of Scotland 1567–1625.

James II, 1633–1701, king of England 1685–88.

James Bay, the S arm of Hudson Bay, in E Canada between Ontario and Quebec provinces. ab. 300 mi. long.

Jameson (jām′sən), *n.* **Sir Leander Starr,** 1853–1917, British colonial administrator.

Jameson Raid, an unsuccessful armed raid into the Boer Republic of Transvaal in 1895 led by Sir L. S. Jameson with the aim of supporting a projected rising of British settlers in Johannesburg.

James River, 1. a river in the U.S., flowing from the W part of Virginia E to Chesapeake Bay. 340 mi. **2.** a river in the U.S., flowing from central North Dakota S through South Dakota to the Missouri river. 710 mi.

Jamestown (jāmz′toun′), *n.* **1.** a ruined village in E Virginia: the first permanent English settlement in North America, 1607. **2.** a seaport in and the capital of St Helena, in the NW part. 1700 (1961).

jam-jar (jăm′jä′), *n.* a jar, usually of glass, for holding jam.

Jammu (jŭm′o͞o), *n.* a town in India, in S Kashmir. 102,738 (1961).

Jammu and Kashmir, official name of **Kashmir** (def. 2).

jammy (jăm′ĭ), *adj.* **1.** of or pertaining to jam. **2.** smeared or covered with jam. **3.** *Slang.* easy; requiring no effort.

Jamnagar (jäm′nŭg′ə), *n.* a town in India, in E Gujarat. 139,652 (1961).

jam session, a meeting of musicians for a spontaneous and improvisatory performance of jazz music, esp. for their own enjoyment.

Jamshedpur (jŭm′shĕd po͞o ə′), *n.* a town in India, in SE Bihar. 291,791 (1961).

Jamshid (jăm shēd′), *n.* *Persian Myth.* the king of the peris who, given a human form as punishment for his boast of immortality, became a powerful and wonder-working Persian king. Also, **Jamshyd.**

Jan., January.

Janáček (yăn′ə chĕk′; *Cz.* yä′nä chĕk), *n.* **Leoš** (*Cz.* lĕ′ŏsh), 1854–1928, Czech composer.

Janet (*Fr.* zhȧ nĕ′), *n.* **Pierre Marie Félix** (*Fr.* pyĕr mȧ rē fĕ lēks′), 1859–1947, French psychologist and neurologist.

jangle (jăng′gl), *v.*, **-gled, -gling,** *n.* **—*v.i.* 1.** to sound harshly or discordantly: *a jangling noise.* **2.** *Archaic.* to speak angrily; wrangle. **—*v.t.* 3.** to cause to sound harshly or discordantly. **4.** to cause to become upset or irritated. **—*n.* 5.** a harsh or discordant sound. **6.** an altercation; quarrel. [ME *jangle(n)*, t. OF: m. *jangler* chatter, tattle; ? of Gmc orig.] **—jan′gler,** *n.*

Janiculum (jə nĭk′yo͞o ləm), *n.* a ridge near the Tiber in Rome.

Janina (yä′nĭ nə), *n.* Serbo-Croat name of **Ioannina.**

janissary (jăn′ĭ sə rĭ), *n.*, *pl.* **-saries. 1.** an infantryman in the Turkish sovereign's personal standing army from the 14th century until 1826. **2.** any Turkish soldier. Also, **janizary** (jăn′ĭ zə rĭ). [t. F: m. *janissaire*, t. Turk.: m. *yeñicheri* new soldiery]

janitor (jăn′ĭ tə), *n.* **1.** a doorkeeper or porter. **2.** *U.S.* a caretaker. [t. L: doorkeeper. See JANUS] **—janitorial** (jăn′ĭ tô′rĭ əl), *adj.* **—janitress** (jăn′ĭ trĭs), *n. fem.*

jankers (jăng′kəz), *n.pl.* *Mil. Slang.* **1.** defaulters' punishment; detention. **2.** punishment cells; prison.

Jan Mayen (yăn mī′ĕn), a volcanic island in the Arctic Ocean between Greenland and Norway: a possession of Norway. 144 sq. mi.

Jansen (jăn′sən; *Du.* yŏn′sə), *n.* **Cornelis** (*Du.* kôr nĕ′lĭs) (*Cornelius Jansenius*), 1585–1638, Dutch Roman Catholic theologian.

Jansenism (jăn′sə nĭz′əm), *n.* the doctrinal system of Cornelis Jansen and his followers, which maintained the radical corruption of human nature and the inability of the will to do good, and that Christ died for the predestined and not for all men. **—Jan′senist,** *n.* **—Jan′-senis′tic,** *adj.*

January (jăn′yo͞o ə rĭ), *n.*, *pl.* **-ries.** the first month of the year, containing 31 days. [t. L: m. s. *Jānuārius* the month of *Janus* (see JANUS); r. ME *Jenever*, t. ONF, and OE *Ianuarius*, t. L]

Janus (jā′nəs), *n.* an ancient Italian (perhaps solar) deity, regarded by the Romans as presiding over doors and gates and over beginnings and endings, commonly represented with two faces in opposite directions. [L]

Janus-faced (jā′nəs fāst′), *adj.* two-faced; deceitful.

Jap (jăp), *adj.*, *n.* *Colloq.* Japanese.

Jap., Japanese.

japan (jə păn′), *n.*, *adj.*, *v.*, **-panned, -panning. —*n.* 1.** any of various hard, durable, black varnishes (orig. from Japan) for coating wood, metal, etc. **2.** work varnished and figured in the Japanese manner. **—*adj.* 3.** of or pertaining to japan. **—*v.t.* 4.** to varnish with japan; lacquer. **5.** to coat with any material which gives a hard, black gloss. [special use of JAPAN]

Japan (jə păn′), *n.* **1.** Japanese, **Nippon.** a constitutional monarchy on a chain of islands off the E coast of Asia: main islands, Hokkaido, Honshu, Kyushu, and Shikoku. 98,281,955 pop. (1965); 141,726 sq. mi. *Cap.*: Tokyo. **2. Sea of,** an arm of the Pacific between Honshu and Hokkaido islands and the mainland of Asia. ab. 405,000 sq. mi.

Japanese (jăp′ə nēz′), *adj.*, *n.*, *pl.* **-nese. —*adj.* 1.** of or pertaining to Japan, its people, or their language. **—*n.* 2.** a native of Japan, or a descendant of one. **3.** the language of Japan (no known congeners).

Japanese cedar, a very tall evergreen pinaceous tree, *Cryptomerica japonica*, of Japan and China.

Japanese ivy, a woody, oriental, climbing shrub, *Parthenocissus tricuspidata.*

Japanese river fever, a group of infectious diseases occurring in Japan, the East Indies, and probably elsewhere, transmitted by the bites of mites. Also, **tsutsugamushi fever.**

Japanese umbrella pine, an evergreen conifer with whorls of stiff leaves, frequently grown for ornament.

Japan laurel, a shrub, *Aucuba japonica*, of eastern Asia, with scarlet berries.

Japan wax, a natural wax obtained from the fruit of certain sumachs, containing a high proportion of palmitin; used in candles and polishes.

jape (jāp), *v.*, **japed, japing,** *n.* **—*v.i.* 1.** *Archaic.* to jest; joke; gibe. **—*n.* 2.** a joke; jest; gibe. [ME; orig. uncert.] **—jap′er,** *n.*

Japheth (jā′fĕth), *n.* *Bible.* the third son of Noah. [ult. t. Heb.: m. *Yepheth*]

Japhetic (jā fĕt′ĭk), *adj.* **1.** of or pertaining to Japheth. **2.** of or pertaining to a hypothetical linguistic family of Europe and W Asia, which was considered by some to have developed before Indo-European and Semitic. **—*n.* 3.** the Japhetic linguistic family.

japonica (jə pŏn′ĭ kə), *n.* **1.** the camellia, *Camellia japonica.* **2.** the Japanese quince, *Chaenomeles lagenaria*, an Asiatic shrub with clusters of scarlet flowers and yellowish fruit. [t. NL, fem. of *Japonicus* of Japan]

Japurá (*Port.* zhȧ po͞o rä′), *n.* a river flowing from the Andes in SW Colombia E through NW Brazil to the Amazon. ab. 1750 mi. Also, **Yapurá.**

Jaques-Dalcroze (*Fr.* zhȧk dȧl krōz′), *n.* **Émile** (*Fr.* ė mēl′), 1865–1950, Swiss composer and inventor of the method of eurhythmics.

jar¹ (jä), *n.* **1.** a broad-mouthed earthen or glass vessel, commonly cylindrical in form. **2.** the quantity contained in it. [t. F: m. *jarre*, t. Pr.: m. *jarro*, or Sp.: m. *jarra*, t. Ar.: m. *jarrah* earthen vessel]

jar² (jä), *v.*, **jarred, jarring,** *n.* **—*v.i.* 1.** to produce a harsh, grating sound; sound discordantly. **2.** to have a harshly unpleasant effect upon the nerves, feelings, etc. **3.** to vibrate audibly; rattle. **4.** to vibrate or shake (without reference to sound). **5.** to be at variance; conflict; clash. **—*v.t.* 6.** to cause to sound harshly or discordantly. **7.** to cause to rattle or shake. **8.** to have a harshly unpleasant effect upon (the feelings, nerves, etc.) (often fol. by *on*). **—*n.* 9.** a harsh, grating sound. **10.** a discordant sound or combination of sounds. **11.** a vibrating movement, as from concussion. **12.** a harshly unpleasant effect upon the mind or feelings due to physical or other shock. **13.** a quarrel; conflict, as of opinions, etc. [cf. OE *cearcian* creak]

jar³ (jä), *n.* **1.** a turn or turning. **2. on the jar,** ajar. [var. of CHAR³. Cf. AJAR¹]

jardinière (zhä′dĭ nyēə′; *Fr.* zhȧr dē nyĕr′), *n.* **1.** an ornamental receptacle or stand for holding plants, flowers, etc. **2.** a variety of glazed, diced, or boiled vegetables, each type cooked separately, and arranged around the main dish in separate groups. [t. F, fem. of *jardinier* gardener, der. *jardin* GARDEN]

jargon¹ (jä′gən), *n.* **1.** unintelligible or meaningless talk or writing; gibberish. **2.** (in contempt) any talk or writing which one does not understand. **3.** the language peculiar to a trade, profession, or other group: *medical jargon.* **4.** a kind of speech abounding in uncommon or unfamiliar words. **5.** debased, outlandish or barbarous language. **—*v.i.* 6.** to utter or talk jargon or a jargon. [ME, t. OF, ult. der. *garg-* throat] **—Syn. 3.** See **language.**

jargon[2] (jä′gŏn), *n.* a colourless-to-smoky semiprecious variety of the mineral zircon. [t. F, t. It.: m. *giargone*, ? ult. t. Pers.: m. *zargūn* gold-coloured. Cf. ZIRCON]

jargonize (jä′gə nīz′), *v.*, **-nized, -nizing.** —*v.i.* **1.** to talk jargon or a jargon. —*v.t.* **2.** to translate into jargon. Also, **jargonise.**

jarl (yäl), *n. Scand. Hist.* a chieftain; an earl. [t. Scand.; cf. Icel. *jarl.* See EARL]

jarosite (jă′rə sīt′), *n.* a yellowish or brownish mineral, $K_2Fe_6(SO_4)_4(OH)_{12}$, occurring in crystals or large masses. [named after Barranco *Jaroso*, in Almeria, south-eastern Spain. See -ITE[1]]

jarrah (jă′rə), *n.* an Australian hardwood, *Eucalyptus marginata.* [t. native Australian]

Jarrow (jă′rō), *n.* a town in England, in County Durham, at the mouth of the Tyne. 28,752 (1961).

Jarry (*Fr.* zhȧ rē′), *n.* **Alfred** (*Fr.* ȧl frĕd′), 1873–1907, French poet and dramatist.

Jas., James.

jasmine (jăs′mĭn, jăz′-), *n.* **1.** any of the fragrant-flowered shrubs constituting the oleaceous genus *Jasminum.* **2.** any of various plants of other genera, as *Gelsemium sempervirens* (**yellow jasmine**), *Gardenia jasminoides* (**Cape jasmine**) and *Plumeria rubra* (**red jasmine,** the frangipani). Also, **jessamine.** [t. F: m. *jasmin*, t. Ar.: m. *yāsmīn*, t. Pers.] —**jas′mine-like′,** *adj.*

Jason (jā′sən), *n. Gk Legend.* the leader of the expedition of the Argonauts in quest of the Golden Fleece. He was the husband of Medea. See **Golden Fleece** and **Medea.**

jasper (jăs′pə), *n.* a compact, opaque, often highly coloured, cryptocrystalline variety of quartz, commonly used in decorative carvings. [ME *jaspre*, t. OF, var. of *jaspe*, t. L: m. s. *iaspis*, t. Gk; of Eastern orig.]

Jassy (jăs′ĭ), *n.* a town in NE Rumania. 126,865 (est. 1963). Rumanian, **Iaşi.**

Jat (jät), *n.* a member of an Indo-Aryan people living mainly in north-western India. In early times they offered vigorous resistance to the Muslim invaders of India. [t. Hind.]

jato (jā′tō), *n. Aeron.* jet-assisted take-off.

jaundice (jôn′dĭs), *n.*, *v.*, **-diced, -dicing.** —*n.* **1.** *Pathol.* a morbid bodily condition due to the presence of increased amounts of bile pigments in the blood, characterized by yellowness of the skin, the whites of the eyes, etc., by lassitude, and by loss of appetite. **2.** the state of feeling in which views are coloured or judgement is distorted. —*v.t.* **3.** to affect with jaundice. **4.** to distort or prejudice, as with pessimism, jealousy, resentment, etc. [ME *jaunes, jaundis*, t. OF: m. *jaunisse*, der. *jaune* yellow, g. L *galbinus* greenish yellow]

jaunt (jônt), *v.i.* **1.** to make a short journey, esp. for pleasure. —*n.* **2.** such a journey. [? nasalized var. of *jot* jog, jolt] —**Syn. 2.** See **excursion.**

jaunting car, a light, two-wheeled, horse-drawn vehicle, popular in Ireland, having seats on each side set back to back and a perch in front for the driver.

Jaunting car

jaunty (jôn′tĭ), *adj.*, **-tier, -tiest. 1.** easy and sprightly in manner or bearing. **2.** smartly trim or effective, as clothing. [earlier *janty*, t. F: m. *gentil.* See GENTLE, GENTEEL] —**jaun′tily,** *adv.* —**jaun′tiness,** *n.*

Jaurès (*Fr.* zhō rĕs′), *n.* **Jean Léon** (*Fr.* zhäN lē ôN′), 1859–1914, French socialist and author.

Jav., Javanese.

Java (jä′və), *n.* an island in Indonesia. with Madura, 63,000,000 pop. (1961); 48,920 sq. mi.

SUMATRA
BORNEO
MOLUCCAS
CELEBES
JAVA
INDIAN OCEAN

Java

Java man, Pithecanthropus.

Javanese (jä′və nēz′), *adj.*, *n.*, *pl.* **-nese.** —*adj.* **1.** of or pertaining to the island of Java, its people, or their language. —*n.* **2.** a member of the native Malayan race of Java, esp. of that branch of it in the central part of the island. **3.** the language of central Java, of the Austronesian family.

Javary (*Port.* zhȧ vȧ rē′), *n.* a river forming part of the boundary between Peru and Brazil, flowing NE to the upper Amazon. ab. 450 mi. Also, **Javari.**

Java Sea, a sea between Java and Borneo.

Java sparrow, a finchlike bird, *Padda oryzivora*, of the East Indies and Malaya, having grey plumage and a pink-tinged belly: a common cagebird.

javelin (jăv′lĭn), *n.* **1.** a spear to be thrown by hand. **2.** *Sport.* a metal or wooden shaft, about 8½ feet long, with a metal point, thrown for distance. —*v.t.* **3.** to strike or pierce with or as with a javelin. [t. F: m. *javeline*; prob. from Celtic]

Javel water (jăv′əl, jə vĕl′), sodium hypochlorite, NaOCl, dissolved in water, used as a bleach, antiseptic, etc. Also, **Javelle water.** [named after *Javel*, district of Paris]

jaw (jô), *n.* **1.** one of the two bones or structures (upper and lower) which form the framework of the mouth. **2.** *Dentistry.* either jawbone containing its complement of teeth and covered by the soft tissues. **3.** the mouth parts collectively, or the mouth. **4.** anything likened to this: *the jaws of a gorge, of death, etc.* **5.** one of two or more parts, as of a machine, which grasp or hold something: *the jaws of a vice.* **6.** *Colloq.* **a.** talkativeness; continual talk. **b.** moralizing or reproving talk. —*v.i.* **7.** *Colloq.* to talk at length; gossip. —*v.t.* **8.** *Colloq.* to talk reprovingly; lecture; admonish. [ME *jawe, jowe*, t. OF: m. *jo(u)e* cheek, jaw] —**jaw′less,** *adj.*

Jawara (jä′wə rə), *n.* **Sir Dauda** (dô′də, dou′də), born 1924, prime minister of Gambia since 1963.

jawbone (jô′bōn′), *n.* **1.** any bone of the jaws; a maxilla or mandible. **2.** the bone of the lower jaw.

jaw-breaker (jô′brā′kə), *n.* **1.** *Colloq.* a word hard to pronounce. **2.** Also, **jaw-crusher.** a machine to break up ore, consisting of a fixed plate and a hinged jaw moved by a toggle joint. —**jaw′-break′ing,** *adj.*

Jaxartes (jăk sä′tēz), *n.* ancient name of **Syr Darya.**

jay (jā), *n.* **1.** any of several crested or uncrested birds of the corvine subfamily *Garrulinae*, all of them robust, noisy, and mischievous, as the **common jay,** *Garrulus glandarius*, of Europe, and the **bluejay,** *Cyanocitta cristata*, of America. **2.** *Slang.* a simple-minded or gullible person; a simpleton. [ME, t. OF. Cf. ML *gaius*, special use of proper name *Gaius*]

Jayhawker (jā′hô′kə), *n. U.S.* **1.** a native of Kansas. **2.** (*l.c.*) *Slang.* a plundering marauder; esp. one of the freebooting guerrillas in Kansas, Missouri, and other states before and during the American Civil War.

jaywalk (jā′wôk′), *v.i. Colloq.* to cross a street otherwise than by a pedestrian crossing or in a heedless manner, as against traffic lights. [f. JAY (see def. 2) + WALK] —**jay′walk′er,** *n.* —**jay′walk′ing,** *n.*

jazz (jăz), *n.* **1.** a type of popular music of American Negro origin, which sprang up in and around New Orleans and is marked by frequent improvisation and syncopated rhythms. **2.** a piece of such music. **3.** dancing or a dance performed to such music, as with violent bodily motions and gestures. **4.** *Slang.* liveliness; noisiness; spirit. **5.** *U.S. Slang.* pretentious or insincere talk. —*adj.* **6.** of the nature of or pertaining to jazz. —*v.t.* **7.** to play (music) in the manner of jazz. **8.** *Slang.* to put vigour or liveliness into (often fol. by *up*). —*v.i.* **9.** to dance to jazz music. **10.** *Slang.* to play or perform jazz music. **11.** *Slang.* to act or proceed with great energy or liveliness. [orig. obscure; said to have been long used by Negroes of the southern U.S., esp. those of Louisiana]

jazz band, a band adapted for or devoted to the playing of jazz.

jazzy (jăz′ĭ), *adj.*, **-zier, -ziest. 1.** *Slang.* pertaining to or suggestive of jazz music; wildly active or lively. **2.** having very bright or glaring colours; vividly patterned.

J.C., 1. Jesus Christ. **2.** Julius Caesar. **3.** jurisconsult.

J.C.D., (L *Juris Civilis Doctor*) Doctor of Civil Law.

J.C.R., Junior Common Room.

jct., junction. Also, **jctn**

J.D., (L *Jurum Doctor*) Doctor of Laws.

jealous (jĕl′əs), *adj.* **1.** feeling resentment against a successful rival or at success, advantages, etc. (fol. by *of*). **2.** characterized by or proceeding from suspicious fears or envious resentment: *jealous intrigues.* **3.** inclined to or troubled by suspicions or fears of rivalry, as in love or aims: *a jealous husband.* **4.** solicitous or vigilant in maintaining or guarding something. **5.** (in biblical use) intolerant of unfaithfulness or rivalry: *the Lord is a jealous God.* **6.** *Obs.* zealous. [ME *gelos, jalous*, t. OF, g. LL *zēlōsus*, der. L *zēlus*, t. Gk: m. *zêlos* ZEAL] —**jeal′ously,** *adv.* —**jeal′ousness,** *n.*

jealousy (jĕl′ə sĭ), *n.*, *pl.* **-ousies. 1.** resentment against a successful rival or the possessor of any coveted advantage. **2.** mental uneasiness from suspicion or fear of rivalry, as in love or aims. **3.** the state or feeling of being jealous. **4.** an instance of jealous feeling.

jean (jēn), *n.* **1.** a stout twilled cotton fabric. **2.** (*pl.*) clothes of this material, esp. close-fitting trousers. [prob. t. F: m. *Gênes* Genoa]

Jean (*Fr.* zhäN), *n.* **Grand Duke,** born 1921, sovereign of Luxembourg since 1964.

Jeanne d'Arc (*Fr.* zhȧn dȧrk′), French name of **Joan of Arc.**

Jeans (jēnz), *n.* **Sir James Hopwood,** 1877–1946, English mathematician, physicist, and astronomer.

Jebb (jĕb), *n.* **Sir Richard Claverhouse** (klăv′ə hous′), 1841–1905, Scottish classical scholar.

jebel (jĕb′l), *n. Arabic.* a mountain.

Jebel Musa (jĕb′l mo͞o′sə), a mountain in NW Morocco, opposite Gibraltar: one of the Pillars of Hercules. ab. 2750 ft.

Jedburgh (jĕd′bə rə, -brə), *n.* a burgh in Scotland, the county town of Roxburgh, on the border with England: ruins of a famous abbey. 3647 (1961).

Jedda (jĕd′ə), *n.* Jidda.

jeep (jēp), *n.* a small (usually $\frac{1}{4}$ ton capacity) military motor vehicle. [? special use of *jeep*, name of fabulous animal in comic strip 'Popeye', or alter. of *G.P.* (for General Purpose Vehicle)]

jeer[1] (jĭə), *v.i.* **1.** to speak or shout derisively; gibe or scoff rudely. —*v.t.* **2.** (often fol. by *at*) to treat with scoffs or derision; make a mock of. **3.** to drive (*out*, *off*, etc.) by jeers. —*n.* **4.** a jeering utterance; a derisive or rude gibe. [? OE *cēir* clamour, der. *cēgan* call out] —**jeer′er,** *n.* —**jeer′ingly,** *adv.* —**Syn. 1.** See **scoff.**

jeer[2] (jĭə), *n.* (*usually pl.*) *Naut.* tackle for hoisting or lowering heavy yards. [? lit., mover, der. GEE, interj.]

jefe (*Sp.* KHĕ′fĕ), *n. Spanish.* leader; commanding officer. [Sp., t. OF: m. *chief*, g. L *caput* head]

Jefferson (jĕf′ə sən), *n.* **Thomas,** 1743–1826, American statesman, writer, and 3rd president of the U.S., 1801–09.

Jefferson City, a city in the U.S., the capital of Missouri, in the central part, on the Missouri river. 28,228 (1960).

Jeffersonian (jĕf′ə sō′nyən), *adj.* **1.** of or pertaining to Thomas Jefferson or his political theories. —*n.* **2.** an adherent of Jefferson.

Jeffrey (jĕf′rĭ), *n.* **Francis** (*Lord Jeffrey*), 1773–1850, Scottish jurist, editor, and critic.

Jeffreys (jĕf′rĭz), *n.* **George, 1st Baron,** 1648–89, English judge, notorious for his injustice and brutality.

jehad (jĭ hăd′), *n.* jihad.

Jehoshaphat (jĭ hŏsh′ə făt′, -hŏs′-), *n.* a king of Judah, son of Asa, who reigned in the 9th century B.C. 1 Kings 22:41–50.

Jehovah (jĭ hō′və), *n.* **1.** a name of God in the Old Testament, an erroneous rendering of the ineffable name, JHVH, in the Hebrew Scriptures. **2.** (in modern Christian use) God.

Jehovah's Witnesses, a sect of Christians who are pacifists, believe in the imminent establishment of God's rule on earth, and do not recognize the authority of the state when it conflicts with religious principles.

Jehovist (jĭ hō′vĭst), *n.* **1.** the author of the earliest major source of the Pentateuch in which God is characteristically referred to as Yahweh (erroneously Jehovah). See **Yahwist. 2.** one who maintains that the vowel points annexed to the word *Jehovah* in Hebrew are the proper vowels of the word, and express the true pronunciation. —*adj.* **3.** characterized by the use of the name Jehovah for God (applied to part of the Pentateuch). —**Jeho′vism,** *n.*

Jehovistic (jē′hō vĭs′tĭk), *adj.* pertaining to or written by a Jehovist. Also, **Yahwistic.**

Jehu (jē′hyo͞o), *n.* **1.** son of Hanani, a prophet of Judah under Jehoshaphat in the 9th century B.C. 1 Kings 16. **2.** (*l.c.*) a fast driver. **3.** (*l.c.*) *Slang.* any driver.

jejune (jĭ jo͞on′), *adj.* **1.** deficient in nourishing or substantial qualities. **2.** unsatisfying to the mind; dull; boring. [t. L: m. s. *jējūnus* fasting, empty, dry, poor] —**jejune′ly,** *adv.* —**jejune′ness, jejunity** (jĭ jo͞o′nĭ tĭ), *n.*

jejunum (jĭ jo͞o′nəm), *n. Anat.* the middle portion of the small intestine, between the duodenum and the ileum. See diag. under **intestine.** [t. NL, prop. neut. of L *jējūnus* empty]

Jekyll and Hyde (jĕk′l, jē′kl), (of a person) having sharply contrasted good and bad qualities. [named after *Dr Jekyll and Mr Hyde*, a novel by R. L. Stevenson]

jell (jĕl), *v.i. Colloq.* **1.** to form a jelly. **2.** to take shape; crystallize; become definite.

Jellicoe (jĕl′ĭ kō′), *n.* **John Rushworth, 1st Earl,** 1859–1935, British admiral.

jellied (jĕl′ĭd), *adj.* **1.** brought to the consistency of jelly. **2.** containing or spread over with jelly.

jellify (jĕl′ĭ fī′), *v.*, **-fied, -fying.** —*v.t.* **1.** to make into a jelly; reduce to a gelatinous state. —*v.i.* **2.** to become gelatinous; turn into jelly. —**jel′lifica′tion,** *n.*

jelly (jĕl′ĭ), *n.*, *pl.* **-lies,** *v.*, **-lied, -lying.** —*n.* **1.** a food preparation of a soft, elastic consistency due to the presence of gelatine, pectin, etc., as fruit juice boiled down with sugar. **2.** anything of the consistency of jelly. —*v.t.*, *v.i.* **3.** to bring or come to the consistency of jelly. [ME *gele*, t. OF: m. *gelee* frost, jelly, g. L *gelāta*, prop. pp. fem., frozen] —**jel′ly-like′,** *adj.*

jellyfish (jĕl′ĭ fĭsh′), *n.*, *pl.* **-fishes,** (*esp. collectively*) **-fish.** any of various marine coelenterates of a soft, gelatinous structure, esp. one with an umbrella-like body and long, trailing tentacles; a medusa.

Jellyfish

jemadar (jĕm′ə dä), *n.* (in India, formerly) **1.** any of various government officials. **2.** the chief of a body of servants. **3.** a native officer in a sepoy regiment, corresponding in rank to a lieutenant. [t. Urdu, t. Pers.: m. *jama'dār*, lit., holder or leader of an aggregation (of men)]

Jemappes (*Fr.* zhə măp′), *n.* a town in SW Belgium: French victory over the Austrians, 1792. 12,950 (1962).

jemmy (jĕm′ĭ), *n.*, *pl.* **-mies,** *v.*, **-mied, -mying.** —*n.* **1.** a short crowbar. —*v.t.* **2.** to force open (a door, etc.) with a jemmy. Also, *U.S.*, **jimmy.** [appar. a form of James]

Jena (yā′nə; *Ger.* yĕ′nä), *n.* a city in East Germany, in Thuringia: Napoleon decisively defeated the Prussians near here, 1806. 83,073 (est. 1955).

je ne sais quoi (*Fr.* zhən sĕ kwä′), *French.* I know not what; an indefinable something.

Jenghis Khan (jĕng′gĭs kän′), Genghis Khan. Also, **Jen′ghiz Khan′.**

Jenin (jĕ nēn′), *n.* a town in NW Jordan. 40,000 (est. 1965).

jenminpi (yĕn′mĭn′pē′), *n.* **1.** the legal tender currency of China. **2.** yuan. [Chinese: people's currency]

Jenner (jĕn′ə), *n.* **1. Edward,** 1749–1823, English physician, discoverer of smallpox vaccine. **2. Sir William,** 1815–98, English physician.

jennet (jĕn′ĭt), *n.* **1.** a small Spanish horse. **2.** a female donkey; jenny ass. Also, **genet, gennet.** [ME *genett*, t. OF: m. *genet*, t. Sp.: m. *jinete* mounted soldier, horse, t. Ar.: m. *Zenāta*, name of Berber tribe noted for cavalry]

jenny (jĕn′ĭ), *n.*, *pl.* **-nies. 1.** a spinning jenny. **2.** female of some animals: *jenny wren.* [prop., woman's name]

Jens (*Ger.* yĕns), *n.* **Walter** (*Ger.* väl′tər), born 1923, German novelist.

jeopardize (jĕp′ə dīz′), *v.t.*, **-dized, -dizing.** to put in jeopardy; risk. Also, **jeopardise;** *U.S.*, **jeop′ard.**

jeopardy (jĕp′ə dĭ), *n.* **1.** hazard or risk of loss or harm. **2.** peril or danger: *for a moment his life was in jeopardy.* **3.** *Law.* the hazard of being found guilty, and of consequent punishment, undergone by criminal defendants on trial. [ME *iuparti*, etc., t. OF: m. *jeu parti*, lit., divided game, even game or chance] —**Syn. 1, 2.** See **danger.**

Jephthah (jĕf′thə), *n.* a judge of Israel. Judg. 11–14.

jequirity (jĭ kwĭ′rĭ tĭ), *n.*, *pl.* **-ties. 1.** the Indian liquorice plant, *Abrus precatorius*, of India and Brazil, whose seed (**jequirity bean**) is used in medicine. **2.** the seeds collectively. [t. F: m. *jéquirity*, t. Tupi-Guarani: m. *jekiriti*]

Jer., 1. Jeremiah. **2.** Jersey.

jerboa (jû bō′ə), *n.* any of various mouselike rodents of North Africa and Asia, as of the genera *Jaculus*, *Dipus*, etc., with long hind legs used for jumping. [t. NL, t. Ar.: m. *yarbū'*]

jereed (jə rēd′), *n.* jerid.

jeremiad (jĕ′rĭ mī′əd), *n.* a lamentation; a lugubrious complaint. [t. F: m. *jérémiade*, der. *Jérémie* Jeremiah; with ref. to the biblical 'Lamentations']

Jerboa, *Jaculus jaculus* (Total length 13 in., tail 8 in.)

Jeremiah (jĕ ′rĭ mī′ə), *n.* **1.** *c.* 650–585 B.C., a major Hebrew prophet. **2.** a book of the Old Testament. **3.** one who denounces wrong-doing and prophesies calamities.

Jerez (*Sp.* KHĕ rĕth′), *n.* a town in SW Spain: noted for its sherry. 140,061 (1965). Also, **Jerez de la Frontera** (*Sp.* dĕ lä frŏn tĕ′rä). Formerly, **Xeres.**

Jericho (jĕ′rĭ kō′), *n.* **1.** an ancient city of Palestine, N of the Dead Sea. **2.** a town in NW Jordan, on the site of the ancient city. 15,000 (est. 1965).

jerid (jə rēd′), *n.* a blunt wooden javelin used in games by horsemen in certain Middle Eastern countries. Also, **jereed, jerreed, jerrid.** [t. Ar.: m. *jarīd* rod, shaft]

Jericho at the time of Christ

Jeritza (*Ger.* yĕ′rĕ tsä), *n.* **Maria** (*Ger.* mä′rĕ ä), born 1887, Austrian soprano.

jerk[1] (jûk), *n.* **1.** a quick, sharp thrust, pull, throw, or the like; a sudden start. **2.** *Physiol.* a sudden movement of an organ or a part. **3.** *U.S. Slang.* a stupid or naive person. **4.** (*pl.*) *U.S.* paroxysms or violent spasmodic muscular movements as resulting from excitement caused by certain religious services. **5.** (*pl.*) See **physical jerks.** —*v.t.* **6.** to give a sudden thrust, pull, or twist to; move or throw with a quick, suddenly arrested motion. **7.** to utter in a broken, spasmodic way (usually fol. by *out*). —*v.i.* **8.** to give a jerk or jerks. **9.** to move with a quick, sharp motion; move spasmodically. [appar. imit.]

jerk[2] (jûk), *v.t.* **1.** to preserve meat, esp. beef (**jerked beef**) by cutting in strips and curing by drying in the sun. —*n.* **2.** jerked meat, esp. beef. [t. Amer. Sp.: m. *charquear*, der. *charque*, *charqui* jerked meat, charqui, t. Quechua]

jerkin (jûʹkĭn), *n.* a close-fitting jacket or short coat, as one of leather worn in the 16th and 17th centuries. [orig. unknown]

Jerkin

jerky (jûʹkĭ), *adj.*, **-kier, -kiest.** characterized by jerks or sudden starts; spasmodic. —**jerkʹily,** *adv.* —**jerkʹiness,** *n.*

Jeroboam (jĕʹrə bōʹəm), *n.* **1.** the first king of the northern kingdom of Israel (def. 5). **2.** (*l.c.*) a wine bottle containing from 2½ to 3 gallons.

Jerome (jĕʹrəm, jə rōmʹ), *n.* **1. Saint** (*Eusebius Sophronius Hieronymus*), A.D. *c.* 340–420, monk and scholar of the Latin Church, maker of the Latin version of the Bible known as the Vulgate. **2. Jerome K(lapka)** (klăpʹkə), 1859–1927, English humorous writer.

jerreed (jə rēdʹ), *n.* jerid. Also, **jerrid.**

jerry (jĕʹrĭ), *n.*, *pl.* **-ries.** *Slang.* a chamber-pot. [appar. m. JEROBOAM]

Jerry (jĕʹrĭ), *n.*, *pl.* **-ries.** *Colloq.* **1.** a German, esp. a German soldier. **2.** (collectively) Germans.

jerry-build (jĕʹrĭ bĭldʹ), *v.t.*, **-built, -building.** to build cheaply, shoddily, and flimsily. —**jerʹry-builtʹ,** *adj.* —**jerʹry-buildʹer,** *n.*

jerry can, a flat can for transporting fluids, esp. motor fuel, and containing between 4½ and 5 gallons. [See JERRY]

jersey (jûʹzĭ), *n.*, *pl.* **-seys.** **1.** a close-fitting knitted heavy woollen garment, as worn by seamen, etc. **2.** a similar garment of knitted wool, silk, etc., worn by women. **3.** jersey cloth. [named after JERSEY, where knitting was a staple industry]

Jersey (jûʹzĭ), *n.* **1.** the largest of the Channel Islands. 63,345 pop. (1961); 45 sq. mi. *Cap.:* St Helier. **2.** New Jersey. **3.** one of a breed of dairy cattle originating on the island of Jersey, whose milk contains a high proportion of butterfat.

Jersey City, a seaport in the U.S., in NE New Jersey, opposite New York City. 276,101 (1960).

jersey cloth, a machine-knitted fabric of wool, silk, or artificial fibre, used for making garments, etc.

Jerusalem (jə rōōʹsə ləm), *n.* an ancient holy city partly in Israel and partly in Israeli-occupied Jordan; place of pilgrimage for Jews, Christians, and Muslims; capital of Israel since 1950; divided between Israel and Jordan 1948–67. 261,700 (est. 1967).

Jerusalem artichoke, **1.** a species of sunflower, *Helianthus tuberosus*, having edible tuberous underground stems or rootstocks. **2.** the tuber itself. [*Jerusalem* t. It.: alter. (by pop. etymology) of *girasole* sunflower, f. s. of *girare* turn + *sole* sun]

Jerusalem cherry, a South American solanaceous shrub with white flowers and red fruits, *Solanum pseudocapsicum*, often grown and sometimes escaping from cultivation.

Jerusalem cross, a cross whose four arms are each capped with a crossbar. See illus. under **cross.**

Jerusalem sage, a hairy labiate shrub with yellow flowers from the Mediterranean region, *Phlomis fruticosa*, often cultivated and sometimes naturalized.

Jespersen (yĕsʹpə sən; *Dan.* yĕsʹbə sən), *n.* **Jens Otto Harry** (*Dan.* yĕns ŏtʹô häʹrē), 1860–1943, Danish philologist.

jess (jĕs), *Falconry.* —*n.* **1.** a short strap fastened round the leg of a hawk and attached to the leash. —*v.t.* **2.** to put jesses on (a hawk). [ME *ges*, t. OF, der. *jeter* throw, g. LL *jectāre*, r. L *jactāre*] —**jessed** (jĕst), *adj.*

jessamine (jĕsʹə mĭn), *n.* jasmine.

jessant (jĕsʹənt), *adj.* *Her.* **1.** shooting up, as a plant. **2.** coming forth; issuant. **3.** lying across.

Jesse (jĕsʹĭ), *n.* father of David. I Sam. 16.

Jesselton (jĕsʹəl tən), *n.* a seaport in Malaysia, the capital of Sabah, on the W coast. 21,714 (1960).

Jesse window, a church window with a genealogical tree showing the descent of Christ from Jesse.

jest (jĕst), *n.* **1.** a witticism, joke, or pleasantry. **2.** a piece of raillery or banter. **3.** sport or fun: *to speak half in jest, half in earnest.* **4.** the object of laughter, sport, or mockery; a laughing-stock. **5.** *Obs.* an exploit. See **gest.** —*v.i.* **6.** to speak in a playful, humorous, or facetious way; joke. **7.** to speak or act in mere sport, rather than in earnest; trifle (*with*). **8.** to utter derisive speeches; gibe or scoff. —*v.t.* **9.** to jest at; deride; banter. [var. of GEST] —**Syn.** **1.** See **joke.**

jester (jĕsʹtə), *n.* **1.** one who is given to witticisms, jokes, and pranks. **2.** a professional fool or clown, kept by a prince or noble, esp. during the Middle Ages.

jesting (jĕsʹtĭng), *adj.* **1.** given to jesting; playful. **2.** fit for joking; unimportant; trivial: *no jesting matter.* —*n.* **3.** pleasantry; triviality. —**jestʹingly,** *adv.*

Jesu (jēʹzyōō), *n.* *Poetic.* Jesus. [t. L, oblique (usually voc.) case form of *Jesus* JESUS]

Jesuit (jĕzʹyōō ĭt), *n.* **1.** a member of a Roman Catholic religious order (**Society of Jesus**) founded by Ignatius Loyola in 1534. **2.** a crafty, intriguing, or equivocating person (in allusion to the methods ascribed to the order by its opponents). —*adj.* **3.** of or pertaining to the Jesuits or Jesuitism. [t. NL: s. *Jēsuita*, f. L. See JESU, -IT(E)[1]]

Jesuitical (jĕzʹyōō ĭtʹĭ kl), *adj.* **1.** (*often l.c.*) sly; crafty; casuistic. **2.** Jesuit. Also, **Jeʹsuitʹic.** —**Jesʹuitʹically,** *adv.*

Jesuitism (jĕzʹyōō ĭ tĭzʹəm), *n.* **1.** the system, principles, or practices of the Jesuits. **2.** (*usually l.c.*) a principle or practice such as casuistry ascribed to the Jesuits by their opponents. Also, **Jesʹuitry.**

Jesuitize (jĕzʹyōō ĭ tīzʹ), *v.t.*, *v.i.*, **-tized, -tizing.** to make Jesuitical or become a Jesuit. Also, **Jesuitise.**

Jesus (jēʹzəs), *n.* born *c.* 6 B.C., crucified *c.* A.D. 29, the founder of the Christian religion. Also, **Jesus Christ.** [ME and OE, t. LL, t. Gk: m. *Iēsoûs*, t. Heb.: m. *Yeshūaʻ*, earlier *Yehōshūaʻ*, lit., Jehovah is salvation]

jet[1] (jĕt), *n.*, *v.*, **jetted, jetting.** —*n.* **1.** a free or submerged stream of fluid produced by efflux from a nozzle, orifice, etc. **2.** that which so issues, as water or gas. **3.** the spout used: *gas jet.* **4.** a jet plane. —*v.i.*, *v.t.* **5.** to shoot forth in a stream; spout. [t. F, der. *jeter*, v.]

jet[2] (jĕt), *n.* **1.** a compact black coal, susceptible of a high polish, used for making beads, jewellery, buttons, etc. **2.** a deep, glossy black. **3.** *Obs.* black marble. —*adj.* **4.** consisting or made of jet. **5.** of the colour jet; black as jet. [ME *gete, iete*, t. OF: m. *jaiet*, g. L *gagātēs*, t. Gk, der. *Gágai*, town in Lycia, Asia Minor]

jet black, deep black: *jet black hair.*

jet-deflection (jĕtʹdĭ flĕkʹshən), *adj.* *Aeron.* (of a jet-propulsion system) having the jets so arranged that they can be deflected downwards to assist take-off and landing.

jet engine, *Aeron.* turbojet (def. 1).

jetliner (jĕtʹlīʹnə), *n.* *Colloq.* a commercial jet plane.

jet plane, an aeroplane operated by jet propulsion.

jet propulsion, a method of producing a propelling force upon an air or water craft through the reaction of a high-velocity jet, usually of heated gases, discharged towards the rear. Also, **reaction propulsion.** —**jetʹ-propelledʹ,** *adj.*

jetsam (jĕtʹsəm), *n.* goods thrown overboard to lighten a vessel in distress, which sink or are washed ashore. See **flotsam.** [var. of *jetson*, syncopated form of *jettison*; assimilated to FLOTSAM]

jet set, (often disparaging) a rich and fashionable social set whose means enable them to travel from resort to resort by jet plane in the pursuit of pleasure.

jet stream, **1.** *Meteorol.* a horizontal cone of air, at altitudes of between about 15,000 and 40,000 ft, extending for great distances along the track of a wind and moving at very high speeds. **2.** *Aeron.* the exhaust of a jet engine or a rocket engine.

jettison (jĕtʹĭ sən, -zən), *n.* **1.** the act of casting cargo, etc., overboard to lighten a vessel or aircraft. **2.** jetsam. —*v.t.* **3.** to throw (cargo, etc.) overboard, esp. to lighten a vessel or aircraft in distress. **4.** to throw off, as an obstacle or burden. [t. AF: m. *getteson*, var. of OF *getaison*, der. *geter* throw]

jetton (jĕtʹn), *n.* an inscribed counter or token. [t. F: m. *jeton*, der. *jeter* throw, cast, cast up (accounts, etc.)]

jetty[1] (jĕtʹĭ), *n.*, *pl.* **-ties.** **1.** a pier or structure of stones, piles, or the like, projecting into the sea or other body of water so as to protect a harbour, deflect the current, etc. **2.** a wharf or landing pier. **3.** the piles or wooden structure protecting a pier. [ME *gette*, t. OF: m. *jetee*, n. use of fem. pp. of *jeter* throw]

jetty[2] (jĕtʹĭ), *adj.* **1.** made of jet. **2.** resembling jet; black as jet, or of the colour jet. [f. JET[2] + -Y[1]]

jeu de mots (*Fr.* zhœd mōʹ), *French.* a pun.

jeu d'esprit (*Fr.* zhœ dĕs prēʹ), *French.* a witticism.

Jevons (jĕvʹənz), *n.* **William Stanley,** 1835–82, English economist and logician.

Jew (jo͞o), *n.* **1.** one of the Hebrew or Jewish people; a Hebrew; an Israelite. **2.** one whose religion is Judaism. **3.** *Colloq.* (used offensively) a usurer; miser; one who drives a hard bargain. —*adj.* **4.** (used offensively) of Jews; Jewish. —*v.t.* **5.** (*l.c.*) *Colloq.* (used offensively) to bargain sharply with; beat (*down*) in price. **6.** (*l.c.*) *Colloq.* (used offensively) to cheat; swindle, or defraud. [ME *Jeu*, *Giu*, t. OF: m. *Juieu*, g. L *Jūdaeus*, t. Gk: m. *Ioudaîos*, prop. one of the tribe of Judah, ult. der. Heb. *Yehūdāh* Judah]

Jew-baiting (jo͞oʹbāʹtĭng), *n.* active anti-Semitism. —**Jewʹ-baitʹer,** *n.*

jewel (jo͞oʹəl), *n.*, *v.*, **-elled, -elling** or (*U.S.*) **-eled, -eling.** —*n.* **1.** a cut and polished precious or semiprecious stone; a gem. **2.** a fashioned ornament for personal adornment, usually set with gems. **3.** a precious possession. **4.** a thing or person of great worth or rare excellence. **5.** a precious stone (or some substitute) used as a bearing of great durability in a watch or delicate instrument. **6.** an ornamental boss of glass, sometimes cut with facets, in stained-glass work. **7.** something resembling a gem in appearance, ornamental effect, etc., as a star, a berry, etc. —*v.t.* **8.** to set or adorn with jewels. [ME *iuel*, t. AF, ult. der. L *jocus* jest, sport] —**jewʹel-likeʹ,** *adj.*

jewelfish (jo͞oʹəl fĭshʹ), *n.*, *pl.* **-fishes,** (*esp. collectively*), **-fish.** a brilliantly coloured aquarium fish, *Hemichromis binaculatus.*

jeweller (jo͞oʹə lə), *n.* one who makes, or deals in, jewels or jewellery. Also, *U.S.*, **jeweler.**

jewellery (jo͞oʹəl rĭ), *n.* jewels; articles made of gold, silver, precious stones, etc., for personal adornment. Also, *Chiefly U.S.*, **jewelry.**

Jewess (jo͞oʹĭs), *n.* a Jewish girl or woman.

jewfish (jo͞oʹfĭshʹ), *n.*, *pl.* **-fishes,** (*esp. collectively*) **-fish.** any of several large marine fishes of the family *Serranidae*, frequenting southern waters, such as the **spotted jewfish** (*Promicropsi taiara*) and the **black jewfish** (*Epinephelus nigritus*) of the south coast of the U.S., West Indies, etc., and the **California jewfish** (*Stereolepsi gigas*), all reaching a weight of several hundred pounds. [appar. f. JEW + FISH]

Jewish (jo͞oʹĭsh), *adj.* **1.** of, pertaining to, or characteristic of the Jews; Hebrew. —*n.* **2.** Yiddish. —**Jewʹishness,** *n.*

Jewish calendar, the lunisolar calendar in use among the Jews, reckoning from the Creation (dated traditionally during the year 3761 B.C.), the year containing 12 or (in intercalary years) 13 months, of 29 or 30 days each, which, beginning during September or October, are as follows: Tishri, Heshvan, Kislev, Tebet, Shebat, Adar, Veadar (occurring only on intercalary years), Nisan, Iyyar, Sivan, Tammuz, Ab, and Elul.

Jewry (jo͞oəʹrĭ), *n.*, *pl.* **-ries.** **1.** the Jewish people collectively. **2.** a district inhabited by Jews; a ghetto. **3.** *Archaic.* Judea. [ME *Jewerie*, t. AF: m. *juerie*, var. of OF *juierie*]

jew's-harp (jo͞ozʹhäpʹ), *n.* a musical instrument consisting of a circular metal frame with a metal tongue which is plucked while the frame is held between the teeth, the varying position of the mouth changing the tone. Also, **jews'-harp.** [appar. jocular in orig., as it is not a harp and has no connection with the Jews]

Jew's-harp (Ab. 3 in.)

Jezebel (jĕzʹə bl), *n.* **1.** the wife of Ahab, king of Israel, notorious for her conduct. I Kings 16:31, 21:25, II Kings, 9:30–37. **2.** a shameless, abandoned woman.

Jezreel (jĕz rēlʹ), *n.* **Plain of,** Esdraelon.

Jhansi (jänʹsĭ), *n.* a town in India, in SW Uttar Pradesh. 140,217 (1961).

Jhelum (jēʹləm), *n.* a river flowing from S Kashmir into the river Chenab in Pakistan. ab. 450 mi.

JHVH. See **Tetragrammaton.** Also, **JHWH.**

jib[1] (jĭb), *n.* *Naut.* **1.** a triangular sail (or either of two triangular sails, **inner jib** and **outer jib**) set in front of the forward (or single) mast. See illus. under **sail.** **2.** any of certain similar sails set beyond the jib proper, as a **flying jib.** **3.** **cut of one's jib,** *Colloq.* one's general appearance. [? akin to GIBBET]

jib[2] (jĭb), *v.i.*, *v.t.*, **jibbed, jibbing.** gybe.

jib[3] (jĭb), *v.*, **jibbed, jibbing,** *n.* —*v.i.* **1.** to move restively sideways or backwards instead of forwards, as an animal in harness; balk. **2.** to hold back or balk at doing something. **3.** **jib at,** be reluctant; show unwillingness. —*n.* **4.** an animal that jibs. [orig. uncert.] —**jibʹber,** *n.*

jib[4] (jĭb), *n.* the projecting arm of a crane; the boom of a derrick. [appar. short for GIBBET]

jib boom, *Naut.* a spar forming a continuation of a bowsprit. See illus. under **bowsprit.**

jib door, a door built flush with the wall in order to be as inconspicuous as possible.

jibe[1] (jīb), *v.*, **jibed, jibing,** *n.* gybe.

jibe[2] (jīb), *v.t.*, *v.i.*, **jibed, jibing,** *n.* gibe. —**jibʹer,** *n.*

jibe[3] (jīb), *v.i.*, **jibed, jibing.** *U.S. Colloq.* to agree; be in harmony or accord. [orig. uncert.]

Jibuti (jĭ bo͞oʹtĭ), *n.* Djibouti.

Jidda (jĭdʹə), *n.* the seaport of Mecca in W Saudi Arabia, on the Red Sea. 150,000 (est. 1965). Also, **Jedda.**

jiffy (jĭfʹĭ), *n.*, *pl.* **-fies.** *Colloq.* a very short time: *to do something in a jiffy.* Also, **jiff.** [orig. unknown]

jig[1] (jĭg), *n.*, *v.*, **jigged, jigging.** —*n.* **1.** a device for holding the work in a machine tool, esp. one for accurately guiding a drill or group of drills so as to ensure uniformity in successive pieces machined. **2.** a device used in fishing, esp. a hook or collection of hooks loaded with metal or having a spoon-shaped piece of bone or other material attached, for drawing through the water. **3.** an apparatus for separating ore from gangue, etc., by shaking in or treating with water. —*v.t.* **4.** to treat, cut, or produce by using any of the mechanical contrivances called jigs. —*v.i.* **5.** to use a jig (mechanical contrivance). [var. of GAUGE. Cf. E *jeg* kind of gauge]

jig[2] (jĭg), *n.*, *v.*, **jigged, jigging.** —*n.* **1.** a rapid, lively, springy, irregular dance for one or more persons, usually in triple rhythm. **2.** a piece of music for, or in the rhythm of, such a dance. **3.** *Obs.* a jest, prank, or a trick. **4.** **the jig is up,** the game is up; there is no further chance. —*v.t.* **5.** to dance (a jig or any lively dance). **6.** to sing or play in the time or rhythm of a jig. **7.** to move with a jerky or bobbing motion; jerk up and down or to and fro. —*v.i.* **8.** to dance or play a jig. **9.** to move with a quick, jerky motion; hop; bob. [appar. var. of JOG, v.] —**jigʹlikeʹ,** *adj.*

jigger[1] (jĭgʹə), *n.* **1.** one who or that which jigs. **2.** *Naut.* **a.** the lowest square sail on a jiggermast. **b.** a jiggermast. **c.** light tackle used about the deck of a ship. **3.** any of various mechanical devices, many of which have a jerky or jolting motion. **4.** a jig for separating ore. **5.** a jig for fishing. **6.** *Golf.* a club (No. 4 iron). **7.** *Billiards.* a bridge. **8.** *U.S.* **a.** a $1\frac{1}{2}$ oz. measure used in cocktail recipes. **b.** a small measure of whisky. [f. JIG[1] + -ER[1]]

jigger[2] (jĭgʹə), *n.* a chigoe.

jiggered (jĭgʹəd), *adj.* *Slang.* a word used as a vague substitute for a taboo word: *I'm jiggered if I know.*

jiggermast (jĭgʹə mästʹ), *n.* *Naut.* the fourth mast of a sailing ship. Also, **jigger.**

jiggery-pokery (jĭgʹə rĭ pōʹkə rĭ), *n.* *Colloq.* dishonest dealing; trickery.

jiggle (jĭgʹl), *v.*, **-gled, -gling,** *n.* —*v.t.*, *v.i.* **1.** to move up and down or to and fro with short, quick jerks. —*n.* **2.** a jiggling movement. [freq. of JIG[2]]

jigsaw (jĭgʹsôʹ), *n.* **1.** a narrow saw mounted vertically in a frame, used for cutting curves, etc. **2.** a jigsaw puzzle.

jigsaw puzzle (jĭgʹsôʹ), small, irregularly shaped pieces of wood or cardboard, which, when correctly fitted together, form a picture.

jihad (jĭ hădʹ), *n.* **1.** a holy war waged by Muslims against unbelievers as a religious duty. **2.** any vigorous campaign on behalf of a principle, etc. Also, **jehad.** [t. Ar.: effort, strife]

Jilolo (jĭ lōʹlō), *n.* Halmahera.

jilt (jĭlt), *v.t.* **1.** to cast off (a lover or sweetheart) after encouragement or engagement. —*n.* **2.** a woman who jilts a lover. [orig. uncert.] —**jiltʹer,** *n.*

Jim Crow (jĭmʹkrōʹ), *U.S.* **1.** (in contemptuous use) Negro. **2.** a practice or policy of segregating Negroes, as in public places, public transport, etc. **3.** (*l.c.*) a tool for bending or straightening railway lines. —**Jim-Crow, jim-crow,** *adj.*

Jiménez (*Sp.* KHē mĕʹnĕth), *n.* **Juan Ramón** (*Sp.* KHwän rä mônʹ), 1881–1958, Spanish poet.

Jiménez de Cisneros (*Sp.* KHē mĕʹnĕth dĕ thēz nĕʹrôs), **Francisco** (*Sp.* frän thēsʹkō), 1436–1517, Spanish cardinal and statesman. Also, **Ximenes, Ximenez.**

jiminy (jĭmʹĭ nĭ), *interj.* (a mild exclamation of surprise.) [alter. of L *Jesu, Domine!* Jesus, Lord!]

jimjams (jĭmʹjămzʹ), *n. pl.* *Slang.* **1.** extreme nervousness. **2.** delirium tremens.

jimmy (jĭmʹĭ), *n.*, *pl.* **-mies,** *v.*, **-mied, -mying.** *U.S.* jemmy.

jimson weed (jĭmʹsən), one of the thorn-apples, *Datura stramonium*, a coarse herb with white flowers and very poisonous leaves, widespread in the Northern Hemisphere. Also, **Jimson weed.** [alter. of *Jamestown weed*; named after *Jamestown*, in Virginia, U.S.A.]

jingal (jĭngʹgl), *n.* a large musket fired from a rest, often mounted on a carriage: formerly used in India, China, etc. Also, **gingal, gingall.** [t. Hind.: m. *janjāl*]

jingle (jĭngʹgl), *v.*, **-gled, -gling,** *n.* —*v.i.* **1.** to make clinking or tinkling sounds, as coins, keys, etc., when struck together repeatedly. **2.** to move or proceed with such sounds. **3.** to sound in a manner suggestive of this, as verse or any sequence of words: *a jingling ballad.* **4.** to make rhymes. —*v.t.* **5.** to cause to jingle. —*n.* **6.** a clinking or tinkling sound, as of small bells or of small pieces of metal struck together repeatedly. **7.** something that makes such a sound, as a small bell or a metal pendant. **8.** a musical succession of like sounds, as in rhyme or alliteration, without particular regard for sense; jingling verse. **9.** a piece of such verse. **10.** (in Ireland and Australia) a covered two-wheeled carriage. [ME *gynglen*, appar. imit.; but cf. D *jengelen*] —**jin′glingly,** *adv.* —**jin′gly,** *adj.*

Jingling Johnny, *Music, U.S.* a crescent (def. 6).

jingo (jĭng′gō), *n., pl.* **-goes,** *adj.* —*n.* **1.** one who boasts of his country's preparedness for war, or who favours an aggressive foreign policy; a chauvinist. **2.** (orig.) a Conservative supporter of Disraeli's Near Eastern policy (1877–78). **3.** *Colloq.* a word used in vehement asseveration in the phrase 'by jingo!' —*adj.* **4.** of jingoes. **5.** characterized by jingoism. [orig. uncert.; first used in conjurer's jargon]

jingoism (jĭng′gō ĭz′əm), *n.* the spirit, policy, or practices of jingoes. —**jin′goist,** *n., adj.* —**jin′gois′tic,** *adj.*

Jinja (jĭn′jə), *n.* a town in Uganda, on the N shore of Lake Victoria. 29,741 (1959).

jinker (jĭng′kə), *n. Austral.* a wheeled conveyance for logs.

jinks (jĭngks), *n.pl. Colloq.* romping games or play; boisterous, unrestrained merrymaking, esp. in the phrase *high jinks.* [cf. d. *chink* to gasp, der. OE *cincung* hearty laughter]

jinn (jĭn), *n.pl., sing.* **jinee. 1.** *Islamic Myth.* a class of spirits lower than the angels, capable of appearing in human and animal forms, and influencing mankind for good and evil. **2.** (*construed as sing. with pl.* **jinns**) a spirit of this class. Also, **djinn.** [t. Ar., pl. of *jinnī* a demon. Cf. GENIE]

Jinnah (jĭn′ə), *n.* **Mohammed Ali** (mō hăm′ĭd ä′lĭ), 1876–1948, Muslim leader in India: governor-general of Pakistan 1947–48.

jinrikisha (jĭn rĭk′shô, -shə), *n.* rickshaw.

Jinsen (jĭn′sĕn′), *n.* Japanese name of **Inchon.**

jinx (jĭngks), *n. Colloq.* a person, thing, or influence supposed to bring bad luck. [var. of *jynx*, t. L: m. *iynx*, t. Gk: bird (wryneck) used in witchcraft, hence, a spell]

jitney (jĭt′nĭ), *n., pl.* **-neys,** *v.,* **-neyed, -neying.** *U.S.* —*n.* **1.** *Colloq.* a motor car which carries passengers, orig. each for a fare of five cents. **2.** *Slang.* a five-cent piece. —*v.t., v.i.* **3.** to carry or ride in a jitney.

jitter (jĭt′ə), *Colloq.* —*n.* **1.** (*pl.*) nervousness; nerves (usually prec. by *the*). **2.** *Electronics.* the rapid fluctuation of a signal caused by instability in a circuit. —*v.i.* **3.** to behave nervously. [var. of *chitter* shiver. Cf. CHATTER]

jitterbug (jĭt′ə bŭg′), *n., v.,* **-bugged, -bugging.** —*n.* **1.** a vigorous dance, popular in the 1940s, performed mainly to boogie-woogie and swing music. **2.** one who dances the jitterbug. **3.** one who is nervous or easily flustered. —*v.i.* **4.** to dance the jitterbug.

jittery (jĭt′ə rĭ), *adj.* nervous; jumpy.

jiujitsu (jo͞o jĭt′so͞o), *n.* jujitsu. Also, **jiujutsu.**

jive (jīv), *n., v.,* **jived, jiving.** —*n.* **1.** *U.S.* jargon used by jazz musicians. **2.** a dance performed to beat music. —*v.i.* **3.** to dance to beat music. [orig. unknown]

JJ., 1. Judges. **2.** Justices.

Jno., John.

jo (jō), *n., pl.* **joes.** *Scot.* sweetheart. Also, **joe.** [var. of JOY]

Joachim (*Ger.* yō′ä KHĭm), *n.* **Joseph** (*Ger.* yō′zĕf), 1831–1907, Hungarian violinist and composer.

Joad (jōd), *n.* **Cyril** (**Edwin Mitchinson**), 1891–1953, English writer, broadcaster, and philosopher.

Joan (jōn), *n.* **1.** mythical female pope about A.D. 855–858. **2.** ('*Fair Maid of Kent*') 1328–85, wife of Edward, the Black Prince, and mother of Richard II.

joannes (jō ăn′ēz), *n., pl.* **-nes.** johannes.

Joan of Arc ('*Maid of Orléans*'), 1412–31, French heroine who aroused the spirit of nationalism in France against the English and was burnt by them as a witch. In 1920 she was canonized. Also, *French,* **Jeanne d'Arc.**

job[1] (jŏb), *n., v.,* **jobbed, jobbing,** *adj.* —*n.* **1.** a piece of work; an individual piece of work done in the routine of one's occupation or trade. **2.** a piece of work of defined character undertaken for a fixed price. **3.** anything one has to do. **4.** *Colloq.* a situation, or post of employment. **5.** *Colloq.* an affair, matter, occurrence, or state of affairs: *to make the best of a bad job.* **6.** the unit or material being worked upon. **7.** the product or result. **8.** a piece of public or official business carried through with a view to improper private gain. **9.** *Colloq.* a difficult task. **10.** *Slang.* a theft or robbery, or any criminal deed. **11. a good job,** *Colloq.* a lucky state of affairs. **12. just the job,** *Colloq.* exactly what is required. **13. on the job,** *Slang.* **a.** busy; occupied. **b.** *Taboo.* engaged in intercourse. —*v.i.* **14.** to work at jobs, or odd pieces of work; do piecework. **15.** to do business as a jobber (def. 2). **16.** to turn public business, etc., improperly to private gain. —*v.t.* **17.** to buy in large quantities and sell to dealers in smaller lots. **18.** to let out (work) in separate portions, as among different contractors or workmen. —*adj.* **19.** of or for a particular job or transaction. **20.** bought or sold together; lumped together: used chiefly in the phrase *job lot.* [orig. uncert.] —**job′less,** *adj.* —**job′lessness,** *n.* —**Syn. 4.** See **position.**

job[2] (jŏb), *v.t., v.i.,* **jobbed, jobbing,** *n.* jab. [ME *jobbe(n)*; ? imit. Cf. JAB]

Job (jōb), *n.* **1.** the much-afflicted hero of an Old Testament book who showed exemplary piety in the face of undeserved suffering. **2.** the book itself. [ult. t. Heb.: m. *Iyyōbh*]

jobber (jŏb′ə), *n.* **1.** a wholesale merchant, esp. one selling to retailers. **2.** a dealer in stock exchange securities. Cf. **broker. 3.** a pieceworker. **4.** one who practises jobbery.

jobbery (jŏb′ə rĭ), *n.* the practice of making improper private gains from public or official business.

jobbing (jŏb′ĭng), *n.* **1.** piecework. **2.** the practice of dealing in stock exchange securities. **3.** jobbery.

job costing, a type of costing in which costs are recorded against each individual job or order.

job lot, 1. any large lot of goods handled by a jobber. **2.** a miscellaneous quantity of goods.

Job's comforter, one who professes to give comfort but who achieves the opposite result.

Job's-tears (jōbz′tĭəz′), *n.pl.* **1.** the hard, nearly globular involucres which surround the female flowers in a species of grass, *Coix lacryma-jobi,* and which when ripe are used as beads. **2.** (*construed as sing., l.c.*) the grass itself, native in Asia but cultivated elsewhere.

Jocasta (jō kăs′tə), *n. Gk Legend.* the wife of Laius, and the mother, and later the wife, of Oedipus.

Jock (jŏk), *n.* nickname for a Scot.

jockey (jŏk′ĭ), *n., pl.* **-eys,** *v.,* **-eyed, -eying.** —*n.* **1.** one who professionally rides horses in races. —*v.t.* **2.** to ride (a horse) as a jockey. **3.** to bring, put, etc., by skilful manoeuvring. **4.** to trick or cheat. **5.** to manipulate trickily. —*v.i.* **6.** to aim at an advantage by skilful manoeuvring (often fol. by *for*). **7.** to act trickily; seek an advantage by trickery. [dim. of *Jock*, Scot. var. of *Jack*] —**jock′eyship′,** *n.*

jockey club, an association for the regulation and promotion of thoroughbred horseracing.

jocko (jŏk′ō), *n., pl.* **-os. 1.** the chimpanzee. **2.** (*cap.*) a familiar name for any monkey. [t. F, from W Afr. name of the chimpanzee, recorded as *engeco, ncheko*]

jockstrap (jŏk′străp′), *n.* a supporter for the genitals worn by male athletes, dancers, etc.

jocose (jə kōs′), *adj.* given to or characterized by joking; jesting; humorous; playful. [t. L: m. s. *jocōsus*] —**jocose′ly,** *adv.* —**jocose′ness,** *n.* —**Syn.** See **jovial.**

jocosity (jō kŏs′ĭ tĭ), *n., pl.* **-ties. 1.** the state or quality of being jocose. **2.** joking or jesting. **3.** a joke or jest.

jocular (jŏk′yo͞o lə), *adj.* given to, characterized by, intended for, or suited to joking or jesting; waggish; facetious. [t. L: s. *joculāris*] —**joc′ularly,** *adv.* —**Syn.** See **jovial.**

jocularity (jŏk′yo͞o lă′rĭ tĭ), *n., pl.* **-ties. 1.** the state or quality of being jocular. **2.** jocular speech or behaviour. **3.** a jocular remark or act.

jocund (jŏk′ənd), *adj.* cheerful; merry; gay; blithe; glad. [ME, t. LL: s. *jocundus* pleasant] —**joc′undly,** *adv.* —**Syn.** See **jovial.**

jocundity (jō kŭn′dĭ tĭ), *n., pl.* **-ties. 1.** the state of being jocund; gaiety. **2.** a jocund remark or act.

Jodhpur (jŏd′po͝oə′), *n.* **1.** Also, **Marwar.** a former state in NW India, now in Rajasthan. **2.** a town in India, in W central Rajasthan. 224,760 (1961).

jodhpurs (jŏd′pəz), *n.pl.* riding breeches reaching to the ankle, and fitting closely from the knee down, worn also in sports, etc. [named after JODHPUR]

Jodrell Bank (jŏd′rəl băngk′), the site, in Cheshire, of a large radio telescope operated by Manchester University.

joe (jō), *n.* jo.

Joe (jō), *n. U.S. Colloq.* a G.I.

Joel (jō′əl), *n.* a Hebrew prophet of the postexilian period, second among the Minor Prophets in the prophetic canon. [ult. t. Heb.: m. *Yō'ēl*]

joey (jō′ĭ), *n., pl.* **-eys.** *Austral.* **1.** any young animal, esp. a kangaroo. **2.** a young child. [t. native Australian: m. *joè*]

Joffre (*Fr.* zhŏ′fr), *n.* **Joseph Jacques Césaire** (*Fr.* zhō zĕf zhák sė zĕr′), 1852–1931, French general in World War I.

jog[1] (jŏg), *v.*, **jogged, jogging,** *n.* —*v.t.* **1.** to move or shake with a push or jerk. **2.** to give a slight push to, as to arouse the attention; nudge. **3.** to stir up by hint or reminder: *to jog a person's memory.* —*v.i.* **4.** to move with a jolt or jerk. **5.** to go or travel with a jolting pace or motion. **6.** to go in a steady or humdrum fashion (fol. by *on* or *along*). —*n.* **7.** a shake; a slight push; a nudge. **8.** a slow, steady walk, trot, etc. **9.** the act of jogging. [b. *jot* jolt and *shog* shake (both now d.)] —**jog′ger,** *n.*

jog[2] (jŏg), *n.* *Chiefly U.S.* an irregularity of line or surface; a projection; a notch. [var. of JAG[1]]

joggle (jŏg′l), *v.*, **-gled, -gling,** *n.* —*v.t.* **1.** to shake slightly; move to and fro as by repeated jerks. **2.** to join or fasten by a joggle or joggles. —*v.i.* **3.** to move irregularly; have a jogging or jolting motion; shake. —*n.* **4.** the act of joggling. **5.** a slight shake; a jolt. **6.** a moving with jolts or jerks. **7.** a projection on one of two joining surfaces, or a notch on the other, to prevent slipping. [freq. of JOG[1]]

Jogjakarta (jŏg′jə kä′tə; *Indon.* jŏg jä kär′tä), *n.* a city in Indonesia, in S Java. 289,400 (1957). Also, **Jokyakarta.**

jogtrot (jŏg′trŏt′), *n.*, *v.*, **-trotted, -trotting.** —*n.* **1.** a slow, regular, jolting pace, as of a horse. **2.** a routine or humdrum mode of procedure. —*v.i.* **3.** to move at a jogtrot.

johannes (jō hăn′ēz), *n.*, *pl.* **-nes.** a Portuguese gold coin of King John (João) V (who reigned 1706–50). Also, **joannes.** [t. NL and ML, var. of LL *Jōannes.* See JOHN]

Johannesburg (jō hăn′ĭs bûg′), *n.* a city in the Republic of South Africa, in S Transvaal: goldmines. with suburbs, 1,152,525 (1960). See map under **South Africa.**

Johannisberger (jō hăn′ĭs bû′gə), *n.* a type of Rhine wine.

john (jŏn), *n.* *Chiefly U.S. Slang.* lavatory.

John (jŏn), *n.* **1.** the Apostle John, to whom is attributed the authorship of the fourth Gospel, three Epistles, and the Book of Revelation. **2.** the fourth Gospel, in the New Testament. **3.** one of the three Epistles of John, referred to as 1, 2, and 3 John. **4.** John the Baptist. Mark 1:4, etc. **5.** any of several characters with this name in the Bible. **6.** name of twenty-three popes. **7.** (*John Lackland*), 1167?–1216, king of England 1199–1216, who signed the Magna Carta in 1215. **8. Augustus Edwyn,** 1879–1961, Welsh painter and etcher. [ME *Iohan* John, OE *Iohannis*, t. ML: m. *Jōhannes*, LL *Jōannes*, t. Gk: m. *Iōánnēs*, t. Heb.: m. *Yōhānān*, lit., Jehovah hath been gracious]

John I (′*the Great*′), 1357–1433, king of Portugal 1385–1433.

John III (*John Sobieski*), 1624–96, king of Poland 1674–96.

John XXIII (*Angelo Giuseppe Roncalli*), 1881–1963, Italian ecclesiastic; pope 1958–63.

John Barleycorn, a facetious personification of barley as used in the brewing of beer.

John Birch Society, an extreme right-wing organization founded in 1958 with the object of combating alleged communist activities in the U.S. [named after *John Birch*, died 1945, U.S. airman]

John Bull, **1.** the English people. **2.** the typical Englishman. [after *John Bull*, the chief character in '*The History of John Bull*' (1712) by John Arbuthnot]

John Doe, a fictitious character in legal proceedings.

John Dory (dô′rĭ), a thin, deep-bodied marine fish, *Zeus faber*, with spiny plates along the base of the dorsal and anal fins. Also, **John Doree.** [f. JOHN + DORY[2] (*doree*), the name of the fish]

Johne's disease (yō′nəz), *Vet. Sci.* a chronic diarrhoeal disease of cattle and sheep caused by infection with an organism related to the tubercle bacillus. [named after H. A. *Johne*, 1839–1910, German scientist]

John F. Kennedy International Airport, the international airport for New York, on SW Long Island. Formerly, **Idlewild.**

johnnycake (jŏn′ĭ kāk′), *n.* *U.S.* a kind of cake or bread made of maize meal, and water or milk. [orig. obscure. The first element may be from obs. *jonakin, jonikin* (appar. of Indian origin) a form of thin griddlecake]

John of Austria ('*Don John*'), 1547–78, Spanish naval commander and general: victor at the battle of Lepanto.

John of Gaunt (gônt). See **Gaunt.**

John of Leyden (lī′dn), 1509?–36, Dutch Anabaptist.

John of Salisbury, died 1180, English ecclesiastic and scholar.

John of the Cross, Saint (*Juan de Yepis y Álvarez*), 1542–91, Spanish mystic: with Saint Theresa founder of the discalced Carmelites. Spanish, **San Juan de la Cruz** (*Sp.* sän KHwän′ dė lä kro͞oth′).

John o'Groat's House (ə grōts′), a place at the northern tip of Scotland, often appearing in the phrase *from Land's End to John o'Groats.*

Johns Hopkins, a men's private university in Baltimore, U.S.A., founded in 1876.

Johnson (jŏn′sən; *Ger.* yón′zŏn *for def.6*), *n.* **1. Amy,** 1904–41, English airwoman. **2. Andrew,** 1808–75, 17th president of the U.S. 1865–69. **3. Lyndon Baines** (lĭn′dən bānz′), born 1908, 36th president of the U.S., 1963–69. **4. Philip,** born 1906, U.S. architect. **5. Samuel** (*Dr Johnson*), 1709–84, English lexicographer, critic, and conversationalist. **6. Uwe** (*Ger.* o͞o′və), born 1934, German author.

Johnsonese (jŏn′sə nēz′), *n.* a literary style characterized by pompous phraseology and many words of Latin origin. [so called from the style of Samuel JOHNSON]

Johnsonian (jŏn sō′nyən), *adj.* of, pertaining to, or characteristic of Samuel Johnson.

Johnston (jŏn′stən), *n.* **1. Albert Sidney,** 1803–62, Confederate general in the American Civil War. **2. Joseph Eggleston** (ĕg′l stən), 1807–91, Confederate general in the American Civil War.

Johnstone (jŏn′stən), *n.* a burgh in Scotland, in Renfrewshire. 18,369 (1961).

Johnstown (jŏnz′toun′), *n.* a town in the U.S., in SW Pennsylvania: disastrous flood, 1889. 53,949 (1960).

John the Baptist, forerunner of Jesus. Matt. 3.

Johore (jō hô′), *n.* a state in Malaysia, on S Malay Peninsula. 1,144,731 pop. (est. 1963); 7330 sq. mi.

Johore Bahru (jō hô′ bä′ro͞o), a town in Malaysia, the capital of Johore, in the S part. 74,909 (1957).

joie de vivre (*Fr.* zhwȧd vē′vr), *French.* joy of living.

join (join), *v.t.* **1.** to bring or put together, in contact or connection. **2.** to come into contact, connection, or union with: *the brook joins the river.* **3.** to bring together in relation, purpose, action, coexistence, etc.: *to join forces.* **4.** to become a member of (a society, party, etc.); enlist in (one of the armed forces). **5.** to come into the company of: *I'll join you later.* **6.** to unite in marriage. **7.** to meet or engage in (battle, conflict, etc.). **8.** to adjoin: *his land joins mine.* **9.** *Geom.* to draw a curve or straight line between. —*v.i.* **10.** to come into or be in contact or connection, or form a junction. **11.** to become united, associated, or combined; associate or ally oneself (fol. by *with*). **12.** to take part with others (often fol. by *in*). **13.** to be contiguous or close; lie or come together; form a junction. **14.** to enlist in one of the armed forces (often fol. by *up*). **15.** *Obs.* to meet in battle or conflict. —*n.* **16.** joining. **17.** a place or line of joining; a seam. [ME *join(en)*, t. OF: m. *joindre*, g. L *jungere* join, yoke] —**join′able,** *adj.*

—**Syn. 1.** link, couple, fasten, attach; conjoin, combine; associate; consolidate, amalgamate. JOIN, CONNECT, UNITE all imply bringing two or more things together more or less closely. JOIN may refer to a connection or association of any degree of closeness, but often implies direct contact: *one joins the corners of a mortise together.* CONNECT implies a joining as by a tie, link, wire, etc.: *one connects two batteries.* UNITE implies a close joining of two or more things so as to form one: *one unites layers of veneer sheets to form plywood.*

joinder (join′də), *n.* **1.** the act of joining. **2.** *Law.* **a.** the joining of causes of action in a suit. **b.** the joining of parties in a suit. **c.** the acceptance by a party to an action of an issue tendered. [t. F: m. *joindre* JOIN]

joiner (joi′nə), *n.* **1.** one who or that which joins. **2.** a craftsman who works in wood already cut and shaped; a worker in wood who constructs the fittings of a house, furniture, etc.

joinery (joi′nə rĭ), *n.* **1.** the art or trade of a joiner. **2.** a joiner's work or his product.

joint (joint), *n.* **1.** the place or part in which two things, or parts of one thing, are joined or united, either rigidly or so as to admit of motion; an articulation. **2.** (in an animal body) **a.** the movable place or part where two bones or two segments join. **b.** the hingelike or other arrangement of such a part. **3.** *Biol.* **a.** a portion, esp. of an animal or plant body, connected with another portion by an articulation, node, or the like. **b.** a portion between two articulations, nodes, or the like. **4.** *Bot.* the part of a stem from which a branch or a leaf grows; a node. **5.** one of the portions into which a carcass is divided by a butcher, esp. one ready for cooking. **6.** *Geol.* a fracture plane in rocks, generally at right angles to the bedding of sedimentary rocks and variously oriented in igneous and metamorphic rocks, commonly arranged in two or more sets of parallel intersecting systems. **7.** *Slang.* **a.** a disreputable bar, restaurant, or nightclub. **b.** any resort or abode. **8. out of joint, a.** dislocated. **b.** out of order; in a bad state. [ME *iointe*, t. OF: m. *joint, jointe* (n. use of pp. of *joindre* JOIN), g. L *junctus, juncta*, prop. pp. of *jungere*]

—*adj.* **9.** shared by or common to two or more. **10.** sharing or acting in common. **11.** joined or associated, as in relation, interest, or action: *joint owners.* **12.** held, done, etc., by two or more in conjunction or in common: *a joint effort.* **13.** *Law.* joined together in obligation or ownership. **14.** *Parl. Proc.* of or pertaining to both branches of a bicameral legislature. **15.** (of a diplomatic action) in which two or more governments are formally united. —*v.t.* **16.** to unite by a joint or joints. **17.** to form or provide with a joint or joints. **18.** to divide at a joint, or separate into pieces. **19.** to prepare (a board, etc.) for fitting in a joint. **20.** to fill up (the joints of stone, interstices in brickwork, etc.) with mortar. [ME, t. OF, pp. of *joindre* JOIN]

joint account, a bank account kept in the names of two or more persons or parties and subject to withdrawals by any one of them.

jointed (join′tĭd), *adj.* **1.** provided with joints. **2.** formed with knots or nodes.

jointer (join′tə), *n.* **1.** one who or that which joints. **2.** a bricklayer's tool used for putting a surface finish on a mortar joint. **3.** *Carp.* a plane for smoothing edges to be joined.

joint ill, *Vet. Sci.* a disease of young foals (horses) characterized by swollen inflamed joints, high fever, and, usually, by death a few days after birth.

jointing (join′tĭng), *n.* **1.** the operation of making joints. **2.** any material used for making a joint between two surfaces pressure-tight, as asbestos, rubber, etc.

jointly (joint′lĭ), *adv.* together; in common.

jointress (join′trĭs), *n.* a woman entitled to a jointure.

joint stock, stock or capital divided into a number of shares.

joint-stock company (joint′stŏk′), a company whose ownership is divided into transferable shares, the object usually being the division of profits among the members in proportion to the number of shares held by each.

jointure (join′chə), *n. Law.* **1.** an estate or property settled on a woman in consideration of marriage, and to be enjoyed by her after her husband's decease. **2.** *Obs.* a joint tenancy limited in favour of a man and his wife. [ME, t. F, g. L *junctūra* a joining]

Joinville (*Fr.* zhwăɴ vēl′), *n.* **Jean de** (*Fr.* zhäɴ′də), *c.* 1224–*c.* 1319, French chronicler.

joist (joist), *n.* **1.** any of the parallel lengths of timber, steel, etc., used for supporting floors, ceilings, etc. —*v.t.* **2.** to furnish with or fix on joists. [ME *giste,* t. OF, der. *gesir* lie, rest, g. L *jacēre* lie; akin to GIST] —**joist′less,** *adj.*

A, Joist; B, Floorboards

Jokai (*Hung.* yô′koi), *n.* **Maurus** (*Hung.* mou′ro͝os) or **Mór** (*Hung.* môr), 1825–1904, Hungarian author.

joke (jōk), *n., v.,* **joked, joking.** —*n.* **1.** something said or done to excite laughter or amusement; a playful or mischievous trick or remark. **2.** an amusing or ridiculous circumstance. **3.** an object of joking or jesting; a thing or person laughed at rather than taken seriously. **4.** a matter for joking about; trifling matter: *the loss was no joke.* —*v.i.* **5.** to speak or act in a playful or merry way. **6.** to say something in mere sport, rather than in earnest. [t. L: m. s. *jocus* jest, sport] —**joke′less,** *adj.* —**jok′ingly,** *adv.*

—**Syn. 1.** witticism, jape; quip, quirk, sally. JOKE, JEST refer to something said (or done) in sport, or to cause amusement. A JOKE is something said or done for the sake of exciting laughter; it may be raillery, a witty remark, or a prank or trick: *to tell a joke.* JEST, today a more formal word, nearly always refers to joking language and is more suggestive of scoffing than is JOKE: *to speak in jest.*

joker (jō′kə), *n.* **1.** one who jokes. **2.** an extra playing card in a pack, used in some games, often counting as the highest card or to represent a card of any denomination or suit the holder wishes. **3.** *Slang.* a fellow or chap. **4.** *Slang.* a hidden clause in any paper, document, etc., which largely changes its apparent nature.

Jokyakarta (jōk′yə kä′tə), *n.* Jogjakarta.

Joliet (jō′lĭ ĕt′; *Fr.* zhō lyĕ′ *for 1 also*), *n.* **1.** Also, **Jolliet, Louis** (*Fr.* lwē), 1645–1700, French explorer. **2.** a town in the U.S., in NE Illinois. 66,780 (1960).

Joliot-Curie (jŏl′ĭ ō kyo͞oə′rĭ; *Fr.* zhō lyō kʏ rē′), *n.* **1. Irène** (*Fr.* ē rĕn′) (*Irène Curie*), 1897–1956, French nuclear physicist (daughter of Pierre and Marie Curie). **2.** her husband, **(Jean) Fréderic** (*Fr.* zhäɴ frè dė rĕk′) (*Jean Frédéric Joliot*), 1900–58, French nuclear physicist.

jollification (jŏl′ĭ fĭ kā′shən), *n.* jolly merrymaking; a jolly festivity. [f. JOLLY, adj. + -FICATION]

jollify (jŏl′ĭ fī′), *v.t., v.i.,* **-lified, -lifying.** *Colloq.* to make or be jolly or merry.

jollity (jŏl′ĭ tĭ), *n., pl.* **-lities. 1.** jolly state, mood, or proceedings. **2.** (*pl.*) jolly festivities.

jolly (jŏl′ĭ), *adj.,* **-lier, -liest,** *v.,* **-lied, -lying,** *n., pl.* **-lies,** *adv.* —*adj.* **1.** in good spirits, gay: *in a moment he was as jolly as ever.* **2.** cheerfully festive or convivial. **3.** *Colloq.* amusing; pleasant. **4.** joyous, glad. —*v.t.* **5.** *Colloq.* to talk or act agreeably to (a person) in order to keep him in good humour, esp. with the purpose of gaining something (often fol. by *along*); cajole; flatter. —*n.* **6.** *Colloq.* a bit of agreeable talk or action to put a person in good humour. —*adv.* **7.** *Colloq.* extremely; very: *jolly well.* [ME *joli(f),* t. OF, ? ult. of Gmc orig.; cf. Icel. *jōl* YULE] —**jol′lily,** *adv.* —**jol′liness,** *n.* —**Syn. 1, 2.** merry, sportive, playful. See **gay.**

jolly-boat (jŏl′ĭ bōt′), *n.* a ship's work boat, smaller than a cutter, hoisted at the stern of a sailing vessel for handy use.

Jolly Roger (rŏj′ə), the pirates' flag.

Jolo (hō lō′), *n.* **1.** one of the Philippine Islands, in the SW part: the main island of the Sulu Archipelago. 137,471 pop. (est. 1958); 345 sq. mi. **2.** a seaport on this island. 22,396 (est. 1959).

jolt (jōlt), *v.t., v.i.* **1.** to jar or shake as by a sudden rough thrust; shake up roughly, as in passing over an uneven road. —*n.* **2.** a jolting shock or movement. [b. *jot* jolt and obs. *joll* knock about] —**jolt′er,** *n.*

jolty (jōl′tĭ), *adj.* full of jolts; uneven; bumpy.

Jonah (jō′nə), *n.* **1.** a Hebrew prophet who for his impiety was thrown overboard from his ship to allay a tempest. He was swallowed by a large fish and lived in its belly three days before he was vomited up. **2.** a book of the Old Testament bearing his name. **3.** any person regarded as bringing bad luck. Also, **Jonas** (jō′nəs).

Jonas (*Ger.* yō′näs), *n.* **Franz** (*Ger.* frants), born 1899, president of Austria since 1965.

Jonathan (jŏn′ə thən), *n.* **1.** son of Saul, and friend of David. 1 Sam. 13, etc. **2. Joseph Leabua** (lĕə′bo͞oə), born 1914, prime minister of Lesotho since 1965. **3.** *Hort.* a variety of red apple that matures in early autumn. **4.** *Archaic.* a generic nickname for Americans, or, esp., New Englanders (often prefaced by *Brother*). [ult. t. Heb.: m. *Yonāthān*]

Jones (jōnz), *n.* **1. Casey** (kā′sĭ) (*John Luther Jones*), ?1864–1900, U.S. train driver whose heroic death in a train crash inspired popular songs about him. **2. Daniel,** 1881–1967, English phonetician. **3. Henry Arthur,** 1851–1929, English dramatist. **4. Inigo** (ĭn′ĭ gō′), 1573–1652, English architect. **5. John Paul,** 1747–92, American naval commander in the War of American Independence, born in Scotland.

Jongkind (*Du.* yông′kĭnt), *n.* **Johan Barthold** (*Du.* yō hōn′ bŏr′tōlt), 1819–91, Dutch landscape and marine painter.

jongleur (zhŏng glû′; *Fr.* zhôɴ glœr′), *n.* (in medieval France and Norman England) an itinerant minstrel or entertainer who sang songs (sometimes of his own composition), and told stories. [t. F, b. OF *jogleor* and *jangler* JANGLE. See JUGGLER]

Jönköping (*Sw.* yœnt′shœ pēng), *n.* a town in S Sweden. 52,732 (1964).

jonquil (jŏng′kwĭl), *n.* a species of narcissus, *Narcissus jonquilla,* with long, narrow, rushlike leaves and fragrant yellow or white flowers. [t. F: m. *jonquille,* t. Sp.: m. *junquillo,* dim. of *junco,* g. L *juncus* a rush]

Jonson (jŏn′sən), *n.* **Ben,** 1573?–1637, English dramatist and poet.

Joppa (jŏp′ə), *n.* ancient name of **Jaffa.**

Jordaens (*Flem.* yôr däns′), *n.* **Jacob** (*Flem.* yä′kôp), 1593–1678, Flemish painter.

jordan (jô′dn), *n. Archaic.* a chamber-pot.

Jordan (jô′dn), *n.* **1.** official name, **Hashemite Kingdom of Jordan.** a country in SW Asia, consisting of what was formerly Trans-Jordan and a part of Palestine. 1,935,440 pop. (est. 1964); 37,264 sq. mi. *Cap.:* Amman. **2.** a river flowing from S Lebanon through the Sea of Galilee and S between Israel and Jordan, then through W Jordan into the Dead Sea. ab. 200 mi.

Jordan

Jordan almond, a large, hard-shelled type of Spanish almond. [ME *jardyne* (t. F: m. *jardin* garden) *almaunde,* i.e. garden almond. See ALMOND]

jorum (jô′rəm), *n.* a large bowl or vessel for holding drink, or its contents: *a jorum of punch.* [said to be named after *Joram,* who brought to David vessels of silver, gold, and brass. See 2 Sam. 8:10]

Joseph (jō′zĭf), *n.* **1.** a Hebrew patriarch, the first son of Jacob by Rachel. His brothers sold him into slavery in

Egypt. Gen. 30:22–24, Gen. 37. **2.** the husband of Mary, the mother of Jesus. Matt. 1:16–25. **3.** (*l.c.*) a long cloak with a cape, worn chiefly in the 18th century, esp. by women. [ult. t. Heb.: m. *Yōsēph*]

Joseph II. See **Franz Josef II.**

Joseph Bonaparte Gulf, an indentation of the Timor Sea on the coast of Australia between Western Australia and Northern Territory. ab. 180 mi. across.

Josephine (jō′zĭ fēn′), *n.* (*Joséphine de Beauharnais*) 1763–1814, first wife of Napoleon Bonaparte.

Joseph of Arimathaea (ăr′ĭ mĭ thē′ə), a rich Israelite who laid the body of Jesus in the tomb. Matt. 27:57–60.

Josephus (jō sē′fəs), *n.* **Flavius** (flā′vyəs), A.D. 37?–c. 100, Jewish historian and general.

josh (jŏsh), *U.S. Slang.* —*v.t., v.i.* **1.** to chaff; banter in a teasing way. —*n.* **2.** a chaffing remark; a piece of banter. [? var. of d. *joss* jostle] —**josh′er,** *n.*

Josh., Joshua.

Joshua (jŏsh′wə), *n.* **1.** the successor of Moses as leader of the Israelites. Exodus 17:9–14. **2.** a book of the Old Testament. [ult. t. Heb.: m. *Yehōshūa'*]

Joshua tree, a tree, *Yucca brevifolia*, growing in arid or desert regions of the south-western U.S. See **yucca.**

joss (jŏs), *n.* a Chinese deity or idol. [pidgin English, t. Pg.: m. *deos*, g. L *deus* god]

joss house, a Chinese temple for idol worship.

joss stick, a slender stick of a dried fragrant paste, burnt by the Chinese as incense, etc.

jostle (jŏs′əl), *v.*, **-tled, -tling,** *n.* —*v.t.* **1.** to strike or push roughly or rudely against; elbow roughly; hustle. **2.** to drive or force by or as by pushing or shoving. —*v.i.* **3.** to collide (fol. by *with*) or strike or push (fol. by *against*) as in passing or in a crowd; push or elbow one's way rudely. **4.** to strive as with collisions, rough pushing, etc., for room, place, or any advantage. —*n.* **5.** a collision, shock, or push. Also, **justle.** [ME *justil*, freq. of *just* JOUST] —**jos′tlement,** *n.* —**jos′tler,** *n.*

jot (jŏt), *n., v.*, **jotted, jotting.** —*n.* **1.** the least part of something; a little bit: *I don't care a jot.* —*v.t.* **2.** to write or mark down briefly (usually fol. by *down*). [t. L: m. *iōta* IOTA]

jota (hō′tə; *Sp.* KHō′tä), *n., pl.* **-tas** (*Sp.* -täs). a fast and lively Spanish dance in triple time, usually performed with castanets.

jotter (jŏt′ə), *n.* **1.** one who jots things down. **2.** a small notebook.

jotting (jŏt′ĭng), *n.* **1.** the act of one who jots. **2.** something jotted down; a brief note or memorandum.

Jotun (yō′to͝on), *n.* *Scand. Myth.* one of a supernatural race of giants. Also, **Jotunn, Jötunn** (*Norw.* yœ′to͝on). [Icel., prop. *jötunn*, c. OE *eoten* giant]

Jotunheim (yō′to͝on hām′), *n.* *Scand. Myth.* the outer world, or realm of giants; Utgard. Also, **Jotunnheim, Jötunnheim** (*Norw.* yœ′to͝on hĕym). [Icel.]

Joubert (zho͞o′bĕə), *n.* **General Petrus Jacobus** (pĕt′rəs jə kō′bəs), 1831–1900, South African soldier and statesman.

joule (jo͞ol), *n.* *Physics.* the derived SI unit of work or energy, defined as the work done when the point of application of a force of one newton is displaced through a distance of one metre in the direction of the force; equal to 10^7 ergs, one watt-second, or approximately 0·74 foot-pounds. *Symbol:* J [named after J. P. JOULE]

Joule (jo͞ol), *n.* **James Prescott,** 1818–89, English physicist.

Joule's law, *Physics.* **1.** the principle that internal energy of a given mass of gas is independent of its volume or pressure and depends only on its temperature. **2.** the principle that the heat produced by an electric current is equal to the product of the resistance of the circuit through which it is passing, the square of the current, and the time for which it flows. [named after J.P. JOULE]

Joule-Thomson effect, *Physics.* the change of temperature exhibited by a gas when it is expanded through a small hole or a porous plug. Also, **Joule-Kelvin effect.** [named after J.P. JOULE and Sir William THOMSON]

jounce (jouns), *v.*, **jounced, jouncing,** *n.* —*v.i., v.t.* **1.** to move violently up and down; bounce. —*n.* **2.** a jouncing movement. [? b. obs. *joll* knock about and BOUNCE]

jour., journal.

Jourdan (*Fr.* zho͞or däN′), *n.* **Jean Baptiste** (*Fr.* zhäN bä tēst′), **Count,** 1762–1833, French marshal.

journal (jû′nəl), *n.* **1.** a daily record, as of occurrences, experiences, or observations; diary. **2.** a register of the daily transactions of a public or legislative body. **3.** a newspaper, esp. a daily one. **4.** any periodical or magazine, esp. one published by a learned society. **5.** *Bookkeeping.* **a.** a daybook. **b.** (in double entry) a book in which all transactions are entered (from the daybook or blotter) in systematic form, to facilitate posting into the ledger. **6.** *Naut.* a log or logbook. **7.** *Mach.* that part of a shaft or axle in actual contact with a bearing. [ME, t. OF, g. LL *diurnālis* DIURNAL]

journalese (jû′nə lēz′), *n.* the style of writing or expression (considered inferior to that of conventional literary work) supposed to characterize newspapers.

journalism (jû′nə lĭz′əm), *n.* **1.** the occupation of writing for, editing, and conducting newspapers and other periodicals. **2.** newspapers collectively.

journalist (jû′nə lĭst), *n.* one engaged in journalism.

journalistic (jû′nə lĭs′tĭk), *adj.* of, pertaining to, or characteristic of journalists or journalism. —**jour′nalis′tically,** *adv.*

journalize (jû′nə līz′), *v.*, **-lized, -lizing.** —*v.t.* **1.** to enter or record in a journal. **2.** to tell or relate, as done in a journal. **3.** (in double-entry bookkeeping) to systematize and enter in a journal, preparatory to posting to the ledger. —*v.i.* **4.** to keep or make entries in a journal. Also, **journalise.**

journey (jû′nĭ), *n., pl.* **-neys,** *v.*, **-neyed, -neying.** —*n.* **1.** a course of travel from one place to another, esp. by land. **2.** a distance travelled, or suitable for travelling, in a specified time: *a day's journey.* —*v.i.* **3.** to make a journey; travel. [ME *jorney*, t. OF: m. *jornee* a day's time, ult. der. L *diurnus* of the day, daily] —**jour′neyer,** *n.* —**Syn. 1.** excursion, jaunt; tour; expedition; pilgrimage. See **trip.**

journeyman (jû′nĭ mən), *n., pl.* **-men. 1.** one who has served his apprenticeship at a trade or handicraft, and who works at it for another. **2.** *Obs.* one hired to do work for another, usually for a day. [f. *journey* a day's work (obs.) + MAN]

journeywork (jû′nĭ wûk′), *n.* **1.** the work of a journeyman. **2.** routine work; hackwork.

joust (joust), *n.* **1.** a combat in which two armoured knights or men-at-arms on horseback opposed each other with lances. **2.** (*pl.*) a tournament. —*v.i.* **3.** to contend in a joust or tournament. Also, **just.** [ME *j(o)uste(n)*, t. OF: m. *j(o)uster*, ult. der. L *juxtā* near] —**joust′er,** *n.*

Jove (jōv), *n.* **1.** Jupiter. **2.** *Poetic.* the planet Jupiter. **3. by Jove,** a mild oath. [t. L: m. s. *Jovis.* See JUPITER]

jovial (jō′vyəl), *adj.* **1.** endowed with or characterized by a hearty, joyous humour or a spirit of good fellowship. **2.** (*cap.*) of or pertaining to the god Jove or Jupiter. [t. L: s. *Joviālis* of Jupiter (in astrology the planet is regarded as exerting a happy influence)] —**jo′vially,** *adv.* —**jo′vialness,** *n.*

—**Syn. 1.** merry, jolly, convivial, gay. JOVIAL, JOCOSE, JOCULAR, JOCUND agree in referring to someone who is in a good humour. JOVIAL suggests a hearty, joyous humour: *a jovial person.* JOCOSE refers to that which causes laughter, it suggests someone who is playful and given to jesting: *with jocose and comical airs.* JOCULAR means humorous, facetious, mirthful, and waggish: *jocular enough to keep up the spirits of all around him.* JOCUND, now a literary word, suggests a cheerful, light-hearted, and sprightly gaiety: *glad and jocund company.* —**Ant. 1.** saturnine, morose, gloomy, staid.

joviality (jō′vĭ ăl′ĭ tĭ), *n.* the state or quality of being jovial; merriment; jollity.

Jovian (jō′vyən), *n.* (*Flavius Claudius Jovianus*), A.D. c. 332–64, Roman emperor A.D. 363–64.

Jovian (jō′vyən), *adj.* **1.** of the god Jupiter. **2.** of the planet Jupiter.

Jowett (jou′ĭt), *n.* **Benjamin,** 1817–93, English scholar.

jowl[1] (joul), *n.* **1.** a jaw, esp. the underjaw. **2.** the cheek. [ME *chawl, chavel*, OE *ceafl* jaw; akin to D *kevel* gum, d. G *Kiefer* jaw, chap, Icel. *kjaptr* mouth, jaw]

jowl[2] (joul), *n.* **1.** a fold of flesh hanging from the jaw, as of a fat person. **2.** the dewlap of cattle. **3.** the wattle of fowls. [ME *cholle*, appar. der. OE *ceole* throat]

joy (joi), *n.* **1.** an emotion of keen or lively pleasure arising from present or expected good; exultant satisfaction; great gladness; delight. **2.** a source or cause of gladness or delight: *a thing of beauty is a joy for ever.* **3.** a state of happiness or felicity. **4.** the manifestation of glad feeling; outward rejoicing; festive gaiety. —*v.i.* **5.** to feel joy; be glad; rejoice. —*v.t.* **6.** *Obs.* to gladden. [ME *joie*, t. OF, g. L *gaudia*, pl. of *gaudium* joy, gladness] —**Syn. 1.** rapture. **3.** bliss. See **pleasure.**

joyance (joi′əns), *n.* *Archaic.* joyous feeling; gladness.

Joyce (jois), *n.* **1. James (Augustine Aloysius),** 1882–1941, Irish author. **2. William** (*'Lord Haw-Haw'*), 1906–46, British traitor, executed for his Nazi propaganda radio broadcasts. —**Joy′cean,** *adj.*

joyful (joi′fəl), *adj.* **1.** full of joy, as a person, the heart, etc.; glad; delighted. **2.** showing or expressing joy, as looks, actions, speech, etc. **3.** causing or bringing joy, as an event, a sight, news, etc.; delightful. —**joy′fully,** *adv.* —**joy′fulness,** *n.* —**Syn. 1.** joyous, happy, blithe; buoyant, elated, jubilant. See **gay.**

joyless (joi′lĭs), *adj.* **1.** destitute of joy or gladness. **2.** causing no joy or pleasure. —**joy′lessly,** *adv.* —**joy′lessness,** *n.* —**Syn. 1.** sad, cheerless; gloomy, dismal.

joyous (joiʹəs), *adj.* joyful. **—joyʹously,** *adv.* **—joyʹousness,** *n.*

joy-ride (joiʹrīdʹ), *n., v.,* **-ride, -riding.** *Colloq.* **—***n.* **1.** a pleasure ride, as in a motor car, esp. when the car is driven recklessly or used without the owner's permission. **—***v.i.* **2.** to take such a ride. **—joyʹ-riʹder,** *n.* **—joyʹ-ridʹing,** *n., adj.*

joystick (joiʹstĭkʹ), *n. Aeron.* the control stick of an aeroplane.

JP, jet propulsion.

J.P., Justice of the Peace.

Jr, Junior. Also, **jr**

Juan de Fuca (jo͞oʹən dĭ fyo͞oʹkə; *Sp.* KHwänʹ dė fo͞oʹkä), a strait between Vancouver island and NW Washington. ab. 100 mi. long; 15–20 mi. wide.

Juan Fernández (jo͞oʹən fə nănʹdĕz; *Sp.* KHwänʹ fĕr nänʹdĕth), a group of three islands in the S Pacific, ab. 400 miles W of and belonging to Chile: Alexander Selkirk, the supposed prototype of 'Robinson Crusoe', was marooned here, 1704.

Juárez (*Sp.* KHwäʹrĕth), *n.* **1. Benito Pablo** (*Sp.* bė nĕʹtō päʹblō), 1806–72, president of Mexico 1853–63, and 1867–72. **2. Ciudad.** See **Ciudad Juárez.**

juba (jo͞oʹbə), *n.* a lively dance developed by plantation Negroes of the U.S.

Juba (jo͞oʹbə), *n.* a river flowing from S Ethiopia S through the Somali Republic to the Indian Ocean. ab. 1000 mi.

Jubal (jo͞oʹbl), *n. Bible.* son of Lamech by Adah, and purported inventor of musical instruments. Gen. 4:21.

jubbah (jo͝obʹə), *n.* a kind of long outer garment with sleeves, worn in Muslim countries. [t. Ar.]

Jubbulpore (jŭbʹl po͝oəʹ), *n.* Jabalpur.

jube (jo͞oʹbĭ), *n. Archit.* **1.** a screen with an upper platform, separating the choir of a church from the nave and often supporting a rood. **2.** a rood loft. [t. L: bid thou, the first word of a formula spoken from the gallery above the rood screen]

jubilant (jo͞oʹbĭ lənt), *adj.* **1.** jubilating; rejoicing; exultant. **2.** expressing or exciting joy; manifesting or denoting exultation or gladness. [t. L: s. *jūbilans,* ppr.] **—juʹbilance, juʹbilancy,** *n.* **—juʹbilantly,** *adv.*

jubilate (jo͞oʹbĭ lātʹ), *v.i.,* **-lated, -lating. 1.** to manifest or feel great joy; rejoice; exult. **2.** to celebrate a jubilee or joyful occasion. [t. L: m. s. *jūbilātus,* pp. of *jūbilāre* shout for joy] **—jubilatory** (jo͞oʹbĭ lə tə rĭ, -trĭ), *adj.*

Jubilate (jo͞oʹbĭ läʹtĭ), *n.* **1.** the 100th Psalm (99th in the Vulgate), used as a canticle in the Anglican liturgy. **2.** the third Sunday **(Jubilate Sunday)** after Easter (when the 66th psalm, 65th in the Vulgate, is used as the introit). **3.** a musical setting of this psalm. [t. L: shout ye, the first word of both psalms in the Vulgate]

jubilation (jo͞oʹbĭ lāʹshən), *n.* **1.** the act of jubilating; rejoicing; exultation. **2.** a joyful or festive celebration.

jubilee (jo͞oʹbĭ lēʹ), *n.* **1.** the celebration of any of certain anniversaries, as the 25th **(silver jubilee),** 50th **(golden jubilee),** or 60th or 75th **(diamond jubilee). 2.** the completion of the 50th year of any continuous course or period, as of existence or activity, or its celebration. **3.** *Rom. Cath. Ch.* an appointed year (or other period) now ordinarily every 25th year, in which remission from the penal consequences of sin is granted upon repentance and the performance of certain religious acts. **4.** (among the ancient Hebrews) a year to be observed every 50th year (see Lev. 25), and to be announced by the blowing of trumpets, during which the fields were to be left untilled, alienated lands to be restored, and Hebrew bondmen to be set free. **5.** any season or occasion of rejoicing or festivity. **6.** rejoicing or jubilation. [ME *jubile,* t. F, t. LL: m. s. *jūbilaeus,* t. Gk: m. *iōbēlaîos,* der. Heb. *yōbēl* ram, ram's horn (used as a trumpet; cf. Lev. 25:9)]

Jud., 1. Judges. **2.** Judith (Apocrypha).

Judaea (jo͞o dĭəʹ), *n.* Judea. **—Judaeanʹ,** *adj., n.*

Judah (jo͞oʹdə), *n.* **1.** the fourth son of Jacob and Leah. Gen. 29:35, etc. **2.** the powerful tribe of his descendants. **3.** an ancient kingdom in S Palestine, including the tribes of Judah and Benjamin. *Cap.:* Jerusalem. See **Israel.** [ult. t. Heb.: m. *Yehūdāh*]

Judaic (jo͞o dāʹĭk), *adj.* **1.** of or pertaining to Judaism. **2.** of or pertaining to the Jews; Jewish. [t. L: s. *Jūdaicus,* t. Gk: m. *Ioudaïkós*]

Judaism (jo͞oʹdā ĭzʹəm), *n.* the religion of the Jews, deriving its authority from the precepts of the Old Testament and the teaching of the rabbis as expounded in the Talmud. It is founded on belief in the one and only God, who is transcendent, the creator of all things, and the source of all righteousness, and in the duty of all Jews to bear witness to this belief.

Judaist (jo͞oʹdā ĭst), *n.* **1.** an adherent of Judaism. **2.** a Jewish Christian in the early Christian Church who followed or advocated Jewish rites or practices. **—Juʹdaisʹtic,** *adj.*

Judaize (jo͞oʹdā īzʹ), *v.,* **-ized, -izing. —***v.i.* **1.** to conform to Judaism in any respect; adopt or affect the manners or customs of the Jews. **—***v.t.* **2.** to bring into conformity with Judaism. Also, **Judaise. —Juʹdaizaʹtion,** *n.* **—Juʹdaizʹer,** *n.*

Judas (jo͞oʹdəs), *n.* **1.** Judas Iscariot, the disciple who betrayed Jesus. Mark 3:19. **2.** one treacherous enough to betray a friend; traitor. **3.** one of the twelve apostles (not Judas Iscariot). Luke 6:16; Acts 1:13; John 14:22. **4.** (*usually l.c.*) Also, **judas hole.** a peephole in a door. **—Juʹdas-likeʹ,** *adj.*

Judas Maccabaeus. See **Maccabaeus.**

Judas tree, 1. a purple-flowered leguminous European and Asiatic tree, *Cercis siliquastrum,* supposed to be the kind upon which Judas hanged himself. **2.** any of various other trees of the same genus, as the redbud.

judder (jŭdʹə), *v.i.* **1.** to vibrate; shake. **—***n.* **2.** a shaking; vibration. [b. JUMP and SHUDDER]

Jude (jo͞od), *n.* a short book, of the New Testament, written by a 'brother of James' (and possibly of Jesus).

Judea (jo͞o dĭəʹ), *n.* the S part of Palestine under the Romans. Also, **Judaea.** See map under **Jericho.**

Judean (jo͞o dĭənʹ), *adj.* **1.** relating to Judea. **—***n.* **2.** a native or inhabitant of Judea. Also, **Judaean.** [f. m. s. L *Jūdaeus* (see JEW) + -AN]

Judg., Judges.

judge (jŭj), *n., v.,* **judged, judging. —***n.* **1.** a public officer authorized to hear and determine causes in a court of law; a magistrate charged with the administering of justice. **2.** a person appointed to decide in any competition or contest; an authorized arbiter. **3.** one qualified to pass a critical judgement: *a judge of horses.* **4.** an administrative head of Israel in the period between Joshua's death and Saul's accession. **—***v.t.* **5.** to try (a person or a case) as a judge does; pass sentence on or in. **6.** to form a judgement or opinion of or upon; decide upon critically; estimate. **7.** to decide or decree judicially or authoritatively. **8.** to infer, think, or hold as an opinion. **9.** (of the Hebrew judges) to govern. **—***v.i.* **10.** to act as a judge; pass judgement. **11.** to form an opinion or estimate. **12.** to make a mental judgement. [ME *juge,* t. OF, g. L *jūdex*] **—judgʹer,** *n.* **—judgeʹless,** *adj.* **—judgeʹlikeʹ,** *adj.* **—judgeʹshipʹ,** *n.*

—Syn. 1. justice. **2.** arbitrator. JUDGE, REFEREE, UMPIRE refer to one who is entrusted with decisions affecting others. JUDGE, in its legal and other uses, implies particularly that one has qualifications and authority for giving decisions in matters at issue: *a judge appointed to the law court.* A REFEREE usually examines and reports on the merits of a case as an aid to a court. An UMPIRE gives the final ruling when arbitrators of a case disagree. **3.** connoisseur, critic. **8.** conclude; consider, deem, regard. See **think**[1]. **10.** adjudge, adjudicate.

judge advocate, *Mil.* an officer appointed to sum up the evidence at an Army or Royal Air Force court martial and to direct the court on questions of law.

judge advocate general, *Mil.* a civilian official, the chief legal officer of the Army and the Royal Air Force, charged with the administration of justice.

judgement (jŭjʹmənt), *n.* **1.** the act of judging. **2.** *Law.* **a.** the judicial decision of a cause in court. **b.** the obligation, esp. a debt, arising from a judicial decision. **c.** the certificate embodying such a decision. **3.** ability to judge justly or wisely, esp. in matters affecting action; good sense; discretion. **4.** the forming of an opinion, estimate, notion, or conclusion, as from circumstances presented to the mind. **5.** the opinion formed. **6.** a misfortune regarded as inflicted by divine sentence, as for sin. **7.** (*often cap.*) the final trial of all mankind, both the living and the dead, at the end of the world (often, **Last Judgement).** Also, **judgment. —Syn. 2.** a verdict, decree. **3.** understanding; discrimination, discernment, perspicacity; sagacity.

Judgement Day, (*sometimes l.c.*) the day of God's final judgement of mankind at the end of the world; doomsday.

Judges (jŭjʹĭz), *n.* a book of the Old Testament, containing the history of Israel under the leaders (judges) from Deborah to Samuel.

judicable (jo͞oʹdĭ kə bl), *adj.* **1.** capable of being judged or tried. **2.** liable to be judged or tried.

judicative (jo͞oʹdĭ kə tĭv), *adj.* having ability to judge; judging: *the judicative faculty.*

judicator (jo͞oʹdĭ kāʹtə), *n.* one who acts as judge or sits in judgement. [t. LL]

judicatory (jo͞oʹdĭ kāʹtə rĭ), *adj., n., pl.* **-tories. —***adj.* **1.** of or pertaining to judgement or the administration of justice: *judicatory power.* **—***n.* **2.** a court of justice; a tribunal. **3.** the administration of justice. [t. LL: m. s. *jūdicātōrius*]

judicature (jo͞oʹdĭ kə chə), *n.* **1.** the administration of justice, as by judges or courts. **2.** the office, function, or authority of a judge. **3.** the extent of jurisdiction of a judge or court. **4.** a body of judges. **5.** the power of administering justice by legal trial and determination. [t. ML: m. s. *jūdicātūra*, der. *jūdicātus*, pp., judged]

judiciable (jo͞o dĭsh′yə bl), *adj.* capable of being judged or tried.

judicial (jo͞o dĭsh′əl), *adj.* **1.** pertaining to judgement in courts of justice or to the administration of justice: *judicial proceedings.* **2.** pertaining to courts of law or to judges: *judicial functions.* **3.** of or pertaining to a judge; proper to the character of a judge; judgelike. **4.** inclined to make or give judgements; critical; discriminating. **5.** decreed, sanctioned, or enforced by a court: *a judicial separation.* **6.** pertaining to judgement or decision in a dispute or contest: *a judicial duel.* **7.** inflicted by God as a judgement or punishment. [ME, t. L: s. *jūdiciālis* of a court of justice] —**judi′cially,** *adv.* —**Syn. 4.** See **judicious.**

judiciary (jo͞o dĭsh′yə rĭ, -dĭsh′ə rĭ), *adj., n., pl.* **-aries.** —*adj.* **1.** pertaining to judgement in courts of justice, or to courts or judges; judicial. —*n.* **2.** the judicial branch of government. **3.** the system of courts of justice in a country. **4.** the judges collectively.

judicious (jo͞o dĭsh′əs), *adj.* **1.** using or showing judgement as to action or practical expediency; discreet, prudent, or politic. **2.** having, exercising, or showing good judgement; wise, sensible, or well-advised: *a judicious selection.* [t. F: m. *judicieux*, der. L *jūdicium* judgement] —**judi′ciously,** *adv.* —**judi′ciousness,** *n.*

—**Syn. 1.** See **practical. 2.** JUDICIOUS, JUDICIAL both refer to a balanced and wise judgement. JUDICIOUS implies the possession and use of discerning and discriminating judgement: *a judicious use of one's time.* JUDICIAL has connotations of judgements made in a courtroom, and refers to a fair and impartial kind of judgement: *cool and judicial in examining the facts.* —**Ant. 1.** unwise.

Judith (jo͞o′dĭth), *n.* **1.** an apocryphal book of the Old Testament. **2.** its heroine, who delivered her people by entering the camp of Holofernes and slaying him in his sleep. [ult. t. Heb.: m. *yehūdhīth* the Jewess]

judo (jo͞o′dō), *n.* a style of self-defence derived from jujitsu, employing less violent methods and emphasizing the sporting element. [t. Jap.: lit., soft art]

judoka (jo͞o′dō kä′), *n.* a competitor in a judo contest. [t. Jap.]

Judy (jo͞o′dĭ), *n.* **1.** the wife of Punch in the puppet show called 'Punch and Judy'. **2.** (*l.c.*) *Slang.* a woman, or girl. [familiar var. of *Judith*, woman's name]

jug (jŭg), *n., v.,* **jugged, jugging.** —*n.* **1.** a vessel in various forms for holding liquids, commonly having a handle, often a spout or lip, and sometimes a lid. **2.** the contents of any such vessel. **3.** *U.S.* a deep vessel, usually of earthenware, with a handle and a narrow neck stopped by a cork. **4.** *Slang.* a prison or jail. —*v.t.* **5.** to put into a jug. **6.** to stew or boil (meat) in a jug or jar. **7.** *Slang.* to commit to jail, or imprison. [? special use of *Jug*, hypocoristic var. of *Joan* or *Joanna*, woman's name]

jugal (jo͞o′gl), *adj.* of or pertaining to the cheek or the cheekbone. [t. L: s. *jugālis*, der. *jugum* a yoke]

jugal bone, 1. (in man) the cheekbone. **2.** a corresponding bone in animals.

jugate (jo͞o′gāt, -gĭt), *adj. Bot.* having the leaflets in pairs, as a pinnate leaf. [t. L: m. s. *jugātus*, pp., joined]

Jugendstil (*Ger.* yo͞o′gən shtēl, -stēl), *n.* See **Art Nouveau.**

jugged hare (jŭgd), hare stewed, as in a stone pot.

Juggernaut (jŭg′ə nôt′), *n.* **1.** Also, **Jagannath, Jagannatha.** an idol of Krishna at Puri in Orissa, India, annually drawn on an enormous car under whose wheels devotees are said to have thrown themselves to be crushed. **2.** (*often l.c.*) anything to which a person blindly devotes himself, or is cruelly sacrificed. **3.** (*often l.c.*) any large, relentless, destructive force. [t. Hind.: m. *Jagannāth*, g. Skt *Jagannātha* lord of the world]

juggins (jŭg′ĭnz), *n. Colloq.* a simpleton; naive person; fool. [orig. surname]

juggle (jŭg′l), *v.,* **-gled, -gling,** *n.* —*v.t.* **1.** to keep (several objects, as balls, plates, knives) in continuous motion in the air at the same time by tossing and catching. **2.** to manipulate or alter by artifice or trickery: *to juggle accounts.* —*v.i.* **3.** to perform feats of manual or bodily dexterity, such as tossing up and keeping in continuous motion a number of balls, plates, knives, etc. **4.** to use artifice or trickery. —*n.* **5.** the act of juggling; a trick; a deception. [ME *jogel(en)*, t. OF: m. *jogler*, g. L *joculārī* jest]

juggler (jŭg′lə), *n.* **1.** one who performs juggling feats, as with balls, knives, etc. **2.** one who deceives by trickery; a trickster. [ME *jugelour*, *jogeler*, t. OF: m. *jogleor*, g. L *joculātor* jester]

jugglery (jŭg′lə rĭ), *n., pl.* **-gleries. 1.** the art or practice of a juggler. **2.** the performance of juggling feats. **3.** any trickery or deception.

juglandaceous (jo͞o′glăn dā′shəs), *adj.* belonging to the *Juglandaceae*, or walnut family of trees. [f. s. L *jūglans* walnut + -ACEOUS]

Jugoslav (yo͞o′gō släv′), *n., adj.* Yugoslav. Also, **Jugo-Slav.** —**Jugoslavic** (yo͞o′gō slăv′ĭk), *adj.*

Jugoslavia (yo͞o′gō slä′vyə), *n.* Yugoslavia. —**Ju′gosla′vian,** *adj., n.*

jugular (jŭg′yo͞o lə), *adj.* **1.** *Anat.* **a.** of or pertaining to the throat or neck. **b.** denoting or pertaining to any of certain large veins of the neck, esp. one (**external jugular vein**) collecting blood from the superficial parts of the head, or one (**internal jugular vein**) receiving blood from within the skull. **2.** (of a fish) having the pelvic fins at the throat, before the pectoral fins. —*n.* **3.** *Anat.* a jugular vein. [t. NL: m. *jugulāris*, der. L *jugulum* collarbone, throat, dim. of *jugum* a yoke]

jugulate (jŭg′yo͞o lāt′), *v.t.,* **-lated, -lating. 1.** to check or suppress (disease, etc.) by extreme measures. **2.** to cut the throat of; kill. **3.** to strangle. [t. L: m. s. *jugulātus*, pp., slain] —**jug′ula′tion,** *n.*

Jugurtha (jo͞o gû′thə), *n.* died 104 B.C., king of Numidia 112?–104 B.C.

juice (jo͞os), *n.* **1.** the liquid part of plant or animal substance. **2.** any natural fluid secreted by an animal body. **3.** any extracted liquid, esp. from a fruit. **4.** essence; strength. **5.** *Slang.* **a.** electric power. **b.** petrol, fuel oil, etc., used to run an engine. [ME *jus*, t. OF, g. L: broth] —**juice′less,** *adj.*

juicy (jo͞o′sĭ), *adj.,* **-cier, -ciest. 1.** full of juice; succulent. **2.** interesting; vivacious; colourful; spicy. —**juic′ily,** *adv.* —**juic′iness,** *n.*

jujitsu (jo͞o jĭt′so͞o), *n.* a Japanese method of defending oneself without weapons in personal encounter, which employs the strength and weight of the opponent to overcome him. Also, **jiujitsu, jiujutsu, jujutsu.** [t. Jap.: soft (or pliant) art]

juju (jo͞o′jo͞o), *n.* (among native tribes of western Africa). **1.** some object venerated superstitiously and used as a fetish or amulet. **2.** the magical power attributed to such an object. **3.** a ban or interdiction effected by it. [t. Hausa]

jujube (jo͞o′jo͞ob), *n.* **1.** the edible plumlike fruit of any of certain Old World trees of the genus *Zizyphus.* **2.** any tree producing this fruit. **3.** a small sweet-flavoured lozenge. [t. F, t. ML: m. *jujuba*, t. LL: m. *zīzyphum*, t. Gk: m. *zízyphon*]

jukebox (jo͝ok′bŏks′), *n.* a coin-operated record-player permitting selection of the record to be played. [f. *juke* (t. Gullah: wicked, bawdy, as in *juke house* brothel) + BOX[1]]

jukskei (yo͝ok′skā), *n. S African.* a team game involving the throwing of a club. [Afrikaans: yoke]

Jul., July.

julep (jo͞o′lĭp), *n.* **1.** a sweet drink, variously prepared and sometimes medicated. **2.** *U.S.* mint julep. [ME, t. OF, t. Ar.: m. *julāb*, t. Pers.: m. *gulāb* rosewater, julep]

Julian (jo͞o′lyən), *n.* (*'the Apostate', Flavius Claudius Julianus*), A.D. 331–363, Roman emperor A.D. 361–363.

Julian (jo͞o′lyən), *adj.* of or pertaining to Julius Caesar.

Juliana (jo͞o′lĭ ä′nə; *Du.* yʏ lē ȧ′nȧ), *n.* (*Juliana Louise Emma Marie Wilhelmina*), born 1909, queen of the Netherlands since 1948.

Julian Alps, a mountain range in NW Yugoslavia. Highest peak, Mt Triglav, 9394 ft.

Julian calendar, the calendar established by Julius Caesar in 46 B.C. which fixed the length of the year at 365 days, with 366 days in every fourth year (leap year), and months similar to today's. Cf. **Gregorian calendar.**

julienne (jo͞o′lĭ ĕn′; *Fr.* zhʏ lyĕn′), *adj.* **1.** (of vegetables) cut into thin strips or small pieces. —*n.* **2.** a clear soup containing vegetables cut into thin strips or small pieces. [t. F, special use of *Julienne*, woman's name]

Julius Caesar (jo͞o′lyəs sē′zə). See **Caesar** (def. 1).

Jullundur (jŭl′ən də), *n.* a town in India, in central Punjab. 222,569 (1961).

July (jo͞o lī′), *n., pl.* **-lies.** the seventh month of the year, containing 31 days. [ME *Julie*, OE *Julius*, t. L; named after JULIUS Caesar, who was born in this month]

jumble (jŭm′bl), *v.,* **-bled, -bling,** *n.* —*v.t.* **1.** to mix in a confused mass; put or throw together without order. **2.** to muddle or confuse mentally. —*v.i.* **3.** to meet or come together confusedly; be mixed up. —*n.* **4.** a confused mixture; a medley. **5.** a state of confusion or disorder. **6.** Also, **jumbal.** a small, flat, sweet cake, usually round, with a hole in the middle. [? b. JOIN and TUMBLE] —**jum′bler,** *n.* —**Syn. 5.** muddle, hotchpotch; farrago; mess; chaos. —**Ant. 5.** order.

jumble sale, a sale of cheap miscellaneous articles, generally second-hand, in aid of charity.

jumbo (jŭm′bō), *n., pl.* **-bos,** *adj. Colloq.* —*n.* **1.** an elephant. **2.** a big, clumsy person, animal, or thing. —*adj.* **3.** very large. [named after *Jumbo*, an elephant at the London Zoo, subsequently sold to Phineas T. Barnum]

jumbuck (jŭm′bŭk′), *n. Austral. Colloq.* a sheep. [Aborigine corruption of *jump up*]

Jumet (*Fr.* zhʏ mĕ′), *n.* a town in SW Belgium. 28,903 (est. 1964).

Jumna (jŭm′nə), *n.* a river in N India, flowing from the Himalayas SE to the Ganges at Allahabad. 860 mi.

jump (jŭmp), *v.i.* **1.** to spring clear of the ground or other support by a sudden muscular effort; propel oneself forwards, backwards, upwards or downwards; leap. **2.** to move or go quickly: *she jumped into a taxi.* **3.** to rise suddenly or quickly: *he jumped from his chair.* **4.** to move suddenly or abruptly, as from surprise or shock; start: *the sudden noise made him jump.* **5.** *Draughts.* to capture an opponent's man by moving over it to an unoccupied square. **6.** to rise suddenly in amount, price, etc. **7.** to pass abruptly, ignoring intervening stages: *to jump to a conclusion.* **8.** to change suddenly: *the traffic lights jumped from green to red.* **9.** to move or change suddenly, haphazardly, or aimlessly: *she kept jumping from one thing to another without being able to concentrate.* **10.** (of a typewriter) to omit letters, etc., because of a defect. **11.** *Colloq.* (of a wound, etc.) to hurt; throb. **12.** *Contract Bridge.* to bid exceptionally and unnecessarily high in order to indicate additional strength. **13.** (of a computer) to leave the sequence of instructions in a program and start obeying a different sequence elsewhere in the program. **14. jump at,** accept eagerly; seize: *he jumped at the chance of a new job.* **15. jump on, upon,** to scold; rebuke; reprimand. **16. jump to it,** *Colloq.* to move quickly; hurry. —*v.t.* **17.** to leap or spring over: *to jump a stream.* **18.** to cause to jump or leap. **19.** to skip or pass over; bypass. **20.** (of a motor vehicle) to ignore or anticipate (a traffic light). **21.** *Chess.* to capture (an opponent's man) by moving over it to an unoccupied square. **22.** *U.S. Colloq.* to attack suddenly without warning. **23.** *Bridge.* to raise (the bid) by more than the necessary overcall. **24.** to abscond from, or evade by absconding: *to jump one's bail.* **25.** to seize or occupy (a mining claim, etc.) on the ground of some flaw in the holder's title. **26.** (of a train) to spring off or leave (the track). **27.** *Taboo Slang.* to have sexual intercourse with. **28. jump the gun,** *Colloq.* to start prematurely; obtain an unfair advantage. **29. jump the queue,** to overtake a queue; obtain something out of one's proper turn.
—*n.* **30.** the act of jumping; a leap. **31.** a space or obstacle or apparatus cleared in a leap. **32.** a descent by parachute from an aeroplane. **33.** a sudden rise in amount, price, etc. **34.** a sudden upward or other movement of an inanimate object. **35.** an abrupt transition from one point or thing to another, with omission of what intervenes. **36.** *U.S. Colloq.* a head start in time or space; advantageous beginning. **37.** *Sport.* any of several athletic games which feature a leap or jump. **38.** *Films.* a break in the continuity of action due to a failure to match action between a long shot and a closer shot of the same scene. **39.** a sudden start, as from nervous excitement. **40.** (*pl.*) a physical condition characterized by such starts; restlessness; anxiety. **41.** *Taboo Slang.* an act of coitus. [appar. imit.]
—**Syn.** **1.** spring, bound; skip, hop. JUMP, LEAP, VAULT imply propelling oneself by a muscular effort of the legs, either into the air or from one position or place to another. JUMP and LEAP are often used interchangeably, but JUMP indicates more particularly the springing movement of the feet in leaving the ground or support: *to jump up and down.* LEAP (which formerly also meant to run) indicates the passage, by a springing movement, from one point or position to another: *to leap across a brook.* VAULT implies leaping over or upon something: *to vault (over) a fence.*

jump ball, *Basketball.* a ball tossed between two opposing players by the referee.

jump bid, *Bridge.* any bid which is higher than that needed to increase the bid made previously.

jump cut, *Films.* a sudden change from one scene to another designed to produce a startling effect.

jumped-up (jŭmpt′ŭp′), *adj. Colloq.* upstart; parvenu; conceited.

jumper[1] (jŭm′pə), *n.* **1.** one who or that which jumps. **2.** a boring tool or device worked with a jumping motion. **3.** *Elect.* **a.** a short length of conductor used to make a connection, usually temporary, between terminals, around a break in a circuit, or around an instrument. **b.** a section of conductor linking the coaches of an electric train. **4.** a kind of sled. [f. JUMP, v. + -ER[1]]

jumper[2] (jŭm′pə), *n.* **1.** a woman's or child's loose-fitting, lightweight pullover. **2.** a loose, outer jacket, worn esp. by sailors. [der. *jump*, nasalized var. of *jup* short coat (t. F: m. *juppe*). See -ER[2]]

jumping bean, the seed of any of certain Mexican euphorbiaceous plants (genus *Sebastiania*, etc.), which is inhabited by the larva of a small moth whose movements cause the seed to move about or jump.

jumping jack, a toy consisting of a jointed figure of a man which is made to jump, or go through various contortions, as by pulling a string attached to its limbs.

jumping-off place (jŭm′pĭng ŏf′), **1.** a place used as a starting point. **2.** *U.S.* an out-of-the-way place; the farthest limit of anything settled or civilized.

jumpy (jŭm′pĭ), *adj.*, **jumpier, jumpiest.** **1.** characterized by or inclined to sudden, involuntary starts, esp. from nervousness, fear, excitement, etc. **2.** causing to jump or start. —**jump′iness,** *n.*

Jun., **1.** June. **2.** junior.

Junc., Junction.

juncaceous (jŭng kā′shəs), *adj.* pertaining or belonging to, or resembling, the *Juncaceae*, or rush family of plants. [f. s. L *juncus* a rush + -ACEOUS]

junction (jŭngk′shən), *n.* **1.** the act of joining; combination. **2.** the state of being joined; union. **3.** a place or station where railway lines meet or cross. **4.** a place of joining or meeting. **5.** *Electronics.* (in a transistor or other semiconductor device) a point or surface where two materials having different electrical properties are in contact. **6.** a cable linking two telephone exchanges. [t. L: s. *junctio* a joining]
—**Syn.** **4.** JUNCTION, JUNCTURE refer to a place, line, or point at which two or more things join. A JUNCTION is a place where things come together: *the junction of two rivers.* A JUNCTURE is a line or point at which two bodies are joined, or a point of exigency or crisis in time: *the juncture of the head and neck, a critical juncture in a struggle.*

junction box, *Elect.* a box in which a connection is made between several electric circuits.

junction rectifier, *Electronics.* a rectifier consisting of two different semiconductors in contact in such a manner that current can flow from one to the other but not back.

junction transistor, *Electronics.* a transistor consisting of several different types of semiconductor material in contact with one another.

juncture (jŭngk′chə), *n.* **1.** a point of time, esp. one made critical or important by a concurrence of circumstances. **2.** a critical state of affairs; a crisis; a critical moment. **3.** the line or point at which two bodies are joined; a joint or articulation; a seam. **4.** the act of joining. **5.** the state of being joined; junction. **6.** something by which two things are joined. [ME, t. L: m. *junctūra* joining, joint] —**Syn.** **3.** See **junction.**

June (jo͞on), *n.* the sixth month of the year, containing 30 days. [ME; OE *Iuni*, t. L: s. *Jūnius*; named after the *Jūnius* gens of Rome]

Juneau (jo͞o′nō), *n.* a seaport in and the capital of Alaska, in the SE part. 6797 (1960).

Juneberry (jo͞on′bĕ′rĭ), *n., pl.* **-ries.** the American serviceberry, *Amelanchier canadensis.*

June bug, **1.** (in the northern U.S.) any of the large, brown scarabaeid beetles of the genus *Phyllophaga* (*Lachnosterna*), which appear about June. **2.** (in the southern U.S.) a large, greenish scarabaeid beetle, *Cotinis nitida.* Also, **June beetle.**

June bug, *Phyllophaga fusca* (Length 1 in.)

Jung (*Ger.* yo͝ong), *n.* **Carl Gustav** (*Ger.* kärl go͞os′täf), 1875–1961, Swiss psychiatrist and psychologist.

Jungfrau (yo͝ong′frou′), *n.* a peak in the Bernese Alps, in S Switzerland. 13,668 ft.

Jungian (yo͝ong′ĭ ən), *adj.* **1.** of or pertaining to the theories of C. G. Jung. —*n.* **2.** a follower of Jung or an advocate of his theories.

jungle (jŭng′gl), *n.* **1.** wild land overgrown with dense, rank vegetation, often nearly impenetrable, as in tropical countries. **2.** a tract of such land. **3.** a tropical rainforest with thick, impenetrable undergrowth. **4.** anything confusing, perplexing, or in disorder. **5.** any place or situation characterized by a struggle for survival, ruthless competition, etc. [t. Hind.: m. *jangal* desert, forest, g. Skt *jangala* dry, desert]

jungle fever, a severe variety of malarial fever occurring in the East Indies and other tropical regions.

jungle fowl, any of various East Indian gallinaceous birds of the genus *Gallus*, certain species of which are supposed to have given rise to the domestic fowl.

junior (jo͞o′nyə), *adj.* **1.** *Chiefly U.S.* younger (often used, esp. as abbreviated *Jr* or *Jun.*, after the name of a person who is the younger of two persons of the same name, as a son having the same name as his father). **2.** of more recent appointment or admission, as to an office or status; of lower rank or standing. **3.** (in American universities, colleges, and schools) denoting or pertaining to the class or year next below that of the senior. **4.** *Law.* subordinate to preferred creditors, mortgagees, and the like. **5.** of later date; subsequent to. **—*n.* 6.** a person who is younger than another. **7.** one who is of more recent entrance into, or of lower standing in, an office, class, profession, etc.; one employed as the subordinate of another. **8.** *U.S.* a student who is in the next to the final year of a course of study. **9.** *Rowing.* an oarsman who has won an open rowing event in a clinker boat but not in a shell. [t. L, contr. of *juvenior*, compar. of *juvenis* young]

junior school, (in England and Wales) a primary school for children aged 7–11.

juniper (jo͞o′nĭ pə), *n.* **1.** any of the coniferous evergreen shrubs or trees constituting the genus *Juniperus*, esp. *J. communis*, whose cones form purple berries used in making gin and in medicine as a diuretic, or *J. virginiana*, a North American species. **2.** a tree mentioned in the Bible. 1 Kings, 19:4. [ME *junipere*, t. L: m. *jūniperus*. See GENEVA and GIN[1]]

Junius (jo͞o′nyəs), *n.* the pen-name of the unknown author of a series of letters (1768–72) attacking the British government.

junk[1] (jŭngk), *n.* **1.** any old or discarded material, as metal, paper, rags, etc. **2.** *Colloq.* anything that is regarded as worthless or mere trash. **3.** old cable or cordage used when untwisted for making gaskets, swabs, oakum, etc. **4.** hard salt meat used for food on shipboard. **5.** tissue in the sperm whale containing spermaceti. **6.** *Slang.* any narcotic drug. **—*v.t.* 7.** *Colloq.* to cast aside as junk; discard as no longer of use. [orig. uncert.]

junk[2] (jŭngk), *n.* a kind of seagoing ship used in Chinese and other waters, having square sails spread by battens, a high stern, and usually a flat bottom. [t. Pg.: m. *junco*, t. Malay: m. *jong*, *ajong*, appar. t. Javanese: (m.) *jong*]

Chinese junk

Junker (yo͝ong′kə), *n.* **1.** a member of a class of aristocratic landholders, esp. in East Prussia, strongly devoted to maintaining the social and political privileges of their group. **2.** a narrow-minded, haughty, overbearing member of the aristocracy of Prussia, etc. [t. G, in MHG *junc herre* young gentleman]

Junkerdom (yo͝ong′kə dəm), *n.* **1.** the body of Junkers. **2.** (*sometimes l.c.*) **a.** the condition or character of a Junker. **b.** the spirit or policy of the Junkers.

Junkerism (yo͝ong′kə rĭz′əm), *n.* (*sometimes l.c.*) the spirit or policy of the Junkers.

junket (jŭng′kĭt), *n.* **1.** a sweet custard-like food of flavoured milk curded with rennet. **2.** a feast or merrymaking; a picnic; a pleasure excursion. **3.** *U.S.* a trip, as by a legislative committee or official body, at public expense and ostensibly to obtain information. **—*v.i.* 4.** to feast; picnic; go on a junket or pleasure excursion. [ME *jonket* basket made of rushes, *joncate* curded food made in a vessel of rushes, t. OF: m. *jonquette*, der. *jonc* a rush, g. L *juncus*] **—jun′keter,** *n.*

junkie (jŭng′kĭ), *n.* *Colloq.* a drug addict.

junk shop, **1.** a shop selling second-hand goods, esp. of inferior quality. **2.** a ship chandler.

Juno (jo͞o′nō), *n.* **1.** *Rom. Myth.* an ancient Roman goddess, the wife of Jupiter, presiding over marriage and women. Cf. **Hera.** **2.** a woman of imposing figure or appearance. **3.** *Astron.* one of the largest and brightest asteroids.

Junoesque (jo͞o′nō ĕsk′), *adj.* (of a woman) stately.

Junot (*Fr.* zhʏ nō′), *n.* **Andoche** (*Fr.* äɴ dōsh′), (*Duc d'Abrantès*), 1771–1813, French marshal.

junta (jŭn′tə), *n.* **1.** a small ruling group in a country, either elected or self-chosen, esp. one which has come to power after a revolution. **2.** a council. **3.** a deliberative or administrative council, esp. in Spain and Latin America. [t. Sp., g. L *juncta*, fem. pp., joined]

junto (jŭn′tō), *n.*, *pl.* **-tos.** junta (def. 1). [erron. var. of JUNTA]

Jupiter (jo͞o′pĭ tə), *n.* **1.** the supreme deity of the ancient Romans, the god of the heavens, manifesting himself esp. in atmospheric phenomena; Jove (Cf. **Zeus**). **2.** the largest planet, fifth in order from the sun. Its period of revolution is 11·86 years, its mean distance from the sun 483,640,000 miles. Its diameter is 88,730 miles, about one tenth that of the sun (11 times that of the earth). It has 12 satellites. [t. L, var. of *Jūppiter*, contr. of *Jovis pater* father Jove]

jupon (zho͞o′pŏn: *Fr.* zhʏ pôɴ′), *n.* a close-fitting tunic, usually padded and bearing heraldic arms, worn over armour. [ME *jupone*, t. F: m. *jupon*, der. *jupe* jacket, t. Ar.: m. *jubbah*]

Jura (jo͝o͞ə′rə; *Fr.* zhʏ rȧ′), *n.* **1.** a department in E France. 225,682 pop. (1962); 1952 sq. mi. *Cap.:* Lons-le-Saunier. **2.** the Jura Mountains.

jural (jo͝o͞ə′rəl), *adj.* **1.** pertaining to law; legal. **2.** pertaining to rights and obligations. [f. s. L *jūs* right, law + -AL[1]] **—ju′rally,** *adv.*

Jura Mountains (jo͝o͞ə′rə; *Fr.* zhʏ rȧ′), a mountain range between France and Switzerland, extending from the Rhine to the Rhone. Highest peak, Crêt de la Neige, 5654 ft. Also, **Jura.**

Jurassic (jo͞o răs′ĭk), *Geol.* **—*adj.* 1.** pertaining to a period of the Mesozoic era, following the Cretaceous and preceding the Triassic. **—*n.* 2.** the Jurassic period. [t. F: m. *jurassique*]

jurat (jo͝o͞ə′răt), *n.* **1.** *Law.* a certificate on an affidavit, by the officer, showing by whom, when, and before whom it was sworn to. **2.** a sworn officer; a magistrate; a member of a permanent jury. [t. ML: s. *jūrātus*, lit., one sworn, *jūrātum*, neut., that which is sworn, prop. pp. of L *jūrāre* swear]

Jur. D., (L *Juris Doctor*) Doctor of Law.

jurel (*Sp.* KHo͞o rĕl′), *n.* any of certain carangoid food fishes of the genus *Caranx* as *C. latus*, a species of the West Indies, etc. [t. Sp., ult. der. Gk *saûros* lizard]

juridical (jo͞oə rĭd′ĭ kl), *adj.* **1.** of or pertaining to the administration of justice. **2.** of or pertaining to law or jurisprudence; legal. Also, **jurid′ic.** [f. s. L *jūridicus* relating to justice + -AL[1]] **—jurid′ically,** *adv.*

juridical days, the days in court on which law is administered; days on which the court can lawfully sit.

jurisconsult (jo͝o͞ə′rĭs kən sŭlt′), *n.* **1.** *Rom. and Civil Law.* one authorized to give legal advice. **2.** *Civil Law.* a master of the civil law. *Abbrev.:* J.C. [t. L: s. *jūrisconsultus* one skilled in the law]

jurisdiction (jo͝o͞ə′rĭs dĭk′shən), *n.* **1.** the right, power, or authority to administer justice by hearing and determining controversies. **2.** power; authority; control. **3.** the extent or range of judicial or other authority. **4.** the territory over which authority is exercised. [ME, t. L: s. *jūrisdictio* administration of the law, authority] **—ju′risdic′tional,** *adj.* **—ju′risdic′tionally,** *adv.*

jurisprudence (jo͝o͞ə′rĭs pro͞o′dns), *n.* **1.** the science or philosophy of law. **2.** a body or system of laws. **3.** a department of law: *medical jurisprudence.* **4.** *Civil Law.* decisions of courts of appeal or other higher tribunals. [t. L: m. s. *jūrisprūdentia* the science of the law] **—jurisprudential** (jo͝o͞ə′rĭs pro͞o dĕn′shəl), *adj.*

jurisprudent (jo͝o͞ə′rĭs pro͞o′dnt), *adj.* **1.** versed in jurisprudence. **—*n.* 2.** one versed in jurisprudence.

jurist (jo͝o͞ə′rĭst), *n.* **1.** one who professes the science of law. **2.** one versed in the law. **3.** one who writes on the subject of law. [t. ML: s. *jūrista*, der. L *jūs* right, law]

juristic (jo͞o rĭs′tĭk), *adj.* of or pertaining to a jurist or to jurisprudence; relating to law; juridical; legal. Also, **juris′tical.** **—juris′tically,** *adv.*

juror (jo͝o͞ə′rə), *n.* **1.** one of a body of persons sworn to deliver a verdict in a case submitted to them; a member of any jury. **2.** one of the panel from which a jury is selected. **3.** one who has taken an oath or sworn allegiance. [ME *jurour*, t. AF, g. L *jūrātor* swearer]

Juruá (*Port.* zho͞o rwȧ′), *n.* a river flowing from E Peru NE through W Brazil to the Amazon. ab. 1200 mi.

jury[1] (jo͝o͞ə′rĭ), *n.*, *pl.* **-ries.** **1.** a body of persons sworn to render a verdict or true answer on a question or questions officially submitted to them. **2.** such a body selected according to law and sworn to inquire into or determine the facts concerning a cause or an accusation submitted to them and to render a verdict. **3.** a body of persons chosen to adjudge prizes, etc., as in a competition. [ME *juree*, t. AF, der. *jure* one sworn, ult. der. L *jūrāre* swear] **—ju′ryless,** *adj.*

jury[2] (jo͝o͞ə′rĭ), *adj.* *Naut.* makeshift, temporary, as for an emergency. [first found in *jury mast*, prob. t. OF: m. *ajurie* relief, help, der. L *adjūtāre* help]

jury-box (jo͝o͞ə′rĭ bŏks′), *n.* an enclosed space in a court of law where members of a jury sit.

juryman (jo͝o͞ə′rĭ mən), *n.*, *pl.* **-men.** a member of a jury.

jury mast, *Naut.* a temporary mast replacing one that has been broken or carried away. [see JURY[2]]

jury-rigged (jo͝o͞ə′rĭ rĭgd′), *adj.* *Naut.* temporarily rigged. [see JURY[2]]

jus[1] (*Fr.* zhʏ), *n.* *French.* juice; gravy. [F, t. L]

jus[2] (jŭs), *n.*, *pl.* **jura** (jo͝o͞ə′rə). *Law.* **1.** a right. **2.** law as a system or in the abstract. [t. L: law, right]

jus canonicum (jŭs′kə nŏn′ĭ kəm), canon law.

jus civile (jŭs′sĭ vē′lĭ), *Rom. Law.* the rules and principles of law derived from the customs and legislation of Rome, as opposed to those derived from the customs of all nations (**jus gentium**) or from fundamental ideas of right and wrong implicit in the human mind (**jus naturale**).

jus divinum (jŭs′ dĭ vē′nəm), *Latin.* divine law.

jus gentium (jŭs′jĕn′tĭ əm). See **jus civile.**

jus naturale (jŭs′năt′yōō rā′lĭ). See **jus civile.**

Jusserand (*Fr.* zhʏs räɴ′), *n.* **Jean Jules** (*Fr.* zhäɴ zhʏl′), 1855–1932, French diplomat and author.

jussive (jŭs′ĭv), *adj. Gram.* **1.** expressing a mild command. The jussive mood occurs in the Semitic languages. —*n.* **2.** a jussive form or construction. [f. s. L *jussus*, pp., commanded + -IVE]

just[1] (jŭst), *adj.* **1.** actuated by truth, justice, and lack of bias: *to be just in one's dealings.* **2.** in accordance with true principles; equitable; even-handed: *a just award.* **3.** based on right; rightful; lawful: *a just claim.* **4.** agreeable to truth or fact; true; correct: *a just statement.* **5.** given or awarded rightly, or deserved, as a sentence, punishment, reward, etc. **6.** in accordance with standards, or requirements; proper, or right: *just proportions.* **7.** (esp. in biblical use) righteous. **8.** actual, real, or genuine. —*adv.* **9.** within a brief preceding time, or but a moment before: *they have just gone.* **10.** exactly or precisely: *that is just the point.* **11.** by a narrow margin; barely: *it just missed the mark.* **12.** only or merely: *he is just an ordinary man.* **13.** *Colloq.* actually; truly; positively: *the weather is just glorious.* [ME, t. L: s. *justus* righteous] —**Syn. 1.** upright; equitable, fair, impartial. **4.** accurate, exact; honest. **5.** rightful, legitimate, deserved, merited, condign. —**Ant. 1.** biased. **4.** untrue.

just[2] (jŭst), *n., v.i.* joust. —**just′er,** *n.*

justice (jŭs′tĭs), *n.* **1.** the quality of being just; righteousness, equitableness, or moral rightness: *to uphold the justice of a cause.* **2.** rightfulness or lawfulness, as of a claim or title; justness of ground or reason: *to complain with justice.* **3.** the moral principle determining just conduct. **4.** conformity to this principle as manifested in conduct; just conduct, dealing, or treatment. **5.** the requital of desert as by punishment or reward. **6.** the maintenance or administration of law, as by judicial or other proceedings: *a court of justice.* **7.** judgement of persons or causes by judicial process: *to administer justice in a community.* **8.** a judicial officer; a judge or magistrate. **9. do justice to, a.** to render or concede what is due to (a person or thing, merits, intentions, etc.); treat or judge fairly. **b.** to exhibit (oneself) in a just light, as in doing something. **c.** to show just appreciation of (something) by action. [ME *justise*, t. OF, t. L: m. s. *justitia*]

justice of the peace, a lay magistrate appointed by the crown to keep the peace within a certain district.

justiceship (jŭs′tĭs shĭp′), *n.* the office of a justice.

justiciable (jŭs tĭsh′ĭ ə bl), *adj.* **1.** capable of being settled by a court of law. **2.** subject to the action of a court of law.

justiciary (jŭs tĭsh′yə rĭ), *adj., n., pl.* **-ries.** —*adj.* **1.** of or pertaining to the administration of justice. —*n.* **2.** Also, **justiciar** (jŭs tĭsh′ĭ ä′). *Hist.* the chief administrator of justice and government from the time of William I to that of Henry III. [t. ML: m. s. *justitiārius* judge, der. L *justitia* justice]

justifiable (jŭs′tĭ fī′ə bl), *adj.* capable of being justified; that can be shown to be, or can be defended as being, just or right; defensible. —**jus′tifi′abil′ity, jus′tifi′ableness,** *n.* —**jus′tifi′ably,** *adv.*

justification (jŭs′tĭ fĭ kā′shən), *n.* **1.** something that justifies; a defensive plea; an excuse; a justifying fact or circumstance. **2.** the act of justifying. **3.** the state of being justified. **4.** *Theol.* the act of God whereby man is made just, or free from the guilt of sin. **5.** *Print.* the equal spacing of words and lines to a given measure.

justificatory (jŭs′tĭ fĭ kā′tə rĭ), *adj.* serving to justify; affording justification. Also, **justificative** (jŭs′tĭ fĭ kā′tĭv).

justifier (jŭs′tĭ fī′ə), *n.* one who or that which justifies.

justify (jŭs′tĭ fī′), *v.,* **-fied, -fying.** —*v.t.* **1.** to show (an act, claim, statement, etc.) to be just, right, or warranted: *the end justifies the means.* **2.** to defend or uphold as blameless, just, or right. **3.** declare guiltless; absolve; acquit. **4.** *Theol.* to declare (a person) free from the penalty of sin. **5.** *Print.* to adjust exactly; make (lines) of the proper length by spacing. —*v.i.* **6.** *Law.* **a.** to show a satisfactory reason or excuse for something done. **b.** to qualify as bail or surety. **7.** *Print.* to conform or fit exactly, as lines of type. [ME *justifie(n)*, t. OF: m. *justifier*, t. LL: m. *justificāre* act justly towards]

Justinian I (jŭs tĭn′ĭ ən), (*'the Great'*, *Flavius Anicius Justinianus*) A.D. 483–565, Byzantine emperor A.D. 527–65, whose leading jurists formulated a code of laws called the **Justinian Code.**

Justin Martyr (jŭs′tĭn mä′tə), **Saint,** A.D. *c.* 100–*c.* 165, Christian saint, philosopher, and martyr, born in Syria.

justle (jŭs′əl), *v.t., v.i.,* **-tled, -tling,** *n.* jostle.

justly (jŭst′lĭ), *adv.* **1.** in a just manner; honestly; fairly. **2.** in conformity to fact or rule; accurately.

justness (jŭst′nĭs), *n.* **1.** the quality or state of being just, equitable, or right; lawfulness. **2.** conformity to fact or rule; correctness; exactness; accuracy.

jut (jŭt), *v.,* **jutted, jutting,** *n.* —*v.i.* **1.** to extend beyond the main body or line; project; protrude (often fol. by *out*). —*n.* **2.** something that juts out; a projection or protruding point. [var. of JET, v.]

jute (jōōt), *n.* **1.** a strong fibre used for making fabrics, cordage, etc., obtained from two tiliaceous East Indian plants, *Corchorus capsularis* and *C. olitorius.* **2.** either of these plants. **3.** any plant of the same genus. **4.** the coarse fabric woven from jute fibres; gunny. [t. Bengali: m. *jhōto*, g. Skt *jūta* braid of hair] —**jute′like′,** *adj.*

Jute (jōōt), *n.* a member of a continental Germanic tribe which invaded Britain in the 5th century and settled in Kent. [t. ML: m. s. *Iutī*, pl., t. OE] —**Jut′ish,** *adj.*

Jutland (jŭt′lənd), *n.* a peninsula comprising the continental portion of Denmark: a major naval engagement between the British and German fleets was fought W of this peninsula, 1916. 1,659,609 pop. (est. 1960); 11,411 sq. mi. Danish, **Jylland.**

Juvarra (*It.* yōō vä′rä), *n.* **Filippo** (*It.* fē lĕp′pō), 1678–1736, Italian architect and draughtsman.

juvenal (jōō′vĭ nəl), *n. Ornithol.* the plumage stage of an altricial bird when it leaves the nest. [t. L: s. *juvenālis*, var. of *juvenīlis* young, pertaining to youth]

Juvenal (jōō′vĭ nəl), *n.* (*Decimus Junius Juvenalis*), A.D. *c.* 60–*c.* 140, Roman satirical poet.

juvenescent (jōō′vĭ nĕs′ənt), *adj.* becoming youthful; growing young again; youthful. [t. L: s. *juvenescens*, ppr., reaching the age of youth] —**ju′venes′cence,** *n.*

juvenile (jōō′vĭ nīl′), *adj.* **1.** pertaining to, suitable for, characteristic of, or intended for young persons: *juvenile behaviour, juvenile books, a juvenile court.* **2.** young. —*n.* **3.** a young person; a youth. **4.** *Theat.* **a.** a youthful male role. **b.** an actor who plays such parts. **5.** *Ornithol.* a young bird in the stage when it has fledged, if altricial, or has replaced down of hatching, if precocial. **6.** a book for young people. [t. L: m. s. *juvenīlis* of youth] —**ju′venile′ly,** *adv.* —**ju′venile′ness,** *n.*

juvenile court, a special court for the trial of children and young persons under the age of 17.

juvenilia (jōō′vĭ nĭl′ĭ ə), *n.pl.* works, esp. writings, produced in youth.

juvenility (jōō′vĭ nĭl′ĭ tĭ), *n., pl.* **-ties. 1.** juvenile state, character, or manner. **2.** (*pl.*) youthful qualities or performances. **3.** young persons collectively.

juxta-, a word element meaning 'near', 'close to', 'beside', [comb. form repr. L *juxtā*, prep., adv.]

juxtapose (jŭks′tə pōz′), *v.t.,* **-posed, -posing.** to place in close proximity or side by side.

juxtaposition (jŭks′tə pə zĭsh′ən), *n.* **1.** a placing close together. **2.** position side by side. [t. F, f. L: *juxtā* JUXTA- + s. *positio* a placing, position]

Jy, July.

Jylland (*Dan.* yʏ′län), *n.* Danish name of **Jutland.**

Jyväskylä (*Finn.* yʏ′väs kʏ lä), *n.* a town in S central Finland. 51,810 (1965).

K

K, k (kā), *n., pl.* **K's** or **Ks, k's** or **ks.** a consonant, the 11th letter of the English alphabet.

K, 1. *Chem.* (L *kalium*) potassium. **2.** *Physics.* kelvin. **3.** *Chess.* king. **4.** Knight.

k., 1. *Elect.* capacity. **2.** karat or carat. **3.** kilogram. **4.** *Chess.* king. **5.** knight. **6.** knot. **7.** kopeck.

kA, *Elect.* kiloamperes.

ka (kä), *n. Egypt. Relig.* a presiding or second spirit supposed to be present in a man or statue. [t. Egypt.]

Kaaba (kä′bə), *n.* a small cube-shaped building in the Great Mosque at Mecca, containing a sacred stone said to have been turned black by the tears of repentant pilgrims or, according to another tradition, by the sins of those who have touched it: the most sacred shrine of the Muslims. Also, **Caaba.** [t. Ar.: m. *ka'ba* a square building, der. *ka'b* cube]

kab (kăb), *n.* cab².

kabala (kə bä′lə), *n.* cabbala. Also, **kabbala.**

kabeljou (kăb′l you′), *n.* a large South African marine food fish, *Otolinthus ruber*; salmon-bass. [t. Afrikaans, t. D: m. *kabeljauw* cod]

kabob (kə bŏb′), *n.* kebab.

kabuki (kə bōō′kĭ), *n.* a form of Japanese popular theatre, with stylized acting, music, and dancing, in which male actors play all dramatic roles.

Kabul (kô′bl), *n.* **1.** the capital of Afghanistan, in the NE part. 450,000 (est. 1965). **2.** a river flowing from NE Afghanistan E to the Indus in Pakistan. ab. 360 mi. See map under **Samarkand.**

Kabyle (kə bīl′), *n.* **1.** one of a branch of the Berber race dwelling in Algeria and Tunisia. **2.** their language, a Berber dialect. [t. Ar.: m. *qabīla* tribe]

Kádar (kä′dä; *Hung.* kȧ′dȧr), *n.* **János** (*Hung.* yȧ′nōsh), born 1912, Hungarian statesman: first secretary 1956–58 and since 1961.

Kaddish (kăd′ĭsh), *n., pl.* **Kaddishim** (kă dĭsh′ĭm). **1.** a Jewish liturgical prayer of three or six verses, recited at given points during each of the three daily services and on certain other occasions. **2.** a five-verse form of this prayer used in observation of the eleven-month period of mourning and on the anniversary of a death.

kadi (kä′dĭ, kā′dĭ), *n., pl.* **-dis.** cadi.

Kadiyevka (*Russ.* kȧ′dĭ yĭf kə), *n.* a town in the S Soviet Union in Europe. 138,000 (est. 1965).

Kaffir (kăf′ə), *n.* **1.** (used disparagingly) a member of a South African Negroid race inhabiting parts of the Cape of Good Hope, Natal, etc. **2.** (used disparagingly) any South African Negro. **3.** a Bantu language; Xhosa. **4.** (*l.c.*) Also, **kaffir corn.** any of certain grain sorghums, varieties of *Sorghum vulgare*, with stout, short-jointed, leafy stalks, cultivated in South Africa. **5.** (*pl.*) *Stock Exchange Slang.* South African mining and other stocks. [t. Ar.: m. *kāfir* unbeliever]

Kaffir beer, *S African Colloq.* an alcoholic drink made from sorghum or millet.

kaffirboom (kăf′ə bōōm′), *n.* a small leguminous tree of S Africa, *Erythrina caffra*, with spikes of bright red flowers.

Kaffraria (kă frēə′rĭ ə), *n.* a region in the S Republic of South Africa; inhabited mostly by Bantus. —**Kaffra′rian,** *adj.*

Kafir (kăf′ə), *n.* **1.** a member of a people of Indo-European speech, in Nuristan. **2.** Kaffir.

Kafiristan (kăf′ĭ rĭ stän′), *n.* former name of **Nuristan.**

Kafka (kăf′kə; *Ger.* kȧf′kȧ), *n.* **Franz** (*Ger.* frȧnts), 1883–1924, Jewish Czech novelist and short-story writer, writing in German. —**Kafkaesque** (kăf′kə ĕsk′), *adj.*

kaftan (kăf′tăn), *n.* caftan.

Kaganovich (*Russ.* kə gȧ nô′vĭch), *n.* **Lazar Moiseevich** (*Russ.* lȧ′zəry mə ĭ syė′yĭ vĭch), born 1893, Soviet politician.

Kagera (kă gĕ′rə), *n.* a river in equatorial Africa, flowing into Lake Victoria from the west: the most remote headstream of the Nile. ab. 430 mi.

Kagoshima (kăg′ō shē′mə), *n.* a seaport in SW Japan, on Kyushu island. 328,446 (1965).

kahawai (kä′hə wī′, kä′wī), *n.* the Australian salmon, or salmon trout, *Ampis salar*, belonging to the family *Arripididae* and abundant off the coasts of southern Australia and New Zealand. [t. Maori]

kahikatea (kə hĭk′ə tīə′, kī′kə-, kä′kə-), *n.* a tall gymnospermous tree with evergreen, brownish green foliage, *Podocarpus dacrydiodes*, a native of New Zealand, where it provides a valuable source of timber. [t. Maori]

Kahn (kän), *n.* **Louis,** born 1901, U.S. architect born in Estonia.

kai (kī), *n. N.Z. Slang.* food. [t. Maori]

kaiak (kī′ăk), *n.* kayak.

Kaieteur (kī′ə tōōə′), *n.* a waterfall in central Guyana, on a tributary of the river Essequibo. 741 ft high.

kaif (kīf), *n.* kef.

Kaifeng (kī′fĕng′), *n.* a city in Honan province, in E China. 318,000 (est. 1958).

Kaikoura (kī kōōə′rə), *adj. Geol.* of or pertaining to the major mountain-building episode in New Zealand, which reached its height at the end of the Tertiary period.

Kaikoura Ranges, a series of mountain ranges in NE South Island, New Zealand. Highest peak, Tapuaenuku, 9465 ft.

kail (kāl), *n.* kale.

Kaimanawa Mountains (kī′mə nä′wə), a high plateau area in central North Island, New Zealand. 4000–5000 ft.

kainite (kī′nīt, kā′-), *n.* a mineral double salt of magnesium sulphate and potassium chloride, $MgSO_4 . KCl_3 . 3H_2O$; a source of potassium salts. [t. G: m. *Kainit.* See CAINO-, -ITE¹]

kainogenesis (kī′nō jĕn′ĭ sĭs), *n.* cainogenesis. —**kainogenetic** (kī′nō jĭ nĕt′ĭk), *adj.* —**kai′nogenet′ically,** *adv.*

Kainozoic (kī′nō zō′ĭk, kā′-), *adj., n.* Cainozoic.

Kairouan (*Fr.* kĕr wäɴ′), *n.* a town in NE Tunisia: a holy city of Islam. 82,299 (1966). Also, **Kairwan** (kī rwän′).

Kaiser (kī′zə), *n.* **1.** a German emperor. **2.** an Austrian emperor. **3.** *Hist.* a ruler of the Holy Roman Empire. **4.** (*l.c.*) an emperor; a Caesar. [t. G, r. ME *caiser(e)*, *keiser(e)*, t. Scand. (cf. Icel. *keisari*); r. ME and OE *cāsere*, ult. t. L: m. *Caesar*] —**kai′sership′,** *n.*

Kaiserslautern (*Ger.* kī zərs lou′tərn), *n.* a town in West Germany, in S Rhineland-Palatinate. 86,700 (est. 1966).

Kajar (kä jä′), *n.* a Persian dynasty which ruled 1794–1925.

kajatehout (kä yä′tĭ hout′, -hōt′), *n.* **1.** either of two large African leguminous trees, *Pterocarpus erinaceus*, or *P. angolensis*, with durable wood resembling teak. **2.** the timber yielded by either of these trees. Also, **kijaat.** [t. Afrikaans]

kaka (kä′kə), *n.* any of certain New Zealand parrots of the genus *Nestor*, esp. *N. meridionalis*, a species about the size of a crow with a mostly greenish, olive brown coloration. [t. Maori]

kaka beak, an evergreen leguminous shrub, *Clianthus puniceus*, with pinnate leaves and clusters of bright red, pointed flowers, a native of New Zealand, but commonly cultivated in cold greenhouses elsewhere. Also, **parrot's bill, glory pea.**

kakapo (kä′kə pō′), *n., pl.* **-pos** (-pōz′). a large, almost flightless, nocturnal parrot, *Strigops habroptilus*, of New Zealand. [t. Maori: f. *kaka* parrot + *po* night]

kakemono (kăk′ĭ mō′nō), *n., pl.* **-nos.** an upright Japanese wall picture, usually long and narrow, painted on silk, paper or other material, and mounted on a roller. [t. Jap.: f. *kake* hang + *mono* thing]

kaki (kä′kĭ), *n., pl.* **-kis. 1.** the Japanese persimmon tree. **2.** its fruit. [t. Jap.]

Kakinada (kăk′ĭ nä′də), *n.* a town in India, in NE Andhra Pradesh. 122,865 (1961).

Kakogawa (kă kō′gə wə, kăk′ō gä′wə), *n.* a town in Japan, in W Honshu island. 101,841 (1965).

kal., kalends.

Kalahari (kăl′ə hä′rĭ), *n.* a desert region in SW Africa, largely in Botswana. ab. 350,000 sq. mi. See map under **Zambezi.**

Kalat (kə lät′), *n.* a region in W Pakistan, in the province of Baluchistan. Also, **Khelat.**

kale (kāl), *n.* **1.** a plant of the mustard family, *Brassica oleracea*, var. *acephala*, with leaves not forming a head, used as a potherb. **2.** *Scot.* cabbage. **3.** *Scot.* a cabbage broth. **4.** *U.S. Slang.* money. Also, **kail.** [ME *cale*, var. of COLE]

kaleidoscope (kə lī′də skōp′), *n.* an optical instrument in which pieces of coloured glass, etc., in a rotating tube are shown by reflection in continually changing symmetrical forms. [f. s. Gk *kalós* beautiful + Gk *eîdo(s)* form + -SCOPE]

kaleidoscopic (kə lī′də skŏp′ĭk), *adj.* **1.** of, pertaining to, or resembling a kaleidoscope. **2.** continually changing, in colour, pattern, relationship, etc. **3.** extremely complex; admitting of many and varied interpretations. Also, **kalei′doscop′ical.** —**kalei′doscop′ically,** *adv.*

kalends (kăl′ĕndz), *n.pl.* calends.

Kalevala (*Finn.* kä′lĕ vä lä), *n.* the national epic of Finland, compiled in 1835–49 from oral traditional poetry by Dr Elias Lönnrot. [t. Finnish: lit., house of a hero]

kaleyard (kāl′yäd′), *n. Scot.* a kitchen garden.

kaleyard school, a school of writers describing homely life in Scotland, with much use of Scottish dialect: in vogue towards the close of the 19th century, when books by J. M. Barrie and others were appearing.

Kalgoorlie (kăl gōōə′lĭ), *n.* a town in S Western Australia: gold-mining. 21,520 (est. 1964).

kali (kăl′ĭ, kā′lĭ), *n., pl.* **kalis.** glasswort. [t. Ar.: m. *qalī* (*qilā*). See ALKALI]

kalian (kăl yän′), *n.* an Eastern tobacco pipe in which the smoke is drawn through water; hookah. [t. Pers.]

Kalidasa (kăl′ĭ dä′sə), *n.* Hindu dramatist and poet of the 6th century or earlier.

Kalimantan (kăl′ĭ măn′tən), *n.* the Indonesian part of the island of Borneo.

Kalinin (*Russ.* kȧ lē′nĭn), *n.* **1. Mikhail Ivanovich** (*Russ.* mĭ KHȧ ēl′ ĭ vȧ′nə vĭch), 1875–1946, president of the Presidium of the Supreme Council of the Soviet Union, 1938–46. **2.** Formerly, **Tver.** a city in the central Soviet Union in Europe, on the Volga. 306,000 (est. 1965).

Kaliningrad (*Russ.* kə lĭn ĭn grȧt′), *n.* a seaport in the W

Soviet Union in Europe; formerly the capital of East Prussia. 253,000 (est. 1965). German, **Königsberg.**

kaliph (kā′lĭf, kăl′ĭf), *n.* caliph.

Kalisz (*Pol.* kä′lēsh), *n.* a town in central Poland. 74,600 (est. 1963). German, **Kalisch** (*Ger.* kä′lĭsh).

kalkoentjie (kăl ko͞on′tyĭ), *n.* **1.** an iridaceous perennial with dark red flowers, *Gladiolus alatus,* of southern Africa. **2.** Also, **Cape longclaw.** a small brown bird, *Macronyx capensis,* family *Motacillidae,* of southern Africa. [t. Afrikaans: small turkey]

Kalmar (*Swed.* käl′mär), *n.* a seaport in SE Sweden, on **Kalmar Sound,** a strait between Öland and the mainland.

kalmia (kăl′mĭ ə), *n.* any plant of the North American ericaceous genus *Kalmia,* comprising evergreen shrubs with showy flowers, as *K. latifolia,* the mountain laurel. [t. NL, after P. *Kalm,* 1715–79, Swedish botanist]

Kalmuck (kăl′mŭk), *n.* **1.** a member of any of a group of Buddhistic Mongol tribes of a region extending from western China to the valley of the lower Volga. **2.** their language, a member of the Mongolian family. Also, **Kalmuk.** [ult. t. Tartar: lit., deserter]

kalong (kä′lŏng), *n.* any of the large fruit-bats or flying foxes, belonging to the genus *Pteropus.* [t. Malay]

kalpak (kăl′păk), *n.* a large black cap of sheepskin or other heavy material, worn by Armenians, Turks, etc. Also, **calpac.** [t. Turk.: m. *qālpāq*]

kalsomine (kăl′sō mīn′, -mĭn), *n., v.t.,* **-mined, -mining.** calcimine. [orig. obscure]

Kaluga (*Russ.* kä lo͞o′gə), *n.* a town in the central Soviet Union in Europe, SW of Moscow. 169,000 (est. 1965).

Kama (*Russ.* kä′mə), *n.* a river flowing from the Ural area in the Soviet Union into the Volga. ab. 1100 mi.

Kama (kä′mə), *n.* *Hinduism.* the god of erotic desire. [t. Skt, personification of *kāma* love]

kamacite (kăm′ə sīt′), *n.* an iron-nickel alloy found in meteorites.

Kamakura (kăm′ə ko͝o′rə), *n.* a town in central Japan, on Honshu island: great statue of Buddha. 118,329 (1965).

kamala (kə mä′lə, kăm′ə lə), *n.* a powder from the capsules of an East Indian euphorbiaceous tree, *Mallotus philippinensis,* used as a yellow dye and in medicine as an anthelmintic. [t. Skt]

Kamarhati (kə mä′rə tĭ), *n.* a town in India, in SE West Bengal. 125,457 (1961).

Kamasutra (kä′mə so͞o′trə), *n.* an ancient Hindu erotic text.

Kamchatka (kăm chăt′kə; *Russ.* kăm chät′kə), *n.* a peninsula in the E Soviet Union in Asia, extending S between the Bering Sea and the Sea of Okhotsk. ab. 750 mi. long; ab. 104,000 sq. mi.

Kamchatka

kame (kām), *n.* **1.** a lead rod for framing a pane in a lattice or stained-glass window. **2.** *Phys. Geog.* a ridge or mound of detrital material, esp. of stratified sand and gravel left by a retreating ice-sheet. **3.** *Scot.* comb. [var. of COMB[1]]

Kamensk-Uralski (*Russ.* kä′mĭnsk o͞o räly′skĭy), *n.* a town in the central Soviet Union. 158,000 (est. 1965).

Kamerad (kăm′ə räd′; *Ger.* kä mə rät′), *n.* *German.* comrade (used as a shout of surrender).

Kamerun (*Ger.* kä mə ro͞on′), *n.* German name of **Cameroons** (def. 1).

Kamikaze (kăm′ĭ kä′zĭ), *n.* **1.** a member of a corps in the Japanese airforce in World War II whose mission was to crash their aircraft, loaded with explosives, into an enemy target, as a ship. *—adj.* **2.** of or pertaining to a Kamikaze. [t. Jap.: divine wind]

Kampala (kăm pä′lə), *n.* the capital of Uganda, in the S central part. 46,735 (1959). See map under **Uganda.**

kampong (kăm′pŏng, kăm pŏng′), *n.* a village or settlement in Malaysia. [t. Malay]

kamseen (kăm sēn′), *n.* khamsin. Also, **kamsin** (kăm′sĭn).

Kan., Kansas.

kana (kä′nə), *n.* the Japanese syllabary, consisting of 73 characters. [t. Jap.: lit., false symbols, so called because KANJI are regarded as real symbols]

Kanaka (kə năk′ə, kăn′ə kə), *n.* **1.** a native Hawaiian. **2.** a South Sea islander. [t. Hawaiian: lit., man]

Kanara (kə nä′rə), *n.* a region in W India, in Maharashtra province. Also, **Canara.**

Kanarese (kăn′ə rēz′), *adj., n., pl.* **-rese.** *—adj.* **1.** of or pertaining to Kanara, or Kannada. *—n.* **2.** an inhabitant of Kanara. **3.** Kannada. Also, **Canarese.**

Kanazawa (kăn′ə zä′wə), *n.* a seaport in central Japan, on Honshu island. 298,967 (1960).

Kanchenjunga (kăn′chən jŭng′gə), *n.* a peak of the E Himalayas, on the boundary between Nepal and Sikkim: third highest peak in the world. 28,146 ft. Also, **Kanchanjanga, Kinchinjunga.**

Kandahar (kăn′də hä′), *n.* a city in S Afghanistan. 115,000 (est. 1962).

Kandinski (kăn dĭn′skĭ; *Russ.* kän dēn′skĭy), *n.* **Vasili** (*Russ.* vä sē′lĭy), 1866–1944, Russian painter and author.

Kandy (kăn′dĭ), *n.* a town in central Ceylon: famous Buddhist temples. 67,768 (1963).

Red kangaroo, *Macropus rufus* (Total length 8½ ft, tail 3½ ft)

kangaroo (kăng′gə ro͞o′), *n., pl.* **-roos,** (*esp. collectively*) **-roo. 1.** any of the family *Macropodidae,* herbivorous marsupials of the Australian region with powerful hind legs developed for leaping, a sturdy tail serving as a support and balance, a small head, and very short forelimbs. **2.** (*pl.*) *Stock Exchange Slang.* Australian mining and other shares. [t. native Australian] **—kan′garoo′-like′,** *adj.*

kangaroo apple, gunyang.

kangaroo court, *Colloq.* an unauthorized or irregular court conducted with disregard for or perversion of legal procedure, as a mock court by prisoners in a jail, or by trade unionists in judging workers who do not follow union decisions.

kangaroo dog, *Austral.* a dog bred for kangaroo-hunting.

Kangaroo Island, an island off the coast of South Australia, the second largest island in Australian waters. 2159 pop. (1954); ab. 90 mi. long and 34 mi. wide.

kangaroo-paw (kăng′gə ro͞o′pô′), *n.* an erect amaryllidaceous perennial of W Australia, *Anigozanthos manglesii,* with narrow leaves and trumpet-shaped flowers, the whole plant covered with short, red, velvety hairs.

kangaroo rat, 1. any of various small jumping rodents of the family *Heteromyidae,* of Mexico and the western U.S., such as those of the genus *Dipodomys.* **2.** an Australian rodent of the genus *Notomys,* found in arid areas.

Kang Te (kăng′tē′). See **Pu-yi.**

kanji (kăn′jĭ, kăn′-), *n.* a system of Japanese writing using Chinese-derived characters. [t. Jap.: *kan* Chinese + *ji* ideograph]

Kankan (*Fr.* käN käN′), *n.* a town in E Guinea. 29,100 (1960).

kanna (kä′nə), *n.* *S African.* ganna.

Kannada (kăn′ə də), *n.* a Dravidian language of Madras state in southern India. Also, **Cannada, Kanarese.**

Kano (kä′nō, kā′nō), *n.* a town in N Northern Nigeria. 130,000 (est. 1963).

Kanpur (kän po͝o′), *n.* a city in N India, on the Ganges. 895,106 (1961). Also, **Cawnpore.**

Kans., Kansas.

Kansas (kăn′zəs), *n.* a state in the central United States. 2,178,611 pop. (1960); 82,276 sq. mi. *Cap.:* Topeka. *Abbrev.:* Kans., or Kan. **—Kan′san,** *adj., n.*

Kansas City, 1. a city in the U.S., in W Missouri at the confluence of the Kansas and the Missouri rivers. 475,539 (1960). **2.** a town in the U.S., in NE Kansas, adjacent to Kansas City, Missouri. 121,901 (1960).

Kansu (kăn′so͞o′), *n.* a province in NW China. 12,800,000 (1958). *Cap.:* Lanchow.

Kant (kănt; *Ger.* känt), *n.* **Immanuel** (ĭ măn′yo͞o əl; *Ger.* ĭ mä′no͞o ĕl), 1724–1804, German philosopher.

kantar (kăn tä′), *n.* (in Muslim countries) a unit of weight corresponding to the hundredweight, but varying in different localities. [t. Ar.: m. *qinṭār,* ult. t. L: m. *centenārium* one hundred (lbs) weight. See QUINTAL]

Kantian (kăn′tĭ ən), *adj.* **1.** of or pertaining to Immanuel Kant or Kantianism. *—n.* **2.** a follower of Kant.

Kantianism (kăn′tĭ ə nĭz′əm), *n.* the doctrine of Immanuel Kant that every attribute is merely a mode in which the mind is affected, and has no application to a thing in itself. A thing in itself is unthinkable, and ideas are of two kinds only: those presented in sensation, and those introduced in the process of thinking. Religious and strict moral ideas are, however, admitted as regulative principles.

Kaohsiung (kou′shyo͝ong′), *n.* a seaport in SW Taiwan. 275,000 (est. 1964). Also, **Takao.**

kaoliang (kā′ō lĭ ăng′), *n.* one of the varieties of grain sorghums, *Sorghum vulgare.* [t. Chinese (Mandarin): f. *kao* tall + *liang* millet]

kaolin (kā′ə lĭn), *n.* a fine white clay used in the manufacture of porcelain and used medically as an absorbent;

china clay. [t. F, t. Chinese: m. *Kao-ling* high hill, name of a mountain in China which yielded the first kaolin sent to Europe]
kaolinite (kā′ə lĭ nīt′), *n.* hydrated aluminium disilicate, $Al_2Si_2O_5(OH)_4$, a very common mineral, the commonest constituent of kaolin.
kaon (kā′ŏn), *n. Physics.* a K-meson. [f. *ka* name of letter K + (MES)ON]
kapai (kăp′ī, kă pī′), *interj. N.Z. Colloq.* (an exclamation of pleasure, approval, etc.) [t. Maori]
Kapellmeister (kă pĕl′mīs′tə), *n., pl.* **-ter.** *German.* **1.** choirmaster. **2.** a conductor of an orchestra. **3.** bandmaster. [G: f. *Kapelle* chapel (choir) + *Meister* master]
Kapfenberg (*Ger.* käp′fĕn bĕrk), *n.* a town in Austria, in NE Styria. 23,894 (1961).
Kapital (*Ger.* kȧ pē tȧl′), *n.* **das** (*Ger.* dȧs), a book (1867) by Karl Marx, on which the beliefs and practices of modern communism are largely based.
kapok (kā′pŏk), *n.* the silky down which invests the seeds of a silk-cotton tree (**kapok tree**), *Ceiba pentandra,* of the East Indies, Africa, and tropical America: used for stuffing pillows, etc., and for sound insulation. [t. Malay: m. *kāpoq*]
kappa (kăp′ə), *n.* the tenth letter of the Greek alphabet (Κ, κ).
kaput (kă po͝ot′), *adj. Slang.* smashed; ruined. [t. G]
karabiner (kă′rə bē′nə), *n. Mountaineering.* a spring-loaded metal clip designed for joining ropes together.
Karachi (kə rä′chĭ), *n.* a seaport in and the former capital of Pakistan, in S West Pakistan, near the Indus delta. 1,912,598 (1961).
Karaganda (*Russ.* kə rȧ gȧn′də), *n.* a city in Kazakhstan, in the SW Soviet Union in Asia. 482,000 (est. 1965).
Karaite (kēə′rə īt′), *n.* one of a Jewish sect which arose in the 8th century in opposition to the Talmud, favouring strict adherence to the Bible. [f. m. Heb. *qārā* to read (the scriptures) + -ITE[1]]
Karajan (*Ger.* kȧ′rȧ yȧn), *n.* **Herbert von** (*Ger.* hĕr′bĕrt fōn), born 1908, Austrian conductor.
karaka (kə răk′ə), *n.* a small evergreen coastal tree of New Zealand, *Corynocarpus laevigata,* family *Anacardiaceae,* having very poisonous seeds and bright orange fruits. [t. Maori]
Karakoram (kă′rə kô′rəm), *n.* **1.** a mountain range in NW India, in N Kashmir. Highest peak, K2, 28,250 ft. **2.** a pass traversing this range, on the route from India to Sinkiang province, China. 18,317 ft.
Karakorum (kă′rə kô′rəm), *n.* the site in the N Mongolian People's Republic of the ancient capital of the Mongol Empire.
karakul (kă′rə kl), *n.* **1.** an Asiatic breed of sheep used primarily for the production of lambskin. Black is the prevailing colour of the lambs, but the fleeces of the old sheep turn to various shades of brown and grey. **2.** caracul (the fur). [orig. place name: (Black Lake), widely used in Turkestan. See CARACUL]
Kara Kum (*Russ.* kȧ rȧ′ ko͞om′), a desert in the SW Soviet Union in Asia, S of the Aral Sea and largely in Turkmenistan. ab. 110,000 sq. mi.
Kara Sea (kä′rə; *Russ.* kȧ′rə), an arm of the Arctic Ocean between Novaya Zemlya and the N Soviet Union.
karat (kă′rət), *n.* carat.
karate (kə rä′tĭ), *n.* a method of defensive fighting, developed in Okinawa, in which hands, elbows, feet, and knees are the only weapons used. [t. Jap.: lit., empty hand]
karbonaatje (kä′bə nä′tyĭ), *n. S African.* a dish of thinly sliced roast meat. [t. Afrikaans]
karee (kə rē′), *n.* a small anacardiaceous tree, *Rhus gueinzii,* of southern Africa. [t. Afrikaans]
Karelia (kə rēl′yə), *n.* a region in the NW Soviet Union, on the border with Finland. **—Kare′lian,** *adj., n.*
Kariba (kə rē′bə), *n.* a gorge and lake of the river Zambezi on the Zambia–Rhodesia border: site of the largest dam and hydro-electric scheme in Africa.
Karl-Marx-Stadt (*Ger.* kȧrl′märks shtȧt), *n.* a city in SE East Germany. 287,400 (1962). Formerly, **Chemnitz.**
Karlovy Vary (*Cz.* kȧr′lŏ vĭ vȧ′rĭ), Czech name of **Carlsbad.**
Karlsbad (käls′băd; *Ger.* kȧrls′bȧt), *n.* German name of **Carlsbad.**
Karlsruhe (kälz′ro͞oə; *Ger.* kȧrls′ro͞o ə), *n.* a city in West Germany, in NW Baden-Württemberg: former capital of former state of Baden. 255,000 (est. 1966).
karma (kä′mə), *n.* **1.** *Hinduism, Buddhism, etc.* the cosmic operation of retributive justice, according to which a person's status in life is determined by his own deeds in a previous incarnation. **2.** *Theosophy.* the doctrine of inevitable consequence. **3.** fate; destiny. [t. Skt: deed, action] **—kar′mic,** *adj.*
Karnak (kä′năk), *n.* a village in Upper Egypt, on the Nile: the N part of the ruins of ancient Thebes.
Kärnten (*Ger.* kĕrn′tən), *n.* German name of **Carinthia.**
karo (kä′rō), *n., pl.* **-ros.** an evergreen shrub or small tree of New Zealand, *Pittosporum crassifolium,* family *Pittosporaceae,* having red flowers and hairy fruit and leaves.
Karoo (kə ro͞o′), *n., pl.* (*for def. 3*) **-roos. 1.** a vast plateau in the S part of the Republic of South Africa, in Cape Province. ab. 100,000 sq. mi.; 3000–4000 ft high. **2.** See **Lower Karoo** and **Upper Karoo. 3.** (*l.c.*) one of the arid tablelands, with red clay soil, in southern Africa. Also, **Karroo.** [later var. of *Karo,* appar. mishearing of Hottentot *toró* karoo or *garo* desert]
kaross (kə rŏs′), *n.* a mantle or blanket of animal skin worn by tribesmen in southern Africa. [t. Afrikaans: m. *karos,* ? t. Hottentot]
karri (kă′rĭ), *n., pl.* **-ris.** a rapidly growing W Australian tree, *Eucalyptus diversicolor,* family *Myrtaceae,* valuable for its hard, durable timber. [t. native Australian]
karst (käst), *n.* a barren region composed of limestone or dolomite and characterized by underground drainage systems, sinkholes, gorges, etc. [named after the *Karst* (region) in NW Yugoslavia]
kart (kät), *n.* a light vehicle, esp. one without bodywork, having a low-powered engine, used for relatively safe racing.
Karviná (*Cz.* kȧr′vē nȧ), *n.* a town in central Czechoslovakia. 66,000 (1965). Also, **Karvinná.**
karyo-, a word element meaning 'nucleus of a cell'. [t. Gk, comb. form of *káryon* nut, kernel]
karyogamy (kă′rĭ ŏg′ə mĭ), *n. Biol.* the fusion of the nuclei of cells, as in fertilization. **—karyogamic** (kă′rĭ ə găm′ĭk), *adj.*
karyokinesis (kă′rĭ ō kĭ nē′sĭs, -kī-), *n. Biol.* **1.** mitosis. **2.** the series of active changes which take place in the nucleus of a living cell in the process of division. [f. KARYO- + Gk *kínēsis* movement] **—karyokinetic** (kă′rĭ ō kĭ nĕt′ĭk, -kī-), *adj.*
karyolymph (kă′rĭ ō lĭmf′), *n. Bot.* the transparent or translucent fluid in a nucleus.
karyolysis (kă′rĭ ŏl′ĭ sĭs), *n. Biol.* the dissolution of a cell nucleus. **—karyolitic** (kă′rĭ ə lĭt′ĭk), *adj.*
karyomitome (kă′rĭ ŏm′ĭ tōm′), *n. Biol.* the network or reticulum in the nucleus of a cell. [f. KARYO- + s. Gk *mítos* thread + *-ome,* var. of -OMA]
karyoplasm (kă′rĭ ō plăz′əm), *n. Biol.* the substance of the nucleus of a cell. **—kar′yoplas′mic,** *adj.*
karyosome (kă′rĭ ō sōm′), *n. Biol.* any of certain irregular or spherical bodies observed in and supposed to be in a portion of the netlike structure in the nucleus of a cell. See diag. under **cell.** [f. KARYO- + -SOME[3]]
karyotin (kă′rĭ ō′tĭn), *n. Biol.* nuclear material; chromatin. [f. s. Gk *karyōtós* nutlike + -IN[2]]
karyotype (kă′rĭ ə tīp′), *n. Biol.* the appearance (size, shape, and number) of the chromosomes in a cell.
Kasavubu (kăs′ə vo͞o′bo͞o), *n.* **Joseph,** 1917?–69, Congolese statesman: president of the Democratic Republic of the Congo 1960–65.
kasbah (kăs′bä), *n.* the older, native quarter of a North African town. Also, **casbah.**
Kashan (kă shän′), *n.* a town in central Iran. 60,505 (est. 1964).
kasher (kä′shə), *adj., n.* kosher.
kashmir (kăsh mĭə′), *n.* cashmere.
Kashmir (kăsh mĭə′), *n.* **1.** an area in SW Asia, sovereignty of which has been in dispute between Pakistan and India since 1947. 92,780 sq. mi. **2.** Official name, **Jammu and Kashmir.** a state in NW India. 3,560,976 pop. (1961); 86,024 sq. mi. *Cap.:* Srinagar. **3.** a territory in NE West Pakistan. ab. 2,000,000 pop.; 6756 sq. mi. *Cap.:* Muzaffarabad. **—Kashmiri** (kăsh mĭə′rĭ), **Kashmirian** (kăsh mĭə′rĭ ən), *adj., n.*
Kashmir rug, an oriental handmade rug, woven flat without pile, and having the pattern which entirely covers its surface embroidered with coloured yarns.
kashrus (kăsh′ro͞os), *Judaism.* **—n. 1.** the body of dietary laws prescribed for Jews. **—adj. 2.** fitness for use according to these laws. Also, **kashrut** (kăsh′ro͞ot).
Kassa (*Hung.* kŏsh′shŏ), *n.* Hungarian name of **Košice.**
Kassala (kə sä′lə), *n.* a town in E Sudan. 49,000 (est. 1964).
Kassel (*Ger.* kȧ′səl), *n.* a town in West Germany, in NE Hesse. 214,100 (est. 1966). Also, **Cassel.**
Kastro (kăs′trō), *n.* **1.** a port in and the capital of the island of Lemnos. 3468 (1967). **2.** former name of **Mytilene.** Also, **Kástron** (kăs′trŏn).
Kastrop-Rauxel (*Ger.* kȧs′trŏp rouk′səl), *n.* Castrop-Rauxel.
Kasugai (kăs′o͞o gī′), *n.* a town in Japan, in SW central Honshu island. 117,384 (1965).

kat (kăt, kät), *n.* an evergreen shrub, *Catha edulis*, of N Africa and Arabia, the leaves of which are chewed or prepared into a drink as a narcotic. Also, **khat, qat.** [t. Ar.: m. *qat*]

kata-, var. of **cata-**. Also, **kat-, kath-.**

katabatic (kăt′ə băt′ĭk), *adj. Meteorol.* (of winds and air currents) blowing downhill, as during the night when air in the upper slopes is cooled by radiation and so becomes denser.

katabolism (kə tăb′ə lĭz′əm), *n.* catabolism.

Katanga (kə tăng′gə), *n.* a province in the E Democratic Republic of the Congo: mining; independent July 1960–December 1961. 1,687,683 pop. (est. 1959); 191,878 sq. mi. *Cap.*: Lubumbashi. —**Katang′an, Katangese** (kăt′-ăng gēz′), *adj., n.*

Katar (kă tä′), *n.* Qatar.

Kathiawar (kăt′ĭ ə wä′), *n.* a peninsula on the W coast of India.

kathode (kăth′ōd), *n.* cathode.

kation (kăt′ī′ən), *n.* cation.

katipo (kăt′ĭ pō′), *n.* a venomous spider of New Zealand, *Latrodectus hasseltii.* [t. Maori]

katjiepiering (kī′tyĭ pĭə′rĭng), *n.* a rubiaceous shrub of southern Africa, *Gardenia thunbergia*, with large, white, solitary flowers. [t. Afrikaans: lit., kitten-saucer]

Katmai (kăt′mī), *n.* **Mount,** an active volcano in SW Alaska: eruption, 1912. ab. 7500 ft: national park, 1700 sq. mi.

Katmandu (kăt′măn dōō′), *n.* the capital of Nepal, in the S part. 195,260 (est. 1961).

Katowice (*Pol.* kä tō vē′tsĕ), *n.* a city in S Poland. 284,000 (est. 1964). German, **Kattowitz** (*Ger.* kä′tō vĭts).

Katrine (kăt′rĭn), *n.* **Loch,** a lake in central Scotland. 8 mi. long.

Katsina (kăt′sĭ nə), *n.* a town in N Northern Nigeria. 53,000 (est. 1963).

Kattegat (kăt′ĭ găt′), *n.* the strait between Jutland and Sweden. 40–70 mi. wide. Also, **Cattegat.**

katydid (kā′tĭ dĭd), *n.* any of the large, usually green, long-horned American grasshoppers of the family *Tettigoniidae*, known for the loud note of the males of some species, notably *Platyphyllum concavum.* [imit. of the sound made]

Katydid, *Tettigonia viridissima* (Length 1½ in.)

Kauai (kä wä′ē), *n.* one of the Hawaiian Islands, in the NW part of the group. 27,922 pop. (1960); 511 sq. mi.

Kaunas (*Russ.* kou′nəs), *n.* a city in the W Soviet Union in Europe. 269,000 (est. 1965). Russian, **Kovno.**

Kaunda (kä ŏŏn′də), *n.* **Kenneth,** born 1924, Zambian statesman: president since 1964.

kauri (kou′ə rĭ), *n., pl.* **-ris. 1.** a tall coniferous tree, *Agathis australis*, of New Zealand, yielding a valuable timber and a resin. **2.** its wood. **3.** kauri resin. **4.** any of various other trees of the genus *Agathis.* [t. Maori]

kauri resin, the resin, used in making varnish, which exudes from the thick bark of the kauri. Masses weighing as much as 100 lbs are found in soil where the trees have grown. Also, **kauri gum, kauri copal.**

kaury (kou′ə rĭ), *n., pl.* **-ries.** kauri.

kava (kä′və), *n.* **1.** a Polynesian shrub, *Piper methysticum*, of the pepper family. Its root has aromatic and pungent qualities. **2.** a fermented, intoxicating beverage made from the roots of the kava. [t. Polynesian]

Kavaphis (*Gk* kä vä′fēs), *n.* **Constantine.** See **Cavafy.**

Kaveri (kô′və rĭ), *n.* Cauvery.

Kawaguchi (kä′wə gōō′chĭ), *n.* a city in central Japan, on Honshu island, near Tokyo. 222,191 (1964).

Kawasaki (kä′wə sä′kĭ), *n.* a seaport in central Japan, on Honshu island, near Tokyo. 789,303 (1964).

Kay (kā), *n.* **Sir,** *Arthurian Legend.* the rude, boastful foster-brother and seneschal of Arthur.

kayak (kī′ăk), *n.* **1.** an Eskimo hunting craft with a skin cover on a light framework, made watertight by flexible closure round the waist of the occupant. **2.** any of various light canoes in imitation of this. Also, **kaiak.** [t. Eskimo]

Eskimo kayak

Kaye (kā), *n.* **Danny** (*Daniel Kominski*), born 1913, U.S. comedian.

Kayes (kās), *n.* a town in SW Mali. 28,500 (est. 1963).

Kayibanda (kä′yĭ băn′də), *n.* **Gregoire** (grĕg′wä), born 1924, president of Rwanda since 1962.

kayo (kā′ō), *n., pl.* **-os,** *v.,* **-oed, -oing.** *Slang.* —*n.* **1.** a knock-out. —*v.t.* **2.** to knock (someone) out. [f. *kay* name of letter K + O, var. of K.O.]

Kayseri (*Turk.* käy′sĕ rē), *n.* a town in central Turkey. 102,596 (1960). Ancient, **Caesarea.**

Kazakh (*Russ.* kä zäKH′), *n.* **1.** a member of a Kirghiz people of central Asia, living mainly in Kazakhstan. —*adj.* **2.** of or pertaining to Kazakhs or Kazakhstan. Also, **Kazak.**

Kazakhstan (*Russ.* kə zäKH stän′), *n.* a constituent republic of the Soviet Union, E and N of the Caspian Sea. 8,500,000 pop. (est. 1956); 1,055,900 sq. mi. *Cap.*: Alma-Ata. Also, **Kazakstan.** Official name, **Kazakh Soviet Socialist Republic.**

Kazan (kə zän′), *n.* **Elia** (ē′lyə), U.S. film director, born 1909.

Kazan (*Russ.* kä zäny′), *n.* a city in the E Soviet Union in Europe, near the Volga. 762,000 (est. 1965).

Kazvin (kăz vēn′), *n.* a town in NW Iran. 77,575 (est. 1964). Also, **Qazvin.**

K.B., **1.** King's Bench. **2.** *Chess.* king's bishop. **3.** Knight Bachelor.

K.B.E., Knight (Commander of the Order) of the British Empire.

kc., kilocycle; kilocycles.

K.C., **1.** King's Counsel. **2.** Knight Commander. **3.** Knights of Columbus.

kcal, kilocalorie.

K.C.B., Knight Commander of the Bath.

K.C.M.G., Knight Commander of the Order of St Michael and St George.

K.C.V.O., Knight Commander of the (Royal) Victorian Order.

kea (kā′ə), *n.* a large, greenish New Zealand parrot, *Nestor notabilis.* [t. Maori]

Kea (kē′ə), *n.* an island of the Cyclades, off the SE coast of Greece. 2373 pop. (1965); 56 sq. mi. Also, **Zea.** Formerly, **Keos.**

Kean (kēn), *n.* **Edmund,** 1787–1833, English tragic actor.

Keats (kēts), *n.* **John,** 1795–1821, English poet.

kebab (kĭ băb′), *n.* **1.** (*sometimes pl.*) an oriental dish consisting of small pieces of meat seasoned and roasted on a skewer, sometimes combined with onions, mushrooms, tomatoes, and peppers. **2.** *Anglo-Indian.* roast meat in general. Also, **kabob, cabob, kabab, kebob.** [t. Ar.: m. *kabāb*]

Keble (kē′bl), *n.* **John,** 1792–1866, English clergyman and religious reformer.

Kechua (kĕch′wə), *n.* Quechua. —**Kech′uan,** *adj., n.*

keck[1] (kĕk), *v.i.* **1.** to retch; be nauseated. **2.** to feel or show disgust or strong dislike. [akin to CHOKE]

keck[2] (kĕk), *n.* **1.** any of several white-flowered, coarse, perennial, umbelliferous herbs, especially cow-parsley and hogweed. **2.** kex. [back-formation from *kecks*, var. of KEX, taken as pl.]

keckle (kĕk′l), *v.t.,* **-led, -ling.** *Naut.* to wind old rope round (a cable or hawser) as a protection against chafing. [orig. unknown] —**keck′ling,** *n.*

Kecskemét (*Hung.* kĕch′kĕ mĕt), *n.* a town in central Hungary. 69,000 (1963).

ked (kĕd), *n.* the sheep tick.

Kedah (kĕd′ə), *n.* a state in Malaysia, on the SW Malay Peninsula. 817,119 pop. (est. 1962); 3660 sq. mi. *Cap.*: Alor Star.

keddah (kĕd′ə), *n.* kheda.

kedge (kĕj), *v.,* **kedged, kedging,** *n.* —*v.t.* **1.** to warp or pull (a ship, etc.) along by means of a rope attached to an anchor. —*v.i.* **2.** to move by being pulled along with the aid of an anchor. —*n.* **3.** Also, **kedge anchor.** a small anchor used in kedging. [ME *cagge(n)* warp, fasten]

kedgeree (kĕj′ə rē′), *n.* a dish of rice, cooked with white or smoked fish. [t. Hindi: m. *khicarī*]

Kedron (kĕd′rŏn), *n.* a ravine in Jordan, E of Jerusalem: in ancient times a brook. Also, **Kidron.**

keef (kĭ ĕf′), *n.* kef (def. 2).

keek (kēk), *v.i., n. Scot.* peep. [ME *kiken*, c. MD, MLG *kīken*]

keel[1] (kēl), *n.* **1.** a longitudinal timber, or combination of timbers, iron plates, or the like, extending along the middle of the bottom of a vessel from stem to stern and supporting the whole frame. See diag. under **gunwale. 2.** a ship. **3.** a part corresponding to a ship's keel in some other structure, as in an aircraft fuselage. **4.** *Bot., Zool.* a longitudinal ridge, as on a leaf or bone; a carina. **5. on an even keel,** in a steady or balanced state or manner. —*v.t., v.i.* **6.** to turn or upset so as to bring the wrong side or part uppermost. **7. keel over,** *Colloq.* to collapse suddenly. [ME *kele*, t. Scand.; cf. Icel. *kjölr*]

keel[2] (kēl), *n.* **1.** a lighter or barge, esp. in eastern England. **2.** a quantity of coal, etc. sufficient to fill a keel. [ME *kele*, t. MD: m. *kiel*; c. OE *cēol* ship]

keel[3] (kēl), *n.* a fatal disease of domestic ducks. [special use of KEEL[1]]

keel[4] (kēl), *n.* **1.** a variety of red ochre used for marking sheep, etc.; ruddle. *—v.t.* **2.** to mark (sheep) with keel. [ME (N dial.) *keyle*; cf. Gael. *cīl*]

keelage (kē′lij), *n.* formerly, dues paid by a vessel to a port owner for occupying a berth or anchorage.

keelboat (kēl′bōt′), *n. Western U.S.* keel[2] (def. 1).

Keele (kēl), *n.* a village in Staffordshire: university, founded 1962.

keelhaul (kēl′hôl′), *v.t.* **1.** *Naut.* to haul (a person) under the keel of a vessel, as for punishment. **2.** *Colloq.* to reprimand severely. [t. D: m. s. *kielhalen*, f. *kiel* keel + *halen* haul]

Keeling Islands (kē′lĭng), Cocos Islands.

keelson (kĕl′sən, kēl′-), *n. Naut.* a strengthening line of timbers or iron plates in a ship, above and parallel with the keel. Also, **kelson.** [der. KEEL[1]; orig. obscure]

Keelung (kē′lo͝ong′), *n.* a seaport on the N coast of Taiwan. 145,200 (est. 1964).

keen[1] (kēn), *adj.* **1.** sharp, or so shaped as to cut or pierce substances readily: *a keen blade.* **2.** sharp, piercing, or biting: *a keen wind, keen satire.* **3.** characterized by strength and distinctness of perception, as the ear or hearing, the eye, sight, etc. **4.** having or showing great mental penetration or acumen: *keen reasoning.* **5.** animated by or showing competitiveness: *keen prices.* **6.** intense, as feeling, desire, etc. **7.** ardent; eager (often fol. by *about*, *for*, etc., or an infinitive). **8.** having a fondness or devotion (for) (fol. by *on*). [ME *kene*, OE *cēne*, c. G *kühn* bold] **—keen′ly,** *adv.* **—keen′ness,** *n.* **—Syn. 1, 4.** See **sharp.**

keen[2] (kēn), *n.* **1.** a wailing lament for the dead. *—v.i.* **2.** to wail in lamentation for the dead. [t. Irish: m. *caoine*, der. *caoinim* I lament] **—keen′er,** *n.*

keep (kēp), *v.*, **kept, keeping,** *n.* *—v.t.* **1.** to maintain in one's action or conduct: *to keep watch, step, or silence.* **2.** to cause to continue in some place, position, state, course, or action specified: *to keep a light burning.* **3.** to maintain in condition or order, as by care and labour. **4.** to hold in custody or under guard, as a prisoner; detain; prevent from coming or going. **5.** to have habitually in stock or for sale. **6.** to maintain in one's service or for one's use or enjoyment. **7.** to associate with: *to keep bad company.* **8.** to have the charge or custody of. **9.** to withhold from the knowledge of others: *to keep a secret.* **10.** to withhold from use; reserve. **11.** to restrain: *for heaven's sake keep him from laughing.* **12.** to maintain by writing, entries, etc.: *to keep a diary.* **13.** to record (business transactions, etc.) regularly: *to keep records.* **14.** to observe; pay obedient regard to (a law, rule, promise, etc.). **15.** to conform to; follow; fulfil: *to keep one's word.* **16.** to observe (a season, festival, etc.) with formalities or rites: *to keep Christmas.* **17.** to maintain or carry on, as an establishment, business, etc.; manage: *to keep house.* **18.** to guard; protect. **19.** to maintain or support (a person, etc.). **20.** to take care of; tend: *to keep sheep.* **21.** to maintain in active existence, or hold, as an assembly, court, fair, etc. **22.** to remain in (a place, etc.). **23.** to maintain one's position in or on. **24.** to continue to follow (a path, track, course, etc.). **25.** to continue to hold or have: *to keep a thing in mind.* **26.** to save, hold, or retain in possession.
—v.i. **27.** to continue in an action, course, position, state, etc.: *to keep in sight.* **28.** to remain, or continue to be, as specified: *to keep cool.* **29.** to remain or stay in a place: *to keep indoors.* **30.** to continue unimpaired or without spoiling: *the milk will keep on ice.* **31.** to admit of being reserved for a future occasion. **32.** to keep oneself or itself (fol. by *away, back, off, out*, etc.): *keep off the grass.* **33.** to restrain oneself: *try to keep from smiling.* *—v.* **34.** Some special verb phrases are:
keep at, to persist in.
keep back, 1. to withhold. **2.** to restrain; hold in check. **3.** to stay away; not advance.
keep in with, *Colloq.* to keep oneself in favour with.
keep on, to persist.
keep time, 1. to record time, as a watch or clock does. **2.** to beat, mark, or observe the rhythmic accents of music, etc. **3.** to perform rhythmic movements in unison.
keep to, 1. to adhere to (an agreement, plan, facts, etc.). **2.** to confine oneself to: *to keep to one's bed.*
keep to oneself, to hold aloof from the society of others.
keep track of, tabs on, to keep account (of).
keep up, 1. to maintain an equal rate of speed, activity, or progress, as with another. **2.** to bear up; continue without breaking down, as under strain.
keep wicket, *Cricket.* to act as wicket-keeper.
—n. **35.** subsistence; board and lodging: *to work for one's keep.* **36.** the innermost and strongest structure or central tower of a medieval castle. **37. for keeps,** *Colloq.* **a.** for keeping as one's own permanently: *to play for keeps.* **b.** permanently; altogether.
[ME *kepen*, OE *cēpan* observe, heed, regard, await, take; akin to Icel. *kōpa* stare]
—Syn. 2. KEEP, RESERVE, RETAIN, WITHHOLD refer to having and holding in possession. KEEP (a common word) and RETAIN (a more formal one) agree in meaning to continue to have or hold, as opposed to losing, parting with, or giving up: *to keep a book for a week.* To RESERVE is to keep for some future use, occasion, or recipient, or to hold back for a time: *to reserve judgement.* To WITHHOLD is generally to hold back altogether: *to withhold help.* **4.** detain, hold, confine.

keeper (kē′pə), *n.* **1.** one who keeps, guards, or watches. **2.** gamekeeper. **3.** wicket-keeper. **4.** shopkeeper. **5.** goalkeeper. **6.** a person in charge of something valuable, as the custodian of a museum, zoo, or any section thereof. **7.** something that keeps, or serves to guard, hold in place, retain, etc. **8.** something that keeps or lasts well, as a fruit. **9.** a guard ring. **10.** *Elect.* a soft iron bar placed across the poles of a permanent magnet in order to prevent loss of magnetism during storage. **—keep′erless,** *adj.* **—Syn. 1.** guard, warden; custodian, guardian.

keeping (kē′pĭng), *n.* **1.** just conformity in things or elements associated together: *his deeds are not in keeping with his words.* **2.** the act of one who or that which keeps; observance, custody, or care. **3.** *Mech.* any of various devices for holding something in position. **4.** maintenance or keep. **5.** holding, reserving, or retaining. **—keep′-ership′,** *n.* **—Syn. 1.** agreement, congruity, harmony. **2.** protection. See **custody.**

keepsake (kēp′sāk′), *n.* anything kept, or given to be kept, for the sake of the giver, as a token of remembrance, friendship, etc.

keeshond (kās′hŏnd, kēs′-), *n.*, *pl.* **-honds** or **-honden** (-hŏn′dən). one of a breed of small dogs, originating in Holland, with ash-grey coat, and a ruff around the neck. [t. D, equiv. to *Kees* (familiar form of proper name *Cornelius*) + *hond* dog]

keeve (kēv), *n.* a kind of large vat, esp. one used for washing tin or copper ores.

Keewatin (kē wŏt′ĭn), *n.* a district in N Canada, in the Northwest Territories. 228,160 sq. mi.

kef (kāf), *n.* (among the Arabs) **1.** a state of drowsy contentment, as from the use of a narcotic. **2.** Also, **keef.** a substance, esp. a smoking preparation of hemp leaves, used to produce this state. Also, **kief, kaif.** [t. Ar.: pleasure]

keg (kĕg), *n.* **1.** a small cask or barrel, usually holding from 5 to 10 gallons. **2.** *Obs.* a unit of weight, equal to 100 lbs, used for nails. [late ME *cag*, t. Scand.; cf. Icel. *kaggi*]

kei apple (kī, kā), **1.** the sour, edible fruit of a small southern African tree, *Dovyalis caffra*, of the family *Flacourtiaceae.* **2.** the tree. [named after the Great *Kei* river in Cape Province]

Keighley (kēth′lĭ), *n.* a town in England, in the West Riding of Yorkshire. 55,845 (1961).

Keijo (kā′jō′), *n.* Japanese name of **Seoul.**

keir (kīə), *n.* kier.

Keitel (*Ger.* kī′təl), *n.* **Wilhelm** (*Ger.* vĭl′hĕlm), 1882–1946, German marshal: chief of Nazi High Command 1938–45.

Keith (kēth), *n.* **Sir Arthur,** 1866–1955, Scottish anthropologist.

Kekkonen (*Finn.* kĕk′kô nĕn), *n.* **Urho** (*Finn.* o͞or′hô), born 1900, president of Finland 1956–68.

Kekulé formula (*Ger.* kĕ′ko͞o lĕ), *Chem.* a structural formula for benzene, in which the six carbon atoms are arranged into a hexagonal ring with alternating single and double bonds between them. [named after F. A. *Kekulé* von Stradonitz, 1829–96, German chemist]

Kelantan (kĕ lăn′tən, kĭ lăn′tăn′), *n.* a state in Malaysia, on the SE Malay Peninsula. 595,293 pop. (est. 1962); 5750 sq. mi. *Cap.:* Kota Bahru.

Keller (kĕl′ə), *n.* **Helen** (**Adams**), 1880–1968, U.S. author, blind and deaf, who learned to speak.

Kelly (kĕl′ĭ), *n.* **Ned,** 1855–80, notorious Australian bushranger.

keloid (kē′loid), *n. Pathol.* a kind of fibrous tumour forming hard, irregular, clawlike excrescences upon the skin. Also, **cheloid.** [*k-* var., f. Gk *kēl(is)* stain + -OID; *ch-* var., f. Gk *chēl(ē)* claw + -OID]

kelp (kĕlp), *n.* **1.** any of the large brown seaweeds belonging to the family *Laminariaceae.* **2.** the ash of such seaweeds. [ME *culp*; ult. orig. unknown]

kelpie[1] (kĕl′pĭ), *n. Scot.* a fabled water spirit, usually in the form of a horse, reputed to give warning of or to cause drowning. [orig. uncert.]

kelpie[2] (kĕl′pĭ), *n.* one of a breed of Australian sheepdogs. [named after one of these dogs]

kelpy (kĕl′pĭ), *n., pl.* **-pies.** kelpie[1].

kelson (kĕl′sən), *n.* keelson.

kelt (kĕlt), *n.* a salmon that has recently spawned. [ME, N dial.]

Kelt (kĕlt), *n.* Celt. **—Kelt′ic,** *n., adj.*

kelter (kĕl′tə), *n. Dial.* good condition; order: *the engine was out of kelter.* Also, *U.S.,* **kilter.**

kelvin (kĕl′vĭn), *n. Physics.* the basic SI unit of temperature, equal to one degree centigrade; the unit of the Kelvin scale. *Symbol:* K [named after Lord KELVIN]

Kelvin (kĕl′vĭn), *n.* **William Thomson, 1st Baron,** 1824–1907, British physicist and mathematician.

Kelvin scale, *Physics.* a scale of temperature (**Kelvin temperature**), based on thermodynamic principles, in which zero is equivalent to −273·16°C or −459·69°F.

Kemal Atatürk (*Turk.* kĕ mäl′ ä tä tʏrk′). See **Atatürk.**

Kemble (kĕm′bl), *n.* **1. Frances Anne,** or **Fanny** (*Mrs Butler*), 1809–93, English actress and author. **2. John Philip,** 1757–1823, English actor.

Kemerovo (*Russ.* kyĕ′mĭ rə və), *n.* a city in the S Soviet Union in Asia. 351,000 (est. 1965).

Kempe (kĕmp), *n.* **Margery,** *c.* 1374–*c.* 1460, English religious writer.

Kempff (*Ger.* kĕmpf), *n.* **Wilhelm (Walter Friedrich)** (*Ger.* vĭl′hĕlm väl′tər frē′drĭkh), born 1895, German pianist.

Kempis (kĕm′pĭs), *n.* **Thomas à** (ə), 1380?–1471, German churchman and author.

ken (kĕn), *n., v.,* **kenned** or **kent, kenning.** **—***n.* **1.** range of sight or vision. **2.** knowledge or cognizance; mental perception. **—***v.t.* **3.** *Archaic.* to see; descry; recognize. **4.** *Scot.* to have acquaintance with. **—***v.i.* **5.** *Archaic or Dial.* to have knowledge of something. [ME *kennen,* OE *cennan,* c. Icel. *kenna* make known, know (cf. later E senses), G *kennen* know; orig. a causative of the verb represented by CAN[1]]

Ken., Kentucky.

Kendal (kĕn′dl), *n.* a town in England, in Westmorland. 18,599 (1961).

Kendal green, 1. a green woollen cloth formerly in use. **2.** green produced by a dye extracted from the woad plant. [named after KENDAL]

kendo (kĕn′dō), *n.* a Japanese style of fencing with bamboo staves.

Kenilworth (kĕn′ĭl wûth′), *n.* a town in England, in Warwickshire: ruined castle. 14,427 (1961).

Kenitra (*Fr.* kė nē trȧ′), *n.* a river port in NW Morocco. 105,000 (est. 1965). Also, **Mina Hassan Tani, Port Lyautey.**

Kennedy (kĕn′ĭ dĭ), *n.* **1. Edward Moore,** born 1932, U.S. politician. **2. John Fitzgerald,** 1917–63, 35th president of the United States, 1961–63. **3. Joseph Patrick,** 1888–1969, U.S. diplomat (father of Edward, John, and Robert). **4. Robert Francis,** 1925–68, U.S. politician. **5. Cape.** Formerly, **Cape Canaveral.** a cape on an island off E Florida: space-vehicle launch complex. **6.** See **John F. Kennedy International Airport.**

kennel (kĕn′əl), *n., v.,* **-nelled, -nelling** or (*U.S.*) **-neled, -neling.** **—***n.* **1.** a house for a dog or dogs. **2.** (*usually pl., construed as sing.*) an establishment where dogs are bred. **3.** (in contemptuous use) a wretched abode. **—***v.t.* **4.** to put into or keep in a kennel. **—***v.i.* **5.** to take shelter or lodge in a kennel. [ME *kenel,* t. ONF, g. VL *canīle,* der. L *canis* dog]

Kennelly (kĕn′ə lĭ), *n.* **Arthur Edwin,** 1861–1939, U.S. electrical engineer.

Kennelly-Heaviside layer (kĕn′ə lĭ hĕv′ĭ sīd′), Heaviside layer. [named after A. E. KENNELLY and O. HEAVISIDE]

kennelmaid (kĕn′əl mād′), *n.* a girl employed to tend dogs in kennels.

kennelman (kĕn′əl măn′), *n., pl.* **-men.** a man employed to tend dogs in kennels.

kenning (kĕn′ĭng), *n.* a descriptive name used for, or in addition to, the usual name of a person or thing. *Example:* 'a wave traveller' for 'a boat' [t. Icel.]

Kenny (kĕn′ĭ), *n.* **Elizabeth** (*Sister Kenny*), 1884?–1952, Australian nurse: developed a method of treating poliomyelitis.

kenogenesis (kē′nō jĕn′ĭ sĭs), *n. Chiefly U.S.* cainogenesis.

kenosis (kĭ nō′sĭs), *n. Theol.* Christ's renunciation of divine privilege at the incarnation in order that He might become entirely man while remaining truly God (based on Phil. 2:6, 7, R.V.). [t. NL, t. Gk: an emptying] **—kenotic** (kĭ nŏt′ĭk), *adj.*

Kensington and Chelsea (kĕn′zĭng tən ən chĕl′sĭ), a SW inner borough of London: a royal borough. 220,600 (1965).

Kent (kĕnt), *n.* **1.** a county in SE England. 1,701,083 pop. (1961); 1525 sq. mi. *Co. town:* Maidstone. **2.** an ancient English kingdom in SE Britain. See map under **Mercia. 3. William,** 1685–1748, English designer, landscape gardener, and architect.

Kentish (kĕn′tĭsh), *adj.* of or pertaining to Kent.

Kentish fire, *Obs.* slow handclapping in unison to express disapproval.

Kentishman (kĕn′tĭsh mən), *n., pl.* **-men.** an inhabitant or native of Kent, traditionally one from west of the river Medway (opposed to a *man of Kent,* from east of the Medway).

kentledge (kĕnt′lĭj), *n. Naut.* pig-iron used as permanent ballast. [orig. obscure]

Kentucky (kĕn tŭk′ĭ), *n.* a state in the E central United States. 3,038,156 pop. (1960); 40,395 sq. mi. *Cap.:* Frankfort. *Abbrev.:* Ky or Ken. **—Kentuck′ian,** *adj., n.*

Kenya (kē′nyə, kĕn′yə), *n.* **1.** an independent state in E Africa: member of the Commonwealth of Nations. 8,626,163 pop. (1962); 219,730 sq. mi. *Cap.:* Nairobi. **2. Mount,** a volcanic mountain in Kenya. 17,040 ft. **—Ken′yan,** *adj.*

Kenyatta (kĕn yăt′ə), *n.* **Jomo** (jō′mō), born 1891, Kenyan statesman: prime minister 1963–64, president since 1964.

Keos (kē′ŏs), *n.* former name of **Kea.**

kep (kĕp), *v.t. Scot.* to catch or intercept.

kephalin (kĕf′ə lĭn), *n. Biochem.* cephalin.

Kephallenia (kĕf′ə lē′nĭ ə), *n.* Greek name of **Cephalonia.**

kepi (kā′pē; *Fr.* kė pē′), *n., pl.* **-pis.** a French military cap with a flat circular top and a horizontal visor. [t. F: m. *képi,* t. d. G: m. *Käppi,* dim. of G *Kappe* cap]

Kepi

Kepler (*Ger.* kĕp′lər), *n.* **Johann** (*Ger.* yō′hän), 1571–1630, German astronomer. **—Keplerian** (kĕp lĭə′rĭ ən), *adj.*

Kepler's laws, *Astron.* three laws of planetary motion stating: **1.** that the planets move in elliptical orbits about the sun, which is situated at one focus of the ellipses. **2.** that the radius vectors joining each planet to the sun describe equal areas in equal times. **3.** that the ratio of the square of the planet's year to the cube of the planet's mean distance from the sun is the same for each planet. [named after J. KEPLER]

kept (kĕpt), *v.* pt. and pp. of **keep.**

Kerala (kĕ′rə lə, kĕ rä′lə), *n.* a state in SW India, comprising the regions of Travancore and Cochin. 16,903,715 pop. (1961); 15,035 sq. mi. *Cap.:* Trivandrum.

keramic (kĭ răm′ĭk), *adj.* ceramic.

keratin (kĕ′rə tĭn), *n. Zool., Anat.* a proteinaceous substance, consisting of the dead outer corneal skin layer, and variously modified into horn, feathers, hair, hoofs. Also, **ceratin.** [f. s. Gk *kéras* horn + -IN[2]]

keratinize (kĭ răt′ĭ nīz′, kĕ′rə tĭ-), *v.t., v.i.,* **-nized, -nizing.** to make or become keratinous. Also, **keratinise. —kera′tiniza′tion,** *n.*

keratinous (kĭ răt′ĭ nəs), *adj.* composed of or resembling keratin.

keratitis (kĕ′rə tī′tĭs), *n.* inflammation of the cornea.

keratogenous (kĕ′rə tŏj′ĭ nəs), *adj.* producing horn or a horny substance. [f. *kerato-* (comb. form repr. Gk *kéras* horn) + -GENOUS]

keratoid (kĕ′rə toid′), *adj.* resembling horn; horny. [t. Gk: m. s. *keratoeidḗs*]

keratoplasty (kĕ′rə tō plăs′tĭ), *n., pl.* **-ties.** a plastic surgical operation upon the cornea; specif., a corneal transplantation.

kerb (kûb), *n.* **1.** a line of joined stones, concrete, or the like at the edge of a street, wall, etc. **2.** *Stock Exchange.* **a.** the pavement or street as a market for the sale of securities. **b.** (*pl.*) dealings conducted after normal hours, orig. in the street. **3.** the fender of a hearth. **4.** the framework round the top of a well. **—***v.t.* **5.** to furnish with, or protect by a kerb. Cf. **curb.** [var. spelling of CURB]

kerb broker, *Stock Exchange.* a broker who is not a member of a stock exchange.

kerbing (kû′bĭng), *n.* the material forming a kerb. Also, *U.S.,* **curbing.**

kerb market, kerb (def. 2).

kerbstone (kûb′stōn′), *n.* one of the stones, or a range of stones, forming a kerb, as along the outer edge of a pavement, etc. Also, *U.S.,* **curbstone.**

Kerch (*Russ.* kyĕrch), *n.* a seaport in the SW Soviet Union, on **Kerch Strait,** a strait connecting the Sea of Azov and the Black Sea. 114,000 (est. 1965).

kerchief (kû′chĭf), *n.* **1.** a cloth worn as a head covering, esp. by women. **2.** a cloth worn or carried on the person. [ME *curchef,* contr. of *coverchef;* t. OF: m. *couvrechief,* f. *couvrir* COVER + *chief* head. Cf. CHIEF]

Kerenski (kə rĕn′skĭ; *Russ.* kyĕ′rĭn skĭy), *n.* **Aleksandr**

Feodorovich (*Russ.* ə lĭk sän′ dər fĭ ô′ də rə vich), 1881–1970, Russian revolutionary leader; prime minister, 1917. Also, **Kerensky.**

Keresan (kĕ′rĭ sən), *n.* a linguistic stock of Pueblo tribes of the Rio Grande valley and neighbouring areas.

kerf (kûf), *n.* **1.** the cut or incision made by a saw or other instrument. **2.** that which is cut. [ME *kerf, kyrf*, OE *cyrf* a cutting, akin to *ceorfan*, v., cut, CARVE]

Kerguelen (kû′gĭ lĭn), *n.* a desolate island in the S Indian Ocean: a possession of France. ab. 1400 sq. mi. French, **Kerguélen** (*Fr.* kĕr gė lĕn′).

Kerkrade (*Du.* kĕrk′rä də), *n.* a town in the SE Netherlands. 50,899 (1965).

Kerkyra (kĕə′kĭ rə), *n.* Greek name of **Corfu.**

Kerman (*Pers.* kėr män′), *n.* a town in SE Iran. 75,228 (est. 1964).

Kermanshah (kû′măn shä′), *n.* a city in W Iran. 125,181 (1956).

kermes (kû′mĭz), *n.* **1.** a red dye formerly prepared from the dried bodies of the females of a scale insect, *Kermes ilices*, which lives on certain oaks of the Mediterranean region. **2.** the small evergreen oak, *Quercus coccifera*, on which it is found. **3.** amorphous antimony trisulphide. [t. Ar., Pers.: m. *qirmiz*. Cf. CARMINE, CRIMSON]

kermesite (kû′mə zīt′, -sīt′), *n.* a mineral antimony oxysulphide, Sb_2S_2O, occurring in red orthorhombic or monoclinic crystals. Also, **pyrostibnite.**

kermis (kû′mĭs), *n.* **1.** (in the Low Countries) an annual fair or festival attended with sports and merrymaking. **2.** *U.S.* a similar entertainment, usually for charitable purposes. Also, **kermess, kirmess.** [t. D, var. of *kermisse, kerkmisse* church mass (on the anniversary of the dedication of a church)]

kern[1] (kûn), *n. Archaic.* **1.** a band of light-armed foot soldiers of ancient Ireland. **2.** (in Ireland or sometimes in the Scottish Highlands) a soldier. **3.** an Irish peasant. Also, **kerne.** [ME *kerne*, t. Irish: m. *ceithern* band of foot soldiers. See CATERAN]

kern[2] (kûn), *Print.* **—*n.*** **1.** a part of the face of a type projecting beyond the body or shank, as in certain italic letters. **—*v.t.*** **2.** to form or furnish with a kern, as a type or letter. [t. F: m. *carne* point, g. s. L *cardo* hinge]

kern[3] (kûn), *Dial.* **—*v.i.*** **1.** (of corn, etc.) to form the hard grains in the ear; to seed. **2.** (of salt, etc.) to crystallize into grains; granulate. **—*v.t.*** **3.** to cause to kern. [ME *kerne, curne*, akin to CORN[1]]

kern[4] (kûn), *n. Engineering.* the central part of an area, through which all compressive forces must pass. [t. G: *Kern* core]

Kern (kûn), *n.* **Jerome (David),** 1885–1945, U.S. composer.

kernel (kû′nəl), *n.*, *v.*, **-nelled, -nelling,** or (*U.S.*) **-neled, -neling. —*n.*** **1.** the softer, usually edible, part contained in the shell of a nut or the stone of a fruit. **2.** the body of a seed within its husk or integuments. **3.** a grain, as of wheat. **4.** the central part of anything; the nucleus; the core. **—*v.t.*** **5.** to enclose as a kernel. [ME *kirnel, curnel*, OE *cyrnel*, dim. of *corn* seed, grain. See CORN[1]] **—ker′nelless,** *adj.*

kernicterus (kə nĭk′tə rəs), *n. Pathol.* a severe form of jaundice in the newborn, usually causing death or permanent brain damage. [t. G: f. *Kern* core (see KERN[4])+ *Icterus* ICTERUS]

kernite (kû′nīt), *n.* a mineral, hydrated sodium borate, $(Na_2B_4O_7 . 4H_2O)$, occurring in transparent colourless crystals. [named after *Kern* County, in California + -ITE[1]]

kerosene (kĕ′rə sēn′), *n.* paraffin oil. Also, **kerosine.** [f. Gk *kērós* wax + -ENE]

Kerouac (kĕ′ro͞o ăk′), *n.* **Jack** (*Jean-Louis Lefris de Kérouac*), 1922–69, U.S. beat novelist, born in Canada.

Kerr effect, *Physics.* the rotation of the plane of polarization of light when it is passed through certain liquids or solids to which a potential difference is applied. [named after John *Kerr*, 1824–1907, Scottish physicist]

Kerr cell, *Physics.* a cell, based on the Kerr effect, which is used as a high-speed camera shutter.

kerry (kĕ′rĭ), *n.*, *pl.* **-ries.** one of a breed of small dairy cattle originating in Kerry.

Kerry (kĕ′rĭ), *n.* a county in the SW Republic of Ireland. 116,458 pop. (1961); 1815 sq. mi. *Co. town:* Tralee.

Kerry blue, one of a breed of large Irish terrier, having a soft, wavy, bluish coat.

kersey (kû′zĭ), *n.*, *pl.* **-seys. 1.** a compact, well-fulled woollen cloth with a fine nap and smooth face. **2.** a coarse twilled woollen cloth with a cotton warp. [ME; ? named after *Kersey*, in Suffolk]

kerseymere (kû′zĭ mĭə′), *n.* a twilled fine woollen cloth of a fancy weave. [f. KERSEY + (CASSI)MERE]

Kesselring (*Ger.* kĕs′əl rĭng), *n.* **Albert** (*Ger.* äl′bĕrt), 1885–1960, German airforce field marshal.

Kesteven (kĕs tē′vən), *n.* an administrative division of Lincolnshire. 134,842 pop. (1961); 722 sq. mi. *Chief town:* Sleaford. Official name, **the Parts of Kesteven.**

kestrel (kĕs′trəl), *n.* a common small falcon, *Falco tinnunculus*, of northern parts of the Eastern Hemisphere, notable for hovering in the air with its head to the wind. [var. of earlier *castrel*. Cf. F *crécerelle*]

ketch (kĕch), *n.* a fore-and-aft rigged vessel with a large mainmast and a smaller mast aft, but forward of the rudder post. [earlier *catch*, appar. der. CATCH, v.]

ketchup (kĕch′əp), *n.* any of several sauces or condiments for meat, fish, etc.: *tomato ketchup; mushroom ketchup.* Also, **catsup, catchup.** [appar. t. Chinese (Amoy d.): m. *kê-tsiap* brine of pickled fish. Cf. Malay *kechop* sauce (? t. Chinese)]

ketene (kē′tēn), *n. Chem.* **1.** a gas, $H_2C = C = O$, with a penetrating smell, obtained from acetic anhydride or acetone. **2.** a class of compounds having the type formulas, $RHC = C = O$ and $R_2C = C = O$. [f. KET(ONE) + -ENE]

keto-enol tautomerism (kē′tō ē′nŏl), *Chem.* a type of tautomerism in which the individual tautomers may be isolated as a keto form and an enol.

keto form (kē′tō), *Chem.* (in a keto-enol tautomeric substance) the form with the characteristics of a ketone.

ketohexose (kĕt′ō hĕk′sōs), *n. Chem.* any of a group of carbohydrates containing six carbon atoms and a ketone group.

ketone (kē′tōn), *n. Chem.* any of a class of organic compounds, having the general formula, RCOR′, containing the carbonyl group, CO, attached to two organic radicals, as acetone, CH_3COCH_3. [t. G: m. *Keton*, with *-e* from *acetone*, of the G equivalent of which *Keton* is a form aphetically der.] **—ketonic** (kĭ tŏn′ĭk), *adj.*

ketone bodies, *Pathol.* acetone and related compounds found in blood, urine, etc., during ketosis; acetone bodies.

ketose (kē′tōs), *n. Chem.* any of the sugars which have a ketone group or its equivalent.

ketosis (kĭ tō′sĭs), *n. Pathol.* the condition of having too much of a ketone in the body, as in diabetes, acidosis, etc. [f. KET(ONE) + -OSIS]

Kettering (kĕt′ə rĭng), *n.* a town in England, in Northamptonshire. 38,659 (1961).

kettle (kĕt′l), *n.* **1.** a portable container with a cover, a spout, and a handle, in which to boil water for making tea and other uses; teakettle. **2.** any of various containers for cooking foods, melting glue, etc. **3.** a fish kettle. **4.** an open vessel for heating metals of low melting point. **5.** a kettleful. **6.** a kettledrum. **7.** a kettle hole. **8. kettle of fish, a.** a mess, muddle, or awkward state of affairs (often preceded ironically by *pretty, fine*, etc.). **b.** any situation or state of affairs: *this is a different kettle of fish altogether.* [ME *ketel*, t. Scand. (cf. Icel. *ketill*, c. OE *cetel*, G *Kessel*), ult. t. L: m. s. *catillus*, dim. of *catinus* bowl, pot]

kettledrum (kĕt′l drŭm′), *n.* a drum consisting of a hollow hemisphere of brass or copper with a skin stretched over it, which can be accurately tuned. **—ket′tledrum′mer,** *n.*

Kettledrum

kettleful (kĕt′l fo͝ol′), *n.* as much as a kettle will hold: *a kettleful of water.*

kettle hole, a kettle-shaped cavity in rock or detrital material, esp. in glacial drift.

keV, *Physics.* kilo-electron-volt(s).

kevel (kĕv′əl), *n. Naut.* a sturdy bit, bollard, etc., on which the heavier hawsers of a ship may be secured. [ME *kevile*, t. ONF: m. *keville* pin, g. L *clāvicula* little key]

Kew (kyo͞o), *n.* a district of the SW outer London borough of Richmond upon Thames: botanical gardens.

Kewpie (kyo͞o′pĭ), *n. Trademark.* a small, very plump doll, usually made of plaster or celluloid.

kex (kĕks), *n. Dial.* **1.** the dry, usually hollow stem or stalk of various herbaceous plants, esp. of large umbelliferous plants, as the cow-parsnip, wild chervil, etc. **2.** the plant itself. [orig. obscure]

key[1] (kē), *n.*, *pl.* **keys,** *adj.*, *v.*, **keyed, keying. —*n.*** **1.** an instrument for fastening or opening a lock by moving its bolt. **2.** a means of attaining, understanding, solving, etc.: *the key to a problem.* **3.** a book or the like containing the solutions or translations of material given elsewhere as exercises. **4.** the system or pattern used to decode a cryptogram, etc. **5.** a systematic explanation of abbreviations, symbols, etc., used in a dictionary, map, etc. **6.** something that secures or controls entrance to a place. **7.** a pin, bolt, wedge, or other piece inserted in a hole or space to lock or hold parts of a mechanism or structure together; a cotter. **8.** *Carp., etc.* a small piece of wood, etc., set across the grain to prevent warping. **9.** a contrivance for grasping and turning a bolt, nut, etc., as for winding a clockwork mechanism, for turning a valve or stopcock.

10. one of a set of levers or parts pressed in operating a telegraph, typewriter, etc. **11.** *Music.* **a.** that part of the lever mechanism of a piano, organ, or woodwind instrument, which a finger operates. **b.** the keynote or tonic of a scale. **c.** the relationship perceived between all notes in a given unit of music to a single note or a keynote; tonality. **d.** the principal tonality of a composition: *symphony in the key of C minor.* **12.** tone or pitch, as of voice: *to speak in a high key.* **13.** strain, or characteristic style, as of expression or thought. **14.** degree of intensity, as of feeling or action. **15.** *Elect.* **a.** a device for opening and closing electrical contacts. **b.** a hand-operated switching device ordinarily formed of concealed spring contacts with an exposed handle or push-button, capable of switching one or more parts of a circuit. **16.** *Bot., Zool.* a systematic tabular classification of the significant characteristics of the members of a group of organisms to facilitate identification and comparison. **17.** *Masonry.* a keystone. **18.** *Bldg Trades.* any grooving or roughness on a surface to improve bond. **19.** the predominant tonal value of a range of colours. **20.** *Bot.* a samara.
—*adj.* **21.** chief; major; fundamental; indispensable: *the key industries of a nation.* **22.** *Photog.* predominant; determining tonal value: *the key tone of a photograph.* **23.** *Advertising, Journalism, etc.* identifying: *a key line, a key number.*
—*v.t.* **24.** to bring to a particular degree of intensity of feeling, excitement, energy, etc. (often fol. by *up*). **25.** to adjust (one's speech, actions, etc.) as if to a particular key, in order to come into harmony with external factors, as the level of understanding of one's hearers. **26.** *Music.* to regulate the key or pitch of. **27.** to fasten, secure, or adjust with a key, wedge, or the like, as parts of a mechanism. **28.** to provide with a key or keys. **29.** (in the layout of publications) to identify by symbols the position on the layout (of artwork, copy, etc.) (often fol. by *up*). **30.** to give (an advertisement) a letter or number to enable replies to it to be identified. **31.** to lock with, or as with, a key. **32.** *Masonry.* to provide (an arch, etc.) with a keystone. **33.** *Bldg Trades.* **a.** to prepare (a surface) by grooving, roughening, etc., to receive paint. **b.** to cause (paint, etc.) to adhere to a surface.
—*v.i.* **34.** *Bldg Trades.* (of paint, etc.) to adhere to a surface. [ME *key(e), kay(e),* OE *cǣg,* c. OFris. *kei, kai*]

key[2] (kē), *n., pl.* **keys.** (in the Caribbean area) a reef or low island; cay. [t. Sp.: m. *cayo*]

keyboard (kē′bôd′), *n.* **1.** the row or set of keys on a piano, typewriter, etc. **2.** any of two or more sets of keys, as on large organs, or harpsichords.

key fruit, *Bot.* a samara.

keyhole (kē′hōl′), *n.* a hole for a key to a lock.

keyhole limpet, a gastropod mollusc of the genus *Fissurela,* which has a hole at the apex of its shell.

keyless (kē′lĭs), *adj.* **1.** without a key. **2.** not requiring a key.

key money, a sum of money paid by a prospective tenant for the opportunity of obtaining an interest in a property.

Keynes (kānz), *n.* **John Maynard** (mā′nəd, -näd), **1st Baron,** 1883–1946, English economist and writer.

Keynesian (kān′zyən), *adj.* **1.** of, pertaining to, or denoting the economic theories, policies, etc., of J. M. Keynes and his followers, esp. the systematic explanation of the determinants of effective demand and the policy of maintaining high employment and of controlling inflation by capital and public investment and by varying taxation and interest rates. —*n.* **2.** one who supports the theories, policies, etc., of Keynes.

keynote (kē′nōt′), *n., v.,* **-noted, -noting.** —*n.* **1.** *Music.* the note on which a key (system of notes) is founded; the tonic. **2.** the determining principle governing the spirit of speech, thought, action, etc. **3.** *U.S.* the line of policy to be followed by a party in a political (or other) campaign, as set forth authoritatively in advance in a public speech or other formal announcement. —*v.t.* **4.** *U.S.* to announce the policy of (a political party, etc.).

key plate, *Print.* (in the offset lithography process where colour separation is not photomechanical) a plate used in multicolour printing to prepare other plates to print each colour.

key punch, *U.S., Computers.* cardpunch.

key ring, a ring, usually of metal, for holding keys, etc.

Keyser (kē′zə, kī′zə; *Du.* kĕy′zər), *n.* **Hendrick de** (*Du.* hĕn′drĭk də), 1565–1621, Dutch architect.

Keyserling (*Ger.* kī′zər lĭng), *n.* **Hermann Alexander** (*Ger.* hĕr′mȧn ȧ lĕ ksȧn′dər), **Count,** 1880–1946, German writer and traveller.

Keys, House of. See **House of Keys.**

key signature, *Music.* (in notation) the group of sharps or flats placed after the clef to indicate the tonality of the music following.

keystone (kē′stōn′), *n.* **1.** the wedge-shaped piece at the summit of an arch, regarded as holding the other pieces in place. See diag. under **arch. 2.** something on which associated things depend.

keyway (kē′wā′), *n. Bldg Trades.* a slot or chase cut in a surface of contact to receive a key to prevent relative movement.

Key West, 1. an island in S Florida, in the Gulf of Mexico. **2.** a seaport on this island: the southernmost town in the U.S.; naval base. 33,956 (1960).

kg, 1. keg; kegs. **2.** kilogram; kilograms.

kg., kilogram; kilograms.

K.G., Knight of the Garter.

K.G.B., the secret police of the Soviet Union. [Russ.: *K(omitet) G(osudarstrennoi) B(ezopasnosti),* lit., Committee of State Security]

Khabarovsk (*Russ.* KHə bȧ rôfsk′), *n.* **1.** Formerly, **Far Eastern Region.** a maritime territory in the E Soviet Union in Asia. 965,400 sq. mi. **2.** the capital of this territory, in the SE part: a port on the river Amur. 408,000 (est. 1965).

Khachaturian (kăch′ə to͝oə′rĭ ən; *Russ.* KHə chə to͞o ryȧn′), *n.* **Aram** (*Russ.* ȧ′rəm), born 1903, Soviet composer born in Armenia.

khaddar (kä′də), *n.* hand-spun, hand-woven cloth produced in India. Also, **khadi** (kä′dĭ). [t. Hind.]

Khaibar Pass (kī′bə), Khyber Pass.

khaki (kä′kĭ), *n., pl.* **-kis,** *adj.* —*n.* **1.** dull yellowish brown. **2.** stout twilled cotton uniform cloth of this colour, worn esp. by soldiers. **3.** a similar fabric of wool. —*adj.* **4.** of the colour of khaki. **5.** made of khaki. [t. Hind.: dusty, der. *khāk* dust]

khaki bush, a naturalized weed of southern Africa, *Althernanthera achyrantha,* originally from Argentina.

khalif (kä lēf′), *n.* caliph. Also, **khalifa** (kä lē′fə).

Khalkidike (*Gk* KHȧl kē dē′kė), *n.* Greek name of **Chalcidice.**

Khama (kä′mə), *n. c.* 1837–1922, king of a South African Bantu tribe, the Bamangwato.

khamsin (kăm′sĭn, kăm sēn′), *n.* a hot southerly wind (varying from SE to SW) that blows regularly in Egypt for about 50 days, commencing about the middle of March. Also, **kamseen, kamsin.** [t. Ar.: lit., fifty]

khan[1] (kän), *n.* **1.** (in the Altaic group of languages) the title borne by hereditary rulers, as: **a.** a hereditary chief of a tribal following. **b.** a hereditary lord of a territorial domain. **2.** the supreme ruler of the Tartar tribes, as well as emperor of China, during the Middle Ages: a descendant of Genghis Khan. **3.** a title of respect in Iran, Afghanistan, Pakistan, etc. [ME, t. Turk. (whence Pers. and Ar.): lord, prince]

khan[2] (kän), *n.* an inn or caravanserai. [t. Pers.]

khanate (kän′āt), *n.* the dominion of a khan.

Khania (kă nĭə′; *Gk* KHȧ nyȧ′), *n.* Greek name of **Canea.**

Kharagpur (kŭ′rəg po͞oə′), *n.* a town in India, in SW West Bengal. 147,253 (1961).

Kharkov (kä′kŏv; *Russ.* KHȧr′kəf), *n.* a city in the S Soviet Union in Europe: former capital of the Ukraine. 1,070,000 (est. 1965). See map under **Ukraine.**

Khartoum (kä to͞om′), *n.* the capital of Sudan, in the W part, at the junction of the White and Blue Nile rivers: besieged, 1895; retaken by the British, 1898. 135,000 (est. 1967). Also, **Khartum.**

Khartoum

khat (kăt, kät), *n.* kat.

Khayyám (kī ăm′), *n.* **Omar.** See **Omar Khayyám.**

kheda (kĕd′ə), *n.* (in India) an enclosure constructed to ensnare wild elephants. Also, **khedah, keddah.**

khedive (kĭ dēv′), *n.* title of the Turkish viceroys in Egypt, 1867–1914. [t. Turk.: m. *khedīv,* t. Pers.: m. *khidīv* lord, sovereign] —**khedi′val, khedivial** (kĭ dē′vyəl), *adj.* —**khedi′vate, khedi′viate,** *n.*

Khelat (kə lät′), *n.* Kalat.

Kherson (*Russ.* KHĭr sôn′), *n.* a city in the SW Soviet Union in Europe: a port on the Dnieper near the Black Sea. 210,000 (est. 1965).

Khios (kī′ŏs; *Gk* KHē′ôs), *n.* Greek name of **Chios.**

Khiva (*Russ.* KHē′və), *n.* a former Asiatic khanate along the Amu Darya river, S of the Aral Sea: now divided between Uzbekistan and Turkmenistan.

Khmer (kmĕə), *n.* **1.** a member of the Cambodian nation, of Mon-Khmer affiliation, which during the Middle Ages produced an important civilization in Indochina. **2.** a language of Cambodia, of the Mon-Khmer family. —*adj.* **3.** Cambodian. **4.** denoting a richly figurative style of architecture developed in Cambodia between the 7th and 13th centuries.

Khorramshahr (kô′rəm shä′), *n.* a town in W Iran. 81,951 (est. 1964). Also, **Mohammerah.**

Khotan (kō′tän′), *n.* **1.** an oasis in W China, in SW Sinkiang. **2.** the chief city in this oasis. 50,000 (est. 1950).

Khrushchev (kro͞os chŏf′; *Russ.* KHro͞o shchôf′), *n.* **Nikita Sergeyevich** (*Russ.* nĭ′kē′tə sĭr gyĕ′yĭ vĭch), born 1894, Soviet statesman: first secretary of the Communist Party 1953–64; premier 1958–64.

Khufu (ko͞o′fo͞o), *n.* Cheops.

Khulna (ko͞ol′nə), *n.* a town in SW East Pakistan. 127,970 (1961).

Khyber Pass (kī′bə), the chief mountain pass between Pakistan and Afghanistan, W of Peshawar. 33 mi. long; 6825 ft high. Also, **Khaibar Pass.**

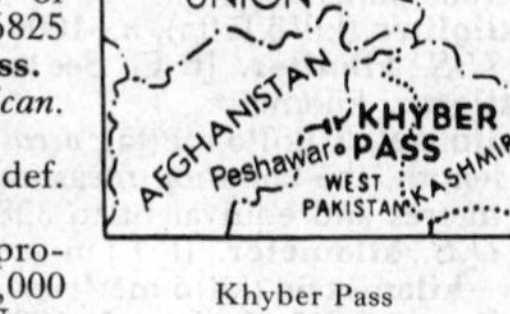

Khyber Pass

kiaat (kyät), *n.* *S African.* kajatehout.

kiang (kĭ ăng′), *n.* onager (def. 1).

Kiangsi (kyăng′sē′), *n.* a province in SE China. 18,610,000 pop. (est. 1957). *Cap.*: Nanchang.

Kiangsu (kyăng′so͞o′), *n.* a maritime province in E China. 45,230,000 pop. (est. 1957). *Cap.*: Nanking.

kia-ora (kĭ′ə ô′rə, kē′ə-), *interj.* *N.Z.* good luck. [t. Maori]

kibble[1] (kĭb′l), *v.t.*, **-bled, -bling.** to grind into small particles. [orig. unknown]

kibble[2] (kĭb′l), *n.* a large iron bucket used in mining. [t. G: m. *Kübel*]

kibbutz (kĭ bo͝ots′), *n.*, *pl.* **-butzim** (-bo͝ot′sĭm, kĭb′-o͞ot sēm′). (in Israel) a communal agricultural settlement. [t. Modern Heb.: m. *qibbūsh* gathering]

kibe (kīb), *n.* *Obs.* a chapped or ulcerated chilblain, esp. on the heel. [ME; cf. Welsh *cibi*]

kibitz (kĭb′ĭts), *v.i.* *Colloq.* to act as a kibitzer.

kibitzer (kĭb′ĭt sə), *n.* *Colloq.* **1.** a spectator at a card game who looks at the players' cards over their shoulders. **2.** a giver of unwanted advice. [t. Yiddish, f. colloq. G *Kiebitz* kibitzer (prop., lapwing) + *-er* -ER[1]]

kiblah (kĭb′lä), *n.* **1.** the point (the Kaaba at Mecca) towards which Muslims turn at prayer. **2.** the facing towards Mecca, wherever orthodox Muslims pray. [t. Ar.: m. *qibla*]

kibosh (kī′bŏsh′), *n.* *Slang.* **1.** nonsense. **2. put the kibosh on,** to render definitely impossible or out of the question. [cf. Yiddish *kibosh* 18 pence]

kick (kĭk), *v.t.* **1.** to strike with the foot. **2.** to drive, force, make, etc., by or as by kicks. **3.** to strike in recoiling. **4.** *Rugby Football.* to score (a goal) by a kick. **5. kick about,** *Colloq.* **a.** to maltreat: *the way they kick that dog about is disgusting.* **b.** to discuss or consider at length or in some detail (an idea, proposal, or the like). **6. kick out,** *Colloq.* to dismiss; get rid of. **7. kick the bucket,** *Slang.* to die. **8. kick up,** *Colloq.* to stir up; to cause (disturbance, trouble, noise, etc.): *to kick up a fuss.* —*v.i.* **9.** to strike out with the foot. **10.** to have the habit of thus striking out, as a horse. **11.** *Colloq.* to resist, object, or complain. **12.** to recoil, as a firearm when fired. **13.** to rise sharply, as a ball after bouncing (often fol. by *up*). **14. kick off, a.** *Football.* to give the ball the first kick, which starts the play. **b.** *Colloq.* to start; commence. **c.** *U.S. Slang.* to die. —*n.* **15.** the act of kicking; a blow or thrust with the foot. **16.** power or disposition to kick. **17.** the right of or a turn at kicking. **18.** a recoil, as of a gun. **19.** *Slang.* an objection or complaint. **20.** *Slang.* any thrill or excitement that gives pleasure; any act, sensation, etc., that gives satisfaction. **21.** *Slang.* a stimulating or intoxicating quality in alcoholic drink. **22.** *Slang.* vigour, energy, or vim. **23.** *Brit. Slang.* sixpence. [ME *kike.* Cf. Icel. *kikna* sink at the knees] —**kick′able,** *adj.* —**kick′er,** *n.*

kickback (kĭk′băk′), *n.* *Colloq.* **1.** a response, usually vigorous. **2.** *U.S.* the practice of an employer, foreman, or person in a supervisory position of taking back a portion of the wages due to workers. **3.** *U.S.* the sum taken. **4.** *U.S.* any sum paid for favours received or hoped for.

kick-off (kĭk′ŏf′), *n.* **1.** *Football.* a kick from a spot in the centre of the field which starts a game or the second half of a game, and in soccer restarts the game after a goal. **2.** *Colloq.* the beginning or initial stage of something.

kick pleat, a short flat pleat, about 3 to 5 inches from the hem at the back of a straight skirt, dress, etc., enabling the wearer to walk freely.

kickshaw (kĭk′shô′), *n.* **1.** any fancy dish in cookery. **2.** any dainty, unsubstantial, or paltry trifle. [t. F: alter. of *quelque chose* something]

kick-sorter (kĭk′sô′tə), *n.* *Electronics.* an apparatus for detecting pulses of electrical energy in a specified intensity range.

kick-start (kĭk′stät′), *v.t.* **1.** to start (a motor) with a kick-starter. —*n.* **2.** a kick-starter.

kick-starter (kĭk′stä′tə), *n.* a starter for an engine, esp. on a motorcycle or lawn-mower, which is operated by the foot. Also, **kick-start.**

kid[1] (kĭd), *n.*, *v.*, **kidded, kidding.** —*n.* **1.** a young goat. **2.** kidskin. **3.** *Slang.* a child or young person. —*v.i.*, *v.t.* **4.** (of a goat) to give birth to (young). [ME, appar. t. Scand.; cf. Icel. *kidh*, Sw. and Dan. *kid*]

kid[2] (kĭd), *v.*, **kidded, kidding,** *n.* *Slang.* —*v.t.* **1.** to tease; banter; jest with. **2.** to humbug or fool. —*v.i.* **3.** to speak or act deceptively, in jest; jest. —*n.* **4.** kidding; humbug; chafing. [? special use of KID[1] (def. 3)] —**kid′der,** *n.*

kid[3] (kĭd), *n.* a tublike wooden vessel in which food is served to sailors. [? var. of KIT[1]]

kid[4] (kĭd), *n.*, *v.*, **kidded, kidding.** —*n.* **1.** a bundle of brushwood, etc., used as a fascine, for burning, or the like. —*v.t.* **2.** to bind into kids. [orig. uncert. Cf. W *cedys*, ? t. E]

Kidd (kĭd), *n.* **William** (*'Captain Kidd'*), 1645–1701, British navigator and privateer, hanged for piracy.

Kidderminster (kĭd′ə mĭn′stə), *n.* **1.** a town in England, in Worcestershire. 41,671 (1961). **2.** a kind of ingrain carpet first made there.

kiddie (kĭd′ĭ), *n.*, *pl.* **-dies.** *Slang.* a child. Also, **kiddy.** [f. KID[1] + IE]

kiddo (kĭd′ō), *n.*, *pl.* **-dos, -does.** *U.S. Slang.* (a familiar form of address.) [f. KID[1] + (*d*)*o*, suffix of association]

kid gloves, 1. gloves made of kidskin. **2. handle with kid gloves,** to handle very gently or tactfully.

kidnap (kĭd′năp′), *v.t.*, **-napped, -napping,** or (*U.S.*) **-naped, -naping.** to steal or abduct (a child or other person); carry off (a person) against his will by unlawful force or by fraud, often with a demand for ransom. [f. KID[1] (def. 3) + *nap*, v., seize] —**kid′nap′per,** *n.*

kidney (kĭd′nĭ), *n.*, *pl.* **-neys. 1.** (in man) either of a pair of bean-shaped glandular organs, about 4 inches in length, in the back part of the abdominal cavity, which excrete urine. **2.** a corresponding organ in other vertebrate animals, or an organ of like function in invertebrates. **3.** the meat of an animal's kidney used as a food. **4.** constitution or temperament. **5.** kind, sort, or class. [ME *kidenei*, f. *kiden-* (orig. and meaning uncert.) + *ey* egg] —**kid′ney-like′,** *adj.*

Human kidney (Section) A, Suprarenal gland; B, Cortex; C, Tubular portion, consisting of cones; D, Papilla; E, Pelvis; F, Ureter

kidney bean, 1. the French bean, *Phaseolus vulgaris.* **2.** its kidney-shaped seed, esp. when it becomes dark in colour.

kidney-shaped (kĭd′nĭ shāpt′), *adj.* having the general shape of a long oval indented at one side.

kidney vetch, an Old World leguminous herb, *Anthyllis vulneraria*, formerly used as a remedy for kidney diseases.

Kidron (kĭ′drŏn), *n.* Kedron.

kidskin (kĭd′skĭn′), *n.* **1.** leather made from the skin of a kid or goat. **2.** a synthetic material in imitation of this.

kief (kēf), *n.* kef.

Kiel (kēl), *n.* a seaport in West Germany, the capital of Schleswig-Holstein, in the NE part, at the Baltic end of the **Kiel Canal,** a ship canal (61 mi. long) connecting the North and Baltic seas. 269,400 (est. 1966). See map under **Schleswig-Holstein.**

Kielce (*Pol.* kyĕl′tsĕ), *n.* a town in S Poland. 102,000 (est. 1965).

kier (kĭə), *n.* a large boiler or vat used in bleaching, etc. Also, **keir.** [t. Scand.; cf. Icel. *ker* tub]

Kierkegaard (*Dan.* kėr′gə gôr), *n.* **Sören Aabye** (*Dan.* sœ′rən ô′bʏ), 1813–55, Danish religious philosopher.

kieselguhr (kē′zəl go͝oə′), *n.* diatomaceous earth. [t. G: f. *Kiesel* flint + *Guhr* earthy deposit]

kieserite (kē′zə rīt′), *n.* a mineral, hydrated magnesium sulphate, found in salt deposits in Germany, used for making Epsom salts. [named after D. G. *Kieser*, died 1862, German physician. See -ITE[1]]

Kiesinger (kē′sĭng ə; *Ger.* kē′zĭng ər), *n.* **Kurt Georg** (*Ger.* ko͝ort gė′ŏrk), born 1904, German statesman: chancellor of West Germany 1966–69.

Kiev (kē′ĕf; *Russ.* kē′yĭf), *n.* a city in the SW Soviet Union in Europe, on the river Dnieper. 1,348,000 (est. 1965). See map under **Ukraine.**

kiewiet (kē′vēt), *n.* *S African.* a crowned lapwing or plover, *Stephanibyx coronatus*, of the family *Charadriidae* of Africa. [t. Afrikaans]

Kigali (kĭ gä′lĭ), *n.* the capital of Rwanda, in the central part. 7000 (est. 1964). See map under **Rwanda.**

kijaat (kyät), *n. S African.* kajatehout. Also, **kyaat, kiaat.** [t. Afrikaans; ult. orig. unknown]

Kikuyu (kĭ ko͞o′yo͞o), *n., pl.* **-yus,** (*esp. collectively*) **-yu.** 1. a member of a Negroid people of Kenya. 2. the language of the Kikuyu.

kil., kilometre; kilometres.

Kildare (kĭl dėə′), *n.* 1. a county in E Republic of Ireland, in Leinster. 64,420 pop. (1961); 654 sq. mi. *Co. town:* Naas.

kilderkin (kĭl′də kĭn), *n.* 1. a unit of capacity, usually equal to half a barrel or two firkins. 2. a container or barrel having such a capacity. [ME, t. MD: m. (by dissimilation) *kyn(d)erkyn,* var. of *kinnekyn,* f. *kinne* (orig. uncert.) + *-kyn* -KIN]

Kilimanjaro (kĭl′ĭ mən jä′rō), *n.* a volcanic mountain in N Tanzania: highest peak of Africa. 19,321 ft.

Kilkenny (kĭl kĕn′ĭ), *n.* 1. a county in the SE Republic of Ireland, in Leinster. 61,668 pop. (1961); 796 sq. mi. 2. its county town. 10,159 (1961).

kill[1] (kĭl), *v.t.* 1. to deprive (any living creature or thing) of life in any manner; cause the death of; slay. 2. to destroy; to do away with; extinguish: *kill hope.* 3. to destroy or neutralize the active qualities of. 4. to spoil the effect of. 5. to pass (the time) idly while waiting for something to come, happen, or the like: *he killed time waiting for the bus to come.* 6. to overcome completely or with irresistible effect. 7. to cancel (a word, paragraph, item, etc.). 8. to defeat or veto (a legislative bill, etc.). 9. *Elect.* to render (a circuit) dead. 10. *Tennis.* to hit (a ball) with such force that its return is impossible. **11. kill off,** to destroy completely and often indiscriminately. *—v.i.* 12. to inflict or cause death. 13. to commit murder. 14. to have an irresistible effect: *dressed to kill.* *—n.* 15. the act of killing (game, etc.). 16. an animal or animals killed. 17. *Tennis.* a stroke of such force that it cannot be returned. [ME *cullen, kyllen;* appar. der. OE *-colla* (in *morgen-colla* morning slaughter)] **—kill′er,** *n.*

—Syn. 1. slaughter, massacre, butcher; hang, electrocute, behead, guillotine, strangle, garrotte. KILL, EXECUTE, MURDER all mean to deprive of life. KILL is the general word, with no implication of the manner of killing, the agent or cause or the nature of what is killed (whether human being, animal, or plant): *to kill a person.* EXECUTE is used of (any means of) putting to death in accordance with a legal sentence: *to execute a criminal.* MURDER is used of killing a human being unlawfully, esp. after premeditation: *he murdered him for his money.*

kill[2] (kĭl), *n. U.S. Dial.* a channel; a creek; a stream; a river. [t. D: m. *kil*]

Killarney (kĭ lä′nĭ), *n.* 1. a town in the SW Republic of Ireland, in Kerry. 6825 (1961). **2. Lakes of,** three lakes nearby.

killed steel, *Metall.* steel that has been fully deoxidized before casting, esp. by the addition of manganese, silicon, and aluminium.

killer whale, a toothed whale, *Oxcinus orca,* 30 ft long, of worldwide distribution.

killick (kĭl′ĭk), *n.* 1. a small anchor or weight for mooring a boat, sometimes consisting of a stone secured by pieces of wood. 2. any anchor. Also, **killock** (kĭl′ək).

Killiecrankie (kĭl′ĭ krăng′kĭ), *n.* a pass in the Grampians in central Scotland: battle, 1689.

killifish (kĭl′ĭ fĭsh′), *n., pl.* **-fishes,** (*esp. collectively*) **-fish.** any of various small fishes, esp. of the genus *Fundulus* (family *Cyprinodontidae*), which abound in shallow bays, channels, rivers, etc., of eastern North America and other regions.

killing (kĭl′ĭng), *n.* 1. the act of one who or that which kills. 2. *Colloq.* a stroke of extraordinary success, as in a successful speculation in stocks. *—adj.* 3. that kills. 4. exhausting. 5. *Colloq.* irresistibly funny. **—kill′ingly,** *adv.*

killjoy (kĭl′joi′), *n.* a person or thing that spoils the joy or enjoyment of others.

Kilmarnock (kĭl mä′nək), *n.* a burgh in Scotland, in Ayrshire. 47,509 (1961).

kiln (kĭln), *n.* 1. a furnace or oven for burning, baking, or drying something, esp. one for calcining limestone or one for baking bricks. *—v.t.* 2. to burn, bake, or treat in a kiln. [ME *kylne,* OE *cyl(e)n,* ult. t. L: m. *culīna* kitchen]

kiln-dry (kĭln′drī′), *v.t.,* **-dried, -drying.** to dry in a kiln.

kilo (kē′lō), *n., pl.* **-los.** 1. a kilogram. 2. a kilometre.

kilo-, a prefix meaning 'thousand', used in the nomenclature of the metric system and of other scientific systems of measurement. [t. F, repr. Gk *chílioi*]

kiloampere (kĭl′ō ăm′pēə), *n. Elect.* a unit of current equal to 1000 amperes.

kilocalorie (kĭl′ō kăl′ə rĭ), *n. Physics.* a large calorie. See **calorie** (def. 1b). Also, **kilogram calorie.**

kilocycle (kĭl′ō sī′kl), *n.* a unit equal to 1000 cycles: used esp. in radio as 1000 cycles per second for expressing the frequency of electromagnetic waves.

kilo-electron-volt (kĭl′ō ĭ lĕk′trŏn vōlt′), *n. Physics.* one thousand electron-volts.

kilogram (kĭl′ō grăm′), *n.* 1. a unit of mass and weight, equal to 1000 grams, and equivalent to 2·2046 lbs avoirdupois. 2. *Physics.* the basic SI unit of mass, based on the international prototype kept at Sèvres, France. *Symbol:* kg Also, **kilogramme.** [t. F: m. *kilogramme.* See KILO-, -GRAM]

kilogram-metre (kĭl′ō grăm′mē′tə), *n.* a unit of work, being the work done by one kilogram of force when its point of application moves a distance of one metre in the direction of the force; equal to about 7·2 foot-pounds.

kilohm (kĭl′ōm′), *n. Elect.* a unit of resistance equal to 1000 ohms.

kilolitre (kĭl′ō lē′tə), *n.* 1000 litres; a cubic metre. Also, *U.S.,* **kiloliter.** [t. F. See KILO-, LITRE]

kilom., kilometre.

kilometre (kĭl′ə mē′tə; *occas.* kĭ lŏm′ĭ tə), *n.* a unit of length, the common measure of distances equal to 1000 metres and equivalent to 3280·8 ft or 0·621 mile. Also, *U.S.,* **kilometer.** [t. F: m. *kilomètre.* See KILO-, -METRE[1]] **—kilometric** (kĭl′ō mĕt′rĭk), **kil′omet′rical,** *adj.*

kiloton (kĭl′ō tŭn′), *n.* 1. 1000 tons. 2. an explosive force equal to that of 1000 tons of TNT.

kilovolt (kĭl′ō vōlt′), *n. Elect.* a unit of electromotive force equal to 1000 volts.

kilowatt (kĭl′ō wŏt′), *n. Elect.* a unit of power, equal to 1000 watts. [f. KILO- + WATT]

kilowatt-hour (kĭl′ō wŏt′ou′ə), *n. Elect.* a unit of energy equivalent to that transferred or expended in one hour by one kilowatt of power, approx. 1·34 HP hour.

kilt (kĭlt), *n.* 1. any short, pleated skirt, esp. one worn by men in the Scottish Highlands. *—v.t.* 2. to draw or tuck up (the skirt, etc.) about one. 3. to pleat (cloth, a skirt, etc.) in deep vertical folds. [ME *kylte,* prob. t. Scand.; cf. Dan. *kilte* tuck up] **—kilt′like′,** *adj.*

kilted (kĭl′tĭd), *adj.* 1. wearing a kilt. 2. pleated.

kilter (kĭl′tə), *n. U.S. Dial.* kelter.

kiltie (kĭl′tĭ), *n. Slang.* one who wears a kilt, esp. a member of a Scottish Highland regiment. Also, **kilty.**

kilting (kĭl′tĭng), *n.* (in a skirt, etc.) an arrangement of flat pleats set close together, each hiding half of the last.

Kimberley (kĭm′bə lĭ), *n.* 1. a town in the Republic of South Africa, in N Cape Province: diamond mines, with suburbs, 79,031 (1960). 2. Also, **the Kimberleys.** a district in Western Australia between the Fitzroy and Ord rivers. ab. 120,000 sq. mi.

Kim Il Sung (kĭm′ ĭl so͝ong′), born 1912, North Korean statesman: prime minister since 1948.

kimono (kĭ mō′nō), *n., pl.* **-nos.** 1. a wide-sleeved robe characteristic of Japanese costume. 2. a woman's loose dressing-gown. [t. Jap.]

kin (kĭn), *n.* 1. one's relatives collectively, or kinsfolk. 2. family relationship or kinship. 3. a group of persons descended from a common ancestor, or constituting a family, clan, tribe, or race. 4. a relative or kinsman. 5. someone or something of the same kind or nature. **6. of kin,** of the same family; related; akin. *—adj.* 7. of kin; related; akin. 8. of the same kind or nature; having affinity. [ME; OE *cynn,* c. OHG *chunni,* Icel. *kyn,* Goth. *kuni;* from Gmc root equivalent to L *gen-,* Gk *gen-,* Skt *jan-* beget, produce] **—kin′less,** *adj.*

-kin, a diminutive suffix, attached to nouns to signify a little object of the kind mentioned: *lambkin, catkin.* [ME; akin to D and LG *-ken,* G *-chen*]

kinaesthesia (kĭ′nĕs thē′zyə, kĭn′-), *n.* the sensation of movement or strain in muscles, tendons, joints. Also, **kin′aesthe′sis;** *Chiefly U.S.,* **kinesthesia, kinesthesis.** [NL, f. Gk: s. *kineîn* move + *-aisthēsia* perception] **—kinaesthetic** (kĭ′nĕs thĕt′ĭk), *adj.*

kinase (kĭ′nās, kĭn′ās, kĭ nās′), *n. Biochem.* one of a group of substances of biological origin which is able to convert a zymogen into an enzyme.

Kinc., Kincardine.

Kincardine (kĭn kä′dĭn), *n.* a county in E Scotland. 48,810 pop. (1961); 379 sq. mi. *Co. town:* Stonehaven. Also, **Kincardineshire** (kĭn kä′dĭn shĭə′, -shə).

Kinchinjunga (kĭn′chĭn jŭng′gə), *n.* Kanchenjunga.

kind[1] (kīnd), *adj.* 1. of a good or benevolent nature or disposition, as a person. 2. having, showing, or proceeding from benevolence: *kind words.* 3. cordial; well-meant: *kind regards.* 4. indulgent, considerate, or helpful (often fol. by *to*): *to be kind to animals.* 5. *Archaic.* loving. [ME *kinde,* OE *gecynde,* der. *gecynd* nature. See KIND[2]]

—Syn. 1. KIND, GRACIOUS, KIND-HEARTED, KINDLY imply a sympathetic attitude towards others, and a willingness to do good or give pleasure. KIND implies a deep-seated characteristic shown either habitually or on occasion by considerate behaviour: *a kind father.* GRACIOUS applies to kindness from a superior or older person to a subordinate, an inferior, a child, etc.: *a gracious old* *lady.* KIND-HEARTED implies an emotionally sympathetic nature, sometimes easily imposed upon: *a kind-hearted old woman.* KINDLY, a mild word, refers usually to general disposition, appearance, manner, etc.: *a kindly face.* **—Ant. 1.** cruel.

kind² (kīnd), *n.* **1.** a class or group of individuals of the same nature or character, esp. a natural group of animals or plants. **2.** nature or character as determining likeness or difference between things: *things differing in degree rather than in kind.* **3.** a person or thing as being of a particular character or class: *he is a strange kind of hero.* **4.** a more or less adequate or inadequate example, or a sort, of something: *the vines formed a kind of roof.* **5.** *Archaic.* the nature, or natural disposition or character: *after one's kind.* **6.** *Obs.* gender; sex. **7. in kind, a.** in something of the same kind in the same way: *to retaliate in kind.* **b.** in goods or natural produce, instead of money. **8. kind of** (used adverbially), *Colloq.* after a fashion; to some extent; somewhat; rather: *the room was kind of dark.* [ME *kinde,* OE *gecynd.* See KIN]

kindergarten (kĭn′də gä′tn), *n.* **1.** a school for furthering the mental, social, and physical development of young children, usually children under the age of five, by means of games, occupations, etc., that make use of their natural tendency to express themselves in action. **2.** any nursery school. [t. G: lit., children's garden, coined by Friedrich Froebel]

kindergartener (kĭn′də gät′nə), *n.* **1.** a child who attends a kindergarten. **2.** a kindergarten teacher. Also, *Chiefly U.S.*, **kindergartner.**

kind-hearted (kīnd′hä′tĭd), *adj.* having or showing a kind heart; kindly. **—kind′-heart′edly,** *adv.* **—kind′-heart′edness,** *n.* **—Syn.** See **kind¹.**

Kindia (*Fr.* kĕn dyȧ′), *n.* a town in W Guinea. 25,000 (1960).

kindle (kĭn′dl), *v.,* **-dled, -dling.** *—v.t.* **1.** to set (a fire, flame, etc.) burning or blazing. **2.** to set fire to, or ignite (fuel or any combustible matter). **3.** to excite; stir up or set going; to animate, rouse, or inflame. **4.** to light up, illuminate, or make bright. *—v.i.* **5.** to begin to burn, as combustible matter, a light, or a fire or flame. **6.** to become roused, ardent, or inflamed. **7.** to become lit up, bright, or glowing, as the sky at dawn or the eyes with ardour. [ME *kindlen,* prob. t. Scand.; cf. Icel. *kynda* kindle, *kyndill* candle, torch] **—kin′dler,** *n.*

—Syn. 1–3. KINDLE, IGNITE, INFLAME imply setting something on fire. To KINDLE is especially to cause something gradually to begin burning; it is often used figuratively: *to kindle someone's interest.* To IGNITE is to set something on fire with a sudden burst of flame: *to ignite dangerous hatreds.* INFLAME, a literary word meaning to set aflame, is now found chiefly in figurative uses, as referring to unnaturally hot, sore, or swollen conditions in the body, or to exciting the mind by strong emotion: *the wound was greatly inflamed.* **—Ant. 1.** quench, smother, extinguish.

kindliness (kīnd′lĭ nĭs), *n.* **1.** the state or quality of being kindly; benevolence. **2.** a kindly deed.

kindling (kĭn′dlĭng), *n.* **1.** material for starting a fire. **2.** the act of one who kindles.

kindly (kīnd′lĭ), *adj.,* **-lier, -liest,** *adv.* *—adj.* **1.** having, showing, or proceeding from a benevolent disposition or spirit; kind-hearted; good-natured; sympathetic: *kindly people.* **2.** gentle or mild, as rule or laws. **3.** pleasant, genial, or benign. **4.** favourable, as soil for crops. *—adv.* **5.** in a kind manner; with sympathetic or helpful kindness. **6.** cordially or heartily: *we thank you kindly.* **7.** with liking; favourably: *to take kindly to an idea.* **8.** obligingly; please: *kindly go away.* [ME *kyndly,* OE *gecyndelic* natural, f. *gecynde* KIND¹ + *-līc* -LY] **—Syn. 1.** See **kind¹.**

kindness (kīnd′nĭs), *n.* **1.** the state or quality of being kind. **2.** a kind act: *his many kindnesses to me.* **3.** kind behaviour: *I will never forget your kindness.* **4.** friendly feeling, or liking. **—Syn. 2.** service, favour.

kindred (kĭn′drĭd), *n.* **1.** a body of persons related to another, or a family, tribe, or race. **2.** one's relatives collectively; kinsfolk; kin. **3.** relationship by birth or descent, or sometimes by marriage; kinship. **4.** natural relationship, or affinity. *—adj.* **5.** associated by origin, nature, qualities, etc.: *kindred languages.* **6.** related by birth or descent, or having kinship: *kindred tribes.* **7.** belonging to kin or relatives: *kindred blood.* [ME *kindrede(n).* See KIN, -RED]

kine (kīn), *n.pl. Archaic.* pl. of **cow.**

kinematics (kī′nĭ măt′ĭks, kĭn′-), *n.* **1.** that branch of mechanics which treats of pure motion, without reference to mass or cause. **2.** the theory of mechanical contrivance for converting one kind of motion into another (**applied kinematics**). [f. s. Gk *kī́nēma* motion + -ICS] **—kin′emat′ic, kin′emat′ical,** *adj.*

kinematic viscosity, *Physics.* the absolute viscosity of a fluid divided by its density, usually measured in stokes.

kinematograph (kī′nĭ măt′ə grăf′, kĭn′-, -gräf′), *n., v.t., v.i.* cinematograph.

kinesthesia (kī′nĕs thē′zyə, kĭn′-), *n. Chiefly U.S.* kinaesthesia. Also, **kinesthesis. —kinesthetic** (kī′nĕs thĕt′ĭk, kĭn′-), *adj.*

kinetic (kĭ nĕt′ĭk, kī-), *adj.* **1.** pertaining to motion. **2.** caused by motion. [t. Gk: m. s. *kīnētikós*]

kinetic art, art (as sculpture, or the like), which is characterized by actual motion.

kinetic energy, *Physics.* the energy which a body possesses by virtue of its motion; the energy which any system possesses by virtue of the motion of its components.

kinetics (kĭ nĕt′ĭks, kī-), *n.* the branch of mechanics which treats of the action of forces in producing or changing the motion of masses.

kinetic theory of gases, *Physics.* a theory that the particles in a gas move freely and rapidly along straight lines but often collide, resulting in variations in their velocity and direction. Pressure is thus interpreted as the force due to the impacts of these particles, and other macroscopic variables are similarly treated.

kinetic theory of heat, *Physics.* a theory that a body's temperature is determined by the average kinetic energy of its particles and that an inflow of heat increases this energy.

kinetic theory of matter, *Physics.* the theory that matter is composed of small particles, all in random motion.

kinfolks (kĭn′fōks′), *n.pl. U.S. Colloq. or Dial.* kinsfolk. Also, **kinfolk.**

king (kĭng), *n.* **1.** a male sovereign or monarch; a man who holds by life tenure (and usually by hereditary right) the chief authority over a country and people. **2.** (*cap.*) God or Christ: *King of Kings, King of Heaven.* **3.** a person or thing pre-eminent in its class: *the lion is the king of beasts, an oil king.* **4.** a playing card bearing the formalized picture of a king, in most games counting as next highest below the ace, or highest, in its suit. **5.** the chief piece in a game of chess, moving one square at a time in any direction. **6.** a piece that has moved entirely across the board in the game of draughts and has been crowned. [ME; OE *cyng, cyning,* c. D *koning,* G *König,* Icel. *konungr,* Sw. *konung,* Dan. *konge*] **—king′less,** *adj.* **—king′like′,** *adj.*

King (kĭng), *n.* **1. Martin Luther,** 1929–68, U.S. Baptist minister and civil rights leader. **2. William Lyon Mackenzie** (mə kĕn′zĭ), 1874–1950, Canadian statesman: prime minister 1921–26, 1926–30, and 1935–48.

kingbolt (kĭng′bōlt′), *n.* **1.** a vertical bolt connecting the body of a horse-drawn vehicle with the fore axle, the body of a railway carriage with a truck, etc. **2.** a kingrod.

King Charles spaniel, a small black-and-tan toy spaniel with a rounded head, short muzzle, full eyes, and well-fringed ears and feet.

king cobra, a large cobra, *Naja hannah,* of south-eastern Asia.

king crab, a horseshoe crab.

kingcraft (kĭng′kräft′), *n.* the art of ruling as king; royal statesmanship.

kingcup (kĭng′kŭp′), *n.* a widespread N temperate ranunculaceous plant of marshes and fens, *Caltha palustris,* which has smooth heart-shaped leaves and large, bright yellow flowers.

kingdom (kĭng′dəm), *n.* **1.** a state or government having a king or queen as its head. **2.** anything conceived as constituting a realm or sphere of independent action or control: *the kingdom of thought.* **3.** a realm or province of nature, esp. one of the three great divisions of natural objects: *the animal, vegetable, and mineral kingdoms.* **4.** the spiritual sovereignty of God or Christ. **5.** the domain over which this extends, whether in heaven or on earth. [ME; OE *cyningdōm*]

—Syn. 1. KINGDOM, MONARCHY, REALM refer to the state or domain ruled by a king or queen. A KINGDOM is a governmental unit ruled by a king or queen: *the kingdom of Norway.* A MONARCHY is primarily a form of government in which a single person is sovereign; it is also the type of power exercised by the monarch: *this kingdom is not an absolute monarchy.* A REALM is the domain (including the subjects) over which the king has jurisdiction; fig., a sphere of power or influence: *the laws of the realm.*

kingdom come, the kingdom of Christ to come; the next world.

kingfish (kĭng′fĭsh′), *n., pl.* **-fishes,** (*esp. collectively*) **-fish. 1.** any of various fishes conspicuous for size or some other quality. **2.** the opah. **3.** the Spanish mackerel.

kingfisher (kĭng′fĭsh′ə), *n.* any of numerous fish- or insect-eating birds of the almost cosmopolitan family *Alcedinidae,* all of which are stout-billed and small-footed, and many of which are crested or brilliantly coloured. Those which eat fish capture them by diving.

kinghood (kĭng′hŏŏd), *n.* kingship.

King Island, an island at the W end of Bass Strait; a municipality of Tasmania. 2727 pop. (1964); 425 sq. mi.

King James Version. See **Authorized Version.**

kingklip (kĭng′klĭp′), *n.* an elongated, edible sea fish of the western waters of southern Africa, *Genypterus capensis.* [part trans. of Afrikaans *koningklip*(*vis*)]

Kinglake (kĭng′lāk′), *n.* **Alexander William,** 1809–91, English historian and traveller.

King Leopold Range, a low mountain range in the N part of Western Australia. Highest point, Mt Ord, 3070 ft.

kinglet (kĭng′lĭt), *n.* **1.** a king ruling over a small country or territory. **2.** any of the diminutive greenish birds constituting the genus *Regulus,* esp. the **firecrest** (*R. ignicapillus*) of Europe, and the **goldcrest** or **golden-covered kinglet** (*R. regulus*) of both Europe and North America.

kingly (kĭng′lĭ), *adj.,* **-lier, -liest,** *adv.* **—***adj.* **1.** having the rank of a king. **2.** consisting of kings or of royal rank. **3.** resembling, suggesting, or befitting a king; kinglike: *he strode into the room with a kingly air.* **4.** pertaining or proper to a king or kings. **—***adv.* **5.** in a kingly manner. **—king′liness,** *n.*

—Syn. 3, 4. princely, sovereign, majestic, august, magnificent, exalted, grand. KINGLY, REGAL, ROYAL refer to that which is closely associated with a king, or is suitable for one. What is KINGLY may either belong to a king, or be befitting, worthy of, or like a king: *a kingly presence, appearance, graciousness.* REGAL is especially applied to the office of kingship or the outward manifestations of grandeur and majesty: *regal authority, bearing, splendour, munificence.* ROYAL is applied especially to what pertains to or is associated with the person of a monarch: *the royal family, word, robes, salute; a royal residence.*

king-maker (kĭng′mā′kə), *n.* one who has sufficient power to influence decisively the appointment or choice made for some important office.

king-of-arms (kĭng′əv ämz′), *n., pl.* **kings-of-arms.** one of certain principal heralds of England and some other kingdoms, having the right and power to grant armorial bearings.

king of the herrings, 1. the shad, genus *Clupea,* said to resemble a large herring. **2.** any of several other fish, as the oarfish, opah, rabbit-fish.

kingpin (kĭng′pĭn′), *n.* **1.** the pin by which a stub axle is articulated to an axle beam or steering head in a motor car; a swivel pin. **2.** *Bowling.* **a.** the pin in the centre when the pins are in place. **b.** the pin at the front apex. **3.** *Colloq.* the principal person in a company, etc. **4.** *Colloq.* the chief element of any system or the like. **5.** kingbolt.

kingpost (kĭng′pōst′), *n.* **1.** a vertical post between the apex of a triangular roof truss and the tie beam. **2.** a stirrup mast stepped on either or both sides of the end of a hatchway fitted with a derrick for the handling of cargoes.

A, Kingpost; B, Tie beam; C, Strut or brace

kingrod (kĭng′rŏd′), *n.* a vertical steel rod connecting the apex of a triangular roof truss and the tie beam in order to support the tie beam when it bears a heavy ceiling load. Also, **kingbolt.**

Kings (kĭngz), *n.pl.* certain books of the Bible which contain the history of the reigns of the kings of Israel and Judah (usually the 11th and 12th books of the Old Testament, called I Kings and II Kings).

King's Bench, (when the reigning monarch is a man) Queen's Bench.

king's chambers, (when the reigning monarch is a man) queen's chambers.

King's Counsel, (when the reigning monarch is a man) Queen's Counsel.

king's English, standard Southern British English, esp. considered as correct or desirable usage. Also, **queen's English.**

king's evidence, (when the reigning monarch is a man) queen's evidence.

king's evil, scrofula: orig. so called because it was supposed to be curable by the touch of the sovereign.

king's highway, (when the reigning monarch is a man) queen's highway.

kingship (kĭng′shĭp), *n.* **1.** kingly state, office, or dignity. **2.** kingly rule. **3.** aptitude for kingly duties. **4.** *Rare.* a title used in referring to a king (prec. by *his, your,* etc.).

king-size (kĭng′sīz′), *adj. Colloq.* larger than the usual size. Also, **king′-sized′.**

Kingsley (kĭngz′lĭ), *n.* **Charles,** 1819–75, English clergyman, novelist, and poet.

King's Lynn (kĭngz′lĭn′), a town in England, in Norfolk. 27,536 (1961).

king snake, any of certain large harmless American snakes, esp. *Lampropeltis getulus,* which feed on other snakes, including rattlesnakes.

king's peace, (when the reigning monarch is a man) queen's peace.

king's proctor, (when the reigning monarch is a man) queen's proctor.

king's remembrancer, (when the reigning monarch is a man) queen's remembrancer.

King's Regulations, (when the reigning monarch is a man) Queen's Regulations.

king's scout, (when the reigning monarch is a man) queen's scout.

king's shilling, 1. (when the reigning monarch was a man) (until 1879) a shilling given to a new recruit to the British army. **2. take the king's shilling,** to enlist. Also (when the reigning monarch was a woman), **queen's shilling.**

King's speech, (when the reigning monarch is a man) Queen's speech.

Kingston (kĭng′stən), *n.* **1.** a seaport in and the capital of Jamaica, in the SE part. 123,313 (1960). **2.** a city in SE Canada: a port at the E end of Lake Ontario; Queen's University founded 1891. 63,419 (1961).

Kingston upon Hull, official name of **Hull** (def. 2).

Kingston upon Thames, a royal outer borough of SW London. 146,300 (1965).

Kingstown (kĭng′stən), *n.* a seaport in and the capital of St Vincent, in the SW part. 15,981 (1960).

Kingtehchen (kĭng′tā′chĕn′), *n.* a city in E China, in Kiangsi province. 266,000 (est. 1958). Also, **Chingtechen.**

king-truss (kĭng′trŭs′), *n.* a truss framed with a kingpost.

kingwood (kĭng′wŏŏd′), *n.* **1.** a Brazilian wood streaked with violet tints, used esp. in cabinetwork. **2.** the tree *Dalbergia cearensis,* which yields it. Also, **violet wood.**

kink (kĭngk), *n.* **1.** a twist or curl, as in a thread, rope, or hair, caused by its doubling or bending upon itself. **2.** a crick, as in the neck or back. **3.** a mental twist; an odd notion; a whim. **4.** a deviation, esp. sexual. **—***v.i., v.t.* **5.** to form or cause to form a kink or kinks, as a rope. [orig. nautical term, prob. t. D: twirl. Cf. Icel. *kinka* nod archly]

kinkajou (kĭng′kə jŏŏ′), *n.* a brownish, soft-furred, arboreal, prehensile-tailed mammal, *Potos flavus,* of Central and South America, related to the raccoon. [t. Canadian F; orig. the same word as CARCAJOU, ult. t. Tupi]

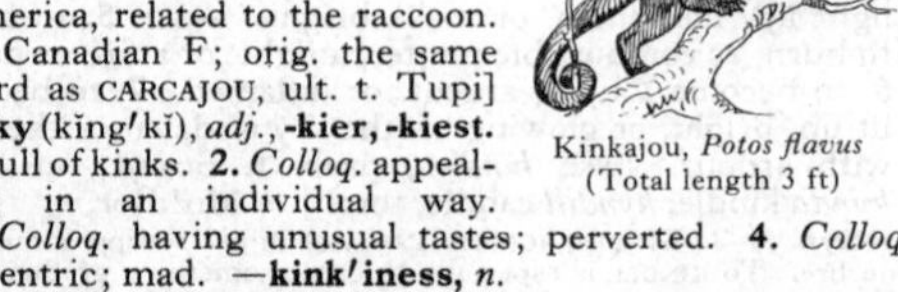
Kinkajou, *Potos flavus* (Total length 3 ft)

kinky (kĭng′kĭ), *adj.,* **-kier, -kiest. 1.** full of kinks. **2.** *Colloq.* appealing in an individual way. **3.** *Colloq.* having unusual tastes; perverted. **4.** *Colloq.* eccentric; mad. **—kink′iness,** *n.*

kinnikinic (kĭn′ĭ kĭ nĭk′), *n.* **1.** a mixture, generally consisting of bark and dried leaves, formerly used by certain North American Indians as a substitute for tobacco or for mixing with it. **2.** any of various plants used in this mixture, such as the bearberry. Also, **kinnikinnick.** [t. Algonquian: lit., that which is mixed]

kino gum (kē′nō), the reddish or black catechu-like inspissated juice or gum of certain tropical trees, esp. that from *Pterocarpus marsupium,* a tall fabaceous tree of India and Ceylon: used in medicine, tanning, etc. [*kino* appar. t. W Afr. (Gambia)]

Kinross (kĭn rŏs′), *n.* **1.** a burgh in Scotland, the county town of Kinross-shire. 2365 (1961). **2.** Kinross-shire.

Kinross-shire (kĭn rŏs′shĭə, -shə), *n.* a county in E Scotland. 6704 pop. (1961); 82 sq. mi. *Co. town:* Kinross. Also, **Kinross.**

Kinsey (kĭn′zĭ), *n.* **Alfred Charles,** 1894–1956, U.S. zoölogist: director of a survey of human sex behaviour.

kinsfolk (kĭnz′fōk′), *n.pl.* relatives or kindred. Also, *U.S. Colloq. or Dial.,* **kinfolks, kinfolk.**

Kinshasa (kĭn shä′zə, -shä′sə), *n.* a river port in and the capital of the Democratic Republic of the Congo, in the SW part, on the river Congo. 1,000,000 (est. 1964). Formerly, **Leopoldville.** See map under **Congo.**

kinship (kĭn′shĭp), *n.* **1.** the state or fact of being of kin; family relationship. **2.** relationship by nature, qualities, etc.; affinity. **—Syn. 1.** See **relationship.**

kinsman (kĭnz′mən), *n., pl.* **-men. 1.** a male blood relative. **2.** (sometimes) a relative by marriage. **3.** a person of the same race. **—kins′wom′an,** *n. fem.*

Kintyre (kĭn tī′ə), *n.* a peninsula of Argyllshire, W Scotland. ab. 40 mi. by 7 mi.

kiosk (kē′ŏsk), *n.* **1.** a small, light structure for the sale of newspapers, cigarettes, etc. **2.** a small cabin containing a public telephone. **3.** a kind of open pavilion or summer-house common in Turkey and Iran. [t. Turk.: m. *kiūsk* pavilion]

Kioto (kĭ ō′tō), *n.* Kyoto.

Kiowa (kī′ə wə), *n., pl.* **-was,** (*esp. collectively*) **-wa. 1.** a member of a North American Indian tribe of western Kansas and eastern Colorado. **2.** the language of the Kiowa, related to Uto-Aztecan.

kip[1] (kĭp), *n.* **1.** the hide of a young or small beast. **2.** a bundle or set of such hides, containing a definite number.

[ME *kipp*, t. MLG: m. *kip* pack (of hides), akin to Icel. *kippi* bundle]

kip[2] (kĭp), *n.* a unit of weight equal to a 1000 lbs. [f. KI(LO)- + P(OUND)]

kip[3] (kĭp), *n.*, *v.*, **kipped, kipping.** *Slang.* —*n.* **1.** sleep. **2.** a bed. **3.** a lodging house. —*v.i.* **4.** to go to bed; sleep. [cf. OE *cip* brothel]

kip[4] (kĭp), *n.* *Austral. Colloq.* a small flat piece of wood used for spinning coins in two-up. [? var. of CHIP]

kip[5] (kĭp), *n.* **1.** the monetary unit of Laos, equivalent to about £0·0017 sterling. **2.** a note of this value. [t. Thai]

Kipling (kĭp′lĭng), *n.* (**Joseph**) **Rudyard** (rŭd′yəd), 1865–1936, English novelist and poet.

kipper[1] (kĭp′ə), *n.* **1.** a kippered fish, esp. a herring. **2.** a method of curing fish by splitting, salting, drying, and smoking. —*v.t.* **3.** to cure (herring, salmon, etc.) by cleaning, salting, etc., and drying in the air or in smoke. [? special use of *kipper*, OE *cypera* spawning salmon]

kipper[2] (kĭp′ə), *n.* *Austral.* an Aborigine youth who has completed the initiation rite. [t. native Australian]

kippersol (kĭp′ə sŏl′), *n.* *S African.* **1.** the umbrella tree, *Musanga smithii.* **2.** any of various trees of southern Africa resembling this. [t. Afrikaans: m. *kiepersol(boom)*]

Kipp's apparatus, *Chem.* an apparatus used in laboratories for the production of a gas which can be made by the action of a liquid on a solid; used esp. for the production of hydrogen sulphide.

Kirchhoff (*Ger.* kĭrKH′hŏf), *n.* **Gustav Robert** (*Ger.* gŏŏs′táf rō′bĕrt), 1824–87, German physicist.

Kirchhoff's laws, *Physics.* two laws relating to electrical circuits which state: **1.** that in any network of wires the algebraic sum of the currents which meet at a point is zero. **2.** that the algebraic sum of the electromotive forces in any closed circuit is equal to the algebraic sum of the products of the resistances of each portion of the circuit and the currents flowing through them. [named after G. R. KIRCHHOFF]

Kirghiz (kû′gĭz), *n.*, *pl.* **-ghiz, -ghizes.** **1.** a member of a widespread people of Mongolian physical type and Turkic speech, dwelling chiefly in west central Asia. **2.** their language.

Kirghizia (kû gĭz′ĭ ə; *Russ.* kĭr gē′zĭ yə), *n.* a constituent republic of the Soviet Union, in the Asiatic part adjoining Sinkiang, China. 2,500,000 pop. (est. 1964); ab. 77,800 sq. mi. *Cap.:* Frunze. Official name, **Kirghiz Soviet Socialist Republic.**

Kirghiz Steppe, a vast steppe in the SW Soviet Union in Asia, in Kazakhstan. Also, **The Steppes.**

Kirin (kē′rĭn′), *n.* **1.** a province in NE China, in Manchuria. 12,550,000 pop. (est. 1957); 45,000 sq. mi. *Cap.:* Changchun. **2.** a city in Kirin province on the river Sungari. 583,000 (est. 1958).

kirk (kûk), *n.* **1.** *Scot. and N Dial.* a church. **2. the Kirk,** the Established Church of Scotland, as distinguished from the Scottish Episcopal Church. [ME, t. Scand.; cf. Icel. *kirkja*, c. CHURCH]

Kirkby in Ashfield (kû′bĭ ĭn ăsh′fēld′), a town in England, in W Nottinghamshire. 21,700 (1961).

Kirkcaldy (kû kô′dĭ), *n.* a seaport in Scotland, in Fife, on the Firth of Forth. 52,371 (1961).

Kirkcud., Kirkcudbrightshire.

Kirkcudbright (kû kōō′brĭ), *n.* **1.** a burgh in Scotland, the county town of Kirkcudbrightshire. 2439 (1961). **2.** Kirkcudbrightshire.

Kirkcudbrightshire (kû kōō′brĭ shĭə′, -shə), *n.* a county in SW Scotland. 28,877 pop. (1961); 896 sq. mi. *Co. town:* Kirkcudbright. *Abbrev.:* Kirkcud. Also, **Kirkcudbright.**

Kirkintilloch (kû′kĭn tĭl′ək), *n.* a burgh in Scotland, in Dunbarton. 18,257 (1961).

kirkman (kûk′mən), *n.*, *pl.* **-men.** **1.** *Scot.* a member or follower of the Kirk. **2.** *Scot. and N Dial.* a churchman; ecclesiastic.

Kirkuk (kû kŏŏk′, kû′kŏŏk), *n.* a town in NE Iraq. 176,794 (est. 1963).

Kirkwall (kûk′wôl′), *n.* a burgh in Scotland, the county town of the Orkney Islands, on Mainland island. 4315 (1961).

Kirman (*Pers.* kėr män′), *n.* a Persian rug marked by ornate flowing designs and light, muted colours. [var. of KERMAN, a town and province in Iran]

kirmess (kû′mĭs), *n.* kermis.

Kirov (*Russ.* kē′rəf), *n.* a town in the E Soviet Union in Europe. 296,000 (est. 1965). Formerly, **Vyatka.**

Kirovabad (*Russ.* kĭ rə vá bát′), *n.* a town in the S Soviet Union in Europe. 166,000 (est. 1965). Formerly, **Elisavetpol** or **Grandzha.**

Kirovograd (*Russ.* kĭ rə vá grát′), *n.* a town in the SW Soviet Union in Europe. 153,000 (est. 1965). Formerly, **Elisavetgrad** or **Zinovievsk.**

kirschwasser (kĭəsh′väs′ə), *n.* a colourless brandy distilled in Germany, Alsace, and Switzerland from wild black cherries. Also, **kirsch.** [t. G: cherry water]

kirtle (kû′tl), *n.* **1.** a woman's gown or skirt. **2.** *Archaic or Dial.* a man's tunic or coat. [ME *kurtel*, OE *cyrtel*, c. Icel. *kyrtill* tunic, ult. der. L *curtus* cut short] —**kir′tled,** *adj.*

Kisangani (kĭs′ăng gä′nĭ), *n.* a town in the NE Democratic Republic of the Congo. 100,000 (est. 1964). Formerly, **Stanleyville.** See map under **Congo.**

kish (kĭsh), *n.* *Metall.* a variety of graphite which sometimes forms on the surface of a molten bath of iron which has a high carbon content.

Kishinev (*Russ.* kĭ shĭ nyôf′), *n.* a town in the SW Soviet Union in Europe, the capital of Moldavia. 282,000 (est. 1965). Rumanian, **Chişinău.**

Kishiwada (kĭ shē′wə də, kē′shĭ wä′də), *n.* a town in Japan, in S Honshu island. 143,710 (1965).

Kislev (kĭs′lĕf), *n.* (in the Jewish calendar) the third month of the year. [t. Heb.]

kismet (kĭz′mĕt, kĭs′-), *n.* fate; destiny. [t. Turk., t. Pers.: m. *qismat*, t. Ar., der. *qasama* divide]

kiss (kĭs), *v.t.* **1.** to touch or press with the lips, while compressing and then separating them, in token of greeting, affection, etc. **2.** to touch gently or lightly. **3.** to put, bring, take, etc., by, or as if by, kissing. **4. kiss the dust, a.** to be killed. **b.** to be humiliated. —*v.i.* **5.** to kiss someone, something, or each other. —*n.* **6.** the act of kissing. **7.** a slight touch or contact. [ME *kysse(n)*, OE *cyssan* (c. G *küssen*), der. *coss* a kiss, c. G *Küss*] —**kiss′able,** *adj.* —**kiss′er,** *n.*

kiss-curl (kĭs′kûl′), *n.* a small curl, esp. on the forehead.

kisser (kĭs′ə), *n.* **1.** one who kisses. **2.** *Slang.* the face.

kiss of death, any act, fact, influence, relationship, etc., which proves disastrous.

kiss of life, artificial respiration performed by the mouth-to-mouth or mouth-to-nose method.

Kistna (kĭst′nə), *n.* a river in S India, flowing from the Western Ghats E to the Bay of Bengal. ab. 800 mi.

Kisumu (kĭ sōō′mōō), *n.* a town in SW Kenya. 23,200 (est. 1962).

kit[1] (kĭt), *n.*, *v.*, **kitted, kitting.** —*n.* **1.** a set or collection of tools, supplies, etc., for a specific purpose: *a first-aid kit.* **2.** a set or collection of parts to be assembled: *a model aircraft kit.* **3.** a case containing tools, parts, etc., or the case with its contents. **4.** *Chiefly Mil.* a set of clothing or personal equipment for a specific purpose: *the soldiers were issued with a complete kit.* —*v.t.* **5.** *Mil.* to provide with kit. [ME *kyt*, *kitt*, appar. t. MD: m. *kitte* kind of tub. Cf. Norw. *kitte* bin]

kit[2] (kĭt), *n.* a kind of small violin, used by dancing masters from the 16th to the 18th century. [orig. uncert.]

kit[3] (kĭt), *n.* shortened form of *kitten.*

Kitakyushu (kē′tä kyōō′shōō), *n.* a city in Japan, in N Kyushu. 1,042,388 (1965).

kitbag (kĭt′băg′), *n.* a long canvas bag in which soldiers, etc., carry their personal belongings.

kitchen (kĭch′ĭn), *n.* **1.** a room or place equipped for or appropriated to cooking. **2.** the culinary department; cuisine. [ME *kitchene*, OE *cycene*, ult. t. L: m. *coquina*]

kitchener (kĭch′ĭn ə), *n.* **1.** one employed in, or in charge of, a kitchen. **2.** an elaborate cooking stove.

Kitchener (kĭch′ĭ nə), *n.* **1. Horatio Herbert** (*Earl Kitchener of Khartoum and of Broome*), 1850–1916, British field marshal and statesman. **2.** a town in Canada, in S Ontario. 74,485 (1961).

kitchenette (kĭch′ĭ nĕt′), *n.* a small kitchen.

kitchen garden, a garden in which vegetables and fruit for the table are grown. —**kitchen gardener.**

kitchen midden, a mound consisting of shells of edible molluscs and other refuse, marking the site of a prehistoric human habitation. [translation of Dan. *kökkenmödding*]

kitchen-sink (kĭch′ĭn sĭngk′), *adj.* (of plays, etc.) dealing realistically with the sordid aspects of contemporary life.

kitchen unit, the fitments of a modern kitchen, including sink, stove, cabinets, etc., arranged in a compact and convenient layout.

kitchenware (kĭch′ĭn wĕə′), *n.* cooking equipment or utensils.

kite (kīt), *n.*, *v.*, **kited, kiting.** —*n.* **1.** a light frame covered with some thin material, to be flown in the wind at the end of a long string. **2.** any of various falconiform birds of the genera *Milvus*, *Elanus*, *Elanoides*, etc., with long, pointed wings, which prey on small quarry, as *Milvus milvus*, the kite of Europe, North Africa, and the Middle East. **3.** a person who preys on others; a sharper. **4.** *Naut.* any light sail that is usually spread in light winds, and furled in a strong breeze. **5.** *Com.* a fictitious negotiable instrument, not representing any actual transaction, used for raising money or sustaining credit. **6.** *Slang.* an aeroplane. **7. to fly a kite,** *Colloq.* to test public opinion by spreading rumours, etc. —*v.i.* **8.** *Colloq.* to fly or move with a rapid or easy motion like that of a kite. **9.** *Com.* to obtain money or credit through kites. —*v.t.* **10.** *Com.* to employ as a kite. [ME *kyte*, OE *cȳta*; akin to G *Kauz* kind of owl]

kite balloon, a captive balloon, used for observation.

kite-mark (kīt′mäk′), *n.* a kite-shaped mark on a manufactured article indicating that it conforms to standards laid down by the British Standards Institution.

kith (kĭth), *n.* one's acquaintances or friends (now chiefly Scot. and N Dial. except in *kith and kin* and often confused in meaning with *kin*). [ME *kitthe*, OE *cȳth*, *cȳththu* knowledge, acquaintance, native land, der. *cūth* known, pp. of *cunnan* CAN[1]]

kith and kin, friends and relatives.

kithara (kĭth′ə rə), *n.* a musical instrument of ancient Greece; cithara. [t. Gk]

kitsch (kĭch), *n.* pretentious or worthless art, literature, etc. [t. G]

kitten (kĭt′n), *n.* **1.** a young cat. **2.** a playful or skittish girl. —*v.t.*, *v.i.* **3.** (of cats) to give birth to; bear. [ME *kitoun*, *kyton*, t. d. OF; cf. OF *chitoun*, *chaton*, dim. of *chat* cat] —**kit′ten-like′**, *adj.*

kittenish (kĭt′n ĭsh), *adj.* kitten-like; artlessly playful. —**kit′tenishly**, *adv.* —**kit′tenishness**, *n.*

Kittikachorn (kĭt′ĭ kä chôn′), *n.* **Thanom** (tŭ nŏm′), born 1911, prime minister of Thailand since 1963.

kittiwake (kĭt′ĭ wāk′), *n.* either of two gulls of the genus *Rissa*, having the hind toe very short or rudimentary. [imit. of its cry]

kittle (kĭt′l), *v.*, **-tled, -tling,** *adj.*, **-tler, -tlest.** *Scot. and Dial.* —*v.t.* **1.** to tickle. **2.** to excite or arouse. —*adj.* **3.** difficult to deal with; risky; ticklish. [t. Scand.; cf. Icel. *kitla* tickle]

kitty[1] (kĭt′ĭ), *n.*, *pl.* **-ties. 1.** a kitten. **2.** a pet name for a cat. [f. KIT[3] + -Y[2]]

kitty[2] (kĭt′ĭ), *n.*, *pl.* **-ties. 1.** a jointly held fund or collection, usually of small amounts of money; savings; accumulation. **2.** a pool into which each player in a card game places a certain sum of money as a stake. **3.** *Bowling.* the jack. [appar. familiar der. of *kitcot*, phonetic var. of *kidcot* prison, f. KID[1] (in sense of slave or criminal) + COT[2]]

Kittyhawk (kĭt′ĭ hôk′), *n.* a village in the U.S., in NE North Carolina: Wright brothers' aeroplane flight, 1903.

Kitwe (kĭt′wā), *n.* a town in NE Zambia. 115,000 (est. 1963).

Kiushu (kyo͞o′sho͞o), *n.* Kyushu.

kiva (kē və), *n.* a large chamber, often wholly or partly underground, in a Pueblo Indian village, used for religious ceremonies and other purposes. [t. N Amer. Ind. (Hopi)]

kiwi (ke′wĭ), *n.*, *pl.* **-wis** (-wĭz). **1.** an apteryx (flightless ratite bird of New Zealand). **2.** *Colloq.* a New Zealander, esp. a sportsman representing New Zealand. [t. Maori]

Kizil Irmak (*Turk.* kĭ zĭl′ĭr mäk), a river flowing through central Turkey N to the Black Sea. ab. 600 mi.

Kjölen (*Swed.* chœ′lən), *n.* a mountain range between Norway and Sweden. Highest peak, Mt Kebnekaise, 7005 ft.

K.K.K., Ku Klux Klan. Also, **KKK.**

K Kt, *Chess.* king's knight.

kl., kilolitre.

Kladno (*Cz.* klȧd′nŏ), *n.* a town in NW Czechoslovakia. 55,000 (est. 1967).

Klagenfurt (*Ger.* klä′gən fo͝ort), *n.* a town in S Austria. 69,218 (1961).

Klaipeda (*Russ.* klȧy′pĭ də), *n.* Lithuanian name of **Memel.**

Klan (klăn), *n.* Ku Klux Klan.

Klang (klăng), *n.* a town in Malaysia, in W Selangor. 75,649 (1957).

Klansman (klănz′mən), *n.*, *pl.* **-men.** a member of the Ku Klux Klan.

Klausenburg (*Ger.* klou′zən bo͝ork), *n.* German name of **Cluj.**

klaxon (klăk′sən), *n.* a type of warning hooter with a strident tone, originally used in motor vehicles. [formerly trademark]

Kléber (*Fr.* klė bĕr′), *n.* **Jean Baptiste** (*Fr.* zhäɴ bȧ tēst′), 1753–1800, French general.

Klebs (*Ger.* klėps), *n.* **Edwin** (*Ger.* ĕt′vēn), 1834–1913, German pathologist and bacteriologist.

Klebs-Löffler bacillus (klĕbz′lûf′lə; *Ger.* klėps′lœf′lər), the bacillus *Corynebacterium diphtheriae*, which causes diphtheria. [named after Edwin KLEBS and F. A. J. *Löffler*, 1852–1915, German bacteriologist]

Klee (*Ger.* klė), *n.* **Paul** (*Ger.* poul), 1879–1940, Swiss painter.

Kleiber (*Ger.* klī′bər), *n.* **Erich** (*Ger.* ė′rĭKH), 1890–1956, Austrian orchestral conductor.

Klein (klīn), *n.* **Felix** (fē′lĭks; *Ger.* fė′-), 1849–1925, German mathematician.

Kleist (*Ger.* klīst), *n.* **Heinrich von** (*Ger.* hīn′rĭKH fŏn), 1777–1811, German dramatist, poet, and moralist.

Klemperer (*Ger.* klĕm′pə rər), *n.* **Otto** (*Ger.* ŏ′tȯ), born 1885, German orchestral conductor.

Klenze (*Ger.* klĕn′tsə), *n.* **Leo von** (*Ger.* lė′ȯ fŏn), 1784–1864, German neoclassical architect.

klepht (klĕft), *n.* a Greek or Albanian brigand, exalted in the war of Greek independence as a patriotic robber; guerrilla. [t. mod. Gk: s. *kléphtēs*, Gk *kléptēs* thief]

kleptomania (klĕp′tō mā′nyə), *n.* an irresistible desire to steal, without regard to personal needs. Also, **cleptomania.** [t. NL, f. Gk: m. s. *kléptēs* thief + *-mania* -MANIA]

kleptomaniac (klĕp′tō mā′nĭ ăk′), *n.* one affected with kleptomania. Also, **cleptomaniac.**

klieg eyes (klēg), inflammation and oedema of the eyes as a result of prolonged exposure to arc lights, as the klieg lights of the film industry.

klieg light, a floodlight with an arc-light source used in film studios to project a beam of high actinic power. [named after J. H. *Kliegl*, 1869–1959, and his brother, Anton T. *Kliegl*, 1872–1927, German-born U.S. inventors]

klipfish (klĭp′fĭsh′), *n.* *S African.* rockfish (def. 3). [part trans. of Afrikaans *klipvis*]

klipspringer (klĭp′sprĭng′ə), *n.* a small, active African antelope, *Oreotragus oreotragus*, of mountainous regions from the Cape of Good Hope to Ethiopia. [t. Afrikaans: lit., rock-springer]

Klondike (klŏn′dīk), *n.* **1.** a region of the Yukon territory in NW Canada: gold rush, 1897–98. **2.** a river in this region, flowing into the Yukon. ab. 90 mi. long. **3.** (*l.c.*) *Cards.* a kind of patience.

Klondike region

kloof (klo͞of), *n.* *S African.* a ravine or gorge. [t. Afrikaans, akin to CLEAVE[2]]

Klopstock (*Ger.* klŏp′shtŏk), *n.* **Friedrich Gottlieb** (*Ger.* frē′drĭKH gŏt′lēp), 1724–1803, German poet.

Klosterneuburg (*Ger.* klȯs tər noʏ′bo͝ork), *n.* a town in Austria, in E Lower Austria, on the Danube. 22,787 (1961).

Kluck (*Ger.* klo͝ok), *n.* **Alexander von** (*Ger.* ȧ lĕ ksȧn′dər fŏn), 1846–1934, German general.

klystron (klĭs′trŏn, klī′strŏn), *n.* **1.** a vacuum tube containing an electron gun, a **buncher resonator** which changes the velocity of the electron beam in accordance with a signal, a **drift tube** in which the electron velocity does not change, a **catcher resonator** which abstracts energy from the electron beam, and a **collector electrode** for the electrons. It has several ultra high frequency applications. **2.** (*cap.*) a trademark for this tube. Cf. **resonator** (def. 4). [appar. der. Gk *klystḗr* syringe]

km, kingdom.

km., kilometre; kilometres.

K-meson (kā′mē′zŏn), *n.* *Physics.* one of a group of mesons all of which have a mass approximately equal to half of that of a proton; they exist in positive, negative, and neutral charged states. Also, **kaon.**

km./sec., kilometres per second.

kn, kronen.

knack (năk), *n.* a faculty or power of doing something with ease as from special skill; aptitude. [ME *knak*; ? akin to *knack*, v., strike (imit.)] —**Syn.** aptness, facility, dexterity.

knacker (năk′ə), *n.* **1.** one who buys old or useless horses for slaughter. **2.** one who buys old houses, ships, etc., to break them up for scrap. [f. obs. *knack*, v. (t. Scand.; cf. Icel. *hnakkr* nape of neck, saddle) + -ER[1]; orig. sense, saddler]

knag (năg), *n.* **1.** a knot in wood. **2.** the base of a branch. [ME, c. G *Knagge* knot, peg]

knaggy (năg′ĭ), *adj.* knotty; rough with knots.

knap (năp), *v.i.*, *v.t.*, **knapped, knapping.** *Chiefly Dial.* **1.** to strike with a hard, short sound; rap. **2.** to break into pieces; chip. [late ME; c. D *knappen* to crack]

Knappertsbusch (*Ger.* knȧ′pərts bo͝osh), *n.* **Hans** (*Ger.* hȧns), 1888–1965, German conductor.

knapsack (năp′săk′), *n.* a leather or canvas case for clothes and the like, carried on the back, esp. by soldiers. [t. LG: f. s. *knappen* bite, eat + *sack* SACK[1]]

knapweed (năp′wēd′), *n.* hardheads.

knar (nä), *n.* a knot on a tree or in wood. [ME *knarre*, c. D *knar*] —**knarred,** *adj.*

knave (nāv), *n.* **1.** an unprincipled or dishonest fellow.

2. *Cards.* a playing card bearing the formalized picture of a prince, in most games counting as next below the queen in its suit; jack. 3. *Archaic.* a male servant or man of humble position. [ME; OE *cnafa*, c. G *Knabe* boy]

—**Syn.** 1. KNAVE, RASCAL, ROGUE, SCOUNDREL are disparaging terms applied to persons considered base, dishonest, or worthless. KNAVE, formerly merely a boy or servant, in modern use emphasizes baseness of nature and intention: *a dishonest and swindling knave.* RASCAL suggests shrewdness and trickery in dishonesty: *a plausible rascal.* A ROGUE is a worthless fellow who sometimes preys extensively upon the community by fraud: *photographs of criminals in a rogues' gallery.* A SCOUNDREL is a blackguard and rogue of the worst sort: *a thorough scoundrel.* RASCAL and ROGUE are often used humorously (*an entertaining rascal, a saucy rogue*) but KNAVE and SCOUNDREL are not.

knavery (nā′və rĭ), *n., pl.* **-ries.** 1. action or practice characteristic of a knave. 2. unprincipled or dishonest dealing; trickery. 3. a knavish act or practice.

knavish (nā′vĭsh), *adj.* 1. like or befitting a knave; dishonest. 2. waggish; mischievous. —**knav′ishly,** *adv.* —**knav′ishness,** *n.*

knawel (nô′əl), *n.* any of several small caryophyllaceous plants of the genus *Scleranthus*, as *S. annuus*, **annual knawel,** widespread in sandy places. [t. G: m. *Knäuel*, lit., ball of yarn]

knead (nēd), *v.t.* 1. to work (dough, etc.) into a uniform mixture by pressing, folding and stretching. 2. to manipulate by similar movements, as the body in massage. 3. to make by kneading. 4. to make kneading motions with. [ME *kneden*, OE *cnedan*, c. G *kneten*] —**knead′er,** *n.*

knee (nē), *n., v.,* **kneed, kneeing.** —*n.* 1. the joint or region in man between the thigh and the lower part of the leg. 2. the joint or region of other vertebrates corresponding or homologous to the human knee, as in the leg of a bird, the hind limb of a horse, etc. 3. a joint or region likened to this but not homologous with it, as the tarsal joint of a bird, or the carpal joint in the forelimb of a horse, cow, etc. 4. the part of a garment covering the knee. 5. something resembling a knee joint, esp. when bent, as a fabricated support or brace with a leg running at an angle to the main member. 6. a piece of wood or metal with an angular bend. 7. **bring someone to his knees,** to compel someone to submit. —*v.t.* 8. to strike or touch with the knee. —*v.i.* 9. *Obs. or Poetic.* to go down on the knees; kneel. [ME *know(e)*, *kne(w)*, OE *cnēo(w)*, c. D *knie*, G *Knie*. Cf. KNEEL]

knee breeches, breeches reaching to or just below the knee.

kneecap (nē′kăp′), *n.* 1. the patella, the flat, movable bone at the front of the knee. 2. a protective covering, usually knitted, for the knee.

knee-deep (nē′dēp′), *adj.* 1. so deep as to reach the knees: *the snow lay knee-deep.* 2. submerged or covered by something having such depth.

knee-high (nē′hī′), *adj.* as high as the knees.

knee-hole (nē′hōl′), *n.* a space into which to fit the knees, as under a desk.

knee jerk, a brisk reflex lifting of the leg induced by tapping the tendon below the kneecap; patellar reflex.

kneel (nēl), *v.,* **knelt** or **kneeled, kneeling,** *n.* —*v.i.* 1. to fall or rest on the knees or a knee. —*n.* 2. the action or position of kneeling. [ME *knele(n)*, *knewlen*, OE *cnēowlian* (c. D *knielen*, LG *knelen*), der. *cnēow* KNEE] —**kneel′er,** *n.*

kneepad (nē′păd′), *n.* a pad to protect the knee.

kneepan (nē′păn′), *n.* the kneecap or patella.

kneepiece (nē′pēs′), *n.* armour for the knee, of hardened leather or of steel. See illus. under **armour.**

knee-sprung (nē′sprŭng′), *adj. Vet. Sci.* (of a horse, mule, etc.) having a forward bowing of the knee caused by inflammatory shortening of the flexor tendons.

knell (nĕl), *n.* 1. the sound made by a bell rung slowly for a death or a funeral. 2. any sound announcing the death of a person or the extinction, failure, etc., of something. 3. any mournful sound. —*v.i.* 4. to sound, as a bell, esp. as a funeral bell. 5. to give forth a mournful, ominous, or warning sound. —*v.t.* 6. to proclaim or summon by, or as by, a bell. [ME *knelle*, *knylle*, OE *cnyllan* strike, ring (a bell), c. Icel. *knylla* beat, strike]

Kneller (nĕl′ə), *n.* **Sir Godfrey,** 1646–1723, English portrait painter, born in Germany.

knelt (nĕlt), *v.* pt. and pp. of **kneel.**

Knesset (nĕs′ĭt), *n.* the parliament of Israel. [t. Heb.: lit., gathering]

knew (nyōō), *v.* pt. of **know.**

Knickerbocker (nĭk′ə bŏk′ə), *n.* 1. a descendant of the Dutch settlers of New York. 2. any New Yorker.

knickerbockers (nĭk′ə bŏk′əz), *n.pl. Orig. U.S.* loosely fitting short breeches gathered in at the knee. [der. KNICKERBOCKER]

knickers (nĭk′əz), *n.pl. Orig. U.S.* 1. a bloomer-like undergarment worn by women. 2. knickerbockers. [shortened form of KNICKERBOCKERS]

knick-knack (nĭk′năk′), *n.* 1. a pleasing trifle; a trinket or gimcrack. 2. a bit of bric-a-brac. Also, **nick-nack.** [dissimilated redupl. of KNACK]

knife (nīf), *n., pl.* **knives,** *v.,* **knifed, knifing.** —*n.* 1. a cutting instrument consisting essentially of a thin blade (usually of steel and with a sharp edge) attached to a handle. 2. a knifelike weapon; a dagger; a short sword. 3. any blade for cutting, as in a tool or machine. 4. **get one's knife into,** to bear a grudge against; desire to hurt. 5. **war to the knife,** war without mercy; relentless hostility. —*v.t.* 6. to apply a knife to; cut, stab, etc., with a knife. 7. *U.S. Slang.* to endeavour to defeat in a secret or underhand way. [ME *knif*, OE *cnīf*, c. Icel. *knīfr*] —**knife′less,** *adj.* —**knife′like′,** *adj.*

knifeboard (nīf′bôd′), *n.* (formerly) 1. a board on which knives were cleaned. 2. a long double bench on the top deck of an open-top bus or tram. —*adj.* 3. of or pertaining to such benches: *knifeboard seating.*

knife edge, 1. the edge of a knife. 2. anything very sharp. 3. a wedge, on the fine edge of which a scale beam, pendulum, or the like, oscillates.

knife-edged (nīf′ĕjd′), *adj.* having a thin, sharp edge.

knife switch, *Elect.* a form of air-switch in which the moving element, usually a hinged blade, enters or embraces the contact clips.

knight (nīt), *n.* 1. *Medieval Hist.* **a.** a mounted soldier serving under a feudal superior. **b.** a man, usually of noble birth, who after an apprenticeship as page and squire was raised to honourable military rank and bound to chivalrous conduct. 2. any person of a rank similar to that of the medieval knight. 3. a man upon whom a certain dignity, corresponding to that of the medieval knight, is conferred by a sovereign because of personal merit or for services rendered to the country. In Britain he holds the rank next below that of a baronet, and the title *Sir* is prefixed to the Christian name, as in *Sir John Smith.* Neither the dignity nor the title is hereditary. 4. *Chess.* a piece shaped like a horse's head, moving one square horizontally or vertically, and then one square obliquely. 5. a member of any order or association of men bearing the name of *Knights.* —*v.t.* 6. to dub or create (a man) a knight. [ME; OE *cniht* boy, manservant; c. D *knecht*, G *Knecht*] —**knight′less,** *adj.*

Knight (nīt), *n.* **Dame Laura,** 1877–1970, English painter.

knight bachelor, the lowest in rank among British knights, not belonging to any special order.

knight banneret, banneret (def. 2).

knight-errant (nīt′ĕ′rənt), *n., pl.* **knights-errant.** *Hist.* a wandering knight; a knight who travelled in search of adventures, to exhibit military skill, etc.

knight-errantry (nīt′ĕ′rən trĭ), *n., pl.* **knight-errantries.** 1. conduct or a performance like that of a knight-errant. 2. quixotic conduct or action.

knightheads (nīt′hĕdz′), *n.pl. Naut.* the top of two heavy timbers built up one on each side of the stern of a sailing ship, to support the bowsprit.

knighthood (nīt′hŏŏd), *n.* 1. the rank or dignity of a knight. 2. the profession or vocation of a knight. 3. knightly character or qualities. 4. the body of knights.

knightly (nīt′lĭ), *adj.* 1. of or belonging to a knight: *knightly deeds.* 2. characteristic of a knight. 3. being or resembling a knight. 4. composed of knights. —*adv.* 5. in a manner befitting a knight. —**knight′liness,** *n.*

Knightsbridge (nīts′brĭj′), *n.* 1. a district in London, S of Hyde Park. 2. a thoroughfare in this district.

Knights Hospitallers. See **Hospitaller** (def. 1).

Knights of Columbus, a Roman Catholic fraternal organization, founded in the U.S. in 1882, aiming to associate members of the church for religious and civic usefulness.

Knights of St John of Jerusalem, Knights Hospitallers. See **Hospitaller** (def. 1).

Knight Templar, *pl.* **Knights Templar, Knights Templars.** Templar (defs 1 and 3).

knit (nĭt), *v.,* **knitted** or **knit, knitting,** *n.* —*v.t.* 1. to make (a garment, fabric, etc.) by interlacing loops of yarn either by hand with knitting needles or by machine. 2. to join closely and firmly together, as members or parts. 3. to contract into folds or wrinkles: *to knit the brow.* —*v.i.* 4. to become closely and firmly joined together; grow together, as broken bones do. 5. to contract, as the brow does. 6. to become closely or intimately united. —*n.* 7. fabric produced by interlooping of a yarn or yarns. [ME *knitte*, OE *cnyttan* tie, der. *cnotta* KNOT[1]] —**knit′ter,** *n.*

knitting (nĭt′ĭng), *n.* 1. the act of a person or thing that knits. 2. the act of forming a fabric by looping a continuous yarn. 3. knitted work.

knitting needle, an instrument for knitting; a straight, slender rod of steel, plastic, etc., with rounded ends.
knitwear (nĭt′wĕə′), *n.* clothing made of knitted fabric.
knives (nīvz), *n.* pl. of **knife.**
knob (nŏb), *n., v.,* **knobbed, knobbing.** —*n.* **1.** a projecting part, usually rounded, forming the handle of a door, drawer, or the like. **2.** a rounded lump or protuberance on the surface or at the end of something, as a knot on a tree trunk, a pimple on the skin, etc. **3.** *Archit.* an ornamental boss, as of carved work. **4.** a rounded hill or mountain, esp. an isolated one. **5.** *Taboo Slang.* the penis. —*v.t.* **6.** to furnish with knobs; produce knobs on. —*v.i.* **7.** to form a knob or knobs. [ME. Cf. G *Knobbe*] —**knobbed,** *adj.* —**knob′like′,** *adj.*
knobble (nŏb′l), *n.* a small knob.
knobbly (nŏb′lĭ), *adj.* full or covered with knobbles; knobby; knotty.
knobby (nŏb′ĭ), *adj.,* **-bier, -biest. 1.** abounding in knobs. **2.** knoblike. —**knob′biness,** *n.*
knobkerrie (nŏb′kĕ′rĭ), *n.* a short, heavy stick or club with a knob on one end, used for both striking and throwing by South African natives. [t. Afrikaans: m. *knopkiri,* f. *knop* knob + Hottentot *kiri* stick, club]
knock (nŏk), *v.i.* **1.** to strike a sounding blow with the fist, knuckles, or anything hard, esp. on a door, window, or the like, as in seeking admittance, calling attention, giving a signal, etc. **2.** (of an internal-combustion engine) to make a metallic noise as a result of faulty combustion. **3.** to collide (usually followed by *against* or *into*). —*v.t.* **4.** to give a sounding or forcible blow to; hit; strike; beat. **5.** to drive, force, or render by a blow or blows: *to knock a man senseless.* **6.** to strike (a thing) against something else. **7.** *Slang.* to criticize; find fault with. —*v.* **8.** Some special verb phrases are:
knock about, 1. to wander in an aimless way; lead an irregular existence. **2.** to treat roughly; maltreat.
knock back, *Colloq.* to drink: *he knocked back two pints of beer.*
knock down, 1. to strike to the ground with a blow. **2.** (in auctions) to signify the sale of (the thing bid for) by a blow with a hammer or mallet; assign as sold to the highest bidder. **3.** to reduce the price of. **4.** to take apart (a motor vehicle, machine, etc.) to facilitate handling.
knock into a cocked hat, knock spots off, *Colloq.* to defeat; get the better of.
knock it off, *Slang.* stop it (usually used to put an end to an argument, fight, criticism, etc.).
knock off, *Colloq.* **1.** to stop an activity, esp. work. **2.** to deduct. **3.** to steal. **4.** to compose (an article, poem, or the like) hurriedly.
knock on, *Rugby Football.* to knock (the ball) forwards in catching it (an infringement of the rules).
knock on the head, to put an end to.
knock out, 1. to defeat (an opponent) in a boxing match by striking him down with a blow after which he does not rise within a prescribed time. **2.** to render senseless. **3.** to destroy; damage severely.
knock the bottom out of, to refute (an argument); render invalid.
knock together, to assemble (something) hastily; put together roughly.
knock up, 1. to arouse; awaken. **2.** to construct (something) hastily or roughly. **3.** *Cricket.* to score (runs). **4.** *Tennis.* to practise.
—*n.* **9.** the act or sound of knocking. **10.** a rap, as at a door. **11.** a blow or thump. **12.** the noise resulting from faulty combustion or from incorrect functioning of some part of an internal-combustion engine. **13.** *Cricket.* an innings. **14.** *Slang.* adverse criticism. **15. take a knock,** suffer a reverse, esp. a financial one.
[ME *knokke,* unexpl. var. of *knoke,* OE *cnocian,* c. Icel. *knoka;* ? imit. in orig.] —**Syn. 1.** See **strike.**
knockabout (nŏk′ə bout′), *n.* **1.** *Naut.* a small handy yacht with a jib and mainsail but no bowsprit. **2.** *Austral. Colloq.* a station hand; odd-job man. —*adj.* **3.** suitable for rough use, as a garment. **4.** characterized by knocking about; rough; boisterous: *knockabout comedy.*
knock-back (nŏk′băk′), *n.* *Austral. Colloq.* a refusal; rejection.
knockdown (nŏk′doun′), *adj.* **1.** such as to knock something down; overwhelming; irresistible: *a knockdown blow.* **2.** constructed in separate parts, so as to be readily knocked down or taken apart, as a boat, a piece of furniture, etc. **3. knockdown price,** the reserve price of an article at an auction, below which it cannot be knocked down. —*n.* **4.** a knockdown object. **5.** the act of knocking down, esp. by a blow. **6.** that which falls or overwhelms.
knocker (nŏk′ə), *n.* **1.** one who or that which knocks. **2.** a hinged knob, bar, etc., on a door, for use in knocking. **3.** *Colloq.* a persistently hostile critic or carping detractor.
knock-for-knock (nŏk′fə nŏk′), *adj.* of or pertaining to a form of agreement between insurance companies whereby when more than one insured person sustains a loss, the insurance companies pay only the amount for which they are liable to their own insured.
knock-knee (nŏk′nē′), *n.* **1.** inward curvature of the legs, causing the knees to knock together in walking. **2.** (*pl.*) such knees. —**knock′-kneed′,** *adj.*
Knockmealdown Mountains (nŏk′mēl doun′), a range of low mountains in the Republic of Ireland, forming the border of Co. Waterford with Tipperary. Highest peak, Knockmealdown, 2609 ft.
knock-on (nŏk′ŏn′), *n.* *Rugby Football.* the act or infringement of knocking on.
knockout (nŏk′out′), *n.* **1.** the act of knocking out. **2.** state or fact of being knocked out. **3.** a knockout blow. **4.** *Slang.* a person or thing of overwhelming success or attractiveness. —*adj.* **5.** that knocks out. **6.** (of a competition) eliminating competitors at each round until only the winner remains. **7.** (of card games) eliminating players under certain circumstances, as on the failure to win a trick.
knock-up (nŏk′ŭp′), *n.* *Tennis, Squash, etc.* practice before a game commences.
knoll[1] (nōl), *n.* a small, rounded hill or eminence; a hillock. [ME *knol,* OE *cnol(l),* c. Norw. *knoll* hillock]
knoll[2] (nōl), *v.t.* *Archaic or Dial.* **1.** to ring a knell for; announce by strokes of a bell or the like. **2.** to ring or toll (a bell). —*v.i.* **3.** to sound, as a bell; ring. **4.** to sound a knell. —*n.* **5.** a stroke of a bell in ringing or tolling. [ME; akin to KNELL]
knop (nŏp), *n.* a small, rounded protuberance; a knob; a boss, stud, or the like, as for ornament. [ME and OE, c. G *Knopf*]
Knossos (nŏs′ŏs), *n.* a ruined city in Crete: capital of the ancient Minoan civilization. Also, **Cnossus.**
knot[1] (nŏt), *n., v.,* **knotted, knotting.** —*n.* **1.** an interlacement of a cord, rope, or the like, drawn tight into a lump or knob, as for fastening two cords, etc., together or to something else. **2.** a piece of ribbon or similar material tied or folded upon itself and used or worn as an ornament. **3.** a cluster of persons or things. **4.** *Bot.* a protuberance in the tissue of a plant; an excrescence on a stem, branch, or root; a node or joint in a stem, esp. when of swollen form. **5.** *Zool.* a hard lump in an animal body as a swelling or the like in a muscle, gland, etc. **6.** the hard, cross-grained mass of wood at the place where a branch joins the trunk of a tree. **7.** a part of this mass showing in a piece of timber, etc. **8.** any of various diseases of trees characterized by the formation of an excrescence, knob, or gnarl. **9.** *Naut.* **a.** one of a series of equal divisions on a log line, marked off by strings knotted through the strands, and made of such a length that the number running out in a certain time will indicate the ship's speed in nautical miles per hour. **b.** a unit of speed of one nautical mile an hour. **c.** nautical mile. **10.** something involved or intricate; a difficulty; a knotty problem. **11.** a bond or tie. —*v.t.* **12.** to tie in a knot or knots; form a knot or knots in. **13.** to secure by a knot. **14.** to form protuberances, bosses, or knobs in; make knotty. —*v.i.* **15.** to become tied or tangled in a knot or knots. **16.** to form knots or joints. [ME *knot(te),* OE *cnotta,* c. D *knot*] —**knot′less,** *adj.* —**Syn. 3.** group, company. **4.** lump, knob, gnarl. **10.** perplexity, puzzle.

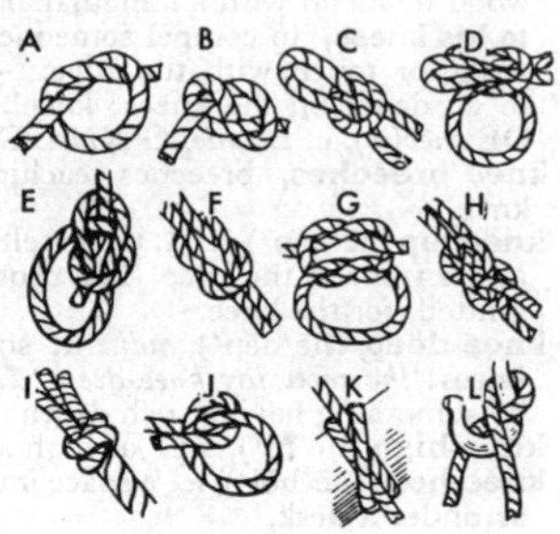

Knot
A, Overhand; B, Figure of eight; C, Slipknot; D, Bow; E, Bowline; F, Reef knot; G, Granny knot; H, Single carrick bend; I, Matthew Walker; J, Half-hitch; K, Clove hitch; L, Blackwall hitch

knot[2] (nŏt), *n.* a wading bird, *Calidris canutus,* of the snipe family. [orig. unknown]
knotgrass (nŏt′gräs′), *n.* **1.** a common polygonaceous weed, *Polygonum aviculare,* with nodes in its stems. **2.** any of certain other species of the genus.
knothole (nŏt′hōl′), *n.* a hole in a board or plank formed by the falling out of a knot or a portion of a knot.
knotted (nŏt′ĭd), *adj.* **1.** knotty. **2.** *Bot.* having many nodes or nodelike swellings; gnarled. **3.** *Zool.* having one or more swellings; nodose.

knotting (nŏt′ĭng), *n.* a solution of shellac in industrial methylated spirits, used in the preparation of wood for covering knots and other resinous areas which might stain or soften a coat of paint.

knotty (nŏt′ĭ), *adj.*, **-tier, -tiest.** **1.** characterized by knots; full of knots. **2.** involved, intricate, or difficult: *a knotty problem.* **—knot′tiness,** *n.*

knotweed (nŏt′wēd′), *n.* any of various knotty-stemmed plants of the polygonaceous genus *Polygonum,* as *P. maritimum* (**seaside knotweed**), a glaucous herb of sandy soils.

knout (nout), *n.* **1.** a kind of whip or scourge formerly used in Russia for flogging criminals. **—***v.t.* **2.** to flog with the knout. [t. F, t. Russ.: m. *knut*]

know (nō), *v.*, **knew, known, knowing,** *n.* **—***v.t.* **1.** to perceive or understand as fact or truth, or apprehend with clearness and certainty. **2.** to have fixed in the mind or memory: *to know a poem by heart.* **3.** to be cognizant or aware of; to be acquainted with (a thing, place, person, etc.), as by sight, experience, or report. **4.** to understand from experience or attainment (fol. by *how* before an infinitive): *to know how to make something.* **5.** to be able to distinguish, as one from another. **6. know the ropes, a.** to know the various ropes about a vessel, as a sailor does. **b.** *Colloq.* to understand the details or methods of any business or the like. **—***v.i.* **7.** to have knowledge, or clear and certain perception, as of fact or truth. **8.** to be cognizant or aware, as of some fact, circumstance, or occurrence; have information, as about something. **—***n.* **9.** the fact of knowing; knowledge: now chiefly in the colloquial phrase **in the know** (having inside knowledge). [ME *knowe(n), knawe(n),* OE (*ge*)-*cnāwan,* c. OHG -*cnāan* know, Icel. *knā* (pres. ind.) know how, can; akin to L (*g*)*nōscere,* Gk *gignṓskein*] **—know′er,** *n.*

—**Syn.** 1. KNOW, COMPREHEND, UNDERSTAND imply being aware of meanings. To KNOW is to be aware of something as a fact or truth: *he knows the basic facts of the subject; I know that he agrees with me.* To COMPREHEND is to know something thoroughly and to perceive its relationships to certain other ideas, facts, etc. To UNDERSTAND is to be fully aware not only of the meaning of something but also its implications: *I could comprehend all he said, but did not understand that he was joking.*

knowable (nō′ə bl), *adj.* that may be known. **—know′ableness,** *n.*

know-all (nō′ôl′), *n. Colloq.* **1.** one who claims to know everything, or everything about a particular subject. **2.** one who appears to know everything.

know-how (nō′hou′), *n.* knowledge of how to do something; faculty or skill for a particular thing.

knowing (nō′ĭng), *adj.* **1.** shrewd, sharp, or astute; often affecting or suggesting shrewd or secret understanding of matters: *a knowing glance.* **2.** having knowledge or information; intelligent; wise. **3.** conscious; intentional; deliberate. **—know′ingly,** *adv.* **—know′ingness,** *n.*

knowledge (nŏl′ĭj), *n.* **1.** acquaintance with facts, truths, or principles, as from study or investigation; general erudition. **2.** familiarity or conversance, as with a particular subject, branch of learning, etc. **3.** acquaintance; familiarity gained by sight, experience, or report: *a knowledge of human nature.* **4.** the fact or state of knowing; perception of fact or truth; clear and certain mental apprehension. **5.** the state of being cognizant or aware, as of a fact or circumstance. **6.** that which is known, or may be known. **7.** the body of truths or facts accumulated by mankind in the course of time. **8.** the sum of what is known. **9.** cognizance of facts, or range of cognizance: *this has happened twice within my knowledge.* **10.** *Law or Archaic.* sexual intercourse: *carnal knowledge.* **11. to one's knowledge, a.** according to one's certain knowledge. **b.** (with a negative) so far as one knows: *I never saw him, to my knowledge.* [ME *knowleche,* der. KNOW]

—Syn. 1. See **information. 4.** understanding. **7.** learning, lore, erudition, scholarship; wisdom, science.

knowledgeable (nŏl′ĭ jə bl), *adj.* possessing knowledge or understanding; intelligent.

known (nōn), *v.* pp. of **know.**

known quantity, *Maths.* a quantity whose value is given: in algebra, etc., frequently represented by a letter from the first part of the alphabet, as *a, b,* or *c.*

Knox (nŏks), *n.* **John,** 1505?–72, leader of the Protestant Reformation in Scotland, preacher, statesman, and historian.

Knoxville (nŏks′vĭl), *n.* a town in the U.S., in E Tennessee, on the Tennessee river. 111,827 (1960).

Knt, Knight.

knuckle (nŭk′l), *n., v.,* **-led, -ling.** **—***n.* **1.** a joint of a finger, esp. one of the joints at the roots of the fingers. **2.** the rounded prominence of such a joint when the finger is bent. **3.** a joint of meat, consisting of the parts about the carpal or tarsal joint of a quadruped. **4.** an angle between two members or surfaces of a vessel. **5.** a cylindrical projecting part on a hinge, through which an axis or pin passes; the joint of a hinge. **6. near the knuckle,** (of a remark, joke, etc.) almost indecent. **—***v.i.* **7.** to hold the knuckles close to the ground in playing marbles (often fol. by *down*). **8.** to apply oneself vigorously or earnestly, as to a task (fol. by *down*). **9.** to yield or submit (often fol. by *down* or *under*). [ME *knokel*; akin to D *kneukel,* G *Knöchel,* dim. of a word repr. by D *knok,* G *Knochen* bone]

knucklebone (nŭk′l bōn′), *n.* **1.** (in man) a bone forming a knuckle of a finger. **2.** (in quadrupeds) a bone homologous with a wrist, ankle, or fingerbone of man, or its knobbed end.

knuckle-duster (nŭk′l dŭs′tə), *n.* a piece of metal fitted across the knuckles, used as a weapon.

knuckle joint, 1. a joint forming a knuckle. **2.** *Mach.* a flexible hinged joint formed by two abutting links.

knur (nû), *n.* an excrescence, esp. on a tree. [ME *knorre,* c. MD, MHG *knorre*]

knurl (nûl), *n.* **1.** a small ridge or the like, esp. one of a series, as on the edge of a thumbscrew to assist in obtaining a firm grip. **—***v.t.* **2.** to make knurls or ridges on. [appar. der. *knur* lump, knot, ME *knurre*]

knurled (nûld), *adj.* **1.** having small ridges on the edge or surface; milled. **2.** having knurls or knots; gnarled.

knurly (nû′lĭ), *adj.*, **-lier, -liest.** having knurls or knots; gnarled.

Knut (kə nyo͞ot′), *n.* Canute.

K.O., knockout. Also, **k.o.**

koala (kō ä′lə), *n.* a sluggish, tailless, grey, furry, arboreal marsupial, *Phascolarctos cinereus,* of Australia, about 2 ft long. Also, **koala bear.** [t. native Australian]

Koala bear, *Phascolarctos cinereus* (28 to 32 in. long)

Kobe (kō′bĭ), *n.* a seaport in Japan, on S Honshu island. 1,216,666 (1965).

København (*Dan.* kœ bən hawn′), *n.* Danish name of **Copenhagen.**

Koblenz (*Ger.* kō′blĕnts), *n.* a town in West Germany in N Rhineland-Palatinate, at the junction of the Rhine and Moselle rivers. 102,600 (est. 1966). Formerly, **Coblenz.**

kobold (kŏb′ōld), *n.* (in German folklore) **1.** a kind of spirit or goblin, often mischievous, that haunts houses. **2.** a spirit that haunts mines or other underground places. [t. G]

Koch (*Ger.* kŏKH), *n.* **Robert** (*Ger.* rō′bĕrt), 1843–1910, German bacteriologist and physician.

Köchel (kû′kl; *Ger.* kœ′KHəl), *n.* **Ludwig von** (*Ger.* lo͞ot′vĭKH fŏn), 1800–77, musician and scholar who compiled the definitive catalogue of Mozart's works.

Kochi (kō′chē′), *n.* a seaport in SW Japan, on Shikoku island. 217,889 (1965).

Koch's bacillus, a bacillus, *Mycobacterium tuberculosis,* that causes tuberculosis.

Kodaira (kō dī′rə), *n.* a town in Japan, in SE central Honshu. 105,353 (1965).

Kodály (kō dī′; *Hung.* kō′dày), *n.* **Zoltán** (zōl′tən; *Hung.* zōl′tán), 1882–1967, Hungarian composer.

Kodiak (kō′dĭ ăk′), *n.* an island in the N Pacific, near the base of the Alaska Peninsula. ab. 100 mi. long.

Kodok (kō′dŏk), *n.* See **Fashoda.**

koel (kō′əl), *n.* a cuckoo of the genus *Eudynamys,* as the **Indian koel,** *E. orientalis.* [t. Hind.: m. *kōil,* der. Skt *kokila*]

Koestler (kûst′lə), *n.* **Arthur,** born 1905, British novelist and essayist born in Hungary.

Kofu (kō′fo͞o, kô′fo͞o), *n.* a town in Japan, in S central Honshu. 172,457 (1965).

koggelmander (kŏg′l măn′də, kŏKH′əl-), *n. S African.* any small lizard or chameleon. [t. Afrikaans]

Kohinoor (kō′ĭ no͝oə′), *n.* one of the world's largest diamonds, 108 carats, first discovered in India and now part of the British crown jewels. [t. Pers.: m. *kōh-i-nūr* mountain of light]

kohl (kōl), *n.* a powder, as finely powdered sulphide of antimony, used in the East to darken the eyelids, make eyebrows, etc. [t. Ar. Cf. ALCOHOL]

Köhler (*Ger.* kœ′lər), *n.* **Wolfgang** (*Ger.* vŏlf′gäng), born 1887, German psychologist.

kohlrabi (kōl′rä′bĭ), *n., pl.* **-bies.** a cultivated variety of *Brassica oleracea,* var. *gongylodes,* whose stem above ground swells into an edible bulblike formation. [t. G, b. G *Kohl* cabbage and It. *cauli* (or *cavoli*) *rape,* pl. of *cavolo rapa* cabbage turnip. Cf. COLE, RAPE[2]]

koilonychia (koi′lō nĭk′ĭ ə), *n. Pathol.* a spoon-shaped depression in the nails. [f. Gk: *koilo-* (comb. form of *koîlos* hollow) + s. *ónyx* nail + *-ia* -IA]

Koine (koiʹnē), *n.* the standard Attic Greek which replaced other dialects and flourished under the Roman Empire. [Gk short for *koinḗ diálektos* common dialect]
Koivisto (*Finn.* kôjʹvēs tô), *n.* **Mauno** (*Finn.* mäwʹnô), born 1923, Finnish statesman: prime minister since 1968.
Kokand (*Russ.* kȧ kȧntʹ), *n.* a city in the SW Soviet Union in Asia, in Uzbekistan: formerly the centre of a powerful khanate. 126,000 (est. 1965).
kokerboom (kōʹkə bo͞omʹ), *n.* the quiver tree, *Aloe dichotoma*. [t. Afrikaans]
kokkewiet (kŏkʹə vētʹ), *n.* **1.** a black-headed, pink-breasted shrike, *Laniarius ferrugineus*, family *Laniidae*, of Africa. **2.** the bokmakierie. [t. Afrikaans]
Koko Nor (kōʹkō nôʹ), a lake in W China, in Chinghai province. ab. 2300 sq. mi.
Kokura (kōʹko͞o räʹ), *n.* a seaport in SW Japan, on Kyushu island. 286,476 (1960).
kola (kōʹlə), *n.* cola.
Kola (*Russ.* kôʹlə), *n.* a peninsula in the NW Soviet Union in Europe between the White and Barents seas.
kola nut (kōʹlə), cola nut.
Kolar Gold Fields (kō läʹ), a town in S India, in E Mysore state: rich mining district. 146,811 (1961).
Kolarovgrad (*Bulg.* kȯ läʹrȯv grȧt), *n.* a town in E Bulgaria. 61,917 (1964). Formerly, **Shumen.**
Kolhapur (kōlʹhä po͞oəʹ), *n.* a town in India, in SW Maharashtra. 187,442 (1961).
kolinsky (kə lĭnʹskĭ), *n.*, *pl.* **-skies. 1.** the red sable, or Siberian mink, *Mustela sibiricus*, about 15 inches long, with a bushy tail 8 or 10 inches long, the fur uniformly buff or tawny, somewhat paler below, varied with black and white on the head. **2.** the fur of such an animal. [t. Russ.: m. *Kolinski*, adj., pertaining to KOLA]
kolkhoz (kŏl hôzʹ), *n.* (in the U.S.S.R.) a collective farm, the holding being common property of all. [t. Russ., f. *kol(lektivnoe)* COLLECTIVE + *khoz(yaistvo)* farm]
Kollwitz (*Ger.* kŏlʹvĭts), *n.* **Käthe** (*Ger.* kĕʹtə), 1867–1945, German designer and sculptress.
Köln (*Ger.* kœln), *n.* German name of **Cologne.**
Kol Nidre (kŏl nĭdʹrĭ, -rə), *Judaism.* a prayer recited on the eve of Yom Kippur asking for the annulment of vows to God and forgiveness for transgressions.
Kolomna (*Russ.* kȧ lômʹnə), *n.* a town in the central Soviet Union in Europe. 130,000 (est. 1965).
Kolozsvár (*Hung.* kȯʹlȯzh vȧr), *n.* Hungarian name of **Cluj.**
Kolrausch's law (kŏlʹroush), *Physics.* the law which states that when ionization is complete the conductivity of an electrolyte is equal to the sum of the conductivities of the ions into which the solute dissociates. [named after F. W. *Kolrausch*, 1840–1910, German physicist]
Kolyma (*Russ.* kə lĭ mȧʹ), *n.* a river in the NE Soviet Union in Asia, flowing NE to the Arctic Ocean. ab. 1000 mi. Also, **Kolima.**
Komati (kə mäʹtĭ, kōʹmə tĭ), *n.* a river in the Republic of South Africa, flowing E through SE Transvaal, through Swaziland, and then to the Crocodile River. ab. 500 mi.
Komintern (kŏmʹĭn tûnʹ), *n.* Comintern.
Kommunarsk (*Russ.* kə mo͞o nȧrskʹ), *n.* a town in the W Soviet Union in Europe. 110,000 (est. 1964).
komodo dragon (kə mōʹdō), a giant monitor, *Varanus komodoensis*, of the island of Komodo in Indonesia: up to 12 ft long.
Kompong Cham (kŏmʹpŏng shămʹ), a town in SE Cambodia. 30,000 (1962).
Komsomol (kŏmʹsō mŏlʹ; *Russ.* kəm sȧ môlʹ), *n.* the communist youth organization in the Soviet Union.
Komsomolsk-on-Amur (kŏmʹsə mŏlskʹŏn ə mo͞oəʹ), *n.* a town in the W Soviet Union in Europe. 204,000 (est. 1965).
Komura (kōʹmo͞o räʹ), *n.* **Marquess Jutaro** (jo͞oʹtä rōʹ), 1855–1911, Japanese statesman and diplomat.
Konakry (*Fr.* kŏ nȧ krēʹ), *n.* Conakry.
konfyt (kŏn fātʹ), *n.* *S African.* a confection of candied peel. [t. Afrikaans, t. D: m. *konfijten*, v., to preserve]
Kongo (kŏngʹgō), *n.* **1.** a Bantu people centred around the lower river Congo. **2.** a member of this people. **3.** the Bantu language spoken by this people.
Königgrätz (*Ger.* kœ nĭKH grĕtsʹ), *n.* a town in NW Czechoslovakia, on the Elbe in Bohemia: the Prussians defeated the Austrians near here in the Battle of Sadowa, 1866. 55,136 (1961).
Königsberg (kûʹnĭgz bĕəgʹ; *Ger.* kœʹnĭKHs bĕrk), *n.* German name of **Kaliningrad.**
Königshütte (*Ger.* kœ nĭKHs hYʹtə), *n.* German name of **Chorzów.**
konini (kə nēʹnĭ, kōʹnĭ nĭ), *n.* the fruit of the fuchsia of New Zealand. [t. Maori]
konometer (kə nŏmʹĭ tə), *n.* an apparatus for measuring the amount of dust in the air (esp. in a mine). Also, **konimeter.**
Konstanz (*Ger.* kŏnʹstȧnts), *n.* German name of **Constance.**
Kon-Tiki (kŏn tēʹkĭ), *n.* a raft of green balsa wood on which an expedition led by Thor Heyerdahl in 1947 floated from Peru to the Marquesas. [named after *Kon-Tiki*, a member of a Peruvian race who, according to legend, floated from Peru to Polynesia]
Konya (*Turk.* kônʹyȧ), *n.* a town in S Turkey. 119,841 (1960). Also, **Konia.** Ancient, **Iconium.**
Koo (ko͞o), *n.* **Wellington** (*Vi Kyuin Wellington Koo*), born 1888, Chinese jurist and diplomat.
koodoo (ko͞oʹdo͞o), *n.*, *pl.* **-doos.** kudu.
kookaburra (ko͝okʹə bŭʹrə), *n.* *Austral.* the laughing jackass. [t. native Australian]
Kooning (*Du.* kȯʹnĭng), *n.* **Wilhelm de** (*Du.* wĭlʹhĕlm də), born 1904, U.S. artist born in Holland.
Kootenay (ko͞oʹtə nāʹ), *n.* a river flowing from SE British Columbia, through NW Montana and N Idaho, swinging back into Canada where it enters **Kootenay Lake** (65 mi. long) and empties into the Columbia river. ab. 400 mi. Also, *U.S.*, **Kootenai.**
kop (kŏp), *n.* *S African.* an isolated hill; a residual rock mass, the result of desert denudation. [t. Afrikaans, t. D: head]
kopeck (kōʹpĕk), *n.* a Russian monetary unit and copper coin, the hundredth part of a rouble. Also, **kopek, copeck.** [t. Russ.: m. *kopeika*]
Kopeisk (*Russ.* kȧ pyĕyskʹ), *n.* a town in the W Soviet Union in Europe. 168,000 (est. 1965).
Kopernik (*Pol.* kŏ pĕrʹnĕk), *n.* Polish name of **Copernicus.**
kopje (kŏpʹĭ), *n.* *S African.* a small kop. Also, **koppie, spitzkoppie.** [t. Afrikaans: dim. of KOP]
kor (kô), *n.* homer². [t. Heb.]
koradji (kŏ räʹjĭ), *n.* *Austral.* a sorcerer. [t. native Australian]
Koran (kô ränʹ), *n.* the sacred scripture of Islam, believed by orthodox Muslims to contain revelations made in Arabic by Allah directly to Mohammed. [t. Ar.: m. *qur'ān* reading, recitation, der. *qara'a* read] —**Koranic** (kô rănʹĭk), *adj.*
korari (kŏʹrə rĭ, kə räʹrĭ), *n.* the flower stalk of the native flax of New Zealand, *Phormium tenax*. [t. Maori]
Korcë (*Alb.* kȯrʹchė), *n.* a town in SE Albania. 42,550 (est. 1964).
Korda (kôʹdə), *n.* **Sir Alexander,** 1893–1956, British film producer, born in Hungary.
Kordofan (kôʹdō fänʹ), *n.* a province in the central Sudan. 2,051,616 pop. (est. 1961); ab. 146,930 sq. mi. *Cap.*: El Obeid.
Korea (kə rĭəʹ), *n.* a country in E Asia, on a peninsula SE of Manchuria and between the Sea of Japan and the Yellow Sea: under Japanese rule, 1910–45; currently divided in the vicinity of 38°N into **South Korea** and **North Korea.** Japanese, **Chosen.**

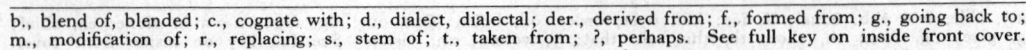

Korea

Korean (kə rĭənʹ), *adj.* **1.** of Korea, its people, or language. —*n.* **2.** a native or inhabitant of Korea. **3.** the language of Korea, of no known linguistic affinity.
Korean War, a war, 1950–53, fought between North Korea supported by Communist China, and South Korea supported by the United Nations.
Korea Strait, the strait between Korea and Japan, connecting the Sea of Japan and the East China Sea. ab. 120 mi. wide.
koromiko (kŏʹrə mēʹkō), *n.* a flowering shrub of New Zealand, *Veronica salicifolia*. [t. Maori]
koruna (kŏ ro͞oʹnə), *n.*, *pl.* **koruny** (kŏ ro͞oʹnĭ), **korun** (kŏ ro͞onʹ). **1.** the monetary unit of Czechoslovakia, equivalent to about £0·0578 sterling. **2.** a copper alloy coin of this value. *Abbrev.*: Kčs. [t. Czech, t. L: m. *corōna* crown]
kos (kōs), *n.*, *pl.* **kos.** (in India) a unit of land distance of various lengths from 1 to 3 mi. Also, **coss.** [t. Hind., g. Skt *krōśa*]
Kos (kŏs), *n.* Cos.
Kosciusko (kŏsʹĭ ŭsʹkō), *n.* **1. Thaddeus** (thădʹĭ əs), (*Tadeusz Kościuszko*), 1746–1817, Polish patriot and general. **2. Mount,** the highest mountain in Australia, in SE New South Wales. 7316 ft.
kosher (kōʹshə), *adj.* **1.** fit, lawful, or ritually permitted, according to the Jewish law: used of food and vessels for food ritually proper for use, esp. of meat slaughtered in accordance with the law of Moses. **2.** (of shops, houses, etc.) selling or using food prepared according to the Jewish law. —*n.* **3.** *Colloq.* kosher food. —*v.t.* **4.** to

prepare (food) according to the Jewish law. Also, **kasher.** [t. Heb.: m. *kāshēr* fit, proper, lawful]

Košice (*Slov.* kō'shē tsĕ), *n.* a town in Czechoslovakia, in SE Slovakia. 99,000 (1965). Hungarian, **Kassa.**

Kosi Lake (kō'sī), a sea lake on the E coast of the Republic of South Africa, in NE Natal.

Kossuth (kŏs'o͞oth; *Hung.* kô'sho͞ot), *n.* **1. Francis** or **Ferencz** (fĕ'rĕnts), 1841–1914, Hungarian statesman. **2.** his father, **Louis** or **Lajos** (*Hung.* lŏ'yŏsh), 1802–94, Hungarian patriot and statesman.

Kostroma (*Russ.* kə strȧ mȧ'), *n.* a town in the central Soviet Union in Europe, on the Volga. 202,000 (est. 1965).

Kosygin (kə sē'gĭn; *Russ.* kȧ sī'gĭn), *n.* **Aleksei Nikolayevich** (*Russ.* ə lĭk syĕy' nĭ kȧ lȧ'yĭ vĭch), born 1904, Soviet statesman: prime minister of the Soviet Union since 1964.

Kotah (kô'tä, kō'tä), *n.* a town in India, in SE Rajasthan. 120,345 (1961).

koto (kō'tō), *n.*, *pl.* **-tos.** a Japanese musical instrument having numerous strings, stretched over a vaulted, wooden sounding-board: plucked with the fingers. [t. Jap.]

kotow (kō'tou'), *v.i.*, *n.* kowtow. **—ko'tow'er,** *n.*

kotukutuku (kō to͞o'ko͞o to͞o'ko͞o), *n.* the tree fuchsia of New Zealand, *Fuchsia excorticata.* [t. Maori]

Kotzebue (*Ger.* kŏt'sə bo͞o), *n.* **August Friedrich Ferdinand von** (*Ger.* ou'go͝ost frē'drĭKH fĕr'dĭ nȧnt fŏn), 1761–1819, German dramatist.

koumis (ko͞o'mĭs), *n.* kumis. Also, **koumiss, koumyss, kumiss.**

Kovar (kō'vä), *n.* *Metall.*, *Trademark.* an alloy of cobalt, iron, and nickel which has a coefficient of expansion similar to glass.

Kovno (*Russ.* kôv'nə), *n.* Russian name of **Kaunas.**

Kovrov (*Russ.* kȧv rôf'), *n.* a town in the central Soviet Union in Europe. 113,000 (est. 1965).

Koweit (kō wāt'), *n.* Kuwait.

kowhai (kō'wī), *n.* a tree of New Zealand, *Sophora microphylla,* noted for its golden, bell-shaped flowers. [t. Maori]

Kowloon (kou'lo͞on'), *n.* **1.** a peninsula in SE China, opposite Hong Kong island: a part of Hong Kong Colony. 1,000,000 pop. (est. 1954); 3 sq. mi. **2.** a seaport on this peninsula.

kowtow (kou'tou'), *v.i.* **1.** to knock the forehead on the ground while kneeling, as an act of reverence, worship, apology, etc. **2.** to act in an obsequious manner; show servile deference. **—*n.* 3.** the act of kowtowing. Also, **kotow.** [t. Chinese (Mandarin): m. *k'o-t'ou*, lit., knock-head] **—kow'tow'er,** *n.*

Kozhikode (kō'zhĭ kō'dĭ), *n.* a town in India, in central Kerala. 192,521 (1961). Formerly, **Calicut.**

KP, *Chess.* king's pawn.

K.P., Knight of the Order of St Patrick.

KR, *Chess.* king's rook.

Kr, *Chem.* krypton.

kr., 1. kreuzer. **2.** krona; kronor. **3.** króna; krónur. **4.** krone[1]; kroner. **5.** krone[2]; kronen.

Kra (krä), *n.* **Isthmus of,** the narrowest part of the Malay Peninsula, between the Bay of Bengal and the Gulf of Siam. ab. 35 mi. wide.

kraal (kräl), *n.* **1.** a village of natives in southern or central Africa, usually surrounded by a stockade or the like and often having a central space for cattle, etc. **2.** the kraal as a social unit. **3.** *S African.* an enclosure for cattle, etc. **—*v.t.*** to shut up in a kraal, as cattle. [t. Afrikaans, t. Pg.: m. *curral* enclosure. Cf. CORRAL]

Krafft-Ebing (*Ger.* krȧft ė'bĭng), *n.* **Richard** (*Ger.* rĭKH'ȧrt), **Baron von,** 1840–1902, German psychiatrist.

kraft paper (kräft), a strong paper, usually brown, processed from wood pulp: used in bags and as wrapping paper. [t. G: *Kraft* strength]

Krag (*Dan.* krȧk), *n.* **Jens Otto** (*Dan.* yĕns ŏt'ô), born 1914: prime minister of Denmark since 1962.

Kragujevac (*Serb.* krȧ'go͞o yĕ vȧts), *n.* a town in Yugoslavia, in central Serbia. 52,792 (1961).

krait (krīt), *n.* any of the extremely venomous snakes of the genus *Bungarus* of south-eastern Asia, esp. *B. coeruleus* of India. [t. Hind.: m. *karait*]

Krakatau (krăk'ə tou'), *n.* a small volcanic island in Indonesia between Java and Sumatra: violent eruption, 1883. Also, **Krakatoa** (krăk'ə tō'ə).

Krakau (*Ger.* krȧ'kou), *n.* German name of **Cracow.**

kraken (krä'kən), *n.* a mythical sea-monster said to appear at times off Norway. [t. Norw.]

Kraków (*Pol.* krȧ'ko͞of), *n.* Polish name of **Cracow.**

Kramatorsk (*Russ.* krə mȧ tôrsk'), *n.* a town in the W Soviet Union in Europe. 135,000 (est. 1965).

kran (krän), *n.* a former monetary unit and silver coin of Iran.

krantz (krănts), *n.* *S. African.* a crag. [t. Afrikaans]

Krasnodar (*Russ.* krəs nȧ dȧr'), *n.* a city in the S Soviet Union in Europe: a port near the Sea of Azov. 385,000 (est. 1965). Formerly, **Ekaterinodar.**

Krasnoyarsk (*Russ.* krəs nȧ yȧrsk'), *n.* a city in the S Soviet Union in Asia, on the Yenisei. 541,000 (est. 1965).

Krebs cycle (krĕbz), citric acid cycle. [named after Sir H. A. *Krebs*, born 1900, British biochemist]

Krefeld (krā'fĕld; *Ger.* krė'fĕlt), *n.* a town in West Germany, in W North Rhine-Westphalia. 223,200 (est. 1966). Also, **Crefeld.**

Kreisler (krīz'lə), *n.* **Fritz** (frĭts), 1875–1962, Austrian violinist, in the U.S.

Kremenchug (*Russ.* krĭ mĭn cho͞ok'), *n.* a city in the SW Soviet Union, on the river Dnieper. 121,000 (est. 1965).

kremlin (krĕm'lĭn), *n.* **1.** the citadel of a Russian town or city. **2.** (*cap.*) the citadel of Moscow, including within its walls the chief office of the Soviet government. [t. Russ.: m. *kreml* citadel]

Krems (*Ger.* krĕms), *n.* a town in Austria, in N Lower Austria. 21,046 (1961).

Kretschmer (*Ger.* krĕch'mər), *n.* **Ernst** (*Ger.* ĕrnst), 1888–1964, German psychiatrist.

kreuzer (kroit'sə), *n.* **1.** a former German coin. **2.** a former Austrian copper coin and monetary unit, equal to one hundredth of a florin. Also, **kreutzer.** [t. G: m. *Kreuzer*, der. *Kreuz* cross (orig. the device on the coin)]

Kriegspiel (krēg'spēl'), *n.* a game designed to teach military science by means of blocks or the like, representing guns, etc., moved on maps or other surfaces. [t. G]

Kriemhild (krēm'hĭlt), *n.* the legendary heroine of the *Nibelungenlied*, wife of Siegfried and avenger of his death: the counterpart of the Scandinavian Gudrun.

krimmer (krĭm'ə), *n.* a lambskin from the Crimean region, dressed as a fur, with wool in loose soft curls and usually whitish or pale grey. Also, **crimmer.** [t. G, der. *Krim* Crimea]

kris (krēs), *n.* a short sword or heavy dagger with a wavy blade, used by the Malays. Also, **crease, creese.** [t. Malay]

Krishna (krĭsh'nə), *n.* the most popular Hindu deity, as an incarnation of Vishnu; the famous teacher in the Bhagavad-gita. [t. Skt, special use of *krishna* black]

Krishna Menon (mĕn'ən), **Vengalil Krishnan** (vĕng'gə lĭl krĭsh'nən), born 1897, Indian statesman.

Kriss Kringle (krĭs'krĭng'gl), *U.S.* Santa Claus. [t. G: m. *Christkindl*, *-del* Christ child, Christmas gift]

Kristiansand (*Norw.* krēs tē ȧn sȧn'), *n.* a seaport in SW Norway. 50,217 (1965). Also, **Christiansand.**

Krivoi Rog (*Russ.* krĭ vôy' rôk'), a city in the SW Soviet Union in Europe. 488,000 (est. 1965).

Królewska Huta (*Pol.* kro͞o lĕf'skȧ ho͞o'tȧ), former name of **Chorzów.**

krombek (krŏm'bĕk), *n.* a small brown warbler of Southern Africa, *Sylvietta rufescens*, subfamily *Sylviinae*; stumptail. Also, **crombec.** [t. Afrikaans: crooked beak]

krona (krō'nə; *Sw.* kro͞o'nȧ), *n.*, *pl.* **-nor** (*Sw.* -nór). **1.** the monetary unit of Sweden, equal to 100 öre, and equivalent to about £0·0805 sterling. **2.** a silver coin of this value. *Abbrev.:* kr. [Sw.: crown]

króna (*Icel.* krōw'nə), *n.*, *pl.* **krónur** (*Icel.* krōw'nĭr). **1.** the monetary unit of Iceland, equivalent to about £0·0084 sterling. **2.** a nickel coin of this value. *Abbrev.:* kr. [Icel.: crown]

krone[1] (krō'nə), *n.*, *pl.* **-ner** (-nə). **1.** the monetary unit of Denmark, equal to 100 öre, and equivalent to about £0·0556 sterling. **2.** a cuprosilver, cupronickel, or copper alloy coin of this value. **3.** the monetary unit of Norway, equal to 100 öre, and equivalent to £0·0058 sterling. *Abbrev.:* kr. **4.** a cupronickel coin of this value. [Dan.: crown]

krone[2] (krō'nə), *n.*, *pl.* **-nen** (-nən). **1.** a former German gold coin equal to 10 marks. **2.** former monetary unit and a silver coin of Austria, equal to 100 heller. *Abbrev.:* kr. [t. G. See KRONE[1]]

Kronos (krō'nŏs), *n.* Cronus.

Kronstadt (krŏn'shtăt; *Russ.* krȧn shtȧt' *for 1* ; *Ger.* krōn'shtȧt *for 2*), *n.* **1.** a seaport in the NW Soviet Union, on an island in the Gulf of Finland, W of Leningrad: naval base. 59,000 (est. 1959). **2.** German name of **Braşov.**

kroon (kro͞on), *n.*, *pl.* **kroons, krooni** (kro͞o'nĭ). a former coin and monetary unit of Estonia equivalent to the Swedish krona. [t. Estonian: crown]

Kropotkin (krŏ pŏt'kĭn; *Russ.* krȧ pôt'kĭn), *n.* **Peter** (*Prince Peotr Alekseevich*), 1842–1921, Russian anarchist, writer, and geographer, in England.

Kruger (kro͞o'gə; *Du.* krY'gər), *n.* **Stephanus Johannes Paulus** (*Du.* stĕ'fȧ no͞os yō hŏ'nəs pȧw'lo͞os) ('*Oom Paul*'), 1825–1904, South African statesman: president of the Transvaal 1883–1900.

Kruger National Park, a park and game reserve in the Republic of South Africa, in E Transvaal, extending from the Crocodile River N to the Limpopo. 8000 sq. mi.

Krugersdorp (kro͞o′gəz dôp′), *n.* a town in the Republic of South Africa, in S Transvaal. with suburbs, 89,947 (1960).

krulgras (kro͝ol′gräs′), *n. S African.* fingergrass. [t. Afrikaans]

Krupp (krŭp; *Ger.* kro͝op), *n.* **Alfred** (*Ger.* äl′frėt), 1812–87, German manufacturer of armaments.

Krupskaya (*Russ.* kro͞op′skə yə), *n.* **Nadezhda Konstantinovna** (*Russ.* nȧ dyĕzh′də kən stȧn tē′nəv nə), 1869–1939, Russian social worker and wife of Nikolai Lenin.

krypton (krĭp′tŏn), *n. Chem.* an inert monatomic gaseous element present in very small amounts in the atmosphere, of some use in high-power, tungsten-filament light bulbs. *Symbol:* Kr; *at. wt:* 83·80; *at. no.:* 36; *weight of one litre at 0° C, and 760 mm. pressure:* 3·708 g. [t. NL, t. Gk, neut. of *kryptós* hidden. See CRYPT]

Kshatriya (kshăt′rĭ yə), *n.* a member of the military caste among the Hindus. [t. Skt, der. *kshatra* rule, n.]

Kt, knight.

kt, **1.** karat; carat. **2.** knot.

K.T., **1.** Knight of the (Order of the) Thistle. **2.** Knight Templar.

K2, a mountain peak in NW India, in the Karakoram range in N Kashmir: second highest peak in the world. 28,250 ft. Also, **Godwin Austen.**

Kuala Lumpur (kwä′lə lo͝om′po͞oə, -pə), the capital of Malaysia, in central Selangor. 450,000 (est. 1965).

Kublai Khan (ko͞o′blī kän′), 1216?–94, Mongol emperor 1259–94, founder of the Mongol dynasty in China.

Kuching (ko͞o′chĭng), *n.* a seaport in Malaysia, the capital of Sarawak, in the SW part. 50,679 (1960).

kudos (kyo͞o′dŏs), *n.* glory; renown. [t. Gk: m. *kŷdos*]

Kudrun (ko͝od′ro͞on, ko͞oth′-), *n.* Gudrun.

kudu (ko͞o′do͞o), *n.* a large handsome African antelope, *Tragelaphus strepsiceros,* the males of which have large corkscrew-like horns. Also, **koodoo.** [t. Hottentot]

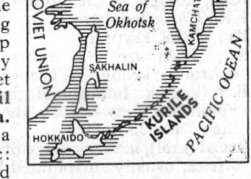

Greater kudu, *Tragelaphus strepsiceros* (5 ft high at shoulder, horns 4 to 5 ft, length 9 ft)

Kuenlun (ko͞on′lo͞on′), *n.* Kunlun.

Kuibyshev (kwē′bĭ shĕf′; *Russ.* ko͞oy′bĭ shəf), *n.* a city in the E Soviet Union in Europe: a port on the Volga. 948,000 (est. 1965). Formerly, **Samara.**

Ku Klux Klan (kyo͞o′ klŭks′ klăn′), **1.** a secret organization in the southern U.S., active for several years after the Civil War, which aimed to suppress the newly acquired powers of the Negroes and to oppose carpetbaggers from the North, and was responsible for many lawless and violent proceedings. **2.** a secret organization (**Knights of the Ku Klux Klan**) inspired by the former, founded in 1915 and active in the southern and other parts of the U.S., admitting to membership none but native-born, white, Gentile, Protestant Americans, and professing Americanism as its object. Also, **Ku Klux.** *Abbrev.:* K.K.K. [? f. m. Gk *kýklos* circle + m. CLAN]

kukri (ko͝ok′rē), *n.* a knife with a curved blade, used by the Gurkhas. [t. Hind.]

kulak (ko͞o′lăk), *n.* (in Russia) **1.** (before the revolution) a hard-fisted merchant or a village usurer. **2.** any peasant who employed hired labour or possessed any machinery. [t. Russ.: fist, tight-fisted person]

Kultur (ko͝ol to͞oə′), *n.* **1.** culture as a social force causing evolutionary development to higher forms of civilization. **2.** a civilization characteristic of a time or a people. [G, t. L: m. s. *cultūra* CULTURE]

Kulturkampf (ko͝ol to͞oə′kämpf′, ko͝ol′tə-), *n.* the conflict between the German imperial government and the Roman Catholic Church from 1872 or 1873 until 1886, chiefly over the control of educational and ecclesiastic appointments. [G: civilization struggle]

Kum (ko͝om), *n.* Qum.

Kumamoto (ko͞o′mä mō′tō), *n.* a city in Japan, on W Kyushu island. 407,052 (1965).

kumara (ko͝om′ə rə), *n.* the New Zealand sweet potato, *Ipomaea batatas.* [t. Maori]

Kumasi (ko͞o măs′ĭ), *n.* a town in central Ghana: ancient capital of the Ashanti kingdom. 190,323 (1960).

Kumba (ko͝om′bä), *n.* a town in E Cameroun. 50,000 (est. 1962).

kumis (ko͞o′mĭs), *n.* **1.** a slightly alcoholic beverage made from fermented mare's or camel's milk, drunk by Asiatic nomads, etc. **2.** a similar drink prepared from other milk, esp. that of the cow, and used for dietetic and medicinal purposes. Also, **koumis, koumiss, koumyss, kumiss.** [t. Russ.: m. *kumys,* t. Tartar: m. *kumiz.* Cf. F *koumis,* G *Kumyss*]

kümmel (ko͝om′əl; *Ger.* kʏm′əl), *n.* a colourless cordial or liqueur flavoured with cumin, caraway seeds, etc., made esp. in the Baltic area. [t. G: *Kümmel* cumin]

kumquat (kŭm′kwŏt), *n.* **1.** a small, round, or oblong citrus fruit with a sweet rind and acid pulp, used chiefly for preserves, being the fruit of *Fortunella japonica* and related species, rutaceous shrubs native in China and cultivated in Japan, Florida, California, etc. **2.** the plant itself. Also, **cumquat.** [t. Chinese, Cantonese pronunciation of Mandarin *kin ku,* lit., gold orange]

Kun (*Hung.* ko͞on), *n.* **Béla** (*Hung.* bė′lŏ), 1885–1937, Hungarian Communist leader.

Kung-fu-tse (ko͝ong′fo͞o′tsä′), *n.* Chinese name of **Confucius.**

Kunlun (ko͞on′lo͞on′), *n.* a lofty mountain system bordering to the N of the Tibetan plateau and extending W across central China. Highest peak, ab. 25,000 ft. Also, **Kuenlun.**

Kunming (ko͞on′mĭng′), *n.* a city in and the capital of Yünnan province, SW China. 900,000 (est. 1958).

kunzite (ko͝onts′īt), *n.* a transparent lilac variety of spodumene, used as a gem. [named after G. F. *Kunz,* 1856–1932, American expert in precious stones. See -ITE[1]]

Kuomintang (kwō′mĭn′tăng′), *n.* a Chinese political party, founded by Sun Yat-sen in 1911 and led since 1925 by Chiang Kai-shek: the dominant party in China until 1948. [t. Chinese (Mandarin): f. *kuo* nation + *min* people + *tang* party]

Kuopio (*Finn.* ko͞o′ô pē ô), *n.* a town in S Finland. 51,051 (1965).

Kura (*Russ.* ko͞o rȧ′), *n.* a river flowing from NE Turkey through the Georgian and Azerbaijan republics of the Soviet Union SE to the Caspian Sea. ab. 810 mi.

Kurashiki (ko͞o rä′shĭ kĭ, ko͝oə′rə shē′kĭ), *n.* a town in Japan, in W Honshu island. 144,461 (1965).

Kurd (kûd), *n.* a member of a pastoral and warlike people speaking an Iranian language and dwelling chiefly in Kurdistan. —**Kurd′ish,** *adj., n.*

Kurdistan (kû′dĭs tăn′; *Pers.* kòr dės tän′), *n.* **1.** a mountain and plateau region in SE Turkey, NW Iran, and N Iraq, peopled largely by Kurds. ab. 74,000 sq. mi. **2.** any of several rugs woven by the Kurds.

Kure (ko͞o′rä′), *n.* a seaport in SW Japan, on Honshu island. 225,013 (1965).

Kurg (ko͝oəg), *n.* Coorg.

Kurgan (*Russ.* ko͝or gȧn′), *n.* a town in the W Soviet Union in Asia. 198,000 (est. 1965).

kuri (ko͝o′rē), *n.* one of a breed of dogs of New Zealand. [t. Maori]

Kurile Islands (ko͞o rēl′), a chain of small islands off the NE coast of Asia, extending from N Japan to the S tip of Kamchatka: renounced by Japan in 1945; under Soviet administration. Also, **Kuril Islands.** Japanese, **Chishima.**

Kurile Islands

Kurland (ko͝oə′lənd), *n.* a former duchy on the Baltic: later a province of Russia, and in 1918 incorporated into Latvia. Also, **Courland.**

Kurnool (ko͝oə no͞ol′), *n.* a town in India, in W Andhra Pradesh. 100,815 (1961).

Kuroki (ko͞o′rō kē′), *n.* **Count Tamemoto** (tä′mĭ mō′tō), 1844–1923, Japanese general.

Kuropatkin (*Russ.* ko͞o rȧ pȧt′kĭn), *n.* **Aleksei Nikolaevich** (*Russ.* ə lĭk syėy′ nĭ kȧ lȧ′yĭ vĭch), 1848–1925, Russian general.

Kurosawa (ko͝oə′rə sä′wə), *n.* **Akira** (ă kē′rə), born 1910, Japanese film director.

kurrajong (kŭ′rə jŏng′), *n.* a malvaceous shrub or tree of Australia and Tasmania, *Plagianthus sidoides.* [t. native Australian]

Kurume (ko͞o ro͞o′mĭ), *n.* a town in Japan, in N Kyushu. 158,974 (1965).

Kursk (*Russ.* ko͞orsk), *n.* a town in the central Soviet Union in Europe. 245,000 (est. 1965).

kurus (ko͞o ro͞osh′), *n.* a Turkish currency unit equal to a hundredth of a lira; piastre. [t. Turk.]

Kustanai (*Russ.* ko͞os tȧ nȧy′), *n.* a town in the W Soviet Union in Asia. 110,000 (est. 1965).

Kutaisi (*Russ.* ko͞o tȧ ē′sĭ), *n.* a town in the S Soviet Union in Europe. 154,000 (est. 1965).

Kutch (kŭch), *n.* Cutch.

Kutuzov (*Russ.* ko͞o to͞o′zəf), *n.* **Mikhail Ilarionovich** (*Russ.* mĭ KHȧ ĕl′ ĭ lə rĭ ȧ nô′vĭch), 1745–1813, Russian general.

Kuwait (ko͞o wāt′), *n.* **1.** an independent state in NE Arabia, on the NW coast of the Persian Gulf. 468,389 pop. (1965); ab. 9375 sq. mi. **2.** a seaport in and the capital of this sheikhdom, in the E part. 210,000 (1962).

Kuwaiti (ko͞o wā′tĭ), *n.* **1.** a native of Kuwait. —*adj.* **2.** of or pertaining to Kuwait or its inhabitants.

Kuyp (koip), *n.* **Aalbert.** See **Cuyp.**

Kuznetsk Basin (*Russ.* ko͞oz nyĕtsk′), an industrial region in the S Soviet Union in Asia: coalfields.

kv., kilovolt.

kv-a., kilovolt ampere.

kvass (kväs), *n.* a Russian beer made from barley, malt, and rye. Also, **kvas, quass.** [t. Russ.: m. *kvas*]

kw., kilowatt.

Kwa (kwä), *n.* a group of languages spoken in coastal W Africa, including Yoruba and Ibo.

Kwakiutl (kwä′kĭ o͞o′tl), *n.* a group of American Indians of Wakashan linguistic stock in SW Canada, esp. British Columbia (including Vancouver island).

Kwangchowan (kwăng′chō wän′), *n.* a territory in S China on the SW coast of Kwangtung province: leased to France, 1898–1945. ab. 250,000 pop.; ab. 190 sq. mi.

Kwangju (kwăng′jo͞o′), *n.* a town in SW South Korea. 343,193 (1964).

Kwangsi (kwăng′sē′), *n.* a region in S China. 19,390,000 (1957). *Cap.:* Yungning. Official name, **Kwangsi Chuang Autonomous Region.**

Kwangtung (kwăng′to͝ong′), *n.* a maritime province in SE China. 37,960,000 (est. 1957). *Cap.:* Canton.

kwashiorkor (kwăsh′ĭ ô′kə), *n.* *Pathol.* a nutritional disease chiefly of children in Africa, associated with a corn diet with its lack of protein, and marked by oedema, potbelly, and changes in skin pigmentation.

Kweichow (kwā′chou′), *n.* a province in S China. 16,890,000 (est. 1957). *Cap.:* Kweiyang.

Kweilin (kwā′lĭn′), *n.* a city in Kwangsi, S China. 145,000 (est. 1955).

Kweisui (kwā′swā′), *n.* former name of **Huhehot.**

Kweiyang (kwā′yăng′), *n.* a city in and the capital of Kweichow province, S China. 530,000 (est. 1958).

kwela (kwā′lə), *n.* a type of music resembling jazz, popular in South Africa among Bantu and Cape Coloured communities, chiefly using simple instruments, as the penny whistle. [ult. der. Bantu: climb up]

kw-h, kilowatt-hour.

Ky, Kentucky.

kyanite (kī′ə nīt′), *n.* cyanite.

kyat (kĭ ät′), *n.* **1.** the monetary unit of Burma, equivalent to £0·075 sterling. **2.** a banknote or coin of this value.

Kyd (kĭd), *n.* **Thomas,** 1558–95, English dramatist.

kylie (kī′lē), *n.* *Austral.* a type of boomerang. [t. native Australian]

kylix (kī′lĭks, kĭl′ĭks), *n.*, *pl.* **kylikes** (kĭl′ĭ kēz′). cylix.

kymograph (kī′mə grăf′, -gräf′), *n.* **1.** an instrument by which variations of fluid pressure, as the waves of the pulse, can be measured and graphically recorded. **2.** an instrument measuring the angular oscillations of an aeroplane in flight with respect to axes fixed in space. Also, **cymograph.** [f. *kymo-* (comb. form of Gk *kŷma* wave) + -GRAPH] —**kymographic** (kī′mə grăf′ĭk), *adj.*

Kymric (kĭm′rĭk), *adj.*, *n.* Cymric.

Kymry (kĭm′rĭ), *n.pl.* Cymry. Also, **Kymrie.**

Kyoto (kĭ ō′tō), *n.* a city in central Japan, in S central Honshu: the capital of Japan, A.D. 784–1868. 1,365,007 (1965). Also, **Kioto.** See map under **Hiroshima.**

kyphosis (kī fō′sĭs), *n.* *Pathol.* a curvature of the spine, convex backwards. [t. NL, t. Gk: bunched state]

Kyrie eleison (kĭ′rĭ ĭ ə lā′sən), **1.** 'Lord, have mercy', a petition used: **a.** in various offices of the Eastern and Roman churches. **b.** as a response in Anglican services. **2.** a musical setting of this. [t. Gk: m. *Kýrie eleēson*]

Kythera (kĭth′ĭ rə), *n.* Cythera.

Kyu (kyo͞o), *n.* *Judo.* **1.** one of the six grades into which inexperienced judo contestants are divided. **2.** a contestant placed in one of such grades. Cf. **Dan**[3].

Kyushu (kyo͞o′sho͞o), *n.* a large island in SW Japan. 12,903,076 pop. (1960); 15,750 sq. mi. Also, **Kiushu.** See map under **Hiroshima.**

Kyzyl Kum (*Russ.* kĭ zĭl ko͞om′), a desert SE of Lake Aral, in the Soviet Union in Asia. ab. 88,000 sq. mi.

L

L[1], **l** (ĕl), *n.*, *pl.* **L's** or **Ls, l's** or **ls. 1.** a consonant, the 12th letter of the English alphabet. **2.** the Roman numeral for 50. See **Roman numerals.**

L[2], *pl.* **L's. 1.** something having a shape like that of the letter L. **2.** ell. **3.** Also, **l.** *Elect.* coefficient of inductance. **4.** Latin. **5.** learner (driver). **6.** *Physics.* length. **7.** (L *libra*) pound; pounds. **8.** *Geog.* (terrestrial) longitude.

L., 1. Lady. **2.** Lake. **3.** large. **4.** Latin. **5.** latitude. **6.** law. **7.** left. **8.** (L *liber*) book. **9.** Liberal. **10.** Low. **11.** *Theat.* stage left.

l., 1. latitude. **2.** law. **3.** leaf. **4.** league. **5.** left. **6.** length. **7.** (L *libra*) pound; pounds. **8.** (*pl.* **ll.**) line; lines. **9.** link. **10.** lira; liras. **11.** litre.

l-, *Chem.* laevo-. Also, **l.**

la[1] (lä), *n.* *Music.* the syllable for the sixth note of a scale, and sometimes for the note A. See **solfa** (def. 1). [See GAMUT]

la[2] (lô), *interj.* (an exclamation of wonder, surprise, etc.) [ME and OE; weak var. of OE *lā* LO]

La, 1. *Chem.* lanthanum. **2.** Louisiana.

laager (lä′gə), *S African.* —*n.* **1.** a camp or encampment, esp. within a circle of wagons. —*v.t.*, *v.i.* **2.** to arrange or encamp in a laager. Also, **lager.** [t. Afrikaans, var. of *lager*, c. G *Lager* camp. Cf. LAIR]

Laaland (*Dan.* lô′lån), *n.* an island of SE Denmark, S of Zealand. 83,170 pop. (1960); 479 sq. mi. Also, **Lolland.**

lab (lăb), *n.* **1.** *Colloq.* laboratory. **2.** labour.

Lab., 1. Labrador. **2.** Labour Party. **3.** Labourite.

Laban (lā′bən), *n.* *Bible.* the father-in-law of Jacob. Gen. 24:29–60.

labarum (lăb′ə rəm), *n.*, *pl.* **-ra** (-rə). **1.** an ecclesiastical standard or banner, as for carrying in procession. **2.** the military standard of Constantine the Great and later Christian emperors of Rome, bearing Christian symbols. [t. L, corresp. to Gk *lábaron*; ult. orig. unknown]

labdanum (lăb′də nəm), *n.* a resinous juice that exudes from various rockroses of the genus *Cistus*: used in perfumery, fumigating substances, medicinal plasters, etc. Also, **ladanum.** [t. ML, m. L *lādanum*, t. Gk: m. *lḗdanon* mastic. Cf. Pers. *lādan* shrub]

labefaction (lăb′ĭ făk′shən), *n.* a shaking or weakening; overthrow; downfall. Also, **labefactation** (lăb′ĭ făk tā′shən). [f. s. L *labefactus*, pp., weakened + -ION]

label (lā′bl), *n.*, *v.*, **-belled, -belling,** or (*U.S.*) **-beled, -beling.** —*n.* **1.** a slip of paper or other material for affixing to something to indicate its nature, ownership, destination, etc. **2.** a short word or phrase of description for a person, group, movement, etc. **3.** a strip or narrow piece of anything. **4.** *Archit.* a moulding or dripstone over a door or window, esp. one which extends horizontally across the top of the opening and vertically downwards for a certain distance at the sides. **5.** *Colloq.* the trade name, esp. of a gramophone record company. —*v.t.* **6.** to affix a label to; mark with a label. **7.** to designate or describe by or on a label: *the bottle was labelled poison.* **8.** to put in a certain class; to describe by a verbal label. **9.** *Physics.* to replace (a stable atom) in a compound by a radioactive isotope of that atom so that its path through a mechanical or biological system can be traced. [ME, t. OF, ? ult. der. Gmc; cf. LAP[1]] —**la′beller,** *n.*

labelled compound, *Physics.* a compound which has been labelled. See **label** (def. 9).

labellum (lə bĕl′əm), *n.*, *pl.* **-bella** (-bĕl′ə). *Bot.* that division of the corolla of an orchidaceous plant which differs more or less markedly from the other divisions, often forming the most conspicuous part. [t. L, dim. of *labrum* lip] —**label′loid,** *adj.*

L

L, Labellum, Lady's-slipper, genus *Cypripedium*

label mould, hood mould.

labia (lā′byə), *n.* pl. of **labium.**

labial (lā′byəl), *adj.* **1.** pertaining to or of the nature of a labium. **2.** *Music.* giving forth sounds produced by the impact of a stream of air upon the sharp edge of a lip, as a flute or pipe organ. **3.** of or pertaining to lips. **4.** *Phonet.* involving lip articulation, as *p*, *v*, *m*, *w*, or a rounded vowel. —*n.* **5.** a labial consonant. [t. ML: s. *labiālis*, der. L *labium* lip] —**la′bially,** *adv.*

labialize (lā′bĭ ə līz′), *v.t.*, **-lized, -lizing.** *Phonet.* to give a labial character to (a sound), e.g. to round (a vowel). Also, **labialise.** —**la′bializa′tion,** *n.*

labial pipes, the fluepipes of an organ.

labiate (lā′bĭ āt′, -ĭt), *adj.* **1.** lipped; having parts which are shaped or arranged like lips. **2.** *Bot.* **a.** belonging to the *Labiatae* (or *Menthaceae*, formerly *Lamiaceae*), the mint family of plants, most of which have bilabiate corollas. **b.** (usually) two-lipped; bilabiate: said of a gamopetalous corolla or gamosepalous calyx. —*n.* **3.** a labiate plant.

A B

Labiate corolla of selfheal, *Prunella vulgaris*
A, seen from the side;
B, laid open, front view

Labiche (*Fr.* là bēsh′), *n.* **Eugène Marin** (*Fr.* œ zhĕn mȧ răɴ′), 1815–88, French dramatist.

labile (lā′bĭl), *adj.* **1.** apt to lapse or change; unstable; lapsable. **2.** *Med.* denoting or pertaining to a mode of application of electricity in which the active electrode is moved over the part to be acted upon. [late ME *labyl*, t. LL: m. s. *lābilis*, der. L *lābi* fall, slide. Cf. LAPSE] —**lability** (lə bĭl′ĭ tĭ), *n.*

labiodental (lā′bĭ ō dĕn′tl), *Phonet.* —*adj.* **1.** with the lower lip close to the upper front teeth, as in *f* or *v*. —*n.* **2.** a labiodental sound.

labionasal (lā′bĭ ō nā′zəl), *Phonet.* —*adj.* **1.** articulated with the lips and given resonance in the nasal passage, as *m*. —*n.* **2.** a labionasal sound.

labiovelar (lā′bĭ ō vē′lə), *Phonet.* —*adj.* **1.** with simultaneous bilabial and velar articulations. —*n.* **2.** a labiovelar sound.

labium (lā′byəm), *n.*, *pl.* **-bia** (-byə). **1.** a lip or liplike part. **2.** *Anat.* **a.** either lip, upper or under, of the mouth, respectively called **labium superiore** and **labium inferiore.** **b.** one of the four 'lips' guarding the orifice of the vulva, including the two outer cutaneous folds (**labia majora**) and the two inner membranous folds (**labia minora**). **3.** *Bot.* the lower lip of a bilabiate corolla. **4.** *Entomol.* the posterior unpaired member of the mouthparts of an insect, formed by the united second maxillae. [t. L: lip]

labor (lā′bə), *n.* *U.S.* labour.

laboratory (lə bŏ′rə tə rĭ, -trĭ), *n.*, *pl.* **-ries,** *adj.* —*n.* **1.** a building or part of a building fitted with apparatus for conducting scientific investigations, experiments, tests, etc., or for manufacturing chemicals, medicines, etc. **2.** any place where or in which similar processes are carried on by natural forces. —*adj.* **3.** serving a function in a laboratory. **4.** relating to techniques of work in a laboratory. [t. ML: m. s. *labōrātōrium* workshop] —**laboratorial** (lə bŏ′rə tô′rĭ əl), *adj.*

laborious (lə bô′rĭ əs), *adj.* **1.** requiring much labour, exertion, or perseverance: *a laborious undertaking*. **2.** requiring labour in construction or execution. **3.** given to or diligent in labour. [ME, t. L: m. s. *labōriōsus*] —**labo′riously,** *adv.* —**labo′riousness,** *n.* —**Syn.** **1.** toilsome, arduous, onerous. **3.** hard-working, industrious, assiduous. —**Ant.** **1.** easy. **3.** lazy.

labor union, *U.S.* a trade union.

labour (lā′bə), *n.* **1.** bodily toil for the sake of gain or economic production. **2.** those engaged in such toil considered as a class: *the rights of labour*. **3.** work, esp. of a hard or fatiguing kind. **4.** a work or task done or to be done: *the twelve labours of Hercules*. **5.** the pangs and efforts of childbirth; travail. **6.** the time during which the pangs and efforts of childbirth take place. —*v.i.* **7.** to perform labour; exert one's powers of body or mind; work; toil. **8.** to work (*for*); strive, as towards a goal. **9.** to be burdened, troubled, or distressed: *you are labouring under a misapprehension*. **10.** to be in travail or childbirth. **11.** to roll or pitch heavily, as a ship. —*v.t.* **12.** to work hard and long at; elaborate: *don't labour the point*. **13.** *Archaic or Poetic.* to work or till (soil, etc.). Also, *U.S.*, **labor.** [ME, t. OF, t. L: m. *labor* toil, distress] —**la′bouringly,** *adv.* —**Syn.** **3.** toil, exertion. See **work.** —**Ant.** **3.** leisure. **7.** rest.

labour camp, a camp where convicts do manual labour.

Labour Day, in many countries a public holiday in honour of labour, often held on May 1st. Also, *U.S.*, **Labor Day.**

laboured (lā′bəd), *adj.* **1.** laboriously formed; made or done with laborious pains or care. **2.** not easy or natural. Also, *U.S.*, **labored.** —**Syn.** **1.** See **elaborate.**

labourer (lā′bə rə), *n.* **1.** one engaged in work which requires bodily strength rather than skill or training: *a day labourer*. **2.** one who labours. Also, *U.S.*, **laborer.**

labour exchange, employment exchange.

Labourite (lā′bə rīt′), *n.* *Colloq.* a supporter of a Labour Party.

labour market, the available supply of labour considered with reference to the demand for it.

Labour Party, **1.** a British political party, formed in 1900 from various socialist and trade union groups, and characterized by its policy of representing the interests of working people, nationalization of key industries, social reform, and social welfare. **2.** any of various similar political parties elsewhere.

labour relations, relations between management and labour, esp. in industry.

labour-saving (lā′bə sā′vĭng), *adj.* saving, or effecting economy in, labour: *labour-saving device*.

Labrador (lăb′rə dô′), *n.* **1.** a peninsula in NE North America between Hudson Bay, the Atlantic, and the Gulf of St Lawrence, containing the Canadian provinces of Newfoundland and Quebec. ab. 500,000 sq. mi. **2.** the portion of Newfoundland in the E part of this peninsula. 13,534 pop. (1961); ab. 120,000 sq. mi. **3.** one of a breed of dogs with black or golden coats, originally bred in Newfoundland.

labradorite (lăb′rə dô′rīt), *n.* a mineral of the plagioclase felspar group, often characterized by a brilliant change of colours with blue and green most common. [f. LABRADOR, where it was discovered + -ITE¹]

labret (lā′brĕt), *n.* a lip ornament worn by primitive tribes, in a pierced hole. [f. s. L *labrum* lip + -ET]

labroid (lăb′roid, lā′broid), *adj.* **1.** belonging to or resembling the *Labridae*, a family of thick-lipped marine fishes including the tautog, etc. —*n.* **2.** a labroid fish. Also, **labrid** (lăb′rĭd). [f. s. L *lābrus* kind of fish + -OID]

Labrouste (*Fr.* là brōōst′), *n.* **Henri** (*Fr.* äɴ rē′), 1801–75, French architect.

labrum (lā′brəm, lăb′rəm), *n.*, *pl.* **labra** (lā′brə, lăb′rə). **1.** a lip or liplike part. **2.** *Zool.* **a.** the anterior unpaired member of the mouthparts of an arthropod, projecting in front of the mouth. **b.** the outer margin of the aperture of a gastropod's shell. **3.** *Anat.* a ring of cartilage about the edge of a joint surface of a bone. [t. L: lip]

La Bruyère (*Fr.* là brʏ yĕr′), **Jean de** (*Fr.* zhäɴ′ də), 1645–96, French moralist and author.

Labuan (lə bōō′ən), *n.* an island off the coast of Sabah, now forming part of the federation of Malaysia. 9253 pop. (est. 1947); 35 sq. mi.

laburnum (lə bû′nəm), *n.* any of several small leguminous trees, having pendulous racemes of yellow flowers, somewhat similar to those of wisteria. *Laburnum anagyroides* of Europe is most common. [t. L]

labyrinth (lăb′ə rĭnth), *n.* **1.** an intricate combination of passages in which it is difficult to find one's way or to reach the exit. **2.** a maze of paths bordered by high hedges, as in a park or garden. **3.** a complicated or tortuous arrangement, as of streets, buildings, etc. **4.** any confusingly intricate state of things or events; an entanglement. **5.** (*cap.*) *Gk Myth.* the Cretan maze constructed by Daedalus, and inhabited by the mythical Minotaur. **6.** *Anat.* **a.** the internal ear, a complex structure including a bony portion (**osseous labyrinth**) and a membranous portion (**membranous labyrinth**) contained in it. **b.** the aggregate of air-chambers in the ethmoid bone, between the eye and the upper part of the nose. **7.** an enclosure for a high-performance loudspeaker which is designed to eliminate unwanted standing waves by means of air chambers. [t. L: s. *labyrinthus*, t. Gk: m. *labýrinthos*]

labyrinthine (lăb′ə rĭn′thīn), *adj.* **1.** pertaining to or forming a labyrinth. **2.** mazy; intricate. Also, **labyrinthian** (lăb′ə rĭn′thĭ ən), **lab′yrin′thic.**

lac¹ (lăk), *n.* a resinous substance deposited on the twigs of various trees in southern Asia by the lac insect, and used in the manufacture of varnishes, sealing wax, etc., and in the production of a red colouring matter. See **shellac.** [t. Hind.: m. *lākh*, g. Skt *lākshā*]

lac² (lăk), *n.* lakh.

Laccadive Islands (lăk′ə dĭv), a group of small islands and coral reefs in the Arabian Sea, off the SW coast of India: centrally administered. 24,108 pop. (1961); ab. 80 sq. mi.

laccolith (lăk′ə lĭth), *n.* *Geol.* a mass of igneous rock formed from lava which when rising from below did not find its way to the surface, but spread out laterally into a lenticular body, thereby causing the overlying strata to bulge upwards. Also, **laccolite** (lăk′ə līt′). [f. m. Gk *lákko(s)* pond + -LITH] —**lac′colith′ic, laccolitic** (lăk′ə lĭt′ĭk), *adj.*

lace (lās), *n.*, *v.*, **laced, lacing.** —*n.* **1.** a netlike ornamental fabric made of threads by hand or machine. **2.** a cord or string for holding or drawing together, as when passed through holes in opposite edges: *shoelaces*. **3.** ornamental cord or braid, as on uniforms. **4.** spirits added to coffee or other beverage. —*v.t.* **5.** to fasten, draw together, or compress by means of a lace. **6.** to pass (a cord, etc.) as a lace, as through holes. **7.** to adorn or trim with lace. **8.** to compress the waist of (a person) by drawing tight the laces of a corset, etc. **9.** to interlace or intertwine. **10.** *Colloq.* to lash, beat, or thrash. **11.** to mark or streak, as with colour. **12.** to intermix, as coffee with spirits. —*v.i.* **13.** to be fastened with a lace. **14. lace into,** to attack (someone) verbally or physically. [ME *las,* t. OF: m. *laz* noose, string, g. L *laqueus* noose, snare. Cf. LASSO] —**lace′like′,** *adj.*

Lacedaemon (lăs′ĭ dē′mən), *n.* ancient Sparta. —**Lacedaemonian** (lăs′ĭ dĭ mō′nyən), *adj., n.*

lace-fern (lās′fûn′), *n.* any of several hothouse ferns with delicate foliage of the genus *Cheilanthes,* esp. *C. gracillima.*

La Ceiba (*Sp.* lä thĕy′bä), a seaport in N Honduras. 24,863 (1965).

lacemaking (lās′mā′kĭng), *n.* the art, act, or process of making lace.

lacerate (*v.* lăs′ə rāt′; *adj.* lăs′ə rāt′, -ə rĭt), *v.,* **-rated, -rating,** *adj.* —*v.t.* **1.** to tear roughly; mangle: *to lacerate the flesh.* **2.** to hurt: *to lacerate a person's feelings.* —*adj.* **3.** lacerated. [t. L: m. s. *lacerātus,* pp.] —**lac′erable,** *adj.* —**lac′erative,** *adv.* —**Syn. 1.** See **maim.**

lacerated (lăs′ə rā′tĭd), *adj.* **1.** mangled; jagged. **2.** *Bot., Zool.* having the edge variously cut as if torn into irregular segments, as a leaf.

laceration (lăs′ə rā′shən), *n.* **1.** the act of lacerating. **2.** the result of lacerating; rough, jagged tear.

lacertilian (lăs′ə tĭl′yən), *adj.* **1.** of or pertaining to the *Lacertilia,* a suborder of reptiles comprising the common lizards and their allies. See **saurian** (def. 1). —*n.* **2.** a lacertilian reptile. Also, **lacertian** (lə sû′shən). [f. s. NL *Lacertilia,* pl. (der. L *lacerta* lizard) + -AN]

lacewing (lās′wĭng′), *n.* any of various neuropterous insects of the family *Chrysopidae,* with delicate lacelike wings, whose larvae prey chiefly on aphids.

La Chaise (*Fr.* lä shĕz′), **Père François d'Aix de** (*Fr.* pĕr fräɴ swä dĕks′ də), 1624–1709, French Roman Catholic priest, confessor to Louis XIV.

laches (lăch′ĭz), *n. Law.* neglect to do a thing at the proper time, esp. such delay as will bar a party from bringing a legal proceeding. [ME *lachesse,* t. AF, var. of *laschesse,* der. *lasche* loose, g. L *laxus* lax]

Lachesis (lăk′ĭ sĭs), *n. Class. Myth.* that one of the three Fates whose duty it was to determine the length of each individual's life, or, sometimes, to decide his fate during life. [t. L, t. Gk: lit., lot, destiny]

Lachlan (lăk′lən), *n.* a river in Australia and chief tributary of the Murrumbidgee, flowing N then W through New South Wales. ab. 920 mi.

Lachryma Christi (lăk′rĭ mə krĭs′tĭ), a strong sweet wine from grapes grown on Vesuvius. [L: tears of Christ]

A

B

Section of a human eye showing A, Lachrymal gland; B, Lachrymal sac

lachrymal (lăk′rĭ məl), *adj.* **1.** of or pertaining to tears; producing tears. **2.** characterized by tears; indicative of weeping. **3.** *Anat., etc.* denoting, pertaining to, or situated near the glands, ducts, or the like, concerned in the secretion or conveyance of tears. —*n.* **4.** (*pl.*) *Anat.* tear-secreting glands. **5.** a lachrymatory. Also, **lacrimal, lacrymal.** [t. ML: s. *lachrymālis, lacrimālis,* der. L *lacrima* tear]

lachrymator (lăk′rĭ mā′tə), *n. Chem.* a substance which causes tears to be shed; a tear gas.

lachrymatory (lăk′rĭ mə tə rĭ, -trĭ), *adj., n., pl.* **-ries.** —*adj.* **1.** of, pertaining to, or causing the shedding of tears. —*n.* **2.** Also, **lachrymal.** a small, narrow-necked vase found in ancient Roman tombs, formerly thought to have been used to hold the tears of bereaved friends.

lachrymose (lăk′rĭ mōs′), *adj.* **1.** given to shedding tears; tearful. **2.** suggestive of or tending to cause tears; mournful. [t. L: m. s. *lac(h)rimōsus,* der. *lac(h)rima* tear] —**lach′rymose′ly,** *adv.*

lacing (lā′sĭng), *n.* **1.** the act of one who or that which laces. **2.** a laced fastening, or a lace for such use. **3.** a trimming of lace or braid. **4.** a thrashing. **5.** spirits added to strengthen or flavour coffee, tea, etc. **6.** *Bldg Trades.* Also, **lacing course.** a course of brickwork in a flint or rubble wall.

Laciniate leaf

laciniate (lə sĭn′ĭ āt′, -ĭt), *adj. Bot., Zool.* cut into narrow, irregular lobes; slashed; jagged. [f. s. L *lacinia* lappet + -ATE¹]

lac insect (lăk), a homopterous insect, *Laccifer lacca,* of India, the females of which produce lac.

lack (lăk), *n.* **1.** deficiency or absence of something requisite, desirable, or customary: *lack of money or skill.* **2.** something lacking or wanting: *skilled labour was the chief lack.* —*v.t.* **3.** to be deficient in, destitute of, or without: *to lack strength.* **4.** to fall short in respect of: *the vote lacks three to be a majority.* —*v.i.* **5.** to be absent, as something requisite or desirable. [ME *lak,* t. MLG or MD: deficiency. Cf. Icel. *lakr* deficient] —**Syn. 1.** want, need, dearth, scarcity, paucity. —**Ant. 1.** surplus.

lackadaisical (lăk′ə dā′zĭ kl), *adj.* sentimentally or affectedly languishing; weakly sentimental; listless. [f. *lackadaisy,* var. of LACKADAY (see ALACK) + -ICAL] —**lack′adai′sically,** *adv.* —**lack′adai′sicalness,** *n.*

lackaday (lăk′ə dā′), *interj. Archaic.* alack.

lacker (lăk′ə), *n., v.t.* lacquer. —**lack′erer,** *n.*

lackey (lăk′ĭ), *n., pl.* **-eys,** *v.,* **-eyed, -eying.** —*n.* **1.** a footman or liveried manservant. **2.** a servile follower. —*v.t.* **3.** to attend as a lackey does. Also, **lacquey.** [t. F: m. *laquais,* t. Sp.: m. *lacayo* foot soldier]

lacklustre (lăk′lŭs′tə), *adj.* **1.** lacking lustre or brightness; dull. —*n.* **2.** a lack of lustre; that which lacks brightness. Also, *U.S.,* **lackluster.**

Laclos (*Fr.* lä klō′), *n.* **Pierre Ambroise François Choderlos de** (*Fr.* pyĕr äɴ brwäz fräɴ swä shō dĕr lō′ də), 1741–1803, French soldier and writer.

Laconia (lə kō′nyə), *n.* an ancient country in the S part of Greece. *Cap.:* Sparta. —**Laco′nian,** *adj., n.*

laconic (lə kŏn′ĭk), *adj.* using few words; expressing much in few words; concise. Also, **lacon′ical.** [t. L: s. *lacōnicus,* t. Gk: m. *lakōnikós* Laconian] —**lacon′ically,** *adv.*

laconism (lăk′ə nĭz′əm), *n.* **1.** laconic brevity. **2.** a laconic utterance or sentence. Also, **laconicism** (lə kŏn′ĭ sĭz′əm). [t. Gk: m. s. *lakōnismós* imitation of Lacedaemonians, who were noted for brief, pithy speech]

La Coruña (*Sp.* lä kō rōō′nyä), Corunna.

lacquer (lăk′ə), *n.* **1.** a protective coating consisting of a resin and/or a cellulose ester dissolved in a volatile solvent, sometimes with pigment added. **2.** any of various resinous varnishes, esp. a natural varnish obtained from a Japanese tree, *Rhus verniciflua,* used to produce a highly polished, lustrous surface on wood, etc. **3.** ware coated with such a varnish, and often inlaid. —*v.t.* **4.** to coat with or as with lacquer. Also, **lacker.** [t. F (obs.): m. *lacre* sealing wax, ult. t. Ar.: m. *lakk,* t. Pers.: m. *lāk;* akin to LAC¹] —**lac′querer,** *n.*

lacquey (lăk′ĭ), *n., pl.* **-eys,** *v.t.,* **-eyed, -eying.** lackey.

lacrimal (lăk′rĭ məl), *adj., n.* lachrymal. Also, **lacrymal.**

lacrosse (lə krŏs′), *n.* a ball game of Amerindian origin, played by two teams of ten players each, who strive to send a ball through a goal by means of long-handled rackets. [t. F: m. *la crosse* the crook (the racket used in the game). See CROSSE]

lact-, a word element meaning 'milk'. Also, **lacto-.** [t. L: m. *lacti-,* comb. form of *lac*]

lactam (lăk′tăm), *n. Biochem.* an organic compound formed from an amino acid by elimination of water from the amino and carboxyl groups. [f. LACT- + AM(MONIA)]

lactase (lăk′tās), *n. Chem.* an enzyme capable of hydrolysing lactose into glucose and galactose.

lactate (lăk′tāt), *n., v.,* **-tated, -tating.** —*n.* **1.** *Chem.* an ester or salt of lactic acid. —*v.i.* **2.** to produce milk.

lactation (lăk tā′shən), *n.* **1.** the secretion or formation of milk. **2.** the period of milk production.

lacteal (lăk′tĭ əl), *adj.* **1.** pertaining to, consisting of, or resembling milk; milky. **2.** *Anat.* conveying or containing chyle. —*n.* **3.** *Anat.* any of the minute lymphatic vessels which convey chyle from the small intestine to the thoracic duct. [f. s. L *lacteus* milky + -AL¹] —**lac′teally,** *adv.*

lacteous (lăk′tĭ əs), *adj.* milky; of the colour of milk.

lactescent (lăk tĕs′ənt), *adj.* **1.** becoming or being milky. **2.** *Bot.* forming a milky juice. **3.** *Entomol.* secreting a milky fluid. [t. L: s. *lactescens,* ppr.] —**lactes′cence,** *n.*

lactic (lăk′tĭk), *adj.* pertaining to or obtained from milk.

lactic acid, *Chem.* an acid, $CH_3CHOHCOOH$, found in sour milk.

lactiferous (lăk tĭf′ə rəs), *adj.* **1.** producing milk; concerned with the secretion of milk. **2.** conveying milk or a milky fluid. [f. LL *lactifer* milk-bearing + -OUS]

lacto-, var. of **lact-,** before consonants.

lactobacillus (lăk′tō bə sĭl′əs), *n., pl.* **-cilli** (-sĭl′ī). any bacterium of the genus *Lactobacillus,* a group of aerobic, long, slender rods which produce large amounts of lactic acid in the fermentation of carbohydrates, esp. in milk. The species most important to man is *Lactobacillus acidophilus.* See **acidophilus milk.**

lactoflavine (lăk′tō flā′vĭn), *n.* riboflavine.

lactometer (lăk tŏm′ĭ tə), *n.* an instrument for determining the specific gravity of milk.

lactone (lăk′tōn), *n. Chem.* one of a class of internal esters derived from hydroxy acids. —**lactonic** (lăk tŏn′ĭk), *adj.*

lactoprotein (lăk′tō prō′tēn), *n.* any protein in milk.

lactose (lăk′tōs), *n. Chem.* a crystalline disaccharide, $C_{12}H_{22}O_{11}$, present in milk, used as a food and in medicine; milk sugar. [f. LACT- + -OSE[2]]

lacuna (lə kyo͞o′nə), *n., pl.* **-nae** (-nē), **-nas. 1.** a pit or cavity; an interstitial or intercellular space as in plant or animal tissue. **2.** *Anat.* one of the numerous minute cavities in the substance of bone, supposed to contain nucleate cells. **3.** *Bot.* an airspace lying in the midst of the cellular tissue of plants. **4.** a gap or hiatus, as in a manuscript. [t. L: gap]

lacunal (lə kyo͞o′nəl), *adj.* **1.** of or pertaining to a lacuna. **2.** having lacunae. Also, **lacunary** (lə kyo͞o′nə rĭ).

lacunar (lə kyo͞o′nə), *adj., n., pl.* **lacunars, lacunaria** (lăk′yo͝o nēə′rĭ ə). *—adj.* **1.** lacunal. *—n.* **2.** *Archit.* **a.** a ceiling, or an undersurface, as of a cornice, formed of sunken compartments. **b.** one of the compartments. [t. L, der. *lacūna* pit, hollow]

lacunose (lə kyo͞o′nōs), *adj.* full of or having lacunae.

lacustrine (lə kŭs′trĭn), *adj.* **1.** of or pertaining to a lake. **2.** living or occurring on or in lakes, as various animals and plants. **3.** formed at the bottom or along the shore of lakes, as geological strata. [f. s. L **lacustris* (der. *lacus* lake, modelled on *palustris* of a swamp) + -INE[1]]

lacy (lā′sĭ), *adj.,* **-cier, -ciest.** resembling lace; lacelike. **—lac′ily,** *adv.* **—lac′iness,** *n.*

lad (lăd), *n.* **1.** a boy or youth. **2.** *Colloq.* (in familiar use) any male. **3.** *Colloq.* a devil-may-care, dashing man; a libertine. [ME *ladde* attendant, OE *Ladda* (nickname), of obscure orig. Cf. Norw. *askeladd* male Cinderella]

Ladakh (lə däk′), *n.* a region of E Jammu and Kashmir in the Himalayas, bordering on Tibet, contains the **Ladakh Range.**

ladanum (lăd′ə nəm), *n.* labdanum.

ladder (lăd′ə), *n.* **1.** a structure of wood, metal, or rope, commonly consisting of two sidepieces between which a series of bars or rungs are set at suitable distances, forming a means of ascent or descent. **2.** something like a ladder. **3.** a line or a place in a stocking, etc., where a series of stitches have slipped out or come undone. **4.** a means of rising, as to eminence: *ladder of success.* **5.** a hierarchical order or rank: *low in the social ladder.* *—v.t.* **6.** to cause a ladder (in a stocking). *—v.i.* **7.** (of a stocking) to develop a ladder. [ME; OE *hlǣder*, c. G *Leiter*]

ladder back, a chair back having a number of horizontal slats between uprights.

ladder stitch, an embroidery stitch in which crossbars at equal distances are produced between two solid ridges of raised work.

laddie (lăd′ĭ), *n. Chiefly Scot.* a young lad; a boy.

lade (lād), *v.,* **laded, laden** or **laded, lading.** *—v.t.* **1.** to put (something) on or in as a burden, load, or cargo; load. **2.** to load oppressively; burden: *laden with responsibilities.* **3.** to fill abundantly: *trees laden with fruit.* **4.** to lift or throw in or out, as a fluid, with a ladle or other utensil. *—v.i.* **5.** to take on a load. **6.** to lade a liquid. [ME *lade(n)*, OE *hladan* load, draw (water), c. D *laden*; akin to G *laden* load. Cf. LADLE]

la-di-da (lä′dĭ dä′), *adj. Slang.* affectedly pretentious, esp. in manner, speech, or bearing. Also, **lah-di-dah.**

ladies (lā′dĭz), *n. Colloq.* a public lavatory for women. Also, **ladies'.**

ladies' fingers, 1. any of various objects fancifully thought to resemble a finger, as a kind of small, crisp, sponge cake. **2.** kidney vetch, *Anthyllis vulneraria.*

ladies' man, a man noted for his attentions to women.

Ladin (lă dēn′), *n.* **1.** a Rhaeto-Romanic language of the southern Tyrol. **2.** Romansh. **3.** a person who speaks Ladin. [t. Romansh, g. L *Latīnus* Latin]

lading (lā′dĭng), *n.* **1.** the act of lading. **2.** that with which something is laden; load; freight; cargo.

Ladino (lə dē′nō), *n.* **1.** a mixed Spanish and Hebrew dialect spoken by Jews of Spanish extraction now living in Turkey and elsewhere. **2.** (in Spanish America) a mestizo. [t. Sp., g. L *Latīnus* Latin]

Ladislaus (lăd′ĭs lôs′) *n.* **Saint,** 1040–95, king of Hungary 1077–95. Also, **Ladislas** (lăd′ĭs lăs′).

ladle (lā′dl), *n., v.,* **-dled, -dling.** *—n.* **1.** a long-handled utensil with a dish-shaped or cup-shaped bowl for dipping or conveying liquids. **2.** *Metall.* a bucket-like container for transferring molten metal. *—v.t.* **3.** to dip or convey with or as with a ladle. [ME *ladel*, OE *hlædel*, der. *hladan* LADE] **—la′dleful′,** *n.* **—la′dler,** *n.*

Ladoga (lăd′ə gə), *n.* a lake in the NW Soviet Union, NE of Leningrad: largest lake in Europe. ab. 7000 sq. mi.

Ladrone Islands (lə drōn′), former name of **Mariana Islands.** Also, **Ladrones** (lə drōnz′; *Sp.* lä drō′nĕs).

lad's-love (lădz′lŭv′), *n.* a shrubby evergreen composite from S Europe, *Artemesia abrotanum*, often cultivated for its fragrant leaves and yellow capitula; old man.

lady (lā′dĭ), *n., pl.* **-dies,** *adj.* *—n.* **1.** a woman of good family or social position, or of good breeding, refinement, etc. (correlative of *gentleman*). **2.** a polite term for any woman. **3.** (*cap.*) **a.** a less formal substitute, often used conversationally, for the specific title and rank of a countess, marchioness, viscountess or baroness, which title she may hold by marriage, by courtesy, or in her own right. **b.** the title, prefixed to the Christian name of daughters of a duke, marquess or earl. **c.** the courtesy title of the wife of a knight or a baronet. **d.** a prefix to a title of honour or respect: *Lady Mayoress.* **4.** a woman: *the tea lady.* **5.** a wife. **6.** a woman who has proprietary rights or authority, as over a manor (correlative of *lord*). **7.** (*cap.*) the Virgin Mary (usually, **Our Lady**). **8.** the mistress of a household: *the lady of the house.* **9.** a woman who is the object of chivalrous devotion. *—adj.* **10.** (*usually cap.*) *Archaic.* **a.** a prefix to the names of allegorical personages: *Lady Luck.* **b.** a prefix to the name of a goddess. **11.** being a lady: *a lady reporter.* **12.** of a lady; ladylike. [ME *lavedi, levedi*, OE *hlæfdige*, ? orig. meaning loaf-kneader, f. *hlāf* LOAF[1] + *-dige*, akin to *dāh* DOUGH. Cf. LORD] **—Syn. 1.** See **woman.**

ladybird (lā′dĭ bûd′), *n.* a beetle of the family *Coccinellidae*, of graceful form and delicate coloration. The larvae feed upon plant-lice and small insects. Also, **lady beetle.** [f. LADY (uninflected poss. case) Virgin Mary + BIRD; i.e., (our) Lady's bird]

Nine-spotted ladybird, *Coccinella novemnotata* ($\frac{1}{4}$–$\frac{1}{3}$ in. long)

lady bountiful, a woman noted for her generosity, which is often slightly ostentatious.

ladybug (lā′dĭ bŭg′), *n. U.S.* ladybird.

Lady Chapel, a chapel dedicated to the Virgin Mary, attached to a church, and generally behind the high altar at the extremity of the apse.

Lady Day, 1. the feast of the Annunciation, March 25th. **2.** one of various days celebrated in honour of the Virgin Mary. **3.** the spring quarter-day, when quarterly rents and accounts are due.

lady-fern (lā′dĭ fûn′), *n.* any of several species of ferns belonging to the genus *Athyrium*, especially *A. filix-femina*, common in woods in the Northern Hemisphere.

ladyfinger (lā′dĭ fĭng′gə), *n.* sponge finger.

lady-in-waiting (lā′dĭ ĭn wā′tĭng), *n., pl.* **ladies-in-waiting.** a lady who is in attendance upon a queen or princess.

lady-killer (lā′dĭ kĭl′ə), *n. Slang.* a man supposed to be dangerously fascinating to women. **—la′dy-kill′ing,** *n., adj.*

ladylike (lā′dĭ līk′), *adj.* **1.** like a lady. **2.** befitting a lady: *ladylike manners.* **—la′dylike′ness,** *n.*

ladylove (lā′dĭ lŭv′), *n.* a beloved lady; sweetheart.

lady orchid, a tuberous orchid with dense spikes of reddish purple flowers, *Orchis purpurea*, found on calcareous soils of Europe and W Asia.

lady's-bedstraw (lā′dĭz bĕd′strô′), *n.* a slender, perennial rubiaceous herb with small yellow flowers, *Galium verum*, widespread on acid soils throughout Europe and W Asia.

ladyship (lā′dĭ shĭp′), *n.* **1.** (*often cap.*) the form used in speaking of or to a woman having the title of *Lady* (prec. by *her, your*, etc.). **2.** the rank of a lady.

lady's maid, a maid who is a lady's personal attendant in dressing, etc.

lady's-mantle (lā′dĭz măn′tl), *n.* any of a number of perennial rosaceous herbs with dense clusters of small green flowers belonging to the genus *Alchemilla.*

Ladysmith (lā′dĭ smĭth′), *n.* a city in the E part of the Republic of South Africa, in Natal: besieged by Boers 1899–1900. 16,413 (est. 1961).

lady's-slipper (lā′dĭz slĭp′ə), *n.* an orchid with creeping rhizomes and erect leafy stems bearing few reddish purple flowers, *Cypripedium calceolus*, confined to woods on limestone in Europe and N Asia. Also, **la′dy-slip′per.**

lady's-smock (lā′dĭz smŏk′), *n.* a cruciferous plant, *Cardamine pratensis*, with white or purple flowers.

lady's-tresses (lā′dĭz trĕs′ĭz), *n.* any of several species of orchid with erect twisted spikes of small flowers belonging to the genus *Spiranthes*, as **autumn lady's-tresses,** *S. spiralis.*

Laënnec (*Fr.* lä ĕ nĕk′), *n.* **René Théophile Hyacinthe** (*Fr.* rə nĕ tĕ ō fēl yä săNt′), 1781–1826, French doctor and inventor of the stethoscope.

Laertes (lā û′tēz), *n. Gk Legend.* father of Odysseus.

Laetare Sunday (lĭ tēə′rĭ), *Rom. Cath. Ch.* the fourth Sunday of Lent, when the introit begins with 'Laetare Jerusalem'. Isaiah 66:10.

laevo-, *Chem.* denoting a substance that rotates the plane of polarized light to the left. *Abbrev.:* l-, l. Also, *U.S.,* **levo-.**

laevoglucose (lē′vō glo͞o′kōs), *n. Chem.* the laevorotatory form of glucose. Also, *U.S.,* **levoglucose.**

laevorotation (lē′vō rō tā′shən), *n. Optics, Chem., etc.* the rotation of the plane of polarization to the left. Also, *U.S.*, **levorotation.**

laevorotatory (lē′vō rō′tə tə rĭ, -trĭ), *adj. Chem.* turning the plane of polarization of light to the left, as certain crystals, etc. Also, *U.S.*, **levorotatory.**

laevulic acid, *Chem.* a hygroscopic acid, CH_3COCH_2-CH_2COOH, obtained industrially from sugar by reaction with hydrochloric acid, and used to clean metals, such as milk cans, to guard against bacterial infection. Also, **laevulinic acid,** *U.S.*, **levulic acid, levulinic acid.**

laevulin (lĕv′yo͞o lĭn), *n. Biochem.* a polysaccharide from which laevulose can be formed, occurring in the tubers of certain species of helianthus, etc.; levan. Also, *U.S.*, **levulin.**

laevulose (lĕv′yo͞o lōs′), *n. Chem.* fructose; fruit sugar. Also, *U.S.*, **levulose.** [f. s. L *laevus* left + -ULE + -OSE²]

Lafayette (lä′fĭ ĕt′; *Fr.* là fà yĕt′), *n.* **1. Marie Joseph Paul Yves Roch Gilbert du Motier** (*Fr.* mà rē zhō zĕf pōl ēv rŏk zhĕl bĕr′ dY mō tyĕ′), **Marquis de,** 1757–1834, French soldier, statesman, and liberal leader, who served on the side of the colonists in the War of American Independence and took a leading part in the French revolutions of 1789 and 1830. **2. Marie-Madeleine** (*Fr.* mà rē màd lĕn′), **Comtesse de,** 1634–93, French novelist.

Lafitte (*Fr.* là fēt′), *n.* **Jean** (*Fr.* zhäN), *c.* 1780–1844, French privateer.

La Follette (lə fŏl′ĭt), **Robert Marion,** 1855–1925, U.S. political leader: U.S. senator, 1906–25.

La Fontaine (*Fr.* là fôN tĕn′), **Jean de** (*Fr.* zhäN′ də), 1621–95, French poet and writer of fables.

lag¹ (lăg), *v.*, **lagged, lagging,** *n.* —*v.i.* **1.** to move slowly; fall behind; hang back (often fol. by *behind*). **2.** to decrease, wane, or flag: *his interest in the project is lagging.* **3.** *Marbles.* to throw one's shooting marble towards a line on the ground in order to decide on the order of play. **4.** *Billiards.* (in deciding the order of play) to drive the cue ball to the end cushion and return, the winner being the one who comes nearest to the head rail. —*n.* **5.** a lagging or falling behind; retardation. **6.** *Mech.* the amount of retardation of some movement. **7.** *Engineering.* the interval by which a periodic signal follows another signal with the same period. **8.** *Marbles, Billiards.* the act of lagging. [t. Scand.; cf. Norw. *lagga* go slowly] —**Syn. 1.** loiter, linger. —**Ant. 1.** hasten.

lag² (lăg), *v.*, **lagged, lagging,** *n. Slang.* —*v.t.* **1.** to send to penal servitude. —*n.* **2.** a convict. **3.** a term of penal servitude. [orig. unknown]

lag³ (lăg), *n.*, *v.*, **lagged, lagging.** —*n.* **1.** one of the staves or strips which form the periphery of a wooden drum, the casing of a boiler, etc. —*v.t.* **2.** to cover, as pipes, to prevent heat loss. [t. Scand.; cf. Sw. *lagg* stave]

lagan (lăg′ən), *n. Law.* anything sunk in the sea, but attached to a buoy, etc., so that it may be recovered. Also, **ligan.** [t. OF; of Scand. orig. and akin to LIE², LAY¹]

Lag b'Omer (lăg bō′mə), a Jewish holiday, the thirty-third day from the second day of Passover. [t. Heb.: *lag* thirty-third (day) in the *'omer* count of forty-nine days from Passover to the Feast of Pentecost]

lager¹ (lä′gə), *n.* a beer matured at very low temperatures and stored for 6 weeks to 6 months before use. Also, **lager beer.** [short for *lager beer*, half adoption, half trans. of G *Lagerbier*]

lager² (lä′gə), *n.*, *v.t.*, *v.i. S. African.* laager.

Lagerkvist (*Swed.* lä′gər kvēst), *n.* **Pär** (*Swed.* pĕr), born 1891, Swedish novelist.

Lagerlöf (*Swed.* lä′gə lœv), *n.* **Selma** (*Swed.* sĕl′mà), 1858–1940, Swedish author.

laggard (lăg′əd), *adj.* **1.** lagging; backward; slow. —*n.* **2.** one who lags; lingerer. —**lag′gardly,** *adv.* —**lag′gardness,** *n.*

lagger (lăg′ə), *n.* one who lags; a laggard.

lagging¹ (lăg′ĭng), *n.* the act of lagging behind. [f. LAG¹ + -ING¹]

lagging² (lăg′ĭng), *n.* **1.** the act of covering a boiler, etc. with heat-insulating material. **2.** the covering formed. **3.** the material used. **4.** (*pl.*) the coverings to the centre of an arch or to the supports in a tunnel, to form a continuous surface. [f. LAG³ + -ING¹]

La Gioconda (lä jĭə′kŏn′də; *It.* là jō kôn′dà). See **Mona Lisa.**

lagniappe (lăn yăp′, lăn′yăp), *n. U.S.* something given with a purchase to a customer, by way of compliment or for good measure. Also, **lagnappe′.** [t. Louisiana F, t. Amer. Sp.: m. *la ñapa* the gift]

lagomorph (lăg′ō môf′), *n.* any of the *Lagomorpha*, an order of mammals resembling the rodents but having two pairs of upper incisors, and including the hares, rabbits, and pikas, formerly classified as a suborder of rodents. [f. Gk *lagō(s)* hare + -MORPH]

lagoon (lə go͞on′), *n.* **1.** an area of shallow water separated from the sea by low banks. **2.** any small, pondlike body of water, esp. one communicating with a larger body of water. Also, **lagune′.** [t. It., Sp.: m. *laguna*, g. L *lacūna* pool, pond]

Lagoon Islands, Ellice Islands.

Lagos (lā′gŏs), *n.* a seaport in and the capital of Nigeria, in the SW part. 450,000 (est. 1963). See map under **Nigeria.**

La Grange (*Fr.* là gräNzh′), **Joseph Louis** (*Fr.* zhō zĕf lwē′), **Count,** 1736–1813, French mathematician and astronomer, born in Italy.

Lagting (läg′tĭng), *n.* See **Storting.** Also, **Lagthing.**

La Guaira (*Sp.* lä gwā′rä), a seaport in N Venezuela: the port of Caracas.

lah-di-dah (lä′dĭ dä′), *adj. Slang.* la-di-da.

La Hogue (*Fr.* là ŏg′), a roadstead off the NW coast of France: naval battle, 1692. Also, **La Hougue** (*Fr.* là o͞og′).

Lahore (lə hô′), *n.* a city in Pakistan, the capital of West Pakistan in the NE part. 1,296,477 (1961).

Lahti (*Finn.* läh′tē), *n.* a town in S Finland. 79,039 (1965).

Laibach (*Ger.* lī′bàKH), *n.* German name of **Ljubljana.**

laic (lā′ĭk), *adj.* **1.** Also, **la′ical.** lay; secular. —*n.* **2.** layman. [t. LL: s. *lāicus*, t. Gk: m. *lāïkós*, der. *lāós* people] —**la′ically,** *adv.*

laicize (lā′ĭ sīz′), *v.t.*, **-cized, -cizing.** to deprive of clerical character. Also, **laicise.** —**la′iciza′tion,** *n.*

laid (lād), *v.* pt. and pp. of **lay¹.**

laidly (lād′lĭ), *adj. Scot.* offensive; hideous; repulsive. [N dial. var. of LOATHLY²]

laid paper, paper with fine parallel and cross lines produced in manufacturing. Cf. **wove paper.**

lain (lān), *v.* pp. of **lie².**

lair (lĕə), *n.* **1.** the den or resting place of a wild beast. **2.** a place in which to lie or rest; a bed. —*v.t.* **3.** to place in a lair. **4.** to serve as a lair for. —*v.i.* **5.** to go to, lie in, or have a lair. [ME *leir*, OE *leger*, c. D and OHG *leger* bed, camp; akin to LIE²]

laird (lĕəd), *n. Scot.* a landed proprietor. [var. of LORD] —**laird′ship,** *n.*

laissez faire (lā′sā fĕə′; *Fr.* lĕ sė fĕr′), **1.** the theory or system of government that upholds the autonomous character of the economic order, believing that government should intervene as little as possible in the direction of economic affairs. **2.** the doctrine of non-interference, esp. in the conduct of others. Also, **lais′ser faire′.** [t. F: lit., allow to act]

laissez-faire (lā′sā fĕə′; *Fr.* lĕ sė fĕr′), *adj.* of or pertaining to the principle of laissez faire. Also, **laisser-faire.**

laitance (lā′tns), *n.* the scum or whitish deposit that rises to the surface of newly placed concrete.

laity (lā′ĭ tĭ), *n.* **1.** laymen, as distinguished from clergymen. **2.** the people outside a particular profession, as distinguished from those belonging to it. [f. LAY³ + -TY²]

Laius (lī′əs), *n. Gk Legend.* a king of Thebes, killed unwittingly by his son Oedipus.

lake¹ (lāk), *n.* **1.** a body of water (fresh or salt) of considerable size, surrounded by land. **2.** some similar body of water or other liquid. [ME; OE *lacu* stream, pool, pond; r. ME *lac*, t. OF, t. L: s. *lacus* lake, tank]

lake² (lāk), *n.* **1.** any of various pigments prepared from animal, vegetable, or coal-tar colouring matters by union (chemical or other) with metallic compounds. **2.** a red pigment prepared from lac or cochineal by combination with a metallic compound. [t. F: m. *laque*, t. Pers.: m. *lāk*. See LAC¹]

Lake District, a picturesque mountainous region abounding in lakes, in NW England; national park.

lake-dweller (lāk′dwĕl′ə), *n.* an inhabitant of a lake-dwelling.

lake-dwelling (lāk′dwĕl′ĭng), *n.* a dwelling, esp. of prehistoric times, built on piles or other support over the water of a lake.

lakefront (lāk′frŭnt′), *n.* the land along the shore of a lake.

lake herring, **1.** Also, **freshwater herring.** the powan, *Coregonus clupeoides*, found in certain lakes of Great Britain. **2.** a cisco (whitefish), *Leucichthys artedi*, of the Great Lakes and small glacial lakes of eastern North America.

Lakeland (lāk′lănd′), *n.* **1.** the English Lake District. **2.** any area having many lakes.

lakeland terrier, one of a breed of small terriers, with harsh, dense coat; tan, black, or white in colour.

Lake Poets, the poets Wordsworth, Coleridge, and Southey; so named from their residence in the Lake District. Also, **Lake School.**

lakh (läk), *n.* (in India) **1.** the sum of 100,000, esp. of rupees. The usual punctuation for sums of Indian money above a lakh is with a comma after the number of lakhs: Rs 30,52,000 (i.e., thirty lakhs and fifty two thousand) instead of 3,052,000. **2.** an indefinitely large number. Also, **lac.** [t. Hind.: *lākh*, g. Skt *laksha* mark, hundred thousand]

laky[1] (lā′kĭ), *adj.* of or like a lake. [f. LAKE[1] + -Y[1]]

laky[2] (lā′kĭ), *adj.* of the colour of a lake pigment. [f. LAKE[2] + -Y[1]]

La Linea (lä lĭn′ĭ ə; *Sp.* lä lē′nė ä), a seaport in S Spain, near Gibraltar. 60,379 (1960).

Lallan (lăl′ən), *adj.* belonging to the Lowlands of Scotland.

Lallans (lăl′ənz), *n.* the Lowland Scottish dialect.

lallation (lă lā′shən), *n.* *Phonet.* a speech defect consisting in pronouncing an *l* sound instead of *r*. [f. s. L *lallāre* sing lullaby + -ATION]

lam[1] (lăm), *v.t.*, **lammed, lamming.** *Slang.* to beat; thrash. [t. Scand.; cf. Icel. *lamdhi*, past tense of *lemja* beat; akin to LAME[1]]

lam[2] (lăm), *n.*, *v.*, **lammed, lamming.** *U.S. Slang.* —*n.* **1.** precipitate escape. **2. on the lam,** escaping or fleeing. **3. take it on the lam,** to flee or escape in great haste. —*v.i.* **4.** to run quickly; run off or away. [special use of LAM[1]. Cf. *beat it* be off]

Lam., Lamentations.

lama (lä′mə), *n.* a priest or monk of the form of Buddhism prevailing in Tibet, Mongolia, etc. [t. Tibetan: m. *blama* (*b-* is silent)]

Lamaism (lä′mə ĭz′əm), *n.* the form of Buddhism in Tibet and Mongolia which has developed an organized hierarchy and a host of deities and saints. —**La′maist,** *n.*

La Mancha (*Sp.* lä män′chä), a barren plateau region in central Spain: the home of Cervantes's Don Quixote.

Lamarck (lä mäk′; *Fr.* lȧ mȧrk′), *n.* **Jean Baptiste Pierre Antoine de Monet de** (*Fr.* zhäɴ bȧ tēst pyĕr äɴ twȧn′ də mō nĕ′ də), 1744–1829, French biologist.

Lamarckian (lä mä′kĭ ən), *adj.* **1.** of or pertaining to Jean de Lamarck or his theory of organic evolution. —*n.* **2.** one who holds this theory.

Lamarckism (lä mä′kĭz′əm), *n.* *Biol.* the theory that characters acquired by habits, use, disuse, or adaptations to changes in environment may be inherited.

Lamartine (*Fr.* lȧ mȧr tēn′), *n.* **Alphonse Marie Louis de** (*Fr.* ȧl fôɴs mȧ rē lwē′ də), 1790–1869, French poet, historian, and statesman.

lamasery (lä′mə sə rĭ), *n.*, *pl.* **-series.** (in Tibet, Mongolia, etc.) a monastery of lamas.

lamb (lăm), *n.* **1.** a young sheep. **2.** the meat of a young sheep. **3.** one who is young, gentle, meek, innocent, etc. **4. the Lamb,** Christ. **5.** one who is easily cheated, esp. an inexperienced speculator. —*v.i.* **6.** to give birth to a lamb. [ME and OE, c. G *Lamm*]

Lamb (lăm), *n.* **Charles** ('*Elia*'), 1775–1834, British essayist and critic.

lambaste (lăm bāst′), *v.t.*, **-basted, -basting.** *Slang.* **1.** to beat severely. **2.** (in sailors' use) to beat with a rope's end. Also, **lambast** (lăm′băst). [appar. f. LAM[1] + BASTE[3]]

lambda (lăm′də), *n.* the eleventh letter of the Greek alphabet (Λ, λ).

lambdacism (lăm′də sĭz′əm), *n.* *Phonet.* excessive use of the sound *l*, its misarticulation, or its substitution for *r*.

lambdoid (lăm′doid), *adj.* having the shape of the Greek capital lambda (Λ). Also, **lambdoi′dal.** [t. NL: s. *lambdoidēs*, t. Gk: m. *lambdoeidēs*. See LAMBDA, -OID]

lambdoidal suture, *Anat.* the suture between the occipital and the two parietal bones of the skull, continued forward between the parietal bones. See diag. under **cranium.**

lambency (lăm′bən sĭ), *n.*, *pl.* **-cies.** **1.** the quality of being lambent. **2.** that which is lambent.

lambent (lăm′bənt), *adj.* **1.** running or moving lightly over a surface: *lambent tongues of flame.* **2.** playing lightly and brilliantly over a subject: *lambent wit.* **3.** softly bright: *a steady, lambent light.* [t. L: s. *lambens*, ppr., licking] —**lam′bently,** *adv.*

lambert (lăm′bət), *n.* *Optics.* the brightness of a perfectly diffusing surface emitting or reflecting one lumen per square centimetre: the c.g.s. unit of brightness. [named after J. H. LAMBERT]

Lambert (lăm′bət *for def. 1*; *Ger.* läm′bĕrt *for def. 2*), *n.* **1. Constant,** 1905–51, English composer and conductor. **2. Johann Heinrich** (*Ger.* yō′hän hīn′rĭKH), 1728–77, German physicist and astronomer.

Lambert's law, *Physics.* the law which states that the illumination of a surface from a point source of light is inversely proportional to the square of the distance between the surface and the source. [named after J. H. LAMBERT]

Lambeth (lăm′bəth), *n.* a S inner London borough. 340,800 (est. 1964).

Lambeth Conference, a convention of Anglican bishops held about every ten years, generally at Lambeth Palace, to confer about doctrine and order.

Lambeth degree, an honorary degree conferred by the Archbishop of Canterbury.

Lambeth Palace, the official residence of the Archbishop of Canterbury, near the Thames in S London.

Lambeth walk, a type of dance popular in the late 1930s.

lambkin (lăm′kĭn), *n.* **1.** a little lamb. **2.** any young and tender creature. [ME *lambkyn.* See LAMB, -KIN]

lamblike (lăm′līk′), *adj.* like a lamb; gentle; meek.

Lamb of God, Christ.

lambrequin (lăm′brĭ kĭn, lăm′bə kĭn), *n.* **1.** a textile fabric worn over a helmet in medieval times to protect it from heat, rust, and sword blows. **2.** a hanging or drapery covering the upper part of an opening, as a door or window, or suspended from a shelf. [t. F, t. Flemish: m. *lamperkin*, dim of *lamper* veil]

lamb's-ear (lămz′ĭə′), *n.* a woolly-leaved, perennial labiate with crimson flowers, *Stachys lanata*, a native of the Caucasus and Iran often used as an edging plant because of its decorative foliage; woolly betony. Also, **lamb's-tongue** (lămz′tŭng′).

lambskin (lăm′skĭn′), *n.* **1.** the skin of a lamb, esp. when dressed with the wool on. **2.** leather made from such skin. **3.** parchment made from such skin. **4.** a kind of cotton cloth having a raised surface and deep nap.

lamb's lettuce, the corn salad, *Valerianella locusta.*

lamb's-tails (lămz′tālz′), *n.pl.* hazel catkins.

lamb's wool, a soft, fluffy wool, with superior spinning qualities, shorn from a lamb of seven months.

lame[1] (lām), *adj.*, **lamer, lamest,** *v.*, **lamed, laming.** —*adj.* **1.** crippled or physically disabled, as a person or animal, esp. in the foot or leg so as to limp or walk with difficulty. **2.** impaired or disabled through defect or injury, as a limb. **3.** defective in quality or quantity; insufficient. —*v.t.* **4.** to make lame or defective. [ME; OE *lama*, c. G *lahm*] —**lame′ly,** *adv.* —**lame′ness,** *n.*

lame[2] (lām; *Fr.* läm), *n.* one of numerous overlapping plates used in building elements of flexible armour. [t. F, g. L *lāmina* thin piece or plate]

lamé (lä′mā; *Fr.* lȧ mė′), *n.* an ornamental fabric in which metallic threads are woven with silk, wool, artificial fibres, or cotton. [t. F: lit., laminated, der. *lame* gold or silver thread or wire]

lame duck (lām), *Colloq.* a person or thing that is disabled, helpless, ineffective, or inefficient.

lamella (lə mĕl′ə), *n.*, *pl.* **-mellae** (-mĕl′ē), **-mellas.** **1.** a thin plate, scale, membrane, or layer, as of bone, tissue, cell walls, etc. **2.** *Bot.* **a.** an erect scale or blade inserted at the junction of the claw and limb in some corollas, and forming a part of their corona or crown. **b.** a gill, one of the radiating vertical plates on the underside of the pileus of an agaric. **c.** (in mosses) a thin sheet of cells standing up along the midrib of a leaf. [t. L, dim. of *lāmina* LAMINA]

lamellar (lə mĕl′ə), *adj.* **1.** referring to a lamella or lamellae. **2.** lamellate.

lamellate (lăm′ĭ lāt′, -lĭt, lə mĕl′āt, -ĭt), *adj.* **1.** composed of or having lamellae. **2.** flat; platelike. Also, **lam′ellat′ed.**

lamellibranch (lə mĕl′ĭ brăngk′), *n.* *Zool.* any of the *Lamellibranchiata*, a class of molluscs comprising the oysters, clams, mussels, scallops, etc., characterized by a bivalve shell enclosing the headless body and lamellate gills. [t. NL: m. *Lāmellibranchia*, pl., f. L *lāmelli-* thin plate + Gk *bránchia* gills] —**lamellibranchiate** (lə mĕl′ĭ brăng′kĭ āt′, -ĭt), *adj.*, *n.*

lamellicorn (lə mĕl′ĭ kôn′), *Entomol.* —*adj.* **1.** having antennae with lamellate and leaf-like terminal segments, as beetles of the group *Lamellicornia*, which includes the scarabaeids and stag-beetles. **2.** (of antennae) having leaf-like terminal segments. —*n.* **3.** a lamellicorn beetle. [t. NL: s. *lāmellicornis*, f. L: *lāmelli-* thin plate + *-cornis* horned]

lamellirostral (lə mĕl′ĭ rŏs′trəl), *adj.* *Ornith.* having a beak equipped with thin plates or lamellae for straining water and mud from food, as the ducks, geese, swans, and flamingos. Also, **lamellirostrate** (lə mĕl′ĭ rŏs′trāt). [f. L *lāmelli-* thin plate + ROSTRAL]

lamellose (lə mĕl′ōs, lăm′ĭ lōs′), *adj.* lamellate.

lament (lə mĕnt′), *v.t.* **1.** to feel or express sorrow or regret for; mourn for or over: *lament his absence, one's folly.* —*v.i.* **2.** to feel, show, or express grief, sorrow, or sad regret. —*n.* **3.** an expression of grief or sorrow. **4.** a formal expression of sorrow or mourning, esp. in verse or song; an elegy or dirge, often played on the bagpipes. [t. L: s. *lāmentārī* wail, weep] —**lament′er,** *n.* —**Ant. 2.** rejoice.

lamentable (lăm′ən tə bl), *adj.* **1.** that is to be lamented: *a lamentable occurrence.* **2.** *Now Rare.* mournful. —**lam′entableness,** *n.* —**lam′entably,** *adv.*

lamentation (lăm′ĕn tā′shən), *n.* **1.** the act of lamenting.

2. a lament. 3. **Lamentations,** a book of the Old Testament, ascribed by tradition to Jeremiah.

lamented (lə mĕn′tĭd), *adj.* 1. mourned for, as one who is dead: *the late lamented Grady.* 2. regretted.

lamia (lā′myə), *n., pl.,* **-mias, -miae** (-mĭ ē′). 1. *Class. Myth.* one of a class of mythical monsters, commonly represented with the head and breast of a woman and the body of a serpent, said to allure youths and children in order to suck their blood. 2. a vampire; a female demon. [ME, t. L, t. Gk]

lamiaceous (lā′mĭ ā′shəs), *adj. Bot.* belonging or pertaining to the mint family (*Lamiaceae, Menthaceae,* or, more commonly, *Labiatae*) including species valued as aromatic and in medicine. See **labiate** (def. 2a). [f. s. NL *Lamiăceae* (der. L *lāmium* dead nettle) + -OUS]

lamina (lăm′ĭ nə), *n., pl.* **-nae** (-nē′), **-nas.** 1. a thin plate, scale, or layer. 2. a layer or coat lying over another: applied to the plates of minerals, bones, etc. See diag. under **vertebrae.** 3. *Bot.* the blade or expanded portion of a leaf. See diag. under **leaf.** [t. L: thin plate, leaf, layer. Cf. LAMELLA]

laminable (lăm′ĭ nə bl), *adj.* capable of being laminated.

laminar (lăm′ĭ nə), *adj.* composed of, or arranged in, laminae. Also, **laminary** (lăm′ĭ nə rĭ).

laminar flow, *Hydraulics.* a flow of a viscous fluid in which neighbouring layers are not mixed.

laminate (*v.* lăm′ĭ nāt′; *adj.* lăm′ĭ nāt′, -nĭt), *v.,* **-nated, -nating,** *adj.* —*v.t.* 1. to separate or split into thin layers. 2. to form (metal) into a lamina, as by beating or rolling. 3. to construct by placing layer upon layer. 4. to cover or overlay with laminae. —*v.i.* 5. to split into thin layers. —*adj.* 6. composed of, or having, a lamina or laminae. [f. LAMIN(A) + -ATE[1]]

laminated (lăm′ĭ nā′tĭd), *adj.* formed of, or set in, thin layers or laminae.

laminated plastic, a stiff board, or glossy surface covering, made from compressed sheets of paper or textile impregnated with a synthetic resin.

lamination (lăm′ĭ nā′shən), *n.* 1. the act or process of laminating. 2. the state of being laminated. 3. laminated structure; arrangement in thin layers. 4. a lamina.

laminitis (lăm′ĭ nī′tĭs), *n. Vet. Sci.* inflammation of sensitive laminae in the hoof of a horse, caused by overwork, overfeeding, etc. [t. NL]

laminose (lăm′ĭ nōs′), *adj.* laminate; laminar.

Lamizana (lăm′ĭ zä′nə), *n.* **Sangoule** (săng′gōōl), born 1916, president of Upper Volta since 1966.

Lammas (lăm′əs), *n.* 1. *Rom. Cath. Ch.* a church festival observed on August 1st in memory of St Peter's imprisonment and miraculous deliverance. 2. (orig.) a harvest festival formerly held in England on August 1st (**Lammas Day**); now a Scottish quarter-day. [ME *Lammasse,* OE *hlāfmæsse* loaf mass. See -MAS]

Lammastide (lăm′əs tīd′), *n.* the season of Lammas.

lammergeyer (lăm′ə gī′ə), *n.* the bearded vulture, *Gypaëtus barbatus,* the largest European bird of prey, ranging in the mountains from southern Europe to China. Also, **lammergeier.** [t. G: m. *Lämmergeier,* lit., lambs' vulture (from its preying on lambs)]

lamp (lămp), *n.* 1. any of various devices for using an illuminant, as gas or electricity, or for heating, as by burning alcohol. 2. a vessel for containing an inflammable liquid, as oil, which is burnt at a wick as a means of illumination. 3. any source as of intellectual or spiritual light. 4. *Poetic.* a torch. 5. *Poetic.* a celestial body, as the moon. 6. a source of intellectual or spiritual light. 7. (*pl.*) *U.S. Slang.* the eyes. [ME *lampe,* t. OF, g. L *lampas,* t. Gk: torch, light, lamp]

lampas (lăm′pəs), *n.* a type of brocaded fabric of silk and cotton, or cotton only, used in upholstery, etc. [ME, t. OFlem.: m. *lampers*]

lampblack (lămp′blăk′), *n.* a fine black pigment consisting of almost pure carbon collected as soot from the smoke of burning oil, gas, etc.

Lampedusa (lăm′pĭ dyōō′zə; *It.* läm pĕ dōō′zä), *n.* a small Italian island in the Mediterranean between Tunisia and Malta.

lamper eel (lăm′pə), lamprey.

lampion (lăm′pyən), *n.* a kind of lamp, often of coloured glass. [t. F, t. It.: m. *lampione* carriage or street lamp, der. *lampa* LAMP]

lamplight (lămp′līt′), *n.* the light shed by a lamp.

lamplighter (lămp′lī′tə), *n.* 1. one who lights street lamps. 2. *U.S.* a contrivance for lighting lamps.

lampoon (lăm pōōn′), *n.* 1. a malicious or virulent satire upon a person, institution, government, etc., in either prose or verse. —*v.t.* 2. to assail in a lampoon. [t. F: m. *lampon,* said to be m. *lampons* let us drink (used in songs or verses), impv. of *lamper*] —**lampoon′er, lampoon′ist,** *n.* —**lampoon′ery,** *n.*

lamppost (lămp′pōst′), *n.* a post, of concrete, steel, or iron, used to support a lamp which lights a street, park, etc.

lamprey (lăm′prĭ), *n., pl.* **-preys.** any of the eel-like cyclostome fishes constituting the group *Hyperoartia.* Some species attach themselves to fishes and rasp a hole in the flesh with their horny teeth so that they can suck the blood of the victim. [ME, t. OF: m. *lampreie,* g. LL *lamprēda*]

Lamprey, *Petromyzon marinus* (21 in. long)

lamprophyre (lăm′prə fī′ə), *n. Geol.* any dark igneous rock having a high proportion of coloured silicates, present both as phenocrysts and groundmass, and little or no felspar; lamprophyres usually occur in dykes. [f. *lampro-* (comb. form repr. Gk *lamprós* clear) + -PHYRE]

lampshade (lămp′shād′), *n.* a covering, often decorative, to diffuse or concentrate the light of a lamp.

lamp-shell (lămp′shĕl′), *n.* a brachiopod.

Lanai (lä nä′ē), *n.* one of the Hawaiian islands, in the central part of the group. 2115 pop. (1960); 141 sq. mi.

Lanark (lăn′ək), *n.* 1. a burgh in Scotland, the county town of Lanarkshire. 8436 (1961). 2. Lanarkshire.

Lanarks., Lanarkshire.

Lanarkshire (lăn′ək shĭə′, -shə), *n.* a county in S Scotland. 1,626,317 pop. (1961); 898 sq. mi. *Co. town:* Lanark. *Abbrev.:* Lanarks. Also, **Lanark.**

lanate (lā′nāt), *adj.* woolly; covered with something resembling wool. [t. L: m. s. *lānātus*]

Lancashire (lăng′kə shĭə′, -shə), *n.* 1. a county in NW England. 5,131,646 pop. (1961); 1878 sq. mi. *Co. town:* Lancaster. *Abbrev.:* Lancs. 2. Lancashire cheese.

Lancashire cheese, a loose, crumbly, whitish yellow cheese; mild in flavour when young, but gaining piquancy in maturity. Also, **Lancashire.**

Lancashire hotpot, a hotpot.

Lancaster (lăng′kə stə; *for 1 also* lăng′kăs′tə), *n.* 1. an English royal house which reigned 1399–1461, descended from John of Gaunt (Duke of Lancaster), and including Henry IV, Henry V, and Henry VI. 2. a town in England, the county town of Lancashire. 48,235 (1961).

Lancastrian (lăng kăs′trĭ ən), *adj.* 1. of or pertaining to the English royal house of Lancaster. 2. of or pertaining to Lancaster or Lancashire. —*n.* 3. an adherent or member of the house of Lancaster, esp. in the Wars of the Roses. 4. a native or resident of Lancashire or Lancaster.

lance (läns), *n., v.,* **lanced, lancing.** —*n.* 1. a long, shafted weapon with a metal head, used by mounted soldiers in charging. 2. a soldier armed with this weapon. 3. an implement resembling the weapon, as a spear for killing a harpooned whale. 4. a lancet. —*v.t.* 5. to open with, or as if with, a lancet: *to lance an abscess.* 6. to pierce with a lance. [ME, t. F, g. L *lancea*]

lance bombardier, a non-commissioned officer in the Royal Regiment of Artillery, corresponding in rank to a lance corporal.

lance corporal, the lowest non-commissioned officer rank in the British Army, below corporal.

lance jack, *Slang.* lance corporal.

lancelet (läns′lĭt), *n.* a small fishlike animal, of the genus *Branchiostoma* (*Amphioxus*), found in sand in shallow waters, related to the vertebrates. [f. LANCE, n. + -LET]

Lancelet, *Branchiostoma pulchellum* (Ab. 2½ in. long)

Lancelot (läns′lət), *n. Arthurian Legend.* the greatest of Arthur's knights, and the lover of Queen Guinevere.

lanceolate (län′sĭ ə lāt′, -lĭt), *adj.* 1. shaped like the head of a lance. 2. (of leaves, etc.) narrow, and tapering towards the apex or (sometimes) each end. [t. L: m. s. *lanceolātus,* der. *lanceola,* dim. of *lancea* lance]

lancer (län′sə), *n.* 1. a mounted soldier armed with a lance. 2. a soldier belonging to one of certain regiments officially called Lancers.

lance rest, (in medieval armour) a support, bolted to the breastplate, upon which the lance rested when couched for use.

Lanceolate leaf

lancers (län′səz), *n.pl.* 1. a form of quadrille (dance). 2. music for such a set of dances.

lance sergeant, a corporal appointed to act as sergeant, without increase in pay; an acting sergeant.

lancet (län′sĭt), *n.* 1. a small surgical instrument, usually sharp-pointed and two-edged, for opening abscesses, etc. 2. *Archit.* a. a lancet arch. b. a lancet window. [late ME *lawnset,* t. OF: m. *lancette,* dim. of *lance* LANCE]

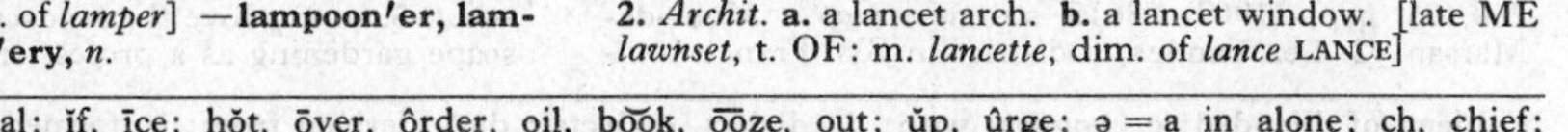

lancet arch, *Archit.* an arch the head of which is acutely pointed.

lanceted (län′sĭ tĭd), *adj.* having a lancet arch or lancet windows.

lancet fish, a large marine fish of the genus *Alepisaurus*, with enormous dagger-like teeth.

lancet window, *Archit.* a high, narrow window terminating in a lancet arch.

lancewood (läns′wo͝od′), *n.* **1.** the tough, elastic wood of any of various trees, as *Oxandra lanceolata*, of tropical America, used for carriage shafts, cabinetwork, etc. **2.** a tree which yields it.

Lanchow (lăn′chou′), *n.* a city in N China, on the Hwang Ho river: capital of Kansu province. 732,000 (est. 1958).

lancinate (län′sĭ nāt′), *v.t.*, **-nated, -nating.** to tear or rend; stab or pierce. [t. L: m. s. *lancinātus*, pp.] —**lan′cina′tion,** *n.*

Lancs., Lancashire.

land (lănd), *n.* **1.** the solid substance of the earth's surface. **2.** the exposed part of the earth's surface, as distinguished from the submerged part: *to travel by land.* **3.** ground, esp. with reference to quality, character, or use: *forest land.* **4.** agricultural areas as opposed to urban. **5.** *Law.* **a.** any part of the earth's surface which can be owned as property, and everything annexed to it, whether by nature or by the hand of man. **b.** any hereditament, tenement, or other interest held in land. **6.** *Econ.* natural resources as a factor of production. **7.** a part of the earth's surface marked off by natural or political boundaries or the like; a region or country. **8.** the people of a country; a nation. **9.** a realm or domain: *the land of the living.* **10.** a surface between furrows, as on a millstone or on the interior of a rifle barrel. **11. see how the land lies,** to investigate a situation, circumstances, etc. —*v.t.* **12.** to bring to or put on land or shore: *to land passengers or goods from a vessel.* **13.** to bring into, or cause to arrive in, any place, position, or condition. **14.** *Colloq.* to catch or capture; gain. **15.** *Angling.* to bring (a fish) to land, or into a boat, etc., as with a hook or a net. —*v.i.* **16.** to come to land or shore: *the boat lands at Cherbourg.* **17.** to go or come ashore from a ship or boat. **18.** to alight upon the ground, as from an aeroplane, a train, or after a jump or the like. **19.** to come to rest or arrive in any place, position, or condition. **20.** to hit or strike and come to rest on the surface of something: *the plane landed in the water.* **21. land on one's feet, a.** to have good luck. **b.** to emerge successfully from an adverse situation. [ME and OE, c. G *Land*]

Land (*Ger.* länt), *n.*, *pl.* **Länder** (*Ger.* lĕn′dər). one of the territorial districts into which West Germany is divided.

land agent, the steward or manager of a landed estate.

land army, the Women's Land Army.

landau (lăn′dô), *n.* **1.** a four-wheeled, two-seated vehicle with a top made in two parts, which may be let down or folded back. **2.** *Archaic.* a sedan-type motor vehicle with a short convertible back. [named after *Landau*, town in Germany]

Landau

Landau (*Russ.* län′dä o͞o), *n.* **Lev Davidovich** (*Russ.* lyĕf dä vē′də vĭch), 1908–68, Soviet physicist.

landaulet (lăn′dô lĕt′), *n.* *Obs.* a motor vehicle having a convertible top for the back seat, with the front seat either roofed or open. Also, **landaulette.**

land breeze, a thermally produced wind blowing during the night from the cool land on to the adjoining warmer sea.

land certificate, a certificate under the seal of a land registry, containing a copy of the registered particulars of a piece of land.

land crab, any of several crabs, esp. of the family *Gecarcinidae*, which are partially adapted to terrestrial life. Land crabs of varied species occur in many tropical regions.

land cress, a biennial cruciferous herb with yellow flowers, *Barbarea verna*, a native of the Mediterranean region but widely naturalized in temperate zones.

landdrost (lăn′drŏst), *n.* *S. African.* a magistrate, esp. in a country district. [t. Afrikaans, t. LG, equiv. to *land* district + obs. *Drost* governor]

landed (lăn′dĭd), *adj.* **1.** owning land: *a landed proprietor.* **2.** consisting of land: *landed property.*

Landes (*Fr.* läɴd), *n.* **1.** a department in SW France. 260,495 pop. (1962); 3615 sq. mi. *Cap.:* Mont-de-Marsan. **2. Les Landes,** a district in SW France comprising low-lying sandy plains bordered by sand-dunes along the Atlantic coast.

landfall (lănd′fôl′), *n.* **1.** an approach to or sighting of land. **2.** the land sighted or reached.

land girl, *Colloq.* a woman member of the Women's Land Army.

landgrave (lănd′grāv′), *n.* **1.** the title of certain princes. **2.** (orig.) a German count having jurisdiction over a considerable territory. [t. G: m. *Landgraf*]

landgraviate (lănd grā′vĭ ĭt, -āt′), *n.* the office, jurisdiction, or territory of a landgrave.

landgravine (lănd′grə vēn′), *n.* **1.** the wife of a landgrave. **2.** a woman of the rank of a landgrave. [t. G: m. *Landgräfin*]

land-holder (lănd′hōl′də), *n.* a holder, owner, or occupant of land. —**land′-hold′ing,** *adj.*

landing (lăn′dĭng), *n.* **1.** the act of one who or that which lands. **2.** a place where persons or goods are landed, as from a ship. **3.** *Archit.* **a.** the floor at the head or foot of a flight of stairs. **b.** a platform between flights of stairs.

landing beam, a radio beam transmitted from an airfield to indicate to a pilot the height and position of his aircraft when approaching to land.

landing card, a card issued to passengers to regulate landing from a boat, aeroplane, etc.

landing craft, a low, flat-bottomed boat, used for landing troops and equipment on a beach.

landing field, an area of land, cleared to allow aircraft to take off and land.

landing gear, the undercarriage of an aircraft.

landing net, a scoop-shaped net, used for lifting a hooked fish out of the water and on to the land or boat.

landing party, a detachment of a ship's crew, sent ashore for exploratory or hostile action.

landing stage, a fixed or floating wharf.

landing strip, an elementary area of flat ground used by aircraft for landing and take-off purposes only.

landlady (lănd′lā′dĭ), *n.*, *pl.* **-dies. 1.** a woman who owns and leases land, buildings, etc. **2.** a woman who owns or runs an inn, lodging house, or boarding house.

landless (lănd′lĭs), *adj.* without land; owning no land.

landlocked (lănd′lŏkt′), *adj.* **1.** shut in more or less completely by land. **2.** living in waters shut off from the sea, as some fish: *a landlocked salmon.*

landlocked salmon. See **salmon** (def. 2).

landlord (lănd′lôd′), *n.* **1.** one who owns and leases land, buildings, etc., to another. **2.** the master of an inn, lodging house, etc. **3.** a landowner.

landlordism (lănd′lô dĭz′əm), *n.* the practice under which property or land which is owned by one person is leased to another for his occupancy or use.

landlubber (lănd′lŭb′ə), *n.* *Naut.* a landsman or raw seaman. —**land′lub′berly,** *adj.* [f. LAND + LUBBER]

landmark (lănd′mäk′), *n.* **1.** a conspicuous object on land that serves as a guide, as to vessels at sea. **2.** a prominent or distinguishing feature, part, event, etc. **3.** something used to mark the boundary of land.

landmine (lănd′mīn′), *n.* **1.** a bomb dropped by parachute, causing widespread damage. **2.** mine (def. 7).

land of milk and honey, 1. a land of great fertility and promise. **2.** (*sometimes cap.*) Israel.

Land of Promise, Canaan, the land promised by God to Abraham. Gen. 12.

Land of the Midnight Sun, 1. any country which contains land within the Arctic Circle, where there is a midnight sun in midsummer. **2.** Lapland.

Land of the Rising Sun, Japan.

Landor (lăn′dô), *n.* **Walter Savage,** 1775–1864, English author.

landowner (lănd′ō′nə), *n.* an owner or proprietor of land. —**land′own′ership′,** *n.* —**land′own′ing,** *n.*, *adj.*

Landowska (lăn dŏf′skə), *n.* **Wanda** (văn′də), 1879–1959, U.S. harpsichordist born in Poland.

land power, 1. a nation having an important and powerful army. **2.** military power on land.

landrace (lăn′drās), *n.* a smallish lop-eared breed of pig, having a coat of short white hairs.

land rail, the corncrake.

land registry, a registry for officially recording the title to, dealings with, and charges on land.

Land Rover, *Trademark.* an adaptable utility vehicle for general commercial and military use, capable of driving cross-country, etc.

landscape (lănd′skāp′), *n.*, *v.*, **-scaped, -scaping.** —*n.* **1.** a view or prospect of rural scenery, more or less extensive, such as is comprehended within the scope or range of vision from a single point of view. **2.** a piece of such scenery. **3.** a picture representing natural inland or coastal scenery. **4.** such pictures as a category. —*v.t.* **5.** to improve the landscape. —*v.i.* **6.** to do landscape gardening as a profession. [earlier *landskip*, *land-*

scap, t. D: m. *landschap*, c. OE *landsceap*, *landscipe*, G *Landschaft* region. See LAND, -SHIP]

landscape architect, one whose profession is to adapt an area of land to give a particular visual effect. —**landscape architecture.**

landscape gardening, the art of arranging trees, shrubbery, paths, fountains, etc., to produce picturesque effects. —**landscape gardener.**

Landseer (lănʹsĭə), *n.* **Sir Edwin Henry,** 1802–73, English painter, esp. of animals.

Land's End, the SW tip of England.

Landshut (*Ger.* lántsʹhōōt), *n.* a town in West Germany, in E central Bavaria. 51,700 (est. 1966).

landsknecht (läntsʹkə nĕktʹ), *n.* lansquenet.

landslide (lăndʹslīdʹ), *n.* **1.** the sliding down of a mass of soil, detritus, or rock on a steep slope. **2.** the mass itself. **3.** an election in which a particular candidate or party receives an overwhelming mass or majority of votes. **4.** any overwhelming victory.

landslip (lăndʹslĭpʹ), *n.* landslide (defs 1 and 2).

Landsmål (*Norw.* làntsʹmòl), *n.* an official language of Norway, based on the dialects of western Norway and Old Norse. Also, **Nynorsk.** Cf. **Riksmål.** [Norw.: country's speech]

landsman (lăndzʹmən), *n.*, *pl.* **-men.** **1.** one who lives, or engages in an occupation, on land (opposed to *seaman*). **2.** *Naut.* **a.** a sailor on his first voyage. **b.** an inexperienced seaman, rated below an ordinary seaman.

Landsting (*Dan.* lànsʹtèng), *n.* the upper house of the Danish Rigsdag in parliament. Also, **Landsthing.** [Dan., f. *lands*, poss. of *land* land + *t(h)ing* parliament]

Landsturm (*Ger.* lăntʹshtōōrm), *n.* (in Germany, Switzerland, etc.) **1.** a general levy of the people in time of war. **2.** the force so called out or subject to such call, consisting of all men capable of bearing arms and not in the army, navy, or Landwehr. [G: land storm]

landward (lăndʹwəd), *adj.* **1.** lying, facing, or tending towards the land or away from the coast: *a landward breeze.* **2.** being in the direction of the land. —*adv.* **3.** landwards.

landwards (lăndʹwədz), *adv.* towards the land or interior. Also, **landward.**

Landwehr (*Ger.* làntʹvèr), *n.* (in Germany, Austria, etc.) formerly that part of the organized military forces of the nation which has completed a certain amount of compulsory training and of which continuous service is required only in time of war. [G: land defence]

lane (lān), *n.* **1.** a narrow way or passage between hedges, fences, walls, or houses. **2.** any narrow or well-defined passage, track, channel, or course. **3.** a fixed route pursued by ocean-going ships or aircraft. **4.** a part of a highway for traffic moving in one line. **5.** (in sprinting or swimming) each of the spaces between the cords or chalked lines which mark the courses of the competitors. **6.** *Tenpin Bowling.* a narrow alley, usually with a polished wooden floor, on which the ball is bowled. [ME and OE, c. D *laan*] —**Syn. 1.** See **path.**

lang (lăng), *adj.*, *n.*, *adv. Scot.* long¹.

Lang (lăng; *Ger.* làng *for 3*), *n.* **1. Andrew,** 1844–1912, Scottish writer. **2. Cosmo Gordon** (kŏzʹmō), 1864–1945, British clergyman: archbishop of Canterbury 1928–42. **3. Fritz** (*Ger.* frĭts), born 1890, German film director.

lang., language.

Langeberg (lăngʹgĭ bûgʹ), *n.* **1.** Also, **Langebergen.** a mountain range in the Republic of South Africa in SW Cape Province between the Little Karoo and the coast. av. height 3000–6000 ft. **2.** a mountain range in the Republic of South Africa in N Cape Province.

Langerhans (lăngʹə hänsʹ), *n.* **islets of.** See **pancreas.**

Langland (lăngʹlənd), *n.* **William,** *c.* 1330–*c.* 1400, English poet: author of *Piers Plowman.* Also, **Langley.**

Langley (lăngʹlĭ), *n.* **1. Batty** (bătʹĭ), 1696–1751, English architectural theorist. **2. Edmund of.** See **York,** 1st Duke of. **3. Samuel Pierpont,** 1834–1906, U.S. astronomer, physicist, and pioneer in aeronautics. **4. William.** See **Langland.**

Langobard (lăngʹgə bädʹ), *n.* a member of an ancient Germanic tribe which finally settled in N Italy. [t. LL: s. *Langobardi*, pl. of Gmc orig.]

Langobardic (lăngʹgə bäʹdĭk), *adj.* **1.** pertaining to the Langobards. —*n.* **2.** the language of the Langobards, a dialect of High German.

langouste (lŏngʹgōōst, lŏng gōōstʹ), *n.* the French gastronomic name for the spiny lobster; prepared and cooked like lobster.

langrage (lăngʹgrĭj), *n.* a kind of shot consisting of bolts, nails, etc., fastened together or enclosed in a case, formerly used for damaging sails and rigging in battles at sea. Also, **langridge.** [orig. unknown]

langsyne (lăngʹsīnʹ), *Scot.* —*adv.* **1.** long since; long ago. —*n.* **2.** time long past. [f. *lang* long + *syne*, contr. of ME *sithen*, OE *siththan* SINCE]

Langton (lăngʹtən), *n.* **Stephen,** *c.* 1150–1228, English cardinal and archbishop of Canterbury.

Langtry (lăngʹtrĭ), *n.* **Lillie** (lĭlʹĭ) (*Emily Charlotte Le Breton, 'the Jersey Lily'*), 1852–1929, English actress.

language (lăngʹgwĭj), *n.* **1.** communication by voice in the distinctively human manner, using arbitrary auditory symbols in conventional ways with conventional meanings. **2.** any set or system of such symbols as used in a more or less uniform fashion by a number of people, who are thus enabled to communicate intelligibly with one another. **3.** the non-linguistic means of communication of animals: *the language of birds.* **4.** communication of meaning in any way: *the language of flowers.* **5.** linguistics. **6.** strong language: *his language shocked us.* **7.** the speech or phraseology peculiar to a class, profession, etc. **8.** form or manner of expression: *in his own language.* **9.** speech or expression of a particular character: *flowery language.* **10.** diction or style of writing. [ME, t. OF: m. *langage*, der. *langue* tongue, g. L *lingua*]

—**Syn. 1.** See **speech. 2.** LANGUAGE, DIALECT, JARGON, VERNACULAR refer to patterns of vocabulary, syntax, and usage characteristic of communities of various sizes and types. LANGUAGE is applied to the general pattern of a people or race: *the English language.* DIALECT is applied to certain forms or varieties of a language, often those which provincial communities or special groups retain (or develop) even after a standard has been established: *Scottish dialect.* A JARGON is an artificial pattern used by a particular (usually occupational) group within a community; or a special pattern created for communication in business or trade between members of the groups speaking different languages: *the jargon of the theatre.* A VERNACULAR is the authentic natural pattern of speech, now usually on the colloquial level, used by persons indigenous to a certain community, large or small.

language laboratory, **1.** a place where languages are taught by tape-recorders and other devices. **2.** the method of teaching languages in this way.

Languedoc (*Fr.* läɴg dŏkʹ), *n.* **1.** a former province in S France. *Cap.*: Toulouse. **2.** an administrative region in S France comprising the departments of Gard, Lozère, Hérault, Aude, and Pyrénées-Orientales. 1,555,021 pop. (1962); 10,714 sq. mi. *Cap.*: Montpellier.

langue d'oc (*Fr.* läɴg dŏkʹ), **1.** the Romance language of medieval southern France. **2.** Provençal. [OF: *'oc'* language, i.e. the language in which *oc* yes was used. See LANGUE D'OÏL]

langue d'oïl (*Fr.* läɴg dŏ ēlʹ), the French of medieval northern France. [OF: *'oïl'* language (OF *oïl* yes). See LANGUE D'OC]

languet (lăngʹgwĕt), *n.* any of various small tongue-shaped parts, processes, or projections. [ME, t. F: m. *languette*, dim. of *langue*, g. L *lingua* tongue]

languette (lăngʹgwĕt), *n. Music.* a thin plate fastened to the mouth of certain organ pipes. [t. F]

languid (lăngʹgwĭd), *adj.* **1.** drooping or flagging from weakness or fatigue; faint. **2.** lacking in spirit or interest; indifferent. **3.** lacking in vigour or activity; slack; dull: *a languid market.* [t. L: s. *languidus*] —**lanʹguidly,** *adv.* —**lanʹguidness,** *n.* —**Syn. 1.** weak, feeble, weary, exhausted. —**Ant. 1.** vigorous. **3.** energetic.

languish (lăngʹgwĭsh), *v.i.* **1.** to become or be weak or feeble; droop or fade. **2.** to lose activity and vigour. **3.** to pine or suffer under any unfavourable conditions: *to languish ten years in a dungeon.* **4.** to pine with desire or longing for. **5.** to assume an expression of tender, sentimental melancholy. —*n.* **6.** the act of languishing. **7.** *Obs.* a languishing expression. [ME *languish(en)*, t. F: m. *languiss-*, s. *languir*, der. L *languēre*] —**lanʹguisher,** *n.*

languishing (lăngʹgwĭ shĭng), *adj.* **1.** becoming languid, in any way. **2.** lingering: *a languishing death.* **3.** expressive of languor; indicating tender, sentimental melancholy: *a languishing sigh.* —**lanʹguishingly,** *adv.*

languishment (lăngʹgwĭsh mənt), *n.* **1.** the act of languishing. **2.** languishing condition. **3.** a languishing expression.

languor (lăngʹgə), *n.* **1.** physical weakness or faintness. **2.** lack of energy; indolence. **3.** emotional softness or tenderness. **4.** lack of spirit. **5.** soothing or oppressive stillness. [t. L; r. ME *langur*, t. OF]

languorous (lăngʹgə rəs), *adj.* **1.** characterized by languor; languid. **2.** inducing languor. —**lanʹguorously,** *adv.*

langur (lŭng gōōəʹ), *n.* any of certain large, slender, long-limbed, long-tailed Asiatic monkeys of the subfamily *Colobinae*, as the entellus (the sacred monkey of India). [t. Hind. Cf. Skt *lāngūlin* having a tail]

laniard (lănʹyəd), *n.* lanyard.

laniary (lănʹĭ ə rĭ), *adj.* **1.** (of teeth) adapted for tearing. —*n.* **2.** a laniary or canine tooth. [t. L: m. s. *laniārius* of a butcher, der. *lanius* butcher]

lank (lăngk), *adj.* **1.** meagrely slim; lean; gaunt: *a tall, lank man.* **2.** (of plants, etc.) unduly long and slender. **3.** *Obs.*

(of a purse, etc.) only partially filled. **4.** (of hair) straight and limp. [OE *hlanc*, akin to OHG *hlanca* loin, side. Cf. FLANK] —**lank′ly,** *adv.* —**lank′ness,** *n.*

Lankester (lăng′kĭ stə), *n.* **Sir Edwin Ray,** 1847–1920, English zoologist.

lanky (lăng′kĭ), *adj.*, **-kier, -kiest.** somewhat lank; ungracefully tall and thin. —**lank′ily,** *adv.* —**lank′iness,** *n.*

lanner (lăn′ə), *n.* **1.** a falcon, *Falco biarmicus*, of southern Europe, northern Africa, and southern Asia. **2.** *Falconry.* the female of this bird. Cf. **lanneret.** [ME *lanere*, t. OF: m. *lanier* cowardly (bird)]

lanneret (lăn′ə rĕt′), *n.* *Falconry.* the male lanner, which is smaller than the female. [ME *lanret*, t. OF, F: m. *laneret*, der. *lanier* LANNER]

lanolin (lăn′ə lĭn), *n.* a fatty substance, extracted from wool, used in ointments. Also, **lanoline** (lăn′ə lĭn, -lēn′). [f. s. L *lāna* wool + -OL[2] + -IN[2]]

Lansbury (lănz′bə rĭ, -brĭ), *n.* **George,** 1859–1940, English politician: leader of the Labour Party 1932–35.

Lansing (lăn′sĭng), *n.* a town in the U.S., the capital of Michigan, in the S part. 107,807 (1960).

lansquenet (lăns′kĭ nĕt′), *n.* mercenary foot soldier, formerly used in the German and other Continental armies. Also, **landsknecht.** [t. F, t. G: m. *Landsknecht*, f. *Lands* land's + *Knecht* manservant. See KNIGHT]

lantana (lăn tā′nə, -tä′-), *n.* any plant of the verbenaceous, mostly tropical genus *Lantana*, including species much cultivated for their aromatic yellow or orange flowers, as *L. camara*. [NL]

lantern (lăn′tən), *n.* **1.** a transparent or translucent case for enclosing a light and protecting it from the wind, rain, etc. **2.** a magic lantern. **3.** the chamber at the top of a lighthouse, surrounding the light. **4.** *Archit.* **a.** a more or less open construction on the top of a tower or crowning a dome. **b.** any light decorative structure of relatively small size crowning a roof. **c.** a raised construction on the roof of a building, designed to admit light. **d.** an open-sided structure on a roof to let out smoke or to assist ventilation. [ME *lanterne*, t. F, t. L: m. *lanterna*, t. Gk: m. s. *lamptḗr* a light, torch, b. with L *lucerna* a lamp]

lantern-fish (lăn′tən fĭsh′), *n.* any small marine fish of the family *Myctophidae*, with rows of luminescent spots, living in the open sea and coming to the surface at night.

lantern-fly (lăn′tən flī′), *n.* any of certain tropical homopterous insects of the family *Fulgoridae*, formerly supposed to emit light.

lantern jaws, long, thin jaws (with sunken cheeks). —**lan′tern-jawed′,** *adj.*

lantern pinion, a wheel used like a pinion consisting essentially of two parallel discs or heads whose peripheries are connected by a series of bars which engage with the teeth of another wheel. Also, **lantern wheel.**

Lantern pinion

lantern slide, slide (def. 12).

lanthanide (lăn′thə nīd′), *n.* *Chem.* any of the closely related metallic elements with atomic numbers 57–71 (see **rare-earth elements,** def. 1). Also, **lanthanon.**

lanthanum (lăn′thə nəm), *n.* *Chem.* a rare-earth, trivalent, metallic element, allied to aluminium, found in certain rare minerals, as monazite. *Symbol:* La; *at. wt:* 138·91; *at. no.:* 57; *sp. gr.:* 6·15 at 20°C. [t. NL, der. Gk *lanthánein* escape notice]

lanthorn (lănt′hôn′, lăn′tən), *n.* *Obs.* lantern.

Lantsang (lăn′tsăng′), *n.* Chinese name of **Mekong.**

lanuginose (lə nyo͞o′jĭ nōs′), *adj.* **1.** covered with lanugo, or soft, downy hairs. **2.** of the nature of down; downy. Also, **lanuginous** (lə nyo͞o′jĭ nəs). [t. L: m. s. *lānūginōsus* woolly]

lanugo (lə nyo͞o′gō), *n.* *Biol.* a coat of delicate, downy hairs, esp. that with which the human foetus or a newborn infant is covered. [t. L: woolly substance]

lanyard (lăn′yəd), *n.* **1.** *Naut.* **a.** a short rope or cord for securing or holding something, esp. a rope rove through deadeyes to secure and tighten rigging. **b. knife lanyard,** a cord to which a knife is attached, worn by seamen around the neck. **2.** *Mil.* a cord with a small hook at one end, used in firing certain kinds of cannon. Also, **laniard.** [b. ME *lanyer* (t. F: m. *lanière* rope) and YARD[1]]

Laoag (lä wäg′), *n.* a seaport in the Philippine Islands, on NW Luzon. 40,800 (1963).

Laocoön (lā ŏk′ō ŏn′), *n.* *Gk Legend.* a priest of Apollo at Troy who warned the Trojans against the Trojan Horse and, with his two sons, was killed by serpents sent by Athena or Apollo.

Laodicea (lā′ō dĭ sĭə′), *n.* an ancient seaport of Syria, on the site of modern Latakia.

Laodicean (lā′ō dĭ sĭən′), *adj.* **1.** lukewarm; indifferent, esp. in religion (like the early Christians of Laodicea). —*n.* **2.** one who is lukewarm or indifferent, esp. in religion.

Laomedon (lā ŏm′ĭ dŏn′), *n.* *Gk Legend.* father of Priam, and founder and king of Troy.

Laon (*Fr.* läɴ), *n.* a town in N France, in Aisne department. 27,268 (1962).

Laos (louz, lous; *Fr.* là ōs′), *n.* a country in south-east Asia; formerly a part of French Indochina. 2,200,000 pop. (est. 1962); 91,500 sq. mi. *Cap.:* Vientiane. See map under **Indochina.** —**Laotian** (lou′shyən), *adj.*, *n.*

Lao-tse (lou′tsā′), *n.* born *c.* 604 B.C., Chinese philosopher, the supposed founder of Taoism. Also, **Lao-tsze, Lao-tzu.**

lap[1] (lăp), *n.* **1.** the part of the clothing that lies on the front portion of the body from the waist to the knees when one sits. **2.** this portion of the body, esp. as the place in or on which something is held or a child is nursed, cherished, etc. **3.** that in which anything rests or reposes, or is nurtured or fostered. **4.** an area of control, charge, or responsibility: *the future is in the lap of Fortune.* **5.** a laplike or hollow place, as a hollow among hills. **6.** the front part of a skirt, esp. as held up to contain something. **7.** a loose border or fold. **8.** a part of a garment which projects or extends over another. [ME *lappe*, OE *læppa*, c. D *lap*; akin to G *Lappen* lap]

lap[2] (lăp), *v.*, **lapped, lapping,** *n.* —*v.t.* **1.** to fold over or about something; wrap or wind round something. **2.** to enwrap in something; wrap up; clothe. **3.** to enfold or hold in or as in the lap; nurse, fondle, or cherish. **4.** to lay (something) partly over something underneath; lay (things) together, one partly over another. **5.** to lie partly over (something underneath). **6.** to get a lap or more ahead of (a competitor) in racing. **7.** to cut or polish (a gem, etc.) with a lap. **8.** to join, as by scarfing, to form a single piece with the same dimensions throughout. —*v.i.* **9.** to be folded over; fold or wind round something. **10.** *Obs.* to lie partly over or alongside something else; lie together, one partly over or beside another. **11.** to lie upon and extend beyond a thing. **12.** to extend beyond a limit. —*n.* **13.** the act of lapping. **14.** the amount of a material required to go round a thing once. **15.** a single round or circuit of the course in racing. **16.** the act of overlapping. **17.** the state of overlapping. **18.** the point or place of overlapping. **19.** an overlapping part. **20.** the extent or amount of overlapping. **21.** a rotating wheel or disc holding an abrasive or polishing powder on its surface, used for gems, cutlery, etc. [ME *lappe(n)*; appar. der. LAP[1]] —**lap′per,** *n.*

lap[3] (lăp), *v.*, **lapped, lapping,** *n.* —*v.t.* **1.** (of water) to wash against or beat upon (something) with a lapping sound. **2.** to take up (liquid) with the tongue; lick up (often fol. by *up*). **3.** to receive and accept avidly. —*v.i.* **4.** (of water) to wash with a sound as of licking up a liquid. **5.** to take up liquid with the tongue; lick up a liquid. —*n.* **6.** the act of lapping liquid. **7.** the lapping of water against something. **8.** the sound of this. **9.** something lapped up, as liquid food for dogs. [ME *lappe*, unexplained var. of *lape*, OE *lapian*, c. MLG *lapen*; akin to L *lambere*, Gk *láptein* lick, lap] —**lap′per,** *n.*

La Palma (*Sp.* là päl′mà), one of the Canary Islands, off the NW coast of Africa. 164,963 (est. 1963); 281 sq. mi. *Cap.:* Santa Cruz de la Palma.

laparotomy (lăp′ə rŏt′ə mĭ), *n.* **1.** a surgical incision through the flank or loin. **2.** any incision into any part of the abdominal wall, usually to establish the diagnosis. [f. *laparo-* (comb. form repr. Gk *lapárā* flank) + -TOMY]

La Paz (*Sp.* là päth′), a city in W Bolivia: seat of the government (Sucre is the nominal capital). 352,912 pop. (1962); ab. 12,000 ft above sea-level. See map under **Titicaca.**

lapboard (lăp′bôd′), *n.* a thin, flat board to be held on the lap for use as a table.

lap-dog (lăp′dŏg′), *n.* a small pet dog.

lapel (lə pĕl′), *n.* part of a garment folded back on the breast, esp. a continuation of a coat collar. [dim. of LAP[1]] —**lapelled′,** *adj.*

lapel microphone, a small microphone which can be attached to a speaker's lapel.

La Perouse (*Fr.* là pě ro͞oz′), **Jean Françoise de Galaup** (*Fr.* zhäɴ fräɴ swà′ də gà lō′), **Count de,** 1741–88?, French naval officer and explorer.

lapful (lăp′fo͝ol′), *n.*, *pl.* **-fuls.** as much as the lap can hold.

lapidary (lăp′ĭ də rĭ), *n.*, *pl.* **-ries,** *adj.* —*n.* **1.** a workman who cuts, polishes, and engraves precious stones. **2.** an old book on the lore of gems. **3.** an expert on gems. —*adj.* **4.** pertaining to the cutting or engraving of precious stones. **5.** of or pertaining to inscriptions cut in stone, or to any formal inscriptions. **6.** characteristic of or suitable for monumental inscriptions. [ME *lapidarie*, t. L: m. *lapidārius* of stones or stone (as n., a stonecutter)]

lapidate (lăp′ĭ dāt′), *v.t.*, **-dated, -dating.** *Rare.* **1.** to pelt with stones. **2.** to stone to death. [t. L: m. s. *lapidātus*, pp.] —**lap′ida′tion,** *n.*

lapidify (lə pĭd′ĭ fī′), *v.t., v.i.*, **-fied, -fying.** to turn to stone; petrify. —**lapid′ifica′tion,** *n.*

lapilli (lə pĭl′ī), *n.pl.*, *sing.* **-pillus** (-pĭl′əs). stony particles or fragments ejected from volcanoes, technically those of rounded shape and less than an inch in diameter. [t. L, dim. of *lapis* a stone]

lapis (lăp′ĭs), *n.*, *pl.* **lapides** (lăp′ĭ dēz′). *Latin.* a stone (used in Latin phrases).

lapis lazuli (lăp′ĭs lăz′yŏŏ lī′), **1.** a deep blue stone containing sodium, aluminium, calcium, sulphur, and silicon, and consisting of a mixture of several minerals. used chiefly for ornamental purposes. **2.** sky blue; azure. [t. ML: f. L *lapis* stone + ML *lazulī*, gen. of *lazulum* lapis lazuli (see AZURE)]

Lapith (lăp′ĭth), *n.*, *pl.* **-iths, -ithae.** *Gk Legend.* a mythical people of Thessaly, who defeated the centaurs in a war which arose at the wedding of Pirithoüs.

lap joint, a joint used where two boards intersect and one or both are cut out to allow for the intersection.

Laplace (*Fr.* là plàs′), *n.* **Pierre Simon** (*Fr.* pyĕr sē môɴ′), **Marquis de,** 1749–1827, French astronomer and mathematician.

Laplace equation, *Maths.* the second-order partial differential equation, $\nabla^2 u = 0$, where the ∇^2 is known as the **Laplace operator** or the **Laplacian,** and u is a function of the independent variable x, y, z. [named after P. S. LAPLACE]

Lapland (lăp′lănd′), *n.* a region inhabited by Lapps in N Norway, N Sweden, N Finland, and the Kola peninsula of the NW Soviet Union.

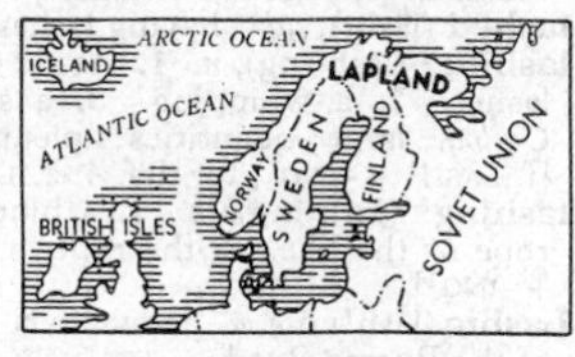

Lapland

La Plata (*Sp.* là plà′tà), **1.** a seaport in E Argentina. 330,310 (1960). **2.** See **Plata, Río de la.**

Lapp (lăp), *n.* **1.** Also, **Laplander** (lăp′lăn′də). one of a Finnic people of northern Norway, Sweden, and Finland, and adjacent regions, characterized by small stature and short, broad heads. **2.** Also, **Lap′pish.** any of the languages of the Lapps, closely related to Finnish. [t. Sw.]

lappet (lăp′ĭt), *n.* **1.** a small lap, flap, or loosely hanging part, esp. of a garment or headdress. **2.** a loose fold of flesh or the like. **3.** a lobe of the ear, etc. **4.** *Ornith.* a wattle or other fleshy process on a bird's head. [dim. of LAP[1]]

lappie (lä′pĭ), *n.* *S African.* a cloth or rag. [t. Afrikaans]

lapsable (lăp′sə bl), *adj.* liable to lapse.

lapse (lăps), *n., v.*, **lapsed, lapsing.** —*n.* **1.** a slip or slight error: *a lapse of memory.* **2.** a failure or miscarriage through some fault, slip, or negligence: *a lapse of justice.* **3.** a gliding or passing away, as of time. **4.** the act of falling, slipping, sliding, etc., slowly or as by degrees. **5.** *Law.* the termination of a right or privilege through neglect to exercise it or through failure of some contingency. **6.** a falling, or sinking to a lower grade, condition, or degree: *a lapse into savagery.* **7.** a moral fall, as from rectitude. **8.** a falling into disuse. —*v.i.* **9.** to pass slowly, silently, or by degrees. **10.** *Law.* **a.** to pass from one to another by lapse. **b.** to become void, as a legacy to one who predeceases the testator. **11.** (of insurance) to cease to be in force. **12.** to fall or sink to a lower grade or condition. **13.** to fall into disuse. **14.** to fall, slip, or glide, esp. downwards. **15.** to deviate from principles, accuracy, etc.; make a slip or error. **16.** to pass away, as time. [late ME, t. L: m. s. *lapsus*, n., a fall, slip] —**laps′er,** *n.*

lapse rate, *Meteorol.* the rate of decrease of atmospheric temperature with increase of elevation vertically above a given location.

lapstreak (lăp′strēk′), *adj.* **1.** (of a boat) built with each plank overlapping the one below it; clinker-built. —*n.* **2.** a lapstreak boat. [f. LAP[2], n. + STREAK]

Laptev Sea (*Russ.* làp′tĭf), an arm of the Arctic Ocean N of the Soviet Union in Asia, between Taimyr peninsula and the New Siberian Islands. Also, **Nordenskjöld Sea.**

Laputa (lə pyōō′tə), *n.* an imaginary flying island described in Swift's *Gulliver's Travels,* whose inhabitants were engaged in all sorts of ridiculous projects.

lapwing (lăp′wĭng′), *n.* a large Old World plover, *Vanellus vanellus,* with strikingly upcurved slender crest, erratic courtship flight and shrill cries; pewit; green plover. [ME *lapwinge,* OE *hlēapewince,* f. *hlēapan* leap + *-wince* (akin to OHG *winkan* waver, totter, and OE *wincian* wink)]

L'Aquila (*It.* là′kwē là), *n.* See **Aquila.**

lar (lä), *n.*, *pl.* **lares** (lēə′rēz), **lars** (läz). See **lares.**

Laramide (lă′rə mīd′), *adj.* *Geol.* of or pertaining to the major mountain-building episode of late Cretaceous and early Tertiary times in North America.

larboard (lä′bəd), *Naut. Obs.* —*n.* **1.** port[2] (def. 1). —*adj.* **2.** port[2] (defs 2 and 3). [early mod. E *larborde* (assimilated to STARBOARD); r. ME *laddeborde,* f. *ladde* (orig. unknown) + *borde,* OE *bord* ship's side]

larcenous (lä′sĭ nəs), *adj.* **1.** of, like, or of the nature of larceny. **2.** guilty of larceny. —**lar′cenously,** *adv.*

larceny (lä′sĭ nĭ), *n.*, *pl.* **-nies.** *Law.* the wrongful taking and carrying away of the personal goods of another with intent permanently to deprive him thereof. [late ME, appar. f. m. AF *larcin* (g. L *latrōcinium* robbery) + -Y[3]]

larch (läch), *n.* **1.** any of the coniferous trees constituting the pinaceous genus *Larix,* characterized by a tough, durable wood. **2.** the wood of such a tree. [t. G: m. *Lärche,* ult. t. L: m. s. *larix*]

lard (läd), *n.* **1.** rendered pig fat, esp. the internal fat of the abdomen. —*v.t.* **2.** to apply lard or grease to. **3.** to prepare or enrich (lean meat, etc.) with pork or bacon, esp. with lardoons. **4.** to intersperse with something for improvement or ornamentation. [ME, t. OF: fat of pork, bacon, g. L *lār(i)dum* fat of pork] —**lard′like′,** *adj.* —**lard′y,** *adj.*

lardaceous (lä dā′shəs), *adj.* lardlike; fatty.

larder (lä′də), *n.* a room or place where food is kept; a pantry. [ME, t. OF: m. *lardier,* der. *lard* LARD]

Lardner (läd′nə), *n.* **Ring** (*Ringgold Wilmer Lardner*), 1885–1933, U.S. writer of short stories.

lardoons (lä dōōnz′), *n.pl.* strips of larding fat (pork or bacon) of varying lengths and thickness, threaded into meat, poultry and game. Also, **lardons** (lä′dnz).

lardy cake (lä′dĭ), a rich, sweet, breadlike cake made with bread dough, lard, sugar, and dried fruit.

lardy-dah (lä′dĭ dä′), *adj.* *Slang.* affected; affecting superiority. Also, **lardy-dardy, la-di-da.**

lares (lä′rēz), *n.*, *pl. of* **lar.** *Rom. Myth.* household or other tutelary gods or spirits. [L]

lares and penates (pĕ nä′tēz), **1.** household gods. See **lares, penates. 2.** the cherished possessions of a family or household.

large (läj), *adj.*, **larger, largest,** *n., adv.* —*adj.* **1.** being of more than common size, amount, or number. **2.** of great scope or range; extensive or broad: *large powers.* **3.** on a great scale: *a large producer.* **4.** grand or pompous. **5.** *Obs.* generous. **6.** *Obs.* unrestrained by decorum. **7.** *Obs.* (of the wind) free; fair. —*n.* **8.** *Music.* the longest note in medieval music; equal to eight semibreves: ⟦note⟧. **9.** *Obs.* freedom; unrestraint. **10. at large, a.** at liberty; free from restraint or confinement: *the murderer is at large.* **b.** at length; to a considerable length: *to discourse at large on a subject.* **c.** as a whole; in general: *the country at large.* **d.** *U.S.* representing the whole of a state, district, or body, not one division or part of it: *a Congressman at large.* **11. in large,** or **in the large,** on a large scale: *viewed in the large.* —*adv.* **12.** *Naut.* before the wind; with the wind free or on the quarter, or in such a direction that all sails will draw. [ME, t. OF, g. L *larga,* fem. of *largus* abundant, liberal] —**large′ness,** *n.* —**Syn. 1.** big, huge, enormous, immense, gigantic, colossal; massive; vast. See **great.** —**Ant. 1.** small.

large calorie. See **calorie** (def. 1b).

large-hearted (läj′hä′tĭd), *adj.* having or showing generosity. —**large′-heart′edness,** *n.*

largely (läj′lĭ), *adv.* **1.** to a great extent; in great part. **2.** in great quantity; much.

large-minded (läj′mīn′dĭd), *adj.* having or showing tolerant views or liberal ideas. —**large′-mind′edness,** *n.*

large-scale (läj′skāl′), *adj.* **1.** very extensive; of great scope. **2.** made to a large scale: *a large-scale map.*

largess (lä jĕs′), *n.* **1.** generous bestowal of gifts. **2.** the gifts or a gift (as of money) so bestowed. **3.** *Archaic.* generosity. Also, **largesse.** [ME *larges,* t. OF: m. *largesse,* der. *large* LARGE]

larghetto (lä gĕt′ō; *It.* lär gĕt′tō), *adj., n., pl.* **-ghettos.** *Music.* —*adj.* **1.** somewhat slow; not so slow as largo, but usually slower than andante. —*n.* **2.** a larghetto movement. [t. It., dim. of *largo* LARGO]

largish (lä′jĭsh), *adj.* rather large.

largo (lä′gō), *adj., n., pl.* **-gos.** *Music.* —*adj.* **1.** slow; in a broad, dignified style. —*n.* **2.** a largo movement. [t. It., g. L *largus* large]

lariat (lă′rĭ ət), *n.* *U.S.* **1.** a long, noosed rope for catching horses, cattle, etc.; a lasso. **2.** a rope or cord for picketing animals while grazing. [t. Sp.: m. *la reata* the rope]

larine (lă′rīn, -rĭn), *adj.* **1.** of the nature of or resembling a gull. **2.** of or pertaining to the suborder *Lari,* family

Laridae, or subfamily *Larinae*, containing the gulls. [t. NL: m. s. *Larinae*, der. LL *larus*, t. Gk: m. *láros* kind of seabird]

Larissa (lə rĭs′ə; *Gk* lä′rē sȧ), *n.* a town in Greece, in E Thessaly. 55,391 (1961). See map under **Thessaly.** Also, **Larisa.**

lark[1] (läk), *n.* **1.** any of numerous oscinine singing birds, mostly of the Old World, of the family *Alaudidae*, characterized by an unusually long, straight hind claw, esp. the skylark, *Alauda arvensis.* **2.** any of various similar birds of other families, as the titlark (*Motacillidae*) of America and Europe. [ME *larke*, OE *lāwerce*, c. G *Lerche*]

lark[2] (läk), *Colloq.* —*n.* **1.** a merry or hilarious adventure; prank. **2.** a frolic. —*v.i.* **3.** to play pranks; have fun. Also, **skylark.** [orig. uncert.] —**lark′er,** *n.* —**larksome** (läk′səm), *adj.*

Larkhall (läk′hôl′), *n.* a town in Scotland, in Lanarkshire. 14,055 (1961).

larkspur (läk′spû′), *n. Bot.* any plant of the genus *Delphinium*, so called from the spur-shaped formation of the calyx and petals. [f. LARK[1] + SPUR]

Larmor precession (lä′mô), *Physics.* the precession of a charged particle in a magnetic field. [named after Sir Joseph *Larmor*, 1857–1947, English physicist]

Larnaca (lä′nə kə), *n.* a seaport in SE Cyprus. 20,000 (est. 1964).

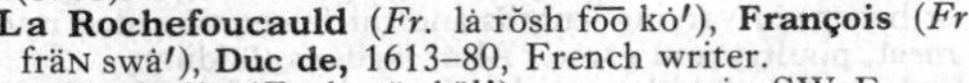

Cross-section of a larkspur flower, *Delphinium consolida*

Larne (län), *n.* a seaport in Northern Ireland, in county Antrim. 16,341 (1961).

La Rochefoucauld (*Fr.* lȧ rŏsh fo͞o kō′), **François** (*Fr.* fräN swȧ′), **Duc de,** 1613–80, French writer.

La Rochelle (*Fr.* lȧ rŏ shĕl′), a seaport in SW France, the capital of Charente-Maritime department, on the Bay of Biscay: besieged as a Huguenot stronghold, 1627–1628. 66,190 (1962).

Larousse (*Fr.* lȧ ro͞os′), *n.* **Pierre Athanase** (*Fr.* pyĕr ȧ tȧ näz′), 1817–75, French grammarian, lexicographer, and encyclopedist.

larrikin (lă′rĭ kĭn), *Chiefly Australian Slang.* —*n.* **1.** a street rowdy; a hoodlum. —*adj.* **2.** disorderly; rowdy. [? f. *Larry* (hypocoristic var. of *Lawrence*) + -KIN] —**lar′rikinism,** *n.*

larrup (lă′rəp), *v.t.*, **-ruped, -ruping.** *Colloq.* to beat; thrash. [cf. D *larpen* thrash] —**lar′ruper,** *n.*

larum (lă′rəm), *n. Archaic.* alarum.

larva (lä′və), *n.*, *pl.* **-vae** (-vē). **1.** *Entomol.* the young of any insect which undergoes metamorphosis. **2.** any animal in an analogous immature form. **3.** the young of any invertebrate animal. [t. NL, special use of L *larva* ghost, spectre, skeleton, mask]

larval (lä′vəl), *adj.* of or in the form of a larva.

larvicide (lä′vĭ sīd′), *n.* an agent for killing larvae.

laryngeal (lă′rĭn jē′əl), *adj.* of or pertaining to the larynx. Also, **laryngal** (lə rĭng′gl). [f. s. NL *laryngeus* (der. *larynges*, pl. of *larynx* LARYNX) + -AL[1]]

laryngitis (lă′rĭn jī′tĭs), *n. Pathol.* inflammation of the larynx. [t. NL; f. LARYNG(O)- + -ITIS] —**laryngitic** (lă′rĭn jĭt′ĭk), *adj.*

laryngo-, a combining form of **larynx.** Also, before vowels, **laryng-.**

laryngoscope (lə rĭng′gə skōp′), *n. Med.* an apparatus for examining the larynx. —**laryngoscopic** (lə rĭng′gə skŏp′ĭk), *adj.*

larynx (lă′rĭngks), *n.*, *pl.* **larynges** (lə rĭn′jēz), **larynxes. 1.** *Anat.* the cavity at the upper end of the human trachea or windpipe containing the vocal cords and acting as the organ of voice. **2.** *Zool.* **a.** a similar vocal organ in other mammals, etc. **b.** a corresponding structure in other animals. [t. NL, t. Gk]

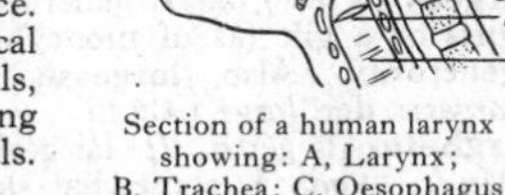

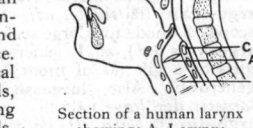

Section of a human larynx showing: A, Larynx; B, Trachea; C, Oesophagus

lasagne (lə zăn′yĭ), *n.* **1.** a form of pasta cut into long ribbons, ½ in. wide. **2.** any of several dishes made with this.

La Salle (*Fr.* lȧ sȧl′), **René Robert Cavelier** (*Fr.* rə nė rŏ bĕr kȧ və lyė′), **Sieur de,** 1643–87, French explorer.

lascar (lăs′kə), *n.* an East Indian sailor. [t. Pg.: m. *laschar*, short for *lasquarin* soldier, t. Hind. (Pers.): m. *lashkari*, adj., military (as n., soldier), der. *lashkar* army, camp]

Lascaux cave (*Fr.* lȧs kō′), a cave near Lascaux in central France, containing Aurignacian wall paintings.

lascivious (lə sĭv′ĭ əs), *adj.* **1.** inclined to lust; wanton or lewd. **2.** inciting to lust or wantonness. [t. LL: m. s. *lascīviōsus*, der. L *lascīvia* wantonness] —**lasciv′iously,** *adv.* —**lasciv′iousness,** *n.*

laser (lā′zə), *Physics.* —*n.* **1.** a device for producing a coherent, monochromatic, high-intensity beam of radiation of a frequency within, or near to, the range of visible light; an optical maser. —*v.t.*, *v.i.* **2.** to operate as a laser. [short for *l*(*ight*) *a*(*mplification by*) *s*(*timulated*) *e*(*mission of*) *r*(*adiation*)]

lash[1] (lăsh), *n.* **1.** the flexible part of a whip; the piece of cord or the like forming the extremity of a whip. **2.** a swift stroke or blow, with a whip, etc., as a punishment: *sentenced to fifty lashes.* **3.** a sharp stroke given to the feelings, etc., as of censure or satire. **4.** a swift dashing or sweeping movement; a switch: *a lash of an animal's tail.* **5.** a violent beating or impact, as of waves, rain, etc., against something. **6.** an eyelash. —*v.t.* **7.** to strike or beat, now usually with a whip or something slender and flexible. **8.** to beat violently or sharply against. **9.** to drive by strokes of a whip or the like. **10.** to dash, fling, or switch suddenly and swiftly. **11.** to assail severely with words, as by censure or satire. —*v.i.* **12.** to strike vigorously at, as with a weapon, whip, or the like (often fol. by *out*). **13.** to move suddenly and swiftly; rush, dash, or flash. **14.** to burst into violent action or speech (fol. by *out*). **15.** to spend money freely (fol. by *out*). [ME *lassh*; orig. obscure] —**lash′er,** *n.*

lash[2] (lăsh), *v.t.* to bind or fasten with a rope, cord, or the like. [special use of LASH[1]] —**lash′er,** *n.*

lashed (lăsht), *adj.* having lashes, or eyelashes.

lashing[1] (lăsh′ĭng), *n.* **1.** the act of one who or that which lashes. **2.** a whipping. **3.** a severe scolding. **4.** (*pl.*) *Colloq.* large quantities; plenty (usually fol. by *of*). [f. LASH[1] + -ING[1]; for def. 4 cf. LASH[1] (def. 15)]

lashing[2] (lăsh′ĭng), *n.* **1.** a binding or fastening with a rope or the like. **2.** the rope or the like used. [f. LASH[2] + -ING[1]]

Lashio (lăsh′ĭ ō′), *n.* a town in N Burma: the SW terminus of the Burma Road.

Lashkar (lŭsh′kə), *n.* a part of a suburb of Gwalior city in N India.

Laski (lăs′kĭ), *n.* **Harold Joseph,** 1893–1950, English socialist leader and writer.

Las Palmas (lăs päl′məs; *Sp.* läs päl′mȧs), a seaport in the Canary Islands, on NE Gran Canaria. 214,854 (1965).

La Spezia (*It.* lȧ spĕt′tsyȧ), a seaport in Italy, in Liguria, on the Ligurian Sea: naval base. 129,383 (1966).

lass (lăs), *n.* **1.** a girl or young woman. **2.** any woman. **3.** a female sweetheart. [ME *lasse*; orig. uncert.]

Lassa (lä′sə), *n.* Lhasa.

Lassalle (*Ger.* lȧ sȧl′), *n.* **Ferdinand** (*Ger.* fĕr′dĭ nȧnt), 1825–64, German socialist and writer.

lassie (lăs′ĭ), *n.* a girl; lass.

lassitude (lăs′ĭ tyo͞od′), *n.* weariness of body or mind from strain, oppressive climate, etc.; languor. [t. L: m. *lassitūdo* weariness]

lasso (lăs′ō; *older* lă so͞o′), *n.*, *pl.* **-sos, -soes,** *v.*, **-soed, -soing.** —*n.* **1.** a long rope or line of hide or other material, with a running noose at one end, used for catching horses, cattle, etc. —*v.t.* **2.** to catch with a lasso. [t. Sp.: m. *lazo*, g. L *laqueus* noose, snare. Cf. LACE] —**las′soer,** *n.*

Lassus (lăs′əs), *n.* **Orlando de** (ô lăn′dō də), 1535–94, Flemish composer.

last[1] (läst), *adj.* **1.** occurring or coming latest, or after all others, as in time, order, or place: *the last line on the page.* **2.** latest; next before the present; most recent: *last week.* **3.** being the only remaining: *one's last penny.* **4.** final: *in his last hours.* **5.** conclusive: *the last word in an argument.* **6.** utmost; extreme. **7.** coming after all others in importance. **8.** coming after all others in suitability or likelihood. **9.** *Eccles.* extreme or final, as to a dying person (applied to the sacraments of penance, viaticum, and extreme unction collectively). **10. on one's last legs,** on the verge of collapse. —*adv.* **11.** after all others. **12.** on the most recent occasion. **13.** in the end; finally; in conclusion. —*n.* **14.** that which is last. **15.** *Colloq.* the final mention or appearance: *to see the last of that woman.* **16.** the end or conclusion. **17. at (long) last,** after much has intervened. **18. breathe one's last,** to die. [ME *last, latst,* syncopated var. of *latest*, OE *latost, lætest*, superl. of *læt* late]

—**Syn. 1.** LAST, FINAL, ULTIMATE refer to what comes as an ending. That which is LAST comes or stands after all others in a stated series or succession; LAST may refer to objects or activities: *a seat in the last row.* That which is FINAL comes at the end, or serves to end or terminate, admitting of nothing further; FINAL is rarely used of objects: *to make a final attempt.* That which is ULTIMATE (literally, most remote) is the last that can be reached, as in progression or regression, experience, or a course of investigation: *ultimate truths.*

last[2] (läst), *v.i.* **1.** to go on, or continue in progress, existence or life; endure: *so long as the world lasts.* **2.** to continue unexpended or unexhausted; be enough (*for*): *while our money lasts.* **3.** to continue in force, vigour, effectiveness, etc.: *to last in a race.* **4.** to continue to remain in a good condition. [ME *lasten*, OE *lǣstan* follow, perform, continue, last (der. *lāst* track), c. OHG *leisten* follow. See LAST[3]] —**last′er,** *n.* —**Syn. 1.** See **continue.**

last[3] (läst), *n.* **1.** a model of the human foot, of wood or other material, on which boots or shoes are shaped, as in the making. —*v.t.* **2.** to shape on or fit to a last. [ME; OE *lǣste* (der. *lāst* sole of foot, track), c. G *Leisten* last] —**last′er,** *n.*

last[4] (läst), *n.* any of various large units of weight or capacity, varying in amount in different localities and for different commodities, often equivalent to 4000 lbs. [ME; OE *hlæst*, c. G *Last* load; akin to LADE]

last-ditch (läst′dĭch′), *adj.* **1.** made in or as a final and desperate effort. **2.** fought with desperate and uncompromising spirit.

lasting (läs′tĭng), *adj.* **1.** that lasts; enduring; permanent; durable. —*n.* **2.** (*pl.*) a strong, durable, closely woven fabric, used for the uppers of shoes, for covering buttons, etc. —**last′ingly,** *adv.* —**last′ingness,** *n.*

Last Judgement. See **judgement** (def. 7).

lastly (läst′lĭ), *adv.* finally, in conclusion, or in the last place.

last-minute (läst′mĭn′ĭt), *adj.* made or occurring at the last possible opportunity.

last post, *Mil.* **1.** a signal on a bugle giving notice to retire for the night. **2.** a similar bugle call sounded at military funerals.

Last Supper, the supper of Jesus and His apostles on the eve of His crucifixion, at which He instituted the sacrament of the Lord's Supper.

last trump, the angelic trumpet call which wakens the dead before the Last Judgement.

Las Vegas (läs vā′gəs), a town in SE Nevada. 64,405 (1960).

lat (lăt), *n., pl.* **lats** (lăts), **latu** (lăt′o͞o). a former monetary unit of Latvia. [abstracted from *Lat*(*vija*) Latvia]

Lat., Latin.

lat., latitude.

Latakia (lăt′ə kē′ə), *n.* **1.** a seaport in NW Syria. 68,498 (1962). Ancient, **Laodicea. 2.** a variety of Turkish tobacco.

latch (lăch), *n.* **1.** a device for holding a door, gate, or the like closed, consisting basically of a bar falling or sliding into a catch, groove, hole, etc. —*v.t.* **2.** to close or fasten with a latch. —*v.i.* **3.** to fasten tightly so that the latch is in position. **4. latch on to,** *Colloq.* **a.** to fasten or attach (oneself) to. **b.** to understand; comprehend. [ME *lacche*, OE *læccan* take hold of, catch, take]

latchet (lăch′ĭt), *n. Archaic.* a strap or lace for fastening a shoe. [ME *lachet*, t. OF, d. var. of *lacet*, dim. of *laz* LACE]

latchkey (lăch′kē′), *n.* a key for drawing back or releasing a latch, esp. on an outer door.

latchstring (lăch′strĭng′), *n.* a string passed through a hole in a door, for raising the latch from the outside.

late (lāt), *adj.*, **later** or **latter, latest** or **last,** *adv.*, **later, latest.** —*adj.* **1.** occurring, coming, or being after the usual or proper time: *late frosts.* **2.** continued until after the usual time or hour; protracted: *a late session.* **3.** far advanced in time: *a late hour.* **4.** belonging to time just before the present: *the latest fashions.* **5.** immediately preceding that which now exists: *his late residence.* **6.** recently deceased: *the late president.* **7.** occurring at an advanced stage in life: *a late marriage.* **8.** belonging to an advanced period or stage in the history or development of something: *Late Latin.* **9. of late,** recently. —*adv.* **10.** after the usual or proper time, or after delay: *to come late.* **11.** until after the usual time or hour; until a late hour at night: *to work late.* **12.** at or to an advanced time, period, or stage. **13.** recently but no longer. [ME; OE *læt* slow, late, c. G *lass* slothful] —**late′ness,** *n.* —**Syn. 1.** tardy; slow, dilatory; delayed, belated. **4.** See **modern.** —**Ant. 1.** early.

late blight, a serious disease of potatoes caused by the fungus *Phytophthora infestans.*

latecomer (lāt′kŭm′ə), *n.* one who arrives late: *latecomers will be excluded from the first act.*

late cut, *Cricket.* a stroke that sends the ball well behind point, in the direction of the slips.

lated (lā′tĭd), *adj. Poetic.* belated.

lateen (lə tēn′), *adj.* pertaining to or having a lateen sail or sails. [t. F: m. (*voile*) *latine* Latin (sail)]

lateen-rigged (lə tēn′rĭgd′), *adj.* having lateen sails.

lateen sail, a triangular sail extended by a long tapering yard, slung at about one quarter the distance from the lower end, which is brought down at the tack: used in xebecs, feluccas, etc., on the Mediterranean.

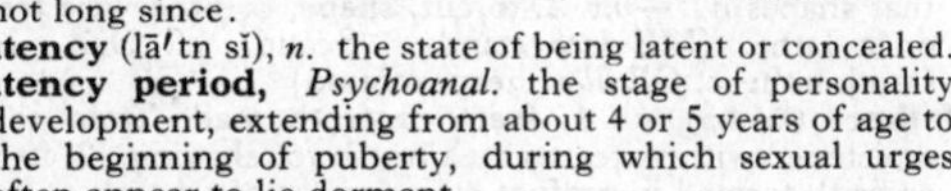
Lateen sail

Late Greek, the Greek of the early Byzantine Empire and of patristic literature, from about A.D. 300 to 700.

Late Latin, the Latin of the late Western Roman Empire and of patristic literature, from about A.D. 300 to 700.

lately (lāt′lĭ), *adv.* of late; recently; not long since.

latency (lā′tn sĭ), *n.* the state of being latent or concealed.

latency period, *Psychoanal.* the stage of personality development, extending from about 4 or 5 years of age to the beginning of puberty, during which sexual urges often appear to lie dormant.

La Tène (*Fr.* lȧ tĕn′), of or pertaining to the late Iron Age culture in central Europe of about 5th to 1st century B.C., which directly followed the Hallstattian culture. [named after *La Tène*, a shallow area at the E end of Lake Neuchâtel, Switzerland, where remains of the culture were found]

latent (lā′tnt), *adj.* **1.** hidden; concealed; present, but not visible or apparent: *latent ability.* **2.** *Pathol.* (of an infectious agent) remaining in a resting or hidden phase; dormant. **3.** *Psychol.* below the surface, but potentially able to achieve expression. **4.** *Bot.* (of buds which are not externally manifest) dormant or undeveloped. [t. L: s. *latens*, ppr., lying hid] —**la′tently,** *adv.*

—**Syn. 1.** LATENT, POTENTIAL refer to powers or possibilities existing but hidden or not yet realized. LATENT emphasizes the hidden character or the dormancy of what is named: *latent qualities, defects, diseases.* That which is POTENTIAL exists in an as yet undeveloped state, but is thought of as capable of coming into full being or activity at some future time: *potential genius, tragedy.* POTENTIAL may be applied also to tangibles: *high-tension wires are a potential source of danger.* —**Ant. 1.** actual, active, effectual.

latent heat, *Physics.* **1.** (of fusion) the heat required to effect the change of state from solid to liquid of 1 gram of a substance at its melting point. **2.** (of vaporization) the heat required to effect the change of state from liquid to gas of 1 gram of a substance at its boiling point.

latent period, 1. *Pathol.* the period that elapses before the presence of a disease is manifested by symptoms. **2.** *Physiol.* the lag between stimulus and reaction.

lateral (lăt′ə rəl), *adj.* **1.** of or pertaining to the side; situated at, proceeding from, or directed to a side: *a lateral view.* **2.** *Phonet.* with the airstream escaping from the mouth on one or both sides of an obstruction formed by the tongue. —*n.* **3.** a lateral part or extension, as a branch or shoot. **4.** *Mining.* a small drift off to the side of a principal one. **5.** *Phonet.* a lateral sound. **6.** a small irrigation channel distributing water from the main canal. [t. L: s. *laterālis*, der. *latus* side] —**lat′erally,** *adv.*

laterality (lăt′ə răl′ĭ tĭ), *n.* the dominance by one side of the body; physical one-sidedness, either left or right.

lateral line, *Ichthyol.* the line of mucous pores, with sensory function, along the sides of fishes.

Lateran Basilica, the church of St John Lateran; the church of the pope as bishop of Rome.

Lateran Council, any of several general councils of the Roman Catholic Church, held in Rome in 1123, 1139, 1179, 1215 and 1512–17, to define points of doctrine.

Lateran Palace, a palace in Rome, the papal residence for nearly a thousand years; rebuilt in 1586 and now used as a museum.

laterite (lăt′ə rīt′), *n. Geol.* **1.** a reddish ferruginous soil formed in tropical regions by the decomposition of the underlying rocks. **2.** a similar soil formed of materials transported by water. **3.** any soil produced by the decomposition of the rocks beneath it. [f. L *later* brick + -ITE[1]] —**lateritic** (lăt′ə rĭt′ĭk), *adj.*

lateritious (lăt′ə rĭsh′əs), *adj.* of the colour of laterite: brick red. Also, **latericeous.**

latescent (lə tĕs′ənt), *adj.* becoming latent. [t. L: s. *latescens*, ppr., hiding oneself] —**lates′cence,** *n.*

latest (lā′tĭst), *adj.* (*superlative of* **late**). **1.** after all others. **2.** current; most up to date. **3. at the latest,** not any later than (a particular time). **4. the latest,** the most recent disclosure, gossip, fashion, advance, development, etc.

latex (lā′tĕks), *n., pl.* **latices** (lăt′ĭ sēz′), **latexes** (lā′tĕk′sĭz). **1.** *Bot.* a milky liquid in certain plants, as milkweeds, euphorbias, poppies, the plants yielding indiarubber, etc., which coagulates on exposure to the air. **2.** any emulsion of particles of synthetic rubber or plastic in water. [t. L: liquid]

lath (läth), *n., pl.* **laths** (läthz, läths), *v.* —*n.* **1.** a thin, narrow strip of wood used with others like it to form a groundwork for supporting the slates or other covering of a roof or the plastering of a wall or ceiling, to construct latticework, and for other purposes. **2.** such strips collectively. **3.** work consisting of such strips. **4.** any material used as a substitute for laths, such as metal lathing or patent lathing. **5.** a thin, narrow, flat piece of wood used for any purpose. —*v.t.* **6.** to cover or line with laths. [ME *la(th)the*, r. ME *latt*, OE *lætt*, c. D *lat*] —**lath′like′,** *adj.*

lathe (lāth), *n., v.,* **lathed, lathing.** —*n.* **1.** a machine for use in working metal, wood, etc., which holds the material and rotates it about a horizontal axis against a tool that shapes it. —*v.t.* **2.** to cut, shape, or otherwise treat on a lathe. [ME *lath* stand, t. Scand.; cf. Dan. *-lad* stand, lathe, c. OE *hlæd* heap, mound]

lather[1] (lă′thə), *n.* **1.** foam or froth made from soap moistened with water, as by a brush for shaving. **2.** foam or froth formed in profuse sweating, as of a horse. —*v.i.* **3.** to form a lather, as soap. **4.** to become covered with lather, as a horse. —*v.t.* **5.** to apply lather to; cover with lather. **6.** *Colloq.* to beat or flog. [ME, OE *lēathor*, c. Icel. *laudhr* washing soda, foam] —**lath′erer,** *n.*

lather[2] (lă′thə), *n.* a workman who puts up laths. [f. LATH, V. + -ER[1]]

lathery (lă′thə rĭ), *adj.* consisting of, covered with, or capable of producing lather.

lathing (lă′thĭng), *n.* **1.** the act or process of applying laths to a wall or the like. **2.** work consisting of laths; laths collectively. Also, **lathwork** (läth′wûk′).

lathy (lă′thĭ), *adj.* lathlike; long and thin.

latices (lăt′ĭ sēz′), *n.* a pl. of **latex.**

laticiferous (lăt′ĭ sĭf′ə rəs), *adj. Bot.* bearing or containing latex. [f. s. L *latex* a liquid + -(I)FEROUS]

latifundium (lăt′ĭ fŭn′dĭ əm), *n., pl.* **-dia** (-dĭ ə). *Rom. Hist.* a great estate. [t. L: f. *lāti-* (comb. form of *lātus* broad) + s. *fundus* estate + *-ium* -IUM]

Latimer (lăt′ĭ mə), *n.* **Hugh,** *c.* 1490–1555, English Protestant Reformation bishop, reformer, and martyr.

Latin (lăt′ĭn), *n.* **1.** the Italic language spoken in ancient Rome, fixed in 2nd-1st century B.C., becoming the official language of the Empire. **2.** one of the forms of literary Latin, as Medieval Latin, Late Latin, Biblical Latin, Liturgical Latin, or of non-classical Latin, as Vulgar Latin. **3.** a native or inhabitant of Latium; an ancient Roman. **4.** a member of any Latin race. **5.** a Roman Catholic. —*adj.* **6.** denoting or pertaining to those peoples (the Italians, French, Spanish, Portuguese, Rumanians, etc.) using languages derived from that of ancient Rome. **7.** denoting or pertaining to the Western Church (which from early times down to the Reformation everywhere used Latin as its official language) or the Roman Catholic Church. **8.** of or pertaining to Latium or its inhabitants. **9.** Roman (def. 4). **10.** Latin-American. [ME and OE, t. L: s. *Latīnus*]

Latina (*It.* lä tē′nä), *n.* See **Littoria.**

Latin America, part of the American continents south of the United States, in which Romance languages are officially spoken.

Latin-American (lăt′ĭn ə mĕ′rĭ kən), *adj.* of or pertaining to Latin America.

Latin Church, the Roman Catholic Church.

Latin cross, an upright bar crossed near the top by a shorter transverse piece. See illus. under **cross.**

Latinism (lăt′ĭ nĭz′əm), *n.* a mode of expression imitating Latin.

Latinist (lăt′ĭ nĭst), *n.* a specialist in Latin.

Latinity (lə tĭn′ĭ tĭ), *n.* **1.** use of the Latin language. **2.** Latin style or idiom.

Latinize (lăt′ĭ nīz′), *v.,* **-nized, -nizing.** —*v.t.* **1.** to cause to conform to the customs, etc., of the Latins or Latin Church. **2.** to intermix with Latin elements. **3.** to translate into Latin. —*v.i.* **4.** to use words and phrases from Latin: *he Latinizes frequently in his poetry.* Also, **Latinise.** —**Lat′iniza′tion,** *n.*

Latin Quarter, the quarter of Paris on the south side of the Seine, frequented for centuries by students and artists. [t. F: trans. of *Quartier Latin*]

latish (lā′tĭsh), *adj.* somewhat late.

latitude (lăt′ĭ tyōōd′), *n.* **1.** *Geog.* **a.** the angular distance north or south from the equator of a point on the earth's surface, measured on the meridian of the point. **b.** a place or region as marked by this distance. **2.** freedom from narrow restrictions; permitted freedom of action, opinion, etc. **3.** *Astron.* the angular distance of a heavenly body from the ecliptic (**celestial latitude**), or from the galactic plane (**galactic latitude**). **4.** *Photog.* the range of exposures over which proportional representation of subject brightness is obtained. [ME, t. L: m. *lātitūdo* breadth] —**Syn. 2.** See **range.**

latitudinal (lăt′ĭ tyōō′dĭ nəl), *adj.* pertaining to latitude. —**lat′itu′dinally,** *adv.*

latitudinarian (lăt′ĭ tyōō′dĭ nĕə′rĭ ən), *adj.* **1.** allowing, or characterized by, latitude in opinion or conduct, esp. in religious views. —*n.* **2.** one who is latitudinarian in opinion or conduct. **3.** *Anglican Ch.* one of those divines in the 17th century who maintained the wisdom of the episcopal form of government and ritual, but denied that they possess divine origin and authority. —**lat′itu′dinar′ianism,** *n.*

latitudinous (lăt′ĭ tyōō′dĭ nəs), *adj.* broad or wide in interpretation, ideas or interests.

Latium (lā′shyəm), *n.* **1.** an ancient country in Italy, SE of Rome. **2.** Italian, **Lazio.** a region in central Italy. 3,922,783 pop. (1961); 6634 sq. mi. *Cap.:* Rome.

Latona (lə tō′nə), *n. Class. Myth.* the Roman name of the Greek goddess Leto, mother of Apollo and Diana.

La Tour (*Fr.* lä tōōr′), **George de,** 1593–1652, French painter.

La Trappe (*Fr.* lä träp′), an abbey in Normandy, France, at which the Trappist order was founded.

latria (lə trī′ə), *n. Rom. Cath. Theol.* that supreme worship which may be offered to God only. Cf. **dulia, hyperdulia.** [t. LL, t. Gk: m. *latreía* service, worship]

latrine (lə trēn′), *n.* a lavatory, esp. in a camp, barracks, a factory, or the like. [t. F, t. L: m. *lātrīna*]

Latrobe (lə trōb′), *n.* **Benjamin,** 1764–1820, American architect.

latten (lăt′n), *n.* **1.** a brasslike alloy, commonly made in thin sheets, formerly much used for church utensils. **2.** tinplate. **3.** any metal in thin sheets. [ME *latoun*, t. OF: m. *laton*, der. *latte.* See LATTICE]

latter (lăt′ə), *adj.* **1.** being the second mentioned of two (opposed to *former*): *I prefer the latter proposition to the former.* **2.** more advanced in time; later: *in these latter days of human progress.* **3.** nearer, or comparatively near, to the end or close: *the latter years of one's life.* **4.** *Poetic.* being the concluding part of. [ME *latt(e)re*, OE *lætra*, compar. of *læt* late]

latter-day (lăt′ə dā′), *adj.* **1.** of a latter or more advanced day or period, or modern: *latter-day problems.* **2.** of the concluding or final days of the world.

Latter-day Saint, a Mormon.

latterly (lăt′ə lĭ), *adv.* **1.** of late; lately. **2.** in the latter or concluding part of a period.

lattermost (lăt′ə mōst′), *adj.* latest; last.

lattice (lăt′ĭs), *n., v.,* **-ticed, -ticing.** —*n.* **1.** a structure of crossed wooden or metal strips with open spaces between, used as a screen, etc. **2.** a window, gate, or the like, so constructed. **3.** Also, **crystal lattice, space lattice.** *Crystall.* the regular network of fixed points about which molecules, atoms, or ions vibrate in a crystal structure. **4.** *Physics.* a structure within a nuclear reactor consisting of discrete bodies of fissile and non-fissile material, the latter usually being the moderator. —*v.t.* **5.** to furnish with a lattice or latticework. **6.** to form into or arrange like latticework. [ME *latis*, t. OF: m. *lattis*, der. *latte* lath, t. Gmc; cf. OE *lætt* lath]

latticework (lăt′ĭs wûk′), *n.* **1.** work consisting of crossed strips with openings between. **2.** a lattice.

latticing (lăt′ĭ sĭng), *n.* **1.** the act or process of furnishing with or making latticework. **2.** latticework.

Latvia (lăt′vĭ ə), *n.* a constituent republic of the Soviet Union in Europe, in the NW part, on the Baltic: an independent state, 1918–49. 2,200,000 pop. (est. 1964); 25,395 sq. mi. *Cap.:* Riga. Lettish, **Latvija** (*Russ.* lät′vĭ yə). Official name, **Latvian Soviet Socialist Republic.** See map under **Memel.**

Latvian (lăt′vĭ ən), *adj.* **1.** of or pertaining to Latvia. —*n.* **2.** a native or inhabitant of Latvia. **3.** Lettish.

laud (lôd), *v.t.* **1.** to praise; extol. —*n.* **2.** music or a song in praise or honour of anyone. **3. lauds, laudes.** *Eccles.* a canonical hour, characterized esp. by psalms of praise which follows, and is usually recited with, matins. [ME *laude*, back-formation from *laudes*, pl., t. L: praises] —**laud′er,** *n.*

Laud (lôd), *n.* **William,** 1573–1645, archbishop of Canterbury and opponent of Puritanism, executed for treason.

laudable (lô′də bl), *adj.* praiseworthy or commendable. —**laud′abil′ity, laud′ableness,** *n.* —**laud′ably,** *adv.*

laudanum (lŏd′nəm), *n.* **1.** tincture of opium. **2.** (formerly) any preparation in which opium was the chief ingredient. [orig. ML var. of LADANUM; arbitrarily used by Paracelsus to name a remedy based on opium]

laudation (lô dā′shən), *n.* the act of lauding; praise.
laudatory (lô′də tə rĭ, -trĭ), *adj.* containing or expressing praise. Also, **laud′ative.**
Lauder (lô′də), *n.* **Sir Harry MacLennan** (mə klĕn′ən), 1870–1950, Scottish ballad singer and comedian.
Laue (*Ger.* lou′ə), *n.* **Max Theodor Felix von** (*Ger.* mäks tė′ō dôr fė′lĭks fon), 1897–1960, German physicist.
laugh (läf), *v.i.* **1.** to express mirth, amusement, derision, etc., by an explosive, inarticulate sound of the voice, facial expressions, etc. **2.** to experience the emotion so expressed. **3.** to utter a cry or sound resembling the laughing of human beings, as some animals do. **4. laugh at, a.** to make fun of; deride; ridicule. **b.** to be sympathetically amused by: *she laughed at his fear of air travel.* **5. laugh in** or **up one's sleeve,** to laugh inwardly at something. **6. laugh on the other** or **wrong side of one's face** or **mouth,** to evince disappointment, chagrin, displeasure, etc. —*v.t.* **7.** to drive, put, bring, etc., by or with laughter. **8.** to utter with laughter. **9. laugh off** or **away,** to dismiss (a situation, criticism, or the like) by treating lightly or with ridicule. **10. laugh out of court,** to dismiss by means of ridicule. —*n.* **11.** the act or sound of laughing, or laughter. **12.** an expression of mirth, derision, etc., by laughing. **13. have the (last) laugh,** to prove ultimately successful; win after an earlier defeat. [ME *laugh(en)*, d. OE *hlæhhan*, OE *hliehhan*, c. Icel. *hlǣja*, Goth. *hlahjan*; akin to G *lachen*] —**laugh′er,** *n.*
—**Syn. 1.** chortle, cackle, cachinnate, hawhaw, guffaw, roar; giggle, snicker, snigger, titter. **11.** LAUGH, CHUCKLE, GRIN, SMILE, refer to methods of expressing mirth, appreciation of humour, etc. A LAUGH may be a sudden, voiceless exhalation, but is usually an audible sound, either soft or loud: *a hearty laugh.* CHUCKLE suggests a barely audible series of sounds expressing private amusement or satisfaction: *a delighted chuckle.* A SMILE is a (usually pleasant) lighting up of the face and an upward curving of the corners of the lips (which may or may not be open); it may express amusement or mere recognition, friendliness, etc.: *a courteous smile.* A GRIN, in which the teeth are usually visible, is like an exaggerated smile, less controlled in expressing the feelings: *a friendly grin.*
laughable (lä′fə bl), *adj.* such as to excite laughter; funny; amusing; ludicrous. —**laugh′ableness,** *n.* —**laugh′ably,** *adv.* —**Syn.** See **funny.**
laughing (lä′fĭng), *n.* **1.** laughter. —*adj.* **2.** that laughs; giving vent to laughter, as persons. **3. no laughing matter,** a serious matter. **4.** uttering sounds like human laughter, as some birds. **5.** suggesting laughter by brightness, etc. —**laugh′ingly,** *adv.*
laughing gas, nitrous oxide, N_2O, which when inhaled sometimes produces exhilarating effects: used as an anaesthetic in dentistry, etc.
laughing hyena, any member of the family *Hyaenidae*; any hyena.
laughing jackass, a harsh-voiced Australian kingfisher, *Dacelo gigas*; a kookaburra.
laughing-stock (lä′fĭng stŏk′), *n.* a butt for laughter; an object of ridicule.
laughter (läf′tə), *n.* **1.** the action or sound of laughing. **2.** an experiencing of the emotion expressed by laughing: *inward laughter.* **3.** an expression or appearance of merriment or amusement. **4.** *Archaic.* a subject or matter for laughing. [ME; OE *hleahtor*]
Laughton (lô′tn), *n.* **Charles,** 1899–1962, English actor.
launce (läns), *n.* sand-launce.
Launceston (lôn′səs tən), *n.* **1.** a town in England, in Cornwall. 4,570 (1961). **2.** a town in N Tasmania. with suburbs, 59,190 (1964).
launch[1] (lônch), *n.* **1.** a heavy open or half-decked boat. **2.** the largest boat carried by a warship. [t. Sp., Pg.: m. *lancha*]
launch[2] (lônch), *v.t.* **1.** to set (a boat) afloat; lower into the water. **2.** to cause (a newly built ship) to move or slide from the stocks into the water. **3.** to start on a course, career, etc. **4.** to set going: *to launch a scheme.* **5.** to send forth; start off (forcefully): *the plane was launched from the deck of the carrier.* **6.** to throw or hurl: *to launch a spear.* —*v.i.* **7.** to burst out or plunge boldly into action, speech, etc. **8.** to start out or forth; push out or put forth on the water. —*n.* **9.** the sliding or movement of a boat or vessel from the land or dock into the water. [ME *launche(n)*, t. ONF: m. *lancher*, var. of central OF *lancier* LANCE, v.] —**launch′er,** *n.*
launch complex, *Aerospace.* the buildings and ancillary equipment required for launching a rocket.
launcher (lôn′chə), *n. Aerospace.* a structure which supports a ballistic or guided missile at the appropriate elevation and bearing before launching.
launch pad, *Aerospace.* a base from which a rocket is launched. Also, **launching pad.**
launch shoe, *Aerospace.* a launcher which carries a missile in its launching position on an aircraft and provides electrical and other services prior to launching. Also, **launching shoe.**
launch vehicle, booster (def. 4b).
launder (lôn′də), *v.t.* **1.** to wash and iron (clothes, etc.). —*v.i.* **2.** to do or wash laundry. —*n.* **3.** (in ore dressing) a passage carrying products of intermediate grade, and residue, which are in water suspension. [ME *lander* one who washes, contr. of *lavender*, t. OF: m. *lavandier* a washer, t. LL: m. s. *lavandārius*, der. L *lavandus*, ger. of *lavāre* wash] —**laun′derer,** *n.*
launderette (lôn′də rĕt′, lôn drĕt′), *n.* **1.** a commercial premises with coin-operated washing machines, spin-dryers, hot-air dryers and often dry-cleaning machines. **2.** (*cap.*) a trademark for this.
laundress (lôn′drĭs), *n.* a woman whose occupation is the washing and ironing of clothes, etc.
laundry (lôn′drĭ), *n., pl.* **-dries. 1.** articles of clothing, etc., to be washed. **2.** a place or establishment where clothes, etc., are laundered. **3.** the act of laundering.
laundryman (lôn′drĭ mən), *n., pl.* **-men. 1.** a man who works in or conducts a laundry. **2.** a man who collects and delivers laundry or works in a laundry.
laundrywoman (lôn′drĭ wŏŏm′ən), *n., pl.* **-women.** a laundress.
lauraceous (lô rā′shəs), *adj.* belonging to the *Lauraceae*, or laurel family of plants. [f. s. L *laurus* laurel + -ACEOUS]
laureate (lô′rĭ ĭt), *adj.* **1.** crowned or decked with laurel as a mark of honour. **2.** specially recognized or distinguished, or deserving of distinction, esp. for poetic merit: *poet laureate.* **3.** consisting of laurel. —*n.* **4.** one crowned with laurel. **5.** a poet laureate. [ME *laureat*, t. L: s. *laureātus* (def. 1)] —**lau′reateship′,** *n.*
laurel (lŏ′rəl), *n., v.t.,* **-relled, -relling.** —*n.* **1.** a small lauraceous evergreen tree, *Laurus nobilis*, of Europe (the **true laurel**); sweet bay. **2.** any tree of the same genus (*Laurus*). **3.** any of various trees or shrubs similar to the true laurel belonging to the ericaceous genus *Kalmia.* **4.** an evergreen shrub with laurel-like leaves of the rosaceous genus *Prunus*, as *P. laurocerasus* (the **cherry laurel**). **5.** an evergreen cornaceous shrub, *Aucuba japonica* (the **spotted laurel**), the female of which has conspicuous yellow spots. **6.** the foliage of the true laurel as an emblem of victory or distinction. **7.** a branch or wreath of it. **8.** (*usually pl.*) honour won, as by achievement. **9. look to one's laurels,** to be aware of the possibility of being excelled by one's rivals. **10. to rest on one's laurels,** to be content with present achievements. —*v.t.* **11.** to adorn or wreathe with laurel. **12.** to honour with marks of distinction. [ME *laurer, laureal*, t. F: m. *laurier*, *lorier*, der. OF *lor*, g. L *laurus* laurel]
Laurel and Hardy (lŏ′rəl ən hä′dĭ), a team of U.S. comic film actors, **Stan Laurel** (*Arthur Stanley Jefferson*), 1890–1965, the thin one, and **Oliver Hardy,** 1892–1957, the fat one.
Laurentian (lô rĕn′shən), *adj.* **1.** of or pertaining to the St Lawrence river. **2.** *Geol.* denoting or pertaining to a series of rocks of the Archaean system, occurring in Canada near the St Lawrence river and the Great Lakes, or the major mountain-building episode to which these rocks were subject in Archaean times.
Laurentian Mountains, a range of low mountains in E Canada between the St Lawrence and Hudson Bay.
lauric acid (lô′rĭk, lŏ′-), *Chem.* a white crystalline insoluble solid, $CH_3(CH_2)_{10}COOH$, occurring as glycerides in milk, palm oil, laurel oil, etc.; used in the manufacture of detergents and cosmetics.
Laurier (lŏ′rĭ ə; *Fr.* lŏ ryė′), *n.* **Sir Wilfrid,** 1841–1919, prime minister of Canada 1896–1911.
laurite (lô′rīt, lŏ′-), *n.* a mineral sulphide of ruthenium and osmium, which occurs as small cubic crystals often associated with platinum.
laurustinus (lŏ′rə stī′nəs), *n.* a caprifoliaceous evergreen garden shrub, *Viburnum tinus*, native in southern Europe, with white or pinkish flowers. [t. NL: f. L *laurus* laurel + *tīnus* kind of plant]
lauryl alcohol (lô′rĭl, lŏ′-), *Chem.* a crystalline solid, $CH_3(CH_2)_{10}CH_2OH$, used in the manufacture of detergents.
Lausanne (lō zăn′; *Fr.* lò zȧn′), *n.* a town in W Switzerland, on Lake Geneva. 132,300 (1964).
laus Deo (lous′dē′ō), *Latin.* praise (be) to God.
Lautrec (*Fr.* lò trĕk′), *n.* See **Toulouse-Lautrec.**
lav (lăv), *n. Colloq.* lavatory.
lava (lä′və), *n.* **1.** the molten or fluid rock (magma), which issues from a volcanic vent. **2.** the igneous rock formed when this solidifies and loses its volatile constituents, occurring in many varieties differing greatly in structure and constitution. [t. It. (Neapolitan): orig., stream, der. *lavare* wash, g. L]
lavabo (lə vā′bō), *n., pl.* **-boes, -bos.** *Eccles.* **1.** the ritual

washing of the celebrant's hands after the offertory in the mass, accompanied in the Roman rite by the recitation of Psalms 26:6–12, or, in the Douay Version, Psalms 25:6–12 (so called from the first word of this passage in the Latin version). **2.** the passage recited. **3.** the small towel or the basin used. **4.** (in many medieval monasteries) a large stone basin from which the water issued by a number of small orifices around the edge, for the performance of ablutions. [t. L: I will wash]

lavage (lăv′ĭj; *Fr.* là vȧzh′), *n.* **1.** a washing. **2.** *Med.* **a.** cleansing by injection or the like. **b.** the washing out of the stomach. [t. F, der. *laver* LAVE]

Laval (*Fr.* là vȧl′), *n.* **Pierre** (*Fr.* pyĕr), 1883–1945, premier of France 1931–32, 1935–36; premier of Vichy France 1942–44; convicted of treason and executed.

lavation (lă vā′shən), *n.* the process of washing. **—lava′tional,** *adj.*

lavatory (lăv′ə tə rĭ, -trĭ), *n., pl.* **-ries. 1.** a room fitted with a water closet or urinal, often with means for washing the hands and face, and often with other toilet conveniences. **2.** a water closet or urinal. **3.** a bowl or basin for washing or bathing purposes. **4.** any place where washing is done. [ME *lavatorie,* t. LL: m. *lavātōrium*]

lavatory paper, toilet paper.

lave (lāv), *v.,* **laved, laving.** *—v.t.* **1.** *Poetic.* to wash; bathe. **2.** *Poetic.* (of a river, the sea, etc.) to wash or flow against. *—v.i.* **3.** *Poetic.* to bathe. [ME; OE *lafian* pour water on, wash. Cf. F *laver,* L *lavāre*]

lavender (lăv′ĭn də), *n.* **1.** a pale, bluish purple colour. **2.** a plant of the menthaceous genus *Lavandula,* esp. *L. officinalis,* a small Old World shrub with spikes of fragrant pale purple flowers, yielding an oil (**oil of lavender**) used in medicine and perfumery. **3.** the dried flowers or other parts of this plant placed among linen, etc., for scent or as a preservative. *—adj.* **4.** pale bluish purple. [ME *lavendre,* t. AF, t. ML: m. s. *lavendula, livendula*; ? der. L *lavāre* wash or L *līvēre* be livid or bluish]

lavender bag, a small bag usually of muslin, filled with dried lavender, used to perfume linen, etc.

lavender water, a perfume made from distilled lavender, alcohol, and ambergris.

laver[1] (lā′və), *n.* **1.** *Old Testament.* a large basin upon a foot or pedestal in the court of the Jewish tabernacle, and subsequently in the temple, containing water for the ablutions of the priests, and for the washing of the sacrifices in the temple service. **2.** *Eccles.* the font or the water of baptism. **3.** any spiritually cleansing agency. **4.** *Archaic.* a basin, bowl, or cistern to wash in. **5.** *Archaic.* any bowl or pan for water. [ME, t. OF: m. *laveoir,* g. LL *lavātōrium* lavatory]

laver[2] (lā′və), *n.* any of several edible seaweeds, esp. of the genus *Porphyra.* [t. L: kind of water plant]

La Vérendrye (*Fr.* là vė räɴ drē′), **Pierre Gaultier de Varennes** (*Fr.* pyĕr gō tyė′ də vȧ rĕn′), **Sieur de,** 1685–1749, French-Canadian explorer of North America.

lavish (lăv′ĭsh), *adj.* **1.** using or bestowing in great abundance or without stint (often fol. by *of*): *lavish of time.* **2.** expended, bestowed, or occurring in profusion: *lavish gifts, lavish spending.* *—v.t.* **3.** to expend or bestow in great abundance or without stint: *to lavish favours on a person.* [late ME, adj. use of obs. *lavish* profusion, t. OF: m. *lavasse* deluge] **—lav′isher,** *n.* **—lav′ishly,** *adv.* **—lav′ishness,** *n.*

—Syn. 1, 2. unstinted, extravagant, excessive. LAVISH, PRODIGAL, PROFUSE refer to that which exists in abundance and is poured out copiously. LAVISH suggests (sometimes excessive) generosity and open-handedness: *lavish hospitality, much too lavish.* PRODIGAL suggests wastefulness, improvidence, and reckless impatience of restraint: *a prodigal extravagance.* PROFUSE emphasizes abundance, but may suggest overemotionalism, exaggeration, and the like: *profuse thanks, compliments, apologies.* **—Ant. 2.** limited.

Lavoisier (*Fr.* là vwȧ zyė′), *n.* **Antoine Laurent** (*Fr.* äɴ twȧn lō räɴ′), 1743–94, French chemist.

law (lô), *n.* **1.** the principles and regulations emanating from a government and applicable to a people, whether in the form of legislation or of custom and policies recognized and enforced by judicial decision. **2.** any written or positive rule, or collection of rules, prescribed under the authority of the state or nation, whether by the people in its constitution, as the **organic law,** or by the legislature in its **statute law,** or by the treaty-making power, or by municipalities in their ordinances or **bylaws. 3.** the controlling influence of such rules; the condition of society brought about by their observance: *to maintain law and order.* **4.** an agent that helps to maintain these rules. **5.** a system or collection of such rules. **6.** the department of knowledge concerned with these rules; jurisprudence: *to study law.* **7.** the body of such rules concerned with a particular subject or derived from a particular source: *commercial law.* **8.** an act of the supreme legislative body of a state or nation, as distinguished from the constitution. **9.** the principles applied in the courts of common law, as distinguished from equity. **10.** the profession which deals with law and legal procedure: *to practise law.* **11.** legal action; litigation. **12.** any rule or principle of proper conduct or collection of such rules. **13.** (in philosophical and scientific use) **a.** a statement of a relation or sequence of phenomena invariable under the same conditions. **b.** a mathematical rule. **14.** a commandment or a revelation from God. **15.** (*often cap.*) a divinely appointed order or system. **16. the Law,** the Mosaic Law (often in contrast to *the Gospel*). **17.** the five books of Moses (the Pentateuch) containing this system and forming the first of the three Jewish divisions of the Old Testament. **18.** the preceptive part of the Bible, esp. of the New Testament, in contradistinction to its promises: *the law of Christ.* **19.** *Sport.* a start given to an animal that is to be hunted, or to a weaker competitor in a race. **20. be a law unto oneself,** to do what one wishes, without regard for established rules and modes of behaviour. **21. lay down the law,** to tell people authoritatively what to do, or state one's opinions authoritatively. **22. take the law into one's own hands,** to seek justice by one's own means, disregarding usual judicial procedures. [ME *law, lagh,* OE *lagu,* t. Scand.; cf. Icel. *lag* layer, pl. *lög* law, lit. that which is laid down; akin to LAY[1], LIE[2]]

Law (lô), *n.* **1. Andrew Bonar** (bŏn′ə), 1858–1923, British politician born in Canada, prime minister of Great Britain 1922–23. **2. John,** 1671–1729, Scottish financier.

law-abiding (lô′ə bī′dĭng), *adj.* abiding by or keeping the law; obedient to law: *law-abiding citizens.*

law-breaker (lô′brā′kə), *n.* one who breaks or violates the law. **—law′-break′ing,** *n., adj.*

law court. See **court** (def. 14a).

Lawes (lôz), *n.* **Harry,** 1596–1662, English songwriter.

lawful (lô′fəl), *adj.* **1.** allowed or permitted by law; not contrary to law. **2.** legally qualified or entitled: *lawful king.* **3.** recognized or sanctioned by law. **4.** valid; legitimate: *a lawful marriage.* **—law′fully,** *adv.* **—law′fulness,** *n.* **—Syn. 1.** legal. **3.** licit.

lawgiver (lô′gĭv′ə), *n.* one who gives or promulgates a law or a code of laws. **—law′giv′ing,** *n., adj.*

lawks (lôks), *interj. Archaic.* (an exclamation of surprise.) [mincing alter. of LORD]

lawless (lô′lĭs), *adj.* **1.** regardless of or contrary to law: *lawless violence.* **2.** uncontrolled by law; unbridled: *lawless passions.* **3.** without law; not regulated by law. **—law′lessly,** *adv.* **—law′lessness,** *n.*

law list, an annual publication containing lists of barristers and solicitors.

Law Lords, those members of the House of Lords who take part in its judicial proceedings; Lords of Appeal in Ordinary.

law-maker (lô′mā′kə), *n.* one who makes or enacts law; a legislator. **—law′-mak′ing,** *n., adj.*

law merchant, the principles and rules, drawn chiefly from custom, determining the rights and obligations of commercial transactions; commercial law.

lawn[1] (lôn), *n.* **1.** a stretch of grass-covered land, esp. one closely mowed, as near a house, etc. **2.** *Archaic or Dial.* a glade. [earlier *laund,* t. OF: m. *la(u)nde* wooded ground; of Celtic orig.] **—lawn′y,** *adj.*

lawn[2] (lôn), *n.* a thin or sheer linen or cotton fabric, either plain or printed. [ME *laun(e), laund(e)*; prob. named after LAON, town in northern France, where much linen was made] **—lawn′y,** *adj.*

lawn-mower (lôn′mō′ə), *n.* a machine for cutting grass.

lawn sleeves, 1. the sleeves of lawn of an Anglican bishop. **2.** the office of an Anglican bishop. **3.** an Anglican bishop or bishops.

lawn tennis, tennis (def. 1) played on a grass court.

law of contradiction, *Logic.* the law which asserts that a proposition cannot at the same time be both true and false, or alternatively that a thing cannot at the same time both have and not have a given property.

Law of Moses, the Pentateuch or Torah.

law of nations, 1. international law. **2.** (in Roman use) the body of rules common to the law of all nations.

Lawrence (lŏ′rəns), *n.* **1. D(avid) H(erbert),** 1885–1930, English novelist and poet. **2. Ernest Orlando,** 1901–58, U.S. physicist: inventor of cyclotron. **3. Sir Thomas,** 1769–1830, English portrait painter. **4. T(homas) E(dward)** ('*Lawrence of Arabia*'; after 1927, *Thomas Edward Shaw*), 1888–1935, British soldier, archaeologist, and writer. **—Lawrentian** (lô rĕn′shən), *adj.*

lawrencium (lŏ rĕn′sĭ əm, lô-), *n. Chem.* a transuranic element produced synthetically. *Symbol:* lw; *at. no.:* 103. [after Ernest O. LAWRENCE]

law report, the published account of a legal proceeding, stating the facts of the case, the principles of law involved, and the reasons given by the court for its decision.

law sitting, the period of the year during which judicial business is conducted.

Law Society, the society which controls and regulates the solicitors' profession, and which sets certain examinations which must be passed before a person can be admitted as a solicitor.

lawsuit (lô′syōōt′), *n.* a suit at law; a prosecution of a claim in a law court.

lawyer (lô′yə), *n.* **1.** one whose profession it is to conduct suits in court or to give legal advice and aid. **2.** *New Testament.* an interpreter of the Mosaic law. **3.** a burbot (so called from the beardlike barbel).

lax[1] (lăks), *adj.* **1.** lacking in strictness or severity; careless or negligent: *lax morals.* **2.** not rigidly exact or precise; vague: *lax ideas of a subject.* **3.** loose or slack; not tense, rigid, or firm: *a lax cord.* **4.** open or not retentive, as the bowels. **5.** having the bowels unduly open, as a person. **6.** loosely cohering; open or not compact, as a panicle of a plant. **7.** *Phonet.* pronounced with relatively relaxed muscles. [ME, t. L: s. *laxus* loose, slack] —**lax′ly,** *adv.* —**lax′ness,** *n.*

lax[2] (lăks), *n.* salmon. [t. Sw. or G: m. *Lachs*; r. OE *leax*]

laxation (lăk sā′shən), *n.* **1.** a loosening or relaxing. **2.** the state of being loosened or relaxed. **3.** a laxative. [ME *laxacion*, t. L: m. s. *laxātio* a widening]

laxative (lăk′sə tĭv), *n.* **1.** *Med.* a laxative medicine or agent. —*adj.* **2.** *Med.* mildly purgative. **3.** *Pathol.* **a.** (of the bowels) subject to looseness. **b.** (of a disease) characterized by looseness of the bowels. [t. L: m. s. *laxātīvus* loosening; r. ME *laxatif*, t. F]

laxity (lăk′sĭ tĭ), *n.* the state or quality of being lax or loose. [t. L: m. s. *laxitas*]

Laxness (*Icel.* läkHs′nĕs), *n.* **Halldór Kiljan** (*Icel.* häl′dōwr kyĭl′yȧn), born 1902, Icelandic novelist.

Laxton superb (lăk′stən), **1.** a variety of apple, firm, juicy, and sweet, having yellowish green skin and white flesh. **2.** a variety of pear having pale yellow skin and whitish flesh, producing a heavy crop.

lay[1] (lā), *v.*, **laid, laying,** *n.* —*v.t.* **1.** to put or place in a position of rest or recumbency: *to lay a book on a desk.* **2.** to bring, throw, or beat down, as from an erect position: *to lay a person low.* **3.** to cause to subside: *to lay the dust.* **4.** to allay, appease, or suppress. **5.** to smooth down or make even: *to lay the nap of cloth.* **6.** to bury. **7.** to bring forth and deposit (an egg or eggs). **8.** to deposit as a wager; stake; bet: *I'll lay you ten to one.* **9.** to put away for future use (fol. by *by*). **10.** to place, set, or cause to be in a particular situation, state, or condition: *to lay hands on a thing.* **11.** to place before a person, or bring to a person's notice or consideration: *he laid his case before the commission.* **12.** to put to; place in contiguity; apply: *to lay a hand on a child.* **13.** to set (a trap, etc.). **14.** to place or locate (a scene): *the scene is laid in France.* **15.** to present, bring forward, or prefer, as a claim, charge, etc. **16.** to impute, attribute, or ascribe. **17.** to impose as a burden, duty, penalty, or the like: *to lay an embargo on shipments of oil.* **18.** to bring down (a stick, etc.), as on a person, in inflicting punishment. **19.** to dispose or place in proper position or in an orderly fashion: *to lay bricks.* **20.** to set (a table). **21.** to form by twisting strands together, as a rope. **22.** to place on or over a surface, as paint; cover or spread with something else. **23.** to devise or arrange, as a plan. **24.** *Naut.* to head a ship towards (an object or compass point), esp. on the closest course she will make to the wind. **25.** to adjust a gun for direction and elevation before firing. **26.** to put (dogs) on a scent. **27.** *Taboo Colloq.* to have sexual intercourse with (a woman). —*v.* **28.** Some special verb phrases are:

lay aboard, *Naut.* (of a boat) to come alongside a ship.

lay down, 1. to put (something) down on the ground; to relinquish. **2. lay down one's arms,** to surrender.

lay hold of or **on,** to grasp; seize; catch.

lay in, 1. to build up a store of (provisions, etc.). **2.** *Naut.* to move along a yard, towards the mast.

lay it on, 1. to exaggerate. **2.** to charge exorbitantly. **3.** to chastise severely.

lay off, 1. to put aside. **2.** to dismiss, esp. temporarily, as a workman. **3.** to mark or plot off. **4.** to hedge (defs 7 and 9). **5.** *Colloq.* to desist.

lay on, to provide or supply.

lay oneself open, to expose oneself (to adverse criticism or the like).

lay out, 1. to extend at length. **2.** to spread out to the sight, air, etc.; spread out in order. **3.** to stretch out and prepare (a body) for burial. **4.** *Slang.* to expend (money) for a particular purpose. **5.** to exert (oneself) for some purpose, effect, etc. **6.** to plot or plan out. **7.** *Naut.* to move along a yard, away from the mast. **8.** to strike down, esp. to knock unconscious.

lay siege to, to besiege.

lay to, *Naut.* **1.** to check the motion of (a ship). **2.** to put (a ship, etc.) in a dock or other place of safety.

lay up, 1. to put away, as for future use; store up. **2.** to cause to remain in bed or indoors through illness.

lay waste, to devastate.

—*v.i.* **29.** to lay eggs. **30.** to wager or bet. **31.** to deal or aim blows (fol. by *on, at, about,* etc.). **32.** to apply oneself vigorously. **33.** *Colloq.* to lie in wait (fol. by *for*). **34.** *Colloq. or Dial.* to plan or scheme (often fol. by *out*). **35.** *Naut.* to take a specified position. **36.** (in substandard use) to lie. —*n.* **37.** the way or position in which a thing is laid or lies. **38.** *Ropemaking.* the quality of a fibre rope characterized by the degree of twist, the angles formed by the strands, and by the fibres in the strands. **39.** a share of the profits or the catch of a whaling or fishing voyage, distributed to officers and crew. **40.** *Taboo Colloq.* **a.** a woman considered as the object of the sexual act. **b.** the sexual act.

[ME *lay(en)*, *legge(n)*, OE *lecgan* (causative of *licgan* LIE[2]), c. D *leggen*, G *legen*, Icel. *leggja*, Goth. *lagjan*] —**Syn. 1.** place; deposit, set. See **put, lie**[2].

lay[2] (lā), *v.* pt. of **lie**[2].

lay[3] (lā), *adj.* **1.** belonging to, pertaining to, or performed by the people or laity, as distinguished from the clergy: *a lay sermon.* **2.** not belonging to, connected with, or proceeding from a profession, esp. the law or medicine. [ME *laye*, t. OF: m. *lai*, g. LL *lāicus* LAIC]

lay[4] (lā), *n.* **1.** a short narrative or other poem, esp. one to be sung. **2.** a song. [ME *lai*, t. OF, ? t. Gmc; cf. OHG *leich* song]

layabout (lā′ə bout′), *n.* one who does not work; a loafer; an idler.

Layamon (lī′ə mən), *n.* fl. *c.* 1200, English chronicler in verse. [modern misspelling of early ME *Laghamon*, ME *Laweman.* See LAW, MAN]

Layard (lĕəd), *n.* **Sir Austen Henry,** 1817–94, English archaeologist, writer, and diplomat.

layback (lā′băk′), *n.* *Mountaineering.* a method of rock-climbing in which the body is held in a nearly horizontal position by pulling with the hands on the near edge of a crack and pushing with the feet on the far side.

lay brother, a man who has taken religious vows and habit, but is employed chiefly in manual work.

lay-by (lā′bī′), *n.* a part of a road or railway where vehicles may draw up out of the stream of traffic.

lay day, one of a certain number of days allowed by a charter party for loading or unloading a vessel without demurrage.

layer (lā′ə), *n.* **1.** a thickness of some material laid on or spread over a surface; a stratum. **2.** something which is laid. **3.** one who or that which lays. **4.** *Hort.* **a.** a shoot or twig placed partly under the ground while still attached to the living stock, for the purpose of propagation. **b.** a plant which has been propagated by layering. —*v.t.* **5.** to make a layer of. **6.** *Hort.* to propagate by layers. [ME, f. LAY[1] + -ER[1]]

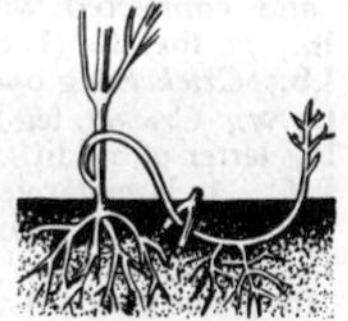
Layer (def. 4)

layer cake, a cake made in layers with a cream or other filling between the layers.

layering (lā′ə rĭng), *n.* *Hort.* a method of propagating plants by causing their shoots to take root while still attached to the mother plant. Also, *Chiefly U.S.*, **layerage** (lā′ə rĭj).

layette (lā ĕt′), *n.* a complete outfit of clothing, toilet articles, etc., for a newborn child. [t. F: box, drawer, layette, dim. of *laie* chest, trough, t. Flemish: m. *laeye*]

lay figure, 1. a jointed model of the human body, usually of wood, from which artists work in the absence of a living model. **2.** a mere puppet or nonentity; a person of no importance. [r. obs. *layman* (t. D: m. *leeman*, f. *lee* joint, limb (c. E *lith*, now d.) + *man* MAN), with *figure* substituted for *man*, to avoid confusion with eccl. term]

layman (lā′mən), *n.*, *pl.* **-men.** one of the laity; one not a clergyman or not a member of some particular profession. [f. LAY[3] + MAN]

lay-off (lā′ŏf′), *n.* **1.** the act of laying off. **2.** an interval of enforced unemployment.

layout (lā′out′), *n.* **1.** a laying or spreading out. **2.** an arrangement or plan. **3.** the plan or sketch of a page, magazine, book, advertisement, or the like, indicating the arrangement of materials.

layover (lā′ō′və), *n.* *U.S.* stopover.

lay reader, 1. *C. of E.* a layman specially commissioned to read the scripture lessons in church services and to preach. **2.** *Rom. Cath. Ch.* a layman who represents the congregation in the sanctuary at mass, reads the epistle, and takes the prayers after the creed.

lay shaft, *Engineering.* a secondary, geared shaft in a gearbox to and from which the drive is transferred.

laywoman (lā′wo͝om′ən), *n.*, *pl.* **-women.** a female member of the laity.

lazar (lăz′ə), *n. Archaic.* **1.** a person, esp. a beggar or poor person, infected with a loathsome disease. **2.** a leper. [ME, t. ML: s. *lazarus*, special use of LAZARUS] —**laz′ar-like′,** *adj.*

lazaretto (lăz′ə rĕt′ō), *n.*, *pl.* **-tos.** **1.** a hospital for those affected with contagious or loathsome diseases. **2.** a building or a ship set apart for quarantine purposes. **3.** *Naut.* a place in some merchant ships, usually near the stern, in which provisions and stores are kept. Also, **lazaret** (lăz′ə rĕt′), **laz′arette′.** [t. It.: m. *lazzaretto*, var. of Venetian *lazareto*, b. *nazareto* (abbr. from name of leper hospital *Santa Maria di Nazaret*) and *lazaro* lazar, leper]

Lazarus (lăz′ə rəs), *n.* **1.** the beggar, 'full of sores', of the parable in Luke 16:19–31. **2.** the brother of Mary and Martha, and friend of Jesus, who raised him from the dead. John 11:1–44; 12:1–18. [t. LL, t. Gk: m. *Lázaros*, t. Heb.: m. *El'āzār* Eleazar]

laze (lāz), *v.*, **lazed, lazing.** —*v.i.* **1.** to be lazy; idle or lounge lazily. —*v.t.* **2.** to pass (time, etc.) lazily (fol. by *away*). —*n.* **3.** the act of lazing. [back-formation from LAZY]

Lazio (*It.* lȧt′tsyȯ), *n.* Italian name for **Latium** (def. 2).

lazulite (lăz′yo͝o līt′), *n.* an azure blue mineral, hydrous magnesium iron aluminium phosphate, (FeMg)-$Al_2P_2O_8(OH)_2$. [f. s. ML *lāzulum* lapis lazuli + -ITE[1]]

lazurite (lăz′yo͝o rīt′), *n.* a mineral, sodium aluminium silicate and sulphide, $Na_5Al_3Si_3O_{12}S_3$, occurring in deep blue crystals and used for ornamental purposes. [f. ML *lāzur* AZURE + -ITE[1]]

lazy (lā′zĭ), *adj.*, **-zier, -ziest.** **1.** disinclined to exertion or work; idle. **2.** slow-moving; sluggish: *a lazy stream.* **3.** *U.S.* denoting a kind of livestock brand which is placed on its side instead of upright. [orig. uncert.] —**la′zily,** *adv.* —**la′ziness,** *n.* —**Syn. 1.** indolent, slothful. See **idle.** —**Ant. 1.** industrious; energetic.

lazybones (lā′zĭ bōnz′), *n. Colloq.* a lazy person.

lazy tongs, a kind of extensible tongs for grasping objects at a distance, consisting of a series of pairs of crossing pieces, each pair pivoted together in the middle and connected with the next pair at the extremities.

Lazy tongs

lb., *pl.* **lbs, lb.** (L *libra*, pl. *librae*) pound (weight).

l.b., *Cricket.* leg bye.

l.b.w., *Cricket.* leg before wicket.

lc, letter of credit. Also, **l/c; l/cr.**

L.C., **1.** Legislative Council. **2.** letter of credit. **3.** Lord Chamberlain. **4.** Lord Chancellor. **5.** Lower Canada.

l.c., **1.** left centre. **2.** letter of credit. **3.** (L *loco citato*) in the place cited. **4.** *Print.* lower case.

L.C.C., London County Council, now the Greater London Council.

l.c.d., lowest common denominator.

L.C.J., Lord Chief Justice.

l.c.m., least or lowest common multiple. Also, **L.C.M.**

LD, **1.** lethal dose. **2.** Low Dutch. Also, **L.D.**

Ld, **1.** Limited. **2.** Lord.

L.D.S., Licentiate in Dental Surgery.

LD-50, median lethal dose.

Le, leone.

lea[1] (lē), *n. Archaic.* a tract of open ground, esp. grassland; a meadow. [ME *ley*, OE *lēa(h)*, c. OHG *lōh*, L *lūcus* grove]

lea[2] (lē), *n.* a measure of yarn of varying quantity, for wool usually 80 yards, cotton and silk 120 yards, linen 300 yards. [ME, ? akin to F *lier* tie]

leach (lēch), *v.t.* **1.** to cause (water, etc.) to percolate through something. **2.** to remove soluble constituents from (ashes, soil, etc.) by percolation. —*v.i.* **3.** (of ashes, soil, etc.) to undergo the action of percolating water. **4.** to percolate, as water. —*n.* **5.** a leaching. **6.** the material leached. **7.** a vessel for use in leaching. [unexplained var. of *letch*, v. (whence d. *letch*, n., bog, etc.), OE *leccan* moisten, wet, causative of LEAK]

leachy (lē′chĭ), *adj.* porous.

Leacock (lē′kŏk′), *n.* **Stephen Butler,** 1869–1944, Canadian humorist and economist.

lead[1] (lēd), *v.*, **led, leading,** *n.* —*v.t.* **1.** to take or conduct on the way; go before or with to show the way. **2.** to conduct by holding and guiding: *to lead a horse by a rope.* **3.** to guide in direction, course, action, opinion, etc.; to influence or induce: *too easily led.* **4.** to conduct or bring (water, wire, etc.) in a particular course. **5.** (of a road, passage, etc.) to serve to bring (a person, etc.) to a place through a region, etc. **6.** to take or bring: *the prisoners were led in.* **7.** to be at the head of, command, or direct (an army, organization, etc.). **8.** to go at the head of or in advance of (a procession, list, body, etc.); to be first in or go before. **9.** to have the directing or principal part in (a movement, proceedings, etc.). **10.** to begin or open, as a dance, discussion, etc. **11.** to act as leader of (an orchestra, etc.). **12.** to go through or pass (life, etc.): *to lead a dreary existence.* **13.** *Cards.* to begin a round, etc., with (a card or suit specified). **14.** to aim and fire a firearm or gun ahead of (a moving target) in order to allow for the travel of the target and time of flight of the bullet or shell in reaching it. **15. lead (someone) a chase** or **dance,** to cause (someone) unnecessary difficulty or trouble. **16. lead (someone) by the nose,** to enforce one's will on (someone), esp. unpleasantly. **17. lead (someone) on,** to induce or encourage (someone) to a detrimental or undesirable course of action. **18. lead the way,** to go in advance of others, esp. as a guide. —*v.i.* **19.** to act as a guide; show the way. **20.** to be led, or submit to being led, as an animal. **21.** to afford passage to a place, etc., as a road, stairway, or the like. **22.** to go first; be in advance. **23.** to take the directing or principal part. **24.** to take the initiative (often fol. by *off*). **25.** *Boxing.* to take the offensive by striking at an opponent. **26.** *Cards.* to make the first play (often fol. by *off*). **27. lead up to,** to prepare gradually for. —*n.* **28.** the first or foremost place; position in advance of others. **29.** the extent of advance. **30.** something that leads. **31.** a thong or line for holding a dog or other animal in check. **32.** a guiding indication. **33.** precedence. **34.** *Theat.* **a.** the principal part in a play. **b.** the person who plays it. **35.** *Cards.* **a.** the act or right of playing first, as in a round. **b.** the card, suit, etc., so played. **36.** *Journalism.* a short summary serving as an introduction to a news story or article. **37.** *Elect.* a single conductor, often flexible and insulated, used in connections between pieces of electrical apparatus. **38.** *Eng.* the interval by which a periodic signal precedes another signal of the same phase. **39.** *Boxing.* the act of taking the offensive by striking at an opponent. **40.** *Naut.* the course of a rope. **41.** an open channel through a field of ice. **42.** *Mining.* **a.** a lode. **b.** an auriferous deposit in an old river-bed. **43.** the act of aiming a firearm or gun ahead of a target moving across the line of fire. [ME *leden*, OE *lǣdan* (causative of *līthan* go, travel), c. D *leiden*, G *leiten*, Icel. *leidha*] —**Syn. 1.** See **guide.**

lead[2] (lĕd), *n.* **1.** *Chem.* a heavy, comparatively soft, malleable bluish grey metal, sometimes found native, but usually combined as sulphide, in galena. *Symbol:* Pb; *at. wt:* 207·19; *at. no.:* 82; *sp. gr.:* 11·34 at 20°C. **2.** something made of this metal or one of its alloys. **3.** a plummet or mass of lead suspended by a line, as for taking soundings. **4. heave the lead,** *Naut.* to take a sounding with a lead. **5. swing the lead,** *Naut.* to pretend to do work which is in fact being shirked. **6.** bullets; shot. **7.** black lead or graphite. **8.** a small stick of it as used in pencils. **9.** Also, **leading.** *Print.* a thin strip of type metal or brass, less than type high, for increasing the space between lines of type. **10.** frames of lead in which panes are fixed, as in windows of stained glass. **11.** (*pl.*) sheets or strips of lead used for covering roofs. **12.** see **red lead, white lead.** —*v.t.* **13.** to cover, line, weight, treat, or impregnate with lead or one of its compounds. **14.** *Print.* to insert leads between the lines of. **15.** to fix (window glass) in position with leads. [ME *lede*, OE *lēad*, c. D *lood*, G *Lot* plummet]

lead acetate (lĕd), *Chem.* a white soluble crystalline salt, $(CH_3COO)_2Pb.3H_2O$, with a sweet taste; used as a mordant and as a drier in paints: sugar of lead.

lead arsenate (lĕd), *Chem.* plumbous arsenate, $Pb_3(AsO_4)_2$, a very poisonous crystalline compound, used as an insecticide.

leaden (lĕd′n), *adj.* **1.** consisting or made of lead. **2.** inertly heavy, or hard to lift or move, as weight, the limbs, etc. **3.** oppressive; burdensome. **4.** sluggish, as the pace. **5.** dull, spiritless, or gloomy, as the mood, thoughts, etc. **6.** of a dull grey: *leaden skies.* —**lead′enly,** *adv.* —**lead′enness,** *n.*

leader (lē′də), *n.* **1.** one who or that which leads. **2.** a guiding or directing head, as of any army, movement, etc. **3.** *Music.* the principal violinist, cornet-player, or singer in an orchestra, band, or chorus, to whom solos are usually assigned. **4.** a horse harnessed in front of a team. **5.** a principal or important editorial article, as in a newspaper. **6.** a featured article of trade, esp. one offered at a low price to attract customers. **7.** *U.S.* a pipe for conveying rainwater, etc. **8.** *Naut.* a piece of metal or wood having apertures for lines to lead them to their proper places. **9.** (*pl.*) *Print.* a row of dots or short lines to lead the eye across a space. **10.** *U.S. Fishing.* **a.** a length of silkworm gut or the like, to which the fly or baited hook is attached. **b.** the net used to direct fish into a weir, pound, etc. **11.** *Films.* a blank strip at the beginning of a reel of film, used to ease threading, and for identification purposes. **12.** *Hort.* the long slender extension shoots of trees, especially of fruit trees, which are cut back in pruning. **13.** *Law.* a Queen's Counsel in charge of a case. **—lead′erless,** *adj.*

leadership (lē′də shĭp′), *n.* **1.** the position, function, or guidance of a leader. **2.** ability to lead.

leader-writer (lē′də rī′tə), *n.* one who writes leaders in a newspaper or the like.

lead-in (lĕd′ĭn′), *n.* **1.** *Radio.* connection between the aerial and a transmitter or receiving set. **2.** an announcer's introduction of a broadcast.

leading[1] (lē′dĭng), *n.* **1.** the act of one who or that which leads; guidance, direction; lead. *—adj.* **2.** directing; guiding. **3.** chief; principal; most important; foremost. [f. LEAD[1] + -ING[1]]

leading[2] (lĕd′ĭng), *n.* **1.** a covering or framing of lead. **2.** *Print.* lead[2] (def. 9). [f. LEAD[2] + -ING[1]]

leading article (lē′dĭng), a principal editorial article in a newspaper; a leader.

leading edge (lē′dĭng), *Aeron.* the edge of an aerofoil or propeller blade facing the direction of motion.

leading light (lē′dĭng), *Colloq.* a person outstanding in a particular sphere.

leading man (lē′dĭng), the principal male actor in a play, film, etc. **—leading lady,** *fem.*

leading note (lē′dĭng), *Music.* the seventh degree of the scale.

leading question (lē′dĭng), a question so worded as to suggest the proper or desired answer.

leading reins (lē′dĭng), (*usually pl.*) **1.** a harness and rein-like strap for leading and supporting a child when learning to walk. **2.** excessively restraining guidance. Also, **leading string.**

lead line (lĕd), *Naut.* a line used in taking soundings.

lead monoxide (lĕd), *Chem.* litharge.

lead-off (lĕd′ŏf′), *n.* an act which starts something; start; beginning.

lead oxide (lĕd), *Chem.* litharge.

lead paint (lĕd), paint containing lead pigment, esp. white lead.

lead pencil (lĕd), an implement for writing or drawing made of graphite in a wooden or metal holder.

lead poisoning (lĕd), *Pathol.* a diseased condition due to the introduction of lead into the system, common among workers in lead or its compounds; plumbism.

lead screw (lĕd), *Mach.* the device by which traversing is effected on a lathe.

leadsman (lĕdz′mən), *n., pl.* **-men.** *Naut.* a man who heaves the lead in taking soundings.

lead tetraethyl (lĕd), *Chem.* a colourless liquid, $Pb(C_2H_5)_4$, used in petrol for internal-combustion engines because of its antiknock properties.

leady (lĕd′ĭ), *adj.* like lead; leaden.

leaf (lēf), *n., pl.* **leaves** (lēvz), *v.* **—n.** **1.** one of the expanded, usually green, organs borne by the stem of a plant. **2.** any similar or corresponding lateral outgrowth of a stem. **3.** a petal: *a rose leaf.* **4.** foliage or leafage. **5. in leaf,** covered with foliage or leaves. **6.** *Bibliog.* a unit generally comprising two printed pages of a book, one on each side, but also applied to blank or illustrated pages. **7.** a thin sheet of metal, etc. **8.** a lamina or layer. **9.** a sliding, hinged, or detachable flat part, as of a door, tabletop, etc. **10.** a single strip of metal in a composite, or leaf, spring. **11.** *Bldg Trades.* one of the two solid outer parts of a cavity wall. **12.** a layer of fat, esp. that about the kidneys of a pig. **13. take a leaf out of someone's book,** to follow someone's example. **14. turn over a new leaf,** to begin a new and better course of conduct or action. **—*v.i.*** **15.** to put forth leaves. **—*v.t.*** **16. leaf through,** to turn the pages of quickly. [ME *leef,* OE *lēaf,* c. G *Laub*] **—leaf′-like′,** *adj.*

A
B
C C

Leaf of heart's-ease, *Viola tricolor*: A, Lamina; B, Petiole; C, Stipule

leafage (lē′fĭj), *n.* foliage.

leaf-hopper (lēf′hŏp′ə), *n.* any of the leaping homopterous insects of the family *Cicadellidae,* including many crop pests.

leaf-lard (lēf′läd′), *n.* lard prepared from the leaf (def. 12) of the pig.

leafless (lēf′lĭs), *adj.* without leaves. **—leaf′lessness,** *n.*

leaflet (lēf′lĭt), *n.* **1.** one of the separate blades or divisions of a compound leaf. **2.** a small leaf-like part or structure. **3.** a small or young leaf. **4.** a small flat or folded sheet of printed matter, as for distribution.

leaf mould, 1. *Hort.* a mass of semi-decayed leaves used as a constituent of potting composts. **2.** *Bot.* any of a number of fungi which attack the foliage of cultivated plants.

leaf spring, a long, narrow, multiple spring composed of several layers of spring metal bracketed together. See illus. under **spring.**

leafstalk (lēf′stôk′), *n.* petiole (def. 1).

leafy (lē′fĭ), *adj.,* **-fier, -fiest.** **1.** abounding in, covered with, or consisting of leaves or foliage: *the leafy woods.* **2.** leaf-like; foliaceous. **—leaf′iness,** *n.*

league[1] (lēg), *n., v.,* **leagued, leaguing,** *adj.* **—n. 1.** a covenant or compact made between persons, parties, states, etc., for the maintenance or promotion of common interests or for mutual assistance or service. **2.** the aggregation of persons, parties, states, etc., associated in such a covenant; a confederacy. **3. in league,** united by or having a compact or agreement; allied (often fol. by *with*). **4.** category or class: *they are not in the same league.* **5.** an association of sporting clubs which arranges matches between teams of approximately similar standard. **6.** (*cap.*) See **Rugby League. —*v.t.*** **7.** to unite in a league; combine. **—*v.i.*** **8.** to join in a league. **—*adj.*** **9.** of or belonging to a league. **10.** of or pertaining to Rugby League. [ME *ligg,* t. OF: m. *ligue,* t. It.: m. *liga, lega,* der. *legare,* g. L *ligāre* bind] **—Syn. 1.** See **alliance.**

league[2] (lēg), *n.* a unit of distance, varying at different periods and in different countries, in English-speaking countries usually estimated roughly at 3 miles. [ME *le(u)ge,* t. LL: m. *leuga, leuca,* said to be of Gallic orig.]

League of Nations, the organization of nations of the world to promote world peace and cooperation which was created by the Treaty of Versailles (1919) and dissolved, April 1946, by action of its 21st assembly.

leaguer[1] (lē′gə), *Archaic.* **—*v.t.*** **1.** to besiege. **—*n.*** **2.** a siege. **3.** a military camp, esp. of a besieging army. [t. D: m. *leger* bed, camp. See LAIR, LAAGER]

leaguer[2] (lē′gə), *n.* a member of a league. [f. LEAGUE[1] + -ER[1]]

Leah (lĭə), *n.* the first wife of Jacob.

leak (lēk), *n.* **1.** an unintended hole, crack, or the like by which fluid, gas, etc., enters or escapes. **2.** any avenue or means of unintended entrance or escape, or the entrance or escape itself. **3.** *Elect.* a point where current escapes from a conductor, as because of poor insulation. **4.** the act of leaking. **5.** an accidental or apparently accidental disclosure of information, etc. **6.** *Slang.* an act of passing water; urination. **—*v.i.*** **7.** to let fluid, gas, etc., enter or escape, as through an unintended hole, crack, permeable material, or the like: *the roof is leaking.* **8.** to pass in or out in this manner, as water, etc.: *gas leaking from a pipe.* **9.** to transpire or become known undesignedly (fol. by *out*). **10.** *Slang.* to pass water; urinate. **—*v.t.*** **11.** to let (fluid, information, etc.) leak in or out. [ME *leke,* t. Scand.; cf. Icel. *leka* drip, leak, c. MD *leken*]

leakage (lē′kĭj), *n.* **1.** the act of leaking; leak. **2.** that which leaks in or out. **3.** the amount that leaks in or out. **4.** *Com.* an allowance for loss by leaking. **5.** *Physics.* the escape of any radiation through a shield round a nuclear reactor.

leakage current, *Elect.* a relatively small current flowing through or across the surface of an insulator when a voltage is impressed upon it.

Leakey (lē′kĭ), *n.* **Louis Seymour Bazett,** born 1903, British archaeologist and anthropologist.

leaky (lē′kĭ), *adj.,* **-kier, -kiest. 1.** allowing fluid, gas, etc., to leak in or out. **2.** *Colloq.* apt to disclose secrets, as a person. **—leak′iness,** *n.*

leal (lēl), *adj.* *Archaic or Scot.* loyal. [ME *lele,* t. OF: m. *leial.* See LOYAL] **—leal′ly,** *adv.*

Leamington (lĕm′ĭng tən), *n.* a town in England, in Warwickshire: spa. 42,561 (1961).

lean[1] (lēn), *v.,* **leant** or **leaned, leaning,** *n.* **—*v.i.*** **1.** to incline or bend from a vertical position or in a particular direction. **2.** to incline in feeling, opinion, action, etc.: *to lean towards socialism.* **3.** to rest against or on something for support: *lean against a wall.* **4.** to depend or rely: *to lean on empty promises.* **5. lean over backwards.** See **backwards** (def. 7). **—*v.t.*** **6.** to incline or bend: *he leant his head forward.* **7.** to cause to lean or rest (fol. by *against, on, upon,* etc.): *lean your arm against the railing.* **—*n.*** **8.** the act of leaning; inclination. [ME *lene(n),* OE *hleonian,* c. G *lehnen*; akin to L *-clīnāre* incline]

lean[2] (lēn), *adj.* **1.** (of persons or animals) scant of flesh; thin; not plump or fat: *lean cattle.* **2.** (of meat) containing little or no fat. **3.** lacking in richness, fullness, quantity, etc.: *a lean diet, lean years.* **4.** (of paint) having a comparatively low oil content. **5.** *Print.* (of letters or strokes) thin; narrow. —*n.* **6.** that part of flesh which consists of muscular tissue rather than fat. **7.** the lean part of anything. [ME *lene*, OE *hlǣne*] —**lean′ly,** *adv.* —**lean′ness,** *n.* —**Syn. 1.** skinny. See **thin.**

Leander (lĭ ăn′də), *n.* See **Hero and Leander.**

lean-face (lēn′fās′), *adj. Print.* (of type) not having the full breadth; thin; narrow. Also, **thin-face.**

leangle (lē′ăng′gl), *n. Austral.* a heavy aboriginal weapon. [t. native Australian]

leaning (lē′nĭng), *n.* inclination; tendency: *strong literary leanings.*

leant (lĕnt), *v.* a pt. and pp. of **lean**[1].

lean-to (lēn′to͞o′), *n., pl.* **-tos.** a shed, or penthouse, with rafters, propped against another building or wall.

leap (lēp), *v.,* **leapt** or **leaped, leaping,** *n.* —*v.i.* **1.** to spring through the air from one point or position to another: *to leap over a ditch.* **2.** to move quickly and lightly: *to leap aside.* **3.** to pass, come, rise, etc., as if with a bound: *to leap to a conclusion.* —*v.t.* **4.** to jump over: *to leap a wall.* **5.** to pass over as if by a leap. **6.** to cause to leap. —*n.* **7.** a spring, jump, or bound; a light springing movement. **8.** the space cleared in a leap. **9.** a place leapt, or to be leapt, over or from. **10.** an abrupt transition, esp. a rise. **11.** *Music.* a melodic interval greater than a second. **12. by leaps and bounds,** very rapidly. **13. leap in the dark,** an action taken without knowledge of the possible outcomes. [ME *lepe(n)*, OE *hlēapan* leap, run, c. G *laufen* run. Cf. LOPE] —**leap′er,** *n.* —**Syn. 1.** See **jump.**

leapfrog (lēp′frŏg′), *n., v.,* **-frogged, -frogging.** —*n.* **1.** a game in which one player leaps over another who is in a stooping posture. —*v.t., v.i.* **2.** to jump over (a person or thing) in, or as in, leapfrog; to move or advance (something) by leaping in this manner over obstacles.

leapt (lĕpt, lēpt), *v.* a pt. and pp. of **leap.**

leap year, a year containing 366 days, or one day (February 29th) more than the ordinary year, to offset the difference in length between the ordinary year and the astronomical year (being, in practice, every year whose number is exactly divisible by 4, as 1948, except centenary years not exactly divisible by 400, as 1900).

Lear (lĭə), *n.* **Edward,** 1812–88, English humorist and painter.

learn (lûn), *v.,* **learnt** or **learned** (lûnd), **learning.** —*v.t.* **1.** to acquire knowledge of or skill in by study, instruction, or experience: *to learn French.* **2.** to memorize. **3.** to become informed of or acquainted with; ascertain: *to learn the truth.* **4.** to acquire (a habit or the like). —*v.i.* **5.** to acquire knowledge or skill: *to learn rapidly.* **6.** to become informed (fol. by *of*): *to learn of an accident.* [ME *lernen*, OE *leornian*, c. G *lernen*; akin to OE *gelǣran* teach] —**learn′er,** *n.*

—**Syn.** 1. LEARN, ASCERTAIN, DETECT, DISCOVER imply adding to one's store of facts. To LEARN is to add to one's knowledge or information: *to learn a language.* To ASCERTAIN is to verify facts by inquiry or analysis: *to ascertain the truth about an event.* To DETECT implies becoming aware of something which had been obscure, secret, or concealed: *to detect a flaw in reasoning.* To DISCOVER is also used with obj. clauses as a synonym of LEARN in order to suggest that the new information acquired is surprising to the learner: *I discovered that she had been married before.*

learned (lû′nĭd), *adj.* **1.** having much knowledge gained by study; scholarly: *a group of learned men.* **2.** of or showing learning. **3.** applied as a term of courtesy to a member of the legal profession: *my learned friend.* —**learn′edly,** *adv.* —**learn′edness,** *n.*

learning (lû′nĭng), *n.* **1.** knowledge acquired by systematic study in any field or fields of scholarly application. **2.** the act or process of acquiring knowledge or skill. **3.** *Psychol.* the modification of behaviour through interaction with the environment.

—**Syn.** 1. LEARNING, ERUDITION, LORE, SCHOLARSHIP refer to knowledge existing or acquired. LEARNING is knowledge acquired by systematic study, as of literature, history, or science: *a body of learning; fond of literary learning.* ERUDITION suggests a thorough, formal, and profound sort of knowledge obtained by extensive research; it is esp. applied to knowledge in fields other than those of mathematics and physical sciences: *a man of vast erudition in languages.* LORE is accumulated knowledge in a particular field, esp. of a curious, anecdotal, or traditional nature; the word is now somewhat poetic: *gipsy lore.* SCHOLARSHIP is the formalized learning which is taught in schools, esp. as actively employed by one trying to master some field of knowledge or extend its bounds: *high standards of scholarship in history.*

learnt (lûnt), *v.* a pt. and pp. of **learn.**

lease (lēs), *n., v.,* **leased, leasing.** —*n.* **1.** an instrument conveying property to another for a definite period, or at will, usually in consideration of rent or other periodical compensation. **2.** the period of time for which it is made. **3. a new lease of life,** a renewed zest for life. —*v.t.* **4.** to grant the temporary possession or use of (lands, tenements, etc.) to another, usually for compensation at a fixed rate; let. **5.** to take or to hold by a lease, as lands. [ME *lese*, t. AF: m. *les* a letting, der. OF *laissier* let; g. L *laxāre* loosen] —**leas′er,** *n.*

leasehold (lēs′hōld′), *n.* **1.** a land interest acquired under a lease. —*adj.* **2.** held by lease.

leaseholder (lēs′hōl′də), *n.* a tenant under a lease.

leash (lēsh), *n.* **1.** a strong lead for a dog. **2.** *Sport.* a set of three, as of hounds. —*v.t.* **3.** to secure or hold in or as in a leash. [ME *lees, lese*, t. OF: m. *laisse*, g. L *laxa*, fem. of L *laxus* loose, lax]

least (lēst), *adj.* **1.** little beyond all others in size, amount, degree, etc.; smallest; slightest: *the least distance.* **2.** *Archaic.* lowest in consideration or dignity. —*n.* **3.** that which is least; the least amount, quantity, degree, etc. **4. at least, a.** at the least or lowest estimate. **b.** at any rate; in any case. **5. in the least,** in the smallest degree. —*adv.* **6.** to the least extent, amount, or degree. [ME *leest(e)*, OE *lǣst*, superl. of *lǣs(sa)* LESS]

least common multiple. See **common multiple.**

least squares, *Statistics.* a method of determining constants from observations, by minimizing squares of residuals between observations and their theoretical expected values.

leastways (lēst′wāz′), *adv. Colloq.* at least; at any rate. Also, **leastwise** (lēst′wīz′).

leat (lēt), *n.* a conduit by which water is conducted on to a waterwheel. [ME, OE *gelǣt*, der. *lǣtan* LET[1]]

leather (lĕth′ə), *n.* **1.** the skin of animals prepared for use by tanning or a similar process. **2.** some article or appliance made of this material. —*v.t.* **3.** to cover or furnish with leather. **4.** *Colloq.* to beat with a leather strap. [ME *lether*, OE *lether* (in compounds), c. D *leder* and G *Leder*, Icel. *ledhr*]

leatherback (lĕth′ə băk′), *n.* a large marine turtle, *Dermochelys coriacea*, with a longitudinally ridged flexible carapace formed of a mosaic of small bony plates embedded in a leathery skin.

leatherette (lĕth′ə rĕt′), *n.* a substitute for leather, used in making bags, suitcases, etc., consisting mostly of vegetable fibre, as paper stock, variously treated. Also, **leatheroid** (lĕth′ə roid′).

Leatherhead (lĕth′ə hĕd′), *n.* a town in England, in Surrey. 35,582 (1961).

leatherjacket (lĕth′ə jăk′ĭt), *n.* a voracious fish of the genus *Aleuteridae*, of Australian coastal waters.

leathern (lĕth′ən), *adj. Archaic.* **1.** made of leather. **2.** resembling leather. [ME and OE *lether(e)n.* See -EN[2]]

leatherneck (lĕth′ə nĕk′), *n. Slang.* a U.S. marine.

leatherwood (lĕth′ə wo͝od′), *n.* **1.** an American shrub, *Dirca palustris*, with a tough bark. **2.** any of various shrubs of Australia belonging to the family *Cunoniaceae.*

leathery (lĕth′ə rĭ), *adj.* like leather; tough and flexible.

leave[1] (lēv), *v.,* **left, leaving.** —*v.t.* **1.** to go away from, depart from, or quit, as a place, a person, or a thing. **2.** to let stay or be as specified: *to leave a door unlocked.* **3.** to desist from, stop, or abandon (fol. by *off*). **4.** to let (a person, etc.) remain in a position to do something without interference: *leave him alone.* **5.** to let (a thing) remain for action or decision. **6.** to omit or exclude (fol. by *out*). **7.** to allow to remain in the same place, condition, etc. **8.** to let remain, or have remaining behind, after going, disappearing, ceasing, etc.: *the wound left a scar.* **9.** to have remaining after death: *he leaves a widow.* **10.** to give in charge; give for use after one's death or departure. **11.** to have as a remainder after subtraction: *2 from 4 leaves 2.* —*v.i.* **12.** to go away, depart, or set out: *we leave for France tomorrow.* **13. leave it at that,** to go no further; do or say nothing more. **14. leave off, a.** not to put on something (as an item of clothing): *he left off his hat.* **b.** to exclude from: *they left her name off the list.* **c.** *Colloq.* to stop; cease doing something: *leave off crying now.* [ME *leve(n)*, OE *lǣfan* (der. *lāf* remainder), c. OHG *leiban*, Icel. *leifa*, Goth. *-laibjan*] —**leav′er,** *n.* —**Syn. 1.** vacate; abandon, forsake, desert. **4.** See **let**[1]. **10.** bequeath, will; devise, transmit.

leave[2] (lēv), *n.* **1.** permission to do something. **2.** permission to be absent, as from duty: *to be on leave.* **3.** the time this permission lasts: *30 days' leave.* **4.** a farewell: *to take leave of someone.* [ME *leve*, OE *lēaf.* Cf. D *(oor)lof*, G *(Ur)laub*, *(Ver)laub* FURLOUGH]

leave[3] (lēv), *v.i.,* **leaved, leaving.** to put forth leaves; leaf. [var. of LEAF, v.i.]

leaved (lēvd), *adj.* having leaves; leafed.

leaven (lĕv′ən), *n.* **1.** a mass of fermenting dough reserved for producing fermentation in a new batch of dough. **2.** any substance which produces fermentation. **3.** an agency which works in a thing to produce a gradual change or modification. —*v.t.* **4.** to produce bubbles of gas in (dough or batter) by means of any of a variety of leavening agents. **5.** to permeate with an altering or transforming influence. [ME *levain*, t. OF, g. L *levāmen* that which raises] —**leav′ening,** *n.*

leaves (lēvz), *n.* pl. of **leaf.**

leave-taking (lēv′tā′kĭng), *n.* the saying of farewell.

leaving (lē′vĭng), *n.* **1.** that which is left; residue. **2.** (*pl.*) remains; refuse.

Leavis (lē′vĭs), *n.* **F(rank) R(aymond),** born 1895, English author and critic.

leavy (lē′vĭ), *adj.*, **-vier, -viest.** *Poetic.* leafy.

Lebanese (lĕb′ə nēz′), *adj.* **1.** of or pertaining to Lebanon. —*n.* **2.** a native of Lebanon.

Lebanon (lĕb′ə nən), *n.* a republic at the E end of the Mediterranean, N of Israel. 1,750,000 pop. (est. 1963); 3927 sq. mi. *Cap.:* Beirut.

Lebanon

Lebanon Mountains, a mountain range extending the length of Lebanon, in the central part. Highest peak, 10,049 ft.

Lebensraum (lā′bənz roum′), *n.* additional territory desired by a nation for expansion of trade, etc. [G: room for living]

Lebombo Mountains (lĕ bŏm′bō), a range of low mountains forming the border between the Republic of South Africa and Mozambique.

Le Bourget (*Fr.* lə bo͞or zhĕ′), one of two international airports for Paris. See **Orly.**

Lebrun (*Fr.* lə brœɴ′), *n.* **1. Albert** (*Fr.* ȧl bĕr′), 1871–1950, president of France 1932–40. **2.** Also, **Le Brun. Charles** (*Fr.* shȧrl), 1619–90, French painter. **3. Marie Anne Élisabeth Vigée** (*Fr.* mȧ rē ȧn ĕ lē zȧ bĕt vē zhĕ′) (*Madame Vigée-Lebrun*), 1755–1842, French painter.

Lecce (*It.* lĕt′chĕ), *n.* a town in Italy, in S Apulia. 78,904 (1966).

Lecco (*It.* lĕk′kō), *n.* a town in Italy, in NW Lombardy. 50,918 (1966).

Le Châtelier's principle (*Fr.* lə shȧ tə lyĕ′), *Chem.* the principle which states that if a system is in equilibrium a change in one of the conditions will shift the equilibrium so that the system tends to return to its original condition. [named after H. L. *Le Châtelier*, 1850–1936, French chemist]

lecher (lĕch′ə), *n.* a man immoderately given to sexual indulgence; a lewd man. [ME *lechur*, t. OF: m. *lecheor* gourmand, sensualist, der. *lechier* lick, live in sensuality, t. Gmc; cf. LICK]

lecherous (lĕch′ə rəs), *adj.* **1.** given to or characterized by lechery. **2.** inciting to lechery. —**lech′erously,** *adv.* —**lech′erousness,** *n.*

lecher wires, *Electronics.* parallel wires of such length and terminations that the system will resonate (i.e., standing waves will appear) if the frequency of the excitation is correct.

lechery (lĕch′ə rĭ), *n.* free indulgence of lust.

lechwe (lĕch′wĭ), *n.* an African antelope, *Kobus leche.*

lecithin (lĕs′ĭ thĭn), *n.* *Biochem.* one of a group of yellow-brown fatty substances, found in animal and plant tissues and egg yolk, composed of units of choline, phosphoric acid, fatty acids, and glycerol. [f. m. s. Gk *lékithos* egg yolk + -IN²]

Lecky (lĕk′ĭ), *n.* **William Edward Hartpole,** 1838–1903, British historian and writer, born in Ireland.

Leclanché cell (*Fr.* lə klăɴ shĕ′), *Physics.* a primary cell with a carbon cathode surrounded by manganese dioxide in a porous pot, and a zinc anode dipping into a solution of ammonium chloride; produces 1·5 volts.

Leconte de Lisle (*Fr.* lə kôɴt də lēl′), **Charles Marie** (*Fr.* shȧrl mȧ rē′), 1818–94, French poet.

Le Corbusier (*Fr.* lə kŏr bʏ zyĕ′), (*Charles Édouard Jeanneret*), 1887–1965, Swiss architect in France.

Le Creusot (*Fr.* lə krœ zō′), a town in E France. 33,002 (1962).

lect., **1.** lecture. **2.** lecturer.

lectern (lĕk′tən), *n.* a reading desk in a church, esp. that from which the lessons are read. [earlier *lecturn*, Latinized and metathetic var. of ME *lettrun*, t. OF, t. ML: m. *lectrum*, der. L *legere* read]

lection (lĕk′shən), *n.* **1.** a reading or version of a passage in a particular copy of a text. **2.** a lesson, or portion of sacred writing, read in divine service. [ME, t. L: s. *lectio* a reading]

lectionary (lĕk′shə nə rĭ), *n.*, *pl.* **-ries.** a book, or a list, of lections for reading in divine service.

lector (lĕk′tô), *n.* a reader, as of lectures in a college or university or of scriptural lessons. [late ME, t. L]

lecture (lĕk′chə), *n.*, *v.*, **-tured, -turing.** —*n.* **1.** a discourse read or delivered before an audience, esp. for instruction or to set forth some subject: *a lecture on Picasso.* **2.** a speech of warning or reproof as to conduct; a long, tedious reprimand. —*v.i.* **3.** to give a lecture. —*v.t.* **4.** to deliver a lecture to or before; instruct by lectures. **5.** to rebuke or reprimand at some length. [ME, t. LL: m. *lectura*, der. L *legere* read]

lecturer (lĕk′chə rə), *n.* **1.** one who lectures. **2.** a regular member of the teaching staff of a college or university, employed to deliver lectures. **3.** *C. of E.* a clergyman holding an office, usually attached to a church in a town, and having the functions of an assistant curate, in addition to certain preaching or teaching responsibilities.

lectureship (lĕk′chə shĭp′), *n.* the office of lecturer.

led (lĕd), *v.* pt. and pp. of **lead¹.**

Leda (lē′də), *n.* *Gk Myth.* the mother by Zeus or by her husband Tyndareus of Helen, Clytemnestra, Castor, and Pollux.

ledge (lĕj), *n.* **1.** any relatively narrow, horizontal projecting part, or any part affording a horizontal shelf-like surface. **2.** a more or less flat shelf of rock protruding from a cliff or slope. **3.** a reef, ridge, or line of rocks in the sea or other water bodies. **4.** *Mining.* **a.** a layer or mass of rock underground. **b.** a lode or vein. [ME *legge* transverse bar, OE *lecg* (exact meaning not clear), der. *lecgan* LAY¹] —**ledged,** *adj.*

ledger (lĕj′ə), *n.* **1.** *Bookkeeping.* an account book of final entry, containing all the accounts. **2.** a horizontal timber fastened to the vertical uprights of a scaffold, to support the putlogs. **3.** a flat slab of stone laid over a grave or tomb. [ME *legger* (book), der. *leggen* LAY¹ (see LEDGE)]

ledger bait, *Angling.* a fishing bait used in ledgering. Also, **leger bait.**

ledger board, the horizontal part of a fence, rail, etc.

ledgering (lĕj′ə rĭng), *n.* *Angling.* any of several fishing methods in which the tackle lies on the bottom so that the fish does not feel the weight of lead when it bites. Also, **legering, ledger-baiting.**

ledger line, **1.** *Music.* a short line added when necessary above or below the lines of a stave to increase the range of the stave. **2.** *Angling.* a line used in ledgering. Also, **leger line.** [f. LEDGER (special use) + LINE¹]

L, Ledger lines

ledger tackle, *Angling.* fishing apparatus set up so that the lead lies on the bottom. Also, **leger tackle.**

Ledoux (*Fr.* lə do͞o′), *n.* **Claude-Nicolas** (*Fr.* klōd nē kō lȧ′), 1736–1806, French architect.

lee¹ (lē), *n.* **1.** shelter. **2.** the side or part that is sheltered or turned away from the wind. **3.** *Chiefly Naut.* the quarter or region towards which the wind blows. —*adj.* **4.** *Chiefly Naut.* pertaining to, situated in, or moving towards the quarter or region towards which the wind blows (opposed to *weather*). [ME; OE *hlēo* shelter]

lee² (lē), *n.* (*usually pl.*) that which settles from a liquid, esp. from wine; sediment; dregs. [ME *lie*, t. OF, g. LL *lia*, of Gallic orig.]

Lee (lē), *n.* **1. Kuan Yew** (kwăn′yo͞o′), born 1923, prime minister of Singapore since 1959. **2. Robert E.,** 1807–1870, Confederate general in the American Civil War. **3. Sir Sidney,** 1859–1926, English biographer and critic.

leeboard (lē′bôd′), *n.* a flat board let down vertically into the water on the leeside of a ship or boat to prevent leeward motion.

leech¹ (lēch), *n.* **1.** any of the bloodsucking or carnivorous, usually aquatic, worms constituting the class *Hirudinea*, certain freshwater species of which were formerly much used by physicians for blood-letting and now occasionally used in eye surgery and the like for reducing bruising. **2.** an instrument used for drawing blood. **3.** a person who clings to another with a view to gain. **4.** *Archaic.* a physician. —*v.t.* **5.** to apply leeches to so as to bleed. **6.** *Archaic.* to cure; heal. [ME *leche*, OE *lǣce* (by confusion with *lǣce* physician); r. ME *liche*, OE *lȳce*, der. *lūcan* draw out, burst out] —**leech′like′,** *adj.*

leech² (lēch), *n.* *Naut.* **1.** either of the perpendicular or sloping edges of a square sail. **2.** the after edge of a fore-and-aft sail. [ME *lek*, *leche*, appar. c. G *Liek* bolt rope, leech rope; akin to Icel. *lik* leech line]

Leeds (lēdz), *n.* a county borough in England, in the West Riding of Yorkshire: university, founded 1904. 510,676 (1961).

leek (lēk), *n.* **1.** a plant of the lily family, *Allium porrum*, allied to the onion but having a cylindrical bulb, and used in cookery. **2.** any of various allied species. **3.** the national emblem of Wales. [ME; OE *lēac*, c. G *Lauch*]

leer (lĭə), *n.* **1.** a side glance, esp. of sly or insulting suggestion or significance. —*v.i.* **2.** to look with a leer. [special use of obs. *leer* cheek, OE *hlēor*] —**leer′ingly,** *adv.*

leery (lĭə′rĭ), *adj. Orig. U.S. Slang.* **1.** doubtful; suspicious. **2.** knowing; sly.
lees (lēz), *n.* pl. of **lee**[2].
lee shore, a shore towards which the wind blows.
leeside (lē′sīd′), *n.* the side of any object which is turned away from the wind.
leet[1] (lēt), *n. Obs.* **1.** a special type of manorial court or its jurisdiction. **2.** the jurisdiction of such a court, and the area over which this extended. Also, **court leet.** [ME *lete*, t. AF, ? t. OE: m. *lǣth* landed property]
leet[2] (lēt), *n. Scot.* a short list.
lee tide, a tidal current running in the direction towards which the wind is blowing. Also, **leeward tide.**
Leeuwarden (*Du.* lē′wŏr də), *n.* a town in the Netherlands, the capital of Friesland, in the N part. 86,246 (1965).
Leeuwenhoek (*Du.* lē′wən hōōk), *n.* **Anton van** (*Du.* ŏn′tôn vŏn), 1632–1723, Dutch naturalist and maker of microscopes. Also, **Leuwenhoek.**
leeward (lē′wəd; *Naut.* lōō′əd), *adj.* **1.** pertaining to, situated in, or moving towards the quarter towards which the wind blows (opposed to *windward*). *—n.* **2.** the leeside; the point or quarter towards which the wind blows. *—adv.* **3.** towards the lee.
Leeward Islands (lē′wəd), **1.** a group of islands in the N Lesser Antilles of the West Indies, extending from Puerto Rico SE to Martinique. **2.** a former British colony now divided into the territories of Antigua, St Kitts, Nevis, Anguilla, Montserrat, and the (British) Virgin Islands. 141,239 (1961).
leeway (lē′wā′), *n.* **1.** the lateral movement of a ship to leeward, or the resulting deviation from her true course. **2.** *Aeron.* the amount an aeroplane is blown off its normal course by cross-winds. **3.** *Naut.* the distance a ship is forced sideways from her course by the wind. **4.** *Colloq.* extra space, time, money, etc.
left[1] (lĕft), *adj.* **1.** belonging or pertaining to the side of a person or thing which is turned towards the west when facing north (opposed to *right*). **2.** belonging or pertaining to the political left. *—n.* **3.** the left side, or what is on the left side. **4.** (in continental Europe) that part of a legislative assembly which sits on the left side of the chamber as viewed by the president, a position customarily assigned to representatives holding socialist or radical views. **5.** (*often cap.*) a party or group holding such views. [ME; special use of d. OE *left* (OE *lyft*) weak, infirm. Cf. MD and MLG *lucht*]
left[2] (lĕft), *v.* pt. and pp. of **leave**[1].
left back, *Soccer, Hockey, etc.* the full-back on the left side of the field of play.
left centre, *Rugby Football.* the left of the two middle players in the three-quarter line.
left half, *Soccer, Hockey, etc.* the left of the three players in the half-back line.
left-hand (lĕft′hănd′), *adj.* **1.** on or to the left: *left-hand drive.* **2.** of, for, or with the left hand.
left-handed (lĕft′hăn′dĭd), *adj.* **1.** having the left hand more serviceable than the right; preferring to use the left hand. **2.** adapted to or performed by the left hand. **3.** situated on the side of the left hand. **4.** moving or rotating from right to left. **5.** ambiguous or doubtful: *a left-handed compliment.* **6.** clumsy or awkward. **7.** morganatic (from the bridegroom's giving the bride his left hand instead of his right as was customary at morganatic weddings). —**left′-hand′edly,** *adv.* —**left′-hand′edness,** *n.*
leftist (lĕf′tĭst), *n.* **1.** a member of a socialist or radical party or a person sympathizing with their views. *—adj.* **2.** having socialist or radical political ideas. [f. LEFT[1] (def. 4) + -IST]
left-luggage office (lĕft′lŭg′ĭj), a room, as at a railway station, where luggage, etc., may be left temporarily for a small fee.
leftover (lĕft′ō′və), *n.* **1.** something left over or remaining. **2.** a remnant of food, as from a meal.
leftward (lĕft′wəd), *adj.* **1.** situated on the left. **2.** directed towards the left. *—adv.* **3.** leftwards.
leftwards (lĕft′wədz), *adv.* towards or on the left. Also, **leftward.**
left wing, **1.** members of a socialist, progressive, or radical political party or section of a party, generally those favouring extensive political reform. **2.** such a group, party, or a group of such parties. **3.** *Sport.* that part of the field of play which forms the left flank of the area being attacked by either team. **4.** *Sport.* a player positioned on the left flank, as the outside left in soccer, the left or the wing three-quarters in Rugby football, etc. —**left′-wing′,** *adj.* —**left′-wing′er,** *n.*
leg (lĕg), *n., v.,* **legged, legging,** *adj. —n.* **1.** one of the members or limbs which support and move the human or animal body. **2.** that part of the limb between the knee and the ankle. **3.** something resembling or suggesting a leg in use, position, or appearance. **4.** that part of a garment, such as a stocking, trousers, or the like, which covers the leg. **5.** one of the supports of a piece of furniture. **6.** one of the sides of a pair of dividers or compasses. **7.** one of the sides of a triangle other than the base or hypotenuse. **8.** a timber, bar, etc., serving to prop or shore up a structure. **9.** one of the distinct portions of any course: *the last leg of a trip.* **10.** *Naut.* **a.** one of the series of straight runs which make up the zigzag course of a sailing ship. **b.** one straight or nearly straight part of a multiple-sided course in a sailing race. **11.** *Sport.* **a.** one of a number of parts of a contest, each of which must be completed in order to determine the winner. **b.** a stage or given distance in a relay race. **12.** *Cricket.* **a.** the leg side. **b.** a fielder on the leg side. **13. a leg up,** assistance in climbing or mounting. **14. have not a leg to stand on,** not to have any good reason at all. **15. pull (one's) leg,** to make fun of (one); to tease. **16. shake a leg,** *Slang.* to hurry up. **17. show a leg,** to make an appearance, as by visiting in the morning. *—v.t.* **18.** *Obsolesc.* to propel (a boat) through a canal tunnel by means of pressing two feet against the top and sides of the tunnel. *—v.i.* **19. leg it,** *Colloq.* to walk or run. *—adj.* **20.** *Cricket.* of, pertaining to, or denoting that part of the field to the left of and behind the batsman as he faces the bowler (whether he is left-handed or right-handed). [ME, t. Scand.; cf. Icel. *leggr*] —**leg′less,** *adj.*
leg., **1.** legal. **2.** legate. **3.** legato. **4.** legislative. **5.** legislature.
legacy (lĕg′ə sĭ), *n., pl.* **-cies.** **1.** *Law.* a gift of property, esp. personal property, as money, by will; a bequest. **2.** anything handed down by an ancestor or predecessor. [ME *legacie*, t. OF: legateship, t. ML: m. s. *lēgātia*, der. L *lēgātus* LEGATE]
legal (lē′gl), *adj.* **1.** appointed, established, or authorized by law; deriving authority from law. **2.** of or pertaining to law: connected with the law or its administration: *the legal profession.* **3.** permitted by law, or lawful: *such acts are not legal.* **4.** recognized by law rather than by equity. **5.** characteristic of the profession of the law: *a legal mind.* **6.** *Theol.* **a.** of or pertaining to the Mosaic Law. **b.** of or pertaining to the doctrine of salvation by good works rather than through free grace. [t. L: s. *lēgālis* pertaining to law] —**le′gally,** *adv.*
legal aid, financial assistance given to persons according to a scale based on income and capital for the purpose of legal proceedings in practically all courts.
legal fiction. See **fiction** (def. 5).
legalism (lē′gə lĭz′əm), *n.* **1.** strict adherence, or the principle of strict adherence, to law or formulated rules. **2.** *Theol.* the doctrine of salvation by good works. —**le′galist,** *n.* —**le′galis′tic,** *adj.*
legality (lĭ găl′ĭ tĭ), *n., pl.* **-ties.** **1.** the state or quality of being in conformity with the law; lawfulness. **2.** attachment to or observance of law. **3.** *Theol.* reliance on good works for salvation, rather than on free grace.
legalize (lē′gə līz′), *v.t.,* **-lized, -lizing.** to make legal; authorize; sanction. Also, **legalise.** —**le′galiza′tion,** *n.*
Le Gallienne (lə găl yĕn′, găl′yən), **Richard,** 1866–1947, English poet and writer.
legal separation, judicial separation.
legal tender, *Law.* currency which may be lawfully tendered or offered in payment of money debts and which may not be refused by creditors.
Legaspi (lĕ găs′pĭ), *n.* a seaport in the Philippine Islands, on SE Luzon. 98,410 (est. 1960). Formerly, **Albay.**
legate (lĕg′ĭt), *n.* **1.** an ecclesiastic delegated by the pope as his representative. **2.** *Rom. Hist.* **a.** an assistant to a general or to a consul or magistrate, in the government of any army or a province; a commander of a legion. **b.** a provincial governor of senatorial rank appointed by the emperor. **3.** an envoy. [ME *legat*, t. L: s. *lēgātus* deputy, prop. pp., deputed] —**leg′ateship′,** *n.* —**legatine** (lĕg′ətīn′), *adj.*
legatee (lĕg′ə tē′), *n.* one to whom a legacy is bequeathed.
legation (lĭ gā′shən), *n.* **1.** a diplomatic minister and his staff when the minister is not of the highest (or ambassadorial) rank. **2.** the official residence or place of business of a minister. **3.** the office or position of a legate. [late ME, t. L: s. *lēgātio* embassy] —**legationary** (lĭ gā′shə nə rĭ), *adj.*
legato (lĭgä′tō; *It.* lĕ gä′tō), *Music. —adj.* **1.** smooth and connected, without breaks between the successive notes. *—adv.* **2.** in a legato manner. Cf. **staccato.** [t. It., pp. of *legare*, g. L *ligāre* bind]
legator (lĕg′ə tô′), *n.* one who bequeaths; a testator. —**legatorial** (lĕg′ə tô′rĭ əl), *adj.*
leg before wicket, *Cricket.* the act of stopping with the

leg or some other part of the body, a pitched ball which would otherwise have hit the wicket, for which a batsman may be declared out. *Abbrev.*: l.b.w.

leg break, *Cricket.* a ball bowled so as to change direction from leg to off when it pitches.

leg bye, *Cricket.* a run scored after the ball has struck part of the batsman's body other than his hand. *Abbrev.*: l.b.

legend (lěj′ənd), *n.* **1.** a non-historical or unverifiable story handed down by tradition from earlier times and popularly accepted as historical. **2.** matter of this kind. **3.** an inscription, esp. on a coin, a coat of arms, a monument, or under a picture, or the like. **4.** explanatory matter in a table or the like forming part of an illustration. **5.** a story of the life of a saint. **6.** *Obs. except Hist.* a collection of such stories. **7.** a collection of stories of any admirable person. [ME *legende*, t. OF, t. ML: m. *legenda*, lit., things to be read, orig. neut. pl. gerundive of L *legere* read]

—Syn. 1. LEGEND, FABLE, MYTH refer to fictitious stories, usually handed down by tradition (though some fables are modern). LEGEND, originally denoting a story concerning the life of a saint, is applied to any fictitious story, sometimes involving the supernatural, and usually concerned with a real person, place, or other subject: *the legend of St Andrew.* A FABLE is specifically a fictitious story (often with animals or inanimate things as speakers or actors) designed to teach a moral: *a fable about industrious bees.* A MYTH is one of a class of stories, usually concerning gods, heroes, imaginary animals, etc., current since primitive times, the purpose of which is to attempt to explain some belief or natural phenomenon: *the Greek myth about Demeter.* **—Ant. 1.** fact.

legendary (lěj′ən də rĭ, -drĭ), *adj., n., pl.* **-ries.** *—adj.* **1.** pertaining to or of the nature of a legend or legends. **2.** celebrated or described in legend. *—n.* **3.** a collection of legends.

Legendre (*Fr.* lə zhäɴ′dr), *n.* **Adrien Marie** (*Fr.* à drē-äɴ mà rē′), 1752–1833, French mathematician.

legendry (lěj′ən drĭ), *n.* legends collectively.

Léger (*Fr.* lė zhė′), *n.* **Fernand** (*Fr.* fĕr näɴ′), 1881–1955, French artist.

legerdemain (lěj′ə də mān′), *n.* **1.** sleight of hand. **2.** trickery; deception. **3.** any artful trick. [ME, t. F: m. *léger de main* light(ness) of hand]

legering (lěj′ə rĭng), *n.* ledgering.

leger line (lěj′ə), *Music.* ledger line.

leges (lē′jēz), *n.* pl. of **lex.**

legged (lěg′ĭd, lěgd), *adj.* having a specified number or kind of legs: *one-legged, long-legged.*

legging (lěg′ĭng), *n.* (*usually pl.*) an extra outer covering for the leg, usually extending from the ankle to the knee, but sometimes higher.

leggy (lěg′ĭ), *adj.* having long legs.

Leghorn (lěg′hôn′ *for 1–3;* lĕ gôn′ *for 4*), *n.* **1.** Livorno. **2.** a fine, smooth, plaited straw. **3.** (*l.c.*) a hat, etc., made of this. **4.** one of a Mediterranean breed of the domestic fowl, characterized by prolific laying of white-shelled eggs.

legible (lěj′ə bl), *adj.* **1.** that may be read or deciphered, esp. with ease, as writing or printing. **2.** that may be discerned or distinguished. [ME, t. LL: m. s. *legibilis*, der. L *legere* read] **—leg′ibil′ity, leg′ibleness,** *n.* **—leg′ibly,** *adv.*

legion (lē′jən), *n.* **1.** an infantry brigade in the army of ancient Rome, numbering from 3000 to 6000 men, and usually combined with from 300 to 700 cavalry. **2.** one of certain military bodies of modern times, as the Foreign Legion. **3.** a military or semi-military unit. **4.** any large body of armed men. **5.** any great host or multitude, whether of persons or of things. *—adj.* **6.** containing or amounting to a great number. [ME, t. OF, t. L: s. *legio*]

legionary (lē′jə nə rĭ), *adj., n., pl.* **-ries.** *—adj.* **1.** pertaining or belonging to a legion. **2.** constituting a legion or legions. *—n.* **3.** *Hist.* a soldier of a legion. **4.** a member of the British Legion.

legionnaire (lē′jyə nĕə′), *n.* **1.** (*often cap.*) *Chiefly U.S.* a member of the American Legion. **2.** a member of a legion. [t. F]

Legion of Honour, a French order of distinction, instituted in 1802 by Napoleon, membership being granted for meritorious civil or military services.

Legis., Legislature.

legislate (lěj′ĭs lāt′), *v.,* **-lated, -lating.** *—v.i.* **1.** to exercise the function of legislation; make or enact laws. *—v.t.* **2.** to effect, bring (*into*), put (*out*), etc., by legislation. [back-formation from LEGISLATION or LEGISLATOR]

legislation (lěj′ĭs lā′shən), *n.* **1.** the act of making or enacting laws. **2.** a law or a body of laws enacted. [t. LL: s. *lēgislātio*, L *lēgis lātio* the proposing of a law]

legislative (lěj′ĭs lə tĭv), *adj.* **1.** having the function of making laws: *a legislative body.* **2.** of or pertaining to legislation: *legislative proceedings.* **3.** ordained by legislation: *a legislative penalty.* **4.** pertaining to a legislature: *a legislative recess.* *—n.* **5.** *Rare.* the legislature. **—leg′islatively,** *adv.*

legislator (lěj′ĭs lā′tə), *n.* **1.** one who gives or makes laws. **2.** a member of a legislative body. [t. L: *legis lātor* bringer of a law] **—legislatress** (lěj′ĭs lā′trĭs), *n. fem.*

legislatorial (lěj′ĭs lə tô′rĭ əl), *adj.* of or pertaining to legislators or legislations.

legislature (lěj′ĭs lā′chə), *n.* the legislative body of a country or state.

legist (lē′jĭst), *n.* one versed in law.

legit (lə jĭt′), *adj. Slang.* legitimate, truthful.

legitim (lěj′ĭ tĭm), *n. Scots Law.* the legal share of the father's free moveable property which must be left on his death to his children. [t. L: s. *lēgitima* (*pars*) lawful (part)]

legitimacy (lĭ jĭt′ĭ mə sĭ), *n.* the state or fact of being legitimate.

legitimate (*adj.* lĭ jĭt′ĭ mĭt; *v.* lĭ jĭt′ĭ māt′), *adj., v.,* **-mated, -mating.** *—adj.* **1.** according to law; lawful. **2.** in accordance with established rules, principles, or standards. **3.** of the normal or regular type or kind. **4.** in accordance with the laws of reasoning; logically inferable; logical: *a legitimate conclusion.* **5.** born in wedlock, or of parents legally married. **6.** resting on or ruling by the principle of hereditary right: *a legitimate sovereign.* **7.** genuine; not spurious. **8.** *Theat.* pertaining to or denoting plays or acting with a serious and literary purpose. *—v.t.* **9.** to make or pronounce lawful. **10.** to establish as lawfully born. **11.** to show or declare to be legitimate or proper. **12.** to authorize; justify. [late ME, t. ML: m. s. *lēgitimātus*, pp. of *lēgitimāre* make lawful, der. L *lēgitimus* lawful] **—legit′imately,** *adv.* **—legit′imateness,** *n.* **—legit′ima′tion,** *n.*

legitimatize (lĭ jĭt′ĭ mə tīz′), *v.t.,* **-tized, -tizing.** to legitimate. Also, **legitimatise.**

legitimist (lĭ jĭt′ĭ mĭst), *n.* a supporter of legitimate authority, esp. of a claim to a throne based on direct descent. **—legit′imism,** *n.* **—legit′imis′tic,** *adj.*

legitimize (lĭ jĭt′ĭ mīz′), *v.t.,* **-mized, -mizing.** to legitimate. Also, **legitimise.** **—legit′imiza′tion,** *n.*

leg-of-mutton (lěg′ə mŭt′n), *adj.* **1.** having the triangular shape of a leg of mutton, as a sail, etc. **2.** (of a sleeve) very full at the shoulder then narrowing so as to be closely fitting at the wrist.

legroom (lěg′ro͞om′), *n.* room to put one's legs in a comfortable position: *there was very little legroom in the back of the car.*

leg-rope (lěg′rōp′), *v.t., v.i. Austral.* to catch and rope (an animal) by the hind leg.

legume (lěg′yo͞om, lĭ gyo͞om′), *n.* **1.** any plant of the family *Leguminosae*, esp. those used for feed, food, or soil-improving crop. **2.** the pod or seed vessel of such a plant, which is usually dehiscent by both sutures, thus dividing into two parts or valves. **3.** any table vegetable of the family *Leguminosae.* [t. F, t. L: m. *legūmen* legume, pulse, lit., something gathered (or picked)]

legumin (lĭ gyo͞o′mĭn), *n. Biochem.* a protein resembling casein, obtained from the seeds of leguminous and other plants. [f. LEGUME + -IN[2]]

leguminous (lĭ gyo͞o′mĭ nəs), *adj.* **1.** pertaining to, of the nature of, or bearing legumes. **2.** belonging or pertaining to the *Leguminosae*, an order or family regarded as comprising the legume-bearing plants, and sometimes subdivided into the bean, senna, and mimosa families. [f. s. L *legūmen* LEGUME + -OUS]

Lehár (lĭ hä′), *n.* **Franz** (frănts), 1870–1948, Hungarian composer of operettas.

Le Havre (lə hä′vrə; *Fr.* lə à′vr), a seaport in N France, in the Seine-Maritime department, at the mouth of the Seine. 183,776 (1962). Also, **Havre.**

lehr (lĭə), *n.* a long tunnel-shaped oven for annealing glass. Also, **leer, lier, lear.** [t. G: pattern]

lei[1] (lā), *n., pl.* **leis.** (in the Hawaiian Islands) a wreath of flowers, leaves, etc., for the neck or head. [t. Hawaiian]

lei[2] (lā), *n.* pl. of **leu.**

Leibnitz (*Ger.* līb′nĭts), *n.* **Gottfried Wilhelm von** (*Ger.* gŏt′frēt vĭl′hĕlm fŏn), 1646–1716, German philosopher, writer, and mathematician. Also, **Leibniz.** **—Leibnitzian** (līb nĭt′sĭ ən), *adj., n.*

Leicester (lěs′tə), *n.* **1. Robert Dudley, Earl of,** 1532?–1588, English statesman: favourite of Queen Elizabeth I. **2.** a county borough in England, the county town of Leicestershire: university, founded 1957. 273,470 (1961). **3.** Leicestershire. **4.** one of an English variety of large early-maturing sheep with coarse, long wool and a heavy mutton yield. **5.** Also, **Leicester cheese.** a rich, russet-coloured mild cheese, flaky and moist when young.

Leicestershire (lěs′tə shĭə′, -shə), *n.* **1.** a county in central England. 682,196 pop. (1961); 832 sq. mi. *Co. town:* Leicester. *Abbrev.:* Leics. Also, **Leicester.** **2.** Leicester cheese.

Leichhard (lĭk′häd, -hät), *n.* a river in Australia flowing N through Queensland to the Gulf of Carpentaria. ab. 300 mi.

Leics., Leicestershire.

Leiden (lī′dn; *Du.* lĕy′də), *n.* a town in the Netherlands, in NW South Holland. 99,360 (1965). Also, **Leyden.**

Leigh (lē), *n.* **1. Vivien,** 1913–67, English actress. **2.** a town in England, in Lancashire. 46,174 (1961).

Leighton (lā′tn), *n.* **Frederick, Baron,** 1830–96, English painter and sculptor.

Leinster (lĕn′stə), *n.* a province in E Republic of Ireland. 1,332,149 pop. (1961); 7580 sq. mi.

leiomyoma (lī′ō mī ō′mə), *n., pl.* **-omata** (-ō′mə tə), **-omas.** a tumour made up of non-striated muscular tissue. Cf. **rhabdomyoma.** [f. *leio-* (t. Gk, comb. form of *leîos* smooth) + MYOMA]

Leipzig (līp′sĭg; *Ger.* līp′tsĭKH), *n.* a city in S East Germany. 595,203 (1964). Also, **Leipsic** (līp′sĭk). See map under **Saxony.**

leister (lē′stə), *n.* **1.** a spear having three or more prongs, used to spear fish, esp. salmon. *—v.t.* **2.** to strike (a fish) with a leister. [t. Scand.; cf. Icel. *ljōstr*, der. *ljōsta* strike]

leisure (lĕzh′ə), *n.* **1.** the condition of having one's time free from the demands of work or duty; ease: *enjoying a life of leisure.* **2.** free or unoccupied time. **3. at leisure, a.** with free or unrestricted time. **b.** without haste. **4. at one's leisure,** when one has leisure. *—adj.* **5.** free or unoccupied: *leisure hours.* **6.** having leisure. [ME *leiser*, t. OF: m. *leisir* (inf.), g. L *licēre* be permitted]

leisured (lĕzh′əd), *adj.* **1.** having leisure: *the leisured classes.* **2.** leisurely.

leisurely (lĕzh′ə lĭ), *adj.* **1.** acting, proceeding, or done without haste; deliberate: *a leisurely stroll.* **2.** showing or suggesting ample leisure; unhurried: *a leisurely manner.* *—adv.* **3.** in a leisurely manner; without haste. **—lei′sureliness,** *n.* **—Syn. 1.** See **slow.**

Leith (lēth), *n.* a seaport in Scotland, in Midlothian, on the Firth of Forth: a suburb of Edinburgh. 81,618 (1961).

leitmotiv (līt′mō tēf′), *n.* (in a music drama) a theme associated throughout the work with a particular person, situation, or idea. Also, **leitmotif.** [t. G: (m.) *Leitmotiv* leading motive]

Leitrim (lē′trĭm), *n.* a county in NW Republic of Ireland, in Connaught. 33,470 pop. (1961); 588 sq. mi. *Co. town:* Carrick-on-Shannon.

Leix (lēsh), *n.* a county in central Republic of Ireland, in Leinster. 45,069 pop. (1961); 633 sq. mi. *Co. town:* Port Laoise.

lek (lĕk), *n.* **1.** the monetary unit of Albania, equivalent to £0·083 sterling. **2.** a note or coin of this value.

Lek (lĕk), *n.* See **Rhine.**

Lely (lē′lĭ; *Du.* lė′lė), *n.* **Sir Peter** (pē′tə; *Du.* pė′tər) (*Pieter van der Faes*), 1618–80, Dutch portrait painter in England.

LEM (lĕm), *n.* lunar excursion module. See **lunar module.**

Lemaître (*Fr.* lə mĕ′tr), *n.* **François Élie Jules** (*Fr.* fräN swȧ ė lē zhYl′), 1853–1915, French critic and writer.

leman (lĕm′ən, lē′mən), *n.* *Archaic.* **1.** a sweetheart. **2.** a mistress. [ME *lemman*, earlier *leofmon*, f. *leof* dear (see LIEF) + *mon* MAN]

Leman (lĕm′ən), *n.* **Lake.** See **Geneva, Lake.**

Le Mans (*Fr.* lə mäN′), **1.** a town in NW France, the capital of Sarthe department. 132,181 (1962). **2.** an international 24-hour motor race held every June at Le Mans. **3. Le Mans start,** a race start in which drivers line up opposite their cars, and run to them at a given signal.

Lemass (lə măs′), *n.* **Seán Francis** (shôn′ frän′sĭs), born 1899, prime minister of the Republic of Ireland 1959–66.

Lemberg (lĕm′bûg; *Ger.* lĕm′bĕrk), *n.* German name of **Lvov.**

lemma[1] (lĕm′ə), *n., pl.* **lemmas, lemmata** (lĕm′ə tə). **1.** a subsidiary proposition introduced in proving some other proposition; a helping theorem. **2.** an argument, theme or subject. **3.** the heading of a gloss, annotation, etc. [t. L, t. Gk: m. *lêmma* premise]

lemma[2] (lĕm′ə), *n., pl.* **lemmas, lemmata** (lĕm′ə tə). *Bot.* a bract in a grass spikelet just below the pistil and stamens. [t. Gk: m. *lémma* shell, husk]

Lemming, *Lemmus lemmus* (6 in. long)

lemming (lĕm′ĭng), *n.* any of various small, mouselike rodents of the genera *Lemmus, Myopus,* and *Dicrostonyx,* of far northern regions, as *L. lemmus,* of Norway, Sweden, and elsewhere. [t. Norw.]

lemniscate (lĕm nĭs′kĭt), *n.* *Geom.* a plane curve in the shape of the figure 8. [t. L: m. s. *lemniscātus* having ribbons, der. Gk *lemnískos* ribbon]

Lemnos (lĕm′nŏs), *n.* a Greek island in the NE Aegean. 22,873 pop. (1965); 186 sq. mi. *Cap.:* Kastro. **—Lemnian** (lĕm′nĭ ən), *adj., n.*

lemon (lĕm′ən), *n.* **1.** the yellowish acid fruit of the subtropical rutaceous tree, *Citrus limon.* **2.** the tree itself. **3.** clear, light yellow colour. **4.** *Slang.* something distasteful, disappointing, or unpleasant. **5.** *Slang.* a foolish, sour, or ugly person. *—adj.* **6.** having a lemon colour. **7.** consisting of, made or flavoured with lemons. [ME *lymon*, t. OF: m. *limon*, t. Ar., Pers.: m. *līmūn*]

lemonade (lĕm′ə nād′), *n.* **1.** a carbonated soft drink made of lemons, sugar, etc. **2.** lemon squash. [t. F: m. *limonade*, der. *limon* LEMON]

lemon curd, a thick, viscous conserve made of pulped and sieved lemons and sugar. Also, **lemon cheese.**

lemon geranium, a hybrid plant, *Pelargonium limoneum*, whose leaves give off a lemon fragrance.

lemon grass, a tufted perennial grass, *Cymbopogon citratus*, cultivated in the tropics as the source of lemon grass oil.

lemon sole, a fine food fish of northern waters, *Pleuronectes microcephalus*, a flat sea fish which rarely grows more than 15 in. long.

lemon squash, a soft drink made of crushed lemons sweetened and diluted with water.

lemon verbena, a verbenaceous garden shrub, *Lippia citriodora*, with long, slender leaves that have a lemon-like fragrance.

lemony (lĕm′ə nĭ), *adj.* *Austral. Slang.* angry; irritable.

Lempert operation (lĕm′pət), *Surg.* fenestration. [named after Julius *Lempert*, born 1890, American otologist who devised it]

lempira (lĕm pĭə′rə), *n.* **1.** the monetary unit of Honduras, equal to 100 centavos, and equivalent to about £0·208 sterling. **2.** a note or silver coin of this value. [t. Amer. Sp.; named after a native chief]

Ring-tailed lemur, *Lemur catta* (Ab. 3½ ft long)

lemur (lē′mə), *n.* any of various small, arboreal, chiefly nocturnal mammals, esp. of the genus *Lemur*, allied to the monkeys, usually having a foxlike face and woolly fur, and found chiefly in Madagascar. [t. NL, der. L *lemures*, pl., ghosts, spectres; so called because of nocturnal habits. Cf. LEMURES] **—le′mur-like′,** *adj.*

lemures (lĕm′yŏŏ rēz′), *n.pl.* (among the ancient Romans) the spirits of the departed. [t. L. Cf. LEMUR]

lemuroid (lĕm′yŏŏ roid′), *adj.* **1.** lemur-like; of the lemur kind. *—n.* **2.** a lemur.

Lena (lē′nə; *Russ.* lyĕ′nə), *n.* a river flowing from near Lake Baikal, in the S Soviet Union in Asia, through the city of Yakutsk, into the Arctic Ocean. ab. 2800 mi. See map under **Baikal.**

Le Nain (*Fr.* lə năN′), **1. Antoine** (*Fr.* äN twȧn′), *c.* 1588–1648, French painter. **2.** his brother, **Louis** (*Fr.* lwē), *c.* 1593–1648, French painter. **3.** their brother, **Mathieu** (*Fr.* mȧ tyœ′), *c.* 1607–77, French painter.

lend (lĕnd), *v.,* **lent, lending.** *—v.t.* **1.** to give the temporary use of (money, etc.) for a consideration. **2.** to grant the use of (something) with the understanding that it (or its equivalent in kind) shall be returned. **3.** to furnish or impart: *distance lends enchantment to the view.* **4.** to give or contribute obligingly or helpfully: *to lend one's aid to a cause.* **5.** to adapt (oneself or itself) to something. **6. lend a hand,** to assist. **7. lend an ear,** *Archaic.* to listen. *—v.i.* **8.** to make a loan or loans. [ME *lende*; r. ME *lene(n)*, OE *lǣnan*, der. *lǣn* loan] **—lend′er,** *n.*

lending library, a library which lends books, records, etc., as a public library or a commercial establishment charging a small fee.

Lend-Lease (lĕnd′lēs′), *n.* a system authorized by Congress (March 11th, 1941) by which the U.S. government gave material aid and other services to the Allies during World War II.

L'Enfant (*Fr.* läN fäN′), *n.* **Pierre Charles** (*Fr.* pyĕr shȧrl′), 1754–1825, French engineer: planned Washington, D.C.

Lenglen (lŏng′lən, lĕng′-; *Fr.* läN läN′), *n.* **Suzanne** (sōō-zăn′; *Fr.* sōō zȧn′), 1899–1938, French tennis player.

length (lĕngth), *n.* **1.** the linear magnitude of anything as measured from end to end: *the length of a river.* **2.** extent from beginning to end of a series, enumeration, account, book, etc. **3.** extent in time; duration: *the length of a battle.* **4.** a distance determined by the length of something specified: *to hold a thing at arm's length.* **5.** a piece or portion of a certain or a known length: *a length of rope.* **6.** a stretch or extent of something, esp. a long stretch. **7.** the extent, or an extent, of going, proceeding, etc. **8.** the quality or fact of being long rather than short: *a journey remarkable for its length.* **9.** the measure from end to end of a horse, boat, etc., as a unit of distance in racing: *a horse wins by two lengths.* **10.** *Pros. and Phonet.* **a.** (of a vowel or syllable) quantity (whether long or short). **b.** the quality of vowels. **11. at length, a.** to or in the full extent. **b.** after a time; in the end. **12. go to any length(s),** to do whatever is necessary, no matter how difficult, dangerous, etc., to achieve something. [ME and OE, der. *lang* LONG[1]. See -TH[1]]

lengthen (lĕng′thən), *v.t.* **1.** to make greater in length. —*v.i.* **2.** to become greater in length.

—**Syn.** 1. LENGTHEN, EXTEND, STRETCH, PROLONG, PROTRACT agree in the idea of making longer. To LENGTHEN is to make longer, either in a material or an immaterial sense: *to lengthen a dress.* To EXTEND is to lengthen beyond some original point or so as to reach a certain point: *to extend a railway line by a hundred miles.* To STRETCH is primarily to lengthen by drawing or tension: *to stretch a rubber band.* Both PROLONG and PROTRACT mean esp. to lengthen in time, and therefore apply to intangibles. To PROLONG is to continue beyond the desired, estimated, or allotted time: *to prolong an interview.* To PROTRACT is to draw out to undue length or to be slow in coming to a conclusion: *to protract a discussion.* —**Ant.** 1. shorten.

lengthways (lĕngth′wāz′), *adv.* in the direction of the length.

lengthwise (lĕngth′wīz′), *adv.* **1.** lengthways. —*adj.* **2.** longitudinal; running lengthways.

lengthy (lĕng′thĭ), *adj.*, **-thier, -thiest.** having or being of great length, esp. speeches, writings, etc. —**length′ily,** *adv.* —**length′iness,** *n.*

leniency (lē′nyən sĭ), *n.* the quality of being lenient. Also, **le′nience.**

lenient (lē′nyənt), *adj.* **1.** mild, clement, or merciful, as in treatment, spirit, or tendency; gentle. **2.** *Archaic.* softening, soothing, or alleviative. [t. L: s. *lēniens*, ppr., softening] —**le′niently,** *adv.*

Lenin (lĕn′ĭn; *Russ.* lyĕ′nĭn), *n.* **Nikolai** (nĭk′ə lī′; *Russ.* nĭ kȧ lȧy′) (*Vladimir Ilich Ulyanov*), 1870–1924, Russian revolutionary leader and writer. He was the chief leader of the 1917 Revolution, and head of the Soviet government from 1917 to 1924.

Leninakan (*Russ.* lĭ nĭ nȧ kȧn′), *n.* a city in the SW Soviet Union, in the Armenian Republic. 127,000 (est. 1965). Formerly, **Aleksandropol.**

Leningrad (lĕn′ĭn grăd′; *Russ.* lĭ nĭn grȧt′), *n.* a seaport in the NW Soviet Union in Europe: capital of the Russian Empire 1703–1917. 3,641,000 (est. 1965). Formerly, **St Petersburg** or **Petrograd.**

Leninism (lĕn′ĭ nĭz′əm), *n.* Russian communism as taught by Nikolai Lenin, with emphasis on the 'dictatorship of the proletariat'.

lenis (lē′nĭs), *adj.*, *n.*, *pl.* **lenes** (lē′nēz). *Phonet.* —*adj.* **1.** pronounced with relatively weak muscular tension and breath pressure, resulting in weak fricative or explosive sound: *v* and *b* are lenis, as compared to fortis *f* and *p*. —*n.* **2.** a lenis consonant. [t. L: gentle]

lenition (lĭ nĭsh′ən), *n.* *Phonet.* a weakening of the articulation of a consonant, often leading, in the historical development of a language, to radical sound changes and even to loss of the sound. [f. LENI(S) + -TION]

lenitive (lĕn′ĭ tĭv), *adj.* **1.** softening, soothing, or mitigating, as medicines or applications. **2.** mildly laxative. —*n.* **3.** a lenitive medicine or application; a mild laxative. **4.** *Rare.* anything that softens or soothes.

lenity (lĕn′ĭ tĭ), *n.*, *pl.* **-ties. 1.** the quality or fact of being mild or gentle, as towards others. **2.** a lenient act. [t. L: m. s. *lēnitas*]

Lennon (lĕn′ən), *n.* **John.** See **Beatles.**

leno (lē′nō), *adj.* (of a weave) having the warp yarns woven in twisted pairs between the filling yarns, usually in a light, gauzy fabric. [t. F: m. *linon*, der. *lin* LINEN, g. L *linum* flax]

Le Nôtre (*Fr.* lə nō′tr), **André** (*Fr.* äɴ drĕ′), 1613–1700, French landscape gardener.

lens (lĕnz), *n.*, *pl.* **lenses. 1.** a piece of transparent substance, usually glass, having two (or two main) opposite surfaces, either both curved or one curved and one plane, used for changing the convergence of light rays, as in magnifying, or in correcting errors of vision.

Lenses (def. 1)
A, Plano-concave; B, Biconcave (concavo-concave); C, Plano-convex; D, Biconvex (convexo-convex); E, The meniscus (converging concavo-convex; converging meniscus); F, Concavo-convex

2. a combination of such pieces. **3.** some analogous device, as for affecting soundwaves, electromagnetic radiation, or streams of electrons. **4.** *Anat.* a part of the eye, a crystalline lens. [t. L: a lentil (which is shaped like a biconvex lens)]

lent (lĕnt), *v.* pt. and pp. of **lend.**

Lent (lĕnt), *n.* **1.** an annual season of fasting and penitence in preparation for Easter, beginning on Ash Wednesday and including the forty weekdays next before Easter, observed by the Roman Catholic, Anglican, and other Churches. **2.** (in the Middle Ages) a period from Martinmas (Nov. 11th) to Christmas, known as St Martin's Lent. **3.** Lent term. [ME *lente(n)*, OE *len(c)ten* spring, Lent; akin to D *lente* spring, G *Lenz*]

lentamente (lĕn′tə mĕn′tĭ; *It.* lėn tȧ mėn′tė), *adv.* *Music.* slowly. [It., der. *lento* LENTO]

lentando (lĕn tăn′dō; *It.* lėn tȧn′dȯ), *adj.* *Music.* becoming slower. [It. ger. of *lentare* slacken, der. L *lentus* slow]

Lenten (lĕn′tən), *adj.* (*often l.c.*) of, pertaining to, or suitable for Lent. [f. LENT + -EN [2]]

lenticel (lĕn′tĭ sĕl′), *n.* *Bot.* a body of cells formed in the periderm of a stem, appearing on the surface of the plant as a lens-shaped spot, and serving as a pore. [t. NL: m. s. *lenticella*, var. of L *lenticula* LENTIL]

lenticular (lĕn tĭk′yŏŏ lə), *adj.* **1.** of or pertaining to a lens. **2.** biconvex. **3.** resembling a lentil (seed) in form. [t. L: s. *lenticulāris* lentil-shaped]

lentigo (lĕn tī′gō), *n.*, *pl.* **-tigines** (-tĭj′ĭ nēz′). *Med.* a freckle. [t. L, der. *lens* a lentil]

lentil (lĕn′tĭl), *n.* **1.** an annual plant, *Lens culinaris*, having flattened, biconvex seeds which constitute a food similar to peas and beans. **2.** the seed. [ME *lentille*, t. F, g. L *lenticula*, dim. of *lens* a lentil]

lentissimo (lĕn tĭs′ĭ mō′; *It.* lėn tēs′sē mȯ), *Music.* —*adj.* **1.** very slow. —*adv.* **2.** very slowly. [It., der. *lento* LENTO]

Lent lily, daffodil.

lento (lĕn′tō; *It.* lĕn′tȯ), *Music.* —*adj.* **1.** slow. —*adv.* **2.** slowly. [It., g. L *lentus*]

lentoid (lĕn′toid), *adj.* having the shape of a biconvex lens.

Lents (lĕnts), *n.pl.* *Rowing.* the annual bumping races held by the Cambridge colleges during the Lent term.

Lent term, (at some universities, etc.) the Hilary term.

Lenz (*Ger.* lĕnts), *n.* **Siegfried** (*Ger.* zēk′frēt), born 1926, German novelist.

Lenz's law (*Ger.* lĕnts), *Physics.* the law which states that when an electric circuit and a magnetic field move relative to each other, the current induced in the circuit will have a magnetic field opposing the motion. [named after H. *Lenz*, 1804–65, German physicist]

Leo (lē′ō), *n.*, *gen.* **Leonis** (lĭ ō′nĭs). **1.** a zodiacal constellation; the Lion. **2.** the fifth sign of the zodiac. See diag. under **zodiac.** [t. L. See LION]

Leo I (lē′ō; *It.* lĕ′ȯ), **Saint** ('*Leo the Great*'), A.D. *c.* 390–461, Italian cleric; pope A.D. 440–461.

Leo III, Saint, A.D. *c.* 750–816, Italian ecclesiastic; pope A.D. 795–816.

Leo X (*Giovanni de' Medici*), 1475–1521, Italian ecclesiastic; pope 1513–21.

Leo XIII (*Gioacchino Pecci*), 1810–1903, Italian ecclesiastic; pope 1878–1903.

Leoben (*Ger.* lė ō′bən), *n.* a town in Austria, in W central Carinthia. 36,257 (1961).

León (*Sp.* lė ȯn′), *n.* **1.** a province in NW Spain: formerly a kingdom. 584,594 pop. (1960); 5936 sq. mi. **2.** the capital of this province. 83,655 (1965). **3.** a city in central Mexico. 275,335 (est. 1965). **4.** a city in W Nicaragua: the former capital. 61,649 (1964).

Leonardesque (lē′ə nä dĕsk′), *adj.* resembling the manner of Leonardo da Vinci.

Leonardo da Vinci (lē′ə nä′dō də vĭn′chĭ; *It.* lė ȯ nȧr′dȯ dȧ vēn′chē), 1452–1519, Italian painter, sculptor, architect, musician, engineer, mathematician, and scientist.

Leoncavallo (lē′ən kə văl′ō; *It.* lė ȯn kȧ vȧl′lȯ), *n.* **Ruggiero** (*It.* rŏŏd jĕ′rȯ), 1858–1919, Italian composer.

leone (lĭ ō′nĭ), *n.* **1.** the monetary unit of Sierra Leone, equal to 100 cents, and equivalent to about £0·005 sterling. **2.** a banknote of this value. *Abbrev.*: Le.

Leoni (*It.*, *Sp.* lė ō′nē), *n.* **1. Giacomo** (*It.* jȧ′kȯ mȯ), *c.* 1686–1746, Italian architect. **2. Raul** (*Sp.* rȧ ŏŏl′), born 1905, president of Venezuela 1964–68.

Leonid (lē′ə nĭd), *n.*, *pl.* **Leonids, Leonides** (lĭ ŏn′ĭ dēz′). *Astron.* any of a shower of meteors occurring about Nov. 15th and appearing to radiate from Leo. [back-formation from *Leonides*, pl., t. L. See LEO, -ID[1]]

Leonidas (lĭ ŏn′ĭ dăs′), *n.* died 480 B.C., Spartan king, 491?–480 B.C., slain in the battle of Thermopylae.

leonine (lē′ə nīn′), *adj.* **1.** of or pertaining to the lion. **2.** lionlike. [ME *leonyne*, t. L: m. s. *leōninus*]

leopard (lĕpʹəd), *n.* **1.** a large, ferocious, spotted Asiatic or African carnivore, *Panthera pardus*, of the cat family, usually tawny, with black markings; the Old World panther. **2.** any of various related animals, as the jaguar (**American leopard**), the cheetah (**hunting leopard**), and the ounce (**snow leopard**). **3.** *Her.* a lion pictured as walking with his head turned towards the spectator, one front paw usually raised. [ME, t. OF, t. LL: s. *leopardus*, t. LGk: m. *leópardos*. See LION, PARD[1]] —**leopardess** (lĕpʹə dĭs), *n. fem.*

Leopard, *Panthera pardus* (Total length 7½ ft, tail 3 ft)

Leopardi (*It.* lĕ ŏ pärʹdē), *n.* **Count Giacomo** (*It.* jäʹkō mō), 1798–1837, Italian poet.

leopard's-bane (lĕpʹədz bānʹ), *n.* any of several species of perennial composite herbs with yellow capitula belonging to the genus *Doronicum*, as *D. plantagineum* of SW Europe, which is frequently cultivated.

Leopold I (lĭəʹpōld), **1.** 1640–1705, emperor of the Holy Roman Empire 1658–1705. **2.** 1790–1865, king of the Belgians 1831–65.

Leopold II, 1. 1747–92, emperor of the Holy Roman Empire 1790–92. **2.** 1835–1909, king of the Belgians 1865–1909.

Leopold III, born 1901, king of the Belgians 1934–51.

Leopoldville (lĭəʹpōld vĭlʹ), *n.* former name of **Kinshasa.** French, **Léopoldville** (*Fr.* lĕ ŏ pōl vēlʹ).

leotard (lĭəʹtäd), *n.* a close-fitting one-piece garment with a low neck and tights, worn by acrobats, dancers, etc.

Lepanto (lĭ pănʹtō; *It.* lĕʹpän tō), *n.* **1.** a seaport in W Greece, on the **Strait of Lepanto,** a strait opening into the Gulf of Corinth: Turkish sea-power was destroyed here in a naval battle, 1571. **2. Gulf of.** See **Corinth, Gulf of.**

leper (lĕpʹə), *n.* a person affected with leprosy. [ME *lepre*, t. OF: leprosy, t. L: m. *lepra*, t. Gk, prop. fem. of *leprós* scaly]

lepido-, a word element meaning 'scale', used esp. in scientific terms. [t. Gk, comb. form of *lepís* scale]

lepidolite (lĭ pĭdʹə lītʹ, lĕpʹĭ də lītʹ), *n.* a mineral of the mica group, potassium lithium aluminium silicate, commonly occurring in lilac, rose-coloured, or greyish white scaly masses. [f. LEPIDO- + -LITE]

lepidopteron (lĕpʹĭ dŏpʹtə rən), *n., pl.* **-tera** (-tə rə). any lepidopterous insect.

lepidopterous (lĕpʹĭ dŏpʹtə rəs), *adj.* belonging or pertaining to the *Lepidoptera*, an order of insects comprising the butterflies and moths, which in the adult state have four membranous wings more or less covered with small scales. Also, **lepʹidopʹteral.** [f. s. NL *Lepidoptera*, pl., having wings + -OUS. See LEPIDO-, -PTEROUS] —**lepʹidopʹteran,** *adj., n.*

lepidosiren (lĕpʹĭ dō sīʹrən), *n.* a lungfish, *Lepidosiren paradoxa*, of the river Amazon, South America, having an eel-shaped body. [t. NL, f. Gk: *lepido-* LEPIDO- + m. *seirēn* siren]

lepidote (lĕpʹĭ dōtʹ), *adj. Bot.* covered with scurfy scales or scaly spots. [t. Gk: m. s. *lepidōtós* scaly]

Lepidus (lĕpʹĭ dəs), *n.* **Marcus Aemilius** (mäʹkəs ē mĭlʹĭ əs), died 13 B.C., Roman politician. Octavian, Antony, and Lepidus formed the second triumvirate.

Lepontine Alps (lĭ pŏnʹtīn), a central range of the Alps in S Switzerland and N Italy. Highest peak, Mt Leone, 11,684 ft.

leporine (lĕpʹə rīnʹ), *adj. Zool.* of, pertaining to, or resembling the hare. [t. L: m. s. *leporinus*]

leprechaun (lĕpʹrə kônʹ), *n. Irish Folklore.* a pygmy, sprite, or goblin. [earlier *lubrican*, t. Irish: m. *lupracān*, metathetic var. of *luchorpān* a pygmy sprite, f. *lu* little + *corpān*, dim. of *corp* body (t. L: m. *corpus*)]

leprosarium (lĕpʹrə sēəʹrĭ əm), *n., pl.* **-saria** (-sēəʹrĭ ə). a centre for the treatment of leprosy.

leprosy (lĕpʹrə sĭ), *n.* a mildly infectious disease due to a micro-organism, *Bacillus leprae*, and variously characterized by ulcerations, tubercular nodules, spots of pigmentary excess or deficit, loss of fingers and toes, anaesthesia in certain nerve regions, etc. Also, **Hansen's disease.** [f. s. L *leprōsus* leprous + -Y[3]]

leprous (lĕpʹrəs), *adj.* **1.** affected with leprosy. **2.** of or like leprosy. [ME, t. LL: m. s. *leprōsus*, der. L *lepra* leprosy. See LEPER] —**lepʹrously,** *adv.*

lepto-, a combining form meaning 'fine', 'small', 'thin', often occurring in terms of zoology and botany. [t. Gk, comb. form of *leptós*]

leptokurtosis (lĕpʹtō kû tōʹsĭs), *n. Statistics.* a distribution curve which has a sharper peak than normal. [f. LEPTO- + Gk *kúrtōsis* bulge, convexity] —**leptokurtic** (lĕpʹtō kûʹtĭk), *adj.*

lepton (lĕpʹtŏn), *n., pl.* **-ta** (-tə). **1.** an ancient Greek coin. **2.** a minor modern Greek coin equal to one hundredth of a drachma. **3.** *Physics.* any one of a group of elementary particles which includes electrons, neutrinos, and muons. [t. Gk, prop. neut. of *leptós* small]

leptophyllous (lĕpʹtō fĭlʹəs), *adj.* having long, slender leaves. [f. LEPTO- + -PHYLLOUS]

leptorrhine (lĕpʹtə rīn), *adj. Anthropol.* having a narrow high-bridged nose. [f. LEPTO- + m. s. Gk *rhís* nose]

Lérida (*Sp.* lĕʹrē dä), *n.* a town in NE Spain. 72,115 (1965).

Lermontov (*Russ.* lyĕrʹmən təf), *n.* **Mikhail Yurievich** (*Russ.* mĭ KHä ēlʹ yōōʹrĭ yĭ vĭch), 1814–41, Russian poet and novelist.

Lerwick (lûʹwĭk), *n.* a burgh in Scotland, the county town of the Shetland Islands. 5906 (1961).

Le Sage (*Fr.* lə sȧzhʹ), **Alain René** (*Fr.* ȧ lăɴ rə nĕʹ), 1668–1747, French novelist and dramatist.

Lesbian (lĕzʹbĭ ən), *adj.* **1.** of or pertaining to Lesbos. **2.** characteristic of or pertaining to lesbianism. **3.** erotic (from the reputed character of the ancient inhabitants of Lesbos and the tone of their poetry). —*n.* **4.** an inhabitant of Lesbos. **5.** (*l.c.*) one given to lesbianism.

lesbianism (lĕzʹbĭ ə nĭzʹəm), *n.* homosexual relations between women.

Lesbos (lĕzʹbŏs), *n.* a Greek island in the NE Aegean. 140,144 pop. (1961); 836 sq. mi. Also, **Mytilene.**

Les Cayes (*Fr.* lĕ kȧyʹ), *n.* a seaport on the SW coast of Haiti. 14,000 (est. 1961). Formerly, **Aux Cayes.**

Lescot (*Fr.* lĕs kōʹ), *n.* **Pierre** (*Fr.* pyĕr), *c.* 1510–78, French architect.

lese-majesty (lēzʹmăjʹĭs tĭ), *n. Law.* (in many continental systems) various crimes or offences against the sovereign power in a state. [t. F: m. *lèse-majesté*, t. L: m. *laesa mājestas* injured sovereignty]

lesion (lēʹzhən), *n.* **1.** an injury; a hurt; a wound. **2.** *Pathol.* any localized, morbid structural change in the body. [late ME, t. ML: s. *lēsio*, L *laesio* an injury]

Lesotho (lə sōʹtō), *n.* (since 1966) an independent kingdom entirely surrounded by the Republic of South Africa. Formerly the British colony of Basutoland. 888,258 pop. (est. 1960); 11,716 sq. mi. *Cap.:* Maseru.

less (lĕs), *adv.* **1.** to a smaller extent, amount, or degree: *less exact.* —*adj.* **2.** smaller in size, amount, degree, etc.; not so large, great, or much: *less speed.* **3.** lower in consideration, dignity, or importance: *no less a person than the manager.* —*n.* **4.** a smaller amount or quantity. —*prep.* **5.** minus; without: *a year less two days.* [ME; OE *l s*(*sa*), c. OFris. *lēs*(*sa*) less; a compar. form (positive lacking, superl. *least*)] —**Syn. 2.** See **fewer, small.**

-less, a suffix of adjectives meaning 'without', as in *childless, peerless.* In adjectives derived from verbs, it indicates failure or inability to perform or be performed, e.g., *resistless, countless.* [ME *-les*, OE *-lēas*, repr. *lēas*, adj., free from, without, c. Icel. *lauss* free, LOOSE]

lessee (lĕ sēʹ), *n.* one to whom a lease is granted. —**lesseeʹship,** *n.*

lessen (lĕsʹən), *v.i.* **1.** to become less. —*v.t.* **2.** to make less. **3.** to represent as less; depreciate; disparage. —**Syn. 1.** decrease, diminish. **3.** reduce.

Lesseps (lĕsʹəps; *Fr.* lĕ sĕpsʹ), *n.* **Ferdinand** (*Fr.* fĕr dē näɴʹ), **Vicomte de,** 1805–94, French engineer, diplomat, promoter of the construction of the Suez Canal.

lesser (lĕsʹə), *adj.* **1.** less; smaller, as in size, amount, importance, etc.: *a lesser evil.* **2.** being the smaller or less important of two. [late ME, f. LESS + -ER[4]]

Lesser Antilles. See **Antilles.**

Lesser Bear, *Astron.* Ursa Minor.

Lesser Dog, *Astron.* Canis Minor.

Lessing (lĕsʹĭng), *n.* **1. Doris** (**May**), born 1919, English novelist and short-story writer. **2. Gotthold Ephraim** (*Ger.* gŏtʹhōlt ĕʹfrä ĭm), 1729–81, German critic and dramatist.

lesson (lĕsʹən), *n.* **1.** something to be learned or studied. **2.** a part of a book or the like assigned to a pupil for study: *the lesson for today is on page 22.* **3.** a length of time during which a pupil or class studies one subject. **4.** a useful or salutary piece of practical wisdom imparted or learned: *this experience taught me a lesson.* **5.** something from which one learns or should learn, as an instructive or warning example: *this experience was a lesson to me.* **6.** a reproof or punishment intended to teach one better ways. **7.** a portion of Scripture or other sacred writing read, or appointed to be read, at divine service. —*v.t.* **8.** to admonish or reprove. [ME, t. OF: m. *leçon*, g. L *lectio* a reading]

lessor (lĕs′ô, lĕ sô′), *n.* one who grants a lease.

lest (lĕst), *conj.* **1.** for fear that; that . . . not; so that . . . not. **2.** (after words expressing fear, danger, etc.) that: *there was danger lest the plan become known.* [ME *leste*, late OE *the lǣste*, earlier *thȳ lǣs the* lest (lit., whereby less that; *the* is the relative particle)]

let[1] (lĕt), *v.*, **let, letting,** *n.* —*v.t.* **1.** to allow or permit. **2.** to allow to pass, go, or come. **3.** to cause or allow to escape. **4.** to grant the occupancy or use of (land, buildings, rooms, space, etc., or movable property) for rent or hire (occasionally fol. by *out*). **5.** to contract for performance: *to let work to a carpenter.* **6.** to cause or make: *to let one know.* **7.** (as an auxiliary used to propose or order): *let me see.* —*v.* **8.** Some special verb phrases are:

let down, 1. to lower. **2.** to disappoint; fail.

let off, 1. to excuse; to exempt from (something arduous, as a punishment, or the like). **2.** to explode (a firework, or other explosive device).

let on, *Colloq.* **1.** to divulge information, esp. indiscreetly. **2.** to pretend: *he let on that he was a detective.*

let out, 1. to divulge. **2.** to make larger (a garment, etc.). **3.** to emit: *he let out a laugh.*

let up, *Colloq.* to slacken or stop.

—*v.i.* **9.** to be rented or leased. —*n.* **10.** a lease. [ME *leten*, OE *lǣtan*, c. D *laten*, G *lassen*; akin to LATE]

—**Syn. 1.** LET, LEAVE, though not synonyms, are often confused, LEAVE being the one used more frequently in both meanings. A further confusion of the verb LEAVE with the noun LEAVE may have helped to perpetuate the misuse. (The noun LEAVE, meaning 'permission', might readily be associated with LET, whose most common meaning is 'permit' or 'allow'. The verb LEAVE, however, does not have a meaning of 'permit' or 'allow'; its most common meaning is 'to go away from'.) In the constructions in which the confusion arises, it should be noted that, although either verb can take a noun object, only LET can take the infinitive (with *to* not expressed). In certain idiomatic expressions, the two verbs are used in parallel constructions, but the meanings differ widely: LET it out means 'allow it to escape' (as the breath), but LEAVE it out means 'omit it' (as a sentence). LET him alone means 'allow him to be without interference' (don't bother him), but LEAVE him alone means 'go away, so that he will be alone'. See **allow.**

let[2] (lĕt), *n.*, *v.*, **letted** or **let, letting.** —*n.* **1.** *Archaic.* hindrance or obstruction; an impediment or obstacle: *without let or hindrance.* **2.** *Tennis, etc.* an interference with the course of the ball (of some kind specified in the rules) on account of which the stroke or point must be played over again. —*v.t.* **3.** *Archaic.* to hinder; stand in the way of. [ME *letten*, OE *lettan* (der. *læt* slow, tardy, LATE), c. Icel. *letja* hinder]

-let, a diminutive suffix, used often for little objects, e.g., *frontlet, bracelet, kinglet.* [t. OF: m. *-elet*, f. *-el* (sometimes g. L *-ellus*, dim. suffix, sometimes g. L *-āle*, neut. See -AL[1]) + *-et* -ET]

l'état, c'est moi (*Fr.* lĕ tȧ′, sĕ mwȧ′), *French.* I am the state (supposed to have been said by Louis XIV).

Letchworth (lĕch′wəth, -wûth′), *n.* a town in England, in Hertfordshire; first English garden city. 25,511 (1961).

letdown (lĕt′doun′), *n.* disillusion or disappointment.

Lethaby (lĕth′ə bĭ), *n.* **William Richard,** 1857–1931, English architect.

lethal (lē′thəl), *adj.* of, pertaining to, or such as to cause death; deadly. [t. L: s. *lēt(h)ālis*]

lethargic (lĭ thä′jĭk), *adj.* **1.** pertaining to or affected with lethargy; drowsy; sluggish. **2.** producing lethargy. Also, **lethar′gical.** —**lethar′gically,** *adv.*

lethargy (lĕth′ə jĭ), *n.*, *pl.* **-gies. 1.** a state of drowsy dullness or suspension of the faculties and energies; apathetic or sluggish inactivity. **2.** *Pathol.* a morbid state or a disorder characterized by overpowering drowsiness or sleep. [t. L: m. s. *lēthargia*, t. Gk: forgetfulness; r. ME *litargie*, t. ML: m. *litargia*]

Lethe (lē′thĭ), *n.* **1.** *Gk Myth.* a river in Hades, whose water caused forgetfulness of the past in those who drank of it. **2.** forgetfulness; oblivion. [t. L, t. Gk: lit., forgetfulness] —**Lethean** (lĭ thē′ən), *adj.*

Leto (lē′tō), *n.* *Gk Myth.* the mother by Zeus of Apollo and Artemis.

Letraset (lĕt′rə sĕt′), *n.* *Trademark.* lettering printed on a special backing sheet, which is transferred to another surface through the application of pressure to the backing sheet: used particularly in the preparation of artwork for printing.

Lett (lĕt), *n.* **1.** one of a people living on and near the eastern coast of the Baltic Sea, closely related to the Lithuanians. **2.** the Lettish language.

letter (lĕt′ə), *n.* **1.** a communication in writing or printing addressed to a person or a number of persons. **2.** one of the marks or signs conventionally used in writing and printing to represent speech sounds; an alphabetic character. **3.** a printing type bearing such a mark or character. **4.** a particular style of type. **5.** such types collectively. **6.** actual terms or wording, as distinct from general meaning or intent. **7.** (*pl.*) literature in general; belles-lettres. **8.** (*pl.*) the profession of literature, or authorship: *a man of letters.* **9. to the letter, a.** with close adherence to the actual wording or the literal meaning. **b.** to the fullest extent. —*v.t.* **10.** to mark or write with letters. [ME, t. OF: m. *lettre*, g. L *littera, lītera*, alphabetic character, pl. epistle, literature] —**let′terer,** *n.*

—**Syn. 7.** See **literature.**

letter-box (lĕt′ə bŏks′), *n.* **1.** a slot in a front door through which letters, etc., are pushed. **2.** pillar-box.

lettered (lĕt′əd), *adj.* **1.** educated or learned. **2.** pertaining to or characterized by polite learning or literary culture. **3.** marked with or as with letters.

letterhead (lĕt′ə hĕd′), *n.* **1.** a printed heading on writing paper, esp. one giving the name and address of a business concern, an institution, etc. **2.** such writing paper.

lettering (lĕt′ə rĭng), *n.* **1.** the act or process of inscribing with or making letters. **2.** the letters themselves.

letter of advice, 1. a document, esp. in commercial shipments, giving specific information as to the consignor's agent in the consignee's territory, his bank, warehouse, etc. **2.** *Com.* a drawer's document, usually forwarded ahead of the bill of lading and other papers giving title to goods shipped by the drawer, stating that a bill has been issued against the drawee.

letter of credit, 1. an order issued by a banker, allowing a person named to draw money to a specified amount from correspondents of the issuer. **2.** an instrument issued by a banker, authorizing a person named to make drafts upon the issuer up to an amount specified.

letter of identification, *Com.* a letter signed by a banker issued together with a letter of credit, also signed by the person in whose favour the credit is issued, thus enabling him to identify himself to the paying agent when cashing drafts drawn under the letter of credit. Also, **letter of indication.**

letter of marque, licence or commission granted by a state to a private citizen to capture and confiscate merchant ships of another nation. Also, **letter of marque and reprisal.**

letter-perfect (lĕt′ə pû′fĭkt), *adj.* **1.** knowing one's part, lesson, or the like, perfectly. **2.** accurate; exact.

letterpress (lĕt′ə prĕs′), *n.* **1.** a method of relief printing in which the type or illustrations to be printed stand above the areas of the printing forme which are not to be printed. **2.** the matter thus printed. **3.** printed text or reading matter, as distinguished from illustrations, etc.

letters of administration, *Law.* an instrument issued by a court or public official authorizing an administrator to take control of and dispose of the estate of the deceased, where the deceased died intestate.

letters of credence, papers formally authorizing a nation's diplomatic agents, issued by the appointing state.

letters patent, *Law.* a written or printed instrument issued by the sovereign power, conferring upon a patentee for a limited time the exclusive right to make, use, and sell his invention.

letters testamentary, *U.S. Law.* grant of probate.

Lettic (lĕt′ĭk), *adj.* **1.** pertaining or related to the Letts. —*n.* **2.** Lettish. **3.** *Obs.* the Baltic group of languages.

Lettish (lĕt′ĭsh), *adj.* **1.** pertaining to the Letts or their language. —*n.* **2.** the language of Latvia.

lettre de cachet (*Fr.* lĕ trə də kȧ shĕ′), *French Hist.* a letter under the seal of the sovereign, esp. one ordering imprisonment, frequently without trial.

lettre de change (*Fr.* lĕ trə de shäNzh′), *French.* a letter or bill of exchange.

lettuce (lĕt′ĭs), *n.* **1.** a composite plant, *Lactuca sativa*, in many varieties, having large, succulent leaves which are much used for salad. **2.** any species of *Lactuca.* [ME *letuse*, t. OF: m. *laitues*, pl., g. L *lactūca*]

let-up (lĕt′ŭp′), *n.* *Colloq.* a slackening; cessation; pause.

leu (lā′o͞o), *n.*, *pl.* **lei** (lā). **1.** the monetary unit of Rumania, equivalent to about £0·06 sterling. **2.** a note or coin of this value.

leucaemia (lyo͞o kē′myə), *n.* leukaemia. Also, *U.S.*, **leucemia** (lyo͞o sē′myə).

Leucas (lo͞o′kəs), *n.* Levkas. Also, **Leukas.**

leucine (lyo͞o′sēn), *n.* *Chem., Biochem.* a white crystalline amino acid, $C_6H_{13}NO_2$, a constituent of proteins. Also, **leucin** (lyo͞o′sĭn). [f. LEUC(O)- + -INE[2]]

leucite (lyo͞o′sīt), *n.* a whitish or greyish mineral, potassium aluminium silicate, $KAlSi_2O_6$, found in certain volcanic rocks. [t. G: m. *Leucit*, f. *leuc-* LEUC(O)- + *-it* -ITE[1]] —**leucitic** (lyo͞o sĭt′ĭk), *adj.*

leuco-, a word element meaning 'white'. Also, before vowels, **leuc-.** [t. Gk: m. *leuko-*, comb. form of *leukós*]

leuco base (lyo͞o′kō), *Chem.* a colourless or slightly coloured compound made by reducing a dye and which is readily oxidized to regenerate the dye.

leucocratic (lyōō′kə krăt′ĭk), *adj. Geol.* composed predominantly of light-coloured minerals. [f. LEUCO- + -CRAT + -IC]

leucocyte (lyōō′kə sīt′), *n. Physiol.* one of the white or colourless corpuscles of the blood, concerned in the destruction of disease-producing micro-organisms, etc.

leucocytic (lyōō′kə sĭt′ĭk), *adj.* **1.** pertaining to leucocytes. **2.** characterized by an excess of leucocytes.

leucocytosis (lyōō′kō sī tō′sĭs), *n. Physiol., Pathol.* the presence of an increased number of leucocytes in the blood, esp. when temporary, as in infection, and not due to leukaemia. [NL. See LEUCOCYTE, -OSIS] **—leucocytotic** (lyōō′kō sī tŏt′ĭk), *adj.*

leucoplast (lyōō′kə plăst′), *n. Bot.* one of the colourless bodies found within the protoplasm of vegetable cells, and serving as points around which starch forms.

leucopoenia (lyōō′kə pē′nyə), *n. Physiol.* a decrease in the number of white cells in the blood. Also, *U.S.*, **leucopenia.**

leucopoiesis (lyōō′kō poi ē′sĭs), *n. Physiol.* the formation and development of the white blood cells.

leucorrhoea (lyōō′kə rē′ə), *n. Pathol.* a whitish discharge from the female genital organs. Also, *Chiefly U.S.*, **leucorrhea.** [NL. See LEUCO-, -RHOEA]

leucosticte (lyōō′kō stĭk′tĭ), *n.* any of several montane finches of the genus *Leucosticte*, commonly called rosy finches.

leucotomy (lyōō kŏt′ə mĭ, lōō-), *n. Surg.* the cutting into or across a lobe of the brain, usually of the cerebrum, to alter brain function, esp. in the treatment of mental disorders. Also, *Chiefly U.S.*, **lobotomy.**

Leuctra (lyōōk′trə), *n.* a town in ancient Greece, in Boeotia: Thebans defeated Spartans here, 371 B.C.

leukaemia (lyōō kē′myə), *n. Pathol.* a disease, usually fatal, characterized by excessive production of white blood cells, which are usually found in greatly increased numbers in the blood. There is an accompanying anaemia, often severe, and the spleen and lymph glands are usually enlarged and in a state of great activity. Also, **leucaemia,** *U.S.*, **leukemia.** [t. NL, f. s. Gk *leukós* white + *-aemia* -AEMIA]

Leuven (*Flem.* lœ′vən), *n.* Flemish name of **Louvain.**

Leuwenhoek (*Du.* lē′wən hōōk), *n.* See **Leeuwenhoek.**

lev (lĕf), *n., pl.* **leva** (lĕv′ə). **1.** the monetary unit of Bulgaria, equivalent to £0·356 sterling. **2.** a note or coin of this denomination.

Lev., Leviticus.

Levalloisian (lĕv′ə loi′zĭ ən), *adj.* of, pertaining to, or characteristic of a tradition of the Middle Palaeolithic era notable for a method of producing stone tools. [f. LEVALLOIS- (PERRET) + -IAN]

Levallois-Perret (*Fr.* lə vȧl wȧ pĕ rĕ′), *n.* a town in N France, in Hauts-de-Seine department, a suburb of Paris, on the Seine. 61,962 (1962).

levan (lē′văn, lĕv′ăn), *n. Biochem.* laevulin.

Levant (lĭ vănt′), *n.* **1.** lands bordering the E shore of the Mediterranean and the Aegean, esp. Syria, Lebanon, and Israel. **2.** (*l.c.*) a superior grade of morocco having a large and prominent grain, orig. made in the Levant, and used for bookbinding; Levant morocco. [t. F, prop. ppr. of (*se*) *lever* rise (with reference to the rising sun). See LEVER]

Levant dollar, a silver coin used for trade purposes, originally minted in Austria, and circulating in Ethiopia, Eritrea, Aden, etc.; Maria Theresa thaler. Its value changes with the price of silver and economic conditions of countries where it is used.

levanter (lĭ văn′tə), *n.* an easterly wind which sometimes blows in the Strait of Gibraltar and in S Spain.

Levantine (lĕv′ən tīn′), *adj.* **1.** of or pertaining to the Levant. *—n.* **2.** a native or a vessel of the Levant. [f. LEVANT + -INE[1]. Cf. F *levantin*]

Levant morocco, levant (def. 2).

levator (lĭ vā′tə, -tô), *n., pl.* **levatores** (lĕv′ə tô′rēz). **1.** *Anat.* a muscle that raises some part of the body. **2.** *Surg.* an instrument used to raise a depressed part of the skull. [t. L: a lifter]

Le Vau (*Fr.* lə vō′), **Louis** (*Fr.* lwē), 1612–70, French baroque architect.

levee[1] (lĕv′ĭ), *n.* **1.** a raised riverside built up naturally by the river by deposition of silt during flooding, as along the Mississippi. **2.** a man-made embankment for preventing the overflowing of a river. **3.** *Agric.* one of the small continuous ridges surrounding fields that are to be irrigated. **4.** *Hist.* a landing place for vessels; a quay. [t. F: m. *levée*, der. *lever* raise. See LEVER]

levee[2] (lĕv′ĭ, lĕv′ā), *n.* **1.** (in Great Britain) a public court assembly, held in the early afternoon, at which men only are received. **2.** a reception held at any time of day. **3.** *Hist.* a reception of visitors held on rising from bed, as formerly by a royal or other personage. [t. F: m. *levé*, *lever* a rising. See LEVER]

levee en masse (lĕv′ĭ ŏn măs′), the enforced conscription of civilians, usually when a country is threatened by invasion, etc. Also, **levy en masse** (lĕv′ĭ ŏn măs′).

level (lĕv′əl), *adj., n., v.*, **-elled, -elling** or (*U.S.*) **-eled, -eling,** *adv.* *—adj.* **1.** having no part higher than another; having an even surface. **2.** being in a plane parallel to the plane of the horizon; horizontal. **3.** on an equality, as one thing with another, or two or more things with one another. **4.** even, equable, or uniform. **5.** mentally well-balanced: *a level head.* **6. one's level best,** *Colloq.* one's very best; one's utmost.

—n. **7.** a device used for determining, or adjusting something to, a horizontal surface. **8.** such a device consisting of a glass tube containing alcohol or ether with a movable bubble which when in the centre indicates horizontalness. **9.** a surveying instrument combining such a device with a mounted telescope. **10.** a measuring of differences in elevation with such an instrument. **11.** an imaginary line or surface everywhere perpendicular to the plumbline. **12.** the horizontal line or plane in which anything is situated, with regard to its elevation. **13.** level position or condition. **14.** a level tract of land, or an extent of country approximately horizontal and unbroken by irregularities. **15.** a level or flat surface. **16.** one of various positions with respect to height; a height: *the water rose to a level of thirty feet.* **17.** a position or plane, high or low: *acting on the level of amateurs.* **18. find one's level,** to find the most suitable place for oneself, esp. with regard to the people around: *he found his level among the older students.* **19. on the level,** sincere; honest.

—v.t. **20.** to make (a surface) level or even: *to level ground before building.* **21.** to raise or lower to a particular level, or position. **22.** to bring (something) to the level of the ground; knock down, as a person: *the city was levelled by one atomic bomb.* **23.** to bring (two or more things) to an equality of status, condition, etc. **24.** to make even or uniform, as colouring. **25.** to aim or point at a mark, as a weapon, criticism, etc. **26.** to turn (looks, etc.) in a particular direction. **27.** *Survey.* to find the relative elevation of different points in (land) as with a level.

—v.i. **28.** to bring things or persons to a common level. **29.** to aim a weapon, etc. **30.** *Survey.* to take levels; use a level. **31.** *Aeron.* to fly at a constant height.

—adv. **32.** *Obs.* in a level, direct or even way or line. [ME *livel*, t. OF, ult. g. L *lībella*, dim. of *lībra* a balance, level] **—lev′elly,** *adv.* **—lev′elness,** *n.*

—Syn. 1, 2. LEVEL, EVEN, FLAT, SMOOTH suggest a uniform surface without marked unevenness. That which is LEVEL is parallel to the horizon: *a level surface; a billiard table must be level.* FLAT is applied to any plane surface free from marked irregularities: *a flat roof.* With reference to land or country, FLAT connotes lowness or unattractiveness; LEVEL does not suggest anything derogatory. That which is EVEN is free from irregularities, though not necessarily level or plane: *an even land surfdce with no hills.* SMOOTH suggests a high degree of evenness in any surface, esp. to the touch and sometimes to the sight: *as smooth as silk.*

level crossing, a place where a road and railway intersect at the same level.

level-headed (lĕv′əl hĕd′ĭd), *adj.* having common sense and sound judgement.

leveller (lĕv′ə lə), *n.* **1.** one who or that which levels. **2.** (*cap.*) *Eng. Hist.* a member of an extremist party originating among the radical supporters of Parliament during the Civil War, who advocated far-reaching constitutional and economic reforms, freedom of worship, and the separation of church and state. Also, *U.S.*, **leveler.**

levelling rod, *Survey.* a graduated rod used for measuring heights in connection with a surveyor's level. Also, **levelling staff**; *U.S.*, **leveling rod.**

Leven (lē′vən), *n.* **Loch,** a lake in E Scotland: ruins of a castle in which Mary, Queen of Scots was imprisoned.

lever (lē′və), *n.* **1.** a bar or rigid piece acted upon at different points by two forces, as a voluntarily applied force (the *power*) and a resisting force (the *weight*), which generally tend to rotate it in opposite directions about a fixed axis or support (the *fulcrum*). **2.** any of various mechanical devices operating on this principle, as a crowbar. *—v.t., v.i.* **3.** to move with or apply a lever. [ME *levere*, t. OF: m. *leveor*, lit., raiser, der. *lever* raise, (refl.) rise, g. L *levāre* lighten, lift, raise] **—lev′er-like′,** *adj.*

Lever (lē′və), *n.* **Charles James** ('*Cornelius O'Dowd*'), 1806–72, Irish novelist.

leverage (lē′və rĭj, -vrĭj), *n.* **1.** the action of a lever. **2.** the mechanical advantage or power gained by using a lever. **3.** power of action; means of influence.

leveret (lĕv′ə rĭt, lĕv′rĭt), *n.* a young hare. [ME, t. OF: m. *levrete*, dim. of *levre*, g. L *lepus* hare]

Leverhulme (lē′və hyo͞om′), *n.* **Viscount** (*William Hesketh Lever*), 1851–1925, English industrialist.

Leverkusen (*Ger.* lā′vər ko͞o zən), *n.* a town in West Germany, in S North Rhine-Westphalia. 106,100 (est. 1966).

Leverrier (*Fr.* lə vĕ ryĕ′), *n.* **Urbain** (*Fr.* ʏʀ băɴ′), 1811–77, French astronomer.

Levi (lē′vī *for 1*; *It.* lĕv′ē *for 2*), *n.* **1.** *Bible.* a son of Jacob and Leah: ancestor of the Levites. Gen. 29:34, etc. **2. Carlo** (*It.* kär′lô), born 1902, Italian writer. [t. Heb.: m. *Lēwī*]

leviable (lĕv′ĭ ə bl), *adj.* **1.** that may be levied. **2.** liable or subject to a levy.

leviathan (lĭ vī′ə thən), *n.* **1.** a sea-monster mentioned in the Old Testament. Job 41. **2.** any huge marine animal, as the whale. **3.** anything, esp. a ship, of huge size. [ME, t. LL, t. Heb.: m. *liwyāthān*, prob. meaning the coiling up (snake)]

levigate (lĕv′ĭ gāt′), *v.t.*, **-gated, -gating. 1.** to rub, grind, or reduce to a fine powder, as in a mortar, with or without the addition of a liquid. **2.** *Chem.* to make a homogeneous mixture of, as gels. [t. L: m. s. *lēvigātus*, pp., made smooth] —**lev′iga′tion,** *n.*

levin (lĕv′ĭn), *n. Archaic.* lightning. [ME *leven(e)*, prob. t. Scand. (cf. OSw. *liughn-* lightning) or repr. OE **lēamne*; c. Goth. *lauhmuni* lightning]

levirate (lĕv′ĭ rĭt), *n.* a custom of the ancient Hebrews, requiring a man under certain circumstances to marry the widow of his brother or nearest kinsman. [f. L *lēvir* husband's brother + -ATE[1]] —**leviratic** (lĕv′ĭ răt′ĭk), **lev′irat′ical,** *adj.*

Levis (lē′vīz), *n.pl. Trademark.* close-fitting jeans, usually made of denim or a similar hard-wearing material and reinforced with copper rivets at the points of stress. [pl. of *Levi* Strauss, name of U.S. manufacturer]

Levit., Leviticus.

levitate (lĕv′ĭ tāt′), *v.*, **-tated, -tating.** —*v.i.* **1.** to rise or float in the air, esp. through some allegedly supernatural power that overcomes gravity. —*v.t.* **2.** to cause to rise or float in the air. **3.** *Med.* to support (a patient) by levitation. [f. LEVIT(Y) + -ATE[1]; modelled on GRAVITATE] —**lev′ita′tor,** *n.*

levitation (lĕv′ĭ tā′shən), *n.* **1.** the act or phenomenon of levitating. **2.** (among spiritualists) the alleged phenomenon of bodies heavier than air being by spiritual means rendered buoyant in the atmosphere. **3.** *Med.* support of a patient on a bed of air by application of the hovercraft principle, used in the treatment of severe burns.

Levite (lē′vīt), *n.* **1.** a descendant of Levi; one of the tribe of Levi. **2.** one of those who assisted the priests in the tabernacle and temple. [ME, t. L: m. s. *levīta, levītes*, t. Gk: (m.) *levītēs*, der. *Leuī* Levite, t. Heb.]

Levitical (lĭ vĭt′ĭ kl), *adj.* of or pertaining to the Levites, the book of Leviticus, or the law (**Levitical law**) contained in the book of Leviticus.

Leviticus (lĭ vĭt′ĭ kəs), *n.* the third book of the Old Testament, containing laws relating to the priests and Levites and to the forms of Jewish ceremonial observance. [t. LL, t. Gk: m. *Leuītikós*, der. *Leuītēs* LEVITE]

levity (lĕv′ĭ tĭ), *n., pl.* **-ties. 1.** lightness of mind, character, or behaviour; lack of proper seriousness or earnestness: *she accused him of levity in his discussion of the divorce law.* **2.** an instance or exhibition of this. **3.** fickleness. **4.** lightness in weight. [t. L: m. s. *levitas*]

Levkas (lĕf kăs′), *n.* an island in the Ionian group, off the W coast of Greece. 28,969 pop. (1961); 114 sq. mi. Also, **Leucas.** Italian, **Santa Maura.**

levo-, *U.S.* var. of **laevo-.**

levoglucose (lē′vō glo͞o′kōs), *n. U.S.* laevoglucose.

levorotation (lē′vō rō tā′shən), *n. U.S.* laevorotation.

levorotatory (lē′vō rō′tə tə rĭ, -trĭ), *adj. U.S.* laevorotatory.

levulin (lĕv′yə lĭn), *n. U.S.* laevulin.

levulinic acid, *U.S.* laevulic acid. Also, **levulic acid.**

levulose (lĕv′yə lōs′), *n. U.S.* laevulose.

levy (lĕv′ĭ), *n., pl.* **-ies,** *v.*, **-ied, -ying.** —*n.* **1.** a raising or collecting, as of money or troops, by authority or force. **2.** that which is raised, as a tax assessment or a body of troops. —*v.t.* **3.** to make a levy of; collect (taxes, contributions, etc.). **4.** to impose (a tax): *to levy a duty on imported wines.* **5.** to raise or enlist (troops, etc.) for service. **6.** to start, or make (war, etc.). —*v.i.* **7.** to make a levy. **8.** *Law.* to seize or attach property by judicial order. [ME, t. F: m. *levée*, der. *lever* raise. See LEVER] —**levier** (lĕv′ĭ ə), *n.*

levy en masse (lĕv′ĭ ŏn măs′; *Fr.* äɴ măs′), levee en masse.

lewd (lo͞od), *adj.* **1.** inclined to, characterized by, or inciting to lust or lechery. **2.** obscene or indecent, as language, songs, etc. **3.** *Obs.* base or vile. [ME *leud*, *lewede*, OE *lǣw(e)de* lay[3]; orig. uncert.] —**lewd′ly,** *adv.* —**lewd′ness,** *n.*

Lewes (lo͞o′ĭs), *n.* **1. George Henry,** 1817–78, English philosophical writer and critic. **2.** a town in England, the county town of Sussex: battle, 1264. 13,645 (1961).

lewis (lo͞o′ĭs), *n.* a device consisting of wedges or curved steel bars for lifting concrete blocks. [named after the inventor (unknown)]

Lewis (lo͞o′ĭs), *n.* **1.** See **Day-Lewis. 2. C(live) S(tables)** (stā′blz), 1898–1963, English novelist and essayist. **3. D(ominic) B(evan) Wyndham** (wĭn′dəm), 1894–1969, British journalist and humorous writer. **4. John L(lewellyn)** (lo͞o ĕl′ĭn), 1880–1969, U.S. labour leader. **5. Matthew Gregory** ('*Monk Lewis*'), 1775–1818, English novelist, dramatist, and poet. **6. Sinclair,** 1885–1951, U.S. novelist, dramatist, and journalist. **7. (Percy) Wyndham,** 1884–1957, English novelist and painter, born in the U.S. **8.** an island of the Outer Hebrides, Ross and Cromarty, Scotland. 16,700 pop. (1961); 632 sq. mi.

Lewis gun, a light air-cooled machine-gun. [named after I. N. *Lewis*, 1858–1931, U.S. army officer]

Lewisham (lo͞o′ĭ shəm), *n.* a SE inner London borough. 291,670 (1965).

lewisite (lo͞o′ĭ sīt′), *n.* a chemical warfare agent, $C_2H_2AsCl_3$, characterized by its vesicant action. [named after W. Lee *Lewis*, 1878–1943, U.S. chemist. See -ITE[1]]

Lewis with Harris (hă′rĭs). See **Harris** (def. 2), **Lewis** (def. 8).

lex (lĕks), *n., pl.* **leges** (lē′jēz). law. [L: the law]

lexical (lĕk′sĭ kl), *adj.* **1.** pertaining to words or to a vocabulary, as that of an author or a language. **2.** pertaining to or of the nature of a lexicon. [f. LEXIC(ON) + -AL[1]]

lexical meaning, *Gram.* that part of the meaning of a linguistic form which does not depend on its membership of a particular form class, esp. (of inflected words) the meaning common to all the members of an inflectional paradigm, e.g., the meaning common to *eat, eats, ate, eaten, eating*, despite their differences in form.

lexicog., 1. lexicographical. **2.** lexicography.

lexicographer (lĕk′sĭ kŏg′rə fə), *n.* a writer or compiler of a dictionary. [f. m. s. LGk *lexikográphos* (f. *lexikó(n)* wordbook + *-gráphos* writer) + -ER[1]]

lexicography (lĕk′sĭ kŏg′rə fĭ), *n.* the writing or compiling of dictionaries. —**lexicographic** (lĕk′sĭ kō grăf′ĭk), **lex′icograph′ical,** *adj.* —**lex′icograph′ically,** *adv.*

lexicology (lĕk′sĭ kŏl′ə jĭ), *n.* the study of the history, form, and meaning of words. —**lexicological** (lĕk′sĭ kə-lŏj′ĭ kl), *adj.* —**lexicologist** (lĕk′sĭ kŏl′ə jĭst), *n.*

lexicon (lĕk′sĭ kən), *n.* **1.** a wordbook or dictionary, esp. of Greek, Latin, or Hebrew. **2.** the list or vocabulary of words belonging to a particular subject, field, or class. [t. ML (much used in Latin titles of dictionaries), t. Gk: m. *lexikón*, neut. of *lexikós* of or for words]

Lexington (lĕk′sĭng tən), *n.* a town in E Massachusetts, NW of Boston: the first battle of the War of American Independence was fought here, April 19th, 1775. 27,691 (1960).

lexis (lĕk′sĭs), *n.* the whole body of words in a language.

lex loci (lĕks′lō′sī), *Latin.* the law of a place.

lex non scripta (lĕks′nŏn skrĭp′tə), *Latin.* unwritten law; common law.

lex scripta (lĕks′skrĭp′tə), *Latin.* written law; statute law.

lex talionis (lĕks′tăl′ĭ ō′nĭs), *Latin.* the law of retaliation, as an eye for an eye, a tooth for a tooth.

ley (lē, lā), *n.* arable land temporarily sown with grass. [var of LEA[1]]

Leyden (lī′dn; *Du.* lĕy′də), *n.* Leiden.

Leyden jar, *Elect.* a device for storing electric charge, consisting essentially of a glass jar lined inside and outside, for about two-thirds of its height, with tinfoil. [named after LEYDEN (LEIDEN)]

Leyland (lā′lənd), *n.* a town in England, in Lancashire: motor works. 19,241 (1961).

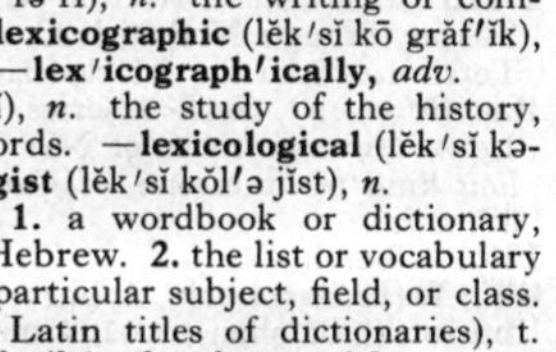

Leyte (lā′tā; *Sp.* lĕy′tĕ), *n.* one of the Philippine Islands, in central part of group: focal point of the U.S. invasion of the Philippines, 1944. 1,146,000 pop. (est. 1965); 3085 sq. mi.

Leyte

Leyton (lā′tn), *n.* a district of the NE outer London borough of Waltham Forest.

l.f., *Radio.* low frequency.

LG, Low German. Also, **L.G.**

LGk, Late Greek. Also, **L.Gk.**

l.h., *Music.* left hand.

Lhasa (läʹsə), *n.* the capital of the Tibetan Autonomous Region, in the SE part: sacred city of Lamaism. 15,000 (est. 1963); ab. 12,000 ft high. Also, **Lassa.**

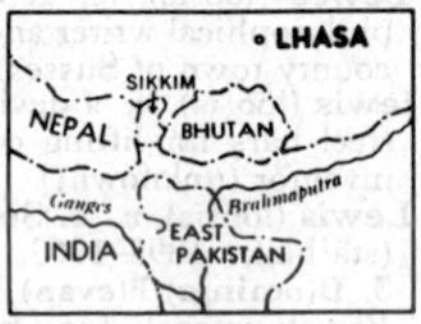

li (lē), *n., pl.* **li** (lē). a Chinese unit of distance, equivalent to about one-third of a mile.

Li, *Chem.* lithium.

liability (līʹə bĭlʹĭ tĭ), *n., pl.* **-ties.** **1.** an obligation, esp. for payment; debt or pecuniary obligations (opposed to *asset*). **2.** something disadvantageous. **3.** the state or fact of being liable: *liability to jury duty, liability to disease.*

liable (līʹə bl), *adj.* **1.** subject, exposed, or open to something possible or likely, esp. something undesirable. **2.** under legal obligation; responsible or answerable. [late ME, f. s. F *lier* bind (g. L *ligāre*) + -ABLE] **—liʹableness,** *n.* **—Syn. 1.** See **likely.**

liaise (lĭ āzʹ), *v.i.,* **-aised, -aising.** to maintain contact and act in concert (usually fol. by *with*). [back-formation from LIAISON]

liaison (lĭ āʹzŏn; *Fr.* lyĕ zónʹ), *n.* **1.** *Mil., etc.* the contact maintained between units, in order to ensure concerted action. **2.** a similar connection or relation maintained between non-military units, bodies, etc. **3.** an illicit sexual relationship between a man and a woman. **4.** *Cookery.* a thickening, as of beaten eggs and cream, for sauces, soups, etc. **5.** *Phonet.* (*esp. in French*) the articulation of a normally silent final consonant in a word as the initial sound of a following word that begins with a vowel or a silent *h.* [t. F, g. L *ligātio* a binding]

Liakoura (lĭ äʹko͞o räʹ), *n.* See **Parnassus, Mount.**

liana (lĭ äʹnə), *n.* a climbing plant or vine. Also, **liane** (lĭ änʹ). [t. F: m. *liane,* earlier *liorne,* b. *viorne* (g. L *viburnum* viburnum) and *lier* bind (g. L *ligāre*)]

liang (lĭ ăngʹ), *n., pl.* **liang.** a Chinese unit of weight, equal to $\frac{1}{16}$ catty, and equivalent to about $1\frac{1}{3}$ ounce.

Liaoning (lyouʹnĭngʹ), *n.* a province in NE China, in Manchuria. 24,090,000 pop. (est. 1957); 25,969 sq. mi. *Cap.:* Shenyang. Formerly, **Fengtien.**

liar (līʹə), *n.* one who lies, or tells lies.

Liard (lēʹäd), *n.* a river in W Canada, flowing from S Yukon through N British Columbia and the Northwest Territories into the Mackenzie river. 550 mi.

lias (līʹəs), *n.* *Geol.* a series of marine sediments, the Lower Jurassic rocks of NW Europe. [ME, t. OF: m. *liois* kind of limestone, of Gmc orig.] **—liassic** (lī ăsʹĭk), *adj.*

Lib., Liberal.

lib., 1. (L *liber*) book. **2.** librarian. **3.** library.

libation (lī bāʹshən), *n.* **1.** a pouring out of wine or other liquid in honour of a deity. **2.** the liquid poured out. [ME, t. L: s. *lībātio*]

Libau (*Ger.* lēʹbou), *n.* German name of **Liepāja.**

Libava (*Russ.* lĭ bäʹvə), *n.* Russian name of **Liepāja.**

libel (līʹbl), *n., v.,* **-belled, -belling** or (*U.S.*) **-beled, -beling.** **—***n.* **1.** *Law.* **a.** defamation by written or printed words, pictures, or in any form other than by spoken words or gestures. **b.** the crime of publishing it. **2.** anything defamatory, or that maliciously or damagingly misrepresents. **3.** *Law.* a formal written declaration or statement, as one containing the allegations of a plaintiff or the ground of a charge. **—***v.t.* **4.** to publish a malicious libel against. **5.** to misrepresent damagingly. **6.** to institute suit against by a libel, as in an admiralty court. [ME, t. L: m. s. *libellus,* dim. of *liber* book]

libellant (līʹbə lənt), *n.* *Law.* one who libels, or institutes suit. Also, *U.S.,* **libelant.**

libellee (līʹbə lēʹ), *n.* *Law.* one against whom a libel instituting a suit has been filed; the respondent. Also, *U.S.,* **libelee.**

libeller (līʹbə lə), *n.* one who libels; one who publishes a libel assailing another. Also, *U.S.,* **libeler.**

libellous (līʹbə ləs), *adj.* containing, constituting, or involving a libel; maliciously defamatory. Also, *U.S.,* **libelous. —liʹbellously,** *adv.*

liber (līʹbə), *n.* *Bot.* phloem. [t. L]

liberal (lĭbʹə rəl, lĭbʹrəl), *adj.* **1.** favourable to progress or reform, as in religious or political affairs. **2.** (*often cap.*) denoting or pertaining to a political party advocating measures of progressive political reform: *the Liberal party.* **3.** favourable to or in accord with the policy of leaving the individual as unrestricted as possible in the opportunities for self-expression or self-fulfilment. **4.** of representational forms of government rather than aristocracies and monarchies. **5.** free from prejudice or bigotry; tolerant. **6.** giving freely or in ample measure: *a liberal donor.* **7.** given freely or abundantly: *a liberal donation.* **8.** not strict or rigorous: *a liberal interpretation of a rule.* **9.** befitting a freeman, a gentleman, or a non-professional person. **—***n.* **10.** a person of liberal principles or views, esp. in religion or politics. **11.** (*often cap.*) a member of a liberal party in politics, esp. of the Liberal Party in Great Britain. [ME, t. L: s. *līberālis* pertaining to a free man] **—libʹerally,** *adv.* **—libʹeralness,** *n.* **—Syn. 7.** See **ample.**

liberal arts, *Chiefly U.S.* the course of instruction at a university, comprising the arts, natural sciences, social sciences, and humanities. [anglicization of L *artēs līberālēs* arts of free men]

liberalism (lĭbʹə rə lĭzʹəm, lĭbʹrə-), *n.* **1.** liberal principles, as in religion or politics. **2.** (*sometimes cap.*) the principles and practices of a liberal party in politics. **3.** a movement in modern Protestantism which emphasizes freedom from tradition and authority, the adjustment of religious beliefs to scientific conceptions, and the spiritual capacities of men. **—libʹeralist,** *n., adj.* **—libʹeralisʹtic,** *adj.*

liberality (lĭbʹə rălʹĭ tĭ), *n., pl.* **-ties. 1.** the quality of being liberal in giving; generosity; bounty. **2.** a liberal gift. **3.** breadth of mind. **4.** liberalism.

liberalize (lĭbʹə rə līzʹ, lĭbʹrə-), *v.t., v.i.,* **-lized, -lizing.** to make or become liberal. Also, **liberalise. —libʹeralizʹer,** *n.*

Liberal Party, 1. a political party in Great Britain, a fusion of Whigs and Radicals, formed in the 1830s, and one of the dominant political parties until after World War I. **2.** any of certain political parties elsewhere.

liberate (lĭbʹə rātʹ), *v.t.,* **-rated, -rating. 1.** to set free, as from bondage; release. **2.** to disengage; set free from combination, as a gas. [t. L: m. s. *līberātus,* pp.] **—libʹeraʹtion,** *n.* **—libʹeraʹtor,** *n.* **—liberatress** (lĭbʹə rāʹtrĭs), *n. fem.*

Liberec (*Cz.* lēʹbĕ rĕts), *n.* a town in W Czechoslovakia. 69,000 (1965).

Liberia (lī bĭəʹrĭ ə), *n.* a republic in W Africa: founded by freed American slaves, 1822. 1,000,000 pop. (est. 1966); ab. 43,000 sq. mi. *Cap.:* Monrovia. See map under **Sierra Leone. —Libeʹrian,** *adj., n.*

libertarian (lĭbʹə tĕəʹrĭ ən), *n.* **1.** one who advocates liberty, esp. with regard to thought or conduct. **2.** one who maintains the doctrine of free will. **—***adj.* **3.** advocating liberty. **4.** maintaining the doctrine of free will. [f. LIBERT(Y) + -ARIAN] **—libʹertarʹianism,** *n.*

liberticide (lĭ bûʹtĭ sīdʹ), *n.* **1.** a destroyer of liberty. **2.** destruction of liberty. [f. LIBERTY + -CIDE] **—liberʹticidʹal,** *adj.*

libertinage (lĭbʹə tĭ nĭj), *n.* libertine conduct, esp. in sexual or religious matters.

libertine (lĭbʹə tīnʹ), *n.* **1.** one free from restraint or control, esp. in moral or sexual matters; a dissolute or licentious man. **2.** a freethinker in religious matters. **—***adj.* **3.** free from moral or sexual restraint; dissolute; licentious. **4.** freethinking in religious matters. [ME, t. L: m. s. *lībertīnus* freedman]

libertinism (lĭbʹə tĭ nĭzʹəm), *n.* libertine practices or habits of life; licentiousness.

liberty (lĭbʹə tĭ), *n., pl.* **-ties. 1.** freedom from arbitrary or despotic government. **2.** freedom from external or foreign rule; independence. **3.** freedom from control, interference, obligation, restriction, hampering conditions, etc.; power or right of doing, thinking, speaking, etc., according to choice. **4.** freedom from captivity, confinement, or physical restraint: *the prisoner soon regained his liberty.* **5.** leave granted to a sailor, esp. in the navy, to go ashore. **6.** the freedom of, or right of frequenting or using a place, etc. **7.** unwarranted or impertinent freedom in action or speech, or a form or instance of it: *to take liberties.* **8. at liberty, a.** free from bondage, captivity, confinement, or restraint. **b.** unoccupied or disengaged. **c.** free, permitted, or privileged to do or be as specified. [ME *libertie,* t. OF: m. *liberte,* t. L: m. s. *lībertas*] **—Syn. 4.** See **freedom.**

liberty cap, a kind of cap used as a symbol of liberty (from the cap of this kind given to a freedman in ancient Rome at his manumission).

Liberty Hall, *Colloq.* a place where a person can do whatever he wishes.

Liberty Island, a small island in New York harbour, where the Statue of Liberty is situated. Formerly, **Bedloe Island.**

Libia (*It.* lēʹbyä), *n.* Italian name of **Libya** (def. 2).

libidinous (lĭ bĭdʹĭ nəs), *adj.* full of lust; lustful; lewd. [ME *lybydynous,* t. L: m. s. *libīdinōsus*] **—libidʹinously,** *adv.* **—libidʹinousness,** *n.*

libido (lĭ bēʹdō), *n.* **1.** *Psychol.* all of the instinctive energies and desires which are derived from the id. **2.** the innate actuating or impelling force in living beings;

the vital impulse or urge. **3.** the sexual instinct. [t. L: pleasure, longing] —**libidinal** (lĭ bĭd′ĭ nəl), *adj.*

libra (lī′brə *for 1*; lē′brä *for 2*), *n., pl.* **-brae** (-brē) *for 1*, **-bras** (-bräs) *for 2.* **1.** the ancient Roman pound (containing 5053 grains). **2.** sol[3] (def. 3). [(def. 1) t. L; (def. 2) t. Sp., g. L]

Libra (lī′brə), *n., gen.* **-brae** (-brē). **1.** *Astron.* the Balance, a zodiacal constellation. **2.** the seventh sign of the zodiac. See diag. under **zodiac.** [t. L: pound, balance, level]

librarian (lī brĕə′rĭ ən), *n.* **1.** a person trained in librarianship. **2.** a person in charge of a library.

librarianship (lī brĕə′rĭ ən shĭp′), *n.* **1.** a profession concerned with organizing collections of books and related materials in libraries and of making these resources available to readers and others. **2.** the position or duties of a librarian.

library (lī′brə rĭ), *n., pl.* **-ries. 1.** a place set apart to contain books and other literary material for reading, study, or reference, as a room, set of rooms, or building where books may be read or borrowed. **2.** a lending library or a public library. **3.** a collection of manuscripts, publications, and other materials for reading, study, or reference. **4.** a series of books of similar character, or alike in size, binding, etc., issued by a single publishing house. [ME *librarie*, t. L: m. *librārium* place to keep books]

Library of Congress, the national library of the U.S. in Washington, D.C., established by Congress in 1800 and receiving copies of all books published in the U.S.

librate (lī′brāt), *v.i.*, **-brated, -brating. 1.** to oscillate; sway. **2.** to be poised or balanced.

libration (lī brā′shən), *n.* *Astron.* a real or apparent oscillatory motion, esp. of the moon. [t. L: s. *librātio* balance, a moving from side to side]

libratory (lī′brə tə rĭ, -trĭ), *adj.* oscillatory.

librettist (lĭ brĕt′ĭst), *n.* the writer of a libretto.

libretto (lĭ brĕt′ō; *It.* lē brĕt′tô), *n., pl.* **-tos, -ti** (-tē). **1.** the text or words of an opera or other extended musical composition. **2.** a book or booklet containing such a text. [t. It., dim. of *libro* book, g. L *liber*]

Libreville (*Fr.* lē brə vēl′), *n.* a port in and the capital of Gabon, in the W part, on the Gulf of Guinea. 31,027 (1961).

libriform (lī′brĭ fôm′), *adj.* *Bot.* having the form of or resembling liber or phloem. [f. LIB(E)R + -(I)FORM]

Libya (lĭb′ĭ ə), *n.* **1.** (in classical times) the part of N Africa W of Egypt. **2.** a constitutional monarchy in N Africa between Tunisia and Egypt. 1,559,399 pop. (1964); 679,400 sq. mi. *Caps:* Tripoli and Benghazi.

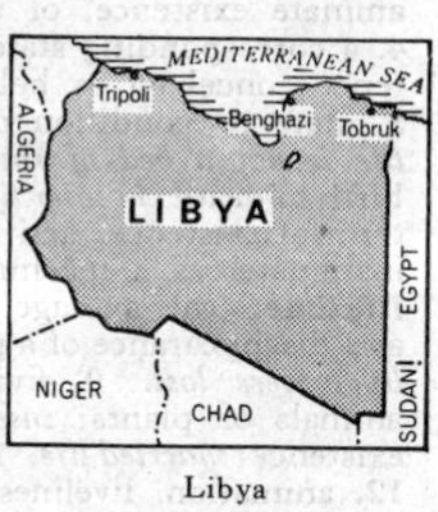

Libyan (lĭb′ĭ ən), *adj.* **1.** of or pertaining to Libya. —*n.* **2.** a native or inhabitant of Libya. **3.** Berber (def. 2), esp. in its ancient form.

Libyan Desert, a part of the Sahara W of the Nile, in E Libya, W Egypt, and NW Sudan.

Libya

lice (līs), *n.* pl. of **louse.**

licence (lī′səns), *n.* **1.** formal permission or leave to do or not to do something. **2.** formal permission from a constituted authority to do something, as to carry on some business or profession, etc. **3.** a certificate of such permission; an official permit. **4.** freedom of action, speech, thought, etc., permitted or conceded. **5.** intentional deviation from rule, convention, or fact, as for the sake of literary or artistic effect: *poetic licence.* **6.** excessive or undue freedom or liberty. **7.** licentiousness. Also, *U.S.*, **license.** [ME, t. OF, t. L: m. s. *licentia*]

license (lī′səns), *v.*, **-censed, -censing,** *n.* —*v.t.* **1.** to grant authoritative permission or licence to; authorize. —*n.* **2.** *U.S.* licence.

licensed victualler, an innkeeper or landlord licensed to sell wines and spirits, etc.

licensee (lī′sən sē′), *n.* one to whom a licence is granted.

licenser (lī′sən sə), *n.* one who grants licences, esp. for the performances of plays or the publication of books.

licentiate (lī sĕn′shĭ ĭt), *n.* **1.** one who has received a licence, as from a university, to practise an art or profession. **2.** the holder of a certain university degree intermediate between that of bachelor and that of doctor, now confined chiefly to certain continental European universities. —**licen′tiateship′**, *n.*

licentious (lī sĕn′shəs), *adj.* **1.** sensually unbridled; libertine; lewd. **2.** unrestrained by law or morality; lawless; immoral. **3.** going beyond customary or proper bounds or limits. [t. ML: m. s. *licentiōsus*] —**licen′tiously,** *adv.* —**licen′tiousness,** *n.*

lichee (lī′chē′), *n.* lychee.

lichen (lī′kən), *n.* **1.** any one of the group *Lichenes*, of the *Thallophyta*, compound plants (fungi in symbiotic union with algae) having a vegetative body (thallus) growing in greenish, grey, yellow, brown, or blackish crustlike patches or bushlike forms on rocks, trees, etc. **2.** *Pathol.* any of various eruptive skin diseases. [t. L, t. Gk: m. *leichēn*] —**li′chen-like′**, *adj.* —**li′chenous,** *adj.*

lichenin (lī′kə nĭn), *n.* *Chem.* a polysaccharide starch, $(C_6H_{10}O_5)_n$, a white gelatinous substance derived from certain mosses. [f. LICHEN + -IN[2]]

lichenoid (lī′kə noid′), *adj.* lichen-like.

lichenology (lī′kə nŏl′ə jĭ), *n.* the branch of botany that treats of lichens. —**lichenological** (lī′kə nə lŏj′ĭ kl), *adj.* —**lichenologist** (lī′kə nŏl′ə jĭst), *n.*

Lichfield (lĭch′fēld′), *n.* a town in England, in Staffordshire: birthplace of Samuel Johnson. 14,087 (1961).

lichgate (lĭch′gāt′), *n.* a roofed gate to a churchyard, under which a bier is set down to await the coming of the clergyman. Also, **lychgate.** [f. *lich* (OE *līc*, c. D *lijk*) body, corpse + GATE]

lichi (lī′chē′), *n., pl.* **-chis.** lychee.

licit (lĭs′ĭt), *adj.* permitted; lawful. [late ME, t. L: s. *licitus*, pp.] —**lic′itly,** *adv.*

lick (lĭk), *v.t.* **1.** to pass the tongue over the surface of (often fol. by *up*, *off*, *from*, etc.). **2.** to make by strokes of the tongue: *to lick the plate clean.* **3.** to pass or play lightly over, as waves or flames do. **4.** *Colloq.* to beat, thrash, or whip, as a punishment, etc. **5.** *Colloq.* to overcome in a fight, etc.; defeat. **6.** *Colloq.* to outdo; surpass. **7. lick into shape,** to bring to a state of completion or perfection; make efficient. **8. lick someone's boots,** to act in a subservient manner; fawn upon. **9. lick the dust.** See **dust** (def. 15). —*n.* **10.** a stroke of the tongue over something. **11.** a small quantity. **12.** a place to which wild animals resort to lick salt occurring naturally there. **13.** *Colloq.* a blow. **14.** *Colloq.* a brief or brisk stroke of activity or endeavour. **15.** *Colloq.* speed. **16. lick and a promise,** a feeble, perfunctory, or superficial attempt at doing something. [ME *licke(n)*, OE *liccian*, c. D *likken*, G *lecken*; akin to L *lingere*] —**lick′er,** *n.*

lickerish (lĭk′ə rĭsh), *adj.* *Archaic.* **1.** eager for choice food. **2.** greedy. **3.** lustful. Also, **liquorish.** [earlier *lickerous* (influenced by *lick* and *liquor*, with substitution of suffix -ISH[1] for -OUS), ME *likerous*, repr. an AF var. of OF *lecheros*, der. *lecheor* gourmand, sensualist. See LECHER]

licking (lĭk′ĭng), *n.* **1.** *Colloq.* **a.** a beating or thrashing. **b.** a defeat; setback. **2.** the act of one who or that which licks.

lickspittle (lĭk′spĭt′l), *n.* an abject toady.

licorice (lĭk′ə rĭs), *n.* liquorice.

lictor (lĭk′tə), *n.* (in ancient Rome) one of a body of attendants on certain magistrates, who preceded them carrying the fasces. [ME, t. L]

lid (lĭd), *n.* **1.** a movable piece, whether separate or hinged, for closing the opening of a vessel, box, etc.; a movable cover. **2.** an eyelid. **3.** (in mosses) **a.** the cover of the capsule; operculum. **b.** the upper section of a pyxidium. **4.** *Slang.* a hat. **5. put the lid on,** to surpass everything; be the climax or culmination of. [ME; OE *hlid*, c. D *lid*, G *Lid*] —**lid′ded,** *adj.*

Liddell Hart (lĭd′l hät′), **Basil Henry,** 1895–1970, English writer on military affairs.

Lidice (lĭd′ĭ chĭ; *Cz.* lē′dye tsĕ), *n.* a village in Czechoslovakia which was destroyed and its male inhabitants murdered by the Nazis in 1942 as a reprisal for the assassination of a high-ranking Nazi official.

lidless (lĭd′lĭs), *adj.* **1.** having no lid. **2.** (of eyes) having no eyelids. **3.** *Poetic.* vigilant.

Lido (lē′dō; *It.* -dô), *n.* **1.** a chain of sandy islands in NE Italy, lying between the Lagoon of Venice and the Adriatic: fashionable beach resort. **2.** (*l.c.*) an open-air public swimming pool.

lie[1] (lī), *n., v.*, **lied, lying.** —*n.* **1.** a false statement made with intent to deceive; an intentional untruth; a falsehood. **2.** something intended or serving to convey a false impression. **3.** the charge or accusation of lying; a flat contradiction. **4. give the lie (to), a.** to charge with lying; contradict flatly. **b.** to imply or show to be false; belie. [ME; OE *lyge*, c. Icel. *lygi*] —*v.i.* **5.** to speak falsely or utter untruth knowingly, as with intent to deceive. **6.** to express what is false, or convey a false impression. —*v.t.* **7.** to bring, put, etc., by lying: *to lie oneself out of a difficulty.* [ME *lien*, OE *lēogan*, c. Goth. *liugan*] —**Syn. 1.** See **falsehood.**

lie[2] (lī), *v.*, **lay, lain, lying,** *n.* —*v.i.* **1.** to be in a recumbent or prostrate position, as on a bed or the ground; recline. **2.** to assume such a position (fol. by *down*): *to lie down on the ground.* **3.** to be buried (in a particular spot). **4.** to rest in a horizontal position; be stretched out or extended: *a book lying on the table.* **5.** to be or remain in a position or state of inactivity, subjection, restraint, concealment, etc.: *to lie in ambush.* **6.** to rest, press, or weigh (fol. by *on* or *upon*): *these things lie upon my mind.* **7.** to depend (fol. by *on* or *upon*). **8.** to be found, occur, or be (where specified): *the fault lies here.* **9.** to be placed or situated: *land lying along the coast.* **10.** to consist or be grounded (fol. by *in*): *the real remedy lies in education.* **11.** to be in or have a specified direction: *the trail from here lies to the west.* **12.** *Law.* to be sustainable or admissible, as an action or appeal. **13.** *Archaic.* to lodge; sojourn. **14. as far as in me lies,** to the best of my ability. **15. let sleeping dogs lie,** to avoid an awkward or controversial topic or action. **16. lie down under,** to accept (abuse, etc.) without protest. **17. lie in, a.** to be confined in childbed. **b.** to stay late in bed. **18. lie in state,** (of a corpse) to be honourably displayed, as in a church, etc. **19. lie low,** to be in hiding. **20. lie off,** (of a ship) to stand some distance away from the shore. **21. lie over,** to be postponed or deferred. **22. lie to,** *Naut.* (of a ship) to lie comparatively stationary, usually with the head as near the wind as possible. **23. lie up, a.** to stay in bed. **b.** (of a ship) to go into dock. **24. lie with, a.** to be the function or responsibility of. **b.** *Archaic.* to have sexual intercourse with. **25. take lying down,** to submit without resistance or protest. *—n.* **26.** manner of lying; the relative position or direction in which something lies: *lie of the land.* **27.** the place where a bird, beast, or fish is accustomed to lie or lurk. **28.** *Golf.* the ground position of the golf ball. [ME *lie(n)*, *liggen*, OE *licgan*, c. D *liggen*, G *liegen*, Icel. *liggja*, Goth. *ligan*]

—Syn. 1. LIE, LAY, often confused, are not synonyms. LIE, meaning 'to recline or rest', does not require an object. Its principal parts, too, are irregular, and are therefore distinctive. LAY (originally *to cause to lie*), with its forms *laid, have laid, laying*, etc., means 'to put or place'. If 'put' or 'place' can be substituted in a contemplated sentence, the verb to use is LAY. Moreover, since one must always 'put' or 'place' *something*, the verb LAY is used only when there is a grammatical object to complete the sense. (It should be noticed, however, that the past tense of LIE is also spelt LAY.)

Lie (lē), *n.* **1. Jonas,** 1880–1940, U.S. painter, born in Norway. **2. Trygve Halvdan** (trĭg′və hälv′dän; *Nor.* tryg′və), 1896–1969, Norwegian statesman: secretary-general of United Nations 1946–53.

Liebfraumilch (*Ger.* lēp′frou mĭlKH), *n.* a hock produced mainly in the Hesse region of West Germany. [t. G, named after *Liebfrauenstift* convent of the Virgin, in Worms, where the wine was first made + *Milch* MILK]

Liebig (*Ger.* lē′bĭKH), *n.* **Justus** (*Ger.* yo͝os′to͝os), **Baron von** (*Ger.* fōn), 1803–73, German chemist.

Liebknecht (*Ger.* lēp′knĕKHt), *n.* **1. Karl** (*Ger.* kärl), 1871–1919, German socialist leader. **2.** his father, **Wilhelm** (*Ger.* vĭl′hĕlm), 1826–1900, German journalist and political leader.

Liechtenstein (lĭk′tən stīn′; *Ger.* lĭKH′tən shtīn), *n.* a small principality in central Europe between Austria and Switzerland. 16,628 pop. (1960); 65 sq. mi. *Cap.:* Vaduz.

Lied (lēd; *Ger.* lēt), *n.*, *pl.* **Lieder** (lē′də; *Ger.* lē′dər). *German.* a German song, lyric, or ballad.

liederkranz (lē′də kränts′), *n.* **1. a.** a cheese mellower than Camembert but not as strong as Limburger. **b.** (*cap.*) a trademark for this cheese. **2.** a German choral society or singing club, esp. of men. [G: garland of songs]

lie detector, an instrument for recording a person's involuntary physiological responses while under interrogation as an indication of the veracity of any statements he makes.

lief (lēf), *adv.* **1.** Also, **lieve.** gladly; willingly. *—adj.* *Archaic.* **2.** willing. **3.** dear. [ME *leef*, OE *lēof*, c. G *lieb*]

liege (lēj), *n.* **1.** a lord entitled to allegiance and service. **2.** a vassal or subject, as of a ruler. *—adj.* **3.** entitled to, or owing, allegiance and service. **4.** pertaining to the relation between vassal and lord. **5.** loyal; faithful. [ME *lige*, t. OF: liege, free, exempt, g. LL *lēticus*, der. *lētus* free man, of Gmc orig.]

Liège (lĭ āzh′; *Fr.* lyĕzh), *n.* **1.** a city in E Belgium, on the river Meuse: one of the first cities attacked in World War I. 153,183 (1962). **2.** a province in E Belgium. 1,003,226 pop. (est. 1963); 1525 sq. mi. *Cap.:* Liège. Flemish, **Luik.**

liegeman (lēj′măn′), *n.*, *pl.* **-men. 1.** a vassal; a subject. **2.** a faithful follower.

Liegnitz (*Ger.* lēg′nĭts), *n.* a town in SW Poland: formerly in Germany. 69,800 (est. 1963). Polish, **Lignica.**

lien[1] (lĭən, lē′ən), *n.* a legal right to hold property or to have it sold or applied for payment of a claim. [t. F, g. L *ligāmen* band, tie]

lien[2] (lĭən), *n.* *Anat.* the spleen.

lientery (lī′ən tə rĭ), *n.* *Pathol.* a form of diarrhoea in which the food is discharged undigested or only partly digested. [t. ML: m. s. *lienteria*, t. Gk: m. *leienteria*] **—lienteric** (lī′ən tĕ′rĭk), *adj.*

Liepāja (lĭ ĕp′ə yə), *n.* a seaport in the W Soviet Union, in the Latvian Republic, on the Baltic. 82,000 (est. 1965). Russian, **Libava.** German, **Libau.**

lier (lī′ə), *n.* one who lies (down, etc.).

lierne (lĭ ûn′), *n.* *Archit.* a short connecting rib in vaulting. [late ME, t. F, var. of *liorne.* See LIANA]

Lierre (*Fr.* lyĕr), *n.* a town in Belgium, in E central Antwerp province. 28,520 (est. 1964).

Lietuva (lĭə to͞o′və), *n.* Lithuanian name of **Lithuania.**

lieu (lyo͞o), *n.* **1.** place; stead. **2. in lieu of,** instead of. [ME *liue*, t. F: m. *lieu*, g. L *locus* place]

lieutenancy (lĕf tĕn′ən sĭ), *n.*, *pl.* **-cies. 1.** the office, authority, incumbency, or jurisdiction of a lieutenant. **2.** lieutenants collectively.

lieutenant (lĕf tĕn′ənt), *n.* **1.** *Mil.* a commissioned officer ranking below a captain and above a second lieutenant. **2.** *Naval.* a commissioned officer ranking below a lieutenant commander and above a sublieutenant. **3.** the rank of either of these. **4.** one who holds an office, civil or military, in subordination to a superior, for whom he acts. [ME *levetenant*, t. F: m. *lieutenant*, f. *lieu* (g. L *locus*) place + *tenant*, ppr. of *tenir* (g. L *tenēre*) hold]

lieutenant colonel, *Mil.* **1.** a commissioned officer ranking below a colonel and above a major. **2.** the rank.

lieutenant commander, *Naval.* **1.** an officer ranking below a commander and above a lieutenant. **2.** the rank.

lieutenant general, *Mil.* **1.** an officer ranking below a general and above a major general. **2.** the rank.

lieutenant governor, 1. a deputy governor. **2.** (in Canada) the governor of a province.

lieve (lēv), *adv.* lief.

life (līf), *n.*, *pl.* **lives. 1.** the condition which distinguishes animals and plants from inorganic objects and dead organisms. The distinguishing manifestations of life are: growth through metabolism, reproduction, and the power of adaptation to environment through changes originating internally. **2.** (collectively) the distinguishing phenomena (esp. metabolism, growth, reproduction, and spontaneous adaptation to environment) of plants and animals, arising out of the energy relationships with protoplasm. **3.** the animate existence, or the term of animate existence, of an individual: *to risk one's life.* **4.** a corresponding state, existence, or principle of existence conceived as belonging to the soul: *eternal life.* **5.** state or condition of existence as a human being: *life is not a bed of roses.* **6.** period of existence from birth to death: *in later life she became more placid.* **7. a.** the term of existence, activity, or effectiveness of something inanimate, as a machine or a lease. **b.** *Physics.* Also, **lifetime.** the average period between the appearance and disappearance of a particle. **8.** a living being: *several lives were lost.* **9.** living things collectively, whether animals or plants: *insect life.* **10.** course or mode of existence: *married life.* **11.** a biography: *a life of Churchill.* **12.** animation, liveliness: *a speech full of life.* **13.** that which makes or keeps alive; the vivifying or quickening principle. **14.** existence in the world of affairs, society, etc. **15.** one who or that which enlivens: *the life of the party.* **16.** effervescence or sparkle, as of wines. **17.** pungency or strong, sharp flavour, as of substances when fresh or in good condition. **18.** the living form or model as the subject or representation in art. **19. a.** a prison sentence covering the rest of the convicted person's natural life. **b.** the maximum possible term of imprisonment that can be awarded by the laws of a state. **20. as large as life,** *Colloq.* actually; in person. **21. come to life, a.** to recover consciousness. **b.** to display liveliness or vigour. **c.** to appear lifelike; be convincing or realistic. **22. for dear life,** urgently, desperately. **23. for the life of one,** with the greatest effort: *for the life of me I can't understand him.* **24. from the life,** (of a drawing, painting, etc.) drawn from a living model. **25. not on your life,** *Colloq.* absolutely not. **26. take one's life in one's hands,** to risk death. **27. the time of one's life,** a very enjoyable occasion. **28. to the life,** being an exact imitation or copy. [ME; OE *līf*, c. D *lijf* body, G *Leib*, Icel. *līf* life, body] **—Syn. 12.** vivacity, sprightliness; spirit. **—Ant. 12.** inertness, dullness.

life assurance, insurance providing payment of a specific sum of money to a named beneficiary upon the death of the assured, or to the assured or to a named beneficiary should the assured reach a specified age. Also, **life insurance.**

lifebelt (līf′bĕlt′), *n.* a belt of buoyant material to keep a person afloat in the water.

lifeblood (līf′blŭd′), *n.* **1.** the blood necessary to life.

2. the element that vivifies, animates or supports anything.

lifeboat (līf′bōt′), *n.* **1.** a shore-based boat especially built for rescuing the occupants of ships in distress along the coast. **2.** a boat, provisioned and equipped for abandoning ship, carried in davits so that it may be lowered quickly.

lifebuoy (līf′boi′), *n.* a buoyant device (in various forms) for throwing, as from a vessel, to persons in the water, to enable them to keep afloat until rescued.

life cycle, the course of development from the fertilization of the egg to the production of a new generation of germ cells.

life expectancy, the probable life span of an individual or class of persons, determined statistically, and affected by such factors as heredity, physical condition, nutrition, occupation, etc.

life-giving (līf′gĭv′ĭng), *adj.* imparting life or vitality; invigorating.

lifeguard (līf′gäd′), *n.* **1.** a man employed on a bathing beach to rescue and give first aid to bathers in distress. **2.** one of a bodyguard of soldiers.

Life Guards, a cavalry regiment of the Household Brigade, distinguished by their scarlet uniform jackets and white helmet plumes.

life history, *Biol.* **1.** the series of living phenomena exhibited by an organism in the course of its development from the egg to its adult state. **2.** a life cycle.

life insurance, life assurance.

life jacket, an inflatable, sleeveless jacket for keeping a person afloat in water.

lifeless (līf′lĭs), *adj.* **1.** not endowed with life: *lifeless matter.* **2.** destitute of living things: *a lifeless planet.* **3.** deprived of life, or dead: *lifeless bodies.* **4.** without animation, liveliness, or spirit: *lifeless performance.* **5.** insensible, as one in a faint. —**life′lessly,** *adv.* —**life′lessness,** *n.* —**Syn. 1.** inanimate, inorganic. **3.** See **dead. 4.** dull; inactive, inert, passive; sluggish, torpid; spiritless. —**Ant. 1, 3.** living. **4.** lively.

lifelike (līf′līk′), *adj.* resembling or simulating real life: *a lifelike picture.* —**life′like′ness,** *n.*

lifeline (līf′līn′), *n.* **1.** a line fired across a vessel by which a hawser for a breeches buoy may be hauled aboard. **2.** a line or rope for saving life, as one attached to a lifeboat. **3.** the line by which a diver is lowered and raised. **4.** any of several lines, which are anchored and used by bathers for support. **5.** a route over which supplies can be sent to an area otherwise isolated. **6.** any vital line of communication.

lifelong (līf′lŏng′), *adj.* lasting or continuing throughout life: *lifelong regret.*

life office, an insurance company specializing in life assurance.

life peer, a peer holding a title which lapses at his death. —**life peeress,** *fem.*

life-preserver (līf′prĭ zû′və), *n.* **1.** a short stick with a loaded head, used for self-defence; bludgeon. **2.** *U.S.* a life jacket, lifebelt, or other device for saving persons in the water from sinking and drowning.

lifer (lī′fə), *n. Slang.* one sentenced to imprisonment for life.

life-saver (līf′sā′və), *n.* **1.** a person who rescues another from danger of death, esp. from drowning. **2.** a lifeguard (def. 1). —**life′-sav′ing,** *adj., n.*

life-size (līf′sīz′), *adj.* of the size of life or the living original: *life-size picture or statue.*

life span, the longest period over which the life of any plant or animal organism or species may extend, according to the available biological knowledge concerning it. Cf. **life expectancy.**

lifetime (līf′tīm′), *n.* **1.** the time that one's life continues; one's term of life: *peace within our lifetime.* **2.** life (def. 7b).

lifework (līf′wûk′), *n.* the work or labour of a lifetime.

Liffey (lĭf′ĭ), *n.* a river in the E Republic of Ireland flowing through Dublin. 50 mi.

Lifford (lĭf′əd), *n.* a town in the Republic of Ireland, the county town of Donegal. 864 (1961).

lift (lĭft), *v.t.* **1.** to move or bring (something) upwards from the ground or other support to some higher position; hoist. **2.** to raise or direct upwards: *to lift the hand, head, or eyes.* **3.** to hold up or display on high. **4.** to raise in rank, condition, estimation, etc.; elevate or exalt. **5.** to make louder or more audible: *to lift the voice.* **6.** to rescind or remove; bring to an end: *to lift the ban on the import of drugs.* **7.** *Colloq.* to steal or plagiarize. **8.** to dig up (root crops). **9.** to perform a facelift on. **10.** *U.S.* to pay off a mortgage, etc. **11.** *Golf.* to pick or take up. —*v.i.* **12.** to go up; give to upward pressure: *the lid won't lift.* **13.** to pull or strain in the effort to lift something: *to lift at a heavy weight.* **14.** to move upwards or rise; rise and disperse, as clouds, fog, etc. **15.** to rise to view above the horizon when approached, as land seen from the sea. —*n.* **16.** the act of lifting, raising, or rising: *the lift of a hand.* **17.** extent of rise, or distance through which anything is raised. **18.** lifting or raising force. **19.** the weight or load lifted. **20.** a moving platform or cage for conveying goods, people, etc., from one level to another, as in a building. **21.** any device or apparatus for lifting. **22.** a helping upwards or onwards. **23.** a ride in a vehicle, esp. one given free of charge to a traveller on foot. **24.** exaltation or uplift, as in feeling. **25.** a rise or elevation of ground. **26.** *Aeron.* the component of the force exerted by the air on an aerofoil having a direction opposite to the force of gravity, and causing an aircraft to stay aloft. **27.** one of the layers of leather forming the heel of a boot or shoe. **28.** *Mining.* a slice or thickness (of ore) mined in one operation. [ME *lifte(n)*, t. Scand.; cf. Icel. *lypta* lift, der. *lopt* air, sky] —**lift′er,** *n.* —**Syn. 1.** See **raise.**

liftboy (lĭft′boi′), *n.* a boy who operates a lift in a hotel, department store, etc.

lifting body, *Aeron.* a wingless aircraft which derives aerodynamic lift from its shape alone.

liftman (lĭft′măn′), *n.* a man who operates a lift in a hotel, department store, etc.

lift-off (lĭft′ŏf′), *n. Aerospace.* the start of a rocket's flight from its launching pad. Also, **blast-off.**

lift-pump (lĭft′pŭmp′), *n.* any pump which merely lifts or raises a liquid (distinguished from *force-pump*).

liftslab (lĭft′slăb′), *n.* a system of erecting multistorey buildings, in which the floor slabs, cast at ground level, are lifted up one by one.

ligament (lĭg′ə mənt), *n., pl.* **ligaments, ligamenta** (lĭg′ə mĕn′tə). **1.** *Anat.* a band of tissue, usually white and fibrous, serving to connect bones, hold organs in place, etc. **2.** a connecting tie; bond. [ME, t. L: s. *ligāmentum* a tie, band]

ligamentous (lĭg′ə mĕn′təs), *adj.* pertaining to, of the nature of, or forming a ligament. Also, **ligamentary** (lĭg′ə mĕn′tə rĭ).

ligan (lī′gən), *n. Law.* lagan.

ligate (lī′gāt), *v.t.*, **-gated, -gating.** to bind, as with a ligature; tie up, as a bleeding artery. [t. L: m. s. *ligātus*, pp.] —**liga′tion,** *n.*

ligature (lĭg′ə chə, -chŏŏə′), *n., v.*, **-tured, -turing.** —*n.* **1.** the act of binding or tying up. **2.** anything that serves for binding or tying up, as a band, bandage, or cord. **3.** a tie or bond. **4.** *Print. and Writing.* a stroke or bar connecting two letters. **5.** *Print.* a character or type combining two or more letters, as *fi, ffl.* **6.** *Music.* **a.** a slur. **b.** a group of notes connected by a slur. **c.** a metal band for adjusting the position of the reed on clarinets and saxophones. **7.** *Surg.* a thread or wire for constriction of blood vessels, etc., or for removing tumours by strangulation. —*v.t.* **8.** to bind with a ligature; tie up; ligate. [ME, t. LL: m. s. *ligātūra*, der. L *ligāre* bind]

liger (lī′gə), *n.* the offspring of a male lion and a female tiger. Cf. **tigon.**

light[1] (līt), *n., adj., v.*, **lit** or **lighted, lighting.** —*n.* **1.** that which makes things visible, or affords illumination: *all colours depend on light.* **2.** *Physics.* **a.** Also, **luminous energy, radiant energy.** electromagnetic radiation to which the organs of sight react, ranging in wavelength from about 4×10^{-7} to $7{\cdot}7 \times 10^{-7}$ metres and propagated at a speed of $2{\cdot}9979 \times 10^{8}$ metres per second. It is considered variously as a wave, corpuscular, or quantum phenomenon. **b.** the sensation produced by it on the organs of sight. **c.** a similar form of radiant energy which does not affect the retina, as ultraviolet or infra-red rays. **3.** an illuminating agent or source, as the sun, a lamp, or a beacon. **4.** the light, radiance, or illumination from a particular source: *the light of a candle.* **5.** the illumination from the sun, or daylight. **6.** daybreak or dawn. **7.** daytime. **8.** measure or supply of light; illumination: *the wall cuts off our light.* **9.** a particular light or illumination in which an object seen takes on a certain appearance: *viewing the portrait in various lights.* **10.** *Art.* **a.** the effect of light falling on an object or scene as represented in a picture. **b.** one of the brightest parts of a picture. **11.** the aspect in which a thing appears or is regarded: *this shows up in a favourable light.* **12.** a gleam or sparkle, as in the eyes. **13.** a means of igniting, as a spark, flame, match, or the like: *could you give me a light?* **14.** state of being visible, exposed to view, or revealed to public notice or knowledge: *to come to light.* **15.** a window, or a pane or compartment of a window. **16.** mental or spiritual illumination or enlightenment: *to throw light on a mystery.* **17.** (*pl.*) information, ideas, or mental capacities possessed: *to act according to one's lights.* **18.** a person who is an illuminating or shining example; a luminary. **19.** a lighthouse. **20.** a traffic light. **21.** *Archaic.* the eyesight. **22. bring to light,** to discover; reveal. **23. come to**

light, to be discovered; become known. **24. in a good (bad) light,** under favourable (unfavourable) circumstances. **25. in the light of,** taking into account; considering. **26. see the light, a.** to come into existence. **b.** to be made public, or published, as a book. **c.** to accept or understand an idea; realize the truth of something. **27. shed** or **throw light on,** to make clear; explain.
—*adj.* 28. having light or illumination, rather than dark: *the lightest room in the entire house.* **29.** pale, whitish, or not deep or dark in colour: *a light red.*
—*v.t.* **30.** to set burning (a candle, lamp, pipe for smoking, etc.); kindle (a fire); ignite (fuel, a match, etc.). **31.** to switch on (an electric light). **32.** to give light to; illuminate; to furnish with light or illumination. **33.** to make bright as with light or colour (usually with *up*): *a huge room lit up with candles.* **34.** to cause (the face, etc.) to brighten or become animated (often fol. by *up*): *a smile lit up her face.* **35.** to conduct with a light: *a candle to light you to bed.*
—*v.i.* **36.** to take fire or become kindled. **37.** to become bright as with light or colour: *the sky lights up at sunset.* **38.** to brighten with animation or joy, as the face, eyes, etc. (often fol. by *up*).
[ME; OE *lēoht*, c. D *licht*, G *Licht*; akin to Icel. *ljōs*, Goth. *liuhath*, also to L *lux* light, Gk *leukós* light, bright]

light[2] (līt), *adj.* **1.** of little weight; not heavy: *a light load.* **2.** of little weight in proportion to bulk; of low specific gravity: *a light metal.* **3.** of less than the usual or average weight: *light clothing.* **4.** weighing less than the proper or standard amount: *that grocer uses light weights.* **5.** of small amount, force, intensity, etc.: *a light rain, light sleep.* **6.** gentle; delicate; exerting only slight pressure. **7.** easy to endure, deal with, or perform: *light duties.* **8.** not profound, serious, or heavy: *light reading.* **9.** of little moment or importance; trivial: *the loss was no light matter.* **10.** easily digested, as food. **11.** not heavy or strong, as wine, etc. **12.** spongy or well leavened, as bread. **13.** porous or friable, as soil. **14.** slender or delicate in form or appearance: *a light, graceful figure.* **15.** airy or buoyant in movement: *light as air.* **16.** nimble or agile: *light fingers.* **17.** free from any burden of sorrow or care: *a light heart.* **18.** cheerful; gay: *a light laugh.* **19.** characterized by lack of proper seriousness; frivolous: *light conduct.* **20.** wanton; immoral. **21.** easily swayed or changing; volatile: *to be light of love.* **22.** dizzy; slightly delirious: *his head is light.* **23.** *Mil.* lightly armed or equipped: *light infantry.* **24.** having little or no cargo: *a ship sailing light.* **25.** adapted by small weight or slight build for small loads or swift movement: *light vessels.* **26.** *Phonet.* **a.** having a less than normally strong pronunciation, as of a vowel or syllable. **b.** (of *l* sounds) resembling a front vowel in quality: *French l is lighter than English l.* **27. make light of,** treat as of little importance.
—*adv.* **28.** lightly. **29.** *Colloq.* with little or no luggage: *to travel light.* [ME; OE *lēoht, līht*, c. D *licht*, G *leicht*]

light[3] (līt), *v.i.*, **lighted** or **lit, lighting. 1.** to get down or descend, as from a horse or a vehicle. **2.** to come to rest, as on a spot or thing; land. **3.** to come by chance, happen, or hit (fol. by *on* or *upon*): *to light on a clue.* **4.** to fall, as a stroke, weapon, vengeance, choice, etc., on a place or person. [ME *liht(en)*, *light(en)*, OE *līhtan* alight, orig. make light, relieve of a weight, der. *līht* LIGHT[2], adj.]

light air, *Meteorol.* a wind of Beaufort scale force 2, i.e. one about 2 miles per hour.

light ale, a pale malt beer of low alcoholic strength, usually bottled; pale ale.

light breeze, *Meteorol.* a wind of Beaufort scale force 3, i.e. one about 5 miles per hour.

light bulb, bulb (def. 3).

lighten[1] (lī′tn), *v.i.* **1.** to become lighter or less dark; brighten. **2.** to shine, gleam, or be bright. **3.** to flash as or like lightning. **4.** to brighten or light up, as the face, eyes, etc. —*v.t.* **5.** to illuminate. **6.** to brighten (the eyes, features, etc.). **7.** to make lighter; make less dark. [ME, f. LIGHT[1], adj. + -EN[1]] —**light′ener,** *n.*

lighten[2] (lī′tn), *v.t.* **1.** to make lighter; lessen the weight of (a load, etc.); reduce the load of (a ship, etc.). **2.** to make less burdensome; mitigate: *to lighten taxes.* **3.** to cheer or gladden. —*v.i.* **4.** to become less burdensome, oppressive, etc. **5.** to become more cheerful or lively. [ME, f. LIGHT[2], adj. + -EN[1]]

lighter[1] (lī′tə), *n.* **1.** one who or that which lights. **2.** a mechanical device for lighting cigarettes, cigars, etc. [ME; f. LIGHT[1], v. + -ER[1]]

lighter[2] (lī′tə), *n.* **1.** a vessel, commonly a flat-bottomed unpowered barge, used in lightening or unloading and also in loading ships, or in transporting goods for short distances. —*v.t.* **2.** to convey in or as in a lighter. [ME, f. LIGHT[2], v. + -ER[1]]

lighterage (lī′tə rĭj), *n.* **1.** the use of lighters. **2.** a fee paid for lighter service.

lighterman (lī′tə mən), *n.* one who navigates a lighter.

lighter-than-air (lī′tə thən ēə′), *adj. Aeron.* **1.** of less specific gravity than the air. **2.** of or pertaining to such aircraft.

lightface (līt′fās′), *n. Print.* a type characterized by thin lines.

lightfast (līt′fäst′), *adj.* (of a pigment, dye, or dyed fabric) not affected by light, esp. not bleached by sunlight.

light-fingered (līt′fĭng′gəd), *adj.* having nimble fingers, esp. in picking pockets; thievish.

light-footed (līt′fo͝ot′ĭd), *adj.* stepping lightly or nimbly. Also, *Poetic*, **light′-foot′.** —**light′-foot′edly,** *adv.* —**light′-foot′edness,** *n.*

light-handed (līt′hăn′dĭd), *adj.* **1.** having a light, skilful, or delicate touch. **2.** carrying little in the hands.

light-headed (līt′hĕd′ĭd), *adj.* **1.** having or showing a frivolous or volatile disposition: *light-headed persons.* **2.** giddy, dizzy, or delirious. —**light′-head′edly,** *adv.* —**light′-head′edness,** *n.*

light-hearted (līt′hä′tĭd), *adj.* carefree; cheerful; gay: *a light-hearted laugh.* —**light′-heart′edly,** *adv.* —**light′-heart′edness,** *n.*

light heavyweight, *Boxing.* a fighter whose weight is not more than 12 st. 7 lbs in professional boxing, or 12 st. 10 lbs in amateur boxing.

light-horseman (līt′hôs′mən), *n.*, *pl.* **-men.** a light-armed cavalry soldier.

lighthouse (līt′hous′), *n.* a tower or other structure displaying a light or lights for the guidance of mariners.

lighting (lī′tĭng), *n.* **1.** the act of igniting or illuminating. **2.** arrangement or method of lights. **3.** the way light falls upon a face, object, etc., esp. in a picture.

lightish[1] (lī′tĭsh), *adj.* rather light in colour.

lightish[2] (lī′tĭsh), *adj.* rather light in weight.

lightless (līt′lĭs), *adj.* **1.** without light; receiving no light; dark. **2.** giving no light.

lightly (līt′lĭ), *adv.* **1.** with little weight, force, intensity, etc.: *to press lightly on a bell.* **2.** to only a small amount or degree. **3.** easily; without trouble or effort: *lightly come, lightly go.* **4.** cheerfully: *to take bad news lightly.* **5.** frivolously: *to behave lightly.* **6.** without due consideration or reason (often with a negative): *an offer not lightly to be refused.* **7.** nimbly: *to leap lightly aside.* **8.** indifferently or slightingly: *to think lightly of one's achievements.* **9.** airily; buoyantly: *flags floating lightly.*

light meter, *Photog.* exposure meter.

light-minded (līt′mīn′dĭd), *adj.* having or showing a light mind; characterized by levity; frivolous. —**light′-mind′edly,** *adv.* —**light′-mind′edness,** *n.*

light music, music produced for popular entertainment, esp. that played by a conventional orchestra.

lightness[1] (līt′nĭs), *n.* **1.** the state of being light, illuminated, or whitish. **2.** thin or pale coloration. [ME *lightnesse*, OE *līhtnes*, f. *līht* LIGHT[1], bright + *-nes* -NESS]

lightness[2] (līt′nĭs), *n.* **1.** the state or quality of being light in weight. **2.** the state or quality of being light as to specific gravity: *the lightness of cork.* **3.** the quality of being agile, nimble, or graceful. **4.** lack of pressure or burdensomeness. **5.** gayness; cheerfulness. **6.** levity in actions, thought, or speech. [f. LIGHT[2], adj. + -NESS]

lightning (līt′nĭng), *n.* a flashing of light, or a sudden illumination of the heavens, caused by the discharge of atmospheric electricity. [var. of *lightening*, f. LIGHTEN[1], v. + -ING[1]]

lightning arrester, a device preventing damage to radio, telephonic, or other electrical equipment from lightning or other high-voltage currents, reducing the voltage of a surge applied to its terminals and restoring itself to its original operating condition.

lightning bug, a firefly.

lightning conductor, a rodlike conductor installed to divert atmospheric electricity away from a structure and protect the structure from lightning by providing a path to earth. Also, **lightning rod.**

light-o'-love (līt′ə lŭv′), *n.* a wanton coquette.

light quantum, *Physics.* a photon.

lights (līts), *n.pl.* the lungs, esp. of sheep, pigs, etc.

lightship (līt′shĭp′), *n.* a ship anchored in a specific location and displaying a light or lights for the guidance of mariners.

lightsome[1] (līt′səm), *adj.* **1.** light, esp. in form, appearance, or movement; airy; buoyant; agile; nimble. **2.** cheerful; gay. **3.** frivolous. [f. LIGHT[2] + -SOME[1]] —**light′somely,** *adv.* —**light′someness,** *n.*

lightsome[2] (līt′səm), *adj.* **1.** luminous. **2.** well-lighted or illuminated. [f. LIGHT[1] + -SOME[1]] —**light′someness,** *n.*

lights out, *Chiefly Mil.* a signal that all or certain lights in a barracks, camp, etc., are to be extinguished.

light-struck (līt′strŭk′), *adj. Photog.* (of film, etc.) injured or fogged by accidental exposure to light.

lightweight (līt′wāt′), *adj.* **1.** light in weight. **2.** unimportant, not serious; trivial. —*n.* **3.** one of less than average weight. **4.** *Colloq.* a person of little mental force or of slight influence or importance. **5.** a boxer or other contestant who weighs between 9 st. 1 lb. and 9 st. 9 lbs.

light-year (līt′yĭə′), *n. Astron.* the distance traversed by light in one year (ab. 5,880,000,000,000 miles): used as a unit in measuring stellar distances.

lign-aloes (līn′ăl′ōz), *n.* the drug aloes; aloes-wood.

ligneous (lĭg′nĭ əs), *adj.* of the nature of or resembling wood; woody. [t. L: m. *ligneus* wooden]

ligni-, var. of **ligno-**.

Lignica (lĭg nĭt′sə), *n.* Polish name of **Liegnitz.**

ligniform (lĭg′nĭ fôm′), *adj.* having the form of wood; resembling wood, as a variety of asbestos.

lignify (lĭg′nĭ fī′), *v.*, **-fied, -fying.** —*v.t.* **1.** to convert into wood. —*v.i.* **2.** to become wood. —**lig′nifica′tion,** *n.*

lignin (lĭg′nĭn), *n. Bot.* an organic substance which, with cellulose, forms the chief part of woody tissue.

lignite (lĭg′nīt), *n.* an imperfectly formed coal, usually dark brown, and often having a distinct woody texture; brown coal. [t. F, der. L *lignum* wood. See -ITE[1]] —**lignitic** (lĭg nĭt′ĭk), *adj.*

lignite wax, montan wax.

ligno-, a word element meaning 'wood'. [comb. form repr. L *lignum*]

lignocellulose (lĭg′nō sĕl′yo͝o lōs′), *n.* any of various compounds of lignin and cellulose found in wood and other fibres.

lignose (lĭg′nōs), *n.* one of the constituents of lignin. [t. L: m. s. *lignōsus* woody]

lignum vitae (lĭg′nəm vī′tē), **1.** the hard, extremely heavy wood of either of two species of guaiacum, *Guaiacum officinale* and *G. sanctum*, used for making pulleys, rulers, etc., and formerly thought to have great medicinal powers. **2.** either tree. **3.** any of various other trees with a similar hard wood. [NL: wood of life]

ligroin (lĭg′rō ĭn), *n. Chem.* a mixture of hydrocarbons of the paraffin series; usually applied to a mixture with a boiling point in the range 70–120° C.

ligula (lĭg′yo͝o lə), *n.*, *pl.* **-lae** (-lē′), **-las. 1.** *Bot., Zool.* a tonguelike or strap-shaped part or organ. **2.** *Bot.* ligule. [t. L: strap, var. of *lingula*, dim. of *lingua* tongue] —**lig′ular,** *adj.*

ligulate (lĭg′yo͝o lĭt, -lāt′), *adj.* **1.** having or forming a ligula. **2.** strap-shaped. See illus. under **corolla.**

ligule (lĭg′yo͞ol), *n. Bot.* **1.** a thin, membranous outgrowth from the base of the blade of most grasses. **2.** a strap-shaped corolla, as in the ray flowers of various composite plants. [t. L: m. *lingula*; see LIGULA]

A, Ligule; B, Stem; C, Leaf blade; D, Leaf sheath

ligure (lĭg′yo͞oə), *n.* an unidentified precious stone mentioned in the Bible. See Ex. 28:19. [ME *ligury*, t. LL: m. s. *ligūrius*, t. Gk: m. *ligýrion* (used to render Heb. *leshem*)]

Liguria (lĭ gyo͞oə′rĭ ə), *n.* a region in NW Italy. 1,717,630 pop. (1961); 2099 sq. mi. *Cap.*: Genoa.

Ligurian (lĭ gyo͞oə′rĭ ən), *n.* **1.** an inhabitant of Liguria. **2.** an Indo-European language spoken in ancient times along the NW coast of the Ligurian Sea. —*adj.* **3.** of or pertaining to Liguria or its inhabitants.

Ligurian Sea, a part of the Mediterranean between Corsica and the NW coast of Italy. See map under **Tuscany.**

Li Hung-chang (lē′ ho͝ong′chăng′), 1823–1901, Chinese statesman.

likable (lī′kə bl), *adj.* likeable.

like[1] (līk), *prep., adj.* (*Archaic.* **liker, likest**), *adv., conj., n.* —*prep.* **1.** similarly to; in a manner characteristic of: *they lived like kings.* **2.** typical or characteristic of: *an act of kindness just like him.* **3.** bearing resemblance to: *he is like his father.* **4.** for example; as; such as: *the basic necessities of life, like food and drink.* **5.** indicating a probability of: *it looks like being a fine day, that seems like a good idea.* **6.** desirous of; disposed to (after *feel*): *I feel like a double whisky.* **7.** introducing an intensive, sometimes facetious, comparison: *like hell, like anything.* —*adj.* **8.** of the same form, appearance, kind, character, amount, etc.: *a like instance.* **9.** corresponding or agreeing in general or in some noticeable respect; similar; analogous: *drawing, painting, and like arts.* **10.** bearing resemblance. **11.** *Archaic or Dial.* likely. —*adv.* **12.** *Colloq.* likely or probably: *like enough.* **13.** *Dial. or Slang.* as it were: *I wish I knew, like.* —*conj.* **14.** *Colloq.* like as, just as, or as. **15.** *Colloq.* as if: *he acted like he was afraid.* —*n.* **16.** something of a similar nature (prec. by *the*): *oranges, lemons, and the like.* **17.** a like person or thing, or like persons or things; a counterpart, match, or equal: *no one has seen his like in a long time.* [ME; OE *gelīc*, c. D *gelijk*, G *gleich*, Icel. *glīkr*, Goth. *galeiks* like, lit. of the same body, or form]

like[2] (līk), *v.*, **liked, liking,** *n.* —*v.t.* **1.** to take pleasure in; find agreeable to one's taste. **2.** to regard with favour, or have a kindly or friendly feeling for (a person, etc.). —*v.i.* **3.** to feel inclined, or wish: *come whenever you like.* **4.** *Dial. or Colloq.* to come near (doing something). **5.** *Obs. or Archaic.* to suit the tastes or wishes. —*n.* **6.** (*usually pl.*) a favourable feeling; preference: *likes and dislikes.* [ME *like(n)*, OE *līcian*, c. D *lijken*, Icel. *līka*]

-like, a suffix of adjectives, use of **like**[1], as in *childlike, lifelike, horselike*, sometimes hyphenated. —**Syn.** See **-ish**[1].

likeable (lī′kə bl), *adj.* readily or easily liked; pleasing. Also, **likable.** —**like′ableness,** *n.*

likelihood (līk′lĭ ho͝od′), *n.* **1.** the state of being likely or probable; probability. **2.** a probability or chance of something: *there is a strong likelihood of his succeeding.* **3.** *Obs. or Archaic.* promising character, or promise. Also, **like′liness.**

likely (līk′lĭ), *adj.*, **-lier, -liest,** *adv.* —*adj.* **1.** probably or apparently going or destined (to do, be, etc.): *likely to happen.* **2.** seeming like truth, fact, or certainty, or reasonably to be believed or expected; probable: *a likely story.* **3.** apparently suitable: *a likely spot to build on.* **4.** promising: *a fine likely boy.* —*adv.* **5.** probably. [ME, t. Scand.; cf. Icel. *līkligr*, f. *līkr* LIKE[1], adj. + *-ligr* -LY]

—**Syn.** 1. LIKELY, APT, LIABLE are not alike in indicating probability; though APT is used colloquially, and LIABLE, mistakenly, in this sense. LIKELY is the only one of these words which means 'probable' or 'to be expected': *it is likely to rain today.* APT refers to a natural bent or inclination; if something is natural and easy, it is often probable; hence APT comes to be associated with LIKELY and to be used informally as a substitute for it: *he is apt at drawing, he is apt to do well at drawing.* LIABLE should not be used to mean 'probable'. When used with an infinitive, it may remind one of LIKELY: *he is liable to be arrested.* But the true meaning, susceptibility to something unpleasant, or exposure to risk, becomes evident when it is used with a prepositional phrase: *he is liable to arrest, liable to error.*

like-minded (līk′mīn′dĭd), *adj.* having a like opinion or purpose. —**like′-mind′edness,** *n.*

liken (lī′kən), *v.t.* to represent as like; compare.

likeness (līk′nĭs), *n.* **1.** a representation, picture, or image, esp. a portrait. **2.** the semblance or appearance of something: *to assume the likeness of a swan.* **3.** the state or fact of being like.

likewise (līk′wīz′), *adv.* **1.** moreover; also; too. **2.** in like manner. [abbrev. of *in like wise.* See LIKE[1], -WISE, n.]

likin (lē′kēn′), *n.* (formerly in China) a provincial duty imposed on articles of trade in transit. [t. Chinese: f. *li* 1/1000 of an ounce + *kin* money]

liking (lī′kĭng), *n.* **1.** preference, inclination, or favour. **2.** pleasure or taste: *much to his liking.* **3.** the state or feeling of one who likes. [ME; OE *līcung*, der. *līcian* please]

lilac (lī′lək), *n.* **1.** any of the oleaceous shrubs constituting the genus *Syringa*, as *S. vulgaris*, the common garden lilac, with large clusters of fragrant purple or white flowers. **2.** pale reddish purple. —*adj.* **3.** having the colour lilac. [t. F (obs.), or t. Sp., t. Ar.: m. *līlak*, t. Pers., var. of *nīlak* bluish, der. *nīl* blue, indigo (c. Skt *nīla* dark blue). Cf. ANIL]

lilaceous (lī lā′shəs), *adj.* of or approaching the colour lilac.

liliaceous (lĭl′ĭ ā′shəs), *adj.* **1.** of or like the lily. **2.** belonging to the *Liliaceae*, or lily family of plants, sometimes subdivided in smaller units such as the *Melanthiaceae, Alliaceae, Convallariaceae, Smilacaceae, Trilliaceae*, etc. [t. LL: m. *liliāceus*, der. L *līlium* LILY]

lilied (lĭl′ĭd), *adj.* **1.** lily-like; white. **2.** abounding in lilies.

Lilienthal (lĭl′ĭ ən thôl′ *for 1; Ger.* lē′lē ən täl *for 2*), *n.* **1. David Ely,** born 1899, U.S. administrator. **2. Otto** (*Ger.* ō′tō), 1848–96, German aeronautical engineer and inventor.

Lilith (lĭl′ĭth), *n.* **1.** *Bible and Talmudic Lit.* a female demon that dwells in deserted places and assaults children. **2.** *Jewish Legend.* Adam's first wife. [t. Heb., ult. t. Akkadian]

Liliuokalani (lē lē′o͞o ō kä lä′nē), *n.* **Lydia Kamekeha** (kä′mä kā′hä), 1838–1917, last queen of the Hawaiian Islands, 1891–93.

Lille (*Fr.* lēl), *n.* a town in N France, the capital of Nord department. 193,096 (1962). Formerly, **Lisle.**

Lillibullero (lĭl′ĭ bə lēə′rō), *n.* **1.** a part of the refrain to a song deriding the Irish Roman Catholics, popular in England during and after the Revolution of 1688. 2. the song, or the tune to which it was sung.

Lilliput (lĭl′ĭ pŭt′, -po͞ot), *n.* an imaginary country inhabited by tiny people, described in Swift's *Gulliver's Travels.*

Lilliputian (lĭl′ĭ pyo͞o′shyən), *adj.* **1.** tiny; diminutive. —*n.* **2.** an inhabitant of Lilliput. **3.** a tiny being. **4.** a person of narrow outlook; a petty-minded person.

Lilongwe (lĭ lŏng′wĭ), *n.* a town in central Malawi. 20,000 (est. 1963).

lilt (lĭlt), *n.* **1.** rhythmic swing or cadence. **2.** a lilting song or tune. —*v.i., v.t.* **3.** to sing or play in a light, tripping, or rhythmic manner. [ME *lulte*; cf. D *lul* pipe]

lily (lĭl′ĭ), *n., pl.* **-ies,** *adj.* —*n.* **1.** any plant of the genus *Lilium*, comprising scaly-bulbed herbs with showy funnel-shaped or bell-shaped flowers of various colours, as *L. candidum* (**Madonna lily**), *L. longiflorum eximium* or *L. harrisii* (the once common **Easter lily**), or *L. philadelphicum* (**orange-cup lily**). **2.** the flower or the bulb of such a plant. **3.** any of various related or similar plants or their flowers, as the mariposa lily or the calla lily. **4.** the fleur-de-lis. —*adj.* **5.** white as a lily. **6.** delicately fair. **7.** pure; unsullied. **8.** pale. [ME and OE *lilie*, t. L: m. *lilium*, t. Gk: m. *leírion*] —**lil′y-like′,** *adj.*

lily iron, a harpoon whose head may be detached.

lily-livered (lĭl′ĭ lĭv′ərd), *adj.* cowardly.

lily-of-the-valley (lĭl′ĭ əv thə văl′ĭ), *n., pl.* **lilies-of-the-valley.** a stemless convallariaceous herb, *Convallaria majalis*, with a raceme of drooping, bell-shaped, fragrant white flowers.

lily pad, the large, floating leaf of a waterlily.

lily-trotter (lĭl′ĭ trŏt′ə), *n.* any of various birds of the family *Jacanidae* having enormously lengthened toes and a long, sharp hind claw, adapted for running on floating vegetation.

lily-white (lĭl′ĭ wīt′), *adj.* as white as a lily.

Lima (lē′mə), *n.* the capital of Peru, in the W part, near the Pacific coast. 1,715,971 (1961).

lima bean (lī′mə), **1.** a kind of bean, including several varieties of *Phaseolus limensis*, with a broad, flat, edible seed. **2.** the seed, much used for food.

limacine (lĭm′ə sīn′, -sĭn, lī′mə-), *adj.* pertaining to, or having the characteristics of, slugs. [f. s. L *līmax* slug, snail + -INE[1]]

Limassol (lĭm′ə sŏl′), *n.* a town in S Cyprus. 47,000 (est. 1964).

limb[1] (lĭm), *n.* **1.** a part or member of an animal body distinct from the head and trunk, as a leg, arm, or wing. **2.** a large or main branch of a tree. **3.** a projecting part or member: *the four limbs of a cross.* **4.** a person or thing regarded as a part, member, branch, offshoot, or scion of something. **5.** *Colloq.* an imp, young scamp, or mischievous child. **6. out on a limb,** in a dangerous or exposed position. [ME and OE *lim*, c. Icel. *limr*] —**limbed** (lĭmd), *adj.* —**limb′less,** *adj.* —**Syn. 1.** See **member. 2.** See **branch.**

limb[2] (lĭm), *n.* **1.** the edge of the disc of the sun, moon, or planet. **2.** the graduated edge of a quadrant or similar instrument. **3.** *Bot.* the upper spreading part of a gamopetalous corolla; the expanded portion of a petal, sepal, or leaf. **4.** *Archery.* the upper or lower portion of a bow. [t. L: s. *limbus* border. Cf. LIMBUS and LIMBO]

limbate (lĭm′bāt), *adj. Bot., Zool.* bordered, as a flower in which one colour is surrounded by an edging of another. [t. LL: m. s. *limbātus*, der. L *limbus* LIMB[2]]

limber[1] (lĭm′bə), *adj.* **1.** bending readily; flexible; pliant. **2.** characterized by ease in bending the body; supple; lithe. —*v.i.* **3.** to make oneself limber (fol. by *up*). —*v.t.* **4.** to make limber. [? akin to LIMB[1]] —**lim′berly,** *adv.* —**lim′berness,** *n.* —**Syn. 1.** See **flexible.**

limber[2] (lĭm′bə), *Mil.* —*n.* **1.** the detachable forepart of a guncarriage, consisting of two wheels, an axle, a pole, etc. —*v.t., v.i.* **2.** to attach the limber to (a gun), in preparation for moving away (usually fol. by *up*). [late ME, ? t. F: m. *limonière*]

limber[3] (lĭm′bə), *n.* (*usually pl.*) *Naut.* one of a series of holes or channels in which seepage collects to be pumped away. [? t. F: alter. of *lumière* hole, lit. light]

limbic (lĭm′bĭk), *adj.* pertaining to or of the nature of a limbus or border; marginal.

limbo (lĭm′bō), *n., pl.* **-bos. 1.** (*often cap.*) a supposed region on the border of hell or heaven, the abode after death of unbaptized infants (**limbo of infants**), or one serving as the temporary abode of the righteous who died before the coming of Christ (**limbo of the fathers** or **patriarchs**). **2.** a place to which persons or things are regarded as being relegated when cast aside, forgotten, past, or out of date. **3.** prison, jail, or confinement. [ME, t. L, abl. of *limbus* border, edge, ML limbo]

Limbourg (*Fr.* lăɴ bo͞or′), *n.* a province in NE Belgium. 631,326 pop. (1966); 929 sq. mi. *Cap.:* Hasselt.

Limburg (lĭm′bûg; *Du.* lĭm′bʏʀᴋʜ), *n.* **1.** a medieval duchy in W Europe: now divided into the provinces of **Limburg** in SE Netherlands and **Limbourg** in NE Belgium. **2.** a province in the SE Netherlands. 980,276 pop. (1966); 851 sq. mi. *Cap.:* Maastricht.

Limburger (lĭm′bû′gə), *n.* a variety of soft cheese of strong odour and flavour. Also, **Limburg cheese.**

limbus (lĭm′bəs), *n., pl.* **-bi** (-bī). **1.** limbo. **2.** (in scientific or technical use) a border, edge, or limb. [t. L]

lime[1] (līm), *n., v.,* **limed, liming.** —*n.* **1.** the oxide of calcium, CaO, a white caustic solid (**quicklime** or **unslaked lime**) prepared by calcining limestone, etc., used in making mortar and cement. When treated with water it produces calcium hydroxide, $Ca(OH)_2$, or **slaked lime. 2.** any calcium compounds for improving crops on lime-deficient soils. **3.** birdlime. —*v.t.* **4.** to treat (soil, etc.) with lime or compounds of calcium. **5.** to smear (twigs, etc.) with birdlime. **6.** to catch with, or as with, birdlime. [ME; OE *līm*, c. D *lijm*, G *Leim*, L *līmus* slime; akin to LOAM]

lime[2] (līm), *n.* **1.** the small, greenish yellow, acid fruit of a tropical tree, *Citrus aurantifolia*, allied to the lemon. **2.** the tree. [t. F, t. Sp.: m. *lima*; akin to LEMON]

lime[3] (līm), *n.* linden. [unexplained var. of obs. *line*, *lind*, ME and OE *lind.* See LINDEN]

lime-burner (līm′bû′nə), *n.* one who makes lime by burning or calcining limestone, etc.

Limehouse (līm′hous′), *n.* a district in the East End of London, in Tower Hamlets.

limekiln (līm′kĭln′), *n.* a kiln or furnace for making lime by calcining limestone or shells.

limelight (līm′līt′), *n.* **1.** (formerly) a strong light, made by heating a cylinder of lime in a flame of mixed gases, thrown upon the stage to illuminate particular persons or objects. **2.** the glare of public interest or notoriety.

limen (lī′mĕn), *n., pl.* **limens, limina** (lĭm′ĭ nə). *Psychol.* threshold (def. 4). [t. L]

limerick (lĭm′ə rĭk), *n.* a kind of humorous verse of five lines, in which the first and second lines rhyme with the fifth line, and the shorter third line rhymes with the shorter fourth. [named after *Limerick*, Ireland; orig., a song with refrain, 'Will you come up to Limerick?']

Limerick (lĭm′ə rĭk), *n.* **1.** a county in SW Republic of Ireland, in Munster. 133,339 pop. (1961); 1037 sq. mi. **2.** its county town: a seaport at the head of the Shannon estuary. 50,786 (1961).

limes (lī′mēz), *n., pl.* **limites** (lĭm′ĭ tēz′). a boundary or frontier, esp. a fortified one. [t. L]

limestone (līm′stōn′), *n.* a rock consisting wholly or chiefly of calcium carbonate, originating principally from the calcareous remains of organisms, and when heated yielding quicklime.

lime tree, the linden.

lime twig, 1. a twig smeared with birdlime to catch birds. **2.** a snare.

limewater (līm′wô′tə), *n.* **1.** an aqueous solution of slaked lime, used medicinally and otherwise. **2.** water containing naturally an unusual amount of calcium carbonate or calcium sulphate.

limey (lī′mĭ), *n., pl.* **-meys,** *adj. U.S. Colloq.* —*n.* **1.** a British sailor or ship. **2.** an Englishman. —*adj.* **3.** British. [from the prescribed use of lime juice against scurvy in British ships in the 18th century]

limicoline (lī mĭk′ə lĭn′, -lĭn), *adj.* shore-inhabiting; of or pertaining to numerous birds of the families *Charadriidae* (plovers) and *Scolopacidae* (sandpipers). [f. s. LL *līmicola* dweller in mud + -INE[1]]

limicolous (lī mĭk′ə ləs), *adj.* living in mud or muddy regions.

liminal (lĭm′ĭ nəl), *adj. Psychol.* of or pertaining to the limen. [f. s. L *līmen* threshold + -AL[1]]

limit (lĭm′ĭt), *n.* **1.** the final or furthest bound or point as to extent, amount, continuance, procedure, etc.: *the limit of vision.* **2.** a boundary or bound, as of a country, tract, district, etc. **3.** *Obs.* an area or region within boundaries. **4.** *Maths.* (of a function) a number such that the value of the function can be made arbitrarily close to this number by restricting its argument to be sufficiently near the point at which the limit is to be taken. **5.** *Games.* the maximum sum by which a bet may be raised at any one time. **6. the limit,** someone or something that exasperates to an intolerable degree. —*v.t.* **7.** to restrict by or as by fixing limits (fol. by *to*): *to limit questions to twenty-five words.* **8.** to confine or keep within limits: *to limit expenditures.* **9.** *Law.* to fix or assign definitely or specifically. [ME *lymyte*, t. OF: m. *limite*, t. L: m. s. *līmes* boundary] —**lim′itable,** *adj.* —**lim′iter,** *n.*

limitary (lĭm′ĭ tə rĭ, -trĭ), *adj.* **1.** of, pertaining to, or serving as a limit. **2.** subject to limits; limited.

limitation (lĭm′ĭ tā′shən), *n.* **1.** that which limits; a limit or bound; a limited condition or circumstance; restriction. **2.** a limiting condition: *one should know one's limitations.* **3.** act of limiting. **4.** state of being limited. **5.** *Law.* the assignment, as by statute, of a period of time within which an action must be brought, or the period of time assigned: *a statute of limitations.*

limitative (lĭm′ĭ tə tĭv), *adj.* limiting; restrictive.

limited (lĭm′ĭ tĭd), *adj.* **1.** confined within limits; restricted, circumscribed, or narrow: *a limited space.* **2.** restricted with reference to governing powers by limitations prescribed in a constitution: *a limited monarchy.* **3.** restricted as to amount of liability. **4.** *U.S.* (of trains, buses, etc.) restricted as to number of passengers, time taken in transit, etc. —*n.* **5.** *U.S.* a limited train, bus, etc. —**lim′itedly,** *adv.*—**lim′itedness,** *n.*

limited company, a company in which the liability of its members is limited by its memorandum of association to the nominal value of the shares they hold in the company.

limited edition, an edition of a book of which there is a limited number of copies available.

limited liability, the liability, either by law or contract, only to a limited amount for debts of a trading company or limited partnership.

limited partnership, a partnership in which at least one partner must be a general or unlimited partner liable for all the debts and obligations of the partnership, the others being liable only to the extent of the amount of capital each has put into the partnership. —**limited partner.**

limiting (lĭm′ĭ tĭng), *adj. Gram.* of the nature of a limiting adjective or a restrictive clause.

limiting adjective, *Gram.* (in English and some other languages) one of a small group of adjectives which modify the nouns to which they are applied by restricting rather than describing or qualifying. *This, some,* and *certain* are limiting adjectives.

limitless (lĭm′ĭt lĭs), *adj.* without limit; boundless.

limmer (lĭm′ə), *n.* **1.** a loose woman; strumpet. **2.** *Obs.* a scoundrel; rogue. [ME (N dial.), akin to LIMB[1] (def. 5)]

limn (lĭm), *v.t.* **1.** to represent in drawing or painting. **2.** *Archaic.* to portray in words. [ME *lymne(n)*, var. of *lumine* illuminate, t. OF: m. *luminer*, ult. der. L *lūmen* light]

limnology (lĭm nŏl′ə jĭ), *n.* the scientific study of bodies of fresh water, as lakes and ponds, with reference to their physical, geographical, biological, and other features. [f. s. Gk *límnē* lake + -(O)LOGY] —**limnological** (lĭm′nə lŏj′ĭ kl), *adj.* —**limnologist** (lĭm nŏl′ə jĭst), *n.*

Limoges (lĭ mōzh′; *Fr.* lē mōzh′), *n.* **1.** a town in central France, the capital of Haute-Vienne department. 117,827 (1962). **2.** Also, **Limoges ware.** a type of porcelain manufactured at Limoges.

limonene (lĭm′ə nēn′), *n. Chem.* a liquid terpene, $C_{10}H_{16}$, occurring in two optically different forms, the dextrorotatory form being present in the essential oils of lemon, orange, etc., and the laevorotatory in Douglas fir needle oil. [f. s. NL *limonum* lemon + -ENE]

limonite (lī′mə nīt′), *n.* an important iron ore, a hydrated ferric oxide, $2Fe_2O_3.3H_2O$, varying in colour from dark brown to yellow. [f. m. Gk *leimṓn* meadow + -ITE[1]] —**limonitic** (lī′mə nĭt′ĭk), *adj.*

Limousin (*Fr.* lē mōō zăN′), *n.* **1.** a former province in central France. **2.** an administrative region in W central France comprising the departments of Haute-Vienne, Creuse, and Corrèze. 733,955 pop. (1962); 10,714 sq. mi. *Cap.:* Limoges.

limousine (lĭm′ōō zēn′, lĭm′ə-, lĭm′ōō zēn′, lĭm′ə-), *n.* any large, luxurious car, esp. a chauffeur-driven one. [t. F, der. LIMOUSIN]

limp[1] (lĭmp), *v.i.* **1.** to walk with a laboured, jerky movement, as when lame; progress with great difficulty. **2.** to proceed in a lame or faltering manner: *his verse limps.* —*n.* **3.** a lame movement or gait. [ME; cf. MHG *limpfen* limp and OE *lempheālt* lame] —**limp′er,** *n.*

limp[2] (lĭmp), *adj.* **1.** lacking stiffness or firmness, as of substance, fibre, structure, or bodily frame: *a limp body.* **2.** tired; lacking vitality. **3.** without proper firmness, force, energy, etc., as of character. [akin to Icel. *limpa* indisposition] —**limp′ly,** *adv.* —**limp′ness,** *n.*

limpet (lĭm′pĭt), *n.* **1.** *Zool.* any of various marine gastropods with a low conical shell open beneath, found adhering to rocks, used for bait and sometimes for food. **2.** one who is reluctant to give up a position or office. **3.** *Eng.* an open caisson shaped so as to fit a dock wall. [ME *lempet*, OE *lempedu*, t. LL: m. *lamprēda* limpet, LAMPREY]

limpet mine, an adhesive mine to be placed against the hull of a ship.

limpid (lĭm′pĭd), *adj.* **1.** clear, transparent, or pellucid, as water, crystal, air, etc. **2.** free from obscurity; lucid: *a limpid style.* [t. L: s. *limpidus*] —**limpid′ity, lim′pidness,** *n.* —**lim′pidly,** *adv.*

limpkin (lĭmp′kĭn), *n.* a large, loud-voiced, wading bird, *Aramus guarauna*, intermediate in size and character between the cranes and the rails, which inhabits Florida, Central America, and the West Indies.

Limpopo River

Limpopo (lĭm pō′pō), *n.* a river rising in S Transvaal, Republic of South Africa, flowing N, then E, forming the border of the Republic with Rhodesia, then S through Mozambique to the Indian Ocean. ab. 1000 mi. Also, **Crocodile River.**

limuloid (lĭm′yōō loid′), *Zool.* —*adj.* **1.** resembling or pertaining to the horseshoe crabs, esp. to *Limulus.* —*n.* **2.** a horseshoe crab. [f. LIMUL(US) + -OID]

limulus (lĭm′yōō ləs), *n., pl.* **-li** (-lī′). a crab of the genus *Limulus*; a horseshoe crab. [t. NL, t. L: somewhat askew, dim. of *līmus* sidelong]

limy (lī′mĭ), *adj.,* **-mier, -miest.** **1.** consisting of, containing, or like lime. **2.** smeared with birdlime.

lin., **1.** lineal. **2.** linear.

linac (lĭn′ăk, lī′năk), *n. Physics.* a linear accelerator.

Linacre (lĭn′ə kə), *n.* **Thomas,** 1460?–1521, English humanist and physician.

linage (lī′nĭj), *n.* **1.** alignment. **2.** number of lines of written or printed matter covered. Also, **lineage.**

linalool (lĭ năl′ō ōl′, lĭn′ə lōōl′), *n. Chem.* a colourless liquid, unsaturated alcohol, $C_{10}H_{17}OH$, related to the terpenes, found in several essential oils. [f. Sp. *linalo(e)* fragrant Mexican wood + -OL[1]]

linarite (lī′nə rīt′), *n.* a mineral, hydrous sulphate of lead and copper, consisting of deep blue crystals resembling azurite.

linchpin (lĭnch′pĭn′), *n.* a pin inserted through the end of an axle to keep the wheel on. [f. *linch-*, OE *lynis* linchpin (c. G *Lünse*) + PIN]

Lincoln (lĭng′kən), *n.* **1.** **Abraham,** 1809–65, 16th president of the U.S., 1861–65. **2.** **Benjamin,** 1733–1810, American general in the War of Independence. **3.** a county borough in England, the county town of Lincolnshire. 77,065 (1961). **4.** a town in the U.S., the capital of Nebraska, in the SE part. 128,521 (1960). **5.** Lincolnshire. **6.** one of a large English variety of mutton sheep, with a heavy fleece of coarse, long wool.

Lincolnshire (lĭng′kən shĭə′, -shə), *n.* a county in E England. 743,383 pop. (1961); 2663 sq. mi. *Co. town:* Lincoln. *Abbrev.:* Lincs. Also, **Lincoln.**

Lincoln's Inn (lĭng′kənz). See **Inns of Court.**

Lincs., Lincolnshire.

linctus (lĭngk′təs), *n.* a medicine for soothing the throat and chest. [t. L: pp. of *lingere* lick]

Lind (lĭnd), *n.* **Jenny** (jĕn′ĭ) (*Johanna Maria Lind Goldschmidt*), 1820–87, Swedish soprano.

Lindbergh (lĭnd′bûg, lĭn′-), *n.* **Charles Augustus,** born 1902, U.S. aviator who made the first non-stop solo transatlantic flight in 1927.

Lindemann (lĭn′də mən), *n.* **Frederick Alexander, Viscount Cherwell** (chä′wĭl), 1866–1957, British scientist and wartime public official.

linden (lĭn′dən), *n.* any of the trees of the genus *Tilia*, which have yellowish or cream-coloured flowers and more or less heart-shaped leaves, as *T. europaea*, a common European species, and *T. americana*, a large American species often cultivated as a shade tree. [n. use of obs. ME and OE adj. *linden* pertaining to a lime tree, f. *lind* lime tree (c. G *Linde*) + -EN[2]]

Lindesnes (*Norw.* lĕn dəs nĕs′), *n.* a cape at the S tip of Norway, on the North Sea. Also, **The Naze.**

Lindisfarne (lĭn′dĭs fän′), *n.* a small island off the coast of Northumberland: monastery. Also, **Holy Island.**

Lindrum (lĭn′drəm), *n.* **Walter,** 1898–1960, Australian billiards player.

line[1] (līn), *n., v.,* **lined, lining.** —*n.* **1.** a mark or stroke long in proportion to its breadth, made with a pen, pencil, tool, etc., on a surface. **2.** something resembling a traced line, as a band of colour, a seam, a furrow, etc.: *lines of stratification in rock.* **3.** a furrow or wrinkle on the face, etc. **4.** something arranged along a line, esp. a straight line; a row or series: *a line of trees.* **5.** a row of people standing side by side. **6.** a row of people standing one behind another; a queue. **7.** a row of written or printed letters, words, etc.: *a page of thirty lines.* **8.** a verse of poetry. **9.** (*pl.*) the spoken words of a drama, etc., or of an actor's part: *the hero forgot his lines.* **10.** a short written message: *a line from a friend.* **11.** an indication of demarcation; boundary; limit: *to draw a line between right and wrong.* **12.** a course of action, procedure, thought, etc.: *the Communist Party line.* **13.** a piece of useful or pertinent information: *get a line on his activities during the war.* **14.** a course of direction; route: *the line of march.* **15.** a continuous series of persons or animals in chronological succession, esp. in family descent: *a line of great kings.* **16.** (*pl.*) outline or contour: *a ship of fine lines.* **17.** (*pl.*) plan of construction, action, or procedure: *two books written on the same lines.* **18.** (*pl.*) *Colloq.* a certificate of marriage. **19.** (*pl.*) one's lot or portion. **20.** a department of activity; a kind of occupation or business: *what line is your father in?* **21. a.** any transport company or system. **b.** a system of public conveyances, as buses, steamers, etc., plying regularly between places. **22.** a strip of railway track, a railway, or a railway system. **23.** *Elect.* a wire circuit connecting two or more pieces of electrical apparatus. **24.** *Television.* one scanning line. **25.** *Fine Arts.* a mark from a crayon, pencil, brush, etc., in a work of graphic art, which defines the limits of the forms employed and is used either independently or in combination with modelling by means of shading. **26.** *Maths.* a continuous extent of length, straight or curved, without breadth or thickness; the trace of a moving point. **27.** a straight line drawn from an observed object to the fovea of the eye: *line of sight.* **28.** a circle of the terrestrial or of the celestial sphere: *the equinoctial line.* **29.** *Geog.* the equator (prec. by *the*). **30.** a supply of commercial goods of the same general class. **31.** *Bridge.* the line drawn between points counting towards game (**below the line**) and bonus, sometimes known as honour points (**above the line**). **32.** *Music.* one of the straight, horizontal, parallel strokes of the stave, or one above or below it. **33.** *Mil.* **a.** a defensive position. **b.** a series of fortifications: *the Maginot line.* **34.** (*pl.*) *Mil.* one of the rows of huts, tents, etc., within a camp. **35.** the line of arrangement of an army or of the ships of a fleet as drawn up ready for battle: *line of battle.* **36.** a body or formation of troops or ships drawn up abreast. **37.** (in the British army) the regular regiments, excluding the Guards, artillery, engineers, etc. **38.** (in the U.S. army) the combatant forces of an army, as distinguished from the supply and ancillary services. **39.** a thread, string, or the like. **40.** clothes line. **41.** a strong cord or slender rope. **42.** a cord, wire, or the like used for measuring or as a guide. **43.** *Naut.* **a.** a length of rope for any purpose. **b.** a pipe or hose: *a steam line.* **44.** a length of cord, nylon, silk, or the like, bearing a hook or hooks, used in fishing. **45.** a wire or cable for a telephone or telegraph. **46.** *Sport.* a mark indicating the boundaries or divisions of a field or court. **47.** *Fencing.* one of the eight imaginary lines forming the target on the fencer's body. **48.** *Fox Hunting.* the trail or scent left by a fox. **49.** (*pl.*) a school punishment, usually consisting of writing out a phrase or sentence a specified number of times. **50.** a unit of length equivalent to $\frac{1}{12}$ inch. **51. bring into line,** to cause or persuade to agree or conform. **52. come (fall) into line,** to agree; conform. **53. draw the line at,** to impose a limit; refuse to do. **54. get a line on,** to obtain information about. **55. hard lines,** *Colloq.* bad luck. **56. in line, a.** straight; in alignment. **b.** in conformity or agreement. **57. line of least resistance,** course of action requiring the minimum of effort or presenting the fewest difficulties. **58. out of line,** not in accord with standard practice, agreement, etc.; deviant. **59. read between the lines,** to find in something spoken or written more meaning than the words appear to express. **60. shoot a line,** *Colloq.* to boast. **61. toe the line,** to conform; obey. —*v.i.* **62.** to take a position in a line; range or queue (often fol. by *up*). —*v.t.* **63.** to bring into a line, or into line with others (often fol. by *up*). **64.** *Colloq.* to get hold of; make available (usually fol. by *up*): *we must line up a chairman for the conference.* **65.** to trace by or as by a line or lines; delineate. **66.** to mark with a line or lines: *to line paper for writing.* **67.** to cover with lines or wrinkles: *a face lined with worry.* **68.** to sketch verbally or in writing; outline. **69.** to arrange a line along. **70.** to form a line along: *people lined the streets.* **71.** to measure or test with a line. [ME *lyne, line,* OE *line* line, row, rule (c. G *Leine* cord, Icel. *līna* line, rope), t. L: m. *līnea* thread, string, der. *līnum* flax] —**line′-like′,** *adj.*

line[2] (līn), *v.t.,* **lined, lining. 1.** to cover or fit on the inner side with something: *to line drawers with paper.* **2.** to provide with a layer of material applied to the inner side: *to line a coat with silk.* **3.** to cover: *walls lined with bookcases.* **4.** to furnish or fill: *to line one's pockets with money.* **5.** to reinforce the back of a book with glued fabric, paper, vellum, etc. [ME *lyne(n)*, der. *line,* n., flax, linen, OE *līn,* t. L: s. *līnum*]

lineage[1] (lĭn′ĭ ĭj), *n.* **1.** lineal descent from an ancestor; ancestry or extraction. **2.** the line of descendants of a particular ancestor; family; race. [f. LINE (AL) + -AGE; r. ME *linage,* t. OF: m. *lignage,* der. *ligne* LINE[1]]

lineage[2] (lī′nĭj), *n.* linage.

lineal (lĭn′ĭ əl), *adj.* **1.** being in the direct line, as a descendant, ancestor, etc., or descent, etc. **2.** of or transmitted by lineal descent. **3.** linear. [ME, t. LL: s. *līneālis,* der. L *līnea* LINE[1]] —**lin′eally,** *adv.*

lineament (lĭn′ĭ ə mənt), *n.* **1.** a feature or detail of a face, body, or figure, considered with respect to its outline or contour. **2.** a distinctive characteristic. [ME, t. L: s. *līneāmentum*]

linear (lĭn′ĭ ə), *adj.* **1.** extended in a line: *a linear series.* **2.** involving measurement in one dimension only; pertaining to length: *linear measure.* **3.** of or pertaining to a line or lines: *linear perspective.* **4.** of or pertaining to a work of art which depends for its effect on the outlines of forms represented. **5.** consisting of or involving lines: *linear design.* **6.** looking like a line: *linear nebulae.* **7.** *Maths.* of the first degree, as an equation. **8.** resembling a thread; narrow and elongated: *a linear leaf.* [t. L: s. *līneāris,* der. *līnea* LINE[1]] —**lin′early,** *adv.*

Linear leaf

Linear A, an undeciphered system of writing found in inscriptions on tablets, pottery, etc., found at Minoan sites on Crete.

linear accelerator, *Physics.* a particle accelerator in which a number of electrodes are so arranged that when a potential difference is applied at an appropriate frequency the particles receive successive increments of energy. *Abbrev.:* linac.

Linear B, an ancient system of writing, found in inscriptions in Crete and S Greece, and generally accepted as being an early form of Greek.

linear motor, *Elect.* a form of induction motor in which the stator and rotor are linear instead of cylindrical, and parallel instead of coaxial.

linear perspective, that branch of perspective which regards only the apparent positions, magnitudes, and forms of objects delineated.

lineate (lĭn′ĭ ĭt, -āt′), *adj.* marked with lines, esp. longitudinal and more or less parallel lines. Also, **lin′eat′ed.** [t. L: m. s. *līneātus,* pp., lined]

lineation (lĭn′ĭ ā′shən), *n.* **1.** a marking with or tracing by lines. **2.** a division into lines. **3.** a line; an outline. **4.** an arrangement or group of lines.

line breeding, *Genetics.* a form of mild inbreeding directed towards keeping the offspring closely related to a highly admired ancestor.

line engraving, 1. style of engraving in which the burin makes curved regular furrows that markedly swell and taper. **2.** a plate so engraved. **3.** a print or picture made from it.

lineman (līn′mən), *n., pl.* **-men.** *U.S.* linesman.

linen (lĭn′ĭn), *n.* **1.** fabric woven from flax yarns. **2.** clothes or other articles made of linen cloth or some substitute, as cotton. **3.** yarn made of flax fibre. **4.** thread made of flax yarns. **5. wash one's dirty linen in public,** to discuss disagreeable personal affairs in public. —*adj.* **6.** made of linen. [ME *lin(n)en,* n. and adj., OE *linnen, līnen,* adj., f. *līn* linen + -EN[2]]

linen draper, one who sells linen and cotton goods.

linenfold (lĭn′ĭn fōld′), *n.* *Archit.* an ornament used on Tudor panelling showing a piece of linen folded vertically.

linen paper, paper made from pure linen or from substitutes which produce a similar paper finish.

line of force, *Physics.* a line in a field of force whose direction at any point is that of the force in the field at that point.

line of sight, *Astron.* an imaginary line between an observer and a celestial body which is coincident with light rays from that body.

line-of-sight velocity, *Astron.* the velocity of a celestial body in a direction which directly approaches, or recedes from the earth. Also, **radial velocity.**

lineolate (lĭn′ĭ ə lāt′), *adj.* *Zool., Bot.* marked with minute lines; finely lineate. Also, **lin′eolat′ed.** [f. s. L *līneola* (dim. of *līnea* LINE[1]) + -ATE[1]]

line-out (līn′out′), *n.* *Rugby Football.* (in Rugby Union) the throw-in of the ball from touch, the forwards of each team forming up in parallel lines at right angles to the touchlines.

line printer, *Computers.* a machine which prints the output from a computer at speeds of up to 1500 lines a minute.

liner[1] (lī′nə), *n.* **1.** one of a commercial line of steamships or aeroplanes. **2.** one who or that which traces by or marks with lines. **3.** a cosmetic used to outline and highlight the eyes. [f. LINE[1] + -ER[1]]

liner[2] (lī′nə), *n.* **1.** one who fits or provides linings. **2.** something serving as a lining. [f. LINE[2] + -ER[1]]

linesman (līnz′mən), *n.*, *pl.* **-men. 1.** *Sport.* an official who assists the referee or umpire. **2.** one who erects or repairs telephone, electric power, or other overhead wires. Also, *U.S.*, **lineman.**

line spectrum, *Physics.* an emission or absorption spectrum consisting of a number of sharply defined lines, as produced by an element in the atomic state. Each line corresponds to a particular wavelength.

line-up (līn′ŭp′), *n.* **1.** a particular order or disposition of persons or things as lined up or drawn up for action, inspection, participation in a game, etc. **2.** the persons or things themselves: *two suspects were included in the police line-up.* **3.** an organization of people, companies, etc., for some common purpose.

liney (lī′nĭ), *adj.*, **-nier, -niest.** liny.

ling[1] (lĭng), *n.*, *pl.* **ling, lings. 1.** an elongated marine ganoid food fish, *Molva molva*, of Greenland and northern Europe. **2.** either of the two species of burbot, freshwater food fishes of north-eastern North America, *Lota maculosa*, and northern Eurasia, *Lota lota.* **3.** any of various other fishes. [ME *ling, lenge*; akin to LONG[1]]

ling[2] (lĭng), *n.* the common heather, *Calluna vulgaris.* [ME *lyng*, t. Scand.; cf. Icel. *lyng*, Dan. *lyng*, Sw. *ljung*]

-ling[1], suffix found in some nouns, often pejorative, denoting one concerned with (*hireling, underling*); also diminutive (*princeling, duckling*). [ME and OE]

-ling[2], an adverbial suffix expressing direction, position, state, etc., as in *darkling, sideling.* [ME and OE]

ling., linguistics.

linga (lĭng′gə), *n.* **1.** *Sanskrit Gram.* the masculine gender. **2.** (in popular Hindu mythology) a phallus, symbol of Shiva. **3.** the male genitals. Also, **lingam** (lĭng′gəm). [t. Skt: *linga* (stem), neut. nom. *lingam*]

Lingayén Gulf (lĭng′gä yĕn′), a gulf on the NW coast of Luzon, in the Philippine Islands.

linger (lĭng′gə), *v.i.* **1.** to remain or stay on in a place longer than is usual or expected, as if from reluctance to leave it. **2.** to remain alive; continue or persist, although tending to cease or disappear: *hope lingers.* **3.** to dwell in contemplation, thought, or enjoyment. **4.** to be tardy in action; delay; dawdle. **5.** to walk slowly; to saunter along. *—v.t.* **6.** to drag out or protract. **7.** to pass (time, life, etc.) in a leisurely or a tedious manner (fol. by *away* or *out*). [ME *lenger*, freq. of *lenge*, OE *lengan* delay, der. *lang* LONG[1]] **—lin′gerer,** *n.*

lingerie (lăn′zhə rē′; *Fr.* lăNzh rē′), *n.* **1.** underwear or other garments of cotton, silk, nylon, lace, etc., worn by women. **2.** *Archaic.* linen goods in general. [t. F, der. *linge* linen, g. L *linum* flax]

lingo (lĭng′gō), *n.*, *pl.* **-goes.** (in contemptuous or humorous use) **1.** language. **2.** peculiar or unintelligible language. **3.** language or terminology peculiar to a particular field, group, etc. [t. Lingua Franca, t. Pr.: m. *lengo*, b. with It. *lingua*, both g. L *lingua* tongue]

lingua (lĭng′gwə), *n.*, *pl.* **-guae** (-gwē). the tongue or a part like a tongue. [t. L]

lingua franca (lĭng′gwə frăng′kə), **1.** any language widely used as a medium among speakers of other languages. **2.** (*cap.*) the Italian-Provençal jargon formerly widely used in E Mediterranean ports. [t. It.: Frankish tongue]

lingual (lĭng′gwəl), *adj.* **1.** of or pertaining to the tongue or some tongue-like part. **2.** pertaining to languages. **3.** *Phonet.* articulated with the tongue, esp. with the tip of the tongue. [t. ML: s. *linguālis*, der. L *lingua* tongue, language] **—lin′gually,** *adv.*

linguiform (lĭng′gwĭ fôm′), *adj.* tongue-shaped. [f. s. L *lingua* tongue + -(I)FORM]

linguist (lĭng′gwĭst), *n.* **1.** a person who is skilled in foreign languages; polyglot. **2.** a person who specializes in linguistics. [f. s. L *lingua* language + -IST]

linguistic (lĭng gwĭs′tĭk), *adj.* **1.** of or belonging to language: *linguistic change.* **2.** of or pertaining to linguistics. Also, **linguis′tical. —linguis′tically,** *adv.*

linguistic form, any meaningful unit of speech, as a sentence, phrase, word, suffix, etc.

linguistics (lĭng gwĭs′tĭks), *n.* the science of language, including among its fields phonetics, phonemics, morphology, and syntax, and having as principal divisions **descriptive linguistics,** which treats the classification and arrangement of the features of language, and **comparative** (or **historical**) **linguistics,** which treats linguistic change, esp. by the study of data taken from various languages.

linguistic stock, 1. a parent language and all its derived dialects and languages. **2.** the people speaking any of these dialects or languages.

lingulate (lĭng′gyo͝o lāt′), *adj.* formed like a tongue; ligulate. [t. L: m. s. *lingulātus*]

liniment (lĭn′ĭ mənt), *n.* a liquid preparation, usually oily, for rubbing on or applying to the skin, as for sprains, bruises, etc. [ME, t. LL: s. *linimentum*]

linin (lī′nĭn), *n. Biol.* the substance forming the net-like structure which connects the chromatin granules in the nucleus of a cell. [f. s. L *līnum* flax + -IN[2]]

lining (lī′nĭng), *n.* **1.** that with which something is lined; a layer of material on the inner side of something. **2.** *Bookbinding.* the material used to strengthen the back of a book after the sheets have been folded, backed, and sewn. **3.** the act of one who or that which lines something. [ME, f. LINE[2] + -ING[1]]

link[1] (lĭngk), *n.* **1.** one of the rings or separate pieces of which a chain is composed. **2.** anything serving to connect one part or thing with another; a bond or tie. **3.** a ring, loop, lock of hair, or the like. **4.** one of a number of sausages in a chain. **5.** cufflink. **6.** one of the 100 wire rods forming the divisions of a surveyor's chain of 66 ft. **7.** the set or effective length of one of these rods used as a measuring unit, equal to 7·92 in. **8.** *Chem.* bond. **9.** *Elect.* fuse link. **10.** *Mach.* a rigid movable piece or rod connected with other parts by means of pivots or the like, for the purpose of transmitting motion. *—v.t., v.i.* **11.** to join by or as by a link or links; unite. [ME *link(e)*, t. Scand.; cf. Sw. *länk*, c. OE *hlence* corselet] **—Syn. 2.** See **bond.**

link[2] (lĭngk), *n.* a torch of tow and pitch or the like. [? t. ML: m. s. *linchinus*, var. of *lichinus* match, wick, t. Gk: m. *lýchnos* lamp]

linkage (lĭng′kĭj), *n.* **1.** the act of linking. **2.** the state or manner of being linked. **3.** a system of links. **4.** *Genetics.* the association of two or more genes located on the same chromosome so that they tend to be passed from generation to generation as an inseparable unit. **5.** *Mech.* any of various mathematical or drawing devices consisting of a combination of bars or pieces pivoted together so as to turn about one another, usually in parallel planes. **6.** *Elect.* the product of the magnetic flux passing through an electric circuit by the number of turns in the circuit.

linkage group, *Genetics.* a group of genes in one chromosome that tend to be inherited as an inseparable unit.

linkboy (lĭngk′boi′), *n.* (formerly) a boy hired to carry a torch for a pedestrian on dark streets. Also, **link′man.**

linked (lĭngkt), *adj. Genetics.* exhibiting linkage.

link motion, a mechanism for operating a valve in a steam-engine, one feature of which is a slotted bar (the **link**) in which slides a block (the **link block**) which terminates the rod working the valve.

Linköping (*Sw.* lĕnt′shœ pĕng), *n.* a town in SE Sweden. 70,752 (1964).

links (lĭngks), *n.pl.* **1.** a golf course. **2.** undulating land near the seashore. [ME *lynkys* slopes, OE *hlincas*, pl. of *hlinc* rising ground, der. *hlin* (cf. *hlinian* lean, recline)]

Link trainer (lĭngk), *Aeron.* a ground training device used in instrument-flight training.

link-up (lĭngk′ŭp′), *n.* a means of contact or communication.

linkwork (lĭngk′wûk′), *n.* **1.** a thing composed of links, as a chain. **2.** a linkage. **3.** *Mach.* a mechanism or device in which motion is transmitted by links.

Linlithgow (lĭn lĭth′gō), *n.* **1.** a burgh in Scotland, the county town of West Lothian. 4327 (1961). **2.** former name of **West Lothian.**

linn (lĭn), *n. Chiefly Scot.* **1.** a waterfall. **2.** a pool of water, esp. one below a waterfall. **3.** a precipice; ravine. [t. Gael.: m. *linne*]

Linnaeus (lĭ nē′əs), *n.* **Carolus** (kăr′rə ləs) (*Carl von Linné*), 1707–78, Swedish botanist.

Linnean (lĭ nē′ən), *adj.* **1.** of or pertaining to Linnaeus, who established the binomial system of scientific nomenclature. **2.** denoting, or pertaining to, a system of botanical classification introduced by him and formerly used (based mainly on the number or characteristics of the stamens and pistils). Also, **Linnaean.**

linnet (lĭn′ĭt), *n.* **1.** a small Old World fringilline song bird, *Carduelis cannabina.* **2.** any of various related birds, as the house finch. [ME *linet*, OE *linete.* Cf. LINTWHITE]

linocut (lī′nō kŭt′), *n.* **1.** a design cut in relief on a block of linoleum. **2.** a print made from such a cut.

linoleic acid (lĭn′ō lē′ĭk), *Chem.* an unsaturated fatty acid, $C_{17}H_{31}COOH$, occurring as a glyceride in fats and drying oils such as linseed oil.

linolenic acid (lĭn′ō lĕn′ĭk, -lē′nĭk), *Chem.* an unsaturated fatty acid, $C_{17}H_{29}COOH$, occurring as a glyceride in linseed oil; used as drying agent in paints.

linoleum (lĭ nō′lyəm), *n.* a floor covering formed by coating hessian or canvas with linseed oil, powdered cork, and rosin, and adding pigments of the desired colour. Also, **lino** (lī′nō). [f. L: s. *linum* flax + *oleum* oil]

Linotype (lī′nō tīp′), *n.* *Trademark.* a kind of type-setting machine, with keyboard, which casts solid lines of type. [orig. phrase, '*line o' type*' line of type]

linsang (lĭn′săng), *n.* a catlike, viverrine carnivore with retractile claws and a long tail, of the genus *Prionodon* (or *Linsang*) of the East Indies, or *Poina* of Africa. [t. Malay]

linseed (lĭn′sēd′), *n.* the seed of flax. [ME *linsed*, OE *līnsǣd*, f. *līn* flax + *sǣd* seed]

linseed cake, crushed linseed, from which the oil has been expressed, used as cattle food.

linseed oil, a drying oil obtained by pressing linseed, used in making paints, printing inks, linoleum, etc.

linsey-woolsey (lĭn′zĭ wo͝ol′zĭ), *n.*, *pl.* **-seys.** **1.** a coarse fabric woven from linen warp and coarse wool filling. **2.** any poor or incongruous mixture. [ME *lynsy wolsye*, f. *lynsy* (f. OE *līn* flax + ME *-sey*, meaningless suffix) + *wolsye* (f. OE *wull* WOOL + ME *-sey*)]

linstock (lĭn′stŏk′), *n.* a staff with one end forked to hold a match, formerly used in firing cannon. [earlier *lyntstock*, t. D: m. *lontstok*, f. *lont* match + *stok* stick]

lint (lĭnt), *n.* **1.** a soft material for dressing wounds, etc., procured by scraping or otherwise treating linen cloth. **2.** bits of thread or fluff. [ME *lyn(e)t* flax, ? OE *linwyrt*, f. *līn* flax + *wyrt* WORT]

lintel (lĭn′tl), *n.* a horizontal supporting member above an opening such as a window or a door. [ME *lyntel*, t. OF: m. *lintel*, *linter*, g. VL *līmitāle*, dim. of L *līmes* boundary, LIMIT]

linter (lĭn′tə), *n.* **1.** (*pl.*) short cotton fibres which stick to seeds after a first ginning. **2.** a machine which removes lint from cloth.

lintwhite (lĭnt′wīt′), *n.* *Chiefly Scot.* the linnet. [ME (N dial.) *lynkwhyte*, r. OE *līnetwige*, equiv. to *līn(e)* flax + *-twīge* plucker]

linty (lĭn′tĭ), *adj.*, **-tier, -tiest.** **1.** full of or covered with lint. **2.** like lint: *linty bits on his coat.*

liny (lī′nĭ), *adj.*, **-nier, -niest.** **1.** full of or marked with lines. **2.** linelike. Also, **liney.**

Linz (*Ger.* lĭnts), *n.* a town in N Austria: a port on the Danube. 196,206 (1961).

lion (lī′ən), *n.* **1.** a large, greyish tan cat, *Panthera leo*, native in Africa and southern Asia, the male of which usually has a mane. **2.** this animal as the national emblem of Great Britain. **3.** a man of great strength, courage, etc. **4.** a person of note or celebrity who is much sought after. **5.** (*cap.*) *Astron.* Leo. **6. the lion's share,** the largest portion of anything. [ME, t. OF, g. s. L *leo*, t. Gk: m. *léōn*. Cf. LEO]

African lion, *Panthera leo* (3 ft high at shoulder, total length up to 9 ft)

lioncel (lī′ən sĕl′), *n.* *Her.* a small or young lion.

lioness (lī′ə nĭs), *n.* a female lion.

lion-hearted (lī′ən hä′tĭd), *adj.* courageous; brave.

lionize (lī′ə nīz′), *v.*, **-nized, -nizing.** —*v.t.* **1.** to treat (a person) as a celebrity. **2.** to visit or exhibit the objects of interest of (a place). —*v.i.* **3.** to visit the objects of interest of a place. Also, **lionise.** —**li′oniza′tion,** *n.*

Lions (lī′ənz), *n.* **Gulf of,** a wide bay of the Mediterranean off the S coast of France. Also, **Gulf of the Lion.** French, **Golfe du Lion** (*Fr.* gŏlf dʏ lyôɴ′).

lip (lĭp), *n.*, *adj.*, *v.*, **lipped, lipping.** —*n.* **1.** either of the two fleshy parts or folds forming the margins of the mouth and performing an important function in speech. **2.** (*pl.*) these parts as organs of speech. **3.** *Slang.* impudent talk. **4.** a liplike part or structure. **5.** *Bot.* either of the two parts (**upper** and **lower**) into which the corolla or calyx of certain plants (esp. the mint family) is divided. **6.** *Zool.* **a.** labium. **b.** the outer or the inner margin of the aperture of a gastropod's shell. **7.** *Music.* the position and arrangement of lips and tongue in playing a wind instrument. **8.** any edge or rim. **9.** a projecting edge, as of a jug. **10.** the edge of an opening or cavity, as of a canyon or wound. **11.** *Carp.* the blade at the end of an auger which cuts the chip after it has been circumscribed by the spur. **12. bite one's lip, a.** to show vexation. **b.** to stifle one's feelings, esp. anger or irritability. **13. curl one's lip,** to show scorn. **14. hang on the lips of,** to listen to very attentively or eagerly. **15. keep a stiff upper lip,** to face misfortune bravely, esp. without outward show of perturbation. **16. smack one's lips,** to show enjoyment or anticipation of something enjoyable, esp. food. —*adj.* **17.** of or pertaining to the lips or a lip. **18.** pertaining to, characterized by, or made with the lips. —*v.t.* **19.** to touch with the lips. **20.** *Golf.* to hit the ball over the rim of (the hole). **21.** to utter, esp. softly. **22.** *Obs.* to kiss. —*v.i.* **23.** to use the lips in playing a musical wind instrument. [ME *lip(pe)*, OE *lippa*, c. D *lip*, G *Lippe*; akin to L *labium*, *labrum*]

lip-, var. of **lipo-,** before vowels, as in *lipectomy*.

Lipari Islands (lĭp′ə rĭ; *It.* lē′pä rē), a group of volcanic islands N of Sicily, belonging to Italy. 11,799 pop. (1951); 44 sq. mi.

lipase (lī′pās, lĭp′ās), *n.* *Biochem.* one of the enzymes produced by the liver, pancreas, and other organs of the digestive system which convert oils or fats into fatty acids and glycerol. [f. LIP(O)- + -ASE]

lipectomy (lĭ pĕk′tə mĭ), *n.*, *pl.* **-mies.** *Surg.* an operation for removal of superficial fat, usually a pendulous abdominal apron of fat, in obese persons.

Lipetsk (*Russ.* lĕ′pĭtsk), *n.* a town in the central Soviet Union in Europe. 226,000 (est. 1965).

lipid (lī′pĭd, lĭp′ĭd), *n.* *Biochem.* any of a group of organic compounds which make up the fats and other esters which have analogous properties. They have a greasy feeling and are insoluble in water, but soluble in alcohols, ethers, and other fat solvents. Also, **lipide** (lī′pīd, lĭp′īd). [f. LIP- + -ID³]

Li Po (lē′ pō′), A.D. *c.* 700–762, Chinese poet. Also, **Li Tai Po.**

lipo-, *Chem.* a word element meaning 'fat', as in *lipochrome*. Also, **lip-.** [t. Gk, comb. form of *lípos* fat]

lipochrome (lĭp′ə krōm′), *n.* *Chem.* any natural pigment containing a lipid, esp. the pigments of butterfat.

lipoclastic (lĭp′ə klăs′tĭk), *adj.* *Chem.* capable of splitting fats, esp. applied to enzymes which are capable of hydrolysing fats; lipolytic.

lipoid (lĭp′oid, lī′poid), *adj.* **1.** fatty; resembling fat. —*n.* **2.** one of a group of fats or fatlike substances such as lecithins, waxes, etc. [f. LIP- + -OID]

lipolysis (lĭ pŏl′ĭ sĭs), *n.* *Chem.* the resolution of fats into fatty acids and glycerol, as by lipase. [f. LIPO- + -LYSIS] —**lipolytic** (lĭp′ō lĭt′ĭk), *adj.*

lipoma (lĭ pō′mə), *n.*, *pl.* **-mata** (-mə tə), **-mas.** *Pathol.* a tumour made up of fat tissue; a fatty tumour. [f. LIP- + -OMA]

lipophilic (lĭp′ō fĭl′ĭk), *adj.* *Chem.* having an affinity for lipids.

lipoprotein (lĭp′ō prō′tēn), *n.* *Biochem.* any of a group of complex compounds of lipids and proteins.

Lippe (*Ger.* lĭp′ə), *n.* a former state in NW Germany; now part of North Rhine-Westphalia in West Germany.

lipped (lĭpt), *adj.* **1.** having lips or a lip. **2.** *Bot.* labiate.

Lippi (*It.* lēp′pē), *n.* **1. Filippino** (*It.* fē lēp pē′nō), 1457?–*c.* 1505, Italian painter. **2.** his father, **Fra Filippo** (*It.* frȧ fē lēp′pō) or **Fra Lippo** (*It.* frȧ lēp′pō), *c.* 1406–69, Italian painter.

Lippmann (lĭp′mən), *n.* **Walter,** born 1889, U.S. journalist and author.

lip-read (lĭp′rēd′), *v.*, **-read** (-rĕd′), **-reading.** —*v.t.* **1.** to understand spoken words by watching the movement of a speaker's lips. —*v.i.* **2.** to read lips.

lip-reading (lĭp′rē′dĭng), *n.* the reading or understanding, as by a deaf person, of the movements of another's lips when forming words. —**lip-reader** (lĭp′rē′də), *n.*

lip-service (lĭp′sû′vĭs), *n.* service with words only; insincere profession of devotion or goodwill.

lipstick (lĭp′stĭck′), *n.* a stick or elongated piece of cosmetic preparation for colouring the lips.

liq., **1.** liquid. **2.** liquor.

liquate (lī′kwāt), *v.t.*, **-quated, -quating.** *Metall.* **1.** to heat (a metal, etc.) sufficiently to melt the more fusible portion and so separate a metal from impurities or other metals. **2.** to separate by such a fusion (often fol. by *out*). [t. L: m. s. *liquātus*, pp., made liquid, melted] —**liquation** (lĭ kwā′shən), *n.*

liquefacient (lĭk′wĭ fā′shənt), *n.* that which liquefies or promotes liquefaction.

liquefaction (lĭk′wĭ făk′shən), *n.* the process of liquefying or making liquid.

liquefy (lĭk′wĭ fī′), *v.t.*, *v.i.*, **-fied, -fying.** to make or become liquid. Also, **liquify.** [late ME, t. L: m. s. *liquefacere* make liquid] —**liq′uefi′able,** *adj.* —**liq′uefi′er,** *n.*

liquescent (lĭ kwĕs′ənt), *adj.* **1.** becoming liquid; melting. **2.** tending towards a liquid state. [t. L: s. *liquescens*, ppr.] —**liques′cence, liques′cency,** *n.*

liqueur (lĭ kyo͝o′ə′; *Fr.* lē kœr′), *n.* any of a class of alcoholic liquors, usually strong, sweet, and highly flavoured, as chartreuse, curaçao, etc.; a cordial. [t. F. See LIQUOR]

liquid (lĭk′wĭd), *adj.* **1.** composed of molecules which move freely among themselves but do not tend to separate like those of gases; neither gaseous nor solid. **2.** of or pertaining to liquids: *liquid measure.* **3.** such as to flow like water. **4.** clear, transparent, or bright: *liquid eyes.* **5.** sounding smoothly or agreeably: *liquid tones.* **6.** *Phonet.* identified with or being either *r* or *l.* **7.** in cash or readily convertible into cash: *liquid assets.* **8. to go liquid,** to realize assets for cash. —*n.* **9.** a liquid substance. **10.** *Phonet.* either *r* or *l.* [ME, t. L: s. *liquidus*] —**liq′uidly,** *adv.* —**liq′uidness,** *n.*

—**Syn. 9.** LIQUID, FLUID agree in referring to that which is not solid. LIQUID commonly refers to substances such as water, oil, alcohol, and the like, which are neither solids nor gaseous: *water ceases to be a liquid when it is frozen or turned to steam.* FLUID is applied to anything that flows, whether liquid or gaseous: *pipes can carry fluids from place to place.*

liquid air, air in its liquid state; an intensely cold, transparent liquid.

liquidambar (lĭk′wĭd ăm′bə; *for genus* -bä), *n.* **1.** any tree of the genus *Liquidambar,* as *L. styraciflua,* a large American tree, having star-shaped leaves and, in warm regions, exuding a fragrant yellowish balsamic liquid used in medicine. **2.** this liquid. See **storax** (def. 2). [t. NL, f. s. L *liquidus* LIQUID + ML *ambar* AMBER]

liquidate (lĭk′wĭ dāt′), *v.,* **-dated, -dating.** —*v.t.* **1.** to settle or pay (a debt, etc.): *to liquidate a claim.* **2.** to reduce (accounts) to order; determine the amount of (indebtedness or damages). **3.** to convert into cash. **4.** to get rid of, esp. by killing or other violent means. **5.** to break up, abolish, or do away with. —*v.i.* **6.** to liquidate debts or accounts; go into liquidation. [t. ML: m. s. *liquidātus,* pp., der. L *liquidus*]

liquidation (lĭk′wĭ dā′shən), *n.* **1.** the process of realizing upon assets and of discharging liabilities in winding up the affairs of a business, estate, etc. **2.** the process of converting securities or commodities into cash for the purpose of taking profits or preventing losses. **3.** liquidated state. **4.** destruction.

liquidator (lĭk′wĭ dā′tə), *n.* a person appointed to carry out the winding up of a company.

liquid crystal, a liquid having different optical properties in different directions and other crystalline characteristics.

liquid fire, flaming petroleum or the like as employed against the enemy in warfare.

liquid glass, waterglass (def. 5).

liquidity (lĭ kwĭd′ĭ tĭ), *n.* **1.** liquid state or quality. **2.** the state of having assets either in cash or readily convertible into cash.

liquidity preference, *Finance.* the choice between holding wealth as idle money or in the form of income-earning assets.

liquidity ratio, the proportion that a bank's liquid assets bear to its liabilities.

liquidize (lĭk′wĭ dīz′), *v.t.,* **-dized, -dizing.** to make liquid; liquefy. Also, **liquidise.**

liquidizer (lĭk′wĭ dī′zə), *n.* a device which converts solids into a fluid state, esp. by chopping or pulverizing. Also, **liquidiser.**

liquid measure, the system of units of capacity ordinarily used in measuring liquid commodities, such as milk, oil, etc.: 4 gills = 1 pint; 2 pints = 1 quart; 4 quarts = 1 gallon.

liquid oxygen, oxygen in its liquid state; a pale blue liquid which boils at −182·9°C; used as an oxidant in rockets. *Abbrev.:* lox.

liquid paraffin, a liquid form of petrolatum used as a laxative.

liquify (lĭk′wĭ fī′), *v.t., v.i.,* **-fied, -fying.** liquefy.

liquor (lĭk′ə), *n.* **1.** spirits (as brandy or whisky) as distinguished from fermented beverages (as wine or beer). **2.** *Chiefly U.S.* any alcoholic drink, esp. spirits. **3.** any liquid substance. **4.** *Pharm.* a solution of a medicinal substance in water. **5.** Also, **liquor amnii** (lī′kôr ăm′nĭ ī′, lī′kwôr-). *Embryol.* liquid contained in the amnion which surrounds the foetus; the waters. **6.** a solution of a substance, esp. a concentrated one used in an industrial process. **7.** *Brewing.* water, when added in brewing processes. —*v.t., v.i.* **8.** *Slang.* to furnish with or imbibe liquor or drink (often fol. by *up*). [t. L: liquid (state), liquid; r. ME *licur, licour,* t. OF]

liquorice[1] (lĭk′ə rĭs), *n.* **1.** a leguminous plant, *Glycyrrhiza glabra,* of Europe and Asia. **2.** the sweet-tasting dried root of this plant, or an extract made from it, used in medicine, confectionery, etc. **3.** any of various related or similar plants. Also, **licorice, liquorish** (lĭk′ə rĭsh). [ME *lycorys,* t. AF, t. LL: m. s. *liquiritia,* L *glycyrrhiza,* t. Gk: m. *glykýrrhiza;* influenced by L *liquor* liquor]

liquorice[2] (lĭk′ə rĭs), *adj.* *Archaic.* lickerish.

liquorice allsorts (ôl′sôts′), variously shaped sweets, liquorice flavoured or having liquorice sections.

lira (lĭə′rə), *n., pl.* **lire** (lĭə′rĭ), **liras. 1.** the monetary unit of Italy, equal to 100 centesimi and equivalent to about £0·00066 sterling. *Abbrev.:* l. **2.** a coin of this value. **3.** a Turkish unit of currency, equal to 100 kurus, and equivalent to about £0·0463 sterling. *Abbrev.:* £T. **4.** a coin of this value. [t. It., d. var. of *lib(b)ra,* g. L *lībra* pound]

liriodendron (lĭr′rĭ ō dĕn′drən), *n., pl.* **-drons, -dra** (-drə). a tree of the magnoliaceous genus *Liriodendron,* of which the tulip tree, *L. tulipifera,* native in eastern North America, is the chief representative. See **tulip tree.** [t. NL, f. m. s. Gk *leírion* lily + *-dendron* -DENDRON]

liripipe (lĭ′rĭ pīp′), *n.* **1.** *Hist.* the tail or pendent part at the back of a hood, as in 14th and 15th century French costume. **2.** a scarf or tippet; a hood. Also, **liripoop** (lĭ′rĭ po͞op′). [t. ML: m. s. *liripipium;* orig. unknown]

Lisbon (lĭz′bən), *n.* a seaport in and the capital of Portugal, on the Tagus estuary. 802,230 (1960). Portuguese, **Lisboa** (*Port.* lēzh bó′ə).

Lisburne (lĭz′bûn′), *n.* a town in Northern Ireland, in Co. Antrim. 17,691 (1961).

lisle (līl), *n.* **1.** knitted goods, as hose, made of lisle thread. —*adj.* **2.** made of lisle thread.

Lisle (lēl), *n.* **1.** See **Leconte de Lisle. 2.** Also, **l'Isle.** See **Rouget de Lisle. 3.** a former name of **Lille.**

lisle thread (līl), a smooth, hard-twisted cotton thread.

Lismore (lĭz′mô′), *n.* a port in the NE part of New South Wales, Australia. 19,000 (1965).

lisp (lĭsp), *n.* **1.** a speech defect consisting in pronouncing *s* and *z* like or nearly like the *th* sounds of *thin* and *this,* respectively. **2.** the act, habit, or sound of lisping. —*v.t., v.i.* **3.** to pronounce or speak with a lisp. [ME *wlispe, lipse,* OE *-wlispian* (in *āwlyspian*), der. *wlisp* lisping. Cf. D *lispen,* G *lispeln*] —**lisp′er,** *n.* —**lisp′ingly,** *adv.*

lis pendens (lĭs′pĕn′dĕnz), *Latin.* **1.** a pending suit. **2.** the rule allowing for registration of land subject to a pending action. **3.** the rule placing property involved in litigation under the court's jurisdiction.

lissom (lĭs′əm), *adj.* **1.** lithe, esp. of body; limber or supple. **2.** agile or active. Also, *Chiefly U.S.,* **lissome.** [var. of LITHESOME] —**lis′somness,** *n.*

lissotrichous (lĭ sŏt′rĭ kəs), *adj.* *Anthropol.* having straight hair. [f. Gk *lissó(s)* smooth + s. Gk *thrix* hair + -OUS]

list[1] (lĭst), *n.* **1.** a record consisting of a series of names, words, or the like; a number of names of persons or things set down one after another. —*v.t.* **2.** to set down together in a list; to make a list of. **3.** to enter in a list with others. **4.** *Archaic.* to enlist. **5.** to register a security on a stock exchange so that it may be traded there. —*v.i.* *Archaic.* **6.** to enlist. [special use of LIST[2]. Cf. F *liste* (t. G) in same sense]

—**Syn. 1.** LIST, CATALOGUE, INVENTORY, REGISTER, ROLL, SCHEDULE imply a definite arrangement of items. LIST denotes a series of names, items, or figures arranged in a row or rows: *a list of groceries.* CATALOGUE adds the idea of alphabetical or other orderly arrangement, and, often, descriptive particulars and details: *a library catalogue.* An INVENTORY is a detailed descriptive list of property, stock, goods, or the like made for legal or business purposes: *a store inventory.* A REGISTER is a list of acts, occurrences, names, etc., kept as a record: *a school register; the parish register of baptisms.* A ROLL is a list of names of members of some defined group: *the electoral roll.* A SCHEDULE is a methodical (esp. official) list, often indicating the time or sequence of certain events: *a train schedule.*

list[2] (lĭst), *n.* **1.** a border or bordering strip of anything (now chiefly or only of cloth). **2.** a selvage. **3.** selvages collectively. **4.** a strip of cloth or other material. **5.** a strip or band of any kind. **6.** *Obs.* a stripe of colour. **7.** a division of the hair or beard. **8.** *U.S.* one of the ridges or furrows of earth thrown up by a lister. —*adj.* **9.** made of selvages or strips of cloth. —*v.t.* **10.** to border or edge. **11.** to apply list or strips of cloth to. **12.** *U.S.* to produce furrows and ridges in (land) by means of a lister. **13.** *U.S.* (in cotton culture) to prepare (land) for the crop by making alternating ridges and furrows. **14.** to shape (a block, stave, etc.) roughly by chopping. [ME *lyst(e),* OE *līste,* c. D *lijst,* G *Leiste*]

list[3] (lĭst), *n.* **1.** a careening, or leaning to one side, as of a ship. —*v.i.* **2.** (of a ship) to careen; incline to one side: *the ship listed to starboard.* —*v.t.* **3.** to cause (a ship) to lean to one side: *the weight of the misplaced cargo listed the ship to starboard.* [orig. obscure]

list[4] (lĭst), *Archaic.* —*v.t.* **1.** to be pleasing to; please. **2.** to like or desire. —*v.i.* **3.** to like; wish; choose. [ME *luste(n),* OE *lystan,* c. G *lüsten,* Icel. *lysta*]

list[5] (lĭst), *Archaic or Poetic.* —*v.i.* **1.** to listen. —*v.t.* **2.** to listen to. [ME *list(e),* OE *hlystan,* der. *hlyst* hearing (c. Icel. *hlust* ear); akin to LISTEN]

listel (lĭs′tl), *n.* *Archit.* a narrow list or fillet. [t. F, t. It.: m. *listello,* dim. of *lista,* t. OHG]

listen (lĭs′ən), *v.i.* **1.** to give attention with the ear; attend closely for the purpose of hearing; give ear. **2.** to give heed; yield to advice. **3.** to wait attentively (fol. by *for*). **4. listen in, a.** to eavesdrop. **b.** to listen to a radio programme. —*v.t.* 5. *Poetic.* to hear; give ear to. [ME *lis(t)ne(n)*, OE *hlysnan*, c. MHG *lüsenen*; akin to LIST[5]] —**lis′tener,** *n.* —**Syn.** 1. See **hear.**

listening post, 1. *Mil.* a post or position, as in advance of a defensive line, established for the purpose of listening to detect the enemy's movements. 2. any position maintained to obtain information.

Lister (lĭs′tə), *n.* **Joseph, 1st Baron,** 1827–1912, English surgeon: the first to use antiseptics in surgery.

lister (lĭs′tə), *n.* *U.S.* a plough with a double mouldboard used to prepare the soil for planting by producing furrows and ridges, and often fitted with attachments for dropping and covering the seeds. Also, **lister plow, lister plough.** [see LIST[2] (def. 8)]

Listerism (lĭs′tə rĭz′əm), *n.* an antiseptic method introduced by Lister, involving the spraying of the parts under operation with a carbolic acid solution.

listless (lĭst′lĭs), *adj.* 1. feeling no inclination towards or interest in anything. 2. characterized by or indicating such feeling: *a listless mood.* [late ME, f. LIST[4] + -LESS] —**list′lessly,** *adv.*

listlessness (lĭst′lĭs nĭs), *n.* 1. the state of being listless. 2. languid inattention. —**Syn.** 2. See **indifference.**

list price, *Com.* price given in a catalogue.

lists (lĭsts), *n.pl.* 1. the barriers enclosing the field of combat at a tournament. 2. the enclosed field. 3. any place or scene of combat. 4. **enter the lists,** to take part in a contest or competition. [ME *liste* boundary, limit (same word as LIST[2])]

Liszt (lĭst), *n.* **Franz** (frănts), 1811–86, Hungarian composer and pianist.

lit (lĭt), *v.* 1. pt. and pp. of **light**[1] and **light**[3]. —*adj.* 2. *Slang.* drunk; intoxicated (often fol. by *up*).

lit., 1. litre. 2. literal. 3. literally. 4. literary. 5. literature.

Li Tai Po (lē′ tī′ pō′), Li Po.

litany (lĭt′ə nĭ), *n., pl.* **-nies.** 1. a ceremonial or liturgical form of prayer consisting of a series of invocations or supplications with responses which are the same for a number in succession. 2. Also, **the Litany.** the general supplication in this form in the Book of Common Prayer. 3. a prolonged recitation; monotonous account. [t. LL: m. s. *litania*, t. Gk: m. *litaneía* litany, an entreating; r. ME *letanie*, t. OF]

litchi (lī′chē′, lĭch′ĭ), *n., pl.* **-tchis.** lychee.

lit de justice (*Fr.* lē də zhʏs tēs′), *French.* 1. the sofa upon which the king of France sat when holding formal sessions of the parliament. 2. such a session.

-lite, a word element used in names of minerals, or fossils: *chrysolite, aerolite.* Cf. **-lith.** [t. F, t. Gk: m. *líthos* stone. Cf. G *-lit(h)*]

liter (lē′tə), *n.* *U.S.* litre.

literacy (lĭt′ə rə sĭ), *n.* the state of being literate; possession of education.

literacy test, (in the U.S. and elsewhere) an examination to determine whether a person meets the literacy requirement for voting, etc.

literae humaniores (lĭt′ə rē′ hyo͞o măn′ĭ ô′rēz), (at Oxford and Cambridge universities) the faculty and school of classical languages and culture. Also, **litterae humaniores.**

literal (lĭt′ə rəl), *adj.* 1. following the letter, or exact words, of the original, as a translation. 2. (of persons) tending to construe words in the strict sense or in an unimaginative way; matter-of-fact; prosaic. 3. in accordance with, involving, or being the natural or strict meaning of the words or word; not figurative or metaphorical: *the literal meaning of a word.* 4. true to fact; not exaggerated: *a literal statement of conditions.* 5. being actually such, without exaggeration or inaccuracy: *the literal extermination of a city.* 6. of or pertaining to the letters of the alphabet. 7. of the nature of letters. 8. expressed by letters. 9. affecting a letter or letters: *a literal error.* —*n.* 10. *Print.* a misprint in printed matter, esp. of one letter only. [ME, t. LL: m. s. *litterālis*, der. *littera* LETTER] —**lit′eralness,** *n.*

literalism (lĭt′ə rə lĭz′əm), *n.* 1. adherence to the exact letter or the literal sense, as in translation or interpretation. 2. a peculiarity of expression resulting from this. 3. exact representation or portrayal, without idealization, as in art or literature. —**lit′eralist,** *n., adj.* —**lit′eralis′tic,** *adj.*

literality (lĭt′ə răl′ĭ tĭ), *n., pl.* **-ties.** 1. the quality of being literal. 2. a literal interpretation.

literalize (lĭt′ə rə līz′), *v.t.,* **-lized, -lizing.** to make literal; interpret literally. Also, **literalise.** —**lit′eraliz′er,** *n.*

literally (lĭt′ə rə lĭ), *adv.* 1. in a literal manner; word for word: *to translate literally.* 2. in the literal sense. 3. actually; without exaggeration or inaccuracy.

literary (lĭt′ə rə rĭ, lĭt′rə rĭ), *adj.* 1. pertaining to or of the nature of books and writings, esp. those classed as literature: *literary history.* 2. versed in or acquainted with literature. 3. engaged in writing books, etc., or in literature as a profession: *a literary man.* 4. pedantic; excessively affected in displaying learning. —**lit′erarily,** *adv.* —**lit′erariness,** *n.*

literate (lĭt′ə rĭt), *adj.* 1. able to read and write. 2. having an education; educated. 3. literary. —*n.* 4. one who can read and write. 5. a learned person. [ME *litterate*, t. L: m. *litterātus, līterātus* lettered]

literati (lĭt′ə rä′tē), *n.pl.* men of learning; men of letters; scholarly or literary people. [t. L]

literatim (lĭt′ə rä′tĭm), *adv.* letter for letter; literally. [t. ML, der. L *littera* LETTER]

literature (lĭt′ə rĭ chə, lĭt′rĭ chə), *n.* 1. writings in which expression and form, in connection with ideas of permanent and universal interest, are characteristic or essential features, as poetry, romance, history, biography, essays, etc.; belles-lettres. 2. the entire body of writings of a specific language, period, people, subject, etc.: *the literature of England.* 3. the writings dealing with a particular subject. 4. the profession of a writer or author. 5. literary work or production. 6. *Colloq.* printed matter of any kind, as circulars or advertising matter. 7. *Rare.* polite learning or literary culture. [ME *litterature*, t. F, t. L: m. *litterātūra* learning]

—**Syn.** 1. LITERATURE, BELLES-LETTRES, LETTERS refer to artistic writings worthy of being remembered. In the broadest sense, LITERATURE includes any type of writings on any subject: *the literature of medicine*; usually, however, it means the body of artistic writings of a country or period which are characterized by beauty of expression and form and by universality or intellectual and emotional appeal: *English literature of the sixteenth century.* BELLES-LETTRES is a more specific term for such writings: *his talent is not for scholarship but for belles-lettres.* LETTERS (rare today except in certain fixed phrases) refers to literature as a domain of study or creation: *a man of letters.*

lith-, a combining form meaning 'stone'. Also, **litho-.** [t. Gk, comb. form of *líthos*]

-lith, a noun termination meaning 'stone', as in *acrolith, megalith, nephrolith, palaeolith*: sometimes occurring in words, as *batholith, laccolith*, that are variants of forms in *-lite.* Cf. **-lite.** [see LITH-]

Lith., 1. Lithuania. 2. Lithuanian.

lith., 1. lithograph. 2. lithography. Also, **litho., lithog.**

litharge (lĭth′äj), *n.* lead monoxide, a yellow earthy substance used in compounding glazes and glasses. [ME *litarge*, t. OF, t. L: m. s. *lithargyrus*, t. Gk: m. *lithárgyros* spume of silver]

lithe (līth), *adj.* bending readily; pliant; limber; supple. Also, **lithesome** (līth′səm). [ME *lith(e)*, OE *lithe*, c. G *lind* mild] —**lithe′ly,** *adv.* —**lithe′ness,** *n.*

lithia (lĭth′ĭ ə), *n.* a white oxide of lithium, Li_2O. [t. NL, der. Gk *líthos* stone]

lithia water, a mineral water, natural or artificial, containing lithium salts.

lithic (lĭth′ĭk), *adj.* 1. pertaining to or consisting of stone. 2. *Pathol.* pertaining to stony concretions, or calculi, formed within the body, esp. in the bladder. 3. *Chem.* of, pertaining to, or containing lithium. [t. Gk: m. s. *lithikós* of stones]

-lithic, an adjective suffix identical with **lithic,** used esp. in archaeology, e.g., *palaeolithic.*

lithium (lĭth′ĭ əm), *n.* *Chem.* a soft silver-white metallic element (the lightest of all metals) occurring combined in certain minerals. *Symbol:* Li; *at. wt:* 6·939; *at. no.:* 3; *sp. gr.:* 0·53 at 20°C. [t. NL, f. s. Gk *líthos* stone + *-ium* -IUM; so named because found in minerals]

litho-, var. of **lith-,** before consonants, as in *lithography.*

litho., 1. lithograph. 2. lithography.

lithog., 1. lithograph. 2. lithography.

lithograph (lĭth′ə grăf′, -gräf′), *n.* 1. a print produced by lithography. —*v.t.* 2. to produce or copy by lithography.

lithographer (lĭ thŏg′rə fə), *n.* a person who works at lithography.

lithography (lĭ thŏg′rə fĭ), *n.* 1. the art or process of producing a picture, writing, or the like, on a flat, specially prepared stone, with some greasy or oily substance, and of taking ink impressions from this as in ordinary printing. 2. a similar process in which a substance other than stone, as aluminium or zinc, is used. —**lithographic** (lĭth′ə grăf′ĭk), **lith′ograph′ical,** *adj.* —**lith′ograph′ically,** *adv.*

lithoid (lĭth′oid), *adj.* stonelike; stony. Also, **lithoi′dal.** [t. Gk: m. s. *lithoeidḗs.* See LITH-, -OID]

lithol., lithology.

lithology (lĭ thŏl′ə jĭ), *n.* 1. the science dealing with the minute mineral characters of rock specimens. 2. *Med. Rare.* the science treating of calculi in the human body. —**lithologic** (lĭth′ə lŏj′ĭk), **lith′olog′ical,** *adj.*

litholopaxy (lĭth′ə lə păk′sĭ, lĭ thŏl′ə-), *n.* *Surg.* the crushing of a bladder stone by a lithotrite, followed by washing out the fragments so produced.

lithomarge (lĭth′ə mäj′), *n.* kaolin (clay) in compact, massive, usually impure form. [t. NL: m. *lithomarga*, f. *litho-* LITHO- + L *marga* marl]

lithophyte (lĭth′ə fīt′), *n.* **1.** *Zool.* a polyp with a hard or stony structure, as a coral. **2.** *Bot.* any plant growing on the surface of rocks. —**lithophytic** (lĭth′ə fĭt′ĭk), *adj.*

lithopone (lĭth′ə pōn′), *n.* a white pigment consisting of zinc sulphide and barium sulphate, used in the manufacture of linoleum and rubber articles. [f. LITHO- + m. s. Gk *pónos* task]

lithosphere (lĭth′ə sfĭə′), *n.* the crust of the earth.

lithotomy (lĭ thŏt′ə mĭ), *n., pl.* **-mies.** *Surg.* the operation or art of cutting for stone in the urinary bladder. [t. LL: m. s. *lithotomia*, t. Gk. See LITHO-, -TOMY] —**lithotomic** (lĭth′ə tŏm′ĭk), **lith′otom′ical,** *adj.* —**lithot′omist,** *n.*

lithotrite (lĭth′ə trīt′), *n.* *Surg.* an instrument for performing lithotrity.

lithotrity (lĭ thŏt′rĭ tĭ), *n., pl.* **-ties.** *Surg.* the operation of crushing stone in the urinary bladder into particles that may be voided. [f. LITHO- + s. L *trītus*, pp., rubbed + -Y³]

Lithuania (lĭth′yōō ā′nyə), *n.* a constituent republic of the Soviet Union in Europe, in the W part, on the Baltic: an independent state 1918–40. 2,880,000 pop. (1963); 24,100 sq. mi. *Cap.:* Vilna. Official name, **Lithuanian Soviet Socialist Republic.** Lithuanian, **Lietuva.** See map under **Memel.** —**Lith′ua′nian,** *adj., n.*

lithy (lī′thĭ), *adj.* *Archaic.* lithe.

litigable (lĭt′ĭ gə bl), *adj.* subject to litigation.

litigant (lĭt′ĭ gənt), *n.* **1.** one engaged in a lawsuit. —*adj.* **2.** litigating; engaged in a lawsuit. [t. L: s. *lītigans*, ppr.]

litigate (lĭt′ĭ gāt′), *v.,* **-gated, -gating.** —*v.t.* **1.** to make the subject of a lawsuit; to contest at law. **2.** to dispute (a point, etc.). —*v.i.* **3.** to carry on a lawsuit. [t. L: m. s. *lītigātus*, pp.] —**lit′iga′tor,** *n.*

litigation (lĭt′ĭ gā′shən), *n.* **1.** the process of litigating. **2.** a lawsuit.

litigious (lĭ tĭj′əs), *adj.* **1.** of or pertaining to litigation. **2.** excessively prone to litigate: *a litigious person.* [ME, t. L: m. s. *lītigiōsus* disputatious] —**liti′giously,** *adv.* —**liti′giousness,** *n.*

litmus (lĭt′məs), *n.* a blue colouring matter obtained from certain lichens, esp. *Roccella tinctoria.* In alkaline solution litmus turns blue, in acid solution red; hence it is widely used as an indicator, esp. in the form of strips of paper impregnated with a solution of the colouring matter (**litmus paper**). [ME *litmose*, t. Scand.; cf. Icel. *litmosi* dyeing-moss]

litotes (lī′tō tēz′), *n., pl.* **-tes.** *Rhet.* a figure in which an affirmative is expressed by the negative of its contrary, as in *not bad at all.* [t. NL, t. Gk: diminution]

litre (lē′tə), *n.* *Metric System.* a unit of capacity equal to the volume of one kilogram of water at its maximum density, or very nearly one cubic decimetre and equivalent to 0·21998 gallons. Also, *U.S.,* **liter.** [t. F, der. *litron* old measure of capacity, der. LL *lītra* measure for liquids, t. Gk: pound]

-litre, a word element meaning litres; of or pertaining to litres, as in *centilitre.* Also, *U.S.,* **-liter.**

litter (lĭt′ə), *n.* **1.** things scattered about; scattered rubbish. **2.** a condition of disorder or untidiness. **3.** a number of young brought forth at one birth. **4.** a framework of canvas stretched between two parallel bars, for the transportation of the sick and the wounded. **5.** a vehicle carried by men or animals, consisting of a bed or couch, often covered and curtained, suspended between shafts. **6.** straw, hay, etc., used as bedding for animals, or as a protection for plants. **7.** the rubbish of dead leaves and twigs scattered upon the floor of the forest. —*v.t.* **8.** to strew (a place) with scattered objects. **9.** to scatter (objects) in disorder. **10.** to be strewn about (a place) in disorder (fol. by *up*). **11.** to give birth to (young): said chiefly of animals. **12.** to supply (an animal) with litter for a bed. **13.** to use (straw, hay, etc.) for litter. **14.** to cover (a floor, etc.) with litter, or straw, hay, etc. —*v.i.* **15.** to give birth to a litter. [ME *litere*, t. AF, der. *lit* bed, g. L *lectus*] —**Syn. 3.** See **brood.**

littérateur (lĭt′ĭ rə tû′; *Fr.* lē tė rȧ tœr′), *n.* a writer of literary works. Also, **litterateur.** [t. F, t. L: m. *litterātor*]

litter-bin (lĭt′ə bĭn′), *n.* a large container, esp. one in a public place, used as a receptacle for litter. Also, **litter-basket** (lĭt′ə bä′skĭt).

littery (lĭt′ə rĭ), *adj.* of or covered with litter; untidy.

little (lĭt′l), *adj.,* **less** or **lesser, least;** or **littler, littlest;** *adv.,* **less, least;** *n.* —*adj.* **1.** small in size; not big or large: *a little child.* **2.** small in extent or duration; short; brief: *a little while.* **3.** small in number: *a little army.* **4.** small in amount or degree; not much: *little hope.* **5.** (by litotes) sufficient to have an effect; appreciable: *having a little trouble.* **6.** being such on a small scale: *little farmers.* **7.** small in force; weak: *a little voice.* **8.** small in consideration, dignity, consequence, etc.: *little discomforts.* **9.** mean, narrow, or illiberal: *a little mind.* **10.** endearingly small or considered as such: *Bless your little heart!* **11.** amusingly small or so considered: *I understand his little ways.* —*adv.* **12.** not at all (before a verb): *he little knows what awaits him.* **13.** in only a small amount or degree; not much: *a zeal little tempered by humanity.* **14.** rarely; infrequently: *I see my mother very little.* —*n.* **15.** that which is little; a small amount, quantity, or degree. **16.** a short distance: *please step back a little.* **17.** a short time: *stay here a little.* **18. little by little,** by degrees; gradually. **19. make little of, a.** to belittle; disparage. **b.** to understand only partially; grasp inadequately: *I can make little of your writing.* **20. not a little,** (by litotes) a very great deal; considerable. [ME and OE *lytel*, c. D *luttel*, d. G *lützel*] —**lit′tleness,** *n.*

—**Syn. 1–4.** LITTLE, DIMINUTIVE, MINUTE, SMALL refer to that which is not large or significant. LITTLE (the opposite of *big*) is very general, covering size, extent, number, quantity, amount, duration, or degree: *a little boy, a little time.* SMALL (the opposite of *large* and of *great*) can many times be used interchangeably with LITTLE, but is especially applied to what is limited or below the average in size: *small oranges.* DIMINUTIVE denotes (usually physical) size that is much less than the average or ordinary; it may suggest delicacy: *the baby's diminutive fingers, diminutive in size but autocratic in manner.* MINUTE suggests that which is so tiny that it is difficult to discern, or that which implies attentiveness to the smallest details: *a minute quantity, examination.*

Little America, the base established 1929 for the Antarctic expeditions of Admiral Richard E. Byrd, on the Bay of Whales, S of the Ross Sea: still in use.

little auk, a small seabird, *Plautus alle*, of N Europe.

Little Bear, *Astron.* a northern constellation containing the stars forming the Little Dipper, the outermost of which (at the end of the tail of the Little Bear) is Polaris, the Pole Star. Also, **Ursa Minor.**

Little Dipper, the Dipper (def. 3b).

Little Dog, *Astron.* the constellation Canis Minor.

Little Englander. See **Englander** (def. 2).

little finger, the finger on the outer edge of a hand, farthest from the thumb; usually the smallest of the fingers.

Little Fox, *Astron.* Vulpecula.

little go, go (def. 43).

Littlehampton (lĭt′l hămp′tən), *n.* a town in England, in W Sussex: seaside resort. 15,647 (1961).

little hours, *Rom. Cath. Ch.* the hours of prime, tierce, sext, and nones, and sometimes also vespers and complin.

Little John, the large, powerful, strong member of Robin Hood's band.

little office, *Rom. Cath. Ch.* a service, resembling the breviary but shorter, in honour of the Virgin Mary.

little people, small legendary beings as elves, pixies, or leprechauns. Also, **little folk.**

Little Rock, a town in the U.S., the capital of Arkansas, in the central part, on the Arkansas river. 107,813 (1960).

Little Russia, an indefinite region in the SW Soviet Union, consisting mainly of the Ukraine, but sometimes including adjacent areas.

Little Russian, a member of a division of the Russian people dwelling in southern and south-western Soviet Union in Europe and in adjoining regions. Cf. **Ruthenian.**

little slam. See **slam²** (def. 1).

little theatre, *U.S.* **1.** a small theatre, producing plays whose effectiveness would be lost in larger houses. **2.** plays that would not draw audiences sufficient to fill the ordinary theatre, esp. as produced by a movement in the early 20th century, identified with various theatrical experiments and innovations. **3.** amateur theatricals.

little toe, the toe on the outer edge of the foot, farthest from the hallux; usually the smallest of the toes.

littoral (lĭt′ə rəl), *adj.* **1.** pertaining to the shore of a lake, sea, or ocean. —*n.* **2.** a littoral region. [t. L: s. *littorālis*]

Littoria (*It.* lēt tŏ′ryȧ), *n.* a town in Italy, in SW Lazio. 62,006 (1966). Also, **Latina.**

liturgical (lĭ tû′jĭ kl), *adj.* **1.** of or pertaining to public worship. **2.** having to do with liturgies or forms of public worship. **3.** of or pertaining to the liturgy or Eucharistic service. **4.** of or pertaining to liturgics. Also, **litur′gic.** [f. m. s. Gk *leitourgikós* ministering + -AL¹] —**litur′gically,** *adv.*

Liturgical Latin, the Latin characteristic of the liturgies of the Western Church.

liturgics (lĭ tû′jĭks), *n.* **1.** the science or art of conducting public worship. **2.** the study of liturgies.

liturgist (lĭt′ə jĭst), *n.* **1.** an authority on liturgies. **2.** a compiler of a liturgy or liturgies. **3.** one who uses, or favours the use of, a liturgy.

liturgy (lĭt′ə jĭ), *n., pl.* **-gies. 1.** a form of public worship; a ritual. **2.** a collection of formularies for public worship.

3. a particular arrangement of services. 4. a particular form or type of the Eucharistic service. 5. the service of the Eucharist, esp. in the Eastern Church. [t. ML: m. s. *līturgia*, t. Gk: m. *leitourgía* public duty, public worship]

Litvinov (*Russ.* lĭt vē′nəf), *n.* **Maksim Maksimovich** (*Russ.* mȧk sēm′ mək sĭ mô′vĭch), 1876–1951, Soviet statesman.

Liu Shao-chi (lyo͞o′shyou′chē′), born 1898, chairman of the People's Republic of China 1959–68.

livable (lĭv′ə bl), *adj.* 1. suitable for living in; habitable. 2. that can be lived with; companionable. 3. worth living; endurable. Also, **liveable.** —**liv′ableness,** *n.*

live[1] (lĭv), *v.*, **lived** (lĭvd), **living.** —*v.i.* 1. to have life, as an animal or plant; be alive; be capable of vital functions. 2. to continue to live; remain alive: *to live long.* 3. to continue in existence, operation, memory, etc.; last: *looks which lived in my memory.* 4. to escape destruction or remain afloat, as at sea. 5. to maintain life; rely for maintenance: *to live on one's income.* 6. to feed or subsist (fol. by *on* or *upon*): *to live on rice.* 7. to dwell or reside: *to live in a cottage.* 8. to pass life (as specified): *they lived happily ever after.* 9. to direct or regulate one's life: *to live by the golden rule.* 10. to experience or enjoy life to the full. 11. **live high,** to live at a high standard; live luxuriously. 12. **live in** (or **out**), to reside at (or away from) the place of one's work. 13. **live with,** to dwell together with, as a husband or wife or lover; to cohabit with. —*v.t.* 14. to pass (life): *to live a life of ease.* 15. to carry out or exhibit in one's life. 16. **live down,** to live so as to cause (something) to lose force or be forgotten: *to live down a mistake.* 17. **live it up,** *Colloq.* to live wildly and exuberantly; go on a spree. 18. **live up to,** to accord with or maintain (expectations or standards). [ME *liv(i)en,* OE *lifian, libban,* c. D *leven,* G *leben*]

live[2] (līv), *adj.* 1. being in life, living, or alive: *live animals.* 2. of or pertaining to life of living beings: *live weight* (the weight of an animal while living). 3. characterized by or indicating the presence of living creatures. 4. full of life, energy, or activity. 5. *Colloq.* alert; wide-awake; up-to-date. 6. *Colloq.* of present interest, as a question or issue. 7. burning or glowing, as a coal. 8. vivid or bright, as colour. 9. flowing freely, as water. 10. fresh, as air. 11. loaded or unexploded, as a cartridge or shell. 12. *Elect.* electrically connected to a source of potential difference, or electrically charged so as to have a potential different from that of earth: *a live wire.* 13. moving, or imparting motion or power: *the live centre on a lathe.* 14. still in use, or to be used, as type set up or copy for printing. 15. (of a radio or TV programme) broadcast or televised at the moment it is being presented at the studio. 16. denoting or pertaining to an actual public performance in the theatre or the like, opposed to a filmed or broadcast performance. —*adv.* 17. (of a radio or TV programme) not taped; at the time of its happening: *this contest is brought to you live from the East Ham public baths.* [aphetic var. of ALIVE, used attributively]

liveable (lĭv′ə bl), *adj.* livable.

livebearer (līv′bēə′rə), *n.* any fish of the viviparous family *Poeciliidae,* esp. those kept in home aquariums.

live centre (līv). See **centre** (def. 8a).

lived (lĭvd), *adj.* having life or a life (as specified): *long-lived.*

livelihood (līv′lĭ ho͝od′), *n.* means of maintaining life; maintenance: *to gain a livelihood.* [earlier *liveliod,* metathetic var. of ME *livilod,* OE *līf(ge)lād* life-support (cf. LIFE, LODE, LOAD); current form influenced by obs. *livelihood* liveliness] —**Syn.** See **living.**

live load (līv), a load that is applied temporarily, as the weight of a train passing over a bridge.

livelong (lĭv′lŏng′), *adj.* 1. long to the full extent (used of time): *the livelong day.* 2. whole or entire. —*n.* 3. a perennial crassulaceous herb with fleshy leaves and clusters of reddish purple flowers, *Sedum telephium,* widespread in woods and hedgerows in N temperate regions. [alter. (by assoc. with LIVE[1]) of *leeve long,* ME *leve longe* dear long. Cf. LIEF, LONG[1]]

lively (līv′lĭ), *adj.*, **-lier, -liest,** *adv.* —*adj.* 1. full or suggestive of life or vital energy; active, vigorous, or brisk: *a lively discussion.* 2. animated, spirited, vivacious, or sprightly: *a lively tune.* 3. eventful, stirring, or exciting: *a lively time.* 4. strong, keen, or distinct: *a lively recollection.* 5. striking, telling, or effective, as an expression or instance. 6. vivid or bright, as colour or light. 7. sparkling, as wines. 8. fresh, as air. 9. riding the sea buoyantly, as a ship. —*adv.* 10. with activity, vigour, or animation; briskly. [ME; OE *līflīc*] —**live′lily,** *adv.* —**live′liness,** *n.*

liven (lī′vən), *v.t.* 1. to put life into; rouse; cheer (often fol. by *up*). —*v.i.* 2. to become more lively; brighten (usually fol. by *up*). —**liv′ener,** *n.*

live oak (līv), 1. an evergreen species of oak, *Quercus virginiana,* of the southern U.S., with a hard wood used in shipbuilding, etc. 2. any of various related trees.

liver[1] (lĭv′ə), *n.* 1. (in man) a large, reddish brown glandular organ (divided by fissures into five lobes) in the upper right-hand side of the abdominal cavity, secreting bile and performing various metabolic functions, and formerly supposed to be the seat of love, desire, courage, etc. 2. an organ in other animals similar to the human liver, often used as food. 3. a disordered state of the liver. 4. a reddish brown colour. —*adj.* 5. of the colour of liver. [ME; OE *lifer,* c. D *lever,* G *Leber,* Icel. *lifr*]

liver[2] (lĭv′ə), *n.* 1. one who lives. 2. one who leads a life (as specified): *an evil liver.* 3. a dweller. [f. LIVE[1] + -ER[1]]

liver extract, an extract of mammalian liver, used to treat anaemia.

liver fluke, a cestode platyhelminth parasitic worm, *Fasciola hepatica,* which lives in the bile ducts of sheep.

liveried (lĭv′ə rĭd), *adj.* clad in livery, as servants.

liverish (lĭv′ə rĭsh), *adj.* 1. having one's liver out of order. 2. disagreeable as to disposition.

liver of sulphur, a red-brown mixture of sulphides obtained by fusing potassium carbonate with sulphur; used as an insecticide, fungicide, and in treating skin diseases. [trans. of L *hepar sulphuris*]

Liverpool (lĭv′ə po͞ol′), *n.* 1. **Robert Banks Jenkinson, 2nd Earl of,** 1770–1828, English statesman: prime minister 1812–27. 2. a city and seaport in England, in Lancashire, on the Mersey estuary: university, founded 1881. 745,750 (1961).

Liverpool Bay, a wide bay between Lancashire in England, and Anglesey in Wales.

Liverpool Range, a mountain range in the E of New South Wales, Australia. Highest point, Oxleys Peak, 4500 ft.

Liverpudlian (lĭv′ə pŭd′lĭ ən), *n.* 1. a native or inhabitant of Liverpool. —*adj.* 2. of or pertaining to Liverpool or a Liverpudlian.

liver sausage, a sausage made with a large percentage of liver. Also, *Chiefly U.S.,* **liverwurst** (lĭv′ə wûst′, -wo͝oəst′).

liverwort (lĭv′ə wût′), *n.* any of the cryptogamic plants which belong to the class *Hepaticae,* comprising mosslike or thalloid plants which grow mostly on damp ground, in water, or on tree trunks.

livery (lĭv′ə rĭ), *n., pl.* **-ries.** 1. a distinctive dress, badge, or device provided for retainers, as of a feudal lord. 2. a kind of uniform worn by servants, now only menservants, of a person or household. 3. a distinctive dress worn by an official, a member of a company or guild, etc. 4. Also, **livery company.** the entire guild company entitled to wear such livery. 5. characteristic dress, garb, or outward appearance: *the green livery of summer.* 6. the keep, or feeding, stabling, etc., of horses for pay. 7. *U.S.* a livery stable. 8. *Law.* an ancient method of conveying a freehold by formal delivery of possession. [ME *livere, levere,* t. AF: m. *liveré,* pp. of *livrer* deliver, g. L *līberāre* liberate]

liveryman (lĭv′ə rĭ mən), *n., pl.* **-men.** 1. a keeper of or an employee in a livery stable. 2. a member of a livery company. 3. *Obs.* a person in livery.

livery stable, a stable where horses and vehicles are cared for or let out for pay.

lives (līvz), *n.* pl. of **life.**

live steam (līv), 1. steam fresh from the boiler and at full pressure. 2. steam which has performed no work or only part of its work.

livestock (līv′stŏk′), *n.* the horses, cattle, sheep, and other useful animals kept or bred on a farm or ranch.

live wire (līv), *Slang.* an energetic, alert person.

livid (lĭv′ĭd), *adj.* 1. having a discoloured bluish appearance due to a bruise, to congestion of blood vessels, etc., as the flesh, face, hands, or nails. 2. dull blue; dark greyish blue. 3. angry; enraged. [t. L: s. *līvidus*] —**liv′idly,** *adv.* —**liv′idness, livid′ity,** *n.*

living (lĭv′ĭng), *adj.* 1. that lives; alive, or not dead. 2. in actual existence or use: *living languages.* 3. active; strong: *a living faith.* 4. burning or glowing, as a coal. 5. flowing freely, as water. 6. (of rock or stone, etc.) in its natural state and place; native, as part of the earth's crust. 7. lifelike, as a picture. 8. of or pertaining to living beings: *within living memory.* 9. pertaining to or sufficient for living: *living conditions.* 10. absolute; entire (used as an intensifier): *to scare the living daylight out of someone.* —*n.* 11. the act or condition of one who or that which lives: *living is very expensive these days.* 12. manner or course of life: *holy living.* 13. means of maintaining life; livelihood: *to earn one's living.* 14. an ecclesiastical benefice. 15. (collectively) those alive at any one given time (often prec. by *the*). —**liv′ingly,** *adv.* —**liv′ingness,** *n.*

—**Syn.** 1. live, quick. 3. lively, vigorous. 13. LIVING, LIVELIHOOD, MAINTENANCE, SUPPORT refer, directly or indirectly, to what is earned or spent for subsistence. LIVING and LIVELIHOOD (a somewhat more formal word), both refer to what one earns to keep (oneself) alive, but are seldom interchangeable within the same phrase: *to earn one's living, to seek one's livelihood.* 'To make a living' suggests making just enough to keep alive, and is particularly frequent in the negative: *you cannot make a living out of that.* 'To make a livelihood out of something' suggests rather making a business of it: *to make a livelihood out of trapping foxes.* MAINTENANCE and SUPPORT refer usually to what is spent for the living of another: *to provide for the maintenance or support of someone.* MAINTENANCE occasionally refers to the allowance itself provided for livelihood: *they are entitled to a maintenance from this estate.*

living death, a life without any hope of happiness; an utterly wretched existence.

living room, a room in a house, flat, etc., used both for entertaining and by the members of the family for relaxing, recreation, etc.; drawing room; sitting room; lounge; parlour.

Livingstone (lĭv′ĭng stən), *n.* **1. David,** 1813–73, Scottish missionary and explorer in Africa. **2.** a town in SW Zambia, on the river Zambezi, near Victoria Falls: the former capital of Northern Rhodesia. 35,400 (est. 1964).

living wage, a wage on which it is possible for a wage-earner to live according to minimum customary standards.

Livonia (lĭ vō′nyə), *n.* a former Russian province on the Baltic: now part of the Latvian and Estonian republics of the Soviet Union.

Livorno (*It.* lē vôr′nô), *n.* a seaport in W Italy, in Tuscany, on the Ligurian Sea. 170,732 (1966). Also, **Leghorn.**

livre (lē′vrə; *Fr.* lē′vr), *n.* an old French money of account and coin, with gradual reductions in value. [t. F, g. L *lībra* pound]

Livy (lĭv′ĭ), *n.* (*Titus Livius*), 59 B.C. – A.D. 17, Roman historian.

lixiviate (lĭk sĭv′ĭ āt′), *v.t.*, **-ated, -ating.** to treat with a solvent; leach. [f. LIXIVI(UM) + -ATE[1]] —**lixiv′ia′tion,** *n.*

lixivium (lĭk sĭv′ĭ əm), *n.*, *pl.* **lixiviums, lixivia** (lĭk sĭv′ĭ ə). **1.** the solution, containing alkaline salts, obtained by leaching wood ashes with water; lye. **2.** any solution obtained by leaching. [t. L, prop. neut. of *lixīvius* made into lye]

lizard (lĭz′əd), *n.* **1.** any of the typical lizards of the Old World family *Lacertidae*, esp. of the genus *Lacerta.* **2.** any reptile of the order *Sauria*, including also larger forms, the monitors, geckos, chameleons, and various limbless forms. **3.** leather made from the skin of any of various lizards, used for making shoes, etc. **4.** *Slang.* an idler or lounger in places of social enjoyment, public resort, etc., esp. one who associates with women; a lounge lizard. **5. The Lizard,** Lizard Point. [ME *lesard*, t. OF (masc.), also *lesarde*, fem., t. L: m. *lacertus*, masc., *lacerta*, fem.]

Common lizard, *Lacerta agilis* (Length up to 8 in.)

lizard fish, any of various large-mouthed fishes (family *Synodontidae*) with lizard-like heads, esp. *Synodus foetens* of the Atlantic coast of the United States and *Synodus lucioceps* of California.

Lizard Point, a promontory in SW England, in Cornwall: the southernmost point in England. Also, **The Lizard.**

Ljubljana (lyo͞o′blĭ ä′nə), *n.* a city in NW Yugoslavia: capital of Slovenia. 135,039 (1961). German, **Laibach.**

'll, a contraction of *will* or *shall.*

ll., 1. lines. 2. (L *loco laudato*) in the place cited.

LL, 1. Late Latin. 2. Low Latin. Also, **L.L.**

llama (lä′mə), *n.* **1.** a woolly-haired South American ruminant of the genus *Lama* (or *Auchenia*), probably a domesticated variety of the guanaco, used as a beast of burden. **2.** the fine, soft fleece of the llama, combined with the wool for coating. [t. Sp., t. Quechua]

Llama, *Lama guanicoe* (4 ft high at shoulder, length 4 to 5 ft)

Llandudno (lăn dĭd′nō), *n.* a town in Wales, in Caernarvonshire: seaside resort. 17,904 (1961).

Llanelly (lă nĕth′lĭ), *n.* a seaport in Wales, in Carmarthenshire. 29,979 (1961).

llano (lä′nō, lyä′nō; *Sp.* lyä′nô), *n.*, *pl.* **-nos** (-nōz; *Sp.* -nôs). (in Spanish America) an extensive grassy plain with few trees. [t. Sp.: a plain, as adj., flat, level, g. L *plānus* PLAIN[1]]

Llano Estacado (lä′nō ĕs′tə kä′dō), a large plateau in W Texas and SE New Mexico: cattle-grazing region. 1000–5000 ft high. Also, **Staked Plain.**

LL.B., (L *Legum Baccalaureus*) Bachelor of Laws.

LL.D., (L *Legum Doctor*) Doctor of Laws.

LL.M., (L *Legum Magister*) Master of Laws.

Lloyd (loid), *n.* **1. Harold (Clayton),** born 1894, U.S. comic film actor. **2. Marie** (mä′rĭ) (*Matilda Alice Victoria Wood*), 1870–1922, English music-hall comedienne.

Lloyd George (loid′ jôj′), **David** (*1st Earl of Dwyfor*), 1863–1945, British statesman: prime minister 1916–22.

Lloyd's (loidz), *n.* an association of English insurance underwriters, founded in 1688, originally to arrange marine insurance, but now issuing policies on nearly all types of insurance. [named after Edward *Lloyd*, 1688–1726, who opened a coffee-house where the original insurers met]

Lloyd's List, a periodical of shipping intelligence, issued by Lloyd's continuously since 1734; now a daily newspaper.

Lloyd's Register of Shipping, 1. an independent society of shipowners, merchants and underwriters, who supervise the construction of ships, and survey them during their use. **2.** an annual register, issued by the society, containing particulars of all known seagoing vessels.

Llyn Tegid (thlĭn′ tā′gĭd), Welsh name of **Bala Lake.**

lm, *Optics.* lumen.

LMP, *Med.* last menstrual period.

L.M.S., 1. London Missionary Society. 2. (before 1948) London, Midland and Scottish (Railway).

L.N.E.R., (before 1948) London and North Eastern Railway.

lo (lō), *interj.* look! see! behold! [ME; OE *lā!* lo! behold! c. Goth. *laian* revile, Icel. *lā* scold]

loach (lōch), *n.* any of various slender European and Asiatic freshwater fishes of the family *Cobitidae*, with several barbels about a small mouth: related to the minnows. [ME *loch*, t. OF: m. *loche*; ? of Celtic orig.]

load (lōd), *n.* **1.** that which is laid on or placed in anything for conveyance. **2.** the quantity that can be or usually is carried, as in a cart; this quantity taken as a unit of measure or weight. **3.** anything upborne or sustained: *the load of fruit on a tree.* **4.** something that weighs down or oppresses like a burden. **5.** the charge of a firearm. **6.** (*pl.*) *Colloq.* a great quantity or number: *loads of people.* **7.** the weight supported by a structure or part. **8.** *Elect.* the power delivered by a generator, motor, power station, or transformer (often fol. by *on*). **9.** *Mech.* the external resistance overcome by an engine, dynamo, or the like, under a given condition, measured by the power required. **10.** *U.S. Slang.* a sufficient quantity of liquor drunk to intoxicate. **11. get a load of,** *Slang.* **a.** to look at; observe. **b.** to listen; to hear. —*v.t.* **12.** to put a load on or in: *to load a cart.* **13.** to supply abundantly or excessively with something: *to load a person with gifts.* **14.** to weigh down, burden, or oppress. **15.** to add to the weight of, often fraudulently, as metals. **16.** to make (dice) heavier on one side than on the others by fraudulent means so as to cause them to fall with a particular face upwards. **17.** *Insurance.* to add to the net premium. See **loading** (def. 5). **18.** to take on as a load: *a vessel loading coal.* **19.** to charge a firearm. **20.** *Physics.* to add additional material to (concrete) containing elements of high atomic number, esp. iron or lead, for use in shielding a nuclear reactor. **21.** *Photog.* to insert a film or plate in a camera. **22. load the dice,** to place in an especially favourable or unfavourable position. —*v.i.* **23.** to put on or take on a load. **24.** to load a firearm. **25.** to become loaded. **26.** to enter a means of conveyance: *the football fans loaded into the special train.* **27.** *Photog.* to load a camera. **28.** *Physics.* to load concrete. [ME *lode*; orig. the same word as LODE (OE *lād* way, source, carrying), but now differential in spelling and sense, and assoc. with LADE] —**load′er,** *n.*

—**Syn. 4.** LOAD, BURDEN referred originally to something placed on a person or animal or put into a vehicle for conveyance; LOAD has still retained this concrete meaning, BURDEN has lost it, except in such fixed phrases as: *beast of burden,* and *a ship of 1500 tons burden* (carrying capacity). Both words have come to be used figuratively to refer to duties, cares, etc., that are oppressively heavy and this is now the main meaning of BURDEN: *you have taken a load off my mind; some children are a burden.*

load displacement, *Naut.* the amount of water displaced by a ship when it is fully loaded.

loaded (lō′dĭd), *adj.* **1.** carrying or bearing a load. **2.** charged with ammunition. **3.** (of a question, statement, etc.) unfair; weighted so as to produce a prejudicial effect. **4.** (of dice) fraudulently weighted so as to produce certain combinations. **5.** *Slang.* very wealthy.

load factor, *Elect.* the ratio of the average load over a designated period of time to the peak load occurring in that period.

loading (lō′dĭng), *n.* **1.** the act of one who or that which loads. **2.** that with which something is loaded; a load; a burden; a charge. **3.** *Elect.* the process of adding inductances to a telephone circuit, radio aerial, etc. **4.** the ratio of the gross weight of an aeroplane to engine power (**power-loading**), wing span (**span-loading**), or wing area (**wing-loading**). **5.** *Insurance.* an addition to the net mathematical premium, to cover expenses and contingencies and to allow for a margin of safety.

loading coil, *Elect.* an inductance coil used to improve the characteristics of a transmission line.

load line, *Naut.* one of several lines on the side of a ship, as the Plimsoll line, established by statute and indicating the maximum legal draught for a certain set of conditions.

loadstar (lōd′stä′), *n.* lodestar.

loadstone (lōd′stōn′), *n.* **1.** a variety of magnetite which possesses magnetic polarity and attracts iron. **2.** a piece of this serving as a magnet. **3.** something that attracts. Also, **lodestone.** [f. LOAD + STONE]

loaf[1] (lōf), *n., pl.* **loaves** (lōvz). **1.** a portion of bread or cake baked in a mass of definite form. **2.** a shaped or moulded mass of food, as of sugar, chopped meat, etc.: *a veal loaf.* **3.** *Slang.* brains; intelligence. [ME *lo(o)f*, OE *hlāf* loaf, bread, c. G *Laib*]

loaf[2] (lōf), *v.i.* **1.** to lounge or saunter lazily and idly. **2.** to idle away time. —*v.t.* **3.** to idle (usually fol. by *away*): *to loaf one's life away.* [back-formation from LOAFER]

loafer (lō′fə), *n.* **1.** an idler; one who does no work. **2.** *U.S.* a casual, moccasin-like shoe. [prob. t. G: m. *(Land)läufer* tramp, vagabond]

loam (lōm), *n.* **1.** a loose soil composed of clay and sand, esp. a kind containing organic matter and of great fertility. **2.** a mixture of clay, sand, straw, etc., used in making moulds for founding, and in plastering walls, stopping holes, etc. **3.** *Archaic.* earth. **4.** *Obs.* clay. —*v.t.* **5.** to cover or stop with loam. [ME *lome, lam(e)*, OE *lām*, c. D *leem*, G *Lehm* loam, clay] —**loam′y,** *adj.*

loan (lōn), *n.* **1.** the act of lending; a grant of the use of something temporarily: *the loan of a book.* **2.** something lent or furnished on condition of being returned, esp. a sum of money lent at interest. —*v.t.* **3.** to make a loan of; lend. **4.** to lend (money) at interest. —*v.i.* **5.** to make a loan or loans. [ME *lon(e), lan(e)*, OE *lān*, appar. t. Scand.; cf. Icel. *lān*, c. OE *lǣn* loan, grant] —**loan′er,** *n.*

loan collection, a number of works of art, lent by their owners for a single or long-term exhibition.

Loanda (lō ăn′də; *Port.* lwən′də), *n.* Luanda.

loan office, **1.** an office for making loans. **2.** a pawnbroker's shop. **3.** a public office for receiving subscriptions to a government loan.

loan shark, *Colloq.* one who loans money at an excessive rate of interest.

loan word, a word of one language adopted into another at any period in history. Examples: *wine* (into Old English from Latin), *blitz* (into Modern English from German). [trans. of G *Lehnwort*]

loath (lōth), *adj.* **1.** reluctant, averse, or unwilling. **2.** **nothing loath,** very willingly. Also, **loth.** [ME *lothe*, OE *lāth* hostile, hateful, c. Icel. *leidhr* loathed, D *leed*, G *Leid* sorrow] —**Syn.** **1.** See **reluctant.**

loathe (lōth), *v.t.* **1.** to feel hatred, disgust, or intense aversion for. **2.** to feel a physical disgust for (food, etc.). [ME *lothien*, OE *lāthian* be hateful, der. *lāth* LOATH] —**loath′er,** *n.* —**Syn.** **1.** abominate, detest.

loathing (lō′thĭng), *n.* **1.** strong dislike mingled with disgust; intense aversion. **2.** physical disgust, as for food. —**loath′ingly,** *adv.* —**Syn.** **1.** See **aversion.**

loathly[1] (lōth′lĭ), *adv.* reluctantly; unwillingly. [f. LOATH + -LY]

loathly[2] (lōth′lĭ), *adj.* *Archaic.* loathsome. [f. LOATHE + -LY]

loathsome (lōth′səm), *adj.* **1.** such as to excite loathing; hateful; disgusting. **2.** physically disgusting; sickening. —**loath′somely,** *adv.* —**loath′someness,** *n.*

loaves (lōvz), *n.* pl. of **loaf**[1].

lob[1] (lŏb), *n., v.,* **lobbed, lobbing.** —*n.* **1.** *Tennis.* a ball struck high to the back of the opponent's court. **2.** *Cricket.* a slow underhand ball. —*v.t.* **3.** *Tennis.* to strike (a ball) high into the air to the back of the opponent's court. **4.** *Cricket.* to bowl with a slow movement. —*v.i.* **5.** *Tennis.* to lob a ball. **6.** *Cricket.* to bowl a lob. [ME *lobbe* pollack; later, bumpkin; as v., move clumsily. See LUBBER]

lob[2] (lŏb), *n.* lobworm.

lobar (lō′bə), *adj.* of or pertaining to a lobe, as of the lungs: *lobar pneumonia.*

lobate (lō′bāt), *adj.* **1.** having a lobe or lobes; lobed. **2.** having the form of a lobe. **3.** *Ornithol.* denoting or pertaining to a foot in which the individual toes have membranous flaps along the sides. Also, **lo′bated.** [t. NL: m. s. *lobātus*, der. LL *lobus* LOBE] —**lo′bately,** *adv.*

lobation (lō bā′shən), *n.* **1.** lobate formation. **2.** a lobe.

lobby (lŏb′ĭ), *n., pl.* **-bies,** *v.,* **-bied, -bying.** —*n.* **1.** a corridor, vestibule, or entrance hall, as in a public building, often serving as an anteroom. **2.** the persons who frequent a legislative lobby or chamber, esp. to influence the members. —*v.i.* **3.** to frequent the lobby of a legislative chamber to influence the members. **4.** to solicit the votes of members of a legislative body in the lobby or elsewhere. —*v.t.* **5.** to influence (legislators), or urge or procure the passage of (a bill), by lobbying. [t. ML: m. s. *lobia, lobium* covered walk; of Gmc origin (cf. G *Laube* an arbour). See LODGE]

lobby correspondent, the parliamentary correspondent of a newspaper, etc.

lobbyism (lŏb′ĭ ĭz′əm), *n.* *U.S.* **1.** the system of lobbying. **2.** the practices of those who lobby. —**lob′byist,** *n.*

lobe (lōb), *n.* **1.** a roundish projection or division, as of an organ, a leaf, etc. **2.** *Anat.* the soft pendulous lower part of the external ear. See diag. under **ear.** **3.** *Electronics.* a part of the energy radiated from a directional aerial. [t. F, t. LL: m. s. *lobus*, t. Gk: m. *lobós*]

lobed (lōbd), *adj.* **1.** having a lobe or lobes; lobate. **2.** *Bot.* (of a leaf) having lobes or divisions extending less than halfway to the middle of the base.

lobelia (lō bē′lyə), *n.* any of the herbaceous plants constituting the genus *Lobelia*, comprising many species, both wild and cultivated, with blue, red, yellow, or white flowers. [t. NL, named after M. de *Lobel*, 1538–1616, Flemish botanist, physician to James I of England]

Lobengula (lō′bən gyōō′lə), *n.* ?1836–94, Matabele king 1868–93.

Lobito (*Port.* lōō bē′tōō), *n.* a seaport in W Angola. 50,164 (1960).

loblolly (lŏb′lŏl′ĭ), *n., pl.* **-ies.** **1.** *Naut.* a thick gruel. **2.** a pine, *Pinus taeda*, of the southern U.S. **3.** the wood of this tree. Also, **loblolly pine** (for defs 2, 3). [prob. f. d. *lob* sup noisily + *lolly* gruel]

loblolly boy, *Obs.* the attendant of a ship's surgeon.

lobo (lō′bō), *n., pl.* **-bos.** a large grey wolf of the western U.S. [t. Sp., g. L *lupus* wolf]

lobola (lō′bə lə), *n.* (in S Africa) the custom among certain native peoples whereby a bridegroom makes a gift of cattle or cash to his prospective parents-in-law. [t. Zulu]

lobotomy (lō bŏt′ə mĭ), *n.* *Surg., Chiefly U.S.* leucotomy.

lobscouse (lŏb′skous′), *n.* *Naut.* a stew of meat, potatoes, onions, ship biscuit, etc. [Cf. Dan. *lapscous*, D *lapskous.* See LOBLOLLY]

lobster (lŏb′stə), *n.* **1.** any of various large, edible, marine, stalk-eyed, decapod crustaceans of the family *Homaridae*, esp. of the genus *Homarus.* **2.** the spiny lobster. **3.** any of various similar crustaceans, as certain crayfishes. [ME *lobster, lop(i)ster*, OE *loppestre*, der. *loppe* spider (both creatures having many projecting parts). See LOP[1], -STER]

Lobster, *Homarus vulgaris* (Up to 20 in. long)

lobster Newburg (nyōō′bûg), sliced cooked lobster, sautéed in butter, cooked in thick cream and sherry.

lobster pot, a trap in which lobsters are caught.

lobster thermidor (thû′mĭ dô′), boiled lobster, replaced in its shell, served with sauce and grated cheese.

lobule (lŏb′yōōl), *n.* **1.** a small lobe. **2.** a subdivision of a lobe. [t. NL: m. s. *lobulus*, dim. of LL *lobus* LOBE] —**lob′ular,** *adj.*

lobworm (lŏb′wûm′), *n.* the lugworm. Also, **lob.**

local (lō′kl), *adj.* **1.** pertaining to or characterized by place, or position in space: *local situation.* **2.** pertaining to, characteristic of, or restricted to a particular place or particular places: *a local custom.* **3.** pertaining to a town or a small district rather than the entire state or country. **4.** pertaining to or affecting a particular part or particular parts, as of a system or object: *a local disease.* **5.** (of an aesthesia or an anaesthetic) acting on only a section of the body, without loss of consciousness. **6.** stopping at all stations: *a local train.* —*n.* **7.** a local train, bus, etc. **8.** a newspaper item of local interest. **9.** *U.S.* a local branch of a union, fraternity, etc. **10.** a public house in the neighbourhood of one's home or place of work. **11.** a local inhabitant. **12.** a local anaesthetic. [ME, t. LL: s. *locālis*, der. L *locus* place]

local authority, the body of people, both elected and paid workers, responsible for the administration of local government.

local colour, 1. distinctive characteristics or peculiarities of a place or period as represented in literature, drama, etc., or observed in reality. 2. the natural colour of any particular object or part in a picture.

locale (lō käl′), *n.* a place or locality, esp. with reference to events or circumstances connected with it. [t. F: m. *local*, n. use of adj. See LOCAL, adj.]

local government, the administration of the local affairs of a town, county, etc., by officers elected by the residents of such a town, county, etc.

localism (lō′kə lĭz′əm), *n.* **1.** a manner of speaking, pronunciation, usage, or inflection that is peculiar to one locality. **2.** a local custom. **3.** attachment to a particular locality. **4.** provincialism.

locality (lō kăl′ĭ tĭ), *n., pl.* **-ties. 1.** a place, spot, or district, with or without reference to things or persons in it. **2.** the place in which a thing is or occurs. **3.** state or condition of being local or having place.

localize (lō′kə līz′), *v.t.*, **-lized, -lizing.** to make local; fix in, or assign or restrict to, a particular place or locality. Also, **localise.** —**lo′caliz′able,** *adj.* —**lo′caliza′tion,** *n.*

localizer beacon, *Aeron.* a directional radio beacon which provides an aircraft with an indication of its lateral position while landing. Also, **approach beacon.**

locally (lō′kə lĭ), *adv.* **1.** in a particular place, or places. **2.** with regard to place. **3.** in a local respect.

local oscillator, *Electronics.* an oscillator in a receiver, whose output is mixed with a signal borne by a carrier wave in order to alter the frequency of the carrier.

local time, the time at any given place on earth as determined from the position of the sun only; it is **local noon** when the sun crosses the meridian and shadows are at their shortest.

Locarno (lō kä′nō; *It.* lȯ kȧr′nȯ), *n.* a town in S Switzerland, on Lake Maggiore: treaty, 1925. 15,000 (est. 1960).

locate (lō kāt′), *v.*, **-cated, -cating.** —*v.t.* **1.** to discover the place or location of: *to locate a leak in a pipe.* **2.** to set, fix, or establish in a place, situation, or locality; place; settle: *to locate one's headquarters in London.* **3.** *U.S.* to enter a claim to (a tract of land); to take up (land). **4.** to refer (something), as by opinion or statement, to a particular place: *locate the garden of Eden in Babylonia.* —*v.i.* **5.** *U.S.* to establish oneself in a place; settle. [t. L: m. s. *locātus*, pp., placed]

location (lō kā′shən), *n.* **1.** a place of settlement or residence: *a good location for a doctor.* **2.** a place or situation occupied: *a house in a fine location.* **3.** a tract of land located, or of designated situation or limits: *a mining location.* **4.** (in South Africa and elsewhere) an area set aside for the native population. **5.** *Films.* a place, outside the studio, affording suitable environment for photographing particular plays, incidents, etc. **6.** the act of locating; state of being located. **7.** *Civil Law.* a letting or lease (from the point of view of the lessor). **8.** *Computers.* a specific register in the high-speed memory of a computer.

locative (lŏk′ə tĭv), *Gram.* —*adj.* **1.** (in some inflected languages) denoting a case, having as chief function indication of place in or at which, as Latin *domī* 'at home'. —*n.* **2.** the locative case. **3.** a word in that case. [t. ML: m. s. *locātīvus.* See LOCATE, -IVE]

locator (lō kā′tə), *n. U.S.* one who fixes the boundaries of a land or mining claim. [t. L]

loc. cit., loco citato.

loch (lŏk, lŏKH), *n. Scot.* **1.** a lake. **2.** Also, **sea loch.** an arm of the sea, esp. when partially landlocked. [t. Gaelic. Cf. LOUGH]

Lochgilphead (lŏk′gĭlp′hĕd′, lŏKH′-), *n.* a burgh in Scotland, the county town of Argyll. 1208 (1961).

lochia (lŏk′ĭ ə), *n.pl. Med.* the liquid discharge from the uterus after childbirth. [t. NL, t. Gk: neut. pl. of *lóchios* pertaining to childbirth] —**lochial** (lŏk′ĭ əl), *adj.*

Lochner (*Ger.* lŏKH′nər), *n.* **Stefan** (*Ger.* shtĕ′fȧn), died 1451, German painter.

Loch Ness monster, a monster supposed to inhabit Loch Ness.

loci (lō′sī), *n.* pl. of **locus.**

lock[1] (lŏk), *n.* **1.** a device for securing a door, gate, lid, drawer, or the like, in position when closed, consisting of a bolt or system of bolts propelled and withdrawn by a mechanism operated by a key, dial, etc. **2.** a device to keep a wheel from rotating, as in descending a hill. **3.** a contrivance for fastening or securing something. **4.** the mechanism in a firearm by means of which it can be kept from operating. **5.** an enclosed portion of a canal, river, etc., with gates at each end, for raising or lowering vessels from one level to another. **6.** any of various grapples or holds in wrestling, esp. any hold in which an arm or leg of one wrestler is held about the body of his opponent. **7.** *Rugby Football.* Also, **lock forward.** the player in the back row of the scrum who binds the second-row forwards together. **8. lock, stock, and barrel,** altogether; completely. —*v.t.* **9.** to fasten or secure (a door, building, etc.) by the operation of a lock. **10.** to shut in a place fastened by a lock or locks, as for security or restraining (fol. by *up, in,* etc.): *to lock a prisoner in a cell.* **11.** to exclude by or as by a lock (usually fol. by *out*). **12.** to make fast or immovable by or as by a lock: *to lock a wheel.* **13.** to fasten or fix firmly, as by engaging parts (often fol. by *up*). **14.** *Print.* to make (type, etc.) immovable in a chase by securing the quoins (fol. by *up*). **15.** to join or unite firmly by interlinking or intertwining: *to lock arms.* **16.** to move (a ship) by means of a lock or locks, as in a canal. **17.** to furnish with locks, as a canal. **18.** to enclose (a waterway) with a lock (fol. by *off*). —*v.i.* **19.** to become locked: *this door locks with a key.* **20.** to become fastened, fixed, or interlocked. **21.** to go or pass by means of a lock or locks, as a vessel. **22.** to construct locks in waterways. [ME; OE *loc* fastening; akin to OE *lūcan*, D *luiken*, Icel. *lūka*, Goth. *galūkan* shut, close]

lock[2] (lŏk), *n.* **1.** a tress or portion of hair. **2.** (*pl.*) the hair of the head. **3.** a flock or small portion of wool, cotton, flax, etc. [ME *locke*, OE *locc* lock of hair, c. Icel. *lokkr*, D *lok* curl, G *Locke*]

lockage (lŏk′ĭj), *n.* **1.** the construction, use, or operation of locks, as in a canal or stream. **2.** passage through a lock or locks. **3.** toll paid for such passage.

Locke (lŏk), *n.* **John,** 1632–1704, English philosopher.

locker (lŏk′ə), *n.* **1.** a chest, drawer, compartment, closet, or the like, that may be locked. **2.** *Naut.* a chest or compartment in which to stow things. **3.** one who or that which locks.

locket (lŏk′ĭt), *n.* a small case for a miniature portrait, a lock of hair, or other keepsake, usually worn on a chain hung round the neck. [ME, t. F: m. *loquet* latch, catch, dim. of OF *loc* lock, t. Gmc; cf. LOCK[1]]

lock-gate (lŏk′gāt′), *n.* a gate at each end of a lock (def. 5).

lockjaw (lŏk′jô′), *n. Pathol.* tetanus in which the jaws become firmly locked together.

locknit (lŏk′nĭt′), *Textiles.* —*n.* **1.** a type of close-knitted fabric designed so that it will not run. —*adj.* **2.** of or pertaining to a locknit fabric. Also, **lock-knit.**

locknut (lŏk′nŭt′), *n.* **1.** a supplementary nut screwed down upon another to prevent it from shaking loose. **2.** a nut in which spontaneous motion is prevented by springs fitting between the threads, or by interlocking parts.

lockout (lŏk′out′), *n.* the closing of a business, or wholesale dismissal of employees by the employer because the employees refuse to accept his terms or because the employer refuses to operate on terms set by a union.

locksmith (lŏk′smĭth′), *n.* one who makes or mends locks.

lockstitch (lŏk′stĭch′), *n.* a sewing-machine stitch in which two threads are locked together at small intervals.

lockup (lŏk′ŭp′), *n.* **1.** a jail. **2.** the act of locking up. **3.** a garage or other storage space, usually rented, capable of being locked up.

Lockyer (lŏk′yə), *n.* **Sir Joseph Norman,** 1836–1920, English astronomer.

loco[1] (lō′kō), *n.* a locomotive.

loco[2] (lō′kō), *n., pl.* **-cos,** *v.*, **-coed, -coing,** *adj. U.S.* —*n.* **1.** locoweed. **2.** *Slang.* a mad or crazy person. —*v.t.* **3.** to poison with locoweed. **4.** to make crazy. —*adj.* **5.** *Slang.* insane; crazy. [t. Sp.: insane, g. L *glaucus* sparkling]

loco citato (lō′kō sī tä′tō), *Latin.* in the place, or passage already mentioned. *Abbrev.:* loc. cit.

loco disease, *U.S.* a disease affecting the brain of animals, caused by eating locoweed.

locomotion (lō′kə mō′shən), *n.* the act or power of moving from place to place. [f. L *locō*, abl. of *locus* place + MOTION]

locomotive (lō′kə mō′tĭv), *n.* **1.** a self-propelled vehicle running on a railway track, designed to pull railway carriages or trucks. **2.** any self-propelled vehicle. —*adj.* **3.** moving or travelling by means of its own mechanism or powers. **4.** serving to produce such movement, or adapted for or used in locomotion: *locomotive organs.* **5.** of or pertaining to movement from place to place. **6.** having the power of locomotion. [f. L *locō*, abl. of *locus* place + MOTIVE, *adj.*]

locomotor (*adj.* lō′kə mō′tə; *n.* lō′kə mō′tə), *adj.* **1.** of or pertaining to locomotion. —*n.* **2.** one who or that which has locomotive power.

locomotor ataxia (ə tăk′sĭ ə), *Pathol.* a degenerative disease of the spinal cord, marked by loss of control over the muscular movements, mainly in walking.

locoweed (lō′kō wēd′), *n.* any of various fabaceous plants of the genera *Astragalus* and *Oxytropis* of the southwestern U.S., producing loco disease in sheep, horses, etc. [f. LOCO[2] + WEED[1]]

Locris (lō′krĭs), *n.* either of two districts in the central part of ancient Greece. —**Locrian** (lō′krĭ ən), *n.*

locular (lŏk′yŏŏ lə), *adj.* having one or more loculi, chambers, or cells. [t. LL: s. *loculāris* kept in boxes, der. L *loculus* box, cell]

loculate (lŏk′yŏŏ lāt′, -lĭt), *adj. Bot.* having one or more loculi. Also, **loc′ulat′ed.** [t. L: m. s. *loculātus* furnished with compartments]

loculus (lŏk′yŏŏ ləs), *n., pl.* **-li** (-lī′). **1.** *Bot., Zool., Anat.* a small compartment or chamber; a cell. **2.** *Bot.* **a.** the cell of a carpel in which the seed is contained. **b.** the cell of an anther in which the pollen is contained. [t. L: a little place, box, dim. of *locus* place]

locum tenens (lō′kəm tē′nĕnz), a temporary substitute, esp. for a clergyman or doctor. Also, **locum.** [ML]

locus (lō′kəs), *n., pl.* **loci** (lō′sī). **1.** a place; a locality. **2.** *Maths.* a curve or other figure considered as generated by a point, line, or surface, which moves or is placed according to a definite law. **3.** *Genetics.* the chromosomal position of a gene as determined by its linear order relative to the other genes on that chromosome. [t. L: place]

locus classicus (lō′kəs klăs′ĭ kəs), *Latin.* a passage commonly cited to illustrate or explain a subject.

locus sigilli (lō′kəs sĭ jĭl′ī), *Latin.* the place of the seal (on a document, etc.). *Abbrev.:* L.S.

locust (lō′kəst), *n.* **1.** any of the grasshoppers with short antennae which constitute the family *Acrididae,* including the notorious migratory species, such as *Locusta migratoria* of the Old World, which swarm in immense numbers and strip the vegetation from large areas. **2.** a thorny-branched, white-flowered American fabaceous tree, *Robinia pseudoacacia.* **3.** its durable wood. **4.** any of various other trees, as the carob and the honey-locust. [ME, t. L: s. *locusta* locust, lobster]

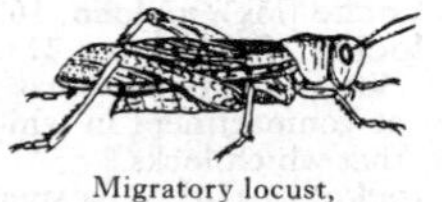
Migratory locust, *Locusta migratoria* (2 in. long)

locusta (lō kŭs′tə), *n., pl.* **-tae** (-tē). *Bot.* the spikelet of grasses. [t. NL, special use of L *locusta* LOCUST]

locution (lō kyōō′shən), *n.* **1.** a particular form of expression; a phrase or expression. **2.** style of speech or verbal expression; phraseology. [ME, t. L: s. *locūtio*]

Loddon (lŏd′n), *n.* a river in Australia flowing N through Victoria to the Little Murray river. 210 mi.

loddon lily (lŏd′n), an amaryllidaceous, bulbous plant with narrow leaves and small groups of pendulous flowers having white, green-tipped perianth parts, *Leucojum aestivum,* found in wet places in Europe and W Asia but frequently cultivated elsewhere.

lode (lōd), *n.* **1.** a veinlike deposit, usually metalliferous. **2.** any body of ore set off from adjacent rock formations. [ME; OE *lād* way, course, carrying (see LOAD), c. OHG *leita* procession, Icel. *leidh* way, course]

lodestar (lōd′stä′), *n.* **1.** a star that shows the way. **2.** Polaris. **3.** something that serves as a guide or on which the attention is fixed. Also, **loadstar.** [ME *loode sterre.* See LOAD, LODE, STAR, n.]

lodestone (lōd′stōn′), *n.* loadstone.

lodge (lŏj), *n., v.,* **lodged, lodging.** —*n.* **1.** a small, slight, or rude shelter or habitation, as of boughs, poles, skins, earth, rough boards, or the like; cabin or hut. **2.** a house used as a temporary abode, as in the hunting season. **3.** *U.S.* a summer cottage. **4.** a house or cottage, as in a park or on an estate, occupied by a gatekeeper, caretaker, gardener, or the like. **5.** a room or rooms in the main gate of a college of a university kept by a porter for inquiries, etc. **6.** a place of abode or sojourn. **7.** the meeting place of a branch of a secret society. **8.** the members composing the branch. **9.** the residence of a college head or master at Cambridge University. **10.** *U.S.* an Indian habitation. **11.** den or habitation of an animal or animals, esp. beavers. —*v.i.* **12.** to have a habitation or quarters, esp. temporarily, as in a place or house. **13.** to live in hired quarters in another's house. **14.** to be fixed or implanted, or be caught in a place or position. —*v.t.* **15.** to furnish with a habitation or quarters, esp. temporarily. **16.** to furnish with a room or rooms in one's house for payment, or have as a lodger. **17.** to serve as a habitation or shelter for, as a house does; shelter; harbour. **18.** to put or deposit, as in a place, for storage or keeping. **19.** to bring or send into a particular place or position: *to lodge a bullet in one's heart.* **20.** to vest (power, etc.). **21.** to lay (information, a complaint, etc.) before a court or the like. **22.** to beat down or lay flat, as vegetation in a storm. **23.** to track (a deer) to its lair. [ME *loge,* t. OF: hut, orig. leafy shelter, t. Gmc (cf. OHG *lauba* arbour)]

Lodge (lŏj), *n.* **1. Henry Cabot** (kăb′ət), 1850–1924, U.S. political leader; senator 1893–1924. **2. Sir Oliver (Joseph),** 1851–1940, English physicist and writer. **3. Thomas,** *c.* 1558–1625, English dramatist and writer.

lodgement (lŏj′mənt), *n.* **1.** act of lodging. **2.** state of being lodged. **3.** something lodged or deposited. **4.** *Mil.* a position or foothold gained from an enemy, or an entrenchment made upon it. **5.** *Rare.* a lodging place; lodgings. Also, *U.S.,* **lodgment.**

lodger (lŏj′ə), *n.* one who lives in hired quarters in another's house.

lodging (lŏj′ĭng), *n.* **1.** accommodation in a house, esp. in rooms for hire: *to furnish board and lodging.* **2.** a place of abode, esp. a temporary one. **3.** (*pl.*) a room or rooms hired for residence in another's house. **4.** (*pl.*) the residence of the head or master of a college at Oxford University.

lodging house, a house in which lodgings are let, esp. a house other than an inn or hotel.

Lodi (*It.* lŏ′dē), *n.* a town in N Italy, in Lombardy: Napoleon defeated the Austrians near here, 1796. 38,321 (1961).

lodicule (lŏd′ĭ kyōōl′), *n. Bot.* a small turgid scale found in some grass flowers.

Lódz (*Pol.* wōōch), *n.* a city in central Poland 740,000 (est. 1965). Russian, **Lodz** (*Russ.* lôdz).

Loeb (lûb; *Ger.* lœb), *n.* **Jacques** (*Ger.* zhȧk), 1859–1924, German physiologist and experimental biologist in U.S.

loess (lō′ĭs; *Ger.* lœs), *n.* a loamy deposit formed by wind, usually yellowish and calcareous, common in Europe and Asia, and in the Mississippi valley in the United States. [t. G]

Lofoten Islands (lō fō′tn; *Norw.* lōō′fōō tən), a group of islands NW of and belonging to Norway: rich fishing grounds. 28,268 pop. (est. 1965); 474 sq. mi.

loft (lŏft), *n.* **1.** the space between the underside of a roof and the ceiling of a room beneath it. **2.** a gallery or upper level in a church, hall, etc., designed for a special purpose: *a choir loft.* **3.** a hayloft. **4.** *U.S.* any upper storey of a warehouse, mercantile building, or factory, esp. of buildings designed for small, light industries. **5.** *U.S.* a building consisting of such lofts. **6.** *Golf.* **a.** the slope of the face of a club backwards from the vertical, tending to drive the ball upwards. **b.** the act of lofting. **c.** a lofting stroke. —*v.t.* **7.** *Golf.* **a.** to slant the face of (a club). **b.** to hit (a ball) into the air or over an obstacle. **c.** to clear (an obstacle) thus. **8.** *U.S.* to provide (a house, etc.) with a loft. —*v.i.* **9.** *Golf.* to loft the ball. [ME *lofte,* late OE *loft,* t. Scand.; cf. Icel. *lopt* the air, sky, an upper room; akin to LIFT²]

lofting iron (lŏf′tĭng), *Golf.* an iron-headed club used in lofting the ball. Also, **loft′er.**

lofty (lŏf′tĭ), *adj.,* **-tier, -tiest. 1.** extending high in the air; of imposing height: *lofty mountains.* **2.** exalted in rank, dignity, or character. **3.** elevated in style or sentiment, as writings, etc. **4.** haughty; proud. —**loft′ily,** *adv.* —**loft′iness,** *n.* —**Syn. 1.** See **high.**

log (lŏg), *n., v.,* **logged, logging.** —*n.* **1.** an unhewn portion or length of the trunk or a large limb of a felled tree. **2.** something inert or heavy. **3.** *Naut.* **a.** a device for determining the speed of and distance covered by a ship. **b. chip log,** a chip (**logchip**) attached to the end of a line (**logline**) thrown over the stern to measure the speed of a ship. **c. patent log,** a screw-shaped implement on the end of a line trailing astern which indicates speed and distance. **4. a.** the official record which a ship's master is obliged by law to keep, of particulars of a ship's voyage, as weather, crew, cargo, etc. **b.** the record which the engine-room and bridge officers keep of the particulars of each watch. **5.** a listing of navigational, meteorological, and other significant data concerning an air journey. **6.** the register of the operation of a machine. **7.** a record kept of development during the drilling of a well, esp. of the geological formations penetrated. —*v.t.* **8.** to cut (trees) into logs. **9.** to cut down the trees or timber on (land). **10.** *Naut.* **a.** to enter in a ship's log. **b.** to record in a ship's log a punishment given to (a seaman). **11.** *Chiefly Naut.* to travel (a distance) according to the indication of a log. —*v.i.* **12.** to cut down trees and get out logs from the forest for timber. [ME *logge*; appar. var. of LUG³ pole]

log., logarithm.

Logan (lō′gən), *n.* **Mount,** a mountain in W Canada, in SW Yukon Territory: the second highest peak in North America. 19,850 ft.

loganberry (lō′gən bə rĭ, -brĭ), *n., pl.* **-ries. 1.** the large, dark red, acid fruit of the plant *Rubus loganobaccus,* with long prostrate canes. **2.** the plant itself. [named after J. H. *Logan,* 1841–1928, of California, by whom first grown]

loganiaceous (lō gā′nĭ ā′shəs), *adj.* belonging to the *Loganiaceae,* a family of herbs, shrubs, and trees of tropical and subtropical regions, including the nux vomica tree and other plants with poisonous properties. [f. s. NL *Logania*, the typical genus (named after James *Logan*, 1674–1751, of Philadelphia) + -ACEOUS]

logaoedic (lŏg′ə ē′dĭk), *Pros.* *—adj.* **1.** composed of dactyls and trochees or of anapaests and iambs, producing a movement somewhat suggestive of prose. *—n.* **2.** a logaoedic verse. [t. LL: s. *logaoedicus*, t. Gk: m. *logaoidikós*, f. s. *lógos* prose + s. *aoidḗ* song + *-ikos* -IC]

logarithm (lŏg′ə rĭth′əm), *n.* *Maths.* the exponent of that power to which a fixed number (called the *base*) must be raised in order to produce a given number (called the *antilogarithm*): *3 is the logarithm of 8 to the base 2.* [t. NL: s. *logarithmus*, f. Gk: s. *lógos* proportion + m. *arithmós* number]

logarithmic (lŏg′ə rĭth′mĭk), *adj.* pertaining to a logarithm or logarithms. Also, **log′arith′mical.** —**log′arith′mically,** *adv.*

logarithmic scale, a scale of measurement in which an increase of one unit represents a logarithmic increase (usually tenfold) in the quantity measured.

logbook (lŏg′bo͝ok′), *n.* **1.** *Naut.* **a.** a book in which are officially recorded the indications of the log. **b.** the record itself. **2.** registration book.

logchip (lŏg′chĭp′), *n.* See **log** (def. 3b). Also, **logship.**

loge (lōzh; *Fr.* lŏzh), *n.* a box in a theatre or opera house. [t. F. See LODGE]

logger (lŏg′ə), *n.* the person who cuts trees into suitable lengths after the trees have been felled.

loggerhead (lŏg′ə hĕd′), *n.* **1.** a thick-headed or stupid person; a blockhead. **2.** Also, **loggerhead turtle.** a large-headed marine turtle, *Caretta caretta*, of all oceans. **3.** Also, **loggerhead shrike.** a common North American butcher-bird, *Lanius ludovicianus*, grey above, white below, with black and white wings and tail and black facial mask. **4.** a ball or bulb of iron with a long handle, used, after being heated, to melt tar, heat liquids, etc. **5.** a rounded post in the stern of a whaleboat, around which the harpoon line is passed. **6. at loggerheads,** engaged in dispute. [back-formation from *loggerheaded*, var. of obs. *log-headed* stupid]

loggia (lŏj′ə, lŏj′ĭ ə; *It.* lôd′jȧ), *n., pl.* **-gias;** *It.* **-gie** (*It.* -jĕ). **1.** a gallery or arcade open to the air on at least one side. **2.** a space within the body of a building but open to the air on one side, serving as an open-air room or as an entrance porch. [t. It. See LODGE, n.]

logging (lŏg′ĭng), *n.* the process, work, or business of cutting down trees and getting out logs from the forest for timber.

logia (lŏg′ĭ ə), *n.* pl. of **logion.**

logic (lŏj′ĭk), *n.* **1.** the science which investigates the principles governing correct or reliable inference. **2.** reasoning or argumentation, or an instance of it. **3.** the system or principles of reasoning applicable to any branch of knowledge or study. **4.** reasons or sound sense, as in utterances or actions. **5.** convincing force: *the irresistible logic of facts.* [ME *logik*, t. ML: m. s. *logica*, t. Gk: m. *logikḗ*, prop. fem. of *logikós* pertaining to reason]

logical (lŏj′ĭ kl), *adj.* **1.** according to the principles of logic: *a logical inference.* **2.** reasoning in accordance with the principles of logic, as a person, the mind, etc. **3.** reasonable; reasonably to be expected: *war was the logical consequence of such threats.* **4.** of or pertaining to logic. —**log′ical′ity, log′icalness,** *n.* —**log′ically,** *adv.*

logical design, *Computers.* the design of a digital computer or other digital equipment out of logical elements. —**logic designer, logical designer.**

logical element, *Computers.* the basic unit from which computers and other digital equipment are built: it operates on signals represented by ones and zeros and acts as a gate, passing or stopping one signal according to whether other signals have certain required values or not.

logical positivism, a philosophy deriving from Auguste Comte and developed by the Vienna Circle in the early twentieth century: it stresses linguistic analysis and teaches that, apart from tautology, only that is true that can, in principle, be verified by observation.

logician (lō jĭsh′ən), *n.* one skilled in logic.

logion (lŏg′ĭ ŏn′), *n., pl.* **logia** (lŏg′ĭ ə). **1.** a traditional saying or maxim, as of a religious teacher. **2.** (*often cap.*) a saying of Jesus (used esp. with reference to sayings of Jesus contained in collections supposed to have been among the sources of the present Gospels, or to sayings ascribed to Jesus but not recorded in the Gospels). [t. Gk: announcement, oracle]

logistic (lō jĭs′tĭk), *adj.* pertaining to military logistics. Also, **logis′tical.** [see LOGISTICS]

logistics (lō jĭs′tĭks), *n.* the branch of military science concerned with the mathematics of transportation and supply, and the movement of bodies of troops. [t. F: m. *logistique*, der. *loger* lodge, or *logis* lodging. See -ICS]

logline (lŏg′līn′), *n.* See **log** (def. 3b).

logo-, a word element denoting speech. [t. Gk, comb. form of *lógos* word, speech]

logogram (lŏg′ō grăm′), *n.* **1.** Also, **logograph.** a conventional abbreviated symbol for a frequently recurring word or phrase. **2.** logogriph. —**logogrammatic** (lŏg′ō grə măt′ĭk), *adj.*

logographic (lŏg′ō grăf′ĭk), *adj.* **1.** consisting of logograms: *logographic writing.* **2.** of or pertaining to logography. Also, **log′ograph′ical.**

logography (lō gŏg′rə fĭ), *n.* **1.** printing with logotypes. **2.** a method of longhand reporting, each of several reporters in succession taking down a few words. [t. Gk: m. s. *logographía* a writing of speeches]

logogriph (lŏg′ō grĭf′), *n.* **1.** an anagram, or a puzzle involving anagrams. **2.** a puzzle in which a certain word, and other words formed from any or all of its letters, must be guessed from indications given in a set of verses. [t. F: m. *logogriphe*, f. Gk: *logo-* LOGO- + m. *grîphos* fishing basket, riddle] —**log′ogriph′ic,** *adj.*

logomachy (lō gŏm′ə kĭ), *n., pl.* **-chies.** **1.** contention about words, or in which words are used as verbiage, regardless of their true meaning. **2.** *U.S.* a game played with cards, each bearing one letter, with which words are formed. [t. Gk: m. s. *logomachía*. See LOGO-, -MACHY] —**logom′achist,** *n.*

logos (lŏg′ŏs), *n.* **1.** (*often cap.*) *Philos.* the rational principle that governs and develops the universe. **2.** (*cap.*) *Theol.* Jesus Christ, the Divine Word (see John, 1:1, 14), the second person of the Trinity. [t. Gk: word, speech, reason, account, reckoning, proportion]

logotype (lŏg′ō tīp′), *n.* *Print.* a single type bearing two or more distinct (not combined) letters, or a syllable or word. Cf. **ligature.** —**log′otyp′y,** *n.*

logroll (lŏg′rōl′), *Chiefly U.S.* *—v.t.* **1.** to procure the passage of (a bill) by logrolling. *—v.i.* **2.** to engage in political logrolling. —**log′roll′er,** *n.*

logrolling (lŏg′rō′lĭng), *n.* **1.** *Chiefly U.S.* (used esp. with reference to legislators) the combining of two or more persons to assist one of them, in consideration of like combined assistance in the interest of each of the others in return. **2.** the action of rolling logs to a particular place. **3.** birling.

Logroño (*Sp.* lô grô′nyô), *n.* a town in N Spain. 69,279 (1965).

logway (lŏg′wā′), *n.* gangway (def. 7).

logwood (lŏg′wo͝od′), *n.* **1.** the heavy brownish red heartwood of a West Indian and Central American caesalpiniaceous tree, *Haematoxylon campechianum*, much used in dyeing. **2.** the tree itself.

logy (lō′gĭ), *adj.*, **-gier, -giest.** *U.S.* heavy; sluggish; dull. [orig. uncert. Cf. D *log* heavy, dull]

-logy, **1.** a combining form naming sciences or bodies of knowledge, as in *palaeontology, theology.* **2.** a termination of many nouns referring to writing, collections, as in *trilogy, martyrology.* [t. Gk: m. s. *-logia*, der. *log-* speak, *lógos* discourse; r. earlier *-logie*, t. F. Cf. G *-logie*]

Lohengrin (lō′ĭn grĭn), *n.* *German Legend.* the son of Parzival, and a knight of the Holy Grail.

loin (loin), *n.* **1.** (*usually pl.*) the part or parts of the body of man or of a quadruped animal on either side of the vertebral column, between the false ribs and hipbone. **2.** a cut of meat from this region of an animal, esp. a portion including the vertebrae of such parts. **3.** *Biblical and Poetic.* the part of the body which should be clothed or girded, or which is regarded as the seat of physical strength and generative power. **4. gird up one's loins,** to make ready or prepare oneself for action of some kind. [ME *loyne*, t. OF: m. *loigne*, ult. der. L *lumbus*]

loin chop, chump chop.

loincloth (loin′klŏth′), *n.* a piece of cloth worn about the loins or hips.

Loire (*Fr.* lwȧr), *n.* **1.** a river flowing from S France into the Atlantic: the longest river in France. ab. 625 mi. **2.** a department in central France. 696,348 pop. (1962); 1853 sq. mi. *Cap.:* St-Étienne.

Loire-Atlantique (*Fr.* lwȧr ȧt läɴ tēk′), *n.* a department in NW France. 803,372 pop. (1962); 2693 sq. mi. *Cap.:* Nantes.

Loiret (*Fr.* lwȧ rĕ′), *n.* a department in N central France. 389,854 pop. (1962); 2629 sq. mi. *Cap.:* Orléans.

Loir-et-Cher (*Fr.* lwȧr ė shĕr′), *n.* a department in N central France. 250,741 pop. (1962); 2478 sq. mi. *Cap.:* Blois.

loiter (loi′tə), *v.i.* **1.** to linger idly or aimlessly in or about a place. **2.** to move or go in a slow or lagging

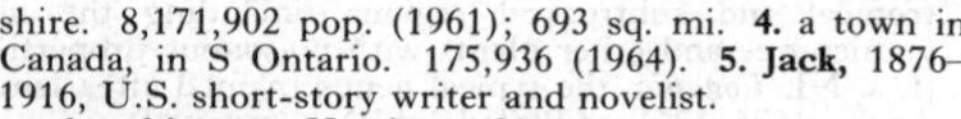

manner: *to loiter along.* **3.** to waste time or dawdle over work, etc. —*v.t.* **4.** to pass (time, etc.) in an idle or aimless manner (fol. by *away*). [ME *lotere*, appar. freq. of obs. *lote* lurk, ME *lotie(n)*, *lutie(n)*, *loyt*. Cf. OE *lūtian* lurk] —**loi′terer,** *n.* —**loi′teringly,** *adv.*

—**Syn. 1.** LOITER, DALLY, DAWDLE, IDLE imply moving or acting slowly, stopping for unimportant reasons, and in general wasting time. To LOITER is to linger aimlessly: *to loiter until late.* To DALLY is to loiter indecisively or to delay sportively as if free from care or responsibility: *to dally on the way home.* To DAWDLE is to saunter, stopping often, and taking a great deal of time, or to fritter away time working in a half-hearted way: *to dawdle over a task.* To IDLE is to move slowly and aimlessly, or to spend a great deal of time doing nothing: *to idle away the hours.*

Lokeren (*Flem.* lō′kə rə), *n.* a town in Belgium in NE East Flanders. 26,243 (est. 1964).

Loki (lō′kĭ), *n.* *Scand. Myth.* the god of destruction, and father of Hel and the serpent of Midgard. [t. Icel.]

loll (lŏl), *v.i.* **1.** to recline or lean in a relaxed or indolent manner; lounge: *to loll on a sofa.* **2.** to hang loosely or droopingly. —*v.t.* **3.** to allow to hang or droop. —*n.* **4.** *Archaic.* act of lolling. **5.** one who or that which lolls. [ME *lolle, lulle.* Cf. MD *lollen* sleep] —**loll′er,** *n.*

Lolland (*Dan.* lŏ′lăn), *n.* Laaland.

Lollard (lŏl′əd), *n.* an English or Scottish follower of the religious teaching of John Wyclif from the 14th to the 16th century. [ME, t. MD.: m. *lollaerd* mumbler, der. *lollen* mumble, hum] —**Lol′lardy, Lol′lardry, Lol′lardism,** *n.*

lollipop (lŏl′ĭ pŏp′), *n.* a kind of boiled sweet or toffee, often a piece on the end of a stick.

lollop (lŏl′əp), *v.i.* to move with bounding, ungainly leaps. [extension of LOLL, in this sense perh. influenced by GALLOP]

lolly (lŏl′ĭ), *n., pl.* **-lies. 1.** a lollipop. **2.** an ice lolly. **3.** *Slang.* money.

Lombard (lŏm′bəd, -bäd; *Fr.* lôɴ băr′), *n.* **Peter** (*Petrus Lombardus*), *c.* 1100–1160 or 1164, Italian theologian; bishop of Paris.

Lombard (lŏm′bəd, -bäd), *n.* **1.** a native or inhabitant of Lombardy. **2.** a Langobard. —*adj.* **3.** Also, **Lombar′dic.** pertaining to the Lombards or Lombardy. [ME, t. OF, t. It.: m. *lombardo*, g. LL *Longobardus*, L *Langobardus*, t. Gmc. See LANGOBARD]

Lombardy

Lombardo (*It.* lòm băr′dò), *n.* **1. Pietro** (*It.* pyĕ′trò), 1435–1515, Italian sculptor and architect. **2.** his sons, **Antonio** (*It.* ăn tŏ′nyò), *c.* 1458–1516? and **Tullio** (*It.* to͞ol′lyò), *c.* 1455–1532, who worked with their father.

Lombard Street, a street in London famous as a financial centre.

Lombardy (lŏm′bə dĭ, lŭm′-), *n.* a region in N Italy: a former kingdom. 7,390,492 pop. (1961); 9190 sq. mi. *Cap.:* Milan.

Lombardy poplar. See **poplar** (def. 1).

Lombok (lŏm′bŏk), *n.* an island in Indonesia, E of Java. 1,500,000 pop. (est. 1966); 1826 sq. mi.

Lombrosian school (lŏm brō′zyən), a school of criminology, holding the theories and employing the methods developed by Lombroso.

Lombroso (*It.* lòm brò′sò), *n.* **Cesare** (*It.* chĕ′ză rè), 1836–1909, Italian physician and criminologist, professor of psychiatry and anthropology.

Lomé (*Fr.* lō mĕ′), *n.* a seaport in and the capital of Togo, on the Gulf of Guinea. 80,000 (est. 1962).

loment (lō′mĕnt), *n.* *Bot.* a legume which is contracted in the spaces between the seeds, and breaks at maturity into one-seeded indehiscent joints. [ME *lomente*, t. L: m. *lōmentum* bean meal] —**lo′ment-like′,** *adj.*

lomentaceous (lō′mĕn tā′shəs), *adj.* *Bot.* of the nature of a loment; loment-like.

lomentum (lō mĕn′təm), *n., pl.* **-ta** (-tə). *Bot.* loment. [t. L]

Lomond (lō′mənd), *n.* **Loch,** the largest lake in Scotland, on the border of Dunbarton and Stirlingshire. 33 sq. mi.

Lomonosov (*Russ.* lə mă nôs′əf), *n.* **Mikhail Vasilievich** (*Russ.* mĭ KHă ĕl′ vă sĕ′lyĭ vĭch), 1711–65, Russian scientist, author, and critic.

lon., longitude.

London (lŭn′dən), *n.* **1.** a metropolis in SE England, on the Thames: capital of the United Kingdom. **2. City of,** an administrative division in the central part of London: the old city and ancient nucleus of the metropolis. 4610 (est. 1962); 1 sq. mi. **3. Greater,** an urban area comprising the City of London, the former London and Middlesex counties, and parts of Essex, Kent, Surrey, and Hertfordshire. 8,171,902 pop. (1961); 693 sq. mi. **4.** a town in Canada, in S Ontario. 175,936 (1964). **5. Jack,** 1876–1916, U.S. short-story writer and novelist.

London Airport, Heathrow Airport.

Londonderry (lŭn′dən dĕ′rĭ), *n.* **1.** a county in Northern Ireland. 111,565 pop. (1961); 804 sq. mi. **2.** its county town: a seaport. 53,744 pop. (1961). Also, **Derry.**

Londoner (lŭn′də nə), *n.* a native or inhabitant of London.

London Gazette, an official government journal, founded 1665, giving government announcements, legal notices etc.: now issued three times weekly.

London pride, a perennial saxifragaceous herb with sprays of pale pink flowers, a commonly cultivated hybrid, between *Saxifraga spathularis* and *S. umbrosa*, of unknown origin.

lone (lōn), *adj.* **1.** being alone; unaccompanied; solitary: *a lone traveller.* **2.** standing apart, or isolated, as a house. **3.** *Poetic.* lonely. **4.** unmarried or widowed. [aphetic var. of ALONE, used attributively] —**Syn. 1.** See **alone.**

lone hand, 1. *Cards.* **a.** a hand which is so strong that it is played without the hand of a partner. **b.** one who plays such a hand. **2.** independent action, often unpopular, taken without outside assistance. **3.** one who takes such action.

lonely (lōn′lĭ), *adj.,* **-lier, -liest. 1.** lone; solitary; without company. **2.** destitute of sympathetic or friendly companionship or relationships: *a lonely exile.* **3.** remote from men or from places of human habitation or resort: *a lonely road.* **4.** standing apart; isolated: *a lonely tower.* **5.** affected with, characterized by, or causing a depressing feeling of being alone; lonesome: *a lonely heart.* —**lone′lily,** *adv.* —**lone′liness,** *n.* —**Syn. 1.** See **alone.**

lonesome (lōn′səm), *adj.* *Now Chiefly U.S.* **1.** lonely in feeling; depressed by solitude or by a sense of being alone: *to feel lonesome.* **2.** attended with or causing such a state of feeling: *a lonesome journey.* **3.** depressingly lonely in situation: *a lonesome road.* —**lone′somely,** *adv.* —**lone′someness,** *n.* —**Syn. 1.** See **alone.**

Lone Star State, Texas (a nickname).

lone wolf. See **wolf** (def. 11).

long[1] (lŏng), *adj.,* **longer** (lŏng′gə), **longest** (lŏng′gĭst), *n., adv.* —*adj.* **1.** having considerable or great extent from end to end; not short: *a long distance.* **2.** having considerable or great extent in duration: *a long visit.* **3.** having many items; of more than average number: *a long list.* **4.** having considerable or great extension from beginning to end, as a series, enumeration, account, book, etc.; not brief. **5.** having a specified extension in space, duration, etc.: *ten feet long.* **6.** continuing too long: *a long speech.* **7.** beyond the normal extension in space, duration, quantity, etc.: *a long hundred* (120). **8.** extending to a great distance in space or time: *a long memory.* **9.** broad; taking in all aspects: *a long look at his future.* **10.** having a long time to run, as a promissory note. **11.** not likely: *a long chance.* **12.** the longest of several or the longer of two. **13.** concentrated; intense: *taking a long look at his faults.* **14.** (of drinks) of considerable or great quantity; thirst-quenching rather than intoxicating, as a diluted alcoholic drink. **15.** *Chiefly Law.* distant or remote in time: *a long date.* **16.** relatively much extended: *a long reach.* **17.** tall. **18.** (of the head or skull) of more than ordinary length from front to back. **19.** *Phonet.* **a.** lasting a relatively long time: *'feed' has a longer vowel than 'feet' or 'fit'.* **b.** belonging to a class of sounds considered as usually longer in duration than another class, such as the vowel of *bought* as compared to *hot*: conventionally, the vowels of *mate, meet, mite, mote, moot* and *mute.* **20.** *Com.* **a.** owning some commodity or stock. **b.** depending for profit on a rise in prices. **21.** (in gambling) **a.** of an exceptionally large difference in proportional amounts on an event: *long odds.* **b.** of or pertaining to the larger number in the odds in betting. **22.** *Cricket.* in the field, near the boundary; deep. **23. in the long run,** after a long course of experience; in the final result. **24. long in the tooth,** *Slang.* elderly. —*n.* **25.** a long time: *before long.* **26.** something that is long. **27. before long,** in the near future; soon. **28. the long and the short of,** the kernel; substance of; gist. —*adv.* **29.** for or through a great extent of space or, esp., time: *a reform long advocated.* **30.** for or throughout a specified extent, esp. of time: *how long did he stay?* **31.** (in elliptical expressions) gone, occupying, delaying, etc., a long or a specified time: *don't be long.* **32.** (for emphasis, after nouns denoting a period of time) throughout the whole length: *all summer long.* **33.** at a point of time far distant from the time indicated: *long before.* **34. so** (or **as**) **long as,** provided that. **35. so long,** *Colloq.* goodbye. [ME *longe*, OE *lang, long*, c. D and G *lang*]

long[2] (lŏng), *v.i.* **1.** to have a prolonged or unceasing

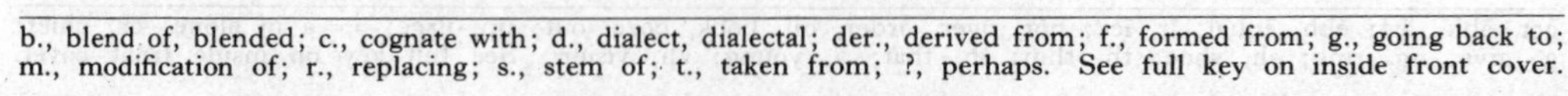

desire, as for something not immediately (if ever) attainable. 2. to have an earnest or strong desire. [ME *longen*, OE *langian* lengthen (impersonal), yearn, der. *lang* LONG[1]]

long., longitude.

longa (lŏng′gə), *n.* a note in medieval music, ╕, equal to two minims: half the length of a large.

longan (lŏng′gən), *n.* 1. the small, one-seeded, greenish brown, pleasant-tasting fruit of the large, evergreen, sapindaceous tree, *Euphoria longan*, native in China and allied to the lychee. 2. the tree. Also, **lungan.** [t. NL: s. *longanum*, t. Chinese: m. *lung-yen* dragon's eye]

Long Beach, a city in the U.S., in SW California, S of Los Angeles: a seaside resort. 344,168 (1960).

longboat (lŏng′bōt′), *n. Naut.* the largest and strongest boat belonging to a sailing ship.

longbow (lŏng′bō′), *n.* 1. the bow drawn by hand and discharging a long feathered arrow. 2. **draw the longbow,** to tell exaggerated stories.

longcloth (lŏng′klŏth′), *n.* 1. a plain or twill coarse cotton cloth, usually manufactured in 36-yard lengths. 2. *U.S.* a kind of muslin, light and soft in texture.

long-distance (lŏng′dĭs′təns), *adj.* 1. extending or travelling over an extensive area of time or space. 2. (of telephone calls) between distant points; trunk.

long division, *Maths.* an algorithm for dividing one number by a second, in which the first step consists of obtaining the first digit of the quotient and the partial remainder by repeated trials. At each step the next digit of the quotient and the partial remainder are derived.

long-drawn (lŏng′drôn′), *adj.* 1. drawn out; prolonged: *a long-drawn narrative.* 2. *Rare.* long.

Long Eaton (ē′tn), a town in England, in W Derbyshire. 30,464 (1961).

longeron (lŏn′jə rən; *Fr.* lôNzh rôN′), *n. Aeron.* a main longitudinal brace or support on an aeroplane. [t. F, der. *long* LONG]

longeval (lŏn jē′vəl), *adj.* long-lived; living to a great age. Also, **longaeval.** [f. m. s. L *longaevus* + -AL[1]]

longevity (lŏn jĕv′ĭ tĭ), *n.* 1. length or duration of life. 2. long life; great duration of life.

longevous (lŏn jē′vəs), *adj.* longeval. [t. L: m. *longaevus* aged]

long face, a dismal or unhappy expression.

Longfellow (lŏng′fĕl′ō), *n.* **Henry Wadsworth** (wŏdz′-wəth), 1807–82, U.S. poet.

Longford (lŏng′fəd), *n.* 1. a county in Leinster, in the Republic of Ireland. 30,643 pop. (1961); 403 sq. mi. 2. its county town. 3558 (1961).

long green, *U.S. Slang.* paper currency.

long-haired (lŏng′hēəd′), *adj.* 1. with long hair. 2. (sometimes disparaging) highbrow; intellectual.

longhand (lŏng′hănd′), *n.* writing of the ordinary kind, in which the words are written out in full (distinguished from *shorthand*).

longhead (lŏng′hĕd′), *n.* a dolichocephalic person.

longheaded (lŏng′hĕd′ĭd), *adj.* 1. dolichocephalic. 2. of great discernment or foresight; far-seeing or shrewd. —**long′-head′edness,** *n.*

Longhena (*It.* lôn gĕ′nä), *n.* **Baldassare** (*It.* bäl däs-sä′rĕ), 1598–1682, Venetian baroque architect.

longhorn (lŏng′hôn′), *n.* 1. one of a kind of cattle predominating on the ranges of northern Mexico and the Great Plains of the U.S. in the early 19th century, developed from Spanish cattle introduced at Vera Cruz about 1521, characterized by long horns and rangy conformation. 2. a small breed of English cattle characterized by excessive horn growth.

long house, 1. a house of great length, particularly a communal dwelling of the Iroquois and of other North American tribes. 2. (*caps*) the league of the Iroquois.

longicorn (lŏn′jĭ kôn′), *adj.* 1. having long antennae, as beetles of the group *Longicornia* (family *Cerambycidae*). 2. belonging to this group. —*n.* 3. a longicorn or long-horned beetle. [t. NL: s. *longicornis*, f. L: *longi-* long + *-cornis* horned]

longing (lŏng′ĭng), *n.* 1. prolonged, unceasing, or earnest desire. 2. an instance of it. —*adj.* 3. having a prolonged or earnest desire. 4. characterized or showing such desire: *a longing look.* —**long′ingly,** *adv.* —**Syn.** 1. See **desire.**

Longinus (lŏn jī′nəs), *n.* **Dionysius Cassius** (dī′ə nĭs′-ĭ əs kăs′ĭ əs), A.D. *c.* 213–273, Greek rhetorician and philosophical critic.

longish (lŏng′ĭsh), *adj.* somewhat long.

Long Island, an island in SE New York: the boroughs of Brooklyn and Queens of New York City are situated at its W end. 118 mi. long; 12–20 mi. wide; 1682 sq. mi.

Long Island Sound, an arm of the Atlantic between Connecticut and Long Island. ab. 110 mi. long.

longitude (lŏn′jĭ tyood′), *n.* 1. *Geog.* angular distance east or west on the earth's surface, measured by the angle contained between the meridian of a particular place and some prime meridian, as that of Greenwich, or by the corresponding difference in time. 2. *Astron.* a. the arc of the ecliptic measured eastwards from the vernal equinox to the foot of the great circle passing through the poles of the ecliptic and the point on the celestial sphere in question (**celestial longitude**). b. the arc on the galactic circle measured from its intersection with the celestial equator (**galactic longitude**). [ME, t. L: m. *longitūdo* length]

longitudinal (lŏn′jĭ tyoo′dĭ nəl), *adj.* 1. of or pertaining to longitude or length: *longitudinal distance.* 2. *Zool.* pertaining to or extending along the long axis of the body, or the direction from front to back, or head to tail. 3. extending in the direction of the length of a thing; running lengthways. See diag. under **section.** —**lon′-gitu′dinally,** *adv.*

longitudinal wave, *Physics.* a wave in which the vibration or displacement is in the direction of propagation.

long johns, *Colloq.* 1. a pair of women's pants reaching nearly to the knee. 2. a pair of men's pants reaching to the ankle.

long jump, *Sport.* 1. a jump in which athletes aim to cover the greatest distance from a given mark. 2. the athletic contest for the longest such jump.

longleaf pine (lŏng′lēf′), 1. an important American pine, *Pinus palustris,* valued as a source of turpentine and for its timber. 2. the wood of this tree.

long-limbed (lŏng′lĭmd′), *adj.* 1. having long limbs. 2. agile; athletic.

long-lived (lŏng′lĭvd′), *adj.* having a long life or existence; functioning for a long time.

long measure, linear measure.

Longobard (lŏng′gə bäd′), *n.* Langobard.

Long Parliament, the parliament which assembled November 3rd, 1640, was expelled by Cromwell in 1653, reconvened in 1659, and was dissolved in 1660.

long pig, (formerly in the South Pacific) human meat eaten by cannibals.

long-playing (lŏng′plā′ĭng), *adj.* (of a gramophone record) having microgrooves, being made of plastic rather than shellac, and being designed to revolve at $33\frac{1}{3}$ r.p.m. *Abbrev.:* LP.

long primer, a printing type (10 points), of a size between bourgeois and small pica.

long-range (lŏng′rānj′), *adj.* 1. extending into the future: *long-range weather forecasts.* 2. designed to project over a great distance: *a long-range gun.*

longshanks (lŏng′shăngks′), *n. Colloq.* a tall man, esp. (*cap.*) as applied to King Edward I.

longship (lŏng′shĭp′), *n.* an ancient Viking ship of war of N Europe, having a long, narrow, open hull, propelled by a small square sail and a number of oars.

longshore (lŏng′shō′), *adj.* existing, found, or employed along the shore: *longshore fisheries.*

longshoreman (lŏng′shô′mən), *n., pl.* **-men.** *U.S.* a docker. [f. *longshore*, aphetic var. of *alongshore* + -MAN]

long shot, 1. an attempt which has little hope of success, but which if successful may offer great rewards. 2. a photograph or a film or television shot taken from some distance.

long-sighted (lŏng′sī′tĭd), *adj.* 1. far-sighted; hypermetropic. 2. having great foresight; foreseeing remote results. Cf. **far-sighted.** —**long′-sight′edness,** *n.*

longstanding (lŏng′stăn′dĭng), *adj.* existing or occurring for a long time: *a longstanding feud.*

long-suffering (lŏng′sŭf′ə rĭng), *adj.* 1. enduring injury or provocation long and patiently. —*n.* 2. long and patient endurance of injury or provocation.

long suit, 1. *Cards.* the suit in a hand which has the most cards. 2. one's strongest point; that field in which one most excels.

long-tailed widowbird (lŏng′tāld′), sakabula. Also, **long-tailed whidah-bird.**

long-term (lŏng′tûm′), *adj.* 1. extending over a period of time of considerable length. 2. maturing over several years or more.

long-term bond (lŏng′tûm′), a bond not maturing for many years.

long tom (tŏm), 1. *Army Slang.* cannon. 2. long heavy cannon formerly carried by small naval vessels.

long ton, a ton of 2240 lbs. Cf. **short ton.**

Longus (lŏng′gəs), *n.* fl. 2nd or 3rd century A.D., Greek writer to whom is attributed *Daphnis and Chloë.*

long vacation, the long summer holiday at universities, etc. Also, **long vac.**

long-waisted (lŏng′wās′tĭd), *adj.* of more than average length from the shoulders to the waist.

longwall mining (lŏng′wôl′), the system by which coal is extracted from a long continuous face.

long wave, *Radio.* an electromagnetic wave with a wavelength of over 1 kilometre. —**long-wave** (lŏng′-wāv′), *adj.*
longways (lŏng′wāz′), *adv.* lengthways. Also, **longwise** (lŏng′wīz′).
longwinded (lŏng′win′dĭd), *adj.* **1.** tediously wordy in speech or writing. **2.** writing or talking tediously and continuously. **3.** able to breathe deeply. —**long′win′-dedly,** *adv.* —**long′win′dedness,** *n.*
Lons-le-Saunier (*Fr.* lôN lə sō nyĕ′), *n.* a town in E France, capital of Jura department. 18,752 (1962).
loo[1] (lōō), *n., pl.* **loos,** *v.,* **looed, looing.** —*n.* **1.** a game of cards in which forfeits are paid into a pool. **2.** the forfeit or sum paid into the pool. **3.** the fact of being looed. —*v.t.* **4.** to subject to a forfeit at loo. [shortened form of *lanterloo,* t. F: meaningless refrain of a song]
loo[2] (lōō), *n. Colloq.* a lavatory. [mincing var. of LAVATORY, but cf. dial. *lew,* OE *hlēow* shelter]
loofah (lōō′fə), *n.* **1.** a tropical, annual, climbing, cucurbitaceous herb, *Luffa cylindrica.* **2.** the fibrous network of its fruit, used as a bath sponge. [t. Ar.]
look (lŏŏk), *v.i.* **1.** to fix the eyes upon something or in some direction in order to see. **2.** to glance or gaze, in a manner specified: *to look questioningly at a person.* **3.** to use the sight in seeking, searching, examining, watching, etc.: *to look through the papers.* **4.** to tend, as in bearing or significance: *conditions look towards war.* **5.** to appear or seem (as specified) to the eye: *to look pale.* **6.** to seem to the mind: *the case looks promising.* **7.** to direct the mental regard or attention: *to look at the facts.* **8.** to have an outlook or afford a view: *the window looks upon the street.* **9.** to face or front: *the house looks east.* —*v.* **10.** Some special verb phrases are:
look after, 1. to follow with the eye, as a person or thing moving away. **2.** to seek, as something desired. **3.** to take care of: *to look after a child.*
look alive, (an expression used to urge speed.)
look down on, to have contempt for; regard with disdain.
look down one's nose, to regard with barely concealed contempt.
look for, 1. to seek, as a person or thing. **2.** to anticipate; expect.
look forward to, to anticipate with pleasure.
look here, (an expression used to attract attention, for emphasis, or the like.)
look in, 1. to take a look into a place. **2.** to come in for a brief visit.
look into, to investigate; examine.
look on, to be a mere spectator.
look out, 1. to look forth, as from a window or a place of observation. **2.** to be on guard. **3.** to take watchful care (fol. by *for*): *to look out for oneself.*
look sharp, (an expression used to urge speed.)
look to, 1. to direct the glance or gaze to. **2.** to give attention to. **3.** to direct the expectations or hopes to, as for something desired. **4.** to look forward expectantly to.
look up, 1. to direct the eyes upwards. **2.** *Colloq.* to rise in amount or value; improve.
look up to, to regard with admiration, or esteem.
—*v.t.* **11.** to try to find; seek (fol. by *up, out,* etc.): *to look a name up in a directory.* **12.** to express or suggest by looks: *to look daggers at a person.* **13.** to view, inspect or examine (fol. by *over*). **14.** to direct a look towards: *she looked him full in the face.* **15.** to have the aspect or appearance appropriate to: *to look one's age, look an idiot.* **16.** to visit or make contact with (fol. by *up*). **17.** *Archaic.* to bring, put, etc., by looks.
—*n.* **18.** the act of looking: *a look of enquiry.* **19.** a visual search or examination. **20.** way of looking or appearing to the eye or to the mind; aspect: *the look of an honest man.* **21.** (*pl.*) general aspect; appearance: *to like the looks of a place, good looks.*
[ME *lōke(n),* OE *lōcian.* Cf. d. G *lugen* look out, spy]
—**Syn. 1.** See **watch. 6.** See **seem.**
looker (lŏŏk′ə), *n.* **1.** one who looks. **2.** *Slang.* an unusually good-looking person.
looker-on (lŏŏk′ər ŏn′), *n., pl.* **lookers-on.** one who looks on; a spectator.
look-in (lŏŏk′ĭn′), *n. Colloq.* a chance of participating: *she was such a good player that he didn't get a look-in.*
looking glass, 1. a mirror made of glass with a metallic or amalgam backing. **2.** such glass as a material.
lookout (lŏŏk′out′), *n.* **1.** the act of looking out. **2.** a watch kept, as for something that may come or happen. **3.** a person or group stationed or employed to keep such a watch. **4.** a station or place from which a watch is kept. **5.** view; prospect; outlook. **6.** *Colloq.* the proper object of one's watchful care or concern.
loom[1] (lōōm), *n.* **1.** a machine or apparatus for weaving yarn or thread into a fabric. **2.** the art or the process of weaving. **3.** the part of an oar between the blade and the handle. —*v.t.* **4.** *Rare.* to weave on a loom. [ME *lome,* OE *gelōma* tool, implement. Cf. HEIRLOOM]
loom[2] (lōōm), *v.i.* **1.** to appear indistinctly, or come into view in indistinct and enlarged form. **2.** to rise before the vision with an appearance of great or portentous size. —*n.* **3.** a looming appearance, as of something seen indistinctly at a distance or through a fog. [cf. d. Sw. *loma* move slowly]
loom[3] (lōōm), *n.* **1.** loon[1]. **2.** a guillemot or murre. [t. Scand.; cf. Icel. *lōmr,* Sw. *lom.* See LOON[1]]
loon[1] (lōōn), *n.* any of several large, short-tailed web-footed, fish-eating diving birds of the Northern Hemisphere, constituting the genus *Gavia,* as the common loon or great northern diver, *Gavia immer,* of the Old and New Worlds. [var. of LOOM[3]]
loon[2] (lōōn), *n.* a worthless, sorry, lazy, or stupid fellow. [ME *lowen, loun.* Cf. Icel. *lūinn* exhausted]
loony (lōō′nĭ), *adj.,* **loonier, looniest,** *n., pl.* **loonies.** —*adj.* **1.** lunatic; crazy. **2.** *Slang.* extremely or senselessly foolish. —*n.* **3.** *Slang.* a lunatic. Also, **looney, luny.** [var. of *luny,* familiar shortening of LUNATIC] —**loon′iness,** *n.*
loony bin, *Slang.* a lunatic asylum.
loop[1] (lōōp), *n.* **1.** a folding or doubling of a portion of a cord, lace, ribbon, etc., upon itself, so as to leave an opening between the parts. **2.** anything shaped more or less like a loop, as a line drawn on paper, a part of a letter, a part of a path, a line of motion, etc. **3.** a curved piece or a ring of metal, wood, etc., used for the insertion of something, or as a handle, or otherwise. **4.** one of the principal ridge-shapes of a fingerprint, consisting of at least one set of ridges crossing themselves at the base of a curve (distinguished from *arch* and *whorl*). **5.** *Railways, etc.* a branch or line that returns to the main line. **6.** *Aeron.* a manoeuvre executed in such a manner that the aeroplane performs a closed curve in a vertical plane. **7.** *Physics.* the part of a vibrating string, column of air, or the like, between two adjacent nodes; antinode. **8.** *Elect.* **a.** a closed electric or magnetic circuit. **b.** a closed curve showing the relation between the magnetizing force and the induction in a ferromagnetic substance when the magnetizing field is carried through a complete cycle. **9.** *Med.* an intra-uterine contraceptive device, formerly made in metal, now in plastic. —*v.t.* **10.** to form into a loop or loops. **11.** to make a loop or loops in. **12.** to enfold or encircle in or with something arranged in a loop. **13.** to fasten by forming into a loop, or by means of something formed into a loop. **14.** to fly (an aeroplane) in a loop or series of loops. **15.** to construct a closed electric or magnetic circuit. —*v.i.* **16.** to make or form a loop or loops. **17.** to move by forming loops, as a measuring worm. [ME *loupe.* Cf. Gaelic and Irish *lub* loop, bend]
loop[2] (lōōp), *n. Archaic.* a small or narrow opening, as in a wall; a loophole. [ME *loupe.* Cf. MD *lūpen* peer]
looper (lōō′pə), *n.* **1.** one who or that which loops something or forms loops. **2.** a measuring worm. **3.** the thread-holder in a sewing machine using two threads.
loophole (lōōp′hōl′), *n., v.,* **-holed, -holing.** —*n.* **1.** a small or narrow opening, as in a wall, for looking through, or for admitting light and air, or particularly, in a fortification, for the discharge of missiles against an enemy outside. **2.** an opening or aperture. **3.** an outlet, or means of escape or evasion. —*v.t.* **4.** to furnish with loopholes. [f. LOOP[2] + HOLE, n.]
loopy (lōō′pĭ), *adj.* **1.** full of loops. **2.** *Slang.* slightly mad or eccentric.
Loos (lōōs), *n.* **Adolf,** 1870–1933, Moravian architect.
loose (lōōs), *adj.,* **looser, loosest,** *adv., v.,* **loosed, loosing.** —*adj.* **1.** free from bonds, fetters, or restraint: *to get one's hand loose.* **2.** free or released from fastening or attachment: *a loose end.* **3.** uncombined, as a chemical element. **4.** not bound together, as papers or flowers. **5.** not put in a package or other container: *loose mushrooms.* **6.** unemployed or unappropriated: *loose funds.* **7.** wanting in retentiveness or power of restraint: *a loose tongue.* **8.** lax, as the bowels. **9.** free from moral restraint, or lax in principle or conduct. **10.** wanton or unchaste: *a loose woman.* **11.** not firm or rigid: *a loose tooth, a loose rein.* **12.** not fitting closely, as garments. **13.** not close or compact in structure or arrangement; having spaces between the parts, or open: *a loose weave.* **14.** (of earth, soil, etc.) not cohering: *loose sand.* **15.** not strict, exact, or precise: *loose thinking.* **16.** free from restraining conditions or factors: *the Commonwealth of Nations is a loose association of sovereign states.* **17. at a loose end, a.** in an unsettled or disorderly condition. **b.** unoccupied; having nothing to do. **18. on the loose,**

a. free from restraint. b. on a spree. —*adv.* 19. in a loose manner; loosely. 20. so as to become free from restraint, independent, etc.: *to cut loose from his family.* —*v.t.* 21. to let loose, or free from bonds or restraint. 22. to release, as from constraint, obligation, penalty, etc. 23. *Chiefly Naut.* to set free from fastening or attachment: *loose a boat from its moorings.* 24. to unfasten, undo, or untie, as a bond, fetter, or knot. 25. to shoot, or let fly. 26. to make less tight; slacken or relax. 27. to render less firmly fixed, or loosen. —*v.i.* 28. to let go a hold. 29. to weigh anchor. 30. to shoot or let fly an arrow, etc. 31. *Obs.* to become loose. [ME *los, loos,* t. Scand.; cf. Icel. *lauss* loose, free, empty, c. D and G *los* loose, free] —**loose′ly,** *adv.* —**loose′ness,** *n.*

loosebox (lo͞os′bŏks′), *n.* a stall for a horse or other large animal, usually in a stable.

loose cover, a cloth cover for a piece of furniture, made so as to be easily removable. Also, *U.S.,* **slip cover.**

loose-jointed (lo͞os′join′tĭd), *adj.* 1. having loose joints. 2. loosely built or framed.

loose-leaf (lo͞os′lēf′), *adj.* (of a book, etc.) having individual leaves that may be inserted or removed without tearing.

loosen (lo͞o′sən), *v.t.* 1. to unfasten or undo, as a bond or fetter. 2. to make less tight; slacken or relax: *to loosen one's grasp.* 3. to make less firmly fixed in place: *to loosen a clamp.* 4. to let loose or set free from bonds, restraint, or constraint. 5. to make less close or compact in structure or arrangement. 6. to make less dense or coherent: *to loosen the soil.* 7. to open, or relieve the costiveness of, (the bowels). 8. to relax in strictness or severity, as restraint or discipline. —*v.i.* 9. to become loose or looser. —**loos′ener,** *n.*

loosestrife (lo͞os′strīf′), *n.* 1. any of various leafy-stemmed herbs of the primulaceous genus *Lysimachia,* as *L. vulgaris,* a common yellow-flowered species (**yellow loosestrife**), and *L. quadrifolia,* a species with leaves in whorls of four or five (**whorled loosestrife**). 2. any of various herbaceous plants of the lythraceous genus *Lythrum,* as *L. salicaria,* a purple-flowered species (**purple loosestrife**). [f. LOOSE, v., + STRIFE, erroneous trans. of L *lysimachia* (actually der. Gk proper name *Lysímachos,* lit., the one loosing (i.e. ending) strife)]

loot (lo͞ot), *n.* 1. spoils or plunder taken by pillaging, as in war. 2. anything dishonestly and ruthlessly appropriated: *a burglar's loot.* 3. the act of looting or plundering: *the loot of a conquered city.* —*v.t.* 4. to take or carry off, as loot. 5. to despoil by taking loot; plunder or pillage (a city, house, etc.), as in war. 6. to rob, as by burglary, corrupt practice in public office, etc. —*v.i.* 7. to take loot; plunder. [t. Hind.: m. *lūt*] —**loot′er,** *n.* —**Syn.** 5. sack, rifle.

lop[1] (lŏp), *v.,* **lopped, lopping,** *n.* —*v.t.* 1. to cut off the branches, twigs, etc., of (a tree or other plant). 2. to cut off the head, limbs, etc., of (a person) or parts of (a thing). 3. to cut off (branches, twigs, etc.) from a tree or other plant. 4. to cut off (the head, limbs, etc.) from a person. —*v.i.* 5. to cut off branches, twigs, etc., as of a tree. 6. to remove parts by or as by cutting. —*n.* 7. parts or a part lopped off. 8. the smaller branches and twigs of trees. [ME (def. 8), etymologically identical with obs. *lop* spider, both objects being marked by many projecting parts] —**lop′per,** *n.*

lop[2] (lŏp), *v.,* **lopped, lopping.** —*v.i.* 1. to hang loosely or limply; droop. 2. to sway, move, or go in a drooping or heavy, awkward way. —*v.t.* 3. to let hang or droop. [der. obs. *lop,* n., lobe (var. of LAP[1] lobe); lit., to behave like a *lop,* i.e., to dangle, hang loosely]

lope (lōp), *v.,* **loped, loping,** *n.* —*v.i.* 1. to move or run with bounding steps, as a quadruped, or with a long, easy stride, as a person. 2. to canter leisurely with a rather long, easy stride, as a horse. —*v.t.* 3. to cause to lope, as a horse. —*n.* 4. the act or the gait of loping. 5. a long, easy stride. [late ME, var. of obs. *loup* leap, t. Scand.; cf. Icel. *hlaupa*] —**lop′er,** *n.*

lop-eared (lŏp′ĭəd′), *adj.* having ears that lop or hang down.

López (lō′pēz), *n.* **Osvaldo** (ŏz văl′dō) (*Osvaldo López Arellano*), born 1921, Honduran general: president since 1965.

lop-grass (lŏp′gräs′), *n.* a variable annual or biennial grass, *Bromus mollis,* widespread in meadows and waste places of temperate regions.

lophobranch (lō′fə brăngk′), *n.* 1. any of the *Lophobranchii,* an order or group of teleostean fishes having gills in tufts, as the seahorses, pipefishes, etc. —*adj.* 2. belonging or pertaining to the *Lophobranchii.* [f. Gk: *lópho(s)* crest + m. s. *bránchia* gills] —**lophobranchiate** (lō′fə brăng′kĭ ĭt, -āt′), *adj., n.*

lophophore (lō′fə fô′), *n.* *Zool.* a ridged or elongated structure bearing ciliate tentacles, in the invertebrate phyla *Bryozoa, Brachiopoda,* and *Phoronidea,* which aids in feeding.

loppy (lŏp′ĭ), *adj.* lopping; limp. [f. LOP[2] + -Y[1]]

lopsided (lŏp′sī′dĭd), *adj.* 1. lopping or inclining to one side. 2. heavier, larger, or more developed on one side than on the other; asymmetrical. —**lop′sid′edly,** *adv.* —**lop′sid′edness,** *n.*

loq., loquitur.

loquacious (lō kwā′shəs), *adj.* 1. talking or disposed to talk much or freely; talkative. 2. characterized by or showing a disposition to talk much: *a loquacious mood.* [f. LOQUACI(TY) + -OUS] —**loqua′ciously,** *adv.* —**Syn.** 1. See **talkative.**

loquacity (lō kwăs′ĭ tĭ), *n.* 1. the state of being loquacious. 2. loquacious flow of talk. Also, **loqua′ciousness.** [t. L: m. s. *loquācitas*]

loquat (lō′kwŏt, -kwət), *n.* 1. a small, evergreen, malaceous tree, *Eriobotrya japonica,* native in China and Japan, but cultivated elsewhere for ornament and for its yellow, plumlike fruit. 2. the fruit. [t. Chinese (Cantonese): m. *luh kwat* rush orange]

loquitur (lŏk′wĭ tə), *v.* *Latin.* he (or she) speaks.

loran (lô′rən), *n.* a device by which a navigator can locate his position by determining the time displacement between radio signals from two known stations. [short for *lo(ng) ra(nge) n(avigation)*]

Lorca (*Sp.* lôr′kä), *n.* 1. See **García Lorca.** 2. a city in SE Spain. 70,998 (1950).

lord (lôd), *n.* 1. one who has dominion over others; a master, chief, or ruler. 2. one who exercises authority from property rights; an owner or possessor of land, houses, etc. 3. a feudal superior; the proprietor of a manor. 4. *Archaic.* a husband. 5. a dominant person; one who is a leader in his own sphere. 6. a titled nobleman, or peer. 7. (*cap.*) the title (in collocation with some other word or words) of certain high officials: *Lord Mayor of London.* 8. (*cap.*) (in ceremonial use) the title of a bishop or archbishop: *Lord Bishop of Durham.* 9. (*cap.*) the title substituted in less formal use for marquess, earl, viscount, or baron: *Lord Kitchener* for *Earl Kitchener.* 10. (*cap.*) the courtesy title of younger sons of a duke or marquess (used as a prefix before the Christian name): *Lord John Russell.* 11. (*cap.*) the title of a Lord of Appeal in Ordinary or a Lord Justice of Appeal; one of the Law Lords. 12. **Lords,** the temporal and spiritual members of the House of Lords. 13. (*cap.*) the Supreme Being, Jehovah, or God. 14. (*cap.*) the Saviour, Jesus Christ. 15. *Astrol.* a planet having dominating influence. —*interj.* 16. (*often cap.*) (the noun Lord (God) used as an exclamation of surprise, etc.) —*v.i.* 17. to play the lord; behave in a lordly manner; domineer (often with indefinite *it*): *to lord it over someone.* [ME *lord, loverd,* OE *hlāford,* f. *hlāf* LOAF[1] + *weard* keeper. Cf. LADY, WARD]

Lord Advocate, the chief Crown lawyer in Scotland.

Lord Chamberlain, the chief officer in the royal household, responsible for arrangements at state occasions, in charge of many royal staff and formerly licenser of plays and public theatres.

Lord Chief Justice, the president of the Queen's Bench division of the High Court of Justice.

Lord High Chancellor, (in Great Britain) the head of the judiciary who is also usually a cabinet minister, Speaker of the House of Lords, keeper of the great seal, etc. Also, **Lord Chancellor.**

Lord Justice of Appeal, an ordinary judge of the Court of Appeal.

lordless (lôd′lĭs), *adj.* having no lord.

Lord Lieutenant, 1. the title of various high officials holding authority deputed from a sovereign. 2. (formerly) the viceroy in Ireland.

lordling (lôd′lĭng), *n.* a little or petty lord.

lordly (lôd′lĭ), *adj.,* **-lier, -liest,** *adv.* —*adj.* 1. suitable for a lord, as things; grand or magnificent. 2. insolently imperious: *lordly contempt.* 3. of or pertaining to a lord or lords. 4. having the character or attributes of a lord, as a person. 5. befitting a lord, as actions. —*adv.* 6. in the manner of a lord. —**lord′liness,** *n.* —**Syn.** 2. haughty, arrogant. —**Ant.** 2. meek.

lord mayor, (in some cities as London, York, etc.) mayor.

Lord of Appeal in Ordinary, a life baron who has held high judicial office for two years or practised at the bar for at least fifteen years, appointed to hear appeals in the House of Lords and the Privy Council; Law Lord.

Lord of Hosts, Jehovah, the Supreme Ruler.

Lord of Misrule, a person formerly chosen to direct revels and sports.

lordosis (lô dō′sĭs), *n.* *Pathol.* forward curvature of the spine. [t. NL, t. Gk: a bending back] —**lordotic** (lô-dŏt′ĭk), *adj.*

Lord President of the Council, the president of the Privy Council who also holds a post bearing special parliamentary duties determined by the prime minister.

Lord Privy Seal, the officer who formerly affixed the privy seal to charters, etc. He is now usually a member of the cabinet but has no official duties.

Lord Protector, protector (def. 2b).

lord provost, provost (def. 2).

Lord's (lôdz), *n.* a cricket ground at St John's Wood, in London; headquarters of the Marylebone Cricket Club.

lords-and-ladies (lôdz′ən lā′dĭz), *n.* the cuckoopint, *Arum maculatum.*

Lord's day, the, Sunday.

lordship (lôd′shĭp), *n.* **1.** (*often cap.*) the form used in speaking of or to a judge or certain noblemen (usually prec. by *his, your,* etc.). **2.** the state or dignity of a lord. **3.** *Hist.* **a.** the authority or power of a lord. **b.** the domain of a lord.

lord spiritual, *pl.* **lords spiritual.** a bishop or archbishop, considered in his capacity of a member of the House of Lords.

Lord's Prayer, the, the prayer given by Jesus to His disciples. Matt. 6:9–13; Luke, 11:2–4.

Lord's Supper, the, 1. the Last Supper of Jesus and His disciples. **2.** the sacrament in commemoration of this; the Eucharist; the communion; the mass.

Lord's table, the, the communion table or the altar.

lord temporal, *pl.* **lords temporal.** one who, by right of birth or elevation is entitled to sit in the House of Lords.

lore[1] (lô), *n.* **1.** the body of knowledge, esp. of a traditional, anecdotal, or popular nature, on a particular subject: *the lore of herbs.* **2.** learning, knowledge, or erudition. **3.** *Archaic.* **a.** teaching or instruction. **b.** that which is taught. [ME; OE *lār,* c. D *leer,* G *Lehre* teaching. Cf. LEARN] **—Syn. 1.** See **learning.**

lore[2] (lô), *n. Zool.* the space between the eye and the bill of a bird, or a corresponding space in other animals, as snakes. [t. L: m. *lōrum* thong]

Lorelei (lô′rə lī′; *Ger.* lō rə lī′), *n. German Legend.* an enchantress who, by her singing, caused sailors to wreck their boats on her rock in the Rhine; created by Clemens Brentano in a poem in 1800. [t. G]

Lorentz (*Du.* lō′rənts), *n.* **Hendrik Antoon** (*Du.* hĕn′drĭk ŏn′tōn), 1853–1928, Dutch physicist.

Lorenzetti (*It.* lō rĕn tsĕt′tē), *n.* **1. Ambrogio** (*It.* äm brŏ′jō), fl. 1319–47, Siennese painter. **2.** his brother, **Pietro** (*It.* pyĕ′trō), fl. 1320–45, Siennese painter.

lorgnette (lô nyĕt′), *n.* **1.** a pair of eyeglasses mounted on a long handle. **2.** opera glasses. [t. F, der. *lorgner* look sidelong at, eye, der. OF *lorgne* squinting]

lorgnon (lô nyŏn′), *n.* **1.** an eyeglass, or a pair of eyeglasses. **2.** opera glasses. [F, der. *lorgner.* See LORGNETTE]

lorica (lŏ rī′kə), *n., pl.* **-cae** (-sē). **1.** *Zool.* a hard protective case or sheath, as the protective coverings secreted by certain infusorians. **2.** a cuirass or corselet, orig. of leather. [t. L: a corselet, a defence]

loricate (lŏ′rĭ kāt′), *adj.* covered with a lorica. Also, **lor′icat′ed.**

Lorient (*Fr.* lō ryäɴ), *n.* a seaport in W France, in Morbihan department. 63,924 (1962).

lorikeet (lŏ′rĭ kēt′, lŏ′rĭ kēt′), *n.* any of various small lories. [f. LORY + (PARA)KEET]

loris (lô′rĭs), *n., pl.* **-ris. 1.** a small, slender, tailless, large-eyed, nocturnal lemur, *Loris gracilis,* of Ceylon (**slender loris**). **2.** any lemur of the related genus *Nycticebus* (**slow loris**). [t. NL, t. D: m. *loeris* booby]

L'Orme (*Fr.* lŏrm), *n.* **Philibert de** (*Fr.* fē lē bĕr′ də), *c.* 1500–70, French architect.

lorn (lôn), *adj.* **1.** *Archaic.* forsaken, desolate, wretched, or forlorn. **2.** *Obs.* lost, ruined, or undone. [ME *lorn,* OE *loren,* pp. of *-lēosan* LOSE (recorded in compounds)]

Lorne (lôn), *n.* **Firth of,** an arm of the sea in Argyll, Scotland. Also, **Lorn.**

Lorrain (lŏ rān′; *Fr.* lō räɴ′), *n.* **Claude** (klôd; *Fr.* klōd) (*Claude Gelée*), 1600–82, French landscape painter. Also, **Lorraine.**

Lorraine (lŏ rān′; *Fr.* lō rĕn′), *n.* **1.** a medieval kingdom in W Europe along the Moselle, Meuse, and Rhine rivers. **2.** a region in NE France, once included in this kingdom: a former province. See **Alsace-Lorraine. 3.** an administrative region in NE France comprising the departments of Moselle, Meurthe-et-Moselle, Meuse, and Vosges. 2,194,151 pop. (1962); 9150 sq. mi. *Cap.:* Metz. **4. Cross of,** a cross having two horizontal arms, the upper one shorter than the other. See illus. under **cross.**

lorry (lŏ′rĭ), *n., pl.* **-ries. 1.** a long, motor-driven wagon, often with low sides, used esp. for heavy work. **2.** any of various vehicles or cars running on rails, as for transporting material in a mine or factory. [cf. d. E *lurry* pull, drag, lug]

lory (lô′rĭ), *n., pl.* **-ries.** any of various parrots (subfamily *Loriinae*) of the Malay Archipelago, Australia, etc., mostly bright-coloured, brush-tongued, and of small size. [t. Malay: m. *lūrī*]

losable (lo͞o′zə bl), *adj.* that may be lost.

Los Angeles (lŏs ăn′jĭ lēz′), a seaport in the U.S., in SW California. 2,479,015 pop. (1960); with suburbs, 5,923,644 (1960); 452 sq. mi.

Loschmidt's number (*Ger.* lŏsh′mĭt), *Physics.* the number of molecules in a cubic centimetre of a perfect gas at N.T.P.; equal to $2{\cdot}687 \times 10^{19}$. [named after Joseph *Loschmidt,* 1821–95, German physicist]

lose (lo͞oz), *v.,* **lost, losing.** *—v.t.* **1.** to come to be without, by some chance, and not know the whereabouts of: *to lose a ring.* **2.** to suffer the loss or deprivation of: *to lose one's life.* **3.** to be bereaved of by death: *to lose a child.* **4.** to fail to keep, preserve, or maintain control of: *to lose one's balance.* **5.** to cease to have: *to lose all fear.* **6.** to bring to destruction or ruin (now chiefly in the passive): *ship and crew were lost.* **7.** to have slip from sight, hearing, attention, etc.: *to lose a face in a crowd.* **8.** to become separated from and ignorant of (the way, etc.). **9.** to leave far behind in a pursuit, race, etc. **10.** to use to no purpose, or waste: *to lose time in waiting.* **11.** to fail to have, get, catch, etc.; miss: *to lose an opportunity.* **12.** to fail to win (a prize, stake, etc.). **13.** to be defeated in (a game, lawsuit, battle, etc.). **14.** to cause the loss of: *the delay lost the battle for them.* **15.** to let (oneself) go astray; become bewildered: *to be lost in a wood.* **16.** to absorb or engross in something to the exclusion of knowledge or consciousness of all else (usually used reflexively or in the passive): *to be lost in thought. —v.i.* **17.** to suffer loss: *to lose on a contract.* **18.** to lose ground, fall behind, or fail to hold one's own, as in a race or other contest. **19.** to fail to win, as in a contest; be defeated. [ME *lose(n),* OE *-leōsan;* r. ME *lese(n),* OE *-lēosan* (cf. *choose,* r. *chese*), c. G *(ver)lieren.* See LOSS] **—los′er,** *n.*

losing (lo͞o′zĭng), *adj.* **1.** that loses. *—n.* **2.** (*pl.*) losses. **—los′ingly,** *adv.*

losel (lō′zəl), *Archaic. —n.* **1.** a worthless person. *—adj.* **2.** worthless; good-for-nothing. [akin to LOSE]

loss (lŏs), *n.* **1.** detriment or disadvantage from failure to keep, have, or get: *to bear the loss of a robbery.* **2.** that which is lost. **3.** amount or number lost. **4.** a being deprived of or coming to be without something that one has had: *loss of friends.* **5.** a bereavement. **6.** the accidental or inadvertent losing of something dropped, misplaced, or of unknown whereabouts: *to discover the loss of a document.* **7.** a losing by defeat, or failure to win: *the loss of a bet.* **8.** failure to make good use of something, as time; waste. **9.** failure to preserve or maintain: *loss of speed.* **10.** destruction or ruin. **11.** *Com.* failure to recover the costs of a transaction or the like, in the form of benefits derived. **12.** *Mil.* **a.** the losing of soldiers by death, capture, etc. **b.** (*often pl.*) the number of soldiers so lost. **13.** *Insurance.* **a.** occurrence of a risk covered by a contract of insurance so as to result in insurer liability. **b.** that which causes such a loss. **c.** an example of such a loss. **14.** *Elect.* the difference between power input and power output in an electric circuit, device, machine, or system incident to the process of electric transmission or energy conversion. **15. at a loss, a.** in a state of bewilderment or uncertainty. **b.** in a state of embarrassment for lack of something: *to be at a loss for words.* [ME; OE *los* destruction, c. Icel. *los* breaking up; akin to LOSE]

loss leader, a popular article which is sold at a loss for the purpose of attracting trade to a shop or store.

loss ratio, *Insurance.* the ratio of paid-in premiums to losses sustained during a certain period.

lost (lŏst), *adj.* **1.** no longer possessed or retained: *lost friends.* **2.** no longer to be found: *lost articles.* **3.** having gone astray or lost the way; bewildered as to place, direction, etc. **4.** not used to good purpose, as opportunities, time, labour, etc.; wasted. **5.** that one has failed to win: *a lost prize.* **6.** attended with defeat: *a lost battle.* **7.** destroyed or ruined: *lost ships.* **8. lost to, a.** no longer belonging to. **b.** no longer possible or open to: *the opportunity was lost to him.* **c.** insensible to: *to be lost to all sense of duty. —v.* **9.** pt. of **lose.**

lost cause, a cause for which defeat has occurred or is inevitable.

lost generation, 1. the men and women who came of age during and just after World War I, considered as spiritually lost in the social upheaval of the times. **2.** the large number of young men who were killed in World War I, considered as a whole generation destroyed.

Lost Pleiad. See **Pleiades** (def. 1).

lost tribes, the ten tribes of ancient Israel which were taken into captivity and were believed never to have returned to Palestine.

lost wax process, a process of casting used esp. for statuary. The figure is modelled in wax and then covered in plaster; when the plaster has set the wax is melted out and replaced by metal.

lot (lŏt), *n.*, *v.*, **lotted, lotting.** —*n.* **1.** one of a set of objects drawn from a receptacle, etc., to decide a question or choice by chance. **2.** the casting or drawing of such objects as a method of deciding something: *to choose a person by lot.* **3.** the decision or choice so made. **4.** allotted share or portion. **5.** the portion in life assigned by fate or providence, or one's fate, fortune, or destiny. **6.** a distinct portion or piece of land; plot. **7.** *Chiefly U.S.* a piece of land forming a part of a district, city, or other community. **8.** *Films.* the site used for film-making, as the studios, locations, etc. **9.** a distinct portion or parcel of anything, as of merchandise. **10.** a number of things or persons collectively. **11.** *Colloq.* a person of a specified sort: *a bad lot.* **12.** (*often pl.*) *Colloq.* a great many or a great deal: *a lot of books.* **13.** *Obs.* a tax or duty. **14. a lot** or **lots,** *Colloq.* a great deal; much: *that is a lot better.* **15. throw in one's lot with,** to give one's entire support to. —*v.t.* **16.** to divide or distribute by lot. **17.** to assign to one as his lot; allot. **18.** to divide into lots, as land. **19.** *Obs.* to cast or draw lots for. —*v.i.* **20.** *Obs.* to draw lots. [ME; OE *hlot*, akin to G *Los*, Icel. *hlutr*, Goth. *hlauts*]

Lot (lŏt), *n. Bible.* the nephew of Abraham. His wife was changed into a pillar of salt for looking back during their flight from Sodom. Gen. 13:1–12, 19. [t. Heb.]

Lot (*Fr.* lŏt), *n.* **1.** a river in S France, flowing W to the Garonne. ab. 300 mi. **2.** a department in S France. 149,929 pop. (1962); 2017 sq. mi. *Cap.:* Cahors.

Lot-et-Garonne (*Fr.* lŏt ė gȧ rŏn′), *n.* a department in SW France. 275,028 pop. (1962); 2078 sq. mi. *Cap.:* Agen.

loth (lōth), *adj.* loath.

Lothair I (lō thĕə′), *c.* 795–855, Holy Roman Emperor 840–855.

Lothair II ('*the Saxon*'), *c.* 1070–1137, Holy Roman Emperor 1125–37.

Lothaire (*Fr.* lō tĕr′), *n.* French name for **Lothair.**

Lothar (*Ger.* lō′tȧr), *n.* German name for **Lothair.**

Lothario (lō thä′rĭ ō′), *n.*, *pl.* **-tharios.** a jaunty libertine; a rake. [named after a character in '*The Fair Penitent*' (1703) by Nicholas Rowe]

Lothians (lō′ŧħyənz), *n.pl.* **The,** three counties in Scotland: East Lothian, Midlothian, West Lothian.

Loti (*Fr.* lō tē′), *n.* **Pierre** (*Fr.* pyĕr) (*Louis Marie Julien Viaud*), 1850–1923, French novelist.

lotion (lō′shən), *n. Pharm., etc.* a watery liquid containing insoluble medicinal matter applied externally to the skin without rubbing. [ME, t. L: s. *lōtio* a washing]

lottery (lŏt′ə rĭ), *n.*, *pl.* **-teries. 1.** a scheme or arrangement for raising money, as for some public, charitable, or private purpose, by the sale of a large number of tickets, certain among which, as determined by chance after the sale, entitle the holders to prizes. **2.** any scheme for the distribution of prizes by chance. **3.** any affair of chance. [t. It.: m. *lotteria*, der. *lotto* lot, t. F: m. *lot*, t. Gmc; cf. LOT]

lotto (lŏt′ō), *n.* a game played by drawing numbered discs from a bag or the like and covering corresponding numbers on cards; bingo. [t. It. See LOTTERY]

Lotto (*It.* lŏt′tō), *n.* **Lorenzo** (*It.* lō rĕn′tsō), *c.* 1480–1556, Italian painter.

lotus (lō′təs), *n.* **1.** a plant, commonly identified with a species of jujube or of elm tree, referred to in Greek legend as yielding a fruit which induced a state of dreamy and contented forgetfulness in those who ate it. **2.** the fruit itself. **3.** either of the two species of waterlilies, *Nelumbium nelumbo* (**sacred lotus of India**) or *N. pentapetalum* (**water chinquapin**). **4.** any of various nymphaeaceous plants, as either of two Egyptian waterlilies *Nymphaea lotus* or *N. caerulea.* **5.** a representation of such a plant, common in Egyptian and Hindu decorative art. **6.** any of the shrubbery herbs, with red, pink, or white flowers, constituting the leguminous genus *Lotus*, certain of which are valued as pasture plants. Also, **lo′tos.** [t. L, t. Gk: m. *lōtós*]

lotus-eater (lō′təs ē′tə), *n.* **1.** an eater of the fruit which induced languor and forgetfulness of home. Homer's *Odyssey*, ix. **2.** one who leads a life of dreamy, indolent ease, indifferent to the busy world.

loud (loud), *adj.* **1.** striking strongly upon the organs of hearing, as sound, noise, the voice, etc.; strongly audible. **2.** making, emitting, or uttering strongly audible sounds: *loud knocking.* **3.** full of sound or noise, or resounding. **4.** clamorous, vociferous, or blatant. **5.** emphatic or insistent: *to be loud in one's praises.* **6.** *Colloq.* strong or offensive in smell. **7.** excessively striking to the eye, or offensively showy, as colours, dress or the wearer, etc.; garish. **8.** obtrusively vulgar, as manners, persons, etc. —*adv.* **9.** loudly. [ME; OE *hlūd*, c. G *laut*] —**loud′ly,** *adv.* —**loud′ness,** *n.*

—**Syn. 1.** resounding; deafening; stentorian. LOUD, NOISY describe a strongly audible sound or sounds. LOUD means characterized by a full, powerful sound or sounds, which make a strong impression on the organs of hearing: *a loud voice, laugh, report.* NOISY refers to a series of sounds, and suggests clamour and discordance, or persistence in making loud sounds which are disturbing and annoying: *a noisy crowd.* **7.** gaudy, flashy, showy. —**Ant. 1.** quiet.

louden (lou′dn), *v.i.*, *v.t.* to make or become louder.

loud-hailer (loud′hā′lə), *n.* a megaphone with a built-in amplifier.

loudish (lou′dĭsh), *adj.* somewhat loud.

loud-mouthed (loud′mouŧħd′), *adj.* loud of voice or utterance; vociferous; blatant.

loud pedal, *Music.* the sustaining pedal on a piano.

loudspeaker (loud′spē′kə), *n.* any of various devices by which speech, music, etc., can be made audible throughout a room, hall, or the like.

lough (lŏk, lŏKH), *n. Irish.* **1.** a lake. **2.** an arm of the sea. [ME, t. Irish: m. *loch.* Cf. LOCH]

Loughborough (lŭf′bə rə, -brə), *n.* a town in England, in Leicestershire. 38,621 (1961).

louis (lo͞o′ĭ), *n.*, *pl.* **louis** (lo͞o′ĭz). louis d'or.

Louis (lo͞o′ĭs), *n.* **Joe** (*Joseph Louis Barrow*), born 1914, U.S. boxer: world heavyweight champion 1937–49.

Louis (lo͞o′ĭ; *Fr.* lwē), *n.* name of 18 kings of France.

Louis I ('*le Débonnaire*', '*the Pious*'), A.D. 778–840, king of France and emperor of the Holy Roman Empire A.D. 814–840 (son of Charlemagne).

Louis II ('*the German*'), A.D. 804?–876, king of all Germany E of Rhine by Treaty of Verdun (A.D. 843). German, **Ludwig II.**

Louis II de Bourbon. See **Condé.**

Louis IV ('*the Bavarian*'), 1287?–1347, king of Germany and emperor of the Holy Roman Empire 1314–47.

Louis V ('*le Fainéant*'), A.D. 967?–987, king of France A.D. 986–987; the last of the Carolingian family of rulers in France.

Louis IX (*Saint Louis*), 1215–70, king of France 1226–1270; canonized in 1297.

Louis XI, 1423–83, king of France 1461–83.

Louis XII ('*Père du Peuple*'), 1462–1515, king of France 1498–1515.

Louis XIII, 1601–43, king of France 1610–43.

Louis XIV ('*the Sun King*'), 1638–1715, king of France 1643–1715.

Louis XV, 1710–74, king of France 1715–74.

Louis XVI, 1754–93, king of France from 1774, deposed in 1792, guillotined in 1793.

Louis XVII, 1785–95, son of Louis XVI. He never reigned, but was called king of France 1793–95, by the monarchists.

Louis XVIII, 1755–1824, king of France 1814–24.

Louisburg (lo͞o′ĭs bûg′), *n.* a seaport in SE Canada, on Cape Breton island, Nova Scotia: French fortress captured by the British, 1745, 1758. 1417 (1961).

louis d'or (lo͞o′ĭ dô′; *Fr.* lwē dŏr′), a French gold coin, issued 1640–1795. Also, **louis.** [F: gold louis]

Louise (lo͝o ēz′), *n.* **Lake,** a glacial lake in the Canadian Rockies, in SW Alberta: resort. 5670 ft high.

Louis heel, a small waisted heel of a woman's boot or shoe.

Louisiana (lo͞o ē′zĭ ăn′ə), *n.* a state in the S United States. 3,257,022 pop. (1960); 48,522 sq. mi. *Cap.:* Baton Rouge. *Abbrev.:* La. —**Loui′sian′an, Louisianian** (lo͞o ē′zĭ ăn′ ĭ ən), *adj.*, *n.*

Louisiana Purchase, The, a huge territory which the United States purchased from France in 1803, extending from the Mississippi to the Rocky Mountains and from the Gulf of Mexico to Canada.

Louis Napoleon, Napoleon III.

Louis Philippe (*Fr.* fē lēp′), 1773–1850, king of France 1830–48.

Louis Quatorze (kă tôz′; *Fr.* kȧ tŏrz′), of the period of Louis XIV of France or the styles of architecture, decoration, etc., prevailing about that time (1650–1700), relying more upon classical models than those of the Louis Treize period, and richly ornamented.

Louis Quinze (*Fr.* kăNz), of the period of Louis XV of France or the styles of architecture, decoration, etc., (known as *rococo*) prevailing about that time (1700–1750), smaller in scale and more delicate in ornament than those of the Louis Quatorze period.

Louis Seize (*Fr.* sĕz), of the period of Louis XVI of France or the styles of architecture, decoration, etc. prevailing about that time (1750–1790), characterized by a recurrence of classical models.

Louis Treize (*Fr.* trĕz), of the period of Louis XIII of France or the styles of architecture, decoration, etc., prevailing about that time (1600–1650), less light and elegant than those of the earlier Renaissance, and employing forms and features based on the classical.

Louisville (lo͞o′ĭ vĭl′), *n.* a city in the U.S., in N Kentucky: a port on the Ohio river. 390,639 (1960).

lounge (lounj), *v.*, **lounged, lounging,** *n.* —*v.i.* **1.** to pass time idly and indolently. **2.** to recline indolently; loll. **3.** to move or go (*about, along, off,* etc.) in a leisurely, indolent manner. —*v.t.* **4.** to pass (time, etc.) in lounging (fol. by *away* or *out*). —*n.* **5.** the living room of a private residence. **6.** a large room in a hotel, etc., used by guests for relaxation purposes. **7.** Also, **lounge bar.** the more expensive part of a public house. **8.** *Chiefly U.S.* chaise longue. **9.** the act or a spell of lounging. **10.** a lounging gait. [? akin to obs. *lungis* laggard, t. OF: m. *longis* one who is long (i.e. slow)] —**loung′er,** *n.*

lounge lizard. See **lizard** (def. 4).

lounge suit, a suit worn by men as informal day wear.

loup (lo͞o), *n.* a cloth mask, often of silk, which covers only half the face. [F: lit., wolf, g. L *lupus*]

loup-garou (*Fr.* lo͞o gȧ ro͞o′), *n., pl.* **loups-garous** (*Fr.* lo͞o-gȧ ro͞o′). *French.* a werewolf; a lycanthrope. [F: f. *loup* wolf (g. L *lupus*) + *garou* werewolf, of Gmc orig.]

louping ill (lou′pĭng, lō′-), an acute, virus-induced infectious disease of sheep, affecting the nervous system, and transmitted by a tick, which also attacks man.

lour (lou′ə), *v.i.* **1.** to be dark and threatening, as the sky or the weather. **2.** to frown, scowl, or look sullen. —*n.* **3.** a dark, threatening appearance, as of the sky, weather, etc. **4.** a frown or scowl. Also, *Chiefly U.S.*, **lower.** [ME *loure(n)* frown, lurk; cf. G *lauern* lurk]

Lourdes (*Fr.* lo͞ord), *n.* a town in SW France: famous shrine. 16,829 (1962).

Lourenço Marques (lə rĕn′sō mäk′, -mäks′; *Port.* lō-rĕɴ′so͞o mȧr′kėsh), a seaport in and the capital of Mozambique, on Delagoa Bay. 93,516 (1960).

lourie (lo͝oə′rĭ), *n.* any bird of the African family *Musophagidae*; touraco. [t. Malay: m. *lūri* LORY]

louse (lous), *n., pl.* **lice** (līs) or (def. 3) **louses;** *v.*, **loused, lousing.** —*n.* **1.** any of the small, wingless, blood-sucking insects of the order *Anoplura,* including several species associated with man, as the **human louse,** *Pediculus humanus* (including the races known as **head louse,** *P. capitis,* and **body louse,** *P. corporis*), and the **crablouse,** *Phthirius pubis.* **2.** any of various other insects parasitic on animals or plants, as those of the order *Mallophaga* (**biting bird lice**) or the homopterous family *Aphididae* (**plant lice**). **3.** *Slang.* a despicable person. —*v.t.* **4.** *Slang.* to spoil (fol. by *up*). [ME *lows(e), lous(e),* OE *lūs* (pl. *lȳs*), c. G *Laus*]

Head louse, *Pediculus capitis* (Length ⅛ in.)

lousewort (lous′wûrt′), *n.* any of the scrophulariaceous herbs constituting the large genus *Pedicularis,* as *P. sylvatica* (**pasture lousewort**), an English species formerly supposed to breed lice in sheep, and *P. canadensis* (**wood betony**).

lousy (lou′zĭ), *adj.*, **lousier, lousiest. 1.** infested with lice. **2.** *Slang.* mean, or contemptible. **3.** *Slang.* well supplied. —**lous′ily,** *adv.* —**lous′iness,** *n.*

lout (lout), *n.* an awkward, stupid person; a boor. [akin to archaic *lout* bow or obs. *lout* lurk]

Louth (louth), *n.* a county in E Ireland, in Leinster. 67,378 pop. (1961); 316 sq. mi. *Co. town.*: Dundalk.

loutish (lou′tĭsh), *adj.* like or characteristic of a lout; boorish. —**lout′ishly,** *adv.* —**lout′ishness,** *n.*

Louvain (*Fr.* lo͞o văɴ′), *n.* a city in central Belgium. 32,474 (1962). Flemish, **Leuven.**

louver (lo͞o′və), *n.* **1.** a turret or lantern on the roof of a medieval building, to supply ventilation or light. **2.** an arrangement of louver-boards or the like closing a window or other opening, or a single louver-board. **3.** one of a number of slitlike openings in the bonnet or body of a motor vehicle for the escape of heated air from within. Also, **louvre.** [ME *lover,* t. OF; orig. obscure]

louver-board (lo͞o′və bôd′), *n.* one of a series of overlapping, sloping boards, slats, or the like, in an opening, so arranged as to admit air but exclude rain. Also, **louvre-board.**

Louvre (*Fr.* lo͞o′vr), *n.* a royal palace (begun 1541) in Paris, largely occupied since 1793 by a famous museum.

Louys (*Fr.* lwē), *n.* **Pierre** (*Fr.* pyĕr), 1870–1925, French author.

lovable (lŭv′ə bl), *adj.* of such a nature as to attract love. Also, **loveable.** —**lov′abil′ity, lov′ableness,** *n.* —**lov′ably,** *adv.*

lovage (lŭv′ĭj), *n.* a European apiaceous herb, *Levisticum officinale,* cultivated in gardens. [ME *loveache,* t. OF: alter. of *levesche,* g. LL *levisticum,* appar. alter. of L *ligusticum,* prop. neut. of *Ligusticus* Ligurian]

love (lŭv), *n., v.*, **loved, loving.** —*n.* **1.** a strong or passionate affection for a person of the opposite sex. **2.** sexual passion or desire, or its gratification. **3.** an object of love or affection; a sweetheart. **4.** (*cap.*) a personification of sexual affection, as Eros or Cupid. **5.** a feeling of warm personal attachment or deep affection, as for a friend (or between friends), parent, child, etc. **6.** strong predilection or liking for anything: *love of books.* **7.** the benevolent affection of God for His creatures, or the reverent affection due from them to God. **8.** *Tennis, etc.* nothing; no score. **9. for love, a.** out of affection. **b.** for nothing; without compensation. **10. for the love of,** for the sake of. **11. in love,** feeling deep affection or passion (often fol. by *with*). **12. make love, a.** to court. **b.** to have sexual intercourse.
—*v.t.* **13.** to have love or affection for. **14.** to have a strong or passionate affection for (one of the opposite sex). **15.** to have a strong liking for; take great pleasure in: *to love music.* —*v.i.* **16.** to have love or affection, esp., to be or fall in love with one of the opposite sex. [ME; OE *lufu,* c. OHG *luba*]
—**Syn. 1, 5.** LOVE, AFFECTION, DEVOTION all mean a deep and enduring emotional regard, usually for another person. LOVE may apply to various kinds of regard: the charity of the Creator, reverent adoration towards God or towards a person, the relation of parent and child, the regard of friends for each other, romantic feelings for one of the opposite sex, etc. AFFECTION is a fondness for persons of either sex, that is enduring and tender, but calm. DEVOTION is an intense love and steadfast, enduring loyalty to a person; it may also imply consecration to a cause. —**Ant. 5.** hate.

loveable (lŭv′ə bl), *adj.* lovable.

love affair, 1. a particular experience of being in love. **2.** a sexual relationship between a man and a woman.

love apple, the tomato.

lovebird (lŭv′bûd′), *n.* **1.** any of various small parrots, esp. of the genera *Agapornis,* of Africa, and *Psittacula,* of South America, remarkable for the fact that the members of each pair keep close together when perching. **2.** *Colloq.* a man or a woman acting lovingly towards a member of the opposite sex.

love child, an illegitimate child.

love feast, 1. (among the early Christians) a meal eaten in token of brotherly love and charity. **2.** *Chiefly U.S.* a rite practised by a few denominations such as Mennonites and Dunkers; a fellowship meal. **3.** a banquet or gathering of persons to promote good feeling.

love-in (lŭv′ĭn′), *n.* a gathering for the display of communal goodwill and brotherly love.

love-in-a-mist (lŭv′ĭn ə mĭst′), *n.* a ranunculaceous plant, *Nigella damascena,* with feathery dissected leaves and whitish or blue flowers.

love-in-idleness (lŭv′ĭn ī′dl nĭs), *n.* the wild pansy, *Viola tricolor.*

love knot, a knot of ribbon as a token of love.

Lovelace (lŭv′lās′), *n.* **Richard,** 1618–58, English poet.

loveless (lŭv′lĭs), *adj.* **1.** devoid of or unattended with love. **2.** feeling no love. **3.** receiving no love. —**love′lessly,** *adv.* —**love′lessness,** *n.*

love-lies-bleeding (lŭv′līz blē′dĭng), *n.* any of several species of amaranth, esp. *Amaranthus caudatus,* with spikes of crimson flowers.

Lovell (lŭv′əl), *n.* **Sir (Alfred Charles) Bernard,** born 1913, English astronomer, director of Jodrell Bank since 1951.

lovelock (lŭv′lŏk′), *n.* **1.** any conspicuous lock of hair. **2.** (formerly) a long, flowing lock or curl, dressed separately from the rest of the hair, worn by courtiers.

lovelorn (lŭv′lôn′), *adj.* forsaken by one's love; forlorn or pining from love. —**love′lorn′ness,** *n.*

lovely (lŭv′lĭ), *adj.*, **-lier, -liest. 1.** charmingly or exquisitely beautiful: *a lovely flower.* **2.** having a beauty that appeals to the heart as well as to the eye, as a person, a face, etc. **3.** *Colloq.* delightful, or highly pleasing: *to have a lovely time.* **4.** of a great moral or spiritual beauty: *lovely character.* [ME *lovelich,* OE *luflic* amiable] —**love′liness,** *n.* —**Syn. 2.** See **beautiful.**

lover (lŭv′ə), *n.* **1.** one who is in love with a person of the opposite sex (now used almost exclusively of the man). **2.** a man who is having a sexual relationship with a woman. **3.** (*pl.*) a man and a woman in love with each other or having a love affair. **4.** one who has a strong predilection or liking for something: *a lover of music.* **5.** one who loves.

Lover (lŭv′ə), *n.* **Samuel,** 1797–1868, Irish novelist, artist, and composer.

love seat, a seat for two persons.

lovesick (lŭv′sĭk′), *adj.* **1.** languishing with love. **2.** expressive of such languishing. —**love′sick′ness,** *n.*

loving (lŭv′ĭng), *adj.* feeling or showing love; affectionate; fond: *loving glances.* —**lov′ingly,** *adv.* —**lov′ingness,** *n.*

loving-cup (lŭv′ĭng kŭp′), *n.* **1.** a large cup, as of silver, commonly with several handles, given as a prize, award, etc.; cup (def. 2). **2.** a similar cup which is filled with wine and passed around an assembly, at a banquet or the like.

loving-kindness (lŭv′ĭng kīnd′nĭs), *n.* kindness arising from love (used primarily of the Deity).

low¹ (lō), *adj.* **1.** situated or occurring not far above the ground, floor, or base: *a low shelf.* **2.** not far above the horizon, as a heavenly body. **3.** lying or being below the general level: *low ground.* **4.** *Print.* (of type or blocks) below the level of the forme surface. **5.** designating or pertaining to regions near the sea-level or sea as opposed to highland or inland regions: *Low Countries.* **6.** prostrate or dead: *to lay one low.* **7.** profound or deep, as a bow. **8.** (of a garment) low-necked. **9.** of small extent upwards, or not high or tall: *low walls.* **10.** rising but slightly from a surface: *low relief.* **11.** of less than average or normal height or depth, as a liquid, stream, etc. **12.** reduced to the least height, depth, or the like: *low tide.* **13.** lacking in strength or vigour; feeble; weak. **14.** affording little strength or nourishment, as diet. **15.** small in amount, degree, force, etc.: *a low number.* **16.** having a small amount of a particular constituent: *low-calorie diet.* **17.** *Cards.* having smaller value than another card. **18.** denoted by a low number: *a low latitude* (one near the equator). **19.** assigning or attributing no great amount, value, or excellence: *a low estimate of something.* **20.** depressed or dejected: *low spirits.* **21.** far down in the scale of rank or estimation; humble: *low birth.* **22.** of inferior quality or character: *a low type of intellect.* **23.** lacking in dignity or elevation, as of thought or expression. **24.** concealed; unnoticeable: *lie low.* **25.** grovelling or abject; mean or base: *a low trick.* **26.** coarse or vulgar: *low company.* **27.** *Biol.* having a relatively simple structure; not complex in organization. **28.** *Music.* produced by relatively low vibrations, as sounds; grave in pitch. **29.** not loud: *a low murmur.* **30.** relatively late or recent, as a date. **31.** holding to Low-Church principles and practices. **32.** *Phonet.* pronounced with the tongue held relatively low in the mouth: *'hot' has a low vowel.* **33.** *Motor vehicles.* of or pertaining to low-transmission gear ratio. —*adv.* **34.** in or to a low position, point, degree, etc. **35.** near the ground, floor, or base; not aloft. **36.** humbly. **37.** at or to a low pitch. **38.** in a low tone; softly; quietly. **39.** far down in time, or late. —*n.* **40.** that which is low; a low level. **41.** *Motor Vehicles.* a transmission gear ratio providing the least forward speed, usually used to start a motor vehicle, or for extra power; first. **42.** *Meteorol.* a pressure system characterized by relatively low pressure at the centre. **43.** *Cards.* **a.** the lowest trump card. **b.** a card of small value. **44.** a point of least value, amount, etc.; nadir: *prices reached an all-time low.* [ME *lowe, lohe,* earlier *lah,* t. Scand.; cf. Icel. *lāgr,* akin to LIE²] —**low′ness,** *n.* —**Syn. 21.** lowly, meek, obscure. **25.** ignoble, degraded, sordid. **26.** See **mean**². **28.** deep. **29.** subdued. —**Ant. 21.** lofty.

low² (lō), *v.i.* **1.** to utter the sound characteristic of cattle; moo. —*v.t.* **2.** to utter by or as by lowing. —*n.* **3.** the act or the sound of lowing. [ME *low(en),* OE *hlōwan,* c. D *loeien*]

Low (lō), *n.* **Sir David,** 1891–1963, British cartoonist, born in New Zealand.

lowan (lō′ən), *n.* the mallee fowl, a light brown speckled bird of central and southern Australia, *Leipoa ocellata,* up to 24 in. long. [t. native Australian]

Low Archipelago (lō), Tuamotu Archipelago.

low area, *Meteorol.* a region where the atmospheric or barometric pressure is lower than that of the surrounding regions: *the low area in the central part of a cyclone.*

lowborn (lō′bôn′), *adj.* of humble birth.

lowboy (lō′boi′), *n. U.S.* a low chest of drawers supported on short legs.

lowbred (lō′brĕd′), *adj.* characterized by or characteristic of low or vulgar breeding.

lowbrow (lō′brou′), *Colloq.* —*n.* **1.** a person of low intellectual calibre or culture. —*adj.* **2.** being a lowbrow. **3.** pertaining or proper to lowbrows.

Low Church, a party in the Anglican Church which lays little stress on sacraments and church authority, etc., and holds evangelical views (opposed to *High Church*). —**Low-Church** (lō′chûch′), *adj.* —**Low′-Church′man,** *n.*

low cloud, *Meteorol.* a cloud with an average height of less than 6500 ft above the ground.

low comedy, comedy which depends on physical action and situation rather than on wit and dialogue.

Low Countries, the lowland region near the North Sea, forming the lower basin of the Rhine, Meuse, and Scheldt rivers, divided in the Middle Ages into numerous small states: corresponding to modern Netherlands, Belgium, and Luxembourg.

low-down (lō′doun′), *n.* **1.** *Slang.* the actual unadorned facts or truth on some subject (prec. by *the*). —*adj.* **2.** *Colloq.* low; dishonourable; mean.

Lowell (lō′əl), *n.* **1. Amy Lawrence,** 1874–1925, U.S. poet and critic. **2. James Russell,** 1819–91, U.S. poet, essayist, and diplomat. **3. Robert,** born 1917, U.S. poet.

lower¹ (lō′ə), *adj.* **1.** compar. of **low**¹. **2.** (*often cap.*) *Geol.* denoting an earlier division of a period, system, or the like: *the Lower Devonian.* —*v.t.* **3.** to reduce in amount, price, degree, force, etc. **4.** to make less loud, as the voice. **5.** to bring down in rank or estimation, degrade, or humble; abase (oneself), as by some sacrifice of dignity. **6.** to cause to descend, or let down: *to lower a flag.* **7.** to make lower in height or level: *to lower the water in a canal.* **8.** *Music.* to make lower in pitch; flatten. —*v.t.* **9.** to become lower or less. **10.** to descend; sink. —**Syn. 3.** decrease, diminish. **5.** humiliate. —**Ant. 3.** raise, increase.

lower² (lou′ə), *v.i., n. Chiefly U.S.* lour.

Lower Austria (lō′ə), a province in NE Austria. 1,374,012 pop. (1961); 7092 sq. mi. German, **Niederösterreich.**

Lower California, a narrow peninsula in NW Mexico between the Gulf of California and the Pacific, forming two territories of Mexico. 604,346 pop. (1960); 55,634 sq. mi. *Cap.:* Mexicali (Northern Territory) and La Paz (Southern Territory). Spanish, **Baja California.**

Lower Canada, the name of Quebec province, 1791–1841.

lower case, *Print.* the lower half of a pair of cases which contains the small letters of the alphabet.

lower-case (lō′ə kās′), *adj., v.,* **-cased, -casing.** —*adj.* **1.** (of a letter) small; minuscule (as opposed to *capital*). **2.** *Print.* pertaining to or belonging in the lower case. See **case**² (def. 8). —*v.t.* **3.** to print or write with a lower-case letter or letters.

lower class, the class of people socially and conventionally regarded as being lower or lowest in the social hierarchy, commonly identified with the working class.

lower-class (lō′ə kläs′), *adj.* belonging or pertaining to the lower class.

lower deck, 1. *Naut.* the deck below a main deck. **2.** (in the Royal Navy) ratings collectively.

Lower Egypt. See **Egypt.**

Lower House, (*often l.c.*) **1.** one of two branches of a legislature, generally more representative and with more members than the upper branch. **2.** the House of Commons.

Lower Hutt (hŭt), a town in New Zealand, on S North Island. 56,600 (est. 1965).

lowering (lou′ə rĭng), *adj.* **1.** dark and threatening, as the sky, clouds, weather, etc. **2.** frowning or sullen, as the face, gaze, etc. —**low′eringly,** *adv.*

Lower Karoo, *Geol.* **1.** pertaining to the Upper Palaeozoic period or system in S Africa, roughly equivalent to the Upper Carboniferous and Permian. **2.** a period or system following the Cape and preceding the Upper Karoo in S Africa. Also, **Lower Karroo.**

lowermost (lō′ə mōst′), *adj.* lowest.

Lower Saxony, a Land in N West Germany. 6,967,200 pop. (est. 1966); 18,298 sq. mi. *Cap.:* Hanover. German, **Niedersachsen.**

lower world, 1. the regions of the dead, conceived by the ancients as lying beneath the earth's surface; Hades. **2.** the earth as distinguished from the heavenly bodies or from heaven.

lowest common multiple. See **common multiple.**

Lowestoft (lōs′tŏft; *locally* -təf), *n.* a seaport in England, in East Suffolk. 45,730 (1961).

low explosive, a relatively slow-burning explosive, usually set off by heat or friction, and used for propelling charges in guns or for ordinary blasting.

low frequency (lō′frē′kwən sĭ), a radio frequency in the range 30 to 300 kilohertz. —**low′-fre′quency,** *adj.*

Low German, 1. the Germanic speech of northern Germany and the Low Countries. **2.** Plattdeutsch.

low-grade (lō′grād′), *adj.* of inferior quality.

lowland (lō′lənd), *n.* **1.** land low with respect to neighbouring country. **2. the Lowlands,** a low, level region in S, central, and E Scotland. —*adj.* **3.** of, pertaining to, or characteristic of lowland or lowlands.

Lowlander (lō′lən də), *n.* **1.** a native of the Lowlands. **2.** (*l.c.*) an inhabitant of lowland or lowlands.

Low Latin, any form of non-classical Latin, as Late Latin, Vulgar Latin, or Medieval Latin.

low-loader (lō′lō′də), *n.* a road or rail vehicle in which the carrying platform is kept low for ease in loading and to give clearance under bridges, etc., for large objects.

lowly (lō′lĭ), *adj.,* **-lier, -liest,** *adv.* —*adj.* **1.** humble in station, condition, or nature: *a lowly cottage.* **2.** low in

growth or position. **3.** humble in spirit; meek. *—adv.* **4.** in a low position, manner, or degree. **5.** in a lowly manner; humbly. **—low′liness,** *n.* **—Syn. 3.** modest.
low mass, a mass said, and not sung, by a priest, assisted by a server only.
low-minded (lō′mīn′dĭd), *adj.* having or showing a low, coarse, or vulgar mind; mean. **—low′-mind′edly,** *adv.* **—low′-mind′edness,** *n.*
low-necked (lō′nĕkt′), *adj.* (of a garment) cut low so as to leave the neck and shoulders exposed; décolleté.
low-pitched (lō′pĭcht′), *adj.* **1.** pitched in a low register or key. **2.** produced by slow vibrations; relatively grave in pitch or soft in sound. **3.** (of a roof) having a low proportion of vertical to lateral dimension.
low-pressure (lō′prĕsh′ə), *adj.* having or involving a low or below-normal pressure (as of steam, etc.).
low-rise (lō′rīz′), *adj.* (of a building) having one or two storeys.
low-spirited (lō′spĭr′ĭ tĭd), *adj.* depressed; dejected. **—low′-spir′itedly,** *adv.* **—low′-spir′itedness,** *n.*
Low Sunday, the Sunday next after Easter.
low-tension (lō′tĕn′shən), *adj. Elect.* **1.** having or designed for use at low voltage, usually less than 750 volts. **2.** the winding of a transformer designed to operate at the lower voltage. *Abbrev.:* L.T. Cf. **high-tension.**
low tide, 1. the tide at low water. **2.** the time of low water. **3.** the lowest point of decline of anything.
low-voltage (lō′vōl′tĭj), *adj.* denoting an electric system with an operating voltage under 250 volts.
low water, water at its lowest level, as in a river.
Low Week, the week after Easter Week.
lox (lŏks), *n. Colloq.* liquid oxygen. [short for L(IQUID) OX(YGEN)]
loxodromic (lŏk′sə drŏm′ĭk), *adj.* pertaining to oblique sailing or sailing on rhumbs (**loxodromic lines**). Also, **lox′odrom′ical.** [f. Gk *loxó(s)* oblique + s. Gk *drómos* a running course + -IC]
loxodromics (lŏk′sə drŏm′ĭks), *n.* the art of oblique sailing. Also, **loxodromy** (lŏk sŏd′rə mĭ).
loyal (loi′əl), *adj.* **1.** faithful to one's allegiance, as to the sovereign, government, or state: *a loyal subject.* **2.** faithful to one's oath, engagements or obligations: *to be loyal to a vow.* **3.** faithful to any leader, party, or cause, or to any person or thing conceived as imposing obligations: *a loyal friend.* **4.** characterized by or showing faithfulness to engagements, allegiance, obligations, etc.: *loyal conduct.* [t. F, g. L *lēgālis* LEGAL] **—loy′ally,** *adv.* **—Syn. 2.** See **faithful.**
loyalist (loi′ə lĭst), *n.* one who is loyal; a supporter of the sovereign of the existing government, esp. in time of revolt. **—loy′alism,** *n.*
loyalty (loi′əl tĭ), *n., pl.* **-ties. 1.** the state or quality of being loyal; faithfulness to engagements or obligations. **2.** faithful adherence to a sovereign or government, or to a leader, cause, or the like.
—Syn. 2. LOYALTY, ALLEGIANCE, FIDELITY all imply a sense of duty or of devoted attachment to something or someone. LOYALTY connotes sentiment and the feeling of devotion which one holds for one's country, creed, family, friends, etc. ALLEGIANCE applies particularly to a citizen's duty to his country, or, by extension, one's obligation to support a party, cause, leader, etc. FIDELITY implies unwavering devotion and allegiance to a person, principle, etc.
Loyang (lō′yăng′), *n.* a city in Honan province, E China. 500,000 (est. 1958).
Loyola (loi ō′lə), *n.* **Ignatius** (ĭg nā′shyəs) (*Iñigo López de Recalde*), 1491–1556, Spanish soldier, priest, and saint, founder of the Jesuit order.
lozenge (lŏz′ĭnj), *n.* **1.** a small flavoured cake or confection of sugar, often medicated, orig. diamond-shaped. **2.** *Geom.* diamond. **3.** *Her.* a shield of this shape. [ME *losenge*, t. OF, appar. der. Pr. *lausa* stone slab]
Lozère (*Fr.* lô zĕr′), *n.* a department of S France. 81,868 pop. (1962); 2000 sq. mi. *Cap.:* Mende.
LP (ĕl′pē′), *adj.* **1.** (of a gramophone record) long-playing. *—n.* **2.** such a record. [initials of LONG-PLAYING]
L.P.S., Lord Privy Seal.
L.R.A.M., Licentiate of the Royal Academy of Music.
L.R.C.P., Licentiate of the Royal College of Physicians.
L.R.C.S., Licentiate of the Royal College of Surgeons.
LSD, *Pharm.* lysergic acid diethylamide, a crystalline solid, $C_{15}H_{15}N_2CON(C_2H_5)_2$, that produces temporary hallucinations and a schizophrenia-like psychotic state, used in medical research into mental disorders. Also, **LSD-25.**
l.s.d., (L *librae, solidi, denarii*) **1.** pounds, shillings, and pence **2.** *Colloq.* money. Also, **£. s. d.**
L.S.E., London School of Economics, a college of the University of London.
l.s.t., *Chiefly U.S.* local standard time.
Lt, Lieutenant.
L.T., low-tension.
l.t., **1.** long ton. **2.** *Chiefly U.S.* local time.
Ltd, limited. See **limited** (def. 3).
Lu, *Chem.* lutetium.
Lualaba (lo͞o′ə lä′bə), *n.* a river in the SE Democratic Republic of the Congo: a headstream of the Congo river. ab. 400 mi.
Luanda (lo͞o ăn′də; *Port.* lwən′də), *n.* a seaport in and the capital of Angola. 225,000 (est. 1960). Also, **Loanda, São Paulo de Loanda.**
Luang Prabang (lo͞o ăng′prä băng′), a town in N Laos, the royal capital. 8000 (est. 1962).
lubber (lŭb′ə), *n.* **1.** a big, clumsy, stupid person. **2.** (among sailors) an awkward or unskilled seaman; landlubber. [ME *lober.* See LOB[1]]
lubberly (lŭb′ə lĭ), *adj.* **1.** like or of a lubber. *—adv.* **2.** in a lubberly manner. **—lub′berliness,** *n.*
lubber's hole, *Naut.* an open space in the platform at the head of a lower mast, through which a sailor may mount and descend without going outside the rim.
Lubbock (lŭb′ək), *n.* **1.** a town in the U.S., in NW Texas. 128,691 (1960). **2. Sir John, Baron Avebury,** 1834–1913, British statesman, scientist, and writer.
Lübeck (*Ger.* lʏ′bĕk), *n.* a seaport in West Germany in NE Schleswig-Holstein: important Baltic port in the medieval Hanseatic League. 241,800 (est. 1966). See map under **Hanseatic League.**
Lübke (*Ger.* lʏp′kə), *n.* **Heinrich** (*Ger.* hīn′rĭKH), born 1894, German politician: president of West Germany 1959–69.
Lublin (*Pol.* lo͞o′blēn), *n.* a city in E Poland. 199,000 (1964). Russian, **Lyublin.**
lubra (lo͞o′brä, -brə), *n.* an aboriginal girl or woman of Australia. [t. native Australian]
lubricant (lo͞o′brĭ kənt), *n.* **1.** a lubricating material. *—adj.* **2.** lubricating.
lubricate (lo͞o′brĭ kāt′), *v.t.,* **-cated, -cating. 1.** to apply some oily, greasy, or other substance to, in order to diminish friction; oil or grease, as parts of a mechanism. **2.** to make slippery or smooth. [t. L: m. s. *lūbricātus*, pp., made slippery] **—lu′brica′tion,** *n.* **—lu′brica′tive,** *adj.*
lubricator (lo͞o′brĭ kā′tə), *n.* a person or a device that lubricates or furnishes lubricant.
lubricious (lo͞o brĭsh′əs), *adj.* lubricous.
lubricity (lo͞o brĭs′ĭ tĭ), *n., pl.* **-ties. 1.** slipperiness or oily smoothness of surface. **2.** capacity for lubrication. **3.** shiftiness. **4.** lewdness. [t. LL: m. s. *lūbricitas*, der. L *lūbricus* lubricous]
lubricous (lo͞o′brĭ kəs), *adj.* **1.** slippery, as of surface; of an oily smoothness. **2.** unstable; uncertain; shifty. **3.** lewd. Also, **lubricious.** [t. L: m. *lūbricus*]
Lubumbashi (lo͞o′bo͝om băsh′ĭ), *n.* a city in the S Democratic Republic of the Congo. 200,000 (est. 1964). Formerly, **Elisabethville.** See map under **Congo.**
Lucan (lo͞o′kən), *n.* (*Marcus Annaeus Lucanus*), A.D. 39–65, Roman poet, born in Spain.
Lucania (lo͞o kā′nyə), *n.* **1.** an ancient region in S Italy, NW of the Gulf of Taranto. **2.** Basilicata.
Lucca (*It.* lo͞ok′kä), *n.* a town in Italy, in NW Tuscany. 90,979 (1966).
luce (lo͞os), *n.* **1.** a freshwater fish, the pike, esp. when full-grown. **2.** *Her.* a device representing a pike.
lucent (lo͞o′sənt), *adj. Archaic.* **1.** shining. **2.** transparent. [t. L: s. *lūcens*, ppr., shining] **—lu′cence, lu′cency,** *n.*
lucerne (lo͞o sûn′), *n.* a European fabaceous forage plant, *Medicago sativa*, with bluish purple flowers; alfalfa. [t. F: m. *luzerne*, t. Pr.: m. *luzerno*, ult. der. L *lux* light]
Lucerne (lo͞o sûn′; *Fr.* lʏ sĕrn′), *n.* **1.** a canton in central Switzerland. 253,446 pop. (1960); 576 sq. mi. **2.** its capital, on **Lake Lucerne** (24 mi. long; 44 sq. mi.). 73,000 (1964). German, **Luzern.**
luces (lo͞o′sēz), *n.* pl. of **lux.**
Lucian (lo͞o′syən), *n.* A.D. *c.* 120–*c.* 180, Greek satirist.
lucid (lo͞o′sĭd), *adj.* **1.** shining or bright. **2.** clear or transparent. **3.** easily understood: *a lucid explanation.* **4.** characterized by clear perception or understanding; rational or sane: *a lucid interval.* [t. L: s. *lūcidus*] **—lucid′ity, lu′cidness,** *n.* **—lu′cidly,** *adv.*
Lucifer (lo͞o′sĭ fə), *n.* **1.** a proud rebellious archangel, identified with Satan, who fell from heaven. **2.** the planet Venus when appearing as the morning star. **3.** (*l.c.*) a friction match. [t. L: the morning star, prop. adj., light-bringing]
luciferase (lo͞o sĭf′ə rās′), *n. Biochem.* an enzyme which is present in the luminous organs of fireflies, etc., and which, acting upon luciferin, produces luminosity. [f. L *lūcifer* light-bringing + -ASE]

luciferin (lo͞o sĭf′ə rĭn), *n. Biochem.* a protein occurring in fireflies, etc., luminous when acted upon by luciferase. [f. L *lūcifer* light-bringing + -IN[2]]

lucifer match, lucifer (def. 3).

luciferous (lo͞o sĭf′ə rəs), *adj.* bringing or giving light. [f. L *lūcifer* light-bringing + -OUS]

Lucina (lo͞o sī′nə), *n.* the Roman goddess of childbirth.

luck (lŭk), *n.* **1.** that which happens to a person, either good or bad, as if by chance, in the course of events: *to have good luck.* **2.** good fortune; advantage or success considered as the result of chance: *to wish one luck.* [ME *lucke*, t. LG or D: m. *luk*, also *Geluk*, c. G *Glück*]

luckily (lŭk′ĭ lĭ), *adv.* by good luck; fortunately: *luckily he had enough money to pay the bill.*

luckless (lŭk′lĭs), *adj.* having no luck. —**luck′lessly,** *adv.* —**luck′lessness,** *n.*

Lucknow (lŭk′nou), *n.* a city in India, the capital of Uttar Pradesh, in the S central part: the British were besieged here for several months (1857–58) during the Mutiny. 559,440 (1961).

lucky (lŭk′ĭ), *adj.*, **-ier, -iest. 1.** having or attended with good luck; fortunate. **2.** happening fortunately: *a lucky accident.* **3.** bringing or presaging good luck, or supposed to do so: *a lucky penny.* —**luck′iness,** *n.* —**Syn. 1.** See **fortunate.**

lucky dip, 1. a large barrel or the like in which articles of more or less value are hidden in sawdust, etc. Participants grope for and select one article as a children's amusement, sideshow at a fair, etc. **2.** the act of dipping into such a barrel and selecting an article. **3.** *Colloq.* a chance; an undertaking of uncertain outcome.

lucrative (lo͞o′krə tĭv), *adj.* profitable; remunerative: *a lucrative business.* [ME, t. L: m. s. *lucrātīvus*] —**lu′cratively,** *adv.* —**lu′crativeness,** *n.*

lucre (lo͞o′kə), *n.* gain or money as the object of sordid desire. [ME, t. L: m. s. *lucrum* gain]

Lucretius (lo͞o krē′shyəs), *n.* (*Titus Lucretius Carus*), *c.* 99–*c.* 55 B.C., Roman poet. —**Lucre′tian,** *adj.*

lucubrate (lo͞o′kyo͝o brāt′), *v.i.*, **-brated, -brating. 1.** to work, write, study, etc., laboriously, esp. at night. **2.** to write learnedly. [t. L: m. s. *lūcubrātus*, pp.] —**lu′cubra′tor,** *n.*

lucubration (lo͞o′kyo͝o brā′shən), *n.* **1.** laborious work, study, etc., esp. at night. **2.** a learned or carefully written production. **3.** (*often pl.*) any literary effort.

luculent (lo͞o′kyo͝o lənt), *adj.* **1.** clear or lucid, as explanations, etc. **2.** convincing. [ME, t. L: s. *lūculentus*] —**lu′culently,** *adv.*

Lucullus (lo͞o kŭl′əs), *n.* **Lucius Licinius** (lo͞o′syəs lĭ sĭn′ĭ əs), *c.* 110–57 B.C., Roman consul and general, famous for his great wealth and luxury. —**Lucul′lan, Lucullean** (lo͞o′kŭ lē′ən), **Lucul′lian,** *adj.*

lucus a non lucendo (lo͞o′kəs ä nŏn′lo͞o kĕn′dō), *Latin.* a grove (so called) from not being light (used as a type of illogical or absurd derivation or reasoning).

Luddite (lŭd′īt), *n.* a member of any of various bands of workmen in England (1811–16) organized to destroy manufacturing machinery, under the belief that its use diminished employment. [named after Ned *Ludd*, fl. 1779, a Leicestershire workman] —**Lud′dism,** *n.*

Ludendorff (lo͞o′dən dôf′; *Ger.* lo͞o′dən dŏrf), *n.* **Erich Friedrich Wilhelm von** (*Ger.* ĕ′rĭKH frē′drĭKH vĭl′hĕlm fŏn), 1865–1937, German general.

Lüdenscheid (*Ger.* lʏ′dən shīt), *n.* a town in West Germany, in central North Rhine-Westphalia. 58,900 (est. 1966).

Lüderitz (*Ger.* lʏ′də rĭts), *n.* a seaport in South-West Africa: diamond-mining centre. 7737 (est. 1968).

Ludhiana (lo͝o′dĭ ä′nə), *n.* a town in India, in central Punjab. 244,032 (1961).

ludicrous (lo͞o′dĭ krəs), *adj.* such as to cause laughter or derision; ridiculous; amusingly absurd: *a ludicrous incident.* [t. L: m. *lūdicrus* sportive] —**lu′dicrously,** *adv.* —**lu′dicrousness,** *n.* —**Syn.** laughable, comical. See **funny.** —**Ant.** solemn, impressive.

ludo (lo͞o′dō), *n.* a children's game played on a board with counters and dice, for up to four players.

Ludwig (*Ger.* lo͞ot′vĭKH), *n.* **Emil** (*Ger.* ĕ′mĕl), 1881–1948, German biographer.

Ludwig II (*Ger.* lo͞ot′vĭKH). See **Louis II.**

Ludwigsburg (*Ger.* lo͞ot′vĭKHs bo͝ork), *n.* a town in West Germany, in central Baden-Württemberg. 77,800 (est. 1966).

Ludwigshafen (*Ger.* lo͞ot′vĭKHs hä fən), *n.* a town in West Germany, in SE Rhineland-Palatinate, on the Rhine opposite Mannheim. 177,500 (est. 1966).

lues (lo͞o′ēz), *n.* syphilis. [t. L: plague]

luff (lŭf), *Naut.* —*n.* **1.** the forward edge of a fore-and-aft sail. —*v.i.* **2.** to bring the head of a sailing vessel closer to or directly into the wind, with sails shaking. **3.** to alter the angle of the jib of a crane, and thus alter the radius of lifting. —*v.t.* **4.** to alter the angle of (the jib of a crane). [early ME *lof*, *loof*, appar. t. OF: m. *lof* a contrivance for altering a ship's course (later, as also D *loef*, the weather side), of Gmc orig.]

luffing crane (lŭf′ĭng), a crane with a jib whose angle, and hence the radius of lifting, can be altered.

luff tackle, *Naut.* a purchase or tackle with a double block at the top and a single one at the bottom.

Luftwaffe (lo͝oft′vä′fə), *n. German.* the German Air Force.

lug[1] (lŭg), *v.*, **lugged, lugging,** *n.* —*v.t.* **1.** to pull along or carry with force or effort. —*v.i.* **2.** to pull; tug. —*n.* **3.** an act of lugging; a forcible pull; a haul. [ME *lugg*(*e*), t. Scand.; cf. Sw. *lugga* pull by the hair]

lug[2] (lŭg), *n.* **1.** *Now Colloq. and Scot.* an ear. **2.** one of the earflaps of a cap. **3.** a projecting piece by which anything is held or supported. **4.** a leather loop hanging down from a saddle, through which a shaft is passed for support. [? special use of LUG[1]]

lug[3] (lŭg), *n.* lugsail. [see LUGSAIL]

lug[4] lŭg), *n.* lugworm. [orig. uncert.; ? t. Irish Gaelic. Cf. Irish *lurg*]

Lugano (*It.* lo͞o gä′nô), *n.* a town in S Switzerland on Lake Lugano: holiday resort.

Lugansk (*Russ.* lo͞o gänsk′), *n.* a town in the S central Soviet Union in Europe. 330,000 (est. 1965). Also, formerly (1935–57), **Voroshilovgrad.**

luggage (lŭg′ĭj), *n.* trunks, suitcases, etc., used in travelling; baggage. [f. LUG[1] + -AGE]

luggage van, a railway van, usually enclosed, or part of a van, used for transporting passengers' luggage.

lugger (lŭg′ə), *n.* a vessel with lugsails. [der. LUGSAIL]

lugsail (lŭg′sāl′; *Naut.* -səl), *n. Naut.* a quadrilateral sail bent upon a yard that crosses the mast obliquely. Also, **lug.** [f. *lug* pole (now d.) + SAIL]

lugubrious (lo͞o go͞o′brĭ əs), *adj.* mournful; doleful; dismal: *lugubrious tones.* [f. L *lūgubri*(*s*) mournful + -OUS] —**lugu′briously,** *adv.* —**lugu′briousness,** *n.*

lugworm (lŭg′wûm′), *n.* any annelid of the genus *Arenicola*, comprising marine worms with tufted gills, which burrow in the sand of the seashore and are much used for bait. Also, **lug.** [f. LUG[4] + WORM]

Luik (*Flem.* lœyk), *n.* Flemish name of **Liège.**

Luke (lo͝ok), *n.* **1.** the Evangelist; an early Christian disciple, probably a gentile, a physician, and companion of St Paul; traditionally, the author of the third Gospel. **2.** the third Gospel, in the New Testament. [t. L: m. *Lūcās*, t. Gk: m. *Loukâs*]

lukewarm (lo͞ok′wôm′), *adj.* **1.** moderately warm; tepid. **2.** having or showing little ardour or zeal; indifferent: *lukewarm applause.* [ME *lukewarme*, f. *luke* tepid (appar. der. *lew* tepid, OE *-hlēow*) + *warme* WARM] —**luke′warm′ly,** *adv.* —**luke′warm′ness,** *n.*

lull (lŭl), *v.t.* **1.** to put to sleep or rest by soothing means: *to lull a child by singing.* **2.** to soothe or quiet. **3.** to lead into a false sense of security. —*v.i.* **4.** to become lulled, quieted, or stilled. —*n.* **5.** a lulled condition; a temporary quiet or stillness: *a lull in a storm.* **6.** a soothing sound: *the lull of falling waters.* [ME *lulle*(*n*). Cf. Sw. *lulla*, G *lullen*, also L *lallāre* sing lullaby]

lullaby (lŭl′ə bī′), *n.*, *pl.* **-bies,** *v.*, **-bied, -bying.** —*n.* **1.** the utterance 'lullaby' or a song containing it; a cradlesong. **2.** any lulling song. —*v.t.* **3.** to lull with or as with a lullaby. [orig. interj., *lulla!* + *by!*]

Lully (lŭl′ĭ; *for 1 also Fr.* lʏ lē′), *n.* **1. Jean Baptiste** (*Fr.* zhäN bȧ tēst′), 1632–87, Italian composer in France. **2. Raymond,** *c.* 1235–1315, Spanish philosopher and missionary.

lumbago (lŭm bā′gō), *n. Pathol.* myalgia in the lumbar region; rheumatic pain in the muscles of the small of the back. [t. LL, der. L *lumbus* loin]

lumbar (lŭm′bə), *adj.* **1.** of or pertaining to the loin or loins. —*n.* **2.** a lumbar vertebra, artery, or the like. See diag. under **spinal column.** [t. NL: s. *lumbāris*, der. L *lumbus* loin]

lumber[1] (lŭm′bə), *n.* **1.** *U.S. and Can.* timber sawn or split into planks, boards, etc. **2.** miscellaneous useless articles that are stored away. —*v.i.* **3.** *U.S. and Can.* to cut timber and prepare it for market. —*v.t.* **4.** to heap together in disorder. **5.** to fill up or obstruct with miscellaneous useless articles; encumber. **6.** *Colloq.* to foist off on or leave with, as with something or someone unwelcome or unpleasant. [orig. uncert.] —**lum′berer,** *n.*

lumber[2] (lŭm′bə), *v.i.* **1.** to move clumsily or heavily, esp. from great or ponderous bulk. **2.** *Obs.* to make a rumbling noise. [ME *lomere*(*n*). Cf. d. Sw. *lomra* resound, *loma* walk heavily]

lumbering[1] (lŭm′bə rĭng), *n. U.S. and Can.* the trade or business of cutting and preparing timber. [f. LUMBER[1] + -ING[1]]

lumbering[2] (lŭm′bə rĭng), *adj.* **1.** moving clumsily or heavily; awkward. **2.** *Obs.* that rumbles. [f. LUMBER[2] + -ING[2]] —**lum′beringly,** *adv.*

lumberjack (lŭm′bə jăk′), *n.* *U.S. and Can.* one who works at lumbering.

lumber-jacket (lŭm′bə jăk′ĭt), *n.* a man's or woman's casual heavy woollen jacket, usually having bold colours and patterns, fastened up to the neck by a zip or the like, as worn originally by lumberjacks.

lumberman (lŭm′bə mən), *n., pl.* **-men. 1.** *U.S. and Can.* one who cuts and prepares timber. **2.** one who deals in lumber.

lumber-room (lŭm′bə ro͝om′, -ro͞om′), *n.* a room in a house used for storing furniture or the like which is not in use; boxroom.

lumberyard (lŭm′bə yäd′), *n.* *U.S. and Can.* a timber-yard.

lumbrical (lŭm′brĭ kl), *n.* *Anat.* one of four wormlike muscles in the palm of the hand and in the sole of the foot. Also, **lumbricalis** (lŭm′brĭ kā′lĭs). [t. NL: s. *lumbrīcālis*, der. L *lumbrīcus* earthworm]

lumbricoid (lŭm′brĭ koid′), *adj.* resembling an earthworm. [f. s. L *lumbrīcus* earthworm + -OID]

lumen (lo͞o′mĭn), *n., pl.* **-mens, -mina** (-mĭ nə). **1.** *Optics.* the derived SI unit of luminous flux; the light emitted in a unit solid angle of one steradian by a point source having a uniform intensity of one candela. *Symbol*: lm. **2.** *Anat.* the canal, duct, or cavity of a tubular organ. **3.** *Bot.* (of a cell) the cavity which the cell walls enclose. [t. L: light, window]

Lumière (lo͞o′mĭ ĕə′; *Fr.* lʏ myĕr′), *n.* **Auguste Marie Louis Nicolas,** 1863–1954, and his brother, **Louis Jean,** 1864–1948, pioneer film directors.

Luminal (lo͞o′mĭ nəl), *n.* *Trademark.* phenobarbitone.

luminance (lo͞o′mĭ nəns), *n.* **1.** the state or quality of being luminous. **2.** *Optics.* a measure of the brightness of a point on a surface equal to the ratio of the luminous intensity, in a given direction, of an infinitesimal element of the surface containing the point, to the orthogonally projected area of the element on a plane perpendicular to the given direction. [f. s. L *lūmen* light + -ANCE]

luminary (lo͞o′mĭ nə rĭ), *n., pl.* **-naries. 1.** a celestial body, as the sun or moon. **2.** a body or thing that gives light. **3.** a person who enlightens mankind or makes some subject clear. [late ME, t. ML: m. s. *lūmināriam* a light, lamp, heavenly body]

luminesce (lo͞o′mĭ nĕs′), *v.i.,* **-nesced, -nescing.** to exhibit luminescence.

luminescence (lo͞o′mĭ nĕs′əns), *n.* an emission of light not due directly to incandescence and occurring at a temperature below that of incandescent bodies: a term including phosphorescence, fluorescence, etc.

luminescent (lo͞o′mĭ nĕs′ənt), *adj.* characterized by or pertaining to luminescence. [f. s. L *lūmen* light + -ESCENT]

luminiferous (lo͞o′mĭ nĭf′ə rəs), *adj.* producing light. [f. s. L *lūmen* light + -(I)FEROUS]

luminosity (lo͞o′mĭ nŏs′ĭ tĭ), *n., pl.* **-ties. 1.** the quality of being luminous. **2.** something luminous. **3.** *Astron.* the amount of light emitted by a star compared to that emitted by the sun.

luminous (lo͞o′mĭ nəs), *adj.* **1.** radiating or reflecting light; shining. **2.** lighted up or illuminated; well lighted. **3.** brilliant intellectually; enlightening, as a writer or his writings. **4.** clear; readily intelligible. [ME *luminose*, t. L: m. *lūminōsus*] —**lu′minously,** *adv.* —**lu′minousness,** *n.*

luminous efficiency, *Optics.* **1.** (of a source) the ratio of the light emitted to the energy input, esp. when expressed as lumens per watt for electric lamps. **2.** (of a radiation) the ratio of the luminous flux to the radiant flux.

luminous energy, 1. light. **2.** *Optics.* the time integral of luminous flux.

luminous flux, rate of transmission of luminous energy; luminous power. Its unit is the lumen.

luminous intensity, *Optics.* (of a light source) the luminous flux emitted per unit solid angle; measured in candelas.

luminous paint, paint which contains a phosphorescent compound and therefore glows after exposure to light.

lumisterol (lo͞o mĭs′tə rōl′), *n.* *Biochem.* a water-soluble compound, $C_{28}H_{44}O$, present in vitamin D_1, produced when ergosterol is irradiated by ultraviolet light.

lummox (lŭm′əks), *n.* *U.S. Colloq.* a clumsy, stupid person.

lump[1] (lŭmp), *n.* **1.** a piece or mass of solid matter without regular shape, or of no particular shape. **2.** a protuberance or swelling: *a lump on the head.* **3.** *Obsolesc.* an aggregation, collection, or mass: *in the lump.* **4.** *Colloq.* a stupid, clumsy person. —*adj.* **5.** in the form of a lump or lumps: *lump sugar.* **6.** including a number of items taken together or in the lump: *a lump sum.* —*v.t.* **7.** to unite into one aggregation, collection, or mass. **8.** to deal with in the lump or mass. **9.** to make into a lump or lumps. **10.** to raise into or cover with lumps. —*v.i.* **11.** to form or raise a lump or lumps. **12.** to move heavily. [ME *lumpe, lomp(e)*. Cf. Dan. *lump(e)* lump, d. Norw. *lump* block]

lump[2] (lŭmp), *v.t.* *Colloq.* to endure or put up with (a disagreeable necessity): *if you don't like it, you can lump it.* [orig. uncert.]

lumper (lŭm′pə), *n.* a labourer employed to load and unload vessels in port.

lumpfish (lŭmp′fĭsh′), *n., pl.* **-fishes,** (*esp. collectively*) **-fish.** lumpsucker.

lumpish (lŭm′pĭsh), *adj.* **1.** like a lump. **2.** clumsy or stupid: *she called him a lumpish boor.* —**lump′ishly,** *adv.* —**lump′ishness,** *n.*

lumpsucker (lŭmp′sŭk′ə), *n.* a clumsy-looking fish, *Cyclopterus lumpus*, with a high, ridged back, of the North Atlantic Ocean. Also, **henfish.**

lumpy (lum′pĭ), *adj.,* **lumpier, lumpiest. 1.** full of lumps: *lumpy gravy.* **2.** covered with lumps, as a surface. **3.** like a lump, as in being heavy or clumsy. **4.** (of water) rough or choppy. —**lump′ily,** *adv.* —**lump′iness,** *n.*

lumpy jaw, *Pathol.* actinomycosis of the jaw.

Lumumba (lə mo͝om′bə), *n.* **Patrice,** 1925–1961, leader of the Congo National Movement and prime minister of the Democratic Republic of the Congo 1960–61.

Luna (lo͞o′nä), *n.* **1.** the moon, personified by the Romans as a goddess. **2.** *Alchemy.* silver. [t. L: moon]

lunacy (lo͞o′nə sĭ), *n., pl.* **-cies. 1.** intermittent insanity. **2.** any form of insanity (usually, except idiocy). **3.** extreme foolishness or an instance of it: *her decision to resign was sheer lunacy.* **4.** *Law.* unsoundness of mind sufficient to incapacitate one for civil transactions. [f. LUN(ATIC) + -ACY]

luna moth, a large American moth, *Tropaea luna*, with light green coloration, purple-brown markings, lunate spots, and long tails. Also, **Luna moth.**

lunar (lo͞o′nə), *adj.* **1.** of or pertaining to the moon: *the lunar orbit.* **2.** measured by the moon's revolutions: *a lunar month.* **3.** resembling the moon; round or crescent-shaped. **4.** of or pertaining to silver. [t. L: s. *lūnāris* of the moon, crescent]

lunar caustic, *Med., Chem.* silver nitrate, $AgNO_3$, esp. in a sticklike mould, used to cauterize tissues.

lunarian (lo͞o nĕə′rĭ ən), *n.* **1.** a supposed inhabitant of the moon. **2.** a selenographer.

lunar module, *Astronautics.* the section of a space vehicle which detaches in lunar orbit and descends to the surface of the moon.

lunar month. See **month** (def. 5).

lunarnaut (lo͞o′nə nôt′), *n.* an astronaut whose destination is the moon.

lunar year. See **year** (def. 4).

lunate (lo͞o′nāt), *adj.* crescent-shaped. Also, **lu′nated.** [t. L: m. s. *lūnātus*]

lunatic (lo͞o′nə tĭk), *n.* **1.** an insane person. —*adj.* **2.** insane or mad; crazy. **3.** indicating lunacy; characteristic of a lunatic. **4.** designated for or used by the insane: *a lunatic asylum.* Also (*for defs 2, 3*), **lunatical** (lo͞o năt′ĭ kl). [ME *lunatik*, t. LL: m. s. *lūnāticus* mad, der. L *lūna* moon] —**lunat′ically,** *adv.*

lunatic fringe, the more extreme members of a community or group.

lunation (lo͞o nā′shən), *n.* the time from one new moon to the next (about 29½ days); a lunar month.

lunch (lŭnch), *n.* **1.** a meal taken at midday or shortly after; luncheon. **2.** a light meal. —*v.i.* **3.** to eat lunch: *we lunched quite late today.* —*v.t.* **4.** to provide lunch for: *they lunched us in regal fashion.* [short for LUNCHEON] —**lunch′er,** *n.*

luncheon (lŭn′chən), *n.* lunch. [b. LUMP[1] and d. *nuncheon* (ME *nonshench*, f. *non* noon + *shench* (OE *scenc*) a drink)]

luncheon meat, a pulverized mixture of meat, usually pork, and cereal in loaf form.

luncheon voucher, 1. a voucher for a specific amount, given by some employers and accepted by some restaurants in payment for lunch. **2.** (*cap.*) a trademark for this.

lunchtime (lŭnch′tīm′), *n.* **1.** the time, usually around or soon after midday, when lunch is eaten. —*adj.* **2.** denoting, pertaining to, or taking place at this time.

lune[1] (lo͞on), *n.* **1.** anything shaped like a crescent or a half-moon. **2.** a crescent-shaped plane figure bounded by two arcs of circles, either on a plane or a spherical surface. **3.** *Rom. Cath. Ch.* lunette (def. 6). [t. F, g. L *lūna* moon]

lune[2] (lo͞on), *n. Falconry.* a line for holding a hawk. [ME; var. of *loigne*, t. OF, g. LL *longia*, der. L *longus* long]

Lüneburg (lo͞o′nĭ bûg′; *Ger.* lʏ′nə bo͝ork), *n.* **1.** a town in West Germany, in NE Lower Saxony. 60,200 (est. 1966). **2. Lüneburg Heath,** the place where all the German forces in Holland, NW Germany including the Frisian Islands, Heligoland, etc., Schleswig-Holstein, and Denmark, surrendered to the Allies in May 1945, at the end of World War II.

Lünen (*Ger.* lʏ′nən), *n.* a town in West Germany, in N central North Rhine-Westphalia. 72,400 (est. 1966).

lunes (lo͞onz), *n.pl. Archaic.* fits of lunacy or madness. [t. ML: pl. m. s. *lūna* fit of lunacy, L moon. See LUNE[1]]

lunette (lo͞o nĕt′), *n.* **1.** any of various objects or spaces of crescent-like or semicircular outline or section. **2.** an arched or rounded aperture or window, as in a vault. **3.** a painting, etc., filling an arched space, usually a semicircle or a flatter chord of a circle. **4.** *Fort.* a work consisting of a salient angle with two flanks and an open gorge. **5.** *Ordn.* a towing ring in the trail-plate of a towed vehicle, as a guncarriage. **6.** *Rom. Cath. Ch.* Also, **lune.** a crescent-shaped fitting to hold the consecrated Host within a monstrance for adoration and benediction. [t. F, dim. of *lune* moon. See LUNE[1]]

Lunéville (*Fr.* lʏ nė vēl′), *n.* a town in NE France: treaty between France and Austria, 1801. 24,463 (1962).

lung (lŭng), *n.* **1.** either of the two saclike respiratory organs in the thorax of man and the higher vertebrates. **2.** an analogous organ in certain invertebrates, as arachnids, terrestrial gastropods, etc. [ME *lunge(n)*, OE *lungen*, c. G *Lunge*; akin to LIGHT[2]]

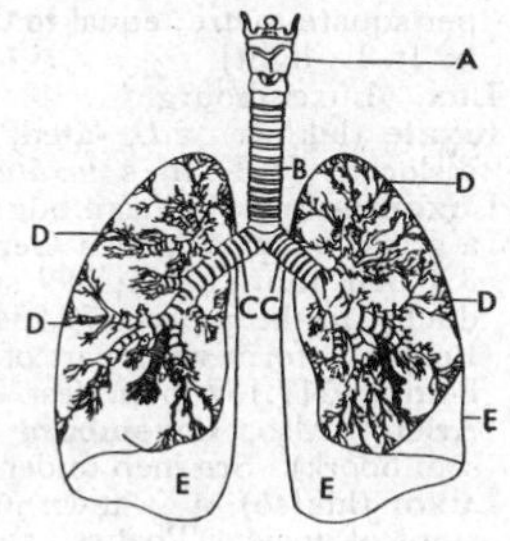

Cross-section of a human lung
A, Larynx; B, Trachea; C, Bronchi; D, Ramifications of bronchial tubes; E, Uncut surface

lungan (lŭng′gən), *n.* longan.

lunge[1] (lŭnj), *n., v.,* **lunged, lunging.** —*n.* **1.** a thrust, as in fencing. **2.** any sudden forward movement; plunge. —*v.i.* **3.** to make a lunge or thrust; move with a lunge. —*v.t.* **4.** to thrust; cause to move with a lunge. [aphetic var. of *allonge* (obs.), t. F, der. *allonger* lengthen, extend, lunge, der. *à* to (g. L *ad*) + *long* long (g. L *longus*)]

lunge[2] (lŭnj), *n., v.,* **lunged, lunging.** —*n.* **1.** a long rope used to guide a horse during training or exercise. **2.** a ring or circular track for such training or exercise. —*v.t.* **3.** to train or exercise (a horse) by the use of a lunge or rope, or on a lunge or track. [t. F: m. *longe* halter, lunge, var. of OF *loigne*. See LUNE[2]]

lungi (lo͝ong′gē), *n.* **1.** a loincloth worn by men in India. **2.** the material of which this is made, also used in turbans and sashes.

lungfish (lŭng′fĭsh′), *n., pl.* **-fishes,** (*esp. collectively*) **-fish.** a dipnoan.

lungworm (lŭng′wûm′), *n.* **1.** any nematode worm of the superfamily *Metastrongylidae*, parasitic in lungs of various mammals. **2.** a nematode worm of the genus *Rhabdias*, parasitic in the lungs of reptiles and amphibians.

lungwort (lŭng′wût′), *n.* a small perennial boraginaceous herb with spotted leaves and blue flowers, *Pulmonaria officinalis*, a native of central and S Europe, frequently cultivated and naturalized elsewhere.

luni-, a word element meaning 'moon'. [comb. form repr. L *lūna*]

lunisolar (lo͞o′nĭ sō′lə), *adj.* pertaining to or based upon the relations or joint action of the moon and sun: *the lunisolar cycle.*

lunitidal (lo͞o′nĭ tī′dl), *adj.* pertaining to that part of the tidal movement dependent on the moon.

lunitidal interval, the period of time between the moon's transit and the next high lunar tide.

lunkhead (lŭngk′hĕd′), *n. U.S. Slang.* a blockhead.

Lunt (lŭnt), *n.* **Alfred,** born 1893, U.S. actor.

lunula (lo͞o′nyo͞o lə), *n., pl.* **-lae** (-lē′). something shaped like a narrow crescent, as the small white area at the base of the human fingernail. Also, **lunule** (lo͞o′nyo͞ol). [t. L, dim. of *lūna* moon]

lunular (lo͞o′nyo͞o lə), *adj.* crescent-shaped: *lunular markings.*

lunulate (lo͞o′nyo͞o lāt′), *adj.* **1.** having lunular markings. **2.** crescent-shaped. Also, **lu′nulat′ed.**

luny (lo͞o′nĭ), *adj.,* **-nier, -niest,** *n., pl.* **-nies.** loony.

Lupercalia (lo͞o′pû kā′lyə), *n.pl.* an ancient Roman festival celebrated annually on February 15th in honour of **Lupercus,** a rustic deity identified with the Roman Faunus and the Greek Pan. [t. L]

lupin (lo͞o′pĭn), *n.* any plant of the leguminous genus *Lupinus*, as *L. albus* (**white lupin**), a European herb with edible seeds cultivated from ancient times, or *L. polyphyllus*, a native of N America often cultivated, with a wide range of flower colours. Also, *Chiefly U.S.*, **lupine.** [ME, t. L: s. *lupīnus, lupīnum.* See LUPINE[2]]

lupine[1] (lo͞o′pĭn), *n. Now Chiefly U.S.* lupin.

lupine[2] (lo͞o′pīn), *adj.* **1.** pertaining to or resembling the wolf. **2.** allied to the wolf. **3.** savage; ravenous. [t. L: m. s. *lupīnus* of a wolf]

lupulin (lo͞o′pyo͞o lĭn), *n.* the glandular hairs of the hop, *Humulus lupulus*, used in medicine. [f. s. NL *lupulus* (dim. of L *lupus* hop) + -IN[2]]

lupus (lo͞o′pəs), *n. Pathol.* a cutaneous disease due to the tubercle bacillus. [t. L: wolf]

lurch[1] (lûch), *n.* **1.** sudden leaning or roll to one side, as of a ship or a staggering person. **2.** a sudden swaying or staggering movement. —*v.i.* **3.** to make a lurch; move with lurches; stagger: *the wounded man lurched across the room at his assailant.* [orig. obscure; first in nautical use]

lurch[2] (lûch), *n.* **1.** the position of one discomfited or in a helpless plight: *to leave someone in the lurch.* **2.** a situation at the close of various games in which the loser scores nothing or is far behind his opponent. [t. F (obs.): m. *lourche* (n.) a game, (adj.) discomfited; ? of Gmc orig.]

lurcher (lû′chə), *n.* **1.** one who lurks or prowls; a petty thief; a poacher. **2.** a crossbred hunting dog.

lure (lyo͝oə), *n., v.,* **lured, luring.** —*n.* **1.** anything that attracts, entices, or allures. **2.** a decoy; a bait, esp. an artificial one, used in angling. **3.** a feathered decoy, sometimes baited, on a long thong, used in falconry to recall the hawk. **4.** a flap or tassel dangling from the dorsal fin of pediculate fish. —*v.t.* **5.** to decoy; entice; allure. **6.** to draw as by a lure. [ME, t. OF: m. *leurre*, t. Gmc; cf. G *Luder* bait] —**lur′er,** *n.*

Lurgan (lû′gən), *n.* a town in Northern Ireland, in County Armagh. 17,873 (1961).

lurid (lyo͝oə′rĭd), *adj.* **1.** lit up or shining with an unnatural or wild (esp. red or fiery) glare: *a lurid sky.* **2.** glaringly vivid or sensational: *lurid tales.* **3.** terrible in fiery intensity, fierce passion, or wild unrestraint: *lurid crimes.* **4.** wan, pallid, or ghastly in hue. [t. L: s. *lūridus* pale yellow, wan] —**lu′ridly,** *adv.* —**lu′ridness,** *n.*

lurk (lûk), *v.i.* **1.** to lie in concealment, as men in ambush; remain in or about a place secretly or furtively. **2.** to go furtively; slink; steal. **3.** to exist unperceived or unsuspected. [ME, freq. of LOUR. Cf. Norw. *lurka* sneak away] —**lurk′er,** *n.* —**lurk′ingly,** *adv.*

—**Syn. 1.** LURK, SKULK, SNEAK, PROWL suggest avoiding observation, often because of a sinister purpose. To LURK is to lie in wait for someone, or to hide about a place, often without motion for periods of time. SKULK suggests cowardliness and stealth of movement. SNEAK emphasizes the attempt to avoid being seen. It has connotations of slinking and of an abject meanness of manner, whether the object is to avoid punishment for some misdeed or whether there is a sinister intent. PROWL implies the definite purpose of seeking for prey; it suggests continuous action in roaming or wandering, slowly and quietly but watchfully, as a cat that is hunting mice.

Lusaka (lo͞o zä′kə, -sä′kə), *n.* the capital of Zambia, in the S part. 112,110 (est. 1962). See map under **Zambia.**

Lusatia (lo͞o sā′shyə), *n.* a region between the Oder and Elbe rivers, in East Germany and SW Poland.

Lusatian (lo͞o sā′shyən), *n.* Sorbian.

luscious (lŭsh′əs), *adj.* **1.** highly pleasing to the taste or smell: *luscious peaches.* **2.** sweet to the senses or the mind. **3.** very luxurious; extremely attractive. **4.** sweet to excess, or cloying. [late ME; ? aphetic var. of DELICIOUS] —**lus′ciously,** *adv.* —**lus′ciousness,** *n.* —**Syn. 2.** See **delicious.**

lush[1] (lŭsh), *adj.* **1.** tender and juicy, as plants or vegetation; succulent; luxuriant. **2.** characterized by luxuriant vegetation. **3.** *Colloq.* characterized by luxury and comfort. [ME *lusch*, prob. var. of *lasch*, t. OF: m. *lasche* loose, slack] —**lush′ly,** *adv.* —**lush′ness,** *n.*

lush[2] (lŭsh), *Now Chiefly U.S. Slang.* —*n.* **1.** intoxicating liquor. **2.** a drunken person. **3.** a drinking bout. —*v.i.* **4.** to drink liquor. —*v.t.* **5.** to drink (liquor). [orig. uncert.]

lushy (lŭsh′ĭ), *adj. Now Chiefly U.S. Slang.* drunk; tipsy.

Lusitania (lo͞o′sĭ tā′nyə), *n.* **1.** an ancient region and Roman province in the Iberian Peninsula, corresponding largely to modern Portugal. **2.** a British steamship sunk by a German submarine in the North Atlantic on May 7th, 1915: one of the events leading up to U.S. entry into World War I.

lust (lŭst), *n.* **1.** passionate or overmastering desire (fol.

by *for* or *of*): *lust for power.* **2.** sexual desire or appetite. **3.** unbridled or lawless sexual desire or appetite. **4.** sensuous desire or appetite considered as sinful. **5.** *Obs.* pleasure or delight. —*v.i.* **6.** to have strong sexual desire. **7.** to have a strong or inordinate desire (often fol. by *for* or *after*). [ME *luste*, OE *lust*, c. D *lust*, G *Lust* pleasure, desire]

luster (lŭs′tə), *n., v.t., v.i.* *U.S.* lustre.

lustful (lŭst′fəl), *adj.* **1.** full of or imbued with lust; libidinous. **2.** *Archaic.* lusty. —**lust′fully,** *adv.* —**lust′fulness,** *n.*

lustihood (lŭst′ĭ ho͝od′), *n. Archaic.* lustiness.

lustral (lŭs′trəl), *adj.* **1.** of, pertaining to, or employed in the lustrum or rite of purification. **2.** occurring every five years. [t. L: s. *lustrālis*]

lustrate (lŭs′trāt), *v.t.*, **-trated, -trating.** to purify by a propitiatory offering or other ceremonial method. [t. L: m. s. *lustrātus*, pp.] —**lustra′tion,** *n.*

lustre[1] (lŭs′tə), *n.* **1.** the state or quality of shining by reflecting light; glitter, glisten, sheen, or gloss: *the lustre of satin.* **2.** some substance used to impart sheen or gloss. **3.** radiant or luminous brightness; radiance. **4.** radiance of beauty, excellence, merit, distinction, or glory: *achievements that add lustre to one's name.* **5.** a shining object. **6.** a chandelier or candle holder, usually ornamented with cut-glass pendants. **7.** a fabric of wool and cotton with a lustrous surface. **8.** *Ceramics.* a shiny, metallic, sometimes iridescent film produced on the surface of pottery or porcelain. **9.** *Mineral.* the nature of the surface of a mineral with respect to its reflecting qualities: *greasy lustre.* —*v.t.* **10.** to finish with a lustre or gloss. —*v.i.* **11.** *Rare.* to shine with lustre. Also, *U.S.*, **luster.** [t. F, t. It.: m. *lustro*, der. *lustrare* to shine, g. L: illuminate] —**Syn. 1.** brightness, brilliance. See **polish.** —**Ant. 1.** dullness.

lustre[2] (lŭs′tə), *n.* lustrum. Also, *U.S.*, **luster.**

lustred (lŭs′təd), *adj.* having a lustre. Also, *U.S.*, **lustered.**

lustrine (lŭs′trĭn), *n.* lutestring.

lustring (lŭs′trĭng), *n.* lutestring. Also, *U.S.*, **lustering** (lŭs′tə rĭng).

lustrous (lŭs′trəs), *adj.* **1.** having lustre; shining; glossy, as silk; bright, as eyes. **2.** brilliant or splendid. —**lus′trously,** *adv.* —**lus′trousness,** *n.*

lustrum (lŭs′trəm), *n., pl.* **-tra** (-trə), **-trums.** **1.** a period of five years. **2.** a lustration or ceremonial purification of the ancient Roman people performed every five years, after the taking of the census. [t. L]

lusty (lŭs′tĭ), *adj.*, **-tier, -tiest.** **1.** full of or characterized by healthy vigour. **2.** hearty, as a meal or the like. [ME; f. LUST, n. + -Y[1]] —**lust′ily,** *adv.* —**lust′iness,** *n.* —**Syn. 1.** robust, strong, sturdy. —**Ant. 1.** feeble.

lusus naturae (lo͞o′so͞os nă to͞oə′rē), *Latin.* a deformed person or thing; a freak. [L: a jest of nature]

Luta (lo͞o′tä), *n.* a seaport on the Yellow Sea, in NE China, in Liaoning province. 210,000 (est. 1954). Formerly, **Port Arthur.**

lutanist (lo͞o′tə nĭst), *n.* lutenist.

lute[1] (lo͞ot), *n., v.,* **luted, luting.** —*n.* **1.** a stringed musical instrument formerly much used, having a long, fretted neck and a hollow, typically pear-shaped body with a vaulted back, the strings being plucked with the fingers of one hand (or struck with a plectrum) and stopped on the frets with those of the other. —*v.i.* **2.** to play on a lute. [ME, t. OF: m. *lut*, t. Pr.: m. *laüt*, t. Ar.: m. *al-'ūd* the lute]

Lute

lute[2] (lo͞ot), *v.t.*, **luted, luting.** *Bldg Trades.* to seal or cement with luting. [ME, n., t. ML: m. s. *lutum* adhesive mud or clay]

lutecium (lo͞o tē′shĭ əm), *n. Chem.* lutetium.

lutenist (lo͞o′tĭ nĭst), *n.* a player on the lute. Also, **lutanist.** [t. ML: m. s. *lūtānista*, der. *lūtāna* lute]

luteolin (lo͞o′tĭ ə lĭn), *n. Chem.* a yellow colouring matter, $C_{15}H_{10}O_6$, obtained from the weed *Reseda luteolar*, used in dyeing silk, etc., and formerly in medicine. [t. F: m. *lutéoline*, der. L *lūteolus* yellowish]

luteous (lo͞o′tĭ əs), *adj.* yellow, generally orangish or reddish. [t. L: m. *lūteus* golden yellow]

lutestring (lo͞ot′strĭng′), *n.* **1.** a kind of glossy silk fabric. **2.** a dress or ribbon made of this. Also, **lustrine, lustring.** [alter. (by folk etymology) of earlier LUSTRINE, t. F. See LUSTRE[1], -INE[1]]

lutetium (lo͞o tē′shĭ əm), *n. Chem.* a lanthanide, or rare-earth, trivalent, metallic element. *Symbol:* Lu; *at wt:* 174·97; *at. no.:* 71. Also, **lutecium.** Formerly, **cassiopeium.** [NL, der. L *Lutetia* Paris]

Luth., Lutheran.

Luther (lo͞o′thə; *Ger.* lo͝ot′ər), *n.* **Martin** (mä′tĭn; *Ger.* măr′tən), 1483–1546, German leader of the Protestant Reformation; theological writer, and translator of the Bible. —**Lu′therism,** *n.*

Lutheran (lo͞o′thə rən), *adj.* **1.** of or pertaining to Luther, adhering to his doctrines, or belonging to one of the Protestant churches which bears his name. —*n.* **2.** a follower of Luther, or an adherent of his doctrines; a member of the Lutheran Church. —**Lu′theranism,** *n.*

luthern (lo͞o′thən), *n.* a dormer window. [unexplained var. of obs. *lucerne*, t. L: m. s. *lucerna* window, light]

Luthuli (lo͞o to͞o′lĭ), *n.* **Albert John,** 1899–1967, Zulu chief: political leader in South Africa.

Lutine bell (lo͞o′tēn, lo͞o tēn′), the ship's bell of the vessel 'Lutine': now kept at Lloyd's and always rung before an important announcement, as of the loss of a vessel.

luting (lo͞o′tĭng), *n. Bldg Trades.* any viscous substance, as clay, concrete or mortar, used for filling gaps or joints.

Luton (lo͞o′tn), *n.* a town in England, in Bedfordshire. 131,583 (1961).

Lutyens (lŭch′ənz), *n.* **Sir Edwin,** 1869–1944, English architect.

Lützen (*Ger.* lʏt′sən), *n.* a town in East Germany, near Leipzig: noted for two battles, 1632, 1813.

Lützow-Holm Bay (lo͝ot′sō hōm′), an inlet of the Indian Ocean on the coast of Antarctica between Queen Maud Land and Enderby Land.

lux (lŭks), *n., pl.* **luces** (lo͞o′sēz). *Optics.* the derived SI unit of illumination, defined as an illumination of one lumen per square metre; equal to 0·0929 foot-candles. *Symbol:* lx [t. L: light]

Lux., Luxembourg.

luxate (lŭk′sāt), *v.t.*, **-ated, -ating.** to put out of joint; dislocate. [t. L: m. s. *luxātus*, pp.] —**luxa′tion,** *n.*

Luxembourg (lŭk′səm bûg′; *Fr.* lʏk säɴ bo͞or′), *n.* **1.** a grand duchy between Germany, France, and Belgium. 330,000 pop. (1964); 999 sq. mi. **2.** the capital of this duchy, in the S part. 77,254 (1965). **3.** a province in SE Belgium: formerly a part of the grand duchy of Luxembourg. 217,157 pop. (est. 1963); 1706 sq. mi. *Cap.:* Arlon. Also, **Luxemburg** (lŭk′səm bûg′; *Ger.* lo͝ok′səm bo͝ork). See map under **Flanders.**

Luxor (lŭk′sô), *n.* a town in Upper Egypt, on the Nile: ruins of ancient Thebes. ab. 15,000 (est. 1968).

luxuriance (lŭg zyo͝oə′rĭ əns), *n.* the condition of being luxuriant; luxuriant growth or productiveness; rich abundance. Also, **luxu′riancy.**

luxuriant (lŭg zyo͝oə′rĭ ənt), *adj.* **1.** abundant or exuberant in growth, as vegetation. **2.** producing abundantly, as soil. **3.** richly abundant, profuse, or superabundant. **4.** florid, as imagery or ornamentation. [t. L: s. *luxurians*, ppr., growing rank] —**luxu′riantly,** *adv.*

luxuriate (lŭg zyo͝oə′rĭ āt′), *v.t.*, **-ated, -ating.** **1.** to indulge in luxury; revel; enjoy oneself without stint. **2.** to take great delight. [t. L: m. s. *luxuriātus*, pp., grown exuberantly, indulged to excess] —**luxu′ria′tion,** *n.*

luxurious (lŭg zyo͝oə′rĭ əs), *adj.* **1.** characterized by luxury; ministering or conducing to luxury: *a luxurious hotel.* **2.** given or inclined to luxury. —**luxu′riously,** *adv.* —**luxu′riousness,** *n.*

luxury (lŭk′shə rĭ), *n., pl.* **-ries,** *adj.* —*n.* **1.** anything conducive to sumptuous living, usually a delicacy, elegance, or refinement of living rather than a necessity. **2.** any form or means of enjoyment. **3.** free indulgence in sumptuous living, costly food, clothing, comforts, etc. **4.** the means of luxurious enjoyment or sumptuous living. —*adj.* **5.** pertaining or conducive to luxury. [ME *luxurie* lust, t. L: m. *luxuria*]

Luzern (*Ger.* lo͞o tsĕrn′), *n.* German name of **Lucerne.**

Luzon (lo͞o zŏn′; *Sp.* lo͞o thôn′), *n.* the chief island of the Philippine Islands, in the N part of the group. 12,000,000 pop. (est. 1960); 40,420 sq. mi. *Cap.:* Manila. See map under **Leyte.**

LV, luncheon voucher.

lw, *Chem.* lawrencium.

l.w.m., low-water mark.

Lvov (*Russ.* lyvôf), *n.* a city in the SW Soviet Union in Europe: formerly in Poland. 496,000 (est. 1965). German, **Lemberg.** Polish, **Lwów** (*Pol.* lvo͞of).

lx, *Optics.* lux.

LXX, Septuagint.

-ly, **1.** the normal adverbial suffix, added to almost any descriptive adjective, e.g., *gladly, gradually.* **2.** the adverbial suffix applied to units of time, meaning 'per', as in *hourly.* [ME *-li, -lich(e)*, OE *-līce*, der. *-lic*. See def. 3] **3.** adjective suffix meaning 'like', e.g., *saintly, manly.* [ME *-li, -ly, lich(e)*, OE *-līc*, c. G *-lich*, repr. a Gmc noun (OE *līc*, etc.) meaning body. See LIKE[1]] —**Syn. 3.** See **-ish**[1].

Lyallpur (lī′əl po͝oə′), *n.* a town in E West Pakistan. 425,248 (1961).
lyard (lī′əd), *adj. Dial.* of a streaked grey. Also, **lyart** (lī′ət). [ME, t. OF: m. *liart*; of obscure orig.]
Lyautey (*Fr.* lyō tĕ′), *n.* **Louis Hubert Gonzalve** (*Fr.* lwē ʏ bĕr gôɴ zȧlv′), 1854–1934, marshal of France, administrator in Morocco.
lycanthrope (lī′kən thrōp′, lī kăn′thrōp), *n.* **1.** a person affected with lycanthropy. **2.** a werewolf or alien spirit in the physical form of a bloodthirsty wolf. [t. Gk: m. s. *lykánthrōpos*, lit., wolf-man]
lycanthropy (lī kăn′thrə pĭ), *n.* **1.** a kind of insanity in which the patient imagines himself to be a wolf or other wild beast. **2.** the supposed or fabled assumption of the form of a wolf by a human being. —**lycanthropic** (lī′kən thrŏp′ĭk), *adj.*
Lycaon (lī kā′ŏn), *n. Gk Myth.* an Arcadian king who tested the divinity of the disguised Zeus by offering him a plate of human flesh. As punishment, Zeus turned him into a wolf.
Lycaonia (lĭk′ə ō′nyə), *n.* an ancient country in S Asia Minor: later a Roman province.
lycée (lē′sā; *Fr.* lē sė′), *n.* (in France) a secondary school maintained by the state. [F, t. L: m. s. *Lycēum* LYCEUM]
lyceum (lī siəm′), *n.* **1.** a building, hall, or the like, devoted to instruction by lectures; a library, etc. **2.** (*cap.*) a public place with covered walks outside ancient Athens, where Aristotle taught. **3.** (*cap.*) the Aristotelian or Peripatetic school of philosophy. **4.** lycée. **5.** *U.S.* an association for discussion and popular instruction by lectures and other means. [t. L, t. Gk: m. *Lýkeion* the Lyceum at Athens (so named from the neighbouring temple of Apollo), prop. neut. of *Lýkeios* an epithet of Apollo]
lychee (lī′chē′), *n.* **1.** the fruit of a Chinese sapindaceous tree, *Litchi chinensis*, consisting of a thin brittle shell, enclosing a sweet jelly-like pulp and a single seed. **2.** the tree. Also, **lichee, lichi, litchi.** [t. Chinese: (m.) *li-tchi*]
lychee nut, the brownish, dried lychee fruit. [t. Chinese]
lychgate (lĭch′gāt′), *n.* lichgate.
lychnis (lĭk′nĭs), *n.* any of the showy-flowered plants constituting the caryophyllaceous genus *Lychnis*, as *L. chalcedonica* (**scarlet lychnis**), cultivated for its flowers, and *L. coronaria*, the rose campion. [t. L, t. Gk]
Lycia (lĭs′ĭ ə), *n.* an ancient country in SW Asia Minor: later a Roman province.
Lycian (lĭs′ĭ ən), *adj.* **1.** of or pertaining to Lycia. —*n.* **2.** an inhabitant of Lycia. **3.** the language of Lycia, probably related to the cuneiform Hittite.
lycopodium (lī′kə pō′dyəm), *n.* **1.** Also, **lycopod** (lī′kə pŏd′). any plant of the genus *Lycopodium*, which comprises erect or creeping, usually mosslike, evergreen-leaved pteridophytic plants, as *L. clavatum*, the common club moss, and *L. obscurum*, the ground pine. **2.** Also, **lycopodium powder.** a highly inflammable powder made from the spores of such a plant, used in making fireworks. [t. NL: f. m. Gk *lýko(s)* wolf + *-podium* -PODIUM]
Lycra (lī′krə), *n. Trademark.* a synthetic elastomer fibre.
Lycurgus (lī kû′gəs), *n.* fl. 9th century B.C., political reformer of Sparta, reputed founder of Spartan constitution.
lyddite (lĭd′īt), *n.* a high explosive consisting chiefly of picric acid. [named after *Lydd*, in Kent. See -ITE[1]]
Lydia (lĭd′ĭ ə), *n.* an ancient kingdom in W Asia Minor: under Croesus, a wealthy empire including most of Asia Minor.
Lydian (lĭd′ĭ ən), *adj.* **1.** of or pertaining to Lydia. **2.** (of music) softly or sensuously sweet; voluptuous. —*n.* **3.** an inhabitant of Lydia. **4.** the language of Lydia, probably Anatolian.
Lydian mode, *Music.* a scale, represented by the white keys of a keyboard instrument, beginning on F.
lye (lī), *n.* any solution resulting from leaching, percolation, or the like. [ME *lie, ley*, OE *lēag*, c. G *Lauge*]
Lyell (lī′əl), *n.* **Sir Charles,** 1797–1875, English geologist.
lying[1] (lī′ĭng), *n.* **1.** the telling of lies; untruthfulness. —*adj.* **2.** that lies; untruthful; false. [der. LIE[1]. See -ING[1], -ING[2]]
lying[2] (lī′ĭng), *v.* pres. part. of **lie.**
lying-in (lī′ĭng ĭn′), *n.* **1.** confinement in childbirth. —*adj.* **2.** pertaining to childbirth: *a lying-in hospital.*
Lyly (lĭl′ĭ), *n.* **John,** 1554?–1606, English writer of romances and plays. See **euphuism.**
Lyme Bay (līm), a wide bay between Devon and Dorset, S England.
lyme grass (līm), a large, glaucous, perennial grass, *Elymus arenarius*, widely distributed on coastal dunes in N temperate regions.
Lymington (lĭm′ĭng tən), *n.* a town in England, in Hampshire. 28,721 (1961).
lymph (lĭmf), *n. Anat., Physiol.* a clear, yellowish, slightly alkaline fluid (which may be regarded as dilute blood minus the red corpuscles) derived from the tissues of the body and conveyed to the bloodstream by the lymphatic vessels. [t. L: s. *lympha* water]
lymph-, a combining form of **lymph,** as in *lymphoid.*
lymphad (lĭm′făd), *n. Archaic.* a galley with one mast and usually a yard upon it. [t. Gaelic: m. *longfhada*]
lymphadenitis (lĭm făd′ĭ nī′tĭs, lĭm′făd ĭ-), *n. Pathol.* inflammation of a lymphatic gland. [f. LYMPH- + ADEN- + -ITIS]
lymphangial (lĭm făn′jĭ əl), *adj.* relating to the lymphatic vessels.
lymphangitis (lĭm′făn jī′tĭs), *n. Pathol.* inflammation of the lymphatic vessels. Also, **lymphangiitis** (lĭm fan′-jĭ ī′tĭs). [t. NL: m. *lymphangiitis*, f. *lymph-* LYMPH- + m. Gk *angeî(on)* vessel + *-itis*, -ITIS]
lymphatic (lĭm făt′ĭk), *adj.* **1.** pertaining to, containing, or conveying lymph: *a lymphatic vessel.* **2.** denoting, pertaining to, or having a temperament characterized by sluggishness of thought and action, formerly supposed to be due to an excess of lymph in the system. —*n.* **3.** a lymphatic vessel. [t. NL: s. *lymphāticus* pertaining to lymph. Cf. L *lymphāticus* mad]
lymph cell, lymphocyte.
lymph gland, any of the glandlike bodies occurring in the lymphatic vessels. Also, **lymph node, lymphatic gland.**
lympho-, var. of **lymph-,** before consonants.
lymphocyte (lĭm′fō sīt′), *n. Anat.* a leucocyte formed in lymphoid tissues, with little cytoplasm and no cytoplasmic granules. Their numbers are increased in certain diseases such as tuberculosis and typhoid fever. Also, **lymph cell.**
lymphoid (lĭm′foid), *adj.* **1.** resembling, of the nature of, or pertaining to, lymph. **2.** denoting or pertaining to a tissue (**lymphoid tissue**) forming the greater part of the lymphatic glands. **3.** pertaining to a lymphocyte.
lyncean (lĭn sē′ən), *adj.* **1.** lynxlike. **2.** sharp-sighted.
lynch (lĭnch), *v.t.* to put (a person) to death (by hanging, burning, or otherwise) by some concerted action without authority or process of law, for some offence known or imputed. [see LYNCH LAW] —**lynch′er,** *n.* —**lynch′ing,** *n.* —**Syn.** See **hang.**
Lynch (lĭnch), *n.* **John,** born 1917, Irish statesman; prime minister of the Republic of Ireland since 1966.
lynch law, the administration of summary punishment, esp. death, upon an offender (actual or reputed) by private persons acting in concert without authority of law. [orig. *Lynch's law*; named after the author, Captain William *Lynch*, 1742–1820, of Virginia]
lynx (lĭngks), *n., pl.* **lynxes,** (*esp. collectively*) **lynx.** any of various wildcats of the genus *Lynx*, having long limbs and short tail, and usually with tufted ears, as *L. rufus*, the **bay lynx,** a common North American species, and *L. canadensis*, a large, densely furred species of Canada and the northern U.S. [ME, t. L, t. Gk] —**lynx′like′,** *adj.*
lynx-eyed (lĭngks′īd′), *adj.* sharp-sighted.
lyo-, a word element meaning 'dispersion', 'solution', 'dissolved', as in, *lyophilic.* [comb. form repr. Gk *lýein* dissolve]
Lyonnais (*Fr.* lē ō nĕ′), *n.* a former province in E France.
lyonnaise (lī′ə nāz′; *Fr.* lē ō nĕz′), *adj.* (of food, esp. fried potatoes) cooked with pieces of onion. [t. F]
Lyonnesse (lī′ə nĕs′), *n. Arthurian Legend.* the mythical region where Sir Tristram was born, situated near Cornwall in SW England, and supposed to have been submerged by the sea. [t. OF: m. *Leonois*]
Lyons (lī′ənz), *n.* a city in E France, in Rhône department, at the confluence of the Rhone and Saône rivers. 528,535 (1962). French, **Lyon** (*Fr.* lyôɴ).
lyophilic (lī′ō fĭl′ĭk), *adj. Chem.* (of a colloid) having dispersed particles with an affinity for the liquid in which they are dispersed.
lyophilize (lī ŏf′ĭ līz′), *v.t.*, **-lized, -lizing.** to freeze-dry. Also, **lyophilise.**
lyophobic (lī′ō fō′bĭk), *adj. Chem.* (of a colloid) having dispersed particles with little or no affinity for the liquid in which they are dispersed.
Lyra (lī′ə rə), *n. Astron.* a northern constellation, containing Vega, one of the brightest stars in the sky. [t. L, t. Gk: lyre]

Lyrate leaf

lyrate (lī′ə rĭt), *adj.* **1.** *Bot.* (of a pinnate leaf) divided transversely into several lobes, the smallest at the base. **2.** *Zool.* lyre-shaped, as the tail of certain birds. Also, **ly′rated.**
lyre (lī′ə), *n.* **1.** a musical instrument of ancient Greece, consisting of a soundbox, with two curving arms carrying a crossbar (yoke) from which strings are stretched to

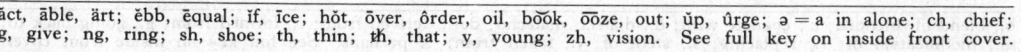

the body, used to accompany the voice in singing and recitation. **2.** (*cap.*) *Astron.* Lyra. [ME *lire*, t. OF, t. L: m. *lyra*, t. Gk]

Lyre

lyrebird (lĭ′ə bûd′), *n.* an Australian passerine bird of the genus *Menura*, the male of which has a long tail which is lyrate when spread.

lyric (lĭ′rĭk), *adj.* Also, **lyr′ical** (for defs 1–6). **1.** (of poetry) having the form and musical quality of a song, and esp. the character of a songlike outpouring of the poet's own thoughts and feelings (as distinguished from *epic* and *dramatic* poetry, with their more extended and set forms and their presentation of external subjects). **2.** pertaining to or writing such poetry: *a lyric poet.* **3.** characterized by or indulging in a spontaneous, ardent expression of feeling. **4.** pertaining to, rendered by, or employing singing. **5.** pertaining, adapted, or sung to the lyre, or composing poems to be sung to the lyre: *ancient Greek lyric odes.* **6.** (of a voice) relatively light of volume and modest in range (most suited for graceful, cantabile melody). **—***n.* **7.** a lyric poem. **8.** (*often pl.*) *Colloq.* the words of a song. [t. L: s. *lyricus*, t. Gk: m. *lyrikós* of a lyre] **—lyr′ically,** *adv.* **—lyr′icalness,** *n.*

Lyrebird, *Menura novaehollandiae* (38 in. long)

lyricism (lĭ′rĭ sĭz′əm), *n.* **1.** lyric character or style, as in poetry. **2.** lyric outpouring of feeling; emotionally expressed enthusiasm. Also, **lyr′ism.**

lyricist (lĭ′rĭ sĭst), *n.* **1.** a lyric poet. **2.** one who writes the words for songs.

lyrist (lĭ′ə rĭst *for 1*; lĭ′rĭst *for 2*), *n.* **1.** one who plays on the lyre. **2.** a lyric poet.

lys-, var. of **lyso-,** before vowels.

Lys (*Fr.* lēs), *n.* a river flowing from N France through W Belgium into the river Scheldt at Ghent. ab. 100 mi.

Lysander (lī săn′də), *n.* died 395 B.C., Spartan naval commander and statesman.

lyse (līs, līz), *v.*, **lysed, lysing.** *Med.*, *Biochem.* **—***v.t.* **1.** to cause dissolution or destruction of cells in by lysins. **—***v.i.* **2.** to undergo lysis. [back-formation from LYSIN]

-lyse, a word element making verbs of processes represented by nouns in *-lysis*, e.g., *catalyse.* Also, *U.S.*, **-lyze.** [back-formation from -LYSIS, influenced by -ISE[1]]

Lysenko (lĭ sĕng′kō; *Russ.* lĭ syĕn′kə), *n.* **Trofim Denisovich** (*Russ.* trä fĕm′ dyĭ nyē′sə vĭch), born 1898, Russian biologist and geneticist.

lysergic acid diethylamide. See **LSD.**

Lysias (lĭs′ĭ ăs′), *n. c.* 450–*c.* 380 B.C., Athenian orator.

Lysimachus (lī sĭm′ə kəs), *n. c.* 360–281 B.C., Macedonian general and king of Thrace, 306–281 B.C.

lysin (lī′sĭn), *n. Med.*, *Biochem.* an antibody or other agent which disintegrates the bacterial cell (bacteriolysis) or the red blood cell (haemolysis). [var. of LYSINE with arbitrary sense-distinction. See -IN[2]]

lysine (lī′sēn, -sĭn), *n. Chem.*, *Biochem.* an essential amino acid, $C_6H_{14}N_2O_2$, occurring in proteins. [f. s. Gk *lýsis* a loosening + -INE[2]]

Lysippus (lī sĭp′əs), *n.* fl. *c.* 360–*c.* 316 B.C., Greek sculptor.

lysis (lī′sĭs), *n.* **1.** *Med.*, *Biochem.* the dissolution or destruction of cells by lysins or other agents. **2.** *Med.* the gradual recession of a disease, as distinguished from the crisis, in which the change is abrupt. [NL, t. Gk: a loosing]

-lysis, a word element, especially scientific, meaning breaking down, decomposition, as in *analysis, electrolysis.* [t. Gk. See LYSIS]

lyso-, a word element meaning 'decomposition'. Also, **lys-.** [t. Gk. See LYSIS]

Lysol (lī′sŏl), *n. Trademark.* a clear, brown, oily liquid, a solution of cresols in soap: used as a disinfectant and antiseptic. [f. s. Gk *lýsis* solution + -OL[2]]

lysosome (lī′sə sōm′), *n. Biol.*, *Biochem.* one of the minute granules, smaller than mitochondria but larger than microsomes, present in living cells, and containing many lytic enzymes. **—lysosomal** (lī′sə sō′məl), *adj.*

lysozyme (lī′sə zīm′), *n. Biochem.* an enzyme present in eggwhite that hydrolyses polysaccharides of bacterial cell walls.

lyssophobia (lĭs′ō fō′byə), *n. Psychiatry.* **1.** morbid fear of rabies. **2.** morbid fear of insanity. [f. s. Gk *lýssa* rage, rabies + -(O)PHOBIA]

-lyte, a word element denoting something subjected to a certain process (indicated by a noun ending in *-lysis*), as in *electrolyte.* [t. Gk: m. *-lytos* that may be or is loosed]

Lytham St Anne's (lĭth′əm sənt ănz′), a town in England, in Lancashire. 36,189 (1961).

lythraceous (lĭth rā′shəs, lī thrā′-), *adj.* belonging to the *Lythraceae*, or loosestrife family of plants.

lytic (lĭt′ĭk), *adj.* pertaining to *-lyte* or *-lysis*, especially adapted in biochemistry to hydrolytic enzyme action. [independent use of -LYTIC]

-lytic, a termination of adjectives corresponding to nouns in *-lysis*, as in *analytic* (*analysis*), *paralytic* (*paralysis*). [t. Gk: m. s. *-lytikós*]

lytta (lĭt′ə), *n.*, *pl.* **lyttas, lyttae** (lĭt′ē). a long, wormlike cartilage in the tongue of the dog and other carnivorous animals. [t. NL, t. Gk: var. of *lýssa* rabies. See LYSSOPHOBIA]

Lytton (lĭt′n), *n.* **1. Edward George Earle Lytton Bulwer-Lytton, 1st Baron,** 1803–73, English novelist, dramatist, and politician. **2.** his son, **Edward Robert Bulwer Lytton, 1st Earl of** (*Owen Meredith*), 1831–91, English diplomat and poet.

Lyublin (*Russ.* lyōō′blĭn), *n.* Russian name of **Lublin.**

M

M (ĕm), *n.*, *pl.* **M's** or **Ms, m's** or **ms. 1.** a consonant, the 13th letter of the English alphabet. **2.** the Roman numeral for 1000. **3.** *Print.* em.

M, 1. Medieval. **2.** Middle. Also, **m**

M., 1. Majesty. **2.** Manitoba. **3.** marquess. **4.** medicine. **5.** meridian. **6.** (L *meridies*) noon. **7.** Monday. **8.** (*pl.* **MM.**) Monsieur. **9.** mountain.

m, metre.

m., 1. maiden over. **2.** male. **3.** mark. **4.** married. **5.** masculine. **6.** *Mech.* mass. **7.** medium. **8.** (L *meridies*) noon. **9.** metre. **10.** mile. **11.** million. **12.** minim. **13.** minute. **14.** modification of. **15.** month. **16.** morning.

M'-, Mac.

M', Mac.

m-, *Chem.* abridgement of **meta-** (def. 2).

ma (mä), *n. Colloq.* mamma; mother.

Ma, 1. *Chem.* masurium. **2.** *Music.* major.

mA, *Elect.* milliampere.

M.A., (L *Magister Artium*) Master of Arts.

ma'am (măm, mäm; *unstressed* məm), *n.* **1.** *Colloq.* madam. **2.** the term of address for a female royal person.

Ma'an (män), *n.* a town in SW Jordan. 21,000 (est. 1965).

maas (mäs), *n. S African.* thick curdled milk, drunk as a tonic, esp. by natives. Also, **amasi.** [t. Zulu: m. *amasi*]

Maas (mäs; *Du.* mäs), *n.* Dutch name for the part of the river **Meuse** in the Netherlands.

maasbanker (mäs′băng′kə), *n. S African.* the horse-mackerel, *Trachurus trachurus.* [t. Afrikaans]

Maastricht (*Du.* mä strĭKHt′), *n.* a town in the Netherlands, the capital of Limburg province, in the S part, on the river Maas. 94,939 (1965). Also, **Maestricht.**

Mabinogion (măb′ĭ nō′gĭ ən), *n.* **The,** a collection of medieval Welsh romances which were translated (1838–49) by Lady Charlotte Guest.

Mabuse (mə byōōz′: *Fr.* mä bYz′), *n.* (*Jan Gossaert*), died *c.* 1533, Dutch painter.

mac (măk), *n. Colloq.* mackintosh.

Mac, a prefix found in many family names of Irish or Scottish Gaelic origin. Also written **Mc-, Mc-,** and **M'-.** [t. Irish and Gaelic: son]

macabre (mə kä′bə, -brə), *adj.* **1.** gruesome; horrible; grim; ghastly. **2.** of or suggestive of the allegorical dance of death. [ME, t. F. ? ult. t. Ar.: m. *maqbara* graveyard]

macadam (mə kăd′əm), *n.* **1.** a macadamized road or pavement. **2.** the broken stone used in making such a road. [named after J. L. *McAdam*, 1756–1836, Scottish inventor]

macadamize (mə kăd′ə mīz′), *v.t.*, **-mized, -mizing.** to construct (a road) by laying and rolling successive layers of broken stone. Also, **macadamise. —macad′amiza′tion,** *n.*

Macao (mə kou′), *n.* **1.** a Portuguese overseas territory in

S China, on a peninsula of **Macao** and two small adjacent islands at the mouth of the Chu-Kiang; 6 sq. mi. **2.** the seaport and capital of this territory. 169,299 (1960). Portuguese, **Macáu** (*Port.* mə kȧw′).

macaque (mə käk′), *n.* any monkey of the genus *Macaca*, chiefly found in Asia, characterized by cheek pouches and, generally, a short tail. [t. F, t. Pg.: m. *macaco*, t. Fiot, a Congolese language]

Stump-tailed macaque, *Macaca speciosa* (Length ab. 1 ft 9 in., tail ab.12 in.)

macaroni (măk′ə rō′nĭ), *n., pl.* **-nis, -nies. 1.** a kind of pasta of Italian origin, prepared from wheat flour, in the form of dried, hollow tubes, to be cooked for food. **2.** an English dandy of the 18th century who affected foreign ways. Also, **maccaroni.** [t. It.: m. *maccaroni*, now *maccheroni*, pl. of *maccarone*, now *maccherone*, ult. der. LGk *makaría* food of broth and pearl barley, orig. happiness]

macaronic (măk′ə rŏn′ĭk), *adj.* Also, **mac′aron′ical. 1.** characterized by a mixture of Latin words with words from another language, or with non-Latin words provided with Latin terminations, as a kind of burlesque verse. **2.** involving a mixture of languages. **3.** *Obs.* mixed; jumbled. —*n.* **4.** (*pl.*) macaronic verses. [t. ML: s. *macarōnicus*, der. It. *maccaroni* MACARONI] —**mac′aron′ically,** *adv.*

macaroni cheese, a dish of macaroni with cheese.

macaroon (măk′ə ro͞on′), *n.* a sweet cake or biscuit made of eggwhites, sugar, little or no flour, and frequently almond paste, coconut, etc. [t. F: m. *macaron*, t. It.: m. *maccarone*, sing., MACARONI]

MacArthur (mə kä′thə), *n.* **Douglas,** 1880–1964, U.S. general.

Macassar (mə kăs′ə), *n.* **1.** a seaport in Indonesia, in SW Celebes. 700,000 (est. 1966). **2. Strait of,** a strait between Borneo and Celebes.

Macassar oil, 1. (originally) an oil for the hair stated to be made from materials obtained from Macassar. **2.** a similar oil or preparation for the hair.

Macaulay (mə kô′lĭ), *n.* **1. Dame Rose,** 1889?–1958, English novelist and poet. **3. Thomas Babington** (băb′ĭng tən), **1st Baron,** 1800–59, English essayist, historian, poet, and statesman.

macaw (mə kô′), *n.* any of various large, long-tailed parrots, chiefly of the genus *Ara*, of tropical and subtropical America, noted for their brilliant plumage and harsh voice. [t. Pg.: m. *macao*; of Brazilian orig.]

Macbeth (mək bĕth′, măk-), *n.* died 1057, king of Scotland 1040–57.

Maccabaeus (măk′ə bē′əs), *n.* **Judas** (jo͞o′dəs), a Jewish patriot; military leader 166–100 B.C.; a leader of the Maccabees.

Maccabean (măk′ə bē′ən), *adj.* of or pertaining to the Macabees or to Judas Maccabaeus.

Maccabees (măk′ə bēz′), *n.pl.* **1.** a family of heroes, deliverers of Judea during the Syrian persecutions of 175–164 B.C. **2.** the last two books of the Apocrypha, recording the struggle of the Maccabees.

maccaboy (măk′ə boi′), *n.* a kind of snuff, usually rose-scented. Also, **maccoboy.** [m. *Macouba*, name of district in Martinique]

maccaroni (măk′ə rō′nĭ), *n., pl.* **-nis, -nies.** macaroni.

Macclesfield (măk′lz fēld′), *n.* a town in England, in Cheshire. 37,644 (1961).

Macdonald (mək dŏn′əld), *n.* **1. Flora,** 1722–90, Scottish patriot who helped the Pretender, Prince Charles, escape from Scotland in 1746. **2. George,** 1824–1905, Scottish novelist and poet. **3. Sir John Alexander,** 1815–91, Canadian statesman: prime minister 1867–73 and 1878–91.

MacDonald (mək dŏn′əld), *n.* **James Ramsay,** 1866–1937, British statesman and leader of the Labour Party: prime minister in 1924 and 1929–35.

Macdonnell Ranges (mək dŏn′əl), a series of mountain ranges in the S of Northern Territory, Australia. Highest point, Mt Ziel, 4955 ft.

mace[1] (mās), *n.* **1.** *Hist.* a clublike weapon of war often with a flanged or spiked metal head. **2.** a staff borne before or by certain officials as a symbol of office. **3.** the bearer of such a staff. **4.** *Billiards.* a light stick with a flat head, formerly used at times instead of a cue. [ME, t. OF. Cf. L *mateola* mallet]

mace[2] (mās), *n.* a spice ground from the layer between a nutmeg shell and its outer husk, resembling nutmeg in flavour. [ME *macis*, t. OF, t. L: m. *mac(c)is* a spice]

mace-bearer (mās′bĕə′rə), *n.* one who carries the mace, as in a procession, before dignitaries.

Maced., Macedonia.

macedoine (măs′ĭ dwän′), *n.* **1.** a mixture of vegetables, served as a salad or otherwise. **2.** a jellied mixture of fruits. **3.** a medley. Also, *French,* **macédoine** (*Fr.* mȧ sė dwȧn′). [t. F: lit., Macedonian]

Macedon (măs′ĭ dən), *n.* Macedonia (def. 1).

Macedonia (măs′ĭ dō′nyə), *n.* **1.** an ancient country in the Balkan Peninsula, N of ancient Greece. **2.** a region in S Europe, including parts of Greece, Bulgaria, and Yugoslavia. **3.** a district in NE Greece. 1,890,654 pop. (1961); 13,380 sq. mi. *Cap.:* Salonika. **4.** a federal unit of S Yugoslavia. 1,406,003 pop. (1961); 10,598 sq. mi. *Cap.:* Skopje. —**Mac′edo′nian,** *adj., n.*

Macedonia (def. 2)

Maceió (*Port.* mȧ sė jŏ′), *n.* a seaport in E Brazil. 170,134 (1960).

macer (mā′sə), *n.* a mace-bearer. [ME *masere*, t. OF: m. *maissier*, der. *masse* MACE[1]]

macerate (măs′ə rāt′), *v.,* **-rated, -rating.** —*v.t.* **1.** to soften, or separate the parts of (a substance) by steeping in a liquid, with or without heat. **2.** to soften or break up (food) by action of a solvent. **3.** to cause to grow thin. —*v.i.* **4.** to undergo maceration. **5.** to become thin; waste away. [t. L: m. s. *mācerātus*, pp.] —**mac′erat′er, mac′era′tor,** *n.* —**mac′era′tion,** *n.*

Macgillycuddy's Reeks (mə gĭl′ĭ kŭd′ĭ), a range of low mountains in county Kerry in the SW Republic of Ireland. Highest peak, Carrauntoohill, 3414 ft.

mach (măk), *n.* a unit of velocity equal to the velocity of sound in the medium, usually air; mach 1 in air is about 760 miles per hour at sea-level. See **mach number.** [named after Ernst *Mach*, 1838–1916, Austrian physicist]

mach., 1. machine. **2.** machinery. **3.** machinist.

Machado (*Sp.* mȧ chȧ′dō), *n.* **1. Antonio,** 1875–1939, Spanish poet and playwright. **2.** his brother, **Manuel,** 1874–1947, Spanish poet and playwright.

Machen (mā′chĭn, mā′kĭn), *n.* **Arthur,** 1863–1947, Welsh novelist and essayist.

ma chère (*Fr.* mȧ shĕr′), *French.* (referring to a woman or girl) my dear.

machete (mə chā′tĭ; *Sp.* mȧ chĕ′tė), *n.* a large, heavy knife used esp. in Latin-American countries as both a tool and a weapon. [t. Sp., ult. der. L *mactāre* slaughter]

Machiavelli (măk′ĭ ə vĕl′ĭ; *It.* mȧ kyȧ vĕl′lē), *n.* **Niccolò di Bernardo** (*It.* nĕk kō lŏ′ dē bĕr nȧr′dō), 1469–1527, Italian statesman and writer on government.

Machiavellian (măk′ĭ ə vĕl′ĭ ən), *adj.* **1.** of, like, or befitting Machiavelli. **2.** being or acting in accordance with Machiavelli's political doctrines, which placed expediency above political morality, and countenanced the use of craft and deceit in order to maintain the authority and effect the purposes of the ruler. **3.** characterized by subtle or unscrupulous cunning; wily; astute. Also, —*n.* **4.** a follower of Machiavelli or his doctrines. Also, **Machiavelian.** —**Mach′iavel′lianism, Mach′iavel′lism,** *n.*

machicolated (mă chĭk′ō lā′tĭd), *adj.* furnished with machicolations. [f. s. ML *machicolātus*, pp. + -ED[2]]

machicolation (mă chĭk′ō lā′shən), *n.* *Archit.* **1.** an opening in the floor between the corbels of a projecting gallery or parapet, as on a wall or in the vault of a passage, through which missiles, molten lead, etc., might be cast upon an enemy beneath. **2.** a projecting gallery or parapet with such openings.

Machicolation

Machida (măch′ĭ də), *n.* a town in Japan, in SE central Honshu. 115,918 (1965).

machinate (măk′ĭ nāt′), *v.,* **-nated, -nating.** to contrive or devise, esp. artfully or with evil purpose. [t. L: m. s. *māchinātus*, pp.] —**mach′ina′tor,** *n.*

machination (măk′ĭ nā′shən), *n.* **1.** the act or process of machinating. **2.** (*usually pl.*) a crafty scheme; evil design; plot.

machine (mə shēn′), *n.*, *v.*, **-chined, -chining.** —*n.* **1.** an apparatus consisting of interrelated parts with separate functions, which is used in the performance of some kind of work: *a sewing machine.* **2.** a mechanical apparatus or contrivance; a mechanism. **3.** something operated by a mechanical apparatus, as a motor vehicle, a bicycle, or an aeroplane. **4.** *Mech.* **a.** a device which transmits and modifies force or motion. **b. simple machines,** the six (sometimes more) elementary mechanisms: the lever, wheel and axle, pulley, screw, wedge, and inclined plane. **5.** a contrivance, esp. in the ancient theatre, for producing stage effects. **6.** some agency, personage, incident, or other feature introduced for effect into a literary composition. **7.** any complex agency or operating system: *the machine of government.* **8.** the body of persons conducting and controlling the activities of a political party or other organization. **9.** a person or agency acting like a mere mechanical apparatus. —*v.t.* **10.** to make, prepare, or finish with a machine. [t. F, t. L: m. *māchina*, t. d. Gk: m. *māchinḗ*, Attic Gk *mēchanḗ*]

machine-gun (mə shēn′gŭn′), *n.*, *v.*, **-gunned, -gunning.** —*n.* **1.** a small arm operated by a mechanism, able to deliver a rapid and continuous fire of bullets as long as the firer keeps pressure on the trigger. —*v.t.* **2.** to shoot at, using a machine-gun.

machine language, *Computers.* the code of symbols used to convey instructions to a digital computer. Also, **machine code.**

machinery (mə shē′nə rĭ), *n.*, *pl.* **-ries. 1.** machines or mechanical apparatus. **2.** the parts of a machine, collectively: *the machinery of a watch.* **3.** contrivances for producing stage effects. **4.** personages, incidents, etc., introduced into a literary composition, as in developing a story or plot. **5.** any system by which action is maintained: *the machinery of government.*

machine shop, a workshop in which metal and other substances are cut, shaped, etc., by machine tools.

machine tool, a power-operated machine, as a lathe, etc., used for general cutting and shaping operations.

machinist (mə shē′nĭst), *n.* **1.** a person who operates machinery, esp. a highly trained and skilled operator of machine tools. **2.** a person, esp. a girl, who operates a sewing machine. **3.** one who makes and repairs machines. **4.** *U.S. Navy.* a junior rank whose duty is to assist the engineer officer in the engine-room. **5.** *Rare.* a person who builds or operates machinery in a theatre.

machmeter (măk′mē′tə), *n.* *Aeron.* an instrument which indicates the mach number of an aircraft when it is in flight.

mach number (măk), a number indicating the ratio between the airspeed of an object and the speed of sound at a given altitude, etc.

-machy, a combining form meaning combat, as in *logomachy.* [t. Gk: m. s. *-machia*, der. *-machos* fighting]

macintosh (măk′ĭn tŏsh′), *n.* mackintosh.

Macintyre (măk′ĭn tī′ə), *n.* a river in E Australia which forms the border with Queensland, and flows into the river Barwon. 350 mi.

Mackay (mə kī′), *n.* a seaport in E Australia, in Queensland. 17,500 (1965).

Mackensen (*Ger.* mȧ′kən zən), *n.* **August von** (*Ger.* ou′go͝ost fŏn), 1849–1945, German field marshal.

Mackenzie (mə kĕn′zĭ), *n.* **1. Sir Alexander,** 1755?–1820, Scottish explorer in Canada. **2. Sir Compton** (kŭmp′tən, kŏmp′-), born 1883, Scottish writer. **3. William Lyon,** 1795–1861, Canadian political leader and journalist, born in Scotland. **4.** a river in NW Canada, flowing from the Great Slave Lake NW to the Arctic Ocean. ab. 900 mi.; with tributaries, ab. 2525 mi. **5.** a district in NW Canada, in the SW part of the Northwest Territories. 527,490 sq. mi.

mackerel (măk′rəl), *n.*, *pl.* **-rel** (*occasionally, esp. with reference to different species*), **-rels. 1.** an abundant food fish of the North Atlantic, *Scomber scombrus*, with wavy cross markings on the back and streamlined for swift swimming. **2.** Spanish mackerel. **3.** any of various other streamlined fishes, as the **pygmy mackerel,** genus *Rastrelliger*, of Indian and Australian waters. [ME *makerel*, t. OF: m. *maquerel*; orig. unknown]

mackerel sky, 1. sky nearly covered with high, small, white, fleecy clouds arranged in bands. **2.** an extensive group of altocumulus clouds arranged in regular waves with blue sky showing in the gaps.

Mackinac (măk′ĭ nô′), *n.* **1. Strait of,** a strait joining Lakes Michigan and Huron. Least width, 4 mi. **2.** an island in Lake Huron at the entrance of this strait: summer resort. 3 mi. long. **3.** a town on this island.

mackinaw (măk′ĭ nô′), *n.* *U.S.* a Mackinaw coat. [shortened form of *Michilli-mackinaw*, name of an island near the strait connecting Lakes Michigan and Huron; said to mean turtle in Ojibwa; cf. *mičimakinak* big turtle]

Mackinaw blanket, a kind of thick blanket, often woven with bars of colour, formerly much used in the northern and western U.S. by Indians, lumbermen, etc.

Mackinaw boat, a flat-bottomed boat with sharp prow and square stern, propelled by oars and sometimes sails, as used on the upper Great Lakes of the United States.

Mackinaw coat, *U.S.* a short coat of a thick, blanket-like, commonly plaid, woollen material.

mackintosh (măk′ĭn tŏsh′), *n.* **1.** a raincoat made of cloth rendered waterproof by indiarubber. **2.** such cloth. **3.** any raincoat. Also, **macintosh.** [named after Charles *Macintosh*, 1766–1843, the inventor]

Mackintosh (măk′ĭn tŏsh′), *n.* **Charles Rennie** (rĕn′ĭ), 1868–1928, Scottish architect; one of the founders of Art Nouveau.

mackle (măk′l), *n.*, *v.*, **-led, -ling.** —*n.* **1.** a blur in printing, as from a double impression. —*v.t.*, *v.i.* **2.** to blur, as from a double impression in printing. Also, **macule.** [t. F: m. *macule*, t. L: m. *macula* spot]

Mackmurdo (mək mû′dō), *n.* **Arthur H.,** 1851–1942, Scottish architect, designer, and illustrator.

macle (măk′l), *n.* *Crystall.* a twin. [t. F, t. L: m. s. *macula* spot]

MacMahon (*Fr.* mȧk mȧ ôɴ′), *n.* **Marie Edme Patrice Maurice** (*Fr.* mȧ rē ĕd mə pȧ trēs mō rēs′), **Count de,** (*Duke of Magenta*), 1808–93, French field marshal: president of France 1873–79.

Macmillan (mək mĭl′ən), *n.* **(Maurice) Harold,** born 1894, British statesman: prime minister 1957–63.

MacNeice (mək nēs′), *n.* **Louis** (lo͞o′ĭ), 1907–63, English poet born in Ireland.

Mâcon (*Fr.* mȧ kôɴ′), *n.* **1.** a town in E central France, the capital of Saône-et-Loire. 27,669 (1962). **2.** Burgundy from this district.

Macpherson (mək fû′sən), *n.* **James,** 1736–96, Scottish author or translator of the poems of 'Ossian'.

Macquarie (mə kwŏ′rĭ), *n.* a river in SE Australia, in New South Wales, flowing NW to the river Darling. ab. 590 mi.

macramé (mə krä′mĭ), *n.* a kind of lace or ornamental work made by knotting thread or cord in patterns. [cf. Turk. *magrama* towel, handkerchief, etc.]

Macready (mə krē′dĭ), *n.* **William Charles,** 1793–1873, English actor.

macro-, a word element meaning 'long', 'large', 'great', 'excessive', used esp. in scientific terminology, contrasting with *micro-*. Also, before vowels, **macr-.** [t. Gk: m. *makro-*, comb. form of *makrós*]

macrocosm (măk′rə kŏz′əm), *n.* the great world, or universe (opposed to *microcosm*). [t. F: m. *macrocosme*, t. ML: m. s. *macrocosmus*, f. *macro-* MACRO- + m. Gk *kósmos* world] —**mac′rocos′mic,** *adj.*

macrocyst (măk′rō sĭst′), *n.* **1.** a cyst of large size, esp. the archicarp of certain *Discomycetes.* **2.** a multinuclear mass of protoplasm enclosed in a cyst.

macrocyte (măk′rō sīt′), *n.* *Pathol.* an abnormally large red blood cell. —**macrocytic** (măk′rō sĭt′ĭk), *adj.*

macrocytic anaemia (măk′rō sĭt′ĭk), *Pathol.* an anaemia characterized by predominance of macrocytes.

macrogamete (măk′rō gă mēt′), *n.* *Biol.* the female (and larger) of two conjugating gametes. Also, **megagamete.**

macrograph (măk′rō grăf′, -gräf′), *n.* a photograph or other image equal to or larger than the original.

macromolecule (măk′rō mŏl′ĭ kyo͞ol′), *n.* *Chem.* a molecule of very large size, as of a synthetic polymer, protein or nucleic acid.

macron (măk′rŏn), *n.* a short horizontal line used as a diacritic over a vowel to indicate that it is a 'long' sound, as in *fāte.* [t. Gk: m. *makrón*, neut., long]

macrophysics (măk′rō fĭz′ĭks), *n.* the part of physics that deals with physical objects large enough to be observed and treated directly.

macroscopic (măk′rō skŏp′ĭk), *adj.* visible to the naked eye (opposed to *microscopic*).

macrosporangium (măk′rō spô răn′jĭ əm), *n.* *Bot.* megasporangium.

macrospore (măk′rō spô′), *n.* *Bot.* megaspore.

macrosporophyll (măk′rō spô′rə fĭl), *n.* *Bot.* megasporophyll.

macrostructure (măk′rō strŭk′chə), *n.* *Metall.* the general crystalline structure of metals and alloys as revealed on an etched surface examined by the naked eye or at low magnification.

macruran (mə kro͞o′ə′rən), *adj.* **1.** belonging or pertaining to the *Macrura*, a group of stalk-eyed decapod crustaceans with long tails, including lobsters, shrimps, etc. —*n.* **2.** a macruran crustacean. [f. s. NL *macrūra*, pl. (f. Gk: s. *makrós* long + m. *ourá* tail) + -AN]

macrurous (mə kro͞oə′rəs), *adj.* long-tailed, as the lobster (opposed to *brachyurous*).

macula (măk′yo͞o lə), *n., pl.* **-lae** (-lē′). a spot on the sun, in the skin, or the like. [ME, t. L] —**mac′ular,** *adj.*

maculate (*v.* măk′yo͞o lāt′; *adj.* măk′yo͞o lĭt), *v.,* **-lated, -lating,** *adj.* —*v.t.* **1.** to mark with a spot or spots; stain. **2.** to sully or pollute. —*adj.* **3.** spotted; stained. **4.** defiled or impure. [late ME, t. L: m. s. *maculātus*, pp.]

maculation (măk′yo͞o lā′shən), *n.* **1.** the act of spotting. **2.** a spotted condition. **3.** a marking of spots, as on an animal. **4.** a disfiguring spot or stain. **5.** defilement.

macule (măk′yo͞ol), *n., v.t., v.i.,* **-uled, -uling.** mackle.

mad (măd), *adj.,* **madder, maddest,** *v.,* **madded, madding.** —*adj.* **1.** disordered in intellect; insane. **2.** *Colloq., Now Chiefly U.S.* moved by anger. **3.** (of wind, etc.) furious in violence. **4.** (of animals) **a.** abnormally furious: *a mad bull.* **b.** affected with rabies; rabid: *a mad dog.* **5.** wildly excited; frantic: *mad haste.* **6.** senselessly foolish or imprudent: *a mad scheme.* **7.** wild with eagerness or desire; infatuated: *to be mad about someone.* **8.** wildly gay or merry: *to have a mad time.* **9. like mad, a.** in the manner of a madman. **b.** with great haste, impetuosity, or enthusiasm. —*v.t.* **10.** *Archaic.* to make mad. —*v.i.* **11.** *Archaic.* to be, become, or act mad. [ME *mad, madd(e)*, OE *gemǣd(d)*, *gemǣded*, pp. of a verb der. from OE *gemād* mad, c. OHG *gameit* foolish]

—**Syn. 1.** demented, lunatic, deranged, maniacal. **2.** furious, exasperated, angry. **6.** MAD, CRAZY, INSANE are used to characterize wildly impractical or foolish ideas, actions, etc. MAD suggests senselessness and excess: *the scheme of selling the bridge was absolutely mad.* CRAZY suggests recklessness and impracticality: *a crazy young couple.* INSANE is used with some opprobrium to express unsoundness and possible harmfulness: *the new traffic system is simply insane.*

Mad., Madam.

Madaba (mə dä′bə), *n.* a town in S central Jordan. 15,000 (est. 1965).

Madag., Madagascar.

Madagascar (măd′ə găs′kə), *n.* an island in the Indian Ocean, ab. 240 mi. off the SE coast of Africa. See **Malagasy Republic.** See map under **Mauritius.** —**Mad′agas′can,** *n., adj.*

madam (măd′əm), *n., pl.* **madams, mesdames** (mā′dăm′; *Fr.* mĕ dȧm′). **1.** a polite term of address used orig. to a woman of rank or authority, but now used to any woman. **2.** the woman in charge of a brothel. [ME *madame*, t. OF, orig. *ma dame* my lady. See DAME]

madame (măd′əm; *Fr.* mȧ dȧm′), *n., pl.* **mesdames** (*Fr.* mĕ dȧm′). a conventional title of respect, orig. for a Frenchwoman of rank, now used distinctively to or of a married woman who is not English-speaking, either separately or prefixed to the name. *Abbrev.:* Mme, *pl.* Mmes. [t. F. See MADAM]

Madariaga (*Sp.* mȧ dȧ ryȧ′gȧ), *n.* **Salvador de** (*Sp.* sȧl bȧ dôr′ dĕ), born 1886, Spanish author and diplomat.

madcap (măd′kăp′), *adj.* **1.** wildly impulsive; lively: *a madcap girl.* —*n.* **2.** a madcap person, esp. a girl.

madden (măd′n), *v.t.* **1.** to make mad or insane. **2.** to infuriate. —*v.i.* **3.** to become mad; act as if mad; rage.

maddening (măd′ən ĭng), *adj.* **1.** driving to madness or frenzy. **2.** infuriating; exasperating. **3.** raging; furious. —**mad′deningly,** *adv.*

madder (măd′ə), *n.* **1.** a plant of the rubiaceous genus *Rubia*, esp. *R. tinctorum*, a European herbaceous climbing plant with panicles of small yellowish flowers. **2.** the root of this plant, used to some extent (esp. formerly) in medicine, and particularly for making dyes which give red and other colours. **3.** the dye or colouring matter itself. **4.** a colour produced by such a dye. [ME *mad(d)er*, OE *mæd(e)re*, c. Icel. *madhra*]

madding (măd′ĭng), *adj.* **1.** mad; acting as if mad: *the madding crowd.* **2.** making mad.

made (mād), *v.* **1.** pt. and pp. of **make.** —*adj.* **2.** produced by making, preparing, etc. **3.** artificially produced. **4.** assured of success or fortune: *a made man.* **5.** *Obs.* invented or made-up.

Madeira (mə dĭə′rə; *Port.* mə dəy′rə), *n.* **1.** a group of five islands off the NW coast of Africa, belonging to Portugal. 310,000 pop. (est. 1966); 308 sq. mi. *Cap.:* Funchal. **2.** the chief island of this group. 280,000 pop. (est. 1966); 286 sq. mi. **3.** (*often l.c.*) a rich strong white wine resembling sherry made there. **4.** a river flowing from W Brazil NE to the Amazon: the chief tributary of the Amazon. ab. 2100 mi. [t. Pg.: lit., wood, timber, g. L *māteria*; so called because island was once a thick forest]

Madeira cake, a rich, yellow cake, containing no fruit, and flavoured only with lemon.

madeleine (măd′ə lĭn, -lān′), *n.* a small, fancy sponge cake baked in a dariole, coated with jam and desiccated coconut.

mademoiselle (măd′mwə zĕl′; *Fr.* mȧd mwȧ zĕl′), *n., pl.* **mesdemoiselles** (*Fr.* mĕd mwȧ zĕl′). the conventional French title of respect for a girl or unmarried woman, either used separately or prefixed to the name. *Abbrev.:* Mlle, *pl.* Mlles. [F., orig. *ma demoiselle* my demoiselle. See DEMOISELLE, DAMSEL]

Maderno (*It.* mȧ dĕr′nō), *n.* **Carlo** (*It.* kȧr′lō), 1556–1629, Italian baroque architect.

made-to-measure (mād′tə mĕzh′ə), *adj.* (of clothes, etc.) made to fit an individual; made to fit individual requirements.

made-up (mād′ŭp′), *adj.* **1.** concocted; invented: *a made-up story.* **2.** wearing facial cosmetics. **3.** put together; finished.

madhouse (măd′hous′), *n.* **1.** an asylum for the insane. **2.** a place of commotion and confusion.

Madhya Pradesh (mŭd′yə prä dĕsh′), a state in central India. 32,372,408 pop. (1961); 171,201 sq. mi. *Cap.:* Bhopal.

Madison (măd′ĭ sən), *n.* **1. James,** 1751–1836, 4th president of the U.S., 1809–17. **2.** a town in the U.S., the capital of Wisconsin, in the S part. 126,706 (1960).

Madison Avenue, a street in New York City on which are concentrated the offices of many advertising and public relations firms and which has, therefore, become a symbol of their attitudes, methods, etc.

madly (măd′lĭ), *adv.* **1.** insanely. **2.** wildly; furiously: *they worked madly to fix the bridge.* **3.** foolishly.

madman (măd′mən), *n., pl.* **-men.** an insane person.

madness (măd′nĭs), *n.* **1.** the state of being mad; insanity. **2.** rabies. **3.** senseless folly. **4.** frenzy; rage.

Madonna (mə dŏn′ə), *n.* **1.** the Virgin Mary (usually prec. by *the*). **2.** a picture or statue representing the Virgin Mary. **3.** *Obs.* (*l.c.*) an Italian title of respect for a woman. [t. It.: my lady. See DONNA]

Madonna lily, a perennial liliaceous herb with long stems bearing pure white flowers, *Lilium candidum*, a native of the E Mediterranean region, but cultivated since early times.

madras (mə drăs′, -dräs′), *n.* **1.** a light cotton fabric with cords set at intervals or with woven stripes or figures, often of another colour, used for shirts, etc. **2.** Also, **madras muslin.** a thin curtain fabric of a light, gauzelike weave with figures of heavier yarns. **3.** a large brightly coloured kerchief, of either silk or cotton, often used for turbans. [named after MADRAS]

Madras (mə dräs′, -drăs′), *n.* **1.** a state in S India: formerly a presidency; boundaries readjusted in 1956 on a linguistic basis. 33,686,963 pop. (1961); 50,110 sq. mi. **2.** a seaport in and the capital of this state, on the Bay of Bengal. 1,729,141 (1961).

madrepore (măd′rĭ pô′), *n.* any of various corals (**madreporarians**) of the genus *Madrepora*, noted for reef-building in tropical seas. [t. F, t. It.: m. *madrepora*, appar. f. *madre* mother (g. L *māter*) + m. *poro* (t. Gk: m. *pôros* kind of stone)] —**madreporic** (măd′rĭ pŏ′rĭk), *adj.*

Madrepore

Madrid (mə drĭd′; *Sp.* mȧ drĕd′), *n.* the capital of Spain, in the central part. 2,558,583 (1965). See map under **Barbary coast.**

madrigal (măd′rĭ gl), *n.* **1.** a lyric poem suitable for musical setting, usually short and often of amatory character (esp. in vogue in the 16th century and later in Italy, France, England, and elsewhere). **2.** a part-song without instrumental accompaniment, usually for five or six voices, and making abundant use of contrapuntal imitation. **3.** any part-song. **4.** any song. [t. It.: m. *madrigale*, g. L *mātricāle* simple, naive, der. *mātrix* womb]

madrigalist (măd′rĭ gə lĭst), *n.* a composer or a singer of madrigals.

madroña (mə drō′nyə), *n.* an ericaceous evergreen tree or shrub, *Arbutus menziesii*, of western North America, having a hard wood and a smooth bark, and bearing a yellow, scarcely edible berry. [t. Sp.: the arbutus or strawberry tree, ult. der. L *mātūrus* ripe]

madroño (mə drō′nyō), *n., pl.* **-ños.** madroña.

Madura (*for 1, Indon.* mȧ do͞o′rȧ; *for 2,* măd′yo͞o rə; *Hind.* mə′do͞o rȧ), *n.* **1.** an island in Indonesia, off the NE coast of Java. pop. (with Java) 51,637,072 (est. 1955); 2112 sq. mi. **2.** Also, **Madurai.** a city in India, in S Madras. 424,810 (1961).

maduro (mə do͞oə′rō), *adj.* (of cigars) strong and darkly coloured. [t. Sp.: mature, g. L *mātūrus*]

madwoman (măd′wo͝om′ən), *n., pl.* **-women.** a mad or insane woman.

madwort (măd′wût′), *n.* **1.** any of several plants, as an alyssum, gold-of-pleasure. **2.** a boraginaceous plant, *Asperugo procumbens.*

Maeander (mē ăn′də), *n.* ancient name of **Menderes** (def. 1).

Maebashi (mä′ĭ băsh′ĭ), *n.* a city in central Japan, on Honshu island. 198,745 (1965).

Maecenas (mē sē′năs), *n.* **1. Gaius Cilnius** (gī′əs sĭl′nĭ əs), between 73 and 63 B.C.–8 B.C., Roman statesman, friend and patron of Virgil and Horace. **2.** a generous patron, esp. of the arts.

Maelstrom (māl′strōm), *n.* **1.** a famous whirlpool off the NW coast of Norway. **2.** (*l.c.*) any great or violent whirlpool. **3.** (*l.c.*) a restless confusion of affairs, influence, etc. [t. early mod. D: now spelt *maalstroom,* f. *malen* grind, whirl + *stroom* stream]

maenad (mē′năd), *n.* **1.** a female attendant of Dionysus; a bacchante. **2.** any frenzied or raging woman. Also, **menad.** [t. L: s. *Maenas,* t. Gk: s. *mainás* a mad woman] —**maenad′ic,** *adj.*

Maesteg (mīs′tĕg), *n.* a town in Wales, in Glamorganshire. 21,652 (1961).

maestoso (mīs tō′sō; *It.* mȧ ės tô′sô), *adj., adv. Music.* with majesty; stately. [It., der. *maesta* majesty, t. L: m. *mājestas*]

maestrale (*It.* mȧ ės trȧ′lė), *n.* a light or moderate north-westerly wind, occurring in the Adriatic Sea in summer.

Maestricht (*Du.* mȧ strĭKHt′), *n.* Maastricht.

maestro (mīs′trō; *It.* mȧ ĕs′trô), *n., pl.* **-tri** (*It.* -trē). **1.** an eminent musical composer, teacher, or conductor. **2.** (*cap.*) a title of respect for addressing such a person. **3.** a master of any art. [It.: master]

Maeterlinck (mā′tə lĭngk′; *Fr.* mȧ tĕr lăNk′), *n.* **Maurice** (*Fr.* mō rēs′), 1862–1949, Belgian dramatist and poet.

Mae West, an inflatable life-preserving jacket for airmen or sailors who fall in the sea. [named after (MAE) WEST]

Mafeking (măf′ĭ kĭng′), *n.* a town in the N part of the Republic of South Africa; besieged for 217 days by the Boers 1899–1900. 8279 (1960).

maffick (măf′ĭk), *v.i.* to celebrate with extravagant public demonstrations. [back-formation from MAFEKING; the relief of the city was celebrated in London with extravagant joy] —**maf′ficker,** *n.*

Mafia (măf′ĭ ə), *n.* **1.** (in Sicily) **a.** (*l.c.*) a popular spirit of hostility to legal restraint and to the law, often manifesting itself in criminal acts. **b.** a 19th-century secret society (similar to the Camorra in Naples) acting in this spirit. **2.** a criminal secret society of Sicilians or other Italians, at home or in foreign countries. Also, **Maffia.** [t. It. (Sicilian): boldness, bravery, der. *Màffio,* var. of *Maffèo,* t. L: m. *Matthaeus* Matthew]

ma foi (*Fr.* mȧ fwȧ′), *French.* my word! really! [F: lit., my faith]

mag., **1.** magazine. **2.** magnetism. **3.** magnitude.

Magalakwena (măg′ə lə kwā′nə), *n.* a river in the Republic of South Africa flowing N through Transvaal to the river Limpopo. ab. 130 mi.

Magallanes (*Sp.* mȧ gȧ lyȧ′nės), *n.* Punta Arenas.

magazine (măg′ə zēn′), *n.* **1.** a periodical publication, usually bound and with a paper cover, containing miscellaneous articles or pieces, in prose or verse, often with illustrations. **2.** a room or place for keeping gunpowder and other explosives, as in a fort or on a warship. **3.** a building or place for keeping military stores, as arms, ammunition, provisions, etc. **4.** a collection of war munitions. **5.** a metal receptacle for a number of cartridges which is inserted into certain types of automatic weapons and which must be removed when empty and replaced by a full receptacle in order to continue firing. **6.** a supply chamber as in a stove, etc. **7.** *Photog.* a light-proof enclosure containing film which enables a camera to be loaded or unloaded in daylight. **8.** a storehouse; warehouse. [t. F: m. *magasin,* t. It.: m. *magazzino* storehouse, t. Ar.: m. *makhāzin,* pl. of *makhzan* storehouse]

magazine-fed (măg′ə zēn fĕd′), *adj.* (of a rifle) loading from a cartridge clip into the magazine.

Magdalena (*Sp.* mȧg dȧ lė′nȧ), *n.* a river flowing from SW Colombia N to the Caribbean. ab. 1060 mi.

Magdalena Bay, a bay on the SW coast of Lower California, Mexico. ab. 17 mi. long.

Magdalene (măg′də lēn′, măg′də lē′nĭ), *n.* **1. the,** Mary Magdalene. Mark 15:40, 16:9; John 20:1–18. **2.** (*l.c.*) a reformed prostitute. Also, **Magdalen** (măg′də lĭn).

Magdalenian (măg′də lē′nyən), *adj.* denoting the period or culture stage in the Old World Stone Age (Upper Palaeolithic) in which Cro-Magnon man reached his highest level of industry and art. [Latinized form of (La) *Madeleine,* France, where implements and art of this period were found. See -IAN]

Magdeburg (măg′də bûg′; *Ger.* mȧk′də bo͝ork), *n.* a town in W East Germany, formerly a member of the Hanseatic League. 265,512 (1962). See map under **Hanseatic League.**

mage (māj), *n. Archaic.* a magician. [ME, t. F, t. L: m. s. *magus*]

Strait of Magellan

Magellan (mə gĕl′ən), *n.* **1. Ferdinand,** *c.* 1480–1521, Portuguese navigator, discoverer of the Strait of Magellan and the Philippine Islands. **2. Strait of,** a strait near the S tip of South America between the mainland of Chile and Tierra del Fuego and other islands, connecting the Atlantic and Pacific oceans. ab. 360 mi. long; 2½–17 mi. wide.

Magellanic (măg′ĭ lăn′ĭk), *adj.* pertaining to or named after Ferdinand Magellan.

Magellanic cloud, *Astron.* either of two bright cloud-like patches of stars in the southern heavens.

magenta (mə jĕn′tə), *n.* **1.** fuchsine. **2.** reddish purple. —*adj.* **3.** of reddish purple colour. [named after MAGENTA; discovered year of battle]

Magenta (mə jĕn′tə), *n.* a town in N Italy, W of Milan: the French and Sardinians defeated the Austrians here 1859. 12,000 (est. 1963).

Maggiore (măj′ĭ ô′rĭ; *It.* mȧd jô′rė), *n.* **Lake,** a lake in N Italy and S Switzerland. 83 sq. mi.

maggot (măg′ət), *n.* **1.** the legless larva of a fly, as of the housefly. **2.** a fly larva living in decaying matter. **3.** an odd fancy; whim. [ME *magot*; orig. uncert.]

maggoty (măg′ə tĭ), *adj.* **1.** infested with maggots, as food. **2.** having queer notions; full of whims.

Magi (mā′jī), *n.pl., sing.* **-gus** (-gəs). **1.** (*also l.c.*) the three wise men who came from the east to Jerusalem to do homage to the infant Jesus. Matt. 2:1–12. **2.** the Zoroastrian priests of ancient Media and Persia, reputed to possess supernatural powers. [See MAGUS] —**Magian** (mā′jĭ ən), *adj.* —**Ma′gianism,** *n.*

magic (măj′ĭk), *n.* **1.** the pretended art of producing effects beyond the natural human power by means of supernatural agencies or through command of occult forces in nature. **2.** the exercise of this art. **3.** the effects produced. **4.** power or influence exerted through this art. **5.** any extraordinary or irresistible influence: *the magic in a great name.* **6.** legerdemain; conjuring. —*adj.* Also, **mag′ical. 7.** employed in magic: *magic spells.* **8.** mysteriously enchanting: *magic beauty.* **9.** of, pertaining to, or due to magic: *magic rites.* **10.** producing the effects of magic; like magic. [ME *magike,* t. LL: m. *magica,* in L *magicē,* t. Gk: m. *magikḗ,* prop. fem. of *magikós* Magian, magic] —**mag′ically,** *adv.*

—**Syn. 1.** enchantment. MAGIC, NECROMANCY, SORCERY, WITCHCRAFT imply producing results through mysterious influences or unexplained powers. MAGIC may have glamorous and attractive connotations; the other terms suggest the harmful and sinister. MAGIC is an art of using some occult force of nature: *fifty years ago television would have seemed to be magic.* NECROMANCY is an art of prediction, supposedly because of communicating with the dead (it is called 'the black art', because Greek *nekro,* dead, was confused with Latin *niger,* black): *necromancy led to violating graves.* SORCERY, originally divination by casting lots, came to mean supernatural knowledge gained through the aid of evil spirits, and often used for evil ends: *spells and charms used in sorcery.* WITCHCRAFT esp. suggests a malign kind of magic, often used by aged and half-crazed women against innocent victims: *those accused of witchcraft were executed.*

magic eye, *Electronics.* a triode valve with a special fluorescent coating, used to tune radio receivers: as the tuning dial is moved the fluorescence varies in proportion to the carrier intensity.

magician (mə jĭsh′ən), *n.* **1.** one skilled in magic arts. **2.** a juggler; conjurer. [ME *magicien,* t. OF, der. L *magicus* MAGIC] —**Syn. 1.** sorcerer, necromancer.

magic lantern, a lantern-slide projector.

magic number, *Physics.* any one of the numbers 2, 8, 20, 28, 50, 82, or 126; atomic nuclei containing these numbers of neutrons or protons have exceptional stability.

Maginot line (măzh′ĭ nō′; *Fr.* mȧ zhē nô′), a zone of French fortifications erected along the French–German border in the years preceding World War II. [named after André *Maginot,* 1877–1932, French minister of war]

magisterial (măj′ĭs tĭə′rĭ əl), *adj.* **1.** of, pertaining to, or befitting a master; authoritative: *a magisterial pronouncement.* **2.** imperious; domineering. **3.** of or befitting a magistrate or his office. **4.** of the rank of a magistrate. [t. ML: s. *magisteriālis,* der. LL *magisterius,* der. L *magister* MASTER] —**mag′iste′rially,** *adv.*

magistracy (măj′ĭs trə sĭ), *n., pl.* **-cies. 1.** the office or function of a magistrate. **2.** a body of magistrates. **3.** the district under a magistrate. Also, **magistrature** (măj′ĭs trə tyo͞oə′).

magistral (măj′ĭs trəl), *adj.* **1.** *Pharm.* prescribed or

prepared for a particular occasion, as a remedy (opposed to *officinal*). **2.** *Fort.* principal. **3.** *Rare.* magisterial. —*n.* **4.** magistral line. [t. L: s. *magistrālis* of a master]
magistral line, *Fort.* the line from which the position of the other lines of fieldworks is determined.
magistrate (măj′ĭs trāt′, -trĭt), *n.* **1.** a person charged with executive functions. **2.** a justice of the peace, paid or unpaid, who officiates in a magistrates' court. [ME *magistrat*, t. L: s. *magistrātus* the office of a chief, a magistrate]
magistrates' court, a court of summary jurisdiction for minor criminal offences which also hears the preliminary investigation into indictable offences and has a few civil and administrative functions.
magma (măg′mə), *n., pl.* **-mata** (-mə tə), **-mas. 1.** any crude mixture of finely divided mineral or organic matters. **2.** *Geol.* molten material under conditions of intense heat and great pressure occurring beneath the solid crust of the earth, and from which igneous rocks are formed. **3.** *Chem., Pharm.* a paste composed of solid and liquid matter. [t. L, t. Gk: a salve] —**magmatic** (măg măt′ĭk), *adj.*
magmatic stoping, *Geol.* stoping.
Magna Carta (măg′nə kä′tə), **1.** the 'great charter' of English liberties, forced from King John by the English barons at Runnymede, June 15th, 1215. **2.** any fundamental constitution or law guaranteeing rights. Also, **Magna Charta.** [t. ML: great charter]
magna cum laude (măg′nä ko͝om lou′dā), *Latin.* with great praise (used chiefly in American universities to grant the middle of three special honours for above-average academic performance).
Magna Graecia (măg′nə grē′shĭ ə), ancient name of the colonial cities of Greece in S Italy.
magnalium (măg nā′lĭ əm), *n. Metall.* a light alloy based on aluminium, containing magnesium and sometimes copper, nickel, tin, or lead.
magnanimity (măg′nə nĭm′ĭ tĭ), *n., pl.* **-ties. 1.** quality of being magnanimous. **2.** a magnanimous act.
magnanimous (măg năn′ĭ məs), *adj.* **1.** generous in forgiving an insult or injury; free from petty resentfulness or vindictiveness. **2.** high-minded; noble. **3.** proceeding from or revealing nobility of mind, etc. [t. L: m. *magnanimus* great-souled] —**magnan′imously,** *adv.* —**magnan′imousness,** *n.* —**Syn. 2.** See **noble.**
magnate (măg′nāt), *n.* **1.** a great or dominant person in a district or, esp. in some field of business: *a property magnate.* **2.** a person of eminence or distinction in any field. **3.** a member of the upper house of certain European parliaments, as formerly in Hungary and Poland. [late ME, t. LL: m. s. *magnas*, der. L *magnus* great]
magnesia (măg nē′shə), *n.* a magnesium oxide, MgO, a white tasteless substance used in medicine as an antacid and laxative. [ME, t. ML (in alchemy), t. Gk: (*hē*) *Magnēsía* (*líthos*), (the) Magnesian (stone); i.e. stone from Magnesia in Thessaly] —**magne′sian, magnesic** (măg nē′sĭk), *adj.*
Magnesia (măg nē′zyə), *n.* ancient name of **Manisa.**
magnesite (măg′nĭ sīt′), *n.* a mineral, magnesium carbonate, $MgCO_3$, usually occurring in white masses.
magnesium (măg nē′zyəm), *n. Chem.* a light, ductile, silver-white metallic element which burns with a dazzling white light, used in lightweight alloys. *Symbol:* Mg; *at. wt:* 24·312; *at. no.:* 12; *sp. gr.:* 1·74 at 20°C. [NL, der. *magnēsia* MAGNESIA]
magnesium light, the strongly actinic white light produced when magnesium is burnt, used in photography, signalling, pyrotechnics, etc.
magnesium oxide, *Chem.* magnesia.
magnesium sulphate, *Chem.* Epsom salts.
magnet (măg′nĭt), *n.* **1.** a body (as a piece of iron or steel) which possesses the property of attracting certain substances, esp. iron; any piece of metal with ferromagnetic properties. **2.** loadstone. **3.** a thing or person that attracts, as by some inherent power or charm. [late ME *magnete*, t. L: m. s. *magnes* loadstone, magnet, t. Gk: *Mágnēs* (*líthos*) (stone) of Magnesia (in Thessaly), loadstone. Cf. MAGNESIA]
magnetic (măg nĕt′ĭk), *adj.* **1.** of or pertaining to a magnet or magnetism. **2.** having the properties of a magnet. **3.** capable of being magnetized or attracted by a magnet. **4.** pertaining to the earth's magnetism: *the magnetic equator.* **5.** exerting a strong attractive power or charm: *a magnetic personality.* Also, **magnet′ical.** —**magnet′ically,** *adv.*
magnetic bearing, *Navig.* the bearing of an object in relation to the magnetic meridian.
magnetic bottle, *Physics.* any configuration of magnetic fields used to contain a plasma in a controlled thermonuclear reaction.
magnetic compass, a compass consisting of a magnetic needle which acts itself along the lines of the earth's magnetic field and thus indicates the direction of the earth's magnetic poles.
magnetic core. See **core** (def. 3c).
magnetic declination, declination (def. 2). Also, **magnetic variation.**
magnetic drum, *Computers.* a memory unit for computers, consisting of a rapidly spinning cylinder on which information is recorded by magnetizing the surface.
magnetic element, any one of the three quantities, magnetic declination, dip, or horizontal intensity, which define the earth's magnetic field at any point on the earth's surface.
magnetic equator, the aclinic line.
magnetic field, a condition of space in the vicinity of a magnet or electric current which manifests itself as a force on magnetic objects within that space.
magnetic flux, 1. the total magnetic induction through a given cross-section. **2.** magnetomotive force divided by reluctance.
magnetic induction, a measure of the magnetic effect at a given point.
magnetic meridian, an imaginary line on the earth's surface which coincides with the horizontal component of the earth's magnetic field.
magnetic mine, a mine designed to be exploded when its mechanism is triggered by the presence of ferrous objects, as the metal hull of a ship.
magnetic moment, a quantity associated with a magnet, equal to the product of its pole strength and its length.
magnetic needle, a slender magnetized steel rod which, when adjusted to swing in a horizontal plane, as in a compass, indicates the direction of the earth's magnetic fields or the approximate north and south.
magnetic north, the direction in which the needle of a compass points, differing in most places from true north.
magnetic pole, 1. a pole of a magnet. **2.** either of the two points on the earth's surface where the dipping needle of a compass stands vertical, one in the Arctic, the other in the Antarctic.
magnetic potential, *Elect.* a scalar quantity analogous to electric potential; the difference in magnetic potential between two points in a magnetic field being the work done in carrying unit magnetic pole from one point to the other.
magnetic recorder, a device for recording sound on magnetic tape; tape-recorder.

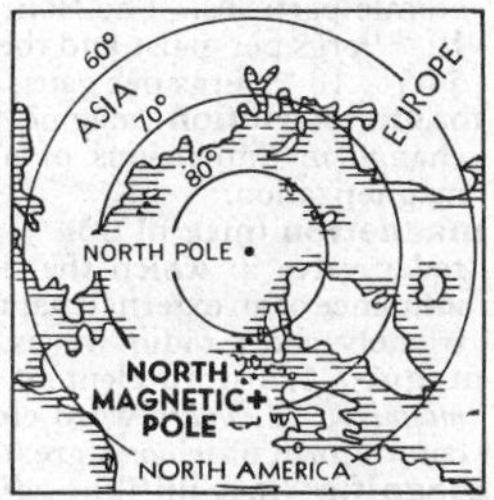

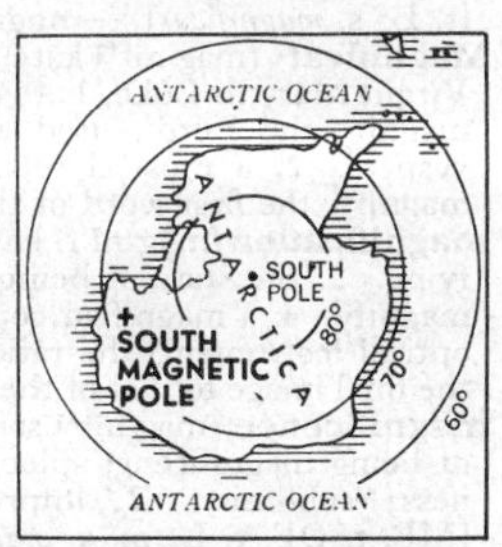

Magnetic poles

magnetic storm, a sudden disturbance in the earth's magnetic field associated with sunspot activity.
magnetic susceptibility, *Elect.* the ratio of the intensity of magnetization produced in a substance to the intensity of the magnetic field to which it is subjected.
magnetic tape, a plastic tape coated with a ferromagnetic powder, esp. iron oxide, used to record sound in a magnetic recorder.
magnetic tape unit, *Computers.* a machine which holds a magnetic tape and transfers information between the tape and a computer.
magnetic variation, magnetic declination. See **declination** (def. 2).
magnetism (măg′nĭ tĭz′əm), *n.* **1.** the characteristic properties possessed by magnets; the molecular properties common to magnets. **2.** the agency producing magnetic phenomena. **3.** the science dealing with magnetic phenomena. **4.** magnetic or attractive power or charm.
magnetite (măg′nĭ tīt′), *n.* a very common black iron oxide, Fe_3O_4, that is strongly attracted by a magnet; an important iron ore.
magnetize (măg′nĭ tīz′), *v.t.,* **-tized, -tizing. 1.** to communicate magnetic properties to. **2.** to exert an attracting or compelling influence upon. **3.** *Obs.* to mesmerize. Also, **magnetise.** —**mag′netiza′tion,** *n.* —**mag′netiz′er,** *n.*

magneto (măg nē′tō), *n.*, *pl.* **-tos.** a small electric generator, the poles of which are permanent magnets, as a hand-operated generator for telephone signalling, or the generator producing sparks in an internal-combustion engine. [short for MAGNETO-ELECTRIC (machine)]

magneto-, a combining form of **magnet** or **magnetic.**

magneto-chemistry (măg nē′tō kĕm′ĭs trĭ), *n.* the study of magnetic and chemical phenomena in their relation to one another. —**magne′to-chem′ical,** *adj.*

magneto-electric (măg nē′tō ĭ lĕk′trĭk), *adj.* pertaining to the induction of electric currents by means of magnets. Also, **magne′to-elec′trical.**

magneto-electricity (măg nē′tō ĭ lĕk′trĭs′ĭ tĭ), *n.* electricity developed by the action of magnets.

magneto-generator (măg nē′tō jĕn′ə rā′tə), *n.* a magneto-electric generator.

magneto-hydrodynamics (măg nē′tō hī′drō dī năm′ĭks), *n.* (*construed as sing.*) *Physics.* **1.** the study of the flow of electrically conducting fluids through a magnetic field. **2.** a method of generating electricity by subjecting the free electrons in a high-temperature, high-velocity flame or plasma to a strong magnetic field. *Abbrev.*: mhd.

magnetometer (măg′nĭ tŏm′ĭ tə), *n.* an instrument for measuring magnetic forces. —**mag′netom′etry,** *n.*

magnetomotive (măg nē′tō mō′tĭv), *adj.* producing magnetic effects, or pertaining to such production.

magnetomotive force, magnetic flux multiplied by reluctance, the force which gives rise to magnetic effects or magnetic flux.

magneton (măg′nĭ tŏn′, măg nī′tŏn), *n.* *Physics.* a unit for measuring the magnetic moments of atomic or subatomic particles. The Bohr magneton is equal to $9{\cdot}27 \times 10^{-21}$ ergs per gauss and the nuclear magneton is equal to $5{\cdot}05 \times 10^{-24}$ ergs per gauss.

magnetostriction (măg nē′tō strĭk′shən), *n.* *Physics.* the change in dimensions of a ferromagnetic substance on magnetization.

magnetron (măg′nĭ trŏn′), *n.* *Electronics.* a two-element radar valve in which the flow of electrons is under the influence of an external magnetic field, used to generate extremely short radio waves. [f. MAGNE(T) + (ELEC)TRON]

magni-, **1.** a word element meaning 'large', 'great', as in *magnify*. **2.** *Zool.* a word element denoting length. [t. L, comb. form of *magnus* great]

magnific (măg nĭf′ĭk), *adj.* *Archaic.* **1.** magnificent; imposing. **2.** grandiose; pompous. Also, **magnif′ical.** [t. L: s. *magnificus*] —**magnif′ically,** *adv.*

Magnificat (măg nĭf′ĭ kăt′), *n.* **1.** the hymn of the Virgin Mary in Luke, 1:46–55, beginning 'My soul doth magnify the Lord', used as a canticle at evensong or vespers. **2.** a musical setting of it. [ME, t. L: doth magnify, the first word of the hymn in the Vulgate]

magnification (măg′nĭ fĭ kā′shən), *n.* **1.** the act of magnifying. **2.** the state of being magnified. **3.** the power to magnify. **4.** a magnified copy or reproduction. **5.** (of an optical instrument) the ratio of the linear dimensions of the final image to that of the object.

magnificence (măg nĭf′ĭ səns), *n.* **1.** the quality or state of being magnificent; splendour; grandeur; impressiveness; sublimity. **2.** impressiveness of surroundings. [ME, t. OF, t. L: m. s. *magnificentia*] —**Syn. 1.** sumptuousness, pomp, state, majesty.

magnificent (măg nĭf′ĭ sənt), *adj.* **1.** making a splendid appearance or show: *a magnificent cathedral.* **2.** extraordinarily fine; superb: *a magnificent opportunity.* **3.** noble; sublime: *a magnificent poem.* **4.** great in deeds (now only as a title): *Lorenzo the Magnificent.* **5.** lavish. [t. OF, t. L: *magnificent-* (recorded in compar., superl., and other forms), for *magnificus*. See MAGNIFIC] —**magnif′icently,** *adv.*

—**Syn. 1, 2.** august, stately, majestic, imposing; sumptuous, grand. MAGNIFICENT, GORGEOUS, SPLENDID, SUPERB are terms of high admiration and all are used colloquially in weak hyperbole. That which is MAGNIFICENT is beautiful, princely, grand, or ostentatious: *a magnificent display of paintings.* That which is GORGEOUS moves one to admiration by the richness and (often colourful) variety of its effects: *a gorgeous array of handsome gifts.* That which is SPLENDID is dazzling or impressive in its brilliance, radiance, or excellence: *splendid jewels, a splendid body of scholars.* That which is SUPERB is above others in, or is of the highest degree of, excellence or elegance (less often, today, of grandeur): *a superb rendition of a song, superb wines.* —**Ant. 1.** modest.

magnifico (măg nĭf′ĭ kō′), *n.*, *pl.* **-coes. 1.** a Venetian grandee. **2.** any grandee or great personage. [t. It., t. L: m. *magnificus* MAGNIFIC]

magnify (măg′nĭ fī′), *v.*, **-fied, -fying.** —*v.t.* **1.** to increase the apparent size of, as a lens does. **2.** to make greater in size; enlarge. **3.** to cause to seem greater or more important. **4.** *Archaic.* to extol; praise. —*v.i.* **5.** to increase or be able to increase the apparent size of an object, as a lens does. [ME *magnifie(n)*, t. L: m. *magnificāre* make much of] —**mag′nifi′er,** *n.* —**Syn. 2.** augment, increase, amplify. **3.** exaggerate, overstate.

magnifying glass, *Optics.* a glass lens, usually convex, or a combination of lenses used to produce a virtual image larger than the object being viewed.

magniloquent (măg nĭl′ə kwənt), *adj.* speaking or expressed in a lofty or grandiose style. [L *magniloquus* + -ENT] —**magnil′oquence,** *n.* —**magnil′oquently,** *adv.*

Magnitogorsk (*Russ.* məg nĭ tä gôrsk′), *n.* a city in the Soviet Union, on the river Ural near the boundary between Europe and Asia. 348,000 (est. 1965).

magnitude (măg′nĭ tyo͞od′), *n.* **1.** size; extent: *to determine the magnitude of an angle.* **2.** great amount, importance, etc.: *affairs of magnitude.* **3.** greatness; great size: *the magnitude of the loss.* **4.** moral greatness: *magnitude of mind.* **5.** *Astron.* the brightness of a star expressed according to an arbitrary numerical system (the brightest degree being the **first magnitude,** and those less bright the **second, third,** or other **magnitude**). Stars brighter than the sixth magnitude are visible to the unaided eye. **6.** *Maths.* a number characteristic of a quantity and forming a basis for comparison with similar quantities. [ME, t. L: m. *magnitūdo* greatness]

magnolia (măg nō′lyə), *n.* **1.** any plant of the genus *Magnolia*, comprising shrubs and trees with large, usually fragrant flowers and an aromatic bark, much cultivated for ornament. **2.** the magnolia blossom. [NL; named from P. *Magnol*, 1638–1715, a French botanist]

magnoliaceous (măg nō′lĭ ā′shəs), *adj.* belonging to the *Magnoliaceae*, or magnolia family of plants, including the magnolias generally, the tulip trees, etc.

magnum (măg′nəm), *n.*, *pl.* **-nums.** a bottle for wine or spirits, holding about 2 quarts. [t. L, neut. of *magnus* great]

magnum opus (ō′pəs), **1.** a great work. **2.** one's chief work, esp. a literary or artistic work. [L]

magpie (măg′pī′), *n.* **1.** any of various noisy, mischievous, corvine birds of the genus *Pica*, having a long, graduated tail and black-and-white plumage, as the **black-billed magpie,** *P. pica*, of Europe and North America. **2.** any of several related corvine birds. **3.** any of several unrelated birds, as those of the genus *Gymnorhina*, of Australia. **4.** a chattering person. **5.** *Archery.* **a.** the third ring or part from the centre of a target, between the inner and the outer. **b.** a shot which strikes this part. **c.** the score value of this part. [f. *Mag*, familiar var. of *Margaret*, woman's name + PIE²]

Magritte (*Fr.* mȧ grĕt′), *n.* **René** (*Fr.* rə nĕ′), 1898–1967, Belgian painter.

maguey (măg′wā; *Sp.* mȧ gĕ′ē), *n.* **1.** any of several species of the amaryllidaceous genus *Agave*, esp. *A. cantala*, or the allied genus *Furcraea*. **2.** the fibre from these plants. [t. Sp., prob. from Haitian]

Magus (mā′gəs), *n.*, *pl.* **-gi** (-jī). **1.** (*also l.c.*) See **Magi** (def. 1). **2.** (*l.c.*) an ancient astrologer or magician. **3.** a Zoroastrian priest. [ME, t. L, t. Gk: m. *Mágos*, t. OPers.: m. *magus*]

Magyar (măg′yä; *Hung.* mŏ′dyŏr), *n.* **1.** a member of the ethnic group, of the Finno-Ugric stock, which forms the predominant element of the population of Hungary. **2.** the Hungarian language. —*adj.* **3.** of or pertaining to the Magyars or their language; Hungarian. [t. Hung.]

Magyarország (*Hung.* mŏ′dyŏr ȯr sȧg), *n.* Hungarian name of **Hungary.**

Mahabharata (mə hä′bä′rə tə), *n.* one of the two chief epics of ancient India. Its central subject is the war between the Kauravas and the Pandavas. Also, **Mahabharatam** (mə hä′bä′rə təm). [t. Skt: f. *mahā-* great + *Bhārata* descendant of a king or a tribe named *Bharata*]

Mahalla el Kubra (mə hä′lə ĕl ko͞o′brə), a town in N Egypt, in the Nile delta. 178,000 (est. 1960).

mahalwari (mə häl′wə rĭ), *n.* one of the principal systems of land tenure in India, in which village communities jointly and severally hold an estate from the government. See **ryotwari, zemindari.** [t. Hind.]

maharaja (mä′hə rä′jə), *n.* the title of certain great ruling princes in India. Also, **maharajah.** [t. Skt: great raja]

maharani (mä′hə rä′nē), *n.* *India.* **1.** the wife of a maharaja. **2.** a female sovereign in her own right. Also, **maharanee.** [t. Hind.: great queen]

Maharashtra (mä′hä răsh′trə), *n.* a state in W India. 39,553,718 pop. (1961); 118,717 sq. mi. *Cap.*: Bombay.

mahatma (mə hăt′mə, -hät′mə), *n.* **1.** an adept in Brahmanism. **2.** a wise and holy leader, esteemed for his saintliness. **3.** *Theosophy.* one of a class of reputed beings with preternatural powers. [t. Skt: m. *mahātman* great-souled] —**mahat′maism,** *n.*

Mahdi (mä′dĭ), *n.*, *pl.* **-dis. 1.** (in Muslim usage) the title of an expected spiritual and temporal ruler destined to establish a reign of righteousness throughout the world. 2. any of various claimants of this title, esp. Mohammed Ahmed (died 1885), who set up in the Egyptian Sudan an independent government which lasted until 1898. [t. Ar.: m. *mahdīy*, lit., the guided or directed one] —**Mahdism** (mä′dĭz′əm), *n.* —**Mah′-dist,** *n.*

mahem (mä′hĕm), *n. S African.* the African crowned crane, *Balearica pavonina.* [t. Zulu: m. *unohemu*]

Mahendra (mə hĕn′drə), *n.* (*Mahendra Bir Bikram*), born 1920, king of Nepal since 1955.

Mahican (mə hē′kən), *n.* Mohican.

mah-jongg (mä′jŏng′), *n.* **1.** a game of Chinese origin, usually for four persons, with 136 (or sometimes 144) domino-like pieces or tiles marked in suits, counters, and dice. —*v.i.* **2.** to win a game of mah-jongg. Also, **mah-jong.** [t. Chinese (Mandarin): m. *ma-ch'iao* sparrow (lit., hemp-bird), pictured on the first tiles of one of the suits]

Mahler (mä′lə; *Ger.* mȧ′lər), *n.* **Gustav** (*Ger.* go͝os′tȧf), 1860–1911, Austrian (Bohemian) composer and conductor.

mahlstick (môl′stĭk′), *n.* a maulstick.

Mahmud II (mä mo͞od′), 1785–1839, sultan of Turkey 1809–39. Also, **Mahmoud.**

mahogany (mə hŏg′ə nĭ), *n., pl.* **-nies,** *adj.* —*n.* **1.** any of certain tropical American meliaceous trees, esp. *Swietenia mahagoni* and *S. macrophylla,* yielding a hard, reddish brown wood highly esteemed for making fine furniture, etc. **2.** the wood itself. **3.** any of various related or similar trees, or their wood. **4.** a reddish brown colour. —*adj.* **5.** pertaining to or made of mahogany. **6.** of the colour mahogany. [? t. some non-Carib W Indian tongue]

Mahomet (mə hŏm′ĭt), *n.* Mohammed. —**Mahom′-etan,** *adj., n.*

mahonia (mə hō′nĭ ə), any of several evergreen berberidaceous shrubs of the genus *Mahonia,* as *M. aquifolium* with pinnate spiny leaves and clusters of yellow flowers.

Mahound (mə hound′, -ho͞ond′), *n.* **1.** *Archaic.* the prophet Mohammed. **2.** *Scot.* the devil. Also, **Mahoun.** [early ME *Mahun, Mahum,* t. OF, shortened form of *Mahomet,* b. with HOUND]

mahout (mə hout′), *n.* (in the East Indies) the keeper and driver of an elephant. [t. Hind.: m. *mahāut*]

Mahratta (mə rä′tə), *n.* Maratha.

Mahratti (mə rä′tĭ), *n.* Marathi.

Mähren (*Ger.* mĕ′rən), *n.* German name of **Moravia.**

Mährisch-Ostrau (*Ger.* mĕ′rĭsh ŏs′trou), *n.* German name of **Moravská Ostrava.**

mahzor (mäKH zô′), *n.* a Hebrew prayer book containing the ritual for festivals. See **siddur.**

Maia (mī′ə), *n. Gk Myth.* the eldest of the Pleiades, mother by Zeus of Hermes.

maid (mād), *n.* **1.** a girl; young unmarried woman. **2.** a spinster (usually in the expression *old maid*). **3.** a female servant. **4. the Maid,** Joan of Arc. [apocopated var. of MAIDEN]

maidan (mī dän′), *n.* (in India) an open space, as a parade ground. [t. Hindi, t. Pers.]

maiden (mā′dn), *n.* **1.** a maid; girl; young unmarried woman; virgin. **2.** Also, **the Maiden.** an instrument resembling the guillotine, formerly used in Edinburgh for beheading criminals. **3.** a maiden speech. **4.** *Cricket.* a maiden over. **5.** a maiden horse. **6.** a maiden race. —*adj.* **7.** of, pertaining to, or befitting a girl or unmarried woman. **8.** unmarried: *a maiden lady.* **9.** made, tried, appearing, etc., for the first time: *maiden voyage.* **10.** (of a horse, etc.) that never has won a race or a prize. **11.** (of a prize or a race) offered for or open only to maiden horses, etc. **12.** untried, as a knight, soldier, or weapon. [ME; OE *mægden,* f. *mægd-* + *-en* -EN⁵]

Maiden Castle, extensive ancient earthwork fortification in Dorset, erected *c.* 250 B.C. over Neolithic and Bronze Age settlements.

maidenhair (mā′dn hĕə′), *n.* any of the ferns constituting the genus *Adiantum.* The cultivated species have fine, glossy stalks and delicate, finely divided fronds.

maidenhair tree, ginkgo.

maidenhead (mā′dn hĕd′), *n.* **1.** maidenhood; virginity. **2.** the hymen.

Maidenhead (mā′dn hĕd′), *n.* a town in England, in Berkshire. 35,411 (1961).

maidenhood (mā′dn ho͝od′), *n.* the state or time of being a maiden; virginity.

maidenly (mā′dn lĭ), *adj.* **1.** pertaining to a maiden: *maidenly years.* **2.** characteristic of or befitting a maiden: *maidenly behaviour.* —**maid′enliness,** *n.*

maiden name, a woman's surname before marriage.

maiden over, *Cricket.* an over in which no runs are made.

maiden pink, a small perennial caryophyllaceous herb with narrow leaves and pink or white flowers, *Dianthus deltoides,* widespread in grassland throughout temperate Europe and Asia.

maiden speech, a first speech, as the first speech of an M.P. in Parliament.

Maid Marian, 1. (orig.) Queen of the May, one of the characters in the old morris dance. **2.** a female personage in a morris dance. **3.** Robin Hood's sweetheart.

maid of honour, 1. the chief unmarried attendant of a bride. **2.** an unmarried woman, usually of noble birth, attendant on a queen or princess. **3.** a small tart with a curd filling.

Maid of Orléans, Joan of Arc.

maidservant (mād′sû′vənt), *n.* a female servant.

Maidstone (mād′stən), *n.* a town in England, the county town of Kent. 59,790 (1961).

maieutic (mā yo͞o′tĭk), *adj.* (of the Socratic mode of enquiry) bringing out ideas latent in the mind. Also, **maieu′tica.** [t. Gk: m. s. *maieutikós* of midwifery]

maigre (mā′gə), *adj.* containing neither flesh nor its juices, as food permissible on days of religious abstinence. [t. F. See MEAGRE]

maihem (mā′hĕm), *n.* mayhem.

mail¹ (māl), *n.* **1.** letters, packages, etc., arriving or sent by post. **2.** the system of transmission of letters, etc., by post. **3.** a train or boat by which postal matter is carried. —*adj.* **4.** of or pertaining to mail: *a mailbag.* —*v.t.* **5.** *Chiefly U.S.* to send by mail; place in a post office or postbox for transmission. [ME *male bag,* t. OF, t. Gmc; cf. OHG *malha* wallet]

mail² (māl), *n.* **1.** flexible armour of interlinked rings, the ends riveted, butted, or soldered. **2.** defensive armour. —*v.t.* **3.** to clothe or arm with mail. [ME *maille,* t. F, g. L *macula* spot, mesh of a net]

Piece of mail² (def. 1)

mailbag (māl′băg′), *n.* a bag in which mail is carried.

mailbox (māl′bŏks′), *n. U.S.* **1.** letter-box. **2.** pillar-box. **3.** postbox.

mailed (māld), *adj.* clad or armed with mail: *the mailed horseman.* [f. MAIL² + -ED²]

mailed fist, armed force, as a threat or fact.

mailing list, a list consisting of the names and addresses of persons to whom information, etc., is sent by post.

Maillart (*Fr.* mȧ yȧr′), *n.* **Robert** (*Fr.* rō bĕr′), 1872–1940, Swiss engineer.

Maillol (*Fr.* mȧ yŏl′), *n.* **Aristide** (*Fr.* ȧ rēs tēd′), 1861–1944, French sculptor and artist.

mailman (māl′măn′), *n., pl.* **-men.** *U.S.* postman.

mail order, 1. an order for goods, etc., received and transmitted by post. **2.** the system of conducting a business by receiving orders and payment by mail and shipping goods to the buyers.

mail-order (māl′ô′də), *v.t.* to send or receive (goods, etc.) by mail order.

maim (mām), *v.t.* **1.** to deprive of the use of some bodily member; mutilate; cripple. **2.** to impair; make essentially defective. —*n.* **3.** *Rare.* an injury or defect. [var. of MAYHEM] —**maim′er,** *n.*

—**Syn. 1.** MAIM, LACERATE, MANGLE, MUTILATE indicate the infliction of painful and severe injuries on the body. To MAIM is to injure by giving a disabling wound, or by depriving a person of one or more members or their use: *maimed in an accident.* To LACERATE is to inflict severe cuts and tears on the flesh or skin: *to wound and lacerate an arm.* To MANGLE is to chop undiscriminatingly or to crush or rend by blows or pressure as if caught in machinery: *bodies mangled in a train wreck.* To MUTILATE is to injure the completeness or beauty of a body, esp. by cutting off an important member: *to mutilate a statue, a tree, a person.*

Maimonides (mī mŏn′ĭ dēz′), *n.* (*Moses ben Maimon*), 1135–1204, Spanish-Jewish scholar and philosopher.

main¹ (mān), *adj.* **1.** chief; principal; leading: *the main office.* **2.** sheer; utmost, as strength, force, etc.: *by main force.* **3.** of or pertaining to a broad expanse: *main sea.* **4.** *Gram.* See **main clause. 5.** *Obs.* strong or mighty. **6.** *Obs.* high-ranking; essential. **7.** *Naut.* pertaining to the mainmast or mainsail. —*n.* **8.** a principal pipe or duct in a system used to distribute water, gas, etc. **9.** the principal wire or cable used to distribute electricity. **10.** strength; force; violent effort: *with might and main.* **11.** the chief or principal part or point. **12.** *Poetic.* the open ocean; high sea. **13.** the mainland. **14. in the main,** for the most part. [ME *meyn,* OE *mægen* strength, power, c. Icel. *megin* strength, main part] —**Syn. 1.** cardinal, prime, paramount.

main² (mān), *n.* a cockfighting match. [orig. obscure]

Main (mān; *Ger.* mīn), *n.* a river flowing from the Bohemian Forest in East Germany W to the Rhine at Mainz in West Germany. 305 mi.

mainbrace (mān′brās′), *n. Naut.* **1.** a pennant and tackle secured to each end of the mainyard and led down to the main deck, used to haul the yard round to trim the mainsail to the wind. **2. splice the mainbrace,** *Slang.* the order to issue a tot of rum to a crew. [def. 2 originated as a rare or unlikely order, the mainbrace being replaced rather than repaired by splicing]

main clause, *Gram.* (in a complex sentence) the clause which may stand syntactically as a sentence by itself; independent clause. For example: in *I was out when he came in,* the main clause is *I was out.*

main deck, the upper deck in a vessel with two decks, and usually the second deck down in a vessel with more than two decks.

Maine (mān), *n.* **1.** a state in the NE United States, on the Atlantic coast. 969,265 pop. (1960); 33,215 sq. mi. *Cap.:* Augusta. *Abbrev.:* Me. **2.** a former province in NW France. *Cap.:* Le Mans.

Maine-et-Loire (*Fr.* mĕn ė lwȧr′), *n.* a department in W France. 556,272 pop. (1962); 2787 sq. mi. *Cap.:* Angers.

mainland (mān′lənd), *n.* the principal land, as distinguished from islands or peninsulas. —**main′lander,** *n.*

Mainland (mān′lənd), *n.* **1.** the largest of the Shetland Islands, NE of Scotland. 13,282 pop. (1961); ab. 200 sq. mi. **2.** Also, **Pomona.** an island N of Scotland: the largest of the Orkney Islands. 13,495 pop. (1961); 190 sq. mi.

main line, a through railway route; a principal line of a railway as contrasted with a branch or secondary line.

mainline (mān′līn′), *v.i.,* **-lined, -lining.** *Slang.* to inject a narcotic drug directly into the vein.

mainliner (mān′lī′nə), *n. Slang.* a drug addict who injects himself or is injected directly into the vein.

mainly (mān′lĭ), *adv.* **1.** chiefly; principally; for the most part. **2.** *Obs.* greatly.

mainmast (mān′mäst′; *Naut.* -məst), *n. Naut.* **1.** the principal mast in a ship or other vessel. **2.** (in a schooner, brig, bark, etc.), the second mast from the bow. **3.** (in a yawl or ketch) the mast nearer the bow.

mainsail (mān′sāl′; *Naut.* -səl), *n. Naut.* **1.** (in a square-rigged vessel) the sail bent to the mainyard. See illus. under **sail. 2.** (in a fore-and-aft rigged vessel) the large sail set abaft the mainmast.

mainsheet (mān′shēt′), *n. Naut.* a sheet of a mainsail.

mainspring (mān′spring′), *n.* **1.** the principal spring in a mechanism, as in a watch. **2.** the chief motive power; the impelling cause.

mainstay (mān′stā′), *n.* **1.** *Naut.* the stay which secures the mainmast forward. **2.** a chief support.

mainstream (mān′strēm′), *n.* **1.** the dominant trend; chief tendency: *she was in the mainstream of fashion.* —*adj.* **2.** *Jazz.* of or pertaining to jazz which lies between traditional and modern in its stage of development.

maintain (mān tān′), *v.t.* **1.** to keep in existence or continuance; preserve; retain: *to maintain good relations with France.* **2.** to keep in due condition, operation, or force; keep unimpaired: *to maintain order, maintain public highways.* **3.** to keep in a specified state, position, etc. **4.** to affirm; assert (with a clause, or with an object and infinitive). **5.** to support in speech or argument, as a statement, etc. **6.** to keep or hold against attack: *to maintain one's ground.* **7.** to provide with the means of existence. [ME *mainten(en),* t. F: m. *maintenir,* g. L *manū tenēre* hold in the hand] —**maintain′able,** *adj.* —**maintain′er,** *n.* —**Syn. 1.** keep up, continue. **4.** contend, claim. **5.** uphold, defend, vindicate. **7.** provide for. See **support.** —**Ant. 1.** break (off). **4.** deny. **5.** contradict.

maintained school, any school financially supported by the state.

maintenance (mān′tĭ nəns), *n.* **1.** the act of maintaining. **2.** the state of being maintained. **3.** means of provision for maintaining; means of subsistence. **4.** *Law.* the money paid either in a lump sum or by way of periodical payments for the support of the other spouse or infant children, usually after divorce. **5.** *Law.* an officious intermeddling in a suit in which the meddler has no interest, by assisting either party with means to prosecute or defend it. —**Syn. 3.** support, livelihood. See **living.**

Maintenon (*Fr.* măNt nôN′), *n.* **Marquise de** (*Françoise d'Aubigne*), 1635–1719, second wife of Louis XIV.

maintop (mān′tŏp′), *n. Naut.* a platform at the head of the lower mainmast.

main-topgallant (mān′tə găl′ənt, -tŏp-), *n.* a sail on the main-topgallant mast. See illus. under **sail.**

main-topgallant mast (mān′tə găl′ənt, -tŏp-), *n. Naut.* the mast next above the main-topmast.

main-topmast (mān′tŏp′məst), *n. Naut.* the mast next above the lower mainmast.

main-topsail (mān′tŏp′səl), *n. Naut.* the sail set on the main-topmast. See illus. under **sail.**

mainyard (mān′yäd′, -yəd), *n. Naut.* the lower yard on the mainmast.

Mainz (*Ger.* mīnts), *n.* a city in West Germany, in E Rhineland-Palatinate: a port at the confluence of the rivers Rhine and Main. 145,400 (est. 1966). French, **Mayence.**

maisonette (mā′zə nĕt′), *n.* **1.** a self-contained flat occupying two floors. **2.** a small house. Also, **maisonnette.**

Maisons-Alfort (*Fr.* mĕ zôN ȧl fôr′), *n.* a town in N France, in Val-de-Marne department. 51,186 (1962).

Maitland (māt′lənd), *n.* **1. Frederic William,** 1850–1906, English legal historian and lawyer. **2.** a town in SE Australia, in New South Wales. 28,100 (est. 1964).

maître d'hôtel (mĕt′rə dō tĕl′), **1.** a steward or butler. **2.** a head waiter. **3.** (of foods) with a sauce of melted butter, minced parsley, and lemon juice or vinegar. [t. F: master of a house]

maize (māz), *n.* **1.** a widely cultivated cereal plant, *Zea mays,* occurring in many varieties, bearing grain in large ears or spikes; Indian corn. **2.** its grain. **3.** a pale yellow colour. —*adj.* **4.** of the colour of maize. [t. Sp.: m. *maíz,* t. Antillean: m. *maysi, mahiz,* t. Arawak: m. *marise*]

Maj., Major.

majestic (mə jĕs′tĭk), *adj.* characterized by or possessing majesty; of lofty dignity or imposing aspect; stately; grand. Also, **majes′tical.** —**majes′tically,** *adv.* —**Syn.** august, regal, imperial.

majesty (măj′ĭs tĭ), *n., pl.* **-ties. 1.** regal, lofty, or stately dignity; imposing character; grandeur. **2.** supreme greatness or authority; sovereignty. **3.** a royal personage, or royal personages collectively. **4.** (*usually cap.*) a title used when speaking of or to a sovereign (prec. by *his, her, your,* etc.). [ME *maieste,* t. F: m. *majesté,* t. L: m. s. *mājestas* greatness, grandeur, majesty]

majolica (mə jŏl′ĭ kə, mə yŏl′-), *n.* **1.** a kind of Italian pottery coated with enamel and decorated, often in rich colours. **2.** a more or less similar pottery made elsewhere. [t. It.: m. *maiolica* MAJORCA]

major (mā′jə), *n.* **1.** *Mil.* a commissioned officer ranking below a lieutenant colonel and above a captain. **2.** one of superior rank in a specified class. **3.** a person of full legal age. **4.** *Music.* a major interval, chord, scale, etc. **5.** *U.S.* a subject or field of study chosen by a student to represent his principal interest and upon which he concentrates a large share of his efforts. —*adj.* **6.** greater, as in size, amount, extent, importance, rank, etc.: *the major part of the town, a major question.* **7.** of or pertaining to the majority. **8.** of full legal age. **9.** *Logic.* broader or more extensive: **a. major term** of a syllogism is the term that enters into the predicate of the conclusion. **b. major premise** is that premise of a syllogism which contains the major term. **10.** *Music.* **a.** (of an interval) being between the tonic and the second, third, sixth, and seventh degrees of a major scale: *the major third, sixth, etc.* **b.** (of a chord) having a major third between the root and the note next above it. **11.** elder; senior; in boys' schools designating the elder of two brothers, the eldest of three, or the second of four. **12.** *U.S.* denoting or pertaining to educational majors: *a major field of study.* —*v.i.* **13.** *U.S.* to pursue a major or principal subject or course of study (fol. by *in*). [ME, t. L: greater, larger, superior, compar. of *magnus* great] —**Syn. 6.** See **capital**[1].

Majorca (mə jô′kə), *n.* a Spanish island in the W Mediterranean: the largest of the Balearic Islands. 350,000 pop. (est. 1966); 1405 sq. mi. *Cap.:* Palma. Spanish, **Mallorca.**

major-domo (mā′jə dō′mō), *n., pl.* **-mos. 1.** a man in charge of a great household, as that of a sovereign; a chief steward. **2.** a steward or butler. [t. Sp.: m. *mayordomo,* or t. It.: m. *maggiordomo,* t. ML: m. *mājor domūs* chief officer of the house]

major general, *Mil.* **1.** an officer ranking below a lieutenant general and above a brigadier general. **2.** the rank. —**ma′jor-gen′eralcy, ma′jor-gen′eralship′,** *n.*

majority (mə jŏ′rĭ tĭ), *n., pl.* **-ties. 1.** the greater part or number: *the majority of mankind.* **2.** a number of voters or votes, jurors, or others in agreement, constituting more than half the total number. **3.** the number by which votes cast for the leading candidate exceed those cast for the next candidate (opposed to *absolute majority*). **4.** *U.S.* absolute majority. **5.** the party or faction with the majority vote. **6.** the state or time of being of full legal age: *to attain one's majority.* **7.** the military rank or office of a major. [t. F: m. *majorité,* t. ML: m. s. *mājōritas,* der. L *mājor* MAJOR]

major key, a key based on a major scale.

major orders. See **order** (def. 15).

Major Prophets. See **prophet** (def. 4b).

major scale, *Music.* a scale whose third tone forms a major third with the root. See illus. under **scale.**

major suit, *Bridge.* hearts or spades (because they have higher point values).

major third, *Music.* an interval of two whole tones.

Majunga (*Fr.* mȧ zhœɴ gȧ′), *n.* a seaport in NW Malagasy Republic. 41,648 (1964).

majuscule (măj′ə skyo͞ol′), *adj.* **1.** large, as letters (whether capital or uncial). **2.** written in such letters (opposed to *minuscule*). —*n.* **3.** a majuscule letter. [t. F, t. L: m. s. *mājusculus* somewhat greater or larger] —**majuscular** (mə jŭs′kyo͝o lə), *adj.*

Makarios (mə kä′rĭ ŏs′), *n.* (*Michael Christedoulos Mouskos*), born 1913, archbishop and patriarch of Cyprus since 1950; president since 1960.

make (māk), *v.*, **made, making,** *n.* —*v.t.* **1.** to bring into existence by shaping material, combining parts, etc.: *to make a dress.* **2.** to produce by any action or causative agency: *to make trouble.* **3.** to cause to be or become; render: *to make an old man young.* **4.** to constitute; appoint: *to make someone a judge.* **5.** to put into proper condition for use: *to make a bed.* **6.** to bring into a certain form or condition: *to make bookcases out of orange boxes.* **7.** to cause, induce, or compel (to do something): *to make a horse go.* **8.** to give rise to; occasion. **9.** to produce, earn, or win for oneself: *to make a fortune.* **10.** to compose, as a poem. **11.** to draw up, as a legal document. **12.** to do; effect: *to make a bargain.* **13.** to fix; establish; enact: *to make laws.* **14.** to become by development; prove to be: *he will make a good lawyer.* **15.** to form in the mind, as a judgement, estimate, or plan. **16.** to judge or infer as to the truth, nature, meaning, etc.: *what do you make of it?* **17.** to estimate; reckon: *to make the distance ten miles.* **18.** (of material or parts) to compose; form: *two and two make four.* **19.** to bring to; bring up the total to: *to make an even dozen.* **20.** to serve for or as: *to make good reading.* **21.** to be sufficient to constitute; be essential to. **22.** to assure the success or fortune of. **23.** to put forth; deliver: *to make a speech.* **24.** *U.S.* to accomplish by travelling, etc.: *to make sixty miles an hour.* **25.** to arrive at or reach: *to make a port.* **26.** to arrive in time for: *to make the first show.* **27.** to achieve a position on or inclusion in (a list of honours, place of honour, or the like). **28.** *Slang.* to seduce or have sexual intercourse with. **29.** *Colloq.* to secure a place on, as a team. **30.** *Cards.* **a.** to name (the trump). **b.** to achieve a trick with (a card). **c.** *Bridge.* to achieve (a bid). **d.** to mix up or shuffle (the cards). **31.** *Sport and Games.* to earn as a score. **32.** to close (an electric circuit).
—*v.i.* **33.** to cause oneself, or something understood, to be as specified: *to make sure.* **34.** to show oneself in action or behaviour: *to make merry.* **35.** to direct or pursue the course; go: *to make for home.* **36.** to rise, as the tide, or as water in a ship, etc. —*v.* **37.** Some special verb phrases are:
make as if or **as though,** to act as if; pretend.
make at, to attack or lunge towards: *he made at me with a knife.*
make away with, 1. to get rid of. **2.** to kill or destroy. **3.** to steal or abduct.
make believe, to pretend.
make do, to operate or carry on using minimal or improvised resources.
make for, 1. to travel towards or attempt to reach. **2.** to help to promote or maintain: *to make for better international relations.*
make heavy weather, 1. *Naut.* to roll and pitch in heavy seas. **2.** to have difficulty; progress laboriously (with) (often fol. by *of*): *to make heavy weather of a simple calculation.*
make it, to achieve one's object.
make off, to run away.
make off with, to steal.
make out, 1. to write out a bill, a cheque, etc. **2.** to prove; establish. **3.** to discern; decipher. **4.** to present as; impute to be: *he made me out a liar.* **5.** *Colloq.* to manage; succeed.
make over, 1. *U.S.* to make anew; alter: *to make over a dress.* **2.** to hand over into the possession or charge of another. **3.** to transfer the title of (property); convey.
make up, 1. (of parts) to constitute; form. **2.** to put together; construct; compile. **3.** to concoct; invent. **4.** to compensate for; make good. **5.** to complete. **6.** to prepare; put in order. **7.** to bring to a definite conclusion, as one's mind. **8.** to settle amicably, as differences. **9.** Also, **make it up.** to become reconciled after a quarrel. **10.** *Print.* to arrange set type, etc., into columns or pages. **11.** to apply cosmetics to, as the face. **12.** to prepare for a part, as on the stage, by appropriate dress, cosmetics, etc. **13.** to adjust or balance, as accounts; to prepare, as statements. **14.** *U.S. Educ.* to repeat a course (or examination in which one has failed) or to take an (examination) from which one has been absent. **15.** to give or work in lieu for; compensate for (time or work lost, etc.).
make up to, 1. *Colloq.* to try to be on friendly terms with; fawn on. **2.** to make advances or pay court to.
make water, to urinate.
—*n.* **38.** style or manner of being made; form; build. **39.** production with reference to the maker: *our own make.* **40.** disposition; character; nature. **41.** the act or process of making. **42. on the make,** *Slang.* intent on gain or one's own advantage. **43.** quantity made; output. **44.** *Cards.* **a.** the act of naming the trump, or the suit named as trump. **b.** the act of shuffling the cards before dealing. **45.** *Elect.* the closing of an electric circuit (opp. to *break*).
[ME *make(n)*, OE *macian*, c. LG and D *maken*, G *machen*]
—**Syn. 1.** form; build; produce; fabricate, create. MAKE, CONSTRUCT, MANUFACTURE mean to put into definite form, to produce, or to put parts together to make a whole. MAKE is the general term: *bees make wax.* CONSTRUCT, more formal, means to put parts together, usually according to a plan or design: *to construct a building.* MANUFACTURE refers to producing from raw materials, now almost entirely by means of machinery: *to manufacture motor vehicles.* The term is used contemptuously of producing imitations of works of art, etc., and is also used abstractly with the same idea of denying genuineness: *to manufacture an excuse.* **6.** convert; transform, change, turn. **9.** get, gain, acquire, obtain. **12.** perform, execute, accomplish. —**Ant. 1.** destroy. **9.** lose.

make and break, *Elect.* a device for alternately making and breaking an electric circuit.

make-believe (māk′bĭ lēv′), *n.* **1.** pretence; feigning; sham. **2.** a pretender; one who pretends. —*adj.* **3.** pretended; feigned; sham.

make-do (māk′do͞o′), *adj.* of a temporary or substitute nature.

makefast (māk′făst′), *n.* *U.S. Naut.* any structure to which a vessel is tied up, as a bollard, buoy, etc.

make-peace (māk′pēs′), *n.* *Rare.* a peacemaker.

maker (mā′kə), *n.* **1.** one who makes. **2.** (*cap.*) God. **3.** *Law.* the party executing a legal instrument, esp. a promissory note. **4.** *Bridge, etc.* **a.** the one who first designates the successful bid. **b.** the person whose turn it is to shuffle. **5.** *Archaic.* a poet.

make-ready (māk′rĕd′ĭ), *n.* the process of preparing a forme for printing by overlays or underlays to equalize the impression.

makeshift (māk′shĭft′), *n.* **1.** a temporary expedient; substitute. —*adj.* **2.** serving as or a makeshift.

make-up (māk′ŭp′), *n.* **1.** cosmetics, as those used by a woman to enhance her features. **2.** the application of such cosmetics. **3.** the total effect achieved by such application. **4.** the way in which an actor or other person dresses himself, paints his face, etc., for a part. **5.** the manner of being made up or put together; composition. **6.** physical or mental constitution. **7.** *Print.* the arrangement of type, illustrations, etc., into columns or pages.

makeweight (māk′wāt′), *n.* **1.** something put in a scale to complete a required weight. **2.** anything added to supply a lack.

Makeyevka (*Russ.* mȧ kyĕ′yĭf kə), *n.* a town in the SW Soviet Union in Europe. 399,000 (est. 1965).

Makhach Kala (*Russ.* mȧkʜ ȧch′ kȧ lȧ′), a seaport in the Soviet Union, on the Caspian Sea. 119,000 (est. 1959).

making (mā′kĭng), *n.* **1.** the act of one who or that which makes. **2.** the process by which something is made to be as it is; origination. **3.** means or cause of success or advancement: *to be the making of someone.* **4.** (*often pl.*) material of which something may be made; potential. **5.** something made. **6.** the quantity made. **7. in the making,** being made; not yet finished.

mako-mako (mä′kō mä′kō), *n.* a small tree, *Aristotelia serrata* of the family *Elaeocarpaceae*, growing in forest clearings in New Zealand. [t. Maori]

mal-, a prefix having attributive relation to the second element, meaning 'bad', 'wrongful', 'ill', as in *maladjustment, malpractice.* [t. F, repr. *mal*, adv. (g. L *male* badly, ill), or *mal*, adj. (g. L *malus*) bad]

Mal., 1. Malachi. **2.** Malayan.

Malabar Coast (măl′ə bä′, măl′ə bä′), a region along the SW coast of India, from the Arabian Sea to the Western Ghats.

Malabar rat, bandicoot.

Malacca (mə lăk′ə), *n.* **1.** a state in Malaysia, on the SW Malay Peninsula. 361,152 pop. (1963); 640 sq. mi. **2.** a seaport in and the capital of this state. 69,848

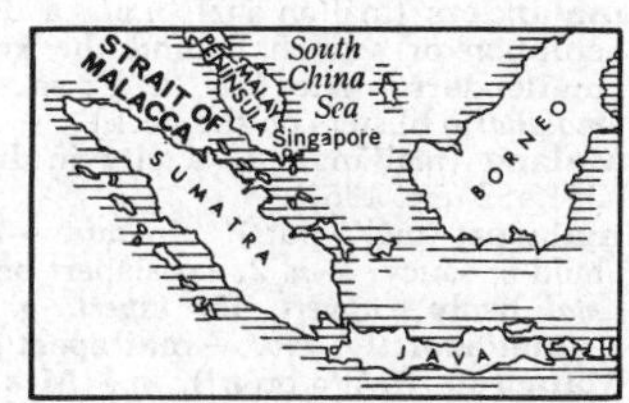

Strait of Malacca

(1957). **3. Strait of,** a strait between Sumatra and the Malay Peninsula. 35–185 mi. wide.

Malacca cane, a cane or walking stick made of the brown, often mottled or clouded stem of an East Indian rattan palm, *Calamus scipionum*, usually highly polished. [named after MALACCA]

malaceous (mə lā′shəs), *adj.* belonging to the *Malaceae*, or apple family of plants, which includes the apple, pear, quince, medlar, loquat, hawthorn, etc. [f. s. L *mālus* apple tree + -ACEOUS]

Malachi (măl′ə kī′), *n.* Hebrew prophet of the 5th century B.C. and author of the last book of the Minor Prophets which bears his name.

malachite (măl′ə kīt′), *n.* a green mineral basic copper carbonate, $Cu_2CO_3(OH)_2$, an ore of copper, also used for making ornamental articles. [t. F, f. s. Gk *maláchē* mallow + *-ite* -ITE[1]]

malacology (măl′ə kŏl′ə jĭ), *n.* the science dealing with the study of molluscs. [f. m. Gk *malakó(s)* soft (with ref. to the soft body of the molluscs) + -LOGY] —**mal′acol′ogist,** *n.*

malacophilous (măl′ə kŏf′ĭ ləs), *adj. Bot.* pollinated by snails or slugs.

malacopterygian (măl′ə kŏp′tə rĭj′ĭ ən), *adj. Zool.* of or pertaining to a division, *Malacopterygii*, of soft-finned teleost fishes. [f. m. Gk *malakó(s)* soft + s. Gk *ptéryx* wing, fin + -IAN]

malacostracan (măl′ə kŏs′trə kən), *adj.* **1.** Also, **mal′acos′tracous.** belonging to the *Malacostraca*, a subclass of crustaceans which have a comparatively complex organization, including lobsters, shrimps, crabs, etc. —*n.* **2.** a malacostracan crustacean. [f. s. NL *Malacostraca* (t. Gk: m. *malakóstraka* (neut. pl.) soft-shelled) + -AN]

maladjusted (măl′ə jŭs′tĭd), *adj.* **1.** badly adjusted. **2.** *Psychol.* suffering from maladjustment.

maladjustment (măl′ə jŭst′mənt), *n.* **1.** a faulty adjustment. **2.** *Psychol.* a failure to function successfully with regard to personal relationships and environment, often a symptom of mental disturbance.

maladminister (măl′əd mĭn′ĭs tə), *v.t.* to manage (esp. public affairs) badly or inefficiently. —**mal′admin′istra′tion,** *n.* —**mal′admin′istra′tor,** *n.*

maladroit (măl′ə droit′), *adj.* lacking in adroitness; unskilful; awkward. [t. F. See MAL-, ADROIT] —**mal′adroit′ly,** *adv.* —**mal′adroit′ness,** *n.*

malady (măl′ə dĭ), *n., pl.* **-dies. 1.** any bodily disorder or disease, esp. one that is chronic or deep-seated. **2.** any form of disorder: *social maladies.* [ME *maladie*, t. OF, der. *malade* sick, g. LL *male habitus*, lit., ill-conditioned] —**Syn. 1.** See **disease.**

mala fide (mā′lə fī′dĭ), *Latin.* in bad faith; not genuine (opposed to *bona fide*).

Málaga (măl′ə gə; *Sp.* mä′lä gä), *n.* a seaport in S Spain, on the Mediterranean. 324,949 (1965).

Malaga (măl′ə gə), *n.* **1.** a sweet strong white wine with a pronounced muscat grape flavour, produced in the province of Málaga, Spain. **2.** any of the grapes grown in or exported from Málaga.

malagas (mä′lə gäs′), *n., pl.* **-gas.** *S African.* the gannet, *Morus capensis.* [? t. Afrikaans]

Malagasy (măl′ə găs′ĭ), *n., pl.* **-gasy, -gasies. 1.** a native of the Malagasy Republic. **2.** an Austronesian language, the language of the Malagasy Republic.

Malagasy Republic, an island republic in the Indian Ocean, ab. 240 mi. off the SE coast of Africa: independent member of the French Community. 5,862,258 pop. (1963); 227,800 sq. mi. *Cap.:* Tananarive. Formerly, **Madagascar.**

malaguena (măl′ə gā′nyə; *Sp.* mä lä gĕ′nyä), *n., pl.* **-guenas** (-gā′nyəz; *Sp.* -gĕ′nyäs). a Spanish dance similar to the fandango, originating in Málaga.

malaise (mă lāz′; *Fr.* mä lĕz′), *n.* a condition of indefinite bodily weakness or discomfort, often marking the onset of a disease. [t. F: f. *mal* ill + *aise* EASE]

Malan (mə län′), *n.* **Daniel,** 1874–1959, South African statesman: prime minister 1948–54.

malanders (măl′ən dəz), *n.pl.* a dry, scabby or scurfy eruption or scratch behind the knee in horses. Also, **mallenders.** [late ME, t. F: m. *malandres*, t. L: m. *malandria* blisters on the neck]

Malang (măl′ăng), *n.* a city in Indonesia, in E Java. 341,452 (est. 1961).

malapert (măl′ə pût′), *Archaic.* —*adj.* **1.** unbecomingly bold or saucy. —*n.* **2.** a malapert person. [ME, t. OF: f. *mal* badly + *appert*, for *espert*, g. L *expertus* EXPERT] —**mal′apert′ly,** *adv.* —**mal′apert′ness,** *n.*

Malaprop (măl′ə prŏp′), *n.* **Mrs,** the 'old weather-beaten she-dragon' of Sheridan's *The Rivals* (1775), noted for her misapplication of words.

malapropism (măl′ə prŏ pĭz′əm), *n.* **1.** the act or habit of ridiculously misusing words. **2.** a word so misused. [named after Mrs MALAPROP. Cf. MALAPROPOS]

malapropos (măl′ăp rə pō′), *adj.* **1.** inappropriate. —*adv.* **2.** inappropriately. [t. F: *mal à propos* not to the point. See MAL-, APROPOS]

malar (mā′lə), *Anat.* —*adj.* **1.** of or pertaining to the cheekbone or cheek. —*n.* **2.** Also, **malar bone.** the cheekbone. [t. NL: s. *mālāris*, der. L *māla* cheekbone, cheek]

Mälar (*Sw.* mĕl′är), *n.* **Lake,** a lake in S Sweden, extending ab. 80 mi. W from Stockholm; ab. 440 sq. mi.

malaria (mə lĕə′rĭ ə), *n.* **1.** any of a group of diseases, usually intermittent or remittent, and characterized by attacks of chills, fever, and sweating: formerly supposed to be due to swamp exhalations, but now known to be caused by a species of parasitic protozoans which are transferred to the human blood by mosquitoes (genus *Anopheles*) and which occupy and destroy the red blood corpuscles. **2.** unwholesome or poisonous air. [t. It.: contr. of *mala aria* bad air] —**malar′ial, malar′ian, malar′ious,** *adj.*

malarkey (mə lä′kĭ), *n. Colloq.* unfounded nonsense, written or spoken, designed to confuse, obscure, or mislead.

malassimilation (măl′ə sĭm′ĭ lā′shən), *n. Pathol.* imperfect assimilation or nutrition.

Malatya (*Turk.* mä lä′tyä), *n.* a town in central Turkey. 83,692 (1960).

malate (măl′āt, mā′lāt), *n. Chem.* a salt or ester of malic acid. [f. MAL(IC) + -ATE[2]]

Malawi (mə lä′wĭ), *n.* **1.** an independent republic in SE central Africa on the W and S shores of Lake Malawi; member of the Commonwealth of Nations. 3,980,890 pop. (est. 1963); 36,065 sq. mi. *Cap.:* Zomba. Formerly, **Nyasaland. 2. Lake,** a lake in SE Africa. ab. 360 mi. long; ab. 11,000 sq. mi. Formerly, **Lake Nyasa.**

Malawi

Malay (mə lā′), *adj.* **1.** of or pertaining to the Malays or their country or language. **2.** denoting or pertaining to the so-called 'brown' race, characterized by short stature, roundish skull, moderate prognathism, and straight black hair. —*n.* **3.** a member of the dominant people of the Malay Peninsula and adjacent islands. **4.** an Austronesian language, widespread in the East Indies as a language of commerce.

Malaya (mə lā′ə), *n.* **1.** the Malay Peninsula. **2.** a country in the S Malay Peninsula; formerly the Federation of Malaya, now, together with Sabah and Sarawak, forming Malaysia. 56,690 sq. mi.

Malayalam (măl′ĭ ä′ləm), *n.* a Dravidian language spoken in extreme south-western India. Also, **Malayalaam.**

Malayan (mə lā′ən), *adj.* **1.** Malay. —*n.* **2.** a Malay.

Malay Archipelago, an extensive archipelago in the Indian and Pacific oceans, SE of Asia: the islands of New Guinea, Indonesia, the Philippines, and the Moluccas. Also, **Malaysia.**

Malayo-Polynesian (mə lā′ō pŏl′ĭ nē′zyən), *adj.* Austronesian.

Malay Peninsula, a peninsula in SE Asia, consisting of Malaya and the S part of Thailand. Also, **Malaya.** See map under **Singapore.**

Malaysia (mə lā′zyə), *n.* **1.** an independent federation of SE Asia, comprising the former Federation of Malaya, Sarawak, and Sabah: member of the Commonwealth of Nations. 9,136,641 pop. (est. 1964); 126,310 sq. mi. *Cap.:* Kuala Lumpur. **2.** Malay Archipelago. —**Malay′sian,** *adj., n.*

malcontent (măl′kən tĕnt′), *adj.* **1.** discontented; dissatisfied. **2.** dissatisfied with the existing administration; inclined to rebellion. —*n.* **3.** a malcontent person. [t. OF. See MAL-, CONTENT[2]]

mal de mer (*Fr.* mäl də mĕr′), *French.* seasickness.

Maldive Islands (môl′dĭv), an independent group of atolls in the Indian Ocean, SW of India. 96,432 pop. (1963); 115 sq. mi. *Cap.:* Malé.

mal du pays (*Fr.* mäl dʏ pĕ ē′), *French.* homesickness.

male (māl), *adj.* **1.** belonging to the sex which begets young, or any division or group corresponding to it. **2.** pertaining to or characteristic of this sex; masculine. **3.** composed of males: *a male choir.* **4.** *Bot.* **a.** designating or pertaining to any reproductive structure which produces or contains elements that bring about the fertilization of the female element. **b.** (of seed plants) staminate. **5.** *Mach.* designating some part, etc., which fits into a corresponding part. **—*n.* 6.** a male human being; a man or boy. **7.** any animal of male sex. **8.** *Bot.* a staminate plant. [ME, t. OF, g. L *masculus*]

—Syn. 1. MALE, MASCULINE, VIRILE are descriptive of one belonging to the paternal sex. MALE always refers to sex, whether of human beings, animals, or plants: *male animals are often larger than the females.* MASCULINE applies to the qualities that properly characterize the male sex: *a masculine love of sports.* The term may be applied to women, also, in either of two ways. It usually suggests some incongruity (as, *a masculine appearance*), but it may be used with complimentary implications: *she has a masculine mind.* VIRILE is a strong and comprehensive term, which formerly emphasized obvious maleness, but now usually implies the vigour, health, and force of mature manhood: *a virile opponent.*

Malé (mə lā′), *n.* chief atoll and capital of the Maldive Islands, in the central part. 10,875 (1963).

maleate (mə lē′ĭt, -lā′-), *n.* *Chem.* a salt or ester of maleic acid.

Malebranche (*Fr.* mȧl bräNsh′), *n.* **Nicolas de** (*Fr.* nē kō lȧ′ də), 1638–1715, French philosopher.

malediction (măl′ĭ dĭk′shən), *n.* **1.** a curse; the utterance of a curse. **2.** slander. [late ME, t. L: s. *maledictio* abuse] **—maledictory** (măl′ĭ dĭk′tə rĭ), *adj.*

malefaction (măl′ĭ făk′shən), *n.* an evil deed.

malefactor (măl′ĭ făk′tə), *n.* **1.** an offender against the law; a criminal. **2.** one who does evil. [late ME, t. L] **—malefactress** (măl′ĭ făk′trĭs), *n. fem.*

male fern, a variable, robust, rhizomatous fern with large dissected leaves, *Dryopteris filix-mas,* widespread in woods of temperate regions.

malefic (mə lĕf′ĭk), *adj.* productive of evil; malign. [t. L: s. *maleficus* evil-doing]

maleficence (mə lĕf′ĭ səns), *n.* **1.** the doing of evil or harm. **2.** maleficent or harmful character.

maleficent (mə lĕf′ĭ sənt), *adj.* doing evil or harm; harmful. [f. L: back-formation from *maleficientia* MALEFICENCE. Cf. BENEFICENT]

Malegaon (mä′lĭ goun′), *n.* a town in India, in NW Maharashtra. 121,408 (1961).

maleic acid (mə lē′ĭk), *Chem.* crystalline dibasic acid, $C_2H_2(COOH)_2$, an isomer of fumaric acid.

Malenkov (măl′ĭn kŏf′; *Russ.* mə lĭn kôf′), *n.* **Georgi Maximilianovich** (*Russ.* gĭ ôr′gĭy mək sĭ mē′lyə nə vĭch), born 1901; Soviet leader: premier of the Soviet Union 1953–55.

Malevich (*Russ.* mȧ′lĭ vĭch), *n.* **Kasimir** (*Russ.* kə zĭ mēr′), 1878–1935, Russian painter, inventor of suprematism.

malevolence (mə lĕv′ə ləns), *n.* the state or feeling of being malevolent; ill will.

—Syn. MALEVOLENCE, MALIGNITY, RANCOUR suggest the wishing of harm to others. MALEVOLENCE is a smouldering ill will: *a vindictive malevolence in his expression.* MALIGNITY is a deep-seated and virulent disposition to injure; it is more dangerous than MALEVOLENCE, because it is not only more completely concealed but it often instigates harmful acts: *the malignity of his nature was shocking.* RANCOUR is a lasting, corrosive, and implacable hatred and resentment.

malevolent (mə lĕv′ə lənt), *adj.* **1.** wishing evil to another or others; showing ill will: *his failure made him malevolent towards others.* **2.** *Astrol.* evil or malign in influence. [t. L: s. *malevolens* wishing ill] **—malev′olently,** *adv.*

malfeasance (măl fē′zəns), *n.* *Law.* the wrongful performance of an act which the actor has no right to perform. [t. F: m. *malfaisance* evil-doing, der. *malfaisant,* f. *mal* evil + *faisant,* ppr. of *faire* do, g. L *facere*] **—malfea′sant,** *adj., n.*

malformation (măl′fô mā′shən), *n.* faulty or anomalous formation or structure, esp. in a living body.

malformed (măl′fômd′), *adj.* faultily formed.

malfunction (măl′fŭngk′shən), *v.i.* **1.** to fail to function properly. **—*n.* 2.** failure to function properly. [f. MAL- + FUNCTION]

Malherbe (*Fr.* mȧl ĕrb′), *n.* **François de** (*Fr.* fräN swȧ′ də), 1555–1628, French poet and critic.

Mali (mä′lĭ), **Republic of,** an independent republic in W Africa: formerly a French territory. 4,100,000 pop. (1960); 463,500 sq. mi. *Cap.:* Bamako. Formerly, **French Sudan.**

malic (măl′ĭk), *adj.* pertaining to or derived from apples. [t. F: m. *malique,* der. L *mālum* apple]

malic acid, *Chem.* a crystalline, dibasic hydroxy acid, $C_2H_3OH(COOH)_2$, occurring in small amounts in almost all living cells as a component of the citric acid cycle, and in greater amounts in apples and other fruits.

malice (măl′ĭs), *n.* **1.** desire to inflict injury or suffering on another. **2.** *Law.* evil intent on the part of one who commits a wrongful act injurious to others. [ME, t. OF, g. L *malitia* badness, spite, malice] **—Syn. 1.** ill will, spite, spitefulness; animosity, enmity; malevolence. See **grudge. —Ant. 1.** benevolence; goodwill.

malice aforethought, *Law.* (in homicide) the distinguishing characteristic between common-law murder and manslaughter, such as an intent to kill, or to do serious bodily harm, except when a killing is committed in the heat of passion from a reasonable provocation.

malicious (mə lĭsh′əs), *adj.* **1.** full of, characterized by, or showing malice; malevolent. **2.** *Law.* motivated by vicious, wanton, or mischievous purposes. **—mali′ciously,** *adv.* **—mali′ciousness,** *n.*

malign (mə līn′), *v.t.* **1.** to speak ill of; slander. **—*adj.* 2.** evil in effect; pernicious; baleful. **3.** having or showing an evil disposition; malevolent. [ME *maligne,* t. OF, t. L: m. *malignus* ill-disposed] **—malign′er,** *n.* **—malign′ly,** *adv.*

malignant (mə lĭg′nənt), *adj.* **1.** disposed to cause suffering or distress; malicious. **2.** very dangerous; harmful in influence or effect. **3.** *Pathol.* deadly; tending to produce death, as a disease, tumour, etc. [t. LL: s. *malignans,* ppr., injuring maliciously] **—malig′nance, malig′nancy,** *n.* **—malig′nantly,** *adv.*

malignity (mə lĭg′nĭ tĭ), *n., pl.* **-ties. 1.** the state or character of being malign; malevolence. **2.** (*pl.*) malignant feelings, actions, etc. [late ME, t. L: m. s. *malignitas*]

malines (mă lēn′; *Fr.* mȧ lēn′), *n.* Mechlin lace. Also, **maline.**

Malines (mă lēn′; *Fr.* mȧ lēn′), *n.* French name of **Mechlin.**

malinger (mə lĭng′gə), *v.i.* to feign sickness or injury, esp. in order to avoid duty, work, etc. [t. F: m. *malingre* sickly, ailing, f. *mal* bad(ly) + OF *heingre* haggard, of Gmc orig.] **—malin′gerer,** *n.*

Malin Head (măl′ĭn), a headland in the Republic of Ireland, in Co. Donegal; the most northerly point of Ireland.

Malinovsky (măl′ĭ nŏf′skĭ; *Russ.* mə lĭ nôf′skĭy), *n.* **Rodion Yakovlevich** (*Russ.* rə dĭ ôn′ yȧ′kəv lĭ vĭch), 1898–1967, Soviet military leader and politician; minister of defence 1957–67.

Malinowski (măl′ĭ nŏf′skĭ), *n.* **Bronislaw Kasper** (brŏn′ĭ släv′ kăs′pə), 1884–1942, Polish anthropologist in the U.S.

malison (măl′ĭ zən, -sən), *n.* *Archaic or Dial.* a curse. [ME, t. OF: m. *maleiçon,* g. L *maledictio* MALEDICTION]

mall (môl, măl), *n.* **1.** a shaded walk, usually public. **2.** the mallet used in the game of pall-mall. **3.** the game. **4.** the place or alley where it was played. [ME *malle,* t. OF: m. *ma(i)l,* g. L *malleus* hammer]

mallard (măl′əd), *n., pl.* **-lards,** (*esp. collectively*) **-lard. 1.** a common, almost cosmopolitan, wild duck, *Anas platyrhynchos,* from which the domestic ducks descended. **2.** a male of this species. [ME, t. OF: m. *malart,* prob. t. Gmc: m. proper name *Madalhart,* given to the duck in a beast epic]

Mallarmé (*Fr.* mȧ lȧr mė′), *n.* **Stéphane** (*Fr.* stė fȧn′), 1842–98, French poet.

malleable (măl′ĭ ə bl), *adj.* **1.** capable of being extended or shaped by hammering or by pressure with rollers. **2.** adaptable or tractable. [ME *malliable,* t. OF: m. *malleable,* der. L *malleāre* beat with a hammer. See -ABLE] **—mal′leabil′ity, mal′leableness,** *n.*

malleable cast iron, white cast-iron castings given a special heat treatment to make them tough.

malleable iron, 1. malleable cast iron. **2.** the purest form of commercial iron, easily welded or forged.

mallee (măl′ē), *n.* **1.** any of various dwarf Australian species of *Eucalyptus,* as *Eucalyptus dumosa* and *E. oleosa,* which sometimes form large tracts of brushwood. **2.** such brushwood. [t. native Australian]

mallee fowl, the lowan.

mallemuck (măl′ĭ mŭk′), *n.* any of various oceanic birds, as the fulmar or albatross. [t. D: m. *mallemok,* f. m. *mal* foolish + *mok* gull]

mallenders (măl′ən dəz), *n.pl.* malanders.

malleolar (mə lē′ə lə), *adj.* *Anat.* pertaining to a malleolus. [f. MALLEOL(US) + -AR[1]]

malleolus (mə lē′ə ləs), *n., pl.* **-li** (-lī′). *Anat.* either of two bony protuberances, one on each side of the ankle, situated in man at the lower end of the fibula and tibia respectively. [t. L, dim. of *malleus* hammer]

mallet (măl′ĭt), *n.* **1.** a hammer-like tool with a head commonly of wood but occasionally of rawhide, plastic, etc., used for driving any tool with a wooden handle, as a chisel. **2.** the wooden implement used to strike the balls in croquet. **3.** the stick used to drive the ball in polo. [ME *maylet,* t. OF: m. *maillet,* dim. of *mail* MALL]

malleus (măl′ĭ əs), *n., pl.* **-lei** (-lĭ ī′). *Anat.* the outermost of three small bones in the middle ear of man and other mammals. See diag. under **ear.** [t. L: hammer]

Mallorca (*Sp.* mä lyôr′kȧ), *n.* Spanish name of **Majorca.**

mallow (măl′ō), *n.* **1.** any plant of the genus *Malva,* comprising herbs with leaves usually angularly lobed or dissected, and purple, pink, or white flowers, as *M. sylvestris*, common in Europe, and *M. neglecta*, the dwarf mallow. 2. any malvaceous plant, as the marsh mallow. [ME *malue*, OE *mealwe*, t. L: m. *malva*]

malm (mäm), *n.* **1.** a kind of soft, friable limestone. **2.** a chalk-bearing soil of the south-eastern part of England. [ME *malme*, OE *mealm*, c. Icel. *mālmr* ore]

Malmédy (*Fr.* mȧl mė dē′), *n.* See **Eupen and Malmédy.**

Malmö (măl′mō; *Sw.* mȧl′mœ), *n.* a seaport in S Sweden, on the Sound opposite Copenhagen, Denmark. 245,803 (1964).

malmsey (mäm′zĭ), *n.* a strong, sweet wine of a strong flavour, orig. made in Greece, but now in Madeira. [ME *malmesey*, t. ML: m. s. *malmasia*, t. NGk: alter. of *Monemvasia* a seaport in southern Greece]

malnutrition (măl′nyo͞o trĭsh′ən), *n.* imperfect nutrition; lack of proper nutrition.

malocclusion (măl′ə klo͞o′zhən), *n.* faulty occlusion, closing, or meeting, as of opposing teeth in the upper and lower jaws.

malodorous (mă lō′də rəs), *adj.* having a bad smell. —**malo′dorously,** *adv.* —**malo′dorousness,** *n.*

malodour (mă lō′də), *n.* a bad smell; a stench. Also, *U.S.*, **malodor.**

Malone (mə lōn′), *n.* **Edmond,** 1741–1812, Irish scholar and editor of Shakespeare.

malonic acid (mə lō′nĭk, -lŏn′ĭk), a dibasic acid, $CH_2(COOH)_2$, easily decomposed by heat. [t. F: m. *malonique*, alter. of *malique* MALIC]

malonic ester, *Chem.* a colourless fluid, $CH_2(COOC_2H_5)_2$, used in organic syntheses.

malonyl (măl′ə nĭl), *n.* *Chem.* a divalent radical, $-OCCH_2CO-$, derived from malonic acid.

malonyl urea, *Chem.* barbituric acid.

Malory (măl′ə rĭ), *n.* **Sir Thomas,** fl. 1470, English translator and compiler of *Morte d'Arthur*.

Malpighi (*It.* mȧl pē′gē), *n.* **Marcello** (*It.* mȧr chĕl′lȯ), 1628–94, Italian anatomist. —**Malpighian** (măl pĭg′ĭ ən), *adj.*

malpighiaceous (măl pĭg′ĭ ā′shəs), *adj.* belonging or pertaining to the *Malpighiaceae*, a large family of tropical plants, certain of which are cultivated for ornamental purposes. [f. s. NL *Malpighia* the typical genus (named after MALPIGHI) + -ACEOUS]

Malpighian bodies, *Anat.* certain small round bodies occurring in the cortical substance of the kidney. Also, **Malpighian corpuscles.**

Malpighian layer, *Anat.* the layer of non-horny cells in the epidermis.

Malpighian tubules, the excretory organs of insects, tubular outgrowths of the alimentary canal near the junction of the ventriculus and intestine. Also, **Malpighian tubes, Malpighian vessels.**

malposition (măl′pə zĭsh′ən), *n.* *Pathol.* faulty or wrong position, esp. of a part or organ of the body or of a foetus in the uterus.

malpractice (măl′prăk′tĭs), *n.* **1.** improper professional action or treatment by a physician, as from reprehensible ignorance or neglect or with criminal intent. **2.** any improper conduct. —**malpractitioner** (măl′prăk tĭsh′ə nə), *n.*

Malraux (*Fr.* mȧl rȯ′), *n.* **André** (*Fr.* äɴ drė′), born 1901, French writer and politician.

malt (môlt), *n.* **1.** germinated grain (usually barley), used in brewing and distilling. **2.** liquor produced from malt by fermentation, as beer or ale. **3.** malt extract. —*v.t.* **4.** to convert (grain) into malt. **5.** to treat or mix with malt or malt product. **6.** to make (liquor) with malt. —*v.i.* **7.** to become malt. **8.** to produce malt from grain. [ME; OE *mealt*, c. G *Malz*; akin to MELT]

Malta (môl′tə), *n.* **1.** an island in the Mediterranean between Sicily and Africa. 319,620 pop. (est. 1961); 95 sq. mi. **2.** an independent state consisting of this island and two small adjacent islands: member of the Commonwealth of Nations. 320,590 pop. (est. 1964); 122 sq. mi. *Cap.*: Valletta.

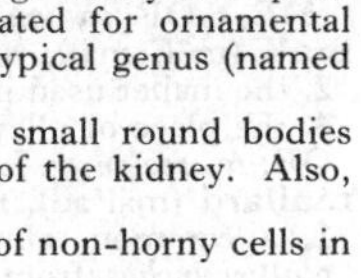

Malta

Malta fever, undulant fever due to *Brucella melitensis*.

maltase (môl′tās, môl tās′), *n.* *Biochem.* an enzyme which converts maltose into dextrose and causes similar cleavage of many other glucosides. [f. MALT + -ASE]

malted milk, **1.** a soluble powder made by dehydrating a mixture of milk and malted cereals. **2.** a beverage made from this powder dissolved, usually, in milk.

Maltese (môl tēz′), *adj.*, *n.*, *pl.* **-tese.** —*adj.* **1.** of or pertaining to Malta, its people, or their language. —*n.* **2.** a native or inhabitant of Malta. **3.** the Arabic dialect spoken in Malta.

Maltese cat, a bluish grey variety of domestic cat.

Maltese cross, a cross having four equal arms that expand in width outwards. See illus. under **cross.**

Maltese dog, one of a breed of toy dogs, with long silky coats, often white in colour.

malt extract, a sweet gummy substance derived from an infusion of malt.

maltha (măl′thə), *n.* **1.** any of various cements or mortars, bituminous or otherwise. **2.** any of various natural mixtures of hydrocarbons, as ozocerite. **3.** a viscous mineral liquid or semiliquid bitumen; a mineral tar. [late ME, t. L, t. Gk: mixture of wax and pitch]

Malthus (măl′thəs), *n.* **Thomas Robert,** 1766–1834, English political economist.

Malthusian (măl thyo͞o′zyən), *adj.* **1.** of or pertaining to T. R. Malthus, who contended that population, tending to increase faster than the means of subsistence, should be checked by social and moral restraints. —*n.* **2.** a follower of Malthus. —**Malthu′sianism,** *n.*

malt liquor, an alcoholic beverage, as beer, fermented from malt.

malt loaf, a loaf made from malt extract, syrup, etc., served sliced with butter.

maltose (môl′tōs, môl tōs′), *n.* *Chem.* a white crystalline sugar, $C_{12}H_{22}O_{11}.H_2O$, formed by the action of diastase (as in malt) on starch. Also, **maltobiose, malt sugar.** [f. MALT + -OSE[2]]

maltreat (măl trēt′), *v.t.* to treat ill; handle roughly or cruelly; abuse. [t. F: m. *maltraiter*. See MAL-, TREAT, v.] —**maltreat′ment,** *n.*

maltster (môlt′stə), *n.* a maker of or dealer in malt.

malty (môl′tĭ), *adj.* of, like, or containing malt.

malvaceous (măl vā′shəs), *adj.* belonging to the *Malvaceae*, or mallow family of plants, which includes the abutilon, althaea, hollyhock, okra, cotton plant, etc. [t. L: m. *malvāceus* of mallows]

malvasia (măl′və sīə′), *n.* a sweet grape from which malmsey wine is made. [t. It. See MALMSEY]

Malvern (môl′vən), *n.* an urban area in W Worcestershire, comprising several small towns and villages on the E slope of the **Malvern Hills**: mineral springs. 27,040 (est. 1962).

malversation (măl′vû sā′shən), *n.* improper or corrupt behaviour in office. [t. F, der. *malverser*, t. L: m. *male versārī* behave wrongly]

malvoisie (măl′voi zĭ, -və-), *n.* **1.** malmsey wine. **2.** malvasia grape. [t. F; r. ME *malvesie* MALMSEY, t. OF]

mama (mə mä′), *n.* mother; mamma.

mamba (măm′bə), *n.* any of the long, slender, arboreal African snakes of the genus *Dendroaspis*, whose bite is almost certain death, and which are said to attack without provocation. [t. Zulu or Xhosa: m. *imamba*]

mambo (măm′bō), *n.*, *pl.* **-bos,** *v.* —*n.* **1.** a ballroom dance of Latin-American origin, somewhat resembling the rumba. —*v.i.* **2.** to dance the mambo. [t. W Ind. Creole]

Mameluke (măm′ĭ lo͞ok′), *n.* **1.** a member of an Egyptian military class, originally slaves, in power from 1250 to 1517, and influential under Turkish rule until destroyed by Mohammed Ali in 1811. **2.** (*l.c.*) (in Muslim countries) a slave. [t. Ar.: m. *mamlūk* slave]

mamey (mă mē′), *n.* mammee.

mamilla (mă mĭl′ə), *n.*, *pl.* **-millae** (-mĭl′ē). **1.** *Anat.* the nipple of the mamma or breast. **2.** any nipple-like process or protuberance. Also, *Chiefly U.S.*, **mammilla.** [t. L: m. *mammilla*, dim. of *mamma* MAMMA[2]]

mamillary (măm′ĭ lə rĭ), *adj.* of, pertaining to, or resembling a mamilla. Also, *Chiefly U.S.*, **mammillary.**

mamillate (măm′ĭ lāt′), *adj.* having a mamilla or mamillae. Also, **mam′illat′ed;** *Chiefly U.S.*, **mammillate.**

mamma[1] (mə mä′), *n.* (esp. in childish use) mother. [redupl. of a syllable common in natural infantile utterance. Cf. F *maman*, L *mamma*, Gk *mámmē*, Russ. and Lith. *mama*]

mamma[2] (măm′ə), *n.*, *pl.* **mammae** (măm′ē), *Anat.*, *Zool.* the organ, characteristic of mammals, which in the female secretes milk; a breast or udder. [OE, t. L: breast, pap]

mammal (măm′əl), *n.* a member of the *Mammalia*, a class of vertebrates whose young feed upon milk from the mother's breast. Most species (except cetaceans) are more or less hairy, all have a diaphragm, and all (except the monotremes) are viviparous. [t. LL: s. *mammālis* of the breast] —**mammalian** (mă mā′lyən), *n.*, *adj.* —**mam′mal-like′,** *adj.*

mammalogy (mă măl′ə jĭ), *n.* the science that deals with mammals. [f. MAMMA(L) + -LOGY]

mammary (măm′ə rĭ), *adj.* *Anat., etc.* of or pertaining to the mamma or breast; mamma-like.

mammee (mă mē′), *n.* **1.** a tall, tropical American resin-yielding tree, *Mammea americana.* **2.** Also, **mammee apple.** its large, edible fruit. **3.** marmalade tree. Also, **mamey.** [t. Sp.: m. *mamey*; from Haitian]

mammiferous (mă mĭf′ə rəs), *adj.* having mammae; mammalian. [f. s. L *mamma* breast + -(I)FEROUS]

mammilla (mă mĭl′ə), *n., pl.* **-millae** (-mĭl′ē). *Chiefly U.S.* mamilla.

mammillary (măm′ĭ lə rĭ), *adj.* *Chiefly U.S.* mamillary.

mammillate (măm′ĭ lāt′), *adj.* *Chiefly U.S.* mamillate.

mammon (măm′ən), *n.* **1.** *New Testament.* riches or material wealth. Matt. 6:24; Luke 16:9, 11, 13. **2.** (*cap.*) a personification of riches as an evil spirit or deity. [t. LL: s. *mammōna*, t. Gk: m. *mamōnâs*, t. Aram.: *māmōn(ā)* riches] —**mam′monish,** *adj.*

mammonism (măm′ə nĭz′əm), *n.* the greedy pursuit of riches. —**mam′monist, mam′monite′,** *n.* —**mam′monis′tic,** *adj.*

Woolly mammoth, *Mammuthus primigenius* (Ab. 10 ft high)

mammoth (măm′əth), *n.* **1.** a large, extinct species of elephant, *Mammuthus primigenius*, the **northern woolly mammoth,** which resembled the present Indian elephant but had a hairy coat and long, curved tusks. **2.** any of various related extinct species of elephant, as the **imperial mammoth,** *Mammuthus imperator*, the largest mammoth. —*adj.* **3.** huge; gigantic: *a mammoth enterprise.* [t. Russ.: m. *mammot′*, now *mamant′*] —**Syn. 3.** See **gigantic.**

mammy (măm′ĭ), *n., pl.* **-mies. 1.** (in childish use) mother. **2.** *Southern U.S.* a coloured female nurse or old family servant.

Mamoré (*Sp.* mȧ mō rĕ′), *n.* a river flowing generally N through Bolivia and joining the Beni on the Brazilian border to form the river Madeira. ab. 700 mi.

man (măn), *n., pl.* **men,** *v.,* **manned, manning.** —*n.* **1.** *Anthropol.* an individual (genus *Homo*, family *Hominidae*, class *Mammalia*) at the highest level of animal development, mainly characterized by his exceptional mentality. **2.** the human creature or being as representing the species or as distinguished from other beings, animals, or things; the human race; mankind. **3.** a human being; a person: *to elect a new man.* **4.** the male human being, as distinguished from woman. **5.** an adult male person. **6.** a husband: *man and wife.* **7.** one; anyone (prec. by *a*): *to give a man a chance.* **8.** a male follower, subordinate, or employee: *officers and men of the army.* **9.** one having manly qualities or virtues. **10.** *Obs.* manly character or courage. **11.** a male servant; a valet. **12.** a word of familiar address to a man. **13.** *Slang.* a term of address to a man or woman. **14.** one of the pieces used in playing certain games, as chess or draughts. **15.** *Hist.* a liegeman; vassal. **16. man and boy,** from childhood. **17. to a man,** all; to the last man. [ME and OE *mann, man* (pl. *menn, men*), c. Icel. *madhr*, D *man*, G *Mann*] —*v.t.* **18.** to furnish with men, as for service or defence. **19.** to take one's place for service, as at a gun, post, etc. **20.** to make manly; brace. **21.** to accustom (a hawk) to the presence of men. [ME *manne(n)*, OE *mannian*]

Man (măn), *n.* **Isle of,** an island in the Irish Sea: one of the British Isles. 48,150 pop. (1961); 227 sq. mi. *Cap.*: Douglas.

Man., Manila.

mana (mä′nə), *n.* *Anthropol.* impersonal, supernatural force which may be concentrated in objects or persons.

man about town, a frequenter of theatres, clubs, etc.

Manabozho (măn′ə bō′zhō), *n., pl.* **-zhos.** the trickster-culture hero of the Ottawa, Chippewa, Potawatomi, and other Central Algonquian tribes.

manacle (măn′ə kl), *n., v.,* **-cled, -cling.** —*n.* (*usually pl.*) **1.** a shackle for the hand; handcuff. **2.** a restraint. —*v.t.* **3.** to handcuff; fetter. **4.** to hamper; restrain. [ME *manicle*, t. OF: handcuff, t. L: m. *manicula*, dim. of *manus* hand]

manage (măn′ĭj), *v.,* **-aged, -aging.** —*v.t.* **1.** to bring about; succeed in accomplishing: *he managed to see the governor.* **2.** to take charge or care of: *to manage an estate.* **3.** to dominate or influence (a person) by tact, address, or artifice. **4.** to handle, direct, govern, or control in action or use. **5.** to wield (a weapon, tool, etc.). **6.** to succeed in accomplishing a task, purpose, etc. **7.** to contrive to get along. **8.** to handle or train (a horse) in the exercises of the manège. **9.** *Obs. or Archaic.* to use sparingly. —*v.i.* **10.** to conduct affairs. [t. It.: m. *maneggiare* handle, train (horses), der. *mano* hand, g. L *manus*; sense influenced by F *manège* act of managing and *ménage* household] —**Syn. 1.** arrange, contrive. **4.** guide, conduct, regulate, engineer. See **rule. 5.** handle, manipulate.

manageable (măn′ĭ jə bl), *adj.* that may be managed; governable; contrivable; tractable. —**man′ageabil′ity, man′ageableness,** *n.* —**man′ageably,** *adv.*

managed currency, a monetary system governed by an administrative organization or according to some specially contrived set of rules (contrasted with the automatic gold standard).

management (măn′ĭj mənt), *n.* **1.** the act or manner of managing; handling, direction, or control. **2.** skill in managing; executive ability. **3.** the person or persons managing an institution, business, etc.: *this shop is under new management.* **4.** executives collectively: *conflicts between labour and management.* —**Syn. 1.** regulation, administration; superintendence, care, charge.

manager (măn′ĭ jə), *n.* **1.** one who manages. **2.** one charged with the management or direction of an institution, a business, or the like. **3.** one who manages resources and expenditures, as of a household. —**man′agership′,** *n.* —**Syn. 1.** administrator, executive, superintendent, supervisor; boss.

manageress (măn′ĭ jə rĕs′, măn′ĭ jə rĕs′), *n.* a female manager.

managerial (măn′ĭ jĭə′rĭ əl), *adj.* pertaining to management or a manager: *managerial functions.* —**man′age′rially,** *adv.*

Managua (*Sp.* mȧ nä′gwȧ), *n.* **1. Lake,** a lake in W Nicaragua. 38 mi. long. **2.** the capital of Nicaragua, in the W part, on Lake Managua. 274,901 (1964).

manakin (măn′ə kĭn), *n.* **1.** any of various songless passerine birds, family *Pipridae*, of the warmer parts of America, mostly small and brilliantly coloured. **2.** manikin. [var. of MANIKIN]

Manama (mə nä′mə), *n.* a town in and the capital of Bahrain, in N Bahrain. ab. 28,000.

mañana (*Sp.* mȧ nyȧ′nȧ), *n., adv.* *Spanish.* tomorrow; the indefinite future.

Manáos (*Port.* mə nȧws′), *n.* a city in N Brazil, on the Rio Negro near its confluence with the Amazon: a seaport ab. 1000 mi. from the Atlantic. 154,040 (1960). Also, **Manaus.**

Manapouri (măn′ə pŏŏə′rĭ), *n.* **1. Lake,** a lake in S South Island, New Zealand. 55 sq. mi. —*adj.* **2.** pertaining to a geological period or system of rocks in New Zealand which correspond with the Pre-Cambrian, Cambrian, Ordovician and Lower Silurian periods or systems.

Manasseh (mə năs′ĭ), *n.* **1.** son of the patriarch Joseph. Gen. 41:51. **2.** one of the ten tribes of Israel. **3.** king of Judah, of the 7th century B.C. II Kings 21.

man-at-arms (măn′ət ämz′), *n., pl.* **men-at-arms. 1.** a soldier. **2.** a heavily armed soldier on horseback.

manatee (măn′ə tē′), *n.* any of various herbivorous, gregarious sirenians constituting the genus *Trichechus* of West Indian and Floridian coast waters, having two flippers in front and a spoon-shaped tail. [t. Sp.: m. *manatí*, t. Carib: m. *manatouï*] —**manatoid** (măn′ə toid′), *adj.*

Florida manatee, *Trichechus manatus* (Ab. 10 ft long)

manatoka (măn′ə tō′kə), *n.* a small exotic tree, *Myoporum insulare*, of southern Africa, having fleshy leaves and small white flowers. [orig. uncert.]

manavelins (mə năv′ĭ lĭnz), *n.pl. Naut. Slang.* miscellaneous pieces of gear and material. Also, **manavilins.**

Manawatu (măn′ə wə to͞o′), *n.* a river of S North Island, New Zealand, flowing S and E to the Tasman Sea. 120 mi.

Manche (*Fr.* mäNsh), *n.* a department of NW France. 446,878 pop. (1962); 2476 sq. mi. *Cap.:* St Lô.

Manchester (măn′chĭs tə), *n.* a city in England, in Lancashire: connected with the Mersey estuary by a ship canal (35½ mi. long): university, founded 1880. 661,791 (1961).

Manchester terrier, one of a breed of medium-sized terriers having short, smooth, glossy black-and-tan coats.

manchineel (măn′chĭ nēl′), *n.* a tropical American euphorbiaceous tree or shrub, *Hippomane mancinella,* with a milky, highly caustic, poisonous sap. [t. F: m. *mancenille,* t. Sp: m. *manzanilla,* dim. of *manzana* apple, g. L (*māla*) *Matiāna* (apples) of Matius (author of a cooking manual)]

Manchu (măn cho͞o′), *n.* **1.** one of a Mongolian people inhabiting Manchuria, who conquered China in the 17th century. **2.** a Tungusic language, spoken by the Manchus. —*adj.* **3.** of or pertaining to the Manchus, their country, or their language.

Manchuria (măn cho͝oə′rĭ ə), *n.* a region in NE China, formerly comprising nine provinces of that country; ancestral home of the Manchus. ab. 413,000 sq. mi. —**Manchu′rian,** *adj.*, *n.*

Manchuria

manciple (măn′sĭ pl), *n.* a steward or purveyor, esp. of a college or Inn of Court, or other institution. [ME, t. OF: slave, servant, t. L: m. s. *manicipium* purchase, possession, a slave]

Mancunian (măng kyo͞o′nĭ ən), *n.* **1.** a native or inhabitant of Manchester. —*adj.* **2.** of, pertaining to, or characteristic of Manchester or its inhabitants.

-mancy, a word element meaning 'divination', as in *necromancy.* [ME *-manci(e), -mancy(e),* t. OF: (m.) *mancie,* g. LL *mantīa* t. Gk: m. *manteia* divination]

Mandaean (măn dē′ən), *n.* **1.** a member of an ancient Gnostic sect still surviving in southern Mesopotamia. **2.** the Aramaic language of the Mandaean sacred books. —*adj.* **3.** of the Mandaeans. [f. m. s. Mandaean *mandayyā* (der. *mandā* knowledge) + -AN]

Mandalay (măn′də lā′), *n.* a city in central Burma, on the river Irrawaddy: the former capital of Upper Burma. 212,873 (est. 1963).

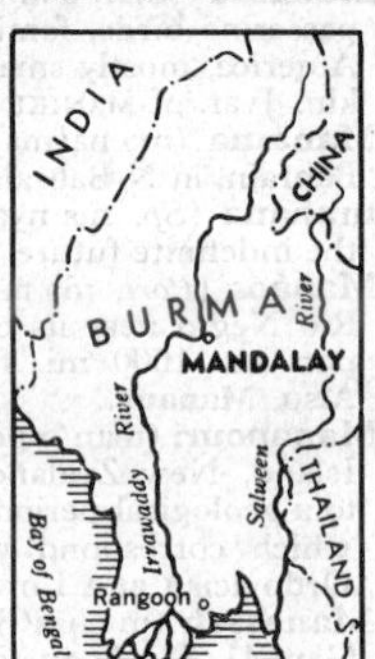

Mandalay

mandamus (măn dā′məs), *n.* **1.** *Law.* a writ from a superior court to an inferior court, or to an officer, a corporation, etc., commanding a specified thing to be done. **2.** (in early English law) any prerogative writ directing affirmative action. —*v.t.* **3.** *Colloq.* to intimidate or serve with such a writ. [t. L: we command]

Mandan (măn′dăn), *n.* a Siouan language.

mandarin (măn′də rĭn), *n.* **1.** (formerly) a member of any of the nine ranks of public officials in the Chinese Empire, each distinguished by a particular kind of button worn on the cap. **2.** an official or bureaucrat, esp. one who is in or makes himself in a high or inaccessible position. **3.** (*cap.*) standard Chinese. **4.** (*cap.*) the language of north China, esp. of Peking. **5.** a small, flattish citrus fruit of which the tangerine is one variety, native in south-western Asia, of a characteristic sweet and spicy flavour. **6.** the tree producing it, *Citrus reticulata,* and related species. [t. Chinese pidgin E, t. Pg.: m. *mandarim,* der. *mandar* to command, b. with Malay and Hind. *mantrī,* g. Skt *mantrin* counsellor, der. *mantra* thought, counsel]

mandarin collar, a type of high, single-piece, stand-up collar on a tunic or dress.

mandarin duck, a crested duck, *Aix galericulata,* with variegated plumage of purple, green, chestnut and white, native in China.

mandarine orange, mandarin (defs 5, 6).

mandatary (măn′də tə rĭ), *n.*, *pl.* **-ries.** a person or nation holding a mandate. Also, **mandatory.** [t. LL: m. s. *mandātārius,* der. L *mandātum* MANDATE]

mandate (*n.* măn′dāt, -dĭt; *v.* măn′dāt), *n.*, *v.*, **-dated, -dating.** —*n.* **1.** a commission given to one nation (the mandatary) by an associated group of nations (such as the League of Nations) to administer the government and affairs of a people in a backward territory. **2.** a mandated territory. **3.** *Politics.* the instruction as to policy given or supposed to be given by electors to a legislative body or to one or more of its members. **4.** a command from a superior court or official to an inferior one. **5.** a command; order. **6.** an order issued by the pope, esp. one commanding the preferment of a certain person to a benefice. **7.** *Roman and Civil Law.* a contract by which one engages gratuitously to perform services for another. **8.** *Roman Law.* an order or decree by the emperor, esp. to governors of provinces. —*v.t.* **9.** to consign (a territory, etc.) to the charge of a particular nation under a mandate. [t. L: m. s. *mandātum,* prop. pp. neut. of *mandāre* commit, enjoin, command]

mandator (măn′dā′tə), *n.* one who gives a mandate.

mandatory (măn′də tə rĭ, -trĭ), *adj.*, *n.*, *pl.* **-ries.** —*adj.* **1.** pertaining to, of the nature of, or containing a mandate. **2.** obligatory. **3.** *Law.* permitting no option. **4.** having received a mandate, as a nation. —*n.* **5.** mandatary.

Mandela (măn dā′lə), *n.* **Nelson Rolihlahla** (rō′lĭ lä′lə), born 1918, South African political leader; imprisoned since 1962.

Mandeville (măn′də vĭl), *n.* **1. Bernard,** 1670?–1733, English philosopher and writer of satires, born in Holland. **2. Sir John,** the ostensible (English) author of a 14th-century book of travels.

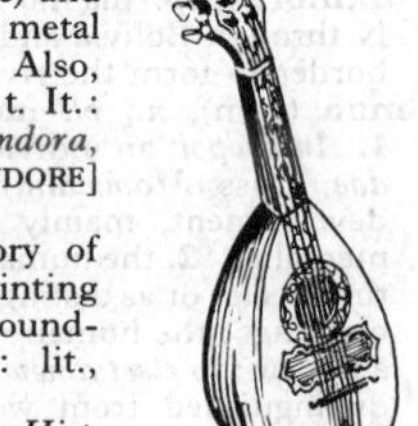

Mandible (def. 1) A, Symphysis; B, Ramus; C, Angle of jaw; D, Ascending ramus; E, Coronoid process; F, Condyle

mandible (măn′dĭ bl), *n.* **1.** the bone of the lower jaw. **2.** (in birds) **a.** the lower part of the beak: the lower jaw. **b.** (*pl.*) the upper and lower parts of the beak; the jaws. **3.** (in arthropods) one of the first pair of mouth-part appendages, typically a jawlike biting organ, but styliform or setiform in piercing and sucking species. [t. LL: m. s. *mandibula, mandibulum* jaw]

mandibular (măn dĭb′yo͞o lə), *adj.* pertaining to or of the nature of a mandible.

mandibulate (măn dĭb′yo͞o lĭt, -lāt′), *adj.* having mandibles.

Mandingo (măn dĭng′gō), *n.*, *pl.* **-gos, -goes,** *adj.* —*n.* **1.** a member of any of a number of Negro peoples forming an extensive linguistic group in western Africa. **2.** one of the principal languages of West Africa. —*adj.* **3.** of the Mandingos or their language.

mandolin (măn′də lĭn′), *n.* a musical instrument with a pear-shaped wooden body (smaller than that of the lute) and a fretted neck, usually having metal strings plucked with a plectrum. Also, **mandoline.** [t. F: m. *mandoline,* t. It.: m. *mandolino,* dim. of *mandola, mandora,* var. of *pandora.* See PANDORA, BANDORE] —**man′dolin′ist,** *n.*

Mandolin

mandorla (măn dô′lə), *n.* a glory of light in an almond shape used in painting and sculpture, usually shown surrounding the figure of Christ. [It.: lit., almond]

mandragora (măn drăg′ə rə), *n.* **1.** *Hist.* mandrake. **2.** a mandrake root. [OE, t. LL, in L *mandragoras,* t. Gk]

mandrake (măn′drāk′), *n.* **1.** a narcotic, short-stemmed European solanaceous herb, *Mandragora officinarum,* with a fleshy, often forked root fancied to resemble a human form. **2.** the May Apple. [ME; popular etymological alter. of MANDRAGORA which was interpreted as MAN + DRAKE²]

mandrel (măn′drəl), *n. Mach.* a spindle, axle, bar, or arbor, usually tapered, pressed into a hole in a piece of work to support the work during the machining process, as between the centres of a lathe. Also, **mandril.** [t. F, dissimilated var. of *mandrin*]

mandrill (măn′drĭl), *n.* a large, ferocious-looking baboon, *Papio sphinx,* of western Africa, the male of which has the face marked with blue and scarlet and the muzzle ribbed. [f. MAN + DRILL⁴]

Mandrill, *Papio sphinx* (Ab. 3 ft long)

manducate (măn′dyōō kāt′), *v.t.*, **-cated, -cating.** *Rare.* to chew; masticate; eat. [t. L: m. s. *mandūcātus*, pp.] —**man′duca′tion,** *n.* —**manducatory** (măn′dyōō-kā′tə rĭ), *adj.*

mane (mān), *n.* **1.** the long hair growing on the back of or about the neck and neighbouring parts of some animals, as the horse, lion, etc. **2.** a long, bushy, often untended head of hair. [ME; OE *manu*, c. G *Mähne*] —**maned** (mānd), *adj.*

man-eater (măn′ē′tə), *n.* **1.** a cannibal. **2.** an animal, esp. a tiger, lion, or shark, that eats or is said to eat men. **3.** the great white shark, *Carcharodon caracharias*, reputedly the most dangerous shark to man.

maned wolf, the largest wild South American dog, *Chrysocyon jubatus*, a red-coated, large-eared, long-legged fox, found in southern Brazil, Paraguay, and northern Argentina.

manège (mă nāzh′), *n.* **1.** the art of training and riding horses. **2.** the action or movements of a trained horse. **3.** a school for training horses and teaching horsemanship. Also, **manege.** [t. F. See MANAGE]

manes (mä′nāz), *n.pl.* **1.** (among the ancient Romans) the deified souls of the dead. **2.** the spirit or shade of a particular dead person. Also, **Manes.** [L]

manet (măn′ĕt), *v.i.* (he or she) remains (used as a stage direction to indicate that one character is to remain on stage, while others exit). [L]

Manet (*Fr.* mȧ nĕ′), *n.* **Édouard** (*Fr.* ė dwȧr′), 1832–83, French impressionist painter.

maneuver (mə nōō′və), *n., v.t., v.i.*, **-vered, -vering.** *U.S.* manoeuvre.

manful (măn′fəl), *adj.* having or showing manly spirit; resolute. —**man′fully,** *adv.* —**man′fulness,** *n.* —**Syn.** See **manly.**

mangabey (măng′gə bĭ), *n.* any primate of the genus *Cercocebus*, monkeys with white eyelids, which live in the forests of central Africa.

Mangalore (măng′gə lô′), *n.* a town in India, in NW Kerala. 142,669 (1961).

manganate (măng′gə nāt′), *n. Chem.* a salt of manganic acid, as potassium manganate, K_2MnO_4.

manganepidote (măn′găn ĕp′ĭ dōt′), *n.* piedmontite.

manganese (măng′gə nēz′), *n. Chem.* a hard, brittle, greyish white metallic element used as an alloying agent with steel and other metals to give them toughness. *Symbol:* Mn; *at. wt:* 54·938; *at. no.:* 25; *sp. gr.:* 7·2 at 20°C. [t. F, t. It., t. ML: m. *magnēsia* MAGNESIA]

manganese bronze, *Metall.* a copper-zinc alloy containing up to 4 per cent manganese.

manganese dioxide, *Chem.* a heavy black powder, MnO_2, occurring naturally as pyrolusite; used as a source of metallic manganese, as an oxidizing agent, and as a catalyst. Also, **manganese peroxide.**

manganese epidote, piedmontite.

manganese steel, a steel alloy containing 10 to 14 per cent of manganese, used for railway points and other devices involving heavy wear and strain.

manganic (măn găn′ĭk), *adj. Chem.* of or containing manganese, esp. in the trivalent state.

manganic acid, *Chem.* an acid, H_2MnO_4, not known in the free state.

manganin (măng′gə nĭn), *n. Trademark.* an alloy based on copper which contains manganese (up to 18 per cent) and nickel (up to 5 per cent); used extensively for electrical purposes as its resistance is only slightly affected by changes in temperature.

manganite (măng′gə nīt′), *n.* **1.** a grey to black mineral, hydrous manganese oxide, MnO(OH), a minor ore of manganese. **2.** *Chem.* any of a series of salts containing tetravalent manganese, and derived from the acids H_4MnO_4 or H_2MnO_3. [f. MANGAN(ESE) + -ITE[1]]

manganous (măng′gə nəs, măn găn′əs), *adj. Chem.* containing divalent manganese.

mange (mānj), *n.* any of various skin diseases due to parasitic mites affecting animals and sometimes man, characterized by loss of hair and scabby eruptions. [late ME *manjewe*, t. OF: m. *manjue* itch, der. *mangier* eat, g. L *mandūcāre* chew]

mangel-wurzel (măng′gl wû′zəl), *n.* a coarse variety of the common beet, *Beta vulgaris*, extensively cultivated as food for cattle, etc. Also, **mangel, mangold, mangold-wurzel.** [t. G, var. of *Mangoldwurzel* beetroot]

manger (mān′jə), *n.* **1.** a box or trough, as in a stable, from which horses or cattle eat. **2.** *Naut.* the deck area between the hawse pipes in the bow of a vessel, and the breakwater built across the cable deck. [ME, t. OF: m. *mangeoire*, der. L *mandūcāre* chew]

mangle[1] (măng′gl), *v.t.*, **-gled, -gling. 1.** to cut, slash, or crush so as to disfigure: *a corpse mangled in battle.* **2.** to mar; spoil: *to mangle a text by poor typesetting.* [ME *mangel(en)*, t. AF: m. *mangler*, ? freq. of OF *mahaignier* MAIM] —**man′gler,** *n.* —**Syn. 1.** See **maim.**

mangle[2] (măng′gl), *n., v.*, **-gled, -gling.** —*n.* **1.** a machine for smoothing or pressing water, etc., out of cloth, household linen, etc., by means of rollers. —*v.t.* **2.** to smooth with a mangle. [t. D: m. *mangel*; ult. akin to MANGONEL]

mango (măng′gō), *n., pl.* **-goes, -gos. 1.** the oblong, slightly acid fruit of a tropical anacardiaceous tree, *Mangifera indica*, which is eaten ripe, or preserved or pickled. **2.** the tree itself. [t. Pg.: m. *manga*, t. Malay: m. *manggā*, t. Tamil: m. *mānkāy*]

mangonel (măng′gə nĕl′), *n.* a large ancient military engine, or powerful crossbow, for throwing arrows, darts, or stones. [ME, t. OF, dim. der. LL *manganum*, t. Gk: m. *mánganon* engine of war]

mangosteen (măng′gō stēn′), *n.* **1.** the juicy edible fruit of an East Indian resin-yielding tree, *Garcinia mangostana*. **2.** the tree itself. [t. Malay: m. *mangustan*]

mangrove (măng′grōv′), *n.* **1.** any tree or shrub of the tropical genus *Rhizophora*, the species of which are mostly low trees remarkable for a copious development of interlacing adventitious roots above the ground. **2.** any of various similar plants, as the **white mangrove,** *Avicennia marina*, a valued source of tannin. [f. m. Sp. *mangle* (ult. t. Taino) + GROVE]

mangy (mān′jĭ), *adj.*, **-gier, -giest. 1.** having, caused by, or like the mange. **2.** contemptible; mean. **3.** squalid; shabby. —**man′gily,** *adv.* —**man′giness,** *n.*

manhandle (măn′hăn′dl), *v.t.*, **-dled, -dling. 1.** to handle roughly. **2.** to move by force of men, without mechanical appliances.

Manhattan (măn hăt′n), *n.* **1.** an island in New York City between the rivers Hudson, East, and Harlem. 13½ mi. long; 2½ mi. greatest width; 22¼ sq. mi. **2.** a borough of New York City approximately coextensive with Manhattan Island: chief business district. 1,698,281 (1960). **3.** a cocktail of whisky and sweet vermouth, often with a dash of bitters and a cherry.

manhole (măn′hōl′), *n.* a hole, usually with a cover, through which a man may enter a sewer, drain, steam boiler, etc., so as to make repairs.

manhood (măn′hŏŏd), *n.* **1.** the state of being a man or adult male person. **2.** manly qualities. **3.** men collectively. **4.** the state of being human.

man-hour (măn′ou′ə), *n.* an hour of work by one man, used as an industrial time unit.

mania (mā′nyə), *n.* **1.** great excitement or enthusiasm; craze. **2.** *Psychol.* a form of insanity characterized by great excitement, with or without delusions, and in its acute stage by great violence. [late ME, t. L, t. Gk: madness]

-mania, a combining form of **mania** (as in *megalomania*), extended to mean exaggerated desire or love for, as *balletomania*.

maniac (mā′nĭ ăk′), *n.* **1.** a raving lunatic; a madman. —*adj.* **2.** raving with madness; mad.

maniacal (mə nī′ə kl), *adj.* of or pertaining to mania or a maniac. —**mani′acally,** *adv.*

manic (măn′ĭk), *adj.* pertaining to mania. [t. Gk: m. s. *manikós* insane]

manic-depressive (măn′ĭk dĭ prĕs′ĭv), *Psychol.* —*adj.* **1.** having a mental disorder marked by cyclothymic manifestations of excitation and depression. —*n.* **2.** one who is suffering from this disorder.

Manichean (măn′ĭ kē′ən), *n.* **1.** an adherent of the religious system of the Persian teacher Mani or Manichaeus (A.D. 216?–276?), composed of Gnostic Christian, Buddhist, Zoroastrian, and various other elements, the principal feature being a dualistic theology which represented a conflict between light and darkness and included belief in the inherent evil of matter. —*adj.* **2.** of or pertaining to Mani or the Manicheans. Also, **Manichaean.** [f. LL: (m.) s. *Manichaeus* (t. LGk: m. *Manichaíos*; from the name of the founder of the sect) + -AN] —**Man′iche′anism, Man′icheism,** *n.*

manicure (măn′ĭ kyŏŏə′), *n., v.*, **-cured, -curing.** —*n.* **1.** professional care of the hands and fingernails. **2.** a manicurist. —*v.t., v.i.* **3.** to care for (the hands and fingernails). [t. F, f. L: m. s. *manus* hand + m. *cura* care]

manicurist (măn′ĭ kyŏŏə′rĭst), *n.* a person who does manicuring.

manifest (măn′ĭ fĕst′), *adj.* **1.** readily perceived by the eye or the understanding; evident; obvious; apparent; plain: *a manifest error.* **2.** *Psychol.* apparent or disguising (used of conscious feelings and ideas which conceal and yet incorporate unconscious ideas and impulses): *the manifest content of a dream as opposed to the latent content which it conceals.* —*v.t.* **3.** to make manifest to the eye or the understanding; show plainly. **4.** to prove; put beyond doubt or question. **5.** to record in a ship's manifest. —*n.* **6.** a list of a ship's cargo, signed by the master, for the information and use of the customs officers. **7.** a list of goods transported by land. **8.** a list of the cargo carried by an aeroplane. [ME, t. L: s. *manifestus* palpable, evident] —**man′ifest′able,** *adj.* —**man′ifest′ly,** *adv.* —**man′ifest′ness,** *n.* —**Syn. 1.** clear, distinct. **3.** reveal. See **display.**

manifestant (măn′ĭ fĕs′tənt), *n.* one who takes part in a public demonstration.

manifestation (măn′ĭ fĕs tā′shən), *n.* **1.** the act of manifesting. **2.** the state of being manifested. **3.** a means of manifesting; indication. **4.** a public demonstration, as for political effect. **5.** *Spiritualism.* a materialization.

manifestative (măn′ĭ fĕs′tə tĭv), *adj.* showing clearly; manifesting.

manifesto (măn′ĭ fĕs′tō), *n., pl.* **-tos** or **-toes.** a public declaration, as of a sovereign or government, or of any person or body of persons taking important action, making known intentions, objects, motives, etc.; a proclamation. [t. It.: manifest, n.]

manifold (măn′ĭ fōld′), *adj.* **1.** of many kinds, numerous and varied: *manifold duties.* **2.** having many different parts, elements, features, forms, etc. **3.** doing or operating several things at once. —*n.* **4.** something having many different parts or features. **5.** a copy or facsimile, as of writing, such as is made by manifolding. **6.** a pipe or chamber with a number of inlets or outlets. **7.** any very fine typing paper. —*v.t.* **8.** to make copies of, as with carbon paper. [ME *monifald,* OE *manigfeald.* See MANY, -FOLD] —**man′ifold′ly,** *adv.* —**man′ifold′ness,** *n.* —**Syn. 1.** See **many.**

manifolder (măn′ĭ fōl′də), *n.* a machine for making manifolds or copies, as of writing.

maniform (măn′ĭ fôm′), *adj.* having the shape of a hand.

manikin (măn′ĭ kĭn), *n.* **1.** a little man; a dwarf; pygmy. **2.** mannequin. **3.** a model of the human body for teaching anatomy, demonstrating surgical operations, etc. Also, **manakin, mannikin.** [t. D: m. *manneken,* dim. of *man* man. Cf. MANNEQUIN]

Manila (mə nĭl′ə), *n.* **1.** a seaport in and the capital of the Republic of the Philippines, on S Luzon island. 1,339,000 (est. 1965). See **Quezon City.** See map under **Bataán. 2.** Manila hemp. **3.** Manila paper.

Manila Bay, a large bay in the Philippine Islands, in W Luzon island: the American fleet under Admiral Dewey defeated the Spanish fleet here, 1898.

Manila hemp, a fibrous material obtained from the leaves of the abaca, *Musa textilis,* used for making ropes, fabrics, etc.

Manila paper, strong light brown paper derived orig. from Manila hemp, but now also from wood-pulp substitutes.

Manila rope, rope manufactured from Manila hemp.

manilla (mə nĭl′ə), *n.* **1.** Manila hemp. **2.** Manila paper.

man in the street, the average citizen.

manioc (măn′ĭ ŏk′), *n.* cassava. [repr. Sp., Pg. *mandioca,* Tupi *manioca,* Guarani *mandio*]

maniple (măn′ĭ pl), *n.* **1.** a subdivision of the Roman legion, consisting of 120 or 60 men. **2.** *Eccles.* one of the Eucharistic vestments, consisting of an ornamental band or strip worn on the left arm near the wrist. [ME, t. OF, t. L: m. s. *manipulus* handful, company]

manipular (mə nĭp′yŏŏ lə), *adj.* **1.** of or pertaining to the Roman maniple. **2.** of or pertaining to manipulation. —*n.* **3.** a soldier belonging to a maniple.

manipulate (mə nĭp′yŏŏ lāt′), *v.t.,* **-lated, -lating. 1.** to handle, manage, or use, esp. with skill, in some process of treatment or performance. **2.** to manage or influence by artful skill: *to manipulate prices.* **3.** to adapt or change (accounts, figures, etc.) to suit one's purpose or advantage. [back-formation from MANIPULATION] —**manip′ula′tive, manip′ula′tory,** *adj.* —**manip′ula′tor,** *n.*

manipulation (mə nĭp′yŏŏ lā′shən), *n.* **1.** skilful or artful management. **2.** the act of manipulating. **3.** the state or fact of being manipulated. **4.** *Med.* a treatment performed in physiotherapy, orthopaedics, and osteopathy to obtain forced passive movement of a joint beyond its active range of movement. [t. F, der. L *manipulus* handful]

Manipur (mŭn′ĭ pŏŏə′), *n.* a centrally administered union territory in NE India between Assam and Burma. 780,037 pop. (1961); 8620 sq. mi. *Cap.:* Imphal.

Manisa (*Turk.* mä′nē sä), *n.* a town in W Turkey, near the Aegean: the Romans defeated Antiochus the Great here, 190 B.C. 59,675 (1960). Ancient, **Magnesia.**

Manitoba (măn′ĭ tō′bə), *n.* **1.** a province in central Canada. 921,686 pop. (1961); 246,512 sq. mi. *Cap.:* Winnipeg. **2.** a lake in the S part of this province. 1817 sq. mi.; ab. 120 mi. long. —**Man′ito′ban,** *adj., n.*

manitou (măn′ĭ tōō′), *n., pl.* **-tos.** (among the Algonquian Indians) a good or evil spirit; a being or object of supernatural power. Also, **manito** (măn′ĭ tō′). [t. Algonquian (Mass. d.): m. *manitto* he is a god]

Manitoulin (măn′ĭ tōō′lĭn), *n.* a Canadian island in N Lake Huron. ab. 80 mi. long.

Manizales (*Sp.* mä nē thä′lĕs), *n.* a town in W Colombia. 221,916 (1964).

mankind (măn′kīnd′ *for 1*; măn′kīnd′ *for 2*), *n.* **1.** the human race; human beings collectively. **2.** men, as distinguished from women.

manlike (măn′līk′), *adj.* **1.** resembling a man. **2.** belonging or proper to a man; manly: *manlike fortitude.*

manly (măn′lĭ), *adj.,* **-lier, -liest,** *adv.* —*adj.* **1.** possessing qualities proper to a man; strong; brave; honourable. **2.** pertaining to or befitting a man: *manly sports.* —*adv.* **3.** *Archaic.* in a manly manner. —**man′lily,** *adv.* —**man′liness,** *n.*

—**Syn. 1.** MANLY, MANFUL, MANNISH mean possessing the qualities of a man. MANLY implies possession of the noblest and most worthy qualities a man can have (as opposed to servility, insincerity, underhandedness, etc.): *a manly man is the noblest work of God.* MANFUL has particular reference to courage, strength, and industry: *manful resistance.* MANNISH applies to that which resembles man: *a boy with a mannish voice.* Applied to a woman, the term is derogatory, suggesting ostentatious imitation of man: *a mannish stride.*

man-made (măn′mād′), *adj.* **1.** made or produced by man. **2.** produced artificially; not deriving from natural processes. **3.** *Textiles.* **a.** (of fibres) manufactured synthetically. **b.** (of fabrics) manufactured from man-made fibres.

Mann (*Ger.* män), *n.* **1. Heinrich** (*Ger.* hīn′rĭKH), 1871–1950, German writer, in the U.S. after 1940 (brother of Thomas). **2. Thomas** (*Ger.* tō′mäs), 1875–1955, German novelist, in the U.S. after 1938.

manna (măn′ə), *n.* **1.** the food miraculously supplied the children of Israel in the wilderness. Ex. 16:14–36. **2.** divine or spiritual food. **3.** anything likened to the manna of the Israelites. **4.** an exudate of the flowering ash, *Fraxinus ornus,* of southern Europe, used in pharmacy. [OE, t. LL, t. Gk, t. Heb.: m. *mān*]

mannequin (măn′ĭ kĭn), *n.* **1.** a model of the human figure made of wood, wax, etc., used by tailors, dress designers, etc., for displaying or fitting clothes. **2.** model (def. 5). [t. F, t. D: m. *manneken.* See MANIKIN]

manner (măn′ə), *n.* **1.** way of doing, being done, or happening; mode of action, occurrence, etc. **2.** characteristic or customary way of doing: *houses built in the Mexican manner.* **3.** (*pl.*) the prevailing customs, modes of living, etc., of a people, class, period, etc. **4.** a person's outward bearing; way of addressing and treating others. **5.** (*pl.*) ways of behaving, esp. with reference to polite standards: *bad manners.* **6.** (*pl.*) good or polite ways of behaving: *have you no manners?* **7.** outward bearing; way of behaving towards others: *the policeman had rather an awkward manner.* **8.** air of distinction: *he had quite a manner.* **9.** kind; sort: *all manner of things.* **10.** characteristic style in art, literature, or the like: *verses in the manner of Spenser.* **11.** mannered style; mannerism. **12.** *Obs.* nature; character; guise. **13. by all manner of means,** by all means; certainly. **14. in a manner,** after a fashion; so to speak; somewhat. **15. in a manner of speaking,** in a way; so to speak. **16. to the manner born, a.** accustomed or destined by birth (to a high position, etc.). **b.** naturally fitted for a position, duty, etc. [ME *manere,* t. AF: orig., way of handling, g. L *manuāria,* fem. of *manuārius* of or for the hand]

—**Syn.** 2. mode, fashion, style; habit, custom. 4. demeanour, deportment. MANNER, AIR, BEARING all refer to one's outward aspect or behaviour. MANNER applies to a distinctive mode of behaviour, or social attitude towards others, etc.: *a gracious manner.* AIR applies to outward appearance insofar as this is distinctive or indicative: *an air of martyrdom.* AIRS imply affectation: *airs and graces.* BEARING applies especially to carriage: *a noble bearing.*

mannered (măn′əd), *adj.* **1.** having (specified) manners: *ill-mannered.* **2.** having mannerisms; affected.

Mannerheim (măn′ə hīm′), *n.* **Baron Carl Gustaf Emil** (käl′ gŏŏs′täf ā′mĕl), 1867–1951, Finnish soldier and statesman.

mannerism (măn′ə rĭz′əm), *n.* **1.** marked or excessive adherence to an unusual manner, esp. in literary work. **2.** a habitual peculiarity of manner. **3.** (*usually cap.*) a style of late 16th-century European art, mainly current in Italy. —**man′nerist,** *n.* —**man′neris′tic,** *adj.*

mannerless (măn′ə lĭs), *adj.* without good manners.

mannerly (măn′ə lĭ), *adj.* **1.** having or showing good manners; courteous; polite. —*adv.* **2.** with good manners; courteously; politely. —**man′nerliness,** *n.*

Mannheim (măn′hīm; *Ger.* män′hīm), *n.* a city in West Germany, in NW Baden-Württemberg, on the Rhine. 329,900 (est. 1966).

mannikin (măn′ĭ kĭn), *n.* manikin.

Manning (măn′ĭng), *n.* **Henry Edward,** 1808–92, English Roman Catholic cardinal and writer.

mannish (măn′ĭsh), *adj.* **1.** (of a woman or her behaviour, etc.) characteristic of or natural to a man. **2.** resembling a man. **3.** imitating a man. —**man′nishly,** *adv.* —**man′nishness,** *n.* —**Syn. 2.** See **manly.**

mannitol (măn′ĭ tōl′), *n. Chem.* a white sweetish crystalline, carbohydrate alcohol, $HOCH_2(CHOH)\ CH_2OH$, occurring in three optically different forms the common one being found in the manna of the ash *Fraxinus ornus,* and in other plants; used in medicine as a diuretic and to assess renal function.

mannose (măn′ōs), *n.* a hexose, $C_6H_{12}O_6$, obtained from the hydrolysis of the ivory nut, and yielding mannitol on reduction. [f. MANN(A) + -OSE²]

manoeuvre (mə no͞o′ vər), *n., v.,* **-vred, -vring.** —*n.* **1.** a planned and regulated movement or evolution of troops, war vessels, etc. **2.** (*pl.*) a series of tactical exercises usually carried out in the field by large bodies of troops in imitation of war. **3.** an adroit move; skilful proceeding, measure, etc. —*v.t.* **4.** to change the position of (troops, etc.) by a manoeuvre. **5.** to bring, put, drive, or make by manoeuvres. **6.** to manipulate with skill or adroitness. —*v.i.* **7.** to perform a manoeuvre or manoeuvres. **8.** to scheme; intrigue. Also, *U.S.*, **maneuver.** [t. F: manipulation, der. *manoeuvrer* work, g. LL *manū operāre* work by hand] —**manoeu′vrable,** *adj.* —**manoeu′vrabil′ity,** *n.* —**manoeu′vrer,** *n.*

man of God, 1. a saint, prophet, etc. **2.** a clergyman.

Man of Sorrows, Jesus Christ. Cf. Isa. 53:3.

man of the world, a sophisticated man.

man-of-war (măn′əv wô′), *n., pl.* **men-of-war. 1.** a warship. **2.** See **Portuguese man-of-war.**

manometer (mə nŏm′ĭ tə), *n.* an instrument for determining the pressure of gases, vapours, or liquids. [t. F: m. *manomètre,* f. Gk *mānó(s)* thin, rare + F *-mètre* METER¹] —**manometric** (măn′ə mĕt′rĭk), *adj.*

manor (măn′ə), *n.* **1.** a landed estate or territorial unit, orig. of the nature of a feudal lordship, consisting of a lord's demesne and of lands within which he has the right to exercise certain privileges and exact certain fees, etc. **2.** the mansion of a lord with the land pertaining to it. **3.** the main house or mansion on an estate. **4.** *Slang.* a police district. [ME *manere,* t. OF: m. *manoir,* n. use of *manoir,* inf., dwell, g. L *manēre* remain] —**manorial** (mə nô′rĭ əl), *adj.*

manor house, the house or mansion of the lord of a manor.

man-o'-war bird, the frigate-bird.

manpower (măn′pou′ə), *n.* **1.** the power supplied by the physical exertions of a man or men. **2.** a unit of power assumed to be equal to the rate at which a man can do mechanical work, commonly taken as $\frac{1}{10}$ horsepower. **3.** rate of work in terms of this unit. **4.** power in terms of men available or required: *the manpower of an army.*

manqué (mŏng′kā; *Fr.* mäɴ kė′), *adj.* failed, unsuccessful; unfulfilled.

manrope (măn′rōp′), *n. Naut.* a rope placed at the side of a gangway, ladder, or the like, to serve as a rail.

mansard roof, (măn′säd, -səd), a roof having two pitches, the upper slopes being flatter than the lower ones. Also, **mansard.** [named after F. MANSART]

Mansard roof

Mansart (*Fr.* mäɴ sär′), *n.* **1. François** (*Fr.* fräɴswȧ′), 1598–1666, French architect. **2.** his great-nephew, **Jules Hardouin** (*Fr.* zh l är dwăɴ′), 1646–1708, French architect.

manse (măns), *n.* **1.** the house and land occupied by a minister or parson. **2.** (orig.) the dwelling of a landholder, with the land attached. [late ME, t. ML: m. s. *mansa* dwelling, orig. pp. fem. of L *manēre* remain]

manservant (măn′sû′vənt), *n., pl.* **menservants.** a male servant.

Mansfield (măns′fēld′), *n.* **1. Katherine** (*Kathleen Beauchamp, Mrs John Middleton Murry*), 1888–1923, English short-story writer, born in New Zealand. **2.** a town in England, in Nottinghamshire. 53,222 (1961).

mansion (măn′shən), *n.* **1.** an imposing or stately residence. **2.** a manor house. **3.** (*pl.*) a block of flats. **4.** *Archaic.* a place of abode. **5.** *Oriental and Medieval Astron.* each of twenty-eight divisions of the ecliptic occupied by the moon on successive days. [ME, t. OF, t. L: s. *mansio* a remaining, dwelling]

Mansion House, the official residence of the Lord Mayor of London.

man-sized (măn′sīzd′), *adj.* of a size or kind suitable for or appropriate to a man.

manslaughter (măn′slô′tə), *n.* **1.** the killing of a human being by a human being; homicide. **2.** *Law.* the killing of a human being unlawfully but without malice aforethought. See **malice aforethought.**

manslayer (măn′slā′ə), *n.* one who kills a human being; a homicide. —**man′slay′ing,** *n., adj.*

Mansur (măn so͞o͝ə′), *n.* See **al Mansur.**

Mansura (măn so͞o͝ə′rə), *n.* El Mansura.

manta (măn′tə; *Sp.* män′tä), *n.* **1.** (in Spain and Spanish America) a cloak or wrap. **2.** the type of blanket or cloth used on a horse or mule. **3.** *Mil.* a movable shelter formerly used to protect besiegers; a mantelet. **4.** a manta ray. [t. Sp., t. Pr.: blanket]

manta ray, a huge tropical ray, reaching a width of twenty feet, with earlike flaps on either side of the head.

manteau (măn′tō; *Fr.* mäɴ tō′), *n., pl.* **-teaus** (-tōz), *Fr.* **-teaux** (*Fr.* -tō′). *Obs.* a mantle or cloak, esp. one worn by women. [t. F. See MANTLE]

Mantegna (*It.* män tĕn′nyä), *n.* **Andrea** (*It.* än drĕ′ä), 1431–1506, Italian painter and engraver.

mantelet (măn′tĭ lĕt′, mănt′lĭt), *n.* **1.** a short mantle. **2.** Also, **mantlet.** *Mil.* **a.** manta (def. 3). **b.** any of various bulletproof shelters or screens. [ME, t. OF, dim. of *mantel* MANTLE]

mantelletta (măn′tĭ lĕt′ə), *n. Rom. Cath. Ch.* a sleeveless vestment of silk or woollen stuff reaching to the knees, worn by cardinals, bishops, abbots, etc. [t. It., dim. of *mantello,* der. L *mantellum* MANTLE]

mantelpiece (măn′tl pēs′), *n.* the more or less ornamental structure above and about a fireplace, usually having a shelf or projecting ledge. Also, **mantle** (măn′tl).

mantelshelf (măn′tl shĕlf′), *n.* **1.** the projecting part of a mantelpiece. **2.** *Mountaineering.* a small ledge on the rock wall.

manteltree (măn′tl trē′), *n.* a wooden beam or arch or a stone arch forming the lintel of a fireplace.

mantic (măn′tĭk), *adj.* **1.** of or pertaining to divination. **2.** having the power of divination. [t. Gk: m. s. *mantikós* prophetic] —**man′tically,** *adv.*

mantilla (măn tĭl′ə), *n.* **1.** a silk or lace headscarf arranged over a high comb and falling over the back and shoulders, worn in Spain, Mexico, etc. **2.** a short mantle or light cape. [t. Sp., dim. of *manta.* See MANTA]

Mantinea (măn′tĭ nĭə′), *n.* an ancient city of Arcadia, in S Greece: battles, 362 B.C., 207 B.C.

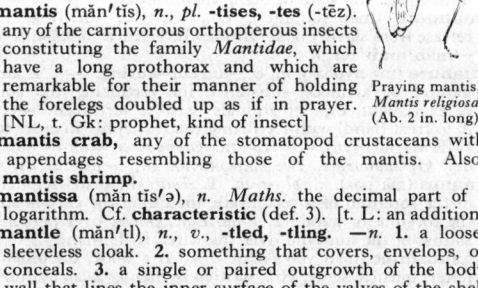

mantis (măn′tĭs), *n., pl.* **-tises, -tes** (-tēz). any of the carnivorous orthopterous insects constituting the family *Mantidae,* which have a long prothorax and which are remarkable for their manner of holding the forelegs doubled up as if in prayer. [NL, t. Gk: prophet, kind of insect]

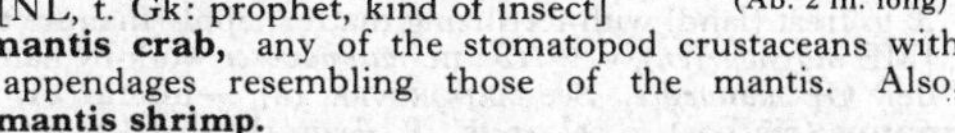

Praying mantis, *Mantis religiosa* (Ab. 2 in. long)

mantis crab, any of the stomatopod crustaceans with appendages resembling those of the mantis. Also, **mantis shrimp.**

mantissa (măn tĭs′ə), *n. Maths.* the decimal part of a logarithm. Cf. **characteristic** (def. 3). [t. L: an addition]

mantle (măn′tl), *n., v.,* **-tled, -tling.** —*n.* **1.** a loose, sleeveless cloak. **2.** something that covers, envelops, or conceals. **3.** a single or paired outgrowth of the body wall that lines the inner surface of the valves of the shell in molluscs and brachiopods. **4.** a gas mantle. **5.** *Ornith.* the back, scapular, and inner wing feathers taken together, esp. when these are all of the same colour. **6.** the outer enveloping masonry of a blast furnace over the hearth. **7.** *Geol.* a band of dense material between the crust of the earth and the core, and generally thought to consist of solid rock. —*v.t.* **8.** to cover with or as with a mantle; envelop; conceal. —*v.i.* **9.** to spread like a mantle, as a blush over the face. **10.** to flush; blush. **11.** (of a hawk) to spread out first one wing and then the other over the corresponding outstretched leg. **12.** (of a liquid) to be or become covered with a coating; foam. [ME *mantel,* OE *mæntel,* t. L: m. s. *mantellum, mantēlum* cloak]

mantle rock, *Phys. Geog.* the layer of disintegrated and decomposed rock fragments, including soil, just above the solid rock of the earth's crust; regolith.

mantlet (mănt′lĭt), *n. Mil.* mantelet (defs 2a, 2b).

man-to-man (măn′tə măn′), *adj.* characterized by frankness or directness: *a man-to-man talk.*

mantrap (măn′trăp′), *n.* **1.** a trap or snare for catching a man, esp. a trespasser. **2.** *Colloq.* a seductive woman.

mantua (măn′tyo͞o ə), *n.* **1.** a kind of loose gown formerly worn by women. **2.** a mantle. [m. MANTEAU due to assoc. with MANTUA in Italy]

Mantua (măn′tyo͞o ə), *n.* a town in Italy, in E Lombardy: birthplace of Virgil. 65,857 (1961). Italian, **Mantova** (*It.* män′tô vä). —**Man′tuan,** *adj., n.*

Manua Islands (mə no͞o′ə), a group of three small islands in the E part of American Samoa. 2695 (1960).

manual (măn′yo͞o əl), *adj.* **1.** of or pertaining to the hand or hands. **2.** done or worked by the hand or hands. **3.** using or involving human energy, power, etc. **4.** of the nature of a manual or handbook. —*n.* **5.** a small book, esp. one giving information or instructions. **6.** *Mil.* prescribed exercises in the handling of a rifle, etc. **7.** *Music.* the keyboard of an organ played with the hands. [t. L: s. *manuālis* (as n., ML *manuāle*) of the hand; r. ME *manuel,* t. OF] —**man′ually,** *adv.*

manual training, training in the various manual arts and crafts, esp. carpentry, metalwork, etc.

manubrium (mə nyo͞o′brĭ əm), *n., pl.* **-bria** (-brĭ ə), **-briums.** **1.** *Anat., Zool.* a segment, bone, cell, etc., resembling a handle. **2.** *Anat.* **a.** the uppermost of the three portions of the sternum. **b.** the long process of the malleus. [t. L: a handle]

manuf., **1.** manufacture. **2.** manufacturer. **3.** manufacturing.

manufactory (măn′yo͞o făk′tə rĭ, -trĭ), *n., pl.* **-ries.** *Archaic.* a factory.

manufacture (măn′yo͞o făk′chə), *n., v.,* **-tured, -turing.** —*n.* **1.** the making of goods or wares by manual labour or by machinery, esp. on a large scale. **2.** the making of anything. **3.** the thing or material manufactured. —*v.t.* **4.** to make or produce by hand or machinery, esp. on a large scale. **5.** to make anything. **6.** to work up (material) into form for use. **7.** to invent fictitiously; concoct; devise. **8.** to produce by mere mechanical industry without inspiration. [t. F, f. L: *manū,* abl. of *manus* hand + m. *factūra* a making] —**man′ufac′turing,** *n.*

—**Syn.** **4.** MANUFACTURE, ASSEMBLE, FABRICATE apply to processes in industry. MANUFACTURE, originally to make by hand, now means to make by machine or by industrial process: *to manufacture rubber tyres.* To ASSEMBLE is to fit together the manufactured parts of something mechanical: *to assemble a motor vehicle.* To FABRICATE is to construct or build by fitting standardized parts together: *to fabricate houses.* See **make.**

manufacturer (măn′yo͞o făk′chə rə), *n.* **1.** one who owns or runs a manufacturing plant. **2.** one who manufactures.

manuka (mä′no͞o kə), *n.* a small, erect, evergreen, myrtaceous shrub, *Leptospermum scoparium,* a native of New Zealand, sometimes cultivated but slow-growing. [t. Maori]

manumission (măn′yo͞o mĭsh′ən), *n.* **1.** the act of manumitting. **2.** the state of being manumitted.

manumit (măn′yo͞o mĭt′), *v.t.,* **-mitted, -mitting.** to release from slavery or servitude. [t. L: m. s. *manūmittere*] —**man′umit′ter,** *n.*

manure (mə nyo͞oə′), *n., v.,* **-nured, -nuring.** —*n.* **1.** any natural or artificial substance for fertilizing the soil. **2.** excrement, esp. of animals used as fertilizer. —*v.t.* **3.** to treat (land) with fertilizing matter; apply manure to. [ME *maynour(en),* v. t. AF: m. *maynoverer* work by hand, der. OF *manuevre.* See MANOEUVRE, n.] —**manur′er,** *n.*

manus (mā′nəs), *n., pl.* **-nus.** **1.** *Anat.* the distal segment of the forelimb of a vertebrate, including the carpus and the forefoot or hand. **2.** *Rom. Law.* power over persons, as that of the husband over the wife. [t. L: hand]

manuscript (măn′yo͞o skrĭpt′), *n.* **1.** a book, document, letter, musical score, etc., written by hand. **2.** an author's copy of his work, written by hand or typewriter, which is used as the basis for typesetting. **3.** writing, as distinguished from print. —*adj.* **4.** written by hand or typed (not printed). [t. ML: s. *manūscriptus,* lit., hand-written] —**man′uscript′al,** *adj.*

Manutius (mə nyo͞o′shyəs), *n.* **Aldus** (ôl′dəs) (*Aldo Manuzio*), 1450–1515, Italian printer.

manward (măn′wəd), *adv.* **1.** Also, **manwards.** towards man. —*adj.* **2.** directed towards man.

Manx (măngks), *adj.* **1.** of or pertaining to the Isle of Man, its inhabitants, or their language. —*n.* **2.** (*construed as pl.*) the inhabitants of the Isle of Man. **3.** the Gaelic of the Isle of Man, virtually extinct. [metathetic and syncopated form of earlier *Maniske*]

manx cat, a tailless variety of the domestic cat.

Manxman (măngks′mən), *n., pl.* **-men.** a native or inhabitant of the Isle of Man.

many (mĕn′ĭ), *adj.,* **more, most.** **1.** constituting or forming a large number: *many people.* **2.** relatively numerous (after *as, so, too,* or *how*): *six may be too many.* **3.** being one of a large number (fol. by *a* or *an*): *many a day.* —*n.* **4.** a great or considerable number (often followed by a noun with *of* expressed or understood): *a great many people.* **5.** (as a collective plural) many persons or things. **6. a good (great) many,** a large number. [ME *mani, manye,* etc., OE *manig,* c. G *manch*]

—**Syn.** **1.** multifarious, multitudinous, myriad. MANY, INNUMERABLE, MANIFOLD, NUMEROUS imply the presence or succession of a large number of units. MANY is a popular and common word for this idea: *many times.* NUMEROUS, a more formal word, refers to a great number, or to containing very many units: *suggestions too numerous to mention.* INNUMERABLE denotes number that is beyond count, or, more loosely, what is extremely difficult to count: *the innumerable stars in the sky.* MANIFOLD implies not only that the number is large but also that there is variety or complexity. —**Ant.** **1.** few, single.

manyplies (mĕn′ĭ plīz′), *n.* *Zool.* the omasum (so called from the many plies or folds of its membrane). [f. MANY + *plies,* pl. of PLY²]

many-sided (mĕn′ĭ sī′dĭd), *adj.* **1.** having many sides. **2.** having many aspects, capabilities, etc.: *a many-sided man.* —**man′y-sid′edness,** *n.*

manzanilla (măn′zə nĭl′ə; *Sp.* män thä nē′lyä), *n.* a pale, very dry Spanish sherry.

Manzoni (*It.* män dzô′nē), *n.* **Alessandro** (*It.* ä lĕs sän′drô), 1785–1873, Italian novelist and poet.

Maori (mou′rĭ, mä′rĭ), *n., pl.* **-ris,** (*esp. collectively*) **-ri,** *adj.* —*n.* **1.** a member of a brown-skinned Polynesian people of New Zealand. **2.** a Polynesian language, the language of the Maoris. —*adj.* **3.** of or pertaining to the Maoris or their language.

Maori chief, a flathead of New Zealand, *Notothena macrocephalus,* with markings resembling a tattoo: usually found in waters below freezing point. Also, **ice fish.**

Mao Tse-tung (mou′tsā to͝ong′), born 1893, Chinese statesman: chairman of the Communist Party since 1943.

map (măp), *n., v.,* **mapped, mapping.** —*n.* **1.** a representation, on a flat surface, of a part or the whole of the earth's surface, the heavens, or a heavenly body. **2.** a maplike representation of anything. **3. off the map,** out of existence, into oblivion: *whole cities were wiped off the map.* **4. put on the map,** to make widely known; make famous. —*v.t.* **5.** to represent or delineate in or as in a map. **6.** to sketch or plan (often fol. by *out*): *to map out a new career.* [t. ML: m. s. *mappa* (*mundī*) map (of the world), in L *mappa* napkin]

—**Syn.** **1.** MAP, CHART, GRAPH refer to representations of surfaces, areas, or facts. MAP most commonly refers to a representation of the surface of the earth or a section of it, or an area of the sky: *a map of England.* A CHART may be an outline map with symbols conveying information superimposed on it, a map designed esp. for navigators on water or in the air, a diagram, or a table giving information in an orderly form: *a chart of the shoals off a coast.* A GRAPH may be a diagram representing a set of interrelated facts by means of dots or lines on a coordinate background; or it may use small figures (people, animals, machines, etc.) appropriate to the facts being represented, each figure standing for a specific number in statistics being given: *a graph of the rise in population from 1900–40.*

Map (măp), *n.* **Walter,** *c.* 1140–*c.* 1209, Welsh ecclesiastic and author. Also, **Mapes** (măps, mā′pēz).

maple (mā′pl), *n.* **1.** any tree of the genus *Acer,* of the north temperate zone, species of which are valued for shade and ornament, for their wood, or for their sap, from which a syrup (**maple syrup**) and a sugar (**maple sugar**) are obtained. **2.** the wood of any such tree. [ME *mapel,* OE *mapel-* in *mapeltrēow* maple tree]

map projection, projection (def. 5).

maquis (*Fr.* mȧ kē′), *n., sing. and pl.* (*often cap.*) a member of one of the French underground groups resisting the Germans in World War II. [F, special use of *maquis, makis* wild, bushy land (Corsican d.)]

mar (mä), *v.t.,* **marred, marring.** **1.** to damage; impair; ruin. **2.** to disfigure; deface. [ME *marre,* OE *merran* hinder, waste, c. OHG *merren,* OS *merrian* hinder]

—**Syn.** **1, 2.** spoil, injure; blot. MAR, DEFACE, DISFIGURE, DEFORM agree in applying to some form of injury. MAR is general, but usually refers to an external or surface injury, if it is a physical one: *the table top was marred by dents and scratches.* DEFACE refers to a surface injury which may be temporary or easily repaired: *a tablecloth defaced by pencilled notations.* DISFIGURE applies to external injury of a more permanent and serious kind: *a birthmark disfigured one side of his face.* DEFORM suggests that something has been distorted or internally injured so severely as to change its normal form or qualities, or that some fault has interfered with its proper development: *deformed by an accident which had crippled him, to deform feet by binding them.* —**Ant.** **2.** enhance, adorn.

Mar., March.

mar., **1.** maritime. **2.** married.

marabou (mă′rə bo͞o′), *n.* **1.** any of three large storks, *Leptoptilus crumeniferus* of Africa, *L. dubius,* the adjutant bird, and *L. javanicus* of the East Indies, having

Marabou, *Leptoptilus crumeniferus* (Ab. 5 ft high)

under the wings and tail soft, downy feathers that are used in millinery and for making a furlike trimming or material. **2.** one of the feathers. **3.** the trimming or material made of them. Also, **marabout.** [t. F: m. *marabout*, orig. a Muslim hermit]

maraca (mə răk′ə), *n.* a gourd filled with pebbles, seeds, etc., and used as a percussion instrument in Latin-American bands.

Maracaibo (mă′rə kī′bō; *Sp.* mä rä kāy′bō), *n.* **1.** a seaport in NW Venezuela. 421,166 (1961). **2. Gulf of,** a gulf on the NW coast of Venezuela. **3. Lake,** a lake in NW Venezuela, connected with the gulf. ab. 100 mi. long; ab. 75 mi. wide.

Maracay (*Sp.* mä rä kāy′), *n.* a town in N Venezuela. 135,353 (1961).

Marajó (*Port.* mä rä zhō′), *n.* an island at the mouth of the Amazon in N Brazil. ab. 20,000 sq. mi.

Marañón (*Sp.* mä rä nyōn′), *n.* a river flowing from W Peru N and then E, joining the Ucayali to form the Amazon. ab. 1000 mi.

Maras (*Turk.* mä′räsh), *n.* a town in S central Turkey. 54,447 (1960).

marasca (mə răs′kə), *n.* a wild cherry, *Prunus cerasus* var. *marasca*, with small, acid, bitter fruit, from which maraschino is made.

maraschino (mă′rə skē′nō), *n.* a cordial or liqueur distilled from marascas. [t. It., der. (*a*)*marasca* kind of cherry, der. *amaro* bitter, g. L *amārus*]

maraschino cherry, a cherry cooked in coloured syrup and flavoured with imitation maraschino.

marasmus (mə răz′məs), *n. Pathol.* gradual loss of flesh and strength, as from malnutrition, old age, etc., rather than from actual disease. [NL, t. Gk: m. *marasmós* a wasting] —**maras′mic,** *adj.*

Marat (*Fr.* mä rä′), *n.* **Jean Paul** (*Fr.* zhäN pōl′), 1743–93, French revolutionary politician; assassinated by Charlotte Corday.

Maratha (mə rä′tə), *n.* a member of a Hindu people inhabiting central and western India. Also, **Mahratta.** [t. Hind.: m. *marhatá*]

Maratha Confederacy, a loose league of states in central and western India, broken up in 1818.

Marathi (mə rä′tĭ), *n.* the language of the Marathas; an Indic language of western India. Also, **Mahratti.**

marathon (mă′rə thən), *n.* **1.** any long-distance race. **2.** a foot race of about 26 miles. **3.** any long contest with endurance as the primary factor: *a dance marathon.* **4.** (*cap.*) a plain in Attica, ab. 20 mi. NE of Athens, Greece: the Athenians defeated the Persians there, 490 B.C. **5.** (*cap.*) an ancient village near this plain. [defs 1–3 from the messenger's running to Athens to carry news of the Greek victory over the Persians (see def. 4)] —**mar′athoner,** *n.*

Marathon (def. 5)

Marathonian (mă′rə thō′nyən), *adj.* **1.** of or pertaining to Marathon. —*n.* **2.** a native or inhabitant of Marathon.

maraud (mə rôd′), *v.i.* **1.** to rove in quest of plunder; make a raid for booty. —*v.t.* **2.** to raid for plunder. —*n.* **3.** the act of marauding. [t. F: s. *marauder*, der. *maraud* rogue, vagabond] —**maraud′er,** *n.* —**maraud′ing,** *adj.*

maravedi (mă′rə vā′dĭ), *n., pl.* **-dis. 1.** a former gold coin struck by the Moors in Spain. **2.** an obsolete Spanish copper coin unit of low value. [t. Sp., t. Ar.: m. *Murābitin* name of the Moorish dynasty of the Almoravides (11th and 12th centuries), pl. of *murābiṭ* member of a religious order]

marble (mä′bl), *n., adj., v.,* **-bled, -bling.** —*n.* **1.** limestone in a more or less crystalline state and capable of taking a polish, occurring in a wide range of colours and variegations, and much used in sculpture and architecture. **2.** a variety of this stone. **3.** a piece of this stone. **4.** a work of art carved in marble. **5.** a marbled appearance or pattern; marbling. **6.** something resembling marble in hardness, coldness, smoothness, etc. **7.** *Games.* **a.** a little ball of stone, baked clay, glass, etc., used in a children's game. **b.** (*pl. construed as sing.*) the game itself. —*adj.* **8.** consisting of marble. **9.** like marble, as being hard, cold, unfeeling, etc. **10.** of variegated or mottled colour. —*v.t.* **11.** to colour or stain like a variegated marble. [dissimilated var. of ME *marbre*, t. OF, g. L *marmor*]

Marble Arch, 1. an ornamental gateway near the NE entrance to Hyde Park, London. **2.** the district adjacent to it.

marble cake, a cake given a marble-like appearance by the use of combinations of dark and light mixture.

marbling (mä′blĭng), *n.* **1.** the act, process, or art of colouring or staining in imitation of variegated marble. **2.** an appearance like that of variegated marble. **3.** *Bookbinding.* marble-like decoration on the paper edges, lining, or binding boards of a book.

marbly (mä′blĭ), *adj.* rigid, cold, etc., like marble.

Marburg (mä′bûg; *Ger.* mär′bo͝ork), *n.* a town in central West Germany. 47,800 (1963).

marc (mäk; *Fr.* mär), *n.* **1.** the grapes contained in the winepress, and the residue (skins and pips) remaining after the juice is expressed. **2.** the brandy distilled from grape pomace. [t. F, der. *marcher* treat, press]

Marc (*Ger.* märk), *n.* **Franz** (*Ger.* fränts), 1880–1916, German expressionist painter.

marcasite (mä′kə sīt′), *n.* **1.** a common mineral (**white iron pyrites**), iron disulphide (FeS_2), of the same composition as pyrite, but differing in crystal system. **2.** (formerly) any of the crystallized forms of iron pyrites, much used in the 18th century for ornaments. **3.** a specimen or ornament of this substance. [t. ML: m. s. *marcasita*, t. Ar.: m. *marqashitā*, from Aram.]

Marceau (*Fr.* mär sō′), *n.* **Marcel** (*Fr.* mär sĕl′), born 1923, French actor and mime.

marcel (mä sĕl′), *v.,* **-celled, -celling,** *n.* —*v.t.* **1.** to wave (the hair) by means of special irons, producing the effect of regular, continuous waves (**marcel waves**). —*n.* **2.** a marcelling. **3.** a marcelled condition. [from *Marcel Grateau*, 1852–1936, French hairdresser, the originator]

Marcellus (mä sĕl′əs), *n.* **Marcus Claudius** (mä′kəs klô′dyəs), 268?–208 B.C., Roman general in the second Punic War.

marcescent (mä sĕs′ənt), *adj. Bot.* withering but not falling off, as a part of a plant. [t. L: s. *marcescens*, ppr., withering] —**marces′cence,** *n.*

march[1] (mäch), *v.i.* **1.** to walk with regular and measured tread, as soldiers; advance in step in an organized body. **2.** to walk in a stately or deliberate manner. **3.** to proceed; advance. —*v.t.* **4.** to cause to march. —*n.* **5.** the act or course of marching. **6.** the distance traversed in a single course of marching. **7.** advance; forward movement: *the march of progress.* **8.** a piece of music with a rhythm suited to accompany marching. **9. steal a march,** to gain an advantage secretly or slyly (often fol. by *on* or *upon*). [t. F: s. *marcher* walk, march, go, earlier trample, der. L *marcus* hammer]

march[2] (mäch), *n.* **1.** a tract of land along a border of a country; frontier. **2.** (*pl.*) the border district between England and Wales. —*v.i.* **3.** to touch at the border; border (fol. by *upon, with,* etc.). [ME *marche*, t. OF, t. Gmc; cf. OHG *marka*]

March (mäch), *n.* the third month of the year, containing 31 days. [ME, t. AF: m. *marche*, c. OF *marz*, g. L *Martius*, lit., month of Mars]

March (*Ger.* märKH), *n.* German name of the **Morava.**

March., Marchioness.

M.Arch., Master of Architecture.

Märchen (*Ger.* mĕr′KHən), *n. German.* fairy story; folktale.

marcher[1] (mä′chə), *n.* one who marches (on foot). [f. MARCH[1] + -ER[1]]

marcher[2] (mä′chə), *n. Hist.* an inhabitant of, or an officer or lord having jurisdiction over, marches or border territory. [f. MARCH[2] + -ER[1]]

Marches (mä′chĭz), *n.* **The,** a region in central Italy, on the Adriatic. 1,347,234 pop. (1961); 3743 sq. mi. *Cap.:* Ancona. Italian, **Le Marche** (*It.* lĕ mär′kĕ).

marchesa (*It.* mär kĕ′zä), *n., pl.* **-se** (*It.* -zĕ). *Italian.* marchioness. [It., fem. of *marchese*]

marchese (*It.* mär kĕ′zĕ), *n., pl.* **-si** (*It.* -zē). *Italian.* marquess.

march fracture, *Med.* fracture of the 2nd, 3rd, or 4th metatarsal bones, occurring after unaccustomed walking or marching.

March hare, a hare in the month of March, the breeding season, proverbially taken as a type of scatterbrained frivolity.

Marcheshvan (mä KHĕsh′văn), *n.* Heshvan.

marching orders, 1. *Mil.* directions to soldiers to proceed in order to take position for battle, etc.: *the brigade received its marching orders shortly after the general's visit.* **2.** *Colloq.* orders to leave; dismissal (from a job, etc.).

marchioness (mä′shə nĭs, mä′shə nĕs′), *n.* **1.** the wife or widow of a marquess. **2.** a lady holding in her own right the rank equal to that of a marquess. [t. ML: m. s. *marchiōnissa*, fem. of *marchio* MARQUESS]

marchpane (mäch′pān′), *n. Obs.* marzipan. [t. F, d. var. of *massepain, marcepain,* t. It.: m. *marzapane,* orig. box of sweets, t. Ar.: m. *martabân* glazed vessel]

march-past (mäch′päst′), *n.* a ceremonial parade or procession, esp. of troops past a saluting base.

Marcionite (mä′shə nīt′), *n.* **1.** an adherent of a 2nd-century heretical sect, which found perfection only in Jesus Christ, regarding all matter pre-existing His incarnation as imperfect and without merit. —*adj.* **2.** of or pertaining to the Marcionites or their doctrines. Also, **Marcionist** (mä′shə nĭst), *n.*

Marconi (mä kō′nĭ; *It.* mȧr kô′nē), *n.* **Guglielmo** (*It.* go͞ol lyĕl′mô), 1874–1937, Italian inventor of the first successful wireless telegraph.

Marco Polo (mä′kō pō′lō). See **Polo, Marco.**

Marcos (mä′kōs), *n.* **Ferdinand** (fû′dĭ nənd), president of the Philippines since 1966.

Marcus Aurelius (mä′kəs ô rē′lyəs) (*Marcus Aurelius Antoninus*), A.D. 121–180, emperor of Rome A.D. 161–180: Stoic philosopher and writer.

Marcuse (mä kyo͞os′), *n.* **Herbert,** born 1898, U.S. political sociologist, born in Germany. —**Marcu′sian,** *adj., n.*

Marcy (mä′sĭ), *n.* **Mount,** a mountain in NE New York, the highest peak of the Adirondack Mountains. 5344 ft.

Mar de Plata (*Sp.* mȧr′ dĕl plȧ′tȧ), a town in E Argentina. 141,886 (est. 1958).

Mardi gras (mä′dĭ grä′), Shrove Tuesday; the last day of carnival: celebrated in Paris, New Orleans, etc., with special festivities. [t. F: meat-eating Tuesday]

Marduk (mä′do͝ok), *n. Babylonian Relig.* the chief of the Babylonian deities. [t. Babylonian]

mardy (mä′dĭ), *adj. Dial.* naughty; mischievous or recalcitrant.

mare[1] (mĕə), *n.* a fully grown female horse. [ME *mare, mere,* OE *mere, myre* (c. Icel. *merr*), fem. of *mearh* horse (c. OHG *marah,* Icel. *marr*). Cf. MARSHAL]

mare[2] (mĕə), *n. Obs.* **1.** the evil spirit supposed to cause bad dreams. **2.** nightmare. [ME and OE, c. Icel. *mara*]

mare[3] (mä′rā), *n., pl.* **maria** (mä′rĭ ə). *Astron.* **1.** any of several large, dark plains on the moon. **2.** any of several dark areas on the planet Mars. [t. L: sea]

mare clausum (mä′rā klou′ro͝om), *Latin.* a closed sea (within the jurisdiction of a particular nation).

mare liberum (mä′rā lē′bə ro͝om), *Latin.* an open sea (to which all countries have unrestricted access).

maremma (mə rĕm′ə), *n., pl.* **-remme** (-rĕm′ē). **1.** a marshy, unhealthy region near the seashore, as in Italy. **2.** the miasma associated with such a region. [t. It., g. L *maritima,* fem. of *maritimus* maritime]

Marengo (mə rĕng′gō), *n.* a village in NW Italy, in Piedmont. Napoleon defeated the Austrians here, 1800.

mare nostrum (mä′rā nŏs′tro͝om), *Latin.* our sea (esp. the Mediterranean, to the Romans and Italians).

mare's-nest (mĕəz′nĕst′), *n.* something imagined to be an extraordinary discovery but proving to be a delusion or a hoax.

mare's-tail (mĕəz′tāl′), *n.* **1.** an erect aquatic Old World plant, *Hippuris vulgaris,* with crowded whorls of narrow, hairlike leaves. **2.** a cirrus cloud resembling a horse's tail.

Margaret of Anjou (mä′gə rĭt, -grĭt), 1430–82, queen of England, wife of Henry VI.

Margaret of Navarre, 1492–1549, queen of Navarre 1544–49, patron of literature, author of stories and poems.

Margaret of Valois, 1553–1615, first queen of Henry IV of France.

margaric acid (mä găr′ĭk), *Chem.* a white fatty acid, $CH_3(CH_2)_{15}COOH$, resembling stearic acid and obtained from lichens or synthetically. [f. s. Gk *márgaron* pearl + -IC]

margarine (mä′jə rēn′), *n.* **1.** a butter-like product made by emulsifying refined vegetable oils in cultured skimmed milk. **2.** oleomargarine. Also, **margarin** (mä′jə rĭn, mä′jə rēn′). [t. F: f. s. Gk *márgaron* white of pearl + *-ine* -INE[2]]

margarite (mä′gə rīt′), *n.* **1.** an aggregate of small crystals, found in a bead-like row in some glassy igneous rocks. **2.** a mineral, hydrated aluminium calcium silicate, occurring in grey or yellow monoclinic crystals.

Margate (mä′gĭt), *n.* a seaside resort in England, in Kent. 45,780 (1961).

margay (mä′gā′), *n.* a small tiger cat, *Felis wiedi,* of tropical America. [t. F: m. *margai,* t. Pg.: m. *maracajá,* t. Tupi: m. *mbaracajá*]

marge[1] (mäj), *n. Poetic.* margin.

marge[2] (mäj), *n. Colloq.* margarine.

margent (mä′jənt), *n. Archaic.* margin.

margin (mä′jĭn), *n.* **1.** a border or edge. **2.** the space bordering the printed or written matter on a page. **3.** a limit, or a condition, etc., beyond which something ceases to exist or be possible: *the margin of consciousness.* **4.** an amount allowed or available beyond what is actually necessary: *a margin of error.* **5.** *Finance.* **a.** a security, as a percentage in money, deposited with a broker as a provision against loss on transactions on behalf of his principal. **b.** the amount representing the customer's investment or equity in such an account. **6.** *Com.* the difference between the cost and the selling price. **7.** *Econ.* the point at which the return from economic activity barely covers the cost of production, and below which production is unprofitable. **8.** *Banking.* the excess value of the relative security over the loan for which it is collateral. —*v.t.* **9.** to provide with a margin or border. **10.** to furnish with marginal notes, as a document. **11.** to enter in the margin, as of a book. **12.** *Finance.* to deposit a margin upon. [ME *margyn,* t. L: m. s. *margo* border, edge] —**Syn. 1.** See **edge.**

marginal (mä′jĭ nəl), *adj.* **1.** pertaining to a margin. **2.** situated on the border or edge. **3.** written or printed in the margin of a page: *a marginal note.* **4.** minimal for requirements; barely sufficient. **5.** *Econ.* **a.** supplying goods at a rate merely covering the cost of production. **b.** of or pertaining to goods produced and marketed at margin: *marginal profits.* **6.** denoting or pertaining to an electoral division in which a poll is likely to result in victory by a narrow margin. **7.** (of land) difficult and unprofitable to cultivate. [t. NL: s. *marginālis,* der. L *margo* MARGIN] —**mar′ginally,** *adv.*

marginalia (mä′jĭ nā′lyə), *n.pl.* marginal notes. [NL]

marginal man, *Sociol.* a person who lives on the margins of two cultural groups, but identifies with neither.

marginate (mä′jĭ nāt′), *adj., v.,* **-nated, -nating.** —*adj.* Also, **mar′ginat′ed. 1.** having a margin. **2.** *Entomol.* having the margin of a distinct colour: *marginate with purple.* —*v.t.* **3.** to furnish with a margin; border. [t. L: m. s. *margināt̄us,* pp.] —**mar′gina′tion,** *n.*

margravate (mä′grə vĭt), *n.* the province of a margrave. Also, **margraviate** (mä grā′vĭ ĭt).

margrave (mä′grāv′), *n.* **1.** the hereditary title of the rulers of certain states. **2.** *Hist.* a hereditary German title, equivalent to *marquess.* **3.** (orig.) a German military governor of a mark, or border province. [t. MD: m. *markgrave* mark or border count]

margravine (mä′grə vēn′), *n.* the wife of a margrave.

marguerite (mä′gə rēt′), *n.* **1.** the common European daisy, *Bellis perennis.* **2.** any of several flowers of the daisy kind, esp. *Chrysanthemum frutescens,* cultivated for its numerous white-rayed, yellow-centred flowers. [t. F: daisy, pearl, t. L: m. *margarita* pearl]

Marheshvan (mä hĕsh′văn), *n.* Heshvan.

mariage de convenance (*Fr.* mȧ ryȧzh′ də kôɴ vnäɴs′), *French.* a marriage of convenience or expediency, usually for money or position.

Marian (mĕə′rĭ ən), *adj.* **1.** of or pertaining to the Virgin Mary. **2.** of or pertaining to some other Mary, as Mary, queen of England, or Mary, queen of Scots. —*n.* **3.** one who has a particular devotion to the Virgin Mary. **4.** an adherent or defender of Mary, Queen of Scots.

Marianao (*Sp.* mȧ ryȧ nȧ′ô), *n.* a city in NW Cuba, near Havana. 229,576 (1960).

Mariana Islands (mă′rĭ ä′nə), a group of fifteen small islands in the Pacific, E of the Philippine Islands: formerly mandated to Japan (except Guam); now under U.S. trusteeship. 10,275 pop. (1964); 453 sq. mi. Also, **Marianas.** Formerly, **Ladrone Islands, Ladrone.**

Marianne (*Fr.* mȧ rē ȧn′), *n.* a popular name for the French Republic personified.

Mariánske Lázně (*Cz.* mȧ′ryȧn skĕ lȧz′nyĕ). See **Marienbad.**

Maria Theresa (mə rē′ə tə rā′zə), 1717–80, archduchess of Austria, queen of Hungary and Bohemia 1740–80. German, **Maria Theresia** (*Ger.* mȧ rē′ȧ tĕ rē′zē ȧ).

Maria Theresa thaler, Levant dollar.

Maribor (mă′rĭ bô′), *n.* a town in N Yugoslavia on the river Drava. 85,144 (1961).

Marie Antoinette (mä′rĭ ŏn′twə nĕt′; *Fr.* mȧ rē äɴ twȧ-nĕt′), 1755–93, queen of France 1774–93; wife of Louis XVI and daughter of Maria Theresa; executed in the French Revolution.

Marie Byrd Land (mä′rĭ bûd′), a part of Antarctica, SE of the Ross Sea: discovered and explored by Adm. Richard E. Byrd; claimed by the U.S.

Marie Galante (*Fr.* mȧ rē gȧ läɴt′), an island in the E West Indies: a dependency of Guadeloupe. 16,341 pop. (1962); 58 sq. mi.

Marie Louise (mä′rĭ lo͞o ēz′; *Fr.* mȧ rē lwēz′), 1791–1847, empress of France, second wife of Napoleon I.

Marienbad (mə rĭən′băd; *Ger.* mȧ rē′ən bȧt), *n.* a spa and resort town in W Czechoslovakia, in Bohemia. 12,813 (1964). Czech, **Mariánske Lázně.**

marigold (mă′rĭ gōld′), *n.* **1.** any of the various chiefly golden-flowered plants esp. of the composite genus *Tagetes*, as *T. erecta*, with strong-scented foliage. See also **marsh marigold. 2.** any of various other plants, esp. of the asteraceous genus *Calendula*, as *C. officinalis*, a common garden plant of some use in dyeing and medicine. [ME, f. MARY (the Virgin) + GOLD]

marigraph (mă′rĭ grăf′, -gräf′), *n.* a device for registering the rise and fall of the tide.

marijuana (mä′rĭ yo͞o ä′nə), *n.* **1.** the Indian hemp, *Cannabis sativa*. **2.** its dried leaves and flowers, used in cigarettes as a narcotic. Also, **marihuana.** [t. Amer. Sp.; ? native word, b. with name *Maria Juana* Mary Jane]

marimba (mə rĭm′bə), *n.* a musical instrument, originating in Africa but popularized and modified in Central America, formed of strips of wood of various sizes (often having resonators beneath to reinforce the sound), struck by hammers or sticks. [t. an E African lang. (cf. Chopi *mbila*)]

Marimba

marina (mə rē′nə), *n.* a boat basin offering dockage and other service for small craft. [It. and Sp.: of the sea]

marinade (*n.* mă′rĭ nād′; *v.* mă′rĭ nād′), *n.*, *v.*, **-naded, -nading.** —*n.* **1.** a seasoned liquid, esp. of vinegar or wine with oil, spices, etc., to steep meat, fish, vegetables, etc., in before cooking. **2.** meat or fish steeped in it. —*v.t.* **3.** to marinate. [t. F, der. *mariner* pickle in brine, der. *marin* MARINE]

marinate (mă′rĭ nāt′), *v.t.*, **-nated, -nating. 1.** to let stand in a seasoned vinegar–oil mixture; marinade. **2.** to apply French dressing to (a salad). [f. s. F *mariner* (see MARINADE) + -ATE¹] —**mar′ina′tion,** *n.*

Marinduque (mä′rĭn do͞o′kĭ), *n.* one of the Philippine Islands, between Luzon and Mindoro islands. 1107,150 pop. (est. 1960); 347 sq. mi.

marine (mə rēn′), *adj.* **1.** of or pertaining to the sea; existing in or produced by the sea. **2.** pertaining to navigation or shipping; nautical; naval; maritime. **3.** serving on shipboard, as soldiers. **4.** of or belonging to the marines. **5.** adapted for use at sea: *a marine barometer.* —*n.* **6.** seagoing vessels collectively, esp. with reference to nationality or class; shipping in general. **7.** one of a class of naval troops serving both on shipboard and on land. **8.** a picture with a marine subject. **9.** naval affairs, or the department of a government (as in France) having to do with such affairs. **10. tell it** (or **that**) **to the marines!** (an expression of disbelief, esp. at an unlikely story.) [ME *maryne*, t. F: m. *marin* (fem. *marine*), g. L *marinus* of the sea]

marine insurance, insurance covering loss or damage to maritime property occasioned by any of the numerous perils on and of the sea.

mariner (mă′rĭ nə), *n.* one who directs or assists in the navigation of a ship; seaman; sailor. [ME, t. AF, der. F *marin* MARINE] —**Syn.** See **sailor.**

Mariolatry (mēə′rĭ ŏl′ə trĭ), *n.* (in opprobrious use) excessive veneration of the Virgin Mary. [f. m. MARY + -OLATRY]—**Mar′iol′ater,** *n.* —**Mar′iol′atrous,** *adj.*

Mariology (mēə′rĭ ŏl′ə jĭ), *n.* the body of belief, doctrine, and opinion concerning the Virgin Mary.

marionette (mă′rĭ ə nĕt′), *n.* a puppet moved by strings attached to its jointed limbs. [t. F, der. *Marion*, dim. of *Marie* Mary]

mariposa lily (mă′rĭ pō′zə, -sə), any of the plants constituting the liliaceous genus *Calochortus*, of the western U.S. and Mexico, having tulip-like flowers of various colours. Also, **mariposa tulip.** [t. Sp.: *mariposa* butterfly, ult. der. *posar* to rest, g. L *pausāre*]

marish (mă′rĭsh), *Archaic or Poetic.* —*n.* **1.** a marsh. —*adj.* **2.** marshy. [ME *mareis*, t. OF. See MORASS]

Marist (mēə′rĭst), *n.* *Rom. Cath. Ch.* a member of the 'Society of Mary', founded in 1816 for missionary and educational work in the name of the Virgin Mary.

Maritain (*Fr.* mȧ rē tăɴ′), *n.* **Jacques** (*Fr.* zhȧk), born 1882, French philosopher and diplomat.

marital (mă′rĭ tl, mə rī′tl), *adj.* **1.** of or pertaining to marriage. **2.** of or pertaining to a husband. [t. L: s. *marītālis* pertaining to married people] —**mar′itally,** *adv.*

maritime (mă′rĭ tīm′), *adj.* **1.** connected with the sea in relation to navigation, shipping, etc.: *maritime law.* **2.** of or pertaining to the sea. **3.** bordering on the sea. **4.** living near the sea. **5.** characteristic of a seaman; nautical. [t. L: m. s. *maritimus* of the sea]

Maritime Alps, a range of the Alps in SE France and NW Italy.

maritime climate, a type of climate characterized by little temperature change, high cloud cover, and precipitation, and associated with coastal areas.

maritime pine, a tall conifer with large cones, *Pinus pinaster*, a native of W and SW Europe on sandy soils near the sea, naturalized in SW England.

Maritime Provinces, the Canadian provinces of Nova Scotia, New Brunswick, and Prince Edward Island.

Maritsa (*Bulg.* mȧ rēt′sȧ), *n.* a river flowing from S Bulgaria along the boundary between Greece and European Turkey into the Aegean. ab. 300 mi.

Mariupol (*Russ.* mə rĭ o͞o′pəly), *n.* Zhdanov.

Marius (mēə′rĭ əs, mă′rĭ əs), *n.* **Gaius** (gī′əs), *c.* 155–86 B.C., Roman general and consul: opponent of Sulla.

Marivaux (*Fr.* mȧ rē vō′), *n.* **Pierre Carlet de Chamblain de** (*Fr.* pyĕr kȧr lĕ′ də shäɴ blăɴ′ də), 1688–1763, French novelist and dramatist.

marjoram (mä′jə rəm), *n.* any plant of the mint family of the genera *Origanum* or *Majorana*, esp. the species *M. hortensis* (**sweet marjoram**) used in cookery, or *O. vulgare*, a wild species native in Europe and naturalized in North America. [ME *majorane*, t. OF, ult. der. L *amāracus*]

mark¹ (mäk), *n.* **1.** a visible trace or impression upon anything, as a line, cut, dent, stain, bruise, etc.: *a birthmark.* **2.** a badge, brand, or other visible sign assumed or imposed. **3.** a symbol used in writing or printing: *a punctuation mark.* **4.** a sign, usually a cross, made by an illiterate person by way of signature. **5.** an affixed or impressed device, symbol, inscription, etc., serving to give information, identify, indicate origin or ownership, attest to character or comparative merit, or the like. **6.** a sign, token, or indication. **7.** a symbol used in rating conduct, proficiency, attainment, etc., as of pupils in a school. **8.** something serving as an indication of position, as a bookmark. **9.** a recognized or required standard: *to be below the mark.* **10.** repute; note; importance, or distinction: *a man of mark.* **11.** a distinctive trait. **12.** (*usually cap.*) a designation for a model of a weapon, an item of military equipment, a motor vehicle, or the like, generally used together with a numeral: *the Mark-4 weapon-carrier.* **13.** an object aimed at, as a target. **14.** an object or end desired or striven for, as a goal. **15.** an object of derision, scorn, hostile schemes, swindling, etc.: *an easy mark.* **16.** *Athletics.* the starting point allotted to a contestant. **17.** *Boxing.* the middle of the stomach. **18.** *Bowls.* See **jack¹** (def. 7). **19.** (on a nautical lead line) one of the measured indications of depth, consisting of a white, blue, or red rag, a bit of leather, or a knot of small line. **20.** a tract of land held in common by a medieval community of freemen. **21.** *Obs. except Hist. and Archaic.* a boundary; frontier. **22.** *Rugby Football.* the place from which a free kick or a penalty kick is taken. **23. beside the mark,** irrelevant. **24. make one's mark,** to become famous or successful. **25. on your mark** or **marks!** (addressed to competitors at the beginning of a race) take your places! **26. up to the mark,** of the required standard. **27. wide of the mark,** inaccurate; irrelevant. —*v.t.* **28.** to be a distinguishing feature of: *a day marked by rain.* **29.** to put a mark or marks on. **30.** to attach or affix to (something) figures or signs indicating price, quality, brand name, etc. **31.** to trace or form by or as by marks (often fol. by *out*). **32.** to indicate or designate by or as by marks. **33.** to single out; destine (often fol. by *out*). **34.** to record, as a score. **35.** to make manifest. **36.** to give heed or attention to. **37.** to notice or observe. **38.** *Sport.* to observe and keep close to (an opponent) with the intention of obtaining advantage.
—*v.i.* **39.** to take notice; give attention; consider.
—*v.* **40.** Some special verb phrases are:
mark down, to reduce the price of.
mark off, to separate, as by a line or boundary.
mark time, 1. to suspend advance or progress temporarily, as while awaiting development. **2.** *Mil.* to move the feet alternately as in marching, but without advancing.
mark up, 1. to mark with notations or symbols. **2.** to increase the price of.
[ME; OE *mearc* boundary, landmark, c. G *Mark*; akin to L *margo* border] —**Syn. 11.** characteristic, feature.

mark² (mäk), *n.* **1.** a former silver coin of Germany, until 1924 the monetary unit. **2.** Deutsche Mark. **3.** Reichsmark. **4. Mark der Deutschen Notenbank,** the monetary unit of East Germany, equal to 100 pfennig, and equivalent to about £0·187 sterling. *Abbrev.:* MDN. **5.** markka. **6.** a former money of account of England, originally worth 13*s.* 4*d.* **7.** an obsolete silver coin of Scotland, originally worth 13*s.* 4*d.* **8.** a former European unit of weight, esp. for gold and silver, generally equal to 8 ounces. [ME; OE *m(e)arc*, c. G *Mark*]

Mark (mäk), *n.* **1.** one of the four Evangelists, traditionally considered the author of the second Gospel. **2.** the second Gospel, in the New Testament. **3. King,** *Arthurian Legend.* ruler of Cornwall, husband of Iseult and uncle to Sir Tristram. [t. L: m. s. *Marcus*]

Mark Antony (mäk′ ăn′tə nĭ). See **Antony.**

markdown (mäk′doun′), *n.* **1.** a reduction in price. **2.** the amount by which a price is reduced.

marked (mäkt), *adj.* **1.** strikingly noticeable; conspicuous: *with marked success.* **2.** watched as an object for suspicion or vengeance: *a marked man.* **3.** having a mark or marks. —**markedly** (mä′kĭd lĭ), *adv.* —**mark′edness,** *n.*

marker (mä′kə), *n.* **1.** one who or that which marks. **2.** something used as a mark or indication, as a bookmark, etc. **3.** one who records a score, as in a game, etc. **4.** a counter used in card-playing.

market (mä′kĭt), *n.* **1.** a meeting of people for selling and buying. **2.** the assemblage of people at such a meeting. **3.** an open space or a covered building where such meetings are held, esp. for the sale of food, etc. **4.** a store for the sale of food. **5.** trade or traffic, esp. as regards a particular commodity. **6.** a body of persons carrying on extensive transactions in a specified commodity: *the cotton market.* **7.** the field of trade or business: *the best shoes on the market.* **8.** demand for a commodity: *an unprecedented market for leather.* **9.** a region where anything is or may be sold: *the foreign market.* **10.** current price or value: *a rising market.* **11. at the market,** at the best obtainable price in the open market. **12. in the market for,** ready to buy; seeking to buy. **13. on the market,** for sale; available. **14. play the market,** to speculate on the Stock Exchange. —*v.i.* **15.** to deal (buy or sell) in a market. —*v.t.* **16.** to carry or send to market for disposal. **17.** to dispose of in a market; sell. [ME and late OE, t. VL: m. s. *marcātus,* L *mercātus* trading, traffic, market]

marketable (mä′kĭ tə bl), *adj.* **1.** readily saleable. **2.** of or pertaining to selling or buying. —**mar′ketabil′ity, mar′ketableness,** *n.*

marketeer (mä′kĭ tĭə′), *n.* one active in or advocating a market as specified: *black marketeer, Common Marketeer.*

market garden, a garden or smallholding where vegetables and fruit are grown for sale. —**market gardener.** —**market gardening.**

Market Harborough (hä′bə rə), a town in England, in S Leicestershire. 12,550 (1961).

marketing (mä′kĭ tĭng), *n.* **1.** the total process whereby goods are put on to the market. **2.** the act of buying or selling in a market.

market order, an order to purchase or sell at the current market price.

marketplace (mä′kĭt plās′), *n.* a place, esp. an open space in a town, where a market is held.

market price, the price at which a commodity, security, or service is selling in the open market. Also, **market value.**

market research, the gathering of information by a firm about the preferences, purchasing powers, etc., of consumers, esp. as a preliminary to putting a product on the market.

market town, a town where a market is held.

Markham (mä′kəm), *n.* **Mount,** a mountain in Antarctica, SW of the Ross Sea. ab. 15,100 ft.

markhor (mä′kô), *n.* the largest of the wild goats, *Capra falconeri,* living in and around the Himalayas. [t. Pers.: lit., snake-eater]

marking (mä′kĭng), *n.* **1.** a mark, or a number or pattern of marks. **2.** the act of one who or that which marks: *the marking of papers.*

marking-ink (mä′kĭng ĭngk′), *n.* an indelible ink used for marking names on linen, etc.

markka (mä′kə), *n., pl.* **-kaa** (-kə). **1.** the monetary unit of Finland, equal to 100 pennia, and equivalent to about £0·099 sterling. **2.** a note or coin of this value. *Abbrev.:* Mk. [t. Finn., t. Sw.: m. *mark*]

Markova (mä kō′və, mä′kə və), *n.* **Alicia** (*Lilian Alicia Marks*), born 1910, English ballet dancer.

Markownikoff's rule, *Chem.* the rule which states that when addition occurs between a hydrogen halide and an unsymmetrical olefine, the halogen atom attaches itself to the carbon atom with the least number of hydrogen atoms. [named after V. V. *Markownikoff,* 1838–1904, Russian chemist]

marksman (mäks′mən), *n., pl.* **-men.** one skilled in shooting at a mark; one who shoots well. —**marks′manship′,** *n.* —**marks′woman,** *n. fem.*

mark-up (mäk′ŭp′), *n.* the amount or percentage added to the cost of the article in fixing the selling price: *a 50 per cent mark-up on cameras.*

marl[1] (mäl), *n.* **1.** a soil or earthy deposit consisting of clay and calcium carbonate, used esp. as a fertilizer. **2.** *Poetic.* earth. —*v.t.* **3.** to fertilize with marl. [ME, t. OF, g. LL *margila,* dim. of L *marga*] —**marlaceous** (mä lā′shəs), **marl′y,** *adj.*

marl[2] (mäl), *v.t. Naut.* to wind (a rope, etc.) with marline, every turn being secured by a hitch. [t. D: s. *marlen,* appar. freq. of *marren* tie. Cf. MARLINESPIKE]

Marl (*Ger.* märl), *n.* a town in West Germany, in W central North Rhine-Westphalia. 75,300 (est. 1966).

Marlborough (mäl′bə rə, -brə, môl′-), *n.* **1. John Churchill, 1st Duke of,** 1650–1722, English military commander. **2.** a town in England, in Wiltshire: public school. 4843 (1961).

marlin (mä′lĭn), *n.* any of the genus *Makaira* of large, powerful fishes with a spearlike snout, as *M. ampla,* of the warm waters of the Atlantic, a favourite big game fish. [short for MARLINESPIKE]

marline (mä′lĭn), *n. Naut.* small cord of two loosely twisted strands, used for seizing. [half adoption, half trans. of D *marlijn,* f. *marr(en)* tie + *lijn* LINE[1]]

marlinespike (mä′lĭn spīk′), *n. Naut.* a pointed iron implement used in marling, separating the strands of rope in splicing, etc. Also, **marlinspike.** [orig. *marling spike.* See MARL[2], SPIKE]

A, Marlinespike; B, Marlinespike separating strands of rope

Marlowe (mä′lō), *n.* **Christopher,** 1564–93, English dramatist and poet.

marmalade (mä′mə lād′), *n.* a jelly-like preserve with fruit (usually citrus) suspended in small pieces. [late ME, t. F: m. *marmelade,* t. Pg.: m. *marmelada,* der. *marmelo* quince, g. L *melimēlum,* t. Gk: m. *melimēlon,* lit. honey apple]

marmalade tree, a sapotaceous tree, *Calocarpum sapota,* of tropical America, with a durable wood resembling mahogany and a fruit used in preserving.

Marmara (mä′mə rə), *n.* **Sea of,** a sea between European and Asiatic Turkey, connected with the Black Sea by the Bosporus, and with the Aegean by the Dardanelles. 4300 sq. mi. See map under **Black Sea.** Also, **Marmora** (mä′mə rə).

marmite (mä′mīt), *n.* **1.** a type of covered cooking pot. **2.** broth cooked in such a pot. **3.** (*cap.*) *Trademark.* a yeast extract used to flavour soups, stews, etc., or as a spread. [t. F: *marmite* pot]

Marmolada (*It.* mä mō lä′dä), *n.* a mountain in N Italy: highest peak in the Dolomites. 11,020 ft.

marmoreal (mä mô′rĭ əl), *adj.* of or like marble. Also, **marmo′rean.** [f. s. L *marmoreus* of marble + -AL[1]]

marmoset (mä′mə zĕt′), *n.* any of various small, squirrel-like South and Central American monkeys, genera *Callithrix* and *Leontocebus,* and allied genera, with soft fur and a long, slightly furry, non-prehensile tail. [ME *marmusette,* t. OF: m. *marmouset* grotesque little figure, der. OF *merme* under age, g. L *minimus* least, b. with Gk *mormōtós* frightful]

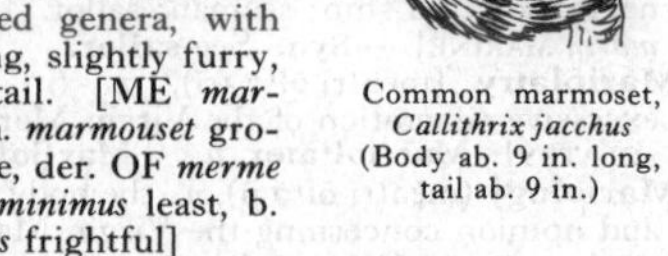

Common marmoset, *Callithrix jacchus* (Body ab. 9 in. long, tail ab. 9 in.)

marmot (mä′mət), *n.* **1.** any of the bushy-tailed, thickset rodents constituting the genus *Marmota,* as the common woodchuck. **2.** any of certain related animals, as the prairie dogs. [t. F: m. *marmotte,* back-formation from *marmottaine,* g. L *mūsmontānus,* f. *mūs* mouse + *montānus* of the mountains]

Marne (män; *Fr.* märn), *n.* **1.** a river in NE France, flowing W to the Seine near Paris; battles, 1914, 1918, 1944. 325 mi. **2.** a department in NE France. 208,446 pop. (1962); 3167 sq. mi. *Cap.:* Châlons-sur-Marne.

marocain (mă′rə kān′), *n.* a ribbed crepe fabric made of silk, wool, or rayon, or a combination of these materials. [t. F: Moroccan]

Hoary marmot, *Marmota caligata* (Ab. 2½ ft long)

Maronite (mă′rə nīt′), *n.* a member of a body of Uniats living chiefly in Lebanon. [t. LL: m. s. *Marōnīta,* named after St *Maron,* 4th-century founder of the sect. See -ITE[1]]

maroon[1] (mə rōōn′), *n.* **1.** dark brownish red. **2.** a firework exploding with a loud report, esp. one used as a

warning or distress signal. —*adj.* **3.** of a dark brownish red colour. [t. F: m. *marron*, t. It.: m. *marrone* chestnut]
maroon[2] (mə ro͞on′), *v.t.* **1.** to put ashore and leave on a desolate island or coast by way of punishment, as was done by buccaneers, etc. **2.** to isolate as if on a desolate island. —*n.* **3.** one of a group of Negroes, orig. fugitive slaves, living in the wilder parts of the West Indies and the Guianas. **4.** one who is marooned. [t. F: m. *marron*. Cf. Sp. *cimarrón* wild, der. *cimarra* bushes]
Maros (*Hung.* mŏ′rŏsh), *n.* Hungarian name of **Mures.**
Marot (*Fr.* mȧ rō′), *n.* **Clément** (*Fr.* klė mäN′), 1495?–1544, French poet.
Marple (mä′pl), *n.* a town in England, in Cheshire. 16,812 (1961).
marplot (mä′plŏt′), *n.* one who mars or defeats a plot, design, or project by officious interference.
Marprelate (mä′prĕl′ĭt), *n.* **Martin** (mä′tĭn), the pseudonym of the writer or writers of satirical Puritan pamphlets circulated in 1588–89 attacking the Church of England.
Marq., Marquess; Marquis.
Marquand (mä′kwənd; *in America* mä kwŏnd′), *n.* **J(ohn) P(hillips),** 1893–1960, U.S. novelist.
marque (mäk), *n.* *Obs.* seizure by way of reprisal. [t. F, t. Pr.: m. *marca*, der. *marcar* seize in reprisal, der. *marc* token of pledge, t. Gmc. See MARK[1]]
marquee (mä kē′), *n.* **1.** a large tent or tentlike shelter, sometimes with open sides, esp. one for temporary use providing refreshment, entertainment, etc. **2.** *U.S.* marquise (def. 4). [assumed sing. of MARQUISE taken as pl.]
Marquesas Islands (mä kā′säs), a group of French islands in the S Pacific. 4170 pop. (1960); 480 sq. mi. See map under **Hawaiian Islands.**
marquess (mä′kwĭs), *n.* a nobleman ranking next below a duke and above an earl or count. Also, **marquis.** [var. of MARQUIS]
marquetry (mä′kĭ trĭ), *n.* inlaid work of variously coloured woods or other materials, esp. in furniture. Also, **marqueterie** (mä′kĭ trĭ). [t. F: m. *marqueterie*, der. *marqueter* mark, chequer, inlay, ult. der. *marque* MARK[1]]
Marquette (*Fr.* mȧr kĕt′), *n.* **Jacques** (*Fr.* zhȧk) (*Père Marquette*), 1637–75, French Jesuit missionary and explorer.
marquis (mä′kwĭs; *Fr.* mȧr kē′), *n.* marquess. [t. F: r. ME *markis*, t. OF: m. *marchis*, der. *marche* MARCH[2]]
Marquis (mä′kwĭs), *n.* **Don(ald Robert Perry),** 1878–1937, U.S. humorist and writer.
marquisate (mä′kwĭ zĭt), *n.* **1.** the rank of a marquess. **2.** the territory ruled by a marquess or a margrave.
marquise (mä kēz′; *Fr.* mȧr kēz′), *n.* **1.** the wife or widow of a marquess. **2.** a lady holding the rank equal to that of a marquess. **3.** a common diamond shape, pointed oval, usually with normal brilliant facets. **4.** a rooflike shelter or canopy, as of glass, projecting above the outer door of a building and over a pavement or terrace. **5.** marquee. [t. F, fem. of MARQUIS]

Marquise (def. 4)

marquisette (mä′kĭ zĕt′, -kwĭ-), *n.* a lightweight open fabric of leno weave in cotton, rayon, silk, or nylon. [t. F, dim. of MARQUISE]
Marrakech (mə răk′ĕsh), *n.* a city in W Morocco, former capital of Southern Sultanate. 255,000 (est. 1965). Also, **Marrakesh, Morocco.**
marram grass (mă′rəm), a stout perennial grass with creeping stems and stiff leaves, *Ammophila arenaria*, abundant in coastal sand-dunes of W Europe.
Marrano (mə rä′nō), *n.*, *pl.* **-nos.** a Spanish or Portuguese Jew converted to Christianity in the late Middle Ages, esp. one converted under duress and who often adhered to Judaism in secret. [t. Sp.: lit., pig, from the Jewish law forbidding the eating of pork]
marriage (mă′rĭj), *n.* **1.** the legal union of a man with a woman for life; state or condition of being married; the legal relation of spouses to each other; wedlock. **2.** the legal or religious ceremony that sanctions or formalizes the decision of a man and woman to live as husband and wife. **3.** any intimate union. [ME *mariage*, t. OF, der. *marier* MARRY[1]]

—**Syn. 1.** MARRIAGE, WEDDING, NUPTIALS are terms for the ceremony uniting couples in wedlock. MARRIAGE is the simple and usual term, without implications as to circumstances and without emotional connotations: *to announce the marriage of a daughter.* WEDDING has strong emotional, even sentimental, connotations, and suggests the accompanying festivities, whether elaborate or simple: *a beautiful wedding, a reception after the wedding.* NUPTIALS is a formal and lofty word applied to the ceremony and attendant social events; it does not have emotional connotations but strongly implies surroundings characteristic of wealth, rank, pomp, and grandeur: *royal nuptials.*

marriageable (mă′rĭ jə bl), *adj.* fit, esp. old enough, for marriage. —**mar′riageabil′ity, mar′riageableness,** *n.*
marriage certificate, a certificate issued compulsorily by a registrar upon the legal marriage of two people.
marriage of convenience, mariage de convenance.
marriage portion, dowry.
marriage settlement, an arrangement for the conveyance of property for the benefit of the parties to, and the prospective children of, a marriage.
married (mă′rĭd), *adj.* **1.** united in wedlock; wedded. **2.** pertaining to marriage or married persons.
marron (mă′rən), *n.* a chestnut; esp. as used in cookery, or candied or preserved in syrup. [t. F. See MAROON[1]]
marrons glacés (*Fr.* mȧ rôN glȧ sė′), *French.* chestnuts glazed or coated with sugar.
marrow[1] (mă′rō), *n.* **1.** a soft, fatty vascular tissue in the interior cavities of bones. **2.** the inmost or essential part. **3.** strength or vitality. **4.** rich and nutritious food. **5.** the oblong fruit of a cultivated variety of *Cucurbita pepo*, widely used as a cooked vegetable; vegetable marrow. [ME *marowe*, *marw(e)*, OE *mearg*, c. G *Mark*]
marrow[2] (mă′rō, -rə), *n.* *Dial.* **1.** a companion; mate; fellow worker. **2.** a husband or wife. **3.** one's like or equal. [late ME *marwe* fellow worker, perh. t. Scand.; cf. Icel. *margr* friendly]
marrowbone (mă′rō bōn′), *n.* **1.** a bone containing edible marrow. **2.** (*pl.*) (in humorous use) the knees. **3.** (*pl.*) crossbones.
marrowfat (mă′rō făt′), *n.* **1.** a tall variety of the pea, with a large seed. **2.** the seed.
marrow squash, *U.S.* any of several squashes with a smooth surface, oblong shape, and hard rind.
marry[1] (mă′rĭ), *v.*, **-ried, -rying.** —*v.t.* **1.** to take in marriage. **2.** to unite in wedlock. **3.** to give in marriage. **4.** to unite intimately. **5.** *Naut.* **a.** to join together, as two ropes, end to end without increasing the diameter. **b.** to force the two parts of (a hatch) into place. —*v.i.* **6.** to take a husband or wife; wed. [ME *marie(n)*, t. F: m. *marier*, g. L *marītāre* wed] —**mar′rier,** *n.*
marry[2] (mă′rĭ), *interj.* *Archaic.* (an exclamation of surprise, etc.) [euphemistic var. of MARY (the Virgin)]
Marryat (mă′rĭ ət), *n.* **Frederick,** 1792–1848, English novelist and naval officer.
Mars (mäz), *n.* **1.** the ancient Roman god of war. **2.** *Astron.* the planet next outside the earth, fourth in order from the sun. Its period of revolution is 686·980 days, its mean distance from the sun about 141,630,000 miles, and its diameter 4220 miles. It has two satellites.
Marsala (mä sä′lə; *It.* mȧr sä′lȧ), *n.* **1.** a seaport in Italy, in W Sicily. 83,304 (1966). **2.** a sweet, dark, fortified wine made near there.
Marseillaise (mä′sə lāz′; *Fr.* mȧr sĕ yĕz′), *n.* the French national anthem, written in 1792 by Rouget de Lisle.
marseilles (mä sālz′), *n.* a stiff cotton fabric woven in figures or stripes, with an embossed effect.
Marseilles (mä sā′; *older* mä sālz′), *n.* a seaport in SE France, the capital of Bouches-du-Rhône department. 778,071 (1962). See map under **Monaco.** French, **Marseille** (*Fr.* mȧr sĕy′).
marsh (mäsh), *n.* a tract of low, wet land; a swamp. [ME *mershe*, OE *mersc*, syncopated var. of *merisc* (c. G *Marsch*), f. *mere* pool + *-isc* -ISH[1]. See MERE[2]]
marshal (mä′shəl), *n.*, *v.*, **-shalled, -shalling** or (*U.S.*) **-shaled, -shaling.** —*n.* **1.** a military officer of the highest rank. In many countries the title is modified by some other term: as in England *field marshal*, and in France *marshal of France.* **2.** *U.S.* an administrative officer of a judicial district who performs duties similar to those of a sheriff. **3.** an officer who attends a judge on the assizes. **4.** the title of various officials having certain police duties. **5.** a high officer of a royal household or court. **6.** a person charged with the arrangement or regulation of ceremonies, etc. **7.** (at Oxford University) a proctor's attendant or bulldog. —*v.t.* **8.** to arrange in due or proper order; set out in an orderly manner. **9.** to array for battle, etc. **10.** to usher or lead. **11.** *Her.* to combine (two or more coats of arms) on a single escutcheon. [ME *mareschal*, t. OF, g. VL *mariscalcus* groom, t. Gmc; cf. OE *mearh* horse, *scealc* servant] —**mar′shalcy, mar′shalship′,** *n.* —**mar′shaller,** *n.* —**Syn. 8.** See **gather.**
Marshall (mä′shəl), *n.* **1. George Catlett** (kăt′lĭt), 1880–1959, U.S. general and statesman: secretary of state 1947–49. **2. John,** 1755–1835, U.S. jurist and statesman: chief justice of the Supreme Court 1801–35.
marshalling yard, *Railways.* a system of parallel tracks, crossings, points, etc., where cars are shunted and made up into trains, and where carriages, locomotives, and other rolling stock are kept when awaiting repairs or when not in use.
Marshall Islands, a group of 24 atolls in the N Pacific:

formerly mandated to Japan; now under U.S. trusteeship. 14,907 pop. (1960); 74 sq. mi. See map under **Hawaiian Islands.**

Marshall Plan, a plan for aiding the economic recovery of European countries after World War II, originated by George C. Marshall in 1947. Later called **European Recovery Programme.** Also, **Marshall Aid.**

Marshal of the Royal Air Force, the highest rank in the Royal Air Force, equivalent to field marshal in the army and admiral of the fleet in the Royal Navy.

Marshalsea (mä′shəl sē′), *n. Hist.* **1.** the court of the marshal of the royal household. **2.** a prison in London, latterly a debtors' prison (abolished in 1849).

marsh elder, 1. *U.S.* any of various composite plants of the genus *Iva*, as *I. frutescens*, which grows in salt marshes. **2.** the cranberry tree.

marsh fern, a fern with a slender creeping rhizome and erect pinnate leaves, *Thelypteris palustris*, widespread in wet places throughout temperate regions.

marsh fleawort, a woolly, biennial, composite herb with yellow capitula, *Senecio palustris*, occurring in fen ditches of northern parts of Europe and W Asia.

marsh gas, a gaseous decomposition product of organic matter, consisting largely of methane.

marsh harrier, an Old World harrier, *Circus aeruginosus*, having a cream-coloured head.

marsh hawk, a slender American hawk, *Circus cyaneus hudsonius*, which frequents marshes and meadows, feeding on frogs, snakes, etc.

marsh hen, any of various rails or rail-like birds.

marshland (mäsh′lănd′), *n.* a district or region characterized by marshes, swamps, etc.

marsh mallow, an Old World mallow, *Althaea officinalis*, with pink flowers, found in marshy places.

marshmallow (mäsh′măl′ō), *n.* **1.** a sweetened paste or confection made from the mucilaginous root of the marsh mallow. **2.** a similar confection with an elastic, spongy texture, sometimes tinted pink or other pastel colours, containing gum arabic or gelatine, sugar, and flavouring. [ME *marshmalue*, OE *merscmealwe*. See MARSH, MALLOW]

marsh marigold, the kingcup, *Caltha palustris*.

marsh wren, either of two American species of marsh-inhabiting wrens, the long-billed (*Telmatodytes palustris*), or the short-billed (*Cistothorus platensis*).

marshy (mä′shĭ), *adj.*, **-shier, -shiest. 1.** like a marsh; soft and wet. **2.** pertaining to a marsh. **3.** consisting of or constituting marsh. **—marsh′iness,** *n.*

marsipobranch (mä′sĭ pō brăngk′), *adj.* **1.** belonging to the *Marsipobrachii* or *Cyclostomata*, a group or class of vertebrates comprising the cyclostomes (the lampreys and hagfishes), characterized by pouchlike gills. —*n.* **2.** a marsipobranch fish.

Marston (mä′stən), *n.* **John,** *c.* 1575–1634, English dramatist and satirical poet.

Marston Moor, a former moor in NE England, W of York: Cromwell's victory over the Royalists, 1644.

marsupial (mä syōō′pyəl), *adj.* **1.** pertaining to, resembling, or having a marsupium. **2.** of or pertaining to the marsupials. —*n.* **3.** any of the *Marsupiala*, the order which includes all of the viviparous, but non-placental mammals, such as the opossums, kangaroos, wombats, bandicoots, etc. Most members have a marsupium containing the mammary glands and serving as a receptacle for the young. [t. NL: s. *marsūpiālis*, der. L *marsūpium*. See MARSUPIUM]

marsupium (mä syōō′pyəm), *n., pl.* **-pia** (-pyə). the pouch or fold of skin on the abdomen of a female marsupial. [t. L: pouch, t. Gk: m. *marsýpion, marsípion*, dim. of *mársipos* bag, pouch]

mart (mät), *n.* **1.** market; trading centre. **2.** *Archaic.* a fair. [t. D, spoken var. of *markt* MARKET]

martagon lily (mä′tə gən), a commonly cultivated liliaceous perennial, *Lilium martagon*, with large, dull purple flowers.

Martel (mä tĕl′; *Fr.* mȧr-), *n.* See **Charles Martel.**

Martello tower (mä tĕl′ō), *Fort.* a circular, tower-like fort with guns on the top. Also, **martello.**

marten (mä′tĭn), *n., pl.* **-tens,** (*esp. collectively*) **-ten. 1.** any of various slender, fur-bearing carnivores of the genus *Martes*, as the American **pine marten,** *M. americana*, of the northern U.S. and Canada. **2.** the fur of such an animal, generally a dark brown. [ME *martren*, t. OF: m. *martrine*, prop. the fur, n. use of *martrin*, adj., der. *martre* marten; ult. t. Gmc (cf. G *Marder*)]

Marten, *Martes americana* (Body ab. 1½ ft long, tail ab. 10 in.)

martensite (mä′tĭn zīt′), *n. Metall.* the hard constituent produced when steel is cooled from the hardening temperature at a greater speed than its critical cooling rate.

Martha (mä′thə), *n. Bible.* the sister of Lazarus, whose house in Bethany Jesus often visited. Luke 10:38–42; John 11:1–44.

Martha's Vineyard, an island in the U.S., off SE Massachusetts: holiday resort. 5800 pop. (1960); 108¾ sq. mi.

martial (mä′shəl), *adj.* **1.** inclined or disposed to war; warlike; brave. **2.** pertaining to or connected with the army and navy. **3.** pertaining to or appropriate for war: *martial music.* **4.** characteristic of or befitting a warrior: *a martial stride.* [ME, t. L: s. *martiālis* of Mars] **—mar′tially,** *adv.* **—mar′tialness,** *n.*

Martial (mä′shəl), *n.* (*Marcus Valerius Martialis*), A.D. *c.* 40–*c.* 102, Roman writer of epigrams, born in Spain.

martial law, the law imposed upon an area by military forces when civil authority has broken down.

Martian (mä′shyən), *adj.* **1.** pertaining to the planet Mars. —*n.* **2.** a supposed inhabitant of the planet Mars. [f. s. L *Martius* of Mars + -AN]

martin (mä′tĭn), *n.* any of the various swallows, as *Chelidon urbica*, the common European **house martin,** which builds its nest about houses, or *Progne subis*, the American **purple martin,** one of the largest birds of the swallow family. [late ME, from *Martin*, man's name]

Martin (mä′tĭn), *n.* **1. Frank,** born 1910, Swiss composer. **2. Saint,** A.D. *c.* 316–397 or 400 French bishop.

Martin du Gard (*Fr.* mȧr tăN dY gȧr′), **Roger** (*Fr.* rō zhė′), 1881–1958, French novelist.

Martineau (mä′tĭ nō′), *n.* **Harriet,** 1802–76, English novelist and economist.

martinet (mä′tĭ nĕt′), *n.* a rigid disciplinarian, esp. a military one. [from General *Martinet*, French drillmaster of the reign of Louis XIV] **—mar′tinet′ish,** *adj.* **—mar′tinet′ism,** *n.*

martingale (mä′tĭn gāl′), *n.* **1.** a strap of a horse's harness passing from the bit or headgear, between the forelegs, to the girth, for holding the head down. **2.** *Naut.* a short, perpendicular spar under the bowsprit end, used for guying down the jib boom. **3.** a gambling system in which the stakes are doubled after each loss. [t. F, t. Pr.: m. *marte(n)galo*, fem. of *marte(n)gan*, inhabitant of Martigue (supposedly noted for stinginess)]

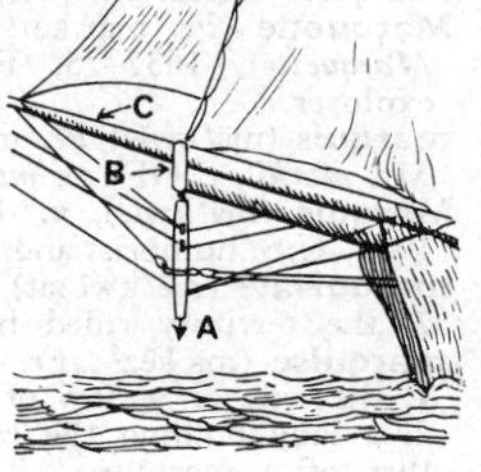

Martingale (def. 2) A, Martingale; B, Bowsprit; C, Jib boom

martini (mä tē′nĭ), *n., pl.* **-nis.** a cocktail of gin and dry vermouth, usually served with an olive or twist of lemon peel.

Martini (mä tē′nĭ; *It.* mȧr tē′nė), *n.* **Simone** (*It.* sē mō′nė), *c.* 1284–1344, Italian painter.

Martinique (mä′tĭ nēk′), *n.* an island in the E West Indies; a department of France. 292,062 pop. (1961); 425 sq. mi. *Cap.:* Fort-de-France.

Martinmas (mä′tĭn məs), *n.* a church festival, November 11th, in honour of St Martin. [f. (Saint) MARTIN + -MAS]

Martinů (mä′tĭ nōō′; *Cz.* mȧr′tyē nōō), *n.* **Bohuslav** (*Cz.* bō′hōō slȧf), 1890–1959, Czech composer.

martlet (mät′lĭt), *n.* **1.** a house martin. **2.** *Her.* a representation of a swallow without legs, used esp. as the fourth son's mark of status. [t. F: m. *martelet*, var. of *martinet*, dim. of *martin* MARTIN]

martyr (mä′tə), *n.* **1.** one who willingly suffers death rather than renounce his religion. **2.** one who is put to death or endures great suffering on behalf of any belief, principle, or cause. **3.** one undergoing severe or constant suffering. —*v.t.* **4.** to put to death as a martyr. **5.** to make a martyr of. **6.** to torment or torture. [ME *marter*, OE *martyr*, t. L, t. Gk: s. *mártys*, orig., witness]

martyrdom (mä′tə dəm), *n.* **1.** the condition, sufferings, or death of a martyr. **2.** extreme suffering.

martyrize (mä′tə rīz′), *v.t.*, **-rized, -rizing. 1.** to make a martyr of. **2.** to torment. Also, **martyrise. —mar′tyriza′tion,** *n.*

martyrology (mä′tə rŏl′ə jĭ), *n., pl.* **-gies. 1.** the branch of knowledge dealing with the lives of martyrs. **2.** an account or history of martyrs. **3.** such histories collectively. **4.** a list of martyrs. **—martyrological** (mä′tə rə lŏj′ĭ kl), *adj.* **—mar′tyrol′ogist,** *n.*

martyry (mä′tə rĭ), *n., pl.* **-ries.** a shrine, chapel, or the

like, erected in honour of a martyr. [t. LL: m. s. *martyrium*, t. LGk: m. *martýrion*]
marula (mə rōō′lə), *n.* a large shrub of southern Africa, *Sclerocarya caffra*, having spiky flowers and walnut-sized drupes. [? t. Tswana]
marvel (mä′vəl), *n.*, *v.*, **-velled, -velling** or (*U.S.*) **-veled, -veling.** —*n.* **1.** a wonderful thing; a wonder or prodigy; something that arouses wonder or admiration. **2.** *Archaic.* the feeling of wonder. —*v.t.* **3.** to wonder at (usually fol. by a clause as object). **4.** to wonder or be curious about (usually fol. by a clause as object). —*v.i.* **5.** to be affected with wonder, as at something surprising or extraordinary. [ME *merveille*, t. F, g. L *mīrābilia* wonderful things, prop. neut. pl. of *mīrābilis* wonderful]
Marvell (mä′vəl), *n.* **Andrew,** 1621–78, English poet.
marvel-of-Peru (mä′vəl əv pə rōō′), *n.* the four-o'clock, *Mirabilis jalapa.*
marvellous (mä′və ləs), *adj.* **1.** such as to excite wonder; surprising, extraordinary. **2.** excellent; superb. **3.** improbable or incredible (often used absolutely in the phrase *the marvellous*). —**mar′vellously,** *adv.* —**mar′vellousness,** *n.*
Marwar (mä′wä), *n.* Jodhpur (def. 1).
Marx (mäks), *n.* **Karl** (käl), 1818–83, German founder of modern socialism and communism.
Marxian (mäk′syən), *adj.* of or pertaining to Karl Marx or his theories. —**Marx′ianism,** *n.*
Marxism (mäk′sĭz′əm), *n.* the system of thought developed by Karl Marx, together with Friedrich Engels, esp. the doctrine that the state throughout history has been a device for the exploitation of the masses by a dominant class, that class struggle has been the main agency of historical change, and that the capitalist state contained from the first the 'seeds of its own decay' and will inevitably, after a transitional period known as 'the dictatorship of the proletariat', be superseded by a socialist order and a classless society.
Marxist (mäk′sĭst), *n.* **1.** an adherent of Karl Marx or his theories. —*adj.* **2.** of Karl Marx or his theories.
Mary (mēə′rĭ), *n.* **1.** *New Testament.* **a.** the mother of Jesus. Matt. 1:18–25. Often called the **Virgin Mary** or **Saint Mary. b.** the sister of Lazarus and Martha. Luke 10:38–42; John 11:1–2. **2.** (*Princess Victoria Mary of Teck*), 1867–1953, queen of England 1910–36, wife of George V. [ME *Marie*, OE *Maria*, t. L, t. Gk, t. Heb.: m. *Miryām*]
Mary I (*'Bloody Mary'*), 1516–58, queen of England 1553–58, and wife of Philip II of Spain. Also, **Mary Tudor.**
Mary II, 1662–94, queen of England 1689–94, joint ruler with her husband, William III.
Maryborough (mēə′rĭ bə rə), *n.* a seaport in Australia, in SE Queensland. 19,500 (est. 1965).
Maryland (mēə′rĭ lănd′, mē′rĭ lənd), *n.* a state in the E United States, on the Atlantic coast. 3,100,689 pop. (1960); 10,577 sq. mi. *Cap.:* Annapolis. *Abbrev.:* Md.
Marylebone Cricket Club, the governing body of cricket in England and the authoritative source of all cricket legislation. *Abbrev.:* M.C.C.
Mary Magdalene, Mary of Magdala, mentioned in Luke 8:2, and traditionally identified with the repentant woman in Luke 7:37–50.
Mary Stuart (styōōət), 1542–87, queen of Scotland 1542–67; beheaded for plotting to assassinate her cousin, Queen Elizabeth of England. Also, **Mary, Queen of Scots.**
marzipan (mä′zĭ păn′), *n.* a confection made of almonds reduced to a paste with sugar, etc., and moulded into various forms, usually diminutive fruits and vegetables. Also, **marchpane.** [t. G. See MARCHPANE]
-mas, a final element in certain names of holidays and Christian feasts, as *Michaelmas.* [comb. form of MASS[2]]
Masaccio (*It.* mȧ zät′chō), *n.* (*Tommaso Guidi*), 1401–28?, Italian painter.
Masai (mä′sī, mä sī′), *n.*, *pl.* **-sais,** (*esp. collectively*) **-sai. 1.** a member of an African people inhabiting the grasslands of Kenya and Tanzania. **2.** their language. —*adj.* **3.** of or pertaining to this people or their language.
Masaryk (măs′ə rĭk; *Cz.* mȧ′sȧ rēk), *n.* **1. Ján** (*Cz.* yän), 1886–1948, Czech statesman (son of Tomáš). **2. Tomáš Garrigue** (*Cz.* tŏ′mȧsh gȧ rēg′), 1850–1937, Czech statesman: first president of Czechoslovakia, 1918–35.
Masbate (măs bä′tĭ), *n.* one of the Philippine Islands, in the central part of the group. 263,550 pop. (est. 1960); 1262 sq. mi.
masc., masculine.
Mascagni (*It.* mȧs kȧn′nyē), *n.* **Pietro** (*It.* pyĕ′trō), 1863–1945, Italian operatic composer.
mascara (măs kä′rə), *n.* a substance used as a cosmetic to colour the eyelashes. [t. Sp.: a mask]
mascle (măs′kl), *n.* *Her.* a lozenge represented as having a lozenge-shaped hole at the centre. [ME, prob. for OF *macle*, g. L *macula* spot, mesh of a net. Cf. MAIL[2]]
mascon (măs′kŏn), *n.* *Astron.* any of several local concentrations of mass below the surface of the moon. [f. MAS(S) + CON(CENTRATION)]
mascot (măs′kət), *n.* a person, animal, or thing supposed to bring good luck. [t. F: m. *mascotte*, dim. of Pr. *masco* witch; of Gmc orig.]
masculine (măs′kyōō lĭn), *adj.* **1.** having manlike qualities; strong; manly: *a masculine voice.* **2.** pertaining to or characteristic of a man or men: *masculine attire.* **3.** *Gram.* denoting or pertaining to one of the three genders of Latin, German, Greek, etc., or one of the two of French, Spanish, etc., so termed because most or all nouns denoting males belong to it, as well as other nouns, as French *crayon* 'pencil' or Spanish *dedo* 'finger'. **4.** (of a woman) mannish. —*n.* **5.** *Gram.* the masculine gender. **6.** a noun or another element marking that gender. [ME *masculin*, t. L: s. *masculinus* male] —**mas′culinely,** *adv.* —**mas′culin′ity, mas′culineness,** *n.* —**Syn. 1.** See **male.**
masculine rhyme, *Pros.* a rhyme of but a single stressed syllable; single rhyme, as in *disdain, complain.*
Masefield (mās′fēld′), *n.* **John,** 1878–1967, English poet, dramatist, and novelist.
maser (mā′zə), *n.* a device for amplifying electrical impulses by stimulated emission of radiation. [short for *m*(*icrowave*) *a*(*mplification by*) *s*(*timulated*) *e*(*mission of*) *r*(*adiation*)]
Maseru (mə sĕə′rōō), *n.* the capital of Lesotho, in the NW part. ab. 10,000 (est. 1967).
mash (măsh), *n.* **1.** a soft, pulpy mass. **2.** pulpy condition. **3.** a mess of boiled grain, bran, meal, etc., fed warm to horses and cattle. **4.** crushed malt or meal of grain mixed with hot water to form wort. **5.** mashed potatoes. **6.** *Obs. Slang.* **a.** sweetheart; object of admiration. **b.** masher. —*v.t.* **7.** to crush. **8.** to reduce to a soft, pulpy mass, as by heating or pressure. **9.** to mix (crushed malt, etc.) with hot water to form wort. **10.** *Obs. Slang.* to flirt with; seek to attract or fascinate (one of the opposite sex). —*v.i.* **11.** *Obs. Slang.* to flirt. [ME *masche*, OE *māsc-* (in compounds), c. G *Maische*]
Masharbrum (mŭsh′ə brōōm′), *n.* a mountain in N India, in the Himalayas. ab. 25,700 ft.
masher (măsh′ə), *n.* **1.** one who or that which mashes. **2.** *Obs. Slang.* a lady-killer, esp. one who dresses showily; a flirtatious dandy.
Mashhad (*Pers.* măsh hăd′), *n.* Meshed.
mashie (măsh′ĭ), *n.* *Golf.* a club (No. 5 iron) having a short head with a sloping face for making lofting shots. Also, **mashy.** [alter. of F *massue* club]
mashlam (măsh′ləm), *n.* maslin.
Mashona (mə shŏn′ə), *n.*, *pl.* **-nas,** (*esp. collectively*) **-na. 1.** a member of an African tribe of no certainly known affinities, inhabiting parts of Rhodesia. **2.** their language. —*adj.* **3.** of or pertaining to the Mashona or their language.
Mashonaland (mə shŏn′ə lănd′), *n.* that part of Rhodesia inhabited by the Mashona.
Masinissa (măs′ĭ nĭs′ə), *n.* *c.* 238–149 B.C., king of Numidia *c.* 210–149. Also, **Massinissa.**
masjid (mŭs′jĭd), *n.* mosque. Also, **musjid.** [t. Ar. See MOSQUE]
mask (mäsk), *n.* **1.** a covering for the face, esp. one worn for disguise; a false face. **2.** a piece of cloth, silk, or plastic material, covering the face of an actor, to symbolize the character he represents: used in Greek and Roman drama and in some modern plays. **3.** anything that disguises or conceals; a disguise; a pretence. **4.** a person wearing a mask. **5.** a masquerade or revel. **6.** a masque (defs 1, 2). **7.** a likeness of a face, as one moulded in plaster after death. **8.** the face or head, as of a fox. **9.** a representation of a face or head, generally grotesque, used as an ornament. **10.** a covering of wire, gauze, tinted glass, cloth, etc., to protect the face, as from splinters, dust, sparks, glare, fumes, polluted air, etc. **11.** a gas-mask. **12.** any of various devices, usually consisting of rubber, glass, and plastic material, used by skin-divers to protect the face. **13.** *Fort.* a screen, as of earth or brush, for concealing or protecting a battery or any military operation. **14.** *Photog.* any device used to limit the amount of light reaching a sensitized surface. —*v.t.* **15.** to disguise or conceal. **16.** to cover with a mask. **17.** *Fort.* to conceal (a battery or any military operation) from the enemy. **18.** to hinder (an army, etc.) from conducting an operation. **19.** *Photog.* to restrict the amount of light reaching (a sensitized surface). —*v.i.* **20.** to put on a mask; disguise oneself. [t. F: m. *masque*, t. It.: m. *maschera*, der. LL *masca*]
Mask (măsk), *n.* **Lough,** a lake in counties Galway and Mayo, Republic of Ireland. ab. 12 mi. long by 3 mi. wide.

maskalonge (măs′kə lŏnj′), *n.* muskellunge.
maskanonge (măs′kə nŏnj′), *n.* muskellunge.
masked ball, a ball at which masks are worn.
masker (mäs′kə), *n.* one who masks; one who takes part in a masque. Also, **masquer.**
masking tape, an adhesive tape used for defining edges and protecting surfaces not to be painted.
maslin (măs′lĭn, măz′-), *n. Dial.* **1.** a mixture of different kinds of grain, esp. rye and wheat. **2.** bread made from such a mixture. Also, **mashlam.** [ME *mastlyoun*, t. MF: m. *mesteillon*, der. *mesteil* mixture]
masochism (măs′ə kĭz′əm), *n. Psychol.* the condition in which sexual gratification depends on suffering, physical pain, and humiliation. [named after Leopold von Sacher *Masoch*, 1836–95, Austrian novelist, who described it] —**mas′ochist,** *n.* —**mas′ochis′tic,** *adj.*
mason (mā′sən), *n.* **1.** one who builds or works with stone. **2.** one who dresses stone. **3.** *U.S.* a bricklayer. **4.** *U.S.* one who dresses bricks. **5.** (*often cap.*) a Freemason. —*v.t.* **6.** to construct of or strengthen with masonry. [ME, t. OF: m. *maçon*, der. LL *maccāre* beat; of Gmc orig.]
mason bee, any of certain bees of the family *Megachilidae*, which construct their nests of clay.
Mason-Dixon line (mā′sən dĭk′sən), the boundary between Pennsylvania and Maryland, partly surveyed by Charles Mason and Jeremiah Dixon between 1763 and 1767, popularly considered before the abolition of slavery as a line of demarcation between free and slave states. Also, **Mason and Dixon's line.**
masonic (mə sŏn′ĭk), *adj.* (*often cap.*) pertaining to or characteristic of Freemasons or Freemasonry.
masonite (mā′sə nīt′), *n.* **1.** a kind of wood-fibre material, pressed in sheets and used for partitions, insulation, etc. **2.** (*cap.*) a trademark for this substance.
masonry (mā′sən rĭ), *n., pl.* **-ries. 1.** the art or occupation of a mason. **2.** work constructed by a mason. **3.** (*often cap.*) freemasonry.
Masora (mə sô′rə), *n.* **1.** the accepted text of the Hebrew scriptures, from which variant readings and inconsistencies had gradually been excised through a succession of centuries. **2.** the collection of critical notes preserving the tradition. Also, **Masorah, Massora, Massorah.** [t. Heb.: (m.) *māsōrāh* tradition]
Masorete (măs′ə rēt′), *n.* **1.** a Hebrew scholar versed in the Masora. **2.** one of the body of Jewish scholars who reduced the Masora to writing. Also, **Masorite** (măs′ə rīt′), **Massorete.**
Masoretic (măs′ə rĕt′ĭk), *adj.* of or pertaining to the Masora, the Masoretes, or their system. Also, **Mas′oret′ical.**
Maspero (*Fr.* mȧs pĕ rō′), *n.* **Sir Gaston Camille Charles** (*Fr.* gȧs tôɴ kȧ mēy shȧrl′), 1846–1916, French Egyptologist.
Masqat (mŭs′kət, -kăt), *n.* Muscat.
masque (mäsk), *n.* **1.** a form of aristocratic entertainment in 16th- and 17th-century England, orig. consisting of pantomime and dancing but later with dialogue and song, in elaborate productions given by amateur and professional actors. **2.** a dramatic composition for such entertainment. **3.** a masquerade; a revel. Also, **mask.** [See MASK]
masquer (mäs′kə), *n.* masker.
masquerade (măs′kə rād′), *n., v.,* **-raded, -rading.** —*n.* **1.** an assembly of persons wearing masks and other disguises, and often elaborate or fantastic costumes, for dancing, etc. **2.** disguise such as is worn at such an assembly. **3.** disguise, or false outward show. **4.** a going about under false pretences. —*v.t.* **5.** to go about under false pretences or a false character. **6.** to disguise oneself. **7.** to take part in a masquerade. [t. F: m. *mascarade*, t. It.: m. *mascherata*, der. *maschera* MASK] —**mas′querad′er,** *n.*
mass[1] (măs), *n.* **1.** a body of coherent matter, usually of indefinite shape and often of considerable size: *a mass of dough.* **2.** an aggregation of incoherent particles, parts, or objects regarded as forming one body: *a mass of sand.* **3.** a considerable assemblage, number, or quantity: *a mass of errors, a mass of troops.* **4.** an expanse, as of colour, light, or shade in a painting. **5.** the main body, bulk, or greater part of anything: *the great mass of British products.* **6.** bulk, size, or massiveness. **7.** *Physics.* that property of a body, commonly but inadequately defined as the measure of the quantity of matter in it, to which its inertia is ascribed: the quotient of the weight of the body and the acceleration due to gravity. **8.** *Pharm.* a preparation of thick, pasty consistency, from which pills are made. **9. in the mass,** in the main; as a whole. **10. the masses,** the great body of the common people; the working classes or lower social orders. —*v.i.* **11.** to come together in or form a mass or masses: *the clouds are massing in the west.* —*v.t.* **12.** to gather into or dispose in a mass or masses; assemble: *the houses are massed in blocks, to mass troops.* [ME *masse*, t. L: m. *massa* mass, lump] —**Syn. 2.** aggregate, aggregation, assemblage. **3.** collection, accumulation, pile, conglomeration. **6.** See **size**[1]. **12.** assemble; collect, gather. —**Ant. 12.** disperse.
mass[2] (măs), *n.* **1.** the celebration of the Eucharist. See **high mass, low mass. 2.** a musical setting of certain parts of this service (now chiefly as celebrated in the Roman Catholic Church), as the Kyrie eleison, Gloria, Credo, Sanctus, and Benedictus, Agnus Dei. Also, **Mass.** [ME *masse*, OE *mæsse*, t. VL: m. *messa*, L *missa*; orig. application of L term uncert.]
Mass., Massachusetts.
Massa (*It.* mȧs′sȧ), *n.* a town in Italy, in NW Tuscany, near the Ligurian Sea. 61,523 (1966).
Massachuset (măs′ə chōō′sĭt), *n., pl.* **-sets,** (esp. collectively) **-set. 1.** a member of an Algonquian Indian people. **2.** the extinct Algonquian language of the Massachusett Indians. Also, **Massachusetts.**
Massachusetts (măs′ə chōō′sĭts), *n.* **1.** a state in the NE United States, on the Atlantic coast. 5,148,578 pop. (1960); 8257 sq. mi. *Cap.:* Boston. *Abbrev.:* Mass. **2.** Massachuset.
Massachusetts Bay, a large, open bay off the E coast of Massachusetts.
Massachusetts Institute of Technology, a U.S. institution of higher education and research at Cambridge, Massachusetts.
massacre (măs′ə kə), *n., v.,* **-cred, -cring.** —*n.* **1.** the unnecessary, indiscriminate killing of a number of human beings, as in barbarous warfare or persecution, or for revenge or plunder. **2.** a general slaughter of human beings. —*v.t.* **3.** to kill indiscriminately or in a massacre. [t. F, der. OF *macecler* to butcher, der. *mache-col* butcher, f. s. *macher* smash (g. *maccāre* to strike; of Gmc orig.) + *col* neck (g. L *collum*); ? also influenced by *masselier* butcher, g. L *macellārius*] —**massacrer** (măs′ə krə), *n.* —**Syn. 3.** See **slaughter.**
massage (măs′äzh, măs′äj), *n., v.,* **-saged, -saging.** —*n.* **1.** the act or art of treating the body by rubbing, kneading, or the like, to stimulate circulation, increase suppleness, etc. —*v.t.* **2.** to treat by massage. [t. F, der. *masser* knead, der. *masse* mass] —**mas′sag′er, mas′sag′ist,** *n.* —**massageuse** (măs′ä zhûz′), *n. fem.*
massasauga (măs′ə sô′gə), *n.* a small rattlesnake, *Sistrurus miliarius*, of the southern U.S.
Massasoit (măs′ə soit′), *n. c.* 1580–1661, American Indian chief (father of King Philip) who negotiated a peace treaty with the Pilgrim Fathers.
Massawa (mə sä′wə), *n.* a seaport in Eritrea, on the Red Sea. ab. 20,000.
mass defect, *Physics.* the difference between the mass of a nucleus and the total mass of its constituent particles, due to the equality of mass and energy.
massé (măs′ĭ), *n. Billiards.* a stroke made by hitting the cue ball with the cue held almost or quite perpendicular to the table. Also, **massé shot.** [t. F, pp. of *masser* strike by a massé, der. *masse* kind of cue, MACE[1]]
Massemba-Débat (mə sĕm′bə dā′bä), *n.* **Alphonse** (ăl′fŏns), born 1921, president of the Republic of Congo 1963–68.
Masséna (*Fr.* mȧ sĕ nȧ′), *n.* **André** (*Fr.* äɴ drĕ′) (*Prince d'Essling*), 1758–1817, French marshal under Napoleon I.
mass-energy equivalence (măs′ĕn′ə jĭ), *Physics.* the theory that mass and energy are connected and equivalent. Equivalent to a given mass is an energy equal to the mass times the square of the velocity of light.
Massenet (*Fr.* mȧs nĕ′), *n.* **Jules Émile Frédéric** (*Fr.* zhYl ĕ mĕl frĕ dĕ rēk′), 1842–1912, French composer.
masseter (mă sē′tə), *n. Anat.* an important masticatory muscle which serves to close the jaws by raising the mandible. [t. NL, t. Gk: m. *masētḗr* a chewer] —**masseteric** (măs′ĭ tĕ′rĭk), *adj.*
masseur (mă sû′), *n.* a man who practises massage. [t. F, der. *masser* to massage] —**masseuse** (mă sûz′), *n. fem.*
Massey (măs′ĭ), *n.* **Vincent,** 1887–1968, Canadian statesman: governor-general of Canada 1952–59.
massicot (măs′ĭ kŏt′), *n.* monoxide of lead, PbO, in the form of a yellow powder, used as a pigment and drier. [t. F, t. Sp: m. *mazacote* soda, t. Ar.: m. *shabb qubṭī* Egyptian alum]
massif (măs′ēf; *Fr.* mȧ sēf′), *n.* **1.** a compact portion of a mountain range, containing one or more summits. **2.** an extensive block of mountain country rising to one or two dominant heights, with longitudinal and transverse valleys, raised or depressed as a unit and bounded by

series of faults; an extensive horst. [t. F, n. use of *massif* MASSIVE]
Massif Central (*Fr.* mȧ sēf säN trȧl′), a plateau region in S central France. ab. 36,000 sq. mi. Highest peak, Puy de Sancy, 6188 ft.
Massine (mă sēn′), *n.* **Léonide** (lā′ŏ nēd′), born 1896, U.S. ballet dancer and choreographer, born in Russia.
Massinger (măs′ĭn jə), *n.* **Philip,** 1583–1640, English dramatist.
Massinissa (măs′ĭ nĭs′ə), *n.* Masinissa.
massive (măs′ĭv), *adj.* **1.** consisting of or forming a large mass; bulky and heavy. **2.** large, as the head or forehead. **3.** solid or substantial; great or imposing. **4.** *Mineral.* without outward crystal form, although perhaps crystalline in internal structure. **5.** *Geol.* homogeneous. **6.** *Med.* affecting a large continuous mass of bodily tissue, as a disease. [ME *massiffe*, t. F: m. *massif*, der. *masse* MASS[1]] **—mas′sively,** *adv.* **—mas′siveness,** *n.*
mass media, the means of communication, as radio, television, newspapers, magazines, etc., that reach large numbers of people.
mass meeting, a large or general assembly to discuss or hear discussed some matter of common interest.
mass number, *Physics.* the integer nearest to the atomic mass of an isotope; the number of nucleons in the nucleus of an atom.
mass observation, research or poll on public opinion and behaviour. *Abbrev.:* M.O.
Massora (mə sô′rə), *n.* Masora.
Massorete (măs′ə rēt′), *n.* Masorete.
massotherapy (măs′ō thĕ′rə pĭ), *n.* *Med.* treatment by massage. [f. F *mass(er)*, v., massage + -o- + THERAPY]
mass-produce (măs′prə dyōōs′), *v.t.*, **-duced, -ducing.** to manufacture in large quantities by standardized mechanical processes.
mass production, the production or manufacture of goods in large quantities by standardized mechanical processes.
mass ratio, *Aeron.* the ratio of the total mass of a rocket to the mass when all the propellant has been consumed.
mass spectrograph, *Physics.* a mass spectrometer with a means of recording photographically the mass spectrum found.
mass spectrometer, *Physics.* a device for separating atoms or molecules of different masses by utilizing the fact that the ions of such entities are deflected in a magnetic field by an amount which depends on the mass. Also, **mass spectroscope.**
massy (măs′ĭ), *adj.*, **-sier, -siest.** massive. **—mass′iness,** *n.*
Massys (mä′sās; *Flem.* mŏ′sĕys), *n.* **Quentin** (kwĕn′tĭn), 1466?–1530, Flemish painter. Also, **Matsys, Metsys.**
mast[1] (mäst), *n.* **1.** a tall spar rising more or less vertically from the keel or deck of a vessel, which supports the yards, sails, etc. **2.** any upright pole, as a support for an aerial, etc. **3.** the upright member in a derrick from which the jib is supported. **4. before the mast,** *Naut.* an unlicensed seaman (named from the quarters of seamen forward of the foremast in the forecastle). *—v.t.* **5.** to provide with a mast or masts. [ME; OE *mæst*, c. G *Mast*; akin to L *mālus*] **—mast′like′,** *adj.*
mast[2] (mäst), *n.* the fruit (acorns, chestnuts, beechnuts, etc.) of certain forest trees, esp. as food for swine. [ME; OE *mæst*, c. G *Mast*; akin to MEAT]
mast-, var. of **masto-,** before vowels, as in *mastectomy.*
mastaba (măs′tə bə), *n.* an ancient Egyptian tomb, rectangular in plan, with sloping sides and a flat roof. Also, **mastabah.** [t. Ar. (Egypt. d.): bench]
mastectomy (măs tĕk′tə mĭ), *n.*, *pl.* **-mies.** *Surg.* the operation of removing the breast or mamma. [f. MAST- + -ECTOMY]
master (mäs′tə), *n.* **1.** one who has the power of controlling, using, or disposing of something: *a master of several languages.* **2.** an employer of workmen or servants. **3.** Also, **master mariner.** the commander of a merchant vessel. **4.** the male head of a household. **5.** an owner of a slave, horse, dog, etc. **6.** a presiding officer. **7.** a male teacher, tutor, or schoolmaster. **8.** a person whose teachings one accepts or follows. **9.** (*cap.*) Christ (prec. by *the, our*, etc.). **10.** a victor. **11.** a workman qualified to teach apprentices and to carry on his trade independently. **12.** a man eminently skilled in something, as an occupation, art, or science. **13.** a title given to a bridge or chess player who has won or been placed high in a certain number of officially recognized tournaments. **14.** one holding this title. **15.** an officer of the Supreme Court of Judicature whose main function is to decide preliminary issues in High Court cases. **16.** *Educ.* one who has been awarded a master's degree. **17.** a boy or young man (used chiefly as a term of address). **18.** the title given to the head of a college at certain universities, to the head of certain corporations, etc. **19.** the title given to the heir apparent of a Scottish viscount or baron. **20.** an original matrix, esp. the first pressing of a gramophone record. **21. be master in one's own house,** to manage one's own affairs without interference. **22. be one's own master,** to be completely free and independent. *—adj.* **23.** being master, or exercising mastery. **24.** chief or principal: *the master bedroom.* **25.** directing or controlling. **26.** dominating or predominant. **27.** being a master carrying on his trade independently, rather than a workman employed by another. **28.** being a master of some occupation, art, etc.; eminently skilled. **29.** characteristic of a master; showing mastery. *—v.t.* **30.** to conquer or subdue; reduce to subjection. **31.** to rule or direct as master. **32.** to make oneself master of; to become an adept in. [ME *maister*, OE *magister*, t. L] **—mas′terdom,** *n.* **—mas′terless,** *adj.*
master-at-arms (mäs′tə rət ämz′), *n.*, *pl.* **masters-at-arms.** *Naut.* **1.** a naval petty officer employed as principal police officer on board ship. **2.** the principal police officer on a merchant vessel.
master builder, 1. a building contractor. **2.** an architect.
masterful (mäs′tə fəl), *adj.* **1.** having or showing the qualities of a master; authoritative; domineering. **2.** showing mastery or skill; masterly. **—mas′terfully,** *adv.* **—mas′terfulness,** *n.*
master hand, 1. an expert. **2.** great expertness.
master key, a key that will open a number of locks whose proper keys are not interchangeable; skeleton key.
masterly (mäs′tə lĭ), *adj.* **1.** like or befitting a master, as in skill or art. *—adv.* **2.** in a masterly manner. **—mas′terliness,** *n.*
master mariner, master (def. 3).
master mason, 1. a Freemason who has reached the third degree. **2.** an expert mason.
master mechanic, a mechanic in charge of other mechanics.
mastermind (mäs′tə mīnd′), *v.t.* **1.** to plan and direct activities skilfully: *the revolt was masterminded by two colonels.* *—n.* **2.** one who originates or is mainly responsible for the carrying out of a particular project, scheme, etc.
Master of Arts, 1. a second university degree, usually in a branch of the humanities or social sciences, normally awarded to one who has completed at least one year's postgraduate study. **2.** one holding this degree. *Abbrev.:* M.A.
master of ceremonies, a person who directs the entertainment at a party, dinner, etc.
master of foxhounds, the person responsible for the conduct of a hunt and to whom all members of the hunt and those connected with it are responsible.
Master of Science, 1. an academic degree similar to the Master of Arts, but taken in the field of natural sciences or mathematics. **2.** one holding this degree. *Abbrev.:* M.Sc.
Master of the Rolls, (in England) the judge responsible for the Public Record Office, the residing judge of the Court of Appeal.
masterpiece (mäs′tə pēs′), *n.* **1.** one's most excellent production, as in an art: *the masterpiece of a painter.* **2.** any production of masterly skill. **3.** a consummate example of skill or excellence of any kind.
master race, a race or nation, as the Germans during the Nazi period, who consider themselves superior to other races or nations and therefore fitted to rule or enslave them.
master's certificate, a certificate of competency entitling the holder to be the master of a merchant vessel.
master sergeant, 1. *U.S. Army, Air Force, Marine Corps.* a non-commissioned officer ranking next to the highest non-commissioned officer. **2.** *U.S. Air Force.* a non-commissioned officer of one of the three highest non-commissioned ranks.
mastership (mäs′tə shĭp′), *n.* **1.** the office, function, or authority of a master. **2.** control. **3.** mastery, as of a subject. **4.** masterly skill or knowledge.
mastersinger (mäs′tə sĭng′ə), *n.* Meistersinger.
master stroke, a masterly action or achievement.
masterwork (mäs′tə wûk′), *n.* a masterpiece.
master workman, 1. a workman in charge. **2.** one who is master of his craft.
master-wort (mäs′tə wût′), *n.* an erect, hairy, umbelliferous perennial with pinkish flowers, *Peucedanum ostruthium*, a native of S Europe which has become naturalized in other temperate areas.
mastery (mäs′tə rĭ), *n.*, *pl.* **-ries. 1.** the state of being master; power of command or control. **2.** command or grasp, as of a subject. **3.** victory. **4.** the action of mastering,

as a subject, etc. **5.** expert skill or knowledge. [f. MASTER + -Y³; r. ME *maistrie*, t. OF, der. *maistre* MASTER]

masthead (mäst′hĕd′), *n.* **1.** the top or head of the mast of a ship or vessel; usually the top of the highest mast in one vertical line. **2.** a statement printed (usually on the editorial page) in all issues of a newspaper, magazine, etc., giving the name, owner, staff, etc. —*v.t. Naut.* **3.** to hoist to the top or head of a mast. **4.** to send to the masthead as a punishment.

mastic (măs′tĭk), *n.* **1.** an aromatic, astringent resin obtained from a small anacardiaceous evergreen tree, *Pistacia lentiscus*, native in the Mediterranean region: used in making varnish. **2.** a similar resin yielded by other trees of the same genus, or a resin likened to it. **3.** a tree yielding a mastic, esp. *Pistacia lentiscus.* **4.** *Bldg Trades.* **a.** any of various preparations used for sealing joints, window frames, etc. **b.** a pasty form of cement used for filling holes in masonry or plastered walls. [ME *mastyk*, t. OF: m. *mastic*, t. L: m. s. *mastichum*, t. Gk: m. *mastíchē*]

masticate (măs′tĭ kāt′), *v.t., v.i.*, **-cated, -cating. 1.** to chew. **2.** to reduce to a pulp by crushing or kneading, as rubber. [t. LL: m. s. *masticātus*, pp., chewed] —**mas′tica′tion,** *n.* —**mas′tica′tor,** *n.*

masticatory (măs′tĭ kə tə rĭ, -trĭ), *adj., n., pl.* **-tories.** —*adj.* **1.** of, pertaining to, or used in or for mastication. —*n.* **2.** a medicinal substance to be chewed, as to promote the secretion of saliva.

Mastiff
(30 in. or more high at the shoulder)

mastiff (măs′tĭf), *n.* one of a breed of large, powerful, short-haired dogs having an apricot, fawn, or brindled coat. [ME, t. OF, b. *mastin* mastiff and *mestif* mongrel]

mastitis (măs tī′tĭs), *n.* **1.** *Pathol.* inflammation of the breast. **2.** *Vet. Sci.* garget. [t. NL; see MAST(O)-, -ITIS]

masto-, a word element meaning the breast, mastoid. Also, **mast-**. [t. Gk, comb. form of *mastós* breast]

Mastodon, *Mammut americanum*
(Up to ab. 9 ft high at the shoulder)

mastodon (măs′tə dŏn′), *n.* any of various species of large, extinct mammals (genus *Mammut*, etc.) of the elephant kind, characterized by nipple-like elevations on the molar teeth. [t. NL, f. Gk: *mast-* MAST- + m. s. *odoús* tooth]

mastoid (măs′toid), *adj.* **1.** resembling a breast or nipple. **2.** denoting the nipple-like process of the temporal bone behind the ear. **3.** of or pertaining to the mastoid process. —*n.* **4.** the mastoid process. [t. Gk: m. s. *mastoeidḗs* like the breast]

mastoidectomy (măs′toi dĕk′tə mĭ), *n., pl.* **-mies.** *Surg.* the removal of part of a mastoid bone.

mastoiditis (măs′toi dī′tĭs), *n. Pathol.* inflammation of the mastoid process of the temporal bone of the skull. [f. MASTOID + -ITIS]

masturbate (măs′tə bāt′), *v.*, **-bated, -bating.** —*v.i.* **1.** to engage in masturbation. —*v.t.* **2.** to practise masturbation upon. —**mas′turba′tor,** *n.*

masturbation (măs′tə bā′shən), *n.* the stimulation by friction of the genitals resulting in orgasm; sexual self-gratification; onanism (def. 2). [t. L: s. *masturbātio*]

Masulipatam (mə so͞o′lĭ pə tăm′), *n.* a seaport in India, in NE Andhra Pradesh. Also, **Bandar.**

Masuria (mə syo͝o′rĭ ə), *n.* a region in NE Poland, formerly in East Prussia, containing the **Masurian Lakes,** near which the Germans defeated the Russians, 1914–15. German, **Masuren** (*Ger.* mä zo͞o′rən).

masurium (mə so͝o′rĭ əm), *n. Chem.* former name of **technetium.** [f. MASUR(IA) + -IUM]

mat¹ (măt), *n., v.,* **matted, matting.** —*n.* **1.** a piece of fabric made of plaited or woven rushes, straw, hemp, or other fibre, or a similar article made of some other material, used to cover a floor, to wipe the shoes on, etc. **2.** a smaller piece of material, often ornamental, set under a dish of food, a lamp, vase, etc. **3.** a thick covering, as of padded canvas, laid on a floor on which wrestlers contend, in order to protect them. **4.** a thickly growing or thick and tangled mass, as of hair or weeds. **5.** a sack made of matting, as for coffee or sugar. **6.** *Print.* **a.** the intaglio (usually of papier-mâché or plastic), impressed from type or cut, from which a stereotype plate is cast or from which plastic and rubber plates are made for letterpress printing. **b.** the brass die used in a linotype, each carrying a letter in intaglio. —*v.t.* **7.** to cover with or as with mats or matting. **8.** to form into a mat, as by interweaving. —*v.i.* **9.** to become entangled; from tangled masses. [ME *matte*, OE *meatt(e)*, t. LL: m. *matta*]

mat² (măt), *n., v.,* **matted, matting.** —*n.* **1.** a piece of cardboard or other material placed round a photograph, painting, etc., to serve as a frame or border. —*v.t.* **2.** to provide (a picture) with a mat. [t. F. See MAT¹, MAT³, adj.]

mat³ (măt), *adj., n., v.,* **matted, matting.** —*adj.* **1.** lustreless and dull in surface. —*n.* **2.** a dull or dead surface, without lustre, produced on metals, etc.; a roughened or frosted surface. **3.** a tool, as a punch, for producing such a surface. —*v.t.* **4.** to finish with a mat surface. Also, **matt;** *U.S.*, **matte.** [t. F, der. *mater* make dull or weak, der. *mat* mated (in chess)]

Matabele (măt′ə bē′lĭ), *n., pl.* **-les,** (*esp. collectively*) **-le. 1.** a member of a Bantu-speaking people of Rhodesia and formerly of the Transvaal. **2.** their language. —*adj.* **3.** of or pertaining to the Matabele or their language.

Matabeleland (măt′ə bē′lĭ lănd′), *n.* that part of southern Africa inhabited or formerly inhabited by the Matabele.

matador (măt′ə dô′), *n.* **1.** the man who kills the bull in bullfights. **2.** one of the principal cards in skat and certain other games. [t. Sp., g. L *mactātor* slayer]

Matagalpa (*Sp.* mä tä gäl′pä), *n.* a town in central Nicaragua. 61,383 (1963).

Mata Hari (măt′ə hä′rĭ) (*Gertrud Margarete Zelle*), 1876–1917, Dutch dancer in France; executed as a spy by the French.

matai (măt′ī), *n.* a coniferous, evergreen tree of New Zealand, *Podocarpus spicatus*, with a bluish bark and small, narrow leaves, reaching a height of 60–80 ft. [t. Maori]

matamata (măt′ə mə tä′), *n.* a common freshwater turtle, *Chelus fimbriata*, of the rivers of Brazil and the Guianas, growing to about 2 ft in length.

Matamoros (măt′ə mô′rəs; *Sp.* mä tä mô′rôs), *n.* a seaport in NE Mexico, on the Rio Grande. 131,576 (est. 1965).

Matanzas (mə tăn′zəs; *Sp.* mä tän′thäs), *n.* a seaport on the NW coast of Cuba. 82,619 (1960).

Matapan (măt′ə păn′, măt′ə păn′), *n.* **Cape,** a cape in S Greece: the S tip of the Peloponnesus.

Mataura (mə tô′rə), *n.* a river in South Island, New Zealand, flowing S into Foveaux Strait. 140 mi.

match¹ (măch), *n.* **1.** a short, slender piece of wood or other material tipped with a chemical substance which produces fire when rubbed on a rough or chemically prepared surface. **2.** a wick, cord, or the like, prepared to burn at an even rate, used to fire cannon, etc. [ME *matche*, t. OF: m. *meiche*; orig. uncert.]

match² (măch), *n.* **1.** a person or thing that equals or resembles another in some respect. **2.** a person or thing that is an exact counterpart of another. **3.** one able to cope with another as an equal: *to meet one's match.* **4.** a corresponding or suitably associated pair. **5.** a contest or game. **6.** an engagement for a contest or game. **7.** a person considered with regard to suitability as a partner in marriage. **8.** a matrimonial compact or alliance. —*v.t.* **9.** to equal, or be equal to. **10.** to be the match or counterpart of: *the colour of the skirt does not match that of the coat.* **11.** to adapt; make to correspond. **12.** to fit together, as two things. **13.** to procure or produce an equal to. **14.** to place in opposition or conflict. **15.** to provide with an adversary or competitor of equal power: *the teams were well matched.* **16.** to encounter as an adversary with equal power. **17.** to prove a match for. **18.** to unite in marriage; procure a matrimonial alliance for. —*v.i.* **19.** to be equal or suitable. **20.** to correspond; be of corresponding size, shape, colour, pattern, etc. **21.** to ally oneself in marriage. [ME *macche*, OE *gemæcca* mate, fellow] —**match′able,** *adj.* —**match′er,** *n.*

matchboard (măch′bôd′), *n.* a board which has a tongue cut along one edge and a groove in the opposite edge: used in making floors, etc., the tongue of one such board fitting into the groove of the next.

matchbox (măch′bŏks′), *n.* a small box, usually of wood, for holding matches, usually with a striking surface on one side.

matchless (măch′lĭs), *adj.* having no equal; peerless: *matchless courage.* —**match′lessly,** *adv.* —**match′lessness,** *n.* —**Syn.** unrivalled, inimitable.

matchlock (măch′lŏk′), *n.* **1.** an old form of gunlock in which the priming was ignited by a slow match. **2.** a hand gun, usually a musket, with such a lock.

matchmaker[1] (măch′mā′kə), *n.* **1.** one who makes, or seeks to bring about, matrimonial matches. **2.** one who makes or arranges matches for athletic contests, etc. [f. MATCH[2] + MAKER] —**match′mak′ing,** *n., adj.*

matchmaker[2] (măch′mā′kə), *n.* one who makes matches for burning. [f. MATCH[1] + MAKER] —**match′mak′ing,** *n., adj.*

match play, *Golf.* play in which the score is reckoned by counting the holes won by each side.

match point, the final point needed to win a contest.

matchstick (măch′stĭk′), *n.* a short, slender fairly rigid length of wood or other similar material, used in making matches.

matchwood (măch′wŏŏd′), *n.* **1.** wood suitable for matches. **2.** splinters.

mate[1] (māt), *n., v.,* **mated, mating.** —*n.* **1.** one joined with another in any pair. **2.** a counterpart. **3.** husband or wife. **4.** one of a pair of mated animals. **5.** a habitual associate; comrade; partner. **6.** an officer of a merchant vessel who ranks below the captain or master (called **first mate, second mate,** etc., when there are more than one on a ship). **7.** an assistant to a tradesman or other functionary on a ship. **8.** *Archaic.* a suitable associate. —*v.t.* **9.** to join as a mate or as mates. **10.** to match or marry. **11.** to pair, as animals. **12.** to join suitably, as two things. **13.** to treat as comparable, as one thing with another. —*v.i.* **14.** to associate as a mate or as mates. **15.** to marry. **16.** to pair. **17.** to consort; keep company. [ME, t. MLG, var. of *gemate*; akin to OE *gemetta* sharer of food, guest. See MEAT]

mate[2] (māt), *n., v.t.,* **mated, mating.** *Chess.* checkmate. [ME *mate(n)*, t. OF: m. *mater*, der. *mat* checkmated, overcome, t. Ar. See MAT[3], CHECKMATE]

mate[3] (mä′tā, măt′ā), *n.* maté.

maté (mä′tā, măt′ā), *n.* **1.** a tealike South American beverage made from the leaves of a species of holly, *Ilex paraguariensis*, native in Paraguay and Brazil. **2.** the plant itself. Also, **mate.** [t. Sp.: prop., a vessel, t. Quechua: m. *mat* calabash]

matelassé (măt lăs′ā), *n.* a heavy type of cloth, with figuring in geometrical forms in a variety of weaves. [t. F: pp. of *matelasser* to quilt]

matelot (măt′ə lō′, măt′lō; *Fr.* mȧt lō′), *n.* *Colloq.* a sailor. [F]

mater (mā′tə), *n.* mother. [L]

mater dolorosa (mā′tə dŏl′ə rō′sə), *Latin.* **1.** the sorrowful mother. **2.** (*cap.*) the mother of Christ sorrowing for her son, esp. as represented in art.

materfamilias (mā′tə fə mĭl′ĭ ăs′), *n.* *Latin.* the mother of a family.

material (mə tĭə′rĭ əl), *n.* **1.** the substance or substances of which a thing is made or composed. **2.** any constituent element of a thing. **3.** anything serving as crude or raw matter for working upon or developing. **4.** information, ideas, or the like on which a report, thesis, etc., is based. **5.** a textile fabric. **6.** (*pl.*) articles of any kind requisite for making or doing something: *writing materials.* —*adj.* **7.** formed or consisting of matter; physical; corporeal: *the material world.* **8.** relating to, concerned with, or involving matter: *material force.* **9.** concerned or occupied unduly with corporeal things or interests. **10.** pertaining to the physical rather than the spiritual or intellectual aspect of things: *material civilization.* **11.** of substantial import or much consequence. **12.** pertinent or essential (fol. by *to*). **13.** *Law.* (of evidence, etc.) likely to influence the determination of a cause. **14.** *Philos.* of or pertaining to matter as distinguished from form. [ME, t. LL: s. *māteriālis*, der. *māteria* matter] —**mate′rialness,** *n.* —**Syn. 1.** See **matter.**

materialism (mə tĭə′rĭ ə lĭz′əm), *n.* **1.** the philosophical theory which regards matter and its motions as constituting the universe, and all phenomena, including those of mind, as due to material agencies. **2.** *Ethics.* the doctrine that the self-interest of the individual is or ought to be the first law of life; egoistic, as opposed to universalistic, hedonism. **3.** devotion to material rather than spiritual objects, needs, and considerations.

materialist (mə tĭə′rĭ ə lĭst), *n.* **1.** an adherent of philosophical materialism. **2.** one absorbed in material interests; one who takes a material view of life. —**mate′rialis′tic,** *adj.* —**mate′rialis′tically,** *adv.*

materiality (mə tĭə′rĭ ăl′ĭ tĭ), *n., pl.* **-ties. 1.** material nature or quality. **2.** something material.

materialize (mə tĭə′rĭ ə līz′), *v.,* **-lized, -lizing.** —*v.t.* **1.** to give material form to. **2.** to invest with material attributes. **3.** to make physically perceptible. **4.** to render materialistic. —*v.i.* **5.** to assume material or bodily form. **6.** to come into perceptible existence; appear. Also, **materialise.** —**mate′rializa′tion,** *n.* —**mate′rializ′er,** *n.*

materially (mə tĭə′rĭ ə lĭ), *adv.* **1.** to an important degree; considerably. **2.** with reference to matter or material things; physically. **3.** *Philos.* with regard to matter or substance as distinguished from form.

materia medica (mə tĭə′rĭ ə mĕd′ĭ kə), **1.** the remedial substances employed in medicine. **2.** the branch of medicine treating of these. [t. ML: medical material]

matériel (mə tĭə′rĭ ĕl′), *n.* **1.** the aggregate of things used or needed in any business, undertaking, or operation (distinguished from *personnel*). **2.** *Mil.* arms, ammunition, and equipment in general. [t. F. See MATERIAL]

maternal (mə tû′nəl), *adj.* **1.** of or pertaining to, befitting, having the qualities of, or being a mother. **2.** derived from a mother. **3.** related through a mother: *his maternal aunt.* [late ME, f. s. L *māternus* of a mother + -AL[1]] —**mater′nally,** *adv.*

maternity (mə tû′nĭ tĭ), *n.* **1.** the state of being a mother; motherhood. **2.** motherliness. —*adj.* **3.** belonging to or characteristic of motherhood or of the period of pregnancy.

maternity hospital, a hospital for the care of women during confinement in childbirth.

matey (mā′tĭ), *Colloq.* —*adj.* **1.** comradely; friendly. —*n.* **2.** comrade; chum.

mat-grass (măt′gräs′), *n.* a small perennial grass with hard, pointed leaves, *Nardus stricta*, occurring on poor, non-alkaline soils in Greenland, Europe, and Asia.

math., **1.** mathematical. **2.** *U.S.* mathematics.

mathematical (măth′ĭ măt′ĭ kl), *adj.* **1.** of, pertaining to, or of the nature of mathematics. **2.** employed in the operations of mathematics. **3.** having the exactness or precision of mathematics. Also, **math′emat′ic.** [f. *mathematic* MATHEMATICS + -AL[1]] —**math′emat′ically,** *adv.*

mathematical expectation, *Statistics.* the average of a set of possible values of a variable, the values weighted by the probabilities associated with these values.

mathematical logic, a modern development of formal logic employing a special notation or symbolism capable of manipulation in accordance with precise rules; symbolic logic.

mathematician (măth′ĭ mə tĭsh′ən), *n.* a student of or an expert in mathematics.

mathematics (măth′ĭ măt′ĭks), *n.* the science that treats of the measurement, properties, and relations of quantities, including arithmetic, geometry, algebra, etc. [pl. of *mathematic*, t. L: s. *mathēmaticus*, t. Gk: m. *mathēmatikós* pertaining to science. See -ICS]

maths, mathematics.

Mathura (mŭ thōō′rə), *n.* a city in India, in W Uttar Pradesh: Hindu shrine and holy city: reputed birthplace of Krishna. 116,959 (1961). Formerly, **Muttra.**

matilda (mə tĭl′də), *n.* *Austral. Colloq.* **1.** swag. **2. to waltz matilda,** to carry a swag. [special use of *Matilda*, girl's name]

matin (măt′ĭn), *n.* **1.** (*pl.*) *Eccles.* **a.** the first of the seven canonical hours, or the service for it, properly beginning at midnight, sometimes at daybreak. **b.** the order for public morning prayer in the Anglican Church. **2.** *Poetic.* a morning song, esp. of a bird. —*adj.* **3.** Also, **mat′inal.** pertaining to the morning or to matins. Also, **mattin.** [ME *matyn* (pl. *matines*), t. OF: m. *matin* morning, g. L *mātūtīnus* of or in the morning]

matinee (măt′ĭ nā′), *n.* an entertainment, esp. a dramatic or musical performance, held in the daytime, usually in the afternoon. Also, *French,* **matinée** (*Fr.* mȧ tē nĕ′). [t. F, der. *matin* morning. See MATIN]

matinee coat, a jacket of wool or warm material for a baby. Also, **matinee jacket.**

Matisse (*Fr.* mȧ tēs′), *n.* **Henri** (*Fr.* äN rē′), 1869–1954, French painter.

Matlock (măt′lŏk′), *n.* a town in England, in Derbyshire. 18,486 (1961).

Mato Grosso (măt′ō grŏs′ō; *Port.* mȧ′tōō grō′sōō), a plateau, a western extension of the plateau of S Brazil, which separates the basins of the Amazon and River Plate; covered by extensive campos at a height of 400 to 3000 ft.

matrass (măt′rəs), *n.* *Chem. Obs.* **1.** a rounded, long-necked glass vessel, used for distilling, etc. **2.** a small glass closed at one end. Also, **mattrass.**

matri-, a word element meaning 'mother'. [t. L, comb. form of *māter*]

matriarch (mā′trĭ äk′), *n.* a woman holding a position analogous to that of a patriarch, as in a family or tribe. [f. MATRI- + -ARCH; modelled on PATRIARCH] —**ma′triar′chal, ma′triar′chic,** *adj.*

matriarchate (mā′trĭ ä′kĭt, -kāt), *n.* **1.** a matriarchal system or community. **2.** *Sociol.* a social order believed to have preceded patriarchal tribal society in the early period of human communal life, embodying rule by the mothers, or by all adult women.

matriarchy (mā′trĭ ä′kĭ), *n., pl.* **-chies.** the matriarchal system; a form of social organization, as in certain primitive tribes, in which the mother is head of the family, and in which descent is reckoned in the female line, the children belonging to the mother's clan.

matrices (mā′trĭ sēz′), *n.* pl. of **matrix.**

matricide (mā′trĭ sīd′), *n.* **1.** one who kills his mother. **2.** the act of killing one's mother. [t. L: m. s. *mātricīdium* (def. 2), *mātri- cīda* (def. 1). See MATRI-, -CIDE] —**ma′tricid′al,** *adj.*

matriculant (mə trĭk′yŏŏ lənt), *n.* one who matriculates; a candidate for matriculation.

matriculate (*v.* mə trĭk′yŏŏ lāt′; *n.* mə trĭk′yŏŏ lĭt), *v.,* **-lated, -lating,** *n.* —*v.i.* **1.** to be admitted to membership, esp. of a college or university. **2.** to pass matriculation (def. 2). —*v.t.* **3.** *Now Chiefly U.S.* to enrol or admit. —*n.* **4.** one who has matriculated. [f. s. LL *mātrīcula,* dim. of *mātrix* public register, roll + -ATE¹] —**matric′ula′tor,** *n.*

matriculation (mə trĭk′yŏŏ lā′shən), *n.* **1.** the process of being formally enrolled in or admitted to certain colleges or universities. **2.** (in Great Britain) a former secondary-school examination, now replaced by the General Certificate of Education (Ordinary Level), in which a required level had to be reached in five or more subjects chosen within a certain range.

matrimonial (măt′rĭ mō′nyəl), *adj.* of or pertaining to matrimony; nuptial. —**mat′rimo′nially,** *adv.*

matrimony (măt′rĭ mə nĭ), *n., pl.* **-nies.** the rite, ceremony, or sacrament of marriage. [ME *matrimonye,* t. L: m. *mātrimōnium* marriage]

matrimony vine, any of the plants constituting the solanaceous genus *Lycium,* species of which are cultivated for their foliage, flowers, and berries; boxthorn.

matrix (mā′trĭks), *n., pl.* **matrices** (mā′trĭ sēz′), **matrixes. 1.** that which gives origin or form to a thing, or which serves to enclose it. **2.** *Anat.* a formative part, as the corium beneath a nail. **3.** *Biol.* the intercellular substance of a tissue. **4.** the rock in which a crystallized mineral is embedded. **5.** *Mining.* gangue. **6.** *Print.* **a.** a mould for casting typefaces. **b.** mat¹ (def. 6). **7.** (in a punching machine) a perforated block upon which the object to be punched is rested. **8.** *Maths, Computers.* a rectangular array of numbers. **9.** *Maths, Computers.* a rectangular array of logical elements acting as a selection system. **10.** *Archaic.* the womb. [t. L: breeding animal, LL womb, source]

matron (mā′trən), *n.* **1.** a married woman, esp. one of ripe years and staid character or established position. **2.** a woman in charge of the domestic arrangements, the sanatorium, etc., in a boarding school. **3.** a woman in charge of nursing, etc., in a hospital. [ME *matrone,* t. OF, t. L: m. *mātrōna* married woman] —**matronal** (mā′trə nəl), *adj.*

matronage (mā′trə nĭj), *n.* **1.** the state of being a matron. **2.** guardianship by a matron. **3.** matrons collectively.

matronly (mā′trən lĭ), *adj.* **1.** like a matron, or having the characteristics of a matron. **2.** characteristic of or suitable for a matron. —**ma′tronliness,** *n.*

matron of honour, a married woman acting as the principal attendant of the bride at a wedding.

Matsu (măt′sōō′), *n.* a Chinese island off the SE coast of China. See **Quemoy.**

Matsue (măt′sŏŏ ĭ), *n.* a town in Japan, in SW Honshu island. 110,534 (1965).

Matsumoto (măt′sŏŏ mō′tō), *n.* a town in Japan, in central Honshu island. 154,131 (1965).

Matsuyama (măt′sŏŏ yä′mə), *n.* a seaport in SW Japan, on Shikoku island. 282,651 (1965).

Matsys (*Flem.* mŏt′sēys), *n.* Massys.

matt (măt), *adj., n., v.* mat³. Also, *U.S.,* **matte.**

Matt., Matthew.

matte (măt), *n. Metall.* an unfinished metallic product of the smelting of certain sulphide ores, esp. those of copper. [t. F. See MAT¹]

matted¹ (măt′ĭd), *adj.* **1.** covered with a dense growth or a tangled mass. **2.** covered with mats or matting. **3.** formed into a mat; entangled in a thick mass. **4.** formed of mats, or of woven material. [f. MAT¹ + -ED²]

matted² (măt′ĭd), *adj.* having a dull finish. [f. MAT³ + -ED²]

Matteotti (*It.* măt tė ŏt′tē), *n.* **Giacomo** (*It.* jä′kō mō), 1885–1924, Italian socialist leader.

matter (măt′ə), *n.* **1.** the substance or substances of which physical objects consist or are composed. **2.** physical or corporeal substance in general (whether solid, liquid, or gaseous), esp. as distinguished from incorporeal substance (as spirit or mind), or from qualities, actions, etc. **3.** whatever occupies space. **4.** a particular kind of substance: *colouring matter.* **5.** some substance excreted by a living body, esp. pus. **6.** the material or substance of a discourse, book, etc., often as distinguished from the form. **7.** things written or printed: *printed matter.* **8.** a thing, affair, or business: *a matter of life and death.* **9.** an amount or extent reckoned approximately: *a matter of ten miles.* **10.** something of consequence: *it is no matter.* **11.** importance or significance: *what matter?* **12.** the trouble or difficulty (prec. by *the*): *there is nothing the matter.* **13.** ground, reason, or cause. **14.** *Philos.* that stuff which by integrative organization forms chemical substances and living things. In Aristotelian tradition *matter* is to *form* as *potentiality* to *actuality.* **15.** *Law.* statement or allegation. **16.** *Print.* **a.** material for work; copy. **b.** type set up. **17. as a matter of fact,** actually; in reality. **18. for that matter,** as far as that is concerned. —*v.i.* **19.** to be of importance; signify: *it matters little.* **20.** to suppurate. [ME *matere,* t. OF, t. L: m. s. *māteria* stuff, material]

—**Syn. 1.** MATTER, MATERIAL, STUFF, SUBSTANCE refer to that of which physical objects are composed (though all these terms are also used abstractly). MATTER, as distinct from mind and spirit, is a broad word which applies to anything perceived, or known to be occupying space: *solid matter, gaseous matter.* MATERIAL usually means some definite kind, quality, or quantity of matter, esp. as intended for use: *woollen material, a house built of good materials.* STUFF, a less technical word, with approximately the same meanings as MATERIAL, is characterized by being of colloquial level when it refers to physical objects (*dynamite is queer stuff*), and of literary or poetic application when it is used abstractly (*the stuff that dreams are made of*). SUBSTANCE is the matter that composes a thing, thought of in relation to its essential properties: *a sticky substance.*

Matterhorn (măt′ə hôn′), *n.* a peak in the Pennine Alps on the Swiss-Italian border. 14,780 ft. French, **Mont Cervin.**

matter of course, the logical and inevitable outcome of a sequence of events.

matter-of-course (măt′ə rəv kôs′), *adj.* occurring or proceeding as if in the natural course of things.

matter-of-fact (măt′ə rəv făkt′), *adj.* adhering to actual facts; not imaginative; prosaic; commonplace.

Matthew (măth′yōō), *n.* **1.** a customs collector at Capernaum summoned to be one of the twelve apostles. Matt. 9:9–13. **2.** the first Gospel in the New Testament. [t. F: m. *Mathieu,* t. LL: m. *Matthaeus,* t. Gk: m. *Matthaîos,* t. Heb.: m. *Mattīthyāh*]

Matthew of Paris, *c.* 1200–59, English chronicler.

Matthews (măth′yōōz), *n.* **Sir Stanley,** born 1915, English professional footballer.

Matthew Walker, a kind of knot. See **knot.**

Matthias (mə thī′əs), *n.* a disciple chosen to take the place of Judas Iscariot as one of the apostles. Acts 1:23–26. [see MATTHEW]

mattin (măt′ĭn), *n., adj.* matin.

matting¹ (măt′ĭng), *n.* **1.** a coarse fabric of rushes, grass, straw, hemp, or the like, used for covering floors, wrapping, etc. **2.** material for mats. [f. MAT¹ + -ING¹]

matting² (măt′ĭng), *n.* a dull, slightly roughened surface, free from polish, produced by the use of the mat. [f. MAT³ + -ING¹]

mattock (măt′ək), *n.* an instrument for loosening the soil in digging, shaped like a pickaxe, but having one end broad instead of pointed. [ME *mattok,* OE *mattuc*]

mattoid (măt′oid), *n.* a person of abnormal mentality bordering on insanity. [t. It.: m. *mattoide,* der. *matto* mad, g. L *mattus* intoxicated]

mattrass (măt′rəs), *n. Chem.* matrass.

mattress (măt′rĭs), *n.* **1.** a case filled with hair, straw, cotton, etc., usually quilted or fastened together at intervals, used as or on a bed. **2.** a mat woven of brush, poles, or similar material used to prevent erosion of the surface of dykes, jetties, embankments, dams, etc. [ME *materas,* t. OF, t. It.: m. *materasso,* t. Ar.: m. (*al*) *maṭraḥ* (the) mat, cushion]

matungulu (mä′tŏŏng gōō′lōō), *n. S African.* the Natal wild plum, *Carissa grandiflora.* Also, **amatungulu.** [t. Zulu: m. *amathungulu*]

maturate (măt′yŏŏ rāt′), *v.i.,* **-rated, -rating. 1.** to suppurate. **2.** to mature. [t. L: m. s. *mātūrātus,* pp., ripened] —**maturative** (mə tyŏŏə′rə tĭv), *adj.*

maturation (măt′yŏŏ rā′shən), *n.* **1.** the act or process of maturating. **2.** *Biol.* the second phase of gametogenesis resulting in the production of mature eggs and sperms from oogonia and spermatogonia.

mature (mə tyo͞oə′), *adj.*, *v.*, **-tured, -turing.** —*adj.* **1.** complete in natural growth or development, as plant and animal forms, cheese, wine, etc. **2.** ripe, as fruit. **3.** fully developed in body or mind, as a person. **4.** pertaining to or characteristic of full development: *a mature appearance.* **5.** completed, perfected, or elaborated in full by the mind: *mature plans.* **6.** *Com.* having reached the limit of its time; having become payable or due, as a note. **7.** *Med.* in a state of perfect suppuration. **8.** *Phys. Geog.* (of topographical features) exhibiting the stage of maximum stream development, as in the process of erosion of a land surface. —*v.t.* **9.** to make mature; esp., to ripen. **10.** to bring to full development. **11.** to complete or perfect. —*v.i.* **12.** to become mature, esp. to ripen. **13.** to come to full development. **14.** *Com.* to become due, as a note. [late ME, t. L: m. s. *mātūrus* ripe, timely, early] —**mature′ly,** *adv.* —**mature′ness,** *n.* —**Syn. 1.** See **ripe.**

maturity (mə tyo͞oə′rĭ tĭ), *n.* **1.** the state of being mature; ripeness. **2.** full development; perfected condition. **3.** *Physiol.* period following attainment of full development of bodily structure and reproductive faculty. **4.** *Com.* **a.** the state of being due. **b.** the time when a note or bill of exchange becomes due.

matutinal (măt′yo͞o tī′nəl), *adj.* pertaining to or occurring in the morning; early in the day. [t. L: s. *mātūtīnālis* of the morning] —**mat′uti′nally,** *adv.*

matzo (măt′sō), *n.*, *pl.* **matzoth** (măt′sōth), **matzos** (măt′sōs). a biscuit of unleavened bread, eaten by Jews during the Feast of Passover. [t. Heb.: m. *matstsāh* cake of unleavened bread]

Maubeuge (*Fr.* mō bœzh′), *n.* a town in N France, on the river Sambre, near the Belgian border. 27,287 (1962).

maud (môd), *n.* **1.** a grey woollen plaid worn by shepherds and others in S Scotland. **2.** a blanket or wrap of like material, used as a travelling rug, etc. [orig. uncert.]

maudlin (môd′lĭn), *adj.* **1.** tearfully or weakly emotional or sentimental. **2.** tearfully or emotionally silly from drink. [from *Maudlin*, familiar var. of *Magdalen* (Mary Magdalene), often represented in art as weeping] —**maud′linly,** *adv.* —**maud′linness,** *n.*

Maugham (môm), *n.* **(William) Somerset,** 1874–1965, English novelist, dramatist, and short-story writer.

maugre (mô′gə), *prep. Archaic.* in spite of; notwithstanding. [ME *maugre*, t. OF: prop., ill will, spite. See MAL-, GREE[2]]

Maui (mou′ĭ), *n.* one of the Hawaiian islands, in the central part of the group. 35,717 pop. (1960); 728 sq. mi.

maul (môl), *n.* **1.** a heavy hammer, as for driving piles. **2.** *Obs.* a heavy club or mace. —*v.t.* **3.** to handle roughly; to injure by rough treatment. **4.** *U.S.* to split with a maul and a wedge, as a rail. [var. of MALL] —**maul′er,** *n.*

Maulmain (moul mān′), *n.* Moulmein.

maulstick (môl′stĭk′), *n.* a painter's stick, held in one hand as a support for the hand which holds the brush. Also, **mahlstick.** [t. D: m. *maalstok*]

Mau Mau (mou′mou′), a political movement among the Kikuyu of Kenya, founded in 1952, which by terrorist activities aimed at driving out European settlers.

Mauna Kea (mou′nə kā′ə, mô′nə kē′ə), an extinct volcano on the island of Hawaii. 13,784 ft.

Mauna Loa (mou′nə lō′ə, mô′nə lō′ə), an active volcano on the island of Hawaii. 13,680 ft.

maund (mônd), *n.* a unit of weight in India and other parts of Asia, varying greatly according to locality: in India, from about 25 to 82·286 lbs (the latter being the government maund). [t. Hind., Pers.: m. *mān*]

maunder (môn′də), *v.i.* **1.** to talk in a rambling, foolish, or imbecile way. **2.** to move, go, or act in an aimless, confused manner. [? t. OF: m. *mendier* beg, g. L *mendīcāre*] —**maun′derer,** *n.*

maundy (môn′dĭ), *n.* **1.** the ceremony of washing the feet of the poor, esp. commemorating Jesus's washing of His disciples' feet on Maundy Thursday. **2.** Also, **maundy money.** money distributed as alms in conjunction with the ceremony of maundy or on Maundy Thursday. [ME *maunde*, t. OF: m. *mande*, t. L: m. s. *mandātum* a command, mandate]

Maundy Thursday (môn′dĭ), the Thursday of Holy Week, commemorating Jesus's Last Supper and His washing of the disciples' feet upon that day. See John 13:5, 14, 34.

Maupassant (*Fr.* mō pȧ säN′), *n.* **(Henri René Albert) Guy de** (*Fr.* äN rə nė ȧl bĕr′ gē′ də), 1850–93, French short-story writer and novelist.

Maurer (*Rum.* mȧw′rər), *n.* **Ion Gheorghe** (*Rum.* yōn gyōr′gė), born 1902, chairman of the Rumanian council of ministers since 1961.

Mauretania (mŏ′rĭ tā′nyə), *n.* an ancient kingdom in NW Africa: it included the territory that is modern Morocco and part of Algeria. Also, **Mauritania.**

Mauriac (*Fr.* mō ryȧk′), *n.* **François** (*Fr.* fräN swȧ′), 1885–1970, French novelist.

Maurice (mŏ′rĭs), *n.* **1.** 1521–53, elector of Saxony. **2. of Nassau,** 1567–1625, Dutch prince and statesman.

Mauritania (mŏ′rĭ tā′nyə), *n.* **1.** a republic in W Africa, largely in the Sahara Desert. 770,000 pop. (est. 1963); 418,120 sq. mi. *Cap.:* Nouakchott. Official name, **Islamic Republic of Mauritania.** See map under **Algeria. 2.** Mauretania. —**Mau′rita′nian,** *n.*, *adj.*

Mauritius (mə rĭsh′əs), *n.* **1.** an island in the Indian Ocean, E of Madagascar. 736,975 pop. (est. 1965); 720 sq. mi. **2.** an independent state consisting of this island and dependencies: member of the Commonwealth of Nations. 741,000 pop. (est. 1965); 809 sq. mi. *Cap.:* Port Louis. Formerly, **Ile de France.** —**Maurit′ian,** *adj.*, *n.*

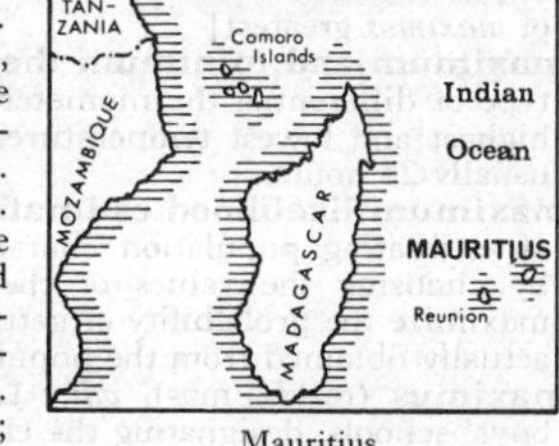

Mauritius

Maurois (*Fr.* mō rwȧ′), *n.* **André** (*Fr.* äN drė′) (*Emile Herzog*), 1885–67, French biographer and novelist.

mausoleum (mô′sə lĭəm′), *n.*, *pl.* **-leums, -lea** (-lĭə′). **1.** a stately and magnificent tomb. **2.** (*cap.*) a magnificent tomb erected at Halicarnassus in Asia Minor in 350 B.C. See **Seven Wonders of the World.** [t. L, t. Gk: m. *mausōleîon* the tomb of Mausolus (king of Caria)] —**mau′solean′,** *adj.*

mauve (mōv), *n.* **1.** pale bluish purple. **2.** a purple dye obtained from aniline, the first of the coal-tar dyes (discovered in 1856). —*adj.* **3.** of the colour of mauve: *a mauve dress.* [t. F: orig., mallow, g. L *malva* MALLOW]

maverick (măv′ə rĭk), *n.* **1.** *U.S.* (in cattle-raising regions) **a.** an animal found without an owner's brand. **b.** a calf separated from its dam. **2.** a dissenter. [prob. named after Samuel *Maverick*, 1803–70, a Texas cattle-raiser who neglected to brand his cattle]

mavis (mā′vĭs), *n.* the European throstle or song thrush, *Turdus philomelus.* [ME *mavys*, t. OF: m. *mauvis*; of Celtic orig.]

Mavor (mā′və), *n.* **Osborne Henry.** See **Bridie.**

mavourneen (mə vo͞oə′nēn), *n. Irish.* my darling. Also, **mavournin.** [t. Irish: m. *mo mhuirnīn*]

maw (mô), *n.* **1.** the mouth, throat, or gullet as concerned in devouring (now chiefly of animals or in figurative use). **2.** the crop or craw of a fowl. **3.** the stomach. [ME *mawe*, OE *maga*, c. G *Magen*]

mawkish (mô′kĭsh), *adj.* **1.** sickly or slightly nauseating. **2.** characterized by sickly sentimentality. [f. *mawk* maggot (t. Scand.; cf. Icel. *madhkr*) + -ISH[1]] —**mawk′ishly,** *adv.* —**mawk′ishness,** *n.*

Mawson (mô′sən), *n.* **Sir Douglas,** 1882–1958, Australian Antarctic explorer, born in England.

max., maximum.

maxilla (măk sĭl′ə), *n.*, *pl.* **maxillae** (măk sĭl′ē). **1.** a jaw or jawbone, esp. the upper. **2.** one of the paired appendages immediately behind the mandibles of arthropods. [t. L: jaw]

maxillary (măk sĭl′ə rĭ), *adj.*, *n.*, *pl.* **-laries.** —*adj.* **1.** of or pertaining to a jaw, jawbone, or maxilla. —*n.* **2.** a maxilla or maxillary bone.

maxim (măk′sĭm), *n.* **1.** an expression, esp. an aphoristic or sententious one, of a general truth, esp. as to conduct. **2.** a principle of conduct. [ME *maxime*, t. OF, t. L: m. *maxima* (*prōpositio*), lit., greatest (proposition)] —**Syn. 1.** See **proverb.**

Maxim (măk′sĭm), *n.* **1. Sir Hiram Stevens,** 1840–1916, British inventor of a machine-gun, born in the U.S. **2.** his brother, **Hudson,** 1853–1927, U.S. inventor.

maxima (măk′sĭ mə), *n.* a pl. of **maximum.**

maximal (măk′sĭ məl), *adj.* of or being a maximum; greatest possible; highest. —**max′imally,** *adv.*

Maximalist (măk′sĭ mə lĭst), *n.* a member of an extremist group or faction of socialists, as of a faction of the Russian Social Revolutionary Party.

Maximilian (măk′sĭ mĭl′yən), *n.* 1832–67, archduke of Austria: emperor of Mexico 1864–67.

Maximilian I, 1459–1519, emperor of the Holy Roman Empire 1493–1519.

Maximilian II, 1527–76, emperor of the Holy Roman Empire 1564–76.

maximite (măk′sĭ mīt′), *n.* a powerful explosive consisting largely of picric acid. [named after Hudson MAXIM. See -ITE[1]]

maximize (măk′sĭ mīz′), *v.t.*, **-mized, -mizing.** to increase to the greatest possible amount or degree. Also, **maximise.** [f. s. L *maximus* greatest + -IZE] —**max′imiza′tion,** *n.* —**max′imiz′er,** *n.*

maximum (măk′sĭ məm), *n., pl.* **-ma** (-mə), **-mums,** *adj.* —*n.* **1.** the greatest quantity or amount possible, assignable, allowable, etc.; the highest amount, value or degree attained or recorded (opposed to *minimum*). **2.** *Maths.* a value of a function at a certain point which is not exceeded in the immediate vicinity of that point. —*adj.* **3.** that is a maximum; greatest possible; highest. **4.** pertaining to a maximum or maximums. [t. L, neut. of *maximus* greatest]

maximum and minimum thermometer, *Meteorol.* a type of differential thermometer, used for measuring the highest and lowest temperatures over a period of time, usually 24 hours.

maximum likelihood estimation, *Statistics.* a method of estimating population characteristics from a sample by choosing the values of the parameters which will maximize the probability of getting the particular sample actually obtained from the population.

maximus (măk′sĭ məs), *adj.* **1.** that is greatest. **2.** in boys' schools, designating the eldest of four brothers.

maxiskirt (măk′sĭ skût′), *n.* a very long skirt (contrasted with *miniskirt*).

Max Müller (măks′mŭl′ə; *Ger.* màks mʏ′lər), **Friedrich.** See **Müller,** Friedrich Max.

maxwell (măks′wəl), *n. Elect.* a unit of magnetic flux, being the flux through a square centimetre in a field in air whose intensity is one gauss. [named after James Clerk MAXWELL]

Maxwell (măks′wəl), *n.* **James Clerk** (kläk), 1831–79, British physicist.

Maxwell-Boltzman distribution (măks′wəl bōlts′mən), *Physics.* a statistical equation for expressing the distribution of particles (or their velocity) in a gas, based on the principle of equi-partition of energy.

may (mā), *v., pres.* 1 **may,** 2 (*Archaic*) **mayest** *or* **mayst,** 3 **may,** *pl.* **may;** *pret.* **might. 1.** used as an auxiliary to express: **a.** possibility, opportunity, or permission: *you may enter.* **b.** wish or prayer: *may you live long.* **c.** contingency, esp. in clauses expressing condition, concession, purpose, result, etc. **d.** *Archaic.* ability or power (more commonly *can*). **2.** *Law, Now Rare.* (in a statute) must (when used not to confer a favour, but to impose a duty). [OE *mæg,* 1st and 3rd pers. sing. pres. ind. of *magan,* c. G *mögen*] —**Syn. 1.** See **can**[1].

May (mā), *n.* **1.** the fifth month of the year, containing 31 days. **2.** the early part of springtime. **3.** the festivities of May Day. **4.** (*l.c.*) the hawthorn. —*v.i.* **5.** to join in the festivities of May Day. **6.** to gather flowers in the spring. [ME; OE *Maius,* t. L]

May (mā), *n.* **Hugh,** 1622–84, English architect.

maya (mī′ə, mä′yə, mä′yä), *n. Hinduism.* the belief that the material universe is an illusion. [t. Skt: *māyā*]

Maya (mä′yə), *n.* **1.** a member of an aboriginal people of Yucatán which had attained a relatively high civilization before the discovery of America. **2.** the historical and modern language of the Mayas, of Mayan stock.

Mayagüez (*Sp.* mà yà gwĕth′), *n.* a seaport in W Puerto Rico. 83,850 (1960).

Mayakovski (*Russ.* mə yà kôf′skĭy), *n.* **Vladimir Vladimirovich** (*Russ.* vlà dē′mĭr vlà dē′mĭ rə vĭch), 1893–1930, Russian poet.

Mayan (mä′yən), *adj.* **1.** of or pertaining to the Mayas. —*n.* **2.** a member of the Mayan tribe. **3.** a linguistic stock of southern Mexico, Guatemala, and British Honduras, including Maya and Quiché, and probably related to Penutian.

May apple, 1. an American perennial herb, *Podophyllum peltatum,* of the family *Podophyllaceae,* bearing an edible, yellowish, egg-shaped fruit. **2.** the fruit.

maybe (mā′bē′), *adv.* perhaps. [short for *it may be*]

May blobs, the kingcup, *Caltha palustris.*

May Day, the first day of May, long celebrated with various festivities, as the crowning of the May queen, dancing round the maypole, etc., and, in recent years, often marked by socialist and labour rallies.

Mayday (mā′dā′), *n.* (according to international radio regulations) the radio telephonic distress signal used by ships or aircraft. [t. F: alter. of *m'aidez* help me]

Mayence (*Fr.* mà yäɴs′), *n.* French name of **Mainz.**

Mayenne (*Fr.* mà yĕn′), *n.* a department in NW France. 250,030 pop. (1962); 1986 sq. mi. *Cap.:* Laval.

Mayfair (mā′fĕə′), *n.* a fashionable district in London, E of Hyde Park.

Mayflower (mā′flou′ə), *n.* **1.** the ship in which the Pilgrim Fathers sailed from Southampton to the New World in 1620. **2.** (*l.c.*) **a.** the hawthorn. **b.** any of various plants that flower in May, esp. (in the U.S.) the trailing arbutus, hepatica, and anemone.

mayfly (mā′flī′), *n.* **1.** any of the *Ephemerida,* an order of delicate-winged insects having the forewings much larger than the hind wings, the larvae being aquatic, and the winged adults being very short-lived; an ephemerid. **2.** an artificial fly made in imitation of this fly.

mayhap (mā′hăp′), *adv. Archaic.* perhaps. [short for *it may hap*]

mayhem (mā′hĕm), *n.* **1.** *Law.* the crime of violently inflicting a bodily injury rendering a man less able to defend himself or to annoy his adversary (now often extended by statute to include any wilful mutilation of another's body). **2.** any tumult, fracas, or fight. Also, **maihem.** [ME *maheym,* t. AF, var. of OF *mahaigne* injury. See MAIM]

Maying (mā′ĭng), *n.* the celebration of May Day.

May lily, a small, rhizomatous liliaceous herb with dense heads of white flowers, *Maianthemum bifolium,* occurring in woods of Europe and N Asia.

Mayo (mā′ō), *n.* **1. Charles Horace,** 1865–1939, U.S. surgeon. **2.** his brother, **William James,** 1861–1939, U.S. surgeon. **3.** a county in NW Republic of Ireland, in Connaught province. 123,330 pop. (1961); 2084 sq. mi. *Co. town:* Castlebar.

Mayon (*Sp.* mà yōn′), *n.* an active volcano in the Philippine Islands, on SE Luzon island. ab. 8000 ft.

mayonnaise (mā′ə nāz′), *n.* a thick dressing of egg yolks, vinegar or lemon juice, seasonings, and oil, used for salads or vegetables. [t. F: earlier *magnonaise, mahonnaise,* ult. der. *Mahon,* a port of the Balearic Islands]

mayor (mĕə), *n.* the principal officer of a municipality; the chief magistrate of a city or borough. [ME *maire,* t. F, g. L *mājor* greater. Cf. MAJOR] —**may′orship′,** *n.*

mayoralty (mĕə′rəl tĭ), *n., pl.* **-ties. 1.** the office of a mayor. **2.** the period of office of a mayor.

mayoress (mĕə′rĭs), *n.* **1.** the wife of a mayor or the deputy of a lady mayor. **2.** a woman mayor.

Mayotte (*Fr.* mà yŏt′), *n.* one of the Comoro Islands, in the Indian Ocean, NW of Madagascar. 27,105 pop. (est. 1965); 143 sq. mi.

maypole (mā′pōl′), *n.* a high pole, decorated with flowers or ribbons, for the merrymakers to dance round at May Day (or May) festivities.

May queen, a girl or young woman crowned with flowers and honoured as queen in the sports of May Day.

May races, intercollegiate boat races held at Cambridge, usually at the beginning of June.

mayst (māst), *v. Archaic.* 2nd pers. sing. pres. indic. of **may.** Also, **mayest.**

Maytime (mā′tīm′), *n.* the month of May. Also, **Maytide** (mā′tīd′).

maytree (mā′trē′), *n.* the hawthorn.

mayweed (mā′wēd′), *n.* a composite herb, *Anthemis cotula,* native in Europe and Asia, and naturalized in America, having pungent, ill-scented foliage, and flower heads with a yellow disc and white rays. [f. obs. *mayth* mayweed (OE *mægtha*) + WEED[1], with loss of *-th*]

May week, the week of the May races at Cambridge, usually in early June.

mazard (măz′əd), *n.* a wild sweet cherry, *Prunus avium,* used as a rootstock for cultivated varieties of cherries. Also, **mazzard.** [earlier *mazer,* t. OF *masere,* t. Gmc (cf. MHG *maser* maple)]

Mazarin (măz′ə rĭn; *Fr.* mà zà răɴ′), *n.* **Jules** (*Fr.* zhʏl) *Giulio Mazarini*), 1602–61, French cardinal and statesman, born in Italy; chief minister of Louis XIV, 1642–61.

Mazar-i-Sharif (mə zä′rĭ shə rēf′), *n.* a town in N Afghanistan. 40,000 (est. 1962).

Mazatlán (*Sp.* mà thà tlàn′), *n.* a seaport in W Mexico. 75,751 (1960).

Mazdaism (măz′də ĭz′əm), *n.* Zoroastrianism. Also, **Mazdeism.**

maze (māz), *n., v.,* **mazed, mazing.** —*n.* **1.** a confusing network of intercommunicating paths or passages; a labyrinth. **2.** a state of bewilderment or confusion. **3.** a winding movement, as in dancing. —*v.t.* **4.** *Archaic or Dial.* to stupefy or daze. [ME *mase(n)*; aphetic var. of AMAZE] —**maze′ment,** *n.* —**maze′like′,** *adj.*

mazurka (mə zû′kə), *n.* **1.** a lively Polish dance in moderate quick triple rhythm. **2.** music for, or in the rhythm of, this dance. Also, **mazourka.** [t. Pol.: equiv. to *Mazur* of Mazovia (district in Poland) + *-ka* fem. adj. suffix]

mazy (mā′zĭ), *adj.,* **-zier, -ziest.** mazelike; full of intricate windings. —**ma′zily,** *adv.* —**ma′ziness,** *n.*

Mazzini (*It.* màt tsē′nē), *n.* **Giuseppe** (*It.* jōō zĕp′pĕ), 1805–72, Italian patriot and revolutionary.

mb, millibar.

M.B., (L *Medicinae Baccalaureus*) Bachelor of Medicine.

Mbabane (əm′bä bä′nĭ), *n.* the capital of Swaziland, in the W part. 8400 (1963).

M.B.E., Member of the Order of the British Empire.

Mboya (əm boi′ə), *n.* **Thomas Joseph** (*Tom*), 1930–69, Kenyan politician.

Mc-, Mac.

M.C., **1.** Master of Ceremonies. **2.** Military Cross

M.C.C., Marylebone Cricket Club.

McCarthy (mə kä′thĭ), *n.* **1. Joseph R(aymond),** 1909–1957, U.S. politician. **2. Mary (Therese),** born 1912, U.S. novelist and critic.

McCarthyism (mə kä′thĭ ĭz′əm), *n. U.S.* **1.** public accusation of disloyalty, esp. of pro-Communist activity, in many instances unsupported by proof or based on slight, doubtful, or irrelevant evidence. **2.** unfairness in investigative technique. **3.** persistent search for and exposure of disloyalty, esp. in government offices. [named after Joseph R. MCCARTHY]

McCartney (mə kät′nĭ), *n.* **Paul.** See **Beatles.**

McCormack (mə kô′mək), *n.* **John,** 1884–1945, Irish-American tenor singer.

McCoy (mə koi′), *n.* **the real,** the best of its kind.

McCullers (mə kŭl′əz), *n.* **Carson,** 1917–67, U.S. authoress.

McDiarmid (mək dĕə′mĭd), *n.* **Hugh** (*Christopher Murray Grieve*), born 1892, Scottish poet.

McDougall (mək dōō′gl), *n.* **William,** 1871–1938, U.S. psychologist and writer, born in England.

McGonagall (mə gŏn′ə gl), *n.* **William,** 1830–?1902, Scottish writer of doggerel.

McKinley (mə kĭn′lĭ), *n.* **1. William,** 1843–1801, 25th president of U.S., 1897–1901. **2. Mount,** a mountain in central Alaska: highest peak of N America. 20,300 ft.

M.C.L., Master of Civil Law.

McLuhan (mə klōōən′), *n.* **(Herbert) Marshall,** born 1911, Canadian writer and teacher.

McMurdo Sound (mək mû′dō), an inlet of the Ross Sea, in Antarctica, N of Victoria Land.

McNamara (măk′nə mä′rə), *n.* **Robert Strange,** born 1916, U.S. politician.

McNaughten rules (mək nô′tn), *Law.* rules laid down in 1843 in R. *v.* McNaughten which provided that to establish insanity the accused must prove either that, as a result of a mental defect he did not know the nature and quality of his act, or that he did not know that it was wrong.

McPherson Range (mək fû′sən), a mountain range forming the E border of Queensland and New South Wales, Australia. Highest point, Mt Superbus, 4525 ft.

M.C.P.S., megacycles per second. Also, **m.c.p.s.**

m.d., **1.** (F *main droite*) right hand. **2.** *Music.* (It. *mano destra*) right hand.

Md, *Chem.* mendelevium.

Md, Maryland.

M.D., **1.** (L *Medicinae Doctor*) Doctor of Medicine. **2.** mental defective. **3.** mental deficiency. **4.** mentally deficient.

MDN, (*Mark der Deutschen Notenbank*). See **mark**[2] (def. 4).

M.D.S., Master of Dental Surgery.

me[1] (mē; *unstressed* mĭ), *pers. pron.* objective case of the pronoun *I.* [ME *mē*, OE *me*, dat. sing. (c. D *mij*, G *mir*); akin to L *mē* (acc.), etc.]

me[2] (mē), *n. Music.* mi.

ME, Middle English. Also, **M.E.**

Me, *Chem.* methyl.

Me, Maine.

M.E., **1.** Marine Engineer. **2.** Mechanical Engineer. **3.** Methodist Episcopal. **4.** Middle English. **5.** Mining Engineer. **6.** Most Excellent.

mead[1] (mēd), *n. Poetic.* a meadow. [ME *mede*, OE *mǣd.* See MEADOW]

mead[2] (mēd), *n.* **1.** an alcoholic liquor made by fermenting honey and water. **2.** *U.S.* any of various non-alcoholic beverages. [ME *mede*, OE *medu*, c. G *Met*]

Mead (mēd), *n.* **Lake,** a lake made by Hoover Dam in the Colorado river, in NW Arizona and SE Nevada: largest artificial lake in world. 115 mi. long; 227 sq. mi.

meadow (mĕd′ō), *n.* **1.** a piece of grassland, whether used for raising of hay or for pasture. **2.** *U.S.* a low, level tract of uncultivated ground, as along a river, producing coarse grass. [ME *medwe*, OE *mǣdw-*, in inflectional forms of *mǣd* (cf. MEAD[1]); akin to G *Matte*]

meadow grass, a variable tufted, perennial grass, *Poa pratensis*, widespread in pastures of the N temperate zone.

meadow lark, a common American songbird of the genus *Sturnella* (family *Icteridae*), esp. the **eastern meadow lark,** *S. magna*, and **western meadow lark,** *S. neglecta*, both of which are robust, yellow-breasted birds about the size of the thrush.

meadow rue, any perennial ranunculaceous herb of the genus *Thalictrum*, as *T. flavum*, the **common meadow rue** of Europe and temperate Asia.

meadow saffron, the autumn crocus, *Colchicum autumnale.*

meadowsweet (mĕd′ō swēt′), *n.* a perennial rosaceous herb, *Filipendula ulmaria*, with dense heads of small, cream-coloured flowers, widespread on wet ground in Europe and temperate Asia.

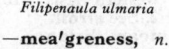

Meadowsweet, *Filipenaula ulmaria*

meadowy (mĕd′ō ĭ), *adj.* pertaining to, resembling, or consisting of meadow.

meagre (mē′gə), *adj.* **1.** deficient in quantity or quality, or without fullness or richness. **2.** having little flesh, lean, or thin. **3.** maigre. —*n.* **4.** a long, thin fish, *Sciaena*, sometimes found in British waters; up to 5 ft long. Also, *U.S.*, **meager.** [ME *megre*, t. OF: m. *maigre*, g. L *macer* lean] —**mea′grely,** *adv.* —**mea′greness,** *n.* —**Syn. 1.** See **scanty.**

meal[1] (mēl), *n.* **1.** one of the regular repasts of the day, as breakfast, lunch, or supper. **2.** the food eaten or served for a repast. [ME; OE *mǣl* measure, fixed time, occasion, meal, c. G *Mal* time, *Mahl* meal]

meal[2] (mēl), *n.* **1.** the edible part of any grain (now usually excluding wheat) or pulse ground to a (coarse) powder and unbolted. **2.** *U.S.* coarse, unbolted grain; cornmeal (def. 2). **3.** any ground or powdery substance, as of nuts or seeds, resembling this. [ME *mele*, OE *melu*, c. G *Mehl*]

mealie (mē′lĭ), *n.* (*usually pl.*) (in South Africa) maize. Also, **mealy.** [t. Afrikaans: m. *milje*]

mealtime (mēl′tīm′), *n.* the usual time for a meal.

mealworm (mēl′wûm′), *n.* the larva of the beetle *Tenebrio molitor*, which infests granaries. It is cultivated in great numbers as food for birds and animals.

mealy (mē′lĭ), *adj.*, **-lier, -liest. 1.** having the qualities of meal; powdery; soft, dry, and crumbly: *mealy potatoes.* **2.** of the nature of, or containing, meal; farinaceous. **3.** covered with or as with meal or powder. **4.** flecked as if with meal, or spotty. **5.** pale, as the complexion. **6.** mealy-mouthed. —**meal′iness,** *n.*

mealy bug, any hemipterous, plant-sucking insect of the family *Coccidae*, so called because of the powdery wax which covers the body.

mealy-mouthed (mē′lĭ mouᵺd′), *adj.* **1.** avoiding the use of plain terms, as from timidity, excessive delicacy, or hypocrisy. **2.** using soft words.

mean[1] (mēn), *v.*, **meant, meaning.** —*v.t.* **1.** to have in the mind as in intention or purpose (often with an infinitive as object): *I mean to talk to him.* **2.** to intend for a particular purpose, destination, etc.: *they were meant for each other.* **3.** to intend to express or indicate: *By 'liberal' I mean . . .* **4.** (of words, things, etc.) to have as the signification; signify. —*v.i.* **5.** to be minded or disposed; have intentions: *he means well.* [ME *mene(n)*, OE *mǣnan*, c. G *meinen*] —**Syn. 1.** purpose, contemplate. See **intend. 4.** import; denote, indicate.

mean[2] (mēn), *adj.* **1.** inferior in grade, quality or character: *he is no mean performer.* **2.** low in station, rank, or dignity. **3.** of little importance or consequence. **4.** unimposing or shabby: *a mean abode.* **5.** without moral dignity; small-minded or ignoble: *mean motives.* **6.** penurious, stingy, or miserly: *a man who is mean about money.* **7.** pettily offensive or unaccommodating; nasty. **8.** *Colloq.* small, humiliated, or ashamed: *to feel mean over some ungenerous action.* **9.** *U.S. Colloq.* in poor physical condition. **10.** *U.S. Colloq.* troublesome or vicious, as a horse. [ME *mene*, aphetic var. of *imene*, OE *gemǣne*, c. G *gemein* common]

—**Syn. 2.** common, humble. **3.** insignificant, petty, paltry. **5.** contemptible, despicable. MEAN, LOW, BASE, SORDID, and VILE all refer to ignoble characteristics worthy of dislike, contempt, or disgust. MEAN suggests pettiness and small-mindedness: *to take a mean advantage.* LOW suggests coarseness and vulgarity: *low company.* BASE suggests selfish cowardice or moral depravity: *base motives.* SORDID suggests a wretched uncleanness, or sometimes an avariciousness without dignity or moral scruples: *a sordid slum, sordid gain.* VILE suggests disgusting foulness or repulsiveness: *a vile insinuation, a vile creature.* —**Ant. 1.** noble, admirable.

mean[3] (mēn), *n.* **1.** (*usually pl. but often construed as sing.*) an agency, instrumentality, method, etc., used to attain an end: *a means of communication.* **2.** (*pl.*) disposable resources, esp. pecuniary resources: *to live beyond one's means.* **3.** (*pl.*) considerable pecuniary resources: *a man of means.* **4.** something intermediate;

that which is midway between two extremes. **5.** *Maths.* **a.** a quantity having a value intermediate between the values of other quantities; an average, esp. the arithmetic mean. **b.** either the second or third term in a proportion of four terms. **6.** *Logic, Obs.* the middle term in a syllogism. **7. by all means, a.** at any cost; without fail. **b.** (in emphasis) certainly: *go, by all means.* **8. by any means,** in any way; at all. **9. by no means, a.** in no way; not at all: *a thing by no means certain.* **b.** on no account; certainly not: *a practice by no means to be recommended.* —*adj.* **10.** occupying a middle position or an intermediate place. **11.** intermediate in kind, quality, degree, time, etc. [ME *mene,* t. OF: m. *meien,* g. LL *mediānus* in the middle] —**Syn. 10.** moderate.

meander (mĭ ăn′də), *v.i.* **1.** to proceed by a winding course. **2.** to wander aimlessly. —*n.* **3.** (*usually pl.*) a turning or winding; a winding path or course. **4.** a circuitous movement or journey. **5.** an intricate variety of fret or fretwork. [t. L, t. Gk: m. *maiandros* a winding, orig. the name of a winding river (now Mendere) in western Asia Minor] —**mean′deringly,** *adv.* —**Syn. 2.** See **stroll.**

mean distance, the arithmetic mean of the greatest and least distances of a planet from the sun, called the semi-major axis, and used in stating the size of an orbit.

mean free path, *Physics.* **1.** the average distance travelled by a particle, atom, or molecule between collisions. **2.** the average distance travelled by a soundwave between successive reflections.

meaning (mē′nĭng), *n.* **1.** that which is intended to be, or actually is, expressed or indicated; signification; import. —*adj.* **2.** intending: *he is very well-meaning.* **3.** expressive or significant: *a meaning look.* —**mean′ingly,** *adv.*

—**Syn. 1.** tenor, gist, drift, trend. MEANING, PURPORT, SENSE, SIGNIFICANCE denote that which is expressed or indicated by something. MEANING is the general word denoting that which is intended to be or actually is expressed or indicated: *the meaning of a word or glance.* SENSE may be used to denote a particular meaning (among others) of a word or phrase: *the word has become obsolete in this sense.* SENSE may also be used loosely to refer to 'intelligible meaning': *there's no sense in what he says.* SIGNIFICANCE refers particularly to a meaning that is implied rather than expressed (*the significance of her glance*); or to a meaning the importance of which may not be easy to perceive immediately: *the real significance of his words was not grasped at the time.* PURPORT is mainly limited to the meaning of a formal document, speech, important conversation, etc., and refers to the gist of something fairly complicated: *the purport of his letter.* **3.** See **expressive.**

meaningful (mē′nĭng fəl), *adj.* full of meaning; significant.

meaningless (mē′nĭng lĭs), *adj.* without meaning or significance. —**mean′inglessly,** *adv.* —**mean′inglessness,** *n.*

meanly (mēn′lĭ), *adv.* in a mean manner; poorly; basely; stingily. [f. MEAN² + -LY]

meanness (mēn′nĭs), *n.* **1.** the state or quality of being mean. **2.** a mean act.

mean noon, *Astron.* the moment when the mean sun's centre crosses the meridian.

mean sea-level, the average level of the sea as calculated from a long series of observations of tidal oscillations taken at equal time intervals.

mean solar time, *Astron.* mean time.

means test, an enquiry into the income of a person in order to ascertain the level of a scale of allowances, grants, etc., to which he is entitled.

mean sun, *Astron.* an imaginary and fictitious sun moving uniformly in the celestial equator and taking the same time to make its annual circuit as the true sun does in the ecliptic.

meant (mĕnt), *v.* pt. and pp. of **mean¹.**

mean time, the time at a given place on earth based on a day of 24 hours; the interval between successive local noons on which local time is based varies and so an average day of 24 hours is used, giving mean time. Also, **mean solar time.**

meantime (mēn′tīm′), *n.* **1.** the intervening time: *in the meantime.* —*adv.* **2.** meanwhile.

meanwhile (mēn′wīl′), *adv.* in the intervening time; during the interval; at the same time.

measled (mē′zəld), *adj.* affected with measles (def. 3).

measles (mē′zəlz), *n.* **1.** an acute infectious disease occurring mostly in children, characterized by catarrhal and febrile symptoms and an eruption of small red spots; rubeola. **2.** any of certain other eruptive diseases, as rubella (**German measles**). **3.** a disease in swine and other animals caused by the larvae of certain tapeworms of the genus *Taenia.* **4.** (*pl.*) the larvae which cause measles. [partly ME *maseles,* c. D *mazelen,* akin to G *Masern* measles, pl. of *Maser* spot; partly ME *mesels,* akin to OHG *māsa* spot]

measly (mēz′lĭ), *adj.,* **-lier, -liest. 1.** infected with measles, as an animal or its flesh. **2.** pertaining to or resembling measles. **3.** (of beef or pork) infected with cysts or tapeworms of the genus *Taenia.* **4.** *Slang.* wretchedly poor or unsatisfactory; very small.

measurable (mĕzh′ə rə bl, mĕzh′rə bl), *adj.* that may be measured. —**meas′urabil′ity, meas′urableness,** *n.* —**meas′urably,** *adv.*

measure (mĕzh′ə), *n., v.,* **-ured, -uring.** —*n.* **1.** the act or process of ascertaining the extent, dimensions, quantity, etc., of something, esp. by comparison with a standard. **2.** size, dimensions, quantity, etc., as thus ascertained. **3.** an instrument, as a graduated rod or a vessel of standard capacity, for measuring. **4.** a unit or standard of measurement. **5.** a definite or known quantity measured out. **6.** a system of measurement. **7.** *Print.* the width of a page or column, usually measured in ems or picas. **8.** any standard of comparison, estimation, or judgement. **9.** a quantity, degree, or proportion. **10.** a limit, or an extent or degree not to be exceeded: *to know no measure.* **11.** reasonable bounds or limits: *beyond measure.* **12.** a legislative bill or enactment. **13.** an action or procedure intended as a means to an end: *to take measures to avert suspicion.* **14.** a short rhythmical movement or arrangement, as in poetry or music. **15.** a particular kind of such arrangement. **16.** a metrical unit. **17.** *Poetic.* an air or melody. **18.** *U.S. Music.* bar (def. 9). **19.** (*pl.*) *Geol.* beds; strata. **20.** *Archaic.* a slow, stately dance or dance movement. **21. for good measure,** as an extra and probably unnecessary act, precaution, etc.: *he padlocked the door for good measure.* —*v.t.* **22.** to ascertain the extent, dimensions, quantity, capacity, etc., of, esp. by comparison with a standard. **23.** to mark or lay off or out, or deal out, with reference to measure (often fol. by *off* or *out*). **24.** to estimate the relative amount, value, etc., of, by comparison with some standard. **25.** to judge of or appraise by comparison with something else. **26.** to serve as the measure of. **27.** to adjust or proportion. **28.** to bring into comparison or competition. **29.** to travel over or traverse. **30. measure up to,** to be adequate for. —*v.i.* **31.** to take measurements. **32.** to admit of measurement. **33.** to be of a specified measure. [ME *mesure(n),* t. OF: m. *mesurer,* g. L *mensūrāre*] —**meas′urer,** *n.*

measured (mĕzh′əd), *adj.* **1.** ascertained or apportioned by measure. **2.** accurately regulated or proportioned. **3.** regular or uniform, as in movement; rhythmical. **4.** deliberate and restrained: *measured speech.* **5.** in the form of metre or verse; metrical. —**meas′uredly,** *adv.*

measureless (mĕzh′ə lĭs), *adj.* without bounds; unlimited; immeasurable: *caverns measureless to man.* —**meas′urelessly,** *adv.* —**meas′urelessness,** *n.*

measurement (mĕzh′ə mənt), *n.* **1.** the act of measuring. **2.** an ascertained dimension. **3.** extent, size, etc., ascertained by measuring. **4.** a system of measuring or of measures. **5.** *Survey.* the estimation by a quantity surveyor, civil engineer, or the like, of the work to be done and billed, and later the measuring on the site of the work done and to be paid for.

measuring worm, the larva of any geometrid moth, which progresses by bringing the rear end of the body forward and then advancing the front end; a looper; an inchworm.

meat (mēt), *n.* **1.** the flesh of animals as used for food. **2.** food in general: *meat and drink.* **3.** the edible part of anything, as a fruit, nut, etc. **4.** the principal meal: *to say grace before meat.* **5.** the main substance of something, as an argument. [ME and OE *mete,* c. OHG *maz*] —**meat′less,** *adj.*

Meath (mēth), *n.* a county in E Republic of Ireland, in Leinster. 65,122 pop. (1961); 902 sq. mi. *Co. town:* Trim.

meatus (mĭ ā′təs), *n., pl.* **-tuses, -tus.** *Anat.* an opening or foramen, esp. in a bone or bony structure, as the opening of the ear, nose, etc. See diag. under **ear.** [t. L: passage]

meaty (mē′tĭ), *adj.,* **-tier, -tiest. 1.** of or like meat. **2.** abounding in meat. **3.** full of substance; pithy. —**mea′tiness,** *n.*

Mecca (mĕk′ə), *n.* **1.** a city in W Saudi Arabia: capital of Hejaz; one of two federal capitals; birthplace of Mohammed; spiritual centre of Islam. 250,000 (est. 1962). **2.** any centre or goal for many people. —**Mec′can,** *adj., n.*

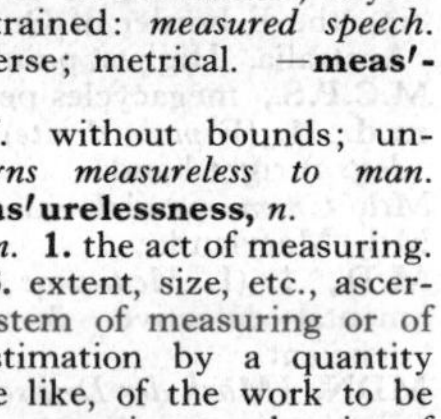

Mecca

Meccano (mĭ kä′nō), *n.* *Trademark.* perforated metal

strips and a kit of components which can be bolted together as a framework for constructing models.

mech., 1. mechanical. 2. mechanics. 3. mechanism.

mechanic (mĭ kăn′ĭk), *n.* **1.** a skilled worker with tools or machines. **2.** one who repairs machinery. [ME, t. L: s. *mēchanicus*, t. Gk: m. *mēchanikós* of machines]

mechanical (mĭ kăn′ĭ kl), *adj.* **1.** having to do with machinery. **2.** of the nature of a device or contrivance for controlling or utilizing material forces, or of a mechanism or machine. **3.** acting or operated by means of such a contrivance, or of a mechanism or machine. **4.** produced by such means. **5.** acting or performed without spontaneity, spirit, individuality, etc. **6.** belonging or pertaining to the subject matter of mechanics. **7.** pertaining to, or controlled or effected by, physical forces. **8. a.** explanatory of phenomena, as due to mechanism (defs 8 and 9). **b.** of or pertaining to those who advocate such explanations, or to their theories. **9.** subordinating the spiritual to the material; materialistic. **10.** involving the material objects or physical conditions: *hindered by mechanical difficulties.* **11.** pertaining to or concerned with the use of tools and the like, or the contrivance and construction of machines or mechanisms. **12.** pertaining to or concerned with manual labour or skill. **13.** exhibiting skill in the use of tools and the like, in the contrivance of machines, etc.: *a mechanical genius.* —**mechan′ically,** *adv.* —**mechan′icalness,** *n.*

mechanical advantage, the ratio of the force performing the work done by a mechanism to the input force.

mechanical drawing, drawing, as of machinery, done with the aid of rulers, scales, compasses, etc.

mechanical engineer, one versed in the design and construction of engines and machines.

mechanical engineering, action, work, or profession of a mechanical engineer.

mechanical equivalent of heat, *Physics.* the number of units of work or energy equivalent to one heat unit, as $4{\cdot}185 \times 10^7$ ergs is equivalent to one calorie.

mechanician (mĕk′ə nĭsh′ən), *n.* one skilled in constructing, working, or repairing machines.

mechanics (mĭ kăn′ĭks), *n.* **1.** the branch of knowledge concerned (both theoretically and practically) with machinery or mechanical appliances. **2.** the science dealing with the action of forces on bodies and with motion, and comprising kinetics, statics and kinematics. **3.** (*construed as pl.*) the mechanical or technical part or aspect. **4.** (*construed as pl.*) methods of operation, procedures, and the like.

mechanism (mĕk′ə nĭz′əm), *n.* **1.** a piece of machinery. **2.** the machinery, or the agencies or means, by which a particular effect is produced or a purpose is accomplished. **3.** machinery or mechanical appliances in general. **4.** the structure, or arrangement of parts, of a machine or similar device, or of anything analogous. **5.** such parts collectively. **6.** the way in which a thing works or operates. **7.** mechanical execution, as in painting or music; technique. **8.** the theory that everything in the universe is produced by matter in motion. Cf. **vitalism**[1]. **9.** *Philos., Biol.* a natural process interpreted as machine-like or as explicable in terms of Newtonian physics. **10.** *Psychoanal.* (used as an analogy drawn from mechanics) the operation and interaction of psychological forces: *the mechanism of sexual desire.* [t. NL: s. *mēchanismus*, f. Gk: s. *mēchanḗ* machine + m. *-ismos* -ISM]

mechanist (mĕk′ə nĭst), *n.* **1.** one who believes in philosophical or biological mechanism (def. 8 and 9). **2.** *Rare.* a mechanician.

mechanistic (mĕk′ə nĭs′tĭk), *adj.* pertaining to mechanists or mechanism, or to mechanics (def. 1), or to mechanical theories in philosophy, etc.

mechanize (mĕk′ə nīz′), *v.t.*, **-nized, -nizing. 1.** to make mechanical. **2.** to operate or perform by or as if by machinery. **3.** to introduce machinery into (an industry, etc.). **4.** *Mil.* to equip with tanks and other armoured motor vehicles. Also, **mechanise.** —**mech′aniza′tion,** *n.*

mechanotherapy (mĕk′ə nō thĕ′rə pĭ), *n.* curative treatment by mechanical means. [f. s. Gk *mēchanḗ* machine + -o- + THERAPY]

Mechlin (mĕk′lĭn), *n.* a town in N Belgium. 65,388 (est. 1964). French, **Malines.** Flemish, **Mechelen** (*Flem.* mĕKH′ə lə).

Mechlin lace, 1. (orig.) handmade bobbin lace with raised cord, made in Flanders. 2. (now) a similar lace copied by machine. Also, **malines.**

Mecklenburg (mĕk′lĭn bûg′; *Ger.* mĕk′lən bo͝ork′), *n.* a former state in NE Germany, formed in 1934 from the two states **Mecklenburg-Schwerin** (*Ger.* mĕk′lən bo͝ork′ shvĕ rēn′) and **Mecklenburg-Strelitz** (*Ger.* mĕk′lən-bo͝ork′ shtrĕ′lĭts).

meconic acid (mĭ kŏn′ĭk), *Chem.* a white crystalline solid, $C_7H_4O_7$, present in opium and used as a test for opium poisoning as it gives a dark red stain with ferric chloride. [*meconic* f. Gk *mḗkōn* poppy + -IC]

med., 1. medical. 2. medicine. 3. medieval. 4. medium.

medal (mĕd′l), *n., v.*, **-alled, -alling** or (*U.S.*) **-aled, -aling.** —*n.* **1.** a flat piece of metal, usually in the shape of a disc, star, cross, or the like, bearing an inscription, device, etc., issued to commemorate a person, action, or event, or given to serve as a reward for bravery, merit, or the like. —*v.t.* **2.** to decorate or honour with a medal. [t. F: m. *médaille*, t. It.: m. *medaglia*, ult. der. L *metallum* metal]

medallic (mĭ dăl′ĭk), *adj.* of or pertaining to medals.

medallion (mĭ dăl′yən), *n.* **1.** a large medal. **2.** *Archit.* **a.** a tablet, usually rounded, often bearing objects represented in relief. **b.** a member in a decorative design resembling a panel. [t. F: m. *médaillon*, t. It.: m. *medaglione*, aug. of *medaglia* MEDAL]

medallist (mĕd′ə lĭst), *n.* **1.** one to whom a medal has been awarded. **2.** a designer, engraver, or maker of medals. Also, *Chiefly U.S.*, **medalist.**

medal play, *Golf.* play in which the score is reckoned by counting the strokes taken to complete the round. Also, **stroke play.**

Medan (*Indon.* mĕ′dăn), *n.* a city in Indonesia, in NE Sumatra. 479,098 (1961).

meddle (mĕd′l), *v.i.*, **-dled, -dling.** to concern or busy oneself with or in something without warrant or necessity; interfere. [ME *medle(n)*, t. OF: m. *medler*, ult. der. L *miscēre* mix] —**med′dler,** *n.*

meddlesome (mĕd′l səm), *adj.* given to meddling. —**med′dlesomely,** *adv.* —**med′dlesomeness,** *n.* —**Syn.** See **curious.**

Mede (mēd), *n.* a native or inhabitant of Media, an ancient kingdom of Asia, south of the Caspian Sea.

Medea (mĭ dĭə′), *n. Gk Legend.* a sorceress, daughter of Aeëtes, king of Colchis, and wife of Jason, whom she assisted in obtaining the Golden Fleece.

Medellín (*Sp.* mĕ dĕ lyĕn′), *n.* a city in W Colombia. 772,887 (1964).

media[1] (mē′dyə), *n.* a pl. of **medium.**

media[2] (mĕd′ĭ ə), *n., pl.* **-diae** (-dĭ ē′). **1.** (in various scientific uses) something medial. **2.** *Anat.* the middle layer of an artery or lymphatic vessel. [t. L: middle (fem. adj.)]

Media (mē′dyə), *n.* an ancient country in W Asia, S of the Caspian Sea, corresponding generally to NW Iran. *Cap.*: Ecbatana.

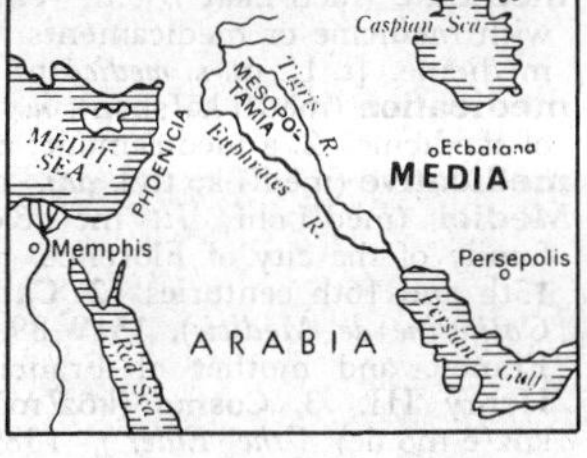

Media

mediacy (mē′dyə sĭ), *n.* the state of being mediate.

mediaeval (mĕd′ĭ-ē′vəl), *adj.* medieval. —**med′iae′valism,** *n.* —**med′iae′valist,** *n.*

medial (mē′dyəl), *adj.* **1.** situated in or pertaining to the middle; median; intermediate. **2.** pertaining to a mean or average; average. **3.** ordinary. **4.** within a word or syllable; neither initial nor final. —*n.* **5.** a medial linguistic element. [t. LL: s. *mediālis*, der. L *medius* middle] —**me′dially,** *adv.*

median (mē′dyən), *adj.* **1.** denoting or pertaining to a plane dividing something into two equal parts, esp. one dividing an animal into right and left halves. **2.** situated in or pertaining to the middle; medial. —*n.* **3.** the middle number in a given sequence of numbers: *4 is the median of 1, 3, 4, 8, 9.* **4.** a line through a vertex of a triangle bisecting the opposite side. [t. L: s. *mediānus* in the middle] —**me′dianly,** *adv.*

Median (mē′dyən), *adj.* **1.** of or pertaining to Media or the Medes. —*n.* **2.** a Mede.

median lethal dose, *Radiobiology.* the dose of ionizing radiation which would kill 50 per cent of a large batch of organisms within a specified period. *Abbrev.*: LD-50.

mediant (mē′dĭ ənt), *n. Music.* the third degree of a scale.

mediastinum (mē′dĭ əs tī′nəm), *n., pl.* **-tina** (-tī′nə). *Anat.* **1.** a median septum or partition between two parts of an organ, or paired cavities of the body. **2.** the partition separating the right and left thoracic cavities, formed of the two inner pleural walls, and, in man, containing all the viscera of the thorax except the lungs. [t. ML, prop. neut. of ML *mediastinus* in the middle, der. L *medius* middle] —**me′diasti′nal,** *adj.*

mediate (*v.* mē′dĭ āt′; *adj.* mē′dĭ ĭt), *v.*, **-ated, -ating,**

adj. —v.t. **1.** to bring about (an agreement, peace, etc.) between parties by acting as mediator. **2.** to settle (disputes, etc.) by mediation; reconcile. **3.** to effect (a result), convey (a gift), etc., as or by an intermediary or medium. —v.i. **4.** to act between parties to effect an agreement, compromise, or reconciliation. **5.** to occupy an intermediate place or position. —adj. **6.** acting through, dependent on, or involving an intermediate agency; not direct or immediate. [ME, t. LL: m. s. *mediātus*, pp., divided, situated in the middle] —**me′diately,** adv.

mediation (mē′dĭ ā′shən), n. **1.** action in mediating between parties, as to effect an agreement or reconciliation. **2.** *Internat. Law.* an attempt to effect a peaceful settlement between disputing nations through the friendly good offices of another power.

mediative (mē′dĭ ə tĭv), adj. mediating; mediatory.

mediatize (mē′dĭ ə tīz′), v.t., **-tized, -tizing.** to annex (a principality) to another state (while allowing certain rights to its former sovereign). Also, **mediatise.** [t. F: m. *médiatiser*, or t. G: m. *mediatisieren*, der. LL *mediātus*, pp., divided] —**me′diatiza′tion,** n.

mediator (mē′dĭ ā′tə), n. **1.** one who mediates. **2.** one who mediates between parties at variance.

mediatory (mē′dĭ ə tə rĭ, -trĭ), adj. **1.** pertaining to mediation. **2.** having the function of mediating. Also, **mediatorial** (mē′dĭ ə tô′rĭ əl).

medic[1] (mĕd′ĭk), n. *Colloq.* a doctor, medical student, or medical orderly.

medic[2] (mĕd′ĭk), n. *Chiefly U.S.* medick.

medicable (mĕd′ĭ kə bl), adj. susceptible of medical treatment; curable. [t. L: m. s. *medicābilis*]

medical (mĕd′ĭ kl), adj. **1.** of or pertaining to the science or practice of medicine. **2.** curative; medicinal; therapeutic: *medical properties.* —n. **3.** a medical examination. [t. LL: s. *medicālis*, der. L *medicus* of healing] —**med′ically,** adv.

medical jurisprudence, the science of the application of medical knowledge to the law. Also, **forensic medicine.**

medical orderly. See **orderly** (def. 8).

medicament (mĭ dĭk′ə mənt, mĕd′ĭ kə-), n. a curative or healing substance. [t. L: s. *medicāmentum*] —**medicamental** (mĕd′ĭ kə mĕn′tl), **med′icamen′tary,** adj.

medicare (mĕd′ĭ kĕə′), n. (in the U.S. and Canada) comprehensive medical or health insurance sponsored by the national government. [b. *medi(cal) care*]

medicate (mĕd′ĭ kāt′), v.t., **-cated, -cating. 1.** to treat with medicine or medicaments. **2.** to impregnate with a medicine. [t. L: m. s. *medicātus*, pp., cured]

medication (mĕd′ĭ kā′shən), n. **1.** the use or application of medicine. **2.** a medicament; a medicinal agent.

medicative (mĕd′ĭ kə tĭv), adj. medicinal.

Medici (mĕd′ĭ chĭ; *It.* mĕ′dē chē), n. **1.** an Italian family of the city of Florence, rich and powerful in the 15th and 16th centuries. **2. Catherine de′** (*It.* dė) (*Fr. Catherine de Médicis*), 1519–89, queen of Henry II of France, and mother of Francis II, Charles IX, and Henry III. **3. Cosmo** (kŏz′mō), or **Cosimo, de′** (*It.* kŏz′ē mō dė) (′*the Elder*′), 1389–1464, Italian banker, statesman, and patron of art and literature. **4. Cosmo,** or **Cosimo, de′** (′*the Great*′), 1519–74, duke of Florence and first grand duke of Tuscany. **5. Giovanni de′** (*It.* jō vän′nē dė). See **Leo X. 6. Giulio de′** (*It.* jōō′lyō dė). See **Clement VII. 7. Lorenzo de′** (*It.* lō rĕn′tsō dė) (′*Lorenzo the Magnificent*′; *Lorenzo I*), 1449–1492, ruler of Florence, patron of art and literature, and poet. **8. Marie de′** (*Fr.* mȧ rė′ də) (*Maria de′*), 1573–1642, queen of Henry IV of France, and regent of France 1610–17. Also, *French,* **Médicis.**

medicinal (mĕ dĭs′ĭ nəl), adj. pertaining to, or having the properties of, a medicine; curative; remedial: *medicinal properties, medicinal substances.* [ME, t. L: s. *medicinālis* of medicine] —**medic′inally,** adv.

medicine (mĕd′sĭn), n., v., **-cined, -cining.** —n. **1.** any substance or substances used in treating disease; a medicament; a remedy. **2.** the art or science of restoring or preserving health or due physical condition, as by means of drugs, surgical operations or appliances, manipulations, etc. (often divided into medicine proper, surgery, and obstetrics). **3.** the art or science of treating disease with drugs or curative substances (distinguished from *surgery* and *obstetrics*). **4.** the medical profession. **5.** any object or practice regarded by savages as of magical efficacy. **6.** any unpleasant treatment or experience, esp. one that is difficult to accept. **7. taste** (or **dose**) **of one′s own medicine,** unpleasant treatment meted out to one who usually punishes or bullies, etc. —v.t. **8.** to administer medicine to. [ME, t. L: m. *medicīna*]

medicine ball, a large, solid, leather-covered ball, thrown from one person to another for exercise.

medicine man, (among American Indians and other primitive peoples) a man supposed to possess mysterious or supernatural powers.

Médicis (*Fr.* mė dē sēs′), n. French name for **Medici.**

medick (mĕd′ĭk), n. any of several small papilionaceous herbs of the genus *Medicago*, as the widespread grassland **black medick,** *M. lupulina.* Also, *Chiefly U.S.*, **medic.** [t. L: m. s. *mēdica*, t. Gk: m. (*póa*) *Mēdikē* Median (grass)]

medico (mĕd′ĭ kō′), n., pl. **-cos.** *Slang.* a doctor. [t. It. and Sp., t. L: m. *medicus* a physician]

medieval (mĕd′ĭ ē′vəl), adj. of or pertaining to, characteristic of, or in the style of the Middle Ages: *medieval architecture.* See **Middle Ages.** Also, **mediaeval.** [f. m. NL *medi(um) aev(um)* middle age + -AL[1]] —**med′ie′vally,** adv.

Medieval Greek, the Greek language of the Middle Ages, usually dated A.D. 700–1500. Also, **Middle Greek.**

medievalism (mĕd′ĭ ē′və lĭz′əm), n. **1.** the spirit, practices, or methods of the Middle Ages. **2.** devotion to or adoption of medieval ideals or practices. **3.** a medieval belief, practice, or the like. Also, **mediaevalism.**

medievalist (mĕd′ĭ ē′və lĭst), n. **1.** an expert in medieval history and affairs. **2.** one in sympathy with the spirit and methods of the Middle Ages. Also, **mediaevalist.**

Medieval Latin, the Latin language of the literature of the Middle Ages (usually dated A.D. 700 to 1500), including many Latinized words from other languages.

Medina (mĕ dē′nə), n. a town in W Saudi Arabia, where Mohammed was first accepted as the supreme Prophet from Allah, and where his tomb is situated. 60,000 (est. 1962).

Medina al Shaab (mĕ dē′nə ăl shäb′), a town in and the capital of South Yemen; 10 mi. NW of Aden.

mediocre (mē′dĭ ō′kə, mē′dĭ ō′kə), adj. of middling quality; of only moderate excellence; neither good nor bad; indifferent; ordinary: *a person of mediocre abilities.* [t. F, t. L: m. *mediocris* in a middle state] —**Syn.** medium, average, commonplace.

mediocrity (mē′dĭ ŏk′rĭ tĭ, mĕd′ĭ-), n., pl. **1.** the state or quality of being mediocre. **2.** mediocre ability or accomplishment. **3.** a person of only moderate ability.

Medit., Mediterranean.

meditate (mĕd′ĭ tāt′), v., **-tated, -tating.** —v.t. **1.** to consider in the mind as something to be done or effected; to intend or purpose. —v.i. **2.** to engage in thought or contemplation; reflect. [t. L: m. s. *meditātus*, pp.] —**med′ita′tor,** n. —**Syn. 1.** contemplate, plan. **2.** ponder, muse, ruminate; cogitate, think.

meditation (mĕd′ĭ tā′shən), n. **1.** the act of meditating. **2.** continued thought; reflection; contemplation.

meditative (mĕd′ĭ tə tĭv), adj. given to, characterized by, or indicative of meditation. —**med′itatively,** adv. —**med′itativeness,** n. —**Syn.** See **pensive.**

Mediterranean (mĕd′ĭ tə rā′nyən), n. **1.** the Mediterranean Sea. —adj. **2.** pertaining to, situated on or near, or dwelling about the Mediterranean Sea. [f. s. L *mediterrāneus* midland, inland + -AN]

Mediterranean climate, a type of climate characterized by sunny, hot summers and warm winters, with rainfall in the winter half of the year; it is associated with the western borders of the continents in middle latitudes.

Mediterranean fever, undulant fever.

Mediterranean race, a Caucasian race division inhabiting the area bordering the Mediterranean Sea, including the ancient Iberians, Ligurians, Minoans, and some Hamites, and most modern Mediterranean peoples except those in the Balkan and Anatolian peninsulas.

Mediterranean Sea, the sea between Africa, Europe, and Asia. ab. 1,145,000 sq. mi.; greatest known depth, 14,436 ft.

medium (mē′dyəm), n., pl. **-dia** (-dyə), **-diums,** adj. —n. **1.** a middle state or condition; a mean. **2.** something intermediate in nature or degree. **3.** *Print.* a size of paper, 18 × 23 inches. **4.** an intervening substance, as air, etc., through which a force acts or an effect is produced. **5.** the element in which an organism has its natural habitat. **6.** one′s environment; surrounding things, conditions, or influences. **7.** an agency, means, or instrument: *newspapers as an advertising medium.* **8.** *Biol.* the substance by which specimens are displayed or preserved. **9.** *Bacteriol.* a nutritive substance containing protein, carbohydrates, salts, water, etc., either liquid or solidified through the addition of gelatine or agar-agar, in or upon which micro-organisms are grown for study. **10.** *Painting.* **a.** a liquid with which pigments are mixed for application. **b.** the material or technique which an artist uses. **11.** a person serving or conceived as serving, as an instrument for the manifestation of another personality or of some alleged supernatural agency: *a spiritualist medium.* —adj. **12.** intermediate in degree, quality, etc.: *a man of medium size.* [t. L: (neut. adj.) middle, intermediate]

medium frequency, *Radio.* a radio frequency of between 30 and 300 kilohertz. *Abbrev.:* m.f.

mediumistic (mē′dyə mĭs′tĭk), *adj.* of or pertaining to a spiritualist medium.

medium wave, *Radio.* an electromagnetic wave with a wavelength of 200–1000 metres. —**medium-wave** (mē′-dyəm wāv′), *adj.*

medlar (mĕd′lə), *n.* **1.** a small malaceous tree, *Mespilus germanica*, the fruit of which resembles an open-topped crab-apple and is not edible until in the early stages of decay. **2.** its fruit. **3.** any of certain other malaceous trees. **4.** the fruit of such a tree. [ME *medler*, t. OF, var. of *meslier* the medlar tree, der. *mesle*, the fruit, g. L *mespilum*, t. Gk: m. *méspilon*]

medley (mĕd′lĭ), *n., pl.* **-leys,** *adj.* —*n.* **1.** a mixture, esp. of heterogeneous elements; a jumble. **2.** a piece of music combining airs or passages from various sources. —*adj.* **3.** mixed; mingled; motley. [ME *medlee*, t. OF, var. of *meslee* a mixing, orig. pp. fem. of *mesler* mix]

medley relay, **1.** *Athletics.* a relay race in which each member of a team runs a different distance. **2.** *Swimming.* a relay race in which each member of a team uses a different stroke.

Médoc (mĕd′ŏk; *Fr.* mė dŏk′), *n.* **1.** a district in SW France, NW of Bordeaux. **2.** a claret wine produced there.

medulla (mĭ dŭl′ə), *n., pl.* **-dullae** (-dŭl′ē). **1.** *Anat.* **a.** the marrow of bones. **b.** the soft marrow-like centre of an organ, such as the kidney, suprarenal, etc. **c.** the medulla oblongata. **2.** *Bot.* the pith of plants. [t. L: marrow, pith]

medulla oblongata (ŏb′lŏng gä′tə), *Anat.* the lowest or hindmost part of the brain, continuous with the spinal cord. [t. NL: prolonged medulla]

medullary (mĭ dŭl′ə rĭ), *adj.* pertaining to, consisting of, or resembling the medulla of an organ or the medulla oblongata.

medullary ray, *Bot.* (in the stems of exogenous plants) one of the vertical bands or plates of parenchymatous tissue which radiate between the pith and the bark.

medullary sheath, **1.** *Bot.* a narrow zone made up of the innermost layer of woody tissue immediately surrounding the pith in plants. **2.** myelin.

medullated (mĕd′ə lā′tĭd, mĭ dŭl′ā tĭd), *adj. Anat.* covered by a medullary substance; possessing myelin sheaths.

medusa (mĭ dyōō′sə), *n., pl.* **-sas, -sae** (-sē). *Zool.* a jellyfish. —**medusoid** (mĭ dyōō′soid), *adj.*

Medusa (mĭ dyōō′zə), *n., pl.* **-sas.** *Gk Legend.* that one of the three Gorgons who was slain by Perseus and whose head was afterwards borne on the aegis or shield of Athena.

medusan (mĭ dyōō′sən), *adj.* **1.** pertaining to a medusa or jellyfish. —*n.* **2.** a medusa or jellyfish.

Medway (mĕd′wā′), *n.* a river in S England flowing through Kent into the Thames estuary. 65 mi.

meed (mēd), *n. Archaic.* a reward or recompense for service or desert (good or bad). [ME *mede*, OE *mēd*, c. G *Miete* hire]

meek (mēk), *adj.* **1.** humbly patient or submissive, as under provocation from others. **2.** unduly patient or submissive; spiritless; tame. **3.** *Obs.* gentle; kind. [ME *meke, meoc*, t. Scand.; cf. Icel. *mjūkr* soft, mild, meek] —**meek′ly,** *adv.* —**meek′ness,** *n.* —**Syn. 1.** forbearing; yielding, docile: humble. See **gentle.** —**Ant. 1.** aggressive.

meelbol (mēl′bŏl′), *n. S African.* a type of infants' gruel prepared from maize. [t. Afrikaans: lit., meal ball]

Meer (mĭə; *Du.* mėr), *n.* **Jan van der** (*Du.* yŏn vŏn dėr). See **Vermeer, Jan.**

meerkat (mĭə′kăt′), *n.* any of several small, burrowing, South African carnivores, esp. *Suricata suricatta*, with dark bands across the back, related to the mongooses. Also, **suricate.** [t. Afrikaans: lit., sea cat]

Meerkat, *Suricata suricatta* (Total length 21 in., tail 9 in.)

meerschaum (mĭə′shəm), *n.* **1.** a mineral hydrous magnesium silicate, $H_4Mg_2Si_3O_{10}$, occurring in white, clay-like masses, used for ornamental carvings, for pipe bowls, etc.; sepiolite. **2.** a tobacco pipe the bowl of which is made of this substance. [t. G: sea foam]

Meerut (mĭə′rət), *n.* a town in India, in W Uttar Pradesh. 200,470 (1961).

meet[1] (mēt), *v.,* **met, meeting,** *n.* —*v.t.* **1.** to come into contact, junction, or connection with. **2.** to come before or to (the eye, gaze, ear, etc.). **3.** to come upon or encounter; come face to face with or into the presence of. **4.** to go to the place of arrival of, as to welcome, speak with, accompany, etc.: *to meet one's guests at the door.* **5.** to come into the company of (a person, etc.) in intercourse, dealings, conference, etc. **6.** to come into personal acquaintance with, as by formal presentation: *to meet the governor.* **7.** to face, eye, etc., directly or without avoidance. **8.** to encounter in opposition or conflict. **9.** to oppose: *to meet charges with countercharges.* **10.** to cope or deal effectively with (an objection, difficulty, etc.). **11.** to satisfy (needs, obligations, demands, etc.): *to meet a cheque.* **12.** to come into conformity with (wishes, expectations, views, etc.). **13.** to encounter in experience: *to meet hostility.* **14. meet (someone) halfway,** to reach an agreed compromise. —*v.i.* **15.** to come together, face to face, or into company: *we met in the street.* **16.** to assemble, as for action or conference as a committee, a legislature, a society, etc. **17.** to become personally acquainted. **18.** to come into contact or form a junction, as lines, planes, areas, etc. **19.** to be conjoined or united. **20.** to concur or agree. **21.** to come together in opposition or conflict, as adversaries, hostile forces, etc. **22. meet with, a.** to encounter; come across. **b.** to experience; undergo; receive (praise, blame, etc.). —*n.* **23.** a meeting, as of huntsmen for a hunt, or cyclists for a ride, etc. **24.** those assembled at such a meeting. **25.** the place of meeting. [ME *mete(n)*, OE *mētan, gemētan*, der. *mōt, gemōt* meeting. See MOOT] —**Syn. 1.** intersect, converge. **7.** confront, face. **11.** settle; discharge, fulfil. **16.** gather, congregate, convene. **22b.** suffer. —**Ant. 1.** diverge.

meet[2] (mēt), *adj.* suitable; fitting; proper. [ME *mete*, repr. d. OE form, r. OE *gemǣte* suitable, c. G *gemäss* conformable]

meeting (mē′tĭng), *n.* **1.** a coming together. **2.** an assembling, as of persons for some purpose. **3.** an assembly or gathering held. **4.** the persons present. **5.** a hostile encounter; a duel. **6.** an assembly for religious worship, esp. of Quakers. **7.** a coming into or being in contact, as of things; junction or union.

meeting house, **1.** a house or building for religious worship. **2.** a house of worship of Quakers.

meetly (mēt′lĭ), *adv.* suitably; fittingly; properly.

mega-, a word element meaning 'great', and, in physics, 1,000,000 times a given unit, as in *megohm, megacycle.* Also, before vowels, **meg-.** [t. Gk, comb. form of *mégas*]

megacephalic (mĕg′ə sĭ făl′ĭk), *adj.* **1.** *Anat.* having a skull with a large cranial capacity or one exceeding the mean. Cf. **microcephalic. 2.** large-headed. Also, **megacephalous** (mĕg′ə sĕf′ə ləs). [f. MEGA- + m. s. Gk *kephalḗ* head + -IC]

megacycle (mĕg′ə sī′kl), *n. Physics.* a million cycles, esp. a million cycles per second. See **kilocycle.**

megadeath (mĕg′ə dĕth′), *n.* the death of a million persons, esp. as the result of an act of nuclear warfare.

Megaera (mĭ jĭə′rə), *n. Gk Myth.* one of the Furies.

megagamete (mĕg′ə gă mēt′), *n.* a macrogamete.

megalith (mĕg′ə lĭth), *n. Archaeol.* a stone of great size, esp. in ancient constructive work (as the Cyclopean masonry) or in primitive monumental remains (as menhirs, dolmens, cromlechs, etc.). —**meg′alith′ic,** *adj.*

megalo-, a word element denoting bigness or exaggeration. [t. Gk, comb. form of s. *mégas* great]

megalocephalic (mĕg′ə lō sĭ făl′ĭk), *adj.* megacephalic. Also, **megalocephalous** (mĕg′ə lō sĕf′ə ləs). —**meg′-aloceph′aly,** *n.*

megalomania (mĕg′ə lō mā′nyə), *n.* **1.** *Psychol.* a form of mental alienation marked by delusions of greatness, wealth, etc. **2.** a mania for big or great things. [t. NL. See MEGALO-, -MANIA]

megalomaniac (mĕg′ə lō mā′nĭ ăk′), *n.* one who is afflicted with megalomania. —**megalomaniacal** (mĕg′-ə lō mə nī′ə kl), *adj.*

megalopolis (mĕg′ə lŏp′ə lĭs), *n.* a large urban region, often consisting of adjoining towns and suburbs which have merged. —**megalopolitan** (mĕg′ə lə pŏl′ĭ tən), *adj.*

megalosaur (mĕg′ə lō sô′), *n.* any of the gigantic carnivorous dinosaurs that constitute the extinct genus *Megalosaurus.* [t. NL: s. *megalosaurus*] —**meg′alo-sau′rian,** *adj., n.*

megaphone (mĕg′ə fōn′), *n.* a device for magnifying sound, or for directing it in increased volume, as a large funnel-shaped instrument used in addressing a large audience out of doors or in calling to a distance. —**megaphonic** (mĕg′ə fŏn′ĭk), *adj.*

megapod (mĕg′ə pŏd′), *adj.* having large feet.

megapode (mĕg′ə pōd′), *n.* any of the *Megapodiidae*, a family of large-footed Australian gallinaceous birds.

Megara (mĕg′ə rə; *Gk* mĕ′gä rä), *n.* a city of ancient

Greece: the capital of **Megaris** (mĕg′ə rĭs), a district between the gulfs of Corinth and Aegina.

megasporangium (mĕg′ə spô răn′jĭ əm), *n.*, *pl.* **-gia** (-jĭ ə). *Bot.* a sporangium containing megaspores.

megaspore (mĕg′ə spô′), *n. Bot.* **1.** the larger of the two kinds of spores produced by some pteridophytes. **2.** the embryo sac of a flowering plant.

megasporophyll (mĕg′ə spô′rə fĭl), *n. Bot.* a sporophyll producing megasporangia only.

megathere (mĕg′ə thĭə′), *n.* any of the huge slothlike animals constituting the extinct genus *Megatherium.* [t. NL: m. s. *megathērium*, f. Gk: *mega-* MEGA- + m. *thērion* beast]

megaton (mĕg′ə tŭn′), *n.* **1.** 1,000,000 tons. **2.** an explosive force equal to that of 1,000,000 tons of TNT.

megavolt (mĕg′ə vōlt′), *n. Elect.* a million volts. *Symbol:* Mv

megawatt (mĕg′ə wŏt′), *n. Elect.* a million watts. *Symbol:* Mw

Megiddo (mə gĭd′ō), *n.* an ancient city in N Israel, on the plain of Esdraelon: scene of many battles; probably the same as Armageddon in the Bible.

megohm (mĕg′ōm′), *n. Elect.* a large unit of resistance, equal to a million ohms.

megrim (mē′grĭm), *n.* **1.** (*pl.*) morbid low spirits. **2.** *Archaic.* a whim or caprice. **3.** *Obs.* migraine. [ME *migraine*, t. F, t. LL: m. *hemicrānia* HEMICRANIA]

Mehemet Ali (mĭ hĕm′ĭt ä′lĭ), 1769–1849, pasha and viceroy of Egypt. Also, **Mohammed Ali.**

Meiji (mā′jē′), *n. Jap. Hist.* the artistic style associated with the reign of the Japanese emperor Mutsuhito, 1867–1912, showing Western influence. [Jap.: lit., enlightened peace]

Meilhac (*Fr.* mĕ yȧk′), *n.* **Henry** (*Fr.* äɴ rē′), 1831–97, French dramatist.

Mein Kampf (mīn′kämpf′), the autobiography of Adolf Hitler, setting forth his political philosophy and his plan for the German conquest of Europe; first published 1925. [G: my struggle]

meiosis (mī ō′sĭs), *n. Biol.* the maturation process of gametes, consisting of chromosome conjugation and two cell divisions, in the course of which the diploid chromosome number becomes reduced to the haploid. [t. Gk: a lessening] —**meiotic** (mī ŏt′ĭk), *adj.*

Meir (mĭ ĭə′, mā-), *n.* **Mrs Golda** (gōl′də), born 1898, Israeli politician: prime minister since 1969.

Meissen (*Ger.* mī′sən), *n.* a town in S East Germany, on the river Elbe: famous for the fine porcelain made there. 131,613 (1965).

Meissonier (*Fr.* mĕ sō nyĕ′), *n.* **Jean Louis Ernest** (*Fr.* zhäɴ lwē ĕr nĕst′), 1815–91, French painter.

Meistersinger (mīs′tə sĭng′ə), *n.*, *pl.* **-singer.** a member of one of the guilds, chiefly of workingmen, established during the 14th, 15th, and 16th centuries in the principal cities of Germany, for the cultivation of poetry and music. Also, **mastersinger.**

Meitner (*Ger.* mīt′nər), *n.* **Lise** (*Ger.* lē′zə), 1878–1968, Austrian nuclear physicist.

Mèknes (*Fr.* mĕk nĕs′), *n.* a town in N Morocco: a former capital. 185,000 (est. 1965).

Mekong (mē′kŏng′), *n.* a river flowing from W China SE along most of the boundary between Thailand and Laos to the South China Sea. ab. 2600 mi. Chinese, **Lantsang.**

melamine (mĕl′ə mēn′), *n. Chem.* a white crystalline solid, $C_3H_6N_6$, used in synthetic resins, esp. with formaldehyde.

melan-, var. of **melano-**, as in *melancholy.*

melancholia (mĕl′ən kō′lyə), *n. Psychol.* mental disease characterized by great depression of spirits and gloomy forebodings. [t. LL. See MELANCHOLY]

melancholiac (mĕl′ən kō′lĭ ăk′), *adj.* **1.** affected with melancholia. —*n.* **2.** one affected with melancholia.

melancholic (mĕl′ən kŏl′ĭk), *adj.* **1.** disposed to or affected with melancholy; gloomy; melancholy. **2.** pertaining to melancholia. —**mel′anchol′ically,** *adv.*

melancholy (mĕl′ən kə lĭ), *n.*, *pl.* **-cholies,** *adj.* —*n.* **1.** a gloomy state of mind, esp. when habitual or prolonged; depression. **2.** sober thoughtfulness; pensiveness. **3.** *Archaic.* **a.** condition of having too much black bile. **b.** the bile itself. —*adj.* **4.** affected with, characterized by, or showing melancholy: *a melancholy mood.* **5.** attended with or inducing melancholy or sadness: *a melancholy occasion.* **6.** soberly thoughtful; pensive. [ME *melancholie*, t. LL: m. *melancholia*, t. Gk: black bile] —**Syn. 1.** dejection, despondency; gloominess; hypochondria. **4.** See **sad.** —**Ant. 5.** happy.

Melanchthon (mĕ lăngk′thŏn; *Ger.* mə lănKH′tŏn), *n.* **Philipp** (*Ger.* fē′lĭp), 1497–1560, German Protestant reformer.

Melanesia (mĕl′ə nē′zyə), *n.* one of the three principal divisions of Oceania, comprising the island groups in the S Pacific, NE of Australia. [f. Gk *méla(s)* black + s. Gk *nêsos* island + -IA ; ? so named from black appearance of the islands seen from the sea]

Melanesian (mĕl′ə nē′zyən), *adj.* **1.** of or pertaining to Melanesia, its inhabitants, or their languages. —*n.* **2.** a member of any of the dark-skinned, frizzy-haired peoples inhabiting Melanesia. **3.** any of the Austronesian languages of Melanesia.

mélange (mā lŏnzh′; *Fr.* mĕ läɴzh′), *n.* a mixture; medley. [t. F, der. *mêler* mix. See MEDDLE]

melanin (mĕl′ə nĭn), *n. Biochem.* the dark pigment in the body of man and certain animals, $C_{17}H_{98}O_{33}N_{14}S$, as that occurring in the hair, epidermis, etc., of coloured races, or one produced in certain diseases. [f. MELAN- + -IN[2]]

melanism (mĕl′ə nĭz′əm), *n. Ethnol., Zool.* the condition of having a high amount of dark or black pigment granules in the skin, hair, and eyes of a human being or the skin and surface structures of any other animal. —**mel′anis′tic,** *adj.*

melanite (mĕl′ə nīt′), *n. Mineral.* a deep-black variety of garnet. [f. MELAN- + -ITE[1]]

melano-, a word element meaning 'black'. [t. Gk, comb. form of *mélas* black]

Melanochroi (mĕl′ə nŏk′rō ī′), *n.pl.* light-complexioned Caucasians with dark hair. [t. NL, repr. coined Gk *melánōchroi* (nom. pl.) black-pale] —**Melanochroid** (mĕl′ə nŏk′roid), *adj.*

melanoid (mĕl′ə noid′), *adj.* **1.** of or characterized by melanosis. **2.** resembling the colour of melanin.

melanoma (mĕl′ə nō′mə), *n.*, *pl.* **-mata** (-mə tə). *Pathol.* a dark-coloured tumour. [t. NL. See MELAN-, -OMA]

melanosis (mĕl′ə nō′sĭs), *n. Pathol.* **1.** morbid deposition or development of black or dark pigment in the tissues, sometimes leading to the production of malignant pigmented tumours. **2.** a discoloration caused by this. [t. NL, t. Gk: a blackening] —**melanotic** (mĕl′ə nŏt′ĭk), *adj.*

melanthaceous (mĕl′ən thā′shyəs), *adj.* belonging to the *Melanthaceae*, a family of monocotyledonous bulbless plants related to and sometimes classified in the lily family, including the bellwort, European white hellebore, etc. [f. s. NL *Melanthāceae* the typical family (f. Gk *mél(as)* black + s. Gk *ánthos* flower + L *-āceae* -ACEAE) + -OUS]

melaphyre (mĕl′ə fī′ə), *n. Obs.* any of various dark-coloured igneous rocks of porphyritic texture. [t. F: f. Gk *méla(s)* black + F *(por)phyre* porphyry]

Melba (mĕl′bə), *n.* **Dame Nellie** (*Mrs Nellie Mitchell Armstrong*), 1861–1931, Australian operatic soprano.

Melba sauce, a sweet sauce made from raspberries.

Melba toast, narrow slices of thin toast.

Melbourne (mĕl′bən), *n.* **1.** a seaport in SE Australia, in Victoria. 2,061,300 (1964). See map under **Canberra. 2. William Lamb, 2nd Viscount,** 1779–1848, British statesman, prime minister in 1834, and 1835–41.

Melbourne Cup, *n.* a major Australian horserace, first run 1861.

Melchior (mĕl′chĭ ô′), *n.* **Lauritz** (lô′rĭts), born 1890, U.S. operatic tenor, born in Denmark.

Melchizedek (mĕl kĭz′ə dĕk′), *n.* **1.** *Old Testament.* a priest-king of Salem. Gen. 14:18. **2.** the higher order of priesthood in the Mormon Church. [t. LL (Vulgate): m. *Melchisedek*, t. Gk (Septuagint), t. Heb.: m. *Malkīsedeq*]

meld[1] (mĕld), *Cards.* —*v.t.*, *v.i.* **1.** to announce and display (a counting combination of cards in the hand) for a score. —*n.* **2.** the act of melding. **3.** any combination of cards to be melded. [t. G: s. *melden* announce]

meld[2] (mĕld), *v.t.*, *v.i.* to merge or blend. [b. MELT + WELD]

Meleager (mĕl′ĭ ā′gə), *n. Gk Legend.* the heroic son of Althaea. He was an Argonaut, and the slayer of the Calydonian boar. It had been prophesied to his mother that as long as a certain brand remained unburnt Meleager would live; after he killed his uncles in argument over the boar, Althaea threw the brand into the fire and so killed her son.

melee (mĕl′ā), *n.* a confused general hand-to-hand fight. Also, *French* **mêlée** (*Fr.* mĕ lĕ′). [t. F. See MEDLEY]

meliaceous (mē′lĭ ā′shyəs), *adj.* belonging to the *Meliaceae*, a family of trees and shrubs including the mahogany, Spanish cedar, etc. [f. s. NL *Melia* the typical genus (t. Gk: ash tree) + -ACEOUS]

melic (mĕl′ĭk), *adj.* **1.** intended to be sung. **2.** denoting or pertaining to the more elaborate form of Greek lyric poetry, as distinguished from iambic and elegiac poetry. [t. Gk: m. s. *melikós*, der. *mélos* song]

melick (mĕl′ĭk), *n.* any of several species of slender, perennial grasses belonging to the genus *Melica*, as the widespread **wood melick,** *M. uniflora*, of shady places. Also, **melic.** [t. NL: m. s. *melica*]

Méliès (*Fr.* mė lyĕs′), *n.* **Georges** (*Fr.* zhôrzh), 1861–1938, pioneer French film director.

Melilla (*Fr.* mė lē yȧ′; *Sp.* mė lē′lyȧ), *n.* a seaport belonging to Spain, on the NE coast of Morocco. 80,520 (1966).

melilot (mĕl′ĭ lŏt′), *n.* any of the clover-like fabaceous herbs constituting the genus *Melilotus.* [ME *mellilot*, t. OF, t. L: m. s. *melilōtos*, t. Gk: a kind of clover]

melinite (mĕl′ĭ nīt′), *n.* a high explosive containing picric acid. [f. s. Gk *mélinos* quince-yellow + -ITE [1]]

meliorate (mē′lyə rāt′), *v.t., v.i.,* **-rated, -rating.** to make or become better; improve; ameliorate. [t. LL: m. s. *meliōrātus*, pp.] **—me′liora′tion,** *n.* **—meliorative** (mē′lyə rə tĭv), *adj.* **—me′liora′tor,** *n.*

meliorism (mē′lyə rĭz′əm), *n.* the doctrine that the world tends to become better, or may be made better by human effort. [f. L *melior* better + -ISM] **—me′liorist,** *n., adj.* **—me′lioris′tic,** *adj.*

meliority (mē′lĭ ŏ′rĭ tĭ), *n.* superiority.

melisma (mĭ lĭz′mə), *n. Music.* a group of notes sung to one syllable.

melliferous (mĭ lĭf′ə rəs), *adj.* yielding or producing honey. [f. L *mellifer* honey-bearing + -OUS]

mellifluent (mĭ lĭf′lo͞o ənt), *adj.* mellifluous. [t. LL: s. *mellifluens* flowing with honey] **—mellif′luence,** *n.* **—mellif′luently,** *adv.*

mellifluous (mĭ lĭf′lo͞o əs), *adj.* **1.** sweetly or smoothly flowing: *mellifluous tones.* **2.** flowing with honey; sweetened with or as with honey. [ME, t. LL: m. *mellifluus* flowing with honey] **—mellif′luously,** *adv.* **—mellif′luousness,** *n.*

mellophone (mĕl′ə fōn′), *n.* a simplified French horn used in dance bands.

mellow (mĕl′ō), *adj.* **1.** soft and full-flavoured from ripeness, as fruit. **2.** well-matured, as wines. **3.** softened, toned down or improved as if by ripening. **4.** soft and rich, as sound, tones, colour, light, etc. **5.** genial; jovial. **6.** friable or loamy, as soil. *—v.t., v.i.* **7.** to make or become mellow; soften by or as by ripening. [ME *mel(o)we*, OE *meru* tender, soft, with change of *r* to *l*, presumably by dissimilation in sequence *melowe fruit*] **—mel′lowly,** *adv.* **—mel′lowness,** *n.* **—Syn. 1.** See **ripe.**

melodeon (mĭ lō′dĭ ən), *n.* **1.** a small reed organ. **2.** a kind of accordion. [pseudo-Gk var. of *melodium* (der. MELODY). Cf. ACCORDION]

melodic (mĭ lŏd′ĭk), *adj.* **1.** melodious. **2.** pertaining to melody as distinguished from harmony and rhythm. **—melod′ically,** *adv.*

melodics (mĭ lŏd′ĭks), *n.* that branch of musical science concerned with the pitch and succession of tones.

melodious (mĭ lō′dyəs), *adj.* **1.** of the nature of or characterized by melody; tuneful. **2.** producing melody or sweet sound. **—melo′diously,** *adv.* **—melo′diousness,** *n.*

melodist (mĕl′ə dĭst), *n.* a composer or a singer of melodies.

melodize (mĕl′ə dīz′), *v.,* **-dized, -dizing.** *—v.t.* **1.** to make melodious. *—v.i.* **2.** to make melody. **3.** to blend melodiously. Also, **melodise.** **—mel′odiz′er,** *n.*

melodrama (mĕl′ə drä′mə), *n.* **1.** a play which does not observe the dramatic laws of cause and effect and which intensifies sentiment and exaggerates passion. **2.** (in the 17th, 18th, and early 19th centuries) a romantic dramatic composition with music interspersed. [t. F: m. *mélodrame*, t. It.: m. *melodramma* musical drama, f. Gk: *mélo(s)* song, music + m. *dráma* DRAMA] **—melodramatize** (mĕl′ə drăm′ə tīz′), *v.t.* **—melodramatist** (mĕl′ə drăm′ə tĭst), *n.*

melodramatic (mĕl′ə drə măt′ĭk), *adj.* **1.** of, like, or befitting melodrama; sentimental and exaggerated. *—n.* **2.** (*pl.*) melodramatic behaviour. **—mel′odramat′ically,** *adv.*

melody (mĕl′ə dĭ), *n., pl.* **-dies.** **1.** musical sounds in agreeable succession or arrangement. **2.** *Music.* **a.** the succession of single notes in musical compositions, as distinguished from harmony and rhythm. **b.** the principal part in a harmonic composition; the air. **c.** a rhythmical succession of single notes producing a distinct musical phrase or idea. **3.** a poem suitable for singing. [ME *melodie*, t. OF, t. LL: m. *melōdia*, t. Gk: m. *melōidía* singing, choral song] **—Syn. 1.** See **harmony.**

meloid (mĕl′oid), *n.* **1.** a blister beetle. *—adj.* **2.** of or pertaining to a blister beetle. [t. NL: s. *Meloïdae* the typical genus, der. *meloē* beetle]

melon (mĕl′ən), *n.* **1.** the fruit of any of various cucurbitaceous plants, as the muskmelon or watermelon. **2. cut a melon,** *U.S. Slang.* to declare a large extra dividend to shareholders. [ME, t. OF, t. LL: s. *mēlo*, t. Gk: short for *mēlopépōn* apple-like gourd]

Melos (mē′lŏs), *n.* an island of the Cyclades group, in the Aegean, S of Greece: statue of **Venus de Milo** found here, 1920. 4913 pop. (est. 1965); 61 sq. mi. Also, **Milo, Milos.**

Melpomene (mĕl pŏm′ĭ nĭ), *n.* the Muse of tragedy. [t. L, t. Gk, prop. ppr. fem. of *mélpesthai* sing]

Melrose (mĕl′rōz′), *n.* a burgh in SE Scotland, on the river Tweed: ruins of a famous abbey. 2133 (1961).

melt (mĕlt), *v.,* **melted, melted** or **molten, melting,** *n.* *—v.i.* **1.** to become liquefied by heat, as ice, snow, butter, metal, etc. **2.** (not in scientific use) to become liquid; dissolve. **3.** to pass, dwindle or fade gradually. **4.** to pass, change, or blend gradually (often fol. by *into*). **5.** to become softened in feeling by pity, sympathy, love, or the like. **6.** *Archaic.* to fail to faint, as the heart or soul, from fear, grief, etc. *—v.t.* **7.** to reduce to a liquid state by heat; fuse. **8.** to cause to pass or fade (*away*). **9.** to cause to pass or blend gradually. **10.** to soften in feeling, as a person, the heart, etc. *—n.* **11.** the act or process of melting. **12.** the state of being melted. **13.** that which is melted. **14.** a quantity melted at one time. **15.** Also, **milt.** the spleen of an animal, esp. a pig, ox, etc. [ME *melte(n)*, OE *meltan*, v.i., *m(i)eltan*, v.t.; akin to Icel. *melta* digest, Gk *méldein* melt] **—melt′er,** *n.*

—Syn. 1. MELT, DISSOLVE, FUSE, THAW imply reducing a solid substance to a liquid state. To MELT is to bring a solid to a liquid condition by the agency of heat: *to melt butter.* DISSOLVE, though sometimes used interchangeably with melt, applies to a different process, depending upon the fact that certain solids, placed in certain liquids, distribute their particles throughout the liquids: *a greater number of solids can be dissolved in water and in alcohol than in any other liquids.* To FUSE is to subject the solid (usually a metal) to a very high temperature; it applies esp. to melting or blending metals together: *bell metal is made by fusing copper and tin.* To THAW is to reduce a frozen substance (whose ordinary condition is liquid) to a liquid or semiliquid by raising its temperature above the freezing point: *sunshine will thaw ice in a lake.*

meltage (mĕl′tĭj), *n.* the amount melted or the result of melting.

melting point, the temperature at which a solid substance melts or fuses.

melting pot, **1.** a pot in which metals or other substances are melted or fused. **2.** any situation in which a mixture of diverse elements or ideas occurs, as a multiracial community.

melton (mĕl′tən), *n.* a smooth heavy woollen cloth, used for coats, hunting jackets, etc. [from MELTON Mowbray]

Melton Mowbray (mĕl′tən mō′brā), a town in England, in Leicestershire. 15,913 (1961).

melt-water (mĕlt′wô′tə), *n. Phys. Geog.* water deriving from melted snow or ice.

Melville (mĕl′vĭl), *n.* **Herman,** 1819–91, U.S. novelist.

Melville Island, **1.** a Canadian island in the Arctic Ocean, N of Canada. ab. 200 mi. long; ab. 130 mi. wide. **2.** the largest island in Australian waters lying off Northern Territory. 2240 sq. mi.

Melville Peninsula, a peninsula in N Canada, SE of the Gulf of Boothia. ab. 250 mi. long.

mem., **1.** member. **2.** memoir. **3.** memorandum.

member (mĕm′bə), *n.* **1.** each of the persons composing a society, party, community, or other body. **2.** each of the persons included in the membership of a legislative body, as Parliament (chiefly the House of Commons). **3.** a part or organ of an animal body; a limb, as a leg, arm, or wing. **4.** a constituent part of any structural or composite whole, as a subordinate architectural feature of a building or the like. **5.** either side of an algebraic equation. [ME *membre*, t. OF, g. L *membrum* limb, part]

—Syn. 3, 4. MEMBER, LIMB refer to an integral part of a larger body. MEMBER is the general term applied to any integral part or vital organ of an organized animal body, or, more widely, to any integral or distinguishable constituent part of a whole which is considered as organic: *the nose, tongue, and arms are members of the body; a member of a facade.* LIMB, which once, like MEMBER, referred to any organ of the body, is now restricted to the legs and arms (particularly of human beings); secondarily applied to the branches of a tree. It has such figurative uses as a *limb of Satan*, or a *limb of the law.* The Victorian 'limb' as a prudish euphemism for 'leg' stimulated further humorous use of the word.

membership (mĕm′bə shĭp′), *n.* **1.** the state of being a member, as of a society. **2.** the status of a member. **3.** the total number of members belonging to a body.

membrane (mĕm′brān), *n.* a thin, pliable sheet or layer of animal or vegetable tissue, serving to line an organ, connect parts, etc. [t. L: m. s. *membrāna* the skin that covers the several members of the body, parchment]

membrane bone, a bone which originates in membranous tissue (distinguished from *cartilage bone*).

membranous (mĕm′brə nəs, mĕm brā′nəs), *adj.* **1.** consisting of, of the nature of, or resembling membrane. **2.** characterized by the formation of a membrane. Also, **membranaceous** (mĕm′brə nā′shyəs).

Memel (mā′məl), *n.* **1.** a seaport in the W Soviet Union, in the Lithuanian Republic. 120,000 (est. 1965). **2.** a territory including this seaport: ceded to Germany by Lithuania, 1939; incorporated into the Soviet Union 1945. 154,694 pop. (1939); 933 sq. mi. **3.** name of the lower course of the river Neman. Lithuanian (for defs 1 and 2), **Klaipeda.**

Memel (def. 1)

memento (mĭ mĕn′tō), *n., pl.* **-tos, -toes. 1.** something that serves as a reminder of what is past or gone. **2.** anything serving as a reminder or warning. **3.** (*cap.*) *Rom. Cath. Ch.* (in the canon of the mass) either of two prayers beginning with the word 'Memento' (remember); the first for persons living, and the second for persons deceased. [t. L, impv. of *meminisse* remember]

memento mori (mĭ mĕn′tō mô′rē), **1.** *Latin.* remember that thou must die (lit., to die). **2.** an object, as a skull or the like, serving as a reminder of death.

Memling (mĕm′lĭng), *n.* **Hans** (hănz), *c.* 1430–*c.* 94, Flemish painter. Also, **Memlinc** (mĕm′lĭngk).

Memnon (mĕm′nŏn), *n.* **1.** a colossal statue near Egyptian Thebes which was said to produce musical sounds when struck by the rays of the morning sun. **2.** *Gk Legend.* an oriental or Ethiopian hero slain by Achilles in the Trojan War. [t. L, t. Gk]

memo (mĕm′ō, mē′mō), *n., pl.* **memos.** *Colloq.* memorandum.

memoir (mĕm′wä), *n.* **1.** (*pl.*) records of facts or events in connection with a particular subject, historical period, etc., as known to the writer or gathered from special sources. **2.** (*pl.*) records of one's own life and experiences. **3.** a biography. **4.** (*pl.*) a collection of reports made to a scientific or other learned society. [t. F: m. *mémoire,* masc., memorandum, memorial, *mémoire,* fem., MEMORY]

memorabilia (mĕm′ə rə bĭl′ĭ ə), *n.pl., sing.* **-rabile** (-răb′ĭ lĭ). matters or events worthy to be remembered. [t. L, neut. pl. of *memorābilis* memorable]

memorable (mĕm′ə rə bl, mĕm′rə bl), *adj.* **1.** worthy to be remembered; notable: *a memorable speech.* **2.** easy to be remembered. [t. L: m. s. *memorābilis*] **—mem′orabil′ity, mem′orableness,** *n.* **—mem′orably,** *adv.*

memorandum (mĕm′ə răn′dəm), *n., pl.* **-dums, -da** (-də). **1.** a note made of something to be remembered, as in future action. **2.** a record or written statement of something. **3.** a note, as one sent from one member of a firm to another, regarding policy or the like. **4.** *Law.* a writing, usually informal, containing the terms of a transaction. **5.** *Diplomacy.* a summary of the state of a question, the reasons for a decision agreed on, etc. **6.** a document which includes the main terms of a shipment of unsold goods and authorizes their return within a specified time. [t. L, neut. of *memorandus* (ger.) that is to be remembered]

memorandum of association, a formal document constituting the charter of incorporation of a company.

memorial (mĭ mô′rĭ əl), *n.* **1.** something designed to preserve the memory of a person, event, etc., as a monument, a periodic observance, etc. **2.** a written statement of facts presented to a sovereign, a legislative body, etc., as the basis of, or expressed in the form of, a petition or remonstrance. *—adj.* **3.** preserving the memory of a person or thing; commemorative: *memorial services.* **4.** of or pertaining to the memory. [ME, t. L: s. *memoriālis* of memory] **—memo′rially,** *adv.*

memorialize (mĭ mô′rĭ ə līz′), *v.t.,* **-lized, -lizing. 1.** to commemorate. **2.** to present a memorial to. Also, **memorialise. —memo′rializa′tion,** *n.* **—memo′rializ′er,** *n.*

memorize (mĕm′ə rīz′), *v.t.,* **-rized, -rizing.** to commit to memory, or learn by heart: *he finally memorized the poem.* Also, **memorise. —mem′oriz′able,** *adj.* **—mem′oriza′tion,** *n.* **—mem′oriz′er,** *n.*

memory (mĕm′ə rĭ), *n., pl.* **-ries. 1.** the mental capacity or faculty of retaining and reviving impressions, or of recalling or recognizing previous experiences. **2.** this faculty as possessed by a particular individual: *to have a good memory.* **3.** the act or fact of retaining mental impressions; remembrance; recollection: *to draw from memory.* **4.** the length of time over which recollection extends: *a time within the memory of living men.* **5.** a mental impression retained; a recollection: *one's earliest memories.* **6.** the reputation of a person or thing, esp. after death. **7.** the state or fact of being remembered. **8.** a person or thing remembered. **9.** commemorative remembrance; commemoration: *a monument in memory of Columbus.* **10.** *Speech.* the step in the classical preparation of a speech in which the wording is memorized. **11.** *Computers.* the part of a digital computer in which data and instructions are held until they are required. [ME *memorie,* t. L: m. *memoria*]

Memphis (mĕm′fĭs), *n.* **1.** a city in the U.S., in SW Tennessee: a port on the Mississippi. 497,524 (1960). **2.** a ruined city in Upper Egypt, on the Nile, S of Cairo: the ancient capital of Egypt. See map under **Media.**

mem-sahib (mĕm′sä′ĭb, -sä′hĭb), *n.* (in India, formerly) a native term of address to a European lady. [t. Hind.: f. *mem* (t. E: m. *ma'am*) + *sāhib* master]

men (mĕn), *n.* pl. of **man.**

Mena (*Sp.* mĕ′nä), *n.* **Juan de** (*Sp.* KH wän′ dĕ), 1411–56, Spanish poet.

menace (mĕn′ĭs), *n., v.,* **-aced, -acing.** *—n.* **1.** something that threatens to cause evil, harm, injury, etc.; a threat. *—v.t.* **2.** to utter or direct a threat against; threaten. **3.** to serve as a probable cause of evil, etc., to. [ME, t. OF, g. L *mināc ia* a threat] **—men′acer,** *n.* **—men′acingly,** *adv.*

menad (mē′năd), *n.* maenad.

ménage (mĕ näzh′; *Fr.* mĕ näzh′), *n.* **1.** a household; a domestic establishment. **2.** housekeeping. Also, **menage.** [t. F, ult. der. L *mansio* MANSION]

menagerie (mĭ năj′ə rĭ), *n.* **1.** a collection of wild or strange animals, esp. for exhibition. **2.** a place where they are kept or exhibited. [t. F: management of a household, menagerie, der. *ménage* MENAGE]

Menai Strait (mĕn′ī), a strait between Anglesey island and the mainland of NW Wales. 14 mi. long.

Menam (mē′năm′), *n.* a river flowing from N Thailand S to the Gulf of Siam. ab. 750 mi. Also, **Chao Phraya.**

Menander (mĭ năn′də), *n.* 342?–291 B.C., Greek writer of comedies.

Mencius (mĕn′shĭ əs), *n.* (*Meng-tse*), 385 or 372–289 B.C., Chinese philosopher.

Mencken (mĕng′kən), *n.* **H(enry) L(ouis),** 1880–1956, U.S. author, editor, and critic.

mend (mĕnd), *v.t.* **1.** to make whole or sound by repairing, as something broken, worn, or otherwise damaged; repair: *to mend clothes, to mend a road.* **2.** to remove or correct defects or errors in. **3.** to remove or correct (a defect, etc.). **4.** to set right; make better; improve: *to mend matters.* *—v.i.* **5.** to progress towards recovery, as a sick person. **6.** (of conditions) to improve. *—n.* **7.** the act of mending; repair or improvement. **8.** a mended place. **9. on the mend, a.** recovering from sickness. **b.** improving in state of affairs. [aphetic var. of AMEND] **—mend′able,** *adj.* **—mend′er,** *n.*

—Syn. 1. MEND, DARN, PATCH mean to repair something and thus renew its usefulness. MEND is an informal and general expression which emphasizes the idea of making whole something damaged: *to mend a broken dish, a tear in an apron.* DARN and PATCH are more specific, referring particularly to repairing holes or rents. To DARN is to repair by means of stitches interwoven with one another: *to darn socks.* To PATCH is to cover a hole or rent (usually) with a piece or pieces of similar material and to secure the edges of these; it implies a more temporary or makeshift repair than the others: *to patch the knees of trousers.*

mendacious (mĕn dā′shəs), *adj.* **1.** false or untrue: *a mendacious report.* **2.** lying or untruthful. [f. MENDACI(TY) + -OUS] **—menda′ciously,** *adv.* **—menda′ciousness,** *n.*

mendacity (mĕn dăs′ĭ tĭ), *n., pl.* **-ties. 1.** the quality of being mendacious. **2.** a falsehood; a lie. [t. LL: m. s. *mendācitas*]

Mendel (*Ger.* mĕn′dəl), *n.* **Gregor Johann** (*Ger.* grĕ′gôr yō′hän), 1822–84, Austrian biologist. **—Mendelian** (mĕn dē′lyən), *adj.*

mendelevium (mĕn′dĭ lē′vĭ əm), *n. Chem.* a synthetic, radioactive element. *Symbol:* Md, Mv; *at. no.:* 101. [f. MENDEL(YE)EV + -IUM]

Mendelism (mĕn′də lĭz′əm), *n.* the theories of heredity advanced by G. J. Mendel. Also, **Mendelianism** (mĕn dē′lĭ ə nĭz′əm).

Mendel's laws, *Genetics.* the basic principles of heredity discovered by Gregor Mendel, showing that alternative hereditary factors of hybrids exhibit a clean-cut separation or segregation from one another, and that different pairs of hereditary traits are independently assorted from each other.

Mendelssohn (mĕn′dl sən; *Ger.* mĕn′dəls zōn), *n.* **1. Felix** (*Ger.* fē′lĭks) (*Jacob Ludwig Felix Mendelssohn-Bartholdy*), 1809–47, German composer. **2.** his grandfather, **Moses** (*Ger.* mō′zĕs), 1729–86, German philosopher.

Mendelyeev (*Russ.* mĭn dĭ lyĕ′yĭf), *n.* **Dmitri Ivanovich** (*Russ.* dmē′trĭy ĭ vän′ə vĭch), 1834–1907, Russian chemist: helped to develop the periodic law. Also, **Mendeleev, Mendeleyev.**

Menderes (*Turk.* mĕn′dĕ rĕs), *n.* **1.** Ancient, **Maeander.** a river in W Asia Minor, flowing into the Aegean near Samos. ab. 240 mi. **2.** Ancient, **Scamander.** a river in NW Asia Minor, flowing across the Trojan plain into the Dardanelles. ab. 65 mi.

Mendès-France (*Fr.* mäɴ dĕs fräɴs′), *n.* **Pierre** (*Fr.* pyĕr), born 1907, French statesman and economist: prime minister 1954–55.

mendicant (mĕn′dĭ kənt), *adj.* **1.** begging, practising begging, or living on alms. **2.** pertaining to or characteristic of a beggar. —*n.* **3.** one who lives by begging; a beggar. **4.** a mendicant friar. [t. L: s. *mendīcans*, ppr., begging] —**men′dicancy,** *n.*

mendicity (mĕn dĭs′ĭ tĭ), *n.* **1.** the practice of begging. **2.** the condition of life of a beggar. [ME *mendicite*, t. L: m. s. *mendīcitas* beggary]

Mendlesohn (*Ger.* mĕn′dəl zōn), *n.* **Erich** or **Eric,** 1887–1953, German expressionist architect.

Mendocino (mĕn′də sē′nō), *n.* **Cape,** a cape in the U.S., in NW California: the westernmost point in California.

Mendoza (*Sp.* mėn dō′thä), *n.* a town in W Argentina. 109,149 (est. 1960).

Mendoza (*Sp.* mėn dō′thä), *n.* **Pedro de** (*Sp.* pė′drō dė), 1487?–1537, Spanish soldier and explorer: founder of Buenos Aires (?1536).

Menelaus (mĕn′ĭ lā′əs), *n. Gk Legend.* a king of Sparta, brother of Agamemnon and husband of Helen; one of the leaders of the Greeks before Troy.

Menelik II (mĕn′ĭ lĭk), 1844–1913, emperor of Ethiopia 1889–1913.

Menéndez de Avilés (*Sp.* mė nėn′dėth dė ä bē lės′), **Pedro** (*Sp.* pė′drō), 1519–74, Spanish admiral and colonizer, esp. in America.

Menes (mē′nēz), *n.* fl. *c.* 3400? B.C., traditional first king of Egypt, founder of 1st dynasty.

Meng-tse (mĕng′tsä′), *n.* Chinese name of **Mencius.**

menhaden (mĕn hā′dn), *n., pl.* **-den.** any marine clupeoid fish of the genus *Brevoortia*, esp. *B. tyrannus*, having the appearance of a shad but with a more compressed body, common along the eastern coast of the U.S., and used for making oil and fertilizer. [t. N Amer. Ind. (Narragansett): they manure]

menhir (mĕn′hĭə), *n. Archaeol.* an upright monumental stone, standing either alone or with others, as in a cromlech, found in various parts of Europe, also in Africa and Asia. [t. Breton: m. *men hir* long stone]

menial (mē′nyəl), *adj.* **1.** pertaining or proper to domestic servants. **2.** servile. —*n.* **3.** a domestic servant. **4.** a servile person. [ME, t. AF, der. *meiniee*, ult. der. L *mansio* household, MANSION] —**me′nially,** *adv.* —**Syn. 2.** See **servile.**

meninges (mĭ nĭn′jēz), *n.pl., sing.* **meninx** (mē′nĭngks). *Anat.* the three membranes (dura mater, arachnoid, and pia mater) investing the brain and spinal cord. [t. NL, pl. of *mēninx*, t. Gk: membrane, esp. of the brain] —**meningeal** (mĭ nĭn′jĭ əl), *adj.*

meningitis (mĕn′ĭn jī′tĭs), *n. Pathol.* inflammation of the meninges, esp. of the pia mater and arachnoid. [t. NL, f. Gk: s. *mēninx* membrane + *-ītis* -ITIS] —**meningitic** (mĕn′ĭn jĭt′ĭk), *adj.*

meniscus (mĭ nĭs′kəs), *n., pl.* **-nisci** (-nĭs′ī). **1.** a crescent or crescent-shaped body. **2.** a lens with a crescent-shaped section. See illus. under **lens. 3.** the convex or concave upper surface of a column of liquid, the curvature of which is caused by capillarity. **4.** a disc of cartilage between the articulating ends of the bones in a joint. [t. NL, t. Gk: m. *mēnískos* crescent, dim. of *mēnē* moon] —**meniscoid** (mĭ nĭs′koid), *adj.*

A B

Menisci (def. 3) A, Concave water meniscus; B, Convex mercury meniscus

menispermaceous (mĕn′ĭ spû mā′shəs), *adj.* belonging to the *Menispermaceae*, a family of dicotyledonous plants, mostly woody climbers, having small, usually three-parted, dioecious flowers, some possessing medicinal properties. See **moonseed.** [f. s. NL *Mēnispermum* the typical genus, moonseed (f. Gk: m. *mēnē* moon + m. *spérma* seed) + -ACEOUS]

Mennonite (mĕn′ə nīt′), *n.* a member of a Protestant denomination opposed to infant baptism, the taking of oaths, the holding of public office, etc. [named after *Menno* Simons, 1492–1559, Frisian founder of the sect]

meno (mĕn′ō; *It.* mė′nō), *adv. Music.* less. [t. It., g. L *minus*]

meno-, a word element meaning 'month'. [t. Gk, comb. form of *mēn*]

menology (mĭ nŏl′ə jĭ), *n., pl.* **-gies. 1.** a calendar of the months. **2.** a record or account, as of saints, arranged in the order of a calendar. [t. NL: m. s. *mēnologium*, t. LGk: m. *mēnológion*, f. *mēno-* MENO- + *lógion* saying]

menopause (mĕn′ō pôz′), *n. Physiol.* the period of irregular menstrual cycles prior to the final cessation of the menses, occurring usually between the ages of 45 and 50. [f. MENO- + PAUSE] —**men′opau′sic,** *adj.*

menorah (mĭ nô′rə), *n. Judaism.* a candelabrum holding nine candles which are lit at the festival of Hanukkah. [t. Heb.]

Menorca (*Sp.* mė nôr′kä), *n.* Spanish name of **Minorca.**

menorrhagia (mĕn′ô rā′jyə), *n. Pathol.* excessive menstrual discharge. [t. NL. See MENO-, -RRHAGIA]

Menotti (*It.* mė nŏt′tē), *n.* **Gian Carlo** (*It.* jän kär′lō), born 1911, Italian operatic composer in the U.S.

mensal[1] (mĕn′səl), *adj.* monthly. [f. s. L *mēnsis* month + -AL[1]]

mensal[2] (mĕn′səl), *adj.* of, pertaining to, or used at the table. [ME, t. LL: s. *mensālis* of a table]

menses (mĕn′sēz), *n.pl. Physiol.* the (approximately) monthly discharge of blood and mucosal tissue from the uterus. [t. L, pl. of *mensis* month]

Menshevik (mĕn′shə vĭk), *n., pl.* **-viki** (-vĭ kē′), **-viks.** a member of a less radical socialistic party or group of the Social Democratic Party opposing the Bolshevik government. [t. Russ.: one of smaller (group), der. *menshe* less] —**Menshevism** (mĕn′shə vĭz′əm), *n.* —**Men′shevist,** *adj.*

mens sana in corpore sano (mĕnz′ sä′nə ĭn kô′pə rā sä′nō), *Latin.* a sound mind in a sound body.

menstrual (mĕn′strŏŏ əl), *adj.* **1.** *Physiol.* of or pertaining to the menses. **2.** monthly. [t. L: s. *menstruālis* monthly]

menstruate (mĕn′strŏŏ āt′), *v.i.,* **-ated, -ating.** to discharge the menses.

menstruation (mĕn′strŏŏ ā′shən), *n.* **1.** the act of discharging the menses. **2.** the period of menstruating.

menstruous (mĕn′strŏŏ əs), *adj.* pertaining to menstruation. [t. L: m. *menstruus* monthly]

menstruum (mĕn′strŏŏ əm), *n., pl.* **-struums, -strua** (-strŏŏ ə). a solvent. [t. ML, prop. neut. of L *menstruus* monthly]

mensurable (mĕn′shə rə bl), *adj.* measurable. [t. LL: m. s. *mensūrābilis*] —**men′surabil′ity,** *n.*

mensural (mĕn′shə rəl), *adj.* pertaining to measure.

mensuration (mĕn′shə rā′shən), *n.* **1.** that branch of mathematics which deals with the determination of length, area, and volume. **2.** the act, art, or process of measuring. [t. LL: s. *mensūrātio*]

mensurative (mĕn′shə rə tĭv), *adj.* adapted for or concerned with measuring.

-ment, a suffix of nouns, often concrete, denoting an action or state resulting (*abridgement, refreshment*), a product (*fragment*), or means (*ornament*). [t. F, t. L: s. *-mentum*, suffix forming nouns, usually from verbs]

mental[1] (mĕn′tl), *adj.* **1.** of or pertaining to the mind. **2.** performed by or existing in the mind: *mental arithmetic.* **3.** pertaining to the intellect; intellectual. **4.** denoting a disorder of the mind. **5.** designated for or pertaining to the care of those with disordered minds: *mental hospital, mental nurse.* **6.** *Slang.* foolish or mad. [ME, t. LL: s. *mentālis*]

mental[2] (mĕn′tl), *adj.* of or pertaining to the chin. [f. s. L *mentum* chin + -AL[1]]

mental age, *Psychol.* the degree of mental development or intelligence of an individual in comparison with the average intelligence of normal children at different ages. It is determined by a graded series of tests, in the form of tasks or questions, designed to measure native ability rather than the result of education: *a child 10 years old with a mental age of 12.*

mental defective, one who is mentally deficient.

mental deficiency, the condition of one who is mentally deficient. It embraces all types of idiocy, imbecility, and moronity.

mental healing, the healing of any ailment or disorder by mental concentration and suggestion.

mental health, the general condition of the mind with reference to sanity and vigour.

mentality (mĕn tăl′ĭ tĭ), *n., pl.* **-ties.** mental capacity or endowment; intellectuality; mind: *she was of average* mentality.

mentally (mĕn′tə lĭ), *adv.* **1.** in or with the mind or intellect; intellectually. **2.** with regard to the mind.

mentally deficient, *Psychol.* characterized by subnormal intelligence which is a handicap to the individual in his school or adult life; feeble-minded.

mentally handicapped, mentally deficient.

menthaceous (mĕn thā′shyəs), *adj.* belonging to the *Menthaceae* (usually included in the *Labiatae*) or mint family of plants, including the horsemint, peppermint, pennyroyal, savory, etc. [f. s. L *mentha* MINT[1] + -ACEOUS]

menthene (mĕn′thēn), *n. Chem.* a colourless liquid, $C_{10}H_{18}$, synthetically obtainable from menthol. [t. G: m. *Menthen*, f. s. L *mentha* MINT[1] + *-en* -ENE]

menthol (mĕn′thŏl), *n.* a colourless, crystalline alcohol, $C_{10}H_{20}O$, present in peppermint oil, used in perfume and confectionery, and for colds and nasal disorders because of its cooling effect on mucous membranes. [t. G: f. s. L *mentha* MINT[1] + *-ol* -OL[1]]

mentholated (mĕn′thə lā′tĭd), *adj.* **1.** covered or treated with menthol. **2.** saturated with or containing menthol.

mention (mĕn′shən), *v.t.* **1.** to refer briefly to; refer to by name incidentally; name, specify, or speak of. **2.** to cite as for some meritorious act. **3. not to mention,** to say nothing of; in addition to. —*n.* **4.** a speaking of or mentioning; a reference, direct or incidental. **5.** recognition, as for a meritorious act or achievement. [t. L: s. *mentio* a calling to mind, mention; r. ME *mencioun*, t. OF] —**men′tionable,** *adj.* —**men′tioner,** *n.*

Menton (mĕn tŏn′; *Fr.* mäN tôN′), *n.* a town in SE France, in Alpes-Maritimes department, on the Mediterranean: resort. 19,308 (est. 1966). Italian, **Mentone** (*It.* mĕn tō′nĕ).

Mentor (mĕn′tô), *n.* **1.** the friend to whom Odysseus, when departing for Troy, gave the charge of his household. **2.** (*l.c.*) a wise and trusted counsellor.

menu (mĕn′yōō; *Fr.* mə nY′), *n.* **1.** a list of the dishes served at a meal; a bill of fare. **2.** the dishes served. [t. F: detailed list, orig. adj., small, g. L *minūtus* MINUTE[2]]

Menuhin (mĕn′yŏŏ ĭn), *n.* **Yehudi** (yə hōō′dĭ), born 1916, U.S. violinist, living in England.

Menzel-Bourguiba (mĕn′zĕl bŏŏə gē′bə), *n.* a town in SE Tunisia. 34,732 (1956).

Menzies (mĕn′zĭz), *n.* **Sir Robert Gordon,** born 1894, Australian statesman; prime minister 1939–41 and 1949–1966.

meow (mĭ ou′, myou), *n., v.i.* miaow.

mepacrine (mĕp′ə krĭn), *n. Pharm.* a substance used in the treatment of malaria and of infestations with worms, such as tapeworms.

Mephistopheles (mĕf′ĭs tŏf′ĭ lēz′), *n. Medieval Demonology.* one of the seven chief devils. He is represented in Goethe's *Faust* as a crafty, sardonic, and scoffing fiend. —**Mephistophelean, Mephistophelian** (mĕf′ĭs tə fē′lyən), *adj.*

mephitic (mĭ fĭt′ĭk), *adj.* **1.** offensive to the smell. **2.** noxious; pestilential; poisonous. —**mephit′ically,** *adv.*

mephitis (mĭ fī′tĭs), *n.* **1.** a noxious or pestilential exhalation, esp. from the earth. **2.** a noisome or poisonous stench. [t. L]

meprobamate (mĕ prō′bə māt′; mĕp′rō băm′āt), *n. Pharm.* a tranquillizer used in the treatment of anxiety states. [f. ME(THYL) + PRO(PYL) + (*car*)*bamate* (see CARBAMIC ACID)]

Merca (mĕə′kə), *n.* a town in the Somali Republic, on the SE coast. 55,553 (est. 1963).

mercantile (mû′kən tīl′), *adj.* **1.** of or pertaining to merchants or to trade; commercial. **2.** engaged in trade or commerce. **3.** *Econ.* of or pertaining to the mercantile system. [t. F, t. It., der. *mercante*, g. L *mercans*, ppr., trading] —**Syn. 1.** See **commercial.**

mercantile agency, a concern which obtains information concerning the financial standing, business reputation, and credit ratings of individuals, firms and companies for the benefit of its subscribers.

mercantile marine, merchant navy.

mercantile paper, negotiable commercial paper, as promissory notes given by merchants for goods purchased, drafts drawn against purchasers, etc.

mercantile system, *Econ.* a system of political and economic policy, evolving with the modern national state, which sought to secure the political supremacy of a state in its rivalry with other states. According to this system, money was regarded as a store of wealth, and the great object of a state was the importation of the precious metals, by exporting the utmost possible quantity of its products and importing as little as possible, thus establishing a favourable balance of trade.

mercantilism (mû′kən tĭ lĭz′əm, -tī lĭz′əm), *n.* **1.** the mercantile spirit. **2.** the mercantile system. —**mer′cantilist,** *n.*

mercaptan (mû kăp′tăn), *n. Chem.* any of a class of sulphur-containing compounds, with the type formula RSH, the low-boiling members of which have an extremely offensive smell, esp. **ethyl mercaptan,** C_2H_5SH, a colourless liquid, with an offensive, garlic-like smell. [t. G: arbitrary abbrev. of L expression (*corpus*) *mer*(*curium*) *captan*(*s*) body-catching mercury]

mercaptide (mə kăp′tīd, mû-), *n. Chem.* the salt of a mercaptan.

Mercator (mû kā′tə; *Flem.* mĕr kä′tôr), *n.* **Gerhardus** (*Flem.* KHĕ′rŏr dəs) (*Gerhard Kremer*), 1512–94, Flemish cartographer and geographer.

Mercator's projection, a map projection with rectangular grid which is conformable and on which any rhumb line is represented as a straight line: particularly useful for navigation, though the scale varies notably with latitude and areal size, and the shapes of large areas are greatly distorted. Also, **Mercator projection.**

Mercator's projection

mercenary (mû′sĭ nə rĭ, -sĭn rĭ), *adj., n., pl.* **-naries.** —*adj.* **1.** working or acting merely for gain. **2.** hired (now only of soldiers serving in a foreign army). —*n.* **3.** a professional soldier serving in a foreign army. **4.** any hireling. [t. L: m. s. *mercēnārius* hired for pay] —**mer′cenarily,** *adv.* —**mer′cenariness,** *n.* —**Syn. 1.** venal, grasping, sordid; acquisitive, avaricious. —**Ant. 1.** unworldly.

mercer (mû′sə), *n.* a dealer in textile fabrics, esp. silks, etc. [ME, t. OF: m. *mercier*, der. OF *merz* goods, wares, g. L *merx*]

mercerize (mû′sə rīz′), *v.t.*, **-rized, -rizing.** to treat (cotton yarns or fabric) with caustic alkali under tension, increasing strength, lustre and affinity for dye. Also, **mercerise.** [from J. *Mercer*, English calico printer, the patentee (1850) of the process. See -IZE] —**mer′ceriza′tion,** *n.*

mercery (mû′sə rĭ), *n., pl.* **-ries. 1.** a mercer's shop. **2.** mercers' wares. [ME *mercerie*, t. OF, der. *mercier* MERCER]

merchandise (mû′chən dīz′), *n., v.,* **-dised, -dising.** —*n.* **1.** goods; commodities; esp. manufactured goods. **2.** the stock of a store. —*v.i.* **3.** to trade. —*v.t.* **4.** to trade in; buy and sell. [ME *marchandise*, t. OF, der. *marchand* MERCHANT] —**mer′chandis′er,** *n.*

merchandising (mû′chən dī′zĭng), *n.* the promotion and planning of the sales of a product, by using all available techniques of display, advertising and marketing.

merchant (mû′chənt), *n.* **1.** one who buys and sells commodities for profit; a wholesaler. **2.** *U.S.* a shopkeeper. —*adj.* **3.** pertaining to trade or commerce: *a merchant ship.* **4.** pertaining to the merchant navy. [ME, t. OF: m. *marcheant*, ult. der. L *mercāri* trade]

merchantable (mû′chən tə bl), *adj.* marketable: *merchantable war-surplus goods.*

merchant bank, a private banking firm engaged chiefly in accepting bills of exchange in foreign trade and underwriting new issues of securities. —**merchant banker.**

merchantman (mû′chənt mən), *n., pl.* **-men.** a trading vessel.

merchant navy, 1. the vessels of a nation engaged in commerce. **2.** the officers and crews of merchant vessels. Also, **mercantile marine, merchant marine.**

merchant prince, a merchant of great wealth, power, or position.

merci (*Fr.* mĕr sē′), *interj. French.* thank (you).

Mercia (mû′shyə), *n.* an early English kingdom in central Britain. —**Mer′cian,** *adj., n.*

merci beaucoup (*Fr.* mĕr-sē bō kōō′), *French.* thank (you) very much.

Mercier (*Fr.* mĕr syĕ′), *n.* **Désiré Joseph** (*Fr.* dĕ zē rĕ zhō zĕf′), 1851–1926, Belgian cardinal and patriot.

Mercia in A.D. 800

merciful (mû′sĭ fəl), *adj.* full of mercy; exercising, or characterized by, mercy; compassionate. —**mer′cifully,** *adv.* —**mer′cifulness,** *n.* —**Syn.** kind, clement, lenient. —**Ant.** hard-hearted.

merciless (mû′sĭ lĭs), *adj.* without any mercy, pitiless. —**mer′cilessly,** *adv.* —**mer′cilessness,** *n.*

mercurate (mû′kyŏŏ rāt′), *v.t.*, **-rated, -rating. 1.** to add mercury to (a compound). **2.** *Obsolesc.* to expose to the action of mercury.

mercurial (mû kyŏŏə′rĭ əl), *adj.* **1.** pertaining to, consisting of or containing, or caused by the metal mercury. **2.** (*cap.*) of or pertaining to the god Mercury or the planet Mercury. **3.** sprightly; volatile. **4.** flighty; fickle; changeable. —*n.* **5.** a preparation of mercury used as a drug. [t. L: s. *mercuriālis* of Mercury] —**mercu′rially,** *adv.* —**mercu′rialness,** *n.*

mercurialism (mû kyŏŏə′rĭ ə lĭz′əm), *n. Pathol.* a morbid condition caused by mercury.

mercurialize (mû kyŏŏə′rĭ ə līz′), *v.t.*, **-lized, -lizing.** **1.** to make mercurial. **2.** to treat or impregnate with mercury or one of its compounds. Also, **mercurialise.** —**mercu′rializa′tion,** *n.*

mercuric (mû kyŏŏə′rĭk), *adj. Chem.* of or containing mercury, esp. in the divalent state.

mercuric chloride, *Chem.* a strongly acrid, highly poisonous, white crystalline soluble salt, $HgCl_2$, prepared by sublimation of chlorine with mercury, much used as an antiseptic; corrosive sublimate. Also, **bichloride of mercury, mercury chloride.**

mercuric oxide, *Chem.* a soluble, poisonous solid, HgO, occurring as a red or yellow powder; used as a pigment and an antiseptic.

mercurous (mû′kyŏŏ rəs), *adj. Chem.* containing monovalent mercury.

mercury (mû′kyŏŏ rĭ), *n., pl.* **-ries.** **1.** *Chem.* a heavy, silver-white metallic element, remarkable for its fluidity at ordinary temperatures; quicksilver. *Symbol:* Hg (for **hydrargyrum**); *at. wt:* 200·59; *at. no.:* 80; *sp. gr.:* 13·546 at 20°C; *freezing point:* −38·9°C; *boiling point:* 357°C. **2.** a preparation of mercury (metal) used in medicine. **3.** (*cap.*) *Astron.* the planet nearest the sun, having a mean distance from the sun of about 36,000,000 miles, and a period of revolution of 87·969 days. Its diameter is 3010 miles. **4.** (*cap.*) a Roman deity, messenger of the gods, and god of commerce, dexterity, and eloquence (identified with *Hermes*). **5.** a messenger, or carrier of news (sometimes used as the name of a newspaper or periodical). **6.** any herb of the euphorbiaceous genus *Mercurialis*, as *M. perennis* (**dog's mercury**), a poisonous weed. [ME, t. L: m. s. *Mercurius* (defs 3, 4; in ML def. 1)]

mercury cell, *Physics.* a primary cell consisting of a zinc anode and a cathode of mercuric oxide mixed with graphite; the electrolyte is potassium hydroxide saturated with zinc oxide. The cell produces about 1·3 volts.

mercury chloride, mercuric chloride.

mercury fulminate, the mercury salt of fulminic acid, $Hg(ONC)_2$, which explodes as a result of very slight friction or shock when dry, used as a detonator.

mercury-vapour lamp (mû′kyŏŏ rĭ vā′pə), a lamp producing a light with a high actinic and ultraviolet content by means of an electric arc in mercury vapour.

mercy (mû′sĭ), *n., pl.* **-cies.** **1.** compassionate or kindly forbearance shown towards an offender, an enemy, or other person in one's power; compassion, pity, or benevolence. **2.** disposition to be merciful: *an adversary wholly without mercy.* **3.** discretionary power as to clemency or severity, pardon or punishment, or the like: *be at the mercy of a conqueror.* **4.** an act of forbearance, compassion, or favour, esp. of God towards his creatures. **5. at the mercy of,** defenceless; unprotected. [ME, t. OF: m. *merci*, fem., favour, mercy; masc., thanks, g. L *merces* pay, ML mercy] —**Syn. 1.** forgiveness, indulgence; clemency, leniency. —**Ant. 1.** cruelty.

mercy killing, euthanasia.

mercy seat, 1. the gold covering on the ark of the covenant, regarded as the resting place of God (see Ex. 25:17–22). **2.** the throne of God.

mere[1] (mĭə), *adj., superl.* **merest.** **1.** being nothing more nor better than what is specified; pure and simple. **2.** *Chiefly Law.* belonging or pertaining to a single individual or group, or sole. **3.** *Obs.* pure or unmixed. **4.** *Obs.* absolute or unqualified. [ME, t. L: m. *merus* pure, unmixed, mere]

—**Syn. 1.** MERE, BARE imply a scant sufficiency. They are often interchangeable, but MERE frequently means 'no more than (enough)'. BARE suggests 'scarcely as much as (enough)'. Thus *a mere livelihood* means enough to live on but no more; *a bare livelihood* means scarcely enough to live on. —**Ant. 1.** abundant.

mere[2] (mĭə), *n.* a lake; a pond. [ME and OE, c. G *Meer*; akin to L *mare* sea]

mere[3] (mĭə), *n. Dial.* a boundary. [ME; OE (*ge*)*mǣre*]

mere[4] (mĭə′rĭ, mĕ′rĭ), *n.* (in New Zealand), a war-club carried by a Maori chief. [t. Maori]

-mere, a word element meaning 'part', as in *blastomere.* [comb. form repr. Gk *méros*]

Meredith (mĕ′rĭ dĭth), *n.* **1. George,** 1828–1909, English novelist and poet. **2. Owen,** pen-name of **Edward Robert Bulwer Lytton.** See **Lytton** (def. 2).

merely (mĭə′lĭ), *adv.* **1.** only as specified, and nothing more; simply: *merely as a matter of form.* **2.** *Obs.* purely. **3.** *Obs.* absolutely or entirely.

meretricious (mĕ′rĭ trĭsh′əs), *adj.* **1.** alluring by a show of false attractions; showily attractive; tawdry. **2.** insincere. **3.** *Archaic.* of, pertaining to, or characteristic of a prostitute. [t. L: m. *meretrīcius* of prostitutes] —**mer′etri′ciously,** *adv.* —**mer′etri′ciousness,** *n.*

merganser (mû găn′sə), *n., pl.* **-sers,** (*esp. collectively*) **-ser.** any of several saw-billed, fish-eating, diving ducks of the subfamily *Merginae*, as the **red-breasted merganser,** *Mergus serrator*, a partial migrant of N Europe. [t. NL, f. s. L *mergus* diver (bird) + *anser* goose]

merge (mûj), *v.*, **merged, merging.** —*v.t.* **1.** to unite or combine. **2.** to cause to be swallowed up or absorbed; to sink the identity of by combination (often fol. by *in* or *into*). —*v.i.* **3.** to become swallowed up or absorbed; lose identity by absorption (often fol. by *in* or *into*). [t. L: m. s. *mergere* dip, plunge, sink] —**mergence** (mû′jəns), *n.*

merger (mû′jə), *n.* **1.** a statutory combination of two or more companies by the transfer of the properties to one surviving company. **2.** any combination of two or more business enterprises into a single enterprise. **3.** the act of merging. [f. MERG(E) + -ER[3]]

mericarp (mĕ′rĭ käp′), *n. Bot.* a single-seeded portion of a schizocarpous fruit, as in umbelliferous plants.

Mérida (*Sp.* mĕ′rē dä), *n.* a town in SE Mexico. 187,015 (est. 1965).

meridian (mə rĭd′ĭ ən), *n.* **1.** *Geog.* **a.** a great circle of the earth passing through the poles and any given point on the earth's surface. **b.** the half of such a circle included between the poles. **2.** magnetic meridian. **3.** *Astron.* the great circle of the celestial sphere which passes through its poles and the observer's zenith. **4.** a point or period of highest development, greatest prosperity, or the like. —*adj.* **5.** of or pertaining to a meridian. **6.** of or pertaining to midday or noon: *the meridian hour.* **7.** pertaining to a period of greatest elevation, prosperity, splendour, etc.; culminating. [t. L: s. *merīdiānus* of midday, of the south; r. ME *meridien*, t. OF]

meridional (mə rĭd′ĭ ə nəl), *adj.* **1.** of, pertaining to, or resembling a meridian. **2.** characteristic of the south or people inhabiting the south, esp. of France. **3.** southern; southerly. —*n.* **4.** an inhabitant of the south, esp. of France. [ME, t. LL: s. *merīdiōnālis* of midday] —**merid′ionally,** *adv.*

Mérimée (*Fr.* mē rē mē′), *n.* **Prosper** (*Fr.* prŏs pĕr′), 1803–70, French short-story writer, novelist, and essayist.

meringue (mə răng′), *n.* **1.** a mixture of sugar and beaten eggwhites formed into small cakes and baked, or spread over pastry, etc. **2.** a dish, cake, or shell made with it. [t. F, ? t. G: m. *Meringe*, lit., cake of Mehringen]

merino (mə rē′nō), *n., pl.* **-nos,** *adj.* —*n.* **1.** one of a variety of sheep, originally in Spain, valued for its fine wool. **2.** wool from such sheep. **3.** a knitted fabric made of wool or wool and cotton. —*adj.* **4.** made of merino wool, yarn, or cloth. [t. Sp., g. L (*ariēs*) *mājōrīnus* (male sheep) of the larger sort, der. *mājor* MAJOR]

Merino, *Ovis aries* (2 ft high at the shoulder)

Merionethshire (mĕ′rĭ ŏn′ĭth shĭə′, -shə), *n.* a county in N Wales. 39,007 pop. (1961); 660 sq. mi. *Co. town:* Dolgelly. Also, **Mer′ion′eth.**

meristem (mĕ′rĭ stĕm′), *n. Bot.* embryonic tissue; undifferentiated, growing, actively dividing cells. [f. Gk: s. *meristós* divided + *-ēm*(*a*), n. suffix] —**meristematic** (mĕ′rĭ stĭ măt′ĭk), *adj.*

merit (mĕ′rĭt), *n.* **1.** claim to commendation; excellence; worth. **2.** something that entitles to reward or commendation; a commendable quality, act, etc.: *the merits of a book or a play.* **3.** (*pl.*) the substantial right and wrong of a matter unobscured by technicalities: *the merits of a case.* **4.** the state or fact of deserving well; good desert. **5.** that which is deserved, whether good or bad. **6.** (*sometimes pl.*) the state or fact of deserving, or desert: *to treat a person according to his merits.* —*v.t.* **7.** to be worthy of; deserve. —*v.i.* **8.** *Chiefly Theol.* to acquire merit. [ME *merite*, t. F, t. L: m. *meritum*, prop. pp. neut., deserved, earned]

—**Syn. 1.** MERIT, DESERT, WORTH refer to the quality in a person, action, or thing which entitles to recognition, esp. favourable recognition. MERIT is usually the excellence which entitles to praise: *a man of great merit.* DESERT is the quality which entitles one to a just reward: *according to his deserts.* WORTH is always used in a favourable sense and signifies inherent value or goodness: *his worth is incalculable.* **—Ant. 1.** worthlessness.

merited (mĕ′rĭ tĭd), *adj.* deserved. **—mer′itedly,** *adv.*

meritocracy (mĕ′rĭ tŏk′rə sĭ), *n.* **1.** persons collectively who have reached positions of authority by reason of real or supposed merit (contrasted with *aristocracy,* etc.). **2.** government or administration by such persons. [f. MERIT + -O- + -CRACY, modelled on ARISTOCRACY]

meritorious (mĕ′rĭ tô′rĭ əs), *adj.* deserving of reward or commendation; possessing merit. [ME, t. ML: m. *meritōrius* meritorious, L serving to earn money] **—mer′ito′riously,** *adv.* **—mer′ito′riousness,** *n.*

Merksem (*Flem.* mĕrk′səm), *n.* a town in Belgium, in NE Antwerp province. 37,382 (est. 1964).

merle[1] (mûl), *n. Chiefly Scot. and Poetic.* the common European blackbird, *Turdus merula.* Also, **merl.** [t. F, g. L *merula, merulus*]

merle[2] (mûl), *adj.* **1.** coloured bluish grey with black mottling, esp. of the coat of an animal, as a dog. **—*n.*** **2.** this colour.

merlin (mû′lĭn), *n.* any of various bold small hawks of the genus *Falco,* esp. the **European merlin,** *F. columbarius aesalon,* and the closely related North American pigeon-hawk, *F. c. columbarius.* [ME *merlion,* t. AF: m. *merilun,* der. OF *esmeril,* t. Gmc; cf. OHG *smirl*]

Merlin (mû′lĭn), *n. Arthurian Legend.* a venerable magician and seer. [t. Welsh: unexplained m. *Myrddin*]

merlon (mû′lən), *n.* (in a battlement) the solid part between two crenels. See illus. under **battlement.** [t. F, t. It.: m. *merlone,* ult. der. L *mergae* fork]

mermaid (mû′măd′), *n.* an imaginary female marine creature typically having the head and trunk of a woman and the tail of a fish. [ME *mermayde.* See MERE[2], MAID]

mermaid's-purse (mû′mădz pûs′), *n.* sea-purse.

merman (mû′măn′), *n., pl.* **-men.** an imaginary man of the sea, corresponding to a mermaid.

meroblastic (mĕ′rō blăs′tĭk), *adj. Embryol.* (of large eggs) undergoing partial cleavage (opposed to *holoblastic*). [f. Gk *méro(s)* part + -BLAST + -IC]

Meroë (mĕ′rō ē′), *n.* a ruined city in the Sudan, on the Nile, NE of Khartoum: a capital of ancient Ethiopia.

merogony (mə rŏg′ə nĭ), *n. Embryol.* the development of egg fragments. [f. Gk *méro(s)* part + -GONY]

Merovingian (mĕ′rō vĭn′jĭ ən), *adj.* designating or pertaining to the Frankish dynasty which reigned in Gaul and Germany from about A.D. 500 to A.D. 751.

merozoite (mĕ′rō zō′īt), *n.* one of the products of reproduction in the asexual phase of parasitic protozoans of the class *Sporozoa,* as malaria parasites. [f. Gk *méro(s)* part + s. Gk *zōḗ* life + -ITE[1]]

Merrimack (mĕ′rĭ măk′), *n.* a river in the U.S., flowing from central New Hampshire through NE Massachusetts into the Atlantic. 110 mi.

merriment (mĕ′rĭ mənt), *n.* **1.** merry gaiety; mirth; hilarity; laughter. **2.** *Obs.* merrymaking. **—Syn. 1.** See **mirth.**

merry (mĕ′rĭ), *adj.,* **-rier, -riest. 1.** full of cheer or gaiety; festive; joyous in disposition or spirit. **2.** laughingly gay; mirthful; hilarious. **3.** *Archaic.* pleasant or delightful: *merry England.* **4.** *Colloq.* slightly intoxicated. **5. make merry,** to be gay or festive. [ME *meri(e), myrie, murie,* OE *myr(i)ge, mer(i)ge* pleasant, delightful] **—mer′rily,** *adv.* **—mer′riness,** *n.* **—Syn. 1.** joyous. See **gay. 2.** jolly, jovial. **—Ant. 1.** sad. **2.** solemn.

merry-andrew (mĕ′rĭ ăn′drōō), *n.* a clown; buffoon.

merry-go-round (mĕ′rĭ gō round′), *n.* **1.** a revolving machine, as a circular platform fitted with wooden horses, etc., on which persons, esp. children, ride for amusement. **2.** any whirl or rapid round.

merrymaker (mĕ′rĭ mā′kə), *n.* one who is making merry.

merrymaking (mĕ′rĭ mā′kĭng), *adj.* **1.** the act of making merry. **2.** a merry festivity; a revel. **—*adj.* 3.** producing mirth; gay; festive.

merrythought (mĕ′rĭ thôt′), *n.* the wishbone of a bird. [from the custom of two persons pulling the bone until it breaks; the person holding the longer (sometimes shorter) piece will supposedly marry first or will be granted a wish made at the time]

Mersey (mû′zĭ), *n.* a river in NW England, forming the border of Lancashire and Cheshire, flowing from Derbyshire W to the Irish Sea. 70 mi.

Mersin (*Turk.* mĕr′sēn), *n.* a seaport in S Turkey. 68,485 (1960).

Merthyr Tydfil (mû′thə tĭd′vĭl), a town in Wales, in Glamorganshire. 59,039 (1961).

Merton (mû′tn), *n.* a S outer borough of London. 188,621 (1964).

mes-, var. of **meso-,** sometimes used before vowels, as in *mesencephalon.*

mesa (mā′sə; *Sp.* mĕ′sȧ), *n.* a land form having a relatively flat top and bounded wholly or in part with steep rock walls, common in arid and semi-arid parts of the south-western U.S. [t. Sp., g. L *mensa* table]

mésalliance (mĕ zăl′ĭ əns; *Fr.* mė zȧl yäNs′), *n.* a marriage with a social inferior; a misalliance. [F: f. *més-* MIS- + *alliance* ALLIANCE]

mesarch (mĕs′äk), *adj.* referring to a strand or cylinder of primary xylem in a stem or root with the xylem other than at the edge.

Mesa Verde (mā′sə vûd′; *Sp.* mĕ′sȧ bĕr′dĕ), a U.S. national park in SW Colorado: ruins of cliff dwellings. 80 sq. mi.

mescal (mĕs kăl′), *n.* **1.** either of two species of cactus, *Lophophora williamsii* or *L. lewinii,* of Texas and northern Mexico, whose button-like tops (**mescal buttons**) are dried and used as a stimulant, esp. by the Indians. **2.** an intoxicating spirit distilled from the fermented juice of certain species of agave. **3.** any agave yielding this spirit. [t. Sp.: m. *mezcal,* t. Nahuatl: m. *mexcalli,* der. *metl* maguey]

mescaline (mĕs′kə lēn′, -lĭn), *n. Pharm.* a white water-soluble crystalline powder, $C_{11}H_{17}NO_3$, obtained from mescal buttons, used in experimental psychology to produce hallucinations. Also, **mescalin.**

mesdames (mā′dăm′; *Fr.* mė dȧm′), *n.* pl. of **madame.**

mesdemoiselles (*Fr.* mĕd mwȧ zĕl′), *n.* pl. of **mademoiselle.** [t. F]

meseems (mĭ sēmz′), *v.impers.*; *pt.* **meseemed.** *Archaic.* it seems to me.

mesembrianthemum (mĕz′ĕm brĭ ăn′thĭ məm, mĭ zĕm′-brĭ-), *n.* a large group of succulent plants, mainly from southern Africa, belonging to the family *Aizoaceae,* often cultivated for their showy flowers. Also, **mesembryanthemum.** [NL, f. Gk: s. *mesēmbria* noon + m. *ánthemon* flower]

mesencephalon (mĕs′ĕn sĕf′ə lŏn′), *n., pl.* **-la** (-lə). *Anat.* the middle segment of the brain; the midbrain. [t. NL. See MES-, ENCEPHALON] **—mesencephalic** (mĕs′ĕn sĭ făl′ĭk), *adj.*

mesenchyme (mĕs′ĕng kīm′), *n. Embryol.* the non-epithelial mesoderm. Also, **mesenchyma** (mĕs ĕng′-kĭ mə). [t. NL, f. Gk: *mes-* MES- + m. *énchyma* infusion] **—mesenchymal** (mĕs ĕng′kĭ məl), **mesenchymatous** (mĕs′ĕng kĭm′ə təs), *adj.*

mesentery (mĕs′ən tə rĭ, mĕz′-), *n., pl.* **-ries.** *Anat.* a fold or doubling of the peritoneum, investing and attaching to the posterior wall of the abdomen. [t. NL: m. s. *mesenterium,* t. Gk: m. *mesentérion* the middle intestine] **—mesenteric** (mĕs′ən tĕ′rĭk, mĕz′-), *adj.*

mesh (mĕsh), *n.* **1.** one of the open spaces of network of a net. **2.** (*pl.*) the threads that bound such spaces. **3.** (*pl.*) means of catching or holding fast: *caught in the meshes of the law.* **4.** a network or net. **5.** a knitted, woven, or knotted fabric, with open spaces between the threads. **6.** light woven or welded interlocking links or wires, as used for reinforcement, for sieves, etc. **7.** *Mach.* **a.** the engagement of gear teeth. **b. in mesh,** with gears engaged. **—*v.t.* 8.** to catch or entangle in or as in the meshes of a net; enmesh. **9.** to form with meshes, as a net. **10.** to cause to coordinate or interlock. **11.** *Mach.* to engage, as gear teeth. **—*v.t.* 12.** to become enmeshed. **13.** to interlock or coordinate. **14.** *Mach.* to become or be engaged, as the teeth of one wheel with those of another. [cf. OE *māx* and *mǣscre* net]

Meshach (mē′shăk), *n.* See **Shadrach.**

Meshed (mĕsh′hĕd; *Pers.* măsh hăd′), *n.* a city in NE Iran: a Muslim shrine. 312,186 (est. 1964). Also, **Mashhad.**

meshuga (mĭ shōōg′ə), *adj. Slang.* crazy; stupid; mad. [t. Yiddish, t. Heb.]

meshugana (mĭ shōōg′ə nə), *n. Slang.* a crazy person. [t. Yiddish: der. *meshuga* MESHUGA]

meshwork (mĕsh′wûk′), *n.* meshed work; network.

meshy (mĕsh′ĭ), *adj.* formed with meshes; meshed.

mesial (mē′zyəl), *adj.* medial. [f. MES- + -IAL] **—me′sially,** *adv.*

mesitylene (mĭ sĭt′ĭ lēn′, mĕs′ĭ tĭ lēn′), *n. Chem.* a colourless, liquid, aromatic hydrocarbon, $C_6H_3(CH_3)_3$, found in coal tar but prepared from acetone. [f. *mesityl* (f. s. Gk *mesítēs* go-between + -YL) + -ENE]

mesmeric (mĕz mĕ′rĭk), *adj.* **1.** hypnotic. **2.** fascinating, spellbinding. **—mesmer′ically,** *adv.*

mesmerism (mĕz′mə rĭz′əm), *n.* **1.** hypnotism. **2.** compelling fascination. [named after F. A. *Mesmer,* 1733–1815, German physician and hypnotist. See -ISM] **—mes′merist,** *n.*

mesmerize (mĕz′mə rīz′), *v.t.,* **-rized, -rizing. 1.** to hypnotize. **2.** to fascinate; dominate; spellbind. Also, **mesmerise.** —**mes′meriza′tion,** *n.* —**mes′meriz′er,** *n.*

mesnalty (mē′nəl tĭ), *n. Law.* the estate of a mesne lord. [t. AF: m. *mesnalte,* der. OF *mesne* MESNE]

mesne (mēn), *adj. Law.* intermediate or intervening. [t. F, altered sp. of AF *meen* MEAN[3]]

mesne lord, a feudal lord who held land of a superior.

meso-, a word element meaning 'middle', used in combination, chiefly in scientific terms. Also, **mes-.** [t. Gk, comb. form of *mésos* middle]

mesoblast (mĕs′ō blăst′), *n. Embryol.* the prospective mesoderm. —**mes′oblas′tic,** *adj.*

mesocarp (mĕs′ō käp′), *n. Bot.* the middle layer of pericarp, as the fleshy part of certain fruits. See diag. under **endocarp.**

mesocephalic (mĕs′ō sĭ făl′ĭk), *adj. Anat.* having a head with a cephalic index between that of dolichocephaly and brachycephaly.

mesocranic (mĕs′ō krā′nĭk), *adj. Anat.* having a skull with a cranial index between that of dolichocranic and brachycranic skulls.

mesoderm (mĕs′ō dûm′), *n. Embryol.* the middle germ layer of a metazoan embryo. —**mes′oder′mal, mes′oder′mic,** *adj.*

mesogastrium (mĕs′ō găs′trĭ əm), *n. Anat.* the mesentery of the embryonic stomach. [t. NL, f. *meso-* MESO- + m. Gk *gastḗr* belly + *-ium* -IUM] —**mes′ogas′tric,** *adj.*

mesoglea (mĕs′ō glē′ə, -glĭə′), *n.* the thin layer between the endoderm and the ectoderm of coelenterates and sponges. [t. NL, f. *meso-* MESO- + m. Gk *gloía* glue]

mesognathous (mĭ sŏg′nə thəs), *adj. Anthropol.* **1.** having medium, slightly protruding jaws. **2.** having a moderate or intermediate gnathic index of from 98 to 103. —**mesog′nathism, mesog′nathy,** *n.*

Mesolithic (mĕs′ō lĭth′ĭk), *adj.* (*sometimes l.c.*) of, pertaining to, or characteristic of an intermediate period between the Palaeolithic and Neolithic periods of the Stone Age.

Mesolonghi (mĕs′ō lŏng′gĭ), *n.* Missolonghi.

mesomorph (mĕs′ō môf′), *n. Physiol.* a person of mesomorphic type.

mesomorphic (mĕs′ō môf′ĭk), *adj. Physiol.* having a muscular or sturdily built body characterized by the relative prominence of structures developed from the embryonic mesoderm (distinguished from *ectomorphic, endomorphic*).

mesomorphous (mĕs′ō mô′fəs), *adj. Chem.* denoting or pertaining to a substance which exists in a state midway between that of a crystalline solid and an amorphous solid.

meson (mē′zŏn), *n. Physics.* any of a group of elementary particles, all of which have rest masses between that of the electron and the proton. Also, **mesotron.**

mesonephros (mĕs′ō nĕf′rŏs), *n. Embryol.* the middle kidney, developing between the pronephros and the metanephros, in proximity with the sex glands. In males of the higher vertebrates, it becomes a part of the epididymis. [t. NL, f. Gk: *meso-* MESO- + *nephrós* kidney] —**mes′oneph′ric,** *adj.*

mesophyll (mĕs′ō fĭl′), *n. Bot.* the parenchyma which forms the interior parts of a leaf, usually containing chlorophyll.

mesophyte (mĕs′ō fīt′), *n. Ecol.* a plant growing under conditions of well-balanced moisture supply. Cf. **hydrophyte** and **xerophyte.** —**mesophytic** (mĕs′ō fĭt′ĭk), *adj.*

Mesopotamia (mĕs′ə pə tā′myə), *n.* **1.** an ancient country in Asia between the rivers Tigris and Euphrates. **2.** a region including the modern state of Iraq, and the whole Tigris and Euphrates valley. —**Mes′opota′mian,** *adj., n.*

mesorrhine (mĕs′ô rīn′, -rĭn′), *adj. Anthropol.* having a moderately broad and high-bridged nose. [f. MESO- + m. s. Gk *rhís* nose]

mesosphere (mĕs′ō sfĭə′), *n.* **1.** the stratum of atmosphere between the ionosphere and the exosphere (250–600 mi.). **2.** the stratum of atmosphere between the top of the stratosphere and an unnamed layer where the minimum of temperature occurs (20–50 mi.); chemosphere. [MESO- + SPHERE] —**mesospheric** (mĕs′ō sfĕ′rĭk), *adj.*

mesothelium (mĕs′ō thē′lyəm), *n., pl.* **-lia** (-lyə). *Anat., Embryol.* epithelium of mesodermal origin, which lines the body cavities. [f. MESO- + *-thelium* as in EPITHELIUM] —**mes′othe′lial,** *adj.*

mesothorax (mĕs′ō thô′răks), *n., pl.* **-raxes, -races** (-rə sēz′). the middle one of three divisions of an insect's thorax, bearing the second pair of legs and first pair of wings. —**mesothoracic** (mĕs′ō thô răs′ĭk), *adj.*

mesothorium (mĕs′ō thô′rĭ əm), *n. Chem.* **1. mesothorium I,** an isotope of radium (though far more radioactive). *at. no.:* 88; *at. wt:* 228; *half life:* 6·7 yrs. **2. mesothorium II,** an isotope of actinium. *at. no.:* 89; *at. wt:* 228; *half life:* 6·13 hrs.

mesotron (mĕs′ə trŏn′), *n. Physics.* meson.

Mesozoic (mĕs′ō zō′ĭk), *Geol.* —*adj.* **1.** pertaining to the geological era of rocks intermediate between Palaeozoic and Cainozoic; the era of reptiles. —*n.* **2.** the era or rocks comprising the Triassic, Jurassic, and Cretaceous periods or systems. [f. MESO- + s. Gk *zōḗ* + -IC]

mesquite (mĕs kēt′, mĕs′kēt), *n.* **1.** a mimosaceous tree or shrub, *Prosopis glandulosa,* of the south-western U.S., Mexico, etc., whose beanlike pods are rich in sugar and form a valuable fodder. **2.** any species of the genus *Prosopis.* [t. Amer. Sp.: m. *mezquite,* t. Nahuatl: m. *mizquitl*]

mess (mĕs), *n.* **1.** a dirty or untidy condition: *the room was in a mess.* **2.** a state of embarrassing confusion: *his affairs are in a mess.* **3.** an unpleasant or difficult situation: *to get into a mess.* **4.** a dirty or untidy mass, litter, or jumble: *a mess of papers.* **5.** a place where service personnel, etc., eat together. **6.** a place used by officers and senior NCOs for eating, recreation, and entertaining. **7.** *Naval.* the living quarters of the crew. **8.** a group regularly taking meals together. **9.** the meal so taken. **10.** *Colloq. or Dial.* a quantity of food, etc., of indefinite amount. **11.** a sloppy or unappetizing preparation of food. **12.** a dish or quantity of soft or liquid food. **13.** *Colloq.* a person whose life is confused or without coherent purpose, often due to psychological difficulties. —*v.t.* **14.** to make dirty or untidy (often fol. by *up*): *mess up a room.* **15.** to make a mess of, or muddle (affairs, etc.). **16.** *Obs.* to supply with meals, as soldiers, etc. **17. mess around** or **about,** *Colloq.* to cause inconvenience to (a person). —*v.i.* **18.** to eat in company, esp. as a member of a mess. **19.** to make a dirty or untidy mess. **20. mess around** or **about,** *Colloq.* **a.** to busy oneself in an untidy or confused way. **b.** to waste time. **c.** to play the fool. **d.** to associate, esp for immoral or illegal purposes (fol. by *with*). **21. mess in,** *Colloq.* to meddle officiously. [ME *mes,* OF: lit., put (on the table), g. L *missum,* pp. neut., sent, put]

message (mĕs′ĭj), *n.* **1.** a communication, as of information, advice, direction, or the like, transmitted through a messenger or other agency. **2.** an official communication, as from a chief executive to a legislative body: *the President's message to Congress.* **3.** an inspired communication of a prophet. **4.** the moral or meaning intended to be conveyed by a book, film, play, or the like. [ME, t. OF, der. *mes* envoy, g. L *missus,* pp., sent]

Messalina (mĕs′ə lī′nə), *n.* **Valeria** (və lĭə′rĭ ə), died A.D. 48, third wife of the Roman emperor Claudius, notorious for her immorality.

messaline (mĕs′ə lēn′, mĕs′ə lēn′), *n.* a thin, soft, silk fabric with a twilled or a satin weave. [t. F]

mess allowance, monies allowed to augment rations in a mess.

mess deck, *Naval.* the deck where the crew eat.

Messene (mĕ sē′nĭ), *n.* a city of ancient Greece: the capital of **Messenia** (mĕs′ĭ nē′ə), a district in the SW Peloponnesus.

messenger (mĕs′in jə), *n.* **1.** one who bears a message or goes on an errand, esp. as a matter of duty or business. **2.** one employed to convey official dispatches or to go on other official or special errands: *a bank messenger.* **3.** *Archaic.* a herald or harbinger. **4.** anything regarded as sent on an errand. **5.** *Naut.* a rope, wire, or chain, forming an endless belt, passing from the capstan to a cable for hauling it in. [ME *messanger, messager,* t. OF: (m.) *messager,* der. *message* MESSAGE] —**Syn. 1.** bearer, courier. **3.** forerunner, precursor.

mess hall, *U.S.* dining hall.

Messiaen (*Fr.* mĕ syäɴ′), *n.* **Olivier Eugène Prosper Charles** (*Fr.* ŏ lē vyĕ œ zhĕn prŏs pĕr shărl′), born 1908, French composer and organist.

Messiah (mĭ sī′ə), *n.* **1.** the title applied to an expected deliverer of the Jewish people, and hence to Jesus (see John 4:25, 26). **2.** any expected deliverer. [var. of L *Messīas* (Vulgate), t. Gk, Hellenized form of Heb. *māshīah* anointed] —**Messi′ahship′,** *n.* —**Messianic** (mĕs′ĭ ăn′ĭk), *adj.*

Messidor (mĕs′ĭ dô′; *Fr.* mĕ sē dŏr′), *n.* (in the calendar of the First French Republic) the tenth month of the year, extending from June 19th to July 18th. [F: f. L *messi(s)* harvest + s. Gk *dōron* gift]

messieurs (mĕs′əz; *Fr.* mĕ syœ′), *n.* pl. of **monsieur.**

Messina (mĕ sē′nə), *n.* **1.** a seaport in NE Sicily: totally destroyed by an earthquake, 1908. 266,440 (1966). **2. Strait of,** a strait between Sicily and Italy. 2½ mi. wide.

Messines (*Fr.* mĕ sēn′), *n.* a village in W Belgium, near Ypres: battles, 1914, 1917.

messing officer, an officer who assists in making mess arrangements.

mess jacket, a short jacket cut to a point at the back

and reaching only to the waist, worn at dinner in the officers' mess on special occasions.

mess kit, 1. formal dress, including a mess jacket, worn by officers on special occasions. 2. *U.S.* a mess tin with knife and fork.

messmate (mĕs′māt′), *n.* a fellow member of a mess.

Messrs, messieurs (used as if a plural of *Mr*).

mess tin, a portable metal dish, used as a plate, cup, and cooking utensil by a soldier in the field.

messuage (mĕs′wĭj), *n.* *Law.* a dwelling house with its adjacent buildings and the lands appropriated to the use of the household. [ME *mesuage*, t. AF: (m.) *me(s)suage*, prob. m. *mesnage*. See MÉNAGE]

messy (mĕs′ĭ), *adj.*, **-sier, -siest.** 1. of the nature of a mess: *a messy concoction.* 2. being in a mess: *a messy table.* 3. attended with or making a mess; dirty; untidy: *messy work.* **—mess′iness,** *n.*

mestee (mĕs tē′), *n.* mustee.

mestizo (mĕs tē′zō), *n.*, *pl.* **-zos, -zoes.** 1. a person of mixed blood. 2. (in Spanish America) one who has Spanish and American Indian blood. 3. one of European and East Indian, Negro, or Malay blood. 4. a Philippine Island native with Chinese blood. [t. Sp., g. LL *mixticius* of mixed race] **—mestiza** (mĕs tē′zə), *n. fem.*

Meštrović (mĕsh′trə vĭch; *Serb.* mĕsh′trô vĕty), *n.* **Ivan** (*Serb.* ē vän′), 1883–1962, Yugoslav sculptor.

met (mĕt), *v.* pt. and pp. of **meet.**

met., 1. metaphor. 2. metaphysics. 3. metropolitan.

meta-, 1. a prefix meaning 'among', 'together with', 'after', 'behind', and often denoting change, found chiefly in scientific words. 2. *Chem.* **a.** a prefix meaning 'containing least water', used of acids and salts, as in *meta-antimonic*, $HSbO_3$, *meta-antimonous*, $HSbO_2$. **b.** a prefix indicating that an organic compound contains a benzene ring substituted in the 1·3 positions. [t. Gk, repr. *metá*, prep., with, after]

metabolism (mĭ tăb′ə lĭz′əm), *n.* *Biol.* the sum of the processes or chemical changes in an organism or a single cell by which food is built up (*anabolism*) into living protoplasm and by which protoplasm is broken down (*catabolism*) into simpler compounds with the exchange of energy. [f. META- + s. Gk *bolḗ* change + -ISM] **—metabolic** (mĕt′ə bŏl′ĭk), *adj.*

metabolite (mĭ tăb′ə līt′), *n.* a substance acted upon or produced in metabolism.

metabolize (mĭ tăb′ə līz′), *v.t.*, **-lized, -lizing.** to subject to metabolism; change by metabolism. Also, **metabolise.**

metacarpal (mĕt′ə kä′pl), *adj.* 1. of or pertaining to the metacarpus. *—n.* 2. a metacarpal bone.

metacarpus (mĕt′ə kä′pəs), *n.*, *pl.* **-pi** (-pī). *Anat.* the part of a hand or forelimb (esp. of its bony structure) included between the wrist or carpus and the fingers or phalanges. [t. NL (see META-, CARPUS); r. *metacarpium*, t. Gk: m. *metakárpion*]

metacentre (mĕt′ə sĕn′tə), *n.* the point where the vertical line through the centre of buoyancy of a floating body (as a ship) in equilibrium meets the vertical line through the new centre of buoyancy when the body is in a slightly inclined position (less than one degree). The equilibrium of the body is stable when this point is above its centre of gravity, and unstable when it is below. Also, *U.S.*, **metacenter.** [t. F: m. *métacentre*, f. Gk: *meta-* META- + m. s. *kéntron* CENTRE] **—met′acen′tric,** *adj.*

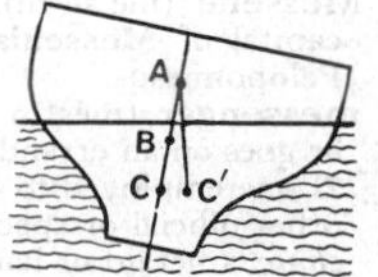

Metacentre of a boat
A, Metacentre; B, Centre of gravity; C, Centre of buoyancy; C′, Centre of buoyancy when boat is displaced

metachromatism (mĕt′ə krō′mə tĭz′əm), *n.* change of colour, esp. that due to variation in the temperature of a body. [f. META- + s. Gk *chrôma* colour + -ISM] **—metachromatic** (mĕt′ə krō măt′ĭk), *adj.*

metagalaxy (mĕt′ə găl′ək sĭ), *n.*, *pl.* **-axies.** *Astron.* the complete system of external galaxies, or extragalactic nebulae.

metage (mē′tĭj), *n.* 1. the official measurement of contents or weight. 2. the charge for it. [f. METE[1] + -AGE]

metagenesis (mĕt′ə jĕn′ĭ sĭs), *n.* *Biol.* reproduction characterized by the alternation of a sexual generation and a generation which reproduces asexually by budding. **—metagenetic** (mĕt′ə jĭ nĕt′ĭk), *adj.*

metagnathous (mĭ tăg′nə thəs), *adj.* *Ornith.* having the tips of the mandibles crossed, as the crossbills. **—metag′nathism,** *n.*

metal (mĕt′l), *n.*, *v.*, **-alled, -alling** or (*U.S.*) **-aled, -aling.** 1. any of a class of elementary substances, as gold, silver, copper, etc., all of which are crystalline when solid and many of which are characterized by opacity, ductility, conductivity, and a peculiar lustre when freshly fractured. 2. an alloy or mixture composed wholly or partly of such substances. 3. *Chem.* **a.** a metal (def. 1) in its pure state, as distinguished from alloys. **b.** an element yielding positively charged ions in aqueous solutions of its salts. 4. formative material; mettle. 5. *Printing, etc.* **a.** type metal. **b.** the state of being set up in type. 6. broken stone used for roads or railway track ballast. 7. (*pl.*) rails. 8. molten glass in the pot or melting tank. 9. *Her.* either of the tinctures gold (*or*) and silver (*argent*). *—v.t.* 10. to furnish or cover with metal. [ME, t. OF, t. L: m. s. *metallum* mine, mineral, metal, t. Gk: m. *métallon* mine]

metal., 1. metallurgical. 2. metallurgy.

metaldehyde (mĭ tăl′dĭ hīd′), *n.* *Chem.* a white, crystalline, poisonous, solid polymer of acetaldehyde; used as a fuel in small heaters.

metall., metallurgy.

metallic (mĭ tăl′ĭk), *adj.* 1. of, pertaining to, or consisting of metal. 2. of the nature of metal: *metallic lustre, metallic sounds.* 3. *Chem.* **a.** (of a metal element) being in the free or uncombined state: *metallic iron.* **b.** containing or yielding metal. **—metal′lically,** *adv.*

metalliferous (mĕt′ə lĭf′ə rəs), *adj.* containing or yielding metal. [f. L *metallifer* yielding metals + -OUS]

metalline (mĕt′ə lĭn′), *adj.* 1. metallic. 2. containing one or more metals or metallic salts.

metallize (mĕt′ə līz′), *v.t.*, **-lized, -lizing.** to make metallic; give the characteristics of metal to. Also, **metallise;** *Chiefly U.S.*, **metalize. —met′alliza′tion,** *n.*

metallography (mĕt′ə lŏg′rə fĭ), *n.* 1. the microscopic study of the structure of metals and alloys. 2. an art or process allied to lithography, in which metallic plates are substituted for stones. **—metallographic** (mĭ tăl′ə grăf′ĭk), *adj.*

metalloid (mĕt′ə loid′), *n.* 1. a non-metal. 2. an element which is both metallic and non-metallic, as arsenic, silicon, or bismuth. *—adj.* 3. of or pertaining to a metalloid. 4. resembling both a metal and non-metal.

metallurgy (mĕt′ə lû′jĭ, mĕ tăl′ə jĭ), *n.* 1. the art or science of separating metals from their ores. 2. the art or science of making and compounding alloys. 3. the art or science of working or heat-treating metals so as to give them certain desired shapes or properties. [t. NL: m. s. *metallurgia*, f. s. Gk *metallourgós* mineworker + *-ia* (suffix)] **—met′allur′gic, met′allur′gical,** *adj.* **—met′allur′gically,** *adv.* **—metallurgist** (mĕt′ə lû′jĭst, mĕ tăl′ə jĭst), *n.*

metalworking (mĕt′l wû′kĭng), *n.* the act of making metal objects. **—met′alwork′,** *n.* **—met′alwork′er,** *n.*

metamere (mĕt′ə mĭə′), *n.* a somite. **—metameral** (mĭ tăm′ə rəl), **metameric** (mĕt′ə mĕ′rĭk), *adj.*

metamerism (mĭ tăm′ə rĭz′əm), *n.* 1. *Zool.* division into metameres, the developmental process of somite formation. 2. *Zool.* the condition of consisting of metameres. 3. *Chem.* a type of isomerism caused by the attachment of different radicals to the same central atom or group, as $(C_2H_5)_2O$ and $CH_3OC_3H_7$.

metamorphic (mĕt′ə mô′fĭk), *adj.* 1. pertaining to or characterized by change of form, or metamorphosis. 2. *Geol.* pertaining to or exhibiting structural change, or metamorphism.

metamorphic rock. See **rock**[1] (def. 2a).

metamorphism (mĕt′ə mô′fĭz′əm), *n.* 1. metamorphosis. 2. *Geol.* a change in the structure or constitution of a rock, due to natural agencies, as pressure and heat, esp. when the rock becomes harder and more completely crystalline.

metamorphose (mĕt′ə mô′fōz), *v.t.*, **-phosed, -phosing.** 1. to transform. 2. to subject to metamorphosis or metamorphism.

metamorphosis (mĕt′ə mô′fə sĭs), *n.*, *pl.* **-ses** (-sēz′). 1. change of form, structure, or substance, as transformation by magic or witchcraft. 2. any complete change in appearance, character, circumstances, etc. 3. a form resulting from any such change. 4. a change of form during the postembryonic or embryonic growth of an animal by which it is adapted temporarily to a special environment or way of living usually different from that of the preceding stage: *the meta-*

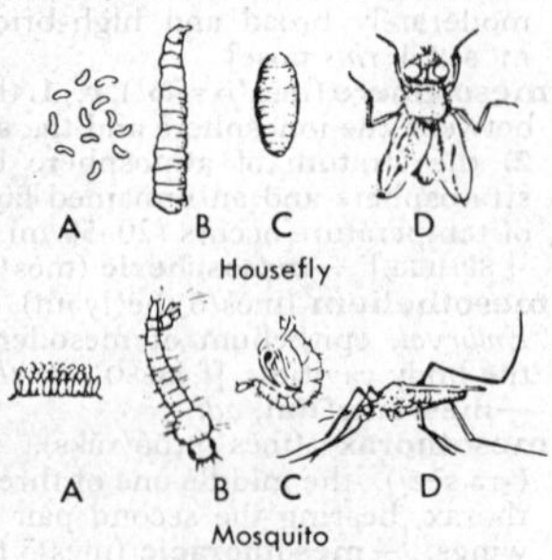

Metamorphosis (def. 4)
A, Eggs; B, Larva; C, Pupa; D, Adult

morphosis of tadpoles into frogs. **5.** *Pathol.* **a.** a type of alteration or degeneration in which tissues are changed: *fatty metamorphosis of the liver.* **b.** the resultant form. **6.** *Bot.* the structural or functional modification of a plant organ or structure during its development. [t. L, t. Gk: transformation]

metamorphous (mĕt′ə mô′fəs), *adj.* metamorphic.

metanephros (mĕt′ə nĕf′rŏs), *n.* *Embryol.* the pelvic kidney, developing from the lowest portion of the renal blastema cords. [t. NL, f. Gk: *meta-* META- + *nephrós* kidney]

metaph., **1.** metaphysical. **2.** metaphysics.

metaphase (mĕt′ə fāz′), *n.* *Biol.* the middle stage in mitotic cell division, in which the chromosomes in the equatorial plane of the cell split.

metaphor (mĕt′ə fə, -fô′), *n.* **1.** a figure of speech in which a term or phrase is applied to something to which it is not literally applicable, in order to suggest a resemblance, as *A mighty fortress is our God.* **2. mixed metaphor,** a figurative expression in which two or more metaphors are employed, producing an incongruous assemblage of ideas, as *The king put the ship of state on its feet.* [t. L: s. *metaphora*, t. Gk: a transfer] —**metaphorical** (mĕt′ə fŏ′rĭ kl), **met′aphor′ic,** *adj.* —**met′aphor′ically,** *adv.*

metaphosphoric acid (mĕt′ə fŏs fŏ′rĭk), *Chem.* an acid, HPO_3, derived from phosphorous pentoxide, and containing the least water of the phosphoric acids. See **phosphoric acid.**

metaphrase (mĕt′ə frāz′), *n.*, *v.*, **-phrased, -phrasing.** —*n.* **1.** a translation. —*v.t.* **2.** to translate, esp. literally. **3.** to change the phrasing or literary form of. [t. NL: m. s. *metaphrasis*, t. Gk: a translation]

metaphys., metaphysics.

metaphysical (mĕt′ə fĭz′ĭ kl), *adj.* **1.** pertaining to or of the nature of metaphysics. **2.** *Philos.* **a.** concerned with abstract thought or subjects, as existence, causality, truth, etc. **b.** concerned with first principles and ultimate grounds, as being, time, substance. **3.** highly abstract or abstruse. **4.** designating or pertaining esp. to that school of early 17th-century English poets of whom John Donne was the chief, whose characteristic style is highly intellectual, philosophical, and crowded with ingenious conceits and turns of wit. **5.** *Archaic.* imaginary. —**met′aphys′ically,** *adv.*

metaphysician (mĕt′ə fĭ zĭsh′ən), *n.* one versed in metaphysics. Also, **metaphysicist** (mĕt′ə fĭz′ĭ sĭst).

metaphysics (mĕt′ə fĭz′ĭks), *n.* **1.** that branch of philosophy which treats of first principles, including the sciences of being (*ontology*) and of the origin and structure of the universe (*cosmology*). It is always intimately connected with a theory of knowledge (*epistemology*). **2.** philosophy, esp. in its more abstruse branches. [t. ML: m. *metaphysica*, t. MGk: m. (*tà*) *metaphysiká* (neut. pl.), repr. *tà metà tà physiká* the (works) after the physics; with reference to the arrangement of Aristotle's writings]

metaplasia (mĕt′ə plā′zĭ ə), *n.* *Pathol.* tissue transformation, as from one form of tissue to another.

metaplasm (mĕt′ə plăz′əm), *n.* **1.** *Biol.* the lifeless matter or inclusions (as starch, pigment, etc.) in the protoplasm of a cell. **2.** a change in the structure of a word by adding, removing, or transposing the sounds of which it is composed or their representation in spelling. **3.** the formation of oblique cases from a stem other than that of the nominative. —**met′aplas′mic,** *adj.*

metaprotein (mĕt′ə prō′tēn), *n.* a hydrolytic derivative of protein, insoluble in water, but soluble in dilute acids or alkalis.

metasomatism (mĕt′ə sō′mə tĭz′əm), *n.* *Geol.* **1.** the processes whereby minerals or rocks are replaced by others of different chemical composition as a result of the introduction of material, usually in very hot aqueous solutions, from sources external to the formation undergoing change. **2.** replacement (def. 3). [f. META- + s. Gk *sôma* body + -ISM]

metastable (mĕt′ə stā′bl), *adj.* **1.** *Chem.* (of a body or system) existing in an apparently stable state although the addition of a small quantity of energy would convert it to a more stable state, as supercooled water will remain liquid below 0°C until a crystal of ice is introduced. **2.** *Physics.* (of an atom or nucleus) being in an excited state for a relatively long period. —**metastability** (mĕt′əstəbĭl′ĭtĭ), *n.*

metastasis (mĭ tăs′tə sĭs), *n.*, *pl.* **-ses** (-sēs′). **1.** *Physiol.*, *Pathol.* transference of a fluid, disease, or the like, from one part of the body to another. **2.** *Chiefly Pathol.* the translocation of cancerous cells to other parts of the body via the circulation, lymphatics, or membranous surfaces. **3.** a transformation. **4.** *Rhet.* a rapid transition, as from one subject to another. [t. LL, t. Gk: removal] —**metastatic** (mĕt′ə stăt′ĭk), *adj.*

metastasize (mĭ tăs′tə sīz′), *v.i.*, **-sized, -sizing.** *Pathol.* (esp. of cells of malignant tumours, or micro-organisms) to spread to other regions by dissemination through the circulation or other channels. Also, **metastasise.**

metatarsal (mĕt′ə tä′səl), *adj.* **1.** of or pertaining to the metatarsus. —*n.* **2.** a metatarsal bone.

metatarsus (mĕt′ə tä′səs), *n.*, *pl.* **-si** (-sī). *Anat.*, *Zool.* **1.** the part of a foot or hind limb (esp. of its bony structure) included between the tarsus and the toes or phalanges. See diag. under **skeleton.** **2.** (in birds) a bone composed of both tarsal and metatarsal elements, extending from the tibia to the phalanges. [NL. See META-, TARSUS]

metatherian (mĕt′ə thĭə′rĭ ən), *n.* a subdivision of the mammals which includes those in which the young are neither hatched from eggs nor nourished by means of a placenta, but are born at a very immature stage and usually carried in a pouch; marsupial.

metathesis (mĭ tăth′ə sĭs), *n.*, *pl.* **-ses** (-sēz′). **1.** the transposition of letters, syllables, or sounds in a word. **2.** *Chem.* a double decomposition, as when two compounds react with each other to form two other compounds. [t. LL, t. Gk: transposition] —**metathetic** (mĕt′ə thĕt′ĭk), **met′athet′ical,** *adj.*

metathorax (mĕt′ə thô′răks), *n.*, *pl.* **-thoraxes, -thoraces** (-thô′rə sēz′). the posterior division of an insect's thorax, bearing the third pair of legs and the second pair of wings. —**metathoracic** (mĕt′ə thô răs′ĭk), *adj.*

metaxylem (mĕt′ə zī′lĕm), *n.* *Bot.* that part of the primary xylem of a vascular strand which is formed after elongation has ceased.

metazoan (mĕt′ə zō′ən), *adj.* **1.** belonging or pertaining to the phylum *Metazoa*, comprising all the animals above the protozoans, i.e., those organisms which, although originating from a single cell, are composed of many cells. —*n.* **2.** any member of this phylum. [t. NL, pl. of *metazōōn*, f. Gk: *meta-* META- + *zôion* animal] —**met′azo′ic,** *adj.*

Metchnikoff (*Fr.* mĕch nē kŏf′), *n.* **Élie** (*Fr.* ė lē′), 1845–1916, Russian biologist and bacteriologist, in France.

mete[1] (mēt), *v.t.*, **meted, meting.** **1.** to distribute or apportion by measure; allot (usually fol. by *out*). **2.** *Archaic.* to measure. [ME; OE *metan*, c. G *messen*]

mete[2] (mēt), *n.* **1.** a limiting mark. **2.** a limit. [ME, t. OF, t. L: m. *mēta* goal-mark, turning post]

metempiric (mĕt′ĕm pĭ′rĭk), *n.* a supporter of the metempirical philosophy. [f. MET(A)- + EMPIRIC]

metempirical (mĕt′ĕm pĭ′rĭ kl), *adj.* **1.** beyond or outside the field of experience. **2.** of or pertaining to metempirics.

metempirics (mĕt′ĕm pĭ′rĭks), *n.* the philosophy of things the existence of which is, even in principle, beyond the field of experience.

metempsychosis (mĕt′ĕmp sĭ kō′sĭs), *n.*, *pl.* **-ses** (-sēz). **1.** the passage of the soul from one body to another. **2.** the rebirth of the soul at death in another body either of human or animal form. [t. L, t. Gk]

metencephalon (mĕt′ĕn sĕf′ə lŏn′), *n.*, *pl.* **-la** (-lə). *Anat.* the segment of the brain including the cerebellum and pons and the upper portion of the medulla oblongata; the hindbrain. [t. NL. See MET(A)-, ENCEPHALON] —**metencephalic** (mĕt′ĕn sĭ făl′ĭk), *adj.*

meteor (mē′tyə), *n.* **1.** a transient fiery streak in the sky produced by a meteoroid passing through the earth's atmosphere; a bolide or shooting star. **2.** any meteoroid or meteorite. **3.** a brief, dazzling success, as of a person or object. **4.** *Obs.* any atmospheric phenomenon, as hail, a typhoon, etc. [late ME, t. NL: s. *meteōrum*, t. Gk: m. *meteōron* (pl. *meteōra* phenomena in the heavens), neut. adj., raised, high in air]

meteor., **1.** meteorological. **2.** meteorology.

meteoric (mē′tĭ ŏ′rĭk), *adj.* **1.** pertaining to or like a meteor. **2.** consisting of meteors: *a meteoric shower.* **3.** flashing like a meteor; transiently brilliant: *a meteoric career.* **4.** swift or rapid. **5.** of the atmosphere; meteorological. —**me′teor′ically,** *adv.*

meteorite (mē′tyə rīt′), *n.* **1.** a mass of stone or metal that has reached the earth from outer space; a fallen meteoroid. **2.** a meteor or a meteoroid. —**meteoritic** (mē′tyə rĭt′ĭk), *adj.*

meteorograph (mē′tyə rə grăf′, -gräf′), *n.* an instrument for automatically recording various meteorological conditions simultaneously, as pressure, temperature, etc.

meteoroid (mē′tyə roid′), *n.* *Astron.* any of the small bodies, often remnants of comets, travelling through space, which, when encountering the earth's atmosphere, are heated to luminosity, thus becoming meteors.

meteorol., **1.** meteorological. **2.** meteorology.

meteorological (mē′tyə rə lŏj′ĭ kl), *adj.* pertaining to meteorology, or to phenomena of the atmosphere or weather. Also, **me′teorolog′ic.** —**me′teorolog′ically,** *adv.*

Meteorological Office, a government department under the Ministry of Defence, having charge of the gathering of the meteorological reports in order to forecast the weather, issue warnings of storms, floods, etc.

meteorology (mē′tyə rŏl′ə jĭ), *n.* the science dealing with the atmosphere and its phenomena, esp. as relating to weather. [t. Gk: m. s. *meteōrologia.* See METEOR, -LOGY] —**me′teorol′ogist,** *n.*

meter[1] (mē′tə), *n.* **1.** an instrument that measures, esp. one that automatically measures and records the quantity of gas, water, electricity, or the like, passing through it or actuating it. —*v.t.* **2.** to measure by means of a meter. [ME; f. METE[1] + -ER[1]]

meter[2] (mē′tə), *n. U.S.* metre[1].

meter[3] (mē′tə), *n. U.S.* metre[2].

-meter[1]**,** a word element used in names of instruments for measuring quantity, extent, degree, etc., e.g., *altimeter, barometer.* [t. NL: m. *-metrum,* t. Gk (see METRE[1]). Cf. METER[1]]

-meter[2]**,** (in words taken from Greek or Latin) a word element denoting a certain poetic measure or rhythmic pattern, depending on the number of feet constituting the verse, as in *pentameter, trimeter.* [See METRE[2]]

-meter[3]**,** *U.S.* -metre.

Meth., Methodist.

methacrylate (mĕth ăk′rĭ lāt′), *n. Chem.* an ester or salt derived from methacrylic acid.

methacrylic acid (mĕth′ə krĭl′ĭk), a colourless liquid acid, $CH_2C(CH_3)COOH$, produced synthetically, the esters of which are used in making plastics.

methaemoglobin (mĕt hē′mō glō′bĭn, mĕ thē′mō-), *n. Biochem.* a brownish compound, a combination of oxygen and haemoglobin, formed in the blood, as by the use of certain drugs. Also, *U.S.,* **methemoglobin.** [f. MET(A)- + HAEMOGLOBIN]

methane (mē′thān), *n. Chem.* a colourless, odourless, inflammable gas, CH_4, the main constituent of marsh gas and the firedamp of coal mines, and obtained commercially from natural gas; the first member of the methane or paraffin series of hydrocarbons. [f. METH (YL) + -ANE]

methane series, *Chem.* a homologous series of saturated aliphatic hydrocarbons, having the general formula $C_nH_{2n}+_2$, as *methane* (CH_4), *ethane* (C_2H_6), etc.; paraffin series; alkanes.

methanol (mĕth′ə nŏl′), *n. Chem.* methyl alcohol, or wood alcohol. [f. METHAN(E) + -OL[1]]

methenamine (mĕ thē′nə mēn′, -mĭn′), *n. U.S.* hexamethylene-tetramine; hexamine.

methinks (mĭ thĭngks′), *v. impers.; pt.* **methought.** *Archaic and Poetic.* it seems to me. [ME *me thinketh,* OE *me thyncth* it seems to me]

methionine (mĕ thī′ə nēn′, -nĭn′), *n. Biochem.* an amino acid, $CH_3SCH_2CH_2CH(NH_2)COOH$, found in such proteins as casein, wool, gelatine, etc.

method (mĕth′əd), *n.* **1.** a mode of procedure, esp. an orderly or systematic mode: *a method of instruction.* **2.** a way of doing something, esp. in accordance with a definite plan. **3.** order or system in doing anything: *to work with method.* **4.** orderly or systematic arrangement. **5.** (*usually cap.*) Also, **Stanislavsky Method, Stanislavsky System.** a way of acting in which the actor first explores the inner motivation of the character to be portrayed and builds his character study outwards: the actor's external reactions are therefore spontaneously created rather than intellectually imposed. —*adj.* **6.** (*usually cap.*) of, pertaining to, or employing the Method. [t. L: s. *methodus* mode of procedure, method, t. Gk: m. *méthodos* a following after, method]

—**Syn.** 1. METHOD, MODE, WAY imply a manner in which a thing is done or in which it happens. METHOD refers to a settled kind of procedure, usually according to a definite, established, logical, or systematic plan: *the open-hearth method of making steel, method of solving a problem.* MODE is a more formal word which implies a customary or characteristic fashion of doing something: *kangaroos have a peculiar mode of carrying their young.* WAY, a word in popular use for the general idea, is equivalent to various more specific words: *a child's way* (manner) *of staring at people; the way* (method) *of rapid calculating; the way* (mode) *of holding a pen.*

methodical (mĭ thŏd′ĭ kl), *adj.* performed, disposed, or acting in a systematic way; systematic; orderly: *a methodical man.* Also, **method′ic.** —**method′ically,** *adv.* —**method′icalness,** *n.* —**Syn.** See **orderly.**

Methodism (mĕth′ə dĭz′əm), *n.* the doctrines, polity, and worship of the Methodist Church.

Methodist (mĕth′ə dĭst), *n.* **1.** a member of one of the Christian denominations which grew out of the revival of religion led by John Wesley. —*adj.* **2.** of or pertaining to the Methodists or Methodism. —**Meth′odis′tic,** *adj.*

methodize (mĕth′ə dīz′), *v.t.,* **-dized, -dizing. 1.** to reduce to method. **2.** to arrange with method. Also, **methodise.** —**meth′odiz′er,** *n.*

methodology (mĕth′ə dŏl′ə jĭ), *n., pl.* **-gies.** the science of method, esp.: **a.** a branch of logic dealing with the logical principles underlying the organization of the various special sciences, and the conduct of scientific enquiry. **b.** *Educ.* a branch of pedagogics concerned with analysis and evaluation of subject matter and methods of teaching.

methought (mĭ thôt′), *v.* pt. of **methinks.**

meths (mĕths), *n. Colloq.* methylated spirits.

Methuselah (mĭ thyōō′zə lə), *n.* **1.** a biblical patriarch before the Flood who according to tradition lived 969 years. Gen. 5:27. **2.** (*l.c.*) a very aged person. **3.** (*l.c.*) a large wine bottle, usually holding 6–8 pints. [t. Heb.: *M'thūshelah*]

methyl (mĕth′ĭl), *n. Chem.* a univalent hydrocarbon radical, CH_3, derived from methane. [t. F: m. *méthyle,* back-formation from *méthylène* METHYLENE]

methyl acetate, *Chem.* a colourless, combustible, volatile liquid, CH_3COOCH_3, having a fragrant odour, used as a solvent; the methyl ester of acetic acid.

methylal (mĕth′ĭ lăl′), *n. Chem.* a liquid compound with a pleasant odour, $CH_2(OCH_3)_2$, used in medicine as a hypnotic. [f. METHYL + AL(COHOL)]

methyl alcohol, *Chem.* a colourless, inflammable, poisonous liquid, CH_3OH, of the alcohol class, formerly obtained by the distillation of wood, but now produced synthetically from carbon monoxide and hydrogen, used as a fuel, solvent, etc.; wood alcohol.

methylamine (mĕth′ĭ lə mĭn′, -mēn′, mĕth′ĭl ăm′ĭn), *n. Chem.* any of three derivatives of ammonia in which one or all of the hydrogen atoms are replaced by methyl radicals; esp., a gas, CH_3NH_2, with an ammonia-like smell, the simplest alkyl derivative of ammonia and, like the latter, forming a series of salts.

methylate (mĕth′ĭ lāt′), *n., v.,* **-lated, -lating.** *Chem.* —*n.* **1.** a methyl alcohol derivative in which the hydrogen of the hydroxyl group has been replaced by a metal. —*v.t.* **2.** to combine with methyl. **3.** to mix with methyl alcohol as in the denaturation of ethyl alcohol: *methylated spirits.* [f. METHYL + -ATE[2]]

methylated spirits, ethyl alcohol denatured with 5–10 per cent of methyl alcohol to prevent its use as a beverage; sometimes also contains pyridine and methyl violet dye although the industrial spirit is normally free of these additives.

methylation (mĕth′ĭ lā′shən), *n. Chem.* the process of replacing a hydrogen atom with a methyl radical.

methyl chloride, *Chem.* chloromethane.

methylene (mĕth′ĭ lēn′), *n. Chem.* a bivalent hydrocarbon radical, CH_2, derived from methane. [t. F: f. s. Gk *méthy* wine + *-yl* -YL + *-ène* -ENE]

methylene blue, *Chem., Pharm.* a thiazine dye, $C_{16}H_{18}ClN_3S.3H_2O$, also used as an antidote for cyanide poisoning.

methylene chloride, *Chem.* dichloromethane.

methyl methacrylate, *Chem.* a colourless volatile liquid, $CH_2C(CH_3)COOCH_3$, which polymerizes to form a clear, transparent thermoplastic. Cf. **Plexiglas, Perspex.**

methylnaphthalene (mĕth′ĭl năf′thə lēn′), *n. Chem.* a compound, $C_{11}H_{10}$, the alpha form of which, a colourless liquid, is used in determining cetane numbers. Cf. **cetane number.**

meticulous (mĭ tĭk′yōō ləs), *adj.* solicitous about minute details; minutely or finically careful: *he was meticulous about his personal appearance.* [t. L: m. s. *meticulōsus* fearful] —**metic′ulousness,** *n.* —**metic′ulously,** *adv.*

metier (mĕt′ĭ ā), *n.* trade; profession; line of work or activity. Also, **métier** (*Fr.* mĕ tyĕ′). [t. F, g. L *ministerium* MINISTRY]

métis (mĕ tēs′), *n.* **1.** any person of mixed ancestry. **2.** *U.S.* a person of one-eighth Negro ancestry; an octoroon. **3.** *Can.* a half-breed of white, esp. French, and Indian parentage. Also, **métif** (mĕ tēf′). [t. F, g. LL *mixtīcius* of mixed blood] —**métisse′,** *n. fem.*

metol (mē′tōl), *n.* a soluble white powder, $C_{14}H_{18}N_2O_2.H_2SO_4$, used as a developer.

Metonic cycle (mĭ tŏn′ĭk), a cycle of nineteen years, after which the new moon recurs on the same day of the year as at the beginning of the cycle. [named after the discoverer, *Meton,* 5th-century B.C. Athenian astronomer. See -IC]

metonym (mĕt′ə nĭm), *n.* a word used in metonymy.

metonymical (mĕt′ə nĭm′ĭ kl), *adj.* having the nature of metonymy. Also, **met′onym′ic.** —**met′onym′ically,** *adv.*

metonymy (mĭ tŏn′ĭ mĭ), *n. Rhet.* the use of the name of one thing for that of another to which it has some logical relation, as 'sceptre' for 'sovereignty', or 'the bottle' for 'strong drink'. [t. LL: m. s. *metōnymia,* t. Gk: a change of name]

metope (mĕt′ōp, mĕt′ə pĭ), *n.* **1.** *Archit.* one of the square spaces, either decorated or plain, between triglyphs in the Doric frieze. **2.** *Anat.* the face, forehead, or frontal surface in general. —**metopic** (mĭ tŏp′ĭk), *adj.* [t. Gk]

A, Metope; B, Triglyph

metre[1] (mē′tə), *n.* the basic SI unit of length equivalent to 39·37 inches. Originally intended to be one ten-millionth of the distance from the equator to the pole measured on a meridian; formerly defined in terms of the distance between two lines on a platinum-iridium bar kept in Paris; redefined in 1960 as 1,650,763·73 wavelengths of the orange-red radiation of krypton-86 under specified conditions. *Symbol:* m Also, *U.S.*, **meter.** [t. F: m. *mètre,* t. Gk: m. *métron* measure]

metre[2] (mē′tə), *n. Pros.* a poetic measure; arrangement of words in regularly measured or patterned or rhythmic lines or verses. Also, *U.S.*, **meter.** [ME, t. F: m. *mètre,* t. L: m. s. *metrum;* r. OE *meter,* t. L: m. s. *metrum* poetic metre, verse, t. Gk: m. *métron* measure]

-metre, a word element meaning metres; of or pertaining to a metre, as in *kilometre.* [See METRE[1]]

metre-kilogram-second system (mē′tə kĭl′ə grăm sĕk′ənd), a system of units used in science, based on the metre, kilogram, and second as the fundamental units of length, mass, and time. *Abbrev.:* MKS system. See **SI unit.**

metric[1] (mĕt′rĭk), *adj.* pertaining to the metre or to the system of measures and weights originally based upon it. [t. F: m. *métrique,* der. *mètre* METRE[1]]

metric[2] (mĕt′rĭk), *adj.* metrical. [t. L: s. *metricus,* t. Gk: m. *metrikós* pertaining to metre or measure]

metrical (mĕt′rĭ kl), *adj.* **1.** pertaining to metre or poetic measure. **2.** composed in metre or verse. **3.** pertaining to measurement. Also, **metric.** —**met′rically,** *adv.*

metrical psalm, a verse translation of a psalm, sung as a hymn.

metrication (mĕt′rĭ kā′shən), *n.* the process of conversion from British or imperial units to the metric system.

metrician (mĕ trĭsh′ən), *n.* a metrist.

metrics (mĕt′rĭks), *n.* **1.** the science of metre. **2.** the art of metrical composition.

metric system, a decimal system of weights and measures, adopted first in France, but now widespread over the world, universally used in science, mandatory for use for all purposes in a large number of countries, and permitted for use in most. The basic units are the metre (39·37 inches) for length, and the gram (15·432 grains) for mass or weight. Derived units are the litre (0·21998 British gallons) for capacity, being the volume of 1000 grams of water under specified conditions; the are (119·6 square yards) for area being the area of a square 10 metres on a side; and the stere (35·315 cubic feet) for volume, being the volume of a cube 1 metre on a side, the term stere being, however, usually restricted to measuring firewood. Names for units larger and smaller than these are formed from the above names by the use of the following prefixes:

kilo	1000	deca	10	centi	0·01
hecto	100	deci	0·1	milli	0·001

To these are often added mega = 1,000,000, myria = 10,000, and micro = 0·000,001. Not all of the possible units are in common use. In many countries names of old units are applied to roughly similar metric units.

metric ton, ton (def. 2).

metrify (mĕt′rĭ fī′), *v.t.*, **-fied, -fying.** to put into metre; compose in verse. [t. F: m. *métrifier,* t. ML: m. s. *metrificāre* put in metre, f. *metri-* (comb. form of *metrum* metre) + *-ficāre* -FY] —**met′rifi′er,** *n.*

metrist (mĕt′rĭst), *n.* one versed in the use of poetic metres. [t. ML: s. *metrista,* der. L *metrum* METRE[2]]

metritis (mĭ trī′tĭs), *n. Pathol.* inflammation of the uterus. [t. NL, f. Gk: s. *mētra* uterus + *-ītis* -ITIS]

metro (mĕt′rō), *n.* an underground railway system in certain cities, esp. Paris. [t. F: m. *métro*]

metrology (mĭ trŏl′ə jĭ), *n., pl.* **-gies.** the science of measures and weights. [f. Gk *métro(n)* measure + -LOGY] —**metrological** (mĕt′rō lŏj′ĭ kl), *adj.* —**metrol′ogist,** *n.*

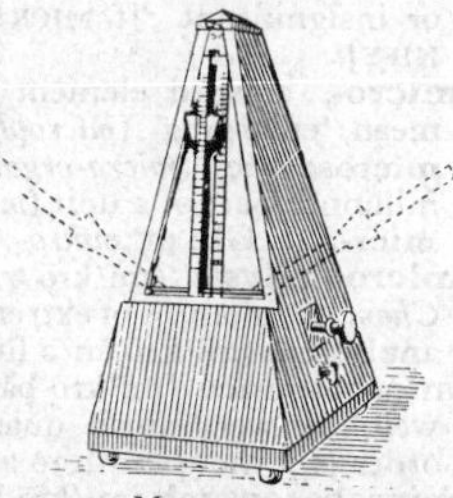
Metronome
(The dotted lines show the extent of vibration of the pendulum)

metronome (mĕt′rə nōm′), *n.* a mechanical contrivance for marking time, as for music. [f. Gk: *métro(n)* measure + m. s. *nómos* law] —**metronomic** (mĕt′rə nŏm′ĭk), *adj.*

metronymic (mĕt′rō nĭm′ĭk), *adj.* **1.** derived from the name of a mother or other female ancestor. —*n.* **2.** a metronymic name. [t. Gk: m. s. *mētrōnymikós* named after one's mother]

metropolis (mĭ trŏp′ə lĭs), *n., pl.* **-lises** (-lĭ sĭz). **1.** the chief city (not necessarily the capital) of a country, state, or region. **2.** a central or principal point, as of some activity. **3.** the mother city or parent state of an ancient Greek (or other) colony. **4.** the chief see of an ecclesiastical province. [t. LL, t. Gk: a mother state or city]

metropolitan (mĕt′rə pŏl′ĭ tən), *adj.* **1.** of, pertaining to, or characteristic of a metropolis or chief city, or of its inhabitants. **2.** pertaining to or constituting a mother country. **3.** pertaining to an ecclesiastical metropolis. —*n.* **4.** an inhabitant of a metropolis or chief city. **5.** one having metropolitan manners, etc. **6.** the next highest rank to patriarch in the Russian Orthodox Church.

metrorrhagia (mē′trô rā′jyə, mĕt′rô-), *n. Pathol.* nonmenstrual discharge of blood from the uterus; uterine haemorrhage. [t. NL, f. Gk: m. s. *mētra* uterus + *-rrhagía* -RRHAGIA]

-metry, a word element denoting the process of measuring, abstract for *-meter,* as in *anthropometry, chronometry.* [t. Gk: m. s. *-metria,* der. *-metros* measuring]

Metsu (*Du.* mĕt′sʏ), *n.* **Gabriel** (*Du.* KHä′brĭ ĕl), 1629–67, Dutch painter.

Metsys (*Flem.* mĕt′sĕys), *n.* Massys.

Metternich (mĕt′ə nĭk; *Ger.* mĕt′ər nĭKH), *n.* **Prince Klemens Wenzel Nepomuk Lothar von** (*Ger.* klĕ′mĕns vĕn′tsəl nĕ′pô mo͝ok lō′tär fōn), 1773–1859, Austrian statesman.

mettle (mĕt′l), *n.* **1.** the characteristic disposition or temper: *to try a man's mettle.* **2.** spirit; courage. **3. on one's mettle,** incited to do one's best. [var. of METAL]

mettlesome (mĕt′l səm), *adj.* spirited; courageous. Also, **mettled** (mĕt′ld).

Metz (mĕts; *Fr.* mĕs), *n.* a fortress city in NE France, in Moselle department: battles, 1870, 1918, 1940, 1944. 102,771 (1962).

meum et tuum (mā′o͞om ĕt to͞o′o͞om), *Latin.* mine and thine.

Meurthe-et-Moselle (*Fr.* mœrt ė mô zĕl′), *n.* a department in NW France. 678,078 pop. (1962); 2038 sq. mi. *Cap.:* Nancy.

Meuse (mûz; *Fr.* mœz), *n.* **1.** Dutch, **Maas.** a river flowing from NE France through E Belgium and S Netherlands into the North Sea. 575 mi. **2.** a department in NE France. 215,985 pop. (1962); 2409 sq. mi. *Cap.:* Bar-le-Duc.

meV, *Physics.* million electron-volts. Also, **mev.**

mew[1] (myo͞o), *n.* **1.** the sound a cat makes. —*v.i.* **2.** to make this sound. [imit.]

mew[2] (myo͞o), *n.* a seagull, esp. the common gull, *Larus canus,* of Europe. [OE, c. G *Möwe*]

mew[3] (myo͞o), *n.* **1.** a cage for hawks, esp. while moulting. **2.** a place of retirement or concealment. **3.** a mews. —*v.t.* **4.** to shut up in or as in a mew; to confine; conceal (often fol. by *up*). [ME *mue,* t. OF, der. *muer* MEW[4]]

mew[4] (myo͞o), *v.t., v.i.* to shed (feathers); to moult. [ME *mewe(n),* t. OF: m. *muer* moult, change, g. L *mūtāre*]

mewl (myo͞ol), *v.i.* to cry, as a young child. [imit.]

mews (myo͞oz), *n.pl., usually construed as sing.* **1.** a set of stables or garages, usually with living accommodation attached, around a yard, court, or alley. **2.** a street, yard, or court lined by buildings originally used as stables and servants' quarters. [orig. pl. of MEW[3]]

Mex., **1.** Mexican. **2.** Mexico.

Mexborough (mĕks′bə rə), *n.* a town in England, in the West Riding of Yorkshire. 17,095 (1961).

Mexicali (mĕk′sĭ kä′lĭ; *Sp.* mė KHē kä′lē), *n.* a town in NW Mexico. 288,601 (est. 1965).

Mexican (mĕk′sĭ kən), *adj.* **1.** of or pertaining to Mexico. —*n.* **2.** a native or inhabitant of Mexico.

Mexican hairless, a medium-sized dog which has hair only on the skull and the end of the tail.

Mexicano (mĕk′sĭ kä′nō), *n.* any Nahuatl language.

Mexican War, the war between the United States and Mexico, 1846–48.

Mexico (mĕk′sĭ kō′; *Sp.* mė′KHė kô), *n.* **1.** a republic in S North America. 34,625,903 pop. (1960); 760,373 sq. mi. *Cap.:* Mexico City. **2. Gulf of,** an arm of the Atlantic between the U.S., Cuba, and Mexico. ab. 716,000 sq. mi.; greatest depth, 12,714 ft.

Mexico City, the capital of Mexico, in the central part. 3,192,804 (est. 1965). ab. 7400 ft high. Official name, **México, Distrito Federal** (mė KHē kô dēs trē′tô fė dė rȧl′).

Meyerbeer (mī′ər bĭə′; *Ger.* mī′ər bĕr), *n.* **Giacomo**

(*Ger.* jä′kô mô) (*Jakob Liebmann Beer*), 1791–1864, German composer.

Meynell (mĕn′əl), *n.* **Alice** (*Alice Christiana Thompson, Mrs Wilfred Meynell*), 1850–1922, English poet and essayist.

mezereon (mĕ zĭə′rĭ ən), *n.* an Old World thymelaeaceous shrub, *Daphne mezereum*, cultivated for its fragrant purplish pink flowers, which appear in early spring. [t. ML, t. Ar.: m. *māzaryūn* the camellia]

Mézières (*Fr.* mė zyĕr′), *n.* a town in NE France, in Ardennes department. 13,328 (1962). See **Charleville-Mézières.**

mezuzah (mĕ zo͞o′zä), *n.*, *pl.* **-zoth** (-zōth). *Judaism.* a piece of parchment inscribed on one side with the passages Deut. 6:4–9 and 11:13–21, and on the other with the word 'Shaddai' (a name applied to God), and so placed in a case that the divine name is visible from the outside, the case being attached to the doorpost of a house in fulfilment of the injunction in each of the passages. Also, **mezuza.** [t. Heb.: doorpost (see Deut. 6:9, 11:20)]

mezzanine (mĕz′ə nēn′, mĕt′sə nēn′), *n.* a low storey between two other storeys of greater height, esp. when the low storey and the one beneath it form part of one composition; an entresol. [t. F, t. It.: m. *mezzanino*, dim. of *mezzano* middle, g. L *mediānus* MEDIAN]

mezzo (mĕt′sō; *It.* mĕd′dzô), *adj.* middle; medium; half. [t. It., g. L *medius* middle]

mezzo-rilievo (mĕt′sō rĭ lē′vō; *It.* mĕd′dzô rē lyĕ′vô), *n.*, *pl.* **-vos** (-vōz), **-vi** (*It.* -vē). middle relief, between alto-rilievo and bas-relief. Also, **mezzo-relievo.** [t. It.]

mezzo-soprano (mĕt′sō sə prä′nō), *n.*, *pl.* **-nos, -ni** (-nē). *Music.* **1.** a voice or voice part intermediate in compass between soprano and contralto. **2.** a person having such a voice. [t. It.]

mezzotint (mĕt′sō tĭnt′), *n.* **1.** a method of engraving on copper or steel by burnishing or scraping away a uniformly roughened surface. **2.** a print produced by this method. —*v.t.* **3.** to engrave in mezzotint. [t. It.: m. *mezzotinto* half-tint]

MF, Middle French. Also, **M.F.**

mf., **1.** *Music.* (It. *mezzoforte*) moderately loud. **2.** microfarad.

m.f., medium-frequency.

mfesi (əm fä′zĭ), *n.* *S African.* the ringhals. [t. Zulu: m. *imfezi*]

mfg, manufacturing.

MFH, master of foxhounds.

mfr., **1.** manufacture. **2.** (*pl.* **mfrs**) manufacturer.

M.Fr., Middle French.

Mg, *Chem.* magnesium.

mg., milligram; milligrams.

m.g., (F *main gauche*) left hand.

M.G.B., (formerly) the Soviet secret police. [t. Russ.: short for *M(inisterstvo) G(osudarstvennoi) B(ezopasnosti)*, lit., Ministry of State Security]

MGk, Medieval Greek.

Mgr, **1.** Monseigneur. **2.** Monsignor.

mgr, manager.

mhd, magneto-hydrodynamics.

MHG, Middle High German.

mho (mō), *n.* *Elect.* a unit of electrical conductivity, equal to the conductivity of a body whose resistance is one ohm; a reciprocal ohm. [coined by Lord Kelvin; reversed spelling of OHM]

mi (mē), *n.* *Music.* the syllable used for the third note of a scale, and sometimes for the note E. See **sol-fa** (def. 1). Also, **me.** [See GAMUT]

mi., **1.** mile; miles. **2.** mill; mills. **3.** minor key.

Miami (mī ăm′ĭ), *n.* **1.** a town in the U.S., in SE Florida: seaside winter resort. 291,688 (1960). See map under **Bermuda. 2.** a river flowing S through W Ohio into the Ohio river. ab. 160 mi.

Miami (mī ăm′ĭ), *n.*, *pl.* **Miamis. 1.** (*pl.*) a North American Indian tribe of the Algonquian family now extinct as a tribe. **2.** a member of this tribe.

mia-mia (mī′ə mī′ə), *n.* an Australian aboriginal's hut. [t. native Australian]

miaow (mĭ ou′, myou), *n.* **1.** the sound a cat makes. —*v.i.* **2.** to make such a sound. Also, **meow, miaou, miaul** (mĭ oul′). [imit.]

miasma (mĭ ăz′mə), *n.*, *pl.* **-mata** (-mə tə), **-mas.** noxious exhalations from putrescent organic matter; poisonous effluvia or germs infecting the atmosphere. [t. NL, t. Gk: pollution] —**mias′mal, miasmatic** (mīəz măt′ĭk), **miasmat′ical, mias′mic,** *adj.*

Mic., Micah.

mica (mī′kə), *n.* any member of a group of minerals, hydrous disilicates of aluminium with other bases, chiefly potassium, magnesium, iron, and lithium, that separate readily into thin, tough, often transparent, and usually elastic laminae. [t. NL, special use of L *mīca* crumb, grain, little bit]

micaceous (mī kā′shəs), *adj.* **1.** consisting of, containing, or resembling mica. **2.** of or pertaining to mica.

Micah (mī′kə), *n.* **1.** a Hebrew prophet of the 8th century B.C. **2.** the sixth book of the 'Minor Prophets', in the Old Testament, which bears his name.

Micanite (mĭk′ə nīt′), *n.* *Trademark.* an insulating material consisting of mica splittings bonded by shellac or synthetic resins.

mice (mīs), *n.* pl. of **mouse.**

M.I.C.E., Member of the Institution of Civil Engineers.

micelle (mĭ sĕl′), *n.* *Phys. Chem.* a colloidal particle formed by the reversible aggregation of dissolved molecules. Electrically charged micelles form colloidal electrolytes, as soaps and detergents. [t. NL: m. *mīcella*, dim. of L *mīca* crumb]

Mich., **1.** Michaelmas. **2.** Michigan.

Michael (mī′kl), *n.* **1.** a militant archangel. Dan. 10:13. **2.** Rumanian, **Mihai** (*Rum.* mē hȧy′), born 1921, king of Rumania 1927–30 and 1940–47.

Michaelmas (mĭk′l məs), *n.* a festival celebrated on September 29th, in honour of the archangel Michael. Also, **Michaelmas Day.** [OE (*Sanct*) *Michaeles mæsse* St Michael's mass]

Michaelmas daisy, any of a number of species of the composite genus *Aster*, with many cultivated varieties and hybrids.

Michaelmas term, an English law sitting and (at some universities, etc.) university term, between variable dates, but usually beginning in October and ending in December.

Michelangeli (*It.* mē kė lȧn′jė lē), *n.* (*Arturo Benedetti Michelangeli*), born 1920, Italian pianist.

Michelangelo (mī′kl ăn′jĭ lō′; *It.* mē kė lȧn′jė lô), *n.* (*Michelangolo, Michelangelo Buonarroti*), 1475–1564, Italian sculptor, painter, architect, and poet.

Michelet (*Fr.* mēsh lĕ′), *n.* **Jules** (*Fr.* zhʏl), 1798–1874, French historian.

Michelozzo di Bartolommeo (*It.* mē kė lôt′tsô dē bȧr tô lô mĕ′ô), 1396–1472, Italian sculptor and architect.

Michelson (mī′kl sən, mĭch′əl sən), *n.* **Albert Abraham,** 1852–1931, U.S. physicist, born in Germany.

Michelson-Morley experiment (mī′kl sən mô′lĭ, mĭch′-əl sən), *Physics.* an experiment carried out in 1887 by A. A. Michelson and E. W. Morley in which they attempted to measure the velocity of the earth relative to the ether, by measuring the effect of this velocity on the velocity of light. No such relative velocity could be detected and this negative result led ultimately to the theory of relativity. [named after A. A. MICHELSON and E. W. *Morley*, 1838–1923, American physicist]

Michigan (mĭsh′ĭ gən), *n.* **1.** a state in the N central United States. 7,823,194 pop. (1960); 58,216 sq. mi. *Cap.:* Lansing. *Abbrev.:* Mich. **2. Lake,** a lake between Wisconsin and Michigan: one of the five Great Lakes. ab. 22,400 sq. mi.

Mick (mĭk), *n.* *Slang.* an Irishman. Also, **Mickey.**

Mickey (mĭk′ĭ), *n.*, *pl.* **-eys. 1.** Also, **Mickey Finn** (fĭn). *Chiefly U.S.* a drink to which a sleeping drug has been added. **2.** Mick. **3.** (*l.c.*) *Austral. Slang.* a young unbranded steer. **4. take the mickey,** to tease; rag.

Mickiewicz (*Pol.* mēts kyĕ′vēch), *n.* **Adam** (*Pol.* ȧ′dȧm), 1798–1855, Polish poet.

mickle (mĭk′l), *adj.* *Scot. and N Dial.* great; large; much. Also, **muckle.** [ME *mikel*, OE *micul*, var. of *micel* MUCH]

Micmac (mĭk′măk), *n.* **1.** (*pl.*) a tribe of Algonquian Indians inhabiting the southern shores of the Gulf of St Lawrence. **2.** a member of this tribe. **3.** the language of the tribe.

Micombero (mĭ kŏm′bə rō′), *n.* **Michel** (mī′kl), born 1940, president of Burundi since 1966.

micra (mī′krə), *n.* a pl. of **micron.**

micrify (mī′krĭ fī′), *v.t.*, **-fied, -fying.** to make small or insignificant. [f. MICR(O)- + -IFY; modelled on MAGNIFY]

micro-, a word element meaning 'very small', used to mean 'enlarging' (*microphone*), as a combining form of **microscopic** (*micro-organism*), and to represent the millionth part of a unit (*microgram*). Also, before vowels, **micr-.** [t. Gk: m. *mīkro-*, comb. form of *mīkrós* small]

microanalysis (mī′krō ə năl′ĭ sĭs), *n.*, *pl.* **-ses** (-sēz′). *Chem.* the analysis of extremely small quantities. —**microanalytical** (mī′krō ăn′ə lĭt′ĭ kl), *adj.*

microbalance (mī′krō băl′əns), *n.* *Chem.* a balance for weighing very small quantities of material, esp. of the order of a thousandth to a millionth of a gram.

microbarograph (mī′krō bă′rə grăf′, -gräf′), *n.* *Meteorol.* a barograph for recording minute fluctuations of atmospheric pressure.

microbe (mī′krōb), *n.* **1.** a micro-organism, usually one of vegetable nature; a germ. **2.** a bacterium, esp. one causing disease. [t. F, f. Gk.: m. *mīkro-* MICRO- + m. s. *bíos* life] —**microbial** (mī krō′byəl), **micro′bic,** *adj.*

microbiology (mī′krō bī ŏl′ə jĭ), *n.* the science concerned with the occurrence, activities, and utilization of the extremely small, microscopic and submicroscopic organisms. —**mi′crobiolog′ical,** *adj.* —**mi′crobiol′ogist,** *n.*

microcephalic (mī′krō sĭ făl′ĭk), *adj.* **1.** *Anat.* having a skull with a small cranial capacity. **2.** *Pathol.* having an abnormally small skull. Also, **microcephalous** (mī′krō sĕf′ə ləs). —**mi′croceph′aly,** *n.*

microchemistry (mī′krō kĕm′ĭs trĭ), *n.* chemistry as concerned with minute or microscopic objects or quantities. —**mi′crochem′ical,** *adj.*

microclimatology (mī′krō klī′mə tŏl′ə jĭ), *n.* a branch of climatology dealing with studies of small-scale climatic conditions, as local climatic changes induced by planting trees as a windbreak.

microcline (mī′krō klīn′), *n.* a mineral of the felspar group, potassium aluminium silicate, $KAlSi_3O_8$, identical in composition with orthoclase but differing in crystal system, used in making porcelain. [t. G: m. *Mikroklin,* f. Gk: *mīkro-* MICRO- + s. *klínein* incline]

micrococcus (mī′krō kŏk′əs), *n., pl.* **-cocci** (-kŏk′sī). any member of the genus *Micrococcus,* comprising globular or oval bacterial organisms, of which certain species cause disease, and others produce fermentation, coloration, etc. [t. NL. See MICRO-, -COCCUS]

microcopy (mī′krō kŏp′ĭ), *n., pl.* **-ies.** a greatly reduced photographic copy of a book page, etc., usually read by enlargement on a ground-glass screen.

microcosm (mī′krō kŏz′əm), *n.* **1.** a little world (opposed to *macrocosm*). **2.** anything regarded as a world in miniature. **3.** man viewed as an epitome of the universe. [t. F: m. *microcosme,* t. LL: m. s. *mīcrocosmus,* t. LGk: m. *mīkrós kósmos* little world] —**mi′crocos′mic, mi′crocos′mical,** *adj.*

microcosmic salt, *Chem.* a phosphate of sodium and ammonium, $NaNH_4HPO_4 . 4H_2O$, orig. obtained from human urine, much used as a blowpipe flux in testing metallic oxides.

microcrystalline (mī′krō krĭs′tə līn′), *adj.* minutely crystalline; composed of microscopic crystals.

microcyte (mī′krō sīt′), *n.* **1.** a minute cell or corpuscle. **2.** *Pathol.* an abnormally small-sized red blood cell, usually deficient in haemoglobin.

microdetector (mī′krō dĭ tĕk′tə), *n.* **1.** an instrument measuring small quantities or changes. **2.** *Elect.* a sensitive galvanometer.

microdont (mī′krō dŏnt′), *adj.* **1.** having small or short teeth. —*n.* **2.** a small or short tooth. —**mi′crodon′tous,** *adj.*

microdot (mī′krō dŏt′), *n.* a microphotograph reduced to the size of a printed or typed dot.

microelectronics (mī′krō ĭ lĕk′trŏn′ĭks), *n.* *Electronics.* the branch of electronics concerned with the development and application of very small circuits, as those formed on a surface by etching.

microfarad (mī′krō fă′răd), *n.* *Elect.* a convenient unit of capacitance in common use, equal to one millionth of a farad.

microfilm (mī′krō fĭlm′), *n.* **1.** a narrow film, esp. of motion-picture stock, on which microcopies are made. **2.** microphotograph.

microgamete (mī′krō gă mēt′), *n.* *Biol.* (in heterogamous reproduction) the smaller of the two gametes, usually the male cell.

microgram (mī′krō grăm′), *n.* a small unit of mass or weight used in microchemistry, equal to a millionth part of a gram. *Abbrev.:* μg.

micrograph (mī′krō grăf′, -gräf′), *n.* **1.** an instrument for executing extremely minute writing or engraving. **2.** a photograph or a drawing of an object as seen through a microscope.

micrography (mī krŏg′rə fĭ), *n.* **1.** the description or delineation of microscopic objects. **2.** examination or study with the microscope. **3.** the art or practice of writing in very small characters. —**micrographic** (mī′krō grăf′ĭk), *adj.*

microgroove (mī′krō grōōv′), *n.* **1.** (in a long-playing gramophone record) a narrow groove which accepts a stylus of the order of thousandths of an inch in diameter. **2.** a record with such grooves.

microinch (mī′krō ĭnch′), *n.* a unit of length equal to a millionth of an inch.

microlitre (mī′krō lē′tə), *n.* a unit of capacity equal to a millionth of a litre, used esp. in microchemistry. *Abbrev.:* μ l or λ. Also, *Chiefly U.S.,* **microliter.**

micrology (mī krŏl′ə jĭ), *n.* excessive attention to petty details or distinctions. [t. Gk: m. s. *mikrología.* See MICRO-, -LOGY]

micrometer (mī krŏm′ĭ tə), *n.* **1.** any of various devices for measuring minute distances, angles, etc., as in connection with a telescope or microscope. **2.** a U-shaped gauge for measuring thicknesses or short lengths in which the gap between the measuring faces is adjusted by a finely threaded screw, the end of which forms one face; a micrometer gauge. [t. F: m. *micromètre,* f. *micro-* MICRO- + *-mètre* -METER[1]]

micrometer screw, a screw with a very fine thread and a graduated head, used in micrometers, etc.

micrometry (mī krŏm′ĭ trĭ), *n.* the method or art of measuring with a micrometer.

micromillimetre (mī′krō mĭl′ĭ mē′tə), *n.* the millionth part of a millimetre; a millimicron.

microminiaturization (mī′krō mĭn′yə chə rī zā′shən), *n.* *Electronics.* the development and application of very small circuits, as those formed on a surface by etching.

micron (mī′krŏn), *n., pl.* **-cra** (-krə), **-crons. 1.** the millionth part of a metre. *Symbol:* μ. **2.** *Phys. Chem.* a colloidal particle whose diameter is between 0·2 and 10 μ. Also, **mikron.** [t. NL, t. Gk: m. *mīkrón* (neut. adj.) small]

Micronesia (mī′krō nē′zyə), *n.* groups of small Pacific islands, N of the equator, E of the Philippine Islands: the main groups included are the Marianas, the Caroline, and the Marshall islands. [f. MICRO- + s. Gk *nêsos* island + -IA]

Micronesian (mī′krō nē′zyən), *adj.* **1.** of Micronesia, its inhabitants, or their languages. —*n.* **2.** a native of Micronesia. **3.** any of the Austronesian languages or dialects spoken in the Micronesian islands.

micro-organism (mī′krō ô′gə nĭz′əm), *n.* a microscopic (animal or vegetable) organism.

microparasite (mī′krō pă′rə sīt′), *n.* a parasitic micro-organism. —**microparasitic** (mī′krō pă′rə sĭt′ĭk), *adj.*

microphone (mī′krə fōn′), *n.* an instrument which is capable of transforming the air-pressure waves of sound into changes in electric currents or voltages. Qualifying adjectives, as *condenser, crystal, velocity,* etc., describe the method of developing the electric quantity. —**microphonic** (mī′krə fŏn′ĭk), *adj.*

microphotograph (mī′krō fō′tə grăf′, -gräf′), *n.* **1.** a small photograph requiring optical enlargement to render it visible in detail. **2.** a film reproduction of a large or bulky publication, as a file of newspapers, used to conserve space or to copy material which is difficult to obtain. **3.** a photomicrograph. —**mi′cropho′tograph′ic,** *adj.* —**microphotography** (mī′krō fə tŏg′rə fĭ), *n.*

micropyle (mī′krō pīl′), *n.* **1.** *Zool.* any minute opening in the coverings of an ovum, through which spermatozoa may gain access to the interior. **2.** *Bot.* the minute orifice or opening in the integuments of an ovule. See diag. under **orthotropous.** [t. F, f. Gk: m. *mīkro-* MICRO- + *pýlē* gate, orifice] —**mi′cropy′lar,** *adj.*

micropyrometer (mī′krō pī rŏm′ĭ tə), *n.* an optical pyrometer for use with small glowing bodies.

micros., microscopy.

microscope (mī′krə skōp′), *n.* an optical instrument having a magnifying lens or a combination of lenses for inspecting objects too small to be seen, or to be seen distinctly and in detail, by the naked eye. [t. NL: m. s. *microscopium,* f. *mīcro-* MICRO- + m. s. Gk *skopeîn* view + *-ium* -IUM]

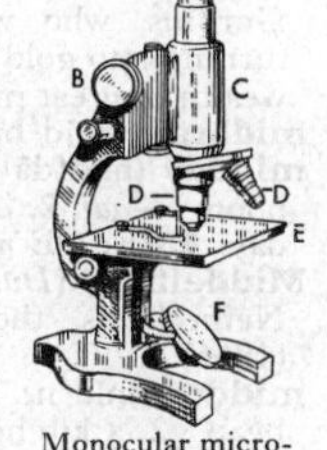

Monocular microscope: A, Eyepiece; B, Adjusting screw; C, Tube; D, Objective; E, Stage; F, Illuminating mirror

microscopic (mī′krə skŏp′ĭk), *adj.* **1.** so small as to be invisible or indistinct without the use of the microscope. **2.** very small; tiny. **3.** of or pertaining to the microscope or its use. **4.** performing the work of a microscope. **5.** suggestive of the use of the microscope: *microscopic exactness.* Also, **mi′croscop′ical.** —**mi′croscop′ically,** *adv.*

microscopy (mī krŏs′kə pĭ), *n.* **1.** the use of the microscope. **2.** microscopic investigation. —**microscopist** (mī krŏs′kə pĭst), *n.*

microsecond (mī′krō sĕk′ənd), *n.* one millionth of a second.

microseism (mī′krō sī′zəm), *n.* *Geol.* a vibration of the ground recorded by seismographs but not believed to be due to an earthquake. [f. MICRO- + s. Gk *seismós* earthquake] —**microseismic** (mī′krō sīz′mĭk), **mi′croseis′mical,** *adj.*

microsome (mī′krō sōm′), *n.* *Biol.* one of the minute granules, smaller than mitochondria and lysosomes, present in living cells, and containing ribonucleic acid and enzymes involved in protein synthesis. [t. NL: m. s. *mīcrosōma.* See MICRO-, -SOME[3]] —**mi′croso′mal,** *adj.*

microsporangium (mī′krō spô răn′jĭ əm), *n.*, *pl.* **-gia** (-jĭ ə). *Bot.* a sporangium containing microspores. [t. NL. See MICRO-, SPORANGIUM]

microspore (mī′krō spô′), *n. Bot.* **1.** the smaller of two kinds of spores produced by some heterosporous pteridophytes. **2.** a pollen grain.

microsporophyll (mī′krō spô′rə fĭl), *n. Bot.* a sporophyll bearing microsporangia.

microstomatous (mī′krō stŏm′ə təs), *adj.* having or pertaining to a very small mouth. Also, **microstomous** (mī krŏs′tə məs). [f. MICRO- + s. Gk *stóma* mouth + -OUS]

microstructure (mī′krō strŭk′chə), *n. Metall.* the structure of metals and alloys as revealed, after polishing and etching, by examination under a microscope.

microtome (mī′krō tōm′), *n.* an instrument for cutting very thin sections, as of organic tissue, for microscopic examination.

microtomy (mī krŏt′ə mĭ), *n.* the cutting of very thin sections, as with the microtome. —**microtomic** (mī′krō tŏm′ĭk), **mi′crotom′ical,** *adj.* —**microt′omist,** *n.*

microtone (mī′krə tōn′), *n. Music.* an interval less than a semitone.

microwaves (mī′krō wāvz′), *n.pl. Electronics.* electromagnetic waves of extremely high frequency, approximately comprising the wavelength range from 50 cm. to 1 mm.

microwave spectroscopy, *Physics.* the measurement of the absorption or emission of electromagnetic radiation, in the waveband 0·1 mm. to 10 cm., by atomic or molecular systems which provides information regarding their structure.

micturate (mĭk′tyo͝o rāt′), *v.i.*, **-rated, -rating.** to pass urine; urinate. [f. s. L *micturīre* desire to urinate + -ATE[1]]

micturition (mĭk′tyo͝o rĭsh′ən), *n.* the act of passing urine. [f. s. L *micturītus*, pp. of *micturīre* desire to urinate + -ION]

mid[1] (mĭd), *adj.* **1.** at or near its middle point: *in mid term.* **2.** occupying a middle place or position: *in the mid nineties of the last century.* **3.** *Phonet.* having a tongue position intermediate between high and low: *beet, bet,* and *bat* have high, mid, and low vowels respectively. **4.** *Cricket.* in the field, midway between the pitch and the boundary, but not behind the wickets. —*n.* **5.** *Archaic.* the middle. [ME; OE *midd*, c. OHG *mitti*, Icel. *midhr*, Goth. *midjis* middle; akin to L *medius*, Gk *mésos*, Skt *madhya* middle]

mid[2] (mĭd), *prep.* amid. Also, **'mid.**

mid-, a combining form of 'middle'.

Mid., midshipman.

mid., middle.

midafternoon (mĭd′ăf′tə no͞on′), *n.* **1.** a point or time about midway through the afternoon, as between 3 p.m. and 4 p.m. —*adj.* **2.** of, pertaining to, or taken at or during midafternoon.

midair (mĭd′ĕə′), *n.* any elevated position above the ground.

Midas (mī′dăs), *n.* **1.** *Gk Legend.* a Phrygian king, son of Gordius, who was given by Dionysus the power of turning into gold whatever he touched. **2.** a man of great wealth or great money-making ability.

midbrain (mĭd′brān′), *n.* the mesencephalon.

midday (mĭd′dā′, mĭd′dā′), *n.* **1.** the middle of the day; noon. —*adj.* **2.** of or pertaining to the middle part of the day. [ME; OE *middæg*]

Middelburg (*Du.* mĭd′əl bʏrKH), *n.* a town in the SW Netherlands, the capital of Zeeland province. 27,996 (1966).

midden (mĭd′n), *n.* **1.** *Archaic or Dial.* a dunghill or refuse heap. **2.** a kitchen midden. [ME *myd(d)yng*, t. Scand.; cf. Dan. *mödding*]

middle (mĭd′l), *adj.*, *n.*, *v.*, **-dled, -dling.** —*adj.* **1.** equally distant from extremes or limits: *the middle point of a line.* **2.** intervening or intermediate: *the middle distance.* **3.** medium: *a man of middle size.* **4.** (*cap.*) (in the history of a language) intermediate between periods classified as Old and New or Modern: *Middle English.* **5.** *Gram.* (in some languages) denoting a voice of verb inflection, in which the subject is represented as acting on or for itself, in contrast to the active voice in which the subject acts, and the passive, in which the subject is acted upon, as in Greek *gráphomai* 'I write for myself', *gráphō* 'I write'. **6.** (*often cap.*) *Geol.* denoting the division intermediate between the Upper and Lower divisions of a period, system, or the like. **7.** *Rare.* at or near its middle. —*n.* **8.** the point, part, etc., equidistant from extremes or limits. **9.** the waist, or middle part of the human body. **10.** something intermediate; a mean. —*v.t.*, *v.i.* **11.** *Chiefly Naut.* to fold in half. [ME and OE *middel*, c. G *Mittel*]
—**Syn. 8.** MIDDLE, CENTRE, MIDST indicate something from which two or more other things are (approximately or exactly) equally distant. MIDDLE denotes the point or part equidistant from or intermediate between extremes or limits in space or in time (activity): *the middle of a road.* CENTRE, a more precise word, is ordinarily applied to a point within circular, globular, or regular bodies, or wherever a similar exactness appears to exist (*the centre of the earth*); it may also be used metaphorically (still suggesting the core of a sphere): *centre of interest.* MIDST usually suggests a point which is closely surrounded or encompassed on all sides, esp. by that which is thick or dense: *the midst of a storm.*

middle age, the period between youth and old age.

middle-aged (mĭd′l ājd′), *adj.* **1.** intermediate in age between youth and old age; commonly, from about 45 to about 60 years old. **2.** characteristic of or suitable for middle-aged people.

Middle Ages, the time in European history between classical antiquity and the Italian Renaissance (from the late 5th century to about A.D. 1350); sometimes restricted to the later part of this period (after 1100); sometimes extended to 1450 or 1500.

middlebrow (mĭd′l brou′), *Colloq.* —*n.* **1.** a person of mediocre or limited intellectual calibre or culture. —*adj.* **2.** being middlebrow. **3.** of or pertaining to middlebrows.

middle C, *Music.* the note indicated by the first ledger line above the bass stave and the first below the treble stave.

middle class, *pl.* **classes.** the class of people socially and conventionally regarded as intermediate between the upper and lower classes, commonly identified with shopkeepers and professional classes.

middle-class (mĭd′l kläs′), *adj.* belonging or pertaining to or characteristic of the middle class; bourgeois.

Middle Congo, a former overseas territory in the SE part of French Equatorial Africa: now an independent republic. See **Congo** (def. 2).

middle distance, *Painting, etc.* the space between the foreground and the background or distance.

middle ear, *Anat.* the tympanum.

Middle East, **1.** the lands from the E shores of the Mediterranean and Aegean to India. **2.** (formerly) the area including Iran, Afghanistan, India, Tibet, and Burma. —**Mid′dle Eas′tern,** *adj.*

Middle English, the English language of the period 1100–1450.

Middle French, the French language of the period 1400–1600.

middle game, *Chess.* that section between the opening and the endgame, characterized by the play of pieces in deployment, while the board is still relatively full.

Middle Greek, Medieval Greek.

Middle High German, the High German language from 1100 to 1450.

Middle Irish, the Irish language from 900 to 1200.

Middle Kingdom, **1.** Also, **Middle Empire.** the second great period in the history of the ancient Egyptian kingdom, about 2200 B.C. to 1690 B.C., comprising dynasties XI–XIV. See **Old Kingdom, New Kingdom.** **2.** the Chinese term for China proper (the 18 inner provinces). **3.** the Chinese Empire (from its supposed position in the centre of the earth).

Middle Low German, Low German of the period 1100–1500.

middleman (mĭd′l măn′), *n.*, *pl.* **-men.** **1.** an intermediary who distributes goods or securities from producer to consumer on his own account and risk. **2.** one who acts as an intermediary between others.

middlemost (mĭd′l mōst′), *adj.* midmost.

middle name, the name between the Christian or first name and the surname.

middle-of-the-road (mĭd′l əv thə rōd′), *adj.* between extremes; moderate.

Middlesbrough (mĭd′lz brə), *n.* a town in England, in the North Riding of Yorkshire. 157,395 (1961).

Middlesex (mĭd′l sĕks′), *n.* a former county in SE England, now an area administered by the Greater London Council and various inner and outer London boroughs. *Abbrev.:* Middx.

Middle Temple. See **Inns of Court.**

middle term, *Logic.* that term of a syllogism which appears twice in the premises, but is eliminated from the conclusion.

Middleton (mĭd′l tən), *n.* **1.** **Thomas,** *c.* 1570–1627, English dramatist. **2.** a town in England, in Lancashire. 56,668 (1961).

middle watch, *Naut.* the watch from midnight to 4 a.m.

middleweight (mĭd′l wāt′), *n.* **1.** one of average weight. **2.** a professional boxer or other contestant intermediate in weight between a light heavyweight and a welterweight, with a maximum weight of 11 st. 6 lbs.

Middle West, that region of the United States bounded on the E and W by the Allegheny Mountains and the Rocky Mountains, and on the S by the Ohio river and the

S extremities of Missouri and Kansas. —**Middle Western.** —**Middle Westerner.**

middling (mĭd′lĭng), *adj.* **1.** medium in size, quality, grade, rank, etc.; moderately large, good, etc. **2.** *Colloq. or Dial.* in fairly good health. —*adv.* **3.** *Colloq. or Dial.* moderately; fairly. —*n.* **4.** (*pl.*) any of various products or commodities of intermediate quality, grade, etc., as the coarser particles of ground wheat mingled with bran. —**mid′dlingly,** *adv.*

Middx, Middlesex.

middy (mĭd′ĭ), *n., pl.* **-dies. 1.** *Colloq.* a midshipman. **2.** a middy blouse.

middy blouse, a loose blouse with a sailor collar, and often extending below the waistline to terminate in a broad band or fold, worn by children, young girls, etc.

Midgard (mĭd′gäd), *n. Scand. Myth.* the abode of humanity, joined to heaven by the rainbow bridge of the gods. Also, **Midgarth** (mĭd′gäth). Icelandic, **Mithgarthr.**

midge (mĭj), *n.* **1.** any of numerous minute flies (order *Diptera*), esp. those of the family *Culicidae.* See **gnat. 2.** a small or diminutive person. [ME *mydge,* OE *mycg,* c. G *Mücke*]

midget (mĭj′ĭt), *n.* **1.** a very small person. **2.** something very small of its kind. [f. MIDGE + -ET]

—**Syn. 1.** MIDGET, DWARF, PYGMY are terms for a very small person. A MIDGET is one perfect in form and normal in function, but like a tiny replica of the ordinary species: *some midgets are like handsome dolls.* A DWARF is one checked in growth, or stunted; he usually has a large head or is in some way not properly formed: *in the past, dwarfs were considered very comical.* A PYGMY is properly a member of one of certain small-sized peoples of Africa and Asia, but the word is often used to mean dwarf or midget.

midgut (mĭd′gŭt′), *n.* the middle part of the alimentary canal.

Midi (*Fr.* mē dē′), *n.* **1.** the south. **2.** the south of France. [F: midday, the south, f. *mi* half (g. L *medius*) + *di* day (g. L *dies*)]

Midian (mĭd′ĭ ən), *n.* the fourth son of Abraham. Gen. 25:2.

Midianite (mĭd′ĭ ə nīt′), *n.* **1.** a member of a desert tribe of north-west Arabia near the Gulf of Aqaba, descended from Midian. Ex. 2:15–22; Judges 6–8. —*adj.* **2.** of or pertaining to the Midianites.

Midi-Pyrénées (*Fr.* mē dē pē rā nā′), *n.* an administrative region in S France comprising the departments of Lot, Aveyron, Tarn-et-Garonne, Tarn, Gers, Haute-Garonne, Ariège, and Hautes-Pyrénées. 2,061,300 pop. (1962); 17,600 sq. mi. *Cap.:* Toulouse.

mid-iron (mĭd′ī′ən), *n. Golf.* an iron (No. 2 iron) whose face has a medium loft, used for far approaches.

midland (mĭd′lənd), *n.* **1.** the middle or interior part of a country. —*adj.* **2.** in or of the midland; inland.

Midlands (mĭd′ləndz), *n.pl.* the central part of England; the midland counties.

mid-leg (mĭd′lĕg′), *n.* **1.** the middle part of the leg. **2.** one of the second pair of legs of an insect. —*adv.* **3.** at the middle of the leg.

Midloth., Midlothian.

Midlothian (mĭd lō′thyən), *n.* a county in SE Scotland. 580,332 pop. (1961); 366 sq. mi. *Co. town:* Edinburgh. *Abbrev.:* Midloth.

midmorning (mĭd′mô′nĭng), *n.* **1.** the period between breakfast and lunch. **2.** a point about halfway through this period, as about 11 a.m. —*adj.* **3.** of, pertaining to or taken at or during midmorning.

midmost (mĭd′mōst′), *adj.* **1.** being in the very middle; middlemost; middle. **2.** at or near its middle point. —*adv.* **3.** in the midmost part; in the midst.

midnight (mĭd′nīt′), *n.* **1.** the middle of the night; 12 o'clock at night. —*adj.* **2.** of or pertaining to midnight. **3.** resembling midnight, as in darkness. **4. burn the midnight oil,** to study or work far into the night. —**mid′night′ly,** *adj., adv.*

midnight sun, the sun visible at midnight in midsummer in arctic and antarctic regions.

midnoon (mĭd′no͞on′), *n.* midday; noon.

mid-off (mĭd′ŏf′), *n. Cricket.* **1.** a fielding position on one off side, near the bowler. **2.** a fielder in this position.

mid-on (mĭd′ŏn′), *n. Cricket.* **1.** a fielding position on one on side near the bowler. **2.** a fielder in this position.

midpoint (mĭd′point′), *n.* **1.** a point midway between the start and the end of a line. **2.** *Geom.* a point at the centre of any geometric figure. **3.** a point in time halfway between the start and the end as of an event, situation.

midrash (mĭd′răsh), *n., pl.* **midrashim** (mĭd rä′shĭm), **midrashoth** (mĭd rä′shōth). *Hebrew Literature.* **1.** the traditional Jewish interpretation of Scripture, whether of its legal or its non-legal portions. **2.** (*cap.*) a series of books, of various titles, containing the traditional Jewish interpretation of Scripture, arranged in the form of commentaries or homilies upon certain books of the Bible or upon selected passages from various books of the Bible. [t. Heb.: commentary]

midrib (mĭd′rĭb′), *n. Bot.* the central or middle rib of a leaf.

M, Midrib

midriff (mĭd′rĭf), *n.* **1.** the diaphragm (in the body). **2.** the middle part of the body, between the chest and the waist. **3.** *U.S.* a dress which exposes this part of the body. —*adj.* **4.** *U.S.* denoting or pertaining to such a dress. [ME *mydryf,* OE *midhrif,* f. *midd* mid + *hrif* belly]

midship (mĭd′shĭp′), *adj.* in or belonging to the middle part of a ship.

midshipman (mĭd′shĭp mən), *n., pl.* **-men. 1.** a probationary rank held by naval cadets before qualifying as officers. **2.** (formerly) one of a class of boys or young men who had various minor duties and who formed the group from which officers were chosen.

midshipmite (mĭd′shĭp mīt′), *n.* (in humorous use) a midshipman.

midships (mĭd′shĭps′), *adv.* amidships.

midst[1] (mĭdst), *n.* **1.** the position of anything surrounded by other things or parts, or occurring in the middle of a period of time, course of action, etc. **2.** the middle point, part, or stage. **3. in our (your, their) midst,** in the midst of us (you, them). [alter. of ME *middes* middle, by assoc. with -EST, superl. suffix] —**Syn. 1.** See **middle.**

midst[2] (mĭdst), *prep. Poetic.* amidst.

midstream (mĭd′strēm′), *n.* the middle of the stream.

midsummer (mĭd′sŭm′ə), *n.* the middle of summer.

Midsummer Day, one of the four quarter-days, celebrated on June 24th.

midsummer madness, *Colloq.* a temporary lapse into folly or foolishness, esp. during the summer.

midsummer-men (mĭd′sŭm ə mĕn′), *n.* (*pl., usually construed as sing.*) a small crassulaceous perennial herb with dense heads of yellow flowers, *Sedum rosea,* widespread on mountain rocks in the N temperate zone; rose-root.

mid-Victorian (mĭd′vĭk tô′rĭ ən), *adj.* **1.** of, pertaining to, or characteristic of the middle portion of the reign of Queen Victoria (reigned 1837–1901) in England: *mid-Victorian writers or ideas.* —*n.* **2.** a person, as a writer, belonging to the mid-Victorian time. **3.** a person of mid-Victorian ideas, tastes, etc.

midway (mĭd′wā′), *adv., adj.* **1.** in or to the middle of the way or distance; halfway. —*n.* **2.** *Obs.* a place or part situated midway. **3.** *U.S.* a place for sideshows and other amusements at any fair or the like. [ME *mydwaye,* OE *midweg*]

Midway Islands, several islets in the N Pacific, ab. 1200 mi. NW of Hawaii: the Japanese were defeated in a naval battle, June 1942. 2356 pop. (1960); 2 sq. mi.

midweek (mĭd′wēk′), *n.* **1.** the middle of the week. **2.** (*cap.*) (among the Quakers) Wednesday. —*adj.* **3.** occurring in the middle of the week.

midweekly (mĭd′wēk′lĭ), *adj.* **1.** midweek. —*adv.* **2.** in the middle of the week.

Midwest (mĭd′wĕst′), *U.S.* —*n.* **1.** Middle West. —*adj.* **2.** Also, **Midwestern** (mĭd′wĕs′tən). Middle Western. —**Mid′west′erner,** *n.*

midwife (mĭd′wīf′), *n., pl.* **-wives** (-wīvz′). a woman who assists women in childbirth. [ME, f. *mid* with, adv. (OE *mid,* c. G *mit*) + WIFE]

midwifery (mĭd′wĭf′ə rĭ), *n.* the art or practice of assisting women in childbirth.

midwinter (mĭd′wĭn′tə), *n.* **1.** the middle of winter. —*adj.* **2.** occurring in the middle of winter.

midyear (mĭd′yĭə′), *n.* **1.** the middle of the year. **2.** (*pl.*) *U.S. Colloq.* midyear examinations. —*adj.* **3.** pertaining to or occurring in midyear.

mielie (mē′lĭ), *n. S African.* mealie; maize.

mien (mēn), *n.* air, bearing, or aspect, as showing character, feeling, etc.: *a man of noble mien.* [der. *demean,* v., influenced by F *mine* aspect, t. Breton: m. *min* beak]

Mies van der Rohe (*Ger.* mēs′ fän dĕr rō′ə), **Ludwig** (*Ger.* lo͞ot′vĭKH), 1886–1969, U.S. architect, born in Germany.

miff (mĭf), *Colloq.* —*n.* **1.** petulant displeasure; a petty quarrel. —*v.t.* **2.** to give offence to; offend. —*v.i.* **3.** to take offence. [? imit. of an exclamation of disgust]

M.I.5, (in Britain) the branch of Military Intelligence which deals with security and counterespionage.

MiG (mĭg), *n.* one of a series of Soviet jet fighter aircraft. Also, **Mig.** [named after *Mi*(*koyan*) and *G*(*urevich*), Soviet aircraft designers]

might[1] (mīt), *v.* pt. of **may.** [ME; OE *mihte*]

might[2] (mīt), *n.* **1.** power to do or accomplish; ability. **2.** effective power or force of any kind. **3.** superior power: *the doctrine that might makes right.* **4. with**

might and main, with utmost strength, vigour, force, or effort. [ME *myghte*, OE *miht*, *meaht*, c. G *Macht*] **—Syn.** **1.** force, puissance. **3.** See **strength.** **—Ant.** **1.** powerlessness.

mightily (mīʹtĭ lĭ), *adv.* **1.** in a mighty manner; powerfully; vigorously. **2.** to a great extent or degree; very much.

mighty (mīʹtĭ), *adj.*, **-tier, -tiest.** **1.** having, characterized by, or showing might or power: *mighty rulers.* **2.** of great size; huge: *a mighty oak.* **3.** *Colloq.* great in amount, extent, degree, or importance. **—*adv.*** **4.** *U.S. Colloq.* very: *to be mighty pleased.* **—mightʹiness,** *n.* **—Syn.** **1.** See **powerful.**

mignon (mĭnʹyŏn; *Fr.* mē nyȯɴʹ), *adj. masc.* small and pretty; delicately pretty. [t. F, der. stem *mign-*, akin to MINION. Cf. Celt. *mino* tender, soft] **—mignonne** (mĭnʹyŏn; *Fr.* mē nyŏnʹ), *adj. fem.*

mignonette (mĭnʹyə nĕtʹ), *n.* **1.** a plant, *Reseda odorata*, common in gardens, having racemes of small, fragrant, greenish white flowers with prominent reddish yellow or brownish anthers. **2.** light green as of reseda plants. [t. F: m. *mignonnette*, dim. of *mignon* MIGNON]

migraine (mēʹgrān), *n.* a paroxysmal headache confined to one side of the head and usually associated with nausea; hemicrania. [t. F. See MEGRIM]

migrant (mīʹgrənt), *adj.* **1.** migrating; migratory. **—*n.*** **2.** one who or that which migrates, as a migratory bird. [t. L: s. *migrans*, ppr.]

migrate (mī grātʹ), *v.i.*, **-grated, -grating.** **1.** to go from one country, region, or place of abode to settle in another. **2.** to pass periodically from one region to another, as certain birds, fishes, and animals. [t. L: m. s. *migrātus*, pp.] **—migraʹtor,** *n.*

—Syn. **1.** MIGRATE, EMIGRATE, IMMIGRATE are used of changing one's abode from one country or part of a country to another. To MIGRATE is to make such a move either once or repeatedly: *to migrate from Ireland to the United States.* To EMIGRATE is to leave a country, usually one's own (and take up residence in another): *each year many people emigrate from Europe.* To IMMIGRATE is to enter and settle in a country not one's own: *there are many inducements to immigrate to Australia.* MIGRATE is applied both to people or to animals that move from one region to another, esp. periodically; the other terms are applied to movements of men.

migration (mī grāʹshən), *n.* **1.** the action of migrating: *the right of migration.* **2.** a migratory movement: *preparations for the migration.* **3.** a number or body of persons or animals migrating together. **4.** *Chem.* a movement or change of place of atoms within a molecule. [t. L: s. *migrātio*] **—migraʹtional,** *adj.*

migration of ions, *Chem.* the movement of ions towards an electrode, during electrolysis.

migratory (mīʹgrə tə rĭ, -trĭ), *adj.* **1.** migrating: *migratory species.* **2.** pertaining to a migration: *migratory movements of birds.* **3.** roving or nomad.

mihrab (mēʹrăb, -rəb), *n.* a niche in a mosque, indicating the direction of Mecca.

mikado (mĭ käʹdō), *n.*, *pl.* **-dos.** (*often cap.*) formerly, a title of the emperor of Japan. [t. Jap.: lit., exalted gate]

mike (mīk), *n. Slang.* a microphone.

Mikoyan (*Russ.* mĭ kȧ yänʹ), *n.* **Anastas Ivanovich** (*Russ.* ə nȧs täsʹ ivänʹə vĭch), born 1895, Soviet president 1964–65.

mikron (mīʹkrŏn), *n.*, *pl.* **-kra, -kras.** micron.

mil (mĭl), *n.* **1.** a unit of length equal to 0·001 of an inch, used in measuring the diameter of wires. **2.** a military unit of angle equal to the angle subtended by an arc of 1/6400 of a circumference. This is the **artillery mil;** it has practically superseded the nearly equivalent **infantry mil,** defined as the angle subtended by an arc of 1/1000 of the radius. **3.** *Pharm.* a millilitre (0·001 of a litre), or cubic centimetre. **4.** a former bronze coin of the mandate of Palestine equal to 0·011 of a pound. [short for L *millēsimus* thousandth]

mil., **1.** military. **2.** militia.

milady (mĭ lāʹdĭ), *n.*, *pl.* **-dies.** a Continental rendering of English *my lady*, used in speaking to or of an English noblewoman. Also, **miladi.**

milage (mīʹlĭj), *n.* mileage.

Milan (mĭ lănʹ), *n.* a city in Italy, in W central Lombardy: famous cathedral. 1,676,559 (1966). Italian, **Milano** (*It.* mē läʹnȯ). See map under **Lombardy.** **—Milanese** (mĭlʹə nēzʹ), *adj.*, *n.*

Milazzo (*It.* mē lätʹtsȯ), *n.* a seaport in Italy, in NE Sicily. 22,013 (1961).

milch (mĭlch), *adj.* (of a cow, goat, or other animal) producing milk; kept for milk-production. [ME *milche*; akin to MILK]

mild (mīld), *adj.* **1.** amiably gentle or temperate in feeling or behaviour towards others. **2.** characterized by or showing such gentleness, as manners, speech, etc. **3.** not cold, severe, or extreme, as air, weather, etc. **4.** gentle or moderate in force or effect: *mild penalties.* **5.** softly shining, as light, etc. **6.** not sharp, pungent, or strong: *mild flavour.* **7.** not acute, as disease, etc. **8.** moderate in intensity, degree, or character: *mild regret.* **9.** easily worked, as soil, stone, wood, etc. **10.** *Obs.* kind or gracious. **—*n.*** **11.** a dark, full-flavoured beer brewed from malt which has been heated on the kiln to a higher temperature than malt for pale ale, which gives it a characteristic burnt flavour. [ME and OE, c. G *mild*] **—mildʹly,** *adv.* **—mildʹness,** *n.* **—Syn.** **2.** See **gentle.** **3.** temperate, moderate, clement. **—Ant.** **1.** forceful.

mild ale, mild (def. 11).

milden (mīlʹdən), *v.t.*, *v.i.* to make or become mild or milder.

mildew (mĭlʹdyōōʹ), *n.* **1.** a plant disease usually characterized by a whitish coating or a discoloration on the surface, caused by any of various parasitic fungi. **2.** any of these fungi. **3.** similar coating or discoloration, due to fungi, on cotton and linen fabrics, paper, leather, etc., when exposed to moisture. **—*v.t.*, *v.i.*** **4.** to affect or become affected with mildew. [ME; OE *mildēaw*, *meledēaw*, lit., honeydew] **—milʹdewʹy,** *adj.*

mild steel, *Metall.* a tough ductile form of steel containing between 0·12 and 0·25 per cent of carbon.

mile (mīl), *n.* **1.** a unit of distance: **a.** the **statute mile,** used as a unit of distances on land in the English-speaking countries, equal to 5280 ft or 1760 yds. **b. nautical, geographical,** or **sea mile,** defined in Great Britain as 6080 ft. **c.** the **international nautical** or **air mile,** a unit of distance in sea and air navigation, equal to 1·852 km. (6076·097 ft), recommended by the International Hydrographic Bureau for international adoption and adopted by a number of countries. **2.** other units of varying length at different periods and in different countries, e.g., the old **Roman mile** having been equivalent to about 1620 yds or the present **Swedish mile** being equal to 10 km. **3.** (*often pl.*) a large distance or interval. [ME *myle*, OE *mīl*, t. L: m. *mīlia* (*passuum*) a thousand (paces)]

mileage (mīʹlĭj), *n.* **1.** the aggregate number of miles made or travelled over in a given time. **2.** length, extent, or distance in miles. **3.** an allowance for travelling expenses at a fixed rate per mile. **4.** a fixed charge per mile, as for railway. **5.** the aggregate number of miles made or travelled over in a given time. **6.** length, extent, of fuel, etc., usually one gallon. Also, **milage.**

mileometer (mī lŏmʹĭ tə), *n.* a device used for measuring the number of miles travelled, as a motor vehicle.

milepost (mīlʹpōstʹ), *n.* **1.** *Racing.* a post marking a point one mile from the finish. **2.** *Chiefly U.S.* a post functioning as a milestone.

miler (mīʹlə), *n.* a participant in a race over one mile, or an athlete specializing in such races.

miles gloriosus (mēʹlās glôʹrĭ ōʹsōōs), *pl.* **milites gloriosi** (mēʹlĭ tāsʹ glôʹrĭ ōʹsī). *Latin.* a braggart soldier.

milestone (mīlʹstōnʹ), *n.* **1.** a stone set up to mark distance by miles, as along a highway or other line of travel. **2.** a birthday or some event regarded as marking a stage in the journey of life.

Miletus (mĭ lēʹtəs), *n.* an ancient city on the Aegean coast of Asia Minor. **—Milesian** (mĭ lēʹzyən), *adj.*, *n.*

milfoil (mĭlʹfoilʹ), *n.* the plant yarrow. [ME, t. OF, g. L *mīlifolium*, *millefolium*, lit., thousand leaves]

Milford Haven (mĭlʹfəd), a seaport in Wales, in Pembrokeshire. 12,802 (1961).

Milhaud (*Fr.* mē yōʹ), *n.* **Darius** (*Fr.* dȧ ryʏsʹ), born 1892, French composer, in the U.S. since 1940.

miliaria (mĭlʹĭ ēəʹrĭ ə), *n. Pathol.* an inflammatory disease of the skin, located about the sweat glands, marked by the formation of vesicles or papules resembling millet seeds; miliary fever. [t. NL, prop. fem. of L *miliārius* MILIARY]

miliary (mĭlʹyə rĭ), *adj.* **1.** resembling a millet seed or seeds. **2.** *Pathol.* accompanied by spots (papules) or vesicles resembling millet seeds: *miliary fever.* [t. L: m. s. *miliārius* of millet]

miliary tuberculosis, *Pathol.* tuberculosis in which the bacilli are spread by the blood from one point of infection, producing small tubercles in other parts of the body.

milieu (mēʹlyû; *Fr.* mē lyœʹ), *n.* medium or environment. [t. F: f. *mi* (g. L *medius*) middle + *lieu* (g. L *locus*) place]

milit., military.

militant (mĭlʹĭ tənt), *adj.* **1.** combative; aggressive: *a militant reformer.* **2.** engaged in warfare; warring. **—*n.*** **3.** one engaged in warfare or strife. **4.** a militant person. [ME, t. L: s. *mīlitans*, ppr., serving as a soldier] **—milʹitancy,** *n.* **—milʹitantly,** *adv.*

militarism (mĭlʹĭ tə rĭzʹəm), *n.* **1.** military spirit or policy. **2.** the principle of keeping a large military establishment. **3.** the tendency to regard military efficiency as the supreme ideal of the state, and to subordinate all other interests to those of the military.

militarist (mĭl′ĭ tə rĭst), *n.* **1.** one imbued with militarism. **2.** one skilled in the art of war. —**mil′itaris′tic,** *adj.* —**mil′itaris′tically,** *adv.*

militarize (mĭl′ĭ tə rīz′), *v.t.*, **-rized, -rizing. 1.** to make military. **2.** to imbue with militarism. Also, **militarise.** —**mil′itariza′tion,** *n.*

military (mĭl′ĭ tə rĭ, -trĭ), *adj.* **1.** of or pertaining to the army, armed forces, affairs of war, or a state of war. **2.** of or pertaining to soldiers. **3.** befitting a soldier. **4.** following the life of a soldier. **5.** having the characteristics of a soldier; soldierly. —*n.* **6.** soldiers generally; the armed forces. [t. L: m. *militāris*] —**mil′itarily,** *adv.* —**Ant. 1.** civilian.

military cross, a decoration awarded since 1914 for bravery to army officers below major and warrant officers. *Abbrev.:* M.C.

military law, rules and regulations applicable to persons in the armed forces.

military police, soldiers who perform police duties within the army. *Abbrev.:* M.P.

militate (mĭl′ĭ tāt′), *v.i.*, **-tated, -tating.** to operate (*against* or *in favour of*); have effect or influence: *every fact militated against his argument.* [t. L: m. s. *mīlitātus*, pp. of *mīlitāre* be a soldier] —**mil′ita′tion,** *n.*

militia (mĭ lĭsh′ə), *n.* **1.** a body of men enrolled for military service, called out periodically for drill and exercise but for actual service only in emergencies. **2.** a body of citizen soldiers as distinguished from professional soldiers. **3.** *U.S.* all able-bodied males who are or are eligible to become citizens, and are more than 18 and not more than 45 years of age. [t. L: military service, soldiery]

militiaman (mĭ lĭsh′ə mən), *n.*, *pl.* **-men.** one serving in the militia.

milium (mĭl′ĭ əm), *n.*, *pl.* **milia** (mĭl′ĭ ə). *Pathol.* a small white or yellowish nodule resembling a millet seed, produced in the skin by the retention of a sebaceous secretion. [t. L: millet]

milk (mĭlk), *n.* **1.** an opaque white or bluish white liquid secreted by the mammary glands of female mammals, serving for the nourishment of their young, and, in the case of the cow and some other animals, used for food or as a source of dairy products. **2.** any liquid resembling this, as the liquid within a coconut, the juice or sap (latex) of certain plants, or various pharmaceutical preparations. **3. cry over spilt milk,** to lament something which cannot be changed. —*v.t.* **4.** to press or draw milk by hand or machine from the udder of (a cow or other animal). **5.** to extract as if by milking; draw. **6.** to extract something from as if by milking. **7.** to drain strength, information, wealth, etc., from; exploit. —*v.i.* **8.** to yield milk, as a cow. **9.** to milk a cow or other animal. [ME; OE *milc, meolc*, c. G *Milch*]

milk and honey, 1. abundance; plenty. **2.** luxury.

milk-and-water (mĭlk′ən wô′tə), *adj.* weak or insipid; wishy-washy.

milk bar, a place, often with an open front, where milk drinks, ice-cream, sandwiches, etc., are sold.

milk chocolate, eating chocolate that has been made with milk.

milker (mĭl′kə), *n.* **1.** one who milks. **2.** milking machine. **3.** a cow or other animal that gives milk.

milk fever, 1. *Pathol.* fever coinciding with the beginning of lactation, formerly believed to be due to lactation, but really due to infection. **2.** *Vet. Sci.* an acute condition often affecting dairy cows immediately after calving, causing somnolence and paralysis.

milkfish (mĭlk′fĭsh′), *n.*, *pl.* **-fishes,** (*esp. collectively*) **-fish.** a herring-like fish, *Chanos chanos*, extensively cultivated in south-eastern Asia.

milk float. See **float** (def. 24).

milking machine, an apparatus for milking cows.

milking stool, a low, three-legged stool with a seat in the shape of a half-circle or three-quarter circle.

milk leg, *Pathol.* a painful swelling of the leg, due to thrombosis of the large veins, occurring most frequently in connection with parturition. Also, **white leg.**

milk loaf, a loaf of white bread made with milk rather than water.

milkmaid (mĭlk′mād′), *n.* a woman who milks cows or is employed in a dairy.

milkman (mĭlk′mən), *n.*, *pl.* **-men.** a man who sells or delivers milk.

milk of magnesia, *Pharm.* an antacid or laxative composed of a magnesium hydroxide, $Mg(OH)_2$, suspension in water.

milk parsley, the hog's fennel, *Peucedanum palustre.*

milk pudding, a hot or cold dish of rice or other grain baked with milk.

milk punch, a beverage containing milk and alcoholic liquor with sugar, flavouring, etc.

milk run, *U.S. Airforce Slang.* a routine or uneventful flight.

milk shake, a frothy drink made of milk, flavouring, and sometimes ice-cream, shaken together.

milk snake, a grey and black non-venomous snake, *Lampropeltis triangulum*, with an arrow-shaped mark over the occiput, found widely in eastern North America.

milksop (mĭlk′sŏp′), *n.* **1.** a dish of bread, etc., soaked in milk, as given to children and invalids. **2.** a soft, unmanly fellow; an effeminate man or youth. —**milk′sopism,** *n.*

milk sugar, lactose.

milk thistle, 1. an annual or biennial composite herb with spiny leaves and reddish purple capitula, *Silybum marianum*, widespread in N temperate grasslands and waste places. **2.** any of several species of the composite genus *Sonchus*, with yellow flower heads and containing a milky juice, as *S. oleraceus*, a widespread weed of cultivated land in temperate regions.

milk tooth, one of the temporary teeth of a mammal which are replaced by the permanent teeth.

milk vetch, 1. a herb, esp. a European species *Astragalus glycyphyllos*, of the fabaceous genus *Astragalus*, reputed to increase the secretion of milk in goats. **2.** any herb of certain allied genera.

milkweed (mĭlk′wēd′), *n.* **1.** any of various plants (mostly with milky juice) of the family *Asclepiadaceae*, esp. those of the genus *Asclepias*, as *A. syriaca* (the **common milkweed**). **2.** any of various plants with a milky juice, as certain spurges.

milk-white (mĭlk′wīt′), *adj.* of a white or slightly blue-white colour, such as that of milk.

milkwort (mĭlk′wût′), *n.* **1.** any of the herbs and shrubs constituting the genus *Polygala*, having (mostly) spikes or spikelike racemes of variously coloured flowers, formerly reputed to increase the secretion of milk. **2.** a primulaceous seaside plant, *Glaux maritima*, having small purplish white flowers (**sea milkwort**).

milky (mĭl′kĭ), *adj.*, **-kier, -kiest. 1.** of or like milk. **2.** of a chalky white. **3.** giving a good supply of milk. **4.** meek, tame, or spiritless. —**milk′iness,** *n.*

Milky Way, *Astron.* the faintly luminous band stretching across the heavens, composed of innumerable stars too faint for unassisted vision; the Galaxy. [trans. of L *via lactea*]

mill[1] (mĭl), *n.* **1.** a building or establishment fitted with machinery, in which any of various mechanical operations or forms of manufacture is carried on, esp. the spinning or weaving of cotton or wool. **2.** a mechanical appliance or a building or establishment equipped with appliances for grinding corn into flour. **3.** a machine for grinding, crushing, or pulverizing any solid substance: *a coffee mill.* **4.** a steel roller for receiving and transferring an impressed design, as to a calico-printing cylinder or a banknote-printing plate. **5.** a machine which does its work by rotary motion, as one used by a lapidary for cutting and polishing precious stones. **6.** any of various other apparatuses for working materials into due form or performing other mechanical operations. **7.** *Slang.* a boxing match or fist fight. **8. go through the mill,** to undergo a gruelling or difficult experience. —*v.t.* **9.** to grind, work, treat, or shape in or with a mill. **10.** to finish the edge of (a coin, etc.) with a series of fine notches or transverse grooves. **11.** to beat or stir, as to a froth: *to mill chocolate.* **12.** *Slang.* to beat or strike; fight; overcome. —*v.i.* **13.** to move confusedly in a circle, as a herd of cattle (often fol. by *about*). **14.** *Slang.* to fight or box. [ME *mille, myln*, OE *mylen*, t. LL: m. s. *molīnum*, der. L *mola* millstone, mill]

mill[2] (mĭl), *n.* a U.S. money of account, equal to one thousandth of a dollar or one tenth of a cent, used in calculating taxes, interest rates, etc. [short for L *millēsimus* thousandth, modelled on CENT]

Mill (mĭl), *n.* **1. James,** 1773–1836, Scottish philosopher, historian, and economist. **2.** his son, **John Stuart,** 1806–73, English philosopher and economist.

Millais (mĭl′ā), *n.* **Sir John Everett,** 1829–96, English painter.

Millay (mĭl′ā), *n.* **Edna St Vincent** (*Mrs Eugen Jan Boissevain*), 1892–1950, U.S. poet.

millboard (mĭl′bôd′), *n.* *Bookbinding.* a strong, thick pasteboard used to make book covers.

milldam (mĭl′dăm′), *n.* a dam built in a stream to furnish a head of water for turning a millwheel.

milled (mĭld), *adj.* **1.** having undergone the operations of a mill. **2.** (of the edge of a coin) serrated.

millefiori (mĭl′ĭ fĭ ô′rĭ), *n.* ornamental glass made by fusing coloured glass rods in a kiln. [t. It., lit., a thousand flowers]

millenarian (mĭl′ĭ nĕə′rĭ ən), *adj.* **1.** of or pertaining to a thousand, esp. the thousand years of the prophesied millennium. —*n.* **2.** a believer in the millennium.

millenary (mĭ lĕn′ə rĭ), *adj.*, *n.*, *pl.* **-ries.** —*adj.* **1.** consisting of or pertaining to a thousand, esp. a thousand years. **2.** pertaining to the millennium. —*n.* **3.** an aggregate of a thousand. **4.** millennium. **5.** millenarian. [t. LL: m. s. *millēnārius* (def. 1)]

millennial (mĭ lĕn′ĭ əl), *adj.* **1.** of or pertaining to a millennium or the millennium. **2.** worthy or suggestive of the millennium. —**millen′nially,** *adv.*

millennium (mĭ lĕn′ĭ əm), *n.*, *pl.* **-niums, -nia** (-nĭ ə). **1.** a period of a thousand years. **2.** a thousandth anniversary. **3.** the period of 'a thousand years' (a phrase variously interpreted) during which Christ is to reign on earth, according to the prophetic statement in Rev. 20:1–7. **4.** a period of general righteousness and happiness, esp. in the indefinite future. [t. NL, f. L: *mille* thousand + *-ennium* as in BIENNIUM]

millepede (mĭl′ĭ pēd′), *n.* millipede.

millepore (mĭl′ĭ pô′), *n.* a coralline hydrozoan of the genus *Millipora*, having a smooth calcareous surface with many perforations. [t. NL: m. s. *millepora*, f. L *mille* thousand + m. *porus* PORE[2]]

miller (mĭl′ə), *n.* **1.** one who keeps or operates a mill, esp. a corn mill. **2.** a milling machine. [ME; r. OE *myle(n)weard* (see MILL[1], WARD)]

Miller (mĭl′ə), *n.* **1. Arthur,** born 1915, U.S. playwright. **2. Henry,** born 1891, U.S. novelist. **3. William,** 1782–1849, U.S. preacher: founder of the Adventist Church.

Millerand (*Fr.* mĕl räN′), *n.* **Alexandre** (*Fr.* à lĕk säN′dr), 1859–1943, president of France 1920–24.

millerite (mĭl′ə rīt′), *n.* a mineral, nickel sulphide (NiS), occurring in bronze-coloured slender crystals, a minor ore of nickel. [named after W. H. *Miller*, 1801–80, English crystallographer. See -ITE[1]]

Millerite (mĭl′ə rīt′), *n.* a member of the Adventist Church founded by William Miller, who taught that the second advent of Christ and the beginning of the millennium were to occur in the immediate future (at first, about 1843).

miller's thumb, any small freshwater European fish of the family *Cottidae*; bullhead.

millesimal (mĭ lĕs′ĭ məl), *adj.* **1.** thousandth. **2.** consisting of thousandth parts. —*n.* **3.** a thousandth part. [f. s. L *millēsimus* thousandth + -AL[1]]

millet (mĭl′ĭt), *n.* **1.** a cereal grass, *Setaria italica*, extensively cultivated in the East and in southern Europe for its small seed or grain (used as a food for man and fowls), but in the U.S. grown chiefly for fodder. **2.** any of various related or similar grasses cultivated as grain plants or forage plants, as **Indian millet,** and **pearl millet. 3.** the grain of any of these grasses. [ME, t. F, dim. of *mil*, g. L *milium*]

Millet (mĭl′ā; *Fr.* mē lĕ′), *n.* **Jean François** (*Fr.* zhäN fräN swá′), 1814–75, French painter.

milli-, a word element meaning 'thousand', used in the metric system for the division of the unit by 1000. [t. L, comb. form of *mille*]

milliard (mĭl′ĭ äd′, mĭl′yäd), *n.* a thousand millions. [t. F, der. L *mille* thousand]

milliary (mĭl′yə rĭ), *adj.* **1.** pertaining to the ancient Roman mile of a thousand paces. **2.** marking a mile. [t. L: m. s. *milliārius* containing a thousand]

millibar (mĭl′ĭ bä′), *n.* *Meteorol.* a widely used unit of atmospheric pressure, equal to 0·001 bar.

millier (*Fr.* mē lyė′), *n.* *French.* 1000 kg.; a metric ton. [F, der. L *mille* thousand]

milligram (mĭl′ĭ grăm′), *n.* a unit of one thousandth of a gram, equivalent to 0·0154 grain. Also, **milligramme.**

Millikan (mĭl′ĭ kən), *n.* **Robert Andrews,** 1868–1953, U.S. physicist.

millilitre (mĭl′ĭ lē′tə), *n.* a unit of capacity in the metric system, equal to one thousandth of a litre, and equivalent to 0·033815 fl. oz., or 0·061025 cu. in. Also, *U.S.*, **milliliter.**

millimetre (mĭl′ĭ mē′tə), *n.* a unit of length in the metric system equal to one thousandth of a metre, and equivalent to 0·03937 in. Also, *U.S.*, **millimeter.** [t. F: m. *millimètre*. See MILLI-, -METRE[1]]

millimicron (mĭl′ĭ mī′krŏn), *n.*, *pl.* **-cra** (-krə). a unit of length, the thousandth part of a micron. *Symbol.*: mμ.

milliner (mĭl′ĭ nə), *n.* one who makes or sells hats for women. [var. of obs. *Milaner* an inhabitant of Milan, a dealer in articles from Milan]

millinery (mĭl′ĭ nə rĭ, -ĭn rĭ), *n.* **1.** articles made or sold by milliners. **2.** the business or trade of a milliner.

milling (mĭl′ĭng), *n.* **1.** the act of subjecting something to the operation of a mill. **2.** the process of producing plane and formed surfaces. **3.** the process of finishing the edge of a coin, etc., with fine notches or transverse grooves. **4.** *Slang.* a thrashing.

milling machine, a machine tool used to produce plane and formed surfaces.

million (mĭl′yən), *n.* **1.** a cardinal number, one thousand times one thousand. **2.** a symbol for this number, as 1,000,000. **3.** the amount of a thousand thousand units of money, as pounds, dollars, or francs. **4.** a very great number. **5.** the multitude, or the mass of the common people (prec. by *the*). —*adj.* **6.** amounting to one million in numbers. [ME *millioun*, t. OF: m. *million*, t. It.: m. *mil(l)ione*, aug. of *mille* thousand, g. L *mille*]

millionaire (mĭl′yə nĕə′), *n.* **1.** a person worth a million or millions, as of pounds, dollars, or francs. **2.** a very rich person. [t. F: m. *millionnaire*, der. *million* MILLION]

millionth (mĭl′yənth), *adj.* **1.** coming last in a series of a million. **2.** being one of a million equal parts. —*n.* **3.** the millionth member of a series; a millionth part, esp. of one (1/1,000,000).

millipede (mĭl′ĭ pēd′), *n.* any one of the many arthropods belonging to the class *Diplopoda*. These are slow-moving, mostly herbivorous, myriapods having a cylindrical body of numerous segments, most of which bear two pairs of legs. Also, **millepede.** [t. L: m. s. *millepeda* wood louse, f. *mille* thousand + m. s. *pēs* foot]

Millipede, *Cambala annulata* (1 in. long)

millisecond (mĭl′ĭ sĕk′ənd), *n.* one thousandth of a second.

millpond (mĭl′pŏnd′), *n.* **1.** a pond for supplying water to drive a millwheel. **2.** an area of very calm water.

millrace (mĭl′rās′), *n.* **1.** the channel in which the current of water driving a millwheel flows to the mill. **2.** the current itself.

millrun (mĭl′rŭn′), *n.* **1.** a millrace. **2.** a test of the mineral content or quality of a rock or ore consisting of the actual milling of a sample. **3.** the mineral so obtained.

mill-run (mĭl′rŭn′), *adj.* **1.** not specially prepared; unsorted as to quality; taken from production. **2.** run-of-the-mill.

Mills bomb (mĭlz), *Mil.* a type of high-explosive grenade weighing about 1·5 lbs. Also, **Mills grenade.** [named after the inventor, Sir William *Mills*, 1856–1932]

millstone (mĭl′stōn′), *n.* **1.** either of a pair of circular stones between which grain or other substance is ground, as in a mill. **2.** something that grinds or crushes. **3.** a heavy burden, esp. in the phrase *a millstone around one's neck* (in allusion to Matt. 18:6).

millstream (mĭl′strēm′), *n.* the stream in a millrace.

millwheel (mĭl′wēl′), *n.* a wheel, esp. a waterwheel, to drive a mill.

millwork (mĭl′wûk′), *n.* **1.** ready-made carpentry work from a mill. **2.** work done in a mill.

millwright (mĭl′rīt′), *n.* one who designs, builds, or sets up mills or mill machinery.

Milne (mĭln), *n.* **A(lan) A(lexander),** 1882–1956, English writer of plays, books for children, and novels.

Milner (mĭl′nə), *n.* **Alfred, 1st Viscount,** 1854–1925, British statesman and colonial administrator.

milo (mī′lō), *n.*, *pl.* **-los.** any of various grain sorghums with heads of white, yellow, or pinkish seeds, grown chiefly in Africa, Asia, and the U.S. [t. a Bantu language of Lesotho]

Milo (mī′lō), *n.* Melos. Also, **Milos** (mē′lŏs).

M.I.Loco.E., Member of the Institute of Locomotive Engineers.

milord (mĭ lôd′), *n.* (a Continental rendering of English *my lord*, used as a term of address.)

milquetoast (mĭlk′tōst′), *n.* *U.S.* a very timid person. [named after Caspar *Milquetoast*, a comic-strip character]

milreis (mĭl′rās′; *Port.* mĕl rĕysh′), *n.*, *pl.* **-reis. 1.** a former Brazilian silver coin and monetary unit, equal to 1000 reis, abandoned in 1942. **2.** a Portuguese gold coin and former monetary unit (superseded in 1911 by the escudo). [t. Pg.: a thousand reis, f. *mil* a thousand (g. L *mille*) + *reis* REIS]

Milstein (mĭl′stīn), *n.* **Nathan,** born 1904, Russian violinist in the U.S.

milt (mĭlt), *n.* **1.** the secretion of the male generative organs of fishes. **2.** the organs themselves. **3.** melt (def. 15). —*v.t.* **4.** to extract the eggs or sperm from (a fish) for artificial spawning. [ME and OE *milte*, c. G *Milz*, etc.; akin to MELT]

milter (mĭl′tə), *n.* a male fish in breeding time.

Miltiades (mĭl tī′ə dēz′), *n.* died *c.* 488 B.C., Athenian general who was victorious over the Persians in the battle of Marathon in 490 B.C.

Milton (mĭl′tən), *n.* **1. John,** 1608–74, English poet.

2. a town in England, in Kent. (with Sittingbourne) 23,616 (1961).

Miltonic (mĭl tŏn′ĭk), *adj.* of or pertaining to the poet Milton or resembling his majestic style. Also, **Miltonian** (mĭl tō′nyən).

Miltown (mĭl′toun′), *n. Trademark.* meprobamate.

Milwaukee (mĭl wô′kĭ), *n.* a city in the U.S., in SE Wisconsin: a port on Lake Michigan. 741,324 (1960).

Milyukov (*Russ.* mĭ lyo͞o kôf′), *n.* **Pavel Nikolaevich** (*Russ.* pȧ′vĭl nĭ kȧ lȧ′yĭ vĭch), 1859–1943, Russian statesman and historian in Paris from 1919.

mime (mīm), *n., v.,* **mimed, miming.** —*n.* **1.** the art or technique of expressing emotion, character, action, etc., by mute gestures and bodily movements. **2.** a play or entertainment in which the performers express themselves by such gestures and movements. **3.** a comedian or clown, esp. one who entertains by mute gesture, facial expression, bodily movement, etc. **4.** a player in an ancient Greek or Roman kind of farce which depended for effect largely upon ludicrous actions and gestures. **5.** such a farce. **6.** the dialogue for such a player. —*v.t.* **7.** to mimic. —*v.i.* **8.** to play a part by mimicry, esp. without words. [t. L: m. s. *mīmus,* t. Gk: m. *mîmos*] —**mim′er,** *n.*

Mimeograph (mĭm′ĭ ə grăf′, -gräf′), *n.* **1.** *Trademark.* a stencil device for duplicating letters, drawings, etc. —*v.t.* **2.** (*l.c.*) to make copies of, using a Mimeograph. [f. *mimeo-* (repr. Gk *mīméomai* I imitate; cf. MIME) + -GRAPH]

mimesis (mĭ mē′sĭs), *n.* **1.** *Rhet.* imitation or reproduction of the supposed words of another, as in order to represent his character. **2.** (in the arts) the imaginative representation of the actions, motives, or natures of men or of their environments. **3.** *Biol.* imitation. **4.** *Zool.* mimicry. **5.** *Pathol.* the imitation of one disease by another; hysterical simulation. [t. NL, t. Gk: imitation]

mimetic (mĭ mĕt′ĭk), *adj.* **1.** characterized by, exhibiting, or of the nature of mimicry or mimesis: *mimetic gestures.* **2.** mimic or make-believe. [t. Gk: m. s. *mīmētikós*] —**mimet′ically,** *adv.*

mimetic diagram, *Elect.* an animated diagram indicating by coloured lights, recorders, and other devices, the state of a large industrial process or other complicated operation.

mimetite (mĭm′ĭ tīt′, mī′mĭ-), *n.* a mineral, lead chloroarsenate, $Pb_5As_3O_{12}Cl$, occurring in yellow to brown prismatic crystals or globular masses: a minor ore of lead. [t. G: m. *Mimetit,* f. s. Gk *mīmētḗs* imitator + *-it* -ITE[1]]

mimic (mĭm′ĭk), *v.,* **-icked, -icking,** *n., adj.* —*v.t.* **1.** to imitate or copy in action, speech, etc., often playfully or derisively. **2.** to imitate unintelligently or servilely; ape. **3.** (of things) to be an imitation of; simulate. —*n.* **4.** one apt at imitating or mimicking the characteristic voice or gesture of others. **5.** one who or that which imitates or mimics; an imitator or imitation. **6.** *Obs.* a mime (def. 3). —*adj.* **7.** being merely an imitation or reproduction of the true thing, often on a smaller scale: *a mimic battle.* **8.** apt at or given to imitating; imitative. [t. L: s. *mīmicus,* t. Gk: m. *mīmikós* belonging to mimes]

mimicry (mĭm′ĭk rĭ), *n., pl.* **-ries. 1.** the act, practice, or art of mimicking. **2.** *Zool.* the close external resemblance, as if from imitation or simulation, of an animal to some different animal or to surrounding objects, esp. as serving for protection or concealment. **3.** an instance, performance, or result of mimicking.

M.I.Min.E., Member of the Institution of Mining Engineers.

Mimir (mē′mĭə), *n. Scand. Myth.* the custodian of the spring of wisdom; his head, cut off by the Vanir, came into Odin's possession and gave him information and advice thenceforth.

mimosa (mĭ mō′sə, -zə), *n.* any plant of the genus *Mimosa,* native in tropical or warm regions, and comprising trees, shrubs, and plants having usually bipinnate and often sensitive leaves, and small flowers in globular heads or cylindrical spikes, esp. the sensitive plant, *M. pudica.* [t. NL, der. L *mīmus* MIME; apparently so named from seeming mimicry of animal life]

mimosaceous (mĭm′ə sā′shəs, mī′mə-), *adj.* belonging to the *Mimosaceae,* or mimosa family of plants, usually treated as part of the larger family *Leguminosae.*

min., 1. mineralogical. **2.** mineralogy. **3.** minim. **4.** minimum. **5.** mining. **6.** minor. **7.** minute; minutes.

mina[1] (mī′nə), *n., pl.* **-nae** (-nē), **-nas.** an ancient unit of weight and value, equal to the sixtieth part of a talent. [t. L, t. Gk: m. *mnâ*; prob. of Babylonian orig.]

mina[2] (mī′nə), *n.* myna.

minacious (mĭ nā′shəs), *adj.* menacing; threatening. [f. s. L *minăciae* threats + -OUS] —**mina′ciously,** *adv.* —**mina′ciousness, minacity** (mĭ năs′ĭ tĭ), *n.*

Mina Hassan Tani (*Fr.* mē nȧ ȧ säɴ tȧ nē′). See **Kenitra.**

minaret (mĭn′ə rĕt′, mĭn′ə rĕt′), *n.* a lofty, often slender, tower or turret attached to a Muslim mosque, surrounded by or furnished with one or more balconies, from which the muezzin calls the people to prayer. [t. Sp.: m. *minarete,* t. Ar.: m. *manāra(t),* orig., lighthouse]

minatory (mĭn′ə tə rĭ, -trĭ), *adj.* menacing; threatening. Also, **minatorial** (mĭn′ə tô′rĭ əl). [t. LL: m. s. *minātōrius,* der. L *minārī* threaten] —**min′atorily,** *adv.*

minbar (mĭn′bä′), *n.* the high pulpit in a mosque.

mince (mĭns), *v.,* **minced, mincing,** *n.* —*v.t.* **1.** to cut or chop into very small pieces. **2.** to subdivide minutely, as land, a subject, etc. **3.** to soften or moderate (one's words, etc.) to a milder form. **4.** to speak of (matters) in polite or euphemistic terms. **5.** to perform or utter with affected elegance. —*v.i.* **6.** to walk or move with short, affectedly dainty steps. **7.** to act, behave, or speak with affected elegance. —*n.* **8.** minced meat. [ME *mynce(n),* t. OF: m. *mincier* make small, ult. der. L *minūtus* small. Cf. MINISH]

Minaret

mincemeat (mĭns′mēt′), *n.* **1.** a mixture composed of minced apples, suet (and sometimes meat), candied peel, etc., with raisins, currants, etc., for filling a pie (mince pie). **2.** minced meat. **3.** anything cut up very small. **4. make mincemeat of,** *Colloq.* assault and do harm to.

mince pie, a covered tart filled with mincemeat (def. 1).

mincer (mĭn′sə), *n.* one who or that which minces, esp. a machine for mincing meat.

Minch (mĭnch), *n.* a sea passage divided into the **North Minch** between the Outer Hebrides and mainland Scotland, and the **Little Minch** between the Outer Hebrides and Skye.

mincing (mĭn′sĭng), *adj.* **1.** affectedly nice or elegant, as the gait, behaviour, air, speech, etc. **2.** walking, acting, or speaking in an affectedly nice or elegant manner. —**min′cingly,** *adv.*

mind (mīnd), *n.* **1.** that which thinks, feels, and wills, exercises perception, judgement, reflection, etc., as in a human or other conscious being: *the processes of the mind.* **2.** *Psychol.* the psyche; the totality of conscious and unconscious activities of the organism. **3.** the intellect or understanding, as distinguished from the faculties of feeling and willing; the intelligence. **4.** a particular instance of the intellect or intelligence, as in a person. **5.** a person considered with reference to intellectual power: *the greatest minds of the time.* **6.** intellectual power or ability. **7.** reason, sanity, or sound mental condition: *to lose one's mind.* **8.** way of thinking and feeling, disposition, or temper: *many men, many minds.* **9.** opinion or sentiments: *to read someone's mind.* **10.** inclination or desire. **11.** purpose, intention, or will. **12.** psychic or spiritual being, as opposed to matter. **13.** a conscious or intelligent agency or being: *the doctrine of a mind pervading the universe.* **14.** remembrance or recollection: *to keep in mind.* **15.** *Rom. Cath. Ch.* commemoration (def. 2). **16.** Some special noun phrases are:

a piece of one's mind, 1. an uncomplimentary opinion. **2.** a reprimand or browbeating.

have a good (or **great**) **mind to,** to firmly intend to.

have half a mind to, to be almost decided to.

make up one's mind, to come to a decision.

presence of mind, alacrity in controlled reaction when faced with danger or difficulty.

put in mind, to cause to remember; remind.

to one's mind, in one's opinion or judgement.

—*v.t.* **17.** to pay attention to, heed, or obey (a person, advice, instructions, etc.). **18.** to apply oneself or attend to: *to mind one's own business.* **19.** to look after; take care of; tend: *to mind the baby.* **20.** to be careful, cautious, or wary concerning: *mind what you say.* **21.** to care about or feel concern at. **22.** (in negative and interrogative expressions) to feel disturbed or inconvenienced by; object to: *would you mind handing me that book?* **23.** to regard as concerning oneself or as mattering: *never mind what he does.* **24.** *Dial.* to perceive or notice. **25.** *Archaic or Dial.* to remember. **26.** *Archaic or Dial.* to remind. —*v.i.* **27.** to take notice, observe, or understand (chiefly in the imperative): *mind you, I think he's wrong.* **28.** to obey. **29.** to be careful or wary. **30.** to care, feel concern, or object (often in negative and interrogative expressions): *mind if I go?* **31.** to regard a thing as concerning oneself or as mattering: *never mind about them.* [ME *mind(e),* OE *gemynd* memory, thought, c. Goth. *gamunds* memory; akin to L *mens* mind]

—**Syn. 1.** MIND, INTELLECT, INTELLIGENCE refer to mental equipment or qualities. MIND is that part of man which thinks, feels, and wills, as contrasted with body: *his mind was capable* *of grasping the significance of the problem.* INTELLECT is reasoning power as distinguished from feeling; it is often used in a general sense to characterize high mental ability: *to appeal to the intellect, rather than the emotions.* INTELLIGENCE is ability to learn and to understand; it is also mental alertness or quickness of understanding: *a dog has more intelligence than many other animals.* **6.** MIND, BRAIN, BRAINS may refer to mental capacity. MIND is the philosophical and general term for the centre of mental activity, and is therefore used of intellectual powers: *a brilliant mind.* BRAIN is properly the physiological term for the organic structure which makes mental activity possible (*the brain is the centre of the nervous system*), but it is often applied, like MIND, to intellectual capacity: *a fertile brain.* The plural BRAINS is the anatomical word (*the brains of an animal used for food*) but, in popular usage, it is applied to intelligence (particularly of a shrewd, practical nature): *that takes brains.*

Mindanao (mĭn′də nou′), *n.* the second largest of the Philippine Islands, in the S part of the group. 4,427,012 pop. (1960); 36,537 sq. mi. See map under **Leyte.**

minded (mīn′dĭd), *adj.* **1.** having a certain kind of mind (usually used in combination): *strong-minded.* **2.** inclined or disposed.

Minden (*Ger.* mĭn′dən), *n.* a town in West Germany, in NE North Rhine-Westphalia. 51,200 (est. 1966).

minder (mīn′də), *n.* one whose occupation is to mind or tend something (usually used in combination): *machine-minder, baby-minder.*

mindful (mīnd′fəl), *adj.* attentive; careful (usually fol. by *of*). **—mind′fully,** *adv.* **—mind′fulness,** *n.*

mindless (mīnd′lĭs), *adj.* **1.** without intelligence; senseless. **2.** unmindful, careless, or heedless. **—mind′lessly,** *adv.* **—mind′lessness,** *n.*

Mindoro (mĭn dô′rō; *Sp.* mēn dō′rō), *n.* one of the Philippine Islands, in the central part of the group. 313,314 pop. (1960); 3922 sq. mi. See map under **Leyte.**

mind-reading (mīnd′rē′dĭng), *n.* reading or discerning of the thoughts in the minds of others, esp. by some apparently supernormal power. **—mind′-rea′der,** *n.*

mind's eye, the imagination.

mind-your-own-business (mīnd′yə rōn bĭz′nĭs), *n.* a small, much-cultivated urticaceous herb, *Helxine soleirolii,* a native of Mediterranean islands; mother-of-thousands.

Mindszenty (*Hung.* mĕnd′sĕn tē), *n.* **Joseph,** born 1892, Hungarian cardinal.

mine[1] (mīn), *pron.* **1.** possessive form of *I,* used predicatively or without a noun following. **2.** the person(s) or thing(s) belonging to me: *that book is mine, a friend of mine.* —*adj.* **3.** *Archaic.* my (used before a vowel or *h,* or after a noun): *mine eyes, lady mine.* [ME; OE *mīn,* poss. adj. and pron. of first person]

mine[2] (mīn), *n., v.,* **mined, mining.** —*n.* **1.** an excavation made in the earth for the purpose of getting out ores, precious stones, coal, etc. **2.** a place where such minerals may be obtained, either by excavation or by washing the soil. **3.** a deposit of such minerals, either under the ground or at its surface. **4.** an abounding source or store of anything: *this book is a mine of information.* **5.** a subterranean passage made to extend under an enemy's works or position, as for the purpose of securing access or of depositing explosives for blowing up the position. **6.** a device containing a large charge of explosive in a watertight casing floating on or moored beneath the surface of the water for the purpose of blowing up an enemy vessel which touches it or passes in close proximity to it. **7.** a similar device used on land; a landmine. —*v.i.* **8.** to dig in the earth for the purpose of extracting ores, coal, etc.; make a mine. **9.** to extract ores, etc., from mines. **10.** to make subterranean passages. **11.** to dig or lay mines, as in military operations. —*v.t.* **12.** to dig in (earth, etc.) in order to obtain ores, coal, etc. **13.** to extract (ores, coal, etc.) from a mine. **14.** to make subterranean passages in or under; burrow. **15.** to make (passages, etc.) by digging or burrowing. **16.** to dig away or remove the foundations of. **17.** to attack, ruin, or destroy by secret or slow methods. **18.** to dig or lay military mines under. [ME, t. OF, of Celtic orig.]

minefield (mīn′fēld′), *n. Mil., Naval.* an area on land or water throughout which mines have been laid.

mine-layer (mīn′lā′ə), *n.* a naval vessel with special equipment for laying mines in water.

miner (mī′nə), *n.* **1.** one who works in a mine, esp. a coalmine. **2.** *Obs.* one who digs or lays military mines.

mineral (mĭn′ə rəl, mĭn′rəl), *n.* **1.** a substance obtained by mining; ore. **2.** any of a class of substances occurring in nature, usually comprising inorganic substances (as quartz, felspar, etc.) of definite chemical composition and definite crystal structure, but sometimes taken to include aggregations of these substances (more correctly called rocks) and also certain natural products of organic origin, as asphalt, coal, etc. **3.** a substance neither animal nor vegetable. **4.** (*usually pl.*) mineral water. —*adj.* **5.** of the nature of a mineral; pertaining to minerals. **6.** impregnated with a mineral or minerals. **7.** neither animal nor vegetable; inorganic: *the mineral kingdom.* [late ME, t. ML: s. *minerālis,* der. *minera* mine, t. OF: m. *miniere,* der. *mine* MINE[2]]

mineral., **1.** mineralogical. **2.** mineralogy.

mineral caoutchouc, elaterite.

mineralize (mĭn′ə rə līz′, mĭn′rə-), *v.,* **-lized, -lizing.** —*v.t.* **1.** to convert into a mineral substance. **2.** to transform (a metal) into an ore. **3.** to impregnate or supply with mineral substances. —*v.i.* **4.** to collect and study mineral specimens, esp. of a particular region. Also, **mineralise.** **—min′eraliza′tion,** *n.* **—min′eraliz′er,** *n.*

mineral jelly, a gelatinous product made from petroleum, used to stabilize some explosives.

mineralogist (mĭn′ə răl′ə jĭst), *n.* a specialist in mineralogy.

mineralogy (mĭn′ə răl′ə jĭ), *n.* the science of minerals. **—mineralogical** (mĭn′ə rə lŏj′ĭ kl), *adj.* **—min′eralog′ically,** *adv.*

mineral oil, any of a class of oils of mineral origin, as petroleum, consisting of mixtures of hydrocarbons, and used as illuminants, fuels, etc., and in medicine.

mineral pitch, asphalt (bituminous substance):

mineral tar, bitumen of the consistency of tar; maltha.

mineral water, **1.** water containing dissolved mineral salts or gases, esp. such water for medicinal use. **2.** carbonated water. **3.** any non-alcoholic effervescent sweetened and flavoured drink, as ginger beer, lemonade, etc.

mineral wax, ozocerite.

mineral wool, an insulating material consisting of woolly fibres made from melted slag.

miner's inch, water-inch.

Minerva (mĭ nû′və), *n.* **1.** *Rom. Myth.* the goddess of wisdom, the arts, and war, identified with the Greek Athena. **2.** a woman of great wisdom or learning.

minestrone (mĭn′ĭ strō′nĭ; *It.* mē nė strō′nė), *n. Italian.* a soup containing vegetables, herbs, pasta, etc., in chicken or meat stock. [It., aug. of *minestra* soup, der. *minestrare,* g. L *ministrāre* MINISTER, v.]

minesweeper (mīn′swē′pə), *n. Naval.* a vessel or ship used for dragging a body of water in order to remove enemy mines.

minette (mĭ nĕt′), *n. Geol.* **1.** a lamprophyre comprised of biotite and orthoclase occurring in dykes associated with major intrusions. **2.** a phosphatic iron ore occurring in the Middle Jurassic of Lorraine and Luxembourg.

Ming (mĭng), *adj.* **1.** denoting or pertaining to the dynasty which ruled China from 1368 to 1644, under which art flourished and there were important revisions of Confucian philosophy. **2.** denoting the objects produced under the Ming dynasty, esp. the fine porcelain produced by the imperial factory before 1620. —*n.* **3.** the Ming dynasty.

mingle (mĭng′gl), *v.,* **-gled, -gling.** —*v.i.* **1.** to become mixed, blended, or united. **2.** to associate or mix in company. **3.** to take part with others; participate. —*v.t.* **4.** to mix or combine; put together in a mixture; blend. **5.** to unite, join, or conjoin: *joy mingled with pain.* **6.** to associate in company. **7.** to form by mixing; compound; concoct. [ME *myngle, mengle,* freq. of *menge(n),* OE *mengan*] **—min′gler,** *n.* **—Syn. 4.** See **mix, mixed.**

mingy (mĭn′jĭ), *adj. Colloq.* mean and stingy. [b. M(EAN[2]) + (ST)INGY]

Minho (*Port.* mē′nyōō), *n.* a river flowing from NW Spain along part of the N boundary of Portugal into the Atlantic. 171 mi. Spanish, **Miño.**

mini (mĭn′ĭ), *Colloq.* —*n.* **1.** something small in size or dimension, as a skirt or motor vehicle. —*adj.* **2.** small; miniature.

mini-, a word element meaning 'small' or 'miniature', as in *miniskirt.* [abbrev. of MINIATURE]

miniature (mĭn′yə chə), *n.* **1.** a representation or image of anything on a very small scale. **2.** greatly reduced or abridged form. **3.** a very small painting, esp. a portrait, on ivory, vellum, or the like. **4.** the art of executing such painting. **5.** an illumination, as in manuscripts. —*adj.* **6.** on a very small scale; reduced. [t. It.: m. *miniatura,* der. L *miniāre* rubricate]

miniature camera, *Photog.* a small camera using film of 35 mm. width or less.

miniaturize (mĭn′yə chə rīz′), *v.t.,* **-rized, -rizing.** to reduce in size; to produce an exact working copy in reduced scale. Also, **miniaturise.** [f. MINIATUR(E) + -IZE] **—min′iaturiza′tion,** *n.*

minibus (mĭn′ĭ bŭs′), *n.* a motor vehicle for carrying between five and ten passengers.

minicab (mĭn′ĭ kăb′), *n.* a small hire car, orig. plying for hire.

minify (mĭn′ĭ fī′), *v.t.,* **-fied, -fying.** **1.** to make less. **2.** to minimize. [f. L *min(us)* less + -(I)FY]

minikin (mĭn′ĭ kĭn), *n.* **1.** a person or object that is delicate or diminutive. **2.** *Obs.* a size of printing type equivalent to 3 point. *—adj.* **3.** delicate; dainty; mincing. [t. MD: m. *minnekijn*, dim. of *minne* love. See -KIN]

minim (mĭn′ĭm), *n.* **1.** the smallest unit of liquid measure, the sixtieth part of a fluid drachm, or about a drop. **2.** *Music.* a note, formerly the shortest in use, but now equivalent in time value to one half of a semibreve. See illus. under **note.** **3.** the least quantity, or a jot, of anything. **4.** something very small or insignificant. **5.** (*cap.*) a member of a mendicant religious order founded in the 15th century by St Francis of Paula. *—adj.* **6.** smallest; very small. [ME, t. L: s. *minimus* least, smallest, superl. of *minor* MINOR]

minimal (mĭn′ĭ məl), *adj.* **1.** pertaining to or being a minimum. **2.** least possible. **3.** smallest; very small. [f. s. L *minimus* least + -AL[1]]

Minimalist (mĭn′ĭ mə lĭst), *n.* a member of a less radical group of socialists, as of a faction of the Russian Social Revolutionary Party. [f. MINIMAL + -IST]

minimize (mĭn′ĭ mīz′), *v.t.*, **-mized, -mizing.** **1.** to reduce to the smallest possible amount or degree. **2.** to represent at the lowest possible estimate; to belittle. Also, **minimise.** —**min′imiza′tion,** *n.* —**min′imiz′er,** *n.*

minimum (mĭn′ĭ məm), *n., pl.* **-mums, -ma** (-mə), *adj.* *—n.* **1.** the least quantity or amount possible, assignable, allowable, etc. **2.** the lowest amount, value, or degree attained or recorded (opposed to *maximum*). **3.** *Maths.* a value of a function at a certain point which is less than or equal to the value attained at nearby points. *—adj.* **4.** that is a minimum. **5.** least possible. **6.** lowest: *a minimum rate.* **7.** pertaining to a minimum or minimums. [t. L, neut. of *minimus.* See MINIM]

minimum wage, the lowest wage, fixed by agreement with a union or by legal authority, payable to employees of a particular group.

minimus (mĭn′ĭ məs), *n.* **1.** a being that is the smallest or least significant. **2.** *Anat.* the little finger or little toe. *—adj.* **3.** youngest; in boys' schools, designating the youngest of three brothers.

mining (mī′nĭng), *n.* **1.** the action, process, or industry of extracting ores, etc., from mines. **2.** the action of laying explosive mines.

minion (mĭn′yən), *n.* **1.** a servile or base favourite of a prince or any patron. **2.** any favourite. **3.** a catamite. **4.** *Print.* a size of type (7 point). *—adj.* **5.** dainty; elegant; trim; pretty. [t. F: m. *mignon* MIGNON]

minish (mĭn′ĭsh), *v.t., v.i.* *Archaic.* to diminish or lessen. [ME *mynyssh(en)*, t. OF: m. *menuisier* make small, g. Rom. *minūtiāre*, der. L *minūtus* MINUTE[2]]

miniskirt (mĭn′ĭ skûrt′), *n.* a very short skirt.

minister (mĭn′ĭs tə), *n.* **1.** one authorized to conduct religious worship; a clergyman; a pastor. **2.** one authorized to administer sacraments, as at mass. **3.** one appointed by (or under the authority of) the sovereign or executive head of a government to some high office of state, esp. to that of head of an administrative department: *the Minister of Labour.* **4.** a diplomatic representative accredited by one government to another ranking below an ambassador, esp. an envoy. See **envoy**[1]. **5.** one acting as the agent or instrument of another. *—v.t.* **6.** to administer or apply. **7.** *Archaic.* to furnish; supply. *—v.i.* **8.** to give service, care, or aid; attend, as to wants, necessities, etc. **9.** to contribute, as to comfort, happiness, etc. [t. L: servant; r. ME *menistre*, t. OF]

ministerial (mĭn′ĭs tĭə′rĭ əl), *adj.* **1.** pertaining to the ministry of religion, or to a minister or clergyman. **2.** pertaining to a ministry or minister of state. **3.** pertaining to or invested with delegated executive authority. **4.** of ministry or service. **5.** instrumental. —**min′iste′rially,** *adv.*

ministerialist (mĭn′ĭs tĭə′rĭ ə lĭst), *n.* *Politics. Obs.* a supporter of the ministry in office.

minister plenipotentiary, *pl.* **ministers plenipotentiary.** plenipotentiary.

minister resident, *pl.* **ministers resident.** a diplomatic representative in a minor country, ranking below an ambassador.

minister without portfolio, *pl.* **ministers without portfolio.** a member of a ministry with no specific departmental responsibilities.

ministrant (mĭn′ĭ strənt), *adj.* **1.** ministering. *—n.* **2.** one who ministers. [t. L: s. *ministrans*, ppr.]

ministration (mĭn′ĭ strā′shən), *n.* **1.** the act of ministering care, aid, religious service, etc. **2.** an instance of it. —**ministrative** (mĭn′ĭ strə tĭv), *adj.*

ministry (mĭn′ĭ strĭ), *n., pl.* **-tries.** **1.** the service, functions, or profession of a minister of religion. **2.** the body or class of ministers of religion; the clergy. **3.** the service, function, or office of a minister of state. **4.** the policy-forming executive officials in a country taken collectively. **5.** any of the administrative departments of state in certain countries. **6.** the building which houses such a department. **7.** the term of office of a minister. **8.** the act of ministering; ministration; service. [ME *ministerie*, t. L: m. *ministerium* office, service]

minitrack (mĭn′ĭ trăk′), *n.* the procedure of tracking the orbit of an artificial satellite and of recording its signals by telemetry.

minium (mĭn′ĭ əm), *n.* red lead, Pb_3O_4. [t. L: native cinnabar, red lead]

miniver (mĭn′ĭ və), *n.* (in medieval times) a fur of white or spotted white and grey used for linings or trimmings. [ME *meniver*, t. OF: m. *menu vair* small vair. See MENU, VAIR]

mink (mĭngk), *n., pl.* **minks,** (*esp. collectively*) **mink.** **1.** a semi-aquatic weasel-like animal of the genus *Mustela*, esp. the North American *M. vison.* **2.** the valuable fur of this animal, brownish with lustrous outside hairs and thick, soft undercoat. [appar. t. Sw.: m. *mänk*]

Mink, *Mustela vison* (Total length 2 ft, tail ab. 8 in.)

Minkowski (*Ger.* mĭng kŏf′skĭ), *n.* **Hermann** (*Ger.* hĕr′män), 1864–1909, German mathematician.

Minkowski world, *Maths.* a four-dimensional space in which the fourth coordinate is time and in which a single element is presented as a point. Also, **Minkowski universe.**

Minn., Minnesota.

Minneapolis (mĭn′ĭ ăp′ə lĭs), *n.* a city in the U.S., in SE Minnesota, on the Mississippi. 482,872 (1960).

minnesinger (mĭn′ĭ sĭng′ə), *n.* one of a class of German lyric poets and singers of the 12th, 13th, and 14th centuries. [t. G: love singer]

Minnesota (mĭn′ĭ sō′tə), *n.* a state in the N central United States. 3,413,864 pop. (1960); 84,068 sq. mi. *Cap.:* St Paul. *Abbrev.:* Minn. —**Min′neso′tan,** *adj., n.*

minnow (mĭn′ō), *n., pl.* **-nows,** (*esp. collectively*) **-now.** **1.** a small European cyprinoid fish, *Phoxinus phoxinus.* **2.** any of various other small silvery fishes. **3.** *U.S.* any fish of the family *Cyprinidae*, mostly small but including some large species, as the carp. **4.** an unimportant, insignificant person or thing. [ME *men(a)we*, late OE *myne* (for *mynu*), c. OHG *munewa* kind of fish]

Miño (*Sp.* mē′nyō), *n.* Spanish name of **Minho.**

Minoan (mĭ nō′ən), *adj.* **1.** of or pertaining to the ancient advanced civilization of Crete, dating (approximately) from 3000 to 1100 B.C. *—adj.* **2.** an inhabitant of ancient Crete. [f. MINO(s) + -AN]

minor (mī′nə), *adj.* **1.** lesser, as in size, extent, or importance, or being the lesser of two: *a minor share, minor faults.* **2.** under legal age. **3.** younger; junior; in boys' schools denoting the younger of two brothers, the second of three, or the third of four. **4.** of or pertaining to the minority. **5.** *Logic.* less broad or extensive: **a. minor term,** (in a syllogism) the term that is the subject of the conclusion. **b. minor premise,** the premise that contains the minor term. **6.** *Music.* **a.** (of an interval) smaller by a semitone than the corresponding major interval. **b.** (of a chord) having a minor third between the root and the note next above it. **7.** *U.S.* denoting or pertaining to educational minors: *a minor subject.* *—n.* **8.** a person under legal age. **9.** one of inferior rank or importance in a specified class. **10.** *Music.* a minor interval, chord, scale, etc. **11.** *U.S.* **a.** a subject or a course of study pursued by a student, esp. a candidate for a degree, subordinately or supplementarily to a major or principal subject or course. **b.** a subject for which less credit than a major is granted in colleges or occasionally in high school. **12.** (*cap.*) a Minorite. *—v.i.* **13.** *U.S.* to pursue a minor or subordinate subject or course of study (fol. by *in*). [t. L: less, smaller, inferior, younger, a compar. form; r. ME *menour*, t. OF] **—Syn.** **1.** smaller, inferior, secondary. **—Ant.** **1.** major.

Minorca (mĭ nô′kə), *n.* **1.** Spanish, **Menorca.** one of the Balearic Islands, in the W Mediterranean. 42,231 pop. (1960); 271 sq. mi. **2.** (*l.c.*) one of a Mediterranean breed of white-skinned domestic fowls of moderate size, notable for prolific laying. —**Minor′can,** *adj., n.*

Minorite (mī′nə rīt′), *n.* a Franciscan friar.

minority (mī nŏ′rĭ tĭ, mĭ-), *n., pl.* **-ties,** *adj.* *—n.* **1.** the smaller part or number; a number forming less than half the whole. **2.** a smaller party or group opposed to a majority, as in voting or other action. **3.** a group having in common ethnic, religious, or other ties different from those of the majority of the inhabitants of a country. **4.** the state or period of being a minor or under legal age. —*adj.* **5.** of or pertaining to a minority.

minor key, *Music.* a key based on a minor scale.

minor order, *Rom. Cath. Ch.* See **order** (def. 15).

minor planet, *Astron.* an asteroid.

Minor Prophets. See **prophet** (def. 4c).

minor scale, *Music.* a scale whose third tone forms a minor third with the root. See illus. under **scale.**

minor suit, *Bridge.* diamonds or clubs.

minor third, *Music.* an interval of three semitones.

Minos (mī′nŏs), *n. Gk Myth.* son of Zeus, and king and lawgiver of Crete: after death, a judge in the lower world. Cf. **Aeacus, Rhadamanthys.**

Minotaur (mĭn′ə tô′), *n. Gk Myth.* a mythical monster, with the head of a bull and body of a man, confined in the Cretan labyrinth and fed with human flesh. It was killed by Theseus, with the help of Ariadne. [t. L: s. *Minōtaurus,* t. Gk: m. *Mīnōtauros,* f. *Mīnō(s)* MINOS + *taûros* bull]

Minsk (*Russ.* mēnsk), *n.* a city in the W Soviet Union in Europe: capital of the White Russian Republic. 717,000 (est. 1965).

minster (mĭn′stə), *n.* **1.** a church actually or originally connected with a monastic establishment. **2.** any large or important church, as a cathedral. [ME and OE *mynster,* c. G *Münster,* of doubtful orig. Cf. LL *monastērium* MONASTERY]

minstrel (mĭn′strəl), *n.* **1.** one of a class of medieval musicians who sang or recited to the accompaniment of instruments. **2.** *Poetic.* any musician, singer, or poet. **3.** one of a troupe of comedians, usually white men made up as Negroes, presenting songs, jokes, etc. [ME *menestral, minstral,* t. OF: m. *menestrel,* orig., servant, g. LL *ministeriālis* ministerial]

minstrelsy (mĭn′strəl sĭ), *n., pl.* **-sies.** **1.** the art or practice of a minstrel. **2.** minstrels' songs, ballads, etc.: *a collection of Scottish minstrelsy.*

M. Inst. T., Member of the Institute of Transport.

mint[1] (mĭnt), *n.* **1.** any plant of the labiate genus *Mentha,* comprising aromatic herbs with opposite leaves and small verticillate flowers, as the spearmint, the peppermint, and the horsemint. **2.** a soft or hard confection flavoured with peppermint or other similar flavouring. —*adj.* **3.** flavoured with or containing mint: *mint sauce.* [ME and OE *minte* (c. OHG *minza*), t. L: m. *ment(h)a,* t. Gk: m. *mínthē*]

mint[2] (mĭnt), *n.* **1.** a place where money is coined by public authority. **2.** a vast amount, esp. of money. —*adj.* **3.** *Philately.* (of a stamp) as issued by the Post Office. **4.** unused. —*v.t.* **5.** to make (coins) by stamping metal. **6.** to coin (money). **7.** to make or fabricate as if by coining: *mint words.* [ME *mynt,* OE *mynet* coin (c. G *Münze*), t. L: m. *monēta* mint, MONEY] —**mint′er,** *n.*

mint[3] (mĭnt), *Archaic or Dial.* —*v.i., v.t.* **1.** to intend. —*n.* **2.** intention. [ME *minten,* OE *gemyntan*; akin to MIND]

mintage (mĭn′tĭj), *n.* **1.** the act or process of minting. **2.** the product or result of minting; coinage. **3.** the charge for or cost of minting or coining. **4.** the output of a mint. **5.** a stamp or character impressed.

mint-bush (mĭnt′bo͝osh′), *n.* any of several strongly scented, evergreen labiate shrubs of the genus *Prostanthera,* natives of Australia and Tasmania.

mint julep, *U.S.* a long drink made of bourbon whiskey, sugar, crushed ice, and sprigs of fresh mint.

minuend (mĭn′yo͞o ĕnd′), *n. Maths.* the number from which another (the subtrahend) is to be subtracted. [t. L: s. *minuendus,* ger. of *minuere* make smaller]

minuet (mĭn′yo͞o ĕt′), *n.* **1.** a slow stately dance of French origin. **2.** a piece of music for such a dance or in its rhythm. [t. F: m. *menuet,* orig. adj., very small (with reference to the small steps taken in the dance), dim. of *menu* small. See MENU]

Minuit (mĭn′yo͞o ĭt), *n.* **Peter,** *c.* 1580–1638, first governor of the Dutch colony of New Netherland, in North America.

minus (mī′nəs), *prep.* **1.** less by the subtraction of; decreased by: *ten minus six.* **2.** lacking or without: *a book minus its titlepage.* —*adj.* **3.** involving or denoting subtraction: *the minus sign.* **4.** algebraically negative: *a minus quantity.* **5.** *Colloq.* lacking: *the profits were minus.* **6.** *Bot.* (in heterothallic fungi) designating, in the absence of morphological differentiation, one of the two strains or mycella which must unite in the sexual process. —*n.* **7.** the minus sign (−). **8.** a minus quantity. **9.** a deficiency or loss. [t. L, adj., neut. of *minor* MINOR]

minuscule (mĭn′ə sko͞ol′), *adj.* **1.** small, as letters not capital or uncial. **2.** written in such letters (opposed to *majuscule*). **3.** very small; tiny. —*n.* **4.** a minuscule letter. **5.** a small cursive script developed in the 7th century from the uncial, which it afterwards superseded. [t. L: m. s. *minusculus* rather small, dim. of *minor* MINOR] —**minuscular** (mĭ nŭs′kyo͞o lə), *adj.*

minus sign, *Maths.* the symbol (−) denoting subtraction or a minus quantity.

minute[1] (mĭn′ĭt), *n., v.,* **-uted, -uting,** *adj.* —*n.* **1.** the sixtieth part of an hour; sixty seconds. **2.** an indefinitely short space of time: *wait a minute.* **3.** a point of time, an instant, or moment: *come here this minute!* **4.** a rough draft, as of a document. **5.** a written summary, note, or memorandum. **6.** (*pl.*) the official record of the proceedings at a meeting of a society, board, committee, council, or other body. **7.** *Geom., etc.* the sixtieth part of a degree, or sixty seconds (often represented by the sign ′), as 12°10′ (twelve degrees and ten minutes). **8. up to the minute,** very modern; latest; most up to date. —*v.t.* **9.** to time exactly, as movements, speed, etc. **10.** to make a draft of (a document, etc.). **11.** to record (something) in a memorandum; note down. **12.** to enter in the minutes of a society or other body. —*adj.* **13.** prepared in a very short time: *minute steak.* [ME, t. OF, t. ML: m. s. *minūta* small part or division, prop. fem. of L *minūtus* MINUTE[2]]

—**Syn.** **2.** MINUTE, INSTANT, MOMENT refer to infinitesimal amounts of time. A MINUTE, properly denoting sixty seconds, is often used loosely for any very short space of time (and may be interchangeable with *second*): *just a minute.* An INSTANT is practically a point in time, with no duration, though it is also used to mean a perceptible amount of time: *not an instant's delay.* MOMENT denotes much the same as INSTANT, though with a somewhat greater sense of duration (but somewhat less than MINUTE): *it will take a moment.*

minute[2] (mī nyo͞ot′), *adj.,* **-nuter, -nutest.** **1.** extremely small, as in size, amount, extent, or degree: *minute differences.* **2.** of very small scope or individual importance: *minute particulars of a case.* **3.** attentive to or concerned with even very small details or particulars: *a minute observer or report.* [ME, t. L: m. s. *minūtus,* pp., made smaller] —**minute′ness,** *n.* —**Syn. 1.** See **little.**

minute gun (mĭn′ĭt), (formerly) a gun fired at intervals of a minute, as in token of mourning or of distress.

minute hand (mĭn′ĭt), the hand that indicates the minutes on a clock or watch.

minutely[1] (mĭn′ĭt lĭ), *adj.* **1.** occurring every minute. —*adv.* **2.** every minute; minute by minute. [f. MINUTE[1] + -LY]

minutely[2] (mī nyo͞ot′lĭ), *adv.* in a minute manner, form, or degree; in minute detail. [f. MINUTE[2] + -LY]

minuteman (mĭn′ĭt măn′), *n., pl.* **-men** (-mĕn′). one of a group of American militiamen just before and during the War of Independence who held themselves in readiness for instant military service.

minutia (mĭ nyo͞o′shĭ ə), *n., pl.* **-tiae** (-shĭ ē′). (*usually pl.*) a small or trivial detail; a trifling circumstance or matter. [t. L: smallness]

minx (mĭngks), *n.* a pert, impudent, or flirtatious girl. [? alter. of *minikins,* f. MINIKIN + hypocoristic *-s*]

Miocene (mī′ə sēn′), *Geol.* —*adj.* **1.** pertaining to a series of the Tertiary period or system. —*n.* **2.** a division of the Tertiary following Oligocene and preceding Pliocene. [f. *mio-* (repr. Gk *meiōn* less) + -CENE]

miosis (mī ō′sĭs), *n. Pathol.* excessive contraction of the pupil of the eye, as the result of disease, drugs, or the like. Also, **myosis.** [t. NL, f. Gk: m. s. *mýein* close (the eyes) + *-ōsis* -OSIS]

miotic (mī ŏt′ĭk), *adj.* **1.** pertaining to, producing, or suffering from miosis. —*n.* **2.** a miotic drug. Also, **myotic.**

Miquelon (mē′kə lŏn′; *Fr.* mē klôɴ′), *n.* See **St Pierre and Miquelon.**

mir (*Russ.* mēr), *n. Russian.* a Russian village commune.

Mirabeau (mĭ′rə bō′; *Fr.* mē rà bō′), *n.* **Honoré Gabriel Victor Riqueti** (*Fr.* ō nō rĕ gà brē ĕl vēk tŏr rēk tē′), **Comte de,** 1749–91, French revolutionary statesman and orator.

mirabile dictu (mĭ răb′ĭ lā dĭk′to͞o), *Latin.* strange to say; marvellous to relate.

mirabilia (mĭ′rə bĭl′ĭ ə), *n.pl. Latin.* marvels; miracles.

miracidium (mĭ′rə sĭd′ĭ əm), *n., pl.* **-cidia** (-sĭd′ĭ ə). the larva that hatches from the egg of a trematode worm or fluke. —**mi′racid′ial,** *adj.*

miracle (mĭ′rə kl), *n.* **1.** an effect in the physical world which surpasses all known human or natural powers and is therefore ascribed to supernatural agency. **2.** a wonderful thing; a marvel. **3.** a wonderful or surpassing example of some quality. **4.** a miracle play. [ME, t. OF, t. L: m. s. *mīrāculum*]

miracle play, a medieval dramatic form dealing with religious subjects such as biblical stories or saints' lives, usually presented in a series or cycle by the craft guilds.

miraculous (mĭ răk′yo͝o ləs), *adj.* **1.** of the nature of a miracle; marvellous. **2.** performed by or involving a supernatural power: *a miraculous cure.* **3.** having power to work miracles or wonders: *miraculous drugs.* [t. ML: m. s. *mīrāculōsus,* der. L *mīrāculum* miracle] —**mirac′ulously,** *adv.* —**mirac′ulousness,** *n.*

—**Syn.** 2. MIRACULOUS, PRETERNATURAL, SUPERNATURAL refer to that which seems to transcend the laws of nature. MIRACULOUS usually refers to an individual event which apparently contravenes known laws governing the universe: *a miraculous answer,* or *success.* PRETERNATURAL suggests the possession of supernormal gifts or qualities: *dogs have a preternatural sense of smell, bats have a sense of hearing that is preternatural.* SUPERNATURAL suggests divine or superhuman properties: *supernatural aid in battle.*

Miraflores (*Sp.* mē rä flō′rĕs), *n.pl.* the locks on the Panama Canal, near the Pacific entrance.

mirage (mĭ′räzh), *n.* **1.** an optical illusion, due to atmospheric conditions, by which reflected images of distant objects are seen, often inverted. **2.** something illusory or unreal. [t. F, der. (*se*) *mirer* look at (oneself) in a mirror, see reflected, g. VL *mīrāre.* See MIRROR, ADMIRE]

mire (mī′ə), *n., v.,* **mired, miring.** —*n.* **1.** a piece of wet, swampy ground. **2.** ground of this kind; wet, slimy soil of some depth, or deep mud. —*v.t.* **3.** to plunge and fix in mire; cause to stick fast in mire. **4.** to involve in difficulties. **5.** to soil with mire or filth; bespatter with mire. —*v.i.* **6.** to sink in mire; stick in mud. [ME *myre,* t. Scand.; cf. Icel. *mȳrr*]

mirepoix (mĭə pwä′; *Fr.* mĕr pwȧ′), *n.* a mixture of carrots, celery, onion, etc., cut into large pieces, fried, and used as a bed on which to braise meat. [after the Duke of *Mirepoix,* 18th-century French diplomat]

mirk (mûk), *n., adj.* murk.

mirky (mû′kĭ), *adj.,* **-kier, -kiest.** murky.

Miró (*Sp.* mē rō′), *n.* **1. Gabriel** (*Sp.* gä bryĕl′), 1879–1930, Spanish poet. **2. Joan** (*Sp.* KHō än′), born 1893, Spanish painter.

mirror (mĭ′rə), *n.* **1.** a reflecting surface, originally polished metal, now usually glass with a metallic or amalgam backing; a looking glass. **2.** such a surface set into an ornamental frame, esp. one with a handle, used chiefly by women. **3.** any reflecting surface, as that of calm water. **4.** *Optics.* a surface (plane, concave, or convex) for reflecting rays of light; a speculum. **5.** something that gives a faithful reflection or true picture of something else. **6.** a pattern for imitation; exemplar. **7.** *Archaic.* a glass, crystal, or the like used by magicians, etc. —*v.t.* **8.** to reflect in or as in a mirror, or as a mirror does. [ME *mirour,* t. OF, der. ML *mīrāre* wonder at, admire, r. L *mīrārī*]

mirror carp, a carp, with reference to its large, shiny scales.

mirror image, 1. the image of an object as viewed in a mirror. **2.** an object reversed in such a way that it bears the same relationship to another object as a right hand bears to a left hand.

mirror writing, backward writing which forms a mirror image of normal writing.

mirth (mûth), *n.* **1.** rejoicing; joyous gaiety; festive jollity. **2.** humorous amusement, as at something ludicrous, or laughter excited by it. [ME; OE *myr(g)th, myrigth,* der. *myrige* MERRY. See -TH[1]]

—**Syn.** 2. MIRTH, GLEE, HILARITY, MERRIMENT refer to the gaiety characterizing people who are enjoying the companionship of others. MIRTH suggests spontaneous amusement or gaiety, manifested briefly in laughter: *uncontrolled outbursts of mirth.* GLEE suggests an effervescence of high spirits or exultation, often manifested in playful or ecstatic gestures; it may apply also to a malicious rejoicing over mishaps to others: *glee over the failure of a rival.* HILARITY implies noisy and boisterous mirth, often exceeding the limits of reason or propriety: *hilarity aroused by practical jokes.* MERRIMENT suggests fun, good spirits, and good nature rather than the kind of wit and sometimes artificial funmaking which cause hilarity: *the house resounded with music and sounds of merriment.* —**Ant.** 1. gloom.

mirthful (mûth′fəl), *adj.* **1.** full of mirth; joyous; jolly; laughingly gay or amused. **2.** affording mirth; amusing. —**mirth′fully,** *adv.* —**mirth′fulness,** *n.*

mirthless (mûth′lĭs), *adj.* without mirth; joyless; gloomy. —**mirth′lessly,** *adv.* —**mirth′lessness,** *n.*

miry (mī′ə rĭ), *adj.,* **-rier, -riest. 1.** of the nature of mire; swampy: *miry ground.* **2.** abounding in mire; muddy. **3.** covered or bespattered with mire. **4.** dirty; filthy. —**mir′iness,** *n.*

mirza (mû′zə; *Pers.* mĕr zä′), *n.* (in Persia) **1.** a royal prince (as a title, placed after the name). **2.** a title of honour for men (prefixed to the name). [t. Pers., apocopated var. of *mīrzād,* f. *mīr* prince (t. Ar.: m. *amīr* EMIR) + *zād* born]

Mirzapur (mû′zə po͝oə′), *n.* a town in India, in SE Uttar Pradesh. 100,097 (1961).

mis-[1], a prefix applied to various parts of speech, meaning 'ill', 'mistaken', 'wrong', or simply negating, as in *mistrial, misprint, mistrust.* [ME and OE *mis(s)-,* c. G *miss-* (see MISS[1], v.); often r. ME *mes-,* t. OF, g. L *minus* (see MINUS)]

mis-[2], var. of **miso-,** before some vowels, as in *misanthrope.*

misaddress (mĭs′ə drĕs′), *v.t.* to address wrongly or mistakenly.

misadventure (mĭs′əd vĕn′chə), *n.* **1.** a piece of ill fortune; a mishap. **2.** ill fortune. **3.** *Law.* an accident, as where a man doing a lawful act, without any intention of hurt, kills another.

misadvise (mĭs′əd vīz′), *v.t.,* **-vised, -vising.** to advise wrongly.

misalliance (mĭs′ə lī′əns), *n.* an improper alliance or association, esp. in marriage; a mésalliance. [half adoption, half trans. of F *mésalliance*]

misally (mĭs′ə lī′), *v.t.,* **-lied, -lying.** to ally improperly or unsuitably.

misanthrope (mĭz′ən thrōp′), *n.* a hater of mankind. Also, **misanthropist** (mĭ zăn′thrə pĭst). [t. Gk: m. s. *misánthrōpos* hating mankind]

misanthropic (mĭz′ən thrŏp′ĭk), *adj.* **1.** of, pertaining to, or characteristic of a misanthrope. **2.** having the character of, or resembling, a misanthrope. Also, **mis′anthrop′ical.** —**mis′anthrop′ically,** *adv.*

misanthropy (mĭ zăn′thrə pĭ), *n.* hatred, dislike, or distrust of mankind.

misapplied (mĭs′ə plīd′), *adj.* mistakenly applied; used wrongly.

misapply (mĭs′ə plī′), *v.t.,* **-plied, -plying.** to make a wrong application or use of. —**misapplication** (mĭs′-ăp′lĭ kā′shən), *n.*

misapprehend (mĭs′ăp′rĭ hĕnd′), *v.t.* to misunderstand. —**mis′ap′prehen′sive,** *adj.* —**mis′ap′prehen′sively,** *adv.* —**mis′ap′prehen′siveness,** *n.*

misapprehension (mĭs′ăp′rĭ hĕn′shən), *n.* misunderstanding.

misappropriate (mĭs′ə prō′prĭ āt′), *v.t.,* **-ated, -ating. 1.** to put to a wrong use. **2.** to apply wrongfully or dishonestly to one's own use, as funds entrusted to one. —**mis′appro′pria′tion,** *n.*

misarrange (mĭs′ə rānj′), *v.t.,* **-ranged, -ranging.** to arrange wrongly. —**mis′arrange′ment,** *n.*

misbecome (mĭs′bĭ kŭm′), *v.t.,* **-came, -come, -coming.** to be unsuitable, unbecoming, or unfit for.

misbegotten (mĭs′bĭ gŏt′n), *adj.* unlawfully or irregularly begotten; illegitimate. Also, **misbegot.**

misbehave (mĭs′bĭ hāv′), *v.t., v.i.,* **-haved, -having.** to behave badly. —**mis′beha′viour,** *n.*

misbelief (mĭs′bĭ lēf′), *n.* **1.** erroneous belief; false opinion. **2.** erroneous or unorthodox religious belief.

misbelieve (mĭs′bĭ lēv′), *v.,* **-lieved, -lieving.** *Obs.* —*v.i.* **1.** to believe wrongly; hold an erroneous belief. —*v.t.* **2.** to disbelieve; doubt. —**mis′believ′er,** *n.*

misbestow (mĭs′bĭ stō′), *v.t.* to bestow improperly.

misc., 1. miscellaneous. **2.** miscellany.

miscalculate (mĭs′kăl′kyo͝o lāt′), *v.t., v.i.,* **-lated, -lating.** to calculate wrongly. —**mis′cal′cula′tion,** *n.*

miscall (mĭs′kôl′), *v.t.* **1.** to call by a wrong name. **2.** *Bridge, etc.* to call incorrectly. **3.** *Dial.* to call by a bad name; abuse; revile; malign.

miscarriage (mĭs kă′rĭj), *n.* **1.** failure to attain the right or desired result: *a miscarriage of justice.* **2.** a transmission of goods not in accordance with the contract of shipment. **3.** failure of a letter, etc., to reach its destination. **4.** premature expulsion of a foetus from the uterus, esp. before it is viable.

miscarry (mĭs kă′rĭ), *v.i.,* **-ried, -rying. 1.** to fail to attain the right end; be unsuccessful. **2.** to go astray or be lost in transit, as a letter. **3.** to have a miscarriage.

miscast (mĭs′käst′), *v.t.,* **-cast, -casting. 1.** *Theat.* to allot an unsuitable part in a play to (an actor), or to select an unsuitable actor or unsuitable actors for (a part or play). **2.** *Metall.* to cast (metal) badly or into a faulty shape.

miscegenation (mĭs′ĭ jĭ nā′shən), *n.* **1.** mixture of races by sexual union. **2.** interbreeding between different races. [f. L *miscē(re)* mix + L *gen(us)* race + -ATION] —**mis′cegenet′ic,** *adj.*

miscellanea (mĭs′ə lā′nyə), *n.pl.* a miscellaneous collection, esp. of literary compositions. [t. L, neut. pl. of *miscellāneus* MISCELLANEOUS]

miscellaneous (mĭs′ə lā′nyəs), *adj.* **1.** consisting of members or elements of different kinds: *miscellaneous volumes.* **2.** of mixed character. **3.** having various qualities or aspects; dealing with various subjects. [t. L: m. *miscellāneus,* der. *miscellus* mixed] —**mis′cella′neously,** *adv.* —**mis′cella′neousness,** *n.*

—**Syn.** 1. MISCELLANEOUS, INDISCRIMINATE, PROMISCUOUS refer to mixture and lack of order, and may imply lack of discernment or taste. MISCELLANEOUS emphasizes the idea of the mixture of things of different kinds or natures: *a miscellaneous assortment of furniture.* INDISCRIMINATE emphasizes lack of discrimination in choice (and consequent confusion): *indiscriminate praise.* PROMISCUOUS is even stronger than INDISCRIMINATE in its emphasis on complete absence of discrimination: *promiscuous in his friendships.*

miscellany (mĭ sĕl′ə nĭ), *n., pl.* **-nies. 1.** a miscellaneous collection of literary compositions or pieces by several authors, dealing with various topics, assembled in a volume or book. **2.** (*often pl.*) a miscellaneous collection of articles or entries, as in a book. [Anglicized var. of MISCELLANEA]

mischance (mĭs chäns′), *n.* ill luck; a mishap or misfortune. [ME *meschance,* t. OF: m. *mescheance.* See MIS-¹, CHANCE]

mischief (mĭs′chĭf), *n.* **1.** conduct such as to tease or cause playfully petty annoyance. **2.** a tendency or disposition to tease or vex. **3.** teasing, vexations, or annoying action. **4.** harm or trouble, esp. as due to an agent or cause. **5.** an injury caused by a person or other agent, or an evil due to some cause. **6.** a cause or source of harm, evil, or annoyance. **7.** *Obs.* the devil. [ME *meschief,* t. OF, der. *meschever* succeed ill, f. *mes-* MIS- + *chever* come to an end, der. *chef* head, end (see CHIEF)] **—Syn. 4.** See **damage.**

mischief-maker (mĭs′chĭf mā′kə), *n.* one who makes mischief; one who stirs up discord, as by tale-bearing. **—mis′chief-mak′ing,** *adj., n.*

mischievous (mĭs′chĭ vəs), *adj.* **1.** fond of mischief, as children. **2.** roguishly or archly teasing, as speeches, glances, etc. **3.** maliciously or playfully annoying, as persons, actions, etc. **4.** harmful or injurious. **—mis′chievously,** *adv.* **—mis′chievousness,** *n.*

mischmetal (mĭsh′mĕt′l), *n.* an alloy of cerium with small amounts of other rare-earth metals; used as a flint in automatic lighters. [t. G: m. *Mischmetall,* equiv. to *misch(en)* MIX + *Metall* METAL]

miscible (mĭs′ĭ bl), *adj.* capable of being mixed. [f. s. L *miscēre* mix + -IBLE] **—mis′cibil′ity,** *n.*

miscolour (mĭs′kŭl′ə), *v.t.* **1.** to give a wrong colour to **2.** to misrepresent. Also, *U.S.,* **miscolor.**

misconceive (mĭs′kən sēv′), *v.t., v.i.,* **-ceived, -ceiving.** to conceive wrongly; misunderstand. **—mis′conceiv′er,** *n.*

misconception (mĭs′kən sĕp′shən), *n.* erroneous conception; a mistaken notion.

misconduct (*n.* mĭs kŏn′dŭkt; *v.* mĭs′kən dŭkt′), *n.* **1.** improper conduct; wrong behaviour. **2.** unlawful conduct by an official in regard to his office, or by a person in the administration of justice, such as a lawyer, witness, or juror. **—*v.t.* 3.** to mismanage. **4.** to misbehave (oneself).

misconstruction (mĭs′kən strŭk′shən), *n.* **1.** wrong construction; misinterpretation. **2.** the act of misconstruing.

misconstrue (mĭs′kən strōō′), *v.t.,* **-strued, -struing.** to construe wrongly; take in a wrong sense; misinterpret; misunderstand.

miscounsel (mĭs′koun′səl), *v.t.,* **-selled, -selling** or (*U.S.*) **-seled, -seling.** to advise wrongly.

miscount (mĭs′kount′), *v.t., v.i.* **1.** to count erroneously or miscalculate. **—*n.* 2.** an erroneous counting or a miscalculation.

miscreance (mĭs′krĭ əns), *n.* *Archaic.* wrong belief; misbelief; false religious faith.

miscreancy (mĭs′krĭ ən sĭ), *n.* *Archaic.* **1.** miscreance. **2.** the state or condition of a miscreant; turpitude.

miscreant (mĭs′krĭ ənt), *adj.* **1.** depraved, villainous, or base. **2.** *Archaic.* misbelieving; holding a false religious belief. **—*n.* 3.** a vile wretch; villain. **4.** *Archaic.* a misbelieving person, as a heretic or an infidel. [ME *miscreaunt,* t. OF: m. *mescreant,* f. *mes-* MIS-¹ + *creant,* ppr. of *creire* believe, g. L *crēdere*]

miscreate (mĭs′krĭ āt′), *v.,* **-ated, -ating,** *adj.* **—*v.t., v.i.* 1.** *Rare.* to create amiss. **—*adj.* 2.** *Archaic.* miscreated. **—mis′crea′tion,** *n.*

miscreated (mĭs′krĭ ā′tĭd), *adj.* wrongly created; misshapen; monstrous.

miscue (mĭs′kyōō′), *n., v.,* **-cued, -cuing. —*n.* 1.** *Billiards, etc.* a slip of the cue, causing it to strike the ball improperly or not at all. **—*v.i.* 2.** to make a miscue. **3.** *Theat.* to fail to answer one's cue or to answer another's cue.

misdate (mĭs′dāt′), *v.,* **-dated, -dating,** *n.* **—*v.t.* 1.** to date wrongly; assign or affix a wrong date to. **—*n.* 2.** a wrong date.

misdeal (mĭs′dēl′), *v.,* **-dealt, -dealing,** *n.* **—*v.t., v.i.* 1.** to deal wrongly, esp. at cards. **—*n.* 2.** a wrong deal. **—mis′deal′er,** *n.*

misdeed (mĭs′dēd′), *n.* an ill deed; a wicked action.

misdeliver (mĭs′dĭ lĭv′ə), *v.t.* to deliver wrongly, as to a wrong address. **—mis′deliv′ery,** *n.*

misdemean (mĭs′dĭ mēn′), *v.t., v.i.* *Archaic.* to misbehave.

misdemeanant (mĭs′dĭ mē′nənt), *n.* *Archaic.* one guilty of misbehaviour.

misdemeanour (mĭs′dĭ mē′nə), *n.* **1.** misbehaviour; a misdeed. **2.** *Law.* any criminal offence, esp. (before 1967) one not classified as a felony or treason. Also, *esp. U.S.,* **misdemeanor.**

misderive (mĭs′dĭ rīv′), *v.t., v.i.,* **-rived, -riving.** to derive wrongly; assign a wrong derivation to.

misdescribe (mĭs′dĭ skrīb′), *v.t., v.i.,* **-scribed, -scribing.** to describe incorrectly or falsely. **—misdescription** (mĭs′dĭ skrĭp′shən), *n.*

misdirect (mĭs′dĭ rĕkt′), *v.t.* to direct or charge wrongly.

misdirection (mĭs′dĭ rĕk′shən), *n.* **1.** a wrong indication, guidance, or instruction. **2.** *Law.* an erroneous charge to the jury by a judge.

misdo (mĭs′dōō′), *v.t., v.i.,* **-did, -done, -doing.** to do wrongly. [ME *misdo(n),* OE *misdōn.* See MIS-¹, DO¹] **—mis′do′er,** *n.*

misdoubt (mĭs dout′), *Archaic.* **—*v.t., v.i.* 1.** to doubt or suspect. **—*n.* 2.** doubt or suspicion.

mise (mēz, mīz), *n.* a settlement or agreement. [late ME, t. AF, der. *mettre* put, set, g. L *mittere* send]

misease (mĭs ēz′), *n.* *Archaic.* **1.** discomfort; distress; suffering. **2.** poverty.

mise en scène (*Fr.* mē zäN sĕn′), *French.* **1.** the act or art of placing a play, scene, etc., on the stage, esp. with regard to the equipment necessary. **2.** stage setting, as of a play. **3.** the surroundings amid which anything is seen.

misemploy (mĭs′ĭm ploi′), *v.t., v.i.* to employ wrongly or improperly; misuse. **—mis′employ′ment,** *n.*

Miseno (*It.* mē zĕ′nô), *n.* a cape in SW Italy, on the N shore of the Bay of Naples: ruins of ancient **Misenum** (mī sē′nəm), a Roman naval station and resort.

miser¹ (mī′zə), *n.* **1.** one who lives in wretched circumstances in order to save and hoard money. **2.** a niggardly, avaricious person. **3.** *Obs.* a wretched or unhappy person. [t. L: wretched, unhappy, sick, bad]

miser² (mī′zə), *n.* a large hand auger. [orig. obscure]

miserable (mĭz′ə rə bl, mĭz′rə-), *adj.* **1.** wretchedly unhappy, uneasy, or uncomfortable. **2.** wretchedly poor; needy. **3.** of wretched character or quality; contemptible; wretchedly bad. **4.** attended with or causing misery: *a miserable existence.* **5.** manifesting misery. **6.** worthy of pity; deplorable: *a miserable failure.* [t. L: m. s. *miserābilis* pitiable] **—mis′erableness,** *n.* **—mis′erably,** *adv.* **—Syn. 1.** forlorn, disconsolate, doleful. See **wretched. 3.** despicable, mean. **6.** pitiable, lamentable. **—Ant. 1.** happy.

misère (mĭ zĕə′), *n.* *Cards.* **1.** a hand which contains no winning card. **2.** a bid made by a player who has such a hand, declaring that he will take no tricks. [t. F: lit., misery]

Miserere (mĭz′ə rēə′rĭ, -rĭə′rĭ), *n.* *Latin.* **1.** the 51st psalm (50th in the Vulgate and Douay versions), one of the penitential psalms. **2.** a musical setting for it. **3.** (*l.c.*) a prayer or expression asking for mercy. **4.** (*l.c.*) misericord (def. 3). [L: have pity; the first word of the psalm in the Vulgate]

misericord (mĭ zĕ′rĭ kôd′), *n.* **1.** a relaxation of a monastic rule. **2.** a room in a monastery where such relaxations are permitted. **3.** a small projection on the underside of a hinged seat of a church stall, which, when the seat was thrown back, gave support to a person standing in the stall. **4.** a medieval dagger, used for the mercy stroke to a wounded foe. Also, **misericorde.** [ME *misericorde,* t. OF, t. L: m. s. *misericordia* mercy]

misericordia (mĭ zĕ′rĭ kô′dĭ ə), *n.* *Latin.* compassion; mercy.

miserly (mī′zə lĭ), *adj.* of, like, or befitting a miser; penurious; niggardly. **—mi′serliness,** *n.*

misery (mĭz′ə rĭ), *n., pl.* **-ries. 1.** great distress of mind; extreme unhappiness. **2.** a cause or source of wretchedness. **3.** distress caused by privation or poverty. **4.** wretchedness of condition or circumstances. **5.** *Dial.* bodily pain. [ME *miserie,* t. L: m. *miseria*] **—Syn. 1.** grief, anguish, woe. See **sorrow.**

misesteem (mĭs′ĭs tēm′), *v.t.* to esteem wrongly; fail to esteem or respect properly.

misestimate (*v.* mĭs′ĕs′tĭ māt′; *n.* mĭs′ĕs′tĭ mĭt), *v.,* **-mated, -mating,** *n.* **—*v.t.* 1.** to estimate wrongly or incorrectly. **—*n.* 2.** wrong estimate.

misfeasance (mĭs fē′zəns), *n.* *Law.* **1.** wrong, actual or alleged, arising from or consisting of affirmative action (contrasted with *nonfeasance*). **2.** the wrongful performance of a normally lawful act; the wrongful and injurious exercise of lawful authority. [AF: m. *mesfesance,* der. *mesfaire* misdo. See MIS-, FEASANCE, and cf. MALFEASANCE]

misfeasor (mĭs fē′zə), *n.* *Law.* one guilty of misfeasance.

misfield (mĭs′fēld′), *v.i., v.t. Cricket.* to fail to stop and return (the ball) cleanly and quickly when fielding.
misfile (mĭs′fīl′), *v.t.*, **-filed, -filing.** to file (papers, etc.) incorrectly or in the wrong place.
misfire (mĭs′fī′ə), *v.*, **-fired, -firing,** *n.* —*v.i.* **1.** (of a gun or projectile, etc.) to fail to fire or explode. **2.** to fail to have a desired effect; be unsuccessful. —*n.* **3.** (of a gun or projectile, etc.) a failure to explode or fire, or to explode or fire properly.
misfit (*v.* mĭs′fĭt′; *n.* mĭs′fĭt′), *v.*, **-fitted, -fitting,** *n.* —*v.t., v.i.* **1.** to fit badly. —*n.* **2.** a bad fit, as an ill-fitting garment, etc. **3.** a badly adjusted person.
misfortune (mĭs fô′chən), *n.* **1.** ill or adverse fortune; ill luck. **2.** an instance of this; a mischance or mishap. —**Syn. 2.** accident; disaster, calamity, catastrophe; reverse; blow. See **affliction.**
misgive (mĭs gĭv′), *v.*, **-gave, -given, -giving.** —*v.t.* **1.** (of one's mind, heart, etc.) to give doubt or apprehension to. —*v.i.* **2.** to be apprehensive.
misgiving (mĭs gĭv′ĭng), *n.* a feeling of doubt, distrust, or apprehension. —**Syn.** See **apprehension.**
misgovern (mĭs′gŭv′ən), *v.t.* to govern or manage badly. —**mis′gov′ernment,** *n.* —**mis′gov′ernor,** *n.*
misguide (mĭs′gīd′), *v.t.*, **-guided, -guiding.** to guide wrongly; mislead. —**mis′guid′ance,** *n.* —**mis′guid′er,** *n.*
misguided (mĭs′gī′dĭd), *adj.* misled. —**mis′guid′edly,** *adv.*
mishandle (mĭs′hăn′dl), *v.t.*, **-dled, -dling. 1.** to handle badly; maltreat. **2.** to mismanage.
mishap (mĭs′hăp), *n.* an unfortunate accident.
mishear (mĭs′hĭə′), *v.t.*, **-heard, -hearing.** to hear incorrectly or imperfectly.
mishit (mĭs′hĭt′), *Cricket, etc.* —*v.t.* **1.** to hit (the ball) faultily, as when batting. —*v.i.* **2.** to make a faulty stroke. —*n.* **3.** a faulty stroke.
mishmash (mĭsh′măsh′), *n.* a hotchpotch, a jumble.
Mishnah (mĭsh′nə), *n., pl.* **Mishnayoth** (mĭsh′nä yōth′). **1.** the collection of oral laws made by Judah ha-Nasi (A.D. *c.* 135–*c.* 220), which forms the basis of the Talmud. **2.** a paragraph of the Mishnah. Also, **Mishna.** [t. Heb.: repetition, study] —**Mishnaic** (mĭsh nā′ĭk), **Mish′nic, Mish′nical,** *adj.*
misinform (mĭs′ĭn fôm′), *v.t.* to give false or misleading information to. —**mis′inform′ant, mis′inform′er,** *n.* —**mis′informa′tion,** *n.*
misinterpret (mĭs′ĭn tû′prĭt), *v.t.* to interpret, explain, or understand incorrectly. —**mis′inter′preta′tion,** *n.*
misjoinder (mĭs join′də), *n. Law.* a joining in one suit or action of causes or of parties not permitted to be so joined.
misjudge (mĭs′jŭj′), *v.t., v.i.*, **-judged, -judging.** to judge or interpret wrongly or unjustly. —**mis′judge′ment, mis′judg′ment,** *n.*
Miskolc (*Hung.* mēsh′kōlts), *n.* a town in N Hungary. 143,364 (1960).
mislay (mĭs lā′), *v.t.*, **-laid, -laying. 1.** to put in a place afterwards forgotten. **2.** to lay or place wrongly; misplace. —**mislay′er,** *n.*
mislead (mĭs lēd′), *v.t.*, **-led, -leading. 1.** to lead or guide wrongly; lead astray. **2.** to lead into error of conduct, thought, or judgement. —**mislead′er,** *n.* —**mislead′ing,** *adj.* —**mislead′ingly,** *adv.*
mislike (mĭs līk′), *v.t.*, **-liked, -liking.** *Archaic.* **1.** to dislike. **2.** to displease. —**mislik′er,** *n.* —**mislik′ing,** *n.*
mismanage (mĭs′măn′ĭj), *v.t., v.i.*, **-aged, -aging.** to manage incompetently or dishonestly. —**mis′man′agement,** *n.*
mismarriage (mĭs mă′rĭj), *n.* an unsuitable or unhappy marriage.
mismatch (mĭs′măch′), *v.t.* **1.** to match badly or unsuitably. —*n.* **2.** a bad or unsatisfactory match.
mismate (mĭs′māt′), *v.t., v.i.*, **-mated, -mating.** to mate amiss or unsuitably.
mismeasure (mĭs′mĕzh′ə), *v.t., v.i.* to measure wrongly. —**mis′meas′urement,** *n.*
mismove (mĭs mo͞ov′), *n.* a wrong move, as in a game or any course of procedure.
misname (mĭs′nām′), *v.t.*, **-named, -naming.** to call by a wrong name.
misnomer (mĭs′nō′mə), *n.* **1.** a misapplied name or designation. **2.** an error in naming a person or thing. [ME *misnoumer*, t. OF: m. *mesnommer*, n. use of inf., f. *mes-* MIS-¹ + *nommer* name, g. L *nōmināre*. See NOMINATE]
miso-, a word element referring to hate. [t. Gk, comb. form of *mīseîn* to hate, *mîsos* hatred]
misogamy (mĭ sŏg′ə mĭ), *n.* hatred of marriage. —**misog′amist,** *n.*
misogyny (mĭ sŏj′ĭ nĭ), *n.* hatred of women. [t. Gk: m. s. *mīsogynía*] —**misog′ynist,** *n.* —**misog′ynous,** *adj.*
misology (mĭ sŏl′ə jĭ, mī-), *n.* hatred of reason or reasoning. [t. Gk: m. s. *mīsologia* hatred of argument] —**misol′ogist,** *n.*
misoneism (mĭs′ō nē′ĭz′əm, mī′sō-), *n.* hatred or dislike of what is new. [t. It.: m. *misoneismo*, f. *miso-* MISO- + s. Gk *néos* new + *-ismo* -ISM] —**mis′one′ist,** *n.*
mispickel (mĭs′pĭk′l), *n.* arsenopyrite. [t. G]
misplace (mĭs′plās′), *v.t.*, **-placed, -placing. 1.** to put in a wrong place. **2.** to place or bestow improperly, unsuitably, or unwisely. —**mis′place′ment,** *n.* —**Syn. 1.** See **displace.**
misplay (mĭs′plā′), *Games.* —*v.t.* **1.** to play wrongly, badly, or against the rules. —*n.* **2.** a wrong play, move or stroke.
misplead (mĭs plēd′), *v.t., v.i.* to plead incorrectly.
mispleading (mĭs plē′dĭng), *n. Law.* a mistake in pleading, as a misjoinder of parties, a misstatement of a cause of action, etc.
misprint (*n.* mĭs′prĭnt′; *v.* mĭs′prĭnt′), *n.* **1.** a mistake in printing. —*v.t.* **2.** to print incorrectly.
misprision[1] (mĭs prĭzh′ən), *n.* **1.** a wrongful action or commission, esp. by a public official. **2.** the act of concealing one's knowledge of a felony. [ME, t. OF, der. *mesprendre* mistake, do wrong, f. *mes-* MIS-¹ + *prendre* take, g. L *prehendere*]
misprision[2] (mĭs prĭzh′ən), *n.* scorn; contempt; low estimation. [f. *misprise* (see MISPRIZE) + -ION]
misprize (mĭs prīz′), *v.t.*, **-prized, -prizing.** to despise; undervalue; slight; scorn. Also, **misprise.** [t. OF: m. *mesprisier*, f. *mes-* MIS-¹ + *prisier* PRIZE²]
mispronounce (mĭs′prə nouns′), *v.t., v.i.*, **-nounced, -nouncing.** to pronounce incorrectly. —**mispronunciation** (mĭs′prə nŭn′sĭ ā′shən), *n.*
mispunctuate (mĭs′pŭngk′tyo͞o āt′), *v.t., v.i.*, **-ated, -ating.** to punctuate wrongly. —**mis′punc′tua′tion,** *n.*
misquote (mĭs′kwōt′), *v.t., v.i.*, **-quoted, -quoting.** to quote incorrectly. —**mis′quota′tion,** *n.*
misread (mĭs′rēd′), *v.t.*, **-read, -reading.** to read wrongly; misinterpret.
misreckon (mĭs′rĕk′ən), *v.t., v.i.* to reckon incorrectly; miscalculate.
misrelate (mĭs′rĭ lāt′), *v.t.*, **-lated, -lating.** to relate incorrectly. —**mis′rela′tion,** *n.*
misrelated participle, *Gram.* a participle related grammatically to a word which it was not intended to modify, as *coming* in: *coming round the corner, the church sprang into view.*
misremember (mĭs′rĭ mĕm′bə), *v.t., v.i.* **1.** to remember incorrectly. **2.** *Dial.* to fail to remember.
misreport (mĭs′rĭ pôt′), *v.t.* **1.** to report incorrectly or falsely. —*n.* **2.** an incorrect or false report. —**mis′report′er,** *n.*
misrepresent (mĭs′rĕp′rĭ zĕnt′), *v.t.* to represent incorrectly, improperly, or falsely. —**mis′rep′resenta′tion,** *n.* —**mis′rep′resent′er,** *n.* —**mis′rep′resen′tative,** *adj.*
misrule (mĭs′ro͞ol′), *n., v.*, **-ruled, -ruling.** —*n.* **1.** bad or unwise rule; misgovernment. **2.** disorder or lawless tumult. —*v.t., v.i.* **3.** to misgovern. —**mis′rul′er,** *n.*
misrun (mĭs′rŭn′), *n. Metall.* a casting marred by premature soldification.
miss[1] (mĭs), *v.t.* **1.** to fail to hit, light upon, meet, catch, receive, obtain, attain, accomplish, see, hear, etc.: *to miss a train.* **2.** to fail to perform, attend to, be present at, etc.: *to miss an appointment.* **3.** to perceive the absence or loss of, often with regret. **4.** to escape or avoid: *he just missed being caught.* **5.** to fail to perceive or understand: *to miss the point of a remark.* **6. miss fire,** to fail to go off, as a firearm; misfire. **7. miss the boat** or **bus,** *Colloq.* to be too late; fail to grasp an opportunity. —*v.i.* **8.** to fail to hit, light upon, receive, or attain something. **9.** to fail of effect or success; be unsuccessful. **10. miss out,** to fail to be present, as at a function, or to fail to receive, esp. something desired (often fol. by *on*). —*n.* **11.** a failure to hit, meet, obtain, or accomplish something. **12.** an omission or neglect, usually deliberate: *give it a miss.* [ME *misse*, OE *missan*, c. D and G *missen*]
miss[2] (mĭs), *n., pl.* **misses. 1.** (*cap.*) the conventional title of respect for an unmarried woman, prefixed to the name. **2.** (without the name) a term of address to an unmarried woman. **3.** a young unmarried woman; a girl. [short for MISTRESS]
Miss., Mississippi.
missal (mĭs′əl), *n. Rom. Cath. Ch.* the book containing the prayers and rites for celebrating mass for a complete year, used by the priest at the altar. [ME, t. ML: s. *missāle*, neut. of *missālis*, der. LL *missa* MASS²]
missay (mĭs sā′), *v.*, **-said, -saying.** *Archaic.* —*v.t.* **1.** to say or speak ill of; abuse; slander. **2.** to say wrongly. —*v.i.* **3.** to speak wrongly.

misseem (mĭs sēm′), *v.t. Archaic.* to misbecome.
missel thrush (mĭs′əl), a large European thrush, *Turdus viscivorus*, which is fond of the berries of the mistletoe. Also, **missel, mistle thrush.** [See MISTLE(TOE), THRUSH[1]]
missend (mĭs′sĕnd′), *v.t.*, **-sent, -sending.** to send wrongly, as to the wrong address.
misshape (mĭs′shāp′), *v.t.*, **-shaped, -shaped** or **-shapen, -shaping.** to shape ill; deform.
misshapen (mĭs′shā′pən), *adj.* badly shaped; deformed. —**mis′shap′enly,** *adv.* —**mis′shap′enness,** *n.*
missile (mĭs′īl), *n.* **1.** an object or weapon that can be thrown, hurled, or shot, as a stone, a bullet, a lance, or an arrow. **2.** a guided missile. —*adj.* **3.** capable of being thrown, hurled, or shot, as from the hand, a gun etc. **4.** that discharges missiles. [t. L: something which can be thrown]
missing (mĭs′ĭng), *adj.* lacking; absent; not found.
missing link, 1. a hypothetical form of animal formerly assumed to have constituted a connecting link between the anthropoid apes and man. **2.** something lacking for the completion of a series or sequence of any kind.
mission (mĭsh′ən), *n.* **1.** a body of persons sent to a foreign country to conduct negotiations, establish relations, or the like. **2.** the business with which an agent, envoy, etc., is charged. **3.** *U.S.* a permanent diplomatic establishment abroad: *chief of mission.* **4.** *Mil.* an operation on land, sea, or in the air, carried out by an armed force against an enemy. **5.** a body of persons sent into a foreign land for religious work among a heathen people, or into any region for the religious conversion or betterment of the inhabitants. **6.** an establishment of missionaries in a foreign land; a missionary post or station. **7.** the district assigned to a missionary priest. **8.** missionary duty or work. **9.** (*pl.*) organized missionary work or activities in any country, region, or field: *foreign missions.* **10.** a district for which no ecclesiastical establishment has been set up, having temporary buildings and offices. **11.** a series of special religious services for increasing piety and converting unbelievers: *to preach a mission.* **12.** a self-imposed or assigned duty. **13.** a sending or being sent for some duty or purpose. **14.** those sent. [t. L: s. *missio* a sending]
missionary (mĭsh′ə nə rĭ), *n., pl.* **-ries,** *adj.* —*n.* **1.** a person sent to work for the propagation of his religious faith in a heathen land or a newly settled district. **2.** one sent on a mission. —*adj.* **3.** pertaining to or connected with religious missions. **4.** engaged in such a mission, or devoted to work connected with missions. [f. MISSION + -ARY[1]]
missioner (mĭsh′ə nə), *n.* the conductor of a crusade or mission designed to stimulate and renew faith in an already Christian context.
missis (mĭs′ĭz, -ĭs), *n. Colloq. or Dial.* **1.** a man's wife. **2.** the mistress of a household. Also, **missus.** [spoken form of MRS]
missish (mĭs′ĭsh), *adj.* prim; affected; prudish.
Mississippi (mĭs′ĭ sĭp′ĭ), *n.* **1.** a state in the S United States. 2,178,141 pop. (1960); 47,716 sq. mi. *Cap.:* Jackson. *Abbrev.:* Miss. **2.** a river flowing from N Minnesota S to the Gulf of Mexico: the principal river of the U.S. 2470 mi.; from the headwaters of the Missouri to the Gulf of Mexico, 3988 mi.
Mississippian (mĭs′ĭ sĭp′ĭ ən), *adj.* **1.** of or pertaining to the state of Mississippi or the Mississippi river. **2.** *U.S. Geol.* pertaining to a late Palaeozoic geological period or a system of rocks in North America equivalent to the Lower Carboniferous. —*n.* **3.** a native or inhabitant of Mississippi. **4.** *U.S. Geol.* the period or system following Devonian and preceding Pennsylvanian; the Lower Carboniferous.
missive (mĭs′ĭv), *n.* **1.** a written message; a letter. —*adj.* **2.** sent, esp. from an official source. [late ME, t. ML: m. s. *missīvus*, der. L *missus*, pp., sent]
Missolonghi (mĭs′ə lŏng′gĭ), *n.* a town in W Greece: Byron died here 1824. 11,266 (1961). Also, **Mesolonghi.**
Missouri (mĭ zo͝oə′rĭ), *n.* **1.** a state in the central United States. 4,319,813 pop. (1960); 69,674 sq. mi. *Cap.:* Jefferson City. *Abbrev.:* Mo. **2.** a river flowing from SW Montana into the Mississippi N of St Louis, Missouri. 2723 mi. **3.** (*pl.*) a North American Indian tribe belonging to the Siouan linguistic stock, situated on the Missouri river in early historic times; now extinct as a tribe. —**Missour′ian,** *adj., n.*
misspeak (mĭs′spēk′), *v.t., v.i.*, **-spoke, -spoken, -speaking.** to speak, utter, or pronounce incorrectly.
misspell (mĭs′spĕl′), *v.t., v.i.*, **-spelt** or **-spelled, -spelling.** to spell incorrectly. —**mis′spell′ing,** *n.*
misspend (mĭs′spĕnd′), *v.t.*, **-spent, -spending.** to spend improperly; squander; waste. —**mis′spend′er,** *n.*
misstate (mĭs′stāt′), *v.t.*, **-stated, -stating.** to state wrongly or misleadingly; make a wrong statement about. —**mis′state′ment,** *n.*
misstep (mĭs′stĕp′), *n.* **1.** a wrong step. **2.** an error or slip in conduct.
missus (mĭs ′əz, -əs), *n. Colloq. or Dial.* missis.
missy (mĭs′ĭ), *n., pl.* **-sies.** *Chiefly U.S. Colloq.* young miss.
mist (mĭst), *n.* **1.** a cloudlike aggregation of minute globules of water suspended in the atmosphere at or near the earth's surface. **2.** *Meteorol.* (by international agreement) a very thin fog in which the horizontal visibility is greater than 1 km. **3.** a cloud of particles resembling a mist. **4.** something which dims, obscures, or blurs. **5.** a hazy appearance before the eyes, as due to tears or to bodily disorders. **6.** a suspension of a liquid in a gas. —*v.i.* **7.** to be or become misty. —*v.t.* **8.** to make misty. [ME and OE, c. D, LG, and Sw. *mist*] —**Syn. 5.** See **cloud.**
mistake (mĭs tāk′), *n., v.*, **-took, -taken, -taking.** —*n.* **1.** an error in action, opinion, or judgement. **2.** a misconception or misapprehension. —*v.t.* **3.** to take or regard as something or somebody else. **4.** to conceive of or understand wrongly; misapprehend; misunderstand. —*v.i.* **5.** to be in error. [ME *mistake(n)*, v., t. Scand.; cf. Icel. *mistaka* take by mistake. See MIS-[1], TAKE]

—**Syn. 1.** MISTAKE, BLUNDER, ERROR, SLIP refer to deviations from right, accuracy, correctness, or truth. A MISTAKE, grave or trivial, is caused by bad judgement or a disregard of rule or principle: *it was a mistake to argue.* A BLUNDER is a careless, stupid, or gross mistake in action or speech, suggesting awkwardness, heedlessness, or ignorance: *through his blunder the message was lost.* An ERROR (often interchanged with MISTAKE) is an unintentional wandering or deviation from accuracy, or right conduct: *an error in addition.* A SLIP is usually a minor mistake made through haste or carelessness: *a slip of the tongue.*

mistakeable (mĭs tā′kə bl), *adj.* that may be mistaken or misunderstood. Also, **mistakable.** —**mista′keably,** *adv.*
mistaken (mĭs tā′kən), *adj.* **1.** wrongly conceived, entertained, or done: *a mistaken notion.* **2.** erroneous; wrong. **3.** having made a mistake; being in error. —**mista′kenly,** *adv.*
misteach (mĭs′tēch′), *v.t.*, **-taught, -teaching.** to teach wrongly or badly.
mister (mĭs′tə), *n.* **1.** (*cap.*) the conventional title of respect for a man, prefixed to the name and to certain official designations (usually written *Mr*). **2.** *Colloq.* (in address, without the name) sir. **3.** the official title used in addressing: **a.** *Mil.* a junior officer, a senior warrant officer, and a cadet in a military academy. **b.** *Naval.* a warrant officer or midshipman. **c.** *Naut.* any officer other than the captain. **4.** (a title used in addressing a surgeon as opposed to *doctor.*) —*v.t.* **5.** *Colloq.* to address or speak of as 'mister' or 'Mr'. [var. of MASTER]
misthink (mĭs thĭngk′), *v.*, **-thought, -thinking.** *Archaic.* —*v.t.* **1.** to think ill of; have a bad opinion of. —*v.i.* **2.** to think unfavourably or wrongly.
Misti (*Sp.* mēs′tē), *n.* El Misti.
mistime (mĭs′tīm′), *v.t.*, **-timed, -timing.** to time wrongly; perform, say, etc., at a wrong time.
mistle thrush, missel thrush.
mistletoe (mĭs′əl tō′), *n.* **1.** a European plant, *Viscum album* (family *Loranthaceae*), with yellowish flowers and white berries, growing parasitically on various trees, much used in Christmas decorations. **2.** any of various other plants of the same family, as *Phoradendron flavescens* of the U.S., also used in Christmas decorations. [ME *mistelto*, OE *misteltān* (c. Icel. *mistilteinn*), f. *mistel* mistletoe + *tān* twig]
mistook (mĭs to͝ok′), *v.* pt. of **mistake.**
mistral (mĭs′trəl, mĭs träl′; *Fr.* mē stràl′), *n.* a cold, dry, northerly wind common in southern France and neighbouring regions. [t. F: lit., master wind, t. Pr.: important, g. L *magistrālis* MAGISTRAL]
Mistral (*Fr., Sp.* mē stràl′), *n.* **1. Frédéric** (*Fr.* frĕ dē rēk′), 1830–1914, French Provençal poet. **2. Gabriela** (*Sp.* gä bryĕ′lä) (*Lucila Godoy de Alcayaga*), 1889–1957, Chilean poet.
mistranslate (mĭs′trăns lāt′, -träns-), *v.t., v.i.*, **-lated, -lating.** to translate incorrectly. —**mis′transla′tion,** *n.*
mistreat (mĭs′trēt′), *v.t.* to treat badly or wrongly. —**mis′treat′ment,** *n.*
mistress (mĭs′trĭs), *n.* **1.** a woman who has authority or control; the female head of a household or some other establishment. **2.** a woman employing, or in authority over, servants or attendants. **3.** a female owner, as of a slave, horse, dog, etc. **4.** a woman who has the power of controlling or disposing of something at pleasure. **5.** something regarded as feminine which has control or supremacy: *England was the mistress of the seas.* **6.** a female teacher; a schoolmistress. **7.** a woman who has a continuing sexual relationship with one man outside marriage.

8. *Archaic or Poetic.* sweetheart. 9. *Archaic or Dial.* a term of address for a woman. Cf. **Mrs** and **Miss.** [ME *maistresse,* t. OF, fem. of *maistre* MASTER]

mistress of ceremonies, a woman who acts as master of ceremonies.

mistrial (mĭs trī′əl), *n. Law.* **1.** a trial terminated without conclusion on the merits because of some error. **2.** *U.S.* an inconclusive trial, as where the jury cannot agree.

mistrust (mĭs′trŭst′), *n.* **1.** lack of trust or confidence; distrust. —*v.t.* **2.** to regard with mistrust; distrust. **3.** *Rare.* to suspect or surmise. —*v.i.* **4.** to be distrustful. —**mis′trust′er,** *n.* —**mis′trust′ingly,** *adv.*

mistrustful (mĭs′trŭst′fəl), *adj.* full of mistrust; suspicious. —**mis′trust′fully,** *adv.* —**mis′trust′fulness,** *n.*

misty (mĭs′tĭ), *adj.,* **-tier, -tiest.** **1.** abounding in or clouded by mist. **2.** of the nature of or consisting of mist. **3.** appearing as if seen through mist; indistinct in form or outline. **4.** obscure; vague. [ME; OE *mistig*] —**mist′ily,** *adv.* —**mist′iness,** *n.*

misunderstand (mĭs′ŭn′də stănd′), *v.t., v.i.,* **-stood, -standing.** **1.** to misinterpret the words or actions of (a person). **2.** to understand wrongly; take (words, statements, etc.) in a wrong sense.

misunderstanding (mĭs′ŭn′də stăn′dĭng), *n.* **1.** disagreement or dissension. **2.** failure to understand; mistake as to meaning.

misunderstood (mĭs′ŭn′də sto͝od′), *adj.* **1.** improperly interpreted. **2.** unappreciated.

misusage (mĭs′yo͞o′zĭj, -sĭj), *n.* **1.** wrong or improper usage, as of words; abusage. **2.** ill-use; bad treatment.

misuse (*n.* mĭs′yo͞os′; *v.* mĭs′yo͞oz′), *n., v.,* **-used, -using.** —*n.* **1.** wrong or improper use; misapplication. **2.** *Obs.* ill-use. —*v.t.* **3.** to use wrongly or improperly; misapply. **4.** to ill-use; maltreat.

misuser (mĭs′yo͞o′zə), *n.* **1.** *Law.* abuse of a liberty or benefit or thing. **2.** one who misuses.

misvalue (mĭs′văl′yo͞o), *v.t.,* **-ued, -uing.** to value wrongly.

misword (mĭs′wûd′), *v.t.* to word wrongly.

miswrite (mĭs′rīt′), *v.t.,* **-wrote, -written, -writing.** to write incorrectly.

M.I.T., Massachusetts Institute of Technology.

Mitaka (mĭ tä′kə), *n.* a town in Japan, in SE central Honshu island. 135,873 (1965).

Mitcham (mĭch′əm), *n.* a district of the S outer London borough of Merton.

Mitchell (mĭch′əl), *n.* **1. Reginald Joseph,** 1895–1937, British aircraft designer: designed the Spitfire fighter. **2.** a river in Australia flowing NW through Queensland to the Gulf of Carpentaria. 350 mi. **3. Mount,** a mountain in W North Carolina: highest peak in eastern U.S. 6684 ft.

mite[1] (mīt), *n.* any of various small arachnids (order *Acari*) with a saclike body, many being parasitic on plants and animals, others living in cheese, flour, unrefined sugar, etc. [ME *myte,* OE *mīte,* c. MD *mīte* (D *mijt*)]

mite[2] (mīt), *n.* **1.** a small contribution, but all that one can afford (in allusion to Mark 12:41–44): *to contribute one's mite.* **2.** a very small sum of money. **3.** a coin of very small value. **4.** a very small object. **5.** a very small creature. **6.** a very small child. —*adv.* **7.** to a limited extent; somewhat (prec. by *a*): *a mite stupid.* [ME, t. MD; ult. identical with MITE[1]]

miter (mī′tə), *n., v.t. U.S.* mitre.

Mitford (mĭt′fəd), *n.* **1. Mary Russell,** 1787–1855, English novelist and dramatist. **2. Nancy,** born 1904, English writer.

mither (mĭth′ə), *n. Scot. and N Dial.* mother.

Mithgarthr (mĭth′gä′thə), *n.* Icelandic name for **Midgard.**

Mithraism (mĭth′rā ĭz′əm), *n.* the ancient Persian religion in which Mithras was worshipped, a major source of Christian beliefs. Also, **Mithraicism** (mĭth rā′ĭ sĭz′əm). —**Mithraic** (mĭth rā′ĭk), **Mith′rais′tic,** *adj.* —**Mith′raist,** *n.*

Mithras (mĭth′răs), *n. Persian Myth.* the god of light and truth, later of the sun. Also, **Mithra** (mĭth′rə). [t. L, t. Gk, t. OPers.: m. *Mithra*]

mithridate (mĭth′rĭ dāt′), *n. Obs. Pharm.* a compound believed to be a universal antidote against every poison and disease. [t. ML: m. s. *mithridatum,* var. of *mithridatium* (neut. sing.) of or pertaining to MITHRIDATES. Cf. MITHRIDATISM]

Mithridates VI (mĭth′rĭ dā′tēz) (*'the Great'*), *c.* 132–63 B.C., king of Pontus 120?–63 B.C., and enemy of Rome.

mithridatism (mĭth′rĭ dā tĭz′əm), *n.* the production of immunity against the action of a poison by taking the poison in gradually increased doses. [named after MITHRIDATES VI, said to have so immunized himself] —**mithridatic** (mĭth′rĭ dăt′ĭk, mĭth′rĭ dā′tĭk), *adj.*

mithridatize (mĭth′rĭ dā′tīz), *v.t.,* **-tized, -tizing.** to induce a state of mithridatism in. Also, **mithridatise.**

mitigate (mĭt′ĭ gāt′), *v.,* **-gated, -gating.** —*v.t.* **1.** to lessen in force or intensity (wrath, grief, harshness, pain, etc.). **2.** to moderate the severity of (anything distressing). **3.** *Rare.* to make milder or more gentle; mollify. —*v.i.* **4.** to become milder; moderate in severity. [ME, t. ML: m. s. *mitigātus,* pp.] —**mit′iga′tive, mitigatory** (mĭt′ĭ gā′tə rĭ), *adj.* —**mit′iga′tor,** *n.*

mitigation (mĭt′ĭ gā′shən), *n.* **1.** the act or fact of mitigating. **2.** *Law.* a reduction or attempt to secure a reduction in damages or punishment, as in a speech made to a judge after a verdict or plea of guilty.

mitis (mī′tĭs, mē′-), *n.* **1.** Also, **mitis metal.** a malleable iron produced by fusing wrought iron with a small amount of aluminium rendering the product fluid enough to cast. —*adj.* **2.** designating or pertaining to mitis. [t. L: mild]

mitochondrion (mī′tō kŏn′drĭ ən), *n., pl.* **-ia** (ĭ ə). *Biol.* one of the minute granules, larger than lysosomes or microsomes, present in living cells, regarded as responsible for respiration and energy production. [f. Gk: m. *mítos* a thread + *chóndrion* granule, dim. of *chóndros* grain] —**mi′tochon′drial,** *adj.*

mitosis (mĭ tō′sĭs, mī-), *n. Biol.* the usual (indirect) method of cell division, characterized typically by the resolving of the chromatin of the nucleus into a threadlike form, which separates into segments or chromosomes, each of which separates longitudinally into two parts, one part of each chromosome being retained in each of two new cells resulting from the original cell. [t. NL, f. s. Gk *mítos* a thread + *-osis* -OSIS] —**mitotic** (mĭ tŏt′ĭk, mī-), *adj.* —**mitot′ically,** *adv.*

mitrailleur (mĭt′rī û′; *Fr.* mē trȧ yœr′), *n. French.* one who operates a mitrailleuse.

mitrailleuse (mĭt′rī ûz′; *Fr.* mē trȧ yœz′), *n. French.* a machine-gun. [F, der. *mitraille* scrap iron, der. OF *mitre, mite* small coin, fragment of metal]

mitral (mī′trəl), *adj.* of or resembling a mitre.

mitral valve, *Anat.* the valve between the left auricle and ventricle of the heart which prevents the blood from flowing back into the auricle.

mitre (mī′tə), *n., v.,* **-tred, -tring.** —*n.* **1.** the ceremonial headdress of a bishop symbolizing his apostolic authority: in the Roman Catholic Church it is by courtesy extended as a mark of distinction to the heads of certain religious houses for men. In the Western Church it can lie flat when not in use and takes the form of a tall divided cap with two ribbons hanging at the back, often richly jewelled and embroidered; in the Eastern Church it takes various forms, but is invariably a solid structure of metal of rounded shape. **2.** the office or rank of bishop; bishopric. **3.** the ceremonial cap of the ancient Jewish high priest. **4.** a kind of headdress formerly worn by Asiatics. **5.** the abutting surface or bevel on either of the pieces joined in a mitre-joint. —*v.t.* **6.** to bestow a mitre upon, or raise to a rank entitled to it. **7.** to join with a mitre-joint. **8.** to make a mitre-joint in; cut to a mitre. Also, *U.S.,* **miter.** [ME *mitre,* t. L: m. *mitra,* t. Gk: belt, headband, headdress]

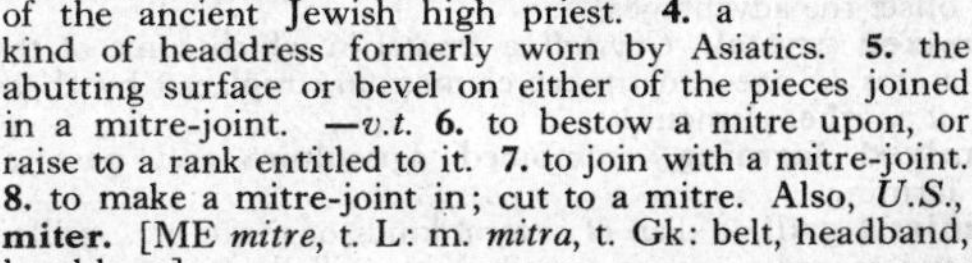

Mitre (def. 1)

mitre box, a box or apparatus for use in cutting mitres (def. 5).

mitred (mī′təd), *adj.* **1.** shaped like a bishop's mitre or having a mitre-shaped apex. **2.** wearing, or entitled or privileged to wear, a mitre. Also, *U.S.,* **mitered.**

mitre-joint (mī′tə joint′), *n.* a joint formed when two pieces of identical cross-section are joined at the ends, and where the joined ends are bevelled at equal angles.

Mitre-joint

mitre wheel, one of a pair of cogwheels each having bevelled faces.

mitrewort (mī′tə wût′), *n.* any of the low herbs which constitute the saxifragaceous genus *Mitella* (so called from the capsule, which resembles a bishop's mitre). Also, *U.S.,* **miterwort.**

mitriform (mī′trĭ fôm′), *adj.* shaped like a mitre.

mitt (mĭt), *n.* **1.** a kind of glove extending only to, or slightly over, the fingers, esp. as worn by women. **2.** *Baseball.* a kind of glove having the side next to the palm of the hand protected by a large, thick mitten-like pad. **3.** a mitten. **4.** *Slang.* a hand. [apocopated var. of MITTEN]

mitten (mĭt′n), *n.* **1.** a kind of hand-covering enclosing the four fingers together and the thumb separately. **2.** a mitt (def. 1). **3.** (*pl.*) *Slang.* boxing gloves. [ME *myteyne,* t. OF: m. *mitaine,* g. Gallo-Rom. *medietāna* half (glove), der. L *medius* middle] —**mit′ten-like′,** *adj.*

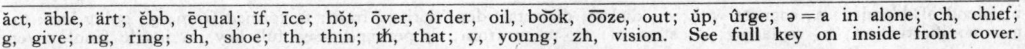

mittimus (mĭtʹĭ məs), *n. Law.* **1.** a warrant of commitment to prison. **2.** a writ for removing a suit or a record from one court to another. [t. L: we send, first word of such a writ in Latin]

Mitty (mĭtʹĭ), *n.* **Walter. 1.** the hero of a short story, *The Secret Life of Walter Mitty* (1940), by James Thurber. **2.** an insignificant man who daydreams that he is someone important.

mitzvah (mĭtsʹvä), *n., pl.* **-voth** (-vōth). *Judaism.* **1.** an order or commandment from the Bible or the rabbis. **2.** a religious act; a meritorious deed. Also, **mitsvah.** [t. Heb.: m. *miswāh* commandment]

mix (mĭks), *v.,* **mixed** or **mixt, mixing,** *n.* —*v.t.* **1.** to put together (substances or things, or one substance or thing with another) in one mass or assemblage with more or less thorough diffusion of the constituent elements among one another. **2.** to put together indiscriminately or confusedly (often fol. by *up*). **3.** to combine, unite, or join: *to mix business and pleasure.* **4.** to put in as an added element or ingredient: *to mix a little baking powder into the flour.* **5.** to form by combining ingredients: *to mix a cake, to mix mortar.* **6.** to crossbreed. **7.** to confuse completely (fol. by *up*). **8. mix up in,** to involve in. —*v.i.* **9.** to become mixed: *oil and water will not mix.* **10.** to associate, as in company. **11.** to be crossbred, or of mixed breeding. **12.** *Slang.* to fight vigorously, as with the fists (sometimes fol. by *it*). **13. mix with,** to associate socially with. —*n.* **14.** a mixing, or a mixed condition; a mixture. **15.** *Colloq.* a muddle or mess. **16.** a commercially prepared blend of ingredients to which it is only necessary to add liquid and stir, before baking, cooking, serving, etc. [back-formation from *mixt* mixed, t. F: m. *mixte*, t. L: m. *mixtus*, pp.]

—**Syn. 1.** MIX, BLEND, COMBINE, MINGLE imply bringing two or more things into more or less intimate association. MIX is the general word for such association: *to mix fruit juices.* BLEND implies such a harmonious joining of two or more types of colours, feelings, etc., that the new product formed displays some of the qualities of each: *to blend fragrances or whiskies.* COMBINE implies such a close or intimate union that distinction between the parts is lost: *to combine forces.* MINGLE usually suggests retained identity of the parts: *to mingle voices.* **2.** jumble, confuse. **10.** consort, mingle.

mixed (mĭkst), *adj.* **1.** put together or formed by mixing. **2.** composed of different constituents or elements. **3.** composed of male and female together: *a mixed school.* **4.** of different kinds combined: *mixed sweets.* **5.** comprising persons of different sexes, or of different classes, status, character, opinions, etc.: *mixed company.* **6.** *Law.* involving more than one issue or aspect: *a mixed question of law and fact.* **7.** *Colloq.* mentally confused (fol. by *up*). **8.** *Phonet.* (of a vowel) central.

—**Syn. 1.** MIXED, MINGLED both refer to intimate association of two or more things. MIXED is generally applied to one noun, MINGLED commonly to two or more: *mixed feelings.*

mixed blessing, an event, thing, situation, etc., which has disadvantages, esp. unexpected disadvantages, which offset the advantages.

mixed crystal, *Crystall.* a crystal in which some of the atoms of one constituent element are replaced by those of another element.

mixed farming, combined agriculture and pastoral farming.

mixed grill, a dish of several kinds of meat, etc., grilled and served together, usually with grilled vegetables.

mixed marriage, a marriage between persons of different religions or races.

mixed metaphor. See **metaphor** (def. 2).

mixed number, a number consisting of a whole number and a fraction, as $4\frac{1}{2}$.

mixed train, a railway train made up partly of passenger carriages and partly of goods wagons.

mixer (mĭkʹsə), *n.* **1.** one who or that which mixes. **2.** *Colloq.* a person with reference to his sociability: *a good mixer.* **3.** a kitchen utensil or electrical appliance used for beating. **4.** an electrical system, as in a broadcasting studio providing for the mixing, etc., of sounds from various sources, as from studio microphones, discs, tapes, etc. **5.** *Radio and Television.* a technician who controls the sound mixer in a studio.

mixing valve, a valve controlling a single outlet receiving water from both hot-water and cold-water pipes. Also, **mixing tap, mixing faucet.**

Mixolydian mode (mĭkʹsō lĭdʹĭ ən), *Music.* a scale represented by the white keys of a keyboard instrument, beginning on G. [f. s. Gk *mixolýdios* mixed LYDIAN + -AN]

mixture (mĭksʹchə), *n.* **1.** a product of mixing. **2.** any combination of differing elements, kinds, qualities, etc.: *a curious mixture of eagerness and terror.* **3.** *Chem., Physics.* an aggregate of two or more substances which are not chemically united, and which exist in no fixed proportion to each other. **4.** a fabric woven of yarns combining various colours: *a heather mixture.* **5.** the act of mixing. **6.** the state of being mixed. **7.** an added element or ingredient; an admixture. **8.** *Music.* a type of organ stop, with several ranks of pipes, giving harmonics. [t. L: m. s. *mixtūra*] —**Syn. 1.** blend, combination; compound. **2.** conglomeration, miscellany, jumble; medley; melange, potpourri, hotchpotch.

mix-up (mĭksʹŭpʹ), *n.* **1.** a confused state of things; a muddle; a tangle. **2.** *Colloq.* a fight.

Miyakonojo (mēʹyə kə nōʹjō), *n.* a town in Japan, in SE Kyushu. 108,220 (1965).

Miyazaki (mĭ yäʹzə kĭ, mēʹyə zäʹkĭ), *n.* a town in Japan, in SE Kyushu. 182,870 (1965).

mizzen (mĭzʹən), *Naut.* —*n.* **1.** the lower sail set on the mizzenmast. **2.** a mizzenmast. —*adj.* **3.** of, relating to, or set on the mizzenmast. Also, **mizen.** See illus. under **sail.** [ME *meseyn*, t. F: m. *misaine*, t. It.: m. *mezzana*, prop. fem. of *mezzano* middle, g. L *mediānus.* See MEDIAN]

mizzenmast (mĭzʹən mästʹ; *Naut.* -məst), *n. Naut.* **1.** the aftermost mast of a three-masted vessel, or the third on a vessel with more than three masts. **2.** the after and shorter of the two masts of a yawl or ketch. Also, **mizenmast.**

mizzle (mĭzʹəl), *v.i.,* **-zled, -zling.** *Dial.* to drizzle.

Mjöllnir (myûlʹnĭə), *n. Scand. Myth.* the hammer of Thor. [t. Icel.]

Mk., markka.

MKS system, the metre-kilogram-second system.

mkt, market.

ML, Medieval Latin. Also, **M.L.**

ml, mail.

ml., millilitre; millilitres.

M.L.A., **1.** Member of the Legislative Assembly. **2.** Modern Language Association.

M.L.C., Member of the Legislative Council.

M.Litt., (L *Magister Litterae*) Master of Letters.

Mlle, *pl.* **Mlles.** Mademoiselle.

MM., Messieurs.

mm., **1.** (L *millia*) thousands. **2.** millimetre; millimetres.

M.M., Military Medal.

Mme, *pl.* **Mmes.** madame.

m.m.f., magnetomotive force.

Mn, *Chem.* manganese.

M.N., Merchant Navy.

MnE, Modern English.

mnemonic (nē mŏnʹĭk), *adj.* **1.** assisting, or intended to assist, the memory. **2.** pertaining to mnemonics or to memory. —*n.* **3.** a verse or the like intended to assist the memory. [t. Gk: m. s. *mnēmonikós* of memory]

mnemonics (nē mŏnʹĭks), *n.* the art of improving or developing the memory. Also, **mnemotechnics** (nēʹmō tĕkʹnĭks).

Mnemosyne (nē mŏzʹĭ nēʹ, -mŏsʹ-), *n. Gk Myth.* the goddess of memory, daughter of Uranus and Gaea, and mother (by Zeus) of the Muses.

Mngr, Monsignor.

mo (mō), *n. Colloq.* a moment.

Mo, *Chem.* molybdenum.

Mo., **1.** Missouri. **2.** Monday.

mo., *pl.* **mos.** month; months.

M.O., **1.** mail order. **2.** Medical Officer. **3.** Also, **m.o.** money order. **4.** mass observation.

-mo, a final member of a series of compounds referring to book sizes by numbering the times the sheets are folded, e.g., *12mo* or *duodecimo.*

moa (mōʹə), *n.* any of various extinct, flightless birds of New Zealand, constituting the family *Dinornithidae*, allied to the apteryx but resembling an ostrich. [t. Maori]

Moa, *Dinornis maximus* (Ab. 10 ft high)

Moab (mōʹăb), *n.* an ancient kingdom E of the Dead Sea, in what is now Jordan. —**Moabite** (mōʹə bītʹ), *n., adj.*

moan (mōn), *n.* **1.** a prolonged, low, inarticulate sound uttered from or as if from physical or mental suffering. **2.** any similar sound: *the moan of the wind.* **3.** *Archaic.* complaint or lamentation. **4.** *Colloq.* a grumble. —*v.i.* **5.** to utter moans, as of pain or grief. **6.** (of the wind, sea, trees, etc.) to make any sound suggestive of such moans. **7.** to utter in lamentation. **8.** *Colloq.* to grumble. —*v.t.* **9.** to lament or bemoan: *to moan one's fate.* [ME *mone*, OE **mān* (inferred from its derivative, OE *mǣnan* complain of, lament)] —**moanʹer,** *n.* —**moanʹingly,** *adv.* —**Syn. 5.** See **groan.**

moat (mōt), *Fort.* —*n.* **1.** a deep, wide trench surrounding a fortified place, as a town or a castle, usually filled with water. See diag. under **bastion.** —*v.t.* **2.** to surround with, or as with, a moat. [ME *mote* moat, (earlier) mound, t. OF: mound, eminence; prob. from Celtic or Gmc]

mob (mŏb), *n.*, *adj.*, *v.*, **mobbed, mobbing.** —*n.* **1.** a disorderly or riotous assemblage of persons. **2.** a crowd bent on or engaged in lawless violence. **3.** *Sociol.* a group of persons stimulating one another to excitement and losing ordinary rational control over their activity. **4.** (often disparagingly) any assemblage or aggregation of persons, animals, or things; a crowd. **5.** the common mass of people; the populace or multitude. —*adj.* **6.** of, pertaining to, characteristic of, or suitable for a mob: *mob violence, mob oratory.* —*v.t.* **7.** to beset or crowd round tumultuously, as from curiosity or with hostile intent. **8.** to attack with riotous violence. [short for L *mōbile vulgus* the movable (i.e., excitable) common people] —**mob′ber,** *n.* —**mob′bish,** *adj.*

Mobangi (mə băng′gĭ), *n.* Ubangi.

mob-cap (mŏb′kăp′), *n. Obs.* a large, full cap fitting down over the ears, formerly much worn indoors by women.

mobile (mō′bĭl), *adj.* **1.** movable; moving readily. **2.** *Mil.* permanently equipped with vehicles for transport. **3.** flowing freely, as a liquid. **4.** changing easily in expression, as features. **5.** quickly responding to impulses, emotions, etc., as the mind; versatile. **6.** characterized by social mobility. **7.** of or pertaining to a mobile. —*n.* **8.** a hanging construction or sculpture of delicately balanced movable parts (of metal, wood, etc.) which describe rhythmic patterns through their motion. [t. L: movable (neut.)]

Mobile (mō bēl′), *n.* a seaport in the U.S., in SW Alabama at the mouth of the **Mobile river,** a river (38 mi.) formed by the Alabama and Tombigbee rivers. 202,779 (1960).

mobility (mō bĭl′ĭ tĭ), *n.* **1.** the quality of being mobile. **2.** *Sociol.* the movement of people in a population, as from place to place, or job to job, or social class to social class.

mobilize (mō′bĭ līz′), *v.*, **-lized, -lizing.** —*v.t.* **1.** to put (armed forces) into readiness for active service. **2.** to organize or adapt (industries, etc.) for service to the government in time of war. **3.** to marshal, as for a task: *to mobilize one's energies.* **4.** to put into motion, circulation, or use: *mobilize the wealth of a country.* —*v.i.* **5.** to be assembled, organized, etc., for war. Also, **mobilise.** [t. F: m. s. *mobiliser*, der. *mobile* MOBILE] —**mo′biliza′tion,** *n.*

möbius strip (mûr′bĭ əs; *Ger.* mœ′bĭ o͞os), *Geom.* a continuous one-sided surface, as formed by half-twisting a strip, as of paper or cloth, and joining the ends. [named after August Ferdinand *Möbius*, 1790–1868, German mathematician]

moble (mŏb′l), *v.t.*, **-bled, -bling.** *Archaic.* to muffle the head or face of, as with a hood.

mobocracy (mŏ bŏk′rə sĭ), *n.*, *pl.* **-cies. 1.** rule by the mob; political control by a mob. **2.** the mob as a ruling class. [f. MOB, n. + -(O)CRACY; modelled on DEMOCRACY, etc.] —**mobocratic** (mŏb′ō krăt′ĭk), **mob′ocrat′ical,** *adj.*

mobster (mŏb′stə), *n. U.S.* a member of a gang of criminals. [f. MOB + -STER]

Mobutu (mə bo͞o′to͞o), *n.* **Joseph** (jō′zĭf), born 1930, Congolese army officer: president of the Democratic Republic of the Congo since 1965.

Moçambique (*Port.* mo͞o səm bē′kə), *n.* Portuguese name of **Mozambique.**

moccasin (mŏk′ə sĭn), *n.* **1.** a shoe made entirely of soft leather, as deerskin, worn originally by the American Indians. **2.** a venomous snake, *Ancistrodon piscivorus*, of the southern U.S., found in or near water (**water-moccasin**). [t. Eastern Algonquian languages (Powhatan and Massachusetts); ? akin to *makak* small case or box]

moccasin flower, 1. the lady's-slipper. **2.** a common cypripedium, *Cypripedium reginae*, of the U.S.

Mocha (mō′kə, mŏk′ə), *n.* **1.** Also, **Mokha.** a seaport in SW Yemen. ab. 5000. **2.** (*l.c.*) a choice variety of coffee, originally coming from Mocha. **3.** (*l.c.*) a flavouring obtained from coffee infusion or combined chocolate and coffee infusion. **4.** (*l.c.*) a glove leather, finer and thinner than doeskin, the best grades of which are made from Arabian goatskins. **5.** (*l.c.*) a cake or pudding flavoured with a combined coffee and chocolate mixture. **6.** (*l.c.*) a dark chocolate colour.

mochila (*Sp.* mô chē′lä), *n. Spanish.* a flap of leather on the seat of a saddle.

mock (mŏk), *v.t.* **1.** to assail or treat with ridicule or derision. **2.** to ridicule by mimicry of action or speech; mimic derisively. **3.** to mimic, imitate, or counterfeit. **4.** to defy; set at naught. **5.** to deceive, delude, or disappoint. **6. mock up,** to build a mock-up. —*v.i.* **7.** to use ridicule or derision; scoff; jeer (often fol. by *at*). —*n.* **8.** a mocking or derisive action or speech; mockery or derision. **9.** something mocked or derided; an object of derision. **10.** imitation. —*adj.* **11.** being an imitation or having merely the semblance of something: *a mock battle.* [ME *mokken*, t. OF: m. *mocquer*; orig. uncert.] —**mock′er,** *n.* —**mock′ingly,** *adv.* —**Syn. 1.** deride; taunt, flout, gibe; tease. See **ridicule. 11.** feigned, pretended, sham, counterfeit.

mockery (mŏk′ə rĭ), *n.*, *pl.* **-ries. 1.** ridicule or derision. **2.** a derisive action or speech. **3.** a subject or occasion of derision. **4.** an imitation, esp. of a ridiculous or unsatisfactory kind. **5.** a mere travesty, or mocking pretence. **6.** something absurdly or offensively inadequate or unfitting.

mock-heroic (mŏk′hĭ rō′ĭk), *adj.* **1.** exaggerating of low or insignificant material in a literary work to heroic proportions or in a heroic style in order to ridicule it. —*n.* **2.** the literary device or style which employs this technique. —**mock′-hero′ically,** *adv.*

mockingbird (mŏk′ĭng bûd′), *n.* **1.** any of several grey, black, and white songbirds of the genus *Mimus*, remarkable for their imitative powers, esp. the celebrated mocker, *M. polyglottos*, of the southern U.S. and Mexico. **2.** any of various allied or similar birds, as the **blue mockingbird,** *Melanotis caerulescens*, of Mexico.

mock moon, paraselene.

mock orange, the common syringa, *Philadelphus coronarius.*

mock sun, parhelion.

mock turtle soup, a brown soup prepared from a calf's head, supposed to resemble real turtle soup.

mock-up (mŏk′ŭp′), *n.* a model, built to scale, of a machine, apparatus, or weapon, used in studying the construction and in testing a new development, or in teaching men how to operate the actual machine, apparatus, or weapon.

mod., 1. moderate. **2.** *Music.* moderato.

mod (mŏd), *Colloq.* —*adj.* **1.** modern. **2.** of or pertaining to a style of dress, furnishing, behaviour, etc., which is fashionable to the point of being unconventional. —*n.* **3.** a young person who dresses in an ultra-fashionable manner and identifies himself (or herself) with others who affect a similar style of dress. Cf. **rocker.**

modal (mō′dl), *adj.* **1.** of or pertaining to mode, manner, or form. **2.** *Music.* **a.** pertaining to mode, as distinguished from key. **b.** based on a scale other than major or minor. **3.** *Gram.* denoting or pertaining to mood. **4.** *Philos.* pertaining to mode as distinguished from substance, matter, or basic attribute. **5.** *Logic.* exhibiting or expressing some phase of modality. [t. ML: s. *modālis*, der. L *modus* MODE[1]] —**mo′dally,** *adv.*

modality (mō dăl′ĭ tĭ), *n.*, *pl.* **-ties. 1.** modal quality or state. **2.** a modal attribute or circumstance. **3.** *Logic.* **a.** that fourfold classification of propositions according to whether the truth of what they assert is either *contingent, possible, impossible* or *necessary.* **b.** (in Kantian logic) that threefold classification of judgements according to whether they are either *problematic, assertoric,* or *apodictic.* **4.** *Med.* the application of a therapeutic agent, usually a physical therapeutic agent.

mod. cons, modern conveniences.

Modder (mŏd′ə), *n.* a river in the Republic of South Africa flowing W through Orange Free State and Cape Province to the Vaal. 186 mi.

mode[1] (mōd), *n.* **1.** manner of acting or doing; a method; a way. **2.** the natural disposition or the manner of existence or action of anything; a form: *heat is a mode of motion.* **3.** *Philos.* appearance, form, or disposition taken by a single reality or by an essential property or attribute of it. **4.** *Logic.* any one of the various forms (four in Scholastic logic, three in Kant) of modal propositions. **5.** *Music.* any of various arrangements of the diatonic notes of an octave, differing from one another in the order of the whole tones and semitones; a scale. **6.** *Gram.* mood. **7.** *Statistics.* (in a statistical population) the category, value, or interval of the variable having the greatest frequency. **8.** *Geol.* the actual mineral composition of a rock, expressed in percentages by weight. **9.** *Engineering.* a resonant oscillation in a system. [ME, t. L: m. s. *modus* measure, due measure, manner] —**Syn. 1.** See **method.**

mode[2] (mōd), *n.* **1.** customary or conventional usage in manners, dress, etc., esp. as observed by persons of fashion. **2.** a prevailing style or fashion. [t. F, t. L: m. s. *modus* MODE[1]]

model (mŏd′l), *n.*, *adj.*, *v.*, **-elled, -elling** or (*U.S.*) **-eled, -eling.** —*n.* **1.** a standard or example for imitation or comparison; a pattern. **2.** a representation, generally in miniature, to show the construction or serve as a copy of something. **3.** an image in clay, wax, or the like to be reproduced in more durable material. **4.** a person, esp. a young woman, who poses for a painter, photographer, sculptor, etc. **5.** one employed to put on articles of apparel to display them to customers; a mannequin. **6.** (euphemistically) a prostitute. **7.** mode of structure or formation. **8.** a typical or specific form or style. *—adj.* **9.** serving as a model. **10.** worthy to serve as a model; exemplary. *—v.t.* **11.** to form or plan according to a model. **12.** to give shape or form to; fashion. **13.** to make a model or representation of. **16.** to fashion in clay, wax, or the like. **17.** to display, esp. by wearing: *to model evening dresses.* *—v.i.* **18.** to make models. **19.** to produce designs in some plastic material. **20.** to assume a typical or natural appearance, as the parts of a drawing in progress. **21.** to serve or be employed as a model. [t. F: m. *modèle*, t. It.: m. *modello*, dim. of *modo*, t. L: m. *modus* MODE[1]] **—mod′eller,** *n.* **—Syn. 1.** paragon; prototype. See **ideal.**

modelling (mŏd′l ĭng, mŏd′lĭng), *n.* **1.** the act or art of one who models. **2.** the process of producing sculptured form with plastic material, usually clay, as for reproduction in a more durable material. **3.** *Graphic Arts.* the process of rendering the illusion of the third dimension. **4.** the undulations of form in sculpture.

Modena (mŏd′ĭ nə; *It.* mô′dĕ nä), *n.* a town in Italy, in central Emilia. 158,049 (1966).

moderate (*adj., n.* mŏd′ə rĭt, mŏd′rĭt; *v.* mŏd′ə rāt′), *adj., n., v.,* **-rated, -rating.** *—adj.* **1.** kept or keeping within due bounds; not extreme, excessive, or intense: *a moderate request.* **2.** of medium quantity, extent, etc.: *a moderate income.* **3.** mediocre; fair: *moderate ability.* **4.** of or pertaining to moderates, as in politics or religion. *—n.* **5.** one who is moderate in opinion or action, or opposed to extreme views and courses, esp. in politics or religion. **6.** (*usually cap.*) a member of a political party advocating moderate reform. *—v.t.* **7.** to reduce the excessiveness of; make less violent, severe, intense, or rigorous. **8.** to preside over or at, as a public meeting. *—v.i.* **9.** to become less violent, severe, intense, or rigorous. **10.** to act as moderator; preside. [ME, t. L: m. s. *moderātus*, pp.] **—mod′erately,** *adv.* **—mod′erateness,** *n.* **—Syn. 7.** See **allay.**

moderate breeze, *Meteorol.* a wind of Beaufort scale force 4, i.e. one about 15 miles per hour.

moderate gale, *Meteorol.* a wind of Beaufort scale force 7, i.e. one about 35 miles per hour.

moderation (mŏd′ə rā′shən), *n.* **1.** the quality of being moderate; restraint; avoidance of extremes; temperance. **2.** (*pl.*) (at Oxford University) the first public honours examination in classics (*literae humaniores*) and certain other subjects. Cf. **greats. 3.** the act of moderating. **4.** *Physics.* the slowing down of neutrons on passing through matter owing to repeated collisions with nuclei. **5. in moderation,** without excess; moderately.

moderato (mŏd′ə rä′tō; *It.* mô dĕ rä′tô), *adj. Music.* moderate; in moderate time. [It.]

moderator (mŏd′ə rā′tə), *n.* **1.** one who or that which moderates. **2.** a presiding officer, as over a public forum, a legislative body, or an ecclesiastical body in the Presbyterian Church. **3.** (at Oxford University) an examiner in moderations. **4.** (at Cambridge University) one of two officers presiding over the examination for the mathematical tripos. **5.** *Physics.* a substance, as graphite or heavy water, used to slow down neutrons from the high energies at which they are released in fission to speeds suitable for further fission. **—mod′era′torship′,** *n.*

modern (mŏd′n), *adj.* **1.** of or pertaining to present and recent time; not ancient or remote. **2.** characteristic of present and recent time; not antiquated or obsolete. **3.** of or pertaining to various styles of jazz, evolved in the 1940s and much developed since then, characterized by complex harmonies and rhythms, free improvisation, and usually small groups. Cf. **bebop. 4.** (of a living language) in its most recent period; in the latest stage of its development; new. **5.** of or denoting school subjects other than Latin or Greek, or a section of a school in which such subjects form the whole or nearly the whole of the curriculum. *—n.* **6.** a person of modern times. **7.** one whose views and tastes are modern. **8.** *Print.* a type style differentiated from *old style* by heavy vertical strokes and straight serifs. [t. LL: s. *modernus*, der. L *modo* just now (orig. abl. of *modus* MODE[1])] **—mod′ernly,** *adv.* **—mod′ernness,** *n.*

—Syn. 1. MODERN, RECENT, LATE apply to that which is near to or characteristic of the present as contrasted with any other time. MODERN is applied to those things which exist in the present age, esp. in contrast to those of a former age or an age long past; hence the word sometimes has the connotation of up-to-date and, thus, good: *modern ideas.* That which is RECENT is separated from the present or the time of action by only a short interval; it is new, fresh, and novel: *recent developments.* LATE may mean nearest to the present moment: *the latest news.*

Modern English, the English language since *c.* 1475.

Modern French, the French language since *c.* 1600.

Modern Greek, the Greek language since *c.* 1500.

Modern Hebrew, the language of modern Israel, a revived form of ancient Hebrew.

modern history, history since the Renaissance.

modernism (mŏd′ə nĭz′əm), *n.* **1.** modern character; modern tendencies; sympathy with what is modern. **2.** a modern usage or characteristic. **3.** *Theol.* **a.** (*cap.*) movement in Roman Catholic thought which sought to interpret the teachings of the church in the light of philosophic and scientific conceptions prevalent in the late 19th and early 20th centuries; condemned by Pope Pius X in 1907. **b.** the liberal theological tendency in Protestantism (opposed to *fundamentalism*).

modernist (mŏd′ə nĭst), *n.* **1.** one who follows or favours modern ways, tendencies, etc. **2.** one who advocates the study of modern subjects in preference to ancient classics. **3.** an adherent of modernism in theological questions. *—adj.* **4.** of modernists or modernism.

modernistic (mŏd′ə nĭs′tĭk), *adj.* **1.** modern. **2.** of or pertaining to modernism or modernists: *a modernistic painting.*

modernity (mŏ dû′nĭ tĭ), *n., pl.* **-ties. 1.** the quality of being modern. **2.** something modern.

modernize (mŏd′ə nīz′), *v.,* **-nized, -nizing.** *—v.t.* **1.** to make modern; give a modern character or appearance to. *—v.i.* **2.** to become modern; adopt modern ways, views, etc. Also, **modernise. —mod′erniza′tion,** *n.* **—mod′erniz′er,** *n.*

modest (mŏd′ĭst), *adj.* **1.** having or showing a moderate or humble estimate of one's merits, importance, etc.; free from vanity, egotism, boastfulness, or great pretensions. **2.** free from ostentation or showy extravagance: *a modest house.* **3.** moderate. **4.** having or showing regard for the decencies of behaviour, speech, dress, etc.; decent. [t. L: s. *modestus* keeping due measure] **—mod′estly,** *adv.*

—Syn. 4. MODEST, DEMURE, PRUDISH imply conformity to propriety and decorum, and a distaste for anything coarse or loud. MODEST implies a becoming shyness, sobriety, and proper behaviour: *a modest, self-respecting person.* DEMURE implied originally a bashful, quiet simplicity, staidness, and decorum; now a modesty either unconscious or cleverly assumed: *a demure young girl.* PRUDISH suggests an exaggeratedly self-conscious modesty or propriety in behaviour or conversation of one who wishes to be thought of as easily shocked, and is often intolerant: *a prudish objection to a harmless remark.* **—Ant. 4.** bold, coarse.

modesty (mŏd′ĭs tĭ), *n., pl.* **-ties. 1.** the quality of being modest; freedom from vanity, boastfulness, etc. **2.** regard for decency of behaviour, speech, dress, etc. **3.** simplicity; moderation.

modicum (mŏd′ĭ kəm), *n.* a moderate or small quantity. [late ME, t. L, neut. of *modicus* moderate]

modification (mŏd′ĭ fĭ kā′shən), *n.* **1.** the act of modifying. **2.** the state of being modified; partial alteration. **3.** a modified form; a variety. **4.** *Biol.* a change in a living organism acquired from its own activity or environment and not transmitted to its descendants. **5.** limitation or qualification. **6.** *Gram.* **a.** the use of a modifier in a construction, or of modifiers in a class of constructions or in a language. **b.** the meaning of a modifier, esp. as it affects the meaning of the word or other form modified: *limitation is one kind of modification.* **c.** a change in the phonemic shape of a morpheme, word, or other form when it functions as an element in a construction, e.g., the change of *not* to *-n't* in the phrase *doesn't.* **d.** the feature of a construction resulting from such a change, e.g., the phrases *doesn't* and *does not* differ in modification. **e.** an adjustment in the form of a word as it passes from one language to another.

modificatory (mŏd′ĭ fĭ kā′tə rĭ), *adj.* modifying. Also, **mod′ifica′tive.**

modifier (mŏd′ĭ fī′ə), *n.* **1.** one who or that which modifies. **2.** *Gram.* a word, phrase, or sentence element which limits or qualifies the sense of another word, phrase, or element in the same construction: *adjectives are modifiers.*

modify (mŏd′ĭ fī′), *v.,* **-fied, -fying.** *—v.t.* **1.** to change somewhat the form or qualities of; alter somewhat. **2.** *Gram.* (of a word or larger linguistic form) to stand in a subordinate relation to (another form called the *head*) usually with descriptive, limiting, or particularizing meaning, as in *a good man, good* modifies the head *man.* **3.** to be the modifier or attribute of. **4.** to change (a vowel) by umlaut. **5.** to reduce in degree; moderate; qualify. *—v.i.* **6.** to change; to become changed. [ME *modifie(n)*, t. L: m. *modificāre, modificārī* set limits to] **—mod′ifi′able,** *adj.*

—Syn. 1. MODIFY, QUALIFY, TEMPER suggest altering an original statement, condition, or the like, so as to avoid anything excessive or extreme. To MODIFY is to alter in one or more particulars, generally in the direction of leniency or moderation: *to modify demands, rates.* To QUALIFY is to restrict or limit by exceptions or conditions: *to qualify one's praise, hopes.* To TEMPER is to alter the quality of something, generally so as to diminish its force or harshness: *to temper the wind to the shorn lamb.*

Modigliani (*It.* mō dēl lyä′nē), *n.* **Amedeo** (*It.* ä mä dĕ′ō), 1884–1920, Italian painter and sculptor.

modillion (mə dĭl′yən), *n. Archit.* one of a series of ornamental blocks or brackets placed under the corona of a cornice in the Corinthian and other orders. [t. It.: m. *modiglione,* ult. der. L *mūtulus*]

Modillion

modiolus (mō dī′ō ləs, mə-), *n., pl.* **-li** (-lī′). *Anat.* the central conical axis round which the cochlea of the ear winds. [t. NL, dim. of L *modius* measure for grain]

modish (mō′dĭsh), *adj.* in accordance with the prevailing mode; fashionable; stylish. —**mo′dishly,** *adv.* —**mo′dishness,** *n.*

modiste (mō dēst′; *Fr.* mō dēst′), *n.* a maker of or dealer in articles of fashionable attire, esp. women's dresses, millinery, etc. [t. F, der. *mode* MODE²]

Modjeska (mō jĕs′kə), *n.* **Helena** (hĕl′ə nə), (*Helena Opid Modrzejewska*), 1840–1909, Polish actress in the U.S.

Modred (mō′drĭd), *n. Arthurian Legend.* the nephew and treacherous killer of Arthur. Also, **Mordred.**

mods (mŏdz), *n.pl. Colloq.* (at Oxford University) moderations.

modular (mŏd′yŏŏ lə), *adj.* of or pertaining to a module or modulus.

modulate (mŏd′yŏŏ lāt′), *v.,* **-lated, -lating.** —*v.t.* **1.** to regulate by or adjust to a certain measure or proportion; soften; tone down. **2.** to alter or adapt (the voice) fittingly in utterance. **3.** *Music.* **a.** to attune to a certain pitch or key. **b.** to vary the volume of (tone). **4.** *Radio.* to cause the amplitude, frequency, phase, or intensity of (the carrier wave) to vary in accordance with the soundwaves or other signals, the frequency of the signal wave usually being very much lower than that of the carrier: frequently applied to the application of soundwave signals to a microphone to change the characteristic of a transmitted radio wave. —*v.i.* **5.** *Radio.* to modulate a carrier wave. **6.** *Music.* to pass from one key to another. [t. L: m. s. *modulātus,* pp., having measured] —**modulative** (mŏd′yŏŏ lə tĭv), *adj.*

modulation (mŏd′yŏŏ lā′shən), *n.* **1.** the act of modulating. **2.** the state of being modulated. **3.** *Music.* transition from one key to another. **4.** *Gram.* **a.** the use of a particular distribution of stress or pitch in a construction, e.g., the use of rising pitch on the last word of *John is here?* **b.** the feature of a construction resulting from such a use, e.g., the question *John is here?* differs from the statement *John is here* only in modulation.

modulator (mŏd′yŏŏ lā′tə), *n.* **1.** one who or that which modulates. **2.** *Radio.* a device for modulating a carrier wave. Cf. **modulate** (def. 4).

module (mŏd′yŏŏl), *n.* **1.** a standard or unit for measuring. **2.** a selected unit of measure, ranging in size from a few inches to several feet, used as a basis for planning and standardization of building materials. **3.** *Archit.* the size of some part, as the semidiameter of a column at the base of the shaft, taken as a unit of measure. **4.** *Electronics.* a small, standard unit which can be used in the construction of a piece of equipment. **5.** *Astronautics.* a detachable section of a space vehicle: *command module.* [t. L: m. s. *modulus,* dim. of *modus* measure, MODE¹]

modulus (mŏd′yŏŏ ləs), *n., pl.* **-li** (-lī′). *Physics.* a coefficient (def. 3). [t. L: a small measure. See MODULE]

modulus of elasticity, the ratio of the stress to the strain in a particular material.

modulus of rigidity, the modulus of elasticity applied to a body under a shearing strain; shear modulus.

modus operandi (mŏd′əs ŏp′ə răn′dē), *Latin.* mode of operating or working.

modus vivendi (mŏd′əs vĭ vĕn′dē), *Latin.* **1.** mode of living. **2.** a temporary arrangement between persons or parties pending a settlement of matters in debate.

Moesia (mē′syə), *n.* an ancient country in S Europe, S of the Danube and N of ancient Thrace and Macedonia: later a Roman province.

Moeskroen (*Du.* mōōs krōōn′), *n.* Mouscron.

Moesogoth (mē′sō gŏth′), *n.* one of the Christianized agricultural Goths who settled in Moesia in the 4th century A.D. —**Moe′sogoth′ic,** *adj.*

mofette (mō fĕt′; *Fr.* mō fĕt′), *n.* **1.** a noxious emanation, consisting chiefly of carbon dioxide, escaping from the earth in regions of nearly extinct volcanic activity. **2.** one of the openings or fissures from which this emanation issues. Also, **moffette.** [t. F, t. It. (Naples d.): m. *mofetta*]

Mogadiscio (*It.* mō gä dēsh′shō), *n.* a seaport in and the capital of the Somali Republic. 120,649 (est. 1963). Also, **Mogadishu** (mŏg′ə dē′shōō). See map under **Somali Republic.**

Mogador (mŏg′ə dô′; *Fr.* mō gä dŏr′), *n.* a seaport in W Morocco. 26,392 (1960).

moggy (mŏg′ĭ), *n. Slang.* a cat. Also, **mog.**

Mogileov (*Russ.* mə gĭ lyôf′), *n.* a town in the W Soviet Union, on the Dnieper. 156,000 (est. 1965).

Mogul (mō′gŭl, mō gŭl′), *n.* **1.** one of the Mongol conquerors of India who ruled from 1526 to 1857 (nominal rulers from 1803 on). **2.** a Mongol or Mongolian. **3.** (*l.c.*) an important person. **4.** (*l.c.*) a steam locomotive, used for hauling heavy trains. —*adj.* **5.** of or pertaining to the Moguls or their empire. [t. Ar. and Pers.: m. *Mughul* Mongol]

M.O.H., Medical Officer of Health.

mohair (mō′hĕə′), *n.* **1.** the coat or fleece of an Angora goat. **2.** a fabric made of yarn from this fleece, in a plain weave for draperies and in a pile weave for upholstery. **3.** a garment made of this fabric. [f. obs. *mo(cayare)* mohair (ult. t. Ar.: m. *mukhayyar*) + HAIR]

Mohaka (mō′hăk′ə, mō hăk′ə), *n.* a river of E North Island, New Zealand, flowing SE to Hawke Bay in the Pacific Ocean. 95 mi.

Moham., Mohammedan.

Mohammed (mō hăm′ĭd), *n.* A.D. 570?–632, Arab prophet, founder of Islam. Also, **Mahomet, Muhammad.**

Mohammed II, 1430–81, sultan of Turkey 1451–81; captured Constantinople in 1453.

Mohammed Ali (ä′lĭ), **1.** 1878–1931, Indian Muslim leader: advocate of Indian independence and associate of Gandhi. **2.** Mehemet Ali. **3.** See **Clay, Cassius.**

Mohammedan (mō hăm′ĭ dən), *adj.* **1.** of or pertaining to Mohammed or his religious system; Islamic; Muslim. —*n.* **2.** a follower of Mohammed; a Muslim. Also, **Mahometan, Muhammadan, Muhammedan.**

Mohammedanism (mō hăm′ĭ də nĭz′əm), *n.* the Mohammedan religion; Islam.

Mohammedanize (mō hăm′ĭ də nīz′), *v.t.,* **-nized, -nizing.** Islamize. Also, **Mohammedanise.**

Mohammed Zahir Shah (mō hăm′ĭd zĭ′ĭə shä′), born 1914, king of Afghanistan since 1933.

Mohammerah (mō hăm′ə rä′), *n.* See **Khorramshahr.**

Mohave (mō hä′vĭ), *n., pl.* **-ves,** (*esp. collectively*) **-ve,** *adj.* —*n.* **1.** a member of a North American Indian tribe belonging to the Yuman linguistic family, formerly situated on both sides of the Colorado river. —*adj.* **2.** of or pertaining to the Mohave tribe. Also, **Mojave.** [t. Amer. Ind. (Yuman), der. *homok* three + *avi* mountain]

Mohave Desert, Mojave Desert.

Mohawk (mō′hôk′), *n., pl.* **-hawks,** (*esp. collectively*) **-hawk.** **1.** a member of a tribe of North American Indians, the most easterly of the Iroquois Five Nations, formerly resident along the Mohawk river, New York. **2.** the Iroquoian language of the Mohawk Indians. **3.** a river flowing E from central New York to the Hudson. 148 mi. [t. N Amer. Ind. (Narragansett): they eat animate things (hence, man-eaters)]

Mohegan (mō hē′gən), *n., pl.* **-gans,** (*esp. collectively*) **-gan.** **1.** a member of a tribe of Algonquian-speaking North American Indians, dwelling chiefly along the Thames river, Connecticut, in the 17th century. **2.** Mohican. [t. N Amer. Ind. (Algonquian): m. *maingan* wolf]

Mohenjo-Daro (mə hĕn′jō dä′rō), *n.* an archaeological site in West Pakistan, near the river Indus; the centre of an ancient Indus civilization.

Mohican (mō′ĭ kən), *n., pl.* **-cans,** (*esp. collectively*) **-can.** **1.** a member of a tribe or confederacy of North American Indians of Algonquian speech, centralized formerly in the upper Hudson valley. **2.** Mohegan (def. 1). Also, **Mahican.** [t. Algonquian: wolf]

Mohock (mō′hŏk′), *n.* one of a class of ruffians, often aristocrats, who infested the London streets at night in the early 18th century. [var. of MOHAWK. Cf. APACHE]

moho (mō′hō′), *n.* the Mohorovicic discontinuity.

Mohole (mō′hōl′), *n. Geol.* any hole drilled through the earth's crust with the intention of penetrating the Mohorovicic discontinuity. [f. MO(HOROVICIC DISCONTINUITY) + HOLE]

Mohorovicic discontinuity (mō′hə rō′vĭ chĭch), *Geol.* the dividing line between the earth's crust and mantle where an abrupt change occurs in the velocity of earthquake waves. Also, **moho.** [named after A. *Mohorovičić,* 1857–1936, Yugoslavian geologist]

Mohs scale (mōz), a scale of hardness used in mineralogy. Its degrees are: talc 1; gypsum 2; calcite 3; fluorite 4;

apatite 5; felspar 6; quartz 7; topaz 8; sapphire 9; diamond 10. Cf. **hardness.** [named after Friedrich *Mohs*, 1773–1839, German mineralogist]

mohur (mō′hə), *n.* a former gold coin of India, introduced in the 16th century. Also, **gold mohur.** [earlier *muhr*, t. Pers.: seal, gold coin]

moidore (moi′dô), *n.* a former gold coin of Portugal and Brazil. [t. Pg.: m. *moeda d'ouro* coin of gold]

moiety (moi′ə tĭ), *n.*, *pl.* **-ties. 1.** a half. **2.** an indefinite portion. **3.** *Anthropol.* one of two units into which a tribe is divided on the basis of unilateral descent. [ME *moit(i)e*, t. OF, g. LL *medietas* half, L the middle]

moil (moil), *v.i.* **1.** to work hard; toil; drudge. **—***n.* **2.** toil or drudgery. **3.** confusion, turmoil, or trouble. [ME *moile(n)*, t. OF: m. *moillier* wet, moisten, ult. der. L *mollis* soft] **—moil′er,** *n.*

moire (mwä), *n.* a watered fabric, as of silk or wool. [t. F, t. E: m. MOHAIR]

moiré (mwä′rā; *Fr.* mwȧ rė′), *adj.* **1.** watered as silk; having a wavelike pattern. **—***n.* **2.** a design pressed on silk, rayon, etc., by engraved rollers. **3.** moire.

Moiseiwitsch (mə zā′vĭch), *n.* **Benno** (bĕn′ō), 1890–1963, British pianist, born in Russia.

moist (moist), *adj.* **1.** moderately or slightly wet; damp; humid. **2.** (of the eyes) tearful. **3.** accompanied by or connected with liquid or moisture. [ME *moiste*, t. OF: moist, mouldy. Cf. L *mūcidus* mouldy, musty] **—moist′ly,** *adv.* **—moist′ness,** *n.* **—Syn. 1.** See **damp.**

moisten (mois′ən), *v.t.*, *v.i.* to make or become moist. **—moist′ener,** *n.*

moisture (mois′chə), *n.* **1.** water or other liquid rendering anything moist. **2.** (*cap.*) **Sea of,** a plain, *Mare Humorum*, on the face of the moon.

moisturize (mois′chə rīz′), *v.*, **-rized, -rizing.** **—***v.t.* **1.** to impart or restore moisture to: *to moisturize one's skin with cream.* **—***v.i.* **2.** to make something moist: *an air-conditioner that moisturizes effectively.*

Mojave (mō hä′vĭ), *n.*, *adj.* Mohave.

Mojave Desert (mō hä′vĭ), a desert in S California: part of the Great Basin. ab. 15,000 sq. mi. Also, **Mohave Desert.**

Moji (mō′jē′), *n.* a seaport in SW Japan, on N Kyushu island. 152,081 (1964).

Mokau (mŏk′ou, mō kou′), *n.* a river in W North Island, New Zealand, flowing W to the Tasman Sea. 85 mi.

moke (mōk), *n.* **1.** *Slang.* a donkey. **2.** *Austral. Slang.* an inferior horse. **3.** *U.S. Slang.* (offensive) a Negro.

Mokha (mŏk′ə), *n.* Mocha.

Mokpo (mŏk′pō′), *n.* a seaport in SW South Korea. 154,241 (1964).

mol (mōl), *n.* *Chem.* the molecular weight of a substance expressed in grams; gram molecule. Also, **mole.** [t. G, der. *Molekül* MOLECULE]

molal (mō′ləl), *adj.* *Chem.* **1.** pertaining to gram-molecular weight, or containing a mol. **2.** pertaining to a solution containing one mol of solute per 1000 grams of solvent.

molality (mō lăl′ĭ tĭ), *n.* *Chem.* the number of mols of solute per 1000 grams of solvent.

molar[1] (mō′lə), *n.* **1.** a tooth adapted for grinding with a broad biting surface as in human dentition. There are twelve molar teeth, three in each quadrant. **—***adj.* **2.** adapted for grinding, as teeth, esp. those in man, with a broad biting surface, situated behind the bicuspids. **3.** pertaining to such teeth. [t. L: s. *molāris* grinder]

molar[2] (mō′lə), *adj.* **1.** *Physics.* pertaining to a body of matter as a whole: contrasted with molecular and atomic. **2.** *Chem.* pertaining to a solution containing one mol of solute per litre of solution. [f. s. L *mōles* mass + -AR[1]]

molarity (mō lă′rĭ tĭ), *n.* *Chem.* the number of mols of solute per litre of solution.

molasses (mə lăs′ĭz), *n.* **1.** the uncrystallized syrup drained from raw sugar. **2.** *U.S.* treacle (def. 1). [t. Pg.: m. *melaço*, g. LL *mellāceum* must, der. *mel* honey]

Mold (mōld), *n.* a town in NE Wales, the county town of Flintshire. 6857 (1961).

mold (mōld), *n.*, *v.t.*, *v.i.* *U.S.* mould.

Moldau (*Ger.* mŏl′dou), *n.* German name of **Vltava.**

Moldavia (mŏl dā′vyə), *n.* **1.** a historic region in NE Rumania; formerly a principality which united with Walachia to form Rumania. *Cap.:* Jassy. **2.** Official name, **Moldavian Soviet Socialist Republic.** a constituent republic of the Soviet Union, in the SW part: formed in 1940 from the former autonomous republic of Moldavia and the ceded Rumanian territory of Bessarabia. 3,500,000 pop. (est. 1965); 13,100 sq. mi. *Cap.:* Kishinev. **—Molda′vian,** *adj.*, *n.*

moldavite (mŏl′də vīt′), *n.* a natural green glass, found in Bohemia and thought to be of possible meteoritic origin. Cf. **tektite.**

moldboard (mōld′bôd′), *n.* *U.S.* mouldboard.

molder (mōl′də), *v.i.*, *v.t.*, *n.* *U.S.* moulder.

molding (mōl′dĭng), *n.* *U.S.* moulding.

molding board, *U.S.* moulding board.

moldy (mōl′dĭ), *adj.* *U.S.* mouldy.

mole[1] (mōl), *n.* **1.** a small congenital spot or blemish on the human skin, usually of a dark colour and slightly elevated, and often hairy. **2.** a pigmented naevus. [ME; OE *māl*, c. OHG *meil* wrinkle, blemish]

European mole, *Talpa europaea* (Up to 6 in. long)

mole[2] (mōl), *n.* any of various small insectivorous mammals, esp. of the family *Talpidae*, living chiefly underground, and having velvety fur, very small eyes, and strong, fossorial forefeet. [ME *molle*, c. MD and MLG *mol*]

mole[3] (mōl), *n.* **1.** a massive structure, esp. of stone, set up in the water, as for a breakwater or a pier. **2.** an anchorage or harbour protected by such a structure. [t. L: m. *mōles* mass, dam]

mole[4] (mōl), *n.* mol.

mole[5] (mōl), *n.* *Pathol.* a fleshy mass in the uterus formed by a haemorrhagic dead ovum. [t. L: m. s. *mola* false conception, millstone]

Molech (mō′lĕk), *n.* Moloch (defs 1, 2).

molecular (mō lĕk′yŏŏ lə), *adj.* pertaining to, caused by or consisting of molecules. [f. s. NL *mōlēcula* MOLECULE + -AR[1]] **—molec′ularly,** *adv.*

molecular beam, *Physics.* a stream of molecules in a vacuum moving in directions almost parallel, produced experimentally by passing the molecules through a series of narrow openings. Also, **molecular ray.**

molecular biology, *Biochem.* the study of the structure and activity of biological macromolecules at a molecular level.

molecular distillation, *Chem.* vacuum distillation in which the mean free path of the distillate molecules is of the same order as the distance between the heating and condensing surfaces; used for isotope separation.

molecular film, *Phys. Chem.* a film or layer one molecule thick.

molecular formula, *Chem.* the formula of a chemical compound showing the number and kind of atoms present in the molecule, but not their arrangement.

molecular volume, *Chem.* the volume occupied by one mol of a substance.

molecular weight, *Chem.* the average weight of a molecule of an element or compound measured in units based on one twelfth of the weight of an atom of carbon-12; the sum of the atomic weights of all the atoms in a molecule.

molecule (mŏl′ĭ kyōōl′), *n.* **1.** *Chem.*, *Physics.* the smallest physical unit of an element or compound, consisting of one or more like atoms in the first case, and two or more different atoms in the second case. **2.** a quantity of a substance, the weight of which, measured in any chosen unit, is numerically equal to the molecular weight; gram molecule. **3.** any very small particle. [t. NL: m. *mōlēcula*, dim. of L *mōles* mass. Cf. MOLE[3], MOL]

molehill (mōl′hĭl′), *n.* **1.** a small mound or ridge of earth raised up by moles burrowing under the ground. **2.** something insignificant, esp. an obstacle or difficulty: *to make a mountain out of a molehill.*

mole-rat (mōl′ răt′), *n.* *S African.* blesmol.

moleskin (mōl′skĭn′), *n.* **1.** the fur of the mole, soft, deep grey in colour, and very fragile. **2.** a stout, napped, twilled cotton fabric used for sportsmen's and labourers' clothing. **3.** (*pl.*) garments, esp. trousers, of this fabric.

molest (mə lĕst′), *v.t.* to interfere with annoyingly, injuriously, or with hostile intent. [ME *moleste(n)*, t. L: m. *molestāre*] **—molestation** (mō′lĕs tā′shən), *n.* **—molest′er,** *n.* **—Syn.** See **attack.**

Molfetta (*It.* mȯl fĕt′tȧ), *n.* a seaport in Italy, in Apulia, on the Adriatic. 64,621 (1966).

Molière (mŏl′ĭ ĕə′; *Fr.* mō lyĕr′), *n.* (*Jean Baptiste Poquelin*), 1622–73, French writer of comedies.

Molina (*Sp.* mȯ lē′nȧ), *n.* **Tirso de** (*Sp.* tēr′sȯ dė), (*Gabriel Téllez*), ?1571–1648, Spanish dramatist.

moll (mŏl), *n.* *Slang.* **1.** the girl friend or mistress of a gangster, thief, etc. **2.** a prostitute. [short for *Molly*, var. of MARY]

mollescent (mō lĕs′ənt), *adj.* producing less hardness or firmness; softening. [t. L: s. *mollescens*, ppr.] **—molles′cence,** *n.*

mollify (mŏl′ĭ fī′), *v.t.*, **-fied, -fying. 1.** to soften in feeling or temper, as a person, the heart or mind, etc. 2. to mitigate or appease, as rage. [ME *mollifie(n)*, t. L: m. s. *mollificāre* soften] —**mol′lifica′tion,** *n.* —**mol′lifi′er,** *n.* —**mol′lify′ingly,** *adv.* —**mol′lifi′able,** *adj.*

mollusc (mŏl′əsk), *n.* any invertebrate of the phylum *Mollusca*, characterized by a calcareous shell (sometimes lacking) of one, two, or more pieces that wholly or partly encloses the soft unsegmented body and including the chitons, snails, bivalves, squids, octopuses, etc. Also, *U.S.*, **mollusk.** [t. NL: m. s. *mollusca*, pl., in L neut. pl. of *molluscus* soft (applied to a thin-shelled nut)] —**molluscan** (mō lŭs′kən), *adj.*, *n.* —**mol′lusc-like′,** *adj.*

molluscoid (mō lŭs′koid), *adj.* denoting or pertaining to an animal group comprising the bryozoans and brachiopods. Also, **molluscoidal** (mŏl′ŭs koi′dl).

molluscum (mō lŭs′kəm), *n.*, *pl.* **-ca** (-kə). *Pathol.* any of various soft, rounded, cutaneous tumours.

molly (mŏl′ĭ), *n.*, *pl.* **mollies.** a livebearing fish of the genus *Mollienisia*, often kept in aquariums. [shortened form of NL *Mollienisia*, named after Comte de *Mollien*, 1758–1850]

mollycoddle (mŏl′ĭ kŏd′l), *n.*, *v.*, **-dled, -dling.** —*n.* 1. a man or boy who is used to being coddled; a milksop. —*v.t.* 2. to coddle; pamper. [f. *Molly* (var. of MARY) + CODDLE] —**mol′lycod′dler,** *n.*

Molnár (*Hung.* mōl′när), *n.* **Ferenc** (*Hung.* fĕ′rĕnts), 1878–1952, Hungarian dramatist and novelist.

Moloch (mō′lŏk), *n.* 1. a Semitic deity, mentioned in the Bible, whose worship was marked by the sacrifice by burning of children offered by their own parents. 2. anything conceived as requiring frightful sacrifice: *the Moloch of war.* 3. (*l.c.*) a spiny Australian lizard, *Moloch horridus.* Also, **Molech** for 1, 2. [t. L (Vulgate), t. Gk (Septuagint), t. Heb.: m. *Mōlek*, orig. *melek* king]

Molokai (mō′lō kä′ĭ), *n.* one of the Hawaiian Islands, in the central part of the group: leper colony. 4744 pop. (1960); 159 sq. mi.

Molopo (mə lō′pō), *n.* an intermittent river of the Republic of South Africa flowing W, then SW, forming the border of Cape Province and Botswana, then S to the river Orange ab. 600 mi.

Molotov (*Russ.* mô′lə təf), *n.* 1. **Viacheslav Mikhailovich** (*Russ.* vyə chĭ släf′ mĭ KHäy′lə vĭch), born 1890, Soviet statesman: commissar for foreign affairs 1939–49 and 1953–56. 2. former name of **Perm.**

Molotov cocktail, an incendiary bomb consisting of a bottle filled with an inflammable liquid, usually petrol, and a saturated wick which is ignited before the bottle is thrown. [named after V. M. MOLOTOV]

molt (mōlt), *v.*, *n.* *U.S.* moult.

molten (mōl′tən), *v.* 1. a pp. of **melt.** —*adj.* 2. liquefied by heat; in a state of fusion. 3. produced by melting and casting: *a molten image.*

Moltke (*Ger.* mōlt′kə), *n.* 1. **Helmuth Karl Bernhard** (*Ger.* hĕl′mōōt kärl bĕrn′härt), **Count von,** 1800–91, German field marshal. 2. his nephew, **Helmuth Johannes Ludwig** (*Ger.* yō hän′əs lōōt′vĭKH), **Count von,** 1848–1916, German general.

molto (mōl′tō), *adv.* *Music.* much; very: *molto allegro.* [It., g. L *multum*]

Moluccas (mō lŭk′əz, mə-), *n.pl.* a group of islands in Indonesia between Celebes and New Guinea. 747,000 pop. (est. 1961); ab. 30,000 sq. mi. Also, **Spice Islands.**

mol. wt, molecular weight.

moly (mō′lĭ), *n.*, *pl.* **molies.** *Class. Myth.* a herb given by Hermes to Odysseus to counteract the spells of Circe. [t. L, t. Gk]

molybdate (mō lĭb′dāt), *n.* *Chem.* a salt of any molybdic acid.

molybdenite (mō lĭb′dĭ nīt′), *n.* a soft, graphite-like mineral, molybdenum sulphide, MoS_2, occurring in foliated masses or scales: principal ore of molybdenum. [f. s. obs. *molybdena* MOLYBDENUM + -ITE[1]]

molybdenous (mō lĭb′dĭ nəs), *adj.* *Chem.* containing divalent molybdenum.

molybdenum (mō lĭb′dĭ nəm), *n.* *Chem.* a silver-white high-melting metalloid, alloyed with iron in making hard, high-speed cutting tools. *Symbol:* Mo; *at. wt:* 95·94; *at. no.:* 42; *sp. gr.:* 10·2. [t. NL, t. L: m. *molybdaena*, t. Gk: m. *molýbdaina* galena]

molybdenum trioxide, *Chem.* a white crystalline powder, MoO_3, which is the anhydride of molybdic acid; used in the manufacture of molybdenum compounds. Also, **molybdic anhydride, molybdic oxide.**

molybdic (mō lĭb′dĭk), *adj.* *Chem.* of or containing molybdenum, esp. in the trivalent or hexavalent states.

molybdic acid, *Chem.* a yellowish crystalline solid, H_2MoO_4.

molybdite (mō lĭb′dīt), *n.* *Chem.* a hydrous ferric molybdate, occurring in molybdenite. Also, **molybdic ochre.**

mom (mŏm), *n.* *Dial.*, *U.S. Colloq.* mother.

Mombasa (mŏm băs′ə), *n.* a seaport on **Mombasa Island** in S Kenya. 179,575 (1962).

moment (mō′mənt), *n.* 1. an indefinitely short space of time; an instant: *wait a moment.* 2. the present or other particular instant: *I cannot recall his name at the moment.* 3. a definite stage, as in a course of events. 4. importance or consequence: *of great moment.* 5. *Statistics.* the average of a given power of the values of a set of variates. 6. *Philos.* an essential or constituent element or factor; momentum. 7. *Mech.* **a.** tendency to produce motion, esp. about an axis. **b.** (of a physical quantity) the product of the quantity and its perpendicular distance from an axis: *moment of area, moment of mass, etc.* [ME, t. L: s. *mōmentum* movement, moment of time, etc.] —**Syn.** 1. See **minute**[1].

momentarily (mō′mən tə rĭ lĭ, -trĭ lĭ), *adv.* 1. for a moment: *to hesitate momentarily.* 2. every moment; from moment to moment: *danger momentarily increasing.* 3. at any moment: *momentarily liable to occur.*

momentary (mō′mən tə rĭ, -trĭ), *adj.* 1. lasting but a moment; very brief: *a momentary glimpse.* 2. occurring at any moment: *to live in fear of momentary exposure.* 3. *Rare.* constant. —**mo′mentariness,** *n.*

momently (mō′mənt lĭ), *adv.* 1. every moment; from moment to moment. 2. for a moment; momentarily.

moment of inertia, *Physics.* the sum of the products of the mass of each element of a body and the square of its distance from an axis about which the body rotates.

moment of truth, 1. the climax of a bullfight when the matador is about to kill the animal. 2. any moment when a person's character, courage, skill, etc., are put to a severe test.

momentous (mō mĕn′təs), *adj.* of great importance or consequence; fraught with serious or far-reaching consequences, as events, decisions, etc. —**momen′tously,** *adv.* —**momen′tousness,** *n.* —**Syn.** See **heavy.**

momentum (mō mĕn′təm), *n.*, *pl.* **-ta** (-tə). 1. *Mech.* the quantity of motion of a moving body, equal to the product of its mass and velocity. 2. impetus, as of a moving body. 3. *Philos.* a moment (def. 6). [t. L. See MOMENT]

Mommsen (mŏm′sən; *Ger.* mŏm′zən), *n.* **Theodor** (*Ger.* tė′ō dōr), 1817–1903, German historian and philologist.

Momus (mō′məs), *n.* 1. *Gk Myth.* the god of censure and ridicule. 2. (*sometimes l.c.*) a faultfinder; a carping critic. [t. L, t. Gk: m. *mômos*, lit., blame, ridicule]

Mon (mōn), *n.* one of the Mon-Khmer languages.

mon-, var. of **mono-,** before vowels.

Mon., 1. Monday. 2. Monmouthshire. 3. Monsignor.

mon., 1. monastery. 2. monetary.

monachal (mŏn′ə kl), *adj.* monastic. [t. ML: s. *monachālis*, der. LL *monachus* MONK]

monachism (mŏn′ə kĭz′əm), *n.* monasticism.

Monaco (mŏn′ə kō′; *It.* mŏ′nä kō; *Fr.* mō nä kō′), *n.* 1. a principality on the Mediterranean coast, bordering SE France. 20,441 pop. (est. 1966); ½ sq. mi. 2. the capital of this principality. 1860 (1951).

Monaco

monad (mŏn′ăd, mō′năd), *n.* 1. *Biol.* **a.** any simple single-celled organism. **b.** a certain type of small, flagellate, colourless, naked amoeboid with one to three flagella. 2. *Chem.* an element, atom or radical having a valency of one. 3. *Philos.* an entity, conceived after the fashion of the self, and regarded as the ultimate unit of being or as a microcosm. 4. a single unit or entity. [t. LL: s. *monas*, t. Gk: unit] —**monadic** (mō năd′ĭk), **monad′ical,** *adj.* —**monad′ically,** *adv.*

monadelphous (mŏn′ə dĕl′fəs), *adj.* *Bot.* 1. (of stamens) united into one bundle or set by their filaments. 2. (of a plant or flower) having the stamens so united. [f. MON- + s. Gk *adelphós* brother + -OUS]

Monadelphous flower of hollyhock, *Althaea rosea*

Monadhliath Mountains (mŏn′ə lĭə′), a range of mountains in the Grampians of Scotland. Highest point, Carn Ban, 3087 ft.

monadism (mŏn′ə dĭz′əm, mō′nə-), *n.* *Philos.* 1. the doctrine of monads as ultimate units of being. 2. the philosophy of Leibnitz. Also, **monadology** (mŏn′ə dŏl′ə jĭ, mō′nə-). —**mon′adis′tic,** *adj.*

monadnock (mə năd′nŏk), *n.* 1. *Phys. Geog.* a residual hill or mountain standing well above the surface of a surrounding peneplain. [from def. 2] **2.** (*cap.*) **Mount,** an isolated peak in SW New Hampshire, U.S. 3186 ft. [t. N Amer. Ind.: (object) standing out; isolated]

Monaghan (mŏn′ə hən), *n.* a county in NE Ireland. 47,088 pop. (1961); 498 sq. mi. *Co. town:* Monaghan.

Mona Lisa (mō′nə lē′zə), a famous portrait by Leonardo da Vinci of a young woman with an enigmatic smile. Also, **La Gioconda.**

monandrous (mŏ năn′drəs), *adj.* **1.** having only one husband at a time. **2.** of or characterized by monandry: *the monandrous system.* **3.** *Bot.* **a.** (of a flower) having only one stamen. **b.** (of a plant) having such flowers. [t. Gk: m. *mónandros* having one husband]

monandry (mŏ năn′drĭ), *n.* the practice or the condition of having only one husband at a time.

monanthous (mŏ năn′thəs), *adj. Bot.* having one flower. [f. MON- + s. Gk *ánthos* flower + -OUS]

Monandrous flower of mare's-tail, *Hippuris vulgaris*

Mona Passage (mō′nə; *Sp.* mô′nȧ), a strait between Hispaniola and Puerto Rico. ab. 80 mi. wide.

monarch (mŏn′ək), *n.* **1.** a hereditary sovereign with more or less limited powers, as a king, queen, emperor, etc. **2.** a sole and absolute ruler of a state. **3.** one who or that which holds a dominating or pre-eminent position. **4.** a large reddish brown butterfly, *Danaus menippe*, having black and white markings, whose larva feeds on milkweed. [late ME, t. LL: s. *monarcha*, t. Gk: m. *monárchēs* ruling alone]

monarchal (mŏ nä′kl), *adj.* **1.** pertaining to, characteristic of, or befitting a monarch. **2.** having the status of a monarch. Also, **monarchial** (mŏ nä′kyəl). —**monar′chally,** *adv.*

Monarchian (mŏ nä′kĭ ən), *Theol.* —*n.* **1.** one who holds that God must be understood as being a single deity, and rejecting the doctrine of the Trinity. Cf. **Unitarian. 2.** an adherent of a 2nd-3rd century heresy teaching this. —*adj.* **3.** denoting or pertaining to this doctrine or heresy. —**Monar′chianism,** *n.*

monarchical (mŏ nä′kĭ kl), *adj.* **1.** of a monarch or monarchy. **2.** characterized by or favouring monarchy. Also, **monar′chic.** —**monar′chically,** *adv.*

monarchism (mŏn′ə kĭz′əm), *n.* **1.** the principles of monarchy. **2.** advocacy of monarchical principles. —**mon′archist,** *n., adj.* —**mon′archis′tic,** *adj.*

monarchy (mŏn′ə kĭ), *n., pl.* **-chies. 1.** a government or state in which the supreme power is actually or nominally lodged in a monarch (known as an **absolute** or **despotic monarchy** when the monarch's authority is not limited by laws or a constitution, and as a **limited** or **constitutional monarchy** when the monarch's authority is so limited). **2.** supreme power or sovereignty wielded by a single person. [ME *monarchie*, t. LL: m. *monarchia*, t. Gk] —**Syn. 1.** See **kingdom.**

monarda (mŏ nä′ də), *n.* any of the labiate genus *Monarda*, of mintlike aromatic erect herbs of North America, including horsemint. [t. NL; named after N. *Monardés*, 1493–1588, Spanish physician and botanist]

monas (mŏn′ăs, mō′năs), *n., pl.* **monades** (mŏn′ə dēz′). monad. [t. LL]

monastery (mŏn′əs tə rĭ, -trĭ), *n., pl.* **-teries. 1.** a house or place of residence occupied by a community of persons, esp. monks, living in seclusion from the world under religious vows. **2.** the community of persons living in such a place. [ME, t. LL: m. s. *monastērium*, t. LGk: m. *monastḗrion* solitary dwelling] —**monasterial** (mŏn′ə stĭə′rĭ əl), *adj.*

monastic (mə năs′tĭk), *adj.* Also, **monastical. 1.** of or pertaining to monasteries: *monastic architecture.* **2.** of, pertaining to, or characteristic of monks, or other persons living in seclusion from the world under religious vows: *monastic vows of poverty, chastity, and obedience.* —*n.* **3.** a member of a monastic community or order; a monk. [t. ML: s. *monasticus*, t. LGk: m. *monastikós* living in solitude] —**monas′tically,** *adv.*

monasticism (mə năs′tĭ sĭz′əm), *n.* the monastic system, condition, or mode of life.

Monastir (mŏn′ə stĭə′), *n.* Turkish name of **Bitolj.**

monatomic (mŏn′ə tŏm′ĭk), *adj. Chem.* **1.** having one atom in the molecule. **2.** containing one replaceable atom or group. **3.** having a valency of one.

monaural (mŏ nô′rəl), *adj.* of or pertaining to one ear.

monaxial (mŏ năk′sĭ əl), *adj. Bot.* **1.** uniaxial. **2.** having flowers that grow on the primary axis.

monazite (mŏn′ə zīt′), *n.* a reddish brown or yellowish brown mineral, a phosphate of cerium and lanthanum, $(Ce,La)PO_4$, the principal ore of thorium. [t. G: m. *Monazit*, f. s. Gk *monázein* be alone + -it -ITE[1]]

Mönchen-Gladbach (*Ger.* mœn′ᴋʜən glăt′bȧᴋʜ), *n.* a town in West Germany, in W North Rhine-Westphalia. 154,200 (est. 1966). Formerly, **München-Gladbach.**

Monck (mŭngk), *n.* **George** (*1st Duke of Albemarle*), 1608–70, English general. Also, **Monk.**

Monday (mŭn′dĭ), *n.* the second day of the week, following Sunday. [ME *Mone(n)day*, OE *mōn(an)dæg* moon's day, used to render LL *Lūnae dies*]

Mond process (mŏnd), *Chem.* a method of extracting pure nickel from the impure metal by reacting carbon monoxide with the metal to form the carbonyl which is decomposed by heating into pure nickel and carbon monoxide. [named after Ludwig *Mond*, 1839–1909, British chemist, born in Germany]

Mondriaan (*Du.* môn′drē ȧn), *n.* **Piet** (*Du.* pēt), 1872–1944, Dutch painter.

monecious (mŏ nē′shəs), *adj.* monoecious.

Monegasque (mŏn′ə găsk′), *adj.* **1.** of or pertaining to Monaco or its inhabitants. —*n.* **2.** a native or inhabitant of Monaco.

Monel metal (mŏ nĕl′), **1.** a non-rusting, silvery-white alloy containing about 67 per cent nickel, 28 per cent copper, and 5 per cent other metals, produced from the nickeliferous ores of the Sudbury district in Canada, and used for a great number of purposes. **2.** a trademark for this metal. Also, **Monell metal.** [named after Ambrose *Monell*, died 1921, of New York]

Monet (*Fr.* mŏ nĕ′), *n.* **Claude** (*Fr.* klōd), 1840–1926, French painter.

monetary (mŭn′ĭ tə rĭ, -trĭ), *adj.* **1.** of or pertaining to the coinage or currency of a country. **2.** of or pertaining to money, or pecuniary: *monetary consideration.* [t. L: m. s. *monētārius* pertaining to the mint] —**mon′etarily,** *adv.* —**Syn. 1.** See **financial.**

monetary unit, the standard unit of value of the currency of a country.

monetize (mŭn′ĭ tīz′), *v.t.*, **-tized, -tizing. 1.** to legalize as money. **2.** to coin into money: *to monetize gold.* **3.** to give the character of money to. Also, **monetise.** —**mon′etiza′tion,** *n.*

money (mŭn′ĭ), *n., pl.* **-eys, -ies. 1.** gold, silver, or other metal in pieces of convenient form stamped by public authority and issued as a medium of exchange and measure of value. **2.** current coin. **3.** coin or certificate (as banknotes, etc.) generally accepted in payment of debts and current transactions. **4.** any article or substance similarly used. **5.** a particular form or denomination of currency. **6.** a money of account. **7.** property considered with reference to its pecuniary value. **8.** an amount or sum of money. **9.** wealth reckoned in terms of money. **10.** (*pl.*) *Archaic or Legal.* pecuniary sums. **11.** pecuniary profit. **12. for one's money,** as far as one's own choice or preference is concerned; in one's own opinion. **13. in the money,** *Slang.* rich. **14. make money,** to become rich. **15. money's worth,** full value; greatest possible advantage. **16. put money into,** to invest in. [ME *moneye*, t. OF: m. *moneie*, g. L *monēta* mint, money, der. *Jūno Monēto* Juno the Adviser, in whose temple at Rome money was coined] —**Syn. 1.** coin, cash, currency, specie, change. **7.** funds, capital, assets.

moneybag (mŭn′ĭ băg′), *n.* **1.** a bag for money. **2.** (*pl. construed as sing.*) a wealthy person.

moneybox (mŭn′ĭ bŏks′), *n.* a closed or locked box into which coins are dropped through a slit, used for savings, collecting contributions to charities, etc.

moneychanger (mŭn′ĭ chān′jə), *n.* one whose business it is to change money at a fixed or official rate.

moneyed (mŭn′ĭd), *adj.* **1.** having money; wealthy. **2.** consisting of or representing money: *moneyed interests.*

money-grubber (mŭn′ĭ grŭb′ə), *n. Colloq.* an avaricous person; one devoted entirely to the making of money. —**mon′ey-grub′bing,** *adj.*

moneylender (mŭn′ĭ lĕn′də), *n.* one whose business it is to lend money at interest.

moneymaker (mŭn′ĭ mā′kə), *n.* **1.** one engaged in or successful at gaining money. **2.** something that yields pecuniary profit. —**mon′eymak′ing,** *n., adj.*

money of account, a monetary denomination used in reckoning, esp. one not issued as a coin.

money order, an order for the payment of money, as one issued by one post office and payable at another.

money-spinner (mŭn′ĭ spĭn′ə), *n. Colloq.* a business enterprise or property which is very profitable.

moneywort (mŭn′ĭ wût′), *n.* a creeping primulaceous herb, *Lysimachia nummularia*, with roundish leaves and yellow flowers.

mong (mŭng), *n. Austral. Colloq.* a mongrel dog.

Monge (*Fr.* mônzh), *n.* **Gaspard** (*Fr.* gȧs pȧr′) (*Comte de Péluse*), 1746–1818, French mathematician.

monger (mŭng′gə), *n.* (usually in compounds) **1.** a

dealer in some commodity: *a fishmonger.* **2.** one who busies himself with something in a sordid or petty way: *a scandalmonger.* [ME *mongere*, OE *mangere* (c. Icel. *mangari*), f. L *mang(o)* trader + *-ere* -ER[1]] —**mon′gering,** *n., adj.*

Mongol (mŏng′gŏl, -gl), *n.* **1.** one of an Asian people now living chiefly in Mongolia. **2.** one having Mongoloid characteristics. **3.** any Mongolian language. **4.** (*often l.c.*) *Pathol.* one afflicted with Mongolism. —*adj.* **5.** Mongolian. **6.** (*often l.c.*) *Pathol.* of or pertaining to Mongolism.

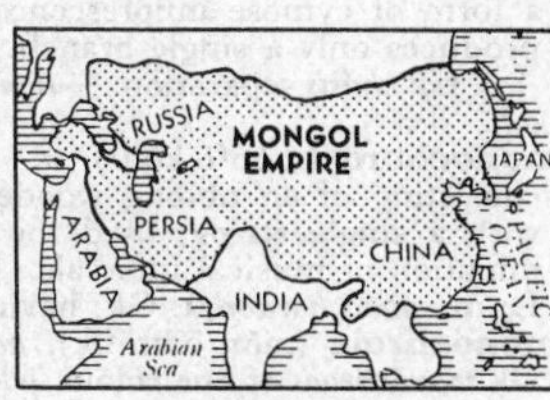

Mongol Empire

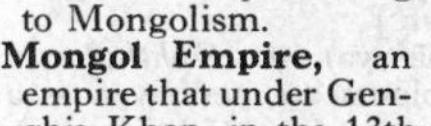

Mongol Empire, an empire that under Genghis Khan, in the 13th century, encompassed the larger part of Asia and extended to the river Dnieper in E Europe.

Mongolia (mŏng gō′lyə), *n.* **1.** a vast region in Asia, including Inner Mongolia, the Mongolian People's Republic, and Tannu Tuva. **2.** **Inner.** Official name, **Inner Mongolian Autonomous Region.** the S part of Mongolia, an autonomous region of China. 9,200,000 (1957). *Cap.*: Huhehot. **3.** **Outer,** former name of **Mongolian People's Republic.**

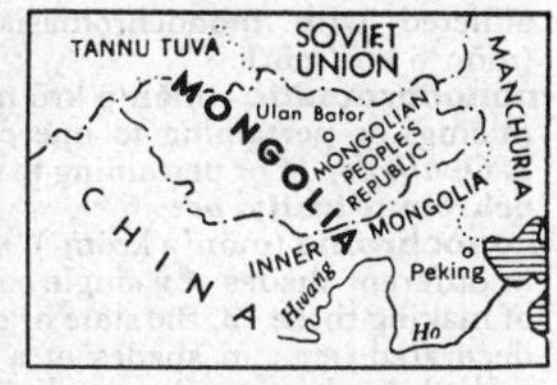

Mongolia

Mongolian (mŏng gō′lyən), *adj.* **1.** pertaining to Mongolia. **2.** of or pertaining to the Mongol people of inner Asia. **3.** *Anthropol.* Mongoloid. **4.** (*often l.c.*) affected with Mongolism. **5.** of or pertaining to Mongolian (def. 9). —*n.* **6.** a member of the Mongoloid peoples of Asia. **7.** a native or inhabitant of Inner Mongolia. **8.** a native or inhabitant of the Mongolian People's Republic. **9.** a subfamily of languages, including the languages of the Mongols, a member of the Altaic linguistic family. **10.** any of the languages of this family.

Mongolian People's Republic, a republic in E central Asia: the N part of Mongolia. 1,044,900 pop. (1964); 604,095 sq. mi. *Cap.*: Ulan Bator. Formerly, **Outer Mongolia.**

Mongolic (mŏng gŏl′ĭk), *adj.* **1.** Mongolian. —*n.* **2.** Mongolian (def. 9).

Mongolism (mŏng′gə lĭz′əm), *n.* (*often l.c.*) *Pathol.* the abnormal condition of a child born with a wide flattened skull, narrow, slanting eyes, and mental deficiency; Down's syndrome.

Mongoloid (mŏng′gə loid′), *adj.* **1.** resembling the Mongols. **2.** *Anthropol.* of, pertaining to, or characteristic of a racial division of mankind, characterized chiefly by yellowish complexion, prominent cheekbones, epicanthic folds about the eyes, short nose, straight black hair, and scanty facial hair, and including the Mongols, Manchus, Chinese, Koreans, Japanese, Annamese, Siamese, Burmese and Tibetans. **3.** (*often l.c.*) *Pathol.* of, pertaining to, or characteristic of Mongolism. —*n.* **4.** a person of a Mongoloid race. **5.** (*often l.c.*) *Pathol.* one afflicted with Mongolism.

Mongoose, *Herpestes edwardsii* (Total length ab. 3 ft, tail ab. 1½ ft)

mongoose (mŏng′-gōōs′), *n., pl.* **-gooses.** a slender ferret-like carnivore, typified by *Herpestes edwardsii*, of India, of the same genus as the common ichneumon, used for destroying rats, etc., and noted for its ability to kill certain venomous snakes. [t. Marathi: m. *mangūs*]

mongrel (mŭng′grəl), *n.* **1.** any animal or plant resulting from the crossing of different breeds or varieties. **2.** any cross between different things. **3.** a dog of mixed or uncertain breed. —*adj.* **4.** of or like a mongrel; of mixed breed, race, origin, nature, etc. [f. obs. *mong* mixture (OE *gemang*) + -REL] —**mon′grelism, mon′grelness,** *n.* —**mon′grelly,** *adv.* —**Syn.** **4.** See **hybrid.** —**Ant.** **1.** thoroughbred.

mongrelize (mŭng′grə līz′), *v.t.,* **-lized, -lizing.** to subject (a breed, race, etc.) to crossbreeding, esp. with a breed or race considered inferior; to make mongrel in race, composition, character, etc. Also, **mongrelise.** —**mon′greliza′tion,** *n.* —**mon′greliz′er,** *n.*

mongst (mŭngst), *prep. Poetic.* amongst.

moniker (mŏn′ĭ kə), *n. Slang.* a person's name; a nickname. Also, **mon′icker.** [b. MONOGRAM and MARKER]

moniliform (mō nĭl′ĭ fôm′), *adj.* **1.** *Bot., Zool.* consisting of or characterized by a series of beadlike swellings alternating with contractions, as certain roots, stems, etc. **2.** resembling a string of beads. [f. s. L *monīle* necklace + -(I)FORM]

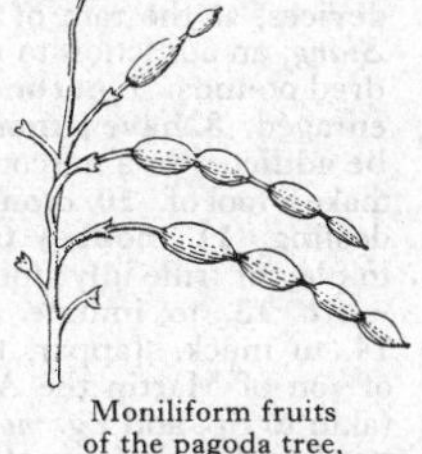
Moniliform fruits of the pagoda tree, *Sophora japonica*

monism (mŏn′ĭz′əm), *n. Philos.* **1.** the doctrine of one ultimate substance or principle, as mind (*idealism*) or matter (*materialism*), or something that is neither mind nor matter but the ground of both. **2.** the theory that reality is one (opposed to ***pluralism***). [t. NL: s. *monismus*, der. Gk *mónos* single] —**mon′ist,** *n.* —**monistic** (mō-nĭs′tĭk), *adj.* —**monis′tically,** *adv.*

monition (mō nĭsh′ən), *n.* **1.** admonition; warning; caution. **2.** an official or legal notice. **3.** *Obs. Law.* a court order summoning a party, either to commence suit by appearance and answer or to answer contempt charges. **4.** a formal notice from a bishop requiring the amendment of an ecclesiastical offence. [ME, t. L: s. *monitio* a reminding]

monitor (mŏn′ĭ tə), *n.* **1.** a pupil appointed to assist in the conduct of a class or school, as to help keep order, etc. **2.** one who admonishes, esp. with reference to conduct. **3.** something that serves to remind or give warning. **4.** a device used to check, observe, or record the operation of a machine or system. **5.** (formerly) an ironclad warship with a low freeboard and one or more revolving turrets, each containing one or more large-calibre guns. **6.** (in hydraulic mining) a nozzle for projecting water at and breaking up sand or gravel; giant. **7.** *U.S.* a raised construction on a roof having windows for lighting or ventilating a building, as a factory or warehouse. **8.** any of the large lizards constituting the genus *Varanus* and family *Varanidae* of Africa, the East Indies, and Australia, supposed to give warning of the presence of crocodiles. **9.** *Television.* a screen or set of screens used, as in a studio, to check the transmission. —*v.t., v.i.* **10.** *Radio, Television.* **a.** to listen to or watch (transmitted signals) using a receiving set in order to check the quality of the transmission. **b.** to listen to (broadcasts) for operating compliance, censorship, propaganda analysis, and similar purposes. **11.** to check, observe, or record, the operation of a machine, etc., without interfering with the operation. **12.** to supervise; observe critically. [t. L] —**mon′itorship′,** *n.*

monitorial (mŏn′ĭ tô′rĭ əl), *adj.* **1.** of or pertaining to a monitor. **2.** monitory.

monitory (mŏn′ĭ tə rĭ, -trĭ), *adj., n., pl.* **-ries.** —*adj.* **1.** serving to admonish or warn; admonitory. **2.** giving monition. —*n.* **3.** Also, **monitory letter.** a letter, as one from a bishop, containing a monition. [late ME, t. L: m. s. *monitōrius*, adj.]

monitress (mŏn′ĭ trĭs), *n.* a girl appointed to help keep order in school or to assist a teacher; a female monitor.

monk (mŭngk), *n.* a man who has withdrawn from the world from religious motives, either as an eremite or, esp., as a member of an order of coenobites living under vows of poverty, chastity, and obedience, according to a rule. [ME; OE *munuc*, ult. t. LL: m. s. *monachus*, t. LGk: m. *monachós*, adj., solitary (as n., monk)]

—**Syn.** MONK, FRIAR refer to special male groups in the Rom. Cath. Church whose lives are devoted to the service of the church. A MONK is properly a member of a monastery, under a superior; he is bound by a vow of stability, and is a co-owner of the community property of the monastery. Since the Reformation, MONK and FRIAR have been used as if they were the same. A FRIAR is, however, strictly speaking, a member of a mendicant order, whose members are not attached to a monastery and own no community property.

Monk (mŭngk), *n.* See **Monck.**

monkery (mŭng′kə rĭ), *n., pl.* **-ries.** **1.** the way of life, behaviour, etc., of monks. **2.** (disparagingly) the practices, beliefs, etc., of monks.

monkey (mŭng′kĭ), *n., pl.* **-keys,** *v.,* **-keyed, -keying.** —*n.* **1.** any member of the mammalian order *Primates*, including the guenons, macaques, langurs, capuchins, etc.,

Rhesus monkey, *Macacus rhesus* (Total length 2 ft, tail ab. 10 in.)

but excluding man, the anthropoid apes, and usually, the lemurs. **2.** a person likened to such an animal, as a mischievous child, a mimic, etc. **3.** the fur of certain species of long-haired monkeys. **4.** any of various mechanical devices, as the ram of a pile-driving apparatus. **5.** *U.S. Slang.* an addiction to narcotic drugs. **6.** *Slang.* five hundred pounds. **7. get one's monkey up,** to become angry or enraged. **8. have a monkey on one's back,** *U.S. Slang.* to be addicted to a narcotic drug. **9. make a monkey of,** to make a fool of. **10. monkey business,** trickery; underhand dealing. **11. monkey tricks,** mischief. *—v.i.* **12.** *Colloq.* to play or trifle idly; fool (often fol. by *about with* or *with*). *—v.t.* **13.** to imitate as a monkey does; ape; mimic. **14.** to mock. [appar. t. LG. Cf. MLG *Moneke* (name of son of Martin the Ape in story of Reynard), f. *mone-* (akin to Sp. and Pg. *mono* ape) + *-ke* (dim. suffix)]

monkey-block (mŭng′kĭ blŏk′), *n. Naut.* a small block that swivels.

monkey-bread (mŭng′kĭ brĕd′), *n.* **1.** the gourdlike fruit of the baobab, eaten by monkeys. **2.** the tree itself.

monkey-faced owl (mŭng′kĭ fāst′), the barn owl, *Tyto alba.*

monkey-flower (mŭng′kĭ flou′ə), *n.* any plant of the scrophulariaceous genus *Mimulus,* which includes species cultivated in gardens and greenhouses, as *M. cardinalis,* having a scarlet corolla.

monkey-gaff (mŭng′kĭ găf′), *n. Naut.* a small gaff for supporting a flag.

monkey-jacket (mŭng′kĭ jăk′ĭt), *n.* **1.** a mess jacket. **2.** a short, close-fitting jacket.

monkey-nut (mŭng′kĭ nŭt′), *n.* peanut.

monkey orchid, a small orchid with spikes of white and red flowers, *Orchis simia,* occurring on chalk grassland in Europe and W Asia.

monkeypot (mŭng′kĭ pŏt′), *n.* the woody, operculate seed vessel of any of certain large South American trees of the genus *Lecythis.*

monkey-puzzle (mŭng′kĭ pŭz′əl), *n.* a South American coniferous tree, *Araucaria araucana,* with candelabra-like branches, stiff sharp leaves, and edible nuts; Chile pine.

monkeyshine (mŭng′kĭ shīn′), *n. U.S. Slang.* a mischievous or clownish trick or prank.

monkey-wrench, a spanner or wrench with an adjustable jaw, for turning nuts of different sizes, etc.

Monkey-wrench

monkfish (mŭngk′fĭsh′), *n.* a thin, flat guitar-shaped fish, *Rhina squatina,* related to the sharks and rays, found in the waters around the British Isles.

Mon-Khmer (mōn′kmĕə′), *adj.* **1.** of or pertaining to a group of related languages of south-east Asia, including Mon and Khmer. *—n.* **2.** these languages collectively.

monkhood (mŭngk′hŏŏd′), *n.* **1.** the condition or profession of a monk. **2.** monks collectively.

monkish (mŭng′kĭsh), *adj.* (often in depreciatory use) of or pertaining to, characteristic of, or resembling a monk. —**monk′ishly,** *adv.* —**monk′ishness,** *n.*

monk's cloth, a heavy cotton fabric in a basket weave, used for curtains, bedspreads, etc.

monkshood (mŭngks′hŏŏd′), *n.* a plant of the genus *Aconitum,* esp. *A. napellus* (so called from the hooded flowers). See **aconite.**

monk's rhubarb, a rhizomatous, polygonaceous perennial, *Rumax alpinus,* a native of the mountains of S Europe and SW Asia, frequently found as an escape from cultivation elsewhere.

Monmouth (mŏn′məth), *n.* **1. James Scott, Duke of,** 1649–85, leader of a rebellion against James II: illegitimate son of Charles II. **2.** Monmouthshire.

Monmouthshire (mŏn′məth shĭə′, -shə), *n.* a county in W England, for administrative purposes included in Wales. 444,679 pop. (1961); 543 sq. mi. *Co. town:* Monmouth. *Abbrev.:* Mon. Also, **Monmouth.**

mono-, a word element: **1.** meaning 'alone', 'single', 'one'. **2.** denoting a monomolecular thickness, as in *monofilm, monolayer,* etc. **3.** adapted in chemistry to apply to compounds containing one atom of a particular element. Also, **mon-.** [t. Gk, comb. form of *mónos* alone]

mono (mŏn′ō), *n., pl.* **monos,** *adj. Colloq. —n.* **1.** a recording not adapted for stereophonic reproduction. *—adj.* **2.** monophonic.

monobasic (mŏn′ō bā′sĭk), *adj.* **1.** *Chem.* (of an acid) containing one replaceable hydrogen atom. **2.** *Biol.* monotypic.

monocable (mŏn′ō kā′bl), *n.* an aerial ropeway with a single moving cable.

monocarp (mŏn′ō kăp′), *n. Bot.* a plant that dies after having once borne fruit.

monocarpellary (mŏn′ō kä′pĭ lə rĭ), *adj. Bot.* consisting of a single carpel.

monocarpic (mŏn′ō kä′pĭk), *adj. Bot.* producing fruit once only and then dying.

monocarpous (mŏn′ō kä′pəs), *adj. Bot.* **1.** having a gynoecium which forms only a single ovary. **2.** monocarpic.

monochasium (mŏn′ō kā′zyəm), *n., pl.* **-sia** (-zyə). *Bot.* a form of cymose inflorescence in which the main axis produces only a single branch. [t. NL: f. *mono-* MONO- + s. Gk *chásis* separation + *-ium* -IUM] —**mon′ocha′sial,** *adj.*

monochord (mŏn′ō kôd′), *n.* an acoustical instrument consisting of an oblong wooden sounding box, usually with a single string, used for the mathematical determination of musical intervals. [ME *monocorde,* t. OF, t. L: m. *monochordon,* t. Gk: having a single string]

monochroic (mŏn′ō krō′ĭk), *adj.* of one colour. [f. s. Gk *monóchroos* of one colour + -IC]

monochromasia (mŏn′ō krō mā′zyə), *n. Ophthalm.* a defect of vision in which all colours are perceived as a single colour. Also, **monochromasy** (mŏn′ō krō′mə sĭ), **monochromatism** (mŏn′ō krō′mə tĭz′əm).

monochromat (mŏn′ō krō′măt), *n. Ophthalm.* one afflicted with monochromasia. Also, **monochromate** (mŏn′ō krō′māt).

monochromatic (mŏn′ō krō măt′ĭk), *adj.* **1.** of, producing, or pertaining to one colour or one wavelength. **2.** *Ophthalm.* of or pertaining to monochromasia. —**mon′ochromat′ically,** *adv.*

monochrome (mŏn′ə krōm′), *n.* **1.** a painting or drawing in different shades of a single colour. **2.** the art or method of making these. **3.** the state or condition of being painted, decorated, etc., in shades of a single colour. **4.** a black and white photograph. *—adj.* **5.** monochromatic. [t. Gk: m. s. *monóchrōmos* of one colour] —**mon′ochro′mic, mon′ochro′mical,** *adj.* —**mon′ochrom′ist,** *n.*

monocle (mŏn′ə kl), *n.* an eyeglass for one eye. [t. F, t. LL: m. s. *monoculus* one-eyed] —**mon′ocled,** *adj.*

monoclinal (mŏn′ō klī′nəl), *Geol. —adj.* **1.** dipping in one direction, as strata. **2.** pertaining to strata which dip in the same direction. *—n.* **3.** monocline. —**mon′ocli′nally,** *adv.*

monocline (mŏn′ō klīn′), *n. Geol.* a monoclinal structure or fold. [f. MONO- + m. s. Gk *klīnein* incline]

monoclinic (mŏn′ō klĭn′ĭk), *adj. Crystall.* denoting or pertaining to crystallization in which the crystals have three unequal axes, with one oblique intersection.

monoclinous (mŏn′ō klī′nəs, mŏn′ō klī′nəs), *adj. Bot.* (of a plant species, etc.) having both the stamens and pistils in the same flower.

monocoque (mŏn′ə kŏk′), *adj. Aeron.* a form of aeroplane fuselage construction in which all or most of the stresses are carried by the skin. [t. F: f. *mono-* MONO- + *coque* shell (t. L: m. s. *coccum*)]

monocotyledon (mŏn′ō kŏt′ĭ lē′dən), *n. Bot.* **1.** a plant with only one cotyledon. **2.** a member of the group *Monocotyledonae,* one of the two subclasses of angiospermous plants, characterized in the main by producing seeds with a single cotyledon or seed leaf, and by an endogenous mode of growth. —**monocotyledonous** (mŏn′ō kŏt′ĭ lē′də nəs), *adj.*

monocracy (mō nŏk′rə sĭ), *n., pl.* **-cies.** government by a single person; autocracy. —**monocratic** (mŏn′ə krăt′ĭk), *adj.*

monocrat (mŏn′ə krăt′), *n.* one favouring monocracy.

monocular (mō nŏk′yŏŏ lə), *adj.* **1.** having only one eye. **2.** pertaining to or intended for one eye: *a monocular microscope.* [f. s. LL *monoculus* one-eyed + -AR[1]]

monoculture (mŏn′ō kŭl′chə), *n. Agric.* the use of land for growing only one kind of crop.

monocyclic (mŏn′ō sī′klĭk), *adj.* **1.** having one cycle. **2.** *Bot.* arranged in a single whorl, as the parts of certain flowers.

monocyte (mŏn′ō sīt′), *n. Anat.* the largest unicellular leucocyte in the blood, having a bean-shaped nucleus.

monocytosis (mŏn′ō sī tō′sĭs), *n. Pathol.* an increase in the circulating monocytes in the blood, found in various bacterial infections, etc.

monodactylous (mŏn′ō dăk′tĭ ləs), *adj. Zool.* having only one digit or claw. Also, **mon′odac′tyl.** [t. Gk: m. *monodáktylos*]

monodic (mō nŏd′ĭk), *adj. Music.* pertaining to monody or homophony. Also, **monod′ical.** [t. Gk: m. s. *monōidikós*] —**monod′ically,** *adv.*

monodrama (mŏn′ō drä′mə), *n.* a dramatic piece for a single performer. —**monodramatic** (mŏn′ō drə măt′ĭk), *adj.*

monody (mŏn′ə dĭ), *n., pl.* **-dies. 1.** a Greek ode sung by a single voice, as in a tragedy; a lament. **2.** a poem in which one person laments another's death. **3.** *Music.* **a.** a style of composition in which one part or melody

predominates; homophony, as distinguished from polyphony. b. a piece in this style. [t. LL: m. s. *monōdia*, t. Gk: m. *monōidía* a solo, lament] —**mon′odist,** *n.*
monoecious (mŏ nē′shəs), *adj.* **1.** *Biol.* having both male and female organs in the same individual; hermaphroditic. **2.** *Bot.* (of a plant species, etc.) having the stamens and the pistils in separate flowers on the same plant. Also, **monecious.** [f. MON- + m. s. Gk *oíkion* house + -OUS]

Branch of a monoecious tree A, Male catkins; B, Female catkins

monofil (mŏn′ə fĭl), *n.* a single strand of synthetic fibre. Also, **monofilament** (mŏn′ə fĭl′ə mənt).
monogamist (mŏ nŏg′ə mĭst), *n.* one who practises or advocates monogamy. —**monog′amis′tic,** *adj.*
monogamous (mŏ nŏg′ə məs), *adj.* **1.** practising or advocating monogamy. **2.** pertaining to monogamy. [t. LL: m. *monogamus*, t. Gk: m. *monógamos*]
monogamy (mŏ nŏg′ə mĭ), *n.* **1.** marriage of one woman with one man. **2.** *Zool.* the habit of having only one mate. **3.** the practice of marrying only once during life.
monogenesis (mŏn′ō jĕn′ĭ sĭs), *n.* **1.** the theoretical descent of all living things from a single ancestral organism. **2.** the theoretical descent of the whole human race from a single pair. **3.** *Biol.* development of an ovum into an organism similar to its parent, without metamorphosis. Also, **monogeny** (mŏ nŏj′ĭ nĭ).
monogenetic (mŏn′ō jĭ nĕt′ĭk), *adj.* **1.** of or pertaining to monogenesis. **2.** having only one generation in the life cycle; without intermediate non-sexual generations: applied to trematode worms of the subclass *Monogenea.* **3.** *Geol.* resulting from one genetic process.
monogram (mŏn′ə grăm′), *n.* a character consisting of two or more letters combined or interlaced, commonly one's initials, often printed on stationery, embroidered on clothing, etc. [t. LL: m. *monogramma*, t. LGk: m. *monógrammon* single-lettered character. See MONO-, -GRAM[1]] —**monogrammatic** (mŏn′ə grə măt′ĭk), *adj.*
monograph (mŏn′ə grăf′, -gräf′), *n.* **1.** a treatise on a particular subject. **2.** an account of a single thing or class of things, as of a species of animals or plants. —**mon′ograph′ic,** *adj.* —**mon′ograph′ically,** *adv.*
monographer (mŏ nŏg′rə fə), *n.* the writer of a monograph.
monogyny (mŏ nŏj′ĭ nĭ), *n.* the practice or the condition of having only one wife at a time. [f. MONO- + m. s. Gk *-gynía*, der. *gynḗ* woman]
monohydric (mŏn′ō hī′drĭk), *adj.* *Chem.* (of a compound, usually an alcohol) having a single hydroxyl radical.
monolatry (mŏ nŏl′ə trĭ), *n.* the worship of one god only, when other gods are recognized as existing. [f. MONO- + m. s. Gk *latreía* worship] —**monolater** (mŏ nŏl′ə tə), **monol′atrist,** *n.* —**monol′atrous,** *adj.*
monolith (mŏn′ə lĭth), *n.* **1.** a single block or piece of stone of considerable size, esp. when used in architecture or sculpture. **2.** an obelisk, column, statue, etc., formed of a single block of stone. **3.** *Engineering.* a concrete, stone, or brick foundation sunk as an open caisson and excavated by a grabbing crane. **4.** something resembling a large block of stone, esp. in having a massive, uniform, or unyielding quality or character. [t. LL: s. *monolithus*, t. Gk: m. *monólithos* made of one stone]
monolithic (mŏn′ə lĭth′ĭk), *adj.* **1.** of or pertaining to a monolith. **2.** made of only one stone or a single block. **3.** characterized by massiveness and uniformity; undifferentiated.
monologue (mŏn′ə lŏg′), *n.* **1.** a prolonged talk or discourse by a single speaker. **2.** any composition, as a poem, in which a single person speaks alone. **3.** a part of a drama in which a single actor speaks alone. **4.** a form of dramatic entertainment by a single speaker. [t. F, t. Gk: m. s. *monólogos* speaking alone] —**monologic** (mŏn′ə lŏj′ĭk), **mon′olog′ical,** *adj.* —**monologist** (mŏn′ə lŏg′ĭst, mə nŏl′ə gĭst), *n.*
monology (mŏ nŏl′ə jĭ), *n.*, *pl.* **-gies.** **1.** the act or habit of soliloquizing. **2.** *Obs.* a monologue. [t. Gk: m. s. *monología*]
monomania (mŏn′ō mā′nyə), *n.* **1.** insanity in which the patient is irrational on one subject only. **2.** an exaggerated zeal for, or interest in, some one thing; a craze. —**monomaniac** (mŏn′ō mā′nĭ ăk′), *n.* —**monomaniacal** (mŏn′ō mə nī′ə kl), *adj.*
monomer (mŏn′ə mə), *n.* *Chem.* a molecule of low molecular weight capable of reacting with identical or indifferent monomers to form a polymer.
monomerous (mŏ nŏm′ə rəs), *adj.* *Bot.* (of flowers) having one member in each whorl. [f. s. Gk *monomerḗs* consisting of one part + -OUS]
monometallic (mŏn′ō mĭ tăl′ĭk), *adj.* **1.** of or using one metal. **2.** pertaining to monometallism.
monometallism (mŏn′ō mĕt′ə lĭz′əm), *n.* **1.** the use of one metal only (as gold or silver) as the monetary standard. **2.** the doctrine or actions supporting such a standard. —**mon′omet′alist,** *n.*
monometer (mŏ nŏm′ĭ tə), *n.* *Pros.* a line of verse having one measure or foot.
monomial (mŏ nō′myəl), *adj.* **1.** *Alg.* consisting of one term only. **2.** *Biol.* denoting or pertaining to a name which consists of a single word or term. —*n.* **3.** *Alg.* a monomial expression or quantity. [irreg. f. MO(NO)- + *-nomial*, after BINOMIAL]
monomolecular (mŏn′ō mə lĕk′yŏŏ lə), *adj.* indicating a thickness of one molecule.
monomorphic (mŏn′ō mô′fĭk), *adj.* **1.** *Biol.* having only one form. **2.** of the same or of an essentially similar type of structure. Also, **mon′omor′phous.**
mononuclear (mŏn′ō nyōō′klĭ ə), *adj.* **1.** *Anat.* having only one nucleus. —*n.* **2.** *Anat.* a cell having only one nucleus, esp. a monocyte. Also, **mononucleate** (mŏn′ō nyōō′klĭ ĭt).
mononucleosis (mŏn′ō nyōō′klĭ ō′sĭs), *n.* *Anat.* monocytosis.
monopetalous (mŏn′ō pĕt′ə ləs), *adj.* *Bot.* **1.** gamopetalous. **2.** having only one petal, as a corolla.
monophagia (mŏn′ō fā′jĭ ə, -jə), *n.* *Med.* the eating of or the desire for only one kind of food.
monophagous (mə nŏf′ə gəs), *adj.* *Med.* eating only one kind of food. —**monoph′agy,** *n.*
monophobia (mŏn′ō fō′byə), *n.* *Psychol.* morbid dread of being alone.
monophonic (mŏn′ō fŏn′ĭk), *adj.* **1.** of or pertaining to monophony. **2.** of or denoting a system of sound reproduction through only one loudspeaker (opposed to *stereophonic*).
monophony (mə nŏf′ə nĭ), *n.* a musical style consisting of a single line of melody without accompaniment.
monophthong (mŏn′əf thŏng′), *n.* a single, simple vowel sound; a monophthongal vowel. [t. Gk: s. *monóphthongos* with one sound]
monophthongal (mŏn′əf thŏng′gl), *adj.* *Phonet.* (of vowels) of unvarying quality; approximately the same from beginning to end.
monophthongize (mŏn′əf thŏng gīz′), *v.*, **-gized, -gizing.** *Phonet.* —*v.t.* **1.** to change into or pronounce as a monophthong. —*v.i.* **2.** to become a monophthong. Also, **monophthongise.**
monophyletic (mŏn′ō fī lĕt′ĭk), *adj.* **1.** of or pertaining to a single tribe or stock. **2.** developed from a single ancestral type, as a group of animals. [f. MONO- + m. s. Gk *phyletikós* belonging to a tribesman]
monophyllous (mŏn′ō fĭl′əs), *adj.* *Bot.* **1.** consisting of one leaf, as a calyx. **2.** having only one leaf. [t. Gk: m. *monóphyllos*]
Monophysite (mŏ nŏf′ĭ sīt′), *n.* *Theol.* one holding that there is in Christ one composite nature, partly divine and partly human. [t. LGk: m. s. *monophysítēs*, f. *mono-* MONO- + *phýs(is)* nature + *-ítēs* -ITE[1]] —**Monophysitic** (mŏn′ō fĭ sĭt′ĭk), *adj.* —**Monoph′ysitism,** *n.*
monoplane (mŏn′ə plān′), *n.* an aeroplane with a single sustaining wing.
monoplegia (mŏn′ō plē′jyə), *n.* *Pathol.* paralysis of only one extremity, muscle, or group of muscles. [t. NL. See MONO-, -PLEGIA] —**monoplegic** (mŏn′ō plē′jĭk), *adj.*
monopode (mŏn′ə pōd′), *adj.* **1.** having only one foot. —*n.* **2.** a creature having only one foot. **3.** one of a legendary race of men having only one leg. **4.** *Bot.* monopodium. [t. Gk: m. s. *monópous* one-footed]
monopodium (mŏn′ə pō′dyəm), *n.*, *pl.* **-dia** (-dyə). *Bot.* a single main axis which continues to extend at the apex in the original line of growth, giving off lateral branches beneath in acropetal succession. [NL, f. Gk: *mono-* MONO- + m. *pódion* foot] —**mon′opo′dial,** *adj.*
monopolism (mə nŏp′ə lĭz′əm), *n.* the existence or prevalence of monopolies.
monopolist (mə nŏp′ə lĭst), *n.* **1.** one who has a monopoly. **2.** an advocate of monopoly. —**monop′olis′tic,** *adj.* —**monop′olist′ically,** *adv.*
monopolize (mə nŏp′ə līz′), *v.t.*, **-lized, -lizing.** **1.** to acquire, have, or exercise a monopoly of. **2.** to obtain exclusive possession of; keep entirely to oneself: *she tried to monopolize his time.* Also, **monopolise.** —**monop′oliza′tion,** *n.* —**monop′oliz′er,** *n.*
monopoly (mə nŏp′ə lĭ), *n.*, *pl.* **-lies.** **1.** exclusive control of a commodity or service in a particular market, or a control that makes possible the manipulation of prices. **2.** an exclusive privilege to carry on a traffic or service,

granted by a sovereign, state, etc. **3.** the exclusive possession or control of something. **4.** something which is the subject of such control; a commodity, service, etc., which is exclusively controlled. **5.** a company or the like having such control. [t. L: m. s. *monopōlium*, t. Gk: m. *monopṓlion* a right of exclusive sale]

monopropellant (mŏn′ō prə pĕl′ənt), *n. Aeron.* a rocket propellant consisting of a single substance, either liquid or solid, which contains both the fuel and oxidant.

monorail (mŏn′ō rāl′), *n.* a railway with coaches running on a single (usually overhead) rail.

monosaccharide (mŏn′ō săk′ə rīd′, -rĭd), *n. Chem.* a simple sugar, such as glucose, fructose, arabinose, and ribose, occurring in nature or obtained by the hydrolysis of glucosides or polysaccharides.

monosepalous (mŏn′ō sĕp′ə ləs), *adj. Bot.* **1.** gamosepalous. **2.** having only one sepal, as a calyx.

monosodium glutamate (mŏn′ō sō′dyəm glo͞o′tə māt′), *Chem.* a white crystalline salt, used to intensify the flavour of foods, esp. meat.

monospermous (mŏn′ō spû′məs), *adj. Bot.* one-seeded. Also, **mon′osper′mal.**

monostable (mŏn′ō stā′bl), *adj. Elect.* denoting a circuit which may have several states, but always reverts to the same state in the absence of external forces.

monostich (mŏn′ə stĭk′), *n.* **1.** a poem or epigram consisting of a single metrical line. **2.** a single line of poetry. [t. LL: s. *monostichum*, t. Gk: m. *monóstichon*, adj. neut., consisting of one line]

monostome (mŏn′ə stōm′), *adj.* having a single mouth, pore, or stoma. Also, **monostomous** (mŏ nŏs′tə məs). [t. Gk: m. *monóstomos* with one mouth]

monostrophe (mŏ nŏs′trə fĭ, mŏn′ə strōf′), *n.* a poem in which all the strophes or stanzas are of the same metrical form. [t. Gk: m. s. *monóstrophos.* See MONO-, STROPHE] —**monostrophic** (mŏn′ə strŏf′ĭk), *adj.*

monostylous (mŏn′ō stī′ləs), *adj. Bot.* having only one style.

monosyllabic (mŏn′ə sĭ lăb′ĭk), *adj.* **1.** having only one syllable, as the word *no.* **2.** having a vocabulary composed exclusively of monosyllables; uncommunicative. **3.** using or uttering monosyllables. —**mon′osyllab′ically,** *adv.*

monosyllabism (mŏn′ə sĭl′ə bĭz′əm), *n.* **1.** monosyllabic character. **2.** use of monosyllables.

monosyllable (mŏn′ə sĭl′ə bl), *n.* a word of one syllable, as *yes* and *no.* [f. MONO- + SYLLABLE. Cf. L *monosyllabon*, t. Gk]

monotheism (mŏn′ō thē ĭz′əm), *n.* the doctrine or belief that there is only one God. [f. MONO- + s. Gk *theós* god + -ISM] —**mon′otheist,** *n., adj.* —**mon′otheis′tic,** *adj.* —**mon′otheis′tically,** *adv.*

Monothelite (mŏn′ŏ thĕl′īt), *Theol.* —*n.* **1.** one who believes that the incarnate Christ had only a single will or faculty of choice. **2.** an adherent of a 7th-century sect holding this opinion. —*adj.* **3.** denoting or pertaining to this opinion. Also, **Monothelete** (mŏn′ə thĕl′ēt). —**Mon′othel′itism, Mon′othel′ism,** *n.*

monothematic (mŏn′ō thĭ măt′ĭk), *adj. Music.* having only a single theme.

monotone (mŏn′ə tōn′), *n.* **1.** a vocal utterance, or series of speech sounds in a single unvaried tone. **2.** a single tone without harmony or variation in pitch. **3.** recitation or singing of words in such a tone. **4.** a person who sings in such manner. **5.** sameness of style, as in composition or writing. —*adj.* **6.** monotonous. —*v.t., v.i.* **7.** to speak, sing, etc., in a monotone. [t. NL: m. s. *monotonus*, t. LGk: m. *monótonos* of one tone]

monotonous (mə nŏt′ə nəs), *adj.* **1.** unvarying in any respect, lacking in variety, or tiresomely uniform. **2.** characterizing a sound continuing on one note. **3.** having very little inflection; limited to a narrow pitch range. [f. MONOTONE + -OUS] —**monot′onously,** *adv.* —**monot′onousness,** *n.* —**Syn. 1.** tedious, humdrum.

monotony (mə nŏt′ə nĭ), *n.* **1.** lack of variety, or wearisome uniformity, as in occupation, scenery, etc. **2.** the continuance of an unvarying sound; monotone. **3.** sameness of tone or pitch, as in utterance. [t. LGk: m. s. *monotonía*]

monotrematous (mŏn′ō trē′mə təs), *adj.* of or pertaining to a monotreme.

monotreme (mŏn′ō trēm′), *n.* any of the *Monotremata*, the lowest order of mammals, restricted to the Australian region and comprising only the duck-billed platypus and the echidnas, oviparous mammals in which the genital, urinary, and digestive organs have a common opening. [f. MONO- + m. Gk *trêma* hole]

monotricha (mŏ nŏt′rĭ kə), *n.pl.* bacteria having the organs of locomotion at one pole. [f. MONO- + s. Gk *thríx* hair + *-a* (repr. of L and Gk neut. pl. suffix *-a*)] —**monotrichic** (mŏn′ō trĭk′ĭk), **monot′richous,** *adj.*

monotropic (mŏn′ō trŏp′ĭk), *adj. Chem.* existing in only one stable physical form.

monotype (mŏn′ə tīp′), *n.* **1.** *Print.* **a.** type composed and cast on separate keyboard and casting machines which produce each character on an individual body. **b.** (*cap.*) a trademark for a machine on which such type is set or cast. **2.** a print from a metal plate on which a picture is painted, as in oil colour or printing ink. **3.** the method of producing such a print. **4.** *Biol.* the only or sole type of its group, as a single species constituting a genus. —**mon′otyp′er,** *n.*

monotypic (mŏn′ō tĭp′ĭk), *adj.* **1.** having only one type. **2.** of the nature of a monotype. **3.** *Biol.* (of genera) established on the basis of a single species or genus.

monovalent (mŏn′ō vā′lənt), *adj.* **1.** *Chem.* having a valency of one; univalent. **2.** *Bacteriol.* (of a serum, tissue, etc.) capable of resisting a specific disease organism because of the presence of the proper antibodies or antigens. [f. MONO- + -VALENT] —**mon′ova′lence, mon′ova′lency,** *n.*

monoxide (mŏ nŏk′sīd), *n. Chem.* an oxide containing one oxygen atom to the molecule.

Monroe (mən rō′), *n.* **James,** 1758–1831, the 5th president of the United States, 1817–25.

Monroe Doctrine, the doctrine, based upon statements contained in the message of President Monroe to the U.S. Congress (December 2nd, 1823), that the interposition of any European power to control the destiny of a Spanish-American state should be looked upon as a manifestation of unfriendly disposition towards the U.S., and that the American continents should no longer be open to colonization by European countries.

Monrovia (mŏn rō′vĭ ə), *n.* a seaport in and the capital of Liberia. 80,000 (est. 1965).

mons (mŏnz), *n. Anat.* a rounded eminence of fatty tissue, covered with hair, over the pubic symphysis of the adult human: called the **mons veneris** in the female, the **mons pubis** in the male.

Mons (*Fr.* mōɴs), *n.* a town in SW Belgium: battle, 1914. 27,144 (est. 1963).

Monseigneur (mŏn′sĕn yû′; *Fr.* mōɴ sĕ nyœr′), *n., pl.* **Messeigneurs** (*Fr.* mė sĕ nyœr′). **1.** a French title of honour given to princes, bishops, and other persons of eminence. **2.** a person bearing this title. Also, **mon′seigneur′.** [t. F: my lord. See SEIGNEUR]

monsieur (mə syû′; *Fr.* mə syœ′), *n., pl.* **messieurs** (*Fr.* mė syœ′). the conventional French title of respect and term of address for a man, corresponding to *Mr* and to *Sir.* [t. F: my lord (orig. applied to men of high station). See SIRE]

Monsignor (mŏn sē′nyə; *It.* mōn sēn nyōr′), *n., pl.* **Monsignors, Monsignori** (*It.* mōn sēn nyō′rē). *Rom. Cath. Ch.* **1.** a title conferred upon certain dignitaries. **2.** a person bearing this title. Also, **monsignor, Monsignore** (*It.* mōn sēn nyō′rė). [t. It.: f. F *mon* my + It. *signor(e)* lord]

monsoon (mŏn so͞on′), *n.* **1.** the seasonal wind of the Indian Ocean and southern Asia, blowing from the south-west in summer, and from the north-east in winter. **2.** the season during which the south-west monsoon blows, commonly marked by heavy rains. **3.** any wind that reverses with the seasons. **4.** any persistent wind established between water and adjoining land. [t. early mod. D: m. *monssœn*, t. Pg.: m. *monçao*, t. Ar.: m. *mausim* time, season]

monster (mŏn′stə), *n.* **1.** a legendary animal compounded of brute and human shape or of the shapes of various brutes, as a centaur, a griffin, or a sphinx. **2.** an animal or a plant of abnormal form or structure, as from marked malformation, the absence of certain parts or organs, etc. **3.** something unnatural or monstrous. **4.** a person who excites horror, as by wickedness, cruelty, etc. **5.** any animal or thing of huge size. —*adj.* **6.** huge; enormous; monstrous. [ME *monstre*, t. OF, t. L: m. s. *monstrum* omen, prodigy, monster]

monstrance (mŏn′strəns), *n. Rom. Cath. Ch.* a receptacle in which the consecrated host is exposed for adoration. [ME, t. ML: m. s. *monstrantia*, der. L *monstrāre* show]

monstrosity (mŏn strŏs′ĭ tĭ), *n., pl.* **-ties. 1.** the state or character of being monstrous. **2.** something monstrous. **3.** a monster. [t. LL: m. s. *monstrōsitas*]

monstrous (mŏn′strəs), *adj.* **1.** huge; extremely great: *a monstrous sum.* **2.** frightful or hideous; extremely ugly. **3.** revolting; outrageous; shocking: *a monstrous proposal.* **4.** deviating greatly from the natural or normal form or type. **5.** having the nature or appearance of a legendary monster. [late ME, t. LL: m. s. *monstrōsus* strange] —**mon′strously,** *adv.* —**mon′strousness,** *n.* —**Syn. 1.** See **gigantic. 2.** horrible, atrocious.

Mont., Montana.

montage (mŏn täzh′; *Fr.* mōɴ tȧzh′), *n.* **1.** the art or method of arranging in one composition pictorial elements borrowed from several sources so that the elements are both distinct and blended into a whole, through techniques such as superimposition. **2.** a picture made in this way. **3.** *Films, Television.* **a.** a technique of film editing in which several shots are juxtaposed or partially superimposed to form a single image. **b.** a method of film-making in which a single idea is expressed by the combining of different elements. **c.** a section of film using either process. [t. F: mounting, putting together]

Montagu (mŏn′tə gyo͞o′), *n.* **Lady Mary Wortley** (wûrt′lĭ) (*Mary Pierrepont*), 1689–1762, English author.

Montaigne (mŏn tān′; *Fr.* mōɴ tĕny′), *n.* **Michel Eyquem** (*Fr.* mē shĕl ē kĕm′), **Seigneur de,** 1533–92, French essayist.

Montale (*It.* mȯn tä′lė), *n.* **Giuseppe** (*It.* jo͞o zĕp′pė), born 1896, Italian poet.

Montana (mŏn tăn′ə), *n.* a state in the NW United States. 674,767 pop. (1960); 147,138 sq. mi. *Cap.*: Helena. *Abbrev.*: Mont. —**Montan′an,** *adj.*, *n.*

montane (mŏn′tān), *Ecol.* —*adj.* **1.** pertaining to mountain conditions. —*n.* **2.** the lower vegetation belt on mountains. [t. L: m. s. *montānus* of a mountain]

montan wax (mŏn′tăn), a dark brown bituminous wax extracted from lignite and peat; used in various polishes. Also, **lignite wax.** [f. *montan* (t. L: s. *montānus* of a mountain) + WAX[1]]

Montauban (*Fr.* mōɴ tō bäɴ′), *n.* a town in S France. 43,401 (1962).

Montauk Point (mŏn′tôk), the E end of Long Island, in SE New York.

Mont Blanc (*Fr.* mōɴ bläɴ′). See **Blanc, Mont.**

Montcalm (mŏnt käm′; *Fr.* mōɴ kȧlm′), *n.* **Louis Joseph** (*Fr.* lwē zhō zĕf′), **Marquis de** (*Louis Joseph, Marquis de Montcalm de Saint-Véran*), 1712–59, French general: defeated by the British under Wolfe at Quebec in 1759.

mont-de-piété (*Fr.* mōɴ də pyė tė′), *n.*, *pl.* **monts-de-piété** (mōɴ-). a public pawnbroking establishment for lending money on reasonable terms, esp. to the poor. [F, t. It.: m. *monte di pietà*, lit., mountain (fund) of pity]

monte (mŏn′tĭ; *Sp.* mȯn′tė), *n.* a gambling game at cards. [t. Sp.: mountain, heap (of cards), g. L *mons* MOUNT[2]]

Monte Carlo (mŏn′tĭ kä′lō; *It.* mȯn tė kär′lȯ), a town in Monaco principality, SE France: gambling; resort. 9430 (1951). See map under **Monaco.**

Monte Cassino (mŏn′tĭ kə sē′nō; *It.* mȯn tė kȧ sē′nȯ). See **Cassino.**

Monte Corno (*It.* mȯn tė kȯr′nȯ), highest peak in the Apennines, in central Italy. 9585 ft.

Montego Bay (mŏn tē′gō), a seaport in NW Jamaica. 23,471 (1960).

monteith (mən tēth′), *n.* a large bowl commonly of silver, often with a rim for suspending drinking glasses in the cool water within the bowl. It is also used as a punchbowl. [orig. proper name]

Montenegro (mŏn′tĭ nē′grō), *n.* a constituent republic of Yugoslavia, in the S part: formerly a kingdom. 471,894 pop. (1961); 5345 sq. mi. *Cap.*: Cetinje. —**Montenegrin** (mŏn′tĭ-nē′grĭn), *adj.*, *n.*

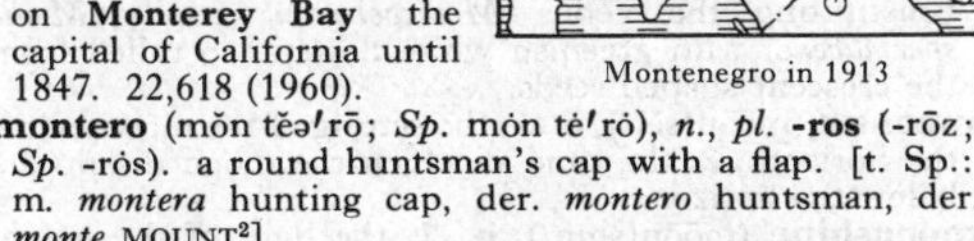

Montenegro in 1913

Monterey (mŏn′tə rā′), *n.* a town in W California, on **Monterey Bay** the capital of California until 1847. 22,618 (1960).

montero (mŏn tėə′rō; *Sp.* mȯn tė′rȯ), *n.*, *pl.* **-ros** (-rōz; *Sp.* -rȯs). a round huntsman's cap with a flap. [t. Sp.: m. *montera* hunting cap, der. *montero* huntsman, der. *monte* MOUNT[2]]

Monterrey (mŏn′tə rā′; *Sp.* mȯn tĕr rėy′), *n.* a city in NE Mexico: battle, 1846. 821,843 (est. 1965).

Montespan (*Fr.* mōɴ tĕs päɴ′), *n.* **Marquise de** (*Françoise Athénaïs de Rochechouart*), 1641–1707, mistress of Louis XIV of France.

Montesquieu (mŏn′tĕs kyo͞o′; *Fr.* mōɴ tĕs kyœ′), *n.* (*Charles Louis de Secondat, Baron de la Brède et de Montesquieu*), 1689–1755, French philosophical writer.

Montessori (mŏn′tĭ sô′rĭ; *It.* mȯn tĕs sŏ′rē), *n.* **Maria,** 1870–1952, Italian educational reformer.

Montessori method, a system for training and instructing young children, of which the fundamental aim is self-education by the children themselves, accompanied by special emphasis on the training of the senses. Also, **Montessori system.**

Monteux (*Fr.* mōɴ tœ′), *n.* **Pierre** (*Fr.* pyĕr), 1875–1964, U.S. orchestral conductor born in France.

Monteverdi (mŏn′tĭ vĕə′dĭ; *It.* mȯn tė vĕr′dē), *n.* **Claudio** (*It.* klȧw′dyȯ), 1567–1643, Italian composer.

Montevideo (mŏn′tĭ vĭ dā′ō; *Sp.* mȯn tė bē dė′ȯ), *n.* a seaport in and the capital of Uruguay. 1,203,700 (est. 1964).

Montezuma II (mŏn′tĭ zo͞o′mə), *c.* 1477–1520, last Aztec emperor of Mexico, 1503–20.

Montfort (mŏnt′fət), *n.* **1. Simon de** (sī′mən də), *c.* 1160–1218, French crusader. **2.** his son, **Simon de,** (*Earl of Leicester*), *c.* 1208–65, English soldier and statesman.

Montgolfier (mŏnt gŏl′fĭ ə; *Fr.* mōɴ gŏl fyė′), *n.* **1. Jacques Étienne** (*Fr.* zhȧk ė tyĕn′), 1745–99, and his brother, **Joseph Michel** (*Fr.* zhō zĕf mē shĕl′), 1740–1810, French inventors of the first balloon to make a successful flight. **2.** (*l.c.*) a balloon raised by heated air from a fire in the lower part.

Montgomery (mənt gŭm′ə rĭ), *n.* **1. Bernard Law, 1st Viscount Montgomery of Alamein,** born 1887, British field marshal. **2.** a city in the U.S., the capital of Alabama, in the central part, on the Alabama river. 134,393 (1960). **3.** a town in Wales, the county town of Montgomeryshire. 970 (1961). **4.** Montgomeryshire.

Montgomeryshire (mənt gŭm′ə rĭ shĭə′, -shə), *n.* a county in central Wales. 44,165 pop. (1961); 797 sq. mi. *Co. town*: Montgomery. Also, **Montgomery.**

month (mŭnth), *n.* **1.** approximately one twelfth of a tropical or solar year (**solar month**). **2.** any of the twelve parts (January, February, etc.) into which the calendar year is divided (**calendar month**). **3.** the time from any day of one calendar month to the corresponding day of the next. **4.** a period of four weeks or 30 days. **5.** the period (**lunar month**) of a complete revolution of the moon with regard to some point, usually the interval (**synodic month**) from one new moon to the next, equivalent to 29 days, 12 hours, 44 minutes, and 2·7 seconds. [ME *mon(e)th*, OE *mōnath*, c. G *Mond* MOON]

Montherlant (*Fr.* mōɴ tĕr läɴ′), *n.* **Henry de** (*Fr.* äɴ rē′ də), born 1896, French novelist, essayist, and dramatist.

monthly (mŭnth′lĭ), *adj.*, *n.*, *pl.* **-lies,** *adv.* —*adj.* **1.** pertaining to a month, or to each month. **2.** done, happening, appearing, etc., once a month, or every month. **3.** continuing or lasting for a month. —*n.* **4.** a periodical published once a month. **5.** *Colloq.* a menstrual period. —*adv.* **6.** once a month; by the month.

month's mind, *Rom. Cath. Ch.* the remembrance of a deceased person, by a Requiem Mass, a month after death.

monticule (mŏn′tĭ kyo͞ol′), *n.* **1.** a small mountain, hill, or mound. **2.** a subordinate volcano cone. [t. F, t. LL: m. s. *monticulus*, dim. of L *mons* MOUNT[2]]

Montluçon (*Fr.* mōɴ lʏ sōɴ′), *n.* a town in central France, in Allier department. 55,184 (1962).

Montmartre (*Fr.* mōɴ mȧr′tr), *n.* a hilly section in the N part of Paris: artists' centre; famous cafes.

Montmorency (mŏnt′mə rĕn′sĭ; *Fr.* mōɴ mŏ räɴ sē′), *n.* **Anne** (*Fr.* ȧn), **Duc de,** 1493–1567, constable of France and French marshal.

Montparnasse (*Fr.* mōɴ pȧr nȧs′), *n.* a district in the S part of Paris: noted for its artists and writers.

Montpelier (mŏnt pē′lĭ ə), *n.* a town in the U.S., the capital of Vermont. 8782 (1960).

Montpellier (*Fr.* mōɴ pə lyė′), *n.* a town in S France, the capital of Hérault department, near the Mediterranean. 123,843 (1962).

Montreal (mŏnt′rĭ ôl′), *n.* a seaport in Canada, in S Quebec, on an island in the St Lawrence. 1,191,062 (1961).

Montreuil (*Fr.* mōɴ trœy′), *n.* a town in N France, in Seine-Saint-Denis department: a suburb of Paris. 92,222 (1962).

Montreux (mŏn trû′; *Fr.* mōɴ trœ′), *n.* a town in Switzerland at the E end of Lake Geneva: a resort. 20,000 (est. 1964).

Montrose (mŏn trōz′), *n.* **1. James Graham, Marques of,** 1612–50, Scottish supporter of Charles I. **2.** a seaport in Scotland, in Angus. 10,702 (1961).

Mont-Saint-Michel (*Fr.* mōɴ săɴ mē shĕl′), *n.* a rocky islet near the coast in NW France, in an inlet of the Gulf of St Malo: famous abbey and fortress.

Montserrat (mŏnt′sĕ răt′ *for 1*; mŏnt′sĕ rät′ *for 2*), *n.* **1.** an island territory in the Leeward Islands in the West Indies. 13,569 pop. (est. 1963); 32½ sq. mi. *Cap.*: Plymouth. **2.** a mountain (4058 ft) in NE Spain, NW of Barcelona: the site of **Monserrat Monastery.**

monument (mŏn′yo͝o mənt), *n.* **1.** something erected in memory of a person, event, etc., as a pillar, statue, or the like. **2.** any building, megalith, etc., surviving from a past age, and regarded as of historical or archaeological importance. **3.** any work, writing, or the like by a person, regarded as a memorial of him after his death. **4.** any enduring evidence or notable example of something. **5.** *U.S.* an object, as a stone shaft, set in the ground to mark the boundaries of real property. **6.** a written document or record; legal instrument. **7.** *Obs.* a tomb; place of burial. **8.** *Obs.* a statue. [ME, t. L: s. *monumentum*]

monumental (mŏn′yo͝o mĕn′tl), *adj.* **1.** resembling a monument; massive or imposing. **2.** *Fine Arts.* of any size larger than that of life. **3.** historically prominent: *a monumental event.* **4.** *Colloq.* conspicuously great or gross. **5.** of a monument or monuments. **6.** serving as a monument. **—mon′umen′tally,** *adv.*

monumentalize (mŏn′yo͝o mĕn′tə līz′), *v.t.*, **-lized, -lizing.** to establish an enduring memorial or record of. Also, **monumentalise.**

mony (mŏn′ĭ), *adj., n. Scot. and N Eng.* many.

-mony, a noun suffix indicating result or condition, as in *parsimony*; but sometimes having the same function as **-ment.** [t. L: m. s. *-mōnia, -mōnium*]

Monza (mŏn′zə; *It.* mȯn′tsȧ), *n.* a town in Italy, in W central Lombardy: motor-racing circuit. 95,495 (1966).

monzonite (mŏn′zə nīt′), *n.* any of a group of granular igneous rocks intermediate in composition between syenite and diorite. [t. G: m. *Monzonit*, f. *Monzoni* (name of mountain in Tyrol) + *-it* -ITE[1]] **—monzonitic** (mŏn′zə nĭt′ĭk), *adj.*

moo (mo͞o), *v.*, **mooed, mooing,** *n., pl.* **moos.** *—v.i.* **1.** to utter the characteristic cry of a cow; low. *—n.* **2.** a mooing sound. **3.** *Slang.* a stupid person, esp. a woman. [imit.]

mooch (mo͞och), *Slang.* *—v.i.* **1.** to skulk or sneak. **2.** to hang or loiter about. **3.** to slouch or saunter along. *—v.t.* **4.** to steal. **5.** to get without paying or at another's expense; cadge. Also, **mouch.** [ME, ? t. OF: m. *muchier*] **—mooch′er,** *n.*

moo-cow (mo͞o′kou′), *n.* (childish) a cow.

mood[1] (mo͞od), *n.* **1.** frame of mind, or state of feeling, as at a particular time. **2.** (*pl.*) fits of uncertainty, gloominess, or sullenness. [ME; OE *mōd* mind, spirit, mood, c. G *Mut* spirit, courage] **—Syn. 1.** disposition.

mood[2] (mo͞od), *n.* **1.** *Gram.* **a.** (in many languages) a set of categories of verb inflection, whose selection depends either on the syntactic relation of the verb to other verbs in the sentence, or on difference in the speaker's attitude towards the action expressed by the verb (e.g., certainty *v.* uncertainty, question *v.* statement, wish *v.* command, emphasis *v.* hesitancy). **b.** (in some languages, including English) a similar set of categories marked by the use of special auxiliary words (Eng. *can, could, may, might,* etc.) instead of by, or in addition to, inflection. **c.** any category of such a set: *the Greek indicative, imperative, optative, and subjunctive moods.* **2.** *Logic.* any of the various forms of valid categorical syllogisms, depending on the quantity and quality of their constituent propositions. [special use of MOOD[1], influenced by MODE[1]]

moody (mo͞o′dĭ), *adj.*, **-dier, -diest. 1.** given to gloomy or sullen moods; ill-humoured. **2.** proceeding from or showing such a mood: *a moody silence.* **3.** exhibiting sharply varied moods; temperamental. **—mood′ily,** *adv.* **—mood′iness,** *n.*

mool (mo͞ol), *n. Scot. and N Dial.* **1.** earth; soil; mould. **2.** soil for a grave. **3.** a grave. [var. of MOULD[3]]

moon (mo͞on), *n.* **1.** the body which revolves around the earth monthly at a mean distance of 238,857 miles, accompanying the earth in its annual revolution about the sun. It is 2159·9 miles in diameter, and its mass is 0·0123 of that of the earth. **2.** this heavenly body during a particular lunar month, or during a certain period of time, or at a certain point of time, regarded as a distinct object or entity. **a. new moon,** the moon when in conjunction with the sun and hence invisible, or the phase so represented, or the moon soon afterwards when visible as a slender crescent. **b. half-moon,** the moon when half its disc is illuminated, occurring when at either quadrature, or quarter. **c. full moon,** the moon when the whole of its disc is illuminated, occurring when in opposition to the sun, or the phase so represented. **d. old moon,** the waning moon. **e. waxing moon,** the moon at any time before it is full, so called because its illuminated area is increasing. **f. waning moon,** the moon at any time after it has been full, so called because its illuminated area is decreasing. **3.** a lunar month, or, in general, a month. **4.** any planetary satellite. **5.** something shaped like an orb or a crescent. **6. once in a blue moon,** seldom; very rarely. *—v.i.* **7.** *Colloq.* to wander about or gaze idly, dreamily, or listlessly (often fol. by *about*). *—v.t.* **8.** to spend (time) idly. [ME *mone*, OE *mōna*, c. OHG *māno*; akin to Gk *mḗnē* moon, *mḗn* month, L *mensis* month]

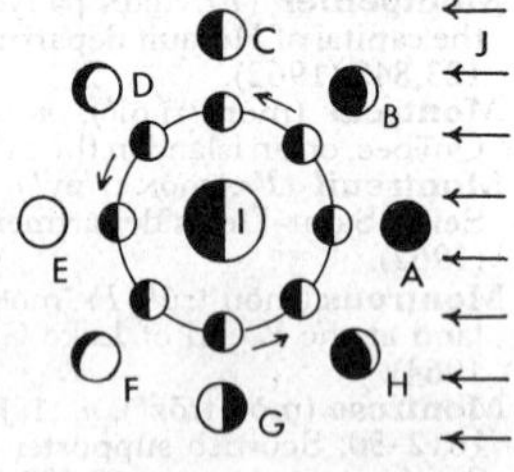

Phases of the moon
The figures on the inner circle show the moon in its orbit round the earth; those on the outer circle represent the moon's corresponding phases as seen from the earth. A, New moon (invisible); B, Waxing crescent; C, First quarter (half-moon); D, Gibbous; E, Full moon; F, Gibbous; G, Last quarter (half-moon); H, Waning crescent; I, Earth; J, Sun's rays

moonbeam (mo͞on′bēm′), *n.* a ray of moonlight.

moon-blind (mo͞on′blīnd′), *adj.* (of horses) afflicted with moon blindness. Also, **moon-eyed** (mo͞on′īd′).

moon blindness, *Vet. Sci.* a specific, probably non-infectious disease of horses, of unknown cause, in which the eyes suffer from recurring attacks of inflammation, and which eventually results in opacity and blindness.

mooncalf (mo͞on′käf′), *n.* a congenital imbecile. [lit., a person influenced by the moon]

moon daisy, a perennial composite herb, *Chrysanthemum leucanthemum,* with single capitula having yellow disc florets and white ray florets; a grassland species of the Old World introduced elsewhere.

mooned (mo͞ond), *adj.* **1.** ornamented with moons or crescents. **2.** shaped like a moon or crescent.

mooneye (mo͞on′ī′), *n.* **1.** a freshwater fish, *Hiodon tergisus,* of central N America with large eyes. **2.** *Vet. Sci.* an eye of a horse affected with moon blindness.

moon-faced (mo͞on′fāst′), *adj.* having a very round face.

moonfish (mo͞on′fĭsh′), *n., pl.* **-fishes,** (*esp. collectively*) **-fish. 1.** any of certain fishes having a deep, sharply compressed, silvery body, as of the carangoid genera *Selene* and *Vomer,* as *S. vomer* and *V. setipinnis* of the warmer coastal waters of North and South America. **2.** the opah. **3.** a minnow, *Platypoecilus maculatus.*

moonflower (mo͞on′flou′ə), *n.* a night-blooming convolvulaceous plant, *Calonyction aculeatum,* with fragrant white flowers.

moonlight (mo͞on′līt′), *n.* **1.** the light of the moon. *—adj.* **2.** pertaining to moonlight. **3.** illuminated by moonlight. **4.** occurring by moonlight, or by night.

moonlighter (mo͞on′lī′tə), *n.* **1.** one who engages in illegal acts by night. **2.** (in Irish history) one who committed agrarian outrages at night in support of rent reduction and peasant-proprietorship. **3.** one who does a job in addition to regular employment.

moonlight flit, *Colloq.* a departure by night with one's possessions in order to avoid payment of rent. Also, **moonlight flitting.**

moonlighting (mo͞on′lī′tĭng), *n.* **1.** the carrying on of activities, esp. illegal ones, by moonlight. **2.** *Colloq.* working at a job in addition to one's regular, full-time employment.

moonlit (mo͞on′lĭt′), *adj.* lit by the moon.

moonraker (mo͞on′rā′kə), *n.* moonsail.

moonrat (mo͞on′răt′), *n.* a hairy hedgehog, *Echinosorex gymnuras,* the largest living insectivores, found in S Asia, Sumatra, and Borneo.

moonrise (mo͞on′rīz′), *n.* **1.** the rising of the moon above the horizon. **2.** the time at which the moon rises above the horizon.

moonsail (mo͞on′səl, -sāl′), *n. Naut.* a small sail carried above the skysail. Also, **moonraker.**

moonseed (mo͞on′sēd′), *n.* any of the climbing herbs constituting the genus *Menispermum* (family *Menispermaceae*) with greenish white flowers, so called from the crescent-shaped seeds.

moonset (mo͞on′sĕt′), *n.* **1.** the setting of the moon below the horizon. **2.** the time at which the moon disappears below the horizon.

moonshine (mo͞on′shīn′), *n.* **1.** the light of the moon. **2.** empty or foolish talk, ideas, etc.; nonsense. **3.** *Colloq.* smuggled or illicitly distilled liquor.

moonshiner (mo͞on′shī′nə), *n. Colloq.* **1.** an illicit distiller. **2.** one who pursues an illegal trade at night.

moonshiny (mo͞on′shī′nĭ), *adj.* **1.** like moonlight. **2.** moonlit. **3.** without sense; fictitious; visionary.

moonshot (mo͞on′shŏt′), *n.* **1.** the launching of a missile to the moon. **2.** the missile itself.

moonstone (mo͞on′stōn′), *n.* a white translucent variety of felspar with a bluish pearly lustre, used as a gem.

moonstruck (mo͞on′strŭk′), *adj.* injuriously affected in mind (or otherwise), supposedly by the influence of the moon; dazed; crazed. Also, **moonstricken** (mo͞on′strĭk′ən).

moonwort (mo͞on′wût′), *n.* **1.** any fern of the genus *Botry-*

chium, esp. *B. lunaria*, whose fronds have crescent-shaped pinnae. **2.** honesty (def. 4).

moony (mo͞o′nĭ), *adj.*, **-nier, -niest. 1.** pertaining to or characteristic of the moon. **2.** resembling the moon in shape. **3.** moonlit. **4.** resembling moonlight. **5.** *Colloq.* mooning, listless, or silly.

moor[1] (mo͝oə), *n.* **1.** a tract of open, peaty, waste land, often overgrown with heath, common in high latitudes and altitudes where drainage is poor; a heath. **2.** a tract of land preserved for shooting game. [ME *more*, OE *mōr*, c. G *Moor* marsh]

moor[2] (mo͝oə), *v.t.* **1.** to secure (a ship, etc.) in a particular place, as by cables and anchors (esp. two or more) or by lines. **2.** to secure, or fix firmly. *—v.i.* **3.** to moor a ship, etc. **4.** to take up a position or be made secure by anchors or the like; as a ship. [late ME *more*, OE *mār-* (in *mārels* mooring rope), c. MD *māren* moor, tie up]

Moor (mo͝oə), *n.* **1.** a Muslim of the mixed Berber and Arab people inhabiting NW Africa. **2.** one belonging to that group of this people which in the 8th century invaded and conquered Spain. **3.** *Archaic.* blackamoor. [ME *More*, t. OF, var. of *Maure*, t. L: m. *Maurus*, t. Gk: m. *Maûros*]

moorage (mo͝oə′rĭj), *n.* **1.** the act of mooring. **2.** the state of being moored. **3.** a place for mooring. **4.** a charge or payment for the use of moorings.

moorcock (mo͝oə′kŏk′), *n.* the male moorfowl.

Moore (mo͝oə), *n.* **1. George,** 1852–1933, Irish novelist, critic, and dramatist. **2. Henry,** born 1898, English sculptor. **3. Sir John,** 1761–1809, British general. **4. Thomas,** 1779–1852, Irish poet.

moorfowl (mo͝oə′foul′), *n.* the red grouse, *Lagopus scoticus.* Also, **moor′bird′**.

moorhen (mo͝oə′hĕn′), *n.* **1.** the female moorfowl. **2.** a common European gallinule, *Gallinula chloropus.*

mooring (mo͝oə′rĭng), *n.* **1.** the act of one who or that which moors. **2.** (*usually pl.*) something by which a ship or the like is moored, as a cable, line, etc. **3.** (*pl.*) the place where a vessel is or may be moored.

mooring buoy, *Naut.* a buoy to which vessels can be moored.

mooring mast, the mast or tower to which a dirigible is moored. Also, **mooring tower.**

Moorish (mo͝oə′rĭsh), *adj.* **1.** of or pertaining to the Moors. **2.** in the style of the Moors, as architecture, decoration, etc.

moorland (mo͝oə′lənd), *n.* land consisting of a moor.

moorwort (mo͝oə′wût′), *n.* a low, ericaceous shrub, *Andromeda polifolia*, with white flowers, native to swamplands in the Northern Hemisphere.

moose (mo͞os), *n.*, *pl.* **moose. 1.** a large animal, *Alces americanus*, of the deer family, inhabiting Canada and the northern U.S., the male of which has enormous palmate antlers, long legs, and a large head. **2.** a similar species, *A. gigas*, found in Alaska. **3.** the European elk, *A. machlis.* [t. N Amer. Ind.; cognate forms in Algonquian, Narragansett, Delaware, etc., meaning 'he strips or eats off']

Moosehead Lake (mo͞os′hĕd′), a lake in central Maine. 36 mi. long; 120 sq. mi.

Moose Jaw, a town in Canada, in S Saskatchewan. 34,500 (est. 1965).

moot (mo͞ot), *adj.* **1.** subject to argument or discussion; debatable; doubtful: *a moot point.* *—v.t.* **2.** to bring forward (any point, subject, project, etc.) for discussion. **3.** *Obs.* to argue (a case, etc.), esp. in a mock court. *—n.* **4.** an early English assembly of the people, exercising political, administrative, and judicial powers. **5.** an argument or discussion, esp. of a hypothetical legal case. [ME *mote*, OE *mōt*, *gemōt* meeting, assembly, c. Icel. *mōt*, D *gemoet*] —**moot′er,** *n.*

moot court, a mock court for the conduct of hypothetical legal cases, as for practice for students of law.

moot hall, (in an English village) a historic building where a moot (def. 4) was once held.

mop (mŏp), *n.*, *v.*, **mopped, mopping.** *—n.* **1.** a bundle of coarse yarn, a piece of cloth, or the like, fastened at the end of a stick or handle, used for washing floors, dishes, etc. **2.** a thick mass, as of hair. *—v.t.* **3.** to rub, wipe, clean, or remove with a mop. **4.** to wipe: *to mop the face with a handkerchief.* **5. mop up,** *Mil.* to clear (ground, trenches, towns, etc.) of scattered or remaining enemy combatants, after attacking forces have gone beyond the place. [earlier *map*, ME *mappe.* Cf. L *mappa* napkin, cloth, ? in ML mop]

mopane (mə pä′nĭ), *n.* an ironwood of southern Africa, *Copaifera mopane*, with durable wood. [? t. Tswana]

mopboard (mŏp′bôd′), *n.* *U.S.* skirting board.

mope (mōp), *v.*, **moped, moping,** *n.* *—v.i.* **1.** to be sunk in listless apathy or dull dejection. *—v.t.* **2.** to make listless and dispirited. *—n.* **3.** a person who mopes or is given to moping. **4.** (*pl.*) low spirits. [var. of obs. *mop* make a wry face. Cf. D *moppen* pout] —**mop′er,** *n.* —**mop′ingly,** *adv.*

moped (mō′pĕd′), *n.* a light, low-powered motorcycle equipped with pedals for starting and assisting the motor.

mopish (mō′pĭsh), *adj.* given to moping; listless and dejected. —**mop′ishly,** *adv.* —**mop′ishness,** *n.*

mopoke (mō′pōk′), *n.* **1.** (in New Zealand) a small owl, *Ninox novaeseelandiae*, which inhabits bush and woodland, and is nocturnal in habit. **2.** (in Australia) the frogmouth, *Podargus strigoides*, a nightjar of the family *Podargidae*, with red-brown or grey-brown feathers and a wide bill. Also, **morepork** (mô′pôk′). [imit.]

moppet (mŏp′ĭt), *n.* **1.** *Obs. or Archaic.* a child or a young girl. **2.** *Colloq.* a doll. [f. (obs.) *mop* baby, rag doll + -ET]

moquette (mŏ kĕt′), *n.* a kind of fabric with a thick velvety pile used for carpets and upholstery. [t. F; orig. uncert.]

Mor (mô), *n.* **Sir Anthonis** (ăn′tə nĭ), *c.* 1519–*c.* 1576, Flemish painter.

mor., morocco.

mora (mô′rə), *n.*, *pl.* **morae** (mô′rē), **moras.** *Pros.* the unit of time equivalent to the ordinary or normal short sound or syllable. [t. L: delay]

moraceous (mô rā′shəs), *adj.* belonging to the *Moraceae*, or mulberry family of plants, which includes the mulberry, breadfruit, fig, hemp, hop, Osage orange, etc. [f. s. L *mōrus* mulberry tree + -ACEOUS]

Moradabad (mô′rə də băd′), *n.* a town in India, in NW central Uttar Pradesh. 180,100 (1961).

moraine (mŏ rān′), *n.* **1.** a ridge, mound, or irregular mass of boulders, gravel, sand, and clay, transported in or on a glacier. **2.** a deposit of such material left on the ground by a glacier. [t. F. Cf. ML *morena* embankment of stakes, It. *mora* cairn] —**morain′al, morain′ic,** *adj.*

moral (mŏ′rəl), *adj.* **1.** pertaining to or concerned with right conduct or the distinction between right or wrong: *moral considerations.* **2.** concerned with the principles or rules of right conduct; ethical: *moral philosophy.* **3.** expressing or conveying truths or counsel as to right conduct, as a speaker, a literary work, etc.; moralizing. **4.** founded on the fundamental principles of right conduct rather than on enactment or custom: *moral rights.* **5.** capable of conforming to the rules of right conduct. **6.** conforming to the rules of right conduct (opposed to *immoral*): *a moral man.* **7.** sexually virtuous; chaste. **8.** of, pertaining to, or producing an effect upon the mind, feelings, or on results generally: *a moral victory*; *moral support.* **9.** depending upon what is observed of human nature and actions or of things generally, rather than upon demonstration: *moral evidence.* **10.** resting upon convincing grounds of probability: *a moral certainty.* *—n.* **11.** the moral teaching or practical lesson contained in a fable, tale, experience, etc. **12.** the embodiment or type of something. **13.** (*pl.*) principles or habits with respect to right or wrong conduct; ethics. **14.** (*pl.*) behaviour or habits in sexual matters. [ME, t. L: s. *mōrālis* relating to manners, customs]
—**Syn. 4.** righteous, just. **6.** virtuous, good. **13.** MORALS, ETHICS refer to rules and standards of conduct and practice. MORALS refers to generally accepted customs of conduct and right living in a society, and to the individual's practice in relation to these: *the morals of our civilization.* ETHICS now implies high standards of honest and honourable dealing, of methods used, and of quality of product, esp. in the professions or in business: *ethics of the medical profession.*

morale (mŏ räl′), *n.* moral or mental condition with respect to cheerfulness, confidence, zeal, etc.: *the morale of troops.* [t. F, fem. of *moral*, adj. See MORAL]

moralism (mŏ′rə lĭz′əm), *n.* **1.** the habit of moralizing. **2.** a moral maxim. **3.** the practice of morality, as distinct from religion.

moralist (mŏ′rə lĭst), *n.* **1.** one who teaches or inculcates morality. **2.** one who practises morality. —**mor′alis′tic,** *adj.*

morality (mə răl′ĭ tĭ), *n.*, *pl.* **-ties. 1.** conformity to the rules of right conduct; moral or virtuous conduct. **2.** sexual virtue; chastity. **3.** moral quality or character. **4.** a doctrine or system of morals; ethics; duties. **5.** moral instruction; a moral lesson or precept; a moralizing discourse or utterance. **6.** morality play. —**Syn. 1.** See **goodness.**

morality play, a form of allegorical drama in vogue from the 14th to the 16th centuries, employing personifications of virtues and vices.

moralize (mŏ′rə līz′), *v.*, **-lized, -lizing.** *—v.i.* **1.** to make moral reflections. *—v.t.* **2.** to explain in a moral sense, or draw a moral from. **3.** to improve the morals of. Also, **moralise.** —**mor′aliza′tion,** *n.* —**mor′aliz′er,** *n.* —**mor′aliz′ingly,** *adv.*

morally (mŏ′rə lĭ), *adv.* **1.** in a moral manner. **2.** from a moral point of view. **3.** virtuously. **4.** virtually; practically.

moral philosophy, ethics.

Moral Rearmament, a worldwide evangelistic and

ideological movement founded by Frank Buchman and emphasizing the practice of absolute honesty, purity, love, and unselfishness in all aspects of life in order to bring about the moral regeneration of mankind. It was earlier known as the Oxford Group. *Abbrev.*: MRA.

moral sense, the ability to distinguish between right and wrong.

moral theology, that branch of theology dealing with principles of moral conduct treated with reference to a divine origin.

moral tutor, (at the colleges of certain English universities) a tutor whose duty is to look after the welfare of the undergraduates entrusted to his charge and to advise them in difficulties, etc.

morass (mə răs′), *n.* **1.** a tract of low, soft, wet ground. **2.** a marsh or bog. **3.** marshy ground. [t. D: m. *moeras*, in MD *maras*, t. OF: m. *marais*, of Gmc orig. See MARSH]

moratorium (mŏr′ə tô′rĭ əm), *n.*, *pl.* **-toria** (-tô′rĭ ə), **-toriums. 1.** a legal authorization to delay payment of money due, as in an emergency. **2.** the period during which such authorization is in effect. **3.** a respite; a temporary cessation of activity, esp. as a result of an agreement. [t. NL, prop. neut. of LL *morātōrius* MORATORY]

moratory (mŏr′ə tə rĭ, -trĭ), *adj.* authorizing delay of payment: *a moratory law.* [t. LL: m. s. *morātōrius* delaying, der. L *morārī* delay]

Morava (mə rä′ və; *Cz.* mŏ′rȧ vȧ), *n.* **1.** German, **March.** a river flowing from N Czechoslovakia S to the Danube. ab. 210 mi. **2.** a river in E Yugoslavia, flowing N to the Danube. ab. 100 mi. **3.** Czech name of **Moravia.**

Moravia (*It.* mȯ rä′vyȧ), *n.* **Alberto** (*It.* äl bĕr′tȯ), born 1907, Italian novelist.

Moravia

Moravia (mə rā′ vyə), *n.* a district in Czechoslovakia, formerly a province. Czech, **Morava.** German, **Mähren.**

Moravian (mə rā′vyən), *adj.* **1.** pertaining to Moravia or its inhabitants. **2.** of or pertaining to the religious body of Moravians. —*n.* **3.** a native or inhabitant of Moravia. **4.** a member of a Protestant denomination, Unity of Brethren (also, **Moravian Brethren**), which traces its origin to John Huss. **5.** a dialect of Czech, spoken in Moravia.

Moravian Gate, a corridor between the Sudeten mountains and the Tatra range of the Carpathians, leading from S Poland into Moravia, Czechoslovakia.

Moravian Gate

Moravská Ostrava (*Cz.* mŏ′rȧf skȧ ŏs′trȧ vȧ), former name of **Ostrava.** German, **Mährisch-Ostrau.**

moray (mŏ rā′), *n.*, *pl.* **-rays.** any of numerous eels of the family *Muraenidae*, esp. those of the genus *Muraena*, as *M. helena*, common in the Mediterranean and valued as a food fish, or *Gymnothorax moringa*, common in West Indian waters (**spotted moray**).

Moray (mŭ′rĭ), *n.* a county in NE Scotland, on **Moray Firth,** an arm of the North Sea. 49,156 pop. (1961); 476 sq. mi. *Co. town:* Elgin. Formerly, **Elgin.**

morbid (mô′bĭd), *adj.* **1.** suggesting an unhealthy mental state; unwholesomely gloomy, sensitive, extreme, etc. **2.** affected by, proceeding from, or characteristic of disease. **3.** pertaining to diseased parts: *morbid anatomy.* [t. L: s. *morbidus* sickly] —**mor′bidly,** *adv.* —**mor′bidness,** *n.*

morbidity (mô bĭd′ĭ tĭ), *n.* **1.** morbid state or quality. **2.** the proportion of sickness in a locality.

morbific (mô bĭf′ĭk), *adj.* causing disease. Also, **morbifical.** [t. NL: s. *morbificus*, der. L *morbus* disease] —**morbif′ically,** *adv.*

Morbihan (*Fr.* mŏr bē äN′), *n.* a department in NW France. 530,833 pop. (1962); 2738 sq. mi. *Cap.:* Vannes.

morbilli (mô bĭl′ī), *n.pl.* measles. [t. ML, pl. of *morbillus*, dim. of L *morbus* disease]

morceau (*Fr.* mŏr sȯ′), *n.*, *pl.* **-ceaux** (*Fr.* -sȯ′). *French.* **1.** morsel. **2.** an excerpt or passage of poetry or music.

mordacious (mô dā′shəs), *adj.* biting; given to biting. [f. *mordaci(ty)* (t. L: m. s. *mordācitas* power of biting) + -OUS] —**morda′ciously,** *adv.* —**mordacity** (mô dăs′ĭ tĭ), *n.*

mordancy (mô′dn sĭ), *n.* mordant quality.

mordant (mô′dnt), *adj.* **1.** caustic or sarcastic, as wit, a speaker, etc. **2.** having the property of fixing colours, as in dyeing. —*n.* **3.** a substance used in dyeing to fix the colouring matter, esp. a metallic compound, as an oxide or hydroxide, which combines with the organic dye and forms an insoluble coloured compound or lake in the fibre. **4.** an acid or other corrosive substance used in etching to eat out the lines, etc. —*v.t.* **5.** to impregnate or treat with a mordant. [ME, t. OF, ppr. of *mordre*, g. L *mordēre* bite] —**mor′dantly,** *adv.*

Mordecai (mô′dĭ kā′ī), *n.* (in the book of Esther) a cousin of Esther, who delivered Esther and the Jews from Haman. Cf. **Purim.**

Mordents
A, Single; B, Double

mordent (mô′dnt), *n.* *Music.* **1.** a melodic embellishment consisting of a rapid alternation of a principal note with a supplementary note a semitone below it, called *single* or *short* when the supplementary note occurs only once, and *double* or *long* when this occurs twice or oftener. **2.** See **inverted mordent.** [t. G, t. It.: m. *mordente*, prop. ppr. of *mordere*, g. L *mordēre* bite]

Mordred (mô′drĕd), *n.* Modred.

more (mô), *adj.*, *superl.* **most,** *n.*, *adv.* —*adj.* **1.** in greater quantity, amount, measure, degree, or number (as the comparative of *much* and *many*, with the superlative *most*): *more money.* **2.** additional or further: *do not lose any more time.* —*n.* **3.** an additional quantity, amount, or number. **4.** a greater quantity, amount, or degree. **5.** something of greater importance. **6.** (*construed as pl.*) a greater number of a class specified, or the greater number of persons. —*adv.* **7.** in or to a greater extent or degree: *more rapid.* **8.** in addition; further; longer; again. **9. more or less,** to a certain extent; approximately. [ME; OE *māra*, c. OS and OHG *mēro.* See MOST]

More (mô), *n.* **1. Hannah,** 1745–1833, English writer on religious subjects. **2. Sir Thomas,** 1478–1535, English statesman and author: canonized in 1935. **3. Glen,** a valley of Inverness-shire, Scotland, in which lies Loch Ness.

Morea (mŏ rĭə′), *n.* Peloponnesus.

Moreau (*Fr.* mŏ rȯ′), *n.* **1. Gustave** (*Fr.* gʏs tȧv′), 1826–98, French painter. **2. Jeanne** (*Fr.* zhȧn), born 1928, French actress. **3. Jean Victor** (*Fr.* zhäN vēk tŏr′), 1763–1813, French general.

Morecambe (mô′kəm), *n.* a seaside resort in England, in Lancashire. (with Heysham) 40,228 (1961).

moreen (mŏ rēn′), *n.* a heavy fabric of wool, or wool and cotton, commonly watered, used for curtains, petticoats, etc. [? akin to MOIRE]

morel (mŏ rĕl′), *n.* an edible mushroom of the genus *Morchella*, an ascomycetous group in which the fruit body has the aspect of a stalked sponge. [ME *morele*, t. OF, der. L *mōrum* a mulberry]

Morelia (*Sp.* mȯ rĕ′lyȧ), *n.* a town in SW Mexico. 127,816 (est. 1965).

morello (mə rĕl′ō), *n.*, *pl.* **-los.** a sour cherry, *Prunus cerasus*, var. *austera*, with a dark-coloured skin and juice. Also, *U.S.*, **amarelle.** [t. It.: dark-coloured (der. L *maurus* moor), ? b. with It. *amarello*, dim. of *amaro* bitter (g. L *amārus*)]

moreover (mô rō′və), *adv.* beyond what has been said; further; besides. —**Syn.** See **besides.**

morepork (mô′pôk′), *n.* *Austral.*, *N.Z.* mopoke.

mores (mô′rēz), *n.pl.* *Sociol.* customs or conventions accepted without question and embodying the fundamental moral views of a group. [t. L: customs]

Moresque (mô rĕsk′), *adj.* Moorish. [t. F, t. It.: m. *moresco*, der. *Moro* MOOR]

Morgain le Fay (mô′gən lə fā′), Morgan le Fay.

Morgan (mô′gən), *n.* **1. Sir Henry,** *c.* 1635–88, English buccaneer. **2. John Pierpont,** 1837–1913, U.S. financier.

morganatic (mô′gə năt′ĭk), *adj.* designating or pertaining to a form of marriage in which a man of high rank takes to wife a woman of lower station with the stipulation that neither she nor the issue (if any) shall have any claim to his rank or property. Also, *Rare*, **morganic** (mô găn′ĭk). [t. NL: s. *morganāticus*, from ML (*mātrimōnium ad*) *morganāticam* (marriage with) morning gift (in lieu of a share in the husband's possessions), der. OHG *morgan* morning. The morning gift was a gift from a husband to his wife the morning after their marriage] —**mor′ganat′ically,** *adv.*

morganite (mô′gə nīt′), *n.* rose beryl. [named after J. P. MORGAN. See -ITE[1]]

Morgan le Fay (mô′gən lə fā′), *Celtic and Arthurian Legend.* the fairy sister of King Arthur. Also, **Morgain le Fay, Morgana** (mô gä′nə).

morgen (mô′gən), *n.* **1.** a unit of land measure equal to about two acres, formerly in use in Holland and the Dutch colonies and still used in South Africa. **2.** a unit equal to about two-thirds of an acre, formerly used in Prussia, Norway, and Denmark. [t. D and G]

morgue (môg), *n.* **1.** a place in which the bodies of persons found dead are exposed for identification. **2.** *Journalism Colloq.* **a.** the reference library of clippings, mats, books, etc., kept by a newspaper, etc. **b.** the room for it. **3.** *Book-publishing Colloq.* the editorial office. [t. F; orig. name of building in Paris so used]

moribund (mŏ′rĭ bŭnd′), *adj.* **1.** in a dying state. **2.** on the verge of extinction or termination. [t. L: s. *moribundus*] —**mor′ibun′dity,** *n.* —**mor′ibund′ly,** *adv.*

Moriguchi (mŏ′rĭ go͞o′chĭ), *n.* a town in Japan, in S Honshu island. 138,856 (1965).

Mörike (*Ger.* mœ′rĭ kə), *n.* **Edward** (*Ger.* ĕ′do͞o ärt), 1804–75, German poet and author.

morion[1] (mô′rĭ ən), *n.* an open helmet with a tall comb and a curved brim merging into a peak at front and back. [t. F, t. Sp.: m. *morrión*, der. *morra* crown of the head]

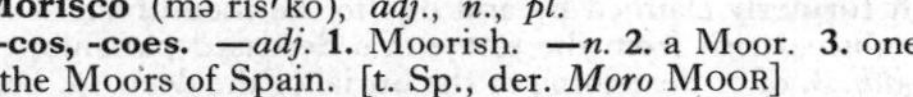
Spanish morion, 16th century

morion[2] (mô′rĭ ən), *n.* a variety of smoky quartz of a dark brown or nearly black colour. [t. L misreading (in early editions of Pliny's Nat. Hist.) of *mormorion*]

Moriori (mô′rĭ ô′rĭ), *n. N.Z.* the people occupying New Zealand during the first Maori invasion in the 14th century. [t. Maori]

Morisco (mə rĭs′kō), *adj., n., pl.* **-cos, -coes.** —*adj.* **1.** Moorish. —*n.* **2.** a Moor. **3.** one of the Moors of Spain. [t. Sp., der. *Moro* MOOR]

morituri te salutamus (mŏ′rĭ to͞oə′rē tā′săl′o͞o tä′mo͞os), *Latin.* we about to die salute thee: said by Roman gladiators as they marched by the Emperor.

Morley (mô′lĭ), *n.* **1. Christopher Darlington,** 1890–1957, U.S. writer. **2. John** (*Viscount Morley of Blackburn*), 1838–1923, English writer and statesman. **3. Thomas,** 1557–1603, English composer and organist. **4.** a town in England, in the West Riding of Yorkshire. 40,338 (1961).

Mormon (mô′mən), *n.* **1.** a member of a religious body founded in the U.S. in 1830 by Joseph Smith and calling itself 'The Church of Jesus Christ of Latter-day Saints'. **2. The Book of Mormon,** a sacred book of the Mormon Church, supposed to be an abridgement by a prophet (**Mormon**) of a record of certain ancient peoples in America, written on golden plates, and discovered and translated (1827–30) by Joseph Smith. —*adj.* **3.** of or pertaining to the Mormons or their religious system: *the Mormon view of Creation.* —**Mor′monism,** *n.*

morn (môn), *n. Poetic.* morning. [ME *morn(e)*, OE *morne* (dat. of *morgen* morning), c. D *morgen* and G *Morgen*]

Mornay (*Fr.* mŏr nĕ′), *n.* **Philippe de** (*Fr.* fē lēp′ də) (*Seigneur du Plessis-Marly*), 1549–1623, French Protestant leader and diplomat.

mornay sauce (mô′nā; *Fr.* mŏr nĕ′), any rich cheese sauce.

morning (mô′nĭng), *n.* **1.** the beginning of day; the dawn. **2.** the first part or period of the day, extending from dawn, or from midnight, to noon. **3.** the first or early period of anything. **4.** (*cap.*) the goddess Eos or Aurora. —*adj.* **5.** of or pertaining to morning: *the morning hours.* **6.** occurring, appearing, coming, used, etc., in the morning: *the morning sun.* [ME. See MORN, -ING[1], modelled on EVENING] —**Syn. 1.** morn, daybreak, sunrise.

morning coat, a black coat with tails, forming part of morning dress.

morning dress, formal dress used in daytime, as at weddings, etc., consisting for men typically of morning coat, light grey striped trousers, a light-coloured top-hat, etc.

morning-glory (mô′nĭng glô′rĭ), *n., pl.* **-ries.** any of various convolvulaceous plants, esp. of the genera *Ipomoea* and *Convolvulus*, as *I. purpurea*, a twining plant with cordate leaves and funnel-shaped flowers of various colours, common in cultivation.

morning room, a room in a house, usually adjoining the kitchen, used esp. for eating breakfast. Also, **breakfast room.**

morning sickness, nausea occurring in the early part of the day, as a characteristic symptom in the first months of pregnancy.

morning star, a bright planet, seen in the east before sunrise.

Moro (mô′rō), *n., pl.* **-ros.** a member of any of the various tribes of Muslim Malays in the southern Philippine Islands. [t. Sp.: a Moor]

Moro (*It.* mŏ′rō), *n.* **Aldo** (*It.* äl′dō), born 1916, Italian lawyer and politician, prime minister 1963–68.

morocco (mə rŏk′ō), *n.* **1.** a fine leather made from goat-skins tanned with sumac, orig. in Morocco. **2.** any leather made in imitation of this. Also, **morocco leather.**

Morocco (mə rŏk′ō), *n.* **1.** a kingdom in NW Africa, formerly a sultanate divided into French, Spanish, and International zones. 11,598,070 pop. (1961); 172,104 sq. mi. *Cap.:* Rabat. See map under **Algeria. 2.** Marrakech. —**Moroccan** (mə rŏk′ən), *adj., n.*

moron (mô′rŏn), *n.* **1.** a person of arrested intelligence whose mentality is judged incapable of developing beyond that of a normal child of 8 to 12 years of age. **2.** *Colloq.* a stupid person. [t. Gk, neut. of *mōrós* dull, foolish] —**moronic** (mô rŏn′ĭk), *adj.* —**mo′ronism, moronity** (mô rŏn′ĭ tĭ), *n.*

morose (mə rōs′), *adj.* gloomily or sullenly ill-humoured, as a person, mood, etc. [t. L: m. s. *mōrōsus* fretful, morose, particular] —**morose′ly,** *adv.* —**morose′ness,** *n.* —**Ant.** good-natured.

morph-, var. of **morpho-** before vowels.

-morph, a word element meaning 'form', as in *isomorph.* [t. Gk: s. *morphḗ* form]

morpheme (mô′fēm), *n. Linguistics.* any of the minimum meaningful elements in a language, not further divisible into smaller meaningful elements, usually recurring in various contexts with relatively constant meaning: either a word, as *girl, world,* or part of a word, as *-ish* or *-ly* in *girlish* and *worldly.* [f. MORPH(O)- + *-eme*, as in *phoneme*]

Morpheus (mô′fyəs, mô′fyo͞os), *n. Gk Myth.* a minor deity, son of the god of sleep; the god of dreams. [ME, t. L, t. Gk, der. *morphḗ* form, in allusion to the forms seen in dreams] —**Mor′phean,** *adj.*

-morphic, a word element used as adjective termination corresponding to **-morph,** as in *anthropomorphic.* [f. s. Gk *morphḗ* form + -IC]

morphine (mô′fēn), *n.* a bitter crystalline alkaloid, $C_{17}H_{19}NO_3 . H_2O$, the most important narcotic principle of opium, used in medicine (usually in the form of a sulphate or other salt) to dull pain, induce sleep, etc. Also, **morphia** (mô′fyə). [t. F, t. G: m. *Morphin*, f. *Morph(eus)* MORPHEUS + *-in* -INE[2]]

morphinism (mô′fĭ nĭz′əm), *n. Pathol.* **1.** a morbid condition induced by the habitual use of morphine. **2.** the habit inducing it.

morpho-, initial word element corresponding to **-morph.**

morphogenesis (mô′fō jĕn′ĭ sĭs), *n. Embryol.* the structural development of an organism or part. Also, **morpho′sis.** —**morphogenetic** (mô′fō jĭ nĕt′ĭk), **morphogenic** (mô′fō jĕn′ĭk), *adj.*

morphology (mô fŏl′ə jĭ), *n.* **1.** the study of form, structure, and the like. **2.** that branch of biology which deals with the form and structure of animals and plants, without regard to functions. **3.** the form of an organism considered as a whole. **4.** *Gram.* **a.** the patterns of word formation in a particular language, including inflection, derivation, and composition. **b.** the study and description thereof. **5.** *Geog.* the study of the physical form of lands, regions, or towns. —**morphologic** (mô′fə lŏj′ĭk), **mor′pholog′ical,** *adj.* —**mor′pholog′ically,** *adv.* —**morphol′ogist,** *n.*

-morphous, a word element used as adjective termination corresponding to **-morph,** as in *amorphous.* [t. Gk: m. *-morphos*, der. *morphḗ* form]

Morris (mŏ′rĭs), *n.* **William,** 1834–96, English poet, artist, and socialist writer.

Morris chair, a large armchair having an adjustable back and loose cushions. [named after William MORRIS]

morris dance, a folk dance, performed by persons in costume, often representing personages of the Robin Hood legend, formerly common in England, esp. in May Day festivities. Also, **mor′ris.** [late ME *moreys daunce* Moorish dance]

Morrison (mŏ′rĭ sən), *n.* **Herbert Stanley, Lord** (*Baron of Lambeth*), 1888–1964, English labour leader and statesman.

morrow (mŏ′rō), *n. Archaic.* **1.** morning. **2.** the day next after this or after some other particular day or night. [ME *morwe*, apocopated var. of *morwen*, OE *morgen* morning. See MORN]

Mors (môz), *n. Rom. Myth.* a deification of death. [t. L]

morse (môs), *n.* **1.** the morse code. —*adj.* **2.** denoting or pertaining to the morse code or the system of communications using it. **3.** pertaining to any code resembling the morse code. [named after S. F. B. MORSE]

Morse (môs), *n.* **Samuel Finley Breeze,** 1791–1872, U.S. inventor of a telegraph system.

morse code, a system of dots, dashes, and spaces, or the corresponding sounds or the like, used in telegraphy and signalling to represent the letters of the alphabet, numerals, etc. Also, **morse alphabet.**

morsel (mô′səl), *n.* **1.** a bite, mouthful, or small portion of food or the like. **2.** a small piece, quantity, or amount of anything; a scrap; a bit. —*v.t.* **3.** to distribute in or divide into tiny portions. [ME, t. OF, dim. of *mors* a bite, g. L *morsum*, pp. neut. of *mordēre* bite]

mort (môt), *n.* **1.** *Hunting.* the note blown on the hunting horn to signify the death of the animal hunted. **2.** *Obs.* death. [ME, t. OF, g. L *mors*]

mortal (mô′tl), *adj.* **1.** liable or subject to death: *all mortal creatures.* **2.** of or pertaining to man as subject to death; human: *this mortal life.* **3.** belonging to this world. **4.** pertaining to death: *mortal throes.* **5.** involving spiritual death (opposed to *venial*): *a mortal sin.* **6.** causing death; fatal: *a mortal wound.* **7.** to the death: *mortal combat.* **8.** deadly or implacable: *a mortal enemy.* **9.** dire, grievous, or bitter: *in mortal fear.* **10.** *Colloq.* long and wearisome. **11.** *Colloq.* extreme; very great: *in a mortal hurry.* **12.** *Colloq.* possible or conceivable: *of no mortal use.* —*n.* **13.** a human being; a being subject to death. [ME, t. L: s. *mortālis* subject to death] —**mor′tally,** *adv.* —**Syn.** **6.** See **fatal.**

mortality (mô tăl′ĭ tĭ), *n., pl.* **-ties.** **1.** the condition of being mortal or subject to death; mortal character, nature, or existence. **2.** mortal beings collectively; humanity. **3.** relative frequency of death, or death rate, as in a district or community. **4.** death or destruction on a large scale, as from war, plague, famine, etc. **5.** *Obs.* death.

mortality table, *Insurance.* an actuarial table compiled from statistics on the life spans of an arbitrarily selected population group or of former policyholders.

mortar[1] (mô′tə), *n.* **1.** a vessel of hard material, having a bowl-shaped cavity, in which drugs, etc., are reduced to powder with a pestle. **2.** any of various mechanical appliances in which substances are pounded or ground. **3.** a cannon very short in proportion to its bore, for throwing shells at high angles. **4.** some similar contrivance, as for throwing pyrotechnic bombs or a lifeline. [ME and OE *mortere*, t. L: m. s. *mortārium* vessel in which substances are pounded, or one in which MORTAR[2] is made; in defs 3 and 4, trans. of F *mortier*]

Mortar and pestle
A, Pestle; B, Mortar

mortar[2] (mô′tə), *n.* **1.** a material which binds bricks, stones, etc., into a compact mass. **2.** a mixture, as of quicklime, cement, etc., sand, and water, which hardens in the air and is used for binding bricks, etc., together. —*v.t.* **3.** to plaster or fix with mortar. [ME *morter*, t. F: m. *mortier*, g. L *mortārium.* See MORTAR[1]]

mortarboard (mô′tə bôd′), *n.* **1.** a board, commonly square, used by masons to hold mortar. **2.** a kind of cap with a close-fitting crown surmounted by a stiff, flat, cloth-covered, square piece, worn by university students, graduates, teachers, etc.

Mortarboard

Morte d'Arthur (môt′ dä′thə), a compilation and translation of French Arthurian romances made by Sir Thomas Malory and printed by Caxton in 1485.

mortgage (mô′gĭj), *n., v.,* **-gaged, -gaging.** *Law.* —*n.* **1.** a conditional conveyance of property to a creditor as security, as for the repayment of money. **2.** the deed by which such a transaction is effected. **3.** the rights conferred by it, or the state of the property conveyed. —*v.t.* **4.** to convey or place (property, esp. houses or land) under a mortgage. **5.** to pledge. [ME *morgage*, t. OF: f. *mort* dead + *gage* pledge, GAGE[1], n.]

mortgage debenture, debenture (def. 2).

mortgagee (mô′gĭ jē′), *n.* one to whom property is mortgaged.

mortgagee clause, a clause attached to a fire-insurance policy, designed to protect the mortgagee against loss or damage.

mortgagor (mô′gĭ jə, mô′gĭ jô′), *n.* one who mortgages property. Also, **mort′gager.**

mortice (mô′tĭs), *n., v.t.,* **-ticed, -ticing.** mortise.

mortician (mô tĭsh′ən), *n.* *U.S.* an undertaker. [f. MORT(UARY) + -ICIAN, modelled on PHYSICIAN]

mortification (mô′tĭ fĭ kā′shən), *n.* **1.** humiliation in feeling, as by some wound to pride. **2.** a cause or source of such humiliation. **3.** the practice of asceticism by penitential discipline to overcome desire for sin and to strengthen the will. **4.** *Pathol.* the death of one part of the body while the rest is alive; gangrene.

mortify (mô′tĭ fī′), *v.,* **-fied, -fying.** —*v.t.* **1.** to humiliate in feeling, as by a severe wound to the pride or self-complacency. **2.** to bring (the body, passions, etc.) into subjection by abstinence, ascetic discipline, or rigorous austerities. **3.** *Pathol.* to affect with gangrene or necrosis. —*v.i.* **4.** to practise mortification or disciplinary austerities. **5.** *Pathol.* to undergo mortification, or become gangrened or necrosed. [ME *mortifie(n)*, t. OF: m. *mortifier*, t. LL: m. *mortificāre* kill, destroy] —**mor′tifi′er,** *n.* —**mor′tify′ingly,** *adv.* —**Syn.** **1.** See **ashamed.**

Mortimer (mô′tĭ mə), *n.* **Roger** (*1st Earl of March*), 1287?–1330, English soldier, the favourite of Queen Isabella, wife of Edward II of England.

mortise (mô′tĭs), *n., v.,* **-tised, -tising.** —*n.* **1.** a rectangular cavity of considerable depth in one piece of wood, etc., for receiving a corresponding projection (tenon) on another piece, so as to form a joint (**mortise and tenon joint**). **2.** *Print.* the portion cut away from a letterpress printing plate for the insertion of type or another plate. —*v.t.* **3.** to fasten by, or as by, a mortise. **4.** to cut or otherwise form a mortise in, to fit a prescribed tenon. **5.** to fasten or join securely. **6.** *Print.* to cut away part of a letterpress printing plate in order to insert type or another plate in its place. Also, **mortice.** [ME *mortas*, t. OF: m. *mortaise*, ? t. Ar.: m. *murtazz* made fast]

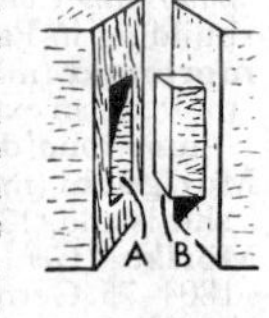

A, Mortise; B, Tenon

mortmain (môt′mān), *n.* *Law.* **1.** the condition of lands or tenements held without right of alienation, as by an ecclesiastical corporation; inalienable ownership. **2.** the holding of land by a corporation or charitable trust beyond the period of time or in violation of the conditions authorized by law. Also, **dead hand.** [ME *mort(e)mayn(e)*, t. OF: m. *mortemain*, trans. of ML *mortua manus* dead hand]

mortuary (mô′tyo͞o ə rĭ), *n., pl.* **-ries,** *adj.* —*n.* **1.** a place for the temporary reception of the dead. **2.** a customary gift formerly claimed by and due to the incumbent of an English parish from the estate of a deceased parishioner. —*adj.* **3.** of or pertaining to the burial of the dead. **4.** pertaining to or connected with death. [ME, t. ML: m. s. *mortuārium*, prop. neut. of L *mortuārius* belonging to the dead]

morula (mŏ′ro͞o lə), *n., pl.* **-lae** (-lē′). *Embryol.* the mass of cells resulting from the cleavage of the ovum before the formation of a blastula. [t. NL, dim. of L *mōrum* mulberry] —**mor′ular,** *adj.*

morwong (mô′wŏng), *n.* a fish of the genus *Cheilodactylidae*, mostly yellowish green in colour, found in Australian waters and widely used as food.

mos, months.

mosaic (mə zā′ĭk), *n.* **1.** a picture or decoration made of small pieces of stone, glass, etc., of different colours, inlaid to form a design. **2.** the process of producing it. **3.** something resembling a mosaic in composition. **4.** *Aerial Surveying.* an assembly of aerial photographs taken vertically and matched in such a way as to show a continuous photographic representation of an area (**mosaic map**). **5.** *Plant Pathol.* a symptom of various virus diseases, a patchy variation of colour. **6.** *Genetics.* an organism, usually animal, composed of a mixture of genetically distinct tissues; chimera. —*adj.* **7.** pertaining to or resembling a mosaic or mosaic work. **8.** composed of diverse elements combined. [ME, t. ML: s. *mosaicus*, var. of *mūsaicus*, lit., of the Muses, artistic] —**mosaicist** (mə zā′ĭ sĭst), *n.*

Mosaic (mə zā′ĭk), *adj.* of or pertaining to Moses or the writings and institutions attributed to him. Also, **Mosa′ical.** [t. NL: s. *Mosaicus*, ? f. after *Hebraicus*]

mosaic gold, **1.** stannic sulphide. **2.** ormolu (def. 1).

mosaicism (mə zā′ĭ sĭz′əm), *n.* *Genetics.* the condition of a mosaic (def. 6).

Mosaic Law, **1.** the ancient law of the Hebrews, attributed to Moses. **2.** the part of the Scripture containing this law; the Pentateuch.

moschate (mŏs′kāt, -kĭt), *adj.* having a musky smell. [t. NL: m. s. *moschātus*, der. ML *moschus* musk]

moschatel (mŏs′kə tĕl′), *n.* a small, inconspicuous plant, *Adoxa moschatellina*, having greenish or yellowish flowers with a musky smell; town-hall clock. [t. F: m. *moscatelle*, t. It.: m. *moscatella*, der. *moscato* musk]

Moscow (mŏs′kō), *n.* the capital of the Soviet Union, in the central part of European Soviet Russia. 6,443,000 (est. 1965). Russian, **Moskva** (*Russ.* măs kvä′). See map under **Volgograd.**

Mosel (mō zĕl′), *n.* Moselle (def. 1).

Moselle (mō zĕl′), *n.* **1.** a river flowing from the Vosges mountains in NE France into the Rhine in W West Germany. 320 mi. **2.** a department in NE France. 919,412 pop. (1962); 2403 sq. mi. *Cap.:* Metz. **3.** a light, sprightly white wine made along the Moselle in West Germany.

Moses (mō′zĭz), *n.* the liberator of the Hebrews from Egypt, leader throughout the years of the desert sojourn, founder of Israel's theocracy, and, according to tradition, its first lawgiver. Ex. 2, Deut. 34. [t. L, t. Gk, t. Heb.: m. *Mōsheh*]

Moses basket, a bassinet.

mosey (mō′zĭ), *v.i.*, **-seyed, -seying.** *U.S. Slang.* **1.** to move or go along or away; make off. **2.** to shuffle along; stroll.

moskonfyt (mŏs′kŏn fāt′), *n.* grape juice syrup prepared in South Africa. [t. Afrikaans: f. *mos* MUST[2] + *konfyt* KONFYT]

Moslem (mŏz′ləm), *adj.*, *n.*, *pl.*, **-lems, -lem.** Muslim. —**Moslemic** (mŏz lĕm′ĭk), *adj.*

Moslemism (mŏz′lə mĭz′-əm), *n.* the Muslim religion; Islam.

Mosley (mōz′lĭ), *n.* **Sir Oswald Ernald** (ûr′nəld), born 1896, British politician, founder of the British Union of Fascists.

mosque (mŏsk), *n.* a Muslim temple or place of worship. [t. F: m. *mosquée*, t. It.: m. *moschea*, t. Ar.: m. *masjid*, der. *sajada* prostrate oneself, worship]

Mosque

mosquito (mə skē′tō), *n.*, *pl.* **-toes, -tos.** any of various dipterous insects of the family *Culicidae* (genera *Culex*, *Anopheles*, etc.), the females of which have a long proboscis, by means of which they puncture the skin of animals (including man) and draw blood, some species transmitting certain diseases, as malaria and yellow fever. [t. Sp., dim. of *mosca*, g. L *musca* a fly]

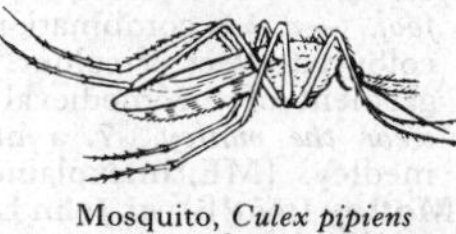
Mosquito, *Culex pipiens* (Body ¼ in. long)

mosquito hawk, a nighthawk (def. 2).

mosquito net, a screen, curtain, or canopy of net, gauze, or the like (**mosquito netting**), for keeping out mosquitoes.

moss (mŏs), *n.* **1.** any of the cryptogamic plants which belong to the class *Musci*, of the bryophytes, comprising small leafy-stemmed plants growing in tufts, sods, or mats on moist ground, tree trunks, rocks, etc. **2.** a growth of such plants. **3.** any of various similar plants, as certain lichens (see **Iceland moss**), the lycopods (see **club moss**), etc. **4.** *Chiefly Scot. and N Dial.* a swamp or peat bog. —*v.t.* **5.** to cover with a growth of moss. [ME *mos(se)*, OE *mos* bog, c. D *mos* moss, G *Moos* bog, moss] —**moss′-like′**, *adj.*

moss agate, a kind of agate or chalcedony containing brown or black mosslike dendritic markings from various impurities.

mossback (mŏs′băk′), *n.* *U.S. Colloq.* **1.** a person attached to antiquated notions. **2.** an extreme conservative.

Mössbauer effect (mŏs′bou′ə; *Ger.* mœs′bou ər), *Physics.* a discovery made in 1957 that in certain cases appreciable fractions of the gamma-ray spectrum emitted by some excited nuclei may be undisturbed by nuclear recoil or lattice vibrations. [named after R. L. *Mössbauer*, born 1922, German physicist]

moss-grown (mŏs′grōn′), *adj.* **1.** overgrown with moss. **2.** old-fashioned.

mossie (mŏs′ĭ), *n.* a bird of southern Africa, *Passer melanurus*, of the family *Ploceidae*, common in the vicinity of human dwellings; Cape sparrow.

mosso (mŏs′ō; *It.* mŏs′sō), *adj. Music.* fast. [t. It., pp. of *muovere* move]

moss rose, a cultivated variety of rose with a mosslike growth on the calyx and stem.

mosstrooper (mŏs′trōō′pə), *n.* **1.** one of the class of marauders who infested the mosses or bogs of the border between England and Scotland in the 17th century. **2.** any marauder. —**moss′troop′ing,** *n.*, *adj.*

mossy (mŏs′ĭ), *adj.*, **-sier, -siest. 1.** overgrown with, or abounding in, moss. **2.** covered with a mosslike growth. **3.** appearing as if covered with moss. **4.** resembling moss. —**moss′iness,** *n.*

mossy cyphel, a small tufted caryophyllaceous perennial herb with minute flowers, *Cherleria sedoides*, occurring on rocky slopes of mountains in Europe.

most (mōst), *adj.*, *superl.* of **more,** *n.*, *adv.* —*adj.* **1.** in the greatest quantity, amount, measure, degree, or number (used as the superlative of *much* and *many*, with the comparative *more*): *the most votes.* **2.** in the majority of instances: *most exercise is beneficial.* **3.** greatest, as in size or extent: *the most part.* —*n.* **4.** the greatest quantity, amount, or degree; the utmost. **5.** the greatest number or the majority of a class specified. **6.** the greatest number. **7.** the majority of persons (*construed as pl.*). —*adv.* **8.** in or to the greatest extent or degree (in this sense much used before adjectives and adverbs, and regularly before those of more than two syllables, to form superlative phrases having the same force and effect as the superlative degree formed by the termination *-est*): *most rapid, most wisely.* **9.** *U.S. and Dial.* almost or nearly. [ME *most(e)*, OE *māst* (r. ME *mest(e)*, OE *mǣst*), c. G *meist*, etc.]

Most (*Cz.* mōst), *n.* a town in W Czechoslovakia. 56,000 (1965).

Mostaganem (*Fr.* mōs tȧ gȧ nĕm′), *n.* a seaport in NW Algeria. 69,000 (1960).

-most, a suffixal use of *most* found in a series of superlatives, e.g., *utmost, foremost.* [ME *-most*, r. ME and OE *-mest*, a double superl. suffix, f. *-ma* + *-est*, both forming superlatives]

mostly (mōst′lĭ), *adv.* **1.** for the most part; in the main: *the work is mostly done.* **2.** chiefly. —**Syn. 2.** especially.

Mosul (mō′səl), *n.* a city in N Iraq on the Tigris, opposite the ruins of Nineveh. 178,222 (1957).

mot (mō), *n.* **1.** a pithy or witty remark. **2.** *Archaic.* a note on a horn, bugle, etc. [t. F: word, saying, note of a horn, etc., g. L *muttum* a mutter, grunt]

M.o.T., Ministry of Transport.

mote[1] (mōt), *n.* a particle or speck, esp. of dust. [ME; OE *mot* speck, c. D *mot* grit, sawdust]

mote[2] (mōt), *v.*, *pt.* **moste** (mōst). *Archaic.* may or might [ME *mot(e)*, OE *mōt*, pres. (c. G *muss*). See MUST, v.]

motel (mō tĕl′), *n.* a roadside hotel which provides parking for travellers' motor vehicles. [b. M(OTOR) and (H)OTEL]

motet (mō tĕt′), *n.* *Music.* a vocal composition in polyphonic style, on a biblical or similar prose text, intended for use in a church service. [ME, t. OF, dim. of *mot* word. See MOT]

moth (mŏth), *n.*, *pl.* **moths** (mŏths). **1.** any of a very large group of lepidopterous insects, generally distinguished from the butterflies by not having their antennae clubbed and by their (mainly) nocturnal or crepuscular habits. **2.** a clothes moth. [ME *motthe*, OE *moththe*, c. G *Motte*]

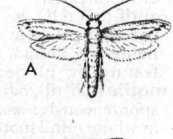

Clothes moth, *Tinea pellionella* A, Adult; B, Larva

mothball (mŏth′bôl′), *n.* **1.** a small ball of naphthalene or (sometimes) camphor which repels moths for the protection of clothing. **2. in mothballs, a.** no longer in use; in reserve. **b.** out of commission, as a ship. —*v.t.* **3.** to put out of use; place in reserve.

moth-eaten (mŏth′ē′tn), *adj.* **1.** eaten or damaged by or as by moths. **2.** decayed. **3.** out of fashion.

mother[1] (mŭth′ə), *n.* **1.** a female parent. **2.** (*often cap.*) one's own mother. **3.** *Colloq.* a mother-in-law, stepmother, or adoptive mother. **4.** a term of familiar address for an old or elderly woman. **5.** the head or superior of a female religious community. **6.** a woman looked upon as a mother, or exercising control or authority like that of a mother. **7.** the qualities characteristic of a mother, or maternal affection. **8.** something that gives rise to, or exercises protecting care over, something else. —*adj.* **9.** that is a mother: *a mother bird.* **10.** pertaining to or characteristic of a mother: *mother love.* **11.** derived from one's mother; native: *mother tongue.* **12.** bearing a relation like that of a mother, as in giving origin or rise, or in exercising protective care: *a mother church.* —*v.t.* **13.** to be the mother of; give origin or rise to. **14.** to acknowledge oneself the author of; assume as one's own. **15.** to care for or protect as a mother does. [ME *moder*, OE *mōdor*, c. D *moeder*, G *Mutter*, Icel. *mōdhir*; akin. to L *māter*, Gk *mḗtēr*, Skt *mātar-*] —**moth′erless,** *adj.*

mother[2] (mŭth′ə), *n.* a stringy, mucilaginous substance formed on the surface of a liquid undergoing acetous fermentation (as wine changing to vinegar), and consisting of the various bacteria, esp. *Mycoderma aceti*, which cause such fermentation. Also, **mother of vinegar.** [special use of MOTHER[1]]

Mother Carey's chicken (kēə′rĭz), any of various small petrels, esp. the stormy petrel, *Hydrobates pelagicus.*

mothercraft (mŭth′ə kräft′), *n.* the knowledge and skill associated with the rearing of children.

Mother Goose, the legendary author of the folk nursery jingles called *Mother Goose's Melodies.*

motherhood (mŭth′ə ho͝od′), *n.* **1.** the state of being a mother; maternity. **2.** mothers collectively. **3.** the qualities or spirit of a mother.

Mother Hubbard (hŭb′əd), **1.** a kind of full, loose gown worn by women. **2.** the heroine of a nursery rhyme.

Mothering Sunday (mŭth′ə rĭng), Mother's Day.

mother-in-law (mŭth′ə rĭn lô′), *n.*, *pl.* **mothers-in-law.** the mother of one's husband or wife.

motherland (mŭth′ə lănd′), *n.* **1.** one's native country. **2.** the land of one's ancestors.

mother lode, *Mining.* a rich or principal lode.

motherly (mŭth′ə lĭ), *adj.* **1.** pertaining to, characteristic of, or befitting a mother: *motherly affection.* **2.** having the character, etc., of a mother. *—adv.* **3.** in the manner of a mother. —**moth′erliness,** *n.*

Mother of God, a designation of the Virgin Mary.

mother-of-pearl (mŭth′ə rəv pûl′), *n.* a hard, iridescent substance which forms the inner layer of certain shells, as that of the pearl oyster; nacre.

mother-of-thousands (mŭth′ə rəv thou′zəndz), *n.* mind-your-own-business, *Helxine soleirolii.*

mother of vinegar, mother[2].

Mother's Day, a day for acts of grateful affection or remembrance by each person towards his mother, observed annually on a Sunday during Lent (in England) or on the second Sunday in May (in the U.S.). Also, **Mothering Sunday.**

mother's help, a girl or woman either living with a family or coming daily, who is paid to help with light housework and look after children.

mother superior, the head of a female religious community.

mother tongue, 1. the language first learned by a person; native language. **2.** a parent language.

Motherwell and Wishaw (mŭth′ə wəl; wish′ô), a burgh in Scotland, in Lanarkshire. 76,249 (est. 1964).

mother wit, common sense.

motherwort (mŭth′ə wût′), *n.* a labiate European plant, *Leonorus cardiaca,* with cut leaves having a close whorl of flowers in the axils, a common U.S. weed.

mothy (mŏth′ĭ), *adj.,* **-ier, -iest. 1.** containing moths. **2.** moth-eaten.

motif (mō tēf′), *n.* **1.** a subject or theme for development or treatment, as in art, literature, or music. **2.** a distinctive figure in a design, as of wallpaper. **3.** a dominant idea or feature. [t. F. See MOTIVE]

motile (mō′tīl), *adj.* **1.** *Biol.* moving, or capable of moving, spontaneously: *motile cells or spores.* *—n.* **2.** *Psychol.* one in whose mind motor images are predominant or especially distinct. [f. s. L *mōtus,* pp., moved + -ILE] —**motility** (mō tĭl′ĭ tĭ), *n.*

motion (mō′shən), *n.* **1.** the process of moving, or changing place or position. **2.** a movement. **3.** power of movement, as of a living body. **4.** the action or manner of moving the body in walking, etc.; gait. **5.** a bodily movement or change of posture; a gesture. **6.** a proposal formally made to a deliberative assembly: *to make a motion to adjourn.* **7.** *Law.* an application made to a court or judge for an order, ruling, or the like. **8.** a suggestion or proposal. **9.** an inward prompting or impulse; inclination: *of one's own motion.* **10.** *Music.* melodic progression, as the change of a voice part from one pitch to another. **11.** *Mach.* **a.** a piece of mechanism with a particular action or function. **b.** the action of such mechanism. **12.** *Med.* faeces (def. 1). **13. in motion,** in active operation; moving. *—v.t.* **14.** to direct by a significant motion or gesture, as with the hand: *to motion a person to a seat.* *—v.i.* **15.** to make a significant motion; gesture, as with the hand for the purpose of directing: *to motion to a person.* [ME, t. L: s. *mōtio* a moving]

—**Syn. 1.** MOTION, MOVE, MOVEMENT refer to change of position in space. MOTION denotes change of position, either considered apart from, or as a characteristic of, that which moves; usually the former, in which case it is often a somewhat technical or scientific term: *perpetual motion.* The chief uses of MOVE are founded upon the idea of moving a piece, in chess or a similar game, for winning the game; and hence the word denotes any change of position, condition, or circumstances for the accomplishment of some end: *a shrewd move to win votes.* MOVEMENT is always connected with the person or thing moving, and is usually a definite or particular motion: *the movements of a dance.*

motionless (mō′shən lĭs), *adj.* without, or incapable of, motion. —**mo′tionlessly,** *adv.* —**mo′tionlessness,** *n.*

motion picture, *Chiefly U.S.* film (def. 4).

motivate (mō′tĭ vāt′), *v.t.,* **-vated, -vating.** to provide with a motive or motives.

motivation (mō′tĭ vā′shən), *n.* a motivating; a providing of a motive; inducement. —**mo′tiva′tional,** *adj.*

motivational research, the application of the knowledge and techniques of the social sciences (esp. psychology and sociology) to understanding consumer attitudes and behaviour: used as a guide in advertising and marketing. Also, **motivation research.**

motive (mō′tĭv), *n., adj., v.,* **-tived, -tiving.** *—n.* **1.** something that prompts a person to act in a certain way or that determines volition; an incentive. **2.** the goal or object of one's actions: *his motive was revenge.* **3.** (in art, literature, and music) a motif. *—adj.* **4.** causing, or tending to cause, motion. **5.** pertaining to motion. **6.** prompting to action. **7.** constituting a motive or motives. *—v.t.* **8.** to provide with a motive. **9.** to motivate. **10.** to relate to a motif or a principal theme or idea in a work of art. [t. ML: m. s. *mōtivum* a moving cause, prop. neut. of *mōtivus* serving to move, der. L *mōtus,* pp., moved; r. ME *motif,* t. OF]

—**Syn. 1.** MOTIVE, INCENTIVE, INDUCEMENT apply to whatever moves one to action. MOTIVE is, literally, that which moves a person; an INDUCEMENT, that which leads him on; an INCENTIVE, that which inspires him. MOTIVE is applied mainly to an inner urge that moves or prompts a person to action, though it may also apply to a contemplated result, the desire for which moves the person: *his motive was a wish to be helpful.* INDUCEMENT is never applied to an inner urge, and seldom to a goal (*the pleasure of wielding authority may be an inducement to get ahead*); it is used mainly of opportunities offered by the acceptance of certain conditions, whether these are offered by a second person or by the factors of the situation: *the salary offered me was a great inducement.* INCENTIVE was once used of anything inspiring or stimulating the emotions or imagination (*incentives to piety*); it has retained of this its emotional connotations, but (rather like INDUCEMENT) is today applied only to something offered as a reward, and offered particularly to stimulate competitive activity: *incentives to greater production.* **2.** See **reason.**

motive power, 1. any power used to impart motion. **2.** a source of mechanical energy. **3.** *Railways.* locomotives, etc., which supply tractive power.

motivity (mō tĭv′ĭ tĭ), *n.* the power of initiating or producing motion.

mot juste (*Fr.* mō zhʏst′), *French.* the exact or appropriate word.

motley (mŏt′lĭ), *adj., n., pl.* **-leys.** *—adj.* **1.** exhibiting great diversity of elements; heterogeneous: *a motley crowd.* **2.** being of different colours combined; particoloured. **3.** wearing a particoloured garment: *a motley fool.* *—n.* **4.** a combination of different colours. **5.** a particoloured effect of colour. **6.** the motley or particoloured garment of the medieval professional fool or jester: *to wear the motley.* **7.** a heterogeneous assemblage. **8.** a medley. [ME, unexplained deriv. of MOTE[1]]

Motley (mŏt′lĭ), *n.* **John Lothrop,** 1814–77, U.S. historian and diplomat.

motmot (mŏt′mŏt), *n.* any of the tropical and subtropical American birds constituting the family *Momotidae,* related to the kingfishers, and having a serrate bill and chiefly greenish and bluish plumage. [t. Amer. Sp.; imit.]

motor (mō′tə), *n.* **1.** a comparatively small and powerful engine, esp. an internal-combustion engine in a motor car, motor boat, or the like. **2.** any self-powered vehicle. **3.** one who or that which imparts motion, esp. a contrivance (as a steam engine), which receives and modifies energy from some natural source in order to utilize it in driving machinery, etc. **4.** *Elect.* a machine which converts electrical energy into mechanical energy: *an electric motor.* **5.** (*pl.*) *Stock Exchange.* motor-vehicle securities. *—adj.* **6.** causing or imparting motion. **7.** pertaining to or operated by a motor. **8.** used in or for, or pertaining to, motor vehicles. **9.** *Physiol.* conveying an impulse that results or tends to result in motion, as a nerve. **10.** *Physiol., Psychol.* denoting the effect or phase of any mental process, as the innervation of muscles and glands. **11.** *Psychol.* pertaining to or involving action: *motor images.* *—v.i.* **12.** to ride or travel in a motor car. *—v.t.* **13.** to convey (someone) by a motor car. [t. L: one who moves]

motorbike (mō′tə bīk′), *n. Colloq.* motorcycle.

motor boat, a boat propelled by its own mechanical power. —**motor-boating** (mō′tə bō′tĭng), *n.*

motorbus (mō′tə bŭs′), *n.* **1.** a bus. **2.** *U.S.* a motor coach.

motorcade (mō′tə kād′), *n.* a procession or parade of motor cars. Also, *U.S.,* **autocade.** [f. MOTOR and (CAVAL)CADE]

motor car, a vehicle, esp. one for passengers, carrying its own power-generating and propelling mechanism, usually an internal-combustion engine, for travel on ordinary roads.

motor coach, a coach (def. 3).

motorcycle (mō′tə sī′kl), *n.* a motor vehicle resembling a bicycle, for one or two riders, sometimes with a sidecar attached. —**motorcyclist** (mō′tə sī′klĭst), *n.*

motor drive, the mechanical system, including an electric motor, used to operate a machine or machines.

motored (mō′təd), *adj.* having a motor or motors, esp. of specified number or type: *a two-motored tape-recorder.*

motor generator, *Elect.* an electric motor coupled to a generator for altering the voltage, frequency, or number of phases of an electric supply.

motorist (mō′tə rĭst), *n.* **1.** one who drives a motor car. **2.** the user of a privately owned motor car.

motorize (mō′tə rīz′), *v.t.,* **-rized, -rizing. 1.** to furnish with a motor or motors, as vehicles. **2.** to supply with motor-driven vehicles in the place of horses and horse-drawn vehicles. Also, **motorise.** —**mo′toriza′tion,** *n.*

motorman (mō′tə mən), *n., pl.* **-men. 1.** one who drives an electric train or tram. **2.** one who operates a motor.

motor scooter, a low-built motorcycle having small wheels, footboards, and an enclosed engine. Also, **scooter.**
motor starter, *Elect.* a device for starting and accelerating an electric motor up to its normal running speed.
motor vehicle, a road vehicle driven by a motor, usually an internal-combustion engine, as a motor car, motorcycle, or the like.
motor vessel, a ship driven by internal-combustion engines, usually diesel. Also, *U.S.*, **motor ship.**
motorway (mō′tə wā′), *n.* a high-speed main road, having separate carriageways for opposite directions and cloverleaf junctions at entry and exit points.
motte (mŏt), *n. U.S. Dial.* a small patch of woods in prairie land. Also, **mott.** [t. F: mound]
M.o.T. test, the regular compulsory testing of motor vehicles under the jurisdiction of the Ministry of Transport after a specified period, to ensure mechanical soundness.
mottle (mŏt′l), *v.*, **-tled, -tling,** *n.* —*v.t.* **1.** to diversify with spots or blotches of a different colour or shade. —*n.* **2.** a diversifying spot or blotch of colour. **3.** mottled colouring or pattern. [back-formation from MOTLEY]
mottled (mŏt′ld), *adj.* spotted or blotched in colouring.
motto (mŏt′ō), *n., pl.* **-toes, -tos. 1.** a maxim adopted as expressing one's guiding principle. **2.** a sentence, phrase, or word attached to or inscribed on anything as appropriate to it. [t. It. See MOT]
mouch (mo͞och), *v.i., v.t. Slang.* mooch.
moue (mo͞o), *n. French.* a pouting grimace. [see MOW[3]]
mouflon (mo͞of′lŏn), *n.* a wild sheep, *Ovis musimon*, inhabiting the mountainous regions of Sardinia, Corsica, etc., the male of which has large curving horns. Also, **moufflon.** [t. F, t. Corsican, g. LL *mufro*]
mouillé (mwē′ā; *Fr.* mo͞o yĕ′), *adj. Phonet.* **1.** palatal or palatalized, esp. referring to sounds spelt *ll* and *ñ* in Spanish, *gl* and *gn* in Italian, etc. **2.** (of French sounds) spelt *l* or *ll* and pronounced as a *y* sound. [t. F, pp. of *mouiller* wet, moisten, der. L *mollis* soft]
moujik (mo͞o′zhĭk), *n.* muzhik.
moulage (mo͞o läzh′), *n.* **1.** the making of a mould in plaster of Paris, etc., of objects, footprints, tyre tracks, etc., esp. for identification. **2.** the mould itself. [t. F]
mould[1] (mōld), *n.* **1.** a hollow form or matrix for giving a particular shape to something in a molten or plastic state. **2.** that on or about which something is formed or made. **3.** something formed in or on a mould: *a mould of jelly.* **4.** the shape imparted to a thing by a mould. **5.** shape or form. **6.** distinctive nature, or native character. **7.** *Archit.* **a.** a moulding. **b.** a group of mouldings. —*v.t.* **8.** to work into a required shape or form; shape. **9.** to shape or form in or on a mould. **10.** *Foundry.* to form a mould of or from, in order to make a casting. **11.** to produce by or as if by shaping material; form. **12.** to fashion; model the character of. **13.** to ornament with mouldings. Also, *U.S.*, **mold.** [ME, t. OF: m. *modle*, g. L *modulus* MODULE] —**mould′-able,** *adj.*
mould[2] (mōld), *n.* **1.** a growth of minute fungi forming on vegetable or animal matter, commonly as a downy or furry coating, and associated with decay. **2.** any of the fungi that produce such a growth. —*v.t., v.i.* **3.** to make or become mould. Also, *U.S.*, **mold.** [ME *mowlde*, appar. var. of *mowled, mouled*, pp. of *moulen*, earlier ME *muwlen*, c. d. Dan. *mugle* grow mouldy]
mould[3] (mōld), *n.* **1.** loose, friable earth, esp. such as is rich in organic matter and favourable to the growth of plants. **2.** *Poetic.* the ground or earth. Also, *U.S.*, **mold.** [ME and OE *molde*, c. OHG *molta* mould, dust]
mouldboard (mōld′bōd′), *n.* the curved board or metal plate in a plough, which turns over the earth from the furrow. Also, *U.S.*, **moldboard.**
moulder[1] (mōl′də), *v.i.* **1.** to turn to dust by natural decay; crumble; waste away. —*v.t.* **2.** to cause to moulder. Also, *U.S.*, **molder.** [freq. of obs. *mold*, v., moulder, crumble away (v. use of MOULD[3]). See -ER[6]]
moulder[2] (mōl′də), *n.* one who moulds; a maker of moulds. Also, *U.S.*, **molder.** [f. MOULD[1], v. + -ER[1]]
moulding (mōl′dĭng), *n.* **1.** the act or process of one who or that which moulds. **2.** something moulded. **3.** *Archit., etc.* **a.** a decorative variety of contour or outline given to cornices, jambs, strips of woodwork, etc. **b.** a shaped member introduced into a structure to afford such variety or decoration. **4.** shaped material in the form of a strip, used for supporting pictures, covering electric wires, etc. Also, *U.S.*, **molding.**
moulding board, the board upon which bread is kneaded. Also, *U.S.*, **molding board.**
mouldy (mōl′dĭ), *adj.* **-dier, -diest. 1.** overgrown or covered with mould. **2.** musty, as from decay or age. Also, *U.S.*, **moldy.** [f. MOULD[2] + -Y[1]] —**mould′iness,** *n.*
moulin (mo͞o′lĭn), *n.* a nearly vertical shaft or cavity worn in a glacier by surface water falling through a crack in the ice. [t. F, g. LL *molīnum* mill. See MILL[1]]
Moulins (*Fr.* mo͞o lăɴ′), *n.* a town in central France, in Allier department. 25,671 (1962).
Moulmein (moul mān′), *n.* a seaport in S Burma at the mouth of the river Salween. 190,000 (est. 1964). Also, **Maulmain.**
moult (mōlt), *v.i.* **1.** (of birds, insects, reptiles, etc.) to cast or shed the feathers, skin, or the like, to be succeeded by a new growth. —*v.t.* **2.** to cast or shed (feathers, etc.) in the process of renewal. —*n.* **3.** the act or process of moulting. Also, *U.S.*, **molt.** [ME *mout*, OE *-mūtian* change (in *bemūtian* exchange for), t. L: m. *mūtāre* change. Cf. MEW[4]] —**moult′er,** *n.*
mound[1] (mound), *n.* **1.** an elevation formed of earth or sand, debris, etc., overlying ruins, a grave, etc. **2.** a tumulus or other raised work of earth dating from a prehistoric or long-past period. **3.** a natural elevation of earth; a hillock or knoll. **4.** an artificial elevation of earth, as for a defence work, a dam or barrier, or any other purpose; an embankment. **5.** a heap or raised mass: *a mound of hay.* **6.** *Baseball.* the slightly elevated ground from which the pitcher delivers the ball and which slopes gradually to the baselines. —*v.t.* **7.** to furnish with a mound of earth, as for a defence. **8.** to form into a mound; heap up. [OE *mund* hand, protection]
mound[2] (mound), *n.* a sovereign's orb. [ME, t. L: m. s. *mundus* world]
Mound-Builder (mound′bĭl′də), *n.* **1.** a member of certain Indian tribes who, in prehistoric and early historic times, erected the burial mounds and other earthworks of the Mississippi drainage basin and south-eastern states of America. **2.** (*l.c.*) a bird of the megapode family, of the E Indies, Australasia, and Polynesia, which deposit their eggs in a mound of sand or decaying vegetation, to be hatched by natural heat. —**mound′-build′ing,** *adj.*
mount[1] (mount), *v.t.* **1.** to go up or ascend: *to mount the stairs.* **2.** to get up on (a platform, a horse, etc.). **3.** to set or place at an elevation: *to be mounted on stilts.* **4.** to furnish with a horse or other mount for riding. **5.** to set on horseback. **6.** to raise or put into position for use, as a gun. **7.** to have or carry (guns) in position for use, as a fortress or a vessel does. **8.** to go or put on (guard), as a sentry or watch. **9.** (of a male animal) to climb up on (a female) for copulation. **10.** to fix on or in a support, backing, setting, etc.: *to mount a photograph.* **11.** to provide (a play, etc.) with scenery, costumes, and other appurtenances for production. **12.** to prepare (an animal body or skeleton) as a specimen. **13.** *Micros.* **a.** to prepare (a slide) for microscopic investigation. **b.** to prepare (a sample, etc.) for examination by a microscope, as by placing it on a slide. —*v.i.* **14.** to rise or go to a higher position, level, degree, etc.; ascend. **15.** to rise in amount (often fol. by *up*): *the costs are steadily mounting.* **16.** to get up on the back of a horse, etc., for riding. **17.** to get up on something, as a platform. —*n.* **18.** the act or manner of mounting. **19.** a horse or other animal (or sometimes a bicycle) used, provided, or available for riding. **20.** an act or occasion of riding a horse, esp. in a race. **21.** a support, backing, setting, or the like, on or in which something is, or is to be, mounted or fixed: *a stamp mount.* **22.** *Micros.* the prepared slide. [ME *monte(n)*, t. OF: m. *monter*, ult. der. L *mons* mountain] —**Syn. 14.** rise, soar. See **climb.**
mount[2] (mount), *n.* a mountain or hill (now chiefly poetic, except in proper names, as *Mount Etna*). [ME *mont, munt*, OE *munt*, t. L: m. s. *mons*]
mountain (moun′tĭn), *n.* **1.** a natural elevation of the earth's surface rising more or less abruptly to a summit, and attaining an altitude greater than that of a hill. **2.** something resembling this, as in size: a *mountain of ice.* **3.** a huge amount. **4. the Mountain,** *French Hist.* a popular name for the extreme revolutionary party led by Danton and Robespierre in the legislatures of the French Revolution, whose members occupied the highest seats. It favoured the ruthless prosecution of the Revolution and Reign of Terror. —*adj.* **5.** of mountains: *mountain air.* **6.** living, growing, or found on mountains: *mountain people, mountain plants.* **7.** resembling or suggesting a mountain, as in size. [ME t. OF: m. *montaigne*, der. *mont* mountain, g. L *mons*]
mountain ash, 1. any of various small trees of the rosaceous genus *Sorbus*, as the European rowan, *S. aucuparia*, and the American *S. americana*, both having pinnate leaves and bearing small white corymbose flowers succeeded by bright red to orange berries. **2.** any of certain other trees, as *Eucalyptus regnans* of Australia.
mountain avens, a prostrate, evergreen rosaceous shrub, *Dryas octopetala*, widespread on mountains of the N temperate zone.
mountain cat, 1. cougar. **2.** bobcat.

mountain chain, 1. a connected series of mountains. 2. two or more mountain ranges of close geographical relation.

mountain dew, *Slang.* 1. Scotch whisky. 2. any whisky, esp. when illicitly distilled.

mountaineer (moun′tĭ nĭə′), *n.* 1. a climber of mountains. 2. an inhabitant of a mountainous district. —*v.i.* 3. to climb mountains. —**moun′taineer′ing,** *n.*

mountain fern, a fern with a short stout rhizome and tufts of pinnate leaves, *Thelypteris limbosperma,* occurring throughout the N temperate zone, particularly on steep banks.

mountain goat, the Rocky Mountain goat.

mountain ibex, the tahr.

mountain lion, the puma.

mountainous (moun′tĭ nəs), *adj.* 1. abounding in mountains. 2. of the nature of a mountain. 3. resembling a mountain or mountains; large and high; huge: *mountainous waves.* —**moun′tainously,** *adv.*

mountain range, 1. a series of more or less connected mountains ranged in a line. 2. a series of mountains, or of more or less parallel lines of mountains, closely related in origin, etc. 3. an area in which the greater part of the land surface is in considerable degree or slope, upland summits are small or narrow, and there are great differences in elevations within the area (commonly over 2000 feet).

mountain sheep, 1. the bighorn, *Ovis canadensis,* found in the Rocky Mountains and in N Asia. 2. any of various wild sheep inhabiting mountains.

mountain sickness, *Pathol.* a morbid condition characterized by difficult breathing, headache, nausea, etc., due to the rarefaction of the air at high altitudes.

Mountain Time, one of the four standard time zones in the U.S. lying on the 105th meridian, seven hours behind **Greenwich Mean Time** and one hour behind **Central Time.**

Mountbatten of Burma (mount′băt′n), **Louis, 1st Earl,** born 1900, British admiral: viceroy of India 1947; governor-general of India 1947–48.

mountebank (moun′tĭ băngk′), *n.* 1. one who sells quack medicines from a platform in public places, appealing to his audience by tricks, storytelling, etc. 2. any charlatan or quack. —*v.i.* 3. to play the mountebank. [t. It.: m. *montambanco,* contr. of *monta in banco* mount-on-(a)-bench] —**mountebankery** (moun′tĭ băng′kə rĭ), *n.*

mounted (moun′tĭd), *adj.* 1. seated or riding on a horse or the like. 2. serving on horseback, or on some special mount, as soldiers, police, etc. 3. *Mil.* permanently equipped with trucks, tanks, or other vehicles, or horses as means of transport. 4. fixed on or in a support, backing, setting, or the like: *mounted gems.* 5. put into position for use, as guns. —**Ant.** 1. afoot.

mounter (moun′tə), *n.* one who or that which mounts.

Mountie (moun′tĭ), *n. Colloq.* a member of the Royal Canadian Mounted Police.

mounting (moun′tĭng), *n.* 1. the act of one who or that which mounts. 2. something that serves as a mount, support, setting, or the like.

Mount Lofty Range, a mountain range in the SE of South Australia. Highest point, Mt Bryan, 3064 ft.

Mount Palomar. See **Palomar, Mount.**

Mount Sinai. See **Sinai, Mount.**

Mount Vernon (vûr′nən), the home and tomb of George Washington in NE Virginia, on the Potomac, 15 mi. below Washington, D.C.

mourn (môn), *v.i.* 1. to feel or express sorrow or grief. 2. to grieve or lament for the dead. 3. to display the conventional tokens of sorrow after a person's death. —*v.t.* 4. to feel or express sorrow or grief over (misfortune, loss, or anything regretted); deplore. 5. to grieve or lament over (the dead). 6. to utter in a sorrowful manner. [ME *mo(u)rne,* OE *murnan,* c. OHG *mornên*] —**Syn.** 1. bewail, bemoan. See **grieve.**

Mourne Mountains (môn), a range of low mountains in Co. Down, N Ireland. Highest peak, Slieve Donard, 2796 ft.

mourner (mô′nə), *n.* 1. one who mourns. 2. one who attends a funeral as a mourning friend or relative of the deceased. 3. *U.S.* (at religious revival meetings) one who professes penitence for sin, with desire for salvation.

mourners' bench, *U.S.* (at religious revival meetings) a bench or seat at the front of the church or room, set apart for mourners or penitent sinners seeking salvation.

mournful (môn′fəl), *adj.* 1. full of, expressing, or showing sorrow or grief, as persons, the tone, etc.; sorrowful; sad. 2. expressing, or used in, mourning for the dead. 3. causing, or attended with, sorrow or mourning: *a mournful occasion.* 4. gloomy, sombre or dreary, as in appearance or character: *mournful shadows.* —**mourn′fully,** *adv.* —**mourn′fulness,** *n.*

mourning (mô′nĭng), *n.* 1. the act of one who mourns; sorrowing or lamentation. 2. the conventional manifestation of sorrow for a person's death, esp. by the wearing of black, the hanging of flags at half-mast, etc. 3. the outward tokens of such sorrow, as black garments, etc. —*adj.* 4. of, pertaining to, or used in mourning. —**mourn′ingly,** *adv.* —**Ant.** 1. rejoicing.

mourning cloak, a European and American butterfly, *Nymphalis antiopa,* having dark wings with a yellow border.

Mouscron (*Fr.* mo͞o krôɴ′, mo͞os-), *n.* a town in Belgium, in SE West Flanders. 37,506 (est. 1964). Flemish, **Moeskroen.**

mouse (*n.* mous; *v.* mouz), *n., pl.* **mice** (mīs), *v.,* **moused, mousing.** —*n.* 1. any of various small rodents of the family *Muridae,* esp. of the genus *Mus,* as *M. musculus,* which infests houses. 2. any similar animal of some other family, as the *Cricetidae.* 3. *Slang.* a black eye. 4. *Colloq.* a person who is very quiet and shy, esp. a girl or woman. —*v.i.* 5. to hunt for or catch mice. 6. to prowl (about, etc.), as if seeking something. 7. to seek or search stealthily or watchfully, as if for prey. —*v.t.* 8. *Chiefly U.S.* to hunt out, as a cat hunts out mice. 9. *Naut.* to secure with a mousing. [ME *mous,* OE *mūs* (pl. *mȳs*), c. G *Maus,* L *mūs*]

Harvest mouse, *Micromys minutus* (Total length 5 in., tail 2½ in.)

mousebird (mous′bûd′), *n.* a coly; any bird of the African family *Coliidae.*

mousedeer (mous′dĭə′), *n.* chevrotain.

mouse-dun (mous′dŭn′), *n.* dark brownish grey.

mouse-ear (mous′ĭə′), *n.* any of various plants with small hairy leaves, as the hawkweed, *Hieracium pilosella,* the forget-me-not, *Myosotis palustris,* etc.

mouser (mou′zə), *n.* 1. an animal that catches mice: commonly used with a qualifying term or with reference to the animal's ability to catch mice. 2. one who mouses, or seeks or prowls as if for prey.

mousetail (mous′tāl′), *n.* any plant of the ranunculaceous genus *Myosurus,* esp. *M. minimus,* the flowers of which have a tail-like torus.

mouse-trap (mous′trăp′), *n.* 1. a trap used for catching mice in houses, usually consisting of a small wooden cage into which the mouse is lured. 2. *Colloq.* an inexpensive, often tasteless, type of cheese.

mousing (mou′zĭng), *n. Naut.* several turns of small rope or the like, uniting the shank and point of a hook.

mousse (mo͞os), *n.* 1. any of various preparations of whipped cream, beaten eggs, gelatine, etc., sweetened and flavoured and chilled. 2. savoury mousse. [t. F: moss, froth, of Gmc orig. See MOSS]

mousseline (*Fr.* mo͞os lĕn′), *n. French.* muslin.

mousseline de laine (*Fr.* mo͞os lĕn də lĕn′), *French.* delaine. [F: lit., woollen muslin]

mousseline de soie (*Fr.* mo͞os lĕn də swȧ′), *French.* a thin, stiff silk or rayon fabric. [F. lit., silken muslin]

mousseline sauce, a hollandaise sauce to which beaten white of egg or thick cream has been added just before serving.

Moussorgsky (mo͞o sôg′skĭ; *Russ.* mo͞o′sərk skĭy), *n.* **Modest Petrovich** (*Russ.* mȧ dyĕst′ pĭt rô′vĭch), 1839–81, Russian composer.

moustache (mə stăsh′), *n.* 1. the hair growing on the upper lip, or on either half of the upper lip, of men. 2. such hair when allowed to grow without shaving, and usually trimmed to a particular shape. 3. hair or bristles growing near the mouth of an animal. 4. a stripe of colour, or elongated feathers, suggestive of a moustache on either side of the head of a bird. Also, *U.S.,* **mustache.** [t. F, t. It.: m. *mostaccio,* ult. t. Gk: *mýstax* upper lip, moustache]

Mousterian (mo͞o stĭə′rĭ ən), *adj. Anthropol.* pertaining to Palaeolithic human relics having the workmanship, finish, and character of the flint scrapers found in the sands of Moustier, France.

mousy (mou′sĭ), *adj.,* **-sier, -siest.** 1. resembling or suggesting a mouse, as in colour, smell, etc. 2. drab and colourless. 3. quiet as a mouse. 4. infested with mice. Also, **mousey.**

mouth (*n.* mouth; *v.* mouth), *n., pl.* **mouths** (mouthz), *v.* —*n.* 1. the opening through which an animal takes in food, or the cavity containing or the parts including the masticating apparatus. 2. the masticating and tasting apparatus. 3. a person or other animal as requiring food. 4. the oral opening or cavity considered as the source of vocal utterance. 5. utterance or expression: *to give mouth to one's thoughts.* 6. a grimace made with the lips. 7. an opening leading out of or into any cavity or hollow place or thing:

the mouth of a cave. **8.** a part of a river or the like where its waters are discharged into some other body of water: *the mouth of the Nile.* **9.** the opening between the jaws of a vice or the like. **10.** the lateral hole of an organ pipe. **11.** the lateral blowhole of a flute. **12. by word of mouth,** orally, as opposed to *in writing.* **13. down in the mouth,** see **down**[1] (def. 28). **14. shut one's mouth,** *Slang.* to be quiet. —*v.t.* **15.** to utter in a sonorous, oratorical, or pompous manner, or with unnecessarily noticeable use of the mouth or lips. **16.** to put or take into the mouth, as food. **17.** to press, rub, or mumble with the mouth or lips. **18.** to accustom (a horse) to the use of the bit and bridle. —*v.i.* **19.** to speak or declaim sonorously and oratorically, or with mouthing of the words. **20.** to grimace with the lips. [ME; OE *mūth,* c. G *Mund*]

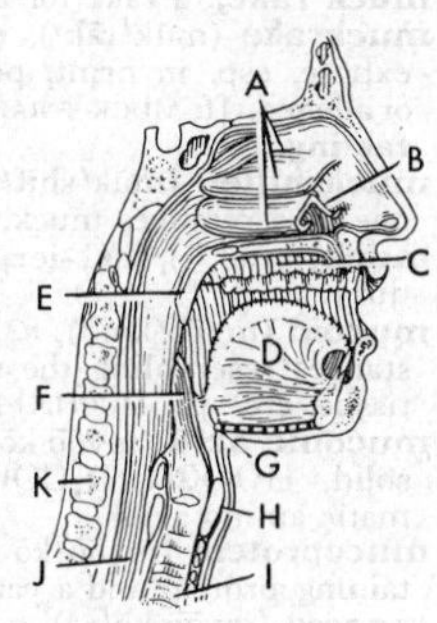

Mouth and nose (section) A, Turbinate bones; B, Lachrymal duct; C, Hard palate; D, Tongue; E, Uvula; F, Epiglottis; G, Hyoid bone; H, Larynx; I, Trachea; J, Oesophagus; K, Cervical vertebrae

mouth-breeder (mouth′brē′də), *n.* any aquarium fish, of the genera *Tilapia* and *Haplochromis,* which care for their young by holding them in the mouth.

mouthful (mouth′fŏŏl′), *n., pl.* **-fuls. 1.** as much as a mouth can hold. **2.** as much as is taken into the mouth at one time. **3.** a small quantity.

mouth organ, a harmonica (def. 1).

mouthpart (mouth′pät′), *n. Zool.* a structure in the region of the mouth of arthropods.

mouthpiece (mouth′pēs′), *n.* **1.** a piece placed at or forming the mouth, as of a receptacle, tube, or the like. **2.** a piece or part, as of an instrument, to which the mouth is applied or which is held in the mouth: *the mouthpiece of a trumpet.* **3.** the part of a bit or bridle, as for a horse, that passes through the animal's mouth. **4.** a person, a newspaper, or the like that voices or communicates the sentiments, decisions, etc., of another or others; a spokesman.

mouth-to-mouth (mouth′ tə mouth′), *adj.* denoting a method of artificial respiration in which air is breathed rhythmically into the mouth of the patient.

mouthwash (mouth′wŏsh′), *n.* a medicated solution used for gargling and cleansing the mouth.

mouth-watering (mouth′wô′tə rĭng), *adj.* (of food, etc.) appetizing: *a mouth-watering smell of cooking.*

mouthy (mou′thĭ), *adj.,* **-thier, -thiest.** loud-mouthed; ranting; bombastic. —**mouth′ily,** *adv.* —**mouth′iness,** *n.*

moutonnée (mōō′tə nā′), *adj. Phys. Geog.* designating scattered knobs of rock rounded and smoothed by glacial action. Also, **moutonnéed.** [t. F: lit., rounded like a sheep's back, pp. fem. of *moutonner,* der. *mouton* sheep. See MUTTON]

movable (mōō′və bl), *adj.* **1.** capable of being moved; not fixed in one place, position, or posture. **2.** changing from one date to another in different years: *movable feast.* **3.** *Law.* moveable. **4.** *Print.* (of type or matrices) separate and capable of being rearranged. —*n.* **5.** an article of furniture which is not fixed in place. **6.** (*usually pl.*) *Law.* moveable. —**mov′ableness, mov′abil′ity,** *n.* —**mov′ably,** *adv.*

move (mōōv), *v.,* **moved, moving,** *n.* —*v.i.* **1.** to change place or position; pass from one place or situation to another. **2.** to change one's abode; go from one place of residence to another. **3.** to advance, progress, or make progress. **4.** to have a regular motion, as an implement or a machine; turn; revolve. **5.** *Com.* to be disposed of by sale, as goods in stock. **6.** *Colloq.* to start off, or depart: *it's time to be moving.* **7.** (of the bowels) to operate. **8.** to be active in a particular sphere: *to move in society.* **9.** to take action, or act, as in an affair. **10.** to make a formal request, application, or proposal: *to move for a new trial.* **11. move heaven and earth,** to do one's utmost. **12. move in,** to take up residence in a new home. **13. move out,** to leave a home. —*v.t.* **14.** to change the place or position of; take from one place, posture, or situation to another. **15.** to set or keep in motion; stir or shake. **16.** to prompt, actuate, or impel to some action: *what moved you to do this?* **17.** to cause (the bowels) to act or operate. **18.** to arouse or excite the feelings or passions of; affect with emotion; excite (*to*). **19.** to affect with tender or compassionate emotion; touch. **20.** to propose formally, as to a court or judge, or for consideration by a deliberative assembly. **21.** to submit a formal request or proposal to (a ruler, a court, etc.). —*n.* **22.** the act of moving; a movement. **23.** a change of abode or residence. **24.** an action towards an end; a step. **25.** *Games, etc.* the right or turn to move. **26. get a move on,** *Colloq.* hurry up. **27. on the move,** moving. [ME *move(n)*, t. AF: m. *mover,* g. L *movēre*] —**mov′er,** *n.* —**Syn. 1.** See **advance. 14.** remove, transfer, shift. **16.** influence; induce, incite, instigate; lead. **22.** See **motion.** —**Ant. 14.** fix.

moveable (mōō′və bl), *adj.* **1.** movable. **2.** *Law.* (of property) **a.** not permanent in place; capable of being moved without injury. **b.** personal, as distinguished from real. —*n.* **3.** movable. **4.** (*usually pl.*) *Law.* an article of personal property not attached to land. —**move′ableness, move′abil′ity,** *n.* —**move′ably,** *adv.*

movement (mōōv′mənt), *n.* **1.** the act or process or result of moving. **2.** a particular manner of moving. **3.** (*chiefly pl.*) an action or activity, as of a person or a body of persons. **4.** *Mil., Naval.* a change of position or location of troops or ships. **5.** rapid progress of events, or abundance of events or incidents. **6.** the progress of events, as in a narrative or drama. **7.** the suggestion of action, as in a painting or the like. **8.** a series of actions or activities directed or tending towards a particular end: *the anti-slavery movement.* **9.** the course, tendency, or trend, of affairs in a particular field. **10.** the price change in the market of some commodity or security. **11.** an evacuation of the bowels. **12.** the material evacuated. **13.** the works, or a distinct portion of the works, of a mechanism, as a watch. **14.** *Music.* **a.** a principal division or section of a sonata, symphony, or the like. **b.** motion; rhythm; time; tempo. **15.** *Pros.* rhythmical structure or character. —**Syn. 1.** See **motion.**

movie (mōō′vĭ), *n. U.S. Colloq.* a motion picture; film (def. 4).

moving (mōō′vĭng), *adj.* **1.** that moves. **2.** causing or producing motion. **3.** actuating, instigating, or impelling: *the moving cause of a dispute.* **4.** that excites the feelings or affects with emotion, esp. touching or pathetic. —**mov′ingly,** *adv.* —**mov′ingness,** *n.*

moving picture, *Chiefly U.S.* film (def. 4).

moving staircase, escalator.

Moviola (mōō′vĭ ō′lə), *n. Trademark.* a film editing machine.

mow[1] (mō), *v.,* **mowed, mown** or **mowed, mowing.** —*v.t.* **1.** to cut down (grass, grain, etc.) with a scythe or a machine. **2.** to cut grass, grain, etc., from. **3.** to cut down, destroy, or kill indiscriminately or in great numbers, as men in battle. —*v.i.* **4.** to cut down grass, grain, etc. **5.** to sweep down men in battle. [ME *mowe(n)*, OE *māwan,* c. G *mähen*] —**mow′er,** *n.*

mow[2] (mou), *n. U.S. and Dial.* **1.** the place in a barn where hay, sheaves of grain, etc., are stored. **2.** a heap or pile of hay or of sheaves of grain in a barn. [ME *mowe,* OE *mūga, mūha,* c. Icel. *mūgi* swath]

mow[3] (mou), *Archaic.* —*n.* **1.** a wry or derisive grimace. —*v.i.* **2.** to make mows, mouths, or grimaces. [ME *mowe,* t. OF: m. *moe* a pouting grimace]

mowe (mou), *n., v.i.,* **mowed, mowing.** *Archaic.* mow[3].

mowing (mō′ĭng), *n.* **1.** the act of levelling or cutting down grass with a mowing machine or scythe. **2.** as much grass as is cut in any specified period.

mowing machine, a machine for mowing or cutting down standing grass, etc.

mown (mōn), *v.* a pp. of **mow**[1].

moyen âge (*Fr.* mwȧ yĕ nȧzh′), *French.* the Middle Ages.

Mozamb., Mozambique.

Mozambique (mō′zəm bēk′), *n.* **1.** Also, **Portuguese East Africa.** a Portuguese overseas territory in SE Africa. 6,592,994 pop. (1960); 297,731 sq. mi. *Cap.:* Lourenço Marques. **2.** a seaport on an island off the NE coast of this territory. 93,516 (1960). Portuguese, **Moçambique.**

Mozambique Channel, a channel between Mozambique and Madagascar. ab. 950 mi. long; 250–550 mi. wide.

Mozart (mōt′sät; *Ger.* mō′tsȧrt), *n.* **Wolfgang Amadeus** (*Ger.* vōlf′gȧng ȧ mȧ dē′ōōs), 1756–91, Austrian composer.

mozzetta (mō zĕt′ə; *It.* mōt sĕt′tȧ), *n. Rom. Cath. Ch.* a short cape which covers the shoulders and can be buttoned over the breast, and to which a hood is attached, worn by the pope and by cardinals, bishops, abbots, and other dignitaries. Also, **mozetta.** [t. It. Cf. AMICE[1], MUTCH]

M.P., 1. melting point. **2.** Member of Parliament. **3.** Metropolitan Police. **4.** Also, **MP.** Military Police. **5.** Also, **MP.** Mounted Police.

m.p., melting point.

m.p.g., miles per gallon.

m.p.h., miles per hour.

M.P.S., 1. Member of the Pharmaceutical Society.

2. Member of the Philological Society. 3. Member of the Physical Society.
m.p.s., miles per second.
Mr (mĭs′tə), *pl.* **Messrs.** mister: a title prefixed to a man's name or position, as in *Mr Lawson, Mr President.* [abbrev. of MISTER]
M.R., Master of the Rolls.
MRA, Moral Rearmament.
M.R.C., Medical Research Council.
M.R.C.P., Member of the Royal College of Physicians.
M.R.C.S., Member of the Royal College of Surgeons.
M.R.C.V.S., Member of the Royal College of Veterinary Surgeons.
Mrs (mĭs′ĭz), mistress: a title prefixed to the name of a married woman: *Mrs Jones.* [var. of MISTRESS. Cf. MISSIS]
MS., *pl.* **MSS.** manuscript. Also, **ms.**
M.S., 1. Master in Surgery. 2. multiple sclerosis.
m.s., modification of the stem of.
M.Sc., Master of Science.
M.S.C., Medical Staff Corps.
Msgr, Monsignor.
M.S.H., Master of Staghounds.
M.S.I., Member of the Chartered Surveyors' Institution.
m'sieur (*Fr.* mə syœ′), *n. French.* contraction of *monsieur.*
m.s.l., mean sea-level.
M.S.T., (in the U.S.) mountain standard time. Also, **MST, m.s.t.**
Ms-Th, *Chem.* mesothorium.
Mt, *pl.* **Mts.** 1. mount: *Mt Everest.* 2. mountain. Also, **mt.**
M.T., 1. mechanical (motor) transport. 2. metric ton.
M.T., m.t., 1. metric ton. 2. (in the U.S.) mountain time.
MTB, motor torpedo-boat.
mtn, mountain.
Mt Rev., Most Reverend.
mu (myo͞o), *n.* the twelfth letter of the Greek alphabet (Μ, μ).
M.U., 1. Mothers' Union. 2. multiple unit.
Mubangi (mə băng′gĭ), *n.* Ubangi.
much (mŭch), *adj.,* **more, most,** *n., adv.* —*adj.* 1. in great quantity, amount, measure, or degree: *much work.* —*n.* 2. a great quantity or amount; a great deal: *much of this is true.* 3. a great, important, or notable thing or matter: *the house is not much to look at.* 4. **to make much of, a.** to treat, represent, or consider as of great importance. **b.** to treat (a person) with great, flattering, or fond consideration. 5. **as much,** the same; precisely that. 6. **much of a muchness,** (of two or more objects, concepts, etc.) very similar; having little to choose between them. —*adv.* 7. to a great extent or degree; greatly; far: *much pleased.* 8. nearly, approximately, or about: *this is much the same as the others.* [ME *muche, moche,* apocopated var. of *muchel, mochel,* OE *mycel;* r. ME *miche(l),* OE *micel* great, much, c. Icel. *mikill,* Goth. *mikils,* Gk *megalo-* great]
muchness (mŭch′nĭs), *n.* greatness, as in quantity, measure, or degree.
mucic acid (myo͞o′sĭk), *Chem.* a dibasic crystalline acid, $HOOC(CHOH)_4COOH$, obtained by oxidizing certain gums, milk sugar, or galactose.
mucid (myo͞o′sĭd), *adj.* mouldy; musty. [t. L: s. *mūcidus*] —**mu′cidness,** *n.*
mucilage (myo͞o′sĭ lĭj), *n.* 1. any of various preparations of gum, glue, or the like, for causing adhesion. 2. any of various gummy secretions or gelatinous substances present in plants. [ME, t. F, t. LL: m. *mucilāgo* a musty juice]
mucilaginous (myo͞o′sĭ lăj′ĭ nəs), *adj.* 1. of the nature of or resembling mucilage; moist, soft, and viscid. 2. *Chiefly U.S.* of, pertaining to, or secreting mucilage.
mucin (myo͞o′sĭn), *n. Biochem.* any of a group of nitrogenous substances found in mucous secretions, etc., and of varying composition according to their source. [f. s. L *mūcus* MUCUS + -IN[2]] —**mu′cinous,** *adj.*
muck (mŭk), *n.* 1. farmyard dung, decaying vegetable matter, etc., in a moist state; manure. 2. a highly organic soil, less than fifty per cent combustible, often used as manure. 3. filth; dirt. 4. *Colloq.* something of no value; trash. 5. *Civ. Eng., Mining, etc.* earth, rock, or other useless matter to be removed in order to get out the mineral or other substances sought. 6. **make a muck of,** *Colloq.* to spoil. —*v.t.* 7. to manure. 8. to make dirty; soil. 9. to remove muck from (often fol. by *out*). 10. *Colloq.* to spoil; make a mess of. 11. **muck in,** *Colloq.* **a.** to share, esp. living accommodation. **b.** to join in. 12. **muck up,** *Colloq.* to spoil. —*v.i.* 13. **muck about,** *Colloq.* to idle; potter; fool about. [ME *muk,* t. Scand.; cf. Icel. *myki* cow dung]
mucker (mŭk′ə), *n.,* 1. a muckshifter. 2. *Slang.* a vulgar, ill-bred person. 3. a friend.
muckle[1] (mŭk′l), *n. U.S. Dial.* a wooden cudgel used to kill fish.
muckle[2] (mŭk′l), *adj.* mickle.
muck rake, a rake for use on muck or filth.
muckrake (mŭk′rāk′), *v.i.,* **-raked, -raking.** *Colloq.* to expose, esp. in print, political or other corruption, real or alleged. [f. MUCK + RAKE] —**muck′rak′er,** *n.* —**muck′rak′ing,** *n.*
muckshifter (mŭk′shĭf′tə), *n. Civ. Eng., Mining, etc.* one who removes muck.
mucky (mŭk′ĭ), *adj.,* **-ier, -iest.** 1. of or like muck. 2. filthy; dirty.
mucoid (myo͞o′koid), *n. Biochem.* any of a group of substances resembling the mucins, occurring in connective tissue, etc. [f. MUC(IN) + -OID]
muconic acid (myo͞o kŏn′ĭk), *Chem.* a white crystalline solid, $HOOC(CH)_4COOH$, formed from certain aromatic amino acids.
mucoprotein (myo͞o′kō prō′tēn), *n.* a compound containing protein and a carbohydrate group.
mucosa (myo͞o kō′sə), *n., pl.* **-sae** (-sē). *Anat.* a mucous membrane. [t. NL, fem. of L *mūcōsus* MUCOUS] —**muco′sal,** *adj.*
mucous (myo͞o′kəs), *adj.* 1. pertaining to, consisting of, or resembling mucus. 2. containing or secreting mucus: *the mucous membrane.* [t. L: m. s. *mūcōsus* slimy] —**mucosity** (myo͞o kŏs′ĭ tĭ), *n.*
mucous membrane, a lubricating membrane lining an internal surface or an organ, such as the alimentary, respiratory, and genito-urinary canals.
mucro (myo͞o′krō), *n., pl.* **mucrones** (myo͞o krō′nēz). *Bot., Zool.* a short point projecting abruptly, as at the end of a leaf. [t. L: point]
mucronate (myo͞o′krō nĭt, -nāt′), *adj. Bot.* having an abruptly projecting point, as a feather, leaf, etc. Also, **muc′ronat′ed.** [t. L: m. s. *mūcrōnātus* pointed]
mucus (myo͞o′kəs), *n.* a viscid secretion of the mucous membranes. [t. L]
mud (mŭd), *n.* 1. wet, soft earth or earthy matter, as on the ground after rain, at the bottom of a pond, or among the discharges from a volcano; mire. 2. **one's name is mud,** *Colloq.* one is in disgrace. 3. **throw (sling) mud at,** *Colloq.* speak ill of; abuse; vilify. [ME *mudde, mode,* c. MLG *mudde*]
mud bath, a bath in mud containing certain salts, for medicinal purposes.
mudcat (mŭd′kăt′), *n.* (in the Mississippi valley) a catfish grown to large size.
mud dauber, any of certain wasps of the family *Sphecidae,* which construct mud cells for their larvae and provision them with insects.
muddle (mŭd′l), *v.,* **-dled, -dling,** *n.* —*v.t.* 1. to mix up or jumble together in a confused or bungling way. 2. to render confused mentally, or unable to think clearly. 3. to render confused or stupid with drink, or as drink does. 4. to make muddy or turbid, as water. 5. *U.S.* to mix or stir. 6. **muddle through,** to come to a satisfactory conclusion without planned direction. —*n.* 7. a muddled condition; a confused mental state. 8. a confused, disordered, or embarrassing state of affairs, or a mess. [f. MUD + *-le,* freq. and dim. suffix]
muddle-head (mŭd′l hĕd′), *n.* a confused or muddled person.
muddle-headed (mŭd′l hĕd′ĭd), *adj.* vague; confused. —**mud′dle-head′edness,** *n.*
muddler (mŭd′lə), *n.* 1. one who muddles or muddles through. 2. *U.S.* a stick for stirring drinks.
muddy (mŭd′ĭ), *adj.,* **-dier, -diest,** *v.,* **-died, -dying.** —*adj.* 1. abounding in or covered with mud. 2. not clear or pure, as colour. 3. dull, as the complexion. 4. not clear mentally. 5. obscure or vague, as thought, expression, literary style, etc. —*v.t.* 6. to make muddy; soil with mud. 7. to make turbid. 8. to render confused or obscure. —*v.i.* 9. to become muddy or turbid. —**mud′dily,** *adv.* —**mud′diness,** *n.*
Mudéjar (*Sp.* mo͞o dĕ′KHär), *n., pl.* **-jares** (*Sp.* -KHä rĕs), *adj.* —*n.* 1. a Spanish Moor, esp. in the Middle Ages. —*adj.* 2. of, or pertaining to a type of early Renaissance Spanish architecture (11th–16th centuries), showing clear Islamic influence. [Sp., t. Ar.: m. *muddajjan* permitted to stay]
mudfish (mŭd′fĭsh′), *n.* a small fish, *Tilapia mossambica,* of southern Africa.
mudflap (mŭd′flăp′), *n.* a flexible appendage to the rear mudguard of a vehicle, hanging down to prevent mud, etc., from being thrown out backwards.
mudflat (mŭd′flăt′), *n.* an area of muddy ground covered by water at high tide.
mudguard (mŭd′gäd′), *n.* a guard or shield so placed as to protect riders or passengers from mud thrown by the wheel of a bicycle, motor vehicle, or the like.
mud pack, a cosmetic preparation for the complexion.

mud puppy, 1. any of the large North American aquatic salamanders of the genus *Necturus*, which have bushy red gills and well-developed limbs. 2. any of various American salamanders of the genus *Ambystoma*.

mudsill (mŭd′sĭl′), *n.* groundsel (def. 2).

mud-slinger (mŭd′slĭng′ə), *n.* *Colloq.* one who abuses or vilifies.

mudstone (mŭd′stōn′), *n.* a clayey rock of nearly uniform texture throughout, with little or no lamination.

mud turtle, any of various freshwater turtles of the U.S., as *Kinosternon subrubrum*, or *Chrysemys picta*.

mud volcano, 1. a cone of mud built up by ejection of hot water and mud from a volcanic vent. 2. a soft slurry of mud caused by an escape of gases through a layer of clay; often associated with oil deposits.

mudwort (mŭd′wût′), *n.* a small annual scrophulariaceous herb, *Limosella aquatica*, found on wet mud at the margins of ponds in N temperate regions.

muezzin (mōō ĕz′ĭn), *n.* (in Muslim communities) the crier who, from a minaret or other part of a mosque, at stated hours five times daily, intones aloud the call summoning the faithful to prayer. [t. Ar.: m. *muazzin*, d. var. of *muadhdhin*]

muff (mŭf), *n.* 1. a kind of thick tubular case covered with fur or other material, in which the hands are placed for warmth. 2. a tuft of feathers on the sides of the head of certain fowls. 3. *Sports.* a failure to hold a ball that comes into one's hands. 4. any failure. —*v.t.* 5. *Colloq.* to perform clumsily, or bungle. 6. *Sports.* to fail to hold (a ball that comes into one's hands). —*v.i.* 7. *Colloq.* to bungle. [t. D: m. *mof*, t. F: m. *moufle*; akin to MUFFLE, n.]

muffin (mŭf′ĭn), *n.* 1. a thick, flat yeast cake made from a soft dough, eaten with butter and usually served hot. 2. *U.S.* a crumpet. [orig. obscure]

muffle (mŭf′əl), *v.*, **-fled, -fling,** *n.* —*v.t.* 1. to wrap or envelop in a cloak, shawl, scarf, or the like disposed about the person, esp. about the face and neck (often fol. by *up*). 2. to wrap with something to deaden or prevent sound: *to muffle drums.* 3. to deaden (sound) by wrappings or other means. —*v.i.* 4. to muffle oneself (*up*) as in garments or other wrappings. —*n.* 5. something that muffles. 6. muffled sound. 7. an oven or arched chamber in a furnace or kiln, used for heating substances without direct contact with the fire: *muffle furnace.* 8. the thick, bare part of the upper lip and nose of ruminants and rodents. [ME *mufle(n)*, appar. t. OF. Cf. OF *emmouflé* wrapped up]

muffler (mŭf′lə), *n.* 1. a heavy neck scarf. 2. anything used for muffling.

mufti (mŭf′tĭ), *n.*, *pl.* **-tis.** 1. civilian dress as opposed to military or other uniform, or as worn by one who usually wears a uniform. 2. a Muslim legal adviser consulted in applying the religious law. 3. (under the Ottoman Empire) the official head of the state religion, or one of his deputies. 4. See **Grand Mufti.** [t. Ar.: lit., one who delivers a judgement; orig. Ar. meaning def. 2. Def. 1 from the fact that a mufti is a civil official]

mug (mŭg), *n.*, *v.*, **mugged, mugging.** —*n.* 1. a drinking cup, usually cylindrical and commonly with a handle. 2. the quantity it holds. 3. *Slang.* the face. 4. *Slang.* the mouth. 5. *Slang.* a grimace. 6. *Slang.* a fool; one who is easily duped. —*v.t.* 7. *Colloq.* to study hard (fol. by *up*). 8. *Slang.* to assault by hitting in the face. 9. *U.S. Slang.* to assault and rob. 10. *U.S. Slang.* to take a photograph of (a person), esp. in compliance with an official or legal requirement. —*v.i.* 11. *Slang.* to grimace. [ME *mogge*, t. Scand.; cf. Sw. *mugg*, D *mugge*]

mugger[1] (mŭg′ə), *n.* one who mugs.

mugger[2] (mŭg′ə), *n.* a broad-snouted crocodile, *Crocodilus palustris*, of India, etc., growing to about 12 ft in length. Also, **mug′gar, mug′gur.** [t. Hind.: m. *magar*]

muggins (mŭg′ĭnz), *n.* 1. a convention in the card game of cribbage in which a player scores points overlooked by an opponent. 2. a game of dominoes in which any player, if he can make the sum of the two ends of the line equal five or a multiple of five, adds the number so made to his score. 3. *Colloq.* a fool. [? orig. surname *Muggins*]

muggy (mŭg′ĭ), *adj.*, **-gier, -giest.** (of the atmosphere, weather, etc.) damp and close; humid and oppressive. [f. d. *mug* mist (t. Scand.; cf. Icel. *mugga*) + -Y[1]] —**mug′giness,** *n.* —**Ant.** dry.

mugwort (mŭg′wût′), *n.* 1. a variable perennial composite herb with aromatic leaves, *Artemisia vulgaris*, widespread in N temperate regions in waste places and hedges. 2. the crosswort, *Galium cruciata.* [ME, OE *mucgwyrt.* See MIDGE, WORT[2]]

mugwump (mŭg′wŭmp′), *n.* *U.S.* 1. (in the presidential campaign of 1884) a Republican who refused to support the party nominee (J. G. Blaine). 2. one who acts as an independent or affects superiority, esp. in politics. [t. Algonquian (Massachusetts): m. *mukquomp* leader, chief, great man, f. m. *moqki* great + *-omp* man] —**mug′wump′ery,** *n.*

Muhammad (mōō hăm′əd), *n.* Mohammed. —**Muham′madan, Muham′medan,** *adj.*, *n.*

Mühlbach (*Ger.* mʏl′bäкн), *n.* **Luise** (*Ger.* lōō ē′zə), (*Klara Müller Mundt*), 1814–73, German novelist.

muishond (mĭs′hŏnt, mās′-), *n.* a nocturnal, aggressive polecat of southern Africa, *Ictonyx capensis.* [t. Afrikaans: mouse dog]

mujik (mōō′zhĭk), *n.* muzhik.

Mukden (mŏŏk′dən), *n.* Shenyang.

mulatto (myōō lăt′ō), *n.*, *pl.* **-tos** or **-toes,** *adj.* —*n.* 1. the offspring of parents of whom one is white and the other a Negro. —*adj.* 2. having a light brown colour (similar to the skin of a mulatto). [t. Sp. and Pg.: m. *mulato*, der. *mulo*, g. L *mūlus* MULE[1]: so called from the hybrid origin]

mulberry (mŭl′bə rĭ, -brĭ), *n.*, *pl.* **-ries.** 1. the edible, berry-like collective fruit of any tree of the genus *Morus.* 2. a tree of this genus, as *M. rubra* (**red** or **American mulberry**), with dark purple fruit, *M. nigra* (**black mulberry**), with dark-coloured fruit, and *M. alba* (**white mulberry**), with fruit nearly white and with leaves especially valued as food for silkworms. 3. a dull, dark, reddish purple colour. [ME *mulberie*, dissimilated var. of *murberie*, OE *mōrberie*, f. s. L *mōrum* mulberry + *berie* BERRY]

mulch (mŭlch), *Hort.* —*n.* 1. straw, leaves, loose earth, etc., spread on the ground or produced by tillage to protect the roots of newly planted trees, crops, etc. —*v.t.* 2. to cover with mulch. [n. use of (obs.) *mulch*, adj., ME *molsh* soft, OE *myl(i)sc* mellow; akin to d. G *molsch* soft, overripe]

mulct (mŭlkt), *n.* 1. a fine; a penalty. —*v.t.* 2. to punish (a person, or formerly, an offence) by fine or forfeiture. 3. to deprive of something as a penalty. 4. to deprive of something by trickery. [t. L: s. *mulcta* fine]

Mule, *Equus asinus x cabbalus* (Ab. 5 ft high at the shoulder)

mule[1] (myōōl), *n.* 1. the offspring of a male donkey and a mare, used esp. as a beast of burden because of its patience, sure-footedness, and hardiness. 2. any hybrid between the donkey and the horse. 3. *Colloq.* a stupid or stubborn person. 4. *Biol.* a hybrid, esp. a hybrid between the canary and some other finch. 5. a machine which spins cotton, etc., into yarn and winds it on spindles. [ME *mule*, t. OF, g. L *mūla*; r. OE *mūl*, t. L: s. *mūlus*]

mule[2] (myōōl), *n.* a kind of slipper which leaves the heel exposed. [ME, t. F]

mule deer, a deer, *Odocoileus hemionus*, with large ears, common in western North America.

mule-skinner (myōōl′skĭn′ə), *n.* *U.S. Colloq.* muleteer.

muleteer (myōō′lĭ tĭə′), *n.* a driver of mules. [t. F: m. *muletier*, der. *mulet*, dim. of OF *mul* MULE[1]]

muley (myōō′lĭ), *adj.*, *n.*, *pl.* **-leys.** —*adj.* 1. (of cattle) hornless; polled. —*n.* 2. any cow. Also, **mulley.** [var. of d. *moiley*, t. Irish: m. *maol*, or t. Welsh: m. *moel*, lit., bald]

Mule deer, *Odocoileus hemionus* ($3\frac{1}{2}$ ft high at the shoulder, total length $5\frac{1}{2}$ ft)

muley saw, *U.S. Colloq.* a saw having a long, stiff blade which is not stretched in a gate but whose motion is directed by clamps at each end mounted on guide rails.

mulga (mŭl′gä, -gə), *n.* *Austral.* 1. dense acacia scrub on the margins of a desert. 2. the bush; back country. 3. the wattle, *Acacia aneura.* 4. an Aborigine's shield. [t. native Australian]

Mulhacén (*Sp.* mōō lä thĕn′), *n.* a mountain in S Spain: the highest peak in Spain. ab. 11,420 ft.

Mülheim an der Ruhr (*Ger.* mʏl′hīm än dĕr rōōr′), a town in West Germany, in W North Rhine-Westphalia, near Essen. 191,200 (est. 1966).

Mulhouse (*Fr.* mʏ lōōz′), *n.* a town in E France, in Haut-Rhin department, near the Rhine. 110,735 (1962). German, **Mülhausen** (*Ger.* mʏl hou′zən).

muliebrity (myōō′lĭ ĕb′rĭ tĭ), *n.* 1. womanly nature or qualities. **2.** womanhood. [t. LL: m. s. *muliebritas*, der. L *muliebris* womanly]

mulish (myōō′lĭsh), *adj.* like a mule; characteristic of a mule; stubborn, obstinate, or intractable. **—mul′ishly,** *adv.* **—mul′ishness,** *n.*

mull[1] (mŭl), *v.t.* **1.** to study or ruminate (*over*), esp. in an ineffective way; ponder upon. **2.** to make a mess or failure of. [? orig. d.: muddle, crumble, t. MD: m. *mail, mol.* See MULLER]

mull[2] (mŭl), *v.t.* to heat, sweeten, and spice for drinking, as ale, wine, etc.: *mulled cider.* [orig. uncert.]

mull[3] (mŭl), *n.* **1.** a soft, thin kind of muslin. **2.** *Bookbinding.* a loosely woven material used to reinforce the spine of a bound book. [earlier *mulmul*, t. Hind.: m. *malmal*]

mull[4] (mŭl), *n. Scot.* a promontory. [t. Scand.; cf. Icel. *múli.* Cf. also Gaelic *maol*]

Mull (mŭl), *n.* an island of the Inner Hebrides, Argyll, Scotland. 1674 pop. (1961); ab. 351 sq. mi.

mullah (mŭl′ə, mōōl′ə), *n.* (in Muslim countries) a title of respect for one who is learned in, teaches, or expounds the sacred law. Also, **mulla.** [t. Turk., Pers., and Hind.: m. *mullā*, t. Ar.: m. *mawlā* patron, lord]

mullein (mŭl′ĭn), *n.* any of a number of plants of the herbaceous scrophulariaceous genus *Verbascum*, as the **dark mullein** (*V. nigrum*), a widespread biennial on calcareous soils in Europe and W Asia. Also, **mullen.** [ME *moleyn*, t. AF: m. *moleine*, t. Celtic. Cf. Breton *melen* yellowish]

muller (mŭl′ə), *n.* **1.** an implement of stone or other substance with a flat base for grinding paints, powders, etc., on a slab of stone or the like. **2.** any of various mechanical devices for grinding. [? orig. meaning powderer (der. ME *mul* powder, OE *myl* dust, c. G *Müll.* See MULL[1])]

Müller (mŭl′ə; *Ger.* mʏ′lər), *n.* **Friedrich Max** (*Ger.* frē′drĭkH mäks), 1823–1900, British Sanskrit scholar and philologist, born in Germany.

mullet (mŭl′ĭt), *n., pl.* **-lets,** (*esp. collectively*) **-let. 1.** any fish of the family *Mugilidae*, which includes various marine and freshwater species with a nearly cylindrical body and generally grey coloration, as the thick-lipped **grey mullet,** *Mugli chelo.* **2.** a goatfish. **3.** a sucker, particularly of the genus *Moxostoma.* **4.** any of various other fishes. [ME *mulet*, t. OF, der. L *mullus* red mullet]

mulley (mŭl′ĭ), *adj., n., pl.* **-leys.** muley.

mulligan stew (mŭl′ĭ gən), *U.S. Slang.* a kind of stew containing meat, vegetables, etc.

mulligatawny (mŭl′ĭ gə tô′nĭ), *n.* a soup of East Indian origin, flavoured with curry. [t. Tamil: m. *milagutannīr* pepper water]

mullion (mŭl′ĭ ən), *Archit.* **—*n.* 1.** a vertical member, as of stone or wood, between the lights of a window, the panels in wainscoting, or the like. **—*v.t.* 2.** to furnish with, or to form into divisions by the use of, mullions. [metathetic var. of *monial*, t. OF; orig. uncert.]

M, Mullion

mullite (mŭl′īt), *n.* a mineral aluminium silicate, $3Al_2O_3 . 2SiO_2$.

mullock (mŭl′ək), *n.* **1.** *Austral., N.Z.* mining refuse; muck. **2.** anything valueless. **—*v.i.* 3.** *Austral. Colloq.* to work in a slipshod way. [f. d. *mull* rubbish (see MULLER) + -OCK]

mulloway (mŭl′ə wā′), *n.* the jewfish of Australia, *Sciaena antarctica*, important as a sporting and food fish.

Mulock (myōō′lŏk), *n.* **Dinah Maria.** See **Craik, Dinah Maria Mulock.**

Multan (mōōl′tän′), *n.* a city in West Pakistan, in W Punjab. 358,201 (1961).

multi-, a word element meaning 'many'. [t. L, comb. form of *multus* much, many]

multicellular (mŭl′tĭ sĕl′yōō lə), *adj.* composed of several or many cells.

multicoil (mŭl′tĭ koil′), *adj.* having more than one coil, as an electrical device.

multicoloured (mŭl′tĭ kŭl′əd), *adj.* of many colours.

multicylinder (mŭl′tĭ sĭl′ĭn də), *adj.* having more than one cylinder, as an internal-combustion or steam engine. Also, **mul′ticyl′indered.**

multidentate (mŭl′tĭ dĕn′tāt), *adj.* having many teeth or toothlike processes.

multifaceted (mŭl′tĭ făs′ĭ tĭd), *adj.* **1.** (of a gem) having many facets. **2.** having many aspects or phases.

multifarious (mŭl′tĭ fēə′rĭ əs), *adj.* **1.** having many different parts, elements, forms, etc. **2.** of many kinds, or numerous and varied; manifold (modifying a pl. n.): *multifarious activities.* [t. L: m. *multifārius* manifold] **—mul′tifar′iously,** *adv.* **—mul′tifar′iousness,** *n.*

multifid (mŭl′tĭ fĭd), *adj.* cleft into many parts, divisions, or lobes. Also, **multifidous** (mŭl tĭf′ĭ dəs). [t. L: s. *multifidus*]

multiflorous (mŭl′tĭ flô′rəs), *adj. Bot.* bearing many flowers, as a peduncle.

multifoil (mŭl′tĭ foil′), *n.* See **foil**[2] (def. 5).

multifoliate (mŭl′tĭ fō′lĭ ĭt, -āt′), *adj. Bot.* having many leaves or leaflets.

multiform (mŭl′tĭ fôm′), *adj.* having many forms; of many different forms or kinds. [t. L: s. *multiformis*] **—multiformity** (mŭl′tĭ fô′mĭ tĭ), *n.*

multigrade (mŭl′tĭ grād′), *adj.* denoting a motor oil with a stable viscosity level over a wide range of temperatures.

Multigraph (mŭl′tĭ grăf′, -gräf′), *n.* **1.** *Trademark.* a rotary typesetting and printing machine, commonly used to reproduce typewritten matter. **—*v.t., v.i.* 2.** to reproduce with such a machine.

multilaminate (mŭl′tĭ lăm′ĭ nĭt, -nāt′), *adj.* having many laminae or layers.

multilateral (mŭl′tĭ lăt′ə rəl, -lăt′rəl), *adj.* **1.** having many sides; many-sided. **2.** *Govt.* denoting an agreement or other instrument in which three or more states participate; multipartite. **3.** *Educ.* (of a school) providing the three main types of secondary education (modern, technical, and grammar). **—mul′tilat′erally,** *adv.*

multilingual (mŭl′tĭ lĭng′gwəl), *adj.* **1.** able to speak one's native language and at least two others with approximately equal facility. **2.** expressed or contained in three or more different languages. **—*n.* 3.** a multilingual person.

multilobular (mŭl′tĭ lŏb′yōō lə), *adj.* having many lobules.

multimillionaire (mŭl′tĭ mĭl′yə nēə′), *n.* one with a fortune of several million pounds, dollars, etc.

multimotored (mŭl′tĭ mō′təd), *adj.* with a number of motors or engines.

multinominal (mŭl′tĭ nŏm′ĭ nəl), *adj.* having many names.

multinuclear (mŭl′tĭ nyōō′klĭ ə), *adj.* having many or several nuclei, as a cell. Also, **mul′tinu′cleate.**

multipara (mŭl tĭp′ə rə), *n., pl.* **-rae** (-rē′). *Obstet.* a woman who has borne two or more children, or who is parturient the second time. [t. NL, fem. of *multiparus* MULTIPAROUS]

multiparous (mŭl tĭp′ə rəs), *adj.* **1.** producing many, or more than one, at a birth. **2.** *Bot.* (of a cyme) having many lateral axes. [t. NL: m. *multiparus.* See MULTI-, -PAROUS]

multipartite (mŭl′tĭ pä′tīt), *adj.* **1.** divided into many parts; having many divisions. **2.** *Govt.* multilateral (def. 2). [t. L: m. s. *multipartītus* much-divided]

multiped (mŭl′tĭ pĕd′), *adj.* **1.** having many feet. **—*n.* 2.** a creature that has many feet. Also, **multipede** (mŭl′tĭ pēd′). [t. L: s. *multipēs*, adj. and n., many-footed]

multiphase (mŭl′tĭ fāz′), *adj. Elect.* having many phases.

multiple (mŭl′tĭ pl), *adj.* **1.** consisting of, having, or involving many individuals, parts, elements, relations, etc.; manifold. **2.** *Elect.* denoting two or more circuits connected in parallel. **3.** *Bot.* (of a fruit) collective. **—*n.* 4.** *Maths.* a number which contains another number some number of times without a remainder: *12 is a multiple of 3.* **5.** *Elect.* **a.** a group of terminals arranged to make a circuit or group of circuits accessible at a number of points at any one of which connection can be made. **b. in multiple,** in parallel. See **parallel** (def. 13). [t. F, t. LL: m. *multiplus* manifold]

multiple alleles, *Genetics.* a series of three or more alternative or allelic forms of a gene, only two of which can exist in any normal, diploid individual.

multiple cropping, *Agric.* the use of the same field for two or more separate crops, whether of the same or of different kinds, successively during a single year.

multiple factors, *Genetics.* a series of two or more pairs of genes responsible for the development of complex, quantitative characters such as size, yield, etc.

multiple neuritis, *Pathol.* inflammation of several nerves at the same time.

multiple sclerosis, *Pathol.* a disease of the nervous system, usually progressive, characterized by remissions and exacerbations, and caused by plaques of demyelization of the white matter of the nervous system. Also, **disseminated sclerosis.** *Abbrev.:* M.S.

multiple star, *Astron.* three or more stars lying close together in the celestial sphere and usually united in a single gravitational system.

multiple store, chain-store.

multiple unit, *Railways.* a train extensively used for local passenger services, some of the coaches of which are capable of self-propulsion. *Abbrev.:* M.U.

multiple voting, casting ballots in more than one constituency in one election, as in England before, and to some extent after, the franchise reform of 1918.

multiplex (mŭl′tĭ plĕks′), *adj.* **1.** manifold; multiple:

multiplex telegraphy. —*v.t.* **2.** *Elect.* to arrange a circuit for use by multiplex telegraphy. [t. L: manifold]
multiplex telegraphy, a system for sending many messages in each direction, simultaneously, over the same wire or communications channel.
multipliable (mŭl′tĭ plī′ə bl), *adj.* that may be multiplied. Also, **multiplicable** (mŭl′tĭ plĭ kə bl).
multiplicand (mŭl′tĭ plĭ kănd′), *n.* *Maths.* the number to be multiplied by another. [t. L: s. *multiplicandus*, gerundive of *multiplicāre* MULTIPLY]
multiplicate (mŭl′tĭ plĭ kāt′), *adj.* multiple; manifold. [ME, t. L: m. s. *multiplicātus*, pp., multiplied]
multiplication (mŭl′tĭ plĭ kā′shən), *n.* **1.** the act or process of multiplying. **2.** the state of being multiplied. **3.** *Arith.* the process of finding the number (the product) resulting from the addition of a given number (the multiplicand) taken as many times as there are units in another given number (the multiplier). **4.** *Maths.* any generalization of this operation applicable to numbers other than integers, such as fractions, irrationals, vectors, etc. **5.** *Physics.* the process by which additional neutrons are produced by a chain reaction in a nuclear reactor. —**mul′tiplica′tional,** *adj.*
multiplication constant, *Physics.* (of a nuclear reactor) the ratio of the average number of neutrons produced by fission per unit time, to the total number of neutrons absorbed or leaking out in the same time.
multiplication table, a table in which the product of any two numbers of a set are given; usually of the integers 1 to 12.
multiplicative (mŭl′tĭ plĭ kā′tĭv, mŭl′tĭ plĭk′ə tĭv), *adj.* **1.** tending to multiply or increase. **2.** having the power of multiplying. —**mul′tiplica′tively,** *adv.*
multiplicity (mŭl′tĭ plĭs′ĭ tĭ), *n., pl.* **-ties.** **1.** a multitude or great number. **2.** the state of being multiplex or manifold; manifold variety. [t. LL: m. s. *multiplicitas*]
multiplier (mŭl′tĭ plī′ə), *n.* **1.** one who or that which multiplies. **2.** *Maths.* the number by which another is to be multiplied. **3.** *Physics.* a device for intensifying some phenomenon.
multiply (mŭl′tĭ plī′), *v.,* **-plied, -plying.** —*v.t.* **1.** to make many or manifold; increase the number, quantity, etc., of. **2.** *Maths.* to take by addition a given number of times; find the product of by multiplication. **3.** to produce (animals or plants) by propagation. **4.** to increase by procreation. —*v.i.* **5.** to grow in number, quantity, etc.; increase. **6.** *Maths.* to perform the process of multiplication. **7.** to increase in number by procreation or natural generation. [ME *multiplie(n)*, t. OF: m. *multiplier*, t. L: m. *multiplicāre*]
multipolar (mŭl′tĭ pō′lə), *adj.* having many poles.
multipurpose (mŭl′tĭ pû′pəs), *adj.* having various different uses.
multiseriate (mŭl′tĭ sē′rĭ ĭt), *adj.* *Bot.* having, or consisting of, more than one row or layer of cells. —**mul′tise′riately,** *adv.*
multistage (mŭl′tĭ stāj′), *adj.* (of a rocket, guided missile, etc.) having more than one stage.
multistorey (mŭl′tĭ stô′rĭ), *adj.* (of a building) having a considerable number of storeys. Also, *Chiefly U.S.*, **multistory.**
multitude (mŭl′tĭ tyōōd′), *n.* **1.** a great number; host: *a multitude of friends.* **2.** a great number of persons gathered together; a crowd or throng. **3. the multitude,** the common people. **4.** the state or character of being many. [ME, t. L: m. *multitūdo*] —**Syn. 2.** See **crowd.**
multitudinous (mŭl′tĭ tyōō′dĭ nəs), *adj.* **1.** forming a multitude or great number, or existing, occurring, or present in great numbers; very numerous. **2.** comprising many items, parts, or elements. **3.** *Poetic.* crowded or thronged. —**mul′titu′dinously,** *adv.* —**mul′titu′dinousness,** *n.*
multivalent (mŭl′tĭ vā′lənt), *adj.* *Chem.* having a valency of three or higher. Cf. **polyvalent.** —**multivalence** (mŭl′tĭ vā′ləns), *n.*
multivibrator (mŭl′tĭ vī brā′tə), *n.* *Electronics.* a circuit consisting of two amplifiers joined to form a loop.
multum in parvo (mōōl′təm ĭn pä′vō), *Latin.* much in little; a great deal in a small space or in brief.
multure (mŭl′chə), *n.* *Obs.* a toll or fee given to the proprietor of a mill for the grinding of grain, usually consisting of a fixed proportion of the grain brought or of the flour made. [ME, t. OF: m. *molture*, g. ML *molitūra* a grinding]
mum[1] (mŭm), *adj.* **1.** silent; not saying a word: *to keep mum.* —*interj.* **2.** Say nothing! Be silent! —*n.* **3.** silence: *mum's the word.* [ME; imit. Cf. G *mumm*]
mum[2] (mŭm), *v.i.,* **mummed, mumming.** **1.** to say 'mum'; call for silence. **2.** to act as a mummer. Also, **mumm.** [v. use of MUM[1]. Cf. OF *momer* mask oneself]
mum[3] (mŭm), *n.* *Colloq.* chrysanthemum.
mum[4] (mŭm), *n.* *Colloq.* mother.
mumble (mŭm′bl), *v.,* **-bled, -bling,** *n.* —*v.i.* **1.** to speak indistinctly or unintelligibly, as with partly closed lips; mutter low, indistinct words. **2.** to chew ineffectively, as from loss of teeth: *to mumble on a crust.* —*v.t.* **3.** to utter indistinctly, as with partly closed lips. **4.** to chew, or try to eat, with difficulty, as from loss of teeth. —*n.* **5.** a low, indistinct utterance or sound. [ME *momele*, freq. of (obs.) *mum*, v., make inarticulate sounds. Cf. G *mummeln*] —**mum′bler,** *n.* —**mum′blingly,** *adv.* —**Syn. 3.** See **murmur.**
mumbo jumbo (mŭm′bō jŭm′bō), **1.** meaningless incantation or ritual. **2.** an object of superstitious awe or reverence. **3.** (*caps.*) a deity formerly worshipped by certain West African tribes. **4.** *Slang.* superstition; witchcraft.
mu-meson (myōō′mē′zŏn), *n.* *Physics.* a meson with a mass 206·77 times that of an electron, which may have either a positive or negative charge, and spin ½; muon.
mu-metal (myōō′mĕt′l), *n.* *Metall.* an alloy of high magnetic permeability containing up to 78 per cent nickel in addition to iron, copper, and manganese.
mumm (mŭm), *v.i.* mum[2].
mummer (mŭm′ə), *n.* **1.** one who wears a mask or fantastic disguise, esp. as formerly and still locally at Christmas and other festive seasons. **2.** (in humorous use) an actor. [late ME, t. OF: m. *momeur*, der. *momer* MUM[2]]
mummery (mŭm′ə rĭ), *n., pl.* **-meries.** **1.** performance of mummers. **2.** any mere theatrical performance or ceremony or empty spectacular pretence, or what is regarded as such. [t. F: m. *momerie*]
mummify (mŭm′ĭ fī′), *v.,* **-fied, -fying.** —*v.t.* **1.** to make (a dead body) into a mummy, as by embalming and drying. **2.** to make like a mummy. —*v.i.* **3.** to dry or shrivel up. —**mum′mifica′tion,** *n.*
mummy[1] (mŭm′ĭ), *n., pl.* **-mies,** *v.,* **-mied, -mying.** —*n.* **1.** the dead body of a human being or animal preserved by the ancient Egyptian (or some similar) method of embalming. **2.** a dead body dried and preserved by the agencies of nature. **3.** a withered or shrunken living being. —*v.t.* **4.** to make into or like a mummy; mummify. [ME *mumie*, t. ML: m. *mumia*, t. Ar.: m. *mūmiya*, from Pers. *mūmiyā* asphalt]
mummy[2] (mŭm′ĭ), *n.* *Colloq.* mother.
mumps (mŭmps), *n.pl., construed as sing.* *Pathol.* a specific infectious viral disease characterized by inflammatory swelling of the parotid and (usually) other salivary glands, and sometimes by inflammation of the testicles, ovaries, etc. [orig. meaning 'grimace'; imit.]
mun (mōōn, mŭn, mən), *aux.v.* must[1]. [t. Scand.; cf. Icel. *muna*, akin to MIND]
mun., municipal.
munch (mŭnch), *v.t.* **1.** to chew with steady or vigorous working of the jaws, and often audibly. —*v.i.* **2.** to chew steadily or vigorously, and often audibly. [ME *monche*, nasalized var. of obs. *mouch* eat, chew; orig. unknown] —**munch′er,** *n.*
Munch (*Norw.* mōōngk), *n.* **Edvard** (*Norw.* ĕd′värd), 1863–1944, Norwegian painter.
München (*Ger.* mʏn′KHən), *n.* German name of **Munich.**
München-Gladbach (*Ger.* mʏn′KHən glät′bäKH), *n.* former name of **Mönchen-Gladbach.**
Münchhausen (*Ger.* mʏnKH′hou zən), *n.* **Karl Friedrich Hieronymus** (*Ger.* kärl frē′drĭKH hē ĕ rō′nʏ mōōs), **Baron von** (*Ger.* fŏn), 1720–97, German soldier and teller of unbelievable tales. English, **Munchausen** (mŭn chô′zən).
mundane (mŭn′dān), *adj.* **1.** of or pertaining to the world, universe, or earth. **2.** of or pertaining to this world or earth as contrasted with heaven; worldly; earthly: *mundane affairs.* [t. L: m. s. *mundānus* of the world; r. ME *mondeyne*, t. OF] —**mun′danely,** *adv.* —**Syn. 2.** See **earthly.**
mungo (mŭng′gō), *n.* shoddy (def. 1). [? der. obs. *mung*, *mong* mixture. Cf. MONGREL]
Munich (myōō′nĭk), *n.* **1.** a city in West Germany, the capital of Bavaria, in the SE part. 1,231,500 (est. 1966). German, **München.** **2.** the Munich Pact.
Munich Pact, the pact signed by Germany, Great Britain, France, and Italy on September 29th, 1938, by which the Sudetenland was ceded to Germany. Also, **Munich Agreement.**
municipal (myōō nĭs′ĭ pl), *adj.* **1.** of or pertaining to the local government of a town or city: *municipal elections.* **2.** pertaining to the internal affairs of a state or nation rather than to international affairs. [t. L: s. *mūnicipālis*, der. *mūniceps* citizen of a privileged (sometimes self-governing) town standing in a certain relation to Rome] —**munic′ipally,** *adv.*

municipality (myo͞o nĭs′ĭ păl′ĭ tĭ), *n., pl.* **-ties.** **1.** a city, town, or other district possessing corporate existence. **2.** a community under municipal jurisdiction. **3.** the governing body of such a district or community.

municipalize (myo͞o nĭs′ĭ pə līz′), *v.t.,* **-lized, -lizing.** **1.** to make a municipality of. **2.** to bring under municipal ownership, direction, or control. Also, **municipalise.** —**munic′ipaliza′tion,** *n.*

munificent (myo͞o nĭf′ĭ sənt), *adj.* **1.** extremely liberal in giving or bestowing; very generous. **2.** (of a gift, or the like) characterized by great generosity. [back-formation from L *mūnificentia* munificence] —**munif′icence,** *n.* —**munif′icently,** *adv.* —**Ant. 1.** niggardly.

muniment (myo͞o′nĭ mənt), *n.* **1.** (*pl.*) *Law.* a document, as a titledeed or a charter, by which rights or privileges are defended or maintained. **2.** a defence or protection. [ME, t. ML: s. *mūnimentum* document, titledeed, L fortification]

munition (myo͞o nĭsh′ən), *n.* **1.** (*usually pl.*) materials used in war, esp. weapons and ammunition. **2.** material or equipment for carrying on any undertaking. —*v.t.* **3.** to provide with munitions. [t. L: s. *mūnītio* fortification]

Munkácsy (*Hung.* mo͞ong′kä chē), *n.* **Mihály von** (*Hung.* mē′häy fôn) (*Michael Lieb*), 1844–1900, Hungarian painter.

munnion (mŭn′yən), *n.* mullion.

Munro (mŭn rō′), *n.* **Sir Hector Hugh** (*Saki*), 1870–1916, Scottish author, born in Burma.

Munster (mŭn′stə), *n.* a province in SW Republic of Ireland. 849,203 pop. (1961); 9316 sq. mi.

Münster (*Ger.* mʏn′stər), *n.* a town in West Germany, in N North Rhine-Westphalia; treaty of Westphalia, 1648. 199,300 (est. 1966).

Münsterberg (mĭn′stə bûg′; *Ger.* mʏn′stər bĕrk), *n.* **Hugo** (hyo͞o′gō; *Ger.* ho͞o′gō), 1863–1916, German psychologist and philosopher, in the U.S.

munt (mŭnt), *n., adj. S African.* (used disparagingly) Bantu. [t. Zulu: m. *umuntu* person]

muntjac (mŭnt′jăk′), *n.* **1.** any of various small deer constituting the genus *Muntiacus,* of southern and eastern Asia and the adjacent islands, esp. *M. muntjac,* of Java, India, etc., having well-developed horns on bony pedicels. **2.** any of the small deer of the related genus *Elaphodus,* of China and Tibet, having minute horns. Also, **muntjak.** [t. Sunda (a language of Indonesia): m. *minchek*]

Muntz metal (mŭnts), *Metall.* an alloy containing approximately 60 per cent copper and 40 per cent zinc, harder and stronger than brass. [after G. F. *Muntz,* 19th-century English metallurgist]

muon (myo͞o′ŏn), *n. Physics.* a mu-meson.

mural (myo͝oə′rəl), *adj.* **1.** of or pertaining to a wall; resembling a wall. **2.** executed on or affixed to a wall (of a decoration, or the like). —*n.* **3.** a mural painting. [t. F, t. L: s. *mūrālis*]

mural crown, a golden crown formed with indentations to resemble a battlement, bestowed among the ancient Romans on the soldiers who first mounted the wall of a besieged place and there lodged a standard.

Murasaki no Shikibu (mo͝oə′rə sä′kĭ nō shē′kĭ bo͞o′), 11th century, first Japanese writer of a novel, the English title of which is *The Tale of Genji.*

Murat (*Fr.* mʏ rä′), *n.* **Joachim** (*Fr.* zhŏ ȧ shăɴ′), 1767–1815, French general, marshal of France, brother-in-law of Napoleon I, and king of Naples 1808–15.

Murat (*Turk.* mo͞o rät′), *n.* a river in E Turkey, flowing W to the Euphrates. 425 mi. Also, **Murad Su** (*Turk.* mo͞o rät′so͞o′).

Murchison (mû′chĭ sən), *n.* a river of Western Australia flowing SW to the Indian Ocean. ab. 440 mi.

Murcia (*Sp.* mo͞or′thyȧ), *n.* **1.** a city in SE Spain. 255,933 (1965). **2.** a region in SE Spain; formerly a kingdom.

murder (mû′də), *n.* **1.** *Law.* the unlawful killing of another human being with malice aforethought. —*v.t.* **2.** *Law.* to kill by an act constituting murder. **3.** to kill or slaughter inhumanly or barbarously. **4.** to spoil or mar by bad execution, representation, pronunciation, etc. —*v.i.* **5.** to commit murder. [ME; var. of MURTHER] —**mur′derer,** *n.* —**mur′deress,** *n. fem.* —**Syn. 2.** See **kill**[1].

murderous (mû′də rəs, -drəs), *adj.* **1.** of the nature of or involving murder: *a murderous deed.* **2.** guilty of, bent on, or capable of murder: *murderous thoughts.* **3.** intentionally deadly. —**mur′derously,** *adv.* —**mur′derousness,** *n.*

Murdoch (mû′dŏk), *n.* **(Jean) Iris,** born 1919, British novelist born in Ireland.

Mures (*Rum.* mo͞o′rĕsh), *n.* a river flowing from the Carpathian Mountains in central Rumania W to the river Tisza in S Hungary. ab. 400 mi. Hungarian, **Maros.**

murex (myo͝oə′rĕks), *n., pl.* **murices** (myo͝oə′rĭ sēz′), **murexes.** **1.** any of the marine gastropods, common in tropical seas, constituting the genus *Murex* or the family *Muricidae,* certain species of which yielded the celebrated purple dye of the ancients. **2.** a shell used as a trumpet, as in representations of Tritons in art. **3.** purplish red. [t. L: the purple fish]

muriate (myo͝oə′rĭ ĭt, -āt′), *n.* (in industry) any chloride, esp. potassium chloride, KCl, used as a fertilizer. [f. s. L *muria* brine + -ATE[2]]

muriated (myo͝oə′rĭ ā′tĭd), *adj. Obsolesc.* charged with or containing a chloride or chlorides, as mineral waters.

Murex, *Murex tenuispina*

muriatic acid (myo͝oə′rĭ ăt′ĭk), the commercial name for hydrochloric acid.

Murillo (myo͞oə rĭl′ō; *Sp.* mo͞o rē′lyō), *n.* **Bartolomé Esteban** (*Sp.* bär tō lō mĕ′ ĕs tĕ′bän), 1617–82, Spanish painter.

murine (myo͝oə′rīn, -rĭn), *adj.* **1.** belonging or pertaining to the *Muridae,* the family of rodents that includes the mice and rats, or to the *Murinae,* the subfamily that includes the domestic species. —*n.* **2.** a murine rodent. [t. L: m. s. *mūrīnus* of a mouse]

murk (mûk), *n.* **1.** darkness, —*adj.* **2.** dark, or with little light, as night, places, etc.; murky. Also, **mirk.** [ME *mirke,* OE *myrce,* c. Icel. *myrkr* gloomy]

murky (mû′kĭ), *adj.,* **-kier, -kiest.** **1.** intensely dark, gloomy, and cheerless. **2.** obscure or thick with mist, haze, or the like, as the air, etc. Also, **mirky.** —**murk′ily,** *adv.* —**murk′iness,** *n.* —**Syn. 1.** See **dark.** —**Ant. 2.** clear.

Murman Coast (*Russ.* mo͞or′mən), an Arctic coastal region in the NW Soviet Union in Europe, on the Kola peninsula.

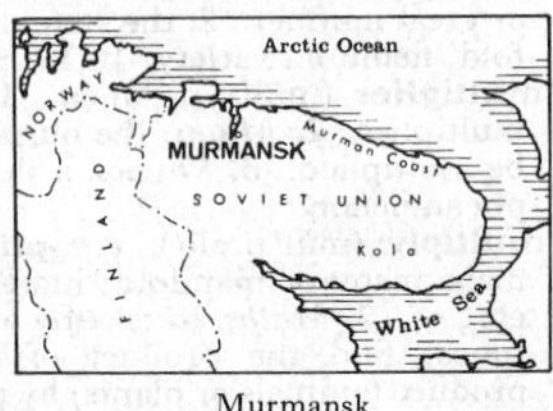

Murmansk

Murmansk (mo͞o-mănsk′; *Russ.* mo͞or′-mənsk), *n.* a seaport (ice-free) and railway terminus in the NW Soviet Union in Europe, on the Murman Coast. 272,000 (est. 1965).

murmur (mû′mə), *n.* **1.** any low, continuous sound, as of a brook, the wind, trees, etc., or of low indistinct voices. **2.** a mumbled or private expression of discontent. **3.** *Med.* an abnormal sound heard on listening over the heart, usually through a stethoscope, produced by vibrations of the valves and walls of the heart and great vessels. [ME, t. L]
—*v.i.* **4.** to make a low or indistinct continuous sound. **5.** to speak in a low tone or indistinctly. **6.** to complain in a low tone, or in private. —*v.t.* **7.** to sound by murmurs. **8.** to utter in a low tone. [ME, t. L: s. *murmurāre*] —**mur′murer,** *n.* —**mur′muring,** *adj., n.* —**mur′muringly,** *adv.*

—**Syn. 8.** MURMUR, MUMBLE, MUTTER mean to make sounds which are not fully intelligible. To MURMUR is to utter sounds or words in a low, almost inaudible tone, as in expressing blandishments, affection, dissatisfaction, etc.: *to murmur disagreement.* To MUMBLE is to utter imperfect or inarticulate sounds with the mouth partly closed, so that the words can be distinguished only with difficulty: *to mumble the answer to a question.* To MUTTER is to utter words in a low, grumbling way, often voicing complaint or discontent, not meant to be fully audible: *to mutter complaints.* **6.** See **complain.**

murmuration (mû′mə rā′shən), *n.* **1.** the act or instance of murmuring. **2.** a flock of starlings.

murmurous (mû′mə rəs), *adj.* **1.** abounding in or characterized by murmurs. **2.** murmuring: *murmurous waters.* —**mur′murously,** *adv.*

murphy (mû′fĭ), *n., pl.* **-phies.** *Slang.* an Irish or white potato. [special use of *Murphy,* Irish surname]

murrain (mŭ′rĭn), *n.* **1.** any of various diseases of cattle, as anthrax, foot-and-mouth disease, etc. **2.** *Archaic.* a plague or pestilence (esp. in curses). [ME *moryne,* t. F: m. *morine* plague, der. L *morī* die]

Murray (mŭ′rĭ), *n.* **1. (Sir George) Gilbert (Aimé)** (ā′mā), 1866–1957, British classical scholar. **2. Sir James Augustus Henry,** 1837–1915, Scottish lexicographer and linguist. **3. Lindley,** 1745–1826, British grammarian, born in America. **4.** Also, **Hume.** a river in SE Australia, flowing along the border between Victoria and New South Wales and through SE South Australia into the Indian Ocean. 1609 mi.

Murray cod, the giant perch, *Macculochella macquariensis,* native to the river Murray.

murre (mû), *n.* **1.** either of two species of diving birds of the genus *Uria,* of northern seas, the thick-billed **Brunnich's murre** (*U. omvia*) or the slender-billed **common murre** (*U. aalge*). **2.** *Colloq.* the razor-billed auk.

murrelet (mû′lĭt), *n.* any of several small, chunky diving birds found chiefly on coasts of the N Pacific, as the **marbled murrelet,** *Brachyramphus marmoratus.*

murrey (mŭ′rĭ), *n.* a dark purplish red colour. [ME *morrey,* t. OF: m. *more,* der. L *mōrum* mulberry]

murrhine (mŭ′rīn, -rĭn), *adj.* **1.** pertaining to a stone or substance of Roman times used for wine cups and other vessels. —*n.* **2.** the substance. Also, **murrine.** [t. L: m. s. *murr(h)inus*]

murrhine glass, 1. any kind of glassware supposed to resemble the Roman cups of murrhine. **2.** a ware composed of glass in which metals, precious stones, or the like are embedded.

Murrumbidgee (mŭ′rəm bĭj′ĭ), *n.* a river in SE Australia, flowing W through New South Wales to the river Murray. ab. 1350 mi.

Murry (mŭ′rĭ), *n.* **John Middleton,** 1889–1957, English writer and critic.

murther (mû′thə), *n., v.t., v.i. Obs.* murder. [ME *morther,* OE *morthor,* c. Goth. *maurthr*]

Mus., 1. museum. **2.** music. **3.** musical. **4.** musician.

musaceous (myōō zā′shəs), *adj.* belonging to the *Musaceae,* or banana family of plants. [f. s. NL *Mūsāceae* (der. *Musa,* the typical genus, t. Ar.: m. *mawza* banana, prob. of East Ind. orig.) + -OUS]

Musashino (mōō sä′shĭ nō′, mōō′sə shē′nō), *n.* a town in Japan, in SE central Honshu island. 133,516 (1965).

Mus.B., (L *Musicae Baccalaureus*) Bachelor of Music. Also, **Mus.Bac.**

muscadel (mŭs′kə dĕl′), *n.* muscatel. Also, **muscadelle.**

muscadet (mōōs′kă dā′; *Fr.* mʏs kȧ dĕ′), *n.* a white wine of the muscatel type from the lower reaches of the Loire.

muscadine (mŭs′kə dĭn, -dīn′), *n.* a grape of the central and southern U.S., having a dull purple, thick-skinned musky fruit.

muscae volitantes (mŭs′sē vŏl′ĭ tăn′tēz), *Pathol.* specks that seem to dance in the air before the eyes, due to defects in the vitreous humour of the eye or other causes. [NL: flies flying about]

muscat (mŭs′kət, -kăt), *n.* **1.** a grape variety with pronounced pleasant sweet aroma and flavour, much used for making wine. **2.** the vine bearing this grape. [t. F, t. Pr., der. LL *muscus* MUSK]

Muscat (mŭs′kət, -kăt), *n.* a seaport in SE Arabia: capital of Muscat and Oman. 5000 (est. 1963). Arabic, **Masqat.**

Muscat and Oman, a sultanate in SE Arabia. 560,000 pop. (est. 1963); ab. 820,000 sq. mi. *Cap.:* Muscat. Also, **Oman.**

muscatel (mŭs′kə tĕl′), *n.* **1.** a sweet wine made from muscat grapes. **2.** the muscat grape. Also, **muscadel, muscadelle.** [ME, t. OF, der. Pr. *muscat* MUSCAT]

muscid (mŭs′ĭd), *adj.* **1.** belonging or pertaining to the *Muscidae,* the family of dipterous insects that includes the common housefly. —*n.* **2.** any muscid fly. [t. NL: s. *Muscidae,* pl., der. L *musca* a fly]

muscle (mŭs′əl), *n., v.,* **-cled, -cling.** —*n.* **1.** a discrete bundle or sheet of contractile fibres having the function of producing movement in the animal body. **2.** the tissue of such an organ. **3.** muscular strength; brawn. —*v.i.* **4.** *Colloq.* to make or shove one's way by sheer brawn or force. **5. muscle in (on),** to force one's way in(to), esp. by violent means, trickery, or in the face of hostility, in order to obtain a share of something. [t. F, t. L: m. s. *musculus* muscle, lit., little mouse (from the appearance of certain muscles)]

muscle-bound (mŭs′əl bound′), *adj.* having muscles enlarged and inelastic, as from excessive exercise.

muscle spindles, *Anat.* the sensory end organs in skeletal muscle.

muscone (mŭs′kōn), *n.* a large cyclic ketone, $C_{16}H_{30}O$, obtained from musk and used in the perfume industry.

muscovado (mŭs′kə vä′dō), *n.* raw or unrefined sugar, obtained from the juice of the sugar cane by evaporation and draining off the molasses. [t. Pg.: m. (*açucar*) *mascavado* (sugar) of inferior quality, pp. of *mascavar* diminish]

Muscovite (mŭs′kə vīt′), *n.* **1.** a native or inhabitant of Moscow. **2.** a native or inhabitant of Muscovy. **3.** *Archaic.* a Russian. **4.** (*l.c.*) common light-coloured mica, essentially $KAl_3Si_3O_{10}(OH)_2$, used as an electrical insulator. —*adj.* **5.** of, pertaining to, or characteristic of Moscow, Muscovy, or the Muscovites.

Muscovy (mŭs′kə vĭ), *n.* **1.** (in Russian history) a principality having as its capital the ancient city of Moscow. **2.** *Archaic.* Moscow. **3.** *Archaic.* Russia. —**Mus′covite′,** *n., adj.* —**Mus′covit′ic,** *adj.*

Muscovy duck, a large, crested, neotropical duck, *Cairina moschata,* which has been widely domesticated. When wild it is glossy black with a large white patch on each wing. [erroneous var. of *musk-duck*]

muscular (mŭs′kyōō lə), *adj.* **1.** of or pertaining to muscle or the muscles. **2.** dependent on or affected by the muscles. **3.** having well-developed muscles; brawny. —**muscularity** (mŭs′kyōō lă′rĭ tĭ), *n.* —**mus′cularly,** *adv.* —**Syn. 3.** sinewy; strong, powerful; stalwart, sturdy.

muscular dystrophy, a disease of unknown origin which produces a progressive muscular deterioration and wasting, robbing the muscles of all vitality until the patient is completely helpless.

musculature (mŭs′kyōō lə chə), *n.* the muscular system of the body or of its parts. [t. F, der. L *musculus* MUSCLE]

Mus.D., (L *Musicae Doctor*) Doctor of Music. Also, **Mus.Doc., Mus.Dr, D.Mus.**

muse (myōōz), *v.,* **mused, musing.** —*v.i.* **1.** to reflect or meditate in silence, as on some subject, often as in a reverie. **2.** to gaze meditatively or wonderingly. —*v.t.* **3.** to meditate on. [ME *muse(n),* t. OF: m. *muser* ponder, loiter, trifle (cf. AMUSE), der. *muse* muzzle] —**mus′er,** *n.*

Muse (myōōz), *n.* **1.** *Class. Myth.* **a.** any of the nine sister goddesses, daughters of Zeus and Mnemosyne, presiding over poetry and song, the drama, dancing, astronomy, etc.: Calliope, Clio, Erato, Euterpe, Melpomene, Polyhymnia, Terpsichore, Thalia, Urania. **b.** some other goddess supposed to preside over a particular art. **2.** (*sometimes l.c.*) the goddess or the power regarded as inspiring a poet. **3.** (*l.c.*) a poet's characteristic genius or powers. [ME, t. OF, t. L: m. *Mūsa,* t. Gk: m. *Moûsa*]

museful (myōōz′fəl), *adj.* deeply thoughtful.

musette (myōō zĕt′), *n., pl.* **-settes. 1.** an ancient French double-reed instrument, resembling a bagpipe, sometimes with a drone and windbag. **2.** a simple tune suitable for a musette. [ME, t. MF, dim. of *muse* bagpipe]

musette bag, *U.S.* a haversack, esp. one used by officers.

museum (myōō zĭəm′), *n.* a building or place for the keeping, exhibition, and study of objects of scientific, artistic, and historical interest. [t. L, t. Gk: m. *mouseîon* seat of the Muses, place of study, library]

museum piece, 1. an object suitable for keeping and exhibiting in a museum. **2.** *Colloq.* anything old-fashioned or which has outlived its usefulness.

Musgrave Ranges (mŭz′grāv′), a series of mountain ranges in N South Australia. Highest point, Mt Woodroffe, 4970 ft.

mush[1] (mŭsh), *n.* **1.** meal, esp. corn meal, boiled in water or milk until it forms a thick, soft mass. **2.** any thick, soft mass. **3.** anything unpleasantly lacking in firmness, force, dignity, etc. **4.** *Colloq.* weak or maudlin sentiment or sentimental language. [b. (obs.) *moose* thick vegetable porridge (t. D: m. *moes*) and MASH, n.]

mush[2] (mŭsh), *v.t.* **1.** to go or travel on foot, esp. over the snow with a dog team. —*interj.* **2.** (an order to start or speed up a dog team.) —*n.* **3.** a journey on foot, esp. over the snow with a dog team. [? t. F: m. *marche* or *marchons,* impv. of *marcher* advance] —**mush′er,** *n.*

mushroom (mŭsh′rōōm, -rŏŏm), *n.* **1.** any of various fleshy fungi including the toadstools, puffballs, coral fungi, morels, etc. **2.** any of certain edible species belonging to the family *Agaricaceae,* usually of umbrella shape. Cf. **toadstool. 3.** the common **meadow mushroom,** *Agaricus campestris,* or related forms grown for the market. **4.** anything of similar shape or correspondingly rapid growth. —*adj.* **5.** of, pertaining to, or made of mushrooms. **6.** resembling or suggesting a mushroom in shape. **7.** of rapid growth and, often, brief duration: *mushroom fame.* —*v.i.* **8.** to gather mushrooms. **9.** to have or assume the shape of a mushroom. **10.** to spread or grow quickly, as mushrooms. [late ME, t. F: m. *mousseron,* g. s. LL *mussirio*]

mushy (mŭsh′ĭ), *adj.,* **-ier, -iest. 1.** mushlike; pulpy. **2.** *Colloq.* weakly sentimental: *a mushy valentine.* —**mush′ily,** *adv.* —**mush′iness,** *n.*

music (myōō′zĭk), *n.* **1.** an art of sound in time which expresses ideas and emotions in significant forms through the elements of rhythm, melody, harmony, and colour. **2.** the tones or sounds employed, occurring in single line (melody) or multiple lines (harmony), and sounded or to be sounded by voice(s) or/and instrument(s). **3.** musical work or compositions for singing or playing. **4.** the written or printed score of a musical composition. **5.** such scores collectively. **6.** any sweet, pleasing, or harmonious sounds or sound; the music of the waves. **7.** appreciation of or responsiveness to musical sounds or harmonies. **8. face the music,** to face the consequences of one's actions; accept responsibility for what one has done. [ME *musik,* t. L: m. s. *mūsica,* t. Gk: m. *mousikḗ* (*téchnē*) orig., any art over which the Muses presided]

musical (myo͞o′zĭ kl), *adj.* **1.** of, pertaining to, or producing music: *a musical instrument.* **2.** of the nature of or resembling music; melodious; harmonious. **3.** fond of or skilled in music. **4.** set to or accompanied by music: *a musical melodrama.* —*n.* **5.** musical comedy. —**mu′sically,** *adv.* —**mu′sical′ity, mu′sicalness,** *n.*

musical box, a box or case containing an apparatus for producing music mechanically, as by means of a comb-like steel plate with tuned teeth sounded by small pegs or pins in the surface of a revolving cylinder or disc. Also, *U.S.*, **music box.**

musical chairs, a children's game in which the players walk to music around a number of chairs (one less than the number of players), with the object of finding a seat when the music stops. The player failing to do so is eliminated, and one chair removed before the next round.

musical comedy, a play or film with music, often of a whimsical or satirical nature, based on a slight plot with singing and dancing in solos and groups.

music drama, that form of opera, as conceived by Richard Wagner, in which the music is used to develop the drama in a symphonic manner, without the use of formal divisions, repeats, etc., and in which themes, characters, etc., are introduced by means of a leitmotiv.

music hall, a theatre or hall for variety entertainment.

musician (myo͞o zĭsh′ən), *n.* **1.** one who makes music a profession, esp. as a performer on an instrument. **2.** one skilled in playing a musical instrument. —**musi′cianly,** *adj.*

musicianship (myo͞o zĭsh′ən shĭp′), *n.* skill and sensitivity in performing or perception in appreciating music.

music of the spheres, a music, imperceptible to human ears, formerly supposed to be produced by the movements of the spheres or heavenly bodies.

musicology (myo͞o′zĭ kŏl′ə jĭ), *n.* the scholarly or scientific study of music, as in historical research, musical theory, the physical nature of sound, etc. —**musicological** (myo͞o′zĭ kə lŏj′ĭ kl), *adj.* —**mu′sicol′ogist,** *n.*

music roll, a roll of perforated paper for use in a mechanical player piano.

music stand, an adjustable stand for holding a music score in position for reading during a performance.

music stool, a stool, usually adjustable, used when playing a piano.

Musil (*Ger.* mo͞os′ĭl), *n.* **Robert** (*Ger.* rō′bĕrt), 1880–1942, Austrian novelist.

musing (myo͞o′zĭng), *adj.* **1.** absorbed in thought; meditative. —*n.* **2.** contemplation. —**mus′ingly,** *adv.*

musjid (mŭs′jĭd), *n.* masjid.

musk (mŭsk), *n.* **1.** a substance secreted in a glandular sac under the skin of the abdomen of the male musk deer, having a strong smell, and used in perfumery. **2.** a synthetic imitation of the substance. **3.** a similar secretion of other animals, as the civet, muskrat, otter, etc. **4.** the smell, or some similar smell. **5.** *Bot.* any of several plants, as the monkey-flower, having a musky fragrance. [ME *muske*, var. of *musco*, t. LL, abl. of *muscus*, t. LGk: m. *móschos*, t. Pers.: m. *mushk*]

musk deer, a small, hornless animal of the deer kind, *Moschus moschiferus*, of central Asia, the male of which secretes musk and has large canine teeth.

musk duck, 1. Muscovy duck. **2.** an Australian duck, *Biziura lobata.*

muskeg (mŭs′kĕg′), *n.* *U.S.* a bog formed in hollows or depressions of the land surface by the accumulation of water and growth of sphagnum mosses. [t. Ojibwa, Kickapoo: grassy bog]

muskellunge (mŭs′kĭ lŭnj′), *n.*, *pl.* **-lunge.** a large game fish, *Esox masquinongy*, of the pike family, of the lakes and rivers of eastern and Middle Western North America. Also, **maskalonge.** [appar. dissimilated var. of *muscanonge, maskinonge*, t. N Amer. Ind. (Ojibwa): m. *mashkinonge*, f. *mash* great + *kinonge* pike]

musket (mŭs′kĭt), *n.* **1.** a hand-gun for infantry soldiers, introduced in the 16th century, the predecessor of the modern rifle. **2.** the male sparrowhawk, *Accipiter nisus.* [t. F: m. *mousquet*, t. It.: m. *moschetto* (orig. sense: def. 2), der. *mosca* a fly, g. L *musca*]

musketeer (mŭs′kĭ tĭə′), *n.* a soldier armed with a musket. [f. MUSKET + -EER, modelled on F *mousquetaire*]

musketry (mŭs′kĭ trĭ), *n.* **1.** *Mil.* instruction in the art of using small arms. **2.** *Obs.* muskets collectively. **3.** *Obs.* troops armed with muskets.

Muskhogean (mŭs kō′gĭ ən), *n.* **1.** a family of American Indian languages of south-eastern U.S., including Choctaw, Chickasaw, and Creek (also called **Muskogee** in Oklahoma and **Seminole** in Florida). **2.** a member of any of the peoples speaking these languages. Also, **Muskogean.**

muskmelon (mŭsk′mĕl′ən), *n.* **1.** a kind of melon, of many varieties, a round or oblong fruit with a juicy, often aromatically sweet, edible flesh (yellow, white, or green). **2.** the plant, *Cucumis melo*, bearing it.

Musk ox, *Ovibos moschatus* (Ab. 5 ft high at the shoulder, total length 8 ft)

Muskogee (mŭs kō′gĭ), *n.* See **Muskhogean.**

musk orchid, a small, tuberous orchid with dense spikes of scented, greenish yellow flowers, *Herminium monorchis*, occurring widely in Europe and temperate Asia on calcareous grassland.

musk ox, a bovine ruminant, *Ovibos moschatus*, between the ox and the sheep in size and anatomy, and having a musky smell, a native of arctic America.

muskrat (mŭsk′răt′), *n.*, *pl.* **-rats,** (*esp. collectively*) **-rat. 1.** a large aquatic North American rodent, *Ondatra zibethica*, with a musky smell. **2.** its thick, light brown fur.

Muskrat, *Ondatra zibethica* (Total length ab. 2 ft, tail 10 in.)

musk rose, a species of rose, *Rosa moschata*, having fragrant white flowers.

musky[1] (mŭs′kĭ), *adj.*, **-kier, -kiest.** of or like musk, as smells; having a smell like that of musk. [f. MUSK + -Y[1]]

musky[2] (mŭs′kĭ), *n.*, *pl.* **-kies.** *Colloq.* muskellunge.

Muslim (mo͝oz′lĭm, mŭz′lĭm), *adj.*, *n.*, *pl.* **-lims, -lim.** —*adj.* **1.** of or pertaining to the religion, law, or civilization of Islam. —*n.* **2.** an adherent of Islam. Also, **Moslem.** [t. Ar.: one who accepts *Islam*, lit., submission]

Muslimism (mo͝oz′lĭ mĭz′əm, mŭz′lĭ-), *n.* the Mohammedan religion; Islam. Also, **Moslemism.**

muslin (mŭz′lĭn), *n.* a cotton fabric made in various degrees of fineness, and often printed, woven or embroidered in patterns; esp., a cotton fabric of plain weave, used for curtains and for a variety of other purposes. [t. F: m. *mousseline*, t. It.: m. *mussolina* muslin, der. *Mussolo* MOSUL, city in Iraq]

Mus. M., (L *Musicae Magister*) Master of Music.

musquash (mŭs′kwŏsh), *n.* muskrat. [t. Algonquian languages of Virginia (Abnaki, Ojibwa): it is red]

muss (mŭs), *n.* *U.S. Colloq.* **1.** a state of disorder or confusion. —*v.t.* **2.** to put into disorder; make untidy or messy; rumple (often fol. by *up*). [alter. of MESS]

mussel (mŭs′əl), *n.* any bivalve mollusc, esp. an edible marine bivalve of the family *Mytilidae* and a freshwater bivalve of the family *Unionidae.* [t. MLG; r. ME and OE *muscle*, t. LL: m. s. *muscula*, var. of L *musculus* MUSCLE, mussel]

Musselburgh (mŭs′əl bə rə, -brə), *n.* a burgh in Scotland, in Midlothian. 17,273 (1961).

Musset (*Fr.* mʏ sĕ′), *n.* **Alfred de** (*Fr.* ȧl frĕd′ də) (*Louis Charles Alfred de Musset*), 1810–57, French poet, dramatist, and writer of stories.

Mussolini (mo͞os′ə lē′nĭ; *It.* mo͞os sō lē′nē), *n.* **Benito** (*It.* bĕ nē′tō) (*Il Duce*), 1883–1945, Italian Fascist leader and prime minister of Italy 1922–43.

Mussorgsky (mo͞o sôg′skĭ; *Russ.* mo͞o′sərk skĭy), *n.* **Modest Petrovich** (*Russ.* mȧ dyĕst′pĭt rô′vĭch), Moussorgsky.

Mussulman (mŭs′əl mən), *n.*, *pl.* **-mans.** a Muslim. [t. Pers.: m. *musulmān*, der. *muslim* MUSLIM, t. Ar. (with the Pers. pl. ending *-ān*)]

mussy (mŭs′ĭ), *adj.*, **-sier, -siest.** *U.S. Colloq.* untidy, messy or rumpled.

must[1] (mŭst; *unstressed* məst, məs), *aux. v.* **1.** to be bound by some imperative requirement to: *I must keep my word.* **2.** to be obliged or compelled to, as by some constraining force or necessity: *man must eat to live.* **3.** may reasonably be supposed to: *she must be nearly fifty.* **4.** to be inevitably certain to: *man must die.* **5.** to have to; ought to; should: *I must go soon.* **6.** *Archaic.* (sometimes used with ellipsis of *go, get*, or some similar verb readily understood from the context): *we must away.* —*n.* **7.** anything necessary or vital: *this law is a must.* [ME *most(e)*, OE *mōste*, pret. (pres. *mōt*); akin to D *moeten*, G *müssen* be obliged]

—**Syn.** 5. MUST, OUGHT, SHOULD express necessity or duty.

MUST expresses necessity, or compulsion: *I must answer this letter, soldiers must obey orders.* OUGHT (weaker than MUST) expresses obligation, duty, desirability: *you ought to tell your mother.* SHOULD expresses obligation, expectation, or probability (*you are not behaving as you should; children should be taught to speak the truth; they should arrive at one o'clock*); it also expresses the conditional (*I should be glad to play if I could*) and future intention (*I said I should be at home next week*).

must[2] (mŭst), *n.* new wine; the unfermented juice as pressed from the grape or other fruit. [ME and OE, t. L: s. *mustum*, short for *vinum mustum* fresh wine]

must[3] (mŭst), *n.* mould; mustiness. [back-formation from MUSTY]

must[4] (mŭst), *n.* musth.

mustache (mə stăsh′), *n. U.S.* moustache.

mustachio (mə stä′shĭ ō′), *n., pl.* **-os.** a moustache.

Mustafa Kemal (mo͞os′tə fə kĕ mäl′), former name of **Kemal Atatürk.**

mustang (mŭs′tăng), *n.* the small, wild or half-wild horse of the American plains, descended from Spanish stock. [t. Sp.: m. *mestengo* wild]

mustard (mŭs′tərd), *n.* **1.** a pungent powder or paste prepared from the seed of the mustard plant, much used as a food seasoning or condiment, and medicinally in plasters, poultices, etc. **2.** any of various brassicaceous plants, esp. *Brassica hirta* (*B. alba*) (**white mustard**), *B. juncea* (**Indian** or **Chinese mustard**), *B. nigra* (**black mustard**), and others cultivated for their seed. [ME, t. OF: m. *moustarde*, orig. powdered mustard seed and must, der. *moust*, g. L *mustum* MUST[2]]

mustard gas, a chemical-warfare agent, $(ClCH_2CH_2)_2S$, stored in liquid form, producing burns, blindness, and death, introduced by the Germans in World War I; yperite.

mustard oil, oil expressed from the seed of mustard, esp. a carbylamine (a drying oil) used in making soap.

mustard plaster, a powdered, black, mustard and rubber solution mixture placed on a cloth and used as a counter-irritant.

mustee (mŭs tē′, mŭs′tē), *n.* **1.** the offspring of a white person and a quadroon. **2.** a half-breed. Also, **mestee.** [t. Sp.: m. *mestizo*]

musteline (mŭs′tĭ līn′, -lĭn), *adj.* **1.** belonging or pertaining to the family *Mustelidae*, including the martens, skunks, minks, weasels, badgers, otters, etc. **2.** weasel-like. **3.** tawny or brown, like a weasel in summer. [t. L: m. s. *mustēlīnus* belonging to a weasel]

muster (mŭs′tə), *v.t.* **1.** to assemble (troops, a ship's crew, etc.), as for battle, display, inspection, orders, discharge, etc. **2.** to gather or summon (often fol. by *up*): *he mustered up all his courage.* **3.** *Naut.* to call the roll of. *—v.i.* **4.** to assemble for inspection, service, etc., as troops or forces. **5.** to come together, collect, or gather. **6. muster in** or **out,** *U.S.* to enlist into or discharge from military service. *—n.* **7.** an assembling of troops or men for inspection or other purposes. **8.** an assemblage or collection. **9** the act of mustering. **10.** Also, **muster roll.** (formerly) a list of the men enrolled in a military or naval unit. **11. pass muster,** to measure up to specified standards. [ME *mostre(n)*, t. OF: m. *mostrer*, g. L *monstrāre* show] **—Syn. 1, 2.** See **gather.**

musth (mŭst), *n.* a condition periodically typical in all mature male elephants and some females, characterized by discharge from a facial gland accompanied by emotional disturbance. Also, **must.** [t. Urdu, t. Pers.: m. *mast*]

musty (mŭs′tĭ), *adj.*, **-tier, -tiest. 1.** having a smell or flavour suggestive of mould, as old buildings, long-closed rooms, food, etc. **2.** made stale by time, or antiquated: *musty laws.* **3.** dull; apathetic. [var. of *moisty* (f. MOIST + -Y[1]), with loss of *i* before *s*] **—mus′tily,** *adv.* **—mus′tiness,** *n.*

mutable (myo͞o′tə bl), *adj.* **1.** liable or subject to change or alteration. **2.** given to changing, or ever changing; fickle or inconstant: *the mutable ways of fortune.* [ME, t. L: m. s. *mūtābilis*] **—mu′tabil′ity, mu′tableness,** *n.* **—mu′tably,** *adv.*

mutant (myo͞o′tnt), *adj.* **1.** undergoing mutation; resulting from mutation. *—n.* **2.** a new type of organism produced as the result of mutation. [t. L: s. *mūtans*, ppr., changing]

mutarotation (myo͞o′tə rō tā′shən), *n. Chem.* a change in the optical rotation of fresh solutions of reducing sugars with time. [f. MUTA(TION) + ROTATION]

mutate (myo͞o tāt′), *v.*, **-tated, -tating.** *—v.t.* **1.** to change; alter. **2.** *Phonet.* to change by umlaut. *—v.i.* **3.** to change; undergo mutation. **—mutative** (myo͞o′tə tĭv, myo͞o tā′tĭv), *adj.*

mutation (myo͞o tā′shən), *n.* **1.** the act or process of changing. **2.** a change or alternation, as in form, qualities, or nature. **3.** *Biol.* **a.** a sudden departure from the parent type, as when an individual differs from its parents in one or more heritable characteristics, caused by a change in a gene or a chromosome. **b.** an individual, species, or the like, resulting from such a departure. **4.** *Phonet.* umlaut. [ME, t. L: m. s. *mūtātio*] **—muta′tional,** *adj.* **—mutative** (myo͞o′tə tĭv, myo͞o tā′tĭv), *adj.*

mutatis mutandis (mo͞o tä′tĭs mo͞o tăn′dĭs), *Latin.* with the necessary changes.

mutch (mŭch), *n. Scot.* a cap worn by women and young children. [late ME, t. MD: m. s. *mutse*, c. G *Mütze* cap]

mutchkin (mŭch′kĭn), *n. Scot.* a unit of liquid measure equal to about three-quarters of an imperial pint. [t. early mod. D: m. *mudseken* a measure]

mute (myo͞ot), *adj., n., v.,* **muted, muting.** *—adj.* **1.** silent; refraining from speech or utterance. **2.** not emitting or having sound of any kind. **3.** incapable of speech; dumb. **4.** *Gram.* (of letters) silent; not pronounced. **5.** *Law.* making no response when arraigned, as a prisoner in **to stand mute,** now resulting in the entry of a plea of not guilty. **6.** *Fox-hunting.* (of a hound) not giving tongue while hunting. *—n.* **7.** one unable to utter words. **8.** an actor whose part is confined to dumb show. **9.** *Law.* a person who makes no response when arraigned. **10.** a hired attendant at a funeral; a professional mourner. **11.** a mechanical device of various shapes and materials for muffling the tone of a musical instrument. **12.** *Phonetics.* a stop. *—v.t.* **13.** to deaden or muffle the sound of (a musical instrument, etc.). **14.** to reduce, as in volume; soften. [t. L: m. s. *mūtus* silent, dumb; r. ME *muet*, t. OF] **—mute′ly,** *adv.* **—mute′ness,** *n.* **—Syn. 3.** See **dumb.**

muti (mo͞o′tĭ), *n. S African.* **1.** curative or magic medicine as dispensed by witchdoctors among the native population. **2.** *Colloq.* medicine. [t. Zulu: m. *umuthi*]

mutilate (myo͞o′tĭ lāt′), *v.t.*, **-lated, -lating. 1.** to deprive (a person or animal, the body, etc.) of a limb or other important part or parts. **2.** to injure, disfigure, or make imperfect by removing or irreparably damaging parts. [t. L: m. s. *mutilātus*, pp., cut off, maimed] **—mu′tila′tion,** *n.* **—mu′tila′tive,** *adj.* **—mu′tila′tor,** *n.* **—Syn. 1.** See **maim.**

mutineer (myo͞o′tĭ nĭə′), *n.* one who mutinies. [t. F (obs.): m. *mutinier*, der. *mutin* rebellious, der. OF *muete* rebellion, orig. pp., der. L *movēre* move]

mutinous (myo͞o′tĭ nəs), *adj.* **1.** disposed to, engaged in, or involving revolt against constituted authority. **2.** characterized by mutiny; rebellious. **—mu′tinously,** *adv.* **—mu′tinousness,** *n.*

mutiny (myo͞o′tĭ nĭ), *n., pl.* **-nies,** *v.,* **-nied, -nying.** *—n.* **1.** revolt, or a revolt or rebellion, against constituted authority, esp. by soldiers or seamen against their officers. *—v.i.* **2.** to commit the offence of mutiny; revolt against constituted authority. [f. (obs.) *mutin*, adj., mutinous (t. F) + -Y[3]]

mutism (myo͞o′tĭz′əm), *n. Psychiatry.* a conscious or unconscious refusal to respond verbally to interrogation, present in some mental disorders. [t. F: m. *mutisme*, der. L *mūtus* mute, adj.]

Mutsuhito (mo͞ot′so͞o hē′tō), *n.* 1852–1912, emperor of Japan 1867–1912.

mutt (mŭt), *n. Slang.* **1.** a dog, esp. a mongrel. **2.** a simpleton; a stupid person. [orig. obscure; ? shortened from *muttonhead*]

mutter (mŭt′ə), *v.i.* **1.** to utter words indistinctly or in a low tone, often in talking to oneself or in making obscure complaints, threats, etc.; murmur; grumble. **2.** to make a low, rumbling sound. *—v.t.* **3.** to utter indistinctly or in a low tone. *—n.* **4.** the act or utterance of one who mutters. [ME *moter(e)*, ? freq. of (obs.) *moot*, v., speak, murmur, OE *mōtian* speak in public. Cf. d. G *muttern*] **—mut′terer,** *n.* **—mut′teringly,** *adv.* **—Syn. 1.** See **murmur.**

mutton (mŭt′n), *n.* **1.** the flesh of sheep, used as food. **2.** the flesh of the well-grown or more mature sheep, as distinguished from lamb. [ME *moton*, t. OF; of Celtic orig.] **—mut′tony,** *adj.*

mutton-bird (mŭt′n bûd′), *n.* any of various species of petrel, including the short-tailed shearwater *Procellaria tenuirostris* which inhabits the Pacific Ocean.

mutton-chops (mŭt′n chŏps′), *n.pl.* side-whiskers narrow at the top, and broad and trimmed short at the bottom, the chin being shaved both in front and beneath. Also, **mutton-chop whiskers.**

mutton-fist (mŭt′n fĭst′), *n.* a large, coarse hand.

mutton-head (mŭt′n hĕd′), *n. Colloq.* a stupid or dull person.

Muttra (mŭt′rə), *n.* former name of **Mathura.**

mutual (myo͞o′cho͞o əl), *adj.* **1.** possessed, experienced, performed, etc., by each of two or more with respect to the other or others; reciprocal: *mutual aid.* **2.** having the same relation each towards the other or others:

mutual foes. **3.** of or pertaining to each of two or more, or common: *mutual acquaintance.* **4.** pertaining to mutual insurance: *a mutual company.* [late ME, f. s. L *mūtuus* reciprocal + -AL[1]] —**mu′tually,** *adv.*

—**Syn. 1.** MUTUAL, RECIPROCAL agree in the idea of an exchange or balance between two or more persons or groups. MUTUAL indicates an exchange of a feeling, obligation, etc., between two or more people, or an interchange of some kind between persons or things: *mutual esteem, in mutual agreement.* It is not properly a synonym for COMMON, though often used in that sense (shared by, or pertaining to two or more things), esp. in the phrase *a mutual friend* (a friend of each of two or more other persons). RECIPROCAL indicates a relation in which one act, thing, feeling, etc., balances or is given in return for another: *reciprocal promises or favours.*

mutual inductance, *Elect.* the ratio of the electromotive force in one circuit to the rate of change of current in another circuit which is magnetically linked to the first circuit; coefficient of mutual induction.

mutual induction, *Elect.* the induction of an electromotive force in one circuit as a result of a changing current in a separate circuit with which it is magnetically linked.

mutual insurance, insurance in which those insured become members of a company who reciprocally engage, by payment of certain amounts into a common fund, to indemnify one another against loss.

mutualism (myo͞o′tyo͞o ə lĭz′əm), *n.* **1.** the attainment of individual and collective well-being through mutual dependence. **2.** *Biol.* symbiosis.

mutuality (myo͞o′tyo͞o ăl′ĭ tĭ), *n.* condition or quality of being mutual; reciprocity; mutual dependence.

mutualize (myo͞o′tyo͞o ə līz′), *v.t., v.i.,* **-lized, -lizing.** *Chiefly U.S.* to make or become mutual. Also, **mutualise.** —**mu′tualiza′tion,** *n.*

mutual savings bank, a non-capitalized savings bank distributing its profits to depositors.

mutule (myo͞o′tyo͞ol), *n.* *Archit.* a projecting flat block under the corona of the Doric cornice, corresponding to the modillion of other orders. [t. F, t. L: m. s. *mūtulus* modillion]

M, Mutule

Muzaffarpur (mo͞o zŭf′ə-po͞oə′), *n.* a town in India, in NW Bihar. 109,048 (1961).

Muzak (myo͞o′zăk), *n.* *Trademark.* recorded background music played, usually continuously, in places of work, hotels, restaurants, etc.

muzhik (mo͞o′zhĭk), *n.* a Russian peasant. Also, **moujik, mujik, muzjik.** [t. Russ.]

muzzle (mŭz′əl), *n., v.,* **-zled, -zling.** —*n.* **1.** the mouth, or end for discharge, of the barrel of a gun, pistol, etc. **2.** the projecting part of the head of an animal, including jaws, mouth, and nose. See illus. under **horse. 3.** a device, usually an arrangement of straps or wires, placed over an animal's mouth to prevent the animal from biting, eating, etc. —*v.t.* **4.** to put a muzzle on (an animal or its mouth) so as to prevent biting, eating, etc. **5.** to restrain from speech or the expression of opinion; gag: *they tried to muzzle him but he insisted on finishing his speech.* [ME *mosel,* t. OF: m. *musel,* dim. of *muse* muzzle; orig. uncert.] —**muz′zler,** *n.*

muzzle-loader (mŭz′əl lō′də), *n.* a firearm which is loaded through the muzzle. —**muz′zle-load′ing,** *adj.*

muzzle velocity, *Ordn.* the speed of a projectile in feet per second as it leaves a gun muzzle.

muzzy (mŭz′ĭ), *adj.,* **-zier, -ziest.** *Colloq.* confused; dazed; tipsy. —**muz′zily,** *adv.* —**muz′ziness,** *n.*

Mv, 1. *Elect.* megavolt. **2.** *Chem.* mendelevium.

M.V., motor vessel.

m.v., (It. *mezza voce*) *Music.* with half the power of the voice; softly.

M.V.D., the internal secret police of the Soviet Union, 1943–53. [Russ. *(M)inisterstvo (V)nutrennikh (D)el,* lit. Ministry of Internal Affairs]

M.V.O., Member (fourth or fifth class) of the Royal Victorian Order.

Mw, *Elect.* megawatt.

Mweru (mwĕə′ro͞o), *n.* a lake in central Africa between the Republic of Congo and Zambia. 68 mi. long.

my (mī), *pron.* **1.** the possessive form corresponding to *I* and *me,* used before a noun: *my house.* —*interj.* **2.** *Colloq.* (an exclamation of surprise): *Oh my!* [ME *mī,* apocopated var. of *mīn,* OE *mīn.* See MINE[1]]

my-, a word element meaning 'muscle'. Also, **myo-.** [t. Gk, comb. form of *mŷs*]

myalgia (mī ăl′jyə), *n.* *Pathol.* pain in the muscles; muscular rheumatism.

myall (mī′ôl), —*n.* **1.** any of several Australian acacias, esp. *Acacia pendula.* **2.** a wild or uncivilized Aborigine. —*adj.* **3.** wild or uncivilized. [t. native Australian]

myasthenia (mī′əs thē′nyə), *n.* *Pathol.* muscle weakness.

myc-, a word element meaning 'fungus'. Also, **myco-.** [comb. form repr. Gk *mýkēs*]

mycelium (mī sē′lĭ əm), *n., pl.* **-lia** (-lĭ ə). *Bot.* the vegetative part or thallus of the fungi, when composed of one or more filamentous elements, or hyphae. [t. NL, der. Gk *mýkēs*] —**myceloid** (mī′sĭ loid′), *adj.*

Mycenae (mī sē′nē), *n.* an ancient city in S Greece, in Argolis: notable ruins.

Mycenaean (mī′sĭ nē′ən), *adj.* **1.** of or pertaining to the ancient city of Mycenae. **2.** denoting or pertaining to the Aegean civilization which flourished at Mycenae (*c.* 1600 B.C. to *c.* 1100 B.C.).

-mycetes, *Bot.* a word element meaning 'fungus', as in *myxomycetes.* [comb. form repr. pl. of Gk *mýkēs* fungus]

mycetoma (mī′sĭ tō′mə), *n.* *Pathol.* localized mycosis of subcutaneous and deeper tissues.

mycetozoan (mī sē′tō zō′ən), *adj.* **1.** of or pertaining to the *Mycetozoa.* —*n.* **2.** any of the *Mycetozoa* (*Myxomycetes,* slime moulds), a group of very primitive organisms lying near the borderline between the plant and animal worlds. [f. *myceto-,* var. of MYC- + -ZOAN]

myco-, var. of **myc-,** before consonants, as in *mycology.*

mycobacterium (mī′kō băk tĭə′rĭ əm), *n., pl.* **-teria** (-tĭə′rĭ ə). any of a group of bacteria, difficult to stain but which, once stained, hold stain tenaciously and are acid- and alcohol-fast. Mycobacteria produce human and bovine or mammalian tuberculosis, avian tuberculosis, tuberculosis of cold-blooded animals, and leprosy. [t. NL. See MYCO-, BACTERIUM]

mycology (mī kŏl′ə jĭ), *n.* **1.** the branch of botany that treats of fungi. **2.** the fungi found in an area. —**mycol′ogist,** *n.*

mycorrhiza (mī′kə rī′zə), *n.* *Biol.* a non-pathogenic association of a fungus with a vascular plant or bryophyte.

mycosis (mī kō′sĭs), *n.* **1.** *Pathol.* the presence of parasitic fungi in or on any part of the body. **2.** a disease caused by them. [t. NL. See MYC-, -OSIS] —**mycotic** (mī kŏt′ĭk), *adj.*

mydriasis (mĭ drī′ə sĭs, mī-), *n.* *Pathol.* excessive dilatation of the pupil of the eye, as the result of disease, drugs, or the like. [t. L, t. Gk]

mydriatic (mĭd′rĭ ăt′ĭk), *adj.* **1.** pertaining to or producing mydriasis. —*n.* **2.** a mydriatic drug.

myel-, a word element meaning 'marrow' or 'of the spinal cord'. Also (before consonants), **myelo-.** [t. Gk, comb. form of *myelós* marrow]

myelencephalon (mī′ĭ lĕn sĕf′ə lŏn′), *n.* *Anat.* the posterior segment of the brain, practically co-extensive with the medulla oblongata; the afterbrain.

myelin (mī′ĭ lĭn), *n.* *Anat.* a soft, white, fatty substance encasing the axis cylinder of certain nerve fibres. Also, **myeline** (mī′ĭ lēn′). [t. G. See MYEL-, -IN[2]]

myelitis (mī′ĭ lī′tĭs), *n.* *Pathol.* **1.** inflammation of the substance of the spinal cord. **2.** inflammation of the bone marrow.

myelocele (mī′ĭ lə sēl′), *n.* *Pathol.* a protrusion of the spinal cord through a defect in the spinal column.

myelocoele (mī′ĭ lə sēl′), *n.* *Anat.* the central cavity of the spinal cord.

myeloid (mī′ĭ loid′), *adj.* *Anat.* **1.** pertaining to the spinal cord. **2.** marrow-like. **3.** pertaining to marrow.

mylonite (mī′lə nīt′, mĭl′ə-), *n.* a rock that has been crushed and rolled out to such an extent that the original structure has been destroyed. [f. Gk *mylṓn* mill + -ITE[1]]

myna (mī′nə), *n.* any of various Asian birds of the starling family (*Sturnidae*), esp. those of the genera *Acridotheres* and *Eulabes,* some of which are well-known cagebirds and learn to talk. Also, **mina, mynah.** [t. Hind.: m. *mainā* a starling]

Mynheer (mə nĭə′; *Du.* mə nėr), *n.* **1.** the Dutch term of address and title of respect corresponding to *sir* and *Mr.* **2.** (*l.c.*) *Colloq.* a Dutchman. [t. D: m. *mijnheer,* f. *mijn* my + *heer* lord, gentleman]

myo-, var. of **my-,** before consonants.

myocardiogram (mī′ō kä′dĭ ə grăm′), *n.* a tracing representing cardiac muscular activity, made by a myocardiograph.

myocardiograph (mī′ō kä′dĭ ə grăf′, -gräf′), *n.* *Physiol.* an apparatus which records the movements of the heart muscle.

myocarditis (mī′ō kä dī′tĭs), *n.* *Pathol.* inflammation of the myocardium. [f. MYOCARD(IUM) + -ITIS]

myocardium (mī′ō kä′dĭ əm), *n.* *Anat.* the muscular substance of the heart. [t. NL. See MYO-, CARDIO-] —**my′ocar′dial,** *adj.*

myoglobin (mī′ō glō′bĭn), *n.* *Biochem.* a muscle protein that, like haemoglobin, can combine reversibly with oxygen.

myogram (mī′ə grăm′), *n.* a tracing representing muscular activity, made by a myograph.

myograph (mī′ə grăf′, -gräf′), *n. Physiol.* an instrument for taking tracings of muscular contractions and relaxations.

myography (mī ŏg′rə fĭ), *n.* **1.** the science of describing muscles; the descriptive aspect of myology. **2.** the process of using a myograph. —**my′ograph′ic,** *adj.*

myology (mī ŏl′ə jĭ), *n.* the science of muscles; the branch of anatomy that treats of muscles.

myoma (mī ō′mə), *n., pl.* **-mata** (-mə tə), **-mas** (-məz). *Pathol.* a tumour composed of muscular tissue. [t. NL. See MY-, -OMA] —**myomatous** (mī ŏm′ə təs, -ō′mə-), *adj.*

myopia (mī ō′pyə), *n. Pathol.* a condition of the eye in which parallel rays are focused in front of the retina, so that only near objects are seen clearly; near-sightedness (opposed to *hypermetropia*). [t. NL: f. s. Gk *mýōps* short-sighted + *ia* -IA] —**myopic** (mī ŏp′ĭk), *adj.*

myoscope (mī′ə skōp′), *n.* an apparatus or instrument for observing muscular contraction.

myosin (mī′ə sĭn), *n. Biochem.* a globulin occurring in muscle plasma. [f. MY- + -OS(E)[2] + -IN[2]]

myosis (mī ō′sĭs), *n. Pathol.* miosis.

myosotis (mī′ə sō′tĭs), *n.* any plant of the boraginaceous genus *Myosotis*, as the common forget-me-not. Also, **myosote** (mī′ə sōt′). [t. L, t. Gk: the plant mouse-ear]

myotic (mī ŏt′ĭk), *adj.* miotic.

Myra (mī′ə rə), *n.* an ancient city in SW Asia Minor, in Lycia.

myriad (mĭr′ĭ əd), *n.* **1.** an indefinitely great number. **2.** a very great number of persons or things. **3.** ten thousand. —*adj.* **4.** of an indefinitely great number; innumerable. **5.** having innumerable phases, aspects, etc.: *the myriad mind of Shakespeare.* **6.** ten thousand. [t. Gk: s. *mȳriás* a number of ten thousand]

myriapod (mĭr′ĭ ə pŏd′), *n.* **1.** any arthropod of the group *Myriapoda*, having an elongated, segmented body with numerous three-jointed legs; formerly treated as a class embracing chiefly the centipedes and millipedes. —*adj.* Also, **myriapodous** (mĭr′ĭ ăp′ə dəs). **2.** belonging or pertaining to the *Myriapoda*. **3.** having very numerous legs. [t. NL: s. *Myriapoda*, pl., f. Gk: *mȳriá(s)* MYRIAD + s. *poús* foot + *-a*, neut. pl. ending]

myrica (mĭ rī′kə), *n.* **1.** the bark of the wax-myrtle. **2.** the bark of the bayberry. [t. L, t. Gk: m. *myríkē*]

myrmeco-, a word element meaning 'ant'. [t. Gk, comb. form of *mýrmēx*]

myrmecology (mû′mĭ kŏl′ə jĭ), *n.* the branch of entomology that treats of ants. —**myrmecological** (mû′mĭ kə lŏj′ĭ kl), *adj.* —**myr′mecol′ogist,** *n.*

myrmecophagous (mû′mĭ kŏf′ə gəs), *adj.* adapted for feeding on ants or termites, as the jaws, teeth, etc., of various anteaters.

myrmecophile (mû′mĭ kō fīl′), *n.* any species of foreign insect that lives more or less permanently in an ant colony.

myrmecophilous (mû′mĭ kŏf′ĭ ləs), *adj.* **1.** of myrmecophiles. **2.** of plants frequented by ants.

Myrmidon (mû′mĭ dən), *n., pl.* **Myrmidons, Myrmidones** (mû mĭd′ə nēz′). **1.** *Class. Legend.* one of the warlike people of ancient Thessaly who accompanied Achilles, their king, to the Trojan War. **2.** (*l.c.*) one who executes without scruple his master's commands.

myrobalan (mī rŏb′ə lən, mĭ-), *n.* the dried plumlike fruit of certain tropical trees of the genus *Terminalia*, used in dyeing and making ink. [t. L: s. *myrobalanum*, t. Gk: m. *myrobálanos* kind of fruit or nut]

Myron (mī′ə rən), *n.* fl. *c.* 450 B.C., Greek sculptor.

myrrh (mû), *n.* an aromatic resinous exudation from certain plants of the genus *Commibhora*, esp. *C. Myrrha*, a spiny shrub, used for incense, perfume, etc. [ME *mirre*, OE *myrre*, t. L: m. *myrrha*, *murra*, t. Gk: m. *mýrra*, ult. from Akkadian *murrû*; cf. Heb. *mor*, akin to *mar* bitter]

myrtaceous (mû tā′shəs), *adj.* **1.** belonging to the *Myrtaceae*, or myrtle family of plants, which includes the myrtle, the clove and allspice trees, the guava, the eucalyptus, etc. **2.** of, pertaining to, or resembling the myrtle. [t. LL: m. *myrtāceus* of myrtle]

myrtle (mû′tl), *n.* **1.** any plant of the genus *Myrtus*, esp. *M. communis*, a shrub of southern Europe with evergreen leaves, fragrant white flowers, and aromatic berries. This plant is used as an emblem of love and was anciently held sacred to Venus. **2.** *U.S.* any of certain plants of other families, as the common periwinkle, *Vinca minor*, and California laurel, *Umbellularia californica*. **3.** Also, **myrtle green.** dark green with bluish tinge. [ME, t. OF: m. *mirtile* myrtle berry, dim. of L *myrtus*, t. Gk: m. *mýrtos* myrtle]

myself (mī sĕlf′), *pron.* **1.** a reflexive form of *me*: *I cut myself.* **2.** an emphatic form of *me* or *I*, used **a.** as object: *I used it for myself.* **b.** in apposition to a subject or object: *I myself did it.* **3.** one's proper or normal self; one's normal state of mind (used after *be*, *become*, or *come to*): *I am myself again.*

Mysia (mĭs′ĭ ə), *n.* an ancient country in NW Asia Minor.

Mysore (mī sô′), *n.* **1.** a state in S India; enlarged in 1956 in conformance with linguistic boundaries. 23,586,772 pop. (1961); 74,326 sq. mi. *Cap.*: Bangalore. **2.** a town in this state, in the S part. 253,865 (1961).

mystagogue (mĭs′tə gŏg′), *n.* one who instructs persons before initiation into religious mysteries or before participation in the sacraments. [t. L: m. s. *mystagōgus*, t. Gk: m. *mystagōgós*] —**mystagogy** (mĭs′tə gŏj′ĭ), *n.* —**mystagogic** (mĭs′tə gŏj′ĭk), *adj.*

mysterious (mĭs tĭə′rĭ əs), *adj.* **1.** full of, characterized by, or involving mystery: *a mysterious stranger.* **2.** of obscure nature, meaning, origin, etc.; puzzling; inexplicable. **3.** implying or suggesting a mystery: *a mysterious smile.* [f. s. L *mystērium* MYSTERY[1] + -OUS] —**myste′riously,** *adv.* —**myste′riousness,** *n.*

—**Syn. 1.** secret, esoteric, occult, cryptic. MYSTERIOUS, INSCRUTABLE, MYSTICAL, OBSCURE refer to that which is not easily comprehended or explained. That which is MYSTERIOUS, by being unknown or puzzling, excites curiosity, amazement, or awe: *a mysterious disease.* INSCRUTABLE applies to that which is impenetrable, so enigmatic that one cannot interpret its significance: *an inscrutable smile.* That which is MYSTICAL has a secret significance, such as that attaching to certain rites, signs, and the like: *mystical symbols.* That which is OBSCURE is discovered or comprehended dimly or with difficulty: *obscure motives.* **2.** unfathomable; enigmatical.

mystery[1] (mĭs′tə rĭ, -trĭ), *n., pl.* **-ries. 1.** anything that is kept secret or remains unexplained or unknown: *the mysteries of nature.* **2.** any affair, thing, or person that presents features or points so obscure as to arouse curiosity or speculation: *a mystery story.* **3.** obscurity, as of something unexplained or puzzling: *proceedings wrapped in mystery.* **4.** obscure, puzzling, or mysterious quality or character. **5.** any truth unknowable except by divine revelation. **6.** (in the Christian religion) **a.** a sacramental rite. **b.** (*pl.*) the consecrated elements. **c.** the eucharist. **7.** an incident or scene in connection with the life of Christ, regarded as of special significance: *the mysteries of the Passion.* **8.** (*pl.*) ancient religions which admitted candidates by secret rites the meaning of which only the initiated might know. **9.** (*pl.*) rites or secrets known only to those specially initiated: *the mysteries of freemasonry.* **10.** a mystery play. [ME *mysterie*, t. L: m. *mystērium*, t. Gk: m. *mystḗrion*]

mystery[2] (mĭs′tə rĭ), *n., pl.* **-ries. 1.** *Archaic.* a craft or trade. **2.** *Archaic or Hist.* a guild, as of craftsmen, merchants, or the like. [ME *misterye*, t. ML: m. *misterium*, L *ministerium* MINISTRY]

mystery play, a medieval religious drama originating in the liturgy and usually dealing with the life, death, and resurrection of Christ.

mystic (mĭs′tĭk), *adj.* **1.** spiritually significant or symbolic, as the dove used in religious art to symbolize the Holy Ghost. **2.** of the nature of or pertaining to mysteries known only to the initiated: *mystic rites.* **3.** of occult character, power, or significance: *a mystic formula.* **4.** of obscure or mysterious character or significance. **5.** of or pertaining to mystics or mysticism. —*n.* **6.** one initiated into mysteries. **7.** one who claims to attain, or believes in the possibility of attaining, insight into mysteries transcending ordinary human knowledge, as by immediate intuition in a state of spiritual ecstasy. [ME *mystik*, t. L: m. s. *mysticus*, t. Gk: m. *mystikós* mystic, secret]

mystical (mĭs′tĭ kl), *adj.* **1.** mystic; occult. **2.** of or pertaining to mystics or mysticism: *mystical doctrines.* **3.** spiritually symbolic. **4.** *Rare.* mysterious; obscure in meaning. —**mys′tically,** *adv.* —**mys′ticalness,** *n.* —**Syn. 1.** See **mysterious.**

mysticism (mĭs′tĭ sĭz′əm), *n.* **1.** the beliefs, ideas, or mode of thought of mystics. **2.** the doctrine of an immediate spiritual intuition of truths believed to transcend ordinary understanding, or of a direct, intimate union of the soul with the Divinity through contemplation and love. **3.** obscure thought or speculation.

mysticize (mĭs′tĭ sīz′), *v.t.,* **-cized, -cizing.** to make mystical; give a mystical significance to. Also, **mysticise.**

mystify (mĭs′tĭ fī′), *v.t.,* **-fied, -fying. 1.** to impose upon (a person) by playing upon his credulity; bewilder purposely. **2.** to involve (a subject, etc.) in mystery or obscurity. [t. F: m. *mystifier*, f. *mysti(que)* mystic + *-fier* -FY] —**mys′tifica′tion,** *n.*

mystique (mĭs tēk′), *n.* **1.** an air of mystery or mystical power surrounding a particular person, object, pursuit, belief, etc. **2.** an incommunicable or esoteric quality; a secret known only to the devotees of a cult, etc. [t. F]

myth (mĭth), *n.* **1.** a traditional story, usually concerning some superhuman being or some alleged person or event, and which attempts to explain natural phenomena; esp., a traditional story about deities or demigods and the creation of the world and its inhabitants. **2.** stories or matter of this kind: *in the realm of myth.* **3.** any invented story. **4.** an imaginary or fictitious thing or person. **5.** *Sociol.* a collective belief that is built up in response to the wishes of the group rather than an analysis of the basis of the wishes. [t. NL: s. *mȳthus*, mod. var. of LL *mȳthos*, t. Gk: word, speech, tale, legend, myth] **—Syn. 1.** See **legend.**

myth., **1.** mythological. **2.** mythology.

mythical (mĭth′ĭ kl), *adj.* **1.** pertaining to, of the nature of, or involving a myth or myths. **2.** dealt with in myth, as a period. **3.** dealing with myths, as a writer. **4.** existing only in myth, as a person. **5.** having no foundation in fact; imaginary; fictitious: *his claim to be of royal blood is completely mythical.* Also, **myth′ic.** **—myth′ically,** *adv.*

mythicize (mĭth′ĭ sīz′), *v.t.*, **-cized, -cizing.** to turn into, or treat or explain as, a myth. Also, **mythicise.**

mytho-, a word element meaning 'myth'. [t. Gk, comb. form of *mȳ̂thos*]

mythol., **1.** mythological. **2.** mythology.

mythological (mĭth′ə lŏj′ĭ kl), *adj.* of or pertaining to mythology. Also, **myth′olog′ic.** **—myth′olog′ically,** *adv.*

mythologist (mĭ thŏl′ə jĭst), *n.* **1.** an expert in mythology. **2.** a writer of myths.

mythologize (mĭ thŏl′ə jīz′), *v.i.*, **-gized, -gizing.** **1.** to classify, explain, or write about myths. **2.** to construct or relate myths. **3.** to make into or explain as a myth; make mythical. Also, **mythologise.** **—mythol′ogiz′er,** *n.*

mythology (mĭ thŏl′ə jĭ), *n.*, *pl.* **-gies.** **1.** a body of myths, as that of a particular people, or that relating to a particular person: *Greek mythology.* **2.** myths collectively. **3.** the science of myths. [ME, t. LL: m. s. *mȳthologia*, t. Gk: legend]

mythomania (mĭth′ō mā′nyə), *n.* *Psychol.* lying or exaggerating to an abnormal degree. **—mythomaniac** (mĭth′ō mā′nĭ ăk′), *n.*, *adj.*

mythopoeic (mĭth′ō pē′ĭk), *adj.* myth-making; pertaining to the making of myths. [f. m. s. Gk *mȳthopoiós* making myths + -IC] **—myth′opoe′ism,** *n.* **—myth′opoe′ist,** *n.*

Mytilene (mĭt′ĭ lē′nĭ; *Gk* mē tē lĕ′nē), *n.* **1.** Formerly, **Kastro.** a port in and the capital of the island of Lesbos, in the Aegean. 25,758 (1961). **2.** Lesbos.

myx-, a word element meaning 'slimy'. Also, **myxo-.** [t. Gk, comb. form of *mýxa* slime, mucus]

myxoedema (mĭk′sĭ dē′mə), *n.* *Pathol.* a disease characterized by thickening of the skin, blunting of the senses and intellect, laboured speech, etc., associated with diminished functional activity of the thyroid gland. Also, *U.S.*, **myxedema.** [t. NL. See MYX-, OEDEMA] **—myxoedematous** (mĭk′sĭ dĕm′ə təs, -dē′mə təs), *adj.* **—myxoedemic** (mĭk′sĭ dĕm′ĭk), *adj.*

myxomatosis (mĭk′sə mə tō′sĭs), *n.* *Vet.* a highly infectious virus disease of rabbits: artificially introduced into Great Britain and Australia to reduce the rabbit population. [f. MYX- + -OMAT(A)+ -OSIS]

myxomycete (mĭk′sō mī sēt′), *n.* any one of the slime moulds (*Myxomycetes, Mycetozoa*), primitive organisms whose characteristics place them at the borderline between the plant and animal kingdoms.

myxomycetous (mĭk′sō mī sē′təs), *adj.* belonging or pertaining to the *Myxomycetes*, or slime moulds (sometimes regarded as a distinct phylum, *Myxophyta*, and sometimes as a class of *Thallophyta*), having characteristics of both animals and plants. [f. s. NL *Myxomycētes*, pl. (see MYXO-, -MYCETES) + -OUS]

Myxophyceae (mĭk′sō fĭs′ĭ ē′), *n.pl.* *Bot.* See **blue-green algae.**

N

N, n (ĕn), *n.*, *pl.* **N's** or **Ns, n's** or **ns.** **1.** a consonant, the 14th letter of the English alphabet. **2.** *Maths.* an indefinite constant whole number, esp. the degree of a quantic or an equation, or the order of a curve. **3.** *Print.* an en. **4.** *Chess.* knight.

N, **1.** *Chem.* nitrogen. **2.** north. **3.** northern.

N., **1.** nationalist. **2.** navy. **3.** new. **4.** noon. **5.** *Chem.* normal (strength solution). **6.** Norse. **7.** north. **8.** northern. **9.** November.

n-, *Chem.* normal (indicating an unbranched carbon chain in an aliphatic molecule).

n., **1.** (L *natus*) born. **2.** nephew. **3.** neuter. **4.** new. **5.** nominative. **6.** noon. **7.** *Chem.* normal (strength solution). **8.** noun. **9.** number.

na (nä, nə), *Obs. except Dial.* (*Chiefly Scot.*). —*adv.* **1.** no. **2.** not. —*conj.* **3.** nor. [Scot. var. of NO]

Na, *Chem.* (L *natrium*) sodium.

N.A., **1.** National Academy. **2.** North America. **3.** *Physics.* numerical aperture.

NAACP, *U.S.* National Association for the Advancement of Coloured People. Also, **N.A.A.C.P.**

Naafi (năf′ĭ), *n.* **1.** an organization which runs canteens, stores, etc., for servicemen and servicewomen at home and overseas. **2.** a canteen, etc., run by this organization. Also, **N.A.A.F.I.** [*N*(*avy*), *A*(*rmy, and*) *A*(*ir*) *F*(*orce*) *I*(*nstitutes*)]

naartjie (nä′tyĭ), *n.* *S African.* a clementine (orange). [t. Afrikaans]

Naas (nās), *n.* a town in the E Republic of Ireland, the county town of Kildare. 4023 (1961).

N.A.A.S., National Agricultural Advisory Service.

nab (năb), *v.t.*, **nabbed, nabbing.** *Colloq.* **1.** to catch or seize, esp. suddenly. **2.** to capture or arrest. [earlier *nap.* Cf. OE *hnæppan* strike]

Nabis (*Fr.* na bē′), *n.pl.* a group of late 19th-century French painters, led by Bonnard. [t. Heb.: m. *nābhi* prophet]

Nablus (nä′bləs), *n.* a town in NW Jordan. 75,000 (est. 1965). Ancient name, **Shechem.**

nabob (nā′bŏb), *n.* **1.** an Englishman who has grown rich in India. **2.** any very wealthy and powerful person. **3.** nawab. [t. Hind.: m. *nawwab.* See NAWAB] **—nabobery** (nā′bŏb′ə rĭ, nā bŏb′ə rĭ), **na′bobism,** *n.* **—na′bobish,** *adj.*

Nabokov (năb′ə kŏf′; *Russ.* ná′bə kəf), *n.* **Vladimir Vladimirovich** (*Russ.* vlă dē′mĭr vlă dē′mĭ rə vĭch), born 1899, U.S. writer and poet, born in Russia.

Naboth (nā′bŏth), *n.* *Bible.* a man of Jezreel whose vineyard was secured for the covetous Ahab by the scheming of Jezebel. I Kings 21.

nacelle (nə sĕl′), *n.* **1.** the enclosed part of an aeroplane, dirigible, etc., in which the engine is housed or passengers, etc., are carried. **2.** the car of a balloon. [t. F, g. LL *nāvicella*, dim. of L *nāvis* ship]

nacre (nā′kə), *n.* mother-of-pearl. [t. F, t. ML: m. *nacrum*, var. of *nacara*, ? t. Pers. (Kurdish): m. *nakára* pearl oyster]

nacreous (nā′krĭ əs), *adj.* **1.** of or pertaining to nacre. **2.** (of minerals) having a lustre resembling that of pearl.

Na-Dene (nə dĕn′), *n.* an American Indian linguistic phylum including Haida, Tlingit, and Athabascan.

nadir (nā′dĭə), *n.* **1.** the point of the celestial sphere vertically beneath any place or observer and diametrically opposite to the zenith. **2.** the lowest point, as of adversity. [ME, ult. t. Ar.: m. *nazīr* corresponding, opposite (i.e., to the zenith)]

nae (nā), *adj.*, *adv.* *Scot.* **1.** no. **2.** not. [var. of NO]

naething (nā′thĭng), *n.*, *adv.* *Scot.* nothing.

naevus (nē′vəs), *n.*, *pl.* **-vi** (-vī). *Dermatology.* any congenital anomaly, including various types of birthmarks and all types of moles. Also, *U.S.*, **nevus.** [t. L] **—naevoid** (nē′void), *adj.*

nag[1] (năg), *v.*, **nagged, nagging.** —*v.t.* **1.** to torment by persistent faultfinding, complaints, or importunities. —*v.i.* **2.** to keep up an irritating or wearisome faultfinding, complaining, or the like (often fol. by *at*). **3.** to cause continual pain, discomfort, or depression, as a headache, feeling of guilt, etc. [cf. MLG *naggen* irritate, provoke, Icel. *nagga* grumble, *nagg* grumbling] **—nag′ger,** *n.* **—nag′gingly,** *adv.*

nag[2] (năg), *n.* **1.** a small horse, or pony, esp. for riding. **2.** *Colloq.* a horse. **3.** an old or inferior horse. [ME *nagge*, c. D *negge*; akin to NEIGH]

nagana (nə gä′nə), *n.* a disease of cattle and other animals produced by the action of *Trypanosoma brucei* and carried by a variety of tsetse fly. It occurs only in certain parts of Africa. [t. Zulu: m. *u*(*lu*)*nakane*]

Nagano (nä gä′nō), *n.* a town in Japan, in central Honshu island. 172,836 (1965).

Nagaoka (nä gä′o͞o kə), *n.* a town in Japan, in N central Honshu island. 154,752 (1965).
Nagari (nä′gə rĭ), *n.* any of a group of Indian scripts, including Devanagari.
Nagasaki (năg′ə sä′kĭ), *n.* a seaport in SW Japan, on Kyushu island: the second military use of the atomic bomb, Aug. 9th, 1945. 252,630 (1940); 174,141 (1946); 405,479 (1965). See map under **Hiroshima.**
Nagercoil (nŭg′ə kĭl′), *n.* a town in India, in SE Kerala. 106,207 (1961).
Nagoya (nä′gə yə), *n.* a city in central Japan, on Honshu island. 1,935,430 (1965). See map under **Hiroshima.**
Nagpur (năg po͝oə′), *n.* a city in India, in NE Maharashtra: former capital of the Central Provinces and Berar. 643,659 (1961).
Naguib (nə gēb′), *n.* See **Neguib.**
Nagy (*Hung.* nŏdy), *n.* **Imre** (*Hung.* ēm′rĕ), 1896–1958, Hungarian statesman: prime minister 1953–55, 1956.
Nagyvárad (*Hung.* nŏdy′vá′rŏd), *n.* Hungarian name of **Oradea.**
Nah., Nahum.
Naha City (nä′hä), a seaport in and the capital of the Ryukyu Islands, on the W coast of S Okinawa island. 250,832 (1960).
Nahuatl (*Sp.* nȧ wȧ′tl), *n.* **1.** a group of peoples of southern Mexico and central America, including the Aztecs. **2.** a member of such peoples. **3.** any of a subgroup of Uto-Aztecan languages of these peoples. *—adj.* **4.** of or pertaining to the Nahuatl language or peoples.
Nahuatlan (nä wät′lən), *n.* **1.** any of the Nahuatl languages. *—adj.* **2.** of or pertaining to Nahuatl or Nahuatlan.
Nahum (nā′həm), *n.* **1.** a Hebrew prophet of the late seventh century B.C. **2.** a book of the Old Testament, the seventh among the Minor Prophets. [t. Heb.]
naiad (nī′ăd), *n., pl.* **-ads, -ades** (-ə dēz′). **1.** (*also cap.*) *Class. Myth.* one of a class of water-nymphs fabled to dwell in and preside over streams and springs. **2.** *Bot.* a plant of the genus *Naias*, or the family *Naiadaceae.* **3.** *Biol.* the aquatic larva or nymph of such insects as dragonflies, mayflies, etc. [t. L: s. *Nāias*, t. Gk]
naïf (nä ēf′), *adj.* naive. [t. F (masc.). See NAIVE]
nail (nāl), *n.* **1.** a slender piece of metal, usually with one end pointed and the other enlarged, for driving into or through wood, etc., as to hold separate pieces together. **2.** a thin, horny plate, consisting of modified epidermis, growing on the upper side of the end of a finger or toe. **3.** a measure of length for cloth, equal to $2\frac{1}{4}$ inches. **4. hard as nails,** (of a person) stern; tough. **5. hit the nail on the head,** to say or do exactly the right thing. **6. on the nail,** *Colloq.* on the spot, or at once. *—v.t.* **7.** to fasten with a nail or nails: *to nail the cover on a box.* **8.** to stud with or as with nails driven in. **9.** to shut (*up*) within something by driving nails in: *to nail goods up in a box.* **10.** to make fast or keep firmly in one place or position: *fear nailed him to the spot.* **11.** *Colloq.* to secure by prompt action; catch or seize. **12.** *Colloq.* to catch (a person) in some difficulty, a lie, etc. **13.** *Colloq.* to detect and expose (a lie, etc.). [ME; OE *nægl*, c. D *nagel* and G *Nagel*] **—nail′er,** *n.*
nailbrush (nāl′brŭsh′), *n.* a small brush with hard bristles, used for scrubbing fingernails.
nailfile (nāl′fīl′), *n.* a small file for trimming or shaping fingernails.
nail scissors, a small pair of scissors, often with a curved blade, used for trimming fingernails, etc.
nail set, a short tapering rod of steel used to drive a nail below, or flush with, the surface. Also, **nail punch, nail sett.**
nail varnish, a varnish, either colourless or of varying shades of pink, orange, or red, used by women to paint their nails. Also, **nail polish.**
nainsook (nān′so͝ok, năn′-), *n.* a fine, soft-finished cotton fabric, usually white, used for lingerie and infants' wear. [t. Hind.: m. *nainsukh*, lit., eye pleasure]
Nairn (nĕən), *n.* **1.** a burgh in Scotland, the county town of Nairnshire. 4899 (1961). **2.** Nairnshire.
Nairns., Nairnshire.
Nairnshire (nĕən′shĭə, -shə), *n.* a county in N Scotland. 8421 pop. (1961); 163 sq. mi. *Co. town:* Nairn. *Abbrev.:* Nairns. Also, **Nairn.**
Nairobi (nī rō′bĭ), *n.* the capital of Kenya, in the S part. 297,000 (est. 1961).
naive (nä ēv′), *adj.* having or showing natural simplicity of nature; unsophisticated; ingenuous. Also, **naïf, naïve.** [t. F, fem. of *naïf*, g. L *nātīvus* native, natural] **—naive′ly,** *adv.* **—Syn.** simple, unaffected; unsuspecting.
naivety (nī ēv′tĭ, nä ēv′tĭ), *n.* **1.** the quality of being naive; artless simplicity. **2.** a naive action, remark, etc. Also, **naiveté, naïveté** (nä ēv′tā). [t. F: m. *naïveté*, der. *naïve*]
naked (nā′kĭd), *adj.* **1.** without clothing or covering; nude. **2.** without adequate clothing. **3.** bare of any covering, overlying matter, vegetation, foliage, or the like: *naked fields.* **4.** bare, stripped, or destitute (*of* something specified): *trees naked of leaves.* **5.** without a sheath or customary covering: *a naked sword.* **6.** without carpets, hangings, or furnishings, as rooms, walls, etc. **7.** (of the eye, sight, etc.) unassisted by a microscope, telescope, or other instrument. **8.** defenceless or unprotected; unguarded; exposed, as to attack or harm. **9.** simple; unadorned: *the naked truth.* **10.** not accompanied or supplemented by anything else: *a naked outline of facts.* **11.** exposed to view or plainly revealed: *a naked vein.* **12.** plain-spoken; blunt. **13.** *Bot.* **a.** (of seeds) not enclosed in an ovary. **b.** (of flowers) without a calyx or perianth. **c.** (of stalks, etc.) without leaves. **d.** (of stalks, leaves, etc.) without hairs or pubescence. **14.** *Zool.* having no covering of hair, feathers, shell, etc. **15.** *Law. Obs.* unsupported, as by authority or consideration: *a naked assertion.* [ME *naked(e)*, OE *nacod*, c. G *nackt*] **—na′kedly,** *adv.* **—na′kedness,** *n.*
naked ladies, the autumn crocus, *Colchicum autumnale.*
Nakuru (nə ko͞o′ro͞o), *n.* a town in W central Kenya. 37,900 (est. 1962).
NALGO (năl′gō), *n.* National and Local Government Officers' Association. Also, **N.A.L.G.O.**
Nama (nä′mə), *n.* **1.** *Geol.* a period or system in southern Africa following the Waterberg-Matsap and preceding the Cape. **2.** a member of a Hottentot people of Namaqualand. **3.** a dialect of Hottentot. *—adj.* **4.** *Geol.* of or pertaining to a lower Palaeozoic period or system in southern Africa, roughly equivalent of Cambrian.
namable (nā′mə bl), *adj.* nameable.
Namangan (*Russ.* nə mȧn gȧn′), *n.* a city in the SW Soviet Union in Asia, in Uzbekistan. 138,000 (est. 1963).
Namaqualand (nə mä′kwə lănd′), *n.* a coastal region in the S part of South-West Africa, extending into Cape Province of the Republic of South Africa: inhabited by Hottentots. Also, **Namaland** (nä′mə lănd′).
Namatjira (nä′mə tyĭə′rə), *n.* **Albert,** 1902–59, Australian Aborigine painter.
namby-pamby (năm′bĭ păm′bĭ), *adj., n., pl.* **-bies.** *—adj.* **1.** weakly simple or sentimental; insipid. *—n.* **2.** namby-pamby verse or prose. **3.** a namby-pamby person. **4.** namby-pamby sentiment. [orig. a nickname, *Namby Pamby*, for Ambrose Philips, d. 1749, English poet; first used by Henry Carey in 1726 as title of poem ridiculing Philips's verses]
name (nām), *n., v.,* **named, naming.** *—n.* **1.** a word or a combination of words by which a person, place, or thing, a body or class, or any object of thought, is designated or known. **2.** mere designation as distinguished from fact: *king in name only.* **3.** an appellation, title, or epithet, applied descriptively, in honour, abuse, etc.: *to call him bad names.* **4.** a reputation of a particular kind given by common report: *a bad name.* **5.** a distinguished, famous, or great reputation; fame: *to seek a name for oneself.* **6.** a widely known or famous person. **7.** a personal or family name as exercising influence or bringing distinction. **8.** a body of persons grouped under one name, as a family or race. **9.** the verbal or other symbolic representation of a thing, event, property, relation, or concept. A **proper name** represents some particular thing or event. A **common name** (e.g. 'man') is the name of anything which satisfies certain indicated conditions. **10. in the name of, a.** with appeal to: *in the name of mercy, stop screaming!* **b.** by the authority of: *open in the name of the law!* **c.** on behalf of: *to vote in the name of others.* **d.** under the name of: *money deposited in the name of a son.* **e.** under the designation of; in the character of: *murder in the name of mercy.* **11. to one's name,** belonging to one: *not a penny to my name.* *—v.t.* **12.** to give a name to: *name a baby.* **13.** to call by a specified name: *to name a child Regina.* **14.** to specify or mention by name: *three persons were named in the report.* **15.** to designate for some duty or office; nominate or appoint: *I have named you for the position.* **16.** to specify: *to name a price.* **17.** to tell the name of: *name the capital of France.* **18.** to speak of. **19.** (in the House of Commons) to cite (a member) for contempt. [ME; OE *nama*, c. G *Name*; akin to L *nōmen*, Gk *ónoma*] **—nam′er,** *n.*

—Syn. 1. NAME, TITLE both refer to the label by which a person is known. NAME is the simpler and more general word, for appellation: *the name is John.* A TITLE is an official or honorary term bestowed on a person or the specific designation of a book, article, etc.: *the title of Doctor; Treasure Island is the title of a book.*

nameable (nā′mə bl), *adj.* that may be named. Also, **namable.**
name-day (nām′dā′), *n.* *Stock Exchange.* the day on which buying brokers pass to selling brokers the names of

the purchasers of the stocks since the last settlement. Also, **ticket day.**

name-dropper (nām′drŏp′ə), *n.* one who introduces casually into a conversation names of prominent people as though they are personal friends, in order to impress. —**name′-drop′ping,** *n.*

nameless (nām′lĭs), *adj.* **1.** unknown to fame; obscure. **2.** having no name. **3.** left unnamed: *a certain person who shall be nameless.* **4.** anonymous: *a nameless writer.* **5.** having no legitimate paternal name, as a child born out of wedlock. **6.** that cannot be specified or described: *a nameless charm.* **7.** too shocking or vile to be specified. —**name′lessly,** *adv.* —**name′lessness,** *n.*

namely (nām′lĭ), *adv.* that is to say; to wit: *two cities, namely, Paris and London.*

Namen (*Flem.* nȧ′mə), *n.* Flemish name of **Namur.**

nameplate (nām′plāt′), *n.* a plate outside a house bearing the name and, usually, the profession of the occupant, as used by doctors, dentists, etc.

namesake (nām′sāk′), *n.* **1.** one having the same name as another. **2.** one named after another. [alter. of *name's sake*]

name tag, a small disc or strip attached to the collar of a dog, cat, or other pet, stating owner, address, etc.

name tape, a tape on an article of clothing bearing the owner's name (used esp. for children at school).

namma (năm′ə), *n. Austral.* a depression in the ground forming a natural reservoir. Also, **namma hole.** [t. native Australian]

Namoi (năm′oi), *n.* a river in E Australia flowing NW through New South Wales to the river Darling. 525 mi.

Namur (nă mo͞oə′; *Fr.* nȧ mʏr′), *n.* **1.** a province in S Belgium. 372,611 pop. (est. 1963); 1413 sq. mi. **2.** a city in and the capital of this province. 32,345 (est. 1963). Flemish, **Namen.**

Nanchang (năn′chăng′), *n.* a city in and the capital of Kiangsi province in SE China. 520,000 (est. 1958).

Nancy (*Fr.* näɴ sē′), *n.* a city in NE France, in Meurthe-et-Moselle department: battles, 1477, 1914, 1944. 208,636 (1962).

Nanda Devi (nŭn′də dē′vĭ), a peak of the Himalayas in N India, in Uttar Pradesh. 25,661 ft.

Nanga Parbat (nŭng′gə pä′bŭt), a peak of the Himalayas in NW Kashmir. 26,660 ft.

nanism (nā′nĭz′əm), *n. Pathol.* a condition of abnormal smallness in size or stature.

nankeen (năng kēn′), *n.* **1.** a firm, durable, yellow or buff fabric, made orig. from a natural-coloured Chinese cotton but now from other cotton and dyed. **2.** (*pl.*) garments made of this material. **3.** a yellow or buff colour. **4.** a type of porcelain, blue on a white background. Also, **nankin.** [named after *Nankin* NANKING]

Nanking (năn′kĭng′), *n.* a city in and the capital of Kiangsu province; a port on the Yangtze in E China. 1,455,000 (est. 1958).

Nan Ling (năn′lĭng′), a mountain range in S China. Also, **Nan Shan.**

Nanning (năn′nĭng′), *n.* a city in and the capital of the Kwangsi Chuang Autonomous Region, S China. 260,000 (est. 1958).

nanny (năn′ĭ), *n., pl.* **-ies.** a nurse for children. [alter. of female Christian name *Ann.* See -Y²]

nannygai (năn′ĭ gī′), *n.* the redfish of Australia, *Centroberyx affinis.*

nanny-goat (năn′ĭ gōt′), *n.* a female goat.

nano-, 1. a prefix indicating one thousand-millionth, as a *nanosecond.* **2.** a prefix indicating very small size, as *nanoplankton.* [comb. form of L *nānus* dwarf; t. Gk: m. *nânos*]

nanoplankton (nā′nō plăngk′tən, năn′ō-), *n.* plankton of such a size that they can be seen only with the aid of a microscope.

nanosecond (năn′ō sĕk′ənd, nā′nō-), *n.* one thousand-millionth part of a second.

Nansen (năn′sən; *Norw.* nän′-), *n.* **Fridtjof** (*Norw.* frĕt′yŏf), 1861–1930, Norwegian arctic explorer, scientist, and diplomat.

Nan Shan (năn′shăn′), **1.** a broad mountain range in W China, in Chinghai and Kansu provinces. **2.** Nan Ling.

Nanterre (*Fr.* näɴ tĕr′), *n.* a town in N France, capital of Hauts-de-Seine department. 83,416 (1962).

Nantes (*Fr.* näɴt), *n.* **1.** a seaport in W France, the capital of Loire-Atlantique department, at the mouth of the river Loire. 240,028 (1962). **2. Edict of,** a law promulgated by Henry IV of France in 1598, granting considerable religious and civil liberty to the Huguenots: revoked by Louis XIV, 1685.

Nantucket (năn tŭk′ĭt), *n.* an island in the U.S., off SE Massachusetts: summer resort. 2804 (1960); 15 mi. long.

Naomi (nā′ə mī), *n. Bible.* the mother-in-law of Ruth. Ruth 1:2, etc. [t. Heb.]

naos (nā′ŏs), *n.* **1.** a temple. **2.** *Archit.* the central chamber, or cella, of an ancient temple. [t. Gk: temple]

nap¹ (năp), *v.,* **napped, napping,** *n.* —*v.i.* **1.** to have a short sleep; doze. **2.** to be off one's guard: *I caught him napping.* —*n.* **3.** a short sleep; a doze. [ME *nappe(n)*, OE *hnappian*, c. MHG *napfen*]

nap² (năp), *n., v.,* **napped, napping.** —*n.* **1.** the short fuzzy ends of fibres on the surface of cloth drawn up in napping. **2.** any downy coating, as on plants. —*v.t.* **3.** to raise a nap on. [ME *noppe*, OE *-hnoppa* (in *wullcnoppa*, mistake for *wullhnoppa* tuft of wool), c. MD and MLG *noppe*; akin to OE *hnoppian* pluck] —**nap′-less,** *adj.*

nap³ (năp), *n.* **1.** *Cards.* **a.** a game in which the players bid for the tricks they propose to win. **b.** a bid in this game to take all five tricks of a hand. **2. go nap,** to undertake to win all five tricks. **3.** napoleon (def. 1). [m. NAPOLEON]

nap⁴ (năp), *n., v.,* **napped, napping.** *Horseracing.* —*n.* **1.** a good tip. —*v.t.* **2.** to name (a certain horse) as the winner of a race. [special use of NAP³]

napalm (nā′päm), *n. Mil.* a highly incendiary jelly-like substance, used in bombs, flame-throwers, etc. [f. NA(PHTHA) + PALM(ITATE)]

nape (nāp), *n.* the back (of the neck). [ME]

napery (nā′pə rĭ), *n.* **1.** table linen; tablecloths, napkins, etc. **2.** linen for household use. [ME *naperie*, t. OF, der. *nape* tablecloth. See NAPKIN]

Naphtali (năf′tə lī′), *n. Bible.* **1.** a son of Jacob. Gen. 30:8. **2.** one of the 12 tribes of Israel. Num. 1:15, 43.

naphtha (năf′thə), *n.* **1.** a colourless, volatile liquid, a petroleum distillate (esp. a product intermediate between gasoline and benzine), used as a solvent, fuel, etc. **2.** any of various similar liquids distilled from other products. **3.** *Obs.* petroleum. [t. L, t. Gk]

naphthalene (năf′thə lēn′), *n. Chem.* a white crystalline hydrocarbon, $C_{10}H_8$, usually prepared from coal tar, used in making dyes, as a moth repellent, etc. Also, **naphthaline, naphthalin** (năf′thə lĭn). [f. NAPHTH(A) + AL(COHOL) + -ENE]

naphthene (năf′thēn), *n. Chem.* any of a group of hydrocarbon ring compounds of the general formula, C_nH_{2n}, derivatives of cyclopentane and cyclohexane, found in certain petroleums.

naphthol (năf′thŏl), *n. Chem.* **1.** either of two isomeric derivatives of naphthalene, having the formula $C_{10}H_7OH$, and occurring in coal tar, used as antiseptics and in dye manufacture. See **beta-naphthol. 2.** any of certain hydroxyl derivatives of naphthalene. Also, **naphtol** (năf′tŏl). [f. NAPHTH(A) + -OL²]

naphthyl group (năf′thĭl), *Chem.* the univalent group $C_{10}H_7$–. Also, **naphthyl radical.**

Napier (nā′pĭə), *n.* **1. Sir Charles James,** 1782–1853, English general. **2.** Also, **Neper. John.** 1550–1617, Scottish mathematician and inventor of logarithms. **3.** a town in E North Island, New Zealand. 28,000 (est. 1965).

Napierian logarithm (nə pĭə′rĭ ən), *Maths.* a logarithm using the number 2·718281828 . . . (*symbol: e*) as a base; natural logarithm. [named after John NAPIER]

Napier of Magdala (măg′də lə), **Robert Cornelis** (kô nē′-lĭs) **Napier, First Baron,** 1810–90, British field marshal.

Napier's bones, a device to facilitate multiplication and division, consisting of rectangular pieces of bone, ivory, or wood, each with one face divided into squares containing digits. [named after John NAPIER, who invented it]

napiform (nā′pĭ fôm′), *adj.* turnip-shaped, as a root. [f. s. L *nāpus* turnip + -(I)FORM]

napkin (năp′kĭn), *n.* **1.** a rectangular piece of linen, cotton cloth or paper, used at table to wipe the lips and hands and to protect the clothes. **2.** a square or oblong piece of linen, cotton cloth or paper for some other purpose: **a.** a towel. **b.** a baby's nappy. **c.** *Now Scot.* a handkerchief. [late ME *napekyn*, dim. of *nape* tablecloth, t. F: m. *nappe*, g. L *mappa* cloth. Cf. MAP]

napkin ring, a ring, band, or the like, in which a table napkin is inserted, esp. when the napkin is to be used again.

Naples (nā′plz), *n.* **1.** a seaport in Italy, in Campania. 1,246,652 (1966). See map under **Salerno. 2. Bay of,** the bay on which Naples is situated. 22 mi. long. Italian, **Napoli.**

Naples yellow, 1. a yellow pigment made from lead antimoniate, originally manufactured in Naples. **2.** the colour of this.

napoleon (nə pō′lyən), *n.* **1.** a former French gold coin, bearing a portrait of Napoleon (I or III). **2.** *Cards.* nap³ (def. 1). [named after NAPOLEON]

Napoleon I (nə pō′lyən) (*Napoleon Bonaparte*), 1769–1821, French general: emperor of France 1804–15. French, **Napoléon** (*Fr.* nȧ pô lē ôɴ′).

Napoleon II, (*Napoleon Bonaparte, Duke of Reichstadt*), 1811–32, son of Napoleon I (never ruled France).

Napoleon III, (*Louis Napoleon Bonaparte*), 1808–73, president of France 1848–52; emperor of France 1852–70 (son of Louis Bonaparte).

Napoleonic (nə pō′lĭ ŏn′ĭk), *adj.* pertaining to, resembling, or suggestive of Napoleon I, or, less often, Napoleon III, or their dynasty.

Napoleonic Code. See **Code Napoléon.**

Napoleonic Wars, a series of wars, 1805–1815, waged by France under Napoleon I against England, Prussia, Austria, and Russia, sometimes individually and sometimes as allies.

Napoli (*It.* nȧ′pȯ lē), *n.* Italian name of **Naples.**

napoo (nă po͞o′), *adj. Slang.* **1.** finished; used up. **2.** doomed; done for. [f. F: alter. of *il n'y a plus* there is no more]

nappe (năp), *n. Geol.* an overturned anticlinal fold of rock strata, often thrust away from its roots by earth movements.

napper[1] (năp′ə), *n.* **1.** one who raises a nap on cloth. **2.** a machine for putting a nap on cloth. [f. NAP[2] + -ER[1]]

napper[2] (năp′ə), *n.* one who naps or dozes. [f. NAP[1] + -ER[1]]

nappy[1] (năp′ĭ), *adj.* **1.** heady or strong, as ale. **2.** *Chiefly Scot.* tipsy. —*n.* **3.** *Chiefly Scot.* liquor, esp. ale. [prob. special use of NAPPY[3]]

nappy[2] (năp′ĭ), *n., pl.* **-pies.** *U.S.* a small dish, usually round and often of glass, with a flat bottom and sloping sides, for food, etc. Also, **nappie.** [orig. obscure]

nappy[3] (năp′ĭ), *adj.,* **-pier, -piest.** covered with nap; downy. [f. NAP[2] + -Y[1]]

nappy[4] (năp′ĭ), *n.* a piece of towelling, usually of muslin, cotton, or some disposable material, used for absorbing and containing a baby's excrement. [alter. of NAPKIN]

naprapathy (nə prăp′ə thĭ), *n. Med.* a system of treatment based on the belief that all diseases are caused by connective tissue and ligament disorders and can be cured by massage. [f. Czech *napra(va)* correction (cf. Russ. *napravit'* direct, guide) + -PATHY] —**naprapath** (năp′rə păth′), *n.*

Nara (nä′rə), *n.* a town in Japan, in S Honshu island. 160,641 (1965).

Narayangunge (nŭ rī′ən gŭnj′), *n.* a town in East Pakistan, in SE East Bengal. 162,054 (1961).

Narbada (nə bŭd′ə), *n.* a river flowing from central India W to the Arabian Sea. ab. 800 mi. Also, **Nerbudda.**

Narbonne (nä bŏn′; *Fr.* nȧr bŏn′), *n.* a town in S France, in Aude department: an important port in Roman times. 35,899 (1962).

narceine (nä′sĭ ĭn), *n. Chem.* a bitter, white, crystalline alkaloid, $C_{23}H_{27}NO_8$, contained in opium, possessing a weak, smooth, muscle-relaxing action. [f. L *narcē* (t. Gk: m. *nárkē* numbness, torpor) + -INE[2]]

narcissism (nä sĭs′ĭz′əm), *n. Psychol.* **1.** sexual excitement through admiration of oneself. **2.** erotic gratification derived from admiration of one's own physical or mental attributes: a normal condition at the infantile level of personality development. **3.** extreme admiration for oneself or one's own attributes; egoism; self-love. Also, **narcism** (nä′sĭz′əm). [t. G: m. *Narzissismus.* See NARCISSUS, -ISM] —**narcis′sist,** *n.* —**nar′cissis′tic,** *adj.*

narcissus (nä sĭs′əs), *n., pl.* **-cissuses, -cissi** (-sĭs′ī). **1.** any plant of the amaryllidaceous genus *Narcissus,* which comprises bulbous plants bearing showy flowers with a cup-shaped corona, as the narcissus, *N. poeticus,* and the wild daffodil, *N. pseudonarcissus.* **2.** (*cap.*) *Gk Legend.* a beautiful youth who fell in love with his own image in water, pined away, and was metamorphosed into the narcissus. [t. L, t. Gk: m. *nárkissos* the plant (so named from its narcotic properties)]

narco-, a word element meaning 'stupor' or 'narcosis'. [f. Gk: m. *nárko-,* comb. form of *nárkē* numbness]

narcolepsy (nä′kə lĕp′sĭ), *n. Pathol.* a condition characterized by an uncontrollable desire for, and short attacks of, sleep on all occasions. [b. NARCO(SIS) and (EPI)LEPSY] —**nar′colep′tic,** *adj.*

narcosis (nä kō′sĭs), *n.* **1.** a state of sleep or drowsiness. **2.** a temporary state of depression produced by a drug, or by heat, cold, or electricity. [t. NL, t. Gk: m. *nárkōsis* a benumbing]

narcosynthesis (nä′kō sĭn′thĭ sĭs), *n.* a treatment for psychiatric disturbances which uses narcotics.

narcotic (nä kŏt′ĭk), *adj.* **1.** having the power to produce narcosis, as a drug. **2.** pertaining to or of the nature of narcosis. **3.** pertaining to narcotics or their use. **4.** for the use or treatment of narcotic addicts. —*n.* **5.** any of a class of substances that blunt the senses, relieving pain, etc., and inducing sleep, and in large quantities producing complete insensibility, often used habitually to satisfy morbid appetite. **6.** an individual inclined towards the habitual use of such substances. [t. Gk: m. s. *narkōtikós* making stiff or numb]

narcotism (nä′kə tĭz′əm), *n.* **1.** the habit of taking narcotics. **2.** the action or influence of narcotics. **3.** narcosis. **4.** an abnormal inclination to sleep.

narcotize (nä′kə tīz′), *v.t.,* **-tized, -tizing.** to subject to a narcotic; stupefy. Also, **narcotise.** —**nar′cotiza′tion,** *n.*

nard (näd), *n.* **1.** an aromatic Himalayan plant, supposedly *Nardostachys jatamansi* (spikenard), the source of an ointment used by the ancients. **2.** the ointment. [ME, t. L: s. *nardus,* t. Gk: m. *nárdos*]

nardoo (nä do͞o′), *n.* **1.** any of the Australian species of the aquatic heterosporous ferns of the genus *Marsilea.* **2.** the spores of such a plant ground into a flour and eaten by Australian Aborigines. [t. native Australian]

nares (nĕə′rēz), *n.pl., sing.* **naris** (nĕə′rĭs). *Anat.* the nostrils or the nasal passages. [t. L, pl. of *nāris*]

Narew (*Pol.* nȧ′rĕf), *n.* a river in NE Poland, flowing into the river Bug a little above its junction with the Vistula: battle, 1915. ab. 290 mi. Russian, **Narev** (*Russ.* nȧ′rĭf).

narghile (nä′gĭ lĭ), *n.* an oriental tobacco pipe in which the smoke is drawn through water before reaching the lips; a hookah. Also, **nargile, nargileh** (nä′gĭ lĭ). [t. Pers.: m. *nārgīleh,* der. *nārgīl* coconut]

narial (nĕə′rĭ əl), *adj. Anat.* of or pertaining to the nares or nostrils. Also, **narine** (nĕə′rĭn, -rīn).

nark (näk), *Slang.* —*n.* **1.** an informer; a spy, esp. for the police. **2.** *Austral., N.Z.* a spoilsport or spiteful person. —*v.t.* **3.** to nag; irritate; annoy. —*v.i.* **4.** to act as an informer. [t. Gipsy: m. *nāk* nose]

Narragansett (nă′rə găn′sĭt), *n.* **1.** a North American Indian tribe of the Algonquian family, formerly found on Rhode Island, now extinct. **2.** a member of this tribe. **3.** the language of this tribe. [f. Algonquian: *naiagons* very small point of land + *et* on, in, along]

Narragansett Bay, an inlet of the Atlantic coast of the U.S., in E Rhode Island. 28 mi. long.

narrate (nă rāt′), *v.,* **-rated, -rating.** —*v.t.* **1.** to give an account of or tell the story of (events, experiences, etc.). —*v.i.* **2.** to relate or recount events, etc., in speech or writing. [t. L: m. s. *narrātus,* pp.] —**narra′table,** *adj.* —**narra′tor,** *n.* —**Syn. 1.** See **describe.**

narration (nă rā′shən), *n.* **1.** an account or story. **2.** the act or process of narrating. **3.** words or matter narrating something. **4.** *Rhet.* (in a classical speech) the third part, the exposition of the question.

narrative (nă′rə tĭv), *n.* **1.** a story of events, experiences, or the like, whether true or fictitious. **2.** narrative matter, as in literary work. **3.** the act or process of narrating. —*adj.* **4.** that narrates: *a narrative poem.* **5.** of or pertaining to narration: *narrative skill.* —**nar′ratively,** *adv.*

—**Syn. 1.** NARRATIVE, ACCOUNT, RECITAL, HISTORY are terms for a story of an event or events. NARRATIVE is the general term (for a story long or short; of past, present, or future; factual or imagined; told for any purpose; and with or without much detail). The other three terms apply primarily to factual stories of time already past. An ACCOUNT is usually told informally, often for entertainment, with emphasis on details of action, whether about an incident or a series of happenings. A RECITAL, an extended narrative usually with an informative purpose, emphasizes accuracy and exhaustive detail. A HISTORY, usually written and at some length, is characterized by a tracing of causes and effects, and by an attempt to estimate, evaluate, and interpret facts.

narrow (nă′rō), *adj.* **1.** of little breadth or width; not broad or wide: *a narrow room.* **2.** limited in extent or space, or affording little room: *narrow quarters.* **3.** limited in range or scope. **4.** lacking breadth of view or sympathy, as persons, the mind, ideas, etc. **5.** limited in amount, small, or meagre: *narrow resources.* **6.** straitened, as circumstances. **7.** barely sufficient or adequate; being barely that: *a narrow escape.* **8.** careful; minute, as a scrutiny, search or inquiry. **9.** *Dial. and Scot.* parsimonious or stingy. **10.** *Phonet.* pronounced with relatively tense muscles. —*v.i.* **11.** to become narrower. —*v.t.* **12.** to make narrower. **13.** to limit or restrict. **14.** to make narrow-minded. —*n.* **15.** a narrow part, place or thing. **16.** (*pl.*) a narrow part of a strait, river, ocean current, etc. [ME; OE *nearu,* c. OS *naru* narrow, D *naar* unpleasant] —**nar′rowly,** *adv.* —**nar′rowness,** *n.*

narrow boat, a long boat not more than 7 ft in the beam, used on certain British canals.

narrow gauge. See **gauge** (def. 14).

narrow-gauge (nă′rō gāj′), *adj.* (of a railway line) having a lesser gauge than standard guage.

narrow-minded (nă′rō mīn′dĭd), *adj.* having or showing a prejudiced mind, as persons, opinions, etc. —**nar′row-mind′edly,** *adv.* —**nar′row-mind′edness,** *n.* —**Syn.** bigoted; intolerant.

narthex (nä′thĕks), *n. Archit.* a vestibule along the facade of an early Christian or Byzantine church. [t. LGk; in Gk, giant fennel]

Narva (*Russ.* nàrʹvə), *n.* a seaport in the W Soviet Union in Europe: the Swedes defeated the Russians here, 1700. 21,300 (1965).

Narváez (*Sp.* nàr väʹěth), *n.* **Pánfilo de** (*Sp.* pänʹfē lō dě), *c.* 1478–1528, Spanish soldier and adventurer in America.

narwhal (näʹwəl), *n.* an arctic cetacean, *Monodon monoceros*, the male of which has a long, spirally twisted tusk extending forwards from the upper jaw. Also, **narwal, narwhale** (näʹwālʹ). [t. Sw. or Dan.: m. *narhval* (f. *nar* + *hval* whale). Cf. Icel. *nāhvalr*, lit., corpse whale (from corpselike colour of belly)]

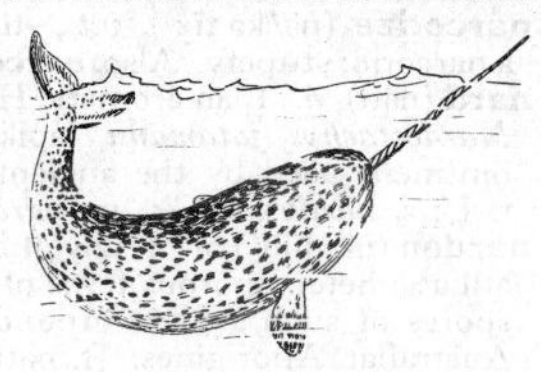
Narwhal, *Monodon monoceros* (Body ab. 12 ft long, tusk ab. 9 ft)

N.A.S.A., *U.S.* National Aeronautics and Space Administration.

nasal[1] (nāʹzəl), *adj.* **1.** of or pertaining to the nose. **2.** *Phonet.* with the voice issuing through the nose, either partly (as in French nasal vowels) or entirely (as in *m*, *n*, or the *ng* of *song*). —*n.* **3.** *Phonet.* a nasal speech sound. [t. NL: s. *nāsālis*, der. L *nāsus* nose. See NOSE] —**nasality** (nā zălʹĭ tĭ), *n.* —**naʹsally,** *adv.*

nasal[2] (nāʹzəl), *n.* a part of a helmet, protecting the nose and adjacent parts of the face. [late ME, t. OF, der. L *nāsus* nose]

nasal feed, the administration of nutrient liquids by means of a tube passed through the nose into the stomach.

nasal index, **1.** *Anat.* (of the skull) the ratio of the distance from the nasion to the lower margin of the nasal aperture to that of the maximum breadth of the nasal aperture. **2.** *Anat.* (of the head) the ratio of the maximum breadth of the external nose to its height from the nasal root to where the septum is confluent with the upper lip.

nasalize (nāʹzə līzʹ), *v.*, **-lized, -lizing.** *Phonet., etc.* —*v.t.* **1.** to pronounce as a nasal sound by allowing some of the voice to issue through the nose. —*v.i.* **2.** to nasalize normally oral sounds. Also, **nasalise.** —**naʹsalizaʹtion,** *n.*

nascent (năsʹənt), *adj.* **1.** beginning to exist or develop: *the nascent republic.* **2.** *Chem.* (of an element) being in the nascent state. [t. L: s. *nascens*, ppr., being born] —**nasʹcence, nasʹcency,** *n.*

nascent state, *Chem.* the condition of an element at the instant it is set free from a combination in which it has previously existed. Also, **nascent condition.**

naseberry (nāzʹbĕ′rĭ), *n.*, *pl.* **-ries.** **1.** the fruit of the sapodilla, *Achras zapota.* **2.** the sapodilla (tree). [t. Sp.: m. *néspera* medlar, g. L *mespila.* See MEDLAR]

Naseby (nāzʹbĭ), *n.* a village in central England, in Northamptonshire: Royalist defeat in the Civil War, 1645.

Nash (năsh), *n.* **1. John,** 1752–1835, English town-planner and architect. **2. Ogden,** born 1902, U.S. humorous poet. **3. Paul,** 1899–1946, English painter. **4. Richard** (*Beau Nash*), 1674–1762, English dandy. **5.** Also, **Nashe. Thomas,** 1567–1601, English author.

Nashville (năshʹvĭl), *n.* a city in the U.S., the capital of Tennessee, in the central part. 170,874 (1960).

Nasik (näʹshĭk), *n.* a town in India, in central Maharashtra. 131,103 (1960).

nasion (nāʹzĭ ən), *n.* *Anat.* the intersection of the internasal suture with the nasofrontal suture, in the midsagittal plane. [t. NL, der. L *nāsus* nose] —**naʹsial,** *adj.*

nasofrontal (nāʹzō frŭnʹtl), *adj.* of or pertaining to the nose and frontal bone.

nasopharynx (nāʹzō făʹrĭngks), *n.*, *pl.* **-pharynges** (-fə rĭnʹjēz), **-pharynxes.** *Anat.* the part of the pharynx behind and above the soft palate, directly continuous with the nasal passages (distinguished from *oropharynx*).

Nassau (năsʹô *for* 1; năsʹou, *Ger.* näʹsou *for* 2), *n.* **1.** a seaport in and the capital of the Bahamas, on the NE coast of New Providence island. 57,858 (1960). **2.** a district in central West Germany: formerly a duchy, now a part of Hesse.

Nasser (näʹsə, năsʹə), *n.* **Gamal Abdel** (gə mälʹ ăbʹdĕl), 1918–70, Egyptian military leader; member of group that dethroned Farouk in 1952; prime minister 1954–70; president of United Arab Republic 1958–70.

nastic (năsʹtĭk), *adj.* *Bot.* of or showing sufficiently greater cellular force or growth on one side of an axis to change the form or position of the axis. [f. s. Gk *nastós* squeezed together + -IC]

-nastic, a suffix forming adjectives of words ending in **-nasty.** [see NASTIC]

nasturtium (nə stûʹshəm), *n.* any of the garden plants constituting the genus *Tropaeolum*, much cultivated for their showy flowers of yellow, red, and other colours, and for their fruit, which is picked and used like capers. [t. L: a kind of cress]

nasty (näsʹtĭ), *adj.*, **-tier, -tiest.** **1.** physically filthy, or disgustingly unclean. **2.** offensive to taste or smell; nauseous. **3.** offensive; objectionable: *a nasty habit.* **4.** morally filthy; obscene. **5.** vicious, spiteful, or ugly: *a nasty dog.* **6.** bad to deal with, encounter, undergo, etc.: *a nasty cut.* **7.** very unpleasant: *nasty weather.* [ME, orig. uncert.] —**nasʹtily,** *adv.* —**nasʹtiness,** *n.*

-nasty, a suffix indicating irregularity of cellular growth because of some pressure. [f. s. Gk *nastós* squeezed together + -Y[3]]

nat., **1.** national. **2.** native. **3.** natural. **4.** naturalist.

N.A.T., National Arbitration Tribunal.

natal (nāʹtl), *adj.* **1.** of or pertaining to one's birth: *one's natal day.* **2.** presiding over or affecting one at birth: *natal influences.* **3.** *Chiefly Poetic.* (of places) native. [ME, t. L: s. *nātālis*]

Natal (nə tălʹ *for* 1; *Port.* nä tälʹ *for* 2), *n.* **1.** a province in the Republic of South Africa, in the E part. 2,979,920 pop. (1960); 35,284 sq. mi. *Cap.:* Pietermaritzburg. **2.** a seaport in E Brazil. 155,860 (1960).

natality (nə tălʹĭ tĭ), *n.* birthrate.

natant (nāʹtnt), *adj.* **1.** swimming; floating. **2.** *Bot.* floating on water, as the leaf of an aquatic plant. [t. L: s. *natans*, ppr.]

natation (nā tāʹshən), *n.* the act or art of swimming. [t. L: s. *natātio*] —**nataʹtional,** *adj.*

natatorial (nāʹtə tôʹrĭ əl), *adj.* pertaining to, adapted for, or characterized by swimming: *natatorial birds.* Also, **natatory** (nāʹtə tə rĭ, -trĭ). [f. s. LL *natātōrius* + -AL[1]]

natatorium (nāʹtə tôʹrĭ əm), *n.*, *pl.* **-toriums, -toria** (-tôʹrĭ ə). *U.S.* a swimming pool. [t. LL]

Natchez (năchʹĭz), *n.* (*sing. and pl.*) a member of an extinct Muskhogean American Indian tribe once living on the lower Mississippi.

nates (nāʹtēz), *n.pl.* the buttocks. [t. L, pl. of *natis*]

Nathan (nāʹthən), *n.* **George Jean,** 1882–1958, U.S. dramatic critic, author, and editor.

natheless (nāthʹlĭs), *Archaic.* —*adv.* **1.** nevertheless. —*prep.* **2.** notwithstanding. Also, **nathless** (năthʹlĭs). [ME *natheles*, OE *nāthēlǣs*, var. of *nāthȳlǣs*, f. *nā* never + *thȳ* for that + *lǣs* less]

nation (nāʹshən), *n.* **1.** an aggregation of persons of the same ethnic family, speaking the same language or cognate languages. **2.** a body of people associated with a particular territory who are sufficiently conscious of their unity to seek or to possess a government peculiarly their own. **3.** a member tribe of an Indian confederation. [ME, t. L: s. *nātio* race, people, nation; orig., birth] —**naʹtionhoodʹ,** *n.* —**naʹtionless,** *adj.* —**Syn. 2.** See **race**[2].

national (năshʹə nəl), *adj.* **1.** of, pertaining to, or maintained by a nation as an organized whole or independent political unit: *national affairs.* **2.** peculiar or common to the whole people of a country: *national customs.* **3.** devoted to one's own nation, its interests, etc.; patriotic. —*n.* **4.** a citizen or subject of a particular nation, entitled to its protection. —**naʹtionally,** *adv.*

National Aeronautics and Space Administration, a civilian agency coordinating U.S. aeronautical and space activities. *Abbrev.:* N.A.S.A.

national anthem, a patriotic hymn played or sung at public gatherings, official ceremonies, etc.

National Assembly, **1.** any of various national legislative bodies, esp. in French-speaking countries. **2.** *French Hist.* the first of the revolutionary assemblies, in session 1789–91.

national assistance, (in Britain) money paid by the state, in special circumstances, to persons (as the aged or unemployed) who are unable to live on other benefits. Now called **supplementary benefits.**

national bank, **1.** a governmentally owned and administered bank, as in some European countries. **2.** *U.S.* a bank chartered by the national government and formerly authorized to issue notes that served as money.

national church, the church established by law in a nation, generally the prevalent religion; established church.

National Convention, *French Hist.* the longest of the revolutionary assemblies, lasting from Sept. 1792 to Oct. 1795.

national debt, the financial indebtedness of a country in respect of money borrowed from individuals for national purposes, as opposed to the personal liabilities of its inhabitants.

National Gallery, a building, esp. that in Trafalgar Square, London, housing a collection of paintings owned by the nation and put on public exhibition.

national guard, **1.** an armed force in France established in 1789 and existing intermittently until 1871. **2.** (*cap.*) state military forces in the U.S., paid by and in part equipped, trained and quartered by the U.S. government, which become an active component of the army when called or ordered into federal service by the president.

National Health Service, the comprehensive health service, which came into force in 1948, enabling every person in Britain to obtain free medical treatment.

national income, *Econ.* the total net value of commodities produced and services rendered by all the people of a nation during a specified period.

national insurance, a scheme of state insurance by which, for weekly contributions paid by both employee and his employer, the employee is insured against sickness, unemployment, retirement, etc.

nationalism (năsh′nə lĭz′əm), *n.* **1.** national spirit or aspirations. **2.** devotion to the interests of one's own nation. **3.** desire for national advancement or independence. **4.** the policy of asserting the interests of a nation, viewed as separate from the interests of other nations or the common interests of all nations.

nationalist (năsh′nə lĭst), *n.* **1.** one inspired with nationalism. **2.** an advocate of national independence. **3.** (*cap.*) a member of a political group, as one advocating national independence or the advancement of one's national or racial group. —*adj.* **4.** Also, **na′tionalis′tic.** of or pertaining to nationalism or nationalists. **5.** (*cap.*) denoting or pertaining to a group or a member of a group advocating national independence. —**na′tionalis′tically,** *adv.*

Nationalist China, a country consisting mainly of the island of Taiwan, off the SE coast of the mainland of China. Official name, **Nationalist Republic of China.** 11,375,085 pop. (1962); 13,890 sq. mi. *Cap.*: Taipeh.

nationality (năsh′ə năl′ĭ tĭ), *n., pl.* **-ties. 1.** the quality of membership in a particular nation (original or acquired): *the nationality of an immigrant.* **2.** relationship of property, etc., to a particular nation, or to one or more of its members: *the nationality of a ship.* **3.** nationalism. **4.** existence as a distinct nation; national independence. **5.** nation or people: *the various nationalities of America.* **6.** national quality or character.

nationalize (năsh′nə līz′), *v.t.*, **-lized, -lizing. 1.** to bring under the control or ownership of a nation, as industries, land, etc. **2.** to make nationwide. **3.** to become naturalized. **4.** to make into a nation. Also, **nationalise.** —**na′tionaliza′tion,** *n.* —**na′tionaliz′er,** *n.*

national park, an area of land which is set aside for the purpose of preserving its natural features and wildlife for the enjoyment of the public.

national service, (in many countries) compulsory service for young men in the armed forces for a period varying from six months to three years.

National Socialism, the principles and practices of Hitler's **Nationalist Socialist German Workers'** (or Nazi) **Party.** See **Nazi.** —**National Socialist.**

National Trust, a charity founded in 1895 to preserve places of natural beauty or historic interest, for the public.

nationwide (nā′shən wīd′), *adj.* extending throughout the nation: *a nationwide campaign against cancer.*

native (nā′tĭv), *adj.* **1.** being the place or environment in which one was born or a thing came into being: *one's native land.* **2.** belonging to a person or thing by birth or nature; inborn; inherent; natural (often fol. by *to*). **3.** belonging by birth to a people regarded as natives, esp. outside the general body of white peoples: *native policemen in India.* **4.** of indigenous origin, growth, or production (often fol. by *to*): *native pottery.* **5.** of, pertaining to, or characteristic of natives: *native customs in Java.* **6.** under the rule of natives: *the native states of India.* **7.** occupied by natives: *the native quarter of Algiers.* **8.** belonging or pertaining to one by reason of one's birthplace or nationality: *one's native language.* **9.** born in a particular place or country: *native Frenchmen.* **10.** remaining in a natural state; unadorned; untouched by art: *native beauty.* **11.** forming the source or origin of a person or thing. **12.** originating naturally in a particular country or region, as animals or plants. **13.** found in nature rather than produced artificially, as a mineral substance. **14.** occurring in nature pure or uncombined, as metals, etc.: *native copper.* **15.** belonging to one as a possession by virtue of his birth: *native rights.* **16.** *Archaic.* closely related, as by birth. —*n.* **17.** one of the original inhabitants of a place or country, esp. as distinguished from strangers, foreigners, colonizers, etc.: *the natives of Chile.* **18.** one born in a particular place or country: *a native of Somerset.* **19.** an animal or plant indigenous to a particular region. **20.** an oyster raised in an artificial bed in British waters. **21.** *Astrol.* one born under a particular planet. [t. L: m. s. *nātīvus* native, innate, natural; r. ME *natif*, t. OF] —**na′tively,** *adv.* —**na′tiveness,** *n.*

native bear, *Austral.* the koala.

native-born (nā′tĭv bôn′), *adj.* born in a place or country indicated.

native companion, the brolga.

nativism (nā′tĭ vĭz′əm), *n.* **1.** the policy of protecting the interests of native inhabitants against those of immigrants. **2.** *Philos.* the doctrine of innate ideas. —**na′tivist,** *n.* —**na′tivis′tic,** *adj.*

nativity (nə tĭv′ĭ tĭ), *n., pl.* **-ties. 1.** birth. **2.** birth with reference to place or attendant circumstances: *of Irish nativity.* **3.** (*cap.*) the birth of Christ. **4.** (*cap.*) the church festival commemorating the birth of Christ; Christmas. **5.** (*cap.*) a representation of the birth of Christ, as in art. **6.** *Astrol.* a horoscope. [ME *nativite*, t. LL: m. s. *nātīvitas*]

NATO (nā′tō), *n.* North Atlantic Treaty Organization.

natrium (nā′trĭ əm), *n. Obs.* sodium.

natrolite (năt′rə līt′, nā′trə-), *n.* a zeolite mineral, a hydrous silicate of sodium and aluminium, $Na_2Al_2Si_3O_{10}.2H_2O$, occurring usually in white or colourless, often acicular, crystals. [f. NATRO(N) + -LITE]

natron (nā′trən), *n.* a mineral, hydrated sodium carbonate, $Na_2CO_3.10H_2O$. [t. F, t. Sp., t. Ar.: m. *natrūn*, t. Gk: m. *nítron* natron. See NITRE]

natter (năt′ə), *v.i.* **1.** *Colloq.* to chatter; gossip. —*n.* **2.** a chat.

natterjack (năt′ə jăk), *n.* a common European toad, *Bufo calamita.*

natty (năt′ĭ), *adj.*, **-tier, -tiest.** neatly smart in dress or appearance; spruce; trim: *a natty white uniform.* [? akin to NEAT[1]] —**nat′tily,** *adv.* —**nat′tiness,** *n.*

natural (năch′rəl), *adj.* **1.** existing in or formed by nature; not artificial: *a natural bridge.* **2.** based on the state of things in nature; constituted by nature: *the natural day.* **3.** of or pertaining to nature or the created universe: *a natural science.* **4.** occupied with the study of natural science. **5.** in a state of nature; uncultivated, as land. **6.** growing spontaneously, as vegetation. **7.** having a real or physical existence, as opposed to one that is spiritual, intellectual, fictitious, etc. **8.** of, pertaining to, or proper to the nature or essential constitution: *natural ability.* **9.** proper to the circumstances of the case. **10.** free from affectation or constraint: *a natural manner.* **11.** essentially pertaining; coming easily or spontaneously: *a manner natural to an aristocrat.* **12.** consonant with the nature or character of. **13.** in accordance with the nature of things: *it was natural that he should hit back.* **14.** based upon the innate moral feeling of mankind: *natural justice.* **15.** having or showing the nature, disposition, feelings, etc., befitting a person. **16.** in conformity with the ordinary course of nature; not unusual or exceptional. **17.** happening in the ordinary course of things, without the intervention of accident, violence, etc.: *a natural death.* **18.** by birth merely, and not legally recognized; illegitimate. **19.** based on what is learned from nature, rather than on revelation: *natural religion.* **20.** true to nature, or closely imitating nature. **21.** unenlightened or unregenerate: *the natural man.* **22.** being such by nature; born such: *a natural fool.* **23.** *Music.* **a.** neither sharp nor flat; without sharps or flats. **b.** changed in pitch by the sign ♮. —*n.* **24.** *Music.* (of horns and trumpets) having no mechanism and thus able to produce only the notes of the harmonic series. **25.** *Colloq.* a thing or a person that is by nature satisfactory or successful. **26.** *Music.* **a.** a white key on the pianoforte, etc. **b.** the sign ♮, placed before a note cancelling the effect of a previous sharp or flat. **c.** a note affected by a ♮, or a note thus represented. **27.** an idiot. [ME, t. L: s. *nātūrālis* by birth, in accordance with nature] —**nat′urally,** *adv.* —**nat′uralness,** *n.*

natural abundance, *Chem.* the abundance of each isotope in an element as it is found in nature.

natural frequency, the frequency of free oscillation of a system.

natural gas, combustible gas formed naturally in the earth, as in regions yielding petroleum, and consisting typically of methane with certain amounts of hydrogen and other gases, used as a fuel, etc.

natural history, **1.** the science or study dealing with all objects in nature. **2.** the aggregate of knowledge connected with such objects.

naturalism (năch′rə lĭz′əm), *n.* **1.** (in literature) **a.** a theory of writing developed originally in France in the late 19th century and used esp. of the novel. It purports to apply scientific methods to the objective description in detail of human actions and character, presenting a determinist view of life. **b.** any writing which represents life, actions, environment, etc., in naturalistic detail. **2. a.** (in the arts) a method of presenting nature in an accurate and lifelike form. **b.** a style of painting characterized by a close fidelity to nature (as distinct from *realism*). **3.** action arising from or based on natural instincts and desires alone. **4.** *Philos.* **a.** the view of the world which takes account only of natural elements and forces, excluding the supernatural or spiritual. **b.** the belief that all phenomena are covered by laws of science and that all teleological explanations are therefore without value. **c.** positivism or materialism. **5.** *Theol.* **a.** the doctrine that mankind apprehends eternal truths only by observation and deduction and never from direct revelation. **b.** the doctrine that man may be saved by his perception of, and actions directed by, verities so revealed to him. **6.** adherence or attachment to what is natural.

naturalist (năch′rə lĭst), *n.* **1.** one who is versed in or devoted to natural history, esp. a zoologist or botanist. **2.** an adherent of naturalism.

naturalistic (năch′rə lĭs′tĭk), *adj.* **1.** imitating nature or usual natural surroundings. **2.** pertaining to naturalists or natural history. **3.** pertaining to naturalism, esp. in art and literature.

naturalize (năch′rə līz′), *v.*, **-lized, -lizing.** —*v.t.* **1.** to invest (an alien) with the rights and privileges of a subject or citizen; confer the rights and privileges of citizenship upon. **2.** to introduce (animals or plants) into a region and cause to flourish as if native. **3.** to introduce or adopt (foreign practices, words, etc.) into a country or into general use: *to naturalize a French phrase.* **4.** to bring into conformity with nature. **5.** to regard or explain as natural rather than supernatural: *to naturalize miracles.* **6.** to adapt or accustom to a place or to new surroundings. —*v.i.* **7.** to become naturalized, or as if native. Also, **naturalise.** —**nat′uraliza′tion,** *n.*

natural law, the expression of right reason or of religion, inhering in nature and man, and having ethically a binding force as a rule of civil conduct.

natural logarithm, Napierian logarithm.

natural philosophy, the branch of physical science which treats of those properties and phenomena of bodies which are unaccompanied by an essential change in the bodies themselves, including the sciences classed under physics, esp. in Scottish universities.

natural region, an area of the earth's surface with general similarity of landscape and characterized by a degree of uniformity of physical characteristics such as structure, relief, climate, and vegetation.

natural resources, the wealth of a country consisting of land, forests, mines, water and energy resources.

natural science, science or knowledge dealing with objects in nature, as distinguished from mental or moral science, abstract mathematics, etc.

natural selection, the elimination of the unfit and the survival of the fit in the struggle for existence, resulting in the adaptation of a species to a specific environment. Cf. **Darwinism.**

natural sine, tangent, etc., *Maths.* the actual value, not the logarithm, of a sine (tangent, etc.).

natural vegetation, the indigenous flora of an area unaltered by man's activities.

nature (nā′chə), *n.* **1.** the particular combination of qualities belonging to a person or thing by birth or constitution; native or inherent character: *the nature of atomic energy.* **2.** the instincts or inherent tendencies directing conduct: *a man of good nature.* **3.** character, kind, or sort: *a book of the same nature.* **4.** a person of a particular character or disposition. **5.** the material world, esp. as surrounding man and existing independently of his activities. **6.** the universe, with all its phenomena. **7.** the sum total of the forces at work throughout the universe. **8.** reality, as distinguished from any effect of art: *true to nature.* **9.** the physical being. **10.** the vital powers: *food sufficient to sustain nature.* **11.** a primitive, wild condition; an uncultivated state. **12.** *Theol.* the moral state as unaffected by grace. **13. by nature,** as a result of inherent qualities. **14. of** or **in the nature of,** having the qualities of. [ME, *natur*, t. L: s. *nātūra* birth, natural character, nature]

nature reserve, (in England and Wales) a region set aside for the preservation of animal and bird life.

nature study, the study of physical nature, esp. in primary schools.

naturism (nā′chə rĭz′əm), *n.* nudism. —**na′turist,** *n., adj.*

Naucratis (nô′krə tĭs), *n.* an ancient Greek city in N Egypt, on the delta of the Nile. Greek, **Naukratis.**

naught (nôt), *n.* **1.** *Now Archaic or Literary.* nothing. **2.** destruction, ruin, or complete failure: *to bring or come to naught.* **3.** *Chiefly U.S.* nought (def. 1). **4. set at naught,** to regard or treat as of no importance. —*adj. Obs. or Archaic.* **5.** worthless; useless. **6.** lost; ruined. **7.** morally bad; wicked. —*adv.* **8.** *Obs. or Archaic.* in no respect or degree. Also, **nought.** [ME; OE *nauht*, *nāwiht*, f. *nā* NO + *wiht* thing. See NOUGHT, WIGHT[1], WHIT]

naughty (nô′tĭ), *adj.*, **-tier, -tiest.** **1.** disobedient; mischievous (esp. in speaking to or about children): *a naughty child.* **2.** improper; obscene: *a naughty word.* **3.** *Obs.* wicked; evil. [ME, f. NAUGHT (def. 7) + -Y[1]] —**naugh′tily,** *adv.* —**naugh′tiness,** *n.*

naumachia (nô mā′kyə), *n.*, *pl.* **-chiae** (-kĭ ē′), **-chias.** **1.** a mock sea-fight, given as a spectacle among the ancient Romans. **2.** a place for presenting such spectacles. [t. L, t. Gk]

naumachy (nô′mə kĭ), *n.*, *pl.* **-chies.** naumachia.

nauplius (nô′plĭ əs), *n.*, *pl.* **-plii** (-plĭ ī′). (in many crustaceans) a larval form with three pairs of appendages and a single median eye, occurring (usually) as the first stage of development after leaving the egg. [t. L: kind of shellfish]

Nauru (nä ōō′rōō), *n.* a Pacific island near the equator, W of the Gilbert Islands: an independent member of the Commonwealth of Nations. 4849 pop. (1962); 8¼ sq. mi. Formerly, **Pleasant Island.**

Nauruan (nä ōō′rōō ən), *adj.* **1.** of or pertaining to Nauru or its inhabitants. —*n.* **2.** an inhabitant of Nauru.

nausea (nô′syə), *n.* **1.** sickness at the stomach; a sensation of impending vomiting. **2.** extreme disgust. **3.** *Obs.* seasickness. [t. L, var. of *nausia*, t. Gk]

nauseate (nô′sĭ āt′), *v.*, **-ated, -ating.** —*v.t.* **1.** to affect with nausea; sicken. **2.** to feel extreme disgust at; loathe. —*v.i.* **3.** to become affected with nausea. [t. L: m. s. *nauseātus*, pp., having been seasick] —**nau′sea′tion,** *n.*

nauseous (nô′syəs), *adj.* **1.** causing nausea, or sickening. **2.** disgusting; loathsome. [t. L: m. s. *nauseōsus*] —**nau′seously,** *adv.* —**nau′seousness,** *n.*

Nausicaä (nô sĭk′ĭ ə), *n.* *Gk Legend.* the daughter of Alcinous, king of the Phaeacians. She led the shipwrecked Odysseus to her father's court.

naut., nautical.

nautch (nôch), *n.* an Indian exhibition of dancing by professional dancing girls (**nautch girls**). [t. Hind.: m. *nāch*, g. Prakrit *nachcha* dancing]

nautical (nô′tĭ kl), *adj.* of or pertaining to seamen, ships, or navigation: *nautical terms.* [f. s. L *nauticus* (t. Gk: m. *nautikós* pertaining to ships or sailors) + -AL[1]] —**nau′tically,** *adv.*

nautical mile, mile (def. 1b).

nautilus (nô′tĭ ləs), *n.*, *pl.* **-luses, -li** (-lī′). **1.** any of the tetrabranchiate cephalopods that constitute the genus *Nautilus*, having a spiral, chambered shell with pearly septa; pearly nautilus. **2.** the paper nautilus or argonaut. [t. L, t. Gk: m. *nautílos*, lit., sailor]

nav., **1.** naval. **2.** navigation.

Navaho (năv′ə hō′), *n.*, *pl.* **-hos, -hoes.** **1.** (*pl.*) the principal tribe of the southern division of the Athabascan stock of North American Indians, found in New Mexico and Arizona, and now constituting the largest tribal group in the U.S. **2.** a member of this tribe. **3.** the language of this tribe. —*adj.* **4.** of or pertaining to the Navaho people, language, etc. Also, **Navajo** (năv′ə hō′). [t. Sp.: m. (*Apaches de*) *Navajo*, t. Tewa: m. *navahu* great fields, applied to former Tewa pueblo and by extension to the Navahos who intruded upon the agricultural pueblos]

naval (nā′vəl), *adj.* **1.** of or pertaining to ships, esp., and now only, ships of war: *a naval battle.* **2.** belonging to, pertaining to, or connected with, a navy: *naval affairs.* **3.** possessing a navy: *the great naval powers.* [t. L: s. *nāvālis* pertaining to a ship]

naval college, a collegiate institution for training naval officers. Also, *U.S.*, **naval academy.**

Navarino (năv′ə rē′nō), *n.* a seaport in SW Greece, in the Peloponnesus: the Turkish and Egyptian fleets were defeated in a naval battle near here, 1827. Greek, **Pilos.**

Navarre (nə vä′), *n.* a former kingdom in SW France and N Spain. Spanish, **Navarra** (*Sp.* nä bär′rä).

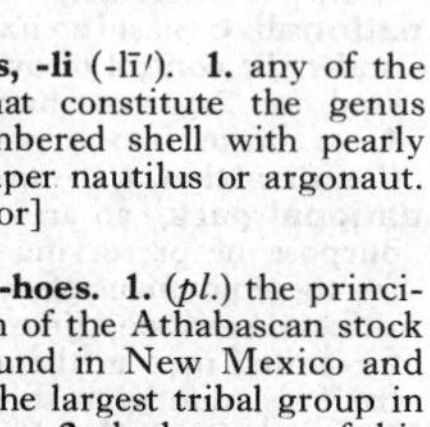

Kingdom of Navarre, 1492

nave[1] (nāv), *n.* the main body, or middle part, lengthwise, of of a church, flanked by the aisles and extending typically from the entrance to the apse or chancel. See diag. under **basilica.** [t. ML: m. s. *nāvis* nave of a church, L ship]

nave[2] (nāv), *n.* **1.** the central part of a wheel; the hub. **2.** *Obs.* the navel. [ME; OE *nafu*, c. G *Nabe*]

navel (nā′vəl), *n.* **1.** a pit or depression in the middle of the surface of the belly; the umbilicus. **2.** the central point or middle of any thing or place. [ME; OE *nafela*, c. G *Nabel*] —**na′vel-like′,** *adj.*

navel orange, a kind of orange having at the apex a navel-like formation containing a small secondary fruit.

navel pipe, *Naut.* a pipe going down through the deck and through which the anchor cable runs. Also, **naval pipe.**

navelwort (nā′vəl wût′), *n.* a perennial, fleshy, saxifragaceous herb with peltate leaves and spikes of small yellow-green flowers, *Umbilicus rupestris*, occurring on rocks and walls in W Europe and Mediterranean regions.

navicert (năv′ĭ sût′), *n.* a certificate granted by a belligerent in wartime, specifying the character of a neutral ship's cargo, etc. [f. L *nāvi(s)* ship + CERT(IFICATE)]

navicular (nə vĭk′yŏŏ lə), *Anat.* —*adj.* **1.** (of certain bones, etc.) boat-shaped. —*n.* Also, **naviculare** (nə vĭk′yŏŏ lä′rĭ). **2.** the bone at the radial end of the proximal row of the bones of the carpus. **3.** the bone in front of the talus, or anklebone, on the inner side of the foot. [t. LL: s. *nāviculāris* relating to ships]

navig., navigation.

navigable (năv′ĭ gə bl), *adj.* that may be navigated, as waters, or vessels or aircraft. —**nav′igabil′ity, nav′igableness,** *n.* —**nav′igably,** *adv.*

navigate (năv′ĭ gāt′), *v.,* **-gated, -gating.** —*v.t.* **1.** to traverse (the sea, a river, etc.) in a vessel, or (the air) in an aircraft. **2.** to direct or manage (a ship, aircraft, etc.) on its course. **3.** to pass over (the sea, etc.), as a ship does. —*v.i.* **4.** to direct or manage a ship, aircraft, etc., on its course. **5.** to travel by using a ship or boat, as over the water; sail. **6.** to pass over the water, as a ship does. [t. L: m. s. *nāvigātus,* pp.]

navigation (năv′ĭ gā′shən), *n.* **1.** the act or process of navigating. **2.** the art or science of directing the course of a ship or aircraft. **3.** an artificial waterway; a canal. —nav′iga′tional, *adj.*

Navigation Acts, a series of acts, the first of which was passed in 1651, aiming at the expansion of British trade and the establishment of Britain as the supreme naval power.

navigator (năv′ĭ gā′tə), *n.* **1.** one who navigates. **2.** one who practises, or is skilled in, navigation, of ships, aircraft, etc. **3.** one who conducts explorations by sea. **4.** a navvy or labourer. [t. L]

Navigators Islands, former name of **Samoa.**

navvy (năv′ĭ), *n., pl.* **-vies.** a labourer employed in making roads, railways, canals, etc. [short for NAVIGATOR]

navy (nā′vĭ), *n., pl.* **-vies.** **1.** the whole body of warships and auxiliaries belonging to a country or ruler. **2.** such a body of warships together with their officers and men, equipment, yards, etc. **3.** Also, **navy blue.** a dark blue, as of a naval uniform. **4.** *Archaic.* a fleet of ships. [ME *navie,* t. OF, der. L *nāvis* ship]

navy yard, *U.S.* a dockyard.

nawab (nə wôb′, nə wäb′), *n.* **1.** a viceroy or deputy governor under the former Mogul empire in India. **2.** an honorary title conferred upon Muslims of distinction in India. Cf. **raja. 3.** nabob. [t. Hind.: m. *nawwāb,* t. Ar.: pl. of *nā′ib* deputy, viceroy]

NAWCH (nôch), *n.* National Association for the Welfare of Children in Hospital.

Naxos (năk′sŏs), *n.* a Greek island in the S Aegean: the largest of the Cyclades group. 18,593 pop. (1951); 169 sq. mi.

nay (nā), *adv.* **1.** no (used in dissent, denial, or refusal). **2.** also; and not only so; but: *many good, nay, noble qualities.* —*n.* **3.** a denial or refusal. **4.** a negative vote or voter. [ME *nai, nei,* t. Scand.; cf. Icel. *nei* no, f. *ne* not + *ei* ever]

Nazarene (năz′ə rēn′), *n.* **1.** a native or inhabitant of the town of Nazareth, as Jesus Christ (**the Nazarene**). **2.** a Christian (so called by the Jews, Muslims, etc.). **3.** one of a sect of early Jewish Christians who retained the Mosaic ritual. —*adj.* **4.** of or pertaining to Nazareth or the Nazarenes. [ME *Nazaren,* t. LL: s. *Nazarēnus,* t. Gk: m. *Nazarēnós,* der. *Nazarét* Nazareth]

Nazareth (năz′ə rĭth), *n.* a town in N Israel: the childhood home of Jesus. 26,400 (est. 1963). See maps under **Galilee** and **Jericho.**

Nazarite (năz′ə rīt′), *n.* **1.** (among the ancient Hebrews) a religious devotee who had taken certain vows. Num. 6. **2.** *Rare.* a Nazarene. **3.** *Rare.* Christian. **4.** *Rare.* Christ. Also, **Nazirite.** [f. L *Nazar(aeus)* (t. Gk: m. *Nazaraîos,* der. Heb. *nāzar* consecrate) + -ITE[1]]

naze (nāz), *n.* headland (def. 1).

Naze (nāz), *n.* **The,** Lindesnes.

Nazi (nät′sĭ), *n., pl.* **-zis,** *adj.* —*n.* **1.** a member of the National Socialist German Workers' party of Germany, which in 1933, under Adolf Hitler, obtained political control of the country, suppressing all opposition and establishing a dictatorship on the principles of one-party control over all cultural, economic, and political activities of the people, belief in the supremacy of Hitler as Führer, anti-Semitism, and the establishment of Germany by superior force as a dominant world power. **2.** one who holds (or held) similar views elsewhere. —*adj.* **3.** of or pertaining to the Nazis. [t. G, short for *Nazi(onalsozialist)* National Socialist]

Nazirite (năz′ə rīt′), *n.* Nazarite.

Nazism (nät′sĭz′əm), *n.* the principles or methods of the Nazis. Also, **Naziism** (nät′sĭ ĭz′əm).

Nb, *Chem.* niobium.

N.B., 1. New Brunswick. **2.** Also, **NB.** nota bene.

n.b., *Cricket.* no ball.

N.C., North Carolina.

N.C.B., National Coal Board.

NCO, non-commissioned officer. Also, **n.c.o.**

Nd, *Chem.* neodymium.

n.d., no date.

N Dak., North Dakota. Also, **N.D.**

Ndola (ən dō′lə), *n.* a town in N Zambia. 80,000 (est. 1963).

Ne, *Chem.* neon.

NE, 1. north-east. **2.** north-eastern. Also, **n.e.**

N.E., 1. New England. **2.** north-east. **3.** north-eastern.

Neagh (nā), *n.* **Lough,** the largest lake in the British Isles, forming the border of counties Antrim, Armagh, Tyrone, and Londonderry in N Ireland. 147 sq. mi.

Neanderthal (nĭ ăn′də täl′), *adj. Anthropol.* of or pertaining to the Neanderthal man.

Neanderthal man, *Anthropol.* the species of primeval man widespread in Europe in the Palaeolithic period. [so called because earliest evidence was discovered at *Neanderthal,* a valley near Düsseldorf, Germany]

Neanderthaloid (nĭ ăn′də tä′loid), *Anthropol.* —*adj.* **1.** characteristic of the Neanderthal man. —*n.* **2.** a species of primeval man, having the characteristics of the Neanderthal man.

neap[1] (nēp), *adj.* **1.** designating those tides, midway between spring tides, which attain the least height. —*n.* **2.** neap tide. See diag. under **tide.** [ME *neep,* OE *nēp,* in *nēpflōd* neap flood]

neap[2] (nēp), *n. U.S. Dial.* the pole or tongue of a wagon, etc. [orig. uncert.]

Neapolitan (nĭə pŏl′ĭ tən), *adj.* **1.** of or pertaining to Naples. **2.** (*l.c.*) variously flavoured and coloured, as ice-cream. —*n.* **3.** a native or inhabitant of Naples. [ME, t. L: s. *Neāpolitānus*]

near (nĭə), *adv.* **1.** close: *near by.* **2.** nigh; at, within, or to a short distance: *to stand near.* **3.** close at hand in time: *New Year's Day is near.* **4.** close in relation; closely with respect to connection, similarity, etc. **5.** *Now Chiefly Colloq. or Dial.* all but; almost: *a period of near thirty years.* **6.** *Naut.* close to the wind. **7. near at hand,** close by. —*adj.* **8.** being close by; not distant: *the near meadows.* **9.** less distant: *the near side.* **10.** short or direct: *the near road.* **11.** close in time: *the near future.* **12.** closely related or connected: *our nearest relation.* **13.** close to an original: *a near translation.* **14.** closely affecting one's interests or feelings: *a matter of near consequence to one.* **15.** intimate or familiar: *a near friend.* **16.** narrow: *a near escape.* **17.** parsimonious or niggardly: *a near man.* **18.** (in riding or driving) on the left (opposed to *off*): *the near wheel.* —*prep.* (*strictly the adverb with 'to' understood*). **19.** at, within, or to a short distance, or no great distance, from: *regions near the equator.* **20.** close upon in time: *near the beginning of the year.* **21.** close upon (a condition, etc.): *a task near completion.* **22.** close to in similarity, resemblance, etc.: *near beer.* **23.** close to (doing something): *this act came near spoiling his chances.* —*v.t., v.i.* **24.** to come or draw near (to); approach. [ME *nere,* OE *nēar,* compar. of *nēah* NIGH] —**near′ness,** *n.*

nearby (nĭə′bī′), *adj.* **1.** close at hand; not far off; adjacent; neighbouring: *a nearby village.* —*adv.* **2.** close at hand; not far off.

Nearctic (nĭ äk′tĭk), *adj.* (in zoogeography) belonging to the northern division of the New World (temperate and arctic North America, with Greenland).

Near East, an indefinite geographical or regional term, usually referring to the Balkan States, Egypt, and the countries of SW Asia.

near-hand (nĭə′hănd′), *adv. Dial and Scot.* **1.** near at hand. **2.** nearly or almost.

nearly (nĭə′lĭ), *adv.* **1.** all but; almost: *nearly dead with cold.* **2.** with close approximation. **3.** with close agreement or resemblance: *a case nearly approaching this one.* **4.** with close kinship, interest, or connection; intimately. **5.** with parsimony. —**Syn. 1.** See **almost.**

near miss, 1. a narrow escape, as from a crash. **2.** a bomb, shell, etc., which does not score a direct hit on a target, but lands close enough to damage it. **3.** *Colloq.* anything which just fails to achieve an object or aim.

nearside (nĭə′sīd′), *adj.* **1.** of or pertaining to the left-hand side of a motor vehicle in a country where traffic drives on the left. **2.** of or pertaining to the side of a road nearer to the footpath. —*n.* **3.** the left-hand side of a vehicle, or the like.

near-sighted (nīə′sī′tĭd), *adj.* seeing distinctly at a short distance only; myopic. —**near′-sight′edly,** *adv.* —**near′-sight′edness,** *n.*

neat[1] (nēt), *adj.* **1.** in a pleasingly orderly condition: *a neat room.* **2.** habitually orderly in appearance, etc. **3.** of a simple, pleasing appearance: *a neat cottage.* **4.** cleverly effective in character or execution: *a neat scheme.* **5.** clever, dexterous, or apt: *a neat characterization.* **6.** unadulterated or undiluted, as liquors. **7.** net: *neat profits.* [t. F: m. *net* clean, g. L *nitidus* bright, fine, neat] —**neat′ly,** *adv.* —**neat′ness,** *n.*

—**Syn.** 1. NEAT, TIDY, TRIM describe orderliness and an attractive appearance. NEAT suggests order and absence of superfluous details: *a neat desk, dress.* TIDY suggests a painstaking orderliness, the result of effort and perhaps of habit, and it may therefore have working-class connotations: *the cottage looked cheerful and tidy.* TRIM suggests a combination of neatness and smartness or stylishness: *a trim new outfit.* —**Ant.** 1. slovenly.

neat[2] (nēt), *n., pl.* **neat.** *Obs.* cattle of the genus *Bos.* [ME *neet,* OE *nēat,* c. Icel. *naut*]

neaten (nē′tn), *v.t.* to make (something) neat.

neath (nēth), *prep. Poetic or Scot.* beneath. Also, **'neath.**

Neath (nēth), *n.* a town in Wales, in Glamorganshire. 30,935 (1961).

neatherd (nēt′hûd′), *n.* a cowherd.

neat's-foot oil (nēts′fo͝ot′), a pale yellow fixed oil made by boiling the feet and shinbones of cattle, used chiefly as a dressing for leather. [see NEAT[2]]

neb (nĕb), *n.* **1.** a bill or beak, as of a bird. **2.** the nose, esp. of an animal. **3.** the tip or pointed end of anything. **4.** the nib of a pen. **5.** *Obs.* a person's mouth. [ME *nebbe,* OE *nebb,* c. MD and MLG *nebbe*]

Neb., Nebraska.

Nebiim (nĕb′ĭ ĭm′), *n.pl.* (in the Hebrew Bible) the Prophets, the books occurring after the Torah and before the Hagiographa. [t. Heb., pl. of *nābhī* prophet]

Nebo (nē′bō), *n.* **Mount.** See **Pisgah, Mount.**

Nebr., Nebraska.

Nebraska (nĭ brăs′kə), *n.* a state in the central United States. 1,411,330 pop. (1960); 77,237 sq. mi. *Cap.:* Lincoln. *Abbrev.:* Nebr. *or* Neb. —**Nebras′kan,** *adj., n.*

nebris (nĕb′rĭs), *n. Gk Antiq.* the skin of a fawn, esp. as worn by Dionysus and later, on festival occasions, by his priests and votaries. [t. L, t. Gk]

Nebuchadnezzar (nĕb′yo͝o kəd nĕz′ə), *n.* a king of Babylonia, 604?–561? B.C., and conqueror of Jerusalem. II Kings 24–25. Also, **Nebuchadrezzar** (nĕb′yo͝o kəd-rĕz′ə).

nebula (nĕb′yo͝o lə), *n., pl.* **-lae** (-lē′), **-las.** **1.** *Astron.* **a.** a cloudlike luminous patch in the sky, consisting of a galaxy of stars, or of the materials from which a galaxy is formed; an extra-galactic nebula. **b.** a small regular disc resembling a planet, consisting of a gaseous envelope enclosing a central star; a planetary nebula. **c.** an irregular, luminous, or dark patch in the sky consisting only of gases and dust; a diffuse nebula, an irregular nebula. **2.** *Pathol.* **a.** a faint opacity in the cornea. **b.** cloudiness in the urine. [t. L: mist, vapour, cloud] —**neb′ular,** *adj.*

nebular hypothesis, *Astron.* the theory that the solar system has been evolved from a mass of nebulous matter (a theory prominent in the 19th century following its precise formulation by Laplace).

nebulize (nĕb′yo͝o līz′), *v.t.,* **-lized, -lizing.** to reduce to fine spray; atomize. Also, **nebulise.** —**neb′uliz′er,** *n.*

nebulose (nĕb′yo͝o lōs′), *adj.* **1.** nebulous; cloudlike. **2.** hazy or indistinct. **3.** having cloudlike markings.

nebulosity (nĕb′yo͝o lŏs′ĭ tĭ), *n., pl.* **-ties.** **1.** nebulous or nebular matter. **2.** nebulous state.

nebulous (nĕb′yo͝o ləs), *adj.* **1.** hazy, vague, indistinct, or confused: *a nebulous recollection.* **2.** cloudy or cloudlike. **3.** nebular. [ME, t. L: m. s. *nebulōsus*] —**neb′ulously,** *adv.* —**neb′ulousness,** *n.*

necessarian (nĕs′ĭ sâə′rĭ ən), *n., adj.* necessitarian. —**nec′essar′ianism,** *n.*

necessarily (nĕs′ĭ sə rĭ lĭ, -ĭs rĭ lĭ), *adv.* **1.** by or of necessity: *you need not necessarily go to the party.* **2.** as a necessary result.

necessary (nĕs′ĭ sə rĭ, -ĭs rĭ), *adj., n., pl.* **-saries.** —*adj.* **1.** that cannot be dispensed with: *a necessary law.* **2.** happening or existing by necessity. **3.** acting or proceeding from compulsion or necessity; not free; involuntary: *a necessary agent.* **4.** *Logic.* **a.** (of propositions) denoting that the denial of that proposition involves a self-contradiction (opp. to *contingent*). **b.** (of inferences or arguments) denoting that it is impossible for the premises of an inference or argument to be true and its conclusion false. **5.** *Archaic.* rendering indispensable or useful services. —*n.* **6.** something necessary, indispensable, or requisite. **7.** (*pl.*) *Law.* food, clothing, etc., required by a dependant or incompetent and varying with his social or economic position or that of the person upon whom he is dependent. [ME, t. L: m. s. *necessārius* unavoidable, indispensable]

—**Syn.** 1. NECESSARY, ESSENTIAL, INDISPENSABLE, REQUISITE indicate something vital for the fulfilment of a need. NECESSARY applies to that which is inevitable to the fulfilment of a condition, or that which is the inevitable as a consequence of certain causes: *food is necessary to life, multiplicity is a necessary result of division.* INDISPENSABLE applies to that which cannot be done without or removed from the rest of a unitary condition: *food is indispensable to living things; he made himself indispensable as a companion.* That which is ESSENTIAL forms a vital necessary condition of something: *air is essential to red-blooded animals, it is essential to understand the matter clearly.* REQUISITE applies to what is thought necessary to fill out, complete, or perfect something: *he had all the requisite qualifications for a position.*

necessitarian (nĭ sĕs′ĭ tēə′rĭ ən), *n.* **1.** one who maintains that the action of the will is a necessary effect of antecedent causes (opposed to *libertarian*). —*adj.* **2.** pertaining to necessitarians or necessitarianism.

necessitarianism (nĭ sĕs′ĭ tēə′rĭ ə nĭz′əm), *n.* the doctrine of the determination of the will by antecedent causes, as opposed to that of the freedom of the will.

necessitate (nĭ sĕs′ĭ tāt′), *v.t.,* **-tated, -tating.** **1.** to make necessary: *the breakdown of the motor necessitated a halt.* **2.** to compel, oblige, or force: *the rise in prices necessitated greater thrift.* —**neces′sita′tion,** *n.* —**necessitative** (nĭ sĕs′ĭ tə tĭv), *adj.*

necessitous (nĭ sĕs′ĭ təs), *adj.* being in or involving necessity; needy; indigent. —**neces′sitously,** *adv.* —**neces′sitousness,** *n.*

necessity (nĭ sĕs′ĭ tĭ), *n., pl.* **-ties.** **1.** something necessary or indispensable: *the necessities of life.* **2.** the fact of being necessary or indispensable; indispensableness. **3.** an imperative requirement or need for something: *necessity for a decision.* **4.** the state or fact of being necessary or inevitable. **5.** an unavoidable compulsion to do something. **6.** a state of being in difficulty or need; poverty. **7.** *Philos.* **a.** constraint viewed as a principle of universal causation, determining even the action of the will. **b.** the relation of the inevitable to the nature of its conditions; inevitable connection. [ME *necessite,* t. L: m. s. *necessitas* exigency] —**Syn.** 1. See **need.**

neck (nĕk), *n.* **1.** that part of an animal's body which is between the head and the trunk and connects these parts. **2.** the part of a garment covering the neck or extending about it. **3.** the length of the neck of a horse or other animal as a measure in racing. **4.** the slender part of a bottle, retort, or any similar object. **5.** that part of a golf club head by which this joins the shaft. **6.** any narrow, connecting, or projecting part suggesting the neck of an animal. **7.** the longer slender part of a violin or the like, extending from the body to the head. **8.** *Anat.* a constricted part of a bone, organ, or the like. **9.** *Dentistry.* the junction between enamel of crown and cementum of the root of a tooth. **10.** *Print.* a beard (def. 5). **11.** *Archit.* the lowest part of the capital of a column, above the astragal at the head of the shaft. See diag. under **column.** **12.** a narrow strip of land, as an isthmus or a cape. **13.** a strait. **14. get it in the neck,** to be reprimanded or punished severely. **15. neck and crop,** entirely; completely. **16. neck and neck,** just even. **17. neck or nothing,** at every risk; desperately. **18. stick one's neck out,** to act, express an opinion, etc., so as to expose oneself to criticism, hostility, danger, etc. **19. win by a neck,** *Racing.* to be first by a head and neck; finish closely. —*v.i.* **20.** *Colloq.* to play amorously. —*v.t.* **21.** to strangle or behead. [ME *nekke,* OE *hnecca,* c. D *nek;* akin to G *Nacken* nape of the neck]

Neckar (*Ger.* nĕk′är), *n.* a river in S West Germany, flowing from the Black Forest S through Baden-Württemberg then N and W to the Rhine at Mannheim. 246 mi.

neckband (nĕk′bănd′), *n.* **1.** a band of cloth at the neck of a garment. **2.** *Obs.* a band worn round the neck.

neckcloth (nĕk′klŏth′), *n. Archaic.* a cravat.

Necker (nĕk′ə; *Fr.* nĕ kĕr′), *n.* **Jacques** (*Fr.* zhȧk), 1732–1804, French statesman, born in Switzerland.

neckerchief (nĕk′ə chĭf), *n.* a cloth worn round the neck by women or men. [f. NECK + KERCHIEF]

necking (nĕk′ĭng), *n.* **1.** *Archit.* **a.** a moulding or group of mouldings between the projecting part of a capital of a column and the shaft. **b.** a gorgerin. **2.** *Colloq.* the act of playing amorously.

necklace (nĕk′lĭs), *n.* an ornament of precious stones, beads, or the like, worn esp. by women round the neck. Also, **necklet** (nĕk′lĭt). [f. NECK + LACE string]

neckline (nĕk′līn′), *n.* the shape at the neck of a woman's garment.

neckpiece (nĕk′pēs′), *n.* a piece of material, fur, etc., covering, bordering, or worn round the neck.

necktie (nĕk′tī′), *n.* **1.** a band of woven or knitted material placed round the neck and tied in front. **2.** *Chiefly U.S.* tie (def. 20). **3.** *U.S. Slang.* a hangman's rope.

neckwear (nĕk′wĕə′), *n.* articles of dress worn round or at the neck.

necr-, a word element meaning 'dead', 'corpse', 'death'. Also, before consonants, **necro-.** [t. Gk: m. *nekr-*, *nekro-*, comb. forms of *nekrós* person, corpse]

necrobacilus (nĕk′rō bə sĭl′əs), *n.* any disease of cattle, horses, sheep, and swine marked by necrotic areas in which a bacillus, *Actinomyces necrophorus,* is found.

necrolatry (nĕ krŏl′ə trĭ), *n.* worship of the dead.

necrology (nĕ krŏl′ə jĭ), *n., pl.* **-gies. 1.** an obituary notice. **2.** a list of persons who have died within a certain time. [t. ML: m. s. *necrologium,* f. Gk (see NECRO-, -LOGY)] **—necrological** (nĕk′rə lŏj′ĭ kl), *adj.* **—nec′rolog′ically,** *adv.* **—necrol′ogist,** *n.*

necromancy (nĕk′rō măn′sĭ), *n.* **1.** magic in general; enchantment; conjuration. **2.** the pretended art of divination through communication with the dead; the black art. [t. L: m. s. *necromantīa,* t. Gk: m. *necromanteía*; r. ME *nigromancie,* t. ML: m. *nigromantīa,* alter. of L *necromantia* by assoc. with L *niger* black. Cf. BLACK ART] **—nec′roman′cer,** *n.* **—nec′roman′tic,** *adj.* **—Syn. 2.** See **magic.**

necromania (nĕk′rō mā′nyə), *n.* necrophilism.

necrophilism (nĕ krŏf′ĭ lĭz′əm), *n.* morbid attraction to corpses. Also, **necrophilia** (nĕk′rō fĭl′ĭ ə), **—necrophiliac** (nĕk′rō fĭl′ĭ ăk′), **necrophilic** (nĕk′rō fĭl′ĭk), *adj.*

necrophobia (nĕk′rō fō′byə), *n.* **1.** morbid fear of death. **2.** a morbid aversion to, or fear of, dead bodies.

necropolis (nĕ krŏp′ə lĭs), *n., pl.* **-lises. 1.** a cemetery, often of large size. **2.** an old or prehistoric burial ground, as of an ancient people. [t. NL, t. Gk: m. *nekrópolis,* lit., city of the dead]

necropsy (nĕk′rŏp sĭ), *n., pl.* **-sies.** the examination of a body after death; an autopsy. Also, **necroscopy** (nĕ krŏs′kə pĭ). [f. NECR- + s. Gk *ópsis* sight + -Y³]

necrose (nĕ krōs′, nĕk′rōs), *v.t., v.i.,* **-crosed, -crosing.** to affect or be affected with necrosis.

necrosis (nĕ krō′sĭs), *n.* **1.** *Pathol.* death of a circumscribed piece of tissue or of an organ. **2.** *Bot.* a diseased condition in plants resulting from the death of the tissue. [t. NL, t. Gk: m. *nékrōsis* a killing] **—necrotic** (nĕ krŏt′ĭk), *adj.*

necrotic enteritis (ĕn′tə rī′tĭs), a disease of swine characterized by extensive ulceration of the intestine.

necrotomy (nĕ krŏt′ə mĭ), *n., pl.* **-mies. 1.** the excision of necrosed bone. **2.** dissection of dead bodies.

nectar (nĕk′tə), *n.* **1.** *Bot.* the saccharine secretion of a plant, which attracts the insects or birds, that pollinate the flower, collected by bees, in whose body it is elaborated into honey. **2.** the drink, or, less properly, the food, of the gods of classical mythology. **3.** any delicious drink. **4.** (*cap.*) **Sea of,** a plain, *Mare Nectaris,* on the face of the moon. [t. L, t. Gk: m. *néktar*]

nectareous (nĕk tĕə′rĭ əs), *adj.* **1.** of the nature of or resembling nectar. **2.** delicious; sweet. Also, **nectar′ean, nectarous** (nĕk′tə rəs). [t. L: m. *nectareus,* t. Gk: m. *nektáreos*]

nectarine (nĕk′tə rĭn, -trĭn), *n.* a form of the common peach, having a skin destitute of down. [n. use of *nectarine,* adj., f. NECTAR + -INE¹]

nectary (nĕk′tə rĭ), *n., pl.* **-ries. 1.** *Bot.* an organ or part, usually of a flower, that secretes nectar. **2.** *Entomol.* one of a pair of small abdominal tubes from which aphids secrete honeydew. **—nectarial** (nĕk-tĕə′rĭ əl), *adj.*

Nectaries (def. 1)
A, Grass-of-Parnassus, *Parnassia palustris*; n, nectary on surface of staminode. B, Toadflax, *Linaria vulgaris*; n, nectary at base of corolla spur. C, Buttercup, *Ranunculus acris*; n, nectary beneath flap at base of petal

N.E.D., New English Dictionary (Oxford English Dictionary).

N.E.D.C., National Economic Development Council.

nee (nā), *adj.* born (placed after the name of a married woman to introduce her maiden name): *Madame de Staël, nee Necker.* Also, **née** (nā; *Fr.* nė). [t. F, fem. of *né,* pp. of *naître* to be born, g. L *nascī*]

need (nēd), *n.* **1.** a case or instance in which some necessity or want exists; a requirement: *to meet the needs of the occasion.* **2.** urgent want, as of something requisite: *he has no need of your kindness.* **3.** necessity arising from the circumstances of a case: *there is no need to worry.* **4.** a situation or time of difficulty; exigency: *a friend in need.* **5.** a condition marked by the lack of something requisite: *the need for leadership.* **6.** destitution; extreme poverty. *—v.t.* **7.** to have need of; require: *to need money.* *—v.i.* **8.** to be necessary: *there needs no apology.* **9.** to be under a necessity (fol. by infinitive, in certain cases without *to*; in the 3rd pers. sing. the form is *need,* not *needs*): *he need not go.* **10.** to be in need or want. [ME *nede,* d. OE *nēd*; r. ME *nud(e),* OE *nȳd, nīed*; akin to G *Not*] **—need′er,** *n.*

—Syn. 2. NEED, NECESSITY imply a want, a lack, or a demand, which must be filled. NEED, a word of Old English origin, has connotations which make it strong in emotional appeal: *the need to be appreciated.* NECESSITY, a word of Latin origin, is more formal and impersonal or objective; though much stronger than NEED in expressing urgency or imperative demand, it is less effective in appealing to the emotions: *water is a necessity for living things.* **6.** See **poverty.**

needful (nēd′fəl), *adj.* **1.** necessary: *needful supplies.* **2.** *Rare.* needy. **—need′fully,** *adv.* **—need′fulness,** *n.*

neediness (nē′dĭ nĭs), *n.* needy state; indigence.

needle (nē′dl), *n., v.,* **-dled, -dling.** *—n.* **1.** a small, slender, pointed instrument, now usually of polished steel, with an eye or hole for thread, used in sewing. **2.** a slender, rodlike implement for use in knitting, or one hooked at the end for use in crocheting, etc. **3.** *Med.* **a.** a slender, pointed, steel instrument used in sewing or piercing tissues. **b.** hypodermic needle. **4.** any of various objects resembling or suggesting a needle. **5.** a small, slender, pointed instrument, usually of polished steel or some other material, used to transmit vibratory motions as from a gramophone record. **6.** magnetic needle. **7.** a pointed instrument used in engraving, etc. **8.** *Bot.* a needle-shaped leaf, as of a conifer: *a pine needle.* **9.** *Zool.* a slender sharp spicule. **10.** *Chem., Mineral.* a needle-like crystal. **11.** a sharp-pointed mass or pinnacle of rock. **12.** an obelisk, or tapering, four-sided shaft of stone. **13.** Also, **needle beam.** *Bldg Trades.* a beam of steel or wood passed through the wall of a house and supported at each end on dead shores. **14. the needle,** *Slang.* extreme nervousness. *—v.t.* **15.** to sew or pierce with or as with a needle. **16.** to prod or goad. **17.** to tease or heckle. *—v.i.* **18.** to form needles in crystallization. **19.** to work with a needle. [ME *nēdle,* d. OE *nēdl*; r. OE *nǣdl,* c. G *Nadel*] **—nee′dle-like′,** *adj.*

needlefish (nē′dl fĭsh′), *n., pl.* **-fishes,** (*esp. collectively*) **-fish. 1.** any fish of the family *Belonidae,* with a long sharp beak and needle-like teeth, found in all warm seas and in some coastal fresh waters. **2.** a pipefish.

needleful (nē′dl fo͝ol′), *n., pl.* **-fuls.** a suitable length of thread for using at one time with a needle.

needle furze, a small spiny papilionaceous shrub with yellow flowers, *Genista anglica,* occurring on dry heathland in W Europe.

needle point, embroidery on canvas worked to cover the area completely with even stitches to resemble tapestry.

needle-point (nē′dl point′), *adj.* denoting a kind of lace (**needle-point lace**) in which a needle works out the design upon parchment or paper.

needless (nēd′lĭs), *adj.* not needed or wanted; unnecessary: *a needless waste of food.* **—need′lessly,** *adv.* **—need′lessness,** *n.*

needle valve, *Mach., Engineering.* a valve with a needle-like part, a fine adjustment, or a small opening; esp., a valve in which the opening is controlled by a needle-like or conical point which fits into a conical seat.

needlewoman (nē′dl wo͝om′ən), *n., pl.* **-women.** a woman who does needlework.

needlework (nē′dl wûk′), *n.* the process or the product of working with a needle as in sewing or embroidery.

needn't (nēd′nt), contraction of *need not.*

needs (nēdz), *adv.* of necessity; necessarily (usually with *must*). [ME *needes,* OE *nēdes,* orig. gen. of *nēd* NEED]

needy (nē′dĭ), *adj.,* **-dier, -diest.** in, or characterized by, need or want; very poor: *a needy family.*

neep (nēp), *n. Scot. and N Dial.* a turnip. [ME *nepe,* d. OE *nēp*; r. OE *nǣp,* t. L: m. s. *nāpus*]

ne'er (nĕə), *adv. Chiefly Poetic.* contraction of *never.*

ne'er-do-well (nĕə′do͞o wĕl′), *n.* **1.** a worthless person. *—adj.* **2.** worthless; good-for-nothing.

nefarious (nĭ fĕə′rĭ əs), *adj.* extremely wicked; iniquitous: *nefarious practices.* [t. L: m. *nefārius* impious] **—nefar′iously,** *adv.* **—nefar′iousness,** *n.*

Nefertiti (nĕf′ə tē′tĭ), *n.* Egyptian queen, wife of Amenhotep IV. Also, **Nofretete.**

neg., **1.** negative. **2.** negatively.

negate (nĭ gāt′), *v.t.,* **-gated, -gating.** to deny; nullify. [t. L: m. s. *negātus,* pp.]

negation (nĭ gā′shən), *n.* **1.** the act of denying. **2.** a denial. **3.** a negative thing; a nonentity. **4.** the absence or opposite of what is actual, positive, or affirmative; denial as opposed to assertion. **5.** a statement, idea, etc., consisting in the absence of something positive.

negative (nĕg′ə tĭv), *adj., n., v.,* **-tived, -tiving.** *—adj.* **1.** expressing or containing negation or denial: *a negative statement.* **2.** expressing refusal to do something. **3.** refusing consent, as to a proposal. **4.** prohibitory, as an order or command. **5.** characterized by the absence of distinguishing or marked qualities or features; lacking positive attributes: *a negative character*. **6.** *Maths, Physics.* **a.** involving or denoting subtraction; minus. **b.** measured or proceeding in the opposite direction to that which is considered as positive. **7.** *Bacteriol.* failing to show a positive result in a test for a specific disease caused by either bacteria or viruses. **8.** *Photog.* denoting an image in which the gradations of light and shade are represented in reverse. **9.** *Physiol.* responding in a direction away from the stimulus. **10.** *Elect.* denoting or pertaining to the kind of electricity developed on resin, amber, etc., when rubbed with flannel, or that present at the pole from which electrons leave an electric generator or battery, having an excess of electrons. **11.** denoting or pertaining to the south-seeking pole of a magnet. **12.** *Chem.* (of an element or radical) tending to gain electrons and become negatively charged. **13.** *Logic.* denoting a proposition or judgement that denies a relation between its terms, or asserts that the predicate applies to the subject. *—n.* **14.** a negative statement, answer, word, gesture, etc. **15.** a refusal of assent. **16.** that side of a question which denies what the opposite side affirms. **17.** the negative form of statement (opposed to *affirmative*). **18.** *Maths.* a negative quantity or symbol. **19.** *Photog.* a negative image, as on a film or plate, used chiefly for printing positive pictures. **20.** *Archaic.* a negative quality or characteristic. **21.** *Obs.* a veto. **22.** *Elect.* the negative plate or element in a voltaic cell. *—v.t.* **23.** to deny; contradict. **24.** to disprove. **25.** to refuse assent or consent to; pronounce against; veto. **26.** to neutralize or counteract. [ME, t. L: m. s. *negātīvus* that denies] **—neg′atively,** *adv.* **—neg′ativeness, neg′ativ′ity,** *n.*

negative catalyst, *Chem.* inhibitor (def. 1).

negative feedback. See **feedback** (def. 2).

negative ion, *Physics, Chem.* an anion.

negative resistance, *Elect.* the property of certain devices in which an increase in the voltage applied causes a decrease in the current passing through them.

negativism (nĕg′ə tĭ vĭz′əm), *n.* **1.** negativistic behaviour. **2.** any system of philosophy in which denial is the prominent feature of its conclusions, as agnosticism, scepticism, etc. **—neg′ativist,** *n.*

negativistic (nĕg′ə tĭ vĭs′tĭk), *adj.* *Psychol.* marked by resistance to a stimulus; tending to react in the opposite way to any suggestion.

negatory (nĕg′ə tə rĭ, nĭ gā′tə rĭ), *adj.* denying; negative.

negatron (nĕg′ə trŏn′), *n.* *Physics, Chem. Rare.* an electron.

Negev (nĕg′ĕv), *n.* a desert area in S Israel. Also, **Negeb** (nĕg′ĕb).

neglect (nĭ glĕkt′), *v.t.* **1.** to pay no attention to; disregard: *a neglected genius.* **2.** to be remiss in care for or treatment of: *to neglect one's family.* **3.** to omit (doing something), through indifference or carelessness. **4.** to fail to carry out or perform (orders, duties, etc.). **5.** to fail to take or use: *to neglect no precaution.* *—n.* **6.** the act or fact of neglecting; disregard. **7.** the fact or state of being neglected; negligence. [t. L: s. *neglectus*, pp., unheeded] **—neglect′er,** *n.*

—Syn. 2. See **slight.** 6, 7. NEGLECT, DERELICTION, NEGLIGENCE, REMISSNESS imply carelessness, failure, or some important omission in the performance of one's duty, a task, etc. NEGLECT and NEGLIGENCE are occasionally interchangeable, but NEGLECT commonly refers to the act, NEGLIGENCE to the habit or trait, of failing to attend to or perform what is expected or required: *gross neglect of duty, negligence in handling traffic problems.* DERELICTION implies culpable or reprehensible neglect or failure in the performance of duty: *dereliction in a position of responsibility.* REMISSNESS implies the omission or the careless or indifferent performance of a duty: *remissness was the cause of tardiness in reporting.* **—Ant.** 6. attention, care.

neglectful (nĭ glĕkt′fəl), *adj.* characterized by neglect; disregardful; careless; negligent (often fol. by *of*). **—neglect′fully,** *adv.* **—neglect′fulness,** *n.*

negligee (nĕg′lĭ zhā′), *n.* **1.** a woman's dressing-gown, esp. a very flimsy one, of nylon, or the like. **2.** easy, informal attire. Also, *French,* **négligé** (*Fr.* nė glē zhė′). [t. F: m. *négligé*, orig. pp. of *négliger* neglect, t. L: m. *negligere*]

negligence (nĕg′lĭ jəns), *n.* **1.** the state or fact of being negligent; neglect. **2.** an instance of being negligent; a defect due to carelessness. **3.** *Law.* the failure to exercise that degree of care which, in the circumstances, the law requires for the protection of those interests of other persons which may be injuriously affected by the want of such care. **—Syn. 1.** See **neglect.**

negligent (nĕg′lĭ jənt), *adj.* guilty of or characterized by neglect, as of duty: *negligent officials.* [ME, t. L: s. *negligens*, ppr., neglecting] **—neg′ligently,** *adv.*

negligible (nĕg′lĭ jə bl), *adj.* that may be neglected or disregarded; very little. **—neg′ligibil′ity, neg′ligibleness,** *n.* **—neg′ligibly,** *adv.*

negotiable (nĭ gō′shyə bl), *adj.* **1.** capable of being negotiated. **2.** (of bills, etc.) transferable by delivery, with or without endorsement, according to the circumstances, the title passing to the transferee. **—nego′tiabil′ity,** *n.*

negotiant (nĭ gō′shyənt), *n.* one who negotiates.

negotiate (nĭ gō′shĭ āt′), *v.*, **-ated, -ating.** *—v.i.* **1.** to treat with another or others, as in the preparation of a treaty, or in preliminaries to a business deal. *—v.t.* **2.** to arrange for or bring about by discussion and settlement of terms: *to negotiate a loan.* **3.** to conduct (an affair, etc.) **4.** to clear or pass (an obstacle, etc.). **5.** to transfer (a bill of exchange, etc.) by assignment, endorsement, or delivery. **6.** to dispose of by sale or transfer: *to negotiate securities.* [t. L: m. s. *negōtiātus.* pp.] **—nego′tia′tor,** *n.*

negotiation (nĭ gō′shĭ ā′shən), *n.* mutual discussion and arrangement of the terms of a transaction or agreement: *the negotiation of a treaty.*

Negri bodies (nā′grĭ, nĕg′rĭ), certain microscopic bodies found in the brain cells of animals affected with rabies.

Negrillo (nĭ grĭl′ō), *n.*, *pl.* **-los.** a Negrito, esp. of the African division; a pygmy. [t. Sp., dim. of *negro* NEGRO]

Negri Sembilan (nĕg′rĭ sĕm bē′lən), a state in Malaysia: formerly one of the Federated Malay States. 355,279 pop. (est. 1962); 2580 sq. mi. *Cap.:* Seremban.

Negritic (nĭ grĭt′ĭk), *adj.* of or pertaining to Negroes or the Negritos.

Negrito (nĭ grē′tō), *n.*, *pl.* **-tos, -toes.** a member of any of certain dwarfish Negroid peoples of south-eastern Asia and of Africa, esp. of Malaya and the Andaman and Philippine Islands. [t. Sp., dim. of *negro* NEGRO]

negritude (nē′grĭ tyōōd′, nĕg′-), *n.* **1.** the fact of being Negro. **2.** the character or spirit of the Negro, in politics, literature, art, etc. Also, **nigritude.** [t. F: m. *négritude*, t. L: m. *nigritūdo* blackness]

Negro (nē′grō), *n.*, *pl.* **-groes,** *adj.* *—n.* **1.** a member of the Negro race. **2.** a person having some Negro ancestry. *—adj.* **3.** of, denoting, or pertaining to the so-called black race of Africa and its descendants elsewhere, characterized by a brown-black complexion, broad and flat nose, projecting jaws, everted lips, and crisp or woolly hair. [t. Sp. and Pg.: a black person, Negro, g. L *niger* black] **—Negress** (nē′grĭs), *n.fem.*

Negro (*Sp.* nė′grȯ; *Port.* nė′grōō), *n.* **Río** (*Sp.* rē′ȯ; *Port.* rē′ōō). **1.** a river flowing from E Colombia through N Brazil into the Amazon. ab. 1400 mi. **2.** a river in S Argentina, flowing from the Andes E to the Atlantic. ab. 700 mi.

Negroid (nē′groid), *adj.* **1.** resembling, or akin to, the Negro race and presumably allied to it in origin. *—n.* **2.** a person of a Negroid race.

Negrophil (nē′grō fĭl), *adj.* **1.** friendly to or liking Negroes. *—n.* **2.** one who is friendly to and likes Negroes. Also, **Negrophile** (nē′grō fīl′). **—Negrophilism** (nē-grŏf′ĭ lĭz′əm, nē-), *n.*

Negrophobe (nē′grō fōb′), *n.* one who fears, or has strong antipathy to, Negroes.

Negrophobia (nē′grō fō′byə), *n.* fear of, or strong antipathy to, Negroes.

Negropont (nĕg′rō pŏnt′), *n.* Euboea.

Negros (nā′grōs; *Sp.* nė′grȯs), *n.* an island of the Philippines, in the central part of the group. 1,850,410 pop. (est. 1960); 4905 sq. mi.

Neguib (nə gēb′), *n.* **Mohammed,** born 1901, Egyptian general; prime minister 1952–54; president 1953–54. Also, **Naguib.**

negus[1] (nē′gəs), *n.* **1.** a royal title in Ethiopia. **2.** (*cap.*) the emperor of Ethiopia. [t. Amharic: king]

negus[2] (nē′gəs), *n.* a beverage made of wine and hot water, with sugar, nutmeg, and lemon. [named after Colonel Francis *Negus*, d. 1732, its reputed inventor]

Neh., Nehemiah.

Nehemiah (nē′ĭ mī′ə), *n.* **1.** a Hebrew leader of the 5th century B.C.: returned to Jerusalem to rebuild its walls. **2.** a book of the Old Testament. [t. Heb.]

Nehru (nĕə′rōō), *n.* **Jawaharlal** (jə wə hə lŭl′), 1889–1964, Hindu political leader in India: prime minister of the republic of India 1947–64.

N.E.I., not elsewhere included.

neigh (nā), *v.i.* **1.** to utter the cry of a horse; whinny. *—n.* **2.** the cry of a horse; a whinny. [ME *neyghe*, OE *hnǣgan*, c. MHG *nēgen.* See NAG[2], n.]

neighbour (nā′bə), *n.* **1.** one who lives near another. **2.** a person or thing that is near another. **3.** a fellow being subject to the obligations of humanity. *—adj.* **4.** *U.S.* living or situated near to another. *—v.t.* **5.** to place or bring near. **6.** to live or be situated near to; adjoin; border on. *—v.i.* **7.** to associate on the terms of neighbours; be neighbourly or friendly (fol. by *with*). **8.** to live or be situated nearby. Also, *U.S.*, **neighbor.** [ME *neighebour*, OE *nēahgebūr*, f. *nēah* nigh + *gebūr* dweller, countryman, c. G *Nachbar*]

neighbourhood (nā′bə ho͝od′), *n.* **1.** the region near or about some place or thing; the vicinity. **2.** a district or locality, often with reference to its character or inhabitants: *a fashionable neighbourhood.* **3.** a number of persons living near one another or in a particular locality: *the whole neighbourhood was there.* **4.** *Archaic.* neighbourly feeling or conduct. **5.** nearness; proximity. **6. in the neighbourhood of,** nearly; about.

neighbouring (nā′bə rĭng), *adj.* living or situated near.

neighbourly (nā′bə lĭ), *adj.* befitting or acting as befits a neighbour; friendly. —**neigh′bourliness,** *n.*

Neisse (*Ger.* nīs′ə), *n.* a river flowing from NW Czechoslovakia N along part of the boundary between East Germany and Poland to the river Oder. ab. 145 mi.

neither (nī′thə), *adj.* **1.** not either; not the one or the other: *neither statement is true.* —*pron.* **2.** not either; not the one or the other: *neither of the statements is true.* —*conj.* **3.** not either (a disjunctive connective preceding a series of two or more alternative words, etc., connected by the correlative *nor*): *neither you nor I nor anybody else knows the answer.* **4.** nor yet: *Ye shall not eat of it, neither shall ye touch it.* [ME *neither* (f. *ne* not + EITHER); r. ME *nauther,* OE *nāwther,* contr. var. of *nāhwæther,* f. *nā* not + *hwæther* either, WHETHER]

Nejd (nĕzhd, nād), *n.* a former sultanate in central Arabia, forming (with dependencies) with Hejaz the kingdom of Saudi Arabia: inhabited by Wahabis. ab. 3,000,000 pop.; ab. 414,000 sq. mi.

Nekrasov (*Russ.* nĭ krȧ′səf), *n.* **Nikolai Alekseevich** (*Russ.* nĭ kȧ lāy′ ə lĭk syė′yĭ vĭch), 1821–77, Russian poet.

nekton (nĕk′tŏn), *n.* the aggregate of actively swimming organisms at the surface of the sea. [t. G, t. Gk: (neut.) swimming] —**nekton′ic,** *adj.*

Nellore (nĕ lô′), *n.* a town in India, in S Andhra Pradesh. 106,776 (1961).

nelson (nĕl′sən), *n.* See **full nelson** and **half nelson.**

Nelson (nĕl′sən), *n.* **1. Viscount Horatio,** 1758–1805, British admiral: famous victories over Napoleon I, esp. Trafalgar (1805). **2.** a river in Canada, flowing from Lake Winnipeg NE to Hudson Bay. ab. 390 mi. **3.** a town in England, in Lancashire. 32,292 (1961). **4.** a town in New Zealand, in N South Island. 26,800 (est. 1965).

nelumbo (nĭ lŭm′bō), *n., pl.* **-bos.** lotus (def. 3). [t. NL, t. Sinhalese: m. *nelumbu*]

Neman (nĕ′mən; *Russ.* nyĕ′mən), *n.* a river in the W Soviet Union, flowing into the Baltic: called **Memel** in its lower course. Also, **Nyeman.** Polish, **Niemen.** Lithuanian, **Nemunas.**

nemat-, a word element referring to threadlike things, especially to *nematodes.* Also, before consonants, **nemato-.** [t. Gk, comb. form of *nêma* thread]

nemathelminth (nĕm′ə thĕl′mĭnth), *n.* any of the *Nemathelminthes,* a phylum of worms (now usually broken up into several phyla), including the nematodes, etc., characterized by an elongated, unsegmented cylindrical body. [f. Gk: s. *nêma* thread + s. *hélmins* worm]

nematocyst (nĕm′ə tə sĭst′), *n.* *Zool.* an organ of offence and defence peculiar to coelenterates, consisting of a minute capsule containing a thread capable of being ejected and of causing a sting.

nematode (nĕm′ə tōd′), *n.* any of the *Nematoda,* the roundworms, a group variously considered a phylum or class. They are elongated smooth worms of cylindroid shape, parasitic or free-living, as ascarids, trichinae, vinegar eels, etc.

nem. con., nemine contradicente.

Nemea (nĭ mĭə′), *n.* a valley in SE Greece, in ancient Argolis. —**Nemean** (nĭ mĭən′), *adj.*

Nemean games, one of the four national festivals of the ancient Greeks. It was celebrated at Nemea in the 2nd and 4th year of each Olympiad.

Nemean lion, *Gk Legend.* a lion said to have been killed by Hercules.

nemertean (nĭ mû′tĭ ən), *n.* **1.** any of the *Nemertinea*; ribbon worm. —*adj.* **2.** belonging or pertaining to the nemerteans. Also, **nemertine** (nĭ mû′tĭn). [f. s. NL *Nemertea,* pl. (der. Gk *Nēmertḗs* name of a nereid) + -AN]

Nemertinea (nĕm′ə tĭn′ĭ ə), *n.pl.* a group of unsegmented marine worms considered either a class of *Platyhelminthes* or an independent phylum, characterized by the long proboscis that can be shot out from the anterior end. Also, **Nemertea.**

nemesia (nə mē′syə), *n.* any of the southern African perennial herbs of the scrophulariaceous genus *Nemesia,* having flowers of a number of pastel shades. [t. NL, t. Gk]

Nemesis (nĕm′ĭ sĭs), *n., pl.* **-ses** (-sēz′). **1.** the goddess of retribution or vengeance. **2.** (*l.c.*) an agent of retribution or punishment. [t. L, t. Gk]

nemine contradicente (nĕm′ĭ nā′ kŏn′trə dĭ kĕn′tā), *Latin.* no one contradicting; unanimously.

nemine dissentiente (nĕm′ĭ nā′ dĭ sĕn′tĭ ĕn′tā), *Latin.* no one dissenting; unanimously.

Nemunas (nyĕm′o͞o näs′), *n.* Lithuanian name of **Neman.**

N Eng., Northern England.

neo-, a word element meaning 'new', 'recent', used in combination, as in *Neo-Darwinism* (a new or modified form of Darwinism), *Neo-Gothic* (Gothic after a new or modern style), *Neo-Hebraic* (pertaining to Hebrew of the modern period). [t. Gk, comb. form of *néos*]

neoarsphenamine (nē′ō äs fĕn′ə mēn′, -fĭ năm′ĭn), *n.* *Pharm.* a yellow-orange medicinal powder, $H_2NC_6H_3(OH)As_2C_6H_3(OH)NHCH_2OSONa$, prepared from, but less toxic than, salvarsan; neosalvarsan.

Neo-Catholic (nē′ō kăth′ə lĭk), *adj.* **1.** (in France) of or pertaining to a person who has left the Roman Catholic Church because of his belief in modernism (def. 3a). —*n.* **2.** a Neo-Catholic person. —**Neo-Catholicism** (nē′ō kə thŏl′ĭ sĭz′əm), *n.*

Neocene (nē′ə sēn′), *Geol.* —*adj.* **1.** of or pertaining to a division of the Tertiary period or system that comprises the Miocene and Pliocene. —*n.* **2.** time or rocks comprising the latter half of the Tertiary period or system. Also, **Neogene.**

neoclassical (nē′ō klăs′ĭ kl), *adj.* belonging or pertaining to a revival of classical style, as in art. Also, **ne′oclas′sic.**

neoclassicism (nē′ō klăs′ĭ sĭz′əm), *n.* a late 18th- and early 19th-century revivalist art and architectural style, deriving directly from classical models.

Neo-Darwinism (nē′ō dä′wĭ nĭz′əm), *n.* *Biol.* the theory of evolution as expounded by later students of Darwin, esp. Weismann, who hold that natural selection accounts for evolution and deny the inheritance of acquired characteristics.

neodymium (nē′ō dĭm′ĭ əm), *n.* *Chem.* a rare-earth, metallic, trivalent element occurring with cerium and other rare-earth metals, and having rose- to violet-coloured salts. *Symbol:* Nd; *at. wt:* 144·24; *at. no.:* 60; *sp. gr.:* 6·9 at 20°C. [t. NL: see NEO-, (DI)DYMIUM]

Neogene (nē′ə jēn′), *adj., n.* Neocene.

neo-impressionism (nē′ō ĭm prĕsh′ə nĭz′əm), *n.* the theory and methods of certain of the later impressionist painters (from about the mid 1880s), characterized by an attempt to make the impressionist methods strictly scientific by employment of the pointillist technique in juxtaposing methodically small dots or squares of pure colours. —**ne′o-impres′sionist,** *n., adj.*

Neo-Lamarckism (nē′ō lə mä′kĭz′əm), *n.* the theory of Lamarckism as expounded by later biologists who hold especially that some acquired characters of organisms may be transmitted to descendants, but that natural selection also is a factor in evolution. —**Neo-Lamarckian** (nē′ō lə mä′kĭ ən), *adj., n.*

Neo-Latin (nē′ō lăt′ĭn), *n.* New Latin.

neolith (nē′ō lĭth), *n.* a neolithic stone implement.

Neolithic (nē′ō lĭth′ĭk), *n.* **1.** the later Stone Age or New Stone Age, characterized by well-finished polished implements of flint and other stone; it includes the Holocene (or Recent) Epoch, i.e., post-glacial time, until the beginning of the Bronze Age. Also, **Neolithic Period.** The earlier part, excluding the last thousand years or so, is often called the **Mesolithic.** —*adj.* **2.** (*sometimes l.c.*) of or pertaining to the Neolithic Period.

neologism (nĭ ŏl′ə jĭz′əm), *n.* **1.** a new word or phrase. **2.** the introduction or use of new words, or new senses of words. **3.** a new doctrine. [t. F: m. *néologisme,* der. *néologie.* See NEO-, -LOGY] —**neol′ogist,** *n.* —**neol′ogis′tic, neol′ogis′tical,** *adj.*

neologize (nĭ ŏl′ə jīz′), *v.i.,* **-gized, -gizing.** to create neologisms. Also, **neologise.**

neology (nĭ ŏl′ə jĭ), *n., pl.* **-gies.** neologism. —**neological** (nē′ə lŏj′ĭ kl), *adj.*

Neo-Melanesian (nē′ō mĕl′ə nē′zyən), *n.* **1.** a pidgin language based on English, spoken in Melanesia and New Guinea. —*adj.* **2.** denoting or pertaining to this language.

neomycin (nē′ō mī′sĭn), *n.* *Med.* a mixture of closely related antibiotics, similar to streptomycin but more effective in combating certain infections, particularly those of the urinary tract.

neon (nē′ən), *n.* *Chem.* a chemically inert gaseous element occurring in small amounts in the earth's atmosphere, and chiefly used in orange-red tubular electrical discharge lamps. *Symbol:* Ne; *at. wt:* 20·183; *at. no.:* 10; *weight of one litre of the gas at* 0°C *and at* 760 *mm. pressure:* 0·9002 gr. [t. NL, t. Gk: (neut.) new]

neonatal (nē′ō nā′tl), *adj.* of or pertaining to a newborn child.

neonate (nē′ō nāt′), *n.* a newborn child.

neon lamp, an electric discharge lamp consisting of a glass tube containing neon gas which gives a red glow when a voltage is applied across the electrodes; widely used in advertising signs.

neophyte (nē′ō fīt′), *n.* **1.** a converted heathen, heretic, etc. **2.** *Primitive Church.* one newly baptized. **3.** *Rom. Cath. Ch.* a novice. **4.** a beginner. [t. LL: m. s. *neophytus*, t. Gk: m. *neóphytos* newly planted] —**neophytic** (nē′ō-fĭt′ĭk), *adj.*

neoplasm (nē′ō plăz′əm), *n. Pathol.* a new growth of different or abnormal tissue; a tumour. —**neoplastic** (nē′ō plăs′tĭk), *adj.*

neoplasticism (nē′ō plăs′tĭ sĭz′əm), *n.* the theory of painting devised by Mondriaan and associated with the modern Dutch movement, De Stijl; characterized by an emphasis on formal structure and primary colours.

neoplasty (nē′ō plăs′tĭ), *n.* the repairing or restoration of a part by plastic surgery.

neoplatonism (nē′ō plā′tə nĭz′əm), *n.* a philosophical system founded chiefly on platonic doctrine and oriental mysticism, later influenced by Christianity. It originated in the 3rd century A.D. Also, **Neo-Platonism.** —**neoplatonic** (nē′ō plə tŏn′ĭk), *adj.* —**ne′opla′tonist,** *n.*

neoprene (nē′ō prēn′), *n.* an oil-resistant synthetic rubber made by polymerizing chloroprene.

neosalvarsan (nē′ō săl′və săn′), *n.* **1.** neoarsphenamine. **2.** (*cap.*) a trademark for it.

Neo-Scholasticism (nē′ō skə lăs′tĭ sĭz′əm), *n.* a contemporary application of scholasticism to modern problems and life. —**Ne′o-Scholas′tic,** *adj.*

neoteny (nĭ ŏt′ə nĭ), *n. Zool.* the capacity or phenomenon of becoming sexually mature in the larval state. Cf. **axolotl.** [t. NL: m. s. *neotēnia*, f. Gk: *neo-* NEO- + m. s. *teínein* extend + *-ia* -IA] —**neot′enous,** *adj.*

neoteric (nē′ō tĕr′ĭk), *adj.* **1.** modern. —*n.* **2.** a modern writer, thinker, etc. [t. LL: s. *neōtericus*, t. Gk: m. *neōterikós* youthful] —**ne′oter′ically,** *adv.*

neotropical (nē′ō trŏp′ĭ kl), *adj. Biol.* belonging to that part of the New World extending from the tropic of Cancer southwards.

neoytterbium (nē′ō ĭ tûr′bĭ əm), *n.* ytterbium.

Neozoic (nē′ō zō′ĭk), *adj.*, *n. Obs.* Cainozoic. [f. NEO- + s. Gk *zōē* life + -IC]

NEP (nĕp), *n.* New Economic Policy. Also, **Nep, N.E.P.**

Nepal (nĭ pôl′), *n.* a constitutional monarchy (since 1959) in the Himalayas between N India and Tibet. 9,500,000 pop. (est. 1964); ab. 54,000 sq. mi. *Cap.:* Katmandu. See map under **Everest.**

nepenthe (nĭ pĕn′thĭ), *n.* **1.** a drug or draught (or the plant yielding it) mentioned by ancient writers as capable of bringing forgetfulness of sorrow or trouble. **2.** anything inducing easeful forgetfulness. Also, **nepenthes** (nĭ pĕn′-thēz). [t. L: m. s. *nēpenthes*, t. Gk: (neut.) banishing sorrow] —**nepen′thean,** *adj.*

neper (nā′pə, nē′pə), *n. Physics.* a unit used to compare two scalar quantities, esp. currents or voltages, defined as the natural logarithm of the ratio of the two quantities. Also, **napier.** [var. of *napier*, named after J. NAPIER]

nephanalysis (nĕf′ə năl′ĭ sĭs), *n. Meteorol.* a map showing cloud patterns and distribution, esp. such a map drawn from photographs taken by artificial satellites. [f. m. s. Gk *néphos* cloud + ANALYSIS]

nepheline (nĕf′ĭ lĭn), *n.* a mineral, essentially sodium aluminium silicate, $NaAlSiO_4$, occurring in alkali-rich volcanic rocks. Also, **nephelite** (nĕf′ĭ līt′). [t. F, f. s. Gk *nephélē* cloud + *-ine* -INE[2]]

nephelinite (nĕf′ĭ lĭ nīt′), *n. Geol.* a fine-grained, dark rock of volcanic origin, essentially a basalt containing nepheline but no felspar and little or no olivine.

nephelometer (nĕf′ĭ lŏm′ĭ tə), *n.* **1.** *Bacteriol.* an apparatus containing a series of barium chloride standards used to determine the number of bacteria in a suspension. **2.** *Chem., etc.* a device for studying the nature of suspensions by the use of diffuse reflected light. [f. s. Gk *nephélē* cloud + -(O)METER[1]]

nephew (nĕv′yōō, nĕf′yōō), *n.* **1.** a son of one's brother or sister. **2.** a son of one's husband's or wife's brother or sister. **3.** (in euphemistic use) an illegitimate son of a celibate ecclesiastic. **4.** *Obs.* a grandson. **5.** *Obs.* a male descendant of more remote degree. [ME *nevew*, t. OF: m. *neveu*, g. L *nepos* grandson, nephew]

nepho-, a word element meaning 'cloud'. [t. Gk, comb. form of *néphos* cloud]

nephogram (nĕf′ə grăm′), *n.* a photograph of a cloud or clouds.

nephograph (nĕf′ə grăf′, -grăf′), *n.* an instrument for photographing clouds.

nephology (nĭ fŏl′ə jĭ), *n.* the branch of meteorology that treats of clouds. —**nephological** (nĕf′ə lŏj′ĭ kl), *adj.*

nephoscope (nĕf′ə skōp′), *n.* an instrument for determining the altitude of clouds and the velocity and direction of their motion.

nephr-, var. of **nephro-,** before vowels.

nephralgia (nĭ frăl′jyə), *n. Pathol.* pain in the kidney or kidneys.

nephrectomy (nĭ frĕk′tə mĭ), *n.*, *pl.* **-mies.** *Surg.* excision or removal of a kidney.

nephric (nĕf′rĭk), *adj.* renal.

nephridium (nĭ frĭd′ĭ əm), *n.*, *pl.* **-phridia** (-frĭd′ĭ ə). *Zool.* the excretory organ of invertebrates consisting of a tubule with an open or closed motile apparatus at its inner end. [t. NL, f. *nephr-* NEPHR- + *-idium* (dim. suffix)] —**nephrid′ial,** *adj.*

nephrism (nĕf′rĭz′əm), *n. Pathol.* the unhealthy state produced by a chronic kidney disease.

nephrite (nĕf′rīt), *n.* a mineral, a compact or fibrous variety of actinolite, varying from whitish to dark green in colour. See **jade**[1] (def. 1). [t. G: m. *Nephrit*, f. *nephr-* NEPHR- + *-it* -ITE[1]]

nephritic (nĭ frĭt′ĭk), *adj.* of, pertaining to, or affected with nephritis. [t. LL: s. *nephrīticus*, t. Gk: m. *nephrītikós* affected with nephritis]

nephritis (nĭ frī′tĭs), *n. Pathol.* inflammation of the kidneys. [t. LL, t. Gk]

nephro-, a word element referring to the kidneys. Also, **nephr-.** [t. Gk, comb. form of *nephrós* kidney]

nephrolith (nĕf′rə lĭth), *n. Pathol.* a renal calculus.

nephrosis (nĭ frō′sĭs), *n. Pathol.* kidney disease, esp. marked by non-inflammatory degeneration of the tubular system. [f. NEPHR- + -OSIS] —**nephrotic** (nĭ frŏt′ĭk), *adj.*

nephrotomy (nĭ frŏt′ə mĭ), *n.*, *pl.* **-mies.** *Surg.* incision into the kidney, as for the removal of a calculus.

ne plus ultra (nā′ plōōs ōōl′trä), *Latin.* **1.** no more beyond; no further (used in prohibiting). **2.** the acme.

nepman (nĕp′mən), *n.*, *pl.* **-men.** *Soviet Hist.* one who, under the NEP, engaged in a private business.

Nepos (nē′pŏs, nĕp′ŏs), *n.* **Cornelius,** *c.* 99–*c.* 24 B.C., Roman biographer and historian.

nepotism (nĕp′ə tĭz′əm), *n.* patronage bestowed in consideration of family relationship and not of merit. [t. F: m. *népotisme*, t. It.: m. *nepotismo*, ult. der. L *nepos* descendant. See -ISM] —**nepotic** (nĭ pŏt′ĭk), *adj.* —**nep′otist,** *n.*

Neptune (nĕp′tyōōn), *n.* **1.** *Rom. Myth.* the Roman god of the sea. Cf. **Poseidon. 2.** the sea or ocean. **3.** *Astron.* the eighth planet in order from the sun. Its period of revolution is 164·8 years, its mean distance from the sun is 2,794,100,000 miles, and its diameter is 27,840 miles. It has two satellites.

Neptunian (nĕp tyōō′nyən), *adj.* **1.** of or pertaining to Neptune or the sea. **2.** of or pertaining to the planet Neptune. **3.** (*often l.c.*) *Geol.* formed by the action of water.

neptunium (nĕp tyōō′nyəm), *n. Chem.* a radioactive transuranic element, not found in nature, produced artificially by the neutron bombardment of U-238. It decays rapidly to plutonium and then to U-235. *Symbol:* Np; *at. no.:* 93; *at. wt:* 237.

Nerbudda (nə bŭd′ə), *n.* Narbada.

Nereid (nĭə′rĭ ĭd), *n.* **1.** (*sometimes l.c.*) *Gk Myth.* any one of the fifty daughters of the ancient sea-god Nereus; a sea nymph. **2.** (*l.c.*) a marine free-living annelid worm of the genus *Nereis*. Also, **Nereis.** [t. L: s. *Nēreïs*, t. Gk]

Nereus (nĭə′rĭ ōōs′), *n.* See **Nereid.**

Neri (nĭə′rĭ; *It.* nĕ′rē), *n.* **Saint Philip** (*Filippo Neri*), 1515–95, Italian priest: founder of the Congregation of the Oratory.

neritic (nĕ rĭt′ĭk), *adj.* of or pertaining to the shallow waters near land.

Nernst heat theorem (nĕənst; *Ger.* nĕrnst), *Thermodynamics.* the theorem which states that there is no change of entropy for chemical reactions involving crystalline solids at the absolute zero of temperature; the third law of thermodynamics. [named after W. B. *Nernst*, 1864–1941, German physicist]

Nero (nĭə′rō), *n.* (*Nero Claudius Caesar Drusus Germanicus, Lucius Domitius Ahenobarbus*), A.D. 37–68, Roman emperor A.D. 54–68, notorious for his cruelty and corruption. —**Neronian** (nĭ rō′nyən), *adj.*

nerol (nĭə′rŏl), *n.* a colourless alcohol, $C_{10}H_{17}OH$, contained in neroli oil.

neroli oil (nĭə′rə lĭ), an essential oil, brown in colour, derived from orange blossoms of the tree *Citrus bigardia*, and consisting of citral, limonene, linalool, etc.: used in the perfume industry. [t. F, t. It.; named after an Italian Princess *Neroli*]

Neruda (*Sp.* nĕ rōō′dä), *n.* **Pablo** (*Sp.* päb′lō), born 1904, Chilean poet.

Nerva (nû′və), *n.* **Marcus Cocceius** (mä′kəs kŏk sē′əs), A.D. 32?–98, Roman emperor A.D. 96–98.

Nerval (*Fr.* nĕr văl′), *n.* **Gérard de** (*Fr.* zhĕ rär′ də), 1808–55, French poet, critic, and essayist.

nervate (nûrʹvāt), *adj. Bot.* (of leaves) having nerves or veins; nerved.
nervation (nû vāʹshən), *n.* venation.
nerve (nûrv), *n., v.,* **nerved, nerving.** —*n.* **1.** one or more bundles of fibres, forming part of a system which conveys impulses of sensation, motion, etc., between the brain or spinal cord and other parts of the body. **2.** *Dentistry.* **a.** the nerve tissue in the pulp of a tooth. **b.** (popularly but incorrectly) pulp tissue of a tooth. **3.** strength, vigour, or energy. **4.** firmness or courage in trying circumstances: *a position requiring nerve.* **5.** (*pl.*) nervousness: *a fit of nerves.* **6.** *Obs.* a sinew or tendon. **7.** *Slang.* impertinent assurance. **8.** *Bot.* a vein, as in a leaf. **9.** a line or one of a system of lines traversing something. **10. get on one's nerves,** to irritate. —*v.t.* **11.** to give strength, vigour, or courage to. [ME, t. L: m. s. *nervus,* akin to Gk *neûron* sinew, tendon, nerve]
nerve cell, *Anat., Physiol.* **1.** any of the cells constituting the cellular element of nervous tissue. **2.** one of the essential cells of a nerve centre. Also, **neurone.**
nerve centre, **1.** *Anat., Physiol.* a group of nerve cells closely connected with one another and acting together in the performance of some function. **2.** (of a large company, movement, or organization) the centre from which plans, policies, and movements are directed.

Nerve cell
A, Cell; B, Nucleus; C, Dendrites; D, Axon

nerve fibre, *Anat., Physiol.* a process, axon, or dendrite of a nerve cell.
nerve impulse, *Physiol.* a wave of electrical and chemical activity progressing along nerve fibres and acting as a stimulus to muscle, gland, or other nerve cells.
nerveless (nûrvʹlĭs), *adj.* **1.** *Anat., Bot., etc.* without nerves. **2.** lacking strength or vigour; feeble; weak. **3.** lacking firmness or courage; spiritless; pusillanimous. —**nerveʹlessly,** *adv.* —**nerveʹlessness,** *n.*
nerve-racking (nûrvʹrăkʹĭng), *adj.* extremely trying.
Nervi (*It.* nĕrʹvē), *n.* **Pier Luigi** (*It.* pyĕr lwēʹjē), born 1891, Italian architect.
nervine (nûrʹvēn), *adj.* **1.** of or pertaining to the nerves. **2.** acting on, or relieving disorders of, the nerves; soothing the nerves. —*n.* **3.** a nervine medicine.
nerving (nûrʹvĭng), *n. Vet. Sci.* the excision of part of a nerve trunk.
nervous (nûrʹvəs), *adj.* **1.** of or pertaining to the nerves. **2.** having or containing nerves of sensation, etc. **3.** affecting the nerves, as diseases. **4.** suffering from, characterized by, or proceeding from disordered nerves. **5.** highly excitable; unnaturally or acutely uneasy or apprehensive. **6.** characterized by or attended with acute uneasiness or apprehension. **7.** *Obs.* sinewy or strong. [ME, t. L: m. s. *nervōsus* sinewy] —**nervʹously,** *adv.* —**nervʹousness,** *n.*
nervous breakdown, any of various psychiatric illnesses, esp. those attended by nervous debility and exhaustion and undefined physical complaints.
nervous system, *Anat., Zool.* **1.** the system of nerves and nerve centres in an animal. **2.** a particular part of this system: **a.** the **central** or **cerebrospinal nervous system,** the brain and spinal cord. **b.** the **peripheral nervous system,** the system of nerves and ganglia derived from the central system, comprising the cranial nerves, the spinal nerves, the various sense organs, etc. **c.** the **autonomic nervous system,** the system of nerves and ganglia which supply the walls of the vascular system and the various viscera and glands.
nervure (nûrʹvyŏŏə), *n. Bot., Zool.* a vein, as of an insect's wing. [t. F, der. L *nervus* NERVE]
nervy (nûrʹvĭ), *adj.,* **-vier, -viest.** **1.** nervous. **2.** excitable; irritable. **3.** requiring nerve. **4.** having or showing courage; audacious; bold. **5.** strong or vigorous.
n.e.s., not elsewhere specified.
nescience (nĕsʹĭ əns), *n.* **1.** lack of knowledge; ignorance. **2.** agnosticism. [t. LL: m. s. *nescientia,* der. L *nesciens,* ppr., being ignorant] —**nesʹcient,** *adj., n.*
ness (nĕs), *n. Archaic, Dial., or in Placenames.* a headland; a promontory; a cape. [ME *nesse,* OE *ness,* c. MLG *ness;* akin to NOSE]
Ness (nĕs), *n.* **1. Loch,** a lake of Inverness-shire, Scotland. ab. 22 mi. long and 1 mi. wide. **2.** See **Loch Ness monster.**
-ness, a suffix used to form, from adjectives and participles, nouns denoting quality or state (also often, by extension, something exemplifying a quality or state), as in *darkness, goodness, kindness, obligingness, preparedness.* [ME *-nes(se),* OE *-nes(s),* c. G *-niss*]
nesselrode (nĕsʹəl rōdʹ), *n. U.S.* a rich and elaborate frozen dessert made from chestnuts, egg yolks, cream, and sometimes candied fruits.
Nesselrode (nĕsʹəl rōdʹ; *Russ.* nĭ sĭl rôʹdə), *n.* **Count Karl Robert** (*Russ.* kärl rä bĕrtʹ *or* rôʹbərt), 1780–1862, Russian diplomat and statesman.
Nessler's solution (nĕsʹləz), *Chem.* a solution of potassium mercuric iodide in potassium hydroxide; used as a test for ammonia, in the presence of which it forms a brown precipitate. [named after Julius *Nessler,* 1827–1905, German chemist]
Nessus (nĕsʹəs), *n. Gk Legend.* a centaur shot by Hercules with a poisoned arrow. Hercules was himself fatally poisoned by a garment stained with the blood of Nessus, sent to him by Deianira, who thought that it would preserve his love for her.
nest (nĕst), *n.* **1.** a structure formed or a place used by a bird for incubation and the rearing of its young. **2.** a place used by insects, fishes, turtles, rabbits, or the like, for depositing their eggs or young. **3.** a number of birds or animals inhabiting one such place. **4.** a snug retreat, or resting place. **5.** an assemblage of things lying or set close together, as a series of tables, trays, etc., that fit within each other. **6.** a place where something bad is fostered or flourishes: *a robbers' nest.* **7.** the occupants or frequenters of such a place. —*v.t.* **8.** to settle or place in or as in a nest. **9.** to fit or place one within another. —*v.i.* **10.** to build or have a nest: *the swallows nested under the eaves.* **11.** to settle in or as in a nest. **12.** to search for nests: *to go nesting.* **13.** to fit together or one within another. [ME and OE, c. G *Nest;* akin to L *nīdus*]
n'est-ce pas (*Fr.* nĕs päʹ), *French.* isn't that so?
nest egg, **1.** an egg (usually artificial) left in a nest to induce a hen to continue laying eggs there. **2.** money saved as the basis of a fund or for emergencies.
nestle (nĕsʹəl), *v.,* **-tled, -tling.** —*v.i.* **1.** to lie close and snug, like a bird in a nest; snuggle or cuddle. **2.** to lie in a sheltered or pleasant situation. **3.** *Obs.* to make or have a nest. —*v.t.* **4.** to provide with or settle in a nest, as birds. **5.** to settle or ensconce snugly. **6.** to put or press confidingly or affectionately. [ME *nestle(n),* OE *nestlian* (c. D *nestelen*), der. *nest* NEST] —**nesʹtler,** *n.*
nestling (nĕstʹlĭng, nĕsʹlĭng), *n.* **1.** a young bird in the nest. **2.** a young child.
Nestor (nĕsʹtô), *n.* **1.** *Gk Legend.* the wisest and oldest of the Greeks in the Trojan War. **2.** a wise old man.
Nestorian (nĕs tôʹrĭ ən), *n.* one of a sect of Christians, followers of Nestorius, who denied the hypostatic union and were represented as maintaining the existence of two distinct persons in Christ. —**Nestoʹrianism,** *n.*
Nestorius (nĕs tôʹrĭ əs), *n.* died A.D. *c.* 451, Syrian churchman; patriarch of Constantinople A.D. 428–31.
net[1] (nĕt), *n., v.,* **netted, netting,** *adj.* —*n.* **1.** a lacelike fabric with a uniform mesh of cotton, silk, rayon, nylon, or other fibre, often forming the foundation of many kinds of lace. **2.** a piece of meshed fabric for any purpose: *a mosquito net.* **3.** a bag or other contrivance of strong thread or cord wrought into an open, meshed fabric, for catching fish, birds, or other animals. **4.** anything serving to catch or ensnare. **5.** a bag of thread or cord wrought into an open meshed fabric, used for carrying. **6.** a hairnet. **7.** any network or reticulated system of filaments, lines, or the like. **8.** *Tennis, etc.* a ball that hits the net. **9.** *Cricket.* a pitch surrounded by netting, used for practice in batting and bowling. **10.** *Soccer, Hockey, etc.* the goal. —*v.t.* **11.** to cover, screen, or enclose with a net or netting. **12.** to take with a net: *to net fish.* **13.** to set or use nets in (a river, etc.), as for fish. **14.** to catch or ensnare. **15.** *Tennis, etc.* to hit (the ball) into the net. **16.** *Soccer, Hockey, etc.* to kick or hit into the goal; score. —*adj.* **17.** made in the form of or resembling a net. [ME *net(te),* OE *net(t),* c. G *Netz*] —**netʹlikeʹ,** *adj.*
net[2] (nĕt), *adj., n., v.,* **netted, netting.** —*adj.* **1.** exclusive of deductions, as for charges, expenses, loss, discount, etc.: *net earnings.* **2.** sold at net prices. **3.** ultimate; conclusive: *the net result.* —*n.* **4.** net income, profits, or the like. —*v.t.* **5.** to gain or produce as clear profit. Also, **nett.** [t. F: clean, clear. See NEAT]
netball (nĕtʹbôlʹ), *n.* a game similar to basketball played, usually by women, by two teams of seven players.
Neth., Netherlands.
nether (nĕthʹə), *adj.* **1.** lying, or conceived as lying, beneath the earth's surface; infernal: *the nether world.* **2.** lower or under: *his nether lip.* [ME; OE *neothera,* earlier *ni(o)ther(r)a* (c. G *nieder*), der. *nither,* adv., downwards, down, a compar. form]
Netherlands (nĕthʹə ləndz), *n.pl.* **The,** a kingdom in W Europe, bordering on the North Sea, West Germany, and Belgium. 11,889,962 pop. (est. 1962); 13,433 sq. mi. *Capitals:* Amsterdam *and* The Hague. Also, **Holland.** —**Nethʹerlander,** *n.*
Netherlands Antilles, possessions of the Netherlands in the West Indies, comprising Curaçao, Aruba, Bonaire,

St Eustatius, Saba, and part of St Martin. Considered an integral part of the Dutch realm. 199,607 pop. (1963); 366 sq. mi. *Cap.*: Willemstad. Also, **Curaçao.** Formerly, **Netherlands West Indies.**

Netherlands East Indies, Dutch East Indies; a former name of **Indonesia.**

Netherlands New Guinea, a former name of **West Irian.** Also, **Dutch New Guinea.**

nethermost (nĕth′ə mōst′), *adj.* lowest.

nether world, 1. hell. **2.** the afterworld.

Néthou (*Fr.* nĕ to͞o′), *n.* **Pic de** (*Fr.* pēk′ də), a mountain in NE Spain: highest peak of the Pyrenees. 11,165 ft. Spanish, **Pico de Aneto.**

netsuke (nĕt′so͝o kĭ), *n.* a small object of ivory, wood, etc., usually carved or decorated, used as a toggle to prevent a pouch or other article, to which it is attached by a cord, from slipping through the girdle. Worn by the Japanese.

nett (nĕt), *adj.*, *n.*, *v.* net².

netting (nĕt′ĭng), *n.* any of various kinds of net fabric: *fish netting, mosquito netting.*

nettle (nĕt′l), *n.*, *v.*, **-tled, -tling.** —*n.* **1.** any plant of the genus *Urtica*, comprising widely distributed herbs armed with stinging hairs. **2.** any of various allied or similar plants. —*v.t.* **3.** to irritate, irk, provoke, or vex. **4.** to sting as a nettle does. [ME; OE *netele*, c. G *Nessel*]

nettlecloth (nĕt′l klŏth′), *n.* a type of heavy cotton fabric finished in lacquer or enamel to imitate leather; used for waist belts, etc.

nettle rash, *Pathol.* urticaria caused by contact with various plants causing local irritation.

net ton, a short ton.

network (nĕt′wûk′), *n.* **1.** any netlike combination of filaments, lines, passages, or the like. **2.** a netting or net. **3.** *Radio.* a group of transmitting stations linked by wire so that the same programme can be broadcast by all. **4.** *Elect.* a system of interconnected electrical elements, units, or circuits.

Neuchâtel (*Fr.* nœ shȧ tĕl′), *n.* **1.** a canton in W Switzerland. 147,633 pop. (1960); 309 sq. mi. **2.** the capital of this canton, on the **Lake of Neuchâtel** (92 sq. mi.). 33,430 (1960). German, **Neuenburg** (*Ger.* noɪ′ən bo͝ork).

Neue Sächlichkeit (*Ger.* noɪ′ə zĕKH′lĭKH kīt), an art movement in Germany in the 1920s, reacting against expressionism and introducing a new regard for realistic representation. [G: new objectivity]

Neufchâtel (*Fr.* nœ shȧ tĕl), *n.* a soft, white cheese similar to cream cheese, made from whole or partly skimmed milk in Neufchâtel, a town in N France.

Neuilly-sur-Seine (*Fr.* nœ yē sʏr sĕn′), *n.* a town in N France, in Hauts-de-Seine department, a suburb of Paris. 73,315 (1962). Also, **Neuilly.**

Neumann (*Ger.* noɪ′män), *n.* **1. Johann Balthasar** (*Ger.* yō′hän bäl′tä zär), 1687–1753, German rococo architect. **2.** See **Von Neumann.**

neume (nyo͞om), *n.* any of various symbols used in medieval musical notation, and still used for noting Gregorian chant, etc. [ME, t. ML: m. s. *neuma*, t. Gk: m. *pneûma* breath] —**neum′ic,** *adj.*

Neumünster (*Ger.* noɪ mʏn′stər), *n.* a town in West Germany, in central Schleswig-Holstein. 74,200 (est. 1966).

neur-, var. of **neuro-,** before vowels.

neural (nyo͝oə′rəl), *adj.* of or pertaining to a nerve or the nervous system. —**neur′ally,** *adv.*

neuralgia (nyo͝o răl′jə), *n.* *Pathol.* sharp and paroxysmal pain along the course of a nerve. [t. NL. See NEUR-, -ALGIA] —**neural′gic,** *adj.*

neurasthenia (nyo͝oə′rəs thē′nyə), *n.* *Pathol.* nervous debility or exhaustion, as from overwork or prolonged mental strain, characterized by vague complaints of a physical nature in the absence of objectively present causes or lesions.

neurasthenic (nyo͝oə′rəs thĕn′ĭk), *adj.* **1.** pertaining to or suffering from neurasthenia. —*n.* **2.** a person suffering from neurasthenia.

neuration (nyo͝o rā′shən), *n.* venation.

neurectomy (nyo͝o rĕk′tə mĭ), *n.*, *pl.* **-mies.** *Surg.* the removal of a nerve or part thereof.

neurilemma (nyo͝oə′rĭ lĕm′ə), *n.* *Anat.* the delicate membranous sheath of a nerve fibre. Also, **neurolemma.** [var. (by assoc. with LEMMA² husk, outer layer) of *neurilema*, f. NEUR- + m. Gk *eílēma* covering]

neuritis (nyo͝o rī′tĭs), *n.* *Pathol.* **1.** inflammation of a nerve. **2.** continuous pain in a nerve associated with its paralysis and sensory disturbances. [NL. See NEUR-, -ITIS] —**neuritic** (nyo͝o rĭt′ĭk), *adj.*

neuro-, a word element meaning 'tendon', 'nerve'. Also, **neur-.** [t. Gk, comb. form of *neûron*]

neuroanatomy (nyo͝oə′rō ə năt′ə mĭ), *n.*, *pl.* **-mies.** *Anat.* the anatomy of the nervous system. —**neur′oan′atom′ical,** *adj.* —**neur′oan′atom′ically,** *adv.* —**neur′oanat′omist,** *n.*

neuroblast (nyo͝oə′rō blăst′), *n.* *Embryol.* one of the cells in the embryonic brain and spinal cord of vertebrates, which eventually give rise to nerve cells.

neurocoele (nyo͝oə′rō sēl′), *n.* *Embryol.* the cavity (ventricles and central canal) of the embryonic brain and spinal cord.

neurofibril (nyo͝oə′rō fī′brĭl), *n.* *Med.* one of many threadlike processes found in the cytoplasm of nerve cells. —**neu′rofi′brilar,** *adj.*

neurofibroma (nyo͝oə′rō fī brō′mə), *n.* *Pathol.* a tumour consisting of nerve and fibrous tissue.

neurogenic (nyo͝oə′rō jĕn′ĭk), *adj.* *Med.* pertaining to the formation of nervous tissue.

neuroglia (nyo͝o rŏg′lĭ ə), *n.* *Anat.* the delicate connective tissue which supports and binds the essential elements of nervous tissue in the central nervous system. [t. NL, f. Gk: *neuro-* NEURO- + *glía* glue]

neurolemma (nyo͝oə′rō lĕm′ə), *n.* neurilemma.

neurology (nyo͝o rŏl′ə jĭ), *n.* the science of the nerves or the nervous system, esp. the diseases thereof. —**neurological** (nyo͝oə′rə lŏj′ĭ kl), *adj.* —**neurol′ogist,** *n.*

neuroma (nyo͝o rō′mə), *n.*, *pl.* **-mata** (-mə tə), **-mas.** *Pathol.* a tumour formed of nervous tissue. [t. NL. See NEUR-, -OMA]

neuromuscular (nyo͝oə′rō mŭs′kyə lə), *adj.* *Med.* concerning both nerves and muscles.

neurone (nyo͝oə′rōn), *n.* a nerve cell. Also, **neuron** (nyo͝oə′rŏn). [t. Gk: m. *neûron* nerve] —**neuronic** (nyo͝o rŏn′ĭk), *adj.*

neuropath (nyo͝oə′rə păth′), *n.* *Psychol.* a person subject to or affected with a functional nervous disease; a neurotic person.

neuropathic (nyo͝oə′rə păth′ĭk), *adj.* neurotic.

neuropathology (nyo͝oə′rō pə thŏl′ə jĭ), *n.* the pathology of the nervous system. —**neu′ropathol′ogist,** *n.*

neuropathy (nyo͝o rŏp′ə thĭ), *n.* disease of the nervous system. [f. NEURO- + -PATHY]

neurophysiology (nyo͝oə′rō fĭz′ĭ ŏl′ə jĭ), *n.* the study of the physiology of the nervous system.

neuropsychiatry (nyo͝oə′rō sī kī′ə trĭ), *n.* the branch of medicine dealing with diseases involving the mind and nervous system. —**neuropsychiatric** (nyo͝oə′rō sī′kĭ ăt′rĭk), *adj.*

neuropsychosis (nyo͝oə′rō sī kō′sĭs), *n.*, *pl.* **-ses** (-sēz). *Pathol.* mental derangement in association with nervous disease.

neuropterous (nyo͝o rŏp′tə rəs), *adj.* belonging to an order of insects, the *Neuroptera*, that includes the antlions and lacewings, characterized by two pairs of membranous wings with netlike venation. [f. NEURO- + s. Gk *pterón* wing + -OUS]

neurosis (nyo͝o rō′sĭs), *n.*, *pl.* **-ses** (-sēz). psychoneurosis; an emotional disorder in which feelings of anxiety, obsessional thoughts, compulsive acts, and physical complaints without objective evidence of disease, in various patterns, dominate the personality.

neurosurgery (nyo͝oə′rō sûr′jə rĭ), *n.* the branch of medicine pertaining to the surgery of the nervous system. —**neu′rosur′gical,** *adj.*

neurotic (nyo͝o rŏt′ĭk), *adj.* **1.** having a neurosis. **2.** pertaining to the nerves or to nervous disease. —*n.* **3.** a person affected with neurosis. —**neurot′ically,** *adv.*

neurotomy (nyo͝o rŏt′ə mĭ), *n.*, *pl.* **-mies.** surgical cutting of a nerve, as to relieve neuralgia.

neurovascular (nyo͝oə′rō văs′kyo͝o lə), *adj.* *Anat.* of or pertaining to both nerves and blood vessels.

Neusatz (*Ger.* noɪ′zäts), *n.* German name of **Novi Sad.**

Neuss (*Ger.* noɪs), *n.* a town in West Germany, in central North Rhine-Westphalia. 113,200 (est. 1966).

Neustria (nyo͞os′trĭ ə), *n.* the W part of the kingdom of the Franks, roughly N and NW France.

neut., neuter.

neuter (nyo͞o′tə), *adj.* **1.** *Gram.* **a.** denoting or pertaining to one of the three genders of Latin, German, Greek, etc., or one of the two of Dutch, Swedish, etc.: so termed because few if any nouns denoting males or females belong to it, or (as in German) purely for traditional reasons. For example: Latin *nōmen* 'name', *cor* 'heart', *bellum* 'war' are all neuter gender. **b.** (of verbs) intransitive. **2.** sexless, apparently sexless, or of indeterminate sex, as a hermaphrodite or castrated person. **3.** *Zool.* having imperfectly developed sexual organs, as the workers among bees and ants. **4.** *Bot.* having neither stamens nor pistils; asexual. **5.** *Archaic.* neutral. —*n.* **6.** *Gram.* **a.** the neuter gender. **b.** a noun of that gender. **c.** another element marking that gender. **d.** an intransitive verb. **7.** an animal made sterile by castration. **8.** a neuter insect.

9. a person of no or of indeterminate sex. 10. *Bot.* a plant with neither stamens nor pistils. 11. *Archaic.* a neutral. —*v.t.* 12. to castrate. [t. L: neither; r. ME *neutre*, t. OF]

Neutra (*Ger.* noʏ′trȧ), *n.* **Richard Joseph** (*Ger.* rĭkh′ärt yō′zĕf), born 1892, Austrian architect in the U.S.

neutral (nyōō′trəl), *adj.* 1. (of a person or state) refraining from taking part in a controversy or war between others. 2. of no particular kind, colour, characteristics, etc.; indefinite. 3. grey; without hue; of zero chroma; achromatic. 4. having no definite colour, so as to match well with other colours. 5. *Phonet.* pertaining to the vowel schwa (ə); pronounced with the tongue in a central position. 6. *Phonet.* pertaining to the lip shape in articulation in which the lips are neither spread nor rounded, as in the vowels of *cat* and *cart.* 7. *Biol.* neuter. 8. *Chem.* exhibiting neither acid nor alkaline qualities: *neutral salts.* 9. *Elect.* neither positive nor negative; not electrified; not magnetized. —*n.* 10. a person or a state that remains neutral, as in a war. 11. a citizen of a neutral nation. 12. *Mach.* the position or state of disengaged gears or other interconnecting parts: *in neutral.* [late ME, t. L: s. *neutrālis* neuter] —**neu′trally,** *adv.*

neutralism (nyōō′trə lĭz′əm), *n.* the policy of remaining strictly neutral in foreign affairs. —**neu′tralist,** *n.*

neutrality (nyōō trăl′ĭ tĭ), *n.* 1. the state of being neutral. 2. the attitude or status of a nation which does not participate in a war between other nations: *the continuous neutrality of Switzerland.* 3. neutral status, as of a seaport during a war.

neutralize (nyōō′trə līz′), *v.t.*, **-lized, -lizing.** 1. to make neutral. 2. to render ineffective; counteract. 3. *Mil.* to put out of action or make incapable of action. 4. to declare neutral; invest with neutrality. 5. *Chem.* to render inert the peculiar properties of. 6. *Elect.* to render electrically neutral. Also, **neutralise.** —**neu′-traliza′tion,** *n.* —**neu′traliz′er,** *n.*

neutretto (nyōō trĕt′ō), *n. Physics.* a neutral meson.

neutrino (nyōō trē′nō), *n., pl.* **-nos.** *Physics.* a neutral particle with zero rest mass. Originally invented to avoid apparent violation of the conservation laws in radioactive disintegrations, it is now known to exist in two forms—the *neutrino* (emitted with positrons) and the *antineutrino* (emitted with negative electrons).

neutron (nyōō′trŏn), *n. Physics.* a neutral particle with approximately the same mass as a proton. [f. NEUTR(AL) neither positive nor negative + *-on* (after ELECTRON, PROTON)]

neutron bomb, a nuclear weapon which releases a shower of neutrons but relatively little blast.

neutron excess, *Physics.* isotopic number.

neutron star, *Astron.* a hypothetical star with an estimated density 10^7 times greater than a white dwarf; postulated as the result of a gravitational collapse in which pressure is so great that electrons and protons coalesce into neutrons.

neutron temperature, *Physics.* the energy of neutrons, in thermal equilibrium with their surroundings, expressed as a temperature on the assumption that they behave as a monotomic gas.

Nev., Nevada.

Neva (nā′və, nē′və; *Russ.* nĭ vä′), *n.* a river in the NW Soviet Union, flowing from Lake Ladoga through Leningrad into the Gulf of Finland: canalized for ships. 40 mi.

Nevada (nĭ vä′də), *n.* a state in the W United States. 285,278 pop. (1960); 110,540 sq. mi. *Cap.:* Carson City. *Abbrev.:* Nev.

Nevadan (nĭ vä′dn), *adj.* 1. of or pertaining to Nevada. 2. *Geol.* of or denoting the major mountain-building episode which occurred in North America at the end of Jurassic times. —*n.* 3. a native or inhabitant of Nevada.

névé (nĕv′ā; *Fr.* nė vė′), *n.* 1. granular snow accumulated on high mountains and subsequently compacted into glacial ice. 2. a field of such snow. Also, **firn.** [t. F, var. of d. F *nevé*, der. O South-eastern F *neif*, g. L *nix* snow]

never (nĕv′ə), *adv.* 1. not ever; at no time. 2. not at all; absolutely not; not even. 3. to no extent or degree. [ME; OE *nǣfre*, f. *ne* not + *ǣfre* EVER]

nevermore (nĕv′ə mô′), *adv.* never again.

never-never (nĕv′ə nĕv′ə), *Colloq.* —*n.* 1. sparsely inhabited desert country; a remote and isolated region. 2. the hire-purchase system. —*adj.* 3. imaginary: *never-never land.*

Nevers (*Fr.* nə vĕr′), *n.* a town in central France, on the river Loire, the capital of Nièvre department. 41,003 (1968).

nevertheless (nĕv′ə thə lĕs′), *adv.* nonetheless; notwithstanding; however. —**Syn.** See **but**[1].

Nevis (nē′vĭs *for 1*; nĕv′ĭs *for 2*), *n.* 1. one of the Leeward Islands in the West Indies. 12,770 pop. (1960); 50 sq. mi. 2. See **Ben Nevis.**

Nevski (nĕv′skĭ, nĕf′-; *Russ.* nyĕf′skĭy), *n.* **Alexander.** See **Alexander Nevski.**

nevus (nē′vəs), *n., pl.* **-vi** (-vī). *U.S.* naevus. —**nevoid** (nē′void), *adj.*

new (nyōō), *adj.* 1. of recent origin or production, or having only lately come or been brought into being: *a new book.* 2. of a kind now existing or appearing for the first time; novel. 3. having only lately or only now come into knowledge: *a new chemical element.* 4. unfamiliar or strange (fol. by *to*): *ideas new to us.* 5. recently arrived: *New Australians.* 6. having only lately come to a position, status, etc.: *a new minister.* 7. unaccustomed (fol. by *to*): *men new to such work.* 8. coming or occurring afresh; further; additional: *new gains.* 9. fresh or unused: *a new sheet.* 10. different and better, physically or morally: *the operation made a new man of him.* 11. other than the former or the old: *a new era.* 12. being the later or latest of two or more things of the same kind: *the New Testament.* 13. (of a language) in its latest known period, esp. as a living language at the present time: *New Latin.* —*adv.* 14. recently or lately. 15. freshly; anew or afresh. —*n.* 16. something new. [ME and OE *newe*, c. G *neu*, L *novus*, Gk *néos*] —**new′ness,** *n.*

—**Syn.** 1. NEW, FRESH, NOVEL describe that which is not old. NEW applies to that which has not been long in existence: *a new broom, dress* (one recently made or bought). FRESH suggests a condition of newness, not yet affected by use or the passage of time: *a fresh towel, dress* (newly clean). NOVEL suggests newness which has an unexpected quality, or is strange or striking, but generally pleasing: *a novel experience, dress* (a dress of unusual design, or the like).

New Amsterdam (ăm′stə dăm′), a former Dutch town on Manhattan Island: the capital of New Netherland; renamed New York by the British, 1664.

Newark (nyōō′ək), *n.* 1. a town in England, in Nottinghamshire. 24,651 (1961). 2. a city in the U.S., in NE New Jersey, on **Newark Bay.** 405,220 (1960).

New Bedford (bĕd′fəd), a seaport in the U.S., in SE Massachusetts: formerly a chief whaling port. 102,477 (1960).

Newbery Award (nyōō′bə rĭ, -brĭ), an annual award for the most distinguished book for children, awarded at the same time as the Caldecott Award. Also, **Newbery Medal.** [named after John *Newbery*, 1713–67, English publisher of books for children]

Newbolt (nyōō′bōlt′), *n.* **Sir Henry (John),** 1862–1938, English poet and naval historian.

newborn (nyōō′bôn′), *adj.* 1. recently or only just born. 2. born anew; reborn.

New Britain (brĭt′n), an island in the S Pacific, NE of New Guinea: the largest island in the Bismark Archipelago. (Including nearby islands) 87,892 pop. (1954); ab. 14,600 sq. mi. *Cap.:* Rabaul.

New Brunswick (brŭnz′wĭk), a province in SE Canada, E of Maine. 623,000 pop. (est. 1965); 27,985 sq. mi. *Cap.:* Fredericton.

Newburn (nyōō′bən), *n.* a town in England, in Northumberland, on the river Tyne. 27,879 (1961).

Newbury (nyōō′bə rĭ, -brĭ), *n.* a town in England, in Berkshire. 20,397 (1961).

New Caledonia (kăl′ĭ dō′nyə), 1. an island in the S Pacific, ab. 800 mi. E of Australia. 6224 sq. mi. 2. an overseas territory of France comprising this island and other smaller islands: formerly a penal colony. 82,500 pop. (est. 1962); 7200 sq. mi. *Cap.:* Nouméa. See map under **Coral Sea.**

New Castile (kăs tēl′), a region in central Spain: formerly a province. 27,933 sq. mi.

Newcastle (nyōō′kä′səl), *n.* 1. **Thomas Pelham-Holles** (pĕl′əm hŏl′ĭs), **1st Duke of,** 1693–1768, British statesman: prime minister 1754–56; 1757–61. 2. Also, **Newcastle-upon-Tyne** (-tīn′). a seaport in NE England, on the Tyne: shipbuilding. 260,750 (est. 1964). See map under **Hadrian's Wall.** 3. a seaport in Australia, in E New South Wales. 219,300 (est. 1964).

Newcastle disease, a specific, virus-induced disease of chickens, etc., marked by loss of egg production in old birds and by paralysis in chicks.

Newcastle-under-Lyme (nyōō′kä səl ŭn′də līm′), *n.* a town in England, in Staffordshire. 75,688 (1961).

new chum, *Austral.* 1. a novice; one inexperienced in some field. 2. *Rare.* an immigrant.

New Church, New Jerusalem Church.

Newcomen (nyōō′kŭm′ən), *n.* **Thomas,** 1663–1729, English blacksmith: inventor of a steam-engine.

newcomer (nyōō′kŭm′ə), *n.* one who has newly come; a new arrival.

New Deal, 1. the principles of the progressive wing of the U.S. Democratic party, esp. those advocated under the leadership of President Franklin D. Roosevelt. 2. the Roosevelt administration. —**New Dealer.**

New Delhi, a city in N India, adjacent to (old) Delhi; the capital of the Republic of India, in the N central part. 261,545 (1961). See map under **India.**

New Economic Policy, a Soviet economic programme, in effect 1921–28, reviving the wage system and private ownership of some factories and businesses, and abandoning grain requisitions. *Abbrev.:* NEP.

newel (nyo͞o′əl), *n.* **1.** a central pillar or upright from which the steps of a winding stair radiate. **2.** a post at the head or foot of a stair, supporting the handrail. [ME *nowell*, t. OF: m. *noiel* kernel, newel (g. LL *nucāle*, neut. of *nucālis* of or like a nut), b. with *noel* bud, trickle-ornament, g. LL *nōdellus*, der. L *nōdus* knot]

New England, six states in the NE United States: Connecticut, Massachusetts, Rhode Island, Vermont, New Hampshire, and Maine. —**New Englander.**

New England Range, a mountain range in Australia, in NE New South Wales. Highest point, Round Mountain, 5300 ft.

newfangled (nyo͞o′făng′gld), *adj.* **1.** new-fashioned; of a new kind: *newfangled ideas.* **2.** fond of novelty. [der. *newfangle*, ME *newfangel*, f. *newe* NEW + *fangel*, der. ME *fangen* take]

new-fashioned (nyo͞o′făsh′ənd), *adj.* lately come into fashion; of a new fashion.

New Forest, a forest region in England, in S Hampshire: national park. 145 sq. mi.

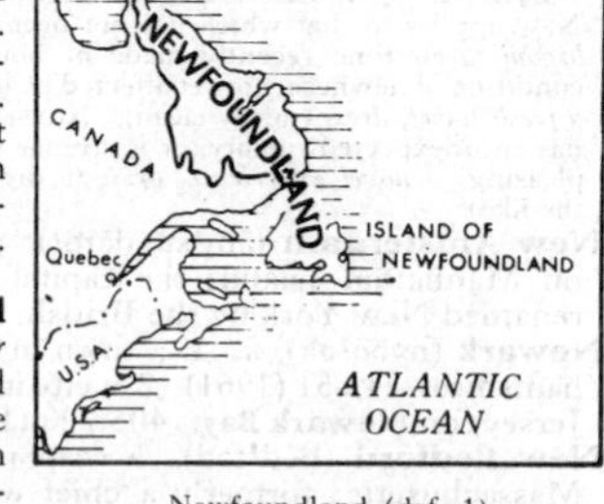

Newfoundland (def. 1)

Newfoundland (nyo͞o′fəndlănd′ *for 1*; nyo͞o found′lənd *for 2*), *n.* **1.** a large island in the eastern part of Canada: became a Canadian province on March 31st, 1949. 498,000 pop. (est. 1965); 42,734 sq. mi. (excluding Labrador). **2.** one of a breed of large, shaggy dogs, orig. from Newfoundland, noted for their sagacity, docility, swimming powers, etc.

Newfoundland (def. 2) (28 in. high at the shoulder)

Newfoundlander (nyo͞o found′lən də), *n.* a native or inhabitant of Newfoundland.

New France, the name of Canada while under French rule, before 1763.

Newgate (nyo͞o′gĭt), *n.* a famous prison in London: destroyed 1902.

New Georgia, 1. a group of islands forming a British protectorate in the Solomon Islands. **2.** the largest of these islands. ab. 50 mi. by 20 mi.

New Granada (grə nä′də), **1.** a former Spanish viceroyalty in NW South America, comprising the present republics of Ecuador, Venezuela, Colombia, and Panama. **2.** early name for Colombia (before the secession of Panama).

New Guinea (gĭn′ĭ), **1.** Also, **Papua.** a large island N of Australia: divided into the Indonesian province of West Irian and the merged Australian territories of Papua and New Guinea. 2,091,373 pop. (est. 1959); ab. 316,000 sq. mi. **2. Territory of,** a territory under the trusteeship of Australia, including NE New Guinea, the Bismarck Archipelago, Bougainville, and other islands: merged with the Territory of Papua, 1945. 1,401,757 (est. 1960); including Papua, 1,905,190 pop. (est. 1960); ab. 93,000 sq. mi. (ab. 69,700 sq. mi. mainland).

Newham (nyo͞o′əm), *n.* an E outer borough of London. 264,000 (1965).

New Hampshire (hămp′shə, -shĭə), a state in the NE United States. 606,921 pop. (1960); 9304 sq. mi. *Cap.:* Concord. *Abbrev.:* N.H.

New Haven (hā′vən), a seaport in the U.S., in Connecticut, on Long Island Sound. 152,048 (1960).

Newhaven (nyo͞o′hā′vən), *n.* a seaport in England, in Sussex. 8325 (1961).

New Hebrides (hĕb′rĭ dēz′), an island group in the S Pacific, ab. 1000 mi. NE of Australia: under joint British and French administration. 62,000 pop. (est. 1962); ab. 5700 sq. mi. *Cap.:* Vila. See map under **Coral Sea.**

Ne Win (nā′wĭn′), born 1911, Burmese soldier and political leader: prime minister 1958–60 and since 1962.

New Ireland, an island in the S Pacific, in the Bismarck Archipelago, NE of New Guinea. (With adjacent islands) 41,465 pop. (1962); ab. 3800 sq. mi.

newish (nyo͞o′ĭsh), *adj.* rather new.

New Jersey (jû′zĭ), a state in the E United States, on the Atlantic coast. 6,066,782 pop. (1960); 7836 sq. mi. *Cap.:* Trenton. *Abbrev.:* N.J. —**New Jerseyite** (jû′zĭ īt′).

New Jerusalem, the heavenly city; the abode of God and His saints. Rev. 21:2.

New Jerusalem Church, the Church composed of the followers of Swedenborg. See **Swedenborgian.**

New Kingdom, the third great period in the history of the ancient Egyptian kingdom, 1580 B.C. to 1085 B.C., comprising dynasties XVIII–XX. Also, **Middle Empire.** See **Old Kingdom, Middle Kingdom.**

new-laid (nyo͞o′lād′), *adj.* **1.** fresh; having just been laid: *new-laid eggs.* **2.** *Slang.* inexperienced; immature in judgement; green.

New Latin, the Latin which became current (notably in scientific literature) after the Renaissance (approximately 1500). Also, **Neo-Latin.**

New Learning, the studies, chiefly in classical literature, of the Renaissance, esp. in the 16th century in England.

New Left, a group of socialist or liberal intellectuals in Britain since the late 1950s and in the U.S. since 1960, characterized by involvement in campaigns for nuclear disarmament, racial equality, and state economic control in various forms, etc.

new look, a complete and radical change in appearance or form.

newly (nyo͞o′lĭ), *adv.* **1.** recently; lately: *a newly wedded couple.* **2.** anew or afresh: *a newly repeated slander.* **3.** in a new manner or form. [ME; OE *nīwlīce*]

Newlyn datum (nyo͞o′lĭn), a fixed level at Newlyn, Cornwall, used as the base to which all other Ordnance Survey levels are related.

newlywed (nyo͞o′lĭ wĕd′), *n.* a recently married person.

Newman (nyo͞o′mən), *n.* **John Henry** (*Cardinal Newman*), 1801–90, English theologian and author.

Newmarket (nyo͞o′mä′kĭt), *n.* **1.** a town in England, in West Suffolk: horseracing. 11,227 (1961). **2.** (*l.c.*) Also, **Newmarket coat.** a long, close-fitting outdoor coat worn by men and women. **3.** (*l.c.*) a kind of card game of the stops family.

New Mexico, a state in the SW United States. 951,023 pop. (1960); 121,666 sq. mi. *Cap.:* Santa Fe. *Abbrev.:* N. Mex. or N.M. —**New Mexican.**

new moon. See **moon** (def. 2a).

New Netherland, a Dutch colony in America on the Hudson (1613) and Delaware rivers: after 1664, included by England in the New York, New Jersey, and Delaware colonies. *Cap.:* New Amsterdam.

New Orleans (ô′lĭ ənz; *older* ô lēnz′), a seaport in the U.S., in SE Louisiana, on the Mississippi: home of traditional jazz. 627,525 (1960).

new penny. See **penny** (def. 1). *Abbrev.:* p.

New Plymouth, a seaport in New Zealand, in W North Island. 31,900 (est. 1965).

Newport (nyo͞o′pôt′), *n.* **1.** a town in England, the county town of Monmouthshire. 108,107 (1961). **2.** a seaport and summer resort in the U.S., in SE Rhode Island: naval base. 47,049 (1960). **3.** a town in England, the chief town of the Isle of Wight. 19,479 (1961).

Newport News, a town in the U.S., in SE Virginia. 113,662 (1960).

new-rich (nyo͞o′rĭch′), *adj.* **1.** characteristic of the nouveau riche. —*n.* **2.** nouveau riche.

news (nyo͞oz), *n.pl.* (*now construed as sing.*) **1.** a report of any recent event, situation, etc. **2.** the report of events published in a newspaper, journal, radio, television, or any other medium. **3.** information, events, etc., considered as suitable for reporting: *it's very interesting, but it's not news.* **4.** information not previously known: *that's news to me.* **5.** newsprint or newspaper. [ME *news*, pl. of ME, OE *newe* that which is new, n. use of *newe*, adj.]

news agency, an organization which collects news and supplies it to newspapers, television and radio stations, etc.

newsagent (nyo͞oz′ā′jənt), *n.* one who deals in newspapers, and usually periodicals, books, stationery, etc.

newsboy (nyo͞oz′boi′), *n.* *Chiefly U.S.* a newspaper-boy.

newscast (nyo͞oz′käst′), *n., v.,* **-cast, -casting.** —*n.* **1.** a radio or television broadcast of news reports. —*v.i.* **2.** to broadcast a news bulletin. —**news′cast′er,** *n.*

newsdealer (nyo͞oz′dē′lə), *n.* *U.S.* a newsagent.

newshawk (nyo͞oz′hôk′), *n.* *Colloq.* a newspaper reporter, esp. one with a keen eye for news. Also, **newshound** (nyo͞oz′hound′).

New Siberian Islands (sī bĭə′rĭ ən), a group of islands in the Arctic Ocean, N of the Soviet Union in Asia: part of the Yakutsk Autonomous Republic.

newsletter (nyo͞oz′lĕt′ə), *n.* **1.** an informal bulletin, as one circulating among people with a common interest. **2.** a confidential report and analysis of the news.

newsman (nyōōz′măn′), *n.* **1.** one who sells or distributes newspapers, periodicals, etc. **2.** a newspaperman; a reporter on a newspaper.

newsmonger (nyōōz′mŭng′gə), *n.* a spreader of news by oral or written means, esp. a gossip.

New South Wales a state in SE Australia. 4,116,706 pop. (1964); 309,433 sq. mi. *Cap.:* Sydney.

New Spain, the former Spanish possessions in the Americas, at one time including Mexico, Central America, the West Indies, and parts of the United States.

newspaper (nyōōs′pā′pə), *n.* **1.** a printed publication issued at regular intervals, usually daily or weekly, and commonly containing news, comment, features, and advertisements. **2.** the organization publishing a newspaper. **3.** a single copy or issue of a newspaper.

newspaper-boy (nyōōs′pā pə boi′), *n.* a boy who sells or delivers newspapers.

newspaperman (nyōōs′pā pə măn′), *n.* a reporter or other employee of a newspaper.

newsprint (nyōōz′prĭnt′), *n.* paper used or made to print newspapers on.

newsreader (nyōōz′rē′də), *n.* one who reads the news bulletin on radio or television.

newsreel (nyōōz′rēl′), *n.* a short film presenting current news events.

newsroom (nyōōz′rŏŏm′, -rōōm′), *n.* **1.** a room in a newspaper office, a television studio, or the like, dealing exclusively with the collection, analysis, and presentation of news. **2.** a room in a library where newspapers, etc., are available for reading.

news-sheet (nyōōz′shēt′), *n.* a short newspaper, usually one printed on a single sheet.

news stall, a bookstall (def. 1).

newsstand (nyōōz′stănd′), *n.* *U.S.* a bookstall (def. 1).

New Stone Age, the neolithic era.

New Style. See **style** (def. 16).

newsvendor (nyōōz′vĕn′də), *n.* a seller of newspapers, etc., esp. one having a regular pitch, as at a street corner.

newsworthy (nyōōz′wûr′thĭ), *adj.* of sufficient interest to appear in a newspaper. **—news′wor′thiness,** *n.*

newsy (nyōō′zĭ), *adj.*, **-sier, -siest,** *n.*, *pl.* **newsies.** *—adj.* **1.** *Colloq.* full of news. *—n.* **2.** *U.S. Colloq.* a newspaperboy. **—news′iness,** *n.*

newt (nyōōt), *n.* a salamander of the genus *Triturus* (or *Triton*), of Europe, North America, and northern Asia. [ME *newte,* for *ewte* (*an ewte* being taken as *a newte*), var. of *evet,* OE *efete.* Cf. EFT[1]]

Crested newt, *Triturus cristatus* (Ab. 6 in. long)

New Test., New Testament.

New Testament, those books in the Bible which were produced by the early Christian Church, and were added to the Jewish scriptures (Old Testament).

newton (nyōō′tn), *n.* *Physics.* the force required to give an acceleration of one metre per second per second to a mass of one kilogram; the derived SI unit of force. *Symbol:* N [named after Sir Isaac NEWTON]

Newton (nyōō′tn), *n.* **Sir Isaac,** 1642–1727, English scientist, mathematician, and philosopher, formulator of the law of gravity. **—Newtonian** (nyōō tō′nyən), *adj.*, *n.*

Newtonabbey (nyōō′tn ăb′ĭ), *n.* a town in Northern Ireland, in Co. Antrim. 37,440 (1961).

Newton Abbot, a town in England, in Devonshire. 18,066 (1961).

Newton Aycliffe (ā′klĭf), a town in England, in Co. Durham. 16,040 (est. 1965).

Newtonian telescope, *Astron.* a telescope employing a reflecting parabolic objective mirror.

Newton-le-Willows (nyōō′tn lə wĭl′ōz), *n.* a town in England, in Lancashire. 21,761 (1961).

Newton's law of gravitation, *Physics.* a law stating that the attractive force of gravitation between any two bodies is proportional to the product of their masses and inversely proportional to the square of the distance between them, the constant of proportionality being known as the **gravitational constant.**

Newton's laws, *Physics.* three laws of motion which form the basis of classical dynamics: **1.** all bodies continue in a state of rest or uniform motion unless they are acted upon by external forces to change that state. **2.** the rate of change of momentum of a body is proportional to the force applied to it. **3.** to every action there is an equal and opposite reaction.

Newton's rings, *Optics.* coloured concentric rings which are produced round the point of contact of a convex lens and a plane reflecting surface.

Newtownards (nyōō′tn ädz′), *n.* a town in Northern Ireland, in Co. Down. 13,090 (1961).

new wave, 1. a movement or trend to break with traditional concepts in art, literature, politics, etc. **2.** nouvelle vague.

New World, The, the Western Hemisphere; the American continents.

new year, 1. the year approaching or newly begun. **2.** (*caps.*) the first day or days of a year. **3.** (*caps.*) New Year's Day.

New Year's Day, the first day of the year; January 1st.

New Year's Eve, the night of December 31st, usually observed with merrymaking.

New York, 1. Also, **New York State.** a state in the NE United States. 16,782,304 pop. (1960); 49,576 sq. mi. *Cap.:* Albany. *Abbrev.:* N.Y. **2.** Also, **New York City.** a seaport in the U.S., in SE New York at the mouth of the Hudson: the largest city in the Western Hemisphere, comprising the boroughs of Manhattan, Queens, Brooklyn, The Bronx, and Staten Island. 7,781,984 (1960). **3. Greater,** New York City and the counties of Nassau, Suffolk, Rockland, Westchester in New York, and the counties of Bergen, Essex, Hudson, Middlesex, Morris, Passaic, Somerset, and Union in New Jersey. 15,404,300 (1960). **—New′ York′er.**

New Zealand (zē′lənd), a country in the S Pacific, a member of the Commonwealth of Nations, consisting of islands (principally North and South Islands). 2,414,984 pop. (1961); 103,416 sq. mi. *Cap.:* Wellington. **—New Zea′lander.**

New Zealand

New Zealand flax, a New Zealand liliaceous plant, *Phormium tenax,* with a rosette of long stiff leaves from which is obtained a fibre used in making rope and twine.

next (nĕkst), *adj.* (*superl. of* **nigh**), *adv.*, *prep.* *—adj.* **1.** immediately following in time, order, importance, etc.: *the next day.* **2.** nearest in place or position: *the next room.* **3.** nearest in relationship or kinship. **4.** *Archaic.* immediately preceding: *the Sunday next before Easter.* *—adv.* **5.** in the nearest place, time, importance, etc. **6.** on the first subsequent occasion: *when next we meet.* *—prep.* **7.** *Archaic.* nearest to: *the house next the church.* [ME *nexte,* OE *nēxt,* var. of *nēhst,* superl. of *nēah* NIGH]

next-door (nĕkst′dôr′), *adj.* **1.** dwelling in or occupying the next house, flat, shop, etc. *—adv.* **2.** at, in, or to the next house, etc.

next friend, *Law.* a person bringing action in a court of law on behalf of a minor or person of unsound mind.

next of kin, 1. a person's nearest relative or relatives. **2.** *Law.* the nearest relative(s), to whom the personal property passes upon the death of an intestate.

nexus (nĕk′səs), *n.*, *pl.* **nexus. 1.** a tie or link; a means of connection. **2.** a connected series. [t. L]

Ney (*Fr.* nĕ), *n.* **Michel** (*Fr.* mē shĕl′) (*Duke of Elchingen, Prince of the Moskova*), 1769–1815, Marshal of France under Napoleon I.

Neyagawa (nā′yə gä′wə), *n.* a town in Japan, in S Honshu island. 113,576 (1965).

Nez Percé (nĕz′ pûs′; *Fr.* nĕ pĕr sĕ′), *pl.* **Nez Percés** (pûr′sĭz; *Fr.* pĕr sĕ′). **1.** (*pl.*) a leading North American Indian tribe of the Shahaptian family. **2.** (formerly as used by the French) a number of tribes supposed to pierce the nasal septum for nose ornaments. **3.** a member of one of these tribes. [t. F: lit., pierced nose]

NF, Norman French.

N.F., **1.** Newfoundland. **2.** Norman French. **3.** (F *nouveau franc*) new franc.

N.F.S., National Fire Service.

N.F.U., National Farmers' Union.

N.G., no good. Also, **n.g.**

ngaio (nī′ō), *n.* a small coastal tree or shrub of New Zealand, *Myoporum laetum,* with narrow leaves and small white flowers marked with purple spots. [t. Maori]

Nganhwei (ən găn′wā′), *n.* Anhwei.

Ngauruhoe (nou′rə hō′ĭ, nă′rə-), *n.* **Mount,** a volcanic peak in the centre of North Island, New Zealand. 7515 ft.

NGk, New Greek. Also, **N. Gk.**

N.H., New Hampshire.

N.H.S., National Health Service.

Ni, *Chem.* nickel.

N.I., Northern Ireland.

niacin (nī′ə sĭn), *n.* **1.** nicotinic acid. **2.** (*cap.*) the trademark for this acid. [f. NI(COTINIC) AC(ID) + -IN[2]]

Niagara (nī ăg′rə, -ăg′ə rə), *n.* **1.** a river in North America, flowing from Lake Erie into Lake Ontario, on the boundary between W New York State and Ontario, Canada. 34 mi. **2.** Niagara Falls.

Niagara Falls, **1.** the falls of the river Niagara: Horseshoe Falls, in Canada, 158 ft high; 2600 ft wide; American Falls, 167 ft high; 1400 ft wide. **2.** a town on the U.S. side of the falls. 102,394 (1960). **3.** a town on the Canadian side. 22,351 (1961).

Niamey (*Fr.* nyȧ mē′), *n.* the capital of Niger, in the SW part. 30,000 (1962).

nib (nĭb), *n.*, *v.*, **nibbed, nibbing.** —*n.* **1.** the point of a pen, esp. a small, tapering metallic device having a split tip for drawing up ink and for writing. **2.** either of the divisions of a nib. **3.** a bill or beak, as of a bird; a neb. **4.** a point of anything. **5.** any pointed extremity. **6.** (*pl.*) crushed cocoa beans. —*v.t.* **7.** to furnish with a nib or point. **8.** *Obs.* to mend or trim the nib of (a quill pen). [OE *nybba* point (in a place name), c. Icel. *nibba* sharp point]

nibble (nĭb′l), *v.*, **-bled, -bling,** *n.* —*v.i.* **1.** to bite off small bits. **2.** to eat or feed by biting off small pieces. **3.** to bite slightly or gently (fol. by *at*). **4.** to evince interest (*at*) without actually accepting. —*v.t.* **5.** to bite off small bits of (a thing). **6.** to eat by biting off small pieces. **7.** to bite (*off*, etc.) in small pieces. —*n.* **8.** a small morsel or bit: *each nibble was eaten with the air of an epicure.* **9.** the act or an instance of nibbling. [late ME; cf. LG *nibbelen*] —**nib′bler,** *n.*

Nibelung (nē′bə lo͝ong′), *n.*, *pl.* **-lungs, -lungen** (lo͝ong′ən). *Germanic Myth.* **1.** one of a race of Northern dwarfs who possessed the treasure later captured by Siegfried. They were named after their king, Nibelung. **2.** one of the followers of Siegfried, who captured the Nibelung's hoard. **3.** (later, in the *Nibelungenlied*) any of the Burgundian kings.

Nibelungenlied (*Ger.* nē′bə lo͝ong ən lēt), *n.* a Middle High German epic, given its present form by an unknown author in south Germany during the first half of the 13th century. [t. G. See NIBELUNG, LIED]

niblick (nĭb′lĭk), *n.* *Golf.* a club (No. 8 iron) with a short, rounded, flat head whose face slopes greatly from the vertical.

nibs (nĭbs), *n.pl.* (*construed as sing.*) *Slang.* **his nibs,** an arrogant or self-important person.

Nicaea (nī sē′ə), *n.* an ancient city in NW Asia Minor: Nicene Creed formulated here, A.D. 325.

Nicaean (nī sē′ən), *adj.* Nicene.

Nicaragua (nĭk′ə răg′yo͞o ə), *n.* **1.** a republic in Central America. 1,559,526 pop. (1964); 57,143 sq. mi. *Cap.:* Managua. **2. Lake,** a lake in SW Nicaragua. 92 mi. long; 34 mi. wide. —**Nic′arag′uan,** *adj.*, *n.*

niccolite (nĭk′ə līt′), *n.* a pale copper-red mineral of a metallic lustre, nickel arsenide (Ni As), usually occurring massive. [f. s. NL *niccolum* nickel + -ITE[1]]

nice (nīs), *adj.*, **nicer, nicest.** **1.** pleasing; agreeable; delightful: *a nice visit.* **2.** amiably pleasant; kind: *they are always nice to strangers.* **3.** characterized by or requiring great accuracy, precision, skill, or delicacy: *nice workmanship.* **4.** requiring or showing tact or care; delicate. **5.** showing minute differences; minutely accurate, as instruments. **6.** minute, fine, or subtle, as a distinction. **7.** having or showing delicate and accurate perception: *a nice sense of colour.* **8.** refined as to manners, language, etc. **9.** suitable or proper: *not a nice song.* **10.** carefully neat as to dress, habits, etc. **11.** dainty or delicious, as food. **12.** dainty as to taste. **13.** *Obs.* coy, shy, or reluctant. **14.** *Obs.* wanton. **15.** *Obs.* foolish. [ME, t. OF: simple, g. L *nescius* not knowing] —**nice′ly,** *adv.* —**nice′ness,** *n.*

Nice (*Fr.* nēs), *n.* a coastal resort in SE France, the capital of Alpes-Maritimes department. 292,958 (1962).

Nicene (nī sēn′), *adj.* of or pertaining to Nicaea. Also, **Nicaean.** [ME, t. LL: m. s. *Nicēnus*, der *Nicēa*, t. Gk: m. *Níkaia*, a town in Bithynia]

Nicene Council, *Eccles.* either of two general ecclesiastical councils which met at Nicaea, the first in A.D. 325 to deal with the Arian heresy, the second in A.D. 787 to consider the question of images.

Nicene Creed, **1.** a formal statement of the chief tenets of Christian belief, adopted by the first Nicene Council. **2.** a later creed of closely similar form referred, perhaps erroneously, to the Council of Constantinople (A.D. 381) and hence sometimes known as the **Niceno-Constantinopolitan Creed,** received universally in the Eastern Church, and, with an addition introduced in the 6th century, accepted generally throughout western Christendom.

nicety (nī′sĭ tĭ), *n.*, *pl.* **-ties.** **1.** a delicate or fine point: *niceties of protocol.* **2.** a fine distinction; subtlety. **3.** (*often pl.*) something nice; a refinement or elegance, as of manners or living. **4.** the quality of being nice. **5.** delicacy of character, as of something requiring care or tact: *a matter of considerable nicety.* **6. to a nicety,** in great detail; with precision. [ME *nycete*, t. OF: m. *nicete*, der. *nice* NICE]

niche (nĭch), *n.*, *v.*, **niched, niching.** —*n.* **1.** an ornamental recess in a wall, etc., usually round in section and arched, as for a statue or other decorative object. **2.** a place or position suitable or appropriate for a person or thing. **3.** *Ecol.* the position or function of an organism in a community of plants and animals. —*v.t.* **4.** to place in a niche. [t. F, der. *nicher* to make a nest, g. Gallo-Rom. *nīdicāre*, der. L *nīdus* nest]

Nicholas (nĭk′ə ləs), *n.* **1.** the name of five popes. **2. Grand Duke,** 1856–1929, Russian general in World War I. **3. Saint, a.** Santa Claus. **b.** fl. 4th cent., bishop in Asia Minor, patron saint of Russia, protector of children.

Nicholas I, **1. Saint,** ('*the Great*') died A.D. 867, Italian ecclesiastic; pope A.D. 858–867. **2.** 1796–1855, tsar of Russia 1825–55.

Nicholas II, 1868–1918, tsar of Russia 1894–1917, executed 1918.

Nicholson (nĭk′l sən), *n.* **Ben,** born 1894, English abstract painter.

Nichrome (nī′krōm), *n.* *Trademark.* a nickel-based alloy, containing chromium and iron, having high electrical resistance and stability at high temperatures.

Nicias (nĭs′ĭ əs), *n.* died 414 B.C., Athenian aristocratic statesman and general.

nick (nĭk), *n.* **1.** a notch, groove, or the like, cut into or existing in a thing. **2.** a hollow place produced in an edge or surface, as of a dish, by breaking. **3.** a small groove on one side of the shank of a printing type, serving as a guide in setting or to distinguish different types. See diag. under **type.** **4.** *Slang.* prison. **5. in the nick of time,** at the vital or last possible moment. —*v.t.* **6.** to make a nick or nicks in; notch. **7.** to record by means of a notch or notches. **8.** to cut into or through. **9.** to incise certain tendons at the root of (a horse's) tail when setting it, to cause him to carry it higher. **10.** to hit, guess, catch, etc., exactly. **11.** *Slang.* to capture or arrest. **12.** to trick, cheat, or defraud. [late ME; cf. OE *gehnycned* wrinkled]

Nick (nĭk), *n.* the devil (usually **Old Nick**). [familiar use of *Nicholas*, proper name]

nickel (nĭk′l), *n.*, *v.*, **-elled, -elling** or (*U.S.*) **-eled, -eling.** —*n.* **1.** *Chem.* a hard, silvery white, ductile and malleable metallic element, allied to iron and cobalt, not readily oxidized, and much used in the arts, in making alloys, etc. *Symbol:* Ni; *at. wt:* 58·71; *at. no.:* 28; *sp. gr.:* 8·9 at 20°C. **2.** *U.S.* a coin composed of or containing nickel, now a five-cent piece. —*v.t.* **3.** to cover or coat with nickel. [t. Sw., short for *kopparnickel* niccolite, t. G: half-trans., half-adoption of *Kupfernickel*, said to mean copper demon, since it looks like copper but yields none]

nickel bloom, annabergite.

nickel carbonyl, *Chem.* a volatile liquid, Ni $(CO)_4$, used in nickel plating and formed in the Mond process for purifying nickel.

nickelic (nĭ kĕl′ĭk), *adj.* *Chem.* of or containing nickel, esp. in the trivalent state.

nickeliferous (nĭk′ə lĭf′ə rəs), *adj.* containing or yielding nickel.

nickelodeon (nĭk′ə lō′dĭ ən), *n.* **1.** *U.S.* (formerly) a place of amusement with a film or variety show, etc., to which the price of admission was five cents. **2.** an early jukebox. [f. NICKEL (def. 2) + *odeon*, var. of ODEUM]

nickelous (nĭk′ə ləs), *adj.* *Chem.* containing bivalent nickel.

nickel plate, a thin coating of nickel deposited on the surface of a piece of metal by electroplating or otherwise.

nickel-plate (nĭk′l plāt′), *v.t.*, **-plated, -plating.** to coat with nickel by electroplating or otherwise.

nickel silver, German silver.

nicker[1] (nĭk′ə), *n.* one who or that which nicks. [f. NICK + -ER[1]]

nicker[2] (nĭk′ə), *v.i.*, *n.* *Scot. and N Dial.* **1.** neigh. **2.** laugh; snicker. [appar. var. of *nicher*, *neigher*, freq. of NEIGH. Cf. LG *gnickern*]

nicker[3] (nĭk′ə), *n.*, *pl.* **nicker.** *Slang.* a pound sterling.

nick-nack (nĭk′năk′), *n.* knick-knack.

nickname (nĭk′nām′), *n.*, *v.*, **-named, -naming.** —*n.* **1.** a name added to or substituted for the proper name of a person, place, etc., as in ridicule or familiarity. **2.** a familiar form of a proper name, as *Jim* for *James.* —*v.t.* **3.** to give a nickname to, or call by a specified nickname. **4.** to call by an incorrect or improper name. [ME *nekename*, for *ekename* (*an ekename* being taken as *a nekename*). See EKE[2], NAME]

Nicobar Islands (nĭk′ō bä′), a group of small islands belonging to India in the Bay of Bengal, W of the Malay Peninsula: a part of the centrally administered territories of Andaman and Nicobar Islands. 12,009 pop. (1951); 635 sq. mi.

Nicolai (*Ger.* nē kō lī′, nĭk′ō lī), *n.* **Carl Otto Ehrenfried** (*Ger.* kärl ōt′ō ĕ′rən frēt), 1810–49, German composer.

Nicolson (nĭk′əl sn), *n.* **Sir Harold (George),** 1886–1968, English diplomat, author, and critic.

Nicosia (nĭk′ə sē′ə, -sĭə′), *n.* the capital of Cyprus, in the central part. 103,000 (est. 1964).

nicotinamide (nĭk′ə tē′nə mīd′), *n. Biochem.* a colourless crystalline solid, $C_6H_4NCONH_2$, the amide of nicotinic acid and a component of the vitamin B complex.

nicotine (nĭk′ə tēn′), *n.* a poisonous alkaloid, $C_{10}H_{14}N_2$, the active principle of tobacco, obtained as a colourless or nearly colourless, oily, acrid liquid. Also, **nicotin** (nĭk′ə tĭn). [t. F, der. Jacques *Nicot*, 1530–1600, who introduced tobacco into France in 1560]

nicotinic acid (nĭk′ə tĭn′ĭk), *Chem.* an acid derived from the oxidation of nicotine, $(C_5H_4N)COOH$, found in fresh meat, yeast, etc.; niacin. The component of the vitamin B complex which counteracts pellagra.

nicotinism (nĭk′ə tē nĭz′əm), *n.* a pathological condition caused by excessive use of tobacco.

Nictheroy (*Port.* nē tė rȯy′), *n.* Niteroi.

nictitate (nĭk′tĭ tāt′), *v.i.*, **-tated, -tating.** to wink. Also, **nictate** (nĭk′tāt). [t. ML: m. s. *nictitātus*, pp. of *nictitāre*, freq. of L *nictāre* wink] —**nic′tita′tion, nicta′tion,** *n.*

nictitating membrane, a thin membrane, or inner or third eyelid, present in many animals, capable of being drawn across the eyeball, as for protection.

Nidaros (*Norw.* nē′dȧ rōs), *n.* former name of **Trondheim.**

niddering (nĭd′ə rĭng), *Archaic.* —*n.* **1.** a cowardly or base person. —*adj.* **2.** cowardly; base. Also, **nidering.** [erroneous var. of *nithing*, t. Scand.; cf. Icel. *nīdhingr*]

nide (nīd), *n.* a nest or brood, esp. of pheasants. [t. L: m. s. *nīdus* nest]

nidicolous (nĭ dĭk′yo͝o ləs), *adj. Ornith.* denoting birds which are helpless when hatched and remain in the nest for some time.

nidificate (nĭd′ĭ fĭ kāt′), *v.i.*, **-cated, -cating.** to build a nest. Also, **nidify.** [t. L: m. s. *nidificātus*, pp.] —**nid′-ifica′tion,** *n.*

nidifugous (nĭ dĭf′yo͝o gəs), *adj. Ornith.* denoting birds which are active soon after hatching and leave the nest almost at once.

nidify (nĭd′ĭ fī′), *v.i.*, **-fied, -fying.** nidificate.

nidus (nī′dəs), *n.*, *pl.* **-di** (-dī). **1.** a nest, esp. one in which insects, etc., deposit their eggs. **2.** a place or point in a living organism where a germ, whether proper or foreign to the organism, normal or morbid, may find means of development. [t. L. See NEST]

Niebuhr (nē′bo͞oə *for 2*; *Ger.* nē′bo͞or), *n.* **1. Barthold Georg** (*Ger.* bär′tōlt gė ōrk′), 1776–1831, German historian. **2. Reinhold** (rīn′hōld), born 1892, U.S. theologian.

niece (nēs), *n.* **1.** a daughter of one's brother or sister. **2.** a daughter of one's husband's or wife's brother or sister. **3.** (in euphemistic use) an illegitimate daughter of a celibate ecclesiastic. [ME *nece*, *nice*, t. OF: m. *niece*, g. VL *neptia*, r. L *neptis* granddaughter, niece]

Niederösterreich (*Ger.* nē′dər œs tə rīKH), *n.* German name of **Lower Austria.**

Niedersachsen (*Ger.* nē′dər zäKH sən), *n.* German name of **Lower Saxony.**

niello (nĭ ĕl′ō), *n.*, *pl.* **nielli** (nĭ ĕl′ĭ), **niellos,** *v.*, **-loed, -loing.** —*n.* **1.** a black metallic composition, consisting of silver, copper, lead, and sulphur, with which an incised design is filled in to produce an ornamental effect. **2.** ornamental work produced by this process. **3.** a specimen of such work. —*v.t.* **4.** to decorate by means of niello; treat with niello or by the niello process. [t. It., g. L *nigellus* blackish]

Nielsen (*Dan.* nėl′sən), *n.* **Carl (August)** (*Dan.* kärl ȧw′go͞ost), 1865–1931, Danish composer.

Niemen (nē′mən; *Pol.* nyĕ′mĕn), *n.* Polish name of **Neman.**

Niemeyer (nē′mī′ə), *n.* **Oscar,** born 1907, Brazilian architect.

Niemöller (nē′mə lə; *Ger.* nē′mœ lər), *n.* **Martin** (mä′-tĭn; *Ger.* mär′tēn), born 1892, German Protestant theologian; prominent anti-Nazi.

Niersteiner (*Ger.* nēr′shtīn ər), *n.* a white Rhine wine. [t. G: f. *Nierstein* place near Mainz + *-er* -ER[1]]

Nietzsche (*Ger.* nē′chə), *n.* **Friedrich Wilhelm** (*Ger.* frē′drĭKH vĭl′hĕlm), 1844–1900, German philosopher.

Nietzscheism (nē′chə ĭz′əm), *n.* the philosophy of Nietzsche, emphasizing self-aggrandizement, or the will to power, as the chief motivating force of both the individual and society. Also, **Nie′tzscheanism.** —**Nie′-tzschean,** *n.*, *adj.*

nieve (nēv), *n. Archaic except Scot. and N Dial.* a fist. [ME *neve*, t. Scand.; cf. Icel. *hnefi* fist]

Nièvre (*Fr.* nyĕ′vr), *n.* a department in central France. 245,921 pop. (1962); 2658 sq. mi. *Cap.:* Nevers.

Ni-Fe accumulator (nī′fē′), *Trademark.* an Edison accumulator. [f. chemical symbols NI + FE]

Niflheim (nĭv′əl hām′), *n.* (in old Scand. cosmogony) the world of eternal darkness and fog in the north; a place of punishment for the dead. Also, **Nifelheim.** [t. Icel.]

nifty (nĭf′tĭ), *adj.*, **-tier, -tiest,** *n.*, *pl.* **-ties.** *Slang.* —*adj.* **1.** smart; stylish; fine. —*n.* **2.** *Chiefly U.S.* something nifty, as a smart or clever remark. [orig. theat. slang]

Niger (nī′jə), *n.* **1.** a river in W Africa rising in S Guinea, flowing NE through Mali, and then SE through Nigeria into the Gulf of Guinea. ab. 2600 mi. **2.** an independent republic in NW Africa; formerly part of French West Africa. 2,400,000 pop. (est. 1959); 458,976 sq. mi. *Cap.:* Niamey.

Nigeria (nī jĭə′rĭ ə), *n.* a republic in W Africa: a member of the Commonwealth of Nations; formerly a British colony and protectorate. 55,653,821 pop. (1963); 360,000 sq. mi. *Cap.:* Lagos. Official name, **Federation of Nigeria.** —**Nige′rian,** *adj.*, *n.*

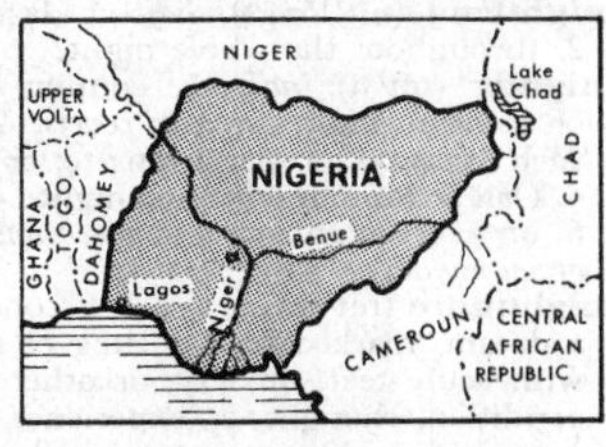

Nigeria

niggard (nĭg′əd), *n.* **1.** an excessively parsimonious or stingy person. —*adj.* **2.** niggardly. [ME, f. (obs.) *nig* niggard (t. Scand.; cf. d. Sw. *nygg*) + -ARD]

niggardly (nĭg′əd lĭ), *adj.* **1.** parsimonious; stingy. **2.** meanly small or scanty: *a niggardly allowance.* —*adv.* **3.** in the manner of a niggard. —**nig′gardliness,** *n.*

nigger (nĭg′ə), *n.* **1.** (offensively) a Negro. **2.** (offensively) a member of any dark-skinned race. **3. nigger in the woodpile,** a hidden snag. —*adj.* **4.** (offensively) denoting or pertaining to a Negro or dark-skinned person. [var. of *neger*, t. F: m. *nègre*, t. Sp.: m. *negro* NEGRO]

niggle (nĭg′l), *v.*, **-gled, -gling.** —*v.i.* **1.** to trifle; work ineffectively. **2.** to make constant petty criticisms. —*v.t.* **3.** to irritate; annoy. [appar. t. Scand.; cf. Norw. *nigla*] —**nig′gler,** *n.*

nigh (nī), *adv.*, *adj.* **nigher, nighest** or **next,** *v.*, *prep.* —*adv.* **1.** near in space, time, or relation. **2.** *Archaic or Dial.* nearly or almost. —*adj.* **3.** being near; not distant; near in relationship. **4.** short or direct. **5.** *Archaic.* (with reference to animals or vehicles) left or near. **6.** *Archaic.* parsimonious. —*v.i.*, *v.t.* **7.** to approach. —*prep.* **8.** near. [ME *nigh(e)*, *neye*, OE *nēah*, *nēh*, c. G *nahe*]

night (nīt), *n.* **1.** the interval of darkness between sunset and sunrise. **2.** nightfall. **3.** the darkness of night; the dark. **4.** a state or time of obscurity, ignorance, misfortune, etc. [ME; OE *niht*, *neaht*, c. G *Nacht*]

night-bird (nīt′bûd′), *n.* **1.** any bird of nocturnal habits. **2.** *Colloq.* one who is habitually up or prowling at night; a nighthawk.

night blindness, nyctalopia (def. 1).

nightcap (nīt′kăp′), *n.* **1.** (formerly) a cap for the head, worn in bed. **2.** *Colloq.* an alcoholic or other drink, esp. a hot one, taken before going to bed.

nightclothes (nīt′klōthz′), *n. pl.* garments designed to be worn in bed.

nightclub (nīt′klŭb′), *n.* a place of entertainment, open until late, offering food, drink, cabaret, dancing, etc.

nightdress (nīt′drĕs′), *n.* **1.** dress or clothing for wearing in bed. **2.** a loose, full-length garment, worn in bed by women and children.

nightfall (nīt′fôl′), *n.* the coming of night.

nightgown (nīt′goun′), *n.* a nightdress or nightshirt.

nighthawk (nīt′hôk′), *n.* **1.** the nightjar or goatsucker. **2.** any of several goatsuckers of the genus *Chordeiles*, all more or less nocturnal, as the **common nighthawk,** mosquito hawk, or bullbat (*C. minor*). **3.** *Colloq.* one who is habitually up or prowling about at night.

night heron, any of certain thick-billed herons of crepuscular or nocturnal habits, of the genus *Nycticorax* and allied genera, as the **black-crowned night heron** (*Nycticorax nycticorax*).

nightie (nī′tĭ), *n.* a nightdress. Also, **nighty.**

nightingale (nī′tĭng gāl′), *n.* a small migratory bird of the thrush family, esp. the common nightingale, *Luscinia megarhyncha*, of Europe, noted for the melodious song of the male given chiefly at night during the breeding season. [ME *nightyngale*, nasalized var. of *nightegale*, OE *nihtegale*, c. G *Nachtigall*, lit., night singer (cf. OE *galan* sing)]

Nightingale, *Luscinia megarhyncha* (6½ in. long)

Nightingale (nī′tĭng gāl′), *n.* **Florence,** 1820–1910, English nurse: reformer of hospital nursing.

nightjar (nīt′jä′), *n.* any goatsucker, esp. the common species, *Caprimulgus europaeus.*

night latch, a spring latch for a door or the like, which when adjusted for use, as at night, prevents the door from being opened from outside except by a key.

night-life (nīt′līf′), *n.* the entertainments and activity of a place at night, as in nightclubs, etc.

night-light (nīt′līt′), *n.* a dim light left burning throughout the night.

nightline (nīt′līn′), *n.* a fishing line left in a river, etc., overnight.

nightlong (nīt′lŏng′), *adj.* **1.** lasting all night. —*adv.* **2.** throughout the whole night.

nightly (nīt′lĭ), *adj.* **1.** coming, occurring, appearing, or active at night: *nightly revels.* **2.** coming or occurring each night. **3.** of, pertaining to, or characteristic of night. **4.** *Obs. or Rare.* resembling night. —*adv.* **5.** at or by night. **6.** on every night: *for one week only, performances will be given nightly.*

nightmare (nīt′mēə′), *n.* **1.** a condition during sleep, or a dream, marked by a feeling of suffocation or distress, with acute fear, anxiety, or other painful emotion. **2.** a condition, thought, or experience suggestive of a nightmare in sleep. **3.** a monster or evil spirit formerly supposed to oppress persons during sleep. [ME. See NIGHT, MARE[2]] —**night′mar′ish,** *adj.*

night owl, *Colloq.* a person who often stays up late.

night-porter (nīt′pô′tə), *n.* a porter or doorkeeper on duty at night.

night raven, **1.** *Now Poetic.* a bird that cries in the night; an ill omen. **2.** a night heron.

nightrider (nīt′rī′də), *n.* *Southern U.S.* one of a band of mounted men committing deeds of violence at night, as for purposes of intimidation or vengeance. —**night′-rid′ing,** *n.*

nightrobe (nīt′rōb′), *n.* **1.** a dressing-gown. **2.** a night-dress.

nights (nīts), *adv.* *Now Colloq. or Dial.* at night.

night school, a school held in the evening, esp. for those who cannot attend a day school; evening classes.

nightshade (nīt′shād′), *n.* **1.** any of various plants of the solanaceous genus *Solanum,* esp. *S. nigrum* (**black nightshade**) or *S. dulcamara* (**woody nightshade,** or bittersweet). **2.** any of various other solanaceous plants, esp. the **deadly nightshade,** *Atropa belladonna.* [ME; OE *nihtscada.* See NIGHT, SHADE]

night shift, **1.** a work period during the night, esp. the shift between 11 p.m. and 6.30 a.m. in the mining industry. **2.** the group of workers working this shift.

nightshirt (nīt′shûrt′), *n.* a knee-length shirt or loose garment worn in bed by men or boys.

night soil, the contents of privies, cesspools, etc., used as manure.

nightstick (nīt′stĭk′), *n.* *U.S.* a heavy stick or long club carried by a policeman at night, and sometimes in the daytime.

night-time (nīt′tīm′), *n.* the time between evening and morning. Also, *Poetic,* **night-tide** (nīt′tīd′).

nightwalker (nīt′wô′kə), *n.* one who walks or prowls about in the night, as a thief, a prostitute, etc. —**night′-wal′king,** *n.*

night watch, **1.** a watch or guard kept during the night. **2.** the person or persons keeping such a watch. **3.** (*usually pl.*) a period or division of the night.

night-watchman (nīt′wŏch′mən), *n., pl.* **-men** (-mən). a man, usually elderly, employed to guard property, etc., at night.

nightwear (nīt′wēə′), *n.* clothes for wearing in bed.

nighty (nī′tĭ), *n., pl.* **nighties.** nightie.

nigrescent (nī grĕs′ənt), *adj.* blackish. [t. L: s. *nigrescens,* ppr., becoming black] —**nigres′cence,** *n.*

nigrify (nĭg′rĭ fī′), *v.t.,* **-fied, -fying.** to make black.

nigritude (nĭg′rĭ tyōōd′), *n.* **1.** blackness. **2.** something black. **3.** negritude. [t. L: m. *nigritūdo*]

nigrosine (nĭg′rə sĭn), *n.* *Chem.* any of a class of black dyestuffs based on the oxidation products of aniline, used as pigments in ink, shoe polish, etc.

nihil (nī′hĭl), *n.* nothing; a thing of no value. [t. L]

nihilism (nī′ĭ lĭz′əm), *n.* **1.** total disbelief in religion or moral principles and obligations, or in established laws and institutions. **2.** *Philos.* **a.** a belief that there is no objective basis of truth. **b.** an extreme form of scepticism, denying all real existence. **c.** nothingness or non-existence. **3.** (*sometimes cap.*) the principles of a Russian revolutionary group, active in the latter half of the 19th century, holding that existing social and political institutions must be destroyed in order to clear the way for a new state of society, and in its extreme measures employing terrorism, assassination, etc. **4.** terrorism or revolutionary activity. [f. L *nihil* nothing + -ISM] —**ni′hilist,** *n.* —**ni′hilis′tic,** *adj.*

nihility (nī hĭl′ĭ tĭ), *n.* nothingness.

nihil obstat (nī′ĭl ŏb′stăt), *Latin.* nothing hinders (used by an official Roman Catholic censor to grant permission for publication of a book containing nothing contrary to faith or morals).

Niigata (nyē′ĭ gä′tə), *n.* a seaport in central Japan, on NW Honshu island. 356,302 (1965).

Niihama (nyē′ĭ hə mə), *n.* a town in Japan, in W Shikoku island. 125,155 (1965).

Nijinsky (nĭ jĭn′skĭ; *Russ.* nĭ zhĭn′skĭy), *n.* **Waslaw** or **Vaslaw** (*Russ.* våts láf′), 1890–1950, Russian ballet-dancer and choreographer.

Nijmegen (nī′mā′gən; *Du.* nĕy′mė KHə), *n.* a town in the Netherlands, in S Gelderland, on the river Waal: peace treaty, 1678. 139,781 (1965). Also, **Nimwegen.**

nikau (nē′kou), *n.* the only palm found in New Zealand, *Rhopalostylus sapida.* [t. Maori]

Nike (nī′kē), *n.* *Gk Myth.* **1.** the goddess of victory, called by the Romans Victoria, represented as a winged maiden, a palm branch in one hand and a garland in the other, or a fillet outstretched in both hands. **2.** the goddess Athena as the giver of victory.

nikethamide (nĭ kĕth′ə mīd′), *n.* *Pharm.* a drug used as a respiratory stimulant.

Nikko (nyĭk′ō), *n.* a town in central Japan, on Honshu island: famous for its shrines and temples. 32,031 (1965).

Nikolaev (*Russ.* nĭ kå lá′yĭf), *n.* a city in the SW Soviet Union in Europe. 280,000 (est. 1965). Formerly, **Vernoleninsk.**

nil (nĭl), *n.* nothing. [t. L, contr. of *nihil*]

Nile (nīl), *n.* **1.** a river in E Africa, flowing N from Lake Victoria to the Mediterranean. 3473 mi. (from the headwaters of the river Kagera, ab. 4000 mi.). **2. Blue,** a tributary of the Nile, flowing from Lake Tana in Ethiopia into the Nile at Khartoum. **3. White,** a part of the Nile above Khartoum.

Nile blue, pale greenish blue.

Nile green, pale bluish green.

nilgai (nĭl′gī), *n., pl.* **-gais,** (*esp. collectively*) **-gai.** a large antelope of E India, *Boselaphus tragocamelus,* the male coloured bluish grey, the hornless female tawny. Also, **nylghau, nylghai.** [t. Hind.: lit., blue cow]

Nilgai, *Boselaphus tragocamelus* ($7\frac{1}{2}$ ft long, up to ab. $4\frac{1}{2}$ ft high at the shoulder)

Nilgiri Hills (nĭl′gĭ rĭ), a group of mountains in S India, in Madras state. Highest peak, Mt Dodabetta, 8760 ft.

nill (nĭl), *v.t., v.i.* *Archaic.* to be unwilling: *will he, nill he.* [ME *nille(n),* OE *nyllan,* f. *ne* not + *willan* will]

Nilometer (nī lŏm′ĭ tə), *n.* a graduated column or the like used to measure the height of the floods of the Nile. [t. Gk: m. s. *Neilométrion*]

Nilotic (nī lŏt′ĭk), *adj.* of or pertaining to the river Nile or the inhabitants of the Nile region. [t. L: s. *Nīlōticus,* t. Gk: m. *Neilōtikós*]

Nilsson (*Sw.* nēl′sŏn), *n.* **Birgit** (*Sw.* bēr′gēt), born 1918, Swedish operatic soprano.

nim[1] (nĭm), *v.t.,* **nam** or **nimmed; nomen, nome,** or **nimmed; nimming.** *Archaic.* **1.** to take. **2.** to steal. [ME; OE *niman,* c. G *nehmen,* Goth. *niman*]

nim[2] (nĭm), *n.* a game in which two players take counters, matches, etc. in turns from piles or patterns, the object being either to draw the last match, etc., or to avoid drawing it. [special use of NIM[1]]

nimble (nĭm′bl), *adj.,* **-bler, -blest.** **1.** quick and light in movement; moving with ease; agile; active; rapid: *nimble feet.* **2.** quick in apprehending, devising, etc.: *nimble wits.* **3.** cleverly contrived. [ME *nymel,* repr. OE var. (unrecorded) of *numol* quick at taking, der. *niman* take] —**nim′bleness,** *n.* —**nim′bly,** *adv.*

nimbostratus (nĭm′bō strā′təs), *n.* *Meteorol.* a low, formless cloud layer, of a nearly uniform dark grey; a layer type of rain cloud. [f. *nimbo-* (comb. form of NIMBUS) + STRATUS]

nimbus (nĭm′bəs), *n., pl.* **-bi** (-bī), **-buses.** **1.** a bright cloud anciently conceived of as surrounding a deity of the classical mythology when appearing on earth. **2.** a cloud or atmosphere of some kind surrounding a person or thing. **3.** *Art.* a disc or otherwise shaped figure representing a radiance about the head of a divine or sacred personage, a medieval sovereign, etc.; a halo. **4.** *Obs.* the type of cloud or mass of clouds, dense, with ragged edges, which yields rain or snow; a rain cloud. [t. L: rainstorm, thunder-cloud]

Nîmes (*Fr.* nēm), *n.* a town in S France, capital of Gard department: Roman ruins. 99,802 (1962).
nimiety (nĭ mī′ə tĭ), *n.* excess. [t. LL: m. s. *nimietas*]
niminy-piminy (nĭm′ĭ nĭ pĭm′ĭ nĭ), *adj.* mincing; affectedly nice or refined. [imit. of a mincing utterance]
n'importe (*Fr.* năɴ pŏrt′), *French.* it does not matter.
Nimrod (nĭm′rŏd′), *n.* **1.** *Bible.* a 'mighty hunter', the great-grandson of Noah. Gen. 10:8, 9. **2.** one expert in or devoted to hunting.
Nimwegen (nĭm′vā′gən), *n.* Nijmegen.
nincompoop (nĭn′kəm po͞op′), *n.* a fool or simpleton.
nine (nīn), *n.* **1.** a cardinal number, eight plus one. **2.** a symbol for this number, as 9 or IX. **3.** a set of nine persons or things. **4.** a team of baseball players. **5.** a playing card with nine pips. **6. dressed (up) to the nines,** *Colloq.* smartly dressed or overdressed. **7. The Nine,** the nine Muses. —*adj.* **8.** amounting to nine in number. [ME; OE *nigen*, var. of *nigon*, c. G *neun*]
nine days' wonder, an event, etc., that arouses great but short-lived popular interest.
ninefold (nīn′fōld′), *adj.* **1.** nine times as much. **2.** having nine parts. —*adv.* **3.** nine times as much.
ninepence (nīn′pəns), *n.* nine pennies.
ninepenny (nīn′pə nĭ), *adj.* of the amount or value of ninepence.
ninepins (nīn′pĭnz′), *n.pl.* **1.** (*construed as sing.*) a game played with nine wooden pins at which a ball is bowled to knock them down; skittles. **2.** the pins used in this game; the skittles.
nineteen (nīn′tēn′), *n.* **1.** a cardinal number, ten plus nine. **2.** a symbol for this number, as 19 or XIX. **3. talk nineteen to the dozen,** to talk very quickly or excitedly. —*adj.* **4.** amounting to nineteen in number. [ME *nintene*, repr. d. OE var. (unrecorded) of OE *nigontȳne*] —**nine′teenth′,** *adj., n.*
nineteenth hole, *Golf Slang.* the bar in a clubhouse.
ninety (nīn′tĭ), *n., pl.* **-ties,** *adj.* —*n.* **1.** a cardinal number, ten times nine. **2.** a symbol for this number, as 90 or XC. **3.** (*pl.*) the numbers from 90 to 99 of a series, esp. with reference to the years of a person's age, or the years of a century, esp. the nineteenth. —*adj.* **4.** amounting to ninety in number. [ME *nineti*, OE *nigontig*] —**ninetieth** (nīn′tĭ ĭth), *adj., n.*
Nineveh (nĭn′ĭ və), *n.* the ancient capital of Assyria: its ruins are opposite Mosul, on the river Tigris, in N Iraq. See map under **Babylon.**
Ningpo (nĭng′pō′), *n.* a seaport in E China, in Chekiang province. 280,000 (est. 1958).
Ningsia (nĭng′shyä′), *n.* an autonomous region in NW China. 1,810,000 (1958). *Cap.:* Yinchuan. Official name, **Ningoia Hui Autonomous egion.** Also, **Ninghsia.**
ninny (nĭn′ĭ), *n., pl.* **-nies.** a fool; a simpleton.
ninon (nē′nŏn, nī′nŏn), *n.* a fine semitransparent silk fabric, used mostly for expensive lingerie.
ninth (nīnth), *adj.* **1.** next after the eighth. **2.** being one of nine equal parts. —*n.* **3.** a ninth part, esp. of one (⅑). **4.** the ninth member of a series. **5.** *Music.* **a.** a note distant from another note by an interval of an octave and a second. **b.** the interval between such notes. **c.** harmonic combination of such notes. —**ninth′ly,** *adv.*
ninth chord, *Music.* a chord formed by the superposition of four thirds.
Ninus (nī′nəs), *n.* *Gk Legend.* the legendary founder of Nineveh: husband of Semiramis.
niobate (nī′ə bāt′), *n.* *Chem.* a salt of any niobic acid. [f. NIOB(IUM) + -ATE[2]]
Niobe (nī′ə bĭ), *n.* *Gk Myth.* the daughter of Tantalus and wife of Amphion of Thebes. She provoked Apollo and Artemis to vengeance by taunting their mother Leto with the number and beauty of her own children. Niobe's children were slain and after Zeus turned her into stone she continued to weep for them.
niobic (nī ō′bĭk, -ŏb′ĭk), *adj.* *Chem.* **1.** containing pentavalent niobium, as *niobic acid*, $Nb_2O_5.nH_2O$. **2.** of or pertaining to niobium.
niobium (nī ō′byəm), *n.* *Chem.* a steel-grey metallic element resembling tantalum in its chemical properties. *Symbol:* Nb; *at. no.:* 41; *at. wt:* 92·906; *sp. gr.:* 8·4 at 20°C. Formerly, **columbium.** [t. NL; named after *Niobe*, daughter of Tantalus, because found with tantalum. See -IUM]
niobous (nī ō′bəs), *adj.* *Chem.* **1.** containing trivalent niobium, as *niobous chloride*, $NbCl_3$. **2.** of or pertaining to niobium.
Niort (*Fr.* nyŏr), *n.* a town in W France, the capital of Deux-Sèvres department. 44,630 (1968).
nip[1] (nĭp), *v.,* **nipped, nipping,** *n.* —*v.t.* **1.** to compress sharply between two surfaces or points; pinch or bite. **2.** to take off by pinching, biting, or snipping (usually fol. by *off*). **3.** to check in growth or development: *to nip a plot in the bud.* **4.** to affect sharply and painfully or injuriously, as cold does. **5.** *Naut.* to secure (a rope) by holding it with a smaller rope. **6.** *Slang.* to snatch or take suddenly or quickly (fol. by *away, up,* etc.). **7.** *Slang.* to steal. —*v.i.* **8.** *Colloq.* to move or go suddenly or quickly, or slip (fol. by *away, off, up,* etc.). —*n.* **9.** the act of nipping; a pinch. **10.** a sharp or biting remark. **11.** a biting quality, as in cold or frosty air. **12.** sharp cold; a sharp touch of frost. **13.** biting taste or tang, as in cheese. **14.** a small bit or quantity of anything. **15.** *Naut.* pressure exerted by pack-ice on the sides of a vessel. **16.** *Naut.* the grip of a rope at the point where it is twisted round something. [ME *nyp(pen)*; akin to obs. *nipe*, c. D *nijpen*]
nip[2] (nĭp), *n., v.,* **nipped, nipping.** —*n.* **1.** a small drink; a sip. **2.** a measure of spirits, in Great Britain usually ⅙ gill. —*v.t., v.i.* **3.** to drink (spirits, etc.) in small sips, esp. repeatedly. [short for *nipperkin*, ? t. D or LG]
Nip (nĭp), *n.* *Slang.* (offensively) a Japanese, esp. a Japanese soldier. [short for NIPPONESE]
nipa (nē′pə, nī′pə), *n.* a palm, *Nipa fruticans*, of the East Indies, the Philippines, etc., whose foliage is much used for thatching, etc. [t. Malay: m. *nīpah*]
nip and tuck, *U.S.* (in a race or other contest) with one competitor equalling the speed or efforts of another; neck and neck.
nipper (nĭp′ə), *n.* **1.** one who or that which nips. **2.** (*usually pl.*) a device for nipping, as pincers or forceps. **3.** one of the large claws of a crustacean. **4.** (*pl.*) *Slang.* handcuffs. **5.** *Naut.* a short length of rope used in the old Royal Navy sailing ships to heave up the anchor with a rope cable. **6.** *Naut.* the boy who did this job. **7.** *Colloq.* a small boy.
nipping (nĭp′ĭng), *adj.* **1.** that nips. **2.** sharp or biting, as cold, etc. **3.** sarcastic. —**nip′pingly,** *adv.*
nipple (nĭp′l), *n.* **1.** a protuberance of the mamma or breast where, in the female, the milk ducts discharge; a teat. **2.** something resembling it, as the mouthpiece of a nursing bottle. **3.** a short piece of pipe with threads on each end, used for joining valves, etc. **4.** *Mach.* a small drilled bush containing a one-way valve through which a lubricant can be supplied to a bearing, esp. by a grease gun. [orig. uncert.]
nipplewort (nĭp′l wûrt′), *n.* a slender, erect annual composite with yellow capitula, *Lapsana communis*, widespread in hedges and waste places of the N temperate zone.
Nippon (nĭp′ŏn), *n.* Japanese name of **Japan.**
Nipponese (nĭp′ə nēz′), *n., pl.* **-ese,** *adj.* Japanese. [f. NIPPON + -ESE]
Nippur (nĭ po͝oə′), *n.* an ancient Sumerian and Babylonian city: site in SE Iraq.
nippy (nĭp′ĭ), *adj.,* **-pier, -piest. 1.** apt to nip; sharp; biting. **2.** *Colloq.* nimble; active.
nirvana (nĭə vä′nə, nû-), *n.* **1.** (*often cap.*) *Buddhism.* **a.** the extinguishing of the restlessness and heat of one's emotions. **b.** the passionless peace of imperturbability, attained through the annihilation of disturbing desires. **2.** freedom from pain, worry, and the external world. [t. Skt: a blowing out (as of a light)]
Niš (nĭsh; *Serb.* nēsh), *n.* a town in Yugoslavia, the capital of Serbia, in the E part. 84,741 (1961). Also, **Nish.**
Nisan (nī′săn; *Heb.* nĭs′än), *n.* (in the Jewish calendar) the seventh month of the civil year and the first of the ecclesiastical year.
Nishapur (*Pers.* nē shä po͝or′), *n.* a town in NE Iran: the birthplace of Omar Khayyam. 39,900 (1966).
Nishinomiya (nē′shĭ nō′mĭ yə), *n.* a city in Japan, in W Honshu island. 336,873 (1965).
nisi (nī′sī), *conj.* **1.** unless. —*adj.* **2.** *Law.* (of a court order, decree, etc.) conditional; not coming into effect unless a person or persons fail to show cause against it within a certain time. [t. L]
nisi prius (nī′sī prī′əs), *Law.* **1.** a trial before a single judge with a jury, either in London or at the assizes: *he was tried at nisi prius.* **2.** denoting such a trial. **3.** (formerly) a trial held at Westminster if it had not previously been held in the proper county. **4.** (formerly) a writ for such a trial. **5.** *U.S.* designating a court of first instance. [t. L: unless previously]
Nissen hut (nĭs′ən), a prefabricated shelter with the shape of a long, slightly flattened cylinder, usually built of steel sheet, esp. for use by soldiers. [named after Colonel P. N. *Nissen*, 1871–1930, the inventor]
Nistru (*Rum.* nē′stro͞o), *n.* Rumanian name of **Dniester.**
nisus (nī′səs), *n., pl.* **-sus.** effort; impulse. [t. L: effort]
nit[1] (nĭt), *n.* **1.** the egg of a parasitic insect attached to a hair, or fibre of clothing; particularly, the egg of a louse. **2.** the insect while young. **3.** *Slang.* a foolish or stupid person. [ME *nite*, OE *hnitu*, c. G *Niss*]
nit[2] (nĭt), *n.* a unit of luminance equal to one candela per square metre. [f. L: m. *nitor* brightness]
Niteroi (*Port.* nē tė rôy′), *n.* a seaport in SE Brazil,

opposite Rio de Janeiro. 245,467 (1960). Also, **Nictheroy.**

nitgrass (nĭtʹgräsʹ), *n.* a small annual tufted grass, *Gastridium ventricosum*, occurring mostly in dry places near the sea in SW Europe and the Mediterranean region.

Nith (nĭth), *n.* a river of SW Scotland flowing from Ayrshire through Dumfriesshire to the Solway Firth. 79 mi.

niton (nīʹtŏn), *n. Chem.* an early name for the element radon. *Symbol:* Nt [t. NL, der. L *nitēre* shine]

nitr-, var. of **nitro-,** before vowels.

nitramine (nīʹtrə mēnʹ, -mĭn), *n. Chem.* any of a class of amines containing a nitro group, and having the general formula $R.NH.NO_2$.

nitrate (nīʹtrāt), *n., v.,* **-trated, -trating.** —*n.* **1.** *Chem.* a salt or ester of nitric acid, or any compound containing the $-NO_3$ radical. **2.** fertilizer consisting of potassium nitrate or sodium nitrate. —*v.t.* **3.** to treat with nitric acid or a nitrate. **4.** to convert into a nitrate. [f. NITRE + -ATE[2]] —**nitraʹtion,** *n.*

nitre (nīʹtə), *n.* **1.** nitrate of potassium, KNO_3, a white salt used in making gunpowder, etc.; saltpetre. **2.** nitrate of sodium, $NaNO_3$; Chile saltpetre. Also, *U.S.,* **niter.** [ME, t. L: m. *nitrum*, t. Gk: m. *nitron* natron, native sodium carbonate]

nitric (nīʹtrĭk), *adj.* **1.** *Chem.* containing nitrogen, usually in the pentavalent state. **2.** of or pertaining to nitre. [t. F: m. *nitrique.* See NITRE, -IC]

nitric acid, a corrosive liquid, HNO_3, with powerful oxidizing properties.

nitric bacteria, nitrobacteria.

nitric ether, *Chem.* ethyl nitrate.

nitric oxide, a colourless gaseous compound of nitrogen and oxygen, NO, formed when copper is treated with dilute nitric acid.

nitride (nīʹtrīd), *n. Chem.* a compound, usually containing two elements only, of which the more electronegative one is nitrogen. Also, **nitrid** (nīʹtrĭd). [f. NITRE + -IDE]

nitriding (nīʹtrīʹdĭng), *n. Metall.* the introduction of nitrogen into the surface of certain types of steel by heating in contact with partially dissociated ammonia: a form of case-hardening.

nitrification (nīʹtrĭ fĭ kāʹshən), *n.* **1.** the act of nitrifying. **2.** the introduction of an NO_2 radical into an organic compound, usually by means of mixed nitric and sulphuric acids.

nitrify (nīʹtrĭ fīʹ), *v.t.,* **-fied, -fying. 1.** to oxidize (ammonia compounds, etc.) to nitrites or nitrates, esp. by bacterial action. **2.** to impregnate (soil, etc.) with nitrates. **3.** to treat or combine with nitrogen or its compounds. **4.** *Obsolesc.* to convert into nitre. [t. F: m. *nitrifier.* See NITRE, -FY]

nitrile (nīʹtrĭl, -trēl, -trīl), *n. Chem.* any of a class of organic compounds with the general formula RCN. Also, **nitril** (nīʹtrĭl). [f. NITR(OGEN) + -ILE]

nitrile rubber, any of a class of synthetic rubbers which are copolymers of butadiene and acrylonitrile, used esp. where oil resistance is required.

nitrite (nīʹtrīt), *n. Chem.* a salt of nitrous acid.

nitro-, *Chem.* **1.** a word element indicating the group NO_2. **2.** a misnomer for the nitrate group (NO_3), as in *nitrocellulose.* Also, **nitr-.** [t. Gk, comb. form of *nítron* native sodium carbonate]

nitrobacteria (nīʹtrō băk tĭəʹrĭ ə), *n.pl.* certain bacteria of the soil, concerned in nitrifying processes. Also, **nitric bacteria.**

nitrobenzene (nīʹtrō bĕnʹzēn), *n. Chem.* a light yellowish liquid, $C_6H_5NO_2$, a derivative of benzene, used in the manufacture of aniline.

nitrocellulose (nīʹtrō sĕlʹyo͝o lōsʹ), *n.* cellulose nitrate.

nitrochalk (nīʹtrō chôkʹ), *n.* a mixture of calcium carbonate and ammonium nitrate, used as a fertilizer.

nitrochloroform (nīʹtrō klōʹrə fômʹ), *n.* chloropicrin.

nitrogen (nīʹtrə jən), *n. Chem.* a colourless, odourless, gaseous element which forms about four-fifths of the volume of the atmosphere and is present (combined) in animal and vegetable tissues, chiefly in proteins. It is used in compounds, as fertilizer, in explosives, and in dyes. *Symbol:* N; *at. wt:* 14·0067; *at. no.:* 7. [t. F: m. *nitrogène.* See NITRO-, -GEN]

nitrogen cycle, the continuous circulation of nitrogen and nitrogen compounds in nature between the atmosphere, the soil, and the various organisms to which nitrogen is essential.

nitrogen dioxide, *Chem.* a dark brown toxic gas, NO_2, used as a nitrating and oxidizing agent; nitrogen peroxide.

nitrogen fixation, 1. any process of combining free nitrogen from the air with other elements, either by chemical means or by bacterial action, used esp. in the preparation of fertilizers, industrial products, etc. **2.** this process as performed by bacteria (**nitrogen fixers**) found in the nodules of leguminous plants, which make the resulting nitrogenous compounds available to their host plants. —**niʹtrogen-fixʹing,** *adj.*

nitrogenize (nī trŏjʹĭ nīzʹ), *v.t.,* **-nized, -nizing.** to combine with nitrogen or add nitrogenous material to. Also, **nitrogenise.**

nitrogenous (nī trŏjʹĭ nəs), *adj.* containing nitrogen.

nitroglycerine (nīʹtrō glĭsʹə rēnʹ), *n.* a colourless, highly explosive oil, $C_3H_5(ONO_2)_3$, a principal constituent of dynamites and certain propellent and rocket powders: a nitration product of glycerine. Also, **nitroglycerin** (nīʹtrō glĭsʹə rĭn).

nitro group, the univalent $-NO_2$ radical.

nitrolic (nī trŏlʹĭk), *adj. Chem.* of or denoting a series of acids of the type, $RC(:NOH)NO_2$, whose salts form deep red solutions. [f. NITR- + -OL[1] + -IC]

nitrometer (nī trŏmʹĭ tə), *n.* an apparatus for determining the amount of nitrogen or nitrogen compounds in a substance or mixture. [f. NITRO- + -METER[1]]

nitroparaffin (nīʹtrō păʹrə fĭn), *n. Chem.* any of a class of compounds derived from the methane series replacing a hydrogen atom by the nitro group.

nitrosamine (nīʹtrōs ə mēnʹ, nīʹtrōs ămʹĭn), *n. Chem.* any of a series of oily compounds with the type formula R_2NNO. Also, **nitrosamin** (nīʹtrōs ămʹĭn).

nitroso (nī trōʹsō), *adj. Chem.* containing the group NO–; nitrosyl.

nitrosyl (nī trōʹsĭl, nīʹtrə sĭl), *adj. Chem.* nitroso.

nitrous (nīʹtrəs), *adj. Chem.* **1.** of or pertaining to compounds obtained from nitre, usually containing less oxygen than the corresponding nitric compounds. **2.** containing nitrogen, usually trivalent. [t. NL: m. s. *nitrōsus* nitrous, L full of natron. See NITRE]

nitrous acid, an acid, HNO_2, known only in solution.

nitrous bacteria, nitrobacteria which convert ammonia derivatives into nitrites by oxidation.

nitrous ether, *Chem.* ethyl nitrite.

nitrous oxide, laughing gas, N_2O, used as an anaesthetic.

nitty (nĭtʹĭ), *adj.,* **-tier, -tiest. 1.** full of nits. **2.** *Slang.* foolish.

nitwit (nĭtʹwĭtʹ), *n.* a slow-witted or foolish person.

Niue (nĭ o͞oʹā), *n.* an island in the S Pacific between Tonga and Cook islands: possession of New Zealand. 5145 pop. (est. 1965); ab. 100 sq. mi. Also, **Savage Island.** —**Niuan** (nĭ o͞oʹən), *adj., n.*

nivation (nĭ vāʹshən), *n. Geol.* the disintegration of rocks around a patch of snow, brought about by alternate freezing and thawing.

niveous (nĭvʹĭ əs), *adj.* snowy; resembling snow. [t. L: m. *niveus*]

Nivernais (*Fr.* nē vĕr nĕʹ), *n.* a former province in central France. *Cap.:* Nevers.

Nivôse (*Fr.* nē vózʹ), *n.* (in the French revolutionary calendar) the fourth month of the year. [t. F, t. L: m. s. *nivōsus* snowy]

nix[1] (nĭks), *Slang.* —*n.* **1.** nothing. —*adv.* **2.** no. —*interj.* **3.** *U.S.* (used as a signal warning of someone's approach): *nix, the cops!* [t. G, var. of *nichts* nothing]

nix[2] (nĭks), *n., pl.* **nixes.** *Folklore.* a water-sprite, usually small and either good or bad. [t. G, var. of *nichs*, OHG *nichus*, c. OE *nicor* fabulous sea-monster] —**nixie** (nĭkʹsĭ), *n. fem.*

Nixon (nĭkʹsən), *n.* **Richard Milhous** (mĭlʹhousʹ), born 1913, president of the U.S. since 1969.

Nizam (nĭ zămʹ), *n.* **1.** the title of the ruler of Hyderabad, India, from *c.* 1700 to 1950. **2.** (*l.c.*) (formerly) a soldier of the Turkish regular army. [t. Hind. and Turk.]

Nizhni Novgorod (*Russ.* nēzhʹnĭy nôvʹgə rət), former name of **Gorki** (def. 2).

Nizhni Tagil (*Russ.* nēzhʹnĭy tá gēlʹ), a city in the W Soviet Union in Asia, on the E slope of the Ural Mts. 370,000 (est. 1965).

N.J., New Jersey.

Njord (nyŏd), *n. Scand. Myth.* the father of Frey and Freya: the dispenser of riches. Also, **Njorth** (nyôth).

Nkomo (əng kōʹmō), *n.* **Joshua,** born 1917, Rhodesian political leader, in confinement since 1963.

Nkongsamba (əngʹkŏng sămʹbə), *n.* a town in E Cameroun. 60,000 (est. 1962).

Nkrumah (əng kro͞oʹmə), *n.* **Kwame** (kwäʹmĭ), born 1909, Ghanaian statesman: prime minister 1957–60; president 1960–66.

N.K.V.D., the secret police of the Soviet Union, 1935–43. [Russ., (*N*)*arodny* (*K*)*omitet* (*V*)*nutrennikh* (*D*)*el*, lit., People's Committee of Home Affairs]

NL, New Latin or Neo-Latin. Also, **NL., N.L.**

n.l., 1. *Print.* new line. **2.** (L *non licet*) it is not permitted. **3.** (L *non liquet*) it is not clear or evident.

N Lat., north latitude.

N.M., New Mexico. Also, **N. Mex.**

NMR, *Physics.* nuclear magnetic resonance.
NNE, north-north-east. Also, **N.N.E.**
n-nonylic acid (nŏ nĭl′ĭk), pelargonic acid.
NNW, north-north-west. Also, **N.N.W.**
no[1] (nō), *adv., n., pl.* **noes.** —*adv.* **1.** a word used: **a.** to express dissent, denial, or refusal, as in response (opposed to *yes*). **b.** to emphasize a previous negative or qualify a previous statement. **2.** not in any degree; not at all (used with a comparative): *he is no better.* **3.** not: *whether or no.* —*n.* **4.** an utterance of the word 'no'. **5.** a denial or refusal. **6.** a negative vote or voter. [ME; OE *nā* (c. Icel. *nei*), f. *ne* not + *ā* ever. See AYE[1]]
no[2] (nō), *adj.* **1.** not any: *no money.* **2.** not at all; very far from being; not at all a: *he is no genius.* [var. of NONE[1]]
No (nō), *n., pl.* **No.** a type of highly stylized Japanese classical drama, first developed in the 15th century, employing music, dancing, a chorus, symbolic scenery, and elaborate costumes and masks. Also, **Noh, Nō.** [t. Jap.: lit., ability]
No, *Chem.* nobelium.
No., **1.** north. **2.** northern. **3.** number. Also, **no.**
N.O., Naval Officer.
Noachian (nō ā′kĭ ən), *adj.* of the patriarch Noah or his time. Also, **Noachic** (nō ăk′ĭk, -ā′kĭk).
Noah (nō′ə), *n.* a Hebrew patriarch, the builder of **Noah's Ark,** in which, with his family and animals of every species, he survived the deluge. Gen. 5–9. [t. Heb.]
nob[1] (nŏb), *n.* **1.** *Slang.* the head. **2.** *Cribbage.* the knave of the same suit as the card turned up, counting one to the holder. [? var. of KNOB]
nob[2] (nŏb), *n.* *Slang.* a person of wealth or social distinction. [? special use of NOB[1]]
no-ball (nō′bôl′), *Cricket.* —*n.* **1.** a ball bowled in a way disallowed by the rules. Such a ball scores one run and a batsman may score from it with risk only of being run out. —*interj.* **2.** (a call by the umpire as the bowler bowls indicating that he has infringed the rules.) Also, **no ball.**
nobble (nŏb′l), *v.t.,* **-bled, -bling.** *Slang.* **1.** to disable (a horse), as by drugging it. **2.** to win (a person, etc.) over by underhand means. **3.** to swindle. **4.** to catch or seize. [back-formation from *nobbler,* var. of HOBBLER (*an 'obbler* being taken as *a nobbler*)] —**nob′bler,** *n.*
nobbut (nŏb′ət), *adv.* *Dial.* only; just; no more than: *he's nobbut a lad.* [ME, f. NO[1] + BUT[1]]
nobby (nŏb′ĭ), *adj.,* **-bier, -biest.** *Slang.* **1.** smart; elegant. **2.** first-rate. [f. NOB[2] + -Y[1]]
Nobel (nō bĕl′), *n.* **Alfred Bernhard** (ăl′frĭd bĕə′näd), 1833–96, Swedish inventor of dynamite and manufacturer of explosives: established Nobel prize awards.
nobelium (nō bē′lyəm), *n.* *Chem.* a synthetic, radioactive element. *Symbol:* No; *at. no.:* 102. [f. NOBEL (*Institute*), where first identified + -IUM]
Nobel prize, one of a number of prizes awarded annually from the bequest of Alfred Nobel for achievement during the preceding year in physics, chemistry, medicine, literature, and the promotion of peace.
Nobeoka (nō bā′ŏŏ kə), *n.* a town in Japan, in SE Kyushu island. 124,000 (1965).
Nobile (*It.* nŏ′bē lė), *n.* **Umberto** (*It.* ōōm bĕr′tŏ), born 1885, Italian airship pioneer.
nobiliary (nō bĭl′yə rĭ), *adj.* of or pertaining to the nobility. [t. F: m. *nobiliaire,* der. L *nōbilis* noble]
nobility (nō bĭl′ĭ tĭ), *n., pl.* **-ties.** **1.** the noble class, or the body of nobles, in a country. **2.** (in Great Britain) the peerage. **3.** the state or quality of being noble. **4.** noble birth or rank. **5.** exalted moral excellence. **6.** grandeur. [ME *nobilite,* t. OF, t. L: m. s. *nōbilitas*]
noble (nō′bl), *adj.,* **nobler, noblest,** *n.* —*adj.* **1.** distinguished by birth, rank, or title. **2.** of or pertaining to persons so distinguished: *noble birth.* **3.** belonging to or constituting a class (the nobility) possessing a hereditary social or political pre-eminence in a country or state. **4.** of an exalted moral character or excellence: *a noble thought.* **5.** admirable in dignity of conception, or in the manner of expression, execution, or composition: *a noble poem.* **6.** imposing in appearance; stately; magnificent: *a noble monument.* **7.** of an admirably high quality; notably superior. **8.** *Chem.* inert; chemically inactive. **9.** (of some metals, as gold and platinum) that are not altered on exposure to the air, do not rust easily, and are much scarcer and more valuable than the so-called useful metals. **10.** *Falconry.* denoting the long-winged falcons which stoop to the quarry at a single swoop (opposed to *ignoble*). —*n.* **11.** a person of noble birth or rank; a nobleman. **12.** (in Great Britain) a peer. **13.** a former English gold coin, worth one third of a pound. [ME, t. OF, g. L *nōbilis* well-known, highborn] —**no′bleness,** *n.*
—**Syn. 4.** NOBLE, HIGH-MINDED, MAGNANIMOUS agree in referring to lofty principles and loftiness of mind or spirit. NOBLE implies a loftiness of character or spirit that scorns the petty, mean, base, or dishonourable: *a noble deed.* HIGH-MINDED implies having elevated principles and consistently adhering to them: *a high-minded devotion to ideals.* MAGNANIMOUS suggests greatness of mind or soul, esp. as manifested in generosity or in overlooking injuries: *magnanimous towards his former enemies.* —**Ant. 4.** base, mean, discreditable, dishonourable.
noble art, boxing.
noble gas, *Chem.* rare gas.
nobleman (nō′bl mən), *n., pl.* **-men.** a man of noble birth or rank; a noble. —**no′blewom′an,** *n. fem.*
noblesse (nō blĕs′), *n.* **1.** noble birth or condition. **2.** the nobility. [ME, t. OF, der. L *nōbilis* noble]
noblesse oblige (*Fr.* nŏ blĕs ŏ blĕzh′), *French.* the nobility has an obligation to display generous and honourable conduct. [lit., nobility obliges]
nobly (nō′blĭ), *adv.* **1.** in a noble manner. **2.** courageously. **3.** splendidly; superbly. **4.** of noble ancestry.
nobody (nō′bə dĭ, nōb′dĭ), *pron., n., pl.* **-bodies.** —*pron.* **1.** no person. —*n.* **2.** a person of no importance, esp. socially.
nocent (nō′sənt), *adj.* *Obs.* **1.** hurtful; harmful; injurious. **2.** guilty. [t. L: s. *nocens,* ppr., harming]
nock (nŏk), *n.* **1.** a metal or plastic piece at the end of an arrow. **2.** a notch or groove at the end of an arrow into which the bowstring fits. **3.** a notch or groove at each end of a bow, to hold the bowstring in place. **4.** *Naut.* the forward upper corner of a fore-and-aft boom sail; throat. —*v.t.* **5.** to furnish with a nock. **6.** to adjust (the arrow) to the bowstring, in readiness to shoot. [ME *nocke;* ? t. D: m. *nok,* or LG: m. *nokk* tip or projection]
noctambulism (nŏk tăm′byŏŏ lĭz′əm), *n.* somnambulism. Also, **noctam′bula′tion.** [f. s. L *nox* night + s. *ambulāre* walk about + -ISM] —**noctam′bulist,** *n.*
nocti-, a word element meaning 'night'. Also (before a vowel), **noct-.** [t. L, comb. form of *nox*]
noctiluca (nŏk′tĭ lōō′kə), *n., pl.* **-cae** (-sē). a pelagic flagellate protozoan, genus *Noctiluca,* notable for its phosphorescence. [t. L: something that shines by night]
noctilucent (nŏk′tĭ lōō′sənt), *adj.* **1.** shining at night; phosphorescent. **2.** *Meteorol.* (of clouds) very high and cirrus-like, visible during the short night of summer and believed to be of meteor dust shining with reflected sunlight. —**noc′tilu′cence,** *n.*
noctivagant (nŏk tĭv′ə gənt), *adj.* wandering at night. [f. L: *nocti-* NOCTI- + s. *vagans,* ppr., wandering]
noctuid (nŏk′tyŏŏ ĭd), *n.* **1.** any of the *Noctuidae,* a large family of dull-coloured moths, the larvae of which include the highly injurious army worms and cutworms. —*adj.* **2.** belonging or pertaining to the *Noctuidae.* [t. NL: s. *Noctuidae,* pl., der. L *noctua* night owl]
noctule (nŏk′tyŏŏl), *n.* a large reddish insectivorous bat, *Nyctalus noctula,* common to Europe and Asia. [t. F, t. It.: *nottola* bat, der. *notte* night, g. L *nox*]
nocturn (nŏk′tûn), *n.* *Rom. Cath. Ch.* one of the divisions of the office of matins, usually three in number.
nocturnal (nŏk tû′nəl), *adj.* **1.** of or pertaining to the night. **2.** done, occurring, or coming by night. **3.** active by night, as many animals. **4.** opening by night and closing by day, as certain flowers. [late ME, t. LL: s. *nocturnālis,* der. L *nocturnus* of or in the night] —**noctur′nally,** *adv.*
nocturne (nŏk′tûn), *n.* *Music.* **1.** a piece appropriate to the night or evening. **2.** an instrumental composition of a dreamy or pensive character. [t. F, t. LL: m. *nocturna* (fem.) of the night]
nocuous (nŏk′yŏŏ əs), *adj.* injurious; noxious. [t. L: m. *nocuus*] —**noc′uously,** *adv.* —**noc′uousness,** *n.*
nod (nŏd), *v.,* **nodded, nodding,** *n.* —*v.i.* **1.** to make a slight, quick inclination of the head, as in assent, greeting, command, etc. **2.** to let the head fall forwards with a sudden, involuntary movement when sleepy. **3.** to grow careless, inattentive, or dull. **4.** (of trees, flowers, plumes, etc.) to droop, bend, or incline with a swaying motion. —*v.t.* **5.** to incline (the head) in a short, quick movement, as of assent, greeting, etc. **6.** to express or signify by such a movement of the head: *to nod assent.* **7.** to summon, bring, or send by a nod of the head. **8.** to incline or cause to lean or sway. **9.** *Soccer.* to head (the ball) with a quick, downward movement. —*n.* **10.** a short, quick inclination of the head, as in assent, greeting, command, or drowsiness. **11.** a nap. **12.** a bending or swaying movement of anything. [ME; orig. obscure] —**nod′der,** *n.*
N.O.D., Naval Ordnance Department.
nodal (nō′dl), *adj.* of or of the nature of a node. —**nodality** (nō dăl′ĭ tĭ), *n.*
nodal point, *Physics.* either of two points on the axis of a lens system, such that if the incident ray passes through one, travelling in a given direction, the emergent ray passes through the other, in a parallel direction.
nodding (nŏd′ĭng), *v.* **1.** present participle of **nod.** —*adj.* **2.** slight; such as to give rise to no more than a brief salutation: *a nodding acquaintance.*

noddle[1] (nŏd′l), *n. Colloq.* the head. [ME *nodel, nodul*; orig. uncert.]

noddle[2] (nŏd′l), *v.t., v.i.,* **-dled, -dling.** to nod lightly or frequently. [freq. of NOD]

noddy (nŏd′ĭ), *n., pl.* **-dies.** **1.** a white-capped dark brown tern, *Anous stolidus*, of warm sea-coasts, usually so fearless of man as to seem stupid. **2.** a fool or simpleton. [? n. use of *noddy*, adj., silly; orig. uncert.]

node (nōd), *n.* **1.** a knot, protuberance, or knob. **2.** a complication; difficulty. **3.** a centring point of component parts. **4.** *Bot.* **a.** a joint in a stem. **b.** a part of a stem which normally bears a leaf. **5.** *Geom.* a point on a curve or surface, at which there can be more than one tangent line or plane. **6.** *Physics.* a point, line, or region in a vibrating medium at which there is comparatively no variation of the disturbance which is being transmitted through the medium. **7.** *Astron.* either of the two points at which the orbit of a heavenly body cuts the plane of the ecliptic, equator, or other properly defined plane (that passed as the body goes to the north being called the **ascending node,** and that passed as it goes to the south being called the **descending node**). **8.** *Pathol.* a circumscribed swelling. [t. L: m. s. *nōdus* knot]

N, Nodes on stem of polygonum

nodical (nō′dĭ kl, nŏd′-), *adj. Astron.* of or pertaining to the nodes: *the nodical month.*

nodose (nō′dōs, nō dōs′), *adj.* having nodes. [m. s. *nōdōsus*] —**nodosity** (nō dŏs′ĭ tĭ), *n.*

no doubt, certainly or almost certainly.

nodous (nō′dəs), *adj.* full of knots. [t. L: m. s. *nōdōsus*]

nodular (nŏd′yŏŏ lə), *adj.* having, relating to, or shaped like nodules.

nodule (nŏd′yōōl), *n.* **1.** a small node, knot, or knob. **2.** a small rounded mass or lump. **3.** *Bot.* a tubercle. [t. L: m. s. *nōdulus*, dim. of *nōdus* node]

nodulous (nŏd′yŏŏ ləs), *adj.* having nodules. Also, **nodulose** (nŏd′yŏŏ lōs′, nŏd′yŏŏ lōs′).

nodus (nō′dəs), *n., pl.* **-di** (-dī). a difficult or intricate point, situation, plot, etc. [t. L: a knot]

Noel (nō ĕl′), *n.* **1.** Christmas. **2.** (*l.c.*) a Christmas song or carol. [t. F: *noël* Christmas carol, *Noël* Christmas, g. L *nātālis* birthday, orig. adj.]

noesis (nō ē′sĭs), *n.* **1.** *Philos.* a thing grasped by the intellect alone. **2.** *Psychol.* cognition; the functioning of the intellect. [t. Gk: a perception]

noetic (nō ĕt′ĭk), *adj.* **1.** of or pertaining to the mind. **2.** originating in and apprehended by the reason.

no-fines (nō′fīnz′), *n.* concrete made without fine aggregate (sand).

Nofretete (nŏf′rə tē′tĭ), *n.* Nefertiti.

nog[1] (nŏg), *n.* **1.** *Chiefly U.S.* any beverage made with beaten eggs, usually with alcoholic liquor; eggnog. **2.** *Obs.* a kind of strong ale. Also, **nogg.** [orig. uncert.]

nog[2] (nŏg), *n.* **1.** a brick-shaped piece of wood built into a wall. **2.** any wooden peg, pin, or block. [orig. uncert.; ? var. of obs. *knag*, ME *knagge* spur, peg]

noggin (nŏg′ĭn), *n.* **1.** a small cup or mug. **2.** a small amount of spirits, usually a gill. **3.** *Colloq.* the head.

nogging (nŏg′ĭng), *n. Bldg Trades.* the brick filling to a wooden-framed partition.

no go, not possible; futile; vain.

no-good (nō′gŏŏd′), *adj. Colloq.* worthless.

Noguchi (nō gōō′chĭ), *n.* **Hideyo** (hē′dĭ yō′), 1876–1928, Japanese physician and bacteriologist in the U.S.

Noh (nō), *n.* No.

no-hoper (nō′hō′pə), *n. Austral. Colloq.* a dead-beat; a complete failure.

nohow (nō′hou′), *adv.* (in substandard use) in no manner; not at all.

noil (noil), *n.* a short fibre of wool or silk separated from the long fibres in combing. [? t. F: m. *noel*, t. ML: *nōdellus*, dim. of L *nōdus* knot, NODE]

noise (noiz), *n., v.,* **noised, noising.** —*n.* **1.** sound, esp. of a loud, harsh, or confused kind: *deafening noises.* **2.** a sound of any kind. **3.** loud shouting, outcry, or clamour. **4.** *Physics.* the combination of a non-harmonious group of frequencies of very short duration. **5.** *Electronics.* interference which degrades the useful information in a signal. **6.** *Archaic.* rumour. **7. big noise,** *Colloq.* an important person. —*v.t.* **8.** to spread the report or rumour of. **9.** to spread (a report, rumour, etc.). —*v.i.* **10.** to talk much or publicly (fol. by *of*). **11.** to make a noise, outcry, or clamour. [ME, t. OF, g. L *nausea* seasickness]

—**Syn. 1.** NOISE, CLAMOUR, DIN, HUBBUB, RACKET refer to (usually loud) unmusical or confused sounds. NOISE is the general word, though it may apply to soft, confused sounds as well: *street noises.* CLAMOUR and HUBBUB are alike in referring to loud noises resulting from shouting, cries, animated or excited tones, and the like; but in CLAMOUR the emphasis is on the meaning of the shouting, and in HUBBUB the emphasis is on the confused mingling of sounds: *the clamour of an angry crowd, his voice could be heard above the hubbub.* DIN suggests a loud, resonant noise, painful if long continued: *the din of a pneumatic drill.* RACKET suggests a loud, confused noise of the kind produced by clatter or percussion: *she always makes such a racket when she washes up.* **3.** See **sound**[1].

noiseless (noiz′lĭs), *adj.* making, or attended with, no noise; silent; quiet: *a noiseless step.* —**noise′lessly,** *adv.* —**noise′lessness,** *n.* —**Syn.** See **still**[1].

noisemaker (noiz′mā′kə), *n.* a person or thing that makes noise, as a hooter, whistle, etc., used in merrymaking. —**noise′mak′ing,** *n., adj.*

noisome (noi′səm), *adj.* **1.** offensive or disgusting, often as to smell. **2.** harmful, injurious, or noxious. [ME, f. obs. or d. *noy* (aphetic var. of ANNOY) + -SOME[1]] —**noi′somely,** *adv.* —**noi′someness,** *n.*

noisy (noi′zĭ), *adj.,* **noisier, noisiest. 1.** making much noise: *a noisy crowd.* **2.** abounding in noise: *a noisy street.* —**nois′ily,** *adv.* —**nois′iness,** *n.* —**Syn. 1.** See **loud.**

Nolan (nō′lən), *n.* **Sydney Robert,** born 1917, Australian painter.

Nolde (*Ger.* nŏl′də), *n.* **Emil** (*Ger.* ĕ′mĕl), 1867–1956, German expressionist painter.

nolens volens (nō′lĕnz vō′lĕnz), *Latin.* willy-nilly.

noli-me-tangere (nō′lĭ mā′tăng′gə rĭ), *n. Latin.* **1.** one who or that which must not be touched or interfered with. **2.** a picture representing Jesus appearing to Mary Magdalene after his resurrection. John 20:17. **3.** the touch-me-not. [L: touch me not]

nolle prosequi (nŏl′ĭ prŏs′ĭ kwī′), *Law.* an entry made upon the records of a court when the plaintiff or prosecutor will proceed no further in a suit or action. [L: to be unwilling to pursue (prosecute)]

nol. pros., nolle prosequi.

nom., nominative.

noma (nō′mə), *n. Pathol.* a gangrenous ulceration of the mouth and cheeks (and sometimes other parts), occurring mainly in debilitated children. [t. NL, t. Gk: m. *nomḗ* a corroding sore]

nomad (nō′măd), *n.* **1.** one of a race or tribe without fixed abode, but moving about from place to place according to the state of the pasturage or food supply. **2.** any wanderer. —*adj.* **3.** nomadic. [t. L: s. *nomas*, t. Gk: roaming (like cattle)] —**no′madism,** *n.*

nomadic (nō măd′ĭk), *adj.* of, pertaining to, or characteristic of nomads. —**nomad′ically,** *adv.*

no-man's-land (nō′mănz lănd′), *n.* a tract of land under dispute, as one between opposing lines of trenches in war.

nomarch (nŏm′äk), *n.* the governor of a nome or a nomarchy. [t. Gk: s. *nomárchēs*]

nomarchy (nŏm′ä kĭ, -ə kĭ), *n., pl.* **-chies.** one of the provinces into which modern Greece is divided. Also, **nome.**

nombles (nŭm′blz), *n. pl. Archaic.* numbles.

nombril (nŏm′brĭl), *n. Her.* the point in an escutcheon between the middle of the base and the fess point. See diag. under **escutcheon.** [t. F: navel]

nom de guerre (*Fr.* nôɴ də gĕr′), *French.* an assumed name; pseudonym. [F: war name]

nom de plume (nŏm′ də plōōm′; *Fr.* nôɴ də plʏm′), pen-name. [coined in E from F words; lit., pen name]

nome (nōm), *n.* **1.** one of the provinces of ancient Egypt. **2.** nomarchy. [t. Gk: m. s. *nomós* territorial division]

nomenclator (nō′mĕn klā′tə), *n.* **1.** one who calls or announces things or persons by their names. **2.** one who assigns names, as in scientific classification. [t. L]

nomenclature (nō mĕn′klə chə), *n.* **1.** a set or system of names of terms, as those used in a particular science or art by an individual or community, etc. **2.** the names or terms forming a set or system. [t. L: m. *nōmenclātūra*] —**nomen′clative, nomenclatorial** (nō mĕn′klə tô′rĭ əl), **nomen′clatural,** *adj.*

nominal (nŏm′ĭ nəl), *adj.* **1.** being such in name only; so-called: *nominal peace.* **2.** (of a price, consideration, etc.) named as a mere matter of form, being trifling in comparison with the actual value. **3.** of, pertaining to, or consisting in a name or names. **4.** *Gram.* **a.** of, pertaining to, or producing a noun or nouns. **b.** used as or like a noun. **5.** assigned to a person by name: *nominal shares of stock.* **6.** containing, bearing, or giving a name or names. **7.** *U.S.* satisfactory; within acceptable limits, as of the launch of a spacecraft. [ME, t. L: s. *nominālis* pert. to names]

nominalism (nŏm′ĭ nə lĭz′əm), *n. Philos.* the doctrine that universals are reducible to names without any objective existence corresponding to them. In the strict sense of the doctrine there are no universals either in the mind or in the external world but words operate as symbols. This doctrine shades into conceptualism. Cf.

terminism. **—nom′inalist,** *n., adj.* **—nom′inalis′tic,** *adj.* **—nom′inalis′tically,** *adv.*

nominally (nŏm′ĭ nə lĭ), *adv.* in a nominal manner; by or as regards name; in name; only in name; ostensibly.

nominal value, book or par value; face value.

nominal wages, *Econ.* wages measured in terms of money and not by their ability to command goods and services. Cf. **real wages.**

nominate (*v.* nŏm′ĭ nāt′; *adj.* nŏm′ĭ nĭt), *v.,* **-nated, -nating,** *adj.* **—*v.t.* 1.** to propose as a proper person for appointment or election to an office. **2.** to appoint for a duty or office. **3.** *Archaic.* to entitle; name. **4.** *Obs.* to specify. **—*adj.* 5.** having a particular name. [t. L: m. s. *nōminātus,* pp., named] **—nom′ina′tor,** *n.*

nomination (nŏm′ĭ nā′shən), *n.* **1.** the act of nominating, esp. to office: *the nomination of candidates for the governorship.* **2.** the state of being nominated.

nominative (nŏm′ĭ nə tĭv, nŏm′nə-), *adj.* **1.** *Gram.* **a.** denoting a case which by its form, position, or function indicates that it serves as the subject of a finite verb, as in Latin *nauta bonus est* 'the sailor is good', *nauta* 'sailor' is in the nominative case. **b.** similar to such a case form in function or meaning. **2.** nominated; appointed by nomination. **—*n.* 3.** *Gram.* the nominative case, a word in that case, or a form or construction of similar function or meaning. [t. L: m. s. *nōminātivus* serving to name; r. ME *nominatif,* t. OF]

nominative absolute, *Gram.* a group of words including a substantive together with a participial modifier, not grammatically related to any other element in the sentence.

nominative of address, *Gram.* a noun naming the person to whom one is speaking. See **vocative.**

nominee (nŏm′ĭ nē′), *n.* **1.** one nominated, as to fill an office or stand for election. **2.** a person appointed by another to act as his agent. [f. NOMIN(ATE) + -EE]

nomism (nō′mĭz′əm), *n.* conduct in a religion based on a law or laws. [f. s. Gk *nómos* law + -ISM] **—nomis′tic,** *adj.*

nomogram (nŏm′ə grăm′, nō′mə-), *n.* a graph containing, usually, three parallel scales graduated for different variables so that when a straight line connects values of any two, the related value may be read directly from the third at the point intersected by the line. Also, **nom′ograph′** (-grăf′, -gräf′). [f. Gk *nomó(s)* law + -GRAM[1]]

nomography (nō mŏg′rə fĭ), *n.* **1.** the art of drawing up laws. **2.** the art of making and using a nomogram for solving a succession of nearly identical problems. [t. Gk: m. *nomographía* a writing of laws] **—nomog′rapher,** *n.* **—nomographic** (nŏm′ə grăf′ĭk), **nom′ograph′ical,** *adj.* **—nom′ograph′ically,** *adv.*

nomology (nō mŏl′ə jĭ), *n.* **1.** the science of law or laws. **2.** the science of the laws of the mind. [f. *nomo-* (t. Gk, comb. form of *nómos* law) + -LOGY] **—nomological** (nŏm′ə lŏj′ĭ kl), *adj.* **—nomol′ogist,** *n.*

nomothetic (nŏm′ə thĕt′ĭk), *adj.* **1.** lawgiving; legislative. **2.** pertaining to or based on laws, esp. religious laws; nomistic. **3.** *Psychol.* of or pertaining to the search for general laws (opposed to *idiographic*). Also, **nom′othet′ical.** [t. Gk: m. s. *nomothetikós*]

-nomy, a final word element meaning 'distribution', 'arrangement', 'management', or having reference to laws or government, as in *astronomy, economy, taxonomy.* [t. Gk: m. s. *-nomía,* der. *nómos* custom, law. See -IA]

non-, a prefix, indicating: **1.** exclusion from a specified class or group: *non-Jew, non-passerine.* **2.** objective negation or opposition: *non-porous, non-recurrent.* **3.** spuriousness or failure to fulfil a claim: *non-event, non-hero.* [repr. L *nōn* not; not a L prefix]

non-access (nŏn ăk′sĕs), *n.* *Law.* the absence of opportunity for sexual intercourse, as when a husband, because of absence, could not have fathered his wife's child.

nonage (nō′nĭj), *n.* **1.** the period of legal minority. **2.** any period of immaturity. [ME *nounage,* t. AF, f. *noun-* NON- + *age* AGE]

nonagenarian (nō′nə jĭ nèə′rĭ ən), *adj.* **1.** of the age of 90 years, or between 90 and 100 years old. **—*n.* 2.** a nonagenarian person. [f. s. L *nōnāgēnārius* containing ninety + -AN]

nonagon (nŏn′ə gən), *n.* a polygon having nine angles and nine sides; enneagon. [f. s. L *nōnus* ninth + *-agon* (after OCTAGON)] **—nonag′onal,** *adj.*

Nonagon

nonanoic acid (nŏn′ə nō′ĭk), pelargonic acid. [ult. der. L *nōnus* ninth. See -ANE, -IC]

non-appearance (nŏn′ə pĭə′rəns), *n.* failure or neglect to appear, as in a court.

nonce (nŏns), *n.* the one or particular occasion or purpose (chiefly in *for the nonce*). [ME *nones,* in phrase *for the nones,* orig., *for then one(s),* lit., for the once]

nonce word, a word coined and used only for the particular occasion.

nonchalance (nŏn′shə ləns, nŏnsh′ləns), *n.* the quality of being nonchalant; cool unconcern or indifference; casualness. [t. F, der. *nonchalant* NONCHALANT]

nonchalant (nŏn′shə lənt, nŏnsh′lənt), *adj.* coolly unconcerned, indifferent, or unexcited; casual. [t. F: f. *non-* NON- + *chalant* (ppr. of *chaloir* have concern for, g. L *calēre* be hot)] **—non′chalantly,** *adv.*

non-claim (nŏn klām′), *n.* *Law.* the failure to make a claim within a time limited by law.

non-collegiate (nŏn′kə lē′jĭ ĭt), *adj.* **1.** belonging to the body of students in a university not attached to any particular college or hall. **2.** below the level usually associated with college or university study. **3.** (of a university) not composed of colleges.

non-com (nŏn′kŏm′), *n.* *Colloq.* a non-commissioned officer.

non-combatant (nŏn kŏm′bə tənt), *n.* **1.** one who is not a combatant; a civilian in time of war. **2.** one connected with a military or naval force in some capacity other than that of a fighter, as a surgeon, a chaplain, etc.

non-commissioned (nŏn′kə mĭsh′ənd), *adj.* not commissioned (applied esp. to military personnel, as sergeants and corporals, ranking below warrant officer).

non-committal (nŏn′kə mĭt′l), *adj.* not committing oneself, or not involving committal, to a particular view, course, or the like: *a non-committal answer.*

non-communicant (nŏn′kə myōō′nĭ kənt), *n.* **1.** one who is not a communicant. **2.** one who does not communicate.

non-compliance (nŏn′kəm plī′əns), *n.* failure or refusal to comply. **—non′-compli′ant,** *adj., n.*

non compos mentis (nŏn′ kŏm′pəs mĕn′tĭs), *Latin.* not of sound mind; mentally incapable.

non-conductor (nŏn′kən dŭk′tə), *n.* a substance which does not readily conduct or transmit heat, sound, electricity, etc.; an insulator. **—non′-conduc′ting,** *adj.*

nonconformance (nŏn′kən fô′məns), *n.* lack of conformity.

nonconformist (nŏn′kən fô′mĭst), *n.* **1.** one who refuses to conform, as to an established Church. **2.** (*often cap.*) one who refuses to conform to the Church of England. **—non′conform′ing,** *adj.*

nonconformity (nŏn′kən fô′mĭ tĭ), *n.* **1.** lack of conformity or agreement. **2.** failure or refusal to conform, as to an established Church. **3.** (*often cap.*) refusal to conform to the Church of England.

---

non′-abra′sive, *adj.*
non′-abra′sively, *adv.*
non′-abra′siveness, *n.*
non′-absorb′ent, *adj., n.*
non′-academ′ic, *adj., n.*
non′-accep′tance, *n.*
non′-adher′ence, *n.*
non′-adher′ent, *n., adj.*
non′-adja′cent, *adj.*
non′-adja′cently, *adv.*
non′-admis′sion, *n.*
non′-aggres′sion, *n., adj.*
non′-aggres′sive, *adj.*
non′-agricul′tural, *adj.*
non′-alcohol′ic, *adj.*
non′-aligned′, *adj.*
non′-align′ment, *n.*
non′-alle′giance, *n.*
non′-alli′ance, *n.*
non′-allel′ic, *adj.*
non′-aquat′ic, *adj.*
non′-arri′val, *n.*
non-Ar′yan, *n., adj.*
non′-assess′able, *adj.*
non′-assim′ila′tion, *n.*
non′-atten′dance, *n.*
non′-automat′ic, *adj., n.*
non-be′ing, *n.*
non′-believ′er, *n.*
non′-believ′ing, *adj.*
non′-believ′ingly, *adv.*
non′-bellig′erent, *n., adj.*
non′-bellig′erency, *n.*
non-break′able, *adj.*
non-can′cellable, *adj.*
non′-canon′ical, *adj.*
non-Cath′olic, *n., adj.*
non-cel′lular, *adj.*
non-cen′tral, *adj.*
non-cen′trally, *adv.*
non-Chris′tian, *adj., n.*
non-civ′ilized′, *adj.*
non-clear′ance, *n.*
non-cle′rical, *adj.*
non′-cogni′tion, *n.*
non′-collap′sible, *adj.*
non′-collec′tion, *n.*
non′-colloid′al, *adj.*
non′-collu′sive, *adj.*
non′-colo′nial, *adj.*
non-com′bat, *n.*
non′-combin′ing, *adj.*
non′-combus′tible, *adj., n.*
non′-combus′tion, *n.*
non′-combus′tive, *adj.*
non′-commer′cial, *adj., n.*
non′-commer′cially, *adv.*
non′-commit′ment, *n.*
non′-commun′icable, *adj.*
non′-commun′ica′tion, *n.*
non′-commun′icative, *adj.*
non′-commun′icatively, *adv.*
non-com′munist, *n., adj.*
non′-compet′itive, *adj.*
non′-comple′tion, *n.*
non′complic′ity, *n.*
non′-compul′sion, *n.*
non′-compul′sory, *adj.*
non′-conceal′ment, *n.*
non′-concur′rence, *n.*
non′-condu′cive, *adj.*
non-con′fidence, *n.*
non-con′gruence, *n.*
non′-consec′utive, *adj.*
non′-consec′utively, *adv.*
non′-consec′utiveness, *n.*
non′-consent′, *n.*
non-con′sequence, *n.*
non′-conser′vative, *adj., n.*

non-content (nŏn′kən tənt′), *n.* not-content.

non-cooperation (nŏn′kō ŏp′ə rā′shən), *n.* **1.** failure or refusal to cooperate. **2.** a method or practice, established in India by Gandhi, of showing opposition to acts or policies of the government by refusing to participate in civic and political life or to obey governmental regulations. —**non-cooperative** (nŏn′kō ŏp′ə rə tĭv), *adj.* —**non′-coop′era′tor,** *n.*

nondescript (nŏn′dĭ skrĭpt′), *adj.* **1.** of no recognized, definite, or particular type or kind: *a nondescript garment.* —*n.* **2.** a person or a thing of no particular type or kind. [f. NON- + s. L *dēscriptus*, pp., described]

non-disjunction (nŏn′dĭs jŭngk′shən), *n. Biol.* the failure of chromosomes to follow normal separation into daughter cells at division.

none[1] (nŭn), *pron.* **1.** no one; not one: *there is none to help.* **2.** not any, as of something indicated: *that is none of your business.* **3.** no part; nothing. **4.** (*construed as pl.*) no, or not any, persons or things: *none come to the feasts.* —*adv.* **5.** to no extent; in no way; not at all: *the supply is none too great.* —*adj.* **6.** *Archaic.* not any; no (in later use only before a vowel or *h*): *Thou shalt have none other gods before me.* [ME *non*, OE *nān*, f. *ne* not + *ān* one]

none[2] (nōn), *n.* sing. of **nones**[2].

non-effective (nŏn′ĭ fĕk′tĭv), *adj.* **1.** not effective. **2.** not fit for duty or active service, as a soldier or sailor. —*n.* **3.** a non-effective person.

non-ego (nŏn ē′gō, -ĕg′ō), *n. Metaphys.* all that is not the ego or conscious self; object as opposed to subject.

nonentity (nŏ nĕn′tĭ tĭ), *n., pl.* **-ties. 1.** a person or thing of no importance. **2.** something which does not exist, or exists only in imagination. **3.** non-existence. [f. NON- + ENTITY]

nones[1] (nōnz), *n. Eccles.* the fifth of the seven canonical hours, or the service for it, orig. fixed for the ninth hour of the day (or 3 p.m.). [pl. of NONE[2], OE *nōn*, t. L: s. *nōna* (*hōra*). See NOON]

nones[2] (nōnz), *n.pl., sing.* **none.** (in the ancient Roman calendar) the ninth day before the ides, both days included, thus being the 7th of March, May, July, and October, and the 5th of the other months. [ME, t. L: m. *nōnae*, orig. fem. pl. of *nōnus* ninth]

non-essential (nŏn′ĭ sĕn′shəl), *adj.* **1.** not essential; not necessary: *non-essential use of petrol.* —*n.* **2.** a non-essential thing or person.

nonesuch (nŭn′sŭch′), *n.* **1.** a person or thing without equal; a paragon. **2.** *Bot.* black medick. Also, **nonsuch.**

nonet (nō nĕt′, nō nĕt′), *n. Music.* **1.** a composition for nine voices or instruments. **2.** a group of nine performers.

nonetheless (nŭn′thə lĕs′), *adv.* however; nevertheless. Also, **none the less.**

non-event (nŏn′ĭ vĕnt′), *n.* an occurrence of little significance or importance, esp. one which was expected to have great importance.

non-existence (nŏn′ĭg zĭs′təns), *n.* **1.** absence of existence. **2.** a thing that has no existence. —**non′-exist′ent,** *adj.*

nonfeasance (nŏn fē′zəns), *n. Law.* the omission of some act which ought to have been performed.

non-fiction (nŏn fĭk′shən), *n.* **1.** a class of writing comprising works dealing with facts and events, rather than imaginative narration: *we publish only non-fiction.* —*adj.* **2.** Also, **non-fic′tional.** denoting or pertaining to writing of this class.

non-forfeiture (nŏn fôr′fĭ chə), *n. Insurance.* a clause written into an insurance policy whereby the policy is not voided by non-payment of a premium.

non-harmonic (nŏn′hä mŏn′ĭk), *adj. Music.* denoting or pertaining to a note sounding with a chord of which it is not a chord note.

nonillion (nō nĭl′yən), *n.* **1.** a cardinal number represented in Great Britain and Germany by one followed by 54 zeroes, and in the U.S. and France by one followed by 30 zeroes. —*adj.* **2.** amounting to one nonillion in number. [t. F: f. *non-* (t. L: s. *nōnus* ninth) + (*m*)*illion* MILLION] —**nonil′lionth,** *n., adj.*

non-inductive (nŏn′ĭn dŭk′tĭv), *adj. Elect.* not inductive: *a non-inductive resistance.*

non-intervention (nŏn′ĭn tə vĕn′shən), *n.* **1.** abstention by a state from interference in the affairs of other states or in those of its own political subdivisions. **2.** failure or refusal to intervene. —**non′-interven′tionist,** *n.*

non-iron (nŏn ī′ən), *adj.* (of clothing) not requiring ironing; drip-dry.

non-joinder (nŏn join′də), *n. Law.* omission to join, as of one who should have been a party to an action.

nonjuror (nŏn jo͝o′rə), *n.* **1.** one who refuses to take a required oath, as of allegiance. **2.** (*often cap.*) one of those clergymen of the Church of England who in 1689 refused to swear allegiance to William and Mary.

non-legal (nŏn lē′gl), *adj.* not (definitely) legal; having

---

non′-consid′era′tion, *n.*
non′-constitu′tional, *adj.*
non′-conta′gious, *adj.*
non′-conta′giously, *adv.*
non′-conta′giousness, *n.*
non′-contem′porary, *adj., n.*
non′-conten′tious, *adj.*
non′-conten′tiously, *adv.*
non′-contin′uance, *n.*
non′-contin′uous, *adj.*
non′-contin′uously, *adv.*
non-con′traband′, *n., adj.*
non′-contradic′tory, *adj., n.*
non′-contrib′utory, *adj., n.*
non′-controver′sial, *adj.*
non′-corro′sive, *adj.*
non′-crea′tive, *adj.*
non′-crea′tively, *adv.*
non′-crea′tiveness, *n.*
non-crit′ical, *adj.*
non-crit′ically, *adv.*
non-crys′talline′, *adj.*
non-cu′mulative, *adj.*
non-cur′dling, *adj.*
non′-decep′tive, *adj.*
non′-decep′tively, *adv.*
non′-decep′tiveness, *n.*
non′-decid′uous, *adj.*
non′-decid′uously, *adv.*
non′-decid′uousness, *n.*
non′-deci′sive, *adj.*
non′-deci′sively, *adv.*
non′-deci′siveness, *n.*
non′-decreas′ing, *adj.*
non-de′ist, *n.*
non′-deliv′ery, *n.*
non′-democrat′ic, *adj., n.*
non′-detach′able, *adj.*
non′-deter′minist, *n., adj.*
non′-deter′rent, *adj.*
non′-destruc′tive, *adj.*
non′-destruc′tively, *adv.*
non′-destruc′tiveness, *n.*
non-dev′iant, *n., adj.*
non′-diplomat′ic, *adj.*
non′-diplomat′ically, *adv.*
non′-direc′tional, *adj.*
non′-direc′tive, *adj.*
non-dir′igible, *adj., n.*
non-dis′ciplinary, *adj.*
non′-discrim′ina′tion, *n.*
non′-discrim′inatory, *adj.*
non′-dispos′able, *adj.*
non′-dispos′al, *n.*
non′-distinc′tive, *adj.*
non′-distribu′tion, *n.*
non′-distrib′utive, *adj.*
non′-distrib′utively, *adv.*
non′-diver′gence, *n.*
non′-diver′gent, *adj.*
non′-diver′gently, *adv.*
non′-divis′ible, *adj.*
non′-dogmat′ic, *adj.*
non′-dramat′ic, *adj.*
non-drink′able, *adj.*
non-drink′er, *n.*
non-driv′er, *n.*
non-dur′able, *adj.*
non-du′tiable, *adj.*
non-ed′ible, *adj., n.*
non-ed′ucable, *adj.*
non′-educa′tional, *adj.*
non′-effi′cient, *adj.*
non′-effi′ciently, *adv.*
non′-elas′tic, *adj.*
non′-elec′tion, *n.*
non′-emo′tional, *adj.*
non′-emo′tionally, *adv.*
non′-enforce′ment, *n.*
non′-equiv′alent, *n., adj.*
non′-equiv′alently, *adv.*
non′-estab′lishment, *n.*
non-eth′ical, *adj.*
non-eth′ically, *adv.*
non′-Euclid′ean, *adj.*
non′-exchange′able, *adj.*
non′-exclu′sive, *adj.*
non′-exemp′tion, *n.*
non′-exist′ing, *adj.*
non′-explo′sive, *adj., n.*
non′-explo′sively, *adv.*
non′-explo′siveness, *n.*
non′-export′able, *adj.*
non′-exporta′tion, *n.*
non-ex′tradit′able, *adj.*
non-fac′tual, *adj.*
non-fac′tually, *adv.*
non-fat′, *adj.*
non-fa′tal, *adj.*
non-fa′tally, *adv.*
non-fed′eral, *adj.*
non-fed′erat′ed, *adj.*
non-fer′rous, *adj.*
non-fes′tive, *adj.*
non-fes′tively, *adv.*
non-feu′dal, *adj.*
non-fi′nite, *adj.*
non-fis′cal, *adj.*
non-fis′cally, *adv.*
non-fis′sile, *adj.*
non-fis′sionable, *adj.*
non-flam′mable, *adj.*
non′-fossilif′erous, *adj.*
non-foul′ing, *adj.*
non-freez′ing, *adj.*
non′-fulfil′ment, *n.*
non-func′tional, *adj.*
non-func′tionally, *adv.*
non-gas′eous, *adj.*
non′-grammat′ical, *adj.*
non-green′, *adj.*
non-hab′itable, *adj.*
non-hab′itably, *adv.*
non′-hered′itary, *adj.*
non′-heret′ical, *adj.*
non′-heret′ically, *adv.*
non-her′itable, *adj.*
non-her′itably, *adv.*
non′-histor′ic, *adj.*
non-hu′man, *adj., n.*
non-hu′morous, *adj.*
non-hu′morously, *adv.*
non′-ideal′, *adj.*
non′-iden′tical, *adj.*
non′-iden′tity, *n.*
non′-idiomat′ic, *adj.*
non′-immu′nity, *n.*
non′-importa′tion, *n.*
non′-impeach′able, *adj.*
non′-impe′rialist, *adj., n.*
non-im′plementa′tion, *n.*
non-im′pregnat′ed, *adj.*
non-in′cident, *n., adj.*
non′-inclu′sive, *adj.*
non′-inclu′sively, *adv.*
non′-indict′able, *adj.*
non′-indict′ment, *n.*
non′-indig′enous, *adj.*
non′-indus′trial, *adj., n.*
non′-indus′trially, *adv.*
non′-infec′tion, *n.*
non′-infec′tious, *adj.*
non′-inflam′mable, *adj.*
non′-inflam′mably, *adv.*
non′-inform′ative, *adj.*
non′-inform′atively, *adv.*
non′-inher′itable, *adj.*
non-in′tercourse′, *n.*
non′-interfer′ence, *n.*
non′-intersec′ting, *adj.*
non′-intox′icant, *adj., n.*
non′-intox′icat′ing, *adj.*
non′-intox′icat′ingly, *adv.*
non-ir′rigable, *adj.*
non-ir′ritant, *adj.*
non-ir′ritat′ing, *adj.*
non-is′suable, *adj.*
non-is′suably, *adv.*
non′-libera′tion, *n.*
non′-life′, *n.*

---

no legal aspect (distinguished from *illegal*): *a completely non-legal controversy.*

non-linear (nŏn lĭn′ĭ ə), *adj. Maths.* (of an equation) not of the first degree. See **linear.**

non-linearity (nŏn′lĭn ĭ ăr′rĭ tĭ), *n. Maths.* the deviation of a mathematical equation from the linear.

non-metal (nŏn mĕt′l), *n. Chem.* **1.** an element not having the character of a metal, as carbon, nitrogen, etc. **2.** an element incapable of forming simple positive ions in solution.

non-metallic (nŏn′mĭ tăl′ĭk), *adj. Chem.* **1.** of or relating to non-metal. **2.** not of a metallic quality: *a non-metallic appearance.*

non-moral (nŏn mŏ′rəl), *adj.* having no relation to morality; neither moral nor immoral: *a completely non-moral problem of society.* **—Syn.** See **amoral.**

non-nitrogenous (nŏn′nī trŏj′ĭ nəs), *adj.* containing no nitrogen.

non-nuclear (nŏn nyōō′klĭ ə), *adj.* not armed with nuclear weapons: *non-nuclear nations.*

Nono (*It.* nō′nō), *n.* **Luigi** (*It.* lwē′jē), born 1924, Italian composer.

non-objective (nŏn′əb jĕk′tĭv), *adj. Fine Arts.* not representing or containing objects known in physical nature; abstract or non-representational.

non obstante (nŏn′ŏb stăn′tĭ), *Latin.* notwithstanding.

nonpareil (nŏn′pə rəl), *adj.* **1.** having no equal; peerless. *—n.* **2.** a person or thing having no equal; something unique. **3.** *Print.* **a.** a size of type (6 point). **b.** a slug occupying 6 points of space between lines. [late ME, t. F: f. *non-* NON- + *pareil* equal (ult. der. L *pār*)]

non-parous (nŏn pă′rəs), *adj. Physiol.* having borne no children.

non-participating (nŏn′pä tĭs′ĭ pā′tĭng), *adj. Insurance.* having no right to dividends or to a distribution of surplus.

non-partisan (nŏn′pä tĭ zăn′), *adj.* **1.** not partisan; objective. **2.** not supporting any of the established or regular parties. Also, **nonpartizan.**

nonplus (nŏn plŭs′), *v.,* **-plussed, -plussing** or (*U.S.*) **-plused, -plusing,** *n. —v.t.* **1.** to bring to a nonplus; puzzle completely. *—n.* **2.** a state of utter perplexity. [t. L: *nōn plūs* not more, no further]

non-polar (nŏn pō′lə), *adj. Chem.* not polar; containing no polar molecules or dipoles.

non possumus (nŏn pŏs′ōō mōōs), *Latin.* we cannot.

non-pro (nŏn prō′), *n., adj. Slang.* non-professional.

non-productive (nŏn′prə dŭk′tĭv), *adj.* **1.** not producing goods directly, as employees in charge of personnel, inspectors, etc. **2.** unproductive. **—non′-produc′-tively,** *adv.* **—non′-produc′tiveness, non′-productiv′-ity,** *n.*

non-profit-making (nŏn prŏf′ĭt mā′kĭng), *adj.* not yielding a return; established or entered into for some motive other than the hope of making a profit. Also, *U.S.,* **non-profit.**

non pros., non prosequitur.

non prosequitur (nŏn′prō sĕk′wĭ tə), *Law.* a judgement entered against the plaintiff in a suit when he does not appear to prosecute it. [L: he does not pursue (prosecute)]

non-provided school, *Obs.* voluntary school.

non-representational (nŏn′rĕp′rĭ zĕn tā′shə nəl), *adj.* not resembling any object in physical nature: *a non-representational painting.*

non-resident (nŏn rĕz′ĭ dənt), *adj.* **1.** not resident in a particular place. **2.** not residing where official duties require one to reside. *—n.* **3.** one who is non-resident. **—non-res′idence, non-res′idency,** *n.*

non-resistant (nŏn′rĭ zĭs′tənt), *adj.* **1.** not resistant; passively obedient. *—n.* **2.** one who does not resist authority or force. **3.** one who maintains that violence should not be resisted by force. **—non′-resist′ance,** *n.*

non-restraint (nŏn′rĭ strānt′), *n.* **1.** *Psychiatry.* the treatment of the mentally ill without mechanical means of restraint. **2.** absence of restraint.

non-restrictive (nŏn′rĭ strĭk′tĭv), *adj.* **1.** not restrictive or limiting: *non-restrictive practices.* **2.** *Gram.* (of a word or clause) purely descriptive rather than limiting in its application to the sentence element it modifies. 'Mr Owen, *who was here yesterday,* is a farmer' illustrates a non-restrictive clause. 'The man who was here yesterday is a farmer' shows the same clause employed to restrict the meaning of *the man.*

non-rigid (nŏn rĭj′ĭd), *adj.* **1.** not rigid. **2.** designating a type of airship having a flexible gas container without a supporting structure and held in shape only by the pressure of the gas within.

non-sectarian (nŏn′sĕk tēə′rĭ ən), *adj.* not affiliated to any specific religious denomination.

nonsense (nŏn′səns), *n.* **1.** that which makes no sense or is lacking in sense. **2.** words without sense or conveying absurd ideas. **3.** senseless or absurd action; foolish conduct, notions, etc.: *to stand no nonsense from a person.* **4.** absurdity: *the nonsense of an idea.* **5.** stuff, trash, or anything useless. **—nonsensical** (nŏn sĕn′sĭ kl), *adj.* **—nonsen′-sically,** *adv.* **—nonsen′sicalness, nonsen′sical′ity,** *n.*

nonsense verse, verse conveying deliberately absurd

---

non-lit′erary, *adj.*
non-lit′erate, *adj.*
non-liv′ing, *adj.*
non-lu′minous, *adj.*
non-lu′minously, *adv.*
non′-magnet′ic, *adj.*
non′-malig′nant, *adj.*
non′-malig′nantly, *adv.*
non-mall′eable, *adj.*
non-man′datory, *adj.*
non′-manufac′turing, *adj.*
non-mar′rying, *adj.*
non-mar′tial, *adj.*
non-mar′tially, *adv.*
non′-mater′ial, *adj.*
non′-math′emati′cian, *n.*
non-meas′urable, *adj.*
non-meas′urably, *adv.*
non′-mechan′ical, *adj.*
non′-mechan′ically, *adv.*
non-med′ical, *adj.*
non-med′ically, *adv.*
non′-medic′inal, *adj.*
non′-medic′inally, *adv.*
non′-melod′ic, *adj.*
non′-melod′ically, *adv.*
non′-melo′dious, *adj.*
non′-melo′diously, *adv.*
non-mel′ting, *adj.*
non-mem′ber, *n.*
non-mem′bership′, *n.*
non-met′rical, *adj.*
non-met′rically, *adv.*
non-mi′gratory, *adj.*
non-mil′itant, *adj.*
non-mil′itantly, *adv.*
non-mil′itary, *adj.*
non-mis′cible, *adj.*
non′-miscibil′ity, *n.*
non-mor′tal, *adj.*
non-mor′tally, *adv.*
non-mo′tile, *adj.*
non-mus′cular, *adj.*
non-mus′cularly, *adv.*
non-mu′sical, *adj.*
non-mu′sically, *adv.*
non-nat′ural, *adj.*
non-nat′urally, *adv.*
non′-nat′uralis′tic, *adj.*
non-nav′igable, *adj.*
non-nav′igably, *adv.*
non-nec′essary, *adj.*
non′-neces′sity, *n.*
non′-nego′tiable, *adj.*
non-neu′tral, *adj.*
non′-nutri′tious, *adj.*
non′-obe′dience, *n.*
non′-oblig′atory, *adj.*
non′-obser′vance, *n.*
non′-occur′rence, *n.*
non-o′dorous, *adj.*
non-o′dorously, *adv.*
non′-offend′er, *n.*
non′-offen′sive, *adj.*
non′-offen′sively, *adv.*
non′-offi′cial, *adj.*
non′-offi′cially, *adv.*
non-orth′odox′, *adj.*
non-orth′odox′ly, *adv.*
non′-parish′ioner, *n.*
non′-parliamen′tary, *adj.*
non′-paro′chial, *adj.*
non′-paro′chially, *adv.*
non′-partic′ipant, *n.*
non′-partic′ipa′tion, *n.*
non-par′ty, *adj.*
non-pas′serine′, *adj.*
non-pay′ing, *adj.*
non-pay′ment, *n.*
non′-perfor′mance, *n.*
non-per′ishable, *adj.*
non-per′manent, *adj.*
non-per′manently, *adv.*
non-per′meable, *adj.*
non′-perpendic′ular, *adj., n.*
non′-perpendic′ularly, *adv.*
non-persis′tence, *n.*
non′-philosoph′ical, *adj.*
non′-philosoph′ically, *adv.*
non′-pina′ceous, *adj.*
non′-poet′ic, *adj.*
non-poi′sonous, *adj.*
non-poi′sonously, *adv.*
non′-polit′ical, *adj.*
non′-polit′ically, *adv.*
non-po′rous, *adj.*
non-pred′atory, *adj.*
non′-predict′able, *adj.*
non′-prehen′sile, *adj.*
non′-prescrip′tive, *adj.*
non′-prio′rity, *n.*
non′-produ′cing, *adj.*
non′produc′tion, *n.*
non′-profes′sional, *adj., n.*
non′-profi′ciency, *n.*
non′-profi′cient, *adj.*
non′-profiteer′ing, *adj.*
non′-progres′sive, *adj.*
non′-progres′sively, *adv.*
non′-propor′tionate, *adj.*
non′-protec′tive, *adj.*
non′-protec′tively, *adv.*
non-pun′ishable, *adj.*
non-ra′cial, *adj.*
non-ra′cially, *adv.*
non′-ra′dioac′tive, *adj.*
non-read′er, *n.*
non′-real′ity, *n.*
non′-recip′rocal, *adj.*
non′-recip′rocally, *adv.*
non′-recogni′tion, *n.*
non′-recur′rent, *adj.*
non′-recur′rently, *adv.*
non′-recur′ring, *adj.*
non′-reduc′tion, *n.*
non′-refill′able, *adj.*
non′-reflect′ing, *adj.*
non′-refu′elling, *adj.*
non-reg′iment′ed, *adj.*
non-reign′ing, *adj.*
non′-reli′gious, *adj.*
non′-reli′giously, *adv.*
non′-remun′erat′ed, *adj.*
non′-remun′erative, *adj.*
non′-remun′eratively, *adv.*
non′-renew′able, *adj.*
non′-residen′tial, *adj.*
non′-restric′ted, *adj.*
non′-restric′tedly, *adv.*
non′-return′able, *adj.*
non′-revers′ible, *adj.*
non′-revers′ibly, *adv.*
non-rhym′ing, *adj.*
non-rhyth′mic, *adj.*
non-ru′ral, *adj.*
non-ru′rally, *adv.*
non-rust′, *adj.*
non-sal′aried, *adj.*
non-sale′able, *adj.*
non-sched′uled, *adj.*
non′-scientif′ic, *adj.*
non-sci′entist, *n.*
non-scrip′tural, *adj.*
non-sea′sonal, *adj.*
non-sec′tional, *adj.*
non-sec′tionally, *adv.*
non′-selec′tive, *adj.*
non′-self-gov′erning, *adj.*
non-sen′sitive, *adj.*
non-sen′sitively, *adv.*
non-sen′suous, *adj.*

---

ideas or using specially coined words, usually humorous.

non seq., non sequitur.

non sequitur (nŏn sĕk′wĭ tə), *Latin.* an inference or a conclusion which does not follow from the premises. [L: it does not follow]

non-skid (nŏn skĭd′), *adj.* having the wheel rim or tyre with a ridged or otherwise skid-resistant surface.

non-slip (nŏn slĭp′), *adj.* designed or constructed in such a way as to minimize danger of slipping.

non-smoker (nŏn smō′kə), *n.* **1.** a person who does not smoke. **2.** a compartment of a railway carriage in which smoking is forbidden. —**non-smo′king,** *adj., n.*

non-starter (nŏn stä′tə), *n.* something which has no chance of success, as an idea that is discounted as inherently impracticable.

non-stick (nŏn stĭk′), *adj.* (of frying pans, etc.) coated on the inside with a substance (as polytetrafluoroethylene) to prevent food sticking during cooking.

non-stop (nŏn′stŏp′), *adj., adv.* without a single stop: *a non-stop flight from New York to Paris.*

non-striated (nŏn′strī ā′tĭd), *adj.* not striated; unstriped, as muscular tissue.

non-striker (nŏn strī′kə), *n.* **1.** one who does not strike. **2.** *Cricket.* the batsman who is at the bowler's wicket. —**non-stri′king,** *n.*

nonsuch (nŭn′sŭch′), *n.* nonesuch.

nonsuit (nŏn syo͞ot′), *Law.* —*n.* **1.** a judgement given against a plaintiff who neglects to prosecute, or who fails to show a legal cause of action or to bring sufficient evidence. —*v.t.* **2.** to subject to a nonsuit.

non-support (nŏn′sə pôt′), *n.* *U.S. Law.* omission to support another, as a wife, child, or other dependant, as required by law.

non troppo (nŏn trŏp′ō), *Music.* not too much: *non troppo lento* (not too slow). [It.]

non-U (nŏn yo͞o′), *adj.* *Colloq.* not appropriate to or characteristic of the upper class. [NON- + *U(pper class)*]

non-union (nŏn yo͞o′nyən), *adj.* **1.** not belonging to, or not in accordance with the rules of, a trade union. **2.** anti-union. —*n.* **3.** *Pathol.* failure of a broken bone to heal.

non-unionism (nŏn yo͞o′nyə nĭz′əm), *n.* disregard of or opposition to trade unions. —**non-un′ionist,** *n.*

non-union shop, a factory or business in which the employer fixes terms and conditions of employment unilaterally without recognizing or dealing with a union.

non-user (nŏn yo͞o′zə), *n.* **1.** one who does not use. **2.** *Law.* ceasing to exercise a right.

noodle[1] (no͞o′dl), *n.* a type of pasta, cut into long, narrow, flat strips, originating in Italy: served in soups or, with a sauce, as a main dish. [t. G: m. *Nudel*]

noodle[2] (no͞o′dl), *n.* **1.** *Slang.* the head. **2.** a simpleton. [? var. of NODDLE[1] (with *oo* from FOOL)]

nook (no͝ok), *n.* **1.** a corner, as in a room. **2.** any secluded or obscure corner. **3.** any small recess. **4.** a remote spot. [ME *noke.* Cf. d. Norw. *nok* hook]

nooky (no͝ok′ĭ), *adj.* **1.** having many nooks. **2.** shaped like a nook. Also, **nookie.**

noon (no͞on), *n.* **1.** midday. **2.** twelve o'clock in the day-time. **3.** the highest, brightest, or finest point or part. [ME *none,* OE *nōn,* t. L: s. *nōna* ninth hour. See NONES[1]]

noonday (no͞on′dā′), *adj.* **1.** of or at noon. —*n.* **2.** midday; noon.

no-one (nō′wŭn′), *pron.* **1.** nobody. —*n.* **2.** no person. Also, **no one.**

nooning (no͞o′nĭng), *n.* **1.** noontime. **2.** an interval at noon for rest or food. **3.** a rest or meal at noon.

noontide (no͞on′tīd′), *n.* **1.** the time of noon; midday. **2.** the highest or best point or part. [ME *nonetyde,* OE *nōntīd*]

noontime (no͞on′tīm′), *n.* the time of noon.

Noordholland (*Du.* nórt hô′lŏnt), *n.* North Holland.

noose (no͞os), *n., v.,* **noosed, noosing.** —*n.* **1.** a loop with a running knot, as in a snare, lasso, hangman's halter, etc., which tightens as the rope is pulled. **2.** a tie or bond; a snare. —*v.t.* **3.** to secure by or as by a noose. **4.** to make a noose with or in (a rope, etc.). [prob. t. OF: m. *nos,* der. *noer* to knit, g. L *nōdāre,* der. *nōdus* knot]

Nootka (no͞ot′kə), *n.* **1.** an American Indian language of Wakashan stock, spoken on Vancouver Island and Cape Flattery, a cape in NW Washington. **2.** a member of an American Indian tribe speaking this language.

nopal (nō′pl), *n.* **1.** any cactus or fruit of the genera *Opuntia* and *Nopalea.* **2.** the prickly pear. [t. Sp., t. Nahuatl.: m. *nopalli* cactus]

no-par (nō′pä′), *adj.* without par, or face, value.

nope (nōp), *adv.* *Colloq.* an emphatic form of **no.**

nor (nô), *conj.* **1.** a negative conjunction used: **a.** as the correlative to a preceding *neither: he could neither read nor write.* **b.** to continue the force of a negative, such as *not, no, never,* etc., occurring in a preceding clause: *he left and I never saw him again, nor did I regret it.* **c.** after an affirmative clause, or as a continuative, in the sense of *and . . . not: they are happy; nor need we mourn.* **d.** *Archaic or Poetic.* with omission of a preceding *neither,* its negative force being understood: *he nor I was there.* **e.** *Now Chiefly Poetic.* instead of *neither,* as correlative to a following *nor: nor he nor I was there.* **2.** *Dial.* than. [ME *nor,* contr. of *nother,* OE *nōther,* f. *ne* not + *ōther* (contr. of *ōhwæther* either)]

nor' (nô), *n., adj., adv.* *Chiefly Naut.* north.

nor-, *Chem.* a word element meaning 'normal'. [short for NORMAL]

Nor., **1.** Norman. **2.** North. **3.** Norway. **4.** Norwegian.

Nord (*Fr.* nŏr), *n.* **1.** an administrative region in N France comprising the departments of Nord and Pas-de-Calais. 3,659,394 pop. (1962); 4834 sq. mi. *Cap.:* Lille. **2.** a department in N France. 2,293,112 pop. (1962); 2228 sq. mi. *Cap.:* Lille.

Nordau (*Ger.* nŏr′dou), *n.* **Max Simon** (*Ger.* māks zē′-mŏn), 1849–1923, Hungarian Jewish writer and leading advocate of Zionism.

Nordenskjöld (*Sw.* no͞or′dən shœld), *n.* **1. Nils Adolf Erik** (*Sw.* nēls ä′dŏlf ĕ′rēk), **Baron,** 1832–1901, Swedish arctic explorer, born in Finland. **2.** his nephew, **Nils Otto Gustaf** (*Sw.* nēls ŏt′o͞o go͝os′tȧv), 1869–1928, Swedish arctic and antarctic explorer.

Nordenskjöld Sea, Laptev Sea.

Nordhausen (*Ger.* nŏrt′hou zən), *n.* a town in SW East Germany: site of a Nazi extermination camp during World War II. 39,200 (est. 1959).

Nordhausen acid, *Chem.* fuming sulphuric acid.

Nordic (nô′dĭk), *adj.* **1.** *Ethnol.* designating, or belonging or pertaining to, a race of men or a Caucasian racial subtype characterized by tall stature, blond hair, blue eyes, and elongated head, exemplified most markedly by Scandinavians and Britons and their descendants. —*n.* **2.** a member of the Nordic race. [t. F: m. *nordique,* der. *nord* north, t. Gmc, and akin to NORTH. See -IC]

---

non-sen′suously, *adv.*
non-sex′ual, *adj.*
non-sex′ually, *adv.*
non′-Shakespea′rian, *adj.*
non-shar′ing, *adj.*
non-shat′ter, *adj.*
non-shrink′, *adj.*
non-shrink′able, *adj.*
non′-signif′icant, *adj.*
non′-signif′icantly, *adv.*
non-so′cial, *adj.*
non-so′cially, *adv.*
non-so′cialist, *adj., n.*
non-sol′vent, *adj.*
non-sol′vency, *n.*
non-spark′ling, *adj.*
non-spe′cialist, *n., adj.*
non-spe′cialized′, *adj.*
non-spi′ritual, *adj.*
non-spi′ritually, *adv.*
non-spore′-form′ing, *adj.*
non-stain′able, *adj.*
non-stain′ing, *adj.*
non-stan′dard, *adj.*
non-stan′dardized′, *adj.*
non-stat′utory, *adj.*
non-stim′ulat′ing, *adj.*
non′-strate′gic, *adj.*
non-stretch′, *adj.*
non′-submis′sive, *adj.*
non′-submis′sively, *adv.*
non′-subscrib′er, *n.*
non′-substan′tial, *adj.*
non′-substan′tially, *adv.*
non′-succes′sive, *adj.*
non′-succes′sively, *adv.*
non′-support′er, *n.*
non′-survi′val, *n.*
non′-sustain′able, *adj.*
non′-sustain′ing, *adj.*
non-swim′mer, *n.*
non-swim′ming, *adj.*
non′-symmet′rical, *adj.*
non′-synthet′ic, *adj.*
non′-systemat′ic, *adj.*
non-tax′able, *adj.*
non-tax′ably, *adv.*
non-teach′able, *adj.*
non-tech′nical, *adj.*
non-tech′nically, *adv.*
non′-terres′trial, *adj.*
non′-territor′ial, *adj.*
non′-territor′ially, *adv.*
non-tex′tual, *adj.*
non-tex′tually, *adv.*
non-ti′dal, *adj.*
non′-total′itar′ian, *adj.*
non-tox′ic, *adj.*
non-trad′ing, *adj.*
non′-tradi′tional, *adj.*
non′-transfer′able, *adj.*
non-tran′sient, *adj.*
non-tran′siently, *adv.*
non-trib′utary, *adj.*
non-trop′ical, *adj.*
non-truth′, *n.*
non-typ′ical, *adj.*
non-typ′ically, *adv.*
non-u′niform′, *adj.*
non′-uni′ted, *adj.*
non′-univer′sal, *adj.*
non′-univer′sally, *adv.*
non′-util′ity, *n.*
non-ut′terance, *n.*
non-ven′omous, *adj.*
non-ven′omously, *adv.*
non-ver′bal, *adj.*
non-ver′bally, *adv.*
non-ver′tical, *adj., n.*
non-ver′tically, *adv.*
non-vi′able, *adj.*
non′-viola′tion, *n.*
non-vi′olence, *n.*
non-vi′olent, *adj.*
non-vi′olently, *adv.*
non-vis′ual, *adj.*
non-vo′cal, *adj.*
non-vo′cally, *adv.*
non′-vocal′ic, *adj.*
non′-voca′tional, *adj.*
non′-voca′tionally, *adv.*
non-vol′atile′, *adj.*
non′-vol′untary, *adj.*
non-vot′er, *n.*
non-vot′ing, *adj.*
non-wes′tern, *adj.*
non-white′, *adj., n.*
non-work′er, *n.*
non-wo′ven, *adj.*
non-yield′ing, *adj.*

Nordkyn Cape (*Norw.* nōōr′KHYn), North Cape.

Nordrhein-Westfalen (*Ger.* nŏrt′rīn vĕst fä′lən), *n.* German name of **North Rhine-Westphalia.**

nor'easter (nôr′ēs′tə), *n.* north-easter.

Norfolk (nô′fək), *n.* **1.** a county in E England. 561,980 pop. (1961); 2054 sq. mi. *Co. town:* Norwich. **2.** a seaport in the U.S., in SE Virginia: naval base. 305,872 (1960).

Norfolk Broads, a low-lying district of East Anglia, in Norfolk, characterized by a series of interconnected lake-like river expansions.

Norfolk Island, an island in the S Pacific between New Caledonia and New Zealand: a territory of Australia. 844 pop. (est. 1961); 13 sq. mi.

Norfolk jacket, a loosely belted single-breasted jacket, with box pleats at front and back.

Norge (*Norw.* nŏr′gə), *n.* Norwegian name of **Norway.**

noria (nô′rĭ ə), *n.* a device consisting of a series of buckets on a wheel, used in Spain and the Orient for raising water. [t. Sp., t. Ar.: m. *nā'ūra*]

Noricum (nŏ′rĭ kəm), *n.* an ancient Roman province in central Europe, roughly corresponding to the part of Austria S of the Danube.

norland (nô′lənd), *n. Chiefly Poetic.* northland. [f. *nor* (apocopated var. of NORTH) + LAND]

norm (nôm), *n.* **1.** a standard, model, or pattern. **2.** *Educ.* **a.** a designated standard of average performance of people of a given age, background, etc. **b.** a standard of average performance by a person. [t. L: s. *norma* carpenter's square, rule, pattern]

Norm., Norman.

normal (nô′məl), *adj.* **1.** conforming to the standard or the common type; regular, usual, natural, or not abnormal: *the normal procedure.* **2.** serving to fix a standard. **3.** *Psychol.* **a.** approximately average in respect to any psychological trait, such as intelligence, personality, emotional adjustment, etc. **b.** without any mental aberrations; sane. **4.** *Maths.* **a.** being at right angles, as a line; perpendicular. **b.** of the nature of or pertaining to a mathematical normal. **5.** *Chem.* **a.** (of a solution) containing one equivalent weight of the constituent in question in one litre of solution. **b.** pertaining to an aliphatic hydrocarbon having a straight unbranched carbon chain, each carbon atom of which is joined to no more than two other carbon atoms. **c.** pertaining to a normal element. **6.** *Biol., Med., etc.* **a.** free from any infection or experimental therapy. **b.** of natural occurrence. —*n.* **7.** the standard or type. **8.** the normal form or state; the average or mean. **9.** *Maths.* a perpendicular line or plane, esp. one perpendicular to a tangent line of a curve, or a tangent plane of a surface, at the point of contact. [t. L: s. *normālis* made according to a carpenter's square or rule]

normal curve, *Statistics.* a bell-shaped curve giving the distribution of probability associated with the different values of a variable.

normalcy (nô′məl sĭ), *n.* the character or state of being normal; normality: *back to normalcy.*

normal element, a galvanic cell of known and reproducible voltage; standard cell.

normality (nô măl′ĭ tĭ), *n.* **1.** the character or state of being normal. **2.** *Psychol.* **a.** the quality of being approximately average with respect to any psychological trait. **b.** sanity; freedom from mental aberration. **3.** *Chem.* the concentration of a solution expressed in gram-equivalents of active reagent per litre of solution. **4.** *Biol., Med., etc.* freedom from infection.

normalize (nô′mə līz′), *v.t.*, **-lized, -lizing. 1.** to make normal. **2.** *Metall.* to heat-treat a steel, in order to relieve its internal stresses, by heating to above the critical temperature and allowing it to cool in air. Also, **normalise.** —**nor′maliza′tion,** *n.* —**nor′maliz′er,** *n.*

normally (nô′mə lĭ), *adv.* as a rule; regularly; according to rule, general custom, etc.

normal school, (in the U.S., France, and elsewhere) a school for the preliminary professional education of teachers. [after F *école normale*]

normal solution, a solution of a chemical substance in water which contains the equivalent weight of that substance in one litre of solution.

Norman (nô′mən), *n.* **1.** a member of that branch of the Northmen or Scandinavians who in the 10th century conquered Normandy. **2.** one of the mixed Scandinavian and French (**Norman French**) race later inhabiting this region, which conquered England in 1066. **3.** a native or inhabitant of Normandy. **4.** Norman French (language). —*adj.* **5.** of or pertaining to the Normans. **6.** of or pertaining to Normandy. **7.** *Archit.* denoting or pertaining to a variety of the Romanesque style of architecture introduced from Normandy into Great Britain before and during the Norman Conquest. [ME, back-formation from OF *Normans*, pl. of *Normant*. See NORTHMAN]

Norman Conquest, the conquest of England by the Normans, under William the Conqueror, in 1066.

Normandy (nô′mən dĭ), *n.* **1.** a region in N France on the English Channel: invaded and settled by Northmen in the 10th century; it became a duchy and later a province; its capital was Rouen. Allied invasion World War II began June 6th, 1944. **2.** See **Basse-Normandie** and **Haute-Normandie.**

Normandy

Norman French, 1. the French of the Normans or of Normandy. **2.** the legal jargon of England, now extinct except in phrases, orig. a dialect of Old French.

Normanize (nô′mə nīz′), *v.i., v.t.*, **-nized, -nizing.** to make or become Norman in customs, language, etc. Also, **Normanise.** —**Nor′maniza′tion,** *n.*

Normanton (nô′mən tən), *n.* a town in England, in the West Riding of Yorkshire. 18,307 (1961).

normative (nô′mə tĭv), *adj.* **1.** concerning a norm, esp. an assumed norm regarded as the standard of correctness in speech and writing. **2.** tending or attempting to establish such a norm, esp. by the prescription of rules: *normative grammar.* **3.** reflecting the assumption of such a norm, or favouring its establishment. —**nor′matively,** *adv.*

norm-formation (nôm′fô mā′shən), *n. Sociol.* the development of common behaviour and beliefs by general agreement within a reference group.

normocyte (nô′mə sīt′), *n. Anat.* a red blood cell of normal size.

normotensive (nô′mō tĕn′sĭv), *adj. Med.* having a normal blood pressure.

Norn (nôn), *n. Scand. Myth.* any one of the goddesses of fate, commonly represented as three in number, whose decrees were irrevocable. [t. Icel.]

Norrköping (*Sw.* nŏrt′shœ pĕng), *n.* a seaport in SE Sweden. 93,161 (1965).

Norse (nôs), *adj.* **1.** belonging or pertaining to Norway, esp. ancient Norway with its colonies (as in Iceland), or to ancient Scandinavia generally. —*n.* **2.** (*construed as pl.*) the Norwegians. **3.** (*construed as pl.*) the ancient Norwegians. **4.** (*construed as pl.*) the Northmen or ancient Scandinavians generally. **5.** the Norwegian language, esp. in its older forms. See **Old Norse.** [prob. t. D: m. *noorsch*, var. of *noordsch*, der. *noord* north. Cf. Norw., Sw., Dan. *Norsk* Norwegian, Norse]

Norseman (nôs′mən), *n., pl.* **-men.** a Northman.

north (nôth), *n.* **1.** a cardinal point of the compass lying in the plane of the meridian and to the right of a person facing the setting sun or west. **2.** the direction in which this point lies. **3.** magnetic north. **4.** (*l.c. or cap.*) a quarter or territory situated in this direction. **5.** (*cap.*) North Country. **6.** (*cap.*) the northern area of the United States, esp. the states which fought with the Union in the Civil War, lying to the north of the Ohio river, Missouri, and Maryland. **7.** *Chiefly Poetic.* the north wind. —*adj.* **8.** lying towards or situated in the north. **9.** directed or proceeding towards the north. **10.** coming from the north, as a wind. **11.** (*cap.*) designating the northern part of a region, nation, country, etc.: *North Atlantic.* —*adv.* **12.** towards or in the north. **13.** from the north. Also, *esp. Naut.*, **nor'** (nô). [ME and OE, c. G *Nord*]

North (nôth), *n.* **1. Christopher,** pen name of **John Wilson. 2. Frederick, 2nd Earl of Guilford,** 1732–92, British statesman: prime minister 1770–82. **3. Sir Thomas,** 1535?–1601?, English translator.

North Africa, that part of Africa abutting on the Mediterranean Sea, generally considered to comprise Morocco, Algeria, Tunisia, Libya, and Egypt. —**North African.**

Northallerton (nô thăl′ə tən), *n.* a town in England, in the North Riding of Yorkshire. 6720 (1961).

North America, the northernmost continent of the Western Hemisphere, extending from Central America to the Arctic Ocean. Highest point, Mt McKinley, 20,300 ft; lowest, Death Valley, 276 ft below sea-level. (including Central America) 261,348,038 pop. (est. 1960); ab. 8,440,000 sq. mi. —**North American.**

Northampton (nô thămp′tən, nôth hămp′-), *n.* a town in England, the county town of Northamptonshire. 106,120 (1961).

Northamptonshire (nô thămp′tən shĭə′, -shə), *n.* a county in central England. 398,132 pop. (1961); 914 sq. mi. *Co. town:* Northampton. *Abbrev.:* Northants.

Northants., Northamptonshire.

North Atlantic Drift, Gulf Stream Drift.

North Atlantic Treaty Organization, a military alliance established in 1949 between the U.S., Canada, Great

Britain, France, Belgium, The Netherlands, Luxembourg, Norway, Denmark, Iceland, Italy, and Portugal, joined in 1951 by Greece and Turkey, and in 1955 by West Germany. *Abbrev.*: NATO.

North Australia, a former division of Australia, now part of Northern Territory.

North Borneo (bô′nĭ ō′), Sabah.

northbound (nôth′bound′), *adj.* travelling towards the north.

North Brabant (brə bănt′), a province in S Netherlands. 2,123,904 pop. (est. 1962); 1965 sq. mi. *Cap.*: 's Hertogenbosch.

north by east, *Navig., Survey.* 11°15′ (one point) east of north. *Abbrev.*: N by E. Also, *esp. Naut.*, **nor' by east.**

north by west, *Navig., Survey.* 11°15′ (one point) west of north; 348°45 from due north. *Abbrev.*: N by W. Also, *esp. Naut.*, **nor' by west.**

North Cape, 1. a point of land on an island at the N tip of Norway: the northernmost point of Europe. **2.** the northern end of North Island, New Zealand.

North Carolina (kăr′ə lī′nə), a state in the SE United States, on the Atlantic coast. 4,556,155 pop. (1960); 52,712 sq. mi. *Cap.*: Raleigh. *Abbrev.*: N.C. —**North Carolinian** (kăr′ə lĭn′ĭ ən).

North Channel, a sea passage between NE Ireland and SW Scotland.

Northcliffe (nôth′klĭf), *n.* **Alfred Charles William Harmsworth, Viscount,** 1865–1922, British newspaper proprietor.

North Country, 1. the part of England north of the river Humber. **2.** Alaska and the Yukon territory of Canada (as a geographical and economic unit). —**north′-coun′try,** *adj.* —**north′-coun′tryman,** *n.*

North Dakota (də kō′tə), a state in the N central United States. 632,446 pop. (1960); 70,665 sq. mi. *Cap.*: Bismarck. *Abbrev.*: N Dak. —**North′ Dako′tan.**

north-east (nôth′ēst′), *n.* **1.** the point or direction midway between north and east. **2.** a region in this direction. —*adv.* **3.** towards or in the north-east. **4.** from the north-east. —*adj.* **5.** lying towards or situated in the north-east. **6.** directed or proceeding towards the north-east. **7.** coming from the north-east, as a wind. Also, *esp. Naut.*, **nor'-east** (nôr′ēst′). —**north′-eas′terner,** *n.*

north-east by east, *Navig., Survey.* 11°15 (one point) east of north-east; 56°15′ from due north. *Abbrev.*: NE by E. Also, *esp. Naut.*, **nor'-east by east.**

north-east by north, *Navig., Survey.* 11°15′ (one point) north of north-east; 33°45′ from due north. *Abbrev.*: NE by N. Also, *esp. Naut.*, **nor'-east by nor'.**

north-easter (nôth′ēs′tə), *n.* a wind or gale from the north-east. Also, *esp. Naut.*, **nor'-easter** (nôr′ēs′tə).

north-easterly (nôth′ēs′tə lĭ), *adj.* **1.** of or situated in the north-east. **2.** towards or from the north-east. —*adv.* **3.** towards or from the north-east. Also, *esp. Naut.*, **nor'-easterly** (nôr′ēs′tə lĭ).

north-eastern (nôth′ēs′tən), *adj.* situated in, proceeding towards, or coming from the north-east. Also, *esp. Naut.*, **nor'-eastern** (nôr′ēs′tən).

North-East Passage, a route for ships along the N coast of Europe and Asia as a possible course for navigation between the Atlantic and the Pacific.

north-eastward (nôth′ēst′wəd), *adv., adj.* **1.** Also, **north′-east′wardly,** *esp. Naut.*, **nor'-eastwardly.** towards the north-east. —*n.* **2.** the north-east. Also, *esp. Naut.*, **nor′-eastward** (nôr′ēst′wəd).

north-eastwards (nôth′ēst′wədz), *adv.* north-eastward. Also, *esp. Naut.*, **nor'-eastwards** (nôr′ēst′wədz).

norther (nô′t͟hə), *n. Now Chiefly Southern U.S.* a wind or storm from the north.

northerly (nô′t͟hə lĭ), *adj.* **1.** moving, directed, or situated towards the north. **2.** coming from the north, as a wind. —*adv.* **3.** towards the north. **4.** from the north. —**nor′therliness,** *n.*

northern (nô′t͟hən), *adj.* **1.** lying towards or situated in the north. **2.** directed or proceeding northwards. **3.** coming from the north, as a wind. **4.** (*cap.*) of or pertaining to the North. **5.** *Astron.* north of the celestial equator or of the zodiac: *a northern constellation.* [ME and OE *northerne.* See -ERN]

Northern Coalsack. See **Coalsack.**

Northern Cross, *Astron.* (in the constellation Cygnus) six stars arranged in the form of a cross.

Northern Crown, *Astron.* the constellation Corona Borealis.

Northerner (nô′t͟hə nə), *n.* (*sometimes l.c.*) a native or inhabitant of a northern country or region, esp. the English North Country or the Northern states of the U.S.

Northern Hemisphere, the half of the earth between the North Pole and the equator.

Northern Ireland, a political division of the United Kingdom, in NE Ireland. 1,435,400 pop. (est. 1962); 5238 sq. mi. *Cap.*: Belfast.

northern lights, the aurora borealis.

northernmost (nô′t͟hən mōst′), *adj.* farthest north.

Northern Rhodesia, former name of **Zambia.**

Northern Territories, a former British protectorate in W Africa; now a part of Ghana, in the N part.

Northern Territory, a territory in N Australia. 32,317 pop. (1964); 523,620 sq. mi. *Cap.*: Darwin.

Northfleet (nôth′flēt′), *n.* a town in England, in Kent, on the river Thames. 22,084 (1961).

North Germanic, the Scandinavian subgroup of Germanic languages.

North Holland, a province in W Netherlands. 2,054,509 pop. (est. 1960); 1163 sq. mi. *Cap.*: Haarlem. Dutch, **Noordholland.**

northing (nô′thĭng), *n.* **1.** northward movement or deviation. **2.** the distance due north made on any course tending northwards.

North Island, the northernmost principal island of New Zealand. 1,684,139 pop. (est. 1961); 44,281 sq. mi. See map under **New Zealand.**

North Korea, a country in E Asia: formed in 1948 after the division of Korea at 38° N. 10,700,000 pop. (est. 1963); 50,000 sq. mi. *Cap.*: Pyongyang. Official name, **Democratic People's Republic of Korea.**

northland (nôth′lənd), *n.* **1.** the land or region in the north. **2.** the northern part of a country. **3.** (*cap.*) the peninsula containing Norway and Sweden. [ME and OE, c. G, Dan., Sw. *nordland*] —**north′lander,** *n.*

Northld, Northumberland.

Northman (nôth′mən), *n., pl.* **-men.** a member of the Scandinavian group which from about the 8th to the 11th century made many raids and settlements on Great Britain, Ireland, and other parts of Europe. Also, **Norseman.**

north-north-east (nôth′nôth ēst′), *Navig., Survey.* —*n.* **1.** the point of the compass midway between north and north-east; 22°30′ from north. —*adj.* **2.** lying or situated in this direction. —*adv.* **3.** to, in, or from this direction. *Abbrev.*: NNE. Also, *esp. Naut.*, **nor'-nor'-east** (nô′nôr ēst′).

north-north-west (nôth′nôth wĕst′), *Navig., Survey.* —*n.* **1.** the point of the compass midway between north and north-west; 337°30′ from north. —*adj.* **2.** lying or situated in this direction. —*adv.* **3.** to, in, or from this direction. *Abbrev.*: NNW. Also, *esp. Naut.*, **nor'-nor'-west** (nô′nô wĕst′).

North Pole, 1. that end of the earth's axis of rotation marking the northernmost point on the earth. **2.** *Astron.* the zenith of the earth's north pole, about 1° distant from the North Star.

North Pole

North Rhine-Westphalia (rīn′wĕst fā′lyə), a Land in W West Germany; formerly a part of Rhine province. 16,835,500 pop. (est. 1966); 13,111 sq. mi. *Cap.*: Düsseldorf. German, **Nordrhein-Westfalen.**

North Riding (rī′dĭng), an administrative division of Yorkshire. 554,102 pop. (1961); 2127 sq. mi. *Chief town*: Northallerton.

North Sea, an arm of the Atlantic between the E of Great Britain and the European mainland. ab. 201,000 sq. mi.; greatest depth, 1998 ft.

North Star, *Astron.* Polaris, the north polar star, situated near the north pole of the heavens; Pole Star.

Northumberland (nô thŭm′bə lənd), *n.* a county in NE England. 818,988 pop. (1961); 2019 sq. mi. *Co. town*: Alnwick. *Abbrev.*: Northld.

Northumbria (nô thŭm′brĭ ə), *n.* an early English kingdom extending from the Humber N to the Firth of Forth. See map under **Mercia.**

Northumbrian (nô thŭm′brĭ ən), *adj.* **1.** of or pertaining to Northumbria, Northumberland, or the inhabitants or dialect of either. —*n.* **2.** a native or inhabitant of Northumbria or Northumberland. **3.** the English dialect of Northumbria or Northumberland.

North Vietnam (vyĕt′năm′), a country in SE Asia, formed by the provisional division in 1954 of Vietnam at about 17°N. 15,916,955 pop. (1960); 63,344 sq. mi. *Cap.*: Hanoi. Official name, **Democratic Republic of Vietnam.** See map under **Vietnam.**

northward (nôth′wəd; *Naut.* nô′t͟həd), *adj.* **1.** moving, bearing, facing, or situated towards the north. —*n.* **2.** the northward part, direction, or point. —*adv.* **3.** northwards. —**north′wardly,** *adj., adv.*

northwards (nôth′wədz), *adv.* towards the north. Also, **northward.**

north-west (nôth′wĕst′), *n.* **1.** the point or direction midway between north and west. **2.** a region in this direction. —*adj.* **3.** lying towards or situated in the north-west. **4.** directed or proceeding towards the north-west. **5.** coming from the north-west, as a wind. —*adv.* **6.** in the direction of a point midway between north and west. **7.** from this direction. Also, *esp. Naut.*, **nor'-west** (nô′wĕst′).

north-west by north, *Navig., Survey.* 11°15′ (one point) north of north-west; 326°15′ from due north. *Abbrev.:* NW by N. Also, *esp. Naut.*, **nor'-west by nor'.**

north-west by west, *Navig., Survey.* 11°15′ (one point) west of north-west; 303°45′ from due north. *Abbrev.:* NW by W. Also, *esp. Naut.*, **nor'-west by west.**

north-wester (nôth′wĕs′tə), *n.* a wind or gale from the north-west. Also, *esp. Naut.*, **nor'-wester** (nô′wĕs′tə).

north-westerly (nôth′wĕs′tə lĭ), *adj., adv.* towards or from the north-west. Also, *esp. Naut.*, **nor'-westerly** (nô′wĕs′tə lĭ).

north-western (nôth′wĕs′tən), *adj.* situated in, proceeding towards, or coming from the north-west. Also, *esp. Naut.*, **nor'-western** (nô′wĕs′tən).

North-West Frontier Province, a former province of Pakistan, now forming part of West Pakistan.

Northwest Passage, ship route along the arctic coast of Canada and Alaska, joining the Atlantic and Pacific oceans.

Northwest Territories, a territory of Canada lying north of the provinces and extending from Yukon territory E to Davis Strait. 22,998 pop. (1961); 1,304,903 sq. mi.

Northwest Territory, *U.S. Hist.* the region north of the Ohio river (Ohio, Indiana, Illinois, Michigan, Wisconsin, and part of Minnesota) organized by Congress in 1787.

north-westward (nôth′wĕst′wəd), *adv., adj.* **1.** Also, **north′-west′wardly,** *esp. Naut.*, **nor'-westwardly.** towards the north-west. —*n.* **2.** the north-west. Also, *esp. Naut.*, **nor'westward** (nô′wĕst′wəd).

north-westwards (nôth′wĕst′wədz), *adv.* north-westward. Also, *esp. Naut.*, **nor'-westwards** (nô′wĕst′wədz).

Northwich (nôth′wĭch), *n.* a town in England, in Cheshire, on the river Weaver. 19,374 (1961).

Norton (nô′tn), *n.* **1. Charles Eliot,** 1827–1908, U.S. scholar. **2. Thomas,** 1532–84, English author.

Norw., **1.** Norway. **2.** Norwegian.

Norway (nô′wā′), *n.* a kingdom in N Europe, in the W part of the Scandinavian Peninsula. 3,654,030 pop. (1963); 124,555 sq. mi. *Cap.:* Oslo. Norwegian, **Norge.** See map under **Baltic.**

Norway spruce, a coniferous tree, *Picea abies,* native of N and central Europe, much planted for forestry elsewhere.

Norwegian (nô wē′jən), *adj.* **1.** of or pertaining to Norway, its inhabitants, or their language. —*n.* **2.** a native or inhabitant of Norway. **3.** the speech of Norway in any of its forms, whether Dano-Norwegian, or the local dialects, or the standard language based on these, all being closely related to one another and to the other Scandinavian languages.

Norwegian elkhound. See **elkhound.**

Norwich (nŏ′rĭj), *n.* a city in England, the county town of Norfolk. 119,904 (1961).

Norwich terrier, a small, short-legged terrier, having a wiry red or black-and-tan coat.

nos-, var. of **noso-,** before vowels.

Nos, numbers. Also, **nos.**

nose (nōz), *n., v.,* **nosed, nosing.** —*n.* **1.** the part of the face or head which contains the nostrils, affording passage for air in respiration, etc. **2.** this part as the organ of smell: *the aroma of coffee greeted his nose.* **3.** the sense of smell: *a dog with a good nose.* **4.** a faculty of perceiving or detecting: *a nose for news.* **5.** the quality of prying or interfering: *keep your nose out of it.* **6.** something regarded as resembling the nose of a person or animal, as a spout or nozzle. **7.** the prow of a ship. **8.** the forward end of an aircraft. **9.** a projecting part of anything. **10.** Some special noun phrases are:

by a nose, *Slang.* by a very narrow margin.

cut off one's nose to spite one's face, to damage one's own interests by a spiteful or vengeful action.

follow one's nose, to find one's own way, as by instinct.

keep someone's nose to the grindstone, to force a person to work without respite.

lead by the nose, to exercise complete control over.

look down one's nose at, to despise; disdain.

pay through the nose, to pay an excessive amount.

put someone's nose out of joint, to thwart or upset a person.

turn one's nose up, to be contemptuous or ungrateful.

under one's nose, in an obvious place.

—*v.t.* **11.** to perceive by or as by the nose or the sense of smell. **12.** to bring the nose close to, as in smelling or examining; sniff. **13.** to move or push forwards. **14.** to touch or rub with the nose; nuzzle. —*v.i.* **15.** to smell or sniff. **16.** to seek as if by smelling or scent (fol. by *after, for,* etc.); pry (fol. by *about, into,* etc.). **17.** to move or push forwards. **18.** to meddle or pry. [ME; OE *nosu,* c. MD and MLG *nose.* Cf. L *nāsus*] —**nose′less,** *adj.*

nosebag (nōz′băg′), *n.* a bag for feeding horses, placed before the mouth with straps around the head.

noseband (nōz′bănd′), *n.* that part of a bridle or halter which passes over an animal's nose. Also, **nosepiece.**

nosebleed (nōz′blēd′), *n.* a bleeding from the nose.

nose-cone (nōz′kōn′), *n. Aeron.* the separable cone-shaped leading end of a rocket, containing equipment or a warhead, built to withstand high temperatures.

nosedive (nōz′dīv′), *n., v.,* **-dived, -diving.** —*n.* **1.** a plunge of an aeroplane with the fore part of the craft vertically downwards. **2.** any sudden drop. —*v.i.* **3.** to execute a nosedive.

nosegay (nōz′gā′), *n.* a bunch of flowers; a bouquet; a posy. [ME; lit., a *gay* (obs., something pretty) for the NOSE (i.e., to smell)]

nosepiece (nōz′pēs′), *n.* **1.** a protective cover for the nose. **2.** the part of a microscope where the object slide is attached. **3.** noseband.

nosey (nō′zĭ), *adj.,* **-sier, -siest.** nosy.

nosh (nŏsh), *Colloq.* —*v.i.* **1.** to eat; have a snack or a meal. —*n.* **2.** anything eaten, esp. a snack. **3.** a titbit eaten between meals. [t. Yiddish; cf. G *naschen* nibble]

no-side (nō′sīd′), *n. Rugby Football.* the end of the period of play.

nosing (nō′zĭng), *n.* a projecting edge, as the part of the tread of a step extending beyond the riser, or a projecting part of a buttress.

noso-, a word element meaning 'disease'. Also, **nos-.** [t. Gk, comb. form of *nósos*]

nosogeography (nŏs′ō jĭ ŏg′rə fĭ), *n.* the study of the causes and occurrence of diseases in terms of geography. —**nosogeographic** (nŏs′ō jĭə grăf′ĭk), **nos′ogeograph′ical,** *adj.* —**nos′ogeograph′ically,** *adv.*

nosography (nŏ sŏg′rə fĭ), *n.* the systematic description of diseases. —**nosog′rapher,** *n.* —**nos′ograph′ic, nos′ograph′ical,** *adj.* —**nos′ograph′ically,** *adv.*

nosology (nŏ sŏl′ə jĭ), *n.* **1.** the systematic classification of diseases. **2.** the knowledge of a disease. —**nosological** (nŏs′ə lŏj′ĭ kl), *adj.* —**nos′olog′ically,** *adv.* —**nosol′ogist,** *n.*

nosophobia (nŏs′ō fō′byə), *n.* morbid fear of disease.

nostalgia (nŏs tăl′jĭ ə), *n.* a longing and desire for home, family and friends, or the past. [t. NL, f. Gk: s. *nóstos* a return to home + *-algia* -ALGIA] —**nostal′gic,** *adj.* —**nostal′gically,** *adv.*

nostoc (nŏs′tŏk), *n.* any of the blue-green freshwater algae constituting the genus *Nostoc,* often found in jelly-like colonies in moist places. [t. NL; coined by Paracelsus]

nostology (nŏs tŏl′ə jĭ), *n.* geriatrics. [f. Gk *nósto(s)* a return to home (with ref. to 'second childhood') + -LOGY] —**nostologic** (nŏs′tə lŏj′ĭk), *adj.*

Nostradamus (nŏs′trə dā′məs), *n.* 1503–66, French astrologer. —**Nos′trada′mic,** *adj.*

nostril (nŏs′trĭl), *n.* one of the external openings of the nose. [ME *nostrill,* OE *nosterl,* var. of *nosthyrl,* f. *nosu* nose + *-thyrel* hole]

nostrum (nŏs′trəm), *n.* **1.** a patent medicine. **2.** a quack medicine. **3.** a medicine made by the person who recommends it. **4.** a pet scheme or device for effecting something. [t. L, neut. of *noster* our, ours (cf. def. 3)]

nosy (nō′zĭ), *adj.,* **-sier, -siest.** *Colloq.* prying; inquisitive. Also, **nosey.** —**nos′ily,** *adv.* —**nos′iness,** *n.*

nosy parker, a person who continually pries; a meddler. Also, **nosey parker.**

not (nŏt), *adv.* (a word expressing negation, denial, refusal, or prohibition): *not far; you must not do that.* [ME, reduced form of *noht, nouht.* See NOUGHT]

nota bene (nō′tə bē′nĭ), *Latin.* note well.

notabilia (nō′tə bĭl′ĭ ə), *n.pl.* **1.** noteworthy things. **2.** noteworthy sayings.

notability (nō′tə bĭl′ĭ tĭ), *n., pl.* **-ties.** **1.** the quality of being notable. **2.** a notable person.

notable (nō′tə bl), *adj.* **1.** worthy of note or notice; noteworthy: *a notable success.* **2.** prominent, important, or distinguished, as persons. **3.** *Archaic.* capable, thrifty, and industrious, as a housewife. —*n.* **4.** a notable person; a prominent or important person. **5.** (*often cap.*) *French Hist.* one of a number of prominent men convoked by the king on special occasions. **6.** *Obs.* a notable thing. [ME, t. L: m. s. *notābilis*] —**no′tableness,** *n.* —**no′tably,** *adv.* —**Syn.** **1.** conspicuous, memorable, great.

notarial (nō tĕə′rĭ əl), *adj.* of or pertaining to, or drawn up or executed by, a notary. **—notar′ially,** *adv.*

notarize (nō′tə rīz′), *v.t.*, **-rized, -rizing.** to authenticate (a contract, etc.). Also, **notarise.**

notary (nō′tə rĭ), *n.*, *pl.* **-ries.** a notary public. [ME, t. L: m. s. *notārius* shorthand writer, clerk, secretary]

notary public, *pl.* **notaries public.** an official, usually a solicitor, authorized to certify contracts, acknowledge deeds, take affidavits, protest bills of exchange, take depositions, etc.

notation (nō tā′shən), *n.* **1.** a system of graphic symbols for a specialized use, other than ordinary writing: *musical notation.* **2.** the process of noting or setting down by means of a special system of signs or symbols. **3.** the act of noting, marking, or setting down in writing. **4.** a note, jotting, or record. [t. L: s. *notātio* a marking] **—nota′tional,** *adj.*

notch (nŏch), *n.* **1.** a more or less angular cut, indentation, or hollow in a narrow object or surface or an edge **2.** a cut or nick made in a stick or other object for record, as in keeping a score. **3.** *U.S.* a deep, narrow opening or pass between mountains. **4.** *Colloq.* a step or degree. *—v.t.* **5.** to cut or make a notch or notches in. **6.** to make notches in by way of record. **7.** to record by a notch or notches. **8.** to score, as in a game. [t. AF: m. *anocher*, var. of OF *enochier*, der. *oche* notch]

notchboard (nŏch′bôd′), *n.* a notched board at the side of a wooden stair, supporting the treads and risers. Also, *U.S.*, **bridgeboard.**

notch graft, *Bot.* a type of graft in which the scion is inserted into a slit in a thicker stock.

not-content (nŏt′kən tĕnt′), *n.* (in the House of Lords) a negative vote or voter. Also, **non-content.**

note (nōt), *n.*, *v.*, **noted, noting.** *—n.* **1.** a brief record of something set down to assist the memory, or for reference or development. **2.** (*pl.*) a record of a speech, statement, testimony, etc., or of one's impressions of something. **3.** an explanatory or critical comment, or a reference to authority quoted, appended to a passage in a book or the like. **4.** a brief written or printed statement giving particulars or information. **5.** *Bibliog.* additional information about a book, such as its special series or some other significant identification, entered on the library catalogue card. **6.** a short informal letter. **7.** a formal diplomatic or official communication in writing. **8.** a paper acknowledging a debt and promising payment; promissory note; note of hand. **9.** a certificate, as of a government or a bank, passing current as money; a banknote. **10.** eminence or distinction: *a man of note.* **11.** importance or consequence: *no other thing of note this year.* **12.** notice, observation, or heed. **13.** a characteristic or distinguishing feature. **14.** a mark, token, or indication of something, or from which something may be inferred. **15.** a sound or tone. **16.** *Music.* a sign or character used to represent a sound, its position and form indicating the pitch and duration. **17.** *Music.* a key, as of a piano. **18.** *Archaic.* a melody, tune, or song. **19.** a sound of musical quality uttered by a bird. **20.** any call, cry, or sound of a bird, fowl, etc. **21.** a tone sounded on a trumpet or other musical instrument as a signal. **22.** a signal, announcement, or intimation: *a note of warning.* **23.** *Colloq.* a new or unexpected element in a situation. **24.** way of speaking or thinking: *to change one's note.* **25.** a mark or sign, as of punctuation, used in writing or printing. *—v.t.* **26.** to mark down, as in writing; make a memorandum of. **27.** to make particular mention of in a writing. **28.** to annotate. **29.** to observe carefully; give attention or heed to. **30.** to take notice of; perceive. **31.** to set down in or furnish with musical notes. **32.** to indicate or designate; signify or denote. [ME, t. L: m. *nota* a mark] **—not′er,** *n.* **—Syn.** 3. See **remark.**

Notes (def. 16)
A, B, Breve; C, Semibreve; D, Minim; E, Crotchet; F, Quaver; G, Semiquaver; H, Demisemiquaver; I, Hemidemisemiquaver

notebook (nōt′bŏŏk′), *n.* **1.** a book of or for notes. **2.** a book in which promissory notes are registered.

notecase (nōt′kās′), *n.* a pocket-book, usually of leather, for carrying banknotes, personal cards, etc.

noted (nō′tĭd), *adj.* **1.** celebrated; famous. **2.** specially observed or noticed. **—not′edly,** *adv.* **—not′edness,** *n.*

noteless (nōt′lĭs), *adj.* **1.** of no note; undistinguished; unnoticed. **2.** unmusical or voiceless.

note of hand, a promissory note.

notepad (nōt′păd′), *n.* a pad of paper for making notes.

notepaper (nōt′pā′pə), *n.* paper used for correspondence.

note-row (nōt′rō′), *n.* (in twelve-tone music) the order in which the 12 semitones are arranged by the composer to form the basis of the composition.

noteworthy (nōt′wû′thĭ), *adj.* worthy of note or notice; notable. **—note′wor′thily,** *adv.* **—note′wor′thiness,** *n.*

not guilty, *Law.* the appropriate plea to an indictment where the prisoner wishes to deny or justify everything and let the prosecution prove what they can.

nothing (nŭth′ĭng), *n.* **1.** no thing; not anything; naught: *say nothing.* **2.** no part, share, or trace (fol. by *of*): *the place shows nothing of its former magnificence.* **3.** that which is non-existent. **4.** something of no importance or significance. **5.** a trivial action, matter, circumstance, thing, or remark. **6.** a person of no importance. **7.** that which is without quantity or magnitude. **8.** a cipher or nought. **9.** Some special noun phrases are:

for nothing, free of charge.

make nothing of, a. to be unable to understand. **b.** to cope easily with; treat lightly.

next to nothing, very little.

nothing doing, *Colloq.* definitely no or not.

nothing for it, no other course of action is open.

—adv. **10.** in no respect or degree; not at all: *it was nothing like what we expected.* [orig. two words. See NO, THING]

nothingness (nŭth′ĭng nĭs), *n.* **1.** the state of being nothing. **2.** that which is non-existent. **3.** non-existence. **4.** unconsciousness. **5.** utter insignificance, emptiness, or worthlessness; triviality. **6.** something insignificant.

notice (nō′tĭs), *n.*, *v.*, **-ticed, -ticing.** *—n.* **1.** information or intelligence: *to give notice of a thing.* **2.** an intimation or warning. **3.** a note, placard, or the like conveying information or warning. **4.** a notification of the termination, at a specified time, of an agreement, as for renting or employment, given by one of the parties to the agreement. **5.** observation, perception, attention, or heed: *worthy of notice.* **6.** interested or favourable attention. **7.** a single observation or perception. **8.** a brief written mention or account, as of a newly published book; a review. *—v.t.* **9.** to pay attention to or take notice of. **10.** to perceive: *did you notice her hat?* **11.** to treat with attention, politeness, or favour. **12.** to acknowledge acquaintance with. **13.** to mention or refer to; point out, as to a person. **14.** *Chiefly U.S.* to give notice to; serve with a notice. [late ME, t. OF, t. L: m. s. *nōtitia* a being known] **—no′ticer,** *n.*

—Syn. 10. NOTICE, DISCERN, PERCEIVE imply becoming aware of, and paying attention to, something. All are 'point-action' verbs. To NOTICE is to become aware of something which has caught one's attention: *to notice the newspaper headline, I'm sorry I didn't notice it.* DISCERN suggests distinguishing (sometimes with difficulty) and recognizing a thing for what it is, discriminating it from its surroundings: *in spite of the fog we finally discerned the outline of the harbour; through her writings he discerned her true character.* PERCEIVE, often used as a formal substitute for 'see' or 'notice', may also convey the idea of understanding meanings and implications: *after examining the evidence he perceived its real meaning.* **—Ant. 9.** ignore.

noticeable (nō′tĭ sə bl), *adj.* that may be noticed; such as to attract notice. **—no′ticeably,** *adv.*

notification (nō′tĭ fĭ kā′shən), *n.* **1.** the act of notifying, making known, or giving notice. **2.** a formal notifying, or informing. **3.** a notice.

notify (nō′tĭ fī′), *v.t.*, **-fied, -fying.** **1.** to give notice to, or inform, of something. **2.** to make known; give information of: *the sale was notified in the newspapers.* [ME *notifie(n)*, t. OF: m. *notifier*, t. L: m. *nōtificāre* make known] **—no′tifi′able,** *adj.* **—no′tifi′er,** *n.*

no time, a very short time: *you'll be fit again in no time.*

notion (nō′shən), *n.* **1.** a more or less general, vague or imperfect conception or idea of something: *notions of beauty.* **2.** an opinion, view, or belief. **3.** conception or idea. **4.** a fanciful or foolish idea; whim. **5.** (*pl.*) *U.S.* small wares, esp. pins, needles, thread, tapes, etc.; haberdashery. [t. L: s. *nōtio* a becoming acquainted, conception, notion]

notional (nō′shə nəl), *adj.* **1.** pertaining to or expressing a notion or idea. **2.** of the nature of a notion. **3.** abstract or speculative, as reflective thought. **4.** ideal or imaginary; not real. **5.** *Now Chiefly U.S.* given to or full of notions, as a person; fanciful. **6.** *Gram.* **a.** relating to the meaning expressed by a linguistic form. **b.** having full lexical meaning, in contrast to relational. **7.** *Semantics.* presentive. **—no′tionally,** *adv.*

notochord (nō′tə kôd′), *n.* *Biol.* a rodlike stiffening structure found in the bodies of the protochordates, e.g., along the back of amphioxus, and also found in the embryos of the vertebrates, and presumed to represent an ancestral stage of the spinal column. [f. *noto-* (t. Gk, comb. form of *nôton* back) + CHORD] **—no′tochord′al,** *adj.*

Notogaea (nō′tə jē′ə), *n.* a biogeographical area of the earth's land area including Australia, New Zealand, part of the East Indies, and the islands of the Pacific. Formerly, Central and South America were also included. [NL, f. Gk: *nóto(s)* the south + m. *gaîa* land, earth] **—No′togae′an,** *n., adj.*

notoriety (nō′tə rī′ə tĭ), *n., pl.* **-ties. 1.** the state or character of being notorious or widely known: *a craze for notoriety.* **2.** a widely known or well-known person.

notorious (nō tô′rĭ əs), *adj.* **1.** widely but unfavourably known: *a notorious gambler.* **2.** publicly or generally known: *notorious crimes.* [t. ML: m. *nōtōrius,* der. L *nōtus,* pp., known] **—noto′riously,** *adv.* **—noto′riousness,** *n.*

notornis (nō tô′nĭs), *n.* any of the rare flightless birds constituting the genus *Notornis,* chiefly of New Zealand. [t. NL, f. Gk: s. *nôtos* the south + *órnis* bird]

not out, *Cricket.* **1.** (of a team) still batting. **2.** (of a batsman) not having been put out by the end of an innings; undefeated. **3.** (of a score) made without the wicket having been taken.

Notre Dame (nō′trə däm′; *Fr.* nŏ trə dȧm′), a famous early Gothic cathedral in Paris (started 1163).

no-trump (nō′trŭmp′), *Bridge.* **—***adj.* **1.** denoting a bid or play without any trump suit. **—***n.* **2.** Also, **no-trumps.** the play, or the bid to play, without any trump suit.

no-trumper (nō′trŭm′pə), *n.* *Bridge.* a game or hand played in no-trumps.

Nottingham (nŏt′ĭng əm), *n.* **1.** a city in England, the county town of Nottinghamshire: university founded 1881. 311,899 (1961). **2.** Nottinghamshire.

Nottinghamshire (nŏt′ĭng əm shĭə′, -shə), *n.* a county in central England. 818,988 pop. (1961); 844 sq. mi. *Co. town:* Nottingham. *Abbrev.:* Notts.

Notts, Nottinghamshire.

notum (nō′təm), *n., pl.* **-ta** (-tə). a scleritic segmental plate on the thorax or back of an insect. [t. NL, t. Gk: m. *nôton* the back] **—no′tal,** *adj.*

notungulate (nō tŭng′gyo͝o lāt′), *adj.* *Palaeontol.* of an order, *Notungulata,* of extinct herbivorous mammals.

notwithstanding (nŏt′wĭth stăn′dĭng, -wĭth-), *prep.* **1.** without being withstood or prevented by; in spite of. **—***adv.* **2.** nevertheless; yet (used after the statement it modifies). **—***conj.* **3.** in spite of the fact that; although. [ME]

—Syn. 1. NOTWITHSTANDING, DESPITE, IN SPITE OF imply that something is true even though there are obstacles or opposing conditions. The three expressions may be used practically interchangeably. NOTWITHSTANDING suggests, however, a hindrance of some kind: *notwithstanding the long delay, I shall still go.* DESPITE, now literary and somewhat archaic, indicates that there is an active opposition: *despite the circulation of slanderous stories about him, the candidate was elected.* IN SPITE OF, the modern equivalent on an informal level, implies meeting strong opposing forces or circumstances which must be taken into account: *he succeeded in spite of all discouragements.*

Nouakchott (*Fr.* nwȧk shŏt′), *n.* the capital of Mauritania, in the SW part. 5807 (1962).

nougat (no͞o′gä), *n.* a hard, pastelike sweet, usually white or pink, containing almonds or other nuts. [t. F, t. Pr., der. *noga,* g. LL *nuca* nut, r. L *nux*]

nought (nôt), *n.* **1.** a cipher (0); zero. **—***adj., adv. Obs. or Archaic.* **2.** naught. [ME *noht, nouht,* OE *nōht,* syncopated var. of *nōwiht*]

noughts-and-crosses (nôts′ən krŏs′ĭz), *n.* a commonly played children's game in which two players set down alternately, in the nine compartments of a figure made of crossed lines, the one a cross, and the other a nought, the object of the game being to be the first to get 3 crosses or 3 noughts in a row. Also, *U.S.,* **tick-tack-toe.**

Nouméa (*Fr.* no͞o mĕ ȧ′), *n.* the capital of New Caledonia, on the SW coast. 35,000 (est. 1963).

noumenon (no͞o′mə nŏn′, nou′-), *n., pl.* **-na** (-nə). **1.** (in Kantian philosophy) that which can be the object only of a purely intellectual (non-sensuous) intuition; essentially, a postulate. **2.** the transexperiential object to which a phenomenon is referred as to the basis or cause of its sense content. **3.** a thing in itself, as distinguished from a phenomenon or thing as it appears to us. [t. Gk: m. *nooúmenon,* neut. ppr. pass., (anything) perceived] **—nou′menal,** *adj.* **—nou′menally,** *adv.* **—nou′menalism,** *n.* **—nou′menalist,** *n.*

noun (noun), *n.* *Gram.* **1.** (in most languages) one of the major form classes, or 'parts of speech', comprising words denoting person, places, things, and such other words as show similar grammatical behaviour, as English *friend, city, desk, whiteness, virtue.* **2.** any such word. **—***adj.* **3.** Also, **noun′al.** pertaining to or resembling a noun. [ME *nowne,* t. AF: m. *noun,* g. L *nōmen* name] **—noun′ally,** *adv.*

nourice (no͞oə′rĭs), *n.* *Obs.* a nurse.

nourish (nŭ′rĭsh), *v.t.* **1.** to sustain with food or nutriment; supply with what is necessary for maintaining life. **2.** to foster or promote. [ME *norische(n),* t. OF: m. *noriss-,* s. *norir,* g. L *nūtrire* suckle, feed, maintain] **—nour′ishable,** *adj.* **—nour′isher,** *n.* **—nour′ishingly,** *adv.* **—Syn. 1.** See **nurse.**

nourishment (nŭ′rĭsh mənt), *n.* **1.** that which nourishes; food, nutriment, or sustenance. **2.** the act of nourishing. **3.** the state of being nourished.

nous (nous), *n.* **1.** *Gk Philos.* mind or intellect. **2.** in Neoplatonism, the absolute reason and absolute subject into which the absolute first differentiates itself. **3.** *Colloq.* common sense.

nouveau riche (*Fr.* no͞o vȯ rēsh′), *pl.* **nouveaux riches** (*Fr.* no͞o vȯ rēsh′). *French.* one who has newly become rich, esp. a boorish person.

nouvelle vague (no͞o′vĕl väg′; *Fr.* no͞o vĕl vȧg′), *pl.* **nouvelles vagues** (no͞o′vĕl väg′; *Fr.* no͞o vĕl vȧg′). *French.* a new style or trend in an art form, esp. the style of film-making current in France after about 1960. [F: lit., new wave]

Nov., November.

nova (nō′və), *n., pl.* **-vas, -vae** (-vē). *Astron.* a new star which makes its appearance suddenly and then gradually grows fainter. [t. NL: (fem.) new]

novaculite (nō văk′yo͝o līt′), *n.* *Geol.* a very hard, compact, siliceous rock, probably sedimentary, used for hones, etc. [f. s. L *novācula* sharp knife, razor + -ITE[1]]

Novalis (*Ger.* nȯ vȧ′lĭs), *n.* pen-name of **Hardenberg, Friedrich von.**

Nova Lisboa (*Port.* nŏ′və lēzh bȯ′ə), a town in W central Angola. 38,745 (1960).

Novara (*It.* nȯ vȧ′rȧ), *n.* a town in Italy, in E Piedmont. 96,457 (1966).

Nova Scotia (no′və skō′shə), a peninsula and province in SE Canada: once a part of the French province of Acadia. 737,007 pop. (1961); 21,068 sq. mi. *Cap.:* Halifax. **—No′va Sco′tian.**

novation (nō vā′shən), *n.* **1.** *Law.* the substitution of a new obligation for an old one, usually by the substitution of a new debtor or of a new creditor. **2.** *Now Rare.* the introduction of something new; an innovation.

Novaya Zemlya (*Russ.* nô′və yə zĭm lyȧ′), two large islands in the Arctic Ocean, N of the Soviet Union in Europe: a part of the Soviet Union. ab. 35,000 sq. mi. Also, **Nova Zembla** (*Russ.* nô′və zĭm blȧ′). See map under **Spitsbergen.**

novel[1] (nŏv′əl), *n.* **1.** a fictitious prose narrative of considerable length, portraying characters, actions, and scenes representative of real life in a plot of more or less intricacy. **2.** (formerly) a short story or a novella. [t. It.: m. s. *novella,* t. L (appar. short for *novella narrātio* new kind of story)]

—Syn. 1. NOVEL, ROMANCE are both long stories. A NOVEL is now a long fictitious story, picturing, in a series of evolving situations, characters and actions that represent real life: *a novel about a drug addict.* A ROMANCE (originally a story told in one of the Romance languages) came to mean a story laid especially in remote or unfamiliar times or places, describing unusual persons, customs, adventures and usually having love as a prominent theme: *a romance about the days of chivalry.*

novel[2] (nŏv′əl), *adj.* of a new kind, or different from anything seen or known before: *a novel idea.* [ME, t. LL: m. s. *novellus* new] **—novelly** (nŏv′əl lĭ), *adv.* **—Syn.** See **new.**

novel[3] (nŏv′əl), *n.* **1.** *Roman Law.* **a.** a constitution with imperial authority, subsequent to publication of a code. **b.** (*pl., cap.*) the constitutions of Justinian and later emperors before A.D. 582, issued after promulgation of the Justinian Code. **2.** *Civil Law.* an amendment to a statute. [t. LL: short for *novella* (*constitūtio*) new (regulation)]

novelette (nŏv′ə lĕt′), *n.* **1.** a short novel, esp. one that is trite and sentimental. **2.** a piece of music like this.

novelettish (nŏv′ə lĕt′ĭsh), *adj.* trite and sentimental, as in a novelette.

novelist (nŏv′ə lĭst), *n.* a writer of novels.

novelistic (nŏv′ə lĭs′tĭk), *adj.* of, pertaining to, or characteristic of novels. **—nov′elis′tically,** *adv.*

novelize (nŏv′ə līz′), *v.t.,* **-lized, -lizing.** to put into the form of a novel. Also, **novelise. —nov′eliza′tion,** *n.*

novella (*It.* nȯ vĕl′lȧ), *n., pl.* **-le** (*It.* -lė). **1.** a tale or short story of the type of those contained in the *Decameron* of Boccaccio, etc. **2.** a short novel, more complex than a short story. [t. It. See NOVEL[1]]

Novello (nə vĕl′ō), *n.* **Ivor** (*Ivor Novello Davies*), 1893–1951, Welsh actor, dramatist, and composer.

novelty (nŏv′əl tĭ), *n., pl.* **-ties. 1.** novel character, newness, or strangeness. **2.** a novel thing, experience, or proceeding. **3.** a new or novel article of trade; a variety of goods differing from the staple kinds. **4.** a decorative and usually worthless trinket. [ME *novelte,* t. OF: m. *novelte,* g. LL *novellitas* newness]

November (nō vĕm′bə), *n.* the eleventh month of the

year, containing 30 days. [ME and OE, t. L: the ninth month of the early Roman year]

novena (nō vē′nə), *n., pl.* **-nae** (-nē). *Rom. Cath. Ch.* a devotion consisting of prayers or services on nine consecutive days. [t. ML, prop. fem. of L *novēnus* nine each]

novercal (nō vû′kl), *adj.* of, like, or befitting a stepmother. [t. L: s. *novercālis*, der. *noverca* stepmother]

Novgorod (*Russ.* nôv′gə rət), *n.* a city in the NW Soviet Union in Europe: a former capital of Russia. 61,000 (1959).

novice (nŏv′ĭs), *n.* **1.** one who is new to the circumstances, work, etc., in which he is placed; a tiro: *a novice in politics.* **2.** one who has been received into a religious order or congregation for a period of probation before taking vows. **3.** a person newly become a church member. **4.** a recent convert to Christianity. **5.** *Sport.* a sportsman who has not qualified for junior or senior status, as an oarsman who has never been a member of a winning crew at an open regatta. [ME *novise*, t. OF: m. *novice*, t. L: m. s. *novīcius* new]

Novi Sad (*Serb.* nô′vē säd′), a town in Yugoslavia, the capital of Voivodina, in the W central part, on the Danube. 110,877 (1961). German, **Neusatz.**

novitiate (nō vĭsh′ĭ ĭt, -āt′), *n.* **1.** the state or period of being a novice of a religious order or congregation. **2.** the quarters occupied by religious novices during probation. **3.** the state or period of being a beginner in anything. **4.** a novice. Also, **novi′ciate.** [t. ML: s. *nōvitiātus*, der. L *novītius* new. See -ATE[3]]

novobiocin (nō′vō bī′ə sĭn), *n.* an antibiotic similar to streptomycin.

novocaine (nō′və kān′), *n.* **1.** a non-irritant local anaesthetic, $C_{13}H_{20}N_2O_2HCl$, a synthetic and much less toxic substitute for cocaine; procaine. **2.** (*cap.*) a trademark for this substance. Also, **novocain.** [f. *novo*- (comb. form repr. L *novus* new) + (CO)CAINE]

Novokuznetsk (*Russ.* nô′və kōōz nyĕtsk′), *n.* a city in the S Soviet Union in Europe: industrial centre. 475,000 (est. 1965). Formerly (1932–61), **Stalinsk.**

Novorossiisk (*Russ.* nə və rȧ sēysk′), *n.* a seaport in the SW Soviet Union, on the Black Sea. 104,000 (est. 1963).

Novosibirsk (*Russ.* nə və sĭ bērsk′), *n.* a city in the W Soviet Union in Asia, on the Ob. 1,029,000 (est. 1965). Formerly, **Novonikolaevsk** (*Russ.* nə və nĭ kä lä′yĭfsk).

Novotný (*Cz.* nŏv′ŏt nē), *n.* **Antonín** (*Cz.* än′tŏ nyēn), born 1904, president of Czechoslovakia 1957–68.

now (nou), *adv.* **1.** at the present time or moment: *he is here now.* **2.** (more emphatically) immediately or at once: *now or never.* **3.** at this time or juncture in some period under consideration or in some course of proceedings described: *the case now passes to the jury.* **4.** at the time or moment only just past: *I saw him just now in the street.* **5.** in these present times; nowadays. **6.** in the present or existing circumstances; as matters stand. **7.** (often used as a preliminary word before some statement, question, or the like): *now, what does he mean?* **8.** (to strengthen a command, entreaty, or the like): *come, now, stop that!* **9. now and again** or **now and then,** occasionally. **10. now that,** inasmuch as. —*conj.* **11.** now that; since, or seeing that. —*n.* **12.** the present time or moment. [ME; OE *nū*, c. Icel. and Goth. *nū*]

nowadays (nou′ə dāz′), *adv.* **1.** at the present day; in these times. —*n.* **2.** the present. [ME; f. NOW + *adays* by day (f. *a* in + *days* by day, adv. gen.)]

noway (nō′wā′), *adv.* in no way, respect, or degree; not at all. Also, *U.S.*, **no′ways′.**

Nowel (nō ĕl′), *n. Archaic.* Noel. [ME, t. OF: m. *no(u)el*, g. L *nātālis* natal]

nowhere (nō′wēə′), *adv.* **1.** Also, *U.S. Dial.*, **no′wheres′.** in, at, or to no place; not anywhere. —*n.* **2.** a state of apparent non-existence; a place unknown: *he disappeared into nowhere.* **3.** a state of anonymity. **4. get nowhere,** to achieve nothing. [ME; OE *nāhwær* (also *nōhwær*)]

nowhither (nō′wĭth′ə), *adv. Archaic.* to no place; nowhere. [ME *nowhider*, OE *nāhwider* (also *nōhwider*)]

nowise (nō′wīz′), *adv.* in no wise; noway; not at all.

nowt[1] (nout), *n. Scot. and N Dial.* cattle or oxen. [ME, t. Scand.; cf. Icel. *naut* NEAT[2]]

nowt[2] (nout), *n. Dial.* naught; nothing.

Nox (nŏks), *n. Rom. Myth.* the goddess of night. [t. L]

noxious (nŏk′shəs), *adj.* **1.** harmful or injurious to health or physical well-being: *noxious vapours.* **2.** morally harmful; pernicious. [t. L: m. *noxius* hurtful] —**nox′iously,** *adv.* —**nox′iousness,** *n.*

noyade (nwä yäd′; *Fr.* nwȧ yȧd′), *n.* destruction or execution by drowning, esp. as practised at Nantes, France, in 1793–94, during the Reign of Terror. [t. F, der. *noyer* drown, g. L *necāre* kill]

noyau (nwī′ō; *Fr.* nwȧ yō′), *n.* a sweet liqueur, either white or pink in colour, originating in France.

Noyes (noiz), *n.* **Alfred,** 1880–1958, English poet.

nozzle (nŏz′əl), *n.* **1.** a projecting spout, terminal discharging pipe, or the like, as of a hose or rocket. **2.** the socket of a candlestick. **3.** the spout of a teapot. **4.** *Slang.* the nose. [f. NOSE + *-le*, dim. suffix]

np, **1.** new penny. **2.** new pence.

N.P., Notary Public.

n.p., **1.** new paragraph. **2.** nisi prius. **3.** no place (of publication).

nr, near.

N.R., North Riding.

N.S., **1.** New Style. **2.** Nova Scotia.

n.s., **1.** not specified. **2.** new series.

N.S.P.C.C., National Society for the Prevention of Cruelty to Children.

N.S.W., New South Wales.

-n't, a combining form of *not*, as in *didn't, won't, can't.*

Nt, *Chem.* niton.

N.T., **1.** National Trust. **2.** New Testament. **3.** Northern Territory.

N.T.P., *Chem.* normal temperature and pressure; a temperature of 0°C and a pressure of 760 mm. of mercury. Also, **S.T.P.**

nth (ĕnth), *adj.* **1.** denoting the last in a series of infinitely decreasing or increasing values, amounts, etc. **2. the nth degree** or **power, a.** a high (sometimes, any) degree or power. **b.** the utmost extent.

nt wt, net weight.

nu (nyōō), *n.* the thirteenth letter (Ν, ν = English N, n) of the Greek alphabet.

Nu (nōō), *n.* **U** (ōō), born 1907, prime minister of Burma 1948–56, 1957–58, 1960–62.

nuance (nyōō äns′; *Fr.* ny äns′), *n.* a shade of colour, expression, meaning, feeling, etc. [t. F, b. OF *muance* variation (der. *muer* to change, g. L *mūtāre*), and *nue* cloud]

nub (nŭb), *n.* **1.** a knob or protuberance. **2.** a lump or small piece. **3.** *Colloq.* the point or gist of anything. [var. of KNOB]

nubbin (nŭb′ĭn), *n. U.S.* **1.** a small lump or piece. **2.** a small or imperfect ear of maize. **3.** an undeveloped fruit. [dim. of NUB]

nubble (nŭb′l), *n.* **1.** a small lump or piece. **2.** a small knob or protuberance. [f. NUB + *-le*, dim. suffix]

nubbly (nŭb′lĭ), *adj.* **1.** full of small protuberances. **2.** in the form of small lumps.

nubia (nyōō′byə), *n.* (formerly) a woman's light knitted woollen scarf. [f. s. L *nūbes* cloud + -IA]

Nubia (nyōō′byə), *n.* a region in what is now S Egypt and the Sudan N of Khartoum, extending from the Nile to the Red Sea.

Nubian (nyōō′byən), *n.* Also, **Nuba** (nyōō′bə). **1.** one of a Negroid people, of mixed descent, inhabiting Nubia. **2.** a language of the Nile valley below Khartoum. **3.** a Nubian or Negro slave. **4.** a Nubian horse. —*adj.* **5.** of or pertaining to Nubia.

Nubian Desert, an arid region in the NE Sudan.

nubile (nyōō′bīl), *adj.* (of a girl or young woman) marriageable, esp. as to age or physical development. [t. L: m. s. *nūbilis*] —**nubility** (nyōō bĭl′ĭ tĭ), *n.*

nubilous (nyōō′bĭ ləs), *adj.* **1.** cloudy or foggy. **2.** obscure; indefinite. [t. L: m. *nūbilus* cloudy]

nucellus (nyōō sĕl′əs), *n., pl.* **-celli** (-sĕl′ī). *Bot.* the central cellular mass of the body of the ovule, containing the embryo sac. [t. NL, dim. of L *nux* nut] —**nucel′lar,** *adj.*

nucha (nyōō′kə), *n., pl.* **-chae** (-kē). the nape of the neck. [ME, t. ML, t. Ar.: m. *nukhā* spinal marrow] —**nu′chal,** *adj.*

nuclear (nyōō′klĭ ə), *adj.* **1.** of, pertaining to, or forming a nucleus. **2.** pertaining to, involving, or powered by atomic energy: *nuclear war, nuclear submarine.* **3.** armed with nuclear weapons: *a nuclear power.*

nuclear energy, *Physics.* atomic energy.

nuclear fission, *Physics.* the breakdown of an atomic nucleus of an element of relatively high atomic number into two or more nuclei of lower atomic number, with conversion of part of its mass into energy.

nuclear fuel, *Physics.* a substance which undergoes nuclear fission in a nuclear reactor.

nuclear fusion, *Physics.* the coming together of two atomic nuclei to form a single nucleus with a consequent release of energy.

nuclear isomer, *Physics.* an atomic nucleus which has the same mass and charge as another nucleus, but a different rate of radioactive decay.

nuclear magnetic resonance, *Physics.* a phenomenon which enables information concerning nuclear properties and the electronic configuration of complex molecules to be obtained spectroscopically, by observing the point of resonance between transitions from one nuclear orientation to another when two externally applied fields at right angles to each other interact with the nuclear magnetic moments.

nuclear physics, the branch of physics dealing with the structure and nature of the atomic nucleus and the behaviour of subatomic particles. **—nu′clear phys′icist.**

nuclear reaction, *Physics.* any reaction which involves a change in the structure or energy state of the nuclei of the interacting atoms.

nuclear reactor, *Physics.* any device in which a self-sustaining chain reaction is maintained and controlled for the production of nuclear energy, fissile material, or radioactive isotopes.

nuclear warhead, a warhead which consists of, or contains, a nuclear weapon.

nuclear weapon, any weapon in which the explosive power is derived from nuclear fission, nuclear fusion, or a combination of both.

nucleate (nyōō′klĭ ĭt, -āt′), *adj., v.,* **-ated, -ating.** **—***adj.* **1.** having a nucleus. **—***v.t.* **2.** to form (something) into a nucleus. **—***v.i.* **3.** to form a nucleus. [t. L: m. s. *nūcleātus* having a kernel or stone]

nuclei (nyōō′klĭ ī′), *n.* pl. of **nucleus.**

nucleic acid (nyōō klē′ĭk, nyōō klā′ĭk), *Biochem.* any of a group of compounds of high molecular weight, yielding on hydrolysis purine and pyrimidine bases, either deoxyribose or ribose and phosphoric acid, that occur in all living cells.

nucleide (nyōō′klĭ īd′), *n.* nuclide.

nuclein (nyōō′klĭ ĭn), *n. Biochem.* any of a class of phosphorus-containing protein substances occurring in cell nuclei.

nucleolar (nyōō klĭə′lə), *adj. Biol.* relating or pertaining to the nucleolus.

nucleolated (nyōō′klĭ ə lā′tĭd), *adj.* containing a nucleolus or nucleoli. Also, **nu′cleolate′.**

nucleolus (nyōō klĭə′ləs), *n., pl.* **-li** (-lī). *Biol.* a conspicuous, often rounded body within the nucleus of a cell. See diag. under **cell.** Also, **nucleole** (nyōō′klĭ ōl′). [t. L: little nut, dim. of *nūcleus.* See NUCLEUS]

nucleon (nyōō′klĭ ŏn′), *n.* one of the elementary particles (protons and neutrons) of atomic nuclei.

nucleonics (nyōō′klĭ ŏn′ĭks), *n.* the techniques of applying nuclear science to industry and to biology, physics, chemistry, and other sciences.

nucleoplasm (nyōō′klĭ ə plăz′əm), *n. Biol.* karyoplasm. [f. *nucleo-* (comb. form of NUCLEUS) + -PLASM] **—nu′cleoplas′mic,** *adj.*

nucleoprotein (nyōō′klĭ ō prō′tēn), *n. Biochem.* any of a group of compounds of high molecular weight containing both nucleic acid and protein.

nucleor (nyōō′klĭ ô′), *n. Physics.* the core of an atomic nucleus.

nucleoside (nyōō′klĭ ə sīd′), *n. Biochem.* any of several compounds of either a purine or a pyrimidine base with either ribose or deoxyribose, and present in combined form in nucleic acids.

nucleotide (nyōō′klĭ ə tīd′), *n. Biochem.* the phosphate of any nucleoside, present in combined form in nucleic acids.

nucleus (nyōō′klĭ əs), *n., pl.* **-clei** (-klĭ ī′), **-cleuses.** **1.** a central part or thing about which other parts or things are grouped. **2.** anything constituting a central part, foundation, or beginning. **3.** *Biol.* a differentiated mass (usually rounded) of protoplasm, encased in a delicate membrane, present in the interior of nearly all living cells and forming an essential element in their growth metabolism and reproduction. See diag. under **cell.** **4.** *Anat.* a mass of grey matter in the brain and spinal cord in which incoming nerve fibres form connections with outgoing fibres. **5.** *Chem.* a fundamental arrangement of atoms, as the benzene ring, which may occur in many compounds by substitution of atoms without a change in structure. **6.** *Physics.* the central core of an atom, composed of protons and neutrons. It has a net positive charge equal to the number of protons. **7.** *Astron.* the more condensed portion of the head of a comet. **8.** *Meteorol.* a particle upon which condensation of water vapour occurs to form water drops. **9.** *Phonet.* the central, vocalic constituent of a syllable, often a vowel, as the *o* sound in *dog.* [t. L: nut, kernel, fruit stone]

nuclide (nyōō′klīd), *n. Physics.* **1.** an atomic species which is characterized by its mass number, atomic number, and energy state. **2.** any individual atom of such a species. Also, **nucleide.**

nude (nyōōd), *adj.* **1.** naked or unclothed, as a person, the body, etc. **2.** without the usual coverings, furnishings, etc.; bare. **3.** *Law.* unsupported; made without a consideration: *a nude pact.* **—***n.* **4. the nude, a.** the condition of being undraped. **b.** the undraped human figure. **5.** a nude figure as represented in art. [t. L: m. s. *nūdus* bare] **—nude′ly,** *adv.* **—nude′ness,** *n.*

nudge (nŭj), *v.,* **nudged, nudging,** *n.* **—***v.t.* **1.** to push slightly or jog, esp. with the elbow, as in calling attention or giving a hint or with sly meaning. **—***n.* **2.** a slight push or jog. [orig. obscure]

nudi-, a word element meaning 'bare'. [t. L, comb. form of *nūdus*]

nudibranch (nyōō′dĭ brăngk′), *n.* a shell-less type of marine snail with external respiratory appendages, noted for its beautiful colouring and graceful form. [t. F: m. *nudibranche,* f. *nudi-* NUDI- + *branche* gills, t. L: m. *branchia* BRANCHIA]

nudicaul (nyōō′dĭ kôl′), *adj. Bot.* having leafless stems. Also, **nu′dicau′lous.** [f. NUDI- + s. L *caulus* stem]

nudism (nyōō′dĭz′əm), *n.* the practice of going nude as a means of healthful living; naturism. **—nud′ist,** *n., adj.*

nudity (nyōō′dĭ tĭ), *n., pl.* **-ties.** **1.** the state or fact of being nude; nakedness. **2.** something nude or naked. **3.** a nude figure, esp. as represented in art.

nudum pactum (nōō′dōōm păk′tōōm), *Law.* a simple contract or promise with no consideration involved.

Nuevo Laredo (*Sp.* nwĕ′bō lä rĕ′dō), a town in E Mexico. 117,728 (est. 1965).

Nuffield (nŭf′ēld), *n.* **William Richard Morris, Viscount,** 1877–1963, English motor manufacturer and philanthropist.

nugae (nyōō′jē), *n.pl. Latin.* jests; trifles.

nugatory (nyōō′gə tə rĭ, -trĭ), *adj.* **1.** trifling; of no real value; worthless. **2.** of no force or effect; futile; vain. [t. L: m. s. *nūgātōrius* worthless]

nugget (nŭg′ĭt), *n.* **1.** a lump of something. **2.** a lump of native gold. **3.** *Austral. Colloq.* a heavy, thick-set, young animal. [appar. der. d. *nug* lump, block]

nuggetty (nŭg′ĭ tĭ), *adj. Austral. Colloq.* short; thick-set.

nuisance (nyōō′səns), *n.* **1.** a highly obnoxious or annoying thing or person. **2.** something offensive or annoying to individuals or to the community, to the prejudice of their legal rights. [ME *nusance,* t. OF: m. *nuisance,* der. *nuire* harm, g. L *nocēre*]

N.U.J., National Union of Journalists.

Nuku'alofa (nōō′kōō ə lō′fə), *n.* the capital of the Tonga Islands, on N coast of Tongatabu Island. 10,600 (1964).

null (nŭl), *adj.* **1.** of no effect, consequence, or significance. **2.** being none, lacking, or non-existent. **3. null and void,** having no legal force or effect. **4.** zero. [t. L: s. *nullus* no, none]

nullah (nŭl′ə), *n.* (in the East Indies) **1.** a ravine. **2.** a watercourse. [t. Hind.: m. *nālā*]

nulla-nulla (nŭl′ə nŭl′ə), *n. Austral.* an aboriginal club. [t. native Australian]

Nullarbor Plain (nŭl′ə bô′, nŭ lä′bə), an arid, limestone plateau in southern Australia, stretching 350 mi. along the Great Australian Bight in Western Australia and South Australia; 150 mi. wide.

nulli-, a word element meaning 'none'. [t. L, comb. form of *nullus*]

nullification (nŭl′ĭ fĭ kā′shən), *n.* **1.** the act of nullifying. **2.** the state of being nullified. **3.** *U.S.* failure of a state to aid in enforcement of federal laws within its limits. **—nul′lifica′tionist,** *n.*

nullifidian (nŭl′ĭ fĭd′ĭ ən), *n.* one who has no faith or religion; sceptic. [f. NULLI- + s. L *fides* faith + -IAN]

nullify (nŭl′ĭ fī′), *v.t.,* **-fied, -fying.** **1.** to make ineffective, futile, or of no consequence. **2.** to render or declare legally void or inoperative: *to nullify a contract.* [t. LL: m. *nullificāre* make null, dispose] **—nil′lifi′er,** *n.*

nullipara (nŭ lĭp′ə rə), *n., pl.* **-rae** (-rē′). *Obstet.* a woman who has never borne a child. [t. NL: f. *nulli-* NULLI- + *-para,* fem. of *parus* -PAROUS] **—nullip′arous,** *adj.*

nullipore (nŭl′ĭ pô′), *n. Bot.* any of the coralline algae with a crustlike plant body. [f. NULLI- + PORE[2]]

nullity (nŭl′ĭ tĭ), *n., pl.* **-ties.** **1.** the state of being null; nothingness; invalidity. **2.** something null. **3.** something of no legal force or validity. [t. ML: m. s. *nullitas*]

Num., Numbers.

num., **1.** numeral. **2.** numerals.

Numantia (nyōō măn′tĭ ə), *n.* an ancient city in N Spain: besieged and taken by Scipio the Younger, 134–133 B.C.

Numa Pompilius (nyōō′mə pŏm pĭl′ĭ əs), d. 672? B.C., 2nd (legendary) king of Rome (715–672 B.C.), said to have introduced religious worship, having been instructed in it by a nymph, Egeria.

numb (nŭm), *adj.* **1.** deprived of or deficient in the power of sensation and movement: *fingers numb with cold.* **2.** of the nature of numbness: *a numb sensation.* **—***v.t.* **3.** to make numb. [ME *nome,* lit., taken, seized, apocopated var. of ME *nomen, numen,* OE *numen,* pp. of *niman* take] **—numb′ly,** *adv.* **—numb′ness,** *n.*

numbat (nŭm′băt′), *n.* the banded anteater, *Myrmecobius fasciatus,* of Australia. [t. native Australian]

number (nŭm′bə), *n.* **1.** the sum, total, count, or aggregate of a collection of units, or any generalization of this concept. **2.** a numeral. **3.** (*pl.*) *Obs.* arithmetic. **4.** the particular numeral assigned to anything in order to fix its place in a series: *a house number.* **5.** a word or symbol, or a combination of words or symbols, used in counting or to denote a total. **6.** one of a series of things distinguished by numerals. **7.** a single part of a book published in parts. **8.** a single issue of a periodical. **9.** any of a collection of poems or songs. **10.** a single part of a programme made up of a number of parts. **11.** the full count of a collection or company. **12.** a collection or company. **13.** a quantity (large or small) of individuals. **14.** a certain collection, company, or quantity not precisely reckoned, but usually considerable or large. **15.** (*pl.*) considerable collections or quantities. **16.** numerical strength or superiority. **17.** quantity as composed of units. **18.** *Gram.* (in many languages) a category of the inflection of nouns, verbs, and related word classes, usually expressing the number of persons or objects referred to: comprising as subcategories the *singular* and *plural* and in some languages one or two intermediate subcategories (the *dual,* referring to two, and the *trial,* referring to three). **19.** (*pl.*) metrical feet, or verse. **20.** (*pl.*) musical periods, measures, or groups of notes. **21.** a distinct part of an extended musical work, or one in a sequence of compositions. **22.** *Obs.* conformity in music or verse to regular beat or measure; rhythm. **23.** an article of merchandise. **24. number one, a.** oneself. **b.** *Naval Colloq.* first officer. **25. one's number is up,** *Slang.* **a.** one is in serious trouble. **b.** one is due to die. **26. without number,** of which the number is unknown or too great to be counted: *stars without number.* —*v.t.* **27.** to ascertain the number of. **28.** to mark with or distinguish by a number or numbers. **29.** to count over one by one. **30.** to mention one by one; enumerate. **31.** to fix the number of, limit in number, or make few in number. **32.** to reckon or include in a number. **33.** to mark with or distinguish by a number or numbers. **34.** to live or have lived (so many years). **35.** to have or comprise in number. **36.** to amount to in number: *a crew numbering fifty men.* **37.** *Obs.* to appoint or allot. —*v.i.* **38.** *Poetic.* to make enumeration; count. **39.** to be numbered or included. [ME *nombre,* t. OF, g. L *numerus*] —**num′berer,** *n.*

—**Syn. 1.** NUMBER, SUM both imply the total of two or more units. NUMBER applies to the result of a count or estimate in which the units are considered as individuals; it is used of groups of persons or things: *a number of persons.* SUM applies to the result of addition, in which only the total is considered: *a large sum of money.*

numberless (nŭm′bə lĭs), *adj.* **1.** innumerable; countless; myriad. **2.** without a number or numbers.

numberplate (nŭm′bə plāt′), *n.* an identifying plate, carried by motor vehicles, bearing a registration number. Also, **registration plate.**

Numbers (nŭm′bəz), *n.* the fourth book of the Old Testament (so called because it relates the numbering of the Israelites after the exodus from Egypt).

number theory, *Maths.* the study of numbers (integers) and of the relations which hold between them.

numbfish (nŭm′fĭsh′), *n., pl.* **-fishes,** (*esp. collectively*) **-fish.** an electric ray (fish): so called from its power of numbing its prey by means of electric shocks.

numbles (nŭm′blz), *n.pl. Archaic.* certain of the inward parts of an animal, esp. of a deer, used as food. Also, **nombles, umbles.** [ME *noumbles,* t. OF: m. *nombles,* g. L *lumbulus,* dim. of *lumbus* loin]

numbskull (nŭm′skŭl′), *n.* numskull.

numen (nyo͞o′mĕn), *n., pl.* **-mina** (-mĭ nə). a deity; a divine power or spirit. [t. L]

numerable (nyo͞o′mə rə bl, nyo͞om′rə bl), *adj.* that may be numbered or counted. [t. L: m. s. *numerābilis*] —**nu′merably,** *adv.*

numeral (nyo͞o′mə rəl, nyo͞om′rəl), *n.* **1.** a word or words expressing a number: *cardinal numerals.* **2.** a letter or figure, or a group of letters or figures, denoting a number: *the Roman numerals.* —*adj.* **3.** of or pertaining to number; consisting of numbers. **4.** expressing or denoting number. [t. LL: s. *numerālis,* der. L *numerus* number]

numerary (nyo͞o′mə rə rĭ, nyo͞om′rə rĭ), *adj.* of or pertaining to a number or numbers.

numerate (nyo͞o′mə rāt′), *v.,* **-rated, -rating,** *adj.* —*v.t.* **1.** to number; count; enumerate. **2.** to read (an expression in numbers). —*adj.* **3.** having some knowledge of or versed in mathematics. [t. L: m. s. *numerātus,* pp.] —**numeracy** (nyo͞o′mə rə sĭ), *n.*

numeration (nyo͞o′mə rā′shən), *n.* **1.** the act, process, or result of numbering or counting. **2.** the process or a method of reckoning or calculating. **3.** the act, art, or method of reading numbers in numerals or figures.

numerator (nyo͞o′mə rā′tə), *n.* **1.** *Maths.* that term (usually written above the line) of a fraction which shows how many parts of a unit are taken. **2.** one who or that which numbers. [t. LL: a counter]

numerical (nyo͞o mĕ′rĭ kl), *adj.* **1.** of or pertaining to number; of the nature of number. **2.** denoting number or a number: *numerical symbols.* **3.** bearing, or designated by, a number. **4.** expressed by a number or figure, or by figures, and not by a letter or letters. **5.** *Maths.* denoting value or magnitude irrespective of sign: *the numerical value of -10 is greater than that of -5.* Also, **numer′ic.** —**numer′ically,** *adv.*

numerical aperture, *Physics.* a measure of the resolving power of a microscope, equal to the product of the refractive index of the medium in which the object is placed and the size of the angle between the axis and the most oblique ray entering the instrument; the resolving power is proportional to the numerical aperture. *Abbrev.:* N.A.

numerology (nyo͞o′mə rŏl′ə jĭ), *n.* the study of numbers (as one's birth year, etc.), supposedly to determine their influence on one's life and future. [f. s. L *numerus* number + -(O)LOGY] —**numerological** (nyo͞o′mə rə lŏj′ĭ kl, nyo͞om′rə-), *adj.*

numerous (nyo͞o′mə rəs, nyo͞om′rəs), *adj.* **1.** very many; forming a great number. **2.** consisting of or comprising a great number of units or individuals. [t. L: m. s. *numerōsus*] —**nu′merously,** *adv.* —**nu′merousness,** *n.* —**Syn. 1.** See **many.**

Numidia (nyo͞o mĭd′ĭ ə), *n.* an ancient country in N Africa, corresponding generally to modern Algeria. —**Numid′ian,** *adj., n.*

Numidian crane, demoiselle (def. 2).

numinous (nyo͞o′mĭ nəs), *adj.* **1.** of or pertaining to a numen. **2.** arousing elevated or religious feelings.

numis., 1. numismatic. **2.** numismatics. Also, **numism.**

numismatic (nyo͞o′mĭz măt′ĭk), *adj.* **1.** of or pertaining to, or consisting of, coins and medals. **2.** pertaining to numismatics. Also, **nu′mismat′ical.** [t. F: m. *numismatique,* der. L *nomisma* coin, t. Gk]

numismatics (nyo͞o′mĭz măt′ĭks), *n.* the science of coins and medals. —**numismatist** (nyo͞o mĭz′mə tĭst), *n.*

numismatology (nyo͞o mĭz′mə tŏl′ə jĭ), *n.* numismatics. —**numis′matol′ogist,** *n.*

nummary (nŭm′ə rĭ), *adj.* **1.** of or pertaining to coins or money. **2.** occupied with coins or money.

nummular (nŭm′yo͝o lə), *adj.* **1.** pertaining to coins or money; nummary. **2.** coin-shaped. [f. s. L *nummulus* (dim. of *nummus* coin) + -AR[1]]

nummulite (nŭm′yo͝o līt′), *n.* any of the foraminifers (mostly fossil) that constitute the family *Nummulitidae,* having a somewhat coinlike shell. [t. NL: m. s. *nummulītēs,* der. L *nummulus,* dim. of *nummus* coin] —**nummulitic** (nŭm′yo͝o lĭt′ĭk), *adj.*

num-num (nŭm′nŭm′), *n.* a spiny apocynaceous shrub, *Carissa arduina,* of southern Africa, bearing scarlet edible berries. [t. Zulu: m. *inamunamu* something sticky, specif. a herb with edible roots]

numskull (nŭm′skŭl′), *n. Colloq.* a dull-witted person; a dunce; a dolt. Also, **numbskull.** [f. NUMB + SKULL]

nun (nŭn), *n.* **1.** a woman devoted to a religious life under vows. **2.** a woman living in a convent under solemn vows of poverty, chastity, and obedience. [ME and OE *nunne,* t. LL: m. *nonna,* fem. of *nonnus* monk]

Nun (no͞on), *n.* the chief mouth of the river Niger, in W Africa.

nunatak (nŭn′ə tăk′), *n.* an isolated rocky peak completely encircled by a glacier or icesheet. [t. Eskimo]

Nunc Dimittis (nŭngk′ dĭ mĭt′ĭs), **1.** the canticle of Simeon (Luke 2:29–32), beginning 'Lord, now lettest thou thy servant depart in peace'. **2.** a musical setting of this. **3.** (*l.c.*) permission to depart; dismissal; departure. [t. L; the first words as given in the Vulgate]

nunciature (nŭn′shĭ ə chə), *n.* the office or the term of service of a papal nuncio. [t. It.: m. *nunziatura,* der. *nunzio* NUNCIO]

nuncio (nŭn′shĭ ō′), *n., pl.* **-cios.** a permanent diplomatic representative of the pope at a foreign court or capital. [t. It., g. L *nuntius* messenger]

nuncle (nŭng′kl), *n. Archaic and Dial.* uncle.

nuncupative (nŭng′kyo͝o pā′tĭv, nŭng kyo͞o′pə tĭv), *adj.* (of wills, etc.) oral, rather than written. [t. LL: m. s. *nuncupātīvus* nominal]

Nuneaton (nŭ nē′tn), *n.* a town in England, in Warwickshire. 57,376 (1961).

nunnery (nŭn′ə rĭ), *n., pl.* **-neries.** a religious house for nuns; a convent.

nun's veiling, a thin, plain-woven, worsted fabric, orig. for nun's veils but now for dresses, etc.

nuptial (nŭp′shəl), *adj.* **1.** of or pertaining to marriage or the marriage ceremony: *the nuptial day.* —*n.* **2.** (*usually* *pl.*) marriage; wedding. [t. L: s. *nuptiālis* pertaining to marriage] **—Syn. 2.** See **marriage.**

N.U.R., National Union of Railwaymen.

nuraghe (nyŏŏ rä′gĭ), *n., pl.* **-ghi** (-gē), **-ghes** (-gĭz). one of a number of large tower-shaped prehistoric stone structures, found in Sardinia.

Nuremberg (nyŏŏə′rəm bûg′), *n.* a city in West Germany, in N central Bavaria; war crimes trials of Nazis, 1945–46. 472,300 (est. 1966). German, **Nürnberg** (*Ger.* nʏrn′bĕrk).

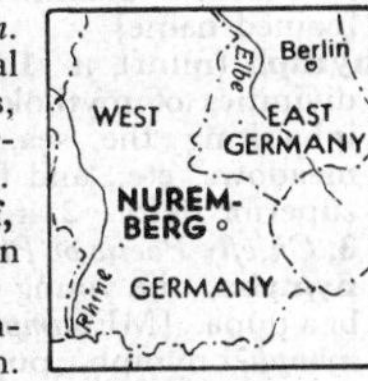

Nuremberg

Nureyev (nŏŏ rä′yĕf), *n.* **Rudolf,** born 1939, ballet dancer, born in the Soviet Union.

Nuristan (nŏŏə′rĭ stän′), *n.* a mountainous region in NE Afghanistan. 5000 sq. mi. Formerly, **Kafiristan.**

nurse (nûs), *n., v.,* **nursed, nursing.** *—n.* **1.** a person (woman or man) who has the care of the sick or infirm. **2.** a woman who has the general care of a child or children. **3.** a woman employed to suckle an infant; wet nurse. **4.** any fostering agency or influence. **5.** a worker that attends the young in a colony of social insects. **6.** *Billiards.* the act of nursing the balls. *—v.t.* **7.** to tend in sickness or infirmity. **8.** to seek to cure (a cold, etc.) by taking care of oneself. **9.** to look after carefully so as to promote growth, development, etc.; foster; cherish (a feeling, etc.). **10.** to treat or handle with adroit care in order to further one's own interests. **11.** to bring up, train, or nurture. **12.** to clasp or handle, as fondly or tenderly. **13.** to suckle (an infant). **14.** to feed and tend in infancy. **15.** *Billiards.* to gather and keep (the balls) together for a series of canons. *—v.i.* **16.** to act as nurse; tend the sick or infirm. **17.** to suckle a child. **18.** (of a child) to take the breast. [ME *norse, nourice,* t. OF, g. LL *nūtrīcia* nurse, prop. fem. of *nūtrīcius* that nourishes] **—nurs′er,** *n.*

—Syn. 14. NURSE, NOURISH, NURTURE may be used practically interchangeably to refer to bringing up the young. NURSE, however, suggests particularly attendance and service; NOURISH emphasizes providing whatever is needful for development; and NURTURE suggests tenderness and solicitude in training mind and manners.

nurseling (nûs′lĭng), *n.* nursling.

nursemaid (nûs′mād′), *n.* a maidservant employed to take care of children. Also, **nurs′erymaid′.**

nursery (nûs′rĭ), *n., pl.* **-eries. 1.** a room or place set apart for young children. **2.** a nursery school. **3.** any place in which something is bred, nourished, or fostered. **4.** any situation, condition, circumstance, practice, etc., serving to foster something. **5.** a place where young trees or other plants are raised for transplanting or for sale.

nurseryman (nûs′rĭ mən), *n., pl.* **-men.** one who owns or conducts a nursery for plants.

nursery rhyme, a short, simple poem or song for children.

nursery school, a school for children between the ages of two and five at which formal instruction is not given.

nursing home, 1. a private hospital or institution where patients pay for their treatment. **2.** a convalescent home. **3.** a private residence equipped for the care of the elderly. **4.** a private maternity unit.

nursling (nûs′lĭng), *n.* **1.** an infant or child under a nurse's care. **2.** any person or thing under fostering care, influences, or conditions. Also, **nurseling.**

nurture (nû′chə), *v.,* **-tured, -turing,** *n. —v.t.* **1.** to feed, nourish, or support during the stages of growth, as children or young; rear. **2.** to bring up; train; educate. *—n.* **3.** upbringing or training. **4.** education; breeding. **5.** nourishment or food. [ME, t. OF, var. of *nourriture,* der. s. *nourrir* to nourish, g. L *nūtrīre*] **—nur′turer,** *n.* **—Syn. 1.** See **nurse.**

N.U.S., 1. National Union of Seamen. **2.** National Union of Students.

nut (nŭt), *n., v.,* **nutted, nutting.** *—n.* **1.** a dry fruit consisting of an edible kernel or meat enclosed in a woody or leathery shell. **2.** the kernel itself. **3.** *Bot.* a hard, indehiscent, one-seeded fruit, as the chestnut or the acorn. **4.** any of various devices or parts supposed in some way to resemble a nut. **5.** a small lump of coal. **6.** a small, hard biscuit. **7.** *Slang.* the head. **8.** *Slang.* an enthusiast. **9.** *Slang.* a foolish or eccentric person. **10.** *Slang.* an insane person. **11.** a perforated block (usually of metal) with an internal thread or female screw, used to screw on the end of a bolt, etc. **12.** (in musical instruments of the violin type) **a.** the ledge, as of ebony, at the upper end of the fingerboard, over which the strings pass. **b.** the movable piece at the lower end of the bow, by means of which the hairs may be slackened or tightened. **13. do one's nut,** *Slang.* to be very angry, anxious, or upset. **14. hard nut to crack, a.** a difficult question, undertaking, or problem. **b.** a person who is difficult to convince, understand, or know. **15. off one's nut,** *Slang.* **a.** mad; insane. **b.** crazy; foolish. *—v.i.* **16.** to look for or gather nuts. *—adj.* **17.** made of or denoting the wood of any nut-bearing tree, as walnut, hickory, etc. [ME *nute,* OE *hnutu,* c. G *Nuss*] **—nut′like′,** *adj.*

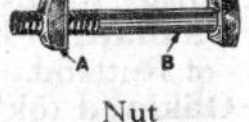

Nut
A, Nut (def. 11);
B, Bolt

N.U.T., National Union of Teachers.

nutant (nyŏŏ′tnt), *adj. Bot.* drooping; nodding. [t. L: s. *nūtans,* ppr.]

nutation (nyŏŏ tā′shən), *n.* **1.** a nodding. **2.** *Bot.* spontaneous movements of plant parts during growth. **3.** *Astron.* the periodic oscillation in the precessional motion of the earth's axis or of the equinoxes. [t. L: s. *nūtātio* a nodding] **—nuta′tional,** *adj.*

nutbrown (nŭt′broun′), *adj.* brown, as many nuts when ripe.

nut case, *Slang.* a foolish or eccentric person.

nutcracker (nŭt′krăk′ə), *n.* **1.** (*often pl.*) an instrument for cracking nuts. **2.** any of several corvine birds of the genus *Nucifraga* which feed on nuts, as the common nutcracker, *N. caryocatactes,* of Europe.

nut-gall (nŭt′gôl′), *n.* **1.** a nutlike gall or excrescence, esp. one formed on an oak. **2.** the Aleppo nut-gall.

nut-grass (nŭt′gräs′), *n. U.S.* any of various sedges of the genus *Cyperus,* esp. *C. rotundus,* bearing small nutlike tubers.

nuthatch (nŭt′hăch′), *n.* any of numerous small short-tailed sharp-beaked birds constituting the family *Sittidae,* which creep on trees and feed on small nuts and insects. [ME *notehache, nuthage, nuthake,* lit., nut-hacker]

nut house, *Slang.* a mental hospital.

nutlet (nŭt′lĭt), *n.* **1.** a small nut; a small nutlike fruit or seed. **2.** the stone of a drupe.

nutmeg (nŭt′mĕg), *n.* **1.** the hard, aromatic seed of the fruit of an East Indian tree, *Myristica fragrans,* used as a spice. **2.** the tree itself. **3.** the similar product of certain other trees of the same genus or other genera. [ME *notemuge,* f. *note* nut + OF *mug(u)e* musk, ult. der. LL *muscus*]

nut oil, edible oil made from nuts.

nut pine, any of various trees of the south-western U.S. and Rocky Mountains, as *Pinus monophylla, P. edulis,* etc., bearing edible nuts.

nutria (nyŏŏ′trĭ ə), *n.* **1.** the coypu. **2.** the fur of this animal, resembling beaver. [t. Sp.: otter, g. L *lūtra* otter, b. with *enitria,* t. Gk: m. s. *énydris*]

nutrient (nyŏŏ′trĭ ənt), *adj.* **1.** containing or conveying nutriment, as solutions or vessels of the body. **2.** nourishing; affording nutriment. *—n.* **3.** a nutrient substance. [t. L: s. *nūtriens,* ppr., nourishing]

nutriment (nyŏŏ′trĭ mənt), *n.* **1.** any matter that, taken into a living organism, serves to sustain it in its existence, promoting growth, replacing loss, and providing energy. **2.** that which nourishes; nourishment, food, or aliment. [t. L: s. *nūtrīmentum*]

nutrition (nyŏŏ trĭsh′ən), *n.* **1.** the act or process of nourishing or of being nourished. **2.** food; nutriment. **3.** the process by which the food material taken into an organism is converted into living tissue, etc. **—nutri′tional,** *adj.* **—nutri′tionally,** *adv.*

nutritionist (nyŏŏ trĭsh′ə nĭst), *n.* one who studies problems of food and nutrition.

nutritious (nyŏŏ trĭsh′əs), *adj.* nourishing, esp. in a high degree. [t. L: m. *nūtrīcius, nūtrītius*] **—nutri′tiously,** *adv.* **—nutri′tiousness,** *n.*

nutritive (nyŏŏ′trĭ tĭv), *adj.* **1.** serving to nourish; affording nutriment. **2.** of or concerned in nutrition. **—nu′tritively,** *adv.* **—nu′tritiveness,** *n.*

nuts (nŭts), *Slang. —interj.* **1.** (an expression of defiance, disgust, etc.) *—adj.* **2.** crazy; insane. **3.** overwhelmingly attracted (fol. by *on* or *over*): *I'm nuts over her.*

nutshell (nŭt′shĕl′), *n.* **1.** the shell of a nut. **2. in a nutshell,** in very brief form; in a few words: *just tell me the story in a nutshell.*

nutter (nŭt′ə), *n.* **1.** one who gathers nuts. **2.** *Slang.* a crazy or foolish person.

nutting (nŭt′ĭng), *n.* the act of seeking or gathering nuts.

nutty (nŭt′ĭ), *adj.,* **-tier, -tiest. 1.** abounding in or producing nuts. **2.** nutlike, esp. in taste. **3.** *Slang.* silly or stupid; crazy. **4.** *Slang.* overwhelmingly attracted (fol. by *over*). **—nut′tiness,** *n.*

nutwood (nŭt′wŏŏd′), *n. Chiefly U.S.* **1.** any one of various species of nut-bearing trees, as walnut, hickory, etc. **2.** a tree or the wood of a tree of such a species. Also, **nut wood.**

nux vomica (nŭks′vŏm′ĭ kə), **1.** the strychnine-containing seed (used in medicine) of the orangelike fruit borne by an East Indian loganiaceous tree, *Strychnos nux-vomica.* **2.** the tree itself. [t. NL: vomiting nut, f. L *nux* nut + NL *vomica,* der. L *vomere* vomit]

nuzzle (nŭz′əl), *v.*, **-zled, -zling.** —*v.i.* **1.** to burrow or root with the nose, as an animal does. **2.** to thrust the nose (fol. by *against, in, up,* etc.): *the pup nuzzled up close to the sick child.* **3.** to snuggle or cuddle up with someone or something. —*v.t.* **4.** to root up with the nose. **5.** to touch or rub with the nose. **6.** to thrust the nose against or into. **7.** to thrust (the nose or head), as into something. [ME *nosele*; freq. of NOSE; to some extent confused with NESTLE]

N.V., (Du. *naamloze vennootschap*) limited-liability company.

NW, 1. north-west. **2.** north-western. Also, **N.W., n.w.**

N.W.T., Northwest Territories (Canada).

N.Y., New York.

nyala (ən yä′lə), *n.* inyala.

Nyasa (nyăs′ə, nī ăs′ə), *n.* **Lake,** former name of **Lake Malawi.**

Nyasaland (nyăs′ə lănd′, nī ăs′ə-), *n.* former name of **Malawi.**

N.Y.C., New York City.

nyckelharpa (nĭk′ĭl hä′pə), *n.* a former Swedish stringed musical instrument, similar to the hurdy-gurdy but sounded with a bow instead of a wheel.

nyct-, a word element meaning 'night'. [t. Gk: m. *nykt-*, comb. form of *nýx*]

nyctaginaceous (nĭk′tə jĭ nā′shəs), *adj.* belonging to the *Nyctaginaceae*, or four-o'clock family of plants. [f. s. NL *Nyctago*, former name for genus *Mirabilis* (der. Gk *nýx* night) + -ACEOUS]

nyctalopia (nĭk′tə lō′pyə), *n.* **1.** a condition of the eyes in which sight is normal in the day or in a strong light, but is abnormally poor or wholly gone at night or in a dim light; night blindness. **2.** hemeralopia, a condition exactly the opposite to night blindness; day blindness. [t. LL, f. m. s. Gk *nyktálōps* blind by night + *-ia* -IA] —**nyctalopic** (nĭk′tə lŏp′ĭk), *adj.*

nyctitropic (nĭk′tĭ trŏp′ĭk), *adj. Bot.* tending to assume at or just before nightfall positions unlike those maintained during the day, as the leaves of certain plants. [f. *nycti-* (var. of NYCT-) + -TROPIC] —**nyctitropism** (nĭk-tĭt′rə pĭz′əm), *n.*

nyctophobia (nĭk′tō fō′byə), *n.* a morbid or abnormal fear of night or darkness.

Nyeman (*Russ.* nyĕ′mən), *n.* Neman.

Nyerere (nĭə rĕə′rĭ), *n.* **Julius Kambarage** (jo͞o′lyəs kăm′bə rä′gĭ), born 1922, African statesman, president of Tanzania since 1964.

Nyíregyháza (*Hung.* nyē′rĕdy hȧ zō), *n.* a town in NE Hungary. 59,000 (est. 1962).

nylghau (nĭl′gô), *n.* nilgai. Also, **nylghai** (nĭl′gī).

nylon (nī′lŏn), *n.* **1.** a synthetic polyamide capable of extrusion when molten into fibres, sheets, etc., of extreme toughness, strength, and elasticity: used for yarn (as for hosiery), for bristles (as for brushes), etc. It is a thermoplastic product, made by interaction of a dicarboxylic acid with a diamine. **2.** (*pl.*) stockings made of nylon. [coined name]

nymph (nĭmf), *n.* **1.** one of a numerous class of inferior divinities of mythology, conceived as beautiful maidens inhabiting the sea, rivers, woods, trees, mountains, meadows, etc., and frequently mentioned as attending a superior deity. **2.** a beautiful or graceful young woman. **3.** *Chiefly Poetic or Playful.* a maiden. **4.** *Entomol.* **a.** Also, **nympha.** the young of an insect without metamorphosis. **b.** a pupa. [ME *nimphe*, t. OF, t. L: m. *nympha*, t. Gk: m. *nýmphē* nymph, pupa] —**nymph′al, nymphean** (nĭm fē′ən), *adj.* —**Syn. 1.** See **sylph.**

nympha (nĭm′fə), *n.*, *pl.* **-phae** (-fē). **1.** (*pl.*) *Anat.* the labia minora (see **labium** def. 2b). **2.** nymph (def. 4a). [t. L. See NYMPH]

nymphaeaceous (nĭm′fĭ ā′shəs), *adj.* belonging to the *Nymphaeaceae*, or waterlily family of plants. [f. s. L *nymphaea* (t. Gk: m. *nymphaía* waterlily, prop. fem. of *nymphaîos* sacred to the nymphs) + -ACEOUS]

nymphalid (nĭm′fə lĭd), *n.* any of the numerous butterflies of the family *Nymphalidae*, characterized by small useless forelegs, and including the fritillaries, etc. [t. NL: s. *nymphălis*, der. L *nympha* NYMPH + *-idae* -IDAE]

nymphet (nĭm′fĭt), *n.* **1.** a young nymph. **2.** a very young girl with strong sexual attraction.

nympho (nĭm′fō), *n.*, *pl.* **-phos.** *Slang.* nymphomaniac.

nympholepsy (nĭm′fə lĕp′sĭ), *n.*, *pl.* **-sies. 1.** an ecstasy supposed to be inspired by nymphs. **2.** a frenzy of emotion, as for something unattainable. [b. NYMPHOLEPT and EPILEPSY] —**nympholeptic** (nĭm′fə lĕp′tĭk), *adj.*

nympholept (nĭm′fə lĕpt′), *n.* one seized with nympholepsy. [t. Gk: s. *nymphólēptos* caught by nymphs]

nymphomania (nĭm′fə mā′nyə), *n. Pathol.* uncontrollable sexual desire in women. [f. Gk *nympho-* NYMPH + MANIA] —**nymphomaniac** (nĭm′fə mā′nĭ ăk′), *adj.*, *n.*

Nynorsk (*Norw.* nʏ′nōrsk), *n.* Landsmål. [Norw.: new Norse]

nystagmus (nĭs tăg′məs), *n. Pathol.* an involuntary oscillation of the eyeball, usually lateral but sometimes rotatory or vertical: occurring esp. among miners and human albinos and in certain diseases. [t. NL, t. Gk: m. *nystagmós* nodding] —**nystag′mic,** *adj.*

Nyx (nĭks), *n. Gk Myth.* a goddess, a personification of night.

N.Z., New Zealand. Also, **N. Zeal.**

O

O¹, o (ō), *n.*, *pl.* **O's** or **Os; o's, os,** or **oes. 1.** a vowel, the 15th letter of the English alphabet. **2.** something resembling the letter O in shape. **3.** the Arabic cipher; zero; nought (0). **4.** a mere nothing.

O² (ō), *interj.*, *n.*, *pl.* **O's.** —*interj.* **1.** (a word used before a name in address, esp., as in solemn or poetic language, to lend earnestness to an appeal): *Praise the Lord, O Jerusalem.* **2.** (an expression of surprise, pain, longing, gladness, etc.) —*n.* **3.** the exclamation 'O'.

o' (ə), *prep.* **1.** an abbreviated form of *of*, now chiefly dialectal or colloquial, except in *o'clock, will-o'-the-wisp,* etc. **2.** an abbreviated form of *on.*

O' (ō), a prefix meaning 'descendant', in Irish family names: *O'Brien, O'Connor.* [repr. Irish *ō* descendant]

O, 1. *Elect.* ohm. **2.** Old. **3.** *Chem.* oxygen.

o-¹, *Chem.* an abridgement of **ortho-.**

o-², var. of **ob-,** before *m*, as in *omission.*

-o-, an ending for the first element of many compounds, originally found in the combining forms of many Greek words, but often used in English as a connective irrespective of etymology, as in *Franco-Italian, speedometer,* etc.

O., 1. Ocean. **2.** octavo. **3.** Ohio. **4.** Old. **5.** Ontario. **6.** Oregon.

o., 1. (L *octavus*) pint. **2.** octavo. **3.** off. **4.** old. **5.** only. **6.** order.

oaf (ōf), *n.* **1.** a simpleton or blockhead. **2.** a lout. **3.** a deformed or mentally deficient child; an idiot. **4.** a changeling. [var. of *auf*, ME *alfe*, OE *ælf* elf, c. G *Alp* nightmare] —**oaf′ish,** *adj.* —**oaf′ishly,** *adv.* —**oaf′ishness,** *n.*

Oahu (ō ä′ho͞o), *n.* the third largest and most important of the Hawaiian Islands. 500,409 pop. (1960); 589 sq. mi.

oak (ōk), *n.* **1.** any tree or shrub of the large fagaceous genus *Quercus*, including many forest trees with hard, durable wood, bearing the acorn as fruit. **2.** the wood of an oak tree. **3.** the leaves of the oak tree, esp. as worn in a chaplet. **4.** anything made of oak, as furniture, a door, etc. **5.** (in Oxford and Cambridge colleges) an outer door to a person's rooms. [ME *ook*, OE *āc*, c. D *eik*, G *Eiche*]

oak-apple (ōk′ăp′l), *n.* any of various roundish galls produced on oaks. Also, **oak-gall** (ōk′gôl′).

oaken (ō′kən), *adj.* **1.** made of oak: *the old oaken bucket.* **2.** of or pertaining to the oak.

oak fern, a fern with solitary leaves and long slender rhizomes, *Thelypteris phegopteris*, widespread in damp shady woods of the N temperate zone.

Oakham (ō′kəm), *n.* a town in England, the county town of Rutland. 4571 (1961).

Oakland (ōk′lənd), *n.* a seaport in the U.S., in W California, on San Francisco Bay. 367,548 (1960).

Oakley (ōk′lĭ), *n.* **Annie, 1.** (*Phoebe Anne Oakley Mozee*), 1860–1926, U.S. markswoman. **2.** *U.S. Slang.* a free ticket of admittance. [def. 2 in allusion to the similarity between a punched ticket and a small target shot through by Annie Oakley]

Oak Ridge, a town in the U.S., in E Tennessee, near Knoxville: a centre of atomic research. 27,169 (1960).

Oaks (ōks), *n.* **The,** (*pl. construed as sing.*) a horserace, founded 1779, run annually at Epsom Downs.

oakum (ō′kəm), *n.* loose fibre obtained by untwisting and picking apart old ropes, used for caulking the seams of ships, etc. [ME *okom(e)*, OE *ācum(a)*, var. of *ācumba*, lit., offcombings. See COMB]

O. and M., organization and method.
OAP, old age pension(er).
oar (ô), *n.* **1.** an instrument for propelling a boat, sometimes used also for steering, consisting of a long shaft of wood with a blade at one end. **2.** something resembling this or used for a similar purpose. **3.** an oarsman. **4. put one's oar in,** to interfere; meddle. **5. rest on one's oars,** to relax; take things easily. *—v.t.* **6.** to propel with or as with oars; row. **7.** to traverse (the sea, etc.), or make (one's way), by or as if by rowing. *—v.i.* **8.** to move or advance as if by rowing. [ME *ore*, OE *ār*, c. Icel. *ār*] **—oar′less,** *adj.* **—oar′like′,** *adj.*
oared (ôd), *adj.* furnished with oars.
oarfish (ô′fĭsh′), *n., pl.* **-fishes,** (*esp. collectively*) **-fish.** any of the pelagic fishes constituting the genus *Regalecus*, characterized by a compressed, tapelike body from 12 to over 20 feet long.
oarlock (ô′lŏk′), *n. Now Chiefly U.S.* rowlock. [ME *orlok*, OE *ārloc*. See OAR, LOCK[1]]
oarsman (ôz′mən), *n., pl.* **-men.** one who rows a boat; a rower.
oarsmanship (ôz′mən shĭp′), *n.* the art of rowing; skill in rowing.
oary (ô′rĭ), *adj. Chiefly Poetic.* oarlike.
OAS, **1.** Organization of American States. **2.** (F *Organisation Armée Secrète*) a secret movement (1961–63) opposing, by the use of violence, the independence of Algeria.
oasis (ō ā′sĭs), *n., pl.* **oases** (-sēz). a fertile place in a desert region where ground water brought to the surface or surface water from other areas provides for humid vegetation. [t. L, t. Gk, ? t. Egyptian: m. *wāh*]
oast (ōst), *n.* a kiln for drying hops or malt. [ME *ost*, OE *āst*, c. D *eest*]
oast-house (ōst′hous′), *n.* a building containing an oast.
oat (ōt), *n.* **1.** (*usually pl.*) a cereal grass, *Avena sativa*, cultivated for its edible seed, which is used in making oatmeal and as a food for horses, etc. **2.** (*pl.*) the seeds. **3.** any species of the same genus, as *A. fatua*, the common **wild oat. 4.** *Poetic.* a musical pipe made of an oat straw. **5. feel one's oats,** *U.S. Slang.* **a.** to feel gay or lively. **b.** to be aware of and use one's importance and power. **6. sow (one's) wild oats,** to indulge in the excesses or follies of youth, esp. in sexual promiscuity. [ME *ote*, OE *āte*]
oatcake (ōt′kāk′), *n.* a cake, usually thin and brittle, made of oatmeal.
oaten (ō′tn), *adj.* **1.** made of oats or of oatmeal. **2.** of or pertaining to the oat. **3.** made of an oat straw.
Oates (ōts), *n.* **Titus** (tī′təs), 1649–1705, English instigator of the Popish Plot scare.
oat grass, **1.** any of certain oatlike grasses. **2.** any wild species of oat.
oath (ōth), *n., pl.* **oaths** (ōt͟hz). **1.** a solemn appeal to God, or to some revered person or thing, in attestation of the truth of a statement or the binding character of a promise: *to testify upon oath.* **2.** a statement or promise strengthened by such an appeal. **3.** a formally affirmed statement or promise accepted as an equivalent. **4.** the form of words in which such a statement or promise is made: *the Hippocratic oath.* **5.** an irreverent or blasphemous use of the name of God or anything sacred. **6.** any profane expression; a curse. **7. on oath, under oath,** *Law.* having sworn on the Bible to tell the truth. [ME *ooth*, OE *āth*, c. G *Eid*]
oatmeal (ōt′mēl′), *n.* **1.** meal made from oats and used in porridge, oatcakes, etc. **2.** oatmeal porridge.
OAU, Organization of African Unity.
Ob (*Russ.* ôpy), *n.* a river in the W Soviet Union in Asia. ab. 2600 mi. long, flowing NW to the **Gulf of Ob** (ab. 600 mi. long), an inlet of the Arctic Ocean.
ob-, a prefix meaning 'towards', 'to', 'on', 'over', 'against', orig. occurring in loan words from Latin, but now used also, with the sense of 'reversely' or 'inversely', to form Neo-Latin and English scientific terms. Also, **o-, oc-, of-, op-.** [t. L, repr. *ob*, prep., towards, to, about, before, on, over, against]
ob., **1.** obiit. **2.** (L *obiter*) incidentally. **3.** oboe.
Obad., Obadiah.
Obadiah (ō′bə dī′ə), *n.* **1.** a Hebrew prophet. **2.** the Old Testament book which bears his name.
Oban (ō′bən), *n.* a seaport in Scotland, on the Firth of Lorne: resort. 6859 (1961).
obb., obbligato
obbligato (ŏb′lĭ gä′tō; *It.* ŏb blē gá′tō), *adj., n., pl.* **-tos, -ti** (*It.* -tē). *Music.* *—adj.* **1.** obligatory or indispensable; so important that it cannot be omitted (opposed to *ad libitum*). *—n.* **2.** an obbligato part or accompaniment. Also, **obligato.** [t. It.: obliged]
obcordate (ŏb kô′dāt), *adj. Bot.* heart-shaped, with the attachment at the pointed end, as a leaf.
obdt, obedient.
obdurate (ŏb′dyo͝o rĭt), *adj.* **1.** hardened against persuasions or tender feelings; hard-hearted. **2.** hardened against moral influence; persistently impenitent: *an obdurate sinner.* [ME, t. L: m. s. *obdūrātus*, pp., hardened] **—obduracy** (ŏb′dyo͝o rə sĭ), **ob′durateness,** *n.* **—ob′durately,** *adj.*
O.B.E., **1.** Officer (of the Order) of the British Empire. **2.** Order of the British Empire.
obeah (ō′bĭə), *n.* obi[2].
obedience (ə bē′dyəns), *n.* **1.** the state or fact of being obedient. **2.** the act or practice of obeying; dutiful or submissive compliance (fol. by *to*). **3.** a sphere of authority, or a body of persons, etc., subject to some particular authority, esp. ecclesiastical. **4.** authority or rule, esp. ecclesiastical, as over those who should obey.
obedient (ə bē′dyənt), *adj.* obeying, or willing to obey; submissive to authority or constraint. [ME, t. L: m. s. *oboediens*, ppr.] **—obe′diently,** *adv.* **—Syn.** compliant, docile, tractable.
obeisance (ō bā′səns, ō bē′-), *n.* **1.** a movement of the body expressing deep respect or deferential courtesy, as before a superior; a bow or curtsy. **2.** deference or homage. [ME *obeisaunce*, t. OF: m. *obeissance* obedience, der. *obeir* OBEY] **—obei′sant,** *adj.*
obelisk (ŏb′ĭ lĭsk), *n.* **1.** a tapering, four-sided shaft of stone, usually monolithic and having a pyramidal apex, of which notable examples are seen among the monuments of ancient Egypt. **2.** something resembling such a shaft. **3.** an obelus. **4.** *Print.* the dagger (†), used esp. as a reference mark. [t. L: m. s. *obeliscus*, t. Gk: m. *obelískos*, dim. of *obelós* OBELUS] **—ob′elis′cal,** *adj.*

Obelisk

obelize (ŏb′ĭ līz′), *v.t.,* **-lized, -lizing.** to mark (a word or passage) with an obelus. Also, **obelise.**
obelus (ŏb′ĭ ləs), *n., pl.* **-li** (-lī′). **1.** a mark (— or ÷) used in ancient manuscripts to point out spurious, corrupt, doubtful, or superfluous words or passages. **2.** *Print.* the obelisk or dagger (†). [t. LL, t. Gk: m. *obelós* spit, pointed pillar, obelus]
Oberammergau (ō′bər ăm′ə gou′; *Ger.* ō bər àm′ər gou), *n.* a village in West Germany, SW of Munich: famous for the passion play performed every ten years.
Oberhausen (*Ger.* ō′bər hou zən), *n.* a town in W West Germany, in W North Rhine-Westphalia, in the lower Ruhr valley. 257,900 (est. 1966).
Oberland (ō′bə lănd′; *Ger.* ō′bər lànt), *n.* a mountain region in central Switzerland, mostly in S Bern canton.
Oberlin (ō′bə lĭn), *n.* a coeducational college in the U.S., in Ohio, founded in 1833.
Oberösterreich (*Ger.* ō′bər œs tə rīKH), *n. German.* Upper Austria.
obese (ō bēs′), *adj.* excessively fat, as a person or animal, the body, etc.; corpulent. [t. L: m. s. *obēsus*, pp.] **—obese′ly,** *adv.* **—obese′ness, obesity** (ō bē′sĭ tĭ, ō bĕs′ĭ-), *n.*
obey (ə bā′), *v.t.* **1.** to comply with or fulfil the commands or instructions of: *obey your parents.* **2.** to comply with or fulfil (a command, etc.). **3.** (of things) to respond conformably in action to: *a ship obeys her helm.* **4.** to submit or conform in action to (some guiding principle, impulse, etc.). *—v.i.* **5.** to be obedient. [ME *obei(en)*, t. OF: m. *obeir*, g. L *oboedīre*] **—obey′er,** *n.*
obfuscate (ŏb′fŭs kāt′), *v.t.,* **-cated, -cating.** **1.** to confuse or stupefy. **2.** to darken or obscure. [t. LL: m. s. *obfuscātus*, pp.] **—ob′fusca′tion,** *n.*
obi[1] (ō′bĭ), *n., pl.* **obis.** a long, broad sash worn by Japanese women and children. [t. Jap.]
obi[2] (ō′bĭ), *n., pl.* **obis.** **1.** a kind of sorcery practised by the Negroes of Africa, the West Indies, etc. **2.** a fetish or charm used in it. Also, **obeah.** [t. a W African lang. (prob. Efik; cf. Efik *abia* practitioner, *ubio* evil charm)]
obiit (ŏb′ĭ ĭt, ō′bĭ-), *Latin.* he (or she) died.
obit (ŏb′ĭt, ō′bĭt), *n.* **1.** the date of a person's death. **2.** an obituary notice. [ME, t. L: s. *obitus* death]
obiter dictum (ŏb′ĭ tə dĭk′təm), *pl.* **obiter dicta** (dĭk′tə). **1.** an incidental opinion; a passing remark. **2.** *Law.* an opinion by a judge in deciding a case, upon a matter not essential to the decision, and therefore not binding. [t. L: (something) said by the way]
obituary (ə bĭt′yo͝o ə rĭ), *n., pl.* **-aries,** *adj.* *—n.* **1.** a notice of the death of a person, often with a brief biographical sketch, as in a newspaper. *—adj.* **2.** pertaining to or recording a death: *an obituary notice.* [t. NL: m. s. *obituārius*, der. L *obitus* death]
obj., **1.** object. **2.** objection. **3.** objective.
object (*n.* ŏb′jĭkt; *v.* əb jĕkt′), *n.* **1.** something that may be perceived by the senses, esp. by sight or touch;

a visible or tangible thing. **2.** a thing or person to which attention or action is directed: *an object of study.* **3.** anything that may be presented to the mind: *objects of thought.* **4.** a thing with reference to the impression it makes on the mind: *an object of curiosity.* **5.** the end towards which effort is directed: *the object of our visit.* **6.** a person or thing which arouses feelings of pity, disgust, etc. **7.** *Gram.* (in English and many other languages) the noun or its substitute which represents the goal of an action (in English either *direct* or *indirect*) or the ending point of a relation (in English expressed by a preposition). For example: in *John kicked the ball, ball* is the goal of the action. In *he came to Venice, Venice* is the ending point of the action. In *he gave the boy a coin, coin* is the direct object, *boy* is the indirect object. **8.** *Metaphys.* that towards which a cognitive act is directed; the non-ego. *—v.i.* **9.** to offer a reason or argument in opposition. **10.** to express or feel disapproval; be averse. *—v.t.* **11.** to bring as a charge; attribute as a fault. **12.** *Obs. or Archaic.* to bring forward or adduce in opposition. [ME, t. ML: s. *objectum*, prop. neut. of L *objectus*, pp., thrown before, presented, exposed, opposed, reproached with] **—objec′tor,** *n.* **—Syn. 5.** purpose, motive, intent. See **aim.**

object., 1. objection. 2. objective.

object ball, *Billiards, etc.* the ball which the striker aims to hit with the cue ball; any ball except the striker's.

object glass, objective (def. 3).

objectify (əb jĕk′tĭ fī′), *v.t.*, **-fied, -fying.** to present as an object, esp. of sense; make objective; externalize. [f. s. ML *objectum* an object + -(I)FY] **—objec′tifica′tion,** *n.*

objection (əb jĕk′shən), *n.* **1.** something adduced or said in disagreement or disapproval; an adverse reason. **2.** the act of objecting. **3.** a ground or cause of objecting. **4.** a feeling of disapproval or dislike.

objectionable (əb jĕk′shə nə bl), *adj.* that may be objected to; unpleasant; offensive: *objectionable remarks; an objectionable smell.* **—objec′tionably,** *adv.*

objective (əb jĕk′tĭv), *n.* **1.** an end towards which efforts are directed; something aimed at. **2.** *Gram.* **a.** the objective case. **b.** a word in that case. **3.** (in a telescope, microscope, etc.) the lens or combination of lenses which first receives the rays from the object and forms the image viewed through the eyepiece or photographed. See diag. under **microscope.** *—adj.* **4.** being the object of perception or thought; belonging to the object of thought rather than to the thinking subject (opposed to *subjective*). **5.** free from personal feelings or prejudice; unbiased. **6.** being the object of one's endeavours or actions. **7.** intent upon or dealing with things external to the mind rather than thoughts or feelings, as a person, a book, etc. **8.** of or pertaining to that which can be known, or to that which is an object or a part of an object. **9.** *Art.* **a.** of or pertaining to an object or objects (opposed to *non-objective* and *non-representational*). **b.** being, or pertaining to, the object whose perspective delineation is required: *an objective plane.* **10.** *Med.* (of a symptom) discernible to others as well as the patient. **11.** *Gram.* **a.** pertaining to the use of a form as object of a verb or preposition. **b.** (in English and some other languages) denoting a case specialized for that use: in *the boy hit him, him* is in the objective case. **c.** similar to such a case in meaning. [t. ML: m. *objectīvus*, adj.] **—objec′tively,** *adv.* **—objec′tiveness,** *n.*

objective complement, *Gram.* a word or a group of words qualifying or modifying a direct object, as *the manager* in *they made him the manager.*

objectivism (əb jĕk′tĭ vĭz′əm), *n.* **1.** a tendency to lay stress on the objective or external elements of cognition. **2.** the tendency to deal with things external to the mind rather than thoughts or feelings, as in a writer. **3.** a doctrine characterized by this tendency. **—objec′tivist,** *n., adj.* **—objec′tivis′tic,** *adj.*

objectivity (ŏb′jĕk tĭv′ĭ tĭ), *n.* **1.** the state or quality of being objective. **2.** intentness on objects external to the mind. **3.** external reality.

objectivize (əb jĕk′tĭ vīz′), *v.t.*, **-vized, -vizing.** to render objective; objectify. Also, **objectivise.**

objectless (ŏb′jĭkt lĭs), *adj.* **1.** having no object. **2.** not directed towards any object; purposeless.

object lesson, 1. a practical illustration of a principle, esp. one serving as a warning. **2.** a lesson in which instruction is conveyed by means of a material object.

objet d'art (*Fr.* ŏb zhĕ dár′), *pl.* **objets d'art** (*Fr.* ŏb zhĕ dár′). *French.* an article of artistic worth.

objurgate (ŏb′jû gāt′), *v.t.*, **-gated, -gating.** to reproach vehemently; upbraid violently; berate. [t. L: m. s. *objurgātus*, pp.] **—ob′jurga′tion,** *n.* **—objurgatory** (ŏb jû′gə tə rĭ, -trĭ), *adj.*

obl., 1. oblique. 2. oblong.

oblanceolate (ŏb lăn′sĭ ə lĭt, -lāt′), *adj. Bot.* inversely lanceolate, as a leaf.

oblast (ŏb′läst), *n.* an administrative subdivision of a republic in the Soviet Union. [t. Russ.]

oblate[1] (ŏb′lāt), *adj.* flattened at the poles, as a spheroid generated by the revolution of an ellipse about its shorter axis (opposed to *prolate*). See diag. under **prolate.** [t. NL: m. s. *oblātus*, f. *ob-* OB- + *-lātus*, modelled on *prolātus* PROLATE] **—ob′lately,** *adv.*

oblate[2] (ŏb′lāt), *n.* **1.** a person offered to the service of a monastery, but not under monastic vows. **2.** a member of any of various Roman Catholic societies devoted to special religious work. [t. ML: m. s. *oblātus*, prop. pp. of *offerre* OFFER]

oblation (ō blā′shən), *n.* **1.** the offering to God of the elements of bread and wine in the Eucharist. **2.** the whole office of the Eucharist. **3.** the act of making an offering, now esp. to God or a deity. **4.** any offering for religious or charitable uses. [ME *oblacion*, t. LL: m. s. *oblātio*] **—oblatory** (ŏb′lə tə rĭ, -trĭ), *adj.*

obligate (*v.* ŏb′lĭ gāt′; *adj.* ŏb′lĭ gĭt, -gāt′), *v.*, **-gated, -gating,** *adj.* *—v.t.* **1.** to oblige or bind morally or legally: *to obligate oneself to fulfil certain conditions.* **2.** *U.S.* to pledge, commit (funds, etc.). *—adj.* **3.** *U.S.* morally or legally bound or constrained. **4.** *U.S.* necessary; essential. **5.** *Biol.* restricted to a particular condition of life, as certain parasites which must live in close association with their usual hosts in order to survive (opposed to *facultative*). [ME, t. L: m. s. *obligātus*, pp.] **—ob′liga′tor,** *n.*

obligation (ŏb′lĭ gā′shən), *n.* **1.** a binding requirement as to action; duty: *to fulfil every obligation.* **2.** the binding power or force of a promise, law, duty, agreement, etc. **3.** a binding promise or the like. **4.** the act of binding oneself by a promise, contract, etc. **5.** *Law.* **a.** an agreement enforceable by law, originally applied to promises under seal. **b.** a document containing such an agreement. **c.** a bond containing a penalty, with a condition annexed for payment of money, performance of covenants, etc. **d.** any bond, note, bill, certificate, or the like, as of a government or a company, serving as security for payment of indebtedness. **6.** a benefit, favour, or service, for which gratitude is due. **7.** a debt of gratitude. **8.** the state or fact of being indebted for a benefit, favour, or service. **—Syn. 1.** See **duty.**

obligato (ŏb′lĭ gä′tō), *adj., n., pl.* **-tos, -ti** (-tē). obbligato.

obligatory (ŏ blĭg′ə tə rĭ, -trĭ), *adj.* **1.** imposing obligation, morally or legally; binding: *an obligatory promise.* **2.** required as a matter of obligation: *a reply is expected but not obligatory.* **3.** incumbent or compulsory (fol. by *on* or *upon*): *duties obligatory on all.* **4.** creating or recording an obligation, as a writing. [ME, t. LL: m. s. *obligātōrius*] **—oblig′atorily,** *adv.*

oblige (ə blīj′), *v.t.*, **obliged, obliging. 1.** to require or constrain, as by law, command, conscience, or necessity. **2.** to bind (a person, etc.) morally or legally, as by a promise, contract, or the like. **3.** to make (an action, course, etc.) incumbent or obligatory. **4.** to place under a debt of gratitude for some benefit, favour, or service. **5.** to favour or accommodate (fol. by *with*): *he obliged us with a song.* *—v.i.* **6.** to do something as a favour: *he'll do anything to oblige.* [ME *oblige(n)*, t. OF: m. *obligier*, t. L: m. *obligāre* bind or tie around] **—oblig′er,** *n.*

—Syn. 5. OBLIGE, ACCOMMODATE imply making a gracious and welcome gesture of some kind. OBLIGE emphasizes the idea of conferring a favour or benefit (and often of taking some trouble to do it): *to oblige someone with a loan.* ACCOMMODATE emphasizes doing a service or furnishing a convenience: *to accommodate someone with lodgings and meals.*

obligee (ŏb′lĭ jē′), *n.* **1.** *Law.* **a.** one to whom another is bound. **b.** the person to whom a bond is given. **2.** one who is under obligation for a benefit or favour.

obliging (ə blī′jĭng), *adj.* **1.** disposed to do favours or services, as a person: *the clerk was most obliging.* **2.** that obliges. **—oblig′ingly,** *adv.* **—oblig′ingness,** *n.* **—Syn. 1.** helpful, kind, friendly, accommodating.

obligor (ŏb′lĭ gô′), *n. Law.* **1.** one who is bound to another. **2.** the person who gives a bond.

oblique (ə blēk′), *adj., v.*, **obliqued, obliquing,** *n.* *—adj.* **1.** neither perpendicular nor parallel to a given line or surface; slanting; sloping. **2.** (of a solid) not having the axis perpendicular to the plane of the base. **3.** designating a method of projection in which neither side of the principal object is parallel to the plane of delineation. **4.** diverging from a given straight line or course. **5.** not straight or direct, as a course, etc. **6.** indirectly stated or expressed: *certain oblique hints.* **7.** indirectly aimed at or reached, as ends, results, etc. **8.** *Rhet.* indirect (applied to discourse in which the original words of a speaker or writer are assimilated to the language of the reporter). **9.** *Gram.* denoting or pertaining to any case of noun inflection except nominative and vocative, or except these two and accusative: *Latin genitive, dative, and ablative cases are said to be oblique.* **10.** morally or mentally wrong; perverse. **11.** *Anat.* pertaining to muscles running obliquely in the body as opposed to those running transversely or longitudinally. **12.** *Bot.* having unequal sides, as a leaf. —*v.i.* **13.** to have or take an oblique direction; slant: *the wall obliques from the gate at a sharp angle.* **14.** *Mil.* to advance obliquely. —*n.* **15.** *Gram.* the oblique case. **16.** something which is oblique. [ME *oblike*, t. L: m. s. *oblīquus*] —**oblique′ly,** *adv.* —**oblique′ness,** *n.*

oblique angle, an angle that is not a right angle.

oblique motion, *Music.* the relative motion of two melodic parts in which one remains in place while the other moves.

oblique sailing, navigation along a course other than directly north, south, east, or west.

obliquity (ə blĭk′wĭ tĭ), *n., pl.* **-ties. 1.** the state of being oblique. **2.** divergence from moral rectitude. **3.** a moral delinquency. **4.** mental perversity. **5.** an instance of mental perversity. **6.** inclination, or degree of inclination. **7.** Also, **obliquity of the ecliptic.** *Astron.* the angle between the plane of the earth's orbit and that of the earth's equator, equal to about 23° 27′. —**obliq′uitous,** *adj.*

obliterate (ə blĭt′ə rāt′), *v.t.,* **-rated, -rating. 1.** to remove all traces of; do away with; destroy. **2.** to blot out or render undecipherable (writing, marks, etc.); cancel; efface. [t. L: m. s. *oblit(t)erātus*, pp., erased] —**oblit′era′tion,** *n.* —**obliterative** (ə blĭt′ə rə tĭv), *adj.* —**Syn. 2.** See **cancel.**

oblivion (ə blĭv′ĭ ən), *n.* **1.** the state of being forgotten, as by the world. **2.** the forgetting, or forgetfulness, of something: *five minutes of oblivion.* **3.** disregard or overlooking: *oblivion of political offences.* [ME, t. L: s. *oblīvio*]

oblivious (ə blĭv′ĭ əs), *adj.* **1.** forgetful; without remembrance: *oblivious of my former failure.* **2.** unmindful; unconscious (fol. by *of* or *to*): *she was oblivious of his adoration.* **3.** inducing forgetfulness. [ME, t. L: m. s. *oblīviōsus*] —**obliv′iously,** *adv.* —**obliv′iousness,** *n.*

obliviscence (ŏb′lĭ vĭs′əns), *n.* the fact or state of having forgotten; forgetfulness.

oblong (ŏb′lŏng), *adj.* **1.** elongated, usually from the square or circular form. **2.** in the form of a rectangle of greater length than breadth. —*n.* **3.** an oblong figure. [ME, t. L: s. *oblongus* rather long, oblong]

Oblong leaf

obloquy (ŏb′lə kwĭ), *n., pl.* **-quies. 1.** the discredit or disgrace resulting from public blame or revilement. **2.** censure, blame, or abusive language aimed at a person, etc., esp. by numbers of persons or by the public generally. [late ME *obloqui*, t. LL: s. *obloquium* contradiction]

obnoxious (əb nŏk′shəs), *adj.* **1.** objectionable; offensive; odious: *obnoxious remarks.* **2.** exposed or liable (to harm, evil, or anything objectionable). **3.** *Obs.* liable to punishment or censure; reprehensible. [t. L: m. *obnoxius* exposed to harm] —**obnox′iously,** *adv.* —**obnox′iousness,** *n.* —**Syn. 1.** See **hateful.**

oboe (ō′bō), *n.* **1.** a woodwind instrument in the form of a slender conical tube, in which the tone is produced by a double reed. **2.** a reed stop in an organ which sounds like an oboe. [t. It., t. F: m. *hautbois* HAUTBOY]

oboist (ō′bō ĭst), *n.* a player on the oboe.

obol (ŏb′ŏl), *n.* an ancient Greek silver coin and weight, $\frac{1}{6}$ of a drachma. [t. L: s. *obolus*, t. Gk: m. *obolós*]

Oboe

Obote (ō bō′tĭ), *n.* **(Apollo) Milton,** born 1924, Ugandan statesman; president of Uganda 1966–71.

obovate (ŏb ō′vāt), *adj.* inversely ovate; ovate with the narrow end at the base.

obovoid (ŏb ō′void), *adj.* inversely ovoid, ovoid with the narrow end at the base, as certain fruits.

Obrenović (*Serb.* ô brĕ′nô vĕty), *n.* **1.** a former ruling family of Serbia. **2.** Alexander I of Serbia.

Obovate leaf

obs., 1. observation. **2.** observatory. **3.** obsolete.

obscene (əb sēn′, ŏb-), *adj.* **1.** offensive to modesty or decency; indecent; inciting to lust or sexual depravity; lewd: *obscene pictures.* **2.** abominable; disgusting; repulsive. [t. L: m. s. *obscēnus, obscaenus* of evil omen, offensive, disgusting] —**obscene′ly,** *adv.* —**obscene′ness,** *n.*

obscenity (əb sĕn′ĭ tĭ, -sē′nĭ-), *n., pl.* **-ties. 1.** obscene quality or character; indecency. **2.** something obscene, as language, a remark, an expression, etc.

obscurant (ŏb skyŏŏə′rənt), *n.* **1.** one who strives to prevent inquiry and enlightenment. **2.** one who obscures. —*adj.* **3.** pertaining to or characteristic of obscurants. [t. L: s. *obscūrans*, ppr.]

obscurantism (ŏb′skyŏŏə răn′tĭz′əm), *n.* **1.** opposition to inquiry and enlightenment. **2.** the principle or practice of obscurants. —**ob′scurant′ist,** *n., adj.*

obscuration (ŏb′skyŏŏə rā′shən), *n.* **1.** the act of obscuring. **2.** the state of being obscured.

obscure (əb skyŏŏə′), *adj.,* **-scurer, -scurest,** *v.,* **-scured, -scuring,** *n.* —*adj.* **1.** (of meaning) not clear or plain; uncertain. **2.** (of language, style, a speaker, etc.) not expressing the meaning clearly or plainly. **3.** inconspicuous or unnoticeable: *the obscure beginnings of a great movement.* **4.** of no prominence, note, or distinction. **5.** not readily seen; remote; retired, as a place. **6.** indistinct to the sight, or to some other sense. **7.** dark, as from lack of light or illumination; murky; dim. **8.** enveloped in, concealed by, or frequenting darkness. **9.** dark, dull, or not bright or lustrous, as colour or appearance. **10.** not clear to the mind; imperfectly understood; ambiguous; uncertain. —*v.t.* **11.** to make obscure, dark, dim, indistinct, etc. —*n.* **12.** darkness or obscurity. [ME, t. L: m. s. *obscūrus* dark, dim, unknown, ignoble] —**obscure′ly,** *adv.* —**obscure′ness,** *n.* —**Syn. 1.** doubtful, dubious, ambiguous. See **mysterious.**

obscurity (əb skyŏŏə′rĭ tĭ), *n., pl.* **-ties. 1.** the state or quality of being obscure. **2.** uncertainty of meaning or expression. **3.** the condition of being unknown. **4.** an unknown or unimportant person or thing. **5.** darkness; dimness; indistinctness.

obsecrate (ŏb′sĭ krāt′), *v.t.,* **-crated, -crating.** to entreat (a person, etc.) solemnly; beseech; supplicate. [t. L: m. s. *obsecrātus*, pp.] —**ob′secra′tion,** *n.*

obsequious (əb sē′kwĭ əs), *adj.* **1.** servilely compliant or deferential: *obsequious servants.* **2.** characterized by or showing servile complaisance or deference: *an obsequious bow.* **3.** *Now Rare.* compliant; obedient; dutiful. [ME, t. L: m. s. *obsequiōsus*] —**obse′quiously,** *adv.* —**obse′quiousness,** *n.* —**Syn. 1.** See **servile.**

obsequy (ŏb′sĭ kwĭ), *n., pl.* **-quies.** (*usually pl.*) a funeral rite or ceremony. [ME *obsequies*, t. ML: m. *obsequiae*, pl., (L *exsequiae*) funeral rites]

observable (əb zû′və bl), *adj.* **1.** that may be or is to be noticed; noticeable; noteworthy. **2.** that may be or is to be followed or kept. —**observ′ably,** *adv.*

observance (əb zû′vəns), *n.* **1.** the action of conforming to, obeying or following: *observance of laws.* **2.** a keeping or celebration by appropriate procedure, ceremonies, etc. **3.** a procedure, ceremony, or rite, as for a particular occasion: *patriotic observances.* **4.** a rule or custom to be observed. **5.** *Rom. Cath. Ch.* **a.** a rule or discipline for a religious house or order. **b.** such a house or order. **6.** observation. **7.** respectful attention or service. **8.** *Archaic.* respectful or courteous attention; deference.

observant (əb zû′vənt), *adj.* **1.** observing or regarding attentively; watchful. **2.** quick to notice or perceive; alert. **3.** careful in the observing of a law, custom, or the like. —*n.* **4.** an observer of law or rule. **5.** Also, **Observantine** (ŏb zû′vən tĭn, -tīn′). (*cap.*) a member of a branch of the Franciscan order which in the 15th century separated from the Conventuals and observes strictly the rule of St Francis. [ME, t. L: s. *observans*, ppr.] —**observ′antly,** *adv.*

observation (ŏb′zə vā′shən), *n.* **1.** the act of noticing or perceiving. **2.** the act of regarding attentively or watching. **3.** the faculty or habit of observing or noticing. **4.** notice: *to escape a person's observation.* **5.** the act of viewing or noting something, for some scientific or other special purpose. **6.** the information or record secured thereby. **7.** that which is learned by observing. **8.** the fact or condition of being observed. **9.** an utterance by way of remark or comment. **10.** *Naut.* **a.** the measurement of the altitude or azimuth of a celestial body to deduce a line of position for a vessel at sea. **b.** the result obtained. **11.** *Obs. or Rare.* observance, as of law, etc. —**Syn. 9.** See **remark.**

observational (ŏb′zə vā′shə nəl), *adj.* of, pertaining to, or founded on observation, esp. as contrasted with experiment.

observation car, a railway carriage usually attached to the rear of a passenger train, designed to afford passengers an unobstructed view of passing scenery.

observation post, *Mil.* a lookout position from which targets may be observed and effective fire directed.

observatory (əb zû′və trĭ), *n., pl.* **-tories. 1.** a place or building designed for making observations of astronomical, meteorological, or other natural phenomena, usually equipped with a powerful telescope. **2.** an institution which controls or carries on the work of an observatory. **3.** a place or structure for affording an extensive view.

observe (əb zûv′), *v.*, **-served, -serving.** —*v.t.* **1.** to see, perceive, or notice. **2.** to regard with attention, so as to see or learn something. **3.** to make or take an observation of; to watch, view, or note for some scientific, official, or other special purpose: *to observe an eclipse.* **4.** to remark; comment. **5.** to keep or maintain in one's action, conduct, etc.: *you must observe the formalities.* **6.** to obey; comply with; conform to: *to observe a law.* **7.** to show regard for by some appropriate procedure, ceremonies, etc.: *to observe a holiday.* **8.** to perform duly, or solemnize (ceremonies, rites, etc.). —*v.i.* **9.** to notice. **10.** to act as an observer. **11.** to remark or comment (commonly fol. by *on* or *upon*). [ME *observe(n)*, t. L: m. *observāre* watch, comply with, observe] —**observ′ingly,** *adv.*

—**Syn. 2.** OBSERVE, WITNESS imply paying strict attention to what one sees or perceives. Both are 'continuative' in action. To OBSERVE is to mark or be attentive to something seen (heard, etc.): to consider carefully; to watch steadily: *to observe the behaviour of birds, a person's pronunciation.* To WITNESS, formerly to be present when something was happening, has added the idea of having observed with sufficient care to be able to give an account as evidence: *to witness an accident.* —**Ant. 1.** disregard, overlook.

observer (əb zû′və), *n.* **1.** one who or that which observes. **2.** one who accompanies the pilot of an aeroplane in order to observe. **3.** one who attends a meeting, etc. but does not take any official part in its activities.

obsess (əb sĕs′), *v.t.* to beset, trouble, or dominate the thoughts, feelings, etc.; haunt: *obsessed by a fear of cancer.* [t. L: s. *obsessus*, pp., besieged, beset] —**obses′sive,** *adj.*

obsession (əb sĕsh′ən), *n.* **1.** the besetting or dominating action or influence of a persistent feeling, idea, or the like, which a person cannot escape. **2.** the feeling or idea itself. **3.** the state of being obsessed. **4.** the act of obsessing. —**obses′sional,** *adj.*

obsessive (əb sĕs′ĭv), *adj.* **1.** of, pertaining to, or resembling an obsession. **2.** causing an obsession. **3.** excessive; extreme.

obsidian (ŏb sĭd′ĭ ən), *n.* a volcanic glass, usually of a very dark colour and with a conchoidal fracture. [t. L: s. *obsidiānus*, prop. *obsiānus*, pertaining to *Obsius*, reputed discoverer of a similar mineral]

obsolesc., obsolescent.

obsolescent (ŏb′sə lĕs′ənt), *adj.* **1.** becoming obsolete; passing out of use, as a word. **2.** tending to become out of date, as machinery, weapons, etc. **3.** *Biol.* gradually disappearing, or imperfectly developed, as organs, marks, etc. [t. L: s. *obsolescens*, ppr.] —**ob′soles′cence,** *n.* —**ob′soles′cently,** *adv.*

obsolete (ŏb′sə lēt′), *adj.* **1.** fallen into disuse, or no longer in use: *an obsolete word.* **2.** of a discarded type; out of date: *an obsolete battleship.* **3.** effaced by wearing down or away. **4.** *Biol.* imperfectly developed or rudimentary in comparison with the corresponding character in other individuals, as of the opposite sex or of a related species. [t. L: m. s. *obsolētus*, pp.] —**ob′solete′ly,** *adv.* —**ob′solete′ness,** *n.*

obstacle (ŏb′stə kl), *n.* something that stands in the way or obstructs progress. [ME, t. OF, t. L: m. s. *obstāculum*]

—**Syn.** OBSTACLE, OBSTRUCTION, HINDRANCE, IMPEDIMENT refer to that which interferes with or prevents action or progress. An OBSTACLE is something, material or non-material, which stands in the way of literal or figurative progress: *lack of imagination is an obstacle to one's advancement.* An OBSTRUCTION is something which more or less completely blocks a passage: *a blood clot is an obstruction to the circulation.* A HINDRANCE keeps back by interfering and delaying: *interruptions are a hindrance to one's work.* An IMPEDIMENT interferes with proper functioning: *an impediment in one's speech.* —**Ant.** help.

obstacle race, a race in which runners have to contend with both natural and artificial obstacles.

obstet., 1. obstetric. **2.** obstetrics.

obstetric (ŏb stĕt′rĭk), *adj.* **1.** of or pertaining to the care and treatment of women in childbirth and during the period before and after delivery. **2.** of or pertaining to obstetrics. Also, **obstet′rical.** [t. NL: s. *obstētricus*, var. of L *obstētricius* pertaining to a midwife] —**obstet′rically,** *adv.*

obstetrician (ŏb′stĕ trĭsh′ən), *n.* one skilled in obstetrics.

obstetrics (ŏb stĕt′rĭks), *n.* the branch of medical art or science concerned with caring for and treating women in, before, and after childbirth; midwifery.

obstinacy (ŏb′stĭ nə sĭ), *n.*, *pl.* **-cies. 1.** the quality or state of being obstinate. **2.** obstinate adherence to purpose, opinion, etc. **3.** stubborn persistence: *the soldiers fought with incredible obstinacy.* **4.** unyielding nature, as of a disease. **5.** an obstinate action; an instance of being obstinate. [ME, t. ML: m. s. *obstinātia*]

obstinate (ŏb′stĭ nĭt), *adj.* **1.** firmly and often perversely adhering to one's purpose, opinion, etc.; not yielding to argument, persuasion, or entreaty. **2.** inflexibly persisted in or carried out: *obstinate resistance.* **3.** not easily controlled: *the obstinate growth of weeds.* **4.** not yielding readily to treatment, as a disease. [ME *obstinat*, t. L: s. *obstinātus*, pp., determined] —**ob′stinately,** *adv.* —**ob′stinateness,** *n.* —**Syn. 1.** mulish, obdurate, unyielding. See **stubborn.**

obstipant (ŏb′stĭ pənt), *n.* a substance that produces obstipation.

obstipation (ŏb′stĭ pā′shən), *n.* obstinate constipation. [t. L: s. *obstipātio*]

obstreperous (əb strĕp′ə rəs, əb strĕp′rəs), *adj.* **1.** resisting control in a noisy manner; unruly. **2.** noisy or clamorous; boisterous. [t. L: m. *obstreperus* clamorous] —**obstrep′erously,** *adv.* —**obstrep′erousness,** *n.*

obstruct (əb strŭkt′), *v.t.* **1.** to block or close up, or make difficult of passage, with obstacles, as a way, road, channel, or the like. **2.** to interrupt, make difficult, or oppose the passage, progress, course, etc., of. **3.** to come in the way of or shut out (a view, etc.). [t. L: s. *obstructus*, pp.] —**obstruct′er, obstruc′tor,** *n.* —**obstruc′tive,** *adj.* —**obstruc′tively,** *adv.* —**obstruc′tiveness,** *n.* —**Syn. 1.** block, stop, close, choke, clog.

obstruction (əb strŭk′shən), *n.* **1.** something that obstructs; an obstacle or hindrance: *obstructions to navigation.* **2.** the act of obstructing. **3.** the retarding of business before a legislative group by parliamentary devices, or an attempt at such a retarding. **4.** the state of being obstructed. **5.** *Football, Hockey, etc.* a foul or infringement whereby a player interposes his body between an opponent and the ball so as to form an obstacle. —**Syn. 1.** See **obstacle.**

obstructionist (əb strŭk′shə nĭst), *n.* a person who obstructs something, esp. legislative business. —**obstruc′tionism,** *n.*

obstruent (ŏb′strōō ənt), *Med.* —*adj.* **1.** (of a substance) producing an obstruction. —*n.* **2.** a medicine that closes the natural passages of the body. [t. L: s. *obstruens*, ppr., blocking up]

obtain (əb tān′), *v.t.* **1.** to come into possession of; get or acquire; procure, as by effort or request: *he obtained a knowledge of Greek.* **2.** *Obs. or Archaic.* to attain or reach. —*v.i.* **3.** to be prevalent, customary, or in vogue; hold good or be valid: *the morals that obtained in Rome.* **4.** *Obs. or Archaic.* to succeed. [ME *obteine(n)*, t. OF: m. *obtenir*, t. L: m. *obtinēre* take hold of, get, prevail, continue] —**obtain′able,** *adj.* —**obtain′er,** *n.* —**obtain′ment,** *n.* —**Syn. 1.** See **get.**

obtect (əb tĕkt′), *adj. Entomol.* denoting a pupa in which the antennae, legs, and wings are glued to the surface of the body by a hardened secretion. Also, **obtected** (əb tĕk′tĭd). [s. L *obtectus*, pp., covered over]

obtest (ŏb tĕst′), *v.t.* **1.** to invoke as witness. **2.** to supplicate earnestly; beseech. —*v.i.* **3.** to protest. [t. L: s. *obtestārī* call as a witness] —**ob′testa′tion,** *n.*

obtrude (əb trōōd′), *v.*, **-truded, -truding.** —*v.t.* **1.** to thrust forward or upon a person, esp. without warrant or invitation: *to obtrude one's opinions upon others.* **2.** to thrust forth; push out. —*v.i.* **3.** to thrust oneself or itself forward, esp. unduly; intrude. [t. L: m. s. *obtrūdere* thrust upon or into] —**obtrud′er,** *n.*

obtrusion (əb trōō′zhən), *n.* **1.** the act of obtruding. **2.** something obtruded.

obtrusive (əb trōō′sĭv), *adj.* **1.** having or showing a disposition to obtrude. **2.** (of a thing) obtruding itself. **3.** projecting. —**obtru′sively,** *adv.* —**obtru′siveness,** *n.*

obtund (ŏb tŭnd′), *v.t.* to blunt; dull; deaden. [ME, t. L: s. *obtundere* beat, strike at] —**obtund′ent,** *adj.*

obturate (ŏb′tyōōə rāt′), *v.t.*, **-rated, -rating. 1.** to stop up; close. **2.** *Ordn.* to close (a hole, joint, or cavity) so as to prevent the flow of gas through it. [t. L: m. s. *obtūrātus*, pp.] —**ob′tura′tion,** *n.* —**ob′tura′tor,** *n.*

obtuse (əb tyōōs′), *adj.* **1.** blunt in form; not sharp or acute. **2.** (of a leaf, petal, etc.) rounded at the extremity. **3.** not sensitive or observant; stupid; dull in perception, feeling, or intellect. **4.** indistinctly felt or perceived, as pain, sound, etc. [t. L: m. s. *obtūsus*, pp., dulled] —**obtuse′ly,** *adv.* —**obtuse′ness,** *n.*

A B C D E

ADE, Obtuse angle; BDE, Right angle; CDE, Straight angle

obtuse angle, an angle exceeding 90 degrees but less than 180 degrees.

obverse (ŏb′vûs), *n.* **1.** that side of a coin, medal etc., which bears the head or principal design (opposed to *reverse*). **2.** the front or principal face of anything. **3.** a counterpart. **4.** *Logic.* a proposition obtained from another by obversion. —*adj.* **5.** turned towards or facing one. **6.** corresponding to something else as a counterpart. **7.** having the base narrower than the top, as a leaf. [t. L: m. s. *obversus*, pp., turned towards or against] —**obverse′ly,** *adv.*

obversion (ŏb vûʹshən), *n.* **1.** the act or result of obverting. **2.** *Logic.* a form of inference in which a negative proposition is inferred from an affirmative or an affirmative from a negative.
obvert (ŏb vûtʹ), *v.t.* **1.** to turn (something) towards an object. **2.** *Logic.* to change (a proposition) by obversion. [t. L: s. *obvertere* turn towards or against]
obviate (ŏbʹvĭ ātʹ), *v.t.*, **-ated, -ating.** to meet and dispose of or prevent (difficulties, objections, etc.) by effective measures: *to obviate the necessity of beginning again.* [t. LL: m. s. *obviātus*, pp., met, opposed, prevented] —**obʹviaʹtion,** *n.*
obvious (ŏbʹvĭ əs), *adj.* **1.** clearly perceptible or evident; easily recognized or understood; open to view or knowledge: *an obvious advantage.* **2.** *Obs.* being or standing in the way. [t. L: m. *obvius* in the way, meeting] —**obʹviously,** *adv.* —**obʹviousness,** *n.* —**Syn. 1.** plain, manifest, evident. See **apparent.**
obvolute (ŏbʹvə lo͞otʹ), *adj.* **1.** rolled or turned in. **2.** *Bot.* denoting or pertaining to a kind of vernation in which two leaves are folded together in the bud so that one half of each is exterior and the other interior. [t. L: m. s. *obvolūtus*, pp., wrapped up] —**obʹvoluʹtion,** *n.* —**obʹvoluʹtive,** *adj.*
oc-, var. of **ob-** (by assimilation) before *c*, as in *Occident.*
Oc., ocean. Also, **oc.**
O.C., Officer Commanding.
o.c., opere citato.
ocarina (ŏkʹə rēʹnə), *n.* a simple musical wind instrument shaped somewhat like an elongated egg, with finger holes. [prob. dim. of It. *oca* goose, with reference to the shape]
O'Casey (ō kāʹsĭ), *n.* **Sean** (shôn), 1884–1964, Irish dramatist.
Occam (ŏkʹəm), *n.* **William of,** died 1349?, English scholastic philosopher. Also, **Ockham.** —**Ocʹcamism,** *n.* —**Ocʹcamist, Ocʹcamiteʹ,** *n.*
Occam's razor, the principle that entities must not be unnecessarily multiplied, on which William of Occam based his rejection of realism. As the principle of economy of hypothesis it is applicable to scientific research.
occas., **1.** occasional. **2.** occasionally.
occasion (ə kāʹzhən), *n.* **1.** a particular time, esp. as marked by certain circumstances or occurrences: *on several occasions.* **2.** a special or important time, event, ceremony, function, etc. **3.** a convenient or favourable juncture or time; opportunity. **4.** the ground, reason, immediate or incidental cause of some action or result. **5.** (*usually pl.*) *Obs.* need or necessity. **6.** (*pl.*) *Obs.* necessary business matters: *to go about one's lawful occasions.* **7. on occasion,** now and then; occasionally. **8. rise to the occasion,** to show oneself equal to a task. —*v.t.* **9.** to give occasion or cause for; bring about. [ME, t. L: s. *occāsio* opportunity, fit time] —**Syn. 4.** See **cause.**
occasional (ə kāʹzhə nəl), *adj.* **1.** occurring or appearing on one occasion or another or now and then: *an occasional visitor.* **2.** intended for use whenever needed: *an occasional table.* **3.** pertaining to, arising out of, or intended for a special occasion, ceremony, etc.: *occasional verses; occasional decrees.* **4.** acting or serving for the occasion or on particular occasions. **5.** serving as the occasion or incidental cause.
occasionalism (ə kāʹzhə nə lĭzʹəm), *n. Philos.* the doctrine that the apparent interaction of mind and matter is to be explained by the supposition that God takes an act of the will as the occasion of producing a corresponding movement of the body, and a state of the body as the occasion of producing a corresponding mental state. —**occaʹsionalist,** *n.*
occasionally (ə kāʹzhə nə lĭ), *adv.* at times; now and then.
Occident (ŏkʹsĭ dənt), *n.* **1.** countries in Europe and America (contrasted with the *Orient*). **2.** the Western Hemisphere. **3.** (*l.c.*) the west; the western regions. [ME, t. L: s. *occidens* the west, sunset, prop. ppr., going down]
occidental (ŏkʹsĭ dĕnʹtl), *adj.* **1.** (*usually cap.*) of, pertaining to, or characteristic of the Occident. **2.** western. —*n.* **3.** (*usually cap.*) a native or inhabitant of the Occident. [ME, t. L: s. *occidentālis* western] —**ocʹcidenʹtally,** *adv.*
Occidentalism (ŏkʹsĭ dĕnʹtə lĭzʹəm), *n.* Occidental character or characteristics. —**Ocʹcidenʹtalist,** *n., adj.*
Occidentalize (ŏkʹsĭ dĕnʹtə līzʹ), *v.t.*, **-lized, -lizing.** to make Occidental. Also, **Occidentalise.** —**Ocʹcidenʹtalizaʹtion,** *n.*
occipital (ŏk sĭpʹĭ tl), *adj.* of or pertaining to the back of the head. [t. ML: s. *occipitālis*, der. *occiput* OCCIPUT]
occipital bone, a compound bone which forms the lower posterior part of the skull. See diag. under **cranium.**
occipito-, a word element meaning 'occiput', as in *occipitofrontal* (pertaining to both occiput and forehead), *occipitohyoid* (pertaining to both the occipital and the hyoid bone), *occipitoparietal, occipitosphenoid.* [comb. form repr. L *occiput*]
occiput (ŏkʹsĭ pŭtʹ), *n., pl.* **occipita** (ŏk sĭpʹĭ tə). *Anat.* the back part of the head or skull. [ME, t. L]
occlude (ə klo͞odʹ), *v.*, **-cluded, -cluding.** —*v.t.* **1.** to close, shut, or stop up (a passage, etc.) **2.** to shut in, out, or off. **3.** *Chem.* (of certain metals and other solids) to absorb and retain gases or liquids, in minute pores. —*v.i.* **4.** *Dentistry.* to shut or close against each other, as the opposing teeth of the upper and lower jaws. [t. L: m. s. *occlūdere* shut up, close up] —**occludʹent,** *adj.*
occluded front, *Meteorol.* the residual front after the cold front of a depression has overtaken the warm front and the warm sector has been lifted. Also, **occlusion.**
occlusion (ə klo͞oʹzhən), *n.* **1.** the action of occluding or fact of being occluded. **2.** *Dentistry.* the contact between the teeth of the upper and lower jaws when the jaws are closed. **3.** *Phonet.* the complete closure of the breath passage in the articulation of a sound. **4.** *Meteorol.* **a.** the forming of an occluded front. **b.** an occluded front.
occlusive (ə klo͞oʹsĭv), *adj.* **1.** occluding or tending to occlude. **2.** *Phonet.* of or pertaining to a consonant made by the complete closure of the breath passage. —*n.* **3.** a consonant made by a complete closure of the breath passage; a plosive or a stop consonant.
occult (ō kŭltʹ), *adj.* **1.** beyond the bounds of ordinary knowledge; mysterious. **2.** not disclosed; secret; communicated only to the initiated. **3.** (in early science) **a.** not apparent on mere inspection but discoverable by experimentation. **b.** of a nature not understood, as physical qualities. **c.** dealing with such qualities; experimental: *occult science.* **4.** of the nature of, or pertaining to, certain reputed sciences, as magic, astrology, etc., involving the alleged knowledge or employment of secret or mysterious agencies. **5.** *Obs. or Rare.* hidden from view. —*n.* **6.** occult studies or sciences. **7.** the supernatural. **8.** anything occult. —*v.t.* **9.** to hide; shut off (an object) from view. **10.** *Astron.* to hide (a body) by occultation. —*v.i.* **11.** to become hidden or shut off from view. **12.** (of a light) to shut off periodically, as in lighthouses, etc. [t. L: s. *occultus*, pp., covered over, concealed] —**occultʹer,** *n.*
occultation (ŏkʹŭl tāʹshən), *n.* **1.** *Astron.* the passage of one celestial body in front of a second, thus hiding the second from view (applied esp. to the moon's coming between an observer and a star or planet). **2.** disappearance from view or notice. **3.** the act of occulting. **4.** the resulting state.
occultism (ŏkʹŭl tĭzʹəm), *n.* the doctrine or study of the occult. —**ocʹcultist,** *n., adj.*
occupancy (ŏkʹyo͞o pən sĭ), *n.* **1.** the fact or condition of being an occupant. **2.** the act of taking possession. **3.** actual possession. **4.** the term during which one is an occupant. **5.** exercise of dominion over a thing which has no owner so as to become legal owner.
occupant (ŏkʹyo͞o pənt), *n.* **1.** one who occupies. **2.** a tenant of a house, estate, office, etc. **3.** *Law.* an owner through occupancy. [t. L: s. *occupans*, ppr.]
occupation (ŏkʹyo͞o pāʹshən), *n.* **1.** one's habitual employment; business, trade, or calling. **2.** that in which one is engaged. **3.** possession, as of a place. **4.** the act of occupying. **5.** the state of being occupied. **6.** tenure, as of an office. **7.** seizure, esp. of the territory of a foreign country, as by invasion. **8.** the period during which a country is under the control of foreign military forces. [ME *occupacion*, t. L: m. s. *occupātio* seizing, employment]
—**Syn. 1.** OCCUPATION, BUSINESS, PROFESSION, TRADE refer to the activity to which one regularly devotes oneself, esp. one's regular work, or means of getting a living. OCCUPATION is the general word: *a pleasant or congenial occupation.* BUSINESS esp. suggests a commercial or mercantile occupation: *the printing business.* PROFESSION implies an occupation requiring special knowledge and training in some field of science or learning: *the profession of teaching.* TRADE suggests an occupation involving manual training and skill: *one of the building trades.*
occupational (ŏkʹyo͞o pāʹshə nəl), *adj.* **1.** of or pertaining to occupation. **2.** of, pertaining to, arising from, or connected with an occupation, trade, or calling: *an occupational disease, occupational guidance, occupational hazard.*
occupational therapy, *Med.* a method of therapy consisting of some kind of light work, such as basketry, carpentry, etc., which provides mental diversion or relaxation for the patient, and frequently serves to exercise an affected part or to give vocational training.
occupy (ŏkʹyo͞o pīʹ), *v.*, **-pied, -pying.** —*v.t.* **1.** to take up (space, time, etc.). **2.** to engage or employ (the mind, attention, etc., or the person). **3.** to take possession of (a place), as by invasion. **4.** to hold (a position, office, etc.). **5.** to be resident or established in (a place) as its

tenant; to tenant. —*v.i.* **6.** *Rare or Obs.* to take or hold possession. [ME *occupie(n)*, t. OF: m. *occuper*, t. L: m. *occupāre* take possession of, take up, employ] —**oc′cupi′er,** *n.* —**Syn. 1–4.** See **have.**

occur (ə kû′), *v.i.*, **-curred, -curring. 1.** to come to pass, take place, or happen. **2.** to be met with or found; present itself; appear. **3.** to suggest itself in thought (usually fol. by *to*): *an idea occurred to me.* [earlier *occurr*, t. L: s. *occurrere* run against, go up to, meet, befall] —**Syn. 1.** See **happen.**

occurrence (ə kŭ′rəns), *n.* **1.** the action or fact of occurring. **2.** something that occurs; an event or incident: *a daily occurrence.* —**occur′rent,** *adj.* —**Syn. 2.** See **event.**

ocean (ō′shən), *n.* **1.** the vast body of salt water which covers almost three fourths of the earth's surface. **2.** any of the geographical divisions of this body (commonly given as five: the Atlantic, Pacific, Indian, Arctic, and Antarctic oceans). **3.** a vast expanse or quantity: *an ocean of grass.* [t. L: s. *ōceanus*, t. Gk: m. *ōkeanós* the ocean, orig. the great stream supposed to encompass the earth (see OCEANUS); r. ME *occean*, t. OF] —**o′cean-like′,** *adj.*

oceanarium (ō′shyə nĕə′rĭ əm), *n.* an enclosed part of the sea or a large salt-water pool, in which dolphins, porpoises, and other sea fauna are kept.

oceanaut (ō′shə nôt′), *n.* an aqualung diver who lives in an underwater shelter for long periods, esp. to study or exploit the resources of the sea.

ocean-going (ō′shən gō′ĭng), *adj.* denoting any vessel designed for sailing on the open sea.

Oceania (ō′shĭ ä′nĭ ə), *n.* the islands of the central and S Pacific, including Micronesia, Melanesia, and Polynesia; sometimes also, Australasia and the Malay Archipelago. Also, **Oceanica** (ō′shĭ ăn′ĭ kə). —**O′cean′ian,** *adj., n.*

oceanic (ō′shĭ ăn′ĭk), *adj.* **1.** of or belonging to the ocean; pelagic. **2.** ocean-like; vast.

oceanics (ō′shĭ ăn′ĭks), *n.* the scientific study of oceans.

Oceanid (ō sē′ə nĭd), *n. Gk Myth.* a daughter of Oceanus; an ocean nymph. [t. Gk: m. s. *Ōkeanís*]

oceanog., oceanography.

oceanography (ō′shyə nŏg′rə fĭ), *n.* the branch of physical geography dealing with the ocean. —**o′ceanog′rapher,** *n.* —**oceanographic** (ō′shyə nō grăf′ĭk), **o′ceanograph′ical,** *adj.* —**o′ceanograph′ically,** *adv.*

Oceanus (ō sīə′nəs), *n. Gk Myth.* **1.** the ocean god, and father of the Oceanids. **2.** the great body of water encircling the plain of the earth.

ocellar (ō sĕl′ə), *adj.* pertaining to an ocellus.

ocellated (ŏs′ĭ lā′tĭd, ō sĕl′ā tĭd), *adj.* **1.** (of a spot or marking) eyelike. **2.** having ocelli, or eyelike spots. Also, **ocellate** (ŏs′ĭ lāt′, ō sĕl′ĭt, -āt). [f. s. L *ocellātus* having little eyes + -ED[2]]

ocellation (ŏs′ĭ lā′shən), *n.* an eyelike spot or marking.

Ocellated marking on a peacock's feather

ocellus (ō sĕl′əs), *n., pl.* **ocelli** (ō sĕl′ī). **1.** a type of eye common to invertebrates, consisting of retinal cells, pigments, and nerve fibres. **2.** an eyelike spot, as on a peacock feather. [t. L, dim. of *oculus* eye]

ocelot (ō′sĭ lŏt′), *n.* a spotted, leopard-like cat, *Felis pardalis*, ranging from the central southern U.S. to central South America. [t. F, t. Nahuatl: m. *ocelotl* field tiger]

och (ŏKH), *interj. Scot. and Irish.* (an expression of surprise, regret, disapproval, impatience, etc.) [Gaelic]

Ocelot, *Felis pardalis* (Total length ab. 4 ft, tail ab. 16 in.)

Ochab (*Pol.* ŏKH′ăp),*n.* **Edward** (*Pol.* ĕd′vărt), born 1906, Polish statesman: president 1964–68.

ocher (ō′kə), *n., adj., v.*, **ochered, ochering.** *U.S.* ochre. —**ocherous** (ō′kə rəs), **ochery** (ō′kə rĭ), *adj.*

ochlocracy (ŏk lŏk′rə sĭ), *n., pl.* **-cies.** government by the mob; mobocracy; mob rule. [t. Gk: m. s. *ochlokratia* mob rule] —**ochlocrat** (ŏk′lə krăt′), *n.* —**och′locrat′ic, och′locrat′ical,** *adj.*

ochone (ə KHōn′), *interj. Irish and Scot.* ohone.

ochre (ō′kə), *n., adj., v.*, **ochred, ochring.** —*n.* **1.** any of a class of natural earths, mixtures of hydrated oxide of iron with various earthy materials, ranging in colour from pale yellow to orange and red, and used as pigments. **2.** the colour of this, ranging from pale yellow to an orangish or reddish yellow. **3.** *Slang.* money, esp. gold coin. —*adj.* **4.** of the colour of ochre. —*v.t.* **5.** to colour or mark with ochre. Also, *U.S.*, **ocher.** [ME *oker*, t. OF: m. *ocre*, t. L: m. *ōchra*, t. Gk: yellow ochre] —**ochreous** (ō′krĭ əs, ō′kə rəs), **ochrous** (ō′krəs), **ochry** (ō′kə rĭ, ō′krĭ), *adj.*

ochrea (ŏk′rĭ ə), *n., pl.* **-reae** (-rĭ ē′). ocrea.

ochroid (ō′kroid), *adj.* yellow as ochre. [t. Gk: m. s. *ōchroeidḗs* pallid]

-ock, a noun suffix used to make descriptive names, as in *ruddock* (lit., the red one); diminutives, as in *hillock*; etc. [ME *-ok*, OE *-oc, -uc*]

Ockenheim (*Du.* ô′kən KHĕm), *n.* Okeghem.

Ockham (ŏk′əm), *n.* **William of.** See **Occam.**

o'clock (ə klŏk′), *adv.* of or by the clock (used in specifying or enquiring the hour of the day): *it is now one o'clock.*

O'Connell (ō kŏn′əl), *n.* **Daniel,** 1775–1847, Irish political agitator and orator.

O'Connor (ō kŏn′ə), *n.* **1. Frank,** 1903–66, Irish writer. **2. Thomas Power,** 1848–1929, Irish journalist, author, and political leader.

ocotillo (ō′kə tē′lyō; *Sp.* ŏ kŏ tē′lyŏ), *n., pl.* **-los.** a spiny woody shrub, *Fouqueria splendens*, of the arid regions of Mexico and the south-western U.S. [t. Mex. Sp., dim. of *ocote* kind of pine, t. Aztec: m. *ocotl*]

ocrea (ŏk′rĭ ə), *n., pl.* **ocreae** (ŏk′rĭ ē′). *Bot., Zool.* a sheathing part, as a pair of stipules united about a stem. Also, **ochrea.** [t. L: greave, legging]

ocreate (ŏk′rĭ ĭt, -āt′), *adj.* having an ocrea or ocreae; sheathed.

oct-, var. of **octa-** or **octo-** before a vowel.

Oct., October.

oct., octavo.

octa-, a word element meaning 'eight'. Also, **oct-, octo-.** [t. Gk, comb. form of *oktṓ*]

O, Ocrea

octad (ŏk′tăd), *n.* **1.** a group or series of eight. **2.** *Chem.* an element, atom, or radical having a valency of eight. [t. LL: s. *octas*, t. Gk: m. *oktás*] —**octad′ic,** *adj.*

octagon (ŏk′tə gən), *n.* a polygon having eight angles and eight sides. [t. Gk: s. *oktágōnos* octangular. See OCTA-, -GON]

octagonal (ŏk tăg′ə nəl), *adj.* having eight angles and eight sides. —**octag′onally,** *adv.*

Octagon

octahedral (ŏk′tə hē′drəl), *adj.* having the form of an octahedron.

octahedrite (ŏk′tə hē′drīt), *n.* anatase.

octahedron (ŏk′tə hē′drən), *n., pl.* **-drons, -dra** (-drə). a solid figure having eight faces. [t. Gk: m. *oktáedron.* See OCT-, -HEDRON]

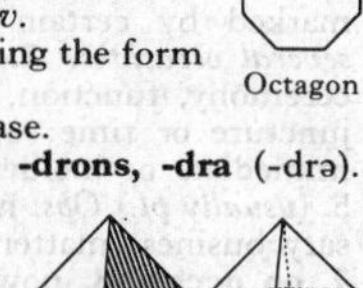

Regular octahedrons

octal (ŏk′tl), *adj. Computers.* of or pertaining to a number system based on the number 'eight'.

octamerous (ŏk tăm′ə rəs), *adj.* **1.** consisting of or divided into eight parts. **2.** *Bot.* (of flowers) having eight members in each whorl. [f. s. Gk *oktamerḗs* of eight parts + -OUS]

octameter (ŏk tăm′ĭ tə), *Pros.* —*adj.* **1.** consisting of eight measures or feet. —*n.* **2.** an octameter verse. [t. LL, t. Gk: m. *oktámetros* of eight measures]

octan (ŏk′tən), *adj.* (of a fever) recurring every eighth day.

octane (ŏk′tān), *n. Chem.* any of eighteen isomeric saturated hydrocarbons, C_8H_{18}, some of which are obtained in the distillation and cracking of petroleum. [f. OCT- + -ANE]

octane number, (of a grade of petrol) a designation of antiknock quality, numerically equal to the percentage of iso-octane by volume in a mixture of iso-octane and normal heptane that matches the given grade of petrol in antiknock characteristics. Also, **octane rating.**

octangular (ŏk tăng′gyŏŏ lə), *adj.* having eight angles. [f. s. L *octangulus* eight-angled + -AR[1]]

Octans (ŏk′tănz), *n. Astron.* the Octant, a southern constellation.

octant (ŏk′tənt), *n.* **1.** the eighth part of a circle. **2.** *Maths.* each of the eighths into which three mutually perpendicular planes with a common point divide space. **3.** an instrument similar to a sextant, having a graduated arc of 45°, used for measuring angles, esp, in navigation. **4.** the position of one heavenly body when 45° distant from another. **5.** (*cap.*) *Astron.* the constellation Octans. [t. L: s. *octans*] —**octantal** (ŏk tăn′tl), *adj.*

octarchy (ŏk′tä′kĭ), *n., pl.* **-chies. 1.** a government by eight persons. **2.** a group of eight states or kingdoms.

octastyle (ŏk′tə stīl′), *adj. Archit.* denoting a portico having eight frontal columns.

octave (ŏk′tāv *for* 6; *otherwise* ŏk′tĭv), *n.* **1.** *Music.* **a.** a note on the eighth degree from a given note (counted as the first). **b.** the interval between such notes. **c.** the harmonic combination of such notes. **d.** a series of notes, or of keys of an instrument, extending through this interval. 2. (in organ building) a stop whose pipes give notes an octave above the normal pitch of the keys used. 3. a series or group of eight. 4. *Pros.* a group or a stanza of eight lines, as the first eight lines of a sonnet. 5. the eighth of a series. 6. *Eccles.* **a.** the eighth day from a feast day (counted as the first). **b.** the period of eight days beginning with a feast day. 7. *Fencing.* **a.** the eighth of eight defensive positions. **b.** one of the divisions of the target area on an opponent's body. —*adj.* **8.** pitched an octave higher. [ME, t. L: m. *octāva* (fem.) eighth] —**octaval** (ŏk tā′vəl, ŏk′tə-), *adj.*

Octavian (ŏk tā′vyən), *n.* See **Augustus.**

octavo (ŏk tā′vō), *n., pl.* **-vos,** *adj. Bookbinding.* —*n.* **1.** a book size (about 6 × 9 inches) determined by printing on sheets folded to form eight leaves or sixteen pages. *Abbrev.:* 8vo or 8°. —*adj.* **2.** in octavo. Also, **eightvo.** [short for NL phrase *in octāvō* in an eighth (of a sheet)]

octennial (ŏk tĕn′yəl), *adj.* **1.** occurring every eight years. **2.** of or for eight years. [f. s. LL *octennium* a period of eight years + AL[1]] —**octen′nially,** *adv.*

octet (ŏk tĕt′), *n.* **1.** a company of eight singers or players. **2.** a musical composition for eight voices or instruments. **3.** *Pros.* **a.** a group of eight lines of verse, esp. the first eight lines (octave) of a sonnet. **4.** *Chem.* a stable group of eight electrons which form a shell surrounding an atomic nucleus. **5.** any group of eight. Also, **octette.** [f. OCT(O)- + *-et* as in *duet*]

octillion (ŏk tĭl′yən), *n.* **1.** a cardinal number represented (in England and Germany) by one followed by 48 zeros or (in the U.S. and France) by one followed by 27 zeros. —*adj.* **2.** amounting to one octillion in number. [t. F: f. *oct-* OCT- + (*m*)*illion* MILLION] —**octil′lionth,** *n., adj.*

octo-, var. of **octa-.**

October (ŏk tō′bə), *n.* the tenth month of the year, containing 31 days. [ME and OE, t. L: the eighth month of the early Roman year]

October Revolution. See **Russian Revolution** (def. 2).

Octobrist (ŏk tō′brĭst), *n.* a member of a Russian political party, so called because it based its policy on Tsar Nicholas II's manifesto of October 1905. [trans. of Russ *oktyabrist*]

octodecimo (ŏk′tō dĕs′ĭ mō′), *n., pl.* **-mos,** *adj.* —*n.* **1.** a book size (about 4 × 6¼ inches) determined by printing on sheets folded to form eighteen leaves or thirty-six pages; eighteenmo. *Abbrev.:* 18mo *or* 18°. —*adj.* **2.** in octodecimo. [short for NL phrase *in octōdecimō* in an eighteenth (of a sheet)]

octogenarian (ŏk′tō jĭ nēə′rĭ ən), *adj.* Also, **octogenary** (ŏk tŏj′ĭ nə rĭ). **1.** of the age of 80 years. **2.** between 80 and 90 years old. —*n.* **3.** an octogenerian person. [f. s. L *octōgēnārius* containing eighty + -AN]

octonary (ŏk′tə nə rĭ), *adj., n., pl.* **-naries.** —*adj.* **1.** pertaining to the number eight. **2.** consisting of eight. **3.** proceeding by eights. —*n.* **4.** a group of eight; an ogdoad. **5.** *Pros.* eight lines, as a stanza. [t. L: m. s. *octōnārius* containing eight]

octopod (ŏk′tə pŏd′), *n.* any of the *Octopoda*, an order or suborder of eight-armed dibranchiate cephalopods that includes the octopuses and paper nautiluses.

octopus (ŏk′tə pəs), *n., pl.* **-puses, -pi** (-pī′). **1.** any animal of the genus *Octopus*, comprising octopods with a soft, oval body and eight sucker-bearing arms, and living mostly on the sea bottom. **2.** a spider (def. 4). **3.** any octopod. **4.** anything likened to an octopus. [t. NL, t. Gk: m. *oktṓpous* eight-footed]

Octopus, *Octopus vulgaris* (Up to 3 ft long)

octoroon (ŏk′tə ro͞on′), *n.* a person having one-eighth Negro ancestry; offspring of a quadroon and a white. [f. OCTO- + *-roon*, modelled on QUADROON]

octosyllable (ŏk′tō sĭl′ə bl), *n.* a word or a line of verse of eight syllables. —**octosyllabic** (ŏk′tō sĭ lăb′ĭk), *adj.*

octroi (ŏk′trwä; *Fr.* ŏk trwȧ′), *n.* **1.** a local tax levied on certain articles, such as foodstuffs, on their admission into a town. **2.** the place at which the tax is collected. **3.** the officials collecting it. [F, der. *octroyer* grant, ult. der. L *auctor* granter, author]

O.C.T.U., *Mil.* Officer Cadets Training Unit.

octuple (ŏk′tyo͞o pl), *adj., v.,* **-pled, -pling.** —*adj.* **1.** eightfold; eight times as great. **2.** having eight effective units or elements. —*v.t.* **3.** to make eight times as great. [t. L: m. s. *octuplus* eightfold]

octuplet (ŏk′tyo͞o plĭt), *n.* **1.** any group or combination of eight related items. **2.** *Music.* a group of eight notes to be played or sung in the time of six.

ocular (ŏk′yo͞o lə), *adj.* **1.** of or pertaining to the eye: *ocular movements.* See diag. under **eye. 2.** of the nature of an eye: *an ocular organ.* **3.** performed or perceived by the eye or eyesight. —*n.* **4.** the eyepiece of an optical instrument. [t. LL: s. *oculāris* of the eyes] —**oc′ularly,** *adv.*

oculist (ŏk′yo͞o lĭst), *n.* a doctor of medicine skilled in the examination and treatment of the eye; an ophthalmologist. [t. F: m. *oculiste,* f. s. L *oculus* eye + *-iste* -IST]

oculomotor (ŏk′yo͞o lō mō′tə), *adj.* moving the eyeball. [f. *oculo-* (comb. form repr. L *oculus* eye) + MOTOR]

oculomotor nerve, *Anat.* either of the two cranial nerves which supply most of the muscles of the eyeball.

od (ŏd), *n.* a hypothetical force formerly held to pervade all nature and to manifest itself in magnetism, mesmerism, chemical action, etc. Also, **odyl, odyle.** [arbitrary name coined by Baron Karl von Reichenbach, 1788–1869, German scientist]

Od (ŏd), *interj. Archaic or Dial.* reduced form of **God,** used interjectionally and in minced oaths. Also, **'Od, Odd.**

O/D, 1. on demand. **2.** overdraft. **3.** overdrawn.

odalisque (ō′də lĭsk), *n.* a female slave or concubine in a harem, esp. in that of the Sultan of Turkey. Also, **odalisk.** [t. F, t. Turk.: m. *ōdalik,* der. *ōdah* room]

Odawara (ō dä′wə rə, ŏd′ə wä′rə), *n.* a town in Japan, in SE central Honshu island. 143,377 (1965).

odd (ŏd), *adj.* **1.** differing in character from what is ordinary or usual: *an odd choice.* **2.** singular or peculiar in a freakish or eccentric way, as persons or their manners, etc. **3.** fantastic or bizarre, as things. **4.** out-of-the-way; secluded. **5.** additional to a whole mentioned in round numbers; being a surplus over a definite quantity; more or less: *she owed him fifty-odd pounds.* **6.** additional to what is taken into account: *ten pounds and a few odd pence.* **7.** being part of a pair, set, or series of which the rest is lacking: *an odd glove.* **8.** (of a pair) not matching: *he was wearing odd shoes.* **9.** leaving a remainder of 1 when divided by 2, as a number (opposed to *even*). **10.** remaining after a division into pairs, or into equal numbers or parts. **11.** left over after the rest have been consumed, used up, etc. **12.** occasional or casual: *odd jobs.* **13.** not forming part of any particular group, set, or class: *odd bits of information.* **14. odd man out,** one left over when the rest have been arranged in pairs, or in a convenient group or groups. —*n.* **15.** that which is odd. **16.** *Golf.* **a.** a stroke more than the opponent has played. **b.** a stroke taken from a player's total score for a hole in order to give him odds. See also **odds.** [ME *odde,* t. Scand.; cf. Icel. *odda-tala* odd number] —**odd′ly,** *adv.* —**odd′ness,** *n.* —**Syn. 1.** See **strange.**

Oddfellow (ŏd′fĕl′ō), *n.* a member of a secret social and benevolent society, the 'Independent Order of Oddfellows', originated in England in the 18th century.

oddish (ŏd′ĭsh), *adj.* rather odd; queer.

oddity (ŏd′ĭ tĭ), *n., pl.* **-ties. 1.** the quality of being odd; singularity or strangeness. **2.** an odd characteristic or peculiarity. **3.** an odd person or thing.

oddment (ŏd′mənt), *n.* **1.** an odd article, bit, remnant, or the like. **2.** an article belonging to a broken or incomplete set. **3.** *Print.* any individual portion of a book excluding the text, as the frontispiece, index, etc.

odd-pinnate (ŏd′pĭn′āt, -ĭt), *adj. Bot.* pinnate with an odd terminal leaflet.

odds (ŏdz), *n.* (*usually construed as pl.*) **1.** an equalizing allowance, as that given to a weaker side in a contest. **2.** the amount by which the bet of one party to a wager exceeds that of the other. **3.** balance of probability in favour of something occurring or being the case. **4.** advantage or superiority on the side of one of two contending parties: *to strive against odds.* **5.** difference in the way of benefit or detriment. **6.** the amount of difference. **7. at odds,** in disagreement; at variance. **8. make no odds,** not to matter; be of no importance. **9. over the odds,** too much. **10. what's the odds?,** *Colloq.* what difference does it make?

odds and ends, odd bits; scraps; remnants; fragments.

odds-on (ŏdz′ŏn′), *adj.* (of a chance) better than even; that is more likely to win, succeed, etc.

ode (ōd), *n.* **1.** a lyric poem typically of elaborate or irregular metrical form and expressive of exalted or enthusiastic emotion. **2.** (orig.) a poem intended to be sung. **3. regular** or **Pindaric ode,** a complex poetic type, consisting of strophes and antistrophes identical in form, with contrasting epodes, the three units being repeated in the poem. **4. irregular, pseudo-Pindaric,** or **Cowleian ode,** a poetic form in the general style of the regular ode, but lacking its strict complex form and written in a series of irregular strophes. **5. Horatian** or **Sapphic ode,** an ode in which one stanzaic form is repeated. [t. F, t. LL: m. *ōda,* t. Gk: m. *ōidḗ,* contr. of *aoidḗ* song]

-ode[1], a suffix of nouns denoting something having some resemblance to what is indicated by the preceding part of the word, as in *phyllode.* [t. Gk: m. *-ōdēs* like, contr. of *-oeidēs* - OID]

-ode[2], a noun suffix meaning 'way', as in *anode, electrode.* [t. Gk: m. *-odos,* der. *hodós* way]

Odelsting (ō′dəls tĭng′), *n.* See **Storting.** Also, **Odelsthing.**

Odense (*Dan.* ô′thən sə), *n.* a seaport in S Denmark, on Fyn island. 111,145 (1960).

Oder (ō′də; *Ger.* ō′dər), *n.* a river flowing from the Carpathians in N Czechoslovakia through SW Poland and along the border between East Germany and Poland and into the Baltic. ab. 550 mi.

Oder-Neisse Line (ō′də nī′sə), present boundary between Poland and East Germany. See **Germany.**

Odessa (ō dĕs′ə; *Russ.* ȧ dyĕ′sə), *n.* a seaport in the SW Soviet Union in Europe, on the Black Sea: the principal export centre of Ukrainian grain. 735,000 (est. 1965).

odeum (ō dē′əm), *n., pl.* **odea** (ō dē′ə). **1.** a hall or structure for musical or dramatic performances. **2.** (in ancient Greece and Rome) a roofed building for musical performances. [t. L, t. Gk: m. *ōideîon* music hall]

odic[1] (ō′dĭk), *adj.* of an ode. [f. ODE + -IC]

odic[2] (ŏd′ĭk), *adj.* of or pertaining to the hypothetical force od. [f. OD + -IC]

Odin (ō′dĭn), *n. Scand. Myth.* the chief deity, being the god of wisdom, culture, war, and the dead. Also, **Othin.** [t. Icel.: m. *Odhinn,* c. E *Woden,* G *Wotan*]

odious (ō′dyəs), *adj.* **1.** deserving of or exciting hatred; hateful or detestable. **2.** highly offensive; disgusting. [ME, t. L: m. s. *odiōsus* hateful] **—o′diously,** *adv.* **—o′diousness,** *n.* **—Syn. 1.** See **hateful.**

odium (ō′dyəm), *n.* **1.** hatred; dislike. **2.** the reproach, discredit, or opprobrium attaching to something hated or odious. **3.** the state of being hated. [t. L: hatred]

Odoacer (ŏd′ō ā′sə), *n.* A.D. 434?–493, first barbarian ruler of Italy, A.D. 476–493. Also, **Odovacar.**

odograph (ŏd′ə grăf′, -gräf′), *n.* **1.** an odometer. **2.** a pedometer. [var. of HODOGRAPH]

odometer (ŏ dŏm′ĭ tə), *n.* an instrument for measuring distance passed over, as by a motor vehicle. Also, **hodometer.** [var. of *hodometer,* f. Gk *hodó(s)* way + -METER[1]] **—odom′etry,** *n.*

odont-, var. of **odonto-** before a vowel.

-odont, a terminal word element equivalent to **odonto-.**

odontalgia (ŏd′ŏn tăl′jyə), *n. Pathol.* toothache. **—od′ontal′gic,** *adj.*

odonto-, a word element meaning 'tooth'. Also, **odont-.** [t. Gk, comb. form of s. *odoús*]

odontoblast (ŏ dŏn′tə blăst′), *n. Anat.* one of a layer of cells which, in the development of a tooth, give rise to the dentine. **—odon′toblas′tic,** *adj.*

odontoglossum (ŏ dŏn′tə glŏs′əm), *n.* any of the epiphytic orchids constituting the genus *Odontoglossum,* natives of the mountainous regions from Bolivia to Mexico. [t. NL, f. Gk: *odonto-* ODONTO- + m. *glôssa* tongue]

odontograph (ŏ dŏn′tə grăf′, -gräf′), *n.* an instrument for marking out the forms of geared teeth or ratchets.

odontoid (ŏ dŏn′toid), *adj.* **1.** denoting a toothlike process, as that of the axis, or second cervical vertebra, upon which the atlas rotates. **2.** resembling a tooth. [t. Gk: m. s. *odontoeidēs* toothlike]

odontology (ŏd′ŏn tŏl′ə jĭ), *n.* **1.** the science or art which treats of the study of the teeth and their surrounding tissues, and of the prevention and cure of their diseases. **2.** dentistry. **—odontological** (ŏ dŏn′tə lŏj′ĭ kl), *adj.* **—od′ontol′ogist,** *n.*

odontophore (ŏ dŏn′tə fō′), *n. Zool.* a structure in the mouth of most molluscs, over which the radula is drawn backwards and forwards in the process of breaking up food. [t. Gk: m. s. *odontophóros* bearing teeth] **—odontophoral** (ŏd′ŏn tŏf′ə rəl), **odontophorine** (ŏd′ŏn tŏf′ə rīn′, -rĭn), **od′ontoph′orous,** *adj.*

odor (ō′də), *n. U.S.* odour.

odoriferous (ō′də rĭf′ə rəs), *adj.* yielding or diffusing an odour, esp. a fragrant one. [ME, f. L *odōrifer* bringing odours + -OUS] **—o′dorif′erously,** *adv.* **—o′dorif′erousness,** *n.*

odorous (ō′də rəs), *adj.* having or diffusing an odour, esp. a fragrant odour. [t. L: m. *odōrus* emitting a scent] **—o′dorously,** *adv.* **—o′dorousness,** *n.*

odour (ō′də), *n.* **1.** that property of a substance which affects the sense of smell: *rank odours.* **2.** an agreeable scent; fragrance. **3.** a bad smell. **4.** a savour or quality characteristic or suggestive of something. **5.** repute or estimation: *in bad odour.* Also, *U.S.,* **odor.** [ME, t. OF, t. L] **—o′dourless,** *adj.*

Odovacar (ŏd′ō vā′kə), *n.* Odoacer.

odyl (ŏd′ĭl), *n.* od. Also, **od′yle.** [f. OD + -YL] **—odylic** (ŏ dĭl′ĭk), *adj.*

-odynia, a word element meaning 'pain'. [t. NL, t. Gk]

Odysseus (ə dĭs′yo͞os), *n. Gk Legend.* the son of Laertes, husband of Penelope, and father of Telemachus: wisest and wiliest of the Greek leaders. Also, **Ulysses.**

Odyssey (ŏd′ĭ sĭ), *n.* **1.** Homer's epic poem describing the ten years' wandering of Odysseus in returning to Ithaca after the Trojan War. **2.** (*also l.c.*) any long series of wanderings. [t. Gk: m. s. *Odýsseia,* der. *Odysseús* Odysseus, Ulysses] **—Odyssean** (ŏd′ĭ sē′ən), *adj.*

OE, Old English. Also, **OE., O.E.**

O.E.C.D., Organization for Economic Cooperation and Development.

oecology (ē kŏl′ə jĭ), *n.* ecology.

oecumenical (ē′kyo͞o mĕn′ĭ kl), *adj.* ecumenical. Also, **oe′cumen′ic.**

O.E.D., Oxford English Dictionary.

oedema (ē dē′mə), *n., pl.* **-mata** (-mə tə). *Pathol.* effusion of serous fluid into the interstices of cells in tissue spaces or into body cavities. Also, **edema.** [NL, t. Gk: m. *oídēma* a swelling] **—oedematous** (ē dĕm′ə təs), **oedematose** (ē dĕm′ə tōs′), *adj.*

Oedipus (ē′dĭ pəs), *n. Gk Legend.* a son of Laius and Jocasta. Reared by the king of Corinth, he slew his father involuntarily and solved the riddle of the Sphinx, thereby becoming King of Thebes and unwittingly winning the hand of his mother in marriage. When the nature of his deeds become apparent, Jocasta hanged herself, and Oedipus tore out his eyes.

Oedipus complex, *Psychol.* **1.** the unresolved desire of a child for sexual gratification through the parent of the opposite sex. This involves, first, identification with and, later, hatred for the parent of the same sex, who is considered by the child as a rival. **2.** sexual desire of the son for the mother. Cf. **Electra complex.**

oeil-de-boeuf (*Fr.* œy də bœf′), *n., pl.* **oeils-de-boeuf** (*Fr.* œy də-). *French.* a comparatively small round or oval window, as in a frieze. [F: eye of ox, bull's eye]

oeillade (û yäd′; *Fr.* œ yȧd′), *n. French.* an amorous glance; ogle. [F, t. It.: m. *occhiata* glance (der. *occhio* eye, g. L *oculus*)]

oenology (ē nŏl′ə jĭ), *n.* the science of viniculture. [f. m. Gk *oîno(s)* wine + -LOGY] **—oenological** (ē′nə lŏj′ĭ kl), *adj.* **—oenol′ogist,** *n.*

oenomel (ē′nə mĕl′), *n.* **1.** a drink made of wine mixed with honey. **2.** something combining strength with sweetness. [t. LL: s. *oenomeli,* t. Gk: m. *oinómeli* wine mixed with honey]

Oenone (ē nō′nĭ), *n. Gk Myth.* a nymph living on Mount Ida near Troy. She was the lover of Paris, who later deserted her for Helen.

o'er (ô), *prep., adv. Poetic or Dial.* over.

oersted (û′stĕd), *n.* **1.** a unit of magnetic intensity equal to the intensity produced by a magnetic pole of unit strength at a distance of one centimetre. **2.** *Obs.* the unit of magnetic reluctance equal to the reluctance of a centimetre cube of vacuum between parallel surfaces. [named after H. C. *Oersted,* 1777–1851, Danish physicist]

oesophageal (ē sŏf′ə jē′əl, -jĭəl′), *adj.* pertaining to the oesophagus. Also, **esophageal.**

oesophagus (ē sŏf′ə gəs), *n., pl.* **-gi** (-gī′). *Anat., Zool.* a tube connecting the mouth or pharynx with the stomach in invertebrate and vertebrate animals; gullet. Also, **esophagus.** See diag. under **intestine.** [t. NL, t. Gk: m. *oisophágos*]

oestradiol (ēs′trə dī′ŏl), *n. Biochem.* the principal oestrogenic hormone, $C_{18}H_{24}O_2$, produced by the ovaries. Also, *U.S.,* **estradiol.**

oestriol (ēs′trĭ ŏl′), *n. Biochem.* an oestrogenic hormone, $C_{18}H_{22}O_3$, occurring in the placenta and in pregnancy urine. Also, *U.S.,* **estriol.**

oestrogen (ēs′trə jən), *n. Biochem.* any one of a group of female sex hormones which induce oestrus in immature or spayed mammals. Also, *U.S.,* **estrogen. —oestrogenic** (ēs′trə jĕn′ĭk), *adj.*

oestrone (ēs′trōn), *n. Biochem.* an oestrogenic hormone, $C_{18}H_{22}O_2$, manufactured by the ovarian follicles and found in pregnancy urine and placental tissue. Also, *U.S.,* **estrone.**

oestrous (ēs′trəs), *adj.* involving or pertaining to the oestrus. Also, *U.S.,* **estrous.**

oestrous cycle, *Zool.* a recurrent series of physiological changes in sexual and other organs in female mammals, extending from one rutting period to the next. Also, *U.S.,* **estrus cycle.**

oestrus (ēs′trəs), *n.* **1.** Also, **oestrum** (ēs′trəm), *U.S.,* **estrus.** the oestrous cycle in mammals, esp. females. **2.** passion or passionate impulse. **3.** a stimulus. [t. L, t. Gk: m. *oîstros* gadfly, sting, frenzy]

oeuvre (*Fr.* œ′vr), *n.*, *pl.* **oeuvres** (*Fr.* œ′vr). *French.* work, esp. a literary or artistic work.

of (ŏv; *unstressed* əv), *prep.* a particle indicating: **1.** distance or direction from, separation, deprivation, riddance, etc.: *within a mile of; to cure of.* **2.** derivation, origin, or source: *of good family; the plays of Shakespeare.* **3.** cause, occasion, or reason: *to die of hunger.* **4.** material, substance, or contents: *a packet of sugar; a suit of mohair.* **5.** a relation of identity: *the city of Paris.* **6.** belonging or possession, connection, or association: *the queen of England; the property of all.* **7.** inclusion in a number, class, or whole: *one of us.* **8.** objective relation: *the ringing of bells.* **9.** reference or respect: *talk of peace.* **10.** qualities or attributes: *a man of tact.* **11.** time: *of an evening.* **12.** *U.S.* to or before (a designated hour of the clock): *twenty minutes of five is 4.40.* **13.** the attribution of a quality to: *it was good of you to come.* **14.** the attribution of a quality with respect to: *fleet of foot.* **15.** *Chiefly Archaic.* the agent by whom something is done: *beloved of all.* [ME and OE, c. G and L *ab*, Gk *apó*. See OFF]

of-, var. of **ob-**, (by assimilation) before *f*, as in *offend.*

OF, Old French. Also, **OF., O.F.**

O'Faoláin (ō fā′loin), *n.* **Sean** (shôn), born 1900, Irish writer.

off (ŏf), *adv.* **1.** away from a position occupied, or from contact, connection, or attachment: *take off one's hat; the handle has come off.* **2.** to or at a distance from, or away from, a place: *to run off.* **3.** away from or out of association or relation: *to cast off.* **4.** deviating from, especially from what is normal or regular. **5.** as a deduction: *10 per cent off on all cash purchases.* **6.** away; distant (in future time): *summer is only a week off.* **7.** out of operation or effective existence; disconnected. **8.** so as to interrupt continuity or cause discontinuance: *to break off negotiations.* **9.** away from employment or service: *we have four days off at Easter.* **10.** so as to exhaust, finish, or complete; completely: *to kill off vermin.* **11.** forthwith or immediately: *right off.* **12.** with prompt or ready performance: *to dash off a letter.* **13.** to fulfilment, or into execution or effect: *the contest came off on the day fixed.* **14.** so as to cause or undergo reduction or diminution: *to wear off.* **15.** on one's way or journey, as from a place: *to see a friend off on a journey.* **16.** *Naut.* away from the land, a ship, the wind, etc. **17. be off,** to depart; leave. **18. off and on, a.** Also, **on and off.** intermittently: *to work off and on.* **b.** *Naut.* on alternate tacks. **19. off with** (anything specified), to remove; take or cut off: *off with his head.* —*prep.* **20.** away from; so as no longer to be or rest on: *to fall off a horse.* **21.** deviating from (something normal or usual): *off one's balance.* **22.** from by subtraction or deduction: *25 per cent off the marked price.* **23.** away or disengaged from (duty, work, etc.). **24.** *Slang.* refraining from (some food, activity, etc.): *to be off gambling.* **25.** distant from: *a village some miles off the main road.* **26.** leading out of: *an alley off the high street.* **27.** *Colloq.* from, indicating source: *I bought it off him.* **28.** from, indicating material: *to make a meal off fish.* **29.** *Naut.* to seaward of. —*adj.* **30.** wide of the truth or fact; in error: *you are off on that point.* **31.** no longer in effect or operation: *the agreement is off.* **32.** as to condition, circumstances, supplies, etc.: *better off.* **33.** (of time) on which work is suspended: *pastime for one's off hours.* **34.** not so good or satisfactory as usual: *an off year for apples.* **35.** below the normal or expected standard; inferior. **36.** (of food) tainted. **37.** of less than the ordinary activity, liveliness, or lively interest: *an off season in the woollen trade.* **38.** (of a chance) remote. **39.** (with reference to animals or vehicles) right (opposed to *near* or *left*). **40.** *Naut.* farther from the shore. **41.** *Cricket.* of, pertaining to, or denoting that part of the field to the right of and behind the batsman as he faces the bowler (whether he is left-handed or right-handed). —*n.* **42.** the state or fact of being off. **43.** *Cricket.* the off side. —*interj.* **44.** be off! stand off! off with you! [ME and OE *of* of, off. See OF]

off., 1. offered. 2. office. 3. officer. 4. official.

offal (ŏf′əl), *n.* **1.** the waste or inedible parts of a butchered animal. **2.** refuse in general. [ME, f. *of* off + *fal* fall]

Offaly (ŏf′ə lĭ), *n.* a county in the Republic of Ireland, in Leinster. 51,533 pop. (1961); 771 sq. mi. *Co. town:* Tullamore.

off-beat (ŏf′bēt′), *adj.* **1.** unusual; unconventional. **2.** (in jazz, etc.) having a strong accent on the second and fourth beat of a four-beat bar. —*n.* **3.** *Music.* the unaccented or less strongly accented beat of a bar.

off break, *Cricket.* a ball bowled so as to change direction from leg to off when it pitches.

off-chance (ŏf′chäns′), *n.* a remote chance or possibility.

off-colour (ŏf′kŭl′ə), *adj.* **1.** defective in colour, as a gem. **2.** *Colloq.* unwell. **3.** *Chiefly U.S.* of doubtful propriety or taste: *an off-colour story.* Also, *U.S.*, **off-color.**

Offenbach (ŏf′ən bäk′; *also, Fr.* ō fĕn bȧk′ *for 1, Ger.* ŏf′ən bȧKH *for 2*), *n.* **1. Jacques** (Fr. zhȧk), 1819–80, French composer. **2.** a town in West Germany, in S Hesse, on the river Main, near Frankfurt. 117,800 (est. 1966).

offence (ə fĕns′), *n.* **1.** a transgression; a wrong; a sin. **2.** any crime. **3.** a crime which is not indictable, but is punishable summarily (**summary offence**). **4.** a cause of transgression or wrong. **5.** something that offends. **6.** the act of offending or displeasing. **7.** the feeling of resentful displeasure caused: *to give offence.* **8.** the act of attacking; attack or assault: *weapons of offence.* **9.** the persons, side, etc., attacking. **10.** *Obs.* injury, harm, or hurt. Also, *U.S.*, **offense.** [ME *offens*, t. L: s. *offensus*] —**Syn. 1.** See **crime.**

offenceless (ə fĕns′lĭs), *adj.* **1.** without offence. **2.** incapable of offence or attack. **3.** unoffending.

offend (ə fĕnd′), *v.t.* **1.** to irritate in mind or feelings; cause resentful displeasure in. **2.** to affect (the sense, taste, etc.) disagreeably. **3.** *Obs.* to violate or transgress. **4.** *Obs.* (in biblical use) to cause to sin. —*v.i.* **5.** to give offence or cause displeasure. **6.** to err in conduct; commit a sin, crime, or fault. [ME *offende(n)*, t. OF: m. *offendre*, t. L: m. *offendere* strike against, displease] —**Syn. 1.** provoke, insult.

offender (ə fĕn′də), *n.* **1.** one who offends. **2.** a criminal; lawbreaker.

offensive (ə fĕn′sĭv), *adj.* **1.** causing offence or displeasure; irritating; highly annoying. **2.** disagreeable to the sense: *an offensive odour.* **3.** repugnant to the moral sense, good taste, or the like; insulting. **4.** pertaining to offence or attack: *offensive movements.* **5.** consisting in or characterized by attack: *offensive warfare.* —*n.* **6.** the position or attitude of offence or attack: *to take the offensive.* **7.** an offensive movement: *the big Soviet offensive.* —**offen′sively,** *adv.* —**offen′siveness,** *n.* —**Syn. 1.** See **hateful. 2.** disagreeable, distasteful, disgusting, repulsive, obnoxious. —**Ant. 1, 2.** pleasing.

offer (ŏf′ə), *v.t.* **1.** to present for acceptance or rejection; proffer: *to offer someone a cigarette.* **2.** to put forward for consideration; *to offer a suggestion.* **3.** to make a show of intention (to do something): *we did not offer to go first.* **4.** to propose or volunteer (to do something): *she offered to accompany me.* **5.** to proffer (oneself) for marriage. **6.** to present solemnly as an act of worship or devotion, as to God, a deity, a saint, etc.; sacrifice. **7.** to present; put forward: *she offered no response.* **8.** to attempt to inflict, do, or make: *to offer battle.* **9.** to do or make (violence, resistance, etc.) actually. **10.** to present to sight or notice. **11.** to present for sale. **12.** to tender or bid as a price: *to offer five pounds for a radio.* **13.** to render (homage, thanks, etc.). —*v.i.* **14.** to make a proposal or suggestion. **15.** to make an offer of marriage; propose. **16.** to present itself; occur: *whenever an occasion offered.* **17.** to present something as an act of worship or devotion; sacrifice. **18.** *Obs. or Rare.* to make an attempt (fol. by *at*). —*n.* **19.** act of offering: *an offer of assistance.* **20.** a proposal of marriage. **21.** a proposal to give or accept something as a price or equivalent for something else; a bid: *an offer of £10,000 for a house.* **22.** the condition of being offered: *an offer for sale.* **23.** something offered. **24.** *Law.* a proposal which requires only acceptance in order to create a contract. **25.** an attempt or endeavour. **26.** a show of intention. [ME *offre(n)*, OE *offrian*, t. L: m. *offerre*] —**of′ferer,** *n.*

—**Syn. 1.** OFFER, PROFFER, TENDER mean to present for acceptance or refusal. OFFER is a common word in general use for presenting something to be accepted or rejected: *to offer assistance.* PROFFER, with the same meaning, is now chiefly a literary word: *to proffer one's services.* TENDER (no longer used in reference to concrete objects) is a ceremonious term for a more or less formal or conventional act: *to tender one's resignation.* —**Ant. 1.** withdraw, withhold.

offering (ŏf′ə rĭng, ŏf′rĭng), *n.* **1.** something offered in worship or devotion, as to God, a deity, etc.; an oblation; a sacrifice. **2.** a contribution given to or through the Church for a particular purpose, as at a service. **3.** anything offered; gift. **4.** the act of one who offers.

offertory (ŏf′ə tə rĭ, -trĭ), *n.*, *pl.* **-ries. 1.** *Rom. Cath. Ch.* the oblation of the unconsecrated elements made by the celebrant in a Eucharistic service. **2.** *Eccles.* **a.** the verses, anthem, or music said, sung, or played while the offerings of the people are received at a religious service. **b.** that part of a service at which offerings are made. **c.** the offerings themselves. [ME *offertorie*, t. LL: m. *offertōrium* place to which offerings were brought, offering, oblation]

offhand (ŏf′hănd′), *adv.* **1.** without previous thought or preparation; extempore: *to decide offhand.* **2.** cavalier, curt, or brusque. —*adj.* Also, **off′hand′ed. 3.** done or made offhand. **4.** informal or casual.

office (ŏf′ĭs), *n.* **1.** a room or place for the transaction of business, the discharge of professional duties, or the like:

the solicitor's office. **2.** the room or rooms in which the clerical work of an industrial or other establishment is done. **3.** a room assigned to a specific person or group of persons in a commercial or industrial organization. **4.** a place where tickets, etc., are sold, information given, etc. **5.** the staff or body of persons carrying on work in a business or other office. **6.** a building or a set of rooms devoted to the business of a branch of a governmental organization: *the post office*. **7.** a position of duty, trust, or authority, esp. in the government or in some company, society, or the like. **8.** the duty, function, or part of a particular person or agency: *the office of adviser*. **9.** official employment or position: *to seek office*. **10.** a service or task to be performed: *little domestic offices*. **11.** *Slang*. (prec. by *the*) hint or signal. **12.** something (good, or occasionally bad) done for another. **13.** *Eccles*. **a.** the prescribed order or form for a service of the Church, or for devotional use, or the services so prescribed. **b.** the prayers, readings from Scripture, and psalms that must be recited every day by all who are in major orders. **c.** a ceremony or rite, esp. for the dead. **14.** a department of government: *the Foreign Office*. **15.** (*pl.*) the parts of a house, as the kitchen, pantry, etc., devoted to household work. **16.** (*pl.*) the stables, barns, cowhouses, etc., of a farm. **17.** a lavatory. [ME, t. OF, t. L: m. s. *officium* service, duty, ceremony] **—Syn. 9.** See **appointment.**

office-bearer (ŏf′ĭs bĕə′rə), *n.* one who holds office.

office block, a large office building.

office boy, a boy employed in an office for errands, etc.

office-holder (ŏf′ĭs hōl′də), *n.* a person filling a governmental position.

office hours, 1. the hours a person spends working in an office. **2.** the hours during which a professional man or an office conducts regular business.

officer (ŏf′ĭ sə), *n.* **1.** one who holds a position of rank or authority in an army, navy, airforce, or any similar organization, esp. one who holds a commission in an army, navy, or airforce. **2.** a policeman or constable. **3.** the master or captain of a merchant vessel or pleasure vessel, or any of his chief assistants. **4.** a person appointed or elected to some position of responsibility and authority in the public service, or in some corporation, society, or the like. **5.** (in some honorary orders) a member of higher rank than the lowest. **6.** *Obs.* an agent. *—v.t.* **7.** to furnish with officers. **8.** to command or direct as an officer does. **9.** to direct, conduct, or manage. [ME, t. OF: m. *officier*, t. ML: m. s. *officiārius*, der. L *officium* office]

officer at arms, a herald. Also, **officer of arms.**

officer of the guard, *Mil.* a junior officer detailed by rota when an officers' guard is called for, who is responsible for the guard carrying out its duties during a prescribed period.

officer of the watch, *Naut.* **1.** the deck officer who during his watch is responsible to the master for the navigation of a ship. **2.** the engineer officer who is in charge of the engine-room during his watch.

office-seeker (ŏf′ĭs sē′kə), *n.* one who seeks public office.

official (ə fĭsh′əl), *n.* **1.** one who holds an office or is charged with some form of official duty. *—adj.* **2.** of or pertaining to an office or position of duty, trust, or authority: *official powers*. **3.** authorized or issued authoritatively: *an official report*. **4.** holding office. **5.** appointed or authorized to act in a special capacity: *an official representative*. **6.** formal or ceremonious: *an official dinner*. **7.** *Pharm.* authorized by the pharmacopoeia. [t. LL: s. *officiālis*, der. L *officium* office] **—offi′cially,** *adv.*

officialdom (ə fĭsh′əl dəm), *n.* **1.** the position or domain of officials. **2.** the entire body of officials.

officialese (ə fĭsh′ə lēz′), *n.* a style of language found in official documents and characterized by pretentiousness, pedantry, obscurity, and the use of jargon.

officialism (ə fĭsh′ə lĭz′əm), *n.* **1.** official methods or systems. **2.** excessive attention to official routine. **3.** officials collectively.

officialize (ə fĭsh′ə līz′), *v.t.*, **-lized, -lizing.** to make official; bring under official control. Also, **officialise.**

Official Receiver, an officer appointed by the Board of Trade to act as an interim receiver and manager of a bankrupt's estate pending the appointment of a trustee in bankruptcy.

Official Referee, *Law.* an official of the High Court who tries in particular cases involving detailed examination of accounts.

Official Solicitor, *Law.* a civil servant who protects the interests of mentally disordered persons, children being adopted, and persons imprisoned for contempt of court.

officiant (ə fĭsh′ĭ ənt), *n.* one who officiates at a religious service or ceremony. [t. ML: s. *officians*, ppr. of *officiāre* OFFICIATE]

officiary (ə fĭsh′yə rĭ), *adj.* **1.** pertaining to or derived from an office, as a title. **2.** having a title or rank derived from an office, as a dignitary.

officiate (ə fĭsh′ĭ āt′), *v.i.*, **-ated, -ating. 1.** to perform the duties of any office or position. **2.** to perform the office of a priest or minister, as at divine worship. [t. ML: m. s. *officiātus*, pp. of *officiāre*, der. L *officium* office] **—offi′cia′tion,** *n.* **—offi′cia′tor,** *n.*

officinal (ŏf′ĭ sī′nəl), *adj.* **1.** kept in stock by apothecaries, as a drug. Cf. **magistral. 2.** recognized by the pharmacopoeia. *—n.* **3.** an officinal medicine. [t. ML: s. *officinālis*, der. L *officīna* workshop, laboratory]

officious (ə fĭsh′əs), *adj.* **1.** forward in tendering or obtruding one's services upon others. **2.** marked by or proceeding from such forwardness: *officious interference*. **3.** *Obs.* ready to serve. [t. L: m. s. *officiōsus* obliging, dutiful] **—offi′ciously,** *adv.* **—offi′ciousness,** *n.*

offing (ŏf′ĭng), *n.* **1.** the more distant part of the sea as seen from the shore, beyond the anchoring ground. **2.** position at a distance from the shore. **3. in the offing, a.** not very distant. **b.** close enough to be seen. **c.** ready or likely to happen, appear, etc.

offish (ŏf′ĭsh), *adj.* *Colloq.* aloof. **—off′ishness,** *n.*

off-licence (ŏf′lī′səns), *n.* **1.** a licence permitting the sale of alcoholic liquors for consumption off the premises. **2.** a shop, etc. having such a licence.

off-limits (ŏf′lĭm′ĭts), *adj.* *U.S.* out of bounds.

off-peak (ŏf′pēk′), *adj.* **1.** of or pertaining to a period of time of less activity than the normal: *off-peak train services*. **2.** *Elect.* (of the load on a power supply system) lower than the maximum.

offprint (ŏf′prĭnt′), *n.* **1.** a reprint in separate form of an article which originally appeared as part of a larger publication. *—v.t.* **2.** to reprint separately, as an article from a larger publication.

off-putting (ŏf′po͝ot′ĭng), *adj.* *Colloq.* disconcerting; discouraging.

offscouring (ŏf′skou′ə rĭng), *n.* (*often pl.*) that which is scoured off; filth; refuse.

off-season (ŏf′sē′zən), *adj.* **1.** denoting a time of year other than the usual or most popular for a specific activity; out of season. *—n.* **2.** an off-season time of year. **3.** a time of reduced activity in business or manufacturing industry.

offset (*v.* ŏf′sĕt′, ŏf′set′; *n., adj.* ŏf′sĕt′), *v.*, **-set, -setting,** *n., adj.* *—v.t.* **1.** to balance by something else as an equivalent: *to offset one thing by another*. **2.** to counterbalance as an equivalent does; compensate for: *the gains offset the losses*. **3.** *Print.* **a.** to make an offset of. **b.** to print by the process of offset lithography. **4.** *Archit.* to build with an offset (def. 16), as a wall. *—v.i.* **5.** to project as an offset or branch. **6.** *Print.* to make an offset. *—n.* **7.** something that offsets or counterbalances; a compensating equivalent. **8.** the start or outset. **9.** a short lateral shoot by which certain plants are propagated. **10.** any offshoot; branch. **11.** an offshoot from a family or race. **12.** a spur of a mountain range. **13.** *Print.* an impression from an inked design or the like on a lithographic stone or metal plate, made on another surface, as a rubber blanket, and then transferred to paper, instead of being made directly on the paper. **14.** *Print.* set-off (def. 4). **15.** *Mach.* a more or less abrupt bend in a pipe, bar, rod, or the like, to serve some particular purpose. **16.** *Archit.* **a.** a reduction in the thickness of a wall, etc. **b.** a flat or sloping projection on a wall, buttress, or the like, below a thinner part. **17.** *Survey.* a short distance measured perpendicularly from a line. *—adj.* **18.** of, denoting, or pertaining to an offset. **19.** *Print.* pertaining to, or printed by, offset.

offshoot (ŏf′sho͞ot′), *n.* **1.** a shoot from a main stem, as of a plant; a lateral shoot. **2.** a branch, or a descendant or scion, of a family or race. **3.** anything conceived as springing or proceeding from a main stock: *an offshoot of a mountain range, a railway, etc.*

offshore (ŏf′shô′), *adv.* **1.** off or away from the shore. **2.** at a distance from the shore. *—adj.* **3.** moving or tending away from the shore: *an offshore wind*. **4.** being or operating at a distance from the shore: *offshore fisheries or fishermen*.

offside (ŏf′sīd′), *adj.* **1.** *Football, Hockey, etc.* illegally between the ball and the opposing team's goal line and outside one's own team's half of the field when the ball is in play. **2.** of or pertaining to the right-hand side of a vehicle where traffic drives on the left. *—n.* **3.** the right-hand side of a vehicle (where traffic drives on the left).

offsider (ŏf′sī′də), *n.* *Austral.* a partner; friend.

offspring (ŏf′sprĭng′), *n.* **1.** children or young of a particular parent or progenitor. **2.** a child or animal in relation to its parent or parents. **3.** a descendant. **4.** descendants collectively. **5.** the product, result, or effect of something: *the offspring of delirium*. [ME and OE *ofspring*. See OFF, SPRING, v.]

offstage (ŏf′stāj′), *adj., adv.* not in view of the audience; backstage, in the wings, etc.

off-street (ŏf′strēt′), *adj.* away from the main street: *off-street parking.*

off-the-record (ŏf′t͟hə rĕk′ôd), *adj.* unofficial; not intended for public quotation: *an off-the-record discussion with the prime minister.* Also (esp. in predicative use), **off the record.**

off-white (ŏf′wīt′), *adj.* white with a slight touch of grey in it.

O'Flaherty (ō flĕə′tĭ), *n.* **Liam** (lē′əm), born 1896, Irish novelist.

O.F.M., (L *Ordo Fratrum Minorum*) Order of Friars Minor (Franciscan).

oft (ŏft), *adv. Chiefly Poetic.* often; frequently. [ME *oft(e)*, OE *oft*, c. G *oft*]

often (ŏf′ən), *adv.* **1.** many times; frequently. **2.** in many cases. —*adj.* **3.** *Archaic.* frequent. [ME *oftin*, var. (before vowels) of *ofte* OFT]

—**Syn. 1, 2.** OFTEN, FREQUENTLY, GENERALLY, USUALLY refer to experiences which are customary. OFTEN and FREQUENTLY may be used interchangeably in most cases, but OFTEN implies numerous repetitions and, sometimes, regularity of recurrence (*we often go there*); FREQUENTLY suggests esp. repetition at comparatively short intervals: *it happens frequently.* GENERALLY refers to place and means 'universally': *it is generally understood; he is generally liked;* but is often used as a colloquial substitute for USUALLY. In this sense, GENERALLY, like USUALLY, refers to time, and means 'in numerous instances'. GENERALLY, however, extends in range from the merely numerous to a majority of possible instances; whereas USUALLY means 'practically always': *the train is generally on time; we usually have hot summers.* —**Ant. 1.** seldom.

oftentimes (ŏf′ən tīmz′), *adv. Archaic.* often. Also, **oft′times′.**

o.g., *Philately.* a stamp with original gum; a mint stamp (having gum as issued by the post office).

Ogaki (ô′gə kĭ), *n.* a town in Japan, in SW central Honshu island. 113,671 (1965).

Ogbomosho (ŏg′bə mō′shō), *n.* a town in W Western Nigeria. 140,000 (est. 1963).

ogdoad (ŏg′dō ăd′), *n.* **1.** the number eight. **2.** group of eight. [t. LL: s. *ogdoas*, t. Gk: the number eight]

ogee (ō′jē), *n.* **1.** a double curve (like the letter S) formed by the union of a concave and a convex line. **2.** *Archit., etc.* a moulding with such a curve for a profile. [var. of OGIVE]

ogee arch, *Archit.* a form of pointed arch, each side of which has the curve of an ogee.

Ogee arch
A, Convex curve;
B, Concave curve

ogham (ŏg′əm), *n.* **1.** an ancient Irish alphabetical script consisting of straight lines drawn or carved perpendicularly or at an angle to a single long line or to the edge of a stone or piece of wood. **2.** a letter of this script. Also, **ogam.** [t. Ir.]

Ogilvie (ō′gl vĭ), *n.* **John,** 1797–1867, Scottish lexicographer.

ogive (ō′jīv), *n. Archit.* **1.** a diagonal groin or rib of a vault. **2.** a pointed arch. **3.** *Statistics.* a curve such that the ordinate for any given value of the abscissa represents the frequency or relative frequency of values of the ordinate less than or equal to the given value. [ME, t. F, also formerly *augive*; orig. uncert.] —**ogi′val,** *adj.*

ogle (ō′gl), *v.*, **ogled, ogling,** *n.* —*v.t.* **1.** to eye with amorous, flirtatious, ingratiating, or impertinently familiar glances. **2.** to eye; look at. —*v.i.* **3.** to cast amorous, ingratiating, or impertinently familiar glances. —*n.* **4.** an ogling glance. [appar. from a freq. (cf. LG *oegeln*, G *äugeln*) of D *oogen* to eye, der. *oog* the eye] —**o′gler,** *n.*

Ogpu (ŏg′pōō), *n.* See **G.P.U.**

ogre (ō′gə), *n.* **1.** a monster, commonly represented as a hideous giant, of fairy tales and popular legends, supposed to live on human flesh. **2.** a person likened to such a monster. [t. F] —**ogreish** (ō′gə rĭsh), **ogrish** (ō′grĭsh), *adj.* —**ogress** (ō′grĭs), *n. fem.*

Ogygia (ō jĭj′ĭ ə), *n. Gk Legend.* the island where Calypso dwelt.

oh (ō), *interj., n., pl.* **oh's, ohs,** *v.* —*interj.* **1.** (an expression denoting surprise, pain, disapprobation, etc., or for attracting attention.) —*n.* **2.** the exclamation 'oh'. —*v.i.* **3.** to utter or exclaim 'oh'.

O'Hara (ō hä′rə), *n.* **John,** born 1905, U.S. author.

O. Henry (ō hĕn′rĭ), pen name of **William S. Porter.**

OHG, Old High German. Also, **OHG., O.H.G.**

O'Higgins (ō hĭg′ĭnz), *n.* **1. Ambrosio** (ăm brō′zĭ ō′), 1720?–1801, Irish soldier and administrator in South America. **2.** his son, **Bernardo** (bû nä′dō), 1778–1842, Chilean soldier and statesman.

Ohio (ō hī′ō), *n.* **1.** a state in the NE central United States: a part of the Midwest. 9,706,397 pop. (1960); 41,222 sq. mi. *Cap.:* Columbus. **2.** a river in the U.S., formed by the confluence of the Allegheny and Monongahela rivers at Pittsburgh, Pennsylvania, flowing SW to the Mississippi in S Illinois. 981 mi. —**Ohi′oan,** *n., adj.*

ohm (ōm), *n. Elect.* the derived SI unit of resistance: the resistance of a conductor in which one volt produces a current of one ampere. *Symbol:* Ω [named after G. S. *Ohm*, 1787–1854, German physicist] —**ohmic** (ō′mĭk), *adj.*

ohmage (ō′mĭj), *n.* electrical resistance expressed in ohms.

ohmmeter (ōm′mē′tə), *n.* an instrument for measuring electrical resistance in ohms.

O.H.M.S., On His (or Her) Majesty's Service.

Ohm's law, *Elect.* the law which states that in any electric circuit the current flowing is proportional to the voltage and inversely proportional to the resistance. [named after G. S. *Ohm.* See OHM]

oho (ō hō′), *interj.* (an exclamation expressing surprise, taunting, exultation, etc.)

ohone (ō hōn′, ō KHōn′), *interj. Irish and Scot.* alas! Also, **ochone.** [t. Irish and Gaelic: m. *ochōn*]

o.h.v., *Mach.* overhead valve.

-oid, a suffix used to form adjectives meaning 'like' or 'resembling', and nouns meaning 'something resembling' what is indicated by the preceding part of the word (and often implying an incomplete or imperfect resemblance), as in *alkaloid, anthropoid, cardioid, cuboid, lithoid, ovoid, planetoid.* [t. Gk: m. s. *-oeidḗs*, f. *-o-* (connective vowel from preceding word element) + *-eidḗs* having the form of, like, der, *eîdos* form. Cf. -ODE[1]]

-oidea, a suffix used in naming zoological classes or entomological superfamilies. [t. NL, der. *-oidēs* -OID]

oidium (ō ĭd′ĭ əm), *n. Biol.* one of a chain of spores budded off from the end of the hyphae of a fungus.

oil (oil), *n.* **1.** any of a large class of substances typically unctuous, viscous, combustible, liquid at ordinary temperatures, and soluble in ether or alcohol but not in water: used for anointing, perfuming, lubricating, illuminating, heating, smoothing waves at sea in a storm, etc. **2.** petroleum (def. 1). **3.** some substance of oily consistency. **4.** *Painting.* **a.** an oil colour. **b.** an oil painting. **5.** *Slang.* flattery; bribery. **6. burn the midnight oil,** to stay up late at night to study, work, etc. **7. pour oil on troubled waters,** to calm; pacify. —*v.t.* **8.** to smear, lubricate, or supply with oil. **9.** to bribe. **10.** to make unctuous or smooth, as in speech. **11.** to convert (butter, etc.) into oil by melting. —*adj.* **12.** pertaining to or resembling oil. **13.** concerned with the production or use of oil. **14.** obtained from oil. **15.** using oil, esp. as a fuel. [ME *olie, oile*, t. OF, g. L *oleum* (olive) oil]

oilbird (oil′bûd′), *n.* the guacharo.

oil-burner (oil′bû′nə), *n.* **1.** a device for atomizing oil and mixing it with air so that a stable flame may be formed; used in industrial and domestic boilers. **2.** a ship, etc., that uses oil as a fuel.

oilcake (oil′kāk′), *n.* a cake or mass of linseed, cottonseed, etc., from which the oil has been expelled used as a food for cattle or sheep, or as soil fertilizer.

oilcan (oil′kăn′), *n.* a can for holding oil, with a long spout or nozzle through which the oil is squirted to lubricate machinery, etc.

oilcloth (oil′klŏth′), *n.* **1.** a cotton fabric made waterproof with oil and pigment, and used for tablecloths, etc. **2.** a piece of it.

oil colour, a colour or paint made by grinding a pigment in oil, usually linseed oil. Also, **oil paint.**

oiled silk, silk cloth treated with oil to make it watertight.

oiler (oi′lə), *n.* **1.** one who oils; a workman employed to oil machinery. **2.** any contrivance for lubricating with oil. **3.** a can with a long spout, used for oiling machinery. **4.** *U.S.* (*often pl.*) an oilskin coat.

oilfield (oil′fēld′), *n.* a place where oil is found.

oil-fired (oil′fī′əd), *adj.* using oil as a fuel.

oilman (oil′mən), *n.* **1.** one who owns or operates oil-wells. **2.** one who deals or trades in oils.

oil of cloves, an oil obtained by distillation from clove and used as a counterirritant and a mild analgesic.

oil of turpentine, a colourless, inflammable, volatile oil, a distillate of turpentine, having a penetrating smell and a pungent bitterish taste: used in paints, varnishes, and the like, and in medicine as a stimulant, diuretic, rubefacient, etc.

oil of vitriol, sulphuric acid.

oil painting, **1.** the art of painting with oil colours. **2.** a work executed in oil colours.

oil-palm (oil′päm′), *n.* an African palm, *Elaeis guineensis*, whose fruits yield palm oil.

oil-paper (oil′pā′pə), *n.* paper made transparent or waterproof by being treated with oil.

oil-press (oil′prĕs′), *n.* a machine for extracting oils from seeds, pulp, etc.

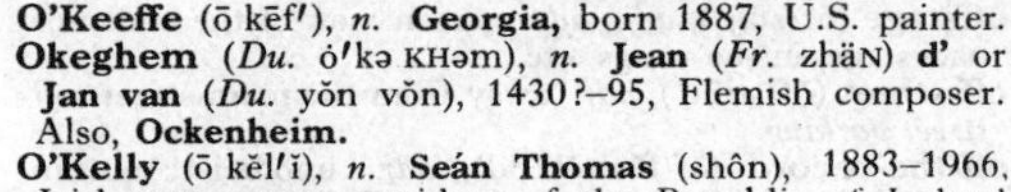

Oil Rivers, a region in W Africa, comprising the vast Niger river delta: formerly a British protectorate; now a part of Nigeria.

oilseed (oil′sēd′), *n.* any of several seeds, as linseed, rapeseed, etc., which yield oil.

oilskin (oil′skĭn′), *n.* **1.** a cotton fabric made waterproof by treatment with oil and used for fishermen's clothing and rain wear. **2.** a piece of this. **3.** (*often pl.*) a garment made of it.

oil slick, a slick or smooth place on the surface of water, caused by the presence of oil.

oilstone (oil′stōn′), *n.* a fine-grained whetstone whose rubbing surface is lubricated with oil.

oilstove (oil′stōv′), *n.* a stove as for cooking, heating, etc., which usually burns paraffin oil.

oil tanker, a ship or motor vehicle for carrying oil in bulk.

oilwell (oil′wĕl′), *n.* a well from which oil is obtained.

oily (oi′lĭ), *adj.*, **oilier, oiliest. 1.** of or pertaining to oil. **2.** full of or containing oil. **3.** smeared or covered with oil, or greasy. **4.** of the nature of or consisting of oil; resembling oil. **5.** smooth, as in manner or speech; bland; unctuous: *an oily hypocrite.* *—adv.* **6.** in an oily manner. **—oil′ily,** *adv.* **—oil′iness,** *n.*

ointment (oint′mənt), *n.* a soft, unctuous preparation, often medicated, for application to the skin; an unguent. [f. obs. *oint* (aphetic var. of ANOINT) + -MENT; r. ME *oignement*, t. OF]

Oireachtas (ĕ′rək thəs), *n.* **1.** the parliament of the Republic of Ireland, consisting of the Dáil Éireann and the Seanad Éireann. **2.** a national assembly or festival held annually in Ireland for the encouragement of the use of the Irish language as a literary medium. [t. Irish: assembly, conference]

Oise (*Fr.* wȧz), *n.* **1.** a river flowing from S Belgium SW through N France to the Seine near Paris. 186 mi. See map under **Compiègne. 2.** a department in N France. 481,289 pop. (1962); 2273 sq. mi. *Cap.:* Beauvais.

Oistrakh (ois′träk; *Russ.* ôy′strəKH), *n.* **1. David** (dā′vĭd), born 1908, Soviet violinist. **2.** his son, **Igor** (ē′gô; *Russ.* ē′gəry), born 1931, Soviet violinist.

Oita (ō′ĭ tə), *n.* a town in Japan, in NE Kyushu. 226,417 (1965).

Ojibwa (ō jĭb′wā), *n.*, *pl.* **-wa, -was. 1.** a large tribe of North American Indians of Algonquian family, divided between the United States and Canada in the Lake Superior region. **2.** a member of the Ojibwa tribe. **3.** their language. Also, **Ojibway, Chippewa.** [t. Amer. Ind. (Algonquian): m. *ojibway* to roast till puckered up, f. *ojib* to pucker up + *ub-way* to roast; with reference to the puckered seam on their moccasins]

Ojukwu (ə jo͞o′kwo͞o), *n.* **Chukwuemeka Odumegwu** (cho͞o′kwo͞o ĕm′ĭ kə ōd′o͞o mĕg′wo͞o), born 1933, Nigerian army officer and politician, leader of Biafra 1967–70.

OK (ō′kā′), *adj.*, *adv.*, *v.*, **OKed, OKing,** *n.*, *pl.* **OKs.** *Colloq.* *—adj.*, *adv.* **1.** all right; correct. *—v.t.* **2.** to put 'OK' on (a proposal, etc.); endorse; approve. *—n.* **3.** an approval or agreement. Also, **ok, O.K., o.k., okay.** [orig. much debated, but prob. abstracted from O.K. Club', formed in 1840 by partisans of Martin Van Buren who allegedly named their organization in allusion to 'Old Kinderhook', his birthplace being Kinderhook, N.Y.]

oka (ō′kə), *n.* **1.** a unit of weight in Turkey and neighbouring countries, equal to about 2¾ lbs. **2.** a unit of liquid measure, equal to about ⅔ of a quart. Also, **oke.** [t. It.: m. *oc*(*c*)*a*, t. Turk.: m. *ōqa*, t. Ar.: m. *ūqiyya*, ult. t. Gk m. *ounkía*, c. L *uncia* OUNCE[1]]

Oka (*Russ.* ȧ kȧ′), *n.* a river in the central Soviet Union in Europe, flowing NE to the Volga at Gorki. ab. 950 mi.

okapi (ō kä′pĭ), *n.*, *pl.* **-pis,** (*esp. collectively*) **-pi.** an African forest mammal, *Okapia johnstoni*, closely related to the giraffe, but smaller and with a much shorter neck. [t. a Central African lang. (Mvuba)]

Okapi, *Okapia johnstoni* (Ab. 5 ft high at the shoulder)

okay (ō′kā′), *adj.*, *adv.*, *v.t.*, *n.* *Colloq.* OK.

Okayama (ō′kə yä′mə), *n.* a seaport in Japan, in W Honshu island. 291,825 (1965).

Okazaki (ō kä′zə kĭ, ō′kə zä′kĭ), *n.* a town in Japan, in SW central Honshu island. 194,409 (1965).

oke (ōk), *n.* oka.

Okeechobee (ō′kĭ chō′bĭ), *n.* a lake in the U.S., in the N part of Everglades, in S Florida. ab. 40 mi. long; ab. 25 mi. wide.

O'Keeffe (ō kēf′), *n.* **Georgia,** born 1887, U.S. painter.

Okeghem (*Du.* ō′kə KHəm), *n.* **Jean** (*Fr.* zhäN) **d'** or **Jan van** (*Du.* yŏn vŏn), 1430?–95, Flemish composer. Also, **Ockenheim.**

O'Kelly (ō kĕl′ĭ), *n.* **Seán Thomas** (shôn), 1883–1966, Irish statesman: president of the Republic of Ireland 1945–59.

Okhotsk (ō kŏtsk′; *Russ.* ȧ KH ôtsk′), *n.* **Sea of,** an arm of the N Pacific enclosed by Kamchatka Peninsula, the Kurile Islands, Sakhalin, and the Soviet Union in Asia. ab. 582,000 sq. mi.; greatest depth, 10,554 ft. See map under **Kamchatka.**

Okinawa (ō′kĭ nä′wə), *n.* the largest of the Ryukyu Islands, in the N Pacific, SW of Japan. 759,000 pop. (est. 1960); 544 sq. mi.

Okla., Oklahoma.

Oklahoma (ō′klə hō′mə), *n.* a state of the S central United States. 2,328,284 pop. (1960); 69,919 sq. mi. *Cap.:* Oklahoma City. *Abbrev.:* Okla. **—O′klaho′man,** *adj.*, *n.*

Oklahoma City, a city in the U.S., the capital of Oklahoma, in the central part. 324,253 (1960).

okra (ō′krə), *n.* **1.** a tall plant of the mallow family, *Hibiscus esculentus*, cultivated for its edible mucilaginous pods, used in soups, etc. **2.** the pod. **3.** the pods collectively. **4.** a dish made with the pods; gumbo. [t. a W African lang. (cf. Twi *ngkuruma*, Igbo *okuro*)]

okta (ŏk′tä), *n.* *Meteorol.* the unit, equal to the area of one eighth of the sky, used in specifying cloud amounts.

-ol[1], a noun suffix used in the names of chemical derivatives, pharmaceutical compounds, commercial products, etc., representing 'alcohol', as in *glycerol*, *naphthol*, *phenol*, or sometimes 'phenol' or less definitely assignable phenol derivatives. [short for ALCOHOL or PHENOL]

-ol[2], var. of **-ole.**

Olaf (ō′ləf; *Nor.* o͞o′läf), *n.* **1. I** (*Olaf Trygvesson*), A.D. 969–1000, king of Norway 995–1000. **2. II, Saint,** A.D. 995–1030, king of Norway 1015–28. **3. V,** born 1903, king of Norway since 1957. Also, **Olav.**

Öland (*Sw.* œ′lȧnd), *n.* an island in SE Sweden, separated from the mainland by Kalmar Sound. 21,702 pop. (1965); 519 sq. mi.

-olatry, a word element meaning 'worship of', as in *demonolatry.* [see LATRIA]

Olbrich (*Ger.* ōl′brĭKH), *n.* **Joseph Maria,** 1867–1908, Austrian architect.

old (ōld), *adj.*, **older, oldest** or **elder, eldest,** *n.* *—adj.* **1.** far advanced in years or life: *a venerable old man.* **2.** of or pertaining to advanced life or persons advanced in years: *to live to a good old age.* **3.** having the appearance or characteristics of advanced age: *prematurely old.* **4.** having reached a specified age: *a man thirty years old.* **5.** advanced in years, in comparison with others or relatively to a scale of age: *the oldest boy.* **6.** having existed long, or made long ago: *old wine.* **7.** long known or in use; familiar: *the same old excuse.* **8.** former, past, or ancient, as time, days, etc.; belonging to a past time: *old kingdoms.* **9.** formerly in use (usually in contrast to something specified as more recent or modern): *he sold his old car in part-exchange for a new one.* **10.** having been so formerly: *the old boys of a school.* **11.** (of colours) dulled, faded or subdued: *old rose.* **12.** deteriorated through age or long use; worn, decayed, or dilapidated. **13.** (*cap.*) (in the history of a language) of or belonging to the earliest stage of development, preceding the period classified as Middle: *Old English.* **14.** *Phys. Geog.* (of topographical features) far advanced in reduction by erosion, etc. **15.** of long experience: *an old hand at the game.* **16.** sedate, sensible, or wise, as if from mature years: *an old head on young shoulders.* **17.** *Often Colloq. or Slang.* (implying long acquaintance or friendly feeling): *good old Henry.* **18.** *Colloq.* carried to great lengths; great: *a fine old spree.* *—n.* **19.** old or former time, often time long past. **20.** old people collectively. **21.** a person or animal of a specified age or age-group: *a class of five-year-olds.* [ME; OE *ald*, *eald*, c. D *oud*, G *alt*; orig. pp., and akin to Icel. *ala* nourish, bring up, and L *alere* nourish] **—old′ness,** *n.*

—Syn. 1. OLD, AGED, ELDERLY all mean advanced in years. An OLD person has lived long, nearly to the end of the usual period of life. An AGED person is very far advanced in years, and is usually afflicted with the infirmities of age. An ELDERLY person is somewhat old, but usually has the mellowness, satisfactions, and joys of age before him. **8.** olden, early, primitive, primeval. **—Ant. 1.** young, youthful.

old age, the period of life (generally) after 65.

old age pension, a pension paid by the state to old people.

Old Bailey (bā′lĭ), the main criminal court of London.

old boy, 1. a former pupil of a specific school. **2.** an old man.

old boy network, the system by which jobs, positions of power or influence, information, etc., are exchanged among persons having a similar background, aims, or interests, esp. among former pupils of a public school or schools.

Oldbury (ōld′bə rĭ, -brĭ), *n.* a town in England, in Worcestershire. 53,948 (1961).

Old Castile (kăs tēl′), a region in N Spain: formerly a province.

Oldcastle (ōld′kä′səl), *n.* **Sir John** (*Baron Cobham*), 1377?–1417, English martyr: leader of a Lollard conspiracy.

Old Catholic, a member of a small national Church holding similar beliefs to, but separated from the Roman Catholic communion, as that which broke away in Holland in 1871 over the doctrine of papal infallibility.

Old Church Slavonic, the extinct language (South Slavic) preserved in religious texts of the Russian Orthodox Church. Also, **Old Church Slavic.**

Old Contemptibles, that part of the British regular army and reserves sent as an expeditionary force to France in 1914.

old country, *U.S.*, *Austral.*, *etc.* the country from which an immigrant or a person's ancestors came, esp. a European country.

olden (ōl′dn), *adj. Archaic.* **1.** old. **2.** of old; ancient: *olden days.* **3.** of or pertaining to former days.

Oldenburg (ōl′dn bûg′; *Ger.* ōl′dən bo͝ork), *n.* **1.** a former state in Germany, including the three scattered provinces of Oldenburg in NW Germany, Birkenfeld in SW Germany, and Lübeck on the Baltic; now a part of Lower Saxony. **2.** a town in NW West Germany, in NW Lower Saxony, formerly capital of Oldenburg. 128,600 (est. 1966).

Old English, 1. the English of periods before 1100; Anglo-Saxon. **2.** *Print.* the form of black-letter used by English printers from the 15th to the 18th century.

Old English sheepdog, one of an English breed of medium-sized dogs having a long, shaggy grey, blue, or blue merle coat, sometimes with white markings.

older (ōl′də), *adj., compar. of* **old.** of greater age.

—Syn. OLDER, ELDER imply having greater age than something or someone else. OLDER is the usual form of the comparative of old: *this building is older than that one.* ELDER, now greatly restricted in application, is used chiefly to indicate seniority in age as between any two people but especially priority of birth as between children born of the same parents: *the elder brother became king.* **—Ant.** newer, younger.

old-fashioned (ōld′făsh′ənd), *adj.* **1.** of an old fashion or a style or type formerly in vogue. **2.** favoured or prevalent in former times: *old-fashioned ideas.* **3.** (of persons) having the ways, ideas or tastes of a former period; out of fashion. **—Syn. 1.** See **ancient.**

old-fogyish (ōld′fō′gĭ ĭsh), *adj.* of or like an old fogy; excessively conservative. Also, **old-fogeyish.**

Old French, the French language of periods before 1400.

old girl, 1. a former pupil of a specific school. **2.** an old woman.

Old Glory, the flag of the United States.

old gold, a dull brownish yellow colour.

Old Guard, 1. the imperial guard created in 1804 by Napoleon. It made the last French charge at Waterloo. **2.** *U.S.* the ultraconservative element of a political party, esp. the Republican Party. **3.** (*usually l.c.*) the ultraconservative members of any group, country, etc. [trans. of F *Vieille Garde*]

Oldham (ōl′dəm), *n.* a town in England, in Lancashire, near Manchester. 115,346 (1961).

Old Harry, *Colloq.* Satan.

old hat, old-fashioned; out-of-date; outmoded.

Old High German, High German of before 1100.

Old Icelandic, the literary language used in Iceland from *c.* 990 to 1300.

Old Irish, the Irish language before the 11th century.

oldish (ōl′dĭsh), *adj.* somewhat old: *an oldish man.*

Old Kingdom, the period in the history of ancient Egypt comprising dynasties III–VI, from 2700 to 2200 B.C.

old lady, *Colloq.* **1.** a mother, usually one's own. **2.** a wife, usually one's own.

old-line (ōld′līn′), *adj. U.S.* **1.** following or supporting conservative or traditional ideas, beliefs, customs, etc. **2.** long established; traditional.

old maid, 1. an elderly or confirmed spinster. **2.** *Colloq.* a person with the alleged characteristics of an old maid, such as primness, prudery, fastidiousness, etc. **3.** a game of cards in which the players draw from one another to match pairs. **—old′-maid′ish,** *adj.*

old man, 1. *Colloq.* a father, usually one's own. **2.** *Colloq.* a husband, usually one's own. **3.** *Colloq.* one in a position of authority, as an employer. **4.** *Austral.* a full-grown male kangaroo. **5.** lad's-love.

old-man's-beard (ōld′mănz′bĭəd′), *n.* a perennial, woody, ranunculaceous climber, *Clematis vitalba,* having white flowers and heads of feathery fruits, found mainly on calcareous soils in Europe, the Caucasus, and N Africa; traveller's joy.

old master, 1. an eminent painter of an earlier period, esp. during the 15th–18th centuries. **2.** a painting by such an artist.

old moon. See **moon** (def. 2d).

Old Nick. See **Nick.**

Old Norse, 1. the language of Scandinavia and Iceland up to the 15th century. **2.** Old Icelandic.

Old Persian, the ancient Iranian of the Persian cuneiforms.

Old Pretender, 1688–1766, James Francis Edward Stuart, son of James II of England.

Old Prussian, a Baltic language extinct since the 17th century.

old rose, rose with a purplish or greyish cast.

Old Sarum. See **Sarum.**

Old Saxon, the Saxon dialect of Low German as spoken before 1100.

old school, advocates or supporters of long-established, esp. conservative policies and practices.

old school tie, 1. a specific tie worn by former members of a school. **2.** the attitudes, manners, accent and bearing associated with former members of English public schools.

old squaw, a lively, voluble sea-duck, *Clangula hyemalis,* of northern regions.

old stager, *Colloq.* a person of long experience; a veteran.

oldster (ōld′stə), *n.* **1.** *Colloq.* an old or older person. **2.** (in the Navy) a midshipman of four years' standing. [f. OLD + -STER, modelled on YOUNGSTER]

Old Stone Age, the Palaeolithic period.

old style, 1. *Print.* a type style differentiated from *modern style* by the more or less uniform thickness of all strokes and the slanted serifs. **2.** (*caps*) See **style** (def. 16). **—old′-style′,** *adj.*

Old Test., Old Testament.

Old Testament, 1. the collection of biblical books comprising the Scriptures of 'the old covenant'. In the Hebrew Bible the three main divisions are the Law, the Prophets, and the Writings. The order in other than Jewish translations follows the Septuagint. In the Vulgate (Latin) translation all but two books of the Apocrypha are included in the Old Testament. **2.** the covenant between God and Israel on Mount Sinai (Ex. 19–24) constituting the basis of the Hebrew religion. See Jer. 31:31–34; also II Cor. 3:6, 14.

old-time (ōld′tīm′), *adj.* belonging to or characteristic of former times; old-fashioned: *old-time dancing.*

old-timer (ōld′tī′mə), *n. Colloq.* **1.** one whose residence, membership, or experience dates from a long time ago. **2.** *U.S.* an old man.

Olduvai Gorge (ōl′dyo͞o vī′), a gorge in Tanzania in which is located a site containing fossils providing evidence of Palaeolithic cultures.

oldwife (ōld′wīf′), *n., pl.* **-wives. 1.** any of various fishes, as the menhaden, or a West Indian fish of the family *Balistidae.* **2.** the old squaw (duck).

old wives' tale, an erroneous idea, superstitious belief, etc., such as is traditionally ascribed to old women.

old woman, *Colloq.* **1.** a wife, usually one's own. **2.** a mother, usually one's own.

old-womanish (ōld′wo͝om′ə nĭsh), *adj.* of or like an old woman; excessively fussy.

Old World, 1. Europe, W Asia, and N Africa. **2.** the Eastern Hemisphere.

old-world (ōld′wûld′), *adj.* **1.** of or pertaining to the ancient world or to a former period of history; of or pertaining to past times. **2.** of or pertaining to the Old World.

-ole, a noun suffix meaning 'oil'. [repr. L *oleum*]

oleaceous (ō′lĭ ā′shəs), *adj.* belonging to the *Oleaceae,* or olive family of plants, which includes the ash, jasmine, etc. [f. s. L *olea* olive + -ACEOUS]

oleaginous (ō′lĭ ăj′ĭ nəs), *adj.* **1.** having the nature or qualities of oil. **2.** containing oil. **3.** producing oil. **4.** oily or unctuous. [t. L: m. *oleāginus* of the olive] **—o′leag′inousness,** *n.*

oleander (ō′lĭ ăn′də), *n. Bot.* any plant of the apocynaceous genus *Nerium,* esp. *N. oleander,* a poisonous evergreen shrub with handsome rose-coloured or white flowers, or *N. odorum,* a species from India with fragrant flowers. [t. ML, ult. g. LL *lorandrum* (var. of L *rhododendron,* t. Gk), influenced by *ole-* oil, or *olea* olive]

oleaster (ō′lĭ ăs′tə), *n.* an ornamental shrub or small tree, *Elaeagnus angustifolia,* of southern Europe and western Asia, with fragrant yellow flowers and an olive-like fruit. [ME, t. L: the wild olive]

oleate (ō′lĭ āt′), *n. Chem.* an ester or a salt of oleic acid.

olecranon (ō lĕk′rə nŏn′, ō′lĭ krā′nən), *n. Anat.* the part of the ulna beyond the elbow joint. [t. Gk: m. *ōlékranon*, short for *ōlenókranon* the point of the elbow]

olefine (ō′lĭ fĭn, -fēn′), *n. Chem.* any of a series of hydrocarbons homologous with ethylene, having the general formula, C_nH_{2n}, also known as alkenes. Also, **olefin** (ō′lĭ fĭn). [f. F *olef(iant)* oil-forming (der. L *oleum* oil) + -INE[2]] —**o′lefin′ic,** *adj.*

oleic (ō lē′ĭk), *adj. Chem.* pertaining to or derived from oleic acid. [f. s. L *oleum* oil + -IC]

oleic acid, *Chem.* an oily liquid, $C_{17}H_{33}COOH$, one of the acids present in fats and oils as the glyceride ester.

olein (ō′lĭ ĭn), *n. Chem.* **1.** a colourless oily compound, the glyceride of oleic acid and the component of olive oil; triolein. **2.** the oily or lower-melting fractions of a fat as distinguished from the solid or higher-melting constituents. [f. s. L *oleum* oil + -IN[2]]

oleo (ō′lĭ ō′), *n.* shortened form of *oleomargarine.*

oleo-, a word element meaning 'oil'. [t. L, comb. form of *oleum*]

oleograph (ō′lĭ ə grăf′, -gräf′), *n.* a kind of chromolithograph printed in oil colours. —**oleographic** (ō′lĭ ə grăf′ĭk), *adj.* —**oleography** (ō′lĭ ŏg′rə fĭ), *n.*

oleomargarine (ō′lĭ ō mä′jə rēn′), *n.* a cooking and table fat made by combining animal oils such as oleo oil and refined lard, and sometimes cotton-seed oil, with milk. See **margarine.**

oleo oil, a product obtained from beef fat, consisting mainly of a mixture of olein and palmitin: used for making butter-like foods.

oleoresin (ō′lĭ ō rĕz′ĭn), *n.* **1.** a natural mixture of an essential oil and a resin. **2.** *Pharm.* an oil holding resin in solution, extracted from a substance (as ginger) by means of alcohol, ether, or acetone.

oleum (ō′lĭ əm), *n. Chem.* fuming sulphuric acid.

O Level, Ordinary Level.

olfaction (ŏl făk′shən), *n.* **1.** the act of smelling. **2.** the sense of smell. [f. (obs.) *olfact* to smell (t. L: s. *olfactāre*) + -ION]

olfactory (ŏl făk′tə rĭ), *adj., n., pl.* **-ries.** —*adj.* **1.** of or pertaining to the sense of smell: *olfactory organs.* —*n.* **2.** (*usually pl.*) an olfactory organ. [t. L: m. s. *olfactōrius,* adj.; only fem. occurs in n. use]

olibanum (ō lĭb′ə nəm), *n.* frankincense. [ME, t. ML, var. of LL *libanus,* t. Gk: m. *líbanos,* of Semitic orig.; cf. Heb. *lĕbhonāh*]

Olifants (ŏl′ĭ fənts), *n.* **1.** a river in the Republic of South Africa flowing E through Transvaal and into the Limpopo in Mozambique. 350 mi. **2.** a river in the Republic of South Africa flowing NW then SW in E Cape Province to the Atlantic Ocean. 170 mi.

olig-, var. of **oligo-** before a vowel.

oligarch (ŏl′ĭ gäk′), *n.* one of the rulers in an oligarchy.

oligarchic (ŏl′ĭ gä′kĭk), *adj.* of, pertaining to, or having the form of an oligarchy. Also, **ol′igar′chical.**

oligarchy (ŏl′ĭ gä′kĭ), *n., pl.* **-chies.** **1.** a form of government in which the power is vested in a few, or in a dominant class or clique. **2.** a state so governed. **3.** the ruling few collectively. [t. Gk: m. s. *oligarchia*]

oligo-, a word element meaning 'few', 'little'. Also, before a vowel, **olig-.** [t. Gk, comb. form of *olígos* small, (pl.) few]

oligocarpous (ŏl′ĭ gō kä′pəs), *adj. Bot.* not bearing much fruit. [f. OLIGO- + -CARP + -OUS]

Oligocene (ŏ lĭg′ō sēn′), *Geol.* —*adj.* **1.** pertaining to an early Tertiary epoch or series. —*n.* **2.** a division of the Tertiary that follows Eocene and precedes Miocene. [f. OLIGO- + m. s. Gk *kainós* new]

oligochaete (ŏl′ĭ gō kēt′), *n.* any of a group of annelids that have locomotory setae sunk directly in the body wall. It includes earthworms and many small freshwater annelids. —**ol′igochae′tous,** *adj.*

oligoclase (ŏl′ĭ gō klās′), *n. Mineral.* a kind of plagioclase felspar occurring commonly in crystals of white colour, sometimes shaded with grey, green, or red. [f. OLIGO- + m. s. Gk *klásis* fracture]

oligocythaemia (ŏl′ĭ go sī thē′myə), *n. Pathol.* a form of anaemia in which there is a reduction in the number of corpuscles in the blood. Also, **oligocythemia.** [f. OLIGO- + CYT(O)- + -(H)AEMIA]

oligopoly (ŏl′ĭ gŏp′ə lĭ), *n.* dearth of sellers in a market. [f. OLIGO- + (MON)OPOLY]

oliguria (ŏl′ĭ gyŏŏə′rĭ ə), *n. Pathol.* scantiness of urine due to diminished secretion. Also, **oliguresis** (ŏl′ĭ gyŏŏ-rē′sĭs). [f. OLIG- + URIA]

olingo (ō lĭng′gō), *n.* any of various raccoons of the genus *Bassaricyon,* living in the forests of South America.

olio (ō′lĭ ō′), *n., pl.* **olios.** **1.** a dish of many ingredients. **2.** any mixture of heterogeneous elements. **3.** a medley or potpourri (musical, literary, or the like); a miscellany. [t. Sp.: m. *olla* pot, stew. See OLLA]

olivaceous (ŏl′ĭ vā′shəs), *adj.* of a deep shade of green; olive. [t. NL: m. *olīvāceus.* See OLIVE]

olivary (ŏl′ĭ və rĭ), *adj.* **1.** shaped like an olive. **2.** *Anat.* denoting or pertaining to either of two oval bodies or prominences (**olivary bodies**), made up of nervous tissue, one on each side of the anterior surface of the medulla oblongata. [t. L: m. s. *olīvārius* of olives]

olive (ŏl′ĭv), *n.* **1.** an evergreen tree, *Olea europaea,* of Mediterranean and other warm regions, cultivated chiefly for its fruit, but yielding also a wood valued for ornamental work. **2.** the fruit, a small oval drupe, esteemed as a relish (pickled in brine when either green or ripe), and valuable as a source of oil. **3.** any of various related or similar trees. **4.** the foliage of the olive tree (*Olea*). **5.** an olive branch. **6.** a wreath of it. **7.** a shade of green or yellowish green. —*adj.* **8.** of, pertaining to, or made of olives, their foliage, or their fruit. **9.** of the colour olive. **10.** tinged with this colour: *an olive complexion.* [ME, t. OF, g. L *olīva*; akin to Gk *elaía* olive tree]

olive branch, **1.** a branch of the olive tree (an emblem of peace). **2.** anything offered in token of peace.

olive drab, **1.** a deep yellowish green. **2.** woollen cloth of this colour used for U.S. army uniforms.

olive green, green with a yellowish or brownish tinge.

olivenite (ō lĭv′ĭ nīt′, ŏl′ĭ vĭ nīt′), *n.* a mineral, basic copper arsenate, $Cu_4As_2O_8(OH)_2$, occurring in crystals and in masses, usually olive green in colour. [f. G *Oliven(erz)* olive ore + -ITE[1]]

olive oil, an oil expressed from the olive fruit, used with food, in medicine, etc.

Oliver (ŏl′ĭ və), *n.* one of the 12 paladins of Charlemagne. See **Roland.** [ME, t. F: m. *Olivier*]

Olives (ŏl′ĭvz), *n.* **Mount of,** a small ridge E of Jerusalem, in what is now Jordan. Highest point, 2737 ft. Also, **Olivet** (ŏl′ĭ vĕt′).

olive shell, **1.** any of various marine gastropods of the family *Olividae,* having an elongated, highly polished shell. **2.** the shell itself.

Olivier (ŏl′ĭ viə′), *n.* **George Borg** (jŏj′bŏj′), born 1911, Maltese statesman: prime minister of Malta since 1964.

Olivier (ə lĭv′ĭ ə), *n.* **Sir Laurence (Kerr)** (lŏ′rəns kä′), born 1907, English actor, producer, and director.

olivine (ŏl′ĭ vēn′, ŏl′ĭ vēn′), *n.* a very common mineral, magnesium iron silicate, $(Mg,Fe)_2SiO_2$, occurring commonly in olive green to grey-green masses as an important constituent of basic igneous rocks; rarely, in one variety, transparent and used as a gem. [f. s. L *olīva* olive + -INE[2]]

olla (ŏl′ə; *Sp.* ō′lyȧ), *n.* (in Spanish-speaking countries) **1.** an earthen pot or jar for holding water or for cooking, etc. **2.** a dish of meat and vegetables cooked in such a pot. [t. Sp.: pot, stew, in LL pot, jar]

olla-podrida (ŏl′ə pō drē′də; *Sp.* ō′lyȧ pȯ drē′dȧ), *n.* **1.** a Spanish stew of meat and vegetables. **2.** any incongruous mixture or miscellaneous collection. [t. Sp.: lit., rotten pot]

olm (ōlm, ŏlm), *n.* a permanently larval form of mud puppy, *Proteus anguinus,* white in colour and about 3 feet long, living in deep caves of S Europe.

ology (ŏl′ə jĭ), *n., pl.* **-gies.** *Colloq.* any science or branch of knowledge. [abstracted from words like BIOLOGY, GEOLOGY where the element -LOGY is preceded by *-o-*. See -O-]

Olomouc (*Cz.* ŏ′lŏ mŏwts), *n.* a town in central Czechoslovakia, in Moravia. 75,000 (est. 1965). German, **Olmütz** (*Ger.* ŏl′mYts).

Olympia (ə lĭm′pĭ ə), *n.* **1.** a plain in ancient Elis, Greece, where the Olympic games were held. **2.** a city in the U.S., the capital of Washington state. 18,427 (1966).

Olympiad (ə lĭm′pĭ ăd′), *n.* (*often l.c.*) **1.** a period of four years reckoned from one celebration of the Olympic games to the next, by which the Greeks computed time from 776 B.C. **2.** a celebration of the modern Olympic games. [ME, t. L: s. *olympias,* t. Gk]

Olympian (ə lĭm′pĭ ən), *adj.* **1.** pertaining to or dwelling on Mount Olympus, as the gods of Classical Greece. **2.** pertaining to Olympia in Elis. **3.** like the gods of Olympus; grand; imposing; superior. —*n.* **4.** an Olympian deity. **5.** a contender in the Olympic games.

Olympic (ə lĭm′pĭk), *adj.* **1.** pertaining to the Olympic games. **2.** pertaining to Olympia, in Greece. **3.** pertaining to Mount Olympus, in Greece. —*n.* **4.** an Olympic game. **5. the Olympics,** the Olympic games.

Olympic games, **1.** the greatest of the games or festivals of ancient Greece, held every four years in the plain of Olympia in Elis, in honour of Zeus. **2.** a modern revival of these games consisting of international competitions in running, jumping, swimming, shooting, etc., held every four years, each time in a different country.

Olympic Mountains, a mountain range in the U.S.,

in NW Washington. Highest peak, Mt Olympus, 7954 ft.
Olympus (ō lĭm′pəs), *n.* **Mount, 1.** a mountain in NE Greece, on the boundary between Thessaly and Macedonia: fabled abode of the greater Grecian gods. 9730 ft. **2.** heaven. **3.** a mountain in the U.S., in NW Washington, highest peak of the Olympic Mountains. 7954 ft.
Olynthus (ō lĭn′thəs), *n.* an ancient city in NE Greece, on Chalcidice Peninsula.
O.M., Order of Merit.
-oma, *pl.* **-omas, -omata.** a suffix of nouns denoting a morbid condition of growth (tumour), as in *carcinoma, glaucoma, sarcoma.* [t. Gk]
Omagh (ō′mə, ō mä′), *n.* a town in Northern Ireland, the county town of Tyrone. 8109 (1961).
Omaha (ō′mə hä′), *n.* **1.** a city in the U.S., in E Nebraska, on the Missouri river. 301,598 (1960). **2.** an Indian of a Siouan tribe, formerly in Nebraska.
Oman (ō män′), *n.* **1.** See **Muscat and Oman. 2. Gulf of,** a NW arm of the Arabian Sea, at the entrance to the Persian Gulf.
Omar Khayyám (ō′mä kī äm′), died 1123?, Persian poet and mathematician, some of whose poems (*The Rubaiyat*) were translated by the English poet Edward FitzGerald.
omasum (ō mā′səm), *n., pl.* **-sa** (-sə). the third stomach of a ruminant, between the reticulum and the abomasum; the manyplies. See diag. under **ruminant.** [t. NL, in L bullock's tripe]
Omayyad (ō mī′ăd), *n.* **1.** a caliph of the dynasty which ruled at Damascus A.D. 661 to 750, claiming descent from Omayya, great-uncle of Mohammed the Prophet. **2.** an emir (A.D. 756–929) or caliph (A.D. 929–1031) of the Omayyad dynasty of Spain. Also, **Ommiad.**
ombre (ŏm′bə), *n.* **1.** a card game, fashionable in the 17th and 18th centuries, played usually by three persons with forty cards. **2.** the player who undertakes to win the pool in this game. Also, *U.S.,* **omber.** [t. F: m. (*h*)*ombre,* t. Sp.: m. *hombre,* lit., man, g. s. L *homo*]
ombrometer (ŏm brŏm′ĭ tə), *n. Meteorol.* a rain gauge.
ombudsman (ŏm′bo͝odz mən), *n.* **1.** (in the Scandinavian countries) an official appointed by parliament to investigate complaints by individuals against the government or the public service. **2.** *Brit. Colloq.* a parliamentary commissioner.
Omdurman (ŏm′dû män′), *n.* a city in the Sudan, on the White Nile opposite Khartoum: British victory 1898. 167,000 (est. 1964).
omega (ō′mĭ gə), *n.* **1.** the last letter (Ω, ω = English long O, o) of the Greek alphabet. **2.** the last of any series; the end. [t. Gk: *ô méga,* lit., great *o.* Cf. OMICRON]
omegatron (ō mĕg′ə trŏn′), *n. Physics.* an instrument used for separating ions of different isotopes of the same element by causing them to move in a spiral path by the application of an electric field at right angles to a constant magnetic field; used for the determination of atomic mass and isotopic and chemical analysis.
omelette (ŏm′lĭt), *n.* a dish consisting of eggs beaten and fried, often with other ingredients. Also, *Chiefly U.S.,* **omelet.** [t. F earlier *amelette,* metathetic form of *alemette,* var. of *alemelle,* lit., thin plate]
omen (ō′mĕn), *n.* **1.** anything perceived or happening that is regarded as portending good or evil or giving some indication as to the future; a prophetic sign. **2.** a prognostic. **3.** prophetic significance; presage: *a bird of ill omen.* —*v.t.* **4.** to be an omen of; portend. **5.** to divine, as if from omens. [t. L] —**Syn. 1.** See **sign.**
omentum (ō mĕn′təm), *n., pl.* **-ta** (-tə). *Anat.* a fold or duplication of the peritoneum passing between certain of the viscera: the **great omentum,** or epiploon (attached to and hanging down from the stomach and the transverse colon); the **lesser omentum** (between the stomach and the liver). [t. L] —**omen′tal,** *adj.*
omer (ō′mə), *n.* **1.** a Hebrew unit of dry measure, the tenth part of an ephah. **2.** (*usually cap.*) *Judaism.* a period of seven weeks from the second day of Passover to the first day of Shabuoth. [t. Heb.: m. *'omer*]
omicron (ō mī′krən), *n.* the fifteenth letter (O, o = English short O, o) of the Greek alphabet. [t. Gk: *ó mīkrón,* lit., small *o.* Cf. OMEGA]
ominous (ŏm′ĭ nəs), *adj.* **1.** portending evil; inauspicious; threatening: *a dull, ominous rumble.* **2.** having the significance of an omen. [t. L: m. s. *ōminōsus* portentous] —**om′inously,** *adv.* —**om′inousness,** *n.*
omissible (ō mĭs′ĭ bl), *adj.* that may be omitted.
omission (ō mĭsh′ən), *n.* **1.** the act of omitting. **2.** the state of being omitted. **3.** something omitted. [ME, t. LL: s. *omissio*]
omissive (ō mĭs′ĭv), *adj.* neglecting; leaving out.
omit (ō mĭt′), *v.t.,* **omitted, omitting. 1.** to leave out: *to omit passages of a text.* **2.** to forbear or fail to do, make, use, send, etc.: *to omit a greeting.* [ME *omitte*(*n*), t. L: m. *omittere* let go, neglect, omit]
ommateum (ŏm′ə tē′əm), *n. Zool.* a compound eye of arthropods.
ommatidium (ŏm′ə tĭd′ĭ əm), *n., pl.* **-tidia** (-tĭd′ĭ ə). *Zool.* one of the radial elements which make up an ommateum. [Latinization of Gk *ommatídion,* f. s. *ómma* eye + *-idion* (dim. suffix)] —**om′matid′ial,** *adj.*
ommatophore (ō măt′ə fô′), *n.* a tentacle or movable stalk bearing an eye, as in certain snails. [f. s. Gk *ómma* eye + -(O)PHORE] —**ommatophorous** (ŏm′ə tŏf′ə rəs), *adj.*
Ommiad (ō mī′ăd), *n., pl.* **-ads, -ades** (-ə dēz′). Omayyad.
omni-, a word element meaning 'all', used in combination as in *omniactive* (all-active, active, everywhere), *omnibenevolent, omnicompetent, omnicredulous, omniprevalent,* and various other words. [t. L, comb. form of *omnis*]
omnia vincit amor (ŏm′nĭ ä vĭng′kĭt ăm′ô), *Latin.* love conquers all.
omnibus (ŏm′nĭ bəs), *n., pl.* **-buses,** *adj.* —*n.* **1.** a bus. **2.** a volume of reprinted works by a single author or related in interest or nature. —*adj.* **3.** pertaining to or covering numerous objects or items at once: *an omnibus clause.* [t. L: lit., for all (dat. pl. of *omnis*)]
omnifarious (ŏm′nĭ fĕə′rĭ əs), *adj.* of all forms, varieties, or kinds. [t. L: m. *omnifārius* of all sorts] —**om′nifar′iousness,** *n.*
omnific (ŏm nĭf′ĭk), *adj.* creating all things.
omnipotence (ŏm nĭp′ə təns), *n.* **1.** the quality of being omnipotent. **2.** (*cap.*) God.
omnipotent (ŏm nĭp′ə tənt), *adj.* **1.** almighty, or infinite in power, as God or a deity. **2.** having unlimited or very great authority. —*n.* **3.** an omnipotent being. **4. the Omnipotent,** God. [ME, t. L: s. *omnipotens* almighty] —**omnip′otently,** *adv.*
omnipresent (ŏm′nĭ prĕz′ənt), *adj.* present everywhere at the same time: *the omnipresent God.* [t. ML: m. s. *omnipraesens.* See OMNI-, PRESENT[1]] —**om′nipres′ence,** *n.*
—**Syn.** OMNIPRESENT, UBIQUITOUS refer to the quality of being everywhere. OMNIPRESENT emphasizes the power, usually divine, of being present everywhere at the same time, as though all-enveloping: *divine law is omnipresent.* UBIQUITOUS is applied to that which seems to appear in many, and all sorts of places, or humorously is 'all over the place', often when unwanted; it is now thus in contrast to the other lofty and dignified expression: *a bore seems to be ubiquitous.*
omniscience (ŏm nĭs′ĭ əns), *n.* **1.** the quality of being omniscient. **2.** infinite knowledge. **3.** (*cap.*) God.
omniscient (ŏm nĭs′ĭ ənt), *adj.* **1.** knowing all things, or having infinite knowledge. —*n.* **2.** an omniscient being. **3. the Omniscient,** God. [f. OMNI- + s. L *sciens,* ppr., knowing] —**omnis′ciently,** *adv.*
omnium-gatherum (ŏm′nĭ əm găth′ə rəm), *n.* a miscellaneous collection. [f. L *omnium* of all + *gatherum* a gathering, pseudo-L deriv. of GATHER]
omnivore (ŏm′nĭ vô′), *n.* an omnivorous person or animal.
omnivorous (ŏm nĭv′ə rəs), *adj.* **1.** eating all kinds of foods indiscriminately. **2.** eating both animal and plant foods. **3.** taking in everything, as with the mind. [t. L: m. *omnivorus*] —**omniv′orously,** *adv.* —**omniv′orousness,** *n.*
omophagia (ō′mə fā′jyə), *n.* the eating of raw flesh or raw food. [t. Gk] —**omophagic** (ō′mə făj′ĭk), **omophagous** (ō mŏf′ə gəs), *adj.* —**omophagist** (ō mŏf′ə jĭst), *n.*
omophorion (ō′mə fô′rĭ ən), *n.* a vestment, resembling a pallium, worn by bishops of the Eastern Church. [t. L Gk *ōmophórion,* equiv. to Gk *ōmo-* (der. *ômos* shoulder) t. LGk *-phorion,* der. Gk *phérein* to bear]
Omphale (ŏm′fə lē′), *n. Gk Legend.* a Lydian queen whom Hercules served in bondage for three years.
omphalos (ŏm′fə lŏs′), *n.* **1.** the navel. **2.** the central point. **3.** *Gk Antiq.* a rounded or conical stone in the temple of Apollo at Delphi, reputed to mark the centre of the earth. [Gk]
Omsk (ŏmsk; *Russ.* ômsk), *n.* a city in the W Soviet Union in Asia, on the river Irtish. 721,000 (est. 1965).
Omuta (ō′mo͞o tä′), *n.* a seaport in SW Japan on W Kyushu island. 193,875 (1965). Also, **Omuda** (ō′mo͞o dä′).
on (ŏn), *prep.* a particle expressing primarily: **1.** position above and in contact with a supporting surface: *on the table.* **2.** contact with any surface: *the picture on the wall; the shoes on my feet.* **3.** immediate proximity: *a house on the coast; to border on absurdity.* **4.** situation, place, etc.: *a scar on the face.* **5.** support, suspension, dependence, reliance; or means of conveyance: *on foot; on wheels.* **6.** state, condition, course, process, etc.: *on the way; on strike.* **7.** ground or basis: *on good authority; a story based on fact; a duty on silk.* **8.** risk or liability: *on pain of death.* **9.** time or occasion: *on Sunday.* **10.** position with reference

to something else: *on the left*; *on the other side.* **11.** direction or end of motion: *to march on the capital.* **12.** encounter: *to happen on a person.* **13.** object or end of action, thought, desire, etc.: *to gaze on a scene.* **14.** membership or association: *on the staff of a newspaper*; *to serve on a jury.* **15.** agency or means: *to speak on the telephone*; *we saw it on television.* **16.** manner: *on the cheap*; *on the sly.* **17.** subject, reference, or respect: *views on public matters.* —*adv.* **18.** on a thing, place, or person: *put the coffee on.* **19.** on oneself or itself: *to put one's coat on.* **20.** fast to a thing, as for support: *to hold on.* **21.** towards a place, point, or object: *to look on.* **22.** forwards, onwards, or along, as in any course or process: *further on.* **23.** with continuous procedure: *to work on.* **24.** into or in active operation or performance: *to turn the gas on.* **25. on and off,** off (def. 18). **26. on and on,** at great length; without interruption. —*adj.* **27.** operating or in use: *the heating is on*; *the handbrake is on.* **28.** occurring; taking place: *is there anything on tomorrow?* **29.** *Cricket.* denoting that part of the playing area to the left and forward of the wicket-keeper (if the batsman is right-handed) (opposed to *leg*). **30. on to,** *Colloq.* in a state of awareness; knowing or realizing the true meaning, nature, etc.: *the police are already on to your little game.* —*n.* **31.** the state or fact of being on. **32.** *Cricket.* the on side. [ME *on, an, o,* OE *on, an* on, in, to, c. D *aan,* G *an,* Icel. *ā,* Goth. *ana*; akin to Gk *aná* up, upon. See ANA-]

On (ŏn), *n.* biblical name of **Heliopolis.**

ON, Old Norse. Also, **ON., O.N.**

onager (ŏn′ə jə), *n., pl.* **-gri** (-grī′), **-gers. 1.** a wild ass, *Equus hemionus,* of south-western Asia; kiang. **2.** an ancient and medieval engine of war for throwing stones. [ME, t. L, t. Gk: m. *ónagros* a wild ass]

Onager, *Equus hemionus* (Ab. $4\frac{1}{2}$ ft high at the shoulder)

onagraceous (ŏn′ə grā′shəs), *adj.* belonging to the *Onagraceae* (or *Oenotheraceae, Ephilobiaceae*), the evening-primrose family, including the widespread ornamental fuchsia, the willow herb, etc.

onanism (ō′nə nĭz′əm), *n.* **1.** (in sexual intercourse) withdrawal before occurrence of orgasm. **2.** masturbation. [from *Onan,* son of Judah: see Gen. 38:9. See -ISM] —**o′nanist,** *n.* —**o′nanis′tic,** *adj.*

O.N.C., Ordinary National Certificate.

once (wŭns), *adv.* **1.** at one time in the past; formerly: *a once powerful nation.* **2.** a single time: *once a day.* **3.** even a single time; at any time; ever: *if the facts once become known.* **4.** by a single degree: *a cousin once removed.* **5. once and for all,** finally and decisively. **6. once in a while,** occasionally. **7. once upon a time,** long ago (a favourite beginning of a children's story, etc.). —*conj.* **8.** if or when at any time; if ever. **9.** whenever. —*n.* **10.** a single occasion: *once is enough.* **11. all at once, a.** suddenly. **b.** immediately. **12. at once, a.** immediately. **b.** at the same time: *do not all speak at once.* [ME *ones,* OE *ānes,* adv. (orig. genitive of *ān* ONE); r. ME *enes,* OE *ǣnes* once, f. *ǣne* once + *-es,* adv. suffix]

once-over (wŭns′ō′və), *n. Colloq.* **1.** a quick or superficial examination, inspection, treatment, etc. **2.** a beating-up; act of physical violence.

oncology (ŏng kŏl′ə jī), *n.* the part of medical science that treats of tumours. [f. m. Gk *ónko(s)* bulk, mass + -LOGY]

oncoming (ŏn′kŭm′ĭng), *adj.* **1.** approaching. —*n.* **2.** the approach: *the oncoming of winter.*

oncost (ŏn′kŏst′), *n.* burden[1] (def. 4).

O.N.D., Ordinary National Diploma.

ondine (ŏn′dīn), *n.* undine.

on dit (*Fr.* ôɴ dē′), *French.* they say; it is said.

ondogram (ŏn′dō grăm′), *n.* a record made on an ondograph.

ondograph (ŏn′dō grăf′, -grăf′), *n.* an instrument for graphically recording oscillatory variations, as in alternating currents. [irreg. f. F *onde* (g. L *unda*) wave + -O- + -GRAPH]

ondometer (ŏn dŏm′ĭ tə), *n.* an instrument for measuring wavelength of radio waves.

one (wŭn), *adj.* **1.** being a single unit or individual, rather than two or more; a single: *one apple.* **2.** being a person, thing, or individual instance of a number or kind indicated: *one member of the party.* **3.** some (day, etc., in the future): *you will see him one day.* **4.** single through union, agreement, or harmony: *all were of one mind.* **5.** of a single kind, nature, or character; the same: *all our pomp of yesterday is one with Nineveh and Tyre!* **6.** a certain (often used in naming a person otherwise unknown or undescribed): *one John Smith was chosen.* **7.** a particular (day, night, time, etc., in the past): *one evening last week.* **8.** a unique or specially remarkable person or thing: *the one man we can rely on.* **9. all one,** (used predicatively) all the same, as in character, meaning, consequence, etc.: *it's all one to me.* —*n.* **10.** the first and lowest whole number, or a symbol, as 1, I, or i, representing it; unity. **11.** a unit; a single person or thing: *to come one at a time.* **12. at one,** in a state of unity, agreement, or accord: *hearts at one.* **13. one and all,** everybody. **14. one by one,** singly and in succession. —*pron.* **15.** a person or thing of number or kind indicated or understood: *one of the poets.* **16.** (in certain pronominal combinations) a person unless definitely specified otherwise: *every one.* **17.** (with a defining clause or other qualifying words) a person or a personified being or agency: *the evil one.* **18.** a person indefinitely; anyone: *as good as one would desire.* **19.** a person of the speaker's kind; such as the speaker himself: *to press one's own claims.* **20.** (to avoid repetition) a person or thing of the kind just mentioned: *the portraits are fine ones.* [ME *oon, oo, o,* OE *ān,* c. G *ein*]

-one, a noun suffix used in the names of chemical derivatives, esp. ketones. [t. Gk, abstracted from fem. patronymics in *-ōnē*]

one another, (referring to each of several reciprocally): *they all began to shout at one another.*

one-armed bandit, a coin-operated gambling machine; a fruit machine.

one-eyed (wŭn′īd′), *adj.* **1.** having only one eye. **2.** *Colloq.* inferior; unimportant.

Onega (ō nyĕg′ə; *Russ.* ȧ nyĕ′gə), *n.* a lake in the NW Soviet Union in Europe: second largest in Europe. 3764 sq. mi.

one-horse (wŭn′hôs′), *adj.* **1.** using or having only a single horse. **2.** *U.S. Colloq.* unimportant; minor; petty.

Oneida (ō nī′də), *n.* **1.** a tribe of the Iroquois confederacy, former inhabitants of the region east of **Oneida Lake,** a lake (20 mi. long; 6 mi. wide) in central New York. **2.** a member of the Oneida tribe. [t. Iroquois: m. *tiionenyote* a rock which something set up and which is still standing (with reference to a boulder near an ancient village)]

O'Neill (ō nēl′), *n.* **1. Eugene,** 1888–1953, U.S. dramatist. **2. Terence Marne,** born 1914, Irish statesman; prime minister of Northern Ireland 1963–69.

oneirocritic (ō nī′ə rō krĭt′ĭk), *n.* **1.** an interpreter of dreams. **2.** oneirocriticism. [t. Gk: m. s. *oneirokritikós,* adj., of or pertaining to the interpretation of dreams] —**onei′rocrit′ical,** *adj.*

oneirocriticism (ō nī′ə rō krĭt′ĭ sĭz′əm), *n.* the art of interpreting dreams.

oneirology (ō′nī rŏl′ə jī), *n.* the study and interpretation of dreams.

oneiromancy (ō nī′ə rō măn′sĭ), *n.* divination through dreams. [f. Gk *oneiro(s)* dream + -MANCY] —**onei′romancer,** *n.*

oneness (wŭn′nĭs), *n.* **1.** the quality of being one; singleness; unity; sameness. **2.** agreement; concord; unity of thought, belief, aim, etc.

one-piece (wŭn′pēs′), *adj.* complete in one piece, as a garment: *a one-piece bathing costume.*

onerous (ŏn′ə rəs), *adj.* burdensome, oppressive, or troublesome: *onerous duties.* [ME, t. L: m. s. *onerōsus*] —**on′erously,** *adv.* —**on′erousness,** *n.*

oneself (wŭn sĕlf′), *pron.* **1.** a person's self (often used for emphasis or reflectively): *one hurts oneself by such methods.* **2.** one's proper or normal self; one's normal state of mind (used after *be, become,* or *come to*). Also, **one's self.**

one-sided (wŭn′sī′dĭd), *adj.* **1.** considering but one side of a matter or question; partial, unjust, or unfair: *a one-sided judgement.* **2.** *Law.* unilateral, as a contract. **3.** unbalanced; unequal: *a one-sided fight.* **4.** existing or occurring on one side only. **5.** having but one side, or but one developed or finished side. **6.** having one side larger or more developed than the other. **7.** having the parts all on one side, as an inflorescence.

onestep (wŭn′stĕp′), *n.* **1.** (formerly) a kind of dance similar to the foxtrot. **2.** music for this dance.

one-time (wŭn′tīm′), *adj.* having been (as specified) at one time; former; quondam: *his one-time partner.*

one-track (wŭn′trăk′), *adj.* **1.** with but a single track. **2.** *Colloq.* restricted: *a one-track mind.*

one-upmanship (wŭn′ŭp′mən shĭp′), *n.* the art or practice of achieving or demonstrating superiority over others by the acquisition of privileges, status symbols, etc.

one-way (wŭn′wā′), *adj.* moving, or allowing motion, in one direction only: *a one-way street.*

onion (ŭn′yən), *n.* **1.** a widely cultivated plant of the lily family, *Allium cepa,* having an edible succulent bulb of pungent taste and smell. **2.** the bulb. **3.** any of certain plants similar to the onion, as *A. fistulosum* (**Welsh onion**). **4. know one's onions,** *Colloq.* to know one's job thoroughly;

be experienced. [ME *onyon*, t. OF: m. *oignon*, g. L *ūnio* large pearl, onion. See UNION] **—on′iony,** *adj.*

Onions (ŭn′yənz), *n.* **Charles Talbut,** 1873–1965, English lexicographer and philologist.

onionskin (ŭn′yən skĭn′), *n.* a translucent, glazed paper.

Onitsha (ō nĭt′shə, ō nē′shə), *n.* a town in S Eastern Nigeria. 77,000 (est. 1963).

on-line (ŏn′līn′), *adj.* *Computers.* (of a computer) able to perform required calculations and present results immediately, without an interval for setting up.

onlooker (ŏn′lo͝ok′ə), *n.* a spectator.

onlooking (ŏn′lo͝ok′ĭng), *adj.* **1.** looking on; observing; perceiving. **2.** looking onwards or foreboding.

only (ōn′lĭ), *adj.* **1.** without others or anything further; alone; solely; exclusively: *only he remained.* **2.** no more than; merely; but; just: *if you would only consent.* **3.** singly; as the only one: *the only begotten Son of God.* **4.** as recently as: *he was here only a moment ago.* **5. only too,** very; extremely: *she was only too pleased to come.* **—adj. 6.** being the single one or the relatively few of the kind, or sole: *an only son.* **7.** single in superiority or distinction. **—conj. 8.** but (introducing a single restriction, restraining circumstance, or the like): *I would have gone, only you objected.* **9.** *Dial.* except that; but or except for: *only for him you would not be here.* [ME *oonli(ch)*, OE *ānlīc*, var. of *ǣnlīc*, f. *ān* ONE + *-līc* -LY]

—Syn. 6. ONLY, SOLE, SINGLE, UNIQUE are all used to refer to an object (or group of objects) as being without counterpart, alone of its kind, whether temporarily or permanently. SINGLE, SOLE, and ONLY all meant originally alone, unaccompanied, and this is still the meaning of SINGLE: *a huge load drawn by a single horse.* SOLE, however, and ONLY have come to refer to a single representative of a type of which no others exist, though this 'type' may be very arbitrarily limited: *the only survivor of a disaster, I am his sole heir.* SOLE, today, is a rather formal word and is infrequent except in a few fixed phrases; in general, it is replaced by ONLY. UNIQUE has always meant existing alone of its kind; today, however, it is mainly used figuratively, to suggest that an object has no equal in excellence, importance, etc.: *a unique occasion.*

o.n.o., or near offer.

onomatopoeia (ŏn′ō măt′ō pē′ə), *n.* **1.** the formation of a name or word by imitating sound associated with the thing designated, e.g., *cuckoo* and *whippoorwill* probably originated in onomatopoeia. **2.** a word so formed. **3.** the use of imitative and naturally suggestive words for rhetorical effect. [t. LL, t. Gk: m. *onomatopoiia* the making of words] **—on′omat′opoe′ic, onomatopoetic** (ŏn′ō măt′ō pō ĕt′ĭk), *adj.* **—on′omat′opoet′ically,** *adv.*

Onondaga (ŏn′ən dä′gə), *n.* **1.** a tribe of the Iroquois confederacy, former inhabitants of the region about **Onondaga Lake,** a salt lake (5 mi. long; 1 mi. wide) in central New York. **2.** a member of the Onondaga tribe. [t. Iroquois: m. *ononytágeh* on top of hill]

onrush (ŏn′rŭsh′), *n.* a strong forward rush, flow, etc.

onset (ŏn′sĕt′), *n.* **1.** an assault or attack: *a violent onset.* **2.** a beginning or start.

onshore (ŏn′shô′), *adv., adj.* ashore.

onside (ŏn′sīd′), *adj.* not offside.

onslaught (ŏn′slôt′), *n.* an onset, assault, or attack, esp. a vigorous or furious one.

onstage (ŏn′stāj′), *adj., adv.* in view of the audience; on or on to the stage.

Ont., Ontario.

Ontario (ŏn tĕə′rĭ ō′), *n.* **1.** a province in S Canada, bordering on the Great Lakes. 6,731,000 (est. 1965); 412,582 sq. mi. *Cap.:* Toronto. **2. Lake,** the smallest of the Great Lakes, between New York and Ontario. ab. 190 mi. long; ab. 7540 sq. mi. **—Ontar′ian,** *adj., n.*

on to, to a place or position on; upon; on: *to get on to a horse.* Also, *Chiefly U.S.,* **onto** (ŏn′to͞o).

ontogeny (ŏn tŏj′ĭ nĭ), *n.* *Biol.* The development of an individual organism (as contrasted with *phylogeny*). Also, **ontogenesis** (ŏn′tō jĕn′ĭ sĭs). [f. Gk *onto-* (comb. form of *ón* being) + -GENY] **—ontogenetic** (ŏn′tō jĭ nĕt′ĭk), *adj.* **—ontog′enist,** *n.*

ontological argument, *Metaphys.* the a priori argument for the being of God, founded on the assumption that existence is a property and one discoverable in the very concept of God, who would fall short of perfection if he had his being in intellect alone instead of in intellect and in reality.

ontologism (ŏn tŏl′ə jĭz′əm), *n.* *Theol.* the doctrine that the human intellect has an immediate cognition of God as its proper object and the principle of all its cognitions.

ontology (ŏn tŏl′ə jĭ), *n.* **1.** the science of being, as such. **2.** the branch of metaphysics that investigates the nature of being and of the first principles, or categories, involved. [t. NL: m. *ontologia*, f. Gk: *onto-* (comb. form of *ṓn* being) + *-logia* -LOGY] **—ontological** (ŏn′tə lŏj′ĭ kl), *adj.* **—ontol′ogist,** *n.*

onus (ō′nəs), *n.* a burden; a responsibility. [t. L: load, burden]

onus probandi (ō′nəs prō băn′dĭ), *Latin.* the burden of proof.

onward (ŏn′wəd), *adj.* **1.** directed or moving onwards or forwards. **—adv. 2.** onwards. [ME. See ON, -WARD]

onwards (ŏn′wədz), *adv.* **1.** towards a point ahead or in front; forwards, as in space or time. **2.** at a position or point in advance. **—Syn. 1.** See **forwards.**

onychophoran (ŏn′ĭ kŏf′ə rən), *n.* **1.** any of the caterpillar-like animals of the genus *Peripatus*, subphylum *Onychophora*, having both arthropod and annelid characteristics. **—adj. 2.** of or pertaining to such an animal. [f. NL: m. *Onychophora*, f. Gk *onycho-* (comb. form of *ónyx* claw) + *-phora* -PHORE]

onyx (ŏn′ĭks), *n.* **1.** a quartz consisting of straight layers or bands which differ in colour, used for ornament. **2.** a nail of a finger or toe. [ME *onix*, t. L: m. *onyx*, t. Gk: nail, claw, veined gem]

oo-, a word element meaning 'egg'. [t. Gk, comb. form of *ōión*]

oocyte (ō′ə sīt′), *n.* *Biol.* a female germ cell in the maturation stage.

oodles (o͞o′dlz), *n.* *Colloq.* a large quantity: *oodles of money.*

oogamy (ō ŏg′ə mĭ), *n.* *Biol.* the fusion during the process of sexual reproduction, of the relatively large female gamete with the small male gamete.

oogenesis (ō′ə jĕn′ĭ sĭs), *n.* *Biol.* the genesis or origin and development of the ovum.

oogonium (ō′ə gō′nĭ əm), *n., pl.* **-nia** (-nĭ ə), **-niums. 1.** *Biol.* one of the female germ cells at the multiplication stage, preceding the maturation or oocyte stage. **2.** *Bot.* the one-celled female reproductive organ in certain thallophytic plants, usually a more or less spherical sac containing one or more eggs. [t. NL; see OO-, -GONIUM]

oolite (ō′ə līt′), *n.* *Geol.* **1.** a limestone composed of minute rounded concretions resembling fish roe, in some places altered to ironstone by replacement with iron oxide. **2.** (*cap.*) an upper division of the European Jurassic, largely composed of oolitic limestone. [t. F: m. *oolithe*, f. *oo-* OO- + *-lithe* -LITE] **—oolitic** (ō′ə lĭt′ĭk), *adj.*

oology (ō ŏl′ə jĭ), *n.* the part of ornithology that treats of birds' eggs. **—oological** (ō′ə lŏj′ĭ kl), *adj.* **—ool′ogist,** *n.*

oolong (o͞o′lŏng), *n.* a variety of semi-fermented brown or amber tea from Taiwan. [t. Chinese: m. *wu-lung*, lit., black dragon]

oomiak (o͞o′mĭ ăk′), *n.* umiak.

oomph (o͞omf), *n.* *Slang.* **1.** vitality; energy. **2.** sex appeal.

oophorectomy (ō′ə fə rĕk′tə mĭ), *n., pl.* **-mies.** *Surg.* the operation of removal of one or both ovaries. [f. *oophor-* (t. NL, comb. form of *oophoron* ovary, t. Gk: lit., egg-bearer) + -ECTOMY]

oophoritis (ō′ə fə rī′tĭs), *n.* *Pathol.* inflammation of an ovary, usually combined with an inflammation of the Fallopian tubes; ovaritis.

oophyte (ō′ə fīt′), *n.* *Biol.* the plant which produces the gametes, in flowerless plants as mosses and ferns which have both sexual and asexual phases during reproduction.

oosphere (ō′ə sfĭə′), *n.* *Bot.* an unfertilized egg within an oogonium.

oospore (ō′ə spô′), *n.* *Bot.* a fertilized egg within an oogonium. Also, *Obs.,* **oosperm** (ō′ə spûm′). **—oosporic** (ō′ə spô′rĭk), **oosporous** (ō ŏs′pə rəs, ō′ə spô′rəs), *adj.*

Oost (*Flem.* ōst), *n.* **1. Jacob van** (*Flem.* yä′kôp vŏn), 1600?–71, Flemish painter. **2.** his son, **Jacob van,** 1639?–1713, Flemish painter.

ootheca (ō′ə thē′kə), *n., pl.* **-cae** (-sē). a case or capsule containing eggs, as that of certain gastropods and insects. [t. NL, f. Gk: *ōo-* OO- + m. *thḗkē* case]

ooze[1] (o͞oz), *v.,* **oozed, oozing,** *n.* **—v.i. 1.** (of moisture, etc.) to percolate or exude, as through pores or small openings. **2.** (of air, etc.) to pass slowly or gradually as if through pores or small openings. **3.** (of a substance) to exude moisture, etc. **4.** (of information, courage, etc.) to leak or pass (*out,* etc.) slowly or imperceptibly. **—v.t. 5.** to make by oozing. **6.** to exude (moisture, etc.). **—n. 7.** the act of oozing. **8.** that which oozes. **9.** an infusion of oak bark, sumach, etc., used in tanning. [ME *wos*, OE *wōs* juice, moisture]

ooze[2] (o͞oz), *n.* **1.** a calcareous mud (chiefly the shells of small organisms) covering parts of the ocean bottom. **2.** soft mud, or slime. **3.** a marsh or bog. [ME *wose*, OE *wāse* mud]

oozy[1] (o͞o′zĭ), *adj.* **1.** exuding moisture. **2.** damp with moisture. [f. OOZE[1] + -Y[1]]

oozy[2] (o͞o′zĭ), *adj.* of or like ooze, soft mud, or slime. [ME *wosie*, der. *wose* mud. See OOZE[2]] **—oo′ziness,** *n.*

op-, var. of **ob-,** (by assimilation) before *p*, as in *oppose.*

op., **1.** opera. **2.** operation. **3.** opposite. **4.** opus.

O.P., **1.** observation post. **2.** (L *Ordo Praedicatorum*)

Order of Preachers (Dominican). **3.** Also, **o.p.** out of print.
OPA, *U.S.* Office of Price Administration.
opacity (ō păs′ĭ tĭ), *n., pl.* **-ties. 1.** the state of being opaque. **2.** something opaque. **3.** *Photog.* the ratio of the incident light and that emerging from a photographic density. **4.** the ability of a coat of paint to obliterate the colours of a surface to which it is applied. **5.** obscurity of meaning. **6.** mental dullness. [t. L: s. *opācitas* shade]
opah (ō′pə), *n.* a large, deep-bodied, brilliantly coloured, oceanic food fish, *Lampris regius.* Also, **moonfish.** [t. a W African lang. (possibly Twi, Fante, or Igbo)]
opal (ō′pl), *n.* a mineral, an amorphous form of silica, (SiO_2 with some water of hydration), not as hard or as heavy as quartz, found in many varieties and colours (often a milky white), certain of which are iridescent and valued as gems. [t. L: s. *opalus*, t. Gk: m. *opállios*]
opalesce (ō′pə lĕs′), *v.i.,* **-lesced, -lescing.** to exhibit a play of colours like that of the opal.
opalescent (ō′pə lĕs′ənt), *adj.* **1.** exhibiting a play of colours like that of the opal. **2.** having a milky iridescence. —**o′pales′cence,** *n.*
opal glass, a translucent or opaque glass.
opaline (ō′pə līn′), *adj.* of or like opal; opalescent.
opaque (ō pāk′), *adj., n., v.,* **opaqued, opaquing.** —*adj.* **1.** impenetrable to light; not able to transmit, or not transmitting, light. **2.** not able to transmit, or not transmitting, radiation, sound, heat, etc. **3.** not shining or bright; dark; dull. **4.** hard to understand; not clear or lucid; obscure. **5.** unintelligent; stupid. —*n.* **6.** something opaque. **7.** *Photog.* a colouring matter, usually black or red, used to darken a part of a negative. —*v.t.* **8.** to cause to become opaque. [ME *opake*, t. L: m. *opācus* shady, darkened] —**opaque′ly,** *adv.* —**opaque′ness,** *n.*
op art, a style of modern painting using special optical effects for emotional or visual stimulation. [shortened form of OP(TICAL) + ART]
Opava (*Cz.* ŏp′ȧ vȧ), *n.* a town in N central Czechoslovakia. 45,000 (1965). German, **Troppau.**
op. cit., (L *opere citato*) in the work cited.
ope (ōp), *adj., v.t., v.i.,* **oped, oping.** *Archaic.* open.
open (ō′pən), *adj.* **1.** not shut, as a door, gate, etc. **2.** not closed, covered, or shut up, as a house, box, drawer, etc. **3.** not enclosed as by barriers, as a space. **4.** that may be entered, used, shared, competed for, etc., by all: *an open session; open competition.* **5.** (of shops, etc.) ready to do business; ready to admit members of the public. **6.** accessible or available (often fol. by *to*): *the only course still open.* **7.** unfilled, as a position. **8.** not engaged, as time. **9.** without prohibition as to hunting or fishing: *open season.* **10.** *U.S. Colloq.* without legal restrictions, or not enforcing legal restrictions, as to saloons, gambling places, etc.: *an open town.* **11.** undecided, as a question. **12.** liable or subject to: *open to question.* **13.** accessible to appeals, ideas, offers, etc. (often fol. by *to*): *to be open to conviction.* **14.** having no cover, roof, etc.: *an open boat.* **15.** not covered or protected; exposed or bare: *to lay open internal parts with a knife.* **16.** unobstructed, as a passage, country, stretch of water, view, etc. **17.** free from ice: *open water in arctic regions.* **18.** free from frost; mild or moderate: *an open winter.* **19.** exposed to general view or knowledge; existing, carried on, etc., without concealment: *open disregard of rules.* **20.** acting publicly or without concealment, as a person. **21.** unreserved, candid, or frank, as persons or their speech, aspect, etc.: *an open face.* **22.** having openings or apertures: *open ranks.* **23.** perforated or porous: *an open texture.* **24.** expanded, extended, or spread out: *an open newspaper.* **25.** generous, liberal, or bounteous: *to give with an open hand.* **26.** *Print.* **a.** (of type) in outline form. **b.** widely spaced or leaded, as printed matter. **27.** not yet balanced or adjusted, as an account. **28.** (of a cheque) uncrossed. **29.** *Music.* **a.** (of an organ pipe) not closed at the far end. **b.** (of a string) not stopped by a finger. **c.** (of a note) produced by such a pipe or string or, on a wind instrument, without the aid of a slide, key, etc. **30.** *Naut.* free from fog. **31.** not constipated, as the bowels. **32.** *Phonet.* **a.** pronounced with a relatively large opening above the tongue: *'cot' has a more open vowel than 'caught'.* **b.** (of a syllable) ending with its vowel.
—*v.t.* **33.** to move (a door, gate, etc.) from a shut or closed position so as to admit of passage. **34.** to make (a house, box, drawer, etc.) open (often fol. by *up*). **35.** to render (any enclosed space) open to passage or access. **36.** to give access to; make accessible or available, as for use. **37.** to recall or revoke, as a judgement or decree, for the purpose of allowing further contest or delay. **38.** to clear of obstructions, as a passage, etc. **39.** to make (bodily passages) clear. **40.** to uncover, lay bare, or expose to view. **41.** to disclose, reveal, or divulge: *to open one's mind.* **42.** to render accessible to knowledge, enlightenment, sympathy, etc. **43.** to expand, extend, or spread out: *to open a map.* **44.** to make less compact, less close together, or the like: *to open ranks.* **45.** to establish for the entrance or use of the public, customers, etc.: *to open an office.* **46.** to set in action, begin, start, or commence (sometimes fol. by *up*): *to open a campaign.* **47.** to cut or break into. **48.** to make an incision or opening in. **49.** to make or produce (an opening) by cutting or breaking, or by pushing aside or removing obstructions: *to open a way through a crowd.* **50.** *Naut.* to come in sight of, or get a view of, as by passing some intervening object. **51.** *Law.* to make the first statement of (a case) to the court or jury. **52.** *Cards.* to begin a hand by making (the first bid) or playing (a card or suit). —*v.i.* **53.** to become open, as a door, building, box, enclosure, etc. **54.** to afford access (into, to, etc.): *a door that opened into a garden.* **55.** (of a building, shop, etc.) to open its doors to the public. **56.** to begin a session or term, as a school. **57.** to begin a season or tour, as a theatrical company. **58.** to have an opening, passage, or outlet (into, upon, etc.): *a room that opens into a corridor.* **59.** to have its opening or outlet (fol. by *towards, to,* etc.). **60.** to come apart or asunder, or burst open, so as to admit of passage or display the interior. **61.** to become disclosed or revealed. **62.** to come into view, or become more visible or plain, as on nearer approach. **63.** to become receptive to knowledge, sympathy, etc., as the mind. **64.** to disclose or reveal one's knowledge, thoughts, feelings, etc. **65.** to spread out or expand, as the hand or a fan. **66.** to open a book, etc.: *open at page 32.* **67.** to become less compact, less close together, or the like: *the ranks opened.* **68.** to begin, start, or commence; start operations. **69.** *Hunting.* (of hounds) to begin to bark, as on the scent of game. **70.** *Law.* to make the first statement of a case to the court or jury. **71.** *Cards.* to make the first bet, bid, lead, etc. **72. open up, a.** to make accessible, as undeveloped land. **b.** to begin firing. —*n.* **73.** an open or clear space. **74.** the open air. **75.** the open water, as of the sea. **76.** the situation of one who does not use or seek concealment. **77.** an opening or aperture. **78.** an opening or opportunity. **79. the open,** the unenclosed or unobstructed country. [ME and OE, c. G *offen*] —**o′pener,** *n.* —**o′penly,** *adv.* —**o′penness,** *n.* —**Syn. 21.** See **frank.** —**Ant. 21.** reticent.
open air, the unconfined atmosphere; outdoor air.
open-air (ō′pən ĕə′), *adj.* existing in, taking place in, or characteristic of the open air; outdoor.
open-and-shut (ō′pən ən shŭt′), *adj.* obvious; easily decided.
open-cast (ō′pən käst′), *adj.* (of a mine) denoting a shallow, open pit, allowing excavation of surface layers only.
open chain, *Chem.* a linking of atoms in an organic molecule which may be represented by a structural formula whose ends do not join to form a ring.
open circuit, *Elect.* an incomplete circuit, preventing the current from flowing.
open city, *Mil.* a city which is officially declared to be of no military importance, either in battle or in the movement of troops and matériel, and is therefore not subject to military attack.
open cluster, *Astron.* a group of stars having a common motion through space in which the stars are not densely packed (as in a globular cluster) but are interspersed with gas and dust clouds.
open day, a day on which certain institutions, as schools, are open to members of the public and special activities, exhibitions, etc., are arranged for their entertainment.
open door, 1. the policy of admitting all nations to a country upon equal terms, esp. for trade. **2.** free admission or access; admission to all upon equal terms.
open-ended (ō′pən ĕn′dĭd), *adj.* organized or arranged so as to allow for various contingencies; without fixed limits.
open-eyed (ō′pən īd′), *adj.* **1.** having the eyes open. **2.** having the eyes wide open as in wonder. **3.** watchful; alert.
open-faced (ō′pən fāst′), *adj.* **1.** having a frank or ingenuous face. **2.** (of a watch) having the dial covered only by the crystal.
open field, *Hist.* the open-field system.
open-field (ō′pən fēld′), *adj. Hist.* having the arable land of a village divided into unenclosed strips and distributed among different cultivators.
open-handed (ō′pən hăn′dĭd), *adj.* generous; free. —**o′pen-hand′edly,** *adv.* —**o′pen-hand′edness,** *n.*
open-hearted (ō′pən hä′tĭd), *adj.* **1.** unreserved, candid, or frank. **2.** kindly. —**o′pen-heart′edly,** *adv.* —**o′pen-heart′edness,** *n.*
open-hearth (ō′pən häth′), *adj. Metall.* denoting a shallow-hearth reverberatory furnace for steel-making, with two openings at each end to admit fuel and air. Combustion takes place over the molten metal charge.

open-hearth process, the steel-making process using an open-hearth furnace.

open house, **1.** a house hospitably open to all friends who may wish to visit it or enjoy its entertainment. **2. keep open house,** to offer hospitality to all; be willing to entertain visitors at any time.

opening (ō′pə nĭng), *n.* **1.** a making or becoming open. **2.** the act of one who or that which opens (in any sense). **3.** an unobstructed or unoccupied space or place. **4.** an open space in solid matter; a gap, hole, or aperture. **5.** *U.S.* a tract of land thinly wooded as compared with adjoining forest tracts. **6.** the act of beginning, starting, or commencing. **7.** the first part or initial stage of anything. **8.** a vacancy. **9.** an opportunity. **10.** a formal or official beginning. **11.** the first performance of a theatrical production; first public showing of something, etc. **12.** *Law.* the statement of the case made by counsel to the court or jury preliminary to adducing evidence. **13.** *Chess, etc.* **a.** a mode of beginning a game. **b.** the first part of a game.

opening time, the time at which public houses are permitted by law to start selling drinks.

open letter, a letter made public by radio, newspaper, or such, but written as though to a specific person.

open-minded (ō′pən mīn′dĭd), *adj.* having or showing a mind open to new arguments or ideas; unprejudiced. **—o′pen-mind′edly,** *adv.* **—o′pen-mind′edness,** *n.*

open-mouthed (ō′pən mouŧħd′), *adj.* **1.** having the mouth open. **2.** gaping with surprise or astonishment. **3.** greedy, ravenous, or rapacious. **4.** clamouring at the sight of game or prey, as hounds. **5.** vociferous or clamorous. **6.** having a wide mouth, as a vessel.

open order, *Mil.* a formation of troops on a ceremonial parade in which the rear rank steps back to allow more space for the inspecting officer, etc., to pass.

open plan, an open-plan system.

open-plan (ō′pən plăn′), *adj.* (of the interior space of a dwelling house, office, etc.) not having walls between areas designed for different uses; having few fixed partitions.

open policy, *Insurance.* a form of marine policy where the value of the subject insured is not stated, and has to be proved when a loss occurs.

open position, *Music.* arrangement of a chord with wide spaces between the parts.

open primary, *U.S.* a direct primary election in which voters need not meet a test of party membership.

open sandwich, a delicacy consisting of meat, cheese, eggs, or the like, placed on thick slices of bread, and garnished.

open sea, the main body of a sea or ocean, esp. that outside territorial waters or not enclosed by headlands or lying between straits.

open secret, something supposedly secret but which is widely known.

open sesame, any very effective method for producing a desired result. [from the use of these words to open the door of the robbers' den in 'Ali Baba and the Forty Thieves', in *The Arabian Nights' Entertainments*]

open verdict, a finding of death by a coroner's jury without stating its cause.

openwork (ō′pən wûk′), *n.* any kind of work, esp. ornamental, as of metal, stone, wood, embroidery, lace, etc., showing openings through its substance.

opera[1] (ŏp′ə rə, ŏp′rə), *n.* **1.** an extended dramatic composition in which music is an essential and predominant factor, consisting of recitatives, arias, choruses, etc., with orchestral accompaniment, scenery, acting, and sometimes dancing; a musical drama. See **comic opera, grand opera.** **2.** the form or branch of musical and dramatic art represented by such compositions. **3.** the score or the words of a musical drama. **4.** a performance of one. **5.** *Colloq.* an opera house. [t. It., t. L: service, work, a work]

opera[2] (ŏp′ə rə), *n.* pl. of **opus.**

operable (ŏp′ə rə bl, ŏp′rə-), *adj.* **1.** that can be put into practice. **2.** admitting of a surgical operation.

opéra bouffe (ŏp′ə rə bo͞of′; *Fr.* ō pĕ rȧ bo͞of′), *French.* a comic opera, esp. of farcical character.

opera-cloak (ŏp′ə rə klōk′, ŏp′rə-), *n.* a cloak for evening wear.

opéra comique (*Fr.* ō pĕ rȧ kō mēk′), *French.* comic opera.

opera glasses, a small, low-power pair of binoculars for use in a theatre, etc. Also, **opera glass.**

opera hat, a man's collapsible tall hat, held open or in shape by springs.

opera house, a theatre devoted chiefly to operas.

operant (ŏp′ə rənt), *adj.* **1.** operating; producing effects. **—***n.* **2.** one who or that which operates. [t. L: s. *operans*]

operate (ŏp′ə rāt′), *v.,* **-rated, -rating.** **—***v.i.* **1.** to work or run, as a machine does. **2.** to work or use a machine, apparatus, or the like. **3.** to act effectively; exert force or influence (often fol. by *on* or *upon*): *now the same causes are operating for war.* **4.** to perform some process of work or treatment. **5.** *Surg.* to perform some manual act or series of acts upon the body of a patient, usually with instruments, to remedy deformity, injury, or disease. **6.** (of medicines, etc.) to produce the effect intended. **7.** *Mil., Naval.* **a.** to carry on operations in war. **b.** to give orders and accomplish military acts, as distinguished from doing staff work. **8.** to carry on transactions in securities, or some commodity, esp. speculatively or on a large scale. **—***v.t.* **9.** to manage or use (a machine, etc.) at work: *to operate a switchboard.* **10.** to keep (a machine, apparatus, factory, industrial system, etc.) working or in operation. **11.** to bring about, effect, or produce, as by action or the exertion of force or influence. [t. L: m. s. *operātus,* pp., having done work, having had effect] **—op′erat′able,** *adj.*

operatic (ŏp′ə răt′ĭk), *adj.* of or pertaining to opera: *operatic music.* **—op′erat′ically,** *adv.*

operating (ŏp′ə rā′tĭng), *adj.* used for or in surgical operations: *operating table*; *operating theatre.*

operating cost, the unit cost, as applied to the costing of services, as transport.

operation (ŏp′ə rā′shən), *n.* **1.** the act, process, or manner of operating. **2.** the state of being operative: *a rule no longer in operation.* **3.** the power of operating; efficacy, influence, or virtue. **4.** exertion of force or influence; agency. **5.** a process of a practical or mechanical nature in some form of work or production: *a delicate operation in watchmaking.* **6.** a course of productive or industrial activity: *building operations.* **7.** a particular course or process: *mental operations.* **8.** a business transaction, esp. one of a speculative nature or on a large scale: *operations in oil.* **9.** *Surg.* a process or method of operating on the body of a patient, as with instruments, to remedy injury, etc. **10.** *Maths.* **a.** a process such as addition. **b.** the action of applying a mathematical process to a quantity or quantities. **11.** *Mil., Naval.* **a.** the conduct of a campaign. **b.** a campaign.

operational (ŏp′ə rā′shə nəl), *adj.* **1.** of or pertaining to an operation or operations. **2.** ready for use; in working order. **3.** *Mil.* of, pertaining to, required for, or involved in military operations.

operationalism (ŏp′ə rā′shə nə lĭz′əm), *n.* *Philos.* the doctrine that scientific concepts secure their meaning from the relevant set of operations involved, stimulated by the relativity theory of Einstein.

operational research, the analysis, usually involving mathematical treatment, of a process, problem, or operation to determine its purpose and effectiveness and to gain maximum efficacy. Also, **operations research.**

operative (ŏp′ə rə tĭv, ŏp′rə-), *n.* **1.** a worker; one engaged, employed, or skilled in some branch of work, esp. productive or industrial work; a workman, artisan, or factory hand. **2.** *U.S.* a secret agent; detective. **—***adj.* **3.** operating, or exerting force or influence. **4.** having force, or being in effect or operation: *laws operative in a community.* **5.** effective or efficacious. **6.** engaged in, concerned with, or pertaining to work or productive activity. **7.** *Med.* concerned with, involving, or pertaining to remedial operations: *operative surgery.* **—op′eratively,** *adv.* **—op′erativeness,** *n.*

operator (ŏp′ə rā′tə), *n.* **1.** a worker; one employed or skilled in operating a machine, apparatus, or the like: *a wireless operator*; *telephone operator.* **2.** one who conducts some working or industrial establishment, enterprise, or system: *the operators of a mine.* **3.** one who deals in shares, currency, etc., esp. speculatively or on a large scale.

operculate (ō pûr′kyo͝o lĭt, -lāt′), *adj.* having an operculum. Also, **oper′cu-lat′ed.**

operculum (ō pûr′kyo͝o-ləm), *n., pl.* **-la** (-lə), **-lums.** **1.** *Bot., Zool., etc.* a part or organ serving as a lid or cover, as a covering flap on a seed vessel. **2.** *Zool.* **a.** the gill cover of fishes and amphibians. **b.** (in many gastropods) a horny plate which closes the opening of the shell when the animal is retracted. [t. L: a cover, lid]

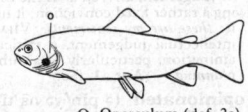

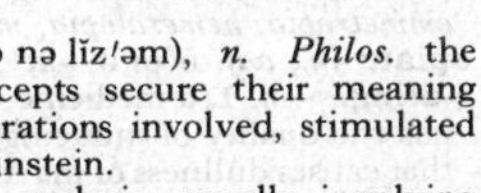

O, Operculum (def. 2a)

opere citato (ŏp′ə rā′sī tä′tō), *Latin.* See **op. cit.**

operetta (ŏp′ə rĕt′ə), *n., pl.* **-ettas, -eretti** (-ə rĕt′ē). a short opera, commonly of a light character. [t. It., dim. of *opera* OPERA]

operose (ŏp′ə rōs′), *adj.* **1.** industrious, as a person. **2.** done with or involving much labour. [t. L: m. s. *operōsus*] **—op′erose′ly,** *adv.* **—op′erose′ness,** *n.*

ophicleide (ŏf′ĭ klīd′), *n.* a musical wind instrument, a development of the old wooden serpent, consisting of a conical metal tube bent double. [t. F, f. Gk: *óphi(s)* serpent + m. s. *kleís* key]

ophidian (ō fĭd′ĭ ən), *adj.* **1.** of, pertaining to, or belonging to the snakes. —*n.* **2.** a snake. [f. s. NL *Ophidia*, pl. (der. Gk *óphis* serpent) + -AN]

ophiolatry (ŏf′ĭ ŏl′ə trĭ), *n.* the worship of snakes. [f. Gk *óphi(s)* snake + -OLATRY] —**oph′iol′atrous,** *adj.*

ophiology (ŏf′ĭ ŏl′ə jĭ), *n.* the study of snakes. —**ophiological** (ŏf′ĭ ə lŏj′ĭ kl), *adj.* —**ophiologist** (ŏf′ĭ ŏl′ə jist), *n.*

Ophir (ō′fə), *n.* a country of uncertain location, possibly southern Arabia or the eastern coast of Africa, from which gold and precious stones and trees were brought for Solomon. I Kings 10:11. [t. Heb.]

ophite (ŏf′īt), *n.* a greenish altered diabase. [t. L: m. s. *ophītēs*, t. Gk: serpent-like, serpentine]

ophitic (ō fĭt′ĭk), *adj.* denoting or pertaining to a rock texture exhibited by certain ophites (diabases), in which elongate felspar crystals are embedded in a matrix.

ophthalm., ophthalmology. Also, **ophthalmol.**

ophthalmia (ŏf thăl′mĭ ə), *n. Pathol.* inflammation of the eye, esp. of its membranes or external structures. [t. LL, t. Gk: a disease of eyes]

ophthalmic (ŏf thăl′mĭk), *adj.* of or pertaining to the eye; ocular.

ophthalmitis (ŏf′thăl mī′tĭs), *n. Pathol.* inflammation of the eye, esp. of the eyeball in both its external and its internal structures. [t. NL]

ophthalmo-, a word element meaning 'eye'. [t. Gk, comb. form of *ophthalmós*]

ophthalmologist (ŏf′thăl mŏl′ə jĭst), *n.* a doctor of medicine skilled in ophthalmology.

ophthalmology (ŏf′thăl mŏl′ə jĭ), *n.* the science dealing with the anatomy, functions, and diseases of the eye. —**ophthalmological** (ŏf thăl′mə lŏj′ĭ kl), *adj.*

ophthalmoscope (ŏf thăl′mə skōp′), *n.* an instrument for viewing the interior of the eye or examining the retina. —**ophthalmoscopic** (ŏf thăl′mə skŏp′ĭk), **ophthal′moscop′ical,** *adj.*

ophthalmoscopy (ŏf′thăl mŏs′kə pĭ), *n.* the use of an ophthalmoscope.

-opia, a word element of nouns denoting a condition of sight or of the visual organs, as in *amblyopia, diplopia, emmetropia, hemeralopia, myopia.* [t. Gk, der. *ōps* eye]

opiate (*n., adj.* ō′pĭ ĭt, -āt′; *v.* ō′pĭ āt′), *n., adj., v.,* **-ated, -ating.** —*n.* **1.** a medicine that contains opium and hence has the quality of inducing sleep; a narcotic. **2.** anything that causes dullness or inaction, or that soothes the feelings. —*adj.* **3.** mixed or prepared with opium. **4.** inducing sleep; soporific; narcotic. —*v.t.* **5.** to subject to an opiate; stupefy. **6.** to dull or deaden. [t. ML: m. s. *opiātus*, der. L *opium* OPIUM]

Opie (ō′pĭ), *n.* **John,** 1761–1807, English painter.

opine (ō pīn′), *v.t., v.i.,* **opined, opining.** to think; deem; hold or express an opinion, or as one's opinion. [t. L: m. s. *opīnārī* think, deem]

opinion (ə pĭn′yən), *n.* **1.** judgement or belief resting on grounds insufficient to produce certainty. **2.** a personal view, attitude, or estimation: *public opinion.* **3.** the expression of a personal view, estimation, or judgement: *to give an opinion on tariffs.* **4.** a formal or professional judgement expressed: *a medical opinion*; *counsel's opinion.* **5.** a judgement or estimate of a person or thing with respect to character, merit, etc. **6.** a favourable estimate; esteem. [ME, t. OF, t. L: s. *opīnio* supposition]

—**Syn. 1.** OPINION, SENTIMENT, VIEW are terms for one's conclusion about something. An OPINION is a belief or judgement which falls short of absolute conviction, certainty or positive knowledge; it is a conclusion that certain facts, ideas, etc., are probably true or likely to prove so: *political opinions; an opinion about art; in my opinion this is true.* SENTIMENT (usually pl.) refers to an opinion or judgement arrived at as the result of deliberation and representing a rather fixed conviction; it usually has a tinge of emotion about it: *these are my sentiments.* VIEW is an estimate of something, an intellectual judgement, a critical survey based on a mental examination, particularly of a public matter: *views on governmental planning.* —**Ant. 1.** fact.

opinionated (ə pĭn′yə nā′tĭd), *adj.* obstinate or conceited with regard to one's opinions; conceitedly dogmatic. —**opin′ionat′edness,** *n.*

opinionative (ə pĭn′yə nā′tĭv), *adj.* **1.** of, pertaining to, or of the nature of opinion. **2.** opinionated. —**opin′iona′tively,** *adv.* —**opin′iona′tiveness,** *n.*

opium (ō′pyəm), *n.* the inspissated juice of a poppy, *Papaver somniferum*, containing morphine and other alkaloids: a stimulant narcotic (in sufficient quantities a powerful narcotic poison) of great value in medicine to relieve pain, induce sleep, etc. [ME, t. L, t. Gk: m. *ópion*, dim. of *opós* juice]

opium den, a place where opium can be bought and smoked.

opiumism (ō′pyə mĭz′əm), *n. Pathol.* **1.** the habit of taking opium. **2.** a morbid condition induced by the habitual use of opium.

opodeldoc (ŏp′ō dĕl′dŏk), *n. Obs.* any of various liniments containing soap, camphor, alcohol, etc. [prob. coined by Paracelsus]

Oporto (ō pô′tō; *Port.* o͞o pôr′to͞o), *n.* a city in NW Portugal: a port near the mouth of the Douro river. 303,424 (1960). Portuguese, **Porto.**

opossum (ə pŏs′əm), *n.* **1.** a prehensile-tailed and pouched marsupial mammal, *Didelphis virginiana*, about the size of a large cat, common in the southern U.S., which feigns death when caught. **2.** any of many neotropical genera of the same family. Also, **possum.** [t. Algonquian; cf. Renape (of Virginia) *apäsum* white beast, Ojibwa *wabāsim* white dog]

Opossum, *Didelphis virginiana* (Total length up to 3 ft, tail ab. 1 ft)

opossum shrimp, any of the small, shrimplike schizopod crustaceans constituting the family *Mysidae.* The females carry their eggs in a pouch between the legs.

opp., **1.** opposed. **2.** opposite.

Oppenheim (ŏp′ən hīm′), *n.* **E(dward) Phillips,** 1866–1946, English novelist.

Oppenheimer (ŏp′ən hī′mə), *n.* **J(ulius) Robert,** 1904–67, U.S. nuclear physicist.

oppidan (ŏp′ĭ dən), *adj.* **1.** of a town; urban. —*n.* **2.** a townsman. **3.** (at Eton College) a pupil who has lodgings in the town. [t. L: s. *oppidānus* belonging to a town]

oppilate (ŏp′ĭ lāt′), *v.t.,* **-lated, -lating.** to stop up; fill with obstructing matter; obstruct. [t. L: m. s. *oppīlātus*, pp.] —**op′pila′tion,** *n.*

opponency (ə pō′nən sĭ), *n.* **1.** the act of opposing. **2.** the state of being an opponent.

opponent (ə pō′nənt), *n.* **1.** one who is on the opposite side in a contest, controversy or the like; an adversary. —*adj.* **2.** being opposite, as in position. **3.** opposing; adverse. **4.** *Anat.* bringing parts into opposition, as the muscles which set the thumb and little finger against each other. [t. L: s. *oppōnens*, ppr., opposing]

—**Syn. 1.** antagonist. OPPONENT, COMPETITOR, RIVAL refer to persons engaged in a contest. OPPONENT is the most impersonal, meaning merely one who opposes; perhaps one who continually blocks and frustrates or one who happens to be on the opposite side in a temporary contest: *an opponent in a debate.* COMPETITOR emphasizes the action in striving against another, or others, for a definite, common goal: *competitors in business.* RIVAL has both personal and emotional connotations; it emphasizes the idea that (usually) two persons are struggling to attain the same object: *rivals for promotion.*

opportune (ŏp′ə tyo͞on′), *adj.* **1.** appropriate or favourable: *an opportune moment.* **2.** occurring or coming at an appropriate time; timely: *an opportune warning.* [ME, t. L: m. *opportūnus*] —**op′portune′ly,** *adv.* —**op′portune′ness,** *n.*

—**Syn. 2.** OPPORTUNE, SEASONABLE, TIMELY refer to that which is particularly fitting or suitable for a certain time. OPPORTUNE refers to that which is well-timed and meets exactly the demands of the time or occasion: *an opportune remark.* That which is SEASONABLE is right or proper for the time or season or occasion: *seasonable weather.* That which is TIMELY occurs or is done at an appropriate time, esp. in time to meet some need: *timely intervention.* —**Ant. 1.** inappropriate.

opportunism (ŏp′ə tyo͞o nĭz′əm), *n.* **1.** the policy or practice, in politics or otherwise, of adapting actions, etc., to expediency or circumstances (often with implication of sacrifice of principle). **2.** an action or proceeding resulting from this policy. —**op′portun′ist,** *n., adj.* —**op′portunis′tic,** *adj.*

opportunity (ŏp′ə tyo͞o′nĭ tĭ), *n., pl.* **-ties.** an appropriate or favourable time or occasion.

opposable (ə pō′zə bl), *adj.* **1.** capable of being placed opposite to something else. **2.** that may be opposed. —**oppo′sabil′ity,** *n.*

oppose (ə pōz′), *v.,* **-posed, -posing.** —*v.t.* **1.** to act or contend in opposition to; drive against; resist; combat. **2.** to stand in the way of; hinder. **3.** to set as an opponent or adversary. **4.** be hostile or adverse to, as in opinion. **5.** to set as an obstacle or hindrance: *to oppose reason to force.* **6.** to set against in some relation, as of offsetting, antithesis, or contrast: *to oppose the advantages to the disadvantages.* **7.** to use or to take as being opposite or contrary: *words opposed in meaning.* **8.** to set (something) over against something else in place, or so as to face or be opposite. —*v.i.* **9.** to be or act in opposition. [ME, t. OF: m. s. *opposer*, b. L *oppōnere* set against and F *poser* POSE[1]] —**oppos′er,** *n.*

—**Syn. 1.** OPPOSE, RESIST, WITHSTAND imply setting up a force against something. The difference between OPPOSE and RESIST is somewhat that between offensive and defensive action: to OPPOSE is mainly to fight against, in order to thwart certain tendencies, procedures, of which one does not approve: *he opposed the passage of the bill.* RESIST suggests that the subject is already threatened by the forces, or by the imminent possibility, against which he struggles: *to resist temptation.* Again, whereas OPPOSE always suggests an attitude of great disapproval, RESIST may imply an inner struggle in which the will is divided: *she tried unsuccessfully to resist his charm.* WITHSTAND generally implies successful resistance; it may refer to endurance that allows one to emerge unharmed (*to withstand a shock*), as well as to active resistance: *the troops bravely withstood the attack.* **—Ant. 9.** comply, submit.

opposite (ŏp′ə zĭt), *adj.* **1.** placed or lying over against something else or each other, or in a corresponding position from an intervening line, space, or thing: *opposite ends of a room.* **2.** contrary or diametrically different, as in nature, qualities, direction, result, or significance. **3.** *Bot.* **a.** situated on diametrically opposed sides of an axis, as leaves when there are two on one node. **b.** having one organ vertically above another; superposed. **4.** *Obs.* adverse or inimical. *—n.* **5.** one who or that which is opposite or contrary. **6.** an antonym. **7.** *Rare.* an opponent. *—prep.* **8.** facing: *she sat opposite me.* **9.** in a complementary role or position: *she played opposite a famous Shakespearian actor.* *—adv.* **10.** on opposite sides. [ME, t. L: m. *oppositus,* pp., put before or against, opposed] **—op′positely,** *adv.* **—op′positeness,** *n.*

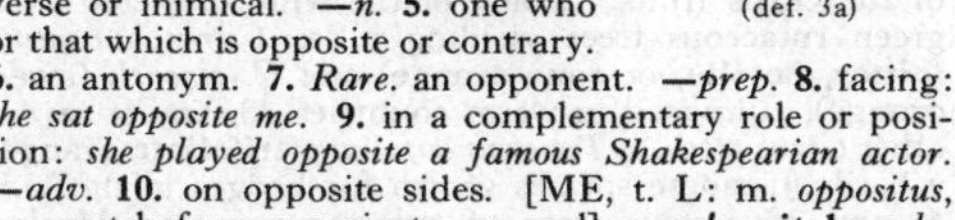

Opposite leaves (def. 3a)

—Syn. 2. OPPOSITE, CONTRARY, REVERSE imply that two things differ from each other in such a way as to indicate a definite kind of relationship. OPPOSITE suggests symmetrical antithesis in position, action, or character: *opposite ends of a pole; sides of a road, views.* CONTRARY sometimes adds to OPPOSITE the idea of conflict or antagonism: *contrary statements; beliefs.* REVERSE suggests that which faces or moves in the opposite direction: *the reverse side of a coin; a reverse gear.* **—Ant. 2.** same, like.

opposite number, a person who holds a corresponding position in another situation; counterpart.

opposition (ŏp′ə zĭsh′ən), *n.* **1.** the action of opposing, resisting, or combating. **2.** antagonism or hostility. **3.** an opposing group or body. **4.** (*usually cap.*) the major political party opposed to the party in power. **5.** the act of placing opposite. **6.** the state or position of being placed opposite. **7.** the act of opposing or the state of being opposed by way of offset, antithesis, or contrast. **8.** *Logic.* the relation with regard to truth and falsehood between two propositions which have the same subject and predicate, but which differ in quantity or quality, or in both. **9.** *Astron.* **a.** the situation of two heavenly bodies when their longitudes or right ascensions differ by 180°. **b.** the opposition of the moon or a planet and the sun, occurring when the earth is directly between them. [t. L: s. *oppositio*; r. ME *opposicioun,* t. OF: m. *opposicion*] **—op′posi′tional,** *adj.*

oppress (ə prĕs′), *v.t.* **1.** to lie heavily upon (the mind, a person, etc.), as care, sorrow, or any disturbing thought does. **2.** to burden with cruel or unjust impositions or restraints; to subject to a burdensome or harsh exercise of authority or power. **3.** to weigh down, as sleep or weariness does. **4.** *Obs.* to put down, subdue or suppress. **5.** *Obs.* to press against or down. [ME *oppresse(n),* t. ML: m. *oppressāre,* freq. of L *opprimere* press against, bear down, subdue] **—oppres′sor,** *n.*

—Syn. 1, 2. OPPRESS, DEPRESS, both having the literal meaning to press down upon, to cause to sink, are today mainly limited to figurative applications. To OPPRESS is usually to subject (a people) to burdens, to undue exercise of authority, and the like; its chief application, therefore, is to a social or political situation: *the tyrant oppressed his subjects.* DEPRESS suggests mainly the psychological effect, upon the individual, of unpleasant conditions, situations, etc., which sadden and discourage: *depressed by the news.* When OPPRESS is sometimes used in this sense, it suggests a psychological attitude of more complete hopelessness: *oppressed by a sense of failure.* **—Ant. 1.** uphold, encourage.

oppression (ə prĕsh′ən), *n.* **1.** the exercise of authority or power in a burdensome, cruel, or unjust manner. **2.** the act of oppressing. **3.** the state of being oppressed. **4.** the feeling of being oppressed by something weighing down the bodily powers or depressing the mind. **—Syn. 1.** tyranny, despotism, persecution.

oppressive (ə prĕs′ĭv), *adj.* **1.** burdensome, unjustly harsh, or tyrannical, as a king, taxes, measures, etc. **2.** causing discomfort because uncomfortably great, intense, elaborate, etc.: *oppressive heat.* **3.** distressing or grievous, as sorrows. **—oppres′sively,** *adv.* **—oppres′siveness,** *n.*

opprobrious (ə prō′brĭ əs), *adj.* **1.** conveying or expressing opprobrium, as language, a speaker, etc.: *opprobrious invectives.* **2.** disgraceful or shameful; contumelious. [ME, t. LL: m. s. *opprōbriōsus*] **—oppro′briously,** *adv.* **—oppro′briousness,** *n.*

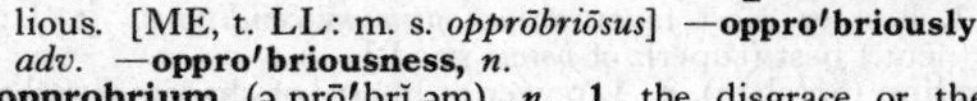

opprobrium (ə prō′brĭ əm), *n.* **1.** the disgrace or the reproach incurred by conduct considered shameful; infamy. **2.** a cause or object of such reproach. [t. L]

oppugn (ŏ pyōōn′), *v.t.* **1.** to assail by criticism, argument, or action. **2.** to call in question (rights, judgement, etc.); dispute (statements, etc.). [ME, t. F: s. *oppugner,* t. L: s. *oppugnāre* fight against] **—oppugn′er,** *n.*

oppugnant (ŏ pŭg′nənt), *adj.* opposing; antagonistic; contrary. **—oppug′nancy,** *n.*

Ops (ŏps), *n. Rom. Myth.* the wife of Saturn and goddess of plenty. [t. L: lit., wealth]

-opsis, a word element indicating apparent likeness, as in *coreopsis.* [t. Gk: appearance, sight]

opsonic (ŏp sŏn′ĭk), *adj. Bacteriol.* of, pertaining to, or influenced by opsonin.

opsonic index, the ratio of the number of bacteria taken up by phagocytes in the blood serum of a patient or test animal, to the number taken up in normal blood serum.

opsonin (ŏp′sə nĭn), *n. Bacteriol.* a constituent of normal or immune blood serum which makes invading bacteria more susceptible to the destructive action of the phagocytes. [f. Gk *opsṓn(ion)* provisions + -IN[2]]

opsonize (ŏp′sə nīz′), *v.t.,* **-nized, -nizing.** *Med.* to increase the susceptibility of (bacteria) to ingestion by phagocytes. Also, **opsonise. —op′soniza′tion,** *n.*

opt (ŏpt), *v.i.* **1.** to make a choice; choose. **2. opt out,** to decide not to participate. [t. F: s. *opter,* t. L: m. *optāre* choose, wish]

opt., 1. optative. **2.** optical. **3.** optician. **4.** optics.

optative (ŏp′tə tĭv), *Gram.* *—adj.* **1.** designating or pertaining to a verb mood (as in Greek) having among its functions the expression of a wish, as Greek *ioimen* 'may we (i.e., we wish we might) go'. *—n.* **2.** the optative mood. **3.** a verb in it. [t. LL: m. s. *optātīvus* serving to express a wish] **—op′tatively,** *adv.*

optic (ŏp′tĭk), *adj.* **1.** pertaining to or connected with the eye as the organ of sight, or sight as a function of the brain. **2.** optical. *—n.* **3.** (*usually pl.*) the eye. [t. ML: s. *opticus,* t. Gk: m. *optikós* of sight]

optical (ŏp′tĭ kl), *adj.* **1.** acting by means of sight or light, as instruments. **2.** constructed to assist the sight, as devices. **3.** pertaining to sight; visual: *an optical illusion.* **4.** pertaining to optics. **5.** dealing with or skilled in optics. **—op′tically,** *adv.*

optical activity, *Phys. Chem.* the property of compounds which consists of rotating the plane of vibration of polarized light.

optical flint glass. See **flint glass.**

optical isomerism, *Chem.* a form of isomerism in which the isomers differ only in their optical activity.

optical maser, *Physics.* a laser.

optical rotation, *Phys. Chem.* the angle through which the plane of polarized light is rotated on passing through an optically active substance.

optic axis, *Crystall.* the direction or directions, uniaxial or biaxial respectively, in a crystal exhibiting double refraction, along which this phenomenon does not occur.

optician (ŏp tĭsh′ən), *n.* **1.** one who makes glasses for remedying defects of vision, in accordance with the prescriptions of oculists. **2.** a maker or seller of optical glasses and instruments. [t. F: m. *opticien,* der. ML *optica* OPTICS. See -ICIAN]

optic nerve, the nerve of sight, connecting the eye with the brain. See diag. under **eye.**

optics (ŏp′tĭks), *n.* the branch of physical science that deals with the properties and phenomena of light and with vision. [pl. of OPTIC. See -ICS]

optic thalamus, thalamus (def. 1).

optimism (ŏp′tĭ mĭz′əm), *n.* **1.** disposition to hope for the best; tendency to look on the bright side of things. **2.** the belief that good ultimately predominates over evil in the world. **3.** the doctrine that the existing world is the best of all possible worlds. **4.** the belief that goodness pervades reality. [t. NL: s. *optimismus,* der. L *optimus* best]

optimist (ŏp′tĭ mĭst), *n.* one given to optimism.

optimistic (ŏp′tĭ mĭs′tĭk), *adj.* **1.** disposed to take a favourable view of things. **2.** of, pertaining to, or characterized by optimism. Also, **op′timis′tical. —op′timis′tically,** *adv.*

optimize (ŏp′tĭ mīz′), *v.,* **-mized, -mizing.** *—v.i.* **1.** to be optimistic. *—v.t.* **2.** to make the best of; make the most effective use of. Also, **optimise. —op′timiza′tion,** *n.*

optimum (ŏp′tĭ məm), *n., pl.* **-ma** (-mə), **-mums,** *adj.* *—n.* **1.** the best or most favourable point, degree, amount, etc., for the purpose, as of temperature, light, moisture, etc., for the growth or reproduction of an organism. *—adj.*

2. best or most favourable: *optimum conditions.* [t. L: (neut.) best (superl. of *bonus* good)]

option (ŏp′shən), *n.* **1.** power or liberty of choosing; right of freedom of choice. **2.** something which may be or is chosen; choice. **3.** the act of choosing. **4.** a privilege acquired, as by the payment of a premium or consideration, of demanding, within a specified time, the carrying out of a transaction upon stipulated terms; the right, conferred by an agreement, to buy (or to decline to buy) a property within a certain time. [t. L: s. *optio* choice] **—Syn. 2.** See **choice.**

optional (ŏp′shə nəl), *adj.* **1.** left to one's choice. **2.** leaving something to choice. **—op′tionally,** *adv.*

optometer (ŏp tŏm′ĭ tə), *n.* any of various instruments for measuring the refractive error of an eye. [f. OPT(IC) + -(O)METER[1]]

optometrist (ŏp tŏm′ĭ trĭst), *n.* one skilled in optometry.

optometry (ŏp tŏm′ĭ trĭ), *n.* the practice or art of testing the eyes by means of suitable instruments or appliances, for defects of vision, in order to supply suitable glasses.

opulence (ŏp′yo͝o ləns), *n.* **1.** wealth, riches, or affluence. **2.** abundance, as of resources, etc. **3.** the state of being opulent. Also, **op′ulency.**

opulent (ŏp′yo͝o lənt), *adj.* **1.** wealthy, rich, or affluent, as persons or places. **2.** richly supplied; abundant or plentiful: *opulent sunshine.* [t. L: s. *opulens, opulentus* rich, wealthy] **—op′ulently,** *adv.* **—Syn. 1.** See **rich.**

opuntia (ō pŭn′shĭ ə), *n.* **1.** any plant of the cactaceous genus *Opuntia,* comprising fleshy herbs, shrubby plants, and sometimes trees, with branches usually composed of flattened or globose joints, and with (usually) yellow flowers and pear-shaped or ovoid, often edible fruit. **2.** a prickly pear. [t. NL, der. L *Opuntius* pertaining to *Opūs,* a town in Locris, Greece]

opus (ō′pəs), *n., pl.* **opera** (ŏp′ə rə). **1.** a work or composition. **2.** a musical composition. **3.** one of the compositions of a composer as numbered according to order of publication. *Abbrev.:* op. [t. L: work, labour, a work]

opuscule (ō pŭs′kyo͞ol), *n.* **1.** a small work. **2.** a literary or musical work of small size. [t. L: m. s. *opusculum,* dim. of *opus* OPUS]

or[1] (ô; *unstressed* ə), *conj.* a particle used: **1.** to connect words, phrases, or clauses representing alternatives: *to be or not to be.* **2.** to connect alternative terms: *the Hawaiian or Sandwich islands.* **3.** often in correlation: *either . . . or; or . . . or; whether . . . or.* [ME *or,* orig. unstressed member of correlative *other . . . or,* earlier *other . . . other,* OE *āther oththe . . . oththe* either . . . or]

or[2] (ô), *prep., conj. Archaic. or Dial.* before; ere. [ME *or* before, OE *ār* soon, early (c. Icel. *ār,* Goth. *air* early); akin to OE *ǣr* soon, before, ERE]

or[3] (ô), *n. Her.* the tincture gold or yellow. [ME, t. F, g. L *aurum* gold]

-or[1], a suffix of nouns denoting a state or condition, a quality or property, etc., as in *error, terror,* and a U.S. alternative of **-our,** as in *color, odor,* etc. [t. L: in some cases, esp. the U.S. variants, r. -OUR]

-or[2], a suffix of nouns denoting one who or that which does something, or has some particular function or office, as in *actor, confessor, creditor, distributor, elevator, emperor, governor, juror, refractor, tailor, traitor.* This suffix occurs chiefly in nouns originally Latin, or formed from Latin stems. In some cases it is used as an alternative or a substitute for **-er**[1], esp. in legal terms (often correlative with forms in **-ee**) or with some other differentiation of use: *assignor, grantor, lessor, sailor, survivor, vendor.* [t. L; in some cases, r. ME *-our,* t. AF: (m.) *-(e)our* (= F *-eur*), g. L *-or, -ātor,* etc.]

orach (ŏ′rĭch), *n.* any of the plants of the genus *Atriplex,* esp. *A. hortensis* (**garden orach**), cultivated for use like spinach. Also, **or′ache.** [ME *orage,* t. OF: m. *arache,* g. L *ātriplex,* t. Gk: m. s. *atráphaxis*]

oracle (ŏ′rə kl), *n.* **1.** (esp. in ancient Greece) an utterance, often ambiguous or obscure, given by a priest or priestess at a shrine as the response of a god to an inquiry. **2.** the agency or medium giving such responses, or a shrine or place at which they were given: *the oracle of Apollo at Delphi.* **3.** a divine communication or revelation. **4.** (*pl.*) the Scriptures. **5.** the holy of holies in the Jewish temple. See I Kings, 6:16, 19–23. **6.** any person or thing serving as an agency of divine communication. **7.** any utterance made or received as authoritative and infallible. **8.** a person who delivers authoritative or highly regarded pronouncements. [ME, t. OF, t. L: m. s. *ōrāculum*]

oracular (ŏ răk′yo͝o lə), *adj.* **1.** of the nature of, resembling, or suggesting an oracle: *an oracular response.* **2.** giving forth utterances or decisions as if by special inspiration or authority. **3.** uttered or delivered as if divinely inspired or infallible; sententious. **4.** ambiguous or obscure. **5.** portentous. **—orac′ularly,** *adv.*

Oradea (*Rum.* ô rá′dyä), *n.* a town in NW Rumania. 110,296 (est. 1963). Also, **Oradea Mare** (*Rum.* mä′rĕ). German, **Grosswardein.** Hungarian, **Nagyvárad.**

oral (ô′rəl), *adj.* **1.** uttered by the mouth; spoken: *oral testimony.* **2.** employing speech, as teachers or methods of teaching. **3.** of or pertaining to the mouth: *the oral cavity.* **4.** done, taken, or administered by the mouth: *an oral dose of medicine.* **5.** *Zool.* pertaining to that surface of polyps and marine animals which contains the mouth and tentacles. **6.** *Phonet.* articulated with none of the voice issuing through the nose: *b* and *v* are oral consonants, and the normal English vowels are oral. **—***n.* **7.** an oral examination in a school, university, etc. [f. s. L *ōs* mouth + -AL[1]] **—o′rally,** *adv.*

—Syn. 1. ORAL, VERBAL may both simply refer to that which is spoken. They may also refer to the spoken as opposed to the written form: *an oral examination, a verbal agreement.* They differ only in their collocations. **—Ant. 6.** nasal.

Oran (ô rän′; *Fr.* ŏ räN′), *n.* a seaport in NW Algeria. 300,000 (est. 1963).

orang (ô răng′), *n.* the orang-utan.

orange (ŏ′rĭnj), *n.* **1.** a globose reddish yellow edible citrus fruit of which there are two principal kinds, the bitter and sweet, the latter comprising the most important of the citrus fruits. **2.** any of the white-flowered evergreen rutaceous trees yielding it, as *Citrus aurantium* (**bitter, Seville,** or **sour orange**) and *C. sinensis* (**sweet orange**), cultivated in warm countries. **3.** any of several other citrus trees, as *Poncirus trifoliata* (**trifoliate orange**), a hardy Japanese species grown for hedges in the U.S. **4.** any of certain trees of other genera, as *Maclura pomifera* (see **Osage orange**), or the fruit. **5.** a colour between yellow and red in the spectrum; reddish yellow. **—***adj.* **6.** of or pertaining to the orange. **7.** made with or prepared from oranges or having the flavour of orange. **8.** reddish yellow. [ME *orange,* t. OF (b. with *or* gold), c. Sp. *naranja,* t. Ar.: m. *nāranj,* t. Pers.: m. *nārang,* t. Skt: m. *nāranja*]

Orange (ŏ′rĭnj), *n.* **1.** a European princely family ruling in England from 1688 to 1694, and in the Netherlands since 1815. **2.** a river in the Republic of South Africa, flowing W from Lesotho, along the border of Orange Free State and Cape Province, and through Cape Province to the Atlantic Ocean. 1360 mi. **3.** a former small principality of W Europe: now in the SE part of France. **4.** a town in Australia, in central New South Wales. 20,000 (est. 1965). **—***adj.* **5.** of or pertaining to Orangemen.

orangeade (ŏ′rĭnj ād′), *n.* an orange-flavoured drink.

orange blossom, the flower of the orange, much worn in wreaths, etc., by brides.

Orange Free State, a province in the central Republic of South Africa: a Boer republic, 1854–1900; a British colony (**Orange River Colony**), 1900–10. 1,386,547 pop. (1960); 49,647 sq. mi. *Cap.:* Bloemfontein.

Orangeism (ŏ′rĭn jĭz′əm), *n.* the principles and practices of the Orangemen. **—Or′angeist,** *n.*

Orangeman (ŏ′rĭnj mən), *n., pl.* **-men. 1.** a member of a secret society formed in the north of Ireland in 1795, having for its object the maintenance of the Protestant religion and political ascendancy. **2.** a Northern Ireland protestant.

orange pekoe, 1. a superior black tea composed of only the smallest top leaves and grown in India and Ceylon. **2.** any Indian or Ceylon tea of good quality.

orangery (ŏ′rĭn jə rĭ), *n., pl.* **-ries.** a place, as a greenhouse, in which orange trees are cultivated. [t. F: m. *orangerie,* der. *oranger* orange tree, der. *orange* ORANGE]

orangewood (ŏ′rĭnj wo͝od′), *n.* the hard, fine-grained, yellowish wood of the orange tree, used in inlaid work and fine turnery.

orang-utan (ô răng′o͞o tăn′), *n.* a large, long-armed anthropoid ape, *Pongo pygmaeus,* of arboreal habits, found in Borneo and Sumatra. Also, **orang-outang** (ô-răng′o͞o tăng′), **orang.** [ult. t. Malay: man of the woods]

Orang-utan, *Pongo pygmaeus* (Up to 5½ ft in height)

Oranje-Nassau (*Du.* ō rŏn′yə nŏs′ōw), *n.* Orange (def. 1).

ora pro nobis (ô′rä prō nō′bĭs), *Latin.* pray for us.

orate (ô rāt′), *v.i.,* **orated, orating.** to make an oration; hold forth. [back-formation from ORATION]

oration (ô rā′shən), *n.* **1.** a formal speech, esp. one delivered on a special occasion, as on an anniversary, at a funeral, or at academic exercises. **2.** a speech characterized by an elevated style, diction, or delivery. [ME *oracion,* t. L: m. s. *ōrātio* speech, discourse, prayer] **—Syn. 1.** See **speech.**

orator (ŏ′rə tə), *n.* **1.** one who delivers an oration; a public speaker, esp. one of great eloquence. **2.** *Law. Obs.* a plaintiff. [t. L: speaker, supplicant; r. ME *oratour,* t. AF] —**oratress** (ŏ′rə trĭs), **oratrix** (ŏ′rə trĭks), *n. fem.*

Oratorian (ŏ′rə tô′rĭ ən), *Rom. Cath. Ch.* —*n.* **1.** a member of the Oratory. —*adj.* **2.** of or pertaining to the Oratorians.

oratorical (ŏ′rə tŏ′rĭ kl), *adj.* **1.** of, pertaining to, or characteristic of an orator or oratory. **2.** given to oratory. —**or′ator′ically,** *adv.*

oratorio (ŏ′rə tô′rĭ ō′), *n., pl.* **-rios.** an extended musical composition, with a text more or less dramatic in character and usually based upon a religious theme, for solo voices, chorus, and orchestra, and performed without action, costume, or scenery. [t. It., g. LL *ōrātōrium* ORATORY[2]; so named from the musical services in the church of the Oratory of St Philip Neri in Rome]

oratory[1] (ŏ′rə tə rĭ, -trĭ), *n.* **1.** the exercise of eloquence; eloquent speaking. **2.** the art of an orator; the art of public speaking. [t. L: m. s. *ōrātōria,* prop. fem. of *ōrātōrius* of an orator]

oratory[2] (ôr′ə tŏr′ĭ, ŏr′-), *n., pl.* **-ries. 1.** a place of prayer, as a small chapel or a room for private devotions. **2.** (*cap.*) any of certain religious societies of the Roman Catholic Church, esp. one (**Oratory of St Philip Neri**) composed of secular priests, not bound by vows, devoted to simple and familiar preaching. [ME, t. LL: m. s. *ōrātōrium* place of prayer, prop. neut. of L *ōrātorius* oratorical]

orb (ôb), *n.* **1.** *Chiefly Poetic.* any of the heavenly bodies: *the orb of day* (the sun). **2.** a sphere or globe. **3.** *Chiefly Poetic.* the eyeball or eye. **4.** a globe bearing a cross; the mound, or emblem of sovereignty, esp. as part of the regalia of England. **5.** *Now Rare.* a circle, or anything circular. **6.** *Astron. Obs.* the orbit of a heavenly body. **7.** *Astrol.* the space within which the influence of a planet, etc., is supposed to act. **8.** *Obs.* the earth. **9.** *Obs.* a range or area of action. —*v.t.* **10.** to form into a circle or a sphere. **11.** *Poetic.* to encircle; enclose. —*v.i.* **12.** to move in an orbit. **13.** *Obs.* to assume the shape of an orb. [t. L: s. *orbis* circle, disc, orb] —**Syn. 2.** See **ball**[1].

orbicular (ô bĭk′yŏŏ lə), *adj.* like an orb; circular; ringlike; spherical; rounded. [ME, t. LL: s. *orbiculāris,* der. L *orbiculus,* dim. of *orbis* ORB] —**orbicularity** (ô bĭk′yŏŏ la′rĭ tĭ), *n.* —**orbic′ularly,** *adv.*

Orbicular leaf

orbiculate (ô bĭk′yŏŏ lĭt, -lāt′), *adj.* orbicular; rounded. Also, **orbic′ulat′ed.** [t. L: m. s. *orbiculātus,* der. *orbiculus.* See ORBICULAR]

orbit (ô′bĭt), *n.* **1.** the elliptical or curved path described by a planet, satellite, etc., about a body, as the earth or sun. **2.** a course regularly pursued, as in life. **3.** *Anat.* **a.** the bony cavity of the skull which contains the eye; the eye socket. **b.** the eye. **4.** *Zool.* the part surrounding the eye of a bird or insect. **5.** an orb or sphere. **6.** *Chem.* the path of an electron around the nucleus of an atom. —*v.t.* **7.** to move or travel in an orbital path. —*v.i.* **8.** to describe an orbit. [t. L: s. *orbita* wheel track, course, circuit] —**or′bital,** *adj.*

orbitale (ô′bĭ tä′lĭ), *n. Anat.* **1.** the lowermost point on the lower margin of the left orbit, located instrumentally on the skull. **2.** the lowermost point on the lower margin of the left orbit, located by palpation on the head. [t. L: of an orbit (neut.)]

orbital electron, *Chem.* an electron contained within an atom which may be thought of as orbiting round the nucleus; a planetary electron.

orbital index, *Anat.* the ratio of the maximum breadth to the maximum height of the orbital cavity.

orbital period, *Aeron.* the time taken by an orbiting object to complete one orbit.

orbital velocity, *Aeron.* the velocity required to overcome the earth's gravitational attraction and so maintain a satellite in orbit.

orby (ô′bĭ), *adj. Rare.* like or pertaining to an orb.

orc (ôk), *n.* **1.** a mythical monster, esp. a sea-monster. **2.** *Obs.* a whale or grampus. [t. L: s. *orca* whale]

orcein (ô′sĭ ĭn), *n. Chem.* a red dye obtained by oxidizing an ammoniacal solution of orcinol, and forming the principal colouring matter of cudbear and orchil. [arbitrary alter. of *orcin.* See ORCINOL]

orch., orchestra.

orchard (ô′chəd), *n.* **1.** a piece of ground, usually enclosed, devoted to the cultivation of fruit trees. **2.** a collection of such trees. [ME *orch(i)ard,* OE *orceard;* r. *ortyard,* ME *ortyerd,* OE *ortgeard* (cf. Goth. *aurtigards* garden), f. *ort-* (cf. L *hortus* garden) + *geard* YARD[2]]

orchardist (ô′chə dĭst), *n.* one who cultivates an orchard.

orchestra (ô′kĭs trə), *n.* **1.** a company of performers on various musical instruments, comprising the four main groups (strings, woodwind, brass and percussion), for playing concert music, as symphonies, operas, and other compositions. **2.** (in a modern theatre) the space reserved for the musicians, usually the front part of the main floor. **3.** (in the ancient Greek theatre) the circular space in front of the stage, allotted to the chorus. **4.** (in the Roman theatre) a similar space reserved for persons of distinction. [t. L, t. Gk: the space on which the chorus danced]

orchestral (ô kĕs′trəl), *adj.* **1.** of or pertaining to an orchestra. **2.** composed for or performed by an orchestra. —**orches′trally,** *adv.*

orchestrate (ô′kĭs trāt′), *v.t., v.i.,* **-trated, -trating.** to compose or arrange (music) for performance by an orchestra. —**or′chestra′tion,** *n.*

orchestrion (ô kĕs′trĭ ən), *n.* a mechanical musical instrument, resembling a barrel organ but more elaborate, for producing the effect of an orchestra.

orchi-, var. of **orchido-.**

orchid (ô′kĭd), *n.* **1.** any plant of the family *Orchidaceae,* comprising terrestrial and epiphytic perennial herbs of temperate and tropical regions, with flowers which are usually beautiful and often singular in form. **2.** purple, varying from bluish to reddish. [t. NL: m. s. *Orchideae* (later *Orchidāceae*), der. L *orchis.* See ORCHIS]

orchidaceous (ô′kĭ dā′shəs), *adj.* belonging to the *Orchidaceae,* or orchid family of plants, as the vanilla.

orchidectomy (ô′kĭ dĕk′tə mĭ), *n., pl.* **-mies.** *Surg.* removal of one or both testicles; castration. Also, **orchiectomy** (ô′kĭ ĕk′tə mĭ).

orchido-. a word element meaning 'orchid' or 'testicle'. Also, **orchi-;** (esp. before vowels), **orchid-.** [*orchid-* (wrongly supposed s. of Gk *órchis* ORCHIS) + -O-]

orchidology (ô′kĭ dŏl′ə jĭ), *n.* the branch of botany or horticulture that deals with orchids.

orchil (ô′chĭl), *n.* **1.** a violet colouring matter obtained from certain lichens, chiefly species of *Roccella.* **2.** any such lichen. Cf. **litmus.** Also, **archil.** [late ME, t. OF]

orchis (ô′kĭs), *n.* **1.** any orchid. **2.** any of various terrestrial orchids (esp. of the genus *Orchis*) of temperate regions, with spicate flowers. **3.** any orchid of an allied genus, esp. *Blephariglottis,* including the fringed orchis. [t. L, t. Gk: orig., testicle; so named with reference to the shape of the root]

orchitis (ô kī′tĭs), *n. Pathol.* inflammation of the testicle.

orcinol (ô′sĭ nŏl′); *n. Chem.* a colourless crystalline compound, formula $CH_3C_6H_3(OH)_2$, found in many lichens, and also prepared synthetically. Also, **orcin** (ô′sĭn). [f. s. NL *orcina* (t. It.: m. *orcello* ORCHIL) + -OL[2]]

Orcus (ô′kəs), *n. Rom. Myth.* **1.** the world of the dead; Hades. **2.** the god of the underworld, Pluto.

Ord (ôd), *n.* a river in NE Western Australia flowing N to the Timor Sea. Ab. 300 mi.

ord., 1. order. 2. ordinal. 3. ordinance. 4. ordinary. 5. ordnance.

ordain (ô dān′), *v.t.* **1.** *Eccles.* to invest with ministerial or sacerdotal functions; confer holy orders upon. **2.** to appoint authoritatively; decree; enact. **3.** *Obs.* to select or appoint for an office. **4.** (of God, fate, etc.) to destine or predestine. [ME *ordeine(n),* t. OF: m. *ordener,* t. L: m. *ordināre* order, arrange, appoint] —**ordain′er,** *n.* —**ordain′ment,** *n.*

ordeal (ô dēl′, ô′dēl), *n.* **1.** any severe test or trial; a trying experience. **2.** a primitive form of trial to determine guilt or innocence, as by the effect of fire, poison, or water upon the accused, the result being regarded as a divine or preternatural judgement. [var. (by correct etym. assoc. with DEAL[1]) of *ordale,* ME and OE *ordāl,* var. of OE *ordēl,* c. G *Urteil* judgement]

order (ô′də), *n.* **1.** an authoritative direction, injunction, command, or mandate. **2.** *Law.* a command of a court or judge. **3.** *Mil.* a command or notice issued by an army, navy, airforce, or a military commander to troops under him. **4.** the disposition of things following one after another, as in space, time, etc.; succession or sequence. **5.** a condition in which everything is in its proper place with reference to other things and to its purpose; methodical or harmonious arrangement. **6.** *Mil.* different dress, equipment, etc., for some special purpose or occasion: *full marching order.* **7.** proper or satisfactory condition: *my watch is out of order.* **8.** state or condition generally: *affairs are in good order.* **9.** *Gram.* **a.** the arrangement of the elements of a construction in a particular sequence, e.g., the placing of *John* before and of *George* after the verb *saw* in the sentence *John saw George.* **b.** the feature of construction resulting from such an arrangement, e.g., the sentences *John saw George* and *George saw John* differs only in order. **10.** any class, kind, or sort, as of persons or things, distinguished from others by nature or character: *talents of a high order.* **11.** the usual major subdivision of a class or subclass, commonly comprising a plurality of families, e.g., the *Hymenoptera* (ants, bees, etc.). **12.** a rank, grade, or class of persons in the community. **13.** a body of persons of the same profession, occupation, or pursuits: *the clerical order.* **14.** a body or society of persons living by common consent under the same religious, moral, or social regulations. **15.** any of the degrees or grades of the clerical office (the number of which varies in different Churches: the Roman Catholic Church, for example, having the **major orders** of bishop, priest, deacon, and subdeacon, and the **minor orders** of acolyte, exorcist, lector, and ostiary, while the Anglican Church recognizes only the three grades of bishop, priest and deacon). **16.** any of the nine grades of angels in medieval angelology (see **angel,** def. 1). **17.** a monastic society or fraternity: *the Franciscan order.* **18.** (*usually pl.*) the rank or status of an ordained Christian minister. **19.** (*usually pl.*) the rite or sacrament of ordination. **20.** a prescribed form of divine service, or of administration of a rite or ceremony. **21.** the service itself. **22.** *Hist.* a society or fraternity of knights, of combined military and monastic character, as in the Middle Ages, as the Knights Templar, etc. **23.** a modern organization or society more or less resembling the knightly orders: *fraternal orders.* **24.** conformity to law or established authority; absence of revolt, disturbance, turbulence, unruliness, etc. **25.** customary mode of procedure, or established usage. **26.** the customary or prescribed mode of proceeding in debates or the like, or in the conduct of deliberative or legislative bodies, public meetings, etc. **27.** conformity to this. **28.** the natural, moral, or spiritual constitution of the world; the prevailing course of things; the established system or regime: *the old order changeth.* **29.** a direction or commission to make, provide or furnish something: *shoes made to order.* **30.** a quantity of goods purchased. **31.** a written direction to pay money or deliver goods. **32.** a pass for admission to a theatre,

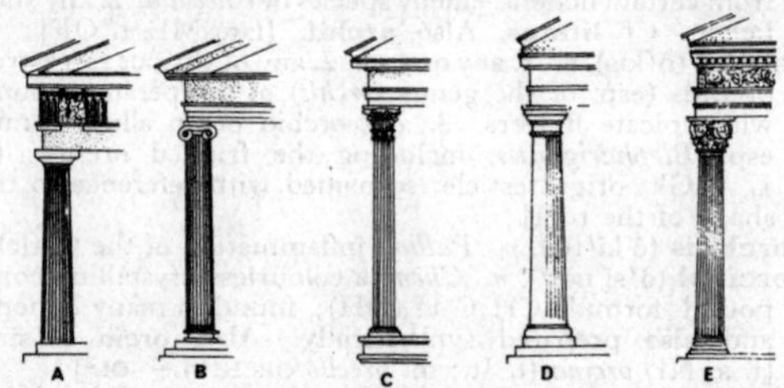

Orders of architecture
A, Doric; B, Ionic; C, Corinthian;
D, Tuscan; E, Composite

museum, or the like. **33.** *Archit.* **a.** a series of columns with their entablature arranged in given proportions. **b.** any one of the typical variations of such an arrangement distinguished by proportion, capital types and other characteristics: *the Doric, Ionic, Corinthian, Tuscan, and Composite orders.* **34.** *Maths.* **a.** degree, as in algebra. **b.** (of a derivative) the number of times a function has been differentiated. **c.** (of a differential equation) the order of the highest derivative in the equation. **35. a tall order,** *Colloq.* a difficult task or requirement. **36. call to order,** to establish or re-establish order at a meeting. **37. in order, a.** in a proper state; correctly arranged; in a state of readiness; functioning correctly. **b.** appropriate; suitable. **c.** correct according to parliamentary procedure. **38. in order that,** to the end that. **39. in order to,** as a means to. **40. in short order,** *U.S.* speedily; promptly. **41. of the order of,** about, approximately. **42. on order,** ordered but not yet received. **43. on the order of,** *U.S.* resembling to a certain extent; similar to. **44. out of order, a.** not functioning properly; broken. **b.** not in accordance with recognized parliamentary rules. —*v.t.* **45.** to give an order, direction, or command to. **46.** to direct or command to go or come (as specified): *to order a person out of one's house.* **47.** to give an order for. **48.** to prescribe: *a doctor orders a medicine for a patient.* **49.** to direct to be made, supplied, or furnished: *we ordered two steaks.* **50.** to regulate, conduct, or manage. **51.** to arrange methodically or suitably. **52.** to ordain, as God or fate does. **53.** to invest with clerical rank or authority. **54. order about,** to keep giving orders to; act in a domineering fashion towards (a person). —*v.i.* **55.** to issue orders. [ME *ordre,* t. OF, t. L: m. s. *ordo* row, rank, regular arrangement] —**or′derer,** *n.* —**Syn. 45.** See **direct.**

order arms, 1. a rifle drill position in which the rifle is held at the right side, with the butt on the ground. **2.** (as an interjection) the command to move the rifle to this position.

order in council, an order issued by the sovereign on the advice of the Privy Council.

orderly (ô′ də lĭ), *adj., adv., n., pl.* **-lies.** —*adj.* **1.** arranged or disposed in order, in regular sequence, or in a tidy manner. **2.** observant of system or method, as persons, the mind, etc. **3.** characterized by or observant of order, rule, or discipline: *an orderly citizen.* **4.** charged with the communication or execution of orders. —*adv.* **5.** according to established order or rule. **6.** *Archaic.* methodically. —*n.* **7.** *Mil.* a private soldier or a non-commissioned officer attending on a superior officer to carry orders, messages, etc. **8.** Also, **medical orderly.** a person employed in a hospital to perform certain general, non-medical duties. —**or′derliness,** *n.*

—**Syn. 1.** ORDERLY, METHODICAL, SYSTEMATIC characterize that which is neat, in order and planned. These three words are sometimes used interchangeably. However, ORDERLY emphasizes neatness of arrangement: *an orderly array of books.* METHODICAL suggests a logical plan, a definite order of actions or method from beginning to end: *a methodical examination of something.* SYSTEMATIC suggests thoroughness, an extensive and detailed plan, together with regularity of action: *a systematic review.* —**Ant. 1.** chaotic, haphazard.

orderly officer, *Mil.* a junior officer detailed by rota to a 24-hour period of duty, which includes the inspection of all buildings in the camp or barracks (notably the cookhouses and dining halls at mealtimes) and of all guards, pickets, and prisoners in the guardroom.

orderly room, *Mil.* the office set aside in a battalion for carrying out clerical duties.

order of the day, 1. (in a legislative body) a programme of business set down for discussion on a particular day. **2.** *Mil.* specific commands, instructions, or notices issued by a commanding officer to the men under his command.

order paper, a schedule of business to be discussed at a session of a legislative assembly.

order statistic, *Statistics.* one of a number of sample observations arranged in order of magnitude.

ordinal[1] (ô′ dĭ nəl), *adj.* **1.** pertaining to an order, as of animals or plants. —*n.* **2.** an ordinal number or numeral. [ME, t. LL: s. *ordinālis,* der. L *ordo* order]

ordinal[2] (ô′ dĭ nəl), *n.* **1.** a directory of ecclesiastical services. **2.** a book containing the forms for the ordination of priests, consecration of bishops, etc. [ME, t. ML: m. *ordināle.* See ORDINAL[1]]

ordinal number, any of the numbers *first, second, third, etc.* (in distinction from *one, two, three, etc.,* which are called **cardinal numbers**). Also, **ordinal numeral.**

ordinance (ô′ dĭ nəns), *n.* **1.** an authoritative rule or law; a decree or command. **2.** a public injunction or regulation. **3.** *Eccles.* **a.** an established rite or ceremony. **b.** a sacrament. **c.** the communion. [ME *ordinaunce,* t. OF: m. *ordenance,* der. *ordener* to order, t. L: m. *ordināre*]

ordinand (ô′ dĭ nănd′), *n. Eccles.* a candidate for ordination.

ordinarily (ô′ dn rĭ lĭ), *adv.* **1.** in ordinary cases; usually: **2.** in the ordinary way. **3.** to the usual extent.

ordinary (ô′ dn rĭ), *adj., n., pl.* **-ries.** —*adj.* **1.** such as is commonly met with; of the usual kind. **2.** not above, but rather below, the average level of quality; somewhat inferior. **3.** customary; normal: *for all ordinary purposes.* **4.** (of jurisdiction, etc.) immediate, as contrasted with that which is delegated. **5.** (of officials, etc.) belonging to the regular staff or the fully recognized class. —*n.* **6.** the ordinary condition, degree, run, or the like: *out of the ordinary.* **7.** something regular, customary, or usual. **8.** *Eccles.* **a.** an order or form for divine service, esp. that for saying mass. **b.** the service of the mass exclusive of the canon. **9.** *Obs. except Hist.* a clergyman appointed to prepare condemned prisoners for death. **10.** *Eccl. Law.* a bishop, archbishop, or other ecclesiastic or his deputy, in his capacity as an *ex officio* ecclesiastical authority. **11.** (in some states of the U.S.) a judge of a court of probate. **12.** a meal regularly served at a fixed price in a restaurant or inn. **13.** a restaurant or inn, or its dining room where such meals are served. **14.** *Her.* **a.** any of the simplest and commonest heraldic charges or bearings, usually bounded by straight lines. **b.** any of the more important of these. **15. in ordinary,** (of officials, etc.) in regular service: *a physician in ordinary to a king.* [ME, t. L: m. s. *ordinārius* of the usual order] —**or′dinariness,** *n.* —**Syn. 1.** See **common.**

Ordinary Level, *Educ.* (in Britain and elsewhere) the first grade of the General Certificate of Education, for which public examinations are taken, usually at fifth-form level. Also, **O Level.**

Ordinary National Certificate, *Educ.* (in Britain and elsewhere) a qualification obtained by apprentices, etc., after a two-year course in technical subjects. *Abbrev.:* O.N.C.

Ordinary National Diploma, *Educ.* (in Britain and elsewhere) a qualification obtained by apprentices, etc., after a two-year, full-time, or sandwich course in technical subjects. *Abbrev.:* O.N.D.

ordinary ray, *Physics.* the part of a doubly refracted ray which obeys the ordinary laws of refraction. Cf. **extraordinary ray.**

ordinary seaman, a seaman who is not sufficiently skilled to be classed as an able-bodied seaman. *Abbrev.:* O.S.

ordinary share, one of the series of shares into which the capital of a company is divided, which rank for dividends after preference shares and before deferred shares, if any such are in issue.

ordinate (ô′dĭ nĭt), *n. Maths.* the *y* Cartesian coordinate. [t. L: m. s. *ordinātus*, pp., ordained]

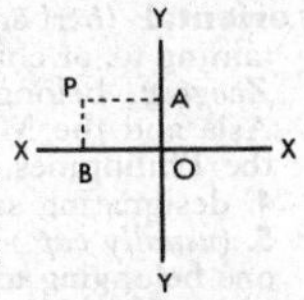

ordination (ô′dĭ nā′shən), *n.* **1.** *Eccles.* the act or ceremony of ordaining. **2.** the fact of being ordained. **3.** a decreeing. **4.** the act of arranging. **5.** the resulting state. [ME *ordinacion*, t. L: m. s. *ordinātio* ordainment, an ordering]

Y P A X X B O Y

Ordinate: P, Any point; AO and PB, Ordinate of P; YY, Axis of ordinate; OB and AP, Abscissa of P; XX, Axis of abscissa

ordn., ordnance.

ordnance (ôd′nəns), *n.* **1.** cannon or artillery. **2.** military weapons of all kinds with their equipment, ammunition, etc. [var. of ORDINANCE]

ordnance datum, the mean sea-level on which heights given in British Ordnance Survey maps are calculated, being mean sea-level at Newlyn, Cornwall, based on observations taken from 1915 to 1921.

Ordnance Survey, 1. the official map-making organization of the British government, which produces maps and large-scale plans of England, Wales, and Scotland. **2.** the official map-making organization of the government of the Republic of Ireland, which produces maps of the whole of Ireland.

ordo (ô′dō), *n., pl.* **ordines** (ô′dĭ nēz′). *Rom. Cath. Ch.* a booklet containing short and abbreviated directions for the contents of the office and mass of each day in the year. [L: row, series, order]

ordonnance (ô′də nəns; *Fr.* ŏr dŏ näNs′), *n.* **1.** arrangement or disposition of parts, as of a building, a picture, or a literary composition. **2.** an ordinance, decree, or law. [t. F. See ORDINANCE]

Ordovician (ô′dō vĭsh′yən), *Geol. —adj.* **1.** pertaining to an early Palaeozoic geological period or system. *—n.* **2.** the period or system following Cambrian and preceding Silurian. [f. s. L *Ordovicēs*, pl., an ancient British tribe in northern Wales + -IAN]

ordure (ô′dyŏŏə), *n.* filth; dung; excrement. [ME, t. OF, der. *ord* filthy, g. L *horridus* horrid]

Ordzhonikidze (*Russ.* ər jə nĭ kēd′zĭ), *n.* a town in the S Soviet Union in Europe, in Caucasia. 208,000 (est. 1965). Also, **Orjonikidze.** Formerly, **Vladikavkaz.**

ore (ô), *n.* **1.** a metal-bearing mineral or rock, or a native metal, esp. when valuable enough to be mined. **2.** a mineral or natural product serving as a source of some non-metallic substance, as sulphur. [ME (*o*)*or* metal, ore, OE *ār* brass]

öre (ûʹrə), *n., pl.* **öre.** a bronze coin and money of account of Denmark, Norway, and Sweden, equal to one hundredth of a krone or krona. [t. Dan., Sw., etc., ult. g. L *aureus* golden (coin)]

Ore., Oregon.

oread (ô′rĭ ăd′), *n. Class. Myth.* a mountain nymph. [t. L: s. *Orēas*, t. Gk: m. *Oreiás*, der. *óros* mountain]

Örebro (*Sw.* œ rə brōō′), *n.* a city in S central Sweden. 79,889 (1964).

orectic (ō rĕk′tĭk), *adj. Philos.* of or pertaining to desire; appetitive. [t. Gk: m. s. *orektikós*]

ore dressing, *Metall.* the art of separating the valuable minerals from an ore without chemical changes.

Oreg., Oregon.

oregano (ə rĕg′ə nō′), *n.* a plant of the mint family of the genus *Origanum*, related to but spicier than marjoram, used in cookery.

Oregon (ŏ′rĭ gən), *n.* a state in the NW United States, on the Pacific coast. 1,768,687 pop. (1960). 96,981 sq. mi. *Cap.:* Salem. *Abbrev.:* Oreg. *or* Ore. **—Oregonian** (ŏ′rĭ gō′nyən), *adj., n.*

Oregon grape, 1. an evergreen shrub, *Mahonia aquifolium*, of the western coast of the U.S. and British Columbia, having small, blue, edible berries. **2.** the berry.

Oregon pine, Douglas fir.

Oregon Trail, a route for westward pioneers in the U.S., starting in Missouri and reaching Oregon, much used in the mid-19th century. ab. 2000 mi. long.

Orel (ō rĕl′; *Russ.* á ryôl′), *n.* a town in the central Soviet Union in Europe. 190,000 (est. 1964).

Orenburg (ŏ′rən bûg′), *n.* a city in the E Soviet Union in Europe. 300,000 (est. 1964). Formerly, **Chkalov.**

Orense (*Sp.* ō rĕn′sĕ), *n.* a town in N Spain. 67,315 (est. 1964).

oreography (ô′rĭ ŏg′rə fĭ), *n.* orography. **—oreographic** (ô′rĭ ə grăf′ĭk), **o′reograph′ical,** *adj.*

oreology (ô′rĭ ŏl′ə jĭ), *n.* orology. **—oreological** (ô′rĭ ə lŏj′ĭ kl), *adj.* **—oreologist** (ô′rĭ ŏl′ə jĭst), *n.*

Orestes (ō rĕs′tēz), *n. Gk Legend.* son of Agamemnon and Clytemnestra, and brother of Electra: slew his mother and Aegisthus, who had slain Agamemnon.

Öresund (*Swed.* œ rə sōōnd′), *n.* Swedish and Danish name of **The Sound.**

Oreti (ə rĕt′ĭ), *n.* a river in South Island, New Zealand, flowing S to Foveaux Strait. 120 mi.

Orff (*Ger.* ŏrf), *n.* **Carl** (*Ger.* kărl), born 1895, German composer and conductor.

orfray (ô′frĭ), *n.* orphrey.

org., 1. organic. **2.** organized.

organ (ô′gən), *n.* **1. a.** a musical instrument (**pipe organ**) consisting of one or more sets of pipes sounded by means of compressed air, played by means of keys arranged in one or more keyboards: in its full modern development the largest and most complicated of musical instruments. **b.** a musical instrument (**electronic** or **electric organ**) resembling a pipe organ but sounded electrophonically. **2.** a reed organ or harmonium. **3.** a barrel organ or hand organ. **4.** *Obs.* any of various musical instruments, esp. wind instruments. **5.** (in an animal or a plant) a part or member, as the heart, having some specific function. **6.** an instrument or means, as of performance. **7.** a means or medium of communicating thoughts, opinions, etc., as a newspaper serving as the mouthpiece of a political party. [ME, t. L: s. *organum*, t. Gk: m. *órganon* instrument, tool, bodily organ, musical instrument]

organdie (ô′gən dĭ), *n., pl.* **-dies.** a fine, thin stiff cotton fabric usually having a durable crisp finish, and either white, dyed or printed; used for dresses, curtains, etc. Also, *U.S.*, **organdy.** [t. F: m. *organdi*; orig. uncert.]

organ-grinder (ô′gən grīn′də), *n.* a street musician who plays a hand organ by turning the crank.

organic (ô găn′ĭk), *adj.* **1.** denoting or pertaining to a class of chemical compounds which formerly comprised only those existing in or derived from living organisms (animal or plant), but which now includes these and all other compounds of carbon except for its oxides, sulphides, and metal carbonates. **2.** characteristic of, pertaining to, or derived from living organisms: *organic remains found in rocks.* **3.** of or pertaining to an organ or the organs of an animal or a plant. **4.** *Philos.* of or pertaining to any physical, mental, intellectual, or other organism. **5.** characterized by the systematic arrangement of parts; organized; systematic. **6.** of or pertaining to the constitution or structure of a thing; constitutional; structural. **7.** *Law.* of or pertaining to the constitutional or essential law or laws organizing the government of a state. [t. L: s. *organicus*, t. Gk: m. *organikós*] **—Syn. 6.** inherent, fundamental, essential.

organically (ô găn′ĭk lĭ), *adv.* **1.** in an organic manner; by or with organs. **2.** with reference to organic structure. **3.** by or through organization.

organic chemistry, the branch of chemistry dealing with the compounds of carbon; originally limited to substances found only in living organisms.

organic disease, a disease in which there is a structural alteration (opposed to *functional disease*).

organicism (ô găn′ĭ sĭz′əm), *n.* **1.** *Biol., Philos.* the theory that vital activities arise not from any one part of an organism but from its autonomous composition. **2.** *Neurol.* the doctrine that all or the majority of the diseases of the nervous system, including those of the mind, are organic, due to demonstrable changes in the brain or spinal cord. **—organicist** (ô găn′ĭ sĭst), *n.*

organic law, See **law** (def. 2).

organism (ô′gə nĭz′əm), *n.* **1.** an individual composed of mutually dependent parts constituted for subserving vital processes. **2.** any form of animal or plant life: *microscopic organisms.* **3.** any organized body or system analogous to a living being. **4.** *Philos.* any structure the parts of which function not only in terms of one another, but also in terms of the whole.

organist (ô′gə nĭst), *n.* one who plays an organ.

organization (ô′gə nĭ zā′shən), *n.* **1.** the act or process of organizing. **2.** the state or manner of being organized. **3.** that which is organized. **4.** organic structure. **5.** any organized whole. **6.** a body of persons organized for some end or work. **7.** the administrative personnel or apparatus of a business. **8.** *U.S.* the functionaries of a political party together with the offices, committees, etc. which they hold or of which they are members. **9.** an organism. Also, **organisation. —or′ganiza′tional,** *adj.*

organization and method, the application of scientific techniques to business problems by measuring the efficiency of work performed. *Abbrev.*: O. and M.

Organization of African Unity, an association of independent African states founded in Addis Ababa in 1963, which pledged itself to a policy which included respect for the sovereignty of member states, the promotion of mutual cooperation, and non-alignment in world affairs. *Abbrev.*: OAU.

Organization of American States, an organization comprising the U.S. and various Central and South American states, formed for the purpose of cooperation in economic, military, and political matters. *Abbrev.*: OAS.

organize (ô′gə nīz′), *v.*, **-nized, -nizing.** —*v.t.* **1.** to form as or into a whole consisting of interdependent or coordinated parts, esp. for harmonious or united action: *to organize a party.* **2.** to systematize: *to organize facts.* **3.** to give organic structure or character to. **4.** to build a trade union among: *to organize workers.* **5.** to enlist the employees of into a trade union: *to organize a factory.* —*v.i.* **6.** to combine in an organized company, party, or the like. **7.** to assume organic structure. Also, **organise.** [ME, t. ML: m. s. *organizāre*, der. L *organum* ORGAN] —**or′ganiz′able,** *adj.*

organized ferment. See **ferment** (def. 1a).

organized labour, *Chiefly U.S.* all workers who are organized in trade unions.

organizer (ô′gə nī′zə), *n.* **1.** one who organizes. **2.** *Embryol.* any part of an embryo that influences the development and differentiation of another part. Also, **organiser.**

organo-, word element meaning 'organ' or 'organic'. [t. Gk, comb. form of *órganon*]

organography (ô′gə nŏg′rə fĭ), *n.* the description of the organs of animals or plants.

organology (ô′gə nŏl′ə jĭ), *n.* **1.** the branch of biology that deals with the structure and functions of the organs of animals or plants. **2.** phrenology.

organometallic (ô găn′ō mĭ tăl′ĭk), *adj. Chem.* of or pertaining to an organic compound in which one or more metal atoms are linked to a carbon atom.

organon (ô′gə nŏn′), *n.*, *pl.* **-na** (-nə), **-nons.** **1.** an instrument of thought or knowledge. **2.** *Philos.* a system of rules or principles of demonstration or investigation. [t. Gk. See ORGAN]

organotherapy (ô′gə nō thĕ′rə pĭ), *n.* that branch of therapeutics which deals with the use of remedies prepared from the organs of animals, as the thyroid gland, the pancreas, the suprarenal bodies, etc. Also, **organotherapeutics** (ô′gə nō thĕ′rə pyōō′tĭks).

organ pipe, **1.** one of the pipes of a pipe organ. **2.** something resembling such a pipe.

organum (ô′gə nəm), *n.*, *pl.* **-na** (-nə), **-nums.** **1.** an organon. **2.** *Music.* **a.** the doubling, or simultaneous singing, of a melody at an interval of either a fourth, fifth, or octave. **b.** the second part in such singing. [t. L. See ORGAN]

organza (ô găn′zə), *n.* a fabric made from a mixture of silk or nylon with cotton: similar to organdie but less fine.

organzine (ô′gən zēn′, ô găn′zēn), *n.* silk yarn used in weaving silk fabrics.

orgasm (ô′găz′əm), *n.* **1.** *Physiol.* a complex series of responses of the genital organs and skin at the culmination of a sexual act. **2.** immoderate excitement. [t. NL: s. *orgasmus*, t. Gk: m. *orgasmós*, der. *orgân* swell, be excited] —**orgastic** (ô găs′tĭk), *adj.*

orgeat (ô′zhä; *Fr.* ŏr zhá′), *n.* a syrup or drink made from almonds (orig. from barley), sugar, and a water prepared from orange flowers. [t. F, t. Pr., der. *orge*, g. L *hordeum* barley]

Orgetorix (ô jĕt′ə rĭks), *n.* fl. *c.* 60 B.C. Helvetian chieftain.

orgiastic (ô′jĭ ăs′tĭk), *adj.* of, pertaining to, or of the nature of orgies. [t. Gk: m. s. *orgiastikós*]

orgy (ô′jĭ), *n.*, *pl.* **-gies.** **1.** wild, drunken, or licentious festivities or revelry. **2.** any proceedings marked by unbridled indulgence of passions: *an orgy of killing.* **3.** (*pl.*) secret rites or ceremonies connected with the worship of certain deities of classical mythology, esp. the rites in honour of Dionysus, celebrated with wild dancing and singing, drinking, etc. [t. L: m. s. *orgia*, pl., t. Gk]

oribi (ŏ′rĭ bĭ), *n.*, *pl.* **-bis.** a small tan-coloured antelope, *Ourebia ourebi*, of southern and eastern Africa, with spikelike horns. [t. Afrikaans, t. Hottentot]

oriel (ô′rĭ əl), *n.* a bay window, usually semi-polygonal, esp. in an upper storey. Also, **oriel window.** [ME, t. OF: m. *oriol* porch, passage, gallery, ult. der. L *aureolus* gilded]

Oriel

orient (*n.*, *adj.* ô′rĭ ənt; *v.* ô′rĭ ĕnt′), *n.* **1. the Orient, a.** the East: the countries to the E (and SE) of the Mediterranean. **b.** the countries of Asia generally, especially E Asia. **2.** *Archaic.* the east; the eastern regions of the heavens or the earth. **3.** the lustre peculiar to the pearl. **4.** an orient pearl. —*adj.* **5.** *Archaic.* rising; appearing as from beneath the horizon: *the orient sun.* **6.** *Now Poetic.* eastern or oriental. **7.** fine or lustrous, as gems, esp. pearls. —*v.t.*, *v.i.* **8.** to orientate. [ME, t. L: s. *oriens* the east, sunrise, n. use of ppr., rising]

oriental (ô′rĭ ĕn′tl), *adj.* **1.** (*sometimes cap.*) of, pertaining to, or characteristic of the Orient or East. **2.** (*cap.*) *Zoogeog.* belonging to a division comprising southern Asia and the Malay Archipelago as far as and including the Philippines, Borneo, and Java. **3.** (of gems) orient. **4.** designating sapphire varieties: *oriental amethyst.* —*n.* **5.** (*usually cap.*) a native or inhabitant of the Orient, esp. one belonging to a native race. [ME, t. L: s. *orientālis*]

orientalism (ô′rĭ ĕn′tə lĭz′əm), *n.* (*sometimes cap.*) **1.** a peculiarity of the oriental peoples. **2.** the character or characteristics of oriental people. **3.** the knowledge and study of oriental languages, literature, etc. —**o′rien′talist,** *n.*

orientalize (ô′rĭ ĕn′tə līz′), *v.t.*, *v.i.*, **-lized, -lizing.** (*sometimes cap.*) to make or become oriental. Also, **orientalise.**

oriental rug, any handmade rug or carpet usually woven in Asia.

orientate (ô′rĭ ĕn tāt′), *v.*, **-tated, -tating.** —*v.t.* **1.** to place so as to face the east, esp. to build (a church) with the chief altar to the east and the chief entrance to the west. **2.** to place in any definite position with reference to the points of the compass or other points: *to orientate a building north and south.* **3.** to adjust with relation to, or bring into due relation to, surroundings, circumstances, facts, etc.: *to orientate one's ideas to new conditions.* **4.** *Survey.* to turn a map or plane-table sheet so that the north direction on the map is parallel to the north direction on the ground. —*v.i.* **5.** to turn towards the east or in specified direction.

orientation (ô′rĭ ĕn tā′shən), *n.* **1.** the act or process of orientating. **2.** the state of being orientated. **3.** *Psychol.* the ability to locate oneself in one's environment with reference to time, place, and people. **4.** the ascertainment of one's true position, as in a novel situation, with reference to new ideas, etc. **5.** *Chem.* **a.** the arrangement of atoms or radicals in a particular position due to electrical charges, etc. **b.** the determination of the position of substituted atoms or radicals in a compound.

Oriente (*Sp.* ò ryèn′tè), *n.* a region in Ecuador, E of the Andes: the border long disputed by Peru.

orienteering (ô′rĭ ĕn tĭə′rĭng), *n.* a sport in which competitors race on foot, skis, cycle, or otherwise over a course consisting of a number of checkpoints which must be located with the aid of maps, compasses, etc.

orifice (ŏ′rĭ fĭs), *n.* a mouth or aperture, as of a tube or pipe; a mouthlike opening or hole; a vent. [t. F, t. L: m. s. *ōrificium*]

oriflamme (ŏ′rĭ flăm′), *n.* **1.** the red banner of St-Denis, near Paris, carried before the early kings of France as a military ensign. **2.** any ensign or standard. [late ME *oriflam*, t. F: m. *oriflamme*, f. OF *orie* golden (g. L *aureus*) + *flamme* FLAME]

orig., **1.** origin. **2.** original. **3.** originally.

origan (ŏ′rĭ gən), *n.* marjoram, esp. the Old World wild marjoram, *Origanum vulgare.* [ME, t. L: s. *orīganum*, t. Gk: m. *orī́ganon*]

Origen (ŏ′rĭ jĕn′), *n.* (*Origenes Adamantius*), A.D. *c.* 185–*c.* 254, Christian theologian, writer, and teacher, at Alexandria.

origin (ŏ′rĭ jĭn), *n.* **1.** that from which anything arises or is derived; the source: *to follow a stream to its origin.* **2.** rise or derivation from a particular source: *these and other reports of like origin.* **3.** the first stage of existence; the beginning: *the date of origin of a sect.* **4.** birth; parentage; extraction: *Scottish origin.* **5.** *Anat.* **a.** the point of derivation. **b.** the more fixed portion of a muscle. **6.** *Maths.* the point of intersection of two or more axes in a system of Cartesian or polar coordinates; the point from which a measurement is taken. [t. L: s. *origo* beginning, source, rise]

original (ə rĭj′ĭ nəl), *adj.* **1.** belonging or pertaining to the origin or beginning of something, or to a thing at its beginning: *the original binding.* **2.** new; fresh; novel: *an original way of advertising.* **3.** arising or proceeding from a thing itself, or independently of anything else. **4.** capable of or given to thinking or acting independently in self-suggested and individual ways: *an original thinker.* **5.** proceeding from a person as the inventor, maker, composer, or author: *original research.* **6.** being that from which a copy, a translation, or the like is made: *the original document is in the British Museum.* —*n.* **7.** a primary form or type from which varieties are derived. **8.** an original work, writing, or the like, as opposed to any copy or imitation. **9.** the person or thing represented by a picture, description, etc. **10.** one who is original in his ways of thinking or acting. **11.** an eccentric person. **12.** *Archaic.* a source of being; an author or originator.

original gum, *Philately.* the gum on the back of a stamp as issued by the post office.

originality (ə rĭj′ĭ năl′ĭ tĭ), *n., pl.* **-ties. 1.** the state or quality of being original. **2.** ability to think or act in an independent, individual manner. **3.** freshness or novelty, as of an idea, method, or performance.

originally (ə rĭj′ĭ nə lĭ), *adv.* **1.** with respect to origin; by origin. **2.** at the origin; at first. **3.** in the first place; primarily. **4.** from the beginning. **5.** in an original, novel, or distinctively individual manner.

original sin, *Theol.* **1.** a depravity, or tendency to evil, held to be innate in mankind and transmitted from Adam to the race in consequence of his sin. **2.** *Rom. Cath. Ch.* the privation of sanctifying grace in consequence of Adam's sin.

originate (ə rĭj′ ĭ nāt′), *v.,* **-nated, -nating.** —*v.i.* **1.** to take its origin or rise; arise; spring. —*v.t.* **2.** to give origin or rise to; initiate; invent. **—orig′ina′tion,** *n.* **—orig′ina′tor,** *n.* **—Syn. 2.** See **discover.**

originative (ə rĭj′ĭ nā′tĭv), *adj.* having or characterized by the power of originating; creative. **—orig′ina′tively,** *adv.*

orinasal (ô′rĭ nā′zəl), *Phonet.* —*adj.* **1.** sounded with the voice issuing through the mouth and nose at the same time, as the nasalized vowels in French. —*n.* **2.** an orinasal sound.

Orinoco (ō′rĭ nō′kō), *n.* a large river in N South America, flowing from S Venezuela into the Atlantic. ab. 1600 mi.

Orinoco River

oriole (ô′rĭ ōl′), *n.* **1.** any bird of the Old World passerine family *Oriolidae,* mostly bright yellow with black on the head, wings, and tail, as the **golden oriole,** *Oriolus oriolus,* of Europe and Africa. **2.** any of various brightly coloured American passerine birds of the family *Iceridae,* not closely related to the true orioles of the Old World, as the Baltimore oriole, *Icterus galbula.* [t. ML: m. s. *oriolus,* var. of L *aureolus* golden]

Orion (ə rī′ən), *n., gen.* **Orionis** (ô′rĭ ō′nĭs). **1.** *Gk Myth.* a giant and a hunter who pursued the Pleiades and was eventually slain by Artemis. He then became the giant constellation. **2.** *Astron.* a constellation, south of Gemini and Taurus, containing the bright stars Betelgeuse and Rigel, and a remarkable gaseous nebula.

orison (ŏ′rĭ zən), *n.* a prayer. [ME, t. OF, g. L *ōrātio* prayer. Cf. ORATION]

Orissa (ŏ rĭs′ə), *n.* a state in E India. 17,548,846 pop. (1961); 60,136 sq. mi. *Cap.:* Cuttack.

-orium. See **-ory².**

Oriya (ŏ rē′yə, -rē′ə), *n.* the Indic language of Orissa.

Orjonikidze (*Russ.* ər jə nĭ kĕd′zĭ), *n.* Ordzhonikidze.

Orkney Islands (ôk′nĭ), an island group off the NE tip of Scotland, comprising a county in Scotland. 18,743 pop. (1961); 376 sq. mi. *Co. town:* Kirkwell.

Orlando (*It.* ọr lȧn′dọ), *n.* **Vittorio Emanuele** (*It.* vēt tŏ′ryọ ė mȧ nwĕ′lė), 1860–1952, Italian statesman.

orle (ôl), *n. Her.* **1.** a narrow band within the shield and following the contour of its edge. **2.** a number of small charges set round the edge of a shield in the manner of an orle. [t. F, g. LL *ōrulum,* dim. of L *ōra* border]

Orléanais (*Fr.* ŏr lė ȧ nĕ′), *n.* a former province in N France. *Cap.:* Orléans.

Orleanist (ô lĭə′nĭst), *n. French Hist.* an adherent of the Orléans family, which is descended from the younger brother of Louis XIV.

Orléans (ô lĭənz′; *Fr.* ŏr lė äN′), *n.* **1.** a city in N France, on the river Loire: siege raised by Joan of Arc, 1428. 84,233 (1962). **2. Louis Philippe Joseph** (*Fr.* lwē fē lēp zhọ zĕf′), **Duc d',** (*Philippe Egalité*) 1747–1793, French political leader.

Orlon (ô′lŏn), *n. Trademark.* a synthetic acrylic textile fibre of light weight and good crease resistance.

orlop (ô′lŏp), *n.* the lowest deck of a ship. [late ME, t. D: m. *overloop,* der. *overloopen* overrun, spread over; so called because it covers the ship's hold]

Orly (*Fr.* ŏr lē′), *n.* one of two international airports in Paris. See **Le Bourget.**

Ormandy (ô′mən dĭ), *n.* **Eugene** (yo͞o′jēn), born 1899, U.S. conductor and violinist, born in Hungary.

Ormazd (ô′məzd), *n. Zoroastrianism.* the cosmic principle, spirit, or person, in ceaseless conflict with the spirit of darkness and evil, Ahriman; Ahura Mazda. Also, **Ormuzd.** [t. Pers., g. Avestan *Ahura Mazda* wise lord]

ormer (ô′mə), *n.* **1.** an abalone, *Haliotis tuberculata,* a gastropod mollusc abundant in the Channel Islands. **2.** any abalone. [t. F: m. *ormier* (g. L *auris maris* sea ear)]

ormolu (ô′mə lo͞o′), *n.* **1.** an alloy of copper and zinc, used to imitate gold. **2. a.** gold prepared for use in gilding. **b.** gilded metal. [t. F: m. *or moulu* ground gold, f. *or* (g. L *aurum* gold) + *moulu,* pp. of *moudre* grind (g. L *molere*]

Ormuz (ô′mŭz), *n.* **Strait of.** See **Hormuz.**

ornament (*n.* ô′nə mənt; *v.* ô′nə mĕnt′), *n.* **1.** an accessory, article, or detail used to beautify the appearance or general effect: *architectural ornaments.* **2.** any adornment or means of adornment. **3.** a person who adds lustre, as to surroundings, society, etc. **4.** the act of adorning. **5.** the state of being adorned. **6.** mere outward display. **7.** *Chiefly Eccles.* any accessory, adjunct, or equipment. **8.** *Music.* a note or group of notes applied as decoration to a principal melody. —*v.t.* **9.** to furnish with ornaments. **10.** to be an ornament to. [t. L: s. *ornāmentum* equipment, ornament; r. ME *ornement,* t. OF]

ornamental (ô′nə mĕn′tl), *adj.* **1.** used for ornament: *ornamental plants.* **2.** such as to ornament; decorative. **3.** of or pertaining to ornament. —*n.* **4.** something ornamental. **5.** a plant cultivated for decorative purposes. **—or′namental′ity,** *n.* **—or′namen′tally,** *adv.*

ornamentation (ô′nə mĕn tā′shən), *n.* **1.** the act of ornamenting. **2.** the state of being ornamented. **3.** that with which a thing is ornamented.

ornate (ô nāt′), *adj.* **1.** elaborately adorned; sumptuously or showily splendid or fine. **2.** embellished with rhetoric, as a style or discourse. [ME, t. L: m. s. *ornātus,* pp., adorned] **—ornate′ly,** *adv.* **—ornate′ness,** *n.*

Orne (*Fr.* ŏrn), *n.* a department in NW France. 280,549 pop. (1962); 2371 sq. mi. *Cap.:* Alençon.

ornery (ô′nə rĭ), *adj. U.S.* **1.** *Colloq.* ugly in disposition or temper. **2.** *Colloq.* stubborn. **3.** *Colloq.* low or vile. **4.** *Chiefly Dial.* ordinary; common. [contr. of ORDINARY]

ornis (ô′nĭs), *n.* an avifauna. [t. G, t. Gk: bird]

ornith., **1.** ornithological. **2.** ornithology.

ornithic (ô nĭth′ĭk), *adj.* of or pertaining to birds. [t. Gk: m. s. *ornithikós* birdlike]

ornithine (ô′nĭ thēn′), *n. Chem., Biochem.* an amino acid, $H_2N(CH_2)_3CH(NH)_2COOH$, obtained by hydrolysis of arginine.

ornitho-, a word element meaning 'bird'. Also, **ornith-.** [t. Gk, comb. form of *órnis*]

ornithoid (ô′nĭ thoid′), *adj.* birdlike.

ornithol., **1.** ornithological. **2.** ornithology.

ornithology (ô′nĭ thŏl′ə jĭ), *n.* the branch of zoology that deals with birds. **—ornithological** (ô′nĭ thə lŏj′ĭ kl), *adj.* **—or′nithol′ogist,** *n.*

ornithopod (ô′nĭ thō pŏd′, ô nĭth′ō pŏd′), *n.* any of the *Ornithopoda,* a group of dinosaurs that walked erect on their hind feet. [t. NL: s. *Ornithopoda,* pl.; or f. ORNITHO- + -POD]

ornithopter (ô′nĭ thŏp′tə), *n.* a heavier-than-air craft sustained in and propelled through the air by flapping wings. [f. ORNITHO- + s. Gk *pterón* wing]

ornithorhynchus (ô′nĭ thō rĭng′kəs), *n.* the duck-billed platypus. [t. NL, f. Gk: *ornitho-* ORNITHO- + m. *rhýnchos* snout, beak]

ornithosis (ô′nĭ thō′sĭs), *n.* a disease of domestic pigeons and other birds, similar to psittacosis, occasionally transmitted to man.

oro-, a word element meaning 'mountain', as in *orography.* [t. Gk, comb. form of *óros*]

orobanchaceous (ô′rō băng kā′shəs), *adj.* belonging to the *Orobanchaceae,* the widespread broomrape family of parasitic herbs. [f. s. L *orobanchē* (t. Gk: broomrape) + -ACEOUS]

orogenesis (ô′rō jĕn′ĭ sĭs), *n. Geol.* the process of mountain-making or upheaval. Also, **orogeny** (ŏ rŏj′ĭ nĭ). **—orogenetic** (ô′rō jĭ nĕt′ĭk), **orogenic** (ô′rō jĕn′ĭk), *adj.*

orographic clouds, *Meteorol.* clouds formed, under suitable conditions, by the passage of air over a mountain or ridge.

orography (ŏ rŏg′rə fĭ), *n.* that branch of physical geography which deals with mountains. Also, **oreography. —orographic** (ŏ′rō grăf′ĭk), **or′ograph′ical,** *adj.*

oroide (ô′rō īd′), *n.* an alloy containing copper, tin, etc., used to imitate gold. [t. F: f. *or* (g. L *aurum*) gold + *-oide* -OID]

orology (ŏ rŏl′ə jĭ), *n.* the science of mountains. Also,

oreology. —**orological** (ŏ′rə lŏj′ĭ kl), *adj.* —**orol′ogist,** *n.*

orometer (ŏ rŏm′ĭ tə), *n.* an aneroid barometer with a scale giving elevations above sea-level, used to determine altitudes of mountains, etc.

Orontes (ŏ rŏn′tēz), *n.* a river flowing from the Lebanon valley N through NW Syria and SW past Antioch, Turkey, into the Mediterranean. ab. 250 mi.

oropharynx (ô′rō fă′rĭngks), *n., pl.* **-pharynges** (-fə rĭn′jēz), **-pharynxes.** *Anat.* **1.** the space immediately beneath the mouth cavity. **2.** the pharynx as distinguished from the nasopharynx. [f. *oro-* (comb. form repr. L *ōs* mouth) + PHARYNX]

orotund (ŏ′rō tŭnd′), *adj.* **1.** (of the voice or utterance) characterized by strength, fullness, richness, and clearness. **2.** (of a style of utterance) pompous or bombastic. [t. L: m. *ōre rotundō*, lit., with round mouth]

Orozco (*Sp.* ȯ rȯth′kȯ), *n.* **José Clemente** (*Sp.* KHȯ sĕ′ klĕ mĕn′tĕ), 1883–1949, Mexican painter.

orphan (ô′fən), *n.* **1.** a child bereaved by death of both parents, or, less commonly, of one parent. —*adj.* **2.** of or for orphans: *an orphan institution.* **3.** bereaved of parents. —*v.t.* **4.** to bereave of parents or a parent. [late ME, t. LL: s. *orphanus*, t. Gk: m. *orphanós* without parents, bereaved] —**or′phanhood′,** *n.*

orphanage (ô′fə nĭj), *n.* **1.** an institution for orphans. **2.** the state of being an orphan. **3.** *Archaic.* orphans collectively.

Orpheus (ô′fĭ əs, -fyōōs), *n. Gk Myth.* a Thracian poet and musician, a son of Apollo and Calliope. He followed his dead wife Eurydice to Hades and was allowed by Pluto, whom he had charmed by his music, to lead her out, provided that he did not look back. At the last moment he did so, and she was lost to him for ever. —**Orphean** (ô fē′ən), *adj.*

Orphic (ô′fĭk), *adj.* **1.** of or pertaining to Orpheus. **2.** resembling the music attributed to Orpheus; entrancing. **3.** pertaining to a religious or philosophical school maintaining a form of the cult of Dionysus or Bacchus, ascribed to Orpheus as founder: *Orphic mysteries.* **4.** (*often l.c.*) mystic; oracular. [t. Gk: m. s. *orphikós*]

Orphism (ô′fĭz′əm), *n.* **1.** the religious or philosophical system of the Orphic school. **2.** Also, **Orphic cubism.** (*often l.c.*) an art movement, dating from 1912, asserting the importance of colour as visual communication, resulting in a form of pure abstract painting.

orphrey (ô′frĭ), *n., pl.* **-phreys. 1.** an ornamental band or border, esp. on an ecclesiastical vestment. **2.** *Now only Hist. or Archaic.* gold embroidery. **3.** *Now only Hist. or Archaic.* rich embroidery of any sort. **4.** a piece of richly embroidered stuff. Also, **orfray.** [ME *orfreis*, t. OF, g. LL *aurifrisium*, for L *aurumphrygium* gold embroidery, lit., Phrygian gold]

orpiment (ô′pĭ mənt), *n.* a mineral, arsenic trisulphide, As_2S_3, found usually in soft yellow foliated masses, used as a pigment, etc. [ME, t. OF, t. L: m. s. *auripigmentum* gold pigment]

orpine (ô′pĭn), *n.* a crassulaceous perennial, *Sedum telephium*, bearing purplish flowers. Also, **or′pin.** [ME, t. F, back-formation from *orpiment* ORPIMENT]

Orpington (ô′pĭng tən), *n.* **1.** one of a breed of large white-skinned domestic fowls. **2.** a town in England, in Kent. 80,293 (1961).

orra (ô′rə, ŏ′rə), *adj. Scot.* odd; extra; occasional.

orrery (ŏ′rə rĭ), *n., pl.* **-reries. 1.** an apparatus for representing the motions and phases of the planets, etc., in the solar system. **2.** any of certain similar machines, as a planetarium. [named after the Earl of *Orrery*, 1676–1731, for whom it was first made]

orris[1] (ŏ′rĭs), *n.* any of certain species of iris, as *Iris florentina*, with a fragrant rootstock. Also, **or′rice.** [unexplained var. of IRIS]

orris[2] (ŏ′rĭs), *n.* embroidery made of gold lace; lace of various patterns of gold and silver. [? var. of ORPHREY]

orrisroot (ŏ′rĭs rōōt′), *n.* the rootstock of the orris, used as a perfume, etc.

Orsat apparatus (ô′sət, -săt), *Chem.* a portable apparatus for determining the amounts of carbon dioxide, carbon monoxide, and oxygen in a flue gas.

Orsk (*Russ.* ôrsk), *n.* a town in the E Soviet Union in Europe, on the Ural river. 210,000 (est. 1965).

ort (ôt), *n.* (*usually pl.*) a fragment of food left at a meal. [ME, c. LG *ort*, early mod. D *oorete*, f. *oor-* rejected (lit., out, from) + *ete* food. Cf. OE *or-*, *ǣt*]

Ortegal (*Sp.* ȯr tĕ găl′), *n.* **Cape,** a cape in NW Spain, on the Bay of Biscay.

Ortega y Gasset (*Sp.* ȯr tĕ′ gȧ ē gȧ sĕt′), **José** (*Sp.* KHȯ sĕ′), 1883–1955, Spanish philosopher and writer.

Orth., Orthodox.

orthite (ô′thīt), *n.* a variety of allanite.

ortho-, 1. a word element meaning 'straight', 'upright', 'right', 'correct', used in combination. **2.** *Chem.* **a.** a prefix indicating that acid of a series which contains most water. Cf. **meta-, pyro-. b.** a prefix applied to a salt of one of these acids: if the acid ends in *-ic*, the corresponding salt ends in *-ate*, as *orthoboric acid* (H_3BO_3) and *potassium orthoborate* (K_3BO_3); if the acid ends in *-ous*, the corresponding salt ends in *-ite*, as *orthoantimonous acid* (H_3SbO_3) and *potassium orthoantimonite* (K_3SbO_3). **c.** a prefix designating the 1.2 position in the benzene ring. [t. Gk, comb. form of *orthós* straight, upright, right, correct]

orthoboric acid (ô′thō bô′rĭk), *Chem.* a white crystalline solid, H_3BO_3, occurring in nature or prepared from borates, used in aqueous solution as a mild antiseptic and in glazes; boric acid.

orthocaine (ô′thə kān′), *n. Chem.* a white crystalline solid, $OH.NH_2.C_6H_3.COOCH_3$, used as a local anaesthetic.

orthocentre (ô′thō sĕn′tə), *n. Geom.* the point of intersection of the altitudes of a triangle.

orthocephalic (ô′thō sĭ făl′ĭk), *adj.* having the relation between the height of the skull and the breadth or the length medium or intermediate. Also, **orthocephalous** (ô′thō sĕf′ə ləs). —**or′thoceph′aly,** *n.*

orthochromatic (ô′thō krō măt′ĭk), *adj. Photog.* **1.** pertaining to or representing the correct relations of colours, as in nature. **2.** designating a film or plate sensitive to yellow and green as well as to blue and violet.

orthoclase (ô′thō klăs′), *n.* a very common mineral of the felspar group, potassium aluminium silicate, $KAlSi_3O_8$, occurring as an important constituent in many igneous rocks: used in the manufacture of porcelain. [f. ORTHO- + m. s. Gk *klâsis* cleavage]

orthodontics (ô′thō dŏn′tĭks), *n.* the branch of dentistry that is concerned with the straightening of irregular teeth. Also, **orthodontia** (ô′thō dŏn′tyə). [t. NL, f. Gk: *orth(o)-* ORTHO- + -ODONT (s. *odoús* tooth) + -ICS] —**or′thodon′tic,** *adj.* —**or′thodon′tist,** *n.*

orthodox (ô′thə dŏks′), *adj.* **1.** sound or correct in opinion or doctrine, esp. theological or religious doctrine. **2.** conforming to the Christian faith as represented in the primitive ecumenical creeds. **3.** (*cap.*) of, pertaining to, or designating the Eastern Church, esp. the Greek Orthodox Church. **4.** (*cap.*) of, pertaining to, or designating Orthodox Jews or Orthodox Judaism. **5.** of, pertaining to, or conforming to the approved or accepted form of any doctrine, philosophy, ideology, etc. **6.** approved; conventional. [t. LL: s. *orthodoxus*, t. Gk: m. *orthódoxos* right in opinion] —**or′thodox′ly,** *adv.*

Orthodox Church, the Christian Church of the countries formerly comprised in the Eastern Roman Empire, and of countries evangelized from it, as Russia; the Church or group of local and national oriental Churches in communion or doctrinal agreement with the Greek patriarchal see of Constantinople.

orthodoxy (ô′thə dŏk′sĭ), *n., pl.* **-doxies. 1.** orthodox belief or practice. **2.** orthodox character.

orthoepy (ô′thō ĕp′ĭ), *n.* the study of correct pronunciation. [t. Gk: m. s. *orthoépeia* correctness of diction] —**orthoepic** (ô′thō ĕp′ĭk), *adj.* —**or′thoep′ist,** *n.*

orthogenesis (ô′thō jĕn′ĭ sĭs), *n.* **1.** *Biol.* the evolution of species in definite lines which are predetermined by the constitution of the germ plasm. **2.** *Sociol.* a hypothetical parallelism between the stages through which any culture necessarily passes, in spite of secondary conditioning factors. —**orthogenetic** (ô′thō jĭ nĕt′ĭk), *adj.*

orthognathous (ô thŏg′nə thəs), *adj. Anat.* straight-jawed; having the profile of the face vertical or nearly so; having a gnathic index below 98. Also, **orthognathic** (ô′thŏg năth′ĭk).

orthogonal (ô thŏg′ə nəl), *adj.* **1.** *Maths.* pertaining to or involving right angles or perpendicular lines: *an orthogonal projection.* **2.** *Crystall.* referable to a rectangular set of axes. [f. obs. *orthogon(ium)* (t. LL, t. Gk: m. *orthogṓnion*, neut., right-angled) + -AL[1]] —**orthog′onally,** *adv.*

orthographer (ô thŏg′rə fə), *n.* **1.** one versed in orthography or spelling. **2.** one who spells correctly. Also, **orthog′raphist.**

orthographic (ô′thə grăf′ĭk), *adj.* **1.** pertaining to orthography. **2.** orthogonal. Also, **or′thograph′ical.** —**or′thograph′ically,** *adv.*

orthography (ô thŏg′rə fĭ), *n., pl.* **-phies. 1.** the art of writing words with the proper letters, according to accepted usage; correct spelling. **2.** that part of grammar which treats of letters and spelling. **3.** manner of spelling. **4.** an orthogonal projection, or an elevation drawn by means of it. [ME *orthographie*, t. L: m. *orthographia*, t. Gk: correct writing]

orthohydrogen (ô′thō hī′drə jən), *n. Chem.* molecular hydrogen in which the spins of the two constituent hydrogen nuclei are parallel.

orthopaedic (ô′thō pē′dĭk), *adj.* pertaining to orthopaedics. Also, *U.S.*, **orthopedic.**

orthopaedics (ô′thō pē′dĭks), *n.* (esp. of children) the correction or cure of deformities and diseases of the spine, bones, joints, muscles, or other parts of the skeletal system. Also, **or′thopae′dy,** *U.S.*, **orthopedics, or′thope′dy.** [f. *ortho-* + m. s. Gk *paîs* child + -ICS]

orthopaedist (ô′thō pē′dĭst), *n.* one skilled in orthopaedics. Also, *U.S.*, **or′thope′dist.**

orthophosphoric acid (ô′thō fŏs fŏr′ĭk), *Chem.* the tribasic acid of pentavalent phosphorus, H_3PO_4, a colourless, crystalline compound, forming phosphates which are used in fertilizers.

orthopsychiatry (ô′thō sī kī′ə trĭ), *n.* the science that concerns itself with the study and treatment of behaviour disorders, esp. of young people. **—orthopsychiatric** (ô′thō sī′kĭ ăt′rĭk), **or′thopsy′chiat′rical,** *adj.* **—or′thopsychi′atrist,** *n.*

orthopteron (ô thŏp′tə rŏn′, -tə rən), *n.* an orthopterous insect.

orthopterous (ô thŏp′tə rəs), *adj.* belonging or pertaining to the *Orthoptera*, an order of insects that includes the crickets, grasshoppers, cockroaches, etc., characterized usually by leathery forewings and longitudinally folded, membranous hind wings. [t. NL: m. *orthopterus*, f. Gk: *ortho-* ORTHO- + m. *-pteros* winged] **—orthop′teran,** *adj.*, *n.*

orthoptic (ô thŏp′tĭk), *adj.* pertaining to or producing normal binocular vision.

orthoptic exercises, a method of exercising the eye and its muscles in order to cure strabismus or improve vision.

orthorhombic (ô′thō rŏm′bĭk), *adj. Crystall.* denoting or pertaining to a system of crystallization characterized by three unequal axes intersecting at right angles.

orthoscopic (ô′thō skŏp′ĭk), *adj.* pertaining to, characterized by, or produced by normal vision; presenting objects correctly to the eye.

orthostichy (ô thŏs′tĭ kĭ), *n.*, *pl.* **-chies.** *Bot.* **1.** a vertical rank or row. **2.** an arrangement of members, as leaves, at different heights on an axis so that their median planes coincide. [f. ORTHO- + m. s. Gk *-stichia* alignment] **—orthos′tichous,** *adj.*

orthotropic (ô′thō trŏp′ĭk), *adj. Bot.* denoting, pertaining to, or exhibiting a mode of growth which is more or less vertical.

orthotropism (ô thŏt′rə pĭz′əm), *n. Bot.* orthotropic tendency or growth.

orthotropous (ô thŏt′rə pəs), *adj. Bot.* (of an ovule) straight and symmetrical, with the chalaza at the evident base and the micropyle at the opposite extremity.

Orthotropous ovule: A, Micropyle; B, Chalaza

Ortler (ôt′lə), *n.* **1.** a range of the Alps in N Italy. **2.** the highest peak of this range. 12,802 ft.

ortolan (ô′tə lən), *n.* **1.** an Old World bunting, *Emberiza hortulana*, esteemed as a table delicacy. **2.** the bobolink. [t. F, t. Pr.: lit., gardener (i.e. frequenting gardens), g. L *hortulānus* of gardens]

Oruro (*Sp.* ō rōō′rō), *n.* a town in W Bolivia: a former capital. 86,985 (1962). over 12,000 ft high.

Orwell (ô′wəl), *n.* **George** (*Eric Arthur Blair*), 1903–1950, English novelist and essayist. **—Orwellian** (ô wĕl′ĭ ən), *adj.*

-ory[1], a suffix of adjectives meaning 'having the function or effect of', as in *compulsory, contributory, declaratory, illusory.* [t. L: m. s. *-ōrius* (neut. *-ōrium*; see -ORY[2]), suffix of adjectives associated esp. with agent nouns in *-or*. See -OR[2]]

-ory[2], a suffix of nouns denoting esp. a place or an instrument or thing for some purpose, as in *directory, dormitory, purgatory.* [t. L: m. s. *-ōrium.* See -ORY[1]]

oryx (ŏ′rĭks), *n.*, *pl.* **oryxes,** (*esp. collectively*) **oryx. 1.** a large African antelope, *Oryx beisa*, greyish with black markings, and having long, nearly straight horns. **2.** gemsbok. [ME, t. L, t. Gk: pickaxe, oryx]

Oryx, *Oryx beisa* (Up to 6½ ft long, ab. 4 ft high at the shoulder)

Os, *Chem.* osmium.

os[1] (ŏs), *n.*, *pl.* **ossa** (ŏs′ə). *Anat.*, *Zool.* a bone. [t. L]

os[2] (ŏs), *n.*, *pl.* **ora** (ô′rə), *Anat.* a mouth, opening or entrance. [t. L: mouth]

os[3] (ōs), *n.*, *pl.* **osar** (ō′sä). *Geol.* an esker, esp. when of great length. [t. Sw.: m. *as* (pl. *asar*) ridge]

o/s, 1. out of stock. **2.** (in banking) outstanding.

O.S., 1. Old Saxon. **2.** old school. **3.** old series. **4.** (of the calendar) Old Style. **5.** ordinary seaman. **6.** Ordnance Survey. **7.** outsize.

o.s., only son.

O.S.A., Order of St Augustine (Augustinian).

Osage (ō sāj′, ō′sāj), *n.*, *pl.* **Osages,** (*esp. collectively*) **Osage. 1.** a Siouan language closely related to Omaha. **2.** a member of an Amerindian people speaking this language. **3.** a river flowing from E Kansas east to the Missouri river in central Missouri. ab. 500 mi.

Osage orange, 1. an ornamental moraceous tree, *Maclura pomifera*, native in Arkansas and adjacent regions, used for hedges. **2.** its fruit, which resembles a warty orange.

Osaka (ō sä′kə), *n.* a seaport in S Japan, on Honshu island. 3,156,222 (1965). See map under **Hiroshima.**

O.S.B., Order of St Benedict (Benedictine).

Osborn (ŏz′bən), *n.* **Henry Fairfield,** 1857–1935, U.S. palaeontologist and author.

Osborne (ŏz′bən), *n.* **John James,** born 1929, English dramatist.

Oscan (ŏs′kən), *n.* **1.** an ancient nationality of south-central Italy constituting a subdivision of the Italic branch (Oscan-Umbrians and Latins) of the Indo-European family. **2.** their language, replaced by Latin. *—adj.* **3.** of or pertaining to the Oscans or their language.

Oscar (ŏs′kə), *n.* one of a group of statuettes awarded annually by the American Academy of Motion Picture Arts for outstanding achievement by a film actor, director, etc.

Oscar II (ŏs′kə), 1829–1907, king of Sweden 1872–1907, and of Norway 1872–1905.

oscillate (ŏs′ĭ lāt′), *v.i.*, **-lated, -lating. 1.** to swing or move to and fro, as a pendulum does; vibrate. **2.** to fluctuate between states, opinions, purposes, etc. **3.** *Physics.* to have, produce, or generate oscillations: *a radio valve oscillates.* [t. L: m. s. *oscillātus*, pp., swung] **—Syn. 1.** See **swing**[1].

oscillation (ŏs′ĭ lā′shən), *n.* **1.** the act or fact of oscillating. **2.** a single swing, or movement in one direction, of an oscillating body, etc. **3.** fluctuation between states, opinions, etc. **4.** *Physics.* **a.** a single forward and backward surge of electric charge. **b.** a rapid change in electromotive force. **c.** one complete cycle of an electric wave.

oscillator (ŏs′ĭ lā′tə), *n.* **1.** a device or machine producing oscillations. **2.** one who or that which oscillates.

oscillatory (ŏs′ĭ lə tə rĭ, -trĭ), *adj.* characterized by or involving oscillation.

oscillograph (ŏ sĭl′ə grăf′, -gräf′), *n.* **1.** an instrument for recording oscillations, esp. electric oscillations. **2.** a device for recording the wave-forms of changing currents, voltages, or any other quantity which can be translated into electrical energy, as, for example, soundwaves. [f. s. L *oscillāre* swing + -(O)GRAPH]

oscilloscope (ŏ sĭl′ə skōp′), *n. Physics.* a device which makes the shape of a voltage or current wave visible on the screen of a cathode-ray tube or other device.

oscinine (ŏs′ĭ nīn′), *adj.* of or pertaining to the *Oscines*, a large group of passerine birds, containing those with the most highly developed vocal organs, and commonly termed the songbirds. Also, **oscine** (ŏs′īn). [back-formation from *Oscines*, t. L]

oscitant (ŏs′ĭ tənt), *adj.* **1.** gaping; yawning. **2.** drowsy; inattentive. **3.** indolent; negligent. [t. L: s. *oscitans*, ppr.] **—os′citancy, os′citance,** *n.*

osculant (ŏs′kyŏŏ lənt), *adj.* **1.** united by certain common characteristics. **2.** *Zool.* adhering closely; embracing. [t. L: s. *osculans*, ppr., kissing]

oscular (ŏs′kyŏŏ lə), *adj.* **1.** pertaining to an osculum. **2.** pertaining to the mouth or kissing. [f. s. L *osculum* little mouth, kiss + -AR[1]]

osculate (ŏs′kyŏŏ lāt′), *v.*, **-lated, -lating.** *—v.t.* **1.** to kiss. **2.** to bring into close contact or union. **3.** *Geom.* to touch so as to have three or more points in common at the point of contact. *—v.i.* **4.** to kiss each other. **5.** to come into close contact or union. **6.** *Geom.* to osculate each other, as two curves. [t. L: m. s. *osculātus*, pp., kissed] **—osculatory** (ŏs′kyŏŏ lə tə rĭ, -trĭ), *adj.*

osculation (ŏs′kyŏŏ lā′shən), *n.* **1.** kissing. **2.** a kiss. **3.** close contact. **4.** *Geom.* the contact between two osculating curves or the like.

osculum (ŏs′kyŏŏ ləm), *n.*, *pl.* **-la** (-lə). a small mouth-like aperture, as of a sponge. [t. L, dim. of *ōs* mouth]

O.S.D., Order of St Dominic (Dominican).

-ose[1], an adjective suffix meaning 'full of', 'abounding in', 'given to', 'like', as in *frondose, globose, jocose, otiose, verbose.* [t. L: m. *-ōsus.* Cf. -OUS]

-ose[2], a noun termination used to form chemical terms, esp. names of sugars and other carbohydrates, as *amylose, fructose, hexose, lactose*, and (rarely) of protein derivatives, as *proteose.* [abstracted from GLUCOSE]

Ösel (*Ger.* œ′zəl), *n.* German name of **Saaremaa.**
O.S.F., Order of St Francis (Franciscan).
Oshogbo (ə shŏg′bō), *n.* a town in W Western Nigeria. 123,000 (est. 1963).
osier (ō′zhə), *n.* **1.** any of various willows, as *Salix viminalis* (the common **basket osier**) and *Salix purpurea* (**red osier**), with tough flexible twigs or branches which are used for wickerwork. **2.** a twig from such a willow. [ME, t. F; akin to ML *ausaria* willow bed]
Osijek (*Serb.* ô′sē yĕk), *n.* a town in Croatia, Yugoslavia. 73,125 (1961). German, **Esseg.**
Osiris (ō sī′ə rĭs), *n.* one of the principal Egyptian gods, brother and husband of Isis, usually represented as a mummy wearing the crown of Upper Egypt.
-osis, *pl.* **-oses.** a noun suffix denoting action, process, state, condition, etc., as in *metamorphosis*, and in many pathological terms, as *tuberculosis*. [t. Gk, suffix forming nouns from verbs with infinitive in *-óein, -oûn*]
-osity, a noun suffix equivalent to **-ose** (or **-ous**) plus **-ity.** [f. -OSE + -ITY, repr. s. L *-ōsitas* and F *-osité*]
Osler (ŏs′lə, ŏz′-), *n.* **Sir William,** 1849–1919, Canadian physician and professor of medicine.
Oslo (ŏz′lō; *Nor.* ōōs′lōō), *n.* a seaport in and the capital of Norway, in the SE part at the head of **Oslo Fiord,** an inlet (ab. 75 mi. long) of the Skagerrak. 483,196 (1965). Formerly, **Christiania.**
Osman (ŏz′mən, ŏz män′; *Turk.* ôs′män), *n.* 1259–1326, Turkish sultan, founder of the Ottoman dynasty of rulers of Turkey.
Osmanli (ŏz măn′lĭ), *n., pl.* **-lis,** *adj.* —*n.* **1.** an Ottoman. **2.** Ottoman Turkish (language). —*adj.* **3.** Ottoman. [t. Turk. See OTTOMAN]
osmic (ŏz′mĭk), *adj. Chem.* of or containing osmium in its higher valencies, esp. the tetravalent state.
osmious (ŏz′mĭ əs), *adj. Chem.* of or containing osmium in its lower valencies.
osmiridium (ŏz′mĭ rĭd′ĭ əm, ŏs′-), *n.* iridosmine.
osmium (ŏz′mĭ əm), *n. Chem.* a hard, heavy, metallic element used for electric-light filaments, etc., having the greatest density of any known material, and forming octavalent compounds, such as OsO_4, OsF_8. *Symbol:* Os; *at. wt:* 190·2; *at. no.:* 76; *sp. gr.:* 22·48 at 20°C. [t. NL, der. Gk *osmḗ* smell, odour; named from the penetrating smell of one of its oxides]
osmometer (ŏz mŏm′ĭ tə), *n. Chem.* an instrument for measuring osmotic pressures.
osmose (ŏz mōs′), *v.,* **-mosed, -mosing.** —*v.i.* **1.** to undergo osmosis. —*v.t.* **2.** to subject to osmosis. —*n.* **3.** osmosis.
osmosis (ŏz mō′sĭs), *n. Phys. Chem., etc.* **1.** the tendency of a fluid to pass through a semipermeable membrane into a solution where its concentration is lower, thus equalizing the conditions on either side of the membrane. **2.** the diffusion of fluids through membranes or porous partitions. Cf. **endosmosis** and **exosmosis.** [t. NL, der. Gk *ōsmós* a thrusting] —**osmotic** (ŏz mŏt′ĭk), *adj.* —**osmot′ically,** *adv.*
osmotic pressure, *Chem.* the pressure which must be applied to a solution in order to prevent the flow of solvent through a semipermeable membrane separating the solution and the pure solvent.
osmund (ŏz′mənd, ŏs′-), *n.* any fern of the genus *Osmunda*, which includes the royal fern.
Osnabrück (ŏz′nə brŏŏk′; *Ger.* ōs nä brʏk′), *n.* a town in West Germany, in SW Lower Saxony. 142,600 (est. 1966).
osnaburg (ŏz′nə bûg′), *n.* a heavy coarse cotton in a plain weave used for grain sacks, etc.
Osorno (*Sp.* ō sôr′nō), *n.* a town in S Chile. 50,909 (est. 1959).
osprey (ŏs′prĭ, ŏs′prā), *n., pl.* **-preys. 1.** a large hawk, *Pandion haliaetus*, which feeds on fish; the fish-hawk. **2.** a kind of feather used to trim hats. [ME *ospray(e)*, t. F: m. *orfraie* (repr. L *ossifraga*), b. with L. See OSSIFRAGE]

Osprey, *Pandion haliaetus* (Ab. 2 ft long)

OSS, *U.S.* Office of Strategic Services.
Ossa (ŏs′ə), *n.* **1.** a mountain in E Greece, in Thessaly. 6490 ft. **2. Mount,** the highest point in Tasmania. 5305 ft.
ossein (ŏs′ĭ ĭn), *n. Biochem.* the organic basis of bone, mainly glycoprotein, which remains after the mineral matter has been removed by treatment with dilute acid. [f. s. L *osseus* bony + -IN[2]]
osseous (ŏs′ĭ əs), *adj.* **1.** composed of, containing, or resembling bone; bony. **2.** ossiferous. [t. L: m. *osseus* bony] —**os′seously,** *adv.*
Ossetia (ŏ sē′shə; *Russ.* ȧ sĕt′yə), *n.* a region in the S Soviet Union in Europe, in Caucasia. —**Osse′tian,** *adj.*
Ossett (ŏs′ĭt), *n.* a town in England, in the West Riding of Yorkshire. 14,729 (1961).
ossia (ō sĭə′), *n. Music.* a simpler version of a difficult passage which may be played as an alternative. [t. It.: *o sia* or let it be]
Ossian (ŏs′ĭ ən), *n. Gaelic Legend.* a hero and poet of the 3rd century A.D.
Ossianic (ŏs′ĭ ăn′ĭk), *adj.* **1.** pertaining to, characteristic of, or resembling the poetry or rhythmic prose published by James Macpherson in 1762–63, as a translation of Ossian. **2.** grandiloquent; bombastic.
ossicle (ŏs′ĭ kl), *n.* a small bone. [t. L: m. s. *ossiculum*, dim. of *os* bone]
Ossietzky (*Ger.* ō sē ĕts′kē), *n.* **Carl von** (*Ger.* kärl′fōn), 1889–1938, German pacifist leader.
ossiferous (ŏ sĭf′ə rəs), *adj.* containing bones.
ossification (ŏs′ĭ fĭ kā′shən), *n.* **1.** the act or process of ossifying. **2.** the resulting state. **3.** that which is ossified.
ossifrage (ŏs′ĭ frĭj), *n.* **1.** the osprey. **2.** the lammergeyer. [t. L: m. s. *ossifragus*, masc., *ossifraga*, fem., lit., bone-breaker]
ossify (ŏs′ĭ fī′), *v.,* **-fied, -fying.** —*v.t.* **1.** to convert into, or harden like, bone. **2.** to render (attitudes, opinions, etc.) rigid or inflexible. —*v.i.* **3.** to become bone or hard like bone. **4.** to become rigid or inflexible in attitudes, opinions, etc. [f. s. L *os* bone + -(I)FY. Cf. F *ossifier*]
ossuary (ŏs′yōō ə rĭ), *n., pl.* **-aries.** a place or receptacle for the bones of the dead. [t. LL: m. s. *ossuārium*, der. L *os* bone]
o.s.t., *Naut.* ordinary spring tides.
osteal (ŏs′tĭ əl), *adj.* osseous. [f. OSTE(O)- + -AL]
osteitis (ŏs′tĭ ī′tĭs), *n. Pathol.* inflammation of the substance of bone. [f. OSTE(O)- + -ITIS]
Ostend (ŏs tĕnd′), *n.* a seaport in NW Belgium. 56,850 (est. 1963). French, **Ostende** (*Fr.* ōs täɴd′).
ostensible (ŏs tĕn′sə bl), *adj.* given out or outwardly appearing as such; professed; pretended. [t. F, f. s. L *ostensus*, pp., displayed + *-ible* -IBLE] —**osten′sibly,** *adv.*
ostensive (ŏs tĕn′sĭv), *adj.* **1.** manifestly demonstrative. **2.** ostensible. —**osten′sively,** *adv.*
ostentation (ŏs′tĕn tā′shən), *n.* **1.** pretentious show; display intended to impress others. **2.** *Obs.* a show or display. Also, **os′tenta′tiousness.** [ME, t. L: s. *ostentātio*] —**Syn. 1.** See **show.**
ostentatious (ŏs′tĕn tā′shəs), *adj.* **1.** characterized by or given to ostentation or pretentious show. **2.** (of actions, manner, qualities exhibited, etc.) intended to attract notice. —**os′tenta′tiously,** *adv.*
osteo-, a word element meaning 'bone'. Also, before vowels, **oste-.** [t. Gk, comb. form of *ostéon*]
osteoarthritis (ŏs′tĭ ō ä thrī′tĭs), *n. Pathol.* a degenerative type of chronic arthritis.
osteoblast (ŏs′tĭ ə blăst′), *n. Anat.* a bone-forming cell.
osteoclasis (ŏs′tĭ ŏk′lə sĭs), *n.* **1.** *Anat.* the breaking down or absorption of osseous tissue. **2.** *Surg.* the fracturing of a bone to correct deformity. [t. NL, f. *osteo-* OSTEO- + m. Gk *klásis* fracture]
osteoclast (ŏs′tĭ ə klăst′), *n.* **1.** *Anat.* one of the large multinuclear cells in growing bone, and concerned in the absorption of osseous tissue, as in the formation of canals, etc. **2.** *Surg.* an instrument for effecting osteoclasis. [f. OSTEO- + m. s. Gk *klastós* broken]
osteogenesis (ŏs′tĭ ə jĕn′ĭ sĭs), *n. Physiol.* the formation of bone.
osteoid (ŏs′tĭ oid′), *adj.* bonelike. [f. OSTE(O)- + -OID]
osteology (ŏs′tĭ ŏl′ə jĭ), *n.* the branch of anatomy that treats of the skeleton and its parts. —**osteological** (ŏs′tĭ ə lŏj′ĭ kl), *adj.* —**os′teol′ogist,** *n.*
osteoma (ŏs′tĭ ō′mə), *n., pl.* **-mas, -mata** (-mə tə). *Pathol.* a tumour composed of osseous tissue. [t. NL. See OSTEO-, -OMA]
osteomalacia (ŏs′tĭ ō mə lā′shyə), *n. Pathol.* a condition due to a deficiency of vitamin D and characterized by a softening of the bones leading to severe deformities: most commonly found in women and often associated with pregnancy.
osteomyelitis (ŏs′tĭ ō mī′ə lī′tĭs), *n. Pathol.* a purulent inflammation of the bone.
osteopath (ŏs′tĭ ə păth′), *n.* one who practises osteopathy. Also, **osteopathist** (ŏs′tĭ ŏp′ə thĭst).
osteopathy (ŏs′tĭ ŏp′ə thĭ), *n.* a theory of disease and a method of treatment resting upon the supposition that most diseases are due to deformation of some part of the body and can be cured by some kind of manipulation. —**osteopathic** (ŏs′tĭ ə păth′ĭk), *adj.*
osteophyte (ŏs′tĭ ə fīt′), *n. Pathol.* a small osseous excrescence or outgrowth on bone. —**osteophytic** (ŏs′tĭ ə fĭt′ĭk), *adj.*

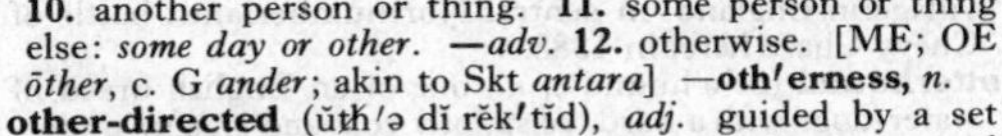

osteoplastic (ŏs′tĭ ə plăs′tĭk), *adj.* **1.** *Surg.* pertaining to osteoplasty. **2.** *Physiol.* pertaining to bone formation.

osteoplasty (ŏs′tĭ ə plăs′tĭ), *n. Surg.* the transplanting or inserting of bone, or surgical reconstruction of bone, to repair a defect or loss.

osteotome (ŏs′tĭ ə tōm′), *n. Surg.* a double-bevelled chisel-like instrument for cutting or dividing bone.

osteotomy (ŏs′tĭ ŏt′ə mĭ), *n., pl.* **-mies.** *Surg.* the dividing of a bone, or the excision of part of it. **—os′teot′omist,** *n.*

Österreich (*Ger.* œ′stə rīKH), *n.* German name of **Austria.**

Ostia (ŏs′tĭ ə; *It.* ôs′tyä), *n.* an ancient city of Latium at the mouth of the Tiber: the port of Rome.

ostiary (ŏs′tĭ ə rĭ), *n., pl.* **-aries. 1.** *Rom. Cath. Ch.* one ordained to the lowest of the four minor orders; a porter. **2.** a doorkeeper, as of a church. [ME, t. L: m. s. *ostiārius* doorkeeper]

ostinato (ŏs′tĭ nä′tō; *It.* ôs tē nä′tô), *n., pl.* **-tos.** *Music.* a constantly recurring melodic fragment. [It.: lit., obstinate]

ostiole (ŏs′tĭ ōl′), *n.* a small opening or orifice. [t. L: m. s. *ostiolum*, dim. of *ostium* door] **—ostiolar** (ŏs′tĭ ə lə, ŏs tī′-), *adj.*

ostler (ŏs′lə), *n.* one who takes care of horses, esp. at an inn. Also, **hostler.**

ostosis (ŏs tō′sĭs), *n. Physiol.* the formation of bone; ossification. [t. NL; see OST(EO)-, -OSIS]

Ostpreussen (*Ger.* ōst′proi̇ sən), *n.* German name of **East Prussia.**

ostracism (ŏs′trə sĭz′əm), *n.* **1.** the act of ostracizing. **2.** the fact or state of being ostracized. [t. Gk: m. s. *ostrakismós*]

ostracize (ŏs′trə sīz′), *v.t.,* **-cized, -cizing. 1.** to banish (a person) from his native country; expatriate. **2.** to exclude by general consent from society, privileges, etc. **3.** *Ancient Gk Hist.* to banish (a citizen) temporarily by popular vote with ballots consisting of potsherds or tablets of earthenware. Also, **ostracise.** [t. Gk: m. s. *ostrakízein* (def. 3), der. *óstrakon* potsherd] **—os′traciz′able,** *adj.* **—os′traciz′er,** *n.*

Ostrava (*Cz.* ôs′trä vä), *n.* a town in Czechoslovakia. 259,000 (est. 1965). Formerly, **Moravská Ostrava.**

ostrich (ŏs′trĭch), *n.* **1.** a large two-toed, swift-footed, flightless bird, *Struthio camelus*, the largest of existing birds, a native of Africa and Arabia, now extensively reared for the plumage. **2.** a rhea (**American ostrich**). [ME *ostrice*, t. OF: m. *ostruce*, g. LL *avi(s) strūthio*, f. *avis* bird + *strūthio* ostrich, t. Gk: m. *strouthíōn*] **—os′trich-like′,** *adj.*

Ostrich, *Struthio camelus* (6 ft long including tail, 8 ft high)

Ostrogoth (ŏs′trə gŏth′), *n.* a member of the easterly division of the Goths, which maintained a monarchy in Italy from A.D. 493 to 555. [t. LL: s. *Ostrogothi*, pl., L *Austrogotī*, t. Goth.] **—Os′trogoth′ic,** *adj.*

Ostrovski (*Russ.* ȧs trôf′skĭy), *n.* **Aleksander Nikolaevich** (*Russ.* ə lĭk sän′dər nĭ kä lä′yĭ vĭch), 1823–86, Russian dramatist.

Ostyak (ŏs′tĭ ăk′), *n.* a language of western Siberia, one of the Ugric languages of the Finno-Ugric family. Also, **Ostiak.**

Oswestry (ŏz′wəs trĭ), *n.* a town in England, in Shropshire. 11,215 (1961).

Oświęcim (*Pol.* ôsh fyĕn′chĕm), *n.* Polish name of **Auschwitz.**

OT, Old Testament. Also, **OT., O.T.**

o/t, overtime.

ot-, var. of **oto-** before vowels.

otalgia (ō tăl′jyə), *n. Pathol.* earache. [t. NL, t. Gk] **—otal′gic,** *adj.*

Otaru (ō tä′ro͞o), *n.* a seaport in N Japan, on W Hokkaido island. 196,771 (1965).

O.T.C., Officers' Training Corps.

O tempora! O mores! (ō tĕm′pə rä′ ō mô′rās), *Latin.* O the times! O the customs!

other (ŭᵺ′ə), *adj.* **1.** additional or further: *he and one other person.* **2.** different or distinct from the one or ones mentioned or implied: *in some other city.* **3.** different in nature or kind: *I would not have him other than he is.* **4.** being the remaining one of two or more: *the other hand.* **5.** (with plural nouns) being the remaining ones of a number: *the other men.* **6.** former: *men of other days.* **7. every other,** every alternate: *a meeting every other week.* **8. the other day (night,** etc.), a day (night, etc.) or two ago. *—pron.* **9.** the other one: *each praises the other.* **10.** another person or thing. **11.** some person or thing else: *some day or other.* *—adv.* **12.** otherwise. [ME; OE *ōther*, c. G *ander*; akin to Skt *antara*] **—oth′erness,** *n.*

other-directed (ŭᵺ′ə dĭ rĕk′tĭd), *adj.* guided by a set of values that is derived from current trends or outward influences rather than from within oneself. **—oth′er-direct′edness,** *n.* **—oth′er-direc′tion,** *n.*

otherguess (ŭᵺ′ə gĕs′), *adj. Archaic or Dial.* of another kind. [assimilatory var. of *othergets*, var. of *othergates* otherwise]

other ranks, the non-commissioned members of a military organization, distinguished from officers, and sometimes also from non-commissioned officers.

otherwhere (ŭᵺ′ə wĕə′), *adv. Archaic or Dial.* elsewhere.

otherwhile (ŭᵺ′ə wīl′), *adv. Archaic or Dial.* **1.** at another time or other times. **2.** sometimes. Also, **oth′erwhiles′.**

otherwise (ŭᵺ′ə wīz′), *adv.* **1.** under other circumstances. **2.** in another manner; differently. **3.** in other respects: *an otherwise happy life.* *—adj.* **4.** other or different; of another nature or kind. [ME *other wis* (two words), OE (*on*) *ōthre wīsan* in other manner. See OTHER, WISE[2]]

other world, the world of the dead; future world.

otherworldly (ŭᵺ′ə wûld′lĭ), *adj.* **1.** of, pertaining to, or devoted to another world, as the world of imagination, or the world to come. **2.** neglectful; impractical. **—oth′erworld′liness,** *n.*

Othin (ō′thĭn), *n. Scand. Myth.* Odin.

Othman (ŏth män′), *n., pl.* **-mans. 1.** Osman. **2.** Ottoman (defs 3, 4).

Otho I (ō′thō), Otto I.

otic (ō′tĭk, ŏt′ĭk), *adj. Anat.* of or pertaining to the ear; auricular. [t. Gk: m. s. *ōtikós*]

-otic, an adjective suffix meaning: **1.** 'suffering from', as in *neurotic.* **2.** 'producing', as in *hypnotic.* **3.** 'resembling', as in *Quixotic.* [t. Gk: m. s. *-ōtikos*]

otiose (ō′shĭ ōs′, ō′tĭ-), *adj.* **1.** at leisure; idle; indolent. **2.** ineffective or futile. **3.** superfluous or useless. [t. L: m. s. *ōtiōsus*] **—o′tiose′ly,** *adv.* **—otiosity** (ō′shĭ ŏs′ĭ tĭ, ō′tĭ-), *n.*

otitis (ō tī′tĭs), *n. Pathol.* inflammation of the ear.

oto-, a word element meaning 'ear'. [t. Gk, comb. form of *oûs*]

otocyst (ō′tə sĭst′), *n. Embryol.* the embryonic auditory vesicle.

otolaryngology (ō′tō lă′rĭng gŏl′ə jĭ), *n.* the branch of medicine dealing with the ear and throat.

otolith (ō′tō lĭth), *n. Anat., Zool.* a calcareous concretion in the internal ear of vertebrates and in the balancing organ of some invertebrates.

otology (ō tŏl′ə jĭ), *n.* the science of the ear and its diseases. **—otol′ogist,** *n.*

Otranto (ō trăn′tō; *It.* ō′trän tô), *n.* **Strait of,** a strait between SE Italy and Albania, connecting the Adriatic and the Mediterranean. 44 mi. wide. See map under **Corfu.**

Otsu (ôt′so͞o), *n.* a town in Japan, in W central Honshu island. 121,041 (1965).

ottava rima (*It.* ôt tä′vä rē′mä), *Pros.* an Italian stanza of eight lines, each of eleven syllables (or, in the English adaptation, of ten or eleven syllables), the first six lines rhyming alternately and the last two forming a couplet with a different rhyme: used in Keats's *Isabella* and Byron's *Don Juan.* [It.: octave rhyme]

Ottawa (ŏt′ə wə), *n.* **1.** the capital of Canada, in SE Ontario. 280,563 (1964). **2.** a river in SE Canada, flowing generally SE along the boundary between Ontario and Quebec into the St Lawrence at Montreal. 685 mi. **3.** (*pl.*) a tribe of Algonquian Indians of Canada, forced into the Lake Superior and Lake Michigan regions by the Iroquois confederacy. **4.** a member of this tribe. [t. Canadian F: m. *Otana, Otawa*, t. d. Ojibwa (Cree, Ottawa, Chippewa): m. *adaawe* to trade]

otter (ŏt′ə), *n., pl.* **-ters,** (*esp. collectively*) **-ter.** any of the various aquatic, furbearing, carnivorous, musteline mammals of the genus *Lutra* and allied genera, with webbed feet adapted for swimming, and a long tail slightly flattened horizontally to act as a rudder, as *L. vulgaris*, of Europe, and *L. canadensis*, of the U.S. and Canada, and the sea-otter. [ME *oter*, OE *oter, ot(o)r*, c. D *otter*, G *Otter*]

Otter, *Lutra lutra* (Length 2½ ft, tail 1½ ft)

Otterburn (ŏt′ə bûn′), *n.* a

village in England, in central Northumberland: battle of Chevy Chase here, in 1388.

otterhound (ŏt′ə hound′), *n.* one of an English breed of water-dogs with a hard, crisp, oily coat and shaggy undercoat, trained to hunt otters.

otter shrew, an insectivorous mammal of W Africa, *Potamogale velox*, about the size of a stoat but resembling an otter in habits and appearance, having brown fur and a flattened tail.

Otto I (ŏt′ō; *Ger.* ŏ′tō) (*'the Great'*), A.D. 912–73, German king A.D. 936–73, and emperor of the Holy Roman Empire A.D. 962–73. Also, **Otho I.**

Otto cycle, the working cycle of a four-stroke internal-combustion engine. [named after N. A. *Otto*, 1832–91, German engineer]

Ottoman (ŏt′ə mən), *adj.*, *n.*, *pl.* **-mans.** *—adj.* **1.** of or pertaining to the Ottoman Empire. **2.** of or pertaining to the lands, peoples, and possessions of the Ottoman Empire. *—n.* **3.** a Turk. **4.** a Turk of the family or tribe of Osman. **5.** (*l.c.*) a kind of divan or sofa, with or without a back. **6.** (*l.c.*) a low cushioned seat without back or arms. **7.** (*l.c.*) a low chest with a padded top. **8.** (*l.c.*) a cushioned footstool. **9.** (*l.c.*) a corded silk or rayon fabric with large cotton cord for filling. Also, **Othman** for 3, 4. [t. F, t. It.: named after the founder of the empire (Ar. *'Othmān*)]

Ottoman Empire, a former Turkish empire, founded about 1300 by Osman, which held sway over large dominions in Asia, Africa, and Europe for more than six centuries until its collapse after World War I. *Cap.*: Constantinople. Also, **Turkish Empire.**

ottrelite (ŏt′rə līt′), *n.* a manganese-bearing mineral. [named after *Ottrez*, Belgium, where it is found. See -LITE]

Otway (ŏt′wā′), *n.* **Thomas,** 1652–85, English dramatist.

ou (ō), *n.* *S African Colloq.* chap; person. [t. Afrikaans: lit., old]

ouabain (wä bä′ĭn), *n.* *Pharm.* a cardiac glucoside derived from the tree, *Strophanthus gratus*.

Ouachita (wŏsh′ĭ tô′), *n.*, *pl.* **-tas,** (*esp. collectively*) **-ta.** **1.** a river in the U.S., flowing from W Arkansas SE through NE Louisiana to the Red River. 605 mi. **2.** a member of a former North American Indian tribe, apparently of the Caddoan stock, of NE Louisiana (not to be confused with the Wichita). Also, **Washita.**

Oubangui (*Fr.* o͞o bäɴ gē′), *n.* French name of the river **Ubangi.**

oubliette (o͞o′blĭ ĕt′), *n.* a secret dungeon with an opening only at the top, as in certain old castles. [t. F, der. *oublier* forget, g. Rom. *oblītāre*, der. L *oblīviscī*]

ouch[1] (ouch), *interj.* (an exclamation expressing sudden pain.) [t. G: m. *autsch*]

ouch[2] (ouch), *Archaic.* *—n.* **1.** a clasp, buckle, or brooch, esp. one worn for ornament. **2.** the setting of a precious stone. *—v.t.* **3.** to adorn with or as with ouches. [ME *ouche*, for *nouche* (*a nouche* being taken as *an ouche*). Cf. LL *nusca*, OHG *nuscha* buckle, ult. of Celtic orig.]

Oud (*Du.* ôwt), *n.* **Jacobus Johannes Pieter** (*Du.* yä kō′bʏs yō hŏn′əs pē′tər), 1890–1963, Dutch architect.

Oudh (oud), *n.* a former part of the United Provinces of Agra and Oudh in N India: now part of Uttar Pradesh.

Ouessant (*Fr.* wĕ säɴ′), *n.* French name of **Ushant.**

Ougadougou (*Fr.* wä gä do͞o go͞o′), *n.* the capital of Upper Volta, in the central part. 51,000 (est. 1960).

ought[1] (ôt), *v. aux.* **1.** was (were) or am (is, are) bound in duty or moral obligation: *every citizen ought to help.* **2.** was (am, etc.) bound or required on any ground, as of justice, propriety, probability, expediency, fitness, or the like (usually fol. by an infinitive with *to* or having the infinitive omitted but understood): *he ought to be punished.* *—n.* **3.** duty or obligation. [ME *ought*, *aught*, etc., OE *āhte*, pret. of *āgan* OWE] **—Syn. 1.** See **must**[1].

ought[2] (ôt), *n.*, *adv.* aught. [var. of NOUGHT, *a nought* being taken as *an ought*]

Ouida (wē′də), *n.* pen-name of **Louise de la Ramée.**

ouija (wē′jä), *n.* a device consisting of a small board on legs, which rests on a larger board marked with words, letters of the alphabet, etc., and which, by moving over the larger board and touching the words, letters, etc., while the fingers of mediums or others rest lightly upon it, is employed to give answers, messages, etc. Also, **ouija board.** [f. F *oui* yes + G *ja* yes]

Oujda (*Fr.* o͞ozh dá′), *n.* a town in NE Morocco. 149,300 (est. 1961).

Oulu (*Finn.* ôw′lo͞o), *n.* a town in W Finland, on the Gulf of Bothnia. 78,545 (1965).

ounce[1] (ouns), *n.* **1.** a unit of weight equal to 437·5 grains or $\frac{1}{16}$ lb. avoirdupois. **2.** a unit of 480 grains, $\frac{1}{12}$ lb. troy or apothecaries' weight. **3.** a fluid ounce. **4.** a small quantity or portion. [ME *unce*, t. OF, g. L *uncia* twelfth part, inch, ounce. Cf. INCH]

ounce[2] (ouns), *n.* a long-haired leopard-like feline, *Panthera uncia*, inhabiting the mountain ranges of central Asia; snow leopard. [ME *once*, t. OF, var. of *lonce* (taken as *l'once* the ounce), g. L *lynx* LYNX]

Ounce, *Panthera uncia* (Ab. 6 ft long, tail 3 ft)

our (ou′ə), *pron. or adj.* the possessive form corresponding to *we* and *us*, used before a noun. Cf. **ours.** [ME *oure*, OE *ure*, gen. pl. See US]

-our, a suffix of nouns denoting state or condition, a quality or property, etc., as in *ardour*, *colour*, *honour*, *labour*. Cf. **-or**[1]. [ME, t. AF (= F *-eur*), g. L *-or* -OR[1]]

ourari (o͞o rä′rĭ), *n.* curare.

Our Lady, the Virgin Mary.

ours (ou′əz), *pron.* **1.** a form of *our* used predicatively or without a noun following. **2.** the person(s) or thing(s) belonging to us: *a friend of ours.*

ourself (ou′ə sĕlf′), *pron.* a form corresponding to *ourselves*, used of a single person, esp. (like *we* for *I*) in the regal or formal style.

ourselves (ou′ə sĕlvz′), *pron. pl.* **1.** a reflexive form of *us*: *we hurt ourselves.* **2.** an emphatic form of *us* or *we* used: **a.** as object: *we used it for ourselves.* **b.** in opposition to a subject or object: *we ourselves did it.*

-ous, 1. an adjective suffix meaning 'full of', 'abounding in', 'given to', 'characterized by', 'having', 'of the nature of', 'like', etc.: *glorious, joyous, mucous, nervous, sonorous, wondrous.* **2.** *Chem.* a suffix used to imply the lower of two possible valencies compared to the corresponding suffix *-ic*; as *stannous chloride*, $SnCl_2$, and *stannic chloride*, $SnCl_4$. Also, **-eous, -ious.** [ME, t. OF, g. L *-ōsus*; often used to repr. L *-us*, adj., Gk *-os*, adj.; in a few words (e.g. *wondrous*) it is attached to native stems]

Ouse (o͞oz), *n.* **1.** a river in NE England, in Yorkshire, flowing SE to the Humber. 57 mi. **2.** Also, **Great Ouse.** a river in E England, flowing from Northamptonshire E, then NE to the Wash. 160 mi.

ousel (o͞o′zəl), *n.* ouzel.

Ouspensky (*Russ.* o͞os pyĕn′skĭy), *n.* **Petr Demianovich** (*Russ.* pyô′tr dĭm yá′nə vĭch), 1878–1947, Russian philosopher and mystic.

oust (oust), *v.t.* **1.** to expel from a place or position occupied. **2.** *Law.* to eject; dispossess. [t. AF: s. *ouster* remove, g. L *obstāre* be in the way, protect against]

ouster (ous′tə), *n.* **1.** *Law.* **a.** ejection; dispossession. **b.** a wrongful exclusion from real property. **2.** one who ousts. [t. AF, n. use of inf. See OUST]

out (out), *adv.* **1.** forth from, away from, or not in a place, position, state, etc.: *out of order.* **2.** away from one's home, country, etc.: *to set out on a journey.* **3.** into the open: *to go out for a walk.* **4.** to exhaustion, extinction, or conclusion; to the end; so as to finish or exhaust or be exhausted; so as to bring to naught or render useless: *to pump out a well.* **5.** to or at an end or conclusion: *to fight it out.* **6.** no longer or not burning or furnishing light; extinguished: *the lamp went out.* **7.** not in vogue or fashion: *that style has gone out.* **8.** into or in public notice or knowledge: *the book came out in May.* **9.** seeking openly and energetically to do or have: *to try out for the team.* **10.** into or in society: *a young girl who came out last season.* **11.** not in present or personal possession or use; let for hire, or placed at interest: *let out for a year.* **12.** on strike: *the miners are coming out.* **13.** so as to project or extend: *to stretch out.* **14.** into or in existence, activity, or outward manifestation: *fever broke out.* **15.** from a source, ground or cause, material, etc. (with *of*): *made out of scraps.* **16.** from a state of composure, satisfaction, or harmony: *to feel put out.* **17.** in or into a state of confusion, vexation, dispute, variance, or unfriendliness: *to fall out about trifles.* **18.** so as to deprive or be deprived (with *of*): *to cheat out of money.* **19.** having used the last (with *of*): *to run out of coal.* **20.** from a number, stock, or store: *to pick out.* **21.** aloud or loudly: *to call out.* **22.** with completeness or effectiveness: *to fit out.* **23.** thoroughly; completely; entirely. **24.** so as to make illegible or indecipherable: *to paint out, ink out.* **25. out and away,** in a pre-eminent degree; by far.

—adj. **26.** torn or worn into holes, as clothing: *his trousers were out at the knees.* **27.** incorrect or inaccurate: *to be out in one's calculations.* **28.** at a pecuniary loss: *to be out by ten pounds.* **29.** lacking; without: *we are completely out of eggs.* **30.** unconscious; senseless: *the boxer was out for about five minutes.* **31.** not in office or employment; unemployed: *out of work.* **32.** finished; ended: *before the month is out.* **33.** *Tennis, etc.* beyond the boundary lines: *the umpire declared the ball out.* **34.** *Cricket.* removed from play by being bowled, l.b.w., stumped, caught, or run out. **35.** *Obs.* external; exterior; outer. **36.** *Obs.* outlying.

—*prep.* **37.** out or forth from (now used chiefly after *from* or in certain expressions): *out the door, out the window.* **38.** *Obs. or Dial.* outside: on the exterior of; beyond. —*interj.* **39.** begone! away! **40.** *Archaic or Dial.* (an exclamation of abhorrence, indignation, reproach, or grief): *out upon you!* —*n.* **41.** projection, or projecting corners: *ins and outs.* **42.** *U.S.* a means of escaping from a place, punishment, retribution, responsibility, etc.: *he always left himself an out.* **43.** *Baseball, etc.* a put-out. **44.** *Printing.* **a.** the omission of a word or words. **b.** that which is omitted. **45.** *Colloq. or Dial.* an outing. —*v.i.* **46.** to go or come out: *murder will out.* **47.** to make known; tell; utter (fol. by *with*). —*v.t.* **48.** to put out; expel; discharge; oust. [ME; OE *ūt*, c. D *uit*, G *aus*, Icel. and Goth. *ūt*]

out-, prefixal use of **out,** adv., prep., or adj., occuring in various senses in compounds, as in *outcast, outcome, outside,* and serving also to form many transitive verbs denoting a going beyond, surpassing, or outdoing in the particular action indicated, as in *outbid, outdo, outgeneral, outlast, outstay, outrate,* and many other words in which the meaning is readily perceived, the more important of these being entered below.

outact (out ăkt′), *v.t.* to outdo or surpass in acting.

out-and-out (out′ənd out′), *adj.* thoroughgoing; thorough; complete; unqualified.

outargue (out ä′gyōō), *v.t.*, **-gued, -guing.** to outdo or defeat in arguing.

outback (out′băk′), *Austral.* —*n.* **1.** remote, sparsely inhabited back country. —*adj.* **2.** of, pertaining to, or located in the back country. —*adv.* **3.** in or to the back country: *to live outback.*

outbalance (out băl′əns), *v.t.*, **-anced, -ancing.** to outweigh.

outbid (out bĭd′), *v.t.*, **-bid, -bidden** or **-bid, -bidding.** to outdo in bidding.

outboard (out′bôd′), *adv., adj. Naut.* on the outside, or away from the centre, of a ship or boat.

outboard motor, a small portable petrol engine with propeller and tiller, clamped on the stern of a boat.

outbound (out′bound′), *adj.* outward bound.

outbox (out bŏks′), *v.t.* to outdo in boxing.

outbrave (out brāv′), *v.t.*, **-braved, -braving. 1.** to defy; stand up to. **2.** to surpass in bravery or daring. **3.** to surpass in beauty, splendour, etc.

outbreak (out′brāk′), *n.* **1.** a breaking out; an outburst. **2.** a sudden and active manifestation. **3.** a public disturbance; a riot; an insurrection.

outbreed (out brēd′), *v.t.*, **-bred, -breeding.** to breed outside the limits of the family, within a breed or variety. —**out′breed′ing,** *n.*

outbuilding (out′bĭl′dĭng), *n.* a detached building subordinate to a main building.

outburst (out′bûst′), *n.* **1.** a bursting forth. **2.** a sudden and violent outpouring: *an outburst of tears.*

outby (out′bī′), *Scot. and N Dial.* —*adv.* **1.** a short distance away. **2.** outside; outdoors. **3.** towards the outside. —*adj.* **4.** outside; outdoor. Also, **outbye.**

outcast (out′käst′), *n.* **1.** a person who is cast out, as from home or society. **2.** a vagabond; homeless wanderer. **3.** *Archaic.* rejected matter; refuse. —*adj.* **4.** cast out, as from one's home or society. **5.** pertaining to or characteristic of an outcast: *outcast misery.* **6.** rejected or discarded.

outcaste (out′käst′), *n.* **1.** a person of no caste. **2.** (in India) one who has forfeited membership in his caste.

outclass (out kläs′), *v.t.* to surpass in class or quality; be distinctly ahead of (a competitor, etc.).

out-clearing (out′klĭə′rĭng), *n.* **1.** a cheque, bill of exchange, etc., presented to a bank through a clearing house or direct by another bank. **2.** the total amount of such items.

outcome (out′kŭm′), *n.* that which results from something; the consequence or issue. —**Syn.** See **end**[1].

outcrop (*n.* out′krŏp′; *v.* out krŏp′), *n., v.*, **-cropped, -cropping.** —*n.* **1.** a cropping out, as of a stratum or vein at the surface of the earth. **2.** the emerging part. **3.** something that occurs unexpectedly, suddenly, or violently: *an outcrop of labour unrest.* —*v.i.* **4.** to crop out, as strata.

outcrossing (out′krŏs′ĭng), *n.* breeding of unrelated animals or plants within a variety or breed. Also, **out′-cross′.**

outcry (*n.* out′krī′; *v.* out krī′), *n., pl.*, **-cries,** *v.*, **-cried, -crying.** —*n.* **1.** a crying out. **2.** a cry of distress, indignation, or the like. **3.** loud clamour. **4.** *Now Chiefly U.S.* an auction. —*v.t.* **5.** to outdo in crying; cry louder than.

outdate (out dāt′), *v.t.*, **-dated, -dating.** to put out of date; make antiquated or obsolete.

outdated (out dā′tĭd), *adj.* made out of date by the passage of time; old-fashioned.

outdistance (out dĭs′təns), *v.t.*, **-tanced, -tancing.** to distance completely; leave far behind; outstrip.

outdo (out dōō′), *v.t.*, **-did, -done, -doing.** to surpass in doing or performance; surpass. —**Syn.** See **excel.**

outdoor (out′dô′), *adj.* **1.** occurring or used out of doors. **2.** given or administered outside or apart from a workhouse, charitable institution, etc.: *outdoor relief.*

outdoors (out′dôz′), *adv.* **1.** out of doors; in the open air. —*n.* **2.** the world outside houses; open air.

outer (ou′tə), *adj.* **1.** farther out; exterior; external; of or pertaining to the outside. —*n.* **2.** *Austral. Colloq.* an open betting place near a racecourse. **3.** *Archery, etc.* **a.** the outermost ring or part of a target. **b.** a shot which strikes this part. **c.** the score value of this part. [compar. of OUT]

outer bar, *Law.* a collective name for all barristers other than Queen's Counsel.

Outer Mongolia, former name of **Mongolian People's Republic.**

outermost (ou′tə mōst′), *adj.* farthest out; remotest from the interior or centre. [f. OUTER + -MOST]

outer space, 1. space beyond the earth's atmosphere. **2.** space beyond the solar system. **3.** space between galaxies.

outface (out fās′), *v.t.*, **-faced, -facing. 1.** to face or stare out. **2.** to face or confront boldly; defy.

outfall (out′fôl′), *n.* the outlet or place of discharge of a river, drain, sewer, etc.

outfield (out′fēld′), *n.* **1.** *Cricket.* the part of the field farthest from the batsman. **2.** *Baseball.* **a.** the part of the field beyond the diamond or infield. **b.** the players stationed in it. **3.** the outlying land of a farm, esp. beyond the enclosed land. **4.** an outlying region.

outfielder (out′fēl′də), *n. Baseball.* one of the players stationed in the outfield.

outfit (out′fĭt′), *n., v.*, **-fitted, -fitting.** —*n.* **1.** an assemblage of articles for fitting out or equipping: *an explorer's outfit.* **2.** a set of articles for any purpose: *a model aircraft outfit.* **3.** a woman's costume, usually including dress, coat, hat, shoes, etc., and matching accessories. **4.** *Orig. U.S.* **a.** a group associated in any undertaking, as a military body, etc. **b.** a business company engaged in a particular kind of work. **c.** a party, company, or set. **5.** the act of fitting out or equipping, as for a voyage, journey, or expedition, or for any purpose. **6.** mental or moral equipment. —*v.t.* **7.** to furnish with an outfit; fit out; equip. —*v.i.* **8.** to furnish oneself with an outfit.

outfitter (out′fĭt′ə), *n.* **1.** one who provides an outfit. **2.** a shopkeeper who sells men's clothes.

outflank (out flăngk′), *v.t.* **1.** to go or extend beyond the flank of (an opposing army, etc.); outmanoeuvre by a flanking movement. **2.** to get the better of (a rival, opponent, etc.).

outflow (out′flō′), *n.* **1.** the act of flowing out. **2.** that which flows out. **3.** any outward movement.

outfly (out flī′), *v.t.*, **-flew, -flown, -flying. 1.** to surpass or outstrip in flying. **2.** *Poetic.* to fly out or forth.

outfoot (out fŏŏt′), *v.t.* **1.** (of one boat) to excel (another) in speed. **2.** to surpass in running, walking, dancing, etc.

outfrown (out froun′), *v.t.* to outdo in frowning; frown down.

outgeneral (out jĕn′ə rəl), *v.t.*, **-alled, -alling** or (*U.S.*) **-aled, -aling.** to outdo in generalship.

outgo (*n.* out′gō′; *v.* out gō′), *n., pl.*, **-goes,** *v.*, **-went, -gone, -going.** —*n.* **1.** a going out. **2.** expenditure. **3.** that which goes out; outflow. —*v.t.* **4.** to outstrip in going; go faster than. **5.** to go beyond or exceed. **6.** to surpass, excel, or outdo. —*v.i.* **7.** *Obs.* to go out.

outgoing (out′gō′ĭng), *adj.* **1.** going out; departing: *outgoing trains.* **2.** interested in and responsive to others: *an outgoing personality.* —*n.* **3.** (*usually pl.*) an amount of

outbar′gain, *v.t.*
outbar′ter, *v.t.*
outbawl′, *v.t.*
outbluff′, *v.t.*
outblus′ter, *v.t.*
outboast′, *v.t.*
outbrag′, *v.t.*, **-bragged, -bragging.**
outbranch′, *v.t.*
outbra′zen, *v.t.*
outbribe′, *v.t.*, **-bribed, -bribing.**
outbuild′, *v.t.*
outcross′, *v.t.*
outdance′, *v.t.*, **-danced, -dancing.**
outdare′, *v.t.*, **-dared, -daring.**
outdaz′zle, *v.t.*, **-zled, -zling.**
outdrink′, *v.t.*, **-drank, -drunk, -drinking.**
outeat′, *v.t.*, **-ate, -eating.**
outfight′, *v.t.*, **-fought, -fighting.**
out′flung′, *adj.*
outfox′, *v.t.*
outgaze′, *v.t.*, **-gazed, -gazing.**
outgen′eral, *v.t.*, **-alled, -alling.**

money expended; outlay; expenses. **4.** a going out. **5.** that which goes out; an effluence.

out-group (out′grōōp′), *n. Sociol.* everyone not belonging to an in-group.

outgrow (out grō′), *v.t.*, **-grew, -grown, -growing. 1.** to grow too large for. **2.** to leave behind or lose in the changes incident to development or the passage of time: *to outgrow a bad reputation.* **3.** to surpass in growing. —*v.i.* **4.** *Rare.* to grow out; protrude.

outgrowth (out′grōth′), *n.* **1.** a natural development, product, or result. **2.** an additional, supplementary result. **3.** a growing out or forth. **4.** that which grows out; an offshoot; an excrescence.

outhaul (out′hôl′), *n. Naut.* a rope used for hauling out a sail on a boom, yard, etc.

out-Herod (out hĕr′əd), *v.t.* to outdo (Herod or any other person) in evil, extravagance or excess.

outhouse (out′hous′), *n.* **1.** an outbuilding. **2.** an outside privy.

outing (ou′tĭng), *n.* **1.** an excursion or pleasure trip. **2.** the part of the sea out from the shore.

outing flannel, a light cotton flannel with a short nap.

outjockey (out jŏk′ĭ), *v.t.*, **-eyed, -eying.** to outmanoeuvre.

outland (*n.* out′lănd′; *adj.* out′lănd′, -lənd), *n.* **1.** *Obs.* outlying land, as of an estate. **2.** *Archaic.* a foreign land. —*adj.* **3.** outlying, as districts. **4.** *Archaic.* foreign. [ME; OE *ūtland*]

outlander (out′lăn′də), **1.** a foreigner; an alien. **2.** *Colloq.* an outsider.

outlandish (out lăn′dĭsh), *adj.* **1.** freakishly or grotesquely strange or odd, as appearance, dress, objects, ideas, practices, etc.; bizarre; barbarous. **2.** foreign-looking. **3.** out-of-the-way, as places. **4.** *Archaic.* foreign. —**outland′ishly,** *adv.* —**outland′ishness,** *n.*

outlast (out läst′), *v.t.* to last longer than.

outlaw (out′lô′), *n.* **1.** one excluded from the benefits and protection of the law. **2.** one under sentence of outlawry. **3.** a habitual criminal. **4.** an untamed or intractable animal. —*v.t.* **5.** to deprive of the benefits and protection of the law. **6.** *U.S.* to remove from legal jurisdiction; deprive of legal force. **7.** to prohibit. [ME *outlawe*, OE *ūtlage*, t. Scand.; cf. Icel. *ūtlagi*]

outlawry (out′lô′rĭ), *n., pl.*, **-ries. 1.** the act or process of outlawing. **2.** the state of being outlawed. **3.** disregard or defiance of the law.

outlay (*n.* out′lā′; *v.* out lā′), *n., v.*, **-laid, -laying.** —*n.* **1.** an expending; an expenditure, as of money. **2.** an amount expended. —*v.t.* **3.** to expend, as money.

outlet (out′lĕt), *n.* **1.** an opening or passage by which anything is let out; a vent or exit. **2.** *Elect.* **a.** a point on a wiring system at which current is taken to supply electrical devices. **b. outlet box,** the metal box or receptacle designed to facilitate connections to a wiring system. **3.** *Com.* **a.** a market for goods. **b.** (of a wholesaler or manufacturer) a shop, merchant, or agency selling one's goods: *he has many good outlets.* **4.** a means of expression; an occasion for releasing energies, etc. **5.** discharge.

outlier (out′lī′ə), *n.* **1.** one who or that which lies outside. **2.** one residing outside the place of his business, duty, etc. **3.** *Geol.* a part of a formation left detached through the removal of surrounding parts by denudation.

outline (out′līn′), *n., v.*, **-lined, -lining.** —*n.* **1.** the line, real or apparent, by which a figure or object is defined or bounded; the contour. **2.** a drawing or a style of drawing with merely lines of contour, without shading. **3.** a general sketch, account or report, indicating only the main features, as of a book, a subject, a project or work, facts, events, etc. **4.** (*pl.*) the essential features or chief characteristics of a subject. —*v.t.* **5.** to draw the outline of, or draw in outline, as a figure or object. **6.** to give an outline of (a subject, etc.); sketch the main features of. —**Syn. 1.** See **form.**

outlive (out lĭv′), *v.t.*, **-lived, -living. 1.** to live longer than; survive (a person, etc.). **2.** to outlast; live or last through: *the ship outlived the storm.* —**Syn. 1.** See **survive.**

outlook (out′lŏŏk′), *n.* **1.** the view or prospect from a place. **2.** the mental view: *one's outlook upon life.* **3.** prospect of the future: *the political outlook.* **4.** the place from which an observer looks out; a lookout. **5.** the act or state of looking out. **6.** a watch kept; watchfulness; vigilance.

outlying (out′lī′ĭng), *adj.* **1.** lying at a distance from the centre or the main body; remote; out-of-the-way. **2.** lying outside the boundary or limit.

outman (out măn′), *v.t.*, **-manned, -manning. 1.** to surpass in manpower. **2.** to surpass in manliness.

outmanoeuvre (out′mə nōō′və), *v.t.* to outdo in or get the better of by manoeuvring. Also, *U.S.*, **maneuver.**

outmatch (out măch′), *v.t.* to surpass; outdo.

outmode (out mōd′), *v.t.*, **-moded, -moding.** to cause to be out of style or become obsolete. —**outmod′ed,** *adj.*

outmost (out′mōst′), *adj.* farthest out; outermost.

outnumber (out nŭm′bə), *v.t.* to exceed in number.

out of bounds. See **bound**³ (def. 5).

out-of-date (out′əv dāt′), *adj.* of a previous style or fashion; obsolete. Also (esp. in predicative use), **out of date.**

out-of-doors (out′əv dôz′), *adj.* **1.** Also, **out-of-door;** (esp. in predicative use), **out of doors.** outdoor. —*adv.*, *n.* **2.** outdoors.

out of play. See **play** (def. 7).

out-of-pocket (out′əv pŏk′ĭt), *adj.* of or pertaining to what has been paid out in cash or outlay incurred: *out-of-pocket expenses.* Also (esp. in predicative use), **out of pocket.**

out of print. See **print** (def. 18).

out-of-the-way (out′əv thə wā′), *adj.* **1.** remote from much-travelled ways or frequented or populous regions; secluded. **2.** unusual. **3.** improper. Also (esp. in predicative use), **out of the way.**

outpace (out pās′), *v.t.* to outstrip or outdo in walking, running, riding, etc.

outpatient (out′pā′shənt), *n.* a patient receiving treatment at a hospital but not being an inmate.

outplay (out plā′), *v.t.* to play better than; defeat.

outpoint (out point′), *v.t.* **1.** to excel in number of points, as in a competition or contest. **2.** *Naut.* to sail closer to the wind than (another vessel).

outport (out′pôt′), *n.* a secondary seaport, auxiliary to another seaport, and generally more accessible to larger vessels.

outpost (out′pōst′), *n.* **1.** a station at a distance from the main body of an army to protect it from surprise attack. **2.** the body of troops stationed there.

outpour (*n.* out′pô′; *v.* out pô′), *n.* **1.** an outflow or overflow; that which is poured out. —*v.t.* **2.** to pour out.

outpouring (out′pô′rĭng), *n.* outflow; effusion.

output (out′pŏŏt′), *n.* **1.** the act of turning out; production. **2.** the quantity or amount produced, as in a given time. **3.** the product or yield, as of a mine. **4.** *Computers.* information obtained from a computer on the completion of a calculation.

outrage (out′rāj′), *n., v.*, **-raged, -raging.** —*n.* **1.** an act of wanton violence; any gross violation of law or decency. **2.** anything that outrages the feelings. **3.** *Obs.* a passionate or violent outbreak. —*v.t.* **4.** to subject to grievous violence or indignity. **5.** to affect with a sense of offended right or decency; shock. **6.** to offend against (right, decency, feelings, etc.) grossly or shamelessly. **7.** to rape (a woman). [ME, t. OF, der. *outrer* push beyond bounds, der. *outre* beyond, g. L *ultrā*]

outrageous (out rā′jəs), *adj.* **1.** of the nature of or involving gross injury or wrong: *an outrageous slander.* **2.** grossly offensive to the sense of right or decency. **3.** passing reasonable bounds; intolerable or shocking: *an outrageous price.* **4.** violent in action or temper. —**outra′geously,** *adv.* —**outra′geousness,** *n.*

Outram (ōō′trəm), *n.* **Sir James,** 1803–63, British general.

outrance (*Fr.* ōō träNs′), *n. French.* the utmost extremity, as in combat. [ME, t. OF, der. *outrer*. See OUTRAGE]

outrange (out rānj′), *v.t.*, **-ranged, -ranging. 1.** to have a longer range than, as a gun. **2.** *Naut.* to outsail.

outrank (out răngk′), *v.t.* to rank above.

outré (ōō′trā; *Fr.* ōō trĕ′), *adj. French.* passing the bounds of what is usual and considered proper. [F, pp. of *outrer*. See OUTRAGE]

outreach (*v.* out rēch′; *n.* out′rēch′), *v.t.* **1.** to reach beyond; exceed. **2.** to reach out; extend. —*v.i.* **3.** to reach out. —*n.* **4.** a reaching out. **5.** length of reach.

outrelief (out′rĭ lēf′), *n. Obs.* public relief given to people not residing in a public or charitable institution.

outremer (*Fr.* ōō trə mĕr′), *adv. French.* beyond the sea.

outride (out rīd′), *v.*, **-rode, -ridden, -riding,** *n.* —*v.t.* **1.** to outdo or outstrip in riding. **2.** (of a ship) to last through a storm. —*v.i.* **3.** to act as an outrider. —*n.* **4.** *Pros.* an unaccented syllable or syllables added to a metrical foot, esp. in sprung rhythm.

outrider (out′rī′də), *n.* **1.** a mounted attendant riding before or beside a carriage. **2.** a motorcyclist who rides ahead of a motor car as an escort, to clear a passage, etc. **3.** one who goes ahead as a member of a vanguard. **4.** one who rides out or forth, esp. as a scout.

---

outjump′, *v.t.*
outleap′, *v.t.*, **-leapt, -leaping.**
outmarch′, *v.t.*
outplease′, *v.t.*, **-pleased, -pleasing.**
outprice′, *v.t.*, **-priced, -pricing.**
outrea′son, *v.t.*
outreign′, *v.t.*
outrig′, *v.t.*, **-rigged, -rigging.**

---

outrigger (out′rĭg′ə), *n.* **1.** a framework extended outboard from the side of a boat, esp., as in South Pacific canoes, supporting a float which gives stability. **2.** a bracket extending outwards from the side of a racing shell, to support a rowlock. **3.** the shell itself. **4.** a spar rigged out from a ship's rail or the like, as for extending a sail. **5.** any of various projecting frames or parts on an aeroplane, as for supporting a rudder, etc. **6.** *Bldg Trades.* a beam projecting from a building and wedged against a ceiling inside the building, used for supporting certain kinds of scaffolding.

Canoe with outrigger

outright (*adj.* out′rīt′; *adv.* out′rīt′), *adj.* **1.** complete or total: *an outright loss.* **2.** downright or unqualified: *an outright refusal.* **3.** *Rare.* directed straight out or on. *—adv.* **4.** completely; entirely. **5.** without restraint, reserve, or concealment; openly. **6.** at once. **7.** *Obs.* straight out or ahead.
outroot (out ro͞ot′), *v.t.* to root out; extirpate.
outrun (out rŭn′), *v.t.*, **-ran, -run, -running.** **1.** to outstrip in running. **2.** to escape by or as by running. **3.** to exceed.
outrunner (out′rŭn′ə), *n.* **1.** one who or that which runs out or outside. **2.** an attendant who runs before or beside a carriage. **3.** the leader of a team of dogs. **4.** a forerunner.
outsail (out sāl′), *v.t.* to outdo or surpass in sailing; outstrip.
outsell (out sĕl′), *v.t.*, **-sold, -selling.** **1.** to outdo in selling; sell more than. **2.** to sell or be sold for more than. **3.** to exceed in value.
outset (out′sĕt′), *n.* the beginning or start.
outshine (out shīn′), *v.*, **-shone, -shining.** *—v.t.* **1.** to surpass in shining. **2.** to surpass in splendour, excellence, etc. *—v.i.* **3.** *Rare.* to shine forth.
outshoot (*v.* out sho͞ot′; *n.* out′sho͞ot′), *v.*, **-shot, -shooting,** *n.* *—v.t.* **1.** to surpass in shooting. **2.** to shoot beyond. **3.** to shoot or send forth. *—v.i.* **4.** to shoot forth; project. *—n.* **5.** a shooting out. **6.** something that shoots out.
outside (out′sīd′), *n.* **1.** the outer side, surface, or part; the exterior. **2.** the external aspect or appearance. **3.** something merely external. **4.** the space without or beyond an enclosure, boundary, etc. **5.** *Rugby Football.* **a.** a back. **b.** any player other than a forward. **6. at the outside,** *Colloq.* the utmost limit: *not more than ten at the outside.* *—adj.* **7.** being, acting, done, or originating beyond an enclosure, boundary, etc.: *outside noises.* **8.** situated on or pertaining to the outside; exterior; external. **9.** not belonging to or connected with an institution, society, etc.: *outside influences.* **10.** extremely unlikely or remote: *an outside chance.* *—adv.* **11.** on or to the outside, exterior, or space without. *—prep.* **12.** on or towards the outside of. **13.** *Colloq., Chiefly U.S.* with the exception of (usually fol. by *of*).
outside-half (out′sīd häf′), *n.* *Rugby Football.* stand-off half. Also, **outside-half-back** (out′sīd häf′băk′).
outside left, *Soccer, Hockey, etc.* a player on the far left wing of the forward line.
outsider (out′sī′də), *n.* **1.** one not within an enclosure, boundary, etc. **2.** one not belonging to a particular group, set, party, etc. **3.** one unconnected or unacquainted with the matter in question. **4.** a racehorse, etc., not included among the favourites.
outside right, *Soccer, Hockey, etc.* a player on the far right wing of the forward line.
outsing (out sĭng′), *v.*, **-sang, -sung, -singing.** *—v.t.* **1.** to sing better than. **2.** to sing louder than. *—v.i.* **3.** to sing out.
out sister, a nun, especially in a coenobite order, who works outside the convent in its service.
outsize (out′sīz′), *n.* **1.** an uncommon or irregular size. **2.** a garment of such a size, esp. when larger. *—adj.* **3.** Also, **out′sized′.** unusually or abnormally large; larger than average: *a display of outsize dresses.*
outskirts (out′skûts′), *n.pl.* outer or bordering parts or districts.
outsmart (out smät′), *v.t.* to prove too clever for; outwit.
outspan (out spăn′), *v.*, **-spanned, -spanning,** *n.* *S African.* *—v.t.* **1.** to unyoke or unhitch, as oxen from a wagon. *—v.i.* **2.** to remove the yoke, harness, etc., from animals. *—n.* **3.** the act of outspanning. **4.** an area on a farm that is required to be kept available for passing travellers. [t. Afrikaans: m. *uitspannen*]
outspeak (out spēk′), *v.*, **-spoke, -spoken, -speaking.** *—v.t.* **1.** to outdo or excel in speaking. **2.** to utter frankly or boldly. *—v.i.* **3.** to speak out.
outspoken (out spō′kən), *adj.* **1.** uttered or expressed with frankness or lack of reserve: *outspoken criticism.* **2.** free or unreserved in speech: *outspoken people.* **—outspo′kenly,** *adv.* **—outspo′kenness,** *n.* **—Syn. 1.** See **frank.**
outspread (*v.* out sprĕd′; *n., adj.* out′sprĕd′), *v.*, **-spread, -spreading,** *adj., n.* *—v.t., v.i.* **1.** to spread out; extend. *—adj.* **2.** spread out; stretched out. **3.** diffused abroad. *—n.* **4.** a spreading out. **5.** that which is spread out; an expanse.
outstand (out stănd′), *v.*, **-stood, -standing.** *Now Rare.* *—v.i.* **1.** to be prominent. **2.** (of a ship) to sail out to sea. *—v.t.* **3.** to stay or remain beyond. **4.** to withstand.
outstanding (out stăn′dĭng), *adj.* **1.** prominent; conspicuous; striking. **2.** that continues in existence; that remains unsettled, unpaid, etc. **3.** standing out; projecting; detached. **4.** that resists or opposes.
outstare (out stēə′), *v.t.*, **-stared, -staring.** **1.** to outdo in staring. **2.** to stare out of countenance.
outstation (out′stā′shən), *n.* an auxiliary station, esp. on the outskirts of a district.
outstay (out stā′), *v.t.* **1.** to stay longer than. **2.** to stay beyond the time or duration of.
outstretch (out strĕch′), *v.t.* **1.** to stretch forth; extend. **2.** to stretch beyond (a limit, etc.). **3.** to stretch out; expand. **4.** *Obs.* to strain.
outstrip (out strĭp′), *v.t.*, **-stripped, -stripping.** **1.** to outdo; surpass; excel. **2.** to outdo or pass in running or swift travel. **3.** to get ahead of or leave behind in a race or in any course of competition.
outstroke (out′strōk′), *n.* **1.** a stroke in an outward direction. **2.** (in an engine) the stroke during which the piston rod moves outwards from the cylinder.
outswinger (out′swĭng′ə), *n.* *Cricket.* a ball bowled so as to swerve from leg to off.
outturn (out′tûn′), *n.* the quantity produced; output.
outvote (out vōt′), *v.t.*, **-voted, -voting.** to outdo or defeat in voting.
outward (out′wəd), *adj.* **1.** being, or pertaining to, what is seen or apparent, as distinguished from the underlying nature, facts, etc., or from what is in the mind: *the outward looks.* **2.** pertaining to the outside of the body. **3.** pertaining to the body as opposed to the mind or spirit: *our outward eyes.* **4.** belonging or pertaining to the external world as opposed to the mind or spirit. **5.** belonging or pertaining to what is external to oneself: *a man's outward relations.* **6.** proceeding or directed towards the outside or exterior. **7.** that lies towards the outside; that is on the outer side: *my outward room.* **8.** of or pertaining to the outside, outer surface, or exterior. **9.** not directly concerned or interested. *—n.* **10.** the outward part; the outside or exterior; the external or material world. **11.** outward appearance. *—adv.* **12.** outwards. **13.** away from port: *a ship bound outward.* [ME; OE *ūtweard*]
outward-bound (out′wəd bound′), *adj.* (of a ship) headed out to sea, esp. from a home port.
outwardly (out′wəd lĭ), *adv.* **1.** as regards appearance or outward manifestation. **2.** towards the outside. **3.** on the outside or outer surface.
outwards (out′wədz), *adv.* towards the outside; out. Also, **outward.**
outwash (out′wŏsh′), *n.* *Geol.* sheets of gravel, sand, and clay, laid down by melt-water streams at the end of a glacier or round the margin of an icesheet.
outwatch (out wŏch′), *v.t.* **1.** to outdo in watching. **2.** to watch until the end of.
outwear (out wēə′), *v.t.*, **-wore, -worn, -wearing.** **1.** to wear or last longer than; outlast. **2.** to outlive or outgrow. **3.** to wear out; consume by wearing. **4.** to exhaust in strength or endurance. **5.** to pass time.
outweigh (out wā′), *v.t.* **1.** to exceed in value, importance, influence, etc.: *the advantages of the plan outweighed its defects.* **2.** to be too heavy or burdensome for. **3.** to exceed in weight.

---

outri′val, *v.t.*, **-rivalled, -rivalling.**
outroar′, *v.t.*
outsay′, *v.t.*, **-said, -saying.**
outsee′, *v.t.*, **-saw, -seen, -seeing.**
outsit′, *v.t.*, **-sat, -sitting.**
outsleep′, *v.t.*, **-slept, -sleeping.**
outsoar′, *v.t.*
outspar′kle, *v.t.*, **-sparkled, -sparkling.**
out′spring′, *n.*
outspring′, *v.*, **-sprang, -sprung, -springing.**
outswear′, *v.t.*, **-swore, -sworn, -swearing.**
outswim′, *v.t.*, **-swam, -swum, -swimming.**
outtalk′, *v.t.*
outthink′, *v.t.*, **-thought, -thinking.**
outtell′, *v.t.*, **-told, -telling.**
outwait′, *v.t.*
outwalk′, *v.t.*

---

outwit (out wĭt′), *v.t.*, **-witted, -witting. 1.** to get the better of by superior ingenuity or cleverness. **2.** *Archaic.* to surpass in intelligence.

outwork (*v.* out wûk′; *n.* out′wûk′), *v.t.*, **-worked** or **-wrought, -working,** *n.* —*v.t.* **1.** to surpass in working; work harder or faster than. **2.** to work out or carry on to a conclusion; finish. —*n.* **3.** *Fort.* a part of the fortifications of a place lying outside the main work.

outworker (out′wû′kə), *n.* one who does work in his home, as for a central factory or organization.

outworn (out wôn′), *adj.* **1.** obsolete; out-of-date as beliefs, customs, etc. **2.** worn out, as clothes. **3.** exhausted in strength or endurance, as persons.

ouzel cock (o͞o′zəl), **1.** a name for members of the thrush family, esp. the blackbird, *Turdus merula.* **2.** ring ouzel. Also, **ousel, ouzel.** [ME *osel,* OE *ōsle,* c. G *Amsel*]

ouzo (o͞o′zō), *n.* an aniseed-flavoured liqueur of Greece.

ova (ō′və), *n.* pl. of **ovum.**

oval (ō′vəl), *adj.* **1.** having the general form, shape, or outline of an egg; egg-shaped. **2.** ellipsoidal or elliptical. —*n.* **3.** any of various oval things. **4.** a body or a plane figure oval in shape or outline. **5.** an elliptical field, or a field on which an elliptical track is laid out, as for athletic contests. [t. NL: s. *ōvālis,* der. L *ōvum* egg. See OVATE] —**o′vally,** *adv.* —**o′valness,** *n.*

ovarian (ō vĕə′rĭ ən), *adj.* of or pertaining to an ovary.

ovariotomy (ō vĕə′rĭ ŏt′ə mĭ), *n., pl.* **-mies.** *Surg.* incision into or removal of an ovary.

ovaritis (ō′və rī′tĭs), *n. Pathol.* oophoritis.

ovary (ō′və rĭ), *n., pl.* **-ries. 1.** *Anat., Zool.* the female gonad or reproductive gland, in which the ova, or eggs, and the hormones that regulate female secondary sex characteristics develop. **2.** *Bot.* the enlarged lower part of the carpel in angiospermous flowers enclosing the ovules. [t. NL: *ōvārium,* der. L *ōvum* egg]

Longitudinal section of ovaries, with ovules A, Larkspur, *Delphinium consolida*; B, Chickweed, *Stellaria media*; C, Buttercup, *Ranunculus bulbosus*; D, Fuchsia, *Fuchsia coccinea*; E, Lily, *Lilium superbum*; F, Maple, *Acer rubrum*

ovate (ō′vāt), *adj.* **1.** egg-shaped. **2.** *Bot.* **a.** having a plane figure like the longitudinal section of an egg. **b.** having such a figure with the broader end at the base, as a leaf. [t. L: m. s. *ōvātus* egg-shaped]

ovation (ō vā′shən), *n.* **1.** an enthusiastic public reception of a person; enthusiastic applause. **2.** a lesser form of triumph accorded to an ancient Roman commander. [t. L: s. *ovātio* rejoicing]

Ovate leaf

oven (ŭv′ən), *n.* a chamber or receptacle for baking or heating, or for drying with the aid of heat. [ME; OE *ofen,* c. G *Ofen*]

ovenbird (ŭv′ən bûd′), *n.* **1.** an American warbler, *Seiurus aurocapillus,* which builds an oven-shaped nest of grasses, etc., on the forest floor. **2.** any of the South American passerine birds of the genus *Furnarius.*

ovenware (ŭv′ən wĕə′), *n.* heat-resistant dishes, casseroles, etc., in which food can be baked in an oven.

ovenwood (ŭv′ən wo͝od′), *n.* brushwood; dead wood fit only for burning.

over (ō′və), *prep.* **1.** above in place or position; higher up than: *the roof over one's head.* **2.** above and to the other side of: *to leap over a wall.* **3.** above in authority, power, etc.; so as to govern, control, or conquer. **4.** on or upon; so as to rest on or cover. **5.** on or on top of: *to hit someone over the head.* **6.** here and there on or in: *at various places over the country.* **7.** through all parts of; all through: *to look over some papers.* **8.** to and fro on or in: *to travel over Europe.* **9.** from side to side of; to the other side of: *to go over a bridge.* **10.** on the other side of: *lands over the sea.* **11.** reaching higher than, so as to submerge. **12.** in excess of, or more than: *over a mile.* **13.** above in degree, etc. **14.** in preference to. **15.** throughout the extent or length of: *over a great distance.* **16.** until after the end of: *to adjourn over the holidays.* **17.** throughout the duration of: *over a long term of years.* **18.** in reference to, concerning, or about: *to quarrel over a matter.* **19.** while engaged on or concerned with: *to fall asleep over one's work.* **20.** by the agency of: *she told me over the phone; we heard the news over the radio.* **21. be all over,** *Colloq.* to show great affection towards; be excessively attentive to: *she was all over him as soon as he entered the room.* **22. over and above,** in addition to; besides. —*adv.* **23.** over the top or upper surface or edge of something. **24.** so as to cover the surface, or affect the whole surface: *to paint a thing over.* **25.** through a region, area, etc.: *to travel all over.* **26.** at some distance, as in a direction indicated: *over by the hill.* **27.** from side to side, or to the other side: *to sail over.* **28.** across any intervening space: *when are you coming over to see us?* **29.** from beginning to end, or all through: *to read a thing over.* **30.** from one person, party, etc., to another: *to make property over to others.* **31.** on the other side, as of a sea, a river, or any space: *over in Ireland.* **32.** so as to bring the upper end or side down or under: *to knock a thing over.* **33.** once more; again: *to do a thing over.* **34.** in repetition: *twenty times over.* **35.** in excess or addition: *to pay the full sum and something over.* **36.** remaining beyond a certain amount: *five goes into seven once, with two over.* **37.** throughout or beyond a period of time: *to stay over till Monday.* **38.** Some adverbial phrases are: **all over, 1.** everywhere. **2.** thoroughly; entirely. **3.** done with; finished.

all over with, done with; finished.

over again, once more; with repetition.

over against, 1. opposite to; in front of. **2.** as contrasted with or distinguished from: *to set truth over against falsehood.*

over and over (again), repeatedly.

—*adj.* **39.** upper; higher up. **40.** higher in authority, station, etc. **41.** serving, or intended, as an outer covering: outer. **42.** in excess or addition; surplus; extra. **43.** too great; excessive. **44.** at an end; done; past: *when the war was over.* **45. all over,** *Colloq.* characteristic; typical: *that's him all over.*

—*n.* **46.** an amount in excess or addition; an extra. **47.** *Mil.* a shot which strikes or bursts beyond the target. **48.** *Cricket.* **a.** the number of balls (six in England, eight in Australia) delivered between successive changes of bowlers. **b.** the part of the game played between such changes.

—*v.t.* **49.** *Rare.* to jump over; leap over. **50.** *Rare.* to get over; pass over.

[ME; OE *ofer,* c. D *over,* G *über,* akin to Skt *upari*]

over-, prefixal use of **over,** *prep., adv.,* or *adj.,* occurring in various senses in compounds, as in *overboard, overcoat, overhang, overlap, overlord, overrun, overthrow,* and especially employed, with the sense of 'over the limit', 'to excess', 'too much', 'too', to form verbs, adjectives, adverbs, and nouns, as *overact, overcapitalize, overcrowd, overfull, overmuch, oversupply, overweight,* and many others, mostly self-explanatory: a hyphen, which is commonly absent from old or well-established formations, being often used in new coinages, or in any words whose compound parts it may be desirable to set off distinctly.

overabound (ō′və rə bound′), *v.i.* to abound to excess.

overabundance (ō′və rə bŭn′dəns), *n.* excessive abundance. —**o′verabun′dant,** *adj.*

overact (ō′vər ăkt′), *v.t., v.i.* to act in an exaggerated manner.

overactive (ō′vər ăk′tĭv), *adj.* active to excess; too active. —**o′veractiv′ity,** *n.*

over-age (ō′vər āj′), *adj.* beyond the proper age. [f. OVER- + AGE, n.]

overall (*adj., n.* ō′vər ôl′; *adv.* ō′vər ôl′), *adj.* **1.** from one extreme limit of a thing to another: *the overall length of a bridge.* **2.** covering or including everything: *an overall estimate.* —*adv.* **3.** covering or including everything; altogether: *the position viewed overall.* —*n.* **4.** (*pl.*) loose, stout trousers, usually with a part extending up over the chest, often worn over other trousers to protect them, as by workmen and others. **5.** a loose-fitting garment covering ordinary clothes, as worn by women doing housework or by small children at play.

overanxious (ō′vər ăngk′shəs), *adj.* excessively anxious. —**overanxiety** (ō′və răng zī′ə tĭ), **o′veranx′iousness,** *n.* —**o′veranx′iously,** *adv.*

overarch (ō′vər ăch′), *v.t.* **1.** to span with or like an arch. —*v.i.* **2.** to form an arch over something.

overarm (ō′vər ăm′), *adj.* thrown or performed with the arm raised above the shoulder.

overawe (ō′vər ô′), *v.t.*, **-awed, -awing.** to restrain or subdue by inspiring awe; intimidate.

o′verabsorb′, *v.t.*
o′verabsorp′tion, *n.*
o′verabste′mious, *adj.*
o′verabste′miously, *adv.*
o′verabste′miousness, *n.*
o′veraccen′tuate′, *v.t.*, **-ated, -ating.**
o′veraccen′tua′tion, *n.*
o′veracid′ity, *n.*
o′verambi′tious, *adj.*
o′verambi′tiously, *adv.*
o′verambi′tiousness, *n.*
o′verassess′ment, *n.*
o′veratten′tive, *adj.*
o′veratten′tively, *adv.*
o′veratten′tiveness, *n.*

overbalance (ō′və băl′əns), *v.*, **-anced, -ancing,** *n.* —*v.t.* **1.** to outweigh. **2.** to cause to lose balance or to fall or turn over. —*v.i.* **3.** to lose (one's balance). —*n.* **4.** an overbalancing weight or amount. **5.** something that more than balances.

overbear (ō′və bĕə′), *v.*, **-bore, -borne, -bearing.** —*v.t.* **1.** to bear over or down by weight or force. **2.** to overcome. **3.** to prevail over or overrule (wishes, objections, etc.). **4.** to treat in a domineering way. **5.** *Naut.* to carry more sail than (another vessel). —*v.i.* **6.** to produce fruit or progeny so abundantly as to impair the health.

overbearing (ō′və bĕə′rĭng), *adj.* domineering; dictatorial; haughtily or rudely arrogant. —**o′verbear′ingly,** *adv.*

overbid (*v.* ō′və bĭd′; *n.* ō′və bĭd′), *v.*, **-bid, -bidden** or **-bid, -bidding,** *n.* —*v.t., v.i.* **1.** to bid more than the value of (a thing). **2.** to outbid (a person, etc.). —*n.* **3.** a higher bid.

overbite (ō′və bīt′), *n.* *Dentistry.* occlusion in which the upper incisor teeth overlap the lower.

overblouse (ō′və blouz′), *n.* a blouse designed to hang loosely over a skirt, slacks, etc., and not to be tucked in at the waist.

overblow (ō′və blō′), *v.*, **-blew, -blown, -blowing.** —*v.t.* **1.** *Archaic.* to blow over, down, or away. **2.** to blow over the surface of, as the wind, sand, or the like does. **3.** *Music.* to increase the pressure of air in (a wind instrument), causing a higher harmonic series to sound. —*v.i.* **4.** *Archaic.* to pass away, as a storm.

overblown (ō′və blōn′), *adj.* **1.** more than full-blown. **2.** inflated to an excessive degree. **3.** turgid; bombastic: *an overblown prose style.*

overboard (ō′və bôd′), *adv.* over the side of a ship or boat, esp. into or in the water: *to fall overboard.*

overbuild (ō′və bĭld′), *v.t.*, **-built, -building.** **1.** to cover or surmount with a building or structure. **2.** to erect too many buildings on (an area). **3.** to build (a structure) on too great or elaborate a scale.

overburden (*v.* ō′və bû′dn; *n.* ō′və bû′dn), *v.t.* **1.** to load with too great a burden; overload. —*n.* **2.** an excessive burden. **3.** waste material, overlying a mineral deposit.

overburdensome (ō′və bû′dn səm), *adj.* excessively burdensome.

overbuy (ō′və bī′), *v.*, **-bought, -buying.** —*v.t., v.i.* **1.** to purchase in excessive quantities, esp. without regard for one's financial means. **2.** *Finance.* to buy on margin in excess of one's ability to provide added security in an emergency, as in a falling market. —*v.i.* **3.** to buy regardless of one's financial ability.

overcall (ō′və kôl′), *v.t.* *Cards.* to bid higher than.

overcapitalize (ō′və kăp′ĭ tə līz′), *v.t.*, **-lized, -lizing.** **1.** to fix the nominal capital (total amount of securities) of a company in excess of the limits set by law or by sound financial policy. **2.** to overestimate the capital value (of a business property or enterprise). **3.** to provide an excessive amount of capital (for a business enterprise). Also, **overcapitalise.** —**o′vercap′italiza′tion,** *n.*

overcast (ō′və käst′), *adj.*, *v.*, **-cast, -casting.** —*adj.* **1.** overspread with clouds, as the sky; cloudy. **2.** dark; gloomy. **3.** *Sewing.* sewn by overcasting. —*v.t.* **4.** to overcloud, darken, or make gloomy. **5.** to sew with stitches passing successively over an edge, esp. long stitches set at intervals to prevent ravelling. —*v.i.* **6.** to become cloudy or dark.

overcasting (ō′və käs′tĭng), *n.* **1.** *Sewing.* the act of sewing along the edges of material with long spaced stitches to prevent ravelling. **2.** *Sewing.* the stitch used to overcast.

overcharge (*v.* ō′və chäj′; *n.* ō′və chäj′), *v.*, **-charged, -charging,** *n.* —*v.t.* **1.** to charge (a person) too high a price. **2.** to charge (an amount) in excess of what is due. **3.** to overload; fill too full. **4.** to exaggerate. —*v.i.* **5.** to make an excessive charge; charge too much for something. —*n.* **6.** a charge in excess of a just price. **7.** an excessive load.

overcheck (ō′və chĕk′), *n.* **1.** a checkrein passed over a horse's head between the ears. **2.** *Textiles.* a prominent check pattern superimposed on another check pattern. **3.** *Textiles.* a fabric having this pattern.

overclothes (ō′və klōz′, -klōthz′), *n.pl.* clothing worn outside other garments.

overcloud (ō′və kloud′), *v.t.* **1.** to overspread with or as with clouds. **2.** to darken; obscure; make gloomy. —*v.i.* **3.** to become clouded over or overcast.

overcoat (ō′və kōt′), *n.* **1.** a coat worn over the ordinary clothing, as in cold weather; a greatcoat; topcoat. **2.** an additional coat of paint applied for protection.

overcome (ō′və kŭm′), *v.*, **-came, -come, -coming.** —*v.t.* **1.** to get the better of in a struggle or conflict; conquer; defeat. **2.** to prevail over (opposition, objections, temptations, etc.). **3.** to surmount (difficulties, etc.). **4.** to overpower (a person, etc.) in body or mind, or affect in an overpowering or paralysing way, as liquor, a drug, excessive exertion, violent emotion, or the like does. **5.** *Archaic.* to overspread or overrun. —*v.i.* **6.** to gain the victory; conquer. [ME; OE *ofercuman*] —**Syn. 1.** See **defeat.**

overcompensation (ō′və kŏm′pĕn sā′shən), *n.* *Psychol.* an exaggerated striving to neutralize and conceal a strong character trait by substituting for it a character trait of an opposite kind.

overconfident (ō′və kŏn′fĭ dənt), *adj.* too confident. —**o′vercon′fidence,** *n.*

overcritical (ō′və krĭt′ĭ kl), *adj.* critical to excess; too critical; hypercritical.

overcrop (ō′və krŏp′), *v.t.*, **-cropped, -cropping.** *Agric.* to crop (land) to excess; exhaust the fertility of by continuous cropping.

overcrowd (ō′və kroud′), *v.t., v.i.* to crowd to excess.

overdevelop (ō′və dĭ vĕl′əp), *v.t.* to develop to excess. —**o′verdevel′opment,** *n.*

overdo (ō′və do͞o′), *v.*, **-did, -done, -doing.** —*v.t.* **1.** to do to excess: *to overdo exercise.* **2.** to carry to excess or beyond the proper limit. **3.** to overact (a part); exaggerate. **4.** to overtax the strength of; fatigue; exhaust. **5.** to cook too much; overcook. —*v.i.* **6.** to do too much. —**overdone** (ō′və dŭn′), *adj.*

overdose (*n.* ō′və dōs′; *v.* ō′və dōs′), *n.*, *v.*, **-dosed, -dosing.** —*n.* **1.** an excessive dose. —*v.t.* **2.** to dose to excess.

overdraft (ō′və dräft′), *n.* **1.** a draft in excess of one's credit balance, or the amount of the excess. **2.** an excess draft or demand made on anything. **3.** the action of overdrawing an account, as at a bank. **4.** overdraught.

overdraught (ō′və dräft′), *n.* **1.** a draught made to pass over a fire, as in a furnace. **2.** a draught passing downwards through a kiln. Also, **overdraft.**

overdraw (ō′və drô′), *v.*, **-drew, -drawn, -drawing.** —*v.t.* **1.** to draw upon (an account, allowance, etc.) in excess of the balance standing to one's credit or at one's disposal. **2.** to draw too far; strain, as a bow, by drawing. **3.** to exaggerate in drawing, depicting, or describing. —*v.i.* **4.** to overdraw an account or the like.

overdress (*v.* ō′və drĕs′; *n.* ō′və drĕs′), *v.*, **-dressed, -dressing,** *n.* —*v.t., v.i.* **1.** to dress to excess or with too much display. —*n.* **2.** a dress worn over another dress.

overdrive (*v.* ō′və drīv′; *n.* ō′və drīv′), *v.*, **-drove, -driven, -driving,** *n.* —*v.t.* **1.** to overwork; push or carry to excess. **2.** to drive too hard. —*n.* **3.** *Mach.* a device containing gearing that provides an extra-high ratio for motor cars when continuous high speed and low fuel consumption are required.

overdue (ō′və dyo͞o′), *adj.* past due, as a belated train or a bill not paid by the assigned date; late; long awaited.

overdye (ō′və dī′), *v.t.*, **-dyed, -dying.** **1.** to dye too much or too long. **2.** to dye over with another colour.

---

o′verbal′last, *v.t.*
o′verbold′, *adj.*
o′verbold′ly, *adv.*
o′verbold′ness, *n.*
o′verbright′, *adj.*
o′verbright′ly, *adv.*
o′verbright′ness, *n.*
o′verbrim′, *v.i.*, **-brimmed, -brimming.**
o′verbus′ily, *adv.*
o′verbus′y, *adj.*
o′verbus′yness, *n.*
o′vercare′ful, *adj.*
o′vercare′fully, *adv.*
o′vercare′fulness, *n.*
o′vercau′tion, *n., v.t.*
o′vercau′tious, *adj.*
o′vercau′tiously, *adv.*
o′vercau′tiousness, *n.*
o′vercen′traliza′tion, *n.*
o′vercen′tralize′, *v.*, **-lized, -lizing.**
o′vercha′ritable, *adj.*
o′vercha′ritableness, *n.*
o′vercha′ritably, *adv.*
o′verchild′ish, *adj.*
o′verchild′ishly, *adv.*
o′verchild′ishness, *n.*
o′vercommer′cializa′tion, *n.*
o′vercommer′cialize′, *v.t.*, **-lized, -lizing.**
o′verconserv′ative, *adj.*
o′verconserv′atively, *adv.*
o′verconserv′ativeness, *n.*
o′vercook′, *v.*
o′vercorrect′, *adj., v.*
o′vercost′ly, *adj.*
o′vercour′teous, *adj.*
o′vercour′teously, *adv.*
o′vercour′teousness, *n.*
o′vercred′ulous, *adj.*
o′vercred′ulously, *adv.*
o′vercred′ulousness, *n.*
o′vercur′ious, *adj.*
o′vercur′iously, *adv.*
o′vercur′iousness, *n.*
o′verdec′orate′, *v.*, **-rated, -rating.**
o′verdec′orative, *adj.*
o′verdec′oratively, *adv.*
o′verdec′orativeness, *n.*
o′verdel′icate, *adj.*
o′verdel′icately, *adv.*
o′verdel′icateness, *n.*
o′verde′tailed, *adj.*
o′verdig′nified′, *adj.*
o′verdiscrim′inat′ing, *adj.*
o′verdiscrim′inat′ingly, *adv.*
o′verdramat′ic, *adj.*

---

overeat (ō′vər ēt′), *v.*, **-ate, -eaten, -eating.** —*v.i.* **1.** to eat too much. —*v.t.* **2.** to eat more than is good for (oneself).

overelaborate (*adj.* ō′və rĭ lăb′ə rĭt, -lăb′rĭt; *v.* ō′və rĭ-lăb′ə rāt′), *adj.*, *v.*, **-rated, -rating.** —*adj.* **1.** excessively elaborate. —*v.t.* **2.** to fill with excessive detail. —*v.i.* **3.** to add excessive details in writing or speaking. —**o′verelab′orately,** *adv.* —**o′verelab′ora′tion, o′verelab′orateness,** *n.*

overestimate (*v.* ō′vər ĕs′tĭ māt′; *n.* ō′vər ĕs′tĭ mĭt), *v.*, **-mated, -mating,** *n.* —*v.t.* **1.** to estimate at too high a value, amount, ratio, or the like. —*n.* **2.** an estimate that is too high. —**o′veres′tima′tion,** *n.*

overexcite (ō′və rĭk sīt′), *v.t.*, **-cited, -citing.** to excite too much. —**o′verexcit′able,** *adj.* —**o′verexcite′ment,** *n.*

overexert (ō′və rĭg zûrt′), *v.t.* to exert too much. —**o′verexer′tion,** *n.*

overexpose (ō′və rĭk spōz′), *v.t.*, **-sposed, -sposing. 1.** to expose too much. **2.** *Photog.* to expose too long.

overfall (ō′və fôl′), *n.* **1.** water made turbulent by a strong current moving over a submerged ridge or by the meeting of contrary currents. **2.** a sudden increase in the depth of the sea. **3.** a device to allow overflow of water from a canal or lock on a river when the water reaches a certain level.

overfill (ō′və fĭl′), *v.t.* **1.** to fill too full so as to cause overflowing. —*v.i.* **2.** to become too full.

overflight (ō′və flīt′), *n.* a flight by an aircraft that passes over a specific area or territory.

overflow (*v.* ō′və flō′; *n.* ō′və flo′), *v.*, **-flowed, -flown, -flowing.** —*v.i.* **1.** to flow or run over, as rivers, water, etc. **2.** to have the contents flowing over, as an overfull vessel. **3.** to pass from one place or part to another as if flowing from an overfull space: *the population overflowed into the adjoining territory.* **4.** to be filled or supplied in overflowing measure (fol. by *with*): *a heart overflowing with gratitude.* —*v.t.* **5.** to flow over; flood; inundate. **6.** to flow over or beyond (the brim, banks, borders, etc.). **7.** to flow over the edge or brim of (a vessel, etc.). **8.** to fill to the point of running over. **9.** to cause to flow over. —*n.* **10.** an overflowing: *the annual overflow of the Nile.* **11.** that which flows or runs over: *to carry off the overflow from a fountain.* **12.** an excess or superabundance. **13.** a portion passing or crowded out from an overfilled place. **14.** an outlet for excess liquid.

overfly (ō′və flī′), *v.t.*, **-flew, -flown, -flying.** to fly over a specific area, territory, etc.

overgarment (ō′və gä′mənt), *n.* outer garment.

overgild (ō′və gĭld′), *v.t.*, **-gilded** or **-gilt, -gilding.** to cover with gilding.

overglance (ō′və gläns′), *v.t.*, **-glanced, -glancing.** *Obs.* to glance over.

overglaze (ō′və glāz′), *n.* a glaze or decoration applied over another glaze on pottery.

overgrow (ō′və grō′), *v.*, **-grew, -grown, -growing.** —*v.t.* **1.** to grow over; cover with a growth of something. **2.** to outdo in growing; choke or supplant by a more exuberant growth. **3.** to grow beyond, grow too large for, or outgrow. —*v.i.* **4.** to grow to excess; grow too large. —**o′vergrown′,** *adj.*

overgrowth (ō′və grōth′), *n.* **1.** a growth overspreading or covering something. **2.** excessive or too exuberant growth.

overhand (ō′və hănd′), *adj.* Also, **o′verhand′ed. 1.** done or delivered overhand. —*adv.* **2.** with the hand over the object. **3.** with the hand raised above the shoulder. **4.** *Sewing.* with close, shallow stitches over two selvages. —*v.t.* **5.** to sew overhand.

overhand knot, a simple knot of various uses which slips easily. See illus. under **knot.**

overhang (*v.* ō′və hăng′; *n.* ō′və hăng′), *v.*, **-hung, -hanging,** *n.* —*v.t.* **1.** to hang or be suspended over. **2.** to extend, project, or jut over: *a dark sky overhangs the earth.* **3.** to impend over, or threaten, as danger or evil: *the sadness which overhung him.* —*v.i.* **4.** to hang over; project or jut out over something below. —*n.* **5.** an overhanging; a projection. **6.** the extent of projection, as of the bow of a vessel. **7.** *Archit.* a projecting upper part of a building as a roof or balcony. **8.** *Aeron.* the amount by which an upper wing of a biplane projects laterally beyond the corresponding lower wing. **9.** *Mountaineering.* a place on a mountain where rock, snow, or ice overhang.

overhaul (*v.* ō′və hôl′; *n.* ō′və hôl′), *v.t.* **1.** to investigate or examine thoroughly, as for repair. **2.** to make necessary repairs to; restore to proper condition. **3.** to gain upon or overtake. **4.** *Naut.* **a.** to slacken (a rope) by hauling in the opposite direction to that in which it was drawn taut. **b.** to release the blocks of (a tackle). —*n.* **5.** a thorough examination.

overhead (*adv.* ō′və hĕd′; *adj.*, *n.* ō′və hĕd′), *adv.* **1.** over one's head; aloft; up in the air or sky, esp. near the zenith: *overhead was a cloud.* —*adj.* **2.** situated, operating, or passing overhead, aloft, or above. **3.** applicable to one and all; general; average. —*n.* **4.** (*pl.*) the general cost of running a business. **5.** (*pl.*) the general cost which cannot be assigned to particular products or orders.

overhead camshaft, a camshaft in an internal-combustion engine which lies across the top of the cylinders and operates directly on to valve stems or rocker arms, rather than on to pushrods.

overhead valve engine, an internal-combustion engine in which the cylinder head contains the inlet and exhaust valves. *Abbrev.*: o.h.v. engine.

overhear (ō′və hĭə′), *v.t.*, **-heard, -hearing.** to hear (speech, etc., or a speaker) without the speaker's intention or knowledge. —**o′verhear′er,** *n.*

overheat (ō′və hēt′), *v.t.* **1.** to heat to excess. —*v.i.* **2.** to become too hot. —*n.* **3.** excessive heat; overheated condition.

overhung (ō′və hŭng′), *v.* **1.** pt. and pp. of **overhang.** —*adj.* **2.** hung from above.

Overijssel (*Du.* ō′vər ĕy səl), *n.* a province in the E Netherlands. 887,261 pop. (1966); 1318 sq. mi. *Cap.*: Zwolle.

overindulge (ō′və rĭn dŭlj′), *v.t.*, *v.i.*, **-dulged, -dulging.** to indulge to excess. —**o′verindul′gence,** *n.* —**o′verindul′gent,** *adj.*

overjoyed (ō′və joid′), *adj.* overcome with joy; made exceedingly joyful.

overkill (ō′və kĭl′), *n.* **1.** the capacity of a nation to destroy, by nuclear weapons, more of an enemy than would be necessary for a military victory. **2.** an instance of such destruction.

overlade (ō′və lād′), *v.t.*, **-laded, -laded** or **-laden, -lading.** to overload (now chiefly in *overladen*, pp.).

overland (*adv.* ō′və lănd′; *adj.* ō′və lănd′), *adv.* **1.** over or across the land. **2.** by land. —*adj.* **3.** proceeding, performed, or carried on overland: *the overland route.* —*v.t.*, *v.i.* **4.** *Austral.* to drive overland for long distances, as sheep or cattle.

overland stage, a stagecoach used in the western U.S. during the mid-nineteenth century.

overlap (*v.* ō′və lăp′; *n.* ō′və lăp′), *v.*, **-lapped, -lapping,** *n.* —*v.t.* **1.** to lap over (something else or each other); extend over and cover a part of. **2.** to cover and extend

---

o′verea′ger, *adj.*
o′verea′gerly, *adv.*
o′verea′gerness, *n.*
o′verear′nest, *adj.*
o′verear′nestly, *adv.*
o′verear′nestness, *n.*
o′vereffu′sive, *adj.*
o′vereffu′sively, *adv.*
o′vereffu′siveness, *n.*
o′verembell′ish, *v.t.*
o′veremo′tional, *adj.*
o′veremo′tionalism, *n.*
o′veremo′tionally, *adv.*
o′verem′phasize′, *v.t.*, **-sized, -sizing.**
o′verenthu′sias′tic, *adj.*
o′verenthu′sias′tically, *adv.*
o′verex′ercise′, *v.*, **-cised, -cising.**
o′verexpand′, *v.*
o′verexpan′sion, *n.*
o′verexpan′sive, *adj.*
o′verexpan′sively, *adv.*
o′verexpan′siveness, *n.*
o′verexplic′it, *adj.*
o′verexplic′itly, *adv.*
o′verfamil′iar, *adj.*
o′verfamil′iarly, *adv.*
o′verfan′ciful, *adj.*
o′verfan′cifully, *adv.*
o′verfan′cifulness, *n.*
o′verfatigue′, *v.*, **-tigued, -tiguing.**
o′verfeed′, *v.*, **-fed, -feeding.**
o′verfish′, *v.t.*
o′verfit′, *adj.*
o′verfond′, *adj.*
o′verfond′ly, *adv.*
o′verfond′ness, *n.*
o′verfre′quent, *adj.*
o′verfre′quently, *adv.*
o′verfull′, *adj.*
o′verful′ly, *adv.*
o′verfull′ness, *n.*
o′vergen′erous, *adj.*
o′vergen′erously, *adv.*
o′vergen′erousness, *n.*
o′vergen′tle, *adj.*
o′vergen′tleness, *n.*
o′vergen′tly, *adv.*
o′vergraze′, *v.*, **-grazed, -grazing.**
o′vergree′dily, *adv.*
o′vergree′diness, *n.*
o′vergree′dy, *adj.*
o′verhas′tily, *adv.*
o′verhas′tiness, *n.*
o′verhas′ty, *adj.*
o′verhelp′ful, *adj.*
o′verhelp′fully, *adv.*
o′verhelp′fulness, *n.*
o′verhigh′, *adj.*
o′verhigh′ly, *adv.*
o′verimag′inative, *adj.*
o′verimag′inatively, *adv.*
o′verimag′inativeness, *n.*
o′verindus′trializa′tion, *n.*
o′verindus′trialize′, *v.*, **-lized, -lizing.**
o′verjeal′ous, *adj.*
o′verjeal′ously, *adv.*
o′verjeal′ousness, *n.*
o′verkind′, *adj.*
o′verkind′ly, *adv.*
o′verkind′ness, *n.*

---

beyond (something else). **3.** to coincide in part with; correspond partly with. —*v.i.* **4.** to lap over. —*n.* **5.** an overlapping. **6.** the extent or amount of overlapping. **7.** an overlapping part. **8.** the place of overlapping.

overlay[1] (*v.* ō′və lā′; *n.* ō′və lā′), *v.*, **-laid, -laying,** *n.* —*v.t.* **1.** to lay or place (one thing) over or upon another. **2.** to cover, overspread, or surmount with something. **3.** to finish with a layer or applied decoration of something: *wood richly overlaid with gold.* **4.** *Print.* to put an overlay upon. —*n.* **5.** something laid over something else; a covering. **6.** a layer or decoration of something applied: *an overlay of gold.* **7.** *Print.* **a.** a shaped piece of paper, or a sheet of paper reinforced at the proper places by shaped pieces, put on the tympan of a press to increase or equalize the impression. **b.** the method of adjusting the impression thus. **c.** a method of preparing material for printing in one or more colours, in which matter to be superimposed is prepared separately on a transparent sheet which is then placed over a key plate, normally one to be printed in black. **d.** a sheet or sheets prepared in this way. **8.** a transparent sheet giving special military information not ordinarily shown on maps, used by being placed over the map on which it is based. **9.** *Scot.* a neckcloth or cravat. [ME, f. OVER- + LAY[1]]

overlay[2] (ō′və lā′), *v.* pt. of **overlie.**

overleaf (ō′və lēf′), *adv.* on the other side of the page or sheet: *continued overleaf.*

overleap (ō′və lēp′), *v.t.* **1.** *Obs.* to leap farther than, or outleap. **2.** to overreach (oneself) by leaping too far. **3.** to pass over or omit. **4.** to leap over or across.

overlie (ō′və lī′), *v.t.*, **-lay, -lain, -lying. 1.** to lie over or upon, as a covering, stratum, etc. **2.** to smother (an infant) by lying upon it, as in sleep.

overlive (ō′və lĭv′), *v.*, **-lived, -living.** *Obs.* —*v.t.* **1.** to live longer than; outlast. —*v.i.* **2.** to survive.

overload (*v.* ō′və lōd′; *n.* ō′və lōd′), *v.t.* **1.** to load to excess; overburden. —*n.* **2.** an excessive load.

overlong (ō′və lŏng′), *adj.*, *adv.* too long.

overlook (ō′və lo͝ok′), *v.t.* **1.** to fail to notice, perceive, or consider: *to overlook a misspelt word.* **2.** to disregard or ignore indulgently, as faults, misconduct, etc. **3.** to look over, as from a higher position. **4.** to afford a view down over: *a hill overlooking the sea.* **5.** to rise above. **6.** to take no notice of; ignore. **7.** to look over in inspection, examination, or perusal. **8.** to look after, oversee, or supervise. **9.** to look upon with the evil eye; bewitch. —**Syn. 1.** See **slight.**

overlooker (ō′və lo͝ok′ə), *n.* overseer.

overlord (ō′və lôd′), *n.* one who is lord over another or over other lords. —**o′verlord′ship,** *n.*

overly (ō′və lĭ), *adv.* *U.S. and Scot.* overmuch; excessively; too: *a voyage not overly dangerous.*

overlying (ō′və lī′ĭng), *v.* ppr. of **overlie.**

overman (*n.* ō′və măn′; *v.* ō′və măn′), *n.*, *pl.* **-men,** *v.*, **-manned, -manning.** —*n.* **1.** a foreman or overseer. **2.** an arbiter or umpire. **3.** *Archaic.* a superman. —*v.t.* **4.** to oversupply with men, esp. for service. [ME]

overmantel (ō′və măn′tl), *n.* an ornamental structure with mirror and shelves set above a mantelpiece.

overmast (ō′və mäst′), *v.t.* *Naut.* to provide with masts that are too high or too heavy.

overmaster (ō′və mäs′tə), *v.t.* to overcome; overpower.

overmatch (ō′və măch′), *v.t.* to outmatch; surpass; defeat.

overmatter (ō′və măt′ə), *n.* *Print.* matter set up in excess of space.

overmuch (ō′və mŭch′), *adj.*, *n.*, *adv.* too much.

overnice (ō′və nīs′), *adj.* too nice or fastidious.

overnight (*adv.* ō′və nīt′; *n.*, *adj.* ō′və nīt′), *adv.* **1.** during the night: *to stay overnight.* **2.** on the previous evening: *preparations were made overnight.* **3.** suddenly; very quickly: *new towns sprang up overnight.* —*adj.* **4.** done, occurring, or continuing during the night: *an overnight stop.* **5.** staying for one night: *overnight guests.* **6.** designed to be used one night or very few nights: *overnight bag.* **7.** of or pertaining to the previous evening. **8.** occurring suddenly or rapidly: *an overnight success.*

overpass (*n.* ō′və päs′; *v.* ō′və päs′), *n.*, *v.*, **-passed** or **-past, -passing.** —*n.* **1.** *U.S.* a flyover. —*v.t.* **2.** to pass over or traverse (a region, space, etc.). **3.** to get over (obstacles, etc.). **4.** to go beyond, exceed, or surpass.

overpay (ō′və pā′), *v.t.*, **-paid, -paying. 1.** to pay more than (an amount due). **2.** to pay in excess. —**o′verpay′ment,** *n.*

overpeople (ō′və pē′pl), *v.t.*, **-pled, -pling.** to overstock with people.

overpersuade (ō′və pə swād′), *v.t.*, **-suaded, -suading. 1.** to bring over by persuasion. **2.** to persuade (a person) against his inclination or intention.

overpitch (ō′və pĭch′), *v.t.* *Cricket.* to bowl (a ball) too far or beyond a good distance.

overplay (ō′və plā′), *v.t.* **1.** to play (a part, etc.) in an exaggerated manner; overemphasize. **2.** to defeat in playing. **3. overplay one's hand,** to overestimate one's chance of success. —*v.i.* **4.** to exaggerate one's part; overact, etc.

overplus (ō′və plŭs′), *n.* *Chiefly U.S.* an excess over a particular amount, or a surplus.

overpopulate (ō′və pŏp′yo͝o lāt′), *v.t.*, **-lated, -lating.** to overpeople. —**o′verpop′ula′tion,** *n.*

overpower (ō′və pou′ə), *v.t.* **1.** to overcome or overwhelm in feeling, or affect or impress excessively. **2.** to overcome, master, or subdue by superior force: *to overpower a maniac.* **3.** to overmaster the bodily powers or mental faculties of: *overpowered with wine.* **4.** to furnish or equip with excessive power. —**Syn. 1.** vanquish, overwhelm, subjugate.

overpowering (ō′və pou′ə rĭng), *adj.* that overpowers; overwhelming. —**o′verpow′eringly,** *adv.*

overprint (*v.* ō′və prĭnt′; *n.* ō′və prĭnt′), *v.t.* **1.** to print additional material or another colour on a forme or sheet previously printed. —*n.* **2.** a quantity of printing in excess of that desired; an overrun. **3.** *Philately.* **a.** any word, inscription or device printed across the face of a stamp altering its use or its locality, or overprinted for a special purpose. **b.** a stamp so marked.

overproduce (ō′və prə dyo͞os′), *v.t.*, *v.i.*, **-duced, -ducing.** to produce excessively or in excess of demand.

overproduction (ō′və prə dŭk′shən), *n.* excessive production; production in excess of the demand.

overproof (ō′və pro͞of′), *adj.* containing a greater proportion of alcohol than proof spirit does.

overproud (ō′və proud′), *adj.* excessively proud.

overrate (ō′və rāt′), *v.t.*, **-rated, -rating.** to rate too highly; overestimate: *his fortune has been overrated.*

overreach (ō′və rēch′), *v.t.* **1.** to reach or extend over or beyond. **2.** to reach for or aim at but go beyond, as a thing sought, a mark, etc. **3.** to stretch (the arm, etc.) to excess, as by a straining effort. **4.** to defeat (oneself) by overdoing matters, often by excessive eagerness or cunning. **5.** to strain or exert (oneself) to the point of exceeding the purpose. **6.** to get the better of (a person, etc.); cheat. **7.** *Obs.* to overtake. —*v.i.* **8.** to reach or extend over something. **9.** to reach too far. **10.** to cheat others. **11.** (of horses, etc.) to strike, or strike and injure, the forefoot with the hind foot.

overrefine (ō′və rĭ fīn′), *v.t.* **-fined, -fining.** to refine excessively.

overrefinement (ō′və rĭ fīn′mənt), *n.* excessive or unnecessary refinement.

override (ō′və rīd′), *v.t.*, **-rode, -ridden, -riding. 1.** to trample underfoot; ride roughshod over. **2.** to pursue one's course in disregard of: *to override one's advisers.* **3.** to prevail over: *a decision that overrides all previous decisions.* **4.** to ride too much. **5.** to exhaust by excessive riding, as a horse. **6.** to pass or extend over. **7.** *Surg.* to overlap, as one piece of a fractured bone over another.

overrider (ō′və rī′də), *n.* **1.** one of a pair of vertical attachments to the bumper of a car, designed to protect the vehicle if in collision with a vehicle having bumpers of differing height. **2.** one who or that which overrides.

overriding (ō′və rī′dĭng), *adj.* prevailing over all other considerations.

overripe (ō′və rīp′), *adj.* too ripe; more than ripe.

overrule (ō′və ro͞ol′), *v.t.*, **-ruled, -ruling. 1.** to rule against or disallow the arguments of (a person). **2.** to

---

o′verlard′, *v.t.*
o′verloud′, *adj.*
o′verloud′ly, *adv.*
o′verloud′ness, *n.*
o′vermea′sure, *n.*
o′vermer′ry, *adj.*
o′vermod′est, *adj.*
o′vermourn′ful, *adj*
o′vermourn′fully, *adv.*
o′vermourn′fulness, *n.*
o′verneat′, *adj.*
o′verneat′ly, *adv.*
o′verneat′ness, *n.*
o′verneg′ligent, *adj.*
o′verneg′ligently, *adv.*
o′verobe′dience, *n.*
o′verobe′dient, *adj.*
o′verobe′diently, *adv.*
o′verop′timism, *n.*
o′verop′timis′tic, *adj.*
o′verop′timis′tically, *adv.*
o′verplease′, *v.*, **-pleased, -pleasing.**
o′verplump′, *adj.*
o′verpop′ulous, *adj.*
o′verpop′ulously, *adv.*
o′verpop′ulousness, *n.*
o′verpow′erful, *adj.*
o′verpow′erfully, *adv.*
o′verpow′erfulness, *n.*
o′verpraise′, *v.t.*, **-praised, -praising.**
o′verprize′, *v.t.*, **-prized, -prizing.**
o′verpropor′tion, *v.t.*, *n.*
o′verpub′licize′, *v.t.*
o′ver-rash′, *adj.*
o′ver-rash′ly, *adv.*
o′ver-rash′ness, *n.*
o′ver-relig′ious, *adj.*
o′ver-relig′iously, *adv.*
o′ver-relig′iousness, *n.*
o′ver-roast′, *v.*

rule or decide against (a plea, argument, etc.); disallow. **3.** to prevail over so as to change the purpose or action. **4.** to exercise rule or influence over.

overrun (*v.* ō′və rŭn′; *n.* ō′və rŭn′), *v.*, **-ran, -run, -running,** *n.* —*v.t.* **1.** to spread over rapidly and occupy (a country), as invading forces: *in 1940 German armies overran the Low Countries.* **2.** to take possession of (an enemy position, etc.): *French troops overran the German gun emplacement.* **3.** to swarm over in great numbers, as animals, esp. vermin. **4.** to spread or grow rapidly over, as plants, esp. vines, weeds, etc. **5.** to spread rapidly throughout, as a new idea, spirit, etc. **6.** to run beyond. **7.** to exceed. **8.** to run over; overflow. **9.** *Print.* to carry over (letters, words, or lines) to the next line, column, or page. **10.** *Archaic.* to outrun; overtake in running. —*v.i.* **11.** to run over; overflow. **12.** to extend beyond the proper or desired limit. **13.** (of an engine) to be driven by the object it normally drives, as the engine of a motor car when going downhill. —*n.* **14.** an overrunning. **15.** an amount overrunning or carried over; excess. **16.** the number by which the quantity manufactured exceeds the amount ordered. [OE *oferyrnan*]

overscore (ō′və skô′), *v.t.*, **-scored, -scoring.** to score over, as with strokes or lines.

overseas (ō′və sēz′), *adv.* **1.** over, across, or beyond the sea; abroad. —*adj.* **2.** of or pertaining to passage over the sea: *overseas travel.* **3.** situated beyond the sea: *overseas lands.* **4.** pertaining to countries beyond the sea; foreign: *overseas military service.* —*n.* **5.** (*construed as sing.*) countries or territories overseas. Also (for defs 1, 2, 3, and 4), **oversea** (ō′və sē′).

oversee (ō′və sē′), *v.t.*, **-saw, -seen, -seeing. 1.** to direct (work or workers); supervise; manage. **2.** to see or observe without being seen. **3.** *Obs.* to survey; watch. **4.** *Obs.* to look over; inspect. [OE *oferseōn*]

overseer (ō′və sĭə′), *n.* **1.** one who oversees; a supervisor. **2.** (formerly) a minor official of a parish (in full, **overseer of the poor**). [ME]

oversell (ō′və sĕl′), *v.t.*, **-sold, -selling. 1.** to sell more of (a stock, etc.) than can be delivered. **2.** to sell to excess.

overset (*v.* ō′və sĕt′; *n.* ō′və sĕt′), *v.*, **-set, -setting,** *n.* —*v.t.* **1.** *Rare.* to upset or overturn; overthrow. **2.** to throw into confusion; disorder physically or mentally. —*v.i.* **3.** *Rare.* to become upset, overturned, or overthrown. **4.** *Print.* (of type or copy) **a.** to set in or to excess. **b.** (of space) to set too much type for. —*n.* **5.** the act or fact of oversetting; overturn. **6.** *Print. U.S.* overmatter. [OE *ofersettan*]

oversew (ō′və sō′, ō′və sō′), *v.t.*, **-sewed, -sewed** or **-sewn, -sewing.** to sew with stitches passing successively over an edge, esp. closely, so as to cover the edge or make a firm seam.

oversexed (ō′və sĕkst′), *adj.* obsessed by, or interested in sex to an abnormal or unusually high degree.

overshade (ō′və shād′), *v.t.*, **-shaded, -shading. 1.** to cast a shade over. **2.** to make dark or gloomy.

overshadow (ō′və shăd′ō), *v.t.* **1.** to diminish the importance of, or render insignificant in comparison. **2.** to tower over so as to cast a shadow over. **3.** to cast a shadow over. **4.** to make dark or gloomy. **5.** to shelter or protect. [OE *ofersceadwian*]

overshine (ō′və shīn′), *v.t.*, **-shone, -shining. 1.** to outshine. **2.** to surpass in splendour, excellence, etc. **3.** *Archaic.* to shine over or upon. [OE *oferscinan*]

overshoe (ō′və shōō′), *n.* *Chiefly U.S.* galoshes.

overshoot (ō′və shōōt′), *v.*, **-shot, -shooting.** —*v.t.* **1.** to shoot or go over or above (something). **2.** to shoot or go beyond (a point, limit, etc.). **3.** to shoot a missile over or beyond (what is aimed at), thus missing: *to overshoot the mark.* **4.** (of an aircraft) to overrun a landing area in attempting to land. **5.** to go further in any course or matter than is intended or proper, or go too far. —*v.t.* **6.** to shoot or go beyond; fly beyond. **7.** to shoot over or too far. [ME]

Overshot waterwheel

overshot (ō′və shŏt′), *adj.* **1.** driven by water passing over from above, as a vertical waterwheel. **2.** having the upper jaw projecting beyond the lower, as a dog; usually considered to be a malformation.

overside (ō′və sīd′), *adv.* **1.** over the side, as of a ship. —*adj.* **2.** effected over the side of a ship. **3.** unloading or unloaded over the side.

oversight (ō′və sīt′), *n.* **1.** failure to notice or take into account. **2.** an omission or mistake due to inadvertence. **3.** supervision; watchful care. [ME] —**Syn. 1, 2.** mistake, blunder, slip. **3.** management, direction, control.

oversize (ō′və sīz′), *adj.* **1.** of excessive size. **2.** of a size larger than is necessary or required. —*n.* **3.** something that is oversize; an oversize article or object. **4.** a size larger than the proper or usual size.

oversized (ō′və sīzd′), *adj.* of excessive size; over the average size; abnormally large.

overskirt (ō′və skût′), *n.* **1.** an outer skirt. **2.** a skirt worn over the skirt of a dress.

oversleep (ō′və slēp′), *v.*, **-slept, -sleeping.** —*v.i.* **1.** to sleep beyond the proper time of waking. —*v.t.* **2.** to sleep beyond (a certain hour). [ME]

oversoul (ō′və sōl′), *n.* a supreme reality or mind, the spiritual unity of all being as conceived by Emerson following Platonic and German idealist philosophy.

overspend (ō′və spĕnd′), *v.*, **-spent, -spending.** —*v.i.* **1.** to spend more than one can afford. —*v.t.* **2.** to spend in excess of. **3.** *Archaic.* to wear out.

overspill (*v.* ō′və spĭl′; *n.* ō′və spĭl′), *v.*, **-spilt** or **-spilled,** *n.* —*v.i.* **1.** to spill over. —*n.* **2.** that which spills out. **3.** excess or surplus population: *new towns were planned to take London's overspill.*

overspread (ō′və sprĕd′), *v.t.*, **-spread, -spreading.** to spread or diffuse over. [OE *ofersprǣdan*]

overstate (ō′və stāt′), *v.t.*, **-stated, -stating.** to state too strongly; exaggerate in statement: *to overstate one's case.* —**o′verstate′ment,** *n.*

overstay (ō′və stā′), *v.t.* to stay beyond the time or duration of; outstay.

oversteer (*v.* ō′və stĭə′; *n.* ō′və stĭə′), *v.i.* **1.** (of a motor vehicle) to tend to turn in a narrower circle than that indicated by the geometry of the wheels. —*n.* **2.** such a tendency.

overstep (ō′və stĕp′), *v.t.*, **-stepped, -stepping.** to step or pass over or beyond.

overstock (*v.* ō′və stŏk′; *n.* ō′və stŏk′), *v.t.* **1.** to stock to excess. —*n.* **2.** a stock in excess of need.

overstrain (*v.* ō′və strān′; *n.* ō′və strān′, ō′və strān′), *v.t.*, *v.i.* **1.** to strain excessively. —*n.* **2.** (esp. of a person) physical or mental deterioration as a result of working too hard, worrying, etc.

overstride (ō′və strīd′), *v.t.*, **-strode, -stridden, -striding. 1.** to stride or step over or across. **2.** to stride beyond. **3.** to surpass. **4.** to bestride. [ME]

overstrung (ō′və strŭng′), *adj.* **1.** too highly strung. **2.** (of pianos) having two sets of strings crossing each other obliquely.

overstudy (*v.* ō′və stŭd′ĭ; *n.* ō′və stŭd′ĭ), *v.*, **-studied, -studying,** *n.* —*v.t.*, *v.i.* **1.** to study too much or too hard. —*n.* **2.** excessive study.

overstuff (ō′və stŭf′), *v.t.* **1.** to force too much into. **2.** *Furnit.* to envelop completely with deep upholstery.

overstuffed (ō′və stŭft′), *adj.* *Furnit.* having the entire frame covered by stuffing and upholstery, so that only decorative woodwork or the like is exposed.

oversubscribe (ō′və səb skrīb′), *v.t.*, **-scribed, -scribing.** to subscribe for in excess of what is available or required. —**oversubscription** (ō′və səb skrĭp′shən), *n.*

oversubscribed (ō′və səb skrībd′), *adj.* (of share issues) having applications to buy exceeding the number of shares available.

oversupply (*n.* ō′və sə plī′; *v.* ō′və sə plī′), *n.*, *pl.* **-plies,** *v.*, **-plied, -plying.** —*n.* **1.** an excessive supply. —*v.t.* **2.** to supply in excess.

overt (ō′vût), *adj.* **1.** open to view or knowledge; not concealed or secret: *overt hostility.* **2.** *Her.* open, as a purse. [ME, t. OF, pp. of *ovrir* open, g. L *aperire* open, with *o-* from *covrir* cover. See COVERT] —**Syn. 1.** plain, manifest, apparent, open, public.

overtake (ō′və tāk′), *v.t.*, **-took, -taken, -taking. 1.** to

o′versalt′, *v.t.*, *adj.*
o′versalt′y, *adj.*
o′versan′guine, *adj.*
o′versan′guinely, *adv.*
o′versan′guineness, *n.*
o′verscep′tical, *adj.*
o′verscep′tically, *adv.*
o′verscru′pulous, *adj.*
o′verscru′pulously, *adv.*
o′verscru′pulousness, *n.*
o′versharp′, *adj.*
o′versimplic′ity, *n.*
o′versim′plify′, *v.*, **-fied, -fying.**
o′versolic′itous, *adj.*
o′versolic′itously, *adv.*
o′versolic′itousness, *n.*
o′verspec′ializa′tion, *n.*
o′verspec′ialize′, *v.*, **-lized, -lizing.**
o′verstim′ulate′, *v.*, **-lated, -lating.**
o′verstress′, *v.t.*
o′verstrict′, *adj.*
o′verstrict′ly, *adv.*
o′verstrict′ness, *n.*
o′versub′tle, *adj.*
o′versub′tlety, *n.*
o′versub′tly, *adv.*
o′versuffi′cient, *adj.*
o′versuffi′ciently, *adv.*
o′versuffi′cientness, *n.*
o′versuscep′tible, *adj.*
o′versuscep′tibleness, *n.*
o′versuscep′tibly, *adv.*
o′versuspi′cious, *adj.*
o′versuspi′ciously, *adv.*
o′versuspi′ciousness, *n.*
o′versweet′, *adj.*
o′versweet′ly, *adv.*

catch up with in travelling or in pursuit. **2.** to come up with or pass in any course of action. **3.** to come upon suddenly or unexpectedly (said esp. of night, storm, death, etc.). **4.** to pass (another vehicle). —*v.i.* **5.** to pass another vehicle. [ME]

overtask (ō′və tăsk′), *v.t.* to impose too heavy a task upon.

overtax (ō′və tăks′), *v.t.* **1.** to tax too heavily. **2.** to make too great demands on: *I had overtaxed my strength.*

over-the-counter (ō′və tħə koun′tə), *adj.* having been dealt in at a place of business other than an exchange, esp. sale and purchase of securities.

overthrow (*v.* ō′və thrō′; *n.* ō′və thrō′), *v.*, **-threw, -thrown, -throwing,** *n.* —*v.t.* **1.** to depose as from a position of power; overcome, defeat, or vanquish. **2.** to put an end to by force, as governments or institutions. **3.** to throw over; upset; overturn. **4.** to knock down and demolish. **5.** to throw (something) too far. **6.** *Obs.* to destroy the sound condition of (the mind). —*n.* **7.** the act of overthrowing. **8.** the resulting state. **9.** deposition from power. **10.** defeat; destruction; ruin. **11.** *Cricket.* **a.** a ball returned by a fielder which is not caught at the wicket. **b.** a run scored as a result of this.

overtime (*n.*, *adv.*, *adj.* ō′və tīm′; *v.* ō′və tīm′), *n.*, *adv.*, *adj.*, *v.*, **-timed, -timing.** —*n.* **1.** time during which one works before or after regularly scheduled working hours; extra time. **2.** pay for such time. —*adv.* **3.** during extra time: *to work overtime.* —*adj.* **4.** of or pertaining to overtime: *overtime pay.* —*v.t.* **5.** to give too much time to, as in photographic exposure.

overtly (ō′vût lĭ), *adv.* openly; publicly.

overtone (ō′və tōn′), *n.* **1.** *Acoustics, Music.* any frequency emitted by an acoustical instrument that is higher in frequency than the fundamental. **2.** (*usually pl.*) additional meaning or implication.

overtop (ō′və tŏp′), *v.t.*, **-topped, -topping.** **1.** to rise over or above the top of. **2.** to rise above in authority; override (law, etc.). **3.** to surpass or excel.

overtrade (ō′və trād′), *v.i.*, **-traded, -trading.** to trade in excess of one's capital or the requirements of the market.

overtrick (ō′və trĭk′), *n. Bridge.* a trick won in addition to the number needed to make a contract.

overtrump (ō′və trŭmp′), *v.t.*, *v.i. Cards.* to trump with a higher trump than has already been played.

overture (ō′və tyŏŏə′), *n.*, *v.*, **-tured, -turing.** —*n.* **1.** an opening of negotiations, or a formal proposal or offer. **2.** *Music.* **a.** an orchestral composition forming the prelude or introduction to an opera, oratorio, etc. **b.** an independent piece of similar character. **3.** an introductory part, as of a poem. **4.** (in Presbyterian churches) **a.** the action of an ecclesiastical court in submitting a question or proposal to other judicatories for consideration. **b.** the proposal or question so submitted. —*v.t.* **5.** to submit as an overture or proposal. **6.** to make an overture or proposal to. [ME, t. OF, g. L *apertūra* opening, n., with *-o-* from *overt* OVERT] —**Syn. 1.** See **proposal.**

overturn (*v.* ō′və tûn′; *n.* ō′və tûn′), *v.t.* **1.** to overthrow; destroy the power of, defeat or vanquish. **2.** to turn over on its side, face, or back; upset. —*v.i.* **3.** to turn on its side, face, or back; upset; capsize. —*n.* **4.** the act of overturning. **5.** the state of being overturned. [ME] —**Syn. 1.** See **upset.**

over-under (ō′vər ŭn′də), *adj.* **1.** (of double-barrelled firearms) with one barrel mounted over the other. —*n.* **2.** such a firearm.

overuse (*v.* ō′və yōōz′; *n.* -yōōs′), *v.*, **-used, -using,** *n.* —*v.t.* **1.** to use too much. —*n.* **2.** too much use.

overvalue (ō′və văl′yōō), *v.t.*, **-ued, -uing.** to value too highly; put too high a value on. —**o′verval′ua′tion,** *n.*

overwatch (ō′və wŏch′), *v.t.* **1.** to watch over. **2.** to weary by watching.

overwear (ō′və wĕə′), *v.t.*, **-wore, -worn, -wearing.** **1.** to wear or use excessively, as clothes. **2.** to tire, exhaust.

overweary (ō′və wĭə′rĭ), *adj.*, *v.*, **-ried, -rying.** —*adj.* **1.** excessively weary; tired out. —*v.t.* **2.** to weary to excess; overcome with weariness.

overween (ō′və wēn′), *v.i.* to be conceited or arrogant. [ME]

overweening (ō′və wē′nĭng), *adj.* **1.** conceited, arrogant, self-opinionated: *an overweening person.* **2.** exaggerated, excessive: *overweening pride.* —**o′verween′ingly,** *adv.*

overweigh (ō′və wā′), *v.t.* **1.** to exceed in weight; overbalance or outweigh. **2.** to weigh down; oppress.

overweight (*n.* ō′və wāt′; *adj.*, *v.* ō′və wāt′), *n.* **1.** extra weight; excess of weight. **2.** too great weight. **3.** greater weight; preponderance. —*adj.* **4.** weighing more than normally or necessarily required. —*v.t.* **5.** to overburden, overload.

overwhelm (ō′və wĕlm′), *v.t.* **1.** to come, rest, or weigh upon overpoweringly; crush. **2.** to overcome completely in mind or feeling. **3.** to vanquish, defeat, esp. by force of numbers. **4.** to load, heap, treat or address with an overpowering or excessive amount of anything. **5.** to cover or bury beneath a mass of something, a flood, or the like, or cover as a mass or flood does. **6.** *Obs.* to overturn; upset. [ME]

overwhelming (ō′və wĕl′mĭng), *adj.* **1.** that overwhelms. **2.** so great as to render opposition useless: *an overwhelming majority.* —**o′verwhelm′ingly,** *adv.*

overwind (ō′və wīnd′), *v.t.*, **-wound, -winding.** to wind beyond the proper limit; wind too far.

overwork (*v.* ō′və wûk′; *n.* ō′və wûk′), *v.*, **-worked** or **-wrought, -working,** *n.* —*v.t.* **1.** to cause to work too hard or too long; weary or exhaust with work (often used reflexively). **2.** to fill (time) too full of work. **3.** to work up, stir up, or excite excessively. **4.** to elaborate to excess. **5.** to work or decorate all over; decorate the surface of. —*v.i.* **6.** to work too hard; work to excess. —*n.* **7.** work beyond one's strength or capacity. **8.** extra work. [OE *oferwyrcan*]

overwrite (ō′və rīt′), *v.t.*, *v.i.*, **-wrote, -written, -writing.** **1.** to cover with writing; write on top of other writing. **2.** to write in a too elaborate, laboured, or diffuse style.

overwrought (ō′və rôt′), *adj.* **1.** wearied or exhausted by overwork. **2.** worked up or excited excessively. **3.** extremely worried; having highly strained nerves. **4.** overworked; elaborated to excess.

overzealous (ō′və zĕl′əs), *adj.* too zealous. —**o′verzeal′ously,** *adv.* —**o′verzeal′ousness,** *n.*

ovi-[1], a word element meaning 'egg', as in *oviferous.* [t. L, comb. form of *ōvum*]

ovi-[2], a word element meaning 'sheep', as in *ovine.* [t. L, comb. form of *ovis*]

Ovid (ŏv′ĭd), *n.* (*Publius Ovidius Naso*) 43 B.C. – A.D. 17?, Roman poet. —**Ovidian** (ō vĭd′ĭ ən), *adj.*

oviduct (ō′vĭ dŭkt′), *n. Anat., Zool.* one of a pair of ducts which lead from the body cavity to the exterior in the female and serve to transport and nourish the ova. In higher forms, the distal ends are fused to form the uterus and vagina. —**o′viduc′al, o′viduct′al,** *adj.* [t. NL: s. *ōviductus*, f. L: *ōvi-* OVI-[1] + s. *ductus* DUCT]

Oviedo (*Sp.* ō vyĕ′dō), *n.* a town in NW Spain. 133,953 (1965).

oviferous (ō vĭf′ə rəs), *adj. Zool.* bearing eggs.

oviform (ō′vĭ fôm′), *adj.* egg-shaped.

ovine (ō′vīn), *adj.* pertaining to, of the nature of, or like sheep. [t. LL: m. s. *ovīnus*, der. L *ovis* sheep]

ovipara (ō vĭp′ə rə), *n.pl.* egg-laying animals. [t. NL, t. L: (neut. pl.) egg-laying]

oviparous (ō vĭp′ə rəs), *adj. Zool.* producing ova or eggs which are matured or hatched after being expelled from the body, as birds, most reptiles and fishes, etc. [t. L: m. *ōviparus* egg-laying] —**oviparity** (ō′vĭ pă′rĭ tĭ), *n.* —**ovip′arously,** *adv.*

oviposit (ō′vĭ pŏz′ĭt), *v.i.* to deposit or lay eggs, esp. by means of an ovipositor. [f. OVI-[1] + s. L *positus*, pp., placed, put] —**oviposition** (ō′vĭ pə zĭsh′ən), *n.*

ovipositor (ō′vĭ pŏz′ĭ tə), *n.* (in certain insects) an organ at the end of the abdomen, by which eggs are deposited. [f. OVI- + L *positor* placer]

O, Ovipositor of a field cricket

ovisac (ō′vĭ săk′), *n. Zool.* a sac or capsule containing an ovum or ova.

ovoid (ō′void), *adj.* **1.** egg-shaped; having the solid form of an egg. **2.** ovate (def. 2). —*n.* **3.** an ovoid body. [f. s. L *ōvum* egg + -OID]

ovolo (ō′və lō′), *n.*, *pl.* **-li** (-lē′). *Archit.* a convex moulding forming or approximating in section a quarter of a circle or ellipse. See diag. under **column.** [t. It., var. (now obs.) of *uovolo*, dim. of *uovo*, g. L *ōvum* egg]

ovoviviparous (ō′vō vī vĭp′ə rəs), *adj. Zool.* producing eggs which are hatched within the body, so that the young are born alive but without placental attachment, as certain reptiles, fishes, etc. [f. *ovo-* (comb. form of OVUM) + VIVIPAROUS]

ovular (ō′vyŏŏ lə), *adj.* pertaining to or of the nature of an ovule. [t. NL: s. *ōvulāris*]

o′versweet′ness, *n.*
o′vertalk′ative, *adj.*
o′vertalk′atively, *adv.*
o′vertalk′ativeness, *n.*
o′vertech′nical, *adj.*
o′vertech′nical′ity, *n.*
o′vertech′nically, *adv.*
o′vertire′, *v.*
o′vertrain′, *v.*
o′vertwist′, *v.*
o′verve′hement, *adj.*
o′verve′hemently, *adv.*
o′verve′hementness, *n.*
o′verven′turesome, *adj.*
o′vervig′orous, *adj.*
o′vervig′orously, *adv.*
o′vervi′olent, *adj.*
o′vervi′olently, *adv.*
o′vervi′olentness, *n.*
o′verwarmed′, *adj.*

ovulate (ō′vyo͝o lāt′), *v.i.*, **-lated, -lating.** *Biol.* to shed eggs from an ovary or ovarian follicle. [f. s. NL *ōvulum* little egg + -ATE[1]] —**o′vula′tion,** *n.*

ovule (ō′vyo͞ol), *n.* **1.** *Biol.* a small egg. **2.** *Bot.* **a.** a rudimentary seed. **b.** the body which contains the embryo sac and hence the female germ cell, and which after fertilization develops into a seed. See diag. under **flower.** [t. NL: m. s. *ōvulum*, dim. of L *ōvum* egg]

ovum (ō′vəm), *n., pl.* **ova** (ō′və). **1.** *Biol.* **a.** an egg, in a broad biological sense. **b.** the female reproductive cell or gamete of plants. **c.** the female reproductive cell of animals, which (usually only after fertilization) is capable of developing into a new individual. **2.** *Archit.* an egg-shaped ornament. [t. L: egg]

owe (ō), *v.*, **owed, owing.** —*v.t.* **1.** to be indebted or beholden for (usually fol. by *to*). **2.** to be under obligation to pay or repay, or to render (often fol. by *to* or a simple dative): *to owe him interest on a mortgage.* **3.** (by omission of the ordinary direct object) to be in debt to: *he owes not any man.* **4.** to have or cherish (a certain feeling) towards a person: *to owe one a grudge.* **5.** *Obs.* to own or possess. —*v.i.* **6.** to be in debt. [ME *owe(n)*, OE *āgan*, c. OHG *eigan.* Cf. OWN, OUGHT[1]]

Owen (ō′ĭn), *n.* **1. Robert,** 1771–1858, British industrialist and social reformer. **2. Wilfred,** 1893–1918, English poet.

Owenism (ō′ĭ nĭz′əm), *n.* the principles and practices of Robert Owen; philanthropic industrial management.

Owen Stanley (ō′ĭn stăn′lĭ), a mountain range in SE New Guinea. Highest peak, Mt Victoria. 13,240 ft.

owing (ō′ĭng), *adj.* **1.** that owes. **2.** owed or due: *to pay what is owing.* **3.** *Obs.* indebted. **4. owing to, a.** on account of; because of. **b.** attributable to.

owl (oul), *n.* **1.** any of numerous birds of prey of the order *Strigiformes*, chiefly nocturnal, with a broad head and with large eyes which are usually surrounded by discs of modified feathers and directed forwards. They feed on mice, small birds and reptiles, etc. **2.** a variety of domestic pigeons of owl-like appearance. **3.** a person of nocturnal habits. **4.** a person of owl-like solemnity or appearance. [ME *oule*, OE *ūle*, c. LG *ūle*; akin to G *Eule*, Icel. *ugla*] —**owl′-like′,** *adj.*

Barn owl, *Tyto alba* (15 in. long)

owlet (ou′lĭt), *n.* a young owl.

owlish (ou′lĭsh), *adj.* owl-like.

own (ōn), *adj.* **1.** belonging, pertaining, or relating to oneself or itself (usually used after a possessive to emphasize the idea of ownership, interest, or relation conveyed by the possessive): *his own money.* **2.** (absolutely, with a possessive preceding) own property, relatives, etc.: *to come into one's own.* **3. get one's own back,** to have revenge. **4. of one's own,** belonging to oneself. **5. on one's own,** *Colloq.* on one's own account, responsibility, resources, etc. **6. be one's own master,** to be independent. [ME *owen*; OE *āgen*, orig. pp. of *āgan* have, possess. See OWE] —*v.t.* **7.** to have or hold as one's own; possess. **8.** to acknowledge or admit: *to own a fault.* **9.** to acknowledge as one's own. —*v.i.* **10.** to confess (often fol. by *up*): *to own to being uncertain.* [ME *ohnien*, OE *agnian*, der. *āgen* OWN, adj.] —**Syn. 7.** See **have.** —**Ant. 7.** lack, need.

owner (ō′nə), *n.* one who owns; a proprietor.

owner-driver (ō′nə drī′və), *n.* one who drives his own car.

owner-occupier (ō′nər ŏk′yo͝o pī′ə), *n.* one who lives in his own dwelling.

ownership (ō′nə shĭp′), *n.* **1.** the state or fact of being an owner. **2.** legal right of possession; proprietorship.

ox (ŏks), *n., pl.* **oxen. 1.** the adult castrated male of the genus *Bos*, used as a draught animal and for food. **2.** any member of the bovine family. [ME *oxe*, OE *oxa*, c. G *Ochse*] —**ox′like′,** *adj.*

Ox., (L *Oxonia*) Oxford.

oxa-, *Chem.* a prefix meaning 'oxygen when it replaces carbon'.

oxalate (ŏk′sə lāt′), *n. Chem.* a salt or ester of oxalic acid. [f. OXAL(IC) + -ATE[2]]

oxalic acid (ŏk săl′ĭk), *Chem.* a white, crystalline, dibasic acid, $(COOH)_2.2H_2O$, first discovered in the juice of a species of oxalis (wood sorrel), used in textile and dye manufacturing, in bleaching, etc. [*oxalic*, t. F: m. *oxalique*, der. L *oxalis* OXALIS]

oxalidaceous (ŏk′săl ĭ dā′shəs), *adj.* belonging to the *Oxalidaceae*, the oxalis family of flowering plants.

oxalis (ŏk′sə lĭs), *n.* any oxalidaceous plant of the large genus *Oxalis*, as *O. acetosella*, the wood sorrel. [t. L, t. Gk: sorrel]

oxazine (ŏk′sə zēn′), *n. Chem.* any of a group of thirteen compounds, C_4H_5NO, containing four carbon atoms, one oxygen atom, and one nitrogen atom, arranged in a six-membered ring. [f. OX(A) + -AZINE]

oxbow (ŏks′bō′), *n.* **1** a bow-shaped piece of wood placed under and around the neck of an ox, with its upper ends inserted in the bar of the yoke. **2.** a former meander of a river remaining as a small bow-shaped lake after the river has straightened its course by cutting through the neck of the meander; cut-off.

Oxbridge (ŏks′brĭj′), *adj., n.* Oxford and Cambridge.

oxcart (ŏks′kät′), *n.* an ox-drawn cart.

oxen (ŏk′sən), *n.* pl. of **ox.**

Oxenstierna (*Sw.* o͞ok′sən shĕr nȧ), *n.* **Count Axel,** (*Sw.* ȧk′səl), 1583–1654, Swedish statesman. Also, **Oxenstiern** (*Sw.* o͞ok′sən shĕrn), **Oxenstjerna.**

oxer (ŏk′sə), *n.* an obstacle in steeplechasing, horse-jumping trials, etc., consisting of a hedge bordered by rails, as a **double oxer** or **reversed oxer.**

oxeye (ŏks′ī′), *n.* any of various plants with flowers composed of a disc with marginal rays, as the mayweed, the oxeye daisy, etc. [ME *oxie*, f. *ox(e)* OX + *ie* EYE]

oxeye daisy. See **daisy** (def. 1).

oxford (ŏks′fəd), *n.* **1.** a low shoe laced or buttoned over the instep. **2.** shirting of cotton or rayon in a basket weave. [named after OXFORD, the city]

Oxford (ŏks′fəd), *n.* **1. Robert Harley, 1st Earl of,** 1661–1724, English statesman. **2.** a city in S England: famous university (founded in the 12th century), the county town of Oxfordshire. 108,880 (est. 1964). **3.** Oxfordshire. **4.** a large English breed of sheep, hornless, with dark brown face and legs, of the mutton type, noted for its relatively large, heavy market lambs, and heavy fleece of relatively coarse wool of medium length. [ME *Oxenford*, OE *Oxenaford*]

Oxford bags, very wide trousers, as fashionable in the 1920s.

Oxford corners, *Print.* ruled border lines about the text of a page, etc., that cross and project slightly at the corners.

Oxford English, a form of standard English, sometimes marked by affectation, supposed by many to be spoken at Oxford.

Oxford Group, Moral Rearmament.

Oxford hollow, *Bookbinding.* a method of reinforcing books in which a tube of kraft paper is inserted in the spine of the book between the case and the backs of the sections.

Oxford Movement, a movement towards High-Church principles in the Church of England, which originated at Oxford University about 1833.

Oxfordshire (ŏks′fəd shĭə′, -shə), *n.* a county in S England. 309,458 pop. (1961); 749 sq. mi. *Co. town:* Oxford. *Abbrev.:* Oxon. Also, **Oxford.**

Oxford shoe, oxford (def. 1).

Oxford Street, a street in the West End of London, noted for the shops.

oxgang (ŏks′găng′), *n. Hist.* a measure of land of various extent, but usually about 20 acres.

oxidant (ŏk′sĭ dənt), *n.* the substance which supplies the oxygen in an oxidation reaction, esp. for the combustion reaction in a rocket. Also, **ox′idiz′er, oxydant.**

oxidase (ŏk′sĭ dās′), *n. Biochem.* any of a group of oxidizing enzymes. [f. OXID(E) + -ASE]

oxidate (ŏk′sĭ dāt′), *v.t., v.i.*, **-dated, -dating.** to oxidize. —**ox′ida′tion,** *n.* —**ox′ida′tive,** *adj.*

oxide (ŏk′sīd), *n. Chem.* a compound, usually containing two elements only, one of which is oxygen, as *mercuric oxide.* [t. F (now *oxyde*), f. *ox(ygène)* oxygen + *(ac)ide* acid]

oxidimetry (ŏk′sĭ dĭm′ĭ trĭ), *n.* a technique of analytical chemistry which utilizes oxidizing agents for titrations.

oxidize (ŏk′sĭ dīz′), *v.*, **-dized, -dizing.** *Chem.* —*v.t.* **1.** to convert (an element) into its oxide; to combine with oxygen. **2.** to cover with a coating of oxide, or rust. **3.** to take away hydrogen from as by the action of oxygen; to add oxygen or any non-metal to. **4.** to increase the valency of (an element) in the positive direction. **5.** to remove electrons from. —*v.t.* **6.** to become oxidized. Also, **oxidise.** —**ox′idiz′able,** *adj.* —**ox′idiza′tion,** *n.* —**ox′idiz′er,** *n.*

oxidizing agent, any substance which brings about an oxidation process.

oxime (ŏk′sēm), *n.* any of a group of compounds with the radical :C:NOH (**oxime group** or **radical**), prepared by the condensation of ketones or aldehydes with hydroxylamine. [f. OX(YGEN) + IM(ID)E]

oxlip (ŏks′lĭp′), *n.* a species of primrose, *Primula elatior*, with pale yellow flowers. [ME; OE *oxanslyppe*, f. *oxan* ox's + *slyppe* slime. See SLIP[2], and cf. COWSLIP]

Oxon (ŏk′sŏn), *n.* Oxfordshire.

Oxon., **1.** (L *Oxonia*) Oxford. **2.** (L *Oxoniensis*) of Oxford.

Oxonian (ŏk sō′nyən), *adj.* **1.** of or pertaining to Oxford or Oxford University. —*n.* 2. a member or graduate of Oxford University. 3. a native or inhabitant of Oxford. [f. s. ML *Oxonia* Oxford + -AN]

oxonium compound (ŏk sō′nĭ əm), *Chem.* the product of reaction between an organic compound containing a basic oxygen atom, and a strong acid.

oxpecker (ŏks′pĕk′ə), *n.* either of two species of African starlings of the genus *Buphagus.*

oxtail (ŏks′tāl′), *n.* the skinned tail of an ox used for soup.

oxter (ŏk′stə), *n. Scot.* the armpit. [appar. der. OE *ōxta*]

oxtongue (ŏks′tŭng′), *n.* 1. the tongue of an ox, used as food. 2. any perennial composite herb covered with stiff hairs of the genus *Picris*, as *P. hieracoides*, the **hawkweed oxtongue.**

Oxus (ŏk′səs), *n.* ancient and modern name of **Amu Darya.**

oxy-[1], a word element meaning 'sharp' or 'acute'. [t. Gk, comb. form of *oxýs* sharp, keen, acid]

oxy-[2], a combining form of **oxygen,** sometimes used as an equivalent of *hydroxy-.*

oxyacetylene (ŏk′sĭ ə sĕt′ĭ lēn′), *adj.* of or pertaining to a mixture of oxygen and acetylene.

oxyacetylene burner, a device for obtaining a high-temperature flame (about 3300°C) for welding or cutting steel, by burning a mixture of oxygen and acetylene in a special jet.

oxyacid (ŏk′sĭ ăs′ĭd), *n. Chem.* an inorganic acid containing oxygen. Also, **oxygen acid.**

oxycalcium (ŏk′sĭ kăl′sĭ əm), *adj.* pertaining to or produced by oxygen and calcium: *the oxycalcium light.*

oxydation (ŏk′sĭ dā′shən), *n.* oxidization.

oxygen (ŏk′sĭ jən), *n. Chem.* a colourless, odourless gaseous element, constituting about one fifth of the volume of the atmosphere and present in a combined state throughout nature. It is the supporter of combustion in air: *weight of 1 litre at 0°C and 760 mm. pressure:* 1·4290 grams. *Symbol:* O; *at. wt:* 15·9994; *at. no.:* 8. [t. F: m. *oxygène*, f. *oxy-* OXY-[1] + *-gène* -GEN]

oxygenate (ŏk sĭj′ĭ nāt′), *v.t.*, **-nated, -nating.** to treat or combine, esp. to enrich, with oxygen. —**ox′ygena′tion,** *n.*

oxygen effect, *Radiobiology.* the increased sensitivity to radiation of biological material when exposed in the presence of oxygen.

oxygenize (ŏk sĭj′ĭ nīz′), *v.t.*, **-nized, -nizing.** oxygenate. Also, **oxygenise.**

oxygen mask, a device covering the nose and mouth used in inhaling oxygen from a cylinder or supply system.

oxygen tent, a small tent for delivering oxygen to a sick person at critical periods.

oxyhaemoglobin (ŏk′sĭ hē′mō glō′bĭn), *n.* the substance formed when haemoglobin proper unites loosely with oxygen, present in arterial blood. See **haemoglobin.**

oxyhydrogen (ŏk′sĭ hī′drĭ jən), *n.* a mixture of oxygen and hydrogen.

oxyhydrogen burner, a similar device to the oxyacetylene burner except that hydrogen is burnt in oxygen instead of acetylene, and the flame temperature is about 2400°C.

oxymoron (ŏk′sĭ mô′rŏn), *n.*, *pl.* **-mora** (-mô′rə). *Rhet.* a figure by which a locution produces an effect by a seeming self-contradiction, as in *cruel kindness* or *to make haste slowly.* [t. NL, t. Gk, neut. of *oxýmōros* pointedly foolish]

oxysalt (ŏk′sĭ sôlt′), *n. Chem.* any salt of an oxyacid. [f. OXY-[2] + SALT]

oxysulphide (ŏk′sĭ sŭl′fīd), *n. Chem.* a sulphide in which part of the sulphur is replaced by oxygen.

oxytocic (ŏk′sĭ tō′sĭk), *Med.* —*adj.* 1. of or causing the stimulation of the involuntary muscle of the uterus. 2. promoting or accelerating parturition. —*n.* 3. an oxytocic medicine or drug. [f. Gk: m. s. *oxytókion* a medicine hastening childbirth + -IC]

oxytocin (ŏk′sĭ tŏs′ĭn, -tō′sĭn), *n. Biochem.* a hormone produced by the pituitary gland, that stimulates contraction of the muscles of the uterus.

oxytone (ŏk′sĭ tōn′), *adj.* 1. (in Greek grammar) having an acute accent on the last syllable. —*n.* 2. an oxytone word. [t. Gk: m. s. *oxýtonos*]

Oyama (ō′yä mä′), *n.* **Iwao** (ē′wä ō′), 1842–1916, Japanese field marshal.

oyer (oi′ə), *n. Law.* 1. the ancient word for assizes. 2. the production in court of some document pleaded by one party and demanded by the other (the party pleading it is said to *make profert* and the other is said to *crave oyer*). [ME, t. AF (prop. inf.), var. of *oir*, g. L *audīre* hear]

oyer and terminer (tû′mĭ nə), *Law.* 1. (in English law) **a.** a commission or writ directing the holding of a court to try offences. **b.** the court itself. 2. *U.S.* any of various higher criminal courts in some of the states. [ME, t. AF: lit., hear and finish]

oyez (ō yĕs′, ō yĕz′), *interj.* 1. hear! attend! (a cry uttered, usually thrice, by a public or court crier to command silence and attention before a proclamation, etc., is made.) —*n.* 2. a cry of 'oyez'. Also, **oyes.** [t. AF: hear ye, 2nd pers. pl. impv. of *oyer.* See OYER]

Oyo (ō′yō), *n.* a town in W Western Nigeria. 72,000 (est. 1963).

oyster (ois′tə), *n.* 1. any of various edible marine bivalve molluscs (family *Ostreidae*), with irregularly shaped shell, found on the bottom or adhering to rocks, etc., in shallow water, some species being extensively cultivated for the market. 2. the oyster-shaped bit of dark meat in the front hollow of the side bone of a fowl. 3. *Slang.* a close-mouthed person. 4. something from which one may extract or derive advantage. —*v.i.* 5. to dredge for or otherwise take oysters. [ME *oistre*, t. OF, t. L: m. s. *ostrea*, *ostreum*, t. Gk: m. *óstreon*]

oyster-bed (ois′tə bĕd′), *n.* a place where oysters breed or are cultivated.

oystercatcher (ois′tə kăch′ə), *n.* any of several long-billed, maritime wading birds constituting the genus *Haematopus*, with a plumage chiefly of black and white, as *H. ostralegus*, the common European species.

oyster-crab (ois′tə krăb′), *n.* a crab, *Pinnotheres*, existing commensally in the mantle cavity of oysters.

oyster-farm (ois′tə fäm′), *n.* an area of oyster-beds.

oysterman (ois′tə mən), *n.*, *pl.* **-men.** *Chiefly U.S.* one who gathers, cultivates, or sells oysters.

oyster plant, the salsify, whose root tastes like oyster.

oyster white, greyish white. Also, **oyster.**

oz., 1. ounce. 2. Also, **ozs.** ounces.

Ozalid (ŏz′ə lĭd, ō′zə-), *n.* 1. *Trademark.* a method of reproducing print, etc., which is on translucent material, used for proofing purposes. 2. (*l.c.*) such reproductions.

Ozark Mountains (ō′zäk), a group of low mountains in S Missouri, N Arkansas, and NE Oklahoma. Also, **Ozarks, Ozark Plateau.**

ozocerite (ō zō′kə rĭt), *n.* waxlike mineral resin; mineral wax. Also, **ozokerite.** [t. G: m. *Ozokerit*, f. Gk *ózō* I smell + s. Gk *kērós* wax + *-iṭ* -ITE[1]]

ozone (ō′zōn), *n.* 1. *Chem.* a form of oxygen, O_3, having three atoms to the molecule, with a peculiar smell suggesting that of weak chlorine, which is produced when an electric spark is passed through air, and in several other ways. It is found in the atmosphere in minute quantities, esp. after a thunderstorm, and is a powerful oxidizing agent, used for bleaching, sterilizing water, etc. 2. *Colloq.* clear, invigorating, fresh air. [t. F, f. s. Gk *ózein* smell + *-one* -ONE] —**ozonic** (ō zŏn′ĭk), *adj.*

ozone layer, *Meteorol.* a rather restricted region in the outer portion of the stratosphere at an elevation of about 20 miles, where much of the atmospheric ozone (O_3) is concentrated. Also, **ozonosphere.**

ozoniferous (ō′zō nĭf′ə rəs), *adj.* containing ozone.

ozonization (ō′zō nĭ zā′shən), *n.* the treatment of a compound with ozone. Also, **ozonisation.**

ozonize (ō′zō nīz′), *v.t.*, **-nized, -nizing.** 1. to impregnate or treat with ozone. 2. to convert (oxygen) into ozone. Also, **ozonise.**

ozonizer (ō′zō nī′zə), *n. Chem.* an apparatus for converting oxygen into ozone. Also, **ozoniser.**

ozonolysis (ō′zō nŏl′ĭ sĭs), *n. Chem.* the reaction of ozone with hydrocarbons.

ozonous (ō′zō nəs), *adj.* of or containing ozone.

ozs, ounces.

P

P, p (pē), *n.*, *pl.* **P's** or **Ps, p's** or **ps.** 1. a consonant, the 16th letter of the English alphabet. 2. *Genetics.* a symbol for parental generation, P_1 indicating parents, P_2 grandparents, etc. 3. **mind one's p's and q's,** to heed one's behaviour.

P, 1. *Chem.* phosphorus. 2. pressure. 3. *Chess.* pawn. 4. *Motor Vehicles.* parking.

p-, *Chem.* para-[1].

P., 1. (L *Pater*) father. 2. (F *Père*) father. 3. president. 4. prince.

p, new penny; new pence.

p., **1.** page. **2.** part. **3.** particle. **4.** past. **5.** (L *pater*) father. **6.** *Chess.* pawn. **7.** pence. **8.** penny. **9.** per. **10.** peseta. **11.** peso. **12.** *Music.* (It. *piano*) softly. **13.** pint. **14.** population. **15.** (L *post*) after.

pa[1] (pä), *n. Colloq.* papa; father.

pa[2] (pä), *n. N.Z.* **1.** a Maori settlement. **2.** (originally) a stockaded village. [t. Maori]

Pa, **1.** Pennsylvania. **2.** protactinium.

PA, **1.** press agent. **2.** public-address (system).

P.A., **1.** personal assistant. **2.** post adjutant. **3.** power of attorney. **4.** Press Association. **5.** purchasing agent.

p.a., **1.** participial adjective. **2.** per annum. **3.** press agent.

pabulum (păb′yo͞o ləm), *n.* **1.** that which nourishes an animal or vegetable organism; food. **2.** nourishment for the mind. [t. L: food, fodder]

Pac., Pacific.

paca (pä′kə, păk′ə), *n.* a large, white-spotted, almost tailless, hystricomorphic rodent, *Agouti paca,* of South and Central America; the spotted cavy. [t. Pg. or Sp., both t. Tupi]

Paca, *Agouti paca* (2½ ft long, 1 ft high)

pace[1] (pās), *n., v.,* **paced, pacing.** —*n.* **1.** rate of stepping, or of movement in general: *a pace of ten miles an hour.* **2.** rate or style of doing anything: *they live at a tremendous pace.* **3.** a linear measurement of variable extent, representing the space naturally measured by the movement of the foot in walking. The pace of a single step (**military pace**) is reckoned in the British Army at 30 inches for quick time (120 paces to the minute). The **geometrical** or **great pace** is 5 feet, representing the distance from the place where either foot is taken up, in walking, to that where the same foot is set down. The **Roman pace,** reckoned like the geometrical pace, was equal to 5 Roman feet, or about 58 English inches. **4.** a single step: *she took three paces across the room.* **5.** the distance covered in a step: *stand six paces inside the gates.* **6.** manner of stepping; gait. **7.** a gait of a horse, etc., in which the feet on the same side are lifted and put down together. **8.** any of the gaits of a horse, etc. **9.** a raised step or platform. **10. put through one's paces,** to cause to perform or show ability. —*v.t.* **11.** to set the pace for, as in racing. **12.** to traverse with paces or steps: *he paced the floor.* **13.** to measure by paces. **14.** to train to a certain pace; exercise in pacing: *to pace a horse.* **15.** (of a horse) to perform as a pace. —*v.i.* **16.** to walk, esp. in a state of nervous excitement (often fol. by *up and down, about*). **17.** to take slow, regular steps. **18.** (of a horse) to go at a pace; amble. [ME *pas,* t. OF, g. L *passus* a step, lit., a stretch (of the leg)]

—**Syn. 8.** step, gait, amble, trot, canter, gallop, walk, run. **12.** PACE, PLOD, TRUDGE refer to a steady and monotonous kind of walking. PACE suggests steady, measured steps as of one completely lost in thought or impelled by some distraction: *to pace up and down.* PLOD implies a slow, heavy, laborious, weary walk: *the ploughman homeward plods his weary way.* TRUDGE implies a spiritless but usually steady and doggedly persistent walk: *the farmer trudged to his village to buy his supplies.* —**Ant. 12.** scamper, scurry, skip.

pace[2] (pā′sĭ), *prep. Latin.* with the permission of (a courteous form used to mention one who disagrees). [L, abl. of *pax* peace, pardon, leave]

paced (pāst), *adj.* **1.** having a specified pace: *slow-paced.* **2.** counted out or measured by paces. **3.** *Racing.* run at a pace determined by a pacemaker.

pacemaker (pās′mā′kə), *n.* **1.** one who sets the pace, as in racing. **2.** a person or group which is followed or imitated on account of its success. **3.** *Physiol.* a collection of nervous tissue which controls the rate of the heartbeat. **4.** *Med.* an instrument implanted beneath the skin to control the rate of the heartbeat. —**pace′mak′ing,** *n.*

pacer (pā′sə), *n.* **1.** one who paces. **2.** a pacemaker. **3.** a horse that paces, or whose natural gait is a pace.

pacha (pä′shə), *n.* pasha.

pachalic (pä′shə lĭk), *n.* pashalik.

pachisi (pə chē′zĭ, pä-), *n.* **1.** a game, somewhat resembling backgammon, for four players played on a cruciform board, with pieces moved according to the throw of a set of six dice. It is much played in India. **2.** ludo. Also, **parcheesi.** [t. Hind.: der. *pachīs* twenty-five (the highest throw in the game)]

Pachmann (*Russ.* päKH′mən), *n.* **Vladimir de** (*Russ.* vlä dē′mĭr də), 1848–1933, Russian pianist.

pachouli (păch′o͝o lĭ, pă cho͞o′lĭ), *n.* patchouli.

Pachuca (*Sp.* pä cho͞o′kä), *n.* a town in central Mexico: silver mines. 70,000 (est. 1960).

pachy-, a word element meaning 'thick', as in *pachyderm.* [t. Gk: comb. form of *pachýs* thick]

pachyderm (păk′ĭ dûm′), *n.* **1.** any of the thick-skinned non-ruminant ungulates, as the elephant, hippopotamus, and rhinoceros. **2.** a person who is not sensitive to criticism, ridicule, etc. [t. F: m. *pachyderme,* t. Gk: m. s. *pachýdermos* thick-skinned] —**pach′yder′matous, pach′yder′mous,** *adj.*

pacific (pə sĭf′ĭk), *adj.* **1.** tending to make peace; conciliatory: *pacific propositions.* **2.** peaceable; not warlike: *a pacific disposition.* **3.** peaceful; at peace: *pacific state of things.* **4.** (*cap.*) designating, or pertaining to, the Pacific Ocean. **5.** (*cap.*) of or pertaining to a region, country, etc., bordering on the Pacific Ocean: *the Pacific states.* —*n.* **6.** (*cap.*) the Pacific Ocean. Also, (defs 1–3), *Obs.,* **pacif′ical.** [t. L: s. *pācificus* peacemaking] —**pacif′ically,** *adv.*

—**Syn. 1.** PACIFIC, PEACEABLE, PEACEFUL describe that which is in a state of peace. That which is PACIFIC tends towards the making, promoting, or preserving of peace: *pacific intentions.* That which is PEACEABLE desires to be at peace or is free from the disposition to quarrel: *peaceable citizens.* That which is PEACEFUL is in a calm state, characteristic of, or characterized by, peace: *a peaceful death.* —**Ant. 1.** warlike, belligerent.

pacificate (pə sĭf′ĭ kāt′), *v.t.,* **-cated, -cating.** to pacify. [t. L: m. s. *pācificātus,* pp.] —**pacification** (păs′ĭ fĭ kā′shən), *n.* —**pacif′ica′tor,** *n.* —**pacificatory** (pə sĭf′ĭ kə tə rĭ, -trĭ), *adj.*

pacificism (pə sĭf′ĭ sĭz′əm), *n. Obs.* pacifism. —**pacif′icist,** *n.*

Pacific Ocean, the largest ocean, between the American continents and Asia and Australia: divided by the equator into the **North Pacific** and the **South Pacific.** ab. 70,000,000 sq. mi.; greatest known depth, 35,433 ft.

Pacific Time, one of the four standard time zones in the U.S., lying on the 120th meridian, eight hours behind **Greenwich Mean Time** and one hour behind **Mountain Time.**

pacifier (păs′ĭ fī′ə), *n.* **1.** one who or that which pacifies. **2.** *U.S.* a baby's dummy. **3.** *U.S.* a teething ring.

pacifism (păs′ĭ fĭz′əm), *n.* **1.** opposition to war or violence of any kind. **2.** the principle or policy of establishing and maintaining universal peace or such relations among all nations that all differences may be adjusted without recourse to war. [f. PACIF(IC) + -ISM]

pacifist (păs′ĭ fĭst), *n.* **1.** one who opposes in principle all war or violence. **2.** a conscientious objector. —*adj.* **3.** Also, **pac′ifis′tic.** of or pertaining to pacifists or pacifism.

pacify (păs′ĭ fī′), *v.t.,* **-fied, -fying.** **1.** to bring into a state of peace; quiet; calm: *pacify an angry man.* **2.** to appease: *pacify one's appetite.* [late ME, t. L: m. *pācificāre* make peace] —**pac′ifi′able,** *adj.*

pack[1] (păk), *n.* **1.** a quantity of anything wrapped or tied up; parcel. **2.** a load or burden, as one carried by an animal. **3.** the quantity of anything put up or packed at one time or in one season: *last season's salmon pack.* **4.** the method, design, materials, etc., used in making a pack or parcel: *a vacuum pack.* **5.** a set or gang (of people): *a pack of thieves.* **6.** a group or unit of wolf cubs in the Boy Scout Movement. **7.** *Rugby Football.* **a.** the forwards of a team collectively, esp. acting together in rushing the ball forward or as a scrum. **b.** the forwards of two opposing teams in a scrum. **8.** a company of certain animals of the same kind: *a pack of wolves.* **9.** *Hunting.* a number of hounds used regularly for hunting together. **10.** Also, **pack wall.** *Mining.* a rubble wall which supports a roof. **11.** a group of things, usually abstract: *a pack of lies.* **12.** a complete set, as of playing cards, usually 52 in number. **13.** a considerable area of pack-ice. **14.** *Med.* **a.** a wrapping of the body in wet or dry cloths for therapeutic purposes. **b.** the cloths so used. **c.** *Obs.* the state of being so wrapped. **15.** a paste or the like consisting of cosmetic materials applied to the skin, esp. of the face, to improve the complexion. **16.** *Obs.* a worthless person.
—*v.t.* **17.** to make into a pack or bundle. **18.** to make into a group or compact mass, as animals, ice, etc. **19.** to fill with anything compactly arranged: *pack a trunk.* **20.** to press or crowd together within; cram: *a packed gallery.* **21.** to put or arrange in suitable form for the market: *pack fruit.* **22.** to make airtight, steamproof, or watertight by stuffing: *to pack the piston of a steam engine.* **23.** to cover or envelop with something pressed closely around. **24.** to load (a horse, etc.) with a pack. **25.** to carry, esp. as a load. **26.** to send off summarily (sometimes fol. by *off, away,* etc.): *packed off to school.* **27.** to put a load upon. **28.** *Slang.* to be capable of (forceful blows). **29.** to treat with a therapeutic pack. **30. pack in** or **up,** to desist from; give up. —*v.i.* **31.** to pack goods, etc., in compact form, as for transportation or storage (often fol. by *up*). **32.** to admit of being compactly stowed: *articles that pack well.* **33.** to

crowd together, as persons, etc. **34.** to become compacted: *wet snow packs readily.* **35.** to collect into a pack: *grouse began to pack.* **36.** to leave hastily (generally fol. by *off*, *away*, etc.). **37.** *Rugby Football.* to form a scrum (often fol. by *down*). **38. send packing,** to dismiss summarily. —*adj.* **39.** transporting, or used in transporting, a pack: *pack animals.* **40.** made up of pack animals. **41.** *Chiefly Scot.* (of animals) tame. **42.** compressed into a pack; packed. **43.** used in or adapted for packing. [ME *packe*, *pakke*, t. Flem., D or LG] **—Syn. 1.** See **package. 8.** See **flock**[1].

pack[2] (păk), *v.t.* to collect, arrange, or manipulate (cards, persons, facts, etc.) so as to serve one's own purposes: *pack a jury.* [? var. of PACT]

package (păk′ĭj), *n.*, *v.*, **-aged, -aging.** —*n.* **1.** a bundle or parcel. **2.** that in which anything is packed, as a case, crate, etc. **3.** the packing of goods, etc. **4.** a unit, group of parts, or the like, considered as a single entity. —*v.t.* **5.** to put into wrappings or a container. **6.** to combine as a single entity.

—Syn. 1. PACKAGE, PACK, PACKET, PARCEL refer to a bundle or to something fastened together. A PACKAGE is a bundle of things packed and wrapped: *a package from the chemist's.* A PACK is a large bundle or bale of things put or fastened together, usually wrapped up or in a bag, case, etc., to be carried by a person or a beast of burden: *a pedlar's pack.* A PACKET, originally a package of letters or dispatches, is a small package or bundle: *a packet of cigarettes.* A PARCEL is an object or objects wrapped up to form a single, small bundle: *a parcel containing two dresses.*

package deal, an agreement in which acceptance of any of the parts of a proposal is contingent upon acceptance of the whole.

packer (păk′ə), *n.* **1.** one whose business is packing food, etc., for the market. **2.** one who or that which packs.

packet (păk′ĭt), *n.* **1.** a small pack or package of anything, orig. of letters. **2.** a definite quantity or measure of something wrapped and retailed: *a packet of biscuits.* **3.** a ship that carries mail, passengers, and goods regularly on a fixed route. **4.** any ship. **5.** *Slang.* a large sum of money. **6.** *Slang.* a heavy or forceful blow, injury, setback, or the like: *he's caught a packet.* —*v.t.* **7.** to bind up in a package or parcel. [dim. of PACK[1]] **—Syn. 1.** See **package.**

packet boat, packet (defs 3 and 4).

packhorse (păk′hôs′), *n.* a horse used for carrying goods, now chiefly in terrain inaccessible to wheeled vehicles.

pack-ice (păk′īs′), *n.* an area in polar seas of large blocks of ice driven together over a long period by winds, currents, etc.

packing (păk′ĭng), *n.* **1.** the act or work of one who or that which packs. **2.** the preparing and packaging of foodstuffs etc. **3.** any material used for packing or making watertight, steamproof, etc., as a fibrous substance closing a joint, a metallic ring round a piston, etc.

packing case, a large container for goods to be transported, usually cube-shaped and made of plywood with reinforced edges.

packing effect, *Physics.* mass defect.

packing fraction, *Physics.* the difference between the mass of an isotope on the physical scale of atomic weights and its mass number, divided by the mass number; often multiplied by 10,000 for convenience.

packing house, *U.S.* an establishment in which provisions, esp. beef and pork, are packed for the market.

packman (păk′mən), *n.*, *pl.* **-men.** a pedlar.

pack rat, a large, bushy-tailed rodent, *Neotoma cinerea*, of North America, noted for carrying away small articles which it keeps in its nest.

packsack (păk′săk′), *n.* *U.S.* a rucksack of canvas or leather.

pack-saddle (păk′săd′l), *n.* a saddle specially designed for supporting the load on a pack animal.

pack-thread (păk′thrĕd′), *n.* a strong thread or twine for sewing or tying up packages.

packtrain (păk′trān′), *n.* a line or group of animals, esp. horses or mules, carrying goods.

pack wall, pack (def. 10).

pact (păkt), *n.* an agreement; a compact. [ME, t. L: s. *pactum*, prop. pp. neut., agreed]

paction (păk′shən), *n.* *Obs.* agreement. [t. L: s. *pactio*]

Pactolus (păk tō′ləs), *n.* a small river in ancient Lydia: famous for the gold washed from its sands.

pad[1] (păd), *n.*, *v.*, **padded, padding.** —*n.* **1.** a cushion-like mass of some soft material, for comfort, protection, or stuffing. **2.** a guard for the leg, containing padding and stiffeners, as worn by the batsmen and wicket-keeper in cricket, the goalkeeper in hockey, etc. **3.** a cushion used as a saddle; saddle of leather and padding without a tree. **4.** a number of sheets of paper held together at the edge to form a tablet. **5.** a soft ink-soaked block of absorbent material for inking a rubber stamp. **6.** one of the cushion-like protuberances on the underside of the feet of dogs, foxes, and some other animals. **7.** the foot of a fox or other beast of the chase. **8.** *Zool.* a pulvillus, as on the tarsus or foot of an insect. **9.** the large floating leaf of the waterlily. **10.** a device built into a road surface through which vehicles passing over it actuate changes of traffic lights. **11.** *Aerospace.* launching pad. **12.** *Slang.* a dwelling, esp. a single room. **13.** *Slang.* a bedroom. **14.** *Slang.* a bed. —*v.t.* **15.** to furnish, protect, fill out, or stuff with a pad or padding. **16.** to expand (writing or speech) with unnecessary words or matter. —*v.i.* **17.** *Slang.* to have one's dwelling (usually fol. by *down*). [special uses of obs. *pad* bundle to lie on, ? b. PACK[1] and BED] —**pad′der,** *n.*

pad[2] (păd), *n.*, *v.*, **padded, padding.** —*n.* **1.** a dull sound, as of footsteps on the ground. **2.** a road horse, distinguished from a hunter or workhorse. **3.** a highwayman. **4.** *Dial.* a path or road. —*v.t.* **5.** to travel along on foot. **6.** *Dial.* to beat down by treading. —*v.i.* **7.** to travel on foot. **8.** to go with the dull sound of footsteps. [t. D or LG (c. PATH); orig. beggars' and thieves' slang] —**pad′der,** *n.*

Padang (*Indon.* pä′däng), *n.* a seaport in Indonesia, in W Sumatra. 143,000 (est. 1961).

padauk (pə douk′, -dôk′), *n.* wood of various papilionaceous trees of the papilionaceous genus *Pterocarpus*, as **Burma padauk** (*P. macrocarpus*).

padded cell, a room in a mental hospital in which a violent patient is prevented from injuring himself.

padding (păd′ĭng), *n.* **1.** material, as cotton or straw, with which to pad. **2.** unnecessary matter used to expand a speech, etc. **3.** the act of one who or that which pads.

Paddington (păd′ĭng tən), *n.* a district of the inner London borough of Westminster.

paddle[1] (păd′l), *n.*, *v.*, **-dled, -dling.** —*n.* **1.** a short oar held in the hands (not resting in the rowlock) and used esp. for propelling canoes. **2.** one of the broad boards on the circumference of a paddlewheel; a float. **3.** a paddlewheel. **4.** one of the similar projecting blades by means of which a waterwheel is turned. **5.** an adjustable shutter that lets waters into or out of a lock, reservoir, or the like. **6.** a flipper or limb of a penguin, turtle, whale, etc. **7.** any of various implements used for beating, stirring, mixing, etc. **8.** the act of paddling. —*v.i.* **9.** to propel a canoe or the like by using a paddle. **10.** to row lightly or gently with oars. **11.** to move by means of paddlewheels, as a steamer. —*v.t.* **12.** to propel (a canoe, etc.) with a paddle. **13.** to stir. **14.** *U.S. Colloq.* to beat with or as with a paddle; spank. **15.** to convey by paddling, as in a canoe. [orig. obscure] —**pad′dler,** *n.*

paddle[2] (păd′l), *v.i.*, **-dled, -dling. 1.** to dabble or play in or as in shallow water. **2.** to toy with the fingers. **3.** to toddle. [orig. uncert.] —**pad′dler,** *n.*

paddle-box (păd′l bŏks′), *n.* a box or casing covering the upper part of the paddlewheel of a vessel.

paddlefish (păd′l fĭsh′), *n.*, *pl.* **-fishes,** (*esp. collectively*) **-fish.** a large ganoid fish, *Polyodon spathula*, remotely allied to the sturgeons, with a long, flat, paddle-like projection of the snout, abundant in the Mississippi and its larger tributaries.

paddle-steamer (păd′l stē′mə), *n.* a steam vessel propelled by paddlewheels.

paddlewheel (păd′l wēl′), *n.* a power-driven wheel with floats or paddles on its circumference, for propelling a vessel over the water.

paddock[1] (păd′ək), *n.* **1.** a small field or enclosure, esp. for pasture, near a stable or house. **2.** *Horseracing.* the enclosure in which horses are saddled and mounted. **3.** *Motor racing.* an area near the pits, in which cars are prepared for a race. **4.** *Austral.* any enclosed field or piece of land. —*v.t.* **5.** to confine or enclose in or as in a paddock. [var. of *parrock*, OE *pearroc* enclosure (orig. fence)]

paddock[2] (păd′ək), *n.* *Now Chiefly Dial. and Scot.* a frog or toad. [ME *paddoke*, f. *pad* toad + *-oke* -OCK]

paddy[1] (păd′ĭ), *n.* **1.** rice. **2.** rice in the husk, uncut or gathered. [t. Malay: m. *pādī*]

paddy[2] (păd′ĭ), *n.* *Colloq.* an intense anger; a rage.

Paddy (păd′ĭ), *n.*, *pl.* **-dies.** an Irishman. [familiar var. of Irish *Padraig* Patrick]

paddymelon (păd′ĭ mĕl′ən), *n.* a small Australian scrub wallaby of the genus *Thylogale.* [alter. (by assoc. with *melon*) of a native Australian word]

paddywhack (păd′ĭ wăk′), *n.* *Colloq.* **1.** a paddy; a rage. **2.** a spanking.

Paderborn (*Ger.* pä dər bŏrn′), *n.* a town in West Germany, in NE North Rhine-Westphalia. 60,100 (est. 1966).

Paderewski (păd′ə rĕv′skĭ; *Pol.* pä dĕ rĕf′skē), *n.* **Ignace** (*Fr.* ē nyäs′) or **Ignacy Jan** (*Pol.* ēg nä′tsĭ yän), 1860–1941, Polish pianist, composer, and statesman.

Padishah (pä′dĭ shä′), *n.* great king; emperor (a title applied esp. to the Shah of Iran, formerly also to the Sultan of Turkey, and in India, to the British sovereign). [t. Pers. (poetical form), f. m. *pati* lord + *shāh* king]

padlock (păd′lŏk′), *n.* **1.** a portable or detachable lock having a pivoted or sliding hasp which passes through a staple, ring, or the like and is then made fast. —*v.t.* **2.** to fasten with or as with a padlock. [late ME, f. *pad*, var. of POD[3], + LOCK[1]]

padnag (păd′năg′), *n.* an ambling nag. [f. PAD[2] + NAG[2]]

padre (pä′drĭ), *n.* **1.** father (used esp. with reference to a priest). **2.** a military or naval chaplain. [t. Sp., Pg., It., g. L *pater* father]

padrone (pə drō′nĭ; *It.* pȧ drô′nĕ), *n., pl.* **-ni** (-nē). **1.** *Italian.* a master, as of a vessel. **2.** *Italian.* an innkeeper. **3.** *U.S.* an employer who exercises control over the private lives of his employees. [It., der. *padre* father]

Padua (păd′yŏŏ ə), *n.* a town in NE Italy. 216,594 (1966). Italian, **Padova** (*It.* pȧ′dô vȧ). —**Pad′uan,** *adj., n.*

paduasoy (păd′yŏŏ ə soi′), *n., pl.* **-soys. 1.** a smooth, strong, rich, silk fabric. **2.** a garment made of it. [appar. alter. of F *pou-de-soie*, by assoc. with *Padua say* serge of PADUA]

Padus (pā′dəs), *n.* ancient name of **Po.**

paean (pē′ən), *n.* **1.** any song of praise, joy, or triumph. **2.** a hymn of invocation or thanksgiving to Apollo or some other Greek deity. Also, **pean.** [t. L, t. Gk: m. *paiā́n* paean, *Paiā́n*, Homer's name for the physician of the gods, later Apollo]

paed-, a word element meaning 'child'. Also, **paedi-, paedo-;** *U.S.*, **ped-.** [t. Gk: m. *paidi-*, comb. form of *paîs*]

paedagogue (pĕd′ə gŏg′, pē′də-), *n.* pedagogue. —**paed′agog′ic,** *adj.* —**paed′agogism,** *n.* —**paed′agog′y,** *n.*

paederast (pĕd′ə răst′), *n.* pederast.

paederasty (pĕd′ə răs′tĭ), *n.* pederasty.

paediatrician (pē′dĭ ə trĭsh′ən), *n.* a physician who specializes in paediatrics. Also, **paediatrist** (pē′dĭ ăt′rist); *U.S.*, **pediatrician.**

paediatrics (pē′dĭ ăt′rĭks), *n.* the study and treatment of the diseases of children. Also, *U.S.*, **pediatrics.** [pl. of *paediatric* (f. PAED- + m. s. Gk: *iātrikós* of medicine). See -ICS] —**pae′diat′ric,** *adj.*

paedobaptism (pē′dō băp′tĭz′əm), *n.* the baptism of infants. Also, *U.S.*, **pedobaptism.** [f. *pedo-* (var. of PAED-) + BAPTISM]

paedogenesis (pē′dō jĕn′ĭ sĭs), *n.* reproduction by animals in the larval state, often by parthenogenesis.

paedology (pē dŏl′ə jĭ), *n.* **1.** the scientific study of the nature and development of children. **2.** paediatrics. Also, *U.S.*, **pedology.** [f. *pedo-* (var. of PAED-) + -LOGY]

paella (pī ĕl′yə; *Sp.* pȧ′lyȧ), *n.* a Spanish dish made from rice, chicken, shellfish, etc. [t. Sp.: orig., the large shallow pan in which it is cooked]

paeon (pē′ən), *n. Class. Pros.* a foot of four syllables, one long (in any position) and three short. [t. L, t. Gk: m. *paiṓn* paeon, hymn, Attic var. of *paiā́n* PAEAN]

Paestum (pĕs′təm), *n.* an ancient coastal city of Lucania, in S Italy: ruins, including three Greek temples and a Roman amphitheatre.

pagan (pā′gən), *n.* **1.** one of a people or community professing some other than the Christian religion (applied to the ancient Romans, Greeks, etc., and sometimes the Jews). **2.** one who is not a Christian, a Jew, or a Muslim. **3.** an irreligious or heathenish person. —*adj.* **4.** pertaining to the worship or worshippers of any religion which is neither Christian, Jewish, nor Muslim. **5.** of, pertaining to, or characteristic of pagans. **6.** heathen; irreligious. [ME, t. L: s. *pāgānus* civilian; so called (by the Christians) because he was not a soldier of Christ] —**pa′ganish,** *adj.* —**Syn. 5.** See **heathen.**

pagandom (pā′gən dəm), *n.* **1.** the pagan world. **2.** pagans collectively.

Paganini (păg′ə nē′nĭ; *It.* pȧ gȧ nē′nē), *n.* **Nicolò** (*It.* nē kô lô′), 1784–1840, Italian violinist.

paganism (pā′gə nĭz′əm), *n.* **1.** pagan spirit or attitude in religious or moral questions. **2.** the beliefs or practices of pagans. **3.** the state of being a pagan.

paganize (pā′gə nīz′), *v.,* **-nized, -nizing.** —*v.t.* **1.** to make pagan. —*v.i.* **2.** to become pagan. Also, **paganise.**

page[1] (pāj), *n., v.,* **paged, paging.** —*n.* **1.** one side of a leaf of a book, manuscript, letter, or the like. **2.** the entire leaf of a book, etc.: *write on both sides of the page.* **3.** any event or period regarded as an episode in history: *a glorious page in English history.* **4.** *Print.* the type set and arranged for a page. —*v.t.* **5.** to paginate. [t. F, g. L *pāgina*]

page[2] (pāj), *n., v.,* **paged, paging.** —*n.* **1.** a boy servant or attendant. **2.** a youth in attendance on a person of rank, sometimes formerly in the course of training for knighthood. **3.** a young male attendant, usually in uniform, in a hotel or the like; a pageboy. **4.** *U.S.* an attendant in a legislative assembly, as Congress. —*v.t.* **5.** to seek (a person) by calling out his name, as a hotel page does. **6.** to attend as a page. [ME, t. OF, t. It.: m. *paggio*, ult. t. Gk: m. *paídion* boy, servant]

page[3] (pāj), *n. Civ. Eng.* a small wedge used to tighten shoring or strutting. [? der. L *pangere* fix]

Page (pāj), *n.* **Sir Frederick Handley,** 1885–1962, English aircraft manufacturer.

pageant (păj′ənt), *n.* **1.** an elaborate public spectacle, whether processional or at some fitting spot, illustrative of the history of a place, institution, or other subject. **2.** a costumed procession, masque, allegorical tableau, or the like, in public or social festivities. **3.** a splendid or stately procession; a showy display. **4.** a specious show. **5.** *Hist.* **a.** a platform or stage, usually moving on wheels, on which scenes from the medieval mystery plays were presented. **b.** a stage bearing any kind of spectacle. [ME *pagent, pagyn*; orig. obscure]

pageantry (păj′ən trĭ), *n., pl.* **-ries. 1.** spectacular display; pomp: *the pageantry of war.* **2.** mere show; empty display. **3.** *Obs.* pageants collectively.

pageboy (pāj′boi′), *n.* **1.** an employee in a hotel who carries luggage, runs errands, etc.; bellboy. **2.** a woman's hairstyle in which the hair falls straight and is rolled under at the bottom.

Paget (păj′ĭt), *n.* **Sir James,** 1814–99, English surgeon and pathologist.

paginal (păj′ĭ nəl), *adj.* **1.** of or pertaining to pages. **2.** consisting of pages. **3.** page for page: *a paginal reprint.* [t. LL: s. *pāginālis*, der. L *pāgina* PAGE[1]]

paginate (păj′ĭ nāt′), *v.t.,* **-nated, -nating.** to indicate the sequence of (pages) by numbers or other characters on each leaf of the book.

pagination (păj′ĭ nā′shən), *n. Bibliog.* **1.** the number of pages or leaves (or both) of a book identified in bibliographical description or cataloguing of the book. **2.** the figures by which pages are numbered. **3.** the act of paginating.

Pagnol (*Fr.* pȧ nyŏl′), *n.* **Marcel** (*Fr.* mȧr sĕl′), born 1895, French dramatist and film producer.

pagoda (pə gō′də), *n.* (in India, Burma, China, etc.) a temple or sacred building, usually more or less pyramidal or forming a tower of many storeys. Also, *Archaic,* **pagod** (păg′əd, pə gŏd′). [t. Pg.: m. *pagode*; orig. uncert.] —**pago′da-like′,** *adj.*

Chinese pagoda

pagoda tree, a deciduous, leguminous tree of China, *Sophora japonica*, with pinnate leaves and greenish white flowers.

Pago Pago (päng′ō päng′ō), the chief harbour and town of American Samoa, on Tutuila island: naval station. 1251 (1960). Also, **Pagopago.**

pagri (pŭg′rĭ), *n.* pugree.

pagurian (pə gyŏŏə′rĭ ən), *adj. Zool.* **1.** belonging or pertaining to the hermit crab family *Paguridae*, esp. aquatic hermit crabs with short antennules. —*n.* **2.** a pagurian crab. [f. s. NL *Pagurus*, the typical genus (t. Gk: m. *págouros* kind of crab) + -IAN]

pagurid (pə gyŏŏə′rĭd, păg′yŏŏ rĭd), *n.* a pagurian.

pah (pä), *interj.* (an exclamation of disgust or disbelief.)

Pahang (pə hŭng′), *n.* a state in Malaysia, in the SE Malay Peninsula. 371,552 pop. (est. 1962); 13,820 sq. mi. *Cap.:* Kuala Lipis.

pahlavi (pä′lə vĭ; *Pers.* păh lă vē′), *n., pl.* **-vis.** an Iranian gold coin worth 100 rials. [t. Pers., named after Riza Shah PAHLAVI]

Pahlavi (pä′lə vĭ; *Pers.* păh lă vē′), *n.* **1. Mohammed** (*Shahansah Mohammed Riza Shah Pahlavi*), born 1919, shah of Iran since 1941. **2.** his father, **Riza** (rē′zä), 1877–1944, shah of Iran 1925–41, founder of the Pahlavi dynasty.

Pahlavi (pä′lə vĭ; *Pers.* păh lă vē′), *n.* the Iranian language of Zoroastrian books, written (3rd–10th centuries) in a Semitic script. Also, **Pehlevi.** [t. Pers.: Parthian]

paid (pād), *v.* pt. and pp. of **pay**[1].

paid-up (pād′ŭp′), *adj.* having paid the dues, initiation fees, etc., required by any organization or association: *the union has a paid-up membership of 60,000.*

paigle (pā′gl), *n.* the cowslip, *Primula veris*, or the oxlip, *P. elatior.*

Paignton (pān′tən), *n.* a seaside resort in England, in S Devonshire. 30,292 (1961).

pail (pāl), *n.* a container of wood, metal, etc., nearly or quite cylindrical, with a semicircular handle, for holding liquids, etc.; a bucket. [ME *payle*, OE *pægel* wine vessel, akin to G *Pegel* water-gauge] —**pailful** (pāl′fŏŏl′), *n.*

paillasse (păl yăs′, păl′yăs), *n.* palliasse. [t. F, der. *paille* straw, g. L *palea* chaff, straw]

paillette (păl yĕt′), *n.* **1.** a spangle used in ornamenting a costume. **2.** a decorative piece of foil used in enamelling. [t. F, dim. of *paille* straw. See PALLET[1]]

pain (pān), *n.* **1.** bodily or mental suffering or distress (opposed to *pleasure*). **2.** a distressing sensation in a particular part of the body. **3.** (*pl.*) laborious or careful efforts; assiduous care: *great pains have been taken.* **4.** (*pl.*) the suffering of childbirth. **5. be at pains to,** to be extremely careful to. **6. on pain of,** liable to the penalty of. **7. pain in the neck,** *Colloq.* an irritating, tedious, or unpleasant person or thing. —*v.t.* **8.** to inflict pain on; hurt; distress. —*v.i.* **9.** to cause pain or suffering. [ME *peine,* t. OF, g. L *poena* penalty, pain, t. Gk: m. *poinē* fine]

—**Syn. 1.** torture, misery. PAIN, ACHE, AGONY, ANGUISH are terms for sensations causing suffering or torment. PAIN and ACHE refer usually to physical sensations (except *heartache*); AGONY and ANGUISH may be physical or mental. PAIN suggests a sudden sharp twinge: *a pain in one's ankle.* ACHE applies to a continuous pain, whether acute or dull: *headache, muscular aches.* AGONY implies a continuous, excruciating, scarcely endurable pain: *in agony from a wound.* ANGUISH suggests not only extreme and long-continued pain, but also a feeling of despair. **3.** See **care. 8.** afflict, torture, torment.

Paine (pān), *n.* **Thomas,** 1737–1809, American writer on government and religion, born in England.

painful (pān′fəl), *adj.* **1.** affected with or causing pain: *painful thoughts.* **2.** laborious; difficult. **3.** *Archaic.* painstaking. —**pain′fully,** *adv.* —**pain′fulness,** *n.* —**Syn. 1.** distressing, torturing, agonizing.

pain-killer (pān′kĭl′ə), *n.* something that relieves pain, esp. an analgesic.

painless (pān′lĭs), *adj.* without pain; causing no pain. —**pain′lessly,** *adv.* —**pain′lessness,** *n.*

painstaking (pānz′tā′kĭng), *adj.* **1.** assiduously careful: *painstaking work.* —*n.* **2.** careful and assiduous effort. —**pains′tak′ingly,** *adv.*

paint (pānt), *n.* **1.** a substance composed of solid colouring matter intimately mixed with a liquid vehicle or medium, and applied as a coating. **2.** the dried surface pigment. **3.** the solid colouring matter alone; a pigment. **4.** application of colour. **5.** *Colloq.* colour, as rouge, used on the face. —*v.t.* **6.** to represent (an object, etc.) in colours or pigment. **7.** to execute (a picture, design, etc.) in colours or pigment. **8.** to depict as if by painting; describe vividly in words. **9.** to describe or represent: *he's not as bad as he's painted.* **10.** to coat, cover, or decorate (something) with colour or pigment. **11.** to colour as if by painting; adorn or variegate. **12.** to apply like paint, as a liquid medicine, etc. **13. paint the town red,** *Colloq.* to have a spree; celebrate. —*v.i.* **14.** to coat or cover anything with paint. **15.** to practise painting. **16.** *Colloq.* to use artificial colours on the face. [ME *peint(en),* t. OF: m. *peint,* pp. of *peindre,* g. L *pingere* paint, adorn]

paintbox (pānt′bŏks′), *n.* a box in which different paints, as watercolours, are kept in separate compartments.

paintbrush (pānt′brŭsh′), *n.* **1.** a brush for applying paint. **2.** any of the figwort family of plants.

painted lady, a brightly coloured butterfly, *Vanessa cardui,* of the family *Nymphalidae,* which inhabits Europe and N Africa.

painted woman, a woman of low morals or promiscuous behaviour.

painter[1] (pān′tə), *n.* **1.** an artist who paints pictures. **2.** one whose occupation is coating surfaces with paint. [ME *peyntour,* t. AF: m. *peintour,* ult. g. L *pictor*]

painter[2] (pān′tə), *n.* a rope, usually at the bow, for fastening a boat to a ship, stake, etc. [? var. of d. *panter* noose, ult. t. OF: m. *pentoir* rope to hang things on, der. *pendre* hang]

painter[3] (pān′tə), *n.* *U.S.* the puma. [var. of PANTHER]

painter's colic, lead poisoning causing intense pain in the intestines.

painting (pān′tĭng), *n.* **1.** a picture or design executed in paints. **2.** the act, art, or work of one who paints.

pair (pēə), *n., pl.* **pairs, pair,** *v.* —*n.* **1.** two things of a kind, matched for use together: *a pair of gloves.* **2.** a combination of two parts joined together: *a pair of scissors.* **3.** a married or engaged couple. **4.** two people, animals, etc., regarded as having a common characteristic: *a pair of fools.* **5.** two mated animals. **6.** a span or team. **7. a.** two members on opposite sides in a deliberative body who for convenience (as to permit absence) arrange together to forgo voting on a given occasion. **b.** the arrangement thus made. **8.** *Cards.* **a.** two cards of the same denomination, without regard to suit or colour. **b.** (*pl.*) two players who are matched together against different contestants. **9.** *Rowing.* a racing shell having two oarsmen, with one oar each. **10.** *Mech.* two parts or pieces so connected that they mutually constrain relative motion **(kinematic pair)**. **11.** *Archaic or Dial.* a set or combination of more than two. —*v.t.* **12.** to arrange in pairs. **13.** to join in a pair; mate; couple. **14.** to cause to mate. —*v.i.* **15.** to separate into pairs (often fol. by *off*). **16.** to form a pair or pairs. **17.** (in a deliberative body) to form a pair to forgo voting. [ME, t. OF: m. *paire,* g. L *pāria,* neut. pl. of *pār* equal]

—**Syn. 1.** PAIR, BRACE, COUPLE, SPAN, YOKE are terms for groups of two. PAIR is used of two things naturally or habitually associated in use, or necessary to each other to make a complete set (*a pair of horses*). It is used also of one thing composed of two similar and complementary parts: *a pair of trousers.* BRACE is a hunter's term, used of a pair of dogs, ducks, etc., a pair of pistols or bullets: *a brace of partridge.* In COUPLE the idea of combination or interdependence has become greatly weakened; it may be used loosely for two of anything (*a couple of apples*), and even for more than two (= several): *I have to see a couple of people.* SPAN is used of a matched pair of horses harnessed together side by side. YOKE applies to two animals hitched together under a yoke for drawing and pulling: *a yoke of oxen.*

pair production, *Physics.* **1.** the simultaneous creation of a positron and an electron as the result of the interaction between a high-energy photon or particle and the field of an atomic nucleus. **2.** the simultaneous creation of any particle and its antiparticle.

paisley (pāz′lĭ), *n., pl.* **-leys. 1.** a soft fabric made from wool and woven with a colourful and minutely detailed pattern. **2.** an article fashioned of paisley. **3.** any pattern similar to that woven on paisley. —*adj.* **4.** made of paisley: *a paisley shawl.*

Paisley (pāz′lĭ), *n.* a burgh in Scotland, in Renfrewshire: shipbuilding; thread factories. 95,753 (1961).

Paiute (pī yo͞ot′), *n.* **1.** a group of North American Indians of Uto-Aztecan family, dwelling in California, Nevada, Utah, and Arizona. **2.** a member of this group. **3.** either of two Shoshonean languages. Also, **Piute.** [orig. name for Corn Creek tribe of Utah]

pajamas (pə jä′məz), *n.pl.* *U.S.* pyjamas.

pakeha (pä′kə hä′, pä kē′ə), *N.Z.* —*n.* **1.** a European; white man. —*adj.* **2.** denoting or pertaining to a white man. [t. Maori]

pakeha Maori, a European who adopts the Maori way of life.

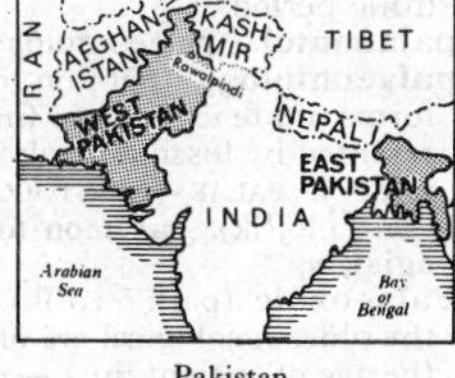

Pakistan

Pakistan (pä′kĭ stän′), *n.* **1.** a republic in S Asia, divided into **West Pakistan** and **East Pakistan,** 900 miles apart and separated by the republic of India; formerly part of India: a member of the Commonwealth of Nations. 93,720,613 pop. (1961); 364,737 sq. mi. *Provisional cap.:* Rawalpindi. **2.** (before 1947) the predominantly Muslim areas of the peninsula of India (as contrasted with *Hindustan,* the predominantly Hindu areas).

Pakistani (pä′kĭ stä′nĭ), *n., pl.* **-nis,** *adj.* —*n.* **1.** a native or inhabitant of Pakistan. —*adj.* **2.** of or pertaining to, or denoting Pakistan or Pakistanis.

pal (păl), *n., v.,* **palled, palling.** *Colloq.* —*n.* **1.** a comrade; a chum. **2.** an accomplice. —*v.i.* **3.** to associate as pals. **4. pal up with,** to become associated or friendly with. [t. Gipsy, dissimilated var. of *plal, pral* brother]

palace (păl′ĭs), *n.* **1.** the official residence of a sovereign, a bishop, or some other exalted personage. **2.** a stately mansion or building. **3.** a large place for exhibitions or entertainment. [ME *palais,* t. OF, g. L *palātium* palace, orig. the Palatine Hill in Rome (on which the emperors resided)]

palace revolution, a seizure of power by those who already hold office or positions of power under the existing government or regime.

Palacio Valdés (*Sp.* pä lä′thyō väl dĕs′), **Armando** (*Sp.* är män′dō), 1853–1938, Spanish novelist and critic.

paladin (păl′ə dĭn), *n.* **1.** one of the legendary twelve peers or knightly champions in attendance on Charlemagne. **2.** any knightly or heroic champion. [t. F, t. It.: m. *paladino,* g. L *palātīnus* PALATINE[1]]

palae-, var. of **palaeo-,** before most vowels, as in *palaeethnology.*

Palaearctic (păl′ĭ äk′tĭk), *adj.* of or pertaining to a biogeographical division of the Holarctic region comprising Europe and N Asia together with N Africa.

palae-ethnology (păl′ĭ ĕth nŏl′ə jĭ), *n.* the branch of ethnology that treats of the earliest or most primitive races of mankind. [f. PALAE- + ETHNOLOGY] —**palaeethnologic** (păl′ĭ ĕth′nə lŏj′ĭk), **pal′ae-eth′nolog′ical,** *adj.* —**pal′ae-ethnol′ogist,** *n.*

palaeo-, a prefix meaning 'old', 'ancient'. Also, **palae-;** *Chiefly U.S.,* **pale-, paleo-.** [t. Gk: m. *palaio-,* comb. form of *palaiós*]

palaeobiology (păl′ĭ ō bī ŏl′ə jĭ), *n.* that branch of palaeontology which deals with fossil plants and animals. —**pal′aeobi′olog′ical,** *adj.* —**pal′aeobiol′ogist,** *n.*

palaeobotany (păl′ĭ ō bŏt′ə nĭ), *n.* the branch of palaeontology that treats of fossil plants. —**palaeobotanical** (păl′ĭ ō bə tăn′ĭ kl), **pal′aeobotan′ic,** *adj.* —**pal′aeobot′anist,** *n.*

Palaeocene (păl′ĭ ō sēn′), *Geol.* —*adj.* **1.** pertaining to the oldest series or epoch of the Tertiary. —*n.* **2.** a division of the Tertiary period or system that precedes Eocene, but which is absent from the British Isles.

palaeoecology (păl′ĭ ō ē kŏl′ə jĭ), *n.* the study of the ecological relationships which prevailed among fossil plants and animals. —**pal′aeoe′colog′ical,** *adj.* —**pal′aeoecol′ogist,** *n.*

palaeog., palaeography.

Palaeogene (păl′ĭ ə jēn′, pā′l-), *adj., n. Geol.* Eogene.

palaeogeography (păl′ĭ ō jĭ ŏg′rə fĭ), *n.* the science of representing the earth's geographic features belonging to any part of the geological past. —**palaeogeographical** (păl′ĭ ō jĭə grăf′ĭ kl), *adj.*

palaeogeology (păl′ĭ ō jĭ ŏl′ə jĭ), *n.* the science of representing geological conditions of some given time in past earth history. —**palaeogeological** (păl′ĭ ō jĭə lŏj′ĭ kl), *adj.*

palaeography (păl′ĭ ŏg′rə fĭ), *n.* **1.** ancient forms of writing, as in documents and inscriptions. **2.** the study of ancient writing, including determination of origin and date, decipherment, etc. —**pal′aeog′rapher,** *n.* —**palaeographic** (păl′ĭ ō grăf′ĭk), **pal′aeograph′ical,** *adj.* —**pal′aeograph′ically,** *adv.*

palaeolith (păl′ĭ ō lĭth), *n.* a palaeolithic stone implement.

Palaeolithic (păl′ĭ ō lĭth′ĭk), *n.* **1.** the earliest part of the Stone Age, the Old Stone Age, characterized by implements of chipped stone; it includes the Pleistocene epoch and precedes the Mesolithic. —*adj.* **2.** (*sometimes l.c.*) of or pertaining to the Palaeolithic period.

Palaeolithic man, *Anthropol.* any of the primitive species of man (Piltdown, Neanderthal, etc.) living in the palaeolithic period.

palaeontol., palaeontology.

palaeontology (păl′ĭ ŏn tŏl′ə jĭ), *n.* the science of the forms of life existing in former geological periods, as represented by fossil animals and plants. [t. F: m. *paléontologie;* f. PALAE- + ONTOLOGY] —**palaeontologic** (păl′ĭ ŏn′tə lŏj′ĭk), **pal′aeon′tolog′ical,** *adj.* —**pal′aeontol′ogist,** *n.*

Palaeozoic (păl′ĭ ō zō′ĭk), *Geol.* —*adj.* **1.** pertaining to the oldest geological era or rocks having abundant fossils; the age of ancient life. —*n.* **2.** the era or rocks comprising divisions from Cambrian to Permian. [f. PALAEO- + s. Gk *zōē* life + -IC]

palaeozoology (păl′ĭ ō zōō ŏl′ə jĭ), *n.* the branch of palaeontology that treats of fossil animals. —**palaeozoological** (păl′ĭ ō zōə lŏj′ĭ kl), *adj.* —**pal′aeozool′ogist,** *n.*

palaestra (pə lĕs′trə, pə lēs′trə), *n., pl.* **-tras, -trae** (-trē). *Gk Antiq.* a public place for training or exercise in wrestling or athletics. Also, **palestra.** [ME, t. L, t. Gk: m. *palaístra*]

palais (păl′ā, păl′ĭ; *Fr.* pȧ lĕ′), *n., pl.* **palais** (păl′āz, -ĭz; *Fr.* pȧ lĕ′). **1.** *French.* a palace. **2.** *Colloq.* a palais de danse.

palais de danse (păl′ĭ də däns′; *Fr.* pȧ lĕ də däNs′), *pl.* **palais de danse** (păl′ĭz də däns′; *Fr.* pȧ lĕ də däNs′). a dance hall, esp. a large and ornately decorated one. [F]

palanquin (păl′ən kēn′), *n.* (in India and other Eastern countries) a covering or boxlike litter borne by means of poles resting on men's shoulders. Also, **palankeen.** [t. Pg. Cf. Skt *palyanka, paryanka* couch, bed; prob. through Telegu]

Palanquin

palatable (păl′ə tə bl), *adj.* **1.** agreeable to the palate or taste; savoury. **2.** agreeable to the mind or feelings. —**pal′atabil′ity, pal′atableness,** *n.* —**pal′atably,** *adv.*

palatal (păl′ə tl), *adj.* **1.** *Anat.* of or pertaining to the palate. **2.** *Phonet.* with the tongue held close to the hard palate: the *y* of *yield* is a palatal consonant. —*n.* **3.** *Phonet.* a palatal sound. [f. PALAT(E) + -AL[1]] —**pal′atally,** *adv.*

palatalize (păl′ə tə līz′), *v.t.,* **-lized, -lizing.** *Phonet.* to pronounce with the tongue held close to the hard palate so that the sound acquires some of the quality of a *y*: in *million* the *l* sound may or may not be palatalized, but is always followed by a *y* sound. Also, **palatalise.** —**pal′ataliza′tion,** *n.*

palate (păl′ĭt), *n.* **1.** the roof of the mouth, consisting of bone (**hard palate**) in front and of a fleshy structure (**soft palate**) at the back. See diag. under **mouth.** **2.** this part of the mouth considered (popularly but erroneously) as the organ of taste. **3.** the sense of taste. **4.** mental taste or liking. [ME *palat,* t. L: s. *palātum*]

palatial (pə lā′shəl), *adj.* pertaining to, of the nature of, or befitting a palace: *palatial homes.* [f. s. L *palātium* PALACE + -AL[1]] —**pala′tially,** *adv.*

Palatinate (pə lăt′ĭ nĭt), *n.* **1. the.** Also, **Lower** or **Rhine Palatinate.** German, **Pfalz.** a district in SW Germany, W of the Rhine, which belonged to Bavaria until 1945; formerly, with portions of the neighbouring territory (the **Upper Palatinate**), it constituted an electorate of the Holy Roman Empire; now part of Rhineland-Palatinate state. See map under **Alsace-Lorraine.** **2.** a native or inhabitant of the Palatinate. **3.** (*l.c.*) the territory under the jurisdiction of a palatine.

palatine[1] (păl′ə tīn′), *adj.* **1.** possessing or characterized by royal privileges: *a count palatine.* **2.** pertaining to a count or earl palatine, or to a county palatine. **3.** of or pertaining to a palace; palatial. **4.** (*cap.*) of or pertaining to the Palatinate. **5.** (*cap.*) of or pertaining to the Palatine Hill. —*n.* **6.** a vassal exercising royal privileges in a province; a count or earl palatine. **7.** an officer of an imperial palace. **8.** a high official of an empire. **9.** (*cap.*) a native or inhabitant of the Palatinate. **10.** (*cap.*) Palatine Hill. **11.** a shoulder cape formerly worn by women. [ME, t. L: m. s. *palātīnus* belonging to the palace, imperial (as n., a palace officer)]

palatine[2] (păl′ə tīn′), *adj.* palatal: *the palatine bones.* [t. F: m. *palatin,* der. L *palātum* PALATE]

Palatine Hill, one of the seven hills on which Rome was built.

Palau Islands (*Sp.* pȧ làw′), a group of Pacific islands in the W part of the Caroline group: formerly a Japanese mandate, now under U.S. trusteeship. 10,280 pop. (1963); 171 sq. mi. Also, **Pelew Islands.**

palaver (pə lä′və), *n.* **1.** a parley or conference, esp. with much talk, as between travellers and primitive natives. **2.** any conference or discussion. **3.** profuse and idle talk. **4.** cajolery or flattery. —*v.i.* **5.** to talk profusely and idly. **6.** to hold a parley or conference. —*v.t.* **7.** to cajole. [t. Pg.: m. *palavra,* g. L *parabola* PARABLE]

Palawan (*Sp.* pȧ lȧ′wȧn), *n.* one of the Philippine Islands, in the SW part of the group. 132,670 pop. (est. 1960); 5697 sq. mi. *Cap.:* Puerto Princesa.

palazzo (pə lăt′sə, -lăd′zə; *It.* pȧ lȧt′tsȯ), *n., pl.* **-lazzi** (*It.* -lȧt′tsĭ). *Italian.* a palace or large building.

pale[1] (pāl), *adj.,* **paler, palest,** *v.,* **paled, paling.** —*adj.* **1.** of a whitish appearance; without intensity of colour: *pale complexion.* **2.** of a low degree of chroma, saturation, or purity; approaching white or grey: *pale yellow.* **3.** lacking in brightness; dim: *the pale moon.* **4.** faint; feeble; lacking vigour. —*v.i., v.t.* **5.** to make or become pale. [ME, t. OF, t. L: m. *pallidus* pallid] —**pale′ly,** *adv.* —**pale′ness,** *n.*

—**Syn. 1.** PALE, PALLID, WAN imply an absence of colour, esp. from the human countenance. PALE implies a faintness or absence of colour, which may be natural when applied to things (*the pale mauve of a violet*) but when applied to the human face, usually unnatural and often temporary as arising from sickness or sudden emotion: *pale cheeks.* PALLID, limited mainly to the human countenance, implies an excessive paleness induced by intense emotion, disease, or death: *the pallid lips of the dying man.* WAN implies a sickly paleness, as after a long illness (*wan and thin*); the suggestion of weakness may be more prominent than that of lack of colour: *a wan smile.* —**Ant. 1.** rosy, ruddy.

pale[2] (pāl), *n., v.,* **paled, paling.** —*n.* **1.** a stake or picket, as of a fence. **2.** any enclosing or confining barrier. **3.** limits or bounds: *outside the pale of the Church.* **4.** the area enclosed by a paling; any enclosed area. **5.** a district or region within fixed bounds. **6.** (*cap.*) Also, **English Pale** or **Irish Pale.** a district in E Ireland included in the Angevin Empire of King Henry II and his successors. **7.** *Her.* a broad vertical stripe in the middle of an escutcheon and one third its width. **8. beyond the pale,** socially or morally unacceptable. —*v.t.* **9.** to enclose with pales; fence. **10.** to encircle. [ME, t. F: m. *pal,* t. L: s. *pālus* stake]

pale-, *Chiefly U.S.* var. of **palae-.** Also, before consonants, **paleo-.** For words beginning with **pale-,** look under the more common British spelling in **palae-.**

palea (pā′lĭ ə), *n., pl.* **-leae** (-lĭ ē′). *Bot.* **1.** a chafflike scale or bract. **2.** the scalelike, membranous organ in the flowers of grasses which is situated upon a secondary axis in the axil of the flowering glume and envelops the stamens and pistil. [t. L: chaff] —**paleaceous** (pā′lĭ ā′shəs), *adj.*

pale ale, light ale.

paleface (pāl′fās′), *n.* a white person (an expression attributed to the American Indians).

Palembang (*Indon.* pȧ lĕm′bȧng), *n.* a city in Indonesia, in SE Sumatra. 474,971 (1961).

Palenque (*Sp.* pȧ lĕn′kĕ), *n.* the ruins of an ancient Mayan city in SE Mexico.

Palermo (pə lû′mō; *It.* pȧ lĕr′mȯ), *n.* a seaport in and the capital of Sicily, in the NW part. 641,838 (1966).

Palestine (păl′ĭ stīn′), *n.* **1.** Also, **Holy Land,** biblical name, **Canaan.** an ancient country in SW Asia, on the E coast of the Mediterranean. **2.** a former British mandate comprising part of this country, now divided between the state of Israel and part of the state of Jordan (**Arab Palestine**). —**Palestinian** (păl′ĭ stĭn′ĭ ən), *adj.*

palestra (pə lĕs′trə, pə lēs′trə), *n., pl.* **-tras, -trae** (-trē). *Gk Antiq.* palaestra.

Palestrina (păl′ĕs trē′nə; *It.* pä lĕs trē′nä), *n.* **Giovanni Pierluigi da** (*It.* jō vän′nē pyĕr lwē′jē dä), 1526?–94, Italian composer of church music.

paletot (păl′tō), *n.* a loose outer garment or coat. [t. F; OF *paltoc*, of uncert. orig.]

palette (păl′ĭt), *n.* **1.** a thin, usually oval or oblong, board or tablet with a thumb hole at one end, used by painters to lay and mix colours on. **2.** the range of colours used by a particular artist. **3.** Also, **pallette.** *Armour.* a small armpit plate. [t. F: palette, flat-bladed implement, ult. der. L *pāla* spade, shovel]

palette knife, a thin, flexible blade set in a handle, used for mixing painters' colours, etc.

palewise (pāl′wīz′), *adv. Her.* in the manner or direction of a pale² (def. 7).

Paley (pā′lĭ), *n.* **William,** 1743–1805, English theologian, philosopher, and clergyman.

palfrey (pôl′frĭ), *n., pl.* **-freys.** *Archaic.* **1.** a riding horse, as distinguished from a warhorse. **2.** a woman's saddle horse. [ME *palefrai*, t. OF: m. *palefrei*, g. LL *paraverēdus*, f. Gk *pará* beside + L *verēdus* light horse, of Celtic orig.]

Palgrave (pôl′grāv′, păl′-), *n.* **Francis Turner,** 1824–97, English critic, poet, and anthologist.

Pali (pä′lĭ), *n.* the Prakrit language of the Buddhist scriptures. [t. Skt: short for *pāli-bhāsā*, lit., canon language]

palikar (păl′ĭ kä′), *n.* a Greek militiaman in the Graeco-Turkish war of 1821–28. Also, **pellekar.** [t. NGk: m. *palikári* lad, der. Gk *pállax* youth]

palimpsest (păl′ĭmp sĕst′), *n.* a parchment or the like from which writing has been partially or completely erased to make room for another text. [t. L: s. *palimpsestus*, t. Gk: m. *palimpsēstos* scraped again]

palindrome (păl′ĭn drōm′), *n.* a word, verse, etc., reading the same backwards as forwards, as *madam, I'm Adam.* [t. Gk: m. s. *palíndromos* running back]

paling (pā′lĭng), *n.* **1.** a fence of pales. **2.** a pale, as in a fence. **3.** pales collectively. **4.** the act of one who builds a fence with pales. [ME, f. PALE² + -ING¹]

palingenesis (păl′ĭn jĕn′ĭ sĭs), *n.* **1.** rebirth; regeneration. **2.** *Biol.* **a.** that development of an individual which reproduces the ancestral features (opposed to *cainogenesis*). **b.** *Obs.* the supposed generation of organisms from others preformed in the germ cells. **3.** baptism in the Christian faith. **4.** the doctrine of transmigration of souls. [f. Gk *pálin* back, again + -GENESIS]

palinode (păl′ĭ nōd′), *n.* **1.** a poem in which the poet retracts something said in a former poem. **2.** a recantation. [t. LL: m. s. *palinōdia*, t. Gk: m. *palinōidía*]

palisade (păl′ĭ sād′), *n., v.,* **-saded, -sading.** —*n.* **1.** a fence of pales or stakes set firmly in the ground, as for enclosure or defence. **2.** one of the pales or stakes, pointed at the top, set firmly in the ground in a close row with others, for defence. **3.** *Bot.* the layer of compact cylindrical cells situated immediately beneath the adaxial epidermis of dorsiventral leaves. **4.** (*pl.*) *U.S.* a line of lofty cliffs. —*v.t.* **5.** to furnish or fortify with a palisade. [t. F: m. *palissade*, der. *palisser* furnish with a paling, der. *palis* paling, der. L *pālus* PALE²]

palish (pā′lĭsh), *adj.* somewhat pale.

pall¹ (pôl), *n.* **1.** a cloth, often of velvet, for spreading over a coffin, bier, or tomb. **2.** something that covers, shrouds, or overspreads, esp. with darkness or gloom. **3.** *Eccles.* **a.** a pallium (vestment). **b.** *Archaic.* a cloth spread upon the altar, esp. a corporal. **c.** a linen cloth, or now usually a square piece of cardboard covered with linen, used to cover the chalice. **4.** *Her.* a bearing representing the front of a pallium (vestment), consisting of a Y-shaped form charged with crosses. **5.** *Obs.* a cloak. —*v.t.* **6.** to cover with or as with a pall. [ME; OE *pæll*, t. L: m. s. *pallium* cloak, covering]

pall² (pôl), *v.i.* **1.** to have a wearying effect (fol. by *on* or *upon*). **2.** to become insipid, distasteful, or wearisome. **3.** to become satiated or cloyed with something. —*v.t.* **4.** to satiate or cloy. **5.** to make vapid, insipid, or distasteful. [ME *palle(n)*; appar. aphetic var. of APPAL]

Palladian¹ (pə lā′dyən), *adj.* **1.** pertaining to, introduced by, or in the style of Andrea Palladio. —*n.* **2.** a follower or admirer of Andrea Palladio, esp. a member of Lord Burlington's circle in 18th-century England.

Palladian² (pə lā′dyən), *adj.* **1.** of or pertaining to the goddess Pallas. **2.** pertaining to wisdom, knowledge, or study.

Palladianism (pə lā′dyə nĭz′əm), *n.* an 18th-century style of English architecture, developed by Lord Burlington, derived from the works of the Renaissance architect, Andrea Palladio.

palladic (pə lăd′ĭk, -lā′dĭk), *adj. Chem.* of or containing palladium, esp. in the tetravalent state.

Palladio (*It.* päl lä′dyō), *n.* **Andrea** (*It.* än drĕ′ä), 1508–1580, Italian architect.

palladium (pə lā′dyəm), *n. Chem.* a rare metallic element of the platinum group, silver-white, ductile and malleable. It is harder than platinum and fuses more readily. *Symbol:* Pd; *at. wt:* 106·4; *at. no.:* 46; *sp. gr.:* 12 at 20°C. [t. NL; named (1803) after the asteroid PALLAS, then recently discovered]

Palladium (pə lā′dyəm), *n., pl.* **-dia** (-dyə). **1.** a statue of Pallas Athene, esp. one on the citadel of Troy on which the safety of the city was supposed to depend. **2.** (*usually l.c.*) anything believed to afford effectual protection or safety. [ME, t. L, t. Gk: m. *Palládion*]

palladous (pə lā′dəs, păl′ə dəs), *adj. Chem.* containing divalent palladium.

Pallas (păl′ăs), *n.* **1.** a name of Athena (often **Pallas Athene**). **2.** *Astron.* one of the asteroids. [t. L, t. Gk]

pallbearer (pôl′bĕə′rə), *n.* one of those who carry or attend the coffin at a funeral.

pallet¹ (păl′ĭt), *n.* **1.** a bed or mattress of straw. **2.** a small or poor bed. [ME *pailet*, t. OF, dim. of *paille* straw, g. L *palea* chaff]

pallet² (păl′ĭt), *n.* **1.** an implement consisting of a flat blade or plate with a handle, used for shaping by potters, etc. **2.** a flat board or metal plate used to support ceramic articles during drying. **3.** *Horol.* a lever with three projections, two of which intermittently lock and receive impulses from the escape wheel, and one which transmits these impulses to the balance. **4.** a lip or projection on a pawl, that engages with the teeth of a ratchet wheel. **5.** *Gilding.* an instrument used to take up the gold leaves from the pillow, and to apply and extend them. **6.** a movable platform on which goods are placed for storage or transportation, esp. one designed to be lifted by a fork-lift truck. **7.** a painter's palette. [t. F: m. *palette* PALETTE]

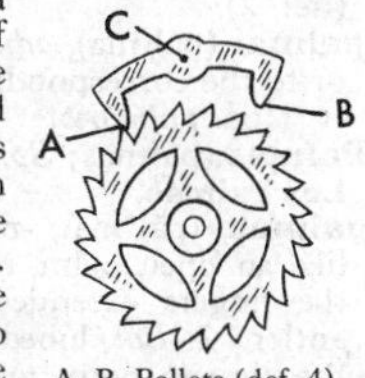

A, B, Pallets (def. 4)
C, Pivot on which pawl oscillates

pallet knife, a blunt, rounded, knifelike instrument, used for lifting cakes from the baking tray, mixing, etc.

pallette (păl′ĭt), *n. Armour.* palette.

palliasse (păl yăs′, păl′yăs), *n.* a mattress of straw or the like. Also, **paillasse.** [See PAILLASSE]

palliate (păl′ĭ āt′), *v.t.,* **-ated, -ating. 1.** to cause (an offence, etc.) to appear less grave or heinous; extenuate; excuse. **2.** to mitigate or alleviate: *to palliate a disease.* [t. L: m. s. *palliātus*, pp., covered with a cloak] —**pal′lia′tion,** *n.* —**pal′lia′tor,** *n.*

palliative (păl′ĭ ə tĭv), *adj.* **1.** serving to palliate. —*n.* **2.** something that palliates. —**pal′liatively,** *adv.*

pallid (păl′ĭd), *adj.* pale; deficient in colour; wan. [t. L: s. *pallidus*] —**pal′lidly,** *adv.* —**pal′lidness,** *n.* —**Syn.** See **pale.**

Palliser (păl′ĭ sə), *n.* **Cape,** a headland forming the most southerly point of North Island, New Zealand.

pallium (păl′ĭ əm), *n., pl.* **pallia** (păl′ĭ ə), **palliums. 1.** *Rom. Antiq.* a voluminous rectangular mantle worn by men, esp. by philosophers. **2.** *Eccles.* **a.** a woollen vestment worn by the pope and conferred by him as an honour on outstanding ecclesiastics, consisting, in its present form, of a narrow ringlike band, which rests upon the shoulders, with two dependent bands or lappets, one in front and one behind. **b.** an altar cloth; a pall. **3.** *Anat.* the entire cortex of the cerebrum. **4.** *Zool.* a mantle. [OE, t. L. See PALL¹]

Pall Mall (păl′măl′), a street in London, famous for its clubs. [See PALL-MALL (def. 2)]

pall-mall (păl′măl′), *n.* **1.** a game formerly played in which a ball of boxwood was struck with a mallet, the object being to drive it through a raised iron ring at the end of an alley. **2.** an alley in which this game was played. [t. F (obs.): m. *pallemaille*, t. It.: m. *pallamaglio* the game, f. *palla* ball (of Gmc orig.; akin to BALL¹) + *maglio* mallet, g. L *malleus* hammer]

pallor (păl′ə), *n.* unnatural paleness, as from fear, ill health, or death; wanness. [t. L]

palm¹ (päm), *n.* **1.** that part of the inner surface of the hand which extends from the wrist to the bases of the fingers. **2.** the corresponding part of the forefoot of an animal. **3.** the part of a glove covering the palm. **4.** a metal shield worn over the palm of the hand by sail-makers to serve instead of a thimble. **5.** a linear measure based on either the breadth of the hand (3 to 4 inches) or its length from wrist to fingertips (7 to 10 inches). **6.** the flat, expanded part of the horn or antler of some deer. **7.** a flat, widened part at the end of an armlike projection. **8.** the blade of an oar. **9.** *Naut.* the inner surface of an anchor fluke. **10. cross, grease,** or **oil someone's palm,** to bribe. —*v.t.* **11.** to conceal in the palm, as in cheating at cards or dice or in juggling. **12.** to touch or stroke with the palm or hand. **13.** *Obs.* to shake hands with. **14. palm off,** to impose (something) fraudulently (fol. by *on* or *upon*): *he tried to palm off the broken watch on me.* [t. L: s. *palma* palm, hand, blade of an oar; r. ME *paume*, t. OF, g. L]

palm[2] (päm), *n.* **1.** any of the plants constituting the large and important *Palmaceae* family, the majority of which are tall, unbranched trees surmounted by a crown of large pinnate or palmately cleft (fan-shaped) leaves. **2.** any of various other trees or shrubs which resemble the palm. **3.** a leaf or branch of a palm tree, esp. as formerly borne as an emblem of victory or as used on festal occasions. **4.** a representation of such a leaf or branch, as on a decoration of honour. **5.** the victor's reward of honour. **6.** victory; triumph. [ME and OE, t. L: s. *palma* palm tree, etymologically identical with PALM[1]] **—palm′-like′,** *adj.*

Palma (păl′mə; *Sp.* päl′mä), *n.* **1. Ricardo** (*Sp.* rē kär′dō), 1833–1919, Peruvian writer. **2.** a seaport in and the capital of the Balearic Islands, on W Majorca. 170,740 (1965).

palmaceous (păl mā′shəs), *adj.* belonging to the palm family of plants.

Palma de Mallorca (*Sp.* päl′mä dē mä lyôr′kä), Palma (def. 2).

palmar (păl′mə), *adj.* pertaining to the palm of the hand, or to the corresponding part of the forefoot of an animal. [t. L: s. *palmāris*]

Palmas (pä′məs; *Sp.* päl′mäs), *n.* **Las** (läs; *Sp.* läs). See **Las Palmas.**

palmate (păl′māt, -mĭt), *adj.* **1.** shaped like an open palm, or like a hand with the fingers extended, as a leaf or an antler. **2.** *Bot.* lobed or divided so that the sinuses point to or reach the apex of the petiole, somewhat irrespective of the number of lobes. **3.** *Zool.* web-footed. Also, **pal′mated.** [t. L: m. s. *palmātus*] **—pal′mately,** *adv.*

Palmate leaf

palmation (păl mā′shən), *n.* **1.** palmate state or formation. **2.** a palmate structure.

Palm Beach (päm), a town in the U.S., in SE Florida: seaside winter resort. 6055 (1960).

palm butter, palm oil in a solid state.

palm-cabbage (päm′kăb′ĭj), *n.* the bud of the cabbage palm.

palm civet, any of various viverrine animals of south-eastern Asia, the East Indies, etc., chiefly arboreal in habit, about the size of the domestic cat, and having a spotted or striped fur and a long curled tail. Also, **palm cat.**

palmer[1] (pä′mə), *n.* **1.** a pilgrim who had returned from the Holy Land, in token of which he bore a palm branch. **2.** any pilgrim. [ME *palmere*, der. PALM[2], translating AF *palmer*, ML *palmārius*, der. L *palma* PALM[2]]

palmer[2] (pä′mə), *n.* one who palms something, as in cheating at cards. [f. PALM[1] + -ER[1]]

Palmer (pä′mə), *n.* **Samuel,** 1805–81, English landscape painter.

Palmerston (pä′mə stən), *n.* **Henry John Temple, 3rd Viscount,** 1784–1865, British statesman: prime minister 1855–58 and 1859–65.

Palmerston North, a city on S North Island, New Zealand. 45,900 (est. 1965).

palmetto (păl mĕt′ō), *n.*, *pl.* **-tos, -toes.** any of various species of palm with fan-shaped leaves such as *Sabal*, *Serenoa*, *Thrinax*, and the only European palm, *Chamaerops.* [t. Sp.: m. *palmito*, dim. of *palma*, g. L *palma* PALM[2]]

palmiet (păl′mĭ ət), *n.* an aloe-like riverside plant, *Prionium palmita*, of the family *Juncaceae*, of southern Africa, having fibrous leaves used for thatching. [t. Afrikaans, t. D: palm-cabbage]

Palmira (*Sp.* päl mē′rä), *n.* a city in W Colombia. 148,510 (est. 1964).

palmistry (pä′mĭs trĭ), *n.* the art or practice of telling fortunes and interpreting character by the lines and configurations of the palm of the hand. [ME *pawmestry*, *palmestrie*, appar. der. *palmester* chiromancer, f. *palme* PALM[1] + -STER] **—palmist** (pä′mĭst), *n.*

palmitate (păl′mĭ tāt′), *n.* *Chem.* a salt or ester of palmitic acid.

palmitic acid (păl mĭt′ĭk), *Chem.* a white crystalline acid, $C_{15}H_{31}COOH$, occurring as a glyceride in palm oil and in most solid fats.

palmitin (păl′mĭ tĭn), *n.* *Chem.* a colourless fatty substance, $(C_{15}H_{13}COO)_3C_3H_5$, the glyceride of palmitic acid, occurring in palm oil and solid fats, and used in soap manufacture. Also, **tripalmitin.** [t. F: m. *palmitine*, der. L *palma* PALM[2]]

palm oil, 1. a yellow, butter-like oil from the fruit of *Elaeis guineensis*, of western Africa, used by the natives as food and employed also for making soap, candles, etc. **2.** oil obtained from various species of palm. **3.** bribery or a bribe.

palm sugar, sugar from the sap of certain palm trees.

Palm Sunday, the Sunday before Easter, celebrated in commemoration of Christ's triumphal entry into Jerusalem.

palmy (pä′mĭ), *adj.*, **-mier, -miest. 1.** glorious, prosperous, or flourishing. **2.** abounding in or shaded with palms: *palmy islands.* **3.** palmlike.

palmyra (păl mī′ə rə), *n.* a tropical Asian fan palm, *Borassus flabellifer.* Also, **palmyra palm.** [t. Pg.: m. *palmeira*, der. L *palma* PALM[2]]

Palmyra (păl mī′ə rə), *n.* an ancient city in Syria, NE of Damascus: reputedly built by Solomon. Biblical name, **Tadmor.**

palolo worm (pə lō′lō), a marine, polychaete, annelid worm of the southern Pacific, *Leodice viridis*, remarkable for the constancy with which it breeds, breaking off the posterior part of the body in the process, on the day of the last quarter of the October–November moon. [*palolo* t. Samoan or Tongan]

Palomar (păl′ə mä′, păl′ə mä′), *n.* **Mount,** the site of an observatory in California, containing a very large optical telescope with a 200-inch reflector.

palomino (păl′ə mē′nō), *n.*, *pl.* **-nos.** a tan or cream-coloured horse, bred chiefly in the SW United States. Also, **palamino.** [t. Sp.]

palooka (pə lo͞o′kə), *n.* *U.S. Slang.* a stupid or clumsy boxer, etc.

Palos (*Sp.* pä′lōs), *n.* a seaport in SW Spain: starting point of Columbus's first voyage westwards. 2280 (1950).

palp (pălp), *n.* **1.** a palpus. —*v.t.* **2.** *Obs.* to touch or feel gently; palpate. [t. F: m. *palpe*, t. L: m. *palpus* a feeler]

palpable (păl′pə bl), *adj.* **1.** readily or plainly seen, heard, perceived, etc.; obvious: *a palpable lie.* **2.** that can be touched or felt; tangible. **3.** *Med.* perceptible by palpation. [ME, t. LL: m. s. *palpābilis*, der. L *palpāre* touch] **—pal′pabil′ity,** *n.* **—pal′pably,** *adv.*

palpate[1] (păl′pāt), *v.t.*, **-pated, -pating.** to examine by the sense of touch, esp. in medicine. [t. L: m. s. *palpātus*, pp., touched, stroked] **—palpa′tion,** *n.*

palpate[2] (păl′pāt), *adj.* *Zool.* having a palpus or palpi. [f. s. L *palpus* a feeler + -ATE[1]]

palpebral (păl′pĭ brəl), *adj.* of or pertaining to the eyelids. [t. LL: s. *palpebrālis*]

palpebrate (păl′pĭ brĭt, -brāt′), *adj.* having eyelids.

palpi (păl′pī), *n.* pl. of **palpus.**

palpitant (păl′pĭ tənt), *adj.* palpitating. [t. L: s. *palpitans*, ppr.]

palpitate (păl′pĭ tāt′), *v.i.*, **-tated, -tating. 1.** to pulsate with unnatural rapidity, as the heart, from exertion, emotion, disease, etc. **2.** to quiver or tremble. [t. L: m. s. *palpitātus*, pp., moved quickly] **—Syn. 1.** See **pulsate.**

palpitation (păl′pĭ tā′shən), *n.* **1.** an act of palpitating. **2.** rapid or violent beating of the heart.

palpus (păl′pəs), *n.*, *pl.* **-pi** (-pī). *Zool.* an appendage attached to an oral part, and serving as an organ of sense, in insects, crustaceans, etc. See diag. under **insect.** [t. NL, t. L: a feeler]

palsgrave (pôlz′grāv′), *n.* a German count palatine. [t. D: m. *paltsgrave* (now *paltsgraaf*), c. G *Pfalzgraf* palace count]

palsgravine (pôlz′grə vēn′), *n.* the wife or widow of a palsgrave.

palstave (pôl′stāv′), *n.* *Archaeol.* a bronze axe fitted into a split wooden handle. [t. Dan.: m. *paalstav*, c. Icel. *pálstafr.* See PALE[2], STAVE]

palsy (pôl′zĭ), *n.*, *pl.* **-sies,** *v.*, **-sied, -sying.** —*n.* **1.** paralysis. —*v.t.* **2.** to paralyse. [ME *parlesie*, t. OF: m. *paralisie*, g. L *paralysis* PARALYSIS] **—pal′sied,** *adj.*

palter (pôl′tə), *v.i.* **1.** to talk or act insincerely; equivocate; deal crookedly. **2.** to haggle. **3.** to trifle. [cf. obs. *palter* mumble, shuffle, b. PALSY and FALTER]

paltry (pôl′trĭ), *adj.*, **-trier, -triest. 1.** trifling; petty: *a paltry sum.* **2.** trashy or worthless: *paltry rags.* **3.** mean or contemptible: *a paltry coward.* [appar. der. d. *palt* rubbish. Cf. LG *paltrig*] **—pal′trily,** *adv.* **—pal′triness,** *n.* **—Syn. 1.** See **petty.**

paludal (pə lyo͞o′dl, păl′yo͝o dl), *adj.* **1.** of or pertaining to marshes. **2.** produced by marshes, as miasma or disease. [f. s. L *palus* marsh + -AL[1]]

paludism (păl′yo͝o dĭz′əm), *n.* *Pathol.* malarial disease.

paly[1] (pā′lĭ), *adj.* *Archaic.* pale. [f. PALE[1] + -Y[1]]

paly[2] (pā′lĭ), *adj.* *Her.* divided palewise, or vertically, into equal parts of alternating tinctures. [t. F: m. *palé*, der. *pal* PALE[2] (see def. 7)]

palynology (păl′ĭ nŏl′ə jĭ), *n.* the study of fossil pollen in peat deposits, the stratification of which provides information about past changes in the land flora. [f. Gk *palýn(ein)* to scatter (akin to *pálē* dust) + -o- + -LOGY] —**palynological** (păl′ĭ nə lŏj′ĭ kl), *adj.* —**pal′ynolog′ically,** *adv.* —**pal′ynol′ogist,** *n.*

pam (păm), *n. Cards.* **1.** the knave of clubs, esp. in a form of loo in which it is the best trump. **2.** the game. [for F *pamphile,* orig. proper name, t. Gk: m. *Pámphilos,* lit., beloved of all]

pam., pamphlet.

Pamirs (pə mĭəz′), *n.pl.* **the,** a lofty plateau in central Asia, where the Hindu Kush, Tien Shan, and Himalayan mountain systems converge. Highest peaks, ab. 25,000 ft. Also, **Pamir.**

pampas (păm′pəz; *Sp.* päm′päs), *n.pl.* the vast grassy plains lying in the rain shadow of the Andes and south of the forested lowlands of the Amazon basin, esp. in Argentina. ab. 400 mi. across. [t. Sp., pl. of *pampa,* t. Quechua] —**pampean** (păm pĭən′, păm′pĭ ən), *adj.*

pampas grass (păm′pəs), any of several species of large, perennial South American grasses of the genus *Cortaderia,* esp. *C. argentea,* which has large feathery inflorescences and is frequently cultivated.

Pampeluna (păm′pĭ lo͞o′nə), *n.* Pamplona.

pamper (păm′pə), *v.t.* **1.** to indulge (a person, etc.) to the full or to excess: *to pamper a child, one's appetite, etc.* **2.** to indulge with rich food, comforts, etc. [ME *pampren.* Cf. Flem. *pamperen,* G *pampen* cram] —**pam′perer,** *n.* —**Syn. 1.** gratify, humour, coddle.

pampero (păm pēə′rō), *n., pl.* **-ros** (-rōz). a cold and dry south-westerly wind that sweeps over the pampas of Argentina and north-eastwards to the Brazilian coast, in the rear of barometric depression. [t. Sp.]

pamph., pamphlet.

pamphlet (păm′flĭt), *n.* **1.** a short treatise or essay, generally controversial, on some subject of temporary interest: *a political pamphlet.* **2.** a complete publication generally less than 80 pages, stitched or stapled and usually enclosed in paper covers. [ME *pamflet,* syncopated var. of *Pamphilet,* popular name for ML poem formally entitled '*Pamphilus, seu dē Amōre*']

pamphleteer (păm′flĭ tĭə′), *n.* **1.** a writer of pamphlets. —*v.i.* **2.** to write and issue pamphlets.

Pamphylia (păm fĭl′ĭ ə), *n.* an ancient country and Roman province in S Asia Minor.

Pamplona (păm plō′nə; *Sp.* päm plô′nä), *n.* a city in N Spain. 115,044 (1965). Also, **Pampeluna.**

pan¹ (păn), *n., v.,* **panned, panning.** —*n.* **1.** a dish commonly of metal, usually broad, shallow and open, used for domestic purposes: *a frying pan.* **2.** any dishlike receptacle or part, as the scales of a balance. **3.** any of various open or closed vessels used in industrial or mechanical processes. **4.** a vessel, usually of cast iron, in which the ores of silver are ground and amalgamated. **5.** a vessel in which gold or other heavy, valuable metals are separated from gravel, etc., by agitation with water. **6.** a depression in the ground, as a natural one containing water, mud, or mineral salts, or an artificial one for evaporating salt water to make salt. **7.** hardpan. **8.** (in old guns) the depressed part of the lock, which holds the priming. **9.** brainpan; the skull or cranium. **10.** kneepan; the patella. **11.** *Slang.* the face. —*v.t.* **12.** to wash (auriferous gravel, sand, etc.) in a pan to separate the gold or other heavy valuable metal. **13.** to separate by such washing. **14.** *U.S.* to cook (oysters, etc.) in a pan. **15.** *Colloq.* to criticize or reprimand severely. —*v.i.* **16.** to wash gravel, etc., in a pan, seeking for gold. **17.** to yield gold, as gravel washed in a pan. **18. pan out,** *Colloq.* to succeed; turn out well. [ME and OE *panne,* c. G *Pfanne*]

pan² (pän), *n.* **1.** the leaf of the betel. **2.** the masticatory of which the betel leaf comprises the wrapper. [t. Hind., g. Skt *parna* feather, leaf]

pan³ (păn), *v.,* **panned, panning.** *Films, Television, etc.* —*v.i.* **1.** (of a camera) to move continuously while shooting in order to record on film a panorama, or to keep a moving person or object in view. **2.** to operate a camera in such a manner. —*v.t.* **3.** to operate (a camera) in such a manner. [shortened form of PANORAMA]

Pan (păn), *n. Gk Myth.* the god of forests, pastures, flocks, and shepherds, represented with the head, chest, and arms of a man, and the legs and sometimes the horns and ears of a goat.

pan-, a word element or prefix meaning 'all', first occurring in words from the Greek, but now used freely as a general formative in English and other languages, esp. in terms implying the union, association, or consideration together, as forming a whole, of all the branches of a race, people, church, or other body, as in *pan-Anglo-Saxon, pan-Celtic, pan-Christian,* and other like words of obvious meaning, formed at will, and tending with longer use to lose the hyphen and the capital, unless these are retained in order to set off clearly the component elements. [t. Gk, comb. form of *pâs* (neut. *pân*)]

Pan., Panama.

panacea (păn′ə sĭə′), *n.* a remedy for all diseases; cure-all. [t. L, t. Gk: m. *panákeia*] —**pan′acean′,** *adj.*

panache (pə năsh′), *n.* **1.** a grand or flamboyant manner; swagger; verve. **2.** an ornamental plume or tuft of feathers, esp. one worn on a helmet or on a cap. [t. F, t. It.: m. *pennacchio,* der. *penna,* g. L: feather]

panada (pə nä′də), *n.* a dish made of bread boiled and flavoured. [t. Sp., Pr., ult. der. L *pānis* bread]

pan-African (păn′ăf′rĭ kən), *adj.* **1.** of or pertaining to all the countries or peoples of Africa. —*n.* **2.** a believer in pan-Africanism. **3.** a member of the Pan-African Congress.

Pan-African Congress, a political movement in various countries of Africa replaced in 1963 by the Organization of African Unity.

pan-Africanism (păn′ăf′rĭ kə nĭz′əm), *n.* advocacy of a political alliance or union of all the countries of Africa.

Panama (păn′ə mä′; *Sp.* pä nä mä′), *n.* **1.** a republic in S Central America, enclosing, but not including, the Panama Canal. 1,075,541 pop. (1960); 28,575 sq. mi. **2.** Also, **Panama City.** the capital of Panama, at the Pacific end of the Panama Canal, though not in the Canal Zone. 306,000 (est. 1963). **3. Isthmus of.** Formerly, **Isthmus of Darien.** an isthmus between North and South America. Least width, ab. 30 mi. **4. Gulf of,** the portion of the Pacific in the bend of the Isthmus of Panama. **5.** (*l.c.*) Panama hat. —**Panamanian** (păn′ə mā′nyən), *adj., n.*

Panama Canal

Panama Canal, a canal extending SE from the Atlantic to the Pacific across the Isthmus of Panama. 40 mi. long.

Panama Canal Zone, Canal Zone.

Panama hat, (*sometimes l.c.*) a fine plaited hat made of the young leaves of a palmlike plant, *Carludovica palmata,* of Central and South America. [named after PANAMA]

pan-American (păn′ə mĕ′rĭ kən), *adj.* of or pertaining to all the countries or peoples of North, Central, and South America.

pan-Americanism (păn′ə mĕ′rĭ kə nĭz′əm), *n.* the idea or advocacy of a political alliance or union of all the countries of North, Central, and South America.

Pan American Union, an organization of the 21 American republics to further understanding and peace.

pan-Arabism (păn′ă′rə bĭz′əm), *n.* the idea or advocacy of a political alliance or union of all Arab states. —**pan′-A′rab,** *n., adj.*

panatella (păn′ə tĕl′ə), *n.* a long, slender cigar, usually tapering to a point. Also, **panetella.** [t. Mex. Sp.: lit., a kind of long, thin biscuit]

Panay (pä nī′; *Sp.* pä näy′), *n.* one of the Philippine Islands, in the central part of the group. 1,813,000 pop. (est. 1965); 4446 sq. mi. *Cap.:* Iloilo. See map under **Leyte.**

pancake (păn′kāk′), *n., v.,* **-caked, -caking.** —*n.* **1.** a thin flat cake of eggs, flour, sugar, and milk, fried in a pan. **2.** make-up compressed into stick form for easy application. **3.** an aeroplane landing made by pancaking. —*v.i.* **4.** (of an aeroplane, etc.) to drop flat to the ground after levelling off a few feet above it. —*v.t.* **5.** to cause (an aeroplane) to pancake.

Pancake Day, Shrove Tuesday, on which pancakes were and are traditionally eaten as the last eggs before Lent.

pancake ice, small, thin slabs of ice which form on the surface of the sea in polar regions when it begins to freeze.

panchromatic (păn′krō măt′ĭk), *adj.* sensitive to light of all colours, as a photographic film or plate. —**panchro′matism,** *n.*

pancratium (păn krā′shyəm), *n., pl.* **-tia** (-shyə). *Gk Antiq.* an athletic contest combining wrestling and boxing. [t. L, t. Gk: m. *pankrátion* complete contest] —**pancratic** (păn krăt′ĭk), *adj.*

pancreas (păng′krĭ əs), *n. Anat., Zool.* a gland situated near the stomach, secreting an important digestive fluid (**pancreatic juice**), discharged into the intestine by one or more ducts. Certain groups of cells (**islets of Langerhans**) also produce a hormone, insulin. See diag. under **stomach.** [t. NL, t. Gk: m. *pánkreas* sweetbread] —**pancreatic** (păng′krĭ ăt′ĭk), *adj.*

pancreatin (păngʹkrĭ ə tĭn), *n.* **1.** *Biochem.* a preparation containing all the enzymes of the pancreatic juice. **2.** a commercial preparation of the enzymes in the pancreas of animals, used as a digestive.

Giant panda, *Ailuropoda melanoleuca* (5 ft long, 2 ft high at the shoulder)

panda (pănʹdə), *n.* either of two mammals of the genus *Carnivora*, largely herbivorous in diet: **1.** the cat-sized **lesser panda,** *Ailurus fulgens*, of the Himalayas, which has reddish brown fur. **2.** the bearlike **giant panda,** *Ailuropoda melanoleuca*, of central China, which is boldly marked in black and white. [said to be the name for the lesser panda current in Nepal]

pandanaceous (pănʹdə nāʹshəs), *adj.* belonging to the *Pandanaceae*, or pandanus family of trees and shrubs.

pandanus (păn dāʹnəs), *n.* any plant of the genus *Pandanus*, comprising tropical trees and shrubs, esp. of the islands of the Malay Archipelago and the Indian and Pacific oceans, having a palmlike or branched stem, long, narrow, rigid, spirally arranged leaves, and aerial roots, and bearing edible fruit; a screw-pine. [t. NL, t. Malay: m. *pandan*]

Pandarus (pănʹdə rəs), *n.* *Gk Legend.* a leader of the Lycians and an ally of the Trojans in the siege of Troy. In Chaucer, other medieval accounts, and Shakespeare, he is represented as the procurer of Cressida for Troilus.

Pandean (păn dēʹən), *adj.* of or pertaining to the god Pan: *Pandean pipes.*

pandect (pănʹdĕkt), *n.* **1.** (*pl.*) a complete body or code of laws. **2.** a comprehensive digest. **3. Pandects.** *Rom. Law.* the Digest. [t. L: s. *pandecta, pandectēs*, t. Gk: m. *pandéktēs*, lit., all-receiver]

pandemic (păn dĕmʹĭk), *adj.* **1.** (of a disease) prevalent throughout an entire country or continent, or the whole world. **2.** general; universal. —*n.* **3.** a pandemic disease. [f. s. Gk *pandēmos* public, common + -IC]

pandemonium (pănʹdĭ mōʹnyəm), *n.* **1.** (*often cap.*) the abode of all the demons. **2.** hell. **3.** a place of riotous uproar or lawless confusion. **4.** wild lawlessness or uproar. [orig. *Pandaemonium*, Milton's name for the capital of hell. See PAN-, DEMON, -IUM] —**pandemoniac** (pănʹdĭ mōʹnĭ ăkʹ), **pandemonic** (pănʹdĭ mŏnʹĭk), *adj.*

pander (pănʹdə), *n.* **1.** a go-between in intrigues of love. **2.** a procurer; pimp. **3.** one who ministers to the weaknesses or baser passions of others. —*v.t.* **4.** to act as a pander for. —*v.i.* **5.** to act as a pander; cater basely. [var. of *pandar*, generalized use of ME *Pandare* PANDARUS]

pandit (pŭnʹdĭt), *n.* (in India) a learned man; a scholar (used as a title of respect). Cf. **pundit.** [t. Hind., g. Skt *pandita* learned]

P. and L., profit and loss.

P. & O., Peninsular and Oriental (Steam Navigation Company).

pandora (păn dôʹrə), *n.* bandore. Also, **pandore** (păn dôʹ, pănʹdô).

Pandora (păn dôʹrə), *n.* *Class. Myth.* the first mortal woman, on whom all the gods and goddesses bestowed gifts. She was given by Zeus to Epimetheus to bring misery to mankind because Prometheus had stolen fire from heaven. [t. L, t. Gk: lit., all-gifted]

Pandora's box, **1.** *Class. Myth.* a box or jar, the gift of Zeus to Pandora, containing all human ills, which escaped when she opened it. According to a later version, the box contained all the blessings of the gods, which would have been preserved for the human race had not Pandora opened it, thus letting all the blessings escape, with the exception of hope. **2.** any source of extensive troubles, esp. one expected at first to yield blessings.

pandour (pănʹdŏŏə), *n.* **1.** one of a force of merciless soldiers raised in the 18th century in Croatia, later made a regiment in the Austrian army. **2.** a brutal, marauding soldier. [t. F, t. Serbo-Croat: m. *pandur* guard]

Pandurate leaf

pandurate (pănʹdyŏŏ rātʹ, -rĭt), *adj.* shaped like a fiddle, as a leaf. Also, **panduriform** (păn dyŏŏəʹrĭ fômʹ). [f. s. LL *pandura* (see BANDORE) + -ATE¹]

pandy (pănʹdĭ), *n.*, *pl.* **-dies,** *v.*, **-died, -dying.** *Chiefly Scot.* —*n.* **1.** a stroke on the palm with a cane or strap as a punishment in schools. —*v.t.* **2.** to strike thus. [said to be t. L: m. *pande*, impv., stretch out]

pane (pān), *n.* **1.** one of the divisions of a window, etc., consisting of a single plate of glass in a frame. **2.** a plate of glass for such a division. **3.** a panel, as of a wainscot, ceiling, door, etc. **4.** a flat section, side, or surface, as one of the sides of a bolthead. [ME *pan*, t. OF, g. L *pannus* a cloth, rag]

paned (pānd), *adj.* having panes: *a diamond-paned window.*

panegyric (pănʹĭ jĭʹrĭk), *n.* **1.** an oration, discourse, or writing in praise of a person or thing; a eulogy. **2.** a formal or elaborate encomium. [t. L: s. *panēgyricus*, t. Gk: m. *panēgyrikós* festival oration, prop. adj.] —**panʹegyrʹical,** *adj.* —**panʹegyrʹically,** *adv.*

panegyrist (pănʹĭ jĭʹrĭst), *n.* one who panegyrizes.

panegyrize (pănʹĭ jĭ rīzʹ), *v.*, **-rized, -rizing.** —*v.t.* **1.** to pronounce or write a panegyric upon; eulogize. —*v.i.* **2.** to indulge in panegyric; bestow praises. Also, **panegyrise.**

panel (pănʹəl), *n.*, *v.*, **-elled, -elling** or (*U.S.*) **-eled, -eling.** —*n.* **1.** a distinct portion or division of a wainscot, ceiling, door, shutter, etc., or of any surface sunk below or raised above the general level, or enclosed by a frame or border. **2.** a pane, as in a window. **3.** a comparatively thin, flat piece of wood or the like. **4.** *Painting.* **a.** a flat piece of wood of varying kinds on which a picture is painted. **b.** a picture painted on such a piece of wood. **5.** a photograph much longer in one dimension than the other. **6.** a broad strip of the same or another material set vertically, as for ornament, in or on a woman's dress, etc. **7.** the section between two bands on the spine of a bound book. **8.** *Elect.* a division of a switchboard containing a set of related cords, jacks, relays, etc. **9.** the portion of a truss between adjacent chord joints. **10.** a surface or section of a machine on which controls, dials, etc., are mounted: *the instrument panel of a car.* **11.** *Law.* **a.** the list of persons summoned for service as jurors. **b.** the body of persons composing a jury. **c.** *Scot. Law.* the person or persons indicted and brought to trial. **12.** any list or group of persons, as one gathered to answer questions, discuss issues, etc. **13.** (in Britain) **a.** a list of patients who under the National Health Service may obtain treatment from a doctor. **b.** a list of doctors in a particular area whom a patient may consult under the National Health Service. **14.** *Aeron.* a subdivision of the surface of an aerofoil or fuselage. **15.** *Mining.* an area of a coal seam, separated for mining purposes from adjacent areas by extra-thick masses or ribs of coal. **16.** the cushion or pad in a saddle separating the framework from the horse's back. See illus. under **saddle.** **17.** *Obs.* a pad or the like serving as a saddle. **18.** a slip of parchment. —*v.t.* **19.** to arrange in, or furnish with, panels. **20.** to ornament with a panel or panels. **21.** to set in a frame as a panel. **22.** to empanel. **23.** *Scot. Law.* to bring to trial. [ME *panel*, t. OF: piece (of anything), ult. der. L *pannus* rag]

panel game, a quiz or the like, as on television, in which selected speakers make guesses, answer questions, etc., for public entertainment.

panel heating, a type of heating in which the heat is diffused through panels in walls, ceilings, etc.

panel lighting, a type of lighting in which the light is diffused through translucent panels.

panelling (pănʹə lĭng), *n.* **1.** wood or other material made into panels. **2.** panels collectively. Also, *U.S.* **paneling.**

panellist (pănʹə lĭst), *n.* a member of a small group organized for public discussion, etc., as on television. Also, *U.S.*, **panelist.**

panel pin, a short, slender nail used in joinery.

panetella (pănʹĭ tĕlʹə), *n.* a panatella.

pang (păng), *n.* **1.** a sudden feeling of mental distress. **2.** a sudden, brief, sharp pain, or a spasm or severe twinge of pain: *the pangs of hunger.* [orig. uncert.]

panga (păngʹgə), *n.* a broad, heavy African knife used as a tool and as a weapon; machete. [t. Swahili]

pangenesis (păn jĕnʹĭ sĭs), *n.* *Biol.* a theory advanced by Darwin, according to which a reproductive cell or body contains gemmules or invisible germs which were derived from the individual cells from every part of the organism, and which are the bearers of hereditary attributes. —**pangenetic** (pănʹjĭ nĕtʹĭk), *adj.*

pan-Germanism (pănʹjûʹmə nĭzʹəm), *n.* the idea or advocacy of a union of all the German peoples in one political organization or state. —**panʹ-Gerʹman,** *adj.*, *n.* —**pan-Germanic** (pănʹjû mănʹĭk), *adj.*

Common pangolin, *Manis pterodactyla* (3 ft long)

pangolin (păng-gōʹlĭn), *n.* any of the scaly anteaters of Africa and tropical Asia, constituting an order of mammals, *Pholidota*, having a covering of broad, overlapping, horny scales. [t. Malay: m. *penggōling* roller]

Pangpu (păng′pōō′), *n.* a city in Anhwei province, in E China. 330,000 (est. 1958).

panhandle[1] (păn′hăn′dl), *n.* **1.** the handle of a pan. **2.** *U.S.* (*sometimes cap.*) a narrow projecting strip of land, esp. part of a state: *the Panhandle of Texas, Alaska, Idaho, etc.*

panhandle[2] (păn′hăn′dl), *v.i.*, **-dled, -dling.** *U.S. Colloq.* to beg (usually in the street). **—pan′han′dler,** *n.*

panhellenic (păn′hĕ lē′nĭk), *adj.* **1.** pertaining to all Greeks or to panhellenism. **2.** *U.S.* of or pertaining to collegiate fraternities and sororities.

panhellenism (păn′hĕl′ĭ nĭz′əm), *n.* the idea or principle of a union of all Greeks in one political body. **—pan′hel′lenist,** *n.* **—pan′hel′lenistic,** *adj.*

panic[1] (păn′ĭk), *n., adj., v.,* **-icked, -icking.** **—***n.* **1.** a sudden demoralizing terror, with or without clear cause, often as affecting a group of persons or animals. **2.** an instance, outbreak, or period of such fear. **3.** *Finance.* a sudden widespread fear concerning financial affairs leading to credit contraction and widespread sale of securities at depressed prices in an effort to acquire cash. **—***adj.* **4.** (of fear, terror, etc.) suddenly destroying the self-control and impelling to some frantic action. **5.** of the nature of, due to, or showing panic: *panic haste.* **6.** (*cap.*) of or pertaining to the god Pan. **—***v.t.* **7.** to affect with panic. **—***v.i.* **8.** to be stricken with panic. [t. F: m. *panique,* t. L: m. *pānicus,* t. Gk: m. *Pānikós* pertaining to or caused by Pan] **—pan′icky,** *adj.* **—panic-stricken** (păn′ĭk strĭk′ən), **panic-struck** (păn′ĭk strŭk′), *adj.* **—Syn. 1.** See **terror.**

panic[2] (păn′ĭk), *n.* **1.** any grass of the genus *Panicum,* many species of which bear edible grain. **2.** the grain. Also, **panic grass.** [OE, t. L: s. *pānicum*]

panic bolt, a bolt on emergency exits, etc., opened by pressure from inside on a horizontal bar.

panicle (păn′ĭ kl), *n. Bot.* **1.** a compound raceme. **2.** any loose, diversely branching flower cluster. [t. L: m. s. *pānicula* tuft on plants, dim. of *pānus* swelling, ear of millet] **—pan′icled,** *adj.*

paniculate (pə nĭk′yŏŏ lāt′, -lĭt), *adj. Bot.* arranged in panicles. **—panic′ulately,** *adv.*

pan-Islamism (păn′ĭz′lə mĭz′əm), *n.* the idea or advocacy of a union of all Muslim nations in one political body. **—pan-Islam** (păn′ĭz′läm), *n.* **—pan-Islamic** (păn′ĭz lăm′ĭk), *adj.*

Branch with panicles

Panjabi (pŭn jä′bĭ), *n., pl.* **-bis.** Punjabi.

panjandrum (păn jăn′drəm), *n.* a mock title for any important or pretentious official. [a made-up word, with prefix PAN- and termination simulating Latin; appar. first used by Samuel Foote, 1720–77, English dramatist and actor]

Pankhurst (păngk′hûst), *n.* **1. Christabel,** 1880–1958, (daughter of Emmeline) English suffragette. **2. Emmeline,** 1857–1928, English suffragette leader. **3. Sylvia,** 1882–1960, (daughter of Emmeline) English suffragette and pacifist.

panlogism (păn′lə jĭz′əm), *n. Philos.* the doctrine that all that is real is intelligible and ultimately of the nature of spirit. The term was coined by J. E. Erdmann to describe the philosophy of Hegel.

Panmunjon (păn′mŏŏn jŏn′), *n.* a small community along the boundary between North Korea and South Korea: site of the truce talks at the close of the Korean War.

panne (păn), *n.* a soft, lustrous, lightweight velvet with flattened pile. [t. F, g. L *penna* feather]

pannier (păn′ĭ ə), *n.* **1.** a basket, esp. one of considerable size, for carrying provisions, etc. **2.** a basket for carrying on a person's back, or one of a pair to be slung across the back of a beast of burden. **3.** one of a pair of bags slung either side of the rear wheel of a motorcycle, used as carriers. **4.** *Obs.* a puffed arrangement of drapery about the hips. **5.** *Obs.* a framework formerly used for distending the skirt of a woman's dress at the hips. [ME *panier,* t. OF, g. L *pānārium* basket for bread]

pannikin (păn′ĭ kĭn), *n.* a small pan or metal cup.

pannikin boss, *Austral. Colloq.* a small-time overseer.

Pannonia (pə nō′nyə), *n.* an ancient country and Roman province in central Europe, S and W of the Danube: now mostly in Hungary and Yugoslavia. **—Panno′nian,** *adj.*

panocha (pə nō′chə), *n.* **1.** Also, **panoche** (pə nō′chĭ). a coarse grade of sugar made in Mexico. **2.** *U.S.* a sweet made of brown sugar, butter, and milk, usually with nuts. [t. Mex. Sp.]

panoply (păn′ə plĭ), *n., pl.* **-plies. 1.** a complete suit of armour. **2.** a complete covering or array of something. [t. Gk: m. s. *panoplía* complete suit of armour] **—panoplied** (păn′ə plĭd), *adj.*

panoptic (păn ŏp′tĭk), *adj.* **1.** permitting the viewing of all parts or elements at once or from one standpoint. **2.** all-embracing; universal: *a panoptic criticism.* Also, **panop′tical. —panop′tically,** *adv.*

panopticon (pă nŏp′tĭ kŏn′, -kən), *n.* a prison or the like in which all parts of the interior are visible from one point. [coined by Jeremy Bentham; f. PAN- + m. Gk *optikón* (adj., neut.) of or pertaining to sight]

panorama (păn′ə rä′mə), *n.* **1.** an unobstructed view or prospect over a wide area. **2.** an extended pictorial representation of a landscape or other scene, often exhibited a part at a time and made to pass continuously before the spectators. **3.** a continuously passing or changing scene. **4.** a comprehensive survey, as of a subject. [f. PAN- + m. Gk *hórāma* view] **—panoramic** (păn′ə răm′ĭk), *adj.* **—pan′oram′ically,** *adv.*

panoramic sight, a sight for guns that can be swung in a complete circle.

panpipe (păn′pīp′), *n.* a primitive wind instrument consisting of a series of pipes of graduated length, the notes being produced by blowing across the upper ends. Also, **Pan's pipes.**

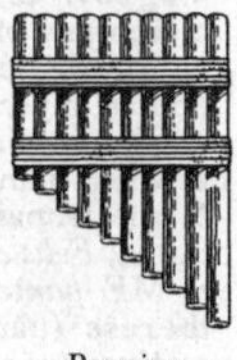

Panpipe

panplegia (păn plē′jĭ ə, -jə), *n. Pathol.* total paralysis.

panpsychism (păn′sī′kĭz′əm), *n. Philos.* the doctrine that there is an inner, psychic nature not only to human beings, animals and plants, but to all matter.

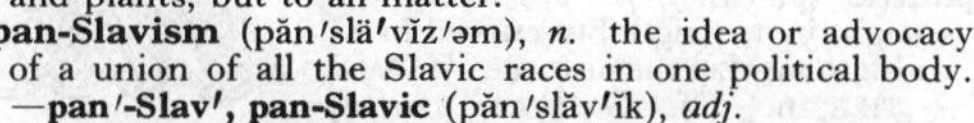

pan-Slavism (păn′slä′vĭz′əm), *n.* the idea or advocacy of a union of all the Slavic races in one political body. **—pan′-Slav′, pan-Slavic** (păn′slăv′ĭk), *adj.*

pansophism (păn′sə fĭz′əm), *n.* the claim or pretension to pansophy. **—pan′sophist,** *n.*

pansophy (păn′sə fĭ), *n.* universal wisdom or knowledge. [f. PAN- + m. s. Gk *sophía* wisdom] **—pansophic** (pănsŏf′ĭk), **pansoph′ical,** *adj.*

pansy (păn′zĭ), *n., pl.* **-sies. 1.** any of several species of herbaceous plants of the genus *Viola,* esp. the **wild pansy,** *V. tricolor,* and the **garden pansy,** *V.* x *wittrockiana,* a hybrid with many cultivated varieties. **2.** its blossom. **3.** *Slang.* **a.** an effeminate man. **b.** a male homosexual. [t. F: m. *pensée* pansy, lit., thought, der. *penser* think. See PENSIVE]

pant (pănt), *v.i.* **1.** to breathe hard and quickly, as after exertion. **2.** to emit steam or the like in loud puffs. **3.** to gasp, as for air. **4.** to long with breathless or intense eagerness: *he panted for revenge.* **5.** to throb or heave violently or rapidly; palpitate. **6.** (of a ship's hull) to vibrate when in heavy seas. **—***v.t.* **7.** to breathe or utter gaspingly. **—***n.* **8.** the act of panting. **9.** a short, quick, laboured effort of breathing; a gasp. **10.** a puff, as of an engine. **11.** a throb or heave, as of the breast. [ME *panten;* appar. akin to OF *pantaisier,* prob. (with ref. to the feeling of oppression in nightmare) ult. der. L *phantasia* phantasm, idea, FANTASY] **—pant′ingly,** *adv.*

—Syn. 1. PANT, GASP suggest breathing with more effort than usual. PANT suggests rapid, convulsive breathing, as from violent exertion or excitement: *to pant after a run for the train.* GASP suggests catching one's breath in a single quick intake, as from amazement, terror, and the like, or a series of such quick intakes of breath as in painful breathing: *to gasp with horror, to gasp for breath.*

Pantagruel (păn tăg′rŏŏ əl; *Fr.* päɴ tȧ gʀʏ ĕl′), *n.* (in Rabelais's *Gargantua and Pantagruel*) the huge son of Gargantua, represented as dealing with serious matters in a spirit of broad and somewhat cynical good humour. [t. F] **—Pantagruelian** (păn′tə grōō ĕl′ĭ ən), *adj.* **—Pantagruelism** (păn′tə grōō′ə lĭz′əm, păn tăg′rŏŏ ə lĭz′əm), *n.* **—Pan′tagru′elist,** *n.*

pantalets (păn′tə lĕts′), *n.pl.* **1.** long drawers with a frill or other finish at the bottom of each leg, and extending below the dress, commonly worn by women and girls in the 19th century. **2.** a pair of separate frilled or trimmed pieces for attaching to the legs of women's drawers. Also, **pan′talettes′.** [alter. of PANTALOON, with dim. -ET(TE) substituted for *-oon*]

pantaloon (păn′tə lōōn′), *n.* **1.** (*pl.*) *Obs.* a man's closely fitting garment for the hips and legs, varying in form at different periods; trousers. **2.** (*often cap.*) (in the modern pantomime) a foolish, vicious old man, the butt and accomplice of the clown. **3.** (*usually cap.*) (in the commedia dell'arte) a lean and foolish old Venetian wearing pantaloons and slippers. [t. F: m. *pantalon,* t. It.: m. *pantalone* buffoon (see def. 3), *Pantalone* a Venetian, from St *Pantaleone* patron of Venice]

pantechnicon (păn těk′nĭ kən), *n.* **1.** a furniture van. **2.** a storage warehouse, esp. for furniture. **3.** *Obs.* a bazaar for everything artistic. [f. PAN- + m. Gk *technikón* (neut. of *technikós* artistic)]

Pantelleria (păn′těl ə rĭə′; *It.* pän těl lĕ rē′ä), *n.* an Italian island in the Mediterranean between Sicily and Tunisia. 10,306 pop. (1951); 32 sq. mi.

pan-Teutonism (păn′tyōō′tə nĭz′əm), *n.* pan-Germanism.

pantheism (păn′thĭ ĭz′əm), *n.* **1.** the doctrine that God is the transcendent reality of which the material universe and man are only manifestations. It involves a denial of God's personality, and expresses a tendency to identify God and nature. Cf. **theism, deism. 2.** any religious belief or philosophical doctrine which identifies the universe with God. [f. PAN- + s. Gk *theós* god + -ISM] **—pan′theist,** *n.* **—pan′theis′tic, pan′theis′tical,** *adj.* **—pan′theis′tically,** *adv.*

Pantheon (păn thē′ən), *n.* **1.** a domed circular temple at Rome, erected A.D. 120–24 by Hadrian using an older porch built by Agrippa 27 B.C., and used as a church since A.D. 609. **2.** (*l.c.*) a public building containing tombs or memorials of the illustrious dead of a nation. **3.** (*l.c.*) a temple dedicated to all the gods. **4.** (*l.c.*) the gods of a particular mythology considered collectively. [ME, t. L, t. Gk: m. *pántheion*, prop. neut. of *pántheios* of all gods]

panther (păn′thə), *n., pl.* **-thers,** (*esp. collectively*) **-ther. 1.** the leopard, *Panthera pardus.* **2.** *U.S.* the cougar or puma, *Felis concolor.* [t. L: s. *panthēra*, t. Gk: m. *pánthēr*; r. ME *pantere* (t. OF) and OE *pandher* (t. L)] **—pantheress** (păn′thə rĭs), *n. fem.*

panties (păn′tĭz), *n.pl.* underpants as worn by women and girls.

pantile (păn′tīl′), *n.* a roofing tile straight in its length but curved in its width to overlap the next tile. [f. PAN[1] + TILE, n. Cf. G *Pfannenziegel*]

Pantiles

panto (păn′tō), *n., pl.* **-tos.** *Colloq.* pantomime.

panto-, a word element or prefix synonymous with **pan-.** [t. Gk, comb. form of s. *pâs*, neut. *pân* all]

pantofle (păn tŏf′əl, -tōō′fəl), *n.* a slipper. Also, **pantoffle** (păn′tŏf′əl), **pantoufle.** [t. F: m. *pantoufle*, t. OIt.: m. *pantufola*, var. of Sicilian *pantofola*, t. Gk: m. *pantóphellos* whole cork, through meaning of cork shoe]

pantograph (păn′tə grăf′, -gräf′), *n.* **1.** an instrument for the mechanical copying of plans, diagrams, etc., upon any desired scale. **2.** *Elect.* a roof-mounted current collector, as on a train, usually a hinged diamond-shaped framework, sprung so as to maintain contact with an overhead wire.

pantology (păn tŏl′ə jĭ), *n.* a systematic view of all human knowledge. **—pantologic** (păn′tə lŏj′ĭk), **pan′tolog′ical,** *adj.* **—pantol′ogist,** *n.*

pantomime (păn′tə mīm′), *n., v.,* **-mimed, -miming.** *—n.* **1.** a form of theatrical entertainment common in England during the Christmas season, originally including a harlequinade, but now based loosely on one of several fairytales, and including stock character types. **2.** a mime (def. 2). **3.** an actor in dumb show, as in ancient Rome. **4.** significant gesture without speech. *—v.t.* **5.** to represent or express by pantomime. *—v.i.* **6.** to express oneself by pantomime. [t. L: m. s. *pantomīmus*, t. Gk: m. *pantómīmos*, lit., all-imitating] **—pantomimic** (păn′tə mĭm′ĭk), *adj.*

pantomime dame, a coarse, ludicrous female character in a pantomime, traditionally played by a man.

pantomimist (păn′tə mī′mĭst), *n.* **1.** one who acts in pantomime. **2.** the author of a pantomime.

pantothenic acid (păn′tə thĕn′ĭk), *Biochem.* an oily hydroxy acid, $HOCH_2C(CH\ )_2CHOHCONHCH_2CH_2$-$COOH$, found in plant and animal tissues, rice bran, etc., and essential for cell growth.

pantoufle (păn′tōō′fəl; *Fr.* päɴ tōō′fl), *n.* pantofle; a slipper.

pantry (păn′trĭ), *n., pl.* **-tries.** a room or cupboard in which bread and other provisions, or silverware, dishes, etc., are kept. [ME *panetrie*, t. AF, der. OF *panetier* servant in charge of bread, der. L *pānis* bread]

pants (pănts), *n.pl.* **1.** underpants. **2.** *U.S. Colloq.* trousers. [familiar abbrev. of PANTALOONS]

pantun (păn tōōn′), *n.* a Malay verse form, usually of four lines, the third rhyming with the first, and the fourth with the second. Also, **pantoum** (păn tōōm′). [t. Malay]

Panurge (pă nûj′; *Fr.* pȧ nʏrzh′), *n.* (in Rabelais's *Gargantua and Pantagruel*) a rascal, companion of Pantagruel. [t. F, t. Gk: m. s. *panoûrgos* ready to do anything]

Panza (păn′zə; *Sp.* pän′thä), *n.* See **Sancho Panza.**

panzer (păn′zə; *Ger.* pän′tsər), *German. —adj.* **1.** armoured: *a panzer division. —n.* **2.** a tank.

Paotow (pou′tou′), *n.* a city in the Inner Mongolian Autonomous Region, in N China. 490,000 (est. 1958).

pap[1] (păp), *n.* **1.** soft food for infants or invalids, as bread soaked in water or milk. **2.** *S African.* a porridge made from mealies. **3.** books, ideas, talk, etc., considered as having no intellectual or permanent value; rubbish; tripe. **4.** *U.S. Slang.* profits or favours secured through official patronage. [ME. Cf. LG *pappe*, ML *pappa*]

pap[2] (păp), *n.* **1.** a teat or nipple. **2.** something resembling a teat or nipple. [ME *pappe*. Cf. d. Norw. and Sw. *pappe*]

papa (pə pä′), *n.* father. [t. F, t. L. Cf. It. *pappa*, Gk *páppas*]

papacy (pā′pə sĭ), *n., pl.* **-cies. 1.** the office, dignity, or jurisdiction of the pope. **2.** the system of ecclesiastical government in which the pope is recognized as the supreme head. **3.** the time during which a pope is in office. **4.** the succession or line of the popes. [ME, t. ML: m. s. *pāpātia*, der. *pāpa* pope, father]

Papadopoulos (păp′ə dŏp′ōō lŏs′; *Gk* pä pä thô′ pōō lôs), *n.* **George** (jôj), born 1919, Greek statesman: prime minister since 1967.

papadum (păp′ə dəm), *n.* a type of Indian wafer, thin and crisp and usually rice-based. Also, **popadum.**

papain (pə pā′ĭn, pā′pə-), *n.* **1.** *Chem.* a proteolytic enzyme contained in the fruit of the papaya tree, *Carica papaya.* **2.** a commercial preparation of this, used as a digestant. [f. PAPA(YA) + -IN[2]]

papal (pā′pl), *adj.* of or pertaining to the pope, the papacy, or the Roman Catholic Church. [ME, t. ML: s. *pāpālis*, der. *pāpa* pope]

papal cross, a cross with three horizontal crosspieces. See illus. under **cross.**

Papal States, a large district in central Italy ruled as a temporal domain by the popes from 755 until the final unification of Italy in 1870: partially annexed by Italy, 1860. Also, **States of the Church.**

Papandreou (păp′ən drā′ōō; *Gk* pä pän thrĕ′ōō), *n.* **George,** 1888–1968, Greek statesman: premier 1944, 1963–65.

papaveraceous (pə pā′və rā′shəs), *adj.* belonging to the *Papaveraceae*, or poppy family of plants, a large group of medicinal importance as the source of opium. [f. L *papāver* poppy + -ACEOUS]

papaverine (pə pā′və rēn′), *n.* a fine, odourless, crystalline, white alkaloid, $C_{20}H_{21}NO_4$, derived from opium, which relaxes the involuntary muscles of the gastro-intestinal tract, and other smooth muscles. Also, **papaverin** (pə pā′və rĭn).

papaw (pə pô′), *n.* **1.** the small fleshy fruit of the temperate North American bush or small tree, *Asimina triloba.* **2.** the tree itself. Also, **pawpaw.** [t. Sp. See PAPAYA]

papaya (pə pī′ə), *n.* **1.** the large yellow melon-like fruit of the tropical American shrub or small tree, *Carica papaya*, of the family *Caricaceae*, much prized for its palatable fruits containing a digestive principle. **2.** the tree itself, which is herbaceous. [t. Sp.: *papaya* the fruit, m. *papayo* the tree; of Carib orig.]

Papeete (pä′pĭ ē′tĭ), *n.* a seaport in the Society Islands on Tahiti: capital of the Society Islands and of French Polynesia. 20,302 (1962).

Papen (pä′pən; *Ger.* pä′pən), *n.* **Franz von** (*Ger.* fränts′ fŏn), 1879–1969, German diplomat and politician: chancellor 1932–33.

paper (pā′pə), *n.* **1.** a substance made from rags, straw, wood, or other fibrous material, usually in thin sheets, for writing or printing on, wrapping things in, etc. **2.** something resembling this substance, as papyrus. **3.** a piece, sheet, or leaf of paper, esp. one bearing writing. **4.** a written or printed document or instrument. **5.** wallpaper. **6.** negotiable notes, bills, etc., collectively: *commercial paper.* **7.** (*pl.*) documents establishing identity, status, etc. **8.** (*pl.*) the documents required to be carried by a ship for the manifestation of her ownership, nationality, destination, etc.; ship's papers. **9.** a set of questions for an examination, or an individual set of written answers to them. **10.** an essay, article, or dissertation on a particular topic. **11.** a newspaper or journal. **12.** *Slang.* a free pass to a place of entertainment. **13. on paper, a.** confirmed in writing. **b.** in the planning or design stage. **c.** in theory rather than practice: *it sounds all right on paper, but will it work?* *—v.t.* **14.** to decorate (a wall, room, etc.) with wallpaper. **15.** to line with paper: *to paper a shelf.* **16.** to fold, enclose, or put up in paper. **17.** to supply with paper. **18.** *Obs.* to write or set down on paper. **19.** *Obs.* to describe in writing. **20.** to sandpaper.

—adj. **21.** made or consisting of paper: *a paper bag.* **22.** paper-like; thin; flimsy; frail. **23.** pertaining to, or carried on by means of, letters, articles, books, etc.: *a paper war.* **24.** written or printed on paper. **25.** existing on paper only and not in reality: *paper profits.* **26.** indicating the first event of a series, as a wedding anniversary. [ME and OE, t. L: m. s. *papyrus* paper, PAPYRUS] **—pa′per-like′,** *adj.*

paperback (pā′pə băk′), *n.* **1.** a book bound in a flexible paper cover, usually cheaper than a hardback of comparable length. *—adj.* **2.** of, denoting, or pertaining to such books or the publishing of such books.

paper birch, the North American birch, *Betula papyrifera*, a tall tree with tough bark and valuable wood.

paperbound (pā′pə bound′), *adj.* paperback.

paperboy (pā′pə boi′), *n.* a boy employed to deliver or sell newspapers, etc.

paperchase (pā′pə chās′), *n.* hare and hounds.

paper chromatography, *Chem.* a method of analysing mixtures which depends on the different rates at which compounds in solution migrate across a sheet of porous paper specially prepared with indicators.

paperclip (pā′pə klĭp′), *n.* a flat wire clip bent so as to hold together papers, etc.

paperer (pā′pə rə), *n.* **1.** a paperhanger. **2.** one who papers.

paperhanger (pā′pə hăng′ə), *n.* one whose business it is to cover or decorate walls with wallpaper. *—***pa′perhang′ing,** *n.*

paperknife (pā′pə nīf′), *n.* a knifelike instrument with a blade of metal, ivory, wood, or the like, for cutting open the leaves of books, folded papers, etc.

paper mulberry, a small moraceous tree of E Asia, *Broussonetia papyrifera*, the inner bark of which was formerly used for making paper in Japan, and is still used in Polynesia for making a kind of cloth.

♦ **paper nautilus,** any dibranchiate cephalopod of the genus *Argonauta*, characterized by the delicate shell of the female; the argonaut.

paper tape, *Computers.* a ribbon of paper through which a pattern of holes is punched to represent information in a form which can be fed into a computer.

paper tiger, one who or that which has the appearance of strength, power, or aggressiveness, but is in fact weak or ineffectual.

paperweight (pā′pə wāt′), *n.* a small, heavy object laid on papers to keep them from being scattered.

paperwork (pā′pə wûk′), *n.* written or clerical work, as the keeping of records, esp. considered as an essential but incidental part of some occupation.

papery (pā′pə rĭ), *adj.* like paper; thin or flimsy.

papeterie (păp′ə trĭ; *Fr.* pȧp trē′), *n., pl.* **-teries** (-trĭz; *Fr.* -trē′). a case or box of paper and other materials for writing. [t. F, der. *papetier* one who makes or sells paper, der. *papier* PAPER]

Paphian (pā′fĭ ən), *adj.* **1.** of or pertaining to Paphos, an ancient city of Cyprus sacred to Aphrodite. **2.** of love, esp. illicit love.

Paphlagonia (păf′lə gō′nyə), *n.* an ancient country and Roman province in N Asia Minor, on the S coast of the Black Sea.

Paphos (pā′fŏs), *n.* an ancient city in SW Cyprus.

Papiamento (*Sp.* pȧ pyȧ mėn′tȯ), *n.* the creolized Spanish of Curaçao, in the Netherlands Antilles.

papier collé (*Fr.* pȧ pyė kŏ lė′), *pl.* **papiers collés** (*Fr.* pȧ pyė kŏ lė′). *French.* an arrangement of various objects and materials pasted on a flat surface to achieve a formal design, used especially in cubism about 1912–14.

papier-mâché (păp′yā măsh′ā; *Fr.* pȧ pyė mȧ shė′), *n.* **1.** a substance made of pulped paper or paper pulp mixed with glue and other materials, or of layers of paper glued and pressed together, moulded when moist to form various articles, and becoming hard and strong when dry. *—adj.* **2.** made of papier-mâché. [t. F: chewed paper]

papilionaceous (pə pĭl′ĭ ə nā′shəs), *adj. Bot.* **1.** having an irregular corolla shaped somewhat like a butterfly, as the pea and other leguminous plants. **2.** belonging to the family *Papilionaceae* (*Fabaceae*), which is often treated as part of the *Leguminosae.* [t. NL: m. *pāpiliōnāceus*, der. L *pāpilio* butterfly]

Papilionaceous flower of bean, *Phaseolus vulgaris* A, Vexillum; B, Wing; C, Keel or Carina

papilla (pə pĭl′ə), *n., pl.* **-pillae** (-pĭl′ē). **1.** any small nipple-like process or projection. **2.** one of certain small protuberances concerned with the senses of touch, taste, and smell: *the papillae of the tongue.* **3.** a small vascular process at the root of a hair. **4.** a papule or pimple. [t. L: nipple]

papillary (pə pĭl′ə rĭ), *adj.* **1.** of or pertaining to, or of the nature of, a papilla or papillae. **2.** provided or furnished with papillae.

papilloma (păp′ĭ lō′mə), *n., pl.* **-mata** (-mə tə), **-mas.** *Pathol.* a tumour of skin or mucous membrane, consisting of a hypertrophied papilla or group of papillae, as a wart or a corn. [f. PAPILL(A) + -OMA]

papillon (păp′ĭ lŏn′), *n.* a variety of toy spaniel having large ears thought to resemble the wings of a butterfly. [t. F: butterfly]

papillose (păp′ĭ lōs′), *adj.* full of papillae. —**papillosity** (păp′ĭ lŏs′ĭ tĭ), *n.*

papillote (păp′ĭ lŏt′), *n.* a decorative curled paper, put at the end of the bone of a cutlet, chop, or the like. [t. F, der. *papillon* butterfly, t. L: m. s. *pāpilio*]

papism (pā′pĭz′əm), *n.* (usually disparaging) Roman Catholicism.

papist (pā′pĭst), *n.* **1.** an adherent of the pope. **2.** a member of the Roman Catholic Church (usually in disparagement). *—adj.* **3.** papistical. [t. NL: s. *pāpista*, der. L *pāpa* POPE]

papistical (pə pĭs′tĭ kl), *adj.* of, pertaining to, or characteristic of papists or papistry (usually in disparagement). Also, **papis′tic.**

papistry (pā′pĭs trĭ), *n.* (usually disparaging) the systems, doctrines, or practices of papists.

papoose (pə po͞os′), *n.* **1.** a North American Indian baby or young child. **2.** *Colloq.* any baby. Also, **pappoose.** [t. Algonquian (New England): m. *papeisses*, der. *peisses* child]

pappose (păp′ōs, pă pōs′), *adj. Bot.* **1.** having or forming a pappus. **2.** downy. Also, **pappous** (păp′əs).

pappus (păp′əs), *n., pl.* **pappi** (păp′ī). *Bot.* a downy, bristly, or tufty appendage of the achene of certain plants, as the dandelion and the thistle. [t. L, t. Gk: m. *páppos* down on seeds, orig. grandfather]

pappy[1] (păp′ĭ), *adj.,* **-pier, -piest.** like pap; mushy.

pappy[2] (păp′ĭ), *n. Chiefly Southern U.S. Dial.* father.

paprika (pă prē′kə, păp′rĭ kə), *n.* **1.** the dried fruit of a cultivated form of *Capsicum frutescens*, ground as a condiment, much less pungent than ordinary red pepper. **2.** the capsicum (fruit or plant). [t. Hung.]

Papua (păp′yo͞o ə), *n.* **1.** New Guinea. **2. Territory of,** an Australian territory in SE New Guinea, including the adjacent islands: merged with the Territory of New Guinea, 1945. 539,553 pop. (1962); 90,540 sq. mi. *Cap.:* Port Moresby. **3. Gulf of,** a large gulf of the Coral Sea, on the SE coast of New Guinea. [t. Malay: lit., frizzled]

Papuan (păp′yo͞o ən), *adj.* **1.** of or pertaining to Papua. **2.** denoting or pertaining to the native negroid race of New Guinea, characterized by a black or sooty brown complexion and crisp, frizzled hair. **3.** of, pertaining to, or denoting any of a number of languages of the south-west Pacific, particularly of New Guinea and New Caledonia. *—n.* **4.** a native or inhabitant of New Guinea. **5.** a Papuan language.

papule (păp′yo͞ol), *n. Pathol.* a small, somewhat pointed elevation of the skin, usually inflammatory but not suppurative. [t. L: m. s. *papula* pustule, pimple]

papyraceous (păp′ĭ rā′shəs), *adj.* papery.

papyrus (pə pī′rəs), *n., pl.* **-pyri** (-pī′ə rī′). **1.** a tall aquatic plant, *Cyperus papyrus*, of the sedge family, of the Nile valley and elsewhere. **2.** a material for writing on, prepared from thin strips of the pith of this plant laid together, soaked, pressed, and dried, used by the ancient Egyptians, Greeks, and Romans. **3.** an ancient document or manuscript written on this material. [ME, t. L, t. Gk: m. *pápȳros* the plant papyrus, something made from papyrus. Cf. PAPER]

par (pä), *n.* **1.** an equality in value or standing; a level of equality: *the gains and the losses are on a par.* **2.** an average or normal amount, degree, quality, condition, or the like: *above par, below par.* **3.** *Com.* **a.** the legally established value of the monetary unit of one country in terms of that of another using the same metal as a standard of value (**mint par of exchange**). **b.** the state of the shares of any business, undertaking, loan, etc., when they may be purchased at the original price (called **issue par**) or at their face value (called **nominal par**). Such shares or bonds are said to be **at par.** Shares or bonds sold or acquired at a premium are said to be **above par,** and at a discount, **below par. 4.** *Golf.* the number of strokes allowed to a hole or course as representing a target standard. *—adj.* **5.** average or normal. **6.** *Com.* at or pertaining to par: *the par value of a bond.* [t. L: equal]

par., **1.** paragraph. **2.** parallel. **3.** parenthesis. **4.** parish.

para (pä′rə), *n., pl.* **-ras, -ra. 1.** a former copper coin of Turkey, worth one fortieth of a kuru. **2.** one hundredth of a dinar (of Yugoslavia). [t. Turk. (Pers.): m. *pārah* piece, portion]

Pará (*Port.* pȧ rȧ′), *n.* **1.** Belém. **2.** an estuary in N Brazil, receiving the Tocantins river and a branch of the Amazon. ab. 200 mi. long; ab. 40 mi. wide. **3.** Pará rubber.

para-[1], **1.** a prefix meaning 'beside', 'near', 'beyond', 'aside', 'amiss', and sometimes implying alteration or modification, occurring orig. in words from the Greek, but used also as a modern formative, chiefly in scientific words. **2.** *Chem.* indicating a compound containing a benzene

ring substituted in the 1·4 positions. Also, before vowels, **par-**. [t. Gk, comb. form of *pará*, prep.]
para-², a prefix of a few words meaning 'guard against', as in *parachute*. [t. F, t. It., impv. of *parāre* defend against, g. L: prepare]
para-³, a prefix meaning 'parachute', as in *paratroops*. [shortened form of PARACHUTE]
Para., Paraguay.
parabiosis (pă′rə bī ō′sĭs), *n. Biol.* experimental or natural union of two individuals with exchange of blood. —**parabiotic** (pă′rə bī ŏt′ĭk), *adj.*
parable (pă′rə bl), *n.* **1.** a short allegorical story, designed to convey some truth or moral lesson. **2.** a discourse or saying conveying the intended meaning by a comparison or under the likeness of something comparable or analogous. [ME *parabil*, t. LL: m. s. *parabola* comparison, parable, proverb, word, t. Gk: m. *parabolḗ* a placing beside, comparison]
parabola (pə răb′ə lə), *n. Geom.* a plane curve formed by the intersection of a right circular cone with a plane parallel to a generator of the cone. [t. NL, t. Gk: m. *parabolḗ*. See PARABLE]

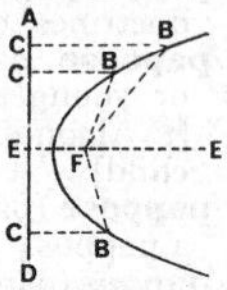

Common parabola: AD, Directrix; F, Focus; B, Point on parabola; BC, Always equal to BF; EE, Axis

parabolic¹ (pă′rə bŏl′ĭk), *adj.* **1.** having the form or outline of a parabola. **2.** pertaining to or resembling a parabola. [ME, t. LL: s. *parabolicus*, t. LGk: m. *parabolikós* figurative]
parabolic² (pă′rə bŏl′ĭk), *adj.* of, pertaining to, or involving a parable. Also, **par′abol′ical.** [see PARABOLIC¹, PARABLE] —**par′abol′ically,** *adv.*
parabolize¹ (pə răb′ə līz′), *v.t.*, **-lized, -lizing.** to explain by means of a parable. Also, **parabolise.**
parabolize² (pə răb′ə līz′), *v.t.*, **-lized, -lizing.** to make paraboloid. Also, **parabolise.**
paraboloid (pə răb′ə loid′), *n. Geom.* a solid or surface generated by the revolution of a parabola about its axis, or one of the second degree some of whose plane sections are parabolas. —**paraboloidal** (pə răb′ə loi′dl), *adj.*
parabrake (pă′rə brāk′), *n.* parachute brake.
Paracelsus (pă′rə sĕl′səs), *n.* **Philippus Aureolus** (fĭl′ĭ pəs ô′rĭ ō′ləs) (*Theophrastus Bombastus von Hohenheim*), 1493?–1541, Swiss-German physician and alchemist. —**Par′acel′sian,** *adj.*
paracentesis (pă′rə sĕn tē′sĭs), *n. Surg.* tapping of fluid from a body cavity.
parachute (pă′rə shōōt′), *n., v.*, **-chuted, -chuting.** —*n.* **1.** an apparatus used in descending safely through the air, esp. from an aircraft, being umbrella-like in form and rendered effective by the resistance of the air, which expands it during the descent and then reduces the velocity of its motion. —*adj.* **2.** dropped by parachute: *parachute troops, a parachute mine.* —*v.t.* **3.** to land (troops, equipment, etc.) by parachute. —*v.i.* **4.** to descend by or as by parachute. [t. F: f. *para-* PARA-² + *chute* a fall. See CHUTE] —**par′achut′ist,** *n.*
parachute brake, *Aeron.* a parachute which opens at the rear of an aircraft or the like to act as a brake on landing. Also, **parabrake.**
paraclete (pă′rə klēt′), *n.* **1.** one called in to aid; an advocate or intercessor. **2.** (*cap.*) the Holy Spirit, or Comforter. [t. LL: m. s. *paraclētus*, t. Gk: m. *paráklētos*]
paracymene (pă′rə sī′mēn), *n.* the most common form of cymene, found in several essential oils, as oil of eucalyptus.
parade (pə rād′), *n., v.*, **-raded, -rading.** —*n.* **1.** show, display, or ostentation: *to make a parade of one's emotions.* **2.** the orderly assembly of troops, boy scouts, or any other body, for inspection, display, or any other purpose. **3.** the troops, etc., so assembled. **4.** *U.S.* a military ceremony involving the marching of troop units and a mass salute at the lowering of the flag at the end of the day. **5.** *U.S.* a parade ground. **6.** a public procession for display, as to draw attention to a political party, celebrate an anniversary, etc. **7.** a promenade; a walk for pleasure or display. **8.** a body of people promenading. **9.** a short street. **10.** a row or block of shops, etc., esp. one having a service road. **11.** *Fort.* the level space forming the interior or enclosed area of a fortification. **12.** *Fencing.* a parry. —*v.t.* **13.** to make parade of; display ostentatiously. **14.** to walk up and down on or in. **15.** to cause to march or proceed for display. **16.** to cause to assemble, as troops. —*v.i.* **17.** to march or proceed with display. **18.** to promenade in a public place to show oneself. **19.** to assemble in military order. [t. F, t. Sp.: m. *parada*, der. *parar*, g. L *parāre* prepare]
parade ground, a place where troops regularly assemble for parade.
paradichlorobenzene (pă′rə dī klô′rō bĕn′zēn), *n. Chem.* a white crystalline compound, $C_6H_4Cl_2$, of the benzene series, used as a moth repellent.
paradigm (pă′rə dīm′), *n.* **1.** *Gram.* **a.** the set of all forms containing a particular element, esp. the set of all inflected forms of a single root, stem, or theme. For example: *boy, boys, boy's, boys'* constitutes the paradigm of the noun *boy.* **b.** a display in fixed arrangement of such a set. **2.** a pattern; an example. [late ME, t. LL: m. *paradīgma*, t. Gk: m. *parádeigma* pattern] —**paradigmatic** (pă′rə dĭg măt′ĭk), **par′adigmat′ical,** *adj.* —**par′adigmat′ically,** *adv.*
paradisaical (pă′rə dĭ sā′ĭ kl), *adj.* paradisiacal. Also, **par′adisa′ic.** —**par′adisa′ically,** *adv.*
paradise (pă′rə dīs′), *n.* **1.** heaven, as the final abode of the righteous. **2.** (according to some) an intermediate place for the departed souls of the righteous awaiting resurrection. **3.** the Garden of Eden. **4.** a place of extreme beauty or delight. **5.** supreme felicity. **6.** See **bird of paradise.** [ME *paradis*, t. LL: s. *paradīsus*, t. Gk: m. *parádeisos* park, t. OPers.: m. *pairidaēza* enclosure]
paradise duck, a brightly coloured game bird of New Zealand, *Cascarea variegata.*
paradise fish, a beautiful fish of either of two species of *Macropodus*, often kept in aquariums.
paradisiacal (pă′rə dĭ sī′ə kl), *adj.* of, like, or befitting paradise. Also, **paradisiac** (pă′rə dĭs′ĭ ăk′). [f. s. LL *paradīsiacus* of paradise + -AL¹] —**par′adisi′acally,** *adv.*
parados (pă′rə dŏs′), *n. Fort.* the bank behind a trench that protects men from fire and from being seen against the skyline. [t. F: f. *para-* PARA-² + *dos* back]
paradox (pă′rə dŏks′), *n.* **1.** a statement or proposition seemingly self-contradictory or absurd, and yet explicable as expressing a truth. **2.** a self-contradictory and false proposition. **3.** any person or thing exhibiting apparent contradictions. **4.** an opinion or statement contrary to received opinion. [t. L: s. *paradoxum*, t. Gk: m. *parádoxon*, neut. of *parádoxos* contrary to received opinion, incredible] —**par′adox′ical,** *adj.* —**par′adox′ically,** *adv.* —**par′adox′icalness,** *n.*
paraesthesia (pă′rēs thē′zyə), *n. Pathol.* abnormal sensation, as prickling, itching, etc. Also, *Chiefly U.S.*, **paresthesia.** [f. PAR(A)-¹ + m. Gk *aisthēsía* sensation] —**paraesthetic** (pă′rēs thĕt′ĭk), *adj.*
paraffin (pă′rə fĭn), *n.* **1.** paraffin oil. **2.** *Chem.* any hydrocarbon of the methane series (**paraffin series**) having a general formula C_nH_{2n+2}; alkane. **3.** *U.S.* paraffin wax. **4.** liquid paraffin. —*v.t.* **5.** to cover or impregnate with paraffin wax. [t. G, f. (by K. von Reichenbach) L *par*(*um*) not enough + L *affīn*(*is*) related; so called from its lack of affinity for other substances]
paraffine (pă′rə fēn′), *n., v.t.*, **-fined, -fining.** paraffin.
paraffin oil, a mixture of liquid hydrocarbons, obtained in the distillation of petroleum, with boiling points in the range 150°–300°C; used for paraffin lamps, oil-burning engines, domestic heaters; kerosene.
paraffin wax, *Chem.* a white translucent solid with a melting point in the range 50°–60°C, consisting of the higher members of the paraffin series; used for candles, waxed papers, polishes, etc.
paraformaldehyde (pă′rə fô măl′dĭ hīd′), *n.* a colourless non-crystalline polymer of formaldehyde, $(CH_2O)_3$, used as an antiseptic. Also, **paraform** (pă′rə fôm′).
paragenesis (pă′rə jĕn′ĭ sĭs), *n. Geol.* the origin and associations of a mineral or a mineral deposit. Also, **paragenesia** (pă′rə jĭ nē′syə). [f. PARA-¹ + GENESIS] —**paragenetic** (pă′rə jĭ nĕt′ĭk), *adj.* —**par′agenet′ically,** *adv.*
paragoge (pă′rə gō′jĭ), *n.* (in linguistic change) the addition of a syllable, phoneme, or other element not originally present, at the end of a word, as the substandard pronunciation of *height* as *height-th*, the standard showing no change. [t. LL, t. Gk: a leading past] —**paragogic** (pă′rə gŏj′ĭk), *adj.*
paragon (pă′rə gən), *n.* **1.** a model or pattern of excellence, or of a particular excellence. **2.** *Print.* a type size (20 points). **3.** an unusually large round pearl. **4.** a perfect diamond weighing 100 carats or more. —*v.t. Archaic.* **5.** to match or parallel. **6.** to compare. **7.** to be a match for; equal; rival. **8.** to surpass. **9.** to regard as a paragon. [t. MF, t. It.: m. *paragone* touchstone, comparison, paragon]
paragraph (pă′rə grăf′, -grâf′), *n.* **1.** a distinct portion of written or printed matter dealing with a particular point, and usually beginning (commonly with indention) on a new line. **2.** a character (now usually ¶) used to indicate the beginning of a distinct or separate portion of a text, or as a mark of reference. **3.** a note, item, or brief article, as in a newspaper. —*v.t.* **4.** to divide into paragraphs. **5.** to write or publish paragraphs about. **6.** to express in a paragraph. [t. LL: s. *paragraphus*, t. Gk: m. *parágraphos* line or mark in the margin]

paragrapher (pă′rə grăf′ə, -grä′fə), *n.* one who writes paragraphs, as for a newspaper. Also, **par′agraph′ist.**

paragraphia (pă′rə grăf′yə), *n. Psychol.* a cerebral disorder marked by the writing of words or letters other than those intended, or the loss of ability to express ideas in writing. [t. NL, f. Gk: *para-* PARA-[1] + *-graphía* writing]

paragraphic (pă′rə grăf′ĭk), *adj.* **1.** of, pertaining to, or forming a paragraph. **2.** divided into paragraphs. **3.** of or pertaining to paragraphia. Also, **par′agraph′ical.** —**par′agraph′ically,** *adv.*

Paraguay (pă′rə gwī′; *Sp.* pä rä gwȧy′), *n.* **1.** a republic in central South America between Bolivia, Brazil, and Argentina. 1,816,890 pop. (1962); 150,515 sq. mi. *Cap.:* Asunción. **2.** a river flowing from W Brazil S through Paraguay to the Paraná. ab. 1500 mi. —**Par′aguay′an,** *adj., n.*

Paraguay tea, maté.

parahydrogen (pă′rə hī′drĭ jən), *n. Chem.* a form of molecular hydrogen in which the spins of the two constituent atoms are antiparallel.

parakeet (pă′rə kēt′), *n.* any of the numerous small, slender parrots, usually with a long, pointed, graduated tail, as the **Australian grass parakeet,** *Melopsittacus undulatus.* Also, **paraquet, paroquet, parrakeet, parroket, parroquet.** [t. It.: m. *parochito,* var. of *parrochetto,* dim. of *parroco* parson]

Slatey-headed parakeet, *Psittacula himalayana* (15 in. long)

paraldehyde (pə răl′dĭ hīd′), *n. Chem.* a colourless liquid, $(CH_3CHO)_3$, formed by polymerization of acetaldehyde, and used as a hypnotic. [f. PAR(A)-[1] + ALDEHYDE]

paralexia (pă′rə lĕk′sĭ ə), *n. Psychol.* inability to read characterized by the substitution or transposition of words or characters. —**par′alex′ic,** *adj.*

paralipsis (pă′rə lĭp′sĭs), *n., pl.* **-ses** (-sēz). *Rhetoric.* a pretended ignoring, for rhetorical effect, of something actually spoken of, as in 'not to mention other faults'. Also, **paraleipsis** (pă′rə līp′sĭs). [t. NL, t. Gk: m. *paráleipsis* a passing over]

parallax (pă′rə lăks′), *n.* **1.** the apparent displacement of an object observed, esp. a heavenly body, due to a change or difference in the position of the observer. **2. diurnal** or **geocentric parallax,** the displacement of a body owing to its being observed from the surface instead of from the centre of the earth. **3. annual** or **heliocentric parallax,** the displacement of a star owing to its being observed from the earth instead of from the sun. **4.** apparent change in the position of crosshairs as viewed through a telescope, when the focusing is imperfect. [t. Gk: s. *parállaxis* change] —**parallactic** (pă′rə lăk′tĭk), *adj.* —**par′allac′tically,** *adv.*

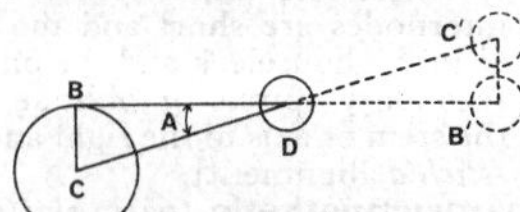

Geocentric parallax of the moon: A, Parallax; B, Observer; C, Centre of earth; D, Moon; C′, Image of C; B′, Image of B

parallel (pă′rə lĕl′), *adj., n., v.,* **-leled, -leling** or **-lelled, -lelling.** —*adj.* **1.** having the same direction, course, or tendency; corresponding; similar; analogous: *parallel forces.* **2.** *Geom.* **a.** (of straight lines) lying in the same plane but never meeting no matter how far extended. **b.** (of planes) having common perpendiculars. **c.** (of a single line, plane, etc.) equidistant from another or others at all corresponding points (fol. by *to* or *with*). **3.** *Music.* **a.** (of two voice parts) progressing so that the interval between them remains the same. **b.** (of a tonality or key) having the same tonic but differing in mode. **4.** *Computers, etc.* denoting or pertaining to a system in which several activities are carried on concurrently. **5.** *Elect.* consisting of or having component parts connected in parallel. —*n.* **6.** anything parallel in direction, course, or tendency. **7.** a parallel line or plane. **8.** *Geog.* **a.** a circle on the earth's surface formed by the intersection of a plane parallel to the plane of the equator, bearing east and west and designated in degrees of latitude north or south of the equator along the arc of any meridian. **b.** the line representing this circle on a chart or map. **9.** a match or counterpart. **10.** correspondence or analogy. **11.** a comparison of things as if regarded side by side. **12.** *Print.* a pair of vertical parallel lines (‖) used as a mark of reference. **13.** *Elect.* a connection of two or more circuits in which all ends having the same instantaneous polarity are electrically connected together, and all ends having the opposite polarity are similarly connected. The element circuits are said to be **in parallel** (opp. to *in series*). **14.** *Fort.* a trench cut in the ground before a fortress, parallel to its defences, for the purpose of covering a besieging force. —*v.t.* **15.** to make parallel. **16.** to furnish a parallel for; find or provide a match for. **17.** to form a parallel to; be equivalent to; equal. **18.** to compare. [t. L: s. *parallēlus,* t. Gk: m. *parállēlos* beside one another]

parallel bars, a gymnasium apparatus consisting of two wooden bars on uprights, adjustable in height, and used for swinging, vaulting, balancing exercises, etc.

parallelepiped (pă′rə lĕl′ĭ pī′pĕd, pă′rə lĕ lĕp′ĭ pĕd′), *n.* a prism with six faces, all parallelograms. Also, **parallelepipedon** (pă′rə lĕl′ĭ pī′pĭ dən). [t. Gk: s. *parallēlepípedon* body with parallel surfaces]

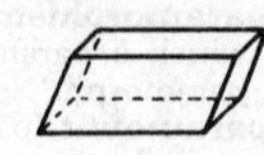
Parallelepiped

parallelism (pă′rə lĕ lĭz′əm), *n.* **1.** the position or relation of parallels. **2.** agreement in direction, tendency, or character. **3.** a parallel or comparison. **4.** a resemblance, or close correspondence. **5.** *Metaphys.* the doctrine that mental and bodily processes are concomitant, each varying with variation of the other, but that there is no causal relation or relation of interaction between the two series of changes.

parallelist (pă′rə lĕl′ĭst), *n.* **1.** a believer in the doctrine of parallelism. **2.** one who draws a parallel or comparison.

parallelogram (pă′rə lĕl′ə-grăm′), *n.* a quadrilateral the opposite sides of which are parallel. [t. Gk: s. *parallēlógrammon,* prop. neut. of *parallēlógrammos* bounded by parallel lines]

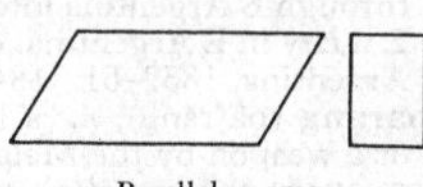
Parallelograms

parallelogram of forces, *Physics.* a parallelogram drawn in such a manner that two adjacent sides represent two forces acting on a body, both in magnitude and direction; the diagonal of this parallelogram then represents the resultant of these two forces.

paralogism (pə răl′ə jĭz′əm), *n. Logic.* **1.** a piece of false or fallacious reasoning, esp. (as distinguished from *sophism*) one of whose falseness the reasoner is not conscious. **2.** reasoning of this kind. [t. Gk: s. *paralogismós* false reasoning] —**paral′ogist,** *n.* —**paral′ogis′tic,** *adj.*

paralyse (pă′rə līz′), *v.t.,* **-lysed, -lysing. 1.** to affect with paralysis. **2.** to bring to a condition of helpless inactivity. Also, *U.S.,* **paralyze.** —**par′alysa′tion,** *n.* —**par′alys′er,** *n.* —**Syn. 2.** stun. See **shock**[1].

paralysis (pə răl′ĭ sĭs), *n., pl.* **-ses** (-sēz′). **1.** *Pathol.* **a.** loss of power of a voluntary muscular contraction. **b.** a disease characterized by this; palsy. **2.** a more or less complete crippling, as of powers or activities: *a paralysis of trade.* [t. L, t. Gk: palsy]

paralysis agitans (ăj′ĭ tănz′), *Pathol.* Parkinson's disease. [L. PARALYSIS + *agitāns* pres. part. of *agitāre* excite]

paralytic (pă′rə lĭt′ĭk), *n.* **1.** one affected with general paralysis. —*adj.* **2.** affected with or subject to paralysis. **3.** pertaining to or of the nature of paralysis. **4.** *Slang.* completely intoxicated with alcoholic drink; very drunk.

paramagnet (pă′rə măg′nĭt), *n.* a body or substance having paramagnetic properties. —**par′amag′netism,** *n.*

paramagnetic (pă′rə măg nĕt′ĭk), *adj.* denoting or pertaining to a class of substances (e.g., liquid oxygen) which are magnetic like iron, though in a much less degree (distinguished from *ferromagnetic* and opposed to *diamagnetic*). [f. PARA-[1] + MAGNETIC]

Paramaribo (*Du.* pä rä mä′rē bō), *n.* a seaport in NE South America: capital of Surinam. 123,000 (est. 1962).

paramatta (pă′rə măt′ə), *n.* a light, twilled dress fabric, having a silk or cotton warp and a woollen weft. Also, **parramatta.** [named after *Parramatta,* town in New South Wales]

paramecium (pă′rə mē′syəm), *n., pl.* **-cia** (-syə). a ciliate infusorian having an oval body and deep long oral groove, inhabiting fresh water and widely distributed in a number of species. [t. NL, der. Gk *paramḗkēs* oblong]

paramedical (pă′rə mĕd′ĭ kl), *adj.* related to the medical profession in a supplementary capacity.

parameter (pə răm′ĭ tə), *n. Maths.* **1.** a variable entering into the mathematical form of any distribution such that the possible values of the variable correspond to different distributions. **2.** a variable which may be kept constant while the effect of other variables is investigated. **3.** one of the independent variables in a set of parametric equations. —**par′amet′ric,** *adj.*

parametric equation, *Maths.* one of two or more equations in which the coordinates of points on a curve or surface are given in terms of one or more variables (parameters, def. 3) of that curve or surface.

parametron (păʹrə mĕtʹrən), *n. Electronics.* a circuit whose behaviour can be varied systematically by a control signal.

paramilitary (păʹrə mĭlʹĭ tə rĭ, -trĭ), *adj.* of, pertaining to, or denoting an organization having a military structure and used as a supplementary force to regular troops.

paramo (păʹrə mōʹ; *Sp.* päʹrä mō), *n., pl.* **-mos** (-mōzʹ; *Sp.* -mōs). a high plateau region in tropical South America, esp. one bare of trees. [t. Sp.]

paramorph (păʹrə môfʹ), *n. Mineral.* a pseudomorph formed by a change in crystal structure but not in chemical composition. **—parʹamorʹphic,** *adj.*

paramorphism (păʹrə môʹfĭzʹəm), *n.* **1.** the process by which a paramorph is formed. **2.** the state of being a paramorph.

paramount (păʹrə mountʹ), *adj.* **1.** above others in rank or authority; superior in power or jurisdiction. **2.** chief in importance; supreme; pre-eminent. **—***n.* **3.** an overlord; a supreme ruler. [t. AF: m. *paramont* above, f. *par* by (g. L *per*) + *amont* upwards, up (g. L *ad montem* to the mountain). Cf. AMOUNT] **—parʹamountʹcy,** *n.* **—Syn. 2.** See **dominant.**

paramour (păʹrə mo͝oəʹ), *n.* **1.** an illicit lover, esp. of a married person. **2.** any lover. **3.** a beloved one. [ME, t. OF, orig. phrase *par amour* by love, by way of (sexual) love, f. *par* by (g. L *per*) + *amour* love (g. L *amor*)]

Paraná (*Sp.* pä rä näʹ; *Port.* pä rə näʹ), *n.* **1.** a river flowing from S Brazil along the SE boundary of Paraguay and through E Argentina into the Rio de la Plata. ab. 2450 mi. **2.** a city in E Argentina, on the river Paraná: the capital of Argentina, 1852–61. 184,000 (est. 1965).

parang (päʹrăng), *n.* a large, heavy knife used as a tool or a weapon by the Malays. [t. Malay]

paranoia (păʹrə noiʹə), *n. Psychol.* mental disorder characterized by systematized delusions and the projection of personal conflicts, which are ascribed to the supposed hostility of others. The disorder often exists for years without any disturbance of consciousness. Also, **paranoea** (păʹrə nēʹə). [t. NL, t. Gk: derangement]

paranoiac (păʹrə noiʹăk), *adj.* **1.** pertaining to or affected with paranoia. **—***n.* **2.** a person affected with paranoia. Also, **parʹanoidʹ, paranoeac** (păʹrə nēʹăk).

paranymph (păʹrə nĭmfʹ), *n.* **1.** a best man or a bridesmaid. **2.** (in ancient Greece) **a.** a friend who accompanied the bridegroom when he went to bring home the bride. **b.** the bridesmaid who escorted the bride to the bridegroom. [ult. t. Gk: s. *paránymphos*, masc., the best man, *paranýmphē*, fem., the bridesmaid]

parapet (păʹrə pĭt), *n.* **1.** *Fort.* **a.** a defensive wall or elevation, as of earth or stone, in a fortification. See diag. under **bastion. b.** an elevation raised above the main wall or rampart of a permanent fortification. **2.** any protective wall or barrier at the edge of a balcony, roof, bridge, or the like. [t. It.: m. *parapetto*, f. *para-* PARA-[2] + *petto*, g. L *pectus* breast] **—parʹapeted,** *adj.*

paraph (păʹrăf), *n.* a flourish made after a signature, as in a document, orig. as a precaution against forgery. [ME *paraf*, t. ML: m. s. *paraphus*, short for L *paragrapus* PARAGRAPH]

paraphernalia (păʹrə fə nāʹlyə), *n.pl.* **1.** personal belongings. **2.** *Law.* the personal articles, apart from dower, reserved by law to a married woman. **3.** (*sometimes construed as sing.*) equipment; apparatus. **4.** (*sometimes construed as sing.*) any collection of miscellaneous articles. [t. ML (prop. neut. pl.), der. LL *parapherna*, t. Gk: bride's belongings other than dowry]

paraphrase (păʹrə frāzʹ), *n., v.,* **-phrased, -phrasing.** **—***n.* **1.** a restatement of the sense of a text or passage, as for clearness; a free rendering or translation, as of a passage. **2.** the act or process of paraphrasing. **—***v.t., v.i.* **3.** to restate; render in, or make, a paraphrase. [t. F, t. L: m. s. *paraphrasis*, t. Gk] **—parʹaphrasʹable,** *adj.* **—parʹaphrasʹer,** *n.* **—Syn. 1.** See **translation.**

paraphrast (păʹrə frăstʹ), *n.* one who paraphrases.

paraphrastic (păʹrə frăsʹtĭk), *adj.* having the nature of a paraphrase. **—parʹaphrasʹtically,** *adv.*

paraphysis (pə răfʹĭ sĭs), *n., pl.* **-ses** (-sēzʹ). *Bot.* one of the sterile, usually filamentous, outgrowths often occurring among the reproductive organs in many cryptogamous plants. [t. NL, t. Gk: offshoot]

paraplegia (păʹrə plēʹjyə), *n. Pathol.* paralysis of both lower or upper limbs. [t. NL, t. Gk: paralysis on one side] **—paraplegic** (păʹrə plēʹjĭk), *adj., n.*

parapodium (păʹrə pōʹdyəm), *n., pl.* **-dia** (-dyə). *Zool.* one of the unjointed lateral locomotor processes or series of rudimentary limbs of many worms, as annelids. [t. NL. See PARA-[1], -PODIUM]

parapsychology (păʹrə sī kŏlʹə jĭ), *n.* a division of psychology which investigates psychic phenomena, as clairvoyance, telepathy, etc. **—parʹapsyʹchologʹical,** *adj.*

paraquet (păʹrə kĕtʹ), *n.* parakeet.

Pará rubber (*Port.* pä räʹ), indiarubber obtained from the euphorbiaceous tree, *Hevea brasiliensis,* and other species of the same genus, of tropical South America.

paras (păʹrəz), *n.pl. Colloq.* paratroops.

parasang (păʹrə săngʹ), *n.* a Persian unit of distance, of varying length, anciently about $3\frac{1}{4}$ miles. [t. L: s. *parasanga*, t. Gk: m. *parasángēs*; of Pers. orig.]

paraselene (păʹrə sĕ lēʹnĭ), *n., pl.* **-nae** (-nē). *Meteorol.* a bright moonlike spot on a lunar halo; a mock moon. Cf. **parhelion.** [t. NL, f. Gk: *para-* PARA-[1] + *selēnē* moon]

parashah (păʹrə shäʹ), *n., pl.* **parashoth** (păʹrə shōthʹ), **parashioth** (păʹrə shēʹōth). **1.** one of the lessons from the Torah or Law read in the Jewish synagogue on Sabbaths and festivals. **2.** one of the subsections into which the weekly lessons read on Sabbaths are divided. Cf. **haphtarah.** [t. Heb.: division]

Parashurama (păʹrə sho͞o räʹmə), *n. Hindu Myth.* first of the three Ramas, and sixth incarnation of Vishnu.

parasite (păʹrə sītʹ), *n.* **1.** an animal or plant which lives on or in an organism of another species (the host), from the body of which it obtains nutriment. **2.** one who lives on others or another without making any useful and fitting return, esp. one who lives on the hospitality of others. **3.** (in ancient Greece) a professional diner-out, who got free meals in return for his amusing or impudent conversation. [t. L: m. s. *parasītus*, t. Gk: m. *parásītos* one who eats at the table of another]

parasitic (păʹrə sĭtʹĭk), *adj.* **1.** living or growing as a parasite; pertaining to or characteristic of parasites. **2.** (of diseases) due to parasites. Also, **parʹasitʹical.** **—parʹasitʹically,** *adv.*

parasiticide (păʹrə sĭtʹĭ sīdʹ), *adj.* **1.** destructive to parasites. **—***n.* **2.** an agent or preparation that destroys parasites.

parasitism (păʹrə sī tĭzʹəm), *n.* **1.** parasitic mode of life or existence. **2.** *Zool., Bot.* the vital relation which a parasite bears to its host; parasitic infestation. **3.** *Pathol.* diseased condition due to parasites.

parasitology (păʹrə sī tŏlʹə jĭ), *n.* a division of biology dealing with parasites and their effects. **—parʹasiʹtologʹical,** *adj.* **—parʹasitolʹogist,** *n.*

parasol (păʹrə sŏlʹ), *n.* a woman's small or light sun umbrella; a sunshade. [t. F, t. It.: m. *parasole*, f. *para-* PARA-[2] + *sole* (g. L *sōl* sun)]

parastichy (pə răsʹtĭ kĭ), *n., pl.* **-chies** (-kĭz). *Bot.* (in a spiral arrangement of leaves, scales, etc., where the internodes are short and the members closely crowded, as in the houseleek and the pine cone) one of a number of secondary spirals or oblique ranks seen to wind round the stem or axis to the right and left. [f. PARA-[1] + m. s. Gk *-stichía* alignment]

parasympathetic (păʹrə sĭmʹpə thĕtʹĭk), *Anat., Physiol.* **—***adj.* **1.** pertaining to that part of the autonomic nervous system which consists of nerves arising from the cranial and sacral regions, and which opposes the action of the sympathetic system, thus inhibiting heartbeat, contracting the pupil of the eye, etc. **—***n.* **2.** a nerve of the parasympathetic system.

parasynapsis (păʹrə sĭ năpʹsĭs), *n. Embryol.* the conjugation of chromosomes side by side; synapsis. **—parʹasynapʹtic,** *adj.*

parasynthesis (păʹrə sĭnʹthĭ sĭs), *n. Gram.* the formation of a word by the addition of an affix to a phrase or compound, as *great-hearted,* which is *great heart* plus *-ed* (not *great* plus *hearted*). [f. PARA-[1] + SYNTHESIS] **—parasynthetic** (păʹrə sĭn thĕtʹĭk), *adj.*

parataxic (păʹrə tăkʹsĭk), *n.* (of emotions, ideas, etc.) ill-adjusted; lacking harmony.

parataxis (păʹrə tăkʹsĭs), *n.* the placing together of sentences, clauses, or phrases without a conjunctive word, as *hurry up, it is getting late; I came—I saw—I conquered.* [t. NL, t. Gk: a placing side by side] **—paratactic** (păʹrə tăkʹtĭk), **parʹatacʹtical,** *adj.* **—parʹatacʹtically,** *adv.*

parathyroid (păʹrə thīʹroid), *Anat.* **—***adj.* **1.** situated near the thyroid gland. **—***n.* **2.** a parathyroid gland.

parathyroid glands, *Anat.* several small glands or oval masses of epithelioid cells, lying near or embedded in the thyroid gland, whose internal secretion governs the calcium content of the blood.

paratrooper (păʹrə tro͞oʹpə), *n.* a soldier who reaches battle, esp. behind enemy lines, by landing from an aeroplane by parachute. [f. PARA-[3] + TROOPER]

paratroops (păʹrə tro͞ops), *n.pl.* paratroops collectively.

paratyphoid (păʹrə tīʹfoid), *adj.* denoting or pertaining to paratyphoid fever.

paratyphoid fever, an infectious disease similar in some ways to typhoid fever but usually milder, and caused by different bacteria.

paravail (păʹrə vālʹ), *adj.* denoting the lowest tenant of a feudal fee. [ME, t. OF: m. *par aval* down, downwards, g. L *per* through + *ad vallem* to the valley]

paravane (păʹrə vānʹ), *n.* a device consisting of a pair of torpedo-shaped vanes towed at the bow of a vessel, usually a minesweeper, at the ends of cables that cut the cable of a moored mine, causing the mine to rise to the surface where it can be destroyed by gunfire.

par avion (*Fr.* pȧr ȧ vyôNʹ), *French.* by aeroplane (as a designation for matter to be sent airmail).

parboil (päʹboilʹ), *v.t.* to boil partially, or for a short time; precook. [ME *parboyle(n)* boil fully (assoc with PART), t. OF: m. *parbouillir*, g. LL *perbullīre.* See PER-, BOIL[1]]

parbuckle (päʹbŭkʹl), *n., v.,* **-led, -ling.** —*n.* **1.** a kind of tackle for raising or lowering a cask or similar object along an inclined plane or a vertical surface, consisting of a rope looped over a post or the like, with its two ends passing round the object to be moved. **2.** a kind of double sling made with a rope, as round a cask to be raised or lowered. —*v.t.* **3.** to raise, lower, or move with a parbuckle. [earlier *parbunkel*; orig. unknown]

Parcae (päʹsē), *n.pl. Rom. Myth.* the Fates. [t. L]

parcel (päʹsəl), *n., v.,* **-celled, -celling** or (*U.S.*) **-celed, -celing,** *adv.* —*n.* **1.** a quantity of something wrapped on put up together; a package or bundle. **2.** a quantity of something, as of a commodity for sale; a lot. **3.** any group or assemblage of persons or things. **4.** a separable, separate, or distinct part or portion or section, as of land. **5.** a part or portion of anything. —*v.t.* **6.** to divide into or distribute in parcels or portions (usually fol. by *out*). **7.** to make into a parcel, or put up in parcels, as goods. **8.** *Naut.* to cover or wrap (a rope, etc.) with strips of canvas. —*adv.* **9.** *Archaic.* partly; in part; partially. [ME *parcelle*, t. OF, t. ML: m. s. *particella*, dim. of L *particula* particle] —**Syn. 1.** See **package.**

parcel post, a branch of a postal service charged with conveying parcels. Also, **parcels post.**

parcenary (päʹsĭ nə rĭ), *n. Law.* coheirship; the undivided holding of land by two or more coheirs.

parcener (päʹsĭ nə), *n. Law.* a joint heir; a coheir. [ME, t. AF, der. *parçon*, g. L *partītio* partition]

parch (päch), *v.t.* **1.** to make dry, esp. to excess, or dry up, as heat, the sun, or a hot wind does. **2.** to make (a person, the lips, throat, etc.) dry and hot, or thirsty, as heat, fever, or thirst does. **3.** *Cookery.* to brown in a dry heat. **4.** (of cold, etc.) to dry or shrivel, like heat. —*v.i.* **5.** to become parched; undergo drying by heat. **6.** to dry (fol. by *up*). **7.** to suffer from heat or thirst. [ME *parche(n)*, *perch(en)*; orig. uncert.]

parcheesi (pä chēʹzĭ), *n.* pachisi.

parchment (pächʹmənt), *n.* **1.** the skin of sheep, goats, etc., prepared for use as a writing material, etc. **2.** a manuscript or document on such material. **3.** a paper resembling this material. [ME *parchemin*, t. OF, b. LL *pergamēna* parchment (der. PERGAMUM, city in Mysia, Asia Minor, whence parchment was brought) and L *parthica* (*pellis*) Parthian (leather)]

parchment paper, a waterproof and grease-resistant paper obtained by treating a paper with concentrated sulphuric acid.

parclose (päʹklōzʹ), *n.* a screen or railing enclosing a shrine, tomb, or chapel separating it from the main body of the church. [ME, t. OF: n. use of fem. pp. of *parclore* completely enclose]

pard[1] (päd), *n. Archaic.* a leopard or panther. [ME, t. OF, t. L: s. *pardus*, t. Gk: m. *párdos*, earlier *párdalis*; of Eastern orig.]

pard[2] (päd), *n. U.S. Slang.* partner; friend. [alter. of PARTNER]

pardi (pä dēʹ), *adv., interj. Archaic.* verily; indeed. Also, **pardie, pardy, perdie.** [ME *parde*, t. OF, t. L: m. *par Deum* by God]

pardner (pädʹnə), *n. U.S. Slang.* partner; friend.

pardon (päʹdn), *n.* **1.** courteous indulgence or allowance, as in excusing fault or seeming rudeness: *I beg your pardon.* **2.** *Law.* **a.** a pardoning; a remission of penalty. **b.** the deed or warrant by which such remission is declared. **3.** forgiveness of an offence or offender. **4.** *Obs.* a papal indulgence. —*v.t.* **5.** to remit the penalty of (an offence): *he will not pardon your transgressions.* **6.** to release (a person) from liability for an offence. **7.** to make courteous allowance for, or excuse (an action or circumstance, or a person): *pardon me, madam.* —*interj.* **8.** (a conventional form of apology for injury or inconvenience.) **9.** (a request for the repetition of something not clearly heard.) [ME *pardone(n)*, t. OF: m. *pardoner*, t. LL: m. *perdōnāre* grant, concede, f. L *per-* PER- + *dōnāre* give] —**parʹdonable,** *adj.* —**parʹdonably,** *adv.* —**Syn. 3.** absolution, remission, amnesty. **5.** forgive, absolve, condone, overlook. **6.** See **excuse.**

pardoner (päʹdə nə), *n.* **1.** one who pardons. **2.** *Hist.* an ecclesiastical official charged with the granting of indulgences.

Pardubice (*Cz.* pȧrʹdo͞o bē tsĕ), *n.* a town in N central Czechoslovakia. 63,000 (1965). German, **Pardubitz** (*Ger.* pȧrʹdo͞o bĭts).

pardy (pä dēʹ), *adv., interj. Archaic.* pardi.

pare (pĕə), *v.t.,* **pared, paring. 1.** to cut off the outer coating, layer, or part of: *to pare apples.* **2.** to remove (an outer coating, layer, or part) by cutting (often fol. by *off* or *away*). **3.** to reduce or remove by, or as if by, cutting; diminish little by little: *to pare down one's expenses.* [ME *pare(n)*, t. OF: m. *parer* prepare, trim, g. L *parāre*] —**Syn. 1.** See **peel**[1].

Paré (*Fr.* pȧ rèʹ), *n.* **Ambroise** (*Fr.* äN brwȧzʹ), 1510–90, French surgeon.

paregoric (păʹrĭ gŏʹrĭk), *Pharm.* —*n.* **1.** a soothing medicine; an anodyne. **2.** a camphorated tincture of opium, intended primarily to check diarrhoea in children. —*adj.* **3.** assuaging pain; soothing. [t. LL: s. *parēgoricus*, t. Gk: m. *parēgorikós* encouraging, soothing]

pareira (pə rēəʹrə), *n.* the root of a South American vine, *Chondodendron tomentosum*, used as a diuretic, etc.; a source of curare. [short for PAREIRA BRAVA]

pareira brava (pə rēəʹrə bräʹvə), pareira. [t. Pg.: m. *parreira brava*, lit., wild vine]

paren., parenthesis.

parenchyma (pə rĕngʹkĭ mə), *n.* **1.** *Bot.* the fundamental (soft) cellular tissue of plants, as in the softer parts of leaves, the pulp of fruits, the pith of stems, etc. **2.** *Anat., Zool.* the proper tissue of an animal organ as distinguished from its connective or supporting tissue. **3.** *Zool.* a kind of jelly-like connective tissue in some lower animals. **4.** *Pathol.* the functional tissue of a morbid growth. [t. NL, t. Gk: lit., something poured in beside] —**parenchymatous** (păʹrĕng kĭmʹə təs), *adj.*

parens, parentheses.

parent (pĕəʹrənt), *n.* **1.** a father or a mother. **2.** a progenitor. **3.** an author or source. **4.** a protector or guardian. **5.** any organism that produces or generates another. [ME, t. L: s. *parens*] —**parʹentless,** *adj.* —**parʹent-likeʹ,** *adj.*

parentage (pĕəʹrən tĭj), *n.* **1.** derivation from parents; birth, lineage, or family; origin: *distinguished parentage.* **2.** parenthood.

parental (pə rĕnʹtl), *adj.* **1.** of or pertaining to a parent: *the parental relation.* **2.** proper to or characteristic of a parent: *parental feelings.* **3.** having the relation of a parent. **4.** *Genetics.* indicating the sequence of generations leading to a particular filial, first parental being shown as P_1, second parental as P_2, etc. —**parenʹtally,** *adv.*

parenteral (pă rĕnʹtə rəl), *adj. Anat., Med., Physiol.* in a manner other than through the digestive canal. [f. PAR(A)-[1] + s. Gk *énteron* intestine + -AL[1]]

parenthesis (pə rĕnʹthĭ sĭs), *n., pl.* **-ses** (-sēzʹ). **1.** the upright curves () collectively, or either of them separately, used to mark off an interjected explanatory or qualifying remark, indicate groupings in mathematics, etc. **2.** *Gram.* a qualifying or explanatory word (e.g., an appositive), phrase, clause (e.g., a descriptive clause), sentence, or other sequence of forms which interrupts the syntactic construction without otherwise affecting it, having often a characteristic intonation, and shown in writing by commas, parentheses, or dashes. Example: *William Smith—you know him well—will be here soon.* **3.** an interval. [t. ML, t. Gk: a putting in beside]

parenthesize (pə rĕnʹthĭ sīzʹ), *v.t.,* **-sized, -sizing. 1.** to insert as or in a parenthesis. **2.** to put between marks of parenthesis: *parenthesize the pronunciation.* **3.** to interlard with parentheses. Also, **parenthesise.**

parenthetic (păʹrən thĕtʹĭk), *adj.* **1.** of, pertaining to, or of the nature of a parenthesis: *several unnecessary parenthetic remarks.* **2.** characterized by the use of parentheses. Also, **parʹenthetʹical.** —**parʹenthetʹically,** *adv.*

parenthood (pĕəʹrənt ho͝odʹ), *n.* the position or relation of, or state of being, a parent.

paresis (pə rēʹsĭs, păʹrĭ sĭs), *n. Pathol.* **1.** incomplete motor paralysis. **2.** See **general paralysis of the insane.** [t. NL, t. Gk: a letting go]

paresthesia (păʹrĕs thēʹzyə), *n. Pathol., Chiefly U.S.* paraesthesia. —**paresthetic** (păʹrĕs thĕtʹĭk), *adj.*

paretic (pə rĕtʹĭk, pə rēʹtĭk), *n.* **1.** one who has general paresis. —*adj.* **2.** pertaining to, or affected with, paresis.

Pareto (*It.* pä rĕʹtō), *n.* **Vilfredo** (*It.* vēl frĕʹdō), 1848–1923, Italian sociologist and economist, in Switzerland.

pareve (päʹrə vĭ), *adj. Judaism.* containing neither milk nor meat in any form, and therefore admissible for use with either according to the dietary laws: *pareve bread.* [t. Yiddish: m. *parev*]

par excellence (pä rĕk′sə ləns; *Fr.* pȧr ĕk sĕ läɴs′), *French.* by excellence or superiority; above all others; pre-eminently.

par exemple (*Fr.* pȧr ĕg zäɴ′pl), *French.* for example.

parfait (pä fā′; *Fr.* pȧr fĕ′), *n.* a rich frozen dessert of whipped cream and egg, variously flavoured. [t. F: lit., perfect]

pargasite (pä′gə sīt′), *n. Mineral.* a variety of hornblende, containing fluorine, sodium, and aluminium. [named after *Pargas*, town in Finland]

parget (pä′jĭt), *n.*, *v.*, **-geted, -geting** or **-getted, -getting.** —*n.* **1.** gypsum or plaster stone. **2.** plaster, esp. a kind of mortar formed of lime, hair, and cow dung. **3.** plasterwork, esp. a more or less ornamental facing for exterior walls. —*v.t.* **4.** to cover or decorate with parget. [ME *pargette(n)*, t. OF: m. *parjeter* throw over a surface, f. *par* over + *jeter* throw]

pargeting (pä′jĭ tĭng), *n.* **1.** the act of one who pargets. **2.** parget. Also, **par′getting.**

parheliacal (pä′hĭ lī′ə kl), *adj.* of or pertaining to or constituting a parhelion or parhelia. Also, **parhelic** (pä hē′lĭk).

parheliacal ring, *Meteorol.* a white horizontal band passing through the sun, either incomplete or extending round the horizon, produced by the reflection of the sun's rays from the vertical faces of ice prisms in the atmosphere. Also, **parhelic circle.**

parhelion (pä hē′lyən), *n.*, *pl.* **-lia** (-lyə). *Meteorol.* a bright circular spot on a solar halo; a mock sun; usually, one of two or more such spots seen on opposite sides of the sun, and often accompanied by additional luminous arcs and bands. [t. L: m. *parēlion* (with etymological *-h-*), t. Gk, var. of *parēlios* f. *para-* PARA-[1] + *hḗlios* sun]

pariah (pă′rĭ ə), *n.* **1.** any person or animal generally despised; an outcast. **2.** (*cap.*) a member of a low caste in southern India. [t. Tamil: m. *paraiyar*, pl. of *paraiyan*, lit., drummer (from a hereditary duty of the caste), der. *parai* a festival drum]

Parian (pĕə′rĭ ən), *adj.* **1.** of or pertaining to Paros, noted for its white marble. **2.** denoting or pertaining to a fine, unglazed porcelain resembling this marble. —*n.* **3.** a native or inhabitant of Paros. **4.** Parian porcelain.

paries (pĕə′rĭ ēz′), *n.*, *pl.* **parietes** (pə rī′ĭ tēz′). (*usually pl.*) *Biol.* a wall, as of a hollow organ; an investing part. [t. L: wall]

parietal (pə rī′ĭ tl), *adj.* **1.** *Anat.* **a.** referring to the side of the skull, or to any wall or wall-like structure. **b.** denoting or pertaining to the parietal bones. **2.** *Biol.* of or pertaining to parietes or structural walls. **3.** *Bot.* pertaining to or arising from a wall: usually applied to ovules when they proceed from or are borne on the walls or sides of the ovary. **4.** *U.S.* pertaining to or having authority over those within the walls or buildings of a college. [t. LL: s. *parietālis*, der. L *pariēs* wall]

parietal bones, *Anat.* a pair of bones of the cranium, right and left, developed in membrane, forming most of the top and sides of the skull vault, between the occipital and the frontal bones. See diag. under **cranium.**

parietal lobe, *Anat.* the middle lobe of the cerebrum.

parimutuel (pă′rĭ myo͞o′tyo͞o əl), *n. Chiefly U.S.* totalizator. [t. F: mutual bet]

paring (pĕə′rĭng), *n.* **1.** the act of one who or that which pares. **2.** a piece or part pared off.

pari passu (pă′rĭ păs′o͞o), *Latin.* **1.** with equal pace or progress; side by side. **2.** fairly and without bias.

paripinnate (pă′rĭ pĭn′āt), *adj. Bot.* **1.** evenly pinnate. **2.** pinnate without an odd terminal leaflet.

Paris (pă′rĭs; *Fr.* pȧ rē′), *n.* **1.** the capital of France, in the N part, on the Seine. 2,790,091 (1962); with suburbs, 6,523,633 (1962). **2.** a department comprising this city. **3.** See **Matthew of Paris. 4.** See **plaster of Paris.** [L *Lutetia Parisiōrum*, LL *Parisiī*, orig. name of the Gallic tribe living there] —**Parisian** (pə rĭz′yən), *adj.*, *n.*

Paris (pă′rĭs), *n. Gk Legend.* a Trojan youth, son of King Priam and Hecuba. His abduction of Helen led to the Trojan War, at the end of which he was killed by Philoctetes. See **apple of discord.**

Paris green, an emerald green pigment prepared from arsenic trioxide and acetate of copper, now used chiefly as an insecticide.

parish (pă′rĭsh), *n.* **1.** an ecclesiastical district having its own church and clergyman. **2.** a local church with its field of activity. **3.** a civil district or administrative division. **4.** the people of a parish (ecclesiastical or civil). **5. on the parish, a.** *Obs.* in receipt of poor relief. **b.** *Colloq.* poor; indigent. [ME, t. OF: m. *paroisse*, g. LL *parochia*, var. of *paroecia*, t. Gk: m. *paroikía*]

parish clerk, a lay officer of the church in a parish whose duties are to keep the register, lead the responses in services, etc.

parish council, a body elected to manage the affairs of a parish.

parishioner (pə rĭsh′ə nə), *n.* one of the community or inhabitants of a parish. [f. earlier *parishion* (t. OF: m. *parochien*) + -ER[1]]

parish pump, a pump forming the common water supply for a small rural community, regarded as the gathering-place for gossip and a symbol of parochialism.

parish register, a record of all births, baptisms, marriages, and deaths in a parish.

parison (pă′rĭ zən), *n. Glassmaking.* a preliminary shape or blank, from which a glass article is to be formed. [t. F: m. *paraison* preparation]

parity[1] (pă′rĭ tĭ), *n.* **1.** equality, as in amount, status, or character. **2.** equivalence; correspondence; similarity or analogy. **3.** *Finance.* **a.** equivalence in value in the currency of another country. **b.** equivalence in value at a fixed ratio between moneys of different metals. **4.** *Physics.* a symmetry property of a wave-function: if the parity is even (+1), the function is not changed by a mirror reflection of the coordinate system; if the parity is odd (−1), the function changes sign. **5.** *Computers.* a method of checking information in a computer, by counting the number of digits present in a binary number. [t. LL: m. s. *pāritas*, der. L *pār* equal]

parity[2] (pă′rĭ tĭ), *n. Obstet.* condition or fact of having borne offspring. [f. s. L *parere* bring forth + -ITY]

park (päk), *n.* **1.** a tract of land set apart, as by a city or a nation, for the benefit of the public: *Hyde Park, the Lake District National Park.* **2.** a considerable extent of land forming the grounds of a country house. **3.** an enclosed tract of land for wild animals. **4.** *Chiefly U.S.* a tract of land set apart for recreation, sports, etc. **5.** *U.S.* a high, plateau-like valley. **6.** *U.S.* a car park. **7.** *Mil.* **a.** the space occupied by the assembled guns, tanks, stores, etc., of a body of soldiers. **b.** the assemblage formed. **c.** complete equipment, as of guns, etc. —*v.t.* **8.** to put or leave (a car, etc.) for a time in a particular place, as at the side of the road. **9.** *Colloq.* to put or leave. **10.** to assemble (artillery, etc.) in compact arrangement. **11.** to enclose in or as in a park. —*v.i.* **12.** to park a car, bicycle, etc. [ME *parc*, t. OF; of Gmc orig., akin to G *Pferch* fold, pen, and OE *pearroc* enclosure, and to PADDOCK[1]] —**park′-like′,** *adj.*

Park (päk), *n.* **Mungo** (mŭng′gō), 1771–1806?, Scottish explorer in Africa.

parka (pä′kə), *n.* **1.** a fur coat, cut like a shirt, worn in north-eastern Asia and in Alaska. **2.** a long woollen shirtlike garment with an attached hood. [t. Russ.]

Park Avenue, a street in New York City, which, because of its large, expensive flats, has come to represent luxury, the height of fashion, etc.

Park Chung Hee (päk′ cho͝ong′ hē′), born 1917, president of South Korea since 1963.

Parker (pä′kə), *n.* **1. Charles Christopher** ('*Charlie*'; '*Bird*'), 1920–55, U.S. jazz saxophonist. **2. Dorothy (Rothschild),** 1893–1967, U.S. writer and wit. **3. Sir Gilbert,** 1862–1932, Canadian novelist and politician in England. **4. Matthew,** 1504–75, English theologian. **5. Theodore,** 1810–60, U.S. preacher, theologian, and reformer.

parkin (pä′kĭn), *n.* a type of ginger cake made with oatmeal, orig. in Yorkshire.

parking (pä′kĭng), *n.* **1.** the act of one who or that which parks. **2.** space in which to park vehicles. **3.** permission to park vehicles. —*adj.* **4.** of, pertaining to, or used for parking.

parking meter, a device for registering and collecting payment for a length of time during which a vehicle may be parked, consisting typically of a clockwork mechanism activated by a coin, mounted on a pole by a parking space.

parking orbit, *Astronautics.* a temporary orbit in which a spacecraft awaits the next phase of its planned mission.

Parkinson's disease (pä′kĭn sənz), *Pathol.* a form of paralysis characterized by tremor, muscular rigidity, and weakness of movement; paralysis agitans; shaking palsy. Also, **Parkinsonism.** [named after James *Parkinson*, 1755–1824, English physician who first described it]

Parkinson's law, either of two ideas, stated facetiously as laws of physics, that **1.** work expands to fill the time allotted to it, and **2.** the staff of an establishment expands even while the productivity remains constant or declines. [devised by C. Northcote *Parkinson*, born 1909, English writer]

park-keeper (päk′kē′pə), *n.* an official whose duty is to maintain a park, prevent breaking of by-laws, etc.

parkland (päk′lănd′), *n.* a grassland region with isolated or grouped trees, usually in temperate regions.

Park Range, a range of the Rocky Mountains in central Colorado. Highest peak, Mt Lincoln, 14,287 ft.

parkway (päk′wā′), *n. Chiefly U.S.* a broad thoroughfare with spaces planted with grass, trees, etc.

parky (pä′kĭ), *adj. Colloq.* cold; chilly. [orig. uncert.]

Parl., 1. Parliament. 2. (*also l.c.*) Parliamentary.

parlance (pä′ləns), *n.* **1.** way of speaking, or language; idiom; vocabulary: *legal parlance.* **2.** *Archaic.* talk; parley. [t. AF, der. *parler* speak, der. L *parabola.* See PARABLE]

parlando (pä lăn′dō; *It.* pȧr lȧn′dȯ), *adj., adv. Music.* (to be sung or played) as though speaking or reciting. [It.]

parlay (pä′lĭ), *U.S.* —*v.t., v.i.* **1.** to bet (an original amount and its winnings) on a subsequent race, contest, etc. —*n.* **2.** such a bet. [alter. of *paroli*, t. F, t. It., possibly der. Neapolitan *paro* pair]

parley (pä′lĭ), *n., pl.* **-leys,** *v.,* **-leyed, -leying.** —*n.* **1.** a discussion; a conference. **2.** an informal conference between enemies under truce, to discuss terms, conditions of surrender, etc. —*v.i.* **3.** to hold an informal conference with an enemy, under a truce, as between active hostilities. **4.** to speak, talk, or confer. Also, *Archaic or Dial.,* **parle.** [t. F: m. *parlée* speech]

Parler (*Ger.* pȧr′lər), *n.* a German family of masons of the 14th and early 15th centuries, the most famous of whom was **Peter** (*Ger.* pė′tər), died 1399.

parliament (pä′lə mənt), *n.* **1.** (*sometimes cap.*) the legislature of Great Britain, historically the assembly of the three estates, now composed of lords spiritual and lords temporal (forming together the House of Lords), and representatives of the counties, cities, boroughs, and universities (forming the House of Commons). **2.** any one of similar legislative bodies in other countries. **3.** (in pre-Revolutionary France) the highest court in each province, succeeding the feudal 'parlements', which were both courts and councils. **4.** a meeting or assembly for conference on public or national affairs. Also, *Obs.,* **parlement.** [ME *parlement*, t. OF, der. *parler* speak. See PARLANCE]

parliamentarian (pä′lə mĕn tēə′rĭ ən), *n.* **1.** one skilled in parliamentary procedure or debate. **2.** a member of Parliament. **3.** (*cap.*) a partisan of the British Parliament in opposition to Charles I. —*adj.* **4.** (*cap.*) of, pertaining to, or in support of the Parliamentarians.

parliamentarianism (pä′lə mĕn tēə′rĭ ə nĭz′əm), *n.* advocacy of a parliamentary system of government.

parliamentary (pä′lə mĕn′tə rĭ, -trĭ), *adj.* **1.** of or pertaining to a parliament. **2.** enacted or established by a parliament. **3.** characterized by the existence of a parliament. **4.** of the nature of a parliament. **5.** in accordance with the rules and usages of parliaments or deliberative bodies: *parliamentary procedure.*

parliament hinge, a hinge with a large projection, which allows a door to open to its fullest extent.

parlor car, *U.S.* a railway carriage for day or evening travel, fitted with individual reserved seats, and more comfortable than ordinary carriages.

parlour (pä′lə), *n.* **1.** a room for the reception and entertainment of visitors; a living room. **2.** a semi-private room in a hotel, club, or the like for relaxation, conversation, etc.; a lounge. **3.** a room in a monastery or a nunnery where conversation is allowed and where visitors are received. **4.** *Orig. U.S.* a room more or less elegantly fitted up for the reception of business patrons or customers: *a beauty parlour.* Also, *U.S.,* **parlor.** [ME *parlur*, t. AF, der. *parler* speak. See PARLANCE]

parlour game, any of a variety of indoor games, as consequences, quizzes, or the like, as played at parties.

parlourmaid (pä′lə mād′), *n.* a maid who waits at table, etc., in a house where menservants are not employed.

parlous (pä′ləs), *Archaic.* —*adj.* **1.** perilous; dangerous. **2.** very great. **3.** clever; shrewd. —*adv.* **4.** very. [ME; var. of PERILOUS] —**par′lously,** *adv.*

parl. proc., parliamentary procedure.

Parma (pä′mə; *It.* pȧr′mȧ), *n.* a city in N Italy. 164,396 (1966).

Parmenides (pä mĕn′ĭ dēz′), *n.* fl. *c.* 475 B.C., Greek Eleatic philosopher, born in Italy.

Parmesan (pä′mĭ zăn′), *adj.* **1.** of or from Parma in northern Italy. —*n.* **2.** a hard, dry, fine-flavoured variety of Italian cheese, made from skimmed milk. [t. F, t. It.: m. *parmigiano*, der. *Parma*]

Parmigianino (*It.* pȧr mē jȧ nē′nȯ), *n.* **Francesco** (*It.* frȧn chĕs′kȯ), 1503–40, early Mannerist Italian painter.

Parnahiba (*Port.* pȧr nȧ ē′bȧ). *n.* a river in NE Brazil, flowing NE to the Atlantic. ab. 900 mi. Also, **Parnahyba.**

Parnassian (pä năs′ĭ ən), *adj.* **1.** pertaining to Mount Parnassus. **2.** pertaining to poetry. **3.** denoting or pertaining to a school of French poets, of the latter half of the 19th century, characterized esp. by emphasis of form and by repression of emotion (so called from *Le Parnasse Contemporain*, the title of their first collection of poems, published in 1866). —*n.* **4.** a member of the Parnassian school of French poets. [f. s. L *Parnās(s)ius*, (der. *Parnās(s)us*) + -AN. Cf. F *Parnassien*]

Parnassus (pä năs′əs), *n.* **1. Mount.** Modern, **Liakoura.** a mountain in central Greece, in ancient Phocis: sacred to Apollo and the Muses, and symbolic of poetic inspiration and achievement. 8068 ft. **2.** a collection of poems or of elegant literature. **3.** the world of poetry, esp. as part of the established literary world.

Parnell (pä nĕl′), *n.* **Charles Stewart,** 1846–91, Irish political leader. —**Parnell′ism,** *n.* —**Parnell′ite,** *n.*

parochial (pə rō′kyəl), *adj.* **1.** of or pertaining to a parish or parishes. **2.** confined to or interested only in one's own parish, or some particular narrow district or field. [ME, t. LL: s. *parochiālis*, der. LL *parochia.* See PARISH] —**paro′chially,** *adv.*

parochialism (pə rō′kyə lĭz′əm), *n.* parochial character, spirit, or tendency; narrowness of interests or view.

parody (păr′ə dĭ), *n., pl.* **-dies,** *v.,* **-died, -dying.** —*n.* **1.** a humorous or satirical imitation of a serious piece of literature or writing. **2.** the kind of literary composition represented by such imitations. **3.** a burlesque imitation of a musical composition. **4.** a poor imitation; a travesty. —*v.t.* **5.** to imitate (a composition, author, etc.) in such a way as to ridicule. **6.** to imitate poorly. [t. L: m. s. *parōdia*, t. Gk: m. *parōidía* burlesque poem] —**par′odist,** *n.* —**Syn. 1.** See **burlesque.**

paroicous (pə roi′kəs), *adj. Bot.* (of certain mosses) having the male and female reproductive organs beside or near each other. Also, **paroecious** (pə rē′shəs). [t. Gk: m. *pároikos* dwelling beside]

parol (pə rōl′), *Law.* —*n.* **1.** *Obs.* the pleadings in a suit. —*adj.* **2.** given by word of mouth; oral; not written (opposed to *documentary*, or given by affidavit): *parol evidence.* [t. AF (legal): m. *parole.* See PAROLE]

parole (pə rōl′), *n., v.,* **-roled, -roling.** —*n.* **1. a.** the liberation of a person from prison, conditional upon good behaviour, prior to the end of the maximum sentence imposed upon that person. **b.** the temporary release of a prisoner. **c.** such release or its duration. **2.** *U.S. Mil.* **a.** the promise of a prisoner of war to refrain from trying to escape, or, if released, to return to custody or to forbear taking up arms against his captors. **b.** a password given by authorized personnel in passing through a guard. **3.** a word of honour given or pledged. **4.** *U.S.* the temporary admission of an alien to the United States at the discretion of the attorney general. **5.** *Law.* parol. —*v.t.* **6.** to put on parole. [t. F, g. L *parabola.* See PARABLE]

parolee (pə rō′lē′), *n.* one who is released on parole.

paronomasia (păr′ə nō mā′syə), *n. Rhet.* **1.** a playing on words; punning. **2.** a pun. [t. L, t. Gk] —**paronomastic** (păr′ə nō măs′tĭk), *adj.* —**par′onomas′tically,** *adv.*

paronychia (păr′ə nĭk′ĭ ə), *n.* an infection of the soft tissues around the nail bed.

paronym (păr′ə nĭm), *n. Gram.* a paronymous word.

paronymous (pə rŏn′ĭ məs), *adj. Gram.* of words having the same root or stem, as *wise* and *wisdom.* [t. Gk: m. *parṓnymos* derivative]

Paroo (pə ro͞o′), *n.* a river in E Australia flowing S through Queensland, then through New South Wales to the river Darling. Course 330 mi.

paroquet (păr′ə kĕt′), *n.* parakeet.

Paros (pēə′rŏs), *n.* a Greek island in the S Aegean: one of the Cyclades; noted for its marble. 7830 pop. (1961); 77 sq. mi.

parotic (pə rŏt′ĭk), *adj. Anat., Zool.* situated about or near the ear.

parotid (pə rŏt′ĭd), *Anat.* —*n.* **1.** either of two saliva-producing glands situated one at the base of each ear. —*adj.* **2.** denoting, pertaining to, or situated near either parotid. [t. L: s. *parōtis*, t. Gk: tumour near the ear]

parotitic (păr′ə tĭt′ĭk), *adj. Pathol.* having the mumps.

parotitis (păr′ə tī′tĭs), *n. Pathol.* mumps. Also, **parotiditis** (pə rŏt′ĭ dī′tĭs). [t. NL; see PAROT(ID), -ITIS]

parotoid (pə rŏt′oid), *Zool.* —*adj.* **1.** resembling a parotid gland. **2.** denoting certain cutaneous glands forming warty masses or excrescences near the ear in certain salientians, as toads. —*n.* **3.** a parotid gland. [f. Gk *parōt(is)* (see PAROTID + -OID]

-parous, an adjective termination meaning 'bringing forth', 'bearing', 'producing', as in *oviparous, viviparous.* [t. L: m. *-parus*, der. *parere* bring forth]

parousia (pə ro͞o′zĭ ə), *n. Theol.* the return of Christ to earth at the end of the world; the Second Advent.

paroxysm (păr′ək sĭz′əm), *n.* **1.** any sudden, violent outburst; a fit of violent action or emotion: *paroxysms of rage.* **2.** *Pathol.* a severe attack, or increase in violence of a disease, usually recurring periodically. [t. ML: s. *paroxysmus*, t. Gk: m. *paroxysmós* irritation] —**par′oxys′mal, par′oxys′mic,** *adj.*

paroxytone (pə rŏk′sĭ tōn′), *Gk Gram.* —*adj.* **1.** having an acute accent on the next to the last syllable. —*n.* **2.** a paroxytone word. [t. Gk: m. s. *paroxýtonos.* See PARA-[1], OXYTONE]

parquet (pä′kā, pä′kĭ), *n.*, *v.*, **-queted** (-kād, -kĭd), **-queting** (-kā ĭng, -kĭ ĭng). —*n.* **1.** composed of short pieces of wood inlaid so as to form a pattern. **2.** *U.S.* the stalls in a theatre. **3.** (in France, etc.) the branch of the administration concerned with the prevention, investigation and punishment of crime. **4.** the official brokers on the Paris Stock Exchange; the stockbrokers collectively. —*v.t.* **5.** to construct (a flooring, etc.) of parquetry. **6.** to furnish with a floor, etc., of parquetry. [t. F: part of a park, flooring, dim. of *parc* PARK]

parquet circle, *U.S.* a space with curving tiers of seats behind and around the parquet of a theatre, etc.

parquetry (pä′kĭ trĭ), *n.* mosaic work of wood used for floors, wainscoting, etc. [t. F: m. *parqueterie*]

Parquetry

parr (pä), *n.*, *pl.* **parrs,** (*esp. collectively*) **parr.** a young salmon, having dark crossbars on its sides. [orig. unknown]

Parr (pä), *n.* **Catherine,** 1512–48, sixth wife of Henry VIII of England.

parrakeet (pă′rə kēt′), *n.* parakeet. Also, **parroket** (pă′rə kēt′), **par′roquet′.**

parramatta (pă′rə măt′ə), *n.* paramatta.

parrel (pă′rəl), *n.* *Naut.* a sliding ring or collar of rope or iron, which confines a yard or the jaws of a gaff to the mast but allows vertical movement. Also, **parral.** [ME *parail,* aphetic var. of *aparail* APPARAL]

parricide (pă′rĭ sīd′), *n.* **1.** one who kills either of his parents or anyone else to whom he owes reverence. **2.** the act or crime of killing a parent or any one else to whom reverence is due. [t. F, t. L: m. *parricīda* (def. 1), *parricīdium* (def. 2), appar. der. *pater* father. See -CIDE, PATRICIDE] —**par′ricid′al,** *adj.*

parrot (pă′rət), *n.* **1.** any of numerous hook-billed, fleshy-tongued, often gaily coloured birds which constitute the order *Psittaciformes,* as the cockatoo, lory, macaw, parakeet, etc., valued as cagebirds because they can be taught to talk. **2.** a person who unintelligently repeats the words or imitates the actions of another. —*v.t.* **3.** to repeat or imitate like a parrot. **4.** to teach to repeat or imitate thus. [t. F: m. *Perrot, Pierrot,* dim. of *Pierre* Peter]

parrot fever, psittacosis. Also, **parrot disease.**

parrotfish (pă′rət fĭsh′), *n.* any of various marine fishes so called because of their colouring or the shape of their jaws, mainly tropical, mostly of the family *Scaridae,* and certain species of the family *Labridae,* esp. *Labrichthys psittacula,* of Australasia and *Halichoeres radiatus* of Florida, the West Indies, etc.

parrot's bill, the kaka beak.

parry (pă′rĭ), *v.*, **-ried, -rying,** *n.*, *pl.* **-ries.** —*v.t.* **1.** to ward off (a thrust, stroke, weapon, etc.), as in fencing. **2.** to turn aside, evade, or avoid. —*v.i.* **3.** to parry a thrust, etc. —*n.* **4.** an act or mode of parrying as in fencing. **5.** a defensive movement in fencing. [prob. t. F: m. *parez,* impv. of *parer,* t. It.: m. *parare* ward off, protect, g. L: make ready, prepare]

Parry (pă′rĭ), *n.* **1. Sir C(harles) Hubert H(astings),** 1848–1918, English composer. **2. Sir William Edward,** 1790–1855, English arctic explorer.

pars, parentheses.

parse (päz), *v.t.*, **parsed, parsing.** to describe (a word or series of words) grammatically, telling the part of speech, inflectional form, syntactic relations, etc. [t. L: m. *pars* part, as in *pars ōrātiōnis* part of speech] —**pars′er,** *n.*

parsec (pä′sĕk′), *n.* *Astron.* a unit of distance corresponding to a heliocentric parallax of one second of an arc, being equal to 206,265 times the distance of the earth from the sun (or about 3·26 light years). [f. PAR(ALLAX) + SEC(OND)[2]]

Parsee (pä sē′), *n.* one of a Zoroastrian sect in India, descendants of the Persians who settled in India in the 8th century to escape Muslim persecution. Also, **Parsi.** [t. Pers. and Hind.: m. *Pārsī* a Persian]

Parseeism (pä′sē ĭz′əm, pä sē′ĭz′əm), *n.* the religion and customs of the Parsees. Also, **Parsiism.**

Parsifal (pä′sĭ fəl), *n.* *German Legend.* Parzival.

parsimonious (pä′sĭ mō′nyəs), *adj.* characterized by or showing parsimony; sparing or frugal, esp. to excess. —**par′simo′niously,** *adv.*

parsimony (pä′sĭ mə nĭ), *n.* extreme or excessive economy or frugality; niggardliness. [ME, t. L: m. s. *parsimōnia, parcimōnia,* lit., sparingness]

parsley (päs′lĭ), *n.* **1.** a garden herb, *Petroselinum crispum,* with aromatic leaves which are much used to garnish or season food. **2.** any of certain allied or similar plants. [ME *persely,* b. OF *per(esil)* (g. LL *petrosilium*) and OE *(peter)silie,* t. LL]

parsley fern, a fern with tufted leaves and short creeping rhizomes, *Cryptogramma crispa,* occurring on mountains in Europe and W Asia.

parsley piert, a small, pale green, rosaceous annual with fan-shaped leaves and minute flowers, *Aphanes arvensis,* a weed of cultivated land throughout N temperate regions.

parsnip (päs′nĭp), *n.* **1.** a plant, *Pastinaca sativa,* cultivated varieties of which have a large, whitish, edible root. **2.** the root. [ME *pasnepe* (influenced by ME *nepe* NEEP), t. OF: m. *pasnaie,* g. L *pastināca*]

parson (pä′sən), *n.* **1.** a clergyman or minister. **2.** the holder or incumbent of a parochial benefice. [ME *persone,* t. ML: m. *persōna* parson, in L person. See PERSON]

parsonage (pä′sə nĭj), *n.* **1.** the residence of a parson or clergyman, as provided by the parish or church. **2.** *Obs. or Legal.* the benefice of a parson.

parson-bird (pä′sən bûd′), *n.* *N.Z.* the tui.

Parsons (pä′sənz), *n.* **Sir Charles Algernon,** 1854–1931, English engineer.

parson's nose, the fatty tail or rump of a fowl when cooked. Also, **pope's nose.**

part (pät), *n.* **1.** a portion or division of a whole, separate in reality, or in thought only; a piece, fragment, fraction, or section; a constituent. **2.** an essential or integral attribute or quality. **3. a.** a section or major division of a work of literature. **b.** a volume. **4.** a portion, member, or organ of an animal body. **5.** each of a number of more or less equal portions composing a whole: *a third part.* **6.** *Maths.* an aliquot part or exact divisor. **7.** an allotted portion; a share. **8.** (*usually pl.*) a region, quarter, or district: *foreign parts.* **9.** one of the sides to a contest, question, agreement, etc. **10.** an extra piece for replacing worn out parts of a tool, machine, etc. **11.** *Music.* **a.** a voice either vocal or instrumental. **b.** the written or printed matter extracted from the score which a single performer or section uses in the performance of concerted music: *a horn part.* **12.** participation, interest, or concern in something. **13.** one's share in some action; a duty, function, or office: *nature didn't do her part.* **14.** a character sustained in a play or in real life; a role. **15.** the words or lines assigned to an actor. **16.** (*usually pl.*) a personal or mental quality or endowment: *a man of parts.* **17.** (*pl.*) the genitals. **18.** a part of speech. **19.** *U.S.* a parting in the hair. **20.** Some special noun phrases are:

for my (his, etc.) **part,** so far as concerns me (him, etc.).

for the most part, with regard to the greatest part; mostly.

in good part, with favour; without offence.

in part, in some measure or degree; to some extent.

part and parcel, an essential part.

play a part, 1. to act deceitfully; dissemble or dissimulate. **2.** to be instrumental.

take part, to participate.

take someone's part, to support or defend.

—*v.t.* **21.** to divide (a thing) into parts; break; cleave; divide. **22.** to comb (the hair) away from a dividing line. **23.** to dissolve (a connection, etc.) by separation of the parts, persons, or things involved: *she parted company with her sisters.* **24.** to divide into shares; distribute in parts; apportion. **25.** to put or keep asunder (two or more parts, persons, etc., or one part, person, etc., from another); draw or hold apart; disunite; separate. **26.** *Obs.* to leave. —*v.i.* **27.** to be or become divided into parts; break or cleave: *the frigate parted amidships.* **28.** to go or come apart or asunder, or separate, as two or more things. **29.** to go apart from each other or one another, as persons: *we'll part no more.* **30.** to be or become separated from something else (usually fol. by *from*). **31.** *Naut.* to break or rend, as a cable. **32.** to depart. **33.** to die. **34. part with, a.** to give up; relinquish: *I parted with my gold.* **b.** to depart from. —*adj.* **35.** in part; partial. —*adv.* **36.** in part; partly. [ME, OE, t. L: s. *pars* piece, portion]

—**Syn. 1.** PART, PIECE, PORTION refer to that which is less than the whole. PART is the general word: *part of a house.* A PIECE suggests a part which is itself a complete unit, often of standardized form: *a piece of pie.* A PORTION is a part allotted or assigned to a person, purpose, etc.: *a portion of food.* —**Ant. 1.** whole.

part., 1. participle. **2.** particular.

partake (pä tāk′), *v.*, **-took, -taken, -taking.** —*v.i.* **1.** to take or have a part or share in common with others; participate (fol. by *in*). **2.** to receive, take, or have a share (fol. by *of*). **3.** to have something of the nature or character (fol. by *of*): *feelings partaking of both joy and regret.* —*v.t.* **4.** to take or have a part in; share. [back formation from *partaking, partaker,* for *part-taking, part-*

taker, trans. of L *participātio, particeps*] —**partak′er,** *n.* —**Syn. 1.** See **share**[1].

partan (pä′tn), *n. Scot.* an edible crab. [t. Gaelic]

parted (pä′tĭd), *adj.* **1.** divided into parts; cleft. **2.** put or kept apart; separated. **3.** *Bot.* (of a leaf) separated into rather distinct portions by incisions which extend nearly to the midrib or the base. **4.** *Archaic.* deceased.

parterre (pä tēə′; *Fr.* pȧr tĕr′), *n.* **1.** an ornamental arrangement of flowerbeds of different shapes and sizes. **2.** *U.S.* the part of the main floor of a theatre, etc., behind the orchestra, often under the galleries. [t. F, f. *par* by, on (g. L *per*) + *terre* earth (g. L *terra*)]

partheno-, a word element meaning 'virgin', 'without fertilization', as in *parthenogenesis.* [comb. form of Gk *parthénos* virgin]

parthenogenesis (pä′thĭ nō jĕn′ĭ sĭs), *n. Biol.* development of an egg without fertilization. —**parthenogenetic** (pä′thĭ nō jĭ nĕt′ĭk), *adj.* —**par′thenogenet′ically,** *adv.*

Parthenon (pä′thĭ nən), *n.* the temple of Athene on the Acropolis of Athens, completed (structurally) about 438 B.C., regarded as the finest example of Doric temple architecture. [t. L, t. Gk, der. *parthénos* virgin (*Athene Parthénos* Athene the Virgin)]

Parthenos (pä′thĭ nŏs′), *n.* maiden or virgin (applied to some Greek goddesses, esp. Athene).

Parthia (pä′thyə), *n.* an ancient country in W Asia, SE of the Caspian Sea: conquered by the Persians, A.D. 226; now a part of NE Iran. —**Par′thian,** *adj., n.*

Parthian shot, 1. a rearward shot by a fleeing mounted archer. **2.** any sharp parting remark.

partial (pä′shəl), *adj.* **1.** pertaining to or affecting a part. **2.** being such in part only; not total or general; incomplete: *partial blindness.* **3.** *Bot.* secondary or subordinate: *a partial umbel.* **4.** being a part; component or constituent. **5.** biased or prejudiced in favour of a person, group, side, etc., as in a controversy. **6.** particularly inclined in fondness or liking (fol. by *to*): *I'm partial to chocolate.* —*n.* **7.** *Music.* a name given to each of the notes of the harmonic series, in ascending order: *first partial, second partial, etc.* [ME, t. LL: s. *partiālis*, der. L *pars* PART, n.] —**par′tially,** *adv.* —**Syn. 5.** one-sided, unfair, unjust.

partial derivative, *Maths.* the derivative of a function with respect to one variable, while the other variables in the function are taken to be constant.

partial fractions, *Alg.* one of the fractions into which a given fraction can be resolved, the sum of such simpler fractions being equal to the given fraction.

partiality (pä′shĭ ăl′ĭ tĭ), *n., pl.* **-ties. 1.** the state or character of being partial. **2.** favourable bias or prejudice: *the partiality of parents for their own offspring.* **3.** a particular liking (often fol. by *for*): *a partiality for society.*

partial pressure, *Physics.* the pressure that one of the gases in a mixture of gases would exert if it was present alone and occupied the same volume as the whole mixture, at the same temperature.

partible (pä′tə bl), *adj.* that may be parted; divisible.

particeps criminis (pä′tĭ kĕps krĭm′ĭ nĭs), *Law.* an accomplice in a crime.

participable (pä tĭs′ĭ pə bl), *adj.* capable of being participated or shared.

participance (pä tĭs′ĭ pəns), *n.* participation.

participant (pä tĭs′ĭ pənt), *n.* **1.** one who participates; a participator. —*adj.* **2.** participating; sharing.

participate (pä tĭs′ĭ pāt′), *v.,* **-pated, -pating.** —*v.i.* **1.** to take or have a part or share, as with others; share (fol. by *in*): *to participate in profits.* —*v.t.* **2.** to take or have a part or share in; share. [t. L: m. s. *participātus*, pp.] —**partic′ipa′tor,** *n.* —**Syn. 1.** See **share**[1].

participation (pä tĭs′ĭ pā′shən), *n.* **1.** the act or fact of participating. **2.** a taking part, as in some action or attempt. **3.** a sharing, as in benefits or profits.

participial (pä′tĭ sĭp′ĭ əl), *Gram.* —*adj.* **1.** of or pertaining to a participle. **2.** similar to or formed from a participle. —*n.* **3.** a participle. [t. L: s. *participiālis*] —**par′ticip′ially,** *adv.*

participle (pä′tĭ sĭ pl), *n. Gram.* (in many languages) an adjective form derived from verbs, which ascribes to a noun participation in the action or state of the verb, in English without specifying person or number of the subject. For example: *burning* in *a burning candle* or *devoted* in *his devoted friend.* [ME, t. OF, der. *participe* (b. with ending *-ple*), t. L: m. s. *participium* a sharing]

particle (pä′tĭ kl), *n.* **1.** a minute portion, piece, or amount; a very small bit: *a particle of dust.* **2.** an elementary particle. **3.** a clause or article, as of a document. **4.** *Rom. Cath. Ch.* **a.** a little piece of the Host. **b.** the small Host given to each lay communicant. **5.** *Gram.* **a.** (in some languages) one of the major form classes, or parts of speech, consisting of words which are neither nouns nor verbs, or of all uninflected words, or the like. **b.** such a word. **c.** a small word of functional or relational use, such as an article, preposition, or conjunction, whether of a separate form class or not. [ME, t. L: m. s. *particula*, dim. of *pars* PART, n.] —**Syn. 1.** mite, whit, iota, jot, tittle.

particle accelerator, *Physics.* an accelerator (def. 6).

particoloured (pä′tĭ kŭl′əd), *adj.* coloured differently in different parts, or variegated: *particoloured dress.* Also, **party-coloured;** *U.S.*, **particolored.**

particular (pə tĭk′yŏŏ lə), *adj.* **1.** pertaining to some one person, thing, group, class, occasion, etc., rather than to others or all; special, not general: *one's particular interests.* **2.** being a definite one, individual, or single, or considered separately: *each particular item.* **3.** distinguished or different from others or from the ordinary; noteworthy; marked; unusual. **4.** exceptional or especial: *to take particular pains.* **5.** being such in an exceptional degree: *a particular friend of mine.* **6.** dealing with or giving details, as an account, description, etc., or a person; detailed; minute; circumstantial. **7.** attentive to or exacting about details or small points: *to be particular about one's food.* **8.** *Logic.* pertaining to a proposition that concerns one or more unspecified members of a class; 'some men are wealthy', 'some man is wealthy', are particular propositions. Cf. **universal** (def. 9); **singular** (def. 6). **9.** *Philos.* partaking of the nature of an unspecified individual as opposed to the universal and to the singular. **10.** *Law.* **a.** denoting an estate which precedes a future or ultimate ownership, as lands devised to a widow during her lifetime, and after that to her children. **b.** denoting the tenant of such an estate. —*n.* **11.** an individual or distinct part, as an item of a list or enumeration. **12.** a point, detail, or circumstance: *a report complete in every particular.* **13.** *Logic.* an unspecified member of a class. **14. in particular,** particularly; especially: *one book in particular.* [t. L: s. *particulāris* of a part, partial; r. ME *particuler*, t. OF]

—**Syn. 1.** See **special. 7.** PARTICULAR, DAINTY, FASTIDIOUS imply great care, discrimination, and taste in choices, in details about one's person, etc. PARTICULAR is the general word implying care and attention to details: *particular about one's clothes.* DAINTY implies delicate taste, and exquisite cleanliness: *a dainty dress.* FASTIDIOUS implies being difficult to please, and critical of small or minor points: *a fastidious taste in shirts.* —**Ant. 7.** careless, slovenly, undiscriminating.

particularism (pə tĭk′yŏŏ lə rĭz′əm), *n.* **1.** exclusive attention or devotion to one's own particular interests, party, etc. **2.** the principle of leaving each state of a federation free to retain its laws and promote its interests. **3.** *Theol.* the doctrine that divine grace is provided only for the elect. —**partic′ularist,** *n.* —**partic′ularis′tic,** *adj.*

particularity (pə tĭk′yŏŏ lă′rĭ tĭ), *n., pl.* **-ties. 1.** the quality or fact of being particular. **2.** special, peculiar, or individual character. **3.** detailed, minute, or circumstantial character, as of description or statement. **4.** attentiveness to details or small points, or special carefulness. **5.** fastidiousness. **6.** that which is particular; a particular or characteristic feature or trait.

particularize (pə tĭk′yŏŏ lə rīz′), *v.,* **-rized, -rizing.** —*v.t.* **1.** to make particular (rather than general). **2.** to mention or indicate particularly. **3.** to state or treat in detail. —*v.i.* **4.** to speak or treat particularly or specifically; mention individuals. Also, **particularise.** —**partic′ulariza′tion,** *n.* —**partic′ulariz′er,** *n.*

particularly (pə tĭk′yŏŏ lə lĭ), *adv.* **1.** in a particular or exceptional degree; especially: *he read it with particularly great interest.* **2.** in a particular manner; specially; individually. **3.** in detail; minutely. —**Syn. 1.** See **especially.**

particulate (pä tĭk′yŏŏ lĭt), *adj.* existing as, composed of, or pertaining to particles.

parting (pä′tĭng), *n.* **1.** the act of one who or that which parts. **2.** division; separation. **3.** leave-taking; departure. **4.** death. **5.** a place of division or separation. **6.** something that serves to part or separate things. **7.** a dividing line formed by combing the hair so that one part falls towards the left and the other towards the right of the head. **8. parting of the ways,** a leave-taking, esp. a final one. —*adj.* **9.** given, taken, done, etc., at parting: *a parting shot.* **10.** of or pertaining to parting, leave-taking, departure, or death. **11.** departing: *the parting day.* **12.** dying. **13.** dividing; separating.

parting strip, a strip, as of wood, used to keep two parts separated, as one in each side of the frame of a window to keep the sashes apart when lowered or raised.

parti pris (*Fr.* pȧr tē prē′), *French.* decision taken; foregone conclusion.

partisan[1] (pä′tĭ′zăn′), *n.* **1.** an adherent or supporter of a person, party, or cause. **2.** *Mil.* a member of a party of light or irregular troops, esp. as forming the indigenous armed resistance to an invader or conqueror; a guerrilla. *—adj.* **3.** pertaining to or carried on by military partisans. **4.** of, pertaining to, or characteristic of partisans. Also, **partizan.** [t. F, t. It.: m. *partigiano*, der. *parte* part, n., g. L *pars*] **—par′tisan′ship,** *n.* **—Syn. 1.** See **follower.**

partisan[2] (pä′tĭ zən), *n.* a shafted weapon with broad blade and curved basal lobes, esp. carried by bodyguards. Also, **partizan.** [t. F: m. *partizane*, t. It.: m. *partigiana* fem., n. use of *partigiano*, adj., PARTISAN[1]]

Head of partisan

partita (pä tē′tə; *It.* pär tē′tä), *n. Music.* an instrumental suite. [t. It.: fem. of *partito* divided into parts]

partite (pä′tīt), *adj.* **1.** divided into parts. **2.** *Bot.* parted. [t. L: m. s. *partītus*, pp.]

partition (pä tĭsh′ən), *n.* **1.** division into or distribution in portions or shares. **2.** separation, as of two or more things. **3.** something that separates. **4.** the date or period of the division of a country into two or more new countries, as that of British India into India and Pakistan in 1947: *before partition.* **5.** a part, division, or section. **6.** an interior wall or barrier dividing a building, enclosure, etc. **7.** a septum or dissepiment, as in a plant or animal structure. **8.** *Law.* **a.** a division of property among joint owners or tenants in common, or a sale of such property followed by a division of the proceeds. **b.** a division of real property held in co-ownership. **9.** *Logic.* the separation of a whole into its integrant parts, i.e. in contradistinction to the division of a genus into species. **10.** *Maths.* a mode of separating a positive whole number into a sum of positive whole numbers. **11.** *Rhet.* (in a speech organized on classical principles) the second part, in which a speaker announces the chief lines of thought he proposes to discuss in support of his theme. *—v.t.* **12.** to divide into parts or portions. **13.** to divide or separate by a partition. **14.** *Law.* to divide property among several owners, either in specie or by sale and division of the proceeds. [ME, t. L: s. *partītio*] **—parti′tioner,** *n.* **—parti′tionist,** *n.* **—parti′tionment,** *n.* **—Syn. 1.** See **division.**

partitive (pä′tĭ tĭv), *adj.* **1.** serving to divide into parts. **2.** *Gram.* denoting part of a whole: *the Latin partitive genitive.* *—n.* **3.** *Gram.* a partitive word or formation, as *of the men* in *half of the men.* **—par′titively,** *adv.*

partizan (pä′tĭ zăn′, pä′tĭ zən), *n., adj.* partisan.

partlet (pät′lĭt), *n. Obs.* a garment for the neck and shoulders. [alter. of *patelet*, t. OF: m. *patelette* band]

partly (pät′lĭ), *adv.* in part; in some measure; not wholly.

partner (pät′nə), *n.* **1.** a sharer or partaker; an associate. **2.** *Law.* **a.** one associated with another or others as a principal or a contributor of capital in a business or a joint venture, usually sharing its risks and profits. **b.** See **limited partner. 3.** See **sleeping partner. 4.** a husband or a wife. **5.** one's companion in a dance. **6.** a player on the same side with another in a game. **7.** (*pl.*) *Naut.* fore-and-aft vertical metal plating fitted underneath a ship's deck to strengthen it where it is cut for a mast, capstan, pump, etc. *—v.t.* **8.** to associate as a partner or partners. **9.** to be, or act as, the partner of. [ME *partener*, var. of PARCENER, appar. by assoc. with PART, n.] **—part′nerless,** *adj.* **—Syn. 1.** colleague, accessory, accomplice.

partnership (pät′nə shĭp′), *n.* **1.** the state or condition of being a partner; participation; association; joint interest. **2.** *Law.* **a.** the relation subsisting between partners. **b.** the contract creating this relation. **c.** an association of persons joined as partners in business. **3.** *Cricket.* the period during which two batsmen stay at the wicket together, usually with reference to the runs scored by them: *a last-wicket partnership of 45.*

part of speech, *Gram.* any of the mutually exclusive major form classes of a language, which taken together include the entire vocabulary: e.g. in Latin, a word is either a *noun, verb, pronoun, adjective, adverb, preposition, conjunction*, or *interjection.*

partook (pä to͝ok′), *v.* pt. of **partake.**

partridge (pä′trĭj), *n., pl.* **-tridges,** (*esp. collectively*) **-tridge. 1.** any of various gallinaceous game birds of the subfamily *Perdicinae*, esp. the **common partridge,** *Perdix perdix*, of Europe. **2.** any of various North American gallinaceous birds as, in New England, the **ruffed grouse** (*Bonasa umbellus*); in Virginia, the **bobwhite quail** (*Colinus virginianus*), etc. **3.** any of various South and Central American tinamous. [ME *pertrich*, t. OF: m. *perdriz*, *perdiz*, g. L *perdix*, t. Gk]

Common partridge, *Perdix perdix* (Length up to 1½ ft)

partridgeberry (pä′trĭj bĕ′rĭ), *n., pl.* **-ries. 1.** a North American, trailing, rubiaceous perennial, *Mitchella repens*, having roundish evergreen leaves, fragrant white flowers, and scarlet berries. **2.** the checkerberry.

partridge-wood (pä′trĭj wo͝od′), *n.* the hard variegated wood of a tropical American papilionaceous tree, *Andira inermis*, sometimes used for cabinet work.

part-song (pät′sŏng′), *n.* a song with parts for several voices, esp. one meant to be sung without accompaniment. **—part′-sing′ing,** *n.*

part time, less than all normal working hours (opposed to *full time*).

part-time (pät′tīm′), *adj.* **1.** of, pertaining to, or occupying less than all normal working hours. **2.** not being one's chief occupation: *a part-time job.* *—adv.* **3.** during less than all normal working hours. **—part′-tim′er,** *n.*

parturient (pä tyo͝o′rĭ ənt), *adj.* **1.** bringing forth or about to bring forth young; in labour. **2.** pertaining to parturition. **3.** bringing forth or about to produce something, as an idea. [t. L: s. *parturiens*, ppr., being in labour] **—partu′riency,** *n.*

parturition (pä′tyo͝o rĭsh′ən), *n.* the act of bringing forth young; childbirth.

party (pä′tĭ), *n., pl.* **-ties,** *adj.* *—n.* **1.** a group gathered together for some purpose, as for amusement or entertainment. **2.** a social gathering or entertainment, as of invited guests at a private house or elsewhere: *to give a party.* **3.** a detachment of troops assigned to perform some particular service. **4.** (*often cap.*) a number or body of persons ranged on one side, or united in purpose or opinion, in opposition to others, as in politics, etc.: *the Labour Party.* **5.** the system or practice of taking sides on public questions or the like. **6.** attachment or devotion to a side or faction; partisanship. **7.** *Law.* **a.** one of the litigants in a legal proceeding; a plaintiff or defendant in a suit. **b.** a signatory to a legal instrument. **c.** one participating in or otherwise privy to a crime. **8.** one who participates in some action or affair. **9.** the person under consideration. **10.** a person in general. *—adj.* **11.** of or pertaining to a party or faction; partisan: *party issues.* **12.** of or for a social gathering: *a party dress.* **13.** *Her.* divided into parts, usually two parts, as a shield. [ME *parti(e)*, t. OF, pp. of *partir* PART, v.] **—Syn. 1.** See **company.**

party-coloured (pä′tĭ kŭl′əd), *adj.* particoloured.

party line, 1. a telephone line shared by two or more subscribers. **2.** the bounding line between adjoining premises. **3.** the authoritatively announced policies and practices of a group, usually followed without exception: *the Communist party line.*

party man, a man belonging to a political party, esp. one who adheres strictly to its principles and policy.

party politics, politics practised with a view to the advancement of a party rather than in the public interest.

party spirit, 1. enthusiastic adherence to a political party. **2.** the mood and feeling of sociability appropriate to a party (def. 2).

party wall, *Law.* a wall used, or useable, as a part of contiguous structures.

parure (pə ro͞o′; *Fr.* pȧ rʏr′), *n.* a set of jewels or ornaments. [ME, t. F, der. *parer* prepare, adorn. See PARE]

parvenu (pä′və nyo͞o′; *Fr.* pȧr və nʏ′), *n.* **1.** one who has risen above his class or to a position above his qualifications; an upstart. *—adj.* **2.** being or resembling a parvenu. **3.** characteristic of a parvenu. [t. F, prop. pp. of *parvenir* arrive, g. L *pervenire*]

parvis (pä′vĭs), *n.* **1.** a vacant enclosed area in front of a church. **2.** a colonnade or portico in front of a church. **3.** a room over a church porch. Also, **parvise** (pä′vĭs). [ME *parvys*, t. OF: m. *parevis*, g. LL *paradīsus* PARADISE]

parvoline (pä′və lēn′), *n. Chem.* any of several oily isomeric, organic bases, $C_9H_{13}N$, one occurring in coal tar and another in decaying mackerel. Also, **parvolin** (pä′və lĭn). [f. s. L *parvus* small (with ref. to its relatively small volatility) + -OL[2] + -INE[2]; modelled on QUINOLINE]

Parzival (*Ger.* pär′tsĭ fäl), *n.* the German counterpart of Percival. Also, **Parsifal.**

pas (pä; *Fr.* pȧ), *n. French.* **1.** a step or movement in dancing, esp. in ballet. **2.** a dance. **3.** precedence; right of preceding. [see PACE[1]]

PAS, *Pharm.* para-amino-salicylic acid, used in the treatment of tuberculosis.

Pasadena (păs′ə dē′nə), *n.* a city in SW California, near Los Angeles. 116,407 (1960).

Pasargadae (pă sär′gə dē′), *n.* an ancient ruined city in S Iran, NE of Persepolis: an early capital of ancient Persia; tomb of Cyrus the Great.

Pasay (pä′sī), *n.* Rizal (def. 2).

Pascal (*Fr.* pȧs kȧl′), *n.* **Blaise** (*Fr.* blĕz), 1623–62, French philosopher, mathematician, and physicist.

Pasch (păsk), *n. Archaic.* **1.** the Passover. **2.** Easter. [ME *pasche*, t. LL: m. *pascha*, t. Gk, t. Heb.: m. *pesaḥ* Passover; var. of PESACH]

paschal (păs′kl), *adj.* **1.** pertaining to the Passover. **2.** pertaining to Easter. [ME *paschall*, t. LL: m. s. *paschālis*, der. *pascha* PASCH]

paschal flower, pasqueflower.

paschal lamb, 1. (among the Jews, during the existence of the Temple) the lamb slain and eaten on the eve of the first day of the Passover. **2.** (*cap.*) Christ. **3.** (*cap.*) any of various symbolical representations of Christ. Cf. **Agnus Dei.**

Paschen series (*Ger.* pȧ′shən), *Physics.* a series of lines occurring in the infra-red region of the hydrogen spectrum. [named after F. *Paschen*, 1865–1947, German physicist]

Pas de Calais (*Fr.* pȧd kȧ lĕ′), **1.** See **Dover, Strait of. 2.** a department in N France. 1,366,282 pop. (1962); 2606 sq. mi. *Cap.*: Arras.

pas de deux (pä′də dû′; *Fr.* pȧ də dœ′), *pl.* **pas de deux.** *French.* a dance by two persons.

pas du tout (*Fr.* pȧ dʏ to͞o′), *French.* not at all.

pash[1] (păsh), *Chiefly Dial.* —*v.t.* **1.** to hurl or dash. **2.** to smash or shatter. —*v.i.* **3.** to dash or strike violently. [ME *pas(s)he(n)*; appar. imit.]

pash[2] (păsh), *n. Chiefly Scot.* the head. [orig. unknown]

pasha (pä′shə), *n.* a title, placed after the name, formerly borne by civil and military officials of high rank in Turkish dominions. Also, **pacha.** [t. Turk., var. of *bāshā*, der. *bash* head, chief]

pashalik (pä′shə lĭk), *n.* the territory governed by a pasha. Also, **pachalic, pashalic.** [t. Turk.: f. *pāshā* PASHA + *-lik*, suffix denoting quality or condition]

Pashto (pŭsh′tō), *n.* Pushtu.

Pasiphaë (pə sĭf′ĭ ē′), *n. Gk Legend.* wife of Minos, and mother of Ariadne. She was the mother of the Minotaur, by the white bull given to Minos by Poseidon.

paso doble (păs′ō dō′blā; *Sp.* pȧ′sȯ dȯ′blĕ), *pl.* **pasos dobles** (păs′ō dō′blāz; *Sp.* pȧs′ȯs dȯ′blĕs). **1.** a quick march often played at the start of bullfights. **2.** a modern ballroom dance in 2/4 time. [*Sp.*: lit., double step]

pasqueflower (păsk′flou′ə), *n.* **1.** an Old World ranunculaceous plant, *Pulsatilla vulgaris*, with purple flowers blooming about Easter. **2.** any of several similar plants, as *Anemone ludoviciana.* [f. *Pasque* (var. spelling of PASCH) + FLOWER (so named by the herbalist Gerarde in 1597); r. *passeflower*, t. F: m. *passe-fleur.* See PASS, v., FLOWER]

pasquil (păs′kwĭl), *n.* a pasquinade.

pasquinade (păs′kwĭ nād′), *n.*, *v.*, **-naded, -nading.** —*n.* **1.** a publicly posted lampoon. —*v.t.* **2.** to assail in a pasquinade or pasquinades. [t. F, t. It.: m. *pasquinata*, der. *Pasquino*, name given to an antique statue dug up in Rome (1501), which was decorated once a year and posted with verses] —**pas′quinad′er,** *n.*

pass (päs), *v.*, **passed** or (*Rare*) **past, passed** or **past, passing,** *n.* —*v.t.* **1.** to go by or move past (something). **2.** to go by without acting upon or noticing; leave unmentioned. **3.** to omit payment of (a dividend, etc.). **4.** to go or get through (a channel, barrier, etc.). **5.** to go across or over (a stream, threshold, etc.); cross. **6.** to undergo successfully (an examination, etc.). **7.** to undergo or get through (an obstacle, experience, ordeal, etc.). **8.** to permit to complete successfully. **9.** to go beyond (a point, degree, stage, etc.); transcend; exceed; surpass. **10.** to cause to go or move onwards; proceed: *to pass a rope through a hole.* **11.** *U.S.* to cause to go by or move past: *to pass troops in review.* **12.** to exist through; live during, as an activity in its own right: *to pass the time of day.* **13.** to cause to go about or circulate; give currency to. **14.** to cause to be accepted or received. **15.** to convey, transfer, or transmit; deliver. **16.** to pronounce; utter: *to pass remarks.* **17.** to pledge, as one's word. **18.** to cause or allow to go through something, as through a test, etc. **19.** to discharge or void, as excrement. **20.** to sanction or approve: *to pass a bill.* **21.** to obtain the approval or sanction of (a legislative body, etc.), as a bill. **22.** to express or pronounce, as an opinion or judgement. **23.** *Law.* to place legal title or interest in (another) by a conveyance, a will, or other transfer. **24.** *Magic.* to perform a pass (def. 61) on (cards, etc.). **25.** *Football, Hockey, etc.* to transmit (the ball, etc.) to another player. —*v.i.* **26.** to go or move onwards; proceed; make one's, or its, way. **27.** to overtake. **28.** to go away or depart. **29.** to elapse, as time. **30.** to come to an end, as a thing in time. **31.** to die. **32.** to go on or take place; happen; occur: *to learn what has passed.* **33.** to go by or move past, as a procession. **34.** to go about or circulate; be current. **35.** to be accepted or received (fol. by *for* or *as*): *material that passed for silk.* **36.** to be transferred or conveyed. **37.** to be interchanged, as between two persons: *sharp words passed between them.* **38.** to undergo transition or conversion: *to pass from a solid to a liquid state.* **39.** to go or get through something, such as a barrier, test, examination, etc., esp. a degree examination without honours. **40.** to go unheeded, uncensured, or unchallenged: *but let that pass.* **41.** to express or pronounce an opinion, judgement, verdict, etc. (usually fol. by *on* or *upon*). **42.** to be voided, as excrement. **43.** to be ratified or enacted, as a bill or law. **44.** *Law.* **a.** to vest title or other legal interest in real or personal property in a new owner. **b.** *U.S.* (of a member of an inquest or other deliberative body) to sit: *to pass on.* **c.** *U.S.* to adjudicate. **45.** to throw a ball from one to another; play catch. **46.** to make a pass, as in football. **47.** *Fencing.* to thrust or lunge. **48.** *Cards.* **a.** to forgo one's opportunity to bid, play, etc. **b.** to throw up one's hand. —*v.* **49.** Some special verb phrases are:

bring to pass, to cause to happen.

come to pass, to occur.

pass away, 1. to cease to be. **2.** to die.

pass off, 1. to put into circulation, or dispose of, esp. deceptively: *to pass off a counterfeit pound.* **2.** to cause to be accepted or received in a false character: *he passed himself off as my servant.* **3.** to end gradually; to cease. **4.** to take place; occur: *the introduction passed off without incident.*

pass on, to die.

pass out, 1. *Colloq.* to faint. **2.** to complete the course, as at a military academy.

pass over, 1. to disregard. **2.** to omit to notice.

pass up, *Colloq.* to refuse; reject.

[ME *passe(n)*, t. OF: m. *passer*, ult. der. L *passus* a step] —*n.* **50.** a narrow route across a relatively low notch or depression in a mountain barrier separating the headwaters of approaching valleys from either side. **51.** a way affording passage, as through an obstructed region. **52.** *U.S.* a navigable channel, as at the mouth or delta of a river. **53.** a permission or licence to pass, go, come, or enter. **54.** *Mil.* **a.** a military document granting the right to cross lines, or to enter or leave a military or naval reservation or other area or building. **b.** written authority given to a soldier to leave a station or duty for a few hours or days. **55.** a free ticket. **56.** the passing of an examination, etc., without honours. **57.** the transference of a ball, etc., from one player to another, as in football. **58.** a thrust or lunge, as in fencing. **59.** *U.S. Slang.* a jab with the arm, esp. one that misses its mark. **60.** *Cards.* an act of not bidding or raising another bid. **61.** *Magic, etc.* **a.** a passing of the hand over, along, or before anything. **b.** the transference or changing of objects by or as by sleight of hand; a manipulation, as of a juggler; a trick. **62.** a stage in procedure or experience; a particular stage or state of affairs: *things have come to a pretty pass.* **63.** the act of passing. **64.** *Archaic.* a sally of wit. **65. make a pass,** to make an amorous overture or gesture (usually fol. by *at*). [ME *passe*; partly n. use of PASS, v.; partly t. F, der. *passer*] —**Syn. 31.** See **die**[1].

pass., 1. passenger. **2.** passive.

passable (pä′sə bl), *adj.* **1.** that may be passed. **2.** that may be proceeded through or over, or traversed, penetrated, crossed, etc., as a road, forest, or stream. **3.** tolerable, fair, or moderate: *a passable knowledge of history.* **4.** that may be circulated, or has valid currency, as a coin. **5.** that may be ratified, or enacted. [ME, t. F, der. *passer* PASS, v.] —**pas′sableness,** *n.*

passably (pä′sə blĭ), *adv.* fairly; moderately.

passacaglia (păs′ə kä′lyə), *n.* **1.** a slow dance of Spanish origin. **2.** the music for this dance, based on an ostinato figure. [t. Sp.: m. *pasacalle*, lit., street-dance; with It. ending *-aglia*]

passade (pă săd′), *n. Manège.* a turn or course of a horse backwards or forwards on the same ground.

passado (pă sä′dō), *n.*, *pl.* **-dos, -does** (-dōz). *Fencing. Obs. or Archaic.* a forward thrust with the sword, one foot being advanced at the same time. [t. Sp.: m. *pasada*, t. It.: m. *passata*, der. *passare* PASS]

passage[1] (păs′ĭj), *n.*, *v.*, **-saged, -saging.** —*n.* **1.** an indefinite portion of a writing, speech, or the like, usually one of no great length; a paragraph, verse, etc.: *a passage of Scripture.* **2.** *Music.* **a.** a scalelike or arpeggio-like series of notes introduced as an embellishment; a run, roulade, or flourish. **b.** a phrase or other division of a piece. **3.** the act of passing. **4.** liberty, leave, or right to pass: *to refuse passage through a territory.* **5.** that by which a person or thing passes; a means of passing; a way, route, avenue, channel, etc. **6.** a corridor, or the like. **7.** movement, transit, or transition, as from one place or state to another. **8.** a voyage across the sea from one port to another: *a rough passage.* **9.** the privilege of conveyance as a passenger: *to secure a passage to Europe.* **10.** lapse, as of time. **11.** progress or course, as of events.

12. the passing into law of a legislative measure. **13.** an interchange of communications, confidences, etc., between persons. **14.** an exchange of blows; an altercation or dispute: *a passage at arms.* **15.** the causing of something to pass; transference; transmission. **16.** an evacuation of the bowels. **17.** *Archaic.* an occurrence, incident, or event. —*v.i.* **18.** to make a passage; cross; pass; voyage. [ME, t. OF, der. *passer* PASS, v.]

passage² (păs′ĭj), *v.*, **-saged, -saging,** *n. Manège.* —*v.i.* **1.** (of a horse) to move sideways, in obedience to pressure by the rider's leg on the opposite side. **2.** (of a rider) to cause a horse to do this. —*v.t.* **3.** to cause (a horse) to passage. —*n.* **4.** the act of passaging. [t. F: m. s. *passager*, t. It.: m. *passeggiare* to pace, walk, der. *passo* pace, g. L *passus* PACE]

passageway (păs′ĭj wā′), *n.* a way for passage, as in a building or among buildings, etc.; a passage.

passant (păs′ənt), *adj. Her.* (of a beast used as a bearing) walking with one paw raised, and looking forward to the dexter side of the escutcheon. [ME, t. F, ppr. of *passer* PASS, v.]

passbook (päs′bŏŏk′), *n.* **1.** a bankbook. **2.** a customer's book in which a merchant or trader makes entries of goods sold on credit. **3.** a record of payments made to a building society.

Passchendaele (păsh′ən dāl′), *n.* a village in NW Belgium: battle of Passchendaele Ridge 1917. 3131 (1965). Also, **Passendale.**

pass degree, (in universities) a degree conferred without honours.

passé (pä′sā, păs′ā; *Fr.* pȧ sĕ′), *adj.* **1.** antiquated, or out-of-date. **2.** passed. **3.** past the prime; aged. [t. F, pp. of *passer* PASS, v.]

passed (päst), *adj.* **1.** that has passed or has been passed. **2.** having passed an examination or test. **3.** *Finance.* denoting a dividend not paid at the usual dividend date.

passementerie (păs mĕn′trĭ; *Fr.* pȧs mäɴ trē′), *n.* trimming made of braid, cord, beads, etc., in various forms. [t. F, der. *passement*, der. *passer* PASS, v.]

passenger (păs′ĭn jə), *n.* **1.** one who travels by some form of conveyance: *the passengers of a ship.* **2.** a wayfarer. **3.** *Colloq.* a member of a team, staff, etc., who does not perform his fair share of work. [ME *passager*, t. OF: m. *passagier*, der. *passage* PASSAGE¹; for *-n-*, cf. MESSENGER, etc.]

passenger pigeon, a wild pigeon, *Ectopistes migratorius*, once extraordinarily common in North America but now extinct.

passe-partout (păs′pä to͞o′; *Fr.* pȧs pȧr to͞o′), *n., pl.* **-touts** (-to͞oz′). **1.** a kind of ornamental mat for a picture. **2.** a frame with such a mat, to receive a photograph or other representation. **3.** a picture frame consisting of a piece of glass, under which the picture is placed, affixed to a backing by means of adhesive strips of paper or other material. **4.** paper, etc., prepared for this purpose. **5.** that which passes, or by means of which one can pass, everywhere. **6.** a master key. [F: lit., pass-everywhere]

passer (pä′sə), *n.* **1.** one that passes or causes something to pass. **2.** a passer-by.

passer-by (pä′sə bī′), *n., pl.* **passers-by.** one who passes by.

passeriform (păs′ə rĭ fôm′), *adj.* belonging or pertaining to the avian order *Passeriformes*; passerine.

passerine (păs′ə rīn′), *adj.* **1.** belonging or pertaining to the *Passeriformes*, an order of birds, typically insessorial (perching), embracing more than half of all birds, and including the finches, thrushes, warblers, swallows, crows, larks, etc. —*n.* **2.** any bird of the order *Passeriformes*. [t. L: m. s. *passerinus* of a sparrow]

pas seul (*Fr.* pȧ sœl′), *French.* a dance performed by one person.

passible (păs′ĭ bl), *adj.* capable of suffering or feeling; susceptible to sensation or emotion. [ME, t. LL: m. s. *passibilis*] —**pas′sibil′ity,** *n.*

passifloraceous (păs′ĭ flô rā′shəs), *adj.* belonging to the *Passifloraceae*, or passionflower family of plants. [f. s. NL *Passiflōra*, the typical genus (f. L: *passi(o)* passion + *-flōra*, fem. adj., flowering) + -ACEOUS]

passim (păs′ĭm), *adv. Latin.* here and there, as in books or writings.

passing (pä′sĭng), *adj.* **1.** going by; elapsing. **2.** fleeting or transitory. **3.** that is now happening; current. **4.** done, given, etc., in passing; cursory: *a passing mention.* **5.** surpassing, pre-eminent, or extreme. **6.** indicating that one has passed: *a passing mark on the test.* —*adv.* **7.** *Archaic.* surpassingly; exceedingly; very. —*n.* **8.** the act of one that passes or causes something to pass. **9.** a means or place of passage; passage. **10. in passing,** in the course of passing, going on, or proceeding.

passing bell, 1. a bell tolled to announce a death or funeral. **2.** a portent or sign of the passing away of anything.

passing modulation, *Music.* a modulation of a temporary nature.

passing note, *Music.* a note foreign to the harmony, introduced between two successive chords in order to produce a melodic transition.

passing-out (pä′sĭng out′), *adj.* (of a ceremony or parade) celebrating the completion of a course or training.

passion (păsh′ən), *n.* **1.** any kind of feeling or emotion, as hope, fear, joy, grief, anger, love, desire, etc., esp. when of compelling force. **2.** strong amorous feeling or desire. **3.** passionate sexual love. **4.** an instance or experience of it. **5.** a person who is the object of such a feeling. **6.** a strong or extravagant fondness, enthusiasm, or desire for anything: *a passion for music.* **7.** the object of such a fondness or desire: *accuracy became a passion with him.* **8.** a passionate outburst: *she broke into a passion of tears.* **9.** violent anger. **10.** *Rare.* the state or fact of being acted upon or affected by something external (opposed to *action*). **11.** (*often cap.*) **a.** the sufferings of Christ on the Cross, or his sufferings subsequent to the Last Supper. **b.** the gospel narrative of the sufferings of Christ, as in Mark 14–15, and parallel passages in the other gospels. **c.** a musical setting of it. **d.** a pictorial representation of Christ's sufferings. **12.** *Archaic.* the sufferings of a martyr. [ME, t. OF, t. L: s. *passio* suffering] —**Syn. 1.** See **feeling.**

passional (păsh′ə nəl), *adj.* **1.** of or pertaining to passion or the passions. **2.** due to passion: *passional crimes.* —*n.* **3.** a book containing descriptions of the sufferings of saints and martyrs, for reading on their festivals.

passionary (păsh′ə nə rĭ), *n., pl.* **-ries.** passional.

passionate (păsh′ə nĭt), *adj.* **1.** affected with or dominated by passion or vehement emotion: *a passionate advocate of socialism.* **2.** characterized by, expressing, or showing vehement emotion; impassioned: *passionate language.* **3.** vehement, as feelings or emotions: *passionate grief.* **4.** easily moved to anger; quick-tempered; irascible. **5.** ardently amorous; easily affected by sexual desire. [late ME *passionat*, t. ML: s. *passionātus*] —**pas′sionately,** *adv.* —**pas′sionateness,** *n.*

passionflower (păsh′ən flou′ə), *n.* any plant of the genus *Passiflora*, which comprises climbing vines or shrubs, mainly American, bearing showy flowers and a pulpy berry or fruit which in some species is edible. [so named from a supposed resemblance of the flower to the wounds, crown of thorns, etc., of Christ]

passionfruit (păsh′ən fro͞ot′), *n.* any edible fruit of a passionflower.

passionless (păsh′ən lĭs), *adj.* without passion; cold; unemotional.

passion play, a dramatic representation of the Passion of Christ, such as that given every ten years at the Bavarian village of Oberammergau.

Passion Sunday, the fifth Sunday in Lent, being the second before Easter.

Passion Week, 1. the week preceding Easter; Holy Week. **2.** the week before Holy Week, beginning with Passion Sunday.

passive (păs′ĭv), *adj.* **1.** not acting, or not attended with or manifested in open or positive action: *passive resistance.* **2.** inactive, quiescent, or inert. **3.** suffering action, acted upon, or being the object of action (opposed to *active*). **4.** receiving or characterized by the reception of impressions from without. **5.** produced by or due to external agency. **6.** suffering, receiving, or submitting without resistance. **7.** characterized by or involving doing this: *passive obedience.* **8.** *Gram.* **a.** (in some languages) denoting a voice, or verb inflection, in which the subject is represented as being acted on. For example: Latin *portātur*, '(he, she, it) is carried', is in the passive voice. **b.** denoting a construction similar to this in meaning, as English *he is carried.* **9.** *Chem.* inactive, esp. under conditions in which chemical activity is to be expected. **10.** (of a metal) having a protective oxide film on the surface rendering it impervious to attack. **11.** (of a communications satellite) only able to reflect signals, and not retransmit them. **12.** *Med.* pertaining to certain unhealthy but insufficiently virulent conditions; inactive (opp. to *active* or *spontaneous*). —*n.* **13.** *Gram.* **a.** the passive voice. **b.** a form or construction therein. [ME, t. L: m. s. *passivus* capable of feeling] —**pas′sively,** *adv.* —**pas′siveness, passiv′ity,** *n.*

passive homing, *Aeron.* a form of missile guidance in which the receiver in the missile utilizes radiations from the target.

passive immunity, *Immunol.* immunity achieved by injecting immune serum from another organism.

passive resistance, the expression of disapproval of authority or of specific laws by various non-violent acts, such as public demonstration or voluntary fasting.

pass key, 1. a master key. 2. a private key. 3. a latchkey. 4. a skeleton key.

Passover (päs′ō′və), *n.* 1. an annual feast of the Jews, instituted to commemorate the passing over or sparing of the Hebrews in Egypt when God smote the firstborn of the Egyptians (see Ex. 12), but used in the general sense of the Feast of Unleavened Bread (Lev. 23: 5–6) in commemoration of the deliverance from Egypt, beginning on the eve of the 15th day of Nisan, and lasting originally seven days but in later Judaism eight days. 2. (*l.c.*) the paschal lamb. 3. (*l.c.*) Christ. [orig. verbal phrase *pass over*]

passport (päs′pôt′), *n.* 1. an official document granting permission to the person specified to visit foreign countries, and authenticating his identity, citizenship and right to protection while abroad. 2. an authorization to pass or go anywhere. 3. a document issued to a ship, esp. to neutral merchant vessels in time of war, granting or requesting permission to proceed without molestation in certain waters. 4. a certificate intended to secure admission. 5. anything that gives admission or acceptance. [t. F: m. *passeport*, f. *passe(r)* PASS + *port* PORT[1] (def. 3)]

passus (päs′əs), *n., pl.* **-sus, -suses.** a section or division of a story, poem, etc.; a canto. [t. ML, in L a step, PACE[2]]

password (päs′wûd′), *n.* a secret word, made known only to authorized persons for their use in passing through a line of guards.

Passy (*Fr.* pȧ sē′), *n.* **Paul Édouard** (*Fr.* pōl ė dwȧr′), 1859–1940, French phonetician.

past (päst), *v. Rare.* 1. pp. and occasional pt. of **pass.** —*adj.* 2. gone by in time. 3. belonging to, or having existed or occurred in time previous to this. 4. gone by just before the present time; just passed: *the past year.* 5. ago. 6. having served a term in an office: *past president.* 7. *Gram.* designating a tense, or other verb formation or construction, which refers to events or states in time gone by. —*n.* 8. the time gone by: *far back in the past.* 9. the events of that time: *to forget the past.* 10. a past history, life, career, etc.: *a glorious past.* 11. a past career which is kept concealed: *a woman with a past.* 12. *Gram.* **a.** the past tense, as *he ate, he smoked.* **b.** another verb formation or construction with past meaning. **c.** a form therein. —*adv.* 13. so as to pass by or beyond; by: *the troops marched past.* —*prep.* 14. beyond in time; after: *past noon.* 15. beyond in position; farther on than: *the house past the church.* 16. beyond in amount, number, etc. 17. beyond the reach, scope, influence, or power of: *past belief.* [see PASS, v.]

pasta (päs′tə; *It.* pȧs′tȧ), *n.* any of several preparations made from flour and egg, the dough of which is used for macaroni, spaghetti, etc.

paste (pāst), *n., v.,* **pasted, pasting.** —*n.* 1. a mixture of flour and water, often with starch, etc., used for causing paper, etc., to adhere. 2. any material or preparation in a soft or plastic mass: *a toothpaste.* 3. dough, esp. when prepared with shortening, as for making pastry. 4. any of various sweet confections of doughlike consistency: *almond paste.* 5. a preparation of fish, tomatoes, or some other article of food reduced to a smooth, soft mass, as for spreading on bread or for seasoning. 6. a mixture of clay, water, etc., for making earthenware or porcelain. 7. a brilliant, heavy glass, used for making artificial gems. 8. an artificial gem of this material. —*v.t.* 9. to fasten or stick with paste or the like. 10. to cover with something applied by means of paste. 11. *Slang.* to strike with a smart blow, or beat soundly, as on the face or body. [ME, t. OF, g. LL *pasta*, t. Gk: m. *pástē* barley porridge]

pasteboard (pāst′bôd′), *n.* 1. a stiff, firm board made of sheets of paper pasted or layers of paper pulp pressed together, used for book covers. 2. *Slang.* a card, as a visiting card or a playing card. 3. *Slang.* a ticket, as for a railway journey. —*adj.* 4. made of pasteboard. 5. unsubstantial or flimsy; sham.

pastel[1] (păs′tl), *n.* 1. a soft, subdued shade. 2. a kind of dried paste used for crayons, made of pigments ground with chalk and compounded with gum water. 3. a crayon made with such paste. 4. the art of drawing with such crayons. 5. a drawing so made. 6. a short, slight prose study or sketch. —*adj.* 7. having a soft, subdued shade. 8. drawn with pastels. [t. F, t. Pr., der. LL *pasta* PASTE]

pastel[2] (păs′tl), *n.* 1. the plant woad. 2. the dye made from it. [t. F, t. It.: m. *pastello*, dim. der. LL *pasta* PASTE]

pastellist (păs′tə lĭst), *n.* an artist who draws with pastels.

paster (pās′tə), *n.* 1. a slip of paper gummed on the back, to be pasted on or over something, as over a name on a ballot. 2. one who or that which pastes.

pastern (păs′tûn), *n.* 1. that part of the foot of a horse, etc., between the fetlock and the hoof. See illus. under **horse.** 2. either of two bones of this part, the upper or first phalanx (**great pastern bone**) and the lower or second phalanx (**small pastern bone**), between which is a joint (**pastern joint**). [ME *pastron*, t. F: m. *pasturon*, der. *pasture* shackle for animal while pasturing]

Pasternak (păs′tə năk′; *Russ.* pəs tĭr nȧk′), *n.* **Boris Leonidovich** (*Russ.* bȧ rēs′ lĭ ȧ nē′də vĭch), 1890–1960, Russian poet, novelist, and translator.

paste-up (pāst′ŭp′), *n. Print.* a sheet of paper on which has been pasted artwork, proofs, etc., as a guide to the page make-up.

Pasteur (păs tû′; *Fr.* pȧs tœr′), *n.* **Louis** (*Fr.* lwē), 1822–1895, French chemist and bacteriologist.

pasteurism (păs′tə rĭz′əm), *n.* 1. a treatment devised by Pasteur for preventing certain diseases, esp. hydrophobia, by inoculations with virus of gradually increasing strength. 2. the act or process of pasteurizing milk, etc. [named after Louis PASTEUR. See -ISM]

pasteurize (păs′tə rīz′), *v.t.,* **-rized, -rizing.** 1. to expose (milk, etc.) to a high temperature, usually about 140° F, in order to destroy certain micro-organisms and prevent or arrest fermentation. 2. to subject to pasteurism in order to prevent certain diseases, esp. hydrophobia. Also, **pasteurise.** —**pas′teuriza′tion,** *n.*

pasticcio (păs tē′chĭ ō′), *n., pl.* **-ci** (-chē). a pastiche. [t. It., der. *pasta* PASTE]

pastiche (păs tēsh′), *n.* any work of art, literature, or music consisting of motifs borrowed from one or more masters or works of art. [t. F, t. It.: m. *pasticcio* PASTICCIO]

pastille (păs′tĭl), *n.* 1. a flavoured or medicated lozenge. 2. a roll or cone of paste containing aromatic substances, burned as a disinfectant, etc. 3. pastel for crayons. 4. a crayon made of it. Also, **pastil** (păs′tĭl). [t. F, t. Sp.: m. *pastilla*, dim. of *pasta* PASTE]

pastime (päs′tīm′), *n.* that which serves to make time pass agreeably; amusement, or sport: *to play cards for a pastime.* [late ME, f. PASS, v. + TIME]

pastiness (pās′tĭ nĭs), *n.* pasty quality.

pasting (pās′tĭng), *n. Slang.* a beating or thrashing.

past master (päst′mä′stə), 1. one who has filled the office of master in a guild, lodge, etc. 2. one who has ripe experience in any profession, art, etc.

Pasto (*Sp.* pȧs′tō), *n.* 1. a city in SW Colombia. 112,876 pop. (1964); ab. 8350 ft high. 2. a volcanic peak near this city. 13,990 ft.

pastor (päs′tə), *n.* 1. a minister or clergyman with reference to his flock. 2. one having spiritual care of a number of persons. 3. a bird, *Sturnus roseus*, of the starling family, found in SE Europe and W Asia, and occasionally in the British Isles. [t. L: shepherd; r. ME *pastour*, t. AF] —**pas′torship′,** *n.*

pastoral (päs′tə rəl, -trəl), *adj.* 1. of or pertaining to shepherds. 2. used for pasture, as land. 3. having the simplicity or charm of such country, as scenery. 4. pertaining to the country or life in the country. 5. portraying the life of shepherds or of the country, as a work of literature, art, or music. 6. pertaining to a minister or clergyman, or to his duties, etc. —*n.* 7. a poem, play, or the like, dealing with the life of shepherds, commonly in a conventional or artificial manner, or with simple rural life generally; a bucolic. 8. a picture or work of art presenting shepherd life. 9. a pastorale. 10. a treatise on the duties of a minister or clergyman. 11. a letter from a spiritual pastor to his people. 12. a letter from a bishop to his clergy or people. 13. a pastoral staff, or crosier. [ME, t. L: s. *pastorālis* pertaining to a shepherd] —**pas′toralism,** *n.* —**pas′toralist,** *n.* —**pas′torally,** *adv.*

pastorale (păs′tə rä′lĭ; *It.* pȧs tō rȧ′lė), *n., pl.* **-li** (*It.* -lē), **-les.** *Music.* 1. an opera, cantata, or the like, with a pastoral subject. 2. a piece of music suggestive of pastoral life. [It., der. *pastore* shepherd, g. L *pastor*]

pastorate (päs′tə rĭt), *n.* 1. the office, or the term of office, of a pastor. 2. a body of pastors.

pastorium (päs tô′rĭ əm), *n. Southern U.S.* a parsonage. [t. NL, der. L *pastor* PASTOR]

pastorship (päs′tə shĭp′), *n.* the dignity or office of a pastor.

past participle, *Gram.* a participle with past or perfect meaning; perfect participle, as *fallen, sung, defeated.*

past perfect, *Gram.* pluperfect.

pastrami (pə strä′mĭ), *n.* a highly seasoned shoulder cut of smoked beef. [t. Yiddish, t. Polish, ult. t. Turkish]

pastry (pās′trĭ), *n., pl.* **-tries.** 1. food made of paste or dough, as the crust of pies, etc. 2. articles of food of which such paste forms an essential part, as pies, tarts, etc. [f. PAST(E) + -RY]

pastry-cook (pās′trĭ kŏŏk′), *n.* a maker or seller of pastries, cakes, etc.

pasturable (päs′chə rə bl), *adj.* capable of affording pasture, as land.

pasturage (päs′chə rĭj), *n.* 1. growing grass or herbage for cattle, etc. **2.** grazing ground. **3.** the act or business of pasturing cattle, etc. [t. F, der. *pasture* PASTURE]

pasture (päs′chə), *n.*, *v.*, **-tured, -turing.** —*n.* **1.** ground covered with grass or herbage, used or suitable for the grazing of cattle, etc.; grassland. **2.** a specific piece of such ground. **3.** grass or herbage for feeding cattle, etc. —*v.t.* **4.** to feed (cattle, etc.) by putting them to graze on pasture. **5.** (of land) to furnish pasturage for. **6.** (of cattle, etc.) to graze upon. **7.** to put cattle, etc., to graze upon (pasture). [ME, t. OF, g. LL *pastūra*, lit., feeding, grazing]

Pasture (*Fr.* pȧ tʏr′), *n.* **Roger de la** (*Fr.* rō zhĕ′də lȧ), French name of **Rogier van der Weyden.**

pasty[1] (pās′tĭ), *adj.*, **-tier, -tiest.** of or like paste in consistency, appearance, etc. [f. PASTE, n. + -Y[1]]

pasty[2] (päs′tĭ), *n.*, *pl.* **pasties.** a pie filled with game, fish, or the like. [ME *pastee*, t. OF, der. *paste* PASTE]

pasty-faced (pās′tĭ fāst′), *adj.* with a pale, pastelike complexion.

pat[1] (păt), *v.*, **patted, patting,** *n.* —*v.t.* **1.** to strike lightly with something flat, as an implement, the palm of the hand, or the foot. **2.** to stroke gently with the palm or fingers as an expression of affection, approbation, etc. **3.** to flatten or smooth into a desired shape, as butter. **4. pat (someone) on the back,** *Colloq.* to congratulate or encourage with praise. —*v.i.* **5.** to strike lightly or gently. **6.** to walk or run with lightly sounding footsteps. —*n.* **7.** a light stroke or blow with something flat. **8.** the sound of a light stroke, or of light footsteps. **9.** a small mass of something, as butter, shaped by patting or other manipulation. **10. a pat on the back,** *Colloq.* a gesture or word of encouragement or congratulation. [ME; akin to PUTT]

pat[2] (păt), *adj.* **1.** exactly to the point or purpose. **2.** apt; opportune; ready. **3.** fluently glib; readily facile. —*adv.* **4.** exactly or perfectly. **5.** aptly; opportunely. **6. stand pat,** *Colloq.* **a.** to stick to one's decision, policy, etc. **b.** *U.S.* (in poker) to play a hand as dealt, without drawing other cards. [appar. akin to PAT[1]] —**pat′ness,** *n.* —**pat′ter,** *n.*

Pat (păt), *n.* *Slang.* an Irishman. [shortened form of christian name *Patrick*]

pat., 1. patent. **2.** patented.

pataca (*Port.* pȧ tȧ′kȧ), *n.* **1.** the monetary unit of Macao, equivalent to £0·0757. **2.** a note of this value. [t. Pg., ult. t. Ar.: m. *abu taqa* coin]

patagium (păt′ə jī′əm), *n.*, *pl.* **-gia** (-jī′ə). **1.** a wing membrane, as of a bat. **2.** the extensible fold of skin of a gliding mammal or reptile, as a flying squirrel. **3.** a membranous fold of skin on the margin of a bird's wing. [t. NL, t. L: a gold border on a woman's tunic]

Patagonia (păt′ə gō′nyə), *n.* **1.** the tableland region constituting the S tip of Argentina. **2.** a region in the extreme S part of South America, extending from the Andes to the Atlantic: mostly in S Argentina, partly in S Chile. —**Pat′ago′nian,** *adj.*, *n.*

Patagonia (def. 2)

patch (păch), *n.* **1.** a piece of material used to mend a hole or break, or strengthen a weak place: *a patch on a sail.* **2.** a piece of material used to cover or protect a wound, an injured part, etc.: *a patch over the eye.* **3.** any of the pieces of cloth sewn together to form patchwork. **4.** a small piece or scrap of anything. **5.** a piece or tract of land. **6.** a small piece of black silk or court plaster worn on the face or elsewhere to hide a defect or to heighten the complexion by contrast. **7.** *U.S.* flash (def. 5). **8.** a period of time. **9. not a patch on,** *Colloq.* not comparable; not nearly so good. —*v.t.* **10.** to mend or strengthen with or as with a patch or patches. **11.** to repair or restore, esp. in a hasty or makeshift way (usually fol. by *up*). **12.** to make by joining patches or pieces together: *to patch a quilt.* **13.** to settle; smooth over: *they patched up their quarrel.* [ME *pacche*; orig. uncert.] —**patch′er,** *n.* —**Syn. 10.** See **mend.**

patch board, *Elect.* a board containing electrical sockets so that any desired combinations of connections can be made up by inserting wires with plugs at each end.

patch cord, *Elect.* an electrical wire with plugs at each end for making connections on a patch board.

patchouli (păch′o͝o lĭ, pă cho͞o′lĭ), *n.* **1.** the East Indian menthaceous plants, *Pogostemon heyneanus* and *P. cablin*, which yield a fragrant oil. **2.** a penetrating perfume derived from it. Also, **pachouli, patchouly.** [t. Tamil: m. *pach-ilai*, lit., green leaf]

patch pocket, a pocket formed by sewing a piece of the material on the outside of a garment.

patchwork (păch′wûk′), *n.* **1.** work made of pieces of cloth or leather of various colours or shapes sewn together, used esp. for covering quilts, cushions, etc. **2.** something made up of various pieces or parts put together: *a patchwork of verses.*

patchy (păch′ĭ), *adj.*, **-ier, -iest. 1.** marked by patches. **2.** occurring in, forming, or like patches. **3.** of unequal quality; irregular; not uniform. —**patch′ily,** *adv.* —**patch′iness,** *n.*

patd, patented.

pate (pāt), *n.* *Archaic.* **1.** the head. **2.** the crown or top of the head. **3.** brains. [ME; ? var. of PATEN]

pâte (*Fr.* pȧt), *n.* porcelain paste used in ceramic work. [see PASTE]

pâté (*Fr.* pȧ tĕ′), *n.* a paste or spread made of finely ground liver, meat, or fish, etc., and served as an hors d'oeuvre.

Patea (pə tī̇ə′), *n.* a river in E North Island, New Zealand, flowing into the Tasman Sea. 75 mi.

pâté de foie gras (*Fr.* pȧ tĕ də fwȧ grȧ′), *French.* a paste made with the livers of specially fattened geese.

patella (pə tĕl′ə), *n.*, *pl.* **-tellae** (-tĕl′ē). **1.** *Anat.* the kneecap. See diag. under **skeleton. 2.** *Bot.*, *Zool.*, *etc.* a panlike or cuplike formation. **3.** *Archaeol.* a small pan or shallow vessel. [t. L: small pan, kneepan, dim. of *patina.* See PATINA[2]] —**patel′lar,** *adj.*

patellate (pə tĕl′ĭt, -āt), *adj.* **1.** having a patella. **2.** patelliform.

patelliform (pə tĕl′ĭ fôm′), *adj.* having the form of a patella; shaped like a saucer, kneecap, or limpet shell. [f. s. L *patella* small pan + -(I)FORM]

paten (păt′ən), *n.* the plate on which the bread is placed in the celebration of the Eucharist. Also, **patin, patine.** [ME *patene*, t. OF, t. L, m. *patena, patina.* See PATINA[2]]

patency (pā′tən sĭ), *n.* **1.** the state of being patent. **2.** *Med.* the condition of not being blocked or obstructed.

Patenir (*Du.* pȧ tē nĕr′), *n.* **Joachim** (*Du.* yō′ȧ KHĭm), died *c.* 1524, Dutch landscape painter. Also, **Patinier, Patinir.**

patent (păt′ənt *for 1–9, 15–19*; *usually* pā′tənt *for 10–14*), *n.* **1.** a government grant to an inventor, his heirs, or assigns, for a stated period of time, conferring upon him a monopoly of the exclusive right to make, use, and vend the invention or discovery. **2.** an invention, process, etc., which has been patented. **3.** an official document conferring some right, privilege, or the like. **4.** the instrument by which the United States conveys the legal fee-simple title to public land. —*adj.* **5.** of a kind specially protected by a patent. **6.** endowed with a patent, as persons. **7.** belonging as if by a proprietary claim; having a trademark. **8.** conferred by a patent, as a right or privilege. **9.** appointed by a patent, as a person. **10.** open to view or knowledge; manifest; evident; plain. **11.** lying open, or not shut in or enclosed, as a place. **12.** *Chiefly Bot.* expanded or spreading. **13.** open, as a door or a passage. **14.** (of plate glass) having been ground and polished on both sides. —*v.t.* **15.** to take out a patent on; obtain the exclusive rights to (an invention) by a patent. **16.** to originate and establish as one's own. **17.** *Rare.* to grant the exclusive right to (an invention) by a patent. **18.** *U.S. Rare.* to grant by a patent (def. 4). **19.** *Metall.* to heat a metal to above its transformation range and subsequently to cool it at a controlled rate in order to produce a structure which facilitates cold working. [ME, t. L: s. *patens*, ppr., lying open; in some senses, through OF] —**pat′entable,** *adj.* —**pat′entabil′ity,** *n.* —**pat′ently,** *adv.* —**Syn. 10.** See **apparent.**

patentee (pā′tən tē′), *n.* one to whom a patent is granted.

patent leather (pā′tnt), **1.** leather lacquered to produce a hard, glossy, smooth finish. **2.** any imitation of this. —**patent-leather** (pā′tnt lĕŧħ′ə), *adj.*

patent log. See **log** (def. 3c).

patent medicine (pā′tnt), a medicine distributed by a company which has a patent on its manufacture.

Patent Office, a government department which issues patents.

patentor (pā′tən tô′), *n.* one who grants a patent.

patent right, the exclusive right created by a patent.

Patent Rolls, the register of patents which have been issued by the Patent Office.

pater (pā′tə *for 1*; păt′ə *for 2, 3*), *n.* **1.** *Slang.* father. **2.** the paternoster or Lord's Prayer. **3.** a recital of it. [ME, t. L: father]

Pater (pā′tə), *n.* **Walter Horatio,** 1839–94, English critic, essayist, and novelist.

paterfamilias (pā′tə fə mĭl′ĭ ăs′), *n.*, *pl.* **patresfamilias** (pā′trās fə mĭl′ĭ ăs′). **1.** the head of a family. **2.** *Roman Law.* a free male citizen who has been freed from patria potestas by death of his father or by emancipation. [t. L: f. *pater* father + *familias*, archaic gen. of *familia* family]

paternal (pə tû′nəl), *adj.* **1.** characteristic of or befitting a father; fatherly. **2.** of or pertaining to a father. **3.** related on the father's side. **4.** derived or inherited from a father. [f. s. L *paternus* fatherly + -AL[1]] —**pater′nally,** *adv.* —**Syn. 1.** See **fatherly.**

paternalism (pə tû′nə lĭz′əm), *n.* the principle or practice, on the part of a government or of any body or person in authority, of managing or regulating the affairs of a country or community, or of individuals, in the manner of a father dealing with his children. —**pater′nalis′tic,** *adj.* —**pater′nalis′tically,** *adv.*

paternity (pə tû′nĭ tĭ), *n.* **1.** derivation from a father. **2.** the state of being a father; fatherhood. **3.** origin or authorship. [ME, t. LL: m. s. *paternitas*, der. L *paternus* fatherly]

paternoster (păt′ə nŏs′tə), *n.* **1.** Also, **Pater Noster.** the Lord's Prayer, esp. in the Latin form. **2.** a recital of this prayer as an act of worship. **3.** one of certain beads in a rosary, usually every eleventh bead, differing in size or material from the rest, and indicating the Lord's Prayer is to be said. **4.** any form of words used as a prayer or charm. **5.** fishing tackle consisting of one or more hooks spaced along a central line, the end of which is weighted. [ME and OE, t. L: our father, the first words of the prayer in the Latin version]

Paterson (păt′ə sən), *n.* a town in the U.S., in NE New Jersey. 143,663 (1960).

path (päth), *n.* **1.** a way beaten or trodden by the feet of men or beasts. **2.** a walk in a garden or through grounds. **3.** a route, course, or track in which something moves. **4.** a course of action, conduct, or procedure. [ME; OE *pæth*, c. G *Pfad*]

—**Syn. 1.** PATH, LANE, TRAIL are passages or routes not so wide as a way or road. A PATH is a way for passing on foot; a track, beaten by feet, not specially constructed, often along the side of a road: *a path through a field.* A LANE is a narrow road or track, generally between fields, often enclosed with fences or trees; sometimes an alley or narrow road between buildings in towns: *a lane leading to a farmhouse; Drury Lane.* A TRAIL is a rough way made or worn through woods or across mountains, or other untravelled regions: *an Indian trail.*

path., 1. pathological. 2. pathology.

Pathan (pə tän′), *n.* **1.** an Afghan. **2.** an Afghan dwelling in Pakistan or India. [t. Pushtu]

pathetic (pə thĕt′ĭk), *adj.* **1.** exciting pity or sympathetic sadness; full of pathos. **2.** affecting or moving the feelings. **3.** pertaining or due to the feelings. **4.** *Colloq.* miserably inadequate: *her vegetables made a pathetic showing at the annual produce fair.* Also, **pathet′ical.** [t. LL: s. *pathēticus*, t. Gk: m. *pathētikós* sensitive] —**pathet′ically,** *adv.*

pathetic fallacy, the crediting of human traits and feelings to nature.

pathfinder (päth′fĭn′də), *n.* **1.** one who finds a path or way, as through a wilderness. **2.** an aircraft sent in advance of a force of bombers to drop flares, etc., to illuminate a target area.

-pathia, an obsolete form of **-pathy.**

-pathic, a word element forming adjectives from nouns ending in *-pathy*, as *psychopathic.* [see -PATHY, -IC]

pathless (päth′lĭs), *adj.* without paths; trackless. —**path′lessness,** *n.*

patho-, a word element meaning 'suffering', 'disease', 'feeling'. [t. Gk, comb. form of *páthos*]

pathogen (păth′ə jĕn′), *n.* a pathogenic or disease-producing organism. Also, **pathogene** (păth′ə jēn′).

pathogenesis (păth′ə jĕn′ĭ sĭs), *n.* the production and development of disease. Also, **pathogeny** (pə thŏj′ĭ nĭ). —**pathogenetic** (păth′ō jĭ nĕt′ĭk), *adj.*

pathogenic (păth′ə jĕn′ĭk), *adj.* disease-producing.

pathognomonic (păth′əg nə mŏn′ĭk), *adj.* *Med.* characteristic of a particular disease.

pathol., 1. pathological. 2. pathology.

pathological (păth′ə lŏj′ĭ kl), *adj.* **1.** of or pertaining to pathology. **2.** due to or involving disease; morbid. Also, **path′olog′ic.** —**path′olog′ically,** *adv.*

pathology (pə thŏl′ə jĭ), *n., pl.* **-gies. 1.** the science of the origin, nature, and course of diseases. **2.** the conditions and processes of a disease. **3.** the study of morbid or abnormal mental or moral conditions. —**pathol′ogist,** *n.*

pathos (pā′thŏs), *n.* **1.** the quality or power, as in speech, music, etc., of evoking a feeling of pity or sympathetic sadness; touching or pathetic character or effect (opposed to *ethos*). **2.** *Obs.* suffering. [t. Gk: suffering, disease, feeling]

pathway (päth′wā′), *n.* a path.

-pathy, a noun element meaning 'suffering', 'feeling', as in *anthropopathy, antipathy, sympathy*, and often, esp. in words of modern formation, 'morbid affection', 'disease', as in *neuropathy, psychopathy*, and hence used also in names of systems or methods of treating disease, as in *homoeopathy, osteopathy.* [t. Gk: m. s. *-pátheia*]

Patiala (pŭt′ĭ ä′lə), *n.* **1.** a former state in NW India, foremost of the Punjab States; now in Punjab. **2.** a town in India in Punjab. 125,234 (1961).

patience (pā′shəns), *n.* **1.** calm and uncomplaining endurance, as under pain, provocation, etc. **2.** calmness in waiting: *have patience a little longer.* **3.** quiet perseverance: *to labour with patience.* **4.** a card game, usually played by one person alone. **5.** *Obs.* sufferance. [t. L: m. s. *patientia*; r. ME *pacience*, t. OF]

—**Syn. 1.** PATIENCE, ENDURANCE, FORTITUDE, STOICISM imply qualities of calmness, stability, and persistent courage in trying circumstances. PATIENCE may denote calm, self-possessed, and unrepining bearing of pain, misfortune, annoyance, or delay; or painstaking and untiring industry or (less often) application in the doing of something: *to bear afflictions with patience.* ENDURANCE denotes the ability to bear exertion, hardship, or suffering (without implication of moral qualities required or shown): *running a marathon requires great endurance.* FORTITUDE implies not only patience but courage and strength of character in the midst of pain, affliction, or hardship: *to show fortitude in adversity.* STOICISM is calm fortitude, with such repression of emotion as to seem almost like indifference to pleasure or pain: *the American Indians were noted for stoicism under torture.*

patient (pā′shənt), *n.* **1.** one who is under medical or surgical treatment. **2.** a person or thing that undergoes action (opposed to *agent*). **3.** *Obs. or Rare.* a sufferer. —*adj.* **4.** quietly persevering or diligent: *patient workers.* **5.** enduring pain, trouble, affliction, hardship, etc., with fortitude, calmness, or quiet submission. **6.** marked by such endurance. **7.** quietly enduring strain, annoyance, etc.: *patient in a traffic jam.* **8.** disposed to or characterized by such endurance. **9.** enduring delay with calmness or equanimity, or marked by such endurance: *be patient.* **10.** having or showing the capacity for endurance (fol. by *of*). **11.** susceptible (fol. by *of*). **12.** *Rare.* undergoing the action of another (opposed to *agent*). [t. L: s. *patiens*, ppr., suffering, enduring; r. ME *pacient*, t. OF] —**pa′tiently,** *adv.* —**Syn. 5.** long-suffering.

patin (păt′ĭn), *n.* paten. Also, **patine.**

patina[1] (păt′ĭ nə), *n.* **1.** a film or encrustation, usually green, caused by oxidization on the surface of old bronze, and esteemed as ornamental. **2.** a similar film or colouring on some other substance. **3.** a surface calcification of implements, usually indicating great age. [t. It., t. L: dish, through meaning tarnish (on metal dish)]

patina[2] (păt′ĭ nə), *n., pl.* **-nae** (-nē′). a broad, shallow dish of the ancient Romans. [t. L]

Patinier (*Du.* pȧ tē nēr′), *n.* See **Patenir.** Also, **Patinir.**

patio (păt′ĭ ō′; *Sp.* pȧ′tyȯ), *n., pl.* **-tios. 1.** a court, as of a house, esp. an inner court open to the sky. **2.** an area, usually paved, adjoining a house, used for outdoor living. [t. Sp.]

patisserie (pə tē′sə rĭ; *Fr.* pȧ tēs rē′), *n., pl.* **-ries** (-rĭz; *Fr.* -rē′). **1.** a fancy cake, often having a cream and fruit filling. **2.** an establishment where such pastries are made and sold. [t. F: m. *pâtisserie*]

Patmore (păt′mô′), *n.* **Coventry (Kersey Dighton)** (kŏv′ən trĭ, kŭv′-, kû′zĭ dī′tn), 1823–96, English poet.

Patmos (păt′mŏs), *n.* one of the Dodecanese Islands, off the SW coast of Asia Minor: St John is supposed to have been exiled on this island. Rev. 1:9. 2564 pop. (1961); 13 sq. mi. Italian, **Patmo** (*It.* pȧt′mȯ).

Patna (păt′nə), *n.* a city in India, the capital of Bihar, in the N part, on the Ganges. 363,700 (1961).

Patna rice, long, thin, highly polished grains of rice, used for curries and savoury dishes.

Pat. Off., Patent Office.

patois (păt′wä; *Fr.* pȧ twȧ′), *n., pl.* **patois** (păt′wäz; *Fr.* pȧ twȧ′). any peasant or provincial form of speech. [t. F, der. OF *patoier* handle clumsily, der. *pate* paw]

Paton (pā′tn), *n.* **Alan (Stewart),** born 1903, South African novelist.

Patras (pə trăs′), *n.* **1.** a seaport in W Greece in the Peloponnesus on the Gulf of Patras. 95,364 (1961). **2. Gulf of,** an inlet of the Ionian Sea in the NW Peloponnesus. 10 mi. long; 25 mi. wide. Greek, **Patrai** (*Gk* pȧ′trĕ).

patri-, a word element meaning 'father'. [t. LL, comb. form of *pater*]

patria potestas (păt′rĭ ä′ pŏ tĕs′tăs), *Roman Law.* the power of a man over his children and descendants, which made all their property his and all their transactions void unless he assented. It ended only with the death of the paterfamilias or with emancipation. [L]

patriarch (pā′trĭ äk′), *n.* **1.** any of the earlier biblical personages regarded as the fathers of the human race, comprising those from Adam to Noah (**antediluvian patriarchs**) and those between the Deluge and the birth of Abraham. **2.** one of the three great progenitors of the Israelites: Abraham, Isaac, or Jacob. **3.** one of the sons of Jacob (the **twelve patriarchs**), from whom the tribes of Israel were descended. **4.** (in the early church) a bishop of high rank, esp. one with jurisdiction over metropolitans. **5.** *Gk Orthodox Ch.* the bishop of the ancient sees of Alexandria, Antioch, Constantinople, and Jerusalem, and in recent years of Russia, Rumania, and Serbia. The bishop of Constantinople is the highest dignitary in the church and bears the title of **ecumenical patriarch.** **6.** a bishop of the highest rank or authority in any of the various non-Orthodox churches in the East. **7.** *Rom. Cath. Ch.* **a.** the pope (**Patriarch of Rome**). **b.** a bishop of the highest rank next after the pope. **8.** one of the highest dignitaries in the Mormon Church who pronounces the blessing of the church; Evangelist. **9.** one of the elders or leading older members of a community. **10.** a venerable old man. **11.** the male head of a family or tribal line. **12.** a person regarded as the father or founder of an order, class, etc. [ME *patriarc*, t. LL: m. s. *patriarcha*, t. Gk: m. *patriárchēs* head of a family] —**pa′triar′chal,** *adj.* —**pa′triar′chally,** *adv.*

patriarchal cross, a cross with two crossbars. See illus. under **cross.**

patriarchate (pā′trĭ ä′kĭt), *n.* **1.** the office, dignity, jurisdiction, province, or residence of an ecclesiastical patriarch. **2.** a patriarchy.

patriarchy (pā′trĭ ä′kĭ), *n.*, *pl.* **-archies.** **1.** a form of social organization in which the father is head of the family, and in which descent is reckoned in the male line, the children belonging to the father's clan. **2.** a community organized and run upon such a system.

patrician (pə trĭsh′ən), *n.* **1.** a member of the original senatorial aristocracy in ancient Rome. **2.** (under the later Roman and Byzantine Empires) a title or dignity conferred by the emperor. **3.** a member of an influential and hereditary ruling class in certain medieval German, Swiss, and Italian free cities. **4.** any noble or aristocrat. —*adj.* **5.** of or belonging to the patrician families of ancient Rome. **6.** of high social rank or noble family. **7.** befitting an aristocrat: *patrician aloofness.* [ME, f. s. L *patricius* of the rank of the *patrēs* senators, patricians (lit., fathers, pl. of *pater* father) + -AN] —**patric′ianly,** *adv.*

patriciate (pə trĭsh′ĭ ĭt, -āt′), *n.* **1.** the patrician class. **2.** patrician rank.

patricide (păt′rĭ sīd′), *n.* **1.** one who kills his father. **2.** the act of killing one's father. [f. PATRI- + -CIDE] —**pat′ricid′al,** *adj.*

Patrick (păt′rĭk), *n.* **Saint,** A.D. *c.* 389–*c.* 461, English missionary and bishop in Ireland; patron saint of Ireland.

patrimony (păt′rĭ mə nĭ), *n.*, *pl.* **-nies.** **1.** an estate inherited from one's father or ancestors. **2.** a heritage. **3.** the estate or endowment of a church, religious house, etc. [t. L: m. s. *patrimōnium* paternal estate; r. ME *patrimoygne*, t. OF: m. *patrimoine*] —**patrimonial** (păt′rĭ mō′nyəl), *adj.*

patriot (pā′trĭ ət, păt′rĭ ət), *n.* a person who loves his country, zealously supporting and defending it and its interests. [t. LL: s. *patriōta*, t. Gk: m. *patriṓtēs* fellow countryman]

patriotic (păt′rĭ ŏt′ĭk), *adj.* **1.** of or like a patriot. **2.** inspired by patriotism. —**pat′riot′ically,** *adv.*

patriotism (păt′rĭ ə tĭz′əm), *n.* the spirit or action of a patriot; devotion to one's country.

patristic (pə trĭs′tĭk), *adj.* of or pertaining to the Fathers of the Christian Church or their writings. Also, **patris′tical.** —**patris′tically,** *adv.*

Patroclus (pə trŏk′ləs), *n.* *Class. Myth.* the friend of Achilles, slain by Hector, whose death led Achilles to return to battle. [t. L, t. Gk: m. *Patroklês, Pátroklos*]

patrol (pə trōl′), *v.*, **-trolled, -trolling,** *n.* —*v.i.* **1.** to go the rounds in a camp or garrison, as a guard. **2.** to traverse a particular district, as a policeman. —*v.t.* **3.** to go about in or traverse for the purpose of guarding or protecting. —*n.* **4.** a person or a body of persons charged with patrolling. **5.** a body of troops or police detailed for reconnaissance. **6.** the act of patrolling. **7.** (in the Boy Scouts and Girl Guides) a unit of about six members. [t. F: m. *patrouiller* patrol, earlier paddle or dabble in mud, orig., paw over, der. OF *pate* paw. Cf. PATOIS] —**patrol′ler,** *n.*

patrol-car (pə trōl′kä′), *n.* a car used by police for patrolling a district.

patrolman (pə trōl′măn′), *n.*, *pl.* **-men.** **1.** a man who patrols. **2.** *U.S.* a member of a police force patrolling a certain district.

patrol wagon, *U.S.* a van used by the police for the conveyance of prisoners.

patron (pā′trən), *n.* **1.** one who supports with his patronage a shop, hotel, or the like. **2.** a protector or supporter, as of a person, cause, institution, art, or enterprise. **3.** one whose support or protection is solicited or acknowledged by the dedication of a book or other work. **4.** a patron saint. **5.** *Rom. Hist.* the protector of a dependant or client, often the ex-master of a freedman, still retaining certain rights over him. **6.** *Eccles.* one who has the right of presenting a clergyman to a benefice. [ME, t. L: s. *patrōnus* patron, ML pattern] —**pa′tronal,** *adj.* —**patroness** (pā′trə nĭs), *n. fem.*

patronage (păt′rə nĭj), *n.* **1.** the financial support afforded a shop, hotel, etc., by customers. **2.** the position, encouragement, or support of a patron. **3.** the control of appointments to the public service or of other political favours. **4.** offices or other favours so controlled. **5.** condescending favour: *an air of patronage.* **6.** the right of presentation to an ecclesiastical benefice.

patronize (păt′rə nīz′), *v.t.*, **-nized, -nizing.** **1.** to favour (a shop, restaurant, etc.) with one's patronage; to trade with. **2.** to treat in a condescending way. **3.** to act as patron towards; support. Also, **patronise.** —**pat′roniz′er,** *n.* —**pat′roniz′ingly,** *adv.*

patron saint, a saint regarded as the special guardian of a person, trade, place, etc.

patronymic (păt′rə nĭm′ĭk), *adj.* **1.** (of names) derived from the name of a father or ancestor, esp. by the addition of a suffix or prefix indicating descent. **2.** (of a suffix or prefix) indicating such descent. —*n.* **3.** a patronymic name, such as *Williamson* (son of William) or *Macdonald* (son of Donald). **4.** a family name; surname. [t. LL: s. *patrōnymicus*, t. Gk: m. *patrōnymikós* pertaining to one's father's name]

patsy (păt′sĭ), *n.* *U.S. Slang.* **1.** a scapegoat. **2.** a person who is easily deceived, swindled, ridiculed, etc.

patten (păt′n), *n.* any of various kinds of footwear, as a wooden shoe, a shoe with a wooden sole, a chopin, etc., to protect the feet from mud or wet. [ME *paten*, t. OF: m. *patin*, der. OF *pate* paw, foot. Cf. PATOIS]

patter[1] (păt′ə), *v.i.* **1.** to strike or move with a succession of slight tapping sounds. —*v.t.* **2.** to cause to patter. **3.** to spatter with something. —*n.* **4.** a pattering sound: *the heavy patter of the rain.* **5.** the act of pattering. [freq. of PAT[1], v.]

patter[2] (păt′ə), *n.* **1.** the glib and rapid speech used by a salesman to praise his wares, by a magician while performing tricks, by a comedian or other entertainer, used to attract attention or amuse. **2.** rapid speech; mere chatter; gabble. **3.** the jargon or cant of any class, group, etc. **4.** *Colloq.* the words of a song. —*v.i.* **5.** to talk glibly or rapidly, esp. with little regard to matter; chatter. **6.** to repeat the paternoster or any prayer, etc., in a rapid, mechanical way. —*v.t.* **7.** to recite or repeat (prayers, etc.) in a rapid, mechanical way. **8.** to repeat or say rapidly or glibly. [var. of PATER (def. 3)] —**pat′terer,** *n.*

patter[3] (păt′ə), *n.* one who or that which pats.

pattern (păt′ən), *n.* **1.** a decorative design, as for china, wallpaper, textile fabrics, etc. **2.** such a design carried out on something. **3.** a style of marking of natural or chance origin: *patterns of frost on the window.* **4.** style or type in general. **5.** an original or model proposed for or deserving of imitation. **6.** anything fashioned or designed to serve as a model or guide for something to be made: *a paper pattern for a dress.* **7.** *U.S.* a sufficient quantity of material for making a garment. **8.** *Metall.* a model or form, usually of wood or metal, used in a foundry to make a mould. **9.** an example or instance. **10.** a sample or specimen. **11.** **a.** the distribution of shot in a target at which a shotgun or the like is fired. **b.** a diagram showing such distribution. —*v.i.* **12.** to model one's conduct, etc. (fol. by *by* or *after*). —*v.t.* **13.** to make after a pattern; model. **14.** to cover or mark with a pattern. **15.** *Rare.* to take as a pattern. [ME *patron.* See PATRON]

Patti (păt′ĭ; *It.*, *Sp.* pät′tē), *n.* **Adelina** (*It.* ä dē lē′nä), 1843–1919, Italian soprano opera singer, born in Spain.

Patton (păt′n), *n.* **George Smith,** 1885–1945, U.S. general.

patty (păt′ĭ), *n.*, *pl.* **-ies.** a little pie; a pasty: *oyster patties.* [t. F: m. *pâté*]

patty pan, a small pan for baking patties, etc.

patulous (păt′yŏŏ ləs), *adj.* **1.** open; gaping; expanded. **2.** *Bot.* **a.** spreading, as a tree or its boughs. **b.** spreading slightly, as a calyx. **c.** bearing the flowers loose or dispersed, as a peduncle. [t. L: m. *patulus* lying open] —**pat′ulously,** *adv.* —**pat′ulousness,** *n.*

Pau (*Fr.* pō), *n.* a town in SW France: winter resort. 59,937 (1962).

P.A.U., Pan American Union.

paua (pou′ə), *n.* a univalve mollusc of the abalone family, *Haliotis iris*, of New Zealand, having edible flesh and an iridescent shell used in ornaments and jewellery. [t. Maori]

paucis verbis (pou′kĭs vû′bĭs), *Latin.* in few words; with or by few words.
paucity (pô′sĭ tĭ), *n.* smallness of quantity; fewness; scantiness: *paucity of material.* [ME, t. L: m. s. *paucitas*]
Paul (pôl *for 1, 2; Ger.* poul *for 3*), *n.* **1. Saint,** died A.D. *c.* 67, the great Christian missionary, apostle to the gentiles, author of several epistles in the New Testament. **2.** name of six popes. **3. Jean.** See **Richter.** [t. L: s. *Paulus*; r. ME *Poul* (t. OF) and OE *Paulus* (t. L)]
Paul I, 1754–1801, tsar of Russia 1796–1801, noted for his great cruelty and brutality.
Paul III, (*Alessandro Farnese*), 1468–1549, Italian ecclesiastic: pope 1534–49.
Paul V, (*Camillo Borghese*), 1552–1621, Italian ecclesiastic: pope 1605–21.
Paul VI, (*Giovanni Battista Montini*), born 1897, Italian ecclesiastic: pope since 1963.
Paul-Boncour (*Fr.* pōl bôɴ ko͞or′), *n.* **Joseph** (*Fr.* zhō zĕf′), born 1873, French statesman: premier 1932–33.
pauldron (pôl′drən), *n.* a piece of armour protecting the shoulder and upper part of the arm. See illus. under **armour.** [late ME *paleron*, t. MF: m. *espalleron* shoulder]
Pauline (pô′līn), *adj.* of or pertaining to the apostle Paul, or his doctrines or writings.
Pauling (pô′lĭng), *n.* **Linus Carl,** born 1901, U.S. chemist.
Pauli's exclusion principle. See **exclusion principle.** [named after Wolfgang *Pauli*, 1900–58, Austrian physicist]
Paulist (pô′lĭst), *n.* **1.** a member of the 'Missionary Society of St Paul the Apostle', a community of Roman Catholic priests founded in New York in 1858. **2.** in Christian India, a name for a Jesuit, from St Paul's church at Goa.
paulownia (pô lō′nyə), *n.* **1.** a tree, *Paulownia tomentosa*, of Japan, bearing showy pale violet or blue flowers, which blossom in early spring. **2.** any other trees of the genus *Paulownia.* [t. NL; named after Anna *Paulovna*, daughter of Tsar Paul I, of Russia]
Paul Pry (pôl′prī′), an inquisitive or nosy person. [play (1825) and its hero, by John Poole, 1786–1872]
Paumotu Archipelago (pou mō′to͞o), Tuamotu Archipelago.
paunch (pônch), *n.* **1.** the belly or abdomen. **2.** a large, prominent belly. **3.** the rumen. [ME *panche*, t. ONF, var. of OE *pance*, der. L *pantex*]
paunchy (pôn′chĭ), *adj.* having a large, prominent belly. —**paun′chiness,** *n.*
pauper (pô′pə), *n.* **1.** a very poor person. **2.** one without means, who is supported by a community. [t. L: poor (man)]
pauperism (pô′pə rĭz′əm), *n.* utter poverty.
pauperize (pô′pə rīz′), *v.t.*, **-rized, -rizing.** to make a pauper of. Also, **pauperise.** —**pau′periza′tion,** *n.*
Pausanias (pô sā′nĭ ăs′), *n.* fl. A.D. *c.* 175, Greek traveller and author.
pause (pôz), *n.*, *v.*, **paused, pausing.** —*n.* **1.** a temporary stop or rest, esp. in speech or action. **2.** a cessation proceeding from doubt or uncertainty. **3.** delay; hesitation; suspense. **4.** a break or rest in speaking or reading as depending on sense, grammatical relations, metrical divisions, etc., or in writing or printing as marked by punctuation. **5.** *Pros.* a caesura. **6.** *Music.* the symbol 𝄐 or 𝄑 placed under or over a note or rest to indicate that it is to be prolonged. **7. give pause,** to cause to hesitate. —*v.i.* **8.** to make a pause; stop; wait; hesitate. **9.** to dwell or linger (fol. by *upon*). [late ME, t. L: m. *pausa*, t. Gk: m. *paûsis* cessation] —**paus′al,** *adj.* —**paus′er,** *n.* —**paus′ingly,** *adv.* —**Syn. 8.** See **stop.**
pavan (păv′ən, pə văn′), *n.* **1.** a stately dance in vogue in the 16th century. **2.** the music for it. Also, **pavane** (păv′ən, pə văn′; *Fr.* pȧ vȧn′), **pavin.** [t. F: m. *pavane*, t. Sp.: m. *pavana*, t. d. It.: Paduan dance]
pave (pāv), *v.t.*, **paved, paving. 1.** to cover or lay (a road, walk, etc.) with stones, bricks, tiles, wood, concrete, etc., so as to make a firm, level surface. **2.** to prepare (the way) for. [ME *pave(n)*, t. OF: m. *paver*, g. Rom. *pavāre*, for L *pavīre* beat down] —**pav′er,** *n.*
pavé (*Fr.* pȧ vĕ′), *n.* *French.* **1.** a pavement. **2.** a setting in which jewels are placed close together so as to show no metal. [orig. pp. of *paver* PAVE]
pavement (pāv′mənt), *n.* **1.** a walk or footway, esp. a paved one, at the side of a street or road. **2.** a surface, ground covering, or floor made by paving. **3.** a material used for paving. **4.** *Obs.* a paved road, etc. [ME, t. OF: a floor beaten down, der. *paver* PAVE]
pavement artist, one who begs for money by drawing pictures on a pavement.
pavement light, a light formed of solid glass blocks, cast into concrete, or set in a cast-iron frame, used over a basement so as to let in daylight. Also, **vault light.**
Pavese (*It.* pȧ vĕ′sĕ), *n.* **Cesare** (*It.* chĕ′zȧ rĕ), 1908–50, Italian novelist.
Pavia (pə vēə′; *It.* pȧ vē′ȧ), *n.* a town in N Italy. 82,858 (1966).
pavid (păv′ĭd), *adj.* frightened; fearful; timid. [t. L: s. *pavidus*]
pavilion (pə vĭl′yən), *n.* **1.** a light, more or less open structure for purposes of shelter, pleasure, etc., as in a park. **2.** a projecting element, architecturally defined, at the front or side of a building. **3.** one of a group of buildings forming a hospital. **4.** a tent. **5.** a large tent on posts. **6.** *Jewellery.* the lower part of the stone, taken from the girdle and including the culet. **7.** *Anat.* the auricle of the ear. —*v.t.* **8.** to set or place in or as in a pavilion. **9.** to furnish with pavilions. [ME *pavilioun*, t. OF, g. L *pāpilio* tent, orig. butterfly]
pavin (păv′ĭn), *n.* pavan.
paving (pā′vĭng), *n.* **1.** a pavement. **2.** material for paving.
paving stone, a stone or concrete block prepared for paving.
paviour (pā′vyə), *n.* **1.** one who or that which paves. **2.** a paving stone or paving tile. Also, *U.S.*, **pavior, paver.**
pavis (păv′ĭs), *n.* a large medieval shield, covering the whole body. Also, **pavise.** [ult. der. PAVIA]
paviser (păv′ĭ sə), *n.* one armed with or bearing a pavis. Also, **pavisor.**
Pavlov (păv′lŏv; *Russ.* pȧv′ləf), *n.* **Ivan Petrovich** (*Russ.* ĭ vȧn′ pĭ trô′vĭch), 1849–1936, Russian physiologist and physician.
Pavlova (păv′lə və; *Russ.* pȧv′lə və), *n.* **Anna** (*Russ.* ȧn′nə), 1885–1931, Russian ballet dancer.
Pavo (pä′vō), *n.* *Astron.* the southern constellation, the Peacock.
pavonine (păv′ə nīn′), *adj.* **1.** of or like the peacock. **2.** resembling the peacock's feathers, as in colouring. [t. L: m. s. *pāvōnīnus* pertaining to a peacock]
paw (pô), *n.* **1.** the foot of an animal with nails or claws. **2.** the foot of any animal. **3.** *Humorous or Contemptuous.* the human hand. —*v.t.* **4.** to strike or scrape with the paws or feet. **5.** *Colloq.* to handle clumsily, rudely, or overfamiliarly. —*v.i.* **6.** to beat or scrape the ground, etc., with the paws or feet. **7.** *Colloq.* to use the hands clumsily or rudely on something. [ME *powe*, t. OF, of Gmc orig.; cf. G *Pfote*]
pawky (pô′kĭ), *adj.*, **-kier, -kiest.** *Scot. and N Dial.* cunning; sly, esp. humorously. [f. *pawk* trick, artifice + -Y¹]
pawl (pôl), *n.* a pivoted bar adapted to engage with the teeth of a ratchet wheel or the like so as to prevent movement or to impart motion. [? t. D: m. *pal*]

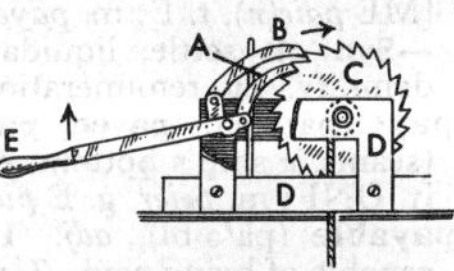

Pawl in hoisting apparatus
A, B, Pawls; C, Ratchet wheel; D, Frame; E, Handle
Arrows indicate direction of motion

pawn¹ (pôn), *v.t.* **1.** to deposit as security, as for money borrowed: *to pawn a watch.* **2.** to pledge or stake: *I pawn my honour.* —*n.* **3.** state of being deposited or held as security: *jewels in pawn.* **4.** something given or deposited as security, as for money borrowed. **5.** any thing or person serving as security. **6.** the act of pawning. [late ME, t. OF: m. *pan.* Cf. G *Pfand*] —**pawner** (pô′nə), *n.*
pawn² (pôn), *n.* **1.** *Chess.* one of the 16 pieces of lowest value, usually moving one square straight ahead, but capturing diagonally. **2.** an unimportant person used as the tool of another. [ME *poune*, t. AF, var. of OF *peon*, g. s. LL *pedo* foot soldier]
pawnbroker (pôn′brō′kə), *n.* one who lends money at interest on pledged personal property. —**pawn′bro′king,** *n.*
Pawnee (pô nē′), *n.* **1.** a member of a confederacy of North American Plains Indians of Caddoan stock now living in northern Oklahoma. **2.** the language of this group. [? der. Pawnee *parika* horn, term used for dressing of scalp lock to resemble a horn]
pawnshop (pôn′shŏp′), *n.* the shop of a pawnbroker where goods can be pawned and unredeemed articles are offered for sale.
pawnticket (pôn′tĭk′ĭt), *n.* a ticket issued by a pawnbroker as a receipt for goods pawned.
pawpaw (pô′pô), *n.* papaw.
pax (păks), *n.* **1.** *Rom. Cath. Ch.* a small tablet bearing a representation of the Crucifixion or some other sacred subject, formerly kissed by the celebrating priest and the congregation at mass. —*interj.* **2.** *Schoolboy Slang.* (a call given as a signal for a desire to cease hostilities.) [ME, t. L: peace]
Pax (păks), *n.* *Rom. Myth.* the goddess of peace, the counterpart of the Greek goddess, Irene.

Paxton (păks′tən), *n.* **Sir Joseph,** 1801–65, English architect: designer of the Crystal Palace.

pax vobiscum (păks′vō bĭs′ko͝om), *Latin.* peace be with you.

paxwax (păks′wăks′), *n. Dial.* neck ligament. [ME *faxwax,* f. OE *feax* hair + *weax(an)* grow]

pay[1] (pā), *v.,* **paid** or (*Obs.* except for def. 1) **payed, paying,** *n., adj.* —*v.t.* **1.** to discharge (a debt, obligation, etc.), as by giving or doing something. **2.** to give (money, etc.) as in discharge of debt or obligation. **3.** to satisfy the claims of (a person, etc.) as by giving money due. **4.** to defray (cost or expense). **5.** to give compensation for. **6.** to yield a recompense or return to; be profitable to: *it pays me to be honest.* **7.** to yield as a return: *the stock pays 4 per cent.* **8.** to requite, as for good, harm, offence, etc. **9.** to give or render (attention, regard, court, compliments, etc.) as if due or fitting. **10.** to make (a call, visit, etc.). **11.** *Naut., etc.* to let out (a rope, etc.) as by slackening (fol. by *out* or *away*).
—*v.i.* **12.** to give money, etc., due: *to pay for goods.* **13.** to discharge debt. **14.** to yield a return or profit; be advantageous or worthwhile. **15.** to give compensation, as for damage or loss sustained. **16.** to suffer, or be punished, as for something; make amends. **17.** *Naut.* to fall (*off*) to leeward.
—*v.* **18.** Some special verb phrases are:
pay off, 1. to retaliate upon or punish. **2.** to discharge a debt in full. **3.** to discharge from one's employ and pay any wages, etc., due. **4.** *Colloq.* to bribe. **5.** to yield a profitable return. **6.** *Naut.* to let fall to leeward.
pay (one's or **its) way, 1.** to pay a fair proportion of one's expenses. **2.** to yield a profit on an investment.
pay out, 1. to disburse; hand out (money). **2.** to retaliate for an injury; punish in revenge.
pay up, 1. to pay upon demand, esp. as when threatened. **2.** to pay fully or promptly.
put paid to, put an end to; prevent.
—*n.* **19.** payment, as of wages. **20.** wages, salary, or stipend. **21.** *Obs. or Obsolesc.* a person in respect to his solvency or reputation for meeting obligations: *he is good pay.* **22.** paid employ: *in the pay of the enemy.* **23.** *Rare.* requital; reward or punishment.
—*adj.* **24.** (of earth, etc.) containing a sufficient quantity of metal or other value to be profitably worked by the miner. **25.** *U.S.* having a mechanism for payment when used: *a pay telephone.*
[ME *paie(n),* t. F: m. *payer,* g. L *pācāre* pacify]
—**Syn. 1.** settle, liquidate. **3.** reward, reimburse, indemnify. **20.** remuneration, emolument, fee.

pay[2] (pā), *v.t.,* **payed, paying.** *Naut.* to coat or cover (seams, a ship's bottom, etc.) with pitch, tar, or the like. [t. ONF: m. *peier,* g. L *picāre* cover with pitch]

payable (pā′ə bl), *adj.* **1.** owed; to be paid; due. **2.** capable of being paid. **3.** profitable. **4.** *Law.* imposing an immediate obligation on the debtor.

pay-as-you-earn (pā′əz yo͞o ûn′), *adj.* denoting a system of collection of income tax by deductions made by the employer from the employee's salary before he receives it.

payday (pā′dā′), *n.* the day when payment is made, or to be made; the day on which wages are paid.

P.A.Y.E., pay-as-you-earn (tax).

payee (pā ē′), *n.* one to whom money is paid or to be paid.

payer (pā′ə), *n.* **1.** one who pays. **2.** the person named in a bill or note who has to pay the holder.

paying guest, a lodger in a private house who pays for his accommodation and food.

paying-in slip (pā′ĭng ĭn′), a printed form filled in by a depositor when he pays an amount of money into his account at a bank.

payload (pā′lōd′), *n.* **1.** the income-producing part of a cargo. **2.** *Astronautics.* the load carried in a rocket or satellite to obtain the results for which the vehicle has been launched.

paymaster (pā′mäs′tə), *n.* an officer or an official responsible for the payment of wages or salaries.

Paymaster-General (pā′mäs tə jĕn′rəl), *n.* **1.** a British government minister and member of the cabinet whose responsibility it is to act as paymaster for government departments. **2.** a similar minister in any of various other governments.

payment (pā′mənt), *n.* **1.** the act of paying. **2.** that which is paid; compensation; recompense. **3.** requital.

paynim (pā′nĭm), *n. Archaic.* **1.** a pagan or heathen. **2.** a Muslim. [ME *painime,* t. OF: m. *paieni(s)me,* g. LL *pāgānismus* heathenism]

pay-off (pā′ŏf′), *n.* **1.** the final settlement of a salary, bet, or debt. **2.** the time when such a payment is made. **3.** a settlement as in retribution. **4.** the climax, as of a joke or routine. **5.** *Colloq.* a final, sometimes unexpected consequence.

payola (pā ō′lə), *n. U.S.* a bribe, esp. for the promotion of a commercial product through the abuse of one's position or influence.

pay-packet (pā′păk′ĭt), *n.* **1.** an envelope or packet containing wages. **2.** the wages themselves.

payroll (pā′rōl′), *n.* **1.** a roll or list of persons to be paid, with the amounts due. **2.** the aggregate of these amounts. **3.** the money that is actually paid out. **4.** the total number of people employed by a firm.

Paysandu (*Sp.* pȧy sȧn do͞o′), *n.* a town in W Uruguay. 60,000 (est. 1964).

Pays de la Loire (*Fr.* pē ē də lȧ lwȧr′), an administrative region in W France comprising the departments of Loire-Atlantique, Vendée, Maine-et-Loire, Mayenne, and Sarthe. 2,461,621 pop. (1962); 12,590 sq. mi. *Cap.:* Nantes.

pay station, *U.S.* a callbox.

payt, payment.

pay tone, *Teleph.* a sound indicating that the call is from a pay-on-answer coin box and that the caller should insert money.

Pb, *Chem.* (L *plumbum*) lead.

P.B., 1. (L *Pharmacopoeia Britannica*) British Pharmacopoeia. **2.** Prayer Book.

PBX, a private telephone exchange, often with outside lines, for routing both internal and external calls in a firm, business, etc. [*P(rivate) B(ranch) (e)X(change)*]

P/C, 1. petty cash. **2.** price current. Also, **p/c.**

pc., 1. (*pl.* **pcs**) piece. **2.** prices.

P.C., 1. Parish Council. **2.** Parish Councillor. **3.** Perpetual Curate. **4.** Police Constable. **5.** Post Commander. **6.** Prince Consort. **7.** Privy Council. **8.** Privy Councillor.

p.c., 1. per cent. **2.** petty cash. **3.** postcard. **4.** price current.

p.c.e., pyrometric cone equivalent.

P.C.S., Principal Clerk of Session.

Pd, *Chem.* palladium.

pd, paid.

P.D., 1. per diem. **2.** Postal District.

p.d., 1. per diem. **2.** potential difference.

P.D.S.A., People's Dispensary for Sick Animals.

P.E., 1. Physical Education. **2.** Presiding Elder. **3.** *Statistics.* probable error. **4.** Protestant Episcopal.

pea (pē), *n., pl.* **peas,** (*Archaic or Dial.*) **pease. 1.** the round, highly nutritious seed of *Pisum sativum,* a hardy plant in wide circulation. **2.** the plant bearing such seeds. **3.** any of various related or similar plants, or their seed, as the chickpea. **4.** something small as a pea. [back-formation from PEASE (orig. sing., but later taken as pl.)] —**pea′like′,** *adj.*

Peabody (pē′bŏd′ĭ), *n.* **George,** 1795–1869, U.S. merchant, banker, and philanthropist in England.

peace (pēs), *n.* **1.** freedom from war or hostilities. **2.** an agreement between contending parties to abstain from further hostilities. **3.** freedom from strife or dissension. **4.** freedom from civil commotion; public order and security: *a justice of the peace.* **5.** freedom from mental disturbance: *peace of mind.* **6.** ease of mind or conscience. **7.** a state of being tranquil or serene. **8.** a state conducive, due to, or characterized by tranquillity or calm. **9.** quiet; stillness; silence. **10. hold one's peace,** to remain quiet; to keep silent. **11. keep the peace,** to refrain from creating a disturbance. **12. make one's peace,** to effect reconciliation for oneself, or for another person. **13. make peace,** to arrange for a stop to hostilities; to end war. —*v.i.* **14.** *Obs.* to be or become silent. [ME *pais,* t. OF, g. L *pax* peace] —**Syn. 2.** armistice, truce. **3.** harmony, amity. **5.** calm, quiet.

peaceable (pē′sə bl), *adj.* **1.** disposed to peace; inclined to avoid strife or dissension: *peaceable intentions.* **2.** peaceful: *a peaceable adjustment.* —**peace′ableness,** *n.* —**peace′ably,** *adv.* —**Syn. 1.** See **pacific.**

Peace Corps, a civilian organization sponsored by the U.S. government to carry out useful, esp. technological, works abroad, esp. in underdeveloped countries.

peaceful (pēs′fəl), *adj.* **1.** characterized by peace; free from strife or commotion; tranquil: *a peaceful reign.* **2.** pertaining to or characteristic of a state of peace: *peaceful uses of atomic energy.* **3.** peaceable. —**peace′fully,** *adv.* —**peace′fulness,** *n.*

—**Syn. 2.** PEACEFUL, PLACID, SERENE, TRANQUIL refer to what is characterized by lack of strife or agitation. PEACEFUL today is rarely applied to persons; it refers to situations, scenes and activities free of disturbances, or, occasionally, of warfare: *a peaceful life.* PLACID, SERENE, TRANQUIL are used mainly of persons; when used of things (usually elements of nature) there is a touch of personification. PLACID suggests an unruffled calm that verges on complacency: *a placid disposition, a placid stream.* SERENE is a somewhat nobler word; when used of persons it suggests dignity, composure, and graciousness (*a serene old age*); when applied to nature there is a suggestion of mellowness (*the serene landscapes of autumn*).

TRANQUIL implies a command of emotions which keeps one unagitated even in the midst of excitement or danger. 3. See **pacific.** —**Ant.** 1. turbulent, disturbed, excited.

peaceful coexistence, the simultaneous existence of two incompatible political systems, without hostilities.

peacekeeping (pēs′kē′pĭng), *n.* **1.** the maintenance of law and order, esp. by the presence of an armed force. —*adj.* **2.** maintaining law and order.

peacemaker (pēs′mā′kə), *n.* one who makes peace, as by reconciling parties at variance.

peace-offering (pēs′ŏf′ə rĭng), *n.* **1.** an offering or sacrifice prescribed by the Levitical law (see Lev. 3, 7) as thanksgiving to God. **2.** any offering made to procure peace.

peace officer, a civil officer appointed to preserve the public peace, as a sheriff or constable.

peace-pipe (pēs′pīp′), *n.* the calumet or pipe smoked by the North American Indians in token or ratification of peace.

Peace River, a river in W Canada, flowing from the Rocky Mountains in E British Columbia NE through Alberta to the Slave river. ab. 1050 mi.

peacetime (pēs′tīm′), *n.* **1.** a period of peace. —*adj.* **2.** of or for such a period: *peacetime uses of atomic energy.*

peach[1] (pēch), *n.* **1.** the sabacid, juicy, drupaceous fruit of a tree, *Prunus persica,* of many varieties, widely cultivated in temperate climates. **2.** the tree itself. **3.** a light pinkish yellow, as of a peach. **4.** *Slang.* a person or thing especially admired or liked. —*adj.* **5.** of the colour peach. **6.** flavoured or cooked with peaches. [ME *peche,* t. OF; r. OE *persic,* t. L: s. *persicum,* t. Gk: m. *Persikón,* lit., Persian (apple)] —**peach′like′,** *adj.*

peach[2] (pēch), *v.i.* **1.** *Now Slang.* to inform against an accomplice or associate. —*v.t.* **2.** *Now Rare.* to inform against. [aphetic var. of *appeach,* ME *apeche(n),* t. AF: m. *apecher,* var. of OF *empechier* hinder. See IMPEACH]

peach-bloom (pēch′blōōm′), *n.* **1.** the powdery surface of a peach. **2.** any surface resembling this, as of human complexion, pottery, etc.

peachblow (pēch′blō′), *n.* a delicate purplish pink. [f. PEACH[1] + BLOW[3], n.]

peach Melba, a dessert consisting of half a peach and vanilla ice-cream, served with Melba sauce.

peachy (pē′chĭ), *adj.,* **-chier, -chiest.** **1.** peachlike, as in colour or appearance. **2.** *Slang.* excellent; wonderful.

peacock (pē′kŏk′), *n., pl.* **-cocks,** (*esp. collectively*) **cock.** **1.** the male of the peafowl, esp. of the common peafowl, *Pavo cristatus,* a native of India but now widely domesticated, distinguished for its long, erectile, ocellated tail coverts with rich iridescent colouring of green, blue, and gold. **2.** any peafowl. **3.** a vain person. **4.** (*cap.*) the southern constellation Pavo. —*v.i.* **5.** to strut like a peacock; make a vainglorious display. —*v.t.* **6.** *Austral., N.Z.* to buy up choice pieces of land, making intervening pieces useless to others. [ME *pecok,* f. *pe* (OE *pea* peafowl, t. L: m. *pavo*) + *cok* COCK[1]] —**pea′cock′ish, pea′cock′y,** *adj.*

Peacock, *Pavo cristatus* (Total length ab. 7 ft)

Peacock (pē′kŏk′), *n.* **Thomas Love,** 1785–1866, English novelist and poet.

peacock blue, a lustrous greenish blue as of certain peacock feathers.

peacock ore, bornite.

pea crab, a small semiparasitic crab of the family *Pinnotheridae,* which inhabits the branchial cavities of molluscs and tunicates.

peafowl (pē′foul′), *n.* any of the gallinaceous birds constituting the genus *Pavo;* a peacock or peahen.

peag (pēg), *n.* wampum (def. 1).

pea green, a medium or yellowish green.

peahen (pē′hĕn′), *n.* the female peafowl.

pea jacket, a short coat of thick woollen cloth worn esp. by seamen. [t. D: anglicization of *pij-jakker*]

peak[1] (pēk), *n.* **1.** the pointed top of a mountain. **2.** a mountain with a pointed summit. **3.** the pointed top of anything. **4.** the highest point: *the peak of his career.* **5.** the maximum point or degree of anything. **6.** *Elect., Mech., etc.* **a.** the maximum value of a quantity during a specified time: *a voltage peak.* **b.** the maximum power consumed or produced by a unit or group of units in a stated period of time. **7.** a projecting point: *the peak of a man's beard.* **8.** widow's peak. **9.** a projecting front piece, or visor, of a cap. **10.** *Naut.* **a.** See **after peak** and **forepeak.** **b.** the upper after-corner of a sail that is extended by a gaff. **c.** the outer extremity of a gaff. —*v.t.* **11.** *Naut.* to raise the after-end of (a yard, gaff, etc.) to or towards an angle above the horizontal. —*v.i.* **12.** to project in a peak. **13.** *Statistics.* to reach a highest point. [b. PIKE[2] (or PICK[1]) and BEAK[1]]

peak[2] (pēk), *v.i.* to become weak, thin, and sickly. [orig. uncert.] —**peak′ily,** *adv.* —**peak′iness,** *n.* —**peak′y,** *adj.*

Peak District, an area of Derbyshire, in central England, around High Peak, 2088 ft; a national park.

peaked[1] (pēkt), *adj.* having a peak. [f. PEAK[1], n. + -ED[2]]

peaked[2] (pēkt), *adj.* thin; emaciated. [f. PEAK[2] + -ED[2]]

peal (pēl), *n.* **1.** a loud, prolonged sound of bells. **2.** any other loud, prolonged sound as of cannon, thunder, applause, laughter, etc. **3.** a set of bells tuned to one another. **4.** a series of changes rung on a set of bells. —*v.t.* **5.** to give forth loudly and sonorously. **6.** *Obs.* to assail with loud sounds. —*v.i.* **7.** to sound forth in a peal; resound. [ME *pele;* akin to *peal, pell,* v., strike, beat]

pean (pē′ən), *n.* paean.

peanut (pē′nŭt′), *n.* **1.** the fruit (pod) or the edible seed of *Arachis hypogaea,* a leguminous plant, the pod of which is forced underground in growing, where it ripens. **2.** the plant. **3.** (*pl.*) *Slang.* any small amount, esp. of money. —*adj.* **4.** of or pertaining to the peanut or peanuts. **5.** made with or from peanuts.

peanut butter, a smooth paste made from finely ground roasted peanuts, used as a spread, etc.

pear (pĕə), *n.* **1.** the edible fruit, typically rounded but elongated and growing smaller towards the stem, of a rosaceous tree, *Pyrus communis,* familiar in cultivation. **2.** the tree itself. [ME *peere,* OE *pere,* t. LL: m. *pirum*]

pear drop, 1. a pear-shaped pendant. **2.** a fruit-flavoured sweet in the shape of a pear.

pearl[1] (pûl), *n.* **1.** a hard, smooth, often highly lustrous concretion, a mass of nacre, white or variously coloured, and rounded, pear-shaped, or irregular (baroque) in form, secreted as a morbid product within the shell of various bivalve molluscs, and often valuable as a gem. **2.** any of various man-made substances that resemble this. **3.** nacre, or mother-of-pearl. **4.** something similar in form, lustre, etc., as a dewdrop or a capsule of medicine. **5.** something precious or choice; the finest example of anything. **6.** a very pale grey approaching white but commonly with a bluish tinge. **7.** *Print.* a size of type (5 point). —*v.t.* **8.** to adorn or stud with or as with pearls. **9.** to make like pearls, as in form or colour. —*v.i.* **10.** to seek for pearls. **11.** to take a pearl-like form or appearance. —*adj.* **12.** of the colour or lustre of pearl; nacreous. **13.** of, pertaining to, or inlaid with pearls or mother-of-pearl. **14.** reduced to small rounded grains: *pearl barley.* [ME *perle,* t. OF, t. ML: m. *perla,* ? b. L *perna* a kind of mussel and *sphaerula* little sphere] —**pearl′er,** *n.*

pearl[2] (pûl), *v.t., v.i., n.* purl[2].

pearl-ash (pûl′ăsh′) *n.* commercial carbonate of potassium.

pearl barley, barley ground into small round grains and used in soups, etc.

pearl blue, a light bluish grey.

pearl button, 1. a button made from mother-of-pearl. **2.** a button made from an artificial pearl.

pearl grey, a very pale bluish grey.

Pearl Harbor, a harbour near Honolulu, on the island of Oahu in the Hawaiian Islands: surprise attack by Japan on the U.S. naval base there December 7th, 1941.

pearlite (pû′līt), *n.* **1.** *Metall.* an iron carbon alloy containing approximately 0·86 per cent carbon, and consisting of alternate layers of ferrite and cementite. **2.** *Geol.* perlite. [f. PEARL[1] + -ITE[1]] —**pearlitic** (pû lĭt′ĭk), *adj.*

pearl millet, a tall grass, *Pennisetum glaucum,* cultivated in Africa, the Orient, and the southern U.S., for its edible seeds and as a forage plant.

pearl oyster, any of the pearl-producing bivalve molluscs of the family *Ostreidae.*

Pearl River, Chu-Kiang.

pearl spar, dolomite.

pearlwort (pûl′wût′), *n.* any of several small herbs of the caryophyllaceous genus *Sagina,* as *S. apetala,* the common pearlwort, an annual widespread on bare soil in temperate regions.

pearly (pû′lĭ), *adj.,* **-lier, -liest,** *n., pl.* **-lies.** —*adj.* **1.** like a pearl or like pearl. **2.** adorned with or abounding in pearls, pearl, or mother-of-pearl. **3.** *Slang.* wearing pearlies. —*n.* **4.** *Slang.* a button, esp. one of large numbers sewn on to the clothes of costermongers for ornament. **5.** *Slang.* a costermonger whose clothes are so ornamented.

Pearly Gates, 1. *Colloq.* the entrance to heaven. **2.** (*l.c.*) *Slang.* teeth.

pearly king, a hereditary title adopted by certain costermongers, originally by a chief stall-holder who protected other traders: now entitling the possessor to dress in costumes decorated with pearl buttons. —**pearly queen,** *fem.*

pearly nautilus, nautilus (def. 1).

pearmain (pĕəʹmān′), *n.* any of several varieties of apple. [ME *parmayn,* t. OF: m. *parmain* pear (? orig. adj., der. *Parma* PARMA]

Pears (pĭəz), *n.* **Peter,** born 1910, English operatic tenor.

Pearson (pĭəʹsən), *n.* **1. Karl,** 1857–1936, English scientist who applied statistics to evolution and heredity. **2. Lester B(owles),** born 1897, prime minister of Canada 1963–68.

peart (pĭət), *adj.* **1.** lively or brisk; cheerful. **2.** clever. [var. of PERT]

Peary (pĭəʹrĭ), *n.* **Robert Edwin,** 1856–1920, U.S. naval officer and explorer: discovered North Pole 1909.

peasant (pĕzʹənt), *n.* **1.** one of a class of persons, as in European countries, of inferior social rank, living in the country and engaged usually in agricultural labour. **2.** a rustic or countryman. **3.** *Colloq.* an unsophisticated person; one unable to appreciate that which is cultured and tasteful; a boor. —*adj.* **4.** of or characteristic of peasants, their crafts, traditions, etc. [late ME, t. AF: m. *paisant,* der. *pais* country, g. LL *pāgensis,* adj., der. L *pāgus* district. Cf. PAGAN]

peasantry (pĕzʹən trĭ), *n.* **1.** peasants collectively. **2.** the status or character of a peasant.

Peasants' Revolt, an insurrection led by Wat Tyler in 1381 in protest against an attempt by landlords to revert to old servile tenures.

pease (pēz), *n., pl.* **pease.** *Archaic or Dial.* **1.** a pea. **2.** (*pl.*) peas collectively. **3.** pl. of **pea.** [ME *pese,* OE *peose, pise,* t. LL: m. *pīsa,* orig. pl. of *pīsum,* t. Gk: m. *píson* pulse, pea]

peasecod (pēzʹkŏd′), *n.* the pod of the pea. Also, **peascod.** [ME; f. PEASE + COD²]

pease pudding, split peas soaked, then boiled and sieved: served with ham or bacon.

peashooter (pēʹshōō′tə), *n.* a tube through which dried peas are blown, as by children.

pea soup, 1. a thick soup made from split peas. **2.** *Slang.* thick, dirty fog.

pea souper, *Slang.* an extremely thick fog.

peat¹ (pēt), *n.* **1.** a highly organic soil (more than fifty per cent combustible) of partially decomposed vegetable matter, in marshy or damp regions, drained and cultivated, cut out and dried for use as fuel. **2.** such vegetable matter as a substance or fuel. [ME *pete* (in Anglo-L *peta*); orig. uncert.] —**peatʹy,** *adj.*

peat² (pēt), *n.* *Archaic.* a pet or darling.

peau de soie (pōʹdə swäʹ; *Fr.* pō də swȧʹ), a fancy reversible silk cloth made on a satin base, having a ribbed appearance. [F]

peavey (pēʹvĭ), *n., pl.* **-veys.** *U.S.* a lumberman's cant dog with a spike at the end. [named after Joseph *Peavey,* the inventor]

peavy (pēʹvĭ), *n., pl.* **-vies.** peavey.

pebble (pĕbʹl), *n., v.,* **-bled, -bling.** —*n.* **1.** a small, rounded stone, esp. one worn by the action of water. **2.** pebbled leather, or its granulated surface. **3.** a transparent, colourless rock crystal used for the lenses of spectacles. **4.** a lens made of it. —*v.t.* **5.** to prepare (leather, etc.) so as to have a granulated surface. **6.** to pelt with or as with pebbles. [ME *puble-,* etc., OE *pæbbel* (in place-names)] —**pebʹbly,** *adj.*

pebble dash, a type of finish used on external walls, formed by throwing or pressing small stones into plaster while it is still plastic.

pecan (pĭ kănʹ), *n.* **1.** a hickory tree, *Carya illinoensis* (*C. pecan*), indigenous to the lower Mississippi valley and grown in the southern U.S. for its oval, smooth-shelled nut with a sweet, oily, edible kernel. **2.** the nut. [t. Amer. Ind. (Algonquian), der. *pukan, pakan* hard-shelled nut]

peccable (pĕkʹə bl), *adj.* liable to sin or err. [t. ML: m. s. *peccābilis*] —**pec′cabilʹity,** *n.*

peccadillo (pĕk′ə dĭlʹō), *n., pl.* **-loes, -los.** a petty sin or offence; a trifling fault. [t. Sp.: m. *pecadillo,* dim. of *pecado,* g. L *peccātum* a sin]

peccant (pĕkʹənt), *adj.* **1.** sinning or offending. **2.** faulty. [t. L: s. *peccans,* ppr., sinning] —**pecʹcancy,** *n.* —**pecʹcantly,** *adv.*

Collared peccary, *Tayassu angulatus* (Ab. 3 ft long; 1½ ft high at the shoulder)

peccary (pĕkʹə rĭ), *n., pl.* **-ries,** (*esp. collectively*) **-ry.** one of two species of gregarious, piglike American ungulates, occurring in the genus *Tayassu,* the **collared peccaries,** and the **white-lipped peccaries,** ranging from Paraguay to Texas and constituting the artiodactylous family *Tayassuidae,* related to the pig. [t. Carib: m. *pakira*]

peccavi (pĕ kāʹvē), *v.* **1.** I have sinned (confession of King David). —*n.* **2.** (*pl.* **-vis**) any avowal of guilt. [t. L]

Pechora (*Russ.* pĭ chôʹrə), *n.* a river in the NE Soviet Union in Europe, flowing from the Ural Mountains into the Arctic Ocean. ab. 1100 mi.

peck¹ (pĕk), *n.* **1.** a dry measure of 8 quarts; the fourth part of a bushel. **2.** a container for measuring this quantity. **3.** a considerable quantity: *a peck of trouble.* [ME *pek,* orig. unknown]

peck² (pĕk), *v.t.* **1.** to strike or indent with the beak, as a bird does, or with some pointed instrument, esp. with quick, repeated movements. **2.** to make (a hole, etc.) by such strokes. **3.** to take (food, etc.) bit by bit, with or as with the beak. **4.** to kiss in a hasty dabbing manner. —*v.i.* **5.** to make strokes with the beak or a pointed instrument. **6.** to pick or nibble at food. **7.** to carp or nag (fol. by *at*). —*n.* **8.** a pecking stroke. **9.** a hole or mark made by or as by pecking. **10.** a hasty kiss. [ME *pekke(n)*; ? var. of PICK¹]

pecker (pĕkʹə), *n.* **1.** one who or that which pecks. **2.** a woodpecker. **3. keep one's pecker up,** *Slang.* to remain cheerful; maintain good spirits, courage, or resolution.

pecking order, 1. the natural hierarchy observable in a flock of poultry or in any gregarious species of birds. **2.** any order of precedence. Also, **peck order.**

peckish (pĕkʹĭsh), *adj.* *Colloq.* having an appetite.

Pecksniffian (pĕk snĭfʹĭ ən), *adj.* making a hypocritical parade of benevolence or high principle. [after Mr *Pecksniff* in Dickens's '*Martin Chuzzlewit*']

Pecos (pāʹkəs; *Sp.* pĕʹkōs), *n.* a river flowing from N New Mexico SE through W Texas to the Rio Grande. 735 mi.

Pécs (*Hung.* pĕch), *n.* a city in SW Hungary. 125,000 (est. 1963). German, **Fünfkirchen.**

pectate (pĕkʹtāt), *n.* *Chem.* a salt of pectic acid.

pecten (pĕkʹtĭn), *n., pl.* **-tens, -tines** (-tĭ nēz′). *Zool., Anat.* **1.** a comblike part or process. **2.** a pigmented vascular membrane with parallel folds suggesting the teeth of a comb, projecting into the vitreous humour of the eye in birds and reptiles. [ME, t. L: a comb]

pectic (pĕkʹtĭk), *adj.* pertaining to pectin. [t. Gk: m. s. *pēktikós* congealing, curdling]

pectic acid, *Chem.* any of several water-insoluble products of the hydrolysis of pectin esters.

pectin (pĕkʹtĭn), *n.* *Chem.* any of the acidic hemicelluloses which occur in ripe fruits, esp. in apples, currants, etc., and which dissolve in boiling water, forming a jelly upon subsequent evaporation. [f. PECT(IC) + -IN²]

pectinate (pĕkʹtĭ nāt′), *adj.* comblike; formed into or with teeth like a comb. Also, **pecʹtinat′ed.** [t. L: m. s. *pectinātus* comblike, pp.] —**pec′tinaʹtion,** *n.*

pectize (pĕkʹtīz), *v.t., v.i.,* **-tized, -tizing.** to change into a jelly; jellify; gel. Also, **pectise.** [f. s. Gk *pēktós* compacted, fixed + -IZE] —**pec′tizaʹtion,** *n.*

pectolite (pĕkʹtə līt′), *n.* a mineral silicate of calcium and sodium which crystallizes in the monoclinic system.

pectoral (pĕkʹtə rəl), *adj.* **1.** of or pertaining to the breast or chest; thoracic. **2.** worn on the breast or chest: *the pectoral cross of a bishop.* **3.** proceeding from the heart or inner consciousness. **4.** *Phonet.* (of a vocal quality) appearing to come from resonance in the chest; full or deep. —*n.* **5.** something worn on the breast for ornament, protection, etc., as a breastplate. **6.** a pectoral fin. [late ME, t. L: s. *pectorālis* pertaining to the breast]

pectoral arch, 1. (in vertebrates) a bony or cartilaginous arch supporting the forelimbs. **2.** (in man) the bony arch, formed by the collarbone and shoulderblade, which attaches the upper extremity to the axial skeleton. Also, **pectoral girdle.**

pectoral fin, (in fishes) either of a pair of fins situated usually behind the head, one on each side, and corresponding to the forelimbs of higher vertebrates.

peculate (pĕkʹyōō lāt′), *v.i., v.t.,* **-lated, -lating.** to embezzle (public money); appropriate dishonestly (money or goods entrusted to one's care). [t. L: m. s. *pecūlātus,* pp., having embezzled] —**pec′ulaʹtion,** *n.* —**pecʹula′tor,** *n.*

peculiar (pĭ kyōōʹlyə), *adj.* **1.** strange, odd, or queer: *a peculiar old man.* **2.** uncommon; unusual: *a peculiar hobby.* **3.** distinguished in nature or character from others. **4.** belonging characteristically (fol. by *to*): *an expression peculiar to Canadians.* **5.** belonging exclusively to a person or thing. —*n.* **6.** *Print.* a special sort. **7.** *Obs.* a peculiar property or privilege. **8.** a particular parish or church which is exempted from the jurisdiction of the ordinary or bishop in whose diocese it lies and is governed by another. [late ME, t. L: s. *pecūliāris* pertaining to one's own, der. *pecūlium* property] —**pecu′liarly,** *adv.* —**Syn.** **1.** eccentric, bizarre. See **strange. 5.** individual, personal, particular, special.

peculiarity (pĭ kyōō′lĭ ă′rĭ tĭ), *n., pl.* **-ties. 1.** an odd trait or characteristic. **2.** singularity or oddity. **3.** peculiar or characteristic quality. **4.** a distinguishing quality or characteristic. —**Syn. 4.** See **feature.**

peculiar people, 1. a modern religious sect that has no priests, preachers, creeds, or organization; characterized by exclusive reliance on prayer to cure disease. **2.** the Jews, considered as God's chosen people.

peculium (pĭ kyōō′lyəm), *n.* **1.** private property. **2.** *Rom. Law.* property given by a paterfamilias to those subject to him, or by a master to his slave, to be treated as though the property of the recipient. [t. L: property]

pecuniary (pĭ kyōō′nyə rĭ), *adj.* **1.** consisting of or given or exacted in money: *pecuniary penalties.* **2.** of or pertaining to money: *pecuniary affairs.* **3.** (of an offence, etc.) entailing a money penalty. [t. L: m. s. *pecūniārius* pertaining to money] —**pecu′niarily,** *adv.* —**Syn. 1.** See **financial.**

ped-[1], var. of **paed-,** as in *pedagogic.*

ped-[2], var. of **pedi-**[1].

-ped, a word element meaning 'foot', serving to form adjectives and nouns, as *aliped, biped, quadruped.* Cf. **-pod.** [t. L, comb. form of *pēs* foot]

ped., 1. pedal. **2.** pedestal.

pedagogic (pĕd′ə gŏj′ĭk), *adj.* of or pertaining to a pedagogue or pedagogy. Also, **ped′agog′ical.** [t. Gk: m. s. *paidagōgikós*, der. *paidagōgós* pedagogue] —**ped′agog′ically,** *adv.*

pedagogics (pĕd′ə gŏj′ĭks), *n.* the science or art of teaching or education; pedagogy.

pedagogism (pĕd′ə gō gĭz′əm), *n.* the principles, manner, or characteristics of pedagogues. Also, **pedagoguism.**

pedagogue (pĕd′ə gōg′), *n.* **1.** a teacher of children; a schoolteacher. **2.** a person who is pedantic, dogmatic, and formal. [ME *pedagoge*, t. OF, t. L: m. *paedagōgus*, t. Gk: m. *paidagōgós* a teacher of boys]

pedagogy (pĕd′ə gŏj′ĭ), *n.* **1.** the function, work, or art of a teacher; teaching. **2.** instruction.

pedal[1] (pĕd′l), *n., v.,* **-alled, -alling** or (*U.S.*) **-aled, -aling,** *adj.* —*n.* **1.** a lever worked by the foot, in various musical instruments, as the organ, piano, and harp, and having various functions. **2.** a keyboard attached to the organ, harpsichord, etc., operated by the feet. **3.** pedal-point. **4.** a lever-like part worked by the foot, in various mechanisms, as the sewing machine, bicycle, motor car, etc.; a treadle. —*v.i., v.t.* **5.** to work or use the pedals (of), as in playing an organ or propelling a bicycle. —*adj.* **6.** of or pertaining to a pedal or pedals. **7.** consisting of pedals: *a pedal keyboard.* [t. F: m. *pédale*, t. It., t. L: (something) pertaining to the foot]

pedal[2] (pē′dl), *adj.* of or pertaining to a foot or the feet. [t. L: s. *pedālis*]

pedalfer (pĭ dăl′fə), *n.* a type of soil lacking in lime but containing accumulations of aluminium and iron components. [f. s. Gk *pedón* ground + AL(UMINIUM) + m. s. L *ferrum* iron]

pedal point (pĕd′l point′), *Music.* **1.** a note sustained by one of the parts (usually the bass) while other parts progress without reference to it. **2.** a passage containing it.

pedant (pĕd′nt), *n.* **1.** one who makes an excessive or tedious show of learning or learned precision; one who possesses mere book-learning without practical wisdom. **2.** *Obs.* a schoolmaster. [t. It.: m. *pedante* teacher, pedant, der. It. *ped-*, *piede* foot (in meaning of servile follower)] —**pedantic** (pĭ dăn′tĭk), **pedan′tical,** *adj.* —**pedan′tically,** *adv.*

pedantry (pĕd′n trĭ), *n., pl.* **-ries. 1.** the character or practice of a pedant; an undue display of learning. **2.** slavish attention to rules, details, etc. **3.** a pedantic expression; an instance of being pedantic.

pedate (pĕd′āt), *adj.* **1.** having feet. **2.** footlike. **3.** having divisions like toes. **4.** *Bot.* (of a leaf) palmately parted or divided with the lateral lobes or divisions cleft or divided. [t. L: m. s. *pedātus* having feet] —**ped′ately,** *adv.*

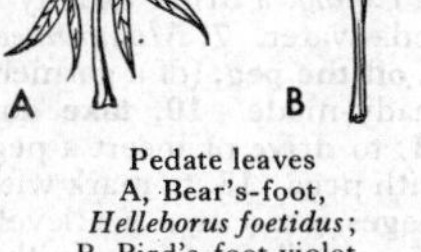

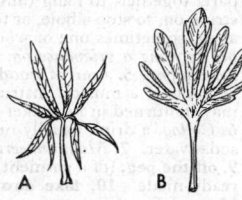

Pedate leaves
A, Bear's-foot, *Helleborus foetidus*;
B, Bird's-foot violet, *Viola pedata*

pedati-, a word element meaning 'pedate'. [comb. form repr. L *pedātus*]

pedatifid (pĭ dăt′ĭ fĭd, -dā′tĭ), *adj. Bot.* pedately cleft.

peddle (pĕd′l), *v.,* **-dled, -dling.** —*v.t.* **1.** to carry about for sale at retail; hawk. **2.** to deal out in small quantities. —*v.i.* **3.** to travel about retailing small wares. **4.** to occupy oneself with trifles; trifle. [appar. a back-formation from PEDLAR, and in part confused with PIDDLE]

peddler (pĕd′lə), *n. U.S.* pedlar.

peddling (pĕd′lĭng), *adj.* trifling; paltry; piddling.

-pede, a word element meaning 'foot', as in *centipede.* [t. F: m. *-pède*, t. L: m. *-peda*, a comb. form of *pēs* foot]

pederast (pĕd′ə răst′), *n.* one, esp. a male adult, who desires or practises pederasty. [t. Gk: m. s. *paiderastḗs* lover of boys]

pederasty (pĕd′ə răs′tĭ), *n.* homosexual relations, esp. those between a male adult and a boy. —**ped′eras′tic,** *adj.* —**ped′eras′tically,** *adv.*

pedestal (pĕd′ĭs tl), *n., v.,* **-talled, -talling** or (*U.S.*) **-taled, -taling.** —*n.* **1.** an architectural support for a column, statue, vase, or the like. **2.** a supporting structure or piece; a base. **3.** one of two supports of a kneehole desk, consisting of a boxlike frame containing drawers. **4. set on a pedestal,** to idealize: *he set her on a pedestal until he discovered her true nature.* —*v.t.* **5.** to set on or supply with a pedestal. [t. F: m. *piédestal*, t. It.: m. *piedestallo*, f. *piè* foot (g. s. L *pēs*) + *di* of (g. L *dē*) + *stallo* (of Gmc orig. Cf. STALL[1])]

pedestrian (pĭ dĕs′trĭ ən), *n.* **1.** one who goes or travels on foot; a walker. —*adj.* **2.** going or performed on foot; walking. **3.** pertaining to walking. **4.** commonplace; prosaic; dull. [f. s. L *pedester* on foot + -IAN]

pedestrian crossing, an area of roadway on which pedestrians have, within legally defined limits, right of way to cross the road. See **zebra crossing.**

pedestrianism (pĭ dĕs′trĭ ə nĭz′əm), *n.* **1.** the exercise or practice of walking. **2.** pedestrian manner or traits.

pedi-[1], a word element meaning 'foot', as in *pediform.* Also, **ped-**[2]. [t. L, comb. form of *pēs*]

pedi-[2], *Chiefly U.S.* var. of **paed-.**

pediatrician (pē′dĭ ə trĭsh′ən), *n. U.S.* paediatrician.

pediatrics (pē′dĭ ăt′rĭks), *n. U.S.* paediatrics. —**pe′diat′ric,** *adj.*

pedicel (pĕd′ĭ sĕl′), *n.* **1.** *Bot.* **a.** a small stalk. **b.** an ultimate division of a common peduncle. **c.** one of the subordinate stalks in a branched inflorescence, bearing a single flower. **2.** *Zool., Anat.* **a.** a small stalk or stalklike part; a peduncle. **b.** a little foot or footlike part. [t. NL: m. s. *pedicellus*, dim. of L *pedīculus* PEDICLE]

A, Pedicel; B, Peduncle

pedicellate (pĕd′ĭ sĕl′āt, pĕd′ĭ sĕl′āt, -ĭt), *adj.* having a pedicel or pedicels.

pedicle (pĕd′ĭ kl), *n. Bot., Zool., etc.* a small stalk or stalklike support; a pedicel or peduncle. [t. L: m. s. *pedīculus*, dim. of *pēs* foot]

pedicular (pĭ dĭk′yŏŏ lə), *adj.* of or pertaining to lice. [t. L: s. *pedīculāris*, der. *pedīculus* louse]

pediculate (pĭ dĭk′yŏŏ lĭt, -lāt′), *adj.* **1.** of or relating to the *Pediculati*, a group of teleost fishes, characterized by the elongated basis of their pectoral fins simulating an arm or penduncle. —*n.* **2.** a member of this group. [f. s. L *pedīculus* footstalk + -ATE[1]]

pediculosis (pĭ dĭk′yŏŏ lō′sĭs), *n. Pathol.* the state of being infested with lice. [t. NL, f. s. L *pedīculus* louse + *-ōsis* -OSIS] —**pediculous** (pĭ dĭk′yŏŏ ləs), *adj.*

pedicure (pĕd′ĭ kyŏŏə′), *n.* **1.** professional care or treatment of the feet. **2.** one who makes a business of caring for the feet; a chiropodist. [t. F, f. L: *pedi-* PEDI-[1] + m. *cūra* care. Cf. MANICURE]

pediform (pĕd′ĭ fôm′), *adj.* in the form of a foot.

pedigree (pĕd′ĭ grē′), *n.* **1.** an ancestral line, or line of descent, esp. as recorded; lineage. **2.** a genealogical table: *a family pedigree.* **3.** a line, family, or race. **4.** derivation, as from a source: *the pedigree of a word.* [ME *pedegru*, appar. t. OF: m. *pied de grue*, lit., foot of crane, said to refer to a mark having three branching lines, used in old genealogical tables]

—**Syn. 2.** PEDIGREE, GENEALOGY refer to an account of ancestry. A PEDIGREE is a table or chart recording a line of ancestors, either of persons or (more especially) of animals, as horses, cattle, and dogs; in the case of animals, such a table is used as proof of superior qualities: *a detailed pedigree.* A GENEALOGY is an account of the descent of a person or family traced through a series of generations, usually from the first known ancestor: *a genealogy that includes a king.*

pedigreed (pĕd′ĭ grēd′), *adj.* having known purebred ancestry.

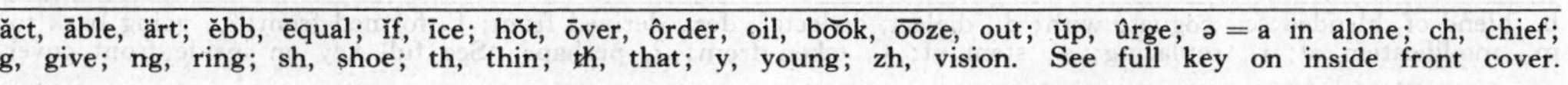

pediment (pĕd′ĭ mənt), *n.* *Archit.* **1.** a low triangular gable crowned with a projecting cornice, in the Greek, Roman, or Renaissance style, esp. over a portico or porch or at the ends of a gable-roofed building. **2.** any member of similar outline and position, as over an opening. [? t. L: m. s. *pedāmentum* a prop for a vine] —**pedimental** (pĕd′-ĭ mĕn′tl), *adj.*

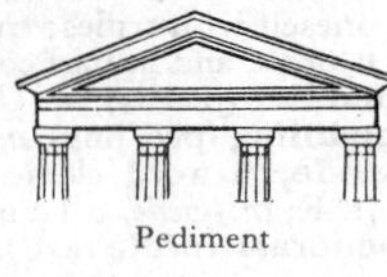
Pediment

pedipalp (pĕd′ĭ pălp′), *n.* the second paired appendage of an arachnid, sometimes used as a weapon or as an organ of touch for feeding.

pedlar (pĕd′lə), *n.* one who peddles. Also, **pedler;** *U.S.,* **peddler.** [ME *pedlere,* appar. der. *pedle,* dim. of *ped* basket]

pedlary (pĕd′lə rĭ), *n.* **1.** the business of a pedlar. **2.** pedlars' wares. **3.** trumpery. Also, *U.S.,* **peddlery.**

pedobaptism (pē′dō băp′tĭz′əm), *n.* *U.S.* paedobaptism.

pedocal (pĕd′ə kăl′), *n.* a type of soil rich in lime, having accumulations of calcium carbonate.

pedology[1] (pĭ dŏl′ə jĭ), *n.* the more fundamental aspects of soil science, particularly the genesis and classification of soils. [f. Gk *pédo(n)* soil + -LOGY]

pedology[2] (pĭ dŏl′ə jĭ), *n.* *U.S.* paedology.

pedometer (pĭ dŏm′ĭ tə), *n.* an instrument for recording the number of steps taken in walking, and thus showing approximately the distance travelled. [t. F: m. *pédomètre,* f. *pedo-* PEDI-[1] + *-mètre* -METER[1]]

pedro (pē′drō), *n., pl.* **-dros.** *U.S. Cards.* **1.** any of several varieties of seven-up in which the five of trumps counts at its face value. **2.** the five of trumps. [t. Sp.: special use of *Pedro* Peter]

peduncle (pĭ dŭng′kl), *n.* **1.** *Bot.* **a.** a flower stalk, supporting either a cluster or a solitary flower. **b.** the stalk bearing the fructification in fungi, etc. **2.** *Zool.* a stalk or stem; a stalklike part or structure. **3.** *Anat.* a stalklike part composed of white matter connecting various regions of the brain. [t. NL: m. s. *pedunculus,* dim. of L *pēs* foot] —**pedun′cled, peduncular** (pĭ-dŭng′kyŏŏ lə), *adj.*

P, Peduncle

peduncúlate (pĭ dŭng′kyŏŏ lĭt, -lāt′), *adj.* **1.** having a peduncle. **2.** growing on a peduncle. Also, **pedun′culat′ed.**

Peebles (pē′blz), *n.* **1.** a burgh in Scotland, the county town of Peeblesshire. 5545 (1961). **2.** Peeblesshire.

Peeblesshire (pē′blz shĭə′, -shə), *n.* a county in S Scotland. 14,117 pop. (1961); 347 sq. mi. *Co. town:* Peebles. Also, **Peebles, Tweeddale.**

peek (pēk), *v.i.* **1.** to peep; peer. —*n.* **2.** a peeking look; a peep. [ME *pike(n),* ? dissimilated var. of *kike* peep; akin to LG *kīken*] —**Syn. 1.** See **peep**[1].

peel[1] (pēl), *v.t.* **1.** to strip off the skin, rind, bark, etc.; decorticate. **2.** to strip off (skin, etc.). **3.** *Croquet.* to send (another player's ball) through a hoop. **4. keep (one's) eye peeled,** *Slang.* to keep a close watch. —*v.i.* **5.** (of skin, etc.) to come off. **6.** to lose the skin, rind, bark, etc. **7.** *Slang.* to undress. —*n.* **8.** the skin or rind of a fruit, etc. [ME *pelen,* phonetic var. of *pilen* PILL[2]]

—**Syn. 1.** PEEL, PARE agree in meaning to remove the skin or rind from something. PEEL means to pull or strip off the natural external covering or protection of something: *to peel an orange.* PARE is used of trimming off chips, flakes, or superficial parts from something, as well as of cutting off the skin or rind: *to pare the nails.*

peel[2] (pēl), *n.* a shovel-like implement for putting bread, pies, etc., into the oven or taking them out. [ME *pele,* t. OF: shovel, g. L *pāla* spade]

peel[3] (pēl), *n.* one of a class of fortified towers, common in the border counties of England and Scotland in the 16th century. [ME *pel,* t. OF: stake, g. L *pālus* PALE[2]]

Peel (pēl), *n.* **1. Sir Robert,** 1788–1850, British statesman; prime minister 1834–35 and 1841–46. **2.** a seaport on the W coast of the Isle of Man: castle; resort. 2487 (1961).

Peele (pēl), *n.* **George,** 1558?–97?, English dramatist.

peeler[1] (pē′lə), *n.* one who or that which peels. [f. PEEL[1] + -ER[1]]

peeler[2] (pē′lə), *n.* *Obsolesc. Slang.* a policeman. [named after Sir Robert PEEL who founded the Irish constabulary and improved it in Britain. Cf. BOBBY]

peeling (pē′lĭng), *n.* **1.** the act of one who or that which peels. **2.** that which is peeled from something, as a piece of the skin or rind of a fruit peeled off.

peen (pēn), *n.* **1.** the sharp, spherical, or otherwise modified end of the head of a hammer, opposite to the face. —*v.t.* **2.** to treat by striking regularly all over with the peen of a hammer. [earlier *pen;* orig. uncert.]

Peenemünde (*Ger.* pē nə mʏn′də), *n.* a village in NE East Germany: centre of German rocket and missile research and development in World War II.

peep[1] (pēp), *v.i.* **1.** to look through or as through a small aperture. **2.** to look slyly, pryingly, or furtively. **3.** to peer, as from a hiding place. **4.** to come partially into view; begin to appear. —*v.t.* **5.** to show or protrude slightly. —*n.* **6.** a peeping look or glance. **7.** the first appearance, as of dawn. **8.** an aperture for looking through. [? assimilated var. of PEEK]

—**Syn. 1, 2.** PEEP, PEEK, PEER mean to look through, over, or around something. To PEEP or PEEK is usually to give a quick look through a narrow aperture or small opening, often furtively, slyly, or pryingly; or to look over or around something curiously or playfully: *to peep over a wall, to peek into a room.* PEEK is often associated with children's games. To PEER is to look continuously and narrowly for some time, esp. in order to penetrate obscurity or to overcome some obstacle: *the sun peers through the clouds.*

peep[2] (pēp), *n.* **1.** a peeping cry or sound. —*v.i.* **2.** to utter the shrill little cry of a young bird, a mouse, etc.; cheep; squeak. **3.** to speak in a thin, weak voice. [ME *pēpe(n),* also *pīpen.* Cf. OF *piper,* L *pīpāre,* D and G *piepen,* all imit.]

peeper[1] (pē′pə), *n.* the maker of a peeping sound. [f. PEEP[2] v. + -ER[1]]

peeper[2] (pē′pə), *n.* **1.** a prying or spying person. **2.** *Slang.* an eye. [f. PEEP[1], v. + -ER[1]]

peephole (pēp′hōl′), *n.* a hole through which to peep.

Peeping Tom, a prying, furtive observer, often for sexual gratification; voyeur. [allusion to the man who peeped at Lady Godiva riding naked through Coventry]

peepshow (pēp′shō′), *n.* **1.** an exhibition of objects or pictures viewed through an aperture usually fitted with a magnifying lens. **2.** any display or spectacle arousing furtive curiosity.

peep sight, a plate containing a small hole through which a gunner peeps in sighting.

peep-toe (pēp′tō′), *adj.* (of shoes) having no covering over part of the big toe and sometimes the other toes.

peepul (pē′pl), *n.* pipal.

peer[1] (pĭə), *n.* **1.** a person of the same civil rank or standing; an equal before the law. **2.** one who ranks with another in respect to endowments or other qualifications; an equal in any respect. **3.** a nobleman. **4.** a member of any of the five degrees of the nobility in Great Britain and Ireland, namely, duke, marquess, earl, viscount, and baron. **5. peer of the realm,** any of a class of peers in Great Britain and Ireland entitled to sit in the House of Lords. **6.** *Obs.* a companion. [ME *per,* t. OF, g. L *pār* equal]

peer[2] (pĭə), *v.i.* **1.** to look narrowly, as in the effort to discern clearly. **2.** to peep out or appear slightly. **3.** to come into view. [late ME, orig. uncert., ? akin to PERK] —**Syn. 1.** See **peep**[1].

peerage (pĭə′rĭj), *n.* **1.** the rank or dignity of a peer. **2.** the body of peers of a country or state. **3.** a book giving a list of peers, with their genealogy, etc.

peeress (pĭə′rĭs), *n.* **1.** the wife of a peer. **2.** a woman having in her own right the rank of a peer.

peerless (pĭə′lĭs), *adj.* having no peer or equal; matchless. —**peer′lessly,** *adv.* —**peer′lessness,** *n.*

peetweet (pēt′wēt), *n.* *U.S.* the spotted sandpiper. See **sandpiper.** [imit. Cf. PEWIT]

peeve (pēv), *v.,* **peeved, peeving,** *n.* —*v.t.* **1.** *Colloq.* to render peevish. —*n.* **2.** an annoyance: *my pet peeve.* [back-formation from PEEVISH]

peevish (pē′vĭsh), *adj.* **1.** cross, querulous, or fretful, as from vexation or discontent. **2.** *Obs.* perverse. [ME *pevysh;* orig. unknown] —**pee′vishly,** *adv.* —**pee′vishness,** *n.* —**Syn. 1.** See **cross.**

peewit (pē′wĭt), *n.* pewit.

peg (pĕg), *n., v.,* **pegged, pegging.** —*n.* **1.** a pin of wood or other material driven or fitted into something, as to fasten parts together, to hang things on, to make fast a rope or string on, to stop a hole, or to mark some point. **2.** *Colloq.* a leg, sometimes one of wood. **3.** an occasion; reason: *a peg to hang a grievance on.* **4.** *Colloq.* a degree: *to come down a peg.* **5.** a pin of wood or metal to which one end of a string of a musical instrument is fastened, and which may be turned in its socket to adjust the string's tension. **6.** *Colloq.* a drink usually made of whisky or brandy and soda water. **7.** *Mountaineering.* a piton. **8.** a clothes peg. **9. off the peg,** (of a garment) available for immediate use; ready-made. **10. take down a peg,** to humble. —*v.t.* **11.** to drive or insert a peg into. **12.** to fasten with or as with pegs. **13.** to mark with pegs. **14.** to maintain (prices, wages, etc.) at a set level by laws or by manipulation. **15.** to strike or pierce with or as with a peg. **16.** *Colloq.* to aim or throw. —*v.i.* **17.** to work persistently, or keep on energetically (fol. by *away, along, on,* etc.). **18.** *Croquet.* to strike a peg. **19. peg out,** to die. [ME *pegge.* Cf. OE *pecg* (in a placename), d. D *peg,* LG *pigge*]

Pegasus

Pegasus (pĕg′ə səs), *n.* **1.** *Class. Myth.* a winged horse, sprung from the blood of Medusa when slain by Perseus, who with a stroke of his hoof caused the spring Hippocrene to open up on Mount Helicon, from which came the modern association with the Muses and poetry. **2.** *Astron.* a northern constellation represented as the forward half of a flying horse.

Pegasus Bay, a wide indentation on the E coast of South Island, New Zealand, divided from the Canterbury Bight by Banks Peninsula.

pegboard (pĕg′bôd′), *n.* a composition board with holes for inserting pegs, hooks, etc.

pegmatite (pĕg′mə tīt′), *n.* **1.** a graphic intergrowth of quartz and felspar; graphic granite. **2.** a coarsely crystalline granite or other rock occurring in veins or dykes. [f. s. Gk *pêgma* something fastened together + -ITE[1]]

peg top, 1. a child's wooden top spinning on a metal peg. **2.** (*pl.*) peg-top trousers. **3.** a peg-top skirt.

peg-top (pĕg′tŏp′), *adj.* shaped like a top, as men's trousers or women's skirts wide at the hips and narrowing to the ankle.

Péguy (*Fr.* pĕ gē′), *n.* **Charles** (*Fr.* shȧrl), 1873–1914, French essayist and poet.

Pehlevi (pā′lə vĭ; *Pers.* păh lă vē′), *n.* the Pahlavi language.

P.E.I., Prince Edward Island.

peignoir (pā′nwä; *Fr.* pĕny wȧr′), *n.* **1.** a dressing-gown. **2.** a negligee. [t. F, der. *peigner,* g. L *pectināre* comb]

Peiping (pā′pĭng′), *n.* former name of Peking; used when city was not capital of China.

Peipus (pī′pəs; *Ger.* -po͞os), *n.* former name of **Chudskoe.** Also, *Estonian,* **Peipsi** (pāp′sĭ).

Peiraeus (pī rē′əs), *n.* Piraeus.

Peiraievs (*Gk* pē rĕ ĕfs′), *n.* Greek name of **Piraeus.**

Peirce (pûs, pĭəs), *n.* **1. Benjamin,** 1809–80, U.S. mathematician and astronomer. **2. Charles Sanders,** 1839–1914, U.S. logician, mathematician, and physicist.

pejorate (pē′jə rāt′), *v.t.* to make worse; deteriorate. —**pe′jora′tion,** *n.*

pejorative (pē′jə rə tĭv, pĭ jŏ′rə tĭv), *adj.* **1.** deprecatory. **2.** having a disparaging force, as certain derivative word forms. —*n.* **3.** a pejorative form or word, as *poetaster.* [f. s. L *pējōrātus,* pp., having been made worse + -IVE] —**pe′joratively,** *adv.*

pekan (pĕk′ən), *n. U.S.* the fisher, *Martes pennanti.* [t. Canadian F, t. Algonquian (Abnaki): m. *pékané*]

peke (pēk), *n. Colloq.* a Pekingese dog.

Pekin (pē′kĭn′), *n.* a hardy yellow-white duck developed in China. [named after PEKING]

Peking (pē′kĭng′), *n.* traditional and present capital of China, in N part. 7,300,000 (est. 1958). See map under **Mongolia.**

Pekingese (pē′kĭng ēz′), *n.* **1.** small, long-haired Chinese dog prized as a pet. **2.** Mandarin. **3.** a native of Peking. —*adj.* **4.** pertaining to Peking. Also, **Pekinese** (pē′kĭ nēz′).

Pekingese (Ab. 8 to 14 in. high at the shoulder)

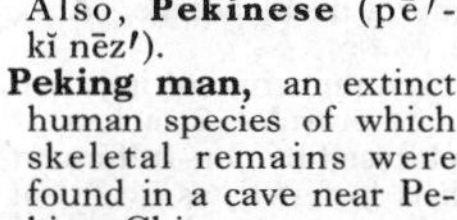

Peking man, an extinct human species of which skeletal remains were found in a cave near Peking, China.

pekoe (pē′kō), *n.* a superior kind of black tea from Ceylon, India, and Java, made from leaves smaller than those used for orange pekoe. [t. Chinese (Amoy dialect): m. *pek-ho* white down]

pelage (pĕl′ĭj), *n.* the hair, fur, wool, or other soft covering of a mammal. [t. F, der. *poil,* g. L *pilus* hair]

Pelagian (pĕ lā′jĭ ən), *n.* a follower of Pelagius, a British monk (fl. about A.D. 400–18), who denied original sin and maintained the freedom of the will and its power to attain righteousness. —**Pela′gianism,** *n.*

pelagic (pĕ lăj′ĭk), *adj.* **1.** of or pertaining to the seas or oceans. **2.** living at or near the surface of the ocean, far from land, as certain animals or plants. [t. L: s. *pelagicus,* t. Gk: m. *pelagikós* pertaining to the sea]

pelargonic acid (pĕl′ə gŏn′ĭk), *Chem.* an oily organic acid, $CH_3(CH_2)_7COOH$, occurring as an ester in a volatile oil in species of pelargonium. Also, **nonanoic acid, n-nonylic acid.**

pelargonium (pĕl′ə gō′nyəm), *n.* any plant of the genus *Pelargonium,* the cultivated species of which are usually called geranium. See **geranium** (def. 2). [t. NL, der. Gk *pelargós* stork]

Pelasgian (pĕ lăz′gĭ ən), *adj.* **1.** of or pertaining to the Pelasgi, an ancient race inhabiting Greece and the islands and coasts of the Aegean Sea and the eastern Mediterranean in prehistoric times. —*n.* **2.** a member of this race.

Pelasgic (pĕ lăz′gĭk), *adj.* Pelasgian.

Pelée (*Fr.* pə lĕ′), *n.* **Mount,** a volcano in the West Indies, on the island of Martinique: eruption 1902. 4428 ft.

pelerine (pĕl′ə rēn′), *n.* a woman's cape, esp. a narrow cape with long descending ends in front. [t. F: pilgrim's cape or mantle, special use of fem. of *pèlerin* pilgrim, g. L *peregrinus* wandering]

Peleus (pē′lyo͞os), *n. Gk Legend.* a king of the Myrmidons, son of Aeacus, and father of Achilles.

Pelew Islands (pē lo͞o′), Palau Islands.

pelf (pĕlf), *n.* (in contemptuous use) money or riches. [ME, t. OF: m. *pelfre* spoil; orig. uncert. Cf. PILFER]

Pelham (pĕl′əm), *n.* **Henry,** 1695?–1754, British statesman: prime minister 1743–54.

Pelias (pē′lĭ ăs′), *n. Gk Legend.* a son of Poseidon, who sent Jason and the Argonauts to recover the Golden Fleece.

pelican (pĕl′ĭ kən), *n.* any of various large, totipalmate birds of the family *Pelecanidae,* having a large fish-catching bill with distensible pouch beneath, into which the young stick their heads when feeding. [ME and OE, t. LL: s. *pelicānus,* var. of *pelecānus,* t. Gk: m. *pelekán*]

European white pelican, *Pelecanus onocrotalus* (Ab. 5 ft long)

Pelion (pē′lĭ ən), *n.* **Mount,** a mountain near the E coast of Greece, in Thessaly. ab. 5330 ft.

pelisse (pĕ lēs′), *n.* **1.** an outer garment lined or trimmed with fur. **2.** a woman's long cloak with arm openings. [t. F, g. LL *pellicia* fur garment, prop. fem. of LL *pelliceus* made of skins]

pelite (pē′līt), *n.* any clay rock. Cf. **psephite** and **psammite.** [f. s. Gk *pēlós* clay, earth + -ITE[1]] —**pelitic** (pĭ lĭt′ĭk), *adj.*

Pella (pĕl′ə), *n.* a ruined city in N Greece, NW of Salonika: the capital of ancient Macedonia; birthplace of Alexander the Great.

pellagra (pə lā′grə, pə lăg′rə), *n. Pathol.* a chronic, non-contagious disease caused by deficient diet, characterized by skin changes, severe nervous dysfunction, and diarrhoea. [t. It., ? orig. *pelle agra* rough skin] —**pella′grous,** *adj.*

pellekar (pĕl′ĭ kä′), *n.* palikar.

Pelles (pĕl′ēz), *n.* **King,** *Arthurian Legend.* the father of Elaine; searcher for the Holy Grail.

pellet (pĕl′ĭt), *n.* **1.** a round or spherical body, esp. one of small size; a little ball, as of food or medicine. **2.** a ball, usually of stone, formerly used as a missile. **3.** a bullet or one of a charge of small shot, as for a shotgun. **4.** an imitation bullet, as of wax or paper. **5.** a boss or raised part on coins or carved ornaments. **6.** undigested remains, as of fur of the prey, which is regurgitated by certain predatory birds. —*v.t. Obs.* **7.** to form into pellets. **8.** to hit with pellets. [ME *pelet,* t. OF: m. *pelote,* der. L *pila* ball]

pellicle (pĕl′ĭ kl), *n.* a thin skin or membrane; a film; a scum. [t. L: m. s. *pellicula,* dim. of *pellis* skin] —**pellicular** (pĕ lĭk′yo͞o lə), *adj.*

pellitory (pĕl′ĭ tə rĭ, -trĭ), *n., pl.* **-ries. 1.** any of several species of urticaceous herbs belonging to the genus *Parietaria,* as **pellitory-of-the-wall,** *P. diffusa,* a branched perennial often found in crevices of rocks and walls in S and W Europe. **2.** an asteraceous plant, *Anacyclus pyrethrum,* of N Africa and S Europe whose root is used as a local irritant (**pellitory of Spain**). [alter. with change of suffix of ME *peletre,* t. AF, g. L *pyrethrum* pellitory of Spain, t. Gk: m. *pýrethron* feverfew]

pell-mell (pĕl′mĕl′), *adv.* **1.** in an indiscriminate medley; in a confused mass or crowd. **2.** in disorderly, headlong haste. —*adj.* **3.** indiscriminate; disorderly; tumultuous. —*n.* **4.** an indiscriminate medley. **5.** violent disorder. Also, **pellmell.** [t. F: m. *pêle-mêle,* in OF *pesle mesle,* appar. der. *mesler* mix]

pellucid (pĕ lyo͞o′sĭd), *adj.* **1.** allowing the passage of light; translucent. **2.** clear or limpid, as water. **3.** clear in meaning. [t. L: s. *pellūcidus* transparent] —**pellucidity** (pĕl/yo͞o sĭd/ĭ tĭ), **pellu/cidness,** *n.* —**pellu/cidly,** *adv.*

Pelmanism (pĕl/mə nĭz/əm), *n.* **1.** a mind-training system promoting powers of memory. **2.** such a system adapted as a card game. [f. *Pelman* (*Institute*), proprietary name, + -ISM]

pelmet (pĕl/mĭt), *n.* a short ornamental drapery or board, placed across the top of a window in order to hide the curtain rail.

Pelopidas (pĕ lŏp/ĭ dăs/), *n.* died 364 B.C., Greek general and statesman of Thebes.

Peloponnesian War, a war between Athens and Sparta from 431 to 404 B.C. which resulted in the transfer of hegemony in Greece from Athens to Sparta.

Peloponnesus (pĕl/ə pə nē/səs), *n.* the S peninsula of Greece: the seat of the early Mycenaean civilization and of the powerful city-states of Sparta, Argos, etc. 1,096,390 (1961); 8356 sq. mi. Also, **Peloponnese** (pĕl/ə pə nēs/), **Peloponnesos** or **Morea.** —**Peloponnesian** (pĕl/ə pənē/shən), *adj.*, *n.*

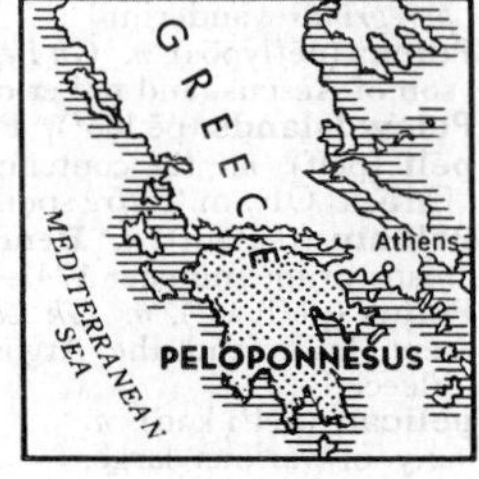

Peloponnesus

Pelops (pē/lŏps), *n. Gk Legend.* a son of Tantalus; restored to life after Tantalus served him as meat to the gods.

peloria (pĕ lô/rĭ ə), *n. Bot.* regularity of structure occurring abnormally in flowers normally irregular. [t. NL, f. Gk: *pélōr* monster + *-ia* -IA] —**peloric** (pĕ lô/rĭk, -lŏ/-), *adj.*

pelorus (pĭ lô/rəs), *n.* a pivoted navigational compass for determining the relative bearings of observed objects. [t. L: named after Cape *Pelōrus* in Sicily]

pelota (pə lŏt/ə), *n.* a Basque and Spanish game played in a court with a ball and a curved wicker racket. [Sp., aug. of *pella*, g. L *pila* ball. Cf. PELLET]

pelt[1] (pĕlt), *v.t.* **1.** to assail with repeated blows or with missiles; to beat or rush against. **2.** to throw (missiles). **3.** to drive, put, etc., by blows or missiles. **4.** to assail with abuse. —*v.i.* **5.** to strike blows; beat with force or violence. **6.** to throw missiles. **7.** to cast abuse. **8.** to hurry. —*n.* **9.** the act of pelting. **10.** a vigorous stroke. **11.** a blow with something thrown. **12.** speed. **13.** a downpour; a repeated beating, as of rain. [orig. uncert.; ? akin to PELLET] —**pelt/er,** *n.*

pelt[2] (pĕlt), *n.* the skin of an animal with or without the hair. [ME, appar. a back-formation from PELTRY] —**Syn.** See **skin.**

peltast (pĕl/tăst), *n.* a soldier of ancient Greece armed with a light shield. [t. L: s. *peltasta*, t. Gk: m. *peltastḗs*]

peltate (pĕl/tāt), *adj. Bot.* (of a leaf, etc.) having the stalk or support attached to the lower surface at a distance from the margin; shield-shaped. [t. L: m. s. *peltātus* armed with a light shield] —**pel/tately,** *adv.*

Peltate leaf

Peltier effect (pĕl/tĭ ā/; *Fr.* pĕl tyĕ/), *Physics.* the heat evolved or absorbed when an electric current flows across the junction between two different metals or semiconductors. [named after C. A. *Peltier*, 1785–1845, French physicist]

pelting (pĕl/tĭng), *adj. Archaic.* paltry; petty; mean. [cf. obs. *peltry*, var. of PALTRY]

Pelton wheel (pĕl/tən), an impulse water turbine, in which specially shaped buckets attached to the rim of a wheel are struck by jets of water from one or more nozzles. [named after L. A. *Pelton*, 1829–1908, American engineer and inventor]

peltry (pĕl/trĭ), *n.*, *pl.* **-ries. 1.** fur skins; pelts collectively. **2.** a pelt. [ME *peltre*, t. OF: m. *peleterie*, ult. der. *pel* skin, g. L *pellis*]

pelvic (pĕl/vĭk), *adj.* of or pertaining to the pelvis.

pelvic arch, 1. (in vertebrates) a bony or cartilaginous arch supporting the hind limbs or analogous parts. **2.** (in man) the arch, formed by the innominate bones, which attaches the lower extremity to the axial skeleton. Also, **pelvic girdle.**

pelvic fin, one of the more posterior paired fins of a fish, on the lower surface of its body.

pelvis (pĕl/vĭs), *n.*, *pl.* **-ves** (-vēz). *Anat.*, *Zool.* **1.** the basin-like cavity in the lower part of the trunk of many vertebrates, formed in man by the innominate bones, sacrum, etc. **2.** the bones forming this cavity. **3.** the cavity of the kidney which receives the urine before it passed into the ureter. [t. L: basin]

Human pelvis, front view
A, Upper base of sacrum;
B, Crest of ilium;
C, Acetabulum;
D, Ischium; E, Pubis;
F, Pubic symphysis

Pemb., Pembrokeshire.

Pemba (pĕm/bə), *n.* an island near the E coast of equatorial Africa: a part of Tanzania. 150,000 pop. (est. (1964); 380 sq. mi.

Pembroke (pĕm/bro͝ok), *n.* **1.** a town in Wales, the county town of Pembrokeshire. 12,751 (1961). **2.** Pembrokeshire. **3.** a variety of the Welsh corgi breed of dogs. See **Welsh corgi.**

Pembrokeshire (pĕm/bro͝ok shĭə/, -shə), *n.* a county in SW Wales. 93,980 pop. (1961); 614 sq. mi. *Co. town.*: Pembroke. Also, **Pembroke.**

Pembroke table, a small, four-legged table with drop leaves and a drawer at one or each end.

pemmican (pĕm/ĭ kən), *n.* dried meat pounded into a paste with melted fat and dried fruits, pressed into cakes, orig. prepared by North American Indians. Also, **pemican.** [t. N Amer. Ind. (Cree): m. *pimikan* manufactured grease, der. *pimikew* he makes grease (by boiling fat)]

pemphigus (pĕm/fĭ gəs, pĕm fī/-), *n. Pathol.* a serious disease, commonly fatal, characterized by vesicles and bullae on the skin and mucous membranes. [t. NL, f. s. Gk *pemphís* bubble + *-us* (n. ending)]

pen[1] (pĕn), *n.*, *v.*, **penned, penning.** —*n.* **1.** any instrument for writing with ink. **2.** a small instrument of steel or other metal, with a split point, used, when fitted into a penholder, for writing with ink; nib. **3.** the pen and penholder together. **4.** a quill pointed and split at the nib, used for writing with ink. **5.** the pen as the instrument of writing or authorship: *the pen is mightier than the sword.* **6.** style or quality of writing. **7.** a writer or author. **8.** the profession of writing or literature: *men of the pen.* **9.** *Ornith.* **a.** a large feather of the wing or tail; a quill feather; a quill. **b.** a pin-feather of a bird. **10.** something resembling or suggesting a feather or quill. **11.** *Zool.* an internal, corneous or chitinous, feather-shaped structure in certain cephalopods, as the squid. —*v.t.* **12.** to write with a pen; set down in writing. [ME *penne*, t. OF, g. L *penna* feather, LL pen]

pen[2] (pĕn), *n.*, *v.*, **penned** or **pent, penning.** —*n.* **1.** a small enclosure for domestic animals. **2.** animals so enclosed. **3.** any place of confinement or safekeeping. —*v.t.* **4.** to confine in or as in a pen. [ME *penne*, OE *penn*; orig. uncert.]

pen[3] (pĕn), *n.* a female mute swan.

Pen., peninsula.

P.E.N., International Association of Poets, Playwrights, Editors, Essayists, and Novelists.

penal (pē/nəl), *adj.* **1.** of or pertaining to punishment, as for offences or crimes. **2.** prescribing punishment: *penal laws.* **3.** constituting punishment: *penal servitude.* **4.** used as a place of punishment: *a penal settlement.* **5.** subject to or incurring punishment: *a penal offence.* **6.** payable or forfeitable as penalty: *a penal sum.* [ME, t. L: m. s. *poenālis* pertaining to punishment]

penal code, *Law.* the aggregate of statutory enactments dealing with crimes and their punishment.

penalize (pē/nə līz/), *v.t.*, **-lized, -lizing. 1.** to subject to a penalty, as a person. **2.** to declare penal, or punishable by law, as an action. **3.** to lay under a disadvantage. Also, **penalise.** —**pe/naliza/tion,** *n.*

penalty (pĕn/əl tĭ), *n.*, *pl.* **-ties. 1.** a punishment imposed or incurred for a violation of law or rule. **2.** a loss or forfeiture to which one subjects himself by non-fulfilment of an obligation. **3.** that which is forfeited, as a sum of money. **4.** consequence or disadvantage attached to any action, condition, etc. **5.** *Sport.* a disadvantage imposed upon a competitor or side for infraction of the rules. **6.** *Soccer.* penalty kick. **7. on** or **under penalty,** with the liability of incurring a penalty in case of non-fulfilment of a specified condition, injunction, etc. [f. PENAL + -TY[2]]

penalty area, *Soccer.* a space 18 yards deep and 44 yards wide in front of each goal, within which any of various infringements by the defending team results in a penalty kick being awarded to the opposing team.

penalty goal, *Soccer.* a goal scored from a penalty kick.

penalty kick, *Soccer.* a free kick taken 12 yards from an opponent's goal, which is defended only by the goalkeeper.

penalty line, *Soccer.* the boundary of the penalty area.

penance (pĕn/əns), *n.* **1.** punishment undergone in token of penitence for sin. **2.** a penitential discipline imposed by church authority. **3.** *Rom. Cath. Ch.* a sacrament minis-tered in consideration of a confession of sin with contrition and the purpose of amendment, followed by the forgiveness of sin. [ME *penaunce*, t. OF: m. *peneance*, g. L *poenitentia*. See PENITENCE]

Penang (pĭ năng′), *n.* **1.** an island in SE Asia, off the W coast of the Malay Peninsula. 350,000 pop. (est. 1964); 110 sq. mi. **2.** a state including this island and parts of the adjacent mainland: part of Malaysia. 696,994 pop. (est. 1964); 400 sq. mi.

Penarth (pĭ näth′), *n.* a town in Wales, in Glamorganshire, on the Severn estuary. 20,897 (1961).

penates (pĕ nä′ tēs), *n.pl. Rom. Myth.* tutelary deities of the household and of the state, worshipped in close association with the lares. Also, **Penates.** [t. L, der. *penus* innermost part of a temple. Cf. PENETRATE]

pence (pĕns), *n.* pl. of **penny,** used esp. when value is indicated: *he gave me twenty-one pence change out of a pound, all in pennies.*

pencel (pĕn′səl), *n. Archaic.* a small pennon, as at the head of a lance. Also, **pennoncel.** [ME, t. AF, contr. of *penoncel*, dim. of *penon* pennon, ult. der. L *penna* feather]

penchant (pĕn′chənt; *Fr.* päN shäN′), *n.* a strong inclination; a taste or liking for something. [t. F, orig. ppr. of *pencher* incline, lean, der. L *pendre* hang]

Penchi (pĕn′chē′), *n.* a city in China in Liaoning province. 449,000 pop. (est. 1958).

pencil (pĕn′səl), *n., v.,* **-cilled, -cilling** or (*U.S.*) **-ciled, -ciling.** —*n.* **1.** a thin tube of wood, etc., with a core of graphite, chalk, the like, for drawing or writing. **2.** style or skill in painting or delineation. **3.** a slender, pointed piece of some marking substance. **4.** a stick of cosmetic colouring material for use on the eyebrows, etc. **5.** a similarly shaped piece of some other substance, as lunar caustic. **6.** a set of lines, light rays, or the like, diverging from or converging to a point. **7.** *Archaic.* an artist's paintbrush, esp. for fine work. —*v.t.* **8.** to use a pencil on. **9.** to execute, draw, or write with or as with a pencil. **10.** to mark or colour with or as with a pencil. [ME *pencel*, t. OF: m. *pincel*, g. VL var. of L *pēnicillum*, dim. of *pēniculus* brush] —**pen′ciller,** *n.*

pencil-sharpener (pĕn′səl shäp′nə), *n.* any device, usually containing a blade, used for sharpening the point of a pencil, crayon, etc.

pend (pĕnd), *v.i.* **1.** to remain undecided. **2.** to hang. **3.** *Obs.* to depend. [late ME, t. L: s. *pendēre* hang, depend]

pendant (pĕn′dənt), *n.* Also, **pendent. 1.** a hanging ornament, as of a necklace or earring. **2.** a chandelier. **3.** a knob or other ornament suspended from the roof, vault, or ceiling. **4.** a match or parallel. **5.** *Naut.* a length of rope or wire fitted to a spar to connect it to a block of a tackle. **6.** pennant (defs 1, 2). —*adj.* **7.** pendent. [ME *pendaunte*, t. OF: m. *pendant*, ppr., hanging, der. *pendre* hang, g. L *pendēre*]

pendant post, a wooden member used in medieval roof framing, placed against a wall, supported by a corbel and with a hammerbeam or tie beam fixed to the top.

pendent (pĕn′dənt), *adj.* Also, **pendant. 1.** hanging or suspended. **2.** overhanging; jutting or leaning over. **3.** impending. **4.** pending or undecided. —*n.* **5.** pendant. [t. L: s. *pendens*, ppr., hanging; r. ME *penda(u)nt*, t. OF: m. *pendant*, g. L] —**pend′ency,** *n.* —**pend′ently,** *adv.*

pendente lite (pĕn dĕn′tĭ lī′tĭ), *Law.* during litigation; while a suit is in progress. [L]

pendentive (pĕn dĕn′tĭv), *n. Archit.* **1.** a triangular segment of the lower part of a hemispherical dome, between two penetrating arches. **2.** a similar segment of a groined vault, resting on a single pier or corbel. [f. PENDENT + -IVE, translating F *pendentif*]

pending (pĕn′dĭng), *prep.* **1.** while awaiting; until: *pending his return.* **2.** in the period before the decision or conclusion of; during: *pending the negotiations.* —*adj.* **3.** remaining undecided; awaiting decision. **4.** hanging; impending. [f. PEND(ENT) + -ING[2]]

pendragon (pĕn drăg′ən), *n.* chief leader (a title of ancient British chiefs). [t. Welsh: f. *pen* head + *dragon* dragon (used as symbol), leader] —**pendrag′onship′,** *n.*

Pendragon (pĕn drăg′ən), *n.* either of two kings of ancient Britain. See **Uther.**

pendulous (pĕn′dyo͝o ləs), *adj.* **1.** hanging. **2.** swinging freely. **3.** vacillating. [t. L: m. *pendulus* hanging, swinging] —**pen′dulously,** *adv.* —**pen′dulousness,** *n.*

pendulum (pĕn′dyo͝o ləm), *n.* **1.** a body so suspended from a fixed point as to move to and fro by the action of gravity and acquired momentum. **2.** a swinging device used for controlling the movement of clockwork. [t. NL, prop. neut. of L *pendulus* hanging, swinging]

Penelope (pĭ nĕl′ə pĭ), *n.* **1.** the wife of Odysseus in the *Odyssey*, who, during her husband's long absence, remained faithful to him in spite of numerous suitors. **2.** a faithful wife.

peneplain (pē′nĭ plān′, pē′nĭ plān′), *n. Geol.* an area reduced almost to a plain by erosion. Also, **peneplane.** [f. L *pēne* almost + PLAIN]

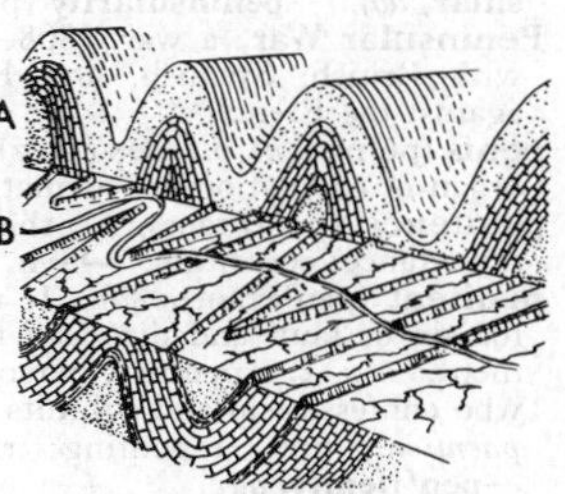

Cross-section of peneplain
A, Original land structure
B, Peneplain with residual ridges

penetrable (pĕn′ĭ trə bl), *adj.* capable of being penetrated. [ME, t. L: m. s. *penetrābilis*] —**pen′etrabil′ity,** *n.* —**pen′etrably,** *adv.*

penetralia (pĕn′ĭ trā′lyə), *n.pl.* the innermost parts or recesses of a place or thing. [t. L, prop. neut. pl. of *penetrālis* inner, orig. penetrating]

penetrate (pĕn′ĭ trāt′), *v.,* **-trated, -trating.** —*v.t.* **1.** to pierce into or through. **2.** to enter the interior of. **3.** to enter and diffuse itself through; permeate. **4.** to affect or impress deeply. **5.** to arrive at the meaning of; understand. —*v.i.* **6.** to enter, reach, or pass through, as by piercing. [t. L: m. s. *penetrātus*, pp.] —**Syn. 1.** See **pierce. 5.** comprehend, fathom.

penetrating (pĕn′ĭ trā′tĭng), *adj.* **1.** that penetrates; piercing; sharp. **2.** acute; discerning. **3.** *Surg.* denoting a wound produced by an agent or missile such that depth is its salient feature, as a wound entering a member. Also, **penetrant** (pĕn′ĭ trənt). —**pen′etrat′ingly,** *adv.* —**Syn. 2.** See **acute.**

penetration (pĕn′ĭ trā′shən), *n.* **1.** the act or power of penetrating. **2.** the extension, usually peaceful, of the influence of one country on the life of another. **3.** mental acuteness, discernment, or insight. **4.** *Firearms.* the depth to which a projectile goes into the target.

penetrative (pĕn′ĭ trə tĭv), *adj.* tending to penetrate; piercing; acute; keen. —**pen′etratively,** *adv.* —**pen′etrativeness,** *n.*

penetrometer (pĕn′ĭ trŏm′ĭ tə), *n.* **1.** a device for measuring the hardness of a material by measuring the extent to which it is penetrated by a given force. **2.** an instrument for measuring the penetrating power of X-rays or other radiations. Also, **radiosclerometer.**

Peneus (pĭ nē′əs), *n.* ancient name of **Salambria.**

penfriend (pĕn′frĕnd′), *n.* a person, esp. one in another country, with whom a friendship is maintained through correspondence.

pengö (pĕng′gû), *n., pl.* **-gö, -gös** (-gû, -gûz). a former silver coin and monetary unit of Hungary equivalent to the present-day forint.

Pengu (pĕn′go͞o′), *n.* Pescadores.

penguin (pĕng′gwĭn), *n.* **1.** any of various flightless aquatic birds of the family *Spheniscidae* of the Southern Hemisphere, with webbed feet, and wings reduced to flippers. **2.** *Obs.* the great auk. **3.** *Aeron.* an aeroplane which merely rolls along the ground, enabling a beginner to learn certain manipulations safely. [cf. F *pingouin*, earlier *penguyn* auk; of disputed orig.]

Emperor penguin, *Aptenodytes forsterii* (Ab. 4 ft high)

penholder (pĕn′hōl′də), *n.* **1.** a holder in which a nib is placed. **2.** a rack or stand for a pen or pens.

penicil (pĕn′ĭ sĭl), *n.* a small brushlike tuft of hairs, as on a caterpillar. [t. L: m. s. *pēnicillus* paintbrush, pencil]

penicillate (pĕn′ĭ sĭl′ĭt, -āt), *adj.* having a penicil or penicils. [t. NL: m. s. *pēnicillātus*, der. L *pēnicillus* pencil] —**pen′icil′lately,** *adv.* —**pen′icilla′tion,** *n.*

penicillin (pĕn′ĭ sĭl′ĭn), *n. Pharm.* **1.** a powerful anti-bacterial substance produced by moulds of the genus *Penicillium.* **2.** any of a group of anti-bacterial substances made synthetically from penicillin. [f. PENICILL(IUM) + -IN[2]]

penicillium (pĕn′ĭ sĭl′ĭ əm), *n., pl.* **-cilliums, -cillia** (-sĭl′ĭ ə). any member of the fungus genus *Penicillium*, known usually as the green moulds, embracing species used in cheese-making (*P. camemberti, P. roqueforti*) and species (especially *P. notatum*) from which penicillin is extracted. [f. s. L *pēnicillus* small brush, lit., small tail + -IUM]

penillion (pĭ nĭl′yən), *n.* an improvisatory Welsh song. Also, **pennillion.** [t. Welsh: pl. of *pennill* verse]

peninsula (pĭ nĭn′syo͞o lə), *n.* **1.** a piece of land almost surrounded by water, esp. one connected with the mainland by only a narrow neck or isthmus. **2. the Peninsula,**

Spain and Portugal; Iberia. [t. L: m. *paeninsula*] —**penin′sular,** *adj.* —**peninsularity** (pĭ nĭn′syŏŏ lă′rĭ tĭ), *n.*

Peninsular War, a war, 1808–14, in Spain and Portugal, with British, Spanish, and Portuguese troops ranged against the French.

penis (pē′nĭs), *n., pl.* **-nes** (-nēz), **-nises** (-nĭ sĭz). the male organ of copulation and urination. [t. L: orig., tail]

penitence (pĕn′ĭ təns), *n.* the state of being penitent; repentance; contrition. —**Syn.** See **regret.**

penitent (pĕn′ĭ tənt), *adj.* **1.** repentant; contrite; sorry for sin or fault and disposed to atonement and amendment. —*n.* **2.** a penitent person. **3.** *Rom. Cath. Ch.* one who confesses sin and submits to a penance. [t. L: m. s. *paenitens*, ppr., repenting; r. ME *penitaunt*, t. AF] —**pen′itently,** *adv.*

penitential (pĕn′ĭ tĕn′shəl), *adj.* **1.** of or pertaining to, proceeding from, or expressive of penitence or repentance. —*n.* **2.** a penitent. **3.** a book or code of canons relating to penance, its imposition, etc. [t. ML: m. s. *poenitentiālis*] —**pen′iten′tially,** *adv.*

penitentiary (pĕn′ĭ tĕn′shə rĭ), *n., pl.* **-ries,** *adj.* —*n.* **1.** *Rom. Cath. Ch.* **a.** an officer appointed to deal with cases of conscience reserved for a bishop or for the Holy See. **b.** an office of the Holy See (presided over by the **cardinal grand penitentiary**) having jurisdiction over such cases. **2.** a place for imprisonment and reformatory discipline. **3.** *U.S.* a prison. —*adj.* **4.** of or pertaining to penance; penitential. **5.** (of an offence) punishable by imprisonment in a penitentiary. **6.** pertaining to or intended for penal confinement and discipline. [ME, t. ML: m. s. *poenitentiārius*, der. L *paenitentia* penitence]

penknife (pĕn′nīf′), *n., pl.* **-knives** (-nīvz′). a small pocketknife, orig. for making and mending quill pens.

penman (pĕn′mən), *n., pl.* **-men. 1.** one who uses a pen. **2.** an expert in penmanship. **3.** a writer or author.

penmanship (pĕn′mən shĭp′), *n.* **1.** the use of the pen in writing; the art of handwriting; a manner of writing. **2.** literary composition; the composing of a document.

Penn (pĕn), *n.* **1. Sir William,** 1621–70, English admiral. **2.** his son, **William,** 1644–1718, English Quaker who founded the colony of Pennsylvania.

Penn., Pennsylvania. Also, **Pa, Penna.**

penna (pĕn′ə), *n., pl.* **pennae** (pĕn′ē). *Ornith.* a contour feather, as distinguished from a down feather, plume, etc. [t. L: feather]

pen-name (pĕn′nām′), *n.* a name assumed to write under; an author's pseudonym; nom de plume.

pennant (pĕn′ənt), *n.* **1.** Also, **pendant, pennon.** a long triangular flag, widest next to the mast, and going almost to a point, borne on naval or other vessels or used in signalling, etc. **2.** *U.S.* any flag serving as an emblem, as of success in an athletic contest. **3.** *U.S. Music.* hook (def. 11). [var. of PENDANT; assoc. also with PENNON]

pennate (pĕn′āt), *adj.* winged; feathered. [t. L: m. s. *pennātus* winged]

Penney (pĕn′ĭ), **Sir William George,** born 1909, English atomic scientist.

penni (pĕn′ĭ), *n., pl.* **pennia** (pĕn′ĭ ə). a Finnish copper coin equivalent to one hundredth of a markka. [Finnish, t. G: m. *Pfennig*]

penniless (pĕn′ĭ lĭs), *adj.* without a penny; destitute of money. —**Syn.** See **poor.**

pennillion (pĭ nĭl′yən), *n.* penillion.

Pennine Alps (pĕn′īn), a mountain range on the Swiss-Italian border. Highest peak, Monte Rosa, 15,217 ft.

Pennines (pĕn′īnz), *n.pl.* a range of low mountains in England extending from the Trent N to the Cheviots. Highest point, Crossfell, 2930 ft. Also, **Pennine Chain.**

penninite (pĕn′ĭ nīt′), *n.* a mineral, magnesium silicate containing combined water, which crystallizes in the monoclinic system.

pennon (pĕn′ən), *n.* **1.** a distinctive flag in various forms (tapering, triangular, swallow-tailed, etc.), orig. one borne on the lance of a knight. **2.** a pennant (def. 1). **3.** any flag or banner. **4.** *Poetic.* a wing or pinion. [ME *penon*, t. OF, der. *penne*, g. L *penna* feather]

pennoncel (pĕn′ən sĕl′), *n.* pencel.

Pennsylvania (pĕn′sĭl vā′nyə), *n.* a state in the E United States. 11,319,366 pop. (1960); 45,333 sq. mi. *Cap.:* Harrisburg. *Abbrev.:* Pa, Penn., or Penna.

Pennsylvania Dutch, 1. the descendants of 18th-century settlers in Pennsylvania from south-western Germany. **2.** a German dialect spoken mainly in eastern Pennsylvania, developed from the language of these settlers. —**Penn′sylva′nia-Dutch′,** *adj.*

Pennsylvanian (pĕn′sĭl vā′nyən), *adj.* **1.** of or pertaining to the state of Pennsylvania. **2.** *U.S. Geol.* pertaining to a late Palaeozoic geological period or a system of rocks in North America equivalent to the Upper Carboniferous. —*n.* **3.** a native or inhabitant of Pennsylvania. **4.** *U.S. Geol.* the period or system following Mississippian and preceding Permian, characterized by abundance of coal deposits; Upper Carboniferous.

penny (pĕn′ĭ), *n., pl.* **pennies,** (*esp. collectively*) **pence. 1.** a bronze coin of the United Kingdom equal to a 100th part of a pound; new penny. *Abbrev.:* p. **2.** (until 1971) a bronze or copper coin equal to one twelfth of a shilling or $\frac{1}{240}$ of a pound. *Abbrev.:* d. **3.** any similar coin of certain other countries. **4.** a bronze coin of Canada, the 100th part of a dollar. **5.** a bronze coin of the U.S. the 100th part of a dollar; a cent. **6.** an unspecified sum of money: *I haven't got a penny.* **7. a bad penny,** a bad, or undesirable person or thing. **8. the penny has dropped,** the explanation or remark has been understood. **9. a pretty penny,** a considerable amount of money. **10. spend a penny,** go to the toilet. **11. turn an honest penny,** earn an honest living; earn money honestly. —*adj.* **12.** of the price or value of a penny. [ME *peni*, OE *penig, pening, pending* c. Icel. *penningr*, G *Pfennig*]

-penny, a suffix forming adjectives that denote price or value, as in *fourpenny, fivepenny*, etc. (as used in *fourpenny nails, fivepenny nails*, etc., formerly meaning 'nails costing fourpence, fivepence, etc., a hundred', but now nails of certain arbitrary sizes).

penny-a-liner (pĕn′ĭ ə lī′nə), *n.* *Archaic.* a hack writer.

penny-cress (pĕn′ĭ krĕs′), *n.* any plant of the cruciferous genus *Thlaspi* as *T. arvense*, the **field penny-cress,** a widespread annual weed of cultivated land in temperate regions.

penny dreadful, a piece of cheap popular sensational literature.

penny-farthing (pĕn′ĭ fä′thĭng), *n.* a high bicycle of an early type with one large wheel in front and one small wheel behind.

penny pincher, a mean, niggardly person. —**pen′ny-pinch′ing,** *adj.*

pennyroyal (pĕn′ĭ roi′əl), *n.* any of several labiate herbaceous plants, as the one found in the Old World, *Mentha pulegium*, or the American **mock pennyroyal,** *Hedeoma pulegioides*, used medicinally and yielding a pungent aromatic oil. [f. *penny* (? alter. of OF *puliol*, der. L *pūlegium* pennyroyal) + ROYAL]

pennyweight (pĕn′ĭ wāt′), *n.* (in troy weight) a unit of 24 grains or one twentieth of an ounce.

penny whistle, a simple and cheap wind instrument, usually consisting of a tin or plastic pipe.

penny-wise (pĕn′ĭ wīz′), *adj.* wise or saving in regard to small sums: *penny-wise and pound-foolish.*

pennywort (pĕn′ĭ wût′), *n.* any of several plants with round or roundish leaves, as the **marsh pennywort,** of the genus *Hydrocotyle*, the navelwort, *Cotyledon umbilicus*, the Kenilworth ivy, *Cymbalaria muralis*, and a small American plant, *Obolaria virginica*, of the gentian family.

pennyworth (pĕn′əth, pĕn′ĭ wûth′), *n.* **1.** as much as may be bought for a penny. **2.** a small quantity. **3.** a bargain.

Penobscot (pə nŏb′skŏt), *n.* **1.** an Algonquian Indian tribe of the Abnaki confederacy situated on both sides of **Penobscot river** and **Bay,** in Maine. **2.** a member of this tribe. **3.** their language. [t. Algonquian, der. *pannawanbskek* it forks on the white rocks; or *penaubsket* it flows on rocks; or *penops* rock (locative); or *penabskat* plenty stones]

penology (pē nŏl′ə jĭ), *n.* **1.** the science of the punishment of crime, in both its deterrent and its reformatory aspects. **2.** the science of the management of prisons. [f. PEN(AL) + -(O)LOGY] —**penological** (pē′nə lŏj′ĭ kl), *adj.* —**penologist** (pē nŏl′ə jĭst), *n.*

pen-pusher (pĕn′pŏŏsh′ə), *n.* *Colloq.* one who works with his pen, considered as a menial or drudge.

Penrith (pĕn′rĭth), *n.* **1.** a town in England, in Cumberland. 10,870 (1961). **2.** a town in SE Australia, in New South Wales. 43,000 (1965).

pensile (pĕn′sīl), *adj.* **1.** hanging, as the nests of certain birds. **2.** building a hanging nest. [t. L (neut.): hanging down] —**pen′sileness, pensility** (pĕn sĭl′ĭ tĭ), *n.*

pension (pĕn′shən; for *3, 4 also* pŏn′syən; *Fr.* päɴ syôɴ′), *n.* **1.** a fixed periodical payment made in consideration of past services, injury or loss sustained, merit, poverty, etc. **2.** an allowance or annuity. **3.** (in France and elsewhere on the Continent) a boarding house, small hotel, or school. **4.** (in France and elsewhere on the Continent) room and board. —*v.t.* **5.** to grant a pension to. **6.** to cause to retire on a pension (fol. by *off*). [t. L: s. *pensio* payment; r. ME *pensioun*, t. OF: m. *pensiun*] —**pen′sionable,** *adj.*

pensionary (pĕn′shə nə rĭ), *n., pl.* **-ries,** *adj.* —*n.* **1.** a pensioner. **2.** a hireling. —*adj.* **3.** of the nature of a pension. **4.** receiving a pension.

pensioner (pĕn′shə nə), *n.* **1.** one who receives a pension. **2.** a hireling. **3.** *Obsolesc.* a student at Cambridge University who pays for his commons, etc., and is not supported by foundation. **4.** *Obs. except Hist.* a gentleman-at-arms.

pensive (pĕn′sĭv), *adj.* **1.** deeply, seriously, or sadly thoughtful. **2.** expressing thoughtfulness or sadness. [t. F (fem.), der. *penser* think; r. ME *pensif*, t. F (masc.)] —**pen′sively,** *adv.* —**pen′siveness,** *n.*

—**Syn. 1.** PENSIVE, MEDITATIVE, REFLECTIVE suggest quiet modes of apparent or real thought. PENSIVE, the weakest of the three, suggests dreaminess or wistfulness, and may involve little or no thought to any purpose: *a pensive, faraway look.* MEDITATIVE involves thinking of certain facts or phenomena—perhaps in the religious sense of 'contemplation'—without necessarily having a goal of complete understanding or of action: *meditative but unjudicial.* REFLECTIVE has a strong implication of orderly, perhaps analytic, processes of thought, usually with a definite goal of understanding: *a careful and reflective critic.*

penstock (pĕn′stŏk′), *n.* **1.** a pipe conducting water from the head gates to a waterwheel. **2.** a conduit for conveying water to a power plant. **3.** a sluicelike contrivance used to control the flow of water.

pent (pĕnt), *v.* **1.** a pt. and pp. of **pen**[2]. —*adj.* **2.** shut in. **3.** confined.

pent-, a word element meaning 'five'. Also, before consonants, **penta-.** [t. Gk, comb. forms of *pénte*]

pentaborane (pĕn′tə bô′rān), *n. Chem.* a liquid, B_5H_9, used as a rocket propellant.

pentacle (pĕn′tə kl), *n.* **1.** a pentagram. **2.** some more or less similar figure, as a hexagram. [prob. t. F, or t. ML: m. *pentaculum.* See PENT(A)-, -CLE]

pentad (pĕn′tăd), *n.* **1.** a period of five years. **2.** *Chem.* a pentavalent element or radical. **3.** a group of five. **4.** the number five. [t. Gk: s. *pentás* a group of five]

pentadactyl (pĕn′tə dăk′tĭl), *adj.* having five digits on each hand or foot.

pentagon (pĕn′tə gən), *n.* **1.** a polygon having five angles and five sides. **2. the Pentagon, a.** the building in Arlington, Virginia, containing most U.S. Defence Department offices. **b.** the U.S. Defence Department. [t. L: s. *pentagōnum,* t. Gk: m. *pentágōnon,* prop. neut. adj. used as noun] —**pentagonal** (pĕn tăg′ə nəl), *adj.* —**pentag′onally,** *adv.*

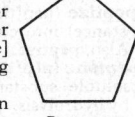

Pentagon

pentagram (pĕn′tə grăm′), *n.* a five-pointed, star-shaped figure made by extending the sides of a regular pentagon until they meet (a symbolical figure used by the Pythagoreans and later philosophers, by magicians and others). [t. Gk: m. s. *pentágrammon* (prop. neut. of adj.) figure consisting of five lines]

Pentagram

pentahedron (pĕn′tə hē′drən), *n., pl.* **-drons, -dra** (-drə). a solid figure having five faces. —**pen′tahe′dral,** *adj.*

pentamerous (pĕn tăm′ə rəs), *adj.* **1.** consisting of or divided into five parts. **2.** *Bot.* (of flowers) having five members in each whorl. [t. NL: m. *pentamerus,* t. Gk: m. *pentamerḗs*]

pentameter (pĕn tăm′ĭ tə), *Pros.* —*n.* **1.** a verse of five feet. **2.** *Anc. Pros.* a verse consisting of two dactyls, one long syllable, two more dactyls, and another single syllable (**elegiac pentameter**). **3.** unrhymed iambic pentameter; heroic verse. —*adj.* **4.** consisting of five metrical feet. [t. L, t. Gk: m. s. *pentámetros*]

pentandrous (pĕn tăn′drəs), *adj.* **1.** (of a flower) having five stamens. **2.** (of a plant) having flowers with five stamens.

pentane (pĕn′tān), *n. Chem.* a hydrocarbon, C_5H_{12}, of the methane series, existing in three isomeric forms. [f. Gk *pént(e)* five + -ANE]

pentangle (pĕn′tăng gl), *n.* pentagram.

pentarchy (pĕn′tä′kĭ), *n., pl.* **-chies. 1.** a government by five persons. **2.** a governing body of five persons. **3.** a group of five states or kingdoms, each under its own ruler. [t. Gk: m. s. *pentarchía*]

pentastich (pĕn′tə stĭk′), *n. Pros.* a strophe, stanza, or poem consisting of five lines or verses. [t. NL: s. *pentastichus,* t. Gk: m. *pentástichos* of five lines]

Pentateuch (pĕn′tə tyōōk′), *n.* the first five books of the Old Testament, regarded as a group. [t. L: s. *Pentateuchus,* t. Gk: m. *pentáteuchos* consisting of five books] —**Pen′tateuch′al,** *adj.*

pentathlon (pĕn tăth′lən), *n.* an athletic contest comprising five different exercises or events, and won by the contestant having the highest total score. [t. Gk]

pentatonic scale (pĕn′tə tŏn′ĭk), *Music.* a five-note scale corresponding to the black notes of a piano octave.

pentavalent (pĕn′tə vā′lənt, pĕn tăv′ə-), *adj. Chem.* possessing a valency of 5: *pentavalent arsenic.*

Pentecost (pĕn′tĭ kŏst′), *n.* **1.** a Christian festival commemorating the descent of the Holy Ghost upon the apostles on the day of the Jewish festival; Whit Sunday. **2.** a Jewish harvest festival observed on the fiftieth day

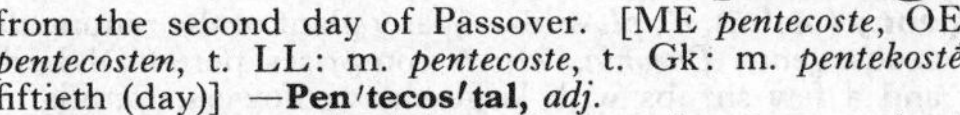

from the second day of Passover. [ME *pentecoste,* OE *pentecosten,* t. LL: m. *pentecoste,* t. Gk: m. *pentekostḗ* fiftieth (day)] —**Pen′tecos′tal,** *adj.*

Pentecostal (pĕn′tĭ kŏs′tl), *n.* **1.** any of various modern non-denominational Christian organizations that lay emphasis on the religious experience, the absolute truth of the Bible, and the possibility of direct contact with the Holy Spirit. —*adj.* **2.** of or pertaining to such an organization.

Pentelicus (pĕn tĕl′ĭ kəs), *n.* a mountain in SE Greece, near Athens: noted for its fine marble. 3640 ft. Also, **Pentelikon** (pĕn tĕl′ĭ kən).

pentene (pĕn′tēn), *n. Chem.* amylene.

penthouse (pĕnt′hous′), *n., pl.* **-houses** (-hou′zĭz). **1.** a separate flat or maisonette on a roof. **2.** a structure on a roof for housing lift machinery, etc. **3.** a shed with a sloping roof, or a sloping roof, projecting from a wall or the side of a building, as to shelter a door. **4.** any roof-like shelter or overhanging part. [ME *pentis,* appar. t. OF: m. *apentis,* der. L *appendere* hang to or on, append]

pentimento (pĕn′tĭ mĕn′tō), *n., pl.* **-ti** (-tē). *Art.* **1.** the reappearance, or visibility under X-ray, of forms that have been painted over in the alteration of a painting. **2.** any of such re-emergent forms. [t. It.: repentance]

Pentland Firth (pĕnt′lənd fûth′), a strait between mainland Scotland and the Orkney Islands, with tidal race. ab. 14 mi. long and 8 mi. wide.

pentlandite (pĕnt′lən dīt′), *n.* a mineral, a sulphide of iron and nickel, which crystallizes in the isometric system; an important ore of nickel.

pentode (pĕn′tōd), *n. Radio.* a radio valve containing five electrodes.

pentomic (pĕn tŏm′ĭk), *adj. U.S. Mil.* of, pertaining to, or characterizing the organization of an army division into five units geared to the requirements of combat with atomic weapons. [PENT- + (AT)OMIC]

pentosan (pĕn′tə săn′), *n. Chem.* any of a class of polysaccharides which occur in plants, humus, etc., and form pentoses upon hydrolysis.

pentose (pĕn′tōs), *n. Chem.* a monosaccharide containing five atoms of carbon, and produced from pentosans by hydrolysis. [f. PENT(A)- + -OSE[2]]

Pentothal sodium (pĕn′tə thŏl′), *Trademark.* sodium pentothal.

pentstemon (pĕnt stĕm′ən, -stē′mən), *n.* any plant of the scrophulariaceous genus *Pentstemon,* chiefly of North America, including species cultivated for their variously coloured flowers with long-tubed corolla. [t. NL, f. Gk: *pént(e)* five + *stḗmon* warp, thread]

pent-up (pĕnt′ŭp′), *adj.* confined; restrained: *pent-up rage.*

penuchle (pē′nŭk′l), *n.* pinochle. Also, **penuckle.**

penult (pĭ nŭlt′), *n.* the last syllable but one in a word. Also, **penultima** (pĭ nŭl′tĭ mə). [t. L: m. *paenultima* (fem.) last but one]

penultimate (pĭ nŭl′tĭ mĭt), *adj.* **1.** next to the last. **2.** of the penult. —*n.* **3.** the penult.

penumbra (pĭ nŭm′brə), *n., pl.* **-brae** (-brē), **-bras.** *Astron.* **1.** the partial or imperfect shadow outside the complete shadow (umbra) of an opaque body, as a planet, where the light from the source of illumination is only partly cut off. **2.** the greyish marginal portion of a sunspot. [t. NL, f. m. L *paene* almost + *umbra* shade, shadow] —**penum′bral,** *adj.*

penurious (pĭ nyŏŏ′rĭ əs), *adj.* **1.** meanly parsimonious; stingy. **2.** extremely poor; destitute. —**penu′riously,** *adv.* —**penu′riousness,** *n.*

penury (pĕn′yŏŏ rĭ), *n.* **1.** extreme poverty; destitution. **2.** dearth or insufficiency. [ME, t. L: m. s. *pēnūria* want, scarcity. Cf. Gk *penía* poverty, need]

Penutian (pĭ nyōō′tĭ ən, -shən), *n.* a tentatively established North American Indian linguistic stock which includes several linguistic families formerly regarded as unrelated, distributed from California northwards through Oregon and British Columbia.

Penza (*Russ.* pyĕn′zə), *n.* a town in the central Soviet Union in Europe. 315,000 (est. 1965).

Penzance (pĕn zăns′), *n.* a town in England, in Cornwall: seaside resort. 19,281 (1961).

peon[1] (pē′ən), *n.* **1.** (in Spanish America etc.) **a.** a day labourer. **b.** one who tends a horse or mule. **2.** *Chiefly Mexico.* one held in servitude to work off debts, etc. [t. Sp.: m. *peón,* g. s. L *pedo* foot soldier. See PAWN[2]]

peon[2] (pyōōn, pē′ən), *n. India.* **1.** a foot soldier. **2.** a messenger or attendant. **3.** a native soldier. [t. Pg.: m. *peão,* and t. F: m. *pion* foot soldier, pedestrian, day labourer. See PEON[1]]

peonage (pē′ə nĭj), *n.* **1.** the condition or service of a peon. **2.** the practice of holding persons in servitude or partial slavery, as to work off debt or (under a convict lease system) a penal sentence. Also, **pe′onism.**

peony (pīə′nĭ), *n.*, *pl.* **-nies. 1.** any plant of the ranunculaceous genus *Paeonia*, which comprises perennial herbs and a few shrubs with large showy flowers, familiar in gardens. **2.** the flower. [t. L: m. s. *paeōnia*, t. Gk: m. *paiōnía*, der. *Paiṓn* the physician of the gods (because the plant was used in medicine); r. ME *pione*, t. ONF, t. L, t. Gk; r. OE *peonie*, t. L, t. Gk]

people (pē′pl), *n.*, *pl.* **-ple, -ples** *for 1*, *v.*, **-pled, -pling.** —*n.* **1.** the whole body of persons constituting a community, tribe, race, or nation: *the people of England.* **2.** the persons of any particular group, company, or number: *the people of a parish.* **3.** persons in relation to a ruler, leader, etc.: *the king and his people.* **4.** one's family or relatives: *to visit one's people.* **5.** the members of any group or number to which one belongs. **6.** the body of enfranchised citizens of a state: *representatives chosen by the people.* **7.** the commonalty or populace: *a man of the people.* **8.** persons indefinitely, whether men or women: *people may say what they please.* **9.** human beings as distinguished from animals. **10.** *Chiefly Poetic.* living creatures. —*v.t.* **11.** to furnish with people; populate. **12.** to stock with animals, inanimate objects, etc. [ME *peple*, t. AF: m. *poeple*, g. L *populus* people] —**peopler** (pē′plə), *n.* —**Syn. 1.** See **race**[2].

People's Charter. See **Chartism.**

People's Republic of China. Official name of **China.**

Peoria (pĭ ô′rĭ ə), *n.* a city in central Illinois, on the Illinois river. 103,162 (1960).

pep (pĕp), *n.*, *v.*, **pepped, pepping.** *Colloq.* —*n.* **1.** spirit or animation; vigour; energy. —*v.t.* **2.** to give spirit or vigour to (fol. by *up*). [short for PEPPER]

Pepin (pĕp′ĭn), *n.* (*'Pepin the Short'*) died A.D. 768, king of the Franks 751–768 (father of Charlemagne).

peplos (pĕp′ləs), *n.* a voluminous outer garment worn draped in folds about the person by women in ancient Greece. Also, **peplus.** [t. Gk]

peplum (pĕp′ləm), *n.*, *pl.* **-lums, -la** (-lə). **1.** a short full flounce or an extension of the waist, covering the hips. **2.** a short skirt attached to a bodice or coat. **3.** a peplos. [t. L: (m.) *peplum*, *peplus.* See PEPLOS]

pepo (pē′pō), *n.*, *pl.* **-pos.** the characteristic fruit of cucurbitaceous plants, having a fleshy, many-seeded interior, and a hard or firm rind, as the gourd, melon, cucumber, etc. [t. L: melon, pumpkin, t. Gk: m. *pépōn* kind of gourd or melon eaten when ripe, orig. adj., ripe]

pepper (pĕp′ə), *n.* **1.** a pungent condiment obtained from various plants of the genus *Piper*, esp. from the dried berries, either whole or ground (affording the **black pepper** and **white pepper** of commerce), of *P. nigrum*, a tropical climbing shrub. **2.** any plant of the genus *Piper* or family *Piperaceae.* **3.** cayenne (**red pepper**), prepared from species of *Capsicum.* **4.** any species of *Capsicum*, esp. *C. frutescens* (the common pepper of the garden) or its fruit (green or red, hot or sweet). —*v.t.* **5.** to season with or as with pepper. **6.** to sprinkle as with pepper; dot; stud. **7.** to sprinkle like pepper. **8.** to pelt with shot or missiles. **9.** to discharge shot or missiles at something. [ME *peper*, OE *piper*, t. L, t. Gk: m. *píperi* pepper; of Eastern orig.]

pepper-and-salt (pĕp′ə rən sôlt′), *adj.* **1.** composed of a fine mixture of black, with white, as cloth. **2.** (of hair) streaked with grey.

pepper-box (pĕp′ə bŏks′), *n.* **1.** *Fives.* (at Eton) an irregular-shaped buttress projecting from the wall of the court. **2.** *Obs.* pepper-pot (def. 1).

peppercorn (pĕp′ə kôn′), *n.* **1.** the berry of the pepper plant, *Piper nigrum*, often dried and used in pickling. **2.** anything very small, insignificant, or trifling. [ME *pepercorn*, OE *piporcorn.* See PEPPER, CORN[1]]

pepper-mill (pĕp′ə mĭl′), *n.* a small, hand-operated apparatus used to crush peppercorns in order to flavour a dish.

peppermint (pĕp′ə mĭnt′), *n.* **1.** a labiate herb, *Mentha piperita*, cultivated for its aromatic pungent oil. **2.** this oil, or some preparation of it. **3.** a lozenge or confection flavoured with it.

pepper-pot (pĕp′ə pŏt′), *n.* **1.** a small, often decorated container with perforations in the top for sprinkling pepper. **2.** a West Indian stew, the principal flavouring of which is cassareep, with meat or fish and vegetables.

pepper saxifrage, a perennial umbelliferous herb with small yellowish flowers, *Silaum silaus*, occurring in grassland in Europe and W Asia.

pepper tree, any of several evergreen trees, members of the genus *Schinus*, mostly native of South America and cultivated in subtropical regions as ornamentals because of their evergreen foliage and bright red fruits.

pepperwort (pĕp′ə wût′), *n.* an annual or perennial cruciferous herb with grey-green foliage, *Lepidium campestre*, occurring in dry places in Europe and W Asia.

peppery (pĕp′ə rĭ), *adj.* **1.** resembling pepper; full of pepper; pungent. **2.** of or pertaining to pepper. **3.** sharp or stinging, as speech. **4.** irascible or irritable, as persons or their temper. —**pep′periness,** *n.*

pep pill, 1. a pill or tablet that consists of a stimulant drug, as amphetamine. **2.** any substance taken as a stimulant.

peppy (pĕp′ĭ), *adj.*, **-pier, -piest.** *Colloq.* energetic. —**pep′piness,** *n.*

pepsin (pĕp′sĭn), *n.* *Biochem.* the proteolytic enzyme produced by the stomach. Also, **pepsine.** [f. s. Gk *pépsis* digestion + -IN[2]]

pepsinate (pĕp′sĭ nāt′), *v.t.*, **-nated, -nating.** to treat, prepare, or mix with pepsin.

pepsinogen (pĕp sĭn′ə jən), *n.* *Biochem.* the inactive precursor of pepsin.

peptic (pĕp′tĭk), *adj.* **1.** pertaining to or concerned in digestion; digestive. **2.** promoting digestion. **3.** of pepsin. —*n.* **4.** a substance promoting digestion. [t. L: s. *pepticus*, t. Gk: m. *peptikós* able to digest]

peptidase (pĕp′tĭ dās′), *n.* *Biochem.* any of a class of enzymes which attack peptide linkages and split off amino acids.

peptide (pĕp′tīd), *n.* *Biochem.* a compound containing two or more amino acids in which the carboxyl group of one acid is linked to the amino group of the other. [f. PEPT(IC) + -IDE]

peptize (pĕp′tīz), *v.t.*, **-tized, -tizing.** to disperse (a substance) into colloidal form, usually in a liquid medium. Also, **peptise.**

peptone (pĕp′tōn), *n.* *Biochem.* any of a class of diffusible, soluble substances into which proteins are converted by hydrolysis. [t. G: m. *Pepton*, t. Gk: (neut. adj.) cooked, digested] —**peptonic** (pĕp tŏn′ĭk), *adj.*

peptonize (pĕp′tə nīz′), *v.t.*, **-nized, -nizing. 1.** to convert into a peptone. **2.** to hydrolyse or dissolve by a proteolytic enzyme, such as pepsin. **3.** to subject (food) to an artificial partial digestion by pepsin or pancreatic extract, to aid digestion. Also, **peptonise.** —**pep′toniza′tion,** *n.*

Pepys (pēps), *n.* **Samuel,** 1633–1703, English government official and diarist. —**Pepysian** (pēp′sĭ ən), *adj.*

Pequot (pē′kwŏt), *n.* a member of a former tribe of Algonquian Indians in southern New England in the early 17th century. [t. Algonquian, contr. of *Paquatauog* destroyers]

per (pû, pə), *prep.* through; by; for each: *per annum* (by the year), *per diem* (by the day), *per yard* (for each yard), etc. [t. L. Cf. PER-]

per-, 1. a prefix meaning 'through', 'thoroughly', 'utterly', 'very', as in *pervert, pervade, perfect.* **2.** *Chem.* a prefix applied: **a.** to inorganic acids to indicate they possess excess of the designated element: *perboric* (HBO_3 or $H_2B_4O_8$), *percarbonic* ($H_2C_2O_5$), *permanganic* ($HMnO_4$), and *persulphuric* ($H_2S_2O_5$) *acids.* **b.** to salts of these acids (the name ending in *-ate*): *potassium perborate* ($K_2B_2O_8$), *potassium permanganate* ($KMnO_4$), and *potassium persulphate* ($K_2S_2O_5$). [t. L (in some words, t. OF or F), repr. *per*, prep., through, by; akin to Gk *pará*]

per., 1. period. **2.** person.

Pera (pĭə′rə), *n.* former name of **Beyoglu.**

per-acid (pûr′ăs′ĭd), *n.* *Chem.* an acid formed by the action of hydrogen peroxide on a normal acid.

peradventure (pə rəd vĕn′chə), *Archaic.* —*adv.* **1.** it may be; maybe; possibly. —*n.* **2.** chance; uncertainty. **3.** doubt or question. [ME *peraventure*, t. OF: m. *par aventure*, f. *par* by (t. L: m. *per*) + *aventure* ADVENTURE]

Peraea (pə rē′ə), *n.* a region in ancient Palestine, E of the Jordan and the Dead Sea. See map under **Jericho.**

Perak (pĕə′rə, pĭə′rə, pĭ răk′), *n.* a state in Malaysia, on the SW Malay Peninsula. 1,449,224 pop. (est. 1962); 7980 sq. mi. *Cap.*: Taiping.

Peralta (*Sp.* pĕ răl′tă), *n.* **Enrique** (*Sp.* ĕn rē′kĕ), born 1908, president of Guatemala 1963–66.

perambulate (pə răm′byŏŏ lāt′), *v.*, **-lated, -lating.** —*v.t.* **1.** to walk through, about, or over; travel through; traverse. **2.** to traverse and examine or inspect. —*v.i.* **3.** to walk or travel about; stroll. [t. L: m. s. *perambulātus*, pp.] —**peram′bula′tion,** *n.* —**perambulatory** (pə răm′byŏŏ-lā′tə rĭ), *adj.*

perambulator (pə răm′byŏŏ lā′tə), *n.* pram.

per an., per annum.

per annum (pər ăn′əm), *Latin.* by the year; yearly.

per ardua ad astra, *Latin.* through difficult steep ways to the stars; the motto of the RAF.

perborate (pə bô′rāt), *n.* *Chem.* a salt of perboric acid, containing the radicals BO_3 or B_4O_8, as *sodium perborate*, $NaBO_3.4H_2O$, used for bleaching, disinfecting, etc. [f. PER- + BORATE]

percale (pə kāl′, pə käl′), *n.* closely woven, smooth-finished cambric, plain or printed. [t. F, t. Pers.: m. *pärgālā*]

percaline (pû′kə lēn′, pû′kə lĭn), *n.* a fine, lightweight cotton fabric, usually finished with a gloss and dyed in one colour: used esp. for linings. [t. F, dim. of *percale* PERCALE]

per capita (pə kăp′ĭ tə), *Latin.* by the individual person.

perceivable (pə sē′və bl), *adj.* capable of being perceived; perceptible. —**perceiv′ably,** *adv.*

perceive (pə sēv′), *v.t.*, **-ceived, -ceiving. 1.** to gain knowledge of through one of the senses; discover by seeing, hearing, etc. **2.** to apprehend with the mind; understand. [ME *perceyve(n)*, t. OF: m. *perceivre*, g. L *percipere* seize, receive, understand] —**perceiv′er,** *n.* —**Syn. 1.** See **notice.**

per cent, 1. by the hundred; for or in every hundred (used in expressing proportions, rates of interest, etc.): *to get 3 per cent interest.* **2.** a proportion; a percentage. **3.** stocks that bear a specified rate of interest. *Symbol:* %. Also, **percent.** [orig. *per cent.*, abbr. of L *per centum* by the hundred]

percentage (pə sĕn′tĭj), *n.* **1.** a rate or proportion per hundred. **2.** an allowance, duty, commission, or rate of interest on a hundred. **3.** a proportion in general. **4.** *Slang.* gain; advantage.

percentile (pə sĕn′tīl), *Statistics.* —*n.* **1.** one of the values of a variable which divides the distribution of the variable into 100 groups having equal frequencies. Thus, there are 100 percentiles: *the first, second, etc., percentile.* —*adj.* **2.** of or pertaining to a percentile or a division of a distribution by percentiles. [f. PER CENT + *-ile*, modelled on BISSEXTILE]

per centum (pə sĕn′təm), *Latin.* per cent.

percept (pû′sĕpt), *n.* **1.** the mental result or product of perceiving, as distinguished from the act of perceiving. **2.** that which is perceived; the object of perception. [t. L: s. *perceptum*, neut. pp., (a thing) perceived]

perceptible (pə sĕp′tə bl), *adj.* capable of being perceived; cognizable; appreciable: *quite a perceptible time.* —**percep′tibil′ity, percep′tibleness,** *n.* —**percep′tibly,** *adv.*

perception (pə sĕp′shən), *n.* **1.** the action or faculty of perceiving; cognition; a taking cognizance, as of a sensible object. **2.** an immediate or intuitive recognition, as of a moral or aesthetic quality. **3.** the result or product of perceiving, as distinguished from the act of perceiving; a percept. **4.** *Psychol.* a single unified meaning obtained from sensory processes while a stimulus is present. [late ME, t. L: s. *perceptio* a receiving, hence apprehension] —**percep′tional,** *adj.*

perceptive (pə sĕp′tĭv), *adj.* **1.** having the power or faculty of perceiving. **2.** of or pertaining to perception. **3.** of ready or quick perception. —**percep′tively,** *adv.* —**perceptivity** (pû′sĕp tĭv′ĭ tĭ), **percep′tiveness,** *n.*

perceptual (pə sĕp′tyo͞o əl), *adj.* pertaining to perception.

Perceval (pû′sĭ vəl), *n.* **1. Spencer,** 1762–1812, British statesman: prime minister 1809–12. **2.** *Arthurian Legend.* Percival.

perch[1] (pûch), *n.* **1.** a pole or rod usually fixed horizontally to serve as a roost for birds. **2.** any thing or place serving for a bird, or for anything else, to alight or rest upon. **3.** an elevated position or station. **4.** a small elevated seat on a vehicle, for the driver. **5.** a pole connecting the fore and hind running parts of a spring carriage or other vehicle. **6.** a rod, or linear measure of $5\frac{1}{2}$ yards or $16\frac{1}{2}$ feet. **7.** a square rod ($30\frac{1}{4}$ square yards). **8.** a solid measure for stone, etc., commonly $16\frac{1}{2}$ feet by $1\frac{1}{2}$ feet by 1 foot. **9.** *Obs. or Dial.* any pole, rod, or the like. —*v.i.* **10.** to alight or rest upon a perch, as a bird. **11.** to settle or rest in some elevated position, as if on a perch. —*v.t.* **12.** to set or place on, or as if on, a perch. [ME *perche*, t. OF, g. L *pertica* pole, measuring rod]

perch[2] (pûch), *n.*, *pl.* **perches,** (*esp. collectively*) **perch. 1.** a spiny-finned freshwater food fish of the genus *Perca*, as *P. fluviatilis* of Europe or *P. flavescens* (**yellow perch**) of the U.S. **2.** any of various other spiny-finned fishes of the same and other families, often marine. [ME *perche*, t. OF, g. L *perca*, t. Gk: m. *pérkē* perch. Cf. Gk *perknós* dark-coloured]

perchance (pə chăns′), *adv. Poetic or Archaic.* **1.** maybe; possibly. **2.** by chance. [ME *per chance*, t. AF: m. *par chance* by chance]

Perche (*Fr.* pĕrsh), *n.* a former division of N France.

percher (pû′chə), *n.* **1.** one who or that which perches. **2.** a bird whose feet are adapted for perching.

Percheron (pû′shə rŏn′), *n.* one of a breed of draught horses, orig. raised in Perche, France. [t. F]

perching birds, the passerines.

perchlorate (pə klô′rāt), *n. Chem.* a salt of perchloric acid, as *potassium perchlorate.*

perchlorethylene (pû′klô rĕth′ĭ lēn′), *n. Chem.* tetrachloroethylene.

perchloric acid (pə klô′rĭk), *Chem.* an acid of chlorine, $HClO_4$, containing one more oxygen atom than chloric acid, and occurring as a colourless syrupy liquid. [f. PER- + CHLOR(INE) + -IC]

perchloride (pə klô′rīd), *n. Chem.* that chloride of any particular element or radical with maximum proportion of chlorine. Also, **perchlorid** (pə klô′rĭd).

perchromic acid (pû krō′mĭk), *Chem.* an unstable acid, $H_3CrO_8.2H_2O$, which forms stable salts called **perchromates.**

percipient (pə sĭp′ĭ ənt), *adj.* **1.** perceiving. **2.** having perception. —*n.* **3.** one who or that which perceives. [t. L: s. *percipiens*, ppr., perceiving] —**percip′ience, percip′iency,** *n.*

Percival (pû′sĭ vəl), *n. Arthurian Legend.* a knight of King Arthur's court who sought the Holy Grail. Also, **Perceval, Percivale.**

percoid (pû′koid), *adj.* **1.** belonging to the *Percoidea*, a group of acanthopterygian fishes comprising the true perches and related families, and constituting one of the largest natural groups of fishes. **2.** resembling a perch. —*n.* **3.** a percoid fish. Also, **percoidean** (pə koi′dĭ ən). [f. s. L *perca* perch + -OID]

percolate (*v.* pû′kə lāt′; *n.* pû′kə lĭt, -lāt′), *v.*, **-lated, -lating,** *n.* —*v.t.* **1.** to cause (a liquid) to pass through a porous body; filter. **2.** (of a liquid) to filter through; permeate. **3.** to make (coffee) in a percolator. —*v.i.* **4.** to pass through a porous substance; filter; ooze: *the coffee started to percolate.* **5.** gradually to become known. —*n.* **6.** a percolated liquid. [t. L: m. s. *percolātus*, pp., strained through] —**per′cola′tion,** *n.*

percolator (pû′kə lā′tə), *n.* **1.** a kind of coffeepot in which boiling water is forced up a hollow stem, filters through ground coffee, and returns to the pot below. **2.** that which percolates.

per contra (pû kŏn′trə), *Latin.* to the opposite side of an account.

percuss (pû kŭs′), *v.t.* **1.** to strike (something) so as to shake or cause a shock to. **2.** *Med.* to strike or tap for diagnostic or therapeutic purposes. [t. L: s. *percussus*, pp., struck through]

percussion (pə kŭsh′ən), *n.* **1.** the striking of one body against another with some violence; impact. **2.** *Med.* the striking or tapping of a part of the body for diagnostic or therapeutic purposes. **3.** the striking of musical instruments to produce notes. **4.** a sharp light blow, esp. one for setting off a cap formerly used to discharge small arms. **5.** the act of percussing. **6.** *Music.* (collectively) the instruments in an orchestra which are played by striking.

percussion cap, a small metallic cap or cup containing fulminating powder, formerly exploded by percussion so as to fire the charge of small arms.

percussion instrument, a musical instrument, as drum, cymbal, piano, etc., which is struck to produce a sound, as distinguished from string or wind instruments.

percussionist (pə kŭsh′ə nĭst), *n.* a musician who plays a percussion instrument.

percussion lock, a gunlock in which a hammer strikes a percussion cap.

percussive (pə kŭs′ĭv), *adj.* of, pertaining to, or characterized by percussion.

Percy (pû′sĭ), *n.* **1. Sir Henry** ('*Hotspur*'), 1364–1403, English military leader, killed near Shrewsbury in a rebellion he led against Henry IV of England. **2. Thomas,** 1729–1811, English bishop who edited a collection of popular ballads.

Perdido (*Sp.* pĕr dē′dō), *n.* **Monte** (*Sp.* mōn′tė), a mountain in NE Spain, a peak of the Pyrenees. 10,994 ft. French, **Mont Perdu.**

perdie (pə dē′), *adv.*, *interj.* pardi.

per diem (pû dĭ′ĕm, -dē′ĕm), **1.** *Latin.* by the day. **2.** a daily allowance, usually for living expenses while travelling in connection with one's work.

perdisulphuric acid (pû′dī′sŭl fyo͞o′rĭk), *Chem.* persulphuric acid (def. 2).

perdition (pû dĭsh′ən), *n.* **1.** a condition of final spiritual ruin or damnation. **2.** the future state of the wicked. **3.** hell. **4.** utter destruction or ruin. [ME, t. L: s. *perditio* act of destroying]

perdu (pû dyo͞o′), *adj.* **1.** hidden or concealed. —*n.* **2.** *Obs.* a soldier placed in a dangerous position. Also, **perdue.** [t. F, pp. of *perdre* lose, g. L *perdere* lose, destroy]

Perdu (*Fr.* pĕr dʏ′), *n.* **Mont** (*Fr.* mōɴ), French name of **Monte Perdido.**

perdurable (pû dyo͝o′rə bl), *adj.* permanent; everlasting; imperishable. [ME, t. LL: m. s. *perdūrābilis*, der. L *perdūrāre* last, hold out] —**perdur′ably,** *adv.*

perdure (pə dyo͝o′), *v.i.*, **-dured, -during.** to continue in existence; endure; last. [ME *perdure(n)*, t. L: m. s. *perdūrāre.* See PER-, DURE[2]]

père (*Fr.* pĕr), *n. French.* **1.** father. **2.** senior: *Dumas père.*

peregrinate (pĕ′rĭ grĭ nāt′), *v.*, **-nated, -nating.** —*v.i.* **1.** to travel or journey. —*v.t.* **2.** to travel over; traverse. [t. L: m. s. *peregrīnātus*, pp., having travelled] —**pe′re-grina′tor,** *n.*

peregrination (pĕ′rĭ grĭ nā′shən), *n.* **1.** travelling from one place to another. **2.** a course of travel; journey.

peregrine (pĕ′rĭ grĭn), *adj.* **1.** foreign; alien; coming from abroad. —*n.* **2.** peregrine falcon. [ME, t. L: m. s. *peregrīnus* coming from foreign parts; as n., a foreigner]

peregrine falcon, a falcon, *Falco peregrinus*, much used in falconry.

pereion (pə rī′ən), *n.*, *pl.* **-reia** (-rī′ə). the thorax of crustaceans.

peremptory (pə rĕmp′tə rĭ, -trĭ), *adj.* **1.** leaving no opportunity for denial or refusal; imperative: *a peremptory command.* **2.** imperious or dictatorial. **3.** *Law.* **a.** that precludes or does not admit of debate, question, etc.: *a peremptory edict.* **b.** decisive or final. **c.** in which a command is absolute: *a peremptory writ.* **4.** positive in speech, manner, etc. [t. L: m. s. *peremptōrius* destructive, decisive] —**peremp′torily,** *adv.* —**peremp′toriness,** *n.*

peremptory plea, *Law.* a plea which attacks the cause of and attempts to quash an action.

perennial (pə rĕn′yəl), *adj.* **1.** lasting for an indefinitely long time; enduring. **2.** *Bot.* having a life cycle lasting more than two years. **3.** lasting or continuing throughout the year, as a stream. **4.** perpetual; everlasting; continuing; recurrent. —*n.* **5.** a perennial plant. **6.** something continuing or recurrent. [f. L *perenni(s)* lasting through the year + -AL[1]] —**peren′nially,** *adv.*

perf., **1.** perfect. **2.** perforated.

perfect (*adj.*, *n.* pû′fĭkt; *v.* pə fĕkt′), *adj.* **1.** in a state proper to a thing when completed; having all essential elements, characteristics, etc.; lacking in no respect; complete. **2.** in a state of complete excellence; without blemish or defect; faultless. **3.** completely suited for a particular purpose or occasion. **4.** completely corresponding to a type or description; exact: *a perfect sphere.* **5.** correct in every detail: *a perfect copy.* **6.** thorough; complete: *perfect strangers.* **7.** pure or unmixed: *perfect yellow.* **8.** absolute; unqualified: *perfect mastery.* **9.** unmitigated or utter. **10.** *Obs.* assured or certain. **11.** *Bot.* **a.** having all parts or members present. **b.** monoclinous. **12.** *Gram.* **a.** denoting action or state brought to a close prior to some temporal point of reference, in contrast to imperfect or uncompleted action. **b.** designating a tense, or other verb formation or construction, with such meaning. **13.** *Music.* **a.** applied to the consonances of unison, octave, fifth, and fourth, as distinguished from those of a third and sixth, which are called imperfect. **b.** applied to the intervals, harmonic or melodic, of an octave, fifth, and fourth in their normal form, as opposed to augmented and diminished. —*n.* **14.** *Gram.* the perfect tense. **15.** *Gram.* any verb formation or construction in the perfect tense. —*v.t.* **16.** to bring to completion, complete, or finish. **17.** to make perfect or faultless, bring to perfection. **18.** to bring nearer to perfection; improve. **19.** to make fully skilled. **20.** *Print.* to print the reverse of (a printed sheet). [t. L: s. *perfectus*, pp., performed, completed; r. ME *parfit*, t. OF] —**perfect′er,** *n.* —**Syn. 1, 2.** See **complete.**

perfect cadence, *Music.* a cadence in which there is a progression from a dominant chord to a tonic chord.

perfect gas, *Physics.* a theoretical concept of a gas which would consist of perfectly elastic molecules which themselves occupy no space and have no forces between them; such a gas would obey the gas laws exactly. Also, **ideal gas.**

perfectible (pə fĕk′tə bl), *adj.* capable of becoming, or being made, perfect. —**perfec′tibil′ity,** *n.*

perfection (pə fĕk′shən), *n.* **1.** the state or quality of being perfect. **2.** the highest degree of proficiency, as in some art. **3.** a perfect embodiment of something. **4.** a quality, trait, or feature of a high degree of excellence. **5.** the highest or most perfect degree of a quality or trait. **6.** the act or fact of perfecting.

perfectionism (pə fĕk′shə nĭz′əm), *n.* **1.** any of various doctrines holding that religious, moral, social or political perfection is attainable. **2.** the desire or endeavour to attain perfection.

perfectionist (pə fĕk′shə nĭst), *n.* **1.** one who adheres to some doctrine concerning perfection. **2.** one who demands nothing less than perfection in any sphere of activity, behaviour, etc. —*adj.* **3.** of, pertaining to, or characterized by perfection or perfectionism.

perfective (pə fĕk′tĭv), *adj.* **1.** tending to make perfect; conducive to perfection. **2.** *Gram.* denoting an aspect of the verb rather than a tense, as in Russian, which indicates completion of the action or state of the verb prior to a temporal point of reference. —*n.* **3.** *Gram.* the perfective aspect. **4.** *Gram.* a verb in the perfective. —**perfec′tively,** *adv.* —**perfec′tiveness,** *n.*

perfectly (pû′fĭkt lĭ), *adv.* **1.** in a perfect manner or degree. **2.** completely.

perfect number, *Maths.* a number which is equal to the sum of its aliquot parts.

perfecto (pə fĕk′tō), *n.*, *pl.* **-tos.** a rather thick medium-sized cigar tapering towards both ends. [t. Sp.: lit., perfect]

perfector (pə fĕk′tə), *n.* *Print.* a printing machine which prints both sides of a sheet of paper during one passage through the machine.

perfect participle, past participle.

perfect pitch, absolute pitch (def. 2).

perfect rhyme, **1.** rhyme of two words spelt or pronounced identically but differing in meaning, as *rain*, *reign*; rich rhyme. **2.** correct or faultless rhyme.

perfervid (pû fû′vĭd), *adj.* very fervid. —**per′fervid′ity, perfer′vidness,** *n.* —**perfer′vidly,** *adv.* —**perfer′vour,** *n.*

perfidious (pû fĭd′ĭ əs), *adj.* guilty of perfidy; deliberately faithless; treacherous. [t. L: m. s. *perfidiōsus*] —**perfid′iously,** *adv.* —**perfid′iousness,** *n.*

perfidy (pû′fĭ dĭ), *n.*, *pl.* **-dies.** a deliberate breach of faith or trust; faithlessness; treachery. [t. L: m. s. *perfidia* faithlessness] —**Syn.** See **disloyalty.**

perfoliate (pə fō′lĭ ĭt, -āt′), *adj.* *Bot.* having the stem apparently passing through the leaf, owing to congenital union of the basal edges of the leaf round the stem: *a perfoliate leaf.* [t. NL: m. s. *perfoliātus*, f. L: *per* through + *foli(um)* leaf + *-ātus* -ATE[1]] —**perfo′lia′tion,** *n.*

Perfoliate leaves

perforate (*v.* pû′fə rāt′; *adj.* pû′fə rĭt), *v.*, **-rated, -rating,** *adj.* —*v.t.* **1.** to make a hole or holes through by boring, punching or other process. **2.** to pierce through or to the interior of; penetrate. —*v.i.* **3.** to make its way through or into something; penetrate. —*adj.* **4.** perforated. [t. L: m. s. *perforātus*, pp., having been pierced through] —**perforative** (pû′fə rə tĭv), *adj.* —**per′fora′tor,** *n.*

perforated (pû′fə rā′tĭd), *adj.* **1.** pierced with a hole or holes. **2.** *Philately.* having perforations by which one stamp can be separated from others in the sheet.

perforation (pû′fə rā′shən), *n.* **1.** a hole, or one of a number of holes, bored or punched through something, as those between individual postage stamps of a sheet to facilitate separation. **2.** a hole made or passing through a thing. **3.** the act of perforating. **4.** the state of being perforated.

perforce (pə fôs′), *adv.* of necessity. [ME *par force*, t. OF: by force, f. *par* by (g. L *per*) + *force* FORCE]

perform (pə fôm′), *v.t.* **1.** to carry out; execute; do: *to perform miracles.* **2.** to go through or execute in due form: *to perform a ceremony.* **3.** to carry into effect; fulfil. **4.** to act (a play, a part, etc.), as on the stage. **5.** to render (music), as by playing or singing. **6.** to execute (any skill or ability) before an audience. **7.** *Obs.* to complete. —*v.i.* **8.** to fulfil a command, promise, or undertaking. **9.** to execute or do something. **10.** to act in a play. **11.** to perform music. **12.** to go through any performance. [ME *parfourme(n)*, t. AF: m. *parfourmer* (appar. for OF *parfournir* complete, accomplish), influenced by *fourme* form, g. L *forma*] —**perform′able,** *adv.* —**perform′er,** *n.*

—**Syn. 1.** PERFORM, DISCHARGE, EXECUTE, TRANSACT mean to carry to completion a prescribed course of action. PERFORM is the general word, often applied to ordinary activity as a more formal expression than *do*, but usually implying regular, methodical, or prolonged application or work: *to perform an exacting task.* DISCHARGE implies carrying out an obligation, often a formal or legal one: *to discharge one's duties as a citizen.* EXECUTE means either to carry out an order, or to carry through a plan or a programme: *to execute a manoeuvre.* TRANSACT, meaning to conduct or manage, has commercial connotations: *to transact business.*

performance (pə fô′məns), *n.* **1.** a musical, dramatic or other entertainment. **2.** the performing of ceremonies, or of music, or of a play, part, or the like. **3.** execution or doing, as of work, acts, or feats. **4.** a particular action, deed, or proceeding. **5.** an action or proceeding of a more or less unusual or spectacular kind. **6.** the act of performing. **7.** the way in which something reacts under certain conditions or fulfils the purpose for which it was intended.

performance test, *Psychol.* a test to be responded to by manual or other behavioural performance rather than verbally.

perfume (*n.* pû′fyŏŏm; *v.* pə fyŏŏm′), *n.*, *v.*, **-fumed, -fuming.** —*n.* **1.** a substance, extract, or preparation for diffusing or imparting a fragrant or agreeable smell. **2.** the scent, odour, or volatile particles emitted by substances that have an agreeable smell. —*v.t.* **3.** (of substances, flowers, etc.) to impart fragrance to. **4.** to impregnate with a sweet odour; scent. [t. F: m. *parfum*, der. *parfumer* to scent, f. *par-* PER- + *fumer* smoke]

—**Syn.** 2. redolence, scent, odour, smell. PERFUME, AROMA, FRAGRANCE all refer to agreeable odours. PERFUME often indicates a strong, rich smell, natural or manufactured: *the perfume of flowers.* FRAGRANCE is best used of fresh, delicate, and delicious odours, esp. from growing things: *fragrance of new-mown hay.* AROMA is restricted to a somewhat spicy smell: *the aroma of coffee.* —**Ant.** 2. stench.

perfumer (pə fo͞o′mə), *n.* **1.** one who or that which perfumes. **2.** a maker or seller of perfumes.

perfumery (pə fo͞o′mə rĭ), *n., pl.* **-ries. 1.** perfumes collectively. **2.** a perfume. **3.** the art or business of a perfumer. **4.** the place of business of a perfumer. **5.** the preparation of perfumes.

perfunctory (pə fŭngk′tə rĭ), *adj.* **1.** performed merely as an uninteresting or routine duty; mechanical; indifferent, careless, or superficial: *perfunctory courtesy.* **2.** acting merely out of duty; formal; official. [t. LL: m. s. *perfunctōrius,* der. L *perfunctus,* pp., performed] —**perfunc′torily,** *adv.* —**perfunc′toriness,** *n.*

perfuse (pə fo͞oz′), *v.t.,* **-fused, -fusing. 1.** to overspread with moisture, colour, etc. **2.** to diffuse (a liquid, etc.) through or over something. [t. L: m. s. *perfūsus,* pp., poured through] —**perfusion** (pə fo͞o′zhən), *n.* —**perfusive** (pə fo͞o′sĭv), *adj.*

Pergamum (pû′gə məm), *n.* an ancient city in W Asia Minor: the capital of ancient Mysia.

pergola (pû′gə lə), *n.* **1.** an arbour formed of horizontal trelliswork supported on columns or posts, over which vines or other plants are trained. **2.** an architectural construction resembling such an arbour. [t. It., t. L: m. *pergula* shed, vine arbour]

Pergolesi (pû′gō lā′zĭ; *It.* pėr gȯ lė′sē), *n.* **Giovanni Battista** (*It.* jȯ vȧn′nē bȧt tēs′tȧ), 1710–36, Italian composer.

perh., perhaps.

Perham (pĕ′rəm), *n.* **Dame Margery** (mä′jə rĭ), born 1895, English writer on colonial affairs.

perhaps (pə hăps′, prăps), *adv.* **1.** maybe; possibly. **2.** *Now Rare.* perchance. [ME *par happes* by chances]

peri (pĭə′rĭ), *n., pl.* **-ris. 1.** one of a race of beautiful fairylike beings of Persian mythology, represented as descended from fallen angels and excluded from paradise till their penance is accomplished. **2.** any lovely, graceful creature. [t. Pers., g. Avestan *pairika* female demon, witch]

peri-, a prefix meaning 'around', 'about', 'beyond', or having an intensive force, occurring in words from the Greek, and used also as a modern formative, esp. in scientific terms. [t. Gk (prefix and prep.)]

perianth (pĕ′rĭ ănth′), *n. Bot.* the envelope of a flower, whether calyx or corolla or both. [short for *perianthium,* t. NL. See PERI-, ANTHO-, -IUM]

periapt (pĕ′rĭ ăpt′), *n.* an amulet. [t. F: m. *périapte,* t. Gk: m. s. *períapton* (neut.), lit., hung around]

periblem (pĕ′rĭ blĕm′), *n. Bot.* the histogen in plants which gives rise to the cortex. [t. Gk: m. *períblēma* anything thrown or put around]

pericardial (pĕ′rĭ kä′dyəl), *adj.* of or pertaining to the pericardium. Also, **pericardiac** (pĕ′rĭ kä′dĭ ăk′).

pericarditis (pĕ′rĭ kä dī′tĭs), *n. Pathol.* inflammation of the pericardium.

pericardium (pĕ′rĭ kä′dyəm), *n., pl.* **-dia** (-dyə). *Anat.* the membranous sac enclosing the heart. [t. NL, t. Gk: m. *perikárdion*]

pericarp (pĕ′rĭ käp′), *n. Bot.* **1.** the walls of a ripened ovary or fruit, sometimes consisting of three layers, the epicarp, mesocarp, and endocarp. **2.** a membranous envelope around the cystocarp of red algae. **3.** a seed capsule. [t. NL: m. s. *pericarpium,* t. Gk: m. *perikárpion* pod, husk] —**pericarpial** (pĕ′rĭ kä′pyəl), *adj.*

A B a b c

Pericarps (def. 1) A, Section and capsule of poppy; B, Section and drupe of plum: a, epicarp; b, endocarp; c, mesocarp

perichaetium (pĕ′rĭ kē′tĭ əm), *n., pl.* **-tia** (-tĭ ə). *Bot.* the sheath of leaves which surrounds the archegonia in mosses.

perichondrium (pĕ′rĭ kŏn′drĭ əm), *n., pl.* **-dria** (-drĭ ə). *Anat.* the membrane of fibrous connective tissue covering the surface of cartilages except at the joints. [f. PERI- + s. Gk *chóndros* cartilage + -IUM] —**per′ichon′drial,** *adj.*

periclase (pĕ′rĭ klās′), *n.* naturally occurring magnesium oxide.

Periclean (pĕ′rĭ klē′ən), *adj.* of or pertaining to Pericles, or his age, the period of the intellectual and material preeminence of Athens.

Pericles (pĕ′rĭ klēz′), *n. c.* 490–429 B.C., Athenian statesman.

periclinal (pĕ′rĭ klī′nəl), *adj. Bot.* parallel to the outer surface of a plant part.

pericline (pĕ′rĭ klīn′), *n.* a mineral, a variety of albite, occurring in large white opaque crystals. [t. Gk: m. s. *periklinēs* sloping on all sides]

pericope (pĕ rĭk′ə pĭ), *n.* an extract or passage from a work, esp. one selected for reading in church. —**pericopic** (pĕ′rĭ kŏp′ĭk), *adj.*

pericranium (pĕ′rĭ krā′nyəm), *n., pl.* **-nia** (-nyə). **1.** *Anat.* the external periosteum of the cranium. **2.** *Obs.* the skull or brain. [t. NL, t. Gk: m. *perikránion* (neut.) around the skull] —**per′icra′nial,** *adj.*

pericycle (pĕ′rĭ sī′kl), *n. Bot.* the outmost cell layer of the stele frequently becoming a multilayered zone. [t. Gk: m. *períkyklos* all around, used as n.]

periderm (pĕ′rĭ dûm′), *n. Bot.* the cork-producing tissue of stems together with the cork layers and other tissues derived from it.

peridium (pĭ rĭd′ĭ əm), *n., pl.* **-ridia** (-rĭd′ĭ ə). *Bot.* the outer enveloping coat of the fruit body in many fungi, sometimes itself differentiated into outer and inner layers, exoperidium and endoperidium respectively. [t. NL, t. Gk: m. *pērídion,* dim. of *pḗra* leather pouch, wallet] —**perid′ial,** *adj.*

peridot (pĕ′rĭ dŏt′), *n.* a green variety of olivine used as a gem. [ME, t. F; orig. uncert.] —**per′idot′ic,** *adj.*

peridotite (pĕ′rĭ dō′tīt), *n.* any of a group of igneous rocks of granitic texture, composed chiefly of olivine with an admixture of various other minerals, but nearly or wholly free from felspar.

perigee (pĕ′rĭ jē′), *n. Astron.* the point in an orbit round the earth that is nearest to the earth (opposed to *apogee*). See diag. under **apogee.** [t. F, t. NL: m. s. *perigēum,* t. Gk: m. *perígeion* (neut.) close around the earth] —**per′igeal, per′igean,** *adj.*

Périgord (*Fr.* pė rē gŏr′), *n.* a former province in SW France.

Périgueux (*Fr.* pė rē gœ′), *n.* a town in SW France, the capital of Dordogne department. 41,134 (1968).

perigynous (pə rĭj′ĭ nəs), *adj. Bot.* **1.** situated around the pistil on the edge of a cuplike receptacle, as stamens, etc. **2.** having stamens, etc., so arranged, as a flower. [t. NL: m. *perigynus,* der. Gk: *peri-* PERI- + *gynḗ* woman, female]

Section of a perigynous flower

perigyny (pə rĭj′ĭ nĭ), *n.* perigynous condition.

perihelion (pĕ′rĭ hē′lyən), *n., pl.* **-lia** (-lyə). *Astron.* the point of the orbit of a planet, comet, or artificial satellite which is nearest to the sun (opposed to *aphelion*). See diag. under **aphelion.** [t. NL: m. *perihēlium,* f. Gk: *peri-* PERI- + m. *hḗlios* sun]

peril (pĕ′rĭl), *n., v.,* **-rilled, -rilling.** —*n.* **1.** exposure to injury, loss, or destruction; risk; jeopardy; danger. —*v.t.* **2.** to imperil. [ME, t. F, g. L *perīculum*] —**Syn. 1.** See **danger.**

perilous (pĕ′rĭ ləs), *adj.* full of or attended with peril; hazardous; dangerous. [ME, t. AF: m. *perillous,* g. L *perīculōsus*] —**per′ilously,** *adv.* —**per′ilousness,** *n.*

perilune (pĕ′rĭ lo͞on′), *n.* the lowest point in the orbit of a body around the moon, measured from the moon's centre.

perilymph (pĕ′rĭ lĭmf′), *n. Anat.* the fluid filling the bony labyrinth of the ear and separating it from the membranous labyrinth.

perimeter (pə rĭm′ĭ tə), *n.* **1.** the circumference, border, or outer boundary of a two-dimensional figure. **2.** the length of such a boundary. **3.** *Ophthalm.* an instrument for determining the extent and defects of the visual field. [t. L: m. *perimetros,* t. Gk] —**perimetric** (pĕ′rĭ mĕt′rĭk), **per′imet′rical,** *adj.* —**per′imet′rically,** *adv.* —**perim′etry,** *n.*

perimorph (pĕ′rĭ môf′), *n.* a mineral enclosing another mineral (opposed to *endomorph* (def. 1)). [f. PERI- + s. Gk *morphḗ* form] —**per′imor′phic, per′imor′phous,** *adj.*

perinephrium (pĕ′rĭ nĕf′rĭ əm), *n. Anat.* the capsule of connective tissue which envelops the kidney. [f. PERI- + s. Gk *nephrós* kidney + -IUM]

perineum (pĕ′rĭ nĭəm′), *n., pl.* **-nea** (-nĭə′). *Anat.* **1.** the urogenital triangle in front of the anus which is bounded by the rami of the pubis, including the vulva or the roots of the penis. **2.** the diamond-shaped area corresponding to the outlet of the pelvis, containing the anus and vulva or the roots of the penis. [t. NL, t. Gk: m. *perínaion*] —**per′ineal′,** *adj.*

perineuritis (pĕ′rĭ nyo͞o rī′tĭs), *n. Pathol.* inflammation of the perineurium.

perineurium (pĕ′rĭ nyo͞oə′rĭ əm), *n., pl.* **-neuria** (-nyo͞oə′rĭ ə). *Anat.* the sheath of connective tissue which encloses a bundle of nerve fibres. [t. NL, f. *peri-* PERI- + s. Gk *neûron* nerve + *-ium* -IUM]

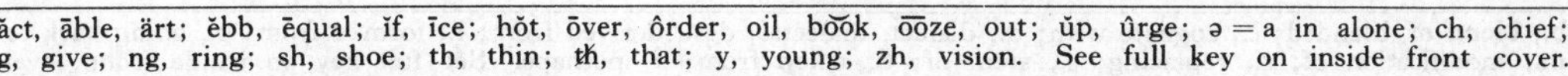

period (pĭəʹrĭ əd), *n.* **1.** an indefinite portion of time, or of history, life, etc., characterized by certain features or conditions. **2.** any specified division or portion of time. **3.** *Educ.* a specific length of time during school hours devoted to a single subject. **4.** *Sport, etc.* a definite, timed part of a game: *a rest between periods.* **5.** *Music.* a division of a composition, usually a passage of eight or sixteen bars, complete or satisfactory in itself, commonly consisting of two or more contrasted or complementary phrases ending with a conclusive cadence. **6.** *Geol.* a main division of a geological era, represented in the earth's crust by systems of rocks laid down during it; it is divided into epochs. **7.** *Physics.* the time of one complete oscillation or cycle of a periodic quantity or motion; the time between a given phase and its next recurrence. **8.** *Astron.* the time in which a planet or satellite revolves about its primary. **9.** *Chem.* a group of elements forming a horizontal row in the periodic table. **10.** a round of time or series of years by which time is measured. **11.** a round of time marked by the recurrence of some phenomenon or occupied by some recurring process of action. **12.** the time during which anything runs its course. **13.** the present time. **14.** the point of completion of a round of time or course of duration or action. **15.** menstruation. **16.** full stop. **17.** a full pause such as is made at the end of a complete sentence. **18.** a complete sentence, esp. an elaborately constructed one. **19.** (*pl.*) rhetorical language. **20.** *Class. Pros.* a group of two or more cola. —*adj.* **21.** pertaining to, denoting, characteristic of, imitating, or representing a past period or the fashions current during a specific period of history: *period costumes.* [ME *peryod*, t. L: m. s. *periodus*, t. Gk: m. *períodos* a going around, cycle, period] **—Syn. 1.** See **age.**

periodate (pû rīʹə dātʹ), *n.* a salt of periodic acid.

periodic (pĭəʹrĭ ŏdʹĭk), *adj.* **1.** characterized by periods or rounds of recurrence. **2.** occurring or appearing at regular intervals. **3.** intermittent. **4.** *Physics.* recurring after equal intervals of time. **5.** *Astron.* **a.** characterized by a series of successive circuits or revolutions, as the motion of a planet or satellite. **b.** of or pertaining to a period, as of the revolution of a heavenly body. **6.** pertaining to or characterized by rhetorical periods or periodic sentences. **7.** (of a sentence) having the sense incomplete until the end is reached. [t. L: s. *periodicus*, t. Gk: m. *periodikós*] **—perʹiodʹically,** *adv.*

periodic acid (pûʹrī ŏdʹĭk), *Chem.* any of a series of acids derived from I_2O_7 by the addition of *n* molecules of water, where *n* has values from 1 to 7. [f. PER- + IODIC]

periodical (pĭəʹrĭ ŏdʹĭ kl), *n.* **1.** a magazine, journal, etc., issued at regularly recurring intervals. —*adj.* **2.** issued at regularly recurring intervals. **3.** of or pertaining to such publications. **4.** periodic.

periodicity (pĭəʹrĭ ə dĭsʹĭ tĭ), *n., pl.* **-ties.** periodic character; tendency to recur at regular intervals.

periodic law (pĭəʹrĭ ŏdʹĭk), *Chem.* **1.** the law that the properties of the elements are periodic functions of their atomic numbers. **2.** (originally) the statement that the chemical and physical properties of the chemical elements recur periodically when the elements are arranged in the order of their atomic weights.

periodic system, *Chem.* a system of classification of the elements based on the periodic law.

periodic table, *Chem.* a table illustrating the periodic system, in which the chemical elements, arranged in the order of their atomic weights (now, atomic numbers) are shown in related groups.

periodide (pû rīʹə dīdʹ), *n. Chem.* an iodide with the maximum proportion of iodine.

periodontics (pĕʹrĭ ō dŏnʹtĭks), *n.* the study of periodontal tissue and its diseases.

periodontitis (pĕʹrĭ ō dŏn tīʹtĭs), *n. Pathol.* inflammation of the periodontium.

periodontium (pĕʹrĭ ō dŏnʹtĭ əm, -tyəm), *n. Anat.* the tissues surrounding the tooth, including the periodontal membrane, the gums, and bone. **—perʹiodonʹtal, perʹiodonʹtic,** *adj.*

periosteum (pĕʹrĭ ŏsʹtĭ əm), *n., pl.* **-tea** (-tĭ ə). *Anat.* the normal investment of bone, made up of a dense outer fibrous tissue layer and a more delicate inner layer which is the layer of bone regeneration. [t. NL, var. of LL *periosteon*, t. Gk: (neut.) around the bones] **—perʹiosʹteal,** *adj.*

periostitis (pĕʹrĭ ŏs tīʹtĭs), *n. Pathol.* inflammation of the periosteum. [f. PERIOST(EUM) + -ITIS] **—periostitic** (pĕʹrĭ ŏs tĭtʹĭk), *adj.*

periotic (pĕʹrĭ ŏtʹĭk), *adj. Anat.* **1.** surrounding the ear. **2.** denoting or pertaining to certain bones or bony elements which form or help to form a protective capsule for the internal ear, being usually confluent or fused, and in man constituting part of the temporal bone. [f. Gk: *peri-* PERI- + m. s. *ōtikós* of the ear]

Peripatetic (pĕʹrĭ pə tĕtʹĭk), *adj.* **1.** of or pertaining to the philosophy or the followers of Aristotle, who taught while walking in the Lyceum of ancient Athens. **2.** (*l.c.*) walking or travelling about; itinerant. —*n.* **3.** a member of the Aristotelian school. **4.** (*l.c.*) one who walks or travels about. [ME, t. L: s. *peripatēticus*, t. Gk: m. *peripatētikós* walking about]

peripatus (pĕ rĭpʹə təs), *n.* onychophoran.

peripeteia (pĕʹrĭ pĭ tīʹə, -tīəʹ), *n.* a sudden reversal or change of fortune, esp. in a dramatic work. [t. Gk]

peripheral (pə rĭfʹə rəl), *adj.* **1.** pertaining to, situated in, or constituting the periphery. **2.** of minor importance; not essential; superficial. **3.** *Anat.* outside of; external (as distinguished from *central*). **—periphʹerally,** *adv.*

peripheral device, *Computers.* a device attached to a computer which transfers information into or out of the computer.

periphery (pə rĭfʹə rĭ), *n., pl.* **-ries. 1.** the external boundary of any surface or area. **2.** the external surface, or outside, of a body. [t. LL: m. s. *peripheria*, t. Gk: m. *periphéreia*]

periphrasis (pə rĭfʹrə sĭs), *n., pl.* **-ses** (-sēzʹ). **1.** a roundabout way of speaking; circumlocution. **2.** a roundabout expression. Also, **periphrase** (pĕʹrĭ frāzʹ). [t. L, t. Gk]

periphrastic (pĕʹrĭ frăsʹtĭk), *adj.* **1.** circumlocutory; roundabout. **2.** *Gram.* **a.** denoting a construction of two or more words with a class meaning which in other languages or in other forms of the same language is expressed by inflectional modification of a single word. For example: *The son of Mr Smith* is periphrastic; *Mr Smith's son* is inflectional. **b.** denoting a class meaning expressed by a construction of two or more words. **—perʹiphrasʹtically,** *adv.*

periplus (pĕʹrĭ pləs), *n.* **1.** a circumnavigation; voyage round a coast. **2.** a narrative of this. [t. L, t. Gk: m. *períplous*]

perique (pə rēkʹ), *n.* a rich-flavoured tobacco produced in Louisiana. [t. Louisiana F]

perisarc (pĕʹrĭ säkʹ), *n. Zool.* the horny or chitinous outer case or covering with which the soft parts of hydrozoans are often protected. [f. PERI- + m. s. Gk *sárx* flesh]

periscope (pĕʹrĭ skōpʹ), *n.* an optical instrument consisting essentially of a tube with an arrangement of prisms or mirrors by which a view at the surface of water, the top of a parapet, etc., may be seen from below or behind. [t. Gk: m. s. *periskopeîn* look around]

periscopic (pĕʹrĭ skŏpʹĭk), *adj.* **1.** (of certain lenses in special microscopes, cameras, etc.) giving distinct vision obliquely, or all around, as well as, or instead of, in a direct line. **2.** pertaining to periscopes or their use. Also, **periscopical.**

perish (pĕʹrĭsh), *v.i.* **1.** to suffer death, or lose life, through violence, privation, etc.: *to perish in battle.* **2.** to pass away; decay and disappear. **3.** to suffer destruction: *whole cities perish in an earthquake.* **4.** to suffer spiritual death. [ME *perisse(n)*, t. OF: m. *periss-*, s. *perir*, g. L *perīre* pass away, perish] **—Syn. 1.** See **die**[1].

perishable (pĕʹrĭ shə bl), *adj.* **1.** liable to perish; subject to decay or destruction. —*n.* **2.** (*usually pl.*) a perishable thing, as food. **—perʹishableness, perʹishabilʹity,** *n.*

perished (pĕʹrĭsht), *adj. Colloq.* weakened or exhausted by cold or hunger.

perisher (pĕʹrĭ shə), *n. Slang.* an annoying or mischievous child.

perishing (pĕʹrĭ shĭng), *adj.* **1.** *Colloq.* bitterly cold. **2.** *Slang.* unpleasant; objectionable. —*adv.* **3.** *Slang.* very; extremely. **—perʹishingly,** *adv.*

perisperm (pĕʹrĭ spûmʹ), *n. Bot.* nutritive tissue which surrounds the embryo in some seeds.

perispore (pĕʹrĭ spôʹ), *n. Bot.* a membrane surrounding a spore.

perissodactyl (pə rĭsʹō dăkʹtĭl), *adj.* **1.** having an uneven number of toes or digits on each foot. —*n.* **2.** any animal of the mammalian order *Perissodactyla*, which comprises the odd-toed hoofed quadrupeds: the tapirs, the rhinoceroses, and horses (*Equidae*), sometimes classified as a suborder of ungulates. Also, **perissodactyle.** [t. NL: s. *perissodactylus*, f. Gk: *perissó(s)* odd, uneven + m. *dáktylos* finger or toe] **—perisʹsodacʹtylous,** *adj.*

peristalsis (pĕʹrĭ stălʹsĭs), *n., pl.* **-ses** (-sēz). *Physiol.* peristaltic movement. [t. NL, f. Gk: *peri-* PERI- + *stálsis* compression]

peristaltic (pĕʹrĭ stălʹtĭk), *adj. Physiol.* denoting or pertaining to the alternate waves of constriction and dilation of a tubular muscle system or cylindrical structure, as the wavelike circular contractions of the alimentary canal. [t. Gk: m. s. *peristaltikós* compressing]

peristerite (pə rĭsʹtə rītʹ), *n.* a white variety of albite, used as a gem.

peristome (pĕʹrĭ stōmʹ), *n.* **1.** *Bot.* the one or two circles of small, pointed, toothlike appendages around the orifice of the capsule or urn of mosses, appearing when the lid is removed. **2.** *Zool.* any of various structures or sets of parts which surround, or form the walls, etc., of a mouth or mouthlike opening. [t. NL: m. *peristoma*, f. Gk: *peri-* PERI- + *stóma* mouth]

peristyle (pĕr′ĭ stīl′), *n.* *Archit.* **1.** a range or ranges of columns surrounding a building, court, or the like. **2.** a space or court so enclosed. [t. F, t. L: m. s. *peristȳlum*, t. Gk: m. *perístȳlon*, neut. of *perístȳlos* having columns all around] —**per′isty′lar,** *adj.*

perithecium (pĕr′ĭ thē′sĭ əm), *n., pl.* **-cia** (-sĭ ə). *Bot.* the fructification of certain fungi, typically a minute, more or less completely closed, globose or flask-shaped body enclosing the asci. [t. NL, f. Gk: *peri-* PERI- + m. *thēkíon*, dim. of *thḗkē* case]

peritoneum (pĕr′ĭ tō nē′əm), *n., pl.* **-nea** (-nē′ə). *Anat.* the serous membrane lining the abdominal cavity and investing its viscera. Also, **peritonaeum.** [t. LL, t. Gk: m. *peritónaion*, lit., stretched over]—**per′itone′al,** *adj.*

peritonitis (pĕr′ĭ tə nī′tĭs), *n.* *Pathol.* inflammation of the peritoneum. [t. NL, f. s. Gk *perítonos* stretched round or over + *-ītis* -ITIS. See PERITONEUM]

peritricha (pə rĭt′rĭ kə), *n.pl.* bacteria having the organs of locomotion all round the body. Cf. **monotricha, amphitricha.** —**perit′richous,** *adj.*

periwig (pĕr′ĭ wĭg′), *n.* a peruke or wig. [alter. of *perruck*, t. F: m. *perruque.* See PERUKE]

periwinkle[1] (pĕr′ĭ wĭng′kl), *n.* **1.** any of various marine gastropods or sea-snails, esp. *Littorina littorea*, used for food. **2.** the shell of any of various other small univalves. [OE *pīnewincle*, f. *pīne* (t. L: m. *pīna* kind of mussel) + *wincle* (c. Dan. *vinkel* snail shell)]

periwinkle[2] (pĕr′ĭ wĭng′kl), *n.* any plant of the apocynaceous genus *Vinca*, as *V. minor* (**lesser periwinkle**) or *V. major* (**greater periwinkle**), trailing evergreen plants with blue flowers. [ME *perwynke*, OE *perwince*, t. L: m. *pervinca*]

perjure (pû′jə), *v.t.*, **-jured, -juring.** to render (oneself) guilty of swearing falsely, or of wilfully making a false statement under oath or solemn affirmation. [late ME, t. L: m. s. *perjūrāre*] —**per′jurer,** *n.*

perjured (pû′jəd), *adj.* **1.** guilty of perjury. **2.** characterized by or involving perjury: *perjured testimony.*

perjury (pû′jə rĭ), *n., pl.* **-ries.** *Law.* the wilful utterance of a false statement under oath or affirmation, before a competent tribunal, upon a point material to a legal inquiry. [ME, t. AF: m. *perjurie*, t. L: m. *perjūrium*]

perk[1] (pûk), *v.i.* **1.** to carry oneself, lift the head, or act in a jaunty manner. **2.** to become lively or vigorous, as after depression or sickness (fol. by *up*). **3.** to put oneself forward briskly or presumptuously. —*v.t.* **4.** to raise smartly or briskly (often fol. by *up*). **5.** to dress smartly, or deck (sometimes fol. by *up* or *out*). —*adj.* **6.** perky. [ME *perke(n)*; ? akin to PEER[2]]

perk[2] (pûk), *v.i., v.t.* *Chiefly U.S.* to percolate.

perk[3] (pûk), *n.* perquisite (def. 2).

Perkin (pû′kĭn), *n.* **Sir William Henry,** 1838–1907, English chemist: first to produce a synthetic dye (1856).

perky (pû′kĭ), *adj.*, **-kier, -kiest.** jaunty; brisk; pert.

perlemon (pĕə′lə mŏn′), *n.* *S African.* abalone. [t. Afrikaans: m. *perlemoen*]

Perlis (pĕə′lĭs, pû′-), *n.* a state in Malaysia, in NW Malaya. 109,102 pop. (est. 1964); 310 sq. mi. *Cap.:* Kangar.

perlite (pû′līt), *n.* *Geol.* a form of obsidian or other vitreous rock, usually appearing as a mass of enamel-like globules. Also, **pearlite.** [t. F] —**perlitic** (pû lĭt′ĭk), *adj.*

perm[1] (pûm), *n.* **1.** permanent wave. —*v.t.* **2.** to give (the hair) a permanent wave.

perm[2] (pûm), *n.* (in football pools) permutation.

Perm (*Russ.* pyĕrmy), *n.* a town in the E Soviet Union in Europe. 764,000 (est. 1965). Formerly, **Molotov.**

permafrost (pû′mə frŏst′), *n.* ground that is permanently frozen, as in arctic regions.

permalloy (pûm′ăl′oi), *n.* **1.** one of a class of alloys of high magnetic permeability, containing 30–90 per cent nickel. **2.** (*cap.*) a trademark for one of these alloys. [f. PERM(EABLE) + ALLOY]

permanence (pû′mə nəns), *n.* the condition or quality of being permanent; continued existence.

permanency (pû′mə nən sĭ), *n., pl.* **-cies. 1.** permanence. **2.** a permanent person, thing, or position.

permanent (pû′mə nənt), *adj.* lasting or intended to last indefinitely; remaining unchanged; not temporary; enduring; abiding. [ME, t. L: s. *permanens*, ppr., remaining throughout] —**per′manently,** *adv.*

Permanent Court of Arbitration, the official name of the **Hague Tribunal.**

permanent gas, *Physics.* a gas which cannot be liquefied by pressure alone.

permanent hardness, hardness of water which is not destroyed by boiling.

permanent magnet, *Physics.* a magnet which retains its magnetism without the presence of an external magnetic field.

permanent wave, a wave set into the hair by a special technique and remaining for a number of months.

permanent way, the ballast, sleepers, and rails which constitute a railway.

permanganate (pə măng′gə nāt′, -nĭt), *n.* *Chem.* a salt of permanganic acid.

permanganic acid (pû′măn găn′ĭk), *Chem.* an acid, $HMnO_4$, containing manganese.

permeability (pû′myə bĭl′ĭ tĭ), *n.* **1.** the property or state of being permeable. **2.** *Physics.* **a.** the ratio of flux density in a material to the magnetizing force producing it (**absolute magnetic permeability**). **b.** the ratio of flux density produced in a material to that which would be produced in a vacuum by the same magnetizing force (**relative magnetic permeability**). **3.** *Aeron.* the rate at which gas is lost through the envelope of a balloon or airship, usually expressed as the number of litres thus diffused in one day through a square metre.

permeable (pû′myə bl), *adj.* capable of being permeated. [t. L: m. s. *permeābilis*]

permeance (pû′mĭ əns), *n.* **1.** the act of permeating. **2.** the conducting power of a magnetic circuit for magnetic flux, or the reciprocal of magnetic reluctance.

permeant (pû′mĭ ənt), *adj.* permeating; pervading.

permeate (pû′mĭ āt′), *v.*, **-ated, -ating.** —*v.t.* **1.** to pass through the substance or mass of. **2.** to penetrate through the pores, interstices, etc., of. **3.** to be diffused through; pervade; saturate. —*v.i.* **4.** to penetrate; become diffused. [t. L: m. s. *permeātus*, pp., passed through] —**per′mea′tion,** *n.* —**permeative** (pû′mĭ ə tĭv), *adj.* —**Syn. 1, 3.** See **pervade.**

per mensem (pû mĕn′səm), *Latin.* by the month.

Permian (pû′mĭ ən), *Geol.* —*adj.* **1.** pertaining to the latest Palaeozoic geological period or system. —*n.* **2.** the period or system following Carboniferous and preceding Triassic, characterized by prominence of salt deposits and, in the Southern Hemisphere, by extensive glaciation. **3.** a subgroup of certain closely related Finno-Ugric languages of Russia, esp. Zyrian and Votyak. [f. PERM (where such strata occur) + -IAN]

per mill, per thousand. Also, **per mil.**

permissible (pə mĭs′ə bl), *adj.* allowable. —**permis′sibil′ity,** *n.* —**permis′sibly,** *adv.*

permission (pə mĭsh′ən), *n.* **1.** the act of permitting; formal or express allowance or consent. **2.** liberty or licence granted to do something. [ME, t. L: s. *permissio*] —**Ant. 2.** restraint, refusal.

permissive (pə mĭs′ĭv), *adj.* **1.** granting permission. **2.** permitted or allowed; optional. **3.** tolerant. **4.** sexually and morally tolerant: *we are living in a permissive society.* —**permis′sively,** *adv.*

permit (*v.* pə mĭt′; *n.* pû′mĭt), *v.*, **-mitted, -mitting,** *n.* —*v.t.* **1.** to allow (a person, etc.) to do something: *permit me to explain.* **2.** to let (something) be done or occur: *the law permits the sale of such drugs.* **3.** to tolerate; agree to. **4.** to afford opportunity for, or admit of: *vents permitting the escape of gases.* —*v.i.* **5.** to grant permission; allow liberty to do something. **6.** to afford opportunity or possibility: *write when time permits.* **7.** to allow or admit (fol. by *of*): *statements that permit of no denial.* —*n.* **8.** a written order granting leave to do something. **9.** an authoritative or official certificate of permission; a licence. **10.** permission. [late ME, t. L: m. s. *permittere* to let go through] —**permit′ter,** *n.* —**Syn. 1.** See **allow.**

permittivity (pû′mĭ tĭv′ĭ tĭ), *n.* *Elect.* **a.** a property of an insulating material equal to the ratio of the capacitance of a capacitor using the material as a dielectric to the capacitance of the same capacitor using air as the dielectric; dielectric constant (**relative permittivity**). **b.** a property of a dielectric medium or space equal to the ratio of the electric displacement to the electric force producing it (**absolute permittivity**).

permonosulphuric acid (pû′mŏn′ō sŭl fyo͝oə′rĭk), *Chem.* persulphuric acid (def. 1).

permutate (pû′myo͞o tāt′), *v.t.*, **-tated, -tating. 1.** to subject (something) to permutation. **2.** to arrange (items) in a different sequence.

permutation (pû′myo͞o tā′shən), *n.* **1.** *Maths.* **a.** the act of changing the order of elements arranged in a particular order (as, *abc* into *acb, bac,* etc.), or of arranging a number of elements in groups made up of equal numbers of the elements in different orders (as, *a* and *b* in *ab* and *ba*). **b.** any of the resulting arrangements or groups. **2.** the act of permuting; alteration.

permute (pə myo͞ot′), *v.t.*, **-muted, -muting. 1.** to alter.

2. *Maths.* to subject to permutation. [ME *permute(n)*, t. L: m. *permūtāre*] —**permut′able,** *adj.*

Pernambuco (pû′năm boo͞′kō; *Port.* pėr nəm boo͞′ko͞o), *n.* Recife.

pernicious (pû nĭsh′əs), *adj.* **1.** ruinous; highly hurtful: *pernicious teachings.* **2.** deadly; fatal. **3.** evil or wicked. [t. L: m. s. *perniciōsus*] —**perni′ciously,** *adv.* —**perni′ciousness,** *n.*

pernicious anaemia, *Pathol.* a macrocytic anaemia produced by deficient maturation of the red blood cells, and associated with subacute degenerative lesions in the posterior and lateral columns of the spinal cord, glossitis, gastric disturbances, and atrophy of the gastric mucosa.

pernickety (pə nĭk′ĭ tĭ), *adj. Colloq.* **1.** fastidious; fussy. **2.** requiring painstaking care. [orig. Scot.]

Pernik (*Bulg.* pĕr′nēk), *n.* former name of **Dimitrovo.**

Pernod (pĕə′nō; *Fr.* pĕr nō′), *n. Trademark.* a French aperitif based on aniseed.

Perón (*Sp.* pė rōn′), *n.* **Juan Domingo** (*Sp.* KHwän dō mēn′gō), born 1895, president of Argentina 1946–55.

peroneal (pĕ′rə nē′əl), *adj. Anat.* pertaining or proximate to the fibula. [f. NL *peronē* fibula (t. Gk: pin, brooch) + -AL[1]]

peroneus (pĕ′rə nē′əs, -nīəs′), *n. Anat.* any of several fibular muscles on the outer side of the leg.

perorate (pĕ′rə rāt′), *v.i.*, **-rated, -rating. 1.** to speak at length; make a speech. **2.** to bring a speech to a close with a formal conclusion. [t. L: m. s. *perōrātus*, pp., spoken at length]

peroration (pĕ′rə rā′shən), *n.* the concluding part of a speech or discourse, in which the speaker or writer recapitulates the principal points and urges them with greater earnestness and force. [late ME, t. L: s. *perōrātio*]

peroxidase (pə rŏk′sĭ dās′), *n. Biochem.* any of a class of enzymes which are capable of catalysing the oxidation of a compound by the decomposition of hydrogen peroxide or any other peroxide.

peroxide (pə rŏk′sīd), *n., adj., v.*, **-ided, -iding.** —*n.* **1.** *Chem.* **a.** an oxide derived from hydrogen peroxide which contains the -O-O- group; generally that oxide of an element or radical which contains an unusually large amount of oxygen. **b.** hydrogen peroxide, H_2O_2. —*adj.* **2.** (of the hair) bleached by peroxide (def. 1b). —*v.t.* **3.** to use peroxide (def. 1b) on (the hair) as a bleach.

peroxidize (pə rŏk′sĭ dīz′), *v.t., v.i.*, **-dized, -dizing.** *Chem.* to convert into a peroxide. Also, **peroxidise.**

peroxyacid (pə rŏk′sĭ ăs′ĭd), *n.* an acid derived from hydrogen peroxide which contains the -O-O group.

peroxyboric acid (pə rŏk′sĭ bô′rĭk), *Chem.* the hypothetical acid, HBO_3, known by its salts (perborates).

peroxydisulphuric acid (pə rŏk′sĭ dī′sŭl fyo͞oə′rĭk), *Chem.* persulphuric acid (def. 2).

peroxymonosulphuric acid (pə rŏk′sĭ mŏn′ō sŭl fyo͞oə′rĭk), *Chem.* persulphuric acid (def. 1).

perpend[1] (pû′pənd), *n. Masonry.* a large stone passing through the entire thickness of a wall so as to show on both sides, and forming a bonder. Also, **perpent.** [t. OF: m. *perpain*, g. LL *perpannius* extending to the visible portion of the wall, influenced by PEND]

perpend[2] (pə pĕnd′), *Archaic.* —*v.t.* **1.** to consider. —*v.i.* **2.** to ponder; deliberate. [t. L: s. *perpendere*]

perpendicular (pû′pən dĭk′yo͞o lə), *adj.* **1.** vertical; upright. **2.** *Geom.* meeting a given line or surface at right angles. **3.** (*cap.*) *Archit.* denoting or pertaining to a style of architecture, the last stage of English Gothic, in which a large proportion of the chief lines of the tracery intersect at right angles. —*n.* **4.** a perpendicular line or plane. **5.** an instrument for indicating the vertical line from any point. **6.** upright position. **7.** rectitude. [t. L: s. *perpendiculāris*; r. ME *perpendiculer*, t. OF] —**perpendicularity** (pû′pən dĭk′yo͞o lă′rĭ tĭ), *n.* —**per′pendic′ularly,** *adv.* —**Syn. 1.** See **upright.**

AB, perpendicular to CD

perpent (pû′pənt), *n. Masonry.* perpend.

perpetrate (pû′pĭ trāt′), *v.t.*, **-trated, -trating.** to perform, execute, or commit (a crime, deception, etc.). [t. L: m. s. *perpetrātus*, pp.] —**per′petra′tion,** *n.* —**per′petra′tor,** *n.*

perpetual (pə pĕt′yo͞o əl), *adj.* **1.** continuing or enduring for ever or indefinitely: *perpetual snows.* **2.** continuing or continued without intermission or interruption: *a perpetual stream of visitors.* **3.** *Hort.* blooming more or less continuously throughout the season or the year. —*n.* **4.** a hybrid rose that is perpetual. [ME *perpetuall*, t. L: m. s. *perpetuālis*] —**perpetuality** (pə pĕt′yo͞o ăl′ĭ tĭ), *n.* —**perpet′ually,** *adv.* —**Syn. 1.** everlasting, permanent. See **eternal. 2.** continuous, ceaseless, incessant, constant.

perpetual motion, the motion of a theoretical machine that would continue to operate for ever without loss of energy and without receiving any energy from outside.

perpetuate (pə pĕt′yo͞o āt′), *v.t.*, **-ated, -ating.** to make perpetual; preserve from oblivion. [t. L: m. s. *perpetuātus*, pp.] —**perpet′ua′tion, perpetuance** (pə pĕt′yo͞o əns), *n.* —**perpet′ua′tor,** *n.*

perpetuity (pû′pĭ tyo͞o′ĭ tĭ), *n., pl.* **-ties. 1.** endless or indefinitely long duration or existence. **2.** something that is perpetual. **3.** an annuity paid for life. **4.** *Law.* (of property) an interest under which property is less than completely alienable for longer than the law allows. **5. in perpetuity,** for ever. [ME *perpetuite*, t. F, t. L: m. s. *perpetuitas*]

Perpignan (*Fr.* pĕr pē nyäN′), *n.* a town in S France, the capital of Pyrénées-Orientales department. 83,025 (1962).

perplex (pə plĕks′), *v.t.* **1.** to cause to be puzzled over what is not understood or certain; bewilder; confuse mentally. **2.** to make complicated or confused, as a matter, question, etc. **3.** to hamper with complications, confusion, or uncertainty. [back-formation from PERPLEXED] —**perplex′ingly,** *adv.* —**Syn. 1.** See **puzzle.**

perplexed (pə plĕkst′), *adj.* **1.** bewildered or puzzled. **2.** tangled; involved. [ME *perplex* intricate, bewildered (t. L: s. *perplexus* involved) + -ED[2]] —**perplexedly** (pə plĕk′sĭd lĭ), *adv.*

perplexity (pə plĕk′sĭ tĭ), *n., pl.* **-ties. 1.** a perplexed or puzzled condition; uncertainty as to what to think or do. **2.** something that perplexes. **3.** tangled, involved, or confused condition.

perquisite (pû′kwĭ zĭt), *n.* **1.** an incidental emolument, fee, or profit over and above fixed income, salary, or wages. **2.** Also, **perk. a.** anything customarily supposed to be allowed or left to an employee or servant as an incidental advantage of the position held. **b.** any fringe benefit, bonus, etc., attaching to a particular post which an employee receives in addition to his normal salary. **3.** something regarded as due by right. [late ME, t. ML: m. s. *perquīsītum*, neut. pp., sought for]

Perrault (*Fr.* pĕ rō′), *n.* **Charles** (*Fr.* shärl), 1628–1703, French writer of fairytales.

Perret (*Fr.* pĕ rĕ′), *n.* **Auguste** (*Fr.* ō gYst′), 1874–1954, French architect.

perron (pĕ′rən; *Fr.* pĕ rōN′), *n. Archit.* an outside platform upon which the entrance door of a building opens, with steps leading to it. [ME *peroun*, t. OF: m. *perron*, der. *pierre* rock, g. L *petra*]

perry (pĕ′rĭ), *n.* a fermented beverage, similar to cider, made from the juice of pears. [ME *pereye*, t. OF, ult. der. L *pirum.* See PEAR]

Perry (pĕ′rĭ), *n.* **Matthew Calbraith** (kăl′brĕth), 1794–1858, U.S. naval officer.

Pers., 1. Persia. 2. Persian.

pers., 1. person. 2. personal.

per-salt (pû′sôlt′), *n. Chem.* (in a series of salts of a given metal or radical) that salt in which the metal or radical has a high, or the highest apparent, valency; a salt corresponding to a per-acid.

perse (pûs), *adj.* of a very deep shade of blue or purple. [ME *pers*, t. OF, g. LL *persus*; orig. uncert.]

per se (pû sā′), *Latin.* by or in itself; intrinsically.

persecute (pû′sĭ kyo͞ot′), *v.t.*, **-cuted, -cuting. 1.** to pursue with harassing or oppressive treatment; harass persistently. **2.** to oppress with injury or punishment for adherence to principles or religious faith. **3.** to annoy by persistent attentions, importunities, or the like. [back-formation from PERSECUTION, conformed to L *persecūtus*, pp., having pursued] —**per′secu′tive, persecutory** (pû′sĭ kyo͞o′tə rĭ), *adj.* —**per′secu′tor,** *n.* —**Syn. 3.** worry, badger, vex.

persecution (pû′sĭ kyo͞o′shən), *n.* **1.** the act of persecuting. **2.** the state of being persecuted. [ME, t. L: s. *persecūtio*] —**per′secu′tional,** *adj.*

Perseid (pû′sĭ ĭd), *n. Astron.* any of a shower of meteors appearing in August, and radiating from a point in the constellation Perseus. [t. Gk: s. *Perseídes*, pl. of *Perseís* daughter of Perseus]

Persephone (pû sĕf′ə nĭ), *n.* **1.** Also, *Latin,* **Proserpina.** *Gk Myth.* daughter of Zeus and Demeter, kidnapped by Pluto (or Hades) to be his wife and queen of the lower world, but allowed to return every year. **2.** a personification of spring.

Persepolis (pû sĕp′ə lĭs), *n.* an ancient capital of Persia: its imposing ruins are in S Iran, ab. 30 mi. NE of Shiraz. See map under **Media.**

Perseus (pû′syo͞os), *n.* **1.** *Gk Myth.* a hero, the son of Zeus and Danaë, who slew the Gorgon Medusa, and afterwards saved Andromeda from a sea-monster. **2.** *Astron.* one of the northern constellations, containing the variable star Algol.

perseverance (pû′sĭ vĭə′rəns), *n.* **1.** steady persistence in a course of action, a purpose, a state, etc. **2.** *Theol.* continuance in a state of grace to the end, leading to eternal salvation. —**per′sever′ant,** *adj.*

—**Syn. 1.** PERSEVERANCE, PERSISTANCE, TENACITY, PERTINACITY imply resolute and unyielding holding on, in following a course of action. PERSEVERANCE commonly suggests activity maintained in spite of difficulties; steadfast and long continued application: *endurance and perseverance combined to win in the end.* It is regularly used in a favourable sense. PERSISTENCE, which may be used in either a favourable or an unfavourable sense, implies unremitting (and sometimes annoying) perseverance: *persistance in a belief, in talking when others wish to be quiet.* TENACITY, with the original meaning of adhesiveness, as of glue, is a dogged and determined holding on. Whether used literally or figuratively it has favourable implications: *a bulldog quality of tenacity, the tenacity of one's memory.* PERTINACITY, unlike its related word, is used chiefly in an unfavourable sense: *the pertinacity of the social climber.*

persevere (pû′sĭ vĭə′), *v.i.*, **-vered, -vering.** to persist in anything undertaken; maintain a purpose in spite of difficulty or obstacles; continue steadfastly. [ME *persevere(n)*, t. F: m. *persévérer*, t. L: m. *persevērāre* continue steadfastly]

persevering (pû′sĭ vĭə′rĭng), *adj.* showing perseverance; steadfast; persistent. —**per′sever′ingly,** *adv.*

Pershing (pû′shĭng), *n.* **John Joseph,** 1860–1948, U.S. general.

Persia (pû′shə), *n.* **1.** an ancient empire situated in W and SW Asia: at its peak it extended from Egypt and the Aegean to India; conquered by Alexander the Great, 334–331 B.C. **2.** former official name (until 1935) of **Iran.**

Persian (pû′shən), *adj.* **1.** of or pertaining to Iran, its people, or their language. —*n.* **2.** a member of the native race of Iran, now a mixed race descended in part from the ancient Iranians. **3.** a citizen of ancient Persia. **4.** an Iranian language, the principal language of Iran, in its historical (Old Persian, Avestan, and Pahlavi) and modern forms. **5.** (*usually pl.*) Persian blinds.

Persian blinds, 1. outside window shutters made of thin, movable horizontal slats. **2.** venetian blinds.

Persian carpet, a large one-piece carpet having a pile of wool, sometimes of silk, twisted by hand with a special knot over the warp.

Persian cat, a variety of domestic cat with long, silky hair and bushy tail, probably originating in Persia.

Persian Gulf, an arm of the Arabian Sea, extending NW between Arabia and Iran. ab. 600 mi. long.

Persian lamb, 1. the lamb of the karakul sheep. **2.** the fur of this animal, having closely curled lustrous hairs, and usually dyed black; caracul.

persiennes (pû′sĭ ĕnz′; *Fr.* pĕr syĕn′), *n.pl.* **1.** Persian blinds. **2.** (*construed as sing.*) a fabric, usually cotton or silk, with a printed or painted pattern. [t. F: pl. of fem. adj.: Persian]

persiflage (pû′sĭ fläzh′; *Fr.* pĕr sē fläzh′), *n.* **1.** light, bantering talk. **2.** a frivolous style of treating a subject. [t. F, der. *persifler* banter lightly, f. *per-* PER- + *siffler* whistle, hiss, g. L *sifilāre, sibilāre*]

persimmon (pû sĭm′ən), *n.* **1.** any of various trees of the genus *Diospyros*, esp. *D. virginiana* of North America, with astringent plumlike fruit becoming sweet and edible when thoroughly ripe, and *D. kaki* of Japan and China, with soft, rich red or orange fruits, often 3 inches across. **2.** the fruit. [t. Algonquian (Delaware): m. *pasimenan* (artificially) dried fruit]

persist (pə sĭst′), *v.i.* **1.** to continue steadily or firmly in some state, purpose, course of action, or the like, esp. in spite of opposition, remonstrance, etc. **2.** to last or endure. **3.** to be insistent in a statement or question. [t. L: s. *persistere* to continue steadfastly]

persistence (pə sĭs′təns), *n.* **1.** the action or fact of persisting. **2.** the quality of being persistent. **3.** continued existence or occurrence. **4.** the continuance of an effect after its cause is removed. Also, **persist′ency.** —**Syn. 1.** See **perseverance.**

persistent (pə sĭs′tənt), *adj.* **1.** persisting, esp. in spite of opposition, etc.; persevering. **2.** lasting or enduring. **3.** continued; constantly repeated. **4.** *Biol.* continuing or permanent. **5.** *Zool.* perennial; holding to morphological character, or continuing in function or activity. —**persist′ently,** *adv.* —**Syn. 1.** indefatigable, pertinacious, tenacious. See **stubborn.**

person (pû′sən), *n.* **1.** a human being, whether man, woman, or child: *the only person in sight.* **2.** a human being as distinguished from an animal or a thing. **3.** *Philos.* a self-conscious or rational being. **4.** the actual self or individual personality of a human being: *to assume a duty in one's own person.* **5.** the living body of a human being, often including the clothes worn. **6.** the body in its external aspect. **7.** a character, part, or role, in a play, story, or in real life, etc. **8.** an individual of distinction or importance. **9.** one not entitled to social recognition or respect. **10.** *Law.* any human being or artificial body of people, having rights and duties before the law. **11.** *Gram.* **a.** (in some languages) a category of verb inflection and of pronoun classification, distinguishing between the speaker (**first person**), the one addressed (**second person**), and anyone or anything else (**third person**), sometimes with further subdivisions of the third; as *I* and *we* (first person), *you* (second person), and *he, she, it* and *they* (third person). **b.** any of these three (or more) divisions. **12.** *Theol.* any of the three hypostases or modes of being in the Trinity (Father, Son, and Holy Ghost). **13. in person,** in one's own bodily presence: *to apply in person.* [ME *persone*, t. OF, g. L *persōna* actor's mask, character acted, personage, being]

—**Syn. 1.** PERSON, INDIVIDUAL, PERSONAGE are terms applied to human beings. PERSON is the most general and common word: *the average person.* INDIVIDUAL views a person (rarely a thing) as standing alone or as a single member of a group: *the characteristics of the individual*; its implication is sometimes derogatory: *a disagreeable individual.* PERSONAGE is used (sometimes ironically) of an outstanding or illustrious person: *a distinguished personage as a visitor.*

persona (pû sō′nə), *n.*, *pl.* **-nae** (-nē). **1.** a person. **2.** (in the psychology of C. G. Jung) the outer or public personality, which is presented to the world and does not represent the inner personality of the individual (contrasted with *anima*).

personable (pû′sə nə bl), *adj.* of pleasing personal appearance; comely; presentable.

personage (pû′sə nĭj), *n.* **1.** a person of distinction or importance. **2.** any person. **3.** a character in a play, story, etc. [late ME, t. OF] —**Syn. 1.** See **person.**

persona grata (pû sō′nə grä′tə), *Latin.* **1.** an acceptable person. **2.** a diplomatic representative acceptable to the government to which he is accredited. [LL]

personal (pû′sə nəl), *adj.* **1.** of or pertaining to a particular person; individual; private: *a personal matter.* **2.** relating to, directed to, or aimed at, a particular person: *a personal favour.* **3.** referring or directed to a particular person in a disparaging or offensive sense or manner: *personal remarks.* **4.** making personal remarks or attacks: *to become personal in a dispute.* **5.** done, affected, held, etc., in person: *a personal conference, personal service.* **6.** pertaining to or characteristic of a person or self-conscious being. **7.** of the nature of an individual rational being: *a personal God.* **8.** pertaining to the person, body, or bodily aspect: *personal cleanliness.* **9.** *Gram.* **a.** denoting grammatical person. For example: in Latin *portō* 'I carry', *portās* 'you carry', *portat* 'he, she or it carries', *-ō*, *-s* and *-t* are said to be personal endings. **b.** denoting a class of pronouns classified as referring to the speaker, the one addressed, and anyone or anything else. **10.** *Law.* denoting or pertaining to estate or property consisting of moveable chattels, money, securities and choses in action (distinguished from *real*). —*n.* **11.** *U.S.* **a.** a short news paragraph in a newspaper, concerning a particular person or particular persons. **b.** a short, confidential notice in a newspaper, often addressed to a particular individual. [ME, t. L: s. *persōnalis*]

personal call, a telephone call over a long distance for which timed charging begins when the required person has been connected. Also, *U.S.*, **person-to-person call** (pû′sən tə pû′sən).

personal column, a part of a newspaper devoted to advertisements of a personal nature.

personal equation, personal tendency to deviation or error, for which allowance must be made.

personalism (pû′sə nə lĭz′əm), *n.* *Philos.* a movement which finds ultimate value and reality in persons, human or divine; usually favouring democracy, self-psychology, theism, and idealism, while opposing naturalism, dualism, and irrationalism. —**per′sonalist,** *n.* —**per′sonalis′tic,** *adj.*

personality (pû′sə năl′ĭ tĭ), *n.*, *pl.* **-ties. 1.** distinctive or notable personal character: *a man with personality.* **2.** a person as an embodiment of an assemblage of qualities. **3.** *Psychol.* **a.** all the constitutional, mental, emotional, social, etc., characteristics of an individual. **b.** an organized pattern of all the characteristics of an individual. **c.** a pattern of characteristics consisting of two or more usually opposing types of behaviour: *multiple personality.* **4.** the quality of being a person; existence as a self-conscious being; personal identity. **5.** the essential character of a person as distinguished from a thing. **6.** application or reference to a particular person or particular persons, often in disparagement or hostility. **7.** a disparaging or offensive statement referring to a particular person. **8.** a well-known or prominent person; celebrity. **9.** *Geog.* the distinguishing or peculiar characteristics of a region. —**Syn. 1.** See **character.**

personality cult, excessive adulation of an individual, esp. a political leader.

personalize (pû′sə nə līz′), *v.t.*, **-lized, -lizing. 1.** to make personal. **2.** to mark in some way so as to identify as the property of a particular person. **3.** to personify. Also, **personalise.**

personally (pû′sə nə lĭ), *adv.* **1.** as regards oneself: *personally I don't care to go.* **2.** as an individual person: *he hates me personally.* **3.** in person. **4.** as if intended for one's own person: *don't take his bluntness personally.*

personal pronoun, *Gram.* any one of the pronouns which indicate grammatical person (*I, we, thou, you, he, she, it, they*).

personalty (pû′sə nəl tĭ), *n., pl.* **-ties.** *Law.* personal estate or property.

persona non grata (pû sō′nə nŏn grä′tə), *Latin.* an unacceptable or unwelcome person, esp. a diplomatic representative.

personate[1] (pû′sə nāt′), *v.*, **-nated, -nating.** *—v.t.* **1.** to act or present (a character in a play, etc.). **2.** to assume the character or appearance of; pass oneself off as, esp. for fraudulent purposes. **3.** (in the arts) to represent in terms of personal properties. *—v.i.* **4.** to act or play a part. [t. L: m. s. *persōnātus,* pp.] **—per′sona′tion,** *n.* **—personative** (pû′sə nə tĭv), *adj.* **—per′sona′tor,** *n.*

personate[2] (pû′sə nĭt, -sə nāt′), *adj. Bot.* **1.** (of a bilabiate corolla) masklike. **2.** having the lower lip pushed upwards so as to close the hiatus between the lips, as in the snapdragon. See illus. under **corolla.** [t. L: m. s. *persōnātus* masked]

personification (pû sŏn′ĭ fĭ kā′shən), *n.* **1.** the attribution of personal nature or character to inanimate objects or abstract notions, esp. as a rhetorical figure. **2.** the representation of a thing or abstraction in the form of a person, as in art. **3.** the person or thing embodying a quality or the like; an embodiment. **4.** an imaginary person or creature conceived or figured to represent a thing or abstraction. **5.** the act of personifying.

personify (pû sŏn′ĭ fī′), *v.t.*, **-fied, -fying. 1.** to attribute personal nature or character to (an inanimate object or an abstraction), as in speech or writing. **2.** to represent (a thing or abstraction) in the form of a person, as in art. **3.** to embody (a quality, idea, etc.) in a real person or a concrete thing. **4.** to be an embodiment of; typify. **5.** to personate. [f. PERSON + -(I)FY, appar. modelled on F *personnifier*] **—person′ifi′er,** *n.*

personnel (pû′sə nĕl′), *n.* the body of persons employed in any work, undertaking, or service (distinguished from *matériel*). [t. F, n. use of adj.]

persorption (pə sôp′shən), *n. Phys. Chem.* adsorption in pores only slightly wider than the diameter of the adsorbed molecule.

perspective (pə spĕk′tĭv), *n.* **1.** the art of depicting on a flat surface, various objects, architecture, landscape, etc., in such a way as to express dimensions and spatial relations. **2.** the relation of parts to one another and to the whole, in a mental view or prospect. **3.** a visible scene, esp. one extending to a distance; a vista. **4.** the appearance of objects with reference to relative position, distance, etc. **5.** a mental view or prospect. **6.** *Obs.* an optical glass. **7. in perspective, a.** according to the laws of perspective. **b.** in true proportion. *—adj.* **8.** of or pertaining to the art of perspective, or represented according to its laws. [ME, t. ML: m. *perspectīva* (*ars*) science of optics, der. L *perspectus* see through] **—perspec′tively,** *adv.*

perspex (pû′spĕks), *n.* **1.** an optically clear thermoplastic resin, polymethyl methacrylate, used as a substitute for glass in certain applications. **2.** (*cap.*) a trademark for this substance.

perspicacious (pû′spĭ kā′shəs), *adj.* **1.** having keen mental perception; discerning. **2.** *Archaic.* having keen sight. [f. PERSPICACI(TY) + -OUS] **—per′spica′ciously,** *adv.*

perspicacity (pû′spĭ kăs′ĭ tĭ), *n.* **1.** keenness of mental perception; discernment; penetration. **2.** *Archaic.* keenness of sight. [t. L: m. s. *perspicācitas*] **—Syn. 1.** See **perspicuity. —Ant. 1.** obtuseness.

perspicuity (pû′spĭ kyōō′ĭ tĭ), *n.* **1.** clearness or lucidity, as of a statement. **2.** the quality of being perspicuous. **3.** perspicacity. [late ME, t. L: m. s. *perspicuitas*]

—Syn. 1. PERSPICUITY and PERSPICACITY are not properly synonyms, but for several centuries the first has been confused with the second, by less careful writers. Both are derived from a Latin word meaning to see through clearly: PERSPICACITY refers to the power of seeing clearly; to clearness of insight or judgement: *a man of acute perspicacity, the perspicacity of his judgement.* PERSPICUITY refers to that which can be seen through, i.e., to lucidity, clearness of style or exposition, freedom from obscurity: *the perspicuity of his argument.* **—Ant. 1.** obscurity.

perspicuous (pə spĭk′yōō əs), *adj.* **1.** clear to the understanding. **2.** clear in expression or statement; lucid. **3.** perspicacious. [late ME, t. L: m. *perspicuus*] **—perspic′uously,** *adv.* **—perspic′uousness,** *n.*

perspiration (pû′spə rā′shən), *n.* **1.** the act or process of perspiring. **2.** that which is perspired; sweat.

—Syn. 2. PERSPIRATION, SWEAT refer (primarily) to moisture exuded (by animals and people) from the pores of the skin. PERSPIRATION is the more refined and elegant word, and is often used over-fastidiously by those who consider SWEAT coarse; but SWEAT is a strong word and in some cases obviously more appropriate: *a light perspiration; the sweat of his brow.* SWEAT is always used when referring to animals or objects: *sweat drips from a dog's tongue*; it may also be used metaphorically of objects: *sweat forms on apples after they are gathered.*

perspiratory (pə spī′ə rə tə rĭ, -trĭ), *adj.* of, pertaining to or stimulating perspiration.

perspire (pə spī′ə), *v.*, **-spired, -spiring.** *—v.i.* **1.** to excrete watery fluid through the pores; sweat. *—v.t.* **2.** to emit through pores; exude. [t. L: m. s. *perspīrāre,* lit., breathe through]

persuade (pə swād′), *v.t.*, **-suaded, -suading. 1.** to prevail on (a person, etc.), by advice, urging, reasons, inducements, etc., to do something: *we could not persuade him to wait.* **2.** to induce to believe; convince. [t. L: m. s. *persuādēre*] **—persuad′able,** *adj.* **—persuad′er,** *n.*

—Syn. 1. PERSUADE, INDUCE, CONVINCE imply influencing someone's thoughts or actions. PERSUADE and INDUCE (followed by the infinitive) are used today mainly in the meaning of winning over a person to a certain course of action: *it was I who persuaded him to call a doctor; I induced him to do it.* They differ in that PERSUADE suggests appealing more to the reason and understanding: *I persuaded him to go back to his wife* (though it is often lightly used: *can't I persuade you to stay to supper?*); INDUCE emphasizes only the idea of successful influence, whether achieved by argument or by promise of reward: *What can I say that will induce you to stay in your job?* Owing to this idea of compensation, INDUCE may be used in reference to the influence of factors as well as of persons: *the prospect of a rise in salary was what induced him to stay.* CONVINCE means to satisfy the understanding of a person with regard to a truth or a statement: *to convince one by quoting statistics.* Only when followed by a *that-* clause may CONVINCE refer to winning a person to a course of action: *I convinced her that she should go.* **—Ant. 1.** dissuade.

persuasible (pə swā′sə bl), *adj.* open to persuasion. **—persua′sibil′ity,** *n.*

persuasion (pə swā′zhən), *n.* **1.** the act of persuading or seeking to persuade. **2.** power of persuading; persuasive force. **3.** the state or fact of being persuaded or convinced. **4.** a conviction or belief. **5.** a form or system of belief, esp. religious belief, or the body of persons adhering to it. **6.** sect or denomination. **7.** *Colloq.* kind or sort. [ME, t. L: s. *persuāsio*]

persuasive (pə swā′sĭv), *adj.* **1.** able, fitted, or intended to persuade. *—n.* **2.** something that persuades. **—persua′sively,** *adv.* **—persua′siveness,** *n.*

persulphate (pû sŭl′fāt), *n. Chem.* a salt of persulphuric acid.

persulphuric acid (pû′sŭl fyōōə′rĭk). *Chem.* **1.** Also, **Caro's acid, permonosulphuric acid, peroxymonosulphuric acid.** a white crystalline solid, H_2SO_5, used as an oxidizing agent. **2.** Also, **perdisulphuric acid, peroxydisulphuric acid.** a white hygroscopic crystalline solid, $H_2S_2O_8$, used in the manufacture of hydrogen peroxide.

pert (pût), *adj.* **1.** bold; forward; impertinent; impudent; saucy. **2.** *Now Dial.* lively; sprightly; in good health. **3.** *Obs.* clever. [ME, aphetic var. of *apert,* appar. b. OF *apert* open (g. L *apertus*) and OF *a(s)pert* skilled (g. L *expertus*)] **—pert′ly,** *adv.* **—pert′ness,** *n.*

pert., pertaining.

pertain (pû tān′), *v.i.* **1.** to have reference or relation; relate: *documents pertaining to the case.* **2.** to belong or be connected as a part, adjunct, possession, attribute, etc. **3.** to belong properly or fittingly; be appropriate. [ME *partene(n),* t. OF: m. *partenir,* g. L *pertinēre* extend, reach, relate]

Perth (pûth), *n.* **1.** a burgh in Scotland, the county town of Perthshire, on the river Tay. 41,199 (1961). **2.** Perthshire. **3.** a city in Australia, the capital of Western Australia, in the SW part. 457,000 (1964).

Perthshire (pûth′shĭə′, -shə), *n.* a county in central Scotland. 127,018 pop. (1961); 1493 sq. mi. *Co. town:* Perth.

pertinacious (pû′tĭ nā′shəs), *adj.* **1.** holding tenaciously to a purpose, course of action, or opinion. **2.** extremely persistent: *pertinacious efforts.* [f. s. L *pertinācia* + -OUS] **—per′tina′ciously,** *adv.* **—per′tina′ciousness,** *n.*

pertinacity (pû′tĭ năs′ĭ tĭ), *n.* the quality of being pertinacious. **—Syn.** See **perseverance.**

pertinent (pû′tĭ nənt), *adj.* pertaining or relating to the matter in hand; relevant; apposite: *pertinent details.* [ME, t. L: s. *pertinens,* ppr.] **—per′tinence, per′tinency,** *n.* **—per′tinently,** *adv.* **—Syn.** See **apt.**

perturb (pə tûb′), *v.t.* **1.** to disturb or disquiet greatly in mind; agitate. **2.** to disturb greatly; throw into disorder; derange. **3.** *Astron.* to induce perturbation of. [ME, t. L: s. *perturbāre*] **—perturb′able,** *adj.*

perturbation (pû′tû bā′shən), *n.* **1.** the act of perturbing. **2.** the state of being perturbed. **3.** mental disquiet or agitation. **4.** a cause of mental disquiet. **5.** *Astron.* deviation of a celestial body from regular motion around its primary due to some force other than the gravitational attraction of a spherical primary.

pertussis (pə tŭs′ĭs), *n.* *Pathol.* whooping cough. [t. NL: f. *per-* PER- + L *tussis* cough] —**pertus′sal,** *adj.*

Peru (pə rōō′; *Sp.* pĕ rōō′), *n.* a republic in W South America. 10,364,620 pop. (1961); 482,258 sq. mi. *Cap.:* Lima. —**Peruvian** (pə rōō′vyən), *adj., n.*

Perugia (pə rōō′jyə; *It.* pĕ rōō′jȧ), *n.* a town in Italy, in N central Umbria. 121,825 (1966).

Perugino, Il (*It.* ēl pĕ rōō jē′nȯ), (*Pietro Vannucci*), 1446–1524, Italian painter.

peruke (pə rōōk′), *n.* a wig, esp. of the kind worn by men in the 17th and 18th centuries; a periwig. [t. F: m. *perruque*, t. It.: m. *perrucca*]

Man wearing a peruke

perusal (pə rōō′zəl), *n.* **1.** a reading. **2.** the act of perusing; survey or scrutiny.

peruse (pə rōōz′), *v.t.*, **-rused, -rusing.** **1.** to read through, as with thoroughness or care. **2.** to read. **3.** *Archaic.* to survey or examine in detail. [late ME; orig., use up, f. PER- + USE, v.] —**perus′able,** *adj.* —**perus′er,** *n.*

Peruvian bark, cinchona (def. 2).

Peruzzi (*It.* pĕ rōōt′tsē), *n.* **Baldassare** (*It.* bȧl dȧs sȧ′rĕ), 1481–1536, Italian architect and painter.

pervade (pû vād′), *v.t.*, **-vaded, -vading.** **1.** to extend its presence, activities, influence, etc., throughout: *spring pervaded the air.* **2.** to go, pass, or spread through. **3.** *Rare.* to go everywhere throughout (a place), as a person. [t. L: m. s. *pervādere*] —**pervad′er,** *n.* —**pervasion** (pû vā′zhən), *n.* —**pervasive** (pû vā′sĭv), *adj.* —**perva′sively,** *adv.* —**perva′siveness,** *n.*

—**Syn. 1.** PERVADE, PERMEATE suggest a slow diffusion and an ultimate saturation of something. PERVADE is now found chiefly in figurative uses: *the perfume of roses pervades the air, a spirit of uneasiness pervaded the city.* PERMEATE is found in both concrete and figurative senses: *water permeated the soil, ideas of democracy permeated the group.*

perverse (pə vûs′), *adj.* **1.** wilfully determined or disposed to go counter to what is expected or desired; contrary. **2.** characterized by or proceeding from such a determination: *a perverse mood.* **3.** wayward; cantankerous. **4.** persistent or obstinate in what is wrong. **5.** turned away from what is right, good, or proper; wicked. [ME, t. L: m. s. *perversus*, pp., turned the wrong way, awry] —**perverse′ly,** *adv.* —**perverse′ness,** *n.* —**Syn. 4.** stubborn, headstrong. See **wilful.**

perversion (pə vû′shən), *n.* **1.** the act of perverting. **2.** the state of being perverted. **3.** a perverted form of something. **4.** *Psychol.* unnatural or abnormal condition of the sexual instincts (**sexual perversion**). **5.** *Pathol.* change to what is unnatural or abnormal: *a perversion of function, taste, etc.*

perversity (pə vû′sĭ tĭ), *n., pl.* **-ties.** **1.** the quality of being perverse. **2.** an instance of it.

perversive (pə vû′sĭv), *adj.* tending to pervert.

pervert (*v.* pə vût′; *n.* pû′vût), *v.t.* **1.** to turn away from the right course. **2.** to lead astray morally. **3.** to lead into mental error or false judgement. **4.** to bring over to a religious belief regarded as false or wrong. **5.** to turn to an improper use; misapply. **6.** to distort. **7.** to bring to a less excellent state, vitiate, or debase. **8.** *Pathol.* to change to what is unnatural or abnormal. **9.** to affect with perversion. —*n.* **10.** *Psychol., Pathol.* one affected with perversion. **11.** one who has been perverted. [ME, t. L: s. *pervertere*] —**pervert′er,** *n.* —**pervert′ible,** *adj.*

perverted (pə vû′tĭd), *adj.* **1.** *Pathol.* changed to or being of an unnatural or abnormal kind: *a perverted appetite.* **2.** turned from what is right; wicked; misguided; misapplied; distorted. **3.** affected with or due to perversion. —**pervert′edly,** *adv.*

pervious (pû′vyəs), *adj.* **1.** admitting of passage or entrance; permeable: *pervious soil.* **2.** accessible to reason, feeling, etc. [t. L: m. *pervius*] —**per′viousness,** *n.*

Pesach (pā′säk), *n.* the Passover. Also, **Pesah.** [t. Heb.: m. *pesah*]

pesante (pə zăn′tĭ; *It.* pĕ sȧn′tĕ), *adv.* *Music.* heavily. [t. It.]

Pesaro (*It.* pĕ′zȧ rȯ), *n.* a seaport in Italy, in The Marches. 75,538 (1966).

Pescadores (pĕs′kə dô′rĭz), *n.pl.* a group of small islands off the SE coast of China, in Taiwan Strait: ceded to Japan, 1895; returned to China, 1945. 110,000 pop. (est. 1965); ab. 50 sq. mi. Also, **Pengu.**

Pescara (*It.* pĕs kȧ′rȧ), *n.* a seaport in Italy, in Abruzzi e Molise. 106,579 (1966).

peseta (pə sĕt′ə, pə sā′tə; *Sp.* pĕ sĕ′tȧ), *n.* **1.** the monetary unit of Spain, equal to 100 céntimos, and equivalent to about £0·006. **2.** a coin of this denomination. *Abbrev.:* pta, p.

Peshawar (pə shô′ə), *n.* a city in N West Pakistan, near the Khyber Pass. 218,691 (1961). See map under **Khyber Pass.**

Peshitta (pĕ shē′tə), *n.* the principal Syriac version of the Bible. Also, **peshito.** [t. Syriac: m. *p'shīttâ* the simple]

pesky (pĕs′kĭ), *adj.*, **-kier, -kiest.** *U.S. Colloq.* troublesome; annoying. [b. *pesty* (der. PEST) and RISKY]

peso (pā′sō; *Sp.* pĕ′sȯ), *n., pl.* **-sos** (-sōz; *Sp.* -sȯs). **1.** the monetary unit of Mexico, equal to 100 centavos, and equivalent to £0·033 sterling. **2.** a note or coin of this denomination. **3.** the monetary unit of Cuba, equal to 100 centavos, and equivalent to about £0·416 sterling. **4.** a banknote of this denomination. **5.** the monetary unit of the Philippines, equal to 100 centavos, and equivalent to about £0·105 sterling. **6.** a note or silver coin of this denomination. **7.** any of various monetary units and coins of Spanish America. **8.** any of certain former Spanish gold or silver coins. *Abbrev.:* p. [Sp.: lit., weight, g. L *pensum*, pp., weighed]

pessary (pĕs′ə rĭ), *n., pl.* **-ries.** *Med.* **1.** an instrument worn in the vagina to remedy uterine displacement. **2.** a vaginal suppository. **3.** a contraceptive device worn in the vagina or cervix. [ME, t. LL: m. s. *pessārium*, der. L *pessus*, t. Gk: m. *pessós*, orig., oval stone used in a game]

pessimism (pĕs′ĭ mĭz′əm), *n.* **1.** disposition to take the gloomiest possible view. **2.** the doctrine that the existing world is the worst of all possible worlds, or that all things naturally tend to evil. **3.** the belief that the evil and pain in the world are not compensated for by the good and happiness. [f. s. L *pessimus* worst + -ISM, modelled on OPTIMISM]

pessimist (pĕs′ĭ mĭst), *n.* **1.** one who looks on the gloomy side of things. **2.** an adherent of pessimism.

pessimistic (pĕs′ĭ mĭs′tĭk), *adj.* pertaining to or characterized by pessimism. —**pes′simis′tically,** *adv.* —**Syn.** See **cynical.**

pest (pĕst), *n.* **1.** a noxious, destructive, or troublesome thing or person; nuisance. **2.** a deadly epidemic disease; a pestilence. **3.** a disease produced by the plague bacillus. **4.** an organism harmful to agriculture. [t. L: s. *pestis* plague, disease]

Pest (pĕst; *Hung.* pĕsht), *n.* See **Budapest.**

Pestalozzi (pĕs′tə lŏt′sĭ; *Ger.* pĕs tȧ lŏt′sĭ), *n.* **Johann Heinrich** (*Ger.* yō′hȧn hīn′rĭKH), 1746–1827, Swiss educational reformer.

pester (pĕs′tə), *v.t.* to harass with petty annoyances, vexing importunities, or the like; torment. [? t. OF: m. *empestrer* hobble (a horse); later associated with PEST]

pesthouse (pĕst′hous′), *n.* *Archaic.* a house or hospital for persons infected with pestilential disease.

pesticide (pĕs′tĭ sīd′), *n.* a chemical substance for destroying pests, such as mosquitoes, flies, etc.

pestiferous (pĕs tĭf′ə rəs), *adj.* **1.** carrying or producing plague. **2.** pestilential. **3.** pernicious in any way. **4.** *Colloq.* mischievous, troublesome, or annoying. [f. L *pestifer* plague-bringing + -OUS] —**pestif′erously,** *adv.*

pestilence (pĕs′tĭ ləns), *n.* **1.** a deadly epidemic disease. **2.** that which produces or tends to produce epidemic disease. **3.** the bubonic plague.

pestilent (pĕs′tĭ lənt), *adj.* **1.** infectious, as a disease; pestilential. **2.** producing or tending to produce infectious disease. **3.** destructive to life; deadly; poisonous. **4.** injurious to peace, morals, etc. **5.** troublesome or annoying. **6.** pernicious or mischievous. [ME, t. L: s. *pestilens*, ppr.] —**pes′tilently,** *adv.*

pestilential (pĕs′tĭ lĕn′shəl), *adj.* **1.** producing or tending to produce pestilence. **2.** pertaining to or of the nature of pestilence, esp. bubonic plague. **3.** pernicious; harmful. [ME, t. ML: s. *pestilentiālis*]

pestle (pĕs′əl), *n., v.*, **-tled, -tling.** —*n.* **1.** an instrument for breaking up and grinding substances in a mortar. See illus. under **mortar.** **2.** any of various appliances for pounding, stamping, etc. —*v.t.* **3.** to pound or triturate with or as with a pestle. —*v.i.* **4.** to work with a pestle. [ME, t. OF: m. *pestel*, ult. der. L *pistum*, pp., pounded]

pet[1] (pĕt), *n., adj., v.*, **petted, petting.** —*n.* **1.** any domesticated or tamed animal that is cared for affectionately. **2.** a person especially cherished or indulged; a favourite. **3.** a thing particularly cherished. —*adj.* **4.** treated as a pet, as an animal. **5.** especially cherished or indulged, as a child or other person. **6.** favourite: *a pet theory.* **7.** principal; most important: *pet aversion.* **8.** showing affection: *a pet name.* —*v.t.* **8.** to treat as a pet; fondle; indulge. **9.** to fondle or caress one of the opposite sex. [? back-formation from *pet lamb* cade lamb, itself ? syncopated var. of *petty lamb* little lamb, where *petty* marks affection. Cf. PETCOCK]

pet[2] (pĕt), *n.* **1.** a fit of peevishness. —*v.i.* **2.** to be peevish; sulk. [appar. back-formation from PETTISH]

Pet., Peter.

Petach Tikva (pĕt′äk tĭk′və, pĕt′äKH), a town in central Israel. 67,000 (est. 1964).

Pétain (*Fr.* pĕ tăN′), *n.* **Henri Philippe** (*Fr.* äN rē fē lēp′), 1856–1951, French general and politician; head of state for the Vichy government 1940–44; convicted of treason 1945.

petal (pĕt′l), *n. Bot.* one of the members of a corolla. See diag. under **flower.** [t. NL: s. *petalum* petal (L metal plate), t. Gk: m. *pétalon* leaf, prop. neut. adj., outspread] —**pet′alled,** *adj.*

petaliferous (pĕt′ə lĭf′ə rəs), *adj.* bearing petals.

petaline (pĕt′ə līn′), *adj.* pertaining to or resembling a petal.

petalody (pĕt′ə lō′dĭ), *n. Bot.* a condition in flowers, in which certain organs, as the stamens in most double flowers, assume the appearance of or become metamorphosed into petals. [f. s. Gk *petalṓdēs* leaf-like + -Y[3]]

petaloid (pĕt′ə loid′), *adj.* having the form or appearance of a petal.

petalous (pĕt′ə ləs), *adj.* having petals.

petard (pĕ täd′), *n.* **1.** an engine of war or an explosive device formerly used to blow in a door or gate, form a breach in a wall, etc. **2.** a kind of firework. **3. hoist with one's own petard,** caught in one's own trap. [t. F, der. *péter* break wind, explode, der. *pet* (noun), g. L *pēditum*, der. *pēdere* break wind]

petasus (pĕt′ə səs), *n.* a low-crowned, broad-brimmed hat worn by ancient Greeks and Romans, often represented as worn by Hermes or Mercury. [t. L, t. Gk: m. *pétasos*]

petcock (pĕt′kŏk′), *n.* a small valve or tap, as for draining off excess or waste material from the cylinder of a steam-engine or for checking the water-level in a boiler. [f. PET(TY) + COCK[1]]

peter[1] (pē′tə), *v.i.* to diminish gradually and then disappear or cease (fol. by *out*). [orig. unknown]

peter[2] (pē′tə), *v.i. Whist.* to signal or call for trumps.

Peter (pē′tə), *n.* **1.** Also, **Simon Peter** or **Saint Peter.** died A.D. 67?, one of the twelve apostles, a fisherman on the Sea of Galilee and leader of the group of apostles. He was the reputed author of two New Testament epistles bearing his name. **2.** one of the two Epistles of Peter. [ME, t. L: m. s. *Petrus*, t. Gk: m. *Pétros* stone, trans. of Syriac *kēfā*]

Peter I, **1.** (*'the Great'*) 1672–1725, tsar of Russia 1682–1725. **2.** (*Peter Karageorgevich*) 1844–1921, king of Serbia 1903–21.

Peter II, born 1923, king of Yugoslavia, 1934–45.

Peter III, 1728–62, the weak-minded husband of Catherine II of Russia: became tsar (1762); assassinated.

Peterborough (pē′tə brə), *n.* **1.** a town in England, in Northamptonshire. 62,340 (1961). **2.** a former administrative division of Northamptonshire, now part of Huntingdonshire. 84 sq. mi.

Peterhead (pē′tə hĕd′), *n.* a seaport in Scotland, in Aberdeenshire. 12,497 (1961).

Peterlee (pē′tə lē′), *n.* a town in England in County Durham: one of the new towns designated in 1948. 17,963 (est. 1965).

Peterloo massacre (pē′tə lo͞o′), an incident at St Peter's Fields near Manchester in 1819, when the crowd at a meeting calling for political and economic reform was charged by soldiers, and people were killed and injured. [*Peterloo*: b. (St) Peter('s Fields) + (WATER)LOO]

Petermann Peak (pē′tə mən; *Ger.* pė′tər män), a mountain in E Greenland. 9645 ft.

Peter Pan (pē′tə păn′), a youthful or immature man: *he is the Peter Pan of politics.* [*Peter Pan* hero of a play (1904) by J. M. Barrie]

peter pan collar, a small, rounded collar on a high, close-fitting neckline, worn by women and children.

Peter principle, the theory that in a hierarchy every employee tends to rise to his own level of incompetence. [from '*The Peter Principle*' (1969) by Dr Laurence F. *Peter* and Raymond Hull]

petersham (pē′tə shəm), *n.* **1.** a kind of heavy woollen cloth used for overcoats, etc. **2.** a kind of heavy overcoat formerly in fashion. **3.** a thick ribbed or corded ribbon used for belts, hatbands, etc. [named after Viscount *Petersham*, 1780–1851]

Peter's pence, **1.** an annual tax or tribute, orig. of a penny from each householder, formerly paid by the people of certain countries to the papal see at Rome. **2.** a voluntary contribution to the pope, made by Roman Catholics everywhere.

Peter the Hermit, *c.* 1050–1115, French monk; a preacher of the first Crusade.

pethidine (pĕth′ĭ dēn′, -dĭn), *n. Pharm.* an analgesic similar to morphine, administered esp. in childbirth.

petiolar (pĕt′ĭ ə lə), *adj. Bot.* of, pertaining to, or growing from a petiole.

petiolate (pĕt′ĭ ə lāt′, -lĭt), *adj. Zool.* having a petiole or peduncle. Also, **pet′iolat′ed.**

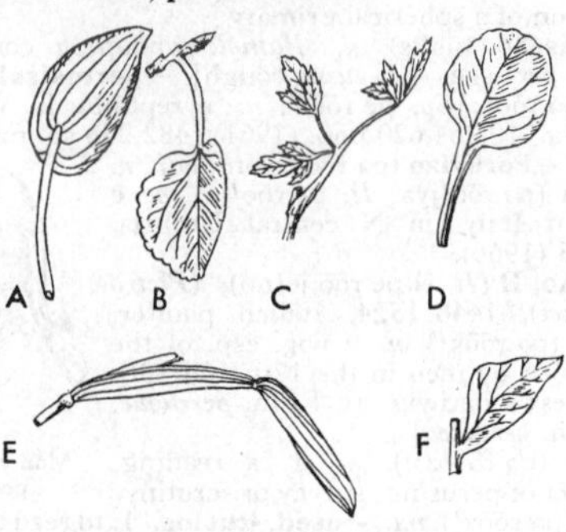

Petioles
A, Terete; B, Flat; C, Dilated at the base; D, Winged; E, Forming a sheath; F, Leaf-like (the so-called phyllode)

petiole (pĕt′ĭ ōl′), *n.* **1.** *Bot.* the slender stalk by which a leaf is attached to the stem; a leafstalk. **2.** *Zool.* a stalk or peduncle, as that connecting the abdomen and thorax in wasps, etc. [t. F, t. L: m. s. *petiolus* little foot, stem, stalk, dim. of *pēs* foot]

petit (pĕt′ĭ; *Fr.* pə tē′), *adj.* (now only in legal phrases) small; petty; minor. [ME, t. F, der. Rom. stem *pit-* small]

petit bourgeois (pə tē′bo͝oə′zhwä; *Fr.* pə tē bo͝or zhwȧ′), a member of the petite bourgeoisie. [t. F; see PETTY, BURGESS] —**petite bourgeoise** (pə tet′ bo͝oə′zhwäz; *Fr.* pə tĕt bo͝or zhwȧz′), *fem.*

petite (pə tēt′), *adj. French.* (of women) little; of small size; tiny.

petite bourgeoisie (pə tēt′ bo͝oə′zhwä zē′; *Fr.* pə tĕt bo͝or zhwȧ zē′), the section of the bourgeoisie having least wealth, status, etc., as shopkeepers, clerks, etc.

petit four (pĕt′ĭ fô′; *Fr.* pə tē fo͞or′), *pl.* **petits fours** (pĕt′ĭ fôz′; *Fr.* pə tē fo͞or′). a small fancy biscuit, eaten esp. with coffee after a meal. [F: little oven]

petition (pĭ tĭsh′ən), *n.* **1.** a formally drawn-up request addressed to a person or a body of persons in authority or power, soliciting some favour, right, mercy, or other benefit. **2.** a request made for something desired, esp. a respectful or humble request, as to a superior or to one or those in authority: *a petition for aid.* **3.** that which is sought by request or entreaty. **4.** *Law.* an application for an order of court or for some judicial action. **5.** a supplication or prayer, as to God. —*v.t.* **6.** to entreat, supplicate, or beg, as for something desired. **7.** to address a formal petition to (a sovereign, a legislative body, etc.). **8.** to ask by petition for (something) (fol. by *that*). —*v.i.* **9.** to present a petition. **10.** to address a formal petition. [ME, t. L: s. *petitio*] —**peti′tioner,** *n.* —**Syn. 9.** See **appeal.**

petitionary (pĭ tĭsh′ə nə rĭ), *adj.* **1.** of the nature of or expressing a petition. **2.** *Obs. or Archaic.* (of a person) petitioning or suppliant.

Petition of Right, a declaration by the English Parliament of the rights and liberties of the people: assented to by Charles I in 1628.

petitio principii (pĭ tĭsh′ĭ ō′ prĭn kĭp′ĭ ī′), *Logic.* a fallacy in reasoning resulting from the assumption of that which in the beginning was set forth to be proved; begging the question. [L, trans. of Gk *tò en archêi aiteîsthai* an assumption at the outset]

petit jury (pĕt′ĭ), petty jury. —**petit juror.**

petit larcency, petty larceny.

petit point (pĕt′ĭ point′; *Fr.* pə tē pwăN′), a tent stitch in embroidery worked over a single-thread canvas.

petits pois (*Fr.* pə tē pwȧ′), *French.* small green peas.

Petra (pĕt′rə, pē′trə), *n.* an ancient city in SW Jordan: unusual ruined buildings, carved out of varicoloured stratified rock.

Petrarch (pĕt′räk), *n.* (*Francesco Petrarca*) 1304–74, Italian poet and scholar.

petrel (pĕt′rəl), *n.* **1.** any of numerous sea-birds of the family *Procellariidae.* **2.** any of various small, long-winged, usually black-and-white oceanic birds known as Mother Carey's chickens, esp. the stormy or storm petrel, *Hydrobates pelagicus.* [t. F, earlier *pétérel*, der. *péter* break wind. See PETARD]

petri dish (pē′trĭ; *Ger.* pė′trē), a shallow, circular dish, usually of glass, used esp. for growing bacteria, etc. [named after J. R. *Petri*, died 1921, German biologist]

Petrie (pē′trĭ), *n.* **Sir Flinders** (flĭn′dəz), 1853–1942, English Egyptologist and archaeologist.

petrifaction (pĕt′rĭ făk′shən), *n.* **1.** the act or process of petrifying. **2.** the state of being petrified. **3.** something petrified. Also, **petrification** (pĕt′rĭ fĭ kā′shən). —**pet′-rifac′tive,** *adj.*

Petrified Forest, a U.S. national monument in E Arizona: forests turned to stone by the action of mineral-laden water. 40 sq. mi.

petrify (pĕt′rĭ fī′), *v.*, **-fied, -fying.** —*v.t.* **1.** to convert into stone or a stony substance. **2.** to make rigid, stiffen, or benumb; deaden; make inert. **3.** to stupefy or paralyse with astonishment, horror, fear, or other strong emotion. —*v.i.* **4.** to become petrified. [t. F: m. s. *pétrifier,* f. *pétri-* (repr. L *petra* rock, stone, t. Gk) + *-fier* -FY]

petrifying liquid, a sealing coat applied to a porous surface before applying an oil-bound water paint; usually consists of an emulsion of drying oil and/or resin in water.

Petrine (pē′trīn), *adj.* of or pertaining to the apostle Peter or the epistles bearing his name.

petro-, a word element meaning 'stone' or 'rock'. [t. Gk, comb. form of *pétra* rock, *pétros* stone]

petrochemical (pĕt′rō kĕm′ĭ kl), *n.* a chemical made from petroleum. [f. PETRO(LEUM) + CHEMICAL]

petrog., petrography.

petrogenesis (pĕt′rō jĕn′ĭ sĭs), *n. Geol.* (of igneous rocks) the mode of formation.

petroglyph (pĕt′rə glĭf′), *n.* a drawing or carving on rock made by prehistoric or primitive people. [t. F: m. *pétroglyphe,* f. Gk: *petro-* PETRO- + *glyphḗ* carving]

Petrograd (pĕt′rō grăd′; *Russ.* pĭ trä grät′), *n.* former name of **Leningrad** (1914–24).

petrography (pĕ trŏg′rə fĭ), *n.* the scientific description and classification of rocks. —**petrog′rapher,** *n.* —**petrographic** (pĕt′rō grăf′ĭk), **pet′rograph′ical,** *adj.* —**pet′-rograph′ically,** *adv.*

petrol (pĕt′rəl), *n.* **1.** a mixture of volatile liquid hydrocarbons, as hexane, heptane, and octane, used as a solvent and extensively as a fuel in internal-combustion engines; gasoline. **2.** *Obs.* petroleum. [t. F: m. *pétrole,* t. ML: m. s. *petroleum* PETROLEUM]

petrol., petrology.

petrolatum (pĕt′rə lā′təm), *n.* a soft or semisolid unctuous substance obtained from petroleum, used as a basis for ointments and as a protective dressing. Also, **petroleum jelly.** [t. NL. See PETROL, -ATE²]

petroleum (pə trō′lyəm), *n.* **1.** an oily, usually dark-coloured liquid (a form of bitumen or mixture of various hydrocarbons), occurring naturally in various parts of the world, and commonly obtained by boring: used (in its natural state or after certain treatment) as a fuel, or separated by distillation into petrol, naphtha, benzine, lubricating oil, paraffin oil, paraffin wax, etc. **2.** petrol. [t. ML: f. *petro-* PETRO- + L *oleum* oil (t. Gk: m. *élaion*)]

petroleum ether, an inflammable low-boiling hydrocarbon mixture produced by the fractional distillation of petroleum, used as a solvent.

petrolic (pĕ trŏl′ĭk), *adj.* relating to, resembling, or produced from petroleum: *petrolic ether.*

petrology (pĕ trŏl′ə jĭ), *n., pl.* **-gies.** the scientific study of rocks, including their origin, structure, changes, etc. —**petrologic** (pĕt′rə lŏj′ĭk), **pet′rolog′ical,** *adj.* —**pet′-rolog′ically,** *adv.* —**petrol′ogist,** *n.*

petrol pump, **1.** a pump at a petrol station. **2.** a pump, electrically or mechanically driven, which delivers petrol to the carburettor of an internal-combustion engine.

petrol station, filling station.

petronel (pĕt′rə nĕl′), *n.* a 16th-century firearm which was fired with the butt resting against the breast. [t. F: m. *petrinal,* orig. adj., for the breast, ult. der. L *pectus* chest]

petronella (pĕt′rə nĕl′ə), *n.* a Scottish country dance.

Petronius (pĕ trō′nyəs), *n.* **Gaius** (gī′əs) ('*Petronius Arbiter*'), died A.D. *c.* 66, Roman writer.

petrosal (pĭ trō′səl), *adj. Anat.* **1.** petrous. —*n.* **2.** a bone forming the pyramidal part of the temporal bone. [f. s. L *petrōsus* stony, rocky + -AL¹. See PETROUS]

petrous (pĕt′rəs, pē′trəs), *adj.* **1.** *Anat.* denoting or pertaining to the hard, dense portion of the temporal bone, containing the internal auditory organs; petrosal. **2.** like stone in hardness; stony; rocky. [t. L: m. *petrōsus,* der. *petra* rock, t. Gk]

Petsamo (*Finn.* pĕt′sä mô), *n.* a seaport in the extreme NW Soviet Union in Europe, on the Arctic Ocean: icefree all the year round: ceded by Finland, 1944.

Petsamo

petticoat (pĕt′ĭ kōt′), *n.* **1.** a skirt, esp. an underskirt, worn by women and children. **2.** any skirtlike part or covering. **3.** *Colloq.* a woman or girl. **4.** *Elect.* the skirt-shaped portion of an insulator. —*adj.* **5.** female or feminine. **6.** wearing petticoats. [ME; see PETTY, COAT]

Petticoat Lane, a street market in Middlesex Street in E London.

pettifog (pĕt′ĭ fŏg′), *v.i.*, **-fogged, -fogging.** **1.** to quibble over petty details. **2.** to carry on a petty or shifty law business. **3.** to practise chicanery of any sort. [back-formation from *pettifogger,* f. PETTY + *fogger* (of obscure orig.)] —**pet′tifog′ger,** *n.* —**pet′tifog′gery,** *n.*

pettifogging (pĕt′ĭ fŏg′ĭng), *adj.* **1.** petty; mean; paltry. **2.** dishonest.

pettish (pĕt′ĭsh), *adj.* peevish; petulant: *a pettish refusal.* [f. PET¹ + -ISH¹, orig., like a spoiled child] —**pet′tishly,** *adv.* —**pet′tishness,** *n.*

pettitoes (pĕt′ĭ tōz′), *n.pl.* **1.** the feet of a pig, esp. as food. **2.** the human feet, esp. those of a child.

petto (*It.* pĕt′tô), *n., pl.* **-ti** (*It.* -tē). *Italian.* the breast. See **in petto.** [It., g. L *pectus* breast]

petty (pĕt′ĭ), *adj.*, **-tier, -tiest.** **1.** of small importance; trifling; trivial: *petty grievances.* **2.** of lesser or secondary importance, merit, etc. **3.** having or showing narrow ideas, interests, etc.: *petty minds.* **4.** mean or ungenerous in small or trifling things: *a petty revenge.* [ME *pety,* t. OF: m. *petit.* See PETIT] —**pet′tily,** *adv.* —**pet′tiness,** *n.*

—**Syn. 1.** PETTY, PALTRY, TRIFLING, TRIVIAL apply to that which is so insignificant as to be almost unworthy of notice. PETTY implies contemptible insignificance and littleness, inferiority and small worth: *petty quarrels.* PALTRY is applied to that which is beneath one's notice, even despicable: *a paltry amount.* That which is TRIFLING is so unimportant and inconsiderable as to be practically negligible: *a trifling error.* That which is TRIVIAL is slight, insignificant, and even in incongruous contrast to that which is significant or important: *a trivial remark, a trivial task.*

petty cash, a small cash fund set aside to meet incidental expenses, as for office supplies.

petty jury, (in a civil or criminal proceeding) a jury, usually of 12 persons, empanelled to determine the facts and render a verdict pursuant to the court's instructions on the law. Also, **petit jury.** —**petty juror.**

petty larceny, **1.** *Law. Obs.* (before 1861) the stealing of a sum of value up to one shilling. **2.** *Colloq.* a minor theft.

petty officer, a naval officer who does not hold a commission.

petty sessions, *Law.* **1.** a meeting of justices of the peace exercising their function as magistrates. **2.** a criminal court of summary jurisdiction.

petty whin, the needle furze, *Genista anglica.*

petulance (pĕt′yo͝o ləns), *n.* **1.** petulant spirit or behaviour. **2.** the state or quality of being petulant. **3.** a petulant speech or action.

petulancy (pĕt′yo͝o lən sĭ), *n., pl.* **-cies.** petulance.

petulant (pĕt′yo͝o lənt), *adj.* moved to or showing sudden, impatient irritation, esp. over some trifling annoyance: *a petulant toss of the head.* [t. L: s. *petulans* forward, pert, wanton, der. *petere* fall on, assail] —**pet′ulantly,** *adv.*

petunia (pĭ tyo͞o′nyə), *n.* **1.** any of the herbs constituting the solanaceous genus *Petunia,* native in tropical America but cultivated elsewhere, bearing funnel-shaped flowers of various colours. **2.** a deep reddish purple. [t. NL, f. Guarani *petun* tobacco + *-ia* -IA]

petuntse (pĭ tŭn′tsĭ, -to͝on′-), *n.* a Chinese rock reduced mechanically to a fine powder and used as one of the ingredients of certain kinds of porcelain. Also, **petuntze.** [t. Chinese: f. *pe* (d. var. of *pai*) white + *tun* mound, stone + *tze* (a formative element)]

pew (pyo͞o), *n.* **1.** (in a church) one of an assemblage of fixed benchlike seats (with backs), accessible by aisles, for the use of the congregation. **2.** an enclosed seat in a church, or an enclosure with seats, appropriated to the use of a family or other worshippers. **3.** *Colloq.* any chair; any place to sit down: *take a pew.* [ME *puwe,* t. OF: m. *puie* balcony, g. L *podia,* pl. of *podium* elevated place, balcony. See PODIUM]

pewit (pē′wĭt), *n.* the lapwing or green plover, *Vanellus vanellus.* Also, **peewit.** [imit. of its cry]

pewter (pyo͞o′tə), *n.* **1.** any of various alloys in which tin is the chief constituent, orig. one of tin and lead. **2.** a vessel or utensil made of such an alloy. **3.** such utensils collectively. —*adj.* **4.** consisting or made of pewter: *a pewter mug.* [ME *peutre,* t. OF; orig. uncert.]

pewterer (pyo͞o′tə rə), *n.* a maker of pewter utensils.

peyote (pā ō′tĭ, pĭ ō′tĭ), *n.* **1.** the mescal, *Lophophora williamsii.* **2.** (in Mexico) any of several related or unrelated cacti. [t. Amer. Sp., t. Nahuatl: m. *peyotl* caterpillar (referring to the downy centre of the peyote button)]

Peyrefitte (*Fr.* pĕr fēt′), *n.* **Roger** (*Fr.* rô zhĕ′), born 1907, French novelist.

Pf., **1.** pfennig. **2.** *Elect.* pico-farad. **3.** preferred.

p.f., (It. *più forte*) *Music.* louder.

Pfalz (*Ger.* pfälts), *n.* German name of the **Palatinate.**

Pfc., *U.S. Mil.* private first class.

pfd, preferred.

pfennig (pfĕn′ĭg, fĕn′ĭg), *n., pl.* **-igs, -ige** (-ĭ gə). a small copper-coated coin of West Germany, the hundredth part of a mark. [G. See PENNY]

pfg, pfennig.

Pforzheim (*Ger.* pfōrts′hīm), *n.* a town in West Germany, in NW Baden-Württemberg. 87,700 (est. 1966).

Pg., **1.** Portugal. **2.** Portuguese.

pg., page.

P.G., paying guest.

Ph, *Chem.* phenyl.

***p*H,** *Chem.* the symbol for the logarithm of the reciprocal of hydrogen ion concentration in gram atoms per litre. For example, a *p*H of 5 indicates a concentration of 0·00001 or 10^{-5} gram atoms of hydrogen ions in one litre of solution.

phacolite (făk′ə līt′), *n.* a mineral of the zeolite group resembling chabazite.

Phaeacia (fē ā′shə), *n. Homeric Legend.* a land visited by Odysseus after the fall of Troy. —**Phaea′cian,** *n., adj.*

Phaedra (fē′drə), *n. Gk Legend.* the daughter of Minos and Pasiphaë, sister of Ariadne, and wife of Theseus. See **Hippolytus.**

Phaedrus (fē′drəs), *n.* fl. A.D. *c.* 40, Roman writer of fables.

Phaëthon (fā′ə thən), *n. Class. Myth.* the son of Helios, the sun-god. For one day he was allowed to drive his father's chariot, but drove too near earth, and had not Zeus struck him down with a thunderbolt, would have set the world on fire. [t. L, t. Gk: lit., shining]

phaeton (fā′tn), *n.* **1.** a light four-wheeled carriage, with or without a top, having one or (more commonly) two seats facing forward, and made in various forms. **2.** (formerly) a motor vehicle of the touring-car type. [t. F: m. *phaéton,* t. L: m. *Phaëthon* PHAËTHON]

Phaeton (def. 1)

-phage, a word element meaning 'eating', 'devouring', used in biology to refer to phagocytes, as in *bacteriophage.* [t. F, t. L: m. s. *-phagus,* t. Gk: m. *-phagos.* See -PHAGOUS]

phagedaena (făj′ĭ dē′nə), *n. Pathol.* a severe destructive eroding ulcer. Also, **phagedena.** [t. L, t. Gk: m. *phagédaina* an eating ulcer]

phago-, a word element corresponding to **-phage.** [t. Gk]

phagocyte (făg′ə sīt′), *n. Physiol.* a blood cell which ingests and destroys foreign particles, bacteria, and other cells. —**phagocytic** (făg′ə sĭt′ĭk), *adj.*

phagocytosis (făg′ə sī tō′sĭs), *n.* the ingestion of particle-like matter by cells, in contrast to the entrance of dissolved substance. [t. NL. See PHAGOCYTE, -OSIS]

-phagous, a word element used as an adjective termination meaning 'eating', 'feeding on', 'devouring', as in *creophagous, hylophagous, rhizophagous.* [t. L: m. *-phagus,* t. Gk: m. *-phagos*]

-phagy, a word element used as a noun termination meaning 'eating', 'devouring', esp. as a practice or habit, as in *allotriophagy, anthropophagy.* [t. Gk: m. s. *-phagia,* der. *-phagos* -PHAGOUS]

phalange (făl′ănj), *n. Anat., etc.* a phalanx. [back-formation from PHALANGES]

phalangeal (fə lăn′jĭ əl), *adj. Anat., etc.* pertaining to, or of the nature of, a phalanx or phalanges.

phalanger (fə lăn′jə), *n.* any of numerous arboreal marsupials constituting the family *Phalangeridae,* of the Australian region, esp. those of the genus *Phalanger* (or *Cuscus*), as *P. maculatus* (**spotted phalanger**). [t. NL, der. Gk *phálanx* bone of finger or toe; with reference to the webbed digits of the hind feet]

phalanges (fă lăn′jēz), *n.* pl. of **phalanx.**

phalanstery (făl′ən stə rĭ, -strĭ), *n., pl.* **-steries. 1.** (in Fourierism) **a.** the buildings occupied by a phalanx. **b.** the community itself. **2.** any similar association, or the buildings they occupy. [t. F: m. *phalanstère,* b. *phalange* phalanx and *monastère* monastery] —**phalansterian** (fă′lən stĭə′rĭ ən), *adj., n.*

phalanx (făl′ăngks), *n., pl.* **phalanxes** (făl′ăngk sĭz), **phalanges** (fă lăn′jēz). **1.** (in ancient Greece) a body of heavily armed infantry formed in ranks and files close and deep, with shields joined and long spears overlapping. **2.** any body of troops in close array. **3.** a compact or closely massed body of persons, animals, or things. **4.** a number of persons, etc., united for a common purpose. **5.** (in Fourierism) a group of about 1800 persons, living together and holding their property in common. **6.** *Anat., Zool.* any of the bones of the fingers or toes. See diag. under **skeleton. 7.** *Bot.* a bundle of stamens, joined by their filaments. [t. L, t. Gk (defs 1, 2, 6)]

phalarope (făl′ə rōp′), *n.* any of three species of small aquatic birds constituting the family *Phalaropodidae,* resembling sandpipers but having lobate toes, as *Phalaropus fulicarius* of both Old and New Worlds. [t. F, t. NL: m. *Phalaropūs* (genus name), f. *phalaro-* (comb. form repr. Gk *phalāris* coot) + *-pūs* (t. Gk: m. *poús* foot)]

phallic (făl′ĭk), *adj.* of or pertaining to the phallus or phallicism. Also, **phal′lical.** [t. Gk: m. s. *phallikós*]

phallicism (făl′ĭ sĭz′əm), *n.* worship of the phallus. Also, **phallism.** —**phal′licist,** *n.*

phallus (făl′əs), *n., pl.* **phalluses, phalli** (făl′ī). **1.** an image of the male reproductive organ, symbolizing in certain religious systems the generative power in nature, esp. that carried in procession in ancient festivals of Dionysus or Bacchus. **2.** *Anat.* the penis, clitoris, or the sexually undifferentiated embryonic organ out of which each develops. [t. L, t. Gk: m. *phallós*]

-phane, a word element indicating apparent similarity to some particular substance. [t. Gk: m. *phan-,* s. *phaínein* shine, (in pass.) appear]

phanerogam (făn′ə rō găm′), *n. Bot.* **1.** any of the *Phanerogamia,* an old primary division of plants comprising those having reproductive organs (stamens and pistils). **2.** a flowering plant or seed plant (opposed to *cryptogam*). [t. NL: s. *phanerogamus,* f. Gk: *phaneró(s)* visible + m. *gámos* marriage] —**phan′erogam′ic, phanerogamous** (făn′ə rŏg′ə məs), *adj.*

phantasm (făn′tăz′əm), *n.* **1.** an apparition or spectre. **2.** a creation of the imagination or fancy. **3.** an illusive likeness of something. **4.** a mental image or representation of a real object. Also, **fantasm.** [t. LL: m. *phantasma,* t. Gk. Cf. PHANTOM] —**Syn. 1.** See **apparition.**

phantasma (făn tăz′mə), *n., pl.* **-mata** (-mə tə). phantasm.

phantasmagoria (făn′tăz mə gô′rĭ ə), *n.* **1.** a shifting series of phantasms, illusions, or deceptive appearances, as in a dream or as created by the imagination. **2.** a changing scene made up of many elements. **3.** an exhibition of optical illusions produced by a magic lantern or the like, as one in which figures increase or diminish in size, dissolve, pass into each other, etc. [t. NL, f. Gk: *phántasma* phantasm + (appar.) m. *agorá* assembly] —**phan′tasmago′rial, phantasmagoric** (făn′tăz mə gŏ′rĭk), **phantasmagorical** (făn′tăz mə gŏ′rĭ kl), *adj.*

phantasmagory (făn′tăz mə gə rĭ), *n., pl.* **-ries.** phantasmagoria.

phantasmal (făn tăz′məl), *adj.* pertaining to or of the nature of a phantasm; unreal; illusive; spectral. Also, **phantas′mic.**

phantasy (făn′tə sĭ), *n., pl.* **-sies.** fantasy.

phantom (făn′təm), *n.* **1.** an image appearing in a dream or formed in the mind. **2.** an apparition or spectre. **3.** a thing or person that is little more than an appearance or show. **4.** an appearance without material substance. —*adj.* **5.** of the nature of a phantom; unreal; illusive; spectral. [ME *fantosme,* t. OF, var. of *fantasme,* g. LL *phantasma* PHANTASM] —**Syn. 1.** See **apparition.**

phantom limb pains, *Pathol.* pains seemingly occurring in part of a limb which has been amputated.

-phany, a noun termination meaning 'appearance', 'manifestation', as of deity or a supernatural being, as in *angelophany, Christophany, epiphany, satanophany.* [t. Gk: m. s. *-pháneia* (sometimes *-phánia*). See -PHANE]

Phar., 1. pharmaceutical. **2.** pharmacopoeia. **3.** pharmacy. Also, **phar.**

Pharaoh (fēə′rō), *n.* a title of the ancient Egyptian kings. [ME *Pharao,* OE *Pharaon,* t. L, t. Gk, t. Heb.: m. *Phar'ōh,* t. Egyptian: m. *per-'o* great house] —**Pharaonic** (fēə rŏn′ĭk), *adj.*

Pharisaic (fă′rĭ sā′ĭk), *adj.* **1.** of or pertaining to the Pharisees. **2.** (*l.c.*) Also, **phar′isa′ical.** *New Testament.* practising or advocating strict observance of external forms and ceremonies of religion without regard to its spirit; self-righteous; hypocritical. —**phar′isa′ically,** *adv.*

Pharisaism (fă′rĭ sā ĭz′əm), *n.* **1.** the doctrine and practice of the Pharisees. **2.** (*l.c.*) rigid observance of external forms of religion without genuine piety; hypocrisy. Also, **Phariseeism** (fă′rĭ sē ĭz′əm).

Pharisee (fă′rĭ sē′), *n.* **1.** one of an ancient Jewish sect which observed strictly the traditions and the written law, seeking its interpretation, its members attempting self-perfection for the coming of the Messiah. **2.** (*l.c.*) a pharisaic, self-righteous, or hypocritical person. [ME *pharise,* ME and OE *farisē,* t. L: (m.) s. *pharisēus,* t. Gk: m. *pharisaîos,* t. Aram.: m. *p'rīshaiyā* separated]

Pharm., 1. pharmaceutic. **2.** pharmacopoeia. **3.** pharmacy. Also, **pharm.**

pharmaceutical (fă′mə syōō′tĭ kl), *adj.* pertaining to pharmacy. Also, **pharmaceutic.** [t. L: s. *pharmaceuticus,* t. Gk: m. *pharmakeutikós*] —**phar′maceu′tically,** *adv.*

pharmaceutics (fä′mə syōō′tĭks), *n.* pharmacy (def. 1). [pl. of PHARMACEUTIC. See -ICS]

pharmacist (fä′mə sĭst), *n.* one skilled in pharmacy; a druggist or pharmaceutical chemist. Also, **pharmaceutist** (fä′mə syōō′tĭst).

pharmacolite (fä′mə kə līt′), *n.* a mineral, hydrous arsenate of calcium, which crystallizes in the monoclinic system.

pharmacology (fä′mə kŏl′ə jĭ), *n.* the science of drugs, their preparation, uses, and effects. [t. NL: m. s. *pharmacologia,* f. Gk: m. *phármako(n)* drug + *-logia* -LOGY] —**pharmacological** (fä′mə kə lŏj′ĭ kl), *adj.* —**phar′macol′ogist,** *n.*

pharmacopoeia (fä′mə kə pē′ə), *n.* **1.** a book, esp. one published by authority, containing a list of drugs and medicines and describing their preparation, properties, uses, etc. **2.** a stock of drugs. [t. NL, t. Gk: m. *pharmakopoiía* art of preparing drugs] —**phar′macopoe′ial,** *adj.*

pharmacy (fä′mə sĭ), *n., pl.* **-cies. 1.** the art or practice of preparing and dispensing drugs and medicines. **2.** the occupation of a druggist. **3.** a dispensary; chemist's shop. [t. LL: m. s. *pharmacia,* t. Gk: m. *pharmakeía* the practice of a druggist; r. ME *fermacie,* t. OF]

Pharos (fêə′rŏs), *n.* **1.** a small peninsula in N Egypt at Alexandria: in ancient times it was an island on which a lighthouse was built. **2.** this lighthouse. See **Seven Wonders of the World. 3.** any lighthouse or beacon to direct seamen.

Pharsalus (fä să′ləs), *n.* an ancient city in central Greece, in Thessaly: site of Pompey's defeat by Caesar, 48 B.C. Modern, **Pharsala** (fä′sə lə).

pharyngeal (fă′rĭn jē′əl), *adj.* of, pertaining to, or connected with the pharynx. Also, **pharyngal** (fə rĭng′gl).

pharyngitis (fă′rĭn jī′tĭs), *n. Pathol.* inflammation of the mucous membrane of the pharynx. [t. NL: f. s. Gk *phárynx* throat + *-ītis* -ITIS]

pharyngo-, a word element meaning 'pharynx'. [t. Gk, comb. form of *phárynx* throat]

pharyngology (fă′rĭng gŏl′ə jĭ), *n.* the science of the pharynx and its diseases.

pharyngoscope (fə rĭng′gə skōp′), *n.* an instrument for inspecting the pharynx.

pharynx (fă′rĭngks), *n., pl.* **pharynges** (fă rĭn′jēz), **pharynxes.** *Anat.* the tube or cavity, with its surrounding membrane and muscles, which connects the mouth and nasal passages with the oesophagus. [t. NL, t. Gk: throat]

phase (fāz), *n.* **1.** any of the appearances or aspects in which a thing of varying modes or conditions manifests itself to the eye or mind. **2.** a stage of change or development. **3.** *Astron.* **a.** the particular appearance presented by a planet, etc., at a given time. **b.** one of the recurring appearances or states of the moon or a planet in respect to the form, or the absence, of its illuminated disc: *the phases of the moon.* **4.** *Biol.* an aspect of or stage in meiosis or mitosis. **5.** *Zool.* any of the stages of development of certain animals which take on a different colour according to the breeding condition. **6.** *Chem.* a mechanically separate, homogeneous part of a heterogeneous system: *the solid, liquid, and gaseous phases of a substance.* **7.** *Physics.* a particular stage or point of advancement in a cycle; the fractional part of the period through which the time has advanced, measured from some arbitrary origin. **8.** *Elect.* one of the circuits in a system or apparatus in which there are two or more alternating voltages displaced in phase (def. 7). —*v.t.* **9.** to plan or order (services, materials, etc.) to be available when required. **10.** to introduce (into a system or the like) in stages. **11.** to adjust or synchronize (with another element in a system). **12. phase in,** to introduce gradually and synchronize into a system, or the like. **13. phase out,** to withdraw (something) gradually from a system. [back-formation from *phases,* pl. of PHASIS]

phase contrast microscope, *Optics.* a type of microscope for examining colourless transparent objects, which depends on phase differences of the transmitted light rays.

phase modulation, *Electronics.* radio transmission in which the carrier wave is modulated by changing its phase to transmit the amplitude and pitch of the signal.

phase rule, *Chem.* a law which states that for a heterogeneous system in equilibrium, the sum of the number of phases and the number of degrees of freedom is equal to the number of components plus 2.

-phasia, a word element referring to disordered speech, as in *aphasia.* Also, **-phasy.** [t. Gk, der. *phánai* speak]

phasis (fā′sĭs), *n., pl.* **-ses** (-sēz). a phase; an appearance; a manner, stage, or aspect of being. [t. L, t. Gk]

Ph.D., (L *Philosophiae Doctor*) Doctor of Philosophy.

pheasant (fĕz′ənt), *n.* **1.** any of various large, long-tailed, gallinaceous birds of the genus *Phasianus* and allied genera, orig. natives of Asia, esp. the **common pheasant** *P. colchicus.* **2.** any of various gallinaceous birds, as, in the southern U.S., the ruffed grouse. [ME *fesant,* t. AF, var. of OF *faisan,* t. Pr., t. L: m. s. *phāsiānus,* t. Gk: m. *phāsiānós* Phasian (bird)]

Common pheasant, *Phasianus colchicus* (Ab. 4 ft long)

pheasant's-eye (fĕz′ənts ī′), *n.* **1.** an annual ranunculaceous herb with bright red flowers, *Adonis autumnalis,* a native of S Europe and SW Asia but sometimes found as a cornfield weed elsewhere. **2.** a subspecies of a variable bulbous amaryllidaceous plant *Narcissus poeticus,* formerly cultivated but now replaced by other forms and hybrids.

Pheidippides (fī dĭp′ĭ dēz′), *n.* the Athenian runner who secured aid from Sparta in the struggle between the Athenians and the Persians, 490 B.C. Also, **Phidippides.**

phellem (fĕl′əm), *n. Bot.* the layer of dead cork cells produced on the outside of a plane by the phellogen.

phelloderm (fĕl′ō dûm′), *n. Bot.* a layer of tissue in certain plants, formed from the inner cells of phellogen, and consisting usually of chlorenchyma. [f. Gk *phellό(s)* cork + -DERM] —**phel′loder′mal,** *adj.*

phellogen (fĕl′ə jən), *n. Bot.* a layer of tissue or secondary meristem external to the true cambium and giving rise to cork tissue on the outside and phelloderm on the inside; cork cambium. [f. Gk *phellό(s)* cork + -GEN] —**phellogenetic** (fĕl′ə jĭ nĕt′ĭk), **phellogenic** (fĕl′ə jĕn′ĭk), *adj.*

phen-, a word element used in chemical terms to indicate derivation from benzene: sometimes used with particular reference to phenol. Also, before consonants, **pheno-.** [t. Gk: m. *phaino-* shining; with reference orig. to products from the manufacture of illuminating gas]

phenacaine (fē′nə kān′, fĕn′ə-), *n. Pharm.* a local anaesthetic, $C_{18}H_{22}N_2O_2HCl$, resembling cocaine in its action, used chiefly for the eye. [f. PHEN- + A(CET)- + (CO)CAINE]

phenacetin (fĭ năs′ĭ tĭn), *n. Pharm.* a crystalline organic compound used as an antipyretic, etc.

phenacite (fĕn′ə sīt′), *n.* a vitreous mineral, beryllium silicate, Be_2SiO_4, occurring in crystals, sometimes used as a gem. Also, **phenakite** (fĕn′ə kīt′). [f. m. s. Gk *phénax* cheat, imposter + -ITE[1]]

phenanthrene (fĭ năn′thrēn), *n. Chem.* a colourless shiny crystalline isomer of anthracene, $C_{14}H_{10}$, derived from coal tar, and used in the dye and drug industries. [f. PHEN- + ANTHR(ACITE) + -ENE]

phenazine (fĕn′ə zēn′), *n. Chem.* a yellowish crystalline organic compound, $C_{12}H_8N_2$, some derivatives of which are important dyes. [f. PHEN- + AZ(O)- + -INE[2]]

phenetidine (fĭ nĕt′ĭ dēn′), *n. Chem.* a liquid organic compound, $C_8H_{11}NO$, a derivative of phenetole, used in making phenacetin, etc. [f. PHENET(OLE) + -ID[2] + -INE[2]]

phenetole (fĕn′ĭ tōl′, -tŏl′), *n. Chem.* the ethyl ether of phenol, $C_6H_5OC_2H_5$, a colourless volatile aromatic liquid. [f. PHEN(YL) + ET(HYL) + -OLE]

phenix (fē′nĭks), *n. U.S.* phoenix.

pheno-, var. of **phen-,** before consonants.

phenobarbitone (fē′nō bä′bĭ tōn′), *n.* a hypnotic, $C_{12}H_{12}O_3N_2$, a white, odourless powder; Luminal. Also, **phenobarbital** (fē′nō bä′bĭ tl).

phenocryst (fē′nə krĭst, fĕn′ə-), *n. Geol.* any of the conspicuous crystals in a porphyritic rock. [f. PHENO- + CRYST(AL)]

phenol (fē′nŏl), *n. Chem.* **1.** carbolic acid, C_6H_5OH, a hydroxyl derivative of benzene used as a disinfectant, antiseptic, and in organic synthesis. **2.** any analogous hydroxyl derivative of benzene. [f. PHEN- + -OL[1]] —**phenolic** (fĭ nŏl′ĭk), *adj.*

phenolate (fē′nə lāt′), *n. Chem.* a salt of phenol.

phenolic resin, any of a class of synthetic thermosetting resins produced by the condensation of phenol or its derivatives with formaldehyde; used in paints, varnishes, adhesives, and plastics.

phenology (fĭ nŏl′ə jĭ), *n.* the science dealing with the influence of climate on the recurrence of such annual phenomena of animal and plant life as bird migrations, budding, etc. [short for PHENOMENOLOGY] —**phenological** (fē′nə lŏj′ĭ kl), *adj.* —**phe′nolog′ically,** *adv.* —**phenol′ogist,** *n.*

phenolphthalein (fē′nŏl fthăl′ĭ ĭn, -fthăl′ēn), *n.* a white crystalline compound, $C_{20}H_{14}O_4$, used as an indicator in acid-base titration and as a laxative.

phenomena (fĭ nŏm′ĭ nə), *n.* pl. of **phenomenon.**

phenomenal (fĭ nŏm′ĭ nəl), *adj.* **1.** extraordinary or prodigious: *phenomenal speed.* **2.** of or pertaining to a phenomenon or phenomena. **3.** of the nature of a phenomenon; cognizable by the senses. —**phenom′en-ally,** *adv.*

phenomenalism (fĭ nŏm′ĭ nə lĭz′əm), *n. Philos.* **1.** the manner of thinking that considers things as phenomena only. Cf. **positivism. 2.** the philosophical doctrine that phenomena are the only objects of knowledge, or that phenomena are the only realities. —**phenom′enalist,** *n.* —**phenom′enalis′tic,** *adj.*

phenomenology (fĭ nŏm′ĭ nŏl′ə jĭ), *n. Philos.* **1.** the science of phenomena, as distinguished from ontology or the science of being. **2.** the school of Husserl, which stresses the careful description of phenomena in all domains of experience without regard to traditional epistemological questions.

phenomenon (fĭ nŏm′ĭ nən), *n., pl.* **-na** (-nə). **1.** a fact, occurrence, or circumstance observed or observable: *the phenomena of nature.* **2.** something that impresses the observer as extraordinary; a remarkable thing or person. **3.** *Philos.* **a.** an appearance or immediate object of awareness in experience. **b.** (in Kantian philosophy) a thing as it appears to, and is constructed by, us, as distinguished from a noumenon, or thing in itself. [t. LL: m. *phaenomenon,* t. Gk: m. *phainómenon,* prop. neut. ppr. (that which is) appearing] —**Syn. 2.** prodigy, marvel, wonder.

phenotype (fē′nō tīp′), *n. Genetics.* the observable hereditary characters arising from the interaction of the genotype with its environment. Organisms with the same phenotype look alike but may breed differently because of dominance. [f. PHENO(MENON) + TYPE]

phenoxide (fĭ nŏk′sīd), *n. Chem.* phenolate.

phenyl (fĕn′ĭl, fē′nĭl), *n. Chem.* a univalent radical, C_6H_5, from benzene. [t. F: m. *phényle.* See PHEN, -YL]

phenyl acetate, *Chem.* a colourless liquid, $C_6H_5COOCH_3$, used as a solvent.

phenylalanine (fĕn′ĭl ăl′ə nēn′), *n. Chem., Biochem.* an amino acid, $C_6H_5CH_2CH(NH_2)COOH$, occurring in proteins.

phenylene (fĕn′ĭ lēn′, fē′nĭ-), *n. Chem.* a bivalent organic radical, C_6H_4, derived from benzene by removal of two of its hydrogen atoms.

phew (fyōō), *interj.* (an exclamation of disgust, impatience, exhaustion, surprise, relief, etc.)

phi (fī), *n.* the twenty-first letter (Φ, φ) of the Greek alphabet.

phial (fī′əl), *n., v.,* **-alled, -alling.** —*n.* **1.** a small vessel as of glass, for liquids. **2.** vial (def. 1). —*v.t.* **3.** to put into or keep in a phial. [ME *fiole,* t. OF, t. LL: m. *fiola,* L *phiala,* t. Gk: m. *phiálē* saucer-like drinking vessel]

Phi Beta Kappa (fī′ bē′tə kăp′ə), a society in the U.S., membership being based on high academic records. It is the oldest American fraternity, founded in 1776.

Phidian (fĭd′ĭ ən), *adj.* of, associated with, or following the style of Phidias, exemplified in the Parthenon.

Phidias (fĭd′ĭ ăs′), *n. c.* 500–*c.* 432 B.C., Greek sculptor.

Phidippides (fĭ dĭp′ĭ dēz′), *n.* Pheidippides.

phil-, a word element meaning 'loving', as in *philanthropy.* Also, **philo-.** [t. Gk, comb. form of *phílos* loving, dear]

-phil, a word element meaning 'loving', 'friendly', or 'lover', 'friend', serving to form adjectives and nouns, as *Anglophil, bibliophil.* Also, **-phile.** [t. L: m. s. *-philus, -phila,* t. Gk: m. *-phílos* dear, beloved, occurring in proper names. Cf. F *-phile*]

Phil., 1. Philemon. 2. Philip. 3. Philippians. 4. Philippine.

phil., 1. philosophical. 2. philosophy.

Phila., Philadelphia.

Philadelphia (fĭl′ə dĕl′fyə), *n.* a city in the U.S., in SE Pennsylvania, on the Delaware river. 2,002,512 (1960).

Philae (fī′lē), *n.* an island in the Nile, in Upper Egypt: the site of ancient temples; submerged except during months the sluices of the Aswan dam are open.

philander (fĭ lăn′də), *v.i.* (of a man) to make love, esp. without serious intentions; carry on a flirtation. [t. Gk: m. s. *phílandros* man-loving (person), later used in fiction as proper name, given to a lover] —**philan′derer,** *n.*

philanthropic (fĭl′ən thrŏp′ĭk), *adj.* of, pertaining to, or characterized by philanthropy; benevolent. Also, **phil′anthrop′ical.** —**phil′anthrop′ically,** *adv.*

philanthropist (fĭ lăn′thrə pĭst), *n.* one who practises philanthropy. [f. PHILANTHROP(Y) + -IST]

philanthropy (fĭ lăn′thrə pĭ), *n., pl.* **-pies. 1.** love of mankind, esp. as manifested in deeds of practical beneficence. **2.** a philanthropic action, work, institution, or the like. [t. LL: m. s. *philanthrōpia,* t. Gk]

philately (fĭ lăt′ə lĭ), *n.* the collecting and study of postage stamps, impressed stamps, stamped envelopes, postmarks, postcards, covers and similar material. [t. F: m. *philatélie,* f. *phil-* PHIL- + m. Gk *atéleia* exemption from charge] —**philatelic** (fĭl′ə tĕl′ĭk), **phil′atel′ical,** *adj.* —**phil′atel′ically,** *adv.* —**philatelist** (fĭ lăt′ə lĭst), *n.*

-phile, var. of **-phil.**

Philem., Philemon.

Philemon (fĭ lē′mŏn), *n.* **1.** *Gk Legend.* See **Baucis and Philemon. 2. the Epistle of Paul to Philemon,** a brief New Testament epistle, written by Paul.

philharmonic (fĭl′ä mŏn′ĭk), *adj.* fond of music; music-loving: used esp. in the name of certain musical societies (**Philharmonic Societies**) and hence applied to their concerts (**philharmonic concerts**). [t. F: m. *philharmonique.* See PHIL-, HARMONIC]

philhellene (fĭl′hĕl′ēn), *n.* a friend or supporter of the Greeks. Also, **philhellenist** (fĭl hĕl′ĭ nĭst). —**philhellenic** (fĭl′hĕ lē′nĭk), *adj.* —**philhellenism** (fĭl hĕl′ĭnĭz′əm), *n.*

philibeg (fĭl′ĭ bĕg′), *n.* filibeg.

Philip (fĭl′ĭp), *n.* **1.** one of the twelve apostles, Mark 3:18; John 1:43–48, 6:5–7, etc. **2.** one of 'the Seven' appointed to oversee the Hellenists in the Jerusalem Church (Acts 6); later an evangelist or missionary (Acts 8:26–40). **3. King** (*Metacom, Metacomet*), died 1676, American Indian chief: leader in a war against the New England colonists 1675–76 (son of Massasoit). **4. Prince** (*Duke of Edinburgh*), born 1921, husband of Queen Elizabeth II of England.

Philip II, 1. 382–336 B.C., king of Macedonia 359–336 B.C. (father of Alexander the Great). **2.** Also, **Philip Augustus.** 1165–1223, King of France 1180–1223. **3.** 1527–98, king of Spain 1556–98, who sent the Armada against England; husband of Mary I of England.

Philip IV ('*Philip the Fair*'), 1268–1314, king of France 1285–1314.

Philip V, 1683–1746, king of Spain 1700–46.

Philip VI, 1293–1350, king of France 1328–50, the first of the Valois family of French rulers.

Philip., Philippians.

Philippe (*Fr.* fē lĕp′), *n.* French name for Philip.

Philippeville (fĭl′ĭp vĭl; *Fr.* fē lĕp vĕl′), *n.* a seaport in NE Algeria. 88,000 (1960).

Philippi (fĭ lĭp′ī), *n.* a ruined city in NE Greece, in Macedonia: Octavian and Mark Antony defeated Brutus and Cassius here, 42 B.C.; the site of one of the first Christian Churches in Europe, founded by St Paul. —**Philippian** (fĭ lĭp′ĭ ən), *adj., n.*

Philippians (fĭ lĭp′ĭ ənz), *n.* the epistle of the apostle Paul to the Christian community in Philippi, in the New Testament.

Philippic (fĭ lĭp′ĭk), *n.* **1.** any of the orations delivered by Demosthenes, the Athenian orator, in the 4th century B.C., against Philip, king of Macedon. **2.** (*l.c.*) any discourse or speech of bitter denunciaton. [t. L: s. *Philippicus,* t. Gk: m. *Philippikós* pertaining to Philip]

philippina (fĭl′ĭ pē′nə), *n.* philopoena. Also, **philippine.**

Philippine (fĭl′ĭ pēn′), *adj.* of or pertaining to the Philippines or their inhabitants. Also, **Filipine.** [t. Sp.: m. *Filipino*]

Philippines (fĭl′ĭ pēnz′), *n.pl.* an archipelago of 7083 islands in the Pacific, SE of China: formerly under the guardianship of the U.S.: now an independent republic. 27,087,685 pop. (1960); 114,830 sq. mi. *Cap.:* Manila. (See **Quezon City**). Also, **Philippine Islands.** Official name, **Republic of the Philippines.**

Philippopolis (fĭl′ĭ pŏp′ə lĭs), *n.* Greek name of **Plovdiv.**

Philips (fĭl′ĭps), *n.* **Ambrose,** 1675?–1749, English poet and dramatist.

Philip the Good, 1396–1467, duke of Burgundy 1419–67.

Philistia (fĭ lĭs′tyə), *n.* an ancient country on the E coast of the Mediterranean.

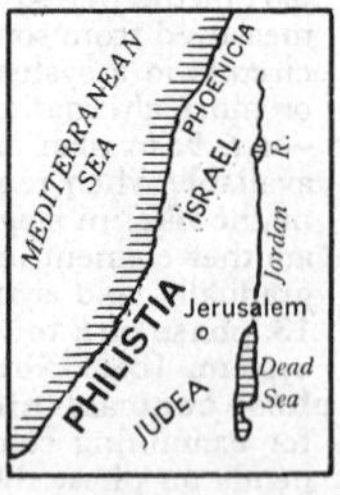

Philistine (fĭl′ĭ stīn′), *n.* **1.** a native or inhabitant of Philistia. **2.** one looked down upon as lacking in and indifferent to culture, aesthetic refinement, etc., or contentedly commonplace in ideas and tastes. —*adj.* **3.** lacking in culture; commonplace. **4.** of or belonging to the ancient Philistines. [ME, t. LL: m. s. *Philistīnī,* pl., t. LGk: m. *Philistînoi,* t. Heb.: m. *p'lishtīm*] —**Philistinism** (fĭl′ĭ stĭ nĭz′əm), *n.*

MEDITERRANEAN SEA
PHOENICIA
ISRAEL
Jordan R.
PHILISTIA
Jerusalem
Dead Sea
JUDEA

Philistia

Phillips (fĭl′ĭps), *n.* **Stephen,** 1868–1915, English poet and dramatist.

philo-, var. of **phil-,** before consonants, as in *philosopher.*

Philoctetes (fĭl′ək tē′tēz), *n. Gk Legend.* the armour-bearer of Hercules, and the archer whose poisoned arrow caused the death of Paris in the Trojan War.

philodendron (fĭl′ə dĕn′drən), *n.* a tropical American climbing plant of the family *Araceae,* usually with smooth, shiny, evergreen leaves, often used as an ornamental house plant. [t. NL. See PHILO-, -DENDRON]

philogyny (fĭ lŏj′ĭ nĭ), *n.* love of women. [t. Gk: m. s. *philogynía*] —**philog′ynist,** *n.* —**philog′ynous,** *adj.*

Philo Judaeus (fī′lō jo͞o dē′əs), *c.* 20 B.C.–A.D. *c.* 50, Jewish philosopher, influenced by Greek philosophy.

philol., 1. philological. 2. philology.

philologian (fĭl′ə lō′jĭ ən), *n.* a philologist.

philology (fĭ lŏl′ə jĭ), *n.* **1.** the study of written records, the establishment of their authenticity and their original form, and the determination of their meaning. **2.** linguistics. [ME *philologie*, t. L: m. *philologia*, t. Gk: love of learning and literature] —**philologic** (fĭl′ə lŏj′ĭk), **phil′olog′ical,** *adj.* —**phil′olog′ically,** *adv.* —**philol′ogist, philol′oger,** *n.*

philomel (fĭl′ə mĕl′), *n. Poetic.* the nightingale. Also, **phil′ome′la.** [ME, t. L: s. *philomēla*, t. Gk]

Philomela (fĭl′ō mē′lə), *n.* **1.** *Gk Legend.* the daughter of a king of Athens. Tereus, her sister Procne's husband, raped her and cut out her tongue. Philomela was turned into a nightingale. **2.** (*l.c.*) philomel. [cf. PHILOMEL]

philopoena (fĭl′ə pē′nə), *n.* **1.** a friendly or playful practice by which when two persons have by agreement shared a nut with two kernels, or the like, the person who fails subsequently to meet certain conditions is bound to pay the other a forfeit. **2.** the thing shared. **3.** the forfeit paid. Also, **philopena, philippina, philippine.** [alter. of G *Vielliebchen* sweetheart, conformed along pseudo-classical lines to PHILO- + L *poena* penalty. Cf. F *philippine*]

philoprogenitive (fĭl′ō prō jĕn′ĭ tĭv), *adj.* **1.** fond of young children, esp. one's own. **2.** inclined towards having offspring.

philos., 1. philosopher. 2. philosophical. 3. philosophy.

philosopher (fĭ lŏs′ə fə), *n.* **1.** one versed in philosophy. **2.** a person who regulates his life, actions, judgements, utterances, etc., by the light of philosophy or reason. **3.** one who is philosophic, esp. in trying circumstances. **4.** an alchemist or occult scientist. [ME *philosophre*, t. AF; r. OE *philosoph*, t. L: s. *philosophus*, t. Gk: m. *philósophos* lover of wisdom]

philosopher's stone, *Alchemy.* an imaginary substance or preparation believed capable of transmuting baser metals into gold or silver, and of prolonging life.

philosopher's wool, *Old Chem.* flocculent zinc oxide.

philosophical (fĭl′ə sŏf′ĭ kl), *adj.* **1.** of or pertaining to philosophy: *philosophical studies.* **2.** versed in or occupied with philosophy, as persons. **3.** proper to or befitting a philosopher. **4.** rationally or sensibly calm in trying circumstances: *a philosophical acceptance of necessity.* **5.** (formerly) of or pertaining to natural philosophy or physical science. Also, **philosophic.** —**phil′osoph′ically,** *adv.*

philosophism (fĭ lŏs′ə fĭz′əm), *n.* **1.** philosophizing. **2.** the affectation of philosophy; spurious philosophy.

philosophize (fĭ lŏs′ə fīz′), *v.i.*, **-phized, -phizing. 1.** to speculate or theorize; moralize. **2.** to think or reason as a philosopher. Also, **philosophise.** —**philos′ophiz′er,** *n.*

philosophy (fĭ lŏs′ə fĭ), *n., pl.* **-phies. 1.** the study or science of the truths or principles underlying all knowledge and being (or reality). **2.** any one of the three branches (natural philosophy, moral philosophy, and metaphysical philosophy) accepted as composing this science. **3.** a system of philosophical doctrine: *the philosophy of Spinoza.* **4.** metaphysical science; metaphysics. **5.** the study or science of the principles of a particular branch or subject of knowledge: *the philosophy of history.* **6.** a system of principles for guidance in practical affairs. **7.** philosophical spirit or attitude; wise composure throughout the vicissitudes of life. [ME *philosophie*, t. L: m. *philosophia*, t. Gk: lit., love of wisdom]

-philous, a word element used as an adjective termination meaning 'loving', as in *anthophilous, dendrophilous, heliophilous.* [t. L: m. *-philus*, t. Gk: m. *-phílos*]

Phil. Soc., Philological Society (of London).

Phil. Trans., the Philosophical Transactions of the Royal Society of London.

philtre (fĭl′tə), *n., v.*, **-tred, -tring.** —*n.* **1.** a potion, drug, or the like, supposed to induce love. **2.** a magic potion for any purpose. —*v.t.* **3.** to charm with a philtre. Also, *esp. U.S.*, **philter.** [t. F: m. *philtre*, t. L: m. *philtrum*, t. Gk: m. *phíltron* love charm]

Phiz (fĭz), *n.* (*Hablot Knight Browne*), 1815–82, English artist and illustrator. [nickname: ? from *phiz*, 19th-century slang abbrev. for physiognomy]

phlebitis (flĭ bī′tĭs), *n. Pathol.* inflammation of a vein. [t. NL, f. Gk: s. *phléps* vein + *-ītis* -ITIS] —**phlebitic** (flĭ bĭt′ĭk), *adj.*

phlebosclerosis (flĕb′ō sklĭə rō′sĭs), *n. Pathol.* sclerosis or hardening of the walls of veins. [f. *phlebo-* (t. Gk, comb. form of *phléps* vein) + SCLEROSIS]

phlebotomize (flĭ bŏt′ə mīz′), *v.t.*, **-mized, -mizing.** to subject to phlebotomy; bleed. Also, **phlebotomise.**

phlebotomy (flĭ bŏt′ə mĭ), *n., pl.* **-mies.** *Med.* the act or practice of opening a vein for letting blood; bleeding. [ME *flebotomie*, t. LL: m. *phlebotomia*, t. Gk] —**phlebot′omist,** *n.*

Phlegethon (flĕg′ĭ thŏn′), *n.* **1.** *Gk Myth.* a fabled river of fire in Hades. **2.** (*cap. or l.c.*) a stream of fire or fiery light. [t. Gk: lit., burning, blazing]

phlegm (flĕm), *n.* **1.** *Physiol.* the thick mucus secreted in the respiratory passages and discharged by coughing, etc., esp. that occurring in the lungs and throat passages during a cold, etc. **2.** (in the old physiology) that one of the four humours supposed when predominant to cause sluggishness or apathy. **3.** sluggishness or apathy. **4.** coolness or self-possession. [ME *fleume*, t. OF, g. LL *phlegma*, t. Gk: flame, clammy humour] —**phlegm′y,** *adj.*

phlegmatic (flĕg măt′ĭk), *adj.* **1.** not easily excited to action or feeling; sluggish or apathetic. **2.** cool or self-possessed. **3.** of the nature of or abounding in phlegm. Also, **phlegmat′ical.** [t. LL: s. *phlegmaticus*, t. Gk: m. *phlegmatikós*] —**phlegmat′ically,** *adv.*

phloem (flō′ĕm), *n. Bot.* that part of a vascular bundle not included in the xylem, including sieve tubes and companion cells, parenchyma, secretory cells, etc.; bast tissue; liber. [t. G, f. Gk: s. *phlóos* bark + *-ēm(a)* (passive suffix)]

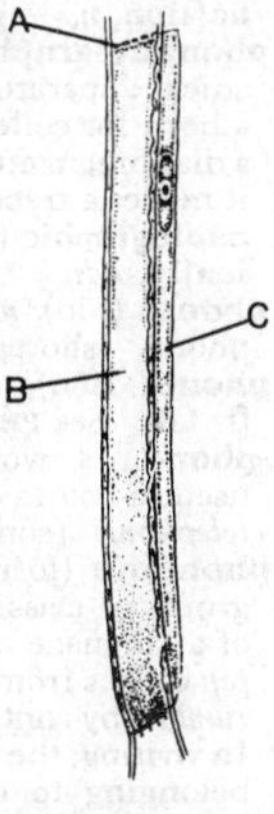

Portions of phloem, showing oblique and transverse striation of the cell walls: A, Sieve plate; B, Sieve tube segment; C, Companion cell

phlogistic (flō jĭs′tĭk), *adj.* **1.** *Pathol.* inflammatory. **2.** *Old Chem.* pertaining to or consisting of phlogiston.

phlogisticated air, *Old Chem.* nitrogen.

phlogiston (flō jĭs′tən), *n. Old Chem.* a non-existent chemical which, previous to the discovery of oxygen, was thought to be released during combustion. [t. NL, t. Gk: (neut.) inflammable]

phlogopite (flŏg′ə pīt′), *n.* a mica, $KMg_3AlSi_3O_{10}(OH)_2$, usually yellowish brown, but sometimes reddish brown. [f. s. Gk *phlogōpós* fiery-looking + ITE[1]]

phlorizin (flô′rĭ zĭn, flŏ′-, flə rī′zĭn), *n. Chem.* a bitter, crystalline glucoside, $C_{21}H_{24}O_{10}$, obtained from the root bark of the apple, pear, cherry, etc., and at one time used as a tonic and antiperiodic. Also, **phlorhizin, phlorrhizin, phloridzin** (flə rĭd′zĭn). [f. s. Gk *phlóos* bark + m. s. Gk *rhiza* root + -IN[2]]

phlox (flŏks), *n. Bot.* **1.** any of the herbs constituting the polemoniaceous genus *Phlox*, native in North America, many of which are cultivated for their showy flowers of various colours. **2.** the flower of these plants. [t. L, t. Gk: kind of plant, orig., flame]

phlyctena (flĭk tē′nə), *n., pl.* **-nae** (-nē). *Pathol.* a small vesicle, blister, or pustule. Also, **phlyctaena.** [t. NL, t. Gk: m. *phlýktaina*]

Phnom Penh (nŏm′ pĕn′), Pnom Penh.

-phobe, a word element used as a noun termination meaning 'one who fears or dreads', and often implying aversion or hatred, as in *Anglophobe, Russophobe.* [t. F, t. L: m. *-phobus* fearing, t. Gk: m. *-phobos*]

phobia (fō′byə), *n.* any obsessing or morbid fear or dread. [independent use of -PHOBIA] —**pho′bic,** *adj.*

-phobia, a word element used as a noun termination meaning 'fear' or 'dread', often morbid, or with implication of aversion or hatred, as in *agoraphobia, Anglophobia, hydrophobia, monophobia.* [t. L, t. Gk]

phocine (fō′sĭn), *adj.* **1.** of or pertaining to the seals. **2.** belonging to the *Phocinae*, the pinniped subfamily that includes the typical seals. [f. s. L *phōca* (t. Gk: m. *phṓkē* seal) + -INE[1]]

Phocion (fō′syən), *n. c.* 402–317 B.C., Athenian statesman and general.

Phocis (fō′sĭs), *n.* an ancient country in central Greece, N of Gulf of Corinth: site of Delphic oracle.

Phoebe (fē′bĭ), *n.* **1.** *Gk Myth.* Artemis (Diana) as goddess of the moon. **2.** *Poetic.* the moon personified. [t. L, t. Gk: m. *Phoíbē*, prop. fem. of *Phoîbos* PHOEBUS]

Phoebus (fē′bəs), *n.* **1.** *Gk Myth.* Apollo as the sun-god. **2.** *Poetic.* the sun personified. [ME *Phebus*, t. L: m. *Phoebus*, t. Gk: m. *Phoîbos*, lit., bright]

Phoenicia (fĭ nĭsh′ĭ ə), *n.* an ancient maritime country on the E coast of the Mediterranean.

Phoenician (fĭ nĭsh′ĭ ən), *n.* **1.** a native or inhabitant of Phoenicia. **2.** the extinct Semitic language of the Phoenicians. —*adj.* **3.** of or pertaining to Phoenicia.

phoenix (fē′nĭks), *n.* **1.** Also, **Phoenix.** a mythical bird of great beauty, the only one of its kind, fabled to live 500 or 600 years in the Arabian wilderness, to burn itself on a funeral pile, and to rise from its ashes in the freshness of youth and live through another cycle of years (often an emblem of immortality). **2.** a person or thing that is restored after death or destruction. **3.** a person or thing of peerless beauty or excellence; a paragon. Also, *U.S.*, **phenix.** [ME and OE *fēnix*, t. ML: m. *phēnix*, L *phoenix*, t. Gk: m. *phoînix*]

Phoenix (fē′nĭks), *n.* a city in the U.S., the capital of Arizona, in the central part. 439,170 (1960).

Phoenix Islands, eight coral islands forming part of the British Gilbert and Ellice Islands colony: two of the group are under British-U.S. control. 70 pop. (1964); 11 sq. mi.

phon (fŏn), *n. Physics.* a unit of loudness equal to the intensity in decibels of a sound of frequency 1000 cycles per second which seems as loud to the ear as the given sound.

phon-, a word element meaning 'voice', 'sound'. Also, **phono-.** [t. Gk, comb. form of *phōnḗ*]

phon., phonetics.

phonate (fō nāt′), *v.t., v.i.,* **-nated, -nating.** to produce (sound) by vibration of the vocal bands; vocalize. **—phona′tion,** *n.* **—phonatory** (fō′nə tə rĭ, -trĭ), *adj.*

phonautograph (fə nô′tə grăf′, -grăf′), *n.* an early mechanical apparatus for recording soundwaves, consisting of a horn for collecting the sound energy which operates on a diaphragm attached to which is a needle arranged so that it makes a trace upon a smoked rotating cylinder. **—phonautographic** (fō nô′tə grăf′ĭk), *adj.* **—phonau′tograph′ically,** *adv.*

phone[1] (fōn), *n., v.t., v.i.,* **phoned, phoning.** *Colloq.* telephone. [short for TELEPHONE]

phone[2] (fōn), *n. Phonet.* an individual speech sound. [t. Gk. See PHON-] **—pho′nal,** *adj.*

-phone, a word element meaning 'sound', especially used in names of instruments, as in *xylophone, megaphone, telephone.* [comb. form repr. Gk *phōnḗ*]

phoneme (fō′nēm), *n. Phonet.* the smallest distinctive group or class of phones in a language. The phonemes of a language contrast with one another; e.g., in English, *pip* differs from *nip, pin, tip, pit, bib,* etc., and *rumple* from *rumble,* by contrast of a phoneme (p) with other phonemes. In writing, the same symbol can be used for all the phones belonging to one phoneme without causing confusion between words: the (r) consonant phoneme includes the voiceless fricative *r* phone of *tree,* the voiced *r* phone of *red,* etc. [t. Gk: m. *phṓnēma* a sound]

phonemic (fō nē′mĭk), *adj.* **1.** of or pertaining to phonemes: *a phonemic system.* **2.** of or pertaining to phonemics; concerning or involving the discrimination of distinctive speech sounds: *a phonemic contrast.*

phonemics (fō nē′mĭks), *n.* the science of phonemic systems and contrasts. **—phonemicist** (fō nē′mĭ sĭst), *n.*

phonet., phonetics.

phonetic (fə nĕt′ĭk), *adj.* **1.** of or pertaining to speech sounds and their production. **2.** agreeing with or corresponding to pronunciation: *phonetic transcription.* Also, **phonetical.** [t. NL: s. *phoneticus,* t. Gk: m. *phōnētikós*] **—phonet′ically,** *adv.*

phonetics (fə nĕt′ĭks), *n.* **1.** the science of speech sounds and their production. **2.** the phonetic system, or the body of phonetic facts, of a particular language. **—phonetician** (fō′nĭ tĭsh′ən), *n.*

phonetist (fō′nĭ tĭst), *n.* one who uses or advocates phonetic spelling.

phoney (fō′nĭ), *adj.,* **-nier, -niest,** *n., pl.* **-nies** or **-neys.** *Slang.* **—***adj.* **1.** not genuine; spurious, counterfeit, or bogus; fraudulent. **—***n.* **2.** a counterfeit or fake. **3.** a faker. Also, **phony.** [var. of *fawney* ring (used in confidence trick), t. Irish: m. *fáinne*]

phonic (fŏn′ĭk, fō′nĭk), *adj.* of or pertaining to speech sounds.

phonics (fŏn′ĭks, fō′nĭks), *n.* **1.** a method of teaching reading, pronunciation, and spelling based upon the phonetic interpretation of ordinary spelling. **2.** *Obs.* phonetics.

phono-, var. of **phon-,** before consonants, as in *phonogram.*

phonogram (fō′nə grăm′), *n.* a unit symbol of a phonetic writing system, standing for a speech sound, syllable, or other sequence of speech sounds, without reference to meaning. **—pho′nogram′ic,** *adj.*

phonograph (fō′nə grăf′, -grăf′), *n. Obs. except U.S.* gramophone. **—phonographic** (fō′nə grăf′ĭk), *adj.* **—pho′nograph′ically,** *adv.*

phonography (fō nŏg′rə fĭ), *n.* **1.** phonetic spelling, writing, or shorthand. **2.** a system of phonetic shorthand invented by Sir Isaac Pitman in 1837.

phonol., phonology.

phonolite (fō′nə līt′), *n.* a fine-grained volcanic rock composed chiefly of alkali felspar and nepheline, some varieties of which split into pieces which ring on being struck. **—phonolitic** (fō′nə lĭt′ĭk), *adj.*

phonologist (fə nŏl′ə jĭst), *n.* a phonetician or phonemicist.

phonology (fə nŏl′ə jĭ), *n.* **1.** phonetics or phonemics, or both together. **2.** the phonetic and phonemic system, or the body of phonetic and phonemic facts, of a language. **—phonologic** (fō′nə lŏj′ĭk), **pho′nolog′ical,** *adj.* **—pho′nolog′ically,** *adv.*

phonon (fō′nŏn), *n. Physics.* a quantum of energy in a solid body.

phonoscope (fō′nə skōp′), *n.* **1.** a device by which sound is indicated by the optical phenomena it is made to produce. **2.** a device for testing the quality of strings for musical instruments.

phonotype (fō′nō tīp′), *n.* **1.** a type bearing a phonetic character or symbol. **2.** phonetic type or print.

phonotypy (fō′nō tī′pĭ), *n.* a phonetic shorthand developed by Sir Isaac Pitman. **—pho′notyp′ist,** *n.*

phony (fō′nĭ), *adj.,* **-nier, -niest,** *n., pl.* **-nies.** phoney.

-phony, a word element used in abstract nouns related to **-phone,** as in *telephony.* [t. Gk: m. s. *-phōnía*]

-phore, a word element used as a noun termination meaning 'bearer', 'thing or part bearing (something)', as in *anthophore, gonophore, ommatophore.* [t. NL: m. s. *-phorus,* t. Gk: m. *-phoros* bearing. Cf. F *-phore*]

-phorous, a word element used as an adjective termination meaning 'bearing', 'having', as in *anthrophorous.* [t. NL: m. *-phorus,* t. Gk: m. *-phoros* bearing]

phosgene (fŏz′jēn), *n. Chem.* carbonyl chloride, $COCl_2$, a poisonous gas used in chemical warfare and in organic synthesis. [f. Gk *phôs* light + -GENE]

phosgenite (fŏz′jĭ nīt′), *n.* a mineral, lead chlorocarbonate, $Pb_2Cl_2CO_3$, occurring in crystals.

phosph-, var. of **phospho-,** before vowels, as in *phosphate.*

phosphagen (fŏs′fə jən), *n. Biochem.* one of the compounds (creatine phosphate in vertebrates and some invertebrates, arginine phosphate in most invertebrates), widely distributed in animal tissues, in which they act as a store of chemical energy. [f. PHOSPHA(TE) + -GEN]

phosphatase (fŏs′fə tās′), *n. Biochem.* any of a group of enzymes that catalyses the hydrolysis of organic phosphates with the production of inorganic phosphate. [f. PHOSPHAT(E) + -ASE]

phosphate (fŏs′fāt), *n.* **1.** *Chem.* **a.** (loosely) a salt or ester of phosphoric acid. **b.** the tertiary salt of orthophosphoric acid: *sodium phosphate.* **2.** *Agric.* a fertilizer containing compounds of phosphorus. [t. F. See PHOSPH-, -ATE[2]]

phosphatic (fŏs făt′ĭk), *adj.* pertaining to, of the nature of, or containing phosphates: *phosphatic slag.*

phosphatide (fŏs′fə tīd′), *n. Biochem.* one of a group of fatty compounds, containing fatty acids, glycerol, phosphoric acid and a nitrogenous compound, as lecithins; phospholipid.

phosphatize (fŏs′fə tīz′), *v.t.,* **-tized, -tizing.** **1.** to treat with phosphates. **2.** to change to phosphate. Also, **phosphatise.**

phosphaturia (fŏs′fə tyŏŏə′rĭ ə), *n. Pathol.* the presence of an excessive quantity of phosphates in the urine. [f. s. NL *phōsphātum* phosphate + -URIA] **—phos′phatu′ric,** *adj.*

phosphene (fŏs′fēn), *n. Physiol.* a luminous image produced by mechanical stimulation of the retina, as by pressing the eyeball with the finger when the lid is closed, [t. F, f. Gk: m. *phôs* light + m. s. *phaínein* show, shine]

phosphide (fŏs′fīd), *n. Chem.* a compound of phosphorus with a basic element or radical.

phosphine (fŏs′fēn), *n. Chem.* **1.** a colourless, poisonous, ill-smelling gas, PH_3, which is spontaneously inflammable. **2.** any of certain organic derivatives of this compound.

phosphite (fŏs′fīt), *n. Chem.* **1.** (loosely) a salt of phosphorous acid. **2.** the tertiary salt of orthophosphorous acid.

phospho-, a word element representing **phosphorus,** as in *phosphoprotein.* Also, **phosph-.**

phospholipid (fŏs′fə lĭp′ĭd), *n. Biochem.* phosphatide.

phosphonium (fŏs fō′nyəm), *n. Chem.* the positively charged radical PH_4^+-, analogous to ammonium (NH_4^+-). [f. PHOSPH(OROUS) + (AMM)ONIUM]

phosphoprotein (fŏs′fō prō′tēn), *n. Biochem.* a protein composed of a molecule of protein linked with a substance other than nucleic acid or phosphatide and containing phosphorus.

phosphor (fŏs′fə), *n.* a substance which is capable of storing energy imparted from ultra-violet or other ionizing radiations, and releasing it later as light; any substance which exhibits luminescence. [special use of PHOSPHOR]

Phosphor (fŏs′fə), *n. Poetic.* the morning star; Lucifer. Also, **Phosphore** (fŏs′fô), **Phos′phorus.** [t. L: s. *Phōsphorus.* See PHOSPHORUS]

phosphorate (fŏs′fə rāt′), *v.t.,* **-rated, -rating.** *Chem.* to combine or impregnate with phosphorus.

phosphor bronze, *Metall.* an alloy of copper, tin, and phosphorus, sometimes also nickel, antimony or lead; a hard, elastic metal with high corrosive resistance.

phosphoresce (fŏs′fə rĕs′), *v.i.*, **-resced, -rescing.** to be luminous without sensible heat, as phosphorus. [f. PHOSPHOR(US) + -ESCE]

phosphorescence (fŏs′fə rĕs′əns), *n.* **1.** the property of being luminous at temperatures below incandescence, as from slow oxidation, in the case of phosphorus, or after exposure to light or other radiation. **2.** this luminous appearance. **3.** any radiation emitted by a substance after the removal of the exciting agent.

phosphorescent (fŏs′fə rĕs′ənt), *adj.* exhibiting phosphorescence.

phosphoretted (fŏs′fə rĕt′ĭd), *adj.* phosphuretted. Also, *U.S.*, **phosphoreted.**

phosphoric (fŏs fŏ′rĭk), *adj. Chem.* pertaining to or containing phosphorus, esp. in its pentavalent state.

phosphoric acid, any of three acids, orthophosphoric acid, H_3PO_4, metaphosphoric acid, HPO_3, or pyrophosphoric acid, $H_4P_2O_7$, derived from phosphorus pentoxide, P_2O_5, with various amounts of water.

phosphorism (fŏs′fə rĭz′əm), *n. Pathol.* condition of chronic phosphorus poisoning.

phosphorite (fŏs′fə rīt′), *n.* **1.** a massive form of the mineral apatite: the principal source of phosphate for fertilizers. **2.** any of various compact or earthy, more or less impure varieties of calcium phosphate.

phosphoroscope (fŏs fŏ′rə skōp′), *n.* an instrument for measuring the duration of evanescent phosphorescence in different substances. [f. PHOSPHOR(US) + -(O)SCOPE]

phosphorous (fŏs′fə rəs, -frəs), *adj. Chem.* containing trivalent phosphorus.

phosphorous acid, a colourless, water-soluble, crystalline acid of phosphorus, H_3PO_3, from which phosphites are derived.

phosphorus (fŏs′fə rəs, -frəs), *n., pl.* **-ri** (-rī′). **1.** *Chem.* a solid non-metallic element existing in at least two allotropic forms, one yellow (poisonous, inflammable, and luminous in the dark), the other red (less poisonous, and less inflammable). *Symbol:* P; *at. wt:* 30·9738; *at. no.:* 15; *sp. gr.:* (yellow) 1·82 at 20°C, (red) 2·20 at 20°C. The element is used in forming smokescreens; its compounds are used in matches and in phosphate fertilizers. It is a necessary constituent in plant and animal life, in bones, nerves, and embryos. The radioactive isotope, **phosphorus-32,** is used as a chemotherapeutic agent. **2.** *Now Rare.* any phosphorescent substance. **3.** *(cap.)* Phosphor. [t. NL, special use of L *Phōsphorus*, the morning star, t. Gk: m. *Phōsphóros*, lit., light-bringer]

phosphorus pentoxide, *Chem.* a deliquescent, colourless crystalline solid, P_2O_5, used as a drying agent and in organic synthesis.

phosphorylase (fŏs fô′rĭ lās′), *n. Biochem.* an enzyme that catalyses the breakdown of carbohydrates with the formation of phosphate compounds.

phosphuretted (fŏs′fyo͝o rĕt′ĭd), *adj. Chem.* combined with phosphorus, esp. in its lowest valency state. Also, **phosphoretted;** *U.S.*, **phosphoreted, phosphureted.** [f. *phosphuret* phosphide (t. NL: m. s. *phosphorētum*, with *-u-* from *phosphure*) + -ED[3]]

phot (fŏt, fōt), *n. Physics.* a unit of illumination, equal to 1 lumen per sq. cm. [t. Gk: s. *phôs* light]

photic (fō′tĭk), *adj.* **1.** of or pertaining to light. **2.** pertaining to the generation of light by organisms, or their excitation by means of light.

photo (fō′tō), *n., pl.* **-tos.** *Colloq.* photograph.

photo-, a word element meaning 'light' (sometimes used to represent 'photographic' or 'photograph'). [t. Gk, comb. form of *phôs* light]

photoactinic (fō′tō ăk tĭn′ĭk), *adj.* emitting radiation having the chemical effects of light and ultraviolet rays, as on a photographic film.

photobathic (fō′tō băth′ĭk), *adj.* in or relating to the stratum of ocean depth penetrated by sunlight.

photocell (fō′tō sĕl′), *n. Electronics.* **1.** a photoelectric cell. **2.** a phototube.

photochemistry (fō′tō kĕm′ĭs trĭ), *n.* the branch of chemistry that deals with the chemical action of light. —**photochemical** (fō′tō kĕm′ĭ kl), *adj.*

photochromy (fō′tō krō′mĭ), *n.* the art of producing photographs showing objects in natural colours.

photochronograph (fō′tō krŏn′ə grăf′, -gräf′), *n.* **1.** a device for taking instantaneous photographs at regular and generally short intervals of time, as of a bird, a horse, a projectile, etc., in motion. **2.** a picture taken by such a device. **3.** a chronograph in which the tracing or record is made by a pencil of light on a sensitized surface. **4.** an instrument for measuring small intervals of time by the photographic trace of a pencil of light.

photocomposition (fō′tō kŏm′pə zĭsh′ən), *n. Print.* filmsetting.

photoconduction (fō′tō kən dŭk′shən), *n. Electronics.* conduction in certain materials stimulated by light.

photoconductive (fō′tō kən dŭk′tĭv), *adj. Electronics.* of or pertaining to a material or device which conducts electricity if exposed to light.

photoconductive cell. See **photoelectric cell.**

photoconductive diode, *Electronics.* a semiconductor diode which conducts more heavily when exposed to light. Also, **photodiode** (fō′tō dī′ōd).

photocopy (fō′tō kŏp′ĭ), *n., pl.* **-copies,** *v.,* **-copied, -copying.** photostat (defs 2 and 3).

photodisintegration (fō′tō dĭs ĭn′tĭ grā′shən), *n. Physics.* any nuclear reaction caused by a photon which results in the emission of charged fragments or neutrons.

photodynamics (fō′tō dī năm′ĭks), *n.* the science dealing with light in its relation to movement in plants.

photoelectric (fō′tō ĭ lĕk′trĭk), *adj.* pertaining to the electronic or other electrical effects produced by light. Also, **photoelectrical.**

photoelectric cell, *Electronics.* **1.** a device incorporated in an electric circuit to make the resistance or electromotive force of part of the circuit variable in accordance with variations in the intensity of light or similar radiation falling upon it, and so to make operations controlled by the circuit dependent on variations in illumination, in a beam of radiation, etc. **2.** a phototube.

photoelectric effect, *Physics.* any effect arising as a result of the transfer of energy from electromagnetic radiation (esp. light) incident upon a substance to electrons within that substance.

photoelectric meter, *Photog.* an exposure meter using a photoelectric cell for the measurement of light intensity.

photoelectron (fō′tō ĭ lĕk′trŏn), *n. Physics.* an electron liberated from a substance as a result of the photoelectric effect.

photoelectrotype (fō′tō ĭ lĕk′trō tīp′), *n.* an electrotype made by the aid of photography.

photoengrave (fō′tō ĭn grāv′), *v.t.*, **-graved, -graving.** to make a photoengraving of. —**pho′toengrav′er,** *n.*

photoengraving (fō′tō ĭn grā′vĭng), *n.* **1.** a process of preparing printing plates for letterpress printing. **2.** a process of photographic reproduction by which a relief-printing surface is obtained for letterpress printing. **3.** a plate so produced.

photo finish, *Racing.* a close race in which the decision is made from a photograph of the contestants as they cross the finishing line.

photofission (fō′tō fĭsh′ən), *n. Physics.* nuclear fission caused by a high-energy photon.

photoflash lamp (fō′tō flăsh′), *Photog.* a flashbulb.

photoflood lamp (fō′tō flŭd′), *Photog.* an incandescent tungsten lamp, in which high intensity is obtained by overloading the voltage.

photog., **1.** photographic. **2.** photography.

photogene (fō′tō jēn′), *n.* an after-image on the retina.

photogenic (fō′tō jĕn′ĭk), *adj.* **1.** *Photog.* (of a person) suitable for being photographed for artistic purposes, etc. **2.** *Biol.* producing or emitting light as certain bacteria; luminiferous; phosphorescent. **3.** *Rare.* produced by light. —**pho′togen′ically,** *adv.*

photogrammetry (fō′tō grăm′ĭ trĭ), *n.* the process of making surveys and maps utilizing photographs. [f. PHOTO- + -GRAM (for -GRAPH) + -METRY]

photograph (fō′tə grăf′, -gräf′), *n.* **1.** a picture produced by photography. —*v.t.* **2.** to take a photograph of. —*v.i.* **3.** to practise photography.

photographer (fə tŏg′rə fə), *n.* one who takes photographs or practises photography.

photographic (fō′tə grăf′ĭk), *adj.* **1.** of or pertaining to photography. **2.** used in or produced by photography. **3.** suggestive of a photograph; extremely realistic and detailed: *photographic accuracy.* **4.** mechanically imitative, with lack of artistic feeling. Also, **pho′tograph′ical.** —**pho′tograph′ically,** *adv.*

photography (fə tŏg′rə fĭ), *n.* the process or art of producing images of objects on sensitized surfaces by the chemical action of light or of other forms of radiant energy, as X-rays, gamma rays, cosmic rays, etc.

photogravure (fō′tə grə vyo͝oə′), *n.* **1.** any of various processes, based on photography, by which an intaglio engraving is formed on a metal plate, from which ink reproductions are made. **2.** the plate. **3.** a print made from it. [t. F: f. *photo-* PHOTO- + *gravure* engraving]

photokinesis (fō′tō kĭ nē′sĭs, -kī-), *n. Physiol.* movement occurring upon exposure to light. —**photokinetic** (fō′tō kĭ nĕt′ĭk, -kī-), *adj.*

photolithograph (fō′tō lĭth′ə grăf′, -gräf′), *n.* **1.** a lithograph printed from a stone, etc., upon which a picture or design has been formed by photography. —*v.t.* **2.** to make a photolithograph of.

photolithography (fō′tō lĭ thŏg′rə fĭ), *n.* the technique or art of making photolithographs. —**photolithographic** (fō′tō lĭth′ə grăf′ĭk), *adj.*

photolysis (fō tŏl′ĭ sĭs), *n.* the breakdown of materials under the influence of light. [t. NL, f. Gk: *phōto-* PHOTO- + *lýsis* a loosing] —**photolytic** (fō′tō lĭt′ĭk), *adj.*

photom., **1.** photometry. **2.** photometrical.

photomechanical (fō′tō mĭ kăn′ĭ kl), *adj.* denoting or pertaining to any of various processes for printing in ink from plates or surfaces prepared by the aid of photography. —**pho′tomechan′ically,** *adv.*

photomeson (fō′tō mē′zŏn), *n. Physics.* a meson produced by the interaction between a photon and an atomic nucleus.

photometer (fō tŏm′ĭ tə), *n.* an instrument for measuring the intensity of light or the relative illuminating power of different lights.

photometry (fō tŏm′ĭ trĭ), *n.* **1.** the measurement of the intensity of light or of relative illuminating power. **2.** the science dealing with this. —**photometric** (fō′tō mĕt′rĭk), **pho′tomet′rical,** *adj.* —**photom′etrist,** *n.*

photomicrograph (fō′tō mī′krə grăf′, -gräf′), *n.* **1.** a photograph of a microscopic object, taken through a microscope. **2.** a microphotograph. —**photomicrography** (fō′tō mī krŏg′rə fĭ), *n.*

photomontage (fō′tō mŏn täzh′), *n. Photog.* a combination of several photographs joined together for artistic effect or to show more of the subject than can be disclosed in a single photograph.

photomultiplier (fō′tō mŭl′tĭ plī′ə), *n. Electronics.* a sensitive instrument which detects light by means of photoelectric effects.

photomural (fō′tō myŏŏ′rəl), *n.* a very large photograph covering most of a wall as decoration.

photon (fō′tŏn), *n. Physics.* a quantum of light energy, the energy being proportional to the frequency of the radiation. [der. PHOTO-; modelled on ELECTRON, PROTON]

photonasty (fō′tō năs′tĭ), *n.* the movement of plant parts in response to changes in light intensity, as the diurnal opening of leaves and flowers.

photoneutron (fō′tō nyŏŏ′trŏn), *n. Physics.* a neutron resulting from photodisintegration.

photo-offset (fō′tō ŏf′sĕt′), *n. Print.* a method of printing similar to offset lithography (see **offset** def. 13), in which the text or designs are impressed on metal plates by photography.

photophilous (fō tŏf′ĭ ləs), *adj.* thriving in strong light, as a plant.

photophobia (fō′tō fō′byə), *n. Pathol.* a morbid dread or intolerance of light, as in iritis. [t. NL. See PHOTO-, -PHOBIA]

photoplay (fō′tō plā′), *n.* film (4b).

photoproton (fō′tō prō′tŏn), *n. Physics.* a proton resulting from photodisintegration.

photo relief, a process in which a model depicting the relief of a tract of country is illuminated by a light situated at the north-west corner, and photographed vertically to produce a map in which the distribution of light and shadow gives a representation of the configuration of hills and valleys.

photosensitive (fō′tō sĕn′sĭ tĭv), *adj.* sensitive to light or similar radiation.

photospectroscope (fō′tō spĕk′trə skōp′), *n.* a spectrograph (def. 2).

photosphere (fō′tō sfĭə′), *n.* **1.** a sphere of light. **2.** *Astron.* the luminous envelope of gas surrounding the sun. —**photospheric** (fō′tō sfē′rĭk), *adj.*

photostat (fō′tō stăt′), *n.* **1.** (*cap.*) *Trademark.* a special camera for making facsimile copies of maps, drawings, pages of books or manuscripts, etc., which photographs directly as a positive on sensitized paper. **2.** Also, **photocopy.** a copy or photograph made with it. —*v.t., v.i.* **3.** Also, **photocopy.** to make a photostatic copy or copies (of). —*adj.* **4.** Also, **pho′tostat′ic.** denoting or pertaining to such a camera or copy.

photosynthesis (fō′tō sĭn′thĭ sĭs), *n. Bot., Biochem.* the synthesis of complex organic materials by plants from carbon dioxide, water, and inorganic salts using sunlight as the source of energy and with the aid of a catalyst such as chlorophyll; commonly used in the more restricted sense of the synthesis of carbohydrates. [t. NL. See PHOTO-, SYNTHESIS] —**photosynthetic** (fō′tō sĭn thĕt′ĭk), *adj.*

phototaxis (fō′tō tăk′sĭs), *n. Biol.* a movement of an organism towards or away from a source of light. Also, **pho′totax′y.** [t. NL. See PHOTO-, -TAXIS]

phototelegraphy (fō′tō tĭ lĕg′rə fĭ), *n.* the electric transmission of facsimiles of photographs, etc.; telephotography. —**phototelegraphic** (fō′tō tĕl′ĭ grăf′ĭk), *adj.*

phototherapeutics (fō′tō thĕ′rə pyŏŏ′tĭks), *n.* that branch of therapeutics which deals with the curative use of light rays. —**pho′tother′apeu′tic,** *adj.*

phototherapy (fō′tō thĕ′rə pĭ), *n.* treatment of disease by means of light rays.

photothermic (fō′tō thûr′mĭk), *adj.* **1.** pertaining to the thermal effects of light. **2.** pertaining to or involving both light and heat.

phototonus (fō tŏt′ə nəs), *n. Biol.* **1.** the normal condition of sensitiveness to light in leaves, etc. **2.** the irritability exhibited by protoplasm when exposed to light of a certain intensity. [t. NL, f. Gk: *phōto-* PHOTO- + m. *tónos* tension] —**phototonic** (fō′tō tŏn′ĭk), *adj.*

phototropic (fō′tō trŏp′ĭk), *adj. Bot.* **1.** taking a particular direction under the influence of light. **2.** growing towards or away from the light. —**pho′totrop′ically,** *adv.*

phototropism (fō tŏt′rə pĭz′əm), *n. Bot.* phototropic tendency or growth.

phototube (fō′tō tyŏŏb′), *n. Electronics.* a two-element valve in which light falling on the light-sensitive cathode causes electrons to be emitted, the electrons being collected by the anode.

phototype (fō′tō tīp′), *n.*, *v.*, **-typed, -typing.** *Print. Obs.* —*n.* **1.** a plate with a (relief) printing surface produced by photography. **2.** any process for making such a plate. **3.** a print made from it. —*v.t.* **4.** to reproduce by phototypy.

phototypesetting (fō′tō tīp′sĕt′ĭng), *n.* filmsetting.

phototypography (fō′tō tī pŏg′rə fĭ), *n. Print. Obs.* the art of making printing surfaces by light or photography, by any of a large number of processes.

phototypy (fō′tō tī′pĭ), *n.* the art or process of producing phototypes.

photovoltaic (fō′tō vŏl tā′ĭk), *adj.* providing a source of electric current under the influence of light or similar radiation.

photovoltaic cell, *Physics.* any type of cell in which an electromotive force is produced as a result of the photovoltaic effect.

photovoltaic effect, *Physics.* a photoelectric effect in which light falling on the junction between certain pairs of substances (esp. a metal and a semiconductor) produces a potential difference across the junction.

phr., phrase.

phrasal (frā′zəl), *adj.* of the nature of, or consisting of, a phrase.

phrase (frāz), *n.*, *v.*, **phrased, phrasing.** —*n.* **1.** *Gram.* **a.** a sequence of two or more words arranged in a grammatical construction and acting as a unit in the sentence. **b.** (in English) such a sequence which is smaller than a clause, e.g., consisting of preposition plus noun or pronoun, adjective plus noun, adverb plus verb, etc. (but not a verb and its subject). **2.** *Speech.* a word or group of spoken words which the mind focuses on momentarily as a meaningful unit and which is preceded and followed by pauses. **3.** way of speaking, mode of expression, or phraseology. **4.** a characteristic, current, or proverbial expression. **5.** a brief utterance or remark. **6.** *Music.* a group of notes forming a recognizable entity. **7.** *Dance.* a sequence of motions making up a choreographic pattern. —*v.t.* **8.** to express or word in a particular way. **9.** to express in words. **10.** *Music.* **a.** to mark off or bring out the phrases of (a piece), esp. in execution. **b.** to group (notes) into a phrase. [back-formation from *phrases*, pl. of LL *phrasis*, t. Gk: speech, phraseology, expression]

phrasebook (frāz′bŏŏk′), *n.* a book of phrases in foreign languages with translations.

phraseogram (frā′zĭ ə grăm′), *n.* a written symbol, as in shorthand, representing a phrase. [f. PHRASEO(LOGY) + -GRAM]

phraseograph (frā′zĭ ə grăf′, -gräf′), *n.* a phrase for which there is a phraseogram.

phraseologist (frā′zĭ ŏl′ə jĭst), *n.* **1.** one who treats of phraseology. **2.** one who affects a particular phraseology.

phraseology (frā′zĭ ŏl′ə jĭ), *n.* **1.** manner or style of verbal expression; characteristic language: *the phraseology of lawyers.* **2.** phrases or expressions: *medical phraseology.* [t. NL: m. s. *phraseologia*, t. Gk] —**phraseological** (frā′zĭ ə lŏj′ĭ kl), *adj.* —**Syn. 1.** See **diction.**

phratry (frā′trĭ), *n.*, *pl.* **-tries. 1.** a grouping of clans or other social units within a tribe. **2.** (in ancient Greece) a subdivision of a phyle. [t. Gk: m. *phratría*]

phren., **1.** phrenological. **2.** phrenology.

phrenetic (frĭ nĕt′ĭk), *adj.* **1.** delirious; insane; frantic; frenzied. **2.** filled with extreme emotion, esp. in religious matters. —*n.* **3.** a phrenetic individual. Also, **frenetic.** [ME *frenetike*, t. OF, t. L: m. *phrenēticus*, t. LGk: m. *phrenētikós*] —**phrenet′ically,** *adv.*

phrenic (frĕn′ĭk), *adj.* **1.** *Anat.* of or pertaining to the diaphragm. **2.** *Physiol.* relating to the mind or mental activity. [t. NL: s. *phrenicus*, f. s. Gk *phrḗn* diaphragm, mind + *-icus* -IC]

phrenol., 1. phrenological. 2. phrenology.
phrenology (frĭ nŏl′ə jĭ), *n.* the theory that one's mental powers are indicated by the shape of the skull. [f. *phreno-* (comb. form repr. Gk *phrḗn* mind) + -LOGY] —**phrenologic** (frĕn′ə lŏj′ĭk), **phren′olog′ical,** *adj.* —**phrenol′ogist,** *n.*
phrensy (frĕn′zĭ), *n., pl.* **-sies,** *v.t.,* **-sied, -sying.** frenzy.
Phrixus (frĭk′səs), *n.* See **Golden Fleece.**
Phrygia (frĭj′ĭ ə), *n.* an ancient country in central and NW Asia Minor. —**Phryg′ian,** *adj., n.*
Phrygian mode, *Music.* a mode which can be represented by a scale of an octave of white keys on the piano from E to E.
PHS, *U.S.* Public Health Service.
phthalein (fthăl′ēn, fthăl′ĭ ĭn), *n. Chem.* any of a group of compounds (certain of whose derivatives are important dyes) formed by treating phthalic anhydride with phenols. [f. (NA)PHTHALE(NE) + -IN[2]]
phthalic (fthăl′ĭk), *adj. Chem.* **1.** denoting or pertaining to any of three isomeric acids, $C_6H_4(COOH)_2$, derived from benzene, esp. one which is prepared by oxidizing naphthalene, which forms an anhydride. **2.** denoting this anhydride. [f. (NA)PHTHAL(ENE) + -IC]
phthalin (fthăl′ĭn), *n. Chem.* any of a group of compounds obtained by reduction of the phthaleins.
phthiocol (thī′ə kŏl′), *n. Biochem.* a yellow pigment, the vitamin K properties of which counteract haemorrhage. [f. PHTHI(SIS) + -O- + -*c*- + -OL[1]]
phthisic (thĭ′sĭk), *n. Pathol.* of the phthisis. [ME *tisike,* t. OF, t. L: m. *phthisica,* fem. of *phthisicus,* t. Gk: m. *phthisikós* consumptive]
phthisical (thĭ′sĭ kl), *adj.* pertaining to, of the nature of, or affected by phthisis. Also, **phthi′sicky.**
phthisis (thī′sĭs), *n. Pathol.* **1.** a wasting away. **2.** tuberculosis of the lungs; consumption. [t. L, t. Gk]
phut (fŭt), *Colloq.* —*adv.* **1. go phut,** to collapse, become ruined. —*interj.* **2.** (an exclamation of annoyance, etc.) Also, **fut.** [t. Hind.: m. *phatnā* to explode]
-phyceae, a combining form used in names of algae. [NL, der. Gk *phŷkos* seaweed]
phycology (fī kŏl′ə jĭ), *n.* the branch of botany that deals with algae. [f. m. Gk *phŷko(s)* seaweed + -LOGY] —**phycol′ogist,** *n.*
phycomycetous (fī′kō mī sē′təs), *adj. Bot.* belonging or pertaining to the *Phycomycetes,* the simplest of the three primary subdivisions of the fungi, whose members more closely resemble algae than do the higher fungi. [f. s. NL *Phycomycētes,* pl., (f. Gk: *phŷko(s)* seaweed + m. pl. of *mýkēs* fungus) + -OUS]
-phyl, var. of **-phyll.**
phylactery (fĭ lăk′tə rĭ), *n., pl.* **-teries. 1.** either of two small leather cases containing slips inscribed with certain texts from the Pentateuch, worn by Jews, one on the head and one on the left arm. during prayer to remind them to keep the law. Deut. 6:8, 11:18. **2.** (in early Christianity) a receptacle containing a holy relic. **3.** a reminder. **4.** an amulet, charm, or safeguard. [t. LL: m. s. *phylactērium,* t. Gk: m. *phylaktḗrion* outpost, safeguard, amulet; r. ME *philaterie,* t. OF]
phyle (fī′lē), *n., pl.* **-lae** (-lē). (in ancient Greece) a tribe or clan, based on supposed kinship. [t. NL, t. Gk]
phyletic (fī lĕt′ĭk), *adj. Biol.* pertaining to race or species; phylogenic; racial. [t. Gk: m. s. *phyletikós*]
-phyll, a word element used as a noun termination meaning 'leaf', as in *chlorophyll, cladophyll, lithophyll.* Also, **-phyl.** [t. Gk: m. s. *phýllon*]
Phyllis (fĭl′ĭs), *n.* a name, orig. in pastoral literature, for a country girl or a sweetheart.
phyllite (fĭl′īt), *n.* a slaty rock with lustrous cleavage planes due to minute scales of mica. [f. PHYLL(O)- + -ITE[1]]
phyllo-, a word element meaning 'leaf'. Also, before vowels, **phyll-.** [t. Gk, combining form of *phýllon*]
phylloclade (fĭl′ō klād′), *n. Bot.* **1.** a flattened stem or branch having the function of a leaf. **2.** cladode. [f. PHYLLO- + m. s. Gk *kládos* branch]
phyllode (fĭl′ōd), *n. Bot.* an expanded petiole resembling, and having the function of, a leaf. [t. F, t. NL: m. s. *phyllōdium,* t. Gk: m. *phyllṓdēs* leaf-like. See -ODE[1]]
phylloid (fĭl′oid), *adj.* leaf-like.
phyllome (fĭl′ōm), *n. Bot.* **1.** a leaf of a plant. **2.** a structure corresponding to it. [t. NL: m. *phyllōma,* t. Gk] —**phyllomic** (fĭ lŏm′ĭk), *adj.*

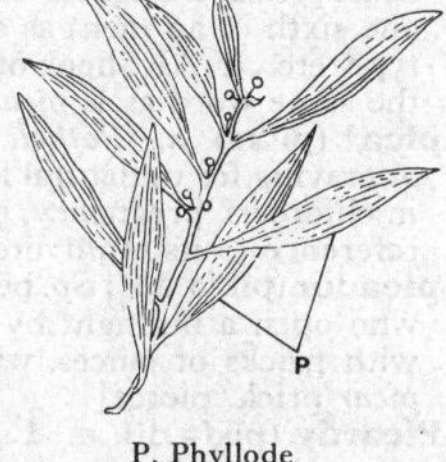

P, Phyllode

phyllopod fĭl′ō pŏd′), *n.* **1.** any of the *Phyllopoda,* an order of crustaceans characterized by leaf-like swimming appendages. —*adj.* **2.** pertaining to the phyllopods. **3.** belonging to the *Phyllopoda.* Also, **phyllopodan** (fĭ lŏp′ə dən). [t. NL: s. *Phyllopoda,* pl. See PHYLLO-, -POD]
phyllotaxis (fĭl′ō tăk′sĭs), *n. Bot.* **1.** the arrangement of leaves on a stem or axis. **2.** the principles governing such arrangement. Also, **phyl′lotax′y.** [t. NL. See PHYLLO-, -TAXIS]
-phyllous, a word element used as an adjective termination meaning 'having leaves', 'leaved', or implying some connection with a leaf, as in *diphyllous, epiphyllous, monophyllous, polyphyllous.* [t. Gk: m. *-phyllos* pertaining to a leaf]
phylloxera (fĭl′ŏk sĭə′rə), *n., pl.* **phylloxerae** (fĭl′ŏk sĭə′rē). any of the plant lice constituting the genus *Phylloxera,* esp. *P. vastatrix,* very destructive to grapevines. [t. NL, f. Gk: *phyllo-* PHYLLO- + m. *xērós* dry]
phylo-, a word element meaning 'tribe'. [t. Gk, comb. form of *phŷlon* race, tribe]
phylogeny (fī lŏj′ĭ nĭ), *n., pl.* **-nies.** *Biol.* the development or evolution of a kind or type of animal or plant; racial history. Cf. **ontogeny.** Also, **phylogenesis** (fī′lō jĕn′ĭ sĭs). —**phylogenetic** (fī′lō jĭ nĕt′ĭk), **phy′logen′ic,** *adj.* —**phy′logenet′ically,** *adv.*
phylum (fī′ləm), *n., pl.* **-la** (-lə). **1.** *Biol.* a primary division of the animal or vegetable kingdom: e.g., the *arthropods,* the *molluscs,* the *spermatophytes.* **2.** (in the classification of languages) a group of linguistic stocks or families having no known congeners outside the group. [t. NL, t. Gk: m. *phŷlon* race, tribe, akin to *phylḗ.* See PHYLE]
-phyre, a word element used to form names of porphyritic rocks, as in *granophyre.* [t. Gk: m. *-phyr,* for *porphyr* porphyry]
phys., 1. physical. 2. physician. 3. physics. 4. physiological. 5. physiology.
phys. chem., physical chemistry.
phys. geog., physical geography.
physic (fĭz′ĭk), *n., v.,* **-icked, -icking.** —*n.* **1.** a medicine that purges; a cathartic. **2.** any medicine; a drug or medicament. **3.** *Archaic.* the medical art or profession. **4.** *Obs.* natural science. —*v.t.* **5.** to treat with physic or medicine. **6.** to treat with or to act upon as, a cathartic; purge. **7.** to work upon as a medicine does; relieve or cure. [ME *fisyke,* t. L: m. *physica* natural (ML medical) science, t. Gk: m. *physikḗ* science of nature, prop. fem. adj., pertaining to nature]
physical (fĭz′ĭ kl), *adj.* **1.** pertaining to the body; bodily: *physical exercise.* **2.** of or pertaining to material nature; material. **3.** denoting or pertaining to the properties of matter and energy other than those that are chemical or peculiar to living matter; pertaining to physics. **4.** denoting or pertaining to the properties of matter and energy other than those peculiar to living matter; pertaining to physical science. [ME, t. ML: s. *physicālis,* der. *physica* PHYSIC] —**phys′ically,** *adv.*
—**Syn. 1.** PHYSICAL, BODILY, CORPOREAL, CORPORAL agree in pertaining to the body. PHYSICAL indicates connected with, pertaining to, the animal or human body as a material organism: *physical strength enough to lift one's own weight.* BODILY means belonging to, concerned with, the human body as distinct from the mind or spirit: *bodily pain or suffering.* CORPOREAL, a more poetic and philosophical word than BODILY, refers esp. to the mortal substance of which the human body is composed as opposed to spirit: *this corporeal habitation.* CORPORAL is now usually reserved for reference to whippings, etc., inflicted on the human body; *corporal punishment.*
physical anthropology, the science concerned with evolutionary changes in man's bodily structure and the classification of modern races, in which mensurational and descriptive techniques are employed.
physical chemistry, that branch of chemistry which deals with the relations between the physical (i.e. electrical, optical, etc.) properties of substances and their chemical composition and transformations.
physical education, instruction given in exercises, gymnastics, sports, etc., for the development and health of the body. Also, **physical training.**
physical geography, that part of geography concerned with natural features and phenomena of the earth's surface, as land forms, drainage features, climates, ocean currents, soils, vegetation, and animal life.
physical jerks, *Colloq.* physical exercises, usually performed without apparatus, to improve the health of the body. Also, **jerks.**
physical science, the study of natural laws and processes other than those peculiar to living matter, as in physics, chemistry, astronomy, etc.
physical therapy, physiotherapy.
physical training, physical education.
physician (fĭ zĭsh′ən), *n.* **1.** one legally qualified to practise medicine. **2.** one engaged in general medical practice as

distinguished from one specializing in surgery. **3.** one who is skilled in the art of healing. [ME *fisicien*, t. OF, der. ML *physica* PHYSIC. See -IAN]

physicist (fĭz'ĭ sĭst), *n.* a person versed in physics and its methods.

physics (fĭz'ĭks), *n.* the science dealing with natural laws and processes, and the states and properties of matter and energy, other than those restricted to living matter and to chemical changes. [pl. of PHYSIC. See -ICS]

physio-, a word element representing **physical, physics.** [t. Gk, comb. form of *phýsis* nature]

physiocrat (fĭz'ĭ ō krăt'), *n.* one of a school of political economists, followers of Quesnay, who recognized an inherent natural order as properly governing society, regarded land as the basis of wealth and taxation, and advocated freedom of industry and trade. [t. F: m. *physiocrate.* See PHYSIO-, -CRAT] —**phys'iocrat'ic,** *adj.*

physiognomy (fĭz'ĭ ŏn'ə mĭ), *n., pl.* **-mies. 1.** the face or countenance, esp. as considered as an index to the character. **2.** the art of determining character or personal characteristics from the features of the face or the form of the body. **3.** the general or characteristic appearance of anything. [t. Gk: m. s. *physiognōmonía* the judging of one's nature; r. ME *fisionomie*, t. ML: m. *phisonomia*] —**physiognomic** (fĭz'ĭ ə nŏm'ĭk), **phys'iognom'ical,** *adj.* —**phys'iognom'ically,** *adv.* —**phys'iogn'omist,** *n.*

physiography (fĭz'ĭ ŏg'rə fĭ), *n.* **1.** physical geography. **2.** the systematic description of nature in general. —**phys'iog'rapher,** *n.* —**physiographic** (fĭz'ĭ ə grăf'ĭk), **phys'iograph'ical,** *adj.*

physiol., 1. physiological. **2.** physiologist. **3.** physiology.

physiological (fĭz'ĭ ə lŏj'ĭ kl), *adj. Physiol.* **1.** of or relating to physiology. **2.** consistent with the normal functioning of an organism. Also, **phys'iolog'ic.** —**phys'iolog'ically,** *adv.*

physiology (fĭz'ĭ ŏl'ə jĭ), *n.* the science dealing with the functioning of living organisms or their parts. [t. L: m. s. *physiologia*, t. Gk] —**phys'iol'ogist,** *n.*

physiotherapy (fĭz'ĭ ō thĕ'rə pĭ), *n.* the treatment of disease or bodily weaknesses or defects by physical remedies, such as massage, gymnastics, etc.

physique (fĭ zēk'), *n.* physical or bodily structure, or development. [t. F, prop. adj., physical, t. L: m. s. *physicus*, t. Gk: m. *physikós*]

physoclistous (fī'sō klĭs'təs), *adj. Ichthyol.* having the air-bladder closed off from the mouth. [f. s. NL *Physōclīstī*, genus name (f. *physō-* (comb. form repr. Gk *phŷsa* bladder) + m. Gk *kleistoí* (pl.) shut) + -OUS]

physostigmine (fī'sō stĭg'mēn), *n. Chem.* a poisonous alkaloid, $C_{15}H_{21}N_3O_2$, constituting the active principle of the Calabar bean, used in medicine as a miotic, etc. [f. m. NL *Phȳsostigma* (f. Gk: m. *phŷsa* bellows + *stígma* stigma) + -INE]

physostomous (fī sŏs'tə məs), *adj. Ichthyol.* having the mouth and air-bladder connected by an air-duct. [f. s. NL *Phȳsostomī*, a genus name (f. Gk: m. *phŷsa* bladder + m. *-stomos* mouthed) + -OUS]

-phyte, a word element used as a noun termination meaning 'a growth', 'plant', as in *epiphyte, halophyte, lithophyte, osteophyte.* [comb. form repr. Gk *phytón*]

Phytin (fī'tĭn), *n. Trademark.* an organic compound containing phosphorus, occurring in seeds, tubers, and rhizomes as a reserve material. [f. PHYT(O)- + -IN²]

phyto-, a word element meaning 'plant'. Also (before vowels), **phyt-.** [t. Gk, comb. form of *phytón* plant]

phytogenesis (fī'tō jĕn'ĭ sĭs), *n.* the origin and development of plants. Also, **phytogeny** (fī tŏj'ĭ nĭ). —**phytogenetic** (fī'tō jĭ nĕt'ĭk), **phy'togenet'ical,** *adj.* —**phy'togenet'ically,** *adv.*

phytogenic (fī'tō jĕn'ĭk), *adj.* of plant origin.

phytogeography (fī'tō jĭ ŏg'rə fĭ), *n.* the science treating of the geographical relationships of plants.

phytography (fī tŏg'rə fĭ), *n.* that branch of botany which deals with the description of plants.

phytology (fī tŏl'ə jĭ), *n. Obs.* botany.

phytopathology (fī'tō pə thŏl'ə jĭ), *n. Bot.* the study of plant diseases.

phytophagous (fī tŏf'ə gəs), *adj.* herbivorous.

pi¹ (pī), *n., pl.* **pis. 1.** the sixteenth letter (Π, π) of the Greek alphabet. **2.** *Maths.* **a.** the letter π, used as the symbol for the ratio (3·141592+) of the circumference of a circle to its diameter. **b.** the ratio itself. [t. Gk, in def. 2 the initial letter of *periphéreia* PERIPHERY]

pi² (pī), *n., v.,* **pied, piing.** *Chiefly U.S.* pie³.

pi³ (pī), *adj. Slang.* pious, esp. hypocritically or smugly so.

P.I., Philippine Islands.

Piacenza (*It.* pyȧ chĕn'tsȧ), *n.* a town in N Italy, on the river Po. 99,388 (1966).

piacular (pī ăk'yŏŏ lə), *adj.* **1.** expiatory. **2.** requiring expiation; sinful; wicked. [t. L: s. *piāculāris*]

Piaf (*Fr.* pyȧf), *n.* **Edith** (*Fr.* ė dēt') (*Edith Giovanna Gassion*), 1914–63, French singer.

piaffe (pĭ ăf'), *v.i.,* **piaffed, piaffing. 1.** (of a horse) to lift each pair of diagonally opposite legs in succession, as in the trot, but without going forwards, backwards, or sideways. **2.** to move slowly forwards, backwards, or sideways in this manner. [t. F. See PIAFFER]

piaffer (pĭ ăf'ə), *n.* the act of piaffing. Also, **piaffe.** [t. F (inf.), t. Pr.: m. *piafá* prance, make merry, b. with *pialhà* scream (der. L *pīca* magpie) and *pifrá* play the bagpipes, ult. of Gmc orig.]

Piaget (*Fr.* pyȧ zhĕ'), *n.* **Jean** (*Fr.* zhäɴ), born 1896, Swiss psychologist.

pia mater (pī'ə mā'tə), *Anat.* the delicate, fibrous, and highly vascular membrane forming the innermost of the three meninges enveloping the brain and spinal cord. [ME, t. ML: tender mother, an inexact rendering of Arabic *umm raqīqah* thin or tender mother. Cf. DURA MATER]

pianissimo (pĭə nĭs'ĭ mō'; *It.* pyȧ nēs'sē mȯ), *adj., adv., n., pl.* **-mos, -mi** (-mē'). *Music.* —*adj.* **1.** very soft. —*adv.* **2.** very softly. —*n.* **3.** a passage or movement played in this way. *Abbrev.:* pp. [It., superl. of *piano*, g. L *plānus*. See PIANO²]

pianist (pĭə'nĭst), *n.* a performer on the piano.

pianistic (pĭə nĭs'tĭk, pyă nĭs'-), *adj.* suitable to or written for the piano.

piano¹ (pĭ ăn'ō), *n.* **1.** a musical instrument in which hammers, operated from a keyboard, strike upon metal strings. **2. grand piano,** a piano with a harp-shaped body supported horizontally, called **concert grand piano** in the largest size. **3. upright piano,** a piano with a rectangular body placed vertically. **4. square piano,** a piano with a rectangular body supported horizontally. [t. It., short for *pianoforte* or *fortepiano* PIANOFORTE]

piano² (pyä'nō), *Music.* —*adj.* **1.** soft; subdued (opposed to *forte*). —*adv.* **2.** softly. *Abbrev.:* p. [It., g. L *plānus* PLAIN¹]

piano accordion, an accordion having a piano-like keyboard for the right hand.

Piano accordion

pianoforte (pyăn'ō fô'tĭ), *n.* the piano. [t. It.: f. *piano* soft + *forte* loud, strong]

Pianola (pĭə nō'lə, pyă nō'-), *n. Trademark.* a player piano.

piassava (pē'ə sä'və), *n.* **1.** a coarse, woody fibre obtained from the palms *Leopoldinia piassaba* and *Attalea funifera* of South America, used in making brooms, etc. **2.** either of these trees. Also, **piassaba.** [t. Pg., t. Tupi: m. *piaçaba*]

piastre (pĭ ăs'tə), *n.* **1.** kurus. **2.** the monetary unit of South Vietnam, equal to 100 cents, and equivalent to about £0·0053 sterling. **3.** a banknote or cupronickel alloy coin of this value. **4.** the old Spanish peso or dollar. **5.** any of the various coins based on it. Also, **piaster.** [t. F: m. *piastre*, t. It.: m. *piastra* metal plate (coin), g. L *emplastrum* a plaster. See PLASTER]

Piave (*It.* pyȧ'vė), *n.* a river in NE Italy, flowing into the Adriatic: scene of bitter fighting 1917–18. 137 mi.

piazza (pĭ ăt'sə, -ăd'zə; *It.* pyȧt'tsȧ), *n., pl.* **piazzas,** *It.* **piazze** (*It.* pyȧt'tsė). **1.** an open square or public place in a city or town. **2.** an arcade or covered walk or gallery, as around a public square or in front of a building. **3.** *U.S.* a veranda of a house. [t. It., g. L *platēa*, t. Gk: m. *plateîa* broad street. See PLACE]

P.I.B., Prices and Incomes Board.

pibroch (pē'brŏk), *n.* (in the Scottish Highlands) a kind of musical piece performed on the bagpipe, comprising a series of variations on a theme, usually martial in character, but sometimes used as a dirge or otherwise. [t. Gaelic: m. *piobaireachd* pipe music, the art of playing a bagpipe, der. *piobair* PIPER]

pica¹ (pī'kə), *n. Print.* **1.** a type (12 point) of a size between small pica and English. **2.** the depth of this type size (about one sixth of an inch) as a unit of linear measurement for type, etc. [t. AL: book of rules for church services, appar. the same word as L *pīca* magpie. See PIE²]

pica² (pī'kə), *n. Pathol.* depraved or perverted appetite or craving for unnatural food, as chalk, clay, etc., common in chlorosis, pregnancy, etc. [t. NL or ML: magpie, with reference to its omnivorous feeding]

picador (pĭk'ə dô'; *Sp.* pē kȧ dȯr'), *n.* one of the horsemen who open a bullfight by irritating and enraging the bull with pricks of lances, without disabling him. [Sp., der. *picar* prick, pierce]

Picardy (pĭk'ə dĭ), *n.* **1.** a region in N France: formerly a province. **2.** an administrative region in N France comprising the departments of Somme, Oise, and Aisne.

1,482,434 pop. (1962); 7581 sq. mi. *Cap.*: Amiens. French, **Picardie** (*Fr.* pē kȧr dē′).

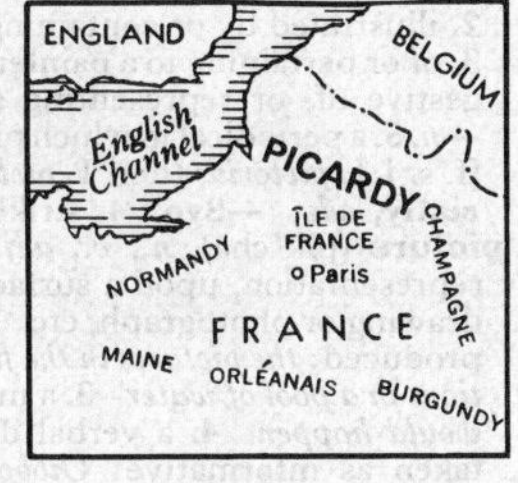

Picardy (def. 1)

picaresque (pĭk′ə rĕsk′), *adj.* of or pertaining to rogues: applied to a type of episodic fiction, of Spanish origin, with a rogue or rogues for hero(es). [t. F, t. Sp.: m. *picaresco*, der. *picaro* rogue, t. F: m. *Picard* native of Picardy]

picaroon (pĭk′ə ro͞on′), *n.* **1.** a rogue, thief, or brigand. **2.** a pirate or corsair. —*v.i.* **3.** to act or cruise as a brigand or pirate. [t. Sp.: m. *picarón*, aug. of *picaro* rogue. See PICARESQUE]

Picasso (pĭ kăs′ō; *Sp.* pē kä′sō), *n.* **Pablo** (*Sp.* pä′blō), born 1881, Spanish painter and sculptor living in France.

picayune (pĭk′ə yo͞on′), *n.* **1.** (formerly in Florida, Louisiana, etc.) the Spanish half real. **2.** *U.S.* any small coin, as a five-cent piece. **3.** *Colloq.* an insignificant person or thing. —*adj.* **4.** *Colloq.* Also, **pic′ayun′ish.** of little value or account; small; petty. [t. F: m. *picaillon*, t. Pr.: m. *picaioun*, old copper coin of Piedmont, ult. der. L *pecūnia* money]

Piccadilly (pĭk′ə dĭl′ĭ), *n.* a main thoroughfare in central London.

piccalilli (pĭk′ə lĭl′ĭ), *n., pl.* **-lis.** a highly seasoned pickle, of East Indian origin, made of chopped vegetables.

piccaninny (pĭk′ə nĭn′ĭ), *n., pl.* **-nies. 1.** a Negro or coloured child. **2.** a small child. Also, **pickaninny.** [t. Negro pidgin E: child, t. Pg.: m. *pequenino* very little]

Piccard (*Fr.* pē kȧr′), *n.* **Auguste** (*Fr.* ō gYst′), 1884–1962, Swiss physicist: stratosphere balloon ascent to 55,500 ft (1932).

piccolo (pĭk′ə lō′), *n., pl.* **-los.** a small flute, sounding an octave higher than the ordinary flute. [t. It.: small]

pice (pīs), *n., pl.* **pice.** (formerly) a British Indian bronze coin and money of account equal to a quarter of an anna. [t. Hind.: m. *paisā*]

piceous (pĭs′ĭ əs, pī′sĭ əs), *adj.* **1.** of, pertaining to, or resembling pitch. **2.** inflammable or combustible. **3.** *Zool.* black or nearly black as pitch. [t. L: m. *piceus*]

pichiciago (pĭch′ĭ sĭ ä′gō, -ā′gō), *n., pl.* **-gos.** the smallest of the armadillos, of the genera *Chlamyphorus* and *Burmeisteria* of southern South America. [t. S Amer. Sp.: m. *pichiciego*, f. Guarani *pichey* small armadillo + Sp. *ciego* blind (g. L *caecus*)]

pick[1] (pĭk), *v.t.* **1.** to choose or select carefully. **2.** to choose (one's way or steps), as over rough ground or through a crowd. **3.** to seek and find occasion for: *to pick a quarrel.* **4.** to seek or find (flaws) in a spirit of faultfinding. **5.** to steal the contents of (a person's pocket, purse, etc.). **6.** to open (a lock) with a pointed instrument, a wire, or the like, as for robbery. **7.** to pierce, indent, dig into, or break up (something) with a pointed instrument. **8.** to form (a hole, etc.) by such action. **9.** to use a pointed instrument, the fingers, the teeth, the beak, etc., on (a thing), in order to remove something. **10.** to clear (a thing) of something by such action: *to pick one's teeth.* **11.** to prepare for use by removing feathers, hulls, or other parts: *to pick a fowl.* **12.** to detach or remove with the fingers, the beak, or the like, esp. with the fingers. **13.** to pluck or gather: *to pick flowers.* **14.** (of birds or other animals) to take up (small bits of food) with the bill or teeth. **15.** to eat in small morsels or daintily. **16.** to separate, pull apart, or pull to pieces (fibres, etc.). **17.** *Music.* **a.** to pluck (the strings of an instrument). **b.** to play (a stringed instrument) by plucking. —*v.i.* **18.** to strike with or use a pointed instrument or the like on something. **19.** to eat with dainty bites. **20.** to choose; make careful or fastidious selection. **21.** to pilfer. —*v.* **22.** Some special verb phrases are:

pick and choose, to choose with great care, esp. fussily.

pick at, *Colloq.* **1.** to find fault with, in a petty way. **2.** to eat very little of: *the child picked at her food.*

pick off, to single out and shoot.

pick on, *Colloq.* **1.** to annoy; tease; criticize or blame. **2.** to chose (a person) indiscriminately, esp. for an unpleasant task.

pick out, 1. to choose. **2.** to distinguish (a thing) from surrounding or accompanying things. **3.** to make out (sense or meaning). **4.** to extract by picking.

pick (someone's) brains, to find out as much as one can, from someone else's knowledge of a subject.

pick to pieces, to criticize, esp. in petty detail.

pick up, 1. to take up: *to pick up a stone.* **2.** to pluck up, recover, or regain (health, courage, etc.). **3.** to learn by occasional opportunity or without special teaching. **4.** to get casually. **5.** to become acquainted with informally or casually. **6.** to take (a person or thing) into a car, ship, etc., or along with one. **7.** to bring into the range of reception, observation, etc.: *to pick up Rome on one's radio.* **8.** to accelerate, esp. in speed. **9.** *Colloq.* to improve. **10.** *Colloq.* to arrest.

—*n.* **23.** choice or selection. **24.** that which is selected. **25.** the choicest or most desirable part, example, or examples. **26.** the right of selection. **27.** an act of picking. **28.** the quantity of a crop picked at a particular time. **29.** *Print.* a speck of dirt, hardened ink, or extra metal on set type or a plate. **30.** a stroke with something pointed. **31.** a plectrum.

[ME *picke* (c. G *picken*), var. of *pike*, v. (now d.), ME *piken.* Cf. OE *pīcung* pricking] —**Syn. 1.** See **choose.**

pick[2] (pĭk), *n.* **1.** a hand tool consisting of an iron bar, usually curved, tapering to a point at one or both ends, mounted on a wooden handle, and used for loosening and breaking up soil, rock, etc. **2.** any pointed or other tool or instrument for picking. [ME *pikk(e)*, OE *pīc*]

pick[3] (pĭk), *Weaving.* —*v.t.* **1.** to cast (a shuttle). —*n.* **2.** (in a loom) one passage of the shuttle. **3.** a single filling yarn. [var. of PITCH[1]]

pickaback (pĭk′ə băk′), *adv.* on the back or shoulders like a pack: *she rode pickaback on her father till he was exhausted.*

pickaninny (pĭk′ə nĭn′ĭ), *n., pl.* **-nies.** piccaninny.

pickaxe (pĭk′ăks′), *n., v.t., v.i.,* **-axed, -axing. 1.** a pick, esp. a mattock. —*v.t.* **2.** to cut or clear away with a pickaxe. —*v.i.* **3.** to use a pickaxe. Also, *U.S.*, **pickax.** [f. PICK[2] + AXE; r. ME *picois*, t. OF (cf. OF *pic*, OE *pīc* PIKE[5])]

picked[1] (pĭkt), *adj.* **1.** specially chosen or selected: *a crew of picked men.* **2.** cleared or cleaned, as of refuse parts, by picking. [f. PICK[1], v. + -ED[2]]

picked[2] (pĭk′ĭd, pĭkt), *adj.* *Now Archaic or Dial.* pointed. [f. PICK[2] + -ED[3]]

picker[1] (pĭk′ə), *n.* **1.** one who picks. **2.** one who plucks or gathers fruit, flowers, etc. [f. PICK[1], v. + -ER[1]]

picker[2] (pĭk′ə), *n.* *Weaving.* **1.** a tool or instrument for picking. **2.** the piece that throws the shuttle of the loom through the warp. **3.** one who works a picker. [f. PICK[3], v. + -ER[1]]

pickerel (pĭk′ə rəl), *n., pl.* **-rels,** (*esp. collectively*) **-rel.** *U.S. and Can.* any of various species of pike, esp. one of the smaller species, as the **chain pickerel,** *Esox niger*, and the **mud pickerel,** *Esox vermiculatus.* [ME *pykerel*, f. PIKE[1] + -REL]

pickerelweed (pĭk′ə rəl wēd′), *n.* any plant of the American genus *Pontederia*, esp. *P. cordata*, a blue-flowered herb common in shallow fresh water.

Pickering (pĭk′ə rĭng), *n.* **1. Edward Charles,** 1846–1919, U.S. astronomer. **2.** his brother, **William Henry,** 1858–1938, U.S. astronomer.

picket (pĭk′ĭt), *n.* **1.** a pointed post, stake, pale, or peg, as for driving into the ground in making a stockade, for placing vertically to form the main part of a fence (**picket fence**), for driving into the ground to fasten something to, etc. **2.** a person or a body of persons stationed by a trade union or the like before a place of work and attempting to dissuade or prevent workers from entering the building during a strike. **3.** *Mil.* a small detached body of troops, posted out from a force to warn against an enemy's approach. —*v.t.* **4.** to enclose, fence, or make secure with pickets. **5.** to fasten or tether to a picket. **6.** to place pickets at, as during a strike. **7.** *Mil.* **a.** to guard, as a camp, by or as pickets. **b.** *Obs.* to post as a picket. —*v.i.* **8.** to stand or march by a place of employment as a picket. [t. F: m. *piquet* pointed stake, military picket, dim. of *pic* a pick; in other senses connected with *piquer* prick, pierce, with dim. suffix. See -ET] —**pick′eter,** *n.*

Pickford (pĭk′fəd), *n.* **Mary** (*Gladys Smith*), born 1893, U.S. film actress, born in Canada.

picking (pĭk′ĭng), *n.* **1.** the act of one who or that which picks. **2.** that which is or may be picked or picked up. **3.** the amount picked. **4.** (*pl.*) things, portions, or scraps remaining and worth picking up or appropriating. **5.** (*pl.*) pilferings, or perquisites obtained by means not strictly honest. [f. PICK[1] + -ING[1]]

pickle (pĭk′l), *n., v.,* **-led, -ling.** —*n.* **1.** (*often pl.*) vegetables, as cucumbers, onions, cauliflowers, etc., preserved in vinegar, brine, etc., and eaten as a relish. **2.** anything preserved in a pickling liquid. **3.** a liquid or marinade prepared with salt or vinegar for the preservation of fish, meat, vegetables, etc., or for the hardening of wood, leather, etc. **4.** a pickled article of food, esp. cucumber. **5.** *Metall.* an acid or other chemical solution in which metal objects are dipped to remove oxide scale or other adhering substances. **6.** *Colloq.* a predicament. **7.** a mischievous child. **8. have a rod in pickle,** have a punishment ready. —*v.t.* **9.** to preserve or steep in pickle. **10.** to clean or treat (objects) in a chemical pickle. [ME *pekille, pykyl*, t. MD or MLG: m. *pekel(e)*. Cf. G *Pökel* brine]

pickled (pĭk′ld), *adj.* **1.** preserved or hardened in pickle. **2.** *Colloq.* drunk.

picklock (pĭk′lŏk′), *n.* **1.** a person who picks locks. **2.** a thief. **3.** an instrument for picking locks.

pick-me-up (pĭk′mē ŭp′), *n. Colloq.* **1.** a stimulating or refreshing drink, esp. alcoholic. **2.** any restorative, such as a meal or drink.

pickpocket (pĭk′pŏk′ĭt), *n.* one who steals from the pockets, handbags, etc., of people in public places.

pickthank (pĭk′thăngk′), *n.* one who curries favour by sycophancy or tale-bearing.

pick-up (pĭk′ŭp′), *n.* **1.** *Slang.* an informal or casual acquaintance, esp. one made in the hope of sexual conquest. **2.** Also, **pick-up truck.** a small, open-bodied delivery lorry, built on a chassis comparable to that of a passenger car. **3.** *Sport.* the act of fielding a ball after it hits the ground. **4.** *Radio.* **a.** the process of receiving sound-waves in the transmitting set in order to change them into electrical waves. **b.** a receiving or recording device as in a tape-recorder; a microphone. **c.** the place at which a broadcast is being transmitted. **d.** interference. **5.** *Television.* **a.** the change of light energy into electrical energy in the transmitting set. **b.** the device used. **6.** Also, **cartridge.** a device which generates electric or acoustic impulses in accordance with the mechanical variations impressed upon a gramophone record (**gramophone pick-up**). **7.** *Motor Vehicles, U.S.* a capacity for rapid acceleration. **8.** a stop made to collect a passenger or item of freight, as by a taxi, bus, etc. **9.** the passenger or item so collected. **10.** *Slang.* a free lift in a motor vehicle. **11.** *U.S. Slang.* **a.** improvement. **b.** pick-me-up.

pick-up arm, the free-swinging arm of a gramophone which contains the pick-up.

Pickwickian (pĭk wĭk′ĭ ən), *adj.* **1.** of, pertaining to, or characteristic of Samuel Pickwick (in Charles Dickens's novel *The Pickwick Papers* the benevolent, naive founder of the Pickwick Club). **2.** (of the use or interpretation of an expression) unusual, or intended to be understood in an unusual sense; recondite.

picnic (pĭk′nĭk), *n., v.,* **-nicked, -nicking. 1.** an outing or excursion, typically one in which those taking part carry food with them and share a meal in the open air. **2.** the meal eaten on such an outing. **3.** *Slang.* an enjoyable experience or time. **4.** *Slang.* an easy undertaking. **5.** *Slang.* an awkward situation; a hullaballoo. —*v.i.* **6.** to hold, or take part in, a picnic. [t. F: m. *pique-nique*; orig. unknown] —**pic′nicker,** *n.*

pico-, a prefix denoting one million millionth, 10^{-12}. [comb. form repr. Sp. *pico* odd number, peak]

Pico della Mirandola (*It.* pē′kō dĕl lä mē rän′ dō lä), **Count Giovanni** (*It.* jō vän′nē), 1463–94, Italian humanist.

Pico de Teide (*Sp.* pē′kō dė tėy′dė). See **Teide.**

picoline (pĭk′ə lēn′, -lĭn), *n. Chem.* any of three isomeric derivatives of pyridine, $CH_3C_5H_4N$, obtained from coal tar as colourless oily liquids with a strong smell. [f. s. L *pix* pitch + L *ol(eum)* oil + -INE[2]]

picot (pē′kō), *n., v.,* **picoted** (pē′kōd), **picoting** (pē′kō ĭng). —*n.* **1.** one of a number of ornamental loops in embroidery, or along the edge of lace, ribbon, etc. —*v.t.* **2.** to make or ornament with, picots. [t. F, dim. of *pic* a pick, something pointed. See PIKE[2]]

picotee (pĭk′ə tē′), *n.* a variety of carnation whose petals have an outer margin of another colour, usually red. [t. F: m. *picoté*, pp. of *picoter* mark with pricks or spots. See PICOT]

picrate (pĭk′rāt, pĭk′rĭt), *n. Chem.* a salt or ester of picric acid.

picric acid (pĭk′rĭk), *Chem.* an intensely bitter yellow acid, $C_6H_2OH(NO_2)_3$ used as a dye and an explosive. [f. m. s. Gk *pikrós* bitter + -IC]

picrite (pĭk′rīt), *n.* a granular igneous rock composed chiefly of olivine and augite, but containing small amounts of felspar. [f. m. s. Gk *pikrós* bitter + -ITE[1]]

Pict (pĭkt), *n.* one of a race of people of disputed origin who formerly inhabited parts of northern Britain, and in the 9th century became united with the Scots. [ME *Pictes*, pl. (t. L: m. *Pictī*, lit., painted); r. ME *Peghttes*, OE *Peohtas*, earlier *Pihtas*, t. L (as above)]

Pictish (pĭk′tĭsh), *n.* **1.** the language of the Picts. —*adj.* **2.** of or pertaining to the Picts.

pictograph (pĭk′tə grăf′, -gräf′), *n.* **1.** a record consisting of pictorial symbols. **2.** a pictorial sign or symbol. [f. s. L *pictus*, pp., painted, represented pictorially + -O- + -GRAPH] —**pictographic** (pĭk′tə grăf′ĭk), *adj.* —**pic′tograph′ically,** *adv.*

pictography (pĭk tŏg′rə fĭ), *n.* the use of pictographs; picture writing.

pictorial (pĭk tô′rĭ əl), *adj.* **1.** pertaining to, expressed in, or of the nature of, a picture or pictures: *pictorial writing.* **2.** illustrated by or containing pictures: *a pictorial history.* **3.** of or pertaining to a painter or maker of pictures. **4.** suggestive of, or representing as if by, a picture; graphic. —*n.* **5.** a periodical in which pictures are the leading feature. [f. s. LL *pictōrius* (der. L *pictor* painter) + -AL[1]] —**picto′rially,** *adv.* —**Syn. 4.** striking, vivid.

picture (pĭk′chə), *n., v., adj.,* **-tured, -turing.** —*n.* **1.** a representation, upon a surface, usually flat, as a painting, drawing or photograph, etc. **2.** any visible image, however produced: *the pictures in the fire, the pictures made by reflections in a pool of water.* **3.** a mental image: *a picture of what would happen.* **4.** a verbal description intended to be or taken as informative: *Gibbon's picture of ancient Rome.* **5.** a tableau, as in theatrical representation. **6.** a very beautiful object, esp. a person: *she looks a picture in her new dress.* **7.** a film (def. 4b). **8. the pictures,** a cinema. **9.** the image or counterpart (of someone else). **10.** an object or person possessing a quality in such a high degree as to seem to embody that quality: *she is a picture of health.* **11.** a situation or set of circumstances: *the employment picture.* **12. get the picture, be in the picture,** to understand the situation. **13.** Also, **clinical picture.** *Pathol.* the overall view of a case. —*v.t.* **14.** to form a mental image of: *he couldn't picture himself doing such a thing.* **15.** to describe, verbally and, usually, plausibly. [MF, t. L: *pictūra*]

picture card, *Cards.* a court card.

picture hat, a woman's hat having a broad flexible brim, often decorated with ostrich feathers, flowers, etc.

picture house, *Colloq., Obs.* a cinema.

picture mould, *Chiefly U.S.* a picture rail. Also, **picture mold, picture moulding, picture molding.**

picture palace, *Obs.* a cinema.

picture rail, a moulding on a wall near the ceiling from which pictures can be hung. See **dado.**

picturesque (pĭk′chə rĕsk′), *adj.* **1:** visually charming or quaint, as resembling or suitable for a picture. **2.** (of written or spoken language) strikingly vivid or graphic. **3.** having pleasing or interesting qualities; strikingly effective in appearance. [f. PICTURE + -ESQUE, modelled on F *pittoresque*, t. It.: m. *pittoresco*, der. *pittore* painter, g. L *pictor*] —**pic′turesque′ly,** *adv.* —**pic′turesque′ness,** *n.*

—**Syn. 2.** PICTURESQUE, GRAPHIC, VIVID apply to descriptions that produce a strong, especially a visual, impression. Of these, PICTURESQUE is the least precise term. A PICTURESQUE account, though striking and interesting, may be inaccurate or may reflect personal ideas: *he gave a picturesque account of the scene.* A GRAPHIC account is more objective and factual; it produces a clear, definite impression, and carries conviction. A VIVID account is told with liveliness and intenseness; the description is so interesting, or even exciting, that the hearer may be emotionally stirred.

picture tube, *Television.* the cathode-ray tube.

picture window, a large window in a house, usually dominating the room, and sometimes designed to focus attention on the view through it.

picture writing, 1. the art of recording events or expressing ideas by pictures or pictorial symbols, as practised by preliterate peoples. **2.** pictorial symbols forming a record or communication.

picul (pĭk′l), *n.* (in the Far East) a weight equal to 100 catties, or from about 133 to about 143 pounds avoirdupois. [t. Malay-Javanese: m. *pikul* a man's load]

piculet (pĭk′yo͞o lĭt), *n.* any of several small short-billed woodpeckers, chiefly of the genus *Picumnus*, lacking stiffened shafts in the tail feathers. [L *pīcu(s)* woodpecker + -LET]

piddle (pĭd′l), *v.i.,* **-dled, -dling.** *Taboo.* **1.** *Colloq.* to urinate. **2.** to do anything in a trifling or ineffective way; dawdle. [cf. Norw. *pydla* pout]

piddling (pĭd′lĭng), *adj.* trifling; petty.

piddock (pĭd′ək), *n.* any of the bivalve molluscs of the genus *Pholas* or the family *Pholadidae*, mostly marine, with long ovate shell, and burrowing in soft rock, wood, etc. [cf. OE *puduc* wart]

pidgin (pĭj′ĭn), *n.* a language which has come into existence through attempts to communicate by speakers of two or more languages, having vocabulary, pronunciation, and syntax selected or developed from both or all the native languages of such speakers. Also, **pigeon.** [? Chinese pron. of BUSINESS]

pidgin English, a pidgin developed from English and any of various other languages, as that formerly much used for commerce in Chinese ports, or in Melanesia, West Africa, etc. Also, **pigeon English.**

pie[1] (pī), *n.* **1.** a baked dish consisting of a sweet or savoury filling of fruit, meat, fish, or the like, enclosed in or covered by pastry. **2.** *U.S.* a tart. **3. have a finger in every pie,** to have an interest in or play a part in many affairs. **4. pie**

in the sky, the illusory prospect of future benefits. [ME; orig. uncert.] —pie′like′, *adj.*

pie² (pī), *n.* magpie. [ME, t. OF, g. L *pīca* magpie]

pie³ (pī), *n., v.,* **pied, pieing.** —*n.* **1.** printing types mixed together indiscriminately. —*v.t.* **2.** to reduce (printing types) to a state of confusion. Also, *Chiefly U.S.,* **pi.** [orig. uncert.]

pie⁴ (pī), *n. Eccles.* (in England before the Reformation) a book of rules for finding the particulars of the service for the day. Also, **pye.** [trans. of L *pīca* magpie; see PICA¹]

pie⁵ (pī), *n.* a former Indian bronze coin, equal to one twelfth of an anna. [t. Hind.: m. *pā'ī*]

piebald (pī′bôld′), *adj.* **1.** having patches of black and white or of other colours; particoloured. **2.** (of a horse) white with black patches. —*n.* **3.** a piebald animal, esp. a horse. [f. PIE² (see PIED) + BALD]

piece (pēs), *n., v.,* **pieced, piecing.** —*n.* **1.** a limited portion or quantity, of something: *a piece of land.* **2.** a quantity of some substance or material forming a mass or body. **3.** one of the more or less definite parts or portions into which something may be divided: *a piece of chocolate.* **4.** one of the parts, fragments, or shreds into which something may be divided or broken: *to tear a letter into pieces.* **5.** one of the parts which, when assembled, form a combined whole: *the pieces of a machine.* **6.** an individual article of a set or collection: *a dinner service of 100 pieces.* **7.** any of the counters, discs, blocks, or the like, of wood, ivory, or other material, used in any of a number of board games, as draughts, backgammon, or chess. **8.** *Chess.* a superior man, as distinguished from a pawn. **9.** a particular length, as of certain goods prepared for sale: *cloth sold by the piece.* **10.** an amount of work forming a single job: *to work by the piece.* **11.** a specimen of workmanship, esp. of artistic production, as a picture or statue. **12.** a literary composition, in prose or verse, usually short. **13.** a play; drama. **14.** a situation or episode: *the villain of the piece.* **15.** a passage of verse, music, or the like, prepared for recitation or performance on a particular occasion. **16.** a musical composition, usually a short one. **17.** an individual thing of a particular class or kind: *a piece of furniture.* **18.** an example, instance, or specimen of something: *a fine piece of workmanship.* **19.** a person, esp. a woman: *she's a nice little piece.* **20.** a woman of loose morals. **21.** *Mil.* **a.** a firearm: *a fowling-piece.* **b.** an item of ordnance. **22.** a coin: *a threepenny piece.* **23.** *Now U.S. Dial.* a distance, esp. a short one. **24. a piece of cake,** *Colloq.* an easily achieved enterprise or undertaking. **25. a piece of one's mind,** outspoken criticism or reproach. **26. go to pieces,** to lose emotional or physical control of oneself. **27. of a piece,** of the same kind; consistent. **28. piece of work, a.** an example or instance of workmanship; something produced. **b.** a person, considered as an example of a specified quality: *a nasty piece of work.* —*v.t.* **29.** to mend (something broken); reassemble (usually fol. by *together*). **30.** to fit together, as pieces or parts. **31.** to make up or form into a whole by or as if by joining pieces (usually fol. by *together*): *to piece together a picture of the situation.* **32.** to patch; to mend (a garment, etc.) by applying a piece or pieces (usually fol. by *up*). **33.** to complete, enlarge, or extend by making additions (usually fol. by *out*). **34.** to add as a piece or part: *to piece new palings into a fence.* [ME *pece,* t. OF, g. Rom. *pettia* broken piece, piece of land, of Celtic orig.] —**Syn. 1.** section, segment, scrap fragment. See **part.**

pièce à thèse (*Fr.* pyĕs à tĕz′), *French.* a play intended to propound a thesis.

pièce de résistance (*Fr.* pyĕs də rė zēs täNs′), *French.* **1.** the principal dish of a meal. **2.** the principal event, incident, article, etc., of a series.

piece-dyed (pēs′dīd′), *adj.* dyed after weaving (opposed to *yarn-dyed*).

piece goods, goods or fabrics woven in lengths suitable for retail sale by the usual linear measure.

piecemeal (pēs′mēl′), *adv.* **1.** piece by piece; gradually. **2.** into pieces or fragments. —*adj.* **3.** done piece by piece; fragmentary. [ME *pecemele* (r. OE *styccemǣlum*). See PIECE]

piecener (pēs′nə), *n.* piecer (def. 1).

piece of eight, the old Spanish dollar or peso, of the value of 8 reals.

piecer (pē′sə), *n.* **1.** Also, **piecener.** *Textiles.* one who joins the ends of threads which break on a mechanical loom. **2.** one who mends, patches, or assembles something. [PIECE + -ER¹]

piece rate, compensation based on output or production, usually a fixed sum per piece of work turned out.

piecework (pēs′wûk′), *n.* work done and paid for by the piece. —**piece′work′er,** *n.*

piecrust (pī′krŭst′), *n.* **1.** the pastry covering of a pie. **2.** the pastry of which the covering of a pie is made. [f. PIE¹ + CRUST]

pied (pīd), *adj.* **1.** having patches of two or more colours, as various birds and other animals. **2.** wearing particoloured clothes. [f. PIE² (with reference to the black-and-white plumage of the magpie) + -ED³]

pied-à-terre (*Fr.* pyė tà tĕr′), *n. French.* a lodging for occasional or temporary use. [F: lit., foot (footing) on ground]

Piedmont (pēd′mŏnt), *n.* **1.** Italian, **Piemonte.** a region in NW Italy. *Cap.:* Turin. 3,899,962 pop. (1961); 11,335 sq. mi. **2.** (*l.c.*) a district lying along or near the foot of a mountain range. **3.** a plateau in the U.S. between the coastal plain and the Appalachian Mountains, including parts of Virginia, North and South Carolina, Georgia, and Alabama. —*adj.* **4.** (*l.c.*) lying along or near the foot of a mountain range. [t. It.: m. *Piemonte,* lit., foothill (region)] —**Piedmontese** (pēd′mŏn tēz′), *adj., n.*

piedmontite (pēd′mŏn tīt′, -mən-), *n.* a mineral silicate of calcium, aluminium, manganese, and hydrogen crystallizing in the monoclinic system. Also, **manganepidote, manganese epidote.**

Pied Piper, 1. the hero of a German legend, popularized in 1842 by Robert Browning. Cf. **Hameln. 2.** (*sometimes l.c.*) one who causes others to follow him, esp. on some foolish venture.

Piemonte (*It.* pyė mōn′tė), *n.* Italian name of **Piedmont** (def. 1).

pier (pĭə), *n.* **1.** a structure built out into the water to serve as a landing place for ships, and, sometimes, protect a harbour, a breakwater or a jetty. **2.** such a structure used as a pleasure promenade. **3.** one of the supports of a span of a bridge or of two adjacent spans. **4.** a square pillar. **5.** a portion of wall between doors, windows, etc. **6.** a pillar or post on which a gate or door is hung. **7.** a support of masonry or the like for sustaining vertical pressure. See diag. under **arch.** [ME *per(e),* t. ML: m. *pera*]

pierce (pĭəs), *v.,* **pierced, piercing.** —*v.t.* **1.** to penetrate or run into or through (something), as a sharp-pointed instrument does; puncture. **2.** to make a hole or opening in. **3.** to bore into or through; tunnel. **4.** to perforate. **5.** to make (a hole, etc.) by or as by boring or perforating. **6.** to force or make a way into or through: *to pierce a wilderness.* **7.** to penetrate with the eye or mind; see into or through. **8.** to affect sharply with some sensation or emotion, as of cold, pain, grief, etc. **9.** to sound sharply through (the air, stillness, etc.) as a cry. —*v.i.* **10.** to force or make a way into or through something; penetrate. [ME *perce(n), persche(n),* t. OF: m. *percier,* ult. der. L *pertūsus,* pp., pierced] —**pierc′er,** *n.* —**pierc′ingly,** *adv.*

—**Syn. 1.** PIERCE, PENETRATE suggest the action of one object passing through another or making a way through and into another. The terms are used both concretely and figuratively. To PIERCE is to perforate quickly, as by stabbing; it suggests the use of a sharp-pointed instrument which is impelled by force: *to pierce the flesh with a knife, a scream pierces one's ears.* PENETRATE suggests a slow or difficult movement: *no ordinary bullet can penetrate an elephant's hide, to penetrate the depths of one's ignorance.*

Pierce (pĭəs), *n.* **1. Benjamin,** 1809–80, U.S. mathematician and astronomer. **2. Franklin,** 1804–69, 14th president of the U.S., 1853–57.

pier glass, 1. a tall mirror such as is used to fill the pier or space between two windows. **2.** any tall window.

Pieria (pī ĭə′rĭ ə), *n.* a coastal region including Mt Olympus, in ancient Macedonia: the legendary birthplace of Orpheus and the Muses.

Pierian (pī ĭə′rĭ ən), *adj.* **1.** of or pertaining to the Muses or to artistic, esp. poetic, inspiration. **2.** of or pertaining to Pieria. [f. s. L *Pīerius* of Pieria + -AN]

pieridine (pī ĕ′rĭ dīn′), *adj.* of or denoting a butterfly of the family *Pieridae,* which includes various white, yellow, and orange species. [t. NL: m. *Pīeridinae,* pl., der. *Pīeris* the typical genus, t. Gk: a Muse]

Piero della Francesca (*It.* pyĕ′rō dĕl lȧ frȧnt chĕs′kȧ), 1410/20–92, Italian painter.

Piero di Cosimo (*It.* pyĕ′rō dē kō′zē mō), *c.* 1462–1521?, Italian painter.

Pierre (pĭə), *n.* a town in the U.S., capital of South Dakota. 10,088 (1960).

Pierrette (pĭə rĕt′; *Fr.* pyĕ rĕt′), *n.* female counterpart of Pierrot; usually accompanying him in entertainments and masquerade.

Pierrot (pĭə′rō; *Fr.* pyĕ rō′), *n.* **1.** a male character in certain French pantomime, having a whitened face and wearing a loose white fancy costume. **2.** (*l.c.*) a masquerader or buffoon so made up. [F, dim. of *Pierre,* man's name. See PETER]

Piers Plowman (pĭəz′ plou′mən) (*The Vision concerning Piers Plowman*), an alliterative poem, written in three main versions (1360–99) by William Langland.

pier table, a table or low bracket for occupying the space against a pier between two windows, often used under a pier glass.

pietà (pĭ′ĕ tä′), *n. Art.* a representation of the Virgin Mary mourning over the body of the dead Christ. [It.: pity, t. L: m. *pietās* PIETY]

Pietermaritzburg (pē′tə mä′rĭts bûg′), *n.* a city in the E Republic of South Africa: the capital of Natal province. with suburbs, 128,598 (1960).

Pietism (pī′ə tĭz′əm), *n.* **1.** a movement originating during the latter part of the 17th century in the Lutheran churches in Germany, that stressed personal piety over religious formality and orthodoxy. **2.** the principles and practices of the Pietists. **3.** (*l.c.*) depth of religious feeling; godliness of life. **4.** (*l.c.*) exaggeration or affectation of piety. [t. NL(G): m. *Pietismus*] —**Pi′etist,** *n.* —**pi′etis′tic,** *adj.*

piety (pī′ə tĭ), *n., pl.* **-ties. 1.** reverence for God, or regard for religious obligations. **2.** the quality or fact of being pious. **3.** dutiful respect or regard for parents or others. **4.** a pious act, remark, belief, or the like. [ME, t. L: m. s. *pietās*] —**Syn. 2.** godliness, devoutness.

piezoelectricity (pī ē′zō ĭ lĕk′trĭs′ĭ tĭ), *n.* electricity produced by pressure, as in a crystal subjected to compression along a certain axis. [f. *piezo-* (comb. form repr. Gk *piézein* press, squeeze) + ELECTRICITY] —**piezoelectric** (pī ē′zō ĭ lĕk′trĭk), *adj.* —**pie′zoelec′trically,** *adv.*

piezometer (pī′ĭ zŏm′ĭ tə), *n.* any of various instruments for measuring pressure. —**piezometric** (pī ē′zō mĕt′rĭk), **pie′zomet′rical,** *adj.*

piezometry (pī′ĭ zŏm′ĭ trĭ), *n.* the measurement of pressure or compressibility.

piffle (pĭf′əl), *n., v.,* **-fled, -fling.** *Colloq.* —*n.* **1.** nonsense; idle talk. —*v.i.* **2.** to talk nonsense. [cf. OE *pyff* PUFF] —**pif′fler,** *n.*

piffling (pĭf′lĭng), *adj. Colloq.* trivial; petty; nonsensical.

pig (pĭg), *n., v.,* **pigged, pigging.** —*n.* **1.** an omnivorous non-ruminant mammal of the family *Suidae*, suborder *Artiodactyla* and order *Ungulata*; a sow, hog, or boar; a swine. Cf. **hog. 2.** a young swine, of either sex, bred for slaughter. **3.** the flesh of swine; pork. **4.** *Colloq.* a person or animal of piggish character or habits. **5.** *Metall.* **a.** an oblong mass of metal that has been run while still molten into a mould of sand or the like, esp. such a mass of iron from a blast furnace; an ingot. **b.** one of the moulds for such masses of metal. **c.** metal in the form of such masses. **6. a pig in a poke,** something purchased without inspection. **7. make a pig of oneself,** to overindulge oneself, as by eating too much. —*v.i.* **8.** to bring forth pigs. **9.** Also, **pig it.** to live, lie, etc., as if in a pigsty; live in squalor. [ME *pigge*, OE *picg* (in *pic(g)-bred* pig-bread, mast). Cf. D *big* young pig]

pig-bed (pĭg′bĕd′), *n. Metall.* a bed of sand for moulding pigs, into which molten metal is poured.

pig-bin (pĭg′bĭn′), *n.* a container for the collection of kitchen refuse which is given to pigs. Also, **pig-bucket** (pĭg′bŭk′ĭt).

pigeon[1] (pĭj′ĭn), *n.* **1.** any bird of the family *Columbidae*, having a compact body and short legs, of which there are several species distributed throughout the world; especially the larger varieties with square or rounded tails. Cf. **dove** (def. 1). **2.** any domesticated member of this family, as bred for racing, exhibiting, etc. **3.** *Colloq.* responsibility; concern: *that's his pigeon.* **4.** *Slang.* a dupe. [ME *pejon*, t. OF: m. *pijon*, g. s. LL *pīpio* squab]

pigeon[2] (pĭj′ĭn), *n.* pidgin.

pigeon breast, *Pathol.* a malformation of the chest in which there is abnormal projection of the sternum and sternal region, often associated with rickets. Also, **pigeon chest.** —**pig′eon-breas′ted,** *adj.* —**pig′eon-breas′tedness,** *n.*

pigeon English, pidgin English.

pigeon-fancier (pĭj′ĭn făn′sĭ ə), *n.* one who keeps, breeds, and sometimes trains domestic pigeons. —**pig′eon-fan′cying,** *n.*

pigeon-hawk (pĭj′ĭn hôk′), *n.* **1.** a hawk that preys on pigeons, as the goshawk. **2.** *U.S.* the American merlin, *Falco columbarius.*

pigeon-hearted (pĭj′ĭn hä′tĭd), *adj.* timid; meek.

pigeonhole (pĭj′ĭn hōl′), *n., v.,* **-holed, -holing.** —*n.* **1.** one of a series of small compartments in a desk, cabinet, or the like, used for papers, etc. **2.** a hole or recess, or one of a series of recesses, for pigeons to nest in. **3.** any series or set of small holes or recesses, as cutaway parts in a boat's superstructure to lead rigging through. —*v.t.* **4.** to put away for reference at some indefinite future time. **5.** to assign a definite place in some orderly system. **6.** to put aside for the present, esp. with the intention of ignoring or forgetting. **7.** to place in a pigeonhole or pigeonholes. **8.** to furnish (a desk, etc.) with pigeonholes. —**Syn. 4.** file. **5.** categorize, catalogue. **6.** postpone, shelve.

pigeon-livered (pĭj′ĭn lĭv′əd), *adj.* meek; spiritless.

pigeon post, a system of sending messages by attaching them to the legs of homing pigeons.

pigeonpox (pĭj′ĭn pŏks′), *n.* a disease affecting pigeons, similar to fowl pox.

pigeon-toed (pĭj′ĭn tōd′), *adj.* having the toes or feet turned inwards.

pigeonwing (pĭj′ĭn wĭng′), *n.* **1.** a fancy step or evolution in dancing. **2.** *U.S.* a particular figure in skating, outlining the spread wing of a pigeon.

pigfish (pĭg′fĭsh′), *n., pl.* **-fishes,** (*esp. collectively*) **-fish.** any of various fishes, as a grunt, *Orthopristis chrysopterus*, a food fish of the S Atlantic coast of the U.S.

piggery (pĭg′ə rĭ), *n., pl.* **-geries. 1.** a place where pigs are kept. **2.** piggishness.

piggin (pĭg′ĭn), *n.* a small wooden pail or tub of staves and hoops with a handle formed by continuing one of the staves above the rim. [? der. *pig* pot, jar]

piggish (pĭg′ĭsh), *adj.* **1.** like or befitting a pig; greedy or filthy. **2.** mean or stubborn. —**pig′gishly,** *adv.* —**pig′gishness,** *n.*

piggy (pĭg′ĭ), *n., pl.* **-gies.** a little pig. Also, **piggie.**

piggyback (pĭg′ĭ băk′), *adv.* **1.** pickaback. —*adj.* **2.** *U.S.* of or pertaining to a lorry trailer, plane, etc., carried part of the way by a larger vehicle.

piggybacking (pĭg′ĭ băk′ĭng), *n. U.S.* the transporting of loaded lorry trailers, especially on flat railway trucks.

piggy bank, *Colloq.* a moneybox shaped like a pig, usually made of china, in which a child might keep his savings; any small money-box.

pig-headed (pĭg′hĕd′ĭd), *adj.* stupidly obstinate.

pig-iron (pĭg′ī′ən), *n.* **1.** iron produced in a blast furnace, poured into special moulds in preparation for making wrought iron, cast iron, or steel. **2.** iron in the unrefined state, before conversion into steel, alloys, etc.

pig Latin, spoken language distorted in one of various ways to make it unintelligible to overhearers.

pig-lead (pĭg′lĕd′), *n.* lead moulded in pigs.

piglet (pĭg′lĭt), *n.* a little pig.

pigling (pĭg′lĭng), *n.* a young or small pig.

pigment (pĭg′mənt), *n.* **1.** a colouring matter or substance. **2.** a dry substance, usually pulverized, which when mixed with a liquid vehicle in which it is insoluble becomes a paint, ink, etc. **3.** *Biol.* any substance whose presence in the tissues or cells of animals or plants colours them. [ME, t. L: s. *pigmentum*]

pigmentary (pĭg′mən tə rĭ, -trĭ), *adj.* of pigment. Also, **pigmental** (pĭg mĕn′tl).

pigmentation (pĭg′mĕn tā′shən), *n. Biol.* coloration with or deposition of pigment.

Pigmy (pĭg′mĭ), *n., pl.* **-mies,** *adj.* Pygmy.

pignut (pĭg′nŭt′), *n.* **1.** the nut of the brown hickory, *Carya glabra*, of North America. **2.** the tree itself. **3.** the tuber of a European plant, *Conopodium denudatum*, a kind of earthnut.

pigpen (pĭg′pĕn′), *n.* **1.** a pigsty. **2.** a dirty place.

pig-rat (pĭg′răt′), *n.* bandicoot.

pig-root (pĭg′ro͞ot′), *v.i. Austral., N.Z.* to plant the forelegs stiffly down and kick up with the hind legs (of a horse).

Pigs (pĭgz), *n.* **Bay of,** a bay on the SW coast of W central Cuba: attempted invasion by U.S.-backed forces 1961.

pigskin (pĭg′skĭn′), *n.* **1.** leather made from the skin of a pig. **2.** any piece of a pig's skin, whether tanned or not. **3.** leather, made from the skins of capybaras, peccaries, etc. **4.** *Colloq.* a saddle. —*adj.* **5.** made of pigskin.

pigstick (pĭg′stĭk′), *v.i.* to hunt wild boar with a spear, on foot or on horseback. —**pig′stick′er,** *n.* —**pig′stick′ing,** *n.*

pigsty (pĭg′stī′), *n., pl.* **-sties.** a sty or pen for pigs.

pig-swill (pĭg′swĭl′), *n.* waste food given to pigs.

pigtail (pĭg′tāl′), *n.* **1.** a braid of hair hanging down the back of the head. **2.** tobacco in a thin twisted roll. **3.** *Elect.* a short flexible wire.

pigwash (pĭg′wŏsh′), *n.* pig-swill.

pika (pī′kə), *n.* any of various small mammals allied to the rabbits and inhabiting alpine regions of the Northern Hemisphere, as *Ochotona princeps* of North America. [t. Tungusic (of Siberia): m. *piika*]

pike[1] (pīk), *n., pl.* **pikes,** (*esp. collectively*) **pike. 1.** any of various large, slender, fierce, voracious freshwater fishes of the genus *Esox*, having a long snout, esp. the **northern pike,** *E. lucius.* **2.** any of various superficially similar fishes, as *Stizostedion vitreum.* [ME, short for *pikefish*, so called from its pointed snout. See PIKE[2]] —**pike′like′,** *adj.*

pike[2] (pīk), *n., v.,* **piked, piking.** —*n.* **1.** *Hist.* an infantry weapon with long shaft and comparatively small metal head. —*v.t.* **2.** to pierce, wound, or kill with or as with a pike. [t. F: m. *pique*, akin to *pic* a pick (cf. PIKE[5]) and *piquer* prick (see PIQUE, v.)]

pike[3] (pīk), *n. U.S.* turnpike.

pike[4] (pīk), *n.* a hill or mountain with a pointed summit. [special use of PIKE[5] Cf. OE *hornpic* pinnacle]

pike[5] (pīk), *n.* **1.** a sharp point; a spike. **2.** the pointed end of anything, as of an arrow or a spear. [ME *pik*, OE *pīc* a pick or pickaxe, a point. See PIKE[2]]

pike[6] (pīk), *v.i.*, **piked, piking.** *Colloq.* to go quickly. [orig. uncert.]

pike dive. See **jackknife dive.**

pikelet (pīk′lĭt), *n. Dial.* a teacake; a crumpet.

pikeman (pīk′mən), *n., pl.* **-men.** a soldier armed with a pike.

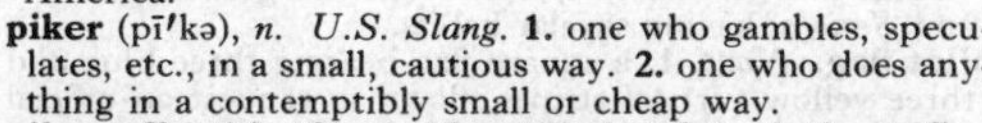

pike-perch (pīk′pûch′), *n.* any of several pikelike fishes of the perch family, as the walleye, *Stizostedion vitreum*, of North America.

Pikeman

piker (pī′kə), *n. U.S. Slang.* **1.** one who gambles, speculates, etc., in a small, cautious way. **2.** one who does anything in a contemptibly small or cheap way.

pikestaff (pīk′stäf′), *n., pl.* **-staffs** (-stäfs′). **1.** the staff or shaft of a pike (weapon). **2. as plain as a pikestaff,** extremely, unmistakably clear.

pilaf (pĭl′ăf), *n.* pilau.

pilaster (pĭ lăs′tə), *n. Archit.* a square or rectangular pillar, with capital and base, engaged in a wall from which it projects. [t. F: m. *pilastre*, t. It.: m. *pilastro*, der. L *pīla* pillar]

Pilate (pī′lət), *n.* **Pontius** (pŏn′tyəs, pŏn′shəs), **1.** Roman procurator of Judea, A.D. 26–36?, concerned in the crucifixion of Christ. **2.** *Colloq.* one who tries to disclaim a moral responsibility.

Pilatus (pĭ lä′təs; *Ger.* pē lä′to͞os), *n.* a mountain of the Alps in central Switzerland, near Lucerne: cable railway. 6998 ft.

Pilaster

pilau (pĭ lou′), *n.* an oriental dish consisting of rice boiled with mutton, fowl, or the like, and flavoured with spices, etc. Also, **pilaf** (pĭl′ăf), **pil′aff, pilao** (pĭ lou′), **pilaw** (pĭ lô′). [t. Pers.: (m). *pilāw*]

pilchard (pĭl′chəd), *n.* **1.** a small marine food fish, *Sardina pilchardus*, resembling the herring, but smaller and plumper; inhabiting the E Atlantic and W Mediterranean. **2.** any of numerous similar fishes, esp. in U.S. and Australasian coastal waters. [earlier *pilcher*, orig. uncert.]

Pilcomayo (*Sp.* pēl kō mä′yō), *n.* a river flowing from S Bolivia SE along the boundary between Paraguay and Argentina to the Paraguay river at Asunción. 1000 mi.

pile[1] (pīl), *n., v.,* **piled, piling.** —*n.* **1.** an assemblage of things laid or lying one upon another in a more or less orderly fashion: *a pile of boxes.* **2.** *Colloq.* a large number, quantity, or amount of anything: *a pile of things to do.* **3.** a heap of wood on which a dead body, a living person, or a sacrifice is burnt. **4.** a lofty or large building or mass of buildings. **5.** *Colloq.* a large accumulation of money. **6.** *Metall.* a bundle of pieces of iron ready to be welded and drawn out into bars; faggot. **7.** *Nuclear Physics.* a latticework of uranium and various moderating substances used to produce plutonium in the original harnessing of atomic energy, essentially a means of controlling the nuclear chain reaction; atomic pile; nuclear reactor. **8.** voltaic pile. **9.** *Mil.* arms arranged systematically. —*v.t.* **10.** to lay or dispose in a pile (often fol. by *up* or *on*). **11.** to accumulate (fol. by *up*). **12.** to cover or load, with a pile or piles. **13. pile arms,** to prop (usually four) rifles, muskets, etc., in the form of a pyramid, with the muzzles pointing upwards. **14. pile on the agony, pile it on,** *Colloq.* to exaggerate. —*v.i.* **15.** to accumulate, as money, debts, evidence, etc. (fol. by *up*). **16.** *Colloq.* to get somewhere (fol. by *in, into, out, off, down,* etc.) in a body and more or less confusedly. **17.** to gather or rise in a pile or piles, as snow, etc. **18.** *Colloq.* (of a vehicle, driver, etc.) to crash (fol. by *up*). [ME, t. OF, t. L: m. *pīla* pillar, pier, mole]

pile[2] (pīl), *n., v.,* **piled, piling.** —*n.* **1.** a heavy timber, stake or pole, sometimes pointed at the lower end, driven vertically into the ground or the bed of a river, etc., to support a superstructure or form part of a wall. **2.** any steel or concrete member similarly used. **3.** *Archery.* the tip of an arrow. **4.** *Her.* a bearing in the form of a wedge, usually with its point downwards. —*v.t.* **5.** to furnish, strengthen, or support with piles. **6.** drive piles into. [ME and OE *pīl* shaft, stake, t. L: s. *pīlum* javelin]

pile[3] (pīl), *n.* **1.** hair, esp. soft, fine hair or down. **2.** wool, esp. of a carpet, fur, or pelage. **3.** a raised surface on cloth, composed of upright cut or looped yarns, as velvet, Turkish towelling, etc. **4.** one of the strands in such a surface. [ME *pilus*, t. L: hair]

pile[4] (pīl), *n.* (*usually pl.*) a haemorrhoid. [ME *pyle*]

pileate (pī′lĭ ĭt, -āt′, pĭl′ĭ-), *adj.* capped, as a mushroom. [t. L: m. s. *pileātus* capped. See PILEUS]

pileated (pī′lĭ ā′tĭd, pĭl′ĭ-), *adj. Ornith.* crested.

pileated woodpecker, a large black-and-white North American woodpecker, *Ceophloeus pileatus*, with prominent red crest.

piled (pīld), *adj.* having a pile, as velvet and other fabrics. [f. PILE[3] + -ED[3]]

pile-driver (pīl′drī′və), *n.* **1.** a machine for driving down piles, usually a tall framework in which a heavy weight of iron is raised between guides to a height, as by steam, and then allowed to fall upon the head of the pile. **2.** *Colloq.* a powerful blow of the fist, kick, stroke, etc.

pile-dwelling (pīl′dwĕl′ĭng), *n.* a dwelling supported on piles so as to be raised above the ground or water; a lake-dwelling.

pileous (pī′lĭ əs), *adj.* **1.** of or pertaining to hair. **2.** hairy. [f. PILE[3] + -OUS]

pileum (pī′lĭ əm, pĭl′ĭ əm), *n., pl.* **pilea** (pī′lĭ ə, pĭl′ĭ ə). the top of the head of a bird, from the base of the bill to the nape. [t. NL, t. L, var. of *pilleum.* See PILEUS]

pile-up (pīl′ŭp′), *n. Colloq.* **1.** a crash or collision, usually involving more than one vehicle. **2.** an accumulation; backlog.

pileus (pī′lĭ əs, pĭl′ĭ əs), *n., pl.* **pilei** (pī′lĭ ī′, pĭl′ĭ ī′). **1.** *Bot.* the horizontal portion of a mushroom, bearing gills, tubes, etc., on its underside; a cap. **2.** *Zool.* the disc-shaped part of a coelenterate which takes the form of a medusa. **3.** a felt skullcap worn by the ancient Romans and Greeks. [t. L, more correctly *pilleus*, also *pilleum* felt cap; akin to L *pilus* hair, Gk *pîlos* felt, felt cap]

pilfer (pĭl′fə), *v.i., v.t.* to steal, esp. in small quantities; obtain by, or practise, petty theft. [appar. t. AF or OF: m. s. *pelfrer* pillage, rob. Cf. PELF] —**pil′ferer,** *n.*

pilferage (pĭl′fə rĭj), *n.* **1.** the act or practice of pilfering; petty theft. **2.** *Archaic.* that which is pilfered.

pilgrim (pĭl′grĭm), *n.* **1.** one who journeys, esp. a long distance, to some sacred place as an act of devotion. **2.** (*cap.*) one of the Pilgrim Fathers. **3.** *Poetic.* a traveller or wanderer. **4.** *Chiefly U.S.* an original settler in a region. **5.** *Western U.S.* a newcomer (person or animal) in a region. [ME *pelegrim*, t. AF (unrecorded), t. ML: m. s. *peregrīnus* pilgrim, L foreigner. See PEREGRINE] —**Syn. 3.** wayfarer, sojourner.

pilgrimage (pĭl′grĭ mĭj), *n.* **1.** a journey, esp. a long one, made to some sacred place, as an act of devotion. **2.** any long journey. [ME, t. AF: m. *pilgrymage*, var. of OF *peligrinage.* See PILGRIM] —**Syn. 1.** See **trip.**

Pilgrimage of Grace, a Catholic rising in N England in 1536, directed against the Reformation. See **Robert Aske.**

Pilgrim Fathers, *U.S. Hist.* the English Puritan separatists who founded the colony of Plymouth, Massachusetts, in 1620.

Pilgrim's Progress, an allegory (1678), by John Bunyan.

pili (pĭ lē′), *n., pl.* **-lis.** **1.** a Philippine burseraceous tree, *Canarium ovatum*, the seeds of which are edible, resembling a sweet almond. **2.** its seeds (**pili-nuts**). [t. Tagalog]

piliferous (pī lĭf′ə rəs), *adj.* having hair. [f. *pili-* (comb. form repr. L *pilus* hair) + -FEROUS]

piliform (pĭl′ĭ fôm′), *adj.* having the form of a hair.

piling (pī′lĭng), *n.* **1.** piles collectively. See **pile**[2]. **2.** a structure composed of piles. [f. PILE[2] + -ING[1]]

pill[1] (pĭl), *n.* **1.** a small globular or rounded mass of medicinal substance, to be swallowed whole; tablet. **2.** something unpleasant that has to be accepted or endured: *a bitter pill to swallow.* **3.** *U.S. Slang., Obs.* a disagreeable or unpleasant person. **4.** *Sports Slang.* a ball, esp. in football, tennis, etc. **5.** (*pl.*) *Slang.* billiards, football, tennis, etc. **6. sugar the pill,** to make bearable some unpleasant experience. **7. the pill,** *Colloq.* oral contraception. —*v.t.* **8.** to dose with pills. **9.** *Slang, Obs.* to blackball. [late ME, prob. t. MD or MLG: s. *pille*, t. L: m. *pilula*, dim. of *pila* ball]

pill[2] (pĭl), *v.t., v.i.* **1.** *Archaic or Dial.* to peel. **2.** *Obs.* to make or become bald. [partly ME *pilen*, OE *pilian* peel, skin, t. L: m. s. *pilāre* deprive of hair; also ME *pille(n)*, *pylle(n)*, t. OF: m. *piller* plunder, mishandle, g. L *pilleāre* flay]

pill[3] (pĭl), *v.t. Archaic.* to rob, plunder, or pillage. [ME, prob. akin to PILL[2]]

pillage (pĭl′ĭj), *v.,* **-laged, -laging,** *n.* —*v.t.* **1.** to strip of money or goods by open violence, as in war; plunder. **2.** to take as booty. —*v.i.* **3.** to rob with open violence; take booty. —*n.* **4.** the act of plundering, esp. in war. **5.** booty or spoil. [ME *pilage*, t. OF: m. *pillage*, der. *piller* PILL[3]] —**pil′lager,** *n.*

pillar (pĭl′ə), *n.* **1.** an upright shaft or structure, of stone, brick, or other material, relatively slender in proportion to its height, and of any shape in section, used as a support. or standing alone, as for a monument. **2.** an upright supporting part. **3.** any natural or accidental object resembling or serving as such a support. **4.** *Horol.* a supporting strut for the framework of a watch or clock. **5.** a person who is a chief support of a state, institution, etc.: *a pillar of society.* **6. from pillar to post, a.** from one predicament or difficulty to another. **b.** aimlessly from place to place. —*v.t.* **7.** to provide or support with pillars. [ME *pylere,* t. OF: m. *piler,* der. L *pīla* pillar, PILE[1]] —**Syn. 1.** See **column.**

pillar-box (pĭl′ə bŏks′), *n.* an iron box, usually cylindrical, about five feet in height, into which letters are deposited for collection and distribution by the postal service; letter-box; mailbox; postbox.

Pillars of Hercules, the two promontories on opposite sides of the E end of the Strait of Gibraltar: the Rock of Gibraltar in Europe, and the Jebel Musa in Africa, supposed to have been raised by Hercules. [trans. of L *Columnae Herculis,* Gk *Hērakleíou stêlai*]

pillbox (pĭl′bŏks′), *n.* **1.** a box, usually shallow and often round, for holding pills. **2.** a small cylindrical hat of similar shape. **3.** a small, low structure of reinforced concrete, enclosing machine-guns, and employed as a minor fortress in warfare.

pill-bug (pĭl′bŭg′), *n.* a terrestrial isopod or woodlouse (genus *Armadillidium*) of Britain and Europe, capable of rolling itself into a ball.

pillion (pĭl′yən), *n.* **1.** a pad or cushion attached behind a saddle, esp. as a seat for a woman. **2.** an extra saddle behind the driver's seat on a motorcycle. —*adj.* **3.** riding on a pillion: *a pillion passenger.* —*adv.* **4.** on a pillion: *to ride pillion.* [appar. t. Gaelic: m. *pillean, pillin,* dim. of *pell* cushion, t. L: s. *pellis* skin, pelt]

pillory (pĭl′ə rĭ), *n., pl.* **-ries,** *v.,* **-ried, -rying.** —*n.* **1.** a wooden framework erected on a post, with holes for securing the head and hands, used to expose an offender to public derision. —*v.t.* **2.** to set in the pillory. **3.** to expose to public ridicule or abuse. [ME *pillori,* t. OF, t. Pr.: m. *espi(ng)lóri,* ? t. ML: alter. of *speculum in glōriam Deī* court (lit., mirror) to the glory of God]

Pillory

pillow (pĭl′ō), *n.* **1.** a bag or case filled with feathers, down, or other soft material, commonly used as a support for the head during sleep or rest. **2.** anything used to support the head; a headrest. **3.** a cushion or pad, as the cushion on which pillow lace is made. **4.** a supporting piece or part, as the block on which the inner end of a bowsprit rests. —*v.t.* **5.** to rest on or as on a pillow. **6.** to support with pillows. **7.** to serve as a pillow for. —*v.i.* **8.** to rest as on a pillow. [ME *pilwe,* OE *pyle, pylu,* pre-E **pulwī(n),* t. L: m. s. *pulvīnus*] —**pil′low-like′,** *adj.* —**Syn. 1.** See **cushion.**

pillow block, *Mach.* a metal box or case for supporting the end of a revolving shaft or journal.

pillowcase (pĭl′ō kās′), *n.* a removable cover, usually of cotton, linen or nylon, drawn over a pillow. Also, **pillowslip** (pĭl′ō slĭp′).

pillow-fight (pĭl′ō fīt′), *n.* a children's game, in which pillows are used as weapons.

pillow lace, lace made on a padded board with threads wound on bobbins.

pillow sham, *Chiefly U.S.* an ornamental cover laid over a bed pillow.

pillowslip (pĭl′ō slĭp′), *n.* a pillowcase.

pillowy (pĭl′ō ĭ), *adj.* pillow-like; soft; yielding: *a pillowy clump of sod.*

pillwort (pĭl′wûrt′), *n.* a small aquatic heterosporous pteridophyte, *Pilularia globulifera,* found on the edges of ponds in Europe and W Asia.

pilocarpine (pī′lō kä′pēn, -pĭn), *n. Chem.* an alkaloid, $C_{11}H_{16}N_2O_2$, obtained from the leaflets of species of a South American shrub, *Pilocarpus* (jaborandi), used as a diaphoretic and diuretic. Also, **pilocarpin** (pī′lō kä′pĭn). [f. s. NL *Pilocarpus* (f. Gk: *pîlo(s)* cap + m. *karpós* fruit) + -INE[2]]

Pilos (pī′lŏs), *n.* Greek name of **Navarino.**

pilose (pī′lōs), *adj.* covered with hair, esp. soft hair; furry. [t. L: m. s. *pilōsus*] —**pilosity** (pī lŏs′ĭ tĭ), *n.*

pilot (pī′lət), *n.* **1.** one duly qualified to steer ships into or out of a harbour or through certain difficult waters. **2.** the steersman of a ship. **3.** *Aeron.* one who controls an aeroplane, balloon, or other aircraft. **4.** a guide or leader. **5.** *Mach.* a smaller element acting in advance of another or principal element, and causing the latter to come into play when desired: *the pilot on a gas stove.* —*v.t.* **6.** to steer. **7.** to guide or conduct, as through unknown places, intricate affairs, etc. **8.** to act as pilot on, in, or over. —*adj.* **9.** experimental; denoting investigation on a small scale designed to assess the practicability of a major commitment. **10.** of or pertaining to pilots. **11.** acting as a guide. [t. F: m. *pilote,* t. It.: m. *pilota,* t. MGk: m. **pēdṓtēs,* der. *pēdá,* pl., rudder]

pilotage (pī′lə tĭj), *n.* **1.** the act of piloting. **2.** the fee paid to a pilot for his services. [t. F]

pilot balloon, a balloon used for the visual observation of upper-air wind currents, etc.

pilot biscuit, *Chiefly U.S.* hardtack. Also, **pilot bread.**

pilot-cloth (pī′lət klŏth′), *n.* a heavy, dark blue, woollen cloth used for overcoats, seamen's clothing, etc.

pilot-fish (pī′lət fĭsh′), *n.* **1.** a small, carangoid, marine fish of warm waters, *Naucrates ductor,* which accompanies and is reputed to act as a guide for the shark. **2.** any of various other similar fish, esp. those of the genus *Naucrates* and *Seriola,* having similar habits.

pilot flag, *Naut.* **1.** a square flag bearing three blue and three yellow vertical stripes, flown to request an official pilot for navigating a harbour, river, etc. **2.** a rectangular flag with its upper half white and its lower half red, or a square flag halved red and white with the white portion next to the mast, indicating that the vessel has a pilot on board, or is a pilot boat.

pilot house, an enclosed place on the deck of a vessel, for the steering gear and the pilot; a wheelhouse.

piloti (*Fr.* pē lō tē′), *n. Archit.* a heavy column or stilt used to carry a structure above ground level. Also, **pilotis.** [F: *piloti(s),* equiv. to *pilot* (aug. of *pile* PILE[1]) + *-is* collective suffix]

pilot lamp, an electric lamp, used in association with a control, which by means of position or colour indicates the functioning of the control; an indicator light or a control light. Also, **pilot light.**

pilot light, 1. a small light kept burning continuously, as beside a large gas burner, to relight a main light whenever desired. **2.** a pilot lamp. Also, **pilot burner.**

pilot officer, the lowest commissioned rank in the Royal Air Force.

pilot plant, a small industrial plant in which processes planned for full-scale operation are tested in advance to eliminate problems, etc.

pilot whale, any of the cetaceans constituting the genus *Globicephala* (family *Delphinidae*), up to twenty-eight feet long, esp. *G. melaena,* of the Atlantic and Pacific oceans.

pilous (pī′ləs), *adj.* hairlike. [t. L: m. s. *pilōsus*]

Pilsen (*Ger.* pĭl′zən), *n.* a city in W Czechoslovakia, in Bohemia. 139,000 (1965). Czech, **Plzeň.**

Pilsner (pĭlz′nə), *n.* a light, pale lager, as one originally brewed at Pilsen. Also, **Pilsener.** [G: adj. from PILSEN]

Pilsudski (*Pol.* pēw sōōt′skē), *n.* **Józef** (*Pol.* yōō′zĕf), 1867–1935, Polish field marshal and statesman: president 1918–22; premier 1926–28, 1930.

Piltdown man (pĭlt′doun măn′), a supposedly very early form of man, *Eoanthropus,* whose existence was inferred from bone fragments found at Piltdown, Sussex, in 1912; these were shown in 1953 to have been assembled as a hoax.

pilular (pĭl′yōō lə), *adj.* of, pertaining to, or characteristic of pills. [f. s. L *pilula* pill + -AR[1]]

pilule (pĭl′yōōl), *n.* a pill; a little pill. [ME, t. L: m. *pilula* pill, dim. of *pila* ball]

Piman (pē′mən), *n.* **1.** a subdivision of the Uto-Aztecan linguistic stock. **2.** (*pl.*) a tribe of North American Indians of southern Arizona and north-western Mexico. —*adj.* **3.** of or pertaining to the Pimans.

pimento (pĭ mĕn′tō), *n., pl.* **-tos. 1.** the dried fruits of *Pimenta officinalis*; allspice. **2.** the tropical American myrtaceous tree yielding it. **3.** the pimiento. [t. Sp.: m. *pimienta* pepper, *pimiento* capsicum, g. L *pigmentum* pigment, in ML spice]

pi-meson (pī′mē′zŏn), *n. Physics.* a meson, which may have positive, negative, or zero charge, and a mass of between 264 and 273 electron masses. Also, **pion.**

pimiento (pĭ myĕn′tō), *n., pl.* **-tos,** a red Spanish pepper with a sweet, pungent flavour, also eaten less ripe, when it is green or yellow. [t. Sp. See PIMENTO]

pimp (pĭmp), *n.* **1.** one who solicits for a prostitute, or brothel; a procurer. **2.** a contemptible person. **3.** *Austral.* an informer; a tale-bearer. —*v.i.* **4.** to procure; pander. **5.** to inform; tell tales. [cf. OE *Pimpern* (place name)]

pimpernel (pĭm′pə nĕl′, -nəl), *n.* a primulaceous herb of the genus *Anagallis,* esp. the **scarlet pimpernel,** *A. arvensis,* a species with scarlet, purplish, or white flowers that close at the approach of bad weather. [ME, t. OF: m. *pimprenele,* earlier *piprenelle,* der. L *piperīnus* consisting of peppercorns; r. OE *pipeneale,* of Rom. orig.]

pimping (pĭm′pĭng), *adj.* **1.** petty. **2.** weak; sickly.

pimple (pĭm′pl), *n.* a small, usually inflammatory swelling or elevation of the skin; a papule or pustule. [ME; cf. OE *piplian* be pimpled]

pimply (pĭm′plĭ), *adj.*, **-plier, -pliest.** having many pimples. Also, **pimpled** (pĭm′pld).

pin (pĭn), *n.*, *v.*, **pinned, pinning.** —*n.* **1.** a small, slender, sometimes tapered or pointed piece of wood, metal, etc., used to fasten, or hold things together, to hang things upon, to stop up holes, or to convey or check motion; a bolt; peg. **2.** a short, slender piece of wire with a point at one end and a head at the other, for fastening things together, as cloth or paper. **3.** any of various forms of fastening or ornament consisting essentially or in part of a pointed penetrating bar: *a safety pin.* **4.** a badge or brooch having a pointed bar or pin attached, by which it is fastened to the clothing. **5.** a linchpin, serving to keep a wheel on its axle. **6.** that part of the stem of a key which enters the lock. **7.** a rolling pin. **8.** a hairpin. **9.** a peg, nail, or stud marking the centre of a target. **10.** one of the bottle-shaped pieces of wood knocked down in ninepins, tenpins, etc. **11.** *Quoits.* the peg over which quoits are thrown. **12.** *Golf.* the flagpole which identifies a hole. **13.** *Colloq.* a leg. **14.** *Music.* a peg. **15.** *Naut.* any of various pegs, fixing devices and axles, as a belaying pin, thole, etc. **16.** *Carpentry.* a dovetail. **17.** a cask containing $4\frac{1}{2}$ gallons. **18.** a very small amount; a trifle. **19.** see **pins and needles.** —*v.t.* **20.** to fasten or attach with a pin or pins, or as if with a pin. **21.** to hold (a man, etc.) fast in a spot or position: *the debris pinned him down.* **22.** to bind or hold to a course of action, a promise, etc. (often fol. by *down*). **23.** to transfix with a pin or the like. **24.** *Chess, Draughts, etc.* to effectively confine your opponent's men. **25.** *Bldg Trades.* Also, **underpin.** to support (masonry, etc.), as by wedges driven in over a beam. [ME; OE *pinn* peg (c. G *Pinne*)]

piña (*Sp.* pē′nyä), *n.* *Spanish.* **1.** piña cloth. **2.** (esp. in Latin America) a pineapple drink. [S Amer. Sp., formerly *pinna*, t. L: m. *pīnea* pine cone]

pinaceous (pī nā′shəs), *adj.* belonging to the *Pinaceae*, or pine family of trees and shrubs, which includes the pine, spruce, fir, etc. [f. s. NL *Pināceae* (der. L *pīnus* pine) the pine family + -OUS]

piña cloth, a fine, sheer fabric, made from the fibre of pineapple leaves.

pinacoid (pĭn′ə koid′), *n.* *Crystall.* a form whose faces are parallel to two of the axes. [f. m. s. Gk *pínax* slab + -OID]

pinafore (pĭn′ə fô′), *n.* **1.** an apron, usually one large enough to cover most of the dress, especially a child's. **2.** a loose dress worn over clothing to protect it during housework, etc. [f. PIN, v., + AFORE, adv.]

Pinar del Río (*Sp.* pē när′ dĕl rē′ō), a city in W Cuba. 87,960 (est. 1951).

pinaster (pī năs′tə, pĭ-), *n.* the maritime pine, *Pinus pinaster.*

pinball (pĭn′bôl′), *n.* any of various games played on a sloping board, the object usually being either to shoot a ball, driven by a spring, up a side passage and cause it to roll back down against pins or bumpers and through channels which electrically record the score, or to shoot a ball into pockets at the back of the board.

pince-nez (păns′nā′, pĭns′-; *Fr.* păNs nĕ′), *n.* a pair of spectacles kept in place by a spring which pinches the nose. [t. F: pinch nose]

pincer movement, *Mil.* a manoeuvre in which both of the enemy's flanks are attacked simultaneously, as if by a pair of pincers.

pincers (pĭn′səz), *n.pl. or sing.* **1.** a gripping tool consisting of two pivoted limbs forming a pair of jaws and a pair of handles (often called a **pair of pincers**). **2.** *Zool.* a grasping organ or pair of organs resembling this. [ME *pynceours*, t. OF, der. *pincier* PINCH]

pinch (pĭnch), *v.t.* **1.** to compress between the finger and thumb, the jaws of an instrument, or any two opposed surfaces. **2.** to compress, constrict, or squeeze painfully, as a tight shoe does. **3.** to cramp within narrow bounds or quarters. **4.** to render (the face, etc.) unnaturally thin and drawn, as pain or distress does. **5.** to nip (plants) injuriously, as frost does. **6.** to affect with sharp discomfort or distress, as cold, hunger, or need does. **7.** to straiten in means or circumstances. **8.** to stint in allowance of money, food, or the like. **9.** to hamper or inconvenience by lack of something specified. **10.** *Dial.* to stint the supply or amount of (a thing). **11.** to put a pinch or small quantity of (a powder, etc.) into something. **12.** *Slang.* to steal. **13.** *Slang.* to arrest. **14.** to move (a heavy object) by means of a pinch or pinch-bar. **15.** *Naut.* to sail (a vessel) so close to the wind that her sails shake slightly and her speed is reduced. **16.** *Hort.* to nip off (part of a shoot, bud, etc.) to improve the shape, quality, etc., of a plant (often fol. by *out*, *off*, or *back*). —*v.i.* **17.** to exert a sharp or painful compressing force. **18.** to cause sharp discomfort or distress: *when hunger pinches.* **19.** to stint oneself; economize unduly; be stingy or miserly. **20.** *Mining.* (of a vein of ore, etc.) to become narrower or smaller, or to give (*out*) altogether. —*n.* **21.** the act of pinching; nip; squeeze. **22.** as much of anything as can be taken up between the finger and thumb: *a pinch of salt.* **23.** a very small quantity of anything. **24.** sharp or painful stress, as of hunger, need, or any trying circumstances. **25.** a situation or time of special stress; an emergency: *any help is useful in a pinch.* **26.** a section of tramway track which veers to the side of the road, as at a stop. **27.** a pinch-bar. **28.** *Slang.* an arrest. **29.** *Slang.* a theft. **30. pinch of salt.** See **grain** (def. 7). **31. at a pinch,** in an emergency, crisis, etc.; if necessary. [ME *pinche(n)*, t. OF: m. *pincier*, g. LL *punctiāre* (der. *punctio* act of pricking), b. with stem *pic-* PIKE[2]]

pinch-bar (pĭnch′bä′), *n.* a kind of crowbar or lever with a projection which serves as a fulcrum.

pinchbeck (pĭnch′bĕk), *n.* **1.** an alloy of copper and zinc, used in imitation of gold. **2.** something spurious. —*adj.* **3.** made of pinchbeck. **4.** sham or spurious. [named after the inventor, Christopher *Pinchbeck* (died 1732), a London clockmaker]

pinchcock (pĭnch′kŏk′), *n.* a clamp for compressing a flexible pipe, as a rubber tube, in order to regulate or stop the flow of a fluid.

pinch effect, *Physics.* the constriction of a stream of charged particles resulting from the magnetic field associated with the current carried by the particles.

pincher (pĭn′chə), *n.* **1.** one who or that which pinches. **2.** (*pl.*) pincers.

pinch-hit (pĭnch′hĭt′), *v.i.*, **-hit, -hitting.** **1.** *Baseball.* to serve as a pinch-hitter. **2.** *U.S.* to substitute for someone.

pinch-hitter (pĭnch′hĭt′ə), *n.* **1.** *Baseball.* a substitute who, usually at some critical moment of the game, bats for another. **2.** any substitute for another, esp. in an emergency.

pinchpenny (pĭnch′pĕn′ĭ), *n.*, *pl.* **-nies,** *adj.* —*n.* **1.** a very mean person. —*adj.* **2.** miserly.

Pinckney (pĭngk′nĭ), *n.* **Charles Cotesworth** (kōts′wûth′), 1746–1825, American patriot and statesman.

pin-curl (pĭn′kûl′), *n.* a curl which is pinned into place by a hairgrip while the hair sets.

pincushion (pĭn′kŏŏsh′ən), *n.* a small cushion in which pins are stuck, in readiness for use.

pindan (pĭn′dăn), *n.* *Austral.* semi-arid country; scrub.

Pindar (pĭn′də), *n.* 518–438 B.C., Greek lyric poet.

Pindaric (pĭn dă′rĭk), *adj.* **1.** of, pertaining to, or after the manner of Pindar. **2.** *Class. Pros.* of elaborate and regular metrical structure. **3.** *Pros.* having an irregular metrical structure, supposedly in imitation of Pindar. —*n.* **4.** an ode or other poem by or in imitation of Pindar. See **ode** (def. 3).

pindling (pĭn′dlĭng), *adj.* *U.S. Dial.* puny; sickly.

Pindus (pĭn′dəs), *n.* a mountain range in central Greece. Highest peak, 7665 ft.

pine[1] (pīn), *n.* **1.** any member of the genus *Pinus*, comprising evergreen coniferous trees varying greatly in size, with long needle-shaped leaves, including many species of economic importance for their timber and as a source of turpentine, tar, pitch, etc. **2.** any of various more or less similar coniferous trees. **3.** the wood of the pine tree. **4.** *Colloq.* the pineapple. [ME; OE *pīn*, t. L: s. *pīnus*] —**pine′like′,** *adj.*

pine[2] (pīn), *v.*, **pined, pining,** *n.* —*v.i.* **1.** to suffer with longing, or long painfully (fol. by *for*). **2.** to fail gradually in health or vitality from grief, regret, or longing. **3.** to languish, droop, or waste away. **4.** to repine or fret. —*v.t.* **5.** *Archaic.* to suffer grief or regret over. —*n.* **6.** *Obs. or Archaic.* painful longing. [ME; OE *pīnian* to torture, der. *pīn*, n., torture, t. VL: m. s. *pēna*, L *poena* punishment]

pineal (pĭn′ĭ əl), *adj.* **1.** pertaining to the pineal body. **2.** resembling a pine cone in shape. [t. NL: s. *pīneālis*, der. L *pīnea* pine cone]

pineal body, a body of unknown function present in the brain of all vertebrates having a cranium, believed to be a vestigial sense organ. Also, **pineal gland.**

pineapple (pĭn′ăp′l), *n.* **1.** the edible juicy fruit (somewhat resembling a pine cone) of a tropical bromeliaceous plant, *Ananas comosus*, being a large collective fruit developed from a spike or head of flowers, and surmounted by a crown of leaves. **2.** the plant itself, a native of tropical South America, now widely cultivated throughout the tropics, having a short stem and rigid, spiny-margined, recurved leaves. **3.** *Mil. Slang.* a bomb or hand grenade esp. of the fragmentation type, resembling a pineapple in appearance.

pine cone, the cone or strobilus of a pine tree.

pine marten, a slender carnivore, *Martes martes*, belonging to the weasel family and inhabiting Britain, much of Europe and part of Asia, and having fine brown fur.

pinene (pī′nēn), *n. Chem.* a terpene, $C_{10}H_{16}$, forming the principal constituent of oil of turpentine and occurring also in other essential oils. [f. PIN(E)[1] + -ENE]

pine needle, the needle-like leaf of the pine tree.

Pinero (pĭ nĭə′rō), *n.* **Sir Arthur Wing,** 1855–1934, English dramatist.

pinery (pī′nə rĭ), *n., pl.* **-eries.** **1.** a place in which pineapples are grown. **2.** a forest or grove of pine trees.

Pines (pīnz), *n.* **Isle of,** an island in the Caribbean, south of and belonging to Cuba. 9812 pop. (1943); 1182 sq. mi.

pine-tar (pīn′tä′), *n.* the residue left after the destructive distillation of pine wood, used medicinally.

pinetum (pī nē′təm), *n., pl.* **-ta** (-tə). an arboretum of pines and coniferous trees. [t. L: pine grove]

piney (pī′nĭ), *adj.,* **-nier, -niest.** piny.

pinfall (pĭn′fôl′), *n. Wrestling.* the fact of being thrown on one's back by an opponent and held down with both shoulder-blades touching the canvas for a count of three. In professional wrestling the first contestant to win the best of three pinfalls, three submissions, or a knockout is declared the winner.

pin-feather (pĭn′fĕth′ə), *n. Ornith.* **1.** an undeveloped feather, before the web portions have expanded. **2.** a feather just coming through the skin.

pinfold (pĭn′fōld′), *n.* **1.** a pound for stray animals. **2.** a fold, as for sheep or cattle. *—v.t.* **3.** to confine in or as in a pinfold. [f. *pin(d)* impound + FOLD[2]; r. ME *ponfold*, OE *pundfald*]

ping (pĭng), *v.i.* **1.** to produce a sharp, ringing, high-pitched sound like that of a bullet striking an object, or of a small bell. *—n.* **2.** a pinging sound. [imit.]

ping-pong (pĭng′pŏng′), *n.* **1.** table tennis. **2.** (*cap.*) a trademark for this game. [der. PING, n., on model of *ding-dong*, etc.]

pinguid (pĭng′gwĭd), *adj.* **1.** fat; oily; unctuous. **2.** (of soil) fertile. [f. s. L *pinguis* fat + -ID[4]] **—pinguid′ity,** *n.*

pinhead (pĭn′hĕd′), *n.* **1.** the head of a pin. **2.** something very small or insignificant. **3.** *Slang.* a stupid person.

pinhole (pĭn′hōl′), *n.* a small hole made by, for, or as by a pin.

pinion[1] (pĭn′yən), *n. Mach.* **1.** a small cogwheel engaging with a larger cogwheel or with a rack. **2.** an arbor or spindle with teeth which engage with a cogwheel. [t. F: m. *pignon* pinion, OF battlement, der. L *pinna* pinnacle]

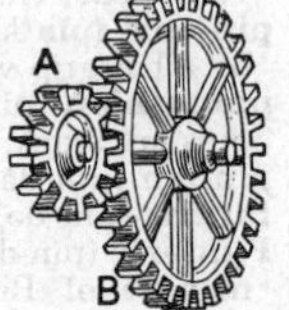

A, Pinion[1] (def. 1)
B, Cogwheel

pinion[2] (pĭn′yən), *n.* **1.** the distal or terminal segment of a bird's wing (the carpus, metacarpus, and phalanges). **2.** the wing of a bird. **3.** a feather. **4.** *Chiefly Poetic.* the flight feathers collectively. *—v.t.* **5.** to cut off the pinion of (a wing) or bind (the wings), as in order to prevent a bird from flying. **6.** to disable or restrain (a bird) thus. **7.** to bind (a person's arms or hands) so as to deprive him of the use of them. **8.** to disable thus; shackle. **9.** to bind or hold fast, as to a thing. [ME, t. OF: m. *pignon* feather, der. L *pinna*]

pinite (pĭn′īt, pī′nīt), *n.* a mica-like material, essentially a hydrous silicate of aluminium and potassium. [t. G: m. *Pinit*; named after the *Pini* mine in Saxony. See -ITE[1]]

pink[1] (pĭngk), *n.* **1.** a light tint of crimson; pale reddish purple. **2.** any plant of the carophyllaceous genus *Dianthus*, as *D. plumarius* (the common **garden pink**), *D. chinensis* (**China pink**), or *D. caryophyllus* (**clove pink,** or carnation). **3.** the flower of such a plant; a carnation. **4.** the highest type or example of excellence. **5.** the highest form or degree: *in the pink of condition.* **6.** (*often cap.*) a person with moderately left-wing or radical political opinions. **7.** scarlet, or scarlet cloth, as worn by fox-hunters. **8.** a fox-hunter. *—adj.* **9.** of the colour pink. **10.** having moderately left-wing or radical political opinions. [orig. uncert.]

pink[2] (pĭngk), *v.t.* **1.** to pierce with a rapier or the like; stab. **2.** to finish at the edge with a scalloped, notched, or other ornamental pattern. **3.** to punch (cloth, leather, etc.) with small holes or figures for ornament. **4.** *Chiefly Brit. Dial.* to deck or adorn (often fol. by *out* or *up*). [ME *pynke(n)* make points (marks) or holes (with a sharp instrument). Cf. OE *pynca* point, der. *pyng-* (s. *pyngan* to prick)]

pink[3] (pĭngk), *n.* a kind of vessel with a narrow stern. [ME *pinck*, t. MD: m. *pincke* fishing boat]

pink[4] (pĭngk), *v.i. Motor Vehicles.* knock (def. 2).

pink champagne, 1. champagne in which the black grape-skins have been left during part of the fermentation period, the drink having as a consequence a pinkish tinge. **2.** a carbonated soft drink alleged to resemble this.

pink elephant, 1. a hallucination, esp. as reputedly experienced by alcoholics. **2.** (*pl.*) *Obsolesc.* delirium tremens.

Pinkerton (pĭng′kə tən), *n.* **Allan,** 1819–84, U.S. detective, born in Scotland.

pinkeye (pĭngk′ī′), *n. Pathol.* a contagious form of conjunctivitis: from the colour of the inflamed eye.

pink gin, a cocktail made from gin and angostura bitters.

pinkie (pĭng′kĭ), *n. U.S. and Dial.* the little (fifth) finger. [orig. uncert.]

pinking shears, shears with notched blades, used for giving a scalloped or notched edge to fabrics to prevent them fraying.

pinkish (pĭng′kĭsh), *adj.* somewhat pink.

pinkroot (pĭngk′ro͞ot′), *n.* **1.** the root of any of various plants of the loganiaceous genus *Spigelia*, which is used as a vermifuge. **2.** any of these plants.

Pinkster (pĭngk′stə), *n. U.S. Dial.* Whitsuntide. [t. D: Easter, ult. t. Gk: alter. of *pentekostē* PENTECOST]

pin money, 1. any small sum set aside for non-essential minor expenditures. **2.** an allowance of money to a wife for personal expenditures.

pinna (pĭn′ə), *n., pl.* **pinnae** (pĭn′ē), **pinnas. 1.** *Bot.* one of the primary divisions of a pinnate leaf. **2.** *Zool.* **a.** a feather, wing, or winglike part. **b.** a fin or flipper. **3.** *Physiol.* the auricle of the ear. [t. L: feather (pl. wing), also fin] **—pin′nal,** *adj.*

pinnace (pĭn′ĭs), *n.* **1.** a light sailing ship, esp. one formerly used in attendance on a larger vessel. **2.** any of various kinds of ship's boats. [t. F: m. *pinace*, t. It.: m. *pinaccia*, or t. Sp.: m. *pinaza*, der. L *pīnus* pine tree]

pinnacle (pĭn′ə kl), *n., v.,* **-cled, -cling.** *—n.* **1.** a lofty peak. **2.** a lofty eminence or position. **3.** the highest or culminating point: *the pinnacle of fame.* **4.** any pointed, towering part or formation, as of rock. **5.** *Archit.* a relatively small upright structure, commonly terminating in a gable, a pyramid, or a cone, rising above the roof or coping of a building or capping a tower, buttress, or other projecting architectural member. *—v.t.* **6.** to place on or as on a pinnacle. **7.** to form a pinnacle on; crown. [ME *pinacle*, t. OF, t. LL: m. *pinnāculum*, dim. of L *pinna* pinnacle, usually identified with *pinna* PINNA] **—Syn. 3.** apex, acme.

pinnate (pĭn′āt, -ĭt), *adj.* **1.** resembling a feather. **2.** having parts arranged on each side of a common axis. **3.** *Bot.* (of a leaf) having leaflets or primary divisions arranged on each side of a common petiole. Also, **pin′nated.** [t. L: m. s. *pinnātus* feathered, pinnate] **—pin′nately,** *adv.*

Pinnate leaf

pinnati-, a word element meaning 'pinnate'. [comb. form repr. L *pinnātus*]

pinnatifid (pĭ năt′ĭ fĭd), *adj. Bot.* (of a leaf) pinnately cleft, with clefts reaching halfway or more to the midrib. [t. NL: s. *pinnātifidus*, f. *pinnāti-* PINNATI- + *-fidus* cleft]

pinnatilobate (pĭ năt′ĭ lō′bāt), *adj. Bot.* (of a leaf) pinnately lobed, with the divisions extending less than halfway to the midrib. Also, **pinnatilobed** (pĭ năt′ĭ lōbd′).

pinnation (pĭ nā′shən), *n. Bot.* pinnate condition or formation.

pinnatiped (pĭ năt′ĭ pĕd′), *adj. Ornith.* having lobate feet.

pinnatisect (pĭ năt′ĭ sĕkt′), *adj. Bot.* (of a leaf) divided in a pinnate manner.

Pinnatifid leaf

pinner (pĭn′ə), *n.* **1.** one who or that which pins. **2.** a headdress with a long hanging flap pinned on at each side. **3.** *Colloq.* a pinafore.

pinnigrade (pĭn′ĭ grād′), *adj.* **1.** moving by means of finlike parts or flippers, as the seals and walruses. *—n.* **2.** a pinnigrade animal.

pinniped (pĭn′ĭ pĕd′), *adj.* belonging to the *Pinnipedia*, a suborder of carnivores with limbs adapted to an aquatic life, including the seals and walruses. [f. *pinni-* (t. L, comb. form of *pinna* feather, fin) + -PED] **—pinnipedian** (pĭn′ĭ pē′dyən), *adj., n.*

pinnula (pĭn′yo͝o lə), *n., pl.* **-lae** (-lē′), **1.** a pinnule. **2.** barb of a feather. [t. L, dim. of *pinna* feather, fin]

pinnulate (pĭn′yo͝o lāt′, -lĭt), *adj.* having pinnules. Also, **pinnulated.**

pinnule (pĭn′yo͞ol), *n.* **1.** *Zool.* **a.** a part or organ resembling the barb of a feather, or a fin or the like. **b.** a finlet. **c.** one of the lateral branchlets of the arms of a crinoid. **2.** *Bot.* a secondary pinna, one of the pinnately disposed divisions of a bipinnate leaf. [t. L: m. *pinnula* PINNULA] **—pinnular** (pĭn′yo͝o lə), *adj.*

pinochle (pē′nŭk′l), *n.* **1.** a card game resembling bezique played by two, three, or four persons, with a 48-card pack. **2.** the combination of the queen of spades and the jack of diamonds in this game. Also, **penuchle, penuckle, pinocle.** See **bezique.** [orig. uncert.]

pinole (pĭ nō′lĭ), *n.* **1.** maize or wheat flour, sweetened with the flour of mesquite beans or with sugar and spice and used as food in Mexico, California, etc. **2.** any of various mixtures or aromatic powders, used as flavouring. [t. Sp., t. Aztec: m. *pinolli*]

pinpoint (pĭn′point′), *n.* **1.** the point of a pin. **2.** a trifle. —*v.t.* **3.** to locate or describe exactly as on the ground or on a map. —*adj.* **4.** exact, precise.

pinprick (pĭn′prĭk′), *n.* **1.** any small puncture made by or as by a pin. **2.** any petty annoyance.

pins and needles, a tingling sensation in the limbs, as that which accompanies the return of feeling after numbness; a form of paraesthesia.

pinstripe (pĭn′strīp′), *n. Textiles.* **1.** a very narrow stripe. **2.** any material having a regular pattern of such stripes.

pint (pīnt), *n.* **1.** a liquid and also dry measure of capacity, equal to one half of a liquid and dry quart respectively. **2.** a pint of beer. [ME *pynte*, t. F: m. *pinte*, t. MD: plug]

pinta[1] (pĭn′tə; *Sp.* pēn′tä), *n.* a disease prevalent in Mexico, Central and South America, and elsewhere, marked by spots of various colours on the skin. [t. Sp.: spot, g. L *pi(n)cta*, fem. pp., painted]

pinta[2] (pĭn′tə), *n. Slang.* a pint of anything, esp. milk. [taken from the advertising slogan *drinka pinta milka day*]

Pinta (pĭn′tə), *n.* one of the three ships under Columbus when he first discovered America.

pintable (pĭn′tā′bl), *n.* a table or board on which pinball is played.

pintail (pĭn′tāl′), *n.* **1.** a long-necked duck, *Anas acuta*, of the Old and New Worlds, having long narrow middle tail feathers. **2.** the pin-tailed sand-grouse, *Pterocles alchata.* **3.** the American ruddy duck, *Erismatura jamaicensis rubida.* **4.** the sharp-tailed grouse, *Pedioecetes phasianellus*, of North America.

Pinter (pĭn′tə), *n.* **Harold,** born 1930, English playwright and actor.

pintle (pĭn′tl), *n.* **1.** a pin or bolt, esp. one upon which something turns, as in a hinge. **2.** a pin, bolt, or hook on the rear of a towing vehicle. [ME and OE *pintel* penis, f. *pint* (c. D *pint* and G *Pint*) + *-el*, dim. suffix]

pinto (pĭn′tō), *adj., n., pl.* **-tos.** —*adj.* **1.** *U.S.* piebald; mottled; spotted: *a pinto horse.* —*n.* **2.** *Western U.S.* a pinto horse. [t. Sp.: painted, short for *pintado*, pp. of *pintar* paint. See PINTA[1]]

Pintsch gas (pĭnch), gas with high illuminating power made from shale oil or petroleum, once widely used in floating buoys, lighthouses, and railway carriages. [named after Richard *Pintsch*, 1840–1919, German inventor]

pint-size (pīnt′sīz′), *adj. Colloq.* of a person, etc., small or insignificant.

pin-up (pĭn′ŭp′), *Colloq.* —*n.* **1.** a picture, typically pinned to the wall by a personally unknown admirer, of an attractive member of the opposite sex, esp. a film star, or a nude or nearly nude girl. **2.** the girl or man depicted. —*adj.* **3.** of or in such a picture: *a pin-up girl.*

pinwheel (pĭn′wēl′), *n.* **1.** a small catherine-wheel. **2.** *Mach.* a wheel with pins, usually on the periphery as cogs. **3.** *Horol.* such a wheel, its pins projecting at right angles to the face, used in an escapement. Also, **pin wheel.**

pinworm (pĭn′wûm′), *n.* a small nematode worm, *Enterobius vermicularis*, infesting the intestine and migrating to the rectum and anus, esp. in children; threadworm.

pinx., pinxit.

pinxit (pĭngk′sĭt), *Latin.* he (or she) painted it.

piny (pī′nĭ), *adj.,* **-nier, -niest. 1.** abounding in or covered with pine trees. **2.** consisting of pine trees. **3.** pertaining to or suggestive of pine trees. Also, **piney.**

pion (pī′ŏn), *n. Physics.* a pi-meson.

pioneer (pī′ə nĭə′), *n.* **1.** one of those who first enter or settle a region, thus opening it for occupation and development by others. **2.** one of those who are first or earliest in any field of inquiry, enterprise, or progress: *pioneers in cancer research.* **3.** one of a body of foot soldiers detailed to make roads, dig entrenchments, etc., in advance of the main body. **4.** *Ecol.* a plant or animal which successfully invades and becomes established in a bare area. —*v.i.* **5.** to act as a pioneer. —*v.t.* **6.** to open or prepare (a way, etc.), as a pioneer does. **7.** to open a way for. **8.** to be a pioneer in. [t. F: m. *pionnier* pioneer, der. OF *peon* foot soldier. See PEON, PAWN[2]]

pious (pī′əs), *adj.* **1.** having or displaying religious fervour or conscientiousness in religious observance. **2.** practised or used from religious motives (real or pretended), or for some good object: *a pious deception.* **3.** sacred as distinguished from secular: *pious literature.* **4.** heartfelt. **5.** respectful or dutiful. **6.** sanctimonious. [t. L: m. *pius*] —**pi′ously,** *adv.* —**pi′ousness,** *n.* —**Syn. 1.** devout, godly. See **religious.**

pip[1] (pĭp), *n.* **1.** one of the spots on dice, playing cards, or dominoes. **2.** each of the small segments into which the surface of a pineapple is divided. **3.** *Mil. Slang.* a badge of rank worn on the shoulders of certain commissioned officers. [earlier *peep*; orig. unknown]

pip[2] (pĭp), *n.* **1.** a contagious disease of birds, esp. poultry, characterized by the secretion of a thick mucus in the mouth and throat. **2.** *Chiefly Humorous.* any minor ailment in a person. **3. give (someone) the pip,** *Colloq.* to annoy; irritate, esp. without intention: *his stupidity gives me the pip.* [ME *pippe*, appar. t. MD, t. VL: m. s. *pipita*, for L *pītuīta* phlegm, pip]

pip[3] (pĭp), *n.* a small seed, esp. of a fleshy fruit, as an apple or orange. [short for PIPPIN]

pip[4] (pĭp), *v.,* **pipped, pipping.** —*v.i.* **1.** to peep or chirp. —*v.t.* **2.** (of a young bird) to crack or chip a hole through (the shell). [var. of PEEP[2]]

pip[5] (pĭp), *v.t. Colloq.* **1.** to beat in a race, etc., esp. by a small margin: *the favourite was pipped at the post.* **2.** to hit with a missile, as by shooting.

pip[6] (pĭp), *n.* **1.** a brief high-pitched sound made by a radio receiver, echo-sounder, or the like. **2.** the signal on the screen of a radar set or the like.

pipa (pĭ pä′, pē′pə), *n.* the Surinam toad, *Pipa pipa*, a tongueless, flat-bodied frog found in the Amazon and Orinoco basins, and noted for its unique practice of hatching its young in pockets in the skin of its back.

pipage (pī′pĭj), *n.* **1.** conveyance, as of water, gas, or oil, by means of pipes. **2.** the pipes so used. **3.** the sum charged for the conveyance.

pipal (pē′pl), *n.* a species of fig tree, *Ficus religiosa*, of India, somewhat resembling the banyan. Also, **pipul, peepul.** Cf. **bo tree.** [t. Hind., g. Skt *pippala*]

pipe[1] (pīp), *n., v.,* **piped, piping.** —*n.* **1.** a hollow cylinder of metal, wood, or other material, for the conveyance of water, gas, steam, etc., or for some other purpose; a tube. **2.** any of various tubular or cylindrical objects, parts, or formations. **3.** a tube of wood, clay, hard rubber, or other material, with a small bowl at one end, used for smoking tobacco, opium, etc. **4.** a quantity, as of tobacco, that fills the bowl. **5.** *Music.* **a.** a tube used as, or to form an essential part of, a musical wind instrument. **b.** a musical wind instrument consisting of a single tube of straw, reed, wood, or other material, as a flute, clarinet, or oboe. **c.** one of the wooden or metal tubes from which the sounds of an organ are produced. **d.** (*pl.*) any musical wind instrument. **e.** (*pl.*) any woodwind instrument. **f.** (*usually pl.*) bagpipe. **g.** (*usually pl.*) a set of flutes, as panpipes. **h.** a small primitive type of flute, played with one hand and usually accompanied by a drum which is struck by the other hand (called a tabor). **6.** *Naut.* **a.** a boatswain's whistle. **b.** the sounding of it as a call. **7.** the note or call of a bird, etc. **8.** *Obs.* the voice, esp. as used in singing. **9.** a tubular organ or passage in an animal body. **10.** (*pl.*) *Colloq.* the respiratory passages. **11.** *Mining.* **a.** a cylindrical vein or body of ore. **b.** one of the vertical cylindrical masses of bluish rock, of eruption origin, in which diamonds are found embedded in South Africa. **12.** *Bot.* the hollow stem of a plant. —*v.i.* **13.** to play on a pipe. **14.** *Naut.* to announce orders, etc., by a boatswain's pipe or other signal. **15.** to speak shrilly. **16.** to make or utter a shrill sound like that of a pipe. **17.** *Mining.* to carve forming a cylindrical cavity. **18.** to form cylindrical or conical holes during moulding, as in casting steel ingots. **19. pipe down,** *Colloq.* to become or keep quiet. **20. pipe up,** *Colloq.* **a.** to begin to talk, esp. unexpectedly. **b.** to make oneself heard. **c.** to speak up, as to assert oneself. —*v.t.* **21.** to convey by means of pipes. **22.** to supply with pipes. **23.** to play (music) on a pipe or pipes. **24.** to summon, order, etc., by sounding the boatswain's pipe or whistle: *all hands were piped on deck.* **25.** to bring, lead, etc., by playing on a pipe. **26.** to utter in a shrill tone. **27.** to trim or finish (a garment, etc.) with piping. [ME and OE *pīpe* (c. LG *pipe*, G *Pfeife*), ult. der. L *pīpāre* chirp] —**pipe′like′,** *adj.*

pipe[2] (pīp), *n.* **1.** a large cask, of varying capacity, for wine, etc. **2.** such a cask as a measure of capacity for wine, etc., equal to 4 barrels, 2 hogsheads, or half a tun, and containing 126 wine gallons (105 imperial gallons). **3.** such a cask with its contents. [t. OF, ult. same as PIPE[1]]

pipeclay (pīp′klā′), *n.* a fine white clay used for making tobacco pipes, whitening parts of military or other dress, etc.

pipe-cleaner (pīp′klē′nə), *n.* any of various devices used for cleaning the inside of the stem of a tobacco pipe, as one consisting of a short, flexible piece of wire encased in tufted fabric.

pipedream (pīp′drēm′), *n. Slang.* a futile hope, far-fetched fancy, or fantastic story.

pipefish (pīp′fĭsh′), *n., pl.* **-fishes,** (*esp. collectively*) **-fish.** an elongate fish belonging to the *Syngnathidae*, a family of lophobranch fishes with an elongated tubular snout and a slender body of angular section, encased in bony armour.

pipeful (pīp′fŏŏl′), *n.*, *pl.* **-fuls.** a quantity sufficient to fill the bowl of a pipe.

pipeline (pīp′līn′), *n.* **1.** a pipe or several pipes together forming a conduit for the transportation of petroleum, petroleum products, natural gas, etc. **2.** a channel of information, usually confidential, direct or privileged. **3. in the pipeline,** on the way; in preparation.

pipe of peace, a calumet.

pipe organ, an organ with pipes, as distinguished from a reed organ. See **organ** (def. 1).

piper (pī′pə), *n.* **1.** one who plays on a pipe. **2.** a bagpiper. **3. pay the piper,** to bear an expense or disadvantage, and so have rights over a corresponding advantage: *he who pays the piper calls the tune.*

piperaceous (pĭp′ə rā′shəs), *adj.* belonging to the *Piperaceae*, or pepper family of plants, which includes the spice-bearing pepper, *Piper nigrum*, the betel and cubeb plants, etc. [f. L *piper* pepper + -ACEOUS]

piperade (*Fr.* pē pē rȧd′), *n.* a French dish of tomatoes, peppers, and eggs combined in a fluffy puree.

piperidine (pĭ pē′rĭ dēn′, -dĭn), *n. Chem.* a volatile liquid, $C_5H_{11}N$, with the smell of an amine, obtained from the alkaloid piperine or from pyridine. [f. L *piper* pepper + ID(E) + -INE[2]]

piperine (pĭp′ə rīn′, -rĭn), *n. Chem.* a white crystalline alkaloid, $C_{17}H_{19}NO_3$, obtained from pepper and other piperaceous plants, and also prepared synthetically. [t. F, t. It.: m. *peperino* a cement of volcanic ashes, der. L *piper* pepper]

piperonal (pĭp′ə rō năl′), *n. Chem.* a white crystalline aldehyde, $C_8H_6O_3$, a benzene derivative, with a smell resembling that of heliotrope: used in perfumery.

pipestem (pīp′stĕm′), *n.* the stem of a tobacco pipe.

pipestone (pīp′stōn′), *n.* a reddish argillaceous stone, used by North American Indians for making tobacco pipes.

pipette (pĭ pĕt′), *n.* a slender graduated tube for measuring and transferring liquids from one vessel to another. Also, **pipet.** [t. F, dim. of *pipe* PIPE[1]]

pipewort (pīp′wût′), *n.* a monocotyledonous plant, *Eriocaulon septangulare*, with narrow, tufted leaves and small unisexual flowers, occurring only in wet situations in W Scotland and Ireland.

pipi (pē′pē), *n. N.Z.* a burrowing mollusc, *Plebidonax deltoides*, used as food or bait. [t. Maori]

piping (pī′pĭng), *n.* **1.** pipes collectively. **2.** material formed into a pipe or pipes. **3.** the act of one who or that which pipes. **4.** the sound of pipes. **5.** shrill sound. **6.** the music of pipes. **7.** a cordlike ornamentation made of icing, used on cakes, pastry, etc. **8.** a tubular band of material, sometimes containing a cord, for trimming garments, etc., as along edges and seams. —*adj.* **9.** playing on a musical pipe. **10.** that pipes. **11.** emitting a shrill sound: *a piping voice.* **12.** *Archaic.* characterized by the music of the peaceful pipe (rather than the martial fife or trumpet). **13. piping hot, a.** very hot. **b.** freshly arrived; brand-new.

pipistrelle (pĭp′ĭ strĕl′), *n.* the commonest and smallest of the species of bats which inhabits Britain, *Pipistrellus pipistrellus*, the range of which also includes much of Europe and Asia.

pipit (pĭp′ĭt), *n.* any of various small passerine birds of the family *Motacillidae*, esp. the genus *Anthus*, bearing a superficial resemblance to the larks. [imit. of its note]

pipkin (pĭp′kĭn), *n.* **1.** a small earthen pot. **2.** *U.S.* a piggin. [? f. PIPE[2] + -KIN]

pippin (pĭp′ĭn), *n.* **1.** any of numerous varieties of apple, generally characterized by substantial roundish, oblate fruit. **2.** *Bot.* a seed. [ME *pipyn*, t. OF: m. *pepin* fruit seed, pip; orig. uncert.]

pipsqueak (pĭp′skwēk′), *n. Colloq.* a small or insignificant person or thing.

pipy (pī′pĭ), *adj.*, **-pier, -piest.** **1.** pipelike; tubular. **2.** piping; shrill.

piquant (pē′kənt), *adj.* **1.** agreeably pungent or sharp in taste or flavour; biting; tart. **2.** agreeably stimulating, interesting, or attractive. **3.** of a smart or racy character: *piquant wit.* **4.** *Archaic.* sharp or stinging, esp. to the feelings. [t. F: pricking, pungent, ppr. of *piquer*. See PIQUE, v.] —**pi′quancy,** *n.* —**pi′quantly,** *adv.*

pique (pēk), *v.*, **piqued, piquing,** *n.* —*v.t.* **1.** to affect with sharp irritation and resentment, esp. by some wound to pride: *to be piqued at a refusal.* **2.** to wound (the pride, vanity, etc.). **3.** to excite (interest, curiosity, etc.). **4.** to affect with a lively interest or curiosity. **5.** to pride or plume (oneself). —*n.* **6.** anger, resentment, or ill feeling, as resulting from a slight or injury, esp. to pride or vanity; offence taken. [t. F: m. s. *piquer* prick, sting] —**Syn.** **1.** offend, sting, nettle, vex. **3.** stimulate, excite, prick, goad.

piqué (pē′kā), *n.* **1.** a fabric, having a corded or similar texture. **2.** fine inlaid work of gold, silver, etc., esp. in points, on tortoiseshell or ivory. —*adj.* **3.** (of glove seams and gloves) stitched through lapping edges. [t. F: stitched, quilted, pp. of *piquer*. See PIQUE]

piquet (pĭ kĕt′), *n.* a card game played by two persons with a pack of 32 cards, the cards from two to six in each suit being excluded. [t. F, orig. uncert.]

piracy (pī′ə rə sĭ), *n.*, *pl.* **-cies.** **1.** robbery or illegal violence at sea or on the shores of the sea. **2.** the unauthorized appropriation or use of a copyrighted or patented work, idea, etc. **3.** the act of operating a pirate bus service, pirate radio station, or the like. [t. ML: m. s. *pirātia*, t. Gk: m. *peirāteía*]

Piraeus (pī rē′əs), *n.* a seaport in SE Greece: the port of Athens. 183,000 (est. 1961). Also, **Peiraeus.** Greek, **Peiraievs.**

piragua (pĭ rä′gwə, -răg′wə), *n.* pirogue. [t. Sp., t. Carib: a dugout. Cf. PIROGUE]

Pirandello (pĭ′rən dĕl′ō; *It.* pē rȧn dĕl′lō), *n.* **Luigi** (*It.* lwē′jē), 1867–1936, Italian dramatist, novelist, and poet.

Piranesi (*It.* pē rȧ nĕ′zē), *n.* **Giovanni Battista** (*It.* jō vȧn′-nē bȧt tēs′tȧ), 1720–78, Venetian architect, engraver and illustrator of architectural fantasies.

piranha (pĭ rä′nyə), *n.* any small (hand-sized) South American characin fish of the subfamily *Serraosalminae*, noted for voracious habits, dangerous even to human swimmers. [t. Pg.]

pirate (pī′ə rət), *n.*, *v.*, **-rated, -rating.** —*n.* **1.** one who robs or commits illegal violence at sea or on the shores of the sea. **2.** a vessel employed by such persons. **3.** any plunderer. **4.** one who appropriates and reproduces, without authorization as for his own profit, the literary, artistic, or other work or any invention of another. **5.** Also, **pirate bus.** a privately owned bus operating in competition with or in substitution for a public bus service. **6.** Also, **pirate radio.** a radio station broadcasting on an unauthorized wavelength, and often operating outside territorial waters or in a foreign country so as to avoid payment of copyright fees or other legal restrictions. —*v.t.* **7.** to commit piracy upon; rob or plunder as a pirate does. **8.** to take by piracy. **9.** to appropriate and reproduce (literary work, etc.) without authorization or legal right. —*v.i.* **10.** to commit or practise piracy. [ME, t. L: m. *pirāta*, t. Gk: m. *peirātḗs*] —**piratical** (pī răt′ĭ kl), *adj.* —**pirat′ically,** *adv.*

Pirithoüs (pī rĭth′ō əs), *n. Class. Myth.* one of the Lapiths and a companion of Theseus. See **Lapithae.**

Pirmasens (*Ger.* pĭr′mȧ zĕns), *n.* a town in West Germany, in S Rhineland-Palatinate, near Mannheim. 51,300 (est. 1966).

pirogue (pĭ rōg′), *n.* **1.** a canoe hollowed from the trunk of a tree. **2.** a native boat, especially an American dugout. **3.** any of various open boats, with or without masts. Also, **piragua.** [t. F, prob. t. Galibi, Carib d. of Cayenne. Cf. PIRAGUA]

pirouette (pĭ′rŏŏ ĕt′), *n.*, *v.*, **-etted, -etting.** —*n.* **1.** a whirling about on one foot or on the points of the toes, as in dancing. —*v.i.* **2.** to perform a pirouette; whirl, as on the toes. [t. F: top, whirligig, whirl, b. with *pivot* pivot and *girouette* weathervane (der. s. *girer* to turn)]

Pisa (pē′zə; *It.* pē′sȧ), *n.* a city in NW Italy, on the river Arno: leaning tower. 100,917 (1966).

pis aller (*Fr.* pē zȧ lĕ′), *French.* the last resort. [F: worst going]

Pisanello (*It.* pē sȧ nĕl′lō), *n.* **Antonio** (*It.* ȧn tŏ′nyō), ?1395–1455/6, Italian painter.

Pisano (*It.* pē sȧ′nō), *n.* **1. Giovanni** (*It.* jō vȧn′nē), *c.* 1245–*c.* 1320, Italian sculptor and architect. **2.** his father, **Niccola** (*It.* nēk kō′lȧ), *c.* 1220–78, Italian sculptor and architect.

piscary (pĭs′kə rĭ), *n.*, *pl.* **-ries.** **1.** *Law.* the right or privilege of fishing in particular waters. **2.** a fishing place. [late ME, t. ML: m. s. *piscāria*, prop. fem. of L *piscārius* pertaining to fish]

piscatorial (pĭs′kə tô′rĭ əl), *adj.* **1.** of or pertaining to fishermen or fishing. **2.** given or devoted to fishing. Also, **piscatory** (pĭs′kə tə rĭ, -trĭ). [f. s. L *piscātorius* + -AL[1]]

Pisces (pĭs′ēz), *n.pl.*, *gen.* **Piscium** (pĭs′ĭ əm). **1.** the Fishes, a northern zodiacal constellation. **2.** the twelfth sign of the zodiac. See diag. under **zodiac.** **3.** *Zool.* the class of vertebrates that includes the fishes (teleosts), exclusive of elasmobranchs, dipnoans, and marsipobranchs. [t. L, pl. of *piscis* fish]

pisci-, a word element meaning 'fish'. [t. L, comb. form of *piscis*]

pisciculture (pĭs′ĭ kŭl′chə), *n.* the breeding, rearing, and transplantation of fish by artificial means.

piscina (pĭs sē′nə), *n.*, *pl.* **-nas, -nae** (-nē). *Eccles.* a basin with a drain used for certain ablutions, now generally in the sacristy. Also, **piscine** (pĭs′ēn). [t. L: orig., fishpond] —**piscinal** (pĭs′ĭ nəl), *adj.*

piscine (pĭs′īn), *adj.* of or pertaining to fish. [f. s. L *piscis* fish + -INE[1]]

Piscis Austrinus (pĭs′ĭs ŏs trī′nəs), *Astron.* a southern constellation between Aquarius and Grus; Southern Fish.

piscivorous (pĭ sĭv′ə rəs), *adj.* fish-eating.

Pisgah (pĭz′gə), *n.* **Mount,** a mountain ridge of ancient Palestine, NE of the Dead Sea (now in Jordan): from its summit, Mt Nebo, Moses viewed the Promised Land.

pish (pĭsh, psh), *interj.* **1.** (an exclamation of contempt or impatience.) —*n.* **2.** an exclamation of 'pish!' —*v.i.* **3.** to say 'pish'. —*v.t.* **4.** to say 'pish' at or to.

Pisidia (pī sĭd′ĭ ə), *n.* an ancient district of S Asia Minor: later a Roman province.

pisiform (pĭs′ĭ fôm′), *adj.* **1.** having the shape of a pea. **2.** *Anat., Zool.* pertaining to the pealike bone on the ulnar side of the carpus. [t. NL: s. *pīsiformis*, f. *pīsi-* (comb. form repr. L *pīsum* pea) + *-formis* -FORM]

Pisistratus (pī sĭs′trə təs), *n. c.* 605–527 B.C., tyrant of Athens.

pismire (pĭs′mī′ə), *n. Dial.* an ant. [cf. Dan. *myre* ant]

pisolite (pī′sō līt′), *n.* limestone composed of rounded concretions about the size of a pea. [t. NL: m. s. *pisolithus*, f. Gk: *píso(s)* pea + m. *-lithos* -LITE] —**pisolitic** (pī′-sō lĭt′ĭk), *adj.*

piss (pĭs), *Colloq., Taboo.* —*v.i.* **1.** to urinate. **2. piss off,** (used offensively) to go away. —*n.* **3.** urine. [t. OF: m. *pisser* t. Rom.: m. *pissare of echoic orig.]

Pissarro (*Fr.* pē sȧ rō′), *n.* **Camille** (*Fr.* kȧ mēy′), 1830?–1903, French impressionist painter.

pissed (pĭst), *adj. Taboo Slang.* drunk.

pistachio (pĭs tä′shĭ ō′), *n., pl.* **-chios. 1.** the stone (nut) of the fruit of a small anacardiaceous tree, *Pistacia vera*, of southern Europe and Asia Minor. **2.** its edible greenish kernel, used for flavouring. **3.** the tree itself. **4.** pistachio nut flavour. **5.** light yellowish green. Also, **pistache** (pĭs tăsh′; *Fr.* pēs tȧsh′). [t. It.: m. *pistacchio*, t. L: m. *pistācium*, t. Gk: m. *pistákion*]

pistareen (pĭs′tə rēn′), *U.S.* —*n.* **1.** (in Spanish America) the old Spanish peseta. —*adj.* **2.** having little value. [appar. a pop. deriv. of Sp. *peseta*, dim. of *peso* PESO]

piste (pēst), *n. Fencing.* a striplike area of specified size upon which bouts take place. [F: path]

pistil (pĭs′tĭl), *n. Bot.* **1.** the ovule-bearing or seed-bearing organ of a flower, consisting when complete of ovary, style and stigma. **2.** such organs collectively, where there are more than one in a flower. **3.** a gynoecium. [t. NL: m. s. *pistillum* pistil, L pestle]

Pistil of lily, *Lilium bulbiferum* A, Stigma; B, Style; C, Ovary

pistillate (pĭs′tĭ lĭt, -lāt′), *adj. Bot.* **1.** having a pistil or pistils. **2.** having a pistil or pistils but no stamens. See illus. under **amentum.**

Pistoia (*It.* pēs tō′yȧ), *n.* a city in N Italy, in Tuscany. 89,360 (1966).

pistol (pĭs′tl), *n., v.,* **-tolled, -tolling** or (*U.S.*) **-toled, -toling.** —*n.* **1.** a short firearm intended to be held and fired with one hand. —*v.t.* **2.** to shoot with a pistol. [t. F: m. *pistole* pistol, also pistole, t. G, t. Czech: m. *pist'al*]

pistole (pĭs tōl′), *n.* **1.** a former gold coin of Spain. **2.** any of various other obsolete European gold coins. [t. F: a coin, transferred use of *pistole* PISTOL, on the analogy of *écu* meaning both shield and coin]

pistoleer (pĭs′tə lĭə′), *n.* one who is armed with or uses a pistol. [t. F: m. *pistolier*]

pistol-grip (pĭs′tl grĭp′), *n.* a handle of a saw, rifle, electric drill, etc., perpendicular to the main axis and thus resembling the stock of a pistol.

piston (pĭs′tən), *n.* **1.** a movable disc or cylinder fitting closely within a tube or hollow cylinder, and capable of being driven alternately forwards and backwards in the tube by pressure, as in an internal-combustion engine, thus imparting reciprocating motion to a rod (**piston rod**) attached to it on one side, or of being driven thus by the rod, as in a pump. **2.** a pumplike valve used to change the pitch in a cornet or the like. [t. F, t. It.: m. *pistone*, der. *pistare* pound, der. L *pistus*, pp., pounded]

piston ring, a metallic ring, usually one of a series, and split so as to be expansible, placed around a piston in order to maintain a tight fit, as inside the cylinder of an internal-combustion engine.

piston rod, the rod which connects the piston of a reciprocating steam-engine to the crosshead.

pit[1] (pĭt), *n., v.,* **pitted, pitting.** —*n.* **1.** a hole or cavity in the ground. **2.** a covered or concealed excavation in the ground to serve as a trap; pitfall. **3.** *Mining.* **a.** an excavation made in digging for some mineral deposit. **b.** the shaft of a coalmine. **c.** the mine itself. **4.** a sunken area in the floor of a garage used for the inspection of vehicles from below. **5.** a hole in the ground used for any of various purposes, as disposal of waste, burning charcoal, making silage, etc. **6.** the abode of evil spirits and lost souls; hell, or a part of it. **7.** a hollow or indentation in a surface. **8.** a natural hollow or depression in the body: *the pit of the stomach.* **9.** a small depressed scar such as one of those left on the skin after smallpox. **10.** an enclosure for combats, as of dogs or cocks. **11.** *U.S.* that part of the floor of an exchange devoted to a special kind of business: *the grain pit.* **12.** (in a theatre) **a.** the ground floor of the auditorium. **b.** the part of the ground floor behind the stalls. **c.** the persons occupying this section. **13.** *Athletics.* an area, typically slightly sunken and filled with sand, which softens the fall of a long jumper, high jumper, etc. **14.** *Motor-racing.* any of the stalls beside the track in which competing cars undergo running repairs, are refuelled, etc., during a race. **15.** *Bot.* a thin place in a cell wall affording communication with another cell. —*v.t.* **16.** to mark with pits or depressions. **17.** to place or bury in a pit. **18.** to set in active opposition, as one against another. **19.** to set (animals) in a pit or enclosure to fight. —*v.i.* **20.** to become marked with pits or depressions. **21.** *Pathol.* to retain for a time the mark of pressure by the finger, etc., as the skin. [ME and OE *pytt*, ult. t. L: m. *puteus* well, pit, shaft]

pit[2] (pĭt), *n., v.,* **pitted, pitting.** *U.S.* —*n.* **1.** the stone of a fruit, as of a cherry, peach, or plum. —*v.t.* **2.** to take out the stone from (a fruit, etc.). [t. D: kernel]

pita (pē′tə), *n.* **1.** a fibre obtained from species of *Agave*, *Aechmea*, or related genera, used for cordage, etc. **2.** one of these plants. [t. Sp., t. Quechua]

pitapat (pĭt′ə păt′), *adv., n., v.,* **-patted, -patting.** —*adv.* **1.** with a quick succession of beats or taps. —*n.* **2.** the movement or the sound of something going pitapat. —*v.i.* **3.** to go pitapat. [imit.]

Pitcairn Island (pĭt kĕən′, pĭt′kĕən′), a small British island in the S Pacific, SE of Tuamotu Archipelago: settled by mutineers of the *Bounty* in 1790. 128 pop. (1962); 2 sq. mi. See map under **Hawaiian Islands.** —**Pit′cairn′ese,** *adj., n.*

pitch[1] (pĭch), *v.t.* **1.** to set up or erect (a tent, camp, etc.). **2.** to put, set, or plant in a fixed or definite place or position (as cricket stumps, etc.). **3.** to set or aim at a certain point, degree, level, etc.: *he pitched his hopes too high.* **4.** *Music.* to set at a particular pitch, or determine the key or keynote of (a tune, etc.). **5.** to throw, fling, or toss. **6.** *Baseball.* to deliver (the ball) to the batter. **7.** *Golf.* to hit (the ball) so that it rises steeply and rolls little on landing. **8.** *Cards.* **a.** to lead (a card of a particular suit), thereby fixing that suit as trumps. **b.** to determine (trumps) thus. **9.** *Bldg Trades.* to dress, work, or place (masonry, etc.). **10. pitch a tale (yarn, etc.),** to tell a story, esp. one that is exaggerated or untrue. —*v.i.* **11.** to plunge or fall forward or headlong. **12.** to lurch. **13.** to throw, fling, or toss. **14.** to slope downwards; dip. **15.** to plunge with alternate fall and rise of bow and stern, as a ship, aeroplane, etc. (opposed to *roll*). **16.** *Aeron.* to change the angle which the longitudinal axis makes relative to the horizontal. **17.** to fix a tent or temporary habitation; encamp. **18.** *Rare.* to settle. **19.** to fix or decide (often fol. by *on* or *upon*), often casually or without particular consideration. **20.** *Golf.* to hit the ball so that it rises steeply and does not roll much on landing. **21.** *Baseball.* **a.** to deliver the ball to the batter. **b.** to fill the position of pitcher. **22. pitch in,** *Colloq.* **a.** to contribute or join in. **b.** to begin vigorously. **23. pitch into, a.** to attack verbally or physically. **b.** to begin to do or work on (something). —*n.* **24.** relative point, position, or degree. **25.** height (now chiefly in certain specific uses): *pitch of an arch.* **26.** the highest point or greatest height: *the pitch of perfection.* **27.** *Music, etc.* degree of height or depth of a note or sound, depending upon the relative rapidity of the vibrations by which it is produced. **28.** a particular tonal standard with which given notes may be compared in respect to their relative level. **29.** *Acoustics.* the apparent predominant frequency of a sound from an acoustical source. **30.** the act or manner of pitching. **31.** a throw or toss. **32.** the pitching movement, or a plunge forward of a ship, aeroplane or the like. **33.** inclination or slope. **34.** degree of inclination or slope; angle. **35.** a sloping part or place. **36.** a quantity of something pitched or placed somewhere. **37. a.** *Sport.* the whole area of play, usually of grass, of cricket, football, hockey, etc. **b.** *Cricket.* the area between the wickets, 22 yards long. **38.** a spot where a person or thing is placed or stationed, esp. the established location of a stall in a street market or of a street pedlar, singer, etc. **39.** a sales talk. **40.** a specific plan of action; way of approaching a problem. **41.** *Geol., Mining.* the inclination of the axis of a fold from the horizontal.

42. *Archit.* the slope or steepness of a roof. **43.** *Mach.* **a.** the distance between corresponding surfaces of adjacent teeth of a gearwheel or the like. **b.** the distance between two things in a regular series, as between threads of a screw, rivets, etc., the distance which a propeller would advance in one revolution, assuming no slip. **44.** *Cards.* a game in which trumps are determined for any one round by the first card led. **45. queer someone's pitch,** *Colloq.* to upset someone's plans. [ME *picche(n)*; ? akin to PICK[1]] —**Syn. 5.** See **throw.**

pitch[2] (pĭch), *n.* **1.** any of various dark-coloured tenacious or viscous substances used for covering the seams of vessels after caulking, for making pavements, etc., as the residuum left after the distillation of coal tar (coal-tar pitch), or a product derived similarly from wood tar (wood pitch). **2.** any of certain bitumens: *mineral pitch* (asphaltum). **3.** any of various resins. **4.** the sap or crude turpentine which exudes from the bark of pines. —*v.t.* **5.** to smear or cover with pitch. [ME *pich*, OE *pic*, t. L: s. *pix*; akin to Gk *pissa*] —**pitch′like′,** *adj.*

pitch-and-toss (pĭch′ən tŏs′), *n.* a game in which players throw coins at a mark, the most accurate player then being allowed to toss all the coins and keep those which come down heads up.

pitchblende (pĭch′blĕnd′), *n.* an impure uraninite, occurring in black pitchlike masses: the principal ore of uranium and radium. [half trans., half adoption of G *Pechblende.* See PITCH[2], BLENDE]

pitch circle, an imaginary circle concentric with the axis of a toothed wheel, at such a distance from the base of the teeth that it is in contact with and rolls upon a similar circle of another toothed wheel engaging with the first.

pitch-dark (pĭch′däk′), *adj.* black or dark as pitch. Also, **pitch-black.**

pitched battle (pĭcht), **1.** a battle following the deliberate choice of time and place, and the orderly arrangement of forces (opposed to a *skirmish*). **2.** a battle fully engaging the resources of the opposing armies. **3.** *Colloq.* any violent fight involving many people.

pitcher[1] (pĭch′ə), *n.* **1.** a container, usually with a handle and spout or lip, for holding and pouring liquids. **2.** *Bot.* **a.** a pitcher-like modification of the leaf of certain plants. **b.** an ascidium. [ME *picher*, t. OF: m. *pichier*; ? akin to BEAKER] —**pitch′er-like′,** *adj.*

pitcher[2] (pĭch′ə), *n.* **1.** one who pitches. **2.** *Baseball.* the player who delivers or throws the ball to the batter. **3.** *Golf.* a lightweight iron golf club (number 7 iron) with a broad, sloping face. [f. PITCH[1], v. + -ER[1]]

pitcher plant, any of various, often insectivorous plants with leaves modified into a pitcher-like receptacle, or ascidium, as the plants of the genera *Sarracenia* and *Darlingtonia.*

Pitcher plant, *Darlingtonia californica*

pitch faced, *Bldg Trades.* (of masonry) composed of stones roughly squared with the pitching tool.

pitchfork (pĭch′fôk′), *n.* **1.** a fork for lifting and pitching hay, etc. —*v.t.* **2.** to pitch or throw with or as with a pitchfork.

pitching (pĭch′ĭng), *n.* **1.** *Bldg Trades.* a carefully laid stone facing of an earth slope or a dam. **2.** *Bldg Trades.* carefully laid stone in the foundations of a road. **3.** *Aeron.* the rotational movement of an aircraft about its lateral axis.

pitching tool, *Bldg Trades.* a chisel for roughly squaring stones.

Pitch Lake, a deposit of asphalt in Trinidad, in the West Indies.

pitch line, 1. a pitch circle. **2.** a corresponding straight line on a toothed rack.

pitchman (pĭch′mən), *n.* *U.S.* **1.** an itinerant salesman of small wares which are usually carried in a case with collapsible legs, allowing it to be set up or removed quickly. **2.** any high-pressure salesman, usually of goods of dubious quality. [f. PITCH[1] + MAN]

pitch pine, any of several species of pine from which pitch or turpentine is obtained.

pitchpipe (pĭch′pīp′), *n.* *Music.* a small pipe, sounded to give the pitch for singing, tuning an instrument, etc.

pitch shot, *Golf.* a shot, used to approach the green, that lifts the ball steeply up, often with backspin applied, to prevent it rolling when it lands.

pitchstone (pĭch′stōn′), *n.* a glassy igneous rock having a resinous lustre and resembling hardened pitch. [f. PITCH[2], n., + STONE, trans. of G *Pechstein*]

pitchy (pĭch′ĭ), *adj.*, **-ier, -iest. 1.** full of or abounding in pitch. **2.** smeared with pitch. **3.** of the nature of pitch; resembling pitch. **4.** black; dark as pitch. —**pitch′iness,** *n.*

piteous (pĭt′ĭ əs), *adj.* **1.** such as to excite or deserve pity, or appealing strongly for pity; pathetic. **2.** *Archaic.* compassionate. [f. *pite* PITY + -OUS; r. ME *pitous*, t. AF, ult. der. L *pietas* piety] —**pit′eously,** *adv.* —**pit′eousness,** *n.* —**Syn. 1.** affecting, distressing, lamentable, woeful, sad. See **pitiful.**

pitfall (pĭt′fôl′), *n.* **1.** a concealed pit prepared as a trap for animals or men to fall into. **2.** any trap or danger for the unwary. —**Syn. 1, 2.** See **trap**[1].

pith (pĭth), *n.* **1.** any soft, spongy tissue or substance: *the pith of an orange.* **2.** *Bot.* the central cylinder of parenchymatous tissue in the stems of dicotyledonous plants. **3.** any of various analogous inner parts or substances, as the centre of a log, a feather, etc. **4.** the important or essential part; essence. **5.** strength, force, or vigour. —*v.t.* **6.** to take the pith from (plants, etc.). **7.** to destroy the spinal cord or brain of. **8.** to slaughter, as cattle, by severing the spinal cord. [ME; OE *pitha* pith. Cf. D *pit* pith, PIT[2]]

pithead (pĭt′hĕd′), *n.* **1.** the top of a mine shaft. **2.** the machinery, offices, etc., on the surface associated with the running of a mine.

pithecanthrope (pĭth′ĭ kăn′thrōp), *n.* a member of the genus *Pithecanthropus.*

Pithecanthropus (pĭth′ĭ kăn thrō′pəs, -kăn′thrə pəs), *n.*, *pl.* **-pi** (-pī′). an extinct genus of apelike men, esp. *Pithecanthropus erectus* of the Pleistocene of Java (**Java man**). [t. NL, f. Gk: m. s. *píthēkos* ape + m. *ánthrōpos* man] —**pith′ecan′thropoid′,** *adj.*

pith helmet, a sun-hat, usually domed with a sloping brim, made of spongewood, and formerly much worn by Europeans in tropical countries; topee.

pithy (pĭth′ĭ), *adj.*, **-ier, -iest. 1.** full of vigour, substance, or meaning; terse; forcible: *a pithy criticism.* **2.** of, like, or abounding in pith. —**pith′ily,** *adv.* —**pith′iness,** *n.*

pitiable (pĭt′ĭ ə bl), *adj.* **1.** deserving to be pitied; such as justly to excite pity; lamentable; deplorable. **2.** such as to excite a contemptuous pity; miserable; contemptible. —**pit′iableness,** *n.* —**pit′iably,** *adv.* —**Syn. 1, 2.** See **pitiful.**

pitier (pĭt′ĭ ə), *n.* one who pities.

pitiful (pĭt′ĭ fəl), *adj.* **1.** such as to excite or deserve pity: *a pitiful fate.* **2.** such as to excite contempt by smallness, poor quality, etc.: *pitiful attempts.* **3.** full of pity or compassion; compassionate. —**pit′ifully,** *adv.* —**pit′ifulness,** *n.*

—**Syn. 1.** lamentable, deplorable, woeful. **1, 2.** PITIFUL, PITIABLE, PITEOUS apply to that which excites pity (with compassion or with contempt). That which is PITIFUL is touching and excites pity or is mean and contemptible: *a pitiful leper; a pitiful exhibition of cowardice.* PITIABLE may mean lamentable, or wretched and paltry; *a pitiable hovel.* PITEOUS refers only to that which exhibits suffering and misery, and is therefore heart-rending: *piteous poverty.*

pitiless (pĭt′ĭ lĭs), *adj.* feeling or showing no pity; merciless. —**pit′ilessly,** *adv.* —**pit′ilessness,** *n.* —**Syn.** See **cruel.**

pitman (pĭt′mən), *n.*, *pl.* **-men** *for 1*, **-mans** *for 2.* **1.** one who works in a pit, as in coal-mining. **2.** *Mach.*, *Chiefly U.S.* a connecting rod. [f. PIT[1] + MAN]

Pitman (pĭt′mən), *n.* **Sir Isaac,** 1813–97, English inventor of a system of shorthand.

pitocin (pĭt′ə sĭn), *n.* *Pharm.* an aqueous solution containing the oxytocic principle of the posterior lobe of the pituitary gland, used to induce labour. [f. PIT(UITARY) + (OXYT)OCIN]

piton (*Fr.* pē tôɴ′), *n.* *Mountaineering.* a metal spike with an eye through which a rope may be passed. Also, **peg.** [F]

Pitot-static tube (pē′tō stăt′ĭk), a combined Pitot and static-pressure tube designed to measure the kinetic and static pressures.

Pitot tube (pē′tō), an instrument for measuring fluid velocity by means of the differential pressure between the tip (dynamic) and side (static) openings.

pit pony, a small pony, formerly used for haulage in coal-mines, etc.

pitsaw (pĭt′sô′), *n.* a saw operated by two men, one above the log and the other below it, in a pit.

pit stop, a stop made at the pits by a racing car during a race.

Pitt (pĭt), *n.* **1. William** (*′the Elder′*, *1st Earl of Chatham*), 1708–78, British statesman. **2.** his son, **William** (*′the Younger′*), 1759–1806, British statesman; prime minister 1783–1801 and 1804–1806. See **Chatham.**

pittance (pĭt′ns), *n.* **1.** a small allowance or sum for living expenses. **2.** a scanty income or remuneration. **3.** any small portion or amount. [ME *pita(u)nce*, t. OF, der. *pitie* pity. See PIETY, PITY]

pitter-patter (pĭt′ə păt′ə), *n.* **1.** a rapid succession of light beats or taps, as of rain. —*adv.* **2.** with a rapid succession of light beats or taps, as of rain.

Pittsburgh (pĭts′bûg′), *n.* a city in SW Pennsylvania: a port where the Allegheny and Monongahela rivers converge to form the Ohio; steel. 604,332 (1960).

pituitary (pĭ tyōō′ĭ tə rĭ, -trĭ), *n., pl.* **-taries,** *adj.* **—***n.* **1.** *Anat.* the pituitary gland. **2.** *Med.* the extract obtained from either the anterior or posterior lobes of the pituitary. The anterior lobe substance regulates growth of the skeleton; that of the posterior lobe increases blood pressure, contracts the smooth muscles, etc. **—***adj. Anat.* **3.** of the pituitary gland. **4.** denoting a physical type of abnormal size with overgrown extremities resulting from excessive pituitary secretion. [t. L: m. s. *pītuītārius* pertaining to, or secreting phlegm]

pituitary gland, *Anat.* a small, oval, endocrine gland attached to the base of the brain and situated in a depression of the sphenoid bone, which secretes several hormones, and was formerly supposed to secrete mucus. Also, **pituitary body.**

pituri (pĭt′yōō rĭ, pĭch′ōō-), *n.* a solanaceous shrub, *Duboisia hopwoodii*, of Australia, the leaves and twigs of which are used by Aborigines as a narcotic. [t. native Australian]

pit viper, any of the snakes of the subfamily *Crotalinae*, with a wide distribution in the Old and New Worlds, having a pit on each side of the head in front of the eye.

pity (pĭt′ĭ), *n., pl.* **pities,** *v.,* **pitied, pitying.** **—***n.* **1.** sympathetic or kindly sorrow excited by the suffering or misfortune of another, often leading one to give relief or aid or to show mercy: *to weep from pity, to take pity on a person.* **2.** a cause or reason for pity, sorrow, or regret: *What a pity you could not go!* **—***v.t.* **3.** to feel pity or compassion for; be sorry for; commiserate. **—***v.i.* **4.** *Obs.* to feel pity. [ME *pite*, t. OF, t. L: m. s. *pietas* piety] **—pit′yingly,** *adv.* **—Syn. 1.** commiseration, sympathy, compassion.

pityriasis (pĭt′ə rī′ə sĭs), *n.* **1.** *Pathol.* any of various skin diseases marked by the shedding of branlike scales of epidermis. **2.** *Vet. Sci.* a skin disease in various domestic animals marked by dry scales. [t. NL, t. Gk: branlike eruption]

più (pyōō), *adv. Music.* more; somewhat. [It.]

Pius (pī′əs), *n.* the name of twelve popes.

Pius II (*Enea Silvio de Piccolomini*), 1405–64, Italian ecclesiastic, poet, and historian (under the name *Aeneas Silvius*); pope 1458–64.

Pius VII (*Luigi Barnaba Chiaramonti*), 1742–1823, Italian ecclesiastic; pope 1800–23.

Pius IX (*Giovanni Maria Mastai-Ferretti*), 1792–1878, Italian ecclesiastic; pope 1846–78.

Pius X (*Guiseppe Sarto*), 1835–1914, Italian ecclesiastic; pope 1903–14.

Pius XI (*Achille Ratti*), 1857–1939, Italian ecclesiastic; pope 1922–39.

Pius XII (*Eugenio Pacelli*), 1876–1958, Italian ecclesiastic; pope 1939–58.

Piute (pī yōōt′), *n.* Paiute.

pivot (pĭv′ət), *n.* **1.** a pin or short shaft on the end of which something rests and turns, or upon and about which something rotates or oscillates. **2.** the end of a shaft or arbor, resting and turning in a bearing. **3.** that on which something turns, hinges, or depends. **4.** the person upon whom a line, as of troops, wheels about. **—***v.i.* **5.** to turn on or as on a pivot. **—***v.t.* **6.** to mount on, attach by, or provide with a pivot or pivots. [t. F; orig. uncert.]

pivotal (pĭv′ə tl), *adj.* **1.** of, pertaining to, or serving as a pivot. **2.** of critical importance. **—piv′otally,** *adv.*

pivot bridge, a swing bridge.

pix (pĭks), *n.* pyx.

pixilated (pĭk′sĭ lā′tĭd), *adj. Colloq.* amusingly eccentric. [der. PIXY, modelled on TITILLATED]

pixy (pĭk′sĭ), *n., pl.* **pixies.** a fairy or sprite. Also, **pixie.** [orig. uncert.]

Pizarro (pĭd zä′rō; *Sp.* pē thär′rō), *n.* **Francisco** (*Sp.* frän thēs′kō), 1471 or 1475–1541, Spanish conqueror of Peru.

pizz., *Music.* pizzicato.

pizza (pēt′sə; *It.* pēt′tsä), *n.* an Italian dish made from yeast dough covered with tomato, grated cheese, anchovies, olives, etc.

pizzicato (pĭt′sĭ kä′tō; *It.* pēt tsē kä′tō), *adj., n., pl.* **-ti** (-tĭ; *It.* -tē). *Music.* **—***adj.* **1.** played by plucking the strings with the finger instead of using the bow, as on a violin. **—***n.* **2.** a note or passage so played. [It., pp. of *pizzicare* pick, twang (a stringed instrument)]

P.J., **1.** presiding judge. **2.** Probate Judge.

pk, **1.** pack. **2.** park. **3.** peak. **4.** peck.

pkg., package.

pkt, packet.

pl., **1.** place. **2.** plate. **3.** plural.

P.L., **1.** partial loss. **2.** (L *Pharmacopoeia londinensis*) London Pharmacopoeia. **3.** poet laureate.

P.L.A., Port of London Authority.

p.l.a., passenger luggage in advance.

placable (plăk′ə bl), *adj.* capable of being placated or appeased; forgiving: *he seemed mild and placable.* [ME, t. L: m. s. *plācābilis*] **—pla′cabil′ity, pla′cableness,** *n.* **—pla′cably,** *adv.*

placard (plăk′äd), *n.* **1.** a written or printed notice to be posted in a public place; a poster. **—***v.t.* **2.** to post placards on or in. **3.** to give notice of by means of placards. **4.** to post as a placard. [t. F, der. *plaque*, t. D: m. *plak* flat board] **—plac′arder,** *n.*

placate (plə kāt′), *v.t.,* **-cated, -cating.** to appease; pacify. [t. L: m. s. *plācātus*, pp.] **—placation** (plə kā′shən), *n.*

placatory (plăk′ə tə rĭ, -trĭ, plə kā′tə rĭ), *adj.* tending or intending to placate. [t. L: m. s. *plācātōrius*]

place (plās), *n., v.,* **placed, placing.** **—***n.* **1.** a particular portion of space, of definite or indefinite extent. **2.** space in general (chiefly in connection with *time*). **3.** the portion of space occupied by anything. **4.** a space or spot, set apart or used for a particular purpose: *a place of worship.* **5.** any part or spot in a body or surface: *a decayed place in a tooth.* **6.** a particular passage in a book or writing. **7.** a space or seat for a person, as in a theatre, train, etc. **8.** the space or position customarily or previously occupied by a person or thing. **9.** position, situation, or circumstances: *if I were in your place.* **10.** a proper or appropriate location or position. **11.** a job, post, or office. **12.** a function or duty. **13.** position or standing in the social scale, or in any order of merit, estimation, etc. **14.** high position or rank. **15.** official employment or position. **16.** a region. **17.** an open space, or square, in a city or town. **18.** a short street, a court, etc. **19.** an area, esp. one regarded as an entity and identifiable by name, used for habitation, as a city, town, or village. **20.** a building. **21.** a part of a building. **22.** a residence, dwelling, or house. **23.** stead or lieu: *use water in place of milk.* **24.** a step or point in order of proceeding: *in the first place.* **25.** a fitting opportunity. **26.** a reasonable ground or occasion. **27.** *Arith.* **a.** the position of a figure in a series, as in decimal notation. **b.** (*pl.*) the figures of the series. **28.** *Drama.* one of three unities. See **unity** (def. 10). **29.** *Astron.* the position of a heavenly body at any instant. **30.** *Sport.* **a.** a position among the leading competitors, usually the first three, at the finish of a race. **b.** the position of the second or third (opposed to *win*). **31.** Some special noun phrases are:

give place, **1.** to make room. **2.** be superseded.

go places, *Slang.* to be successful in one's career.

know one's place, to recognize one's (low) social rank and behave accordingly.

out of place, **1.** not in the proper position. **2.** inappropriate, unsuitable.

pride of place, the highest or most important position.

put in one's place, to humble (an arrogant person, etc.).

take one's place, to sit down, or take up a position, as of right.

take place, to happen.

take the place of, to be a substitute for; oust.

—*v.t.* **32.** to put in a particular place; set. **33.** to put in an appropriate position or order. **34.** to put into a suitable or desirable place for some purpose, as money for investment, an order or contract, etc. **35.** to fix (confidence, esteem, etc.) in a person or thing. **36.** to appoint (a person) to a post or office. **37.** to find a place, situation, etc., for (a person). **38.** to determine or indicate the place of. **39.** to assign a certain position or rank to. **40.** to direct or aim with precision. **41.** to assign a position to (a horse, etc.) among the leading competitors, usually the first three, at the finish of a race. **42.** to put or set in a particular place, position, situation, or relation. **43.** to identify by connecting with the proper place, circumstances, etc.: *to be unable to place a person.* **44.** to sing or speak with consciousness of the bodily point of emphasis of resonance of each note or register. **—***v.i.* **45.** *U.S. Racing.* to finish among the three winners, usually second; to be placed.

[ME; OE *plætse, plæce*, t. L: m. s. *platēa* street, area, t. Gk: m. *plateîa* broad way, prop. fem. of *platýs* broad] **—Syn. 11.** See **position. 32.** See **put.**

placebo (plə sē′bō), *n., pl.* **-bos, -boes.** **1.** *Med.* a medicine which performs no physiological function but may benefit the patient psychologically. **2.** *Rom. Cath. Ch.* the vespers of the office for the dead, so called from the initial word of the first antiphon, taken from Psalm 114:9 of the Vulgate. [ME, t. L: I shall be pleasing, acceptable]

place-card (plās′käd′), *n.* a card put by each place at a dinner table, etc., indicating who is to sit there.

placekick (plās′kĭk′), *n. Rugby Football, etc.* a kick made when the ball has been placed on the ground, at a predetermined spot. Cf. **drop kick** and **punt**[1].

placeman (plās′mən), *n., pl.* **-men.** one who holds a place or office, esp. under a government (often depreciatory).

placement (plās′mənt), *n.* **1.** the act of placing. **2.** the act of an employment exchange or employer in filling a position. **3.** the state of being placed. **4.** location; arrangement.

placename (plās′nām′), *n.* the name of a place. Cf. **toponym.**

placenta (plə sĕn′tə), *n., pl.* **-tas, -tae** (-tē). **1.** *Zool., Anat.* the organ formed in the lining of the mammalian uterus by the union of the uterine mucous membrane with the membranes of the foetus to provide for the nourishment of the foetus and the elimination of its waste products. **2.** *Bot.* **a.** that part of the ovary of flowering plants which bears the ovules. **b.** (in ferns, etc.) the tissue giving rise to sporangia. [t. NL: something having a flat circular form, L a cake, t. Gk: m. *plakoûnta*, acc. of *plakoûs* flat cake] —**placen′tal,** *adj.*

placentate (plə sĕn′tāt), *adj.* having a placenta.

placentation (plăs′ĕn tā′shən), *n.* **1.** *Zool., Anat.* **a.** the formation of a placenta. **b.** the manner of the disposition or construction of a placenta. **2.** *Bot.* the disposition or arrangement of a placenta or placentas.

placentography (plăs′ĕn tŏg′rə fī), *n. Med.* an X-ray examination to show the site of the placenta in the uterus.

placer[1] (plăs′ə), *n. Mining.* **1.** a superficial gravel or similar deposit containing particles of gold or the like (distinguished from *lode*). **2.** a place where such a deposit is washed for gold, etc. (**placer mining**). [t. Amer. Sp.: sandbank; akin to *plaza.* See PLACE]

placer[2] (plā′sə), *n.* one who places. [f. PLACE, v. + -ER[1]]

placet (plā′sĕt), *n.* an expression or vote of assent or sanction by the Latin word *placet* it pleases.

placid (plăs′ĭd), *adj.* pleasantly calm or peaceful; unruffled; tranquil; serene. [t. L: s. *placidus*] —**placidity** (plă sĭd′ĭ tĭ), **plac′idness,** *n.* —**plac′idly,** *adv.* —**Syn.** See **peaceful.**

placket (plăk′ĭt), *n.* an opening at the top of a skirt, or in a dress or blouse, to facilitate putting it on and off.

placoid (plăk′oid), *adj.* **1.** platelike, as the scales or dermal investments of sharks. **2.** relating to the *Placoidae.* —*n.* **3.** a member of the *Placoidae*, a group of fishes including the sharks and rays, and distinguished by irregular bony scales. [f. m. s. Gk *pláx* something flat, tablet + -OID]

plafond (*Fr.* plà fôɴ′), *n. Archit.* a ceiling, whether flat or arched, esp. one of decorative character. [t. F: f. *plat* flat + *fond* bottom. See PLATE[1], FUND]

plagal (plā′gl), *adj. Gregorian Music.* (of a mode) having the final in the middle of the compass. Cf. **authentic** (def. 4). [t. ML: s. *plagālis*, der. *plaga* plagal mode, appar. back-formation from *plagius*, t. MGk: m. *plágios*, in Gk, oblique]

plagal cadence, *Music.* a cadence in which there is a progression from a subdominant chord to a tonic chord.

plagiarism (plā′jyə rĭz′əm), *n.* **1.** the appropriation or imitation of another's ideas and manner of expressing them, as in art, literature, etc., to be passed off as one's own. **2.** something appropriated and passed off as one's own in this manner. —**pla′giarist,** *n.* —**pla′giaris′tic,** *adj.*

plagiarize (plā′jyə rīz′), *v.,* **-rized, -rizing.** —*v.t.* **1.** to appropriate by plagiarism. **2.** to appropriate ideas, passages, etc., from by plagiarism. —*v.i.* **3.** to commit plagiarism. Also, **plagiarise.** —**pla′giariz′er,** *n.*

plagiary (plā′jyə rĭ), *n., pl.* **-ries. 1.** plagiarism. **2.** a plagiarist. [t. L: m. s. *plagiārius* one who abducts the child or slave of another]

plagioclase (plā′jĭ ō klās′), *n.* any of the felspar minerals varying in composition from $NaAlSi_3O_8$ to $CaAl_2Si_2O_8$, important constituents of many igneous rocks. [f. Gk: *plágio(s)* oblique + m. *klásis* fracture] —**plagioclastic** (plā′jĭ ō klăs′tĭk), *adj.*

plagioclimax (plā′jĭ ō klī′măks), *n. Ecol.* final and stable stage in the ecological succession of a plant-animal community, differing from the natural climax as a result of interference from some extraneous factor, such as human activity.

plagiotropic (plā′jĭ ō trŏp′ĭk), *adj. Bot.* denoting, pertaining to, or exhibiting a mode of growth which is more or less divergent from the vertical. [f. Gk: *plágio(s)* oblique + m. s. *tropikós* inclined] —**pla′giotrop′ically,** *adv.*

plagiotropism (plā′jĭ ŏt′rə pĭz′əm), *n. Bot.* plagiotropic tendency or growth.

plague (plāg), *n., v.,* **plagued, plaguing.** —*n.* **1.** an epidemic disease of high mortality; a pestilence. **2.** an infectious, epidemic disease, occurring in several forms (**bubonic, pneumonic,** and **septicaemic**), known in history as the **Black Death** of the 14th century, the **Great Plague of London** in 1664–65, and the **Oriental Plague. 3.** an affliction, calamity, or evil, esp. one regarded as a visitation from God: *the ten plagues.* **4.** any cause of trouble or vexation. —*v.t.* **5.** to trouble or torment in any manner. **6.** to annoy, bother, or pester. **7.** to smite with a plague. **8.** to infect with a plague. **9.** to afflict with any evil. [ME *plage*, t. L: m. *plāga* blow, wound, LL affliction, pestilence; akin to Gk *plēgḗ* stroke] —**pla′guer,** *n.* —**Syn. 4.** nuisance, trouble, bother. **6.** harass, vex. See **bother.**

plaguy (plā′gĭ), *Archaic.* —*adj.* **1.** such as to plague, torment, or annoy; vexatious. —*adv.* **2.** vexatiously or excessively. —**pla′guily,** *adv.*

plaice (plās), *n., pl.* **plaice. 1.** a European flatfish, *Pleuronectes platessa*, an important food fish. **2.** any of various American flatfishes or flounders. [ME *plais*, t. OF, g. LL *platessa* flatfish, der. Gk *platýs* flat]

plaid (plăd), *n.* **1.** any fabric woven of different coloured yarns in a cross-barred pattern. **2.** a pattern of this kind. **3.** a long, rectangular piece of cloth, usually with such a pattern, worn about the shoulders by Scottish Highlanders. —*adj.* **4.** having the pattern of a plaid. [t. Gaelic: m. *plaide* blanket, plaid]

plaided (plăd′ĭd), *adj.* **1.** wearing a plaid. **2.** made of plaid, or having a similar pattern.

plain[1] (plān), *adj.* **1.** clear or distinct to the eye or ear: *leaving a plain trail.* **2.** clear to the mind; evident, manifest, or obvious: *to make one's meaning plain.* **3.** conveying the meaning clearly or simply; easily understood: *plain talk.* **4.** downright; sheer: *plain folly.* **5.** free from ambiguity or evasion; candid; outspoken; honest. **6.** without special pretensions, superiority, elegance, etc.: *plain people.* **7.** not beautiful; unattractive: *a plain face.* **8.** without intricacies or difficulties. **9.** ordinary, simple, or unostentatious. **10.** with little or no embellishment, decoration, or enhancing elaboration: *plain clothes.* **11.** without pattern, device, or colouring. **12.** unruled, as paper. **13.** not rich, highly seasoned, or elaborately prepared, as food. **14.** flat or level: *plain country.* **15.** unobstructed, clear, or open, as ground, a space, etc. **16.** *Cards.* **a.** not a court card. **b.** not a trump. **17.** (of knitting) consisting of plain stitches. —*adv.* **18.** simply; absolutely. **19.** clearly or intelligibly. —*n.* **20.** an area of land not significantly higher than adjacent areas and with relatively minor differences in elevation within the area (commonly less than 500 feet). **21.** the simplest stitch in knitting. **22. the Plain,** a popular name for the more moderate party in the legislatures of the French Revolution. **23. The Plains,** the Great Plains. [ME, t. OF, g. L *plānus* flat, level, plane] —**plain′ly,** *adv.* —**plain′ness,** *n.* —**Syn. 5.** blunt. **10.** See **simple.**

plain[2] (plān), *v.i. Archaic.* to complain. [ME *plei(g)ne*, t. OF: m. s. *plaindre*, g. L *plangere* beat (the breast, etc.), lament]

plainchant (plān′chänt′), *n.* plainsong.

plain chocolate, chocolate that has been made with little or no milk.

plain-clothes (plān′klōz′, -klōthz′), *adj.* wearing civilian clothes rather than a uniform, as a detective.

plain dealing, honesty; straightforwardness. —**plain-dealer** (plān′dē′lə, plān′dē′lə), *n.*

plain-laid (plān′lād′), *adj.* (of a rope) made by laying three strands together with a right-handed twist.

plain sailing, 1. sailing on a plain course, free from obstruction or difficulty. **2.** an easy and unhindered course of action. Also, **plane sailing.**

Plains Indian, a member of any of the American Indian tribes which once inhabited the Great Plains, of the Algonquian, Athabascan, Caddoan, Kiowa, Siouan, and Uto-Aztecan linguistic stocks. All were more or less nomadic, following the buffalo in their movements, and were often in touch with one another, so that the development among them of common culture traits is evident. Also, **Buffalo Indian.**

plainsman (plānz′mən), *n., pl.* **-men.** a man or inhabitant of the plains.

Plains of Abraham, a high plain adjoining the city of Quebec in Canada: battlefield where the English under Wolfe defeated the French under Montcalm, 1759.

plainsong (plān′sŏng′), *n.* the unisonal liturgical music used in the Christian Church from the earliest times; Gregorian chant. Also, **plainchant.** [trans. of ML *cantus plānus*]

plain-spoken (plān′spō′kən), *adj.* candid; blunt.

plaint (plānt), *n.* **1.** a complaint. **2.** *Law.* a statement of grievance made to a court for the purpose of asking redress. **3.** *Archaic and Poetic.* lament. [ME *plainte*, t. OF, g. L *planctus* lamentation. See PLAIN]

plaintiff (plān′tĭf), *n. Law.* one who brings an action in a civil case. [ME *plaintif* complaining, t. OF. See PLAINTIVE]

plaintive (plān′tĭv), *adj.* expressing sorrow or melancholy discontent; mournful: *plaintive music.* [ME *plaintif*, t. OF. See PLAINT]—**plain′tively,** *adv.* —**plain′tiveness,** *n.* —**Syn.** wistful, sorrowful, sad.

plaister (plās′tə), *n., v.t. Obs.* plaster.

plait (plăt), *n.* **1.** a braid, as of hair or straw. **2.** a pleat or fold, as of cloth. *—v.t.* **3.** to braid (hair, etc.). **4.** to make (a mat, etc.) by braiding. **5.** to pleat (cloth, etc.). Also, **plat.** [ME *pleyt*, t. OF: m. *pleit*, g. L *plicitum*, pp. neut., folded. See PLY²]

plan (plăn), *n.*, *v.*, **planned, planning.** *—n.* **1.** a scheme of action or procedure: *a plan of operations.* **2.** a design or scheme of arrangement. **3.** a project or definite purpose: *plans for the future.* **4.** a drawing made to scale to represent the top view or a horizontal cut of a structure or a machine, as a floor plan of a building. **5.** a representation of a thing drawn on a plane, as a map or diagram: *a town plan.* **6.** one of several planes in front of a represented object, and perpendicular to the line between the object and the eye. *—v.t.* **7.** to arrange a plan or scheme for (any work, enterprise, or proceeding). **8.** to form a plan, project, or purpose of: *to plan a visit.* **9.** to draw or make a plan of (a building, etc.). *—v.i.* **10.** to make plans. [t. F, n. use of *plan* flat, plane, t. L: s. *plānus.* See PLANE¹, PLAIN¹]

—Syn. **1.** PLAN, PROJECT, DESIGN, SCHEME imply a formulated method of doing something. PLAN refers to any method of thinking out acts and purposes beforehand: *what are your plans for today?* A PROJECT is a proposed or tentative plan, often elaborate or extensive: *an irrigation project.* DESIGN suggests art, dexterity or craft (sometimes evil and selfish) in the elaboration or execution of a plan, and often tends to emphasize the purpose in view: *a misunderstanding brought about by design.* A SCHEME is often used of either a speculative, possibly impractical, plan, or a selfish or dishonest one: *a scheme to swindle someone.*

plan-, var. of **plano-,** before vowels, as in *planarian.*

planarian (plə nĕə′rĭ ən), *n. Zool.* a free-living flatworm having a trifid intestine. [f. s. NL *Plānāria*, the typical genus (prop. fem. of LL *plānārius* level, flat, der. L *plānus*) + -AN]

planch (plänch), *n.* **1.** a flat piece of metal, stone, or baked clay, used as a tray in an enamelling oven. **2.** *Dial.* **a.** a floor. **b.** a plank. [ME *plaunche*, t. OF: m. *planche.* See PLANK]

planchet (plän′chĭt), *n.* a flat piece of metal for stamping as a coin; a coin blank. [f. PLANCH + -ET]

planchette (plän shĕt′), *n.* a small board on two castors and a vertical pencil, said to write messages without conscious effort by persons whose fingers rest lightly on the board. [t. F, dim. of *planche* PLANCH]

Planck (*Ger.* plängk), *n.* **Max** (*Ger.* mäks), 1858–1947, German physicist: formulated the quantum theory.

Planck's constant, *Physics.* a universal constant (approx. $6{\cdot}624 \times 10^{-27}$ erg-seconds; *Symbol: h*) expressing the proportion of the energy of any form of wavelike radiation to its frequency.

plane¹ (plān), *n.*, *adj.*, *v.*, **planed, planing.** *—n.* **1.** a flat or level surface. **2.** *Maths.* a surface containing all the straight lines which pass through a fixed point and which intersect a straight line in space. **3.** a level of dignity, character, existence, development, or the like: *a high moral plane.* **4.** an aeroplane or a hydroplane. **5.** *Aeron.* a thin, flat, or curved, extended member of an aeroplane or a hydroplane, affording a supporting surface. *—adj.* **6.** flat or level, as a surface. **7.** of plane figures: *plane geometry.* *—v.i.* **8.** to glide. **9.** to lift partly out of water when running at high speed, as a racing boat does. [t. L: m. s. *plānum* level ground. See PLAIN¹] **—plane′ness,** *n.*

plane² (plān), *n.*, *v.*, **planed, planing.** *—n.* **1.** a tool with an adjustable blade for paring, truing, smoothing, or finishing the surface of wood, etc. **2.** a tool resembling a trowel for smoothing the surface of the clay in a brick mould. *—v.t.* **3.** to smooth or dress with or as with a plane or a planer. **4.** to remove by or as by means of a plane (fol. by *away* or *off*). *—v.i.* **5.** to work with a plane. **6.** to function as a plane. [ME, t. F, g. LL *plāna*]

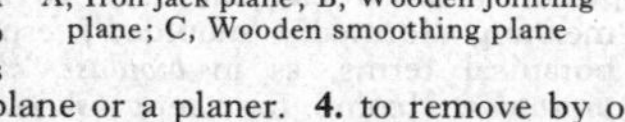

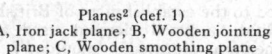

Planes² (def. 1)
A, Iron jack plane; B, Wooden jointing plane; C, Wooden smoothing plane

plane³ (plān), *n.* a plane tree. [ME, t. F, g. L *platanus*, t. Gk: m. *plátanos*, der. *platýs* broad (with reference to the leaves)]

plane angle, *Maths.* an angle between two intersecting lines.

plane figure, *Geom.* a figure whose parts all lie in one plane.

plane geometry, *Maths.* the geometry of figures whose parts all lie in one plane.

planer (plā′nə), *n.* **1.** one who or that which planes. **2.** *Carp.* a power machine for removing the rough or excess surface from a board. **3.** *Print.* a flat piece of wood laid on top of printing type which is in a chase, and tapped with a wooden mallet to ensure that the type stands level.

planer saw, *Carp.* a type of circular saw which saws so smoothly that planing is unnecessary.

plane sailing, plain sailing.

planet (plăn′ĭt), *n.* **1.** *Astron.* **a.** a solid body revolving around the sun, or a similar body revolving around a star other than the sun; planets are only visible by reflected light. Around the sun (in the solar system) there are nine **major planets** (Mercury, Venus, the Earth, Mars, Jupiter, Saturn, Uranus, Neptune, and Pluto, in their order from the sun) and thousands of **minor planets** or asteroids between the orbit of Mars and Jupiter. **Inferior planets** are those nearer to the sun than the earth is; **superior planets** are those farther from the sun than the earth is. **b.** (orig.) a celestial body moving in the sky, as distinguished from a fixed star, formerly applied also to the sun and moon. **2.** *Astrol.* a heavenly body regarded as exerting influence on mankind and events. [ME *planete*, t. LL: m. *planēta*, t. Gk: m. *planḗtēs*, lit. wanderer]

plane table, *Surveying.* a drawing-board mounted on a tripod by means of which survey data may be obtained and plotted in the field.

plane-table (plān′tā′bl), *v.i.*, *v.t.*, **-bled, -bling.** to survey with a plane table.

planetarium (plăn′ĭ tĕə′rĭ əm), *n.*, *pl.* **-tariums, -taria** (-tĕə′rĭ ə). **1.** an apparatus or model representing the planetary system. **2.** an optical device which projects a representation of the heavens upon a dome through the use of many stereopticons in motion. **3.** the structure in which such a planetarium is housed. [t. NL, prop. neut. of L *planētārius* planetary]

planetary (plăn′ĭ tə rĭ, -trĭ), *adj.* **1.** of, pertaining to, of the nature of, or resembling a planet or the planets. **2.** wandering or erratic. **3.** terrestrial or mundane. **4.** *Mach.* denoting or pertaining to a form of transmission (consisting of an epicyclic train of gears) for varying the speed in motor vehicles. [t. L: m. s. *planētārius*]

planetesimal (plăn′ĭ tĕs′ĭ məl), *adj.* **1.** of or pertaining to minute bodies in the solar system or in similar systems, which, according to the **planetesimal hypothesis,** move in planetary orbits and gradually unite to form the planets and satellites of the system. *—n.* **2.** one of the minute bodies of the planetesimal hypothesis. [der. PLANET modelled on INFINITESIMAL]

planetoid (plăn′ĭ toid′), *n.* a minor planet; an asteroid. **—plan′etoi′dal,** *adj.*

plane tree, any tree of the genus *Platanus*, esp. the S European *P. orientalis*, the N American *P. occidentalis*, and the widely planted hybrid between these two species.

planet-struck (plăn′ĭt strŭk′), *adj.* **1.** stricken by the supposed influence of a planet; blasted. **2.** panic-stricken. Also, **planet-stricken** (plăn′ĭt strĭk′ən).

planet wheel, any of the wheels in an epicyclic train, whose axes revolve round the common centre.

plangent (plăn′jənt), *adj.* **1.** beating or dashing, as waves. **2.** resounding loudly. [t. L: s. *plangens*, ppr., beating, lamenting. Cf. PLAIN²] **—plan′gency,** *n.*

plani-, var. of **plano-,** as in *planimeter.*

planimeter (plă nĭm′ĭ tə), *n.* an instrument for measuring mechanically the area of plane figures.

planimetry (plă nĭm′ĭ trĭ), *n.* the measurement of plane areas. **—planimetric** (plăn′ĭ mĕt′rĭk), **plan′imet′rical,** *adj.*

planish (plăn′ĭsh), *v.t.* **1.** to flatten or smooth (metal) by hammering, rolling, etc. **2.** to finish off (metal, paper, etc.) with a polished surface. [ME, t. F (obs.): m. *planiss-*, s. *planir*, for *planner.* See PLANE², v.] **—plan′isher,** *n.*

planisphere (plăn′ĭ sfĭə′), *n.* **1.** a map of half or more of the celestial sphere with a device for indicating the part visible at a given time. **2.** a projection or representation of the whole or a part of a sphere on a plane. [f. PLANI- + SPHERE; r. ME *planisperie*, t. ML: m. *plānisphaerium*]

plank (plăngk), *n.* **1.** a long, flat piece of timber thicker than a board. **2.** timber in such pieces. **3.** something to stand on or to cling to for support. **4.** *U.S.* a principle of a party expressed on a political platform. **5. to walk the plank,** to be compelled, as by pirates, to walk to one's death by stepping off a plank extending from a ship's side over the water. *—v.t.* **6.** to lay, cover, or furnish with planks. **7.** *Colloq.* to lay, put, or pay (fol. by *down*, etc.). **8.** *U.S.* to cook (and usually to serve) meat or fish on a special wooden board of well-seasoned hardwood, of long or oval shape. [ME *planke*, t. ONF, g. L *planca.* Cf. PLANCH]

planking (plăng′kĭng), *n.* **1.** planks collectively, as in a floor. **2.** the act of laying or covering with planks.

plank-sheer (plăngk′shĭə′), *n. Naut.* a timber around a vessel's hull at the deck line.

plankton (plăngk′tən), *n. Biol.* the small animal and plant organisms that float or drift in the water, esp. at or near the surface. Cf. **nekton.** [t. G, t. Gk: (neut.) wandering] —**planktonic** (plăngk tŏn′ĭk), *adj.*

planned obsolescence, the deliberate policy of making a product become rapidly out of date or unserviceable, as by changing minor characteristics of a model, in order to ensure continued sales of new goods.

planner (plăn′ə), *n.* one who plans.

planning permission, permission which must be given by a government authority before property may be developed.

plano-, a word element meaning 'flat', 'plane'. Also, **plan-, plani-.** [comb. form repr. L *plānus*]

plano-concave (plā′nō kŏn kāv′), *adj.* (of lenses) plane on one side and concave on the other. See **lens.**

plano-convex (plā′nō kŏn vĕks′), *adj.* (of lenses) plane on one side and convex on the other. See **lens.**

planogamete (plăn′ə gə mēt′), *n. Biol.* a motile gamete.

planography (plə nŏg′rə fĭ), *n. Print.* one of the basic printing processes in which the printing areas are in the same plane as the non-printing areas. The areas to print are ink-attracting and the remaining areas are ink-repellent.

planometer (plă nŏm′ĭ tə), *n.* a flat plate, usually of cast iron, used as a gauge for plane surfaces. —**planometric** (plăn′ə mĕt′rĭk), *adj.*

plant (plänt), *n.* **1.** any member of the vegetable group of living organisms. **2.** a herb or other small vegetable growth, in contrast to a tree or a shrub. **3.** a seedling or a growing slip, esp. one ready for transplanting. **4.** the equipment, including the fixtures, machinery, tools, etc., and often the buildings, necessary to carry on any industrial business: *a manufacturing plant.* **5.** the complete equipment or apparatus for a particular mechanical process or operation: *the power plant of a factory.* **6.** *U.S.* the buildings, equipment, etc., of an institution: *the sprawling plant of the university.* **7.** *Slang.* something or someone intended to trap, decoy, or lure, as criminals. **8.** *Slang.* a scheme to trap, trick, swindle, or defraud. —*v.t.* **9.** to put or set in the ground for growth, as seeds, young trees, etc. **10.** to furnish or stock (land) with plants. **11.** to implant (ideas, sentiments, etc.); introduce and establish (principles, doctrines, etc.). **12.** to introduce (a breed of animals) into a country. **13.** to deposit (young fish, or spawn) in a river, lake, etc. **14.** to bed (oysters). **15.** to insert or set firmly in or on the ground or some other body or surface. **16.** to put or place. **17.** *Slang.* to deliver (a blow, etc.). **18.** to post or station. **19.** to locate or situate. **20.** to establish or set up (a colony, city, etc.); found. **21.** to settle (persons), as in a colony. **22.** *Slang.* to hide or conceal, as stolen goods. **23.** *Slang.* to put (gold dust, ore, etc.) in a mine or the like to create a false impression of the value of the property. —*v.i.* **24.** to plant trees, colonies, etc.
[ME and OE *plante*, t. L: m. *planta* sprout, slip, graft]

Plantagenet (plăn tăj′ĭ nĭt), *n.* one of the line of English sovereigns from Henry II to Richard III. [t. F: lit., sprig of broom]

plantain[1] (plăn′tĭn), *n.* **1.** a tropical herbaceous plant, *Musa paradisiaca.* **2.** its fruit, very similar to the banana, usually requiring cooking. [t. Sp.: m. *plántano* plantain, also plane tree, t. L: m. *pla(n)tanus.* See PLANE[3]]

plantain[2] (plăn′tĭn), *n.* any plant of the widespread genus *Plantago*, esp. *P. major*, a common weed with large, spreading leaves close to the ground and long, slender spikes of small flowers. [ME *planteine*, t. OF: m. *plantain*, g. s. L *plantāgo*]

plantain-eater (plăn′tĭn ē′tə), *n.* any of several African birds of the family *Musophagidae*, as the **blue-crested plantain-eater,** *Tauraco hartlaubi*, related to the cuckoos.

plantar (plăn′tə), *adj. Anat., Zool.* of or pertaining to the sole of the foot. [t. L: s. *plantāris*]

plantation (plăn tā′shən), *n.* **1.** a farm or estate, esp. in a tropical or semitropical country, on which cotton, tobacco, coffee, sugar, or the like is cultivated, usually by resident labourers. **2.** a group of planted trees or plants. **3.** *Hist.* **a.** a colony. **b.** the establishment of a colony, etc. **4.** *Rare.* the planting of seeds, etc. [late ME, t. L: s. *plantātio* a planting]

planter (plăn′tə), *n.* **1.** one who plants. **2.** an implement or machine for planting seeds in the ground. **3.** the owner or occupant of a plantation. **4.** *Hist.* a colonist. **5.** *U.S.* a decorative container, of a variety of sizes and shapes, for plants, ferns, etc.

plantigrade (plăn′tĭ grād′), *adj.* **1.** walking on the whole sole of the foot, as man, the bears, etc. —*n.* **2.** a plantigrade animal. [t. NL: m. s. *plantigradus*, f. L: m. *planta* sole + *-gradus* walking]

plant-louse (plänt′lous′), *n., pl.* **-lice.** aphid.

planula (plăn′yŏŏ lə), *n., pl.* **-lae** (-lē′). *Zool.* the ciliate, free-swimming larva of a coelenterate, characterized by the solid interior. [t. NL, dim. of L *plānus* flat, plane] —**plan′ular,** *adj.*

plaque (plăk, pläk), *n.* **1.** a thin, flat plate or tablet of metal, porcelain, etc., intended for ornament, as on a wall, or set in a piece of furniture. **2.** a platelike brooch or ornament, esp. one worn as the badge of an honorary order. **3.** *Anat., Zool.* a small flat, rounded formation or area. [t. F, t. D: m. *plak* flat board. See PLACK]

plash[1] (plăsh), *n.* **1.** a splash. **2.** a pool or puddle. —*v.t., v.i.* **3.** to splash. [ME *plasch*, OE *plæsc*, c. D and LG *plas*, prob. of imit. orig.]

plash[2] (plăsh), *v.t.* **1.** to interweave (branches, etc., bent over and often cut partly through), as for a hedge or an arbour. **2.** to make or renew (a hedge, etc.) by such interweaving. [ME, t. OF: m. *plaissier*, der. L *plectere* plait. Cf. PLEACH]

plashy (plăsh′ĭ), *adj.*, **-ier, -iest. 1.** marshy; wet. **2.** splashing.

-plasia, a word element meaning 'biological cellular growth', as in *hypoplasia.* Also, **-plasy.** [t. NL, der. Gk *plásis* a moulding]

-plasm, a word element used as a noun termination meaning 'something formed or moulded' in biological and other scientific terms, as in *bioplasm, metaplasm, neoplasm, protoplasm.* [comb. form repr. Gk *plásma*]

plasma (plăz′mə), *n.* **1.** *Anat., Physiol.* the liquid part of blood or lymph, as distinguished from the corpuscles. **2.** *Biol.* protoplasm. **3.** wheỳ. **4.** a green, faintly translucent chalcedony. **5.** *Physics.* a highly ionized gas which, because it contains an approximately equal number of positive ions and electrons, is electrically neutral and highly conducting. Also, **plasm** (plăz′əm). [t. LL, t. Gk: something formed or moulded] —**plasmatic** (plăz măt′ĭk), **plas′mic,** *adj.*

plasma engine, *Aeron.* a reaction engine using magnetically accelerated plasma as a propellant.

plasmagene (plăz′mə jēn′), *n. Biol.* a protein particle in the cytoplasm of a cell; believed to affect heredity.

plasmochin (plăz′mə kĭn), *n. Pharm.* **1.** a synthetic antimalarial drug, $C_{19}H_{29}N_3O$. **2.** (*cap.*) a trademark for this substance.

plasmodium (plăz mō′dyəm), *n., pl.* **-dia** (-dyə). **1.** *Biol.* a mass or sheet of protoplasm formed by the fusion or contact of a number of amoeboid bodies. **2.** *Zool.* a parasitic protozoan organism of the genus *Plasmodium* (malaria parasites). [t. NL, f. *plasma* PLASMA + *-ōdium* -ODE[1]]

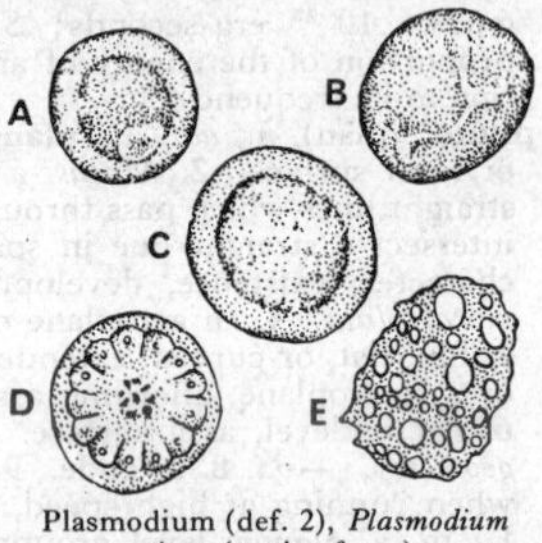

Plasmodium (def. 2), *Plasmodium vivax* (tertian form)
A, Young form with a red corpuscle; B, Developing pigmented form within corpuscle; C, Full-grown body; D, Segmenting body; E, Degenerating form undergoing vacuolation

plasmolysis (plăz mŏl′ĭ sĭs), *n. Bot.* contraction of the protoplasm in a living cell when water is removed by exosmosis. [f. *plasmo-* (comb. form repr. Gk *plásma* PLASMA) + -LYSIS]

plasmosome (plăz′məsōm′), *n. Biol.* a true nucleolus which is stained by cytoplasmic dyes. Cf. **karyosome.** [f. *plasmo-* (comb. form repr. Gk *plásma* PLASMA) + m. Gk *sôma* body]

Plassey (plăs′ĭ), *n.* a village in NE India, ab. 80 mi. N of Calcutta: Clive's victory over a Bengal army here (1757) led to the establishment of British power in India.

-plast, a word element used as a noun termination, meaning 'formed', 'moulded', esp. in biological and botanical terms, as in *bioplast, chloroplast, mesoplast, protoplast.* [comb. form repr. Gk *plastós*]

plaster (pläs′tə), *n.* **1.** a pasty composition, as of lime, sand, water, and often hair, used for covering walls, ceilings, etc., where it hardens in drying. **2.** gypsum powdered but not calcined. **3.** calcined gypsum (**plaster of Paris**), a white powdery material which swells when mixed with water and sets rapidly, used for making casts, moulds, etc. **4.** a solid or semisolid preparation for spreading upon cloth or the like and applying to the body for some remedial or other purpose. **5.** sticking plaster. —*v.t.* **6.** to cover (walls, etc.) with plaster. **7.** to treat with gypsum or plaster of Paris. **8.** to lay flat like a layer of plaster. **9.** to daub or fill with plaster or something similar. **10.** to apply a plaster to (the body, etc.). **11.** to overspread with anything, esp. thickly or to excess: *a wall plastered with posters.* **12.** *Colloq.* to hit hard and often. **13.** *Colloq.* to bomb heavily. [ME and OE, t. VL and ML: m. s. *plastrum* plaster (both medical and builder's senses), g. L *emplastrum*, t. Gk: m. *émplastron* salve] —**plas′terer,** *n.* —**plas′tering,** *n.* —**plas′tery,** *adj.*

plasterboard (pläs′tə bôd′), *n.* plaster in paper-covered sheets, used for walls.

plaster cast, 1. any piece of sculpture cast in plaster of Paris. **2.** *Surg.* See **cast** (def. 45).

plastered (pläs′təd), *adj. Slang.* drunk.

plastic (plăs′tĭk), *adj.* **1.** concerned with or pertaining to moulding or modelling: *plastic arts.* **2.** capable of being moulded or of receiving form: *plastic substances.* **3.** produced by moulding: *plastic figures.* **4.** having the power of moulding or shaping formless or yielding material. **5.** *Biol.*, *Pathol.* formative. **6.** Also, **anaplastic.** *Surg.* concerned with or pertaining to the remedying or restoring of malformed, injured, or lost parts: *plastic surgery.* **7.** pliable; impressionable: *the plastic mind of youth.* **8.** made of or consisting of plastic: *a plastic bag.* —*n.* **9.** any of a group of synthetic or natural organic materials which may be shaped when soft and then hardened, including many types of resins, resinoids, polymers, cellulose derivatives, casein materials, and proteins. Plastics are used in place of such other materials as glass, wood, and metals in construction and decoration, for making many articles, as coatings, and, drawn into filaments, for weaving. They are usually known by trademarks such as *Bakelite*, *Vinylite*, *Perspex*, etc. [t. L: s. *plasticus* that may be moulded, t. Gk: m. *plastikós*] —**plas′tically,** *adv.*

-plastic, a word element forming adjectives related to *-plast*, *-plasty*, as in *protoplastic.* [see PLASTIC]

plastic bomb, a bomb, often home-made, consisting of a plastic putty-like explosive, as cyclonite, manually moulded around a detonator: used, either by direct adhesion (without a container) or in any rudimentary form of container as an old sock, esp. in guerrilla warfare, by commandos, or in civil disturbances.

plastic bronze, *Metall.* a bronze containing a high proportion of lead (8–20 per cent) in addition to copper, tin, and sometimes zinc, nickel, or phosphorus; used for bearing surfaces.

plastic deformation, *Metall.* a permanent change in the shape of a piece of metal as a result of a mechanical stress.

plasticine (plăs′tĭ sēn′), *n.* **1.** a plastic modelling compound, in various colours. **2.** (*cap.*) a trademark for this substance.

plasticity (plăs tĭs′ĭ tĭ), *n.* **1.** the quality of being plastic. **2.** capability of being moulded, receiving shape, or being brought to a definite form.

plasticize (plăs′tĭ sīz′), *v.t.*, *v.i.*, **-cized, -cizing.** to make or become plastic. Also, **plasticise.**

plasticizer (plăs′tĭ sī′zə), *n.* **1.** any of a group of substances which are used in plastics, mortar, or the like, to impart softness and viscous quality to the finished product. **2.** a non-volatile substance added to paints, etc., to prevent brittleness when dry. Also, **plasticiser.**

plastid (plăs′tĭd), *n. Biol.* **1.** a morphological unit consisting of a single cell. **2.** any of certain small specialized masses of protoplasm (as chloroplasts, chromoplasts, etc.) in certain cells. See diag. under **cell.** [t. G, short for *plastidion*, f. Gk: *plast(ós)* formed + *-idion*, dim. suffix]

plastral (plăs′trəl), *adj. Zool.* relating to the plastron.

plastron (plăs′trən), *n.* **1.** *Armour.* a medieval metal breastplate worn under the hauberk. **2.** a protective shield of leather for the breast of a fencer. **3.** an ornamental front piece of a woman's bodice. **4.** the starched front of a shirt. **5.** *Zool.* the ventral part of the shell of a tortoise or turtle. [t. F, t. It.: m. *piastrone*, aug. of *piastra* metal plate. See PLASTER. Cf. PIASTRE]

-plasty, a word element used as a noun termination meaning 'formation', occurring in the names of processes of plastic surgery, as *autoplasty*, *cranioplasty*, *dermatoplasty*, *neoplasty*, *rhinoplasty*, and occasionally in other words, as *galvanoplasty.* [t. Gk: m. s. *-plastia*, comb. form der. *plastós* formed]

-plasy, var. of **-plasia.**

plat[1] (plăt), *n.*, *v.*, **platted, platting.** —*n.* **1.** a plot of ground, usually small. **2.** *U.S.* a plan or map, as of land. —*v.t.* **3.** *U.S.* to make a plat of; plot. [ME (in place-names), c. Goth. *plat* patch]

plat[2] (plăt), *n.* plait or braid. [var. of PLAIT]

plat., 1. plateau. **2.** platoon.

Plata (*Sp.* plä′tä), *n.* **Río de la** (*Sp.* rē′ō dĕ lä), Spanish name of **River Plate.**

Plataea (plă tē′ə), *n.* an ancient Boeotian city NW of Athens: Greeks defeated Persians here, 479 B.C.

platan (plăt′ən), *n.* a plane tree.

platanna (plə tăn′ə), *n.* a frog, *Xenopus laevis*, of southern Africa, having clawed feet; used in pregnancy testing. [t. Afrikaans, said to be alter. of *plathander* lit., flat-hander]

plat du jour (*Fr.* plȧ dʏ zho͞or′), a dish recommended or specially available on a certain day in a restaurant. [t. F: dish of the day]

plate[1] (plāt), *n.*, *v.*, **plated, plating.** —*n.* **1.** a shallow, usually circular dish, now usually of earthenware or porcelain, from which food is eaten. **2.** the contents of such a dish. **3.** a service of food for one person at table. **4.** an entire course: *a cold plate.* **5.** domestic dishes, utensils, etc., of gold or silver. **6.** a dish, as of metal or wood, used for collecting offerings in a church, etc. **7.** a thin, flat sheet or piece of metal or other material, esp. of uniform thickness. **8.** metal in such sheets. **9.** a flat, polished piece of metal on which something may be or is engraved. **10.** a sheet of metal for printing from, formed by stereotyping or electrotyping a page of type, or metal or plastic formed by moulding, etching, or photographic development. **11.** a printed impression from such a piece, or from some similar piece, as a woodcut. **12.** such a piece engraved to print from. **13.** a full-page inserted illustration forming part of a book. **14.** plated metallic ware. **15.** wrought metal, or a piece of it, used in making armour. **16.** armour composed of such pieces. **17.** *Dentistry.* a piece of metal, vulcanite, or plastic substance, with artificial teeth attached, to replace lost or missing natural teeth. **18.** *Baseball.* the home base, at which the batter stands and which he must return to and touch, after running round the bases, in order to score a run. **19.** plate glass. **20.** *Photog.* a sensitized sheet of glass, metal, etc., on which to take a photograph or make a reproduction by photography. **21.** *Anat.*, *Zool.*, *etc.* a platelike part, structure, or organ. **22.** *U.S. Electronics.* the anode of a radio valve. **23.** *Elect.* an electrode in an accumulator. **24.** *Archit.* a timber laid horizontally, as in a wall, to receive the ends of other timbers. **25.** a gold or silver cup or the like awarded as a prize in horseracing, etc. **26.** a horserace or other contest for such a prize. **27.** a light metal shoe, as worn by a horse in a race. **28.** a plate rail. **29. on a plate,** already attended to; with no difficulties remaining. **30. on one's plate,** waiting to be dealt with; pending. —*v.t.* **31.** to coat (metal) with a thin film of gold, silver, nickel, etc., by mechanical or chemical means. **32.** to cover or overlay with metal plates for protection, etc. **33.** *Print.* to make a stereotype or electrotype plate from (type).
[ME, t. OF: flat piece, plate, prob. der. OF *plat* flat, g. LL *plattus*, t. Gk: m. *platýs* broad, flat] —**plate′like′,** *adj.*

plate[2] (plāt), *n. Obs.* a coin, esp. of silver. [ME, t. OF; etymologically same as PLATE[1]]

Plate (plāt), *n.* **River,** an estuary on the SE coast of South America between Argentina and Uruguay, formed by the rivers Uruguay and Paraná: British naval victory over the Germans, 1939. ab. 185 mi. long. Spanish, **Plata.**

plateau (plăt′ō), *n.*, *pl.* **-eaus, -eaux** (-ōz). **1.** a tabular surface of high elevation, often of considerable extent. **2.** *Psychol.* a period of little or no progress in an individual's learning, marked by temporary constancy in speed, number of errors committed, etc., and indicated by a flat stretch on a graph. [t. F, in OF flat object, der. *plat* flat]

plated (plā′tĭd), *adj.* (of a knitted fabric) made of two yarns, as wool on the face and cotton on the back.

plateful (plāt′fo͝ol′), *n.*, *pl.* **-fuls.** as much as a plate will hold.

plate glass, a soda-lime-silica glass formed by rolling the hot glass into a plate which is subsequently ground and polished: used in large windows, mirrors, etc.

platelayer (plāt′lā′ə), *n.* one who lays and maintains the rails of a railway track.

platelet (plāt′lĭt), *n.* a microscopic disc occurring in profusion in the blood: important aid in coagulation. [f. PLATE[1] + -LET]

plate-mark (plāt′mäk′), *n.* hallmark.

platen (plăt′ən), *n.* **1.** a variety of printing press in which the sheet of paper to be printed is held on a flat metal surface and pressed against the inked type or plates which are also held on a flat surface. **2.** the surface on which the paper is held. **3.** *Mach.* the work-table of a machine tool, which may be slotted to allow the use of clamping bolts. **4.** the roller of a typewriter. [ME *plateyne*, t. OF: m. *platine* flat piece of metal, also pop. alter. of *patene* paten, from its form]

plater (plā′tə), *n.* **1.** one who or that which plates. **2.** an inferior racehorse. **3.** a selling-plater.

plate rack, a rack for holding plates and other crockery, esp. for draining after washing.

plate rail, (formerly) a flanged wheel track, as used for colliery tracks. Also, **plate.**

plateresque (plăt′ə rĕsk′), *adj.* denoting an ornate style of architecture much used in 16th-century Spain, characterized by many ornamental motifs. [f. *plater-* (s. Sp. *platero* silversmith) + -ESQUE]

platform (plăt′fôm′), *n.* **1.** a raised flooring or structure, as in a hall or meeting place, for use by public speakers, performers, etc. **2.** the raised area between or alongside the tracks of a railway station, from which the train is entered. **3.** the open entrance area at the end of a bus or the like. **4.** a level place for mounting guns, as in a fort. **5.** a flat elevated piece of ground. **6.** a body of principles on which a party or the like takes its stand in appealing to the public. **7.** a public statement of the principles and policy of a political party, esp. as put forth by the representatives of the party. **8.** a plan or set of principles. **9.** *Now Rare.* a scheme of religious principles or doctrines. [t. F: m. *plateforme*, lit., flat form, plan, flat area, terrace. See PLATE[1]] **—Syn. 1.** stage, dais, rostrum, pulpit.

platform ticket, a ticket allowing the purchaser to go beyond the barrier on to a railway platform.

platina (plăt′ĭ nə, plə tē′nə), *n.* a native alloy of platinum with palladium, iridium, osmium, etc. [t. NL or Sp. See PLATINUM]

plating (plā′tĭng), *n.* **1.** a thin coating of gold, silver, etc. **2.** an external layer of metal plates. **3.** the act of one who or that which plates.

platinic (plə tĭn′ĭk), *adj. Chem.* of or containing platinum, esp. in its tetravalent state.

platiniridium (plăt′ĭ nĭ rĭd′ĭ əm), *n.* a natural alloy composed chiefly of platinum and iridium. [f. PLATIN(UM) + IRIDIUM]

platinize (plăt′ĭ nīz′), *v.t.*, **-nized, -nizing.** to coat or plate with metallic platinum. Also, **platinise.**

platinized asbestos, *Chem.* asbestos which has been treated with finely divided platinum, used as a catalyst.

platino-, a combining form of **platinum.**

platinocyanic acid (plăt′ĭ nō sī ăn′ĭk), *Chem.* an acid containing platinum and the radical cyanogen.

platinocyanide (plăt′ĭ nō sī′ə nīd′), *n. Chem.* a salt of platinocyanic acid.

platinoid (plăt′ĭ noid′), *adj.* **1.** resembling platinum: *the platinoid elements.* —*n.* **2.** any of the metals (palladium, iridium, etc.) with which platinum is usually associated. **3.** an alloy of copper, zinc, and nickel, to which small quantities of such elements as tungsten or aluminium have been added; used in electrical work, etc.

platinotype (plăt′ĭ nō tīp′), *n. Photog.* **1.** a process of printing in which a platinum salt is employed yielding more permanent prints than those obtainable with silver salts. **2.** a print made by such a process.

platinous (plăt′ĭ nəs), *adj. Chem.* containing divalent platinum.

platinum (plăt′ĭ nəm), *n.* **1.** *Chem.* a heavy, greyish white, highly malleable and ductile metallic element, resistant to most chemicals, practically unoxidizable save in the presence of bases, and fusible only at extremely high temperatures, used esp. for making chemical and scientific apparatus, as a catalyst in the oxidation of ammonia to nitric acid, and in jewellery. *Symbol:* Pt; *at. wt:* 195·09; *at. no.:* 78; *sp. gr.:* 21·5 at 20°C. **2.** a light metallic grey with very slight bluish tinge when compared with silver. [t. NL, earlier *platina*, t. Sp., der. *plata* silver]

platinum black, a black powder consisting of very finely divided metallic platinum, used as a catalyst, esp. in organic synthesis.

platinum thermometer, *Physics.* an instrument for measuring temperatures up to about 1200°C; consists of a coil of platinum wire enclosed within a protective tube, changes of temperature being indicated by a change in the resistance of the platinum wire.

platitude (plăt′ĭ tyo͞od′), *n.* **1.** a flat, dull, or trite remark, esp. one uttered as if it were fresh and profound. **2.** flatness, dullness, or triteness. [t. F, der. *plat* flat. Cf. F and E *latitude, altitude.* See PLATE[1], -TUDE]

platitudinize (plăt′ĭ tyo͞o′dĭ nīz′), *v.i.*, **-nized, -nizing.** to utter platitudes. Also, **platitudinise.**

platitudinous (plăt′ĭ tyo͞o′dĭ nəs), *adj.* **1.** characterized by or given to platitudes. **2.** of the nature of a platitude.

Plato (plā′tō), *n.* 427?–347 B.C., Greek philosopher.

Platonic (plə tŏn′ĭk), *adj.* **1.** of or pertaining to Plato or his doctrines: *the Platonic philosophy.* **2.** of or pertaining to love which, in Platonic philosophy, transcends the feeling for the individual and rises to a contemplation of the ideal. **3.** (*l.c. or cap.*) purely spiritual; free from sensual desire: *platonic love.* **4.** (*l.c. or cap.*) (of persons) feeling or professing such love. —**Platon′ically,** *adv.*

Platonism (plā′tə nĭz′əm), *n.* **1.** the philosophy or doctrines of Plato or his followers. **2.** a Platonic doctrine or saying. **3.** the belief that physical objects are but impermanent representations of unchanging ideas, and that these ideas alone give true knowledge as they are known by the mind. **4.** (*l.c. or cap.*) the doctrine or the practice of platonic love. —**Pla′tonist,** *n., adj.*

Platonize (plā′tə nīz′), *v.*, **-nized, -nizing.** —*v.i.* **1.** to follow the opinions or doctrines of Plato. **2.** to reason like Plato. —*v.t.* **3.** to give a Platonic character to. **4.** to explain in accordance with Platonic principles. Also, **Platonise.**

platoon (plə to͞on′), *n.* **1.** a military unit consisting of two or more sections, being part of a company. **2.** a company or group of persons. [t. F: m. *peloton* little ball, group, platoon, dim. of *pelote* ball. See PELLET]

Plattdeutsch (*Ger.* plät′doĭch), *n.* the colloquial Low German of northern Germany. [G: f. *platt* flat (see PLATE[1]) + *deutsch* German]

Plattensee (*Ger.* plät′ən zē), *n.* German name of **Lake Balaton.**

platter (plăt′ə), *n.* a large, shallow dish, commonly oval, for holding or serving meat, etc. [ME *plater*, t. AF, der. OF *plat* plate, dish]

platyhelminth (plăt′ĭ hĕl′mĭnth), *n.* a member of the *Platyhelminthes*, a phylum of worms, the flatworms, having bilateral symmetry and a soft, solid, usually flattened body, including the planarians, flukes, tapeworms, and others. [t. NL: s. *Platyhelmintha*, f. Gk: m. *platýs* broad, flat + m. s. *hélmins* worm]

platypus (plăt′ĭ pəs), *n., pl.* **-puses, -pi** (-pī′). the duck-billed platypus. [t. NL, t. Gk: m. *platýpous* flat-footed]

platyrrhine (plăt′ĭ rīn′), *adj. Zool., Anthropol.* having a broad, flat-bridged nose; belonging to one of the two divisions of primates (opposed to *catarrhine*). [f. *platy-* (t. Gk, comb. form of *platýs* broad) + m. s. Gk *rhis* nose]

plaudit (plô′dĭt), *n.* (*usually pl.*) **1.** a demonstration or round of applause, as for some approved or admired performance. **2.** any enthusiastic expression of approval. [t. L: alter. of *plaudite*, impv., APPLAUD]

Plauen (*Ger.* plou′ən), *n.* a town in S East Germany. 81,250 (1966).

plausible (plô′zə bl), *adj.* **1.** having an appearance of truth or reason; seemingly worthy of approval or acceptance; specious: *a plausible story.* **2.** fair-spoken and apparently worthy of confidence: *a plausible adventurer.* [t. L: m. s. *plausibilis*] —**plau′sibil′ity, plau′sibleness,** *n.* —**plau′sibly,** *adv.*

—**Syn. 1.** PLAUSIBLE, SPECIOUS describe that which has a fair appearance but is completely deceptive. The person or thing that is PLAUSIBLE strikes the superficial judgement favourably; it may or may not be intentionally deceptive: *a plausible argument* (one which omits or glosses over important points). SPECIOUS definitely implies deceit or hypocrisy; the surface appearances are quite different from what is beneath: *a specious pretence of honesty, a specious argument* (one deliberately deceptive, probably for selfish or evil purposes). —**Ant. 1.** honest, sincere.

plausive (plô′sĭv), *adj.* **1.** *Rare.* applauding. **2.** *Obs.* plausible.

Plautus (plô′təs), *n.* **Titus Maccius** (tī′təs măk′sĭ əs), *c.* 254–*c.* 184 B.C., Roman comic dramatist.

play (plā), *n.* **1.** a dramatic composition or piece; a drama. **2.** a dramatic performance, as on the stage. **3.** exercise or action by way of amusement or recreation. **4.** fun, jest, or trifling, as opposed to earnest: *he said it merely in play.* **5.** the playing, or carrying on, of a game. **6.** manner or style of playing. **7.** the state, as of a ball, of being played with or in use in the active playing of a game: *in play; out of play.* **8.** a playing for stakes; gambling. **9.** *Obs.* (except in *fair play*, etc.) action, conduct, or dealing of a specified kind. **10.** action, activity, or operation: *the play of fancy.* **11.** brisk movement or action: *a fountain with a leaping play of water.* **12.** elusive change, as of light or colours. **13.** a space in which a thing, as a piece of mechanism, can move. **14.** freedom of movement, as within a space, as of a part of a mechanism. **15.** freedom for action, or scope for activity: *full play of the mind.* **16.** *U.S.* an act or performance in playing: *a stupid play.* **17.** *U.S.* turn to play: *it is your play.* [ME; OE *plega, plæga*] —*v.t.* **18.** to act the part of (a person or character) in a dramatic performance: *to play Lady Macbeth.* **19.** to perform (a drama, etc.) on or as on the stage. **20.** to act or sustain (a part) in a dramatic performance or in real life. **21.** to sustain the part or character of in real life: *to play the fool.* **22.** *U.S.* to give performances in, as a theatrical company does: *to play the larger cities.* **23.** to engage in (a game, pastime, etc.). **24.** to contend against in a game. **25.** to employ (a player, etc.) in a game. **26.** to move or throw (an object) in a game: *he played the card reluctantly.* **27.** to use as if in playing a game, as for one's own advantage: *play off one person against another.* **28.** to play an extra game or round in order to settle (a tie) (fol. by *off*). **29.** to stake or wager, as in playing. **30.** to lay a wager or wagers on (something). **31.** to

represent or imitate in sport: *to play school.* **32.** to perform on (a musical instrument). **33.** to perform (music) on an instrument. **34.** to do, perform, bring about, or execute: *to play tricks.* **35.** to cause to move or change lightly or quickly: *play coloured lights on a fountain.* **36.** to operate, or cause to operate, esp. continuously or with repeated action: *to play a hose on a fire.* **37.** to allow (a hooked fish) to exhaust itself by pulling on the line. **38.** to bring to an end; use up (fol. by *out*). —*v.i.* **39.** to exercise or employ oneself in diversion, amusement, or recreation. **40.** to do something only in sport, which is not to be taken seriously. **41.** to amuse oneself or toy; trifle (fol. by *with*). **42.** to take part or engage in a game. **43.** to take part in a game for stakes; gamble. **44.** to act, or conduct oneself, in a specified way: *to play fair.* **45.** to act on or as on the stage; perform. **46.** to perform on a musical instrument. **47.** (of the instrument or the music) to sound in performance. **48.** to move freely, as within a space, as a part of a mechanism. **49.** to move about lightly or quickly. **50.** to present the effect of such motion, as light or the changing colours of an iridescent substance. **51.** to operate continuously or with repeated action, often on something: *the noise played on his nerves.* —*v.* **52.** Some special verb phrases are:
play at, to take part in (a game, hobby, etc.), often without serious attention.
play ball, to co-operate.
play down, to minimize.
play for time, to gain time for one's own purposes by prolonging something unduly.
play into the hands of, to act in such a way as to give an advantage to.
play on or **upon,** to work on (the feelings, weaknesses, etc., of another) for one's own purpose.
play the game, *Colloq.* **a.** to play in accordance with the rules. **b.** to play one's part.
play up, to behave naughtily or annoyingly.
play up to, to attempt to get into the favour of.
[ME *pleye(n)*, OE *plegan*, c. MD *pleyen* dance, leap for joy, G *pflegen* take care of, look after]
—**Syn.** 3. PLAY, GAME, SPORT refer to forms of diverting activity. PLAY is the general word for any such form of activity, often undirected, spontaneous, or random; *childhood should be a time for play.* GAME refers to a recreational contest, mental or physical, usually governed by set rules: *a game of chess.* Besides referring to an individual contest, GAME may refer to a pastime as a whole: *golf is a good game.* If, however, the pastime is one (usually an outdoor one) depending chiefly on physical strength, though not necessarily a contest, the word SPORT is applied: *football is a vigorous sport.* 10. movement, action, exercise. 20. personate, impersonate. 39. sport, frolic, romp, revel. —**Ant.** 3. work, toil.

playa (plä′yə), *n.* **1.** the sandy, salty, or mud-caked floor of a desert basin with interior drainage, usually occupied by a shallow lake during the rainy season or after prolonged, heavy rains. **2.** the lake itself. [t. Sp.: shore, beach, g. LL *plāgia*, der. *plāga* region, tract]

playable (plā′ə bl), *adj.* **1.** capable of or suitable for being played. **2.** (of ground) fit to be played on.

play-act (plā′ăkt′), *v.i.* to pretend; to behave theatrically or melodramatically. —**play′-act′ing,** *n.*

playback (plā′băk′), *n.* **1.** a device on a tape-recorder, by which a recording can be reproduced. **2.** such a reproduction. —*adj.* **3.** of, pertaining to, or denoting a device used in reproducing a recording.

playbill (plā′bĭl′), *n.* a programme or announcement of a play.

playboy (plā′boi′), *n.* a wealthy, carefree man who spends most of his time at parties, nightclubs, etc.

playday (plā′dā′), *n.* a holiday.

played-out (plād′out′), *adj. Colloq.* exhausted; used up.

player (plā′ə), *n.* **1.** one who or that which plays. **2.** one who takes part or is skilled in some game. **3.** a person engaged in playing a game professionally. **4.** one who plays parts on the stage; an actor. **5.** one who plays a musical instrument. **6.** a mechanical device by which a musical instrument, esp. a piano, is played automatically. **7.** a gambler.

player piano, a piano fitted with a mechanism by which it can be played automatically.

playfellow (plā′fĕl′ō), *n.* a playmate.

playful (plā′fəl), *adj.* **1.** full of play; sportive; frolicsome. **2.** pleasantly humorous: *a playful remark.* —**play′fully,** *adv.* —**play′fulness,** *n.*

playgoer (plā′gō′ə), *n.* one who often or habitually attends the theatre.

playground (plā′ground′), *n.* **1.** ground used specifically for open-air recreation, as one attached to a school. **2.** any place of open-air recreation. **3.** an area where swings, etc., are provided for children.

playhouse (plā′hous′), *n.* **1.** a theatre. **2.** a small house for children to play in. [OE *gleghūs* theatre]

playing card, **1.** one of the conventional set of 52 cards, in 4 suits (diamonds, hearts, spades, and clubs), used in playing various games of chance and skill. **2.** one of any set or pack of cards used in playing games.

playing field, a field or open space used for sports, athletics, etc., esp. by schools.

playlet (plā′lĭt), *n.* a short play.

playmate (plā′māt′), *n.* a companion in play.

play-off (plā′ŏf′), *n.* the playing off of a tie, as in games or sports.

play on words, a pun.

playpen (plā′pĕn′), *n.* a small enclosure in which a young child can play safely without constant supervision.

playroom (plā′ro͝om′, -ro͞om′), *n.* a room in a house set aside for children to play in.

play school, a school for children of pre-school age; nursery school; kindergarten.

playsuit (plā′syo͞ot′), *n.* an outfit worn by women and children for sports and leisure wear, consisting of shorts with a top.

plaything (plā′thĭng′), *n.* a thing to play with; a toy.

playtime (plā′tīm′), *n.* time for play or recreation.

playwright (plā′rīt′), *n.* a writer of plays; a dramatist. [f. PLAY + WRIGHT]

plaza (plä′zə), *n.* a public square or open space in a city or town. [t. Sp., g. L *platēa.* See PLACE]

plea (plē), *n.* **1.** that which is alleged, urged, or pleaded in defence or justification. **2.** an excuse; a pretext. **3.** *Law.* **a.** an allegation made by, or on behalf of, a party to a legal suit, in support of his claim or defence. **b.** (in courts of equity) a plea which admits the truth of the declaration, but alleges special or new matter in avoidance. **c.** a suit or action at law: *to hold pleas (to try actions at law).* **d.** *Archaic.* statement of defence. **4.** an appeal or entreaty: *a plea for mercy.* [ME *plaid, plai,* t. OF, g. L *placitum* (thing which) seemed good, prop. pp. neut., pleased; in ML, court, plea. See PLEASE]

pleach (plēch), *v.t.* **1.** to plash or interweave (growing branches, vines, etc.), as for a hedge or arbour. **2.** to interlace or entwine. [ME *pleche(n),* var. of PLASH[2]]

plead (plēd), *v.,* **pleaded** or **plead** (plĕd) or, *U.S. and Scot. Law,* **pled, pleading.** —*v.i.* **1.** to make earnest appeal or entreaty: *to plead for help.* **2.** to use arguments or persuasions, as with a person, for or against something. **3.** to afford an argument or appeal: *his youth pleads for him.* **4.** *Law.* **a.** to make any allegation or plea in an action at law. **b.** to address a court as an advocate. **c.** *Obs.* to prosecute a suit or action at law. —*v.t.* **5.** to allege or urge in defence, justification, or excuse: *to plead ignorance.* **6.** *Law.* **a.** to maintain (a cause, etc.) by argument before a court. **b.** to allege or set forth (something) formally in an action at law. **c.** to allege or cite in legal defence: *to plead a statute of limitations.* [ME *plaide(n),* t. OF: m. *plaidier* go to law, plead, g. VL *placitāre,* der. L *placitum* thing which pleases]

pleadable (plē′də bl), *adj.* capable of being pleaded.

pleader (plē′də), *n.* one who pleads, esp. at law.

pleading (plē′dĭng), *n.* **1.** the act of one who pleads. **2.** *Law.* **a.** the advocating of a cause in a court of law. **b.** the art or science of setting forth or drawing pleas in legal causes. **c.** a formal statement (now usually written) setting forth the cause of action or the defence of a case at law. **d.** (*pl.*) the successive statements delivered alternately by plaintiff and defendant until issue is joined. —**plead′ingly,** *adv.*

pleasance (plĕz′əns), *n.* **1.** a space laid out with trees, walks, etc. **2.** *Archaic.* pleasure. [ME, t. OF: m. *plaisance* der. *plaisant* PLEASANT]

pleasant (plĕz′ənt), *adj.* **1.** pleasing, agreeable, or affording enjoyment; pleasurable: *pleasant news.* **2.** (of persons, manners, disposition, etc.) agreeable socially. **3.** (of weather, etc.) fair. **4.** gay, sprightly, or merry. **5.** jocular or facetious. [ME *pleasaunt,* t. OF: m. *plaisant,* ppr. of OF *plaisir* PLEASE] —**pleas′antly,** *adv.* —**pleas′antness,** *n.* —**Syn.** 2. delightful, congenial.

Pleasant Island, former name of **Nauru.**

pleasantry (plĕz′ən trĭ), *n., pl.* **-tries.** **1.** good-humoured raillery; pleasant humour in conversation. **2.** a humorous or jesting remark. **3.** a humorous action.

please (plēz), *v.,* **pleased, pleasing.** —*v.t.* **1.** to act to the pleasure or satisfaction of: *to please the public.* **2.** to be the pleasure or will of; seem good to: *may it please God.* **3.** (as a polite addition to requests, etc.) if you are willing: *please come here.* **4.** to find something agreeable; like, wish, or choose: *go where you please.* —*v.i.* **5.** to be agreeable; give pleasure or satisfaction. **6. if you please, a.** if you like; if it be your pleasure. **b.** (in stating some surprising fact): *in his pocket, if you please, was the letter.* [ME *plese,* t. OF: m. *plaisir,* g. L *placēre* please, seem good]

pleasing (plē′zĭng), *adj.* that pleases; giving pleasure; agreeable; gratifying; likeable. —**pleas′ingly,** *adv.* —**pleas′ingness,** *n.* —**Syn.** See **interesting.**

pleasurable (plĕzh′ə rə bl, plĕzh′rə bl), *adj.* such as to give pleasure; agreeable; pleasant. —**pleas′urableness,** *n.* —**pleas′urably,** *adv.*

pleasure (plĕzh′ə), *n., v.,* **-ured, -uring.** —*n.* **1.** the state or feeling of being pleased. **2.** enjoyment or satisfaction derived from what is to one's liking; gratification: delight. **3.** worldly or frivolous enjoyment: *the pursuit of pleasure.* **4.** sensual gratification. **5.** a cause or source of enjoyment or delight: *it was a pleasure to see you.* **6.** pleasurable quality. **7.** one's will, desire, or choice: *to make known one's pleasure.* —*v.t.* **8.** to give pleasure to; gratify; please. —*v.i.* **9.** to take pleasure; delight. **10.** *Colloq.* to seek pleasure, as by taking a holiday. [ME *plesir,* t. OF: m. *plaisir* PLEASE]

—**Syn.** 1. happiness, gladness, delectation. PLEASURE, ENJOYMENT, DELIGHT, JOY refer to the feeling of being pleased and happy. PLEASURE is the general term: *to take pleasure in beautiful scenery.* ENJOYMENT is a quiet sense of well-being and pleasurable satisfaction: *enjoyment at sitting in the shade on a warm day.* DELIGHT is a high degree of pleasure, usually leading to active expression of it: *delight at receiving a hoped-for letter.* JOY is a feeling of delight so deep and so lasting that one radiates happiness and expresses it spontaneously: *joy at unexpected good news.* —**Ant.** 1. discomfort, sorrow, grief.

pleasure principle, *Psychol.* an automatic mental drive or instinct seeking to avoid pain and to obtain pleasure. Also, **pleasure-pain principle.**

pleat (plēt), *n.* **1.** a fold of definite even width made by doubling cloth or the like upon itself, and pressing, stitching, or otherwise fastening in place. —*v.t.* **2.** to fold or arrange in pleats. [var. of PLAIT]

pleb (plĕb), *n.* a plebeian or commoner.

plebeian (plĭ bē′ən), *adj.* **1.** belonging or pertaining to the Roman plebs. **2.** belonging or pertaining to the common people. **3.** common, commonplace, or vulgar. —*n.* **4.** a member of the Roman plebs. **5.** a plebeian person. [f. s. L *plēbēius* belonging to the plebs + -AN] —**plebe′ianism,** *n.*

plebiscite (plĕb′ĭ sĭt), *n.* **1.** a direct vote of the qualified electors of a state in regard to some important public question. **2.** the vote by which the people of a political unit determine autonomy or affiliation with another country. [t. L: m. s. *plēbiscītum*]

plebs (plĕbz), *n., pl.* **plebes** (plē′bēz). **1.** (in ancient Rome) the commons as contrasted with the patricians, the later senatorial nobility, or the equestrian order. **2.** the common people; the populace. [t. L]

plectognath (plĕk′tŏg năth′), *adj.* belonging to the *Plectognathi,* a group of teleost fishes having the jaws extensively ankylosed and including the filefish, globefish, etc. [t. NL: s. *Plectognathī,* pl., f. Gk: m. *plektó(s)* plaited, twisted + m. *gnáthos* jaw]

plectron (plĕk′trən), *n., pl.* **-tra** (-trə). plectrum.

plectrum (plĕk′trəm), *n., pl.* **-tra** (-trə), **-trums.** a small piece of wood, metal, ivory, etc., for plucking strings of a lyre, mandolin, guitar, etc. [t. L, t. Gk: m. *plêktron*]

pled (plĕd), *v. U.S. and Scot. Law.* a pt. and pp. of **plead.**

pledge (plĕj), *n., v.,* **pledged, pledging.** —*n.* **1.** a solemn promise of something, or to do or refrain from doing something: *a pledge of aid.* **2.** a piece of personal property delivered as security for the payment of a debt or the discharge of some obligation, and liable to forfeiture. **3.** the state of being given or held as security: *to put a thing in pledge.* **4.** *Law.* **a.** the act of delivering goods, etc., to another for security. **b.** the resulting legal relationship. **5.** anything given or regarded as a security of something. **6.** *Obs.* **a.** a hostage. **b.** one who becomes bail or surety for another. **7.** an assurance of support or goodwill conveyed by drinking a person's health; a toast. **8.** the solemn, formal vow to abstain from intoxicating drink: *to take the pledge.* —*v.t.* **9.** to bind by or as by a pledge: *to pledge hearers to secrecy.* **10.** to promise solemnly, or engage to give, maintain, etc.: *to pledge one's support.* **11.** to give or deposit as a pledge; pawn. **12.** to plight or stake, as one's honour, etc. **13.** to secure by a pledge; give a pledge for. **14.** to drink a health or toast to. [ME *plege,* t. OF, g. ML *plevium, plebium;* of Gmc orig.] —**pledg′er,** *n.*

pledgee (plĕj ē′), *n.* the person with whom something is deposited as a pledge.

pledget (plĕj′ĭt), *n.* a small, flat mass of lint, absorbent cotton, or the like, for use on a wound, sore, etc.

pledgor (plĕj ô′), *n. Law.* one who deposits personal property as a pledge.

-plegia, a word element used as a noun termination in pathological terms denoting forms of paralysis, as in *paraplegia.* [t. Gk, comb. form der. *plēgē* blow, stroke]

Pleiad (plī′əd), *n.* any of the Pleiades.

Pleiades (plī′ə dēz′), *n.pl.* **1.** *Class. Myth.* the seven daughters of Atlas and a nymph, pursued by Orion and transformed into the group of stars bearing their name (one star, missing, being the traditional **Lost Pleiad**). **2.** *Astron.* a conspicuous group or cluster of stars in the constellation Taurus, commonly spoken of as seven, though only six are plain to the average naked eye.

plein-air (plān′ĕə′; *Fr.* plĕn ĕr′), *adj.* pertaining to a movement in art, originating in France about 1870 and concerned with rendering effects of atmosphere and light in nature, as seen outside, rather than in the artificial light of studios. [F: *plein air* open air]

Pleiocene (plī′ō sēn′), *adj., n. Geol.* Pliocene.

Pleistocene (plīs′tō sēn′), *Geol.* —*adj.* **1.** pertaining to the earlier division of the Quaternary period or system (the glacial epoch or ice age). —*n.* **2.** the epoch or series of the Quaternary that follows Pliocene and precedes Recent. [f. Gk *pleîsto(s)* most (superl. of *polýs* much) + -CENE]

plenary (plē′nə rĭ), *adj.* **1.** full; complete; entire; absolute; unqualified. **2.** attended by all qualified members, as a council; fully constituted. [late ME, t. LL: m. s. *plēnārius*] —**ple′narily,** *adv.*

plenary indulgence, *Rom. Cath. Ch.* remission of the total temporal punishment which is still due to sin after sacramental absolution. See **indulgence** (def. 5).

plenipotent (plĕ nĭp′ə tənt), *adj.* invested with or possessing full power. [t. LL: s. *plēnipotens,* f. L *plēni-* full + *potens* potent]

plenipotentiary (plĕn′ĭ pə tĕn′shə rĭ, -tĕnsh′rĭ), *n., pl.* **-ries,** *adj.* —*n.* **1.** a person, esp. a diplomatic agent, invested with full power or authority to transact business. —*adj.* **2.** invested with full power or authority, as a diplomatic agent. **3.** bestowing full power, as a commission. **4.** absolute or full, as power. [t. ML: m. s. *plēnipotentiārius,* der. LL *plēnipotens*]

plenish (plĕn′ĭsh), *v.t. Chiefly Scot.* to fill up; stock; furnish. [late ME *plenyss,* t. OF: m. *pleniss-,* s. *plenir,* der. *plen-,* g. L *plēnus* full]

plenitude (plĕn′ĭ tyōōd′), *n.* **1.** fullness in quantity, measure, or degree; abundance. **2.** the condition of being full. [t. L: m. *plēnitūdo*]

pleno jure (plē′nō jōōə′rĭ), *Latin.* with full right.

plenteous (plĕn′tyəs), *adj.* **1.** plentiful; copious; abundant: *a plenteous supply of corn.* **2.** yielding abundantly. —**plen′teously,** *adv.* —**plen′teousness,** *n.*

plentiful (plĕn′tĭ fəl), *adj.* **1.** existing in great plenty. **2.** amply supplied with something. **3.** yielding abundantly. —**plen′tifully,** *adv.* —**plen′tifulness,** *n.* —**Syn.** **1.** bountiful, ample.

plenty (plĕn′tĭ), *n., pl.* **-ties,** *adj., adv.* —*n.* **1.** a full or abundant supply: *there is plenty of time.* **2.** abundance: *resources in plenty.* **3.** a time of abundance. —*adj.* **4.** *Now Chiefly Colloq.* existing in ample quantity or number (usually in the predicate): *this is plenty.* —*adv.* **5.** *Colloq.* fully: *plenty good enough.* [ME *plente(th),* t. OF: m. *plente(t),* g. s. L *plēnitas* fullness, abundance]

—**Syn.** 2. plenteousness, copiousness. PLENTY, ABUNDANCE, PROFUSION refer to a large quantity or supply. PLENTY suggests a supply that is fully adequate to any demands: *plenty of money.* ABUNDANCE implies a great plenty, an ample and generous oversupply: *an abundance of rain.* PROFUSION applies to such a lavish and excessive abundance as often suggests extravagance or prodigality: *luxuries in great profusion.*

Plenty (plĕn′tĭ), *n.* **Bay of,** a wide indentation of the Pacific Ocean on the N coast of North Island, New Zealand. ab. 95 mi. long.

plenum (plē′nəm), *n., pl.,* **-nums, -na** (-nə). **1.** a container of air, or other gas, under greater than the surrounding pressure. **2.** the whole of space regarded as being filled with matter. **3.** a full assembly, as a joint legislative assembly. [t. L, prop. neut. of *plēnus* full, filled, complete, abundant]

pleochroic (plē′ō krō′ĭk), *adj.* (of a biaxial crystal) exhibiting different colours in three different directions when viewed by transmitted light. [f. m. Gk *pleiōn* more + Gk *chrô(s)* colour + -IC] —**pleochroism** (plĭ ŏk′rō ĭz′əm), *n.*

pleonasm (plē′ə năz′əm), *n.* **1.** the use of more words than are necessary to express an idea; redundancy. **2.** an instance of this. **3.** a redundant word or expression. [t. L: s. *pleonasmus,* t. Gk: m. *pleonasmós*] —**ple′onas′tic,** *adj.* —**ple′onas′tically,** *adv.*

pleopod (plē′ō pŏd′), *n. Zool.* a swimmeret. [f. Gk *pléo(n),* ppr., swimming + -POD]

plesiosaur (plē′sĭ ə sô′), *n.* any member of the extinct genus *Plesiosaurus* (and of the order *Sauropterygia*), comprising marine reptiles with small head, very long neck, short tail, and four large flippers, which existed in the Jurassic and Cretaceous. Also, **plesiosaurus**

(plē′sĭ ə sôr′əs). [t. NL: s. *plēsiosaurus*, f. Gk: *plēsio(s)* near + m. *saûros* lizard]

plessor (plĕs′ə), *n.* plexor.

plethora (plĕth′ə rə), *n.* **1.** overfullness; superabundance. **2.** *Pathol., Obs.* a morbid condition due to excess of red corpuscles in the blood or increase in the quantity of blood. [t. NL, t. Gk: m. *plēthṓrē* fullness]

plethoric (plĕ thŏ′rĭk), *adj.* **1.** overfull; turgid; inflated. **2.** characterized by plethora. **—plethor′ically,** *adv.*

pleur-, a word element meaning 'side', 'pleura', sometimes 'rib'. Also, before consonants, **pleuro-.** [t. Gk, comb. form of *pleurá* side, rib, or *pleurón* rib; or abstracted from PLEURA]

pleura (plo͝oə′rə), *n., pl.* **pleurae** (plo͝oə′rē). a delicate serous membrane investing each lung in mammals and folded back as a lining of the corresponding side of the thorax. [t. NL, t. Gk: rib, side] **—pleu′ral,** *adj.*

pleurisy (plo͝oə′rĭ sĭ), *n.* *Pathol.* inflammation of the pleura, with or without a liquid effusion. [ME, t. OF: m. *pleurisie*, t. LL: m. *pleurisis*, for L *pleuritis*, t. Gk] **—pleuritic** (plo͝oə rĭt′ĭk), *adj.*

pleurisy root, 1. a North American milkweed, *Asclepias tuberosa*, whose root was used as a popular remedy for pleurisy; butterfly weed (def. 1). **2.** the root.

pleurodont (plo͝oə′rō dŏnt′), *adj.* **1.** ankylosed or attached to the inner edge of the jaw, as a tooth. **2.** having teeth so ankylosed, as certain lizards. **—***n.* **3.** a pleurodont animal. [f. PLEUR- + -ODONT]

pleuron (plo͝oə′rŏn), *n., pl.* **pleura** (plo͝oə′rə). *Entomol.* the lateral plate or plates of a thoracic segment of an insect. [t. Gk: side]

pleuropneumonia (plo͝oə′rō nyo͞o mō′nyə), *n.* *Pathol.* pleurisy conjoined with pneumonia.

Pleven (*Bulg.* plĕv′ĕn), *n.* a town in N Bulgaria: siege of 143 days, 1877. 80,179 (1964). Also, **Plevna** (*Bulg.* plĕv′nȧ).

plexiform (plĕk′sĭ fôm′), *adj.* in the form of a plexus. [f. PLEX(US) + -(I)FORM]

Plexiglas (plĕk′sĭ gläs′), *n.* *Trademark.* a thermoplastic notable for its permanent transparency, light weight, and resistance to weathering. It can be bent to any shape when hot, but returns to its original shape when reheated. Also, **plexiglass.**

pleximeter (plĕk sĭm′ĭ tə), *n.* *Med.* a small, thin plate, as of ivory, to receive the blow of a plexor. [f. Gk *plêxi(s)* stroke, percussion + -METER[1]]

plexor (plĕk′sə), *n.* *Med.* a small hammer with a soft rubber head or the like, used in percussion for diagnostic purposes. Also, **plessor.** [f. Gk *plêx(is)* stroke, percussion + -OR[2]]

plexus (plĕk′səs), *n., pl.,* **plexuses, plexus.** a network, as of nerves or blood vessels. [t. L: an interweaving, twining] **—plex′al,** *adj.*

plf, plaintiff. Also, **plff.**

pliable (plī′ə bl), *adj.* **1.** easily bent; flexible; supple. **2.** easily influenced; yielding; adaptable. [t. F, der. *plier* fold, bend. See PLY[2]] **—pli′abil′ity, pli′ableness,** *n.* **—pli′ably,** *adv.*

pliant (plī′ənt), *adj.* **1.** bending readily; flexible; supple. **2.** easily inclined or influenced; yielding; compliant. [ME, t. OF, ppr. of *plier* fold, bend. See PLY[2]] **—pli′ancy, pli′antness,** *n.* **—pli′antly,** *adv.* **—Syn. 1, 2.** See **flexible.**

plica (plī′kə), *n., pl.* **plicae** (plī′sē). **1.** *Zool., Anat.* a fold or folding. **2.** *Pathol.* a matted, filthy condition of the hair, caused by disease, etc. [t. ML: a fold, der. L *plicāre* fold]

plicate (plī′kāt), *adj.* folded like a fan; pleated. Also, **pli′cated.** [t. L: m. s. *plicātus*, pp., folded] **—pli′cately,** *adv.*

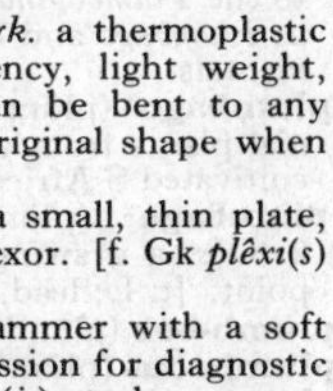

plication (plī kā′shən, plĭ-), *n.* **1.** a folding or fold. **2.** plicate form or condition. Also, **plicature** (plĭk′ə chə).

plié (plē′ā; *Fr.* plē ė′), *n.* *Ballet.* a position in which the knees are bent and the back kept straight. [F: pp. of *plier* to bend]

Plicate leaf

plier (plī′ə), *n.* **1.** (*pl., sometimes construed as sing.*) small pincers with long jaws, for bending wire, holding small objects, etc. (often called **a pair of pliers**). **2.** one who or that which plies.

plight[1] (plīt), *n.* condition, state, or situation (usually bad). [ME *plit*, t. AF, var. of OF *pleit* fold, manner of folding, condition (see PLAIT); ? influenced by PLIGHT[2] in archaic sense of danger] **—Syn.** See **predicament.**

plight[2] (plīt), *v.t.* **1.** to pledge (one's troth) in engagement to marry. **2.** to bind by a pledge, now esp. of marriage. **3.** to give in pledge; pledge (one's honour, etc.). **—***n.* **4.** *Now Rare.* pledge. [ME; OE *pliht* danger, risk, c. G *Pflicht* duty, obligation] **—plight′er,** *n.*

plim (plĭm), *v.t., v.i.,* **plimmed, plimming.** *Dial.* to swell; inflate; grow or make plump. [akin to ME *plume(n)* rise]

plimsoll (plĭm′səl), *n.* a rubber-soled canvas shoe, laced to fit the foot, worn esp. for gymnastics, sports, etc.

Plimsoll (plĭm′səl), *n.* **Samuel,** 1824–98, English politician and social reformer.

Plimsoll line (plĭm′səl), a line or mark required to be placed on the hull of all British merchant vessels, showing the depth to which they may be submerged through loading. Also, **Plimsoll mark.** [named after Samuel PLIMSOLL]

plinth (plĭnth), *n.* *Archit.* **1.** the lower square part of the base of a column. See diag. under **column. 2.** a square base or a lower block, as of a pedestal. **3.** a course of stones, as at the base of a wall, forming a continuous plinthlike projection. [t. L: s. *plinthus*, t. Gk: m. *plínthos* plinth, squared stone] **—plinth′like′,** *adj.*

Pliny (plĭn′ĭ), *n.* **1.** ('*the Elder*', *Gaius Plinius Secundus*), A.D. 23–79, Roman naturalist, encyclopedist, and writer. **2.** his nephew ('*the Younger*', *Gaius Plinius Caecilius Secundus*), A.D. 62?–*c.* 113, Roman writer, statesman, and orator.

Pliocene (plī′ō sēn′), *Geol.* **—***adj.* **1.** pertaining to the latest principal division of the Tertiary period or system. **—***n.* **2.** the epoch or series of the Tertiary that follows Miocene and precedes Pleistocene. Also, **Pleiocene.** [f. m. Gk *pleíon* more (compar. of *polýs* much) + -CENE]

plod (plŏd), *v.,* **plodded, plodding,** *n.* **—***v.i.* **1.** to walk heavily; trudge; move laboriously. **2.** to work with dull perseverence; drudge. **—***v.t.* **3.** to walk heavily over or along. **—***n.* **4.** the act or a course of plodding. **5.** a sound of or as of a heavy tread. [? imit.] **—plod′der,** *n.* **—plod′dingly,** *adv.* **—Syn. 1.** See **pace**[1].

Ploeşti (*Rum.* plò yĕshty′), *n.* a city in S Rumania: the centre of a rich oil-producing region. 133,711 (1964).

-ploid, a word element used in cytology and genetics referring to the number of chromosomes as *diploid.* [f. s. Gk *-ploos* (equivalent to E suffix *-fold*) + -(O)ID]

plonk[1] (plŏngk), *v.t.* **1.** to place or drop heavily or suddenly (often fol. by *down*). **—***v.i.* **2.** to drop heavily or suddenly (often fol. by *down*). **—***n.* **3.** the act or sound of plonking. **—***adv.* **4.** with a plonking sound. **5.** *Colloq.* exactly. [imit.]

plonk[2] (plŏngk), *n.* *Austral., N.Z. Colloq.* cheap wine. [? var. of F (*vin*) *blanc* white (wine)]

plop (plŏp), *v.,* **plopped, plopping,** *n.* **—***v.i.* **1.** to make a sound like that of a flat object striking water without a splash. **2.** to fall plump with such a sound. **—***n.* **3.** a plopping sound or fall. **4.** the act of plopping. **—***adv.* **5.** with a plop. [imit.]

plosion (plō′zhən), *n.* *Phonet.* the audible end of a stop consonant at break of closure.

plosive (plō′sĭv), *adj., n.* *Phonet.* a stop consonant that ends with an explosion.

plot[1] (plŏt), *n., v.,* **plotted, plotting. —***n.* **1.** a secret plan or scheme to accomplish some purpose, esp. a hostile, unlawful, or evil purpose. **2.** the plan, scheme, or main story of a play, novel, poem, or the like. **3.** *Artillery.* the position of a target and the fall of shot correctly indicated on a map or graph. **—***v.t.* **4.** to plan secretly (something hostile or evil): *to plot mutiny.* **5.** to mark on a plan, map, or chart, as a ship's course, etc. **6.** to make a plan or map of, as a tract of land, a building, etc. **7.** to determine and mark (points), as on graph paper, by means of measurements or co-ordinates. **8.** to draw (a curve) by means of points so marked. **9.** to represent by means of such a curve. **10.** to make (a calculation) by graph. **—***v.i.* **11.** to form secret plots; conspire. [aphetic var. of COMPLOT] **—plot′ter,** *n.*

—Syn. 1. intrigue, conspiracy, cabal. **4.** devise, contrive, concoct. **11.** PLOT, CONSPIRE, SCHEME imply secret, cunning, and often unscrupulous planning to gain one's own ends. To PLOT is to contrive a secret plan of a selfish and often treasonable kind: *to plot against someone's life.* To CONSPIRE is to unite with others in an illicit or illegal machination: *to conspire to seize a government.* To SCHEME is to plan ingeniously, subtly, and often craftily for one's own advantage: *to scheme how to gain power.*

plot[2] (plŏt), *n., v.,* **plotted, plotting. —***n.* **1.** a small piece or area of ground: *a garden plot.* **2.** *Chiefly U.S.* a plan, map, or diagram, as of land, a building, etc. **—***v.t.* **3.** to divide (land) into plots. [ME and OE; orig. uncert.]

Plotinus (plŏ tī′nəs), *n.* A.D. 205?–270?, neoplatonic philosopher in Rome, born in Egypt.

plotting paper, graph paper.

plough (plou), *n.* **1.** an agricultural implement for cutting and turning over the soil. **2.** any of various implements resembling this, as a plane for cutting grooves or a device for snow clearance. **3.** a device on a tram, formerly used for collecting current from a conductor in a conduit.

4. (*cap.*) *Astron.* a group of seven stars in the constellation of the Great Bear. 5. *Colloq.* ploughed land. 6. *Colloq.* an examination failure. —*v.t.* 7. to make furrows in or turn up (the soil) with a plough. 8. to make (a furrow, etc.) with a plough. 9. to furrow, remove, etc., or make (a furrow, groove, etc.) with or as with a plough. 10. *Naut.* a. to cleave the surface of (the water). b. to make (a way) or follow (a course) thus. 11. *Colloq.* a. to fail (someone) in an examination. b. to fail (an examination). 12. **plough back,** to reinvest (profits of a business) in that business. —*v.i.* 13. to till the soil with a plough; work with a plough. 14. to take ploughing in a specified way: *land that ploughs easily.* 15. to move through anything in the manner of a plough. 16. to work at something slowly and with perseverance (usually fol. by *through*). 17. to move through water by cleaving the surface. 18. *Colloq.* to fail an examination. Also, *Chiefly U.S.*, **plow.** [ME; OE *plōh* ploughland, c. G *Pflug* plough] —**plough′er,** *n.*

ploughboy (plou′boi′), *n.* 1. a boy who leads or guides a team drawing a plough. 2. a country boy. Also, *Chiefly U.S.*, **plowboy.**

ploughman (plou′mən), *n., pl.* **-men.** 1. a man who ploughs. 2. a farm labourer or a rustic. Also, *Chiefly U.S.*, **plowman.**

ploughman's spikenard, an erect composite herb with dull yellow capitula, *Inula conyza*, found on calcareous soils in England and Wales, central and SE Europe.

ploughshare (plou′shĕə′), *n.* the share of a plough which cuts the slice of earth and raises it to the mouldboard. Also, *Chiefly U.S.*, **plowshare.**

Plovdiv (*Bulg.* plŏv′dēf), *n.* a city in S Bulgaria, on the river Maritsa. 206,069 (1964). Greek, **Philippopolis.**

plover (plŭv′ə), *n.* 1. any of various limicoline birds of the family *Charadriidae*, esp. those with a short tail and a bill like that of a pigeon, as the **golden plover,** *Choradrius apricarius.* 2. any of various shorebirds, as the **upland plover,** *Bartramia longicauda*, of the New World. [ME, t. AF, der. L *pluvia* rain (cf. PLUVIAL); the connection of the bird with rain being uncert.]

plow (plou), *n., v.t., v.i.* *Chiefly U.S.* plough.

ploy[1] (ploi), *n.* a manoeuvre or stratagem, as in conversation, to gain the advantage. [t. F: s. *ployer*, g. L *plicāre* fold]

ploy[2] (ploi), *n.* *Scot. and N Dial.* a game or hobby. [aphetic var. of EMPLOY]

plu., plural.

pluck (plŭk), *v.t.* 1. to pull off or out from the place of growth, as fruit, flowers, feathers, etc. 2. to give a pull at. 3. to pull with sudden force or with a jerk. 4. to pull by force (fol. by *away, off, out,* etc.). 5. to pull off the feathers, hair, etc., from. 6. *Slang.* to rob, plunder, or fleece. 7. to sound (the strings of a musical instrument) by pulling at them with the fingers or a plectrum. 8. *Slang.* to reject, as after an examination. 9. **pluck up,** a. to pull up; uproot; eradicate. b. to rouse (courage, spirit, etc.) —*v.i.* 10. to pull sharply; tug (*at*). 11. to snatch (*at*). —*n.* 12. the act of plucking; a pull, tug, or jerk. 13. the heart, liver, and lungs, esp. of an animal used for food. 14. courage or resolution in the face of difficulties. [ME *plukke*, OE *pluccian*, c. MLG *plucken*; akin to G *pflücken*] —**pluck′er,** *n.*

plucky (plŭk′ĭ), *adj.*, **-ier, -iest.** having or showing pluck or courage; brave. —**pluck′ily,** *adv.* —**pluck′iness,** *n.*

plug (plŭg), *n., v.,* **plugged, plugging.** —*n.* 1. a piece of wood or other material used to stop up a hole or aperture, to fill a gap, or to act as a wedge. 2. *Elect.* a. a tapering piece of conducting material designed to be inserted between contact surfaces and so establish connection between elements of an electric current connected to the respective surfaces. b. a device to which may be attached the conductors of a cord and which by insertion in a jack, or by screwing into a receptacle, establishes contact. 3. a sparking plug. 4. a fireplug. 5. a cake of pressed tobacco. 6. a piece of tobacco cut off for chewing, etc. 7. *Colloq.* the favourable mention of a product or the like on radio, television, etc.; an advertisement, esp. unsolicited. 8. *Colloq.* a worn-out or unsaleable article. 9. *Slang.* a punch. 10. *Chiefly U.S. Slang.* a worn-out or inferior horse. 11. *Orig. U.S. Angling.* an artificial bait with hooks attached. 12. *U.S. Slang.* a man's tall silk hat (**plug hat**). —*v.t.* 13. to stop or fill with or as with a plug. 14. to insert or drive a plug into. 15. to secure by a plug. 16. to insert (something) as a plug. 17. *Colloq.* to mention (a product or the like) favourably and, often, repetitively as in a lecture, radio show, etc. 18. *Slang.* to punch. 19. *Slang.* to shoot. 20. to connect (an electrical device) with an outlet (fol. by *in*). —*v.i.* 21. *Colloq.* to work steadily or doggedly. 22. *Slang.* to strike; shoot. [t. MD: m. *plugge* (D *plug*) plug, peg; akin to G *Pflock*] —**plug′ger,** *n.*

plug board, *Elect.* patch board.

plug-ugly (plŭg′ŭg′lĭ), *n., pl.* **-lies.** *U.S. Slang.* 1. a ruffian; a rowdy; a tough. —*adj.* 2. characteristic of or pertaining to ruffians or the like.

plum[1] (plŭm), *n.* 1. the drupaceous fruit of any of various trees of the rosaceous genus *Prunus*, closely related to the cherry but with an oblong stone. 2. a tree bearing such fruit. 3. any of various other trees with a plum-like fruit. 4. the fruit itself. 5. a sugarplum. 6. a raisin as in a cake or pudding. 7. anything resembling a plum, as in taste or shape. 8. Also, **displacer.** *Bldg Trades.* a large stone put in as filling to economize on concrete. 9. a deep purple varying from bluish to reddish. 10. a good or choice thing, as one of the best parts of anything, a fine situation or appointment, etc. [ME; OE *plūme* (c. G *Pflaume*), ult. t. Gk: m. *proûmnon*] —**plum′like′,** *adj.*

plum[2] (plŭm), *adj., adv.* plumb (defs 3–7).

plumage (plōō′mĭj), *n.* 1. the entire feathery covering of a bird. 2. feathers collectively. [late ME, t. OF: f. *plume* feather + *-age* -AGE]

plumate (plōō′māt, -mĭt), *adj.* *Zool.* resembling a feather, as a hair or bristle which bears smaller hairs. [t. L: m. s. *plūmātus*, pp., covered with feathers]

plumb (plŭm), *n.* 1. a small mass of lead or heavy material, used for various purposes. 2. the position of a plumbline when freely suspended; the perpendicular: *out of plumb.* —*adj.* 3. true according to a plumbline; perpendicular. 4. *Colloq.* downright or absolute. —*adv.* 5. in a perpendicular or vertical direction. 6. exactly, precisely, or directly. 7. *Colloq.* completely or absolutely. —*v.t.* 8. to test or adjust by a plumbline. 9. to make vertical. 10. to sound (the ocean, etc.) with, or as with, a plumbline. 11. to measure (depth) by sounding. 12. to sound the depths of, or penetrate to the bottom of. 13. to seal with lead. —*v.i.* 14. *Colloq.* to work as a plumber. Also, **plum** for 3–7. [ME *plumbe*, t. OF: m. *plomb*, g. L *plumbum* lead]

plumbaginaceous (plŭm băj′ĭ nā′shəs), *adj.* belonging to the *Plumbaginaceae* family of plants, certain of which, as *Plumbago* and *Statice*, are in wide cultivation as ornamentals.

plumbago[1] (plŭm bā′gō), *n.* a genus of annual or perennial plants from warm regions, including the frequently cultivated S African climbing shrub *P. capensis.*

plumbago[2] (plŭm bā′gō), *n., pl.* **-gos.** 1. graphite. 2. *Obs.* a drawing made by an instrument with a lead point. [t. L: lead, ore]

plumb-bob (plŭm′bŏb′), *n.* plummet (def. 1).

plumbeous (plŭm′bĭ əs), *adj.* leaden. [t. L: m. *plumbeus*]

plumber (plŭm′ə), *n.* 1. one who installs and repairs piping, fixtures, appliances, and appurtenances in connection with the water supply, drainage systems, etc., both in and out of buildings. 2. a worker in lead or similar metals. [ME, t. OF: m. *plombier*, g. LL *plumbārius*, der. L *plumbum* lead]

plumbery (plŭm′ə rĭ), *n., pl.* **-ries.** 1. a plumber's workshop. 2. plumber's work.

plumbic (plŭm′bĭk), *adj.* *Chem.* containing lead, esp. in the tetravalent state. [f. s. L *plumbum* lead + -IC]

plumbiferous (plŭm bĭf′ə rəs), *adj.* yielding or containing lead. [f. s. L *plumbum* lead + -(I)FEROUS]

plumbing (plŭm′ĭng), *n.* 1. the system of pipes and other apparatus for conveying water, liquid wastes, etc., as in a building. 2. the work or trade of a plumber. 3. the act of one who plumbs, as in ascertaining depth.

plumbism (plŭm′bĭz′əm), *n.* *Pathol.* chronic lead poisoning.

plumbline (plŭm′lĭn′), *n.* 1. a string to one end of which is attached a metal bob, used to determine perpendicularity, find the depth of water, etc. 2. a plumb-rule.

plumbous (plŭm′bəs), *adj.* *Chem.* containing divalent lead. [t. L: m. s. *plumbōsus*]

plumb-rule (plŭm′rōōl′), *n.* a device used by builders, etc., for determining perpendicularity, consisting of a narrow board fitted with a plumbline and bob.

plumbum (plŭm′bəm), *n.* *Chem.* lead. *Symbol:* Pb [t. L]

plum duff, a kind of flour pudding containing raisins or currants, steamed, or boiled in a cloth.

plume (plōōm), *n., v.,* **plumed, pluming.** —*n.* 1. a feather. 2. a large, long, or conspicuous feather: *the plume of an ostrich.* 3. a soft, fluffy feather. 4. any plumose part or formation. 5. a feather, a tuft of feathers, or some substitute, worn as an ornament on the hat, helmet, etc. 6. an ornament; a token of honour or distinction. 7. *Now Chiefly Poetic.* plumage. —*v.t.* 8. to furnish, cover, or adorn with plumes or feathers. 9. (of a bird) to preen itself or its feathers). 10. to display or feel satisfaction with or pride in (oneself); pride (oneself) complacently (fol. by *on* or *upon*). [t. OF, g. L *plūma* feather; r. OE *plūm*, t. L: s. *plūma*] —**plume′like′,** *adj.*

plumelet (plōōm′lĭt), *n.* a small plume.

plummet (plŭm′ĭt), *n.* **1.** Also, **plumb-bob.** a piece of lead or some other weight attached to a line, used for determining perpendicularity, for sounding, etc.; the bob of a plumbline. **2.** a plumb-rule. **3.** *Angling.* an apparatus consisting of a weight attached to a line, used to determine the depth of water. **4.** something that weighs down or depresses. —*v.i.* **5.** to plunge. [ME *plomet*, t. OF: m. *plommet*, *plombet*, dim. of *plomb* lead]

plummy (plŭm′ĭ), *adj.* **1.** full of or resembling plums. **2.** *Colloq.* choice, good, or desirable. **3.** (of a voice) deep or vibrant, esp. excessively or affectedly so.

plumose (plōō′mōs), *adj.* **1.** having feathers or plumes; feathered. **2.** feathery or plumelike. [t. L: m. s. *plūmōsus*] —**plumosity** (plōō mŏs′ĭ tĭ), *n.*

plump[1] (plŭmp), *adj.* **1.** well filled out or rounded in form; somewhat fleshy or fat; chubby. —*v.i.* **2.** to become plump (often fol. by *up* or *out*). —*v.t.* **3.** to make plump (fol. by *up* or *out*). [ME *plompe* dull, rude, c. MLG *plump* blunt, thick, rude] —**plump′ly,** *adv.* —**plump′ness,** *n.* —**Syn. 1.** See **stout.**

plump[2] (plŭmp), *v.i.* **1.** to fall heavily or suddenly and directly; drop, sink, or come abruptly, or with direct impact. **2.** to vote exclusively for or choose one out of a number (often fol. by *for*). —*v.t.* **3.** to drop or throw heavily or suddenly. **4.** to utter or say bluntly (often fol. by *out*). —*n.* **5.** a heavy or sudden fall. —*adv.* **6.** with a heavy or sudden fall or drop. **7.** directly or bluntly, as in speaking. **8.** straight. **9.** with sudden encounter. **10.** with direct impact. —*adj.* **11.** direct; downright; blunt. [ME *plumpen*, c. D *plompen*; prob. imit.]

plump[3] (plŭmp), *n. Archaic or Dial.* a group or cluster. [orig. uncert.]

plumper[1] (plŭm′pə), *n.* **1.** a plumping or falling heavily. **2.** the vote of one who plumps. **3.** a voter who plumps. [f. PLUMP[2], v. + -ER[1]]

plumper[2] (plŭm′pə), *n.* **1.** something that plumps, or makes plump. **2.** something carried in the mouth to fill out hollow cheeks. [f. PLUMP[1], v. + -ER[1]]

plum pudding, Christmas pudding.

plumule (plōō′myōōl), *n.* **1.** *Bot.* the bud of the ascending axis of a plant while still in the embryo. **2.** *Ornith.* a down feather. [t. L: m. *plūmula*, dim. of *plūma* feather]

plumy (plōō′mĭ), *adj.* **1.** having plumes or feathers. **2.** adorned with a plume or plumes: *a plumy helmet.* **3.** plumelike or feathery.

P, Plumules in A, Rhubarb, *Rheum moorcroftianum*; B, Bean, *Vicia faba*; C, Sedge, *Cyperus niculata*

plunder (plŭn′də), *v.t.* **1.** to rob of goods or valuables by open force, as in war, hostile raids, brigandage, etc: *to plunder a town.* **2.** to rob, despoil, or fleece: *to plunder the public treasury.* **3.** to take by pillage or robbery. —*v.i.* **4.** to take plunder; pillage. —*n.* **5.** plundering, pillage, or spoliation. **6.** that which is taken in plundering; loot. **7.** anything taken by robbery, theft, or fraud. [t. G: m. *plündern*] —**plun′derer,** *n.*

plunderage (plŭn′də rĭj), *n.* **1.** the act of plundering; pillage. **2.** *Maritime Law.* **a.** the embezzlement of goods on board ship. **b.** the goods embezzled.

plunge (plŭnj), *v.*, **plunged, plunging,** *n.* —*v.t.* **1.** to cast or thrust forcibly or suddenly into a liquid, a penetrable substance, a place, etc.; immerse; submerge: *to plunge a dagger into one's heart.* **2.** to bring into some condition, situation, etc.: *to plunge a country into war.* **3.** to immerse mentally, as in thought. —*v.i.* **4.** to cast oneself, or fall as if cast, into water, a deep place, etc. **5.** to rush or dash with headlong haste: *to plunge through a doorway.* **6.** *Slang.* to bet or speculate recklessly. **7.** to throw oneself impetuously or abruptly into some condition, situation, matter, etc.: *to plunge into war.* **8.** to descend abruptly or precipitously, as a cliff, a road, etc. **9.** to pitch violently forward, esp. with the head downwards, as a horse, ship, etc. —*n.* **10.** the act of plunging. **11.** a leap or dive into water or the like. **12.** a headlong or impetuous rush or dash. **13.** a sudden, violent pitching movement. **14.** *U.S.* a place for plunging or diving, as a swimming pool. **15. take the plunge,** to resolve to do something (usually unpleasant) and to act straightaway. [ME, t. OF: m. *plungier*, ult. der. L *plumbum* lead] —**Syn. 1.** See **dip.**

plunger (plŭn′jə), *n.* **1.** *Mach.* a device or a part of a machine which acts with a plunging or thrusting motion; a piston; a ram. **2.** one who or that which plunges; a diver. **3.** *Slang.* a reckless better or speculator.

plunging (plŭn′jĭng), *adj.* **1.** that plunges. **2.** *Mil.* (of fire) directed downwards from pieces situated above the plane of the object fired at.

plunk (plŭngk), *v.t.* **1.** to pluck (a stringed instrument or its strings); twang. **2.** to throw, push, put, etc., heavily or suddenly. **3.** *Colloq.* to shoot at. —*v.i.* **4.** to give forth a twanging sound. **5.** to drop down heavily or suddenly; plump. —*n.* **6.** the act or sound of plunking. **7.** a direct, forcible blow. **8.** *U.S. Slang.* a dollar. —*adv.* **9.** with a plunking sound. **10.** *Colloq.* exactly; plump. Also (for defs 2, 5, 6, 7, 9, 10), **plonk.** [imit.]

pluperfect (plōō′pû′fĭkt), *Gram.* —*adj.* **1.** perfect with respect to a temporal point of reference in the past. Example: In 'He had done it when I came', *had done* is pluperfect (completed action) in relation to *came.* **2.** designating a tense, or other verb formation or construction, with such meaning. Latin *portāveram* 'I had carried' etc., is in the pluperfect tense. —*n.* **3.** the pluperfect tense, or other verb formation or construction with such meaning. **4.** a form therein. [t. L, contr. of *plūs quam perfectum* more than perfect]

plupf., pluperfect.

plur., **1.** plural. **2.** plurality.

plural (plŏŏə′rəl), *adj.* **1.** consisting of, containing, or pertaining to more than one. **2.** pertaining to or involving a plurality of persons or things. **3.** being one of such a plurality: *a plural wife.* **4.** *Gram.* (in many languages) designating the number category that normally implies more than one person, thing, or collection, as English, *men, things, they.* —*n.* **5.** *Gram.* the plural number. **6.** a form therein. [ME, t. L: s. *plūrālis*]

pluralism (plŏŏə′rə lĭz′əm), *n.* **1.** *Philos.* a theory or system that recognizes more than one ultimate substance or principle. Cf. **monism, dualism. 2.** the holding by one person of two or more offices, esp. ecclesiastical benefices, at the same time. **3.** the character of being plural. —**plu′ralist,** *n.* —**plu′ralis′tic,** *adj.*

plurality (plŏŏə răl′ĭ tĭ), *n., pl.* **-ties. 1.** more than half of the whole; the majority. **2.** *U.S.* majority (def. 3). **3.** a number greater than unity. **4.** the fact of being numerous. **5.** a large number, or a multitude. **6.** the state or fact of being plural. **7.** pluralism (def. 2). **8.** any of the offices or benefices so held.

pluralize (plŏŏə′rə līz′), *v.t.,* **-lized, -lizing. 1.** to make plural. **2.** to express in the plural form. Also, **pluralise.**

plurally (plŏŏə′rə lĭ), *adv.* as a plural; in a plural sense.

plural voting, 1. a system by which a person is allowed to vote more than once in an election. **2.** the system in Britain before 1948 when certain people could vote in more than one constituency in parliamentary elections.

pluri-, a word element meaning 'several', 'many'. [t. L, comb. form of *plūrēs*, pl.]

plus (plŭs), *prep.* **1.** more by the addition of; increased by: *ten plus two.* **2.** with the addition of; with. —*adj.* **3.** involving or denoting addition. **4.** positive: *a plus quantity.* **5.** *Colloq.* with something in addition. **6.** more (by a certain amount). **7.** *Elect.* positive or to be connected to the positive: *the plus terminal.* **8.** *Bot.* designating, in the absence of morphological difference, one of the two strains or mycelia in fungi which must unite in the sexual process. —*n.* **9.** a plus quantity. **10.** the plus sign (+). **11.** something additional. **12.** a surplus or gain. [t. L: more]

plus-fours (plŭs′fōz′), *n.* baggy trousers, covering the knee and strapping below it.

plush (plŭsh), *n.* **1.** a fabric of silk, cotton, wool, etc., having a longer pile than that of velvet. —*adj.* **2.** Also, **plush′y.** denoting something, esp. a room, furnishings, or the like, luxurious and costly. [t. F: m. *pluche*, *peluche*, ult. der. L *pilus* hair]

plus sign, the symbol (+) indicating summation or a positive quantity.

Plutarch (plōō′täk), *n.* A.D. *c.* 46–*c.* 120, Greek biographer.

Pluto (plōō′tō), *n.* **1.** *Gk Myth.* **a.** Hades, the lord of the dead and the lower world. **b.** a nymph, mother of Tantalus. **2.** *Astron.* the ninth and outermost planet from the sun, discovered in 1930. Its period of revolution is 248·2 years, its mean distance from the sun 3,661,000,000 miles, and its diameter 3600 miles. [t. L, t. Gk: m. *Ploutōn*]

plutocracy (plōō tŏk′rə sĭ), *n., pl.* **-cies. 1.** the rule or power of wealth or of the wealthy. **2.** a government or state in which the wealthy class rules. **3.** a class or group ruling, or exercising power or influence, by virtue of its wealth. [t. Gk: m. *ploutokratía.* See -CRACY]

plutocrat (plōō′tə krăt′), *n.* a member of a plutocracy.

plutocratic (plōō′tə krăt′ĭk), *adj.* of, pertaining to, or indicative of a plutocracy or plutocrats. Also, **plu′tocrat′ical.**

pluton (plōō′tŏn), *n. Geol.* any body of igneous rock that solidified far below the earth's surface. [named after PLUTO]

ăct, āble, ärt; ĕbb, ēqual; ĭf, īce; hŏt, ōver, ôrder, oil, bŏŏk, ōōze, out; ŭp, ûrge; ə = a in alone; ch, chief; g, give; ng, ring; sh, shoe; th, thin; ŧh, that; y, young; zh, vision. See full key on inside front cover.

Plutonian (plōō tō′nyən), *adj.* **1.** of or pertaining to Pluto; infernal. **2.** (*cap. or l.c.*) *Geol.* pertaining to the theory that the present condition of the earth's crust is mainly due to igneous action.

plutonic (plōō tŏn′ĭk), *adj.* **1.** *Geol.* denoting a class of igneous rocks which have solidified far below the earth's surface. **2.** (*cap. or l.c.*) Plutonian.

plutonium (plōō tō′nyəm), *n.* *Chem.* a radioactive element, capable of self-maintained explosive fission, isolated during research on the atomic bomb in 1940. It is formed by deuteron bombardment of neptunium, and has an isotope of major importance, $^{239}_{94}$Pu, which is fissionable and can be produced in chain-reacting units from uranium-238, by neutron capture followed by the spontaneous emission of two beta particles. *Symbol:* Pu; *at. no.:* 94. [f. m. Gk *Ploútōn* PLUTO + -IUM]

Plutus (plōō′təs), *n.* *Class. Myth.* a personification of wealth, the son of Demeter, and associated with peace. [t. L, t. Gk: m. *Ploûtos* god of riches, lit., wealth]

pluvial[1] (plōō′vyəl), *adj.* **1.** of or pertaining to rain; rainy. **2.** *Geol.* due to rain. [t. L: s. *pluviālis*]

pluvial[2] (plōō′vyəl), *n.* cope[2] (def. 1).

pluviometer (plōō′vĭ ŏm′ĭ tə), *n.* an instrument for measuring rainfall. [f. s. L *pluvia* rain + -(O)METER[1]] —**pluviometric** (plōō′vĭ ə mĕt′rĭk), **plu′viomet′rical,** *adj.* —**plu′viom′etry,** *n.*

Pluviôse (plōō′vĭ ōz′; *Fr.* plY vyōz′), *n.* (in the calendar of the first French republic) the fifth month of the year, extending from January 20th to February 18th. [t. F, t. L: m. *pluviōsus* rainy]

pluvious (plōō′vyəs), *adj.* **1.** rainy. **2.** pertaining to rain. [t. L: m. *pluviōsus*]

ply[1] (plī), *v.*, **plied, plying.** —*v.t.* **1.** to use; employ busily, or work with or at: *to ply the needle.* **2.** to carry on, practise, or pursue: *to ply a trade.* **3.** to treat with something repeatedly applied: *I plied the fire with fresh fuel.* **4.** to assail persistently: *to ply horses with a whip.* **5.** to supply with something pressingly offered: *to ply a person with drink.* **6.** to address persistently or importunately, as with questions, solicitations, etc.; importune. **7.** to traverse (a river, etc.), esp. on regular trips. —*v.i.* **8.** to travel or run regularly over a fixed course or between certain places, as a boat, a stage, etc. **9.** to perform one's or its work or office busily or steadily: *to ply with the oars.* **10.** to pursue or direct the course, on the water or otherwise. **11.** *Naut.* to make way windward by tacking. [ME *plye(n)*, aphetic var. of ME *aplye(n)* APPLY]

ply[2] (plī), *n.*, *pl.* **plies,** *v.*, **plied, plying.** —*n.* **1.** a fold; a thickness. **2.** a strand of yarn: *single ply.* **3.** bent, bias, or inclination. —*v.t.* **4.** *Now Chiefly Dial.* to bend, fold, or mould. —*v.i.* **5.** *Obs.* to bend, incline, or yield. [ME *plien*, t. OF: m. *plier* fold, bend, g. L *plicāre* fold]

-ply, suffixal use of **ply**[2] (thickness), as in *three-ply.*

Plymouth (plĭm′əth), *n.* **1.** a city and seaport in England, in S Devonshire: naval base. 204,409 (1961). **2.** a town in the U.S., in SE Massachusetts: the oldest town in New England; founded by the Pilgrim Fathers, 1620. 6488 (1960).

Plymouth Brethren, a religious sect which originated in the 1820s in Plymouth, Bristol, and Dublin, having no formal creed and no order of ministers.

Plymouth Colony, the colony established in SE Massachusetts by the Pilgrim Fathers in 1620.

Plymouth Rock, **1.** a rock at Plymouth, Massachusetts, on which the Pilgrim Fathers are said to have landed in 1620. **2.** one of an American breed of medium-sized domestic fowls.

plywood (plī′wŏŏd′), *n.* a material consisting of an odd number of thin sheets or strips of wood glued together with the grains (usually) at right angles, used in building, cabinetwork, and aeroplane construction.

Plzeň (*Cz.* pəl′zěny), *n.* Czech name of **Pilsen.**

P.M., **1.** Past Master. **2.** Paymaster. **3.** Police Magistrate. **4.** Postmaster. **5.** post-mortem. **6.** Prime Minister. **7.** Provost Marshal.

p.m., **1.** (L *post meridiem*) after noon. **2.** the period from 12 noon to 12 midnight. **3.** post-mortem.

P.M.G., **1.** Postmaster General. **2.** Provost Marshal General.

P.N., promissory note. Also, **p.n.**

P.N.E.U., Parents' National Educational Union.

pneum., **1.** pneumatic. **2.** pneumatics.

pneuma (nyōō′mə), *n.* *Gk Philos., etc.*, the vital spirit; the soul. [t. Gk]

pneumatic (nyōō măt′ĭk), *adj.* **1.** of or pertaining to air, or gases in general. **2.** pertaining to pneumatics. **3.** operated by air, or by pressure or exhaustion of air. **4.** containing air; filled with compressed air, as a tyre. **5.** *Theol.* of or pertaining to the spirit; spiritual. **6.** *Zool.* containing air or air cavities. [t. L: s. *pneumaticus*, t. Gk: m. *pneumatikós*] —**pneumat′ically,** *adv.*

pneumatic brake, a system of braking used on some railway trains in which compressed air is used to operate brake cylinders throughout the train simultaneously.

pneumatic drill, a hard rock, or road, drill which is operated by compressed air.

pneumatics (nyōō măt′ĭks), *n.* the branch of physics that deals with the mechanical properties of air and other gases. [pl. of PNEUMATIC, adj. See -ICS]

pneumatic trough, *Chem.* a vessel used in laboratories for the collection of gases.

pneumato-, a word element, used chiefly in scientific terms, referring to air, breath, spirit. [t. Gk, comb. form of *pneûma*]

pneumatology (nyōō′mə tŏl′ə jĭ), *n.* **1.** *Theol.* **a.** the doctrine of the Holy Spirit. **b.** the belief in intermediary spirits between men and God. **2.** the doctrine or theory of spiritual beings. **3.** *Archaic.* psychology. **4.** *Obs.* pneumatics.

pneumatolysis (nyōō′mə tŏl′ĭ sĭs), *n.* *Geol.* the process by which minerals and ores are formed by the action of vapours given off from igneous magmata.

pneumatolytic (nyōō′mə tō lĭt′ĭk), *adj.* *Geol.* pertaining to or formed by pneumatolysis.

pneumatometer (nyōō′mə tŏm′ĭ tə), *n.* *Physiol.* an instrument for measuring the quantity of air inhaled or exhaled during a single inspiration or expiration, or the force of inspiration or expiration.

pneumatophore (nyōō′mə tō fô′), *n.* **1.** *Bot.* a specialized structure developed from the root in certain plants growing in swamps and marshes, and serving as a respiratory organ. **2.** *Zool.* the air-sac of a siphonophore, serving as a float.

pneumatotherapy (nyōō′mə tō thĕ′rə pĭ), *n.* the use of compressed or rarefied air in treating disease.

pneumo-, a word element referring to the lungs or to respiration. [comb. form repr. Gk *pneúmōn* lung, or, less often, *pneûma* wind, air, breath]

pneumobacillus (nyōō′mō bə sĭl′əs), *n.*, *pl.* **-cilli** (-sĭl′ī). a bacillus, *Streptococcus pneumoniae*, the causative agent of certain respiratory diseases, esp. pneumonia. [t. NL. See PNEUMO-, BACILLUS]

pneumococcus (nyōō′mō kŏk′əs), *n.*, *pl.* **-cocci** (-kŏk′sī). a bacterium, *Micrococcus lanceolatus*, a rather large pear-shaped coccus, occurring in pairs and surrounded by a wide capsule: the cause of acute lobar pneumonia and **pneumococcal meningitis.** [t. NL. See PNEUMO-, COCCUS]

pneumoconiosis (nyōō′mō kŏn′ĭ ō′sĭs), *n.* *Pathol.* a disease of the lungs caused by the inhalation of dust.

pneumodynamics (nyōō′mō dī năm′ĭks), *n.* pneumatics.

pneumonectomy (nyōō′mō nĕk′tə mĭ), *n.*, *pl.* **-mies.** the total or partial removal of lung tissue by surgery. [f. Gk *pneúmōn* lung + -ECTOMY]

pneumonia (nyōō mō′nyə), *n.* *Pathol.* **1.** inflammation of the lungs. **2.** an acute affection of the lungs, **croupous pneumonia** or **lobar pneumonia,** regarded as due to the pneumococcus. [t. NL, t. Gk]

pneumonic (nyōō mŏn′ĭk), *adj.* **1.** of, pertaining to, or affecting the lungs; pulmonary. **2.** pertaining to or affected with pneumonia.

pneumothorax (nyōō′mō thô′răks), *n.* *Pathol.* the presence of air or gas in the pleural cavity.

Pnom Penh (nŏm′pĕn′), a city in SE Asia, capital of Cambodia. 403,000 (1962). Also, **Pnom-Penh, Phnom Penh, Pnom penh.**

pnxt, pinxit.

Po (pō), *n.* a river flowing from the Alps in NW Italy E to the Adriatic. 418 mi. Ancient, **Padus.**

Po, *Chem.* polonium.

P.O., **1.** petty officer. **2.** pilot officer. **3.** postal order. **4.** post office.

poaceous (pō ā′shəs), *adj.* belonging to the *Poaceae* (or *Gramineae*), the grass family of plants. [f. s. NL *Poa* the typical genus (t. Gk: grass) + -ACEOUS]

poach[1] (pōch), *v.i.* **1.** to trespass on another's land, etc., esp. in order to steal game. **2.** to take game or fish illegally. **3.** to encroach on another's rights; take something belonging to another. **4.** (of land) to become broken up or slushy by being trampled. —*v.t.* **5.** to trample. **6.** to mix with water and reduce to a uniform consistency, as clay. [t. MF: m. *pocher* thrust or put out (eyes), dig out with the fingers, prob. t. Gmc; akin to POKE[1]]

poach[2] (pōch), *v.t.* to cook (an egg) by dropping it whole (without the shell) into boiling water and simmering till done. [t. F: m. s. *pocher*; cf. *poche* cooking spoon, g. LL *popia*, of Gaelic orig.; ult. c. L *coquere* to cook]

poacher[1] (pō′chə), *n.* one who trespasses on another's land, to steal game.

poacher[2] (pō′chə), *n.* a pan or the like for poaching eggs.
P.O.B., post office box. Also, **POB.**
Pocahontas (pŏk′ə hŏn′təs), *n.* (*Rebecca Rolfe*) 1595?–1617, American Indian girl said to have prevented the execution of Captain John Smith.
pochard (pō′chəd), *n.* **1.** an Old World diving duck, *Aythya ferina*, with a chestnut-red head. **2.** any of various related ducks. [orig. uncert.]
pochette (pō shĕt′), *n.* **1.** a small handbag, without handles, clutched in the hand. **2.** a kit[2]. [F: dim. of *poche* pocket]
Po Chü-i (pō′cho͞o′ē′), A.D. 772–846, Chinese poet.
pock (pŏk), *n.* **1.** a pustule on the body in an eruptive disease, as smallpox. **2.** a mark or spot left by or resembling such a pustule. [ME *pokke*, OE *poc*, c. G *Pocke*; ? akin to OE *pocca* bag. See POKE[2]]
pocket (pŏk′ĭt), *n.* **1.** a small bag inserted in a garment, for carrying a purse or other small articles. **2.** a bag or pouch. **3.** money, means, or financial resources. **4.** any pouchlike receptacle, hollow, or cavity. **5.** a small isolated area: *a pocket of resistance.* **6.** a cavity in the earth, esp. one containing gold or other ore. **7.** a small ore body or mass of ore, frequently isolated. **8.** *Mining Dial.* **a.** a bin for ore or rock storage. **b.** a raise or small slope fitted with chute gates. **9.** a small bag or net at the corner or side of a billiard table. **10.** *Racing.* a position in which a contestant is so hemmed in by others that his progress is impeded. **11.** See **air-pocket. 12. in one's pocket,** under one's control. **13. in pocket,** having money or a profit, esp. after some transaction. **14. line one's pockets,** to gain, esp. financially, at the expense of others. **15. out of pocket,** without money or having made a loss, esp. after some transaction. —*adj.* **16.** suitable for carrying in the pocket: *a pocket edition of a novel.* **17.** small enough to go in the pocket; diminutive. —*v.t.* **18.** to put into one's pocket. **19.** to take possession of as one's own, often dishonestly. **20.** to submit to or endure without protest or open resentment. **21.** to conceal or suppress: *to pocket one's pride.* **22.** to enclose or confine as in a pocket. **23.** to drive (a ball) into a pocket, as in billiards. **24.** *U.S.* (of the President or a legislative executive) to retain (a bill) without action on it and thus prevent it from becoming a law. **25.** to hem in (a contestant) so as to impede progress, as in racing. [ME *poket*, t. AF: m. *pokete*, dim. of ONF *poke*, var. of F *poche* bag. See POKE[2], POUCH]
pocket battleship, a small, heavily armed and armoured warship serving as a battleship because of limitations imposed by treaty.
pocket billiards. See **pool**[2] (def. 8).
pocket-book (pŏk′ĭt bo͝ok′), *n.* **1.** a wallet. **2.** a small notebook.
pocket borough, a borough whose parliamentary representation (before 1832) was practically in the hands of one person or family.
pocketful (pŏk′ĭt fo͝ol′), *n., pl.* **-fuls.** as much as a pocket will hold.
pocket-handkerchief (pŏk′ĭt hăng′kə chĭf), *n.* a handkerchief carried in the pocket.
pocket-knife (pŏk′ĭt nīf′), *n., pl.* **-knives** (-nīvz′). a knife with one or more blades which fold into the handle, suitable for carrying in the pocket.
pocket-money (pŏk′ĭt mŭn′ĭ), *n.* a small weekly allowance of money, as given to a child by his parents.
pocket veto, *U.S.* **1.** the retaining, without action, past the time of the adjournment of Congress, by the President of the U.S., of a bill presented to him for signature within ten days of the end of a session, which is equivalent to a veto. **2.** a similar action on the part of any legislative executive.
pockmark (pŏk′mäk′), *n.* a mark or pit left by a pustule in smallpox or the like. —**pock′marked′,** *adj.*
pocky (pŏk′ĭ), *adj.* having pocks; marked by pocks.
poco (pō′kō; *It.* pŏ′kō), *adj. Music.* somewhat: *poco presto* (*somewhat fast*). [It.: little, g. L *paucus* few]
poco a poco (pō′kō ä pō′kō), *Music.* gradually. [It.]
pococurante (pō′kō kyo͞o răn′tĭ; *It.* pō kō ko͞o rän′tė), *n.* **1.** a careless or indifferent person. —*adj.* **2.** caring little; indifferent; nonchalant. [t. It.: f. *poco* little + *curante* caring, g. s. L *curans*, ppr.] —**pococurantism** (pō′kō kyo͞o răn′tĭz′əm), *n.*
pod[1] (pŏd), *n., v.,* **podded, podding.** —*n.* **1.** a more or less elongated, two-valved seed vessel, as that of the pea or bean. **2.** a dehiscent fruit or pericarp with several seeds. **3.** *Aeron.* a streamlined structure suspended under the wing of an aircraft for housing a jet engine, cargo, missiles, or other weapons. —*v.i.* **4.** to produce pods. **5.** to swell out like a pod. —*v.t.* **6.** to remove the shell from. [appar. back-formation from *podder* peasecod-gatherer. Cf. *podder*, var. of *podware*, unexplained var. of *codware* podded vegetables (f. COD[2] pod, bag + *-ware* crops, vegetables)]
pod[2] (pŏd), *n.* **1.** a small herd or school, esp. of seals or whales. **2.** a small flock of birds. [orig. uncert.]
pod[3] (pŏd), *n.* the straight groove or channel in the body of certain augers or bits. [cf. OE *pād* covering, cloak]
pod-, a word element meaning 'foot', as in *podiatry*. Also, before consonants, **podo-.** [t. Gk, comb. form of *poús*]
-pod, a word element meaning 'footed', as in *cephalopod*. Cf. **-poda.** [t. Gk: s. *-podos*, der. *poús* foot]
-poda, pl. of **-pod,** as in *Cephalopoda.*
podagra (pə dăg′rə), *n.* gout in the foot. [t. L, t. Gk: lit., a trap for the feet]
poddy (pŏd′ĭ), *n.* **1.** *Austral.* a hand-fed calf. **2.** *Slang.* pot-bellied.
poddy-dodger (pŏd′ĭ dŏj′ə), *n. Austral. Colloq.* one who steals unbranded calves.
podesta (pō dĕs′tə; *It.* pō dĕs tä′), *n.* any of certain magistrates in Italy, as a chief magistrate in medieval towns and republics. [t. It., g. L *potestas* power, magistrate]
podge (pŏj), *n. Colloq.* a podgy person.
Podgorica (*Serb.* pôd gô′rē tsä), *n.* former name of **Titograd.**
Podgorny (*Russ.* păd gôr′nĭy), *n.* **Nikolai Viktorovich** (*Russ.* nĭ kä lăy′ vēk′tə rə vĭch), born 1903, president of the Soviet Union since 1965.
podgy (pŏj′ĭ), *adj.,* **-ier, -iest.** short and fat; plump. Also, **pudgy.** [orig. obscure] —**podg′ily,** *adv.* —**podg′iness,** *n.*
podiatry (pō dī′ə trĭ), *n. Med.* the investigation and treatment of foot disorders. [f. POD- + -IATRY] —**podi′atrist,** *n.*
podium (pō′dĭ əm), *n., pl.* **-dia** (-dĭ ə). **1.** a small platform for the conductor of an orchestra, for a public speaker, etc. **2.** *Archit.* **a.** a continuous projecting base of a building usually of considerable height and forming the front of the basement of the foundation behind it. **b.** a low continuous structure serving as a base or terrace wall. **c.** the stylobate or the structure under the stylobate of a temple. **d.** a raised platform surrounding the arena of an ancient amphitheatre. **3.** *Zool., Anat.* a foot. **4.** *Bot.* a footstalk or stipe. [t. L: elevated place, balcony, t. Gk: m. *pódion*, dim. of *poús* foot. Cf. PEW]
-podium, a word element meaning 'footlike', used in nouns. [t. NL. See PODIUM]
podophyllin (pŏd′ō fĭl′ĭn), *n.* a resin obtained from podophyllum and used as a cathartic and in the treatment of some skin diseases.
podophyllum (pŏd′ō fĭl′əm), *n.* the dried rhizome of the May apple, *Podophyllum peltatum*, used in the treatment of warts. [t. NL, f. Gk: *podo-* (see POD-) + m. *phýllon* leaf]
-podous, a word element used as an adjective termination, corresponding to *-pod*. [t. Gk: m. *-podos* footed, der. *poús* foot]
podzol (pŏd′zŏl), *n.* a forest soil, notably acidic, having an upper layer that is greyish white or ash-coloured and depleted of colloids and iron and aluminium compounds, and a lower layer, brownish in colour, in which these have accumulated; an infertile soil difficult to cultivate, found over vast areas in northern North America and Eurasia. Also, **podsol.** [t. Russ.: adj., resembling ashes] —**podzol′ic,** *adj.*
podzolize (pŏd′zŏ līz′), *v.t., v.i.,* **-lized, -lizing.** to form podzol. Also, **podsolize, podsolise, podzolise.**
Poe (pō), *n.* **Edgar Allan,** 1809–49, U.S. poet, writer and critic.
Poelzig (*Ger.* pœl′tsĭKH), *n.* **Hans** (*Ger.* häns), 1869–1936, German architect.
poem (pō′ĭm), *n.* **1.** a composition in verse, esp. one characterized by artistic construction and imaginative or elevated thought: *a lyric poem.* **2.** a composition which, though not in verse, is characterized by beauty of language or thought: *a prose poem.* **3.** a work in poetry rather than prose. **4.** something having qualities suggestive of or likened to those of poetry. [t. L: s. *poēma*, t. Gk: m. *poíēma* poem, something made]
poenology (pē nŏl′ə jĭ), *n.* penology.
poesy (pō′ĭ zĭ), *n., pl.* **-sies. 1.** *Poetic.* poetry in general. **2.** *Archaic.* the work or the art of poetic composition. **3.** *Archaic.* poetry or verse. **4.** *Obs.* a verse or poetry or the like used as a motto. See **posy** (def. 2). **5.** *Obs.* a poem. [ME *poesie*, t. OF, t. L: m. *poēsis*, t. Gk: m. *poíēsis* poetic composition, poetry, a making]
poet (pō′ĭt), *n.* **1.** one who composes poetry. **2.** one having the gift of poetic thought, imagination, and creation, together with eloquence of expression. [ME *poete*, t. L: m. *poēta*, t. Gk: m. *po(i)ētēs* poet, maker]
poet., 1. poetic. 2. poetical. 3. poetry.
poetaster (pō′ĭ tăs′tə), *n.* an inferior poet; a writer of indifferent verse. [t. ML or NL. See POET, -ASTER]
poetess (pō′ĭ tĭs), *n.* a female poet.

poetic (pō ĕt′ĭk), *adj.* Also, **poetical.** **1.** possessing the qualities or the charm of poetry: *poetic descriptions of nature.* **2.** of or pertaining to a poet or poets. **3.** characteristic of or befitting a poet: *poetic feeling.* **4.** endowed with the faculty or feeling of a poet, as a person. **5.** having or showing the sensibility of a poet. **6.** of or pertaining to poetry: *poetic licence.* **7.** of the nature of poetry: *a poetic composition.* **8.** celebrated in poetry, as a place. **9.** affording a subject for poetry. **10.** of or pertaining to literature in verse form. —*n.* **11.** poetics. [t. L: s. *poēticus*, t. Gk: m. *po(i)ētikós*] —**poet′ically,** *adv.*

poetic justice, an ideal distribution of rewards and punishments such as is common in poetry and fiction.

poetic licence, licence or liberty taken by a poet in deviating from rule, conventional form, logic, or fact, in order to produce a desired effect.

poetics (pō ĕt′ĭks), *n.* **1.** literary criticism treating of the nature and laws of poetry. **2.** a treatise on poetry: *the 'Poetics' of Aristotle.*

poetize (pō′ĭ tīz′), *v.*, **-tized -tizing.** —*v.i.* **1.** to compose poetry. —*v.t.* **2.** to write about in poetry; express in poetic form. **3.** to make poetic: *he poetized his letter to her.* Also, **poetise.**

poet laureate, *pl.* **poets laureate.** **1.** (in Great Britain) an officer of the royal household, of whom no special duty is required, but who formerly was expected to write odes, etc., in celebration of court and national events. **2.** (formerly) a title given to any eminent poet.

poetry (pō′ĭ trĭ), *n.* **1.** the art of rhythmical composition, written or spoken, for exciting pleasure by beautiful, imaginative, or elevated thoughts. **2.** literary work in metrical form; verse. **3.** prose with poetic qualities. **4.** poetic qualities however manifested. **5.** poetic spirit or feeling. **6.** something suggestive of or likened to poetry. [ME *poetrie*, t. LL: m. *poētria*]

—**Syn.** **2.** POETRY, VERSE agree in referring to the work of a poet. The difference between POETRY and VERSE is usually the difference between substance and form. POETRY is lofty thought or impassioned feeling expressed in imaginative words: *Elizabethan poetry.* VERSE is any expression in words which conforms to accepted metrical rules and structure: *the differences between prose and verse.* —**Ant.** **2.** prose.

pogge (pŏg), *n.* a common small fish of the N Atlantic, *Agonus cataphractus*; the armed bullhead.

pogonia (pə gō′nyə), *n.* a plant of the genus *Pogonia*, comprising terrestrial orchids of North America. [t. NL, t. Gk: m. *pōgōnías* bearded (with reference to the frequently fringed lip)]

pogonophora (pŏg′ə nŏf′ə rə, pō′gə-), *n.* a phylum of wormlike sedentary invertebrates which have no alimentary canal and which live on the seabed.

pogo stick, (pō′gō), a metal stick on a spring, with handles at the top and footrests near the base, on which children jump up and down.

pogrom (pŏg′rəm), *n.* an organized massacre, esp. of Jews. [t. Russ.: devastation, destruction]

pogy (pō′gĭ, pŏg′ĭ), *n.*, *pl.* **-gies.** **1.** a porgy. **2.** a viviparous perch, *Holconotus rhodoterus*, caught in the surf of the West Coast of the U.S. **3.** the menhaden.

Pohai (pō′hī′), *n.* a NW arm of the Yellow Sea, forming a gulf on the NE coast of China.

pohutakawa (pə hoo′tə kä′wə), *n.* the New Zealand Christmas tree, *Metrosideros tomentosa*, having brilliant red flowers in summer. [t. Maori]

poi[1] (poi, pō′ĭ), *n.* a Hawaiian dish made of the root of the taro baked, pounded, moistened, and fermented.

poi[2] (poi), *n.* *N.Z.* a small light ball on a string, used by Maori women in ceremonial dances as the **Poi dance.** [t. Maori]

-poiesis, a word element meaning 'making', 'creation', 'genesis', as in *erythropoiesis.* [t. Gk: *poíēsis* act of making]

-poietic, a word element meaning 'productive', as in *haematopoietic.* [t. Gk: m. s. *poiētikós* creative, active]

poignant (poin′ənt, poi′nyənt), *adj.* **1.** keenly distressing to the mental or physical feelings: *poignant regret, poignant suffering.* **2.** keen or strong in mental appeal: *a subject of poignant interest.* **3.** pungent to the taste or smell. [ME *poynaunt*, t. OF: m. *poignant*, ppr. of *poindre*, g. L *pungere* prick, pierce. Cf. PUNGENT] —**poign′ancy,** *n.* —**poign′antly,** *adv.*

poikilothermal (poi′kĭ lō thû′məl), *adj.* *Zool.* having a body temperature that fluctuates with the temperature of the environment. [f. Gk *poikílo(s)* various + THERMAL]

poilu (pwä′loo; *Fr.* pwȧ lʏ′), *n.* a French common soldier. [t. F: hairy, der. *poil* hair, g. L *pilus*]

Poincaré (*Fr.* pwăɴ kȧ rĕ′), *n.* **1.** **Jules Henri** (*Fr.* zhʏl äɴ rē′), 1854–1912, French mathematician. **2.** his cousin, **Raymond** (*Fr.* rĕ mōɴ′), 1860–1934, French statesman; president of France 1913–20.

poinciana (poin′sĭ ä′nə), *n.* **1.** a plant of the caesalpiniaceous genus *Poinciana*, of the warmer parts of the world, comprising trees or shrubs with showy orange or scarlet flowers. **2.** a tree, *Delionix regia* (**royal poinciana**), native in Madagascar but now widely cultivated, remarkable for its showy scarlet flowers. [t. NL, named after M. de *Poinci*, governor of the French West Indies in the 17th century]

poind (poind), *Scot.* —*v.t.* **1.** to seize and sell property of a debtor under a warrant. **2.** to impound. —*n.* **3.** a distraint. [ME (Scot. d.) *pund, poynd*, OE *pyndan* enclose. See POUND[2], n.]

poinsettia (poin sĕt′ĭ ə), *n.* a euphorbiaceous perennial, *Euphorbia* (*Poinsettia*) *pulcherrima*, native to Mexico and Central America, with variously lobed leaves and brilliant scarlet bracts. [t. NL, named after J. R. *Poinsett*, 1779–1851, U.S. minister to Mexico, who discovered the plant there in 1828]

point (point), *n.* **1.** a sharp or tapering end, as of a dagger. **2.** a projecting part of anything. **3.** a tapering extremity, as a cape. **4.** something having a sharp or tapering end. **5.** a pointed tool or instrument, as an etching needle. **6.** a mark made as with the sharp end of something. **7.** a mark of punctuation. **8.** full stop. **9.** a decimal point, etc. **10** *Phonet., etc.* a diacritical mark indicating a vowel or other modification of sound. **11.** one of the embossed dots used in certain systems of writing and printing for the blind. **12.** something that has position but not extension, as the intersection of two lines. **13.** a place of which the position alone is considered; a spot. **14.** any definite position, as in a scale, course, etc.: *the boiling point.* **15.** **a.** each of the 32 positions indicating direction marked at the circumference of the card of a compass. **b.** the interval of 11° 15′ between any two adjacent positions. **16.** a degree or stage: *frankness to the point of insult.* **17.** a particular instant of time. **18.** critical position in a course of affairs. **19.** a decisive state of circumstances. **20.** the important or essential thing: *the point of the matter.* **21.** the salient feature of a story, epigram, joke, etc. **22.** a particular aim, end, or purpose: *he carried his point.* **23.** a hint or suggestion: *points on getting a job.* **24.** a single or separate article or item, as in an extended whole; a detail or particular. **25.** an individual part or element of something: *noble points in her character.* **26.** a distinguishing mark or quality, esp. one of an animal, used as a standard in stockbreeding, etc. **27.** (*pl.*) the extremities of a horse, pig, etc. **28.** a single unit, as in counting, measuring rations allowed, etc. **29.** a unit of count in the score of a game. **30.** *Cricket.* **a.** the position of the fielder who stands a short distance in front and to the offside of the batsman. **b.** the player himself. **31.** *Boxing.* the tip of the chin. **32.** *Hunting.* the position taken by a pointer or setter when it finds game. **33.** a branch of an antler of a deer. **34.** one of the narrow tapering spaces marked on a backgammon board. **35.** *Elect.* **a.** either of a pair of contacts tipped with tungsten or platinum that make or break current flow in a distributor. **b.** an outlet or socket. **36.** *Com.* a unit of price quotation in share transactions on the stock exchange: *copper advanced two points yesterday.* **37.** *Mil.* **a.** the stroke in bayonet drill or battle. **b.** *U.S.* a patrol or reconnaissance unit that goes ahead of the advance party of an advance guard, or follows the rear party of the rearguard. **38.** *Print.* a unit of measurement being about, 1/72 (0·0138 +) of an inch. **39.** a vaccine point. **40.** point lace. **41.** (*usually pl.*) *Railways.* a device for shifting moving trains, etc., from one track to another, commonly consisting of a pair of movable rails. **42.** the act of pointing. **43.** *Obs. or Rare.* an end or conclusion. **44.** *Obs.* condition. **45.** any lace made by hand. **46.** *Obs.* a pointed weapon, as a dagger. **47.** *Archaic.* a tagged ribbon or cord, formerly much used in dress, as for tying or fastening parts. **48.** Some special noun phrases are:

at, on, or **upon the point of,** close to; on the verge of.

in point, pertinent; relevant: *the case in point.*

in point of, as regards: *in point of fact.*

make a point of, to consider as important; insist upon.

off the point, not relevant.

stretch a point, to make a special concession; depart from the normal procedure.

to the point, pertinent; relevant.

[ME, t. OF (two words): *point* dot, mark, place, moment (g. L *punctum*) and *pointe* sharp end (g. L *puncta*); both L words prop. pp. forms of *pungere* prick, stab]

—*v.t.* **49.** to direct (the finger, a weapon, the attention, etc.) at, to, or upon something. **50.** to indicate the presence or position of, as with the finger (usually fol. by *out*). **51.** to direct attention to (fol. by *out*). **52.** to furnish with a point or points; sharpen. **53.** to mark with one or more points, dots, or the like. **54.** to punctuate, as writing. **55.** *Phonet., etc.* to mark (letters) with points. **56.** to

separate (figures) by dots or points (usually fol. by *off*). **57.** to give point or force to (speech, action, etc.). **58.** *Hunting.* (of a pointer or setter) to indicate game by standing rigid, with the muzzle usually directed towards it. **59.** to fill the joints of (brickwork, etc.) with mortar or cement, smoothed with the point of the trowel.
—*v.i.* **60.** to indicate position or direction, or direct attention, with or as with the finger. **61.** to direct the mind or thought in some direction: *everything points to his guilt.* **62.** to aim. **63.** to have a tendency, as towards something. **64.** to have a specified direction. **65.** to face in a particular direction, as a building. **66.** *Hunting.* (of a pointer or setter) to point game. **67.** *Naut.* to sail close to the wind. **68.** (of an abscess) to come to a head. [ME, t. OF: m. *pointer*, der. *point(e)*, n.]

point-blank (point′ blăngk′), *adj.* **1.** aimed or fired straight at the mark at close range; direct. **2.** straightforward, plain, or explicit. —*adv.* **3.** with a direct aim at close range; directly; straight. **4.** bluntly. [f. POINT, v. + BLANK (def. 17)]

point d'appui (*Fr.* pwăN dȧ pwē′), *French.* **1.** a prop; a stay **2.** *Mil.* a point of support for a battle line.

point-device (point′dĭ vīs′), *Archaic.* —*adv.* **1.** completely; perfectly; exactly. —*adj.* **2.** perfect; precise; scrupulously nice or neat. [ME *at poynt devys* (cf. OF or AF *devis* devised, arranged). See POINT, DEVISE]

point duty, traffic control by a policeman at a road junction, etc.

pointed (poin′tĭd), *adj.* **1.** having a point or points: *a pointed arch.* **2.** sharp or piercing: *pointed wit.* **3.** having point or force: *pointed comment.* **4.** directed; aimed. **5.** directed particularly, as at a person. **6.** marked; emphasized. —**point′edly,** *adv.* —**point′edness,** *n.*

pointed fox, a red fox fur having badger hairs glued to the fur near the skin, in order to simulate silver fox.

pointer (poin′tə), *n.* **1.** one who or that which points. **2.** a long, tapering stick used by teachers, lecturers, etc., in pointing things out on a map, blackboard, or the like. **3.** the hand on a watch, machine, or instrument. **4.** one of a breed of short-haired hunting dogs trained to point game. **5.** a hint or suggestion; piece of advice. **6.** (*cap., pl.*) *Astron.* the two outer stars of the Great Bear, the line joining which points towards the Pole Star. **7.** *U.S. Mil. and Naval.* one whose function is to control the aim, elevation, etc., of a gun.

Pointer
(Ab. 2 ft high at the shoulder)

pointillism (pwăn′tĭ lĭz′əm, poin′tĭ lĭz′əm), *n.* a method of painting in which luminosity is produced by laying on the colours in points or small dots of unmixed colour in close proximity, which are then fused by the eye into an optical mixture of their constituents. [t. F: m. *pointillisme*, der. *pointiller* mark with points] —**poin′tillist,** *n.*

pointing (poin′tĭng), *n. Music.* (in psalm-singing) a method of showing how to fit irregular lines to a regular tune.

point lace, lace made with a needle rather than with bobbins; needle point.

pointless (point′lĭs), *adj.* **1.** without a point. **2.** blunt, as an instrument. **3.** without force, meaning, or relevance, as a remark. **4.** without a point scored, as in a game. —**point′lessly,** *adv.* —**point′lessness,** *n.*

point of honour, something that affects one's honour, reputation, etc.

point of order, *Parl. Proc.* a question raised as to whether proceedings are in order, or in conformity with parliamentary law.

point of view, 1. a point from which things are viewed. **2.** a mental position or viewpoint.

point shoe, blocked shoe.

pointsman (points′mən), *n.* **1.** one in charge of railway points. **2.** a policeman on point duty.

point source, *Physics.* the theoretical concept of a source of radiation which emanates from a point.

point system, 1. *Print.* a system for grading the sizes of type bodies, leads, etc., which employs the point as a unit of measurement. See **point** (def. 38). **2.** any of certain systems of writing and printing for the blind which employ embossed symbols for letters, etc.

point-to-point (point′tə point′), *n.* a cross-country horse race from one specified place to another.

poise[1] (poiz), *n.*, *v.*, **poised, poising.** —*n.* **1.** a state of balance or equilibrium, as from equality or equal distribution of weight; equipoise. **2.** composure; self-possession. **3.** steadiness; stability. **4.** suspense or indecision. **5.** the way of being poised, held, or carried. **6.** a state or position of hovering: *the poise of a bird in the air.* —*v.t.* **7.** to balance evenly; adjust, hold, or carry in equilibrium. **8.** to hold supported or raised, as in position for casting, using, etc.: *to poise a spear.* **9.** to hold or carry in a particular manner. **10.** *Obs.* to weigh. —*v.i.* **11.** to be balanced; rest in equilibrium. **12.** to hang supported or suspended. **13.** to hover, as a bird in the air. [late ME, t. OF: m. *peser* (OF 3rd pers. sing. pres. ind. *poise*), g. L *pensāre*, freq. of *pendere* weigh]

poise[2] (pwäz), *n. Phys. Chem.* a unit of viscosity in the centimetre-gram-second system, defined as the tangential force per unit area required to maintain unit difference in velocity between two parallel planes separated by one centimetre of fluid. [named after J. L. M. *Poiseuille*, 1799–1869, French physician]

poised (poizd), *adj.* **1.** self-possessed; self-assured; confident; dignified. **2.** in a state of balance or equilibrium. **3.** wavering. **4.** hovering; suspended.

poison (poi′zən), *n.* **1.** any substance (liquid, solid, or gaseous) which by reason of an inherent deleterious property tends to destroy life or impair health. **2.** anything harmful, fatal, baneful, or highly pernicious, as to character, happiness, or well-being: *the poison of slander.* **3.** *Physics.* a substance which absorbs neutrons in a nuclear reactor, either added deliberately or formed as a fission product. —*v.t.* **4.** to administer poison to (a person or animal). **5.** to kill or injure with poison, or as poison does. **6.** to put poison into or upon; impregnate with poison: *to poison food.* **7.** to ruin, vitiate, or corrupt: *to poison the mind.* **8.** *Phys. Chem.* to destroy or diminish the activity of (a catalyst, enzyme, or a nuclear reaction). —*adj.* **9.** poisonous; causing poisoning. [ME, t. OF: potion, draught, poison, g. L *pōtio.* See POTION] —**poi′soner,** *n.*

—**Syn. 1.** POISON, TOXIN, VENOM, VIRUS are terms for any substance that injures the health or destroys life when absorbed into the system, esp. of a higher animal. POISON is the general word: *a poison for insects.* A TOXIN is a poison produced in animal tissues by the action of micro-organisms; it is a medical term for the albuminous secretion of microbes, which causes certain diseases: *a toxin produces diphtheria.* VENOM is esp. used of the poisons secreted by certain animals, usually injected by bite or sting: *the venom of a snake.* VIRUS is a medical term for the active organic element or poison which infects with and produces contagious disease: *the virus of scarlet fever.*

poison dogwood, poison sumac. Also, **poison elder.**

poison gas, any of various toxic gases, esp. those used in warfare, as chlorine, phosgene, etc.

poison ivy, any of several North American shrubs of the anacardiaceous genus *Rhus*, or *Toxicodendron*, poisonous to the touch, with shiny trifoliate leaves, green flowers, and whitish berries, esp. a climbing species, *R. radicans*, growing on fences, rocks, trees, etc.

poison oak, 1. any of several shrubs of the genus *Rhus* (or *Toxicodendron*). **2.** poison sumac. **3.** common poison ivy.

poisonous (poi′zə nəs), *adj.* **1.** full of or containing poison. **2.** having the properties or effects of a poison. **3.** unpleasant; offensive. —**poi′sonously,** *adv.* —**poi′sonousness,** *n.*

poison-pen (poi′zən pĕn′), *adj.* denoting a letter, note, etc., usually anonymous, sent with malicious intent.

poison sumach, a highly poisonous N American shrub or small tree, *Rhus* (or *Toxicodendron*) *vernix*, a sumach with pinnate leaves and whitish berries, growing in swamps.

Poisson distribution (*Fr.* pwȧ sôN′), *Statistics.* a limiting form of the binomial probability distribution for small values of the probability of success and for large numbers of trials. It is particularly useful in industrial quality-control work and in radiation and bacteriological problems. [named after Siméon Denis *Poisson*, 1781–1840, French mathematician]

Poisson's ratio (pwä′sənz), *Physics.* an elastic constant of a material, defined as the ratio of lateral strain to the longitudinal strain.

Poitiers (*Fr.* pwȧ tyĕ′), *n.* a city in W France, the capital of Vienne department: Roman ruins; battles A.D. 507, 732, 1356. 62,178 (1962).

Poitou (*Fr.* pwȧ to͞o′), *n.* **1.** a former province in W France. *Cap.:* Poitiers. **2. Gate of,** a wide pass near Poitiers.

Poitou-Charente (*Fr.* pwȧ to͞o shȧ räNt′), *n.* an administrative region in W France comprising the departments of Vienne, Deux-Sèvres, Charente, and Charente-Maritime. 1,451,292 pop. (1962); 10,144 sq. mi. *Cap.:* Poitiers.

poke[1] (pōk), *v.*, **poked, poking,** *n.* —*v.t.* **1.** to thrust against or into (something) with the finger or arm, a stick, etc.; prod: *to poke a person in the ribs.* **2.** to make (a hole, one's way, etc.) by or as by thrusting. **3.** to thrust or push: *he poked his head through the door.* **4.** to force or drive (*away, in, out*, etc.) by or as by thrusting or pushing.

5. to thrust obtrusively. —*v.i.* **6.** to make a thrusting or pushing movement with the finger, a stick, etc. **7.** to extend or project; protrude (often fol. by *out*). **8.** to thrust oneself obtrusively. **9.** to pry; search curiously (often fol. by *about* or *around*). **10. poke fun at,** to ridicule or mock, esp. covertly or slyly. **11. poke one's nose into,** to interfere; pry; show too much curiosity. —*n.* **12.** a thrust or push. [ME *poken*, c. LG and D *poken*. Cf. POACH[1]]

poke[2] (pōk), *n.* **1.** *Now Chiefly Dial.* a bag or sack. **2.** *Archaic.* a pocket. **3. to buy a pig in a poke.** See **pig** (def. 6). [ME *poke*, c. MD *poke*; akin to OE *pocca*, *pohha* pocket, bag. Cf. ONF *poke* (t. D) and *pouche* POUCH]

poke[3] (pōk), *n.* **1.** a projecting brim at the front of a woman's bonnet or hat. **2.** a bonnet (**poke bonnet**) or hat with such a brim. [appar. special use of POKE[1]]

Poke[3] (def. 2)

poke[4] (pōk), *n.* pokeweed. [t. Algonquian (Virginia): m. *puccoon* plant used in dyeing]

pokeberry (pōk′bə rĭ, -brĭ), *n.*, *pl.* **-ries. 1.** the berry of the pokeweed. **2.** the plant. [f. POKE[4] + BERRY]

poker[1] (pō′kə), *n.* **1.** one who or that which pokes. **2.** a metal rod for poking or stirring a fire. [f. POKE[1], v. + -ER[1]]

poker[2] (pō′kə), *n.* a card game played by two or more persons, in which the players bet on the value of their hands, the winner taking the pool. [orig. uncert. Cf. G *Pochspiel*, a similar game, der. *pochen* POKE[1]]

poker dice, 1. dice marked on their faces with symbols representing the six highest playing cards instead of spots. **2.** any of various gambling games played with such dice.

poker face, *Colloq.* an expressionless face. —**poker-faced** (pō′kə fāst′), *adj.*

pokerwork (pō′kə wûk′), *n.* ornamentation of wood by burning a design into it with a heated point.

pokeweed (pōk′wēd′), *n.* a tall herb, *Phytolacca americana*, of North America, having juicy purple berries and a purple root used in medicine, and young edible shoots resembling asparagus. Also, **pokeroot** (pōk′ro͞ot′), **poke.** [f. POKE[4] + WEED[1]]

poky (pō′kĭ), *adj.*, **-kier, -kiest. 1.** (of a person) pottering; concerned with petty matters. **2.** (of a place) small and cramped. [f. POKE[1] + -Y[1]]

Pol., 1. Poland. **2.** Polish.

pol., 1. political. **2.** politics.

Pola (pō′lə; *It.* pô′lȧ), *n.* Italian name of **Pula.**

polacca[1] (pə lăk′ə), *n.* any of various three-masted sailing vessels, formerly used in the Mediterranean. Also, **polac′re.**

polacca[2] (pə lăk′ə), *n.* a Polish dance in 3/4 time; a polonaise.

Polack (pō′lăk), *n.* **1.** (in contemptuous use) a person of Polish descent. **2.** *Archaic.* a Pole.

Poland (pō′lənd), *n.* a republic in central Europe. 31,340,000 pop. (est. 1965); 120,359 sq. mi. *Cap.:* Warsaw. Polish, **Polska.** See map under **Baltic.**

Poland China, one of an American breed of black pigs with white markings.

polar (pō′lə), *adj.* **1.** of or pertaining to a pole, as of the earth, a magnet, an electric cell, etc. **2.** opposite in character or action. **3.** existing as ions; ionized. **4.** central. **5.** analogous to the Pole Star as a guide; guiding. [t. ML: s. *polāris*, der. L *polus* POLE[2]]

polar axis, a line about which a body rotates, or about which a rotation is measured.

polar bear, a large white bear, *Thalarctos maritimus*, of the arctic regions.

Polar bear, *Thalarctos maritimus* (7 to 8 ft long)

polar body, *Biol.* one of the minute cells arising by the very unequal meiotic divisions of the ovum at or near the time of fertilization.

polar circles, the Arctic and Antarctic circles.

polar coordinates, *Maths.* a system of plane coordinates in which the position of a point is determined by the length of its radius vector from a fixed origin and the angle this vector makes with a fixed line.

polar distance, *Astron.* codeclination.

polar front, the transition region, or belt, between the cold polar easterly winds and the relatively warm southwesterly winds of the middle latitudes.

polarimeter (pō′lə rĭm′ĭ tə), *n.* **1.** an instrument for measuring the amount of polarized light, or the extent of polarization, in the light received from a given source. **2.** a form of polariscope for measuring the angular rotation of the plane of polarization. [f. ML *polāri(s)* polar + -METER[1]]

Polaris (pō lä′rĭs, pō lă′rĭs), *n.* **1.** *Astron.* the Pole Star. **2.** a U.S. intermediate-range ballistic missile developed for firing from a submarine. [short for ML *stella polāris* polar star]

polariscope (pō lă′rĭ skōp′), *n.* an instrument for exhibiting or measuring the polarization of light, or for examining substances in polarized light.

polarity (pō lă′rĭ tĭ), *n.* **1.** *Physics.* **a.** the possession of an axis with reference to which certain physical properties are determined; the possession of two poles. **b.** the power or tendency of a magnetized bar, etc., to orientate itself along the lines of force. **c.** positive or negative polar condition. **2.** the possession or exhibition of two opposite or contrasted principles or tendencies.

polarization (pō′lə rī zā′shən), *n.* **1.** *Optics.* a state, or the production of a state, in which rays of light, or similar radiation, exhibit different properties in different directions, e.g. when they are passed through a crystal of tourmaline, which transmits rays in which the vibrations are confined to a single plane. **2.** *Elect.* the process by which gases produced during electrolysis are deposited on the electrodes of a cell. **3.** *Chem.* the separation of a molecule into positive and negative ions. **4.** the production or acquisition of polarity. Also, **polarisation.**

polarize (pō′lə rīz′), *v.*, **-rized, -rizing.** —*v.t.* **1.** to cause polarization in. **2.** to give polarity to. —*v.i.* **3.** to become polarized. Also, **polarise.** [f. POLAR + -IZE] —**po′lariz′able,** *adj.* —**po′lariz′er,** *n.*

polar lights, the aurora borealis or the aurora australis.

polar molecule, *Chem.* a molecule which has a permanent electric dipole as a result of the configuration of the electric charges within it.

polarograph (pō lă′rə grăf′, -gräf′), *n.* an instrument that automatically measures and records the concentration, solubility, constituents, equilibrium, etc., of an electrolytic solution.

Polaroid (pō′lə roid′), *n. Trademark.* a material which polarizes light, consisting of a pane compounded of a sheet of plastic holding orientated iodo-quinine crystals between two panes of protecting glass.

polar regions, the regions within the Arctic and Antarctic circles.

polder (pōl′də, pŏl′də), *n.* a tract of low land, esp. in the Netherlands, reclaimed from the sea or other body of water and protected by dykes. [t. D]

pole[1] (pōl), *n.*, *v.*, **poled, poling.** —*n.* **1.** a long, rounded, usually slender piece of wood, metal, etc. **2.** the long tapering piece of wood extending from the front axle of a vehicle, between the animals drawing it. **3.** *Naut.* a light spar. **4.** a unit of length equal to 16½ ft; a rod. **5.** a square rod, 30¼ sq. yds. **6.** the lane of a race track nearest the inner boundary. **7. under bare poles,** *Naut.* (of a sailing ship) having all sails furled. **8. up the pole,** *Colloq.* **a.** in a predicament. **b.** slightly mad. —*v.t.* **9.** to furnish with poles. **10.** to push, strike, propel, etc., with a pole. **11.** *Metall.* to stir (a molten bath or copper) with green wood poles, thus introducing carbon which reacts with the oxygen present to effect deoxidization. —*v.i.* **12.** to propel a boat, etc., with a pole. [ME; OE *pāl*, t. L: s. *pālus* stake. Cf. PALE[2]]

pole[2] (pōl), *n.* **1.** each of the extremities of the axis of the earth or of any more or less spherical body. **2.** each of the two points in which the extended axis of the earth cuts the celestial sphere, about which the stars seem to revolve (**celestial pole**). **3.** *Physics.* each of the two regions or parts of a magnet, electric battery, etc., at which certain opposite forces are manifested or appear to be concentrated. **4.** *Biol.* **a.** either end of an ideal axis in a nucleus, cell, or ovum, about which parts are more or less symmetrically arranged. **b.** either end of a spindle-shaped figure formed in a cell during mitosis. **5.** *Anat.* the point in a nerve cell where a process forming an axis cylinder begins. **6.** one of two completely opposed or contrasted principles, tendencies, etc. **7. poles apart,** having completely opposite or widely divergent views, interests, etc. [ME *pol*, t. L: s. *polus*, t. Gk: m. *pólos* pivot, axis, pole]

Pole (pōl), *n.* a native or inhabitant of Poland. [t. G, sing. of *Polen*, t. Pol.: m. *Poljane* Poles, lit., field-dwellers, der. *pole* field]

Pole (pōl), *n.* **Reginald,** 1500–58, English cardinal and last Roman Catholic archbishop of Canterbury.

poleaxe (pōl′ăks′), *n.*, *v.*, **-axed, -axing.** —*n.* **1.** a medieval shafted weapon with blade combining axe, hammer, and apical spike, used for fighting on foot. **2.** an axe, usually with a hammer opposite the cutting edge, used in felling or stunning animals. **3.** an axe formerly much used in naval warfare, to help in boarding vessels, cutting rigging, etc. —*v.t.* **4.** to fell with a poleaxe. Also, *U.S.*, **poleax.** [ME *pollax*, lit., head-axe. Cf. MLG *polexe* and see POLL[1] (def. 10)]

Polecat, *Mustela putorius*
(Body 1½ ft long, tail 7 in. long)

polecat (pōl′kăt′), *n.* **1.** a European mammal, *Mustela putorius*, of the weasel family, having blackish brown fur, and giving off an offensive smell. **2.** any of various North American skunks. [ME *polcat*; *pol-* of uncert. orig.]

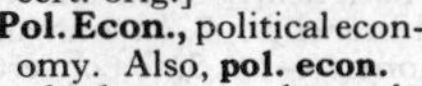

Pol. Econ., political economy. Also, **pol. econ.**

pole horse, a horse harnessed alongside the pole of a vehicle; a poler; wheeler.

pole jump, pole vault.

pole-jump (pōl′jŭmp′), *v.i.* pole-vault. —**pole′-jump′-er,** *n.*

polemic (pŏ lĕm′ĭk), *n.* **1.** a controversial argument; argumentation against some opinion, doctrine, etc. **2.** one who argues in opposition to another; a controversialist. —*adj.* **3.** Also, **polem′ical.** of or pertaining to disputation or controversy; controversial. [t. Gk: m. s. *polemikós* of or for war] —**polem′ically,** *adv.*

polemics (pŏ lĕm′ĭks), *n.* the art or practice of disputation or controversy, esp. in theology.

polemist (pŏl′ĭ mĭst), *n.* one engaged or versed in polemics. Also, **polemicist** (pŏ lĕm′ĭ sĭst).

polemoniaceous (pŏl′ĭ mō′nĭ ā′shəs), *adj.* belonging to the *Polemoniaceae*, a family of plants including the Jacob's-ladder, phlox, etc. [f. s. NL *Polemōnium*, the typical genus (t. Gk: m. *polemṓnion* kind of plant) + -ACEOUS]

polenta (pŏ lĕn′tə), *n.* a thick porridge eaten in Italy, usually made from maize. [t. It., g. L: pearl barley]

poler (pō′lə), *n.* **1.** one who or that which poles. **2.** a pole horse.

Pole Star (pōl′stä′), **1.** *Astron.* Also, **North Star, Polaris.** a star of the second magnitude situated close to the north pole of the heavens, in the constellation Ursa Minor. **2.** (*l.c.*) a centre of attraction. **3.** (*l.c.*) a guiding principle.

pole vault, *Sport.* a leap over a horizontal bar with the help of a long pole.

pole-vault (pōl′vôlt′), *v.i.* to execute a pole vault. —**pole′-vault′er,** *n.*

police (pə lēs′), *n.*, *v.*, **-liced, -licing.** —*n.* **1.** an organized civil force for maintaining order, preventing and detecting crime, and enforcing the laws. **2.** (*construed as pl.*) the members of such a force. **3.** the regulation and control of a community, esp. with reference to the maintenance of public order, safety, health, morals, etc. **4.** the department of the government concerned with this, esp. with the maintenance of order. **5.** any body of men officially maintained or employed to keep order, enforce regulations, etc. **6.** *Mil.* (in the U.S. Army) **a.** the cleaning and keeping clean of a camp, post, station, etc. **b.** the condition of a camp, post, station, etc., with reference to cleanliness. —*v.t.* **7.** to regulate, control, or keep in order by police or as a police force does. **8.** *U.S. Mil.* to clean and keep clean (a camp, etc.). [t. F: government, civil administration, police, t. ML: m. *polītia*, var. of L *polītia* POLITY. Cf. POLICY[1]]

police constable, a policeman of the lowest regular rank.

police court, magistrates' court.

police dog, any dog used or trained to assist the police.

policeman (pə lēs′mən), *n.*, *pl.* **-men.** a member of a body or force of police. —**police′wom′an,** *n. fem.*

police state, a country in which the police, esp. the secret police, are employed to detect and suppress any form of opposition to the government in power.

police station, the headquarters of a local police force.

policy[1] (pŏl′ĭ sĭ), *n.*, *pl.* **-cies.** **1.** a definite course of action adopted as expedient or from other considerations: *a business policy.* **2.** a course or line of action adopted and pursued by a government, ruler, political party, or the like: *the foreign policy of a country.* **3.** action or procedure conforming to, or considered with reference to, prudence or expediency: *it was good policy to consent.* **4.** prudence, practical wisdom, or expediency. **5.** sagacity; shrewdness. **6.** *Rare.* government; polity. **7.** (in Scotland) the grounds around a country house. [ME *policie*, t. OF: government, civil administration, t. L: m. *polītia* POLITY Cf. POLICE]

policy[2] (pŏl′ĭ sĭ), *n.*, *pl.* **-cies.** **1.** a document embodying a contract of insurance. **2.** *U.S.* a method of gambling in which bets are made on numbers to be drawn by lottery. [t. F: m. *police*, t. It.: m. *polizza*, g. ML *apodixa*, ult. t. Gk: m. *apódeixis* a showing or setting forth]

policyholder (pŏl′ĭ sĭ hōl′də), *n.* the person in whose name an insurance policy is written; the insured.

poling board, one of a row of vertical planks, held in position by a wale, used to hold back the earth in an excavation.

polio (pō′lĭ ō), *n.* poliomyelitis.

poliomyelitis (pō′lĭ ō mī′ə lī′tĭs), *n.* *Pathol.* an acute viral disease, most common in infants but often attacking older children and even adults, characterized by inflammation of the nerve cells, mainly of the anterior horns of the spinal cord, and resulting in motor paralysis, followed by muscular atrophy, and often by permanent deformities. [t. NL, f. Gk: *polió(s)* grey + s. *myelós* marrow + *-ītis* -ITIS]

-polis, a word element meaning 'city', as in *metropolis* (lit., 'the mother city'). [t. Gk, comb. form of *pólis*]

polish (pŏl′ĭsh), *v.t.* **1.** to make smooth and glossy, esp. by friction: *to polish metal.* **2.** to render finished, refined or elegant: *his speech needs polishing.* **3.** to take or bring to a different state by smoothing or refining (often fol. by *away*, *off*, *out*, etc.). **4.** *Slang.* to finish, or dispose of quickly (fol. by *off*): *to polish off an opponent.* **5.** *Colloq.* to improve (fol. by *up*). —*v.i.* **6.** to become smooth and glossy; take on a polish. **7.** *Archaic.* to become refined or elegant. —*n.* **8.** a substance used to give smoothness or gloss: *shoe polish.* **9.** the act of polishing. **10.** the state of being polished. **11.** smoothness and gloss of surface. **12.** superior or elegant finish imparted; refinement; elegance: *the polish of literary style.* [ME *polische(n)*, t. F: m. *poliss-*, s. *polir*, g. L *polīre*] —**pol′isher,** *n.*

—**Syn.** **11.** POLISH, GLOSS, LUSTRE, SHEEN refer to a smooth, shining or bright surface from which light is reflected. POLISH suggests the smooth and shining quality given to a surface by friction: *a high polish on a varnished surface.* GLOSS suggests a superficial, hard smoothness such as characterizes a lacquered surface: *a gloss on oilcloth.* LUSTRE denotes the characteristic quality of the light reflected from the surfaces of certain materials (pearls, silk, wax, freshly cut metals, etc.): *an opaline lustre.* SHEEN, sometimes poetical, is a glistening brightness such as that reflected from the surface of silk or velvet, or from furniture oiled and hand-polished: *a rich velvety sheen.*

Polish (pō′lĭsh), *adj.* **1.** of or pertaining to Poland, its inhabitants, or their language. —*n.* **2.** a Slavic language, the principal language of Poland.

Polish Corridor, 1938

Polish Corridor, a strip of land near the mouth of the river Vistula, formerly separating Germany from East Prussia: given to Poland in the Treaty of Versailles 1919 to provide her with access to the Baltic.

polished (pŏl′ĭsht), *adj.* **1.** made smooth and glossy. **2.** naturally smooth and glossy. **3.** refined, cultured, or elegant. **4.** flawless or excellent. **5.** (of rice) milled, so that the husk, etc., is removed.

polit., **1.** political. **2.** politics.

Politburo (pŏ lĭt′byo͝oə rō′), *n.* a former committee in the Communist Party of the Soviet Union, which examined every question before it was referred to the government, and sometimes issued orders independently.

polite (pə līt′), *adj.* **1.** showing good manners towards others, as in behaviour, speech, etc.; courteous; civil: *a polite reply.* **2.** refined or cultured: *polite society.* **3.** of a refined or elegant kind: *polite learning.* [late ME, t. L: m. s. *polītus*, pp., polished] —**polite′ly,** *adv.* —**polite′ness,** *n.* —**Syn.** **1.** well-bred, gracious. See **civil.**

polit. econ., political economy.

politesse (pŏl′ĭ tĕs′; *Fr.* pō lĕ tĕs′), *n.* *Now chiefly as French.* politeness. [F, t. It.: m. *pulitezza*, der. *pulito* polished, pp. of *pulire*, g. L *polīre*]

Politian (pŏ lĭsh′ən), *n.* (*Angelo Poliziano*), 1454–94, Italian classical scholar, teacher, and poet.

politic (pŏl′ĭ tĭk), *adj.* **1.** sagacious; prudent. **2.** shrewd; artful. **3.** expedient; judicious. **4.** political (now chiefly in *body politic*, which see). [ME, t. L: s. *politicus*, t. Gk: m. *polītikós* pertaining to citizens or to the state] —**pol′iticly,** *adv.* —**Syn.** **1.** See **diplomatic.**

political (pə lĭt′ĭ kl), *adj.* **1.** pertaining to or dealing with the science or art of politics: *political writers.* **2.** pertaining to or connected with a political party, or its principles, aims, activities, etc.: *a political campaign.*

3. exercising or seeking power in the governmental or public affairs of a state, municipality, or the like: *a political party.* **4.** of or pertaining to the state or its government: *political measures.* **5.** affecting or involving the state of government: *a political offence.* **6.** engaged in or connected with civil administration: *political office.* **7.** having a definite policy or system of government: *a political community.* **8.** of or pertaining to citizens: *political rights.* —**polit′ically,** *adv.*

political economy, **1.** a social science dealing with the relationship between political and economic policies and their influence on social institutions. **2.** (in the 17th and 18th centuries) the control of society, especially with regard to the wealth of a government. **3.** (in the 19th century) a social science similar to modern economics, but concerned mainly with social policy.

political science, the science of politics, or of the principles and conduct of government.

politician (pŏl′ĭ tĭsh′ən), *n.* **1.** one who is active in party politics. **2.** one skilled in political government or administration; a statesman. **3.** one who holds a political office. **4.** *U.S.* a seeker or holder of public office who is more concerned to win favour or to retain power than to maintain principles. **5.** one who seeks power or advancement within an organization by unscrupulous or dishonest means. **6.** *Now Rare.* an expert in politics or political government.
—**Syn. 2.** POLITICIAN, STATESMAN refer to one skilled in politics. These terms differ particularly in their connotations; POLITICIAN is more often derogatory, and STATESMAN laudatory. POLITICIAN may suggest the schemes and devices of one who engages in (esp. small) politics for party ends or his own advantage: *a scheming politician.* STATESMAN suggests the eminent ability, foresight, and unselfish devotion to the interests of his country of one dealing with (esp. important or great) affairs of state: *a distinguished statesman.*

politicize (pə lĭt′ĭ sīz′), *v.,* **-cized, -cizing.** —*v.t.* **1.** to make political. —*v.i.* **2.** to engage in, or talk about politics. Also, **politicise.**

politico (pə lĭt′ĭ kō′), *n., pl.* **-cos.** *Chiefly U.S.* a politician. [t. It. or Sp.]

politico-, a word element meaning 'political', used in combination, as in *politico-military* (political and military), *politico-religious, politico-social.* [comb. form repr. Gk *politikós*]

politics (pŏl′ĭ tĭks), *n.* (*construed as sing. or pl.*) **1.** the science or art of political government. **2.** the practice or profession of conducting political affairs. **3.** political affairs. **4.** political methods or manoeuvres. **5.** political principles or opinions. **6.** the use of underhand or unscrupulous methods in obtaining power or advancement within an organization.

polity (pŏl′ĭ tĭ), *n., pl.* **-ties.** **1.** a particular form or system of government (civil, ecclesiastical, or other). **2.** the condition of being constituted as a state or other organized community or body. **3.** government or administrative regulation. **4.** a state or other organized community or body. [t. F (obs.): m. *politie,* t. L: m. *polītia,* t. Gk: m. *polīteia* citizenship, government, form of government, commonwealth]

polje (pŏl′yĕ), *n., pl.* **polja** (pŏl′yə). *Geol.* (in limestone country or karst regions) an extensive elliptical depression, usually flat-floored and sometimes having a small lake or marsh. [t. Serbo-Croat: lit., field]

Polk (pōk), *n.* **James Knox,** 1795–1849, the 11th president of the United States, 1845–49.

polka (pŏl′kə), *n., v.,* **-kaed, -kaing.** —*n.* **1.** a lively round dance of Bohemian origin, with music in duple time. **2.** a piece of music for such a dance or in its rhythm. —*v.i.* **3.** to dance the polka. [t. F and G, t. Czech: m. *pulka* half-step]

polka dot, **1.** a dot or round spot (printed, woven, or embroidered) repeated to form a pattern on a textile fabric. **2.** a pattern of, or a fabric with such dots.

poll[1] (pōl), *n.* **1.** the registering of votes, as at an election. **2.** the voting at an election. **3.** the number of votes cast. **4.** the numerical result of the voting. **5.** an enumeration or a list of individuals, as for purposes of taxing or voting. **6.** (*usually pl.*) the place where votes are taken. **7.** a poll tax. **8.** a person or individual in a number or list. **9.** an analysis of public opinion on a subject, usually by selective sampling. **10.** the head, esp. the part of it on which the hair grows. **11.** the back of the head. **12.** the broad end or face of a hammer. —*v.t.* **13.** to receive at the polls, as votes. **14.** to enrol in a list or register, as for purposes of taxing or voting. **15.** to take or register the votes of, as persons. **16.** to deposit or cast at the polls, as a vote. **17.** to bring to the polls, as voters. **18.** to cut off or cut short the hair, etc., of (a person, etc.); crop; clip; shear. **19.** to cut off or cut short (hair, etc.). **20.** to cut off the top of (a tree, etc.); pollard. **21.** to cut off or cut short the horns of (cattle). —*v.i.* **22.** to vote at the polls; give one's vote. [ME *pol(le),* c. MD and LG *polle.* Cf. d. Sw. *pull* crown of the head, Dan. *puld*] —**poll′able,** *adj.*

poll[2] (pŏl), *n.* a parrot.

poll[3] (pŏl), *n.* (formerly at Cambridge University) **1.** the body of students who read for or obtained a degree without honours. **2.** Also, **poll degree.** the degree so awarded; pass degree. [appar. t. Gk: s. *polloí,* in *hoi polloí* the many]

pollack (pŏl′ək), *n., pl.* **-acks,** (*esp. collectively*) **-ack.** a darkly coloured North Atlantic food fish, *Pollachius virens,* of the cod family. Also, **pollock.** [Scot. d. *podlock,* of unknown orig.]

Pollaiuolo (*It.* pŏl lāy wŏ′lŏ), *n.* **1. Antonio** (*It.* än tŏ′nyŏ), *c.* 1432–98, Italian painter, sculptor, engraver, and goldsmith. **2.** his brother, **Piero** (*It.* pyĕ′rŏ), *c.* 1441–96, Italian painter, sculptor, and goldsmith. Also, **Pollaiolo, Pollajuolo.**

pollard (pŏl′əd), *n.* **1.** a tree cut back nearly to the trunk, so as to produce a dense mass of branches. **2.** an animal, as a stag, ox, or sheep, without horns. —*v.t.* **3.** to convert into a pollard. [appar. f. POLL[1], v. + -ARD]

polled (pōld), *adj.* hornless, as the Aberdeen Angus.

pollen (pŏl′ĭn), *n.* **1.** the fertilizing element of flowering plants, consisting of fine, powdery, yellowish grains or spores, sometimes in masses. —*v.t.* **2.** to pollinate. [t. L: fine flour, dust]

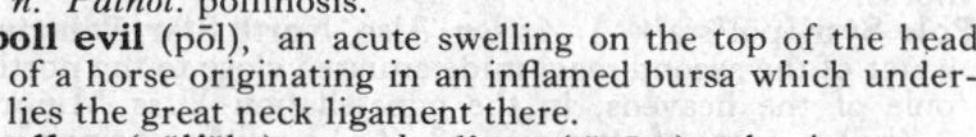

Grains of pollen
A, Evening primrose, *Oenothera biennis*; B, Scots pine, *Pinus sylvestris*; C, Chicory, *Cichorium intybus*; D, Hibiscus, *Hibiscus moscheutos*; E, Passionflower, *Passiflora caerulea*

pollen analysis, palynology.

pollen basket, an area on the leg of a bee adapted for carrying pollen.

pollen count, a measure of pollen in the air published as a guide to sufferers from hay fever.

pollenosis (pŏl′ĭ nō′sĭs), *n. Pathol.* pollinosis.

poll evil (pōl), an acute swelling on the top of the head of a horse originating in an inflamed bursa which underlies the great neck ligament there.

pollex (pŏl′ĕks), *n., pl.* **-lices** (-ĭ sēz′). the innermost digit of the forelimb; the thumb. [t. L: thumb]

pollinate (pŏl′ĭ nāt′), *v.t.,* **-nated, -nating.** *Bot.* to convey pollen for fertilization to; shed pollen on.

pollination (pŏl′ĭ nā′shən), *n. Bot.* the transfer of pollen from the anther to the stigma.

polling booth (pō′lĭng), a booth in which voters cast their votes.

polling day, the day appointed for the recording of votes in an election.

polling station, a place where voters go to record their votes in an election.

polliniferous (pŏl′ĭ nĭf′ə rəs), *adj.* **1.** *Bot.* producing or bearing pollen. **2.** *Zool.* fitted for carrying pollen. [f. s. L *pollen* dust + -I- + -FEROUS]

pollinium (pə lĭn′ĭ əm), *n., pl.* **-linia** (-lĭn′ĭ ə). *Bot.* an agglutinated mass or body of pollen grains, characteristic of orchidaceous and asclepiadaceous plants. [t. NL: f. s. L *pollen* dust + *-ium* -IUM]

pollinosis (pŏl′ĭ nō′sĭs), *n. Pathol.* hay fever. Also, **pollenosis.** [t. NL: f. s. L *pollen* dust + *-ōsis* -OSIS]

polliwog (pŏl′ĭ wŏg′), *n. U.S. and Dial.* a tadpole. Also, **pollywog.** [cf. ME *polwygle,* f. POLL[1] (def. 10) + WIGGLE]

pollock (pŏl′ək), *n.* pollack.

Pollock (pŏl′ək), *n.* **1. Jackson,** 1912–56, U.S. action painter. **2. Sir Frederick,** 1845–1937, English legal scholar and author.

pollster (pōl′stə), *n.* one whose occupation is the taking of public opinion polls.

poll tax, a capitation tax, the payment of which is a prerequisite to exercise of the right of suffrage.

poll-taxer (pōl′tăk′sə), *n. U.S. Slang.* **1.** an advocate of the poll tax. **2.** a congressman from a state having a poll tax.

pollutant (pə lo͞o′tənt), *n.* that which pollutes; a polluting agent.

pollute (pə lo͞ot′), *v.t.,* **-luted, -luting.** **1.** to make foul or unclean; dirty. **2.** to make morally unclean; defile. **3.** to render ceremonially impure; desecrate. [t. L: m. s. *pollūtus,* pp.] —**pollut′er,** *n.* —**pollution** (pə lo͞o′shən), *n.*

polluted (pə lo͞o′tĭd), *adj.* made impure or unclean; tainted; contaminated.

Pollux (pŏl′əks), *n.* **1.** *Gk Myth.* See **Castor and Pollux.**

2. *Astron.* the brightest star in the constellation Gemini. [t. L, t. Gk: m. *Polydeúkēs*]

pollywog (pŏl′ĭ wŏg′), *n.* polliwog.

polo (pō′lō), *n.* **1.** a game resembling hockey, played on horseback with long-handled mallets and a wooden ball. **2.** some game more or less resembling this, as water polo. [t. Baltī (language of Kashmir) c. Tibetan *pulu* ball] —**po′loist,** *n.*

Polo (pō′lō), *n.* **Marco** (mä′kō), *c.* 1254–*c.* 1324, Venetian traveller in Asia, esp. at the court of Kublai Khan.

polonaise (pŏl′ə nāz′), *n.* **1.** a slow dance of Polish origin, in triple rhythm, consisting chiefly of a march or promenade in couples. **2.** a piece of music for, or in the rhythm of, such a dance. **3.** a woman's overdress combining a bodice and a cutaway overskirt. [t. F: (fem.) Polish]

polo-neck (pō′lō nĕk′), *adj.* **1.** of or denoting a sweater, etc., having a closely fitting, doubled-over collar. —*n.* **2.** such a collar. **3.** a garment having such a collar.

polonium (pə lō′nyəm), *n.* *Chem.* a radioactive element discovered by Pierre and Marie Curie in 1898. *Symbol:* Po; *at. no.:* 84; *at. wt of most stable isotope:* 210. Also, **radium F.** [f. ML *Polon(ia)* Poland + -IUM]

Polska (*Pol.* pŏl′skȧ), *n.* Polish name of **Poland.**

Poltava (*Russ.* pȧl tȧ′və), *n.* a town in the SW Soviet Union in Europe: Russian defeat of Swedes 1709. 170,000 (est. 1965).

poltergeist (pŏl′tə gīst′), *n.* a ghost or spirit which manifests its presence by noises, knockings, movement of physical objects, etc. [t. G: lit., noise-ghost]

Poltoratsk (*Russ.* pəl tȧ rȧtsk′), *n.* former name of **Ashkhabad.**

poltroon (pŏl trōōn′), *n.* a wretched coward; a craven. [t. F: m. *poltron,* t. It.: m. *poltrone,* der. *poltro* lazy (as n., bed; cf. *poltrire* lie lazily in bed), t. Gmc; cf. OHG *polstar* BOLSTER]

poltroonery (pŏl trōō′nə rĭ), *n.* cowardice.

poly-, a word element or prefix, meaning 'much', 'many', first occurring in words from the Greek (as *polyandrous*), but now used freely as a general formative, esp. in scientific or technical words. Cf. **mono-.** [t. Gk, comb. form of *polýs* much, many; akin to L *plēnum* full, and to FULL[1]]

poly., polytechnic.

polyadelphous (pŏl′ĭ ə dĕl′fəs), *adj.* *Bot.* (of stamens) united by their filaments into three or more bundles or sets.

polyamide (pŏl′ĭ ăm′īd, -ĭd), *n.* *Chem.* any polymer in which the units are linked by amide or thio-amide groups.

polyandrous (pŏl′ĭ ăn′drəs), *adj.* **1.** of, pertaining to, or characterized by polyandry. **2.** *Bot.* having the stamens indefinitely numerous.

polyandry (pŏl′ĭ ăn′drĭ), *n.* **1.** the practice or the condition of having more than one husband at one time. **2.** *Bot.* the fact of being polyandrous. [t. Gk: m. s. *polyandria*]

polyanthus (pŏl′ĭ ăn′thəs), *n.* **1.** a hybrid primrose, *Primula polyantha.* **2.** a narcissus, *Narcissus tazetta,* in many varieties, bearing small white or yellow flowers. [t. NL, t. Gk: m. *polýanthos* having many flowers]

polybasic (pŏl′ĭ bā′sĭk), *adj.* *Chem.* (of an acid) having two or more atoms of replaceable hydrogen.

polybasite (pŏl′ĭ bā′sīt, pə lĭb′ə sīt′), *n.* a blackish mineral, Ag_9SbS_6: a minor ore of silver. [t. G: m. *Polybasit.* See POLY-, BASIS, -ITE[1]]

Polybius (pŏ lĭb′ĭ əs), *n.* *c.* 205–*c.* 123 B.C., Greek historian who wrote a history of Rome.

Polycarp (pŏl′ĭ kăp′), *n.* **Saint,** A.D. 69?–155, bishop of Smyrna and Christian martyr.

polycarpic (pŏl′ĭ kä′pĭk), *adj.* *Bot.* producing fruit many times a year or year after year. Also, **pol′ycar′pous.**

polychaete (pŏl′ĭ kēt′), *Zool.* —*n.* **1.** any of the *Polychaeta,* a group or division of annelids having unsegmented swimming appendages with many chaetae or bristles, and including most of the common marine worms. —*adj.* **2.** Also, **pol′ychae′tous.** pertaining to the polychaetes. [t. NL: m. s. *Polychaeta,* t. Gk: m. *polychaítēs* having much hair]

polychasium (pŏl′ĭ kā′zyəm), *n., pl.* **-sia** (-zyə). *Bot.* a form of cymose inflorescence in which each axis produces more than two lateral axes. [t. NL, f. *poly-* POLY- + s. Gk *chásis* separation + *-ium* -IUM]

polychromatic (pŏl′ĭ krō măt′ĭk), *adj.* having many colours; exhibiting a variety of colours. Also, **polychromic** (pŏl′ĭ krō′mĭk). —**polychromatism** (pŏl′ĭ krō′mə tĭz′əm), *n.*

polychrome (pŏl′ĭ krōm′), *adj.* **1.** being of many or various colours. **2.** decorated or executed in many colours, as a statue, a vase, a mural painting, a printed work, etc. [t. F, t. Gk: m. *polýchrōmos* many-coloured]

polychromy (pŏl′ĭ krō′mĭ), *n.* polychrome colouring; decoration or execution in many colours.

polyclinic (pŏl′ĭ klĭn′ĭk), *n.* a clinic or a hospital dealing with various diseases; a general hospital.

Polyclitus (pŏl′ĭ klī′təs), *n.* fl. *c.* 450–*c.* 420 B.C., Greek sculptor. Also, **Polycleitus, Polycletus** (pŏl′ĭ klē′təs).

polyconic projection (pŏl′ĭ kŏn′ĭk), *Cartog.* a conic projection in which the parallels are arcs of circles that are not concentric but are equally spaced along the central straight meridian, all other meridians being curves equally spaced along the parallels.

Polycrates (pə lĭk′rə tēz′), *n.* died 522? B.C., Greek tyrant of Samos.

polycyclic (pŏl′ĭ sī′klĭk), *adj.* *Chem.* of or pertaining to a molecule which contains more than one ring.

polycyesis (pŏl′ĭ sī ē′sĭs), *n.* *Med.* multiple pregnancy.

polydactyl (pŏl′ĭ dăk′tĭl), *adj.* **1.** having many or several digits. **2.** having more than the normal number of fingers or toes. —*n.* **3.** a polydactyl animal. —**pol′ydac′tylism,** *n.*

polydipsia (pŏl′ĭ dĭp′sĭ ə), *n.* *Pathol.* excessive thirst.

Polydorus (pŏl′ĭ dô′rəs), *n.* fl. 1st century B.C., Greek sculptor.

polyembryony (pŏl′ĭ ĕm′brĭ ə nĭ), *n.* *Embryol.* the production of more than one embryo from one egg.

polyester (pŏl′ĭ ĕs′tə), *n.* *Chem.* a synthetic polymer in which the structural units are linked by ester groups, formed by condensing carboxylic acids with alcohols.

polyethylene (pŏl′ĭ ĕth′ĭ lēn′), *n.* polythene.

polyfoil (pŏl′ĭ foil′), *Archit.* —*adj.* **1.** having many, esp. more than five, foils: *a polyfoil window.* —*n.* **2.** a polyfoil ornament or decorative feature.

polygala (pə lĭg′ə lə), *n.* any of the herbs and shrubs, commonly known as milkworts, which constitute the genus *Polygala.* [t. Gk, pl. of *polýgalon* milkwort]

polygamist (pə lĭg′ə mĭst), *n.* one who practises or favours polygamy.

polygamous (pə lĭg′ə məs), *adj.* **1.** of, pertaining to, characterized by, or practising polygamy. **2.** *Bot.* bearing both unisexual and hermaphrodite flowers on the same or on different plants. [t. Gk: m. *polýgamos*] —**polyg′amously,** *adv.*

polygamy (pə lĭg′ə mĭ), *n.* **1.** the practice or condition of having many or several spouses, esp. wives, at one time. **2.** *Zool.* the habit of mating with more than one of the opposite sex.

polygenesis (pŏl′ĭ jĕn′ĭ sĭs), *n.* *Biol.* the descent of a species or race from more than one ancestral species.

polygenetic (pŏl′ĭ jĭ nĕt′ĭk), *adj.* **1.** *Biol.* relating to or exhibiting polygenesis. **2.** formed by several different causes, in several different ways, or of several different parts.

polygenic inheritance (pŏl′ĭ jĕn′ĭk), *Genetics.* the heredity of complex characters based on their development from a large number of genes, each one ordinarily with a relatively small effect.

polyglot (pŏl′ĭ glŏt′), *adj.* **1.** knowing many or several languages, as a person. **2.** containing, made up of, or in several languages: *a polyglot Bible.* —*n.* **3.** a mixture or confusion of languages. **4.** a person with a command of a number of languages, whether as to reading or speaking, or both. **5.** a book or writing, esp. a Bible, containing the same text in several languages. [t. ML: m. s. *polyglōttus,* t. Gk: m. *polýglōttos* many-tongued]

Polygnotus (pŏl′ĭg nō′təs), *n.* fl. *c.* 450 B.C., Greek painter.

polygon (pŏl′ĭ gən), *n.* a figure, esp. a closed plane figure, having many (more than four) angles and sides. [t. L: s. *polygōnum,* t. Gk: m. *polýgōnon* (neut.) many-angled] —**polygonal** (pə lĭg′ə nəl), *adj.* —**polyg′onally,** *adv.*

polygonaceous (pŏl′ĭ gə nā′shəs, pə lĭg′ə-), *adj.* belonging to the *Polygonaceae,* or buckwheat family of plants, including the knotgrass, dock, etc.

polygonum (pə lĭg′ə nəm), *n.* a plant of the genus *Polygonum,* which consists chiefly of herbs, often with knotty, jointed stems, and which includes the knotgrass, bistort, etc. [t. NL, t. Gk: m. *polýgonon* knotgrass]

polygraph (pŏl′ĭ grăf′, -gräf′), *n.* **1.** an apparatus for producing copies of a drawing or writing. **2.** a prolific or versatile author. **3.** *Med.* an instrument for recording certain bodily activities, as pulse beats, respiratory movements, etc. [t. Gk: s. *polygráphos* writing much] —**polygraphic** (pŏl′ĭ grăf′ĭk), *adj.*

polygynous (pə lĭj′ĭ nəs), *adj.* **1.** of, pertaining to, characterized by, or practising polygyny. **2.** characterized by plurality of wives for one husband. **3.** *Bot.* having many pistils or styles.

polygyny (pə lĭj′ĭ nĭ), *n.* **1.** the practice or the condition of having more than one wife at one time. **2.** the habit or condition of mating with more than one female. **3.** *Bot.* the fact of having many pistils or styles. [f. Gk *polygýn(aios)* having many wives + -Y[3]]

polyhedral (pŏl′ĭ hē′drəl), *adj.* many-faced.
polyhedron (pŏl′ĭ hē′drən), *n., pl.* **-drons, -dra** (-drə). a solid figure having many faces. [t. Gk: m. *polýedron* (neut.) having many bases. See -HEDRON]
polyhistor (pŏl′ĭ hĭs′tə), *n.* a person of great and varied learning. —**polyhistoric** (pŏl′ĭ hĭs tŏ′rĭk), *adj.*
polyhydric alcohol (pŏl′ĭ hī′drĭk), *Chem.* an alcohol which contains two or more hydroxyl groups in the molecule.
polyhydroxy (pŏl′ĭ hī drŏk′sĭ), *adj. Chem.* containing a number of hydroxyl groups.
Polyhymnia (pŏl′ĭ hĭm′nĭ ə), *n.* the Muse of sublime hymns or serious sacred songs. [t. L, t. Gk: m. *Polýmnia* to agree with L *hymnus* HYMN]
polyisoprene (pŏl′ĭ ī′sə prēn′), *n. Chem.* a polymer of isoprene which is the primary constituent of natural rubber.
polymath (pŏl′ĭ măth), *n.* a person of great and varied learning. [t. Gk: s. *polymathḗs*]
polymer (pŏl′ĭ mə), *n. Chem.* **1.** a compound of high molecular weight derived either by the combination of many smaller molecules or by the condensation of many smaller molecules eliminating water, alcohol, etc. **2.** any of two or more polymeric compounds. **3.** a product of polymerization. [t. Gk: s. *polymerḗs* of many parts]
polymeric (pŏl′ĭ mĕ′rĭk), *adj. Chem.* (of compounds, or of one compound in relation to another) having the same elements combined in the same proportions by weight, but differing in molecular weight: more recently extended to include high molecular weight substances resulting from condensation.
polymerism (pə lĭm′ə rĭz′əm, pŏl′ĭ mə-), *n.* **1.** *Chem.* polymeric state. **2.** *Biol., Bot.* polymerous state.
polymerization (pə lĭm′ə rī zā′shən, pŏl′ĭ mə rī-), *n. Chem.* **1.** the act or process of forming a polymer or polymeric compound. **2.** the union of two or more molecules of a compound to form a more complex compound with a higher molecular weight. **3.** the conversion of one compound into another by such a process. Also, **polymerisation.**
polymerize (pŏl′ĭ mə rīz′, pə lĭm′ə rīz′), *v.t., v.i.,* **-rized, -rizing. 1.** to combine so as to form a polymer. **2.** to subject to or undergo polymerization. Also, **polymerise.**
polymerous (pə lĭm′ə rəs), *adj.* **1.** *Biol.* composed of many parts. **2.** *Bot.* having numerous members in each whorl.
polymethyl methacrylate (pŏl′ĭ mĕth′ĭl), *Chem.* perspex.
polymorph (pŏl′ĭ môf′), *n.* **1.** *Zool., etc.* a polymorphous organism or substance. **2.** *Crystall.* one of the forms assumed by a polymorphous substance. **3.** *Anat.* a type of white blood cell. [t. Gk: s. *polýmorphos*, adj., multiform]
polymorphism (pŏl′ĭ mô′fĭz′əm), *n.* **1.** polymorphous state or condition. **2.** *Crystall.* crystallization into two or more chemically identical but crystallographically distinct forms. **3.** *Zool., Bot.* existence of an animal or plant in several form or colour varieties.
polymorphous (pŏl′ĭ mô′fəs), *adj.* having, assuming, or passing through many or various forms, stages, or the like. Also, **pol′ymor′phic.**
Polynesia (pŏl′ĭ nē′zyə), *n.* one of the three principal divisions of Oceania, comprising those island groups in the Pacific lying E of Melanesia and Micronesia and extending from the Hawaiian Islands S to New Zealand. [t. NL, t. F: m. *Polynésie*, f. *poly-* POLY- + *-nésie*, der. Gk *nêsos* island]
Polynesian (pŏl′ĭ nē′zyən), *adj.* **1.** of or pertaining to Polynesia, its inhabitants, or their languages. —*n.* **2.** a member of any of a number of brown-skinned peoples, variously classified as to race, of distinctive customs, speaking closely related Austronesian languages, and inhabiting Polynesia. **3.** the easternmost group of the Austronesian languages, including Maori, Tahitian, Samoan, Hawaiian, and the language of Easter Island.
Polynices (pŏl′ĭ nī′sēz), *n. Gk Legend.* the son of Oedipus. The expedition of the Seven against Thebes was organized to restore him to the throne of Thebes.
polynomial (pŏl′ĭ nō′myəl), *adj.* **1.** consisting of or characterized by many or several names or terms. —*n.* **2.** a polynomial name or the like. **3.** *Alg.* an expression consisting of two or more terms, as $2x^3 = 7x^2 + 4x + 2$. **4.** *Zool., Bot.* a species name containing more than two terms. [f. POLY- + *-nomial* as in BINOMIAL]
polynuclear (pŏl′ĭ nyōō′klĭ ə), *adj.* multinuclear.
polyp (pŏl′ĭp), *n.* **1.** *Zool.* **a.** a sedentary type of animal form characterized by a more or less fixed base, columnar body, and free end with mouth and tentacles, esp. as applied to coelenterates. **b.** an individual zooid of a compound or colonial organism. **2.** *Pathol.* a projecting growth from a mucous surface, as of the nose, being either a tumour or a hypertrophy of the mucous membrane. [t. F: m. *polype*, t. L: m. s. *polypus*, t. Gk: m. *polýpous* octopus, also polyp (def. 2)]
polypary (pŏl′ĭ pə rĭ), *n., pl.* **-ries.** the common supporting structure of a colony of polyps, as corals.
polypeptide (pŏl′ĭ pĕp′tīd), *n. Chem., Biochem.* one of a group of compounds having two or more amino acids and one or more peptide radicals. See **peptide.**
polypetalous (pŏl′ĭ pĕt′ə ləs), *adj. Bot.* having many or (commonly) separate petals. See illus. under **corolla.**
polyphagia (pŏl′ĭ fā′jyə), *n.* **1.** *Pathol.* excessive desire to eat. **2.** *Zool.* the habit of subsisting on many different kinds of food. [t. NL, t. Gk] —**polyphagous** (pə lĭf′ə gəs), *adj.*
polyphase (pŏl′ĭ fāz′), *adj. Elect.* **1.** having more than one phase. **2.** denoting or pertaining to a system combining two or more alternating currents which differ from one another in phase.
Polyphemus (pŏl′ĭ fē′məs), *n. Gk Legend.* a chief among the Cyclopes, blinded by Odysseus who thus escaped him.
polyphone (pŏl′ĭ fōn′), *n. Phonet.* a polyphonic letter or symbol.
polyphonic (pŏl′ĭ fŏn′ĭk), *adj.* **1.** consisting of many voices or sounds. **2.** *Music.* **a.** having two or more voices or parts, each with an independent melody, but all harmonizing; contrapuntal (opposed to *homophonic*). **b.** of or pertaining to music of this kind. **c.** capable of producing more than one note at a time, as an organ or a harp. **3.** *Phonet.* having more than one phonetic value, as a letter. [f. s. Gk *polýphōnos* having many tones + -IC]
polyphony (pə lĭf′ə nĭ), *n.* **1.** *Music.* polyphonic composition; counterpoint. **2.** *Phonet.* representation of different sounds by the same letter or symbol. [t. Gk: m. s. *polyphōnía* variety of tones or speech] —**polyph′onous,** *adj.*
polyphyletic (pŏl′ĭ fī lĕt′ĭk), *adj.* developed from more than one ancestral type, as a group of animals. [f. POLY- + m. s. Gk *phyletikós* of the same tribe]
polyploid (pŏl′ĭ ploid′), *Genetics.* —*n.* **1.** an organism with more than twice the haploid number of chromosomes. —*adj.* **2.** of a chromosome number which is some multiple of the haploid number. —**pol′yploi′dy,** *n.*
polypody (pŏl′ĭ pə dĭ), *n., pl.* **-dies.** any fern of the genus *Polypodium*, as *P. vulgare*, a common species with creeping rootstocks, deeply pinnatifid evergreen fronds, and round, naked sori. [t. L: m. s. *polypodium*, t. Gk: m. *polypódion*]
polypoid (pŏl′ĭ poid′), *adj.* of, pertaining to, or resembling a polyp.
polypropylene (pŏl′ĭ prō′pĭ lēn′), *n. Chem.* a plastic polymer of propylene, similar to polythene but of greater strength; used as a substitute for jute in making bags, etc.
polyptych (pŏl′ĭp tĭk), *n.* a painted or sculptured ensemble, usually an altarpiece, composed of several connected panels. Cf. **diptych.** [t. LL: s. *polyptycha* (neut. pl.) account books, t. Gk: having many folds]
polypus (pŏl′ĭ pəs), *n., pl.* **-pi** (-pī′). *Pathol.* a polyp. [t. L. See POLYP]
polysaccharide (pŏl′ĭ săk′ə rīd′, -rĭd), *n. Chem.* a carbohydrate, as starch, inulin, cellulose, etc., containing more than three monosaccharide units per molecule, the units being attached to each other in the manner of acetals, and therefore capable of hydrolysis by acids or enzymes to monosaccharides.
polysepalous (pŏl′ĭ sĕp′ə ləs), *adj. Bot.* having the sepals separate from one another.
polystyle (pŏl′ĭ stīl′), *adj.* having many columns.
polystyrene (pŏl′ĭ stī′ə rēn′), *n. Chem.* a clear, plastic polymer of styrene possessing good electrical properties.
polysulphide (pŏl′ĭ sŭl′fīd), *n. Chem.* a sulphide containing more than the ordinary quantity of sulphur.
polysyllabic (pŏl′ĭ sĭ lăb′ĭk), *adj.* **1.** consisting of many, or more than three, syllables, as a word. **2.** characterized by such words, as language, etc. Also, **pol′ysyllab′ical.** [f. s. ML *polysyllabus* (t. Gk: m. *polysýllabos* of many syllables) + -IC]
polysyllable (pŏl′ĭ sĭl′ə bl), *n.* a polysyllabic word.
polysyllogism (pŏl′ĭ sĭl′ə jĭz′əm), *n. Logic.* a number of syllogisms arranged in a series, so that the conclusion of one (a **prosyllogism**) serves as the premise of another (an **episyllogism**).
polysyndeton (pŏl′ĭ sĭn′dĭ tən), *n. Rhet.* the use of a number of conjunctions in close succession, as in Rom. 8:38, 39. Cf. **asyndeton.** [t. NL, f. Gk: *poly-* POLY- + *sýndeton* (neut.) bound together]
polysynthesism (pŏl′ĭ sĭn′thĭ sĭz′əm), *n.* **1.** the synthesis of various elements. **2.** the combining of several words in a sentence into a single word.
polysynthetic (pŏl′ĭ sĭn thĕt′ĭk), *adj.* (of a language) having many word elements in a sentence combined into

one word, as in a number of American Indian languages.

polytechnic (pŏl′ĭ tĕk′nĭk), *adj.* **1.** of, pertaining to, or dealing with scientific or technical subjects. **—***n.* **2.** an institute of higher education in which instruction is given chiefly in scientific and technical subjects. [t. F: m. *polytechnique*, f. s. Gk *polýtechnos* + *-ique* -IC]

polytetrafluoroethylene (pŏl′ĭ tĕt′rə flo͝oə′rō ĕth′ĭ lēn′), *n. Chem.* the plastic produced by the polymerization of tetrafluoroethylene, with a very low coefficient of friction and good resistance to temperature: noted for non-stick properties. *Abbrev.:* PTFE

polytheism (pŏl′ĭ thē ĭz′əm), *n.* the doctrine of, or belief in, many gods or more gods than one. [t. F: m. *polythéisme*, f. s. Gk *polýtheos* of many gods + *-isme* -ISM] **—pol′ytheist,** *n.* **—pol′ytheis′tic,** *adj.*

polythene (pŏl′ĭ thēn′), *n. Chem.* a plastic polymer of ethylene used for containers, electrical insulation, packaging, etc. Also, **polyethylene.**

polytonality (pŏl′ĭ tō năl′ĭ tĭ), *n. Music.* the use of more than one key at the same time.

polytypic (pŏl′ĭ tĭp′ĭk), *adj.* having or involving many or several types. Also, **pol′ytyp′ical.**

polyurethane (pŏl′ĭ yo͝oə′rə thān′), *n. Chem.* a polymer of urethane used in making rigid foam products for insulation, decoration, etc.

polyuria (pŏl′ĭ yo͝oə′rĭ ə), *n. Pathol.* the passing of an excessive quantity of urine, as in diabetes, certain nervous diseases, etc. [t. NL. See POLY, -URIA] **—pol′yu′ric,** *adj.*

polyvalent (pŏl′ĭ vā′lənt, pə lĭv′ə lənt), *adj.* **1.** *Chem.* having more than one valency. **2.** *Bacteriol.* denoting a serum which contains antibodies against a group of similar diseases and is capable of attacking their different antigens. [f. POLY- + -VALENT] **—pol′yva′lence,** *n.*

polyvinyl acetate (pŏl′ĭ vī′nĭl), *Chem.* a transparent thermoplastic resin, produced by the polymerization of vinyl acetate, used as an adhesive, in inks and lacqueurs, etc. *Abbrev.:* PVA

polyvinyl chloride, *Chem.* a colourless thermoplastic resin, produced by the polymerization of vinyl chloride, with good resistance to water, acids, and alkalis. *Abbrev.:* PVC

polyvinylidene chloride (pŏl′ĭ vī nĭl′ĭ dēn′), *Chem.* a white thermoplastic material, produced by the polymerization of vinylidene chloride, used alone or as a copolymer with vinyl chloride for a variety of purposes.

Polyxena (pō lĭk′sĭ nə), *n. Gk Legend.* daughter of Priam and Hecuba and bride of Achilles.

polyzoan (pŏl′ĭ zō′ən), *adj., n.* bryozoan. [f. POLY- + -ZO(A) + -AN]

polyzoarium (pŏl′ĭ zō ĕə′rĭ əm), *n., pl.* **-aria** (-ĕə′rĭ ə). *Zool.* a bryozoan colony, or its supporting skeleton.

polyzoic (pŏl′ĭ zō′ĭk), *adj.* **1.** (of a bryozoan colony) composed of many zooids. **2.** (of a spore) producing many sporozoites.

pom (pŏm), *n.* pommy.

Pom (pŏm), *n.* a Pomeranian dog.

pomace (pŭm′ĭs), *n.* **1.** the pulpy residue from apples or similar fruit after crushing and pressing, as in cider-making. **2.** any crushed or ground pulpy substance. [ME, t. ML: m. s. *pōmācium* cider, der. L *pōmum* fruit]

pomaceous (pō mā′shəs), *adj.* pertaining to pomes, as the apple, pear, and quince. [t. NL: m. *pōmāceus*, der. L *pōmum* fruit]

pomade (pə mäd′), *n., v.,* **-maded, -mading.** **—***n.* **1.** a scented ointment, used for the scalp and hair. **—***v.t.* **2.** to anoint or dress with pomade. [t. F: m. *pommade*, t. It.: m. *pomata* (so called because orig. made with apples), der. L *pōmum* fruit. Cf. POMATUM]

pomander (pō măn′də), *n.* **1.** a mixture of aromatic substances, often in the form of a ball, formerly carried on the person for perfume or as a guard against infection. **2.** the container in which it is carried. [earlier *pomeamber*, f. POME + AMBER]

pomatum (pə mā′təm), *n.* pomade. [t. NL, der. L *pōmum* fruit]

pome (pōm), *n. Bot.* the characteristic fruit of the apple family, as an apple, pear, quince, etc. [ME, t. OF, g. LL *pōma* (neut. pl.) fruit] **—pome′like′,** *adj.*

pomegranate (pŏm′grăn′ĭt), *n.* **1.** a several-chambered, many-seeded, globose fruit of medium size, with a tough rind (usually red) and surmounted by a crown of calyx lobes, the edible portion consisting of pleasantly acid flesh developed from the outer seed coat. **2.** the shrub or small tree, *Punica granatum*, which yields it, native in south-western Asia but widely cultivated in warm regions. [ME *pomegarnet*, t. OF: m. *pome grenate* (f. *pome* apple, fruit + *grenate*, t. L: m. *grānāta* (fem.) having grains or seeds). See POME, GRAIN]

pomelo (pŏm′ĭ lō′), *n., pl.* **-los. 1.** grapefruit. **2.** shaddock. [t. D: m. (along pseudo-Spanish lines) *pompelmoes*]

Pomerania (pŏm′ə rā′nyə), *n.* a former province of NE Germany, now mostly in NW Poland. German, **Pommern.**

Pomeranian (pŏm′ə rā′nyən), *adj.* **1.** of or pertaining to Pomerania. **—***n.* **2.** one of a breed of small dogs with erect ears, and long, thick silky hair. **3.** a native or inhabitant of Pomerania.

Pomeranian (Ab. 14 in. high at the shoulder)

Pomfret cake (pŭm′frĭt), Pontefract cake.

pomiculture (pŏm′ĭ kŭl′chə), *n.* the cultivation or growing of fruit. [f. *pōmi-* (comb. form of L *pōmum* fruit) + CULTURE] **—pom′i-cul′turist,** *n.*

pomiferous (pō mĭf′ə rəs), *adj. Bot.* bearing pomes or pomelike fruits. [f. L *pōmifer* fruit-bearing + -OUS]

pommel (pŭm′əl), *n., v.,* **-melled, -melling** or (*U.S.*) **-meled, -meling.** **—***n.* Also, **pummel. 1.** a terminating knob, as on the top of a tower, hilt of a sword, etc. **2.** the protuberant part at the front and top of a saddle. See illus. under **saddle.** **—***v.t.* **3.** pummel. [ME *pomel*, t. OF, ult. der. L *pōmum* fruit]

Pommern (*Ger.* pŏm′ərn), *n.* German name of **Pomerania.**

pommy (pŏm′ĭ), *n., pl.* **-mies.** *Austral., N.Z.* an Englishman.

pomology (pō mŏl′ə jĭ), *n.* the science that deals with fruits and fruit-growing. [t. NL: m. s. *pōmologia*. See POME, -LOGY] **—pomological** (pŏm′ə lŏj′ĭ kəl), *adj.* **—pomol′ogist,** *n.*

Pomona (pə mō′nə), *n.* **1.** *Rom. Myth.* the goddess of fruit trees. **2.** Mainland (def. 2).

pomp (pŏmp), *n.* **1.** stately or splendid display; splendour; magnificence. **2.** ostentatious or vain display, esp. of dignity or importance. **3.** (*pl.*) pompous displays or things. **4.** *Obs.* a stately or splendid procession; pageant. [ME *pompe*, t. OF, t. L: m. *pompa*, t. Gk: m. *pompḗ*, orig., a sending] **—Syn. 1.** See **show.**

pompadour (pŏm′pə do͝oə), *n.* **1.** an arrangement of a woman's hair, popular in the early 18th century, in which it is raised above the forehead, often over a pad. **2.** a shade of pink or of crimson. **3.** *Textiles.* **a.** a fabric, esp. silk, often in red, having a small floral design. **b.** the design. [named after the Marquise de POMPADOUR]

Pompadour (*Fr.* pôɴ pȧ do͞or′), *n.* **Marquise de** (*Jeanne Antoinette Poisson Le Normant D'Étoiles*), 1721–64, mistress of Louis XV of France.

pompano (pŏm′pə nō′), *n., pl.* **-nos. 1.** a deep-bodied food fish of the genus *Trachinotus*. **2.** a prized food fish, *Palometus simillimus*, of California. [t. Sp.: m. *pampano*, g. L *pampinus*]

Pompeian red, a greyish yellow shade of red.

Pompeii (pŏm pā′ē), *n.* an ancient city in SW Italy at the foot of Mount Vesuvius: buried by an eruption, A.D. 79. **—Pompeian** (pŏm pā′ən, -pē′ən), *adj., n.*

Pompey (pŏm′pĭ), *n.* ('*The Great*', *Gnaeus Pompeius Magnus*), 106–48 B.C., Roman general and statesman: a member of the first triumvirate.

Pompidou (*Fr.* pôɴ pē do͞o′), *n.* **Georges** (*Fr.* zhôrzh), born 1911, French statesman: president of France since 1969.

pompom (pŏm′pŏm), *n.* an automatic anti-aircraft cannon. [imit.]

pompon (pŏm′pŏn; *Fr.* pôɴ pôɴ′), *n.* **1.** an ornamental tuft or ball of feathers, wool, or the like, used in millinery, etc. **2.** a tuft of wool or the like worn on a shako, a sailor's cap, etc. **3.** *Hort.* a form of small, globe-shaped flower head that characterizes a class or type of various flowering plants, especially chrysanthemums and dahlias. [t. F, ult. der. *pompe* POMP]

pomposity (pŏm pŏs′ĭ tĭ), *n., pl.* **-ties. 1.** the quality of being pompous. **2.** pompous parade of dignity or importance. **3.** ostentatious loftiness of language, style, behaviour, etc. [ME, t. ML: m. s. *pompōsitas*]

pompous (pŏm′pəs), *adj.* **1.** characterized by an ostentatious parade of dignity or importance: *a pompous bow*. **2.** (of language, style, etc.) ostentatiously lofty. **3.** characterized by pomp, stately splendour, or magnificence. [ME, t. LL: s. *pompōsus*] **—pomp′ously,** *adv.* **—pomp′ousness,** *n.*

ponce (pŏns), *n., v.,* **ponced, poncing.** *Slang.* **—***n.* **1.** a pimp. **—***v.i.* **2.** to act as a pimp.

Ponce (*Sp.* pôn′thė), *n.* a seaport in S Puerto Rico. 145,586 (1960).

Ponce de León (pŏns′ də lē′ən; *Sp.* pôn′thė dė lė ôn′), **Juan** (*Sp.* KHwän), *c.* 1460–1521, Spanish explorer.

poncho (pŏn′chō), *n., pl.* **-chos.** a blanket-like cloak with a hole in the centre to put over the head. [t. S Amer. Sp., t. Araucanian: m. *pontho*]

pond (pŏnd), *n.* a body of water smaller than a lake, often one artificially formed. [ME, anomalous var. of POUND[3]]

ponder (pŏn′də), *v.i.* **1.** to consider deeply; meditate. —*v.t.* **2.** to weigh carefully in the mind, or consider carefully. [ME *pondre(n)*, t. OF: m. *ponderer*, t. L: m. *ponderāre* ponder, weigh] —**Syn. 1.** reflect, cogitate, deliberate, ruminate.

ponderable (pŏn′də rə bl, -drə bl), *adj.* capable of being weighed; having appreciable weight. —**pon′derabil′ity,** *n.*

ponderous (pŏn′də rəs, -drəs), *adj.* **1.** of great weight; heavy; massive: *a ponderous mass of iron.* **2.** without graceful lightness or ease; dull: *a ponderous dissertation.* [ME, t. L: m. s. *ponderōsus*] —**pon′derously,** *adv.* —**pon′derousness, ponderosity** (pŏn′də rŏs′ĭ tĭ), *n.*

Pondicherry (pŏn′dĭ chĕ′rĭ), *n.* **1.** a former province of French India, on the Coromandel Coast; now a union territory of India. With Mahé, Karikal, and Yanaon, 369,079 pop. (1961); 186 sq. mi. **2.** a seaport in and capital of the territory. 40,421 (1961). Also, **Pondichéry** (*Fr.* pôɴ dē shė rē′). See **French India.**

pond lily, a waterlily.

pondok (pŏn′dŏk), *n.* (in S Africa) a primitive kind of house, made of tin sheet, reeds, etc., and used esp. by the Hottentots of SW Africa. [t. Malay: leaf-house]

pond scum, any free-floating freshwater alga that forms a green scum on water.

pond-skater (pŏnd′skā′tə), *n.* water-strider.

pondweed (pŏnd′wēd′), *n.* any of the aquatic plants constituting the genus *Potamogeton*, most of which grow in ponds and quiet streams.

pone[1] (pōn), *n. Southern U.S.* **1.** Also, **pone bread.** baked or fried bread made of maize. **2.** an oval-shaped loaf or cake of it. [t. Powhatan: m. *äpan* something baked]

pone[2] (pōn, pō′nĭ), *n. Cards.* the player on the dealer's right.

pong (pŏng), *Slang.* —*n.* **1.** a stink; unpleasant smell. —*v.i.* **2.** to stink.

pongee (pŏn jē′), *n.* **1.** silk of a plain weave made from filaments of wild silk woven in natural tan colour. **2.** a cotton or rayon fabric imitating it. [? t. North Chinese: m. *pun-chī*, Mandarin *pun-kī* own loom]

pongid (pŏn′jĭd), *n.* **1.** one of the great apes of the family *Pongidae*, which includes the chimpanzee, gorilla, and orang-utan. —*adj.* **2.** belonging or pertaining to the *Pongidae*. [t. NL: s. *Pongidae*, the family, equiv. to *Pongo*, the typical genus (t. Congo: m. *mpungu* ape) + *-idae* -IDAE]

Pongola (pŏng′gə lə), *n.* a river of southern Africa forming the border of Transvaal and Natal, then flowing NE and on through Mozambique to the Indian Ocean. ab. 350 mi.

poniard (pŏn′yəd), *n.* **1.** a dagger. —*v.t.* **2.** to stab with a poniard. [t. F: m. *poignard*, der. *poing*, g. L *pugnus* fist]

pons (pŏnz), *n., pl.* **pontes** (pŏn′tēz). *Anat.* a connecting part. [t. L: bridge]

pons asinorum (pŏnz′ ăs′ĭ nô′rəm), the geometrical proposition (Euclid, 1:5) that if a triangle has two of its sides equal, the angles opposite these sides are also equal: so named from the difficulty experienced by beginners in mastering it. [L: bridge of asses]

pons Varolii (pŏnz′ və rō′lĭ ī′), *Anat.* a band of nerve fibres in the brain connecting the lobes of the cerebellum, as well as the medulla and cerebrum. [named after Costanzo *Varolio*, 1543–75, Italian anatomist]

pont (pŏnt), *n.* (in South Africa) a floating bridge; pontoon.

Ponta Delgada (*Port.* pôn′tə dĕl gä′də), a seaport in the Azores, on SW São Miguel island. 22,419 (1960).

Pontchartrain (pŏn′chə trān′), *n.* **Lake,** a shallow extension of the Gulf of Mexico in SE Louisiana, N of New Orleans. ab. 40 mi. long; ab. 22 mi. wide.

Pontefract (pŏn′tĭ frăkt′), *n.* a town in England, in the West Riding of Yorkshire: ruins of a 12th-century castle. 27,128 (1961).

Pontefract cake, a small disc of liquorice eaten as a sweet. Also, **Pomfret cake.**

Ponti (*It.* pôn′tē), *n.* **Gio** (*It.* jô), born 1891, Italian designer and architect.

Pontic (pŏn′tĭk), *adj.* pertaining to the Pontus Euxinus (Black Sea) or to Pontus (an ancient country south of it). [t. L: s. *Ponticus*, t. Gk: m. *Pontikós*]

pontifex (pŏn′tĭ fĕks′), *n., pl.* **pontifices** (pŏn tĭf′ĭ sēz′). a member of the principal college of priests in ancient Rome, whose head was the **Pontifex Maximus,** or chief priest. [L: a Roman high priest]

pontiff (pŏn′tĭf), *n.* **1.** an ancient Roman pontifex. **2.** a high or chief priest. **3.** *Eccles.* **a.** a bishop. **b.** the bishop of Rome (the pope). [t. L: m. *pontifex*]

pontifical (pŏn tĭf′ĭ kl), *adj.* **1.** of, pertaining to, or characteristic of a pontiff; papal. —*n.* **2.** (in the Western Church) a book containing the forms for the sacraments and other rites and ceremonies to be performed by a bishop. **3.** (*pl.*) the vestments and insignia of a bishop, proper to his liturgical functions. [ME, t. L: s. *pontificālis*] —**pontif′ically,** *adv.*

Pontifical College, 1. the chief body of priests in ancient Rome. **2.** the chief hieratic body of the Roman Catholic Church.

Pontifical Mass, a mass conducted by a bishop with full ceremonial.

pontificate (*n.* pŏn tĭf′ĭ kĭt; *v.* pŏn tĭf′ĭ kāt′), *n., v.,* **-cated, -cating.** —*n.* **1.** the office, or term of office, of a pontiff. —*v.i.* **2.** to speak in a pompous manner. **3.** to serve as a pontiff or bishop, esp. in a Pontifical Mass. [t. ML: m. s. *pontificātus*, pp.]

pontil (pŏn′tĭl), *n.* punty.

Pontine Marshes (pŏn′tīn), an area in W Italy, SE of Rome: formerly marshy, now drained.

Pontius (pŏn′tyəs, pŏn′shəs), *n.* family name of **Pilate.**

pontlevis (pŏnt lĕv′ĭs; *Fr.* pôɴ lə vē′), *n.* a drawbridge.

pontonier (pŏn′tə nĭə′), *n.* **1.** *U.S. Mil.* an officer or soldier in charge of bridge equipment or construction of pontoon bridges. **2.** one in charge of a bridge or ferry. Also, **pontoneer.** [t. F: m. *pontonnier*, der. *ponton* PONTOON[1]]

pontoon[1] (pŏn to͞on′), *n.* **1.** *Mil.* a boat, or some other floating structure, used as one of the supports for a temporary bridge over a river. **2.** a floating construction serving as a temporary dock or a floating bridge. **3.** a watertight box or cylinder used in raising a submerged vessel, etc. **4.** a seaplane float. Also, **ponton** (pŏn′tən). [t. F: m. *ponton*, g. s. L *ponto* bridge, pontoon, punt]

pontoon[2] (pŏn to͞on′), *n. Cards.* a gambling game, the object of which is to obtain from the dealer cards whose total values add up to, or nearly add up to, 21, but do not exceed it. [(? humorous) mispron. of F *vingt-et-un* twenty-one]

pontoon bridge, a bridge supported by pontoons.

Pontormo (*It.* pôn tôr′mô), *n.* **Jacopo** (*It.* yä′kô pô), 1494–1556, Italian painter.

Pontus (pŏn′təs), *n.* an ancient country in NE Asia Minor, bordering on the Black Sea: became a Roman province A.D. 62.

Pontus Euxinus (yo͝ok sī′nəs), ancient name of the **Black Sea.**

Pontypool (pŏn′tĭ po͞ol′), *n.* a town in Monmouthshire. 38,879 (1961).

Pontypridd (pŏn′tĭ prēth′), *n.* a town in Wales, in Glamorganshire. 35,494 (1961).

pony (pō′nĭ), *n., pl.* **-nies,** *v.,* **-nied, -nying.** —*n.* **1.** a horse of a small type, usually not more than 13 or 14 hands high. **2.** a horse of any small type or breed. **3.** *U.S. Slang.* crib (def. 13). **4.** *Colloq.* a small glass for spirits. **5.** *Colloq.* the amount of liquid it will hold. **6.** *Slang.* the sum of £25. —*v.t., v.i. U.S. Slang.* **7.** to prepare (lessons) by means of a crib. **8.** to pay (money), as in settling an account (fol. by *up*). [var. of *powney*, t. F: m. *poulenet*, ult. der. L *pullus* young animal. See FOAL]

pony express, a former system in the American West of carrying mail rapidly by relays of riders mounted on ponies, esp. that operating in 1860–61, between Missouri and California.

ponytail (pō′nĭ tāl′), *n.* a woman's hairstyle in which the hair is drawn back tightly and tied at the back of the head and then hangs loose.

pooch (po͞och), *n. Slang.* a dog.

pood (po͞od), *n.* a Russian weight equal to about 36 pounds avoirdupois. [t. Russ., t. LG or Scand.: m. *pund* POUND[2]]

poodle (po͞o′dl), *n.* one of a breed of intelligent pet dogs, of several varieties, with thick curly hair often trimmed in an elaborate manner. [short for *poodle dog*, half adoption, half trans. of G *Pudelhund*, lit., splash-dog (because the poodle is a water-dog). Cf. PUDDLE]

Poodle (15 in. or more high at the shoulder)

poof (po͞of), *n. Slang.* a male homosexual. Also, **poove, pouf, pouffe.**

pooh (po͞o), *interj.* **1.** (an exclamation of disdain or contempt (often repeated).) —*n.* **2.** an exclamation of 'pooh'.

pooh-pooh (po͞o′po͞o′), *v.t.* to express disdain or contempt for; make light of; dismiss as unworthy of consideration.

pool[1] (po͞ol), *n.* **1.** a small body of standing water; pond. **2.** a puddle. **3.** any small collection of liquid on a surface: *a pool of blood.* **4.** a still, deep place in a stream. **5.** a swimming pool. [ME and OE *pōl*, c. G *Pfuhl*]

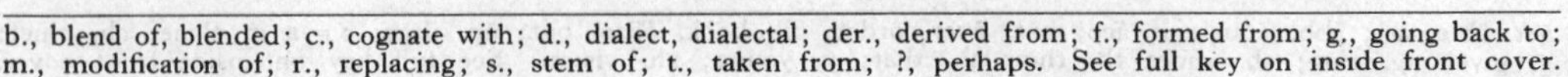
b., blend of, blended; c., cognate with; d., dialect, dialectal; der., derived from; f., formed from; g., going back to; m., modification of; r., replacing; s., stem of; t., taken from; ?, perhaps. See full key on inside front cover.

pool[2] (po͞ol), *n.* **1.** an association of competitors who agree to control the production, market, and price of a commodity for mutual benefit, although they appear to be rivals. **2.** *Chiefly U.S. Finance.* a combination of persons to manipulate one or more securities. **3.** a combination of interests, funds, etc., for common advantage. **4.** the combined interests or funds. **5.** a facility or service that is shared by a number of people: *a typing pool.* **6.** the persons or parties involved. **7.** the stakes in certain games. **8.** Also, **pocket billiards.** any of various games played on a billiard table in which the object is to drive all the balls into the pockets with the cue ball. **9.** the total amount staked by a combination of betters, as on a race, to be awarded to the successful better or betters. **10.** the combination of such betters. **11.** *Fencing.* a match in which each team-mate successively plays against each member of the opposite team. *—v.t.* **12.** to put (interests, money, etc.) into a pool, or common stock or fund, as for a financial venture, according to agreement. **13.** to form a pool of. **14.** to make a common interest of. *—v.i.* **15.** to enter into or form a pool. [t. F: m. *poule,* lit., hen; prob. at first slang for booty]

Poole (po͞ol), *n.* a seaport and resort in England, in Dorset: large natural harbour. 92,111 (1961).

poolroom (po͞ol′ro͞om′, -ro͝om′), *n. U.S.* **1.** an establishment or room in which pool or billiards is played. **2.** a place in which betting is carried on.

pools (po͞olz), *n.pl.* football pools.

pool table, a billiard table with six pockets, on which pool is played.

poon (po͞on), *n.* **1.** any of several East Indian trees of the tropical genus *Calophyllum,* which yield a light, hard wood used for masts, spars, etc. **2.** the wood. [t. Sinhalese or Telugu: m. *puna*]

Poona (po͞o′nə), *n.* a city in India, in W Maharashtra. 597,562 (1961).

poop[1] (po͞op), *n.* **1.** the enclosed space in the aftermost part of a ship, above the main deck. **2.** a deck above the ordinary deck in that part, often forming the roof of a cabin, etc. *—v.t.* **3.** (of a wave) to break over the stern of (a ship). **4.** to take (seas) over the stern. [ME *pouppe,* t. OF: m. *poupe,* t. It.: m. *poppa,* g. L *puppis*]

poop[2] (po͞op), *v.t. Slang.* to tire or exhaust. [ME *poupe(n),* lit., blow]

poop deck, a raised deck built on the stern of a ship above the main deck.

Poopó (*Sp.* pō ō pō′), *n.* a lake in SW Bolivia, in the Andes. ab. 80 mi. long; ab. 12,000 ft high.

poor (po͝oə, pô), *adj.* **1.** having little or nothing in the way of wealth, goods, or means of subsistence. **2.** (of a country, institution, etc.) meagrely supplied or endowed with resources or funds. **3.** (of the circumstances, life, home, dress, etc.) characterized by or showing poverty. **4.** deficient or lacking in something specified: *a region poor in mineral deposits.* **5.** faulty or inferior, as in construction. **6.** deficient in desirable ingredients, qualities, or the like: *poor soil.* **7.** lean or emaciated, as cattle. **8.** of an inferior, inadequate, or unsatisfactory kind; not good: *poor health.* **9.** deficient in aptitude or ability: *a poor cook.* **10.** deficient in moral excellence; cowardly, abject, or mean. **11.** scanty, meagre, or paltry in amount or number: *a poor pittance.* **12.** humble: *deign to visit our poor house.* **13.** unfortunate or hapless (much used to express pity): *the poor mother was in despair.* *—n.* **14.** poor persons collectively (usually prec. by *the*). [ME *povere,* t. OF: m. *povre,* g. L *pauper.* Cf. PAUPER] —**poor′ness,** *n.*

—Syn. 1. needy, indigent, necessitous, straitened, destitute, penniless, poverty-stricken. POOR, IMPECUNIOUS, IMPOVERISHED, PENNILESS refer to those lacking money. POOR is the simple term for the condition of lacking means to obtain the comforts of life: *a very poor family.* IMPECUNIOUS often suggests that the poverty is a consequence of unwise habits: *an impecunious actor.* IMPOVERISHED often implies a former state of greater plenty, from which one has been reduced: *the impoverished aristocracy.* PENNILESS may mean destitute, or it may apply simply to a temporary condition of being without funds: *the widow was left penniless with three small children.* **—Ant. 1.** rich, wealthy.

poor-box (po͝oə′bŏks′, pô′-), *n.* a box in which money may be placed for distribution to the poor.

poor farm, *U.S.* a farm maintained at public expense for the housing and support of paupers.

poorhouse (po͝oə′hous′, pô′-), *n.* a house in which paupers are maintained at the public expense.

poor law, a law or system of laws providing for the relief or support of the poor at the public expense.

poorly (po͝oə′lĭ, pô′lĭ), *adv.* **1.** in a poor manner or way. *—adj.* **2.** in poor health; somewhat ill.

poor-spirited (po͝oə′spĭ′rĭ tĭd, pô′-), *adj.* having or showing a poor, cowardly, or abject spirit.

poort (po͝oət, pôt), *n.* a narrow pass through a step in the side of the southern African plateau.

poor white, (*usually collective or pl.*) (often used derogatorily) an ignorant, shiftless, poverty-stricken white, in the southern U.S., southern Africa, and elsewhere.

poor white trash, (derogatory) poor whites collectively.

poove (po͞ov), *n.* poof. Also, **pouf, pouffe.**

pop[1] (pŏp), *v.,* **popped, popping,** *n., adv.* *—v.i.* **1.** to make a short, quick, explosive sound or report: *the cork popped.* **2.** to burst open with such a sound, as chestnuts or corn in roasting. **3.** to come or go quickly, suddenly, or unexpectedly (fol. by *in, into, out,* etc.). **4.** to shoot with a firearm: *to pop at a mark.* **5. pop off,** *Slang.* **a.** to depart, esp. abruptly. **b.** to die, esp. suddenly. *—v.t.* **6.** to cause to make a sudden, explosive sound. **7.** to cause to burst open with such a sound. **8.** to put or thrust quickly, suddenly, or unexpectedly. **9.** *Colloq.* to fire (a gun, etc.). **10.** to shoot (fol. by *off,* etc.). **11.** *Slang.* to pawn. **12. pop the question,** *Colloq.* to propose marriage. *—n.* **13.** a short, quick, explosive sound. **14.** a popping. **15.** a shot with a firearm. **16.** an effervescent beverage, esp. an unintoxicating one. *—adv.* **17.** with a pop or explosive sound. **18.** quickly, suddenly, or unexpectedly. [ME; imit.]

pop[2] (pŏp), *Colloq.* *—adj.* **1.** popular. **2.** denoting or pertaining to a type of tune or song having great but ephemeral popularity, esp. among the young, and usually characterized by an insistent rhythmic beat. **3.** denoting or pertaining to a singer or player of such music. *—n.* **4.** a pop tune or song. [short for POPULAR]

pop[3] (pŏp), *n. Colloq.* father.

pop., 1. popular. **2.** popularly. **3.** population.

popadum (pŏp′ə dəm), *n.* papadum.

pop art, modern painting using the elements of popular culture and mass media.

popcorn (pŏp′kôn′), *n.* **1.** any of several varieties of maize whose kernels burst open and puff out when subjected to dry heat. **2.** popped corn.

pope[1] (pōp), *n.* **1.** (*often cap.*) the bishop of Rome as head of the Roman Catholic Church. **2.** one considered as having or assuming a similar position or authority. [ME; OE *pāpa,* t. ML: bishop, pope, orig. father, t. Gk: m. *pápas,* var. of *páppas* father]

pope[2] (pōp), *n.* a rough-skinned freshwater fish of the genus *Acerina,* found in N Europe and the southern half of Great Britain; ruffe.

Pope (pōp), *n.* **Alexander,** 1688–1744, English poet.

popedom (pōp′dəm), *n.* **1.** the office or dignity of a pope. **2.** the tenure of office of a pope. **3.** the papal government. **4.** a system resembling the papacy.

popery (pō′pə rĭ), *n.* (usually derogatory) the doctrines, customs, etc., of the Roman Catholic Church.

pope's nose, parson's nose.

popeyed (pŏp′īd′), *adj.* having prominent, bulging, or staring eyes.

popgun (pŏp′gŭn′), *n.* a child's toy gun from which a pellet is shot with a loud pop by compressed air.

popinjay (pŏp′ĭn jā′), *n.* **1.** a vain, chattering person; a coxcomb; a fop. **2.** a figure of a parrot formerly used as a target. **3.** a woodpecker, esp. the green woodpecker, *Picus viridis,* of Europe. **4.** *Archaic.* a parrot. [ME *papejay,* t. OF: m. *papegai* parrot, t. Sp.: m. *papagayo,* t. Ar.: m. *babbaghā',* t. Pers.]

popish (pō′pĭsh), *adj.* (usually derogatory) of or pertaining to the Roman Catholic Church. —**pop′ishly,** *adv.* —**pop′ishness,** *n.*

Popish Plot, a plot by Roman Catholics to murder King Charles II and his ministers and establish Roman Catholicism in England, which Titus Oates claimed to have discovered in 1678.

poplar (pŏp′lə), *n.* **1.** any of various rapidly growing trees constituting the salicaceous genus *Populus,* yielding a useful, light, soft wood, as *P. nigra* v. *italica* (**Lombardy poplar**), a tall tree of striking columnar or spire-shaped outline due to the fastigiate habit of its branches. **2.** the wood itself. **3.** the wood of any such tree. [ME *popler,* t. OF: m. *poplier;* r. OE *pōpul,* t. L: s. *pōpulus*]

Poplar (pŏp′lə), *n.* a district of E London.

poplin (pŏp′lĭn), *n.* a strong, finely ribbed, mercerized cotton material, used for dresses, blouses, children's wear, etc. [t. F: m. *popeline,* t. It.: m. *papalina,* fem. of *papalino* papal; so called from being made at the papal city of Avignon]

popliteal (pŏ plĭt′ĭ əl, pŏp′lĭ tē′əl), *adj. Anat.* of or pertaining to the ham, or part of the leg behind the knee. [f. s. NL *popliteus* (der. L *poples* the ham) + -AL[1]]

Popocatepetl (pŏp′ə kăt′ĭ pĕt′l; *Sp.* pō pō kä tĕ′pĕ tl), *n.* a volcano in S central Mexico, ab. 40 mi. SE of Mexico City. 17,887 ft.

popover (pŏp′ō′və), *n. Cooking.* an individual batter pudding served with roast beef.

poppa (pŏp′ə), *n. U.S. Colloq.* father.

Poppaea Sabina (pŏ pē′ə sə bī′nə), died A.D. 65?, second wife of the Roman emperor Nero.

Pöppelmann (*Ger.* pœ′pəl män), *n.* **Matthaeus Daniel** (*Ger.* mä tĕ′o͞os dä′nē ĕl), 1662–1736, German baroque architect.

popper (pŏp′ə), *n.* **1.** one who or that which pops. **2.** a utensil for popping maize. **3.** *Colloq.* a press-stud.

poppet (pŏp′ĭt), *n.* **1.** Also, **poppet valve.** a valve which in opening is lifted bodily from its seat instead of being hinged at one side. **2.** *Naut.* a piece of shaped wood fitted to close up the slot cut in a boat's gunwhale and top strake for shipping an oar. **3.** a term of endearment for a girl or child. [earlier form of PUPPET]

poppied (pŏp′ĭd), *adj.* **1.** covered or adorned with poppies. **2.** affected by or as by opium; listless.

popping crease (pŏp′ĭng), *Cricket.* See **crease** (def. 3).

popple (pŏp′l), *v.*, **-pled, -pling,** *n.* —*v.i.* **1.** to move in a tumbling, irregular manner, as boiling water. —*n.* **2.** a poppling motion. [ME *pople(n)*; prob. imit.]

poppy (pŏp′ĭ), *n., pl.* **-pies. 1.** any plant of the genus *Papaver*, comprising herbs with showy flowers of various colours, as *P. somniferum*, the source of opium. **2.** an extract, as opium, from such a plant. **3.** an orangeish red; scarlet. **4.** *Archit.* poppyhead (def. 2). [ME; OE *popæg, papig*, t. VL: m. *papāvum*, for L *papāver*]

poppycock (pŏp′ĭ kŏk′), *n.* *Colloq.* nonsense; bosh.

poppyhead (pŏp′ĭ hĕd′), *n.* **1.** the seed capsule of the poppy. **2.** Also, **poppy.** *Archit.* a finial or other ornament, often richly carved, as at the top of the upright end of a bench or pew.

poppy seed, seed of the poppy plant, used as a topping for breads, rolls, and biscuits.

pop-shop (pŏp′shŏp′), *n.* *Slang.* a pawnshop.

popsy (pŏp′sĭ), *n.* *Slang.* a girl, esp. a sexually attractive one.

populace (pŏp′yo͞o ləs), *n.* the common people of a community, as distinguished from the higher classes. [t. F, t. It.: m. *popolaccio*, pejorative of *popolo* PEOPLE]

popular (pŏp′yo͞o lə), *adj.* **1.** regarded with favour or approval by associates, acquaintances, the general public, etc.: *a popular preacher.* **2.** of, pertaining to, or representing the people, or the common people: *popular discontent.* **3.** prevailing among the people generally: *a popular superstition.* **4.** suited to or intended for the general mass of people: *popular music.* **5.** adapted to the ordinary intelligence or taste: *popular lectures on science.* **6.** suited to the means of ordinary people: *popular prices.* [t. L: s. *populāris*] —**Syn. 1.** favourite, approved. **2.** common, prevailing, current. See **general.**

popular front, an alliance of left-wing or progressive political parties, often formed against a common opponent, as fascism.

popularity (pŏp′yo͞o lăr′ĭ tĭ), *n.* **1.** the quality or fact of being popular. **2.** favour enjoyed with the people, the public generally, or a particular set of people.

popularize (pŏp′yo͞o lə rīz′), *v.t.*, **-rized, -rizing.** to make popular. Also, **popularise.** —**pop′ulariza′tion,** *n.* —**pop′ulariz′er,** *n.*

popularly (pŏp′yo͞o lə lĭ), *adv.* **1.** by the people as a whole; generally. **2.** in a popular manner.

populate (pŏp′yo͞o lāt′), *v.t.*, **-lated, -lating. 1.** to inhabit. **2.** to furnish with inhabitants, as by colonization; people. [t. ML: m. s. *populātus*, pp., inhabited]

population (pŏp′yo͞o lā′shən), *n.* **1.** the total number of persons inhabiting a country, town, or any district or area. **2.** the body of inhabitants of a place. **3.** the number or body of inhabitants of a particular race or class in a place. **4.** *Statistics.* an aggregate of statistical items. **5.** *Ecol.* **a.** all the individuals of one species in a given area. **b.** the assemblage of plants or animals living in a given area. **6.** the act or process of populating.

population parameter, *Statistics.* a variable entering into the mathematical form of the distribution of a population such that the possible values of the variable correspond to different distributions: *the mean and variance of a population are population parameters.*

population pyramid, *Sociol.* a graph showing the distribution of a population in terms of sex, age, etc.

populous (pŏp′yo͞o ləs), *adj.* full of people or inhabitants, as a region; well populated. —**pop′ulously,** *adv.* —**pop′ulousness,** *n.*

porbeagle (pô′bē′gl), *n.* a shark of the genus *Lamna*, esp. *L. nasus*, a large voracious species of the North Atlantic and North Pacific oceans. [t. Cornish]

porcelain (pôs′lĭn), *n.* **1.** a vitreous, more or less translucent, ceramic material; china. **2.** a vessel or object made of this material. [t. F: m. *porcelaine*, t. It.: m. *porcellana* orig., a kind of shell, der. *porcella*, dim. of *porca*, of uncert. orig. (? akin to PORK)]

porcelain enamel, *U.S.* vitreous enamel.

porch (pôch), *n.* **1.** an exterior appendage to a building, forming a covered approach or vestibule to a doorway. **2.** *U.S.* a veranda. **3.** a portico. **4. the Porch,** a public ambulatory in ancient Athens to which the Stoic philosopher Zeno of Citium and his followers resorted. [ME *porche*, t. OF, g. L *porticus* porch, portico]

porcine (pô′sīn), *adj.* **1.** of or resembling swine. **2.** swinish, hoggish, or piggish. [t. L: m. s. *porcinus*]

Porcupine, *Erethizon dorsatum* (Total length 3 to 3½ ft, tail 6 to 8 in.)

porcupine (pô′kyo͞o-pīn′), *n.* any of various rodents covered with stout, erectile spines or quills, as the **crested porcupine,** *Hystrix cristata*, of S Europe and N Africa, with long spines, and the common porcupine of North America, *Erethizon dorsatum*, with short spines or quills partially concealed by the fur. [ME *porkepyn*, t. OF: m. *porcespin*, lit., spine-pig. See PORK, SPINE]

porcupine anteater, an echidna, or spiny anteater.

pore[1] (pô), *v.t.*, **pored, poring. 1.** to meditate or ponder intently (usually fol. by *over, on,* or *upon*). **2.** to gaze earnestly or steadily. **3.** to read or study with steady attention or application. [ME *pouren, puren*; orig. uncert.]

pore[2] (pô), *n.* **1.** a minute opening or orifice, as in the skin or a leaf, for perspiration, absorption, etc. **2.** a minute interstice in a rock, etc. [ME, t. F, t. L: m. *porus*, t. Gk: m. *póros* passage]

Pori (*Finn.* pô′rē), *n.* a seaport in SW Finland. 59,543 (est. 1965).

poriferan (pô rĭf′ə rən), *n.* **1.** any animal of the phylum *Porifera*, comprising the sponges. —*adj.* **2.** belonging to or pertaining to the *Porifera.*

poriferous (pô rĭf′ə rəs), *adj.* bearing or having pores. [f. s. L *porus* pore + -(I)FEROUS]

porion (pô′rĭ ən), *n., pl.* **poria** (pô′rĭ ə). *Anat.* the most lateral point in the roof of the bony external auditory meatus (or earhole). [t. NL, der. Gk *póros* passage, way]

porism (pô′rĭz′əm), *n.* *Maths.* a form of proposition among the Greeks which has been variously defined, esp. as a proposition affirming the possibility of finding such conditions as will render a certain problem indeterminate, or capable of innumerable solutions. [t. L: m. *porisma*, t. Gk: a corollary, a problem]

pork (pôk), *n.* **1.** the flesh of pigs used as food. **2.** *U.S. Slang.* appropriations, appointments, etc., by the government for political reasons rather than for public necessity, as for public buildings, river improvements, etc. [ME *porc*, t. OF, g. L *porcus* hog, pig. See FARROW[1]] —**pork′-like′,** *adj.*

pork barrel, *U.S. Slang.* a government appropriation, bill, or policy which supplies funds for local improvements designed to ingratiate legislators with their constituents.

porker (pô′kə), *n.* a pig, esp. one fattened for killing.

pork-pie (pôk′pī′), *n.* **1.** a pie made of minced, seasoned pork. —*adj.* **2.** (of a hat) having a round, flat crown and an upturned brim.

porky (pô′kĭ), *adj.* **1.** porklike. **2.** fat.

pornographer (pô nŏg′rə fə), *n.* one who writes or sells pornography.

pornography (pô nŏg′rə fĭ), *n.* obscene literature, art, or photography, designed to excite sexual desire. [f. s. Gk *pornográphos* writing of prostitutes + -Y[3]] —**pornographic** (pô′nə grăf′ĭk), *adj.*

porosity (pô rŏs′ĭ tĭ), *n.* state or quality of being porous. [ME, t. ML: m. s. *porōsitas*]

porous (pô′rəs), *adj.* **1.** full of pores. **2.** permeable by water, air, or the like. —**po′rousness,** *n.*

porphyria (pô fĭ′rĭ ə), *n.* *Pathol.* a metabolic disorder associated with excess porphyrin in the blood and urine.

porphyrin (pô′fĭ rĭn), *n.* *Biochem.* any of a group of pyrrole derivatives, iron-free or magnesium-free, decomposition products of haematin and chlorophyll. They are found in all plant and animal protoplasm.

porphyritic (pô′fĭ rĭt′ĭk), *adj.* **1.** of, pertaining to, containing, or resembling porphyry. **2.** denoting, pertaining to, or resembling the texture or structure characteristic of porphyry.

porphyroid (pô′fĭ roid′), *n.* **1.** a rock resembling porphyry. **2.** a sedimentary rock which has been altered by some metamorphic agency so as to take on a slaty and more or less perfectly developed porphyritic structure.

porphyry (pôʹfĭ rĭ), *n.*, *pl.* **-ries.** **1.** a very hard rock, quarried in ancient Egypt, having a dark, purplish red groundmass containing small crystals of felspar. **2.** any rock of similar texture. [ME *porfirie*, t. AF, ult. der. Gk *pórphyros* purple. Cf. L *porphyrītēs* porphyry, t. Gk]

porpoise (pôʹpəs), *n.*, *pl.* **-poises,** (*esp. collectively*) **-poise.** **1.** any of the gregarious cetaceans constituting the genus *Phocaena* (family *Delphinidae*), five to eight feet long, usually blackish above and paler beneath, and having a blunt, rounded snout, esp. the common porpoise, *P. phocaena*, of both the North Atlantic and Pacific. **2.** a name used erroneously for other cetaceans, mostly in the U.S. [ME *porpeys*, t. OF: m. *porpeis*, g. LL *porcus piscis* hogfish, for L *porcus marīnus*]

Porpoise, *Phocaena phocaena* (Ab. 6 ft long)

porridge (pŏrʹĭj), *n.* a breakfast dish, originating in Scotland, consisting of oatmeal, or the like, water, or milk. [var. of POTTAGE]

porringer (pŏrʹĭn jə), *n.* a dish or basin from which soup, porridge, etc., may be eaten. [alter. of earlier *potager*, t. OF, der. *potage* POTTAGE]

Porsena (pôʹsĭ nə), *n.* **Lars** (läz), a legendary Etruscan king, said to have attacked Rome in order to restore the banished Tarquinius Superbus to the throne. Also, **Porsenna** (pô sĕnʹə).

port[1] (pôt), *n.* **1.** a town or place where ships load or unload. **2.** a place along the coast where ships may take refuge from storms. **3.** *Law.* any place where persons and merchandise are allowed to pass (by water or land) into and out of a country and where customs officers are stationed to inspect or appraise imported goods; port of entry. [ME and OE, t. L: s. *portus* harbour, haven] **—Syn. 1.** See **harbour.**

port[2] (pôt), *Naut.* **—***n.* **1.** the left-hand side of a ship or aircraft facing forward (opp. to *starboard*). See illus. under **aft.** **—***adj.* **2.** pertaining to the port. **3.** on the left side of a ship or aircraft. **—***v.t.*, *v.i.* **4.** to turn or ship to the port or left side. [orig. uncert.; ? because the larboard side was customarily next to the shore in port]

port[3] (pôt), *n.* any of a class of very sweet wines, mostly dark red, originally from Portugal. [from *Oporto* (Pg. *o porto* the port), city in Portugal]

port[4] (pôt), *n.* **1.** *Naut.* a porthole. **2.** a steel door in the side of a ship for loading and discharging cargo and baggage. **3.** *Mech.* an aperture in the surface of a cylinder, for the passage of steam, air, water, etc. **4.** *Mil.* gunport. **5.** a position in arms drill when the rifle is held across the body for inspection. **6.** *Elect.* a point in a circuit where an external connection is made. **7.** the curved mouthpiece of certain bits. **8.** *Chiefly Scot.* a gate or portal, as of a town or fortress. [ME and OE, t. L: s. *porta* gate]

port[5] (pôt), *v.t.* **1.** *Mil.* to carry (a rifle, etc.) with both hands, in a slanting direction across the front of the body, with the barrel or like part near the left shoulder. **—***n.* **2.** *Mil.* the position of a rifle or other weapon when ported. **3.** manner of bearing oneself; carriage or bearing. [t. F: s. *porter*, g. L *portāre* carry; ult. akin to FARE]

Port., **1.** Portugal. **2.** Portuguese.

portable (pôʹtə bl), *adj.* **1.** capable of being transported or conveyed. **2.** easily carried or conveyed by hand. **3.** *Obs.* endurable. **—***n.* **4.** something that is portable. [ME, t. LL: m. s. *portābilis*] **—portʹabilʹity,** *n.*

Portadown (pôʹtə dounʹ), *n.* a town in Northern Ireland, in County Antrim. 18,605 (1961).

portage (pôʹtĭj), *n.* **1.** the act of carrying; carriage. **2.** the carrying of boats, goods, etc., overland from one navigable water to another. **3.** place or course over which this is done. **4.** cost of carriage. [ME, t. F, der. *porter* carry]

portal[1] (pôʹtl), *n.* **1.** a door, gate, or entrance, esp. one of imposing appearance, as in a palace. **2.** Also, **portal frame.** a stiff, rectangular frame used as the skeleton for buildings and other structures. [ME *portale*, t. ML, der. L *porta* gate]

portal[2] (pôʹtl), *Anat.* **—***adj.* **1.** denoting or pertaining to the transverse fissure of the liver. **—***n.* **2.** portal vein. [t. ML: s. *portālis* of a gate]

portal vein, *Anat.* the large vein conveying blood to the liver from the veins of the stomach, intestine, spleen, and pancreas.

portamento (pôʹtə mĕnʹtō; *It.* pŏr tä mĕnʹtō), *n.*, *pl.* **-ti** (-tē). *Music.* a passing or gliding from one pitch or note to another with a smooth progression. [It.: a bearing, carrying, der. *portare* carry, g. L]

portance (pôʹtns), *n.* *Archaic.* bearing; behaviour. [t. F (obs.)]

Port Arthur (äʹthə), former name of **Luta.**

portative (pôʹtə tĭv), *adj.* **1.** portable. **2.** having or pertaining to the power or function of carrying. **—***n.* **3.** (formerly) a small, portable organ. [ME *portatif*, t. OF, der. *porter* carry. See -IVE]

Port-au-Prince (pôʹtō prĭnsʹ; *Fr.* pŏr tō prăNsʹ), *n.* a seaport in and the capital of Haiti, in the S part. 25,000 (est. 1965).

Port Blair (blĕə), a seaport in and the capital of the Andaman and Nicobar Islands. 14,075 (1961).

portcullis (pôt kŭlʹĭs), *n.* a strong grating, as of iron, made to slide in vertical grooves at the sides of a gateway of a fortified place, and let down to prevent passage. [ME *portcullise*, t. OF: m. *porte coleice*, f. porte PORT[4] (def. 8) + *coleice*, fem. of *coleis* flowing, sliding, ult. der. L *cōlātus*, pp., filtered]

Portcullis

Porte (pôt), *n.* the Ottoman Turkish court and government. Official name, **Sublime Porte.** [short for *Sublime Porte*, lit. High Gate, F trans. of the Turkish official title, with reference to the palace gate at which justice was administered]

porte-cochere (pôtʹkō shĕəʹ), *n.* **1.** a covered carriage entrance, leading into a courtyard. **2.** a porch at the door of a building for sheltering persons entering and leaving carriages. Also, *French*, **porte-cochère** (*Fr.* pŏrt kō shĕrʹ). [t. F: gate for coaches]

Port Elizabeth (ĭ lĭzʹə bəth), a seaport in the Republic of South Africa, in SE Cape Province. 290,693 (1960).

portend (pô tĕndʹ), *v.t.* **1.** to indicate beforehand, or presage, as an omen does. **2.** *Obs.* to signify; mean. [ME, t. L: s. *portendere* point out, indicate, portend]

portent (pôʹtĕnt), *n.* **1.** an indication or omen of something about to happen, esp. something momentous. **2.** ominous significance: *an occurrence of dire portent.* **3.** a prodigy or marvel. [t. L: s. *portentum*, prop. neut. pp., presaged] **—Syn. 1.** See **sign.**

portentous (pô tĕnʹtəs), *adj.* **1.** of the nature of a portent; momentous. **2.** ominous; ominously indicative. **3.** marvellous; amazing; prodigious. **—portenʹtously,** *adv.* **—portenʹtousness,** *n.*

porter[1] (pôʹtə), *n.* **1.** one employed to carry burdens or luggage, as at a railway station, hotel, etc. **2.** *U.S.* a railway carriage attendant. [ME *portour*, t. OF: m. *porteour*, ult. der. L *portāre* carry]

porter[2] (pôʹtə), *n.* **1.** one who has charge of a door or gate; a doorkeeper; a janitor. **2.** (in certain English universities) a college servant with responsibility for regulating entry and answering enquiries. **3.** *Rom. Cath. Ch.* an ostiary. [ME, t. AF, g. LL *portārius*, der. L *porta* gate]

porter[3] (pôʹtə), *n.* a heavy, dark brown beer made with malt browned by drying at a high temperature. [short for *porter's ale*, appar. orig. brewed for porters]

Porter (pôʹtə), *n.* **1. Cole,** 1893–1964, U.S. composer. **2. Katherine Anne,** born 1894, U.S. writer. **3. William Sidney** (*O. Henry*), 1862–1910, U.S. short-story writer.

porterage (pôʹtə rĭj), *n.* **1.** the work of a porter or carrier. **2.** the charge for such work.

porterhouse (pôʹtə housʹ), *n.* **1.** Also, **porterhouse steak.** a choice cut of beef from between the prime ribs and the sirloin. **2.** *Archaic.* a house where porter and other liquors are retailed. **3.** *Archaic.* a chophouse.

Port-Étienne (*Fr.* pŏr tĕ tyĕnʹ), *n.* a seaport in NW Mauritania. 1200 (est. 1963).

portfolio (pôtʹfōʹlyō), *n.*, *pl.* **-lios.** **1.** a portable case for loose papers, prints, etc. **2.** such a case for carrying documents of a state department. **3.** the office or post of a minister of state or member of a cabinet. **4.** an itemized account; the securities, discount paper, etc., of an investment organization, bank, or other investor. [t. It.: m. *portafoglio*, f. *porta*, impv. of *portare* (g. L) carry + *foglio* (g. L *folium*) leaf, sheet]

Port Glasgow, a seaport in Scotland, in Renfrewshire, near Glasgow: shipbuilding. 22,551 (1961).

Port Harcourt (häʹkət), a seaport in S Eastern Nigeria. 72,000 (est. 1963).

porthole (pôtʹhōlʹ), *n.* an aperture in the side of a ship, for admitting light and air.

Portici (*It.* pŏrʹtē chē), *n.* a seaport in Italy, in Campania. 62,313 (1966).

portico (pôʹtĭ kōʹ), *n.*, *pl.* **-coes, -cos.** a structure consisting of a roof supported by columns or piers, forming the entrance to a temple, church, house, etc. [t. It., t. L: m. *porticus* porch, portico]

portiere (pôʹtĭ ĕəʹ), *n.* a curtain hung at a doorway, either to replace the door or merely for decoration. Also, *French*, **portière** (*Fr.* pŏr tyĕrʹ). [t. F]

portion (pô′shən), *n.* **1.** a part of any whole, whether actually separated from it or not: *a portion of the manuscript is illegible.* **2.** the part of a whole allotted to or belonging to a person or group; a share. **3.** a quantity of food served for one person. **4.** the part of an estate that goes to an heir or next of kin. **5.** the money, goods, or estate which a woman brings to her husband at marriage; a dowry. **6.** that which is allotted to a person by God or fate. —*v.t.* **7.** to divide into or distribute in portions or shares; parcel (often fol. by *out*). **8.** to furnish with a portion, inheritance, or dowry. **9.** to provide with a lot or fate. [ME *porcion*, t. OF, t. L: m. s. *portio* share, part; akin to L *pars* part] —**por′tionless,** *adj.* —**Syn. 1.** See **part.**

Port Jackson (jăk′sən), an inlet of the Pacific in SE Australia, forming the harbour of Sydney.

Portland (pôt′lənd), *n.* **1. William Henry Cavendish Bentinck** (kăv′ən dĭsh bĕn′tĭngk), **3rd Duke of,** 1738–1809, British statesman: prime minister 1783, 1807–09. **2.** a seaport in the U.S., in NW Oregon at the confluence of the Willamette and Columbia rivers. 372,676 (1960).

Portland cement, a kind of hydraulic cement usually made by burning a mixture of limestone and clay in a kiln. [named after the Isle of *Portland*, Dorset]

Portland stone, a type of limestone, used in building, quarried on the Isle of Portland.

Port Laoise (pôt′lē′shə), a town in the Republic of Ireland, the county town of Leix. 3133 (1961).

Port Louis (lo͞o′ĭs, lo͞o′ĭ), a seaport in and the capital of Mauritius, in the Indian Ocean, E of Madagascar. 128,450 (1965).

Port Lyautey (*Fr.* pŏr lyō tē′). See **Kenitra.**

portly (pôt′lĭ), *adj.*, **-lier, -liest. 1.** large in person; stout; corpulent. **2.** stately, dignified, or imposing. [f. PORT[5], n. + -LY] —**port′liness,** *n.*

portmanteau (pôt′măn′tō), *n., pl.* **-teaus, -teaux.** a case or bag to carry clothing, etc., while travelling, esp. a leather case which opens into two halves. [t. F: m. *portemanteau* cloak-carrier. See PORT[5], MANTLE]

portmanteau word, a word made by telescoping or blending two other words, as *brunch* for *breakfast* and *lunch.* See **blend** (def. 8).

Port Moresby (môz′bĭ), a seaport in SE New Guinea: capital of the merged Australian territories of Papua and New Guinea. 23,600 (est. 1964).

Porto (*Port.* pȯr′to͞o), *n.* Portuguese name of **Oporto.**

Porto Alegre (*Port.* pȯr′to͞o ȧ lĕ′grē), a seaport in S Brazil. 617,629 (1960).

Portobello (pô′tō bĕl′ō), *n.* a small seaport on the Caribbean coast of Panama, NE of Colón: harbour discovered and named by Columbus, 1502; a principal city of Spanish colonial America.

port of call, a port where ships stop briefly to take on stores or undergo repairs.

port of entry, port[1] (def. 3).

Port-of-Spain (pôt′əv spān′), *n.* a seaport in the West Indies, in NW Trinidad, the capital of Trinidad and Tobago. 93,954 (1960).

Porto Novo (pô′tō nō′vō), a seaport in and the capital of Dahomey, in the SE part. 65,000 (est. 1963).

Porto Rico (pô′tō rē′kō), Puerto Rico.

Port Philip Bay (fĭl′ĭp), a bay in SE Australia: the harbour of Melbourne. 31 mi. long; ab. 20 mi. wide.

portrait (pô′trĭt), *n.* **1.** a likeness of a person, especially of the face, usually made from life. **2.** a verbal picture, usually of a person. [t. F, orig. pp. of *portraire*, g. L *prōtrahere* portray, bring forward]

portraitist (pô′trĭ tĭst), *n.* a portrait painter.

portraiture (pô′trĭ chə), *n.* **1.** the art of portraying. **2.** a pictorial representation; a portrait. **3.** a verbal picture. [ME *purtreyture*, t. OF: m. *portraiture*, der. *portrait* PORTRAIT]

portray (pô trā′), *v.t.* **1.** to represent by a drawing, painting, carving, or the like. **2.** to represent dramatically, as on the stage. **3.** to depict in words; describe graphically. [ME, t. OF: s. *portraire*, g. LL *prōtrahere* depict, L draw forth] —**portray′able,** *adj.* —**portray′er,** *n.* —**Syn. 1, 3.** picture, delineate. See **depict.**

portrayal (pô trā′əl), *n.* **1.** the act of portraying. **2.** a representation portraying something.

portress (pô′trĭs), *n.* a female porter or doorkeeper.

Port Royal (roi′əl), **1.** a village in S South Carolina, on **Port Royal island**: colonized by French Huguenots, 1562. **2.** a historic town in SE Jamaica at the entrance of Kingston harbour: a former capital of Jamaica. **3.** former name of **Annapolis Royal.**

Port Said (sä′ēd, sīd), a seaport in NE Egypt at the Mediterranean end of the Suez Canal. 244,000 (est. 1960). See map under **Suez.**

Port-Salut (pô′sə lo͞o′; *Fr.* pŏr sȧ lY′), *n.* a semi-hard, mild cheese, made originally in W France, formed into a flat, round shape weighing 3–4 lbs.

Portsmouth (pôts′məth), *n.* **1.** a city and seaport in England, in Hampshire: naval establishment. 215,198 (1961). **2.** a seaport in the U.S., in SE Virginia: naval dockyard. 114,773 (1960).

Port Sudan, a seaport in NE Sudan, on the Red Sea. 57,000 (est. 1964).

Port Talbot (pôt′tôl′bət, -tăl′-), a seaport in Wales, in Glamorganshire. 51,322 (1961).

Portugal (pô′tyo͝o gl; *Port.* po͞or to͞o gȧl′), *n.* a republic in SW Europe, on the Iberian Peninsula W of Spain. (Including the Azores and the Madeira Islands) 8,889,392 pop. (1960); 35,414 sq. mi. *Cap.*: Lisbon. See map under **Barbary Coast.**

Portuguese (pô′tyo͝o gēz′), *adj.* **1.** of or pertaining to Portugal, its people, or their language. —*n.* **2.** a native or inhabitant of Portugal. **3.** the Romance language of Portugal and Brazil.

Portuguese East Africa, Mozambique (def. 1).

Portuguese Guinea, a Portuguese overseas province on the W coast of Africa between Guinea and Senegal. 519,229 pop. (1960); 13,948 sq. mi. *Cap.*: Bissao. See map under **Senegal.**

Portuguese India, a former Portuguese overseas territory on the W coast of India, consisting of the districts of Goa, Daman, and Diu: annexed by India 1961. *Cap.*: Goa.

Portuguese man-of-war, any of several large oceanic hydrozoans of the genus *Physalia*, having a large, bladder-like structure by which they are buoyed up and from which are suspended numerous processes.

Portuguese West Africa, Angola.

portulaca (pô′tyo͝o lăk′ə, -lā′kə), *n.* any plant of the genus *Portulaca*, which comprises herbs with thick, succulent leaves and variously coloured flowers, as *P. grandiflora*, cultivated in gardens, and *P. oleracea*, the common purslane. [NL, t. L: purslane]

portulacaceous (pô′tyo͝o lə kā′shəs), *adj.* belonging to the *Portulacaceae*, or portulaca family of plants.

Porz (*Ger.* pŏrts), *n.* a town in West Germany, in S North Rhine-Westphalia. 68,500 (est. 1966).

pos., 1. positive. **2.** possessive.

posada (*Sp.* pō sä′dȧ), *n. Spanish.* an inn.

pose[1] (pōz), *v.*, **posed, posing,** *n.* —*v.i.* **1.** to affect a particular character as with a view to the impression made on others. **2.** to present oneself before others: *to pose as a judge of literature.* **3.** to assume or hold a position or attitude for some artistic purpose. —*v.t.* **4.** to place in a suitable position or attitude for a picture, tableau, or the like: *to pose a group for a photograph.* **5.** to assert, state, or propound: *to pose a hard problem.* **6.** *Archaic.* to put or place. —*n.* **7.** attitude or posture of body: *her pose had a kind of defiance in it.* **8.** attitude assumed in thought or conduct. **9.** the act or period of posing, as for a picture. **10.** a position or attitude assumed in posing, or exhibited by a figure in a picture, sculptural work, tableau, or the like. **11.** a studied attitude or mere affectation, as of some character, quality, sentiment, or course: *his liberalism is all a pose.* [ME, t. OF: m. *poser*, g. LL *pausāre* lay down (a sense due to confusion with L *pōnere* place, put), in L halt, cease] —**Syn. 7.** See **position.**

pose[2] (pōz), *v.t.*, **posed, posing. 1.** to embarrass by a difficult question or problem. **2.** *Obs.* to examine by putting questions. [aphetic var. of obs. *appose*, var. of OPPOSE, used in sense of L *appōnere* put to]

Poseidon (pŏ sī′dən), *n.* the Greek god of the sea, identified by the Romans with Neptune.

Posen (*Ger.* pō′zən), *n.* German name of **Poznań.**

poser[1] (pō′zə), *n.* one who poses. [f. POSE[1] + -ER[1]]

poser[2] (pō′zə), *n.* a question or problem that puzzles. [f. POSE[2] + -ER[1]]

poseur (pō zû′; *Fr.* pō zœr′), *n.* one who affects a particular pose (def. 11) to impress others. [t. F, der. *poser* POSE[1]]

posh (pŏsh), *Colloq.* —*adj.* **1.** elegant; luxurious; smart; first-class. —*v.t.* **2.** to make smart or elegant (fol. by *up*). —**posh′ly,** *adv.* —**posh′ness,** *n.*

posigrade rocket (pō′sĭ grād′), *Aerospace.* a small rocket which fires in the direction of flight, often used to separate an expended stage from a multistage rocket.

posit (pŏz′ĭt), *v.t.* **1.** to place, put, or set. **2.** to lay down or assume as a fact or principle; affirm; postulate. [t. L: s. *positus*, pp., placed]

position (pə zĭsh′ən), *n.* **1.** condition with reference to place; location. **2.** a place occupied or to be occupied; site: *a fortified position.* **3.** proper or appropriate place: *out of position.* **4.** situation or condition, esp. with relation to circumstances: *to be in an awkward position.* **5.** status or standing. **6.** high standing, as in society.

7. a post of employment: *a position in a bank.* **8.** manner of being placed, disposed, or arranged: *the relative position of the hands of a clock.* **9.** posture or attitude of body. **10.** mental attitude; way of viewing a matter; stand: *one's position on a public question.* **11.** condition (of affairs, etc.). **12.** the act of positing. **13.** that which is posited. **14.** *Class. Pros.* the situation of a short vowel before two or more consonants or their equivalent, making the syllable metrically long. **15.** *Music.* **a.** one of the points on the fingerboard of a stringed instrument. **b.** a shift of the slide of a trombone. —*v.t.* **16.** to put in a particular or appropriate position; place. **17.** to determine the position of; locate. [ME, t. L: s. *positio.* Cf. POSIT, POSE[1]] —**posi′tional,** *adj.*

—**Syn. 1.** station, place, locality, spot. **7.** POSITION, JOB, PLACE, SITUATION refer to a post of employment. POSITION is any employment, though usually above manual labour: *position as clerk.* JOB is colloquial for POSITION, and applies to any work from lowest to highest in an organization: *a job as fireman, as manager.* PLACE and SITUATION are both mainly used today in reference to a POSITION that is desired or being applied for; SITUATION is the general word in the business world: *Situations Wanted;* PLACE is used rather of domestic employment: *she is looking for a place as a housekeeper.*

—**Syn. 9.** POSITION, POSTURE, ATTITUDE, POSE refer to an arrangement or disposal of the body or its parts. POSITION is the general word for the arrangement of the body: *in a sitting position.* POSTURE is usually an assumed arrangement of the body: *an erect posture, a relaxed posture.* ATTITUDE is often a posture assumed for imitative effect or the like, but may be one adopted for a purpose (as that of a fencer or a tightrope walker): *an attitude of prayer.* A POSE is an attitude assumed, in most cases, for artistic effect: *an attractive pose.*

positive (pŏz′ə tĭv), *adj.* **1.** explicitly laid down or expressed: *a positive declaration.* **2.** arbitrarily laid down; determined by enactment or convention (opposed to *natural*): *positive law.* **3.** admitting of no question: *positive proof.* **4.** stated; express; emphatic. **5.** confident in opinion or assertion, as a person; fully assured. **6.** overconfident or dogmatic. **7.** without relation to or comparison with other things; absolute (opposed to *relative* and *comparative*). **8.** *Colloq.* downright; out-and-out. **9.** possessing an actual force, being, existence, etc. **10.** *Philos.* concerned with or based on matters of experience: *positive philosophy.* See **positivism** (def. 2). **11.** practical; not speculative or theoretical. **12.** characterized by optimism or hopefulness: a *positive attitude.* **13.** consisting in or characterized by the presence or possession of distinguishing or marked qualities or features (opposed to *negative*): *light is positive, darkness negative.* **14.** denoting the presence of such qualities, as a term. **15.** measured or proceeding in a direction assumed as that of increase, progress, or onward motion. **16.** *Elect.* denoting or pertaining to the kind of electricity developed on glass when rubbed with silk, or the kind of electricity present at that pole where electrons enter, or return to, an electric generator; having a deficiency of electrons. **17.** *Chem.* (of an element or radical) basic. **18.** *Photog.* showing the lights and shades as seen in the original, as a print from a negative. **19.** *Gram.* being, denoting, or pertaining to the initial degree of the comparison of adjectives and adverbs, as English *smooth* in contrast to *smoother* and *smoothest.* **20.** *Maths.* denoting a quantity greater than zero. **21.** *Biol.* orientated or moving towards the focus of excitation: *a positive tropism.* **22.** *Bacteriol.* (of blood, affected tissue, etc.) showing the presence of an organism which causes a disease. **23.** *Mach.* denoting or pertaining to a process or machine part having a fixed or certain operation, esp. as the result of elimination of play, free motion, etc.: *positive lubrication.*
—*n.* **24.** something positive. **25.** a positive quality or characteristic. **26.** a positive quantity or symbol. **27.** *Photog.* a positive picture. **28.** *Gram.* **a.** the positive degree. **b.** a form in it.
[t. L: m. s. *positivus;* r. ME *positif,* t. OF] —**pos′itiveness,** *n.* —**Syn. 1.** See **sure.**

positive feedback. See **feedback** (def. 2).

positively (pŏz′ə tĭv lĭ), *adv.* absolutely; undoubtedly; decidedly; definitely.

positive organ, (formerly) a kind of small fixed organ (opposed to *portative*).

positivism (pŏz′ə tĭ vĭz′əm), *n.* **1.** the state or quality of being positive; definiteness; assurance. **2.** a philosophical system founded by Comte, concerned with positive facts and phenomena, and excluding speculation upon ultimate causes or origins. —**pos′itivist,** *adj., n.* —**pos′itivis′tic,** *adj.*

positron (pŏz′ĭ trŏn′), *n. Physics.* a particle of positive electricity with a mass equal to that of the electron. [f. POSIT(IVE) + (ELECT)RON]

positronium (pŏz′ĭ trō′nyəm), *n. Physics.* an unstable unit, resembling an atom of hydrogen, except that it consists of a positron and an electron: it decays in less than 10^{-7} seconds into three photons.

posology (pə sŏl′ə jĭ), *n.* the branch of medicine dealing with the determination of dosage. [f. Gk *póso(s)* how much + -LOGY]

poss., 1. possession. 2. possessive. 3. possible. 4. possibly.

posse (pŏs′ĭ), *n. Now Chiefly U.S.* **1.** posse comitatus. **2.** a body or force armed with legal authority. [t. ML: power, force, n. use of L inf., to be able, have power. See POTENT]

posse comitatus (pŏs′ĭ kŏm′ĭ tä′təs), **1.** the body of men that a sheriff is empowered to call to assist him in preserving the peace, and serving writs. **2.** a body of men so called into service. [ML: force of the county]

possess (pə zĕs′), *v.t.* **1.** to have as property; to have belonging to one. **2.** to have as a faculty, quality, or the like: *to possess courage.* **3.** to have knowledge of. **4.** to impart; inform; familiarize. **5.** to keep or maintain (oneself, one's mind, etc.) in a certain state, as of peace, patience, etc. **6.** to maintain control over (oneself, one's mind, etc.). **7.** (of a spirit, esp. an evil one) to occupy and control, or dominate from within, as a person. **8.** (of a feeling, idea, etc.) to dominate or actuate after the manner of such a spirit. **9.** to make (one) owner, holder, or master, as of property, information, etc. **10.** to cause to be dominated or influenced, as by a feeling, idea, etc.; imbue (*with*). **11.** (of a man) to have sexual intercourse with. **12.** *Obs.* to occupy or hold. **13.** *Archaic.* to seize or take. **14.** *Archaic.* to gain or win. [back-formation from *possessor,* ME *possessour,* t. L: m. *possessor*] —**posses′sor,** *n.* —**posses′sorship′,** *n.*

possessed (pə zĕst′), *adj.* **1.** moved by a strong feeling, madness, or some supernatural agency; frenzied (often fol. by *by, of,* or *with*). **2.** self-possessed; calm; poised. **3. possessed of,** having; possessing.

possession (pə zĕsh′ən), *n.* **1.** the act or fact of possessing. **2.** the state of being possessed. **3.** ownership. **4.** *Law.* actual holding or occupancy, either with or without rights of ownership. **5.** a thing possessed. **6.** (*pl.*) property or wealth. **7.** a territorial dominion of a state. **8.** control over oneself, one's mind, etc. **9.** domination or actuation by a feeling, idea, etc. **10.** the feeling or idea itself. [ME, t. L: s. *possessio*] —**Syn. 2.** See **custody.**

possessive (pə zĕs′ĭv), *adj.* **1.** of or pertaining to possession or ownership. **2.** exerting or seeking to exert excessive influence on the affections, behaviour, etc., of others: *a possessive wife.* **3.** *Gram.* **a.** indicating possession, ownership, origin, etc. **b.** denoting a case that indicates possession, ownership, origin, etc. —*n. Gram.* **4.** the possessive case. **5.** a form in the possessive. —**posses′sively,** *adv.* —**posses′siveness,** *n.*

possessory (pə zĕs′ə rĭ), *adj.* **1.** pertaining to a possessor or to possession. **2.** arising from possession: *a possessory interest.* **3.** having possession.

posset (pŏs′ĭt), *n.* a drink made of hot milk curdled with ale, wine, or the like, often sweetened and spiced. [late ME *poshote, possot,* ? OE **poswǣt* drink good for cold, f. *pos* cold in the head + *wǣt* drink]

possibility (pŏs′ə bĭl′ĭ tĭ), *n., pl.* **-ties. 1.** the state or fact of being possible: *the possibility of error.* **2.** a possible thing or person.

possible (pŏs′ə bl), *adj.* **1.** that may or can be, exist, happen, be done, be used, etc.: *no possible cure.* **2.** that may be true or a fact, or may perhaps be the case, as something concerning which one has no knowledge to the contrary: *it is possible that he went.* [ME, t. L: m. s. *possibilis*]

—**Syn. 1.** POSSIBLE, FEASIBLE, PRACTICABLE refer to that which may come about or take place without prevention by serious obstacles. That which is POSSIBLE is naturally able or even likely to happen, other circumstances being equal: *a new source of plutonium may be possible.* FEASIBLE refers to the ease with which something can be done and implies a high degree of desirability for doing it: *this plan is the most feasible.* PRACTICABLE applies to that which can be done with the means which are at hand, and conditions being what they are: *we ascended the slope as far as was practicable.*

possibly (pŏs′ə blĭ), *adv.* **1.** perhaps or maybe. **2.** in a possible manner. **3.** by any possibility.

possie (pŏz′ĭ), *n. Austral., N.Z. Colloq.* a place; position.

possum (pŏs′əm), *n.* **1.** *Colloq.* opossum. **2. play possum,** *Colloq.* to dissemble; feign illness or death. **3.** *Austral.* any of many kinds of phalangers, esp. of the genus *Trichosurus.*

post[1] (pōst), *n.* **1.** a strong piece of timber, metal, or the like, set upright as a support, a point of attachment, a mark, a place for displaying notices, etc. **2.** *Horseracing.* a pole on a racecourse marking the starting or finishing point for races. —*v.t.* **3.** to affix (a notice, etc.) to a post, wall, or the like. **4.** to bring to public notice by or as by a placard: *to post a reward.* **5.** to denounce by a public notice or declaration: *to post a person as a coward.* **6.** to enter the name of in a published list. **7.** to publish the name of (a ship) as missing or lost. **8.** to placard (a wall, etc.) with notices or bills. [ME and OE, t. L: s. *postis*]

post[2] (pōst), *n.* **1.** a position of duty, employment, or trust to which one is assigned or appointed: *a diplomatic post.* **2.** the station, or round of a soldier, sentry, or other person on duty. **3.** a military station with permanent buildings. **4.** *U.S.* the body of troops occupying a military station. **5.** *U.S.* a local unit of a veterans' organization. **6.** a trading post. **7.** *Mil.* either of two bugle calls (**first post** and **last post**) giving notice of the hour for retiring, as for the night. *—v.t.* **8.** to station at a post or place as a sentry or for some other purpose. **9.** *Mil., Naval.* to transfer away to another unit or command. [t. F: m. *poste*, t. It.: m. *posto*, g. L *positus*, pp., placed, put. Cf. POSITION] **—Syn. 1.** See **appointment.**

post[3] (pōst), *n.* **1.** a single collection or delivery of letters, packages, etc. **2.** the letters, packages, etc., themselves; mail. **3.** an established service or system for the conveyance of letters, etc., esp. under government authority. **4.** a post office. **5.** a pillar-box. **6.** one of a series of stations along a route, for furnishing relays of men and horses for carrying letters, etc. **7.** one who travels express, esp. over a fixed route with letters, etc. **8.** any of three sizes of paper: **large post,** 16½ × 21 inches, **small post,** 15¼ × 19 inches, and **pinched post,** 14½ × 18½ inches. *—v.t.* **9.** to place (a letter, etc.) in a postbox, post office, etc., for transmission. **10.** *Bookkeeping.* **a.** to transfer (an entry or item), as from the journal to the ledger. **b.** to enter (an item) in due place and form. **c.** to make all the requisite entries in (the ledger, etc.). **11.** to supply with up-to-date information; inform. *—v.i.* **12.** to travel with relays of horses. **13.** to travel with speed; go or pass rapidly; hasten. *—adv.* **14.** by post or courier. **15.** with post-horses, or by posting. **16.** with speed or haste; posthaste. [t. F: m. *poste*, t. It.: m. *posta*, g. *posita*, pp. fem., placed, put. Cf. POST[2]]

post-, a prefix meaning 'behind', 'after', occurring orig. in words from the Latin, but now freely used as an English formative: *post-Elizabethan, postfix, postgraduate.* Cf. **ante-** and **pre-.** [t. L, repr. *post*, adv. and prep.]

Post (pōst; *Du.* pôst *for def. 3*), *n.* **1. Emily Price,** 1873?–1960, U.S. writer on social etiquette. **2. George Browne,** 1837–1913, U.S. architect. **3. Pieter** (*Du.* pē′tər), 1608–1669, Dutch architect.

postage (pōs′tĭj), *n.* the charge for the conveyance of a letter or other matter sent by post, usually prepaid by means of a stamp or stamps.

postage stamp, an official stamp on an envelope, postcard, etc., in the form of a printed, adhesive label, as evidence of prepayment of a designated postage.

postal (pōs′tl), *adj.* **1.** of or pertaining to the post office or the carriage of mails. *—n.* **2.** *U.S. Colloq.* a postal card.

postal card, *U.S.* **1.** a card sold by the post office with a stamp already printed on it, which can usually be posted at a lower rate than letters in envelopes. **2.** a postcard.

postal order, a money order which is bought from and cashed at a post office.

postal union, an agreement among governments of many countries for the regulation of international post office business.

postaxial (pōst′ăk′sĭ əl), *adj.* *Anat., Zool.* behind the body axis, as the posterior part of the limb axis.

post-bag (pōst′băg′), *n.* **1.** a mailbag. **2.** (considered collectively) letters received.

post bellum (pōst′bĕl′əm), after the war. [L]

post-bellum (pōst′bĕl′əm), *adj.* occurring after the war, esp. the American Civil War.

postbox (pōst′bŏks′), *n.* a receptacle in which letters are deposited for posting.

postboy (pōst′boi′), *n.* **1.** a boy or man who rides post or carries letters. **2.** a postilion.

postcard (pōst′käd′), *n.* a card of standard size, often having a photograph, picture, etc., on one side, on which a message may be written and sent by post.

postchaise (pōst′shāz′), *n.* a hired coach drawn by horses changed at each stage used for rapid travelling in the 18th and early 19th centuries.

postcibal (pōst′sī′bl), *adj.* *Med.* occurring after the taking of food. [f. POST- + s. L *cibus* food + -AL[1]]

postclassical (pōst′klăs′ĭ kl), *adj.* denoting or occurring during a period after a classical period, as of literature, language, etc.

postdate (pōst′dāt′), *v.t.*, **-dated, -dating. 1.** to give a later date to than the true date. **2.** to date (an instrument such as a cheque or invoice) with a date later than the current date. **3.** to follow in time.

postdiluvian (pōst′dĭ lōō′vyən), *adj.* **1.** existing or occurring after the Flood. *—n.* **2.** one who has lived since the Flood.

poster[1] (pōs′tə), *n.* **1.** a placard or bill posted or for posting in some public place. **2.** one who posts bills, etc. [f. POST[1], v. + -ER[1]]

poster[2] (pōs′tə), *n.* *Obs.* a post-horse. [f. POST[3] + -ER[1]]

poste restante (pōst′rĕs′tŏnt; *Fr.* pŏst rĕs tä**N**t′), a department in a post office where letters may be kept until they are called for. [F: standing post]

posterior (pŏs tĭə′rĭ ə), *adj.* **1.** situated behind, or hinder (opposed to *anterior*). **2.** coming after in order, as in a series. **3.** coming after in time; later; subsequent (sometimes fol. by *to*). **4.** *Zool.* pertaining to the caudal end of the body. **5.** *Anat.* of or pertaining to the dorsal side of man. **6.** *Bot.* (of an axillary flower) on the side next to the main axis. *—n.* **7.** (*sometimes pl.*) the hinder parts of the body; the buttocks. [t. L, compar. of *posterus* coming after] **—poste′riorly,** *adv.* **—Syn. 1.** See **back**[1].

posteriority (pŏs tĭə′rĭ ŏ′rĭ tĭ), *n.* posterior position or date.

posterity (pŏs tĕ′rĭ tĭ), *n.* **1.** succeeding generations collectively. **2.** descendants collectively. [ME *posterite*, t. L: m. s. *posteritas*]

postern (pŏs′tûn), *n.* **1.** a back door or gate. **2.** any lesser or private entrance. *—adj.* **3.** like or pertaining to a postern. [ME, t. OF: m. *posterne*, for *posterle*, g. LL *posterula*, dim. of L *posterus* behind]

post exchange, *U.S. Mil.* a retail store in a military camp or base selling general merchandise, etc. *Abbrev.:* PX.

postexilian (pōst′ĭg zĭl′ĭ ən), *adj.* subsequent to the Babylonian exile or captivity of the Jews. Also, **post′-exil′ic.**

postfix (*v.* pōst fĭks′; *n.* pōst′fĭks), *v.t.* **1.** to affix at the end of something; append; suffix. *—n.* **2.** something postfixed. **3.** *Rare.* a suffix. [f. POST- + FIX, modelled on PREFIX]

post-free (pōst′frē′), *adj., adv.* **1.** Also, **postpaid.** with the postage prepaid. **2.** free of postal charges.

postglacial (pōst′glā′shəl), *adj.* denoting or occurring during a period following a glacial epoch.

postgraduate (pōst′grăd′yŏŏ ĭt), *adj.* **1.** pertaining to or pursuing a course of study after graduation. *—n.* **2.** a postgraduate student.

posthaste (pōst′hāst′), *adj.* **1.** with all possible speed or promptness: *to come posthaste.* *—n.* **2.** *Archaic.* great haste. [f. POST[3] + HASTE]

post hoc, ergo propter hoc (pōst′hŏk′, û′gō prŏp′tə hŏk′), *Latin.* after this, therefore because of it (a formula designating an error in logic: taking for a cause something merely earlier in time).

post-horn (pōst′hôn′), *n.* a simple brass instrument without keys, formerly used by coachmen on postchaises.

post-horse (pōst′hôs′), *n.* (formerly) a horse kept for the use of persons riding post or for hire by travellers.

posthumous (pŏs′tyŏŏ məs), *adj.* **1.** published after the death of the author. **2.** born after the death of the father. **3.** arising, existing, or continuing after one's death. [t. L: m. *posthumus*, erroneously (by assoc. with *humus* earth, ground, as if referring to burial) for *postumus* last, posthumous (superl. adj.)] **—post′humously,** *adv.*

posthypnotic (pōst′hĭp nŏt′ĭk), *adj.* **1.** of or pertaining to the period following a hypnotic trance. **2.** (of a suggestion) made during a hypnotic trance so as to be effective when the subject awakes.

postiche (pŏs tēsh′), *adj.* **1.** superadded, esp. inappropriately, as a sculptural or architectural ornament. **2.** artificial, counterfeit, or false. *—n.* **3.** an imitation or substitute. **4.** pretence. **5.** a hairpiece. [F, t. It.: m. (*ap*)*posticcio*, g. L *appositīcius* put on, factitious, false]

posticous (pŏs tē′kəs, -tī′-), *adj.* *Bot.* hinder; posterior. [t. L: m. *postīcus*]

postilion (pŏs tĭl′yən), *n.* one who rides the near horse of the leaders when four or more horses are used to draw a carriage, or who rides the near horse when only one pair is used. Also, **postillion.** [t. F: m. *postillon*, t. It.: m. *postiglione*, der. *posta* POST[3]]

post-impressionism (pōst′ĭm prĕsh′ə nĭz′əm), *n.* the varied doctrines and methods of certain modern painters developed between 1875 and 1890, which rejected the casual and momentary effects and the naturalistic tendency of the impressionists, but accepted their use of pure colour as a means of intensifying permanence and solidity (Cézanne), movement (Van Gogh), pattern (Gauguin), etc. **—post′-impres′sionist,** *n., adj.* **—post′-impres′sionis′tic,** *adj.*

posting (pōs′tĭng), *n.* the transfer of service personnel away to another unit or command.

postliminy (pōst′lĭm′ĭ nĭ), *n.* *Internat. Law.* the right by which persons and things taken in war are restored to their former status when coming again under the power of the nation to which they belonged. [t. L: m. s. *postlīminium*]

postlude (pōst′lōōd′), *n.* *Music.* **1.** a concluding piece or movement. **2.** a voluntary at the end of a church service. [f. POST- + m. s. L *lūdus* game; modelled on PRELUDE]

postman (pōst′mən, pōs′mən), *n.*, *pl.* **-men. 1.** a postal employee who sorts and delivers letters and parcels, or collects letters from postboxes. **2.** *Obs.* courier.

postmark (pōst′mäk′, pōs′mäk′), *n.* **1.** an official mark stamped on letters or other mail, to cancel the postage stamp, indicate the place and date of sending or of receipt, etc. —*v.t.* **2.** to stamp with a postmark.

postmaster (pōst′mäs′tə, pōs′mäs′tə), *n.* **1.** the official in charge of a post office. **2.** *Obs.* the master of a station for furnishing post-horses for travellers. —**post′mas′ter-ship′**, *n.*

postmaster general, *pl.* **postmasters general.** the minister at the head of the postal system of a country.

postmedieval (pōst′mĕd′ĭ ē′vəl), *adj.* after the Middle Ages. Also, **postmediaeval.**

postmeridian (pōst′mə rĭd′ĭ ən), *adj.* **1.** occurring after noon. **2.** of or pertaining to the afternoon.

post meridiem (pōst′mə rĭd′ĭ ĕm′), after noon: used in specifying the hour, usually in the abbreviated form p.m. [L]

postmillennial (pōst′mĭ lĕn′ĭ əl), *adj.* of or pertaining to the period following the millennium.

postmillennialism (pōst′mĭ lĕn′ĭ ə lĭz′əm), *n.* the doctrine or belief that the second coming of Christ will follow the millennium. —**post′millen′nialist,** *n.*

postmistress (pōst′mĭs′trĭs, pōs′mĭs′trĭs), *n.* a woman in charge of a post office.

post-mortem (pōst′mô′təm, pōs′mô′təm), *adj.* **1.** subsequent to death, as an examination of the body. —*n.* **2.** a post-mortem examination. **3.** an examination of the causes of failure of a plan, project, or the like. [t. L: after death]

post-mortem examination, *Med.* an autopsy.

postnatal (pōst′nā′tl), *adj.* **1.** subsequent to birth. —*n.* **2.** a postnatal examination (of the mother).

postnuptial (pōst′nŭp′shəl), *adj.* of or pertaining to the period after marriage.

post-obit (pōst′ō′bĭt, -ŏb′ĭt), *adj.* effective after a particular person's death. [short for POST OBITUM]

post-obit bond, a bond paying a sum of money after the death of some specified person.

post obitum (pōst′ŏb′ĭ təm), *Latin.* after death.

post office, 1. a department of government responsible for a country's postal and telecommunications services. **2.** a local office of this department for receiving, distributing, and transmitting mail, selling postage stamps, providing telecommunications services, etc. —**post′-of′fice,** *adj.*

post-office box, 1. (in a post office) a numbered compartment into which letters addressed to a particular individual or firm are put until called for. *Abbrev.*: P.O.B., POB. **2.** *Elect.* a portable type of Wheatstone bridge in which the resistances are contained in a box and variations in the resistance of the arms are made by inserting and removing plugs.

post-operative (pōst′ŏp′ə rə tĭv), *adj.* of or pertaining to the period of time following a surgical operation.

postorbital (pōst′ô′bĭ tl), *adj.* *Anat., Zool.* situated behind the orbit or socket of the eye.

postpaid (pōst′pād′), *adj.* post-free (def. 1).

post partum (pä′təm), *Med.* after childbirth.

postpone (pōst pōn′, pōs pōn′), *v.*, **-poned, -poning.** —*v.t.* **1.** to put off to a later time; defer: *he postponed his departure an hour.* **2.** to place after in order of importance or estimation; subordinate: *to postpone private ambitions to the public welfare.* [t. L: m. s. *postpōnere*] —**postpon′-able,** *adj.* —**postpone′ment,** *n.* —**postpon′er,** *n.* —**Syn.** **1.** See **defer.**

postposition (pōst′pə zĭsh′ən), *n.* **1.** the act of placing after. **2.** the state of being so placed. **3.** *Gram.* a word placed after another as a modifier or to show its relation to other parts of the sentence. Examples: *attorney general, the man afloat.* [f. POST- + POSITION. Cf. PREPOSITION]

postpositive (pōst′pŏz′ə tĭv), *Gram.* —*adj.* **1.** placed after. —*n.* **2.** a postposition. —**post′pos′itively,** *adv.*

postprandial (pōst′prăn′dĭ əl), *adj.* after a meal, esp. after dinner. [f. POST- + s. L *prandium* meal + -AL^1]

postrevolutionary (pōst′rĕv′ə lōō′shə nə rĭ), *adj.* after a revolution.

postrider (pōst′rī′də), *n.* one who rides post; a mounted mail carrier.

postroad (pōst′rōd′), *n.* **1.** (formerly) a road with stations for furnishing horses for postriders, mail coaches, or travellers. **2.** a road or route over which mail is carried.

postscript (pōs′skrĭpt′), *n.* **1.** a paragraph, sentence, etc., added to a letter which has already been concluded and signed by the writer. **2.** any supplementary part. [t. L: s. *postscriptum*, pp. neut., written after]

post-tensioned (pōst′tĕn′shənd), *adj.* (in prestressed concrete) having the reinforcement stretched after the concrete is cast. Cf. **pre-tensioned.**

postulancy (pŏs′tyōō lən sĭ), *n.* the period or condition of being a postulant, esp. in a religious order.

postulant (pŏs′tyōō lənt), *n.* **1.** one who asks or applies for something. **2.** a candidate, esp. for admission into a religious order. [t. L: s. *postulans*, ppr., demanding]

postulate (*v.* pŏs′tyōō lāt′; *n.* pŏs′tyōō lĭt), *v.*, **-lated, -lating,** *n.* —*v.t.* **1.** to ask, demand, or claim. **2.** to claim or assume the existence or truth of, esp. as a basis for reasoning. **3.** to assume without proof, or as self-evident; take for granted. **4.** *Geom.* to assume; to take as an axiom. **5.** *Eccles.* to nominate to a position, subject to the approval of a higher authority. —*n.* **6.** something postulated or assumed without proof as a basis for reasoning or as self-evident. **7.** a fundamental principle. **8.** a necessary condition; a prerequisite. [t. L: m. s. *postulātum*, prop. pp. neut., thing requested] —**pos′tula′tion,** *n.*

posture (pŏs′chə), *n.*, *v.*, **-tured, -turing.** —*n.* **1.** the relative disposition of the various parts of anything. **2.** the position of the body and limbs as a whole: *a change in posture, a sitting posture.* **3.** an affected or unnatural attitude, or a contortion of the body: *antic postures and gestures.* **4.** mental or spiritual attitude. **5.** position, condition, or state, esp. of affairs. —*v.t.* **6.** to place in a particular posture or attitude; dispose in postures. —*v.i.* **7.** to assume a particular posture. **8.** to assume affected or unnatural postures; bend or contort the body in various ways, specif. in public performing. **9.** to act in an affected or artificial way, as if for show; pose for effect. [t. F, g. L *positūra*] —**pos′tural,** *adj.* —**pos′turer,** *n.* —**Syn.** **2.** See **position.**

posturize (pŏs′chə rīz′), *v.i.*, **-rized, -rizing.** to posture; pose. Also, **posturise.**

postwar (pōst′wô′), *adj.* of or pertaining to the period following a war: *postwar trade.*

posy (pō′zĭ), *n.*, *pl.* **-sies. 1.** a flower; a nosegay or bouquet. **2.** *Archaic.* a brief motto or the like, such as is inscribed within a ring. [syncopated var. of POESY]

pot^1 (pŏt), *n.*, *v.*, **potted, potting.** —*n.* **1.** an earthen, metallic, or other container, usually round and deep, used for domestic or other purposes. **2.** such a vessel with its contents. **3.** a potful. **4.** a potful of liquor. **5.** liquor or other drink. **6.** a wicker vessel for trapping fish or crustaceans. **7.** a round or oval refractory container in which glass is melted. **8.** *Slang.* a large sum of money. **9.** the aggregate of bets at stake at one time, as in card games, esp. poker. **10.** *Slang.* (in horseracing) a heavily backed horse; favourite. **11.** a pot shot. **12.** a liquid measure, usually equal to a pint or quart. **13.** *Colloq.* an important person: *a big pot.* **14.** *Colloq.* a potbelly. **15.** a chamber-pot. **16.** *Colloq.* a trophy or prize in a contest, esp. a silver cup. **17.** (*pl.*) *Colloq.* a large quantity. **18.** *Slang.* marijuana. **19. go to pot,** to deteriorate. —*v.t.* **20.** to put into a pot. **21.** to preserve (food) in a pot. **22.** to cook in a pot. **23.** to plant in a pot of soil. **24.** *Hunting.* **a.** to shoot (game birds) on the ground or water, or (game animals) at rest, instead of in flight or running. **b.** to shoot for food, not for sport. **25.** *Colloq.* to capture, secure, or win. **26.** *Billiards.* to pocket. **27.** *Colloq.* to put (a young child) on a chamber-pot. —*v.i.* **28.** *Slang.* to take a pot shot; shoot. [ME and OE *pott*, c. MLG *pot.* Cf. F *pot* (? t. G)]

pot^2 (pŏt), *n.* *Scot. and N Dial.* a deep hole; a pit. [ME; ? same as POT^1]

pot., 1. potential. **2.** potentiometer.

potable (pō′tə bl), *adj.* **1.** fit or suitable for drinking. —*n.* **2.** (*usually pl.*) anything drinkable. [t. LL: m. s. *pōtābilis*, der. L *pōtāre* drink]

potage (pō täzh′; *Fr.* pō tȧzh′), *n.* *French.* soup.

potamic (pō tăm′ĭk), *adj.* of or pertaining to rivers. [f. s. Gk *potamós* + -IC]

potash (pŏt′ăsh′), *n.* **1.** potassium carbonate, esp. the crude impure form obtained from wood ashes. **2.** caustic potash. **3.** the oxide of potassium, K_2O. **4.** potassium: *carbonate of potash.* [earlier *pot-ashes*, pl., trans. of early D *potasschen*]

potassic (pə tăs′ĭk), *adj.* of, pertaining to, or containing potassium.

potassium (pə tăs′yəm), *n.* *Chem.* a silvery white metallic element, which oxidizes rapidly in the air, and whose compounds are used as fertilizer and in special hard glasses. *Symbol*: K; *at. wt*: 39·102; *at. no.*: 19; *sp. gr.*: 0·86 at 20°C. [f. s. NL *potassa* (t. F: m. *potasse*, a former equivalent of POTASH) + -IUM]

potassium-argon dating (pə tăs′yəm ä′gŏn), a method of dating rocks which depends on the ratio of potassium-40 to radiogenic argon-40 which they contain.

potassium bicarbonate, *Chem.* a white powder, $KHCO_3$, used in cookery and medicine.

potassium bromide, a white crystalline compound, KBr, used in photography and medicinally as a sedative.

potassium carbonate, a white solid, K_2CO_3, used in the manufacture of glass, etc.

potassium cyanide, a white, crystalline, poisonous compound, KCN, used in metallurgy and photography.

potassium dichromate, an orange-red crystalline compound, $K_2Cr_2O_7$, used in dyeing, photography, etc.

potassium ferricyanide, *Chem.* a red crystalline solid, $K_3Fe(CN)_6$, used in the manufacture of pigments.

potassium ferrocyanide, *Chem.* a yellow crystalline solid, $K_4Fe(CN)_6.3H_2O$, used in dyeing and metallurgy.

potassium hydroxide, a white caustic solid, KOH, used in making soft soap, etc.

potassium nitrate, saltpetre; a crystalline compound, KNO_3, used in gunpowder, fertilizers, preservatives, and medicinally as a diaphoretic. It is produced by nitrification in soil.

potassium permanganate, a nearly black crystalline compound, $KMnO_4$, forming red-purple solutions in water: used as an oxidizing agent, disinfectant, etc.

potation (pō tā′shən), *n.* **1.** the act of drinking. **2.** a drink or draught, esp. of an alcoholic beverage. [t. L: s. *pōtātio*; r. ME *potacioun*, t. OF]

potato (pə tā′tō), *n., pl.* **-toes. 1.** the edible tuber (**white potato** or **Irish potato**) of a cultivated plant, *Solanum tuberosum.* **2.** the plant itself. **3.** sweet potato. [t. Sp.: m. *patata* white potato, var. of *batata* sweet potato, t. Haitian]

potato beetle. See **Colorado beetle.** Also, *Chiefly U.S.*, **potato bug.**

potato chip, 1. a deep-fried finger of potato. **2.** *U.S.* a crisp.

potatory (pō′tə tə rĭ, -trĭ), *adj.* **1.** of, pertaining to, or given to drinking. **2.** *Rare.* potable. [t. L: m. s. *pōtātōrius*]

pot-au-feu (*Fr.* pŏ tō fœ′), *n.* a traditional French dish of meat and vegetables. [F: lit., pot on the fire]

potbelly (pŏt′bĕl′ĭ), *n., pl.* **-lies.** a distended or protuberant belly. **—pot′bel′lied,** *adj.*

potboiler (pŏt′boi′lə), *n. Colloq.* an inferior work of literature, etc., produced merely for financial gain.

potboy (pŏt′boi′), *n.* a youth employed in a public house to serve beer.

poteen (pŏ tēn′), *n.* (in Ireland) illicitly distilled whiskey. Also, **potheen.** [t. Irish: m. *poitīn* small pot, dim. of *pota* pot]

Potemkin (pŏ tĕm′kĭn; *Russ.* pȧ tyôm′kĭn), *n.* **Prince Grigori Aleksandrovich** (*Russ.* grĭ gô′rĭy ə lĭk sȧn′drə vĭch), 1739–91, Russian statesman and favourite of Catherine II.

potence (pō′tns), *n.* potency.

potency (pō′tn sĭ), *n., pl.* **-cies. 1.** the quality of being potent. **2.** power or authority. **3.** powerfulness or effectiveness. **4.** strength or efficacy, as of a drug. **5.** a person or thing exerting power or influence. **6.** *Obs.* capability of development, or potentiality. Also, **potence.** [t. L: m. s. *potentia*]

potent (pō′tnt), *adj.* **1.** powerful; mighty. **2.** cogent, as reasons, motives, etc. **3.** producing powerful physical or chemical effects, as a drug. **4.** possessed of great power or authority. **5.** exercising great moral influence. **6.** having sexual power. [t. L: s. *potens*, ppr., being able, powerful] **—po′tently,** *adv.* **—po′tentness,** *n.* **—Syn. 1.** See **powerful.**

potentate (pō′tn tāt′), *n.* one who possesses great power; a sovereign, monarch, or ruler. [t. LL: m. s. *potentātus* potentate, L power, dominion]

potential (pə tĕn′shəl), *adj.* **1.** possible as opposed to actual. **2.** capable of being or becoming; latent. **3.** *Gram.* expressing possibility, as of a mode or model construction, as, I *can* go. **4.** *Physics.* potential energy. **5.** *Rare.* potent. *—n.* **6.** a possibility or potentiality. **7.** *Gram.* a potential mode or construction, or a form therein. **8.** *Elect.* **a.** the electrification of a point near or within an electrified body, represented by the work hypothetically necessary to bring a unit of positive electricity from an infinite distance to that point. **b.** the relative electrification of a point or body with respect to some other electrification, e.g., that of the ground nearby or of the earth in general, taken as a base of reference. **9.** *Maths., Physics.* a type of function from which the intensity of a field may be derived, usually by differentiation. [ME, t. ML: s. *potentiālis*] **—Syn. 2.** See **latent.**

potential difference, *Elect.* the difference in potential between two points, defined as the work performed when unit positive charge is moved from one point to the other. *Abbrev.:* p.d. Also, **voltage drop.**

potential divider, *Elect.* a voltage divider.

potential energy, *Physics.* energy which is due to position rather than motion, as a coiled spring or a raised weight (opposed to *kinetic energy*).

potentiality (pə tĕn′shĭ ăl′ĭ tĭ), *n., pl.* **-ties. 1.** potential state or quality; possibility; latent power or capacity. **2.** something potential. [t. ML: m. s. *potentiālitas*]

potentially (pə tĕn′shə lĭ), *adv.* not actually, but possibly.

potentilla (pō′tən tĭl′ə), *n.* any plant of the rosaceous genus *Potentilla*, comprising herbs, or small shrubs, abundant in north temperate regions. [t. NL, f. s. L *potens* potent + *-illa* (dim. suffix)]

potentiometer (pə tĕn′shĭ ŏm′ĭ tə), *n. Elect.* **1.** an instrument for measuring electromotive force or difference in potential. **2.** a voltage divider. [f. POTENTI(AL), n., + -(O)-METER[1]] **—potentiometric** (pə tĕn′shĭ ō mĕt′rĭk), *adj.*

Potenza (*It.* pō tĕn′tsȧ), *n.* a town in S Italy, the capital of the Basilicata region. 47,700 (est. 1964).

potful (pŏt′fo͝ol′), *n.* the amount that can be carried in a pot.

pot glass, glass melted in a pot rather than a tank furnace.

potheen (pŏ thēn′), *n.* poteen.

pother (pŏth′ə), *n.* **1.** commotion; uproar. **2.** a disturbance or fuss. **3.** a choking or suffocating cloud, as of smoke or dust. *—v.t., v.i.* **4.** to worry; bother. [orig. uncert.]

potherb (pŏt′hûb′), *n.* any herb prepared as food by cooking in a pot, or added as seasoning in cookery, as thyme.

pothole (pŏt′hōl′), *n.* **1.** a deep hole; a pit. **2.** a more or less cylindrical hole formed in rock by the grinding action of the detrital material in eddying water. **3.** Also, **sinkhole.** a hole formed in soluble rock by the action of water, serving to conduct water to an underground passage. **4.** a hole in the surface of a road.

potholing (pŏt′hō′lĭng), *n.* the exploration of potholes and underground passages. **—pot′hol′er,** *n.*

pothook (pŏt′ho͝ok′), *n.* **1.** a hook for suspending a pot or kettle over an open fire. **2.** an iron rod, usually curved, with a hook at the end, used to lift hot pots, irons, stove lids, etc. **3.** an S-shaped stroke in writing, esp. as made by children in learning to write.

pothouse (pŏt′hous′), *n.* an alehouse.

pothunter (pŏt′hŭn′tə), *n.* **1.** one who hunts merely for food or profit, regardless of the rules of sport. **2.** one who takes part in contests merely to win prizes.

potiche (pŏ tēsh′), *n., pl.* **-tiches** (-tēsh′). a vase or jar, as of porcelain, with rounded or polygonal body narrowing at the top. [t. F, der. *pot* POT[1]]

potion (pō′shən), *n.* **1.** a drink or draught, esp. one of a medicinal, poisonous, or magical kind. **2.** *Rare.* a beverage. [t. L: s. *pōtio*; r. ME *pocioun*, t. OF]

potlatch (pŏt′lăch′), *n.* **1.** (among some American Indians of the northern Pacific coast) a ceremonial festival at which gifts are bestowed on the guests and property destroyed in a competitive show of wealth. **2.** a celebration; party. [t. N Amer. Ind.: metathetic var. of Chinook *potshatl* gift]

potluck (pŏt′lŭk′), *n.* **1.** whatever food happens to be at hand without special preparation or buying. **2.** *Colloq.* a random or haphazard choice.

potman (pŏt′mən), *n., pl.* **-men.** a man employed in a public house; barman.

pot marigold, the common marigold, *Calendula officinalis*, the flower heads of which are sometimes used in cookery for seasoning.

pot metal, 1. an alloy of copper and lead formerly used in plumbing fixtures. **2.** (in glass-making) glass coloured while it is being fused.

Potomac (pə tō′mək), *n.* a river in the U.S., flowing SE from the Allegheny Mountains past Washington, D.C., into Chesapeake Bay. 287 mi. long.

potoroo (pō′tə ro͞o′), *n.* kangaroo rat.

Potosí (pŏt′ō sē′; *Sp.* pō tō sē′), *n.* a city in S Bolivia: once a rich silver-mining centre. 57,000 (est. 1965); 13,022 ft high.

potpie (pŏt′pī′), *n. U.S.* a baked meat pie.

potpourri (pō po͝o′ə′rĭ; *Fr.* pō po͞o rē′), *n., pl.* **-ris. 1.** a mixture of dried petals of roses or other flowers with spices, etc., kept in a jar for the fragrance. **2.** a musical medley. **3.** a collection of miscellaneous literary extracts. **4.** any mixture of unrelated things. [t. F: rotten pot, trans. of Sp. *olla podrida.* See OLLA]

pot roast, meat which is browned, then cooked slowly in a covered pot, with very little water.

Potsdam (pŏts′dăm′; *Ger.* pŏts′dȧm), *n.* a city in central East Germany, near Berlin: formerly the residence of the German emperors. 109,867 (1964).

potsherd (pŏt′shûd′), *n. Archaic.* a fragment or broken piece of pottery. [f. POT[1] + *sherd*, var. of SHARD]

pot shot, 1. a shot fired at game merely for food, with little regard to skill or the rules of sport. **2.** a shot at an animal or person within easy range, as from ambush. **3.** a random or aimless shot.

potstone (pŏt′stōn′), *n.* a kind of soapstone, sometimes used for making pots and other household utensils.

pottage (pŏt′ĭj), *n.* a thick soup made of vegetables, without or with meat. [ME *potage*, t. OF, der. *pot* pot]

potted (pŏt′ĭd), *adj.* **1.** placed in a pot. **2.** preserved or cooked in a pot. **3.** *Colloq.* abridged, summarized, or condensed. **4.** *U.S. Slang.* drunk.

potter[1] (pŏt′ə), *n.* one who makes earthen pots or other vessels. [ME; OE *pottere*, f. *pott* POT[1] + *-ere* -ER[1]]

potter[2] (pŏt′ə), *v.i.* **1.** to busy or occupy oneself in an ineffective manner. **2.** to move or go with ineffective action or little energy or purpose (fol. by *about, along,* etc.). **3.** to move or go slowly or aimlessly; loiter. —*n.* **4.** pottering or ineffective action; dawdling. Also, *U.S.*, **putter.** [appar. freq. of obs. or prov. *pote* push, poke, OE *potian* push, thrust. See PUT] —**pot′terer,** *n.* —**pot′teringly,** *adv.*

Potter (pŏt′ə), *n.* **1. Beatrix,** 1866–1943, English writer of children's stories. **2. Paul,** 1625–54, Dutch painter.

Potteries (pŏt′ə rĭz), *n.* **the,** a district in Staffordshire where pottery is a major industry.

Potters Bar, a town in England, in Hertfordshire. 23,376 (1961).

potter's field, a piece of ground reserved as a burial place for strangers and the friendless poor. See Matt. 27:7.

potter's wheel, a device with a rotating horizontal disc upon which clay is moulded by a potter.

pottery (pŏt′ə rĭ), *n., pl.* **-teries. 1.** ware fashioned from clay or other earthy material and hardened by heat. **2.** a place where earthen pots or vessels are made. **3.** the art or business of a potter; ceramics. [late ME, t. F: m. *poterie*, der. *potier* potter, der. *pot* pot]

pottle (pŏt′l), *n.* **1.** a former liquid measure equal to two quarts. **2.** a pot or tankard of this capacity. **3.** the wine, etc., in it. **4.** alcoholic beverages. **5.** a small container or basket, as for fruit or the like. [ME *potel*, t. OF, dim. of *pot* POT[1]]

potto (pŏt′ō), *n.* a member of the loris family, *Perodicticus potto*, with nocturnal habits, living in the forest belt of central Africa. [t. some W African language]

Pott's disease (pŏts), *Pathol.* caries of the bodies of the vertebrae, often resulting in marked curvature of the spine, and usually associated with a tuberculosis infection. [named after Percival *Pott*, 1714–88, English surgeon, who described it]

potty[1] (pŏt′ĭ), *adj. Colloq.* **1.** foolish; crazy. **2.** paltry; petty.

potty[2] (pŏt′ĭ), *n. Colloq.* a chamber-pot, esp. one for a child.

pot-valiant (pŏt′văl′yənt), *adj.* brave only when drunk.

pot-walloper (pŏt′wŏl′ə pə), *n.* (before 1832, in some English boroughs) a man qualified for a parliamentary vote as a householder, the test being possession of his own fireplace. [alter. of *potwaller*, lit., potboiler, after *wallop*, v., boil vigorously]

pouch (pouch), *n.* **1.** a bag, sack, or similar receptacle, esp. one for small articles. **2.** a small moneybag. **3.** a bag or case of canvas, leather, etc., used by soldiers for carrying ammunition. **4.** a bag for carrying mail. **5.** something shaped like or resembling a bag or pocket. **6.** *Chiefly Scot.* a pocket in a garment. **7.** a baggy fold of flesh under the eye. **8.** *Zool.* a baglike or pocket-like part; a sac or cyst, as the sac beneath the bill of pelicans, the saclike dilation of the cheeks of gophers, or (esp.) the receptacle for the young of marsupials. **9.** *Bot.* a baglike cavity. —*v.t.* **10.** to put into or enclose in a pouch, bag, or pocket; pocket. **11.** to arrange (something) in the form of a pouch. **12.** (of a fish or bird) to swallow. —*v.i.* **13.** to form a pouch or a cavity resembling a pouch. [ME *pouche*, t. ONF, var. of OF *poche*, also *poque*, *poke* bag. Cf. POKE[2]]

pouched (poucht), *adj.* having a pouch, as the pelicans, gophers, and marsupials.

pouf (po͞of), *n.* **1.** a kind of headdress worn by women in the latter part of the 18th century. **2.** an arrangement of the hair over a pad. **3.** a puff of material as an ornament in a dress or headdress. **4.** a stuffed cushion of thick material forming a low seat. **5.** poof. Also, **pouffe.** [t. F. Cf. PUFF]

poulard (po͞o′läd), *n.* **1.** a hen spayed to improve the flesh for use as food. **2.** a fatted hen. [t. F, der. *poule* hen. See PULLET]

Poulenc (*Fr.* po͞o lăɴk′), *n.* **Francis** (*Fr.* frăɴ sĕs′), 1899–1963, French composer.

poult (pōlt), *n.* the young of the domestic fowl, the turkey, the pheasant, or a similar bird. [ME *pult(e)*, syncopated var. of PULLET]

poulterer (pōl′tə rə, -trə), *n.* a dealer in poultry, game, etc. [f. *poulter* poultry dealer (t. F: m. *pouletier*) + -ER[1]]

poultice (pōl′tĭs), *n., v.,* **-ticed, -ticing.** —*n.* **1.** a soft, moist mass of bread, meal, linseed, etc., applied as a medicament to the body. —*v.t.* **2.** to apply a poultice to. [orig. *pultes*, appar. pl. of L *puls* thick pap]

poultry (pōl′trĭ), *n.* domestic fowls collectively, as chickens, turkeys, guineafowls, ducks, and geese. [ME *pult(e)rie*, t. OF: m. *pouleterie*, ult. der. *poulet* PULLET]

pounce[1] (pouns), *v.,* **pounced, pouncing,** *n.* —*v.i.* **1.** to swoop down suddenly and lay hold, as a bird does on its prey. **2.** to spring, dash, or come suddenly. —*v.t.* **3.** to seize with the talons. **4.** to swoop down upon and seize suddenly, as a bird of prey does. —*n.* **5.** the claw or talon of a bird of prey. **6.** a sudden swoop, as on prey. [orig. uncert.]

pounce[2] (pouns), *v.t.,* **pounced, pouncing.** to emboss (metal) by hammering on an instrument applied on the reverse side. [prob. same as POUNCE[1]]

pounce[3] (pouns), *n., v.,* **pounced, pouncing.** —*n.* **1.** a fine powder, as of cuttlebone, formerly used to prevent ink from spreading in writing, as over an erasure or an unsized paper, or to prepare parchment for writing. **2.** a fine powder, usually charcoal, rubbed through a perforated pattern, for transferring a design. —*v.t.* **3.** to sprinkle, smooth, or prepare with pounce. **4.** to trace (a design) with pounce. **5.** to finish the surface of (hats) by rubbing with sandpaper or the like. [t. F: m. *ponce*, ult. g. L *pūmex* PUMICE] —**pounc′er,** *n.*

pounce box, a small box with perforated lid for holding pounce powder for transferring designs, or for use in writing.

pouncet box (poun′sĭt), *Archaic.* a small perfume box with a perforated lid. [der. POUNCE[2] or POUNCE[3]]

pound[1] (pound), *v.t.* **1.** to strike repeatedly and with great force, as with an instrument, the fist, heavy missiles, etc. **2.** to produce (sound) by striking or thumping, or with an effect of thumping (often fol. by *out*): *to pound out a tune on a piano.* **3.** to force (a way) by battering. **4.** to crush by beating, as with an instrument; bray, pulverize, or triturate. —*v.i.* **5.** to strike heavy blows repeatedly: *to pound on a door.* **6.** to beat or throb violently, as the heart. **7.** to give forth a sound of or as of thumps: *the drums pounded loudly.* **8.** to walk or go with heavy steps; move along with force or vigour. —*n.* **9.** the act of pounding. **10.** a heavy or forcible blow. **11.** a thump. [ME *pounen*, OE *pūnian*; akin to D *puin* rubbish, LG *pün* fragments] —**pound′er,** *n.* —**Syn. 1.** See **beat.**

pound[2] (pound), *n., pl.* **pounds,** (*collectively*) **pound. 1.** a unit of weight and of mass, varying in different periods and countries. **2.** (in English-speaking countries) either of two legally fixed units, the **pound avoirdupois** (of 7000 grains, divided into 16 ounces) used for ordinary commodities, or the **pound troy** (of 5760 grains, divided into 12 ounces) used for gold, silver, etc., and also serving as the basis of apothecaries' weight. **3.** a British money of account (**pound sterling**) of the value of 100 new pence (denoted by the symbol £ before the numeral or sometimes *l.* after it, and orig. equivalent to a pound of silver). **4.** the monetary unit of various countries, as Cyprus, Egypt, the Republic of Ireland, Israel, Lebanon, Libya, Nigeria, Sudan, and Syria. **5.** a former money of account (**pound Scots**) orig. the equivalent of the pound sterling, but at the union of the crowns of England and Scotland in 1603 worth only one twelfth of the pound sterling. **6.** a note or coin of any of these denominations. **7.** (formerly) the Turkish lira. [ME and OE *pund*, t. L: m. *pondo* a pound, orig. *libra pondō* a pound in weight]

pound[3] (pound), *n.* **1.** an enclosure maintained by public authorities for confining stray or homeless animals. **2.** an enclosure for sheltering, keeping, confining, or trapping animals. **3.** an enclosure or trap for fish. **4.** a place of confinement or imprisonment. —*v.t.* **5.** to shut up in or as in a pound; impound; imprison. [ME and OE *pund-*. Cf. obs. *pind*, v., enclose, OE *pyndan*]

Pound (pound), *n.* **Ezra** (**Loomis**), born 1885, U.S. poet.

poundage[1] (poun′dĭj), *n.* a tax, commission, rate, etc., of so much per pound sterling or per pound weight. [f. POUND[2] + -AGE]

poundage[2] (poun′dĭj), *n.* **1.** confinement within an enclosure or within certain limits. **2.** the fee demanded to free animals from a pound. [f. POUND[3] + -AGE]

poundal (poun′dl), *n. Physics.* a unit of force: the force which, acting on a mass of one pound, gives it an acceleration of one foot per second per second.

poundcake (pound′kāk′), *n.* a rich, sweet cake originally made with a pound each of butter, sugar, and flour.

pounder[1] (poun′də), *n.* one who or that which pounds, pulverizes, or beats. [f. POUND[1] + -ER[1]]

pounder[2] (poun′də), *n.* **1.** a person or thing having, or associated with, a weight or value of a pound or a specified number of pounds. **2.** a gun that discharges a missile of a specified weight in pounds. **3.** a person possessing, receiving an income of, or paying a specified number of pounds. [f. POUND[2] + -ER[1]]

pound-foolish (pound′fo͞o′lĭsh), *adj.* foolish in regard to large sums. Cf. **penny-wise.**

pound net, a trap for catching fish consisting of an arrangement of netting having a pound or enclosure with a contracted opening.

pour (pô), *v.t.* **1.** to send (a liquid or fluid, or anything in loose particles) flowing or falling, as from a container or into, over, or on something. **2.** to emit or discharge, esp. continuously or rapidly. **3.** to send forth (words, etc.) as in a stream or flood (often fol. by *out* or *forth*). —*v.i.* **4.** to issue, move, or proceed in great quantity or number. **5.** to flow forth or along. **6.** to rain heavily. —*n.* **7. a.** the act or process of pouring molten metal into a mould. **b.** the amount poured. **8.** an abundant or continuous flow or stream. **9.** a heavy fall of rain; downpour. [ME *poure(n)*; orig. uncert.] —**pour′er,** *n.* —**pour′ingly,** *adv.*

pourboire (po͞oə′bwä; *Fr.* po͞or bwȧr′), *n.* a tip or gratuity. [F: lit., for drinking]

pourparler (po͞oə pä′lā; *Fr.* po͞or pȧr lĕ′), *n.* an informal preliminary conference. [F, n. use of OF *pourparler* discuss, f. *pour-* for, before (g. L *prō*) + *parler* speak]

pourpoint (po͞oə′point′), *n.* a stuffed and quilted doublet worn by men from the 14th to 17th centuries. [t. F, orig. pp. of *pourpoindre* quilt, perforate, f. *pour-*, for *par-* (g. L *per ad*) through + *poindre* (g. L *pungere* prick, pierce); r. ME *purpont*, t. ML: m. s. *purpuntum*, for *perpunctum*]

pourpresture (po͞oə prĕs′chə), *n.* purpresture.

pousse-café (*Fr.* po͞os kȧ fė′), *n., pl.* **-fés** (-fė′). **1.** a small glass of liqueur served after coffee. **2.** a glass of various liqueurs arranged in layers. [F: lit., coffee-pusher]

poussette (po͞o sĕt′), *n., v.,* **-setted, -setting.** —*n.* **1.** a dance step in which a couple or several couples dance around the ballroom, holding hands, used in country dances. —*v.i.* **2.** to perform a poussette, as a couple in a country dance. [t. F, der. *pousser* push]

poussin (*Fr.* po͞o săɴ′), *n. Cookery.* a chicken killed when young to preserve its flavour and tenderness. [t. F]

Poussin (*Fr.* po͞o săɴ′), *n.* **Nicolas** (*Fr.* nē kō lȧ′), 1594–1655, French painter.

pou sto (po͞o′ stō′, pou′), **1.** a place to stand on. **2.** a basis of operation. [Gk: where I may stand; from the alleged saying of Archimedes, 'Give me where I may stand, and I will move the earth.']

pout[1] (pout), *v.i.* **1.** to thrust out or protrude the lips, esp. in displeasure or sullenness. **2.** to look sullen. **3.** to swell out or protrude, as lips. —*v.t.* **4.** to protrude (lips, etc.). **5.** to utter with a pout. —*n.* **6.** a protrusion of the lips, as in pouting. **7.** a fit of sullenness. [ME *poute(n)*, c. d. Sw. *puta* be inflated]

pout[2] (pout), *n., pl.* **pouts,** (*esp. collectively*) **pout. 1.** the horned pout. **2.** an eelpout. **3.** the bib. [OE *-pūte* in *ælepūte* eelpout, c. D *puit* frog]

pouter (pou′tə), *n.* **1.** one who pouts. **2.** one of a breed of long-legged domestic pigeons characterized by the habit of puffing out the crop.

poverty (pŏv′ə tĭ), *n.* **1.** the condition of being poor with respect to money, goods, or means of subsistence. **2.** deficiency or lack of something specified: *poverty of ideas.* **3.** deficiency of desirable ingredients, qualities, etc.: *poverty of soil.* **4.** scantiness; scanty amount. [ME *poverte*, t. OF, g. s. L *paupertas*. Cf. POOR, PAUPER]

—**Syn. 1.** POVERTY, DESTITUTION, NEED, WANT imply a state of privation and lack of necessities. POVERTY denotes serious lack of the means for proper existence: *living in a state of extreme poverty.* DESTITUTION, a somewhat more literary word, implies a state of having absolutely none of the necessaries of life: *widespread destitution in countries at war.* NEED emphasizes the fact that help or relief is necessary: *most of the people were in great need.* WANT emphasizes privations, esp. lack of food and clothing: *families were suffering from want.* —**Ant. 1.** riches, wealth, plenty.

poverty-stricken (pŏv′ə tĭ strĭk′ən), *adj.* suffering from poverty; very poor: *poverty-stricken exiles.*

pow (pō, pou), *n. Scot. and N Dial.* the poll; the head. [var. of POLL[1]]

POW, prisoner of war. Also, **P.O.W.**

powan (pou′ən), *n.* a freshwater fish resembling a herring, *Coregonus clupeoides*, found in some Scottish lochs.

powder[1] (pou′də), *n.* **1.** any solid substance in the state of fine, loose particles, as produced by crushing, grinding, or disintegration; dust. **2.** a preparation in this form for some special purpose, as gunpowder, a medicinal powder, a cosmetic or toilet powder, etc. —*v.t.* **3.** to reduce to powder; pulverize. **4.** to sprinkle or cover with powder. **5.** to apply powder to (the face, skin, etc.) as a cosmetic. **6.** to sprinkle or strew as with powder. **7.** to ornament with small objects scattered over a surface. —*v.i.* **8.** to use powder as a cosmetic. **9.** to become pulverized. [ME *poudre*, t. OF, g. s. L *pulvis* dust] —**pow′derer,** *n.*

powder[2] (pou′də), *v.i. Dial.* to rush. [orig. uncert.]

powder blue, pale blue diluted with grey.

powdered sugar, *U.S.* icing sugar.

powder flask, a flask or case for gunpowder.

powder horn, a powder flask made of horn.

powder magazine, a compartment for the storage of ammunition and explosives.

powder metallurgy, the art or science of manufacturing useful articles by compacting metal and other powders in a die, followed by sintering.

powder monkey, 1. a boy formerly employed on warships, etc., to carry powder. **2.** a man in charge of explosives in any operation requiring their use.

powder puff, a soft, feathery ball or pad, as of down, for applying powder to the skin.

powder room, a women's lavatory in a restaurant or other public building.

powdery (pou′də rĭ), *adj.* **1.** of the nature of, or consisting of, powder. **2.** easily reduced to powder. **3.** sprinkled or covered with powder.

power (pou′ə), *n.* **1.** ability to do or act; capability of doing or effecting something. **2.** (*usually pl.*) a particular faculty of body or mind. **3.** political or national strength: *the balance of power in Europe.* **4.** great or marked ability to do or act; strength; might; force. **5.** the possession of control or command over others; dominion; authority; ascendancy or influence. **6.** political ascendancy or control in the government of a country, etc.: *the party in power.* **7.** legal ability, capacity, or authority. **8.** delegated authority; authority vested in a person or persons in a particular capacity. **9.** a written statement, or document, conferring legal authority. **10.** one who or that which possesses or exercises authority or influence. **11.** a state or nation having international authority or influence: *the great powers of the world.* **12.** a military or naval force. **13.** (*often pl.*) a deity or divinity. **14.** (*pl.*) *Theol.* an order of angels. **15.** *Colloq.* a large number or amount. **16.** *Physics.* the time rate of transferring or transforming energy; work done, or energy transferred, per unit of time. **17.** *Mech.* energy or force available for application to work. **18.** mechanical energy as distinguished from hand labour. **19.** a particular form of mechanical energy. **20.** *Maths.* the product obtained by multiplying a quantity by itself one or more times: *4 is the second, 8 the third, power of 2.* **21.** *Optics.* the magnifying capacity of a microscope, telescope, etc., expressed as ratio of diameter of image to object. **22. the powers that be,** those in authority. —*v.t.* **23.** to supply with electricity or other means of power. **24.** (of an engine, etc.) to provide the force or motive power to operate (a machine). [ME *poër*, t. AF, prop. inf., be able, g. VL *potēre*, for L *posse*] —**Syn. 4.** See **strength.**

powerboat (pou′ə bōt′), *n.* **1.** a boat propelled by mechanical power. **2.** a motor boat.

power cable, *Elect.* a cable for conducting electricity, esp. high-voltage electricity.

power-dive (pou′ə dīv′), *n., v.,* **-dived, -diving.** *Aeron.* —*n.* **1.** a steep dive by an aircraft with engines at full power. —*v.i.* **2.** to perform a power-dive.

power drill, a drill operated by a motor.

powered (pou′əd), *adj.* having, exerting or producing, or propelled by, mechanical energy.

power factor, *Elect.* the ratio of the power dissipated in an electrical circuit to the product of the E.M.F. and the current. In single- and three-phase circuits it is equal to the cosine of the phase angle between the E.M.F. and the current.

powerful (pou′ə fəl), *adj.* **1.** having or exerting great power or force. **2.** strong physically, as a person. **3.** producing great physical effects, as a machine or a blow. **4.** potent, as a drug. **5.** having great influence, as a speech, speaker, description, reason, etc. **6.** having great power, authority, or influence, as a nation; mighty. **7.** *Dial.* great in number or amount: *a powerful lot of money.* —**pow′erfully,** *adv.* —**pow′erfulness,** *n.*

—**Syn. 1.** POWERFUL, MIGHTY, POTENT suggest great force or strength. POWERFUL suggests capability of exerting great force or overcoming strong resistance: *a powerful machine like a bulldozer.* MIGHTY, now chiefly rhetorical, implies uncommon or overwhelming strength of power: *a mighty army.* POTENT, a dignified word, implies great natural or inherent power: *a potent influence.* **5.** convincing, forcible, cogent. —**Ant. 1.** weak.

powerhouse (pou′ə hous′), *n. Elect.* a generating station.

powerless (pou′ə lĭs), *adj.* **1.** lacking power or ability; unable to produce any effect. **2.** lacking power to act; helpless. —**pow′erlessly,** *adv.* —**pow′erlessness,** *n.*

power-loading (pou′ə lō′dĭng), *n. Aeron.* See **loading** (def. 4).

power loom, a loom worked by mechanical power.

power of appointment, *Law.* the right granted by one person (the donor) to another (the donee or appointer) to dispose of the donor's property or create rights therein.

power of attorney, *Law.* a written document given by one person or party to another authorizing the latter to act for the former.

power pack, *Radio.* the unit in an electronic device which supplies power at the required voltages to the rest of the circuit.

power plant, 1. a plant (including engines, dynamos, etc., with the building or buildings) for the generation of power. 2. the apparatus for supplying power for a particular mechanical process or operation.

power politics, international diplomacy based on the use, or threatened use, of military power.

power reactor, a nuclear reactor designed to produce electric power.

power station, *Elect.* a generating station.

Powhatan (pou′hə tăn′), *n. c.* 1550–1618, Indian chief in Virginia, father of Pocahontas.

powwow (pou′wou′), *n.* 1. (among North American Indians) a ceremony, esp. one accompanied by magic, feasting, and dancing, performed for the cure of disease, success in a hunt, etc. 2. a council or conference of or with Indians. 3. *Colloq.* any conference or meeting. —*v.i.* 4. to hold a powwow. 5. *Colloq.* to confer. [t. Algonquian (Narragansett): m. *pow wah* or *po-wah*]

Powys (pō′ĭs), *n.* 1. **John Cowper** (ko͞o′pə), 1872–1963, English author. 2. his brother, **Llewelyn** (lo͞o ĕl′ĭn), 1884–1939, English author. 3. his brother, **Theodore Francis,** 1875–1953, English author.

pox (pŏks), *n.* 1. a disease characterized by multiple skin pustules, as smallpox. 2. syphilis (**great pox** or **French pox**). [for *pocks*, pl. of POCK]

Poyang (pō′yăng′), *n.* a lake in E China, in Kiangsi province. ab. 90 mi. long; ab. 20 mi. wide.

Poznań (*Pol.* pŏz′nāyn), *n.* a city in W Poland, on the river Warta. 434,000 (est. 1964). German, **Posen.**

Pozsony (*Hung.* pô′zhôny), *n.* Hungarian name of **Bratislava.**

pozzuolana (pŏt′swə lä′nə), *n.* a porous variety of volcanic tuft or ash used in making hydraulic cement. Also, **pozzolana** (pŏt′sə lä′nə). [t. It., n. use of adj., belonging to POZZUOLI (L *Puteolī*), lit., little springs]

Pozzuoli (*It.* pôt tswô′lē), *n.* a seaport in Italy, in Campania, near Naples: Roman ruins. 59,130 (1966).

pp., 1. pages. 2. past participle. 3. pianissimo. 4. privately printed.

P.P., Parish Priest.

p.p., 1. parcel post. 2. past participle. 3. postpaid.

P.P.E., Philosophy, Politics, and Economics.

ppl., participle.

P.P.M., *Chem.* parts per million. Also, **p.p.m.**

ppr., present participle. Also, **p.pr.**

P.PS., (L *post postscriptum*) a second postscript.

P.P.S., 1. parliamentary private secretary. 2. principal private secretary.

P.Q., Province of Quebec.

p.q., previous question.

Pr, *Chem.* praseodymium.

Pr., 1. preferred (stock). 2. Priest. 3. Prince. 4. Provençal.

pr, 1. pair. 2. paper. 3. power.

pr., 1. pair. 2. pairs. 3. paper. 4. power. 5. preference. 6. preferred (stock). 7. present. 8. price. 9. priest. 10. printing. 11. pronoun.

P.R., 1. Proportional Representation. 2. public relations. 3. Puerto Rico.

p.r., (L *per rectum*) *Med.* taken through the rectum, as a suppository.

P.R.A., President of the Royal Academy.

practic (prăk′tĭk), *adj. Archaic.* practical. [ME *practik*, t. LL: m. s. *practicus*, t. Gk: m. *praktikós* practical]

practicable (prăk′tĭ kə bl), *adj.* 1. capable of being put into practice, done, or effected, esp. with the available means or with reason or prudence; feasible. 2. capable of being used or traversed, or admitting of passage: *a practicable road.* [f. s. ML *practicāre* PRACTISE + -ABLE] —**prac′ticabil′ity, prac′ticableness,** *n.* —**prac′ticably,** *adv.*

—**Syn.** 1. See **possible.** PRACTICABLE, PRACTICAL, though not properly synonyms, often cause confusion. PRACTICABLE means possible or feasible, able to be done, capable of being put into practice or of being used: *a practicable method of communication.* PRACTICAL (applied to persons) means sensible and businesslike, (applied to things) efficient and workable, as contrasted with theoretical: *practical measures.* —**Ant.** 1. unfeasible; inefficient, theoretical.

practical (prăk′tĭ kl), *adj.* 1. pertaining or relating to practice or action: *practical mathematics.* 2. consisting of, involving, or resulting from practice or action: *a practical application of a rule.* 3. pertaining to or connected with the ordinary activities, business, or work of the world: *practical affairs.* 4. adapted for actual use: *a practical method.* 5. engaged or experienced in actual practice or work: *a practical politician.* 6. inclined towards or fitted for actual work or useful activities: *a practical man.* 7. mindful of the results, usefulness, advantages or disadvantages, etc., of action or procedure. 8. matter-of-fact; prosaic. 9. being such in practice or effect; virtual: *a practical certainty.* [f. PRACTIC(E) + -AL[1]] —**prac′tical′ity, prac′ticalness,** *n.*

—**Syn.** 1. See **practicable.** 7. PRACTICAL, JUDICIOUS, SENSIBLE refer to good judgement in action, conduct, and the handling of everyday matters. PRACTICAL suggests the ability to adopt means to an end or to turn what is at hand to account: *to adopt practical measures for settling problems.* JUDICIOUS implies the possession and use of discreet judgement, discrimination and balance: *a judicious use of one's time.* SENSIBLE implies the possession and use of sound reason and shrewd common sense: *a sensible suggestion.* —**Ant.** 7. ill-advised, unwise, foolish.

practical joke, a trick played upon a person, often involving some physical action.

practically (prăk′tĭk lĭ), *adv.* 1. in effect; virtually. 2. in a practical manner. 3. from a practical point of view. 4. nearly; almost.

practice (prăk′tĭs), *n., v.,* **-ticed, -ticing.** —*n.* 1. habitual or customary performance: *normal business practice.* 2. a habit or custom. 3. repeated performance or systematic exercise for the purpose of acquiring skill or proficiency: *practice makes perfect.* 4. skill gained by experience or exercise. 5. the action or process of performing or doing something (opposed to *theory* or *speculation*). 6. the exercise of a profession or occupation, esp. law or medicine. 7. the business of a professional man: *a doctor with a large practice.* 8. *Law.* the established method of conducting legal proceedings. 9. deceitful or dishonest dealing or procedure; trickery: *sharp practice.* 10. (*usually pl.*) *Archaic.* a plot or intrigue. 11. **make a practice of,** to do (something) habitually or usually. —*v.t., v.i.* 12. *U.S.* practise. [n. use of PRACTISE, v., substituted for earlier *practic*, n.] —**Syn.** 2. See **custom.** 3. See **exercise.**

practician (prăk tĭsh′ən), *n.* one who works at a profession or occupation; practitioner.

practise (prăk′tĭs), *v.,* **-tised, -tising.** —*v.t.* 1. to carry out, perform, or do habitually or usually. 2. to follow, observe, or use habitually or in customary practice. 3. to exercise or pursue as a profession, art, or occupation: *to practise law.* 4. to perform or do repeatedly in order to acquire skill or proficiency. 5. to exercise (a person, etc.) in something in order to give proficiency; train or drill. —*v.i.* 6. to act habitually; do something habitually or as a practice. 7. to pursue a profession, esp. law or medicine. 8. to exercise oneself by performance tending to give proficiency: *to practise shooting.* 9. *Archaic.* to plot or conspire. Also, *U.S.,* **practice.** [ME, t. OF: s. *pra(c)tiser*, ult. der. LL *practicus* PRACTICAL] —**prac′tiser,** *n.*

practised (prăk′tĭst), *adj.* 1. experienced; expert; proficient. 2. acquired or perfected through practice.

practitioner (prăk tĭsh′ə nə), *n.* 1. one engaged in the practice of a profession or the like: *a medical practitioner.* 2. one who practises something specified. [f. m. *practician* (f. PRACTIC + -IAN) + -ER[1]]

prae-, var. of **pre-.**

praedial (prē′dyəl), *adj.* 1. of, pertaining to, or consisting of land or its products; real; landed. 2. arising from or consequent upon the occupation of land. 3. attached to land. Also, **predial.** [t. ML: s. *praediālis*, der. L *praedium* farm, estate]

praefect (prē′fĕkt), *n.* prefect.

praemunire (prē′myo͝o nī′ə rĭ), *n. Law.* 1. a writ charging the offence of resorting to a foreign court or authority, as that of the pope, and thus calling in question the supremacy of the English Crown. 2. the offence. 3. the penalty of forfeiture, imprisonment, outlawry, etc., incurred. [t. ML: a word used in the writ (by confusion with L *praemūnīre* fortify, protect) for L *praemonēre* forewarn, admonish. See PREMONISH]

praenomen (prē′nō′mĕn), *n., pl.* **-nomina** (-nŏm′ĭ nə). the first or personal name of a Roman citizen, as 'Gaius' in 'Gaius Julius Caesar'. [t. L: f. *prae* before + *nōmen* name] —**praenominal** (prē′nŏm′ĭ nəl), *adj.*

praepostor (prē′pŏs′tə), *n.* (at various English public schools) a prefect or monitor. Also, **prepositor, prepostor.** [t. ML: m. *praepositor*, der. L *praepositus*, pp., set before]

praetor (prē′tə), *n. Rom. Hist.* 1. the title of a consul as leader of the army. 2. one of a number of elected magistrates, engaged chiefly in the administration of justice. Also, **pretor.** [ME, t. L: leader, chief, head] —**praetorial** (prē tô′rĭ əl), *adj.*

praetorian (prē tô′rĭ ən), *adj.* 1. of or pertaining to a praetor. 2. (*often cap.*) denoting or pertaining to the Praetorian Guard. —*n.* 3. a man having the rank of a praetor or ex-praetor. 4. (*often cap.*) a soldier of the Praetorian Guard. Also, **pretorian.**

Praetorian Guard, *Rom. Hist.* the bodyguard of a Roman military commander, esp. the imperial guard in Rome.

pragmatic (prăg măt′ĭk), *adj.* Also, **pragmatical** (for defs 3, 5, 6, 7). **1.** treating historical phenomena with special reference to their causes, antecedent conditions, and results. **2.** *Philos.* of or pertaining to pragmatism. **3.** concerned with practical consequences or values. **4.** pertaining to the affairs of a state or community. **5.** busy or active. **6.** officiously busy; meddlesome. **7.** conceited; opinionated; dogmatic. —*n.* **8.** a pragmatic sanction. [t. L: s. *pragmaticus*, t. Gk: m. *pragmatikós* active, versed in state affairs; as n., a man of business or action] —**pragmat′ically,** *adv.*

pragmatic sanction, *Hist.* any of various decrees issued by those European countries which followed Roman law as an expression of the will of the sovereign, defining the limits of his power or regulating the succession to the throne, and having the effect of fundamental law, as the decree of Charles VII of France in 1438 or that of Charles VI of Austria in 1713.

pragmatism (prăg′mə tĭz′əm), *n.* **1.** character or conduct which emphasizes practical values or attention to facts; practicality. **2.** *Philos.* the doctrine of C. S. Peirce that difference of meaning depends on difference of practice. It has been interpreted by some as the doctrine that both truth and conduct are to be judged by practical consequences. **3.** officiousness; dogmatism; pedantry. —**prag′matist,** *n., adj.*

Prague (präg), *n.* the capital of Czechoslovakia, in the W part, on the Moldau: also the capital of Bohemia. 1,020,000 (est. 1965). Czech, **Praha** (*Cz.* prȧ′hȧ). German, **Prag** (*Ger.* prȧk).

Praia (*Port.* prȧ′yə), *n.* the capital of the Cape Verde Islands, on SE São Tiago Island. 3628 (1960).

Prairial (*Fr.* prĕ rē ȧl′), *n.* (in the French Revolutionary calendar) the ninth month of the year, extending from May 20th to June 18th. [F, der. *prairie* meadow. See PRAIRIE]

prairie (prĕə′rĭ), *n.* **1.** an extensive or slightly undulating treeless tract of land, characterized by highly fertile soil and originally grassland, which occurs in the interior of continents in temperate latitudes, as that of the upper Mississippi valley and Canada. **2.** a meadow. **3.** (in the southern U.S.) a tract of grassland often covered with water; marshland. [t. F, der. *pré* field, g. L *prātum* meadow]

prairie chicken, a North American gallinaceous bird, *Tympanuchus cupido*, inhabiting prairies and valued as game. Also, **prairie hen.**

prairie dog, any of certain gregarious burrowing rodents (genus *Cynomys*) of North American prairies, which utter a barklike cry.

prairie oyster, a drink made primarily from a raw egg, the yolk of which remains unbroken and is said to resemble an oyster: given to invalids and those suffering from a hangover.

Prairie dog, *Cynomys ludovicianus* (14 to 16 in. long; tail 2½ to 3 in.)

Prairie Provinces, the provinces of Manitoba, Saskatchewan, and Alberta, in W Canada.

prairie schooner, a small covered wagon used by pioneers in crossing the prairies and plains of North America.

prairie wolf, the coyote.

praise (prāz), *n., v.,* **praised, praising.** —*n.* **1.** the act of expressing approval or admiration; commendation; laudation. **2.** the offering of grateful homage in words or song, as an act of worship. **3.** state of being approved or admired. **4.** *Archaic.* a ground for praise, or a merit. **5.** *Obs.* an object of praise. —*v.t.* **6.** to express approval or admiration of; commend; extol. **7.** to offer grateful homage to (God or a deity), as in words or song. [ME *preise(n)*, t. OF: m. *preisier* value, prize, ult. der. L *pretium* price. Cf. PRIZE²] —**prais′er,** *n.* —**Syn. 1.** acclamation, plaudit, compliment. **6.** See **approve. 7.** glorify, magnify, exalt.

praiseworthy (prāz′wûr′thĭ), *adj.* deserving of praise; laudable. —**praise′wor′thily,** *adv.* —**praise′wor′thiness,** *n.*

Prakrit (prä′krĭt), *n.* any of the vernacular Indic languages of the ancient and medieval periods, as distinguished from Sanskrit. [t. Skt: m. *prākrta* natural, common, vulgar. Cf. SANSKRIT]

praline (prä′lēn), *n.* **1.** a confection of nuts and caramelized sugar, often used as a centre for chocolates and to decorate puddings. **2.** a French sweet consisting of an almond encased in sugar. [t. F; named after Comte de Plessis-*Praslin*, 1598–1675, whose cook invented them]

pralltriller (präl′trĭl′ə), *n. Music.* See **inverted mordent.** [G: lit., rebounding quaver]

pram (prăm), *n.* a small, four-wheeled vehicle used for carrying a baby, pushed from behind. [shortened form of PERAMBULATOR]

prance (präns), *v.,* **pranced, prancing,** *n.* —*v.i.* **1.** to spring, or move by springing, from the hind legs, as a horse. **2.** to ride on a horse doing this. **3.** to ride gaily, proudly, or insolently. **4.** to move or go in an elated manner; swagger. **5.** to caper or dance. —*v.t.* **6.** to cause to prance. —*n.* **7.** the act of prancing; a prancing movement. [ME *pra(u)nce*, ? alliterative alter. of DANCE. Cf. *prick and prance* (Gower)] —**pranc′er,** *n.* —**pranc′ingly,** *adv.*

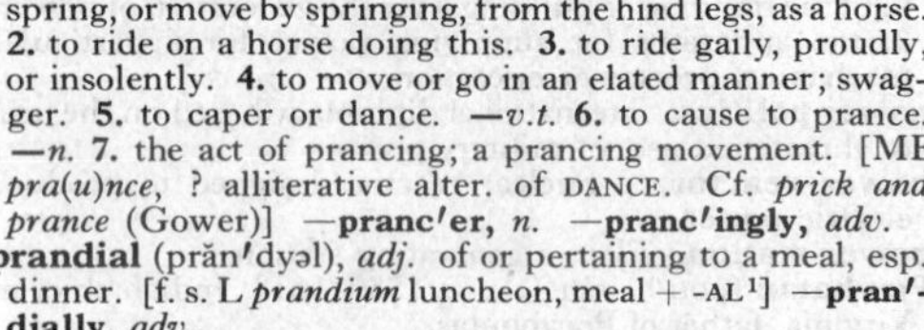

prandial (prăn′dyəl), *adj.* of or pertaining to a meal, esp. dinner. [f. s. L *prandium* luncheon, meal + -AL¹] —**pran′dially,** *adv.*

prang (prăng), *Slang.* —*v.t.* **1.** to crash-land (an aircraft); damage; destroy. **2.** to bomb or damage by bombing (a town, etc.). **3.** to crash (a car or the like. —*v.i.* **4.** to have a crash. —*n.* **5.** an achievement. **6.** an aircraft crash. **7.** a bombing raid by aircraft. **8.** a crash, esp. a minor one, in a motor vehicle or the like.

prank¹ (prăngk), *n.* **1.** a trick of a playful nature. **2.** a trick of a malicious nature. [orig. uncert.]

prank² (prăngk), *v.t.* **1.** to dress or deck in a showy manner; adorn. —*v.i.* **2.** to make an ostentatious show or display. [cf. D *pronk* show, finery, MLG *prank* pomp]

prankish (prăng′kĭsh), *adj.* **1.** of the nature of a prank. **2.** full of pranks.

prankster (prăngk′stə), *n.* a practical joker; mischievous or malicious person.

Prasad (prə säd′), *n.* **Rajendra** (rə jĕn′drə), 1884–1963, Indian statesman: president 1950–62.

prase (prāz), *n.* a leek-green cryptocrystalline variety of chalcedony. [ME, t. F, t. L: m. s. *prasius* a leek-green stone, t. Gk: m. *prásios* leek-green]

praseodymium (prā′zĭ ō dĭm′ĭ əm), *n. Chem.* a rare-earth, metallic, trivalent element: so named from its green salts. *Symbol:* Pr; *at. wt:* 140·907; *at. no.:* 59; *sp. gr.:* 6·5 at 20°C. [f. *praseo-* (comb. form repr. PRASE) + (DI)DYMIUM]

prate (prāt), *v.,* **prated, prating,** *n.* —*v.i.* **1.** to talk too much; talk foolishly or pointlessly; chatter; babble. —*v.t.* **2.** to utter in empty or foolish talk. —*n.* **3.** the act of prating. **4.** empty or foolish talk. [late ME *prate*, c. D and LG *praten*] —**prat′er,** *n.* —**prat′ingly,** *adv.*

pratincole (prăt′ĭng kōl′, prā′tĭng-), *n.* any bird of the Old World family *Glareolidae*, somewhat resembling swallows in appearance and habits. [t. NL: m. *prātincola*, f. s. L *prātum* meadow + *incola* inhabitant]

pratie (prā′tĭ), *n. Irish.* a potato.

pratique (prăt′ēk; *Fr.* prȧ tēk′), *n. Com.* licence or permission to use a port, given to a ship after quarantine or on showing a clean bill of health. [t. F: lit., practice, t. ML: m. *practica*]

Prato (*It.* prȧ′tō), *n.* a town in Italy, in N central Tuscany. 129,153 (1966).

Pratolini (*It.* prȧ tō lē′nē), *n.* **Vasco** (*It.* vȧs′kō), born 1913, Italian novelist.

prattle (prăt′l), *v.,* **-tled, -tling,** *n.* —*v.i.* **1.** to talk or chatter in a simple-minded or foolish way; babble. —*v.t.* **2.** to utter by chattering or babbling. —*n.* **3.** the act of prattling. **4.** chatter; babble. **5.** a babbling sound. [freq. and dim. of PRATE] —**prat′tler,** *n.* —**prat′tlingly,** *adv.*

prau (prou), *n.* proa.

prawn (prôn), *n.* **1.** any of various shrimplike decapod crustaceans of the genera *Palaemon*, *Penaeus*, etc. (suborder *Macrura*), certain of which are used as food. —*v.i.* **2.** to catch prawns, as for food. [ME *pra(y)ne*; orig. unknown] —**prawn′er,** *n.*

Prawn, *Palaemon serratus* (3 to 4 in. long)

praxis (prăk′sĭs), *n.* **1.** practice, esp. as opposed to theory. **2.** habit; custom. **3.** a set of examples for practice. [t. ML, t. Gk]

Praxiteles (prăk sĭt′ĭ lēz′), *n.* fl. *c.* 350 B.C., Greek sculptor.

pray (prā), *v.t.* **1.** to make earnest petition to (a person, etc.). **2.** to make devout petition to (God or an object of worship). **3.** to make petition or entreaty for; crave. **4.** to offer (a prayer). **5.** to bring, put, etc., by praying. —*v.i.* **6.** to make entreaty or supplication, as to a person or for a thing. **7.** to make devout petition to God or to an object of worship. **8.** to enter into spiritual communion with God or an object of worship through prayer. [ME *preie(n)*, t. OF: m. *preier*, ult. g. L *precārī* beg, pray; akin to OE *fricgan*, G *fragen* ask]

prayer¹ (prĕə), *n.* **1.** a devout petition to, or any form of spiritual communion with, God or an object of worship. **2.** the act, action, or practice of praying to God or an object of worship. **3.** a spiritual communion with God or an object of worship, as in supplication, thanksgiving, adoration, or confession. **4.** a form of words used in or appointed for praying: *the Lord's Prayer.* **5.** a religious observance, either public or private, consisting wholly or mainly of prayer. **6.** that which is prayed for. **7.** a petition or entreaty. **8.** the section of a bill in equity, or of a petition, setting forth the complaint or the action desired. [ME *preiere,* t. OF, g. Rom. *precāria,* orig. neut. pl. of L *precārius* obtained by entreaty]

prayer² (prā′ə), *n.* one who prays. [f. PRAY + -ER¹]

prayer book (prĕə), **1.** a book of forms of prayer. **2.** (*usually caps*) the Book of Common Prayer.

prayerful (prĕə′fəl), *adj.* given to, characterized by, or expressive of prayer; devout. —**prayer′fully,** *adv.* —**prayer′fulness,** *n.*

prayer meeting, (in some Protestant churches) a meeting at which those present offer up individual prayers to God.

prayer rug, a small rug on which Muslims kneel and prostrate themselves during prayer. Also, **prayer mat.**

prayer wheel (prĕə), a wheel or cylinder inscribed with or containing prayers, used chiefly by Buddhists of Tibet as a mechanical aid to continual praying, each revolution counting as an uttered prayer.

praying mantis, the mantis.

pre-, a prefix applied freely to mean 'prior to', 'in advance of' (*prewar*), also 'early', 'beforehand' (*prepay*), 'before', 'in front of' (*preoral, prefrontal*), and in many figurative meanings, often attached to stems not used alone (*prevent, preclude, preference, precedent*). [t. L: m. *prae-,* repr. *prae,* prep., adv.]

preach (prēch), *v.t.* **1.** to advocate or inculcate (religious or moral truth, right conduct, etc.) in speech or writing. **2.** to proclaim or make known by sermon (the gospel, good tidings, etc.). **3.** to deliver (a sermon or the like). —*v.i.* **4.** to deliver a sermon. **5.** to give earnest advice, as on religious subjects. **6.** to do this in an obtrusive or tedious way. [ME *preche(n),* t. OF: m. *preëchier,* g. LL *praedicāre.* See PREDICATE]

preacher (prē′chə), *n.* **1.** one whose occupation or function it is to preach the gospel. **2.** one who preaches. **3.** (*cap.*) the author of the Book of Ecclesiastes.

preachify (prē′chĭ fī′), *v.i.,* **-fied, -fying.** *Chiefly U.S.* (usually disparaging) to preach in an obtrusive or tedious way. [f. PREACH + -(I)FY]

preaching (prē′chĭng), *n.* **1.** the act or practice of one who preaches. **2.** the art of delivering sermons. **3.** a sermon. **4.** a public religious service with a sermon. —**preach′ingly,** *adv.*

preachment (prēch′mənt), *n.* **1.** the act of preaching. **2.** a sermon or other discourse, esp. when obtrusive or tedious.

preadamite (prē′ăd′ə mīt′), *n.* **1.** a person supposed to have existed before Adam. **2.** a person who believes that there were men in existence before Adam. —*adj.* **3.** existing before Adam. **4.** of the preadamites.

preadolescence (prē′ăd′ə lĕs′əns), *n.* the period immediately preceding adolescence.

preadolescent (prē′ăd′ə lĕs′ənt), *adj.* pertaining to the period just before adolescence.

preadult (prē′ăd′ŭlt), *adj.* of or pertaining to the period before adulthood.

preallotment (prē′ə lŏt′mənt), *n.* an allotment given in advance.

prealtar (prē′ôl′tə), *adj.* in front of the altar.

preamble (prē′ăm′bl), *n.* **1.** an introductory statement; a preface; an introduction. **2.** the introductory part of a statute, deed, or the like, stating the reasons and intent of what follows. **3.** a preliminary or introductory fact or circumstance. [ME, t. F: m. *préambule,* t. ML: m. s. *praeambulum,* prop. neut. of LL *praeambulus* walking before]

preamplifier (prē′ăm′plĭ fī′ə), *n.* a device in the amplifier circuit of a radio or gramophone which increases the strength of a weak signal for detection and amplification. Also, **preamp** (prē ămp′), **preselector.**

prearrange (prē′ə rānj′), *v.t.,* **-ranged, -ranging.** to arrange beforehand. —**pre′arrange′ment,** *n.*

preaxial (prē′ăk′sĭ əl), *adj. Anat., Zool.* situated before the body axis; pertaining to the radial side of the upper limb and the tibial side of the lower limb.

prebend (prĕb′ənd), *n.* **1.** a stipend allotted from the revenues of a cathedral or a collegiate church to a canon or member of the chapter. **2.** the land yielding such a stipend. **3.** a prebendary. [ME *prebende,* t. ML: m. *prēbenda,* var. of *praebenda* prebend, LL allowance, prop. neut. pl. ger. of L *prae(hi)bēre* offer, furnish] —**prebendal** (prĭ bĕn′dl), *adj.*

prebendary (prĕb′ən də rĭ, -drĭ), *n., pl.* **-daries.** a canon or clergyman who for special services at a cathedral or collegiate church is entitled to a prebend.

prec., **1.** preceded. **2.** preceding.

Pre-Cambrian (prē′kăm′brĭ ən), *Geol.* —*adj.* **1.** pertaining to time or systems of rocks older than the Cambrian. —*n.* **2.** geological period, era, or systems of rocks older than the Cambrian, characterized by almost complete lack of fossils.

precancel (prē′kăn′səl), *v.,* **-celled, -celling** or (*U.S.*) **-celed, -celing,** *n. Philately.* —*v.t.* **1.** to cancel a stamp before placing it on postal matter. —*n.* **2.** a precancelled stamp.

precarious (prĭ kĕə′rĭ əs), *adj.* **1.** dependent on circumstances beyond one's control; uncertain; unstable; insecure: *a precarious livelihood.* **2.** dependent on the will or pleasure of another; liable to be withdrawn or lost at the will of another: *precarious tenure.* **3.** exposed to or involving danger; dangerous; perilous; risky: *a precarious life.* **4.** having insufficient, little, or no foundation: *a precarious assumption.* [t. L: m. *precārius* obtained by entreaty or by mere favour, hence uncertain, precarious] —**precar′iously,** *adv.* —**precar′iousness,** *n.* —**Syn. 1.** See **uncertain.**

precast (prē′käst′), *adj., v.,* **-cast, -casting.** *Bldg Trades.* —*adj.* **1.** (of concrete parts) cast before being put into position in a structure. —*v.t.* **2.** to cast (concrete parts) before putting them into position in a structure.

precatory (prĕk′ə tə rĭ, -trĭ), *adj.* pertaining to, or of the nature of, or expressing entreaty or supplication. Also, **precative** (prĕk′ə tĭv). [t. LL: m. s. *precātōrius*]

precaution (prĭ kô′shən), *n.* **1.** a measure taken beforehand to ward off possible evil or secure good results. **2.** caution employed beforehand; prudent foresight. [t. LL: m. s. *praecautio,* der. L *praecavēre* guard against]

precautionary (prĭ kô′shə nə rĭ), *adj.* **1.** pertaining to or of the nature of precaution or a precaution. **2.** expressing or advising precaution. Also, **precau′tional.**

precautious (prĭ kô′shəs), *adj.* using or displaying precaution.

precede (prĭ sēd′), *v.,* **-ceded, -ceding.** —*v.t.* **1.** to go before, as in place, order, rank, importance, or time. **2.** to introduce by something preliminary; preface. —*v.i.* **3.** to go or come before. [ME *precede(n),* t. L: m. *praecēdere*]

precedence (prĭ sē′dns, prĕs′ĭ dəns), *n.* **1.** the act or fact of preceding. **2.** priority in order, rank, importance, etc. **3.** priority in time. **4.** the right to precede others in ceremonies or social formalities. **5.** the order to be observed ceremonially by persons of different ranks. Also, **precedency** (prĭ sē′dn sĭ, prĕs′ĭ dən sĭ).

precedent¹ (prĕs′ĭ dənt), *n.* **1.** a preceding instance or case which may serve as an example for or a justification in subsequent cases. **2.** *Law.* a legal decision or form of proceeding serving as an authoritative rule or pattern in future similar or analogous cases. [n. use. of PRECEDENT²]

precedent² (prĭ sē′dnt, prĕs′ĭ dənt), *adj.* preceding. [ME, t. L: m. s. *praecēdens* going before]

precedential (prĕs′ĭ dĕn′shəl), *adj.* **1.** of the nature of or constituting a precedent. **2.** having precedence.

preceding (prĭ sē′dĭng), *adj.* that precedes; previous.

precent (prĭ sĕnt′), *v.t.* **1.** to lead as a precentor in singing. —*v.i.* **2.** to act as precentor. [back-formation from PRECENTOR]

precentor (prĭ sĕn′tə), *n.* **1.** one who leads a church choir or congregation in singing. **2.** the member of a cathedral chapter in charge of the music. [t. LL: m. *praecentor* leader in music, der. L *praecinere* sing before] —**precentorial** (prē′sĕn tô′rĭ əl), *adj.* —**precen′torship′,** *n.*

precept (prē′sĕpt), *n.* **1.** a commandment or direction given as a rule of action or conduct. **2.** an injunction as to moral conduct; a maxim. **3.** a rule, as for the performance of some technical operation. **4.** *Law.* **a.** a writ or warrant. **b.** a written order issued pursuant to law, as a sheriff's order for an election. **5.** an order for the collection of money under a rate. [ME, t. L: m. s. *praeceptum,* prop. neut. pp., instructed]

preceptive (prĭ sĕp′tĭv), *adj.* **1.** of the nature of or expressing a precept; mandatory. **2.** giving instructions; instructive. —**precep′tively,** *adv.*

preceptor (prĭ sĕp′tə), *n.* **1.** an instructor; a teacher; a tutor. **2.** the head of a preceptory. [t. L: m. *praeceptor*] —**preceptorate** (prĭ sĕp′tə rĭt), *n.* —**preceptorial** (prē′sĕp tô′rĭ əl), **precep′toral,** *adj.* —**preceptress** (prĭ sĕp′trĭs), *n. fem.*

preceptory (prĭ sĕp′tə rĭ), *n., pl.* **-ries.** a subordinate house or community of the Knights Templar. [t. ML: m. s. *praeceptōria,* der. L *praeceptor* PRECEPTOR]

precession (prĭ sĕsh′ən), *n.* **1.** the act or fact of preceding; precedence. **2.** *Astron.* **a.** the precession of the equinoxes. **b.** the related motion of the earth's axis of rotation. **3.** the motion of a rotating body which, as a result of an applied couple whose axis is perpendicular to the axis of rotation, also involves rotation about a third mutually perpendicular axis. [ME, t. LL: m. s. *praecessio*, der. L *praecessus*, pp., gone before]

precessional (prĭ sĕsh′ə nəl), *adj.* of, pertaining to, characterized by, or resulting from precession.

precession of the equinoxes, *Astron.* the earlier occurrence of the equinoxes in each successive sidereal year because of a slow retrograde motion of the equinoctial points along the ecliptic, caused by the combined action of the sun and moon on the mass of matter accumulated about the earth's equator. A complete revolution of the equinoxes requires about 26,000 years.

pre-Christian (prē′krĭs′chən), *adj.* of, pertaining to, or belonging to a period of time before the Christian era.

precinct (prē′sĭngkt), *n.* **1.** a place or space of definite or understood limits. **2.** (*often pl.*) an enclosing boundary or limit. **3.** (*pl.*) the parts or regions immediately about any place; the environs: *the precincts of a town.* **4.** the ground immediately surrounding a church, temple, or the like. **5.** a walled or otherwise bounded or limited space within which a building or place is situated. **6.** an area in a town whose use is in some way restricted: *a shopping precinct, a pedestrian precinct.* **7.** *U.S.* a district, as of a town, defined for governmental, administrative, or other purposes: *a police precinct.* **8.** *U.S.* one of a number of districts, each containing a polling place, into which a town is divided for electoral purposes. [ME, t. ML: m. s. *praecinctum*, prop. neut. of L *praecinctus*, pp., girded about, surrounded]

preciosity (prĕsh′ĭ ŏs′ĭ tĭ), *n.*, *pl.* **-ties.** fastidious or carefully affected refinement, as in language, style, or taste. [ME *preciosite*, t. OF, t. L: m. s. *pretiōsitas*]

precious (prĕsh′əs), *adj.* **1.** of great price or value; valuable; costly: *precious metals.* **2.** of great moral or spiritual worth. **3.** dear or beloved. **4.** choice; fine; great (used ironically). **5.** egregious; arrant, or gross. **6.** affectedly or excessively delicate, refined, or nice. —*n.* **7.** precious one; darling. —*adv.* **8.** *Colloq.* extremely; very. [ME, t. OF: m. *precios*, t. L: m. s. *pretiōsus* costly] —**pre′ciously,** *adv.* —**pre′ciousness,** *n.* —**Syn. 1.** See **valuable.**

precious stone, a gem distinguished for its beauty and rarity, used in jewellery, etc.

precipice (prĕs′ĭ pĭs), *n.* **1.** a cliff with a vertical, or nearly vertical, or overhanging face. **2.** a situation of great peril. [t. F, t. L: m. s. *praecipitium*]

precipitancy (prĭ sĭp′ĭ tən sĭ), *n.*, *pl.* **-cies. 1.** the quality or fact of being precipitant. **2.** headlong or rash haste. **3.** (*pl.*) hasty or rash acts. Also, **precip′itance.**

precipitant (prĭ sĭp′ĭ tənt), *adj.* **1.** falling headlong. **2.** rushing headlong, rapidly, or hastily onwards. **3.** hasty; rash. **4.** unduly sudden or abrupt. —*n.* **5.** *Chem.* anything that causes precipitation. [t. L: m. s. *praecipitans*, ppr., falling headlong] —**precip′itantly,** *adv.*

precipitate (*v.* prĭ sĭp′ĭ tāt′; *adj.*, *n.* prĭ sĭp′ĭ tĭt), *v.*, **-tated, -tating,** *adj.*, *n.* —*v.t.* **1.** to hasten the occurrence of; bring about in haste or suddenly: *to precipitate a quarrel.* **2.** *Chem.* to separate (a substance) in solid form from a solution, as by means of a reagent. **3.** *Physics, Meteorol.* to condense (moisture) from a state of vapour in the form of rain, dew, etc. **4.** to cast down headlong; fling or hurl down. **5.** to cast, plunge, or send, violently or abruptly: *to precipitate oneself into a struggle.* —*v.i.* **6.** to separate from a solution as a precipitate. **7.** *Physics, Meteorol.* to be condensed as rain, dew, etc. **8.** to be cast down or falling headlong. —*adj.* **9.** headlong. **10.** rushing headlong or rapidly onwards. **11.** proceeding rapidly or with great haste: *a precipitate retreat.* **12.** exceedingly sudden or abrupt. **13.** acting, or done or made, in sudden haste, or without due deliberation; overhasty; rash. —*n.* **14.** *Chem.* a substance precipitated from a solution. **15.** *Physics, Meteorol.* moisture condensed in the form of rain, dew, etc. [t. L: m. s. *praecipitātus*, pp., cast headlong] —**precip′itately,** *adv.* —**precip′itateness,** *n.* —**precip′itative,** *adj.* —**precip′ita′tor,** *n.*

precipitation (prĭ sĭp′ĭ tā′shən), *n.* **1.** the act of precipitating. **2.** the state of being precipitated. **3.** a casting down or falling headlong. **4.** a hastening or hurrying in movement, procedure, or action. **5.** sudden haste. **6.** unwise or rash rapidity. **7.** *Chem., Physics.* the precipitating of a substance from a solution. **8.** *Meteorol.* **a.** falling products of condensation in the atmosphere, as rain, snow, hail. **b.** the amount precipitated at a given place within a given period, usually expressed in inches of rain or snow, etc. **9.** *Spiritualism.* materialization.

precipitin (prĭ sĭp′ĭ tĭn), *n.* *Med., Biochem.* a substance developed in certain blood serums, capable of precipitating proteinaceous substances, etc. [f. PRECIPIT(ATE) + -IN²]

precipitous (prĭ sĭp′ĭ təs), *adj.* **1.** of the nature of a precipice, or characterized by precipices: *a precipitous wall of rock.* **2.** extremely or impassably steep. **3.** precipitate. [f. PRECIPIT(ATE), adj., + -OUS] —**precip′itously,** *adv.* —**precip′itousness,** *n.*

precis (prā′sē), *n.*, *pl.* **-cis,** *v.* —*n.* **1.** an abstract or summary. —*v.t.* **2.** to make a precis of. Also, **précis.** [t. F, n. use of adj., cut short, PRECISE]

precise (prĭ sīs′), *adj.* **1.** definite or exact; definitely or strictly stated, defined, or fixed: *precise directions.* **2.** being exactly that, and neither more nor less: *the precise amount.* **3.** being just that, and not some other. **4.** definite or exact in statement, as a person. **5.** carefully distinct, as the voice. **6.** exact in measuring, recording, etc., as an instrument. **7.** excessively or rigidly particular; puritanical. [t. L: m. s. *praecīsus*, pp., cut short, brief] —**precise′ly,** *adv.* —**precise′ness,** *n.* —**Syn. 1.** See **correct.**

precisian (prĭ sĭzh′ən), *n.* **1.** one who adheres punctiliously to the observance of rules or forms, esp. in matters of religion. **2.** one of the English Puritans of the 16th and 17th centuries. —**preci′sianism,** *n.*

precision (prĭ sĭzh′ən), *n.* **1.** the quality or state of being precise. **2.** accuracy; exactness. **3.** mechanical exactness. **4.** punctiliousness. —*adj.* **5.** of, pertaining to, or characterized by precision or accuracy; adapted for fine measurement: *precision instruments, precision tools.* —**preci′sionist,** *n.*

precision bombing, aerial bombing in which bombs are dropped as accurately as possible on a narrowly defined target area.

preclassical (prē′klăs′ĭ kəl), *adj.* of, pertaining to, or characteristic of a time preceding the classical era.

preclinical (prē′klĭn′ĭ kəl), *Med.* —*adj.* **1.** pertaining to the period prior to the appearance of the symptoms. —*n.* **2.** a preliminary course in anatomy and physiology taken by medical students before actual medical or surgical work in a hospital.

preclude (prĭ klōōd′), *v.t.*, **-cluded, -cluding. 1.** to shut out or exclude; prevent the presence, existence, or occurrence of; make impossible. **2.** to shut out, debar, or prevent (a person, etc.) from something. [t. L: m. s. *praeclūdere* shut off, close] —**preclusion** (prĭ klōō′zhən), *n.* —**preclusive** (prĭ klōō′sĭv), *adj.* —**preclu′sively,** *adv.*

precocial (prĭ kō′shəl), *adj.* (of birds) active, down-covered, and able to move about freely when hatched. [f. PRECOCI(OUS) + -AL¹]

precocious (prĭ kō′shəs), *adj.* **1.** forward in development, esp. mental development, as a child. **2.** prematurely developed, as the mind, faculties, etc. **3.** pertaining to or showing premature development. **4.** *Bot.* **a.** flowering, fruiting, or ripening early, as plants or fruit. **b.** bearing blossoms before leaves, as plants. **c.** appearing before leaves, as flowers. [f. PRECOCI(TY) (t. F: m. *précocité* early maturity) + -OUS] —**preco′ciously,** *adv.* —**preco′ciousness, precocity** (prĭ kŏs′ĭ tĭ), *n.*

precognition (prē′kŏg nĭsh′ən), *n.* foreknowledge; knowledge of future events, esp. through extrasensory means. —**precognitive** (prē′kŏg′nĭ tĭv), *adj.*

pre-Columbian (prē′kə lŭm′bĭ ən), *adj.* of, pertaining to, or belonging to the period before the discovery of America by Columbus: *pre-Columbian civilizations.*

preconceive (prē′kən sēv′), *v.t.*, **-ceived, -ceiving.** to conceive beforehand; form an idea of in advance.

preconception (prē′kən sĕp′shən), *n.* **1.** a conception or opinion formed beforehand. **2.** bias; predilection.

preconcert (prē′kən sûrt′), *v.t.* to arrange beforehand.

precondemn (prē′kən dĕm′), *v.t.* to condemn beforehand, esp. before a fair and objective trial.

precondition (prē′kən dĭsh′ən), *n.* a prior or pre-existing condition; a condition necessary to a subsequent result; prerequisite.

preconize (prē′kə nīz′), *v.t.*, **-nized, -nizing. 1.** to proclaim; commend publicly. **2.** to summon publicly. **3.** *Rom. Cath. Ch.* (of the pope) to declare solemnly in consistory the appointment of (a new bishop). Also, **preconise.** [ME, t. ML: m. *praecōnizāre*, der. L *praeco* crier, herald]

preconscious (prē′kŏn′shəs), *adj.* **1.** *Psychoanal.* absent from the conscious mind but capable of being easily recalled to it. **2.** of or pertaining to a state before the development of consciousness. —*n.* **3.** the preconscious part of the mind. —**pre′con′sciously,** *adv.* —**pre′con′sciousness,** *n.*

precontract (*n.* prē′kŏn′trăkt; *v.* prē′kən trăkt′), *n.* **1.** a pre-existing contract, esp. of marriage. —*v.t.* **2.** to engage (a person) beforehand, esp. in a contract of marriage. **3.** to establish (an agreement) by prior contract. —*v.i.* **4.** to enter into a contract in advance.

precook (prē′kŏŏk′), *v.t.* to cook partly or wholly beforehand.

precritical (prē′krĭt′ĭ kəl), *adj.* *Med.* anteceding a crisis.

precursor (prĭ kû′sə), *n.* **1.** one who or that which precedes; a predecessor. **2.** one who or that which indicates the approach of another or something else. [t. L: m. *praecursor*]

precursory (prĭ kû′sə rĭ), *adj.* **1.** of the nature of a precursor; introductory. **2.** indicative of something to follow. Also, **precursive** (prĭ kû′sĭv).

pred., predicate.

predacious (prĭ dā′shəs), *adj.* predatory. Also, **preda′ceous.** [f. m. s. L *praedārī* take booty + -ACIOUS] —**preda′ciousness, predacity** (prĭ dăs′ĭ tĭ), *n.*

predate (prē′dāt′), *v.t.*, **-dated, -dating. 1.** to date before the actual time: *he predated the cheque by three days.* **2.** to precede in date.

predator (prĕd′ə tə), *n.* a predatory person, organism, or thing. [t. L: m. *praedātor*]

predatory (prĕd′ə tə rĭ, -trĭ), *adj.* **1.** of, pertaining to, or characterized by plundering, pillaging, or robbery. **2.** addicted to or living by plundering or robbery: *predatory bands.* **3.** *Zool.* habitually preying upon other animals. [t. L: m. s. *praedātōrius*] —**pred′atorily,** *adv.* —**pred′atoriness,** *n.*

predecease (prē′dĭ sēs′), *v.t.*, **-ceased, -ceasing.** to die before (a person or an event).

predecessor (prē′dĭ sĕs′ə), *n.* **1.** one who precedes another in an office, position, etc. **2.** anything succeeded or replaced by something else. **3.** an ancestor or forefather. [ME *predecessour*, t. LL: m. *praedēcessor*]

predefine (prē′dĭ fīn′), *v.t.*, **-fined, -fining.** to define or delimit beforehand.

predella (prĭ dĕl′ə; *It.* prē dĕl′lä), *n.* **1.** *Archit.* the base step of an altar. **2.** *Painting.* a long, narrow, painted panel, at the base of an altarpiece. [It.: slab, ult. der. Gmc]

predesignate (prē′dĕz′ĭg nāt′), *v.t.*, **-nated, -nating.** to designate beforehand. —**pre′des′igna′tion,** *n.*

predestinarian (prĭ dĕs′tĭ nâ′rĭ ən), *adj.* **1.** of or pertaining to predestination. **2.** believing in predestination. —*n.* **3.** one who holds the doctrine of predestination. —**predes′tinar′ianism,** *n.*

predestinate (*v.* prĭ dĕs′tĭ nāt′; *adj.* prĭ dĕs′tĭ nĭt, -tĭ nāt′), *v.*, **-nated, -nating,** *adj.* —*v.t.* **1.** to foreordain; predetermine. **2.** *Theol.* to foreordain by divine decree or purpose. —*adj.* **3.** foreordained. [ME, t. L: m. s. *praedestinātus*, pp., appointed beforehand]

predestination (prĭ dĕs′tĭ nā′shən, prē′dĕs-), *n.* **1.** the act of predestinating or predestining. **2.** the resulting state. **3.** fate or destiny. **4.** *Theol.* **a.** the action of God in foreordaining from eternity whatever comes to pass. **b.** the decree of God by which men are foreordained to everlasting happiness (election) or misery.

predestine (prĭ dĕs′tĭn), *v.t.*, **-tined, -tining.** to destine beforehand; foreordain; predetermine: *he seemed almost predestined for the ministry.*

predeterminate (prē′dĭ tû′mĭ nĭt), *adj.* determined beforehand.

predetermine (prē′dĭ tû′mĭn), *v.t.*, **-mined, -mining. 1.** to determine or decide beforehand. **2.** to ordain beforehand; predestine. **3.** to direct or impel beforehand to something. —**pre′deter′mina′tion,** *n.* —**pre′deter′minative,** *adj.*

predial (prē′dyəl), *adj.* praedial.

predicable (prĕd′ĭ kə bl), *adj.* **1.** that may be predicated or affirmed; assertable. —*n.* **2.** that which may be predicated; an attribute. **3.** *Logic.* any one of the various kinds of predicate that may be used of a subject (in Aristotelian logic: genus, species, difference, property, and accident). —**pred′icabil′ity, pred′icableness,** *n.* —**pred′icably,** *adv.*

predicament (prĭ dĭk′ə mənt), *n.* **1.** an unpleasant, trying, or dangerous situation. **2.** a particular state, condition, or situation. **3.** one of the classes or categories of logical predications. [ME, t. LL: m. s. *praedicāmentum*, der. L *praedicāre* proclaim] —**predicamental** (prĭ dĭk′ə mĕn′tl), *adj.*

—**Syn. 1.** PREDICAMENT, DILEMMA, PLIGHT, QUANDARY refer to unpleasant or puzzling situations. PREDICAMENT and PLIGHT stress more the unpleasant nature, QUANDARY and DILEMMA the puzzling nature of the situation. PREDICAMENT and PLIGHT are sometimes interchangeable; PLIGHT, however, though originally meaning peril, danger, has today lost its full force of meaning, and is used lightly: *when his suit failed to come from the cleaners, he was in a terrible plight.* PREDICAMENT, though likewise capable of being used lightly, may also refer to a really crucial situation: *unexpected company for supper, and no food: what a predicament!* DILEMMA, in popular use, means a position of doubt or perplexity in which one is faced by two equally undesirable alternatives: *the dilemma of one who must choose between waiting with a badly injured companion on the mountainside in the hope of rescue, and leaving him while going to seek help.* QUANDARY (hardly used except in the expression *to be in a quandary*) is the state of mental perplexity of one faced with a difficult situation: *there seemed to be no way out of the quandary.*

predicant (prĕd′ĭ kənt), *adj.* **1.** preaching. —*n.* **2.** *Obs.* a preacher, esp. a member of a predicant order. **3.** a predikant.

predicate (*n.*, *adj.* prĕd′ĭ kĭt; *v.* prĕd′ĭ kāt′), *v.*, **-cated, -cating,** *adj.*, *n.* —*v.t.* **1.** to proclaim; declare; affirm or assert. **2.** to affirm or assert (something) of the subject of a proposition. **3.** to connote or imply. **4.** *U.S.* to found or base (a statement, action, etc.) on something. —*v.i.* **5.** to make an affirmation or assertion. —*adj.* **6.** predicated. **7.** *Gram.* belonging to the predicate: *a predicate noun.* —*n.* **8.** *Gram.* (in many languages) the active verb in a sentence or clause together with all the words it governs and those which modify it, e.g., *is here* in *Jack is here.* **9.** *Logic.* that which is predicated or said of the subject in a proposition. [t. L: m. s. *praedicātus*, pp., declared publicly, asserted, LL preached] —**pred′ica′tion,** *n.* —**predicative** (prĭ dĭk′ə tĭv), *adj.* —**predic′atively,** *adv.*

predicative adjective, (in English and certain other languages, when one of a particular group of verbs is used) an adjective of the predicate bearing a kind of attributive relation to the subject (e.g., *he is dead*) or to the direct object (e.g., *it made him sick*).

predicate noun, (in English and some other languages) a noun following one of a certain group of verbs and designating the same entity as the subject (he is *the king*) or the direct object (they made him *king*).

predicatory (prĕd′ĭ kā′tə rĭ, prĕd′ĭ kā′tə rĭ), *adj.* pertaining to preaching.

predict (prĭ dĭkt′), *v.t.* **1.** to foretell; prophesy. —*v.i.* **2.** to foretell the future. [t. L: m. s. *praedictus*, pp.] —**predict′able,** *adj.* —**predic′tive,** *adj.* —**predic′tively,** *adv.* —**predic′tor,** *n.*

—**Syn. 1.** PREDICT, PROPHESY, FORESEE, FORECAST mean to know or tell (usually correctly) beforehand what will happen. To PREDICT is usually to foretell with precision of calculation, knowledge, or shrewd inference from facts or experience: *the astronomers can predict an eclipse*; it may, however, be used quite lightly: *I predict she'll be a success at the party.* PROPHESY may have the solemn meaning of predicting future events by the aid of divine or supernatural inspiration: *Merlin prophesied that the two knights would meet in conflict*; this verb, too, may be used loosely: *I prophesy he'll soon be back in the old job.* To FORESEE refers specifically not to the uttering of predictions but to the mental act of seeing ahead; there is often (but not always) a practical implication of preparing for what will happen: *he was clever enough to foresee this shortage of materials.* FORECAST has much the meaning of FORESEE, except that conjecture rather than real insight is apt to be involved; it is used particularly of the weather: *rain is forecast for tonight.*

prediction (prĭ dĭk′shən), *n.* **1.** the act of predicting. **2.** an instance of this; a prophecy.

predictive (prĭ dĭk′tĭv), *adj.* having the character or quality of predicting or indicating the future. —**predic′tively,** *adv.* —**predic′tiveness,** *n.*

predigest (prē′dĭ jĕst′, -dī-), *v.t.* to treat (food) by an artificial process similar to digestion, in order to make it more easily digestible. —**pre′diges′tion,** *n.*

predikant (prĕd′ĭ kănt′), *n.* a minister of the Dutch Reformed Church, esp. in South Africa.

predilection (prē′dĭ lĕk′shən), *n.* a predisposition of the mind in favour of something; a partiality; preference. [f. PRE- + s. L *dīlectio* love, choice]

predispose (prē′dĭs pōz′), *v.*, **-posed, -posing. 1.** to give a previous inclination or tendency to. **2.** to render subject, susceptible, or liable: *poor health predisposed them to infection.* **3.** to dispose beforehand. —*v.i.* **4.** to give or furnish a tendency or inclination.

predisposition (prē′dĭs′pə zĭsh′ən), *n.* **1.** the condition of being predisposed. **2.** *Pathol.* the condition of being particularly susceptible to a certain disease.

prednisone (prĕd′nĭ sōn′), *n.* *Pharm.* a hydrogenated product of cortisone having the basic steroid structure.

predominance (prĭ dŏm′ĭ nəns), *n.* the quality of being predominant; prevalence over others. Also, **predom′inancy.**

predominant (prĭ dŏm′ĭ nənt), *adj.* **1.** having ascendancy, power, authority, or influence over others; ascendant. **2.** prevailing. —**predom′inantly,** *adv.* —**Syn. 1, 2.** See **dominant.**

predominate (prĭ dŏm′ĭ nāt′), *v.*, **-nated, -nating.** —*v.i.* **1.** to be the stronger or leading element; preponderate; prevail. **2.** to have or exert controlling power (often fol. by *over*). **3.** to surpass others in authority or influence. **4.** to be more noticeable or imposing than something else. —*v.t.* **5.** to dominate or prevail over. [f. PRE- + m. s. L *dominātus*, pp., ruled, dominated] —**predom′inat′ingly,** *adv.* —**predom′ina′tion,** *n.* —**predom′ina′tor,** *n.*

predynastic (prē′dĭ năs′tĭk), *adj.* of or pertaining to the period in Egypt before the first dynasty, generally taken as before 3200 B.C.

pre-election (prē′ĭ lĕk′shən), *adj.* occurring before an election.

pre-eminence (prĭ ĕmʹĭ nəns), *n.* the state or character of being pre-eminent.

pre-eminent (prĭ ĕmʹĭ nənt), *adj.* eminent before or above others; superior to or surpassing others; distinguished beyond others. [ME, t. L: m. s. *praeēminens*, ppr., standing out, rising above] —**pre-emʹinently,** *adv.* —**Syn.** See **dominant.**

pre-empt (prĭ ĕmptʹ), *v.t.* **1.** to occupy (land) in order to establish a prior right to buy. **2.** to acquire or appropriate beforehand. —*v.i.* **3.** *Bridge.* to make a pre-emptive bid. [back-formation from PRE-EMPTION] —**pre-emptory** (prĭ-ĕmpʹtə rĭ), *adj.* —**pre-emptor** (prĭ ĕmpʹtô, -tə), *n.*

pre-emption (prĭ ĕmpʹshən), *n.* the act or right of purchasing before or in preference to others. [f. PRE- + s. L *emptio* a buying]

pre-emptive (prĭ ĕmpʹtĭv), *adj.* **1.** of or pertaining to pre-emption. **2.** *Bridge.* of or pertaining to an unnecessarily high bid, made to deter one's opponents from bidding.

preen (prēn), *v.t.* **1.** to trim or dress with the beak, as a bird does its feathers. **2.** to prepare, dress, or array (oneself) carefully in making the toilet. **3.** to pride (oneself) on an achievement, etc. [prob. var. of PRUNE[3]] —**preenʹer,** *n.*

pre-engage (prēʹĭn gājʹ), *v.t., v.i.,* **-gaged, -gaging.** to engage beforehand. —**preʹ-engageʹment,** *n.*

pre-English (prēʹĭngʹglĭsh), *n.* **1.** the ancient Germanic dialect which by differentiation from its sister dialects eventually became English. **2.** the languages current in Britain before the English settlement. —*adj.* **3.** pertaining to the ancestral Germanic dialect from which English grew, and to its speakers. **4.** pertaining to the languages and peoples of Britain before the English settlement.

pre-establish (prēʹĭs tăbʹlĭsh), *v.t.* to establish beforehand. —**preʹ-estabʹlishment,** *n.*

pre-examination (prēʹĭg zămʹĭ nāʹshən), *adj.* before an examination: *pre-examination nerves.* Also, *Colloq.*, **preʹ-examʹ.**

pre-exilian (prēʹĕg zĭlʹĭ ən), *adj.* before the Babylonian exile or captivity of the Jews. Also, **preʹ-exilʹic.** [f. PRE- + s. L *exilium* exile + -AN]

pre-exist (prēʹĭg zĭstʹ), *v.i.* **1.** to exist beforehand. **2.** to exist in a previous state. —**preʹ-existʹence,** *n.* —**preʹ-existʹent,** *adj.*

pref., **1.** preface. **2.** prefaced. **3.** preference. **4.** preferred. **5.** prefix. **6.** prefixed.

prefab (prēʹfăbʹ), *n.* a prefabricated house.

prefabricate (prēʹfăbʹrĭ kātʹ), *v.t.,* **-cated, -cating. 1.** to fabricate or construct beforehand. **2.** to manufacture (houses, etc.) in standardized parts or sections ready for rapid assembling and erection. —**preʹfabʹricatʹed,** *adj.* —**preʹfabʹricaʹtion,** *n.*

preface (prĕfʹĭs), *n., v.,* **-aced, -acing.** —*n.* **1.** a preliminary statement by the author or editor of a book, setting forth its purpose and scope, expressing acknowledgment of assistance from others, etc. **2.** an introductory part, as of a speech. **3.** something preliminary or introductory. **4.** *Eccles.* a prayer of thanksgiving, the introduction to the canon of the mass, ending with the Sanctus. —*v.t.* **5.** to provide with or introduce by a preface. **6.** to serve as a preface to. [ME, t. OF, t. ML: m. *prēfātia*, r. L *praefātio* a saying beforehand] —**Syn. 1.** See **introduction.**

prefatory (prĕfʹə tə rĭ, -trĭ), *adj.* of the nature of a preface; preliminary. —**prefʹatorily,** *adv.*

prefect (prēʹfĕkt), *n.* **1.** a person appointed to any of various positions of command, authority, or superintendence, as a chief magistrate in ancient Rome, or the chief administrative official of a department of France and Italy. **2.** (in many English schools) one of a body of senior pupils with authority for maintaining order and discipline; praepostor. **3.** the dean in a Jesuit school or college. Also, **praefect.** [ME, t. L: m. s. *praefactus* overseer, director, prop. pp., appointed as a superior]

prefectorial (prēʹfĕk tôʹrĭ əl), *adj.* of, pertaining to, or characteristic of a prefect.

prefecture (prēʹfĕk tyo͝oəʹ), *n.* **1.** the office, jurisdiction, territory, or official residence of a prefect. **2.** the administrative centre of a French region. [t. L: m. *praefectūra*] —**prefectural** (prē fĕkʹtyo͝o rəl), *adj.*

prefer (prĭ fûʹ), *v.t.,* **-ferred, -ferring. 1.** to set or hold before or above other persons or things in estimation; like better; choose rather: *to prefer Dickens to Thackeray.* **2.** *Law.* to give priority, as to one creditor over another. **3.** to put forward or present (a statement, suit, charge, etc.) for consideration or sanction. **4.** to put forward or advance, as in rank or office. [ME *preferre*, t. L: m. *praeferre* bear before, set before, prefer] —**preferʹrer,** *n.* —**Syn. 1.** See **choose.**

preferable (prĕfʹə rə bl, prĕfʹrə bl), *adj.* **1.** worthy to be preferred. **2.** more desirable. —**prefʹerabilʹity, prefʹerableness,** *n.* —**prefʹerably,** *adv.*

preference (prĕfʹə rəns, prĕfʹrəns), *n.* **1.** the act of preferring; estimation of one thing above another; prior favour or choice. **2.** the state of being preferred. **3.** that which is preferred; the object of prior favour or choice. **4.** a practical advantage given to one over others. **5.** a prior right or claim, as to payment of dividends, or to assets upon dissolution. **6.** the favouring of one country or group of countries by granting special advantages over others in international trade. —**Syn. 3.** See **choice.**

preference shares, shares which rank before ordinary shares in the entitlement to dividends, usually at a fixed rate of interest. Also, *U.S.*, **preferred stock.**

preference stock, stock in a company which entitles the holder to preferential rights in respect of dividends over holders of other classes of stock or shares, as ordinary or deferred.

preferential (prĕfʹə rĕnʹshəl), *adj.* **1.** pertaining to or of the nature of preference. **2.** showing or giving preference. **3.** receiving or enjoying preference. —**prefʹerenʹtialism,** *n.* —**prefʹerenʹtialist,** *n.* —**prefʹerenʹtially,** *adv.*

preferential voting, a system of voting which enables the voter to indicate his order of preference for the candidates on the ballot.

preferment (prĭ fûʹmənt), *n.* **1.** the act of preferring. **2.** the state of being preferred. **3.** advancement or promotion, as in rank. **4.** a position or office giving social or pecuniary advancement.

preferred stock, *U.S.* preference shares.

prefiguration (prēʹfĭg yo͞o rāʹshən), *n.* **1.** the act of prefiguring. **2.** that in which something is prefigured.

prefigure (prēʹfĭgʹə), *v.t.,* **-ured, -uring. 1.** to represent beforehand by figure or type; foreshow; foreshadow. **2.** to figure or represent to oneself beforehand. [late ME, t. LL: m. s. *praefigūrāre.* See PRE-, FIGURE, v.] —**prefigurative** (prēʹfĭgʹyo͞o rə tĭv), *adj.* —**preʹfigʹurement,** *n.*

prefix (*n.* prēʹfĭks; *v.* prē fĭksʹ, prēʹfĭks), *n.* **1.** *Gram.* an affix which is put before a word, stem, or word element to add to or qualify its meaning (as *un-* in *unkind*), strictly speaking an inseparable form, but usually applied to prepositions and adverbs also, as in German *mitgehen.* **2.** something prefixed, as a title before a person's name. —*v.t.* **3.** to fix or put before or in front. **4.** *Gram.* to add as a prefix. **5.** *Rare.* to fix, settle, or appoint beforehand. [ME, t. L: m. s. *praefixus*, pp., fixed before] —**prefixal** (prēʹfĭk səl, prē fĭkʹsəl), *adj.* —**preʹfixally,** *adv.*

preform (prēʹfômʹ), *v.t.* to form beforehand.

preformation (prēʹfô māʹshən), *n.* **1.** previous formation. **2.** *Biol.* a theoretical concept according to which the individual, with all its parts, pre-exists in the germ and grows from microscopic to normal proportions during embryogenesis (opposed to *epigenesis*).

prefrontal (prēʹfrŭnʹtl), *Anat.* —*adj.* **1.** in front of the frontal bone or gyrus. —*n.* **2.** the middle portion of the ethmoid bone.

preglacial (prēʹglāʹsyəl), *adj.* existing or occurring before a glacial epoch, esp. the Pleistocene.

pregnable (prĕgʹnə bl), *adj.* **1.** capable of being taken or won by force, as a fortress. **2.** open to attack; assailable. [late ME *prenable*, t. OF, der. s. *prendre*, g. L *pre(he)ndere* seize, take] —**pregʹnabilʹity,** *n.*

pregnancy (prĕgʹnən sĭ), *n., pl.* **-cies.** the condition or quality of being pregnant.

pregnant (prĕgʹnənt), *adj.* **1.** being with child or young, as a woman or female mammal; having a foetus in the womb. **2.** fraught, filled, or abounding (fol. by *with*): *words pregnant with meaning.* **3.** fertile or rich (fol. by *in*): *a mind pregnant in ideas.* **4.** full of meaning; highly significant: *a pregnant utterance.* **5.** full of possibilities, involving important issues or results, or momentous. **6.** teeming with ideas or imagination: *a pregnant wit.* [ME, t. L: m. s. *praegnans*] —**pregʹnantly,** *adv.*

preheat (prēʹhētʹ), *v.t.* to heat before using or before submitting to some process.

prehensile (prĭ hĕnʹsĭl), *adj.* **1.** adapted for seizing, grasping, or laying hold of anything. **2.** fitted for grasping by folding or wrapping round an object. [t. F, f. s. L *prehensus*, pp., seized + *-ile* -ILE] —**prehensility** (prēʹhĕn sĭlʹĭ tĭ), *n.*

prehension (prĭ hĕnʹshən), *n.* **1.** the act of seizing, grasping, or taking hold. **2.** mental apprehension. [t. L: s. *prehensio*]

prehistoric (prēʹhĭs tŏʹrĭk), *adj.* of or belonging to a period prior to that of recorded history. Also, **preʹhistorʹical.** —**preʹhistorʹically,** *adv.*

prehistory (prēʹhĭsʹtə rĭ), *n.* **1.** the history of man in the period before recorded events, known mainly through archaeological research; an account or study of prehistoric man. **2.** a history of events leading up to a particular incident, situation, etc.

prehuman (prēʹhyo͞oʹmən), *adj.* before the advent or evolution of man.

pre-ignition (prē′ĭg nĭsh′ən), *n.* ignition of the charge in an internal-combustion engine earlier in the cycle than is compatible with proper operation.

pre-industrial (prē′ĭn dŭs′trĭ əl), *adj.* before the growth of modern industrial processes; before the Industrial Revolution.

prejudge (prē′jŭj′), *v.t.*, **-judged, -judging.** **1.** to judge beforehand. **2.** to pass judgement on prematurely or in advance of due investigation. **—pre′judg′er,** *n.* **—pre′-judge′ment,** *n.*

prejudice (prĕj′o͝o dĭs), *n.*, *v.*, **-diced, -dicing.** **—***n.* **1.** an unfavourable opinion or feeling formed beforehand or without knowledge, thought, or reason. **2.** any preconceived opinion or feeling, favourable or unfavourable. **3.** disadvantage resulting from some judgement or action of another. **4.** resulting injury or detriment. **5. without prejudice,** *Law.* without dismissing, damaging, or otherwise affecting a legal interest or demand. **—***v.t.* **6.** to affect with a prejudice, favourable or unfavourable: *these facts prejudiced us in his favour.* **7.** to affect disadvantageously or detrimentally. [ME, t. F, t. L: m. s. *praejūdicium*] **—Syn. 1.** See **bias.**

prejudicial (prĕj′o͝o dĭsh′əl), *adj.* causing prejudice or disadvantage; detrimental. **—prej′udi′cially,** *adv.*

prelacy (prĕl′ə sĭ), *n.*, *pl.* **-cies.** **1.** the office or dignity of a prelate. **2.** the order of prelates. **3.** the body of prelates collectively. **4.** (often derogatory) the system of church government by prelates.

prelate (prĕl′ĭt), *n.* an ecclesiastic of a high order, as an archbishop, bishop, etc.; a church dignitary. [ME *prelat*, t. ML: m. s. *praelātus*, a civil or ecclesiastical dignitary; in L, pp., set before, preferred] **—prel′ateship′,** *n.* **—prelatic** (prĭ lăt′ĭk), *adj.*

prelatism (prĕl′ĭ tĭz′əm), *n.* prelacy or episcopacy. **—prel′atist,** *n.*

prelature (prĕl′ĭ chə), *n.* **1.** the office of a prelate. **2.** the order of prelates. **3.** prelates collectively. [t. ML: m. *praelātūra*, der. L *praelātus*. See PRELATE]

prelect (prĭ lĕkt′), *v.i.* to lecture or discourse publicly. **—prelection** (prĭ lĕk′shən), *n.* **—prelec′tor,** *n.*

prelibation (prē′lī bā′shən), *n.* a foretaste. [t. LL: m. s. *praelībātio*, der. L *praelībāre* taste beforehand]

prelim., preliminary.

prelim (prē′lĭm), *n.* **1.** *Colloq.* a preliminary examination. **2.** (*pl.*) *Print.* the pages at the beginning of a book preceding the actual text.

preliminary (prĭ lĭm′ĭ nə rĭ, -lĭm′nə-), *adj.*, *n.*, *pl.* **-naries.** **—***adj.* **1.** preceding and leading up to the main matter or business; introductory; preparatory. **—***n.* **2.** something preliminary; introductory or preparatory step, measure, sporting contest, or the like. [t. NL: m. *praelīmindruis*, f. L: *prae-* PRE- + *līmināris* of a threshold] **—prelim′-inarily,** *adv.*

—Syn. 1. PRELIMINARY, INTRODUCTORY both refer to that which comes before the principal subject of consideration. That which is PRELIMINARY is in the nature of preparation or of clearing away details which would encumber the main subject or problem; it often deals with arrangements and the like, which have to do only incidentally with the principal subject: *preliminary negotiations.* That which is INTRODUCTORY leads with natural, logical, or close connection, directly into the main subject of consideration: *introductory steps.* **—Ant. 1.** concluding.

preliterate (prē′lĭt′ə rĭt), *adj.* not leaving or having written records: *a preliterate culture.*

prelude (prĕl′yo͞od), *n.*, *v.*, **-uded, -uding.** **—***n.* **1.** a preliminary to an action, event, condition, or work of broader scope and higher importance. **2.** preliminary action, remarks, etc. **3.** *Music.* **a.** a relatively short, independent instrumental composition, free in form and of an improvised character. **b.** a piece which precedes a more important movement. **c.** the overture to an opera. **d.** an independent piece, of moderate length, sometimes used as an introduction to a fugue. **e.** music opening a church service; an introductory voluntary. **—***v.t.* **4.** to serve as a prelude or introduction to. **5.** to introduce by a prelude. **6.** to play as a prelude. **—***v.i.* **7.** to serve as a prelude. **8.** to give a prelude. **9.** to play a prelude. [t. F, t. ML: m. s. *praelūdium*, der. L *praelūdere* play beforehand] **—preluder** (prĕl′yo͞o də, prĭ lyo͞o′də), *n.*

prelusion (prĭ lyo͞o′zhən), *n.* a prelude. [t. L: m. s. *praelūsio*]

prelusive (prĭ lyo͞o′sĭv), *adj.* introductory. Also, **prelusory** (prĭ lyo͞o′sə rĭ). **—prelu′sively,** *adv.*

prem., premium.

premarital (prē′mă′rĭ tl), *adj.* before marriage.

premature (prĕm′ə tyo͞oə′, prĕm′ə tyo͞oə′), *adj.* **1.** coming into existence or occurring too soon. **2.** mature or ripe before the proper time. **3.** overhasty, as in action. [t. L: m. s. *praemātūrus*] **—prem′ature′ly,** *adv.* **—prem′-ature′ness, prem′atu′rity,** *n.*

premaxilla (prē′măk sĭl′ə), *n.*, *pl.* **-maxillae** (-măk sĭl′ē). *Zool.* one of a pair of bones of the upper jaw of vertebrates, situated in front of and between the maxillary bones. [t. NL: m. *praemaxilla*, f. L: *prae-* PRE- + *maxilla* jawbone] **—premaxillary** (prē′măk sĭl′ə rĭ), *adj.*

premed (prē′mĕd′), *n.* *Colloq.* **1.** premedication. **2.** premedical.

premedical (prē′mĕd′ĭ kl), *adj.* **1.** pertaining to the preparation for the study of medicine. **—***n.* **2.** in medical training, a course of study in basic sciences to be completed prior to the preclinical studies.

premedication (prē′mĕd′ĭ kā′shən), *n.* the giving of drugs prior to an operation, to sedate and prepare a patient.

premeditate (prĭ mĕd′ĭ tāt′), *v.t.*, *v.i.*, **-tated, -tating.** to meditate, consider, or plan beforehand. [t. L: m. s. *praemeditātus*, pp., meditated beforehand] **—premed′-itat′edly,** *adv.* **—premed′ita′tive,** *adj.* **—premed′ita′-tor,** *n.* **—Syn.** See **deliberate.**

premeditation (prē′mĕd ĭ tā′shən, prĭ mĕd′ĭ-), *n.* **1.** the act of premeditating. **2.** *Law.* sufficient forethought to impute deliberation and intent to commit the act.

premenstrual tension (prē′mĕn′stro͝o əl), symptoms of physiological and emotional upset, as headache, pelvic discomfort, and breast enlargement, experienced by women in the week prior to menstruation.

premier (prĕm′yə), *n.* **1.** the prime minister, or first minister of state; the head of the administration of a state. **—***adj.* **2.** first in rank; chief; leading. **3.** earliest. [t. F: first, g. L *prīmārius* of the first rank] **—premiership** (prĕm′yə shĭp′), *n.*

premiere (prĕm′ĭ ĕə′, prĕm′ĭ ə), *n.* **1.** a first public performance of a play, etc. **2.** the leading woman, as in a drama. Also, *French*, **première** (*Fr.* prə myĕr′). [t. F: lit., first (fem.)]

premillenarian (prē′mĭl′ĭ neə′rĭ ən), *n.* a believer in premillennialism. **—pre′mil′lenar′ianism,** *n.*

premillennial (prē′mĭ lĕn′ĭ əl), *adj.* of or pertaining to the period preceding the millennium.

premillennialism (prē′mĭ lĕn′ĭ ə lĭz′əm), *n.* the doctrine or belief that the second coming of Christ will precede the millennium. **—pre′millen′nialist,** *n.*

premise (prĕm′ĭs), *n.*, *v.*, **-ised, -ising.** **—***n.* **1.** (*pl.*) **a.** the property forming the subject of a conveyance. **b.** a tract of land. **c.** a house or building with the grounds, etc., belonging to it. **2.** Also, **premiss.** *Logic.* a proposition (or one of several) from which a conclusion is drawn. **3.** *Law.* **a.** a basis, stated or assumed, on which reasoning proceeds. **b.** an earlier statement in a document. **c.** (in a bill in equity) the statement of facts upon which the complaint is based, the parties, etc. **—***v.t.* **4.** to set forth beforehand, as by way of introduction or explanation. **5.** to assume, whether explicitly or implicitly, a proposition as a premise for some conclusion. **—***v.i.* **6.** to set down, as a preface. **7.** to state or assume as a premise. [ME *premiss*, t. ML: m. s. *praemissa*, prop. fem. pp., sent before]

premium (prē′myəm), *n.* **1.** a prize to be won in a competition. **2.** a bonus, gift, or sum additional to price, wages, interest, or the like. **3.** a bonus, prize, or the like, offered as an inducement to buy a product. **4.** the amount paid or agreed to be paid, in one sum or periodically, as the consideration for a contract of insurance. **5.** *Econ.* the excess value of one form of money over another of the same nominal value. **6.** a sum above the nominal or par value of a thing. **7.** *Stock Market.* the amount that a buyer is prepared to pay for the right to subscribe for a new or rights issue of stocks or shares in a company. **8.** a fee paid for instruction in a trade or profession. **9. at a premium, a.** in high esteem; in demand. **b.** at a high price. [t. L: m. *praemium* profit]

Premium Savings Bonds, bonds issued by the Treasury in units of £1, which, instead of earning interest, are put in a monthly draw for cash prizes. Also, **premium bonds.**

premolar (prē′mō′lə), *adj.* **1.** denoting or pertaining to certain of the permanent teeth in mammals (in man, usually called bicuspid teeth) in front of the molar teeth. **—***n.* **2.** a premolar tooth. **3.** a bicuspid.

premonish (prĭ mŏn′ĭsh), *v.t.* to forewarn. [f. s. L *praemonēre* forewarn + -ISH, modelled on ADMONISH]

premonition (prē′mə nĭsh′ən), *n.* **1.** a forewarning. **2.** a presentiment. [t. F (obs.), t. LL: m. s. *praemonitio*]

premonitory (prĭ mŏn′ĭ tə rĭ, -trĭ), *adj.* giving premonition; serving to warn beforehand.

premorse (prĭ môs′), *adj.* *Biol.* having the end irregularly truncate, as if bitten or broken off. [t. L: m. s. *praemorsus*, pp., bitten off in front]

premotion (prē mō′shən), *n.* an action by God believed to determine the will of man.

prenatal (prē′nā′tl), *adj.* antenatal. **—pre′na′tally,** *adv.*

prenominate (prĭ nŏm′ĭ nĭt), *adj.* *Archaic.* forementioned. [t. L: m. s. *praenōminātus*, pp., named before]

prenotion (prē nō′shən), *n.* a preconception. [t. L: m. s. *praenōtio*]

prentice (prĕn′tĭs), *n.*, *v. Archaic.* apprentice. [ME]

preoccupancy (prĭ ŏk′yŏŏ pən sĭ), *n.* **1.** previous occupancy. **2.** the state of being preoccupied; engrossed in thought.

preoccupation (prĭ ŏk′yŏŏ pā′shən), *n.* **1.** the state of being preoccupied. **2.** the act of preoccupying. **3.** that with which one is preoccupied.

preoccupied (prĭ ŏk′yŏŏ pīd′), *adj.* **1.** completely engrossed in thought; absorbed. **2.** occupied previously. **3.** *Biol.* already used as a name for some species, genus, etc., and not available as a designation for any other.

preoccupy (prĭ ŏk′yŏŏ pī′), *v.t.*, **-pied, -pying. 1.** to absorb or engross to the exclusion of other things. **2.** to occupy or take possession of beforehand or before others. —**preoc′cupant, preoc′cupi′er,** *n.*

preoral (prē′ô′rəl), *adj. Zool.* situated in front of or before the mouth. —**pre′o′rally,** *adv.*

preordain (prē′ô dān′), *v.t.* to ordain beforehand; foreordain. —**pre′ordain′ment, preordination** (prē′ô′dĭ nā′shən), *n.*

prep (prĕp), *Colloq.* —*adj.* **1.** preparatory: *a prep school.* —*n.* **2.** a preparatory school. **3.** preparation (def. 3).

prep., 1. preparation. **2.** preparatory. **3.** preposition.

preparation (prĕp′ə rā′shən), *n.* **1.** a proceeding, measure, or provision by which one prepares for something: *preparations for a journey.* **2.** any proceeding, experience, or the like considered as a mode of preparing for the future. **3.** homework, or, esp. in a boarding school, individual work supervised by a teacher. **4.** the act of preparing. **5.** the state of being prepared. **6.** something prepared, manufactured, or compounded. **7.** a specimen, as an animal body, prepared for scientific examination, dissection, etc. **8.** *Music.* **a.** the preparing of a dissonance, by introducing the dissonant note as a consonant note in the preceding chord. **b.** the note so introduced. **9.** the day before the Jewish Sabbath, or any other major Jewish festival. **10.** (in the Eastern European and Orthodox churches) the day before the Christian Sabbath.

preparative (prĭ pă′rə tĭv), *adj.* **1.** preparatory. —*n.* **2.** something that prepares. **3.** a preparation.

preparatory (prĭ pă′rə tə rĭ, -trĭ), *adj.* **1.** serving or designed to prepare or make ready: *preparatory arrangements.* **2.** preliminary or introductory. **3.** of or pertaining to education which prepares a child for public school, etc. —**prepar′atorily,** *adv.*

preparatory school, an independent school, often boarding, for pupils under about 13 years of age, before entering a public school.

prepare (prĭ pĕə′), *v.*, **-pared, -paring.** —*v.t.* **1.** to make ready, or put in due condition, for something. **2.** to get ready for eating, as a meal, by due assembling, dressing, or cooking. **3.** to manufacture, compound, or compose. **4.** *Music.* to lead up to (a discord, an embellishment, etc.) by some preliminary note or notes. —*v.i.* **5.** to put things or oneself in readiness; get ready: *to prepare for war.* [t. L: m. s. *praeparāre* make ready beforehand] —**preparedly** (prĭ pĕə′rĭd lĭ, -pĕəd′lĭ), *adv.* —**prepar′er,** *n.*

—**Syn. 1.** Prepare, contrive, devise imply planning for, and making ready for something expected or thought possible. To prepare is to make ready beforehand for some approaching event, need, and the like: *to prepare a room, a speech.* Contrive and devise emphasize the exercise of ingenuity and inventiveness. The first word suggests a shrewdness that borders on trickery, but this is absent from devise: *to contrive a means of escape; to devise a time-saving method.*

preparedness (prĭ pĕə′rĭd nĭs, -pĕəd′nĭs), *n.* the state of being prepared; readiness.

prepay (prē′pā′), *v.t.*, **-paid, -paying. 1.** to pay beforehand. **2.** to pay the charge upon in advance. —**pre′pay′able,** *adj.* —**pre′pay′ment,** *n.*

prepense (prĭ pĕns′), *adj.* premeditated: *malice prepense.* [earlier *prepenst, prepensed,* pp. of obs. *prepense* meditate beforehand; r. ME *purpense,* t. OF]

preponderance (prĭ pŏn′də rəns, -drəns), *n.* the quality or fact of being preponderant; superiority in weight, power, number, etc. Also, **prepon′derancy.**

preponderant (prĭ pŏn′də rənt, -drənt), *adj.* superior in weight, force, influence, number, etc.; preponderating; predominant. —**prepon′derantly,** *adv.*

preponderate (prĭ pŏn′də rāt′), *v.i.*, **-rated, -rating. 1.** to exceed something else in weight; be the heavier. **2.** to incline downwards or descend, as one scale or end of a balance, because of greater weight; be weighed down. **3.** to be superior in power, force, influence, number, amount, etc.; predominate. [t. L: m. s. *praeponderātus,* pp. See ponder] —**prepon′derat′ing,** *adj.* —**prepon′derat′ingly,** *adv.* —**prepon′dera′tion,** *n.*

preposition (prĕp′ə zĭsh′ən), *n. Gram.* **1.** (in some languages) one of the major form-classes, or parts of speech, comprising words placed before nouns to indicate their relation to other words or their function in the sentence. *By, to, in, from* are prepositions in English. **2.** any such word, as *by, to, in, from.* **3.** any word or construction of similar function or meaning, as *on top of* (=*on*). [ME, t. L: m. s. *praepositio*] —**prep′osi′tional,** *adj.* —**prep′osi′tionally,** *adv.*

prepositive (prĭ pŏz′ĭ tĭv), *adj.* **1.** put before; prefixed. —*n.* **2.** *Gram.* a word placed before another as a modifier or to show its relation to other parts of the sentence. *Red* in *red book* is a prepositive adjective. *John's* in *John's book* is a prepositive genitive.

prepositor (prē pŏz′ĭ tə), *n.* praeposter. Also, **prepostor** (prē pŏs′tə). —**prepositorial** (prē pŏz′ĭ tô′rĭ əl), *adj.*

prepossess (prē′pə zĕs′), *v.t.* **1.** to possess or dominate mentally beforehand, as a prejudice does. **2.** to prejudice or bias, esp. favourably. **3.** to impress favourably beforehand or at the outset.

prepossessing (prē′pə zĕs′ĭng), *adj.* that prepossesses, esp. favourably. —**pre′possess′ingly,** *adv.*

prepossession (prē′pə zĕsh′ən), *n.* **1.** the state of being prepossessed. **2.** a prejudice, esp. in favour of a person or thing.

preposterous (prĭ pŏs′tə rəs, -trəs), *adj.* directly contrary to nature, reason, or common sense; absurd, senseless, or utterly foolish. [t. L: m. *praeposterus* with the hinder part foremost] —**prepos′terously,** *adv.* —**prepos′terousness,** *n.* —**Syn.** See **absurd.**

prepotency (prĭ pō′tn sĭ), *n. Genetics.* the ability of one parent to impress its hereditary characters on its progeny because it possesses more homozygous, dominant, or epistatic genes.

prepotent (prĭ pō′tnt), *adj.* **1.** pre-eminent in power, authority, or influence; predominant. **2.** *Genetics.* denoting, pertaining to, or having prepotency. [t. L: m. s. *praepotens,* ppr., having superior power. See potent] —**prepo′tently,** *adv.*

preprint (prē′prĭnt′), *n.* an advance printing, usually of a portion of a book or of an article in a periodical.

prepublication (prē′pŭb′lĭ kā′shən), *adj.* before publication, as a specially reduced price of a book before the official date of publication.

prepuce (prē′pyōōs), *n. Anat.* the fold of skin which covers the head of the penis or clitoris; foreskin. [ME, t. F, t. L: m. s. *praepūtium*] —**preputial** (prē pyōō′shəl), *adj.*

Pre-Raphaelite (prē′răf′ə līt′), *n.* **1.** one of a group of English artists (the **Pre-Raphaelite Brotherhood,** formed in 1848, and including Holman Hunt, John Everett Millais, and Dante Gabriel Rossetti) who aimed to revive the style and spirit of the Italian artists before the time of Raphael. Their work was delicate in colour and finish and imbued with poetic sentiment. —*adj.* **2.** of, pertaining to, or characteristic of the Pre-Raphaelites. —**Pre′-Raph′aelitism,** *n.*

prerecord (prē′rĭ kôd′), *v.t.* to record beforehand, for playing back at a subsequent date.

prerelease (prē′rĭ lēs′), *n.* the release of something before the scheduled date, as a film, record, etc.

prerequisite (prē′rĕk′wĭ zĭt), *adj.* **1.** required beforehand; requisite as an antecedent condition. —*n.* **2.** something prerequisite: *a knowledge of French was the only prerequisite for admission to the course.*

prerogative (prĭ rŏg′ə tĭv), *n.* **1.** an exclusive right or privilege attaching to an office or position. **2.** a right or privilege attached to a specific person or group of persons. **3.** royal prerogative. **4.** a prior, peculiar, or exclusive right or privilege. **5.** *Obs.* precedence. —*adj.* **6.** having or exercising a prerogative. **7.** pertaining to, characteristic of, or existing by virtue of, a prerogative. [ME, t. L: m. *praerogātīva,* prop. fem. adj., voting first] —**Syn. 1.** See **privilege.**

prerogative court, a former ecclesiastical court in England and Ireland for the trial of certain testamentary cases.

prerogative order, *Law.* a command by a higher court that a lower court shall not exercise jurisdiction in a particular case. Formerly, **writ of prohibition.**

Pres., President.

pres., 1. present. **2.** presidency.

presa (prĕs′ä), *n.*, *pl.* **prese** (prĕs′ā). *Music.* a mark, as :S:, +, or ※, used in a canon, round, etc., to indicate where the successive voice parts are to take up the theme. [It.: a taking, fem. of *preso,* pp. of *prendere* take, g. L *prehendere*]

presage (*n.* prĕs′ĭj; *v.* prĕs′ĭj, prĭ sāj′), *n.*, *v.*, **-saged, -saging.** —*n.* **1.** a presentiment or foreboding. **2.** a prophetic impression. **3.** something that portends or foreshadows a future event; an omen, prognostic, or warning indication. **4.** prophetic significance; augury. **5.** a forecast or prediction. —*v.t.* **6.** to have a presentiment of. **7.** to portend, foreshadow. **8.** to forecast; predict. —*v.i.* **9.** to have a presentiment. **10.** to make a prediction. [ME, t. L: m. s. *praesāgium*] —**presag′er,** *n.*

Presb., Presbyterian.
presbyopia (prĕz′bĭ ō′pyə), *n.* *Pathol.* a defect of vision incident to advancing age, in which near objects are seen with difficulty. [f. *presby-* (t. Gk, comb. form of *présbys* old man) + -OPIA] —**presbyopic** (prĕz′bĭ ŏp′ĭk), *adj.*
presbyter (prĕz′bĭ tə), *n.* **1.** (in the early Christian church) an office-bearer exercising teaching, priestly, and administrative functions. **2.** (in hierarchical churches) a priest. [t. LL, t. Gk: s. *presbýteros*, prop. adj., older] —**presbyteral** (prĕz bĭt′ə rəl), *adj.*
presbyterate (prĕz bĭt′ə rĭt), *n.* **1.** the office of presbyter or elder. **2.** a body of presbyters.
presbyterial (prĕz′bĭ tĭə′rĭ əl), *adj.* **1.** of or pertaining to a presbytery. **2.** presbyterian (def. 1).
presbyterian (prĕz′bĭ tĭə′rĭ ən), *adj.* **1.** pertaining to or based on the principle of ecclesiastical government by an elected body of lay elders. **2.** (*cap.*) designating or pertaining to various churches having this form of government and holding more or less modified forms of Calvinism. —*n.* **3.** (*cap.*) a member or adherent of a Presbyterian church. [f. s. L *presbyterium* presbytery + -AN]
Presbyterianism (prĕz′bĭ tĭə′rĭ ə nĭz′əm), *n.* **1.** church government by presbyters or elders, equal in rank and organized into graded administrative courts. **2.** the doctrines of Presbyterian churches.
presbytery (prĕz′bĭ tə rĭ, -trĭ), *n.*, *pl.* **-teries.** **1.** a body of presbyters or elders. **2.** (in Presbyterian churches) a judicatory consisting of all the ministers (teaching elders) and representative lay or ruling elders from the congregations within a district. **3.** the churches under the jurisdiction of a presbytery. **4.** the part of a church, east of the choir, in which the high altar is situated. **5.** (now only in Roman Catholic use) a clergyman's or priest's house. [ME, t. LL: m. s. *presbyterium*, t. Gk: m. *presbytérion*]
preschool (prē′sko͞ol′), *adj.* denoting, pertaining to, or taught prior to compulsory school age of 5 years.
prescience (prĕs′ĭ əns), *n.* knowledge of things before they exist or happen; foreknowledge; foresight. [ME, t. LL: m. *praescientia*, der. L *praesciens*, ppr., knowing before] —**pre′scient,** *adj.* —**pre′sciently,** *adv.*
prescientific (prē′sī′ən tĭf′ĭk), *adj.* before the widespread development of a scientific culture.
prescind (prĭ sĭnd′), *v.t.* **1.** to separate in thought; abstract. **2.** to remove. —*v.i.* **3.** to withdraw the attention (*from*). **4.** to turn aside in thought. [t. L: m. s. *praescindere* cut off in front]
prescribe (prĭ skrīb′), *v.*, **-scribed, -scribing.** —*v.t.* **1.** to lay down, in writing or otherwise, as a rule or a course to be followed; appoint, ordain, or enjoin. **2.** *Med.* to designate or order for use, as a remedy or treatment. —*v.i.* **3.** to lay down rules, direct, or dictate. **4.** *Med.* to designate remedies or treatment to be used. **5.** *Law.* to claim a right or title by virtue of long use and enjoyment (esp. with *for* or *to*). [t. L: m. s. *praescrībere* write before, direct] —**prescrib′er,** *n.*
prescript (*adj.* prĭ skrĭpt′, prē′skrĭpt; *n.* prē′skrĭpt), *adj.* **1.** prescribed. —*n.* **2.** that which is prescribed; a rule; a regulation. [t. L: m. s. *praescriptum*, n. use of pp., (thing) prescribed]
prescriptible (prĭ skrĭp′tə bəl), *adj.* **1.** subject to effective prescription. **2.** depending on or derived from prescription, as a claim or right.
prescription (prĭ skrĭp′shən), *n.* **1.** *Med.* **a.** a direction (usually written) by the doctor to the pharmacist for the preparation and use of a medicine or remedy. **b.** the medicine prescribed. **2.** the act of prescribing. **3.** that which is prescribed. **4.** *Law.* **a.** a long or immemorial use of some right with respect to a thing so as to give a right to continue such use. **b.** the process of acquiring rights by uninterrupted assertion of the right over a long period of time. [ME, t. L: m. s. *praescriptio*]
prescriptive (prĭ skrĭp′tĭv), *adj.* **1.** that prescribes; giving directions or injunctions. **2.** depending on or arising from effective prescription, as a right or title. —**prescrip′tively,** *adv.*
preselect (prē′sĭ lĕkt′), *v.t.* **1.** to select in advance. —*v.i.* **2.** to use or be used as a preselector.
preselector (prē′sĭ lĕk′tə), *n.* **1.** *Radio.* a preamplifier. **2.** *Mach.* a type of gearbox for motor vehicles in which the gear ratio is selected before it is actually required. —*adj.* **3.** denoting or pertaining to a preselector.
presence (prĕz′əns), *n.* **1.** the state or fact of being present, as with others or in a place. **2.** attendance or company. **3.** immediate vicinity; close proximity: *in the presence of witnesses.* **4.** the immediate personal vicinity of a great personage giving audience or reception. **5.** personal appearance or bearing, esp. of a dignified or imposing kind: *a man of fine presence.* **6.** a person, esp. of dignified or fine appearance. **7.** a divine or spiritual being. **8.** *Obs.* a presence chamber. [ME, t. OF, t. L: m. *praesentia*]
presence chamber, the room in which a great personage, as a sovereign, receives guests, etc.
presence of mind, alert, calm state of mind enabling one to act quickly in emergencies.
present[1] (prĕz′ənt), *adj.* **1.** being, existing, or occurring at this time or now: *the present ruler.* **2.** for the time being: *articles for present use.* **3.** *Gram.* **a.** denoting action or state in process at the moment of speaking. Example: *'knows' is a present form in 'he knows that'.* **b.** designating a tense, or other verb formation or construction, with such meaning. **4.** being with one or others, or in the specified or understood place (opposed to *absent*): *to be present at a wedding.* **5.** being here or there, rather than elsewhere. **6.** existing in a place, thing, combination, or the like: *carbon is present in many minerals.* **7.** being actually here or under consideration. **8.** being before the mind. **9.** *Obs. or Rare.* mentally alert or calm, esp. in emergencies. **10.** *Obs.* immediate or instant. —*n.* **11.** the present time. **12.** *Gram.* the present tense, or other verb formation or construction with present meaning, or a form therein. **13.** (*pl.*) *Law.* the present writings, or this document, used in a deed of conveyance, a lease, etc., to denote the document itself: *know all men by these presents.* **14.** *Obs.* the matter in hand. [ME, t. L: m. s. *praesens*, ppr., lit., being before (one)] —**Syn. 1.** See **current.**
present[2] (*v.* prĭ zĕnt′; *n.* prĕz′ənt), *v.t.* **1.** to furnish or endow with a gift or the like, esp. by formal act: *to present someone with a gold watch.* **2.** to bring, offer, or give, often in a formal or ceremonious way: *to present a message, one's card, etc.* **3.** afford or furnish (an opportunity, possibility, etc.). **4.** to hand or send in, as a bill or a cheque for payment. **5.** to bring (a person, etc.) before, or into the presence of another, esp. a superior. **6.** to introduce (a person) to another. **7.** to bring before or introduce to the public: *to present a new play.* **8.** to come to show (oneself) before a person, in or at a place, etc. **9.** to show or exhibit. **10.** to bring before the mind; offer for consideration. **11.** to set forth in words: *to present arguments.* **12.** to represent, impersonate, or act, as on the stage. **13.** to direct, point, or turn to something or in a particular way. **14.** to level or aim (a weapon, esp. a firearm). **15.** to offer or recommend (a clergyman) to the bishop for institution to a benefice. —*n.* **16.** a thing presented as a gift; a gift: *Christmas presents.* [ME *presente(n)*, t. OF: m. *presenter*, t. L: m. *praesentāre*] —**present′er,** *n.*
—**Syn. 1.** See **give. 5.** See **introduce. 16.** PRESENT, GIFT, DONATION, BONUS refer to something freely given. PRESENT and GIFT are both used of something given as an expression of affection, friendship, interest, or respect. PRESENT is the less formal; GIFT is generally used of something conferred (esp. with ceremony) on an individual, a group, or an institution: *a birthday present; a gift to a bride.* DONATION applies to an important gift, usually of considerable size, though the term is often used, to avoid the suggestion of charity, in speaking of small gifts to or for the needy: *a donation to an endowment fund, to the Red Cross.* BONUS applies to something given in addition to what is due, esp. to employees who have worked for a long time or particularly well: *a bonus at the end of the year.*
presentable (prĭ zĕn′tə bəl), *adj.* **1.** that may be presented. **2.** suitable as in appearance, dress, manners, etc., for being introduced into society or company. **3.** of sufficiently good appearance, or fit to be seen. —**present′abil′ity, present′ableness,** *n.* —**present′ably,** *adv.*
present arms, *Mil.* position in which the rifle is held in both hands vertically in front of the body, with the muzzle up and the trigger side of the gun forward.
presentation (prĕz′ən tā′shən), *n.* **1.** the act of presenting. **2.** the state of being presented. **3.** introduction, as of a person at court. **4.** exhibition or representation, as of a play. **5.** offering, delivering, or bestowal, as of a gift. **6.** a gift. **7.** *Com.* the presentment of a bill, note, or the like. **8.** *Med.* the appearance of a particular part of the foetus at the mouth of the uterus during labour. **9.** *Eccles.* the act or the right of presenting a clergyman to the bishop for institution to a benefice.
presentational (prĕz′ən tā′shə nəl), *adj.* **1.** of or pertaining to presentation. **2.** presentive.
presentationism (prĕz′ən tā′shə nĭz′əm), *n.* the doctrine that perception is an immediate cognition of ideas. —**pres′enta′tionist,** *n.*, *adj.*
presentative (prĭ zĕn′tə tĭv), *adj.* **1.** having the power of presenting a notion to the mind. **2.** *Eccles.* admitting of or pertaining to presentation.
present-day (prĕz′ənt dā′), *adj.* current.
presentee (prĕz′ən tē′), *n.* **1.** one to whom something is presented. **2.** one who is presented.
presentiment (prĭ zĕn′tĭ mənt), *n.* a feeling or impression of something about to happen, esp. something evil; a foreboding. [t. F (obs.), der. L *praesentīre* perceive beforehand] —**presentimental** (prĭ zĕn′tĭ mĕn′tl), *adj.*
presentive (prĭ zĕn′tĭv), *adj.* *Semantics.* (esp. formerly) belonging to a class of words which express clear concepts,

as distinct from *symbolic* words, which express relations between concepts; notional. —**presen′tively,** *adv.* —**presen′tiveness,** *n.*

presently (prĕz′ənt lĭ), *adv.* **1.** in a little while or soon. **2.** *Archaic or Dial.* immediately. —**Syn.** See **immediately.**

presentment (prĭ zĕnt′mənt), *n.* **1.** the act of presenting. **2.** the state of being presented. **3.** presentation. **4.** a representation, pictures, or likeness. **5.** *Com.* the presenting of a bill, note, or the like, as for acceptance or payment. **6.** *Law.* the written statement of an offence by a jury, of their own knowledge or observation, when no indictment has been laid before them. [ME, t. OF: m. *presentement*, der. *presenter* PRESENT[2]]

present participle, a participle with present meaning, e.g. *growing* in 'a growing boy'.

present perfect, 1. (in English) the tense form constructed by using the present tense of *have* with a past participle, and denoting that the action of the verb was completed prior to the present, e.g. *I have finished.* **2.** (in some other languages) a tense form of similar construction. **3.** a verb in this tense.

preservative (prĭ zû′və tĭv), *n.* **1.** something that preserves or tends to preserve. **2.** a chemical substance used to preserve foods, etc., from decomposition or fermentation. **3.** a medicine that preserves health or prevents disease. —*adj.* **4.** tending to preserve.

preserve (prĭ zûv′), *v.*, **-served, -serving,** *n.* —*v.t.* **1.** to keep alive or in existence; make lasting. **2.** to keep safe from harm or injury; save. **3.** to keep up; maintain. **4.** to keep possession of; retain: *to preserve one's composure.* **5.** to prepare (food or any perishable substance) so as to resist decomposition or fermentation. **6.** to prepare (fruit, etc.) by cooking with sugar. **7.** to keep (game, etc.) undisturbed for personal use in hunting or fishing. —*v.i.* **8.** to preserve fruit, etc.; make preserves. **9.** to maintain a preserve for game animals. —*n.* **10.** something that preserves. **11.** that which is preserved. **12.** (*usually pl.*) fruit, etc., prepared by cooking with sugar. **13.** a place set apart for the protection and propagation of game or fish for sport, etc. [ME *preserve(n)*, t. LL: m. *praeservāre*, f. L *prae-* PRE- + *servāre* keep] —**preserv′able,** *adj.* —**preservation** (prĕz′ə vā′shən), *n.* —**preserv′er,** *n.* —**Syn.** **2.** See **defend.**

preset (prē′sĕt′), *v.*, **-set, -setting,** *adj.* —*v.t.* **1.** to set in advance: *to preset an oven to roast a joint four hours later.* —*adj.* **2.** determined in advance to follow a certain course or the like: *a preset ICBM.*

preshrunk (prē′shrŭngk′), *adj.* (of a fabric or garment) having been subjected to a shrinking process so that it will not shrink further when washed.

preside (prĭ zīd′), *v.i.*, **-sided, -siding. 1.** to occupy the place of authority or control, as in an assembly; act as chairman or president. **2.** to exercise superintendence or control. [t. L: m. s. *praesidēre* sit before, guard, preside over] —**presid′er,** *n.*

presidency (prĕz′ĭ dən sĭ), *n.*, *pl.* **-cies. 1.** the office, function, or term of office of a president. **2.** *Mormon Ch.* **a.** a local governing body consisting of a council of three. **b.** the highest administrative body (**First Presidency**), composed of the prophet and his two councillors. **3.** the former designation of any of the three original provinces of British India: Bengal, Bombay, and Madras.

president (prĕz′ĭ dənt), *n.* **1.** (*often cap.*) the highest official in a republic. **2.** an officer appointed or elected to preside over an organized body of persons, as a council, society, etc. **3.** *U.S.* the chief officer of a college or university, or the chairman of a company, etc. **4.** one who presides over a meeting, conference, or the like. [ME, t. L: m. s. *praesidens*, ppr., presiding, ruling]

president-elect (prĕz′ĭ dənt ĭ lĕkt′), *n.* a president after election but before induction into office.

presidential (prĕz′ĭ dĕn′shəl), *adj.* **1.** of or pertaining to a president or presidency. **2.** of the nature of a president. [t. ML: m. s. *praesidentiālis*]

presidential primary, *U.S.* a direct primary for the choice of state delegates to a national party convention and the expression of preference for a presidential nominee.

presidentship (prĕz′ĭ dənt shĭp′), *n.* presidency.

presidio (prĭ sĭd′ĭ ō′; *Sp.* prĕ sē′dyô), *n.*, *pl.* **-sidios** (-sĭd′ĭ ōz′; *Sp.* -sē′dyôs). **1.** a garrisoned fort; a military post. **2.** a penal settlement. [t. Sp., g. L *praesidium* guard, garrison, post] —**presid′ial, presidiary** (prĭ sĭd′ĭ ə rĭ), *adj.*

presidium (prĭ sĭd′ĭ əm), *n.* (in the Soviet Union) an administrative committee, usually permanent and governmental. [t. L: m. *praesidium* a sitting before]

presignify (prē′sĭg′nĭ fī′), *v.t.*, **-fied, -fying.** to signify or indicate beforehand; foretell. [t. L: m. *praesignificāre*]

press[1] (prĕs), *v.t.* **1.** to act upon with weight or force. **2.** to move by weight or force in a certain direction or into a certain position. **3.** to compress or squeeze, as to alter in shape or size. **4.** to weigh heavily upon; to subject to pressure. **5.** to subject to heavy weights, as a method of fatal punishment. **6.** to make flat by subjecting to weight: *she pressed the flowers between the pages of a book.* **7.** to hold closely, as in an embrace; clasp. **8.** to iron (clothes, etc.). **9.** to extract juice, etc., from by pressure. **10.** to squeeze out or express, as juice. **11.** to form hot glass into ware (**pressed ware**) by means of iron mould and plunger, operated by hand or mechanically. **12.** to beset or harass. **13.** to oppress or trouble; to put to straits, as by lack of something: *they were pressed for time.* **14.** to urge or impel, as to a particular course; constrain or compel. **15.** to urge onwards; hurry; hasten. **16.** to urge (a person, etc.), importune, beseech, or entreat. **17.** to insist on: *to press the payment of a debt, to press one's theories.* **18.** to plead with insistence: *to press a claim.* **19.** to push forward. **20.** *Archaic.* to crowd upon or throng. —*v.i.* **21.** to exert weight, force, or pressure. **22.** to iron clothes, etc. **23.** to bear heavily, as upon the mind. **24.** to compel haste: *time presses.* **25.** to demand immediate attention. **26.** to use urgent entreaty: *to press for an answer.* **27.** to push forward with force, eagerness, or haste. **28.** to crowd or throng. [ME *pressen*, v., der. *presse*, n.; but cf. OF *presser*, g. L *pressāre*, freq. of *premere* press]

—*n.* **29.** printed publications collectively, esp. newspapers and periodicals. **30.** the body or class of persons engaged in writing for or editing newspapers or periodicals. **31.** the critical comment of newspapers, etc., on some matter of current public interest. **32.** *Print.* **a.** machine used for printing, as a **flat-bed cylinder press,** one in which a flat bed holding the printing form moves against a revolving cylinder which carries the paper. **b. rotary press,** one in which the types or plates to be printed are fastened upon a rotating cylinder and are impressed on a continuous roll of paper. **33.** an establishment for printing books, etc. **34.** the process or art of printing. **35.** any of various instruments or machines for exerting pressure. **36.** the act of pressing; pressure. **37.** a pressing or pushing forward. **38.** a pressing together in a crowd, or a crowding or thronging. **39.** a crowd, throng, or multitude. **40.** pressed state. **41.** pressure or urgency, as of affairs or business. **42.** an upright case, or piece of furniture, for holding clothes, books, etc. **43.** a framework secured by screws for holding tennis rackets, and the like, when not in use. **44.** *Obs.* a crease caused by pressing. **45. go to press,** to begin to be printed. [ME *presse*, OE *press*, t. ML: s. *pressa*]

press[2] (prĕs), *v.t.* **1.** to force into service, esp. naval or military service; to impress. **2.** to make use of in a manner different from that intended or desired. —*n.* **3.** impressment into service, esp. naval or military service. [back-formation from *prest*, pp. of obs. *prest*, v., take (men) for military service, v. use of obs. *prest*, n., enlistment, loan, t. OF, der. *prester* furnish, lend, g. L *praestāre* perform, vouch for, excel]

press agency, an organization that collects news for distribution to the newspapers, radio, etc.

press agent, a person employed to attend to the advertising and publicity of a theatre, performer, etc., through advertisements and other notices in the press.

press-box (prĕs′bŏks′), *n.* a shelter or stand for reporters at sports matches, etc.

Pressburg (*Ger.* prĕs′bo͝ork), *n.* German name of **Bratislava.**

press conference, an interview of a famous person, public official, etc., with the press, often to make an important announcement or to answer questions.

press-cutting (prĕs′kŭt′ĭng), *n.* an article or the like cut from a newspaper. Also, **press′-clip′ping.**

pressed steel, sheet steel, pressed hot or cold into various shapes as car bodies, doorframes, etc.

presser (prĕs′ə), *n.* one who or that which presses, or applies pressure.

press-gang (prĕs′găng′), *n.* a body of men under the command of an officer, formerly employed to impress other men for service, esp. in the navy or army. [f. PRESS[2] + GANG[1]]

pressing (prĕs′ĭng), *adj.* **1.** urgent; demanding immediate attention: *a pressing need.* —*n.* **2.** an act or instance of one who or that which presses. **3. a.** a run of gramophone records produced at one time. **b.** a gramophone record. —**press′ingly,** *adv.*

pressing board, a wooden board with a metal edge used to give books a pronounced groove when they dry under pressure after binding.

pressman (prĕs′mən), *n.*, *pl.* **-men. 1.** a man who operates or has charge of a printing press. **2.** a newspaper reporter.

pressmark (prĕs′măk′), *n.* a mark put upon a volume to indicate its place in a library, etc.

press office, an office maintained by government departments, institutions, large companies, etc., which releases information about its activities to the press. **—press officer.**

press of sail, *Naut.* as much sail as the wind, etc., will permit a ship to carry. Also, **press of canvas.**

pressor (prĕs′ə), *adj. Physiol.* increasing pressure, as in the circulatory system.

pressor nerve, *Physiol.* a nerve whose stimulation causes an increase of blood pressure.

press release, an item of news prepared for and distributed to the press.

pressroom (prĕs′ro͞om′, -ro͝om′), *n.* the room in a printing establishment containing the presses.

press-stud (prĕs′stŭd′), *n.* a metal fastener, used esp. on clothing, in which two parts are pressed together.

press-up (prĕs′ŭp′), *n.* an exercise in which one raises one's body from a prone position to the full extent of the arms and then lowers it, the feet remaining on the ground and the body and legs in a straight line.

pressure (prĕsh′ə), *n.* **1.** the exertion of force upon a body by another body in contact with it; compression. **2.** *Physics.* the force per unit area exerted at a given point. **3.** *Elect.* electromotive force. **4.** the act of pressing. **5.** the state of being pressed. **6.** harassment; oppression. **7.** a state of trouble or embarrassment. **8.** a constraining or compelling force or influence. **9.** urgency, as of affairs or business. **10.** *Obs.* that which is impressed. [ME, t. F (obs.), t. L: m. *pressūra*]

pressure contour, *Meteorol.* a line drawn on a chart indicating the altitude at which a specified pressure occurs in the atmosphere.

pressure cooker, a strong, closed vessel in which stews, meats, vegetables, etc., may be cooked above the normal boiling point under pressure.

pressure drag, *Aeron.* that part of the drag due to the resolved component of the pressure normal to the surface of a moving body.

pressure gauge, 1. an apparatus for measuring the pressure of gases or liquids, as of steam in a boiler. **2.** an instrument used to determine the pressure in the bore or chamber of a gun when the charge explodes.

pressure gradient, *Meteorol.* the decrease in atmospheric pressure per unit of horizontal distance in the direction in which pressure decreases most rapidly.

pressure group, a group, in politics, business, etc., which attempts to protect or advance its own interests.

pressure head, *Physics.* the pressure of a fluid at a given point in a system divided by the unit weight of the fluid.

pressure suit, *Aeron.* a garment designed to provide body pressure and air, for use in conditions, as in high-flying aircraft and spacecraft, where the ambient pressure is low. Also, **pressurized suit.**

pressurize (prĕsh′ə rīz′), *v.t., v.i.,* **-rized, -rizing. 1.** to maintain normal air pressure in (the cockpit or cabin of) an aeroplane designed to fly at high altitudes. **2.** to compress (a gas or liquid) to a pressure greater than normal. Also, **pressurise. —pres′suriza′tion,** *n.*

pressurized water reactor, *Physics.* a type of nuclear reactor in which water under high pressure is used as both coolant and moderator. *Abbrev.:* P.W.R.

presswork (prĕs′wûrk′), *n.* **1.** the working or management of a printing press. **2.** the work done by it.

prest[1] (prĕst), *adj. Obs.* ready. [ME, t. OF, g. VL or LL *praestus*]

prest[2] (prĕst), *n. Obs.* an advance of money; a loan.

Presteign (prĕs tēn′), *n.* a town in Wales, the county town of Radnorshire. 1190 (1961). Also, **Presteigne.**

Prester John (prĕs′tə), a supposed Christian monk and potentate of the Middle Ages, said to have had a kingdom in some remote part of Asia or Africa and associated with fabulous narratives of travel. [*Prester* priest, ME, t. OF: m. *prestre*]

prestidigitation (prĕs′tĭ dĭj′ĭ tā′shən), *n.* sleight of hand; legerdemain. [t. F, der. s. L *praestigiātor* juggler, b. with *preste* lively (t. It.: m. *presto*, g. L *praestō*) and with L *digitus* finger] **—pres′tidig′ita′tor,** *n.*

prestige (prĕs tēzh′), *n.* **1.** reputation or influence arising from success, achievement, rank, or other circumstances. **2.** distinction or reputation attaching to a person or thing and dominating the mind of others or of the public. **—*adj.* 3.** characteristic of one who has attained success, wealth, etc. [t. F: illusion, glamour, t. L: m. s. *praestīgium* illusion, der. *praestigiae*, pl., jugglers' tricks] **—prestigious** (prĕs tĭj′əs), *adj.*

prestissimo (prĕs tĭs′ĭ mō′; *It.* prĕs tĕs′sē mō), *adv. Music.* in the most rapid tempo. [t. It., superl. of *presto* PRESTO]

presto (prĕs′tō; *It.* prĕs′tō), *adv., adj., n., pl.* **-tos. —*adv.* 1.** quickly, rapidly, or immediately. **2.** *Music.* in quick tempo. **—*adj.* 3.** quick or rapid. **4.** *Music.* in quick tempo. **—*n.* 5.** *Music.* a movement or piece in quick tempo. [t. It.: quick, quickly, g. LL *praestus*, adj., ready, L *praestō*, adv., at hand]

Preston (prĕs′tən), *n.* a seaport in England, in Lancashire. 113,341 (1961).

Prestonpans (prĕs′tən pănz′), *n.* a town in SE Scotland, E of Edinburgh: battle, 1745. 3188 (est. 1966).

prestress (prē′strĕs′), *v.t.* to induce an initial stress, as in concrete, to cancel out stresses resulting from applied loads. **—pre′stressed′,** *adj.*

prestressed concrete, compressed concrete strengthened with tensioned wires to increase its efficiency.

Prestwich (prĕst′wĭch), *n.* a town in England, in Lancashire. 34,209 (1961).

Prestwick (prĕst′wĭk′), *n.* a burgh in Scotland, in Ayrshire, on the Firth of Clyde: international airport. 12,564 (1961).

presumable (prĭ zyo͞o′mə bl), *adj.* capable of being taken for granted; probable. **—presum′ably,** *adv.*

presume (prĭ zyo͞om′), *v.,* **-sumed, -suming. —*v.t.* 1.** to take for granted, assume, or suppose: *I presume you're tired.* **2.** *Law.* to assume as true in the absence of proof to the contrary. **3.** to undertake, with unwarrantable boldness. **4.** to undertake or venture (to do something) as by taking a liberty: *to presume to speak for another.* **—*v.i.* 5.** to take something for granted; suppose. **6.** to act or proceed with unwarrantable or impertinent boldness. **7.** to rely (*on* or *upon*) in acting unwarrantably or taking liberties. [ME, t. L: m. s. *praesūmere* take beforehand, venture] **—presumedly** (prĭ zyo͞o′mĭd lĭ), *adv.* **—presum′er,** *n.*

presumption (prĭ zŭmp′shən), *n.* **1.** the act of presuming. **2.** assumption of something as true. **3.** belief on reasonable grounds or probable evidence. **4.** that which is presumed; an assumption. **5.** a ground or reason for presuming or believing. **6.** *Law.* an inference required or permitted by law as to the existence of one fact from proof of the existence of other facts. **7.** unwarrantable, unbecoming, or impertinent boldness.

presumptive (prĭ zŭmp′tĭv), *adj.* **1.** affording ground for presumption. **2.** based on presumption: *a presumptive title.* **3.** regarded as such by presumption: *an heir presumptive.* **—presump′tively,** *adv.*

presumptuous (prĭ zŭmp′tyo͞o əs), *adj.* **1.** full of, characterized by, or showing presumption or readiness to presume in conduct or thought. **2.** unwarrantedly or impertinently bold; forward. **3.** *Obs.* presumptive. [ME *presumptuose*, t. LL: m. *praesumptuōsus*, var. of *praesumptiōsus*] **—presump′tuously,** *adv.* **—presump′tuousness,** *n.* **—Syn. 2.** See **bold.**

presuppose (prē′sə pōz′), *v.t.,* **-posed, -posing. 1.** to suppose or assume beforehand; to take for granted in advance. **2.** (of a thing) to require or imply as an antecedent condition: *an effect presupposes a cause.* **—presupposition** (prē′sŭp′ə zĭsh′ən), *n.*

presurmise (prē′sû mīz′), *n.* a surmise previously formed.

pret., preterite.

pretence (prĭ tĕns′), *n.* **1.** pretending or feigning; make-believe: *my sleepiness was all pretence.* **2.** a false show of something: *a pretence of friendship.* **3.** a piece of make-believe. **4.** the act of pretending or alleging, now esp. falsely. **5.** an alleged or pretended reason or excuse, or a pretext. **6.** insincere or false profession. **7.** the putting forth of a claim. **8.** the claim itself. **9.** pretension (fol. by *to*): *destitute of any pretence to wit.* **10.** pretentiousness. Also, *U.S.,* **pretense.** [MF, t. AF: m. *pretensse*, t. ML: m. *praetensa*, prop. fem. (r. L *praetenta*) of pp. of *praetendere* pretend]

pretend (prĭ tĕnd′), *v.t.* **1.** to put forward a false appearance of; feign: *to pretend illness.* **2.** to venture or attempt falsely (to do something). **3.** to allege or profess, esp. insincerely or falsely. **—*v.i.* 4.** to make believe. **5.** to lay claim (fol. by *to*). **6.** to make pretensions (fol. by *to*). **7.** to aspire, as a suitor or candidate (fol. by *to*). [ME *pretende(n)*, t. L: m. *praetendere* stretch forth, put forward, pretend]

—Syn. 1. PRETEND, AFFECT, ASSUME, FEIGN imply an attempt to create a false appearance. To PRETEND is to create an imaginary characteristic or to play a part: *to pretend to be ill.* To AFFECT is to make a consciously artificial show of having qualities which one thinks would look well and impress others: *to affect shyness.* To ASSUME is to take on or put on a specific outward appearance, often (but not always) with intent to deceive: *to assume an air of indifference.* To FEIGN implies using ingenuity in pretence, and some degree of imitation of appearance or characteristics: *to feign surprise.*

pretended (prĭ tĕn′dĭd), *adj.* **1.** insincerely or falsely professed. **2.** feigned, fictitious, or counterfeit. **3.** alleged or asserted; reputed. **—pretend′edly,** *adv.*

pretender (prĭ tĕn′də), *n.* **1.** one who pretends; one who makes false professions. 2. an aspirant or candidate. 3. a claimant to a throne.

pretense (prĭ təns′), *n. U.S.* pretence.

pretension (prĭ tĕn′shən), *n.* 1. a laying claim to something. 2. a claim or title to something. 3. (*often pl.*) a claim made, esp. indirectly or by implication, or right to some quality, merit, or the like: *pretensions to superior judgement.* 4. claim to dignity, importance, or merit. 5. pretentiousness. 6. the act of pretending or alleging. 7. an allegation. 8. a pretext.

pre-tensioned (prē′tĕn′shənd), *adj.* (in prestressed concrete) having the reinforcement stretched before the concrete is cast. Cf. **post-tensioned.**

pretentious (prĭ tĕn′shəs), *adj.* 1. full of pretension. 2. characterized by assumption of dignity or importance. 3. making an exaggerated outward show; ostentatious. [f. m. L *praetenti(o)* pretension + -OUS] —**preten′tiously,** *adv.* —**preten′tiousness,** *n.*

preter-, a prefix meaning 'beyond', 'more than'. [t. L: m. *praeter-*, repr. *praeter*, adv., prep.]

preterhuman (prē′tə hyōō′mən), *adj.* beyond what is human.

preterist (prĕt′ə rĭst), *n. Theol.* one who believes that biblical prophecies (esp. those in the Apocalypse) have already been fulfilled.

preterite (prĕt′ə rĭt, prĕt′rĭt), *n.* 1. *Gram.* (esp. in Germanic grammar) **a.** past. **b.** a preterite tense. **c.** a verb form in this tense. —*adj.* 2. *Gram.* denoting past action or state. 3. bygone; past. Also, **preterit.** [ME, t. L: m. s. *praeteritus*, pp., gone by]

preterition (prĕt′ə rĭsh′ən), *n.* 1. the act of passing by or over; omission; neglect. 2. *Law.* the passing over by a testator of an heir otherwise entitled to a portion. 3. *Calvinistic Theol.* the passing over by God of those not elected to salvation or eternal life. [t. LL: m. s. *praeteritio* a passing over. See PRETERITE]

preteritive (prĭ tĕ′rĭ tĭv), *adj.* 1. preterite. 2. (of verbs) limited to past tenses.

pretermit (prē′tə mĭt′), *v.t.*, **-mitted, -mitting.** 1. to let pass without notice; disregard. 2. to leave undone; neglect; omit. 3. to leave off for a short time. [t. L: m. s. *praetermittere* let pass] —**pretermission** (prē′tə mĭsh′ən), *n.*

preternatural (prē′tə năch′rəl), *adj.* 1. out of the ordinary course of nature; abnormal. 2. supernatural. —**pre′ternat′uralism,** *n.* —**pre′ternat′urally,** *adv.* —**Syn.** 1. See **miraculous.**

pretext (prē′tĕkst), *n.* 1. that which is put forward to conceal a true purpose or object; an ostensible reason. 2. an excuse; a pretence. [t. L: m. s. *praetextus*]

pretor (prē′tə), *n. Rom. Hist.* praetor. —**pretorian** (prē tô′rĭ ən), *adj.*, *n.*

Pretoria (prĭ tô′rĭ ə), *n.* a city in the NE Republic of South Africa: the capital of Transvaal and seat of the executive government of the Republic of South Africa. 422,590 (1960). See map under **South Africa.**

Pretorius (prĭ tô′rĭ əs; *Afrik.* prė tȯ′rĭ ʏs), *n.* **Andries Wilhelmus Jacobus** (*Afrik.* ŏn′drēs wĭl′hĕl mʏs yȧ kȯ′bʏs), 1799–1853, and his son, **Marthinus Wessels** (*Afrik.* mȧr tē′nʏs wĕs′əls), 1819–1901, Boer soldiers and statesmen in South Africa.

prettify (prĭt′ĭ fī′), *v.t.*, **-fied, -fying.** to make pretty (often in a disparaging sense). [f. PRETT(Y) + -(I)FY]

pretty (prĭt′ĭ), *adj.*, **-tier, -tiest,** *n.*, *pl.* **-ties,** *adv.* —*adj.* 1. fair or attractive to the eye in a feminine or childish way: *a pretty face.* 2. (of things, places, etc.) pleasing to the eye, esp. without grandeur. 3. pleasing to the ear: *a pretty tune.* 4. pleasing to the mind or aesthetic taste: *some pretty little story.* 5. fine, pleasant, or excellent (much used ironically): *a pretty mess.* 6. *Colloq. or Dial.* considerable; fairly great. 7. *Archaic or Scot.* brave; hardy. 8. *Archaic.* smart; elegant. 9. **pretty penny,** a considerable sum of money. —*n.* 10. (*usually pl.*) a pretty thing, as a trinket or ornament. 11. a pretty one (used esp. in address). —*adv.* 12. moderately: *her work was pretty good.* 13. quite; very: *the wind blew pretty hard.* 14. *Chiefly Dial.* prettily. 15. **sitting pretty,** in a satisfactory and unchallenged position. —*v.t.* 16. to make pretty: *she prettied herself up for her boyfriend.* [ME *prety, praty*, OE *prættig* cunning, wily, der. OE *prætt*, n., wile, trick; akin to D *part* trick, prank, Icel. *prettr* trick, *prettugr* tricky] —**pret′tily,** *adv.* —**pret′tiness,** *n.* —**pret′tyish,** *adj.* —**Syn.** 1. See **beautiful.**

pretypify (prē′tĭp′ĭ fī′), *v.t.*, **-fied, -fying.** to typify beforehand; prefigure.

pretzel (prĕt′səl), *n.* a crisp, dry biscuit, usually in the form of a knot or stick, salted on the outside. [t. G, var. of *Bretzel.* Cf. ML *bracellus* bracelet]

Preussen (*Ger.* proɪ′sən), *n.* German name of **Prussia.**

prevail (prĭ vāl′), *v.i.* 1. to be widespread or current; to exist everywhere or generally: *dead silence prevailed.* 2. to appear or occur as the more important or frequent feature or element; predominate: *green tints prevail in the picture.* 3. to be or prove superior in strength, power, or influence. 4. to operate effectually; to be efficacious. 5. to use persuasion or inducement successfully (fol. by *on, upon,* or *with*). [ME *prevaylle(n)*, t. L: m. *praevalēre* be more able]

prevailing (prĭ vā′lĭng), *adj.* 1. predominant. 2. generally current. 3. having superior power or influence. 4. effectual. —**prevail′ingly,** *adv.* —**prevail′ingness,** *n.* —**Syn.** 2. See **current.**

prevalent (prĕv′ə lənt), *adj.* 1. widespread; of wide extent or occurrence; in general use or acceptance. 2. *Rare.* having the superiority or ascendancy. 3. *Now Rare.* effectual or efficacious. [t. L: m. s. *praevalens*, ppr., prevailing] —**prev′alence,** *n.* —**prev′alently,** *adv.* —**Syn.** 1. See **current.**

prevaricate (prĭ vă′rĭ kāt′), *v.i.*, **-cated, -cating.** to act or speak evasively; equivocate; quibble. [t. L: m. s. *praevāricātus*, pp., walked crookedly, deviated] —**prevar′ica′tion,** *n.* —**prevar′ica′tor,** *n.*

prevenient (prĭ vē′nyənt), *adj.* 1. coming before; antecedent. 2. anticipatory. [t. L: m. s. *praeveniens*, ppr.] —**prevenance** (prĕv′ĭ nəns), **prevenience** (prĭ vē′nyəns), *n.*

prevent (prĭ vĕnt′), *v.t.* 1. to keep from occurring; hinder. 2. to hinder (a person, etc.), as from doing something: *there is nothing to prevent us from going.* 3. *Rare.* to cut off beforehand or debar (a person, etc.), as from something. 4. *Obs.* to precede. 5. *Obs.* to anticipate. —*v.i.* 6. to interpose a hindrance: *he will come if nothing prevents.* [ME, t. L: m. s. *praeventus*, pp., lit., come before] —**prevent′able, prevent′ible,** *adj.*

—**Syn.** 1. PREVENT, HAMPER, HINDER, IMPEDE refer to complete or partial stoppage of action or progress. To PREVENT is to stop something effectually by forestalling action and rendering it impossible: *to prevent the sending of a message.* To HAMPER is to clog or entangle or put an embarrassing restraint upon: *to hamper preparations for a trip.* To HINDER is to keep back by delaying or stopping progress or action: *to hinder the progress of an expedition.* To IMPEDE is to make difficult the movement or progress of anything by interfering with its proper functioning: *to impede a discussion by demanding repeated explanations.* —**Ant.** 1. help, assist.

preventer (prĭ vĕn′tə), *n.* 1. one who or that which prevents. 2. *Naut.* a supplementary rope or stay, supporting a mast.

prevention (prĭ vĕn′shən), *n.* 1. the act of preventing; effectual hindrance. 2. a preventive.

preventive (prĭ vĕn′tĭv), *adj.* 1. *Med.* warding off disease. 2. serving to prevent or hinder. 3. of or pertaining to the customs and excise service: *a preventive officer.* —*n.* 4. *Med.* a drug, etc., for preventing disease. 5. a preventive agent or measure. 6. a contraceptive. Also, **preventative** (prĭ vĕn′tə tĭv). —**preven′tively,** *adv.* —**preven′tiveness,** *n.*

preventive detention, a prison sentence for certain persistent offenders over the age of 30, lasting between 5 and 14 years.

Prévert (*Fr.* prė vĕr′), *n.* **Jacques** (*Fr.* zhȧk), born 1900, French poet.

preview (prē′vyōō′), *n.* 1. a previous view; a view in advance, as of a film. —*v.t.* 2. to view beforehand or in advance.

previous (prē′vyəs), *adj.* 1. coming or occurring before something else; prior. 2. *Colloq.* done, occurring, etc., before the proper time; premature. [t. L: m. *praevius*] —**pre′viously,** *adv.* —**pre′viousness,** *n.*

previous question, *Parl. Proc.* the question whether a vote shall be taken on a main question, moved before the main question is put, resorted to in order to cut off debate.

previse (prĭ vīz′), *v.t.*, **-vised, -vising.** 1. to foresee. 2. to forewarn. [t. L: m. s. *praevīsus*, pp., foreseen]

prevision (prĭ vĭzh′ən), *n.* 1. foresight, foreknowledge, or prescience. 2. an anticipatory vision or perception. [f. PRE- + VISION] —**previ′sional,** *adj.*

Prévost (*Fr.* prė vȯ′), *n.* **Marcel** (*Fr.* mȧr sĕl′), 1862–1941, French novelist and dramatist.

Prévost d'Exiles (*Fr.* prė vȯ dĕg zēl′), **Antoine François** (*Fr.* äɴ twȧn fräɴ swȧ′) ('*Abbé Prevost*'), 1697–1763, French novelist.

prewar (prē′wô′), *adj.* before a war, esp. World War II.

prey (prā), *n.* 1. an animal hunted or seized for food, esp. by a carnivorous animal. 2. a person or thing that falls a victim to an enemy, a disease, or any adverse agency. 3. the action or habit of preying: *beast of prey.* 4. *Rare.* booty or plunder. —*v.i.* 5. to seek for and seize prey, as an animal does. 6. to take booty or plunder. 7. to make profit by activities on a victim. 8. to exert a harmful or destructive influence: *these worries preyed upon his mind.* [ME *preye*, t. OF, g. L *praeda* booty, prey] —**prey′er,** *n.*

Priam (prī′əm), *n. Gk Legend.* son of Laomedon, husband of Hecuba, and father of Hector and Paris. He was the last king of Troy, at the capture of which he was slain.

priapism (prī′ə pĭz′əm), *n. Pathol.* persistent painful erection of the penis.

Priapus (prī ā′pəs), *n. Gk and Rom. Relig.* the personification as a god of the male procreative power. He is the deity of gardens and vineyards, but is a comparatively late addition to the pantheon. [t. L, t. Gk: m. *Priāpos*] —**Priapean** (prī′ə pē′ən), *adj.*

Pribilof Islands (prĭb′ĭ ləf; *Russ.* prĭ bĭ lôf′), a group of islands in the Bering Sea, SW of Alaska, and belonging to the U.S.: the breeding ground of fur seals.

price (prīs), *n., v.,* **priced, pricing.** —*n.* **1.** the sum or amount of money or its equivalent for which anything is bought, sold, or offered for sale. **2.** a sum offered for the capture of a person alive or dead: *a price on a man's head.* **3.** the sum of money, or other consideration, for which a person's support, consent, etc., may be obtained: *he has his price.* **4.** that which must be given, done, or undergone in order to obtain a thing: *to gain a victory at a heavy price.* **5.** *Archaic.* value; worth. **6.** betting odds. **7. at a price,** at a somewhat high price. **8. at any price,** at any cost, no matter how great. **9. beyond** or **without price,** unobtainable; priceless. **10. what price,** *Colloq.* **a.** what is the chance of. **b.** what do you think. —*v.t.* **11.** to fix the price of. **12.** *Colloq.* to ask the price of. [ME, t. OF: m. *pris,* g. L *pretium* price, value, worth]

—**Syn. 1, 4.** PRICE, CHARGE, COST, EXPENSE refer to outlay or expenditure required in buying or maintaining something. PRICE is used mainly of single, concrete objects offered for sale; CHARGE, of services: *what is the price of that coat? a small charge for posting parcels.* COST is mainly a purely objective term, often used in financial calculations: *the cost of building a new annex was estimated at £40,000.* EXPENSE suggests cost plus incidental expenditure: *the expense of the journey was more than the contemplated cost.* Only CHARGE is not used figuratively. PRICE, COST, and sometimes EXPENSE may be used to refer to the expenditure of mental energy, what one 'pays' in anxiety, suffering, etc.

price-cutting (prīs′kŭt′ĭng), *n.* the act of selling an article at a price under the usual or advertised price.

price discrimination, the selling of identical goods to different buyers at different prices.

price index, an indicator used to show the general level of prices.

priceless (prīs′lĭs), *adj.* **1.** having a value beyond all price; invaluable: *she was a priceless help to him.* **2.** *Colloq.* delightfully amusing; absurd.

price-list (prīs′lĭst′), *n.* a list of articles for sale, with prices.

price ring, an agreement whereby suppliers of goods or services agree to charge uniform prices.

price-tag (prīs′tăg′), *n.* a label attached to an item offered for sale, showing its price.

pricey (prī′sĭ), *adj. Colloq.* expensive.

prick (prĭk), *n.* **1.** a puncture made by a needle, thorn, or the like. **2.** the act of pricking: *the prick of a needle.* **3.** the state or sensation of being pricked. **4.** *Obs.* a small or minute mark; a dot or a point. **5.** *Archaic.* a goad for oxen. **6.** *Obs.* any pointed instrument or weapon. **7.** *Taboo Slang.* **a.** the penis. **b.** an unpleasant or despicable person. **8. kick against the pricks,** to hurt oneself by vain resistance. [ME *prike,* OE *prica* dot, c. LG *prik* point]
—*v.t.* **9.** to pierce with a sharp point; puncture. **10.** to affect with sharp pain, as from piercing. **11.** to cause sharp mental pain to; sting, as with remorse or sorrow: *his conscience pricked him suddenly.* **12.** to urge on with, or as with, a goad or spur: *my duty pricks me on.* **13.** to mark (a surface) with pricks or dots in tracing something. **14.** to mark or trace (something) on a surface by pricks or dots. **15.** to cause to stand erect or point upwards: *to prick up one's ears.* **16.** *Farriery.* **a.** to lame (a horse) by driving a nail improperly into its hoof. **b.** to nick: *to prick a horse's tail.* **17.** to measure (distance, etc.) on a chart with dividers (fol. by *off*). **18.** to transplant (seedlings, etc.) from their original beds to larger boxes (fol. by *out*). —*v.i.* **19.** to perform the action of piercing or puncturing something. **20.** to have a sensation of being pricked. **21.** to rise erect or point upwards, as the ears of an animal (fol. by *up*). **22.** *Archaic.* to spur or urge a horse on; ride rapidly. **23. prick up one's ears,** to listen, esp. at something unexpected or of particular interest. [ME *priken,* OE *prician,* der. *prica* puncture] —**prick′er,** *n.* —**prick′ingly,** *adv.*

pricket (prĭk′ĭt), *n.* **1.** a sharp metal point on which to stick a candle. **2.** a candlestick with one or more such points. **3.** a buck in his second year. [ME, f. PRICK + -ET]

prickle (prĭk′l), *n., v.,* **-led, -ling.** —*n.* **1.** a sharp point. **2.** a small, pointed process growing from the bark of a plant; a thorn. **3.** *Colloq.* a pricking sensation. —*v.t.* **4.** to prick. **5.** to cause a pricking sensation in. —*v.i.* **6.** to rise or stand erect like prickles. **7.** to tingle as if pricked. [ME *prykel,* OE *pricel,* f. *pric(a)* prick + *-el,* n. suffix]

prickly (prĭk′lĭ), *adj.,* **-lier, -liest. 1.** full of or armed with prickles. **2.** full of troublesome points. **3.** prickling; smarting. **4.** sensitive; easily angered. —**prick′liness,** *n.*

prickly ash, a rutaceous shrub or small tree, *Zanthoxylum americanum,* of North America, with aromatic leaves and branches usually armed with strong prickles.

prickly comfrey, a tall, bristly, boraginaceous perennial, *Symphytum asperum,* having blue flowers.

prickly heat, *Pathol.* a cutaneous eruption accompanied by a prickling and itching sensation, due to an inflammation of the sweat glands.

prickly pear, 1. the pear-shaped or ovoid, often prickly and sometimes edible, fruit of any of certain species of cactus (genus *Opuntia*). **2.** the plant itself.

prickly poppy, a tropical American papaveraceous herb, *Argemone mexicana,* having spiny leaves and yellow flowers: now naturalized in other warm parts of the world and believed to have medicinal properties.

prickly thrift, any of several plants of the plumbaginaceous genus *Acantholimon,* small perennials with stiff narrow leaves and spikes of showy flowers, frequently grown in sunny rock-gardens.

prick-song (prĭk′sŏng′), *n. Archaic or Hist.* written music, esp. a descant.

pride (prīd), *n., v.,* **prided, priding.** —*n.* **1.** high or inordinate opinion of one's own dignity, importance, merit, or superiority, whether as cherished in the mind or as displayed in bearing, conduct, etc. **2.** the state or feeling of being proud. **3.** becoming or dignified sense of what is due to oneself or one's position or character; self-respect; self-esteem. **4.** pleasure or satisfaction taken in something done by or belonging to oneself or conceived as reflecting credit upon oneself: *civic pride.* **5.** that of which a person or a body of persons is proud: *he was the pride of the family.* **6.** the best or most admired part of anything. **7.** the most flourishing state or period: *in the pride of manhood.* **8.** a company of lions. **9.** mettle in a horse. **10.** *Archaic.* splendour, magnificence, or pomp. **11.** *Archaic.* ornament or adornment. **12.** *Obs.* sexual desire, esp. in a female animal. —*v.t.* **13.** to indulge or plume (oneself) in a feeling of pride (usually fol. by *on* or *upon*). [ME; OE *prȳde* (c. Icel. *prȳdhi* bravery), der. *prūd* proud] —**pride′ful,** *adj.* —**pride′fully,** *adv.*

—**Syn. 1.** PRIDE, CONCEIT, SELF-ESTEEM, VANITY imply an unduly favourable idea of one's own appearance, advantages, achievements, etc., and often apply to offensive characteristics. PRIDE is a lofty and often arrogant assumption of superiority in some respect: *pride must have a fall.* CONCEIT implies an exaggerated estimate of one's own abilities or attainments, together with pride: *blinded by conceit.* SELF-ESTEEM implies an estimate of oneself more complimentary than that held by others: *a ridiculous self-esteem.* VANITY implies self-admiration and an excessive desire to be admired by others: *his vanity was easily flattered.* —**Ant. 1.** humility.

Pride (prīd), *n.* **Thomas,** died 1658, English soldier and regicide.

pride of place, the highest or most important position.

Pride's Purge, the exclusion from the House of Commons in December 1648, of about 100 members who favoured compromise with the Royalist party. It was carried out by a force under Colonel Thomas Pride.

prie-dieu (prē′dyû′; *Fr.* prē dyœ′), *n.* a piece of furniture for kneeling on during prayer, having a rest above, as for a book. [F: pray God]

Prie-dieu
(19th century)

prier (prī′ə), *n.* one who looks or searches curiously or inquisitively into something. Also, **pryer.** [f. PRY + -ER[1]]

priest (prēst), *n.* **1.** one whose office it is to perform religious rites, and esp. to make sacrificial offerings. **2.** (in Christian use) **a.** one ordained to the sacerdotal or pastoral office; a clergyman; a minister. **b.** (in hierarchal churches) a clergyman of the order next below that of bishop, authorized to carry out the Christian ministry. **3.** a minister of any religion. **4.** a club or mallet used for killing fish. [ME *preest,* OE *prēost,* ult. (through VL) t. L: m. *presbyter.* See PRESBYTER]

priestcraft (prēst′kräft′), *n.* priestly arts.

priestess (prēs′tĭs), *n.* a woman who officiates in sacred rites.

priest-hole (prēst′hōl′), *n. Hist.* a hiding-place for a priest in a house, as when Roman Catholic priests were proscribed in England.

priesthood (prēst′ho͝od′), *n.* **1.** the condition or office of a priest. **2.** priests collectively. [ME; OE *prēosthād.* See PRIEST, -HOOD]

Priestley (prēst′lĭ), *n.* **1. J(ohn) B(oynton)** (boin′tən), born 1894, English novelist. **2. Joseph,** 1733–1804, English chemist, author, and clergyman.

priestly (prēst′lĭ), *adj.*, **-lier, -liest. 1.** of or pertaining to a priest; sacerdotal. **2.** characteristic of or befitting a priest. —**priest′liness,** *n.*

priest-ridden (prēst′rĭd′n), *adj.* managed or governed by priests; dominated by priestly influence.

prig[1] (prĭg), *n.* one who is precise to an extreme in attention to principle or duty, esp. in a self-righteous way. [formerly, coxcomb; ? akin to PRINK]

prig[2] (prĭg), *v.*, **prigged, prigging,** *n.* —*v.t.* **1.** *Slang.* to steal. **2.** *Scot. and N Dial.* to haggle. —*v.i.* **3.** *Scot. and N Dial.* to make entreaty. —*n.* **4.** *Slang.* a thief. [orig. cant]

priggery (prĭg′ə rĭ), *n.*, *pl.* **-geries.** the conduct or character of a prig.

priggish (prĭg′ĭsh), *adj.* excessively precise, esp. in an affectedly superior or high-minded way. —**prig′gishly,** *adv.* —**prig′gishness,** *n.*

priggism (prĭg′ĭz′əm), *n.* priggish character or ideas.

prim (prĭm), *adj.*, **primmer, primmest,** *v.*, **primmed, primming.** —*adj.* **1.** affectedly precise or proper, as persons, behaviour, etc.; stiffly neat. —*v.i.* **2.** to draw up the mouth in an affectedly nice or precise way. —*v.t.* **3.** to make prim, as in appearance. **4.** to purse (the mouth, etc.) into a prim expression. [orig. obscure] —**prim′ly,** *adv.* —**prim′ness,** *n.*

prim., 1. primary. **2.** primate. **3.** primitive.

primacy (prī′mə sĭ), *n.*, *pl.* **-cies. 1.** the state of being first in order, rank, importance, etc. **2.** *Eccles.* the office, rank, or dignity of a primate. **3.** *Rom. Cath. Ch.* the jurisdiction of the pope as supreme bishop. [ME, t. ML: m. s. *primātia,* der. L *prīmas* PRIMATE]

prima donna (prē′mə dŏn′ə; *It.* prē mȧ dôn′nȧ), *pl.* **prima donnas, prime donne** (*It.* prē mė dôn′nė). **1.** a first or principal female singer of an operatic company. **2.** *Colloq.* a temperamental, petulant person. [t. It.: first lady]

prima facie (prī′mə fā′shĭ), *Latin.* at first appearance; at first view, before investigation.

prima-facie evidence, *Law.* evidence sufficient to establish a fact, or to raise a presumption of fact, unless rebutted.

primage (prī′mĭj), *n.* a small allowance formerly paid by a shipper to the master and crew of a vessel for the loading and care of the goods: now charged with the freight and retained by the shipowner. [f. PRIME, v., load + -AGE]

primal (prī′məl), *adj.* **1.** first; original; primeval. **2.** of first importance; fundamental. [t. ML: s. *prīmālis,* der. L *prīmus* first]

primarily (prī′mə rĭ lĭ, prīm′rĭ lĭ), *adv.* **1.** in the first place; chiefly; principally. **2.** in the first instance; at first; originally.

primary (prī′mə rĭ), *adj.*, *n.*, *pl.* **-ries.** —*adj.* **1.** first or highest in rank or importance; chief; principal. **2.** first in order in any series, sequence, etc. **3.** first in time; earliest; primitive. **4.** constituting, or belonging to, the first stage in any process. **5.** of the nature of the ultimate or simpler constituents of which something complex is made up. **6.** original, not derived or subordinate; fundamental; basic. **7.** immediate or direct, or not involving intermediate agency. **8.** *Ornith.* pertaining to any of the set of flight feathers situated on the distal segment of a bird's wing. **9.** *Elect.* denoting or pertaining to the inducing circuit, coil, or current in an induction coil or the like. **10.** *Chem.* **a.** involving, or obtained by replacement of one atom or radical. **b.** denoting or containing a carbon atom united to no other or to only one other carbon atom in a molecule. **11.** *Gram.* **a.** (of derivation) with a root or other unanalysable element as underlying form. **b.** (of Latin, Greek, Sanskrit tenses) having reference to present or future time. **12.** *Educ.* denoting or pertaining to the education given in primary schools. —*n.* **13.** that which is first in order, rank, or importance. **14.** *U.S. Politics.* **a.** a meeting of the voters of a political party in an election district for nominating candidates for office, choosing delegates for a convention, etc. **b.** a preliminary election in which voters of each party nominate candidates for office, party officers, etc. **15.** one of any set of primary colours. See **primary colours. 16.** *Ornith.* a primary feather. **17.** *Elect.* a primary circuit or coil. **18.** *Astron.* a body in relation to a smaller body or smaller bodies revolving round it, as a planet in relation to its satellites. **19.** *Chem.* a substance obtained directly from natural or crude raw materials by extraction and purification. [late ME, t. L: m. s. *prīmārius* of the first rank. See PRIME, -ARY] —**Syn. 4.** See **elementary.**

primary accent, *Phonet.* the principal or strongest stress of a word. Also, **primary stress.**

primary cell, *Elect.* a cell designed to produce electric current through an electrochemical reaction which is not efficiently reversible and hence the cell, when discharged, cannot efficiently be recharged by an electric current.

primary colours, red, green, and blue lights, which when properly selected and mixed can produce any hue, even white, greys, and purples. These are the **additive primary colours.** In mixing dyes and pigments the colours act subtractively; the **subtractive primary colours** are carelessly named as red, yellow, and blue, but actually the red must be a purple and the blue must be a blue-green. More than 100 different hues have been detected in the spectrum, but only four of them (red, yellow, green, and blue) contain no suggestion of another hue. From the viewpoint of sensation, therefore, these four may be considered primary colours. To these, white and black may be added for the same reason.

primary education, education for children aged 5–11.

primary election, primary (def. 13b).

primary group, *Sociol.* a group of individuals living in close, intimate, and personal relationship.

primary school, a state school for full-time elementary instruction from the age of 5 to about 11. Formerly, **elementary school.**

primate (prī′mĭt *for 1 and 3*; prī′māt *for 2*), *n.* **1.** *Eccles.* an archbishop or bishop ranking first among the bishops of a province, country, etc. **2.** any mammal of the order *Primates,* that includes man, the apes, the monkeys, the lemurs, etc. **3.** *Rare.* a chief or leader. [ME, t. ML: m. s. *prīmas* chief bishop, in LL, chief, head, n. use of L *prīmas,* adj., of first rank] —**pri′mateship′,** *n.* —**primatial** (prī mā′shəl), *adj.*

Primaticcio (*It.* prē mȧ tēt′chô), *n.* **Francesco** (*It.* frȧn chĕs′kô), 1504/5–70, Italian decorative painter and sculptor who worked mainly in France.

prime (prīm), *adj.*, *n.*, *v.*, **primed, priming.** —*adj.* **1.** first in importance, excellence, or value. **2.** first or highest in rank, dignity, or authority; chief; principal; main: *the prime minister.* **3.** first in comparison with others. **4.** of the first grade or best quality: *prime ribs of beef.* **5.** first in order of time, existence, or development; earliest; primitive. **6.** original; fundamental. **7.** *Maths.* **a.** not divisible without remainder by any number except itself and unity: *5 is a prime number.* **b.** having no common divisor except unity: *2 is prime to 9.* [late ME, t. L: m. s. *prīmus* first (superl. of *prior* PRIOR[1])]
—*n.* **8.** the most flourishing stage or state. **9.** the time of early manhood or womanhood: *prime of youth.* **10.** the period or state of greatest perfection or vigour of human life: *in the prime of life.* **11.** the choicest or best part of anything. **12.** the beginning or earliest stage of any period. **13.** the spring of the year. **14.** the first hour or period of the day, after sunrise. **15.** *Eccles.* the second of the seven canonical hours or the service for it, orig. fixed for the first hour of the day. **16.** *Maths.* **a.** a prime number. **b.** one of the equal parts into which a unit is primarily divided. **c.** the mark (′) indicating such a division (also variously used as a distinguishing mark). **17.** *Fencing.* the first of eight defensive positions. **18.** *Music.* (in a scale) the tonic or keynote. [ME; OE *prīm* (def. 15), t. L: s. *prīma* (*hōra*) first (hour). Cf. F *prime*]
—*v.t.* **19.** to prepare or make ready for a particular purpose or operation. **20.** to supply (a firearm) with powder for communicating fire to a charge. **21.** to lay a train of powder to (any charge, a mine, etc.). **22.** to pour water into (a pump) so as to swell the sucker and so act as a seal, making it work effectively. **23.** to cover (a surface) with a preparatory coat or colour, as in painting. **24.** to supply or equip with information, words, etc., for use. **25.** (of a boiler or a steam-engine) to operate so that water is carried over into the cylinder with the steam. [orig. doubtful] —**prime′ness,** *n.*

—**Syn. 5.** PRIME, PRIMEVAL, PRIMITIVE have reference to that which is first. PRIME means first in numerical order or order of development: *prime meridian; prime cause.* PRIMEVAL means belonging to the first or earliest ages: *the primeval forest.* PRIMITIVE suggests the characteristics of the origins or early stages of a development, and hence implies the simplicity of original things: *primitive tribes, conditions, ornaments, customs, tools.*

prime cost, that part of the cost of a commodity deriving from the labour, materials, and expense directly involved in its construction.

primely (prīm′lĭ), *adv. Colloq.* excellently.

prime meridian, a meridian from which longitude east and west is reckoned, usually that of Greenwich, England.

prime minister, (*often cap.*) the first or principal minister of certain governments: the chief of the cabinet or ministry. —**prime ministry.**

prime mover, 1. *Mech.* a. the initial agent which puts a machine in motion, as wind, electricity, etc. b. a machine, as a waterwheel or steam-engine, which receives and modifies energy as supplied by some natural source. 2. means of towing a cannon, as an animal, tractor, etc. 3. *Aristotelian Philos.* that which is the first cause of all movement and does not itself move.

prime number, *Maths.* See **prime** (def. 7).

primer[1] (prī′mə *for 1 and 2*; prĭm′ə *for 3 and 4*), *n.* 1. an elementary book for teaching children to read. 2. any small book of elementary principles: *a primer of phonetics.* 3. great primer. 4. long primer. [ME, t. ML: m. s. *prīmārium*, prop. neut. adj., PRIMARY]

primer[2] (prī′mə), *n.* 1. one who or that which primes. 2. a cap, cylinder, etc., containing a compound which may be exploded by percussion or other means, used for firing a charge of powder. See diag. under **cartridge.** 3. the first complete coat of paint applied to an unpainted surface. 4. any preliminary coating or preparation applied before a final surface finish. [f. PRIME, v. + -ER[1]]

primero (prĭ mēə′rō), *n.* a card game fashionable in England in the 16th and 17th centuries. [t. Sp.: alter. of *primera*, fem. of *primero* first, g. L *prīmārius* PRIMARY]

primeval (prī mē′vəl), *adj.* of or pertaining to the first age or ages, esp. of the world: *primeval forms of life.* Also, **primaeval.** [f. m. s. L *prīmaevus* young + -AL[1]] —**prime′vally,** *adv.* —**Syn.** See **prime.**

primigenial (prī′mĭ jē′nyəl), *adj.* 1. of a primitive type; primordial. 2. *Obs.* first generated or produced. [f. s. L *prīmigenius* original + -AL[1]]

primine (prī′mĭn), *n. Bot.* the outer integument of an ovule. Cf. **secundine.** [f. s. L *prīmus* first + -INE[2]]

priming (prī′mĭng), *n.* 1. the powder or other material used to ignite a charge. 2. the act of one who or that which primes. 3. primer[2] (def. 3). [see PRIME, v.]

primipara (prī mĭp′ə rə), *n.*, *pl.* **-rae** (-rē′). *Obstet.* a woman who has borne only one child or who is parturient for the first time. [t. L: f. *prīmi-* (comb. form of *prīmus* first) + *-para* (fem.) -PAROUS] —**primiparity** (prī′mĭ pă′rĭ tĭ), *n.* —**primip′arous,** *adj.*

primitive (prĭm′ĭ tĭv), *adj.* 1. being the first or earliest of the kind or in existence, esp. in an early age of the world: *primitive forms of life.* 2. early in the history of the world or of mankind. 3. characteristic of early ages or of an early state of human development: *primitive art.* 4. *Anthropol.* of or pertaining to a race, group, etc., having cultural or physical similarities with their early ancestors. 5. unaffected or little affected by civilizing influences. 6. being in its or the earliest period; early. 7. old-fashioned. 8. original or radical (as opposed to *derivative*): *a primitive word.* 9. primary (as opposed to *secondary*). 10. *Biol.* a. rudimentary; primordial. b. denoting species, etc., only slightly evolved from early antecedent types. c. of early formation and temporary, as a part that subsequently disappears. 11. *Theol.* belonging to a minority group detached from one of the protestant sects which seeks to return to the original simplicity of the gospel message: *primitive Baptist, primitive Methodist.* —*n.* 12. something primitive. 13. *Art.* a. an artist, esp. a painter, belonging to an early period in the development of a style, esp. that preceding the Renaissance. b. a provincial or naive painter. c. a work of art by such an artist. 14. *Maths.* a geometrical or algebraic form or expression from which another is derived. 15. the form from which a given word or other linguistic form has been derived, by either morphological or historical processes, as *take* in *undertake.* [t. L: m. s. *prīmitīvus* first of its kind; r. ME *primitif*, t. OF] —**prim′itively,** *adv.* —**prim′itiveness,** *n.* —**Syn.** 1. See **prime.**

primitivism (prĭm′ĭ tĭ vĭz′əm), *n.* a recurrent theory or belief, as in philosophy, art, etc., that the qualities of primitive or chronologically early cultures are superior to those of contemporary civilization. —**prim′itivist,** *n.*

Primo de Rivera (*Sp.* prē′mō dĕ rē bĕ′rä), 1. **José Antonio** (*Sp.* KHō sĕ′ än tō′nyō), 1903–39, Spanish politician: founder of the Falange. 2. his father, **Miguel** (*Sp.* mē gĕl′), 1870–1930, Spanish general: dictator of Spain.

primogenitor (prī′mō jĕn′ĭ tə), *n.* 1. a first parent or earliest ancestor. 2. a forefather or ancestor. [t. ML, f. L: *prīmō* at first + *genitor* male parent]

primogeniture (prī′mō jĕn′ĭ chə), *n.* 1. the state or fact of being the firstborn among the children of the same parents. 2. *Law.* the principle of inheritance or succession by the firstborn, specif. the eldest son. [t. ML: m. *prīmōgenitūra*, der. L *prīmōgenitus* firstborn]

primordial (prī mô′dyəl), *adj.* 1. constituting a beginning; giving origin to something derived or developed; original; elementary. 2. *Biol.* primitive; initial; first. 3. pertaining to or existing at or from the very beginning: *primordial matter.* [ME, t. LL: s. *prīmordiālis*, der. L *prīmordium* beginning] —**primor′dially,** *adv.*

primordium (prī mô′dyəm), *n.*, *pl.* **-dia** (-dyə). *Embryol.* the first recognizable, histologically undifferentiated stage in the development of an organ. [prop. neut. of L *prīmordius* original]

primp (prĭmp), *v.t.* 1. to dress or deck with nicety. —*v.i.* 2. *Dial. or Colloq.* to primp oneself; to prink. [akin to PRIM, v.]

primrose (prĭm′rōz′), *n.* 1. any plant of the genus *Primula* (family *Primulaceae*), comprising perennial herbs with variously coloured flowers, as *P. vulgaris*, a common yellow-flowered European species cultivated in many varieties, or *P. sinensis*, with flowers of various colours. 2. evening primrose. 3. pale yellow. —*adj.* 4. pertaining to the primrose. 5. abounding in primroses. 6. pleasant; being that of pleasure: *the primrose path.* 7. of a pale yellow. [ME *primerose*, t. ML: m. *prīma rosa* first rose]

primula (prĭm′yŏŏ lə), *n.* a primrose (def. 1). [t. ML: kind of flower; short for *prīmula vēris*, lit., first (flower) of spring]

primulaceous (prĭm′yŏŏ lā′shəs), *adj.* belonging to the *Primulaceae*, a family of plants of which the primrose or primula is the type. [f. PRIMUL(A) + -ACEOUS]

primum mobile (prī′mŏŏm mō′bĭ lĭ), *Latin.* 1. *Ptolemaic Astronomy.* the outermost of the ten concentric spheres of the universe, making a complete revolution every twenty-four hours and causing all the others to do likewise. 2. a prime mover. [L: lit., first moving thing]

primus[1] (prī′məs), *n.* the presiding bishop of the Scottish Episcopal Church, without metropolitan authority. [t. L: first]

primus[2] (prī′məs), *n.* 1. a portable cooking stove burning paraffin. 2. (*cap.*) a trademark for this.

prin., principal.

prince (prĭns), *n.* 1. a non-reigning male member of a royal family. 2. a sovereign or monarch; a king. 3. (in Great Britain) a son, or a grandson (if the child of a son), of a king or queen. 4. the English equivalent of certain titles of nobility of varying importance or rank in certain continental European (or other) countries. 5. the holder of such a title. 6. the ruler of a small state, as one actually or nominally subordinate to a suzerain. 7. one who or that which is chief or pre-eminent in any class, group, etc.: *a merchant prince.* [ME, t. OF, t. L: m. s. *princeps* principal person, prop. adj., first, principal] —**prince′liness,** *n.*

Prince Albert, a double-breasted, long frockcoat.

prince consort, 1. a prince who is the husband of a reigning female sovereign. 2. (*caps*) **Albert,** 1819–61, Prince of Saxe-Coburg-Gotha, husband of Queen Victoria.

princedom (prĭns′dəm), *n.* 1. the position, rank, or dignity of a prince. 2. a principality (territory). 3. (*pl.*) the principalities (angels).

Prince Edward Island, an island in the Gulf of St Lawrence, forming a province of Canada: fox farms. 108,000 pop. (est. 1965); 2184 sq. mi. *Cap.*: Charlottetown.

prince imperial, the eldest son of an emperor.

princekin (prĭns′kĭn), *n.* a little or minor prince. Also, **princelet** (prĭns′lĭt), **princeling** (prĭns′lĭng).

princely (prĭns′lĭ), *adj.*, **-lier, -liest.** 1. greatly liberal; lavish. 2. like or befitting a prince; magnificent. 3. of or pertaining to a prince; royal; noble; magnificent. —**prince′liness,** *n.*

Prince of Darkness, the devil; Satan.

Prince of Peace, Christ. Is. 9:6.

Prince of Wales, 1. a title conferred on the eldest son, or heir apparent, of the British sovereign. 2. **Cape,** a cape in W Alaska, on Bering Strait opposite the Soviet Union: the westernmost point of North America.

prince regent, a prince who is regent of a country.

prince royal, the eldest son of a king or queen.

Prince Rupert (rōō′pət), a seaport and railway terminus in W Canada, in British Columbia. 11,987 (1961).

prince's-feather (prĭn′sĭz fĕth′ə), *n.* 1. a tall, showy, garden annual, a variety of *Amaranthus hybridus*, bearing thick crowded spikes of small red flowers. 2. a tall, tropical, polygonaceous annual, *Polygonum orientale*, with long pendulous inflorescences.

princess (prĭn sĕs′), *n.* 1. a non-reigning female member of a royal family. 2. a female sovereign. 3. the consort of a prince. 4. (in Great Britain) a daughter, or a granddaughter (if the child of a son), of a king or queen. [ME *princesse*, t. F, fem. of *prince* PRINCE]

princess line (prĭn sĕs′, prĭn′sĕs), a style of woman's dress which is cut in an unbroken line from shoulder to hem, usually close-fitting down to the hips then flaring out.

princess royal, a title which may be conferred on the eldest daughter of the British sovereign.

Princeton (prĭns′tən), *n.* a borough in central New Jersey: university for men, founded 1746. 11,890 (1960).

principal (prĭn′sĭ pl), *adj.* 1. first or highest in rank, importance, value, etc.; chief; foremost. 2. of the nature of principal, or a capital sum. —*n.* **3.** a chief or head. **4.** a governing or presiding officer, as of a school or college. **5.** one who takes a leading part; a chief actor or doer. **6.** the first player of a division of instruments in an orchestra (excepting the leader of the first violins). **7.** something of principal or chief importance. **8.** *Law.* **a.** a person authorizing another (an agent) to represent him. **b.** a person directly responsible for a crime, either as actual perpetrator or as abetter present at its commission. Cf. **accessory** (def. 3). **9.** a person primarily liable for an obligation, in contrast, e.g., with an endorser. **10.** the main body of an estate, etc., as distinguished from income. **11.** *Com.* a capital sum, as distinguished from interest or profit. **12.** *Music.* **a.** an organ stop otherwise called diapason. **b.** the subject of a fugue (opposed to *answer*). **13.** the central structure of a roof which determines its shape and supports it. **14.** each of the combatants in a duel, as distinguished from the seconds. [ME, t. L: s. *principālis* first, chief] —**prin′cipalship′,** *n.* —**Syn. 1.** prime, paramount, leading, main. See **capital[1].**

principal axis, *Optics.* the straight line passing through both the centre of the surface of a lens or mirror and its centre of curvature.

principal boy, the hero of a pantomime, a part traditionally played by a woman dressed as a boy.

principal clause, main clause.

principal focus, *Optics.* focal point.

principality (prĭn′sĭ păl′ĭ tĭ), *n., pl.* **-ties. 1.** a state ruled by a prince, usually a relatively small state or a state that falls within a larger state such as an empire. **2.** the position or authority of a prince or chief ruler; sovereignty; supreme power. **3.** the rule of a prince of a small or subordinate state. **4. the principality,** (*often cap.*) Wales. **5.** (*pl.*) *Theol.* an order of angels. See **angel** (def. 1). **6.** *Obs.* pre-eminence.

principally (prĭn′sĭp lĭ), *adv.* chiefly; mainly. —**Syn.** See **especially.**

principal parts, *Gram.* a set of inflected forms of a verb from which all the other inflected forms can be inferred (theoretically, the smallest such set) as *sing, sang, sung; smoke, smoked.*

principal points, *Optics.* two points on the principal axis of a thick lens or lens system, such that if the object distance is measured from one and the image distance from the other, the equations relating object-image distance and focal length are similar to those for a simple thin lens.

principate (prĭn′sĭ pĭt), *n.* chief place or authority.

principium (prĭn sĭp′ĭ əm), *n., pl.* **-cipia** (-sĭp′ĭ ə). a principle. [t. L]

principle (prĭn′sĭ pl), *n.* **1.** an accepted or professed rule of action or conduct: *a man of good principles.* **2.** a fundamental, primary, or general truth, on which other truths depend: *the principles of government.* **3.** a fundamental doctrine or tenet; a distinctive ruling opinion: *the principles of the Stoics.* **4.** (*pl.*) right rules of conduct. **5.** guiding sense of the requirements and obligations of right conduct: *a man of principle.* **6.** fixed rule or adopted method as to action. **7.** a rule or law exemplified in natural phenomena, in the construction or operation of a machine, the working of a system, or the like: *the principle of capillary attraction.* **8.** the method of formation, operation, or procedure exhibited in a given case: *a community organized on the principle of one great family.* **9.** a determining characteristic of something; essential quality of character. **10.** an originating or actuating agency or force. **11.** an actuating agency in the mind or character, as an instinct, faculty, or natural tendency. **12.** *Chem.* a constituent of a substance, esp. one giving to it some distinctive quality or effect. **13.** *Obs.* beginning or commencement. **14. in principle,** according to the rule generally followed. **15. on principle, a.** according to fixed rule, method, or practice. **b.** according to the personal rule for right conduct, as a matter of moral principle. [ME, f. F *principe* (t. L: m. *principium*) + *-le,* n. suffix (cf. SYLLABLE, etc.)]

—**Syn. 1, 2.** PRINCIPLE, CANON, RULE imply something established as a standard or test, for measuring, regulating, or guiding conduct or practice. A PRINCIPLE is a general and fundamental truth which may be used in deciding conduct or choice: *to adhere to principle.* CANON, originally referring to an edict of the Church (a meaning which it still retains), is used of any principle, law, or critical standard which is officially approved, particularly in aesthetics and scholarship: *canons of literary criticism.* A RULE, usually something adopted or enacted, is often the specific application of a principle: *the golden rule.*

principled (prĭn′sĭ pld), *adj.* imbued with or having principles: *high-principled.*

prink (prĭngk), *v.t.* **1.** to deck or dress for show. —*v.i.* **2.** to deck oneself out. **3.** to fuss over one's dress, esp. before the looking glass. [appar. akin to PRANK[2], v.] —**prink′er,** *n.*

print (prĭnt), *v.t.* **1.** to produce (a text, a picture, etc.) by applying inked types, plates, blocks, or the like, with direct pressure to paper or other material. **2.** to cause (a manuscript, etc.) to be reproduced in print. **3.** to write in letters like those commonly used in print. **4.** to indent or mark (a surface, etc.) by pressing something into or on it. **5.** to produce or fix (an indentation, mark, etc.) as by pressure. **6.** to impress on the mind, memory, etc. **7.** to apply (a thing) with pressure so as to leave an indentation, mark, etc. **8.** *Photog.* to produce a positive picture from (a negative) by the transmission of light. **9.** *Computers.* to produce (a result, data, etc.) in a legible form on paper (often fol. by *out*).
—*v.i.* **10.** to take impressions from type, etc., as in a press. **11.** to produce books, etc., by means of a press. **12.** to give an impression on paper, etc., as types, plates, etc. **13.** to write in characters such as are used in print. **14.** to follow the craft of a printer. **15.** *Computers.* to produce results in a legible form on paper (often fol. by *out*).
—*n.* **16.** the state of being printed. **17. in print, a.** in printed form; published. **b.** (of a book, etc.) still available for purchase from the publisher. **18. out of print,** (of a book, etc.) no longer available for purchase from the publisher; sold out by the publisher. **19.** printed lettering, esp. with reference to character, style, or size. **20.** printed matter. **21.** a printed publication, as a newspaper. **22.** newsprint. **23.** a picture, design, or the like, printed from an engraved or otherwise prepared block, plate, etc. **24.** an indentation, mark, etc., made by the pressure of one body or thing on another. **25.** something with which an impression is made; a stamp or die. **26.** a design, usually in colour, pressed on woven cotton with engraved rollers. **27.** the cloth so treated. **28.** something that has been subjected to impression, as a pat of butter. **29.** *Photog.* a picture made from a negative. —*adj.* **30.** made of printed material, esp. cotton. [ME *priente,* t. OF: impression, print, pp. of *preindre,* g. L *premere* press] —**print′able,** *adj.*

print., printing.

printanier (prĭn tä′nĭ ā′; *Fr.* prăɴ tȧ nyĕ′), *n.* a mixture of vegetables scooped into small balls, or cut into small dice, cooked and served with butter. [t. F: f. m. *printemps* spring + *-ier* -IER]

printed circuit, *Radio.* a circuit forming part of electronic equipment in which the wiring between components, and some components themselves, are printed, or etched, on to an insulating board.

printer (prĭn′tə), *n.* **1.** one who or that which prints. **2.** a person or a firm engaged in the printing industry. **3.** *Computers.* a machine that prints on paper information sent by means of electrical or mechanical signals.

printer's devil (prĭn′təz), devil (def. 4).

printery (prĭn′tə rĭ), *n., pl.* **-ries.** *Chiefly U.S.* **1.** an establishment for typographic printing. **2.** an establishment for the printing of calico or the like.

printing (prĭn′tĭng), *n.* **1.** the art, process, or business of producing books, newspapers, etc., by impression from movable types, plates, etc.; typography. **2.** the act of one who or that which prints. **3.** words, etc., in printed form. **4.** printed matter. **5.** the whole number of copies of a book, etc., printed at one time. **6.** writing in which the letters are like those commonly used in print.

printing press, a machine for printing on paper or the like from type, plates, etc. Cf. **press** (def. 32).

printless (prĭnt′lĭs), *adj.* making, retaining, or showing no print or impression.

print-out (prĭnt′out′), *n.* *Computers.* results, data, or the like printed automatically by a computer in legible form.

print shop, 1. a shop where prints or engravings are sold. **2.** *Colloq.* an establishment for typographical printing.

prior[1] (prī′ə), *adj.* **1.** preceding in time, or in order; earlier or former; anterior or antecedent: *a prior agreement.* **2. prior to,** preceding: *prior to that time.* —*adv.* **3.** previously (fol. by *to*). [t. L: former, earlier]

prior[2] (prī′ə), *n.* **1.** an officer in a monastic order or religious house, sometimes next in rank below an abbot. **2.** the superior of certain monastic orders and houses. **3.** a chief magistrate, as in the medieval republic of Florence. [ME and OE, t. ML: superior, head] —**pri′orship′,** *n.*

Prior (prī′ə), *n.* **Matthew,** 1664–1721, English poet.

priorate (prī′ə rĭt), *n.* **1.** the office, rank, or term of office of a prior. **2.** a priory.

prioress (prī′ə rĭs), *n.* a woman holding a position corresponding to that of a prior, sometimes ranking next below an abbess.

priority (prī ŏ′rĭ tĭ), *n., pl.* **-ties. 1.** the state of being earlier in time, or of preceding something else. **2.** precedence in order, rank, etc. **3.** the having of certain rights before another.

priory (prī′ə rĭ), *n., pl.* **-ries.** a religious house governed by a prior or prioress, often dependent upon an abbey. [ME *priorie,* t. ML: m. *priōria*]

Pripet (prĭp′ĭt), *n.* a river in W Russia flowing E then SE to the Dnieper through the extensive **Pripet Marshes.** ab. 500 mi. Also, **Pripyat.**

Priscian (prĭsh′ĭ ən), *n.* fl. A.D. *c.* 500, Latin grammarian.

prise (prīz), *v.*, **prised, prising,** *n.* —*v.t.* **1.** to raise, move, or force with or as with a lever. —*n.* **2.** leverage. **3.** *Dial.* a lever. Also, **prize;** *Chiefly U.S.*, **pry.** [ME *prise*, t. F: a taking hold, ult. g. L *pre(he)nsa*, fem. pp., seized]

prism (prĭz′əm), *n.* **1.** *Optics.* a transparent prismatic body (esp. one with triangular bases) used for decomposing light into its spectrum or for reflecting light beams. **2.** *Geom.* a solid whose bases or ends are any congruent and parallel polygons, and whose sides are parallelograms. **3.** *Crystall.* **a.** a form consisting of faces which are parallel to the vertical axis and intersect the horizontal axes. **b.** a dome (**horizontal prism**). [t. LL: m. *prisma*, t. Gk: lit., something sawed]

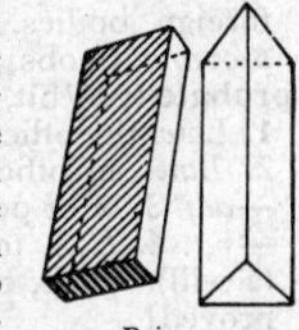
Prisms

prismatic (prĭz măt′ĭk), *adj.* **1.** of, pertaining to, or like a prism. **2.** formed by, or as if by, a transparent prism. **3.** varied in colour; brilliant. Also, **prismat′ical.** —**prismat′ically,** *adv.*

prismatic colours, the components of ordinary white or near-white light as separated by a prism.

prismatic instrument, *Optics.* an instrument, as binoculars, in which a right-angled prism is used to invert the inverted image produced by the objective.

prison (prĭz′ən), *n.* **1.** a public building for the confinement or safe custody of criminals and others committed by law. **2.** a place of confinement or involuntary restraint. **3.** imprisonment. [ME, t. OF, g. s. L *pre(he)nsio* seizure, arrest]

prison-camp (prĭz′ən kămp′), *n.* a camp for prisoners of war, political prisoners, etc.

prisoner (prĭz′ə nə, prĭz′nə), *n.* **1.** one who is confined in prison or kept in custody, esp. as the result of legal process. **2.** one taken by an enemy in war (**prisoner of war**). **3.** one who or something that is deprived of liberty or kept in restraint.

prisoner's base, an old game variously played, esp. by boys.

prissy (prĭs′ĭ), *adj.*, **-sier, -siest.** *Colloq.* precise; prim; affectedly nice. [b. PRIM and SISSY]

pristine (prĭs′tīn), *adj.* **1.** of or pertaining to the earliest period or state; original; primitive. **2.** having its original purity. [t. L: m. s. *pristinus* early]

prithee (prĭth′ĭ), *interj.* *Archaic.* (I) pray thee.

priv., privative.

privacy (prī′və sĭ, prĭv′ə sĭ), *n.*, *pl.* **-cies.** **1.** the state of being private; retirement or seclusion. **2.** secrecy. **3.** *Rare.* a private place. [f. PRIV(ATE) + -ACY]

Privas (*Fr.* prē vȧ′), *n.* a town in France, the capital of Ardèche department. 9207 (1968).

Privatdocent (*Ger.* prē vȧt′ dȯ tsĕnt′), *n.* (in German and certain other universities) a private teacher or lecturer recognized by the university but receiving no compensation from it, being remunerated by fees. Also, **Privatdozen.** [G: private instructor]

private (prī′vĭt), *adj.* **1.** belonging to some particular person or persons; belonging to oneself; being one's own: *private property.* **2.** pertaining to or affecting a particular person or a small group of persons; individual; personal: *for your private satisfaction.* **3.** confined to or intended only for the person or persons immediately concerned; confidential: *a private communication.* **4.** not holding public office or employment, as a person. **5.** not of an official or public character: *to retire to private life.* **6.** (of a company) restricting the right to transfer its shares, limiting the number of its members to 50, and prohibiting public subscription for its shares or debentures. **7.** removed from or out of public view or knowledge; secret. **8.** not open or accessible to people in general: *a private road.* **9.** without the presence of others; alone; secluded. **10. a.** of or pertaining to a person receiving individual medical treatment apart from that given free, as for example under the National Health Service in Britain. **b.** of or pertaining to such treatment or to the place it is given. **11.** (of a member of parliament) not holding a government post. **12.** of lowest military rank. —*n.* **13.** a private soldier. **14.** *U.S. Army.* a soldier of one of the three lowest ranks (**private 1, private 2, private first class**). **15. in private,** in secret; not publicly. [ME, t. L: m. s. *prīvātus*, pp., lit., separated] —**pri′vately,** *adv.* —**pri′vateness,** *n.*

private bar, a small room in a public house, originally mainly used for private parties. Cf. **public bar, saloon bar.**

privateer (prī′və tĭə′), *n.* **1.** a privately owned and manned armed vessel, commissioned by a government in time of war to fight the enemy, esp. his commercial shipping. **2.** the commander, or one of the crew, of such a vessel. —*v.i.* **3.** to cruise as a privateer. [f. PRIVATE + -EER, modelled on VOLUNTEER]

privateersman (prī′və tĭəz′mən), *n.*, *pl.* **-men.** *U.S.* an officer or seaman of a privateer.

private eye, a detective working for an individual person.

private hotel, a hotel or boarding house, usually unlicensed and often residential, where guests are accepted at the proprietor's discretion.

private means, an income which does not depend on a salary or the like. Also, **independent means.**

private parts, the external sex organs. Also, **privy parts.**

private practice, medical practice involving care for the health of private patients, for which charges to the individual are made.

private school, a school which is privately financed and managed, and is outside the state system of education.

private secretary, a person who handles the individual or confidential correspondence, etc., of a person or business organization.

privation (prī vā′shən), *n.* **1.** lack of the usual comforts or necessaries of life, or an instance of this: *to lead a life of privation.* **2.** a depriving. **3.** the state of being deprived. [ME *privacion*, t. L: m. s. *prīvātio*] —**Syn. 1.** See **hardship.**

privative (prĭv′ə tĭv), *adj.* **1.** having the quality of depriving. **2.** consisting in or characterized by the taking away of something, or the loss or lack of something properly present. **3.** *Gram.* indicating negation or absence. —*n.* **4.** *Gram.* a private element, as *a-* in *asymmetric* = *without symmetry.* **5.** that which is privative. [t. L: m. s. *prīvātivus*] —**priv′atively,** *adv.*

privet (prĭv′ĭt), *n.* **1.** a European oleaceous shrub, *Ligustrum vulgare*, with evergreen leaves and small white flowers, much used for hedges. **2.** any of various other species of the genus *Ligustrum.* [orig. uncert.]

privilege (prĭv′ĭ lĭj), *n.*, *v.*, **-leged, -leging.** —*n.* **1.** a right or immunity enjoyed by a person or persons beyond the common advantages of others. **2.** a special right or immunity granted to persons in authority or office; a prerogative. **3.** a prerogative, advantage, or opportunity enjoyed by anyone in a favoured position (as distinct from a right). **4.** a grant to an individual, a company, etc., of a special right or immunity, sometimes in derogation of the common right. **5.** the principle or condition of enjoying special rights or immunities. **6.** any of the more sacred and vital rights common to all citizens under a modern constitution. **7.** *Stock Exchange.* a speculative contract covering a call, put, spread, or double option. —*v.t.* **8.** to grant a privilege to. **9.** to exempt (fol. by *from*). **10.** to authorize or to license (something otherwise forbidden). [ME *privileg(i)e*, t. L: m. *prīvīlēgium*, orig., a law in favour of or against an individual]

—**Syn. 1.** PRIVILEGE, PREROGATIVE refer to some special advantage which one person has over others. A PRIVILEGE is a benefit or advantage conferred or attained justly or unjustly: *the privilege of paying half-fare.* A PREROGATIVE is a particular or official privilege assumed or granted as a right, and thought suitable and proper for one of a certain rank, descent, office, etc.: *a king's prerogative.*

privily (prĭv′ĭ lĭ), *adv.* *Archaic.* in a privy manner; secretly.

privity (prĭv′ĭ tĭ), *n.*, *pl.* **-ties.** **1.** participation in the knowledge of something private or secret, esp. as implying concurrence or consent. **2.** *Law.* the relation between privies. **3.** *Obs.* privacy. [ME *privete, privite*, t. OF, der. L *prīvus* private. See PRIVATE, -ITY]

privy (prĭv′ĭ), *adj.*, *n.*, *pl.* **privies.** —*adj.* **1.** participating in the knowledge of something private or secret (usually fol. by *to*): *many persons were privy to the plot.* **2.** private; assigned to private uses: *the privy purse.* **3.** belonging or pertaining to some particular person or persons, now esp. with reference to a sovereign. **4.** *Archaic.* secret, concealed, hidden, or secluded. **5.** *Archaic.* acting or done in secret. —*n.* **6.** an outhouse serving as a lavatory. **7.** *Law.* one participating directly in a legal transaction, or claiming through or under such a one. [ME, t. OF: m. *prive*, adj. and n., g. L *prīvātus*, pp., separated, private]

privy chamber, **1.** a private apartment in a royal residence. **2.** *Archaic.* a room reserved for the private or exclusive use of some particular person or persons.

privy council, (*sometimes cap.*) **1.** a board or select body of personal advisers, as of a sovereign. **2.** (in Great Britain) a body of advisers, selected theoretically by the sovereign, whose function of advising the Crown in matters of state is, except in a formal sense, now discharged by the cabinet, committees, etc. **3.** any similar body, as one appointed to assist the governor of a British dominion. —**privy councillor.**

privy parts, private parts.

privy purse, (*sometimes cap.*) (in Great Britain) a sum of money voted by Parliament for the private expenses of the sovereign.

privy seal, (*sometimes cap.*) (in Great Britain) formerly, the seal affixed to grants, etc., which afterwards had to pass the great seal, and to documents which did not require the great seal.

prix (*Fr.* prē), *n. French.* prize.

prize[1] (prīz), *n.* **1.** a reward of victory or superiority, as in a contest or competition. **2.** that which is won in a lottery or the like. **3.** anything striven for, worth striving for, or much valued. **4.** a taking or capturing at sea. **5.** a capturing. **6.** something seized or captured, esp. an enemy's ship with the property in it taken at sea under the law of war. **7.** *Archaic.* a contest or match. *—adj.* **8.** that has gained a prize. **9.** worthy of a prize. **10.** given or awarded as a prize. [ME *prise,* t. OF: a taking, pp. of *prendre* take, capture, g. L *pre(he)ndere;* influenced by ME *pris, prise* reward, prize, PRICE] **—Syn. 1.** See **reward.**

prize[2] (prīz), *v.t.,* **prized, prizing. 1.** to value or esteem highly. **2.** to estimate the worth or value of. [ME *prise(n),* t. OF: m. *prisier* praise, g. L *pretiāre* prize] **—Syn. 1.** See **appreciate.**

prize[3] (prīz), *v.t.,* **prized, prizing,** *n.* prise.

prize court, a court whose function it is to adjudicate on prizes taken in war.

prize-day (prīz′dā′), *n.* the annual giving of prizes, as for academic merit, to pupils in a school. Also, **prize-giving** (prīz′gĭv′ĭng).

prize fight, a contest between boxers for a prize. **—prize′-fight′er,** *n.* **—prize′-fight′ing,** *n., adj.*

prize money, 1. money won as a prize in a competition. **2.** a portion of the money from the sale of a prize, esp. an enemy's vessel, divided among the captors.

prizer (prī′zə), *n. Archaic.* a competitor for a prize.

prize ring, 1. a ring or enclosed square area for prize-fighting. **2.** prize-fighting.

p.r.n., (L *prō rē nāta*) (used in prescriptions) as and when needed.

pro[1] (prō), *adv., n., pl.* **pros.** *—adv.* **1.** in favour of a proposition, opinion, etc. (oppsed to *con*). *—n.* **2.** a proponent of an issue; one who upholds the affirmative in a debate. **3.** an argument, consideration, vote, etc., for something. [t. L: prep., in favour of, for]

pro[2] (prō), *n., pl.* **pros,** *adj. Colloq.* professional.

pro[3] (prō), *n. Slang.* a prostitute.

P.R.O., 1. Public Records Office. **2.** public relations officer.

pro-[1], **1.** prefix indicating favour for some party, system, idea, etc., without identity with the group, e.g., *pro-British, pro-communist, proslavery,* having *anti-* as its opposite. **2.** prefix of priority in space or time having especially a meaning of advancing or projecting forwards or outwards, having also extended figuration meanings, including substitution, attached widely to stems not used as words, e.g., *provision, prologue, proceed, produce, protract, procathedral, proconsul.* [t. L, repr. *prō,* prep., before, for, in favour of, on behalf of]

pro-[2], a prefix identical in meaning with **pro-**[1], occurring in words taken from Greek (as *prodrome*) or formed of Greek (and occasionally Latin) elements. [t. Gk, repr. *pró* for, before, in favour of]

proa (prō′ə), *n.* **1.** any of various types of South Pacific boat. **2.** a swift Malay sailing boat built with the leeside flat and balanced by a single outrigger. Also, **prau.** [t. Malay: m. *prāū*]

prob., 1. probably. **2.** problem.

probabilism (prŏb′ə bĭ lĭz′əm), *n.* **1.** *Philos.* the doctrine that certainty is impossible, and that probability suffices to govern faith and practice. **2.** *Rom. Cath. Theol.* a theory that in cases of doubt as to the lawfulness or unlawfulness of an action, it is permissible to follow a soundly probable opinion favouring its lawfulness. **—prob′abilist,** *n., adj.*

probability (prŏb′ə bĭl′ĭ tĭ), *n., pl.* **-ties. 1.** the quality or fact of being probable. **2.** a likelihood or chance of something: *there is a probability of his coming.* **3.** a probable event, circumstance, etc.: *to regard a thing as a probability.* **4.** *Statistics.* the relative frequency of the occurrence of an event as measured by the ratio of the number of cases or alternatives favourable to the event to the total number of cases or alternatives. **5. in all probability,** likely; very probably.

probability curve, *Statistics.* **1.** a curve which describes the distribution of probability over the values of a variable. **2.** the normal curve.

probable (prŏb′ə bl), *adj.* **1.** likely to occur or prove true. **2.** having more evidence for than against, or evidence which inclines the mind to belief but leaves some room for doubt. **3.** affording ground for belief: *probable evidence.* [ME, t. L: m. s. *probābilis*]

probable cause, *Law.* reasonable ground for a belief, esp. as a defence to an action for malicious prosecution.

probable error, *Statistics.* a value such that the error in an error distribution is equally likely to be greater or smaller than it.

probably (prŏb′ə blĭ), *adv.* in a probable manner; with probability; in all likelihood.

probang (prō′băng), *n. Surg.* a long, slender, elastic rod with a sponge, ball, or the like, at the end, formerly introduced into the oesophagus, etc., as for removing foreign bodies, or for introducing medication. [orig. *provang,* b. obs. *prov(et)* probe and (F)ANG, n. or v.]

probate (prō′bĭt, prō′bāt), *n., adj., v.,* **-bated, -bating.** *—n.* **1.** *Law.* the official proving of a will as authentic or valid. **2.** *Law.* an officially certified copy of a will so proved. *—adj.* **3.** of or pertaining to probate or a court of probate. *—v.t.* **4.** *U.S.* to establish the authenticity or validity of (a will). [ME, t. L: m. s. *probātum,* neut. pp., (a thing) proved]

probate court, a special court limited to the administration of estates of deceased persons, the probate of wills, etc., in England now forming part of the Probate, Divorce, and Admiralty Division of the High Court of Justice.

probation (prə bā′shən), *n.* **1.** the act of testing. **2.** the testing or trial of a person's conduct, character, qualifications, or the like. **3.** the state or period of such testing or trial. **4.** *Law.* **a.** a method of dealing with offenders, esp. young persons guilty of minor crimes or first offences, by allowing them to go at large conditionally under supervision, as that of a person (**probation officer**) appointed for such duty. **b.** the state of having been conditionally released. **5.** a trial period in which a person can redeem failures, misconduct, etc. **6.** the testing or trial of a candidate for membership in a religious body or order, for holy orders, etc. **7.** *Rare.* proof. [ME *probacion,* t. L: m. s. *probātio*] **—proba′tional, probationary** (prə bā′shə nə rĭ), *adj.*

probationer (prə bāsh′nə), *n.* one undergoing probation or trial. **—proba′tionership′,** *n.*

probation officer, a person appointed to advise and supervise offenders under probation.

probative (prō′bə tĭv), *adj.* **1.** serving or designed for testing or trial. **2.** affording proof or evidence. Also, **probatory** (prō′bə tə rĭ, -trĭ).

probe (prōb), *v.,* **probed, probing,** *n.* *—v.t.* **1.** to search into or examine thoroughly; question closely. **2.** to examine or explore as with a probe. *—v.i.* **3.** to penetrate or examine with or as with a probe. *—n.* **4.** the act of probing. **5.** a slender surgical instrument for exploring the depth or direction of a wound, sinus, or the like. **6.** *Electronics.* an electronic circuit connected to a long thin rod, used for monitoring otherwise inaccessible points in an electronic system. **7.** *Aeron.* a spacecraft capable of exploring, examining any testing conditions in space and radioing back the results. **8.** *U.S.* an investigation or inquiry, esp. by a legislative committee, of suspected illegal activity. [t. ML: m. *proba* test, LL proof. See PROOF] **—prob′er,** *n.*

probity (prō′bĭ tĭ), *n.* integrity; uprightness; honesty. [t. L: m. s. *probitas*]

problem (prŏb′ləm), *n.* **1.** any question or matter involving doubt, uncertainty, or difficulty. **2.** a question proposed for solution or discussion. **3.** *Maths.* a question requiring a mathematical solution. *—adj.* **4.** difficult to train or guide; unruly: *a problem child.* **5.** *Literature.* dealing with choices of action difficult either for an individual or for society at large: *a problem play.* [ME *probleme,* t. L: m. *problēma,* t. Gk]

problematic (prŏb′lĭ măt′ĭk), *adj.* **1.** of the nature of a problem; doubtful; uncertain; questionable. **2.** *Logic.* denoting a proposition or judgement which claims that it may or may not be true. See **modality** (def. 3b). Also, **problematical. —prob′lemat′ically,** *adv.*

pro bono publico (prō bō′nō pōōb′lĭ kō′), *Latin.* for the public good or welfare.

proboscidean (prō′bə sĭd′ĭ ən), *adj.* **1.** pertaining to or resembling a proboscis. **2.** having a proboscis. **3.** belonging or pertaining to the *Proboscidea,* the order of mammals that consists of the elephants and their extinct allies. Also, **proboscidian.** [f. m. s. NL *Proboscidea,* pl. (see PROBOSCIS) + -AN]

proboscis (prə bŏs′ĭs), *n., pl.* **-boscises** (-bŏs′ĭ sĭz), **-boscides** (-bŏs′ĭ dēz′). **1.** an elephant's trunk. **2.** any long flexible snout, as of the tapir. **3.** *Entomol.* **a.** an elongate but not rigid feeding organ of certain insects formed of the mouthparts, as in the *Lepidoptera* and *Diptera.* **b.** any elongate or snoutlike feeding organ. **4.** *Humorous.* the human nose. [t. L, t. Gk: m. *proboskís*]

proboscis monkey, a powerfully built monkey, *Nasalis larvatus,* of Borneo, having a long, bulbous nose.

proc., 1. procedure. 2. proceedings. 3. process.

procaine (prō kān′, prō′kān), *n.* novocaine. [f. PRO-¹ + (CO)CAINE]

procambium (prō kăm′bĭ əm), *n. Bot.* the meristem from which vascular bundles are developed. [t. NL. See PRO-¹, CAMBIUM] —**procam′bial,** *adj.*

procarp (prō′kärp′), *n. Bot.* a carpogonium plus certain cells intimately associated with it.

procathedral (prō′kə thē′drəl), *n.* a church used temporarily as a cathedral.

procedure (prə sē′jə), *n.* **1.** the act or manner of proceeding in any action or process; conduct. **2.** a particular course or mode of action. **3.** mode of conducting legal, parliamentary, or other business, esp. litigation and judicial proceedings. [t. F, der. *procéder* PROCEED] —**proce′dural,** *adj.* —**Syn. 2.** See **process.**

proceed (*v.* prə sēd′; *n.* prō′sēd), *v.i.* **1.** to move or go forwards or onwards, esp. after stopping. **2.** to go on with or carry on any action or process. **3.** to go on (to do something). **4.** to continue one's discourse. **5.** *Law.* **a.** to begin and carry on a legal action. **b.** to take legal proceedings (fol. by *against*). **6.** to be carried on, as an action, process, etc. **7.** to go or come forth; issue. **8.** to arise, originate, or result. —*n.* **9.** (*usually pl.*) the sum derived from a sale or other transaction. **10.** that which results or accrues. [ME *procede(n)*, t. L: m. *prōcēdere*] —**Syn. 1.** See **advance.**

proceeding (prə sē′dĭng), *n.* **1.** a particular action or course of action. **2.** action, course of action, or conduct. **3.** the act of one who or that which proceeds. **4.** (*pl.*) records of the doings of a society. **5.** *Law.* **a.** the instituting or carrying on of an action at law. **b.** a legal step or measure: *to institute proceedings against a person.* —**Syn. 1, 2, 4.** See **process.**

proceleusmatic (prŏs′ĭ lōōs măt′ĭk), *adj.* **1.** inciting, animating, or inspiriting. **2.** *Pros.* **a.** denoting a metrical foot of four short syllables. **b.** pertaining to or consisting of feet of this kind. —*n.* **3.** *Pros.* a proceleusmatic foot. [t. LL: s. *proceleusmaticus*, t. Gk: m. *prokeleusmatikós*]

process (prō′sĕs), *n.* **1.** a systematic series of actions directed to some end: *the process of making butter.* **2.** a continuous action, operation, or series of changes taking place in a definite manner: *the process of decay.* **3.** *Law.* **a.** the summons, mandate, or writ by which a defendant or thing is brought before court for litigation. **b.** the total of such summoning writs. **c.** the whole course of the proceedings in an action at law. **4.** *Photog.* **a.** photomechanical or photoengraving methods collectively. **b.** a system of superimposing background in a film, or otherwise creating a picture by combining elements not ordinarily united: *a process shot.* **5.** *Biol.* a natural outgrowth, projection, or appendage: *a process of a bone.* **6.** a prominence or protuberance. **7.** the action of going forward or on. **8.** the condition of being carried on. **9.** course or lapse, as of time. **10. in (the) process of,** during the course of; in the middle of. —*v.t.* **11.** to treat or prepare by some particular process, as in manufacturing. **12.** to convert (an agricultural commodity) into marketable form by some special process. **13.** to institute a legal process against. **14.** to serve a process or summons on. **15.** *Computers.* (of data) to manipulate in order to abstract the required information. —*adj.* **16.** prepared or modified by an artificial process. **17.** pertaining to, made by or using, or used in, photomechanical or photoengraving methods. [ME *proces*, t. F, t. L: m. s. *prōcessus* a going forward]

—**Syn. 1.** PROCESS, PROCEDURE, PROCEEDING apply to something which goes on or takes place. A PROCESS is a series of progressive and interdependent steps by which an end is attained: *a chemical process.* PROCEDURE usually implies a formal or set order of doing a thing, a method of conducting affairs: *parliamentary procedure.* PROCEEDING (usually pl.) applies to what goes on or takes place on a given occasion, to a certain behaviour, or transaction (or, the records of a transaction): *Proceedings of the Royal Academy of Sciences.*

process control, the control of a complex industrial or chemical process usually by electronic means.

process costing, a method of costing used to ascertain the cost of the product at each stage of manufacture.

procession (prə sĕsh′ən), *n.* **1.** the proceeding or moving along in orderly succession, in a formal or ceremonious manner, of a line or body of persons, animals, vehicles, or other things. **2.** the line or body of persons or things moving along. **3.** *Eccles.* an office, litany, etc., said or sung in a religious procession. **4.** *Theol.* the relation of the Holy Spirit to the Father and later, in the Western Church, to the Son; distinguished from the 'generation' of the Son and the 'unbegottenness' of the Father. John 15, 26. **5.** the act of proceeding forth from a source. —*v.i.* **6.** to go in procession. [early ME, t. ML: s. *prōcessio* a religious procession, L a marching on]

processional (prə sĕsh′ə nəl), *adj.* **1.** of or pertaining to a procession. **2.** of the nature of a procession. **3.** characterized by processions. **4.** sung or recited in procession, as a hymn. —*n.* **5.** a processional hymn. **6.** an office book containing hymns, litanies, etc., for use in religious processions.

process printing, a method of printing practically any colour by using four separate halftone plates for red, yellow, blue, and black ink.

process-server (prō′sĕs sû′və), *n. Law.* one who serves legal documents such as a subpoena, writ, or warrant, etc., requiring appearance in court or before a notary public, etc.

procès-verbal (*Fr.* prŏ sĕ vĕr bȧl′), *n., pl.* **-baux** (-bō′). **1.** a report of proceedings, as of an assembly. **2.** *French Law.* an authenticated written account of facts in connection with a criminal or other charge. [F]

prochein (prō′shĕn), *adj. Law.* nearest: *prochein ami* (next friend). Also, *French,* **prochain** (*Fr.* prŏ shăN′). [t. F: m. *prochain*, ult. der. L *prope* near]

proclaim (prə klām′), *v.t.* **1.** to announce or declare publicly or officiously: *to proclaim one's opinions.* **2.** to announce or declare, publicly and officially: *to proclaim war.* **3.** (of things) to indicate or make known. **4.** to declare (a district, etc.) subject to particular legal restrictions. **5.** to declare to be an outlaw, evildoer, or the like. **6.** to denounce or prohibit publicly. —*v.i.* **7.** to make proclamation. [ME *proclame(n)*, t. L: m. *proclāmāre*] —**proclaim′er,** *n.* —**Syn. 1.** See **announce.**

proclamation (prŏk′lə mā′shən), *n.* **1.** that which is proclaimed; a public and official announcement. **2.** the act of proclaiming.

proclitic (prō klĭt′ĭk), *Gram.* —*n.* **1.** an element similar to a prefix but of more independent status, approaching that of a separate word. —*adj.* **2.** having the nature of a proclitic. [t. NL: s. *procliticus*, der. Gk *proklínein* lean forward. Cf. ENCLITIC]

proclivity (prə klĭv′ĭ tĭ), *n., pl.* **-ties.** natural or habitual inclination or tendency; propensity; predisposition: *a proclivity to fault-finding.* [t. L: m. *prōclīvitas* tendency, propensity. Cf. F *proclivité*]

Procne (prŏk′nĭ), *n. Gk Legend.* the wife of Tereus and sister of Philomela, later turned into a swallow.

proconsul (prō′kŏn′səl), *n.* **1.** (among the ancient Romans) a governor or military commander of a province with duties and powers similar to those of a consul. **2.** any appointed administrator over a dependency or an occupied area. [ME, t. L] —**pro′con′sular,** *adj.*

proconsulate (prō′kŏn′syŏŏ lĭt), *n. Hist.* the office or term of office of a proconsul. Also, **pro′con′sulship′.**

Procopius (prō kō′pyəs), *n.* A.D. *c.* 490–*c.* 562, Greek historian of the Byzantine Empire.

procrastinate (prō krăs′tĭ nāt′), *v.,* **-nated, -nating. 1.** to defer action; delay: *to procrastinate until an opportunity is lost.* —*v.t.* **2.** to put off till another day or time; defer; delay. [t. L: m. s. *prōcrastinātus*, pp., put off till the morrow] —**procras′tina′tion,** *n.* —**procras′tina′tor,** *n.*

procreant (prō′krĭ ənt), *adj.* **1.** procreating; generating. **2.** pertaining to procreation. [t. L: s. *prōcreans*, ppr.]

procreate (prō′krĭ āt′), *v.t.,* **-ated, -ating. 1.** to beget or generate (offspring). **2.** to produce; bring into being. [t. L: m. s. *prōcreātus*, pp.] —**pro′crea′tion,** *n.* —**pro′crea′tive,** *adj.* —**pro′crea′tor,** *n.*

Procrustean (prō krŭs′tĭ ən), *adj.* **1.** pertaining to or suggestive of Procrustes. **2.** tending to produce conformity by violent or arbitrary means.

Procrustes (prō krŭs′tēz), *n. Gk Legend.* a robber who stretched or mutilated his victims to make them conform to the length of his bed.

proctology (prŏk tŏl′ə jĭ), *n.* the branch of medicine dealing with the rectum and anus. [f. *procto-* (comb. form repr. Gk *prōktós* anus) + -LOGY] —**proctological** (prŏk′tə lŏj′ĭ kl), *adj.* —**proctol′ogist,** *n.*

proctor (prŏk′tə), *n.* **1.** (in certain universities) an official charged with various duties, esp. with the maintenance of discipline among undergraduates. **2.** *Law.* (formerly) a person employed to manage another's cause in a court of civil or ecclesiastical law, or to collect tithes for the owner of them. **3.** *C. of E.* a representative of the clergy in convocation. [contracted var. of PROCURATOR] —**proctorial** (prŏk tô′rĭ əl), *adj.* —**proc′torship′,** *n.*

proctoscope (prŏk′tə skōp′), *n.* an instrument for examining the interior of the rectum. [f. *procto-* (t. Gk: m. *prōkto-*, comb. form of *prōktós* anus) + -SCOPE]

procumbent (prō kŭm′bənt), *adj.* **1.** lying on the face; prone; prostrate. **2.** *Bot.* (of a plant or stem) lying along the ground, but without putting forth roots. [t. L: s. *prōcumbens*, ppr., falling forward]

procurable (prə kyŏŏ′rə bl), *adj.* obtainable.

procurance (prə kyŏŏ′rəns), *n.* the act of bringing something about; agency.

procuration (prŏk′yŏŏ rā′shən), *n.* **1.** the appointment of a procurator, agent, or attorney. **2.** the authority given. **3.** a document whereby the authority is given. **4.** the act of obtaining or getting; procurement. **5.** the act of procuring for the gratification of lust or purposes of prostitution. **6.** *Obs.* management for another; agency.

procurator (prŏk′yŏŏ rā′tə), *n.* **1.** *Rom. Hist.* any of various imperial officers with fiscal or administrative powers. **2.** *Law. Now Rare.* an agent, deputy, or attorney. [ME *procuratour*, t. L: m. *prōcūrātor*] —**procuratorial** (prŏk′yŏŏ rə tô′rĭ əl), **procuratory** (prŏk′yŏŏ rə tə rĭ, -trĭ), *adj.*

procurator-fiscal (prŏk′yŏŏ rā′ tə fĭs′kl), *n.* the public prosecutor in Scotland, who also exercises the function of coroner.

procure (prə kyŏŏə′), *v.*, **-cured, -curing.** —*v.t.* **1.** to obtain or get by care, effort, or the use of special means: *to procure evidence.* **2.** to effect; cause; bring about, esp. by unscrupulous or indirect means: *to procure a person's death.* **3.** to obtain for the gratification of lust or purposes of prostitution. —*v.i.* **4.** to act as a procurer or pimp. [ME, t. L: m. s. *prōcūrāre* take care of, manage] —**procure′ment,** *n.* —**Syn. 1.** acquire, gain, win, secure. See **get.**

procurer (prə kyŏŏə′rə), *n.* **1.** one who procures, esp. a pander or pimp. —**procuress** (prə kyŏŏə′rĭs), *n. fem.*

Procyon (prō′syən), *n. Astron.* a star of the first magnitude in the constellation Canis Minor.

prod (prŏd), *v.*, **prodded, prodding,** *n.* —*v.t.* **1.** to poke or jab with something pointed: *to prod an animal with a stick.* **2.** to seek to rouse or incite as if by poking. —*n.* **3.** the act of prodding; a poke or jab. **4.** any of various pointed instruments, as a goad. [cf. OE *prod-* in *prodbor* auger] —**prod′der,** *n.*

prod., **1.** produce. **2.** produced. **3.** product.

prodigal (prŏd′ĭ gl), *adj.* **1.** wastefully or recklessly extravagant: *prodigal expenditure.* **2.** giving or yielding profusely; lavish (fol. by *of*): *prodigal of smiles.* **3.** lavishly abundant; profuse. —*n.* **4.** one who spends, or has spent, his money or substance with wasteful extravagance; a spendthrift. [back-formation from PRODIGALITY] —**prod′igally,** *adv.* —**Syn. 1.** See **lavish.**

prodigality (prŏd′ĭ găl′ĭ tĭ), *n., pl.* **-ties. 1.** quality or fact of being prodigal; wasteful extravagance in spending. **2.** an instance of it. **3.** lavish abundance. [ME *prodigalite*, t. ML: m. s. *prōdigālitas*]

prodigious (prə dĭj′əs), *adj.* **1.** extraordinary in size, amount, extent, degree, force, etc.: *a prodigious noise.* **2.** wonderful or marvellous: *a prodigious feat.* **3.** abnormal; monstrous. **4.** *Obs.* ominous. [t. L: m. *prōdigiōsus*] —**prodi′giously,** *adv.* —**prodi′giousness,** *n.* —**Syn. 1.** enormous, immense, huge. **2.** amazing, stupendous.

prodigy (prŏd′ĭ jĭ), *n., pl.* **-gies. 1.** a person, esp. a child, endowed with extraordinary gifts or powers: *a musical prodigy.* **2.** a marvellous example (fol. by *of*): *that prodigy of learning.* **3.** something wonderful or marvellous; a wonder. **4.** something abnormal or monstrous. **5.** *Rare.* something extraordinary regarded as of prophetic significance. [t. L: m. s. *prōdigium* prophetic sign]

prodrome (prŏd′rōm), *n. Pathol.* a premonitory symptom. [t. F, t. NL: m. s. *prodromus*, t. Gk: m. *pródromos* running before] —**prodromal** (prŏd′rə məl), *adj.*

produce (*v.* prə dyōōs′; *n.* prŏd′yōōs), *v.*, **-duced, -ducing,** *n.* —*v.t.* **1.** to bring into existence; give rise to; cause: *to produce steam.* **2.** to bring into being by mental or physical labour, as a work of literature or art. **3.** *Econ.* to create (something having an exchangeable value). **4.** to bring forth; bear; give birth to. **5.** to yield; provide, furnish, or supply: *a mine producing silver.* **6.** to cause to accrue: *money producing interest.* **7.** to bring forward; present to view or notice; exhibit. **8.** to bring (a play, film, etc.) before the public. **9.** to extend or prolong, as a line. —*v.i.* **10.** to bring forth or yield offspring, products, etc. **11.** *Econ.* to create value; bring crops, goods, etc., into a state in which they will command a price. —*n.* **12.** that which is produced; yield; product. **13.** agricultural or natural products collectively. [t. L: m. s. *prōdūcere* lead or bring forward, extend, prolong, bring forth, produce] —**produc′ible,** *adj.* —**Syn. 11.** See **crop.**

producer (prə dyōō′sə), *n.* **1.** one who produces. **2.** *Econ.* one who creates value, or produces goods and services (opposed to *consumer*). **3.** a person who exercises general supervision over a film, television, or radio production, having particular responsibility for all administrative and financial aspects of the production. **4.** *Theat.* a person responsible for the presentation of a play, including the interpretation of the author's script, the direction of actors at rehearsals, the use of costumes, etc. **5.** an apparatus for making producer gas.

producer gas, a vaporous fuel produced by gasifying cheap solid fuel with steam, used in the place of petrol, natural gas, etc.: the chief constituents are carbon monoxide, hydrogen, and nitrogen.

producer goods, *Econ.* goods that are used in the process of creating final consumer goods, as machinery, raw materials, etc.

product (prŏd′əkt, prŏd′ŭkt), *n.* **1.** a thing produced by any action or operation, or by labour; an effect or result. **2.** something produced; a thing produced by nature or by a natural process. **3.** *Chem.* a substance obtained from another substance through chemical change. **4.** *Maths.* the result obtained by multiplying two or more quantities together. [ME, t. L: s. *prōductum*, neut. pp., (thing) produced]

production (prə dŭk′shən), *n.* **1.** the act of producing; creation; manufacture. **2.** that which is produced; a product. **3.** *Econ.* the creation of value; the producing of articles having an exchangeable value. **4.** the total amount produced. **5.** a work of literature or art. **6.** the act of exhibiting or displaying. **7.** the artistic direction and interpretation of a play. [ME, t. L: s. *prōductio*]

productive (prə dŭk′tĭv), *adj.* **1.** having the power of producing; generative; creative. **2.** producing readily or abundantly; fertile; prolific. **3.** *Econ.* producing or tending to produce goods and services having exchangeable value. —**produc′tively,** *adv.* —**productivity** (prŏd′ŭk tĭv′ĭ tĭ), **produc′tiveness,** *n.*

—**Syn.** 2. PRODUCTIVE, FERTILE, FRUITFUL apply to that which is capable of generating or producing (abundantly). PRODUCTIVE, meaning that which produces, refers to continued activity, past, present, and future: *productive soil, a productive influence.* FERTILE refers to that in which seeds may be expected to take root: *fertile soil, a fertile suggestion.* FRUITFUL refers to that which has produced: *fruitful soil, discovery, theory. Fertile soil, properly cultivated, has become fruitful, and is now steadily productive.* —**Ant.** 2. sterile.

production reactor, *Physics.* a nuclear reactor whose main function is the production of fissile material.

proem (prō′ĕm), *n.* an introductory discourse; an introduction; a preface; a preamble. [t. L: m. s. *prooemium*, t. Gk: m. *prooímion*; r. ME *proheme*, t. OF] —**proemial** (prō ē′myəl), *adj.*

proembryo (prō ĕm′brĭ ō′), *n.* the group of cells produced by division of a zygote before differentiation of the embryo proper.

prof (prŏf), *n. Colloq.* professor.

Prof., Professor.

profanation (prŏf′ə nā′shən), *n.* the act of profaning; desecration; defilement; debasement.

profanatory (prə făn′ə tə rĭ, -trĭ), *adj.* tending to desecrate; profaning.

profane (prə fān′), *adj.*, *v.*, **-faned, -faning.** —*adj.* **1.** characterized by irreverence or contempt for God or sacred things; irreligious, esp. speaking or spoken in manifest or implied contempt for sacred things. **2.** not sacred, or not devoted to sacred purposes; unconsecrated; secular: *profane history.* **3.** unholy; heathen; pagan. **4.** not initiated into religious rites or mysteries, as persons. **5.** common or vulgar. —*v.t.* **6.** to misuse (anything that should be held in reverence or respect); defile; debase; employ basely or unworthily. **7.** to treat (anything sacred) with irreverence or contempt. [ME *prophane*, t. F, t. L: m. *profānus*, lit., before (outside) the temple] —**profane′ly,** *adv.* —**profane′ness,** *n.* —**profan′er,** *n.*

profanity (prə făn′ĭ tĭ), *n., pl.* **-ties. 1.** the quality of being profane; irreverence. **2.** profane conduct or language; a profane act or utterance.

profert (prō′fət), *n. Law.* an exhibition of a record or paper in open court. [L: he brings forward]

profess (prə fĕs′), *v.t.* **1.** to lay claim to (a feeling, etc.), often insincerely; pretend to: *he professed extreme regret.* **2.** to declare openly; announce or affirm; avow or acknowledge: *to profess one's satisfaction.* **3.** to affirm faith in or allegiance to (a religion, God, etc.). **4.** to declare oneself skilled or expert in; claim to have knowledge of; make (a thing) one's profession or business. **5.** to receive or admit into a religious order. —*v.i.* **6.** to make profession. **7.** to take the vows of a religious order. [back-formation from PROFESSED]

professed (prə fĕst′), *adj.* **1.** alleged; pretended. **2.** avowed; acknowledged. **3.** professing to be qualified; professional (rather than amateur). **4.** having taken vows of or been received into a religious order. [ME (def. 4), f. s. L *professus*, pp., + -ED[2]]

professedly (prə fĕs′ĭd lĭ), *adv.* **1.** allegedly. **2.** avowedly. **3.** ostensibly.

profession (prə fĕsh′ən), *n.* **1.** a vocation requiring knowledge of some department of learning or science, esp. one of the three vocations of theology, law, and medicine (formerly known specifically as **the professions** or **the learned professions**): *a lawyer by profession.* **2.** any vocation, occupation, etc. **3.** the body of persons engaged in an occupation or calling: *to be respected by the medical profession.* **4.** the act of professing; avowal; a declaration, whether true or false: *professions of love.* **5.** the declaration of belief in or acceptance of religion or a faith: *the profession of Christianity.* **6.** a religion or faith professed. **7.** the declaration made on entering a religious order. [ME, t. L: s. *professio*] **—Syn. 1.** See **occupation.**

professional (prə fĕsh′ə nəl), *adj.* **1.** following an occupation as a means of livelihood or for gain: *a professional actor.* **2.** pertaining or appropriate to a profession: *professional studies.* **3.** engaged in one of the learned professions: *a professional man.* **4.** following as a business an occupation ordinarily engaged in as a pastime: *a professional golfer.* **5.** making a business of something not properly to be regarded as a business: *a professional politician.* **6.** undertaken or engaged in as a means of livelihood or for gain: *professional football.* **—***n.* **7.** one belonging to one of the learned or skilled professions. **8.** one who makes a business of an occupation, etc., esp. of an art or sport, in which amateurs engage for amusement or recreation. **9.** an expert in a game, hired by a sports club to instruct members. **—profes′sionally,** *adv.*

professionalism (prə fĕsh′ə nə lĭz′əm), *n.* **1.** professional character, spirit, or methods. **2.** the standing, practice, or methods of a professional as distinguished from an amateur.

professionalize (prə fĕsh′ə nə līz′), *v.*, **-lized, -lizing.** **—***v.t.* **1.** to give a professional status or character to. **—***v.i.* **2.** to become professional. Also, **professionalise.**

professor (prə fĕs′ə), *n.* **1.** a teacher of the highest rank, usually holding a chair in a particular branch of learning, in a university or college. **2.** a teacher. **3.** an instructor in some popular art, as singing, etc. **4.** one who professes his sentiments, beliefs, etc. [ME, t. L] **—professorial** (prŏf′ĕ sô′rĭ əl), *adj.* **—prof′esso′rially,** *adv.*

professorate (prə fĕs′ə rĭt), *n.* **1.** the office or the period of service of a professor. **2.** a group of professors.

professoriate (prŏf′ĕ sô′rĭ ĭt), *n.* **1.** a group of professors. **2.** the office or post of professor.

professorship (prə fĕs′ə shĭp′), *n.* the office or post of a professor.

proffer (prŏf′ə), *v.t.* **1.** to put before a person for acceptance; offer. **—***n.* **2.** the act of proffering. **3.** an offer. [ME *profre(n)*, t. AF: m. *profrer*, var. of OF *poroffrir*, f. *por-* PRO-¹ + *offrir* (g. LL *offerire*, var. of L *offerre* offer)] **—Syn. 1.** See **offer.**

proficiency (prə fĭsh′ən sĭ), *n.*, *pl.* **-cies.** the state of being proficient; skill; expertness: *proficiency in music.*

proficient (prə fĭsh′ənt), *adj.* **1.** well advanced or expert in any art, science, or subject; skilled. **—***n.* **2.** an expert. [t. L: s. *prōficiens*, ppr., making progress. See PROFIT] **—profi′ciently,** *adv.*

profile (prō′fīl), *n.*, *v.*, **-filed, -filing.** **—***n.* **1.** the outline or contour of the human face, esp. as seen from the side. **2.** a drawing, painting, etc., of the side view of the head. **3.** the outline of something seen against a background. **4.** *Archit., Engin.* a drawing of a section, esp. a vertical section, through something. **5.** a vivid and concise sketch of the biography and personality of an individual. **—***v.t.* **6.** to draw a profile of. **7.** to shape as to profile. [t. It.: m. *profilo*, der. *profilare* draw in outline, f. L *pro-* PRO-¹ + LL *filāre* spin]

profile drag, *Aeron.* the drag of a body excluding that due to lift: it comprises the sum of the form drag (which depends on the shape of the body) and the skin friction (which depends on the nature of its surface).

profit (prŏf′ĭt), *n.* **1.** (*often pl.*) pecuniary gain resulting from the employment of capital in any transaction: **a. gross profit,** gross receipts less the immediate costs of production. **b. net profit,** amount remaining after deducting all costs from gross receipts. **c.** the ratio of such pecuniary gain to the amount of capital invested. **2.** (*often pl.*) returns, proceeds, or revenue, as from property or investments. **3.** *Econ.* the surplus left to the producer or employer after deducting wages, rent, cost of raw materials, etc. **4.** (*usually pl.*) such additional benefits as interest on capital, insurance, etc. **5.** advantage; benefit; gain. **—***v.i.* **6.** to gain advantage or benefit. **7.** to make profit. **8.** to be of advantage or benefit. **9.** to take advantage. **10.** *Obs.* to make progress. **—***v.t.* **11.** to be of advantage or profit to. [ME, t. OF, g. L *prōfectus* progressed, profited] **—prof′itless,** *adj.* **—Syn. 2.** dividend, revenue, proceeds, returns. **5.** good, welfare. See **advantage.**

profitable (prŏf′ĭ tə bl), *adj.* **1.** yielding profit; remunerative. **2.** beneficial or useful. **—prof′itableness,** *n.* **—prof′itably,** *adv.*

profit and loss, the gain and loss arising from commercial or other transactions, applied esp. to an account in bookkeeping showing gains and losses in business. **—prof′it-and-loss′,** *adj.*

profiteer (prŏf′ĭ tĭə′), *n.* **1.** one who seeks or exacts exorbitant profits, as by taking advantage of public necessity. **—***v.i.* **2.** to act as a profiteer. **—prof′iteer′ing,** *n.*

profiterole (prŏf′ĭ tə rōl′, prŏf′ĭ tə rōl′, prə fĭt′ə rōl), *n.* a small ball of choux pastry cooked, then filled with cream, jam, cheese, or the like. [t. F]

profit sharing, the sharing of profits, as between employer and employee, esp. in such a way that the labourer receives, in addition to his wages, a share in the profits of the business. **—prof′it-shar′ing,** *adj.*

profligacy (prŏf′lĭ gə sĭ), *n.* **1.** shameless dissoluteness. **2.** reckless extravagance. **3.** great abundance.

profligate (prŏf′lĭ gĭt), *adj.* **1.** utterly and shamelessly immoral; thoroughly dissolute. **2.** recklessly prodigal or extravagant. **—***n.* **3.** a profligate person. [t. L: m. s. *prōflīgātus*, pp., overthrown, ruined] **—prof′ligately,** *adv.* **—prof′ligateness,** *n.*

profluent (prŏf′lo͞o ənt), *adj.* flowing smoothly along. [ME, t. L: s. *prōfluens*, ppr., flowing forth]

pro forma (prō fô′mə), *Latin.* according to form; as a matter of form.

profound (prə found′), *adj.* **1.** penetrating or entering deeply into subjects of thought or knowledge: *a profound thinker.* **2.** intense; extreme: *profound sleep.* **3.** being or going far beneath what is superficial, external, or obvious: *profound insight.* **4.** of deep meaning; abstruse: *a profound book.* **5.** extending, situated, or originating far down, or far beneath the surface. **6.** low: *a profound bow.* **7.** deep. **—***n. Poetic.* **8.** that which is profound. **9.** the deep sea; ocean. **10.** depth; abyss. [ME, t. OF: m. *profond*, g. L *profundus*] **—profound′ly,** *adv.* **—profound′ness,** *n.*

profundity (prə fŭn′dĭ tĭ), *n.*, *pl.* **-ties.** **1.** quality of being profound; depth. **2.** a profoundly deep place; an abyss. **3.** (*pl.*) profound or deep matters. [ME *profundite*, t. LL: m. s. *profunditas*]

profuse (prə fyo͞os′), *adj.* **1.** spending or giving freely and in large amount, often to excess; extravagant (often fol. by *in*). **2.** made or done freely and abundantly: *profuse apologies.* **3.** abundant; in great amount. [ME, t. L: m. s. *profūsus*, pp., poured forth] **—profuse′ly,** *adv.* **—profuse′ness,** *n.* **—Syn. 1.** See **lavish.**

profusion (prə fyo͞o′zhən), *n.* **1.** abundance; abundant quantity. **2.** a great quantity or amount (often fol. by *of*). **3.** lavish spending; extravagance. **—Syn. 1.** See **plenty.**

prog (prŏg), *n. Colloq.* proctor (def. 1).

Prog., Progressive.

prog., **1.** progress. **2.** progressive.

progenitive (prō jĕn′ĭ tĭv), *adj.* producing offspring; reproductive.

progenitor (prō jĕn′ĭ tə), *n.* **1.** a direct ancestor; forefather. **2.** an originator, as of an artistic movement. [ME *progenitour*, t. L: m. *prōgenitor*]

progeny (prŏj′ĭ nĭ), *n.*, *pl.* **-nies.** offspring; issue; descendants. [ME *progenie*, t. OF, t. L: m. *prōgenies*]

progesterone (prō jĕs′tə rōn′), *n. Biochem.* a hormone of the corpus luteum of the ovary, $C_{21}H_{30}O_2$, which prepares the uterus for the fertilized ovum and helps to maintain pregnancy. Also, **progestine** (prō jĕs′tĭn). [f. PRO-¹ + GE(STATION) + STER(OL) + -ONE]

proglottis (prō glŏt′ĭs), *n.*, *pl.* **-glottides** (-glŏt′ĭ dēz′). *Zool.* one of the segments or joints of a tapeworm, containing complete reproductive systems, usually both male and female. Also, **proglottid** (prō glŏt′ĭd). [t. NL, t. Gk: m. *proglōssis* point of the tongue (with reference to shape)] **—proglot′tic,** *adj.*

prognathous (prŏg nā′thəs), *adj.* **1.** (of a jaw) protruding; with a gnathic index over 103. **2.** (of a skull or a person) having protrusive jaws. Also, **prognathic** (prŏg năth′ĭk). [f. PRO-² + s. Gk *gnáthos* jaw + -OUS] **—prognathism** (prŏg′nə thĭz′əm), **prognathy** (prŏg′nə thĭ), *n.*

prognosis (prŏg nō′sĭs), *n.*, *pl.* **-noses** (-nō′sēz). *Med.* **1.** a forecasting of the probable course and termination of a disease. **2.** a particular forecast made. [t. LL, t. Gk: foreknowledge]

prognostic (prŏg nŏs′tĭk), *adj.* **1.** of or pertaining to prognosis. **2.** indicating something in the future. **—***n.* **3.** a forecast or prediction. **4.** a portent or omen. [t. L: s. *prognōsticon*, t. Gk: m. *prognōstikón* a prognostic; r. ME *pronostike*, t. F]

prognosticate (prŏg nŏs′tĭ kāt′), *v.*, **-cated, -cating.** **—***v.t.* **1.** to forecast or predict (something future) from present indications or signs; to prophesy. **—***v.i.* **2.** to make a forecast; to prophesy. **—prognosticative** (prŏg nŏs′tĭ kə tĭv), *adj.* **—prognos′tica′tor,** *n.*

prognostication (prŏg nŏs′tĭ kā′shən), *n.* **1.** the act of prognosticating. **2.** a forecast or prediction.

program (prō′grăm), *n.*, *v.*, **-grammed, -gramming** or (*U.S.*) **-gramed, -graming.** —*n.* **1.** *Computers.* See **computer program. 2.** *U.S.* a programme. —*v.t.* **3.** *Computers.* to organize and arrange (data, etc.) relevant to a problem so that it can be solved by a computer. **4.** *U.S.* to schedule as part of a programme. —*v.i.* **5.** *U.S.* to plan a programme.

programme (prō′grăm), *n.*, *v.*, **-grammed, -gramming.** —*n.* Also, *U.S.*, **program. 1.** a plan or policy to be followed. **2.** a list of things to be done; agenda. **3.** a list of items, pieces, performers, etc., in a musical, theatrical, or other entertainment; playbill. **4.** an entertainment with reference to its pieces or numbers. **5.** (in radio or television) a particular item or production. **6.** a prospectus or syllabus. —*v.t.*, *v.i.* **7.** program. [t. LL: m. *programma*, t. Gk: public notice in writing]

programmer (prŏ′grăm′ə), *n.* *Computers.* one who prepares data, etc., for a computer.

programme music, music intended to convey an impression of a definite series of images, scenes, or events (opposed to *absolute music*).

progress (*n.* prō′grĕs; *v.* prə grĕs′), *n.* **1.** a proceeding to a further or higher stage, or through such stages successively: *the progress of a scholar in his studies.* **2.** advancement in general. **3.** growth or development; continuous improvement. **4.** *Sociol.* the development of an individual or group in a direction considered as beneficial and to a degree greater than that yet attained. **5.** *Biol.* increasing differentiation and perfection in the course of ontogeny or phylogeny. **6.** forward or onward movement. **7.** course of action, of events, of time, etc. **8. in progress,** taking place; under way; happening. —*v.i.* **9.** to advance. **10.** to go forwards or onwards. [ME, t. L: s. *prōgressus* a going forward] —**Syn. 9.** develop, improve, grow.

progress chaser, a person employed to see that work is completed according to schedule, as in a factory, etc.

progression (prə grĕsh′ən), *n.* **1.** the act of progressing; forward or onward movement. **2.** a passing successively from one member of a series to the next; succession; sequence. **3.** *Astron.* (of a planet) direct, as opposed to retrograde, motion. **4.** *Maths.* a succession of quantities in which there is a constant relation between each member and the one succeeding it. Cf. **arithmetic progression** and **geometric progression. 5.** *Music.* the manner in which notes or chords follow one another. —**progres′sional,** *adj.*

progressionist (prə grĕsh′ə nĭst), *n.* one who believes in or advocates progress, as of mankind, society, etc. —**progres′sionism,** *n.*

progressist (prə grĕs′ĭst), *n.* one favouring progress, as in politics; a progressive.

progressive (prə grĕs′ĭv), *adj.* **1.** favouring or advocating progress, improvement, or reform, esp. in political matters. **2.** progressing or advancing; making progress towards better conditions, more enlightened or liberal ideas, the use of new and advantageous methods, etc.: *a progressive community.* **3.** characterized by such progress, or by continuous improvement. **4.** going forwards or onwards; passing successively from one member of a series to the next; proceeding step by step. **5.** denoting or pertaining to a form of taxation in which the rate increases with certain increases in the taxable income. **6.** *Gram.* denoting a verb aspect, or other verb category, which indicates action or state going on at a temporal point of reference: *the progressive form of 'is doing' in 'he is doing it'.* **7.** *Med.* continuously increasing in extent or severity, as a disease. —*n.* **8.** one who is progressive, or who favours progress or reform, esp. in political matters. **9.** *Gram.* the progressive aspect of a verb. —**progres′sively,** *adv.* —**progres′siveness,** *n.*

progressive jazz, any style of modern jazz which is marked by progressive characteristics, either in its use of unconventional instrumentation, harmony, or rhythm, or in a combination of these elements.

progressivism (prə grĕs′ĭ vĭz′əm), *n.* the principles and practices of progressives.

prohibit (prə hĭb′ĭt), *v.t.* **1.** to forbid (an action, a thing) by authority: *smoking is prohibited.* **2.** to forbid (a person) from doing something. **3.** to prevent; to hinder. [ME, t. L: s. *prohibitus*, pp., held back, restrained] —**Syn. 1.** See **forbid.**

prohibition (prō′ĭ bĭsh′ən), *n.* **1.** the act of prohibiting. **2.** a law or decree that forbids. **3.** the interdiction by law of the manufacture and sale of alcoholic drinks for common consumption, esp. in the U.S. between 1919 and 1933. —**Syn. 2.** interdiction.

prohibitionist (prō′ĭ bĭsh′ə nĭst), *n.* one who favours or advocates the prohibition of the manufacture and sale of alcoholic drinks for common consumption. —**pro′hibi′tionism,** *n.*

Prohibition Party, a U.S. political party advocating prohibition: founded 1869.

prohibitive (prə hĭb′ĭ tĭv), *adj.* **1.** that prohibits or forbids something. **2.** serving to prevent the use, purchase, etc., of something: *the prohibitive price of meat.* —**prohib′itively,** *adv.*

prohibitory (prə hĭb′ĭ tə rĭ, -trĭ), *adj.* prohibitive.

project (*n.* prŏj′ĕkt; *v.* prə jĕkt′), *n.* **1.** something that is contemplated, devised, or planned; a plan; a scheme; an undertaking. —*v.t.* **2.** to propose, contemplate, or plan. **3.** to throw, cast, or impel forwards or onwards. **4.** to set forth; present. **5.** to communicate; convey; make known (an idea, impression, etc.). **6.** to throw or cause to fall upon a surface or into space, as a ray of light, a shadow, etc. **7.** to cause (a figure or image) to appear as on a background. **8.** to visualize and regard (an idea, etc.) as an objective reality. **9.** to cause to jut out or protrude. **10.** to throw forwards (a figure, etc.) by straight lines or rays (parallel or from a centre) which pass through all points of it and reproduce it on a surface or other figure. **11.** to delineate by any system of correspondence between points. **12.** to transform the points of (one figure) into those of another by any correspondence between points. —*v.i.* **13.** to extend or protrude beyond something else. **14.** to communicate or convey an idea or impression. [ME, t. L: s. *prōjectum*, pp. neut., (thing) thrown out] —**Syn. 1.** See **plan.**

projectile (*n.* prŏj′ĭk tīl′, prə jĕk′tīl; *adj.* prə jĕk′tīl), *n.* **1.** *Mil.* an object fired from a gun with an explosive propelling charge, such as a bullet, shell, rocket, or grenade. **2.** an object set in motion by an exterior force which then continues to move by virtue of its own inertia. —*adj.* **3.** impelling or driving forwards, as a force. **4.** caused by impulse, as motion. **5.** capable of being impelled forwards, as a missile. **6.** *Zool.* protrusile, as the jaws of a fish. [t. NL, neut. of *prōjectilis*, adj., projecting]

projection (prə jĕk′shən), *n.* **1.** a projecting or protruding part. **2.** the state or fact of jutting out or protruding. **3.** a causing to jut out or protrude. **4.** *Geom., etc.* the act, process, or result of projecting. **5.** Also, **map projection.** *Cartog.* a systematic drawing of lines representing the meridians of longitude and parallels of latitude on a plane surface: on the grid or graticule so produced the earth's surface (or celestial sphere) or some portion of it may be drawn. **6.** *Photog.* **a.** the projection of an image by optical means, as in the projection of slides or films on to a screen or the making of enlargements. **b.** the image so formed. **7.** the act of visualizing and regarding an idea or the like as an objective reality. **8.** that which is so visualized and regarded. **9.** *Psychol.* **a.** the tendency to attribute to another person, or to the environment, what is actually within oneself. **b.** *Psychoanal.* (usually) such an attribution relieving the ego of guilt feelings. **10.** the act of planning or scheming. **11.** *Alchemy.* the casting of the powder of the philosopher's stone upon metal in fusion, to transmute it into gold or silver. [t. L: s. *prōjectio*]

projectionist (prə jĕk′shə nĭst), *n.* one who operates a cinema projector.

projective (prə jĕk′tĭv), *adj.* **1.** of or pertaining to projection. **2.** produced, or capable of being produced, by projection. **3.** *Psychol.* **a.** pertaining to projection. **b.** of, pertaining to, or denoting a technique for revealing the hidden motives or underlying personality structure of an individual by using certain test materials that allow him to express himself freely. —**projectivity** (prŏj′ĕk tĭv′ĭ tĭ), *n.*

projective geometry, the geometric study of projective properties.

projective property, a geometric property which is unaltered by projection.

projector (prə jĕk′tə), *n.* **1.** an apparatus for throwing an image on a screen, as of a slide; a film projector, etc. **2.** a device for projecting a beam of light. **3.** one who forms projects or plans; a schemer.

projet (prōzh′ā; *Fr.* prō zhĕ′), *n.* **1.** a project. **2.** a draft of a proposed treaty or other instrument. [F. See PROJECT, n.]

Prokofiev (prə kŏf′ĭ ĕf′; *Russ.* prä kôf′yĭf), *n.* **Sergei Sergeevich** (*Russ.* sĭr gyĕy′ sĭr gyĕ′yĭ vĭch), 1891–1953, Russian composer.

Prokopievsk (*Russ.* prä kôp′yĭfsk), *n.* a town in the S Soviet Union in Asia, SE of Novosibirsk. 291,000 (est. 1965).

prolactin (prō lăk′tĭn), *n.* *Biochem.* an anterior pituitary hormone which regulates milk secretion in mammals and the activity of the crop glands in birds.

prolamine (prō′lə mēn′, -mĭn), *n.* *Biochem.* one of a group of water-insoluble proteins which are soluble in 70–90 per cent alcohol.

prolapse (*n.* prō′lăps; *v.* prō lăps′), *n.*, *v.*, **-lapsed, -lapsing.** —*n.* Also, **prolapsus** (prō lăp′səs). **1.** *Pathol.* a falling down of an organ or part, as the uterus, from its normal position. —*v.i.* **2.** *Chiefly Pathol.* to fall or slip down or out of place. [t. LL: m. s. *prōlapsus* a falling down]

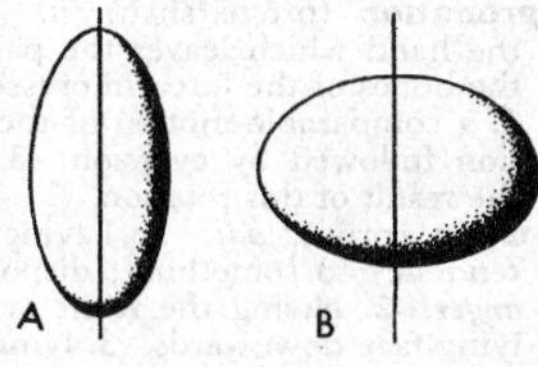

Spheroids
A, Prolate; B, Oblate

prolate (prō′lāt), *adj.* elongated along the polar diameter, as a spheroid generated by the revolution of an ellipse about its longer axis (opposed to *oblate*). [t. L: m. s. *prōlātus*, pp., brought forward, extended]

prole (prōl), *n. Colloq.* a member of the proletariat.

proleg (prō′lĕg′), *n.* one of the abdominal ambulatory processes of caterpillars and other larvae, as distinct from the true or thoracic legs. [f. PRO-[1] + LEG]

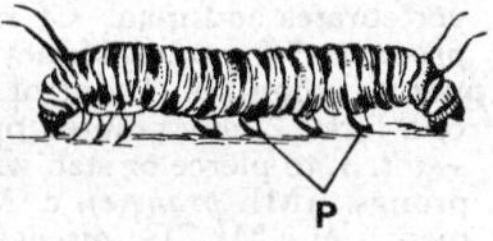

P, Prolegs of larva of monarch butterfly, *Danaus menippe*

prolegomenon (prō′lĕ gŏm′ĭ nən), *n., pl.* **-gomena** (-gŏm′ĭ nə). a preliminary observation, as on the subject of a book (usually pl., as applied to an introduction to a book). [t. NL, t. Gk: (neut. ppr. pass.) being said beforehand]

prolegomenous (prō′lĕ gŏm′ĭ nəs), *adj.* **1.** prefatory; preliminary. **2.** characterized by unnecessary or lengthy prologuizing.

prolepsis (prō lĕp′sĭs), *n., pl.* **-ses** (-sēz). **1.** *Rhet.* an anticipation of objections in order to answer them in advance. **2.** the assigning of an event, etc., to a period earlier than its actual date. **3.** the use of an epithet in anticipation of its becoming applicable. [t. L, t. Gk: anticipation, preconception] —**prolep′tic,** *adj.*

proletarian (prō′lĭ tĕə′rĭ ən), *adj.* **1.** pertaining or belonging to the proletariat. **2.** (in ancient Rome) belonging to the lowest or poorest class of people. —*n.* **3.** a member of the proletariat. [f. s. L *prōlētārius* a Roman citizen of the lowest class + -AN]

proletariat (prō′lĭ tĕə′rĭ ət), *n.* **1.** the unpropertied class; that class which is dependent for support on the sale of its labour. **2.** the working class, or wage-earners in general. [t. F, f. s. L *prōlētārius* a Roman citizen of the lowest class + *-at* -ATE[3]]

proletary (prō′lĭ tə rĭ), *adj., n., pl.* **-ries.** proletarian.

proliferate (prə lĭf′ə rāt′), *v.i., v.t.,* **-rated, -rating.** to grow or produce by multiplication of parts, as in budding or cell division. —**prolif′era′tion,** *n.*

proliferous (prə lĭf′ə rəs), *adj.* **1.** proliferating. **2.** *Bot.* **a.** producing new individuals by budding or the like. **b.** producing an organ or shoot from an organ which is itself normally the last, as a shoot or a new flower from the midst of a flower. [f. ML *prōlifer* (f. L *prōli-* offspring + *-fer* bearing) + -OUS]

prolific (prə lĭf′ĭk), *adj.* **1.** producing offspring, young, fruit, etc., esp. abundantly; fruitful. **2.** producing much or abundantly: *a prolific writer.* **3.** abundantly productive of or fruitful in something specified. **4.** characterized by, involving, or causing abundant production. [t. ML: s. *prōlificus,* f. L *prōli-* offspring + *-ficus* -FIC] —**prolificacy** (prə lĭf′ĭ kə sĭ), **prolif′icness,** *n.* —**prolif′ically,** *adv.*

proline (prō′lēn, -lĭn), *n. Biochem.* an alcohol-soluble amino acid, NHC_4H_7COOH, found in all proteins. [contr. of *pyrroline,* f. PYRROLE + -INE[2]]

prolix (prō′lĭks), *adj.* **1.** extended to great, unnecessary, or tedious length; long and wordy. **2.** speaking or writing at great or tedious length. [ME, t. L: s. *prōlixus* extended, long] —**prolixity** (prō lĭk′sĭ tĭ), **prolix′ness,** *n.* —**prolix′ly,** *adv.*

prolocutor (prō lŏk′yŏŏ tə), *n.* **1.** a presiding officer of an assembly; a chairman. **2.** *C. of E.* the chairman of the lower house of a convocation. [t. L] —**proloc′utorship′,** *n.*

prologue (prō′lŏg), *n., v.,* **-logued, -loguing.** —*n.* **1.** an introductory speech, often in verse, calling attention to the theme of a play. **2.** the actor who delivers it. **3.** an introductory act of a dramatic performance. **4.** a preliminary discourse; a preface or introductory part of a discourse, poem, or novel. **5.** any introductory proceeding, event, etc. —*v.t.* **6.** to introduce with, or as with, a prologue. [ME *prolog,* t. L: s. *prōlogus,* t. Gk: m. *prólogos*]

prologuize (prō′lŏ gīz′), *v.i.,* **-gized, -gizing.** to compose or deliver a prologue. Also, **prologize** (prō′lŏ gīz′), **prologuise.** —**pro′loguiz′er,** *n.*

prolong (prə lŏng′), *v.t.* **1.** to lengthen out in time; to extend the duration of; to cause to continue longer: *to prolong one's life.* **2.** to make longer in spatial extent: *to prolong a line.* [late ME *prolonge(n),* t. LL: m. *prolongāre*] —**prolong′er,** *n.* —**prolong′ment,** *n.* —**Syn. 1.** See **lengthen.**

prolongate (prō′lŏng gāt′), *v.t.,* **-gated, -gating.** *Rare.* to prolong.

prolongation (prō′lŏng gā′shən), *n.* **1.** the act of prolonging: *the prolongation of a line.* **2.** the state of being prolonged. **3.** a prolonged or extended form. **4.** an added part.

prolonge (prə lŏnj′; *Fr.* prŏ lôNzh′), *n. Mil.* a rope having a hook at one end and a toggle at the other, used for various purposes, as to draw a guncarriage. [t. F, der. *prolonger* PROLONG]

prolusion (prə lōō′zhən), *n.* **1.** a preliminary written article. **2.** an essay preliminary to a more profound work, or of an introductory or slight nature. [t. L: s. *prōlūsio* preliminary exercise]

prolusory (prə lōō′sə rĭ), *adj.* **1.** serving for prolusion. **2.** of the nature of a prolusion.

prom (prŏm), *n.* **1.** a promenade concert. **2.** *U.S. Colloq.* a formal dance, esp. at a school or college. [short for PROMENADE]

prom., promontory.

pro memoria (prō′mĕ mô′rĭ ə), *Latin.* for memory (used in diplomacy to recall rights which have lapsed for a long time).

promenade (prŏm′ĭ näd′; prŏm′ĭ näd′ *for defs 3, 5, and 8*), *n., v.,* **-naded, -nading.** —*n.* **1.** a walk, esp. in a public place, as for pleasure or display. **2.** an area suitable for leisurely walking, esp. one along the seafront at a seaside resort; esplanade. **3.** a march of dancers in folk or square-dancing. —*v.i.* **4.** to take a promenade. **5.** to dance a promenade. —*v.t.* **6.** to take a promenade through or about. **7.** to take or conduct on or as on a promenade; parade. **8.** to dance (a promenade). [t. F, der. *promener* lead out, take for a walk or airing] —**prom′enad′er,** *n.*

promenade concert, a concert at which part of the audience have no seats, and stand or move about.

promenade deck, a deck on a liner for use as a promenade by the passengers.

Promethean (prə mē′thyən), *adj.* **1.** of or suggestive of Prometheus. **2.** creative; boldly original. —*n.* **3.** one who resembles Prometheus in spirit or actions.

Prometheus (prə mē′thyōōs), *n. Gk Myth.* a Titan fabled to have made men out of clay, to have stolen fire for them from Olympus, and to have taught them various arts, in punishment for which he was chained by order of Zeus to a rock in the Caucasus, where his liver was daily gnawed by a vulture. He was freed when Hercules killed the vulture.

promethium (prə mē′thyəm), *n. Chem.* a radioactive, rare-earth, metallic, trivalent element. *Symbol:* Pm; *at. no.:* 61.

prominence (prŏm′ĭ nəns), *n.* **1.** Also, **prominency.** the state of being prominent; conspicuousness. **2.** that which is prominent; a projection or protuberance: *the prominence of a rock or cliff, the prominences of a face.* **3.** *Astron.* a cloud of gas high above the surface of the sun, especially when seen in silhouette at the sun's edge.

prominent (prŏm′ĭ nənt), *adj.* **1.** standing out so as to be easily seen; conspicuous; especially noticeable: *a prominent feature.* **2.** standing out beyond the adjacent surface or line; projecting. **3.** important; leading; well-known: *a prominent citizen.* [t. L: s. *prōminens,* ppr., jutting out] —**prom′inently,** *adv.*

promiscuity (prŏm′ĭs kyōō′ĭ tĭ), *n., pl.* **-ties.** **1.** the state of being promiscuous. **2.** promiscuous sexual union. **3.** indiscriminate mixture.

promiscuous (prə mĭs′kyŏŏ əs), *adj.* **1.** characterized by or involving indiscriminate mingling or association, esp. indulging in sexual intercourse with a number of partners. **2.** consisting of parts, elements, or individuals of different kinds brought together without order. **3.** indiscriminate; without discrimination. **4.** casual; without particular plan or reason. [t. L: m. *prōmiscuus*] —**promis′cuously,** *adv.* —**promis′cuousness,** *n.* —**Syn. 2.** See **miscellaneous.**

promise (prŏm′ĭs), *n., v.,* **-ised, -ising.** —*n.* **1.** a declaration made, as to another person, with respect to the future, giving assurance that one will do, not do, give, not give, etc., something. **2.** an express assurance on which expectation is to be based. **3.** something that has the effect of an express assurance; indication of what may be expected. **4.** indication of future excellence or achievement: *a writer that shows promise.* **5.** that which is promised. —*v.t.* **6.** to engage or undertake by promise (with an infinitive or a clause): *to promise not to interfere.* **7.** to make a promise of: *to promise help.* **8.** to make a promise of (something) to. **9.** to afford ground for expecting. **10.** to engage to join in marriage. **11.** to assure (used in emphatic declarations). —*v.i.* **12.** to afford ground for expectation (often fol. by *well* or *fair*). **13.** to make a promise. [ME, t. L: m. s. *prōmissum* a promise, prop. neut. pp. of *prōmittere* to promise] —**prom′iser;** *Law,* **promisor** (prŏm′ĭ sôr′), *n.*

Promised Land, 1. Canaan; the land promised by God to Abraham and his descendants. Gen. 12:7. **2.** Heaven.

promisee (prŏm′ĭ sē′), *n. Law.* one to whom a promise is made.

promising (prŏm′ĭ sĭng), *adj.* giving promise; likely to turn out well: *a promising young man.* —**prom′isingly,** *adv.*

promissory (prŏm′ĭ sə rĭ), *adj.* **1.** containing or implying a promise. **2.** of the nature of a promise. **3.** *Insurance.* of or denoting preliminary agreements and representations, made in drawing up a contract of insurance. [t. ML: m. s. *prōmissōrius,* der. L *prōmissor*]

promissory note, a written promise to pay a specified sum of money to a person designated or to his order, or to the bearer, at a time fixed or on demand.

promontory (prŏm′ən trĭ), *n., pl.* **-ries. 1.** a high point of land or rock projecting into the sea or other water beyond the line of coast; a headland. **2.** *Anat.* a prominent or protuberant part. [t. ML: m. s. *prōmontōrium,* for L *prōmunturium*]

promote (prə mōt′), *v.t.,* **-moted, -moting. 1.** to advance in rank, dignity, position, etc. **2.** to further the growth, development, progress, etc., of; encourage. **3.** to help to found; originate; organize; launch (a financial undertaking, publicity campaign, etc.). [ME, t. L: m. s. *prōmōtus,* pp., moved forward, advanced]

promoter (prə mō′tə), *n.* **1.** one who initiates or takes part in the organizing of a company, development of a project, etc. **2.** one who or that which promotes. **3.** *Chem.* a substance which increases the activity of a catalyst. **4.** *Obs.* an informer.

promotion (prə mō′shən), *n.* **1.** advancement in rank or position. **2.** furtherance or encouragement. **3.** the act of promoting. **4.** the state of being promoted.

promotive (prə mō′tĭv), *adj.* tending to promote.

prompt (prŏmpt), *adj.* **1.** done, performed, delivered, etc., at once or without delay: *a prompt reply.* **2.** ready in action; quick to act as occasion demands. **3.** ready and willing. —*v.t.* **4.** to move or incite to action. **5.** to suggest or induce (action, etc.); inspire or occasion. **6.** to assist (a person speaking) by suggesting something to be said. **7.** *Theat.* to supply (an actor or reciter) with his cue from offstage if he has missed it, or his line if he has forgotten it. —*v.i.* **8.** *Theat.* to supply offstage cues and effects. —*n.* **9.** *Com.* **a.** a limit of time given for payment for merchandise purchased, the limit being stated on a note of reminder called a **prompt note. b.** the contract setting the time limit. **10.** the act of prompting. **11.** something that prompts. [ME, t. L: s. *promptus,* pp., taken out, at hand] —**prompt′ly,** *adv.* —**prompt′ness,** *n.*

prompt-book (prŏmpt′bŏŏk′), *n. Theat.* the script of a play, containing cues, etc., used by a prompter.

prompt-box (prŏmpt′bŏks′), *n. Theat.* the place where a prompter sits.

prompt-copy (prŏmpt′kŏp′ĭ), *n.* a prompt-book.

prompter (prŏmp′tə), *n.* **1.** *Theat.* one who follows offstage a play in progress from the book, to repeat missed cues and supply actors with forgotten lines. **2.** one who or that which prompts.

promptitude (prŏmp′tĭ tyōōd′), *n.* promptness. [late ME, t. LL: m. *promptitūdō*]

prompt neutron, *Physics.* a neutron emitted during a nuclear fission process without measurable delay, i.e., in less than a millionth of a second.

prompt-side (prŏmpt′sīd′), *n. Theat.* that part of the stage to the actor's left as he faces the audience.

promulgate (prŏm′əl gāt′), *v.t.,* **-gated, -gating. 1.** to make known by open declaration; to publish; to proclaim formally or put into operation (a law or rule of court or decree). **2.** to set forth or teach publicly (a creed, doctrine, etc.). [t. L: m. s. *prōmulgātus,* pp., made publicly known, published] —**promulgation** (prŏm′əl gā′shən), *n.* —**promulgator** (prŏm′əl gā′tə), *n.*

promulge (prō mŭlj′), *v.t.,* **-mulged, -mulging.** *Archaic.* to promulgate.

promycelium (prō′mī sē′lyəm), *n., pl.* **-lia** (-lyə). *Bot.* a short filament produced in the germination of a spore, which bears small spores and then dies. —**pro′myce′lial,** *adj.*

pron., 1. pronominal. **2.** pronoun. **3.** pronounced. **4.** pronunciation.

pronate (prō nāt′), *v.,* **-nated, -nating.** *Physiol.* —*v.t.* **1.** to render prone; to rotate or place (the hand or forearm) so that the surface of the palm is downward when the limb is stretched forward horizontally. Cf. **supinate.** —*v.i.* **2.** to become pronated. [t. LL: s. *prōnātus,* pp., bent forward, der. L *prōnus* PRONE] —**prona′tor,** *n.*

pronation (prō nā′shən), *n. Physiol.* **1.** a rotation of the hand which leaves the palm facing downwards and the bones of the forearm crossed (opposed to *supination*). **2.** a comparable motion of the foot consisting of abduction followed by eversion. **3.** the position assumed as the result of this rotation.

prone (prōn), *adj.* **1.** having a natural inclination or tendency to something; disposed; liable: *to be prone to anger.* **2.** having the front or ventral part downwards; lying face downwards. **3.** lying flat; prostrate. **4.** having a downward direction or slope. **5.** having the palm downwards, as the hand. [ME, t. L: m. s. *prōnus* turned or leaning forwards, inclined downwards, disposed, prone] —**prone′ly,** *adv.* —**prone′ness,** *n.*

pronephros (prō nĕf′rŏs), *n. Embryol.* a primitive kidney functioning in lower vertebrates but vestigial in higher vertebrates and man. Cf. **mesonephros.** [t. NL, f. Gk: *pro-* PRO-[2] + *nephrós* kidney]

prong (prŏng), *n.* **1.** one of the pointed divisions or tines of a fork. **2.** any pointed projecting part, as of an antler. —*v.t.* **3.** to pierce or stab with a prong. **4.** to supply with prongs. [ME *prang(e),* c. MLG *prange* pinching instrument; cf. ML G *pfrengen* press, Goth. *anaprangan* oppress]

pronged (prŏngd), *adj.* having prongs.

pronghorn (prŏng′hôn′), *n.* a fleet, antelope-like ruminant, *Antilocapra americana,* of the plains of western North America.

Pronghorn, *Antilocapra americana* (3 ft high at the shoulder, length 5½ ft)

pronk (prŏngk), *v.i. S African.* to make a series of spirited leaps and bounds, as springboks at certain seasons of the year. [t. Afrikaans: show off]

pronominal (prō nŏm′ĭ nəl), *adj.* pertaining to or having the nature of a pronoun. [t. LL: s. *prōnōminālis,* der. L *prōnōmen* pronoun] —**pronom′inally,** *adv.*

pronoun (prō′noun′), *n. Gram.* **1.** (in many languages) one of the major form classes, or parts of speech, comprising words used as substitutes for nouns. **2.** any such word, as *I, you, he, this, who, what.* **3.** a word of similar function or meaning, whether member of a special form class or not. [t. F: m. *pronom,* t. L: m. *prōnōmen*]

pronounce (prə nouns′), *v.,* **-nounced, -nouncing.** —*v.t.* **1.** to enunciate or articulate (words, etc.). **2.** to utter or sound in a particular manner in speaking. **3.** to declare (a person or thing) to be as specified. **4.** to utter or deliver formally or solemnly. **5.** to announce authoritatively or officially. —*v.i.* **6.** to pronounce words, etc. **7.** to make a statement or assertion, esp. an authoritative statement (often fol. by *on*). **8.** to give an opinion or decision (usually fol. by *on*). [ME, t. OF: m. *prononcier,* t. L: m. *prōnuntiāre* proclaim, announce, recite, utter] —**pronounce′able,** *adj.* —**pronounc′er,** *n.*

pronounced (prə nounst′), *adj.* **1.** strongly marked. **2.** clearly indicated. **3.** decided; definite: *to have very pronounced views.* —**pronouncedly** (prə nounst′lĭ), *adv.*

pronouncement (prə nouns′mənt), *n.* **1.** a formal or authoritative statement. **2.** an opinion or decision. **3.** the act of pronouncing.

pronto (prŏn′tō), *adv. Slang.* promptly; quickly. [t. Sp. (adj. and adv.), g. L *promptus.* See PROMPT]

pronucleus (prō nyōō′klĭ əs), *n., pl.* **-clei** (-klĭ ī′). *Embryol.* either of the gametic nuclei which after fertilization unite and form a double nucleus.

pronunciamento (prə nŭn′sĭ ə mĕn′tō), *n., pl.* **-tos.** a proclamation; manifesto. [t. Sp.: f. *pronuncia(r)* (t. L: m. *prōnuntiāre* proclaim) + *-mento* (noun suffix)]

pronunciation (prə nŭn′sĭ ā′shən), *n.* the act or the result of producing the sounds of speech, including articulation, vowel and consonant formation, accent, inflection, and intonation, often with reference to the correctness or acceptability of the speech sounds. [ME, t. L: m. s. *prōnuntiātio*] —**pronun′cia′tional,** *adj.*

proof (prōōf), *n.* **1.** evidence sufficient to establish a thing as true, or to produce belief in its truth. **2.** anything serving as such evidence. **3.** the act of testing or making trial of anything; test; a trial: *to put a thing to the proof.* **4.** the establishment of the truth of anything; demonstration. **5.** *Law.* (in judicial proceedings) evidence having probative weight. **6.** the effect of evidence in convincing the mind. **7.** an arithmetical operation serving to check the correctness of a calculation. **8.** a test to determine the quality, etc., of materials used in manufacture. **9.** the state of having been tested and approved. **10.** proved strength, as of armour. **11. a.** the arbitrary standard strength, as of alcoholic liquors. **b.** strength with reference to this standard, indicated on a scale on which '100 proof' signifies a proof spirit. **12.** *Photog.* a trial print from a negative. **13.** *Print.* **a.** a trial impression as of composed type, taken to correct errors and make alterations. **b.** one of a number of early and superior impressions taken before the printing of the ordinary issue. **14.** *Engraving, etc.* an impression taken from a plate or the like to show its state during the process of execution. *—adj.* **15.** impenetrable, impervious, or invulnerable: *proof against temptation.* **16.** of tested or proved strength or quality: *proof armour.* **17.** used for testing or proving; serving as proof. **18.** of standard strength, as an alcoholic liquor. *—v.t.* **19.** to treat or coat (a material) in order to make it resistant to deterioration or damage, impervious to water, etc. **20.** *Print., etc.* to take a trial impression of (type, etc.). [ME *preove,* t. OF: m. *prueve,* g. LL *proba* proof, der. L *probāre* PROVE] **—Syn. 1.** See **evidence.**

-proof, a suffix meaning 'insulated from', 'impervious to', 'not affected by', etc., as in *waterproof.*

proofing (pro͞o′fĭng), *n.* **1.** the act or process of making a thing resistant to deterioration, damage, etc. **2.** a chemical used in manufacture to make materials waterproof.

proofread (pro͞of′rēd′), *v.t., v.i.,* **-read, -reading.** to read (printers' proofs, etc.) in order to detect and mark errors to be corrected. **—proof′read′er,** *n.* **—proof′read′ing,** *n.*

proof sheet, a printer's proof.

proof spirit, 1. an alcoholic liquor, or mixture of alcohol and water, containing 49·28 per cent ethyl alcohol by weight or 57·10 per cent by volume, and having a specific gravity of 0·91976 at 60°F. **2.** *U.S.* one having 50 per cent alcohol by volume and a specific gravity of 0·93353.

prop[1] (prŏp), *v.,* **propped, propping,** *n.* *—v.t.* **1.** to support, or prevent from falling, with or as with a prop (often fol. by *up*): *to prop a roof.* **2.** to rest (a thing) against support. **3.** to support or sustain. *—n.* **4.** a stick, rod, pole, beam, or other rigid support. **5.** a person or thing serving as a support or stay. [ME *proppe,* c. MD *proppe* prop, support; orig. uncert.]

prop[2] (prŏp), *n.* *Theat.* property (def. 8).

prop[3] (prŏp), *n.* *Colloq.* a propeller.

prop[4] (prŏp), *v.i.* *Austral., N.Z.* to stop suddenly and change direction.

prop., 1. properly. **2.** property. **3.** proposition.

propaedeutic (prō′pē dyo͞o′tĭk), *adj.* Also, **pro′paedeu′tical. 1.** pertaining to or of the nature of preliminary instruction. **2.** introductory to some art or science. *—n.* **3.** a propaedeutic subject or study. **4.** (*pl.*) the preliminary body of knowledge and rules necessary for the study of some art or science. [f. PRO-[2] beforehand + m. s. Gk *paideutikós* pertaining to teaching]

propagable (prŏp′ə gə bl), *adj.* capable of being propagated.

propaganda (prŏp′ə găn′də), *n.* **1.** false, distorted, or misleading information, rumours, etc. deliberately spread in order to help or harm a person, group, institution, country, etc. **2.** the deliberate spreading of such information, rumours, etc. **3.** the particular doctrines or principles propagated by an organization or movement. **4. College of Propaganda,** a committee of cardinals, established in 1622 by Pope Gregory XV, having supervision of the foreign missions of the Roman Catholic Church and of the training of priests for these missions. [t. NL: short for *congregātio dē propāgandā fidē* congregation for propagating the faith]

propagandism (prŏp′ə găn′dĭz′əm), *n.* zealous propagation of particular doctrines or principles.

propagandist (prŏp′ə găn′dĭst), *n.* **1.** one devoted to the propagation of particular doctrines or principles. *—adj.* **2.** pertaining to propaganda or propagandists.

propagandize (prŏp′ə găn′dīz), *v.,* **-dized, -dizing.** *—v.t.* **1.** to propagate or spread (principles, etc.) by propaganda. *—v.i.* **2.** to spread propaganda. Also, **propagandise.**

propagate (prŏp′ə gāt′), *v.,* **-gated, -gating.** *—v.t.* **1.** to cause (plants, animals, etc.) to multiply by any process of natural reproducing from the parent stock. **2.** to reproduce (itself, its kind, etc.), as a plant or an animal does. **3.** to transmit (traits, etc.) in reproduction, or through offspring. **4.** to spread (a report, doctrine, practice, etc.) from person to person; disseminate. **5.** to cause to increase in number or amounts. **6.** to cause to extend to a greater distance, or transmit through space or a medium: *to propagate sound.* *—v.i.* **7.** to multiply by any process of natural reproduction, as plants or animals; to breed. [t. L: m. s. *propāgātus,* pp., propagated (orig. referring to plants by layers or slips)] **—prop′aga′tive,** *adj.* **—prop′aga′tor,** *n.*

propagation (prŏp′ə gā′shən), *n.* **1.** the act of propagating. **2.** the fact of being propagated. **3.** multiplication by natural reproduction. **4.** transmission; dissemination.

propane (prō′pān), *n.* *Chem.* a gaseous hydrocarbon, C_3H_8, of the methane series, found in petroleum. [f. PROP(IONIC) + -ANE]

propanol (prō′pə nōl′), *n.* *Chem.* propyl alcohol.

proparoxytone (prō′pə rŏk′sĭ tōn′), *Class. Gk Gram.* *—adj.* **1.** having an acute accent on the antepenultimate syllable. *—n.* **2.** a proparoxytone word. [t. Gk: m. s. *proparoxýtonos*] **—proparoxytonic** (prō′pə rŏk′sĭ tŏn′ĭk), *adj.*

pro patria (prō′ păt′rĭ ä′), *Latin.* for one's country.

propel (prə pĕl′), *v.t.,* **-pelled, -pelling. 1.** to drive, or cause to move, forwards: *a boat propelled by oars.* **2.** to impel or urge onwards. [t. L: m. s. *prōpellere*]

propellant (prə pĕl′ənt), *n.* **1.** a propelling agent. **2.** *Mil.* the charge of explosive used in a gun to fire the projectile. **3.** *Aeron.* one or more substances used in rocket motors for the chemical generation of gas at the controlled rates required to provide thrust. **4.** the compressed gas used in an aerosol container to expel the liquid product through a fine jet, in the form of a spray.

propellent (prə pĕl′ənt), *adj.* **1.** propelling; driving forward. *—n.* **2.** a propelling agent.

propeller (prə pĕl′ə), *n.* **1.** a device having a revolving hub with radiating blades, for propelling a ship, aircraft, etc. **2.** one who or that which propels.

propend (prō pĕnd′), *v.i.* *Obs.* to incline or tend. [t. L: s. *prōpendēre*]

propene (prō′pēn), *n.* *Chem.* propylene.

propenol (prō′pĭ nōl′), *n.* *Chem.* allyl alcohol.

propensity (prə pĕn′sĭ tĭ), *n., pl.* **-ties. 1.** natural or habitual inclination or tendency: *a propensity to find fault.* **2.** *Obs.* favourable disposition or partiality. Also, *Rare,* **propension** (prə pĕn′shən).

proper (prŏp′ə), *adj.* **1.** adapted or appropriate to the purpose or circumstances; fit; suitable: *the proper time to plant.* **2.** conforming to established standards of behaviour or manners; correct or decorous. **3.** fitting; right. **4.** strictly belonging or applicable: *the proper place for a stove.* **5.** belonging or pertaining exclusively or distinctly to a person or thing. **6.** strict; accurate. **7.** strictly so-called; in the strict sense of the word (now usually following the noun): *shellfish do not belong to the fishes proper.* **8.** *Gram.* **a.** (of a name, noun, or adjective) designating a particular person or thing, written in English with an initial capital letter: *John, London, Monday, French.* **b.** having the force or function of a proper name: *a proper adjective.* **9.** normal or regular. **10.** *Her.* (of an object used as a bearing) represented in its natural colour or colours: *an eagle proper.* **11.** *Eccles.* used only on a particular day or festival: *the proper introit.* **12.** *Colloq.* complete or thorough: *a proper thrashing.* **13.** *Archaic or Dial.* **a.** excellent; capital; fine. **b.** good-looking or handsome. **14.** *Archaic.* belonging to oneself or itself; own. **15.** *Archaic.* of good character; respectable. *—n.* **16.** *Eccles.* a special office or special parts of an office appointed for a particular day or time. [ME *propre,* t. OF, t. L: m. s. *proprius* one's own]

proper fraction, *Maths.* a fraction having the numerator less, or lower in degree, than the denominator.

properly (prŏp′ə lĭ), *adv.* **1.** in a proper manner. **2.** correctly. **3.** appropriately. **4.** decorously. **5.** accurately. **6.** justifiably. **7.** *Colloq.* completely.

proper motion, *Astron.* the component of a star's motion in space which is perpendicular to the line of sight.

proper name. See **name** (def. 9).

proper noun, *Gram.* a noun that is not usually preceded by an article or other limiting modifier, in meaning applicable only to a single person or thing, or to several persons or things which constitute a unique class only by virtue of having the same name: *Gladstone, London,* in contrast to *man, city.* See **common noun.**

propertied (prŏp′ə tĭd), *adj.* owning property.

Propertius (prə pû′shyəs), *n.* **Sextus** (sĕk′stəs), *c.* 50–*c.* 15 B.C., Roman poet.

property (prŏp′ə tĭ), *n., pl.* **-ties. 1.** that which one owns; the possession or possessions of a particular owner. **2.** goods, lands, etc., owned: *a man of property.* **3.** a piece of land owned: *property in Chelsea.* **4.** ownership; right of possession, enjoyment, or disposal of anything, esp. of something tangible: *to have property in land.* **5.** something at the disposal of a person, a group of persons, or the community or public: *the secret became common property.* **6.** an essential or distinctive attribute or quality of a thing. **7.** *Logic.* **a.** any attribute or characteristic. **b.** (according to Aristotelian usage) one of the five ways in which a predicate can be related to a subject. **8.** Also, **prop.** *Theat.* an item of furniture, ornament, or decoration in a stage setting; any object handled or used by an actor in performance. [ME *proprete*, f. *propre* PROPER (defs 5 and 14) + *-te* -TY[2]]

—**Syn. 1.** PROPERTY, CHATTELS, EFFECTS, ESTATE, GOODS are terms for material things which are owned. PROPERTY is the general word: *he owns a great deal of property (land, etc.); he said that the umbrella was his property.* CHATTELS is a term for pieces of personal property or movable possessions; it may be applied to livestock, motor vehicles, etc.: *his goods and chattels.* EFFECTS is a legal term for personal property, including even things of the least value: *all his effects were insured against fire.* ESTATE refers to property of any kind which has been, or is capable of being handed down to descendants or disposed of otherwise in a will: *he left most of his estate to his nephew.* It may consist of personal estate (money, valuables, securities, chattels, etc.), or real estate (land and buildings). GOODS refers to household possessions or other movable property, esp. that comprising the stock in trade of a business: *a store arranges its goods conveniently for sale.* **6.** See **quality.**

property man, *Theat.* a man in charge of stage properties.

prophase (prō′fāz′), *n. Biol.* the first stage of mitosis during which the chromosomes progressively contract and become thicker and the nuclear membrane begins to disappear.

prophecy (prŏf′ĭ sĭ), *n., pl.* **-cies. 1.** foretelling or prediction (orig. by divine inspiration) of what is to come. **2.** that which is declared by a prophet; a prediction. **3.** divinely inspired utterance or revelation. **4.** the action, function, or faculty of a prophet. [ME *prophecie*, t. OF, t. LL: m. *prophētia*, t. Gk: m. *prophēteía*]

prophesy (prŏf′ĭ sī′), *v.,* **-sied, -sying.** —*v.t.* **1.** to foretell or predict: *to prophesy a storm.* **2.** to indicate beforehand. **3.** to declare or foretell by or as by divine inspiration. **4.** to utter in prophecy or as a prophet. —*v.i.* **5.** to make predictions. **6.** to make inspired declarations of what is to come. **7.** to speak as a mediator between God and man or in God's stead. **8.** to teach religious subjects or material. [v. use of and var. of PROPHECY] —**proph′esi′er,** *n.* —**Syn. 1.** See **predict.**

prophet (prŏf′ĭt), *n.* **1.** one who speaks for God or a deity, or by divine inspiration. **2.** a member of a recognized order in the early Church, inspired to utter revelations and predictions. 1 Cor. 12: 28. **3. the Prophet, a.** Mohammed, the founder of Islam. See **Koran. b.** *Mormon Ch.* Joseph Smith. **4. the Prophets,** the books which form the second of the three Jewish divisions of the Old Testament, comprising **a.** Joshua, Judges, I and II Samuel, and I and II Kings; **b.** Isaiah, Jeremiah, and Ezekiel (**Major Prophets**); **c.** Hosea, Joel, Amos, Obadiah, Jonah, Micah, Nahum, Habakkuk, Zephaniah, Haggai, Zechariah, and Malachi (**Minor Prophets**). Group **a** is called the **Former Prophets;** groups **b** and **c** together the **Latter Prophets.** Cf. **law** (def. 17), **Hagiographa. 5.** one regarded as, or claiming to be, an inspired teacher or leader. **6.** one who foretells or predicts what is to come: *a weather prophet.* **7.** a spokesman or proclaimer of some doctrine, cause, or the like. [ME *prophete*, t. L: m. *prophēta*, t. Gk: m. *prophḗtēs* spokesman, interpreter, prophet] —**prophetess** (prŏf′ĭ tĭs), *n. fem.* —**proph′ethood′,** *n.*

prophetic (prə fĕ′tĭk), *adj.* **1.** of or pertaining to a prophet: *prophetic inspiration.* **2.** of the nature of or containing prophecy: *prophetic writings.* **3.** having the function or powers of a prophet, as a person. **4.** predictive; presageful; ominous. Also, **prophetical.** —**prophet′ically,** *adv.*

prophylactic (prŏf′ĭ lăk′tĭk), *adj.* **1.** defending or protecting from disease, as a drug. **2.** preventive; preservative; protective. —*n.* **3.** a prophylactic medicine or measure. **4.** a contraceptive. [t. Gk: m. s. *prophylaktikós*]

prophylaxis (prŏf′ĭ lăk′sĭs), *n.* **1.** the preventing of disease. **2.** the prevention of a specific disease, as by studying the biological behaviour, transmission, etc., of its causative agent and applying a series of measures against it. **3.** prophylactic treatment. [t. NL, f. Gk: *pro-* PRO-[2] + *phýlaxis* a watching, guarding]

propinquity (prə pĭng′kwĭ tĭ), *n.* **1.** nearness in place; proximity. **2.** nearness of relation; kinship. **3.** affinity of nature; similarity. **4.** nearness in time. [ME *propinquite*, t. L: m. s. *propinquitas*]

propionate (prō′pĭ ə nĭt), *n. Chem.* an ester or salt of propionic acid.

propionic acid (prō′pĭ ŏn′ĭk), *Chem.* a liquid organic acid, C_2H_5COOH. [f. PRO-[2] + Gk *píōn* fat + -IC]

propitiate (prə pĭsh′ĭ āt′), *v.t.,* **-ated, -ating.** to make favourably inclined; appease; conciliate. [t. L: m. s. *propitiātus*, pp.] —**propitiable** (prə pĭsh′ĭ ə bl), *adj.* —**propitiative** (prə pĭsh′ĭ ə tĭv), *adj.* —**propi′tia′tor,** *n.* —**Syn.** See **appease.**

propitiation (prə pĭsh′ĭ ā′shən), *n.* **1.** the act of propitiating; conciliation. **2.** that which propitiates.

propitiatory (prə pĭsh′ĭ ə tə rĭ, -trĭ), *adj.* **1.** serving or intended to propitiate. **2.** making propitiation; conciliatory. —*n.* **3.** the mercy seat.

propitious (prə pĭsh′əs), *adj.* **1.** presenting favourable conditions; favourable: *propitious weather.* **2.** indicative of favour: *propitious omens.* **3.** favourably inclined; disposed to bestow favours or forgive. [late ME *propicius*, t. L: m. *propitius*] —**propi′tiously,** *adv.* —**propi′tiousness,** *n.*

propjet (prŏp′jĕt′), *n. Aeron.* a turboprop.

propolis (prŏp′ə lĭs), *n.* a reddish resinous cement collected by bees from the buds of trees, used to stop up crevices in the hives, strengthen the cells, etc. [t. L, t. Gk]

proponent (prə pō′nənt), *n.* **1.** one who puts forward a proposition or proposal. **2.** *Law.* one who argues in favour of; specif., one who seeks to obtain probate of a will. **3.** one who supports a cause or doctrine.

proportion (prə pô′shən), *n.* **1.** comparative relation between things or magnitudes as to size, quantity, number, etc.; ratio: *a house tall in proportion to its width.* **2.** proper relation between things or parts. **3.** relative size or extent. **4.** (*pl.*) dimensions: *a rock of gigantic proportions.* **5.** a portion or part in its relation to the whole: *a large proportion of the total.* **6.** a portion or part. **7.** symmetry; harmony; balanced relationship. **8.** *Maths.* **a.** a relation of four quantities such that the first divided by the second is equal to the third divided by the fourth; the equality of ratios. **b.** the rule of three. **9.** *Archaic.* comparison; analogy. —*v.t.* **10.** to adjust in proper proportion or relation, as to size, quantity, etc. **11.** to adjust the proportions of. [ME *proporcioun*, t. L: m. s. *prōportio*] —**propor′tioner,** *n.*

proportionable (prə pô′shə nə bl), *adj.* being in due proportion; proportional.

proportional (prə pô′shə nəl), *adj.* **1.** having due proportion; corresponding. **2.** being in or characterized by proportion. **3.** of or pertaining to proportion; relative. **4.** *Maths.* having the same or a constant ratio or relation. —**proportionality** (prə pô′shə năl′ ĭ tĭ), *n.* —**propor′tionally,** *adv.*

proportional representation, a method of voting by which political parties are given legislative representation in proportion to their popular strength.

proportionate (*adj.* prə pô′shə nĭt; *v.* prə pô′shə nāt′), *adj., v.,* **-nated, -nating.** —*adj.* **1.** proportioned; being in due proportion; proportional. —*v.t.* **2.** to make proportionate. —**propor′tionately,** *adv.* —**propor′tionateness,** *n.*

proportionment (prə pô′shən mənt), *n.* **1.** the act of proportioning. **2.** the state of being proportioned.

proposal (prə pō′zəl), *n.* **1.** the act of proposing for acceptance, adoption, or performance. **2.** a plan or scheme proposed. **3.** an offer, esp. of marriage.

—**Syn. 2.** PROPOSAL, OVERTURE, PROPOSITION refer to something in the nature of an offer. A PROPOSAL is a plan, a scheme, an offer to be accepted or rejected: *to make proposals for peace.* An OVERTURE is a friendly approach, an opening move (perhaps involving a proposal) tentatively looking towards the settlement of a controversy, or else preparing the way for a proposal, etc.: *to make overtures to an enemy.* PROPOSITION, used in mathematics to refer to a formal statement of truth, and often including the proof or demonstration of the statement, has something of this same meaning when used non-technically (particularly in business): a PROPOSITION is a PROPOSAL in which the terms are clearly stated and their advantageous nature emphasized: *his proposition involved a large discount to the retailer.*

propose (prə pōz′), *v.,* **-posed, -posing.** —*v.t.* **1.** to put forward (a matter, subject, case, etc.) for consideration, acceptance, or action: *to propose a new method; to propose a toast.* **2.** to put forward or suggest as something to be done: *he proposed that a messenger be sent.* **3.** to present (a person) for some position, office, membership, etc. **4.** to put before oneself as something to be done; to design; to intend. **5.** to present to the mind or attention; state. **6.** to propound (a question, riddle, etc.). —*v.i.* **7.** to make a proposal, esp. of marriage. **8.** to form or entertain a purpose or design. [ME, t. F: m. s. *proposer*, f. *pro-* PRO-[1] + *poser* put (see POSE[1]), but assoc. with derivatives of L *prōpōnere* set forth] —**propos′er,** *n.* —**Syn. 4.** See **intend.**

proposition (prŏp′ə zĭsh′ən), *n.* **1.** the act of proposing, or a proposal of, something to be considered, accepted, adopted, or done. **2.** a plan or scheme proposed. **3.** an offer of terms for a transaction, as in business. **4.** a thing, matter, or person considered as something to be dealt with or encountered. **5.** anything stated or affirmed for discussion or illustration. **6.** *Logic.* a statement in which something (a predicate) is affirmed or denied of a subject, or in which membership of a class is affirmed or denied of something, or in which a relation is affirmed or denied to hold between two or more things. **7.** *Maths.* a formal statement of either a truth to be demonstrated or an operation to be performed; a theorem or a problem. **8.** a proposal for sexual intercourse. **9.** *Archaic.* a statement of the subject of a discourse or argument; the introductory part of a speech, literary work, etc. —*v.t.* **10.** to propose a plan, deal, etc., to. **11.** to propose sexual intercourse to. [ME *proposicioun*, t. L: s. *prōpositio* a setting forth] —**prop′osi′tional,** *adj.* —**prop′osi′tionally,** *adv.* —**Syn.** 2. See **proposal.**

propound (prə pound′), *v.t.* **1.** to put forward for consideration, acceptance, or adoption. **2.** to demand probate of (a will) in solemn form. [later var. of ME *propone*, t. L: m. s. *prōpōnere* set forth. Cf. COMPOUND, EXPOUND] —**propound′er,** *n.*

propraetor (prō prē′tə), *n. Rom. Hist.* an officer who, after having served as praetor in Rome, was sent to govern a province with praetorial authority. Also, **propre′tor.** [t. L]

proprietary (prə prī′ə tə rĭ, -trĭ), *adj., n., pl.* **-taries.** —*adj.* **1.** belonging to a proprietor or proprietors. **2.** being a proprietor or proprietors; holding property: *the proprietary class.* **3.** pertaining to property or ownership: *proprietary rights.* **4.** belonging or controlled as property. **5.** manufactured and sold only by the owner of the patent, formula, brand name, or trademark associated with the product: *proprietary medicine.* —*n.* **6.** an owner or proprietor. **7.** a body of proprietors. **8.** *Amer. Hist.* the grantee or owner, or one of the grantees or owners, of a proprietary colony. **9.** ownership. **10.** something owned. **11.** a proprietary medicine. [ME, t. LL: m. s. *proprietārius*, der. L *proprietas* ownership]

proprietary colony, *Amer. Hist.* a colony granted by the British Crown to particular persons, with full rights of government.

proprietor (prə prī′ə tə), *n.* **1.** the owner of a business establishment, a hotel, newspaper, etc. **2.** one who has the exclusive right or title to something; an owner, as of property. **3.** proprietary (def. 7). [f. PROPRIET(Y) (in obs. sense of property) + -OR[2]] —**propri′etorship′,** *n.* —**proprietress** (prə prī′ə trĭs), *n. fem.*

propriety (prə prī′ə tĭ), *n., pl.* **-ties. 1.** conformity to established standards of behaviour or manners. **2.** appropriateness to the purpose or circumstances; suitability. **3.** rightness or justness. **4. the proprieties,** the conventional standards or requirements of proper behaviour. **5.** *Obs.* a property. **6.** *Obs.* a peculiarity, or characteristic of something. [ME *propriete*, t. L: m. s. *proprietas* peculiarity, ownership] —**Syn. 1.** See **etiquette.**

proprioceptive (prō′prĭ ə sĕp′tĭv), *adj. Physiol.* pertaining to sensory excitations originating in muscles, tendons and joints. [f. *proprio-* (comb. form of L *proprius* one's own) + (RE)CEPTIVE]

proprioceptor (prō′prĭ ə sĕp′tə), *n. Physiol.* the sensory end organ in muscles, tendons and joints responding to certain activities of these parts. [f. PROPRIOCEPT(IVE) + -OR[2]]

prop root, *Bot.* a root that supports the plant, as the aerial roots of the mangrove tree or of maize.

proptosis (prŏp tō′sĭs), *n. Med.* forward displacement of the eyeball. [t. NL, t. Gk: a fall forward]

propulsion (prə pŭl′shən), *n.* **1.** the act of propelling or driving forward or onward. **2.** the state of being propelled. **3.** propulsive force; impulse given. [f. s. L *prōpulsus*, pp., driven forward + -ION] —**propulsive** (prə pŭl′sĭv), *adj.*

propulsion reactor, *Physics.* a nuclear reactor designed to provide energy for propulsion, as in a ship or submarine.

propyl (prō′pĭl), *n. Chem.* the univalent radical, C_3H_7, derived from propane. [f. PROP(IONIC) + -YL]

propylaeum (prŏp′ĭ lē′əm), *n., pl.* **-laea** (-lē′ə). (*commonly pl.*) a vestibule or entrance to a temple area or other enclosure, esp. when elaborate or of architectural importance. Also, **propylon.** [t. L, t. Gk: m. *propýlaion* (neut.) before the gate]

propyl alcohol, *Chem.* a colourless liquid alcohol, C_3H_7OH, used in organic synthesis and as a solvent. Also, **propanol.**

propylene (prō′pĭ lēn′), *n. Chem.* a colourless, unsaturated, gaseous hydrocarbon gas, C_3H_6. Also, **propene.**

propylite (prŏp′ĭ līt′), *n. Geol.* an altered form of andesite or some allied rock, usually containing secondary minerals such as chlorite and calcite. [f. s. Gk *própylon* gateway + -ITE[1]; so named because supposed to open the tertiary volcanic epoch]

pro rata (prō rä′tə), in proportion; according to a certain rate. [ML: according to rate]

pro-rata (prō′rä′tə), *adj.* proportionately calculated.

prorate (prō rāt′, prō′rāt′), *v.,* **-rated, -rating.** *U.S.* —*v.i.* **1.** to make an arrangement on a basis of proportional distribution. —*v.t.* **2.** to divide or distribute proportionately. [der. PRO RATA] —**prorat′able,** *adj.*

pro re nata (prō′rā nä′tə), *Latin.* for an unexpected contingency.

prorogation (prō′rə gā′shən), *n.* **1.** the act of proroguing. **2.** the time during which a legislative body is prorogued.

prorogue (prə rōg′), *v.t.* **-rogued, -roguing. 1.** to discontinue meetings of (parliament or a similar legislative body) until the next session. **2.** *Rare.* to defer; postpone. [late ME *proroge*, t. F: m. s. *proroguer*, t. L: m. *prōrogāre* prolong, protract, defer]

pros., prosody.

prosaic (prō zā′ĭk), *adj.* **1.** commonplace or dull; matter-of-fact or unimaginative: *a prosaic mind.* **2.** having the character or spirit of prose as opposed to poetry, as verse or writing. Also, **prosa′ical.** [t. ML: s. *prōsaicus*, der. L *prōsa* PROSE] —**prosa′ically,** *adv.* —**prosa′icness,** *n.*

prosaism (prō′zĭ ĭz′əm), *n.* **1.** prosaic character. **2.** a prosaic expression. Also, **prosaicism** (prō zā′ĭ sĭz′əm), *n.*

proscenium (prō sē′nyəm), *n., pl.* **-nia** (-nyə). **1.** (in the modern theatre) the decorative arch or opening between the stage and the auditorium. **2.** (in the ancient theatre) the stage. [t. L, t. Gk: m. *proskḗnion*]

proscribe (prō skrīb′), *v.t.,* **-scribed, -scribing. 1.** to denounce or condemn (a thing) as dangerous; to prohibit. **2.** to put outside the protection of the law; to outlaw. **3.** to banish or exile. **4.** to announce the name of (a person) as condemned to death and subject to confiscation of property. [t. L: m. s. *prōscrībere* write before, publish, proscribe] —**proscrib′er,** *n.*

proscription (prō skrĭp′shən), *n.* **1.** the act of proscribing. **2.** the state of being proscribed. **3.** outlawry; interdiction. —**proscriptive** (prō skrĭp′tĭv), *adj.* —**proscrip′tively,** *adv.*

prose (prōz), *n., adj., v.,* **prosed, prosing.** —*n.* **1.** the ordinary form of spoken or written language, without metrical structure (as distinguished from poetry or verse). **2.** matter-of-fact, commonplace, or dull expression, quality, discourse, etc. **3.** *Liturgy.* a hymn sung after the gradual, originating from a practice of setting words to the jubilatio of the alleluia. —*adj.* **4.** consisting of or pertaining to prose. **5.** prosaic. —*v.t.* **6.** to turn into prose. —*v.i.* **7.** to write or talk in a dull or prosy manner. [ME, t. F, t. L: m. *prōsa* (*ōrātio*), lit., straightforward (speech), fem. of *pro(r)sus*, for *prōversus*, pp., turned forward]

prosect (prō sĕkt′), *v.t. Med.* to dissect (a cadaver) for anatomical demonstration.

prosector (prō sĕk′tə), *n. Med.* one who dissects cadavers for the illustration of anatomical lectures or the like. [t. LL: anatomist, der. L *prōsectus*, pp., cut off]

prosecute (prŏs′ĭ kyōōt′), *v.,* **-cuted, -cuting.** —*v.t.* **1.** *Law.* **a.** to institute legal proceedings against (a person, etc.). **b.** to seek to enforce or obtain by legal process. **c.** to conduct criminal proceedings in court against. **2.** to follow up or go on with something undertaken or begun: *to prosecute an inquiry.* **3.** to carry on or practice. —*v.i.* **4.** *Law.* **a.** to institute and carry on a legal prosecution. **b.** to act as prosecutor. [ME, t. L: m. s. *prōsecūtus*, pp., pursued, continued]

prosecution (prŏs′ĭ kyōō′shən), *n.* **1.** *Law.* **a.** the institution and carrying on of legal proceedings against a person. **b.** the body of persons by whom such proceedings are instituted and carried on. **2.** the following up of any matter in hand; pursuit.

prosecutor (prŏs′ĭ kyōō′tə), *n.* **1.** *Law.* **a.** one who institutes and carries on legal proceedings in a court of justice, esp. in a criminal court. **b.** an officer charged with the conduct of criminal prosecution in the interest of the public: *public prosecutor.* **2.** one who prosecutes.

proselyte (prŏs′ĭ līt′), *n., v.,* **-lyted, -lyting.** —*n.* **1.** one who has come over or changed from one opinion, religious belief, sect, or the like to another; a convert. —*v.t.* **2.** to make a proselyte of; convert. —*v.i.* **3.** to make proselytes. [ME, t. LL: m. s. *prosēlytus*, t. Gk: m. *prosḗlytos* newcomer, proselyte]

proselytism (prŏs′ĭ lĭ tĭz′əm), *n.* **1.** the state or condition of a proselyte. **2.** the practice of making proselytes.

proselytize (prŏs′ĭ lĭ tīz′), *v.t., v.i.,* **-tized, -tizing.** proselyte. Also, **pros′elytise′.**

prosencephalon (prŏs′ĕn sĕf′ə lŏn′), *n., pl.* **-la** (-lə). *Anat.* **1.** the anterior segment of the brain, consisting of the cerebral hemispheres (or their equivalent) and certain adjacent parts. **2.** the forebrain. [t. NL, f. Gk: *prós* before + m. *enképhalon* brain] —**prosencephalic** (prŏs′ĕn sĭ făl′ĭk), *adj.*

prosenchyma (prŏs ĕng′kĭ mə), *n. Bot.* the tissue characteristic of the woody and bast portions of plants, consisting typically of long, narrow cells with pointed ends. [t. NL, f. Gk: *prós* towards, to + *énchyma* infusion;

modelled on PARENCHYMA] —**prosenchymatous** (prŏs′ĕng kĭm′ə təs), *adj.*
prose poem, a composition written as prose but having many of the characteristics of poetry.
proser (prō′zə), *n.* one who talks or writes prosaically.
Proserpina (prə sû′pĭ nə), *n.* the Roman counterpart of Persephone. Also, **Proserpine** (prŏs′ə pīn′). [t. L, t. Gk: alter. of *Persephónē*]
prosit (prō′sĭt), *interj. Latin.* (as a toast) may it do good!
proslavery (prō′slā′və rĭ), *adj.* **1.** favouring slavery. **2.** *U.S. Hist.* favouring the continuance of the institution of Negro slavery, or opposed to interference with it. —*n.* **3.** the favouring or support of slavery.
prosodist (prŏs′ə dĭst), *n.* one versed in prosody.
prosody (prŏs′ə dĭ), *n.* **1.** the science or study of poetic metres and versification. **2.** a particular or distinctive system of metrics and versification: *Milton's prosody.* [late ME, t. L: m. s. *prosōdia*, t. Gk: m. *prosōidía* tone or accent, modulation of voice, song sung to music] —**prosodiac** (prə sō′dĭ ăk′), **prosodiacal** (prŏs′ə dī′ə kl), **prosodic** (prə sŏd′ĭk), **prosod′ical,** *adj.*
prosopopoeia (prŏs′ə pə pē′ə), *n. Rhet.* **1.** personification, as of inanimate things. **2.** representation of an imaginary or absent person as speaking or acting. Also, **prosopopeia.** [t. L: m. *prosōpopoeia*, t. Gk: m. *prosōpopoiía*]
prospect (*n.* prŏs′pĕkt; *v.* prə spĕkt′), *n.* **1.** (*usually pl.*) an apparent probability of advancement, success, profit, etc. **2.** a mental looking forward, or contemplation of something future or expected. **3.** the outlook for the future: *good business prospects.* **4.** something in view as a source of profit. **5.** a prospective customer, as in business. **6.** a view or scene presented to the eye, esp. of scenery. **7.** outlook or view over a region or in a particular direction. **8.** a mental view or survey, as of a subject or situation. **9.** *Mining.* **a.** an apparent indication of metal, etc. **b.** a spot giving such indications. **c.** excavation or workings in search of ore. **10.** *Archaic.* sight; range of vision. **11. in prospect,** in view; under consideration. —*v.t.* **12.** to search or explore (a region), as for gold. **13.** to work (a mine or claim) experimentally in order to test its value. —*v.i.* **14.** to search or explore a region for gold or the like. [ME, t. L: s. *prōspectus* outlook, view] —**prospector** (prə spĕk′tə), *n.* —**Syn. 6.** See **view.**
prospective (prə spĕk′tĭv), *adj.* **1.** of or in the future. **2.** potential; likely; expected. —**prospec′tively,** *adv.*
prospectus (prə spĕk′təs), *n.* **1.** a statement which describes or advertises a forthcoming literary work, a new enterprise, or the like. **2.** a pamphlet issued by a school giving details about itself. [t. L: outlook, view]
prosper (prŏs′pə), *v.i.* **1.** to be prosperous or successful; to thrive. —*v.t.* **2.** to make prosperous or successful. [late ME, t. L: s. *prosperāre* make prosperous] —**Syn. 1.** See **succeed.**
prosperity (prŏs pĕ′rĭ tĭ), *n.*, *pl.* **-ties. 1.** prosperous, flourishing, or thriving condition; good fortune; success. **2.** (*pl.*) prosperous circumstances.
prosperous (prŏs′pə rəs, -prəs), *adj.* **1.** having or characterized by continued good fortune; flourishing; successful: *a prosperous business.* **2.** well-to-do or well-off: *a prosperous family.* **3.** favourable or propitious. [late ME, t. L: m. *prosperus*] —**pros′perously,** *adv.* —**pros′perousness,** *n.*
prostate (prŏs′tāt), *Anat.* —*n.* **1.** the prostate gland. —*adj.* **2.** designating or pertaining to the prostate gland. [t. ML: m. *prostata*, t. Gk: m. *prostátēs* one standing before] —**prostatic** (prŏ stăt′ĭk), *adj.*
prostatectomy (prŏs′tə tĕk′tə mĭ), *n. Surg.* removal of the prostate gland.
prostate gland, *Anat.* the composite gland which surrounds the urethra of males at the base of the bladder.
prostatitis (prŏs′tə tī′tĭs), *n. Pathol.* inflammation of the prostate gland.
prosthesis (prŏs′thĭ sĭs), *n. Surg.* the addition of an artificial part to supply a defect of the body. [t. LL, t. Gk: a putting to, addition] —**prosthetic** (prŏs thĕt′ĭk), *adj.*
prosthetic group, *Biochem.* a non-protein group of atoms which is combined with a protein, as the haem group in haemoglobin.
prosthion (prŏs′thĭ ŏn′), *n. Anat.* the most forward projecting point of the anterior surface of the upper jaw (maxilla), in the mid-sagittal plane. [t. Gk: m. *prosthéōn* running forward]
prosthodontics (prŏs′thə dŏn′tĭks), *n.* the branch of dentistry concerned with the reconstruction and replacement of missing teeth. Also, **prosthodontia** (prŏs′thə dŏn′tyə). [f. Gk *prósth(en)* forwards + -ODONT + -ICS] —**prosthodontist** (prŏs′thə dŏn′tĭst), *n.*
prostitute (prŏs′tĭ tyōōt′), *n.*, *v.*, **-tuted, -tuting.** —*n.* **1.** a woman who engages in sexual intercourse for money as a livelihood; whore; harlot. **2.** one who debases himself or allows his talents to be used in an unworthy way, usually for financial gain. —*v.t.* **3.** to submit to sexual intercourse for money as a livelihood. **4.** to put to any base or unworthy use. [t. L: m. s. *prōstitūtus*, pp., placed before, exposed publicly, prostituted] —**pros′titu′tor,** *n.*
prostitution (prŏs′tĭ tyōō′shən), *n.* **1.** the act or practice of engaging in sexual intercourse for money. **2.** any base or unworthy use of talent, ability, etc.
prostrate (*v.* prŏs trāt′; *adj.* prŏs′trāt), *v.*, **-trated, -trating,** *adj.* —*v.t.* **1.** to cast (oneself) down in humility, submission, or adoration. **2.** to lay flat, as on the ground. **3.** to throw down level with the ground. **4.** to overthrow, overcome, or reduce to helplessness. **5.** to reduce to physical weakness or exhaustion. —*adj.* **6.** lying flat or at full length, as on the ground. **7.** lying with the face to the ground, as in token of submission or humility. **8.** overthrown, overcome, or helpless: *a prostrate country.* **9.** in a state of physical weakness or exhaustion. **10.** submissive. **11.** disconsolate; depressed; dejected. **12.** *Bot.* (of a plant or stem) lying flat on the ground. [ME *prostrat*, t. L: s. *prōstrātus*, pp., spread out]
prostration (prŏs trā′shən), *n.* **1.** the act of prostrating. **2.** the state of being prostrated. **3.** extreme mental depression or dejection. **4.** extreme physical weakness or exhaustion: *nervous prostration.*
prostyle (prō′stīl), *Archit.* —*adj.* **1.** having a portico in front, standing out from the walls of the building, as a temple. —*n.* **2.** a prostyle building. [t. L, t. Gk: m. *próstylos*, adj., equiv. to *pro-* PRO-² + *stŷlos* pillar]
prosy (prō′zĭ), *adj.*, **-sier, -siest. 1.** of the nature of or resembling prose. **2.** prosaic; commonplace, dull, or wearisome. —**pros′ily,** *adv.* —**pros′iness,** *n.*
prot-, var. of **proto-,** before some vowels, as in *protamine.*
Prot., Protestant.
protactinium (prō′tăk tĭn′ĭ əm), *n. Chem.* a radioactive, metallic element. *Symbol:* Pa; *at. no.:* 91. Formerly, **protoactinium.** [f. PROT(O)- + ACTINIUM]
protagonist (prō tăg′ə nĭst), *n.* **1.** the leading character in a play, novel, etc. **2.** any leading character or personage in a movement, cause, etc. **3.** a champion, or supporter of a movement, cause, idea, etc.; advocate; spokesman. [t. Gk: s. *prōtagōnistḗs*]
Protagoras (prō tăg′ə răs′), *n. c.* 481–411? B.C., Greek philosopher.
protamine (prō′tə mēn′), *n. Biochem.* any of a group of basic, simple proteins which do not coagulate by heat, are soluble in ammonia, and upon hydrolysis form amino acids. [f. PROT- + AMINE]
protandry (prō tăn′drĭ), *n.* (in a hermaphrodite animal or plant) a condition in which the development and maturation of the male organs takes place before that of the female organs. —**protandrous** (prō tăn′drəs), *adj.*, —**protan′drously,** *adv.*
protanopia (prō′tə nō′pĭ ə), *n. Ophthalm.* a form of dichromatic vision in which colours can be matched by a mixture of yellow and blue stimuli, but in which red and orange vision is much less than normal; red-blindness.
protasis (prŏt′ə sĭs), *n.* **1.** the clause expressing the condition in a conditional sentence, in English usually beginning with *if.* Cf. **apodosis. 2.** (in ancient drama) the first part of the play, in which the characters are introduced and the subject is proposed. [t. L, t. Gk]
protea (prō′tĭ ə), *n.* any of the shrubs or trees of the southern African family *Proteaceae*, as the **giant protea,** *Protea cynaroides.* [t. NL, t. Gk: named after PROTEUS] —**proteaceous** (prō′tĭ ā′shəs), *adj.*
protean (prō tē′ən), *adj.* **1.** readily assuming different forms or characters; exceedingly variable. **2.** (*cap.*) of, like, or suggestive of Proteus.
protease (prō′tĭ ās′), *n. Biochem.* any enzyme that acts upon proteins. [f. PROTE(IN) + -ASE]
protect (prə tĕkt′), *v.t.* **1.** to defend or guard from attack, invasion, annoyance, insult, etc.; cover or shield from injury or danger. **2.** *Econ.* to guard (a country's industry) from foreign competition by imposing import duties. **3.** *Com.* to provide funds for the payment of (a draft, etc.). —*v.i.* **4.** to provide, or be capable of providing protection. [t. L: s. *prōtectus*, pp., covered over] —**Syn. 1.** See **defend.**
protection (prə tĕk′shən), *n.* **1.** the act of protecting. **2.** the state of being protected. **3.** preservation from injury or harm. **4.** something that protects. **5.** *Insurance.* coverage. **6.** *Colloq.* money paid to criminals as a guarantee against threatened violence. **7.** *Econ.* the system or theory of fostering or developing home industries by protecting them from foreign competition through duties imposed on imports from foreign countries. **8.** a treaty, safe-conduct, passport, or other writing which secures from molestation the person, persons, or property specified in it. **9.** patronage. —**Syn. 4.** See **cover.**

protectionism (prə tĕk′shə nĭz′əm), *n.* the economic system or theory of protection. —**protec′tionist,** *n.*

protective (prə tĕk′tĭv), *adj.* **1.** having the quality of protecting. **2.** tending to or designed to protect. **3.** of, pertaining to, or designed for economic protection. —**protec′tively,** *adv.*

protective colouring, colouring assumed by various animals in their natural surroundings, rendering them inconspicuous to their enemies.

protective tariff, a tariff for the protection of domestic production, rather than for revenue.

protector (prə tĕk′tə), *n.* **1.** one who or that which protects; a defender; a guardian. **2.** *Hist.* **a.** one in charge of a kingdom during the sovereign's minority, incapacity, or absence. **b.** (*cap.*) the title (more fully **Lord Protector**) of the head of government during the period of the Protectorate (held by Oliver Cromwell, 1653–58, and by Richard Cromwell, 1658–59). **3.** a man who keeps a mistress. —**protec′toral,** *adj.* —**protec′torship′,** *n.* —**protectress** (prə tĕk′trĭs), *n. fem.*

protectorate (prə tĕk′tə rĭt, -trĭt), *n.* **1.** the relation of a strong state towards a weaker state or territory which it protects and partly controls. **2.** a state or territory so protected. **3.** the office or position, or the term of office, of a protector. **4.** the government of a protector. **5.** (*cap.*) *Hist.* the period during which Oliver and Richard Cromwell held the title of Lord Protector.

Protectorate of South Arabia. See **South Arabia, Protectorate of.**

protectory (prə tĕk′tə rĭ), *n., pl.* **-ries.** an institution for the care of destitute or delinquent children.

protégé (prō′tĭ zhā′; *Fr.* prō tĕ zhĕ′), *n., pl.* **-gés.** one who is under the protection or friendly patronage of another. [t. F, pp. of *protéger* protect, t. L: m. *prōtegere*] —**protégée,** *n. fem.*

protein (prō′tēn), *n.* **1.** *Biochem.* any of a group of nitrogenous organic compounds of high molecular weight, synthesized by plants from simple substances, and undergoing hydrolysis by enzymes to yield amino acids, which in animal metabolism are required for all life processes. **2.** (formerly) a substance thought to be the essential nitrogenous component of all organic bodies. Also, **proteid** (prō′tēd). [t. G, f. m. s. Gk *prōteîos* primary + *-in* -IN^{2}]

proteinase (prō′tĭ nās′), *n.* *Biochem.* any of several enzymes which are capable of hydrolysing proteins.

proteinuria (prō′tĭ nyŏŏə′rĭ ə), *n.* *Pathol.* a condition marked by the presence of protein in the urine.

pro tem (prō tĕm′), pro tempore.

pro tempore (prō tĕm′pə rĭ), *Latin.* **1.** temporarily; for the time being. **2.** temporary.

proteolysis (prō′tĭ ŏl′ĭ sĭs), *n.* *Biochem.* the hydrolysis or breaking down of proteins into simpler compounds, as in digestion. [f. *proteo-* (comb. form repr. PROTEIN) + -LYSIS] —**proteolytic** (prō′tĭ ə lĭt′ĭk), *adj.*

proteose (prō′tĭ ōs′), *n.* *Biochem.* any of a class of soluble compounds derived from proteins by the action of gastric juice, etc. [f. PROTE(IN) + -OSE^{2}]

Proterozoic (prŏt′ə rō zō′ĭk), *Geol.* —*adj.* **1.** of or pertaining to a geological era or rocks preceding the Palaeozoic; the late Pre-Cambrian. —*n.* **2.** the era or rocks intervening between Archaeozoic and Palaeozoic, presumed to be characterized by relative prominence of sedimentary rocks in a few of which fossils of early primitive organisms occur. [f. Gk *prótero(s)* being before + s. Gk *zōḗ* life + -IC]

protest (*n.* prō′tĕst; *v.* prə tĕst′), *n.* **1.** a formal expression or declaration of objection or disapproval, often in opposition to something which one is powerless to prevent or avoid: *to submit under protest.* **2.** *Com.* **a.** a formal notarial certificate attesting the fact that a cheque, note, or bill of exchange has been presented for acceptance or payment and that it has been refused. **b.** the action taken to fix the liability for a dishonoured bill of exchange or note. **3.** *Law.* **a.** (upon one's payment of a sum of money) a formal statement disputing the legality of the demand. **b.** a written and attested declaration made by the master of a ship stating the circumstances in which some injury has happened to the ship or cargo, or other circumstances involving the liability of the officers, crew, etc. **4.** *Sport.* a formal expression of objection or complaint placed with an official. [ME, t. ML: s. *prōtestum* declaration] —*v.i.* **5.** to give formal expression to objection or disapproval; remonstrate. **6.** to make solemn declaration. —*v.t.* **7.** to make a protest or remonstrance against. **8.** to say in protest or remonstrance. **9.** to declare solemnly or formally; affirm; assert. **10.** to make a formal declaration of the non-acceptance or non-payment of (a bill of exchange or note). **11.** *Obs.* to call to witness. [late ME, t. F: s. *protester,* t. L: m. *prōtestārī* declare publicly] —**protest′er,** *n.* —**protest′ingly,** *adv.* —**Syn. 6.** See **declare.**

Protestant (prŏt′ĭs tənt), *n.* **1.** any Western Christian not an adherent of the Roman Catholic Church. **2.** an adherent of any of those Christian bodies which separated from the Church of Rome at the Reformation, or of any group descended from them. **3.** (orig.) any of the German princes who protested against the decision of the Diet of Speyer in 1529, which had denounced the Reformation. **4.** (*l.c.*) one who protests. —*adj.* **5.** belonging or pertaining to Protestants or their religion. **6.** (*l.c.*) protesting. [sing. of *protestants* for L *prōtestantēs,* pl. ppr. of *prōtestārī* protest]

Protestant Episcopal Church, the church in the United States inheriting the doctrine, discipline, and worship of the Church of England: it became an independent body within the Anglican communion.

Protestantism (prŏt′ĭs tən tĭz′əm), *n.* **1.** the religion of Protestants. **2.** the Protestant churches, collectively. **3.** adherence to Protestant principles.

Protestant Reformation, reformation (def. 3).

protestation (prō′tĕs tā′shən), *n.* **1.** the act of protesting or affirming. **2.** a solemn declaration or affirmation. **3.** the formal expression of objection or disapproval; protest.

Proteus (prō′tyŏŏs), *n.* **1.** a sea-god of classical mythology who was able to assume different forms. **2.** a person or thing capable of taking on various aspects or characters.

prothalamion (prō′thə lā′mĭ ən), *n., pl.* **-mia** (-mĭ ə). a song or poem written to celebrate a marriage. Also, **prothalamium** (prō′thə lā′mĭ əm). [f. PRO-^{2} + s. Gk *thálamos* bridal chamber + -ION; coined by Spenser, after Gk *epithalámion* EPITHALAMIUM]

prothallium (prō thăl′ĭ əm), *n., pl.* **-thallia** (-thăl′ĭ ə). *Bot.* **1.** the gametophyte of ferns, etc. **2.** the analogous rudimentary gametophyte of seed-bearing plants. [NL, f. Gk: *pro-* PRO-^{2} + m. *thallíon,* dim. of *thallós* young shoot] —**prothal′lial,** *adj.*

prothesis (prŏth′ĭ sĭs), *n.* **1.** the addition of a phoneme or syllable at the beginning of a word, as in Spanish *escala* (ladder) from Latin *scala.* **2.** *Gk Orth. Ch.* **a.** the preparation and preliminary oblation of the eucharistic elements. **b.** the table on which this is done. **c.** the part of the bema or sanctuary where this table stands. [t. LL, t. Gk: a putting before] —**prothetic** (prō thĕt′ĭk), *adj.* —**prothet′ically,** *adv.*

prothonotary (prō′thə nō′tə rĭ, prō thŏn′ə tə rĭ, -trĭ), *n., pl.* **-taries.** **1.** a principal clerk in some courts of law. **2.** Also, **prothonotaries apostolic(al).** *Rom. Cath. Ch.* a member of the college of twelve prelates which records papal acts, canonizations, beatifications, etc. **3.** the principal ecclesiastical secretary of a patriarch of the Eastern Church. Also, **protonotary.** [t. ML: m. s. *prōthonotārius,* LL *prōtonotārius,* t. Gk: m. *prōtonotários*] —**prothonotarial** (prō thŏn′ə tĕə′rĭ əl), *adj.*

prothorax (prō thô′răks), *n., pl.* **-thoraxes, -thoraces** (-thô′rĭ sēz′). the anterior division of an insect's thorax, bearing the first pair of legs. See illus. under **coleopteron.** —**prothoracic** (prō′thô răs′ĭk), *adj.*

prothrombin (prō thrŏm′bĭn), *n.* *Biochem.* one of the clotting factors in blood, the forerunner of thrombin.

protist (prō′tĭst), *n.* *Biol.* any of the single-celled organisms, including all the unicellular animals and plants. [t. NL: s. *protista,* pl., t. Gk: m. *prṓtistos* the very first, superl. of *prôtos* first] —**protistan** (prō tĭs′tən), *adj., n.* —**protis′tic,** *adj.*

protium (prō′tyəm), *n.* *Chem.* the common isotope of hydrogen, of atomic weight 1·008. *Symbol:* H^1.

proto-, a word element meaning 'first', 'earliest form of', used in chemistry of the first of a series of compounds, or of one containing the minimum amount of an element. Also, **prot-.** [t. Gk, comb. form of *prôtos* first]

protoactinium (prō′tō ăk tĭn′ĭ əm), *n.* *Chem.* protactinium.

protochordate (prō′tō kô′dāt), *n.* *Zool.* any of the nonvertebrate chordates, as the tunicates, cephalochordates, and hemichordates.

protocol (prō′tə kŏl′), *n.* **1.** the customs and regulations dealing with the ceremonies and etiquette of the diplomatic corps and others at a court or capital. **2.** an original draft, minute, or record from which a document, esp. a treaty, is prepared. **3.** a supplementary international agreement. **4.** an agreement between states. **5.** an annex to a treaty giving data relating to it. —*v.i.* **6.** to issue a protocol. —*v.t.* **7.** to record in a protocol. [earlier *protocoll,* t. ML: s. *prōtocollum,* t. LGk: m. *prōtókollon,* orig., a first leaf glued to the front of a manuscript containing notes as to contents]

protogine (prō′tə jĭn, -jēn′), *n.* a gneissoid granite, occurring chiefly in the Alps. [t. F, irreg. f. Gk: *prōto-* PROTO- + *gíne(sthai)* be born or produced]

protogyny (prō tŏj′ĭ nĭ), *n.* (in a hermaphrodite animal or plant) a condition in which the development and maturation of the female organs takes place before that of the male organs. —**protogynous** (prō tŏj′ĭ nəs), *adj.*

protolithic (prō′tō lĭth′ĭk), *adj. Anthropol.* denoting or pertaining to stone implements selected according to fitness of form, and shaped by wear without definite shaping on the part of the user.

protomartyr (prō′tō mä′tə), *n.* **1.** the first Christian martyr (Stephen). **2.** the first martyr in any cause.

protomorphic (prō′tō mô′fĭk), *adj. Biol.* having a primitive character or structure. —**pro′tomorph′**, *n.*

proton (prō′tŏn), *n. Physics, Chem.* a subatomic particle which has a positive charge equal in magnitude to the negative charge of a single electron, and which is one of the fundamental constituents of every atomic nucleus, the number of protons in the nucleus being different for each element and called the *atomic number* of that element. [t. Gk, neut. of *prôtos* first]

protonema (prō′tə nē′mə), *n., pl.* **-mata** (-mə tə). *Bot.* a primary, usually filamentous structure produced by the germination of the spore in mosses and certain related plants, and upon which the leafy plant which bears the sexual organs arises as a lateral or terminal shoot. [t. NL, f. Gk: *prōto-* PROTO- + *nêma* thread]

protonotary (prō′tə nō′tə rĭ, prō tŏn′ə tə rĭ, -trĭ), *n., pl.* **-teries.** prothonotary.

protopathic (prō′tə păth′ĭk), *adj. Physiol.* **1.** denoting general non-discriminating sensory reception (opposed to *epicritic*). **2.** primitive; primary.

protoplasm (prō′tə plăz′əm), *n. Biol.* **1.** a complex substance (typically colourless and semifluid) regarded as the physical basis of life, having the power of spontaneous motion, reproduction, etc.; the living matter of all vegetable and animal cells and tissues. **2.** (formerly) cytoplasm. [t. NL: m. *prōtoplasma*, ML first thing made, first creature, f. Gk: *prōto-* PROTO- + *plásma* something formed] —**pro′toplas′mic,** *adj.*

protoplast (prō′tə plăst′), *n.* **1.** *Biol.* **a.** the protoplasm within a cell considered as a fundamental entity. **b.** the primordial living unit or cell. **2.** one who or that which is first formed; the original. **3.** the hypothetical first individual or one of the supposed first pair of a species or the like. [t. LL: s. *prōtoplastus* the first man, t. Gk: m. *prōtóplastos* formed first] —**pro′toplas′tic,** *adj.*

protostele (prō′tə stē′lĭ, -stēl′), *n. Bot.* the solid stele of most roots, having a central core of xylem enclosed by phloem. —**protostelic** (prō′tə stē′lĭk), *adj.*

prototrophic (prō′tə trŏf′ĭk), *adj.* (of certain micro-organisms) having no specific nutritional requirements for growth. [f. PROTO- + s. Gk *trophḗ* nourishment + -IC]

prototype (prō′tə tīp′), *n.* **1.** the original or model after which anything is formed. **2.** *Biol.* an archetype; a primitive form regarded as the basis of a group. [t. NL: m. s. *prōtotypon*, t. Gk: (neut.) original, primitive] —**prototypal** (prō′tə tī′pl), **prototypic** (prō′tə tĭp′ĭk), *adj.*

protoxide (prō tŏk′sīd), *n. Chem.* the oxide of an element which contains the least number of oxygen atoms, when that element forms more than one oxide.

protoxylem (prō′tə zī′ləm), *n. Bot.* the part of the primary xylem that develops first, consisting of narrow, thin-walled cells. [f. PROTO- + XYLEM]

protozoan (prō′tə zō′ən), *adj.* **1.** Also, **protozoic.** belonging to or pertaining to the phylum *Protozoa*, comprising animals consisting of one cell or of a colony of like or similar cells. —*n.* **2.** any of the *Protozoa.* [f. NL *prōtozōa* (pl. of *prōtozōon*, f. Gk: *prōto-* PROTO- + m. *zôion* animal) + -AN]

protract (prə trăkt′), *v.t.* **1.** to draw out or lengthen in time; extend the duration of; prolong. **2.** *Anat., etc.* to extend or protrude. **3.** *Survey., etc.* to plot; to draw by means of a scale and protractor. [t. L: s. *prōtractus*, pp., drawn forth, drawn out] —**protrac′tive,** *adj.* —**Syn. 1.** See **lengthen.** —**Ant. 1.** shorten.

protractile (prə trăk′tīl), *adj.* capable of being protracted, lengthened, or protruded.

protraction (prə trăk′shən), *n.* **1.** the act of protracting. **2.** extension in time or space. **3.** that which is protracted.

protractor (prə-trăk′tə), *n.* **1.** one who or that which protracts. **2.** *Maths, etc.* an instrument, a graduated arc, for plotting or measuring angles on paper.

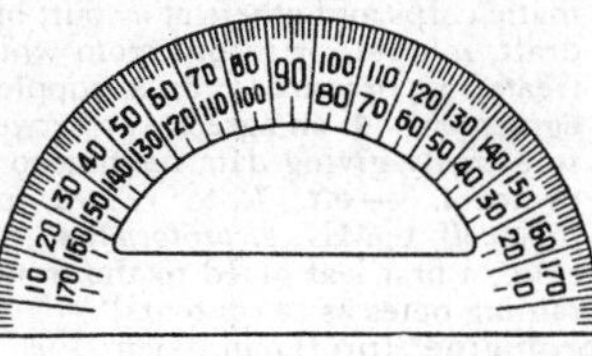

Protractor (def. 2)

protrude (prə-trōōd′), *v.,* **-truded, -truding.** —*v.i.* **1.** to project. —*v.t.* **2.** to thrust forward; cause to project. [t. L: m. s. *prōtrūdere*] —**protrud′ent,** *adj.* —**protrusible** (prə trōō′sə bl), *adj.*

protrusile (prə trōō′sĭl), *adj.* capable of being thrust forth or extended, as a limb, etc. [f. s. L *prōtrūsus*, pp., thrust forth + -ILE]

protrusion (prə trōō′zhən), *n.* **1.** the act of protruding. **2.** the state of being protruded. **3.** that which protrudes.

protrusive (prə trōō′sĭv), *adj.* **1.** thrusting forward. **2.** obtrusive. **3.** projecting. —**protru′sively,** *adv.*

protuberance (prə tyōō′bə rəns, -brəns), *n.* **1.** protuberant state or form. **2.** a protuberant part; a rounded projection.

protuberancy (prə tyōō′bə rən sĭ, -brən sĭ), *n., pl.* **-cies.** protuberance.

protuberant (prə tyōō′bə rənt, -brənt), *adj.* bulging out beyond the surrounding surface. [t. LL: s. *prōtūberans*, ppr., swelling] —**protu′berantly,** *adv.*

protyle (prō′tīl), *n.* a hypothetical primitive matter from which all the chemical elements are supposed to have been formed. [irreg. f. Gk: *prōto-* PROT(O)- + (*h*)*ýlē* matter, wood]

proud (proud), *adj.* **1.** feeling pleasure or satisfaction over something conceived as highly honourable or creditable to oneself (often fol. by *of*, an infinitive, or a clause). **2.** having or cherishing, or proceeding from or showing, a high, esp. an inordinately high, opinion of one's own dignity, importance, or superiority. **3.** having or showing self-respect or self-esteem. **4.** highly gratifying to the feelings or self-esteem. **5.** highly honourable or creditable: *a proud achievement.* **6.** (of things) stately, majestic, or magnificent: *proud cities.* **7.** of lofty dignity or distinction: *a proud name, proud nobles.* **8.** *Poetic.* full of vigour or spirit. **9.** *Obs.* brave. —*adv.* **10. do (someone) proud, a.** to be a source of credit to (a person). **b.** to entertain (someone) generously or lavishly. [ME; late OE *prūd*, c. Icel. *prūdhr* magnificent, stately, gallant, appar. t. VL. Cf. OF *prud*, *prod* gallant, g. L *prōd-* in *prōdesse* be of worth] —**proud′ly,** *adv.*

—**Syn. 2.** PROUD, ARROGANT, HAUGHTY imply a consciousness of, or a belief in, one's superiority in some respect. PROUD implies sensitiveness, lofty self-respect, or jealous preservation of one's dignity, station, and the like. (It may refer to an affectionate admiration or a justifiable pride concerning someone else: *proud of his son.*) ARROGANT applies to insolent or overbearing behaviour, arising from an exaggerated belief in one's importance: *arrogant rudeness.* HAUGHTY implies lofty reserve and confident, often disdainful assumption of superiority over others: *the haughty manner of an aristocrat.* —**Ant. 1.** humble. **2.** modest.

proud flesh, *Pathol.* granulation tissue.

Proudhon (*Fr.* prōō dôɴ′), *n.* **Pierre Joseph** (*Fr.* pyĕr zhō zĕf′), 1809–65, French socialist and writer.

Proust (*Fr.* prōōst), *n.* **Marcel** (*Fr.* mȧr sĕl′), 1871–1922, French novelist. —**Proustian** (prōōs′tyən), *adj.*

proustite (prōōs′tīt), *n. Mineral.* a mineral, silver arsenic sulphide, Ag_3AsS_3, occurring in scarlet crystals and masses: a minor ore of silver; ruby silver. [named after J. L. *Proust*, 1754–1826, French chemist. See -ITE[1]]

Prov., **1.** Provençal. **2.** Provence. **3.** Proverbs. **4.** Province. **5.** Provost.

prov., **1.** province. **2.** provincial. **3.** provisional. **4.** proverbially.

prove (prōōv), *v.,* **proved, proved** or **proven, proving.** —*v.t.* **1.** to establish the truth or genuineness of, as by evidence or argument: *to prove one's contention.* **2.** *Law.* to establish the authenticity or validity of (a will or testament). **3.** to give demonstration of by action. **4.** to put to the test; try or test. **5.** to show (oneself) to have the character, ability, courage, etc., expected of one, esp. through one's actions. **6.** to show (oneself) to be as specified. **7.** *Maths.* to verify the correctness of (some statement). **8.** proof (def. 20). **9.** to determine the characteristics of by scientific analysis: *to prove ore.* **10.** *Cookery.* to cause (dough) to rise in a warm place before baking. **11.** *Archaic.* to experience. —*v.i.* **12.** to turn out: *the report proved to be false.* **13.** to be found by trial or experience, or in the event, to be. **14.** (of dough) to rise in a warm place before baking. [ME, t. OF: m. *prover*, g. L *probāre* try, test, prove, approve] —**prov′able,** *adj.* —**prov′er,** *n.*

provenance (prŏv′ĭ nəns), *n.* the place of origin, as of a work of art, etc. [t. F, der. *provenir*, t. L: m. *prōvenīre* come forth]

Provençal (prŏv′ŏn säl′; *Fr.* prō väɴ sȧl′), *adj.* **1.** of or pertaining to Provence, its people, or their language. —*n.* **2.** a native or inhabitant of Provence. **3.** a Romance language, formerly widely spoken and written, of SE France. [t. F, der. *Provence*, g. L *prōvincia* province]

Provençale (prŏv′ŏn säl′; *Fr.* prō väɴ sȧl′), *adj.* **1.** fem. form of **Provençal.** **2. à la Provençale,** *Cookery.* characterized by the use of a mixture of tomato and garlic, or sometimes of garlic alone.

Provence (prō vôns′; *Fr.* prō väNs′), *n.* **1.** a region in SE France, bordering on the Mediterranean: formerly a province; famous in the Middle Ages for poetry and chivalry. **2.** Official name, **Provence-Côte d'Azur-Corse** (*Fr.* prō väNs′ kōt dȧ zʏr′ kôrs′). an administrative region in SE France, comprising the departments of Bouches-du-Rhône, Vaucluse, Hautes-Alpes, Basses-Alpes, Alpes-Maritimes, Corsica, and Var. 2,818,992 pop. (1962); 12,057 sq. mi. *Cap.:* Marseilles.

provender (prŏv′ĭn də), *n.* **1.** dry food for livestock, as hay; fodder. **2.** food or provisions. [ME *provendre*, t. OF, var. of *provende* prebend, provender, g. LL *prōbenda*, b. *praebenda* prebend and *prōvidēre* look out for] **—Syn. 1.** See **feed.**

provenience (prō vē′nyəns), *n.* provenance; origin. [der. *provenient*, t. L: s. *prōveniens*, ppr., coming forth]

proverb (prŏv′ûb), *n.* **1.** a short popular saying, long current, embodying some familiar truth or useful thought in expressive language. **2.** a wise saying or precept; a didactic sentence. **3.** a person or thing that is commonly regarded as the embodiment of some quality; byword. **4.** *Bible.* a profound saying or oracular utterance requiring interpretation. **5. Proverbs,** one of the books of the Old Testament, made up of sayings of wise men of Israel, including Solomon. *—v.t.* **6.** to utter in the form of a proverb. **7.** to make (something) the subject of a proverb. **8.** to make a byword of. [ME *proverbe*, t. OF, t. L: m. s. *prōverbium*]

—Syn. 1. PROVERB, MAXIM are terms for short pithy sayings. A PROVERB is such a saying popularly known and repeated, usually expressing simply and concretely, though often metaphorically, a truth based on common sense or the practical experience of mankind: *A stitch in time saves nine.* A MAXIM is a brief statement of a general and practical truth, esp. one that serves as a rule of conduct or a precept: *It is wise to risk no more than one can afford to lose.*

proverbial (prə vû′byəl), *adj.* **1.** pertaining to or characteristic of a proverb: *proverbial brevity.* **2.** expressed in a proverb or proverbs: *proverbial wisdom.* **3.** of the nature of or resembling a proverb: *proverbial sayings.* **4.** having been made the subject of a proverb. **5.** having become an object of common mention or reference. **—prover′bially,** *adv.*

provide (prə vīd′), *v.*, **-vided, -viding.** *—v.t.* **1.** to furnish or supply. **2.** to afford or yield. **3.** *Law.* to arrange for or stipulate beforehand, as by a provision or proviso. **4.** *Archaic.* to get ready, prepare, or procure beforehand. *—v.i.* **5.** to take measures with due foresight (usually fol. by *for* or *against*). **6.** to make arrangements for supplying means of support, money, etc. (usually fol. by *for*). **7.** to supply means of support, etc. (often fol. by *for*). [ME, t. L: m. s. *prōvidēre* foresee, look after, provide for] **—provid′er,** *n.*

provided (prə vī′dĭd), *conj.* it being stipulated or understood (that); on the condition or supposition (that): *to consent, provided* (or *provided that*) *all the others agree.* **—Syn.** See **if.**

providence (prŏv′ĭ dəns), *n.* **1.** the foreseeing care and guardianship of God over His creatures. **2.** (*cap.*) God. **3.** a manifestation of the divine care or direction. **4.** provident or prudent management of resources; economy. **5.** *Rare.* foresight; provident care.

Providence (prŏv′ĭ dəns), *n.* **1.** a seaport in the U.S., the capital of Rhode Island, in the NE part, at the head of Narragansett Bay. 207,498 (1960). **2. Cape,** the SW tip of South Island, New Zealand.

provident (prŏv′ĭ dənt), *adj.* **1.** having or showing foresight; careful in providing for the future. **2.** characterized by or proceeding from foresight: *provident care.* **3.** mindful in making provision (usually fol. by *of*). **4.** economical or frugal. [ME, t. L: s. *prōvidens*, ppr., looking for, providing] **—prov′identy,** *adv.*

provident club, a type of hire-purchase or credit-payment system run by large stores, mail order organizations, etc.

providential (prŏv′ĭ dĕn′shəl), *adj.* **1.** of, pertaining to, or proceeding from divine providence: *providential care.* **2.** opportune, fortunate, or lucky: *a providential occurrence.* **—prov′iden′tially,** *adv.*

provident society, 1. a friendly society. **2.** a provident club.

providing (prə vī′dĭng), *conj.* provided. **—Syn.** See **if.**

province (prŏv′ĭns), *n.* **1.** an administrative division or unit of a country: *the provinces of Spain.* **2. the provinces,** the parts of a country outside the capital or the largest cities. **3.** a country, territory, district, or region. **4.** *Geog.* an area lower in rank than a region. **5.** a department or branch of learning or activity: *the province of mathematics.* **6.** the sphere or field of action of a person, etc.; one's office, function, or business. **7.** (formerly) a major subdivision of British India. **8.** an ecclesiastical territorial division, as that within which an archbishop or a metropolitan exercises jurisdiction. **9.** (formerly) **a.** any of the North American colonies of Great Britain now forming major administrative divisions of Canada. **b.** certain of those colonies which after the War of Independence came together to form the United States. **10.** *Rom. Hist.* a country or territory outside Italy, brought under the ancient Roman dominion, and administered by a governor sent from Rome. [ME, t. F, t. L: m. s. *prōvincia* province, official charge]

Provincetown (prŏv′ĭns toun′), *n.* a town in the U.S., in SE Massachusetts, at the tip of Cape Cod: the first landing place of the Pilgrim Fathers in the New World, 1620. 3346 (1960).

provincial (prə vĭn′shəl), *adj.* **1.** belonging or peculiar to some particular province or provinces; local: *provincial customs.* **2.** of or pertaining to the provinces: *the provincial press.* **3.** having or showing the manners characteristic of inhabitants of a province or the provinces; countrified; rustic; unsophisticated; narrow or illiberal. **4.** *Hist.* of or pertaining to any of the British provinces in North America. *—n.* **5.** one who lives in or comes from the provinces. **6.** a countrified, unsophisticated, or narrow-minded person. **7.** *Eccles.* **a.** the head of an ecclesiastical province. **b.** a member of a religious order presiding over his order in a given district or province. **—provin′cially,** *adv.*

provincialism (prə vĭn′shə lĭz′əm), *n.* **1.** narrowness of outlook or interests resulting from provincial life. **2.** manner, habit of thought, etc., characteristic of a province or the provinces. **3.** a word, expression, or mode of pronunciation peculiar to a province. **4.** devotion to one's own province before the nation as a whole.

provinciality (prə vĭn′shĭ ăl′ĭ tĭ), *n.*, *pl.* **-ties. 1.** provincial character. **2.** a provincial characteristic.

proving ground, any place or area for conducting experiments or testing something, as a piece of scientific equipment, a new theory, etc.

proving stand, *Aeron.* an apparatus for testing reaction engines, as rocket engines.

provision (prə vĭzh′ən), *n.* **1.** a clause in a legal instrument, a law, etc., providing for a particular matter; stipulation; proviso. **2.** the providing or supplying of something, as of food or other necessities. **3.** arrangement or preparation beforehand, as for the doing of something, the meeting of needs, the supplying of means, etc. **4.** something provided; a measure or other means for meeting a need. **5.** a supply or stock of something provided. **6.** (*pl.*) supplies of food. **7.** *Eccles.* **a.** appointment to an ecclesiastical office. **b.** appointment by the pope to a see or benefice not yet vacant. *—v.t.* **8.** to supply with provisions, or stores of food. [ME, t. L: s. *prōvīsio*] **—provi′sioner,** *n.* **—Syn. 6.** See **food.**

provisional (prə vĭzh′ə nəl), *adj.* Also, **provi′sionary. 1.** serving for the time being only; existing until permanently replaced; temporary; conditional; tentative: *a provisional agreement.* *—n.* **2.** *Philately.* a stamp which serves temporarily pending the appearance of the regular issue, or during a temporary shortage of the regular stamps. **—provi′sionally,** *adv.*

proviso (prə vī′zō), *n.*, *pl.* **-sos, -soes. 1.** a clause in a statute, contract, or the like, by which a condition is introduced. **2.** a stipulation or condition. [late ME, t. ML: *prōvīsō* (*quod*) it being provided that]

provisory (prə vī′zə rĭ), *adj.* **1.** provisional. **2.** containing a proviso or condition; conditional.

provitamin (prō vĭt′ə mĭn), *n.* *Biochem.* a substance which an organism can transform into a vitamin, as carotene, which is converted into vitamin A in the liver.

provo (prō′vō), *n.* in Holland, a young person who disapproves of the rules and morality of present-day society, and seeks to defy them and assert his own individuality. [t. D, t. F: shortened form of *provocateur*]

provocation (prŏv′ə kā′shən), *n.* **1.** the act of provoking. **2.** something that incites, instigates, angers, or irritates. **3.** *Crim. Law.* words or conduct leading to a killing in hot passion and without deliberation. [ME, t. L: s. *prōvocātio* a calling forth]

provocative (prə vŏk′ə tĭv), *adj.* **1.** tending or serving to provoke; inciting, stimulating, irritating, or vexing. *—n.* **2.** something provocative. **—provoc′atively,** *adv.* **—provoc′ativeness,** *n.*

provoke (prə vōk′), *v.t.*, **-voked, -voking. 1.** to anger, enrage, exasperate, or vex. **2.** to stir up, arouse, or call forth. **3.** to incite or stimulate (a person, etc.) to action. **4.** to give rise to, induce, or bring about. **5.** *Obs.* to summon. [ME, t. L: m. *prōvocāre* call forth, challenge, provoke] **—provok′er,** *n.* **—provok′ing,** *adj.* **—provok′ingly,** *adv.* **—Syn. 1.** See **irritate.**

provost (prŏv′əst), *n.* **1.** a person appointed to superintend or preside. **2.** an officer in a Scottish burgh corresponding to mayor. **3.** *Eccles.* **a.** the senior clergyman responsible for any cathedral of recent foundation. **b.** the head officer of a chapter or governing body, esp. of a religious foundation, next below an abbot. **4.** the head of certain colleges, schools, etc. **5.** *U.S.* an administrative officer in a university having responsibility for curriculum, faculty appointments, etc. **6.** *Hist.* a feudal overseer. **7.** *Obs.* a prison warder. [ME; OE *profost*, t. ML: m. s. *prōpositus*, lit., one placed before, president] **—prov′ostship′,** *n.*

provost marshal (prə vō′), **1.** (in the army) an officer acting as head of military police in a camp or area, and charged with the maintenance of order, etc. **2.** (in the navy) a master-at-arms.

provost sergeant (prə vō′), a senior non-commissioned officer of the military police.

prow (prou), *n.* **1.** the forepart of a ship or boat; the bow. **2.** *Poetic.* a ship. [t. F: m. *proue*, t. d. It. (Genoese): m. *proa*, g. L *prōra*, t. Gk: m. *prôira*]

prowess (prou′ĭs), *n.* **1.** valour; bravery. **2.** outstanding ability: *prowess at shooting.* **3.** *Obs.* a valiant or daring deed. [ME *prowesse*, t. OF: m. *proec(c)e*, der. *proue* good, valiant, g. L *prōd-* in *prōdesse* be useful]

prowl (proul), *v.i.* **1.** to rove or go about stealthily in search of prey, plunder, etc. **—***v.t.* **2.** to rove over or through in search of what may be found. **—***n.* **3.** the act of prowling. [ME *proll(en)*; orig. uncert.] **—prowl′er,** *n.* **—Syn. 1.** See **lurk.**

prowl car, *U.S.* a police patrol car.

prox., (L *proximo* [*mense*]) next month; proximo.

proximal (prŏk′sĭ məl), *adj.* situated towards the point of origin or attachment, as of a limb or bone (opposed to *distal*). [f. s. L *proximus* next + -AL[1]] **—prox′imally,** *adv.*

proximate (prŏk′sĭ mĭt), *adj.* **1.** next; nearest. **2.** closely adjacent; very near. **3.** fairly accurate; approximate. **4.** next in a chain of relation. [t. LL: m. s. *proximātus*, pp., approached] **—prox′imately,** *adv.*

proximity (prŏk sĭm′ĭ tĭ), *n.* nearness in place, time, or relation. [late ME, t. L: m. s. *proximitas*]

proximity fuse, a device for causing a missile to explode when it is in the immediate vicinity of its target, triggered by heat, light, etc., emitted from the target. Also, **variable time fuse.**

proximo (prŏk′sĭ mō′), *adv.* in or of the next or coming month: *on the 1st proximo.* Cf. **ultimo.** *Abbrev.*: prox. [L: in the next (month), abl. of *proximus* next. See PROXIMAL]

proxy (prŏk′sĭ), *n.*, *pl.* **proxies. 1.** the agency of a person deputed to act for another. **2.** the person so deputed; an agent; a substitute. **3.** a written authorization empowering another to vote or act for the signer. [ME *prokecye*, contr. of *procuracy* (see PROCURATOR)]

prs, pairs.

prude (prōōd), *n.* a person who affects extreme modesty or propriety. [t. F: a prude, as adj., prudish, back-formation from OF *preudefeme, prodefeme* worthy or respectable woman]

prudence (prōō′dns), *n.* **1.** cautious practical wisdom; good judgement; discretion. **2.** the quality or fact of being prudent. **3.** regard for one's own interests. **4.** provident care in management; economy or frugality. **—Syn. 1.** PRUDENCE, CALCULATION, FORESIGHT, FORETHOUGHT imply attempted provision against possible contingencies. PRUDENCE is care, caution, and good judgement, as well as wisdom in looking ahead: *sober prudence in handling one's affairs.* CALCULATION suggests a disposition to get a large return for as small an outlay as possible (lit. or fig.) and willingness to benefit at the expense of others (lit. and fig.): *cold calculation.* FORESIGHT implies a prudent looking ahead rather far into the future: *admirable foresight in planning.* FORETHOUGHT emphasizes the adequacy of preparation for the future: *complete forethought.* **—Ant. 1.** rashness.

prudent (prōō′dnt), *adj.* **1.** wise, judicious, or wisely cautious in practical affairs, as a person; sagacious or judicious; discreet or circumspect. **2.** careful of one's own interests; provident, or careful in providing for the future. **3.** characterized by or proceeding from prudence, as conduct, action, etc. [ME, t. L: s. *prūdens* foreseeing, knowing, contr. of *prōvidens* PROVIDENT] **—pru′dently,** *adv.*

prudential (prōō dĕn′shəl), *adj.* **1.** of, pertaining to, or characterized by prudence. **2.** exercising prudence. **3.** *U.S.* having discretionary charge of certain matters. **—pruden′tially,** *adv.*

prudery (prōō′də rĭ), *n.*, *pl.* **-ries. 1.** extreme modesty or propriety. **2.** prudish action or speech.

prudish (prōō′dĭsh), *adj.* **1.** extremely modest or proper. **2.** characteristic of a prude. **—prud′ishly,** *adv.* **—prud′ishness,** *n.* **—Syn. 1.** See **modest.**

pruinose (prōō′ĭ nōs′), *adj.* *Biol.* covered with a frostlike bloom or powdery secretion, as a plant surface. [t. L: m. s. *pruīnōsus* frosty]

prune[1] (prōōn), *n.* **1.** the purplish black dried fruit of any of several varieties of plum tree, used for eating, cooked or uncooked. **2.** such a fruit, whether dried or not. **3.** a variety of plum tree bearing such fruit. **4.** *Obs.* any plum. [late ME, t. F, g. LL *prūna*, for L *prūnum* plum (*prūnus* plum tree), t. Gk: m. *proûnon* plum]

prune[2] (prōōn), *v.t.*, **pruned, pruning. 1.** to cut or lop off (twigs, branches, or roots). **2.** to cut or lop superfluous or undesired twigs, branches, or roots from; to trim. **3.** to rid or clear of (anything superfluous or undesirable). **4.** to remove (superfluities, etc.). [ME *prouyne(n)*, t. OF: m. *proignier* prune (vines), g. L *prōvīneāre*, der. *vīnea* vine] **—prun′er,** *n.*

prune[3] (prōōn), *v.t.*, **pruned, pruning.** *Archaic.* to preen. [ME *prune(n)*, *pruyne(n)*, *proyne(n)*]

pruning hook, an implement with a hooked blade, used for pruning vines, etc.

pruning knife, a short knife with a curved blade used for pruning.

pruning shears, secateurs.

prurient (prōōə′rĭ ənt), *adj.* **1.** inclined to or characterized by lascivious thought. **2.** morbidly uneasy, as desire or longing. **3.** itching. **4.** *Bot.* causing itching. [t. L: s. *prūriens*, ppr., itching] **—pru′rience, pru′riency,** *n.* **—pru′riently,** *adv.*

pruriginous (prōō rĭj′ĭ nəs), *adj.* *Med.* itching. [t. LL: m. s. *prūrīginōsus*]

prurigo (prōō rī′gō), *n.* *Pathol.* a skin affection characterized by itching papules. [t. L: an itching]

pruritus (prōō rī′təs), *n.* *Pathol.* itching. [t. L: an itching. See PRURIENT] **—pruritic** (prōō-rĭt′ĭk), *adj.*

Prus., 1. Prussia. **2.** Prussian.

Prussia, 1871–1914

Prussia (prŭsh′ə), *n.* a former state in N Germany: as a former kingdom (with its capital at Berlin) it was the central state in the formation of the German Empire: dissolved March, 1947. German, **Preussen.**

Prussian (prŭsh′ən), *adj.* **1.** of or pertaining to Prussia or its inhabitants. **—***n.* **2.** a native or inhabitant of Prussia. **3.** any of the German dialects of East or West Prussia. **4.** Old Prussian. **5.** (orig.) one of a Lettic people formerly inhabiting territory along and near the coast at the south-eastern corner of the Baltic Sea.

Prussian blue, a dark blue, crystalline, insoluble pigment, $Fe_4[Fe(CN)_6]_3.10H_2O$, formed in testing for the ferric ion, and produced by ageing **soluble Prussian blue,** $KFe_2(CN)_6$.

Prussianism (prŭsh′ə nĭz′əm), *n.* **1.** the spirit, system, policy, or methods of the Prussians. **2.** Prussian militarism and the despotic characteristics attributed to it, especially since Frederick the Great (ruled 1740–86).

prussiate (prŭsh′ĭ ĭt), *n.* *Chem.* a salt of prussic acid; a cyanide. [t. F: f. *prussi(que)* PRUSSIC + *-ate* -ATE[2]]

prussic acid (prŭs′ĭk), *Chem.* hydrocyanic acid. [*prussic*, t. F: m. *prussique*, der. *Prusse* Prussia]

Prut (*Russ.* prōōt), *n.* a river flowing from the Carpathian Mountains in the SW Soviet Union SE along the border between the Soviet Union and Rumania into the Danube. ab. 500 mi. German, **Pruth** (*Ger.* prōōt). See map under **Walachia.**

pry[1] (prī), *v.*, **pried, prying,** *n.*, *pl.* **pries. —***v.i.* **1.** to look closely or curiously, peer, or peep. **2.** to search or inquire curiously or inquisitively into something: *to pry into the affairs of others.* **—***v.t.* **3.** to ferret or find (*out*) by curious searching or inquiry. **—***n.* **4.** the act of prying; a prying glance. **5.** an inquisitive person. [ME *prye(n)*, *prie(n)*; orig. uncert.]

pry[2] (prī), *v.t.*, **pried, prying,** *n.*, *pl.* **pries.** *Chiefly U.S.* prise. [back-formation from PRISE, n. (taken as pl.)]

pryer (prī′ə), *n.* prier.

prying (prī′ĭng), *adj.* **1.** that pries; looking or searching curiously. **2.** unduly curious; inquisitive. **—pry′ingly,** *adv.* **—Syn. 2.** See **curious.**

Prynne (prĭn), *n.* **William,** 1600–69, English pamphleteer and Puritan.

Przemyśl (*Pol.* pshĕ′mĭ syəl), *n.* a city in SE Poland: occupied by the Russians, 1915. 50,000 (est. 1965).

Przewalski's horse (pû′zhə văl′skĭz), a variety of wild horse, *Equus caballus przewalskii*, of Mongolia.

Ps., Psalm; Psalms.

ps, pieces.
P.S., 1. Also, **p.s.** postscript. 2. Privy Seal.
Psa., Psalm; Psalms.
psalm (säm), *n.* **1.** a sacred or solemn song, or hymn. **2.** (*cap.*) any of the 150 songs, hymns, and prayers which together form a book of the Old Testament (**Book of Psalms**). **3.** a metric version or paraphrase of any of these. **4.** a poem of like character. —*v.t.* **5.** to celebrate in psalms; hymn. [ME *psalme*, OE *ps(e)alm, sealm*, t. LL: m. s. *psalmus*, t. Gk: m. *psalmós* song sung to the harp, orig., a plucking, as of strings]
psalmist (säʹmĭst), *n.* **1.** the author of a psalm or psalms. **2. the Psalmist,** David, the traditional author of the Psalms.
psalmody (säʹmə dĭ, sălʹmə dĭ), *n., pl.* **-dies. 1.** the arrangement of psalms for singing. **2.** psalms or hymns collectively. **3.** the act, practice, or art of singing psalms or hymns. [ME, t. LL: m. s. *psalmōdia*, t. Gk: m. *psalmōidía* singing to the harp] —**psalʹmodist,** *n.*
Psalter (sôlʹtə), *n.* **1.** the Book of Psalms. **2.** (*sometimes l.c.*) a book containing the Psalms for liturgical or devotional use. [t. LL: m. s. *psaltērium* the Psalter, L a psaltery, t. Gk: m. *psaltḗrion* a stringed instrument; r. ME *sauter* (t. AF) and OE *saltere* (t. LL: m. s. *psaltērium*)]
psalterium (sôl tĭəʹrĭ əm), *n., pl.* **-teria** (-tĭəʹrĭ ə). *Zool.* the omasum or manyplies. [t. LL: the Psalter (the folds of the omasum being likened to the leaves of a book), t. Gk: m. *psaltḗrion*]
psaltery (sôlʹtə rĭ), *n., pl.* **-teries. 1.** an ancient musical instrument consisting of a flat sounding box with numerous strings which were plucked with the fingers or struck with a plectrum. **2.** (*cap.*) the Psalter. [t. L: m. s. *psaltērium* psaltery, LL the Psalter, t. Gk: m. *psaltḗrion* psaltery, later the Psalter; r. ME *sautrie*, t. OF]

Man playing a psaltery (12th century)

psammite (sămʹīt), *n. Geol.* any sandstone (contrasted with *psephite* and *pelite*). [f. s. Gk *psámmos* sand + -ITE¹] —**psammitic** (să mĭtʹĭk), *adj.*
p's and q's, behaviour; manners: *mind one's p's and q's.*
psephite (sēʹfīt), *n. Geol.* any coarse fragmental rock, as breccia (contrasted with *psammite* and *pelite*). [f. s. Gk *psêphos* pebble + -ITE¹] —**psephitic** (sē fĭtʹĭk), *adj.*
psephology (sĕ fŏlʹə jĭ), *n.* the study of elections, their results, trends, etc. [f. Gk *psêpho-* (comb. form of *psêphos* a pebble (used in Athens for voting) + -LOGY] —**psephological** (sĕfʹə lŏjʹĭ kl), *adj.* —**psephʹologʹically,** *adv.* —**psepholʹogist,** *n.*
pseud (syo͞od), *n. Colloq.* a person who pretends to be what he is not.
pseud., pseudonym.
pseudaxis (syo͞o dăkʹsĭs), *n. Bot.* sympodium. [f. PSEUD(O)- + AXIS]
pseudepigrapha (syo͞oʹdə pĭgʹrə fə), *n.pl.* certain writings (other than the canonical books and the Apocrypha) professing to be biblical in character, but not considered canonical or inspired. [NL, t. Gk, neut. pl. of *pseudepígraphos* falsely inscribed, bearing a false title] —**pseudepigraphic** (syo͞oʹdə pĭ grăfʹĭk), **pseudepigraphous** (syo͞oʹdə pĭgʹrə fəs), *adj.*
pseudo (syo͞oʹdō), *adj.* **1.** false; counterfeit; spurious; sham; pretended. —*n.* **2.** a person who pretends to be what he is not. [ME; independent use of PSEUDO-]
pseudo-, a word element meaning 'false', 'pretended', freely used as a formative; in scientific use, denoting close or deceptive resemblance to the following element, used sometimes in chemical names of isomers. Also, before vowels, **pseud-**. [t. Gk, comb. form of *pseudḗs* false]
pseudoaquatic (syo͞oʹdō ə kwătʹĭk), *adj.* not aquatic but indigenous to moist regions.
pseudocarp (syo͞oʹdō kärpʹ), *n. Bot.* a fruit which includes other parts besides the mature ovary and its contents, as the apple, pineapple, etc. —**pseuʹdocarʹpous,** *adj.*
pseudoclassic (syo͞oʹdō klăsʹĭk), *adj.* falsely or spuriously classic. —**pseudoclassicism** (syo͞oʹdō klăsʹĭ sĭzʹəm), *n.*
pseudolearned (syo͞oʹdō lûʹnĭd), *adj.* **1.** characterized by erroneous or defective learning. **2.** exhibiting unnecessary or misguided antiquarianism, as in adding *b* in the spelling of *debt* after the Latin source *debitum*, for Middle English *det.*
pseudomorph (syo͞oʹdō môfʹ), *n.* **1.** a false or deceptive form. **2.** *Mineral.* a mineral which takes its external appearance from another mineral which it has replaced in chemical action. —**pseuʹdomorʹphic, pseuʹdomorʹphous,** *adj.* —**pseuʹdomorʹphism,** *n.*
pseudonym (syo͞oʹdə nĭm), *n.* an assumed name adopted by an author to conceal his identity; pen-name. [t. Gk: s. *pseudṓnymon* false name]
pseudonymity (syo͞oʹdə nĭmʹĭ tĭ), *n.* **1.** pseudonymous character. **2.** the use of a pseudonym.
pseudonymous (syo͞o dŏnʹĭ məs), *adj.* **1.** bearing a false name. **2.** writing or written under an assumed name. [t. Gk: m. *pseudṓnymos*] —**pseudonʹymously,** *adv.*
pseudopodium (syo͞oʹdō pōʹdyəm), *n., pl.* **-dia** (-dyə). a temporary protrusion of the protoplasm of a protozoan, serving as an organ of locomotion, prehension, etc. Also, **pseudopod** (syo͞oʹdō pŏdʹ). [NL, f. Gk: *pseudo-* PSEUDO- + m. *pódion*, dim. of *poús* foot]
pseudoscalar (syo͞oʹdō skāʹlə), *adj. Physics.* describing a scalar quantity which changes sign in the transition from a right-handed to a left-handed system of coordinates.
pseudoscorpion (syo͞oʹdō skôʹpyən), *n.* any of a number of widely distributed small arthropods belonging to the order *Chelonethida*, which superficially resemble scorpions but are more closely related to the mites.
p.s.f., pounds per square foot.
pshaw (pshô), *interj.* **1.** (an exclamation expressing impatience, contempt, etc.) —*n.* **2.** an exclamation of 'pshaw!' —*v.i.* **3.** to say 'pshaw'. —*v.t.* **4.** to say 'pshaw' at or to.
psi (psī), *n.* the twenty-third letter (Ψ, ψ) of the Greek alphabet.
p.s.i., pounds per square inch.
psilanthropism (sī lănʹthrə pĭzʹəm), *n.* the doctrine that Jesus Christ was a mere man. Also, **psilanʹthropy.** [f. s. Gk *psilánthrōpos* merely human + -ISM] —**psilanʹthropist,** *n.*
psilomelane (sī lŏmʹĭ lānʹ), *n.* a common mineral, a hydrated barium manganate, occurring in smooth, black to steel-grey, botryoidal or stalactitic forms and in masses: an ore of manganese. [f. Gk: *psiló(s)* bare, mere + m. *mélan* (neut.) black]
Psiloriti (psēʹlô rēʹtĭ), *n.* **Mount.** See **Ida, Mount** (def. 2).
psilosis (sī lōʹsĭs), *n. Pathol.* sprue. [NL, t. Gk]
psittacosis (psĭtʹə kōʹsĭs), *n.* a severe infectious disease characterized by high fever and pulmonary involvement, a disease of parrots, also known to affect other species of birds, easily transmissible to man; parrot fever. [NL, f. m. s. Gk *psittakós* parrot + *-ōsis* -OSIS]
Pskov (*Russ.* pskôf), *n.* **1.** a lake in the W Soviet Union in Europe, forming the S part of Lake Peipus. **2.** a city near this lake. 10,000 (est. 1964).
psoas (sōʹəs), *n. Anat.* a muscle of the loin, arising internally from the sides of the spinal column and fitting into the upper end of the thighbone. [NL, t. Gk: acc. pl. of *psóa* a muscle of the loins]
psoralea (sō rāʹlyə), *n.* any plant of the leguminous genus *Psoralea*, esp. the breadroot, *P. esculenta.* [NL, t. Gk: (neut. pl.) scabby; with reference to the glandular dots on the plant]
psoriasis (sō rīʹə sĭs), *n. Pathol.* a common chronic skin disease characterized by scaly patches. [t. NL, t. Gk] —**psoriatic** (sôʹrĭ ătʹĭk), *adj.*
P.SS., (L *postscripta*) postscripts. Also, **p.ss.**
P.S.T., (in the U.S.) Pacific Standard Time. Also, **PST, p.s.t.**
P.S.V., Public Service Vehicle.
psych-, var. of **psycho-,** before some vowels, as in *psychasthenia.*
psych., 1. psychological. 2. psychology.
psychasthenia (sīʹkăs thēʹnyə, -thĭ nīʹə), *n.* **1.** *Psychiatry.* a neurosis marked by fear, anxiety, phobias, etc. **2.** *Pathol.* mental weakness or exhaustion. [NL. See PSYCH-, ASTHENIA] —**psychasthenic** (sīʹkăs thĕnʹĭk), *adj.*
psyche (sīʹkĭ), *n.* **1.** the human soul, spirit, or mind. **2.** (*cap.*) *Gk Myth.* the soul, sometimes represented in art as a butterfly or a tiny winged being, and in the late classical era as a beautiful girl loved by Eros or Cupid. **3.** *Philos.* by Homer, identified with life itself; by Plato, as immortal and akin to the gods; and by neoplatonism, as the animating principle of the body, but inferior to the nous and the logos. [t. L, t. Gk: lit., breath]
psychedelic (sīʹkĭ dĕlʹĭk), *adj.* **1.** denoting or pertaining to a mental state of enlarged consciousness, involving a sense of aesthetic joy and increased perception transcending verbal concepts. **2.** denoting or pertaining to any of a group of drugs inducing such a state, esp. LSD. **3.** *Colloq.* intensely pleasurable or fashionable. **4.** *Colloq.* having bright colours and imaginative patterns, as materials. [f. PSYCHE + *-delic* (der. Gk *dēlóein* to show, reveal)]
psychiatrist (sī kīʹə trĭst), *n.* one who is versed in or practises psychiatry. Also, *Obs.*, **psychiater** (sī kīʹə tə).
psychiatry (sī kīʹə trĭ), *n.* the practice or the science of treating mental diseases. [f. PSYCH- + m. s. Gk *iatreía* healing] —**psychiatric** (sīʹkĭ ătʹrĭk), **psyʹchiatʹrical,** *adj.* —**psyʹchiatʹrically,** *adv.*
psychic (sīʹkĭk), *adj.* Also, **psyʹchical. 1.** of or pertaining to the human soul or mind; mental (opposed to *physical*). **2.** *Psychol.* pertaining to super- or extra-sensory

mental functioning, such as clairvoyance, telepathy. See **parapsychology.** **3.** exerted by or proceeding from non-physical agency. **4.** of the nature of such an agency. **5.** associated with or attributed to such agencies, as phenomena, etc. **6.** of or pertaining to the class of phenomena associated with such agencies: *psychic research.* **7.** specially susceptible to psychic influences. —*n.* **8.** a person specially susceptible to psychic influences. [t. Gk: m. s. *psȳchikós* of the soul] —**psy′chically,** *adv.*

psychic bid, *Bridge.* a bid based on intuition rather than on the strength of one's hand.

psycho (sī′kō), *Slang.* —*adj.* **1.** psychopathic. —*n.* **2.** a psychopath.

psycho-, a word element representing 'psyche' (as in *psychological*) and 'psychological' (as in *psychoanalysis*). Also, **psych-.** [t. Gk, comb. form of *psȳchḗ* breath, spirit, soul, mind]

psychoanal., psychoanalysis.

psychoanalysis (sī′kō ə năl′ĭ sĭs), *n.* **1.** a systematic structure of theories concerning the relation of conscious and unconscious psychological processes. **2.** a technical procedure for investigating unconscious mental processes, and for treating neuroses. —**psychoanalytic** (sī′kō ăn′ə lĭt′ĭk), **psy′choan′alyt′ical,** *adj.* —**psy′choan′alyt′ically,** *adv.*

psychoanalyst (sī′kō ăn′ə lĭst), *n.* one who is versed in or practises psychoanalysis.

psychoanalyse (sī′kō ăn′ə līz′), *v.t.*, **-lysed, -lysing.** to investigate or treat by psychoanalysis. Also, *U.S.*, **psychoanalyze.** —**psy′choan′alys′er,** *n.*

psychobiology (sī′kō bī ŏl′ə jĭ), *n.* **1.** that branch of biology which treats of the relations or interactions between body and mind, esp. as exhibited in the nervous system, receptors, effectors, or the like. **2.** psychology as studied by biological methods or in terms of biology. —**psychobiological** (sī′kō bī′ə lŏj′ĭ kl), *adj.* —**psy′chobiol′ogist,** *n.*

psychodrama (sī′kō drä′mə), *n. Psychiatry.* **1.** a type of group therapy used in treating patients in a mental hospital, in which the patients act out a theme of their own choosing, thereby having an opportunity to express and resolve their own personal conflicts. **2.** the drama itself. —**psychodramatic** (sī′kō drə măt′ĭk), *adj.*

psychogenesis (sī′kō jĕn′ĭ sĭs), *n.* **1.** genesis of the psyche. **2.** the origin of physical or psychological states, normal or abnormal, out of the interplay of conscious and unconscious psychological forces. —**psychogenetic** (sī′kō jĭ nĕt′ĭk), *adj.* —**psy′chogenet′ically,** *adv.*

psychogenic (sī′kō jĕn′ĭk), *adj.* of psychic origin, or dependent on psychic conditions or processes, as a mental disorder.

psychognosis (sī kŏg′nə sĭs), *n. Psychiatry.* a complete examination of the mind.

psychograph (sī′kə grăf′, -gräf′), *n. Psychol.* the graphic representation of the relative strength of the various traits of a personality. —**psychographic** (sī′kə grăf′ĭk), *adj.* —**psy′chograph′ically,** *adv.* —**psychography** (sī kŏg′rə fĭ), *n.*

psychol., **1.** psychological. **2.** psychology.

psychological (sī′kə lŏj′ĭ kl), *adj.* **1.** of or pertaining to psychology. **2.** pertaining to the mind or to mental phenomena, esp. as the subject matter of psychology. Also, **psy′cholog′ic.** —**psy′cholog′ically,** *adv.*

psychological moment, the most appropriate moment for effect on the mind; the critical moment: *at the psychological moment he announced his resignation.*

psychologism (sī kŏl′ə jĭz′əm), *n.* **1.** a tendency to attach preponderating importance to the psychological aspect of things and affairs. **2.** *Philos.* a tendency in some German philosophy of the nineteenth century to base philosophy wholly or mainly upon psychological concepts and principles.

psychologist (sī kŏl′ə jĭst), *n.* one trained in psychology.

psychologize (sī kŏl′ə jīz′), *v.i.*, **-gized, -gizing.** to make psychological investigations or speculations. Also, **psychologise.**

psychology (sī kŏl′ə jĭ), *n.*, *pl.* **-gies.** **1.** the science of mind, or of mental states and processes; the science of human nature. **2.** the science of human and animal behaviour. **3.** the mental states and processes of a person or of a number of persons, esp. as determining action: *the psychology of the fighting man in war.* [t. NL: m. s. *psȳchologia*, f. Gk: *psȳcho-* PSYCHO- + *-logia* -LOGY]

psychomancy (sī′kō măn′sĭ), *n.* occult communication between souls or with spirits.

psychometry (sī kŏm′ĭ trĭ), *n.* **1.** Also, **psychometrics** (sī′kō mĕt′rĭks). *Psychol.* the measurement of mental states, mental processes, and their relationships. **2.** the alleged art or faculty of divining the properties of an object, or matters associated with it, through contact with or proximity to it. —**psychom′eter,** *n.* —**psychometric** (sī′kō mĕt′rĭk), *adj.* —**psy′chomet′rically,** *adv.*

psychomotor (sī′kō mō′tə), *adj.* of or pertaining to voluntary movement.

psychoneurosis (sī′kō nyōō rō′sĭs), *n.*, *pl.* **-ses** (-sēz). neurosis. —**psychoneurotic** (sī′kō nyōō rŏt′ĭk), *adj.*

psychopath (sī′kō păth′), *n.* one affected with psychopathy or a psychopathic personality.

psychopathic (sī′kō păth′ĭk), *adj.* **1.** denoting a personality outwardly normal but characterized by a diminished sense of social responsibility, inability to establish deep human relationships, and sometimes, abnormal or dangerous acts. **2.** pertaining to or of the nature of, affected with, or engaged in treating psychopathy. **3.** pertaining to a psychosis or neurosis, or to any other mental disorder.

psychopathology (sī′kō pə thŏl′ə jĭ), *n.* mental pathology; the science of diseases of the mind. —**psychopathological** (sī′kō păth′ə lŏj′ĭ kl), *adj.* —**psy′chopathol′ogist,** *n.*

psychopathy (sī kŏp′ə thĭ), *n.* **1.** mental disease or disorder. **2.** a psychopathic personality. **3.** the treatment of disease by mental or psychological influence.

psychophysics (sī′kō fĭz′ĭks), *n.* that department of psychology which deals with the measurement of relationships between attributes of the stimulus and of the sensation. —**psychophysical** (sī′kō fĭz′ĭ kl), *adj.* —**psy′chophys′ically,** *adv.* —**psychophysicist** (sī′kō fĭz′ĭ sĭst), *n.*

psychophysiology (sī′kō fĭz′ĭ ŏl′ə jĭ), *n.* the branch of physiology which deals with the mind and its functions. —**psychophysiological** (sī′kō fĭz′ĭ ə lŏj′ĭ kl), *adj.* —**psy′chophys′iol′ogist,** *n.*

psychopomp (sī′kō pŏmp′), *n.* one who conducts spirits or souls to the other world, as Hermes or Charon. [f. PSYCHO- + s. Gk *pompós* conductor]

psychoprophylaxis (sī′kō prŏf′ĭ lăk′sĭs), *n. Obstet.* a method of conditioning pregnant women for child-bearing by training in labour technique, breathing control, etc. —**psy′choproph′ylac′tic,** *adj.*

psychosis (sī kō′sĭs), *n.*, *pl.* **-ses** (-sēz). **1.** *Pathol.* any major, severe form of mental affection or disease. **2.** *Rare.* the state of consciousness at a given time. [t. NL, t. LGk] —**psychotic** (sī kŏt′ĭk), *adj.*, *n.*

psychosomatic (sī′kō sō măt′ĭk), *adj.* denoting a physical disorder which is caused by or notably influenced by the emotional state of the patient.

psychosomatic medicine, the application of the principles of psychology in the study and treatment of physical diseases.

psychotherapeutics (sī′kō thĕ′rə pyōō′tĭks), *n.* therapeutics concerned with the treatment of disease by psychological influence, as by mental suggestion. —**psy′chother′apeu′tic,** *adj.* —**psy′chother′apeu′tically,** *adv.* —**psy′chother′apeu′tist,** *n.*

psychotherapy (sī′kō thĕ′rə pĭ), *n.* the science or art of curing psychological abnormalities and disorders by psychological techniques. —**psy′chother′apist,** *n.*

psychrometer (sī krŏm′ĭ tə), *n.* an instrument used to determine atmospheric humidity by the reading of two thermometers, the bulb of one of which is kept moistened and ventilated; wet-and-dry bulb hygrometer. [f. *psychro-* (t. Gk, comb. form of *psȳchrós* cold) + -METER[1]] —**psychrometric** (sī′krō mĕt′rĭk), *adj.*

psychrometry (sī krŏm′ĭ trĭ), *n.* the measurement of the humidity of the atmosphere.

Pt, *Chem.* platinum.

pt, **1.** part. **2.** *Med.* patient. **3.** payment. **4.** pint; pints. **5.** point. **6.** port.

pt., preterite.

P.T., **1.** (in the U.S.) Pacific time. **2.** Physical Training. **3.** Pupil Teacher.

p.t., **1.** past tense. **2.** pro tempore.

pta, *pl.* **ptas.** peseta.

P.T.A., **1.** Parent-Teacher Association. **2.** Passenger Transport Authority.

Ptah (ptä, tä), *n.* an ancient Egyptian deity of high rank, worshipped especially at Memphis, and reverenced as the creative force. [t. Egypt.]

ptarmigan (tä′mĭ gən), *n.* any of various species of grouse of the genus *Lagopus*, characterized by feathered feet, and found in mountainous and cold regions. [t. Gaelic: m. *tarmachan*; orig. unknown]

PT boat, *U.S.* M.T.B.

pteridology (tĕ′rĭ dŏl′ə jĭ), *n.* the branch of botany that treats of ferns. [f. *pterido-* (comb. form repr. Gk *pterís* fern) + -LOGY] —**pteridological** (tĕ′rĭ dō lŏj′ĭ kl), *adj.* —**pter′idol′ogist,** *n.*

pteridophyte (tĕ′rĭ dō fīt′), *n.* any of the *Pteridophyta*, a primary division of the vegetable kingdom comprising plants (as the ferns and fern allies) which are without seeds, have vascular tissue, and are differentiated into root, stem, and leaf. It includes ferns, horsetails, and club mosses. [t. NL: m. *Pteridophyta*, pl., f. Gk: *pterido-* (comb. form repr. Gk *pterís* fern) + m. *phytá* plants] —**pteridophytic** (tě′rĭ dō fĭt′ĭk), **pteridophytous** (tě′-rĭ dŏf′ĭ təs), *adj.*

pterion (tĭə′rĭ ən, tě′rĭ ən), *n. Craniom.* the craniometric point at the side of the sphenoidal fontanelle.

ptero-, a word element meaning 'wing', as in *pterodactyl.*

pterocarpous (tě′rō kä′pəs), *adj. Bot.* having a winged fruit.

pterodactyl (tě′rō dăk′tĭl), *n.* any member of the *Pterosauria*, an order of extinct (Jurassic to Cretaceous) flying reptiles, having the outside digit of the forelimb greatly elongated and supporting a wing membrane. [t. NL: s. *Pterodactylus*, genus name, f. Gk: m. *pteró(n)* wing + m. *dáktylos* digit]

pteropod (tě′rə pŏd′), *adj.* belonging or pertaining to the *Pteropoda*, a group of molluscs which have the lateral portions of the foot expanded into winglike lobes. [t. NL: s. *Pteropoda*, pl., t. Gk, neut. pl. of *pterópous* wing-footed]

-pterous, an adjectival word element meaning 'winged', as in *dipterous.* [t. Gk: m. *-pteros*, comb. form der. *pterón* feather, wing]

pterygoid (tě′rĭ goid′), *adj.* **1.** winglike. **2.** *Anat.* denoting or pertaining to the pterygoid process. —*n.* **3.** *Anat.* the muscles, nerves, blood vessels, etc., of the pterygoid process. [t. Gk: m. s. *pterygoeidḗs* winglike]

pterygoid process, *Anat.* **1.** either of two processes descending, one on each side, from the point where the body of the sphenoid bone joins a bone of a temporal wing, each process consisting of two plates (**external pterygoid plate** and **internal pterygoid plate**) separated by a notch. **2.** either of these two plates.

PTFE, polytetrafluoroethylene.

ptg, printing.

P.T.I., Physical Training Instructor.

ptisan (tĭ zăn′), *n.* a nourishing decoction, often having a slight medicinal quality, originally one made from barley. [t. L: s. *ptisana*, t. Gk: m. *ptisánē* peeled barley, barley water; r. ME *tisane*, t. F]

p.t.o., please turn over. Also, **P.T.O.**

Ptolemaic (tŏl′ĭ mā′ĭk), *adj.* of or pertaining to Ptolemy.

Ptolemaic system, *Astron.* a system elaborated by Ptolemy and subsequently modified by others, according to which the earth was the fixed centre of the universe, with the heavenly bodies moving about it.

Ptolemaist (tŏl′ĭ mā′ĭst), *n.* a believer in the Ptolemaic system of astronomy.

Ptolemy (tŏl′ĭ mĭ), *n.* **1.** (*Claudius Ptolemaeus*), fl. A.D. 127–151, Greek mathematician, astronomer, and geographer, at Alexandria. **2.** any of a Macedonian family of rulers of Egypt, 323–30 B.C.

Ptolemy I (surnamed *Soter*), 367?–283 B.C., king of Egypt 306–285 B.C., born in Macedonia, founder of Macedonian dynasty in Egypt.

Ptolemy II (surnamed *Philadelphus*), 309?–247? B.C., king of Egypt 285–247? B.C. (son of Ptolemy I).

ptomaine (tō′mān), *n.* any of a class of basic nitrogenous substances, some of them very poisonous, produced during putrefaction of animal or plant proteins. Also, **pto′main.** [t. It.: m. *ptomaina*, f. Gk *ptôma* dead body + *-ina* -INE[2]]

ptomaine poisoning, **1.** a toxic condition caused by the consumption of ptomaines. **2.** (formerly) food poisoning.

ptosis (tō′sĭs), *n. Pathol.* a dropping of the upper eyelid. [NL, t. Gk: a falling] —**ptotic** (tō′tĭk), *adj.*

pts, **1.** parts. **2.** payments. **3.** pints. **4.** points. **5.** ports.

ptyalin (tī′ə lĭn), *n. Biochem.* an enzyme in the saliva of man and certain of the lower animals, possessing the property of converting starch into dextrin and maltose; salivary amylase. [f. s. Gk *ptýalon* spittle, saliva + -IN[2]]

ptyalism (tī′ə lĭz′əm), *n. Pathol.* excessive secretion of saliva. [t. Gk: s. *ptyalismós* expectoration]

pub (pŭb), *n. Colloq.* a public house.

pub., **1.** public. **2.** publication. **3.** published. **4.** publisher. **5.** publishing.

puberty (pyōō′bə tĭ), *n.* sexual maturity; the earliest age at which a person is capable of procreating offspring (in common law, presumed to be 14 years in the male and 12 years in the female). [ME *puberte*, t. L: m. s. *pūbertas*]

pubes (pyōō′bēz), *n., pl.* **-bes** (-bēz). *Anat.* **1.** the lower part of the abdomen, esp. the region between the right and left iliac regions. **2.** the hair appearing on the lower part of the abdomen at puberty. [t. L: pubic hair, groin]

pubescent (pyōō bĕs′ənt), *adj.* **1.** arriving or arrived at puberty. **2.** *Bot., Zool.* covered with down or fine short hair. [t. L: s. *pūbescens*, ppr., reaching puberty, becoming hairy or downy] —**pubes′cence,** *n.*

pubic (pyōō′bĭk), *adj.* pertaining to the pubes or pubis.

pubis (pyōō′bĭs), *n., pl.* **-bes** (-bēz), **-bises** (-bĭ sēz′). *Anat.* that part of either innominate bone which, with the corresponding part of the other, forms the front of the pelvis. See diag. under **pelvis.** [short for NL *os pūbis* bone of the pubes]

public (pŭb′lĭk), *adj.* **1.** of, pertaining to, or affecting the people as a whole or the community, state, or nation: *public affairs.* **2.** done, made, acting, etc., for the people or community as a whole: *a public prosecutor.* **3.** open to all the people: *a public meeting.* **4.** pertaining to or engaged in the affairs or service of the community or nation: *a public official.* **5.** maintained at the public expense, under public control, and open to the public generally: *a public library.* **6.** open to the view or knowledge of all; existing, done, etc., in public: *the fact became public.* **7.** having relations with or being known to the public generally: *a public character.* —*n.* **8.** the people constituting a community, state, or nation. **9.** a particular section of the people: *the novel-reading public.* **10.** public view or access: *in public.* **11.** *Colloq.* a public bar. [t. L: s. *pūblicus*; r. ME *publique*, t. F (fem.)]

public-address system (pŭb′lĭk ə drĕs′), an electronic system consisting of microphone, amplifier, and a loudspeaker, or a number of each of these units, which serves to amplify sound, as for use in a public hall, for speech or music.

publican (pŭb′lĭ kən), *n.* **1.** the keeper of a public house. **2.** *Roman Hist.* one who farmed the public revenues; a tax-gatherer. **3.** any collector of toll, tribute, or the like. [ME, t. L: s. *pūblicānus*]

publication (pŭb′lĭ kā′shən), *n.* **1.** the publishing of a book, periodical, map, piece of music, engraving, or the like. **2.** the act of publishing. **3.** the state or fact of being published. **4.** that which is published, as a book or the like. [ME, t. L: s. *pūblicātio*]

public bar, a room in a public house where drinks are cheaper than in the saloon bar, and which is less comfortably furnished. Cf. **saloon bar, private bar.**

public company, a company having shares offered for public subscription, advertising itself by prospectus and having not less than 50 shareholders.

public convenience, a room, building, etc., having lavatories, washbasins, etc., for public use.

public domain, *U.S. Law.* **1.** the status of a writing or an invention upon which the copyright or patent has expired or of works which have been published without copyright protection. **2.** land owned by the government.

public enemy, **1.** a person who is a danger or menace to the public, usually as shown by his criminal record. **2.** a nation or government at war with one's own.

public funds, government securities which comprise the national debt.

public house, a place where alcoholic beverages are sold to be drunk on the premises, usually having more than one bar; tavern.

publicist (pŭb′lĭ sĭst), *n.* **1.** one who is expert in or writes on current public or political affairs. **2.** an expert in public or international law. **3.** a press agent or public relations man.

publicity (pŭb lĭs′ĭ tĭ), *n.* **1.** the state of being public, or open to general observation or knowledge. **2.** public notice as the result of advertising or other special measures. **3.** the state of being brought to public notice by announcements (apart from advertisements) by mention in the press, on the radio, or any means serving to effect the purpose. **4.** the measures, process, or business of securing public notice. **5.** advertisement matter, as leaflets, films, etc., intended to attract public notice.

publicize (pŭb′lĭ sīz′), *v.t.,* **-cized, -cizing.** to give publicity to; bring to public notice; advertise: *they publicized the meeting as best they could.* Also, **publicise.**

public liability insurance, insurance which protects the policyholder against risks involving liability to the public for legal damages occasioned by negligence.

publicly (pŭb′lĭk lĭ), *adv.* **1.** in a public or open manner. **2.** by the public. **3.** in the name of the community. **4.** by public action or consent.

public opinion, an opinion held by a wide section of a community: *public opinion was against disarmament.*

public opinion poll, a poll by sampling to predict election results or to estimate public attitudes on issues.

public orator, an officer in certain English universities having the duty of making speeches, usually in Latin, on certain occasions.

public prosecutor, an officer of the state who is required to prosecute in certain important legal cases: in England called **Director of Public Prosecutions.**

Public Record Office, the place where the general records of the realm are kept.

public relations, **1.** the practice of promoting goodwill among the public for a company, government body, individual or the like; the practice of working to present a favourable image. **2.** the techniques used.

public school, **1.** (in Britain) any of certain large, endowed boarding schools, patronized esp. by the wealthy, which prepare pupils mainly for the universities or public service. **2.** (in the U.S.) a school maintained at the public expense for the education of the children and youth of a community or district, as part of a system of public (and usually free) education, commonly forming one of a series of graded schools including primary schools, grammar schools, and high schools. The primary schools and grammar schools together are known as elementary or common schools; the high schools, as distinguished from these, are known as secondary schools.

public servant, a civil servant, or one holding a government office.

public service vehicle, a bus, taxi, or the like licensed to carry passengers.

public-spirited (pŭb′lĭk spĭr′ĭ tĭd), *adj.* having or showing an unselfish desire for the public good: *a public-spirited citizen.*

public trustee, a government-appointed official who acts as executor or trustee if required, thus ensuring continuity of service.

public utility, an organization performing an essential public service, as supplying gas, electricity or transport, and operated or regulated either by a company, the state, or local government.

public works, constructions as roads, dams, post offices, etc., out of government funds for public use.

publish (pŭb′lĭsh), *v.t.* **1.** to issue, or cause to be issued, in copies made by printing or other processes, for sale or distribution to the public, as a book, periodical, map, piece of music, engraving, or the like. **2.** to issue to the public the works of (an author). **3.** to announce formally or officially; proclaim; promulgate. **4.** to make publicly or generally known. **5.** *Law.* (in the law of defamation) to communicate (the defamatory statement in some form) to some person or persons other than the person defamed. —*v.i.* **6.** to issue a periodical or the like, esp. regularly: *they publish on Fridays.* **7.** to have one's writing published by a particular publishing house: *with whom does he publish?* [ME, f. F *publ(ier)* + -ISH²] —**pub′lishable,** *adj.* —**Syn. 3.** See **announce.**

publisher (pŭb′lĭ shə), *n.* **1.** one whose business is the publishing of books, periodicals, engravings, or the like. **2.** *U.S.* the proprietor of a newspaper, etc., or his representative.

publishing (pŭb′lĭ shĭng), *n.* the business of a publisher.

publishment (pŭb′lĭsh mənt), *n.* publication.

Puccini (po͞o chē′nĭ; *It.* po͞ot chē′nē), *n.* **Giacomo** (*It.* jä′kō mō), 1858–1924, Italian operatic composer.

puccoon (pə ko͞on′), *n.* **1.** any of certain plants which yield a red dye, as the bloodroot (*Sanguinaria canadensis*) and certain herbs of the boraginaceous genus *Lithospermum.* **2.** the dye itself. [t. Algonquian]

puce (pyo͞os), *adj.* **1.** of a dark or purplish brown. —*n.* **2.** dark or purplish brown. [t. F: lit., flea, g. L *pūlex*]

puck (pŭk), *n.* a flat rubber disc used in place of a ball in ice hockey. [var. of POKE¹]

Puck (pŭk), *n.* **1.** a mischievous sprite, fairy, or goblin (called also Hobgoblin and Robin Goodfellow) who appears as a character in Shakespeare's *Midsummer Night's Dream.* **2.** (*l.c.*) a malicious or mischievous demon or spirit; a goblin. [ME *pouke*, OE *pūca*, c. Icel. *pūki* a mischievous demon]

pucka (pŭk′ə), *adj.* pukka.

pucker (pŭk′ə), *v.t., v.i.* **1.** to draw or gather into wrinkles or irregular folds. —*n.* **2.** a wrinkle; an irregular fold. **3.** a puckered part, as of cloth tightly or crookedly sewn. **4.** *Archaic.* a state of agitation or perturbation. [appar. a freq. form connected with POKE² (bag). Cf. PURSE, v.]

puckery (pŭk′ə rĭ), *adj.* **1.** puckered. **2.** puckering. **3.** tending to pucker.

puckish (pŭk′ĭsh), *adj.* (*also cap.*) mischievous; impish.

pud (po͝od), *n. Colloq.* pudding.

pudding (po͝od′ĭng), *n.* **1.** a sweet or savoury dish made in many forms and of various ingredients, as flour (or rice, tapioca, or the like), milk, and eggs, with fruit, meat, or other ingredients. **2.** a course in a meal following the main or meat course; dessert; sweet. **3.** a skin filled with seasoned minced meat, oatmeal, blood, etc., and cooked; a kind of sausage. **4.** anything resembling a pudding (def. 1), as in texture, etc. **5.** *Colloq.* a small, fat person. **6.** *Colloq.* a stupid person. [ME *puddyng, poding*; orig. uncert. Cf. LG *puddewurst* black pudding]

pudding face, *Colloq.* a round, fat, smooth face. —**pudding-faced** (po͝od′ĭng fāst′), *adj.*

pudding fender, *Naut.* a cylindrical canvas bag covered with coir matting, filled with small pieces of cork, used as a fender (def. 4).

pudding head, *Colloq.* a stupid person. —**pudding-headed** (po͝od′ĭng hĕd′ĭd), *adj.*

pudding stone, *Geol.* a conglomerate.

puddle (pŭd′l), *n., v.,* **-dled, -dling.** —*n.* **1.** a small pool of water, esp. dirty water, as in a road after rain. **2.** a small pool of any liquid. **3.** clay, or a similar material, which has been mixed with water and tempered, used as a watertight canal lining, etc. **4.** *Rowing.* the swirl of water left by the blade of an oar after a stroke. —*v.t.* **5.** to mark or fill with puddles. **6.** to wet with dirty water, etc. **7.** to make (water) muddy or dirty. **8.** to muddle or confuse. **9.** to make (clay, etc.) into puddle. **10.** to cover with pasty clay or puddle. **11.** to subject (molten iron) to the process of puddling. **12.** *Hort.* to dip (the roots of a tree, shrub, etc.) into a mixture of loam and water to retard drying out during transplanting. [ME *puddel, podel*, appar. der. OE *pudd* ditch] —**pud′dler,** *n.* —**pud′dly,** *adj.*

puddling (pŭd′lĭng), *n.* **1.** the act of one who puddles. **2.** the conversion of pig-iron into wrought iron by heating and stirring the molten metal in a reverberatory furnace, with an oxidizing agent. **3.** the act or method of making puddle of clay or a similar material. **4.** puddle (def. 3).

pudency (pyo͞o′dn sĭ), *n.* shamefacedness; modesty. [t. LL: m. s. *pudentia*]

pudendum (pyo͞o dĕn′dəm), *n., pl.* **-da** (-də). (*also pl.*) *Anat.* the external genital organs, esp. those of the female; the vulva. [t. L, prop. neut. ger., that about which one should have a feeling of modesty]

pudgy (pŭj′ĭ), *adj.,* **pudgier, pudgiest.** podgy. [orig. obscure] —**pudg′ily,** *adv.* —**pudg′iness,** *n.*

Pudsey (pŭd′zĭ), *n.* a town in England, in the West Riding of Yorkshire. 34,851 (1961).

Puebla (*Sp.* pwĕ′blä), *n.* a town in S central Mexico. 338,685 (est. 1965).

pueblo (pwĕb′lō; *also for 3, 4, Sp.* pwĕ′blō), *n., pl.* **-los.** **1.** *U.S.* **a.** a communal habitation of certain Indians of the south-western U.S.; the communal house or group of houses, built of adobe or stone. **b.** (*cap.*) any sedentary, farming, peace-loving Indians of four linguistic groups (Tanoan, Keresan, Zuñi, Hopi), living prehistorically and now in pueblos in New Mexico and Arizona. **2.** an Indian village. **3.** (in Spanish America) a town or village. **4.** (in the Philippines) a town or a township. [t. Sp.: people, g. L *populus*]

Pueblo (pwĕb′lō), *n.* a city in central Colorado. 91,181 (1960).

puerile (pyo͞o′ə rĭl), *adj.* **1.** of or pertaining to a child or boy. **2.** childishly foolish, irrational, or trivial: *a piece of puerile writing.* [t. L, neut. of *puerīlis*] —**pu′erilely,** *adv.*

puerilism (pyo͞o′ə rĭ lĭz′əm), *n. Psychol.* childishness (the stage following infantilism).

puerility (pyo͞oə rĭl′ĭ tĭ), *n., pl.* **-ties.** **1.** the quality of being puerile; childish foolishness or triviality. **2.** something puerile; a puerile act, idea, remark, etc.: *an inexcusable puerility.*

puerperal (pyo͞o û′pə rəl), *adj.* **1.** of or pertaining to a woman in childbirth. **2.** pertaining to or consequent on childbirth: *puerperal fever.* [t. NL: s. *puerperālis*, der. L *puerperus* bringing forth children]

puerperal fever, an infection occurring during the puerperium; childbed fever.

puerperium (pyo͞oə pĭə′rĭ əm), *n. Obstet.* the period following childbirth during which the organs of reproduction are returning to normal, usually lasting 6 weeks. [t. L]

Puerto Rico (pwû′tō rē′kō; *Sp.* pwĕr′tō rē′kō), an island in the West Indies: a commonwealth associated with the U.S. 2,513,200 (est. 1963); 3435 sq. mi. *Cap.:* San Juan. Former official name (until 1932), **Porto Rico.** See map under **Haiti.** —**Puer′to-Ri′can,** *adj., n.*

puff (pŭf), *n.* **1.** a short, quick blast, as of wind or breath. **2.** an abrupt emission of air, vapour, etc. **3.** a single inhalation and exhalation, as of a cigarette. **4.** the sound of an abrupt emission of air, etc. **5.** a small quantity of vapour, smoke, etc., emitted at one blast. **6.** an inflated or distended part of a thing; a swelling; a protuberance. **7.** a commendation, esp. an exaggerated one, of a book, an actor's performance, etc. **8.** inflated or exaggerated praise, esp. as uttered or written from interested motives; seller's talk. **9.** a powder puff. **10.** a form of light pastry with a filling of cream, jam, or the like. **11.** a portion of material gathered and held down at the edges but left full in the middle, as in a dress, etc. **12.** a cylindrical roll of hair. **13.** *Chiefly U.S.* an eiderdown quilt. **14.** *Slang.* a male homosexual. **15.** *Dial.* a puffball. —*v.i.* **16.** to blow with short, quick blasts, as the wind. **17.** to be emitted in a puff. **18.** to emit a puff or puffs; to breathe quick and hard, as after violent exertion. **19.** to go with puffing or panting. **20.** to emit puffs or whiffs of vapour or smoke. **21.** to move with such puffs. **22.** to take puffs at a cigar, etc. **23.** to become inflated or distended (usually fol. by *up*). **24.** *Auctioneering.* (of an auctioneer's accomplice) to make artificial bids in order to inflate the price of an object. **—*v.t.* 25.** to send forth (air, vapour, etc.) in short quick blasts. **26.** to drive or impel by puffing, or with a short quick blast. **27.** to extinguish with a puff; blow out (fol. by *out*): *to puff out a light.* **28.** to smoke (a cigar, etc.). **29.** to inflate or distend, esp. with air. **30.** to inflate with pride, etc. **31.** to praise in exaggerated language. **32.** to advertise with exaggerated commendation. **33.** to apply powder to (the face, etc.) with a powder puff. **34.** to apply (powder) with a powder puff. **35.** to arrange in puffs, as the hair. **36.** *Auctioneering.* to inflate the price of artificially, as by having an accomplice in the audience who makes false bids. [ME, OE *pyff*; of imit. orig.]

puff adder, a large, venomous African snake, *Bitis arietans*, which puffs up its body when irritated.

puffball (pŭf′bôl′), *n.* any of various basidiomycetous fungi, esp. genus *Lycoperdon* and allied genera, characterized by a ball-like fruit body which emits a cloud of spores when broken.

puffed (pŭft), *adj.* **1.** distended or inflated. **2.** *Colloq.* out of breath.

puffed-up (pŭft′ŭp′), *adj. Colloq.* self-important.

puff bird, any bird of the tropical American family *Bucconidae*, usually brownish in colour, with long bills.

puffer (pŭf′ə), *n.* **1.** one who or that which puffs. **2.** any of various fishes of the family *Tetraodontidae*, capable of inflating the body with water or air until it resembles a globe, with the spines in the skin erected. **3.** *Auctioneering.* an auctioneer's accomplice who makes false bids in order to inflate prices artificially. **4.** *Childish Slang.* a steam locomotive.

puffery (pŭf′ə rĭ), *n., pl.* **-eries. 1.** act of praising unduly. **2.** exaggerated commendation.

puffin (pŭf′ĭn), *n.* any of various seabirds (genera *Fratercula* and *Lunda*) of the auk family, with a curious bill, as *F. arctica*, the common species, which abounds on the coasts of the northern Atlantic, nesting in holes in the ground. [ME *poffin, pophyn*; orig. uncert.]

Common puffin, *Fratercula arctica* (Ab. 1 ft long)

puffing adder (pŭf′ĭng), the hognose snake of the U.S.

puff pastry, rough puff pastry. Also, *U.S.*, **puff paste.**

puff pipe, *Plumbing.* a pipe with access to the open air, connected to a waste pipe to prevent siphonic action from occurring.

puffy (pŭf′ĭ), *adj.*, **puffier, puffiest. 1.** gusty. **2.** short-winded. **3.** inflated or distended. **4.** fat. **5.** conceited. **6.** bombastic. **—puff′iness,** *n.*

pug[1] (pŭg), *n.* **1.** one of a breed of dogs, having a short, smooth coat of silver, fawn, or black, a deeply wrinkled face, and a tightly curled tail. **2.** a pug nose. **3.** a fox. **4.** a small locomotive used for shunting. [orig. unknown]

Pug[1] (def. 1) (1 ft high at the shoulder)

pug[2] (pŭg), *v.t.*, **pugged, pugging. 1.** to knead (clay, etc.) with water to make it plastic, as in brick-making. **2.** to stop or fill in with clay or the like. **3.** to pack or cover with mortar, etc., to deaden sound. **4.** to mix with water, forming a paste. [orig. uncert.]

pug[3] (pŭg), *n. Slang.* pugilist. [short for PUGILIST]

pug[4] (pŭg), *n., v.*, **pugged, pugging.** *Anglo-Indian.* **—*n.* 1.** a footprint, as of an animal. **—*v.t.* 2.** to track (game, etc.) by following footprints. [t. Hind.: m. *pag*]

pugdog (pŭg′dŏg′), *n.* pug[1] (def. 1).

puggaree (pŭg′ə rĭ), *n.* pugree. Also, **pugaree.**

pugging (pŭg′ĭng), *n.* **1.** the action of one who pugs. **2.** material of various kinds, commonly used for deadening sound, as in floors.

pugh (pōō, pŏŏ), *interj.* pooh.

pugilism (pyōō′jĭ lĭz′əm), *n.* the art or practice of fighting with the fists; boxing. [f. L *pugil* boxer (akin to *pugnus* fist, and *pugnāre* fight) + -ISM]

pugilist (pyōō′jĭ lĭst), *n.* one who fights with the fists; a boxer, usually a professional. **—pu′gilis′tic,** *adj.* **—pu′gilis′tically,** *adv.*

Pugin (pyōō′jĭn), *n.* **Augustus Welby Northmore** (ô gŭs′təs wĕl′bĭ nôth′mô), 1812–52, English architect.

Puglia (*It.* pōōl′lyä), *n.* Italian name of **Apulia.**

pugnacious (pŭg nā′shəs), *adj.* given to fighting; quarrelsome; aggressive. [f. *pugnaci(ty)* (t. L: m. s. *pugnācitas* combativeness) + -OUS] **—pugna′ciously,** *adv.* **—pugnacity** (pŭg năs′ĭ tĭ), **pugna′ciousness,** *n.*

pug nose, a short nose turning abruptly up at the tip. **—pug-nosed** (pŭg′nōzd′), *adj.*

pugree (pŭg′rĭ), *n.* **1.** a light turban worn by natives in India. **2.** a scarf of silk or cotton wound round a hat or helmet and falling down behind, as a protection against the sun. Also, **pagri, puggaree, puggree, puggery, pugri.** [t. Hind.: m. *pagrī* turban]

puisne (pyōō′nĭ), *adj. Law.* younger; inferior in rank; junior, as in appointment. [archaic form of PUNY, t. OF: f. *puis* after (g. var. of L *posteā*) + *ne* born, pp. of *naistre* come into existence (g. L *nascere*)]

puissance (pyōō′ĭ səns), *n. Archaic.* power, might, or force. [ME, t. OF, der. *puissant* PUISSANT]

puissant (pyōō′ĭ sənt), *adj. Archaic.* powerful; mighty; potent. [ME, t. OF, ppr. of *pouvoir* be able, g. var. of L *potens*, ppr., being able, having power] **—pu′issantly,** *adv.*

puke (pyōōk), *v.i., v.t.*, **puked, puking,** *n.* vomit. [orig. uncert.]

pukeko (pōō kĕk′ō, pōō′kĕk′ə), *n.* the swamphen of New Zealand, *Porphyrio melanotus.* [t. Maori]

pukka (pŭk′ə), *adj.* **1.** *Anglo-Indian.* reliable; good; genuine. **2.** *Colloq.* of colonial, esp. Anglo-Indian, origin, behaviour, etc. Also, **pucka.** [t. Hind.: m. *pakkā* cooked, ripe, mature]

puku (pōō′kōō), *n.* a medium-sized foxy-red antelope, *Cobus vardoni* or *Adenota vardonii*, of southern Africa, now rare except in Zambia. [t. Tonga (a language of Zambia): m. *mpuku*]

Pula (*Serb.* pōō′lä), *n.* a seaport in NW Yugoslavia, on the Istrian peninsula. 37,403 (1961). Formerly, **Pulj** (pōōly). Italian name, **Pola.**

pulchritude (pŭl′krĭ tyōōd′), *n.* beauty; comeliness. [ME, t. L: m. *pulchritūdo*]

pulchritudinous (pŭl′krĭ tyōō′dĭ nəs), *adj.* beautiful.

pule (pyōōl), *v.i.*, **puled, puling.** to cry in a thin voice, as a child; whimper; whine. [? of imit. orig.] **—pul′er,** *n.*

puling (pyōō′lĭng), *adj.* whining: *a puling child.* **—pul′ingly,** *adv.*

Pulitzer (pōōl′ĭt sə), *n.* **Joseph,** 1847–1911, U.S. journalist and publisher, born in Hungary.

Pulitzer Prize, one of a group of annual prizes in journalism and letters established by Joseph Pulitzer.

pull (pōōl), *v.t.* **1.** to draw or haul towards oneself or itself, in a particular direction, or into a particular position: *to pull a sledge up a hill.* **2.** to draw or tug at with force: *to pull a person's hair.* **3.** to draw, rend, or tear (apart, to pieces, etc.). **4.** to draw or pluck away from a place of growth, attachment, etc.: *to pull a tooth.* **5.** to strip of feathers, hair, etc., as a bird, a hide, etc. **6.** *Slang.* to draw out for use, as a knife or a pistol. **7.** *Slang.* to put or carry through (something attempted): *to pull a fast one.* **8.** to cause to form, as a grimace: *to pull a face.* **9.** *Golf.* to play (the ball) with a curve to the left (or, if a left-handed player, to the right). **10.** *Print.* to take (an impression or proof) from type, etc. **11.** to propel by rowing, as a boat. **12.** to be provided with, or rowed with (a certain number of oars), as a boat: *a racing shell pulls eight oars.* **13.** to strain, as a ligament. **14.** *Racing.* to hold in or check (a horse), esp. so as to keep it from winning. **15.** *Boxing.* to deliver (a punch) without full force; check or restrain. **16.** *Cricket.* to hit (a ball pitched on the wicket or on the off side) to the on side. **—*v.i.* 17.** to exert a drawing, tugging, or hauling force (often fol. by *at*). **18.** to inhale through a pipe, cigarette, etc. **19.** to become or come as specified, by pulling: *a rope pulls apart.* **20.** to row. **21.** to proceed by rowing. **22.** *Cricket, Golf.* to pull the ball. **—*v.* 23.** Some special verb phrases are:

pull a fast one, *Colloq.* to deceive; to play a sly trick.

pull ahead, to move towards the front, or begin to win in a race or other contest.

pull apart, 1. to rend in pieces. **2.** to analyse critically in detail.

pull down, 1. to lower; draw downwards: *to pull down the blinds.* **2.** to demolish. **3.** to reduce or make lower: *to pull down prices in a sale.*

pull in, 1. (of a vehicle, driver, etc.) to move to the side of the road, into a lay-by, or the like, as in order to stop. **2.** to arrive at a destination, stopping place, etc.: *the train pulled in to Waterloo.* **3.** *Slang.* to arrest (a person).

pull off, *Colloq.* to succeed in achieving or performing something.

pull one's punches, 1. *Boxing.* to deliver punches without full force. **2.** to act with more show than effect, as by failing to follow through an initial move.

pull oneself together, to recover one's self-control.

pull one's weight, to make a full and fair contribution to

a task or undertaking, as in rowing or any other activity.
pull out, **1.** to leave; depart: *a train pulling out of a station.* **2.** (of a vehicle, driver, etc.) to move out of a lane or stream of traffic, as in preparing to overtake. **3.** *Colloq.* to withdraw, as from an agreement or enterprise. **4.** (of an aircraft) to return to level flight after a dive.
pull over, (of a vehicle, driver, etc.) to move towards the side of the road, or in some other direction as specified.
pull round, *Colloq.* to recover, as from an illness, period of adversity, or the like.
pull someone's leg, to tease a person.
pull strings, *Colloq.* to seek the advancement of oneself or another by using social contacts and other means not directly connected with one's ability or suitability.
pull the wool over someone's eyes, *Colloq.* to deceive; hoodwink.
pull through, *Colloq.* **1.** to recover, as from an illness, period of adversity, or the like. **2.** to make one's way through, as by a pull or effort.
pull together, to cooperate, as in a team.
pull to pieces, **1.** to rend in pieces; destroy completely. **2.** to analyse critically in detail.
pull up, **1.** to stop. **2.** to cause to stop. **3.** to correct or rebuke. **4.** to improve; bring to a higher or required standard. **5.** to uproot or pull out of the ground. **6.** *Colloq.* to gain ground, as a horse in a race.
—n. **24.** the act of pulling or drawing. **25.** force used in pulling; pulling power. **26.** a drawing of a liquid into the mouth: *he took a long pull at his glass of beer.* **27.** an inhalation of tobacco, as from a pipe or cigarette. **28.** a part or thing to be pulled, as a handle or the like. **29.** an instrument or device for pulling something. **30.** a spell at rowing. **31.** a stroke of an oar. **32.** a pulling of the ball in cricket or golf. **33.** *Slang.* an advantage over another or others. **34.** *Slang.* influence, as with persons able to grant favours. [ME *pulle(n)*, OE *pullian* pull, pluck. Cf. MLG *pūlen* strip off husks, pick, Icel. *pūla* work hard] —**pull′er,** *n.* —**Syn.** **2.** See **draw.** —**Ant.** **2.** push.

pullback (po͝ol′băk′), *n.* *Mach.* a device for pulling a moving part back to its original position.

pullet (po͝ol′ĭt), *n.* a young hen, less than one year old. [ME *poullet*, t. OF: m. *poulette* young hen, dim. of *poule* hen, g. LL *pulla* young animal, chicken]

pulley (po͝ol′ĭ), *n., pl.* **-leys.** **1.** a wheel with a grooved rim for carrying a line, turning in a frame or block and serving to change the direction of or transmit power, as in pulling at one end of the line to raise a weight at the other end. **2.** a combination of such wheels in a block, or of such wheels or blocks in a tackle, to increase the power applied. **3.** a wheel driven by or driving a belt or the like, as in the transmission of power. [ME, t. OF: m. *poulie*, ult. from a deriv. of Gk *pólos* axle]

pull-in (po͝ol′ĭn′), *n.* **1.** a place by the roadside where vehicles may pull in and stop; a lay-by. **2.** a roadside café.

Pullman (po͝ol′mən), *n., pl.* **-mans.** **1.** a railway carriage with luxury fittings. **2.** a fast train of such carriages, with dining cars, etc. [named after George M. *Pullman*, 1831–1897, the American originator]

pullorum disease (po͞o lô′rəm), an egg-transmitted bacterial disease, frequently a cause of heavy death losses in very young poultry. [*pullorum*, gen. pl. of L *pullus* cockerel]

pull-on (po͝ol′ŏn′), *n.* **1.** an article of clothing that is pulled on, as a sweater. *—adj.* **2.** denoting such an article.

pullover (po͝ol′ō′və), *n.* a sweater which is drawn over the head when it is put on.

pullulate (pŭl′yo͞o lāt′), *v.i.,* **-lated, -lating.** **1.** to come forth in growth; sprout. **2.** to send forth sprouts, buds, etc. **3.** to spring up abundantly. **4.** to breed; multiply; teem. **5.** to be produced as offspring. [t. L: m. s. *pullulātus*, pp., sprouted] —**pul′lula′tion,** *n.*

pulmonary (pŭl′mə nə rĭ), *adj.* **1.** of or pertaining to the lungs. **2.** of the nature of a lung; lunglike. **3.** affecting the lungs. **4.** having lungs or lunglike organs. **5.** pertaining to or affected with disease of the lungs. [t. L: m. s. *pulmōnārius*, der. *pulmo* lung, akin to Gk *pleúmōn*, later *pneúmōn* lung]

pulmonary artery, an artery conveying (venous) blood from the right ventricle of the heart to the lungs. See diag. under **heart.**

pulmonary vein, a vein conveying (arterial) blood from the lungs to the left auricle of the heart. See diag. under **heart.**

pulmonate (pŭl′mə nĭt), *adj.* **1.** having lungs or lunglike organs. **2.** belonging to the *Pulmonata*, an order or group of gastropod molluscs usually breathing by means of a lunglike sac, and including most of the terrestrial snails and the slugs and certain aquatic snails. *—n.* **3.** a pulmonate gastropod. [t. NL: m. s. *pulmōnātus*, der. L *pulmo* lung]

pulmonic (pŭl mŏn′ĭk), *adj.* **1.** pulmonary. **2.** pneumonic. [t. F: m. *pulmonique*, der. L *pulmo* lung]

Pulmotor (pŭl′mō′tə, po͝ol′-), *n.* *Trademark.* a mechanical device for artificial respiration where respiration has ceased through asphyxiation, drowning, etc., which forces oxygen into the lungs. [f. L *pul(mo)* lung + MOTOR]

pulp (pŭlp), *n.* **1.** the succulent part of a fruit. **2.** the pith of the stem of a plant. **3.** a soft or fleshy part of an animal body. **4.** the inner substance of the tooth containing arteries, veins, and lymphatic and nerve tissue which communicate with their respective vascular and lymph and nerve systems of the body. See diag. under **tooth.** **5.** any soft, moist, slightly cohering mass, as that into which linen, wood, etc., are converted in the making of paper. **6.** anything worthless, as a magazine containing sensational and lurid stories, articles, etc.; trash. **7.** *Mining.* **a.** ore pulverized and mixed with water. **b.** dry crushed ore. *—v.t.* **8.** to reduce to pulp. **9.** to remove the pulp from. *—v.i.* **10.** to become reduced to pulp. [t. L: s. *pulpa*]

pulpit (po͝ol′pĭt), *n.* **1.** a platform or raised structure in a church, from which the priest delivers a sermon, etc. **2. the pulpit, a.** the clergy collectively. **b.** the Christian ministry. **3.** preaching. [ME, t. L: s. *pulpitum* stage, platform, ML pulpit]

pulpiteer (po͝ol′pĭ tĭə′), *n.* a preacher by profession (usually contemptuous). Also, **pulpiter** (po͝ol′pĭ tə).

pulpwood (pŭlp′wo͝od′), *n.* spruce or other soft wood suitable for making paper.

pulpy (pŭl′pĭ), *adj.,* **pulpier, pulpiest.** of the nature of or resembling pulp; fleshy; soft. —**pulp′iness,** *n.*

pulque (po͝ol′kĭ; *Sp.* po͞ol′kė), *n.* a fermented milky drink made from the juice of the agave in Mexico. [Mex. Sp.]

pulsar (pŭl′sä), *n.* *Astron.* one of a number of sources of pulsed radio signals detected within the galaxy but outside the solar system. [PULS(ATING ST)AR]

pulsate (pŭl sāt′), *v.i.,* **-sated, -sating.** **1.** to expand and contract rhythmically, as the heart; beat; throb. **2.** to vibrate; quiver. [t. L: m. s. *pulsātus*, pp., pushed, struck, beaten. See PULSE[1]]
—**Syn.** **1.** PULSATE, BEAT, PALPITATE, THROB refer to the recurrent vibratory movement of the heart, the pulse, etc. To PULSATE is to move in a definite rhythm, temporarily or for a longer duration: *blood pulsates in the arteries.* To BEAT is to repeat a vibration or pulsation regularly for some time: *one's heart beats many times a minute.* To PALPITATE is to beat at a rapid rate, often producing a flutter: *to palpitate with excitement.* To THROB is to beat with so much force as often to cause pain: *to throb with terror.*

pulsatile (pŭl′sə tīl′), *adj.* pulsating; throbbing.

pulsatilla (pŭl′sə tĭl′ə), *n.* a small group of ranunculaceous perennial herbs usually included in the genus *Anemone*, differing from related plants in having persistent, feathery styles, as *A. pulsatilla*, the pasque flower.

pulsation (pŭl sā′shən), *n.* **1.** the act of pulsating; beating or throbbing. **2.** a beat or throb, as of the pulse. **3.** vibration or undulation. **4.** a single vibration.

pulsative (pŭl′sə tĭv), *adj.* pulsating.

pulsator (pŭl sā′tə), *n.* **1.** something that pulsates, beats, or strikes. **2.** a pulsometer (def. 2). [t. L: striker]

pulsatory (pŭl′sə tə rĭ, -trĭ), *adj.* pulsating; throbbing.

pulse[1] (pŭls), *n., v.,* **pulsed, pulsing.** *—n.* **1.** the regular throbbing of the arteries caused by the successive contractions of the heart, esp. as felt in an artery at the wrist. **2.** a single beat or throb of the arteries or the heart. **3.** the rhythmic recurrence of strokes, vibrations, or undulations. **4.** a single stroke, vibration, or undulation. **5.** a throb of life, emotion, etc. **6.** vitality. **7.** feeling, sentiment, or tendency. **8.** a brief increase in the magnitude of a quantity whose value is usually constant, as a current or voltage. **9.** an intermittent signal from a radio transmitter, radar apparatus or the like. *—v.i.* **10.** to beat or throb; pulsate. **11.** to beat, vibrate, or undulate. [t. L: m. *pulsus* a pushing, beating, pulse; r. ME *pous*, t. OF]

pulse[2] (pŭls), *n.* **1.** the edible seeds of certain leguminous plants, as peas, beans, lentils, etc. **2.** a plant producing such seeds. [ME *puls*, t. OF: m. *po(u)ls*, g. L *puls* thick pap of meal, pulse, etc. Cf. POULTICE]

pulse-jet (pŭls′jĕt′), *n.* *Aeron.* a type of ramjet engine in which the combustion process is discontinuous and is arranged to occur at intervals between which the pressure in the combustion chamber is allowed to build up, as used in the flying bombs of World War II. Also, **pul′sojet′.**

pulse-time modulation, *Electronics.* radio transmission in which the carrier is modulated to produce a series of pulses timed to transmit amplitude and pitch of the signal.

pulse-train (pŭls′trān′), *n.* a finite sequence of regular electrical pulses.

pulse-wave (pŭls′wāv′), *n.* the wave of blood flowing along an artery as the result of a heartbeat.

pulsimeter (pŭl sĭm′ĭ tə), *n.* an instrument for measuring the strength or quickness of the pulse. [f. *pulsi-* (comb. form repr. PULSE[1]) + -METER[1]]

pulsojet (pŭl′sə jĕt′), *n.* a pulse-jet.

pulsometer (pŭl sŏm′ĭ tə), *n.* **1.** a pulsimeter. **2.** a vacuum pump. [f. *pulso-* (comb. form repr. PULSE[1]) + -METER[1]]

pulverable (pŭl′və rə bl), *adj.* pulverizable.

pulverize (pŭl′və rīz′), *v.*, **-rized, -rizing.** —*v.t.* **1.** to reduce to dust or powder, as by pounding, grinding, etc. **2.** to demolish. **3.** *Slang.* to defeat overwhelmingly, as a fighter. —*v.i.* **4.** to become reduced to dust. Also, **pulverise.** [ME, t. LL: m. s. *pulverizāre*, der. L *pulvis* dust] —**pul′veriz′able,** *adj.* —**pul′veriza′tion,** *n.* —**pul′veriz′er,** *n.*

pulverulent (pŭl vĕ′ro͝o lənt), *adj.* **1.** consisting of dust or fine powder. **2.** crumbling to dust. **3.** covered with dust or powder. [t. L: s. *pulverulentus* dusty]

pulvillus (pŭl vĭl′əs), *n.*, *pl.* **-villi** (-vĭl′ī). *Entomol.* a cushion-like pad or process on an insect's foot. [t. L, dim. of *pulvīnus* cushion]

pulvinar (pŭl vī′nə), *adj.*, *n.*, *pl.* **-nars, -naria** (pŭl′vĭ nĕə′rĭ ə). —*adj.* **1.** cushion-like. **2.** of or pertaining to a pulvinus. —*n.* **3.** *Roman Antiq.* **a.** a cushioned couch, as one kept in readiness for a visitation by a god. **b.** a cushioned seat at a circus. **c.** any cushioned seat or sofa. [t. L: couch]

pulvinate (pŭl′vĭ nāt′), *adj.* **1.** cushion-shaped. **2.** having a pulvinus. Also, **pulvinated.** [t. L: m. s. *pulvīnātus* made into or like a cushion]

pulvinus (pŭl vī′nəs), *n.*, *pl.* **-ni** (-nī). *Bot.* a cushion-like swelling at the base of a leaf or leaflet, at the point of junction with the axis. [t. L: cushion]

puma (pyo͞o′mə), *n.* **1.** a large tawny feline, *Felis concolor*, of North and South America; the cougar; panther; mountain lion. **2.** its fur. [t. Sp., t. Quechua]

Puma, *Felis concolor* (Total length 7 ft, tail 2½ ft)

pumice (pŭm′ĭs), *n.*, *v.*, **-iced, -icing.** —*n.* **1.** Also, **pumice stone.** a porous or spongy form of volcanic glass, used, esp. when powdered, as an abrasive, etc. —*v.t.* **2.** to rub, smooth, clean, etc., with pumice. [ME *pomis*, t. OF, g. s. L *pūmex*; r. OE *pumic(stān)* pumice (stone), from L] —**pumiceous** (pyo͞o mĭsh′əs), *adj.*

pummel (pŭm′əl), *v.*, **-melled, -melling** or (*U.S.*) **-meled, -meling,** *n.* —*v.t.* Also, *Chiefly U.S.*, **pommel. 1.** to beat or thrash with rapid blows, as with the fists or, orig., a pommel. —*n.* **2.** a pommel.

pump[1] (pŭmp), *n.* **1.** an apparatus or machine for raising, driving, exhausting, or compressing fluids, as by means of a piston, plunger, or rotating vanes. —*v.t.* **2.** to raise, drive, etc., with a pump. **3.** to free from water, etc., by means of a pump (sometimes fol. by *out*). **4.** to inflate by pumping (often fol. by *up*): *to pump up a tyre.* **5.** to operate by action like that on a pump handle. **6.** to supply with air, as an organ, by means of a pumplike device. **7.** to drive, force, etc., as if from a pump: *they pumped ten bullets into him.* **8.** to seek to elicit information from, as by artful questioning. **9.** to elicit (information) by questioning. —*v.i.* **10.** to work a pump; raise or move water, etc., with a pump. **11.** to operate as a pump does. **12.** to gush out in spurts, as if driven by a pump: *blood pumping from a wound.* **13.** to move up and down like a pump-handle. **14.** to exert oneself in a manner likened to pumping. **15.** to seek to elicit information from a person. [ME *pumpe*, c. G *Pumpe*; orig. uncert.] —**pump′able,** *adj.* —**pump′er,** *n.* —**pump′like′,** *adj.*

pump[2] (pŭmp), *n.* **1.** a low, light, black, patent-leather shoe worn by men for ballroom dancing, with formal dress, etc. **2.** a low, slipper-like shoe worn by women, as for dancing. [orig. uncert.]

pumpernickel (pŭm′pə nĭk′l; *Ger.* po͝om′pə nĭk əl), *n.* a coarse, slightly sour bread made with wholemeal rye. [t. G]

pump gun, a repeating shotgun, operated by sliding a handle backwards and forwards along the magazine.

pumpkin (pŭmp′kĭn), *n.* **1.** the large edible fruits of species of coarse cucurbitaceous plants, esp. *Cucurbita maxima* in Europe, and *C. pepo* and its varieties in the U.S. **2.** the plants. [alter. of *pumpion*, t. F: m. *pompon* a melon, ult. der. L *pepo*, t. Gk: m. *pépōn*]

pumpkin-seed (pŭmp′kĭn sēd′), *n.* **1.** the seed of the pumpkin. **2.** a freshwater sunfish, *Lepomis gibbosus*, of eastern North America.

pumpman (pŭmp′mən), *n.*, *pl.* **-men** (-mən). a man who operates a power-driven pump.

pumproom (pŭmp′ro͝om′, -ro͞om′), *n.* a room in a spa where medicinal water is dispensed.

pumpwell (pŭmp′wĕl′), *n.* a well having a pump.

pun (pŭn), *n.*, *v.*, **punned, punning.** —*n.* **1.** the humorous use of a word in such a manner as to bring out different meanings or applications, or of words alike or nearly alike in sound but different in meaning; a play on words. —*v.i.* **2.** to make puns. [orig. uncert.]

puna (*Sp.* po͞o′nä), *n.* a high, cold, arid plateau, as in the Peruvian Andes. [t. Amer. Sp., t. Quechua]

Punakha (po͞o′nə kə), *n.* the winter capital of Bhutan. Cf. **Thimphu.**

punch[1] (pŭnch), *n.* **1.** a thrusting blow, esp. with the fist. **2.** *Slang.* a vigorous, telling effect or force. —*v.t.* **3.** to give a sharp thrust or blow to, esp. with the fist. **4.** *Western U.S.* to drive (cattle). **5.** to poke or prod, as with a stick. —*v.i.* **6.** to deliver blows: *he punches cleanly.* [? var. of POUNCE[1]] —**punch′er,** *n.*

punch[2] (pŭnch), *n.* **1.** a tool or apparatus for piercing, perforating, or stamping materials, impressing a design, forcing nails beneath a surface, driving bolts out of holes, etc. **2.** the solid tool used in a punching machine in conjunction with a corresponding hollow die for blanking out shaped pieces of sheet metal; the upper die. —*v.t.* **3.** to cut, stamp, pierce, form, or drive with a punch (tool). [short for PUNCHEON[2] (def. 3)]

punch[3] (pŭnch), *n.* **1.** a beverage consisting of wine or spirits mixed with water, milk, etc., and flavoured with sugar, lemon, spices, etc. **2.** a beverage of two or more fruit juices, sugar and water, often carbonated. [? short for PUNCHEON[1]; if so, a metonymic use]

Punch (pŭnch), *n.* **1.** the chief character in the puppet show called 'Punch and Judy', a grotesque, hook-nosed, hunchbacked figure who strangles his child, beats his wife (Judy) to death, etc. **2. pleased as Punch,** delighted; highly pleased. [short for PUNCHINELLO]

punchball (pŭnch′bôl′), *n.* **1.** Also, **punchbag** (pŭnch′-băg′). an inflated or stuffed ball or bag, usually suspended, punched with the fists as exercise or training. **2.** *U.S.* a game resembling baseball in which a rubber ball is thrown in the air and punched rather than hit with a bat.

punchbowl (pŭnch′bōl′), *n.* **1.** a bowl in which punch is mixed, and from which it is served by means of a ladle. **2.** devil's punchbowl.

punch-drunk (pŭnch′drŭngk′), *adj.* **1.** having cerebral concussion so that one's movements resemble those of a drunken person, a condition sometimes found in boxers. **2.** *Colloq.* dull-witted; stupid or dazed.

punched card, *Computers.* a standard-sized card through which a pattern of holes is punched to represent information in a form which can be read by a computer or business machine. Also, **punch card.**

punched paper tape, *Computers.* See **paper tape.**

puncheon[1] (pŭn′chən), *n.* **1.** a large cask of varying capacity, but usually 111·6 gals. **2.** its volume as a measure. [t. F, ult. identical with PUNCHEON[2]]

puncheon[2] (pŭn′chən), *n.* **1.** a slab of timber, or a piece of a split log, with the face roughly dressed, used for flooring, etc. **2.** a short upright timber in a framing. **3.** (in goldsmith work) **a.** any of various pointed instruments; a punch. **b.** a stamping tool. [ME *punchon*, t. OF: m. *po(i)nchon*, ult. der. L *punctus*, pp., pricked, pierced. Cf. PUNGENT]

Punchinello (pŭn′chĭ nĕl′ō), *n.*, *pl.* **-los, -loes. 1.** the chief character in a puppet show of Italian origin, being the prototype of Punch. **2.** (*l.c.*) any similar grotesque or absurd person or thing. [t. It.: m. *Pulcinella*, prob. orig. dim. of *pulcino* chicken, ult. der. L *pullus* young animal]

punching bag, *Chiefly U.S.* punchball. Also, **punching ball.**

punching machine, *Mach.* a power-driven machine used to cut, draw, or otherwise shape material, esp. metal sheets, with dies, under pressure or by heavy blows. Also, **punching press;** *U.S.*, **punch press.**

punch line, the culminating sentence, line, phrase, or the like of a joke, esp. that on which the whole joke depends.

punch-up (pŭnch′ŭp′), *n.* *Colloq.* a fight.

punchy (pŭn′chĭ), *adj.* **-chier, -chiest.** *Colloq.*, *Chiefly U.S.* **1.** punch-drunk. **2.** forceful; vigorously effective.

punctate (pŭngk′tāt), *adj.* marked with points or dots; having minute spots or depressions. Also, **punctated.** [t. NL: m. s. *punctātus*, der. L *punctum* point]

punctation (pŭngk tā′shən), *n.* **1.** punctate condition or marking. **2.** one of the marks or depressions.

punctilio (pŭngk tĭl′ĭ ō′), *n.*, *pl.* **-tilios. 1.** a fine point, particular, or detail, as of conduct, ceremony, or procedure. **2.** strictness or exactness in the observance of forms. [t. It.: m. *puntiglio*, t. Sp.: m. *puntillo*, dim. of *punto* point, t. L: m. *punctum*]

punctilious (pŭngk tĭl′ĭ əs), *adj.* attentive to punctilios; strict or exact in the observance of forms in conduct or actions. —**punctil′iously,** *adv.* —**punctil′iousness,** *n.* —**Syn.** See **scrupulous.**

punctual (pŭngk′tyo͞o əl), *adj.* **1.** strictly observant of an appointed or regular time; not late. **2.** prompt, as an action; made at an appointed or regular time: *punctual payment.* **3.** of or pertaining to a point: *punctual coordinates* (the coordinates of a point). **4.** *Obs.* punctilious. [ME, t. ML: s. *punctuālis*, der. L *punctus* a pricking, a point] —**punc′tually,** *adv.* —**punc′tualness,** *n.*

punctuality (pŭngk′tyo͞o ăl′ĭ tĭ), *n.* **1.** the quality or state of being punctual. **2.** strict observance in keeping engagements, etc.; promptness.

punctuate (pŭngk′tyo͞o āt′), *v.*, **-ated, -ating.** —*v.t.* **1.** to mark or divide with punctuation marks, as a sentence, etc., in order to make the meaning clear. **2.** to interrupt at intervals, as a speech by cheers. **3.** to give point or emphasis to. —*v.i.* **4.** to insert or use marks of punctuation. [t. ML: m. s. *punctuātus*, pp., pointed, der. L *punctus* a point] —**punc′tua′tor,** *n.*

punctuation (pŭngk′tyo͞o ā′shən), *n.* **1.** the practice, art, or system of inserting marks or points in writing or printing in order to make the meaning clear; the punctuating of written or printed matter with commas, semicolons, colons, full stops, etc. (**punctuation marks**). **2.** the act of punctuating.

puncture (pŭngk′chə), *n.*, *v.*, **-tured, -turing.** —*n.* **1.** the act of pricking or perforating as with a pointed instrument or object. **2.** a mark or hole so made. **3.** *Zool.* a small pointlike depression. —*v.t.* **4.** to prick, pierce, or perforate: *to puncture the skin with a pin.* **5.** to make (a hole, etc.) by pricking or perforating. **6.** to make a puncture in: *to puncture a tyre.* —*v.i.* **7.** to admit of being punctured. [t. L: m. *punctūra*] —**punc′turable,** *adj.*

pundit (pŭn′dĭt), *n.* **1.** *Colloq.* one who sets up as an expert. **2.** pandit. [See PANDIT]

punga (pŭng′ə), *n.* a tall tree fern with large, leathery bi- or tripinnate leaves, *Cyathea medullaris*, a native of Australia and New Zealand. [t. Maori]

pungent (pŭn′jənt), *adj.* **1.** sharply affecting the organs of taste, as if by a penetrating power; biting; acrid. **2.** acutely distressing to the feelings or mind; poignant. **3.** caustic, biting, or sharply expressive, as speech, etc. **4.** mentally stimulating or appealing. **5.** *Biol.* piercing or sharp-pointed. [t. L: s. *pungens*, ppr., pricking. Cf. POIGNANT, POINT, PUNCHEON², etc.] —**pun′gency,** *n.* —**pun′gently,** *adv.*

Punic (pyo͞o′nĭk), *adj.* **1.** of or pertaining to the ancient Carthaginians. **2.** treacherous; perfidious (as applied by the Romans to the Carthaginians). —*n.* **3.** the language of ancient Carthage, a form of late Phoenician. [t. L: s. *Pūnicus*, earlier *Poenicus* Carthaginian, prop. Phoenician, t. Gk: m. *Phoînix*]

Punic Wars, the three wars waged by Rome against Carthage, 264–241, 218–201, and 149–146 B.C., resulting in the overthrow and annexation of Carthage to Rome.

punish (pŭn′ĭsh), *v.t.* **1.** to subject to a penalty, or to pain, loss, confinement, death, etc., for some offence, transgression, or fault: *to punish a criminal.* **2.** to inflict a penalty for (an offence, fault, etc.): *to punish theft.* **3.** to handle severely or roughly, as in a fight. **4.** to put to painful exertion, as a horse in racing. **5.** *Colloq.* to make a heavy inroad on (a supply, etc.). —*v.i.* **6.** to inflict punishment. [ME *punische(n)*, t. OF: m. *puniss-*, s. *punir*, g. L *pūnīre*] —**pun′isher,** *n.*

—**Syn.** 1. PUNISH, CORRECT, DISCIPLINE refer to making evident, by penalties, public or private disapproval of violations of law, wrongdoing, or refusal to obey rules or regulations. To PUNISH is chiefly to inflict penalty or pain as a retribution for misdeeds, with little or no expectation of a correction or improvement: *to punish a thief.* To CORRECT is to reprove or inflict punishment for faults, specifically with the idea of bringing about improvement: *to correct a rebellious child.* To DISCIPLINE is to give a kind of punishment which will educate or will establish useful habits: *to discipline a schoolboy.* —**Ant.** 1. reward.

punishable (pŭn′ĭ shə bl), *adj.* liable to or deserving punishment. —**pun′ishabil′ity,** *n.*

punishment (pŭn′ĭsh mənt), *n.* **1.** the act of punishing. **2.** the fact of being punished, as for an offence or fault. **3.** that which is inflicted as a penalty in punishing. **4.** severe handling or treatment.

punitive (pyo͞o′nĭ tĭv), *adj.* serving for, concerned with, or inflicting punishment: *punitive laws.* Also, **punitory** (pyo͞o′nĭ tə rĭ, -trĭ).

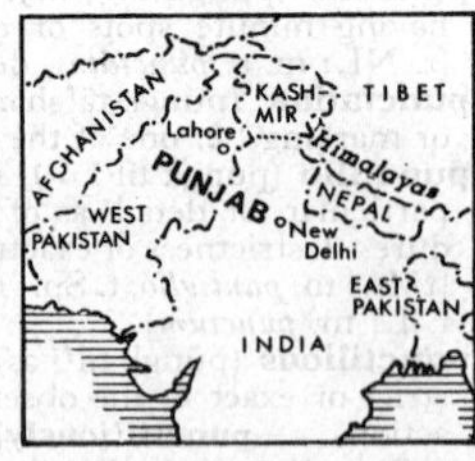

Punjab

Punjab (pŭn jäb′, pŭn′jäb), *n.* **1.** a former province in NW India: now divided between Punjab (in India) and West Punjab (in Pakistan). **2.** a state in NW India. 20,306,812 pop. (1961); 47,456 sq. mi. *Cap.:* Chandigarh.

Punjabi (pŭn jä′bĭ), *n.* **1.** a native of the Punjab. **2.** an Indic language of the Punjab. —*adj.* **3.** of or pertaining to the Punjab, Punjabis or their language. Also, **Panjabi.** [t. Hind.: m. *Panjābī*]

Punjab States, a former group of states in NW India; amalgamated with Punjab state (in India) in 1956.

punk¹ (pŭngk), *n.* *Chiefly U.S.* **1.** a preparation that will smoulder, used in sticks, as for lighting fireworks. **2.** decayed wood used as tinder. [orig. uncert. Cf. Lenape *punk* living ashes, Shawnee *pekwi* ashes, Ojibwa *pinkoš* sandfly]

punk² (pŭngk), *Slang.* —*n.* **1.** something or someone worthless, degraded, or bad. **2.** a petty criminal. **3.** a catamite. **4.** *Archaic.* a prostitute. —*adj.* **5.** worthless, degraded, or of poor quality. [orig. unknown]

punkah (pŭng′kə), *n.* (in India and elsewhere) a fan, esp. a large, swinging, screenlike fan hung from the ceiling and kept in motion by a servant or by machinery. Also, **punka.** [t. Hind.: m. *pankhā* a fan, g. Skt *pakshaka*]

punnet (pŭn′ĭt), *n.* a small, shallow basket, as for strawberries. [dim. of d. *pun* POUND²]

punster (pŭn′stə), *n.* one given to making puns.

punt¹ (pŭnt), *n.* **1.** *Rugby Football.* a kick given to a dropped ball before it touches the ground. **2.** *Soccer.* a light, rising shot. **3.** a shallow, flat-bottomed, square-ended boat, usually propelled by thrusting with a pole against the bottom of the river, etc. —*v.t.* **4.** *Rugby Football.* to kick (a dropped ball) before it touches the ground. **5.** *Soccer.* to kick the ball so that it rises. **6.** to propel (a punt or other boat) by thrusting with a pole against the bottom. **7.** to convey (a person, etc.) in, or as in, a punt. —*v.i.* **8.** to punt a football. **9.** to propel, or travel in, a punt. [OE *punt*, t. L: m. *ponto* punt, PONTOON] —**punt′er,** *n.*

punt² (pŭnt), *v.i.* **1.** to lay a stake against the bank, as at faro. **2.** to gamble; wager; lay bets. —*n.* **3.** one who lays such a stake. **4.** a wager; bet. [t. F: m. s. *ponter*, der. *ponte* punter, t. Sp.: m. *punto* point, t. L: m. *punctum*] —**punt′er,** *n.*

Punta Arenas (*Sp.* po͞on′tä ä rĕ′näs), a seaport in S Chile, on the Strait of Magellan: the southernmost town in the world. 34,440 (1960). Also, **Magallanes.**

punty (pŭn′tĭ), *n.*, *pl.* **-ties.** an iron rod used in glass-making for handling the hot glass. Also, **pontil.** [t. It.: m. *ponte* bridge]

puny (pyo͞o′nĭ), *adj.*, **-nier, -niest.** **1.** of less than normal size and strength; weakly. **2.** petty; insignificant. **3.** *Obs.* puisne. [var. of PUISNE] —**pu′nily,** *adv.* —**pu′niness,** *n.*

P.U.O., *Med.* pyrexia of unknown origin.

pup (pŭp), *n.*, *v.*, **pupped, pupping.** —*n.* **1.** a young dog, under one year; a puppy. **2.** a young seal. **3.** a conceited or empty-headed boy or young man. **4. be sold a pup,** *Colloq.* to be the victim of some deception. —*v.i.* **5.** to bring forth pups. [apocopated var. of PUPPY]

pupa (pyo͞o′pə), *n.*, *pl.* **-pae** (-pē), **-pas.** an insect in the nonfeeding, usually immobile, transformation stage between the larva and the imago. See illus. under **metamorphosis.** [NL, in L girl, doll, puppet. Cf. PUPIL, PUPPET] —**pu′pal,** *adj.*

puparium (pyo͞o pĕə′rĭ əm), *n.* *Entomol.* a pupal case formed of the cuticula of a preceding larval instar. [NL: f. *pupa* PUPA + *-ārium*; modelled on HERBARIUM]

pupate (pyo͞o pāt′), *v.i.*, **-pated, -pating.** to become a pupa. —**pupa′tion,** *n.*

pupil¹ (pyo͞o′pl), *n.* **1.** one who is under an instructor or teacher; a student. **2.** *Civil Law.* a person under twenty-five (under puberty, in Roman law), orphaned or emancipated, and under the care of a guardian. [ME *pupille*, t. OF, t. L: m. *pūpillus* (masc.) *pūpilla* (fem.) orphan, ward, dims of *pūpus* boy, *pūpa* girl]

—**Syn.** 1. PUPIL, DISCIPLE, SCHOLAR, STUDENT refer to one who is studying, usually in a school. A PUPIL is one under the close supervision of a teacher, either because of his youth or of specialization in some branch of study: *a grammar-school pupil, the pupil of a famous musician.* A DISCIPLE is one who follows the teachings or doctrines of a person whom he considers to be a master or authority: *a disciple of Swedenborg.* SCHOLAR, once meaning the same as PUPIL, is today usually applied to one who has acquired wide erudition in some field of learning: *a great Latin scholar.* A STUDENT is one attending a higher institution of learning, or one who has devoted much attention to a particular problem: *a university student, a student of politics.*

pupil² (pyo͞o′pl), *n.* *Anat.* the expanding and contracting opening in the iris of the eye, through which light passes to the retina. [t. L: m. s. *pūpilla*, lit., little doll. See PUPA]

pupillage (pyo͞o′pĭ lĭj), *n.* the state or period of being a pupil. Also, *Chiefly U.S.*, **pupilage.**

pupillary¹ (pyo͞o′pĭ lə rĭ), *adj.* pertaining to a pupil or student. Also, **pupilary.** [t. L: m. *pūpillāris*]

pupillary² (pyo͞o′pĭ lə rĭ), *adj.* *Anat.* pertaining to the pupil of the eye. Also, **pupilary.** [f. s. L *pūpilla* PUPIL² + -ARY¹]

pupiparous (pyo͞o pĭp′ə rəs), *adj.* bringing forth young which are already developed to the pupal phase, as in certain parasitic insects. [t. NL: m. *pūpiparus*, f. *pūpi-* PUPA + *-parus* -PAROUS]

puppet (pŭp′ĭt), *n.* **1.** a doll. **2.** an artificial figure with jointed limbs, moved by wires, etc., as on a miniature stage; a marionette. **3.** a person whose actions are prompted and controlled by another or others. [earlier *poppet*, ME *popet*, appar. der. MLG *poppe* doll, of Rom. orig.; cf. LL *puppa*]

puppeteer (pŭp′ĭ tĭə′), *n.* one who manipulates puppets; a puppet-master.

puppet-master (pŭp′ĭt mäs′tə), *n.* one who manipulates puppets; puppeteer.

puppetry (pŭp′ĭ trĭ), *n., pl.* **-ries. 1.** the art of making puppets perform. **2.** the action of puppets. **3.** a mummery; mere show. **4.** puppets collectively.

puppet state, a state whose government is more or less controlled by a more powerful state.

puppy (pŭp′ĭ), *n., pl.* **-pies. 1.** a young dog. **2.** the young of certain other animals, as the shark. **3.** a presuming, conceited, or empty-headed young man. [t. F: m. *poupée* doll, ult. der. LL *puppa.* See PUPPET]

pur (pû), *v.i., v.t.,* **purred, purring,** *n.* purr.

Purana (pōō rä′nə), *n.* one of a class of sacred poems in Sanskrit which tells the mythology of the Hindus. [t. Skt: ancient]

Purbeck marble (pû′bĕk), a dark limestone quarried in the **Purbeck Hills,** Dorset, capable of receiving a high polish.

purblind (pû′blīnd′), *adj.* **1.** nearly blind; partially blind; dim-sighted. **2.** dull in discernment or understanding. **3.** *Obs.* totally blind. [ME *pur blind* completely blind. See PURE, formerly used as adv., entirely] **—pur′blind′ly,** *adv.* **—pur′blind′ness,** *n.* **—Syn. 2.** See **blind.**

Purcell (pû′səl), *n.* **Henry,** 1658?–95, English composer.

purchasable (pû′chə sə bl), *adj.* **1.** capable of being bought. **2.** that may be won over by bribery; venal. **—pur′-chasabil′ity,** *n.*

purchase (pû′chəs), *v.,* **-chased, -chasing,** *n.* **—***v.t.* **1.** to acquire by the payment of money or its equivalent; buy. **2.** to acquire by effort, sacrifice, flattery, etc. **3.** to win over by a bribe. **4.** (of things) to be sufficient to buy. **5.** *Law.* to acquire, as an estate in lands, otherwise than by inheritance. **6.** to haul, draw, or raise, esp. by the aid of a mechanical power. **7.** to get a leverage on. **8.** *Obs.* to procure, acquire, or obtain. **—***n.* **9.** acquisition by the payment of money or its equivalent; buying, or a single act of buying. **10.** something which is purchased or bought. **11,** a (good, bad, etc.) bargain. **12.** *Law.* the acquisition of an estate in lands, etc., otherwise than by inheritance. **13.** acquisition by means of effort, sacrifice, etc. **14.** a means of increasing power or influence. **15.** the annual return or rent from land. **16.** a tackle, lever, or other device to increase power in raising or moving a heavy object. **17.** an effective hold or position for applying leverage. **18.** a firm grasp or foothold. **19.** *Obs.* booty. [ME, t. AF: m. *purchacer* seek to obtain, procure, f. *pur-* PRO-[1] + *chacer* CHASE] **—pur′chaser,** *n.* **—Syn. 1.** See **buy. —Ant. 1.** sell.

purchase tax, a tax added to the retail price of certain non-essential articles.

purdah (pû′dä), *n.* (in India, Pakistan, and elsewhere). **1.** a screen hiding women from the sight of men or strangers. **2.** the system of such seclusion. [t. Urdu: curtain, t. Pers.: m. *pardah*]

pure (pyŏŏə), *adj.,* **purer, purest. 1.** free from extraneous matter, or from mixture with anything of a different, inferior, or contaminating kind: *pure gold.* **2.** unmodified by an admixture; simple or homogeneous: *a pure colour.* **3.** of unmixed descent. **4.** free from foreign or inappropriate elements: *pure Attic Greek.* **5.** (of language) idiomatic, and unmixed with foreign elements. **6.** (of literary style) straightforward; unaffected. **7.** abstract or theoretical (opposed to *applied*): *pure science.* **8.** without discordant quality; clear and true. **9.** *Phonet.* monophthongal. **10.** unqualified; absolute; utter; sheer: *pure ignorance.* **11.** being that and nothing else; mere: *a pure accident.* **12.** clean, spotless, or unsullied: *pure hands.* **13.** clear; free from blemish: *a pure complexion.* **14.** untainted with evil; innocent; chaste: *pure in heart.* **15.** ceremonially clean. **16.** free or without guilt; guiltless. **17.** independent of sense or experience: *pure knowledge.* **18.** *Biol., Genetics.* **a.** homozygous. **b.** containing but one characteristic for a trait. [ME *pur*, t. OF, g. L *pūrus* clean, unmixed, plain, pure] **—pure′ness,** *n.* **—Syn. 1.** unmixed, unadulterated, unalloyed. See **clean. 4.** genuine, faultless. **14.** virtuous, undefiled.

purebred (pyŏŏə′brĕd′), *adj.* **1.** denoting an animal the ancestors of which are all of the same standard breed over many generations. **—***n.* **2.** such an animal.

pure culture, a nutrient medium and a single bacterial or other species cultivated on it.

puree (pyŏŏə′rā), *n., v.,* **-reed, -reeing. —***n.* **1.** a cooked and sieved vegetable or fruit used for soups or other foods. **—***v.t.* **2.** to make a puree of. Also, *French,* **purée** (*Fr.* pʏ rĕ′). [t. F, der. *purer* strain, der. *pur* PURE]

pure line, *Genetics.* a uniform strain of organisms which is relatively pure genetically because of continued inbreeding coupled with selection.

purely (pyŏŏə′lĭ), *adv.* **1.** in a pure manner; without admixture. **2.** merely; entirely: *purely accidental.* **3.** exclusively. **4.** cleanly; innocently; chastely.

pure tone, *Physics.* a sound consisting of a wave of a single frequency.

purfle (pû′fəl), *v.,* **-fled, -fling,** *n.* **—***v.t.* **1.** to finish with an ornamental border. **—***n.* **2.** Also, **purfling.** an ornamental border, as one of inlaid wood around the edge of a violin table. [ME *purfile(n)*, t. OF: m. *porfiler*, f. *por-* PRO-[1] + *filer* spin, der. *fil* thread, g. L *filum*]

purgation (pû gā′shən), *n.* the act of purging.

purgative (pû′gə tĭv), *adj.* **1.** purging; cleansing; specif., causing evacuation of the bowels. **—***n.* **2.** a purgative medicine or agent. [ME, t. LL: m. s. *purgātīvus*, pp., cleansed] **—pur′gatively,** *adv.*

purgatorial (pû′gə tô′rĭ əl), *adj.* **1.** removing sin; purifying. **2.** of, pertaining to, or like purgatory.

purgatory (pû′gə tə rĭ, -trĭ), *n., pl.* **-ries,** *adj.* **—***n.* **1.** (in the belief of Roman Catholics and others) a condition or place in which the souls of those dying penitent are purified from venial sins, or undergo the temporal punishment which, after the guilt of mortal sin has been remitted, still remains to be endured by the sinner. **2.** any condition, situation, or place of temporary suffering, expiation, or the like. **—***adj.* **3.** serving to purge, cleanse, or purify; expiatory. [ME *purgatorye*, t. LL: m. *purgātōrius*, adj., der. *purgāre* cleanse]

purge (pûj), *v.,* **purged, purging,** *n.* **—***v.t.* **1.** to cleanse; rid of whatever is impure or undesirable; purify. **2.** to rid or clear (fol. by *of*) or free (fol. by *from*): *to purge a party of undesirable members.* **3.** to eliminate, as by killing, an unwanted person, as a political opponent or potential opponent. **4.** to clear (a person, etc.) of imputed guilt. **5.** to clear away or wipe out legally (an offence, accusation, etc.) by atonement or other suitable action. **6.** to remove by cleansing or purifying (often fol. by *away, off,* or *out*). **7.** to clear or empty (the bowels, etc.) by causing evacuation. **8.** to cause evacuation of the bowels of (a person). **—***v.i.* **9.** to become cleansed or purified. **10.** to undergo or cause purging of the bowels. **—***n.* **11.** the act or process of purging. **12.** something that purges, as a purgative medicine or dose. **13.** the elimination from political activity, as by killing, of political opponents and others. **14.** the period when such an elimination takes place: *He disappeared in Stalin's great purge of 1936–38.* [ME, t. OF: m. *purgier*, g. L *purgāre* cleanse] **—purg′er,** *n.*

Puri (pōō′rē, pōō rē′), *n.* a seaport in E India, on the Bay of Bengal: a place of pilgrimage (temple of Krishna). See **Juggernaut** (def. 1b).

purificator (pyŏŏə′rĭ fĭ kā′tə), *n.* a cloth used at Holy Communion to wipe the chalice and paten, and also the celebrant's fingers and lips.

purify (pyŏŏə′rĭ fī′), *v.,* **-fied, -fying. —***v.t.* **1.** to make pure; free from extraneous matter, or from anything that debases, pollutes, or contaminates: *to purify metals.* **2.** to free from foreign or objectionable elements: *to purify a language.* **3.** to free from whatever is evil or base. **4.** to clear or purge (fol. by *of* or *from*). **5.** to make ceremonially clean. **—***v.i.* **6.** to become pure. [ME *puryfie(n)*, t. OF: m. *purifier*, t. L: m. *pūrificāre*] **—pu′rifica′tion,** *n.* **—purificatory** (pyŏŏə′rĭ fĭ kā′tə rĭ), *adj.* **—pu′rifi′er,** *n.*

Purim (pyŏŏə′rĭm), *n.* a Jewish festival, observed in February or March, in commemoration of the deliverance of the Jews from the massacre planned by Haman. Esther 9. [t. Heb., pl. of *pūr*, said to mean lot]

purine (pyŏŏə′rēn), *n.* *Chem.* a white crystalline compound, $C_5H_4N_4$, regarded as the parent substance of a group of compounds including uric acid, xanthine, caffeine, etc. Also, **purin** (pyŏŏə′rĭn). [b. PURE and URINE, modelled on G *Purin*]

purine base, *Biochem.* any of several compounds related to purine present in combined form in nucleic acids.

purism (pyŏŏə′rĭz′əm), *n.* **1.** scrupulous or excessive observance of or insistence on purity in language, style, etc. **2.** an instance of this. [f. PURE + -ISM] **—pur′ist,** *n.* **—puris′tic,** *adj.*

Puritan (pyŏŏə′rĭ tən), *n.* **1.** one of a class of Protestants who arose in the 16th century within the Church of England, demanding further reforms in doctrine and worship, and greater strictness in religious discipline, and during part of the 17th century constituting a powerful political party. **2.** (*l.c.*) one who affects great purity or strictness of life in moral and religious matters. **—*adj.* 3.** of or pertaining to the Puritans or (*l.c.*) puritans. [f. LL *pūrit(as)* purity + -AN]

puritanical (pyŏŏə′rĭ tăn′ĭ kl), *adj.* **1.** having the character of a puritan; excessively strict, rigid, or austere. **2.** of, pertaining to, or characteristic of puritans or (*cap.*) the Puritans. Also, **pu′ritan′ic.** —**pu′ritan′ically,** *adv.* —**pu′ritan′icalness,** *n.*

Puritanism (pyŏŏə′rĭ tə nĭz′əm), *n.* **1.** the principles and practices of the Puritans. **2.** (*l.c.*) strictness in matters of conduct or religion; puritanical austerity.

purity (pyŏŏə′rĭ tĭ), *n.* **1.** the condition or quality of being pure; freedom from extraneous matter or from anything that debases or contaminates: *the purity of drinking water.* **2.** freedom from any admixture or modifying addition. **3.** freedom from foreign or inappropriate elements; careful correctness: *purity of language.* **4.** (of colour) chroma; saturation; degree of freedom from white. **5.** cleanness or spotlessness, as of garments. **6.** ceremonial cleanness. **7.** freedom from evil or guilt; innocence; chastity. [t. L: m. s. *pūritas*; r. ME *pur(e)te*, t. OF]

purl[1] (pûl), *v.i.* **1.** to flow with curling or rippling motions, as a shallow stream does over stones. **2.** to flow with a murmuring sound. **3.** to pass in a manner or with a sound likened to this. **—*n.* 4.** the action or sound of purling. **5.** a circle or curl made by the motion of water; a ripple; eddy. [cf. Norw. *purla* bubble up, gush]

purl[2] (pûl), *v.t., v.i.* **1.** to knit with inversion of the stitch. **2.** to finish with loops or a looped edging. **—*n.* 3.** a stitch used in hand knitting to make a rib effect. **4.** one of a series of small loops along the edge of lace braid. **5.** thread made of twisted gold or silver wire. Also, **pearl.** [orig. uncert. Cf. obs. or dial. *pirl* twist (threads, etc.) into a cord]

purl[3] (pûl), *Chiefly Dial.* **—*v.i.* 1.** to spin round. **2.** to fall headlong, as from a horse. **—*v.t.* 3.** to cause to fall or spin round. **—*n.* 4.** a heavy or headlong fall, as from a horse. [orig. obscure; ? special use of PURL[2]]

purler (pû′lə), *n. Chiefly Dial.* a headlong or heavy fall or throw.

purlieu (pû′lyōō), *n.* **1.** a piece of land on the border of a forest. **2.** any bordering, neighbouring, or outlying region or district. **3.** *Hist.* a piece of land which, after having been included in a royal forest, was restored to private ownership, though still subject in some respects to the operation of the forest laws. **4.** (*pl.*) neighbourhood. **5.** a place where one may range at large; one's bounds. **6.** one's haunt or resort. [alter. (simulating F *lieu* place) of earlier *purlewe, purley, puraley* purlieu of a forest, t. AF: m. *purale(e)* a going through]

purlin (pû′lĭn), *n.* a timber or piece laid horizontally on the principal rafters of a roof to support the common rafters. Also, **pur′line.** [orig. uncert.]

purloin (pû loin′), *v.t.* **1.** to take dishonestly or steal. **—*v.i.* 2.** to commit theft. [ME *purloyne(n)*, t. AF: m. *purloigner* put off, remove, der. *pur-* PRO-[1] + *loin* far off (g. L *longē*)] —**purloin′er,** *n.*

purple (pû′pl), *n., adj., v.,* **-pled, -pling.** **—*n.* 1.** any colour having components of both red and blue, esp. a dark shade of such a colour. **2.** *Hist.* crimson. **3.** cloth or clothing of this hue, esp. as formerly worn distinctively by persons of imperial, royal, or other high rank: *born to the purple.* **4.** the rank or office of a cardinal, in allusion to his scarlet official dress. **5.** the office of a bishop. **6.** imperial or lofty rank or position. **—*adj.* 7.** of the colour of purple. **8.** imperial or regal. **9.** brilliant or gorgeous. **10.** full of literary devices and effects: *a purple passage.* **—*v.t., v.i.* 11.** to make or become purple. [ME *purpel*, OE (Northumbrian) *purpl(e)*, var. of OE *purpur(e)*, t. L: m. *purpura*, t. Gk: m. *porphýra* kind of shellfish yielding purple dye]

purple emperor, any purple-brown butterfly of the genus *Apatura*, as *A. iris*, occasionally found in oak woods in Britain.

purple-fringed orchid (pû′pl frĭnjd′), either of two orchids of genus *Habenaria* (*Blephariglottis*) of eastern North America, the smaller (*H. psychodes*) having dark purple fringed flowers, and the larger (*H. fimbriata*) lighter flowers.

purple gallinule, a purple, blue, green, and white gallinule, *Porphyrula martinica*, having a bright red, yellow, and blue bill, and lemon-yellow legs and feet, and inhabiting warmer parts of the New World.

purple heart, 1. a heart-shaped purple pill containing an addictive drug consisting of dexamphetamine and amylobarbitone. **2.** the drug.

Purple Heart, *U.S. Army.* a medal awarded to anyone wounded by enemy action while in service.

purple medic, lucerne or alfalfa.

purple of Cassius, a purple pigment consisting of a mixture of colloidal gold and stannic acid; used for making ruby glass and ceramic glazes. [named after A. *Cassius*, 17th-century German physician]

purplish (pû′plĭsh), *adj.* of a somewhat purple hue. Also, **pur′ply.**

purport (*v.* pû pôt′, pû′pət; *n.* pû′pôt, -pət), *v.t.* **1.** to profess or claim: *a document purporting to be official.* **2.** to convey to the mind as the meaning or thing intended; express; imply. **—*n.* 3.** tenor, import, or meaning. **4.** purpose or object. [late ME, t. AF: s. *purporter* convey, f. *pur-* PRO-[1] + *porter* (g. L *portāre*) carry] **—Syn. 3.** See **meaning.**

purpose (pû′pəs), *n., v.,* **-posed, -posing.** **—*n.* 1.** the object for which anything exists or is done, made, used, etc. **2.** an intended or desired result; end or aim. **3.** intention or determination. **4.** that which one puts before oneself as something to be done or accomplished. **5.** the subject in hand; the point at issue: *to the purpose.* **6.** practical result, effect, or advantage: *to good purpose.* **7. on purpose, a.** by design; intentionally. **b.** with the particular purpose specified. **—*v.t.* 8.** to put before oneself as something to be done or accomplished; propose. **9.** to determine on the performance of; design; intend. **10.** to be resolved. [ME *purpos*, t. OF, der. *purposer*, var. of *proposer* PROPOSE] —**pur′poseless,** *adj.* —**pur′poselessly,** *adv.* —**pur′poselessness,** *n.* **—Syn. 1.** See **intention.**

purposeful (pû′pəs fəl), *adj.* **1.** having a purpose. **2.** determined; resolute. —**pur′posefully,** *adv.* —**pur′posefulness,** *n.*

purposely (pû′pəs lĭ), *adv.* **1.** intentionally: *to do a thing purposely.* **2.** with the particular purpose specified; expressly.

purposive (pû′pə sĭv), *adj.* **1.** acting with, characterized by, or showing a purpose, intention, or design. **2.** adapted to a purpose or end. **3.** serving some purpose. **4.** characterized by purpose, determination, or resolution. **5.** of or of the nature of purpose. —**pur′posively,** *adv.* —**pur′posiveness,** *n.*

purpresture (pû prĕs′chə), *n. Law.* anything done to the nuisance or hurt of the Queen's demesnes, or the highways, by enclosure or building. Also, **pourpresture.**

purpura (pû′pyōō rə), *n. Pathol.* a disease characterized by purple or livid spots on the skin or mucous membrane, caused by the extravasation of blood. [t. NL, special use of L *purpura.* See PURPLE]

purpure (pû′pyŏŏə), *n., adj. Her.* purple. [OE, t. L: m. *purpura.* See PURPLE]

purpurin (pû′pyōō rĭn), *n. Chem.* a reddish crystalline dye, $C_{14}H_8O_5$ (isomeric with flavopurpurin).

purr (pû), *v.i.* **1.** to utter a low, continuous murmuring sound expressive of satisfaction, as a cat does. **2.** (of things) to make a sound suggestive of the purring of a cat. **—*v.t.* 3.** to express by, or as if by, purring. **—*n.* 4.** the act of purring. **5.** the sound of purring. Also, **pur.** [imit.]

purse (pûs), *n., v.,* **pursed, pursing.** **—*n.* 1.** a small bag, pouch, or case for carrying money on the person. **2.** *U.S.* a handbag. **3.** a purse with its contents. **4.** money, resources, or wealth. **5.** a sum of money collected as a present or the like. **6.** a sum of money offered as a prize. **7.** any baglike receptacle. **—*v.t.* 8.** to contract into folds or wrinkles; pucker. **9.** *Rare.* to put into a purse. [ME and OE *purs*, b. *pusa* bag and *burs*, t. LL: s. *bursa* bag, t. Gk: m. *býrsa* hide, leather]

purse-proud (pûs′proud′), *adj.* proud of one's wealth.

purser (pû′sə), *n.* an officer, esp. on board a ship, charged with keeping accounts, etc.

purse seine, *U.S.* a large seine, generally drawn by two boats, which can be closed into a baglike net around a school of fish.

purse strings, 1. the strings by which a purse is closed. **2.** the power to spend or withhold money.

purslane (pûs′lĭn), *n.* **1.** a widely distributed, yellow-flowered species of portulaca, *Portulaca oleracea*, used as a salad plant and potherb. **2.** any other portulacaceous plant. [ME *purcelan(e)*, t. OF: m. *porcelaine*, appar. b. L *porcilāca* (for *portulāca* purslane) and It. *porcellana* porcelain]

pursuance (pə syōō′əns), *n.* the following or carrying out of some plan, course, injunction, or the like.

pursuant (pə syōō′ənt), *adj.* **1.** proceeding conformably (fol. by *to*). **2.** pursuing. **—*adv.*** Also, **pursuantly. 3.** according (fol. by *to*): *to do something pursuant to an agreement.* **4.** in a manner conformable (fol. by *to*).

pursue (pə syōō′), *v.,* **-sued, -suing.** **—*v.t.* 1.** to follow with the view of overtaking, capturing, killing, etc.; chase. **2.** to follow close upon; go with; attend: *bad luck pursued him.* **3.** to strive to gain; seek to attain or accomplish (an end, object, purpose, etc.). **4.** to proceed in accordance with (a method, plan, etc.). **5.** to carry on (a course of action, train of thoughts, etc.). **6.** to prosecute (inquiries, studies, etc.). **7.** to practise (an occupation, pastime, etc.). **8.** to continue to discuss (a subject, topic, etc.). **9.** to follow (a path, etc.). **10.** to continue on (one's way, course, etc.); go on with or continue (a journey, etc.). —*v.i.* **11.** to follow in pursuit. **12.** to continue. [ME *pursue(n)*, t. AF: m. *pursuer*, g. L *prōsequī* follow, continue. Cf. PROSECUTE] —**pursu′able,** *adj.*

pursuer (pə syo͞o′ə), *n.* **1.** one who pursues. **2.** *Scot. Law.* the plaintiff.

pursuit (pə syo͞ot′), *n.* **1.** the act of pursuing: *in pursuit of the fox.* **2.** the effort to secure; quest: *the pursuit of happiness.* **3.** any occupation, pastime, or the like, regularly or customarily pursued: *literary pursuits.* [ME *pursuit*, t. AF: m. *purseute*, der. *pursuer* PURSUE]

pursuivant (pû′sĭ vənt), *n.* **1.** a heraldic officer of the lowest class, ranking below a herald. **2.** an official attendant on heralds. **3.** any attendant. [ME *purs(ev)aunt*, t. OF: m. *poursuivant*, prop. ppr. of *poursuivre* PURSUE]

pursy (pû′sĭ), *adj.*, **-sier, -siest. 1.** short-winded, esp. from corpulence or fatness. **2.** corpulent or fat. [earlier *pursive*, ME *pursif*, t. AF: m. *porsif*, var. of OF *polsif*, der. *polser* pant, heave. See PUSH] —**pur′siness,** *n.*

purtenance (pû′tĭ nəns), *n. Archaic.* the heart, liver, and lungs of an animal. [ME; aphetic var. of APPURTENANCE]

purulence (pyo͝oə′ro͞o ləns), *n.* **1.** the condition of containing or forming pus. **2.** pus. Also, **purulency.**

purulent (pyo͝oə′ro͞o lənt), *adj.* **1.** full of, containing, forming, or discharging pus; suppurating: *a purulent sore.* **2.** attended with suppuration: *purulent appendicitis.* **3.** of the nature of or like pus: *purulent matter.* [t. L: s. *pūrulentus*] —**pu′rulently,** *adv.*

Purús (*Port.* po͞o ro͞os′), *n.* a river flowing from E Peru NE through W Brazil to the Amazon. ab. 2000 mi.

purvey (pû vā′), *v.t.* to provide, furnish, or supply (esp. food or provisions). [ME *porveie(n)*, t. AF: m. *porveier*, g. L *prōvidēre* foresee, provide for]

purveyance (pû vā′əns), *n.* **1.** the act of purveying. **2.** that which is purveyed, as provisions. **3.** *Law, Hist.* a prerogative of the crown, abolished in 1660, of taking provisions, supplies or services for the sovereign or the royal household at an appraised value.

purveyor (pû vā′ə), *n.* **1.** one who purveys, provides, or supplies. **2.** *Law, Hist.* an officer who, by purveyance, provided or exacted provisions, etc., for the sovereign under the prerogative of purveyance.

purview (pû′vyo͞o′), *n.* **1.** range of operation, activity, concern, etc. **2.** range of vision; view. **3.** that which is provided or enacted in a statute, as distinguished from the preamble. **4.** the full scope or compass of a statute or law, or of any document, statement, book, subject, etc. [ME *purveu*, t. AF: provided, pp. of *porveier* PURVEY]

pus (pŭs), *n.* a yellow-white, more or less viscid substance produced by suppuration and found in abscesses, sores, etc., consisting of a liquid plasma in which leucocytes, etc., are suspended. [t. L; akin to Gk *pýon* pus. See PYIN, FOUL] —**pus′like′,** *adj.*

Pusan (po͞o′săn′), *n.* a seaport in SE South Korea. 1,391,000 (1963). Formerly, **Fusan.**

Pusey (pyo͞o′zĭ), *n.* **Edward Bouverie** (bo͞o′və rĭ), 1800–1882, English clergyman.

Puseyism (pyo͞o′zĭ ĭz′əm), *n.* Tractarianism. —**Puseyite** (pyo͞o′zĭ īt′), *n.*, *adj.*

push (po͝osh), *v.t.* **1.** to exert force upon or against (a thing) in order to move it away. **2.** to move (*away, off*, etc.) by exerting force thus; shove; thrust; drive. **3.** to make by thrusting obstacles aside: *to push one's way through the crowd.* **4.** to press or urge (a person, etc.) to some action or course. **5.** to press (an action, etc.) with energy and insistence. **6.** to carry (an action or thing) further, to a conclusion or extreme, too far, etc. **7.** to press the adoption, use, sale, etc., of. **8.** to peddle (narcotics). **9.** to press or bear hard upon (a person, etc.) as in dealings. **10.** to depend excessively on: *you're pushing your luck.* **11.** to put to straits (often fol. by *for*): *we're pushed for time.* **12.** to dismiss: *he was pushed last week.* **13.** *Cricket, Golf, etc.* to make a stiff, lunging stroke at (the ball). —*v.i.* **14.** to exert a thrusting force upon something. **15.** to use steady force in moving a thing away; shove. **16.** to make one's way with effort or persistence, as against difficulty or opposition. **17.** to put forth vigorous or persistent efforts. **18.** *Cricket, Golf, etc.* to make a pushing stroke.
—*v.* **19.** Some special verb phrases are:

push off, 1. to move away from the shore, etc., as the result of a push. **2.** *Colloq.* to leave; go away.

push on, to continue; proceed.

push up daisies, *Slang.* to be dead and buried.

—*n.* **20.** the act of pushing; a shove or thrust. **21.** a contrivance or part to be pushed in order to operate a mechanism. **22.** a vigorous onset or effort. **23.** a determined pushing forward or advance. **24.** the pressure of circumstances. **25.** an emergency. **26.** *Cricket, Golf, etc.* a stiff, lunging stroke. **27.** *Colloq.* persevering energy; enterprise. **28.** *Slang.* a crowd, company, or set of persons. **29.** *Slang.* dismissal; the sack.
[ME *posshe(n)*, t. OF: m. *poulser*, g. L *pulsāre.* See PULSATE]

—**Syn. 1.** PUSH, SHOVE, THRUST is to move or attempt to move something by exerting force against it. To PUSH is to move or attempt to move something in the direction in which a force is exerted: *to push a wheelbarrow.* To SHOVE, a more colloquial word, is to cause to move by sliding, or to push roughly: *to shove a person aside.* To THRUST is a formal word, meaning to shove with one quick, strong movement, usually with the effect of penetrating into or through something: *to thrust a sword through a body.*

pushball (po͝osh′bôl′), *n.* **1.** a game played with a large, heavy ball, usually about 6 feet in diameter, which two sides of players endeavour to push towards opposite goals. **2.** the ball used in this game.

pushbike (po͝osh′bīk′), *n. Colloq.* a bicycle.

push-button (po͝osh′bŭt′n), *n.* **1.** a device designed to close or open an electric circuit when a button or knob is depressed, and to return to a normal position when it is released. —*adj.* **2.** operated by, or as by, push buttons.

pushcart (po͝osh′kät′), *n. U.S.* a street vendor's barrow.

pushchair (po͝osh′chĕə′), *n.* a light, folding chair on wheels, used for carrying small children.

pusher (po͝osh′ə), *n.* **1.** one who or that which pushes. **2.** a small child's table implement for pushing food on to a spoon. **3.** an aggressively ambitious person. **4.** a pedlar of narcotics. **5.** *Aeron.* **a.** a former type of aeroplane which had its propeller behind the main supporting planes. **b.** the propeller. **6.** *Slang.* a girl or woman.

pushing (po͝osh′ĭng), *adj.* **1.** that pushes. **2.** enterprising; energetic. **3.** aggressive; presuming. —*adv.* **4.** nearly; almost (a specified age, etc.): *pushing forty.*

Pushkin (po͝osh′kĭn; *Russ.* po͝osh′kĭn), *n.* **Aleksander Sergeevich** (*Russ.* ə lĭk sän′dər sĭr gyė′yĭ vĭch), 1799–1837, Russian poet and short-story writer.

push-over (po͝osh′ō′və), *n. Slang.* **1.** anything done easily. **2.** an easily defeated person or team.

pushpin (po͝osh′pĭn′), *n.* **1.** a children's game played with pins. **2.** child's play; triviality.

push-pull (po͝osh′po͝ol′), *Electronics.* —*n.* **1.** a two-valve symmetrical arrangement in which the grid excitation voltages are opposite in phase. —*adj.* **2.** denoting or pertaining to such an arrangement or a device having such an arrangement.

pushrod (po͝osh′rŏd′), *n.* a rod which operates a rocker from a tappet of an internal-combustion engine when the camshaft is in the crankcase.

Pushtu (pŭsh′to͞o), *n.* an Iranian language, the principal language of Afghanistan. Also, **Pashto.**

pusillanimity (pyo͞o′sĭ lə nĭm′ĭ tĭ), *n.* the state or condition of being pusillanimous; timidity; cowardliness.

pusillanimous (pyo͞o′sĭ lăn′ĭ məs), *adj.* **1.** lacking strength of mind or courage; faint-hearted; cowardly. **2.** proceeding from or indicating a cowardly spirit. [t. LL: m. *pusillanimis*, f. L: s. *pusillus* very small, petty + *-animis* -spirited] —**pu′sillan′imously,** *adv.*

puss[1] (po͝os), *n.* **1.** a cat. **2.** a hare. **3.** *Slang.* a girl or woman. [cf. D *poes*, LG *puus-katte*, d. Sw. *katte-pus*]

puss[2] (po͝os), *n. Slang.* **1.** face. **2.** mouth. [orig. obscure]

pussy[1] (po͝os′ĭ), *n.*, *pl.* **pussies. 1.** a cat. **2.** the game of tipcat. **3.** the tapering piece of wood, the cat, used in it. [dim. of PUSS[1]]

pussy[2] (pŭs′ĭ), *adj. Med.* puslike. [f. PUS + -Y[1]]

pussyfoot (po͝os′ĭ fo͝ot′), *v.i.* **1.** to go with a soft, stealthy tread like that of a cat. **2.** to act cautiously or timidly, as if afraid to commit oneself on a point at issue. —*n.* **3.** a person with a catlike, or soft and stealthy tread. **4.** one who pussyfoots. **5.** a teetotaler.

pussywillow (po͝os′ĭ wĭl′ō), *n.* **1.** a small salicaceous tree or shrub, *Salix discolor*, with silky catkins. **2.** any of various similar willows.

Pussy-willow, *Salix discolor*

pustulant (pŭs′tyo͝o lənt), *adj.* **1.** causing the formation of pustules. —*n.* **2.** a medicament or agent causing pustulation. [t. LL: s. *pustulans*, ppr.]

pustular (pŭs′tyo͝o lə), *adj.* **1.** of, pertaining to, or of the nature of pustules. **2.** characterized by pustules. [t. NL: s. *pustulāris*]

pustulation (pŭs′tyo͝o lā′shən), *n.* the formation or breaking out of pustules.

pustule (pŭs′tyo͞ol), *n.* **1.** *Pathol.* a small elevation of the skin containing pus. **2.** any pimple-like or blister-like swelling or elevation. [ME, t. L: m. *pustula*]

put (po͝ot), *v.*, **put, putting,** *n.* —*v.t.* **1.** to move or place (anything) so as to get it into or out of some place or position: *to put money in one's purse.* **2.** to bring into some relation, state, etc.: *put*

everything in order. **3.** to place in the charge or power of a person, etc.: *to put oneself under a doctor's care.* **4.** to subject to the endurance or suffering of something: *to put a person to death.* **5.** to set to a duty, task, action, etc.: *to put one to work.* **6.** to force or drive to some course or action: *to put an army to flight.* **7.** to render or translate, as into another language. **8.** to assign or attribute: *to put a certain construction upon an action.* **9.** to set at a particular place, point, amount, etc., in a scale of estimation: *he puts the distance at five miles.* **10.** to wager; bet. **11.** to express or state: *to put a thing in writing.* **12.** to apply, as to a use or purpose. **13.** to set, give, or make: *to put an end to a practice.* **14.** to propose or submit for answer, consideration, deliberation, etc.: *to put a question.* **15.** to impose, as a burden, charge, or the like: *to put a tax on an article.* **16.** to lay the blame of (fol. by *on, to*, etc.). **17.** to invest: *to put £100 into Consols.* **18.** to throw or cast, esp. with a forward motion of the hand when raised close to the shoulder: *to put the shot.* —*v.i.* **19.** to go, move, or proceed: *to put to sea.* **20.** *U.S. Colloq.* to make off: *to put for home.*
—*v.* **21.** Some special verb phrases are:
put about, 1. to propagate; disseminate (a rumour, etc.). **2.** to inconvenience; upset. **3.** *Naut.* to change direction, as on a course.
put across, to communicate; cause to be understood; explain effectively.
put aside, away, or **by,** to save or store up.
put down, 1. to write down. **2.** to repress or suppress. **3.** to ascribe or attribute (usually fol. by *to*). **4.** to pay as a lump sum, esp. the down payment on an article to be bought by hire-purchase. **5.** to land an aircraft or in an aircraft. **6.** to destroy (an animal), esp. mercifully, as for reasons of old age, disease, etc.
put forth, 1. to bring out or bear: *a plant puts forth new shoots.* **2.** to set out: *to put forth from the shore.*
put forward, 1. to suggest or propose. **2.** to nominate.
put in, 1. *Naut.* to enter a port or harbour, esp. in turning aside from the regular course for shelter, repairs, provisions, etc. **2.** to interpose; say as an intervention. **3.** to apply (often fol. by *for*). **4.** to enter as a candidate, contestant, or the like (often fol. by *for*). **5.** to devote, as time, work, etc.: *I have put in a great deal of work on this project.*
put it across (someone), *Slang.* to deceive or outwit.
put off, 1. to postpone. **2.** to bid or cause to wait until later. **3.** to get rid of (a person, demand, etc.) by delay or evasive shifts. **4.** to lay aside. **5.** to set down, as from a bus. **6.** to disconcert or distract (from): *to put someone off his work.* **7.** to disgust or cause to dislike: *the smell puts me off curry.* **8.** *Naut.* to start out, as on a voyage.
put on, 1. to assume: *to put on airs.* **2.** to assume insincerely or falsely: *his sorrow is only put on.* **3.** to don; dress in (clothing). **4.** to impose on or take advantage of. **5.** to produce; stage. **6.** to cause to speak on the telephone: *she asked them to put on the manager.*
put out, 1. to extinguish (fire, etc.). **2.** to confuse or embarrass. **3.** to distract, disturb, or interrupt. **4.** to subject to inconvenience. **5.** to annoy, irritate, or vex. **6.** *Cricket, etc.* to cause to be removed from an opportunity to score. **7.** *Naut.* to go out to sea.
put over, 1. to put across. **2.** *U.S.* to postpone. **3.** *U.S.* to accomplish.
put paid to, *Colloq.* to destroy finally: *bankruptcy put paid to his hopes of becoming a millionaire.*
put through, 1. to connect by telephone. **2.** to organize or carry into effect.
put up, 1. to erect. **2.** to preserve (jam, etc.). **3.** to arrange (hair) in some style so that it does not hang down. **4.** to provide (money, etc.). **5.** to lodge. **6.** to give lodging to. **7.** to show. **8.** to stand as a candidate. **9.** to nominate as a candidate. **10.** to persuade to do (fol. by *to*). **11.** *Archaic.* to sheathe one's sword; stop fighting.
put upon, to impose on or take advantage.
put up with, to endure; tolerate; bear.
—*n.* **22.** a throw or cast, esp. one made with a forward motion of the hand when raised close to the shoulder. **23.** *Finance.* the privilege of delivering a certain amount of stock, at a specified price, within a specified time to the maker of the contract. [ME *putten, puten* push, thrust, put. Cf. OE *putung* an impelling, inciting, *potian* push, thrust, also Dan. *putte* put, put in]
—**Syn. 1.** PUT, PLACE, LAY, SET mean to bring or take an object (or cause to go) to a certain place or position, there to leave it. PUT is the general word: *to put the dishes on the table, to put one's hair up.* PLACE is a more formal word, suggesting precision of movement or definiteness of location: *he placed his hand on the Bible.* LAY, meaning originally to cause to lie, and SET, meaning originally to cause to sit, are used particularly to stress the position in which an object is put: LAY usually suggests putting an object rather carefully into a horizontal position: *to lay out a design.* SET usually means to place upright: *to set a child on a horse.*

putamen (pyo͞o tā′mĕn), *n., pl.* **-tamina** (-tăm′ĭ nə). *Bot.* a hard or stony endocarp, as a peach stone. [t. L: that which is removed in pruning]
putative (pyo͞o′tə tĭv), *adj.* commonly regarded as such; reputed; supposed. [late ME, t. LL: m. s. *putātīvus*, der. L *putāre* think] —**pu′tatively,** *adv.*
putlog (pŭt′lŏg′), *n.* one of the short horizontal timbers that support the floor of a scaffolding. Also, **putlock.**
put-out (po͝ot′out′), *n. Baseball.* an act or instance of putting out a batter.
putrefaction (pyo͞o′trĭ făk′shən), *n.* the act or process of putrefying; rotting. —**pu′trefac′tive,** *adj.*
putrefy (pyo͞o′trĭ fī′), *v.,* **-fied, -fying.** —*v.t.* **1.** to render putrid; cause to rot or decay with an offensive smell. —*v.i.* **2.** to become putrid; rot. **3.** to become gangrenous. [ME *putrefie(n)*, t. OF: m. *putrefier*, t. L: m. *putrefierī* rot] —**Syn. 2.** See **decay.** —**pu′trefi′er,** *n.*
putrescent (pyo͞o trĕs′ənt), *adj.* becoming putrid; in process of putrefaction. [t. L: s. *putrescens*, ppr., growing rotten] —**putres′cence,** *n.*
putrescible (pyo͞o trĕs′ĭ bl), *adj.* **1.** liable to become putrid. —*n.* **2.** a putrescible substance. —**putres′cibil′ity,** *n.*
putrescine (pyo͞o trĕs′ēn, -ĭn), *n. Biochem.* a colourless, liquid ptomaine, $C_4H_{12}N_2$, with a disagreeable smell, derived from decayed animal tissue.
putrid (pyo͞o′trĭd), *adj.* **1.** in a state of foul decay or decomposition, as animal or vegetable matter; rotten. **2.** attended with or pertaining to putrefaction. **3.** having the smell of decaying flesh. **4.** thoroughly corrupt, depraved, or bad. **5.** offensively or disgustingly objectionable or bad. [t. L: s. *putridus*] —**putrid′ity, pu′tridness,** *n.* —**pu′tridly,** *adv.*
putrilage (pyo͞o′trĭ lĭj), *n.* putrid matter. [t. L: m. s. *putrilāgo* putrefaction] —**putrilaginous** (pyo͞o′trĭ lăj′ĭ nəs), *adj.*
Putsch (*Ger.* po͝och), *n. German.* a revolt or uprising.
putt (pŭt), *Golf.* —*v.t., v.i.* **1.** to strike (the ball) gently and carefully so as to make it roll along the putting green into the hole. —*n.* **2.** an act of putting. **3.** a stroke made in putting. [var. of PUT]
puttee (pŭt′ĭ), *n.* **1.** a long strip of cloth wound spirally round the leg from ankle to knee, formerly worn by sportsmen, soldiers, etc., as a protection or support. **2.** a kind of gaiter or legging of leather or other material, worn by soldiers, riders, etc. Also, **putty.** [t. Hind.: m. *paṭṭī* bandage. Cf. Skt *paṭṭa* strip of cloth, bandage]
putter[1] (pŭt′ə), *v.i., n. U.S.* potter[2].
putter[2] (pŭt′ə), *n. Golf.* **1.** one who putts. **2.** a club with a relatively short, stiff shaft and a wooden or iron head, used in putting. [f. PUTT + -ER[1]]
putter[3] (po͝ot′ə), *n.* **1.** one who puts. **2.** an athlete who puts the shot; shot-putter.
puttier (pŭt′ĭ ə), *n.* one who putties, as a glazier.
putting green (pŭt′ĭng), *n. Golf.* **1.** that part of the course within 20 yards or more or less of a hole, excepting hazards. **2.** a practice area for putting.
putty[1] (pŭt′ĭ), *n., pl.* **-ties,** *v.,* **-tied, -tying.** —*n.* **1.** a kind of cement, of doughlike consistency, made of whiting and linseed oil and used for securing panes of glass, stopping up holes in woodwork, etc. **2.** any of various more or less similar preparations, prepared from other ingredients and used for the same or other purposes. **3.** a substance consisting of linseed oil and various other materials (as ferric oxide and red and white lead), employed in sealing the joints of tubes, pipes, etc. **4.** *Plastering, etc.* a very fine cement made of lime only. **5.** any person or thing easily moulded, influenced, etc. **6.** light brownish or yellowish grey. —*adj.* **7.** of a yellowish or light brownish grey colour. —*v.t.* **8.** to secure, cover, etc., with putty. [t. F: m. *potée*, prop., a potful]
putty[2] (pŭt′ĭ), *n., pl.* **-ties.** puttee.
putty knife, a tool having a thin, flexible blade for laying on putty.
putty powder, stannic oxide used for glass-polishing.
Putumayo (*Port.* po͞o to͞o mä′yo͞o), *n.* a river forming the boundary between S Colombia and N Peru, flowing into the Amazon in NW Brazil. ab. 900 mi. Called **Iça** in Brazil.
put-up (po͝ot′ŭp′), *adj. Colloq.* planned beforehand in a secret or crafty manner: *a put-up job.*
put-upon (po͝ot′ə pŏn′), *adj.* much subject to impositions; ill-used.
Puvis de Chavannes (*Fr.* pY vē də shȧ vän′), **Pierre Cécile** (*Fr.* pyĕr sė sĕl′), 1824–98, French painter.
puy (pwē), *n. Geog.* in France, a small extinct volcano cone.
Puy-de-Dôme (*Fr.* pwē də dōm′), *n.* **1.** a department in S central France. 508,928 pop. (1962); 3090 sq. mi. *Cap.:* Clermont-Ferrand. **2.** a mountain in central France. 4805 ft.
Pu-yi (po͞o′yē′), *n.* **Henry,** 1906–67, as Hsiian T'ung,

last emperor of China 1908–12; as Kang Te, emperor of Manchukuo 1934–45.

puzzle (pŭz′əl), *n.*, *v.*, **-zled, -zling.** —*n.* **1.** a toy or other contrivance designed to amuse by presenting difficulties to be solved by ingenuity or patient effort. **2.** something puzzling; a puzzling matter or person. **3.** puzzled or perplexed condition. —*v.t.* **4.** to cause to be at a loss; bewilder; confuse. **5.** to perplex or confound, as the understanding. **6.** to exercise (oneself, one's brain, etc.) over some problem or matter. **7.** to make, as something obscure, by careful study or effort (fol. by *out*): *to puzzle out the meaning of a sentence.* —*v.i.* **8.** to be in perplexity. **9.** to ponder or study over some perplexing problem or matter. [ME *poselet* puzzled, confused, OE *puslian* pick (out), c. D *peuzelen* pick, piddle, Norw. *pusla* be careful or fussy. For meaning, cf. E slang *fussed* confused]

—**Syn.** **2.** PUZZLE, RIDDLE, ENIGMA refer to something baffling or confusing which is to be solved. A PUZZLE is a question or problem, intricate enough to be perplexing to the mind; it is sometimes a contrivance made purposely perplexing to test one's ingenuity: *the reason for their behaviour remains a puzzle; a crossword puzzle.* A RIDDLE is an intentionally obscure statement or question, the meaning of or answer to which is to be arrived at only by guessing: *the riddle of the Sphinx.* ENIGMA, originally meaning riddle, now refers to some baffling problem with connotations of mysteriousness: *he will always be an enigma to me.* **4.** PUZZLE, BEWILDER, PERPLEX imply mental confusion and consequent inability to decide or to act. PUZZLE suggests mental embarrassment amid a complexity of possible decisions: *one may be puzzled over a problem.* BEWILDER suggests complete bafflement, the mind being lost in a multiplicity of considerations and alternatives: *bewildered by an unexpected situation.* PERPLEX suggests such an entanglement of one's judgement that one is uncertain as to what to think or how to act: *perplexed as to a decision.*

puzzlement (pŭz′əl mənt), *n.* **1.** puzzled state; perplexity. **2.** something puzzling.

puzzler (pŭz′lə), *n.* **1.** a person who puzzles. **2.** a baffling question or problem.

p.v., (L *per vaginam*) *Med.* taken through the vagina, as a suppository.

PVA, *Chem.* polyvinyl acetate.

PVC, *Chem.* polyvinyl chloride.

Pvt., Private.

P.W.A., *U.S.* Public Works Administration.

P.W.D., Public Works Department.

P.W.R., *Physics.* pressurized water reactor.

pwt, pennyweight.

PX, Post Exchange.

P.X., **1.** part exchange. **2.** please exchange.

pxt, pinxit.

pya (pyä, pĭ ä′), *n.* a copper coin of Burma, the 100th part of a kyat.

pyaemia (pī ē′myə), *n.* *Pathol.* the growth, in different tissues, of multiple metastatic abscesses, developing from emboli disseminated in the bloodstream as fragments of a disintegrating thrombus. Also, **pyemia.** [NL. See PYO-, -AEMIA]

pycnidium (pĭk nĭd′ĭ əm), *n.*, *pl.* **-nidia** (-nĭd′ĭ ə). *Bot.* (in certain ascomycetes and *Fungi imperfecti*) an asexual (imperfect) fruit body, commonly globose or flask-shaped and bearing conidia on conidiophores. [t. NL, f. Gk: PYCN(O)- + m. *-idion* (dim. suffix)]

pycno-, a word element meaning 'dense', 'close', 'thick', as in *pycnometer.* Also, **pykno-;** before vowels, **pych-.** [t. NL, comb. form repr. Gk *pyknós*]

pycnometer (pĭk nŏm′ĭ tə), *n.* a flask holding a definite volume, used in determining relative density or specific gravity. Also, **pyknometer.** [PYCNO- + -METER[1]]

pycnostyle (pĭk′nə stīl′), *adj.* *Archit.* having columns set 1½ diameters apart.

Pydna (pĭd′nə), *n.* an ancient town of Pieria, in Macedonia, W of the Gulf of Salonika: decisive Roman victory over the Macedonians, 168 B.C.

pye (pī), *n.* *Eccles.* pie[4].

pyelitis (pī′ĭ lī′tĭs), *n.* *Pathol.* inflammation of the pelvis or outlet of the kidney. —**pyelitic** (pī′ĭ lĭt′ĭk), *adj.* [t. NL, f. Gk. See PYELO-, -ITIS]

pyelo-, a word element used with the meaning 'pelvis' in the formation of compound words, as in *pyelogram.* Also, before vowels, **pyel-.** [t. NL, comb. form repr. Gk *pýelos* basin. Cf. L *pelvis* basin, PELVIS]

pyelogram (pī′ə lō grăm′), *n.* an X-ray produced by pyelography. Also, **pyelograph** (pī′ə lō grăf′, -gräf′).

pyelography (pī′ə lŏg′rə fĭ), *n.* the art of making photographs of the kidneys and ureter by means of X-rays, after the injection of an opaque solution or of a radio-opaque dye. —**pyelographic** (pī′ə lō grăf′ĭk), *adj.*

pyelonephritis (pī′ə lō nĭ frī′tĭs), *n.* *Pathol.* inflammation of the kidney and the pelvis of the ureter.

pyemia (pī ē′myə), *n.* *Pathol.* pyaemia.

pygal (pī′gl), *adj.* of or pertaining to the posterior or rump of an animal. [f. s. Gk *pȳgḗ* rump + -AL[1]]

pygidium (pī jĭd′ĭ əm, pī gĭd′-), *n.*, *pl.* **-gidia** (-jĭd′ĭ ə, -gĭd′-). the posterior part of the body in certain invertebrates. [t. NL, f. Gk: *pȳg(ḗ)* rump + m. *-idion* dim. suffix]

pygmaean (pĭg mē′ən, -mī′ən′), *adj.* pygmy. Also, **pygmean.**

Pygmalion (pĭg mā′lyən), *n.* *Gk Legend.* a sculptor and king of Cyprus, who fell in love with an ivory statue which he had made and which came to life in answer to his prayer. Cf. **Galatea.**

Pygmy (pĭg′mĭ), *n.*, *pl.* **-mies.** **1. a.** a member of a Negroid race of small stature inhabiting equatorial Africa. **b.** a Negrito of south-eastern Asia, or of the Andaman and Philippine Islands. **2.** (*l.c.*) a small or dwarfish person. **3.** (*l.c.*) anything very small of its kind. **4.** (*l.c.*) one who is of small importance, or who has some quality, etc., in very small measure. **5.** one of a race of dwarfs in ancient history and tradition. —*adj.* **6.** (*often l.c.*) of or pertaining to the Pygmies. **7.** (*l.c.*) of very small size, capacity, power, etc. Also, **pigmy.** [ME *pigmey*, t. L: m. s. *Pygmaeī*, pl., t. Gk: m. *Pygmaîoi*, prop. pl. of *pygmaîos* dwarfish] —**Syn.** **2.** See **midget.**

pyin (pī′ĭn), *n.* *Biochem.* an albuminous constituent of pus. [f. s. Gk *pýon* pus + -IN[2]]

pyjamas (pə jä′məz), *n.* (*construed as pl.*) **1.** nightclothes consisting of loose trousers and jacket. **2.** loose trousers, usually of silk or cotton, worn by both sexes in oriental countries. Also, *U.S.*, **pajamas.** [t. Hind., t. Pers.: m. *pāejāmah*, lit., leg garment] —**pyjama,** *adj.*

pyknic (pĭk′nĭk), *adj.* **1.** (of a physical type) characterized by stocky build, with a large chest and abdomen, and a tendency to obesity. —*n.* **2.** a person of the pyknic type. [f. Gk: s. *pyknós* thick + -IC]

pylon (pī′lən), *n.* **1.** a steel tower or mast carrying high-tension, telephonic or other cables and lines. **2.** a relatively tall structure at either side of a gate, bridge, or avenue, marking an entrance or approach. **3.** an architectural form of a projecting nature which flanks an entrance. **4.** a marking post or tower for guiding pilots, frequently used in races. **5.** *Egypt. Archit.* **a.** a monumental gateway to an Egyptian temple or edifice, in the shape of a truncated pyramid through which the passage for the gate was pierced. **b.** a combination of two such truncated pyramidal structures connected by a lower architectural member, in which was the gate proper. **6.** *Aeron.* a structure supporting an engine or fuel tank. [t. Gk: gateway]

pylorectomy (pī′lô rĕk′tə mĭ), *n.*, *pl.* **-mies.** *Surg.* removal of the pylorus. [f. PYLOR(US) + -ECTOMY]

pylorus (pī lô′rəs), *n.*, *pl.* **-lori** (-lô′rī). *Anat.* the opening between the stomach and the intestine. [t. LL, t. Gk: m. *pylōrós*, lit., gatekeeper] —**pyloric** (pī lŏ′rĭk), *adj.*

Pym (pĭm), *n.* **John,** 1584–1643, English statesman: championed rights of Parliament against King Charles I.

pyo-, a word element meaning 'pus'. [t. Gk, comb. form of *pýon*]

pyogenesis (pī′ə jĕn′ĭ sĭs), *n.* *Pathol.* the generation of pus; the process of the formation of pus.

pyogenic (pī′ə jĕn′ĭk), *adj.* *Pathol.* **1.** producing or generating pus. **2.** pertaining to the formation of pus.

pyoid (pī′oid), *adj.* *Pathol.* pertaining to pus; puslike. [t. Gk: m. s. *pyoeidḗs* puslike]

Pyongyang (pyŏng′yăng′), *n.* the capital of North Korea, in the SW part. 940,000 (est. 1962). See map under **Korea.**

pyorrhoea (pī′ə rīə′), *n.* *Pathol.* a disease occurring in various forms and degrees of severity, characterized in its severe forms by the formation of pus in the pockets between the root of the tooth and its surrounding tissues, and frequently accompanied by the loss of the teeth; Riggs' disease. Also, **pyorrhea.** [t. NL. See PYO-, -(R)RHOEA] —**py′orrhoeal′,** *adj.*

pyosis (pī ō′sĭs), *n.* *Pathol.* the formation of pus; suppuration. [NL, t. Gk]

pyr-, var. of **pyro-,** used occasionally before vowels or *h*, as in *pyran.*

pyracantha (pī′rə kăn′thə), *n.* any evergreen shrub of the rosaceous genus *Pyracantha*, as *P. coccinea*, the firethorn with clusters of bright red fruits.

pyralid (pĭ′rə lĭd), *n.* **1.** any of numerous slender-bodied, long-legged moths of the family *Pyralidae.* —*adj.* **2.** of, pertaining to, or belonging to the family *Pyralidae.*

pyramid (pĭ′rə mĭd), *n.* **1.** *Archit.* a massive structure built of stone, with square (or polygonal) base, and sloping sides meeting at an apex, such as those built by the ancient Egyptians as royal

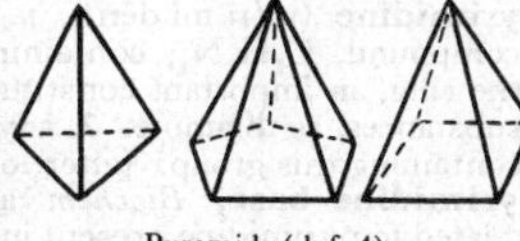

Pyramids (def. 4)

tombs or by the Mayas as platforms for their sanctuaries. **2.** anything of such form. **3.** a number of things heaped up or arranged in this form. **4.** *Geom.* a solid having a triangular, square, or polygonal base, and triangular sides which meet in a point. **5.** *Crystall.* any form the planes of which intersect all three of the axes. **6.** *Anat., Zool.* any of various parts or structures of pyramidal form. **7.** a tree pruned, or trained to grow, in pyramidal form. **8.** (*pl.*) a form of billiards played with 15 coloured balls, initially arranged in the form of a triangle, and one cue ball. —*v.i.* **9.** to be disposed in the form or shape of a pyramid. —*v.t.* **10.** to arrange in the form of a pyramid. **11.** to raise or increase (costs, wages, etc.) by increasing additions, as if building up a pyramid. [t. L: s. *pyramis*, t. Gk, of Egypt. orig.; r. ME *pyramis*, t. L] —**pyr′amid-like′,** *adj.*

pyramidal (pĭ răm′ĭ dl), *adj.* **1.** of or pertaining to a pyramid: *the pyramidal form.* **2.** of the nature of a pyramid; pyramid-like. —**pyram′idally,** *adv.*

pyramidical (pĭ′rə mĭd′ĭ kl), *adj.* pyramidal. Also, **pyramidic.** [f. m. s. Gk *pyramidikós* + -AL[1]] —**pyr′amid′ically,** *adv.*

Pyramus and Thisbe (pĭ′rə məs), *Class. Myth.* two young lovers of Babylon. Pyramus killed himself when he mistakenly thought Thisbe to be dead, and she committed suicide on discovering his body.

pyran (pī′răn, pī răn′), *n. Chem.* either of two compounds, C_5H_6O, containing one oxygen and five carbon atoms arranged in a six-membered ring. [f. PYR- + -AN. Cf. PYRONE]

pyrargyrite (pī rä′jĭ rīt′), *n.* a blackish mineral, silver antimony sulphide ($AgSbS_3$), showing (when transparent) a deep ruby red colour by transmitted light; an ore of silver. [t. G: m. *Pyrargyrit*, f. Gk *pŷr* fire + s. Gk *árgyron* silver + *-it* -ITE[1]]

pyre (pī′ə), *n.* **1.** a pile or heap of wood or other combustible material. **2.** such a pile for burning a dead body. [t. L: m. *pyra*, t. Gk]

pyrene (pī′rēn), *n.* **1.** *Bot.* a putamen or stone, esp. when there are several in a single fruit; a nutlet. **2.** *Chem.* a yellow crystalline tetracyclic hydrocarbon, $C_{16}H_{10}$, found in coal tar. **3.** (*cap.*) *Trademark.* a fire-extinguishing liquid consisting of carbon tetrachloride. [t. NL: m. *pȳrēna*, t. Gk: m. *pȳrḗn* fruit stone]

Pyrenees (pĭ′rə nēz′), *n.pl.* a mountain range between Spain and France. Highest peak, Pic de Néthou, 11,165 ft. —**Pyr′ene′an,** *adj.*

Pyrénées-Orientales (*Fr.* pē rĕ nĕ ō rē äɴ tȧl′), *n.* a department in S France. 251,231 pop. (1962); 1598 sq. mi. *Cap.*: Perpignan.

pyrethrin (pī rē′thrĭn), *n. Chem.* either of two compounds, $C_{21}H_{28}O_3$ (**pyrethrin-1**), or $C_{22}H_{28}O_5$ (**pyrethrin-2**), which are obtained from pyrethrum flowers and are used as contact insecticides.

pyrethrum (pī rē′thrəm), *n.* **1.** a name given by horticulturalists to certain species of the composite genus *Chrysanthemum*, esp. *C. roseum* and its many cultivated varieties. **2.** an insecticide prepared from the dried heads of *C. roseum.*

pyretic (pī rĕt′ĭk), *adj.* of, pertaining to, affected by, or producing fever. [t. NL: s. *pyreticus*, der. Gk *pyretós* fever]

pyretology (pĭ′rə tŏl′ə jĭ, pī′rə-), *n.* the branch of medicine that treats of fevers. [f. Gk *pyretó(s)* fever + -LOGY]

Pyrex (pī′rĕks, pī′ə rĕks′), *n. Trademark.* a heat-resistant glassware for baking, frying, etc.

pyrexia (pī rĕk′sĭ ə), *n. Pathol.* **1.** fever. **2.** feverish condition. [NL, t. Gk: m. *pýrexis* feverishness] —**pyrex′ial, pyrex′ic,** *adj.*

pyrheliometer (pə hē′lĭ ŏm′ĭ tə), *n. Astrophysics.* an instrument for measuring the total intensity of the sun's energy radiation. [f. Gk *pŷr* fire + HELIO- + -METER[1]]

pyridine (pĭ′rĭ dēn′), *n. Chem.* a liquid organic base, C_5H_5N, with a pungent smell, found in coal tar, bone oil, etc., and the parent substance of many compounds: used as a solvent and as an amine. [f. Gk *pŷr* fire + -ID[2] + -INE[2]] —**pyridic** (pī rĭd′ĭk), *adj.*

pyridoxine (pĭ′rĭ dŏk′sēn), *n. Biochem.* a derivative of pyridine that, together with the closely related compounds **pyridoxal** and **pyridoxamine,** is known as vitamin B_6, deficiency of which may lead to dermatitis and anaemia. [f. PYR- + -ID[2] + OX(YGEN) + -INE[2]]

pyriform (pĭ′rĭ fôm′), *adj.* pear-shaped. [t. NL: s. *pyriformis*, f. *pyri-* (for *piri-* pear) + *-formis* -FORM]

pyrimidine (pĭ′rĭ mĭ dēn′), *n. Chem.* **1.** a heterocyclic compound, $C_4H_4N_2$, containing two nitrogen atoms in the ring, an important constituent of several biochemical substances, as thiamine. **2.** any of a group of compounds containing this group. [alter. of PYRIDINE]

pyrimidine base, *Biochem.* any of several compounds related to pyrimidine present in combined form in nucleic acids.

pyrite (pī′ə rīt′), *n.* a very common brass-yellow mineral, iron disulphide (FeS_2), with a metallic lustre, burnt to sulphur dioxide in the manufacture of sulphuric acid; fool's gold. Also, **pyrite, iron pyrites.** [t. L: m. *pyrītēs.* See PYRITES] —**pyritic** (pī rĭt′ĭk), **pyrit′ical,** *adj.*

pyrites (pī rī′tēz), *n.* **1.** pyrite (sometimes called **iron pyrites**). **2.** marcasite (**white iron pyrites**). **3.** any of various other sulphides, as of copper, tin, etc. [t. L, t. Gk: orig. adj., of or in fire]

pyro-, a word element used: **1.** *Chem.* **a.** before the name of an inorganic acid, indicating that its water content is intermediate between that of the corresponding ortho- (more water) and meta- (least water) acids: *pyroantimonic*, $H_4Sb_2O_7$, *pyroarsenic*, $H_4As_2O_7$, and *pyrosulphuric*, $H_2S_2O_7$, *acids.* **b.** applied to salts of these acids. If the acid ends in *-ic*, the corresponding salt ends in *-ate*, as *pyroboric acid*, $H_2B_4O_7$ and *potassium pyroborate*, $K_2B_4O_7$. If the acid ends in *-ous*, the corresponding salt ends in *-ite*: *pyrophosphorous acid*, $H_4P_2O_5$, *potassium pyrophosphite*, $K_4P_2O_5$. **2.** *Geol.* in the names of minerals, rocks, etc., indicating a quality produced by the action of fire. **3.** to mean 'of, relating to, or concerned with fire'. Also, before vowels, **pyr-.** [t. Gk, comb. form of *pŷr* fire]

pyrocatechol (pī′rō kăt′ĭ kŏl′), *n.* catechol. Also, **pyrocatechin** (pī′rō kăt′ĭ kĭn).

pyrochemical (pī′rō kĕm′ĭ kl), *adj.* pertaining to or producing chemical change at high temperatures. —**py′rochem′ically,** *adv.*

pyrochroite (pī′rō krō′īt), *n. Chem.* a mineral hydroxide of manganese crystallizing in the trigonal system.

pyroclastic (pī′rō klăs′tĭk), *adj. Geol.* composed chiefly of fragments of volcanic origin, as agglomerate, tuff, and certain other rocks.

pyrocrystalline (pī′rō krĭs′tə līn′), *adj. Geol.* crystallized from a molten magma or highly heated solution.

pyroelectric (pī′rō ĭ lĕk′trĭk), *adj.* of, subject to, or manifesting, pyroelectricity.

pyroelectricity (pī′rō ĭ lĕk′trĭs′ĭ tĭ), *n.* the electrified state, or electric polarity, in some crystals produced by and changing with temperature.

pyrogallate (pī′rō găl′āt), *n. Chem.* a salt or ester of pyrogallol.

pyrogallol (pī′rō găl′ŏl), *n. Chem.* a white crystalline phenolic compound, $C_6H_3(OH)_3$, obtained by heating gallic acid, and used as a photographic developer. Also, **pyrogallic acid.** —**py′rogal′lic,** *adj.*

pyrogen (pī′rō jĕn′), *n.* a substance which produces a rise of temperature in an animal body.

pyrogenic (pī′rō jĕn′ĭk), *adj.* **1.** producing heat or fever. **2.** produced by fire, as igneous rocks.

pyrogenous (pī rŏj′ĭ nəs), *adj. Geol.* produced by the action of heat or fire.

pyrognostics (pī′rŏg nŏs′tĭks), *n.pl.* those properties of a mineral which it exhibits when heated, alone or with fluxes, in the blowpipe flame, as the fusibility, intumescence, or other phenomena of fusion, flame coloration, etc. [pl. of *pyrognostic*, f. PYRO- + m. s. Gk *gnōstikós* pertaining to knowledge. See -ICS]

pyrography (pī rŏg′rə fĭ), *n.* the process of burning designs on wood, leather, etc., with a heated tool. —**pyrog′rapher,** *n.* —**pyrographic** (pī′rə grăf′ĭk), *adj.*

pyroligneous (pī′rō lĭg′nĭ əs), *adj.* produced by the distillation of wood. Also, **pyrolignic.** [f. PYRO- + m. L *ligneus* of wood]

pyroligneous acid, an acidic distillate obtained from wood and containing about 10 per cent acetic acid.

pyroligneous alcohol, methyl alcohol.

pyrolusite (pī′rō lo͞o′sīt), *n.* a common mineral, manganese dioxide, MnO_2, the principal ore of manganese, used in various manufactures, as a decolorizer of brown or green tints in glass, as a depolarizer in dry-cell batteries, etc. [f. PYRO- + m. s. Gk *loûsis* washing + -ITE[1]]

pyrolysis (pī rŏl′ĭ sĭs), *n. Chem.* the subjection of organic compounds to very high temperatures and the resulting decomposition. —**pyrolytic** (pī′rō lĭt′ĭk), *adj.*

pyromagnetic (pī′rō măg nĕt′ĭk), *adj.* **1.** pertaining to or depending upon the combined action of heat and magnetism. **2.** relating to magnetic properties as changing with the temperature.

pyromancy (pī′rō măn′sĭ), *n.* divination by fire, or by forms appearing in fire. [ME *piromancie*, t. ML: m. *pyromantīa*, t. Gk: m. *pyromanteía*]

pyromania (pī′rō mā′nyə), *n.* a mania for setting things on fire. —**py′roma′niac′,** *n.* —**pyromaniacal** (pī′rōmə nī′ə kl), *adj.*

pyrometallurgy (pī′rō mĕt′ə lû′jĭ), *n.* the practice of refining ores by the use of heat which serves to accelerate chemical reactions or to melt the metallic or non-metallic content.

pyrometer (pī rŏm′ĭ tə), *n.* an apparatus for determining high temperatures which depends commonly on observation of colour or measurement of electric current produced by heating of dissimilar metals. —**pyrometric** (pī′rō mĕt′rĭk), **py′romet′rical,** *adj.*

pyrometric cone, Seger cone.

pyrometric cone equivalent, *Chem.* a measure of the melting point of refractory materials, based on the use of Seger cones. *Abbrev.*: p.c.e.

pyromorphite (pī′rō mô′fīt), *n.* a mineral, lead chlorophosphate, $Pb_5P_3O_{12}Cl$, occurring in crystalline and massive forms and of a green, yellow, or brown colour: a minor ore of lead. [t. G: m. *Pyromorphit.* See PYRO-, MORPH-, -ITE[1]]

pyrone (pī′rōn, pī rōn′), *n.* *Chem.* either of two heterocyclic ketones, $C_5H_4O_2$. [f. PYR- + -ONE]

pyrope (pī′rōp), *n.* a mineral, magnesium-aluminium garnet, $Mg_3Al_2Si_3O_{12}$, occurring in crystals of varying shades of red, and frequently used as a gem. [ME *pirope,* t. OF, t. L: m. *pyrōpus* gold-bronze, t. Gk: m. *pyrōpós* fiery (eyed), gold-bronze. Cf. G *Pyrop*]

pyrophoric alloy (pī′rō fŏ′rĭk), *Metall.* an alloy which emits sparks when scraped or struck; used as a flint in automatic lighters.

pyrophosphoric acid (pī′rō fŏs fŏ′rĭk), *Chem.* the acid $H_4P_2O_7$, formed by the union of one molecule of phosphorus pentoxide with two molecules of water. It is a water-soluble, crystalline powder.

pyrophotometer (pī′rō fō tŏm′ĭ tə), *n.* a form of pyrometer which measures temperature by optical or photometric means.

pyrophyllite (pī′rō fĭl′īt), *n.* a mineral, hydrous aluminium silicate, $AlSi_2O_5(OH)_4$, usually having a white or greenish colour, and occurring in either foliated or compact masses, the latter variety being used like soapstone. [t. G: m. *Pyrophyllit*; so called from its exfoliating when heated. See PYRO-, PHYLL(O)-, -ITE[1]]

pyrostat (pī′rə stăt′), *n.* a thermostat for high temperatures.

pyrostibnite (pī′rō stĭb′nīt), *n.* kermesite.

pyrosulphate (pī′rō sŭl′fāt), *n.* *Chem.* a salt of pyrosulphuric acid.

pyrosulphuric acid (pī′rō sŭl fyŏŏə′rĭk), *Chem.* fuming sulphuric acid.

pyrotechnic (pī′rō tĕk′nĭk), *adj.* **1.** of or pertaining to pyrotechnics. **2.** pertaining to, resembling, or suggesting fireworks. Also, **py′rotech′nical.**

pyrotechnics (pī′rō tĕk′nĭks), *n.* **1.** the art of making fireworks. **2.** the making and use of fireworks for display, military purposes, etc. **3.** a brilliant or sensational display, as of rhetoric, etc. Also, **py′rotech′ny** for defs 1, 2.

pyrotechnist (pī′rō tĕk′nĭst), *n.* one skilled in pyrotechnics.

pyrotoxin (pī′rō tŏk′sĭn), *n.* pyrogen.

pyroxene (pī′rŏk sēn′), *n.* a very common group of minerals of many varieties, silicates of magnesium, iron, calcium, and other elements, occurring as important constituents of many kinds of rocks, chiefly igneous. [t. F, f. Gk: *pyro-* PYRO- + m. s. *xénos* stranger; orig. supposed to be a foreign substance when found in igneous rocks] —**pyroxenic** (pī′rŏk sĕn′ĭk), *adj.*

pyroxenite (pī rŏk′sĭ nīt′), *n.* any rock composed essentially, or in large part, of pyroxene of any kind.

pyroxylin (pī rŏk′sĭ lĭn), *n.* a nitrocellulose compound containing fewer nitro groups than guncotton and used as collodion, and in the artificial silk, leather, oilcloth industries, etc. Also, **pyroxyline.** [f. PYRO- + s. Gk *xýlon* wood + -IN[2]]

Pyrrha (pĭ′rə), *n.* *Gk Legend.* wife of Deucalion.

Pyrrhic (pĭ′rĭk), *adj.* of or pertaining to Pyrrhus, king of Epirus.

pyrrhic[1] (pĭ′rĭk), *Pros.* —*adj.* **1.** consisting of two short or unaccented syllables. **2.** composed of or pertaining to pyrrhics. —*n.* **3.** a pyrrhic foot. [t. L: m. s. *pyrrhichius,* t. Gk: m. *pyrrhíchios* pertaining to the *pyrrhíchē* PYRRHIC[2]]

pyrrhic[2] (pĭ′rĭk), *n.* **1.** an ancient Grecian warlike dance in which the motions of actual warfare were imitated. —*adj.* **2.** of or pertaining to this dance. [t. L: m. s. *pyrrhicha,* t. Gk: m. *pyrríchē* a dance; said to be named after *Pyrrhichus,* the inventor]

Pyrrhic victory, a victory gained at too great a cost, as that of Pyrrhus over the Romans at Apulum (modern Ascoli Satriano in SE Italy) in 279 B.C.

Pyrrho (pĭ′rō), *n.* *c.* 365–*c.* 275 B.C., Greek philosopher.

Pyrrhonism (pĭ′rə nĭz′əm), *n.* **1.** the Sceptic doctrines or system of Pyrrho and his followers. **2.** absolute or extreme scepticism.

pyrrhotite (pĭ′rə tīt′), *n.* a common mineral, iron sulphide (nearly FeS), occurring in crystalline and massive forms, of a bronze colour and metallic lustre, and generally slightly magnetic. Also, **pyrrhotine** (pĭ′rə tīn′). [for earlier *pyrrhotine,* f. s. Gk *pyrrhótēs* redness + -INE[2]]

pyrrhuloxia (pĭ′rə lŏk′sĭ ə), *n.* a cardinal-like grosbeak, *Pyrrhuloxia sinuata,* inhabiting the south-western U.S. and Mexico, and having a bill superficially resembling that of a parrot.

Pyrrhus (pĭ′rəs), *n.* **1.** *c.* 318–272 B.C., king of Epirus *c.* 300–272 B.C. **2.** *Gk Legend.* son of Achilles.

pyrrole (pĭ′rōl, pĭ rōl′), *n.* *Chem.* a five-membered ring system, C_4H_5N, containing four carbon atoms and a nitrogen atom. Chlorophyll, haemin, and many other important naturally occurring substances are built up of pyrrole rings. [f. Gk *pyrr(hós)* red + -OLE]

pyrrolidine (pĭ rŏl′ĭ dēn′), *n.* *Chem.* a compound, C_4H_9N, derived from proline and some alkaloids, and present in tobacco.

pyrroline (pĭ′rə lĭn′, -lĭn), *n.* *Chem.* a colourless liquid, C_4H_7N, derived from pyrrole.

pyruvic acid (pī rōō′vĭk), *Chem., Biochem.* an acid, $CH_3COCOOH$, important in many biochemical processes, prepared by heating tartaric acid. [f. PYR(O)- + L *ūv(a)* grape + -IC + ACID]

pyruvic aldehyde, *Chem.* an organic compound, CH_3COCHO, containing both an aldehyde and a ketone group, usually obtained in a polymeric form.

Pythagoras (pī thăg′ə rəs), *n.* *c.* 582–*c.* 500 B.C., Greek philosopher, mathematician, and religious reformer.

Pythagoras's theorem, *Geom.* the theorem which states that in a right-angled triangle the square on the hypotenuse is equal to the sum of the squares on the other two sides.

Pythagorean (pī thăg′ə rē′ən), *adj.* **1.** pertaining to Pythagoras, who is thought to have viewed philosophy more as a means to a way of life than as a mere search for knowledge, and to have taught metempsychosis. —*n.* **2.** a follower of Pythagoras. —**Pythag′ore′anism,** *n.*

Pythia (pĭth′ĭ ə), *n.* *Gk Myth.* the priestess of Apollo at Delphi who delivered the oracles. [t. L, t. Gk, prop. fem. of *Pýthios* Pythian]

Pythiad (pĭth′ĭ ăd′), *n.* the period of four years between two celebrations of the Pythian games.

Pythian (pĭth′ĭ ən), *adj.* Also, **Pythic. 1.** of or pertaining to Delphi in ancient Greece. **2.** of or pertaining to Apollo, with reference to his oracle at Delphi. —*n.* **3.** a Pythian priestess. [f. s. L *Pȳthius* (t. Gk: m. *Pýthios* of Delphi) + -AN]

Pythian games, one of the great national festivals of ancient Greece, held every four years at Delphi in honour of Apollo.

Pythias (pĭth′ĭ ăs′), *n.* See **Damon.**

python[1] (pī′thən), *n.* **1.** a possessing spirit or demon. **2.** one who is possessed by a spirit and prophesies by its aid. [t. LGk; relation to PYTHON not clear]

python[2] (pī′thən), *n.* any of various large, non-venomous, Old World snakes, of the genus *Python,* which kill by constriction. [t. L, t. Gk]

Python (pī′thən), *n.* *Gk Myth.* a huge servant or monster which guarded a chasm, fabled to have been slain by Apollo near Delphi.

pythoness (pī′thə nĕs′), *n.* **1.** a woman supposed to be possessed by a soothsaying spirit, as the priestess of Apollo at Delphi. **2.** a woman with power of divination; a witch. [f. PYTHON[1] + -ESS; r. ME *phytonesse,* t. OF]

pythonic[1] (pī thŏn′ĭk), *adj.* prophetic; oracular. [t. L: s. *pythōnicus,* t. Gk: m. *pythōnikós* prophetic]

pythonic[2] (pī thŏn′ĭk), *adj.* **1.** of or pertaining to pythonus. **2.** python-like. [f. PYTHON[2] + -IC]

pyuria (pī yŏŏə′rĭ ə), *n.* *Pathol.* the presence of pus in the urine. [f. PY(O)- + -URIA]

pyx (pĭks), *n.* **1.** *Eccles.* **a.** the box or vessel in which the reserved Eucharist or Host is kept. **b.** a watch-shaped container for carrying the Eucharist to the sick. **2.** a box or chest at a mint, in which specimen coins are deposited and reserved for trial by weight and assay. Also, **pix.** [ME, t. L: s. *pyxis,* t. Gk: a box, orig., made of boxwood]

pyxidium (pĭk sĭd′ĭ əm), *n., pl.* **pyxidia** (pĭk sĭd′ĭ ə). *Bot.* a seed vessel which dehisces transversely, the top part acting as a lid, as in the purslane. [NL, t. Gk: m. *pyxídion,* dim. of *pyxis* box]

Pyxidium

pyxie (pĭk′sĭ), *n.* **1.** either of two trailing, shrubby, evergreen plants, *Pyxidanthera barbulata* or *P. brevifolia,* of the eastern U.S., bearing numerous small, starlike blossoms. **2.** *Bot.* pyxidium. [short for NL *Pyxidanthera,* equiv. to *pyxid-* (s. L *pyxis* box; see PYX) + *anthera* ANTHER]

pyxis (pĭk′sĭs), *n., pl.* **pyxides** (pĭk′sĭ dēz′), **1.** a small box or boxlike vase. **2.** a casket. **3.** *Bot.* a pyxidium. [ME, t. L. See PYX]

P.Z.I., protamine zinc insulin, a type of insulin used in the treatment of diabetes mellitus.

Q, q (kyōō), *n., pl.* **Q's** or **Qs, q's** or **qs.** a consonant, the 17th letter of the English alphabet.

Q, 1. *Physics.* heat. **2.** *Chess.* queen. **3.** *Physics.* Q-value.

Q., 1. quarto. **2.** Quebec. **3.** Queen. **4.** question.

q., 1. (L *quadrans*) farthing. **2.** quart; quarts. **3.** query. **4.** question. **5.** quintal. **6.** quire.

Q.A.R.A.N.C., Queen Alexandra's Royal Army Nursing Corps.

qat (kăt, kät), *n.* kat.

Qatar (kă tä'), *n.* **1.** a peninsula in E Arabia extending into the SW Persian Gulf. **2.** a sheikhdom coextensive with this peninsula: under British protection. 60,000 pop. (est. 1965); ab. 8000 sq. mi. *Cap.:* Doha. Also, **Katar.**

Qazvin (kăz vēn'), *n.* Kazvin.

QB, *Chess.* queen's bishop.

Q.B., Queen's Bench.

Q.B.D., Queen's Bench Division.

QBP, *Chess.* queen's bishop's pawn.

Q.C., Queen's Counsel.

q.e., (L *quod est*) which is.

Q.E.D., quod erat demonstrandum.

Q.E.F., quod erat faciendum.

Q-fever (kyōō'fē'və), *n.* a fever exhibiting pneumonia-like symptoms, and caused by *Rickettsia burnetii.*

qintar (kĭn tä', kĭn'tä), *n.* a coin of Albania, equal to a hundredth of a lek.

Qishm (kĭsh'əm), *n.* an island S of, and belonging to, Iran, in the Strait of Hormuz. ab. 25,000 pop.; 68 mi. long; ab. 510 sq. mi.

QKt, *Chess.* queen's knight.

QKtP, *Chess.* queen's knight's pawn.

ql, quintal.

q.l., (L *quantum libet*) (in prescriptions) as much as you like.

Q.M., Quartermaster.

Q. Mess., Queen's Messenger.

Q.M.G., Quartermaster-General.

Q.M.S., Quartermaster-Sergeant.

QNP, *Chess.* queen's knight's pawn.

QP, *Chess.* queen's pawn.

q. pl., (L *quantum placet*) as much as you please.

qq. v., (L *quae vide*) which (words, etc.) see.

QR, *Chess.* queen's rook.

qr, quarter.

qr., *pl.* **qrs. 1.** (L *quandrans, pl. quadrantes*) farthing. **2.** quire.

QRP, *Chess.* queen's rook's pawn.

Q.S., quarter sessions.

q.s., 1. quantum sufficit. **2.** quarter section.

Q-ship (kyōō'shĭp'), *n.* (in World War I) a naval vessel disguised as a merchant ship or fishing boat in order to lure enemy submarines within range of its guns. Also, **Q-boat** (kyōō'bōt').

qt, *pl.* **qt, qts.** quart.

qt., quantity.

q.t., *Colloq.* **1.** quiet. **2. on the q.t.,** secretly.

q.t.r., 1. quarter. **2.** quarterly.

qu., 1. quart. **2.** quarter. **3.** quarterly. **4.** queen. **5.** query. **6.** question.

qua (kwā, kwä), *adv.* as; as being; in the character or capacity of. [t. L, orig. abl. fem. of *qui* who]

quack[1] (kwăk), *v.i.* **1.** to utter the cry of a duck, or a sound resembling it. —*n.* **2.** the cry of a duck, or some similar sound. [imit. Cf. D *kwaken,* G *quacken*]

quack[2] (kwăk), *n.* **1.** an ignorant or fraudulent pretender to medical skill. **2.** one who pretends professionally or publicly to skill, knowledge, or qualifications which he does not possess; a charlatan. **3.** *Colloq.* any medical practitioner. —*adj.* **4.** being a quack: *a quack doctor.* **5.** falsely claiming curative powers: *quack medicine.* **6.** of, pertaining to, or befitting a quack. **7.** involving quackery: *quack methods.* —*v.i.* **8.** to play the quack. —*v.t.* **9.** to treat in the manner of a quack. [short for QUACKSALVER]

quackery (kwăk'ə rĭ), *n., pl.* **-eries. 1.** the practice or methods of a quack. **2.** an instance of this.

quack grass, couch-grass, *Agropyron repens.* [var. of QUITCH OR QUICK GRASS]

quacksalver (kwăk'săl'və), *n.* **1.** a quack in medicine. **2.** *Archaic.* a charlatan. [t. early mod. D. Cf. QUACK[1], SALVE]

quad[1] (kwŏd), *n. Colloq.* a quadrangle, orig. of a college. [short for QUADRANGLE; orig. university slang]

quad[2] (kwŏd), *n. Print.* a piece of type metal of less height than the lettered types, serving to cause a blank in printed matter, used for spacing, etc. [short for QUADRAT]

quad[3] (kwŏd), *n. Slang.* quod.

quad[4] (kwŏd), *n. Colloq.* quadruplet.

quad[5] (kwŏd), *adj.* denoting a size of printing paper having four times the area of the size specified: *quad crown.* [short for QUADRUPLE]

quad., quadrangle.

quadr-, var. of **quadri-,** before vowels, as in *quadrangle.*

Quadragesima (kwŏd'rə jĕs'ĭ mə), *n.* **1.** the first Sunday in Lent (more fully, **Quadragesima Sunday**). **2.** *Obs.* the forty days of Lent. [ML, short for L *quadrāgēsima dies* fortieth day]

Quadragesimal (kwŏd'rə jĕs'ĭ məl), *adj.* **1.** pertaining to, or suitable for, Lent. **2.** (*sometimes l.c.*) lasting forty days, as the fast of Lent.

quadrangle (kwŏd'răng'gl), *n.* **1.** a plane figure having four angles and four sides, as a square. **2.** a quadrangular space or court wholly or nearly surrounded by a building or buildings, as in a college, etc. **3.** the building or buildings about such a space or court. [ME, t. LL: m. s. *quadrangulum* (neut.), lit., four-cornered (thing)] —**quadrangular** (kwŏ drăng'gyōō lə), *adj.*

quadrant (kwŏd'rənt), *n.* **1.** the quarter of a circle; an arc of 90°. **2.** the area included between such an arc and two radii drawn one to each extremity. **3.** something shaped like a quarter of a circle, as a part of a machine. **4.** *Geom.* one of the four parts into which a plane is divided by two perpendicular lines. **5.** an instrument, usually containing a graduated arc of 90°, used in astronomy, navigation, etc., for measuring altitudes. [ME, t. L: s. *quadrans* fourth part] —**quadrantal** (kwŏ drăn'tl), *adj.*

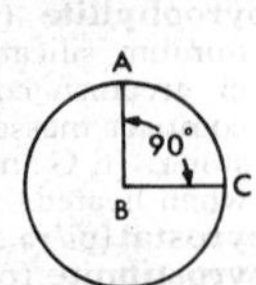

Quadrants
Arc AC (def. 1)
Segment ABC (def. 2)

quadrat (kwŏd'rət), *n.* **1.** *Print.* a quad[2]. **2.** *Ecol.* a rectangular plot of land selected at random for the study of plants and animals within it. [var. of QUADRATE]

quadrate (*adj., n.* kwŏd'rĭt; *v.* kwŏ drāt'), *adj., n., v.,* **-rated, -rating.** —*adj.* **1.** square; rectangular. **2.** *Zool.* of or pertaining to the quadrate. —*n.* **3.** a square, or something square or rectangular. **4.** *Zool.* one of a pair of bones in the skulls of many lower vertebrates, to which the lower jaw is articulated. —*v.t.* **5.** to cause to conform; adapt. —*v.i.* **6.** to agree; conform. [ME *quadrat,* t. L: s. *quadrātus,* pp., made square]

quadratic (kwə drăt'ĭk), *adj.* **1.** square. **2.** *Alg.* involving the square and no higher power of the unknown quantity; the second degree: *a quadratic equation.* —*n.* **3.** *Alg.* a quadratic polynomial or equation.

quadratics (kwə drăt'ĭks), *n.* (*construed as sing.*) the branch of algebra that treats of quadratic equations.

quadrature (kwŏd'rə chə), *n.* **1.** the act of squaring. **2.** the act or process of finding a square equal in area to a given surface, esp. a surface bounded by a curve. **3.** *Astron.* **a.** the situation of two heavenly bodies when their longitudes differ by 90°. **b.** either of the two points in the orbit of a body, as the moon, midway between the syzygies. **c.** (of the moon) one of the points or moments at which a half-moon is visible. **4.** *Electronics.* the relationship between two waves which are out of phase by 90°. [t. L: m. *quadrātūra*]

quadrature of the circle, *Maths.* the geometrically insoluble problem of constructing a square equal in area to a given circle.

quadrennial (kwŏ drĕn'ĭ əl), *adj.* **1.** occurring every four years. **2.** of or for four years. [earlier *quadriennial,* f. L *quadrienni(s)* + -AL[1]] —**quadren'nially,** *adv.*

quadrennium (kwŏd rĕn'ĭ əm), *n., pl.* **-renniums, -rennia** (-rĕn'ĭ ə). a period of four years. [NL, alter. of L *quadriennium*]

quadri-, a word element meaning 'four'. Also, before vowels, **quadr-.** [t. L; cf. L *quattuor* four]

quadric (kwŏd'rĭk), *Maths.* —*adj.* **1.** of the second degree: said esp. of functions with more than two variables. —*n.* **2.** a surface such as an ellipsoid or paraboloid as defined by a second degree equation in three real variables. [f. s. L *quadra* a square + -IC]

quadricentennial (kwŏd'rĭ sĕn tĕn'yəl), *adj.* **1.** pertaining to, consisting of, or marking the completion of, a period of 400 years. —*n.* **2.** *U.S.* a quatercentenary.

quadriceps (kwŏd′rĭ sĕps′), *n.* *Anat.* the great muscle of the front of the thigh, which extends the leg and is considered as having four heads or origins. [NL, f. L: *quadri-* QUADRI- + *-ceps* headed. Cf. BICEPS]

quadricycle (kwŏd′rĭ sī′kl), *n.* a vehicle similar to the bicycle and tricycle but having four wheels.

quadrifid (kwŏd′rĭ fĭd), *adj.* cleft into four parts or lobes. [t. L: s. *quadrifidus.* See QUADRI-, -FID]

quadriga (kwə drē′gə), *n., pl.* **-gae** (-jē). *Class. Antiq.* a two-wheeled chariot drawn by four horses harnessed abreast. [L, earlier pl., *quadrigae*, contr. of *quadrijugae* a team of four]

quadrilateral (kwŏd′rĭ lăt′ə rəl, -lăt′rəl), *adj.* **1.** having four sides. —*n.* **2.** a plane figure having four sides and four angles. **3.** something of this form. **4.** *Geom.* a figure formed by four straight lines which have six points of intersection (**complete quadrilateral**). **5.** the space enclosed between and defended by four fortresses. [f. s. L *quadrilaterus* four-sided + -AL[1]]

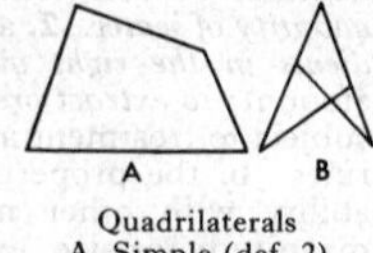

Quadrilaterals
A, Simple (def. 2)
B, Complete (def. 4)

quadrilingual (kwŏd′rĭ lĭng′gwəl), *adj.* using or involving four languages. [f. QUADRI- + s. L *lingua* tongue + -AL[1]]

quadrille[1] (kwə drĭl′), *n.* **1.** a square dance for four couples, consisting of five parts or movements, each complete in itself. **2.** the music for such a dance. [t. F, t. Sp.: m. *cuadrilla* company, troop, dim. of *cuadra* square, g. L *quadra*]

quadrille[2] (kwə drĭl′), *n.* a card game played by four persons. [t. F, t. Sp.: m. *cuartillo*, der. *cuarto* fourth, g. L *quartus*]

quadrillion (kwŏ drĭl′yən), *n.* **1.** (in Britain and Germany) a cardinal number represented by one followed by 24 zeros. **2.** (in the U.S. and France) a cardinal number represented by one followed by 15 zeros. —*adj.* **3.** amounting to one quadrillion in number. [f. QUADR- + (M)ILLION]

quadrinomial (kwŏd′rĭ nō′myəl), *Alg.* —*adj.* **1.** consisting of four terms. —*n.* **2.** a quadrinomial expression.

quadripartite (kwŏd′rĭ pä′tīt), *adj.* **1.** divided into or consisting of four parts. **2.** involving four participants: *a quadripartite treaty.* [t. L: m. s. *quadripartitus*]

quadriplegia (kwŏd′rĭ plē′jyə), *n.* *Pathol.* a condition in which the arms and legs are paralysed. —**quadriplegic** (kwŏd′rĭ plē′jĭk), *n., adj.*

quadrisyllable (kwŏd′rĭ sĭl′ə bl), *n.* a word of four syllables. —**quadrisyllabic** (kwŏd′rĭ sĭ lăb′ĭk), *adj.*

quadrivalent (kwŏd′rĭ vā′lənt, kwŏ drĭv′ə-), *adj.* *Chem.* **1.** having a valency of four; tetravalent. **2.** exercising four different valencies, as antimony with valencies 5, 4, 3, and -3. —**quad′riva′lency, quad′riva′lence,** *n.*

quadrivial (kwŏ drĭv′ĭ əl), *adj.* **1.** having four ways or roads meeting in a point. **2.** (of ways or roads) leading in four directions. [ME, t. ML: s. *quadriviālis*, der. L *quadrivium.* See QUADRIVIUM]

quadrivium (kwŏ drĭv′ĭ əm), *n.* (during the Middle Ages) the more advanced division of the seven liberal arts, comprising arithmetic, geometry, astronomy, and music. [t. LL, special use of L *quadrivium* place where four ways meet]

quadroon (kwŏ dro͞on′), *n.* a person who is one-fourth Negro; the offspring of a mulatto and white. [t. Sp.: m. *cuarterón*, der. *cuarto* fourth, g. L *quartus*]

quadrumane (kwŏd′ro͝o mān′), *n.* a quadrumanous animal, as a monkey.

quadrumanous (kwŏ dro͞o′mə nəs), *adj.* four-handed; having all four feet adapted for use as hands, as animals of the monkey kind. [t. NL: m. *quadrumanus*]

quadruped (kwŏd′ro͝o pĕd′), *adj.* **1.** four-footed. —*n.* **2.** an animal, esp. a mammal, having four feet. [t. L: s. *quadrupēs*] —**quadrupedal** (kwŏ dro͞o′pĭ dl, kwŏd′ro͝o-pĕd′l), *adj.*

quadruple (kwŏd′ro͝o pl, kwŏ dro͞o′pl), *adj., n., v.,* **-pled, -pling.** —*adj.* **1.** fourfold; consisting of four parts: *a quadruple alliance.* **2.** four times as great. —*n.* **3.** a number, amount, etc., four times as great as another. —*v.t., v.i.* **4.** to make or become four times as great. [ME, t. L: m. s. *quadruplus*]

quadruplet (kwŏd′ro͝o plĭt), *n.* **1.** any group or combination of four. **2.** (*pl.*) four children born at a birth. **3.** one of four such children. **4.** *Music.* a group of four notes of equal length in a beat of different tempo. [f. QUADRUPLE + -ET, modelled on TRIPLET]

quadruple time, **1.** a measure consisting of four beats or pulses with accent on the first and third. **2.** the rhythm created by use of this measure.

quadruplex (kwŏd′ro͝o plĕks′), *adj.* **1.** fourfold; quadruple. **2.** denoting or pertaining to a system of telegraphy by which four messages may be transmitted simultaneously over a single wire or communications channel. [t. L]

quadruplicate (*v.* kwŏ dro͞o′plĭ kāt′; *adj., n.,* kwŏ dro͞o′-plĭ kĭt), *v.,* **-cated, -cating,** *adj., n.* —*v.t.* **1.** to make fourfold; quadruple. —*adj.* **2.** fourfold; quadruple. —*n.* **3.** one of four identical things. [t. L: m. s. *quadruplicātus*, pp., quadrupled] —**quadru′plica′tion,** *n.*

quaere (kwĭə′rĭ), *v. imperative.* **1.** ask; enquire (used to introduce or suggest a question). —*n.* **2.** a query or question. [L, impv. of *quaerere* seek, ask. Cf. QUERY]

quaestor (kwēs′tə), *n.* *Rom. Hist.* **1.** one of two subordinates of the consuls serving as public prosecutors in certain criminal cases. **2.** (later) one of the public magistrates in charge of the state funds, as treasury officers or attached to the consuls and provincial governors. [t. L] —**quaestorial** (kwēs tô′rĭ əl), *adj.* —**quaes′torship′,** *n.*

quaff (kwäf), *v.i.* **1.** to drink a beverage, esp. an alcoholic one in large draughts, as with hearty enjoyment. —*v.t.* **2.** to drink (a beverage, etc.) copiously and heartily. —*n.* **3.** a quaffing. [earlier *quaft*, b. QUENCH and DRAUGHT] —**quaff′er,** *n.*

quag (kwăg), *n.* a quagmire.

quagga (kwăg′ə), *n.* an equine mammal of southern Africa, *Equus quagga*, extinct since about 1875, related to the zebra, but striped only on the forepart of the body and the head. [prob. t. Hottentot; akin to Xhosa *iqwara*]

quaggy (kwăg′ĭ), *adj.,* **-gier, -giest.** of the nature of or resembling a quagmire; boggy.

quagmire (kwăg′mī′ə, kwŏg′-), *n.* **1.** a piece of miry or boggy ground whose surface yields under the tread; a bog. **2.** a situation from which extrication is difficult. Also, **quag.** [f. *quag-* (? b. QUAKE and SAG) + MIRE]

quahog (kwä′hŏg′), *n.* an edible American clam, *Venus mercenaria*, the **round clam** or **hard clam** of the Atlantic coast. Also, **quahaug.** [t. N Amer. Ind. (Narragansett), aphetic var. of *poquauhock*]

Quai d'Orsay (*Fr.* kĕ dŏr sē′), **1.** the quay along the south bank of the Seine in Paris, on which are the department of foreign affairs and other government offices. **2.** the French foreign office, or the government in general. [F: lit., quay of Orsay (a French general)]

quail[1] (kwāl), *n., pl.* **quails,** (*esp. collectively*) **quail. 1.** a small migratory Old World gallinaceous game bird, *Coturnix coturnix.* **2.** any of several other birds of the genus *Coturnix* and allied genera. [ME *quaille*, t. OF; of Gmc orig. Cf. D *kwakkel* quail, and MD, MLG *quackele*, akin to QUACK[1]]

Quail,
Coturnix coturnix
(8 in. long)

quail[2] (kwāl), *v.i.* to lose heart or courage in difficulty or danger; shrink with fear. [ME; orig. uncert.]

quaint (kwānt), *adj.* **1.** strange or odd in an interesting, pleasing, or amusing way: *the quaint streets of York.* **2.** oddly picturesque; having an old-fashioned attractiveness or charm: *a quaint old house.* **3.** strange; odd; whimsical. **4.** *Archaic.* wise; skilled. [ME *queinte*, t. OF, var. of *cointe* pretty, pleasing, g. L *cognitus*, pp., known] —**quaint′ly,** *adv.* —**quaint′ness,** *n.*

quake (kwāk), *v.,* **quaked, quaking,** *n.* —*v.i.* **1.** (of persons) to shake from cold, weakness, fear, anger, or the like. **2.** (of things) to shake or tremble, as from shock, internal convulsion, or instability. —*n.* **3.** an earthquake. **4.** a trembling or tremulous agitation. [ME; OE *cwacian* shake, tremble] —**Syn. 1.** shudder, tremble. See **shiver**[1].

Quaker (kwā′kə), *n.* a member of the Society of Friends. [f. QUAKE, V. + -ER[1]; first used because George Fox, the founder, bade them 'tremble at the word of the Lord'] —**Quak′eress,** *n. fem.* —**Quak′erish,** *adj.*

Quaker gun, a dummy gun, as in a ship or fort (so called in allusion to the Quakers' opposition to war).

Quakerism (kwā′kə rĭz′əm), *n.* the beliefs, principles, and customs of the Quakers.

Quakerly (kwā′kə lĭ), *adj.* **1.** like a Quaker. —*adv.* **2.** in the manner of the Quakers.

quaking grass, any grass of the genus *Briza*, esp. *B. media*, an erect perennial with slender, spreading inflorescences which are readily shaken by the wind.

quaky (kwā′kĭ), *adj.* inclined to quake; shaky.

qualification (kwŏl′ĭ fĭ kā′shən), *n.* **1.** a quality, accomplishment, etc., which fits for some function, office, etc. **2.** a required circumstance or condition for acquiring or exercising a right, holding an office, or the like. **3.** the act of qualifying. **4.** the state of being qualified. **5.** modification, limitation, or restriction; an instance of this: *to assert a thing without any qualification.*

qualified (kwŏl′ĭ fīd′), *adj.* **1.** possessed of qualities or accomplishments which fit one for some function or office. **2.** having qualifications required by law or custom. **3.** modified, limited, or restricted in some way: *a qualified statement.* —**qual′ified′ly,** *adv.*

qualifier (kwŏl′ĭ fī′ə), *n.* **1.** one who or that which qualifies. **2.** *Gram.* a word which qualifies the meaning of another, as an adjective or adverb.

qualify (kwŏl′ĭ fī′), *v.,* **-fied, -fying.** —*v.t.* **1.** to invest with proper or necessary qualities, skills, etc.; make competent. **2.** to attribute some quality or qualities to; characterize, call, or name. **3.** to modify in some way; limit; make less strong or positive: *to qualify a statement.* **4.** *Gram.* to modify. **5.** to make less violent, severe, or unpleasant; moderate; mitigate. **6.** to modify or alter the strength or flavour of. —*v.i.* **7.** to make or show oneself competent for something. **8.** to obtain authority, licence, power, etc., as by fulfilling necessary conditions or taking an oath. **9.** *Sport.* to demonstrate the necessary ability in an initial contest. **10.** *Mil.* to pass a test in one's branch of the service to achieve a higher standard of efficiency. [t. ML: m. s. *quālificāre.* See -FY] —**Syn. 1.** fit. **3.** See **modify. 5.** reduce, diminish, temper, soften.

qualitative (kwŏl′ĭ tə tĭv), *adj.* pertaining to or concerned with quality or qualities. —**qual′itatively,** *adv.*

qualitative analysis, *Chem.* the analysis of a substance in order to ascertain the nature of its constituents.

quality (kwŏl′ĭ tĭ), *n., pl.* **-ties. 1.** a characteristic, property, or attribute. **2.** character or nature, as belonging to or distinguishing a thing. **3.** character with respect to excellence, fineness, etc., or grade of excellence: *food of poor quality, silk of the finest quality.* **4.** high grade; superior excellence: *goods of quality.* **5.** native excellence or superiority. **6.** an accomplishment or attainment. **7.** good or high social position: *a man of quality.* **8.** the superiority or distinction associated with high social position. **9.** *Acoustics.* the texture of a note, dependent on its overtone content, which distinguishes it from others of the same pitch and loudness. **10.** *Phonet.* the timbre or tonal colour of a speech sound. **11.** *Logic.* the character of a proposition as affirmative or negative. **12.** *Archaic.* social status or position. **13.** *Archaic.* persons of high social position. [ME *qualite,* t. L: m. s. *quālitas*]

—**Syn.** 1. trait, character, feature. QUALITY, ATTRIBUTE, PROPERTY agree in meaning a particular characteristic (of a person or thing). A QUALITY is a characteristic, innate or acquired, which, in some particular, determines the nature and behaviour of a person or thing: *kindness as a quality, the quality of cloth.* An ATTRIBUTE was originally a quality attributed, usually to a person or something personified; more recently it has meant a fundamental or innate characteristic: *an attribute of God, attributes of a logical mind.* PROPERTY applies only to things; it means a characteristic belonging specifically in the constitution of, or found (invariably) in, the behaviour of a thing: *a property of hydrogen, of limestone.* 3. nature, kind, grade.

quality control, a method of sampling the output of an industrial process, based on the theory of probability, with the object of detecting and controlling any variations in quality.

qualm (kwäm), *n.* **1.** an uneasy feeling or a pang of conscience as to conduct. **2.** a sudden misgiving, or feeling of apprehensive uneasiness. **3.** a sudden sensation of faintness or illness, esp. of nausea. [OE *cwealm* torment, pain, plague]

qualmish (kwä′mĭsh), *adj.* **1.** inclined to have, or having, qualms, esp. of nausea. **2.** characterized by qualms. **3.** of the nature of a qualm. **4.** apt to cause qualms. —**qualm′ishly,** *adv.* —**qualm′ishness,** *n.*

quamash (kwŏm′ăsh, kwə măsh′), *n.* camass.

quandary (kwŏn′də rĭ), *n., pl.* **-ries.** a state of embarrassing perplexity or uncertainty, esp. as to what to do; a dilemma. [orig. obscure] —**Syn.** See **predicament.**

quandong (kwŏn′dŏng′), *n.* **1.** a santalaceous tree, *Fusanus acuminatus,* of Australia, yielding an edible drupaceous fruit whose seed (**quandong nut**) has an edible kernel. **2.** the fruit, or the seed or nut. Also, **quandang** (kwŏn′dŏng′). [t. native Australian]

quant (kwŏnt), *Dial.* —*n.* **1.** a pole having a flange near its tip, used for punting. —*v.t., v.i.* **2.** to propel or be propelled with the aid of a quant.

quanta (kwŏn′tə), *n.* pl. of **quantum.**

Quanthlamba (kwŭn thlŭm′bə), *n.* Drakensberg.

quantic (kwŏn′tĭk), *n. Maths.* a rational, integral, homogeneous function of two or more variables. [f. s. L *quantus* how great + -IC]

quantifier (kwŏn′tĭ fī′ə), *n. Logic.* an expression, such as 'all' or 'some', which indicates the quantity of a proposition.

quantify (kwŏn′tĭ fī′), *v.t.,* **-fied, -fying. 1.** to determine the quantity of; measure. **2.** *Logic.* to make explicit the quantity of. [t. ML: m. s. *quantificāre.* See -FY] —**quan′tifica′tion,** *n.*

quantitative (kwŏn′tĭ tə tĭv), *adj.* **1.** that is or may be estimated by quantity. **2.** of or pertaining to the describing or measuring of quantity. **3.** of or pertaining to the metrical system in classical poetry based on feet of long and short, rather than accented and unaccented, syllables. **4.** of or pertaining to the length or quantity of a vowel. —**quan′titatively,** *adv.* —**quan′titativeness,** *n.*

quantitative analysis, *Chem.* the analysis of a substance in order to determine the amounts and proportions of its constituents.

quantity (kwŏn′tĭ tĭ), *n., pl.* **-ties. 1.** a particular, indefinite, or considerable amount of anything: *a small quantity of water.* **2.** amount or measure: *to mix the ingredients in the right quantities.* **3.** considerable or great amount: *to extract ore in quantity.* **4.** *Maths.* **a.** an entity subject to treatment in accordance with a set of consistent rules. **b.** the property of magnitude involving comparability with other magnitudes. **c.** something having magnitude, or size, extent, amount, or the like. **d.** magnitude, size, volume, area, or length. **5.** *Music.* the length or duration of a note. **6.** *Logic.* the character of a proposition as either universal, or particular, or (with Kant) singular. **7.** *Philos.* that which can be augmented or diminished, and the augmentation or diminution of which is directly measurable either in terms of its own kind (as length, duration, weight) or, if at all, in terms of something else (as pain, pleasure, beauty, loudness, brightness). **8.** *Pros., Phonet.* (of sounds or syllables) character as to being longer or shorter, with reference to the time required in uttering them. **9.** *Law.* the duration of an estate, or interest. [ME *quantite,* t. L: m. s. *quantitas*]

quantity surveyor, one who estimates the materials and labour required for the construction of a building, etc., in order to prepare a bill of quantities.

quantize (kwŏn′tīz), *v.t.,* **-tized, -tizing.** *Physics.* **1.** to restrict (a variable) to a discrete value rather than a set of continuous values. **2.** to assign (a discrete value), as a quantum, to the energy content or level of a system. **3.** *Electronics.* to convert a continuous signal waveform into a waveform which can have only a finite number (usually two) of values. Also, **quantise.** —**quan′tiza′tion,** *n.*

quantum (kwŏn′təm), *n., pl.* **-ta** (-tə). **1.** quantity or amount. **2.** a particular amount. **3.** a share or portion. **4.** *Physics.* **a.** one of the discrete quantities of energy or momentum of an atomic system which are characteristic of the quantum theory. **b.** this amount of energy regarded as a unit. [t. L: (neut.) how great, how much]

quantum electronics, the study of the generation or amplification of microwave power in solid crystals, in accordance with the laws of quantum mechanics.

quantum mechanics, *Physics.* the system of mechanics, based on quantum theory, which has replaced Newtonian mechanics as a means of interpreting physical phenomena on the atomic scale.

quantum number, *Physics.* one of a set of integers or half-integers which defines the energy state of a system, or its components, in quantum mechanics.

quantum optics, *Physics.* the branch of optics which deals with light in terms of a stream of photons.

quantum statistics, *Physics.* statistics of the distribution of elementary particles of a specified type in relation to their quantized energies.

quantum sufficit (kwăn′to͝om so͞of′ĭ kĭt), *Latin.* as much as suffices; enough.

quantum theory, *Physics.* a theory that energetic physical processes, especially changes of energy in molecules and atoms, are discontinuous, involving discrete quantities of energy called quanta.

quar., **1.** quarter. **2.** quarterly.

quarantine (kwŏ′rən tēn′), *n., v.,* **-tined, -tining.** —*n.* **1.** a strict isolation designed to prevent the spread of disease. **2.** a period, orig. forty days, of detention or isolation imposed upon ships, persons, etc., on arrival at a port or place, when liable or suspected to be bringing some infectious or contagious disease. **3.** a system of measures maintained by public authority at ports, on frontiers, etc., for preventing the spread of disease. **4.** a place or station at which such measures are carried out. **5.** the detention or isolation enforced. **6.** the port or place where the ships are detained. **7.** the place (esp. a hospital) where people are detained. **8.** a period of forty days. —*v.t.* **9.** to put in or subject to quarantine. **10.** to isolate politically and commercially. [t. It.: m. *quarantina,* der. *quaranta,* g. L *quadrāgintā* forty]

quark[1] (kwäk), *n.* (used in cables, etc.) a question mark. [b. QU(ESTION M)ARK]

quark[2] (kwäk), *n. Physics.* one of three hypothetical particles with three corresponding antiparticles which have been postulated as the basis of all other particles in the universe. [special use of *quark* in 'Three quarks for

Muster Mark', from '*Finnegan's Wake*' by James Joyce]

Quarles (kwôlz), *n.* **Francis,** 1592–1644, English poet.

Quarnero (*It.* kwär nĕ′rô), *n.* **Gulf of,** an arm of the Adriatic Sea, E of Istria, in NW Yugoslavia.

quarrel[1] (kwŏ′rəl), *n., v.,* **-relled, -relling** or (*U.S.*) **-reled, -reling.** —*n.* **1.** an angry dispute or altercation; a disagreement marked by a break in friendly relations. **2.** a cause of complaint or hostile feeling against a person, etc. —*v.i.* **3.** to disagree angrily, squabble, or fall out. **4.** to dispute angrily; wrangle. **5.** to raise a complaint, or find fault. [ME *querele*, t. OF, g. L *querēl(l)a* complaint] —**quar′reller,** *n.*

—**Syn. 1.** dispute, contention, disagreement, controversy, dissension. QUARREL, FEUD apply to a more or less hostile demonstration or a situation of enmity existing between individuals or groups. A QUARREL varies in degrees of seriousness from a slight, brief, and petty difference or dispute (usually between individuals), to an angry, violent altercation resulting in deep-seated hostility: *a domestic quarrel.* A FEUD is an enduring hostility between families or groups (rarely individuals), often resulting in acts of violence and efforts at retaliation and revenge: *a bitter feud between the Montagues and Capulets.* **3.** disagree, differ, bicker, squabble.

quarrel[2] (kwŏ′rəl), *n.* **1.** a square-headed bolt or arrow, formerly used with a crossbow. **2.** a small square or diamond-shaped pane of glass, as used in latticed windows. **3.** any of certain tools, as a stonemason's chisel. [ME *quarel*, t. OF, t. ML: m. s. *quadrellus*, dim. of L *quadrus* square]

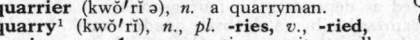

Quarrel[2] (def. 2)

quarrelsome (kwŏ′rəl səm), *adj.* inclined to quarrel. —**quar′relsomely,** *adv.* —**quar′relsomeness,** *n.*

quarrier (kwŏ′rĭ ə), *n.* a quarryman.

quarry[1] (kwŏ′rĭ), *n., pl.* **-ries,** *v.,* **-ried, -rying.** —*n.* **1.** an excavation or pit, usually open to the air, from which building stone, slate, or the like is obtained by cutting, blasting, etc. —*v.t.* **2.** to obtain (stone, etc.) from, or as from, a quarry. **3.** to make a quarry in. [ME *quarey*, t. ML: m. s. *quareia*, var. of *quareria*, VL *quadrāria* place where stone is squared, der. L *quadrāre* to square]

quarry[2] (kwŏ′rĭ), *n., pl.* **-ries. 1.** an animal or bird hunted or pursued. **2.** game, esp. game hunted with hounds or hawks. **3.** any object of pursuit or attack. [ME *querre*, t. OF: m. *cuiree*, der. *cuir* skin, hide, g. L *corium*]

quarry[3] (kwŏ′rĭ), *n., pl.* **-ries. 1.** a square stone or tile. **2.** quarrel[2] (def. 2). [n. use of obs. *quarry*, adj., square, t. OF: m. *quarre*]

quarryman (kwŏ′rĭ mən), *n.* one who quarries stone. Also, **quarrier.**

quart[1] (kwôt), *n.* **1.** a liquid or dry measure of capacity, equal to a quarter of a gallon or one eighth of a peck respectively (of varying content in different systems, places, and times). **2.** a vessel or measure holding a quart. [ME, t. F: m. *quarte*, t. ML: m. *quarta* (fem.) fourth]

quart[2] (kät), *n.* **1.** *Cards.* (in piquet) **a.** a sequence of four cards. **b. quart major,** the sequence of the highest four cards in any suit. **2.** *Fencing.* quarte. [t. F: m. *quarte* (fem.) fourth, g. L *quarta*]

quart., 1. quarter. **2.** quarterly.

quartal harmony (kwô′tl), *Music.* harmony based on chords constructed of fourths instead of thirds.

quartan (kwô′tn), *adj.* **1.** (of a fever, ague, etc.) characterized by paroxysms which recur every fourth day, both days of consecutive occurrence being counted. —*n.* **2.** a quartan fever or ague. [ME *quartaine*, t. F, g. L (*febris*) *quartāna* quartan fever, (fever) of the fourth]

quarte (kät; *Fr.* kȧrt), *n. Fencing.* the fourth of eight defensive positions. Also, **carte, quart.** [t. F, t. It.: m. *quarta* fourth]

quarter (kwô′tə), *n.* **1.** one of the four equal or equivalent parts into which anything is or may be divided: *a quarter of an apple.* **2.** *U.S. and Can.* one fourth of a dollar (25 cents). **3.** a silver coin of this value. **4.** one fourth of an hour (15 minutes). **5.** the moment marking this period. **6.** one fourth of a year. **7.** *Astron.* **a.** a fourth of the moon's period or monthly revolution, being that portion of its period or orbital course between a quadrature and a syzygy. **b.** either quadrature of the moon. **c. first quarter,** that fourth of the moon's period coming between the new moon and the last half-moon. See diag. under **moon. d. last quarter,** that fourth of the moon's period coming between the second half-moon and the new moon. See diag. under **moon. 8.** (in certain schools, colleges, and universities) one of the periods into which instruction is organized, generally 10 to 12 weeks in length. **9.** *Sport.* any one of the four periods that make up certain games, as baseball. **10.** one fourth of a lb. **11.** a fourth of a mile; two furlongs. **12.** the fourth part of a yard; 9 inches. **13.** a unit of weight, the fourth part of a hundredweight: in Britain equal to 28 lbs and in the U.S. to 25 lbs. **14.** a measure of capacity for grain, etc., equal to 8 bushels, or, locally, to more or less than this. **15.** the region of any of the four principal points of the compass or divisions of the horizon. **16.** such a point or division. **17.** any point or direction of the compass. **18.** a region, district, or place. **19.** a particular district of a city or town, esp. one appropriated to or occupied by a particular class or group of people. **20.** (*usually pl.*) **a.** a place of stay; lodgings; residence. **b.** *Mil.* the buildings, houses, barracks, or rooms occupied by military personnel or their families. **21.** a part or member of a community, government, etc., which is not specified: *information from a high quarter.* **22.** mercy or indulgence, esp. as shown to a vanquished enemy in sparing his life and accepting his surrender. **23.** one of the four parts, each including a leg, of the body or carcass of a quadruped. **24.** *Vet. Sci.* either side of a horse's hoof, between heel and toe. **25.** *Shoemaking.* the part of a boot or shoe on either side of the foot, from the middle of the back to the vamp. **26.** *Naut.* **a.** the after part of a ship's side, usually from about the aftermost mast to the stern. **b.** the general horizontal direction 45° from the stern of a ship on either side: *land in sight on the port quarter.* **c.** one of the stations to which crew members are called for battle, emergencies, or drills. **d.** the part of a yard between the slings and the yardarm. **27.** *Her.* **a.** one of the four (or more) parts into which a shield may be divided by horizontal and vertical lines. **b.** a charge occupying one fourth of the shield, placed in chief. **c.** a quartering, or one of various coats of arms marshalled upon one shield. —*v.t.* **28.** to divide into four equal or equivalent parts. **29.** to divide into parts fewer or more than four. **30.** to cut the body of (a person) into quarters, esp. in executing for treason or the like. **31.** *Mach.* to make holes in, fix, etc., a quarter of a circle apart. **32.** to provide with lodgings in a particular place. **33.** to impose (soldiers) on persons, etc., to be lodged and fed. **34.** to assign to a particular position for living purposes, action, etc., as on a ship. **35.** to traverse (the ground) from left to right and right to left while advancing, as dogs in search of game. **36.** *Her.* **a.** to divide a shield into four (or more) parts by horizontal and vertical lines. **b.** to place or bear quarterly upon a shield, as different coats of arms. **c.** to add (a coat of arms) thus to one's own. —*v.i.* **37.** to take up or be in quarters; lodge. **38.** to range to and fro, as dogs in search of game. **39.** *Naut.* to sail so as to have the wind or the sea on the quarter. —*adj.* **40.** being one of the four equal (or approximately equal) parts into which anything is or may be divided. **41.** being equal to only about one fourth of the full measure. [ME, t. OF, g. L *quartārius* fourth part]

Heraldic quarter (def. 27b)

quarterage (kwô′tə rĭj), *n.* a quarterly payment, charge, or allowance. [ME, t. OF]

quarter-day (kwô′tə dā′), *n.* one of the four days (in England), Lady Day, Midsummer Day, Michaelmas, and Christmas or (in Scotland), Candlemas, Whitsunday, Lammas, and Martinmas, regarded as marking off the quarters of the year, on which tenancies begin and end, quarterly payments fall due, etc.

quarterdeck (kwô′tə dĕk′), *n. Naut.* the upper deck between the mainmast and the poop or stern.

quartered (kwô′təd), *adj.* **1.** divided into quarters. **2.** furnished with quarters or lodging. **3.** (of timber) quartersawn. **4.** *Her.* **a.** divided or arranged quarterly. **b.** (of a cross) having a square piece missing in the centre.

Quartered arms (def. 4a)

quarterfinal (kwô′tə fī′nəl), *adj. Sport.* **1.** of or pertaining to the contests preceding the semifinals in a tournament. —*n.* **2.** such a contest. —**quar′terfin′alist,** *n.*

quartering (kwô′tə rĭng), *n.* **1.** the act of one who or that which quarters. **2.** the assigning of quarters or lodgings. **3.** *Her.* **a.** the division of a shield into (four or more) quarters. **b.** the marshalling of various coats of arms upon one shield, as to indicate family alliances. **c.** (*chiefly pl.*) one of the coats so marshalled. —*adj.* **4.** that quarters. **5.** lying at right angles. **6.** *Naut.* (of a wind) blowing on a ship's quarter.

quarterly (kwô′tə lĭ), *adj., n., pl.* **-lies,** *adv.* —*adj.* **1.** occurring, done, etc., at the end of every quarter of a year. **2.** pertaining to or consisting of a quarter. —*n.* **3.** a periodical issued every three months. —*adv.* **4.** by quarters; once in a quarter of a year. **5.** *Her.* **a.** with division into quarters. **b.** in the quarters of a shield.

quartermaster (kwô′tə mäs′tə), *n.* **1.** *Mil.* a regimental officer in charge of quarters, rations, clothing, equipment, and transport. **2.** *Naval.* a petty officer having charge of signals, navigating apparatus, etc. *Abbrev.*: Q.M.

quartermaster-general (kwôʹtə mäsʹtə jĕnʹə rəl, -jĕnʹ-rəl), *n.* a senior staff officer at the Ministry of Defence in charge of the department controlling the quartering of troops, their rations, clothing, transportation, and equipment. *Abbrev.:* Q.M.G.

quartermaster-sergeant (kwôʹtə mäsʹtə säʹjənt), *n.* a regimental non-commissioned officer assisting the quartermaster and ranking as a staff sergeant. *Abbrev.:* Q.M.S.

quartern (kwôʹtən), *n.* a quarter, or fourth part, esp. of certain weights and measures, as of a pound, ounce, peck, or pint. [ME *quarteroun*, t. OF: m. *quarteron*, der. *quart* fourth. See QUART[1]]

quarter note, *U.S. Music.* a crotchet.

quarter-phase (kwôʹtə fāzʹ), *adj. Elect.* denoting a combination of circuits energized by alternating electromotive forces which differ in phase by a quarter of a cycle; diphase.

quarter point, the fourth part of the distance between any two adjacent points of the 32 marked on a compass, being 2° 48′ 45″.

quartersaw (kwôʹtə sôʹ), *v.t.*, **-sawed, -sawn** or **-sawed, -sawing.** to saw (timber) into quarters so that the faces coincide with radii of the log.

quarter section, *U.S.* (in surveying, etc.) a square tract of land, half a mile on each side, thus containing ¼ sq. mi. or 160 acres.

quarter sessions, *Law.* **1.** a criminal court which tries certain indictable offences and hears appeals from the magistrates' court (petty sessions). **2.** *U.S.* a court having limited criminal jurisdiction.

quarterstaff (kwôʹtə stäfʹ), *n., pl.* **-staves** (-stāvzʹ, -stävzʹ). **1.** a former weapon consisting of a stout pole 6 to 8 feet long, tipped with iron. **2.** exercise or fighting with this weapon.

quarter tone, *Music.* an interval equivalent to half a semitone.

quarter-wave plate, *Optics.* a plate of doubly refracting material cut parallel to the optic axis of the crystal, of such a thickness that a phase difference of a quarter of a period is introduced between the ordinary and extraordinary rays travelling normally through the plate.

quartet (kwô tĕtʹ), *n.* **1.** any group of four persons or things. **2.** a group of four singers or players. **3.** a musical composition for four voices or instruments. Also, **quartette.** [t. F: m. *quartette*, t. It.: m. *quartetto*, der. *quarto* fourth, g. L *quartus*]

quartile (kwôʹtīl), *adj.* **1.** *Astrol.* denoting or pertaining to the aspect of two heavenly bodies when their longitudes differ by 90°. —*n.* **2.** *Astrol.* a quartile aspect. **3.** *Statistics.* (in a frequency distribution) one of the values of a variable which divides the distribution of the variable into four groups having equal frequencies. [t. ML, neut. of *quartīlis*, der. L *quartus* fourth]

quarto (kwôʹtō), *n., pl.* **-tos,** *adj.* —*n.* **1.** a volume printed from sheets folded twice to form four leaves or eight pages; book size about 9½ × 12 inches. *Abbrev.:* 4to or 4°. —*adj.* **2.** in quarto. [short for NL *in quartō* in fourth]

quartz (kwôts), *n.* one of the commonest minerals, silicon dioxide, SiO_2, having many varieties which differ in colour, lustre, etc., occurring in crystals (rock crystal, amethyst, citrine, etc.) or massive (agate, bloodstone, chalcedony, jasper, etc.), an important constituent of many rocks. It is piezoelectric and is cut into wafers used to control the frequencies of radio transmitters. [t. G: m. *Quarz*; orig. unknown]

quartz clock, a very accurate clock which is controlled by a quartz crystal regulating the frequency of the alternating current which drives the clock motor.

quartz glass, a glass composed entirely of silica.

quartziferous (kwôt sĭfʹə rəs), *adj.* containing quartz; consisting of quartz. [f. QUARTZ + -(I)FEROUS]

quartzite (kwôtsʹīt), *n.* a granular rock consisting essentially of quartz in interlocking grains.

quartz plate, *Elect.* a carefully cut quartz crystal which is piezoelectrically active. See **crystal** (def. 10).

quasar (kwāʹsä), *n. Astron.* one of many extragalactic, very massive sources of high-energy, radio-frequency, electromagnetic radiation of unknown constitution or structure. [short for *qua(si-stell)ar (source)*]

quash[1] (kwŏsh), *v.t.* to put down or suppress completely; subdue. [ME *quasche(n)*, t. OF: m. *quasser*, t. L: m. *quassāre* shake, freq. of *quatere*]

quash[2] (kwŏsh), *v.t.* to make void, annul, or set aside (a law, indictment, decision, etc.). [ME *quasche(n)*, t. OF: m. *quasser*, t. L: m. *quassāre* shake, but influenced by LL *cassāre* annul, der. L *cassus* empty, void]

quasi (kwäʹzī), *adj.* **1.** resembling; as it were. —*adv.* **2.** seemingly, but not actually. [ME, t. L]

quasi-, a prefix form of 'quasi', *adj.* and *adv.*, as in **quasi-official, quasi-deify.**

quasi contract, *Law.* an obligation imposed by law in the absence of a contract to prevent unjust enrichment; an implied contract.

quasi-judicial (kwäʹzī jo͞o dĭshʹəl), *adj.* having characteristics of a judicial act but performed by an administrative agency.

Quasimodo (*It.* kwȧ zēʹmȯ dȯ), *n.* **Salvatore** (*It.* säl vȧ-tōʹrĕ), 1908–68, Italian poet.

quass (*Russ.* kfȧs), *n.* kvass.

quassia (kwŏshʹə), *n.* **1.** a plant of the simaroubaceous genus *Quassia*, esp. *Q. amara*, a tree of tropical America. **2.** the bitter wood of this tree and certain other trees. **3.** a medicinal preparation made from it. [NL; named after *Quassi*, a Surinam Negro, who (ab. 1730) used the bark as a fever remedy]

quatercentenary (kwătʹə sĕn tēʹnə rī), *adj., n., pl.* **-naries.** —*adj.* **1.** of or pertaining to a 400th anniversary. —*n.* **2.** a 400th anniversary. **3.** its celebration. **4.** a period of 400 years.

quaternary (kwə tûʹnə rī), *adj., n., pl.* **-ries.** —*adj.* **1.** consisting of four. **2.** arranged in fours. **3.** (*cap.*) *Geol.* pertaining to the most recent geological period or system of rocks, which constitutes the later principal division of the Cainozoic era. —*n.* **4.** a group of four. **5.** the number four. **6.** (*cap.*) *Geol.* the period or system following the Tertiary. [ME, t. L: m. s. *quaternārius*]

quaternary ammonium compound, *Chem.* any of a class of compounds with the general formula, NR_4OH, theoretically derived from ammonium hydroxide.

quaternion (kwə tûʹnyən), *n.* **1.** a group or set of four persons or things. **2.** *Maths.* **a.** the quotient of two vectors considered as depending on four geometrical elements and as expressible by an algebraic quadrinomial. **b.** (*pl.*) the calculus of such quantities. [ME, t. LL: s. *quaternio* the number four, a group of four, der. L *quaternī* four together]

quatrain (kwŏtʹrān), *n.* a stanza or poem of four lines, usually with alternate rhymes. [t. F, der. *quatre* four. See QUATRE]

quatre (kătʹrə; *Fr.* kȧʹtr), *n.* **1.** four. **2.** the four at cards, dice, or the like. [t. F, g. L *quattuor* four]

Quatre Bras (kătʹrə bräʹ; *Fr.* kȧ trə brȧʹ), a village in central Belgium, near Brussels: a battle preliminary to the battle of Waterloo was fought here, 1815.

quatrefoil (kătʹrə foilʹ), *n.* **1.** a leaf composed of four leaflets, as sometimes a leaf of clover. **2.** *Archit.* an ornament or decorative feature having four foils or lobes. [late ME *quater foyl(e)*, f. MF. See QUATRE, FOIL[2]]

Quatrefoils (def. 2)

quattrocento (kwătʹrō chĕnʹtō; *It.* kwȧt trȯ chĕnʹtȯ), *n.* the 15th century, used in reference to Italian art of that time. [It.: four hundred, short for *mille quattrocento* one thousand four hundred]

quaver (kwāʹvə), *v.i.* **1.** to shake tremulously, quiver, or tremble (now said usually of the voice). **2.** to sound, speak, or sing tremulously. **3.** to perform quavers, shakes, or trills in singing or on a musical instrument. —*v.t.* **4.** to utter, say, or sing with a quavering or tremulous voice. —*n.* **5.** a quavering or tremulous shake, esp. in the voice. **6.** a quavering tone or utterance. **7.** *Music.* a note equal in length to half a crotchet. See illus. under **note.** [ME; b. QUAKE and WAVER] —**quaʹvery,** *adj.*

quay (kē), *n.* an artificial landing place, as of masonry built along navigable water, for vessels unloading or loading cargo, etc. [later spelling (after F *quai*) of earlier *kay*, also *key* (whence the mod. pronunciation), t. OF: m. *kay, cay*; akin to Sp. *cayo* shoal. See KEY[2]]

quayage (kēʹĭj), *n.* **1.** quays collectively. **2.** space appropriated to quays. **3.** a charge for the use of a quay or quays. [t. F, der. *quay* QUAY]

Que., Quebec.

quean (kwēn), *n.* **1.** a bold, impudent woman; a shrew; a hussy. **2.** a prostitute. **3.** *Scot. and Dial.* a girl or young woman, esp. one of robust appearance. **4.** *Slang.* a male homosexual. [ME *quene*, OE *cwene*, c. OHG *quena* woman; akin to Gk *gynḗ* woman. Cf. QUEEN]

queasy (kwēʹzī), *adj.*, **-sier, -siest.** **1.** inclined to nausea, as the stomach, a person, etc. **2.** tending to cause nausea, as articles of food. **3.** uneasy or uncomfortable, as feelings, the conscience, etc. **4.** squeamish; excessively fastidious. [late ME; orig. obscure] —**queaʹsily,** *adv.* —**queaʹsiness,** *n.*

Quebec (kwĭ bĕkʹ), *n.* **1.** a province in E Canada. 5,259,211 pop. (1961); 594,860 sq. mi. **2.** the capital of this province: a seaport on the St Lawrence; the capital of New France from 1663 to 1759, when it was taken by the English. 171,979 (1961). with suburbs, 357,568 (1961).

quebracho (kā bräʹchō; *Sp.* kĕ brȧʹchȯ), *n., pl.* **-chos.**

1. the anacardiaceous trees *Schinopsis lorentzii* and *S. balansae*, the wood and bark of which are important in tanning and dyeing. **2.** the apocynaceous tree *Aspidosperma quebrachoblanco*, yielding a medicinal bark. **3.** any of several hard-wooded South American trees. **4.** the wood or bark of any of these trees. [t. Sp., der. *quebrar* break, g. L *crepāre* burst]

Quechua (kĕch′wə), *n.* **1.** a language spoken by Indians in Peru, Bolivia, and Ecuador, formerly the language of the Incas. **2.** a member of an Indian people of Peru speaking Quechua. Also, **Kechua.** —**Quechuan** (kĕch′wən), *adj., n.*

queen (kwēn), *n.* **1.** the wife or consort of a king. **2.** a female sovereign or monarch. **3.** a woman, or something personified as a woman, that is chief or pre-eminent in any respect: *a beauty queen.* **4.** a playing card bearing the formalized picture of a queen, in most games counting as next below the king in its suit. **5.** *Chess.* the most powerful piece, moving any distance in any straight or diagonal line. **6.** a fertile female of ants, bees, wasps, or termites. **7.** *Slang.* a male homosexual. —*v.i.* **8.** to reign as queen. **9.** to have queenly pre-eminence; behave in an overbearing or pretentious manner (usually fol. by indefinite *it*). [ME *quene*, OE *cwēn* wife, queen, c. OS *quān*, Goth. *qēns* woman, wife; akin to QUEAN]

Queen Anne, denoting or pertaining to a style of architecture which obtained in England in the reign of Queen Anne (1702–14), combining classical designs and plans with baroque decorative motifs.

Queen Anne's lace, an umbelliferous plant, *Daucus carota*, with large lacy umbels of minute, white flowers, the central one usually dark purple.

queen cake, a small, light, rich cake containing dried fruit and cooked in patty tins or paper cases.

Queen Charlotte Islands (shä′lət), a group of islands in British Columbia, off the W coast of Canada. 3014 pop. (1961); 3970 sq. mi.

queen consort, the wife of a reigning king.

queendom (kwēn′dəm), *n.* **1.** the position or dignity of a queen. **2.** the realm of a queen.

queen dowager, the widow of a king.

queenhood (kwēn′hŏŏd′), *n.* the rank or dignity of a queen.

queenly (kwēn′lĭ), *adj.*, **-lier, -liest,** *adv.* —*adj.* **1.** belonging or proper to a queen: *queenly rank.* **2.** befitting, or suggestive of, a queen: *queenly dignity.* —*adv.* **3.** in a queenly manner. —**queen′liness,** *n.*

Queen Mab (măb), *Irish and English Folklore.* a mischievous, tantalizing fairy who governs and produces the dreams of men.

Queen Maud Land (môd), a large coastal region of Antarctica, S of Africa: Norwegian explorations.

Queen Maud Range (môd), a mountain range S of the Ross Sea, in Ross Dependency, Antarctica.

queen mother, a queen dowager who is also mother of a reigning sovereign.

queen of pudding, a pudding made of custard and breadcrumbs with a meringue top.

queen of the meadow, meadowsweet.

queen olive, **1.** any large-fruited, meaty olive suitable for pickling or processing. **2.** such an olive from the area of Seville, Spain.

queen post, one of a pair of timbers or posts extending vertically upwards from the tie beam of a roof truss or the like, one on each side of the centre.

Queen-post roof
A, Queen post; B, Tie beam; C, Strut; D, Straining beam

queen regent, a queen who rules on behalf of another.

queen regnant, a queen who reigns in her own right.

Queens (kwēnz), *n.* a borough of E New York City, on Long Island. 1,809,578 pop. (1960); 113 sq. mi.

Queen's Bench, **1.** a division of the High Court with jurisdiction over all matters, civil or criminal, formerly within the exclusive jurisdiction of the Court of Queen's Bench, Court of Common Pleas, or Court of Exchequer, such as contract and tort. **2.** (formerly) one of the three original common law courts, in which the sovereign sat in person. Cf. **King's Bench.**

Queensberry rules (kwēnz′bə rĭ, -brĭ), a set of rules followed in modern boxing. [named after the 8th Marquess of *Queensberry*, 1844–1900, English sportsman]

queen's chambers, that portion of the sea around the coasts of Great Britain which is enclosed by an imaginary line from one headland to another and is part of the crown's territorial waters. Cf. **king's chambers.**

Queen's Counsel, **1.** a barrister appointed counsel to the crown on the recommendation of the Lord High Chancellor, usually as a mark of professional distinction. **2.** the title. *Abbrev.*: Q.C. Cf. **King's Counsel.**

queen's English, (sometimes used when the reigning monarch is a woman) king's English.

queen's evidence, *Law.* evidence given by an accomplice in a crime on behalf of the Crown against the other defendants. Cf. **king's evidence.**

queen's highway, any portion of land or passage which every subject of the kingdom has a right to use. Cf. **king's highway.**

Queensland (kwēnz′lənd), *n.* a state in NE Australia. 1,518,859 pop. (1961); 667,000 sq. mi. *Cap.*: Brisbane.

Queensland maple, an evergreen tree of Australia, *Flindersia baileyana*, of the family *Flindersiaceae*, having small flowers and a conelike fruit, the timber of which is widely used for furniture.

queen's peace, the law relating to public order generally: *a breach of the queen's peace.* Cf. **king's peace.**

queen's proctor, *Law.* the Treasury solicitor who represents the crown in the Probate, Divorce, and Admiralty division of the High Court of Justice. Cf. **king's proctor.**

Queen's Regulations, a volume dealing with all aspects of military law, in peace and war. It also embodies the Army Act and contains advice to regimental officers on the conduct of court martial procedure, punishments, etc. Cf. **King's Regulations.**

queen's remembrancer, **1.** (formerly) an official of the Court of Exchequer, responsible for the collection of debts due to the sovereign. **2.** an official, who is also the senior master of the Supreme Court, who performs certain ceremonial duties. Cf. **king's remembrancer.**

queen's scout, a boy scout who has achieved the greatest degree of proficiency in scouting. Cf. **king's scout.**

queen's shilling, (when the reigning monarch was a woman) (until 1879) king's shilling.

Queen's speech, a speech read by the sovereign to the assembled members of both houses of Parliament at the beginning of each new parliamentary session, reviewing the nation's affairs and outlining the government's programme of legislation for the new session. Cf. **King's speech.**

Queenstown (kwēnz′toun′), *n.* former name of **Cóbh.**

queer (kwĭə), *adj.* **1.** strange from a conventional point of view; singular or odd: *a queer notion.* **2.** *Colloq.* of questionable character; suspicious; shady. **3.** out of the normal state of feeling physically; giddy, faint, or qualmish: *to feel queer.* **4.** *Colloq.* mentally unbalanced or deranged. **5.** *Slang.* bad, worthless, or counterfeit. **6. queer for,** *Slang.* having an inordinate craving for. **7.** *Slang.* homosexual. —*v.t.* **8.** *Slang.* to spoil; jeopardize; ruin. —*n.* **9.** *Slang.* a male homosexual. [t. G: m. *quer* oblique, cross, adverse] —**queer′ly,** *adv.* —**queer′ness,** *n.* —**Syn.** **1.** curious.

queer street, (*often caps.*) *Colloq.* a state of financial embarrassment.

quell (kwĕl), *v.t.* **1.** to suppress (disorder, mutiny, etc.); put an end to; extinguish. **2.** to vanquish; subdue. **3.** to quiet or allay (feelings, etc.). [ME; OE *cwellan* kill, causative of *cwelan* die; akin to D *kwellen*, G *quälen*] —**quell′er,** *n.* —**Syn.** **1.** crush, quash, overpower.

Quelpart (kwĕl′pät′), *n.* Cheju.

Quemoy (kĕ moi′), *n.* an island off the SE coast of China; with Matsu remained part of Nationalist China after the Communist conquest of the mainland. with Matsu: 56,349 pop. (est. 1956); ab. 67 sq. mi.

quench (kwĕnch), *v.t.* **1.** to slake, as thirst; allay; satisfy. **2.** to put out or extinguish (fire, flames, etc.). **3.** to cool suddenly, as by plunging into water, as steel in tempering it. **4.** to suppress; stifle; subdue; overcome. **5.** *Electronics.* to suppress (an oscillation) in a circuit, or (a discharge) in a valve or counter tube. **6.** *Physics.* to reduce (the duration of phosphorescence) in a luminescent material by the addition of a suitable substance. [ME *quench(en)*, OE *-cwencan*, causative of *-cwincan*. Cf. Fris. *kwinka* be put out] —**quench′able,** *adj.* —**quench′er,** *n.*

quenchless (kwĕnch′lĭs), *adj.* that cannot be quenched; inextinguishable.

quenelle (kə nĕl′), *n.* *Cookery.* a preparation of fish, meat, or poultry, cooked and sieved, blended with egg, and cooked in stock or fried as croquettes. [t. F, t. G: m. *Knödel*]

quercetin (kwûr′sĭ tĭn), *n.* *Chem.* a yellow crystalline powder, $C_{15}H_{10}O_7$, obtained from the bark of the quercitron and from other vegetable substances: used as a yellow dye. [appar. f. s. L *quercētum* oak wood + -IN[2]] —**quercetic** (kwû sĕt′ĭk, -sē′tĭk), *adj.*

quercine (kwû′sīn), *adj.* of or pertaining to the oak. [t. LL: m. s. *quercīnus*, der. L *quercus* oak]

quercitol (kwû′sĭ tŏl′), *n.* *Chem.* a colourless crystalline solid, $C_6H_7(OH)_5$, found in oak wood and acorns.

quercitron (kwûʹsĭtʹrən), *n.* **1.** a species of oak, *Quercus velutina,* of eastern North America, whose inner bark yields a yellow dye. **2.** the bark itself. **3.** the dye obtained from it. [abbr. for *querci-citron,* f. *querci-* (comb. form repr. L *quercus* oak) + CITRON]

Queredo (*Sp.* kė rėʹdō), *n.* **Francisco de** (*Sp.* frän thēsʹkō dė), 1580–1645, Spanish novelist.

querist (kwĭəʹrĭst), *n.* one who puts a query. [f. m. s. L *quaerere* ask + -IST]

quern (kwûn), *n.* a hand mill for grinding corn. [ME; OE *cweorn*; c. OHG *quirn,* Icel. *kvern*]

querulous (kwĕʹrŏŏ ləs), *adj.* **1.** full of complaints; complaining. **2.** characterized by, or uttered in, complaint; peevish: *a querulous tone.* [t. L: m. *querulus*] —**querʹulously,** *adv.* —**querʹulousness,** *n.*

query (kwĭəʹrĭ), *n., pl.* **-ries,** *v.,* **-ried, -rying.** —*n.* **1.** a question; an enquiry. **2.** doubt; uncertainty. **3.** *Print.* a question or interrogation mark (?), esp. as added on a manuscript, proofs or the like, with reference to some point in the text. —*v.t.* **4.** to ask or enquire about. **5.** to question (a statement, etc.) as doubtful or obscure. **6.** *Print.* to mark with a query. **7.** to ask questions of. [earlier *quere,* t. ML, for L *quaere,* impv. of *quaerere* ask]

ques., question.

Quesnay (*Fr.* kė nĕʹ), *n.* **François** (*Fr.* fräN swäʹ), 1694–1774, French economist and physician.

quest (kwĕst), *n.* **1.** a search or pursuit made in order to find or obtain something: *a quest for gold.* **2.** *Medieval Legend.* a knightly expedition undertaken to secure or achieve something: *the quest of the Holy Grail.* **3.** those engaged in such an expedition. **4.** *Dial.* an inquest. **5.** a jury of inquest. —*v.i.* **6.** to search; seek (often fol. by *for* or *after*). **7.** to go on a quest. **8.** *Hunting.* (of dogs, etc.) **a.** to search for game. **b.** to bay or give tongue in pursuit of game. —*v.t.* **9.** to search or seek for; pursue. [ME *queste,* t. OF, g. L *quaesītus,* pp., sought, asked] —**questʹer,** *n.*

question (kwĕsʹchən), *n.* **1.** a sentence in an interrogative form, addressed to someone in order to elicit information. **2.** a problem for discussion or under discussion; a matter for investigation. **3.** a matter or point of uncertainty or difficulty; a case (fol. by *of*): *to be a question of time.* **4.** a subject of dispute or controversy. **5.** a proposal to be debated or voted on, as in a meeting or a deliberative assembly. **6.** *Law.* **a.** a controversy which is submitted to a judicial tribunal or administrative agency for decision. **b.** the interrogation by which information is secured. **c.** *Obs.* judicial examination or trial. **7.** the act of asking or enquiring; interrogation; query. **8.** enquiry into or discussion of, some problem or doubtful matter. **9. beyond question,** beyond dispute; indisputably. **10. call in** or **into question, a.** to dispute; challenge. **b.** to cast doubt upon. **11. in question, a.** under consideration. **b.** in dispute. **12. out of the question,** not to be considered; impossible. —*v.t.* **13.** to ask a question or questions of; interrogate. **14.** to ask or enquire. **15.** to make a question of; doubt. **16.** to challenge; dispute. —*v.i.* **17.** to ask a question or questions. [ME *questiun,* t. AF, t. L: m. s. *quaestio*] —**quesʹtioner,** *n.* —**Syn. 14.** See **enquire.**

questionable (kwĕsʹchə nə bl), *adj.* **1.** of doubtful propriety, honesty, morality, respectability, etc. **2.** open to question or dispute; doubtful or uncertain: *whether this is true is questionable.* **3.** open to question as to being such: *a questionable privilege.* —**quesʹtionableness, quesʹtionabilʹity,** *n.* —**quesʹtionably,** *adv.* —**Syn. 2.** debatable, disputable, controvertible.

questionary (kwĕsʹchə nə rĭ), *n., pl.* **-aries.** a questionnaire.

questioning (kwĕsʹchə nĭng), *adj.* **1.** expressing or implying a question. **2.** characterized by curiosity; enquiring; inquisitive. —**quesʹtioningly,** *adv.*

questionless (kwĕsʹchən lĭs), *adj.* **1.** unquestionable. **2.** unquestioning. —*adv.* **3.** without question.

question mark, a mark indicating a question: usually, as in English, the mark (?) placed after the question; interrogation mark.

question-master (kwĕsʹchən mäsʹtə), *n.* one who puts questions to the members of a brains trust, contestants in a quiz game, etc.

questionnaire (kwĕs/tyə nēəʹ, kĕs/-), *n.* a list of questions, usually printed on a form as for statistical purposes, or for use, or to obtain opinions on some subject. [t. F]

question time, *Parl. Proc.* a period during which ministers reply to questions submitted by members.

Quetta (kwĕtʹə), *n.* a city in W central West Pakistan; almost totally destroyed by an earthquake, 1935. 106,633 (1961).

quetzal (kĕtʹsəl), *n.* **1.** a Central American bird, *Pharomachrus mocinno,* having golden-green and scarlet plumage, and, in the male, long flowing upper tail coverts (the national bird of Guatemala). **2.** the monetary unit of Guatemala, equal to 100 centavos, and equivalent to about £0·417 sterling. **3.** a note of this value. Also, **quezal** (kė sälʹ). [t. Sp., t. Aztec: m. *quetzalli* tail-feather of the bird *quetzaltototl*]

Quetzalcoatl (kĕtʹsəl kō ătʹl; *Sp.* kėtʹ thäl kō ä tl), *n.* the feathered serpent god of the Aztec and Toltec cultures.

queue (kyōō), *n., v.,* **queued, queuing.** —*n.* **1.** a file or line of people, vehicles, etc., waiting in turn to obtain something, enter a place, proceed along a road, etc. **2.** a braid of hair worn hanging down behind. —*v.i.* **3.** to form in a line while waiting; line up (often fol. by *up*). [t. F, g. L *cōda* tail, r. *cauda*] —**queuʹer,** *n.*

Quezaltenango (*Sp.* kė thäl tė nänʹgō), *n.* a town in SW Guatemala: earthquake, 1902. 56,921 (1964).

Quezon City (kāʹzŏn), a city in the Philippines, on Luzon island NE of Manila; designated the national capital in 1948, though Manila remains the traditional capital and centre of administration. 397,990 (1960).

Quezon y Molina (kāʹzŏn ē mō lēʹnə; *Sp.* kė thōnʹ ē mō lēʹnä), **Manuel Luis** (*Sp.* mä nwĕlʹ lwēs), 1878–1944, Filipino political leader; 1st president of the Philippine Commonwealth, 1935–44.

quibble (kwĭbʹl), *n., v.,* **-bled, -bling.** —*n.* **1.** a use of ambiguous, prevaricating, or irrelevant language or arguments to evade a point at issue. **2.** the use of such arguments. **3.** trivial, petty, or carping criticism. —*v.i.* **4.** to use a quibble or quibbles; evade the point or the truth by a quibble. [? der. *quib* gibe, appar. var. of QUIP] —**quibʹbler,** *n.* —**Syn. 1.** evasion, equivocation, sophism, shift.

quibbling (kwĭbʹl ĭng), *adj.* **1.** characterized by quibbles; petty; carping. —*n.* **2.** an instance of quibbling.

Quiberon (*Fr.* kē brôNʹ), *n.* a peninsula (6 mi. long) in NW France, on the S coast of Brittany, partially enclosing **Quiberon Bay**: British naval victory over the French, 1759.

quiche (kēsh), *n.* a savoury custard tart, a speciality of Alsace and Lorraine. [t. F (Alsace d.), t. G: m. *Kuchen* cake]

Quiché (*Sp.* kē chėʹ), *n.* a Mayan language of Guatemala.

quick (kwĭk), *adj.* **1.** done, proceeding, or occurring with promptness or rapidity, as an action, process, etc.; prompt; immediate: *a quick answer.* **2.** that is over or completed within a short space of time. **3.** moving with speed. **4.** swift or rapid, as motion. **5.** hasty; impatient: *a quick temper.* **6.** lively or keen, as feelings. **7.** prompt in action; acting with swiftness or rapidity. **8.** prompt or swift (to do something): *quick to respond.* **9.** prompt to perceive: *a quick eye.* **10.** prompt to understand, learn, etc.; of ready intelligence. **11.** consisting of living plants: *a quick hedge.* **12.** brisk, as fire, flames, heat, etc. **13.** *Finance.* readily convertible into cash; liquid, as assets. **14.** *Mining.* containing ore, or productive, as veins. **15.** *Archaic or Dial.* endowed with life. **16.** *Archaic or Dial.* living, as persons, animals, plants, etc. **17.** *Rare.* having a high degree of vigour, energy, or activity. —*n.* **18.** living persons: *the quick and the dead.* **19.** living plants (esp. hawthorn) as set to form a hedge. **20.** a single such plant. **21.** the tender sensitive flesh of the living body, esp. that under the nails: *nails bitten down to the quick.* **22.** the vital or most important part. **23. cut to the quick,** to hurt deeply the feelings of. —*adv.* **24.** quickly. [ME; OE *cwic, cwicu* living, c. OS *quik,* G *queck, keck,* Icel. *kvikr*; akin to L *vīvus* living] —**quickʹness,** *n.*

—**Syn. 3.** QUICK, FAST, SWIFT, RAPID describe speedy tempo. QUICK applies particularly to something practically instantaneous, an action or reaction, perhaps, of very brief duration: *to give a quick look round, to make a quick change of clothes.* FAST and SWIFT refer to actions, movements, etc., which continue for a time, and usually to those which are uninterrupted; when used of communication, transport, and the like, they suggest a definite goal and a continuous trip. SWIFT, the more formal—even poetic—word suggests the greater speed: *a fast train, a swift message.* RAPID, less speedy than the others, applies to a rate or movement or action, and usually to a series of actions or movements, related or unrelated: *rapid calculation, a rapid walker.* **10.** See **sharp.**

quick assets, *Accounting.* liquid assets including cash, receivables and marketable securities.

quick-change (kwĭkʹchānj/), *adj.* quickly changing from one thing to another, as an entertainer, actor, etc., who changes costumes, etc., during a performance.

quicken (kwĭkʹən), *v.t.* **1.** to make more rapid; accelerate; hasten: *she quickened her pace.* **2.** to make quick or alive; restore life to. **3.** to give or restore vigour or activity to; stir up, rouse, or stimulate: *to quicken the imagination.* —*v.i.* **4.** to become more active, sensitive, etc. **5.** to become alive; receive life. **6.** (of the mother) to enter that stage of pregnancy in which the child gives indications of life. **7.** (of a child in the womb) to begin to manifest signs of life. —**quickʹener,** *n.*

quick fire, rapid fire.

quick-firing (kwĭkʹfīʹə rĭng), *adj.* shooting, or capable of shooting, rapidly.

quick-freeze (kwĭk′frēz′), *v.t.*, **-froze, -frozen, -freezing.** to subject (cooked or uncooked food) to rapid refrigeration, permitting it to be stored almost indefinitely at freezing temperatures. —**quick-frozen** (kwĭk′frō′zən), *adj.*

quick grass, 1. couch-grass, *Agropyron repens.* 2. a fine, widely cultivated grass, *Cynodon dactylon*, of southern Africa. [*quick*: def. 1 var. of QUITCH; def. 2 t. Afrikaans: *kweek* cultivation]

quickie (kwĭk′ĭ), *n. Slang.* 1. a book, story, film, etc., usually trivial in quality, requiring only a short time to produce. 2. anything of extremely short duration.

quicklime (kwĭk′līm′), *n.* unslaked lime. See **lime.**

quickly (kwĭk′lĭ), *adv.* with speed; rapidly; very soon.

quick march, a march in quick time.

quicksand (kwĭk′sănd′), *n.* an area of soft or loose wet sand of considerable depth, as on a coast or inland, yielding under weight and hence apt to engulf persons, animals, etc., coming upon it.

quickset (kwĭk′sĕt′), *n.* 1. a plant or cutting (esp. of hawthorn) set to grow, as in a hedge. 2. such plants collectively. 3. a hedge of such plants. —*adj.* 4. formed of quickset, or of growing plants.

quick-setting (kwĭk′sĕt′ĭng), *adj.* made so as to set more quickly than usual, as cement, paint, etc.

quicksilver (kwĭk′sĭl′və), *n.* the metallic element mercury. [ME *qwyksilver*, OE *cwicseolfor* living silver, c. G *Quecksilber*, after L *argentum vīvum* living silver]

quickstep (kwĭk′stĕp′), *n.* 1. (formerly) a lively step used in marching. 2. music adapted to such a march, or in a brisk march rhythm. 3. a rapid ballroom dance step.

quick-tempered (kwĭk′tĕm′pəd), *adj.* easily moved to anger.

quick time, 1. a quick rate of marching. 2. *Mil.* a normal rate of marching in which 120 paces are taken in a minute (as opposed to the ceremonial *slow march*).

quick trick, *Bridge.* a card, or group of cards, that will probably win the first or second trick in a suit, regardless of who plays it or at what declaration.

quick-witted (kwĭk′wĭt′ĭd), *adj.* having a nimble, alert mind. —**quick′-wit′tedly,** *adv.* —**quick′-wit′tedness,** *n.*

quid[1] (kwĭd), *n.* a portion of something, esp. tobacco, for holding in the mouth and chewing. [OE *cwidu* CUD]

quid[2] (kwĭd), *n., pl.* **quid.** *Slang.* a £1 note. [orig. uncert.]

quiddity (kwĭd′ĭ tĭ), *n., pl.* **-ties.** 1. that which makes a thing what it is; the essential nature. 2. a trifling nicety or subtle distinction, as in argument. [t. ML: m. s. *quidditas*, der. L *quid* what]

quidnunc (kwĭd′nŭngk′), *n.* one who is curious to know all the news and gossip. [t. L: *quid nunc* what now?]

quid pro quo (kwĭd′ prō kwō′), *Latin.* one thing in return for another. [L: something for something]

quiescent (kwī ĕs′ənt), *adj.* being at rest, quiet, or still; inactive or motionless. [t. L: s. *quiescens*, ppr., keeping quiet] —**quies′cently,** *adv.* —**quies′cence, quies′cency,** *n.*

quiet[1] (kwī′ət), *n.* 1. freedom from disturbance or tumult; tranquillity; rest; repose: *to live in quiet.* 2. peace; peaceful condition of affairs. [ME *quiet(e)*, t. L: s. *quies* rest, repose, quiet]

quiet[2] (kwī′ət), *adj.* 1. making no disturbance or trouble; not turbulent; peaceable. 2. free from disturbance or tumult; tranquil; peaceful: *a quiet life.* 3. free from disturbing emotions, etc.; mentally peaceful. 4. being at rest. 5. refraining or free from activity, esp. busy or vigorous activity: *a quiet evening at home.* 6. motionless or still; moving gently: *quiet waters.* 7. making no noise or sound, esp. no disturbing sound: *quiet neighbours.* 8. free, or comparatively free, from noise: *a quiet street.* 9. silent: *be quiet!* 10. restrained in speech, manner, etc.; saying little. 11. said, expressed, done, etc., in a restrained or unobtrusive way. 12. of an inconspicuous kind; not showy; subdued. 13. *Com.* commercially inactive. 14. **on the quiet,** *Colloq.* secretly. —*v.t.* 15. to make quiet. 16. to make tranquil or peaceful; pacify. 17. to calm mentally, as a person. 18. to allay, as tumult, doubt, fear, etc. 19. to silence. —*v.i.* 20. to become quiet. [ME, t. L: s. *quiētus*, pp., rested] —**qui′eter,** *n.* —**qui′etly,** *adv.* —**qui′etness,** *n.* —**Syn.** 8. See **still**[1].

quieten (kwī′ə tn), *v.i.* 1. to become quiet. —*v.t.* 2. to make quiet.

quietism (kwī′ə tĭz′əm), *n.* 1. a form of religious mysticism taught by Molinos, a Spanish priest, in the latter part of the 17th century, requiring extinction of the will, withdrawal from worldly interests, and passive meditation on God and divine things. 2. some similar form of religious mysticism. 3. quietness of mind or life. [t. It.: m. *quietismo*] —**qui′etist,** *n.*

quietude (kwī′ĭ tyōōd′), *n.* the state of being quiet; tranquillity; calmness; stillness; quiet. [t. LL: m. *quiētūdo*, der. L *quiētus*]

quietus (kwī ē′təs), *n.* 1. a finishing stroke; anything that effectually ends or settles: *to give a quietus to a rumour.* 2. discharge or release from life. [t. ML: quit (in *quiētus est* he is quit, a formula of acquittance), L he is quiet, at rest. See QUIET[2], adj. Cf. QUIT, adj.]

quiff (kwĭf), *n.* a lock or curl of hair on the forehead. [orig. unknown]

quill (kwĭl), *n.* 1. one of the large feathers of the wing or tail of a bird. 2. the hard, tubelike part of a feather of a bird, nearest the body, extending to the superior umbilicus. 3. a feather, as of a goose, formed into a pen for writing. 4. one of the hollow spines on a porcupine or hedgehog. 5. a device for plucking the strings of a musical instrument (as of a harpsichord), made from the quill of a feather. 6. a roll of bark, as of cinnamon, as formed in drying. 7. a reed or other hollow stem on which yarn is wound. 8. a bobbin or spool. 9. *Archaic.* a musical pipe, esp. one made from a hollow stem. 10. *Mach.* any object that resembles the quill of a bird, as a **quill bit** for boring in wood or a quill shaft. —*v.i.* 11. *Textiles.* to form work into the shape of a quill. [ME *quil.* Cf. LG *quiele*, G *Kiel*]

quillai (kĭ lī′), *n.* soapbark (def. 1). [t. Araucanian]

quillai bark, soapbark (def. 2).

Quiller-Couch (kwĭl′ə kōōch′), *n.* **Sir Arthur Thomas** ('*Q*'), 1863–1944, English novelist and critic.

quillet (kwĭl′ĭt), *n. Archaic.* a subtlety; a quibble.

quillon (kē′yŏn; *Fr.* kē yôɴ′), *n.* either of the two arms forming the cross-guard of a sword.

quill shaft, *Mach.* a hollow shaft revolving on an inner spindle.

quillwort (kwĭl′wût′), *n.* any of the aquatic and paludal pteridophytic plants constituting the genus *Isoëtes*, characterized by clustered, quill-like leaves bearing sporangia in their bases.

quilt (kwĭlt), *n.* 1. a coverlet for a bed, made by stitching together two thicknesses of fabric with a padding of some soft substance, as wool, down, etc., between them, the padding being kept in place by stitching passing through both thicknesses. 2. anything quilted or resembling a quilt. 3. a bedspread or counterpane. 4. *Obs.* a kind of mattress. —*v.t.* 5. to stitch together (two pieces of cloth with a soft interlining), usually in an ornamental pattern. 6. to sew up between pieces of material. 7. to pad or line with some material. —*v.i.* 8. to make quilts or quilted work. [ME *quilte*, t. OF: m. *cuilte*, g. L *culcita* mattress, cushion] —**quil′ter,** *n.*

quilted (kwĭl′tĭd), *adj.* 1. resembling a quilt, as in texture, design, etc. 2. filled or padded like a quilt.

Quilter (kwĭl′tə), *n.* **Roger,** 1877–1953, English composer.

quilting (kwĭl′tĭng), *n.* 1. the act of one who quilts. 2. material for making quilts.

quilting bee, *U.S.* a social gathering where women make quilts.

Quimper (*Fr.* kăɴ pĕr′), *n.* a seaport in NW France, the capital of Finistère department. 45,989 (1962).

quin (kwĭn), *n. Colloq.* a quintuplet.

quinacrine (kwĭn′ə krēn′), *n.* atabrine.

quinary (kwī′nə rĭ), *adj.* 1. pertaining to or consisting of five. 2. arranged in fives. 3. of, pertaining to, or denoting a numeral system based on the number 5. —*n.* 4. a number in a quinary system. [t. L: m. s. *quinārius* containing five]

quince (kwĭns), *n.* 1. the hard, yellowish, acid fruit of a small, hardy, rosaceous tree, *Cydonia oblonga.* 2. the tree itself. [ME *qwince*, appar. orig. pl., taken as sing., of ME *quyne, coyn*, t. OF: m. *cooin*, g. L *cotōneum*, for *cydōnium*, t. Gk: m. *kydṓnion* quince, lit., (apple) of *Cydonia* (ancient city of Crete)]

quincentenary (kwĭn′sĕn tē′nə rĭ), *adj., n., pl.* **-naries.** —*adj.* 1. of or pertaining to a 500th anniversary. —*n.* 2. a 500th anniversary. 3. its celebration. 4. a period of 500 years.

quincentennial (kwĭn′sĕn tĕn′yəl), *adj.* quincentenary.

quincuncial (kwĭn kŭn′shəl), *adj.* 1. consisting of or resembling a quincunx. 2. *Bot.* denoting a five-ranked arrangement of leaves.

quincunx (kwĭn′kŭngks), *n.* 1. an arrangement of five objects (as trees) in a square or rectangle, one at each corner and one in the middle. 2. *Bot.* an imbricated arrangement of five petals or leaves, in which two are interior, two are exterior, and one is partly interior and partly exterior. [t. L: orig., five twelfths (a Roman coin worth five twelfths of the as, and marked with a quincunx of spots)]

quindecagon (kwĭn dĕk′ə gən), *n. Geom.* a polygon with fifteen angles and fifteen sides. [f. L *quindec(im)* fifteen + *-agon* (abstracted from DECAGON)]

quindecennial (kwĭn′dĭ sĕn′yəl), *adj.* 1. of or pertaining to a period of fifteen years or the fifteenth occurrence of a series, as an anniversary. —*n.* 2. a fifteenth anniversary. [f. L *quindec(im)* fifteen + *-ennial*, as in DECENNIAL]

quinic acid (kwĭn′ĭk), *Chem.* a white crystalline organic acid, $C_6H_7(OH)\ CO_2H$, present in cinchona bark, coffee beans, and the leaves of many plants. [f. Sp. *quin(a)*, (t. Quechua: m. *kina* bark) + -IC + ACID]

quinidine (kwĭn′ĭ dēn′), *n. Pharm.* a colourless crystalline alkaloid isomeric with quinine, $C_{20}H_{24}N_2O_2$, derived from the bark of species of *Cinchona*: used to regulate the heart rhythm, and to treat malaria.

quinine (kwĭ nēn′), *n. Chem.* **1.** a bitter colourless alkaloid, $C_2\ H_{24}N_2O_2$, having needle-like crystals, which is used in medicine as a stimulant and to treat malaria; originally derived from the bark of species of *Cinchona*. **2.** a salt of this alkaloid, esp. the sulphate. [f. Sp. *quin(a)* (t. Quechua: m. *kina* bark) + -INE[2]]

quinoid (kwĭn′oid), *n. Chem.* a quinonoid substance.

quinol (kwĭn′ŏl), *n. Chem.* hydroquinone.

quinoline (kwĭn′ə lēn′, -lĭn′), *n. Chem.* a nitrogenous organic base, C_9H_7N, a colourless liquid with a pungent odour, occurring in coal tar, and obtained by oxidation of a mixture of aniline and glycerol, and used in preparing other compounds. Also, **quinolin** (kwĭn′ə lĭn). [f. *quinole* (f. Sp. *quin(a)* quinine bark + -OLE) + -INE[2]]

quinone (kwĭ nōn′, kwĭn′ōn), *n. Chem.* **1.** Also, **benzoquinone.** a yellow crystalline unsaturated cyclic diketone, $C_6H_4O_2$, formed by oxidizing aniline or hydroquinone, and used in tanning leather. **2.** any of a class of compounds based on this structure. [f. Sp. *quin(a)* quinine bark + -ONE]

quinonoid (kwĭn′ə noid′, kwĭ nō′noid), *adj. Chem.* of or resembling quinone. [f. QUINON(E) + -OID]

quinoxaline (kwĭ nŏk′sə lēn′), *n. Chem.* **1.** a colourless, crystalline solid, $C_8H_6N_2$, consisting of a benzene ring condensed with a diazine ring. **2.** any of a class of compounds based on this structure.

quinquagenarian (kwĭng′kwə jĭ nâr′ĭ ən), *adj.* **1.** of the age of 50 years. **2.** between 50 and 60 years old. —*n.* **3.** a quinquagenarian person. [f. s. L *quinquāgēnārius* consisting of fifty + -AN]

Quinquagesima (kwĭng′kwə jĕs′ĭ mə), *n.* the Sunday before Lent (more fully, **Quinquagesima Sunday**), being the fiftieth day before Easter (reckoning inclusively); Shrove Sunday. [ME, t. ML, short for L *quinquāgēsima dies* fiftieth day]

quinque-, a word element meaning 'five'. [t. L, comb. form of *quinque*]

quinquefoliolate (kwĭng′kwĭ fō′lĭ ə lĭt), *adj. Bot.* having five leaves or leaflets.

quinquennial (kwĭng kwĕn′ĭ əl), *adj.* **1.** of or for five years. **2.** occurring every five years. —*n.* **3.** something that occurs every five years. **4.** a fifth anniversary. **5.** a five-year term in office. [late ME, f. L *quinquenni(s)* of five years + -AL[1]]

quinquennium (kwĭng kwĕn′ĭ əm), *n.*, *pl.* **-quenniums, -quennia** (-kwĕn′ĭ ə). a period of five years. Also, **quinquenniad** (kwĭng kwĕn′ĭ ăd′). [t. L]

quinquepartite (kwĭng′kwĭ pä′tīt), *adj.* divided into or consisting of five parts.

quinquereme (kwĭng′kwĭ rēm′), *n.* an ancient ship having five banks of oars.

quinquevalent (kwĭng′kwĭ vā′lənt, kwĭng kwĕv′ə lənt), *adj. Chem.* **1.** pentavalent. **2.** exercising five different valencies, as phosphorus with valencies 5, 4, 3, 1, and -3. —**quinquevalence** (kwĭng′kwĭ vā′ləns, kwĭng kwĕv′ə-ləns), **quin′queva′lency,** *n.*

quinsy (kwĭn′zĭ), *n.*, *pl.* **-sies.** *Pathol.* a suppurative inflammation of the tonsils; suppurative tonsillitis. [ME *qwinaci*, t. ML: m. *quinancia*, der. LL *cynanchē*, t. Gk: m. *kynánchē* sore throat]

quint[1] (kwĭnt *for 1*, kĭnt *for 2*), *n.* **1.** an organ stop sounding a fifth higher than the corresponding digitals. **2.** *Piquet.* a series of five cards, all of the same suit. [t. F: m. *quinte* (fem.), t. L: m. *quinta* fifth]

quint[2] (kwĭnt), *n. U.S. Colloq.* a quintuplet.

Quintain

quintain (kwĭn′tĭn), *n.* **1.** (during the Middle Ages and later) a post, or an object mounted on a post, for tilting at as a knightly or other exercise. **2.** such exercise or sport. [ME *quyntain*, t. OF: m. *quintaine*, t. ML: m. *quintāna* quintain, L street in a camp]

quintal (kwĭn′tl), *n.* **1.** a unit of weight in the metric system, equal to 100 kilograms, and equivalent to 220·462 avoirdupois pounds. **2.** a hundredweight. [late ME, t. ML: s. *quintāle*, t. Ar.: *qinṭār* weight of a hundred pounds, prob. ult. der. L *centēnārius*, der. *centum* hundred. Cf. KANTAR]

quintan (kwĭn′tən), *adj.* **1.** (of a fever, ague, etc.) characterized by paroxysms which recur every fifth day, both days of consecutive occurrence being counted. —*n.* **2.** a quintan fever or ague. [t. L: s. *quintāna (febris)* (fever) belonging to the fifth]

quinte (*Fr.* kăNt), *n. Fencing.* the fifth of eight defensive positions. [F]

Quintero (*Sp.* kēn tĕ′rō), *n.* See **Álvarez Quintero.**

quintessence (kwĭn tĕs′əns), *n.* **1.** the pure and concentrated essence of a substance. **2.** the most perfect embodiment of something. **3.** the fifth essence or element of ancient and medieval philosophy (in addition to earth, water, air, and fire), supposed to constitute the heavenly bodies, to permeate the material world, and to be capable of extraction. [ME, t. ML: alter. of *quinta essentia* fifth essence] —**quintessential** (kwĭn′tĭ sĕn′shəl), *adj.*

quintet (kwĭn tĕt′), *n.* **1.** any set or group of five persons or things. **2.** a set of five singers or players. **3.** a musical composition for five voices or instruments. Also, **quintette.** [t. F: (m.) *quintette*, t. It.: m. *quintetto*, der. *quinto* fifth, g. L *quintus* fifth]

quintic (kwĭn′tĭk), *Maths.* —*adj.* **1.** of the fifth degree or order. —*n.* **2.** a quantity of the fifth degree.

quintile (kwĭn′tĭl), *Astrol.* —*adj.* **1.** pertaining to the aspect of two heavenly bodies distant from each other the fifth part of the zodiac, or 72°. —*n.* **2.** a quintile aspect. [t. L, neut. of *quintīlis* fifth]

Quintilian (kwĭn tĭl′yən), *n.* (*Marcus Fabius Quintilianus*), A.D. *c.* 35–*c.* 95, Roman rhetorician.

quintillion (kwĭn tĭl′yən), *n.* **1.** (in Britain and Germany) a cardinal number represented by one followed by 30 zeros. **2.** (in the U.S. and France) a cardinal number represented by one followed by 15 zeros. —*adj.* **3.** amounting to one quintillion in number. [f. s. L *quintus* fifth + (M)ILLION]

quintuple (kwĭn′tyŏŏ pl, kwĭn tyŏŏ′pl), *adj.*, *n.*, *v.*, **-pled, -pling.** —*adj.* **1.** fivefold; consisting of five parts. **2.** five times as great. —*n.* **3.** a number, amount, etc., five times as great as another. —*v.t.*, *v.i.* **4.** to make or become five times as great. [t. F, f. *quint* fifth + *-uple* (abstracted from *quadruple* QUADRUPLE)]

quintuplet (kwĭn′tyŏŏ plĭt, kwĭn tyŏŏ′plĭt), *n.* **1.** any group or combination of five. **2.** (*pl.*) five offspring born at a birth. **3.** one of five children born at a birth. **4.** *Music.* a group of five notes of equal length in a beat of different tempo.

quip (kwĭp), *n.*, *v.*, **quipped, quipping.** —*n.* **1.** a sharp, sarcastic remark; a cutting jest. **2.** a clever or witty saying. **3.** a quibble. **4.** an odd or fantastic action or thing. —*v.i.* **5.** to utter quips. [back formation from *quippy* quip, t. L: m. *quippe* indeed]

quipster (kwĭp′stə), *n.* one given to making quips.

quipu (kē′pōō, kwĭp′ōō), *n.* (among the ancient Peruvians) a device consisting of a cord with knotted strings of various colours attached, for recording events, keeping accounts, etc. [t. Quechua: lit., knot]

quire[1] (kwī′ə), *n.* **1.** a set of 24 uniform sheets of paper. **2.** *Bookbinding.* the section of leaves or pages in proper sequence after the printed sheet or sheets have been folded; a gathering. [ME *quayer*, t. OF: m. *quaier*, g. VL **quaternum* set of four sheets, der. L *quaternī* four each]

quire[2] (kwī′ə), *n.*, *v.i.*, *v.t.*, **quired, quiring.** *Archaic.* choir.

Quirinal (kwĭ′rĭ nəl), *n.* **1.** one of the Seven Hills on which ancient Rome was built. **2.** the Italian civil authority or government (as distinguished from the Vatican). —*adj.* **3.** denoting or pertaining to the Quirinal. **4.** of or pertaining to Quirinus. [t. L: s. *Quirīnālis*, der. *Quirīnus* an ancient Italian war god identified by the Romans with Romulus]

Quirinus (kwĭ rī′nəs), *n.* an early Roman god of war, identified with the deified Romulus.

Quirites (kwĭ rī′tēz), *n.pl.* the citizens of ancient Rome considered in their civil capacity. [t. L, pl. of *Quirīs*, orig. an inhabitant of the Sabine town *Cures*, later a Roman citizen]

quirk (kwûk), *n.* **1.** a trick or peculiarity. **2.** a shift or evasion; a quibble. **3.** a sudden twist, turn, or curve. **4.** a flourish, as in writing. **5.** an acute angle or a channel, as one separating a convex part of a moulding from a fillet. —*adj.* **6.** formed with a quirk or channel, as a moulding. [orig. obscure] —**quirk′y,** *adj.*

quirt (kwût), *U.S.* —*n.* **1.** a riding whip consisting of a short, stout stock and a lash of braided leather. —*v.t.* **2.** to strike with a quirt. [t. Sp.: m. *cuerda* cord]

quisling (kwĭz′lĭng), *n.* a person who betrays his own country by helping an occupying enemy force; a fifth columnist. [from Vidkun *Quisling*, 1887–1945, pro-Nazi Norwegian leader]

quit (kwĭt), *v.*, **quitted** or **quit, quitting,** *adj.* —*v.t.* **1.** to stop, cease, or discontinue. **2.** to depart from; leave. **3.** to give up; let go; relinquish. **4.** to let go one's hold of (something grasped). **5.** *Archaic.* to acquit (oneself).

—*v.i.* **6.** to cease from doing something; stop. **7.** to depart or leave. **8.** to give up one's job or position; resign. —*adj.* **9.** released from obligation, penalty, etc.; free, clear, or rid (usually fol. by *of*). [ME *quitte(n)*, *quite(n)*, t. OF: m. *quit(t)er*, t. ML: m. *quittāre*, *quiētāre*, release, discharge, LL QUIET[2], v.] —**Syn. 6.** See **stop.**

quitch (kwĭch), *n.* couch-grass. Also, **quitch grass.** [OE *cwice*, c. D *kweek*, Norw. *kvike*; akin to QUICK, adj.]

quitclaim (kwĭt′klām′), *n. Law.* **1.** a transfer of all one's interest, as in a parcel of real estate. **2. quitclaim deed,** the instrument making such a transfer (as distinguished from a *warranty deed*). —*v.t.* **3.** to quit or give up claim to (a possession, etc.). [ME *quitclayme*, t. AF: m. *quiteclame*, der. *quiteclamer* declare quit. See QUIT, adj., CLAIM]

quite (kwīt), *adv.* **1.** completely, wholly, or entirely: *quite the reverse.* **2.** actually, really, or truly: *quite a sudden change.* **3.** *Colloq.* to a considerable extent or degree: *quite pretty.* —*interj.* **4.** (an expression of agreement, etc.). [ME; adv. use of ME *quite*, adj., QUIT]

Quito (kē′tō; *Sp.* kē′tō), *n.* the capital of Ecuador, in the N part. 348,151 (est. 1962); 9348 ft high.

quitrent (kwĭt′rĕnt′), *n.* rent paid by a freeholder or copyholder in lieu of services which might otherwise have been required of him. [f. QUIT, adj., + RENT[1]]

quits (kwĭts), *adj.* **1.** on equal terms by repayment or retaliation. **2. call it quits, a.** to abandon an activity, esp. temporarily. **b.** to give up a quarrel, rivalry, etc.; agree to end a dispute, competition, etc. [cf. QUIT, adj.; *-s* of uncert. orig.]

quittance (kwĭt′ns), *n.* **1.** recompense or requital. **2.** an acquittance.

quitter (kwĭt′ə), *n. U.S. Colloq.* one who quits or gives up easily.

quittor (kwĭt′ə), *n. Vet. Sci.* any of various infections of the foot in which tissues degenerate and form a slough, possibly involving tendons and bone as well as skin. [ME, t. OF: m. *cuiture* cooking]

quiver[1] (kwĭv′ə), *v.i.*, *v.t.* **1.** to shake with a slight but rapid motion; vibrate tremulously; tremble. —*n.* **2.** the act or state of quivering; a tremble; a tremor. [ME; c. MD *quiveren* tremble] —**quiv′ery,** *adj.* —**Syn. 1.** See **shake.**

quiver[2] (kwĭv′ə), *n.* **1.** a case for holding arrows. **2.** the contents of such a case. [ME, t. AF: m. *quiveir*, var. of OF *quivre*; ? of Gmc orig.; cf. OE *cocer* quiver]

quiver tree, a tall, multi-branched aloe, *Aloe dichotoma*, of southern Africa, the hollowed stems of which were used by the Bushmen as quivers.

qui vive (*Fr.* kē vēv′), *French.* **1.** who goes there? **2. on the qui vive,** on the alert. [F: (long) live who?—as if calling for such a reply as *Vive le roi!* Long live the king!]

Quixote (kwĭk′sət; *Sp.* kē KHō′tĕ), *n.* See **Don Quixote.**

quixotic (kwĭk sŏt′ĭk), *adj.* **1.** (*sometimes cap.*) resembling or befitting Don Quixote. **2.** extravagantly chivalrous or romantic; visionary; impracticable. Also, **quixotical.** [f. (DON) QUIXOTE + -IC] —**quixot′ically,** *adv.*

quixotism (kwĭk′sə tĭz′əm), *n.* **1.** (*sometimes cap.*) quixotic character or practice. **2.** a quixotic idea or act.

quiz (kwĭz), *v.*, **quizzed, quizzing,** *n.*, *pl.* **quizzes.** —*v.t.* **1.** to question closely. **2.** *U.S.* to examine or test (a student or class) informally by questions. **3.** *Obs.* to make fun of; ridicule; chaff. **4.** *Obs.* to look at or stare at mockingly or impudently. —*n.* **5.** a general knowledge test, esp. as an entertainment on radio, television, etc. **6.** a questioning. **7.** *U.S.* an informal examination or test of a student or class. **8.** *Obs.* a practical joke; hoax. [orig. uncert.] —**quiz′zer,** *n.*

quizmaster (kwĭz′mäs′tə), *n.* one who puts questions to competitors in a quiz, esp. in radio or television programmes.

quizzical (kwĭz′ĭ kl), *adj.* **1.** odd, queer, or comical. **2.** quizzing, ridiculing, or chaffing: *a quizzical smile.* —**quiz′zically,** *adv.*

Qum (kōōm), *n.* a city in central Iran. 96,499 (est. 1964). Also, **Kum.**

quod (kwŏd), *n. Slang.* a prison. [orig. unknown]

quod erat demonstrandum (kwŏd ĕ′răt dĕm′ən străn′-dōōm), *Latin.* which was to be shown or proved. *Abbrev.:* Q.E.D.

quod erat faciendum (kwŏd ĕ′răt făk′ĭ ĕn′dōōm), *Latin.* which was to be done. *Abbrev.:* Q.E.F.

quoddy boat (kwŏd′ē), *U.S.* a type of small boat once used for fishing off New England coasts. [named after (*Passama*)*quoddy* (*Bay*), on the New England coast of the U.S.]

quodlibet (kwŏd′ lĭ bĕt), *n.* **1.** a sophisticated or complex problem or point of argument, esp. one which arises in the study of philosophy or theology. **2.** a thesis or debate devoted to a problem of this type. **3.** *Music.* a composition, often lighthearted in character, consisting of a combination of well-known tunes blended together melodically. [ME, g. L *quod libet* what pleases] —**quod′libet′ical,** *adj.* —**quod′libet′ically,** *adv.*

quoin (koin), *n.* **1.** an external solid angle of a wall or the like. **2.** one of the stones forming it; a cornerstone. **3.** a wedge-shaped piece of wood, stone, or other material, used for any of various purposes. **4.** *Print.* a wedge of wood or metal for securing type in a chase, etc. —*v.t.* **5.** to provide with quoins, as a corner of a wall. **6.** to secure or raise with a quoin or wedge. [var. of COIN]

Quoins

quoit (koit), *n.* **1.** a flattish ring of iron or some other material thrown in play to encircle a peg stuck in the ground or to come as close to it as possible. **2.** (*pl.*, *construed as sing.*) the game so played. —*v.t.* **3.** to throw as or like a quoit. Cf. **deck quoit.** [ME *coyte*; orig. unknown]

quokka (kwŏk′ə), *n.* a small wallaby, *Setonix brachyurus*, found on Rottnest Island, Western Australia. [t. native Australian]

quondam (kwŏn′dăm), *adj.* that formerly was or existed; former: *his quondam partner.* [t. L: formerly]

quonset hut (kwŏn′sĭt), *U.S.* a type of temporary prefabricated shed of corrugated metal, consisting of a half-cylinder with its ends closed, used for storage or for housing soldiers. [orig. trademark]

quorum (kwô′rəm), *n.* **1.** the number of members of a body required to be present to transact business legally (in the House of Commons 40 members). **2.** a particularly chosen group. [t. L: of whom; from a use of the word in commissions written in Latin]

quot., quotation.

quota (kwō′tə), *n.* **1.** the proportional part or share of a total which is due from, or is due or belongs to, a particular district, area, person, etc. **2.** a proportional part or share of a fixed total amount or quantity. **3.** the number of persons of a particular group allowed to immigrate to a country, join an institution, etc. [t. ML, short for L *quota pars* how great a part?]

quotable (kwō′tə bl), *adj.* **1.** able to be quoted; easily or effectively quoted. **2.** suitable or appropriate for quotation.

quotation (kwō tā′shən), *n.* **1.** that which is quoted; a passage quoted from a book, speech, etc. **2.** the act or practice of quoting. **3.** *Com.* **a.** the statement of the current or market price of a commodity or security. **b.** the price so stated.

quotation mark, one of the marks used to indicate the beginning and end of a quotation, in English usually consisting of an inverted comma (‘) at the beginning and an apostrophe (’) at the end, or, for a quotation within a quotation, of double marks of this kind: *‘He said,* “*I will go*”.’ Double marks are still sometimes used instead of single, the latter then being used for a quotation within a quotation.

quote (kwōt), *v.*, **quoted, quoting,** *n.* —*v.t.* **1.** to repeat (a passage, etc.) from a book, speech, etc., as the words of another, as by way of authority, illustration, etc. **2.** to repeat words from (a book, author, etc.). **3.** to bring forward, adduce, or cite. **4.** to enclose (words) within quotation marks. **5.** *Com.* **a.** to state (a price). **b.** to state the current price of. —*v.i.* **6.** to make a quotation or quotations, as from a book or author. —*n.* **7.** a quotation. **8.** a quotation mark. [ME, t. ML: m. *quotāre* divide into chapters and verses, der. L *quot* how many] —**quot′able,** *adj.*

quoth (kwōth), *v.t. Archaic.* said (used with nouns, and with first and third person pronouns, and always placed before the subject): *quoth the raven,* ‘*Never more*’. [pret. of *quethe* (otherwise obs.), OE *cwethan* say. Cf. BEQUEATH]

quotha (kwō′thə), *interj. Archaic.* indeed! (used ironically or contemptuously in quoting another). [for *quoth a* quoth he]

quotidian (kwŏ tĭd′ĭ ən), *adj.* **1.** daily. **2.** everyday; ordinary. **3.** (of a fever, ague, etc.) characterized by paroxysms which recur daily. —*n.* **4.** something recurring daily. **5.** a quotidian fever or ague. [t. L: s. *quotīdiānus* daily; r. ME *cotidien*, t. OF]

quotient (kwō′shənt), *n. Maths.* the result of division; the number of times one quantity is contained in another. [ME, t. L: m. *quotiens* how many times]

quo warranto (kwō′wŏ răn′tō), *Law.* **1.** an ancient writ calling upon a person to show by what warrant he claims an office, privilege, franchise, or liberty. **2.** (now) a similar proceeding upon an information of this nature of quo warranto or under statutory provisions. [ML: by what warrant]

q.v., (L *quod vide*) which see.

Q-value (kyōō′văl′yōō), *n. Physics.* the net energy released in a nuclear reaction; usually expressed in millions of electron volts. *Abbrev.:* Q.

qy, query.

R

R, r (ä), *n., pl.* **R's** or **Rs, r's** or **rs. 1.** the 18th letter of the English alphabet. **2.** See **the three R's.**
R, 1. *Physics., Chem.* gas constant. **2.** *Chem.* radical. **3.** Rand. **4.** *Maths.* ratio. **5.** *Elect.* resistance. **6.** *Chess.* rook. **7.** (*pl.* **Rs**) rupee.
r, 1. *Elect.* resistance. **2.** röntgen. **3.** rouble.
R., 1. rabbi. **2.** Radical. **3.** radius. **4.** railway. **5.** Réaumur (thermometer). **6.** rector. **7.** redactor. **8.** Regina or Rex. **9.** Republican. **10.** response. **11.** *Theat.* stage right. **12.** River. **13.** Road. **14.** rouble. **15.** Royal.
r., 1. radius. **2.** rare. **3.** *Com.* received. **4.** recipe. **5.** replacing. **6.** residence. **7.** right. **8.** rises. **9.** river. **10.** road. **11.** rod. **12.** rouble. **13.** rule(d). **14.** *Cricket, Baseball.* runs. **15.** (*pl.* **rs**) rupee.
Ra (rä), *n.* the great sun-god of the Egyptians, the sovereign god of historical Egypt, in art typically represented as a hawk-headed man bearing on his head the solar disc and the royal uraeus. Also **Re.** [t. Egypt.]
Ra, *Chem.* radium.
R.A., 1. Rear Admiral. **2.** *Astron.* right ascension. **3.** Royal Academician. **4.** Royal Academy. **5.** Royal Artillery.
R.A.A., Royal Academy of Arts.
R.A.A.F., Royal Australian Air Force.
Raabe (*Ger.* rä′bə), *n.* **Wilhelm** (*Ger.* vĭl′hĕlm), ('*Jacob Corvinus*'), 1831–1910, German poet and novelist.
Rabat (rə bät′), *n.* a seaport in and the capital of Morocco, in the NW part. 261,450 (est. 1964).
rabbet (răb′ĭt), *n., v.,* **-beted, -beting.** —*n.* **1.** a cut, groove, or recess made on the edge or surface of a board or the like, as to receive the end or edge of another board or the like similarly shaped. **2.** a joint so made. —*v.t.* **3.** to cut or form a rabbet in (a board, etc.). **4.** to join by rabbets. —*v.i.* **5.** to join by a rabbet (fol. by *on* or *over*). Also, **rebate.** [ME *rabit*, prob. t. OF: m. *rabat* a beating down, or *rabot* a joiner's plane]

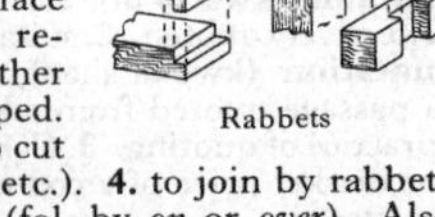
Rabbets

rabbet plane, a plane for cutting rabbets, having its blade either at right angles or diagonal to the direction of motion.
rabbi (răb′ī), *n., pl.* **-bis.** *Judaism.* **1.** the principal religious official of a synagogue, equivalent to the Christian minister of religion; the spiritual leader of a Jewish community. **2.** a Jewish scholar; an expounder of the Jewish law. **3.** (*cap.*) a title of respect accorded to such an official or scholar. **4.** any of the early Jewish scholars who contributed to the formation of the Talmud. [ME and OE, t. L, t. Heb.: my master]
rabbin (răb′ĭn), *n.* rabbi. [t. ML: s. *rabbinus*]
rabbinate (răb′ĭ nĭt), *n.* **1.** the status or tenure of office of a rabbi. **2.** rabbis collectively, esp. the rabbis of a particular place or region.
Rabbinic (rə bĭn′ĭk), *n.* the Hebrew language as used by the rabbis in their writings; the later Hebrew.
rabbinical (rə bĭn′ə kl), *adj.* of or pertaining to the rabbis or their learning, writings, etc. Also, **rabbin′ic.**
rabbinist (răb′ĭ nĭst), *n.* (among the Jews) one who accepts the teaching of the Talmud and the tradition of the rabbis. Also, **rab′binite′.** —**rab′binism,** *n.* —**rab′binis′tic, rab′binis′tical,** *adj.*
rabbit[1] (răb′ĭt), *n., v.i.,* **-bited, -biting.** —*n.* **1.** a small, long-eared, burrowing lagomorph, *Oryctolagus cuniculus*, of the hare family. **2.** any of various rodent-like lagomorph mammals, as *Sylvilagus floridanus*, the eastern cottontail rabbit of North America. **3.** the skin of any member of the rabbit family. **4.** its flesh, used as food. **5.** *Colloq.* a poor performer at some sport, as tennis or golf. —*v.i.* **6.** to hunt rabbits. [ME *rabet.* Cf. Walloon *robett*, Flem. *robbe*] —**rab′biter,** *n.*

European wild rabbit, *Oryctolagus cuniculus* (13 to 18 in. long)

rabbit[2] (răb′ĭt), *n. Physics.* a small container in which samples are passed through a nuclear reactor for irradiation. [orig. uncert.]
rabbit fever, *Med.* tularaemia.
rabbit-fish (răb′ĭt fĭsh′), *n.* **1.** a deep-water fish of the Atlantic, *Chimaera monstrosa*, whose large cutting teeth resemble those of a rabbit. **2.** any of various other fishes said to resemble the rabbit. See **king of the herrings.**
rabbit punch, a short sharp blow to the nape of the neck or the lower part of the skull.
rabbitry (răb′ĭ trĭ), *n., pl.* **-tries. 1.** a collection of rabbits. **2.** a place where rabbits are kept.
rabbit's-foot (răb′ĭts fo͝ot′), *n.* a clover, *Trifolium arvense*, having soft-haired, cylindrical flowering heads.
rabbit-warren (răb′ĭt wŏ′rən), *n.* warren.
rabble[1] (răb′l), *n., v.,* **-bled, -bling.** —*n.* **1.** a disorderly crowd; a mob. **2.** (in contemptuous use) the lowest class of people (prec. by *the*). —*v.t.* **3.** to beset as a rabble does; mob. [ME *rabel*; ? akin to RABBLE[3]]
rabble[2] (răb′l), *n., v.,* **-bled, -bling.** *Metall.* —*n.* **1.** a tool or mechanically operated device used for stirring or mixing a charge in a roasting furnace. —*v.t.* **2.** to stir (the charge) in a roasting furnace. [t. F: m. *râble*, g. L *rutābulum* fire-shovel] —**rab′bler,** *n.*
rabble[3] (răb′l), *v.t., v.i.,* **-bled, -bling.** *Scot. and N Dial.* to utter, read, or speak in a rapid, confused manner. [late ME *rable*, c. G *rabbeln*]
rabble-rouser (răb′l rou′zə), *n.* a demagogue.
Rabelais (răb′ə lā′; *Fr.* rȧ blĕ′), *n.* **François** (*Fr.* fräN-swȧ′), *c.* 1490–1553, French satirist and humorist.
Rabelaisian (răb′ə lā′zĭ ən, -zhən), *adj.* **1.** of, pertaining to, or suggesting François Rabelais, whose work is characterized by broad, coarse humour and keen satire. —*n.* **2.** one who admires or studies the works of Rabelais. **3.** a person resembling in some way, esp. coarse humour or grossness, a character created by Rabelais.
rabid (răb′ĭd), *adj.* **1.** irrationally extreme in opinion or practice: *a rabid isolationist.* **2.** furious or raging; violently intense: *rabid hunger.* **3.** affected with or pertaining to rabies; mad. [t. L: s. *rabidus* raving, mad] —**rabid′ity, rab′idness,** *n.* —**rab′idly,** *adv.*
rabies (rā′bēz), *n.* a fatal, infectious disease of the brain which occurs in all warm-blooded animals including man, and is due to a specific virus which occurs in saliva and is transmitted to new victims by the bite of an afflicted animal, generally the dog; hydrophobia. [t. L: madness, rage]
R.A.C., 1. Royal Agricultural College. **2.** Royal Armoured Corps. **3.** Royal Automobile Club.
raccoon (rə ko͞on′), *n.* **1.** any of several small nocturnal carnivores of the genus *Procyon*, esp. the North American *Procyon lotor*, arboreal in habit, and having a sharp snout and a bushy ringed tail. **2.** the thick grey to brown underfur of the raccoon, with silver-grey guard hairs tipped with black. Also, **racoon.** [t. N Amer. Ind. (Algonquian, Virginia): m. *ärähkunem* he scratches with the hands)]

Raccoon, *Procyon lotor* (Up to 3 ft long, tail ab. 10 in.)

raccoon dog, a small wild dog of eastern Asia, of the genus *Nyctereutes* having dark marks around the eyes that give it some resemblance to a raccoon.
race[1] (rās), *n., v.,* **raced, racing.** —*n.* **1.** a contest of speed, as in running, riding, driving, sailing, etc. **2.** (*pl.*) a series of races, esp. horseraces or greyhound races run at a set time over a regular course. **3.** any contest or competition: *an armament race, the race for the presidency.* **4.** *Geol.* **a.** a strong or rapid current of water, as in the sea or a river. **b.** the channel or bed of such a current, or of any stream. **5.** an artificial channel, leading water to or from a place where its energy is utilized. **6.** the current of water in such a channel. **7.** a narrow passageway for livestock, as one leading to a sheep dip. **8.** *Mach.* a channel, groove, or the like, for a sliding or rolling part, as for ball-bearings. **9.** *Archaic.* onward movement; an onward or regular course. **10.** *Archaic.* the course of time. **11.** *Archaic.* the course of life, or of a part of life. —*v.i.* **12.** to engage in a contest of speed; run a race. **13.** to run horses in races; engage in or practise horseracing. **14.** to run, move, or go swiftly. **15.** (of an engine, wheel, etc.) to run with undue or uncontrolled speed when the load is diminished without corresponding diminution of fuel, power, etc. —*v.t.* **16.** to run a race with; try to beat in a contest of speed. **17.** to cause to run in a race or races. **18.** to cause to run, move, or go swiftly: *to race a motor.* [ME *ras(e)*, t. Scand.; cf. Icel. *rās* a running, race, rush of liquid, c. OE *rǣs* a running, rush]

race[2] (rās), *n.* **1.** a group of persons connected by common descent, blood, or heredity. **2.** a population so connected. **3.** *Ethnol.* a subdivision of a stock, characterized by a more or less unique combination of physical traits which are transmitted in descent. **4.** a group of tribes or peoples forming an ethnic stock. **5.** the state of belonging to a certain ethnic stock. **6.** the distinguishing characteristics of special ethnic stocks. **7.** the human race or family, or mankind. **8.** *Zool.* a variety; a subspecies. **9.** a natural kind of living creature: ***the human race, the race of fishes.*** **10.** any group, class, or kind, esp. of persons. **11.** *Archaic.* (of speech, writing, etc.) characteristic quality, esp. liveliness or piquancy; raciness. **12.** the characteristic taste or flavour of wine. [t. F, t. It.: m. *razza* race, breed, lineage; orig. uncert.]

—Syn. 1. RACE, NATION, PEOPLE are terms for a large body of persons who may be thought of as a unit because of common characteristics. RACE refers to a large body of persons, animals, or plants characterized by community of descent: *the white race.* NATION considers a body of persons as living under an organized government, occupying a fixed area, and dealing as a unit in matters of peace and war with other similar groups: *the English nation.* Whereas NATION is more or less objective, PEOPLE has emotional connotations similar to those of *family.* PEOPLE refers to the persons composing a race, nation, tribe, etc., as members of a body with common interests and a unifying culture: *we are one people, any people on any continent, the peoples of the world.*

race[3] (rās), *n.* a root (of ginger). [ME, t. OF: m. *rais,* g. L *rādix* root]

Race (rās), *n.* **Cape,** a cape at the SE extremity of Newfoundland.

race-card (rās′käd′), *n.* the programme for a race meeting. Also, **card.**

racecourse (rās′kôs′), *n.* **1.** a piece of ground on which horseraces are held for public entertainment. **2.** any place where races are held. **3.** a millrace or the like.

race ginger, whole ginger.

race-hatred (rās′hā′trĭd), *n.* animosity engendered by racial differences, esp. as between Whites and Negroes.

racehorse (rās′hôs′), *n.* a horse bred or kept for racing.

raceme (rə sēm′), *n. Bot.* **1.** a simple indeterminate inflorescence in which the flowers are borne on short pedicels lying along a common axis, as in the lily-of-the-valley. **2.** a compound inflorescence in which the short pedicels with single flowers of the simple raceme are replaced by racemes (**compound raceme**). [t. L: m. s. *racēmus* cluster of grapes. See RAISIN] **—racemiferous** (răs′ĭ mĭf′ə rəs), *adj.*

Raceme of lily-of-the-valley, *Convallaria majalis*

race meeting, an organized series of races, esp. between horses.

racemic (rə sē′mĭk, -sĕm′ĭk), *adj. Chem.* denoting or pertaining to any of various organic compounds in which racemism occurs. [f. s. L *racēmus* cluster of grapes + -IC]

racemic acid, *Chem.* an isomeric modification of tartaric acid, which is sometimes found in the juice of grapes in conjunction with the common dextrorotatory form, and which is optically inactive, but can be separated into the two usual isomeric forms, dextrorotatory and laevorotatory.

racemism (răs′ĭ mĭz′əm, rə sē′mĭz′əm), *n. Chem.* the character of an optically inactive substance (as racemic acid) separable into two other substances, of the same chemical composition as the original substance, one of which is dextrorotatory and the other laevorotatory.

racemization (răs′ĭ mī zā′shən), *n. Chem.* the conversion of substances which are optically active into ones which are optically inactive. Also, **racemisation.**

racemose (răs′ĭ mōs′), *adj. Bot.* **1.** having the form of a raceme. **2.** arranged in racemes. [t. L: m. s. *racēmōsus* clustering]

racer (rā′sə), *n.* **1.** one who or that which races, or takes part in a race, as a racehorse, or a bicycle, yacht, etc., used for racing. **2.** anything having great speed. **3.** a mounting on which a heavy gun is turned.

race relations, the reciprocal behaviour of two or more races of people, esp. in a single society.

race riot, an act of mob violence resulting from racial animosity.

race suicide, the extinction of a race or people which tends to result when, through the unwillingness or forbearance of its members to have children, the birth-rate falls below the death rate.

racetrack (rās′trăk′), *n.* **1.** a track on which races, esp. motor races, are held. **2.** *U.S.* a racecourse.

raceway (rās′wā′), *n. U.S.* a passage or channel for water, as a millrace.

Rachel (rā′chəl), *n. Bible.* Jacob's favourite wife, and mother of Joseph and Benjamin. Gen. 29–35.

rachis (rā′kĭs), *n., pl.* **rachises** (rā′kĭ sĭz), **rachides** (răk′ĭ dēz′, rā′kĭ-). **1.** *Bot.* **a.** the axis of an inflorescence when somewhat elongated, as in a raceme. **b.** (in a pinnately compound leaf or frond) the prolongation of the petiole along which the leaflets are disposed. **c.** any of various axial structures. **2.** *Zool.* the shaft of a feather, esp. that part, anterior to the superior umbilicus, bearing the web, as distinguished from the quill. **3.** *Anat.* the spinal column. Also, **rhachis.** [NL, t. Gk]

R, Rachis (def. 1b)

rachitis (rə kī′tĭs), *n. Pathol.* rickets. [NL, t. Gk: disease of the spine] **—rachitic** (rə kĭt′ĭk), *adj.*

Rachmaninov (răk măn′ĭ nŏf′; *Russ.* răкн mä′nĭ nəf), *n.* **Sergei Vassilievich** (*Russ.* sĭr gyĕy′ vä sĕl′jĭ vĭch), 1873–1943, Russian pianist and composer. Also, **Rachmaninoff.**

Rachmanism (răk′mə nĭz′əm), *n.* **1.** a system of extortionate landlordism involving overcrowding of slum properties, esp. with coloured people, exploitation of racial prejudice and other pressures to drive out existing tenants, and, finally, summary eviction before renovating the property and letting it at higher rents. **2.** any form of morally reprehensible and extortionate landlordism. [named after Perec (Peter) *Rachman,* 1920–1962, British property-owner born in Poland]

racial (rā′shəl), *adj.* **1.** pertaining to or characteristic of race or extraction, or a race or races. **2.** pertaining to the relations between people of different races. **—ra′cially,** *adv.*

racialism (rā′shə lĭz′əm), *n.* **1.** the belief that human races have distinctive characteristics which determine their respective cultures, usually involving the idea that one's own race is superior and has the right to rule or dominate others. **2.** offensive or aggressive behaviour to members of another race stemming from such a belief. **3.** a policy or system of government and society based upon it. Also, **racism. —ra′cialist,** *n., adj.*

Racine (rä sēn′; *Fr.* rä sēn′), *n.* **Jean Baptiste** (*Fr.* zhäɴ bȧ tēst′), 1639–99, French tragic dramatist.

racing (rā′sĭng), *adj.* **1.** of, pertaining to, designed for, or used in races, speed tests, etc.: *a racing car.* **—n. 2.** the act of taking part in or attending races, esp. horse-races.

racism (rā′sĭz′əm), *n.* racialism. **—rac′ist,** *n., adj.*

rack[1] (răk), *n.* **1.** a framework of bars, wires, or pegs on which articles are arranged or deposited (used esp. in composition): *a shoe rack.* **2.** a spreading framework, fixed or movable, for carrying hay, straw, or the like in large loads, esp. for fodder. **3.** *Print.* an upright framework with side cleats or other supports for the storing of cases or galleys of type, etc. **4.** *Mach.* **a.** a bar with teeth on one of its sides, adapted to engage with the teeth of a pinion or the like, as for converting circular into rectilinear motion or vice versa. **b.** a similar bar with notches over which the projections of such devices as pawls operate. **5.** an apparatus or instrument formerly in use for torturing persons by stretching the body. **6.** a cause or state of intense suffering of body or mind. **7.** torment, anguish. **8.** violent strain. **9. on the rack, a.** in great pain, distress, or anxiety. **b.** under the strain of great effort. **—v.t. 10.** to torture; distress acutely; torment. **11.** to strain in mental effort: *to rack one's brains.* **12.** to strain by physical force or violence; shake violently. **13.** to strain beyond what is normal or usual. **14.** to stretch the joints of (a person) in torture by means of a rack. **15.** to furnish with, or put on or in a rack. **16.** *Bldg Trades.* to leave (a wall) with unfinished ends for later additions. [ME *rekke, rakke,* t. MD or MLG] **—Syn. 7, 10.** See **torment.**

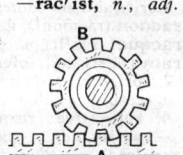

A, Rack[1] (def. 4); B, with pinion gear

rack[2] (răk), *n.* **1.** wreck; destruction. **2. rack and ruin,** disrepair or collapse, esp. owing to neglect; dilapidation. [var. of WRACK]

rack[3] (răk), *n.* **1.** the gait of a horse in which the legs move in lateral pairs but not quite simultaneously. **2.** pace (def. 7). **—v.i. 3.** (of a horse) to go with a gait, similar to a pace, in which the legs move in lateral pairs but not quite simultaneously. **4.** to pace. [? var. of ROCK[2], v.]

rack[4] (răk), *n.* **1.** flying, broken clouds; a mass of clouds driven by the wind. **—v.i. 2.** to drive or move, esp. before the wind. [ME *rak, rakke*; prob. t. Scand.; cf. Icel. *reki* drift, wreckage, *reka* drive]

rack[5] (răk), *v.t.* to draw off (wine, cider, etc.) from the lees. [late ME; cf. obs. F *raqué* of wine, pressed from the marc of grapes, Pr. *arracar* to rack, *raca* dregs]

rack[6] (răk), *n. Dial.* the neck portion of mutton, pork, or veal. [Cf. G *Rachen* throat]

rack-and-pinion (răk′ən pĭn′yən), *adj.* denoting or pertaining to a railway operated on a steep incline with a rack-rail and a pinion.

racket[1] (răk′ĭt), *n.* **1.** a loud noise, esp. of a disturbing of confusing kind; din; uproar; clamour or noisy fuss. **2.** social excitement, gaiety, or dissipation. **3.** *Slang.* an organized illegal activity such as the extortion of money by threat or violence from legitimate businessmen: *the protection racket.* **4.** *Slang.* a dishonest scheme, trick, etc. **5.** *Slang.* one's legitimate business or occupation: *he's in the advertising racket.* —*v.i.* **6.** to make a racket or noise. **7.** to indulge in social gaiety or dissipation. [metathetic var. of d. *rattick.* See RATTLE[1]] —**Syn. 1.** See **noise.**

racket[2] (răk′ĭt), *n.* **1.** a light bat having a network of cord or catgut stretched in a more or less elliptical frame, used in tennis, etc. **2.** (*pl. construed as sing.*) a game of ball, played in a walled court, in which such bats are used. **3.** a snowshoe made in the manner of a tennis racket. —*v.t.* **4.** to strike with a racket. Also, **rackett, racquet.** [t. F: m. *raquette*; orig. uncert.]

racketeer (răk′ĭ tĭə′), *Orig. U.S.* —*n.* **1.** one engaged in a racket. —*v.i.* **2.** to engage in a racket. [f. RACKET[1] (defs 3, 4) + -EER] —**rack′eteer′ing,** *n., adj.*

rackety (răk′ĭ tĭ), *adj.* **1.** making or causing a racket; noisy. **2.** fond of excitement or dissipation.

Rackham (răk′əm), *n.* **Arthur,** 1867–1939, English illustrator and water-colourist.

rack-rail (răk′rāl′), *n.* (in an inclined-plane or mountain-climbing railway) a rail between the running rails having cogs or teeth with which cogwheels on the locomotive engage.

rack-railway (răk′rāl′wā′), *n.* a steep railway fitted with a rack-rail.

rack-rent (răk′rĕnt′), *n.* **1.** a rent for land equal or nearly equal to its full annual value. **2.** an exorbitant rent. —*v.t.* **3.** to exact the highest possible rent for. **4.** to demand rack-rent from. [f. RACK[1], v. + RENT[1]] —**rack′-rent′er,** *n.*

rackwork (răk′wûk′), *n.* a mechanism in which a rack is used; a rack and pinion or the like.

racon (rā′kŏn), *n.* a radio beacon. [b. RA(DIO BEA)CON)]

raconteur (răk′ŏn tû′), *n.* a person skilled in relating stories and anecdotes. [t. F. See RECOUNT]

racoon (rə ko͞on′), *n.* raccoon.

racquet (răk′ĭt), *n.* racket[2].

racy (rā′sĭ), *adj.,* **-cier, -ciest. 1.** vigorous; lively; spirited. **2.** sprightly; piquant; pungent: *a racy style.* **3.** having an agreeably peculiar taste or flavour, as wine, fruits, etc. **4.** suggestive; risqué: *a racy story.* [f. RACE[1] + -Y[1]] —**rac′ily,** *adv.* —**rac′iness,** *n.*

rad (răd), *n. Physics.* the unit of dose of ionizing radiation; 100 ergs of absorbed energy per gram of irradiated material. [short for RADIATION]

rad, *Maths.* radian.

Rad., 1. Radical. **2.** Radnorshire.

rad., 1. *Maths.* radical. **2.** radix.

RADA (rä′də), *n.* Royal Academy of Dramatic Art.

radar (rā′dä), *n. Electronics.* a device to determine the presence and location of an object by measuring the time for the echo of a radio wave to return from it, and the direction from which it returns. [short for *ra*(*dio*) *d*(*etecting*) *a*(*nd*) *r*(*anging*)]

radarscope (rā′dä skōp′), *n.* the viewing screen of radar equipment.

R.A.D.C., Royal Army Dental Corps.

Radcliffe (răd′klĭf), *n.* **1.** a town in England, in Lancashire. 26,724 (1961). **2.** a women's university college in the U.S., in Cambridge, Massachusetts, founded in 1879. **3. Mrs Ann,** 1764–1823, English novelist.

raddle[1] (răd′l), *v.t.,* **-dled, -dling,** *n. N Dial.* —*v.t.* **1.** to interweave; wattle. —*n.* **2.** a lath or wattle. **3.** a fence or the like made of wattles. [v. use of *raddle* lath, t. AF: m. *reidele* thick stick]

raddle[2] (răd′l), *n., v.t.,* **-dled, -dling.** reddle.

Radetzky (*Ger.* rä dĕt′skē), *n.* **Count Joseph** (*Ger.* yō′zĕf), 1766–1858, Austrian field marshal.

Radhakrishnan (rä′də krĭsh′nən), *n.* **Sir Sarvepalli** (sä′vĭ pä′lĭ), born 1888, president of India 1962–67.

radial (rā′dyəl), *adj.* **1.** arranged like radii or rays. **2.** having spokes, bars, lines, etc., arranged like radii, as a machine. **3.** *Zool.* pertaining to structures that radiate from a central point, as the arms of a starfish. **4.** of, like, or pertaining to a radius or a ray. **5.** *Anat.* referring to the radius or more lateral of the two bones of the forearm. [t. ML: s. *radiālis,* f. L: s. *radius* RADIUS + *-ālis* -AL[1]] —**ra′dially,** *adv.*

Radial arrangement of spokes of a wheel

radial engine, an engine having cylinders grouped so that they resemble equally spaced radii of a circle.

radial-ply tyre, a pneumatic tyre with flexible walls achieved by having the casing cords running radially and with additional plies strengthening the tread only.

radial velocity, *Astron.* the velocity, usually expressed in kilometres per second, with which a celestial body approaches or recedes from the observer. Also, **line-of-sight velocity.**

radian (rā′dyən), *n.* the supplementary SI unit of plane angle, defined as the angle at the centre of a circle, subtending an arc of the circle equal in length to the radius: equal to 57·2958°. *Symbol:* rad

radiance (rā′dyəns), *n.* **1.** radiant brightness or light: *radiance of the tropical sun, radiance lit her face.* **2.** radiation. Also, **radiancy.**

radiant (rā′dyənt), *adj.* **1.** emitting rays of light; shining; bright: *the radiant sun, radiant colours.* **2.** bright with joy, hope, etc.: *radiant smiles.*. **3.** *Physics.* emitted in rays, or by radiation. —*n.* **4.** a point or object from which rays proceed. **5.** *Astron.* the point in the heavens from which a shower of meteors appears to radiate. [late ME, t. L: s. *radians,* ppr., emitting rays] —**ra′diantly,** *adv.* —**Syn. 1.** See **bright.**

radiant energy, *Physics.* the energy propagated through a medium as a wave, as heat, light, sound, etc.

radiant flux, *Physics.* power emitted, transferred, or received in the form of radiant energy.

radiant heat, *Physics.* heat energy transmitted by electromagnetic radiation; infra-red radiation.

radiate (rā′dĭ āt′), *v.,* **-ated, -ating,** *adj.* —*v.i.* **1.** to spread or move like rays or radii from a centre. **2.** to emit rays, as of light or heat; irradiate. **3.** to issue or proceed in rays. —*v.t.* **4.** to emit in rays; disseminate as from a centre. **5.** (of persons) to exhibit abundantly (good humour, benevolence, etc.). —*adj.* **6.** radiating from a centre. **7.** represented with rays proceeding from it, as a head on a coin, in art, etc. [t. L: m. s. *radiātus,* pp.] —**radiative** (rā′dĭ ə tĭv), *adj.*

radiation (rā′dĭ ā′shən), *n.* **1.** *Physics.* **a.** the emission and diffusion of rays of particles, electromagnetic waves, or soundwaves. **b.** radiant energy or a particular form of it. **c.** the emission of rays by a radioactive substance, which may consist either of particles or electromagnetic waves. **2.** the act or process of radiating. **3.** that which is radiated; a ray or rays. **4.** radial arrangement of parts.

radiation potential, *Physics.* the energy in electron-volts required to transfer an electron from its normal position in an atom to a position of greater energy.

radiation sickness, illness caused by exposure to ionizing radiations or the consumption of radioactive materials.

radiative (rā′dĭ ə tĭv), *adj.* emitting radiation.

radiative capture, *Physics.* the capture of a particle by an atomic nucleus which causes the prompt emission of gamma radiation.

radiative collision, *Physics.* a collision between charged particles in which part of the kinetic energy is converted into electromagnetic radiation.

radiator (rā′dĭ ā′tə), *n.* **1.** one who or that which radiates. **2.** any of various heating devices, as a series or coil of pipes through which steam or hot water passes. **3.** a device constructed from thin-walled tubes and metal fins, used for cooling circulating water, as in the cooling system of a motor-car engine, etc. **4.** *Radio.* a type of aerial.

radical (răd′ĭ kl), *adj.* **1.** going to the root or origin; fundamental: *a radical change.* **2.** thoroughgoing or extreme, esp. towards reform. **3.** (*often cap.*) **a.** favouring drastic political, social or other reforms. **b.** belonging or pertaining to a political party holding such views. **4.** forming the basis or foundation. **5.** existing inherently in a thing or person: *radical defects of character.* **6.** *Maths.* **a.** pertaining to or forming a root. **b.** denoting or pertaining to the radical sign. **7.** *Gram.* of or pertaining to a root. **8.** *Bot.* of or arising from the root or the base of the stem. —*n.* **9.** one who holds or follows extreme principles, esp. left-wing political principles; an extremist. **10.** (*often cap.*) **a.** one who advocates fundamental and drastic political reforms or changes. **b.** a member of a radical (political) party. **11.** *Maths.* **a.** a quantity expressed as a root of another quantity. **b.** a radical sign. **12.** *Chem.* an atom or group of atoms regarded as an important constituent of a molecule, which remains unchanged and behaves as a unit in many reactions. **13.** *Gram.* a root. [ME, t. LL: s. *rādīcālis,* der. L *rādix* root] —**rad′icalness,** *n.*

—**Syn. 2.** RADICAL, EXTREME, FANATICAL denote that which goes beyond moderation or even to excess in opinion, belief, action, etc. RADICAL emphasizes the idea of going to the root of a matter, and this often seems immoderate in its thoroughness or completeness: *radical ideas, radical changes, reforms.* EXTREME applies to excessively biased ideas, intemperate conduct, or repressive legislation: *to use extreme measures.* FANATICAL is applied to a person who has extravagant views, esp. in matters of religion or morality, which render him incapable of sound judgements; and excessive zeal which leads him to take violent action against those who have other views: *fanatical in persecuting others.*

radical axis, *Geom.* (of two circles) the line such that tangents drawn from any point of the line to the two circles are equal in length.

radicalism (răd′ĭ kə lĭz′əm), *n.* **1.** the holding or following of radical or extreme views or principles, esp. left-wing political principles. **2.** the principles or practices of radicals.

radically (răd′ĭ klĭ), *adv.* **1.** with regard to origin or root. **2.** in a complete or fundamental manner.

radical sign, *Maths.* the symbol √ or $\sqrt{}$ (initially the first letter of *radix*) indicating extraction of a root of the following quantity: $\sqrt{a^2} = \pm a$, $\sqrt[3]{a^3 b^3} = ab$.

radicel (răd′ĭ sĕl′), *n. Bot.* a minute root; a rootlet. [t. NL: m. s. *rādicella*, dim. of L *rādix* root]

radicle (răd′ĭ kl), *n. Bot.* **1.** the lower part of the axis of an embryo; the primary root. **2.** a rudimentary root; a radicel or rootlet. **3.** *U.S. Chem.* a radical. **4.** *Anat.* a small rootlike part, as the beginning of a nerve fibre. [t. L: m. *rādicula*, dim. of *rādix* root]

radii (rā′dĭ ī′), *n.* pl. of **radius.**

radio (rā′dĭ ō′), *n., pl.* **-dios,** *adj., v.,* **-dioed, -dioing.** —*n.* **1.** wireless telegraphy or telephony: *speeches broadcast by radio.* **2.** an apparatus for receiving radio broadcasts; a wireless. **3.** a message transmitted by radio. —*adj.* **4.** pertaining to, used in, or sent by radio. **5.** pertaining to or employing radiations, as of electrical energy. —*v.t.* **6.** to transmit (a message, etc.) by radio. **7.** to send a message to (a person) by radio. —*v.i.* **8.** to transmit a message, etc., by radio. [short for *radiotelegraphic* (or *-telephonic*) *instrument, message,* or *transmission*]

radio-, a word element meaning: **1.** radio. **2.** radial. **3.** radium, radioactive, or radiant energy. [orig. comb. form of RADIUS]

radioactivate (rā′dĭ ō ăk′tĭ vāt′), *v.t.,* **-vated, -vating.** *Physics.* to make radioactive. —**ra′dioac′tiva′tion,** *n.*

radioactive (rā′dĭ ō ăk′tĭv), *adj. Physics, Chem.* possessing, pertaining to, or caused by radioactivity.

radioactive age, *Physics.* the age of a mineral, fossil, or wooden object as estimated from its content of radioactive isotopes.

radioactive series, *Physics, Chem.* the series of isotopes of various elements through which a radioactive substance decays before it reaches a stable state. The three known spontaneous series start with thorium and two different isotopes of uranium and each ends at a stable isotope of lead.

radioactive standard, *Physics.* a specimen of a material containing a radioactive isotope of known rate of decay; used for calibrating instruments for measuring radiation.

radioactive tracer. See **tracer** (def. 5).

radioactivity (rā′dĭ ō ăk tĭv′ĭ tĭ), *n. Physics, Chem.* the property of spontaneous disintegration possessed by certain elements due to changes in their atomic nuclei. The disintegration is accompanied by the emission of alpha-, beta-, or gamma-radiation.

radio altimeter, *Aeron.* an electronic altimeter which indicates the height of an aircraft by measuring the time taken for an emitted radio wave to travel to the ground and back again.

radioastronomy (rā′dĭ ō ə strŏn′ə mĭ), *n.* the branch of astronomy based on the radio-frequency radiation (as distinct from light) which is received on the earth. —**radioastronomical** (rā′dĭ ō ăs′trə nŏm′ĭ kl), *adj.*

radioautograph (rā′dĭ ō ô′tə grăf′, -gräf′), *n.* autoradiograph.

radio beacon, a radio transmitter emitting a characteristic signal so as to enable ships or aircraft to determine their position or bearing by a receiving instrument (**radio compass).**

radio beam, beam (def. 13).

radiobiology (rā′dĭ ō bī ŏl′ə jĭ), *n.* the branch of biology concerned with the effects of radiation on living organisms and the behaviour of radioactive materials, or the use of radioactive tracers, in biological systems.

radiocarbon dating (rā′dĭ ō kä′bən), the determination of the age of objects of plant or animal origin by means of their content of radioactive carbon ($^{14}_{6}C$). Also, **carbon dating.**

radio channel, a band of frequencies assigned for a specific communication purpose.

radiochemistry (rā′dĭ ō kĕm′ĭs trĭ), *n.* the chemical study of radioactive elements, both natural and artificial, and their use in the study of other chemical processes.

radio-compass (rā′dĭ ō kŭm′pəs), *n.* any device, as a radio receiver with a directional aerial, which can be used for position-finding.

radio control, 1. the remote control of an apparatus, as a pilotless aircraft or the like, by means of signals from a radio transmitter. **2.** the direction of a vehicle, as a police car or taxi, by instructions from a radio transmitter. —**ra′dio-controlled′,** *adj.*

radio direction-finder. See **direction-finder.**

radioelement (rā′dĭ ō ĕl′ĭ mənt), *n.* **1.** an element which is naturally radioactive. **2.** a radioisotope.

radiofrequency (rā′dĭ ō frē′kwən sĭ), *n., pl.* **-cies. 1.** the frequency of the transmitting waves of a given radio message or broadcast. **2.** a frequency within the range of radio transmission, i.e. from about 10,000 to 3×10^{11} hertz. —*adj.* **3.** pertaining to, denoting, or operating at a radiofrequency. Also, **radio frequency.**

radiofrequency heating, industrial dielectric or induction heating when the frequency of the alternating field exceeds about 25 kilohertz.

radiofrequency welding, a method of welding thermoplastic materials in which the necessary heat is generated by the application of a radiofrequency field to the material.

radio galaxy, *Astron.* a galaxy which is observed to emit electromagnetic radiation of radiofrequencies.

radiogenic (rā′dĭ ō jĕn′ĭk), *adj. Physics.* resulting from radioactive decay.

radiogram (rā′dĭ ō grăm′), *n.* **1.** a combined radio and gramophone. **2.** a message transmitted by radiotelegraphy. **3.** a radiograph or X-ray photograph.

radiograph (rā′dĭ ō grăf′, -gräf′), *Chiefly U.S.* —*n.* **1.** an image or picture produced by the action of X-rays or other rays (as from radioactive substances) on a photographic plate; an X-ray photograph. —*v.t.* **2.** to make a radiograph of.

radiography (rā′dĭ ŏg′rə fĭ), *n.* the production of radiographs. —**ra′diog′rapher,** *n.* —**radiographic** (rā′dĭ ō-grăf′ĭk), *adj.*

radio interferometer, *Astron.* a type of radio telescope, based on the principle of the optical interferometer but operating on radiofrequencies. It consists of two or more aerials all receiving electromagnetic radiation from the same source and connected to the same receiver, thus producing an analysable interference pattern.

radioisotope (rā′dĭ ō ī′sə tōp′), *n.* a radioactive isotope, usually artificially produced, of a normally inert chemical element, used in physical and biological research, therapeutics, etc.

radiolarian (rā′dĭ ō lĕə′rĭ ən), *n.* any of the *Radiolaria*, an extensive group or order of minute marine protozoans, having amoeba-like bodies with fine radiating pseudopodia, and usually elaborate skeletons. [f. s. NL *Radiolāria*, pl., (der. L *radiolus*, dim. of *radius* ray) + -AN]

radio link, a radio communication circuit, comprising transmitters, receivers, and aerials, often used to join land-line circuits.

radiolocation (rā′dĭ ō lə kā′shən), *n. Elect.* radar.

radiological (rā′dĭ ō lŏj′ĭ kl), *adj.* **1.** involving radioactive materials: *radiological warfare.* **2.** pertaining to radiology.

radiology (rā′dĭ ŏl′ə jĭ), *n.* **1.** the science dealing with X-rays or rays from radioactive substances, esp. for medical uses. **2.** the examining or photographing of organs, etc., with such rays. —**ra′diol′ogist,** *n.*

radiolucent (rā′dĭ ō lo͞o′sənt), *adj.* permitting the passage of X-rays with little hindrance.

radioluminescence (rā′dĭ ō lo͞o′mĭ nĕs′əns), *n. Physics.* luminescence caused by radiation from a radioactive material.

radiolysis (rā′dĭ ŏl′ĭ sĭs), *n. Chem.* the chemical decomposition of a substance as a result of irradiation.

radiometeorograph (rā′dĭ ō mē′tyə rə grăf′, -gräf′), *n.* radiosonde.

radiometer (rā′dĭ ŏm′ĭ tə), *n.* **1.** an instrument for indicating the transformation of radiant energy into mechanical work, consisting of an exhausted glass vessel containing vanes which revolve about an axis when exposed to radiant energy. **2.** an instrument based on the same principle, but used for detecting and measuring small amounts of radiant energy. —**radiometric** (rā′dĭ ō mĕt′rĭk), *adj.* —**ra′diom′etry,** *n.*

Radiometer (def. 1)

radiomicrometer (rā′dĭ ō mī krŏm′ĭ tə), *n. Physics.* a sensitive instrument for measuring heat radiation, consisting of a thermocouple connected directly into a single copper loop which forms the coil of a galvanometer.

radionuclide (rā′dĭ ō nyo͞o′klīd), *n. Physics.* a radioactive nuclide.

radio-opaque (rā′dĭ ō ō pāk′), *adj.* opaque to radiation, hence, visible in X-ray photographs and under fluoroscopy. Also, **radiopaque** (rā′dĭ ō pāk′). —**radio-opacity** (rā′-dĭ ō ō păs′ĭ tĭ), *n.*

radioparent (rā′ dĭ ō pā′ rənt), *adj.* permitting the passage of X-rays without hindrance.

radiophone (rā′dĭ ō fōn′), *n.* **1.** any of various devices for producing sound by the action of radiant energy. Thus, light falling on a phototube will vary an electric current which can actuate a loudspeaker. **2.** a radiotelephone.

radio receiver, a device which converts the information conveyed by radio waves into soundwaves.

radio relay, a system which receives radio signals and retransmits them, thus establishing radio communication between two points which could not otherwise communicate directly.

radiosclerometer (rā′dĭ ō sklĭə rŏm′ĭ tə), *n. Physics.* a penetrometer (def. 2).

radioscopy (rā′dĭ ŏs′kə pĭ), *n.* the examination of opaque objects by means of the X-rays or rays emitted by radioactive substances. —**radioscopic** (rā′dĭ ō skŏp′ĭk), **ra′-dioscop′ical,** *adj.*

radio set, a radio receiver or transceiver.

radio signal, any electromagnetic wave emitted by a radio transmitter.

radiosonde (rā′dĭ ō sŏnd′), *n. Meteorol.* an instrument carried aloft by a balloon and sending back information, by means of a small radio transmitter, about the atmospheric temperature, pressure, and humidity encountered. [f. RADIO- + SONDE]

radio source, *Astron.* any cosmic source of electromagnetic radiation of radio frequency.

radio spectrum, the wavelength range of electromagnetic waves (approximately 30,000 metres to 1 millimetre or 10 kilohertz to 300,000 megahertz).

radio star, *Astron.* a discrete source of radiofrequency electromagnetic radiation outside the solar system.

radio station, 1. a combination of devices for radio transmitting and/or receiving. **2.** a complete installation for radio broadcasting, including transmitting apparatus, broadcasting studios, etc. **3.** an organization engaged in broadcasting, on a fixed frequency or frequencies, programmes of news, entertainment, propaganda, etc.

radiotelegram (rā′dĭ ō tĕl′ĭ grăm′), *n.* a message transmitted by radiotelegraphy.

radiotelegraph (rā′dĭ ō tĕl′ĭ grăf′, -gräf′), *n.* **1.** a radiotelegram. —*v.t., v.i.* **2.** to telegraph by radiotelegraphy. —**radiotelegraphic** (rā′dĭ ō tĕl′ĭ grăf′ĭk), *adj.*

radiotelegraphy (rā′dĭ ō tĭ lĕg′rə fĭ), *n.* telegraphy without wires or cables, in which messages are transmitted through space by means of the radiated energy of electromagnetic waves; wireless telegraphy.

radiotelephone (rā′dĭ ō tĕl′ĭ fōn′), *n., v.,* **-phoned, -phoning.** —*n.* **1.** a telephone in which the signal is transmitted by radiotelephony; wireless telephone. —*v.t., v.i.* **2.** to telephone by radiotelephony. —**radiotelephonic** (rā′-dĭ ō tĕl′ĭ fŏn′ĭk), *adj.*

radiotelephony (rā′dĭ ō tĭ lĕf′ə nĭ), *n.* a system of transmitting and receiving voice messages by means of radio; wireless telephony.

radio telescope, a large parabolic reflector, or a radio interferometer, used to gather radio signals emitted by celestial bodies or spacecraft and focus them for reception by a receiver. See **radio astronomy.**

radiotherapy (rā′dĭ ō thĕ′rə pĭ), *n.* treatment of disease by means of X-rays or of radioactive substances.

radiothermy (rā′dĭ ō thû′mĭ), *n.* therapy which utilizes the heat from a short-wave radio apparatus or diathermy machine.

radiothorium (rā′dĭ ō thô′rĭ əm), *n.* a disintegration product of thorium. [NL. See RADIO-, THORIUM]

radio transmitter, an apparatus which emits electromagnetic radiation modulated by signals.

radio valve, valve (def. 7). Also, **radio tube.**

radio wave, *Radio.* an electromagnetic wave of radiofrequency.

radish (răd′ĭsh), *n.* **1.** the crisp, pungent, edible root of a cruciferous plant, *Raphanus sativus.* **2.** the plant. [late ME; OE *rædic,* t. L: m. s. *rādix* root, radish]

radium (rā′dyəm), *n. Chem.* a naturally occurring radioactive metallic element with chemical properties resembling those of barium. *Symbol:* Ra; *at. wt of most stable isotope:* 226; *at. no.:* 88. [NL, der. L *radius* ray]

radium A, a substance, formed from radon by disintegration, which gives rise to radium B.

radium B, an isotope of lead, formed from radium A by disintegration, which gives rise to an isotope of bismuth called **radium C,** from which **radium D, radium E,** and **radium F** (polonium) are derived.

radium emanation, *Chem.* radon.

radius (rā′dyəs), *n., pl.* **-dii** (-dĭ ī′), **-diuses, 1.** a straight line extending from the centre of a circle or sphere to the circumference or surface. **2.** the length of such a line. **3.** any radial or radiating part. **4.** a circular area of an extent indicated by the length of the radius of its circumscribing circle: *every house within a radius of fifty miles.* **5.** field or range of operation or influence. **6.** extent of possible operation, travel, etc., as under a single supply of fuel: *the flying radius of an aeroplane.* **7.** *Anat.* that one of the two bones of the forearm which is on the thumb side. **8.** *Zool.* a corresponding bone in the forelimb of other vertebrates. **9.** *Mach.* the throw of an eccentric wheel or cam. [t. L: staff, rod, spoke of a wheel, radius, ray or beam of light]

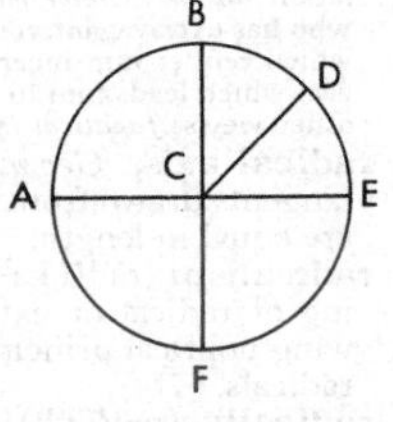

Radii: CA, CB, CD, CE, CF

radius of curvature, *Maths.* the radius of the circle or sphere of which a curve or surface forms part.

radius of gyration, *Physics.* the square root of the quotient of the moment of inertia of a body, about a given axis, and its mass.

radius vector (vĕk′tə), *pl.* **radii vectores** (vĕk tô′rēz), **radius vectors. 1.** *Maths.* the length of the line segment joining a fixed point or origin to a variable point. **2.** *Astron.* a line (or distance) from the sun or the like taken as a fixed point or origin, to a planet or the like as a variable point. [see RADIUS, VECTOR]

radix (rā′dĭks), *n., pl.* **radices** (rā′dĭ sēz′), **radixes. 1.** *Maths.* a number taken as the base of a system of numbers, logarithms, or the like. **2.** *Bot.* a root; a radical. **3.** *Gram.* a root (def. 11). [t. L: root]

Radnorshire (răd′nə shĭə′, -shə), *n.* a county in E Wales. 18,431 pop. (1961); 471 sq. mi. *Co. town:* Presteign. Also, **Radnor.**

Radom (*Pol.* rȧ′dŏm), *n.* a town in E Poland. 141,000 (est. 1964).

radome (rā′dōm′), *n.* a domed cover over an aerial system designed to allow the free passage of radio waves.

radon (rā′dŏn), *n. Chem.* a rare, chemically inert, radioactive gaseous element produced in the disintegration of radium. *Symbol.:* Rn; *at. no.:* 86; *at. wt:* 222. Also, **radium emanation.** [f. RAD(IUM) + *-on,* modelled on ARGON, NEON]

radula (răd′yŏŏ lə), *n., pl.* **-lae** (-lē′). a chitinous band in the mouth of most molluscs, set with numerous minute horny teeth, and drawn backwards and forwards over the odontophore in the process of breaking up food. [t. L: a scraper] —**rad′ular,** *adj.*

Raeburn (rā′bûn′), *n.* **Sir Henry,** 1756–1823, Scottish portrait painter.

R.A.E.C., Royal Army Educational Corps.

RAF, Royal Air Force. Also, **R.A.F.**

raf (răf), *n. Colloq.* the Royal Air Force.

raff (răf), *n.* **1.** the riffraff; the rabble. **2.** *Scot. and N Dial.* refuse, rubbish. [appar. abstracted from RIFFRAFF]

raffia (răf′ĭ ə), *n.* **1.** a species of palm, *Raphia pedunculata,* of Madagascar, bearing long, plume-like, pinnate leaves, the leafstalks of which yield an important fibre. **2.** the fibre, much used for tying plants, cut flowers, small parcels, etc., and for making matting, baskets, hats, and the like. **3.** some other palm of the same genus. **4.** its fibre. [t. Malagasy]

raffinose (răf′ĭ nōs′), *n. Chem.* a colourless crystalline trisaccharide, $C_{18}H_{32}O_{16}.5H_2O$, with little or no sweetness, occurring in the sugar beet, cottonseed, etc., and breaking down to fructose, glucose, and galactose on hydrolysis. [f. s. F *raffiner* refine + -OSE[2]]

raffish (răf′ĭsh), *adj.* **1.** disreputable, rakish. **2.** vulgar, tawdry. [f. RAFF + -ISH[1]] —**raff′ishly,** *adv.* —**raff′-ishness,** *n.*

raffle[1] (răf′əl), *n., v.,* **-fled, -fling.** —*n.* **1.** a lottery in which the prizes are usually goods rather than money. —*v.t.* **2.** to dispose of by a raffle (sometimes fol. by *off*): *to raffle off a watch.* —*v.i.* **3.** to take part in a raffle. [ME *rafle,* t. OF: m. *raffle* kind of game at dice, net, plundering, der. *rafler* scratch, t. D: m. *rafelen* ravel] —**raf′fler,** *n.*

raffle[2] (răf′əl), *n.* **1.** rubbish. **2.** *U.S. Naut.* shakings. [der. RAFF (def. 2)]

Raffles (răf′əlz), *n.* **Sir Thomas Stamford** (stăm′fəd), 1781–1826, English colonial administrator; founded Singapore.

rafflesia (ră flē′zhĭ ə, -zĭ ə), *n.* one of the genus *Rafflesia* of Malaysian parasitic plants, as *R.arnoldi* which has fleshy flowers 18 inches across. [named after Sir Thomas RAFFLES]

raft[1] (räft), *n.* **1.** a more or less rigid floating platform made of buoyant materials, assembled for ease of transport or for the conveyance of people, their possessions, etc. **2.** such a platform for use in an emergency, often collapsible. **3.** a slab of reinforced concrete extending entirely under a building used to spread the weight of the building over the whole area, esp. on yielding soils. —*v.t.* **4.** to transport on a raft. **5.** to form (logs, etc.) into a raft. **6.** to navigate by a raft. —*v.i.* **7.** to use a raft; go or travel on a raft. [ME *rafte* beam, rafter, t. Scand.; cf. Icel. *raptr* log]

raft[2] (räft), *n. U.S. Colloq.* a great quantity or number: *a raft of trouble.* [var. of *raff* large number (ME abundance, plenty). See RAFF]

rafter (räf′tə), *n.* **1.** one of the sloping timbers or members substaining the outer covering of a roof. —*v.t.* **2.** to furnish with rafters. See diag. under **curb roof.** [ME; OE *ræfter*, c. MLG *rafter*. See RAFT[1]]

raftsman (räfts′mən), *n., pl.* **-men.** a man who manages, or is employed on, a raft.

R.A.F.V.R., Royal Air Force Volunteer Reserve.

rag[1] (răg), *n.* **1.** a comparatively worthless fragment of cloth, esp. one resulting from tearing or wear. **2.** (*pl.*) ragged or tattered clothing. **3.** a shred, scrap, or fragmentary bit of anything. **4.** *Colloq.* an article of cloth, paper, etc., such as a handkerchief, a theatre curtain, or a piece of paper money. **5.** *Colloq.* a newspaper or magazine, esp. one considered as being of little value. **6.** *Colloq.* a wretched or worthless person or thing. **7.** *Colloq.* a song or a piece of instrumental music in ragtime. **8.** *Bot.* the axis and carpellary walls of a citrus fruit. **9.** *Bldg Trades.* a stone or slate left rough on one side or edge. **10. chew the rag,** *Slang.* to argue or grumble. **11. glad rags,** *Colloq.* fine clothes. [ME *ragg(e)*, t. Scand.; cf. Icel. *rögg* shag]

rag[2] (răg), *v.,* **ragged, ragging,** *n. Slang.* —*v.t.* **1.** to scold. **2.** to tease; torment. **3.** to play rough jokes on. —*n.* **4.** any disorderly or high-spirited conduct, esp. by a group of young people. **5.** (in certain student communities) an organized display of grotesque or absurd behaviour publicizing a collection of money for charity, or the like. [cf. Icel. *ragna* curse, swear]

ragamuffin (răg′ə mŭf′ĭn), *n.* **1.** a ragged, disreputable person; a tatterdemalion. **2.** a ragged child.

rag-and-bone man (răg′ən bōn′), a dealer in discarded clothing, furniture, household articles, etc. Also, **rag-and-bone merchant.**

ragbag (răg′băg′), *n.* **1.** a bag for scraps of fabric. **2.** a slovenly or unkempt person.

rag bolt, a foundation bolt with a long, tapered, jagged head around which molten lead or concrete can be poured to provide an anchorage.

rage (rāj), *n., v.,* **raged, raging.** —*n.* **1.** angry fury; violent anger: *to fall into a rage.* **2.** fury or violence of wind, waves, fire, disease, etc. **3.** violence of feeling, desire, or appetite: *the rage of thirst.* **4.** a violent desire or passion. **5.** ardour; fervour; enthusiasm: *poetic rage.* **6.** the object of widespread enthusiasm: *chess became all the rage.* **7.** *Obs.* insanity. —*v.i.* **8.** to act or speak with fury; show or feel violent anger. **9.** to move, rush, dash, or surge furiously. **10.** to proceed, continue, or prevail with great violence: *the battle raged ten days.* **11.** (of feelings, etc.) to hold sway with unabated violence. [ME, t. OF, g. VL *rabia*, for L *rabies* madness, rage. See RABIES] —**Syn. 1.** frenzy, passion. See **anger. 6.** vogue, fad, fashion, craze. **8.** rave, fume.

ragged (răg′ĭd), *adj.* **1.** clothed in tattered garments. **2.** torn or worn to rags; tattered: *ragged clothing.* **3.** shaggy, as an animal, its coat, etc. **4.** having loose or hanging shreds or fragmentary bits: *a ragged wound.* **5.** full of rough or sharp projections; jagged: *ragged stones.* **6.** in a wild or neglected state: *a ragged garden.* **7.** rough, imperfect, or faulty: *a ragged piece of work.* **8.** irregular: *a ragged volley of shots.* **9.** harsh, as sound, the voice, etc. —**rag′gedly,** *adv.* —**rag′gedness,** *n.*

ragged robin, a caryophyllaceous plant, *Lychnis flos-cuculi*, bearing pink or white flowers with dissected petals, widespread in Europe and Asia.

ragged school, (formerly) a charity school for poor children.

raggle-taggle (răg′l tăg′l), *adj.* motley; unkempt.

ragi (răg′ĭ), *n.* a cereal grass, *Eleusine coracana*, cultivated in Asia, etc., for its grain. Also, **raggee, raggy.** [t. Hind.: m. *rāgī*]

raglan (răg′lən), *n.* **1.** a loose overcoat the sleeves of which are cut so as to continue up to the collar. —*adj.* **2.** (of a coat or sleeve) tailored in such a manner. [named after Lord *Raglan*, 1788–1855, British field marshal]

ragman (răg′măn′, -mən), *n., pl.* **-men** (-mĕn′, -mən). a man who gathers, or deals in, rags.

Ragnarok (răg′nə rŏk′), *n. Scand. Myth.* the destruction of the gods and all things in a great battle with evil powers. Also, **Ragnarök** (răg′nə rŏk′).

ragout (răg′ōō), *n., v.,* **-gouted** (răg′ōōd), **-gouting** (răg′ōō ĭng). —*n.* **1.** a highly seasoned stew of poultry or meat and vegetables, usually flavoured with mushrooms, tomatoes, port wine, etc. —*v.t.* **2.** to make into a ragout. [t. F, der. *ragoûter* restore the appetite of, der. *re-* RE- + *à* (g. L *ad*) to + *goût* (g. L *gustus*) taste]

rag-picker (răg′pĭk′ə), *n.* one who picks up rags and other waste material from the streets, refuse heaps, etc., for a livelihood.

ragtag and bobtail (răg′tăg′), riffraff or rabble.

ragtime (răg′tīm′), *n. Music.* **1.** rhythm marked by frequent syncopation, such as is common in early American Negro piano music. **2.** music in this rhythm. [prob. alter. of *ragged time*]

rag trade, *Colloq.* the clothes-manufacturing trade.

Ragusa (rə gōō′zə; *It.* rä gōō′zä), *n.* **1.** Italian name of **Dubrovnik. 2.** a town in Italy, in S Sicily. 59,805 (1966).

ragweed (răg′wēd′), *n.* **1.** any of the composite herbs constituting the genus *Ambrosia*, whose airborne pollen is the most prevalent cause of autumnal hay fever, as the common ragweed, *A. artemisiifolia*, and the **giant ragweed,** *A. trifida.* **2.** the ragwort.

ragwort (răg′wût′), *n.* any of various composite plants of the genus *Senecio*, as *S. jacobaea*, a yellow-flowered Old World herb with irregularly lobed leaves, or a North American species, *S. aureus* (**golden ragwort**), also bearing yellow flowers.

rah (rä), *interj.* (an exclamation.) [short for HURRAH]

Rahman Putra Al-Haj (rä′mən pōō′trə äl häj′), **Tunku Abdul** (tŏŏng′kōō äb′dōōl), born 1903, Malaysian statesman: prime minister of Malaya 1957–59, 1959–63, and prime minister of Malaysia since 1964.

raia (rä′yə, rī′ə), *n. Obs.* rayah.

raid (rād), *n.* **1.** a sudden onset or attack, as upon something to be seized or suppressed: *a police raid on a gambling house.* **2.** *Mil.* a sudden attack on the enemy, esp. by air or by a small force. —*v.t.* **3.** to make a raid on. —*v.i.* **4.** to engage in a raid. [ME *raide*, OE *rād* expedition, lit., riding. See ROAD] —**raid′er,** *n.* —**Syn. 2.** incursion, invasion, inroad.

Raikes (rāks), *n.* **Robert,** 1735–1811, English founder of a Sunday school movement.

rail[1] (rāl), *n.* **1.** a bar of wood or metal fixed more or less horizontally for any of various purposes, as for a support, barrier, fence, railing, etc. **2.** a fence; a railing, esp. (*pl.*) at a racecourse. **3.** one of a pair of steel bars that provide a guide and running surface for the wheels of vehicles. **4.** the railway, as a means of transportation: *to travel by rail.* **5.** (*pl.*) *Stock Exchange.* stocks, shares, etc., of railways. **6.** *Naut.* the upper part of the bulwarks of a ship. **7.** a horizontal timber or piece in a framework or in panelling. **8. off the rails,** in an abnormal condition; insane; out of control. —*v.t.* **9.** to furnish with a rail or rails. **10.** to enclose with a fence, rail or rails (usually fol. by *in* or *off*). [ME *raylle*, t. OF: m. *reille*, g. L *rēgula* rule, straight stick, bar. See RULE]

rail[2] (rāl), *v.i.* **1.** to utter bitter complaint or vehement denunciation (often fol. by *at* or *against*): *to rail at fate.* —*v.t.* **2.** to bring, force, etc., by railing. [late ME, t. F: m. s. *railler* deride, t. Pr.: m. *ralhar* chatter, ult. der. L *ragere* shriek] —**rail′er,** *n.*

rail[3] (rāl), *n.* any of numerous wading birds constituting the subfamily *Rallinae* (family *Rallidae*), characterized by short wings, a narrow body, strong legs, long toes, and a harsh cry, and abounding in marshes in most parts of the world, as the European **water-rail** (*Rallus aquaticus*). [late ME, t. OF: m. *raale*, c. Pr. *rascla*, prob. ult. der. L *rādere* scratch]

Water-rail, *Rallus aquaticus* (Length 11 in.)

railcar (rāl′kä′), *n.* **1.** Also, **railcoach** (rāl′kōch′). a self-propelled railway carriage. **2.** *U.S.* a railway carriage.

railhead (rāl′hĕd′), *n.* **1.** the farthest point to which a railway has been laid. **2.** *Chiefly Mil.* a railway depot at which supplies are unloaded to be distributed or forwarded by other means.

railing (rā′lĭng), *n.* **1.** (*often pl.*) a barrier made of rails, rails and supports, etc. **2.** rails collectively.

raillery (rā′lə rĭ), *n., pl.* **-ries. 1.** good-humoured ridicule; banter. **2.** a bantering remark. [t. F: m. *raillerie.* See RAIL[2]]

railman (rāl′măn′), *n., pl.* **-men** (-mĕn′). a railway worker.

railroad (rāl′rōd′), *U.S.* —*n.* **1.** a railway. —*v.t.* **2.** to transport by means of a railway. **3.** to supply with railways. **4.** *Colloq.* to send or push forward with great or undue speed: *to railroad a bill through Congress.* **5.** to force or compel, esp. by unfair means: *he was railroaded out of office.* **6.** *Slang.* to convict (a person) unjustly or with undue haste.

railway (rāl′wā′), *n.* **1.** a permanent road or way, laid or provided with rails of steel, iron, etc., commonly in one or more pairs of continuous lines forming a track or tracks, on which vehicles run for the transporting of passengers, goods, and mail. **2.** such a road together with its rolling stock, buildings, etc.; the entire railway plant, including fixed and movable property. **3.** the company of persons owning or operating it. **4.** any line or lines of rails forming a track for flanged-wheel equipment.

railway curve, one of a set of templates used by draughtsmen for marking curves to scale; French curve.

railwayman (rāl′wā mən), *n., pl.* **-men.** a railway worker.

raiment (rā′mənt), *n. Archaic or Poetic.* clothing; apparel; attire. [ME *rayment,* aphetic var. of *arrayment.* See ARRAY]

rain (rān), *n.* **1.** water in drops falling from the sky to the earth, being condensed from the aqueous vapour in the atmosphere. **2.** a rainfall, rainstorm, or shower. **3.** (*pl.*) the seasonal rainfalls, or the rainy or wet season, in some regions, as India. **4.** a large quantity of anything falling thickly: *a rain of blows.* **5. right as rain,** perfectly all right. **6. Sea of Rains,** a plain, *Mare Imbrium,* on the face of the moon. *—v.i.* **7.** (of rain) to fall: *it rained all night.* **8.** to fall like rain: *tears rained from her eyes.* **9.** to send down or let fall rain (said of God, the sky, the clouds, etc.). *—v.t.* **10.** to send down, scatter, or sprinkle (rain, etc.). **11.** to offer, bestow, or give abundantly: *to rain blows upon a person.* **12. rain cats and dogs,** to rain heavily. **13. rained off,** prevented from taking place by rain. [ME *rein,* OE *regn,* c. D *regen,* G *Regen,* Icel. *regn*]

rainband (rān′bănd′), *n. Physics.* a dark band in the solar spectrum, due to water-vapour in the atmosphere.

rainbow (rān′bō′), *n.* **1.** a bow or arc of prismatic colours appearing in the sky opposite the sun, due to the refraction and reflection of the sun's rays in drops of rain. **2.** a similar bow of colours, esp. one appearing in the spray of cataracts, etc. **3.** any array of many bright colours. **4.** the spectrum. **5. Bay of Rainbows,** a plain, *Sinus Iridium,* on the face of the moon. *—adj.* **6.** multicoloured. [ME *reinbowe,* OE *regnboga,* c. OHG *reginbogo,* Icel. *regnbogi*]

rainbow trout, a trout, *Salmo gairdnerii,* native to North America in the coastal waters and streams from Lower California to Alaska but introduced elsewhere.

raincheck (rān′chĕk′), *n. U.S.* **1.** a ticket for future use given to spectators at a baseball game, sports meeting, etc., stopped by rain. **2.** *Colloq.* a postponement (as of an invitation, etc.).

raincoat (rān′kōt′), *n.* a waterproof coat, worn as a protection from rain.

raindrop (rān′drŏp′), *n.* a drop of rain.

rainfall (rān′fôl′), *n.* **1.** a fall or shower of rain. **2.** the amount of water falling as rain, snow, etc., within a given time and area, ordinarily expressed as a hypothetical depth of coverage: *a rainfall of 70 inches a year.*

rainforest (rān′fŏ′rĭst), *n.* dense forest found in tropical and temperate areas with high humidity and heavy rainfall occurring throughout the year.

rain gauge, an instrument for measuring rainfall. Also, *U.S.,* **rain gage.**

Rainier (rā′nĭ ə, rā nĭə′, rə nĭə′), *n.* **Mount,** a mountain in the U.S., in W Washington, in the Cascade Range. 14,408 ft. Also, **Mount Tacoma.**

Rainier III (rā′nĭ ā′), **Rainier Louis Henri Maxence Bertrand de Grimaldi** (*Fr.* rĕ nyĕ′ lwē äN rē măk sāNs bĕr trăN′ də grē măl dē′), **Prince of Monaco,** born 1923, reigning prince of Monaco since 1949.

rainproof (rān′pro͞of′), *adj.* **1.** proof against rain; impervious to rain. *—v.t.* **2.** to make impervious to rain.

rain shadow, a drier area to the lee of a mountain range in the path of rain-bearing winds.

rainstorm (rān′stôm′), *n.* a storm accompanied by heavy rain.

rainwater (rān′wô′tə), *n.* water fallen as rain, and thus relatively free of impurities.

rainy (rā′nĭ), *adj.,* **-nier, -niest.** **1.** characterized by rain: *rainy weather, a rainy region.* **2.** wet with rain: *rainy streets.* **3.** bringing rain: *rainy clouds.* **4. a rainy day,** a time of need or emergency in the future. **—rain′iness,** *n.*

Raipur (rī′po͝oə), *n.* a town in India, in SE Madhya Pradesh. 139,792 (1961).

raise (rāz), *v.,* **raised, raising,** *n.* *—v.t.* **1.** to move to a higher position; lift up; elevate: *to raise one's hand.* **2.** to set upright; lift up. **3.** to cause to rise or stand up. **4.** *Archaic.* to rouse. **5.** to build; erect: *to raise a monument.* **6.** *U.S.* to set up the framework of (a house, etc.). **7.** to cause to project; bring into relief. **8.** to cause to be or appear: *to raise a tempest.* **9.** *Chiefly U.S.* to cultivate, produce, breed (crops, plants, animals, etc.). **10.** to bring up; rear (children, etc.). **11.** to give rise to; bring up or about (a question, issue, etc.); put forward (an objection, etc.). **12.** *Law.* to institute (a lawsuit, etc.). **13.** to restore to life: *to raise the dead.* **14.** to stir up: to raise a rebellion. **15.** to give vigour to; animate (the mind, spirits, hopes). **16.** to advance in rank, dignity, etc.: *to raise someone to the peerage.* **17.** to gather together; collect: *to raise an army, raise funds.* **18.** to increase in height or thickness. **19.** to cause (dough, etc.) to rise and become light, as by the addition of yeast. **20.** to increase in degree, intensity, pitch, or force. **21.** to utter (a cry, etc.) esp. in a loud voice. **22.** to make (the voice) louder. **23.** to express, as in protest, agreement, or the like. **24.** to increase in amount, as rent, prices, wages, etc. **25.** to increase the price of (a commodity, stock, etc.). **26.** *Poker, etc.* to bet more than (another player, or previous bet). **27.** *Mil.* to end (a siege or blockade), by withdrawing or repelling the besieging forces. **28.** to remove (a prohibition, etc.). **29.** *Naut.* to come in sight of (as by its rising above the horizon in coming nearer); sight. **30.** *Maths.* to multiply (a number) by itself for a stated number of times: *100 is 10 raised to the power of 2.* **31.** *Colloq.* to establish communication with, as by two-way radio: *we tried in vain to raise headquarters.* **32. raise Cain** or **hell,** to create a disturbance, nuisance, or trouble. **33. raise the roof,** *Colloq.* to cause a great noise, excitement, etc. *—n.* **34.** *Chiefly U.S.* a rise (in wages). **35.** *Chiefly U.S.* the amount of such an increase. **36.** a raising, lifting, etc. [ME *reise(n),* t. Scand.; cf. Icel. *reisa,* c. OE *rǣran* raise, causative of OE *rīsan* RISE. See REAR²] **—raise′able,** *n.* **—rais′er,** *n.*

—Syn. 1, 2. RAISE, LIFT, HEAVE, HOIST imply bringing something up above its original position. RAISE, the most general word, may mean to bring something to or towards an upright position with one end resting on the ground; or it may be used like LIFT of moving an object generally a comparatively short distance upwards, but breaking completely its physical contact with the place where it has been: *to raise a ladder; to lift a package.* HEAVE implies lifting with effort or exertion: *to heave a huge box on to a lorry.* HOIST implies lifting slowly and gradually something of considerable weight, usually with mechanical help, such as a crane or derrick: *to hoist steel beams to the top of the framework of a building.* See **rise.** **—Ant. 1.** lower.

raised beach, *Phys. Geog.* an ancient wave-cut platform cut into a cliff, and now above sea-level as a result of a relative fall in sea-level.

raised pie, a pie made with hot-water crust pastry which becomes firm during baking and retains its shape, usually served cold, filled with stock which sets into a jelly.

raisin (rā′zən), *n.* **1.** a grape of any of various sweet varieties dried in the sun or artificially, and used in cookery, etc. **2.** dark bluish purple. [ME *razin,* t. OF, g. L *racēmus* cluster of grapes]

raison d'état (*Fr.* rĕ zôN dē tä′), *French.* reason of state; for the good of the country as a whole.

raison d'être (*Fr.* rĕ zôN dĕ′tr), *French.* reason or justification for being or existence.

raj (räj), *n.* (in India) rule; dominion: *the British raj.*

raja (rä′jə), *n.* **1.** (in India) **a.** a king or prince. **b.** a chief or dignitary. **c.** an honorary title conferred on Hindus in India. **2.** a title of rulers, princes, or chiefs in Java, Borneo, etc. Also, **rajah.** [t. Hind.: m. *rājā,* c. L *rex* king]

Rajahmundry (rä′jə mo͞on′drĭ), *n.* a town in India, in NE Andhra Pradesh. 130,002 (1961).

Rajasthan (rä′jə stän′), *n.* a state in NW India; formerly Rajputana and a group of small states. 20,155,602 pop. (1961); 132,078 sq. mi. *Cap.*: Jaipur.

Rajkot (räj′kōt), *n.* a town in India, in Gujarat. 193,498 (1961).

Rajput (räj′po͝ot), *n.* a member of a Hindu race claiming descent from the ancient Kshatriya or warrior caste and noted for their military spirit. Also, **Rajpoot.** [t. Hind., f. Skt *rāj* king + *put(ra)* son. See RAJAH, RAJ]

Rajputana (räj′po͝o tä′nə), *n.* a former region in NW India, now making up the preponderant part of Rajasthan state.

Rakaia (rə kī′ə), *n.* a river in New Zealand, in South Island, flowing SE to the Canterbury Bight in the Pacific Ocean. 90 mi.

rake¹ (rāk), *n., v.,* **raked, raking.** *—n.* **1.** a long-handled tool with teeth or tines for gathering together hay or the like, breaking and smoothing the surface of ground, etc. **2.** a similar implement used in agriculture, esp. one drawn by a tractor. **3.** any of various implements having a similar form or function, as a croupier's implement for gathering in money on a gaming table. **4.** a long, forcible sweep or onset. —*v.t.* **5.** to gather together, draw, or remove with a rake: *to rake dead leaves from a lawn.* **6.** to clear, smooth, or prepare with a rake: *to rake a garden bed.* **7.** to clear (a fire, etc.) by stirring with a poker or the like. **8.** to gather or collect abundantly (often fol. by *in*): *to rake in the money.* **9.** to collect, esp. with difficulty (often fol. by *up*). **10.** to reveal, as to discredit someone (usually fol. by *up*): *to rake up an old scandal.* **11.** to search thoroughly through. **12.** to scrape; scratch; graze. **13.** to traverse with gunfire, the length of (a place, ship, a body of troops, etc.). **14.** to sweep with the eyes. —*v.i.* **15.** to use a rake. **16.** to search as with a rake. **17.** to scrape or sweep (fol. by *against, over,* etc.). [ME; OE *raca*]

rake[2] (rāk), *n.* a profligate or dissolute man, esp. one in fashionable society; a roué. [short for RAKEHELL]

rake[3] (rāk), *v.*, **raked, raking,** *n.* —*v.i.* **1.** to incline from the vertical (as a mast) or from the horizontal (as a stage). —*n.* **2.** inclination or slope away from the perpendicular or the horizontal, as of a ship's mast. **3.** *Aeron.* the angle measured between the tip edge of an aerofoil and the plane of symmetry. **4.** *Mach.* the angle between the cutting face of a tool and a plane perpendicular to the surface of the work at the cutting point. **5.** *Theat.* the slope of a stage down to the footlights. [orig. uncert.]

rake[4] (rāk), *v.i.*, **raked, raking. 1.** *Hunting.* **a.** (of a hawk) to fly along after the game, or to fly wide of it. **b.** (of a dog) to hunt with the nose close to the ground. **2.** *Dial.* to go or proceed, esp. with speed. [OE *racian* go, proceed, hasten, c. Sw. *raka* run, rush]

rakehell (rāk′hĕl′), *n. Archaic.* a roué; a rake. [f. RAKE[1] (def. 11) + HELL; r. ME *rakel*, adj., rash, rough, coarse, hasty, der. RAKE[4]]

rakehelly (rāk′hĕl′ĭ), *adj. Archaic.* profligate.

rake-off (rāk′ŏf′), *n. Slang.* **1.** a share or portion, as of a sum involved or of profits. **2.** a share or amount taken or received illicitly.

raki (rä kē′, răk′ĭ), *n.* an alcoholic spirit drink distilled from grain, grapes, plums, etc., flavoured with aniseed and mastic, in south-eastern Europe and the Near East. [t. Turk.: m. *rāqī*]

raking (rā′kĭng), *adj.* going swiftly, as a horse, or its stride.

raking shore, one of a set of sloping timbers used to support a wall that is bulging or a ship on the stocks.

rakish[1] (rā′kĭsh), *adj.* **1.** smart; jaunty; dashing. **2.** like a rake; dissolute. [f. RAKE[2] + -ISH[1]] —**rak′ishly,** *adv.* —**rak′ishness,** *n.*

rakish[2] (rā′kĭsh), *adj.* (of ships) having an appearance suggestive of speed and dash. [f. RAKE[3] + -ISH[1]]

râle (räl), *n. Pathol.* an abnormal sound accompanying the normal respiratory murmur, as in pulmonary diseases. [t. F, der. *râler* rattle when breathing, der. *râle* RAIL[3]]

Raleigh (rô′lĭ), *n.* **1.** Also, **Ralegh. Sir Walter,** 1552?–1618, English explorer and author, favourite of Queen Elizabeth I. **2.** a city in the U.S., the capital of North Carolina. 93,931 (est. 1960).

rall., rallentando.

rallentando (răl′ĕn tăn′dō; *It.* räl lĕn tän′dô), *adj. Music.* slackening; becoming slower. [It., ppr. of *rallentare* abate]

ralliform (răl′ĭ fôm′), *adj. Zool.* rail-like in shape, anatomy, etc. [t. NL: s. *ralliformis.* See RAIL[3]]

ralline (răl′īn, -ĭn), *adj.* belonging or pertaining to the subfamily *Rallinae,* or the family *Rallidae,* which includes the rails and their near relatives. [f. s. NL *Rallus* typical genus of rails + -INE[1]]

rally[1] (răl′ĭ), *v.*, **-lied, -lying,** *n., pl.* **-lies.** —*v.t.* **1.** to bring together or into order again: *to rally an army.* **2.** to draw or call (persons) together for common action. **3.** to concentrate or revive, as one's strength, spirits, etc. —*v.i.* **4.** to come together for common action. **5.** to come together or into order again. **6.** to come to the assistance of a person, party, or cause. **7.** to recover partially from illness. **8.** to acquire fresh strength or vigour: *the stock market rallied today.* **9.** *Tennis, etc.* to engage in a rally. —*n.* **10.** a recovery from dispersion or disorder, as of troops. **11.** a renewal or recovery of strength, activity, etc. **12.** a partial recovery of strength during illness. **13.** a drawing or coming together of persons, as for common action, as in a mass meeting. **14.** *Finance.* a sharp rise in price and active trading, after a declining market. **15.** *Tennis, etc.* the return of the ball by both sides a number of times consecutively. **16.** *Boxing.* an exchange of blows. **17.** a motor-car competition, mainly over public roads, in which speed is less important than skill and consistency in adhering to specified rules and schedules. **18.** *Theat.* to quicken the pace of a performance. [t. F: m. s. *rallier.* See RE-, ALLY]

rally[2] (răl′ĭ), *v.t.*, **-lied, -lying.** to ridicule (someone) good-humouredly; banter. [t. F: m. s. *railler* RAIL[2]]

ram (răm), *n., v.*, **rammed, ramming.** —*n.* **1.** an uncastrated male sheep. **2.** (*cap.*) the zodiacal constellation or sign Aries. **3.** any of various devices for battering, crushing, driving, or forcing something. **4.** a battering ram. **5.** a heavy beak or spur projecting from the bow of a warship, for penetrating an enemy's ship. **6.** a vessel so equipped. **7.** the heavy weight which strikes the blow in a pile-driver or the like. **8.** a piston, as on a hydraulic press. **9.** a hydraulic ram. —*v.t.* **10.** to drive or force by heavy blows. **11.** to strike with great force; dash violently against. **12.** to cram; stuff. **13.** to push firmly. **14.** to force (a charge) into a firearm, as with a ramrod. [ME and OE, c. D and LG *ram,* G *Ramm*]

ram-, an intensive prefix, as in *ramshackle.* [cf. Icel. *ram-* very, special use of *rammr* strong, akin to RAM]

R.A.M., Royal Academy of Music.

Rama (rä′mə), *n.* the name of three avatars of Vishnu and heroes of Hindu mythology: Balarama, Parashurama, and Ramachandra (esp. the last). [Skt]

Ramachandra (rä′mə chŭn′drə), *n.* the hero of the Ramayana, and a character in the Mahabharata.

Ramadan (răm′ə dän′), *n.* **1.** the ninth month of the Muslim year. **2.** the daily fast which is rigidly enjoined from dawn until sunset during this month. [t. Ar.: m. *Ramadān*]

Ramakrishna (rä′mə krĭsh′nə), *n.* **Sri** (srē), 1834–86, Hindu yogi and religious reformer, and founder of an international Vedanta movement.

Raman effect (rä′mən), *Physics.* the appearance of additional lines in the spectrum of light which has been scattered on passing through a transparent medium. [named after Sir C. V. *Raman,* born 1888, Indian physicist]

Ramat Gan (răm′ăt găn′), a town in W Israel. 102,600 (1966).

Ramayana (rä mī′ə nə), *n.* one of the two great epics of India (the other being the Mahabharata). It is ascribed to the poet Valmiki, and was probably composed early in the Christian era. [Skt]

ramble (răm′bl), *v.*, **-bled, -bling,** *n.* —*v.i.* **1.** to wander about in a leisurely manner, without definite aim or direction; walk for pleasure. **2.** to have an aimless or meandering course, as a stream or path. **3.** to grow or extend in an unsystematic fashion, as a plant or building. **4.** to talk or write discursively, without sequence of ideas, or incoherently. —*n.* **5.** a walk without a definite route, taken for pleasure. [? freq. of ROAM but cf. Icel. *ramba* sway to and fro] —**Syn. 1.** stroll, saunter. See **roam.**

rambler (răm′blə), *n.* **1.** one who or that which rambles. **2.** any of various climbing roses, esp. the many cultivated hybrids, as *Rosa wichuraiana* and *Rosa multiflora.*

rambling (răm′blĭng), *adj.* **1.** wandering about aimlessly. **2.** taking an irregular course; straggling. **3.** spread out irregularly in various directions: *a rambling mansion.* **4.** straying from one subject to another.

Rambouillet (rŏm′bŏŏ yā′, răm′bŏŏ lā′; *Fr.* räN bōō yĕ′), *n.* a variety of Merino sheep yielding good mutton and wool, esp. common in the western U.S. [named after *Rambouillet,* a town in France]

rambunctious (răm bŭngk′shəs), *adj. U.S. Colloq.* **1.** boisterous; noisy. **2.** obstreperous; perverse; unruly. [var. of RUMBUSTIOUS]

rambutan (răm bōō′tn), *n.* **1.** the bright red, oval, edible fruit of a Malayan sapindaceous tree, *Nephelium lappaceum,* covered with soft spines or hairs. **2.** the tree. [t. Malay]

R.A.M.C., Royal Army Medical Corps.

Rameau (*Fr.* rä mō′), *n.* **Jean Philippe** (*Fr.* zhä fē lēp′), 1683–1764, French composer.

Ramée (rä mā′), *n.* **Louise de la** ('*Ouida*'), 1839–1908, English novelist.

ramekin (răm′ĭ kĭn, răm′kĭn), *n.* **1.** a small, separately cooked portion of some savoury preparation, or other food mixture, baked in a small dish. **2.** the dish. Also, **ramequin.** [t. F: m. *ramequin,* t. D. Cf. G *Rahm* cream]

Rameses (răm′ĭ sēz′), *n.* Ramses.

rami (rā′mī), *n.* pl. of **ramus.**

ramie (răm′ĭ), *n.* **1.** an Asiatic urticaceous shrub, *Boehmeria nivea,* yielding a fibre used in making textiles, etc. **2.** the fibre itself. [t. Malay: m. *rāmī*]

ramification (răm′ĭ fĭ kā′shən), *n.* **1.** the act, process, or manner of ramifying. **2.** a branch: *the ramifications of a nerve.* **3.** a division or subdivision springing or derived from a main stem or source: *to pursue a subject in all its ramifications.* **4.** *Bot.* **a.** a structure formed of branches. **b.** a configuration of branching parts.

ramiform (răm′ĭ fôm′), *adj.* **1.** having the form of a branch; branchlike. **2.** branched. [f. *rami-* (t. L, comb. form of *rāmus* branch) + -FORM]

ramify (răm′ĭ fī′), *v.t.*, *v.i.*, **-fied, -fying.** to divide or spread out into branches or branchlike parts. [t. F: m. s. *ramifier*, t. ML: m. *rāmificāre*, f. L: *rāmi-* (comb. form of *rāmus* branch) + *-ficāre* make]

ramjet (răm′jĕt′), *n. Aeron.* a jet-propulsion engine operated by the injection of fuel into a stream of air compressed by the forward speed of the aircraft.

ramkie (răm′kĭ), *n.* a hybrid lutelike musical instrument of the Hottentots of South Africa, having three to six plucked strings stretched over a body made of calabash, wood, or an empty tincan. [t. Portuguese: m. *rabequinha* a little violin]

rammer (răm′ə), *n.* one who or that which rams.

rammish (răm′ĭsh), *adj.* **1.** like a ram. **2.** rank² (def. 3).

ramose (rā′mōs, ră mōs′), *adj.* **1.** having many branches. **2.** branching. [t. L: m. s. *rāmōsus*]

ramous (rā′məs), *adj.* **1.** ramose. **2.** like branches.

ramp (rămp), *n.* **1.** a sloping surface connecting two different levels. **2.** a short concave slope or bend, as one connecting the higher and lower parts of a bannister at a landing or of the top of a wall. **3.** any extensive sloping walk or passageway. **4.** the act of ramping. **5.** a swindle, esp. one depending on a rise in prices. [t. F: m. *rampe*]
—*v.i.* **6.** to rise or stand on the hind legs, as a quadruped, esp. a lion (often one represented in heraldry or sculpture). **7.** to rear as if to spring. **8.** to leap or dash with fury (fol. by *about*, etc.). **9.** to act violently; rage; storm. [ME, t. F: s. *ramper* creep, crawl, climb]

rampage (*n.* răm pāj′, răm′pāj′; *v.* răm pāj′), *n.*, *v.*, **-paged, -paging.** —*n.* **1.** violent or furious behaviour. **2.** an instance of this: *to go on the rampage.* —*v.i.* **3.** to rush, move, or act furiously or violently. [orig. Scot.; appar. dissimilated var. of *ramp-rage.* See RAMP (def. 8), RAGE (def. 10)]

rampageous (răm pā′jəs), *adj.* violent; unruly; boisterous. —**rampa′geousness,** *n.*

rampancy (răm′pən sĭ), *n.* rampant condition or position.

rampant (răm′pənt), *adj.* **1.** violent in action, spirit, opinion, etc.; raging; furious. **2.** in full sway; unchecked: *the rampant growth of anarchy.* **3.** luxurious, as a plant. **4.** lustful. **5.** standing on the hind legs; ramping. **6.** *Her.* (of a lion, bear, etc.) standing on its left hind leg with the forelegs elevated, the right higher than the left, and, unless otherwise specified, with the head in profile. **7.** *Archit.* (of an arch or vault) springing at one side from one level of support and resting at the other on a higher level. [ME *rampaunt*, t. OF: m. *rampant*, ppr. of *ramper* climb, RAMP] —**ramp′antly,** *adv.*

Rampant (def. 6)

rampart (răm′pät′), *n.* **1.** *Fort.* **a.** a broad elevation or mound of earth raised as a fortification about a place, and usually having a stone or earth parapet built upon it. **b.** such an elevation together with the parapet. **2.** anything serving as a bulwark or defence. —*v.t.* **3.** to furnish with or as with a rampart. [t. F: m. *rempart*, der. *remparer* fortify] —**Syn. 2.** bulwark, breastwork, barricade.

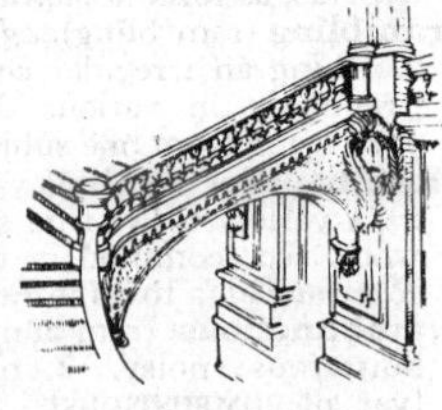

Rampant arch in staircase

rampion (răm′pyən), *n.* **1.** a European campanula, *Campanula rapunculus*, having an edible white tuberous root used for salad. **2.** any of the plants of the campanulaceous genus *Rhyteuma*, bearing heads or spikes of blue flowers. [cf. It. *ramponzolo*]

Rampur (răm′po͝oə), *n.* a city in India, in N Uttar Pradesh. 135,407 (1961).

ramrod (răm′rŏd′), *n.* **1.** a rod for ramming down the charge of a muzzle-loading firearm. **2.** a cleaning rod for the barrel of a rifle, etc. **3.** any person or thing considered as exemplifying or exercising stiffness or unyielding rigidity.

Ramsay (răm′zĭ), *n.* **1. Allan,** 1686–1758, Scottish poet. **2. James Andrew Brown.** See **Dalhousie. 3. Sir William,** 1852–1916, English chemist.

Ramsbottom (rămz′bŏt′əm), *n.* a town in England, in Lancashire. 13,813 (1961).

Ramsden eyepiece (rămz′dən), *Optics.* an eyepiece used in optical instruments, often when a crosshair or scale is required; consists of two plano-convex lenses (curved surfaces inwards) of equal focal length, f, separated by a distance of ⅔f. [named after Jesse *Ramsden*, 1735–1800, English maker of optical instruments]

Ramses (răm′sēz), *n.* the name of twelve kings of ancient Egypt. Also, **Rameses, Ramesses.**

Ramses II, died 1225? B.C., a king of ancient Egypt.

Ramses III, died 1167? B.C., a king of ancient Egypt.

Ramsey (răm′zĭ), *n.* **1. Arthur Michael,** born 1904, Archbishop of Canterbury since 1961. **2.** a seaport in the NW Isle of Man. 3764 (1961).

Ramsgate (rămz′gĭt), *n.* a seaport in England, in Kent: seaside resort. 37,380 (est. 1962).

ramshackle (răm′shăk′l), *adj.* loosely made or held together; rickety; shaky: *a ramshackle house.* [earlier *ramshackled*, f. RAM- + *shackled*, pp. of *shackle*, freq. of SHAKE, v.]

ramson (răm′sən, -zən), *n.* **1.** a species of garlic, *Allium ursinum*, with broad leaves. **2.** (*usually pl.*) its bulbous root, used as a relish. [orig. pl. taken as sing.; ME *ramsyn*, OE *hramsan*, pl. of *hramsa* kind of garlic]

ramulose (răm′yo͝o lōs′), *adj. Bot., Zool.* having many small branches. Also, **ramulous** (răm′yo͝o ləs). [t. L: m. s. *rāmulōsus*]

ramus (rā′məs), *n., pl.* **-mi** (-mī). *Bot., Anat., etc.* a branch, as of a plant, a vein, a bone, etc. [t. L]

ran¹ (răn), *v.* pt. of **run.**

ran² (răn), *n.* a measure of twine or netting. [orig. unknown]

Ran (rän), *n. Scand. Myth.* the sea-goddess, who caught drowning men in her net; wife of Aegir.

R.A.N., Royal Australian Navy.

rana (rā′nə), *n.* any of the family of the true frogs, *Ranidae*, having approximately 2500 species with worldwide distribution. [NL: genus name]

Rancagua (*Sp.* rȧn kȧ′gwȧ), *n.* a town in central Chile. 50,719 (est. 1959).

rance (răns), *n.* a variety of marble from Belgium, dull red with white and blue graining. [t. F]

ranch (rănch), *n.* **1.** a farm for cattle, horses, sheep, or the like, generally having extensive grazing land, as in America and Australia. **2.** the establishment, staff, buildings, etc., of such a farm. **3.** *U.S.* any farm or farming establishment. —*v.i.* **4.** to own, manage, or work on, a ranch. [t. Sp.: m. *rancho.* See RANCHO]

rancher (răn′chə), *n. Austral., U.S., etc.* one who owns or works on a ranch.

ranchero (răn chĕə′rō; *Sp.* rȧn chė′rȯ), *n., pl.* **-cheros** (-chĕə′rōz; *Sp.* -chė′rȯs). (in Spanish America and the south-western U.S.) a rancher. [t. Sp.]

ranch house, 1. the main building on a ranch, where the owner lives. **2.** *U.S.* a long, single-storey house, often having an open-plan interior layout.

Ranchi (răn′chĭ), *n.* a town in NE India, in Bihar. 122,416 (1961).

ranchman (rănch′mən), *n., pl.* **-men.** *U.S.* a rancher.

rancho (răn′chō; *Sp.* rȧn′chȯ), *n., pl.* **-choes** (-chōz; *Sp.* -chȯs). (in Spanish America and the south-western U.S.) **1.** a hut or collection of huts for herdsmen, labourers, or travellers. **2.** a ranch. [t. Sp.: mess, group of persons who eat together, in Sp. Amer. applied to the huts occupied by herdsmen and labourers]

rancid (răn′sĭd), *adj.* **1.** having a rank, unpleasant, stale smell or taste: *rancid butter.* **2.** rank in this manner: *a rancid smell.* [t. L: s. *rancidus*] —**ran′cidness,** *n.*

rancidity (răn sĭd′ĭ tĭ), *n.* **1.** rancid state or quality. **2.** a rancid smell or taste.

rancorous (răng′kə rəs), *adj.* full of or showing rancour. —**ran′corously,** *adv.* —**ran′corousness,** *n.*

rancour (răng′kə), *n.* bitter, rankling resentment or ill will; hatred; malice. Also, *U.S.*, **rancor.** [ME, t. OF, g. LL *rancor* rank smell or taste, der. L *rancere* to be rank] —**Syn.** See **malevolence.**

rand¹ (rănd), *n.* **1.** *Shoemaking.* a strip of leather, for levelling, set in a shoe at the heel before the lifts are attached. **2.** *Scot. or Dial.* a border, margin, or strip. **3.** *S African.* a rocky ridge. [ME and OE, c. D *rand*, G *Rand* border, margin]

rand² (rănd), *n., pl.* **rand. 1.** the monetary unit of the Republic of South Africa, South West Africa, Lesotho, Botswana, and Swaziland, equal to 100 cents and equivalent to £0·583 sterling. **2.** a banknote or silver coin of this value. *Abbrev.*: R. [t. Afrikaans: special use of *rand* RAND¹]

Rand (rănd), *n.* **The,** Witwatersrand.

R & D, research and development.

randan (răn dăn′), *n. Colloq. and Dial.* a boisterous or noisy occasion; a spree. [? der. RANDOM]

R. & I., 1. (L *Regina et Imperatrix*) Queen and Empress. **2.** (L *Rex et Imperator*) King and Emperor.

Randers (*Dan.* rȧn′ərs), *n.* a seaport in Denmark, in E Jutland. 42,238 (1960).

random (răn′dəm), *adj.* **1.** going, made, occurring, etc., without definite aim, purpose, or reason. **2.** not according to a pattern or method. **3.** *Bldg Trades.* (of slates, blocks, paving stones, etc.) irregular in size or arrangement.

—*n.* **4. at random,** in a haphazard way; without definite aim, purpose, or method. [ME *randon*, t. OF: rushing movement, disorder] —**ran′domly,** *adv.* —**Syn. 1.** haphazard, chance, casual, stray, aimless.

random-access (răn′dəm ăk′sěs), *adj.* denoting or pertaining to an information-storage device designed to reduce the effect of variation of access time for an arbitrary sequence of addresses.

random sampling, *Statistics.* the drawing of a sample from a statistical population in which all members of the population have equal probabilities of being included in the sample.

randy (răn′dĭ), *adj.* **1.** *Slang.* lecherous. **2.** *Scot. and N Dial.* loud; boisterous. [f. *rand* (var. of RANT)+-Y[1]]

ranee (rä′n, rä nē′), *n.* rani.

rang (răng), *v.* pt. of **ring[2].**

range (rānj), *n., adj., v.,* **ranged, ranging.** —*n.* **1.** the extent to which, or the limits between which, variation is possible: *the range of prices for a commodity.* **2.** the extent or scope of the operation or efficacy of something: *within range of vision.* **3.** the distance to which a projectile is or may be sent by a weapon, etc. **4.** the distance of the target from the weapon. **5.** an area in which shooting at targets is practised either with guns or with missiles. **6.** the distance which an aircraft, ship, or land vehicle can travel without refuelling. **7.** the distance of something to be located from some point of operation, as in sound-ranging. **8.** *Statistics.* the difference between the smallest and largest varieties in a statistical distribution. **9.** the compass of a musical instrument or a voice. **10.** *Survey.* **a.** the extension or prolongation of a line to intersect a transit line usually employed for location of physical features. **b.** a line established by markers on shore for the location of soundings. **11.** (in U.S. public-land surveys) one of a series of divisions numbered east or west from the principal meridian of the survey, and consisting of a row of townships, each six miles square, which are numbered north or south from a baseline. **12.** a rank, class, or order. **13.** a row or line, as of persons or things. **14.** a set or series. **15.** the act of ranging, or moving about, as over an area or region. **16.** an area or tract that is or may be ranged over. **17.** the region over which something is distributed, is found, or occurs: *the range of a plant.* **18.** a chain of mountains; a mountain range. **19.** *U.S.* an extensive stretch of grazing ground. **20.** a form of large stove, portable or stationary, for cooking, now usually having one or more ovens, and openings on the top for heating various articles at once. —*adj.* **21.** of, or grazing on, a range (def. 19). [ME, t. OF, der. *ranger* RANGE, V.] —*v.t.* **22.** to draw up or dispose (persons or things) in a row or line, in rows or lines, or in a particular position, company, or group (often fol. by *in, among, alongside,* etc.). **23.** to dispose systematically; set in order; arrange. **24.** to place in a particular class; classify. **25.** to make straight, level, or even, as lines of type. **26.** to pass over or through (an area or region) in all directions, as in exploring or searching. **27.** to pasture (cattle) on a range. **28.** to train, as a telescope, upon an object. **29.** to obtain the range of (something aimed at or to be located). **30.** *Naut.* to lay out (an anchor cable) so that the anchor may descend smoothly. —*v.i.* **31.** to vary within certain limits: *prices ranging from £5 to £10.* **32.** to have range of operation. **33.** to have a particular range, as a gun or a projectile. **34.** to find the range, as of something aimed at or to be located. **35.** to stretch out or extend in a line. **36.** to extend, run or go in a certain direction: *a boundary ranging east and west.* **37.** to lie or extend in the same line, or the same plane, as one thing with another or others. **38.** to take up a position in a line or in order. **39.** to take up or occupy a particular place or position. **40.** to move about or through a region in all directions, as persons, animals, etc. **41.** to rove, roam, or wander: *the talk ranged over a variety of matters.* **42.** to extend, be found, or occur over an area or throughout a period, as animals, plants, etc.: *a plant which ranges from Canada to Mexico.* [ME *range(n)*, v., t. OF: m. *ranger* arrange in line, der. *reng* line. See RANK[1]] —**Syn. 1.** RANGE, COMPASS, LATITUDE, SCOPE refer to extent or breadth, with or without limits. RANGE emphasizes extent and diversity: *the range of one's interests.* COMPASS suggests definite limits: *within the compass of one's mind.* LATITUDE emphasizes the idea of freedom from narrow confines; thus breadth or extent: *granted latitude of action.* SCOPE suggests great freedom but a proper limit: *the scope of one's activities or of one's obligations.* **41.** See **roam.**

rangefinder (rānj′fīn′də), *n.* any of various instruments for determining the range or distance of an object, as in order that a gun may be accurately sighted when firing at it, or to focus a camera.

ranger (rān′jə), *n.* **1.** *Chiefly U.S.* a warden employed to patrol a tract of forest. **2.** *Chiefly U.S.* one of a body of troops, usually mounted, employed in policing a region. **3.** (*cap.*) *U.S.* a commando. **4.** a keeper of a royal forest or park. **5.** one who or that which ranges. —**rang′-ership′,** *n.*

Rangitaiki (răng′gĭ tī′kĭ), *n.* a river in N North Island, New Zealand, flowing N to the Pacific Ocean at the Bay of Plenty. 95 mi.

Rangitata (răng′gĭ tä′tə), *n.* a river in South Island, New Zealand, flowing SE to the Pacific Ocean at Canterbury Bight. 75 mi.

Rangitikei (răng′gĭ tē′kā), *n.* a river in S North Island, New Zealand, flowing SW to the Tasman Sea. 130 mi.

rangitira (răn′gĭ tĭ′rə), *n. N.Z.* a chief or member of the Maori aristocracy. [t. Maori]

Rangoon (răng gōōn′), *n.* a seaport in and the capital of Burma, in the S part. 1,530,434 (est. 1964). See map under **Mandalay.**

rangy (rān′jĭ), *adj.,* **-gier, -giest. 1.** slender and long-limbed, as animals or persons. **2.** given to or fitted for ranging or moving about, as animals. **3.** *Austral.* having a mountain range; mountainous.

rani (rä′nĭ, rä nē′), *n., pl.* **-nis.** (in India and elsewhere) **1.** the wife of a raja, king, or prince. **2.** a reigning queen or princess. Also, **ranee.** [t. Hind.: m. *rānī*]

Ranjit Singh (rŭn′jĭt sĭng′) (*'Lion of the Punjab'*), 1780–1839, Indian maharaja: established the Sikh kingdom in the Punjab.

rank[1] (răngk), *n.* **1.** a number of persons forming a separate class in the social scale or in any graded body: *men of every rank and station.* **2.** position or standing in the social scale or in any graded body: *the rank of colonel.* **3.** high position or station in the social or some similar scale: *pride of rank.* **4.** a class in any scale of comparison. **5.** relative position or standing: *a writer of the highest rank.* **6.** a row, line, or series of things or persons. **7.** (*pl.*) the lines or body of an army or other force or organization. **8.** the general body of any party, society, or organization apart from the officers or leaders. **9.** orderly arrangement; array. **10.** a line of persons, esp. soldiers, standing abreast (distinguished from *file*). **11.** (*pl.*) the members of an army, etc., other than and distinguished from commissioned officers; other ranks: *to rise from the ranks.* **12.** *Chess.* one of the horizontal lines of squares on a chessboard. **13. pull (one's) rank (on),** to resort to use of a position of authority, esp. military authority, to compel some action or behaviour. —*v.t.* **14.** to arrange in a rank or row, or in ranks, as things or persons. **15.** to dispose in suitable order; arrange; classify. **16.** to assign to a particular position, station, class, etc. **17.** *U.S.* to outrank. —*v.i.* **18.** to form a rank or ranks. **19.** to stand in rank. **20.** to take up or occupy a place in a particular rank, class, etc. **21.** *U.S.* to be the senior in rank: *the major ranks here.* [t. F (obs.): m. *ranc*, OF *renc, reng*, of Gmc orig.; cf. OE *hring* RING[1]]

rank[2] (răngk), *adj.* **1.** growing with excessive luxuriance; vigorous and tall of growth: *tall rank grass.* **2.** producing an excessive and coarse growth, as land. **3.** having an offensively strong smell or taste: *a rank cigar.* **4.** offensively strong, as smell or taste. **5.** utter; unmistakable: *a rank outsider, rank treachery.* **6.** highly offensive; disgusting. **7.** grossly coarse or indecent. [ME; OE *ranc* proud, bold, c. Icel. *rakkr* erect] —**rank′ly,** *adv.* —**rank′ness,** *n.*

rank and file, the body of an army, or any other organization or group, apart from officers or leaders.

Ranke (*Ger.* răng′kə), *n.* **Leopold von** (*Ger.* lĕ′ō pōlt fōn), 1795–1886, German historian.

ranker (răng′kə), *n.* **1.** a soldier in the ranks. **2.** a commissioned officer promoted from the ranks. **3.** one who ranks. [f. RANK[1], n., + -ER[1]]

Rankine scale (răng′kĭn), *Physics.* an absolute scale of temperature based on the Fahrenheit degree in which the absolute zero is equal to −459·69°F. [named after W. J. M. *Rankine*, 1820–70, Scottish physicist]

rankle (răng′kl), *v.i.,* **-kled, -kling.** (of unpleasant feelings, experiences, etc.) to produce or continue to produce within the mind keen irritation or bitter resentment; fester; be painful. [ME *rancle(n)*, t. OF: m. *(d)raoncler*, der. ML *dracunculus* ulcer, dim. of L *draco* serpent, DRAGON]

ransack (răn′săk′), *v.t.* **1.** to search thoroughly or vigorously through (a house, receptacle, etc.). **2.** to search (a place, etc.) for plunder; pillage. [ME *ransake(n)*, t. Scand.; cf. Icel. *rannsaka* search (a house), f. *rann* house + *-saka*, akin to *sœkja* SEEK] —**ran′-sack′er,** *n.*

ransom (răn′səm), *n.* **1.** the redemption of a prisoner, slave, kidnapped person, captured goods, etc., for a price. **2.** the sum or price paid or demanded. **3.** a means of delivering or rescuing, esp., in religious use, from sin and its consequences. **4. hold to ransom, a.** to confine (a person or thing) until redeemed at a price.

b. to attempt to compel (someone) to accede to one's demands. **5. king's ransom,** any very large sum of money or valuables. —*v.t.* **6.** to redeem from captivity, bondage, detention, etc., by paying a price demanded. **7.** to release or restore on receipt of a ransom. **8.** to deliver or redeem from sin and its consequences. [ME *ransome,* t. OF: m. *rançon,* g. s. L *redemptio* REDEMPTION] —**ran′somer,** *n.* —**Syn. 6.** See **redeem.**

rant (rănt), *v.i.* **1.** to speak or declaim extravagantly or violently; talk in a wild or vehement way: *a ranting actor.* —*v.t.* **2.** to utter or declaim in a ranting manner. —*n.* **3.** ranting, extravagant, or violent declamation. **4.** a ranting utterance. [t. MD: s. *ranten* rave, c. G *ranzen* frolic] —**rant′er,** *n.* —**rant′ing,** *adj.*

ranunculaceous (rə nŭng′kyo͝o lā′shəs), *adj.* belonging to the *Ranunculaceae,* the crowfoot or buttercup family of plants, which includes also the kingcup, aconite, black hellebore, anemone, hepatica, clematis, columbine, larkspur, peony, etc. [f. RANUNCUL(US) + -ACEOUS]

ranunculus (rə nŭng′kyo͝o ləs), *n., pl.* **-luses, -li** (-lī′). any plant of the large and widely distributed genus *Ranunculus,* comprising herbs with leaves mostly divided and flowers, commonly yellow, with five petals; a crowfoot; a buttercup. [t. L, orig., dim. of *rana* frog]

R.A.O.C., Royal Army Ordnance Corps.

Raoul (*Fr.* rȧ o͞ol′), *n.* Bluebeard.

rap[1] (răp), *v.,* **rapped, rapping,** *n.* —*v.t.* **1.** to strike, esp. with a quick, smart, or light blow, as to attract attention, communicate in code, etc. **2.** to produce or announce by raps (fol. by *out,* and used esp. of communications ascribed to spirits). **3.** to utter sharply or vigorously (usually fol. by *out*): *to rap out an oath.* **4. rap over** or **on the knuckles,** *Colloq.* to reprimand sharply; reprove. —*v.i.* **5.** to knock smartly or lightly, esp. so as to make a noise: *to rap on a door.* —*n.* **6.** a quick, smart, or light blow. **7.** the sound so produced. **8.** *Slang.* punishment or blame: *to take the rap.* **9.** (in modern spiritualism) a sound as of knocking, ascribed to the agency of disembodied spirits. [ME; cf. Sw. *rappa* beat, drub, G *rappeln* rattle]

rap[2] (răp), *n.* **1.** the least bit: *I don't care a rap.* **2.** a counterfeit coin, worth about half a farthing, which formerly passed current in Ireland for a halfpenny. [cf. Anglo-Irish *rap* bad halfpenny]

rapacious (rə pā′shəs), *adj.* **1.** given to seizing for plunder or the satisfaction of greed. **2.** inordinately greedy; predatory; extortionate: *a rapacious disposition.* **3.** (of animals) subsisting by the capture of living prey; predacious. [f. RAPACI(TY) (t. L: m. s. *rāpācitas* greediness) + -OUS] —**rapa′ciously,** *adv.* —**rapacity** (rə păs′ĭ tĭ), **rapa′ciousness,** *n.*

Rapallo (rə păl′ō; *It.* rȧ pȧl′lō), *n.* a seaport in NW Italy, on the Gulf of Genoa: treaties, 1920, 1922. 15,639 (1961).

Rapa Nui (rä′pä no͞o′ĭ), native name of **Easter Island.**

R.A.P.C., Royal Army Pay Corps.

rape[1] (rāp), *n., v.,* **raped, raping.** —*n.* **1.** the crime of having sexual intercourse with a woman against her will. **2.** the act of having sexual intercourse with any other person against his or her will. **3.** the act of forcing someone to consent to anything against his or her will. **4.** an act of aggression by which one state seizes the territory of another. —*v.t.* **5.** to commit the crime or act of rape on. **6.** to seize, take, or carry off by force. **7.** to plunder (a place). —*v.i.* **8.** to commit rape. [ME *rape(n),* t. L: m. *rapere* seize, carry off] —**rap′ist,** *n.*

rape[2] (rāp), *n.* a variable cruciferous herb, *Brassica napus,* widely cultivated as a fodder plant and for the seeds, which yield rapeseed oil. [ME, t. L: m. *rāpum, rāpa* turnip]

rape[3] (rāp), *n.* the refuse of grapes, after the juice has been extracted, used as a filter in making vinegar. [t. F, g. LL *raspa,* der. *raspāre* grate, t. Gmc; cf. OHG *raspōn*]

rape-cake (rāp′kāk′), *n.* cattle food made of the husks of rapeseed remaining after the extraction of the oil.

rapeseed (rāp′sēd′), *n.* **1.** the seed of the rape. **2.** the plant itself.

rapeseed oil, a brownish yellow oil obtained from rapeseed, used as a lubricant, etc.; colza oil. Also, **rape oil.**

Raphael (răf′ā əl), *n.* **1.** (*Raffaello Santi* or *Sanzio*) 1483–1520, Italian painter. **2.** one of the archangels. [(def. 2) ult. t. Heb.: m. *Rĕfā'ēl* God healed]

raphe (rā′fĭ), *n., pl.* **-phae** (-fē). **1.** *Anat.* a seamlike union between two parts or halves of an organ or the like. **2.** *Bot.* **a.** (in certain ovules) a ridge connecting the hilum with the chalaza. **b.** a median line or slot on a cell wall of a diatom. [NL, t. Gk: seam, suture]

raphides (răf′ĭ dēz′), *n.pl. Bot.* acicular crystals, usually composed of calcium oxalate, which occur in bundles in the cells of many plants. [NL (pl.), t. Gk: needles]

rapid (răp′ĭd), *adj.* **1.** occurring with speed; coming about within a short time: *rapid growth.* **2.** moving or acting with great speed; swift: *a rapid worker.* **3.** characterized by speed, as motion. —*n.* **4.** (*usually pl.*) a part of a river where the current runs very swiftly, as over a steep slope in the bed. [t. L: s. *rapidus*] —**rap′idly,** *adv.* —**Syn. 2.** See **quick.**

rapid fire, fast firing, as used against a moving target.

rapid-fire (răp′ĭd fī′ə), *adj.* **1.** characterized by or delivered or occurring in rapid procedure, esp. in speech: *rapid-fire questions.* **2.** *Ordn.* denoting or pertaining to any of various mounted guns of moderate calibre which can be fired rapidly. **3.** *Mil.* firing shots in rapid succession. Also, **rapid-firing.** —**rap′id-fir′er,** *n.*

rapidity (rə pĭd′ĭ tĭ), *n.* rapid state or quality. —**Syn.** swiftness, fleetness, speed, velocity, celerity.

rapid-transit (răp′ĭd trăn′sĭt), *adj.* (of a transport system) involving or pertaining to high-speed urban railways.

rapier (rā′pĭ ə), *n.* **1.** a sword, with elaborate hilt, and long, slender, pointed blade, used only for thrusting. **2.** (orig.) a long, narrow, two-edged sword, used chiefly for thrusting. [t. F: m. *rapière,* orig. adj., der. *râpe* grater. See RAPE[3]]

rapine (răp′ĭn), *n.* the violent seizure and carrying off of property of others; plunder. [ME, t. L: m. *rapina*]

rapparee (răp′ə rē′), *n.* **1.** an armed Irish freebooter or plunderer, esp. of the 17th century. **2.** a freebooter or robber. [t. Irish: m. *rapaire*]

rappee (ră pē′), *n.* a strong snuff made by rasping the darker and ranker kinds of tobacco leaves. [t. F: m. *râpé* grated, pp. of *râper.* See RAPE[3], RASP]

rappel (ră pĕl′), *n., v.,* **-pelled, -pelling.** —*n.* **1.** *Mountaineering.* abseil. **2.** a beat of a drum formerly used to call soldiers to arms. —*v.i.* **3.** *Mountaineering.* to descend by rappel. [t. F: lit., a recall]

rapper (răp′ə), *n.* one who or that which performs the act or produces the sound of rapping or knocking. [f. RAP[1] + -ER[1]]

rapport (ră pô′; *Fr.* rȧ pŏr′), *n.* relation; connection, esp. harmonious or sympathetic relation (usually in the phrases *to be en,* or *in, rapport with*). [t. F, der. *rapporter* bring back, refer, f. *re-* RE- + *apporter* (t. L: m. *apportāre* bring to)]

rapprochement (ră prŏsh′mŏng; *Fr.* rȧ prŏsh mäɴ′), *n.* an establishment or re-establishment of harmonious relations. [F, der. *rapprocher* bring near. See APPROACH]

rapscallion (răp skăl′yən), *n. Obs.* a rascal; rogue; scamp. [ult. der. RASCAL]

rapt (răpt), *adj.* **1.** deeply engrossed or absorbed: *rapt in thought.* **2.** transported with emotion; enraptured: *rapt with joy.* **3.** showing or proceeding from rapture: *a rapt smile.* **4.** carried off to another place, sphere of existence, etc. [first used as pp., ME, t. L: s. *raptus,* pp., seized, transported. See RAPE[1]]

raptor (răp′tə), *n.* a bird of the order *Raptores,* consisting of birds of prey, as the eagles, hawks, etc. [t. L: robber, plunderer]

raptorial (răp tô′rĭ əl), *adj.* **1.** preying upon other animals; predatory. **2.** adapted for seizing prey, as the beak or claws of a bird. **3.** belonging or pertaining to the raptors. [f. s. NL *Raptōrēs* (pl. of L *raptor* robber, plunderer) + -(I)AL]

Head and foot of raptorial bird, Golden eagle, *Aquila chrysaëtos*

rapture (răp′chə), *n.* **1.** ecstatic joy or delight; joyful ecstasy. **2.** (*often pl.*) an utterance or expression of ecstatic delight. **3.** the carrying of a person to another place or sphere of existence. **4.** *Obs.* the act of carrying off. **5. in raptures,** delighted; full of enthusiasm. [f. RAPT + -URE]

rapturous (răp′chə rəs, -chrəs), *adj.* **1.** full of, feeling, or manifesting ecstatic joy or delight. **2.** characterized by, attended with, or expressive of, such rapture: *rapturous surprise.* —**rap′turously,** *adv.* —**rap′turousness,** *n.*

rara avis (rĕə′rə ā′vĭs), *pl.* **rarae aves** (rĕə′rē ā′vēz). *Latin.* a rare person or thing. [L: a rare bird]

rare[1] (rĕə), *adj.,* **rarer, rarest. 1.** coming or occurring far apart in space or time; unusual; uncommon: *rare occasions, a rare smile, a rare disease.* **2.** few in number. **3.** thinly distributed over an area, or few and widely separated: *rare lighthouses.* **4.** having the component parts not closely compacted; of low density or pressure: *rare mountain air.* **5.** remarkable or unusual, esp. in excellence or greatness: *rare tact, a rare find; sympathetic to a rare degree.* [ME, t. L: m. s. *rārus* thin, not dense] —**rare′ness,** *n.*

—**Syn.** 1. RARE, SCARCE characterize that which is hard to find, exists in small quantities, or is uncommon. A thing is RARE which is seldom to be met with and is therefore often sought after; the word often implies exceptional quality or value: *a rare book; a rare beauty.* SCARCE is applied to that of which there is an insufficient supply; it usually implies a previous or usual condition of greater abundance: *food is scarce, fruit is scarce this year.* —**Ant.** 1. abundant.

rare[2] (rĕə), *adj.*, **rarer, rarest.** (of meat) not thoroughly cooked; underdone. [ME *rere*, OE *hrēr* lightly boiled (said of eggs)]

rarebit (rĕə′bĭt), *n.* Welsh rarebit.

rare book, a book which is distinctive by virtue of its early printing date, limited copies, special character of the edition, binding, historical interest, or the like.

rare earth, *Chem.* the oxide of any of the rare-earth elements, contained in various minerals.

rare-earth elements (rĕər′ûth′), *Chem.* **1.** a group of closely related metallic elements of atomic number 57 to 71 inclusive, often divided into three groups: **cerium metals** (lanthanum, cerium, praseodymium, neodymium, promethium, and samarium), **terbium metals** (europium, gadolinium, and terbium), and **yttrium metals** (dysprosium, holmium, erbium, thulium, yttrium, ytterbium, and lutetium); lanthanides. **2.** this group of sixteen elements together with the element scandium.

raree show (rĕə′rē), *Obs.* **1.** a peepshow. **2.** any show or spectacle. [? repr. foreigners' pronunciation of *rare show*]

rarefaction (rĕə′rĭ făk′shən), *n.* **1.** the act or process of rarefying. **2.** the state of being rarefied. —**rar′efac′tive,** *adj.*

rarefy (rĕə′rĭ fī′), *v.*, **-fied, -fying.** —*v.t.* **1.** to make rare, more rare, or less dense. **2.** to make less gross; refine. —*v.i.* **3.** to become rare or less dense; become thinned. [t. L: m. *rārēfacere*]

rare gas, *Chem.* any of the gases, helium, neon, argon, krypton, xenon or radon; chemically inactive, although some compounds have been reported. Also, **inert gas, noble gas.**

rarely (rĕə′lĭ), *adv.* **1.** on rare occasions; infrequently; in few instances: *he is rarely late.* **2.** exceptionally; in an unusual degree. **3.** unusually or remarkably well or excellent.

raring (rĕə′rĭng), *adj.* ready; eager. [ppr. of d. *rare*, var. of REAR]

rarity (rĕə′rĭ tĭ), *n.*, *pl.* **-ties. 1.** something rare, unusual, or uncommon. **2.** something esteemed or interesting as being rare, uncommon, or curious. **3.** rare state or quality. **4.** rare occurrence; infrequency. **5.** unusual excellence. **6.** thinness, as of air or a gas.

Rarotonga (rĕə′rə tong′gə), *n.* one of the Cook Islands, in the S Pacific. 8676 pop. (1961); 26 sq. mi.

R.A.S., 1. *Naut.* refuelling at sea. 2. Royal Agricultural Society. 3. Royal Asiatic Society. 4. Royal Astronomical Society.

Ras al Khaimah (răs′ăl kī′mä). See **Trucial States.**

R.A.S.C., Royal Army Service Corps.

rascal (răs′kl), *n.* **1.** a base, dishonest person. **2.** (mildly or affectionately reproving) any person or animal: *you little rascal.* **3.** *Obs.* a person belonging to the rabble. —*adj.* **4.** *Obs.* knavish; dishonest. **5.** *Obs.* belonging to or being the rabble. [ME *rascayl*, t. OF: m. *rascaille* rabble, ult. der. L *rādere* scratch] —**Syn. 1.** See **knave.**

rascality (răs kăl′ĭ tĭ), *n.*, *pl.* **-ties. 1.** rascally or knavish character or conduct. **2.** a rascally act.

rascally (răs′kə lĭ), *adj.* **1.** being, characteristic of, or befitting a rascal or knave; dishonest; mean: *a rascally trick.* **2.** (of places, etc.) wretchedly bad or unpleasant. —*adv.* **3.** in a rascally manner.

rase (rāz), *v.t.*, **rased, rasing.** raze.

rash[1] (răsh), *adj.* **1.** acting too hastily or without due consideration. **2.** characterized by or showing too great haste or lack of consideration: *rash promises.* [ME *rasch*, c. D and G *rasch* quick, brisk] —**rash′ly,** *adv.* —**rash′ness,** *n.* —**Syn. 1.** hasty, impetuous, reckless.

rash[2] (răsh), *n.* an eruption or efflorescence on the skin. [t. F: m. *rache*, ult. der. L *rādere* scratch]

rasher (răsh′ə), *n.* a thin slice of bacon. [cf. OE *ræscettan* crackle]

Rask (*Dan.* råsg), *n.* **Rasmus Christian** (*Dan.* rås′mo͞os krĕs′dján), 1787–1832, Danish philologist.

Rasmussen (*Dan.* rås′mo͞o sən), *n.* **Knud Johan Victor** (*Dan.* kno͞oth yô hän′ vĕk′tôr), 1879–1933, Danish arctic explorer.

rasorial (rə sô′rĭ əl), *adj.* given to scratching the ground for food, as poultry; gallinaceous. [f. NL *Rasōrēs* (pl.) lit., scratchers, der. L *rāsus* scratched + -(I)AL]

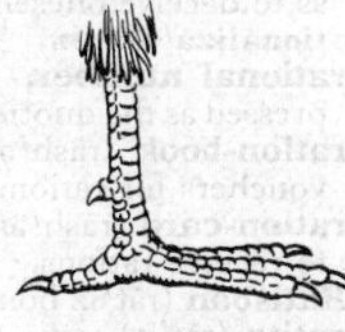

Foot of rasorial bird

rasp (räsp), *v.t.* **1.** to scrape or abrade with a rough instrument. **2.** to scrape or rub roughly. **3.** to grate upon or irritate (the nerves, feelings, etc.). **4.** to utter with a grating sound. —*v.i.* **5.** to scrape or grate. **6.** to make a grating sound. —*n.* **7.** the act of rasping. **8.** a rasping sound. **9.** a coarse form of file, having separate pointlike teeth. **10.** any similar surface. [ME *raspe(n)*, t. OF: m. *rasper* scrape, grate, t. Gmc; cf. obs. G *raspen* grate]

raspberry (räz′bə rĭ, -brĭ), *n.*, *pl.* **-ries. 1.** the fruit of several shrubs of the rosaceous genus *Rubus*, consisting of small juicy drupelets, red, black, or pale yellow, forming a detachable cap about a convex receptacle, being thus distinguished from the blackberry. **2.** one of these plants, as the **red raspberry,** *R. idaeus*, of Europe. **3.** dark reddish purple. **4.** *Slang.* a sound expressing derision or contempt made with the tongue and lips. [f. *rasp(is)* raspberry (orig. uncert.) + BERRY]

rasper (räs′pə), *n.* one who or that which rasps, as a machine for rasping sugar cane.

rasping (räs′pĭng), *adj.* harsh: *a rasping voice.*

Rasputin (răs pyo͞o′tĭn; *Russ.* rȧs po͞o′tĭn), *n.* **Grigori Efimovich** (*Russ.* grĭ gô′rĭy yĭ fē′mə vĭch), 1871–1916, Siberian peasant who posed as a monk and exerted great and malign influence over Tsar Nicholas II.

raster (răs′tə), *n.* *Electronics.* a series of parallel sweeps by an electronic scanning device. [t. G, t. L: m. *rastrum* a rake]

rat (răt), *n.*, *v.*, **ratted, ratting.** —*n.* **1.** any of certain long-tailed rodents of the genus *Rattus* and allied genera (family *Muridae*), resembling but larger than the mouse, as the **brown rat,** *R. norvegicus.* **2.** any rodent of the same family, or any of various similar animals. **3.** *Slang.* one who abandons his friends or associates, esp. in time of trouble. **4.** *Slang.* a person considered as wretched or despicable. **5. smell a rat,** *Colloq.* to be suspicious. —*interj.* **6.** (*pl.*) *Slang.* (an exclamation of annoyance, incredulity, denial, or disappointment.) —*v.i.* **7.** *Slang.* to desert one's party or associates, esp. in time of trouble: *a man who would rat on his friends.* **8.** *Slang.* **a.** to behave like a mean, cowardly person. **b.** to inform (on); betray. **9.** to hunt or catch rats. [ME *ratte*, OE *ræt*, c. G *Ratz, Ratte*]

rata (rä′tə), *n.* any of several flowering trees of the genus *Metrosideros* of New Zealand. [t. Maori]

ratable (rā′tə bl), *adj.* rateable. —**rat′abil′ity, rat′ableness,** *n.* —**rat′ably,** *adv.*

ratafia (răt′ə fĭə′), *n.* **1.** a cordial or liqueur flavoured with fruit-kernels, fruit, or the like. **2.** a flavouring essence made with the essential oil of almonds. **3.** an almond biscuit or cake. Also, **ratafee** (răt′ə fē′). [t. F]

ratafia biscuit, a type of sweet biscuit usually flavoured with ratafia essence, similar to a macaroon, but smaller.

ratal (rā′tl), *n.* the amount on which rates or taxes are assessed. [f. RAT(E)[1] + -AL[1]]

ratan (rə tăn′), *n.* rattan.

rataplan (răt′ə plăn′), *n.*, *v.*, **-planned, -planning.** —*n.* **1.** a sound of or as of the beating of a drum; a rub-a-dub. —*v.t.*, *v.i.* **2.** to play by or play a rataplan. [t. F]

ratatouille (*Fr.* rȧ tȧ to͞oy′), *n.* a type of vegetable casserole or stew, originating in Provence.

ratbag (răt′băg′), *n.* *Slang.* a rascal; rogue.

ratbite fever (răt′bīt′), a relapsing fever, widely distributed geographically, caused by infection with a spirillum transmitted by rats. Also, **ratbite disease.**

ratcatcher (răt′kăch′ə), *n.* one who catches and destroys rats, esp. as a profession.

ratch (răch), *n.* ratchet. [var. of RATCHET. Cf. G *Ratsche*]

ratchet (răch′ĭt), *n.* **1.** a toothed bar with which a pawl engages. **2.** the pawl used with such a device. **3.** a mechanism consisting of such a bar or wheel with the pawl. **4.** a ratchet wheel. [t. F: m. *rochet* ratchet, bobbin, t. It.: m. *rocchetto*, der. *rocca* distaff, t. Gmc; cf. obs. E *rock* distaff]

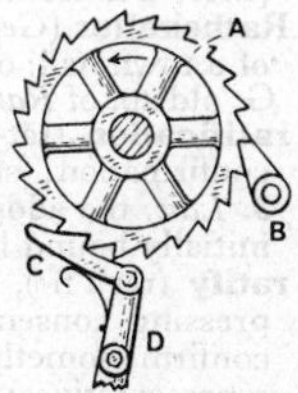

Ratchet wheel A, wheel; B, Pawl preventing reversal of motion; C, Pawl conveying motion to wheel; D, Reciprocating lever

ratchet wheel, a wheel with teeth on the edge, in which a pawl catches, as to prevent reversal of motion or convert reciprocating into rotatory motion.

rate[1] (rāt), *n.*, *v.*, **rated, rating.** —*n.* **1.** a certain quantity or amount of one thing considered in relation to a unit of another thing and used as a standard or measure: *at the rate of 60 miles an hour.* **2.** a fixed charge per unit of quantity: *a rate of sixpence in the pound.* **3.** the amount of a charge or payment with reference to some basis of calculation: *the rate of interest.* **4.** price: *to cut rates.* **5.** degree of speed, of travelling, working, etc.: *to work at a rapid*

rate. **6.** degree or relative amount of action or procedure: *the rate of increase.* **7.** relative condition or quality; grade, class, or sort. **8.** assigned position in any of a series of graded classes; rating. **9.** *U.S.* a charge by a common carrier for transport, sometimes including certain services involved in operating such transport. **10.** (*usually pl.*) a tax on property, imposed by a local authority and used for the maintenance of local services, etc. **11. at any rate, a.** under any circumstances; in any case; at all events. **b.** at least. **12. at this rate,** if the present circumstances continue.
—*v.t.* **13.** to estimate the value or worth of; appraise. **14.** to esteem, consider, or account: *he was rated one of the rich men of the city.* **15.** to fix at a certain rate, as of charge or payment. **16.** to value for purposes of taxation, etc. **17.** to make subject to the payment of a certain rate or tax. **18.** to deserve. **19.** *Chiefly Naut.* to place in a certain class, etc., as a ship or a seaman; give a certain rating to. **20.** *U.S.* to arrange for the conveyance of (goods) at a certain rate. —*v.i.* **21.** to have value, standing, etc. **22.** to have position in a certain class.
[ME, t. ML: m. *rata* fixed amount or portion, rate, prop. fem. of L *ratus*, pp., fixed by calculation, determined. See RATIO]

rate² (rāt), *v.t., v.i.*, **rated, rating.** to chide vehemently; scold. [ME; appar. c. Sw. *rata* find fault]

rateable (rā′tə bl), *adj.* **1.** capable of being rated or appraised. **2.** proportional. **3.** liable to payment of rates or local taxes. Also, **ratable.** —**rate′abil′ity, rate′ableness,** *n.* —**rate′ably,** *adv.*

rateable value, the value of a property assessed by a local authority on which the amount of rate charged is based.

rateen (ră tēn′), *n.* **1.** an all-wool lining serge, similar to frieze. **2.** ratine. [t. F: m. *ratine.* See RATINE]

ratel (rā′tl), *n.* a badger-like carnivore, *Mellivora capensis*, of Africa and India. [t. Afrikaans]

Ratel, *Mellivora capensis* (Total length 3 ft, tail 9 in.)

rate of exchange, the ratio at which the unit of currency of one country can be exchanged for the unit of currency of another country. Also, **exchange rate.**

ratepayer (rāt′pā′ə), *n.* one who pays rates on property, esp. a householder.

ratguard (răt′gäd′), *n.* a large, thin circular piece of metal fitted round a ship's mooring ropes to prevent rats climbing up them to get on board.

rathe (rāth), *adj.* **1.** *Archaic and Poetic.* growing, blooming, or ripening early in the year or season. —*adv.* **2.** *Archaic.* quickly. **3.** *Archaic and Dial.* early. [ME; OE *hrǣth*, c. OHG *hrad*, Icel. *hradhr* quick]

Rathenau (*Ger.* rä′tə nou), *n.* **Walther** (*Ger.* väl′tər), 1867–1922, German industrialist, writer, and statesman (assassinated).

rather (rä′thə; *def. 8. sometimes* rä′thû′), *adv.* **1.** more so than not; to a certain extent; somewhat: *rather good.* **2.** (with verbs) in some degree (used either literally to modify a statement, or ironically to lend emphasis). **3.** more properly or justly; with better reason: *the contrary is rather to be supposed.* **4.** sooner or more readily or willingly: *to die rather than yield, I would rather go today.* **5.** in preference; as a preferred or accepted alternative. **6.** more properly or correctly speaking; more truly. **7.** on the contrary. **8.** (as a response, a colloquial equivalent of an emphatic affirmative): *Is it worth going to? Rather!* [ME; OE *hrathor*, compar. of *hrathe* quickly]

Rathskeller (*Ger.* räts′kĕ lər), *n.* (in Germany) the cellar of a town hall, often used as a beer hall or restaurant. [t. G, old sp. of *Ratskeller*, lit., town-hall cellar]

ratification (răt′ĭ fĭ kā′shən), *n.* **1.** the act of ratifying; confirmation; sanction. **2.** the state of being ratified. **3.** *Law.* the adoption of a contract or the like by one not initially bound by it.

ratify (răt′ĭ fī′), *v.t.*, **-fied, -fying. 1.** to confirm by expressing consent, approval, or formal sanction. **2.** to confirm (something done or arranged by an agent or by representatives) by such action. [ME *ratifie(n)*, t. OF: m. *ratifier*, t. ML: m. *ratificāre*, f. *rati-* (comb. form repr. L *ratus* fixed; see RATE¹) + L *-ficāre* make] —**rat′ifi′er,** *n.*

ratine (ră tēn′), *n.* **1.** a rough woollen cloth, formerly in use chiefly for travelling coats. **2.** a coarse fabric made from fine warp-yarn cotton. **3.** rateen (def. 1). Also, **rateen, ratiné** (răt′ĭ nā′). [t. F]

rating¹ (rā′tĭng), *n.* **1.** classification according to grade or rank. **2.** *Naut.* **a.** assigned position in a particular class or grade, or relative standing, as of a ship or a seaman. **b.** *Naval.* a sailor who has no commissioned rank. **3.** a person's or firm's credit standing. **4.** an amount fixed as a municipal rate; the act of assessing this. **5.** a proportion of £1 or some other monetary unit payable in tax. **6.** *Elect.* (of a machine, apparatus, etc.) a designated limit of operating characteristics, as voltage, amperes, frequency, etc., based on definite conditions. **7.** a measure of success, as of a television programme, based on an assessment of audience size. **8.** *Rowing.* the rate of striking, usually in strokes per minute. [f. RATE¹ + -ING¹]

rating² (rā′tĭng), *n.* angry reprimand or rebuke; a scolding. [f. RATE² + -ING¹]

ratio (rā′shĭ ō′), *n., pl.* **-tios. 1.** the relation between two similar magnitudes in respect to the number of times the first contains the second: *the ratio of 5 to 2, which may be written* 5 : 2, *or* ⁵/₂. **2.** proportional relation; rate; quotient of two numbers. **3.** *Finance.* the relative value of gold and silver in a bimetallic currency system, fixed by the government of a country. [t. L: reckoning, relation, reason]

ratiocinate (răt′ĭ ŏs′ĭ nāt′), *v.i.*, **-nated, -nating.** to reason; carry on a process of reasoning; think logically. [t. L: m. s. *ratiōcinātus*, pp., calculated] —**ra′tioc′ina′tor,** *n.*

ratiocination (răt′ĭ ŏs′ĭ nā′shən), *n.* reasoning, or a process of reasoning; logical thought or thinking. —**ratiocinative** (răt′ĭ ŏs′ĭ nə tĭv), *adj.*

ration (răsh′ən), *n.* **1.** a fixed allowance of provisions of food: *rations of coal and coffee.* **2.** (*usually pl.*) the fixed allowance supplied to a soldier or sailor. —*v.t.* **3.** to apportion or distribute as rations or by some method of allowance. **4.** to put on, or restrict to, rations. **5.** to supply with rations, as of food: *to ration an army.* [t. F, t. ML: s. *ratio* allowance of provisions, L account. See RATIO] —**ra′tioning,** *n.* —**Syn. 1.** See **food.**

rational (răsh′ə nəl), *adj.* **1.** agreeable to reason; reasonable; sensible. **2.** having or exercising reason, sound judgement, or good sense. **3.** being in or characterized by full possession of one's reason; sane; lucid: *the patient appeared perfectly rational.* **4.** endowed with the faculty of reason: *man is a rational animal.* **5.** of or pertaining to reason: *the rational faculty.* **6.** proceeding or derived from reason, or based on reasoning: *a rational explanation.* **7.** *Maths.* **a.** expressible as the quotient of two integers. **b.** (of functions) expressible as the quotient of two polynomials. **8.** *Gk and Lat. Pros.* capable of measurement in terms of the metrical unit (mora). [t. L: s. *ratiōnālis*] —**ra′tionally,** *adv.* —**Syn. 2.** intelligent, wise, judicious, discreet. **6.** See **reasonable.**

rationale (răsh′ə näl′), *n.* **1.** a statement of reasons. **2.** a reasoned exposition of principles. **3.** the fundamental reasons serving to account for something. [t. L, neut. of *ratiōnālis* rational]

rationalism (răsh′ə nə lĭz′əm), *n.* **1.** the principle or habit of accepting reason as the supreme authority in matters of opinion, beliefs, or conduct. **2.** *Philos.* **a.** the theory that reason is in itself a source of knowledge independently of the senses (distinguished from *empiricism*, def. 2). **b.** the theory that even sense experience is possible only because of a rational element supplied by reason (distinguished from *sensationalism*, def. 5). **3.** *Theol.* the doctrine that revelation and scriptural tradition are to be accepted only so far as, in principle, they conform with reason. —**ra′tionalist,** *n., adj.* —**ra′tionalis′tic, ra′tionalis′tical,** *adj.* —**ra′tionalis′tically,** *adv.*

rationality (răsh′ə năl′ĭ tĭ), *n., pl.* **-ties. 1.** the quality of being rational. **2.** the possession of reason. **3.** reasonableness. **4.** the exercise of reason. **5.** a rational or reasonable view, practice, etc.

rationalize (răsh′ə nə līz′), *v.*, **-lized, -lizing.** —*v.t.* **1.** *Psychol.* to invent a rational, acceptable explanation for behaviour which has its origin in the unconscious; to justify unconscious behaviour. **2.** to remove unreasonable elements from. **3.** to make rational or conformable to reason. **4.** to treat or explain in a rational or rationalistic manner. **5.** to reorganize (resources, the components of a business, etc.) to promote efficiency, economy, etc. —*v.i.* **6.** to employ reason; think in a rational or rationalistic manner. **7.** to reorganize and integrate (an industry). **8.** to justify one's behaviour by plausible explanations, as to deceive oneself or others. Also, **rationalise.** —**ra′tionaliza′tion,** *n.* —**ra′tionaliz′er,** *n.*

rational number, *Maths.* a number which can be expressed as the quotient of two positive or negative integers.

ration-book (răsh′ən bo͝ok′), *n.* a book of coupons or vouchers for rationed goods.

ration-card (răsh′ən käd′), *n.* a card entitling the holder to receive rations.

Ratisbon (răt′ĭz bŏn′), *n.* Regensburg.

ratite (răt′īt), *adj.* **1.** without a carina, as a breastbone. **2.** having a flat breastbone, as the ostrich, cassowary, emu, moa, etc. (contrasted with *carinate*). [f. s. L *ratis* raft + -ITE[2]]

rat-kangaroo (răt′kăng′gə roo͞′), *n.* any of various small, Australian kangaroos, as the bilby, *Thalacomis lagotis.*

ratline (răt′lĭn), *n. Naut.* **1.** any of the small ropes or lines which traverse the shrouds horizontally, serving as steps for going aloft. **2.** the kind of rope or line from which these are made. Also, **ratlin.** [late ME *ratling, radelyng*; orig. uncert.]

R, Ratline; S, Shroud

ratoon (ră to͞on′), *n.* **1.** a sprout or shoot from the root of a plant (esp. a sugar cane) after it has been cropped. —*v.i., v.t.* **2.** to put forth or cause to put forth ratoons. Also, **rattoon.** [t. Sp.: m. *retoño*, t. Hind.: m. *ratun*]

rat-race (răt′rās′), *n.* the struggle for success, esp. in career, fiercely competitive and often unscrupulous.

ratsbane (răts′bān′), *n.* **1.** rat poison. **2.** the trioxide of arsenic. [earlier *rats bane.* See RAT, BANE]

rattan (rə tăn′), *n.* **1.** any of various climbing palms of the genus *Calamus*, or allied genera. **2.** the tough stems of such palms, used for wickerwork, canes, etc. **3.** a stick or switch of this material. Also, **ratan.** [var. of *rotang*, t. Malay: m. *rōtan*]

ratteen (ră tēn′), *n. Obs.* ratine.

ratter (răt′ə), *n.* **1.** one who or that which catches rats, as a terrier. **2.** *Slang.* a deserter or betrayer.

Rattigan (răt′ĭ gən), *n.* **Terence (Mervyn),** born 1911, English dramatist.

rattish (răt′ĭsh), *adj.* **1.** of, pertaining to, characteristic of, or resembling a rat. **2.** infested with rats.

rattle[1] (răt′l), *v.*, **-tled, -tling,** *n.* —*v.i.* **1.** to give out a rapid succession of short sharp sounds, as in consequence of agitation and repeated concussions: *the windows rattled in their frames.* **2.** to be filled with such sounds, as a place: *the hall was rattling with excitement.* **3.** to move or go, esp. rapidly, with such sounds. **4.** to talk rapidly; chatter. —*v.t.* **5.** to cause to rattle: *he rattled the doorknob violently.* **6.** to drive, send, bring, etc., esp. rapidly, with rattling. **7.** to utter or perform in a rapid or lively manner: *to rattle off a speech.* **8.** *Colloq.* to disconcert or confuse (a person). **9.** *Hunting.* to stir up (a cover). —*n.* **10.** a rapid succession of short, sharp sounds, as from the collision of hard bodies. **11.** an instrument contrived to make a rattling sound, as a child's toy. **12.** a device consisting of a wooden frame with a wheel and clapper, which when swung round emits a loud clacking noise, as used by football fans to encourage players, express emotions, etc. **13.** any plant with a dry capsule in which the seeds rattle, as the **red-rattle,** *Pedicularis palustris*, and **yellow-rattle,** *Rhinanthus minor.* **14.** the series of horny pieces or rings at the end of a rattlesnake's tail, with which it produces a rattling sound. **15.** a rattling sound in the throat, as the death rattle. [ME *ratele(n)*, c. D *ratelen*, G *rasseln*; imit.]

rattle[2] (răt′l), *v.t.*, **-tled, -tling.** *Naut.* to furnish with ratlines (usually fol. by *down*). [back-formation from RATLINE, taken as a verbal n.]

rattlebrain (răt′l brān′), *n.* a giddy, empty-headed chatterer. Also, **rattlehead** (răt′l hĕd′), **rattlepate** (răt′l-pāt′).

rattler (răt′lə), *n.* **1.** a rattlesnake. **2.** one who or that which rattles. **3.** *Colloq.* a person regarded as extremely good or extremely bad.

rattlesnake (răt′l snāk′), *n.* any of various venomous American snakes of the genera *Crotalus* and *Sistrurus*, having several loosely articulated horny pieces or rings at the end of the tail, which produce a rattling or whirring sound when shaken.

rattletrap (răt′l trăp′), *n.* **1.** a shaky, rattling object, as a rickety vehicle. **2.** *Slang.* a garrulous person. **3.** *Slang.* the mouth.

rattling (răt′lĭng), *adv.*, *adj. Colloq.* extremely (good).

rattly (răt′lĭ), *adj.* **1.** apt to rattle. **2.** making or having a rattling sound.

rattoon (ră to͞on′), *n.*, *v.i.*, *v.t.* ratoon.

rat-trap (răt′trăp′), *n.* **1.** a device for catching rats. **2.** a difficult and involved set of circumstances. **3.** a bicycle pedal having deep serrations to prevent the foot slipping.

ratty (răt′ĭ), *adj.*, **-tier, -tiest. 1.** full of rats. **2.** of or characteristic of a rat. **3.** wretched; shabby. **4.** *Slang.* annoyed; irritable.

raucous (rô′kəs), *adj.* hoarse; harsh-sounding, as a voice. [t. L: m. *raucus*] —**rau′cously,** *adv.* —**rau′cousness, raucity** (rô′sĭ tĭ), *n.*

Raukumara Range (rou′ko͝o mä′rə), a range of mountains in NE North Island, New Zealand. Highest peak, Mount Hikurangi, 5753 ft.

raupo (rou′pō), *n.* the giant bulrush, *Typha angustifolia*, of New Zealand. [t. Maori]

rauwolfia (rô wo͝ol′fĭ ə), *n.* **1.** *Bot.* any tree or shrub of the genus *Rauwolfia*, family *Apocynaceae*, esp. *R. vomitoria*, a species of tropical Africa. **2.** *Pharm.* an extract from the roots of the rauwolfia with many medicinal uses in its various purified forms. [named after Leonhart *Rauwolf*, 16th-century German botanist and physician]

ravage (răv′ĭj), *n.*, *v.*, **-aged, -aging.** —*n.* **1.** devastating or destructive action. **2.** havoc; ruinous damage: *the ravages of war.* —*v.t.* **3.** to work havoc upon; damage or mar by ravages: *a face ravaged by grief.* —*v.i.* **4.** to work havoc; do ruinous damage. [t. F, der. *ravir.* See RAVISH] —**rav′ager,** *n.*

—**Syn. 3.** RAVAGE, DEVASTATE, LAY WASTE all refer, in their literal application, to the wholesale destruction of a countryside by an invading army (or something comparable). LAY WASTE has remained the closest to the original meaning of destruction of land: *the invading army laid waste the towns along the coast;* but RAVAGE and DEVASTATE (the Latin equivalent of LAY WASTE) are used in reference to other types of violent destruction and may also have a purely figurative application. RAVAGE is often used of the results of epidemics: *the Black Death ravaged 14th-century Europe,* and even of the effect of disease or suffering on the human countenance: *a face ravaged by grief.* DEVASTATE, in addition to its concrete meaning (*vast areas devastated by bombs*), may be used figuratively: *a devastating wit.*

R.A.V.C., Royal Army Veterinary Corps.

rave (rāv), *v.*, **raved, raving,** *n.*, *adj.* —*v.i.* **1.** to talk wildly, as in delirium. **2.** (of wind, water, storms, etc.) to make a wild or furious sound; rage. **3.** *Colloq.* to talk or write with extravagant enthusiasm. **4.** *Slang.* to act boisterously or enthusiastically. **5.** *Slang.* to adopt fashionable ways with great enthusiasm. —*v.t.* **6.** to utter as if in madness. —*n.* **7.** an act of raving. **8.** extravagantly enthusiastic praise. **9.** *Slang.* a wild or hectic party or the like. —*adj.* **10.** praising with extravagant enthusiasm: *a rave review.* [ME, prob. t. OF: m. s. *raver* wander, be delirious]

ravel (răv′əl), *v.*, **-elled, -elling** or (*U.S.*) **-eled, -eling,** *n.* —*v.t.* **1.** to tangle or entangle. **2.** to involve; confuse; perplex. **3.** to disengage the threads or fibres of (a woven or knitted fabric, a rope, etc.). **4.** to make plain or clear (often fol. by *out*). —*v.i.* **5.** to become disjoined thread by thread or fibre by fibre; fray. **6.** to become tangled. **7.** to become confused or perplexed. **8.** *Civ. Eng.* (of a road surface) to lose aggregate because of wear. —*n.* **9.** a tangle or complication. [appar. t. MD: s. *ravelen* entangle] —**rav′eller,** *n.*

Ravel (ră vĕl′; *Fr.* rȧ vĕl′), *n.* **Maurice** (*Fr.* mō rēs′), 1875–1937, French composer.

ravelin (răv′lĭn), *n. Fort.* a triangular outwork, outside the main ditch, having two embankments forming a projecting angle. [t. F, earlier *revellin*, t. D: m. *regeling* framework]

ravelling (răv′ə lĭng), *n.* something ravelled out, as a thread drawn from a knitted or woven fabric. Also, *Chiefly U.S.*, **raveling.**

ravelment (răv′əl mənt), *n.* entanglement; confusion.

Raven, *Corvus corax* (Ab. 2 ft long)

raven[1] (rā′vən), *n.* **1.** any of several large corvine birds with lustrous black plumage and raucous voice, esp. the raven, *Corvus corax*, of the New and Old Worlds, which has from time immemorial been considered a bird of ill-omen. **2.** (*cap.*) *Astron.* the southern constellation Corvus. —*adj.* **3.** lustrous black: *raven locks.* [ME; OE *hræfn*, c. OHG *hraban*, MD *rāven*]

raven[2] (răv′ən), *v.i.* **1.** to seek plunder or prey. **2.** to eat or feed voraciously or greedily. **3.** to have a ravenous appetite. —*v.t.* **4.** to seize as spoil or prey. **5.** to devour voraciously. —*n.* **6.** rapine; robbery. **7.** plunder or prey. Also, **ravin.** [ME *ravine*, t. F, g. L *rapina* RAPINE]

ravening (răv′ə nĭng), *adj.* **1.** rapacious; voracious. —*n.* **2.** rapacity. —**Syn. 1.** See **ravenous.**

Ravenna (rə vĕn′ə; *It.* rȧ vĕn′nȧ), *n.* a city in NE Italy: the capital of Italy under the Byzantine Empire; tomb of Dante. 127,181 (1966).

ravenous (răv′ĭ nəs), *adj.* **1.** extremely hungry. **2.** extremely rapacious. **3.** voracious or gluttonous. **4.** given to seizing prey in order to devour, as animals. [ME, t. OF: m. *ravinos.* See RAVEN[2]] —**rav′enously,** *adv.* —**rav′enousness,** *n.*

—**Syn. 1.** RAVENOUS, RAVENING, VORACIOUS suggest a greediness for food and usually intense hunger. RAVENOUS implies extreme hunger, or a famished condition: *ravenous wild beasts.* RAVENING adds the idea of fierceness and savagery, esp. as shown in a violent manner of acquiring food: *ravening wolves.* VORACIOUS implies the eating of a great deal of food, or the disposition to eat a great deal, without reference to the degree of hunger (*a voracious small boy incessantly eating*) or figuratively (*a voracious reader*).

raver (rāʹvə), *n.* **1.** one who or that which raves. **2.** *Slang.* an enthusiastic person, usually a young one, as a fan of a pop singer. **3.** *Slang.* a homosexual.

ravin (răvʹĭn), *n., v.t., v.i.* raven[2]

ravine (rə vēnʹ), *n.* a long, deep, narrow valley, esp. one worn by water. [t. F: torrent of water, ravine]

raving (rāʹvĭng), *adj.* **1.** that raves; delirious; frenzied. **2.** *Colloq.* extraordinary or remarkable: *she's no raving beauty.* —*n.* **3.** irrational, incoherent talk.

ravioli (răvʹĭ ōʹlĭ; *It.* rȧ vyȯʹlē), *n. pl.* small pieces of pasta, cut square or otherwise, enclosing forcemeat (and often spinach), cooked, and served in a tomato sauce. [t. It., der. d. It. *rava*, ult. g. L *rāpum* turnip, beet]

ravish (răvʹĭsh), *v.t.* **1.** to fill with strong emotion, esp. joy. **2.** to seize and carry off by force. **3.** to carry off (a woman) by force. **4.** to rape (a woman). [ME *ravisshe(n)*, t. OF: m. *raviss-*, s. *ravir*, der. L *rapere* seize, carry off. Cf. RAPE[1], RAPTURE] —**ravʹisher,** *n.*

ravishing (răvʹĭ shĭng), *adj.* entrancing; enchanting. —**ravʹishingly,** *adv.*

ravishment (răvʹĭsh mənt), *n.* **1.** rapture or ecstasy. **2.** violent removal. **3.** the forcible abduction of a woman. **4.** rape.

raw (rô), *adj.* **1.** uncooked, as articles of food. **2.** not having undergone processes of preparing, dressing, finishing, refining, or manufacture: *raw silk.* **3.** unnaturally or painfully exposed, as flesh, etc., by removal of the skin or natural integument. **4.** painfully open, as a sore, wound, etc. **5.** crude in quality or character; not tempered or refined by art or taste. **6.** ignorant, inexperienced, or untrained: *a raw recruit.* **7.** brutally or grossly frank: *a raw portrayal of human passions.* **8.** *Educ.* denoting a score, level of achievement, etc., as in a test, before adjustments for age, etc., have been made. **9.** *Slang.* brutally harsh or unfair: *a raw deal.* **10.** disagreeably damp and chilly, as the weather, air, etc. **11.** *Chiefly U.S.* not diluted, as spirits. —*n.* **12.** unrefined sugar, etc. **13. the raw, a.** sore or naked flesh. **b.** a particularly sensitive place, point, topic, or the like. [ME; OE *hrēaw*, *hrǣw*, c. D *rauw*, G *roh*; akin to L *crūdus* raw, *cruor* blood, Gk *kréas* raw flesh] —**rawʹish,** *adj.* —**rawʹly,** *adv.* —**rawʹness,** *n.*

—**Syn.** **1.** RAW, CRUDE, RUDE refer to something not in a finished or highly refined state. RAW applies particularly to material not yet changed by a process, by manufacture, or by preparation for consumption: *raw cotton, leather.* CRUDE refers to that which still needs refining: *crude oil.* RUDE refers to what is still in a condition of rough simplicity or in a makeshift form: *rude agricultural implements.* —**Ant.** **1.** manufactured, polished, refined.

Rawalpindi (rôl pĭnʹdĭ), *n.* a city in Pakistan, in W Punjab: provisional capital of Pakistan. 340,175 (1961).

raw-boned (rôʹbōndʹ), *adj.* having little flesh; gaunt.

rawhide (rôʹhīdʹ), *n., adj. v.*, **-hided, -hiding.** —*n.* **1.** untanned skin of cattle or other animals. **2.** a rope or whip made of this. —*adj.* **3.** made of or pertaining to rawhide. —*v.t.* **4.** to whip with a rawhide.

Rawlinson (rôʹlĭn sən), *n.* **1. George,** 1812–1902, English historian. **2.** his brother, **Sir Henry Creswicke** (krĕzʹĭk), 1810–95, English archaeologist, diplomat, and soldier.

Rawlplug (rôlʹplŭgʹ), *n.* *Trademark.* a small drilled plug, usually of wood fibre, inserted into a hole in a wall as a fixing for a nail or screw.

raw material, 1. unprocessed or partly processed material for processing and manufacture. **2.** an untrained recruit or a group of such recruits.

Rawsthorne (rôsʹthônʹ), *n.* **Alan,** born 1905, English composer.

Rawtenstall (rôʹtn stôlʹ), *n.* a town in England, in S Lancashire. 23,890 (1961).

ray[1] (rā), *n.* **1.** a narrow beam of light. **2.** a gleam, or slight manifestation, of intelligence, comfort, etc.: *a ray of hope.* **3.** a raylike line or stretch of something. **4.** *Poetic.* light or radiance. **5.** a line of sight. **6.** *Physics.* **a.** any of the lines or streams in which light or radiant energy appears to issue from a luminous object. **b.** the straight line perpendicular to the wavefront in the propagation of radiant energy. **c.** a stream of material particles moving in the same line. **7.** *Maths.* one of a system of straight lines emanating from a point. **8.** any of a system of parts radially arranged. **9.** *Zool.* **a.** one of the branches or arms of a starfish or other radiate animal. **b.** one of the jointed supports of the soft fins of fishes. **10.** *Bot.* **a.** a ray flower. **b.** one of the branches of an umbel. **c.** a medullary ray. **d.** (in certain composite plants) the marginal part of the flower head. **11.** *Astron.* one of many long bright streaks radiating from the large lunar craters. —*v.i.* **12.** to emit rays. **13.** to issue in rays. —*v.t.* **14.** to send forth in rays. **15.** to throw rays upon; irradiate. **16.** to subject to the action of rays, as in radiotherapy. **17.** to furnish with rays or radiating lines. [ME *raye*, t. OF: m. *rai*, g. L *radius.* See RADIUS] —**Syn. 1.** See **gleam.**

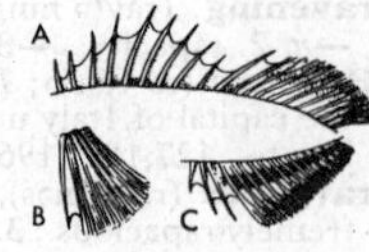

Rays on fin of fish A, Dorsal, with 10 spines; B, Ventral, with 1 spine; C, Anal, with 3 spines

ray[2] (rā), *n.* an elasmobranch fish, with flat (depressed) body fitted for life on the sea bottom, distinguished by having the gill openings on the lower surface. [ME *raye*, t. F: m. *raie*, g. L *raia*]

Ray (rā), *n.* **1. Man,** born 1890, U.S. surrealist painter and photographer. **2. Satyajit** (sătʹyə jĭt, sŭtʹ-), born 1922, Indian film director.

rayah (rīʹə), *n.* (formerly) any subject of the Sultan of Turkey who was not a Muslim. Also, **raya.** [t. Ar.: m. *ra-'īyah* flock, peasants]

ray flower, *Bot.* one of the marginal florets surrounding the disc of tubular florets in the flower heads of certain composite plants. Also, **ray floret.**

ray-grass (rāʹgräsʹ), *n.* the rye-grass *Lolium perenne.*

Rayleigh (rāʹlĭ), *n.* **1. John William Strutt** (strŭt), **3rd Baron,** 1842–1919, English physicist. **2.** a town in England, in Essex. 19,044 (1961).

Rayleigh disc, *Physics.* a small disc hung by a fine thread in the path of a soundwave so that the extent to which the disc is deflected is a measure of the intensity of the soundwave. [named after Lord RAYLEIGH]

rayless (rāʹlĭs), *adj.* **1.** without rays. **2.** unillumined, dark, or gloomy.

rayon (rāʹŏn), *n.* **1.** any textile made from cellulose by passing an appropriate solution of it through spinnerets to form filaments which are used in yarns for making cloth; artificial silk. **2.** fabric made with the product. [t. F: ray, der. OF *rai* RAY[1]]

raze (rāz), *v.t.*, **razed, razing. 1.** to tear down, demolish, or level to the ground. **2.** *Obs.* to scratch or graze. Also, **rase.** [ME *rase(n)*, t. F: m. *raser*, g. VL *rāsāre*, der. L *rāsus*, pp., scraped] —**razʹer,** *n.* —**Syn.** See **destroy.**

razee (rā zēʹ), *n., v.*, **-zeed, -zeeing.** *Obs.* —*n.* **1.** a ship, esp. a warship, reduced in height by the removal of the upper deck. —*v.t.* **2.** to cut down (a ship) by removing the upper deck. [t. F: m. *rasé*, pp. of *raser* RAZE]

razoo (rə zōōʹ), *n.* *Austral., N.Z. Colloq.* a small coin.

razor (rāʹzə), *n.* **1.** a sharp-edged instrument used esp. for shaving hair from the skin. **2.** an electrically powered device, as one having rotating or reciprocating blades behind a foil, used for the same purpose. —*v.t.* **3.** to apply a razor to. **4.** to shave. [ME *rasour*, t. OF: m. *rasor*, der. *raser* scrape, shave, RAZE]

razorback (rāʹzə băkʹ), *n.* **1.** a finback or rorqual. **2.** a wild or semi-wild pig with a ridgelike back, common in the southern U.S.

razorbill (rāʹzə bĭlʹ), *n.* a shorebird, *Alca torda*, of rocky coasts of the North Atlantic, having a flattened, slightly hooked bill.

razorshell (rāʹzə shĕlʹ), *n.* an elongated marine bivalve mollusc of the family *Solenidae*, as *Ensis ensis*, common on sandy shores in Europe.

razz (răz), *U.S. Slang.* —*v.t.* **1.** to deride; make fun of. —*n.* **2.** severe criticism; derision. [short for RASPBERRY]

razzia (răzʹĭ ə), *n.* a raid for plunder. [t. F, t. Ar. (Algerian): m. *ghāzya*]

razzle-dazzle (răzʹl dăzʹl), *n.* *Slang.* noisy and showy activity; razzmatazz.

razzmatazz (răzʹmə tăzʹ), *n.* *Slang.* **1.** noisy and showy activity. **2.** any traditional style of jazz.

Rb, *Chem.* rubidium.

R.C., 1. Red Cross. **2.** Roman Catholic.

R.C.A.F., Royal Canadian Air Force.

R.C.M., Royal College of Music.

R.C.M.P., Royal Canadian Mounted Police.

R.C.N., Royal Canadian Navy.

R.C.O., Royal College of Organists.

r-coloured (äʹkŭlʹəd), *adj.* *Phonet.* as of vowels, pronounced with a special articulation, usually retroflex, which produces an *r* quality. —**rʹ-colʹour,** *n.*

R.C.P., Royal College of Physicians.

R.C.S., Royal College of Surgeons.

Rd, Road.

rd, 1. rendered. **2.** road. **3.** rod; rods. **4.** round.

R.D.C., Rural District Council.

R.D.F., radio direction-finding.

RDX, *Chem.* cyclonite.

re[1] (rā, rē), *n.* *Music.* the syllable used for the second degree of the scale in solfa notation and sometimes for the note D. See **sol-fa.** [See GAMUT]

re[2] (rē), *prep.* in the case of; with reference to. [t. L, abl. of *rēs* thing, matter]
Re (rā), *n.* Ra.
Re, *Chem.* rhenium.
're, a contracted form of *are*: **we're** (wē ə, wiə), **you're** (yo͞o ə, yo͝oə, yô), **they're** (thā ə, thēə).
re-, **1.** a prefix indicating repetition, as in *reprint, rebirth.* **2.** a prefix indicating withdrawal or backward motion, often figurative like 'back', applied often to stems not used as words, as in *revert, retract.* [t. L]
Re, rupee. Also, **re.**
R.E., **1.** Reformed Episcopal. **2.** Right Excellent. **3.** Royal Engineers.
reach (rēch), *v.t.* **1.** to get to, or get as far as, in moving, going, travelling, etc.: *the boat reached the shore.* **2.** to come to or arrive at in some course of progress, action, etc.: *his letter reached me.* **3.** to succeed in touching or seizing with an outstretched hand, a pole, etc.: *to reach a book on a high shelf.* **4.** to stretch or hold out; extend. **5.** to stretch or extend so as to touch or meet: *the bookcase reaches the ceiling.* **6.** to establish communication with. **7.** to amount to, as in the sum or total: *the cost will reach millions.* **8.** to penetrate to (a point, etc.). **9.** to succeed in striking or hitting, as with a weapon or missile. **10.** to succeed in influencing, impressing, interesting, convincing, etc. —*v.i.* **11.** to make a stretch, as with the hand or arm. **12.** to become outstretched, as the hand or arm. **13.** to make a movement or effort as if to touch or seize something: *to reach for a weapon.* **14.** to extend in operation or effect: *power that reaches throughout the land.* **15.** to stretch in space; extend in direction, length, distance, etc.: *a coat reaching to the knee.* **16.** to extend or continue in time. **17.** to get or come to a specified place, person, condition, etc. (often fol. by *to*). **18.** to amount (fol. by *to*): *sums reaching to a considerable total.* **19.** to penetrate. **20.** *Naut.* **a.** to sail on a reach. **b.** to sail with the wind from somewhere near abeam, i.e., neither ahead nor dead astern. —*n.* **21.** the act of reaching: *to make a reach for a weapon.* **22.** the extent or distance of reaching: *within reach of his voice.* **23.** range of effective action, power, or capacity. **24.** a continuous stretch or extent of something: *a reach of woodland.* **25.** a level portion of a canal, between locks. **26.** a portion of a river between bends. **27.** *Naut.* a point of sailing where the wind is coming from within a few points of abeam. In a **close reach** the wind is forward of the beam; in a **broad reach** it is abaft the beam; in a **beam reach** it is abeam or nearly so; in a **head reach** it is very nearly dead ahead. **28.** the pole connecting the rear axle of a wagon to the transverse bar or bolster over the front axle supporting the wagon bed. [ME *reche*, OE *rǣcan*, c. G *reichen*] —**reach'er,** *n.* —**Syn.** 22, 23. See **grasp.**
reach-me-down (rēch'mĭ doun'), *n. Colloq.* **1.** an article of clothing handed down or acquired at second hand. **2.** a cheap, ready-made garment. Also, *Chiefly U.S.*, **hand-me-down.**
react (rĭ ăkt'), *v.i.* **1.** to act in return on an agent or influence; act reciprocally upon each other, as two things. **2.** to act in a reverse direction or manner. **3.** to act in opposition, as against some force. **4.** to respond to a stimulus in a particular manner. [f. RE- (def. 2) + ACT, v.]
re-act (rē ăkt'), *v.t.* to act or perform again; re-enact. [f. RE- (def. 1) + ACT, v.]
reactance (rĭ ăk'təns), *n. Elect.* that part of the impedance of an alternating-current circuit which is due to inductance and capacity. [f. REACT + -ANCE]
reactant (rĭ ăk'tənt), *n. Chem.* a substance which takes part in a chemical reaction.
reaction (rĭ ăk'shən), *n.* **1.** a reverse movement or tendency. **2.** action in a reverse direction or manner. **3.** action in response to some influence, event, etc.: *his reaction to the president's speech.* **4.** a political tendency or movement in the direction of extreme conservatism, esp. in opposition to radical or socialist policies. **5.** *Physiol.* action in response to a stimulus, as of the system, or of a nerve, muscle, etc. **6.** *Med.* **a.** the action caused by the resistance to another action. **b.** a return to the opposite physical condition, as after shock, exhaustion, or chill. **7.** *Bacteriol., Immunol.* the specific cellular effect produced by a foreign matter, as in testing for allergies. **8.** *Chem.* the reciprocal action of chemical agents upon each other; a chemical change. **9.** nuclear reaction. **10.** *Mech.* a force called into existence together with another force, being equal and opposite to it. **11.** *Com.* a drop in the market after an advance in prices.
reactionary (rĭ ăk'shə nə rĭ, -shən rĭ), *adj., n., pl.* **-aries.** —*adj.* **1.** of, pertaining to, marked by, or favouring reaction, as in politics. —*n.* **2.** one who favours or inclines to reaction. Also, **reac'tionist.**
reaction engine, *Aeron.* an engine that develops thrust by reaction to the ejection of a substance from it, esp. an engine that ejects a stream of gases created by the burning of fuel within itself as a rocket or jet engine. Also, **reaction motor.**
reaction product, *Chem.* a substance formed as the result of a chemical or nuclear reaction.
reaction propulsion, *Aeron.* jet propulsion.
reaction turbine. See **turbine.**
reactive (rĭ ăk'tĭv), *adj.* **1.** tending to react. **2.** *Chem.* chemically active; readily entering into a chemical reaction. **3.** pertaining to or characterized by reaction. **4.** *Elect.* characterized by or pertaining to reactance.
reactor (rĭ ăk'tə), *n.* **1.** a substance or person undergoing a reaction. **2.** *Elect.* a device, the primary purpose of which is to introduce reactance into a circuit. **3.** *Immunol., Vet. Sci.* a patient or animal that reacts positively towards a foreign matter. **4.** *Physics.* nuclear reactor.
read[1] (rēd), *v.*, **read** (rĕd), **reading** (rē'dĭng), *n.* —*v.t.* **1.** to observe, and apprehend the meaning of (something written, printed, etc.): *to read a book.* **2.** to utter aloud; render in speech (something written, printed, etc.). **3.** to have such knowledge of (a language) as to be able to understand things written in it: *to be able to read French.* **4.** to apprehend the meaning of (signs, characters, etc.) otherwise than with the eyes, as by means of the fingers. **5.** to make out the significance of, by scrutiny or observation: *to read the sky.* **6.** to foresee, foretell, or predict: *to read a person's fortune.* **7.** to make out the character, etc., of (a person, etc.), as by the interpretation of outward signs. **8.** to understand or take (something read or observed) in a particular way. **9.** to introduce (something not expressed or directly indicated) into what is read or considered. **10.** to adopt or give as a reading in a particular passage: *for 'one thousand' another version reads 'ten thousand'.* **11.** to register or indicate, as a thermometer or other instrument. **12.** (of a computer) to take (information) from a peripheral device, as a set of punched cards, into the central computer. **13.** to study, as by perusing books: *to read law.* **14.** to learn by, or as if by, perusal: *to read a person's thoughts.* **15.** to bring, put, etc., by reading: *to read oneself to sleep.* **16.** to give one (a lecture or lesson) by way of admonition or rebuke. **17.** to discover or explain the meaning of (a riddle, a dream, etc.). —*v.i.* **18.** to read or peruse writing, printing, etc., or papers, books, etc. **19.** to utter aloud, or render in speech, written or printed words that one is perusing: *to read to a person.* **20.** to give a public reading or recital. **21.** to inspect and apprehend the meaning of written or other signs or characters. **22.** to occupy oneself seriously with reading or study, esp. in a specific course of study: *to read for holy orders.* **23.** to obtain knowledge or learn of something by reading. **24.** to admit of being read, esp. properly or well. **25.** to have a certain wording. **26.** to admit of being read or interpreted (as stated): *a rule that reads two different ways.* **27.** (of a computer) to take in information. **28. read oneself in,** *C. of E.* to take possession of a benefice by publicly reading the Thirty-nine Articles. —*n.* **29.** the act or process of reading: *I just lay in bed and had a good read.* [ME *rede(n)*, OE *rǣdan* counsel, consider, read, c. D *raden*, G *raten*, Icel. *rādha* REDE]
read[2] (rĕd), *adj.* having knowledge gained by reading: *a widely read person.* [prop. pp. of READ[1]]
Read (rēd), *n.* **Sir Herbert,** born 1893, English poet and critic.
readable (rē'də bl), *adj.* **1.** easy or interesting to read. **2.** capable of being read; legible. —**read'abil'ity, read'ableness,** *n.* —**read'ably,** *adv.*
Reade (rēd), *n.* **Charles,** 1814–84, English novelist.
reader (rē'də), *n.* **1.** one who reads. **2.** a schoolbook for instruction and practice in reading. **3.** one employed to read and report on manuscripts, etc., submitted for publication. **4.** one who reads or recites before an audience; an elocutionist. **5.** one authorized to read the lessons, etc., in a church service. **6.** a university teacher ranking next below a professor, being a recognized authority on some

---

re'absorb', *v.t.*
re'absorp'tion, *n.*
re'accede', *v.t.*, -ceded, -ceding.
re'accel'erate', *v.*, -rated, -rating.
re'accept', *v.t.*
re'acces'sion, *n.*
re'accom'modate', *v.t.*, -dated, -dating.
re'accom'pany, *v.t.*, -nied, -nying.
re'accuse', *v.t.*, -cused, -cusing.
re'accus'tom, *v.t.*
re'acknowl'edge, *v.t.*, -ledged, -ledging.
re'acquire', *v.t.*, -quired, -quiring.
re'ac'tivate', *v.t.*, -vated, -vating.
re'adapt', *v.t.*
re'ad'apta'tion, *n.*
re'address', *v.t.*

---

subject but not normally in charge of a department. 7. *U.S.* an assistant to a professor. 8. a proofreader.

readership (rē′də shĭp′), *n.* 1. the readers collectively of a publication, esp. a newspaper or periodical. 2. the position, duty, or profession of a university or other reader. 3. the fact or state of being a reader.

readily (rĕd′ĭ lĭ), *adv.* 1. promptly; quickly; easily. 2. in a ready manner; willingly.

readiness (rĕd′ĭ nĭs), *n.* 1. the condition of being ready. 2. ready action or movement; promptness; quickness; ease; facility. 3. willingness; inclination; cheerful consent: *a readiness to help others.*

reading (rē′dĭng), *n.* 1. the action or practice of one who reads. 2. ability to read; the oral interpretation of written language. 3. the rendering given to a dramatic part, musical composition, etc., by a particular person. 4. the extent to which one has read; literary knowledge: *a man of wide reading.* 5. matter read or for reading: *a novel that makes good reading.* 6. the form or version of a given passage in a particular text: *the various readings of a line in Shakespeare.* 7. an interpretation given to anything: *what is your reading of the situation?* 8. the indication of a graduated instrument. 9. *Parl. Proc.* the formal presentation of a bill to a legislative body. —*adj.* 10. pertaining to, or used for, reading. 11. given to reading: *the reading public.*

Reading (rĕd′ĭng), *n.* 1. **Rufus Daniel Isaacs, 1st Marquess of,** 1860–1935, Lord Chief Justice of England 1913–21; viceroy of India 1921–26. 2. a county borough in England, the county town of Berkshire. 119,937 (1961). 3. a town in the U.S., in SE Pennsylvania. 98,177 (1960).

reading desk (rē′dĭng), 1. a desk for use in reading, esp. by a person standing. 2. (in church) a lectern.

reading room, a room appropriated to reading, as in a library or a club.

readjust (rē′ə jŭst′), *v.t.* to adjust again or anew; rearrange. —**re′adjust′er,** *n.*

readjustment (rē′ə jŭst′mənt), *n.* 1. a readjusting or state of being readjusted. 2. *Finance.* important changes in the financial structure of a company (often less drastic than in *reorganization*).

ready (rĕd′ĭ), *adj.*, **readier, readiest,** *v.*, **readied, readying,** *n.* —*adj.* 1. completely prepared or in due condition for immediate action or use: *troops ready for battle, dinner is ready.* 2. duly equipped, completed, adjusted, or arranged, as for the occasion or purpose. 3. willing: *ready to forgive.* 4. prompt or quick in perceiving, comprehending, speaking, writing, etc. 5. proceeding from or showing such quickness: *a ready reply.* 6. prompt or quick in action, performance, manifestation, etc. 7. inclined, disposed, or apt: *too ready to criticize others.* 8. in such a condition as to be about; likely or liable at any moment (to do something): *a tree ready to fall.* 9. immediately available for use: *ready money.* 10. pertaining to prompt payment. 11. present or convenient (to hand, to the hand, etc.): *to lie ready to one's hand.* —*v.t.* 12. to make ready; prepare. —*n.* 13. *Colloq.* ready money. 14. the condition or position of being ready: *to bring a rifle to the ready.* [ME *redy*, early ME *rædig*, f. OE *rǣde* ready + *-ig* -Y[1]]

ready-made (rĕd′ĭ mād′), *adj.* 1. made for sale to any purchaser, rather than to order: *ready-made shoes.* 2. made for immediate use. 3. perfectly suited; apt. 4. unoriginal; conventional. —*n.* 5. a ready-made article, esp. of clothing.

ready-mix (rĕd′ĭ mĭks′), *n.* 1. any preparation, as food, in which the ingredients are already mixed for immediate use. 2. concrete mixed and delivered in wet form to a site. —*adj.* 3. of or pertaining to a preparation in which the contents are already mixed.

ready reckoner, a collection of mathematical and other tables for rapid calculation.

ready-to-wear (rĕd′ĭ tə wĕə′), *adj.* (of clothing) made in standard sizes to fit a large number of people.

ready-witted (rĕd′ĭ wĭt′ĭd), *adj.* having a quick wit or intelligence.

reafforest (rē′ə fŏ′rĭst), *v.t.* to replant with forest trees. Also, **reforest.** —**re′affo′resta′tion,** *n.*

reagent (rē ā′jənt), *n.* a substance which, on account of the reactions it causes, is used in chemical analysis.

real[1] (rĭəl), *adj.* 1. true (rather than merely ostensible, nominal, or apparent): *the real reason for an act.* 2. existing or occurring as fact; actual (rather than imaginary, ideal, or fictitious): *a story taken from real life.* 3. being an actual thing, with objective existence (rather than merely imaginary). 4. being actually such (rather than merely so called): *a real victory.* 5. genuine; not counterfeit, artificial, or imitation: *a real antique, a real diamond, real silk.* 6. unfeigned or sincere: *real sympathy.* 7. *Philos.* a. existent or pertaining to the existent as opposed to the non-existent. b. actual as opposed to possible or potential. c. independent of experience as opposed to phenomenal or apparent. 8. *Law.* denoting or pertaining to immoveable property of a freehold type, as lands and tenements excluding leaseholds (opposed to *personal*). 9. *Optics.* (of an image) formed by the actual convergence of rays, as the image produced in a camera (opposed to *virtual*). 10. *Maths.* of or pertaining to a real number. —*adv.* 11. *Colloq.* very. —*n.* 12. **the real, a.** that which is real or actually exists. b. reality in general. [ME, t. LL: s. *reālis*, der. L *rēs* thing, matter] —**real′ness,** *n.*

—**Syn.** 2. REAL, ACTUAL, TRUE suggest a faithful rendering of facts, whether those existing in nature or those created by human action. REAL applies particularly to facts rooted in nature: *sunshine and rain are real.* ACTUAL applies to facts as they now are or have become, implying that one may have previously had a different idea of them or that the facts themselves may have been changed by circumstances: *the actual facts of natural science are different today since new elements have been created.* TRUE may be used of that which conforms to either the real or the actual.

real[2] (rā äl′; *Sp.* rĕ äl′), *n., pl.* **reals** (rā älz′), *Sp.* **reales** (rĕ ä′lĕs). 1. a former silver coin of Spain and certain Spanish-American countries, equal to one eighth of a peso. 2. a former Spanish monetary unit equal to one quarter of a peseta. [t. Sp.: lit., royal, g. L *rēgālis* regal]

real[3] (*Port.* ryäl), *n.* sing. of **reis.**

real estate, real property.

realgar (rĭ äl′gə), *n.* arsenic disulphide, As_2S_2, found native as an orange-red mineral and also prepared artificially: used in pyrotechnics. [ME, t. ML, t. Ar.: m. *rehj alghār* powder of the mine]

realism (rĭə′lĭz′əm), *n.* 1. interest in or concern for the actual or real as distinguished from the abstract, speculative, etc. 2. the taking of a practical rather than a moral view in human problems, etc. 3. the tendency to view or represent things as they really are. 4. the treatment of subjects in literature or art with fidelity to nature or to real life (opposed to *idealism*). 5. a 19th-century movement in painting and literature characterized by fidelity to life or to nature, particularly the squalid and depressing, as a reaction against romanticism. 6. *Philos.* a. the doctrine that universals have a real objective existence (**medieval realism**). Cf. **nominalism** and **conceptualism.** b. the doctrine that objects of sense perception have an existence independent of the act of perception. Cf. **idealism.**

realist (rĭə′lĭst), *n.* 1. one who tends to view or represent things as they really are, esp. a writer or artist. 2. one who takes a practical rather than a moral view in human problems, etc. 3. an adherent of philosophical or literary or artistic realism. —*adj.* 4. of, pertaining to, denoting, or characteristic of artistic or literary realism.

realistic (rĭə lĭs′tĭk), *adj.* 1. interested in or concerned with what is real or practical. 2. taking a practical rather than a moral view in human problems, etc. 3. pertaining to, characterized by, or given to the representation in literature or art of things as they really are: *a realistic novel.* 4. of or pertaining to realists or realism in philosophy. —**realis′tically,** *adv.*

reality (rĭ äl′ĭ tĭ), *n., pl.* **-ties.** 1. the state or fact of being real. 2. resemblance to what is real. 3. a real thing or fact. 4. *Philos.* a. that which exists independently of ideas concerning it. b. that which exists independently of all other things; an ultimate thing which produces derivatives. 5. that which is real. 6. that which constitutes the real or actual thing, as distinguished from that which is merely apparent. 7. **in reality,** really; actually; in fact or truth.

realization (rĭə′lĭ zā′shən), *n.* 1. the making or being made real of something imagined, planned, etc. 2. the result of such a process: *the realization of a project.* 3. the act of realizing. 4. the state of being realized. 5. an instance or result of realizing. 6. *Music.* a. the act of realizing a piece of music. b. the work so realized. Also, **realisation.**

realize (rĭə′lĭz), *v.*, **-lized, -lizing.** —*v.t.* 1. to grasp or understand clearly. 2. to make real, or give reality to (a hope, fear, plan, etc.). 3. to bring vividly before the mind. 4. to convert into cash or money: *to realize securities.* 5. to obtain as a profit or income for oneself by trade, labour, or investment. 6. to bring as proceeds, as from a sale: *the goods realized £1000.* 7. *Music.* a. to

re′adjourn′, *v.*
re′adjourn′ment, *n.*
re′admin′ister, *v.t.*
re′admis′sion, *n.*
re′admit′, *v.*, **-mitted, -mitting.**
re′admit′tance, *n.*
re′adopt′, *v.t.*
re′adop′tion, *n.*
re′adorn′, *v.t.*
re′advance′, *v.*, **-vanced, -vancing.**
re′ad′vertise′, *v.*, **-tised, -tising.**
re′affirm′, *v.t.*
re′af′firma′tion, *n.*
re′align′, *v.*
re′align′ment, *n.*
re′al′locate′, *v.t.*, **-cated, -cating.**

create, as an orchestral work, from parts or a part left by a composer. **b.** to create a complete work from. —*v.i.* **8.** to convert property or goods into cash or money. **9.** to realize a profit. Also, **realise.** —**real′izable,** *adj.* —**real′izer,** *n.* —**Syn. 1.** conceive, comprehend. **3.** See **imagine.**

really (rĭə′lĭ), *adv.* **1.** in reality; actually: *to see things as they really are.* **2.** genuinely or truly: *a really honest man.* **3.** indeed: *really, this is too much.*

realm (rĕlm), *n.* **1.** a royal domain; kingdom: *the realm of England.* **2.** the region, sphere, or domain within which anything rules or prevails: *the realm of dreams.* **3.** the special province or field of something: *the realm of physics.* [ME *realme,* t. OF: m. *reialme,* der. *reial* regal, g. L *rēgālis*] —**Syn. 1.** See **kingdom.**

real number, *Maths.* a rational number or the limit of a sequence of rational numbers, as opposed to complex numbers.

Realpolitik (*Ger.* rė ȧl′pō lē tēk′), *n.* *German.* political realism, esp. policy based on power rather than on ideals.

Real Presence, *Theol.* the doctrine of the Roman Catholic and Orthodox Churches that in the liturgy, under the semblance of bread and wine, the actual body and blood of the Saviour are present on the altar.

real property, land and whatever by nature or artificial annexation is a part of it or is the means of its enjoyment, as minerals, trees, buildings, fences, etc.

real tennis, an ancient form of tennis played in a walled court, points being scored by hitting the ball so that it lands between certain lines marked on the walls, or in certain openings in the walls. Also, **royal tennis;** *Chiefly U.S.,* **court tennis.** [ME *real* royal (t. OF) + TENNIS]

realtor (rĭəl′tə, -tô), *n.* *U.S.* an estate agent. [f. REALT(Y) + -OR²]

realty (rĭəl′tĭ), *n.* real property. [f. REAL¹ (def. 8) + -TY²]

real wages, wages estimated not in money but in their purchasing power. Cf. **nominal wages.**

ream¹ (rēm), *n.* **1.** a standard quantity among paper dealers meaning 20 quires or 500 sheets (formerly 480 sheets). A **printer's ream** consists of 484–516 sheets. **2.** (*pl.*) *Colloq.* a large quantity: *to write reams and reams of poetry.* [ME *rem,* t. OF: m. *rayme,* through Sp., t. Ar.: m. *razmah, rizmah* bundle or bale]

ream² (rēm), *v.t.* to enlarge (a hole or opening) to size by means of a reamer. [ME *reme,* OE *rēman* open up]

reamer (rē′mə), *n.* one of many rotating finishing tools with spiral or straight fluted cutting edges for finishing a hole to size and shape. [f. REAM² + -ER¹]

A

B

Reamers
A, Head of machinist's reamer; B, Head of flatsided reamer or broach

reanimate (rē ăn′ĭ māt′), *v.t.,* **-mated, -mating. 1.** to restore to life; resuscitate. **2.** to give fresh vigour, spirit, or courage to. **3.** to stimulate to renewed activity. —**re′animа′tion,** *n.*

reap (rēp), *v.t.* **1.** to cut (grain, etc.) with a sickle or other implement or a machine, as in harvest. **2.** to gather or take (a crop, harvest, etc.). **3.** to get as a return, recompense, or result: *to reap large profits.* —*v.i.* **4.** to reap grain, etc. [ME *repe(n),* OE *repan,* c. MLG *repen* ripple (flax); akin to RIPE]

reaper (rē′pə), *n.* **1.** a machine for cutting standing grain; a reaping machine. **2.** one who reaps.

reaping machine, a machine for reaping corn.

rear¹ (rĭə), *n.* **1.** the back of anything, as opposed to the front. **2.** the space or position behind anything. **3.** the behind; buttocks. **4.** the hindmost portion of an army, fleet, etc. —*adj.* **5.** situated at or pertaining to the rear: *the rear door.* [aphetic var. of ARREAR, n.] —**Syn. 5.** See **back¹.**

rear² (rĭə), *v.t.* **1.** to care for and support up to maturity: *to rear a child.* **2.** to raise by building; erect. **3.** to raise to an upright position: *to rear a ladder.* **4.** to lift or hold up; elevate; raise. —*v.i.* **5.** to rise on the hind legs, as a horse or other animal. **6.** (of persons) to start up in angry excitement, hot resentment, or the like (commonly fol. by *up*). **7.** to rise high or tower aloft, as a building. [ME *rere(n),* OE *rǣran* RAISE, c. Goth. *-raisjan,* Icel. *reisa*]

rear admiral, a naval officer next in rank below a vice-admiral.

rearguard (rĭə′gäd′), *n.* a part of an army or military force detached from the main body to bring up and guard the rear from surprise attack, esp. in a retreat.

rearm (rē′äm′), *v.t.* **1.** to arm again. **2.** to furnish with new or better weapons: *they rearmed the troops as soon as possible.* —*v.i.* **3.** to arm oneself again. —**rearmament** (rē′ä′mə mənt), *n.*

rearmost (rĭə′mōst′), *adj.* farthest in the rear; last.

rear sight, the sight nearest the breech of a firearm.

rearview mirror (rĭə′vyōō′), a mirror on a motor vehicle placed so that the driver can see traffic approaching from behind.

rearward (rĭə′wəd), *adj., adv.* towards or in the rear.

rearwards (rĭə′wədz), *adv.* rearward.

reason (rē′zən), *n.* **1.** a ground or cause, as for a belief, action, fact, event, etc.: *the reason for declaring war.* **2.** a statement in justification or explanation of belief or action. **3.** the mental powers concerned with drawing conclusions or inferences. **4.** sound judgement or good sense. **5.** normal or sound powers of mind; sanity. **6.** *Logic.* a premise of an argument. **7.** *Philos.* intellect as opposed to sensibility. In Kantianism it is superior to understanding and a source of a priori principles. **8. by reason of,** on account of; because of. **9. in** or **within reason,** in accordance with reason; justifiable or proper. **10. it stands to reason,** it is obvious or logical. —*v.i.* **11.** to think or argue in a logical manner. **12.** to draw conclusions or inferences from facts or premises. **13.** to urge reasons which should determine belief or action. —*v.t.* **14.** to think out (a problem, etc.) logically (often fol. by *out*). **15.** to conclude or infer (fol. by *that*). **16.** to bring, persuade, etc., by reasoning. **17.** to support with reasons. [ME *reisun,* t. OF: m. *raison,* g. L *ratio* reckoning, account] —**rea′soner,** *n.*

—**Syn. 1.** REASON, CAUSE, MOTIVE are terms for a circumstance (or circumstances) which brings about or explains certain results. A REASON is an explanation of a situation or circumstance which made certain results seem possible or appropriate: *the reason for the robbery was the victim's display of his money.* The CAUSE is the way in which the circumstances produce the effect; that is, make a specific action seem necessary or desirable: *the cause was the robber's extreme need of money.* A MOTIVE is the hope, desire, or other force which starts the action (or an action) in an attempt to produce specific results: *the motive was to get money to buy food for his family.*

reasonable (rē′zə nə bl, rēz′nə-), *adj.* **1.** endowed with reason. **2.** agreeable to reason or sound judgement: *a reasonable choice.* **3.** not exceeding the limit prescribed by reason; not excessive: *reasonable terms.* **4.** moderate, or moderate in price: *the coat was reasonable but not cheap.* —**rea′sonableness, rea′sonabil′ity,** *n.* —**rea′sonably,** *adv.*

—**Syn. 1.** REASONABLE, RATIONAL refer to the faculty of reasoning. RATIONAL is the more technical or more abstract term, concerned always with pure reason. It is applied to statements, etc., which reflect or satisfy highly logical thinking: *her conclusions are always of a rational, never an emotional, nature.* REASONABLE has taken on more and more the pragmatic idea of simple common sense: *a reasonable supposition is one which appeals to our common sense.*

reasoned (rē′zənd), *adj.* **1.** guided by reason: *a carefully reasoned decision.* **2.** logically thought out and presented: *a reasoned reply.*

reasoning (rē′zə nĭng), *n.* **1.** the act or process of one who reasons. **2.** the process of drawing conclusions or inferences from facts or premises. **3.** the reasons, arguments, proofs, etc., resulting from this process.

reasonless (rē′zən lĭs), *adj.* **1.** not according to reason: *an utterly reasonless display of temper.* **2.** not endowed with reason. —**rea′sonlessly,** *adv.* —**rea′sonlessness,** *n.*

reassure (rē′ə shŏŏə′, -shô′), *v.t.,* **-sured, -suring. 1.** to restore (a person, etc.) to assurance or confidence: *his remarks reassured me.* **2.** to assure again. **3.** to reinsure. —**re′assur′ance,** *n.* —**re′assur′er,** *n.* —**re′assur′ing,** *adj.* —**re′assur′ingly,** *adv.*

---

re′allot′, *v.t.,* **-lotted, -lotting.**
re′an′alyse′, *v.t.,* **-lysed, -lysing.**
re′anal′ysis, *n.*
re′appeal′, *v.t.*
re′appear′, *v.i.*
re′appear′ance, *n.*
re′ap′plica′tion, *n.*
re′apply′, *v.,* **-plied, -plying.**
re′appoint′, *v.t.*
re′appoint′ment, *n.*
re′apprai′sal, *n.*
re′ap′prehend′, *v.t.*
re′ap′prehen′sion, *n.*
re′approach′, *v.*
re′appro′priate′, *v.t.,* **-ated, -ating.**
re′appro′pria′tion, *n.*
re′ar′gue, *v.t.,* **-gued, -guing.**
re′arrange′, *v.t.,* **-ranged, -ranging.**
re′arrange′ment, *n.*
re′arrest′, *v.t., n.*
re′artic′ulate′, *v.,* **-lated, -lating.**
re′artic′ula′tion, *n.*
re′ascend′, *v.*
re′ascent′, *n.*
re′assem′ble, *v.,* **-sembled, -sembling.**
re′assem′bly, *n.*
re′assert′, *v.t.*
re′asser′tion, *n.*
re′assess′, *v.t.*
re′assess′ment, *n.*
re′assign′, *v.t.*
re′assign′ment, *n.*
re′assim′ilate′, *v.,* **-lated, -lating.**
re′assim′ila′tion, *n.*
re′asso′ciate′, *v.,* **-ated, -ating.**
re′assume′, *v.t.,* **-sumed, -suming.**
re′assump′tion, *n.*

Réaum., Réaumur (thermometer).

Réaumur (*Fr.* rė ō mʏr′), *n.* **René Antoine Ferchault de** (*Fr.* rə nė äɴ twȧn fĕr shō′ də), 1683–1757, French physicist and inventor.

Réaumur (rā′ə myo͞oə′), *adj.* designating, or in accordance with, the thermometric scale introduced by de Réaumur in which the freezing point of water is at 0°, and the boiling point at 80°. See illus. under **thermometer.** *Abbrev.*: R. Also, **Reaumur.**

reave[1] (rēv), *v.t.*, **reaved** or **reft, reaving.** *Archaic.* to deprive forcibly, strip, or rob. [ME *reve(n)*, OE *rēafian*, c. G *rauben* ROB]

reave[2] (rēv), *v.t., v.i.*, **reaved** or **reft, reaving.** *Archaic.* to rend; break; tear. [appar. special use of REAVE[1] by assoc. with RIVE]

rebarbative (rĭ bä′bə tĭv), *adj.* unattractive; fearsome or repellent. [t. F: m. *rébarbatif*, der. *rébarber*, equiv. to *ré-* RE- + *barbe* beard + *-atif* -ATIVE]

rebate[1] (*n.* rē′bāt; *v.* rĭ bāt′), *n., v.*, **-bated, -bating.** —*n.* **1.** a return of part of an original amount paid for some service or merchandise; repayment, as of a part of charges. —*v.t.* **2.** to allow as a discount. **3.** to deduct (a certain amount), as from a total. **4.** *Obs.* to reduce the effectiveness of (a thing) or the vigour of (a person). **5.** *Obs.* to make blunt (the edge of a weapon, etc.) [ME, t. OF: m. *rabatre* beat or put down, f. *re-* RE- + *abatre* ABATE[1]]

rebate[2] (rē′bāt, răb′ĭt), *n., v.t., v.i.*, **-bated, -bating.** rabbet. [var. of RABBET]

rebec (rē′bĕk), *n.* a small medieval fiddle having commonly a pear-shaped body and three strings, and played with a bow. Also, **rebeck.** [t. F; r. ME *ribibe*, ult. t. Ar.: m. *rabāb* primitive one- or two-stringed viol]

Rebecca (rĭ bĕk′ə), *n.* *Bible.* the sister of Laban, wife of Isaac, and mother of Esau and Jacob. Gen. 24–27. Also, **Rebekah.**

rebel (*n., adj.* rĕb′l; *v.* rĭ bĕl′), *n., adj., v.*, **-belled, -belling.** —*n.* **1.** one who refuses allegiance to, resists, or rises in arms against, the established government or ruler. **2.** one who or that which resists any authority or control. **3.** one who rejects traditional or established customs, culture, etc. —*adj.* **4.** rebellious. **5.** of or pertaining to rebels. —*v.i.* **6.** to rise in arms or active resistance against one's government or ruler. **7.** to resist any authority. **8.** to manifest or feel utter repugnance: *her very soul rebelled at going back.* [ME *rebell(en)*, t. OF: m. *rebeller*, t. L: m. *rebellāre* wage war again (as conquered people)] —**Syn. 1.** insurgent, insurrectionist, mutineer. **6.** revolt, mutiny.

Rebec

rebeldom (rĕb′l dəm), *n.* **1.** a region controlled by rebels. **2.** rebels collectively. **3.** rebellious conduct.

rebellion (rĭ bĕl′yən), *n.* **1.** open, organized, and armed resistance to one's government or ruler. **2.** resistance against or defiance of any authority or control. **3.** rejection of traditional or established customs, culture, etc. **4.** the act of rebelling. [ME, t. L: s. *rebellio*] —**Syn. 1.** insurrection, mutiny, sedition, revolution. See **revolt. 2.** insubordination, disobedience.

rebellious (rĭ bĕl′yəs), *adj.* **1.** defying lawful authority; insubordinate; disposed to rebel. **2.** pertaining to or characteristic of rebels or rebellion. **3.** (of things) resisting treatment; refractory. [ME, f. REBELLI(ON) + -OUS] —**rebel′liously,** *adv.* —**rebel′liousness,** *n.* —**Syn. 1.** insurgent, mutinous, seditious.

rebirth (rē′bûth′), *n.* **1.** being born again; a second birth. **2.** a renaissance; a new activity or growth.

reboant (rĕb′ō ənt), *adj.* resounding loudly. [t. L: s. *reboans*, ppr., bellowing in return]

rebop (rē′bŏp′), *n.* *Jazz.* bebop.

rebore (rē′bô′), *v.*, **-bored, -boring,** *n.* —*v.t.* **1.** to bore again. **2.** to bore out (the cylinders of an internal-combustion engine). —*n.* **3.** the process of reboring or being rebored.

reborn (rē′bôn′), *adj.* born again.

rebound (*v.* rĭ bound′; *n.* rē′bound′, rĭ bound′), *v.i.* **1.** to bound or spring back from force of impact. —*v.t.* **2.** to cause to bound back; cast back. —*n.* **3.** the act of rebounding; recoil. **4. on the rebound, a.** in the act of bouncing back. **b.** during a period of reaction, as after being rejected: *she married him on the rebound after an unhappy love affair.* [ME, t. OF: m. s. *rebondir*]

rebuff (rĭ bŭf′), *n.* **1.** a blunt or abrupt check, as to one making advances. **2.** a peremptory refusal of a request, offer, etc.; a snub. **3.** a check to action or progress. —*v.t.* **4.** to give a rebuff to; check; repel; refuse; drive away. [t. F (obs.): m. *rebuffe*, t. It.: m. *ribuffo*]

rebuke (rĭ byo͞ok′), *v.t.*, **-buked, -buking,** *n.* —*v.t.* **1.** to reprove or reprimand. —*n.* **2.** a reproof; a reprimand. [ME, t. AF: m. *rebuker*, var. of OF *rebuchier* beat back] —**rebuke′able,** *adj.* —**rebuk′er,** *n.* —**Syn. 1.** censure, upbraid, chide. See **reproach.**

rebus (rē′bəs), *n.* an enigmatical representation of a word or phrase by pictures, symbols, etc., suggesting the word elements or words: *two gates and a head is a rebus for Gateshead.* [t. L, abl. pl. of *rēs* thing]

rebut (rĭ bŭt′), *v.t.*, **-butted, -butting. 1.** to refute by evidence or argument. **2.** to oppose by contrary proof. [ME *rebute(n)*, t. AF: m. *reboter*, f. *re-* RE- + *boter* BUTT, v.] —**rebut′table,** *adj.*

rebuttal (rĭ bŭt′l), *n.* the act of rebutting, esp. in law.

rebutter[1] (rĭ bŭt′ə), *n.* one who or that which rebuts. [REBUT + -ER[1]]

rebutter[2] (rĭ bŭt′ə), *n.* *Law.* a defendant's answer to a plaintiff's surrejoinder. [t. AF: m. *rebuter*, inf. used as noun]

rec., **1.** receipt. **2.** recipe. **3.** record. **4.** recorder.

recalcitrant (rĭ kăl′sĭ trənt), *adj.* **1.** resisting authority or control; not obedient or compliant; refractory. —*n.* **2.** a recalcitrant person. [t. L: s. *recalcitrans*, ppr., lit., kicking back] —**recal′citrance, recal′citrancy,** *n.*

recalcitrate (rĭ kăl′sĭ trāt′), *v.i.*, **-trated, -trating.** to make resistance or opposition; show strong objection or repugnance. —**recal′citra′tion,** *n.*

recalesce (rē′kə lĕs′), *v.i.*, **-lesced, -lescing.** *Metall.* to become hot again (said esp. of cooling iron, which glows with increased brilliancy upon passing certain temperatures). [t. L: m. s. *recalescere*] —**re′cales′cence,** *n.* —**re′cales′cent,** *adj.*

recall (rĭ kôl′), *v.t.* **1.** to recollect or remember. **2.** to call back; summon to return. **3.** to bring back in thought or attention, as to present circumstances. **4.** to revoke, take back, or withdraw: *to recall a promise.* **5.** to deprive (a public official) of office. **6.** *Poetic.* to revive. —*n.* **7.** the act of recalling. **8.** memory; recollection. **9.** the act or possibility of revoking something. **10.** *U.S.* the removal, or the right of removal, of a public official from office by a vote of the people taken upon petition of a specified number of the qualified electors. **11.** a signal flag used to recall a boat to a ship, etc. —**recall′able,** *adj.* —**Syn. 1.** See **remember.**

Récamier (*Fr.* rė kȧ myė′), *n.* **Madame** (*Jeanne Françoise Julie Adélaïde Bernard*), 1777–1849, French social leader in the literary and political circles of Paris.

recant (rĭ kănt′), *v.t.* **1.** to withdraw or disavow (a statement, etc.), esp. formally; retract. —*v.i.* **2.** to disavow an opinion, etc., esp. formally. [t. L: s. *recantāre*] —**recantation** (rē′kăn tā′shən), *n.* —**recant′er,** *n.*

recap[1] (rē′kăp′), *n., v.*, **-capped, -capping.** *Colloq.* —*n.* **1.** a recapitulation. —*v.t., v.i.* **2.** to recapitulate.

recap[2] (rē′kăp′, rē kăp′), *v.t.*, **-capped, -capping.** *U.S.* to retread.

recapitalization (rē kăp′ĭ tə lī zā′shən), *n.* a revision of a company's capital structure by an exchange of securities. Also, **recapitalisation.**

recapitalize (rē kăp′ĭ tə līz′), *v.t.*, **-lized, -lizing.** to renew or change the capital of. Also, **recapitalise.**

recapitulate (rē′kə pĭt′yo͞o lāt′), *v.*, **-lated, -lating.** —*v.t.* **1.** to review by way of an orderly summary, as at the end of a speech or discourse. **2.** *Zool.* (of a young animal) to repeat (ancestral evolutionary stages) in its development. **3.** *Music.* to restate (an original musical argument) in a sonata-form movement. —*v.i.* **4.** to sum up statements or matters. [t. LL: m. s. *recapitulātus*, pp] —**Syn. 1.** See **repeat.**

recapitulation (rē′kə pĭt′yo͞o lā′shən), *n.* **1.** the act of recapitulating. **2.** the state or fact of being recapitulated. **3.** a review or summary, as at the end of a speech or discourse. **4.** *Zool.* the repetition of ancestral evolutionary stages in the development of an individual. **5.** the theory that such repetition takes place, as in the embryonic development of an individual. **6.** *Music.* (in a sonata-form movement) the restatement of the original musical argument. —**recapitulative** (rē′kə pĭt′yo͞o lə tĭv), **recapitulatory** (rē′kə pĭt′yo͞o lə tə rĭ, -trĭ), *adj.*

---

re′attach′, *v.t.*
re′attach′ment, *n.*
re′attain′, *v.t.*
re′attain′ment, *n.*
re′attempt′, *v.t.*
re′au′dit, *v., n.*
re′audi′tion, *v., n.*
re′au′thorize′, *v.t.*, **-rized, -rizing.**
re′awa′ken, *v.*
re′awa′kening, *n.*
re′bait′, *v.t.*
re′bap′tism, *n.*
re′baptize′, *v.t.*, **-tized, -tizing.**
re′bid′, *v.*, **-bade** or **-bid, -bidding.**
re′bind′, *v.t.*, **-bound, -binding.**
re′board′, *v.t.*
re′broad′cast, *v.t.*, **-cast** or **-casted, -casting,** *n.*
re′build′, *v.*, **-built, -building.**
re′bu′ry, *v.t.*, **-buried, -burying.**
re′cal′culate′, *v.*
re′calk′, *v.t.*

---

b., blend of, blended; c., cognate with; d., dialect, dialectal; der., derived from; f., formed from; g., going back to; m., modification of; r., replacing; s., stem of; t., taken from; ?, perhaps. See full key on inside front cover.

recaption (rĭ kăp′shən), *n. Law.* the remedy of retaking one's goods, wife, child, or servant, without a breach of the peace, from one who has taken them.

recapture (rē/kăp′chə), *v.*, **-tured, -turing,** *n.* —*v.t.* **1.** to capture again; recover by capture; retake. **2.** *U.S.* (of the government) to take by recapture. **3.** to evoke anew or repeat (an experience, sensation, achievement, or the like). —*n.* **4.** recovery or retaking by capture. **5.** *U.S.* the taking by the government of a fixed part of all earnings in excess of a certain percentage of property value, as in the case of a railway. **6.** the fact of being recaptured.

recast (*v.* rē/käst′; *n.* rē/käst′, rē′käst/), *v.*, **-cast, -casting,** *n.* —*v.t.* **1.** to cast again or anew. **2.** to provide a new or altered cast for (a play, etc.). **3.** to form, fashion, or arrange again. **4.** to remodel or reconstruct (a literary work, a document, a sentence, etc.). —*n.* **5.** a recasting. **6.** a new form produced by recasting. —**re/cast′er,** *n.*

recce (rĕk′ĭ), *n. Mil. Slang.* reconnaissance.

recd, received. Also, **rec'd.**

recede (rĭ sēd′), *v.i.*, **-ceded, -ceding. 1.** to go or move back, to or towards a more distant point. **2.** to become more distant. **3.** to slope backwards: *a receding chin.* **4.** to draw back or withdraw from a position taken in a matter, or from an undertaking, promise, etc. [ME, t. L: m. s. *recēdere* go back]

re-cede (rē sēd′), *v.t.*, **-ceded, -ceding.** to cede back; yield or grant to a former possessor. [f. RE- + CEDE]

receipt (rĭ sēt′), *n.* **1.** a written acknowledgement of having received money, goods, etc., specified. **2.** (*pl.*) the amount or quantity received. **3.** the act of receiving. **4.** the state of being received. **5.** that which is received. **6.** a recipe. —*v.t.* **7.** to acknowledge in writing the payment of (a bill). **8.** to give a receipt for (money, goods, etc.). —*v.i.* **9.** to give a receipt, as for money or goods. [ME *receite*, t. AF, g. L *recepta*, fem. pp., received]

receiptor (rĭ sē′tə), *n. Chiefly U.S.* **1.** one who receipts. **2.** *U.S. Law.* a person to whom attached property is delivered for safekeeping in return for a bond to produce it when the litigation ends.

receivable (rĭ sē′və bl), *adj.* **1.** fit for acceptance. **2.** awaiting receipt of payment: *accounts receivable.* **3.** capable of being received.

receive (rĭ sēv′), *v.*, **-ceived, -ceiving.** —*v.t.* **1.** to take into one's hand or one's possession (something offered or delivered). **2.** to have (something) bestowed, conferred, etc.: *to receive an honorary degree.* **3.** to have delivered or brought to oneself: *to receive a letter.* **4.** to get or learn: *to receive notice, to receive news.* **5.** to become the support of; sustain. **6.** to hold or contain. **7.** to take into the mind; apprehend mentally. **8.** to take from another by hearing or listening: *a priest received his confession.* **9.** to meet with; experience: *to receive attention.* **10.** to suffer or undergo: *to receive an affront.* **11.** to have inflicted upon one: *to receive a broken arm.* **12.** to be at home to (visitors). **13.** to greet or welcome (guests, etc.) upon arriving. **14.** to admit (a person) to a place. **15.** to admit to a state or condition, a privilege, membership, etc.: *to receive someone into the Church.* **16.** to accept as authoritative, valid, true, or approved: *a principle universally received.* —*v.i.* **17.** to receive something. **18.** to receive visitors or guests. **19.** *Radio.* to convert incoming electromagnetic waves into the original signal, as soundwaves or light on a television screen. **20.** to receive the Eucharist. [ME *receve*, t. ONF: m. *receivre*, ult. g. L *recipere* take back, take to one's self, receive]

Received Standard English, the dialect of English which has won general acceptance in England and certain other places as 'correct'; the speech of the southern middle classes, the B.B.C., and the universities, historically deriving chiefly from the south-east Midland dialect of Middle English.

receiver (rĭ sē′və), *n.* **1.** one who or that which receives. **2.** a device or apparatus which receives electrical signals, waves, or the like, and renders them perceptible to the senses, as the part of a telephone held to the ear, a radio receiving set, or a television receiving set. **3.** *Law.* a person appointed, usually by a court, to take charge of a business or property of others, pending litigation. **4.** *Com.* one appointed to receive money due. **5.** one who, for purposes of profit or concealment, knowingly receives stolen goods. **6.** a receptacle; a device or apparatus for receiving or holding something. **7.** *Chem. Obs.* a vessel for collecting and containing a distillate.

receiver-general (rĭ sē′və jĕn′ə rəl, -jĕn′rəl), *n.* (in Great Britain) an officer in each county who receives the taxes and remits the money to the Treasury.

receivership (rĭ sē′və shĭp/), *n. Law.* **1.** the condition of being in the hands of a receiver. **2.** the position or function of being a receiver in charge of administering the property of others.

receiving set, *Radio.* a mechanism for the reception of electromagnetic waves.

recension (rĭ sĕn′shən), *n.* **1.** a revision of an early work on the basis of critical examination of the text and the sources used. **2.** a version of a text resulting from such revision. [t. L: s. *recensio*]

recent (rē′sənt), *adj.* **1.** of late occurrence, appearance, or origin; lately happening, done, made, etc.: *recent events.* **2.** not long past, as a period. **3.** belonging to such a period; not remote or primitive. **4.** (*often cap.*) *Geol.* pertaining to the later division of the Quaternary period or system, succeeding the Pleistocene, and regarded as the present or existing geological division. [t. L: s. *recens*] —**re′cency, re′centness,** *n.* —**re′cently,** *adv.* —**Syn. 1.** See **modern.**

recept (rē′sĕpt), *n. Psychol.* an idea formed by the repetition of similar percepts, as successive percepts of the same object. [t. L: s. *receptum*, neut. pp., taken back]

receptacle (rĭ sĕp′tə kl), *n.* **1.** that which serves to receive or hold something; a repository; a container. **2.** *Bot.* the modified or expanded portion of an axis, which bears the organs of a single flower or the florets of a flower head. **3.** *Elect., U.S.* a socket outlet. [late ME, t. L: m. s. *receptāculum*]

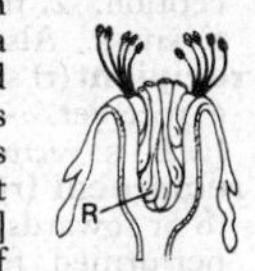

R, Receptacle (Longitudinal section)

reception (rĭ sĕp′shən), *n.* **1.** the act of receiving. **2.** the fact of being received. **3.** a manner of being received: *the book met with a favourable reception.* **4.** a function or occasion when people are formally received. **5.** a place, office, desk, or the like where callers are received, as in an office or hotel. **6.** *Radio.* the quality or fidelity attained in receiving under given circumstances. [ME *recepcion*, t. L: m. s. *receptio*]

reception centre, a place provided by local authorities where homeless persons are received.

receptionist (rĭ sĕp′shə nĭst), *n.* a person employed to receive callers, as in an office or hotel.

reception room, a room for receiving visitors, clients, etc.

receptive (rĭ sĕp′tĭv), *adj.* **1.** having the quality of receiving, taking in, or admitting. **2.** able or quick to receive ideas, etc.: *a receptive mind.* **3.** having, or characterized by, a disposition to receive a suggestion, offer, or the like with favour: *a receptive person.* **4.** of or pertaining to reception or receptors: *a receptive end organ.* —**recep′tively,** *adv.* —**receptivity** (rē/sĕp tĭv′ĭ tĭ), **recep′tiveness,** *n.*

receptor (rĭ sĕp′tə), *n. Physiol.* one of or a group of the end organs of sensory or afferent neurons, specialized to be sensitive to stimulating agents. [t. L: a receiver]

recess (*n.* rĭ sĕs′, rē′sĕs; *v.* rĭ sĕs′), *n.* **1.** a part or space that is set back or recedes, as a bay or an alcove in a room. **2.** an indentation in a line or extent of coast, hills, forest, etc. **3.** (*usually pl.*) a secluded inner area or part: *in the recesses of the palace.* **4.** *Chiefly U.S.* withdrawal or cessation for a time from the usual occupation, work, or activity. **5.** *Chiefly U.S.* a period of such withdrawal, as the mid-morning break between school classes. —*v.t.* **6.** to place or set in a recess. **7.** to set or form as or like a recess; make a recess or recesses in: *to recess a wall.* —*v.i.* **8.** *Chiefly U.S.* to take a recess. [t. L: s. *recessus* a going back]

recession[1] (rĭ sĕsh′ən), *n.* **1.** the act of receding or withdrawing. **2.** a receding part of a wall, etc. **3.** a procession at the end of a church service. **4.** a decline in business. [t. L: s. *recessio*]

recession[2] (rē sĕsh′ən), *n.* the returning of ownership to a former possessor. [f. RE- + CESSION]

recessional (rĭ sĕsh′ə nəl), *adj.* **1.** of or pertaining to a recession of the clergy and choir after a church service. **2.** of or pertaining to a recess, as of a legislative body. —*n.* **3.** a recessional hymn, or music for it.

recessional hymn, a hymn sung at the close of a church service while the clergy and choir retire from the chancel to the vestry.

recessive (rĭ sĕs′ĭv), *adj.* **1.** tending to recede; receding. **2.** *Biol.* pertaining to or exhibiting a recessive, as opposed to a dominant. **3.** (of accent) showing a tendency to recede from the end towards the beginning of a word. —*n. Biol.* **4.** a hereditary character resulting from a gene which possesses less biochemical activity than another termed the dominant, and hence is suppressed more or less completely by it when in a heterozygous condition. **5.** an individual exhibiting such character. —**recess′ively,** *adv.* —**recess′iveness,** *n.*

---

re/car′pet, *v.t.*
re/car′ry, *v.t.*, **-carried, -carrying.**
re/cel′ebrate/, *v.*, **-rated, -rating.**
re/cel′ebra′tion, *n.*
re/cer′tify/, *v.t.*, **-fied, -fying.**

---

réchauffé (*Fr.* rė shō fė′), *n.*, *pl.* **-fés** (-fė′). *French.* **1.** a warmed-up dish of food. **2.** anything old or stale brought out again. [F: warmed again]

recherché (rə shĕə′shā; *Fr.* rə shĕr shė′), *adj.* **1.** sought out with care. **2.** rare or choice. **3.** of studied refinement or elegance. [t. F, pp. of *rechercher.* See RESEARCH, v.]

recidivism (rĭ sĭd′ĭ vĭz′əm), *n.* **1.** repeated or habitual relapse into crime. **2.** *Psychol.* the chronic tendency towards repetition of criminal or antisocial behaviour patterns. [f. s. L *recidīvus* relapsing + -ISM] **—recid′ivist,** *n.* **—recid′ivis′tic, recid′ivous,** *adj.*

Recife (*Port.* rė sē′fĕ), *n.* a seaport in E Brazil. 788,569 (1960). Also, **Pernambuco.**

Recife (rĭ sē′fĭ), *n.* **Cape,** a headland in the Republic of South Africa at the E extremity of the S coast of Cape Province.

recipe (rĕs′ĭ pē′), *n.* **1.** any formula, esp. one for preparing a dish in cookery. **2.** a medical prescription. **3.** a method to attain a desired end. [ME, t. L: take, impv. of *recipere* (see RECEIVE), as used at the head of prescriptions]

recipience (rĭ sĭp′ĭ əns), *n.* **1.** the act of receiving; reception. **2.** the state or quality of being receptive; receptiveness. Also, **recip′iency.**

recipient (rĭ sĭp′ĭ ənt), *n.* **1.** one who or that which receives; a receiver. **—*adj.* 2.** receiving or capable of receiving. [t. L: s. *recipiens,* ppr., receiving]

reciprocal (rĭ sĭp′rə kl), *adj.* **1.** given, felt, etc., by each to or towards each; mutual: *reciprocal affection.* **2.** given, performed, felt, etc., in return: *reciprocal aid.* **3.** *Gram.* expressing mutual relation, as *each other, one another,* etc. (sometimes opposed to, but often including, *reflexive* when referring to plural subjects). **4.** *Maths.* denoting or pertaining to relations or functions which involve reciprocals. **—*n.* 5.** a thing that is reciprocal to something else; an equivalent; a counterpart; a complement. **6.** *Maths.* that by which a given quantity is multiplied to produce unity. [f. s. L *reciprocus* returning, reciprocal + -AL[1]] **—recip′rocal′ity,** *n.* **—recip′rocally,** *adv.* **—Syn. 2.** See **mutual.**

reciprocal ohm, *Elect.* a mho.

reciprocal translocation, *Genetics.* an atypical interchange of parts of two or more pairs of non-homologous chromosomes, ordinarily giving a ring of such chromosomes.

reciprocate (rĭ sĭp′rə kāt′), *v.*, **-cated, -cating.** **—*v.t.* 1.** to give, feel, etc., in return. **2.** to give and receive reciprocally; interchange: *to reciprocate favours.* **3.** to cause to move alternately backwards and forwards. **—*v.i.* 4.** to make return, as for something given. **5.** to make interchange. **6.** to be correspondent. **7.** to move alternately backwards and forwards. [t. L: m. s. *reciprocātus,* pp.] **—reciprocative** (rĭ sĭp′rə kə tĭv), *adj.* **—recip′roca′tor,** *n.*

reciprocating engine, an engine characterized by the movement of the pistons in the cylinders back and forth in a straight line.

reciprocation (rĭ sĭp′rə kā′shən), *n.* **1.** the act or fact of reciprocating. **2.** a making return for something. **3.** a mutual giving and receiving. **4.** the state of being reciprocal or corresponding.

reciprocity (rĕs′ĭ prŏs′ĭ tĭ), *n.* **1.** reciprocal state or relation. **2.** reciprocation; mutual exchange. **3.** that relation or policy in commercial dealings between countries by which corresponding advantages or privileges are granted by each country to the citizens of the other.

recision (rĭ sĭzh′ən), *n.* an invalidating or rescinding. [t. L: s. *recīsio*]

recit., *Music.* recitative.

recital (rĭ sī′tl), *n.* **1.** a musical or other entertainment given usually by a single performer, or consisting of selections from a single composer. **2.** the act of reciting. **3.** a detailed statement. **4.** an account, narrative, or description. **5.** *Law.* mention in a deed or instrument of that which has gone before. **—Syn. 4.** See **narrative.**

recitation (rĕs′ĭ tā′shən), *n.* **1.** the act of reciting. **2.** a reciting or repeating of something from memory, esp. formally or publicly. **3.** an elocutionary delivery of a piece of poetry or prose, without the text, before an audience. **4.** a piece so delivered or for such delivery. **5.** *U.S.* a reciting of a prepared lesson by pupils before a teacher. **6.** *U.S.* a separate part of classroom instruction. [t. L: s. *recitātio*]

recitative[1] (rĭ sī′tə tĭv), *adj.* pertaining to or of the nature of recital, as of facts. [f. RECITE + -ATIVE]

recitative[2] (rĕs′ĭ tə tēv′), *Music.* **—*adj.* 1.** of the nature of or resembling recitation or declamation. **—*n.* 2.** a style of vocal music intermediate between speaking and singing. **3.** a passage, part, or piece in this style. [t. It.: m. *recitativo,* der. *recitare* RECITE]

recitativo (rĕs′ĭ tə tē′vō), *adj., n., pl.* **-vi** (-vē), **-vos.** *Music.* recitative[2]. [It.]

recite (rĭ sīt′), *v.*, **-cited, -citing.** **—*v.t.* 1.** to repeat the words of, as from memory, esp. in a formal manner: *to recite a lesson.* **2.** to repeat (a piece of poetry or prose) before an audience, as for entertainment. **3.** to give an account of: *to recite one's adventures.* **4.** to enumerate. **—*v.i.* 5.** to recite or repeat something from memory. **6.** *U.S.* to recite a lesson, or part of a lesson, before a teacher. [late ME, t. L: m. s. *recitāre* read aloud, repeat] **—recit′er,** *n.* **—Syn. 2, 3.** See **relate.**

reck (rĕk), *v.i.* **1.** to have care, concern, or regard (often fol. by *of, with,* or a clause). **2.** to take heed. **3.** *Archaic.* to be of concern or importance, or matter: *it recks not.* **—*v.t.* 4.** to have regard for; mind; heed. [ME *rekke(n),* OE *reccan,* var. of *rēcan,* c. G *(ge)ruhen* deign]

reckless (rĕk′lĭs), *adj.* **1.** utterly careless of the consequences of action; without caution (fol. by *of*). **2.** characterized by or proceeding from such carelessness: *reckless extravagance.* [ME *rekles,* OE *recceléas,* var. of *rēceléas* careless (c. G *ruchlos*)] **—reck′lessly,** *adv.* **—reck′lessness,** *n.*

Recklinghausen (*Ger.* rĕk lĭng hou′zən), *n.* a town in West Germany, in central North Rhine-Westphalia. 127,900 (1966).

reckon (rĕk′ən), *v.t.* **1.** to count, compute, or calculate as to number or amount. **2.** to esteem or consider (as stated): *to be reckoned a wit.* **3.** *Colloq. or U.S. Dial.* to think or suppose. **—*v.i.* 4.** to count; make a computation or calculation. **5.** to settle accounts, as with a person. **6.** to count, depend, or rely (*on*), as in expectation. **7.** to deal (*with*), as with something to be taken into account or entering into a case. **8. reckon without,** to fail to take into account: *they reckoned without his strong sense of duty when they tried to bribe him.* [ME *reken(e),* OE *(ge)recenian,* c. G *rechnen*] **—Syn. 1.** enumerate. **2.** regard, account, deem.

reckoner (rĕk′ə nə), *n.* **1.** one who reckons. **2.** a ready reckoner.

reckoning (rĕk′ə nĭng), *n.* **1.** count, computation, or calculation. **2.** the settlement of accounts, as between parties. **3.** a statement of an amount due; bill. **4.** an accounting, as for things received or done: *a day of reckoning.* **5.** See **dead reckoning.**

reclaim (rĭ klām′), *v.t.* **1.** to bring (wild, waste, or marshy land) into a condition for cultivation or other use. **2.** to recover (substances) in a pure or usable form from refuse matter, articles, etc. **3.** to bring back to more socially, morally, or religiously acceptable courses, living, principles, ideas, etc. **—*n.* 4.** reclamation: *beyond reclaim.* [ME *reclaime(n),* t. OF: m. *reclaimer,* g. L *reclāmāre* cry out against] **—reclaim′able,** *adj.* **—reclaim′er,** *n.* **—Syn. 2.** See **recover.**

re-claim (rĭ klām′), *v.t.* to claim or demand the return or restoration of. [f. RE- + CLAIM]

reclaimant (rĭ klā′mənt), *n.* a person who makes appeals to reclaim.

reclamation (rĕk′lə mā′shən), *n.* **1.** the reclaiming of waste, desert, marshy, or submerged land for cultivation or other use. **2.** the act or process of reclaiming. **3.** the state of being reclaimed. **4.** the process or industry of deriving usable materials from waste products. [t. L: s. *reclāmātio*]

réclame (*Fr.* rė klȧm′), *n.* *French.* **1.** publicity; advertisement. **2.** a seeking for publicity.

reclassify (rē′klăs′ ĭ fī′), *v.t.* **-fied, -fying.** **1.** to put into a new or another category. **2.** to classify again; reassess. **—re′clas′sifica′tion,** *n.*

recline (rĭ klīn′), *v.*, **-clined, -clining.** **—*v.i.* 1.** to lean or lie back; rest in a recumbent position. **—*v.t.* 2.** to cause to lean back on something; place in a recumbent position. [late ME, t. L: m. s. *reclīnāre*] **—reclin′able,** *adj.* **—reclin′er,** *n.* **—reclination** (rĕk′lĭ nā′shən), *n.*

recluse (rĭ kloōs′), *n.* **1.** a person who lives in seclusion or apart from society, often for religious meditation. **2.** a religious voluntarily immured or remaining for life within a cell; incluse. **—*adj.* 3.** shut off or apart from the world, or living in seclusion, often for religious reasons.

---

re′chal′lenge, *v.t.*, **-lenged, -lenging.**
re′chan′nel, *v.t.*, **-nelled, -nelling.**
re′charge′, *v.*, **-charged, -charging.**
re′charge′able, *adj.*
re′charg′er, *n.*
re′chart′, *v.t.*
re′chart′er, *v.t., n.*
re′check′, *v.*
re′check′, *n.*
re′choose′, *v.t.*, **-chose, -chosen, -choosing.**
re′chris′ten, *v.t.*
re′cir′cle, *v.*, **-circled, -circling.**
re′cir′culate′, *v.t.*, **-lated, -lating.**
re′cir′cula′tion, *n.*
re′clasp′, *v.t.*
re′class′, *v.t.*
re′clothe′, *v.t.*, **-clothed** or **-clad, -clothing.**

---

4. characterized by seclusion. [ME *reclus*, t. OF, g. LL *reclūsus*, pp., shut up] —**reclu′sive,** *adj.*
reclusion (rĭ klōō′zhən), *n.* **1.** the condition or life of a recluse. **2.** a shutting or a being shut up in seclusion.
recognition (rĕk′əg nĭsh′ən), *n.* **1.** the act of recognizing. **2.** the state of being recognized. **3.** the perception of something as identical with something previously known or in the mind. **4.** the perception of something as existing or true; realization. **5.** the acknowledgement of something as valid or as entitled to consideration: *the recognition of a claim.* **6.** the acknowledgement of kindness, service, merit, etc. **7.** the expression of this by some token of appreciation. **8.** formal acknowledgement conveying approval or sanction. **9.** *U.S.* acknowledgement of right to be heard or given attention. **10.** *Internat. Law.* an official act by which one state acknowledges the existence of another state or government, or of belligerency or insurgency. [late ME, t. L: s. *recognitio*] —**recognitive** (rĭ kŏg′nĭ tĭv), **recognitory** (rĭ kŏg′nĭ tə rĭ, -trĭ), *adj.*
recognizance (rĭ kŏg′nĭ zəns), *n.* **1.** the act of recognizing; recognition. **2.** *Law.* **a.** a bond or obligation of record entered into before a court of record or a magistrate, binding a person to do a particular act. **b.** the sum pledged as surety on such a bond. Also, **recognisance.** [ME *reconissance*, t. OF. See RECOGNIZE]
recognize (rĕk′əg nīz′), *v.t.*, **-nized, -nizing. 1.** to know again; perceive to be identical with something previously known: *he had changed so much that one could scarcely recognize him.* **2.** to identify from knowledge of appearance or character. **3.** to perceive as existing or true; realize: *to be the first to recognize a fact.* **4.** to acknowledge formally as existing or as entitled to consideration: *one government recognizes another.* **5.** to acknowledge or accept formally as being something stated: *to recognize a government as a belligerent.* **6.** to acknowledge or treat as valid: *to recognize a claim.* **7.** to acknowledge acquaintance with (a person, etc.) as by a salute. **8.** to show appreciation of (kindness, service, merit, etc.) as by some reward or tribute. **9.** *U.S.* to acknowledge as the person entitled to speak at the particular time. Also, **recognise.** [appar. f. *recogn(ition)* + -IZE; r. late ME (Scot.) *racunnys*, t. OF] —**rec′ogniz′able,** *adj.* —**rec′ogniz′ably,** *adv.* —**rec′ogniz′er,** *n.*
recognizee (rĭ kŏg′nĭ zē′), *n. Law.* one to whom a person who enters into a recognizance is bound. Also, **recognisee.**
recognizor (rĭ kŏg′nĭ zôr′), *n. Law.* one who enters into a recognizance. Also, **recognisor.**
recoil (rĭ koil′ *for 1–4*; rē koil′, rē′koil′ *for 5–7*), *v.i.* **1.** to draw back; start or shrink back, as in alarm, horror, or disgust. **2.** to spring or fly back, as in consequence of force of impact or the force of the discharge, as a firearm. **3.** to spring or come back; react (fol. by *on* or *upon*). **4.** *Physics.* (of an atom, nucleus, or particle) to undergo a change of momentum as a result of ejection of another particle or photon. —*n.* **5.** the act of recoiling. **6.** the length through which a weapon moves backwards after its discharge. **7.** *Physics.* the motion acquired by an atom, nucleus or particle through ejecting another particle or photon. [ME *recuyel(l)e(n)*, t. OF: m. *reculer*, der. L *re-* RE- + *cūlus* the buttocks]
recoilless (rĭ koil′lĭs), *adj.* without recoil: *recoilless artillery.*
recollect (rĕk′ə lĕkt′), *v.t.* **1.** to recall to mind, or recover knowledge of by an act or effort of memory; remember. **2.** to concentrate or absorb (the mind, etc.), as in preparation for mystical contemplation. —*v.i.* **3.** to have a recollection; remember. [from the same source as RE-COLLECT, but distinguished in sense and pronunciation] —**rec′ollec′tive,** *adj.* —**rec′ollec′tively,** *adv.* —**Syn. 1.** See **remember.**
re-collect (rē′kə lĕkt′), *v.t.* **1.** to collect, gather together, or assemble again (what is scattered). **2.** to rally (one's faculties, powers, spirits, etc.); recover or compose (oneself). [orig. t. L: s. *recollectus*, pp., collected again, but later taken as f. RE- + COLLECT]
recollection (rĕk′ə lĕk′shən), *n.* **1.** the act or power of recollecting, or recalling to mind; remembrance. **2.** that which is recollected: *recollections of one's childhood.* [f. RECOLLECT + -ION]
re-collection (rē′kə lĕk′shən), *n.* **1.** the act of re-collecting, or gathering together again. **2.** the state of being re-collected. [f. RE-COLLECT + -ION]
recommend (rĕk′ə mĕnd′), *v.t.* **1.** to commend by favourable representations; present as worthy of confidence, acceptance, use, etc.: *to recommend a book.* **2.** to represent or urge as advisable or expedient: *to recommend caution.* **3.** to advise (a person, etc., to do something): *to recommend one to wait.* **4.** to make acceptable or pleasing: *a plan that has very little to recommend it.* [ME *recommende(n)*, t. ML: m. *recommendāre*, f. L: *re-* RE- + *commendāre* commend] —**rec′ommend′able,** *adj.* —**rec′ommend′er,** *n.*
recommendation (rĕk′ə mĕn dā′shən), *n.* **1.** the act of recommending. **2.** a letter or the like recommending a person or thing. **3.** representation in favour of a person or thing. **4.** anything that serves to recommend a person or thing or induce acceptance or favour.
recommendatory (rĕk′ə mĕn′də tə rĭ, -trĭ), *adj.* **1.** serving to recommend; recommending. **2.** serving as, or of the nature of, a recommendation.
recommit (rē′kə mĭt′), *v.t.*, **-mitted, -mitting. 1.** to commit again. **2.** to refer again to a committee. —**re′commit′ment, re′commit′tal,** *n.*
recompense (rĕk′əm pĕns′), *v.*, **-pensed, -pensing,** *n.* —*v.t.* **1.** to make compensation to (a person, etc.); repay, remunerate, reward, or requite for service, aid, etc. **2.** to make compensation for; make a return or requital for. —*v.i.* **3.** to make compensation for something; repay or reward a person for service, aid, etc. —*n.* **4.** compensation made, as for loss, injury, or wrong: *to make recompense.* **5.** repayment or requital. **6.** remuneration or a reward. [ME, t. LL: m. *recompensāre*, f. L: *re-* RE- + *compensāre* compensate] —**Syn. 6.** See **reward.**
recompose (rē′kəm pōz′), *v.t.*, **-posed, -posing. 1.** to compose again; reconstitute; rearrange. **2.** to restore to composure or calmness. —**recomposition** (rē′kŏm pə-zĭsh′ən), *n.*
reconcilable (rĕk′ən sī′lə bl), *adj.* that can be reconciled; capable of reconciliation. —**rec′oncil′abil′ity, rec′oncil′ableness,** *n.* —**rec′oncil′ably,** *adv.*
reconcile (rĕk′ən sīl′), *v.t.*, **-ciled, -ciling. 1.** to render no longer opposed; bring to acquiescence (fol. by *to*): *to reconcile someone to his fate.* **2.** to win over to friendliness: *to reconcile a hostile person.* **3.** to compose or settle (a quarrel, difference, etc.). **4.** to bring into agreement or harmony; make compatible or consistent: *to reconcile differing statements.* [ME, t. L: m. s. *reconciliāre*] —**rec′oncile′ment,** *n.* —**rec′oncil′er,** *n.*
reconciliation (rĕk′ən sĭl′ĭ ā′shən), *n.* **1.** the act of reconciling. **2.** the state of being reconciled. **3.** the process of making consistent or compatible.
reconciliatory (rĕk′ən sĭl′yə tə rĭ, -trĭ), *adj.* tending to reconcile.
recondite (rĭ kŏn′dīt), *adj.* **1.** dealing with abstruse or profound matters: *a recondite treatise.* **2.** removed from ordinary knowledge or understanding; abstruse; profound: *recondite principles.* **3.** little known; obscure. [earlier *recondit*, t. L: s. *reconditus*, pp., put away, hidden] —**recon′ditely,** *adv.* —**recon′diteness,** *n.*
recondition (rē′kən dĭsh′ən), *v.t.* to restore to a good or satisfactory condition; repair; overhaul.
reconnaissance (rĭ kŏn′ĭ səns), *n.* **1.** the act of reconnoitring. **2.** *Mil.* a search made for useful military information in the field, esp. by examining the ground. **3.** *Civ. Eng.* a preliminary examination of a region as to its general natural features, before a more exact survey for triangulation, etc. **4.** *Geol.* an examination or survey of the general geological characteristics of a region. [t. F. See RECOGNIZANCE]
reconnoitre (rĕk′ə noi′tə), *v.*, **-tred, -tring.** —*v.t.* **1.** to inspect, observe, or survey (the enemy, the enemy's strength or position, a region, etc.) in order to gain information for military purposes. **2.** to examine or survey (a region, etc.) for engineering, geological, or other purposes. —*v.i.* **3.** to make a reconnaissance. —*n.* **4.** the act of reconnoitring; a reconnaissance. Also, *U.S.*, **reconnoiter.** [t. F: m. *reconnoitre*, earlier form of *reconnaître* reconnoitre, RECOGNIZE] —**rec′onnoi′trer,** *n.*
reconsider (rē′kən sĭd′ə), *v.t.* **1.** to consider again. **2.** to consider again with a view to a change of decision or action:

---

re′co′difica′tion, *n.*
re′co′dify′, *v.t.*, **-fied, -fying.**
re′coin′, *v.t.*
recoin′age, *n.*
re′col′onize′, *v.t.*, **-nized, -nizing.**
re′col′our, *v.t.*
re′comb′, *v.t.*
re′com′bina′tion, *n.*
re′combine′, *v.*, **-bined, -bining.**
re′commence′, *v.*, **-menced, -mencing.**
re′commence′ment, *n.*
re′commis′sion, *v.t.*
re′com′plicate′, *v.t.*, **-cated, -cating.**
re′compute′, *v.t.*, **-puted, -puting.**
re′conceal′, *v.t.*
re′con′centrate′, *v.*, **-trated, -trating.**
re′con′centra′tion, *n.*
re′con′densa′tion, *n.*
re′condense′, *v.t.*, **-densed, -densing.**
re′confirm′, *v.t.*
re′confront′, *v.t.*
re′connect′, *v.t.*
re′connec′tion, *n.*
re′con′quer, *v.t.*
re′con′quest, *n.*
re′con′secrate′, *v.t.*, **-crated, -crating.**
re′con′secra′tion, *n.*

---

to reconsider a refusal. —*v.i.* **3.** to reconsider a matter. —**re′consid′era′tion,** *n.*

reconsign (rē′kən sīn′), *v.t.* to consign again.

reconsignment (rē′kən sīn′mənt), *n.* a consigning again.

reconstitute (rē′kŏn′stĭ tyo͞ot′), *v.t.*, **-tuted, -tuting.** to constitute again; reconstruct; recompose. —**re′constitu′tion,** *n.*

reconstruct (rē′kən strŭkt′), *v.t.* **1.** to construct again; rebuild. **2.** to re-create or re-enact past events or another place: *to reconstruct a crime, the scene of a crime.* **3.** *Linguistics.* to suggest hypothetical forms for (a language, or parts of a language, for which no documentary evidence survives) by comparison of related languages or forms for which such evidence is available.

reconstruction (rē′kən strŭk′shən), *n.* **1.** the act of reconstructing. **2.** something reconstructed, as a model, or a re-enactment of past events. **3.** (*cap.*) *U.S. Hist.* the process by which the states which had seceded were reorganized as a part of the Union after the Civil War.

reconstructive (rē′kən strŭk′tĭv), *adj.* tending to reconstruct.

record (*v.* rĭ kôd′; *n., adj.* rĕk′ôd), *v.t.* **1.** to set down in writing or the like, as for the purpose of preserving evidence. **2.** to cause to be set down or registered: *to record one's vote.* **3.** to indicate or state: *they recorded a protest by sitting down in the streets.* **4.** to serve to relate or to tell of, as a written statement. **5.** to set down or register in some permanent form, as instruments. **6.** to set down, register, or fix by characteristic marks, incisions, magnetism, etc., for the purpose of reproduction by a gramophone or tape-recorder. **7.** to play or read for the purposes of making a recording: *the orchestra recorded a symphony.*
—*v.i.* **8.** to record something.
—*n.* **9.** the act of recording. **10.** the state or fact of being recorded, as in writing. **11.** an account in writing or the like preserving the memory or knowledge of facts or events. **12.** information or knowledge preserved in writing or the like. **13.** *Computers.* a self-contained group of data, as a punched card or a line of print. **14.** a report, list, or aggregate of actions or achievements, as in the case of a person, an organization, a horse, a ship, etc.: *to have a good record.* **15.** any thing or person serving as a memorial. **16.** the tracing, marking, or the like made by a recording instrument. **17.** a disc or, formerly, a cylinder, or other device having characteristic markings for reproducing sound, esp. for use with a gramophone; gramophone record. **18.** the highest or farthest recorded degree attained; the best rate, amount, etc., attained, as in some form of sport: *to break the record in the high jump.* **19.** an official writing intended to be preserved. **20.** *Law.* **a.** the commitment to writing, as authentic evidence, of something having legal importance, esp. as evidence of the proceedings or verdict of a court. **b.** evidence preserved in this manner. **c.** an authentic or official written report of proceedings of a court of justice. **21. off the record,** unofficially; without intending to be quoted. **22. on record,** recorded in a publicly available document: *he is on record as having said that he would launch a war against China.*
—*adj.* **23.** making or affording a record. **24.** notable in the degree of attainment; surpassing all others: *a record year for sales.*
[ME *recorde(n)*, t. OF: m. *recorder*, g. L *recordārī* call to mind, remember]

record-changer (rĕk′ôd chān′jə), *n.* a device which automatically changes the records on a gramophone.

recorded delivery, a postal service by which a letter or parcel is delivered only after signature of a receipt by the addressee.

recorder (rĭ kô′də), *n.* **1.** one who records, esp. as an official duty. **2.** *Law.* a barrister of five years' standing, appointed by the Crown, who is sole judge of Quarter Sessions. **3.** a recording or registering apparatus or device. **4.** See **tape-recorder.** **5.** a soft-toned flute with a plug in the mouthpiece, played in vertical position. —**record′ership′,** *n.*

recording (rĭ kô′dĭng), *n.* **1.** the act or practice of making a record. **2.** *Electronics.* a record of music, speech or the like made on magnetic tape or similar medium for purposes of reproduction; a record or tape.

recording head, 1. (in the manufacture of gramophone records) an electromagnetic device which cuts the original track in the master wax record from which the stampers are made. **2.** an inductance coil in a tape-recorder for recording the signal on a magnetic tape.

recording instrument, any measuring instrument which is so constructed that it makes a permanent record of the measurements it makes, as a recording barograph.

record-player (rĕk′ôd plā′ə), *n.* a gramophone, esp. a small one.

recount (rĭ kount′), *v.t.* **1.** to relate or narrate; tell in detail; give the facts or particulars of. **2.** to narrate in order. **3.** to tell one by one; enumerate. [late ME *recompte(n)*, t. AF: m. *reconter* repeat, relate, f. *re-* RE- + *conter* tell, COUNT[1]] —**Syn. 1.** See **relate.**

re-count (*v.* rē′kount′; *n.*, rē′kount′, rē′kount′), *v.t.* **1.** to count again. —*n.* **2.** a second or additional count, as of votes in an election. [f. RE- + COUNT[1]]

recountal (rĭ koun′tl), *n.* the act of recounting.

recoup (rĭ ko͞op′), *v.t.* **1.** to obtain an equivalent for; compensate for: *to recoup one's losses.* **2.** to regain or recover. **3.** to yield in return; return an amount equal to. **4.** to reimburse or indemnify: *to recoup a person for expenses.* **5.** *Law.* to withhold (a portion of something due) having some rightful claim to do so. —*v.i.* **6.** to obtain an equivalent, as for something lost. —*n.* **7.** the act of recouping. [ME, t. F: s. *recouper* cut again, f. *re-* RE- + *couper* cut] —**recoup′ment,** *n.*

recourse (rĭ kôs′), *n.* **1.** resort or application to a person or thing for help or protection, as when in difficulty: *to have recourse to someone.* **2.** a person or thing resorted to for help or protection. **3.** *Com.* the right to resort to a person for pecuniary compensation. An endorsement **without recourse** is one by which a payee or holder of a negotiable instrument, by writing 'without recourse' with his name, merely transfers the instrument without assuming any liability upon it. [ME *recours*, t. OF, g. L *recursus* a running back]

recover (rĭ kŭv′ə), *v.t.* **1.** to get again, or regain (something lost or taken away): *to recover lost property.* **2.** to make up for or make good (loss, damage, etc., to oneself). **3.** to regain the strength, composure, balance, etc., of (oneself). **4.** *Law.* **a.** to obtain by judgement in a court of law, or by legal proceedings: *to recover damages for a wrong.* **b.** to acquire title to through judicial process: *to recover land.* **5.** to reclaim from a bad state, practice, etc. **6.** to regain (a substance) in usable form, as from refuse material or from a waste product or by-product of manufacture; reclaim. **7.** *Mil.* **a.** to bring back (a weapon) to a certain position, as after use. **b.** to bring back (equipment, etc.) from a battlefield after an action. —*v.i.* **8.** to regain health after sickness, a wound, etc. (often fol. by *from*): *to recover from an illness.* **9.** to regain a former (and better) state or condition: *the city soon recovered from the effects of the explosion.* **10.** to regain one's composure, balance, etc. **11.** *Law.* to obtain a favourable judgement in a suit. **12.** *Fencing, Rowing, etc.* to make a recovery. [ME *recovere*, t. AF: m. *recoverer*, g. L *recuperāre* recuperate] —**recov′erable,** *adj.* —**recov′erer,** *n.*

—**Syn. 1.** RECOVER, RECLAIM, RETRIEVE is to regain literally or figuratively something or someone. To RECOVER is to obtain again what one has lost possession of: *to recover a stolen watch.* To RECLAIM is to bring back from error or wrongdoing, or from an undeveloped state: *to reclaim desert land by irrigation.* To RETRIEVE is to bring back or restore, esp. something to its former, prosperous state: *to retrieve one's fortune.* —**Ant. 1.** lose.

re-cover (rē′kŭv′ə), *v.t.* to cover again or anew.

recovery (rĭ kŭv′ə rĭ), *n., pl.* **-eries. 1.** the act of recovering. **2.** the regaining of something lost or taken away, or the possibility of this. **3.** restoration or return to health from sickness. **4.** restoration or return to a former (and better) state or condition. **5.** time required for recovery. **6.** that which is gained in recovering. **7.** the regaining of substances in usable form, as from refuse material or waste products. **8.** *Law.* the obtaining of right to something by verdict or judgement of a court of law. **9.** *Fencing.* the movement to the position of guard after a lunge. **10.** *Rowing.* a return to a former position for making the next stroke. **11.** *Athletics.* the movement in running of the leg when it is not touching the ground.

recreant (rĕk′rĭ ənt), *adj.* **1.** cowardly or craven. **2.** unfaithful, disloyal, or false. —*n.* **3.** a coward or craven. **4.** an apostate; a traitor. [ME, t. OF, der. *recreire*, yield in a contest, f. *re-* back + *creire*, g. L *crēdere* believe] —**rec′reance, rec′reancy,** *n.* —**rec′reantly,** *adv.*

---

re′consol′idate′, *v.*, **-dated, -dating.**	**re′contract′,** *v.*	**re′conver′gence,** *n.*	**-copied, -copying.**
re′consol′ida′tion, *n.*	**re′contrac′tion,** *n.*	**re′conver′sion,** *n.*	**re′cor′ona′tion,** *n.*
re′con′tact, *v., n.*	**re′convene′,** *v.*, **-vened, -vening.**	**re′convert′,** *v.t.*	**re′correct′,** *v.t.*
re′contend′, *v.i.*	**re′converge′,** *v.i.*,	**re′convey′,** *v.t.*	**re′crate′,** *v.t.*,
re′contest′, *v.t.*	**-verged, -verging.**	**re′convey′ance,** *n.*	**-crated, -crating.**
		re′cop′y, *v.t.*,	**re′cross′,** *v.*

---

recreate (rĕk′rĭ āt′), *v.*, **-ated, -ating.** —*v.t.* **1.** to refresh by means of relaxation and enjoyment, as after work. **2.** to restore or refresh physically or mentally. —*v.i.* **3.** to take recreation. [late ME, t. L: m. s. *recreātus*, pp. of *recreāre* restore, f. *re-* RE- + *creāre* create]

re-create (rē′krĭ āt′), *v.t.*, **-ated, -ating.** to create anew. [f. RE- + CREATE]

recreation (rĕk′rĭ ā′shən), *n.* **1.** refreshment by means of some pastime, agreeable exercise, or the like. **2.** a pastime, diversion, exercise, or other resource affording relaxation and enjoyment. **3.** the act of recreating. **4.** the state of being recreated. [ME, t. L: s. *recreātio*] —**rec′rea′tional,** *adj.*

re-creation (rē′krĭ ā′shən), *n.* **1.** the act of creating anew. **2.** a thing created anew. [f. RE- + CREATION]

recreation ground, an area, esp. one in a town, set aside for recreation and usually having swings, slides, and the like for children.

recrement (rĕk′rĭ mənt), *n.* *Physiol.* a secretion which, after having been separated from the blood, is returned to it, as the saliva. —**rec′remen′tal,** *adj.*

recriminate (rĭ krĭm′ĭ nāt′), *v.*, **-nated, -nating.** —*v.i.* **1.** to bring a countercharge against an accuser. —*v.t.* **2.** to accuse in return. [t. ML: m. s. *recrīminātus*, pp.] —**recrim′ina′tion,** *n.* —**recriminative** (rĭ krĭm′ĭ nə tĭv), **recriminatory** (rĭ krĭm′ĭ nə tə rĭ, -trĭ), *adj.* —**recrim′ina′tor,** *n.*

recrudesce (rē′kroo dĕs′), *v.i.*, **-desced, -descing.** to break out afresh, as a sore or a disease, or anything that has been quiescent. [t. L: m. s. *recrūdescere*]

recrudescence (rē′kroo dĕs′əns), *n.* a breaking out afresh, or into renewed activity; revival or reappearance in active existence. Also, **re′crudes′cency.** —**re′crudes′cent,** *adj.*

recruit (rĭ kroot′), *n.* **1.** a newly enlisted member of the armed forces. **2.** a newly secured member of any body or class. —*v.t.* **3.** to enlist (men) for service in the armed forces. **4.** to raise (a force) by enlistment. **5.** to strengthen or supply (an army, etc.) with new men. **6.** to furnish or replenish with a fresh supply; renew. **7.** to renew or restore (the health, strength, etc.). —*v.i.* **8.** to enlist or raise men for service in the armed forces. **9.** to recover health, strength, etc. **10.** to gain new supplies of anything lost or wasted. [t. F: m. s. *recruter*, der. *recrue* a new growth, prop. pp. of *recroître* grow again, f. *re-* RE- + *croître* (g. L *crescere*) grow] —**recruit′able,** *adj.* —**recruit′er,** *n.* —**recruit′ment,** *n.*

rect, receipt.

rect., **1.** receipt. **2.** rector. **3.** rectory.

recta (rĕk′tə), *n.* plural of **rectum.**

rectal (rĕk′tl), *adj.* of or pertaining to the rectum. —**rec′tally,** *adv.*

rectangle (rĕk′tăng′gl), *n.* a parallelogram with all its angles right angles. [t. LL: m. s. *rectangulum*, neut. of *rectangulus* right-angled]

Rectangle

rectangular (rĕk tăng′gyoo lə), *adj.* **1.** shaped like a rectangle. **2.** having the base or section in the form of a rectangle. **3.** having right angles or a right angle. **4.** forming a right angle. —**rectangularity** (rĕk tăng′gyoo lăr′ĭ tĭ), *n.* —**rectan′gularly,** *adv.*

recti (rĕk′tī), *n.* plural of **rectus.**

recti-, a word element meaning 'straight', 'right'. Also, before vowels, **rect-.** [t. L, comb. form of *rectus*]

rectifier (rĕk′tĭ fī′ə), *n.* **1.** one who or that which rectifies. **2.** *Elect.* an apparatus or contrivance which changes an alternating current into a direct current, without an intermediate transformation of energy. **3.** *Chem.* an apparatus used in chemical rectifying for collecting the most volatile distillate.

rectify (rĕk′tĭ′fī), *v.t.*, **-fied, -fying.** **1.** to make, put, or set right; remedy; correct. **2.** to put right by adjustment or calculation, as an instrument or a course at sea. **3.** *Chem.* to purify (esp. a spirit or liquor) by repeated distillation. **4.** *Elect.* to change (an alternating current) into a direct current. **5.** to determine the length of (a curve). **6.** *Astron.*, *Geog.* to adjust (a globe) for the solution of any proposed problem. [ME, t. LL: m. s. *rectificāre*. See RECTI-, -FY] —**rec′tifi′able,** *adj.* —**rectification** (rĕk′tĭ fĭ kā′shən), *n.* —**Syn. 2.** adjust, regulate.

rectilinear (rĕk′tĭ lĭn′ĭ ə), *adj.* **1.** forming a straight line. **2.** formed by straight lines. **3.** characterized by straight lines. **4.** moving in a straight line. Also, **rectilineal.** —**rec′tilin′early,** *adv.*

rectitude (rĕk′tĭ tyood′), *n.* **1.** rightness of principle or practice: *the rectitude of one's motives.* **2.** correctness: *rectitude of judgement.* **3.** *Rare.* straightness. [ME, t. LL: m. *rectitūdo*, der. L *rectus*. See RECTI-, -TUDE]

recto (rĕk′tō), *n.*, *pl.* **-tos.** *Print.* a right-hand page of an open book or manuscript; the front of a leaf (opposed to *verso*). [t. L, short for *rectō* (*foliō*) on right-hand (leaf)]

rectocele (rĕk′tō sēl′), *n.* a hernia of the rectum into the vagina. [f. *recto-* (comb. form of RECTUM) + -CELE[1]]

rector (rĕk′tə), *n.* **1.** *Rom. Cath. Ch.* an ecclesiastic in charge of a college, religious house, or congregation. **2.** *C. of E.* a clergyman who has the charge of a parish with full possession of all its rights, tithes, etc. **3.** the permanent head in certain universities, colleges, and schools. **4.** *U.S.* a clergyman in charge of a parish in the Protestant Episcopal Church. [ME, t. L: ruler] —**rectorial** (rĕk tô′rĭ əl), *adj.*

rectorate (rĕk′tə rĭt), *n.* the office, dignity, or term of a rector.

rectory (rĕk′tə rĭ), *n.*, *pl.* **-ries.** **1.** a rector's house; a parsonage. **2.** a benefice held by a rector.

rectrix (rĕk′trĭks), *n.*, *pl.* **rectrices** (rĕk trī′sēz). *Ornith.* a large tail feather of a bird. [t. L: fem. of *rector* director]

rectum (rĕk′təm), *n.*, *pl.* **-ta** (-tə). *Anat.* the comparatively straight terminal section of the intestine, ending in the anus. See diag. under **intestine.** [t. NL, short for L *rectum intestinum* straight intestine]

rectus (rĕk′təs), *n.*, *pl.* **-ti** (-tī). *Anat.* any of several straight muscles, as of the abdomen, thigh, eye, etc. [NL, short for L *rectus musculus* straight muscle]

recumbent (rĭ kŭm′bənt), *adj.* **1.** lying down; reclining; leaning. **2.** inactive; idle. **3.** *Zool.*, *Bot.* denoting a part that leans or reposes upon anything. —*n.* **4.** a recumbent person, animal, plant, etc. [t. L: s. *recumbens*, ppr.] —**recum′bency,** *n.* —**recum′bently,** *adv.*

recuperate (rĭ kyoo′pə rāt′, -prāt), *v.*, **-rated, -rating.** —*v.i.* **1.** to recover from sickness or exhaustion; regain health or strength. **2.** to recover from pecuniary loss. —*v.t.* **3.** to restore to health, vigour, etc. [t. L: m. s. *recuperātus*, pp., regained, recovered] —**recu′pera′tion,** *n.*

recuperative (rĭ kyoo′pə rə tĭv, -prə tĭv), *adj.* **1.** that recuperates. **2.** having the power of recuperating. **3.** pertaining to recuperation: *recuperative powers.* Also, **recuperatory** (rĭ kyoo′pə rə tə rĭ, -prə trĭ). —**recu′perativeness,** *n.*

recuperator (rĭ kyoo′pə rā′tə), *n.* **1.** one who or that which recuperates. **2.** a system of thin-walled refractory ducts for exchange of heat between gases, esp. for heating the incoming air required by a furnace with the exhaust gases.

recur (rĭ kû′), *v.i.*, **-curred, -curring.** **1.** to occur again, as an event, experience, etc. **2.** to return to the mind: *recurring ideas.* **3.** to come up again for consideration, as a question. **4.** to return in action, thought, etc.: *to recur to a subject.* **5.** *Maths.* to repeat a figure or a series of figures in a decimal. **6.** *Rare.* to have recourse. [late ME, t. L: m. s. *recurrere* run back]

recurrence (rĭ kŭ′rəns), *n.* **1.** the act or fact of recurring. **2.** return to a state, habit, subject, etc. **3.** recourse.

recurrent (rĭ kŭ′rənt), *adj.* **1.** that recurs; occurring or appearing again, esp. repeatedly or periodically. **2.** *Anat.*, *etc.* turned back so as to run in a reverse direction, as a nerve, artery, branch, etc. [t. L: s. *recurrens*] —**recur′rently,** *adv.*

recurring decimal, *Maths.* a decimal in which a series of digits is repeated ad infinitum, as 0·147232323.

recurring fraction, *Maths.* continued fraction.

recurvate (rĭ kû′vĭt, -vāt), *adj.* recurved. [t. L: m. s. *recurvātus*, pp.]

recurve (rĭ kûv′), *v.t.*, *v.i.*, **-curved, -curving.** to curve or bend back or backwards.

recusancy (rĕk′yoo zən sĭ), *n.* **1.** the state of being recusant. **2.** obstinate refusal or opposition. [der. RECUSANT. See -CY]

recusant (rĕk′yoo zənt), *adj.* **1.** refusing to submit, comply, etc. **2.** obstinate in refusal. **3.** *Hist.* refusing to attend services of the Church of England. —*n.* **4.** one who is recusant. **5.** *Hist.* a person, esp. a Roman Catholic, who refused to attend the services of the Church of England when it was legally compulsory. [t. L: s. *recūsans*, ppr., refusing]

red (rĕd), *adj.*, **redder, reddest,** *n.* —*adj.* **1.** of a spectral hue beyond orange in the spectrum. **2.** distinguished by being red, wearing red, having red clothing, etc. **3.** (*often cap.*) ultraradical politically, esp. communist. —*n.* **4.** any of the hues adjacent to orange in the spectrum, such as scarlet, vermilion, cherry. **5.** something red. **6.** (*often cap.*) an ultraradical in politics, esp. a communist. **7.** *Archery.* a ring on a target coloured red, scoring seven points. **8. paint the town red,** *Colloq.* to celebrate, esp. wildly and extravagantly. **9. see red,** *Colloq.* to become angry or

---

re′crown′, *v.t.*
re′crys′tallize′, *v.*, -lized, -lizing.
re′cul′tivate′, *v.t.*, -vated, -vating.
re′cul′tiva′tion, *n.*
re′cut′, *v.t.*, -cut, -cutting.

infuriated. **10. the red, a.** red ink as used in bookkeeping and accounting practice for recording losses and deficits in financial statements. **b.** loss or deficit: *to be in or out of the red.* [ME *red(e)*, OE *rēad*, c. G *rot*, akin to L *rūfus*, *ruber*]

-red, a noun suffix denoting condition, as in *hatred*, *kindred*. [ME *-rede*, OE *-rǣden*]

redact (rĭ dăkt′), *v.t.* **1.** to bring into presentable literary form; revise; edit. **2.** to draw up or frame (a statement, etc.). [t. L: s. *redactus*, pp., brought back, reduced] **—redac′tion,** *n.* **—redac′tor,** *n.*

red admiral, a common butterfly, *Vanessa atalanta*, having wings bearing reddish bands.

red algae, algae of the class *Rhodophyceae*, in which the chlorophyll is masked by a red or purplish pigment.

redan (rĭ dăn′), *n. Fort.* a work consisting of two parapets forming a salient angle. [t. F, var. of *redent*, a double notching or jagging, f. *re-* RE- + *dent* tooth, g. s. L *dens*]

Red Army, the official name of the Soviet Army.

red-backed sandpiper (rĕd′băkt′), dunlin.

red-baiting (rĕd′bā′tĭng), *n. Chiefly U.S. Colloq.* the act of denouncing or deprecating political opponents who are radical or left-wing. **—red′-bait′er,** *n.*

red belt, *Judo.* **1.** a belt worn by an experienced contestant ranking from the ninth to the eleventh Dan. **2.** a contestant entitled to wear this.

red biddy, 1. a kind of cheap red wine. **2.** a drink made of red wine mixed with methylated spirits.

redbill (rĕd′bĭl′), *n.* any of various birds having a red bill, as the sakabula, or the **red-billed teal,** *Anas erythrorhyncha*, of southern Africa.

red-blindness (rĕd′blīnd′nĭs), *n.* protanopia.

red-blooded (rĕd′blŭd′ĭd), *adj.* vigorous; virile. **—red′-blood′edness,** *n.*

red brass, *Metall.* an alloy of zinc and copper containing 15–20 per cent zinc.

redbreast (rĕd′brĕst′), *n.* the European robin, *Erithacus rubecula*, so called from the colour of the breast feathers.

redbrick (rĕd′brĭk′), *adj.* **1.** denoting or pertaining to British universities of comparatively recent foundation, esp. those which emphasize technical subjects, as opposed to Oxford and Cambridge. *—n.* **2.** such universities collectively.

Redbridge (rĕd′brĭj′), *n.* a NE outer borough of London. 248,600 (1965).

redbud (rĕd′bŭd′), *n.* the leguminous American Judas tree, *Cercis canadensis*, bearing small, budlike, pink flowers.

redbug (rĕd′bŭg′), *n. U.S.* a chigger.

red cabbage, a purplish variety of cabbage, used for cooking, pickling, etc.

redcap (rĕd′kăp′), *n.* **1.** *Colloq.* a military policeman. **2.** the European goldfinch, *Carduelis carduelis*. **3.** *U.S.* a luggage porter, esp. at a railway station.

Redcar (rĕd′kä′), *n.* a seaside resort in England, in the North Riding of Yorkshire. 31,460 (1961).

red carpet, 1. a red strip of carpet laid for important persons to walk on when entering or leaving a building, etc. **2.** highly favoured or deferential treatment.

red cedar, 1. any of several coniferous trees, esp. a juniper, *Juniperus virginiana*, with a fragrant reddish wood used for making pencils, etc., and an arbor vitae, *Thuja plicata*, both of North America. **2.** the wood of these trees.

red cent, *U.S. Colloq.* a cent (used esp. in negative expressions): *not worth a red cent.*

Red China, China (def. 1).

red clover, the common clover, *Trifolium pratense*, a leguminous plant with red flowers, widely cultivated as a forage plant.

redcoat (rĕd′kōt′), *n.* **1.** (formerly) a British soldier. **2.** a member of the staff at certain holiday camps whose duties are to lead holiday-makers in collective activities.

Red Crescent, the Muslim organization functioning as the Red Cross, esp. in Turkey.

Red Cross, 1. an international philanthropic organization (**Red Cross Society**) formed, in consequence of the Geneva Convention of 1864, to care for the sick and wounded in war, and secure the neutrality of nurses, hospitals, etc., and active also in relieving suffering occasioned by a pestilence, floods, fire, and other calamities. **2.** a branch of it: *the British Red Cross.* **3.** the English national emblem of St George's cross, which was also the emblem of the crusaders. **4.** Geneva cross.

redcurrant (rĕd′kŭ′rənt), *n.* **1.** the small, red, edible fruit of the shrub *Ribes sativum*. **2.** the shrub itself.

redd (rĕd), *v.t.*, **redd, redded, redding.** *Now Chiefly U.S. Colloq.* to put in order; tidy. [special use of obs. *redd* to free, rescue (OE *hreddan*), confused with obs. *rede*, OE *rǣdan* put in order. Cf. READY]

red deer, a species of deer, *Cervus elaphus*, native in the forests of Europe and Asia, and formerly very abundant in England.

redden (rĕd′n), *v.t.* **1.** to make or cause to become red. *—v.i.* **2.** to become red. **3.** to blush; flush.

reddendum (rĕ dĕn′dəm), *n. Law.* a clause specifying the rent in a lease. [L: gerund of *reddere* return]

red devil, *Slang.* a member of a special section of the Parachute Regiment.

reddish (rĕd′ĭsh), *adj.* somewhat red; tending to red; tinged with red. **—red′dishness,** *n.*

Redditch (rĕd′ĭch), *n.* a town in England, in Worcestershire. 29,000 (est. 1965).

reddle (rĕd′l), *n., v.*, **-led, -ling.** *—n.* **1.** ruddle. *—v.t.* **2.** to paint with ruddle. **3.** to colour coarsely. Also, **raddle.** [var. of RUDDLE]

Red Duster, *Colloq.* Red Ensign.

rede (rēd), *v.t. Archaic or Dial.* **1.** to counsel; advise. **2.** to explain. **3.** to tell. *—n.* **4.** counsel; advice. **5.** a plan; scheme. **6.** a tale; story. **7.** interpretation. [ME *rede(n)*, OE *rǣdan*; the same word as READ[1]]

red earth, a clayey, tropical soil formed by intensive chemical weathering, and usually highly leached and coloured red by iron compounds.

redeem (rĭ dēm′), *v.t.* **1.** to buy or pay off; clear by payment: *to redeem a mortgage.* **2.** to buy back, as after a tax sale or a mortgage foreclosure. **3.** to recover (something pledged or mortgaged) by payment or other satisfaction: *to redeem a pawned watch.* **4.** to convert (paper money) into specie. **5.** to discharge or fulfil (a pledge, promise, etc.). **6.** to make up for; make amends for: *a redeeming feature.* **7.** to obtain the release or restoration of, as from captivity, by paying a ransom. **8.** *Theol.* to deliver from sin and its consequences by means of a sacrifice offered for the sinner. [late ME, t. L: m. *redēm-*, perfect s. of *redimere* buy back]

—Syn. 1. REDEEM, RANSOM mean literally to buy back. REDEEM is wider in its application than RANSOM, and means to buy back or regain possession of anything; as by money, endeavour, devotion, sacrifice, or the like: *to redeem one's property.* To RANSOM is to redeem a person from captivity by paying a stipulated price, or (theol.) to redeem by sacrifice: *to ransom a kidnapped child.* **—Ant. 1.** abandon.

redeemable (rĭ dē′mə bl), *adj.* **1.** capable of being redeemed. **2.** that is to be redeemed: *bonds redeemable in five years' time.* Also, **redemptible** (rĭ dĕmp′tə bl). **—redee′mably,** *adv.*

redeemer (rĭ dē′mə), *n.* **1.** one who redeems. **2.** (*cap.*) Jesus Christ.

redeliver (rē′dĭ lĭv′ə), *v.t.* **1.** to deliver again. **2.** to deliver back; return. **—re′deliv′ery,** *n.*

redemand (rē′dĭ mänd′), *v.t.* **1.** to demand again. **2.** to demand back; demand the return of.

redemption (rĭ dĕmp′shən), *n.* **1.** the act of redeeming. **2.** the state of being redeemed. **3.** deliverance; rescue. **4.** *Theol.* deliverance from sin and its penalties; salvation. **5.** repurchase, as of something sold. **6.** paying off, as of a mortgage, bond, or note. **7.** recovery by payment, as of something pledged. **8.** convertibility of paper money into specie. [ME *redempcio(u)n*, t. L: m. s. *redemptio*, der. *redemptus*, pp. of *redimere* buy back]

redemptive (rĭ dĕmp′tĭv), *adj.* **1.** serving to redeem. **2.** denoting or pertaining to religions of which redemption is a major doctrine.

Redemptorist (rĭ dĕmp′tə rĭst), *n. Rom. Cath. Ch.* a member of the Congregation of the Most Holy Redeemer, founded by St Alphonsus Liguori in 1732.

redemptory (rĭ dĕmp′tə rĭ), *adj.* **1.** of or pertaining to redemption. **2.** redemptive.

Red Ensign, a red flag with the Union Jack in canton, the ensign of the British merchant navy.

redeploy (rē′dĭ ploi′), *v.t.* **1.** to rearrange, reorganize, or transfer (a person, department, military unit, or the like), as in order to promote greater efficiency. *—v.i.* **2.** to

re′darn′, *v.t.*
re′date′, *v.t.*, **-dated, -dating.**
re′debate′, *n., v.t.*, **-bated, -bating.**
re′dec′orate′, *v.t.*, **-rated, -rating.**
re′dec′ora′tion, *n.*
re′ded′icate′, *v.t.*, **-cated, -cating.**
re′ded′ica′tion, *n.*
re′defeat′, *v.t., n.*
re′defend′, *v.t.*
re′define′, *v.t.*, **-fined, -fining.**
re′def′ini′tion, *n.*
re′defy′, *v.t.*, **-fied, -fying.**
re′delib′erate′, *v.t.*, **-rated, -rating.**
re′delib′era′tion, *n.*
re′dem′onstrate′, *v.t.*, **-strated, -strating.**
re′dem′onstra′tion, *n.*
re′deni′al, *n.*
re′deny′, *v.t.*, **-nied, -nying.**
re′depos′it, *v., n.*

carry out a reorganization or rearrangement. —**re′-deploy′ment,** *n.*

redevelop (rē′dĭ vĕl′əp), *v.t.* **1.** to develop (something) again. **2.** *Photog.* to intensify or tone by a second developing process. —*v.i.* **3.** to develop again. —**re′-devel′oper,** *n.* —**re′devel′opment,** *n.*

redevelopment area, an urban area designated as being below certain sanitary and other standards and scheduled for improvement but not demolition.

red-faced (rĕd′fāst′), *adj.* **1.** having a naturally red face. **2.** having a face reddened with embarrassment, anger, etc. —**red′-faced′ly,** *adv.*

redfin (rĕd′fĭn′), *n.* any of various small freshwater minnows with red fins, esp. a shiner, *Natropis umbratilis,* of eastern and central North America.

red fir, 1. any of certain pinaceous trees, as *Abies magnifica* and *Pseudotsuga taxifolia* of North America and *Larix potanini* of China. **2.** their wood. **3.** Douglas fir.

red fire, any of various combustible preparations (as one containing strontium nitrate) burning with a vivid red light, used in pyrotechnic displays, signalling, etc.

redfish (rĕd′fĭsh′), *n., pl.* **-fishes,** (*esp. collectively*) **-fish. 1.** one of the Pacific salmon, the red or sockeye salmon, *Oncorhynchus nerka.* **2.** the rosefish. **3.** the nannygai.

red flag, 1. the recognized symbol of a socialist or revolutionary party. **2.** a socialist revolutionary song. **3.** a danger signal. **4.** something certain to arouse anger, etc.

red giant, *Astron.* one of a class of stars in an intermediate stage of stellar evolution, characterized by a large volume and a low surface temperature.

Redgrave (rĕd′grāv′), *n.* **1. Sir Michael (Scudamore)** (skyōō′də mô′), born 1908, English actor. **2.** his daughter, **Vanessa,** born 1937, English actress.

red grouse. See **grouse¹.**

Red Guard, 1. a member of a militant youth movement in China (**Red Guards**) formed to spread the works of Mao Tse-tung and effect the Cultural Revolution. **2.** a member of any of various extreme left-wing organizations elsewhere, usually Trotskyite.

red-handed (rĕd′hăn′dĭd), *adj., adv.* in the very act of a crime or other deed: *catch a thief red-handed.*

red hat, 1. the official hat of a cardinal. **2.** the office or dignity of a cardinal. **3.** a cardinal. **4.** *Mil. Slang.* a staff officer.

redhead (rĕd′hĕd′), *n.* a person having red hair.

red-headed (rĕd′hĕd′ĭd), *adj.* **1.** having red hair, as a person. **2.** having a red head, as a bird.

red heat, 1. the temperature of a red-hot body. **2.** the condition of being red-hot.

red herring, 1. something to divert attention; a false clue. **2.** a smoked herring.

red-hot (rĕd′hŏt′), *adj.* **1.** red with heat; very hot. **2.** very excited or enthusiastic. **3.** violent; furious: *red-hot anger.* **4.** fresh; new; most recent: *a red-hot tip for a horserace.*

red-hot poker, any plant of the liliaceous genus *Kniphofia,* frequently cultivated handsome perennial herbs from S and E Africa, with rosettes of long leaves and tall erect spikes of colourful flowers.

redia (rē′dĭ ə), *n., pl.* **-diae** (rē′dĭ ē′). larva produced asexually by previous larval stage of trematodes; rediae reproduce giving rise to cercariae or to more rediae.

Red Indian, an aborigine of North America; Amerindian.

redingote (rĕd′ĭng gōt′), *n.* **1.** a full-length double-breasted coat with skirts sometimes cut away in front. **2.** a man's outer coat of similar cut, worn in the 18th century. [t. F, t. E: m. *riding coat*]

redintegrate (rĕ dĭn′tĭ grāt′), *v.t.,* **-grated, -grating.** to make whole again; restore to a perfect state; renew; re-establish. [t. L: m. s. *redintegrātus,* pp. See RE-, INTEGRATE] —**redintegrative** (rĕ dĭn′tĭ grə tĭv), *adj.*

redintegration (rĕ dĭn′tĭ grā′shən), *n.* **1.** the act or process of redintegrating. **2.** *Psychol.* the tendency, when a response has occurred to a complex stimulus, to make that same response later to any part of that stimulus.

redirect (rē′dĭ rĕkt′), *v.t.* **1.** to direct again. **2.** to re-address. —*adj.* **3.** *U.S. Law.* pertaining to the examination of a witness by the party calling him, after cross-examination. —**re′direc′tion,** *n.*

rediscount (rē dĭs′kount), *v.t.* **1.** to discount again. —*n.* **2.** an act of rediscounting. **3.** (*usually pl.*) commercial paper which is discounted a second time.

redistrict (rē dĭs′trĭkt), *v.t.* *U.S.* to divide anew into districts, as for administrative or electoral purposes.

red lattice, *Archaic.* an alehouse.

red lead (lĕd), a heavy, earthy substance, Pb_3O_4, orange to red in colour, used as a paint pigment and in the manufacture of glass and glazes; minium.

red-lead ore (rĕd′lĕd′), crocoite.

red-letter day (rĕd′lĕt′ə), **1.** a day marked by red letters in the Church calendar, on which judges wear red robes. **2.** a memorable or especially happy occasion: *a red-letter day for someone.*

red light, 1. a red lamp, used as a signal to mean 'stop'. **2.** an order to stop. **3.** a warning signal. **4.** the symbol of a brothel.

red-light district, a neighbourhood with many brothels, sometimes, esp. formerly, indicated by red lights.

red man, a North American Indian.

red meat, meat that is dark-coloured, as beef, lamb, venison, etc. (distinguished from *white meat*).

red millet, a tufted annual grass of warm and temperate regions, *Digitaria ischaemum,* which occurs rarely in sandy fields in England.

Redmond (rĕd′mənd), *n.* **John Edward,** 1856–1918, Irish political leader.

red mullet, a common food fish, *Mullus surmuletus,* of European waters, esp. the Mediterranean.

redneck (rĕd′nĕk′), *n.* *U.S. Colloq.* (disparaging) a southern U.S. white farm labourer, esp. one who is ill-educated or ignorant.

redness (rĕd′nĭs), *n.* the quality or state of being red.

red oak, 1. any of several oak trees, as *Quercus velutina,* common to North America. **2.** the hard cross-grained wood of these trees.

red ochre, any of the red natural earths, mixtures of haematites, which are used as pigments.

redolent (rĕd′ō lənt), *adj.* **1.** having a pleasant smell; fragrant. **2.** odorous or smelling (fol. by *of*). **3.** suggestive; reminiscent (fol. by *of*): *stories redolent of mystery.* [ME, t. L: s. *redolens,* ppr., giving back a smell] —**red′-olence,** *n.* —**red′olently,** *adv.*

red osier, any willow of the genus *Salix,* with red twigs used for basketwork.

redouble (rĭ dŭb′l), *v.,* **-led, -ling,** *n.* —*v.t.* **1.** to double or increase greatly: *to redouble one's efforts.* **2.** to repeat: *to redouble an attack.* **3.** to echo or re-echo. **4.** *Bridge.* to double the double of (an opponent). —*v.t.* **5.** to be doubled; become greatly increased. **6.** to be echoed; resound. **7.** *Bridge.* to double the double of an opponent. —*n.* **8.** *Bridge.* the act of doubling one's opponent's double. [late ME, t. F: m. *redoubler*]

redoublement (rĭ dŭb′l mənt), *n.* *Fencing.* an attack immediately following one that has failed but which has not brought a riposte.

redoubt (rĭ dout′), *n.* *Fort.* **1.** an isolated work forming a complete enclosure of any form used to defend a prominent point. **2.** an independent earthwork built within a permanent fortification to reinforce it. [t. F: m. *redoute,* t. It.: m. *ridotto,* g. LL *reductus* a refuge, L, pp., retired; with intrusive *-b-* due to assoc. with REDOUBTABLE]

redoubtable (rĭ dou′tə bl), *adj.* **1.** that is to be feared; formidable. **2.** commanding respect. [ME *redoutable,* t. OF, der. *redouter* fear, der. *douter* DOUBT] —**redoubt′-ableness,** *n.* —**redoubt′ably,** *adv.*

redoubted (rĭ dou′tĭd), *adj.* **1.** dreaded; formidable. **2.** respected; renowned.

redound (rĭ dound′), *v.i.* **1.** to have an effect or result, as to the advantage, disadvantage, credit, or discredit of a person or thing. **2.** to result or accrue, as to a person. **3.** to come back or recoil, as upon a person. **4.** to proceed, issue, or arise. —*v.t.* **5.** *Archaic.* to reflect; cast: *to redound dishonour on someone's head.* —*n.* **6.** the fact of redounding or resulting. [ME *redounde,* t. OF: m. *redonder,* t. L: m. *redundāre* overflow]

redowa (rĕd′ə və, -wə), *n.* a Bohemian dance in two forms, the more common resembling the waltz or the mazurka, the other resembling the polka. [G, t. Czech: m. *reydovák,* der. *reydovati* turn or whirl round]

red pepper, 1. the condiment cayenne. **2.** any of the hot peppers, *Capsicum frutescens* and botanical varieties,

---

re′descend′, *v.*
re′descent′, *n.*
re′describe′, *v.t.,*
-scribed, -scribing.
re′descrip′tion, *n.*
re′design′, *v.t.*
re′des′ignate′, *v.t.,*
-nated, -nating.
re′des′igna′tion, *n.*
re′deter′mine, *v.,*
-mined, -mining.
re′diffuse′, *v.,*
-fused, -fusing.
re′diffu′sion, *n.*
re′digest′, *v.t.*
re′dis′cipline, *v.t.,*
-plined, -plining.
re′discov′er, *v.t.*
re′discov′ery, *n.*
re′discuss′, *v.t.*
re′disper′sal, *n.*
re′disperse′, *v.,*
-persed, -persing.
re′display′, *v.t.*
re′dissolve′, *v.,*
-solved, -solving.
re′distil′, *v.t.,*
-tilled, -tilling.
re′dis′tilla′tion, *n.*
re′distrib′ute, *v.t.,*
-buted, -buting.
re′dis′tribu′tion, *n.*
re′divide′, *v.,*
-vided, -viding.
re′do′, *v.t.,* **-did,**
-done, -doing.

the yellow or red pods of which are used for flavouring, sauces, etc.

red pine, rimu.

redpoll (rĕd′pōl′), *n.* **1.** any of various small fringilline birds of the genus *Acanthis*, the adults of which usually have a crimson crown patch, such as the **lesser redpoll,** *Acanthis flammea*, of Europe, including Britain. **2.** (*cap.*) one of a breed of polled, red, good-quality beef and milk cattle, having a coat of short hair.

redraft (rē′dräft′), *n.* **1.** a second draft or drawing. **2.** *Com.* a draft on the drawer or endorser of a dishonoured and protested bill of exchange for the amount of the bill plus the costs and charges.

red rag, something that excites a person's anger or passion.

red-rattle (rĕd′răt′l), *n.* a semiparasitic, annual, scrophulariaceous herb of Europe and W Asia, *Pedicularis palustris*, with purplish pink flowers, occurring in wet grassy places.

redress (rĭ drĕs′), *n.* **1.** the setting right of what is wrong: *redress of abuses.* **2.** relief from wrong or injury. **3.** compensation for wrong or injury. *—v.t.* **4.** to set right; remedy or repair (wrongs, injuries, etc.). **5.** to correct or reform (abuses, evils, etc.). **6.** to remedy or relieve (suffering, want, etc.). **7.** to adjust evenly again, as a balance. [ME *redresse*, t. F. See RE-, DRESS] —**redress′er, redres′sor,** *n.*

—Syn. 1. REDRESS, REPARATION, RESTITUTION suggest making amends or giving indemnification for a wrong. REDRESS may refer either to the act of setting right an unjust situation (as by some power), or to satisfaction sought or gained for a wrong suffered: *the redress of grievances.* REPARATION means compensation or satisfaction for a wrong or loss inflicted. The word may have the moral idea of amends (*to make reparation for one's neglect*), but more frequently it refers to financial compensation (which is asked for, rather than given): *the reparations demanded of the aggressor nations.* RESTITUTION means literally the restoration of what has been taken from the lawful owner (*he demanded restitution of his land*); it may also refer to restoring the equivalent of what has been taken: *the servant convicted of robbery made restitution to his employer.*

re-dress (rē′drĕs′), *v.t., v.i.* to dress again.

Red River, 1. a river in the U.S. flowing from NW Texas along the S boundary of Oklahoma into the Mississippi in E Louisiana. ab. 1200 mi. **2.** Also, **Red River of the North.** a river in the U.S. flowing along the Minnesota-North Dakota boundary N to Lake Winnipeg in S Canada. 545 mi.

redroot (rĕd′ro͞ot′), *n.* **1.** a North American plant, *Lachnanthes caroliana*, having sword-shaped leaves, woolly flowers, and a red root. **2.** any of various other plants with red roots, as the alkanet, *Alkanna tinctoria.*

red rose, *Hist.* See **rose** (def. 9b).

Redruth (rĕd′ro͞oth′), *n.* a town in England, in Cornwall. with Camborne 36,090 (1961).

Red Sea, a long narrow arm of the Indian Ocean, extending NW between Africa and Arabia: connected with the Mediterranean by the Suez Canal. ab. 1450 mi. long; ab. 178,000 sq. mi.; greatest depth, 7254 ft.

Red Sea

red setter, a variety of Irish setter.

redshank (rĕd′shăngk′), *n.* either of two wading birds of the genus *Tringa*, as the **common redshank,** *T. totanus*, or **spotted redshank,** *T. erythio.*

red-shank (rĕd′shăngk′), *n.* a polygonaceous annual herb with cylindrical heads of pale pink flowers, *Polygonum persicaria*, widespread in waste places and cultivated land through the Northern Hemisphere.

red shift, *Astrophysics.* the shift of light observed in a spectrometer from the galaxies towards longer wavelengths: interpreted as indicating that the galaxies are receding and the universe expanding. See **Doppler effect.**

red-short (rĕd′shôt′), *adj. Metall.* brittle when at a red heat, as iron or steel containing too much sulphur. [t. Sw.: m. *rödskört* (sc. *jern* iron), neut. of *rödskör*, f. *röd* red + *skör* brittle]

redskin (rĕd′skĭn′), *n., adj.* North American Indian.

red squirrel, a reddish arboreal rodent, *Sciurus vulgaris* (family *Sciuridae*), of Europe and northern and central Asia.

redstart (rĕd′stät′), *n.* a small European bird, *Phoenicurus phoenicurus*, with reddish brown tail. [f. RED + *start* tail, OE *steort*]

red tape, 1. tape of a reddish colour, much used for taping up official papers. **2.** excessive attention to formality and routine. —**red′-tape′,** *adj.*

reduce (rĭ dyo͞os′), *v.*, **-duced, -ducing.** *—v.t.* **1.** to bring down to a smaller extent, size, amount, number, etc. **2.** to lower in degree, intensity, etc.: *to reduce speed.* **3.** to bring down to a lower rank, dignity, etc. **4.** to lower in price. **5.** to bring to a certain state, condition, arrangement, etc.: *to reduce glass to powder.* **6.** to bring under control or authority; subdue. **7.** *Photog.* to treat so as to make less dense, as a negative. **8.** to adjust or correct by making allowances, as an astronomical observation. **9.** *Maths.* to change the denomination or form of. **10.** *Chem.* **a.** to deoxidize. **b.** to add hydrogen to. **c.** to change (a compound) so that the valency of the positive element is lower. **11.** *Chem., Metall.* to bring into the metallic state by separating from non-metallic constituents; smelt. **12.** to lower the proof of wines or spirits by adding water. **13.** to thin (paints, etc.) with oil or turpentine. **14.** *Biol.* to cause (a cell) to undergo meiotic division. **15.** *Surg.* to restore to the normal place, relations, or condition, as a dislocated organ or a fractured bone with separation of the fragment ends. *—v.i.* **16.** to become reduced. [ME, t. L: m. *redūcere* bring back, restore, replace] —**reduc′ible,** *adj.* —**reduc′ibil′ity,** *n.* —**reduc′ibly,** *adv.* —**Syn. 1.** diminish, decrease, shorten, abridge, curtail, retrench.

reduced (rĭ dyo͞ost′), *adj.* **1.** that is or has been reduced. **2.** *Maths.* denoting an equation in which the second highest power is missing.

reducer (rĭ dyo͞o′sə), *n.* **1.** one who or that which reduces. **2.** *Photog.* **a.** an oxidizing solution used to reduce a negative in density. **b.** a developing agent. **3.** *Bldg Trades.* a special fitting for connecting pipes of varying diameter.

reducing agent, *Chem.* a substance that causes another substance to undergo reduction and is oxidized in the process.

reductase (rĭ dŭk′tās), *n. Biochem.* any enzyme that catalyses a chemical reduction. [f. REDUCT(ION) + -ASE]

reductio ad absurdum (rĭ dŭk′tĭ ō ăd′ăb sû′dəm), *Latin.* a reduction to an absurdity; the refutation of a proposition by demonstrating the absurd inevitable conclusion to which it would logically lead.

reduction (rĭ dŭk′shən), *n.* **1.** the act of reducing. **2.** the state of being reduced. **3.** the amount by which something is reduced or diminished. **4.** a form produced by reducing; a copy on a smaller scale. **5.** *Biol.* meiosis. **6.** *Chem.* the converse of oxidation. [t. L: s. *reductio*] —**reduc′tional,** *adj.* —**reduc′tive,** *adj.*

reductor (rĭ dŭk′tə), *n.* a tube with a stopcock at one end, filled with granulated zinc, for reducing iron to a ferrous state for analysis.

redundancy (rĭ dŭn′dən sĭ), *n., pl.* **-cies. 1.** the state of being redundant. **2.** a redundant thing, part, or amount; a superfluity. **3.** the payment made to a redundant employee. Also, **redun′dance.**

redundant (rĭ dŭn′dənt), *adj.* **1.** being in excess; exceeding what is usual or natural: *a redundant part.* **2.** characterized by or using too many words to express ideas: *a redundant style.* **3.** denoting or pertaining to an employee who is or becomes superfluous to the needs of his employer, and who in Great Britain is entitled to compensatory payment for the loss of his job. **4.** having some unusual or extra part or feature. **5.** characterized by superabundance or superfluity. **6.** *Electronics.* of or pertaining to elements in a system which are not normally used, but come into operation if an active element fails. **7.** *Engineering.* (of a structure) having members which do not have a force acting through them. [t. L: s. *redundans*, ppr., overflowing] —**redun′dantly,** *adv.*

redupl., reduplication.

reduplicate (*v.* rĭ dyo͞o′plĭ kāt′; *adj.* rĭ dyo͞o′plĭ kĭt), *v.*, **-cated, -cating.** *—v.t.* **1.** to double; repeat. **2.** *Gram.* to form (a derivative or inflected form) by doubling a specified syllable or other portion of the primitive, sometimes with fixed modifications, as in Greek *léloipa* 'I have left'; *leipo* 'I leave'. *—v.i.* **3.** to become doubled. **4.** *Gram.* to become reduplicated. *—adj.* **5.** doubled. **6.** *Bot.* valvate, with the edges folded back so as to project outwards. [t. LL: m. s. *reduplicātus*, pp., doubled. See REDUPLICATE]

reduplication (rĭ dyo͞o′plĭ kā′shən), *n.* **1.** the act of reduplicating. **2.** the state of being reduplicated. **3.** something resulting from reduplicating. **4.** *Gram.* **a.** reduplicating as a grammatical pattern. **b.** the added element in a reduplicated form. **c.** a form containing a reduplicated element.

reduplicative (rĭ dyo͞o′plĭ kə tĭv), *adj.* **1.** tending to

---

re′drain′, *v.t.*
re′draw′, *v.t.* **-drew, -drawn, -drawing.**
re′drill′, *v.t.*
re′drop′, *v.*, **-dropped, -dropping.**
re′dry′, *v.*, **-dried, -drying.**
re′dye′, *v.t.*, **-dyed, -dying.**
re′-earn′, *v.*
re′-ed′ify′, *v.t.*, **-fied, -fying.**
re′-ed′it, *v.t.*

reduplicate. **2.** pertaining to or marked by reduplication. **3.** *Bot.* reduplicate.

red valerian, an erect valerianaceous perennial herb with dense heads of small, spurred, red (rarely pink or white) flowers, *Centranthus ruber*, a native of S Europe and Asia Minor, but widely naturalized elsewhere.

redware (rĕd′wĕə′), *n. Obs.* a large brown seaweed, *Laminaria digitata*, common off northern Atlantic coasts. [f. RED + *ware* (ME; OE *wār*) seaweed]

redwing (rĕd′wĭng′), *n.* a European thrush, *Turdus musicus*, having chestnut-red flank and axillary feathers.

redwood (rĕd′wo͝od′), *n.* **1.** a coniferous tree, *Sequoia sempervirens*, of California, remarkable for its height (commonly from 200 to over 300 feet). **2.** its valuable brownish red timber. **3.** a red-coloured wood. **4.** any of various trees with a reddish wood. **5.** any tree whose wood produces a red dyestuff. **6.** its wood.

Ree (rē), *n.* **Lough,** a lake in the Republic of Ireland dividing counties Longford and Westmeath from Roscommon, in the middle of the river Shannon. ab. 17 mi. long.

re-echo (rē ĕk′ō), *v.*, **-echoed, -echoing,** *n.*, *pl.* **-echoes.** —*v.i.* **1.** to echo back, as a sound. **2.** to give back an echo; resound. —*v.t.* **3.** to echo back. **4.** to repeat like an echo. —*n.* **5.** a repeated echo.

reed (rēd), *n.* **1.** the straight stalk of any of various tall grasses, esp. of the genera *Phragmites* and *Arundo*, growing in marshy places. **2.** the stalk of *Phragmites communis*. **3.** any of the plants themselves. **4.** such stalks or plants collectively. **5.** anything made from such a stalk or from something similar, as an arrow. **6.** *Music.* **a.** a pastoral or rustic musical pipe made from a reed or from the hollow stalk of some other plant. **b.** a small flexible piece of cane or metal which, attached to the mouths of some wind instruments (**reed instruments**), is set into vibration by a stream of air and, in turn, sets into vibration the air column enclosed in the tube of the instrument. **c.** any instrument with such a device, as the oboe, clarinet, etc. **7.** *Archit., Carp., etc.* a small convex moulding. **8.** (in a loom) the series of parallel strips of wires which force the weft up to the web and separate the threads of the warp. **9.** *Bible.* a Hebrew unit of length, equal to 6 cubits. **10. broken reed,** one who is too weak to be relied upon. —*v.t.* **11.** to decorate with reed. **12.** to thatch with or as with reed. [ME; OE *hrēod*, c. D *riet* and G *Riet*]

Reed (rēd), *n.* **1. Sir Carol,** born 1906, English film director. **2. John,** 1887–1920, U.S. journalist and poet.

reedbird (rēd′bûd′), *n.* the American bobolink.

reedbuck (rēd′bŭk′), *n.*, *pl.* **-bucks,** (*esp. collectively*) **-buck.** any of various yellowish African antelopes, genus *Redunca*, about the size of a small deer. The males have short, forward-curving horns. [trans. of Afrikaans *rietbok*]

reed bunting. See **bunting[2].**

Reed College, a university for men and women in the U.S., in Portland, Oregon, founded 1909.

reed-grass (rēd′gräs′), *n.* **1.** a widespread, waterside grass, *Phalaris arundinacea*. **2.** a tall perennial grass, *Glyceria maxima*, common in wet places.

reeding (rē′dĭng), *n.* **1.** a small convex or semicylindrical moulding, resembling a reed. **2.** a set of such mouldings, as on a column, where they resemble small convex fluting. **3.** ornamentation consisting of such mouldings. **4.** vertical grooves on the edge of a coin. [f. REED, v. + -ING[1]]

reedling (rēd′lĭng), *n.* a small European bird, *Panurus biarmicus*, frequenting reedy places, and characterized in the male by a tuft of black feathers on each side of the chin; bearded tit. [f. REED, n. + -LING[1]]

reed mace, the cat's-tail (def. 1).

reed organ, a musical keyboard instrument resembling the pipe organ but having the notes produced by small metal reeds.

reed pipes, the pipes of a reed organ.

reedstop (rēēd′stŏp′), *n.* a set of reed pipes (opposed to *fluestop*).

re-educate (rē′ĕd′yo͞o kāt′), *v.t.*, **-cated, -cating. 1.** to educate again. **2.** to educate for resumption of normal activities, as a cripple. —**re′-ed′uca′tion,** *n.*

reedwarbler (rēēd′wô′blə), *n.* a small Old World warbler, *Acrocephalus scirpaceus*, inhabiting marshy places, and occurring as a summer migrant in southern Britain.

reedy (rē′dĭ), *adj.*, **reedier, reediest. 1.** full of reeds. **2.** consisting or made of a reed or reeds: *a reedy pipe.* **3.** like a reed or reeds: *reedy grass.* **4.** denoting or having a tone like that of a reed instrument. —**reed′iness,** *n.*

reef[1] (rēf), *n.* **1.** a narrow ridge of rocks or sand, often of coral debris, at or near the surface of water. **2.** *Mining.* a lode or vein. [earlier *riff(e)*, t. D or LG: m. *rif*, t. Scand.; cf. Icel. *rif* rib, reef]

reef[2] (rēf), *Naut.* —*n.* **1.** a part of a sail which is rolled and tied down to reduce the area exposed to the wind. —*v.t.* **2.** to shorten (sail) by tying in one or more reefs. **3.** to reduce the length of (a topmast, a bowsprit, etc.), as by lowering, sliding inboard, or the like. [ME *riff*, t. Scand.; cf. Icel. *rif* rib, reef]

reef band, *Naut.* a strip of canvas stitched over a sail to strengthen it where the reef points are secured.

reefer[1] (rē′fə), *n.* **1.** *Naut.* one who reefs. **2.** a short coat or jacket of thick cloth. [f. REEF[2] + -ER[1]]

reefer[2] (rē′fə), *n. Colloq.* a marijuana cigarette. [same as REEF[2], in generalized sense of rolled object]

reef knot, *Naut.* a kind of knot, so called because it is used in tying reef points. See illus. under **knot.**

reef point, *Naut.* a short piece of line fastened through a sail, used to tie in a reef.

reek (rēk), *n.* **1.** a strong, unpleasant smell. **2.** vapour or steam. —*v.i.* **3.** to smell strongly and unpleasantly. **4.** to be strongly pervaded with something unpleasant or offensive. **5.** to give off steam, smoke, etc. **6.** to be wet with sweat, blood, etc. —*v.t.* **7.** to expose to or treat with smoke. **8.** to emit (smoke, fumes, etc.). [ME *rek(e)*, OE *rēc*, c. G *Rauch*] —**reek′er,** *n.* —**reek′y,** *adj.*

reel[1] (rēl), *n.* **1.** a cylinder, frame, or other device, turning on an axis, on which to wind something. **2.** a rotatory device attached to a fishing rod at the butt, for winding up or letting out the line. **3.** a small cylinder of wood or other material, now typically expanded at each end and having a hole lengthwise through the centre, on which thread is wound. **4.** a quantity of something wound on a reel. **5. a.** the spool, usually metal, on which film is wound. **b.** a roll of celluloid bearing a series of photographs to be exhibited with a film projector. **c.** the standard length of cinema film for projection (about 1000 ft). —*v.t.* **6.** to wind on a reel, as thread, yarn, etc. **7.** to draw with a reel, or by winding: *to reel in a fish.* **8.** to say, write, or produce in an easy, continuous way (fol. by *off*). [ME *rele*, OE *hrēol*] —**reel′er,** *n.*

reel[2] (rēl), *v.i.* **1.** to sway or rock under a blow, shock, etc.: *to reel under a heavy blow.* **2.** to fall back; waver, as troops. **3.** to sway about in standing or walking, as from dizziness, intoxication, etc.; stagger. **4.** to turn round and round; whirl. **5.** to have a sensation of whirling: *his brain reeled.* —*v.t.* **6.** to cause to reel. —*n.* **7.** the act of reeling; a reeling or staggering movement. [ME *rele(n)*, der. *rele* REEL[1]] —**Syn. 3.** See **stagger.**

reel[3] (rēl), *n.* **1.** a lively dance popular in Scotland. **2.** music for this. [special use of REEL[2] (def. 7)]

re-enforce (rē′ĭn fôs′), *v.t.*, **-forced, -forcing.** to enforce again.

re-enter (rē′ĕn′tə), *v.t.* **1.** to come or go into again. **2.** to record again, as in a list or account. —*v.i.* **3.** to come or go into again. —**re-entrance** (rē′ĕn′trəns), *n.*

re-entering angle, an angle directed back inwards, rather than extending outwards, as an exterior angle of less than 180° in a closed polygon.

R, Re-entering angle

re-entering polygon, a polygon having one or more re-entering angles.

re-entrant (rē ĕn′trənt), *adj.* **1.** re-entering: *a re-entrant angle.* —*n.* **2.** a re-entering angle or part.

re-entry (rē ĕn′trĭ), *n.*, *pl.* **-tries. 1.** the act of re-entering.

---

re′-eject′, *v.t.*
re′-elect′, *v.t.*
re′elec′tion, *n.*
re′-el′evate′, *v.t.*, **-vated, -vating.**
re′-el′eva′tion, *n.*
re′-embark′, *v.*
re′-embel′lish, *v.t.*
re′-embrace′, *v.*, **-braced, -bracing.**
re′-emerge′, *v.i.*, **-merged, -merging.**
re′-emer′gence, *n.*
re′-emer′gent, *adj.*
re′-em′igrate′, *v.i.*, **-grated, -grating.**
re′-em′igra′tion, *n.*
re′-emis′sion, *n.*
re′-emit′, *v.t.*, **-mitted, -mitting.**
re′-em′phasis, *n.*, *pl.*, **-ses′.**
re′-em′phasize′, *v.t.*, **-sized, -sizing.**
re′-employ′, *v.t.*
re′-employ′ment, *n.*
re′-enact′, *v.t.*
re′-enact′ment, *n.*
re′-enclose′, *v.t.*, **-closed, -closing.**
re′-encoun′ter, *v.t.*, *n.*
re′-encour′age, *v.t.*, **-raged, -raging.**
re′-encour′agement, *n.*
re′-endorse′, *v.t.*, **-dorsed, -dorsing.**
re′-endorse′ment, *n.*
re′-endow′, *v.t.*
re′-endow′ment, *n.*
re′-en′ergize′, *v.t.*, **-gized, -gizing.**
re′-engage′, *v.*, **-gaged, -gaging.**
re′-engage′ment, *n.*
re′-engrave′, *v.t.*, **-graved, -graving.**
re′-engross′, *v.t.*
re′-enjoin′, *v.t.*
re′-enlarge′, *v.t.*, **-larged, -larging.**
re′-enlarge′ment, *n.*
re′-enlist′, *v.*
re′-enlist′ment, *n.*
re′-enslave′, *v.t.*, **-slaved, -slaving.**
re′-enun′ciate′, *v.t.*, **-ated, -ating.**

2. *Law.* the retaking of possession under a right reserved in a prior conveyance. 3. Also, **re-entry card.** *Whist and Bridge.* a card which will win a trick and thereby permit one to take the lead once again. 4. *Aeron.* the return of a spacecraft, rocket, etc., into the earth's atmosphere.

reeve[1] (rēv), *n.* 1. *Hist.* an administrative officer of a town or district. 2. *Hist.* one of high rank representing the crown. 3. a bailiff, steward, or overseer. 4. (in Canada) the presiding officer of a village or town council. [ME *ireve*, OE *gerēfa* high official, lit., head of a *rōf* array, number (of soldiers)]

reeve[2] (rēv), *v.t.*, **reeved** or **rove, reeving.** *Naut.* 1. to pass (a rope, etc.) through a hole, ring, or the like. 2. to fasten by placing through or around something. 3. to pass a rope through (a block, etc.). [? t. D: m. *rēven* REEF[2]]

reeve[3] (rēv), *n.* the female of the European ruff, *Philomachus pugnax.*

re-examine (rē'ĭg zăm'ĭn), *v.t.*, **-ined, -ining.** 1. to examine again. 2. *Law.* to examine (a witness) again after he has been cross-examined by the other party's advocate. —**re'-exam'ina'tion,** *n.* —**re'-exam'iner,** *n.*

re-export (*v.* rē'ĭks pôt'; *n.* rē'ěks'pôt'), *v.t.* 1. to export again, as imported goods. —*n.* 2. a re-exporting. 3. that which is re-exported. —**re'-ex'porta'tion,** *n.*

ref., 1. referee. 2. reference. 3. referred. 4. reformation. 5. reformed.

reface (rē'fās'), *v.t.*, **-faced, -facing.** 1. to renew, restore, or repair the face or surface of (buildings, stone, etc.). 2. to provide (a garment, etc.) with a new facing.

Ref. Ch., Reformed Church.

refect (rĭ fěkt'), *v.t. Archaic.* to refresh, esp. with food or drink. [t. L: s. *refectus*, pp., restored]

refection (rĭ fěk'shən), *n.* 1. refreshment, esp. with food or drink. 2. a portion of food or drink; repast. [ME, t. L: s. *refectio*]

refectory (rĭ fěk'tə rĭ), *n., pl.* **-ries.** a dining hall in a religious house, a university or other institution. [t. ML: m. s. *refectōrium*, der. L *reficere* restore]

refectory table, a long, narrow, wooden dining table supported on two pillar-like legs.

refer (rĭ fû'), *v.*, **-ferred, -ferring.** —*v.t.* 1. to direct the attention or thoughts of: *the asterisk refers the reader to a footnote.* 2. to direct for information or for anything required: *to refer students to books on a subject.* 3. to return (a thesis, examination paper or the like) to a candidate in order that he may improve the thesis, retake the examination, etc., in order to reach the required standard. 4. to allow (a candidate) who did not reach the required standard in an examination, etc., to take it again. 5. to hand over or submit for information, consideration, decision, etc.: *to refer a cause to arbitration.* 6. to assign to a class, period, etc.; regard as belonging or related. —*v.i.* 7. to direct attention, as a reference mark does. 8. to direct anyone for information, esp. about one's character, abilities, etc.: *to refer to a former employer.* 9. to have relation; relate; apply. 10. to have recourse or resort; turn, as for aid or information: *to refer to one's notes.* 11. to direct a remark or mention; make reference or allusion, as a speaker or writer does. [ME *referre*, t. L: lit., carry back] —**referable** (rĭ.fû'rə bl), *adj.* —**refer'ral,** *n.* —**refer'rer,** *n.* —**Syn.** 6. attribute, ascribe. 11. advert, allude.

referee (rěf'ə rē'), *n., v.*, **-reed, -reeing.** —*n.* 1. one to whom something is referred, esp. for decision or settlement; arbitrator; umpire. 2. a judge in certain games having functions fixed by the rules. 3. *Law.* **a.** a person selected by a court to take testimony in a case and return it to the court with recommendations as to the decision. **b.** a person selected to hear and decide controversies pending before administrative agencies. 4. See **Official Referee.** 5. reference (def. 8). —*v.t.* 6. to preside over as referee; act as referee in. —*v.i.* 7. to act as referee. —**Syn.** 1. See **judge.**

reference (rěf'rəns), *n.* 1. the act or fact of referring. 2. direction of the attention: *marks of reference.* 3. a mention; allusion. 4. a direction in a book or writing to some book, passage, etc.: *to look up a reference.* 5. a note indicating this. 6. direction or a direction to some source of information. 7. use or recourse for purposes of information: *a library for public reference.* 8. a person to whom one refers for testimony as to one's character, abilities, etc. 9. a written testimonial as to character, abilities, etc. 10. relation, regard, or respect: *all persons, without reference to age.* 11. *Law.* **a.** the proceedings before a referee. **b.** the act of submitting a matter to a referee for investigation or judgement. 12. **terms of reference,** the scope allowed to an investigating body. 13. **with reference to,** concerning; with regard to.

reference book, a publication consulted to identify certain facts or for background information, as an encyclopedia, dictionary, atlas, etc.

reference group, *Sociol.* 1. a group or class of persons with which an individual wishes to conform and which sanctions attitudes and standards of behaviour. 2. a group which is used as a standard for the purposes of self-perception.

reference library, a library of reference books which may be consulted but generally not borrowed or taken away.

reference mark, a sign, as *, †, etc., used in a publication to direct the reader's attention from the text to a footnote.

referendum (rěf'ə rěn'dəm), *n., pl.* **-da** (-də). 1. the principle or procedure of referring or submitting measures proposed or passed by a legislative body to the vote of the electorate for approval or rejection. 2. an instance of this procedure. [t. L, gerund (or neut. gerundive) of *referre* refer]

referent (rěf'ə rənt), *n.* 1. *Rhet., Semantics.* **a.** the object to which a term of discourse refers. **b.** the object of thought, alternatively as viewed by the thinker or by a supposedly all-knowing mind. 2. *Logic.* any related term from which the relation proceeds, e.g., in 'John loves Mary', 'John' is the referent.

refill (*v.* rē'fĭl'; *n.* rē'fĭl'), *v.t.* 1. to fill again. —*n.* 2. the material replacing a used-up product which was in an original purchase: *a refill for a lipstick.* —**re'fill'able,** *adj.*

refinance (rē'fĭ'năns, rē'fĭ năns'), *v.i., v.t.*, **-nanced, -nancing.** to sell securities in order to redeem (existing bonds or preferred stock).

refine (rĭ fīn'), *v.*, **-fined, -fining.** —*v.t.* 1. to bring to a fine or a pure state; free from impurities: *to refine metal, sugar, petroleum, etc.* 2. to purify from what is coarse, vulgar, or debasing; make elegant or cultured. 3. to bring by purifying, as to a finer state or form. 4. to make more fine, nice, subtle, or minutely precise. —*v.i.* 5. to become pure. 6. to become more fine, elegant, or polished. 7. to make fine distinctions in thought or language. 8. **refine on** or **upon, a.** to reason or discourse with subtlety. **b.** to improve (*on*) by superior fineness, excellence, etc. [f. RE- + FINE[1], v.] —**refin'er,** *n.*

refined (rĭ fīnd'), *adj.* 1. imbued with or showing nice feeling, taste, etc.: *refined people.* 2. freed or free from coarseness, vulgarity, etc.: *refined taste.* 3. freed from impurities: *refined sugar.* 4. subtle: *refined distinctions.* 5. minutely precise; exact.

refinement (rĭ fīn'mənt), *n.* 1. fineness of feeling, taste, etc. 2. elegance of manners or language. 3. an instance of refined feeling, manners, etc. 4. the act of refining. 5. the state of being refined. 6. improvement on something else. 7. an instance or result of this. 8. a subtle point or distinction. 9. subtle reasoning. 10. an improved, higher, or extreme form of something.

refinery (rĭ fī'nə rĭ), *n., pl.* **-eries.** an establishment for refining something, as metal, sugar, or petroleum.

refit (rē'fĭt'), *v.*, **-fitted, -fitting,** *n.* —*v.t.* 1. to fit, prepare, or equip again. —*v.i.* 2. to renew supplies or equipment. 3. to get refitted. —*v.* 4. the act of refitting.

refl., 1. reflection. 2. reflective. 3. reflex. 4. reflexive.

reflate (rē flāt'), *v.*, **-flated, -flating.** —*v.i.* 1. to increase the amount of money and credit in circulation by relaxing government controls over economic restriction. —*v.t.* 2. to increase (money and credit) again by relaxing government controls over restrictions.

reflation (rē flā'shən), *n.* the relaxation of government controls over economic restrictions, with a view to improving a country's economy.

reflect (rĭ flěkt'), *v.t.* 1. to cast back (light, heat, sound,

---

re'-equip', *v.t.*, -quipped, -quipping.
re'-erect', *v.t.*
re'-erec'tion, *n.*
re'-erupt', *v.i.*
re'-estab'lish, *v.t.*
re'-estab'lishment, *n.*
re'-es'timate', *v.t.*, -mated, -mating.
re'-es'timate, *n.*
re'-evac'uate', *v.*, -ated, -ating.
re'-evac'ua'tion, *n.*
re'-eval'uate', *v.t.*, -ated, -ating.
re'-eval'ua'tion, *n.*
re'-ex'cavate', *v.t.*, -vated, -vating.
re'-ex'cava'tion, *n.*
re'-ex'ecute', *v.t.*, -cuted, -cuting.
re'-exhib'it, *v.t.*
re'-expand', *v.*
re'-expan'sion, *n.*
re'-expel', *v.t.*, -pelled, -pelling.
re'-explain', *v.t.*
re'-ex'plana'tion, *n.*
re'-ex'plora'tion, *n.*
re'-explore', *v.t.*, -plored, -ploring.
re'-expose', *v.t.*, -posed, -posing.
re'-ex'posi'tion, *n.*
re'-expo'sure, *n.*
re'-express', *v.t.*
re'-expul'sion, *n.*
re'-fash'ion, *v.t.*
re'-fas'ten, *v.t.*
re'-fer'tilize', *v.t.*, -lized, -lizing.
re'file', *v.t.*, **-filed, -filing.**
re'film', *v.t.*
re'fil'ter, *v.t.*

---

etc.) after incidence. **2.** to give back or show an image of; mirror. **3.** to throw or cast back; cause to return or rebound. **4.** to reproduce; show: *followers reflecting the views of the leader.* **5.** to serve to cast or bring (credit, discredit, etc.). **6.** to think carefully; meditate on. *—v.i.* **7.** to be turned or cast back, as light. **8.** to cast back light, heat, etc. **9.** to be reflected or mirrored. **10.** to give back or show an image. **11.** to serve or tend to bring reproach or discredit. **12.** to serve to give a particular aspect or impression: *his speech reflects no credit on his candidacy.* **13.** to think, ponder, or meditate. [late ME, t. L: s. *reflectere* bend back] **—Syn. 6.** ruminate, ponder, deliberate, muse, consider, cogitate, contemplate. See **study.**

reflectance (rĭ flĕk′təns), *n. Physics.* the ratio of the luminous flux reflected by a surface to the incident luminous flux. Also, **reflection factor.**

reflecting telescope, a telescope using a mirror instead of a lens to form the principal image.

reflection (rĭ flĕk′shən), *n.* **1.** the act of reflecting. **2.** the state of being reflected. **3.** an image; representation; counterpart. **4.** a fixing of the thoughts on something; careful consideration. **5.** a thought occurring in consideration or meditation. **6.** an unfavourable remark or observation. **7.** the casting of some imputation or reproach. **8.** *Physics.* **a.** the casting back, or the change of direction, of light, heat, sound, etc., after striking a surface. **b.** something so reflected, as heat, or esp., light. Also, **reflexion.** **—reflec′tional,** *adj.* **—Syn. 4.** meditation, rumination, deliberation, cogitation, study. **6.** imputation, aspersion.

reflective (rĭ flĕk′tĭv), *adj.* **1.** that reflects; reflecting. **2.** of or pertaining to reflection. **3.** cast by reflection. **4.** given to or concerned with meditation. **—reflec′tively,** *adv.* **—reflec′tiveness, reflectivity** (rē′flĕk tĭv′ĭ tĭ), *n.* **—Syn. 4.** See **pensive.**

reflector (rĭ flĕk′tə), *n.* **1.** one who or that which reflects. **2.** a body, surface, or device that reflects light, heat, sound, or the like. **3.** a reflecting telescope. **4.** *Physics.* a layer of material surrounding the core of a nuclear reactor which reflects back into the core some of the neutrons which would otherwise escape. **5.** a piece of red glass or metal attached to the rear of a cycle or motor vehicle, or used to mark the edge of a road near road hazards.

reflet (rə flā′), *n.* an effect of lustre, colour, or iridescence on an object (as a piece of pottery) due to reflection of light. [F: reflection]

reflex (*adj., n.* rē′flĕks; *v.* rĭ flĕks′), *adj.* **1.** *Physiol.* denoting or pertaining to an involuntary response in which an impulse evoked by a stimulus is transmitted along an afferent nerve to a nerve centre, and from there through one or more synapses to an efferent nerve, calling into play muscular or other activity. **2.** occurring in reaction; responsive. **3.** designating a radio apparatus in which the same part performs two functions, as in a **reflex klystron,** in which one resonator acts as buncher and catcher. **4.** cast back; reflected, as light, etc. **5.** bent or turned back. *—n.* **6.** *Physiol.* a reflex action or movement. **7.** *Psychol.* an immediate response to a stimulus, inborn and often unaccompanied by consciousness, as blinking, perspiring, sneezing, etc. **8.** the reflection or image of an object, as exhibited by a mirror or the like. **9.** a reproduction as if in a mirror. **10.** a copy; adaptation. **11.** reflected light, colour, etc. **12.** a reflex radio receiving apparatus or set. *—v.t.* **13.** to bend, turn, or fold back. [t. L: s. *reflexus,* pp., reflected, bent back]

reflex angle, *Geom.* an angle greater than 180° but less than 360°.

reflex camera, *Photog.* a camera containing a pivoted mirror which allows the image of the object which is to be photographed to be viewed and focused on a ground-glass screen up to the moment of exposure.

reflexion (rĭ flĕk′shən), *n.* **1.** *Chiefly Anat.* the bending or folding back of a thing upon itself. **2.** reflection.

reflexive (rĭ flĕk′sĭv), *adj. Gram.* **1.** (of a verb) having identical subject and object, as *shave* in *he shaved himself.* **2.** (of a pronoun) indicating identity of object with subject, as *himself* in the example above. *—n.* **3.** a reflexive verb or pronoun, as *himself* in *he deceived himself.* **—reflex′ively,** *adv.* **—reflex′iveness, reflexivity** (rē′flĕk sĭv′ĭ tĭ), *n.*

refluent (rĕf′lo͞o ənt), *adj.* flowing back; ebbing, as the waters of a tide. [ME, t. L: s. *refluens,* ppr.] **—ref′luence,** *n.*

reflux (rē′flŭks), *n.* a flowing back; ebb. [f. RE- + FLUX. Cf. F *reflux*]

reflux condenser, *Chem.* a condenser attached to a vessel containing a boiling liquid so that the condensed vapour flows back into the vessel, thus preventing it from boiling dry.

reforest (rē fŏ′rĭst), *v.t.* reafforest. **—re′foresta′tion,** *n.*

reform (rĭ fôm′), *n.* **1.** the improvement or amendment of what is wrong, corrupt, etc.: *social reform.* **2.** an instance of this. **3.** the amendment of conduct, etc. *—v.t.* **4.** to restore to a former and better state; improve by alteration, substitution, abolition, etc. **5.** to cause (a person) to abandon wrong or evil ways of life or conduct. **6.** to put an end to (abuses, disorders, etc.). *—v.i.* **7.** to abandon evil conduct or error. [ME *reforme,* t. L: m. *reformāre*] **—reform′able,** *adj.* **—reform′ative,** *adj.* **—reform′er,** *n.* **—Syn. 4.** better, rectify, correct.

re-form (rē′fôm′), *v.t., v.i.* to form again.

reformation (rĕf′ə mā′shən), *n.* **1.** the act of reforming. **2.** the state of being reformed. **3.** (*cap.*) the great religious movement in the 16th century which had for its object the reform of the Roman Catholic Church, and which led to the establishment of the Protestant Churches. **—ref′orma′tional,** *adj.* **—Syn. 1.** improvement, betterment, correction.

reformatory (rĭ fô′mə tə rĭ, -trĭ), *adj., n., pl.* **-ries.** *—adj.* **1.** serving or designed to reform: *reformatory schools.* *—n.* **2.** Also, **reform school.** a penal institution for the reformation of young offenders; approved school.

Reform Bill, *Eng. Hist.* any one of the bills passed by Parliament in 1832, 1867, 1884, which reformed the House of Commons by increasing the number of voters in elections and redistributing many seats.

reformed (rĭ fômd′), *adj.* **1.** amended by removal of faults, abuses, etc. **2.** improved in conduct, morals, etc. **3.** (*cap.*) denoting or pertaining to Protestant Churches, esp. Calvinist as distinguished from Lutheran.

refract (rĭ frăkt′), *v.t.* **1.** to subject to refraction. **2.** to determine the refractive condition of (an eye, a lens). [t. L: s. *refractus,* pp., broken up]

refracting telescope, a telescope consisting essentially of a lens for forming an image and an eyepiece for viewing it. See **telescope** (def. 1).

refraction (rĭ frăk′shən), *n.* **1.** *Physics.* the change of direction of a ray of light, heat, or the like, in passing obliquely from one medium into another in which its speed is different. **2.** *Optics.* **a.** the ability of the eye to refract light which enters it so as to form an image on the retina. **b.** the determining of the refractive condition of the eye. **—refrac′tional,** *adj.*

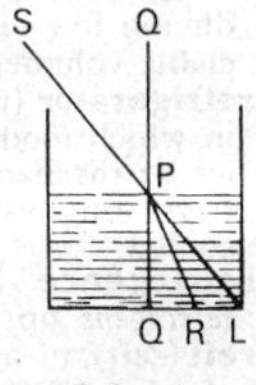

S Q P Q R L

Refraction SP, Ray of light; SPL, Original direction; SPR, Refracted ray; QQ, Perpendicular

refraction correction, *Astron.* the small correction which has to be made to the observed altitude of a celestial body due to the refraction by the earth's atmosphere of the light which it emits or reflects.

refractive (rĭ frăk′tĭv), *adj.* **1.** of or pertaining to refraction. **2.** having power to refract. **3.** refracting. **—refrac′tively,** *adv.* **—refrac′tiveness, refractivity** (rē′frăk tĭv′ĭ tĭ), *n.*

refractive index, *Physics.* a specific property of a material equal to the ratio of the velocity of light in a vacuum to its velocity in that material.

refractivity (rē′frăk tĭv′ĭ tĭ), *n. Physics.* **1.** the difference between the refractive index of a material and unity. **2.** this difference divided by the density of the material (**specific refractivity**). **3.** the specific refractivity multiplied by the molecular weight of the material (**molecular refractivity**).

refractometer (rē′frăk tŏm′ĭ tə), *n. Physics.* an instrument for determining the refractive index of a material. [f. REFRACT + -O- + -METER[1]]

refractor (rĭ frăk′tə), *n.* **1.** something that refracts. **2.** a refracting telescope.

refractory (rĭ frăk′tə rĭ), *adj., n., pl.* **-ries.** *—adj.* **1.** stubborn; unmanageable: *a refractory child.* **2.** resisting ordinary methods of treatment. **3.** difficult to fuse, reduce, or work, as an ore or metal. *—n.* **4.** a material having the ability to retain its physical shape and chemical identity when subjected to high temperatures. **5.** (*pl.*) bricks of various shapes used in lining furnaces. **6.** *Physiol.* a momentary state of reduced excitability following a

---

re′fire′, *v.t.,* **-fired, -firing.**
re′fix′, *v.t.*
re′float′, *v.t.*
re′flores′cence, *n.*
re′flow′, *v.i.*
re′fo′cus, *v.,* **-focussed, -focussing.**
re′fold′, *v.*
re′forge′, *v.t.,* **-forged, -forging.**
re′for′mulate′, *v.t.,* **-lated, -lating.**
re′for′tify′, *v.t.,* **-fied, -fying.**
re′for′ward, *v.t.*
re′frac′ture, *v.,* **-tured, -turing.**
re′frame′, *v.t.,* **-framed, -framing.**

response: *the refractory period of a nerve.* —**refrac'torily,** *adv.* —**refrac'toriness,** *n.*

refrain[1] (rĭ frān'), *v.i.* **1.** to keep oneself from. —*v.t.* **2.** *Rare.* to curb. [ME *refreyne(n)*, t. OF: m. *refrener*, t. L: m. *refrēnāre* to bridle] —**refrain'er,** *n.*

refrain[2] (rĭ frān'), *n.* **1.** a phrase or verse recurring at intervals in a song or poem, esp. at the end of each stanza; chorus. **2.** a musical setting for the refrain of a poem. [ME *refreyne*, t. OF: m. *refrain*, der. *refraindre*, g. VL *refrangere*, r. L *refringere* refract]

refrangible (rĭ frăn'jĭ bl), *adj.* capable of being refracted, as rays of light. [f. RE- + s. L *frangere* break + -IBLE] —**refran'gibleness, refran'gibil'ity,** *n.*

refresh (rĭ frĕsh'), *v.t.* **1.** to reinvigorate by rest, food etc. (often reflexive). **2.** to stimulate (the memory). **3.** to make fresh again; reinvigorate or cheer (a person, the mind, spirits, etc.). **4.** to freshen in appearance, colour, etc., as by a restorative. —*v.i.* **5.** to take refreshment, esp. food or drink. **6.** to become fresh or vigorous again; revive. [ME, t. OF: m. s. *refrescher*, der. *re-* RE- + *fresche* FRESH] —**refresh'ing,** *adj.* —**refresh'ingly,** *adv.*

refresher (rĭ frĕsh'ə), *adj.* **1.** serving as a review of material previously studied: *a refresher course.* —*n.* **2.** one who or that which refreshes. **3.** a fee paid to a counsel in addition to that marked on his brief.

refreshing (rĭ frĕsh'ĭng), *adj.* **1.** capable of reinvigorating, cooling, restoring energy, etc. **2.** interesting because of unique or unusual qualities.

refreshment (rĭ frĕsh'mənt), *n.* **1.** that which refreshes, esp. food or drink. **2.** (*pl.*) articles or portions of food or drink, esp. for a light meal. **3.** the act of refreshing. **4.** the state of being refreshed.

refrigerant (rĭ frĭj'ə rənt), *adj.* **1.** refrigerating; cooling. **2.** reducing bodily heat or fever. —*n.* **3.** a refrigerant agent, as in a drug. **4.** a liquid capable of vaporizing at a low temperature, as ammonia, used in mechanical refrigeration. **5.** a cooling substance, as ice, solid carbon dioxide, etc., used in a refrigerator.

refrigerate (rĭ frĭj'ə rāt'), *v.t.*, **-rated, -rating. 1.** to make or keep cold or cool. **2.** to freeze (food, etc.) for preservation. [t. L: m. s. *refrīgerātus*, pp., made cool again] —**refrigerative** (rĭ frĭj'ə rə tĭv), **refrigeratory** (rĭ frĭj'ə rə-tə rĭ, -trĭ), *adj.*

refrigeration (rĭ frĭj'ə rā'shən), *n.* **1.** the process of producing low temperatures, usually throughout an appreciable volume. **2.** the resulting state.

refrigerator (rĭ frĭj'ə rā'tə), *n.* **1.** a box, room, or cabinet in which food, drink, etc., are kept cool, as by means of ice or mechanical refrigeration. **2.** the element of a refrigerating system consisting of the space or medium to be cooled.

refringence (rĭ frĭn'jəns), *n.* refraction. [t. L: m. *refringens*, ppr.] —**refrin'gent,** *adj.*

reft (rĕft), *v.* a pt. and pp. of **reave.**

refuel (rē fyōō'əl), *v.*, **-elled, -elling** or (*U.S.*) **-eled, -eling.** —*v.t.* **1.** to supply again with fuel: *to refuel an aeroplane.* —*v.i.* **2.** to take on a fresh supply of fuel: *they refuelled at Paris and flew on.*

refuge (rĕf'yōōj), *n.*, *v.*, **-uged, -uging.** —*n.* **1.** shelter or protection from danger, trouble, etc.: *to take refuge from a storm.* **2.** a place of shelter, protection, or safety. **3.** anything to which one has recourse for aid, relief, or escape. **4.** a platform in the centre of a street for the use of pedestrians in crossing; island (def. 5). —*v.t.* **5.** *Archaic.* to afford refuge to. —*v.i.* **6.** *Archaic.* to take refuge. [ME, t. OF, t. L: m. s. *refugium*] —**Syn. 2.** asylum, retreat, sanctuary.

refugee (rĕf'yōō jē'), *n.* one who flees for refuge or safety, esp. to a foreign country, as in time of political upheaval, war, etc. [t. F: m. *refugié*, pp. of *refugier* take refuge, der. *refuge* REFUGE]

refulgent (rĭ fŭl'jənt), *adj.* shining; radiant; glowing. [t. L: s. *refulgens*, ppr.] —**reful'gence,** *n.* —**reful'gently,** *adv.*

refund[1] (*v.* rĭ fŭnd'; *n.* rē'fŭnd'), *v.t.* **1.** to give back or restore (esp. money); repay. **2.** to make repayment to; reimburse. —*v.i.* **3.** to make repayment. —*n.* **4.** a repayment. [ME, t. L: s. *refundere*, lit., pour back]

refund[2] (rē'fŭnd'), *v.t.* **1.** to fund anew. **2.** *Finance.* **a.** to meet (a matured debt structure) by new borrowing, esp. through issuance of bonds. **b.** to replace (an old issue) with a new, esp. with one bearing a lower rate of interest. [f. RE- + FUND]

refurbish (rē'fû'bĭsh), *v.t.* to furbish again; renovate; polish up again; brighten.

refusal (rĭ fyōō'zəl), *n.* **1.** the act of refusing. **2.** priority in refusing or taking something; option.

refuse[1] (rĭ fyōōz'), *v.*, **-fused, -fusing.** —*v.t.* **1.** to decline to accept (something offered): *to refuse an office.* **2.** to decline to give; deny (a request, demand, etc.). **3.** to express a determination not (to do something): *to refuse to discuss the question.* **4.** to decline to submit to. **5.** (of a horse) to decline to leap over (a fence, water, etc.). **6.** *Obs.* to renounce. —*v.i.* **7.** to decline acceptance, consent, or compliance. [ME, t. OF: m. *refuser*, g. VL *refusāre*, der. L *refusus*, pp., lit., poured back] —**refus'er,** *n.*

—**Syn. 1.** REFUSE, DECLINE, REJECT, SPURN all imply non-acceptance of something. To DECLINE is milder and more courteous than to REFUSE, which is direct and often emphatic in expressing determination not to accept what is offered or proposed: *to refuse a bribe, to decline an invitation.* To REJECT is even more positive and definite than refuse: *to reject a suitor.* To SPURN is to reject with scorn: *to spurn a bribe.* —**Ant. 1.** accept, welcome.

refuse[2] (rĕf'yōōs), *n.* **1.** that which is discarded as worthless or useless; rubbish. —*adj.* **2.** rejected as worthless; discarded: *refuse matter.* [ME, t. OF: m. *refus*, pp., refused. See REFUSE[1]]

refutation (rĕf'yōō tā'shən), *n.* the act of refuting a statement, charge, etc.; disproof. Also, **refutal** (rĭ fyōō'tl).

refute (rĭ fyōōt'), *v.t.*, **-futed, -futing. 1.** to prove to be false or erroneous, as an opinion, charge, etc. **2.** to prove (a person) to be in error. [t. L: m. s. *refūtāre* repel, refute] —**refutable** (rĕf'yōō tə bl, rĭ fyōō'tə bl), *adj.* —**ref'utably,** *adv.* —**refut'er,** *n.* —**Syn. 1.** disprove, rebut.

Reg., **1.** Regent. **2.** Regina.

reg., **1.** regiment. **2.** register. **3.** registered. **4.** registrar. **5.** registry. **6.** regular. **7.** regularly. **8.** regulation.

regain (rĭ gān'), *v.t.* **1.** to get again; recover. **2.** to succeed in reaching again; get back to: *to regain the shore.* —**regain'er,** *n.*

regal[1] (rē'gl), *adj.* **1.** of or pertaining to a king; royal: *the regal power.* **2.** befitting or resembling a king. **3.** stately; splendid. **4.** (of a woman) tall, dignified, and elegant. [ME, t. L: s. *rēgālis*] —**re'gally,** *adv.* —**Syn. 2.** See **kingly.**

regal[2] (rē'gl), *n.* a small portable reed organ, of the 16th and 17th centuries. [t. MF: m. *régale*; connection with REGAL[1] obscure]

regale (rĭ gāl'), *v.*, **-galed, -galing,** *n.* —*v.t.* **1.** to entertain agreeably; delight. **2.** to entertain with choice food or drink. —*v.i.* **3.** to feast. —*n.* **4.** a choice feast. **5.** a choice article of food or drink. **6.** refreshment. [t. F: s. *régaler*, der. OF *regale* feast, der. *gale* pleasure, t. MD: m. *wale* wealth] —**regale'ment,** *n.*

regalia (rĭ gā'lyə), *n.pl.* **1.** the rights and privileges of a king. **2.** the ensigns or emblems of royalty, as the crown, sceptre, etc. **3.** the decorations or insignia of any office or order. [t. ML, prop. neut. pl. of L *rēgālis* regal]

regality (rē găl'ĭ tĭ), *n.*, *pl.* **-ties. 1.** royalty, sovereignty, or kingship. **2.** a right or privilege pertaining to a king. **3.** a kingdom. **4.** *Hist.* (in Scotland) **a.** a territorial jurisdiction of a royal nature conferred by the king. **b.** a territory subject to such jurisdiction.

regard (rĭ gäd'), *v.t.* **1.** to look upon or think of with a particular feeling: *to regard a person with favour.* **2.** to have or show respect or concern for. **3.** to think highly of. **4.** to take into account; consider. **5.** to look at; observe. **6.** to relate to; concern. **7.** *Obs.* to show attention to; guard. —*v.i.* **8.** to pay attention. **9.** to look or gaze. —*n.* **10.** reference; relation: *to err in regard to facts.* **11.** a point or particular: *quite satisfactory in this regard.* **12.** thought; attention; concern. **13.** look; gaze. **14.** respect; deference: *due regard to authority.* **15.** kindly feeling; liking. **16.** (*pl.*) sentiments of esteem or affection: *give them my regards.* **17.** *Obs.* aspect. **18. with regard to,** concerning. [ME *regard*, n., t. F, der. *regarder*, v., f. *re-* RE- + *garder* GUARD] —**Syn. 3.** esteem, respect.

regardant (rĭ gä'dnt), *adj.* *Her.* looking backwards. [t. F, ppr. of *regarder* REGARD]

regardful (rĭ gäd'fəl), *adj.* **1.** observant; attentive; heedful (often fol. by *of*). **2.** considerate or thoughtful; respectful. —**regard'fully,** *adv.* —**regard'fulness,** *n.*

regarding (rĭ gä'dĭng), *prep.* with regard to; respecting; concerning: *he knew nothing regarding the lost watch.*

regardless (rĭ gäd'lĭs), *adj.* **1.** having or showing no regard; heedless; unmindful; careless (often fol. by *of*). **2.** without regard to expense, danger, etc. —*adv.* **3.** anyway. **4.** without regard for. —**regard'lessly,** *adv.* —**regard'lessness,** *n.* —**Syn. 1.** inattentive, negligent, neglectful, indifferent.

regatta (rĭ găt'ə), *n.* **1.** a boat race, as of rowing boats, yachts, or other vessels. **2.** an organized series of such races. **3.** (orig.) a gondola race in Venice. **4.** a coloured, striped cotton cloth with a twill weave. [t. It. (Venetian): m. *regata*, der. *regatare* compete]

---

re'freeze', *v.*, **-froze, -frozen, -freezing.**
re'func'tion, *v.i.*
re'furl', *v.t.*
re'fur'nish, *v.t.*
re'gal'vanize', *v.t.*, **-nized, -nizing.**
re'gar'rison, *v.t.*

regelate (rē′jĭ lāt′), *v.i.*, **-lated, -lating.** to freeze together, as two pieces of ice pressed together near the freezing point. [t. L: m. s. *regelātus*] —**re′gela′tion,** *n.*

regency (rē′jən sĭ), *n.*, *pl.* **-cies,** *adj.* —*n.* **1.** the office, jurisdiction, or control of a regent or body of regents exercising the ruling power during the minority, absence, or disability of a sovereign. **2.** a body of regents. **3.** a government consisting of regents. **4.** a territory under the control of a regent or regents. **5.** the term of office of a regent. **6.** (*cap.*) in Britain, the period (1811–20) during which George (later, George IV) was regent. **7.** (*cap.*) in France, the period (1715–23) during which Philip, Duke of Orleans, was regent, in the minority of Louis XV. **8.** the office or function of a regent or ruler. —*adj.* **9.** pertaining to a regency. **10.** (*cap.*) of or pertaining to the Regency in French or English history or to the styles popular at those times.

regeneracy (rĭ jĕn′ə rə sĭ), *n.* regenerate state.

regenerate (*v.* rĭ jĕn′ə rāt′; *adj.* rĭ jĕn′ə rĭt), *v.*, **-rated, -rating,** *adj.* —*v.t.* **1.** to effect a complete moral reform in. **2.** to re-create, reconstitute, or make over, esp. in a better form or condition. **3.** to generate or produce anew; bring into existence again. **4.** *Physics.* to restore (a substance) periodically to a favourable thermal state or physical condition from which it later departs while performing a desired function. **5.** *Electronics.* to magnify the amplification of, by relaying part of the output circuit power into the input circuit. **6.** *Theol.* to cause to be born again spiritually. —*v.i.* **7.** to come into existence or be formed again. **8.** to reform; become regenerate. **9.** to produce a regenerative effect. —*adj.* **10.** reconstituted in a better form. **11.** reformed. **12.** *Theol.* born again spiritually. [late ME, t. L: m. s. *regenerātus*, pp., made over, produced anew]

regeneration (rĭ jĕn′ə rā′shən), *n.* **1.** the act of regenerating. **2.** the state of being regenerated. **3.** *Electronics.* a feedback process in which energy fed back to the grid circuit reinforces the input. **4.** *Biol.* the restitution of a lost part by an organism. **5.** *Theol.* spiritual rebirth.

regenerative (rĭ jĕn′ə rə tĭv), *adj.* **1.** pertaining to regeneration. **2.** tending to regenerate. —**regen′eratively,** *adv.*

regenerative braking, *Elect.* a method of braking electric motors in which they are operated as generators, the power produced being returned to the supply source.

regenerative cooling, **1.** *Aeron.* the cooling of a rocket combustion chamber wall by the circulation of a propellant before its injection into the chamber. **2.** *Chem.* the cooling of a gas by allowing a portion of it to expand rapidly.

regenerative furnace, a furnace in which the hot combustion products pass into a chamber containing a lattice structure of firebricks (the regenerator). The direction of the gas flow is periodically reversed so that the hot bricks in the regenerator can be used to preheat the incoming cold gas.

regenerator (rĭ jĕn′ə rā′tə), *n.* **1.** one who or that which regenerates. **2.** *Mech.* (in a regenerative furnace, etc.) a device for heating the incoming air or fuel gas.

Regensburg (*Ger.* rė′gəns bo͝ork), *n.* a town in West Germany, in E Bavaria: battle, 1809. 125,300 (est. 1966). Also, **Ratisbon.**

regent (rē′jənt), *n.* **1.** one who exercises the ruling power in a kingdom during the minority, absence, or disability of the sovereign. **2.** (formerly in some universities) a member of certain governing and teaching bodies. **3.** *U.S.* a member of the governing board of certain universities and other institutions. **4.** *U.S.* a university officer who exercises a general supervision over the conduct and welfare of the students. **5.** *Rare.* a ruler or governor. —*adj.* **6.** acting as regent of a country. **7.** exercising vicarious ruling authority: *a prince regent.* **8.** *U.S.* holding the position of a regent in a university. **9.** *Rare.* ruling. [ME, t. L: s. *regens*, ppr., ruling] —**re′gentship′,** *n.*

Regent's Park, a park in London: zoological gardens.

Regent Street, a street in the West End of London, noted for its shops.

Reggio di Calabria (*It.* rĕd′jō dē kȧ lȧ′brē ȧ), a seaport in S Italy, on the Strait of Messina: almost totally destroyed by an earthquake, 1908. 160,816 (1966).

Reggio nell'Emilia (*It.* rĕd′jō nĕl ė mē′lyȧ), a town in N Italy. 124,656 (1966). Also, **Reggio Emilia** (*It.* rĕd′jō ė mē′lyȧ).

regicide (rĕj′ĭ sīd′), *n.* **1.** one who kills a king; one responsible for the death of a king (esp. applied to the judges who condemned Charles I of England to death). **2.** the killing of a king. [f. *regi-* (comb. form repr. L *rex* king) + -CIDE] —**reg′icid′al,** *adj.*

regime (rā zhēm′), *n.* **1.** a mode or system of rule or government. **2.** a ruling or prevailing system. **3.** *Med.* regimen. **4.** the variation in the volume of a river with the season. **5.** the seasonal pattern of a climate. Also, **régime.** [t. F, t. L: m. *regimen* direction, government]

regimen (rĕj′ĭ mĕn′), *n.* **1.** *Med.* a regulated course of diet, exercise, or manner of living, intended to preserve or restore health or to attain some result. **2.** rule or government. **3.** a particular form or system of government. **4.** a prevailing system. **5.** *Gram. Obsolesc.* government: *the regimen of the verb by its subject.* [ME, t. L]

regiment (*n.* rĕj′ĭ mənt; *v.* rĕj′ĭ mĕnt′), *n.* **1.** *Mil.* a unit of ground forces, commanded by a lieutenant colonel, consisting of two or more battalions, a headquarters unit, and certain supporting units. **2.** *Obs.* government. —*v.t.* **3.** to form into a regiment or regiments. **4.** to assign to a regiment or group. **5.** to form into an organized body or group; organize or systematize. **6.** to group together and treat in a uniform manner; subject to strict discipline. [ME, t. LL: s. *regimentum* rule] —**reg′imenta′tion,** *n.*

regimental (rĕj′ĭ mĕn′tl), *adj.* **1.** of or pertaining to a regiment. —*n.* **2.** (*pl.*) the uniform of a regiment.

regina (rĭ jī′nə), *n.* (*often cap.*) reigning queen. [t. L]

Regina (rĭ jī′nə), *n.* a town in SW Canada: the capital of Saskatchewan. 126,700 (est. 1965).

region (rē′jən), *n.* **1.** any more or less extensive, continuous part of a surface or space. **2.** a part of the earth's surface (land or sea) of considerable and usually indefinite extent: *tropical regions.* **3.** a district without respect to boundaries or extent. **4.** a part or division of the universe, as the heavens: *celestial regions.* **5.** one of the administrative divisions into which a territory or country, as Italy, is divided. **6.** *Geog.* a large faunal area of the earth's surface, sometimes one regarded as a division of a larger area. **7.** *Anat.* a place in, or a division of, the body or a part of the body: *the abdominal region.* [ME, t. L: s. *regio* line, district]

regional (rē′jə nəl), *adj.* **1.** of or pertaining to a region of considerable extent; not merely local. **2.** of or pertaining to a particular region, district, area, or part; sectional; local. —**re′gionally,** *adv.*

regionalism (rē′jə nə lĭz′əm), *n.* **1.** *Politics.* the theory, principles, and practice of dividing a country into administrative regions. **2.** regional patriotism.

register (rĕj′ĭs tə), *n.* **1.** a book in which entries of acts, occurrences, names, or the like are made for record. **2.** any list of such entries; a record of acts, occurrences, etc. **3.** an entry in such a book, record, or list. **4.** *Com.* a ship's official document of identification which must be produced when a ship is entering or leaving a port. **5.** registration or registry. **6.** a mechanical device by which certain data are automatically recorded, as a cash register. **7.** *Music.* **a.** the compass or range of a voice or an instrument. **b.** a particular series of tones, esp. of the human voice, produced in the same way and having the same quality: *the head register.* **c.** (in an organ) a stop. **8.** *Linguistics.* a section of the vocabulary of a language according to the cultural or occupational area in which the words are used; occupational dialect. **9.** a contrivance for regulating the passage of warm air, or the like, esp. a closable perforated plate in a duct of a heating or ventilating system. **10.** *Photog.* the proper relationship between two plane surfaces in photography, as corresponding plates in photoengraving, etc. **11.** *Print., etc.* **a.** a precise adjustment or correspondence, as of lines, columns, etc., esp. on the two sides of a leaf. **b.** correct relation or exact superimposition, as of colours in colour printing. **12.** *Computers.* a device capable of holding digital information until it is required. —*v.t.* **13.** to enter or have entered formally in a register. **14.** to cause to be recorded for purposes of safety, as letters or parcels at a post office, for security in transmission, by payment of a special fee. **15.** to indicate by a record, as instruments do. **16.** to indicate or show, as on a scale. **17.** *Print, etc.* to adjust so as to secure exact correspondence; cause to be in register. **18.** *Mil.* to adjust (fire) on a known point. **19.** to show (surprise, joy, anger, etc.), as by facial expression or by actions. **20.** *Music.* to select the stops appropriate for (a piece of music for the organ). —*v.i.* **21.** to enter one's name, or cause it to be entered, in a register; enrol. **22.** *U.S.* to apply for and obtain inclusion of one's name on the list of voters. **23.** *Print., etc* to be in register. **24.** to show surprise, joy, etc. **25.** *Colloq.* to make an impression. [ME *registre*, t. ML: m. *registrum*, for *regestum*, neut. of L *regestus*, pp., recorded] —**reg′isterer,** *n.* —**reg′istrable,** *adj.* —**Syn.** **2.** roll, roster, catalogue.

---

re′gath′er, *v.*
re′gauge′, *v.t.*, **-gauged, -gauging.**
re′gear′, *v.t.*
re′gel′, *v.i.*, **-gelled, -gelling.**
re′ger′minate′, *v.t.*, **-nated, -nating.**
re′ger′mina′tion, *n.*
re′gild′, *v.t.*, **-gilded, -gilt, -gilding.**
re′gird′, *v.t.*, **-girt** or **-girded, -girding.**

---

registered (rĕj′ĭs tәd), *adj.* **1.** recorded, as in a register or book; enrolled. **2.** *Com.* officially listing the owner's name with the issuing company and suitably inscribing the certificate, as with bonds to evidence title. **3.** officially or legally certified by a government officer or board: *a registered patent.* **4.** denoting cattle, horses, dogs, etc., having pedigrees verified and filed by authorized associations of breeders.

register of wills, *U.S.* (in some states) the official charged with the probate of wills or with the keeping of the records of the probate court.

registrar (rĕj′ĭs trä′), *n.* **1.** one who keeps a record; an official recorder. **2.** the chief administrative official in a university. **3.** a doctor in a hospital next below a consultant, who is training to be a specialist. **4.** *Law.* an official in a court, subordinate to a judge, who deals with interlocutory matters, but who may also hear certain cases. **5.** an employee of a limited company who is responsible for registering the issues of securities. [f. REGISTER, v. + -AR[3]]

Registrar-General (rĕj′ĭs trä jĕn′ә rәl, -jĕn′rәl), *n.* an official responsible for the registration of all births, deaths, and marriages.

Registrar of Companies, an official appointed by the Board of Trade for the purpose of keeping the register of companies, that of mortgages and charges executed by companies, etc.

registration (rĕj′ĭs trā′shәn), *n.* **1.** the act of registering. **2.** an instance of this. **3.** an entry in a register. **4.** *Music.* the selection of stops used in playing the organ.

registration book, a document issued by a local taxation authority for a motor vehicle, containing particulars of that vehicle, a record of ownership, etc.; logbook.

registration plate, a numberplate.

registry (rĕj′ĭs trĭ), *n., pl.* **-tries. 1.** the act of registering; registration. **2.** a place where a register is kept; an office of registration. **3.** a register.

registry office, 1. Official name, **register office.** an office where births, marriages and deaths are recorded, and civil marriages take place. **2.** *Obs.* an employment bureau, esp. of domestic staff.

regius (rē′jyәs), *adj.* **1.** of or belonging to a king. **2.** (of a professor in a British university) holding a chair founded by the sovereign. [t. L]

reglet (rĕg′lĭt), *n.* **1.** *Archit.* a narrow, flat moulding. **2.** *Print.* **a.** a thin strip, usually of wood, less than type-high, used to produce a blank in or about a page of type. **b.** such strips collectively. [t. F, dim. of *regle*, g. L *rēgula* rule]

regma (rĕg′mә), *n., pl.* **-mata** (-mә tә). *Bot.* a dry fruit consisting of three or more carpels which separate from the axis at maturity. [NL, t. Gk: m. *rhēgma* rupture]

regnal (rĕg′nәl), *adj.* of or pertaining to reigning, sovereignty, or a reign: *the second regnal year.* [t. ML: s. *regnālis*, der. L *regnum* kingdom]

regnant (rĕg′nәnt), *adj.* **1.** reigning; ruling: *a queen regnant.* **2.** exercising sway or influence; predominant. **3.** prevalent; widespread. [t. L: s. *regnans*, ppr., ruling] **—regnancy** (rĕg′nәn sĭ), *n.*

regolith (rĕg′ә lĭth), *n. Phys. Geog.* mantle rock. [f. m. Gk *rhēgo(s)* blanket covering + -LITH]

regorge (rĭ gôj′), *v.*, **-gorged, -gorging.** *—v.t.* **1.** to disgorge; cast up again. *—v.i.* **2.** to rush back again; gush: *the waters regorged.* [t. F: m. s. *regorger*, or f. RE- + GORGE, v., after L *regurgitāre* regurgitate]

regrate (rĭ grāt′), *v.t.*, **-grated, -grating. 1.** to buy up (grain, provisions, etc.) in order to sell again at a profit in or near the same market. **2.** to sell again (commodities so bought); retail. [ME, t. OF: m. *regrater*, ? der. *grater* GRATE[2]] **—regrat′er,** *n.*

regress (*v.* rĭ grĕs′; *n.* rē′grĕs), *v.i.* **1.** to move in a backward direction; go back. *—n.* **2.** the act of going back; return. **3.** backward movement or course; retrogression. [ME, t. L: s. *regressus* a going back] **—regres′sive,** *adj.* **—regres′sively,** *adv.*

regression (rĭ grĕsh′әn), *n.* **1.** the act of going back; return; backward movement. **2.** retrogradation; retrogression. **3.** *Biol.* reversion to an earlier or less advanced state or form or to a common or general type. **4.** *Psychol.* the reversion to a chronologically earlier or less adapted pattern of behaviour and feeling. **5.** the disappearance of the symptoms or signs of a disease.

regression coefficient, *Statistics.* a constant by which a given value of a variable may be multiplied to obtain the best estimate of the value of a second variable corresponding to this value.

regret (rĭ grĕt′), *v.*, **-gretted, -gretting,** *n.* *—v.t.* **1.** to feel sorry about (anything disappointing, unpleasant, etc.). **2.** to think of with a sense of loss: *to regret one's vanished youth.* *—n.* **3.** a sense of loss, disappointment, dissatisfaction, etc. **4.** the feeling of being sorry for some fault, act, omission, etc., of one's own. **5.** (*pl.*) feelings of sorrow over what is lost, gone, done, etc. **6.** (*pl. or sing.*) a polite and formal expression of regretful feelings. [ME *regrette*, t. OF: m. *regretter*, der. Gmc **grētan*; cf. OE *grǣtan* GREET[2]] **—regret′table,** *adj.* **—regret′tably,** *adv.* **—regret′ter,** *n.*

—Syn. 2. deplore, lament. **4.** REGRET, PENITENCE, REMORSE imply a sense of sorrow about events in the past, usually wrongs committed or errors made. REGRET is distress of mind, sorrow for what has been done: *to have no regrets.* PENITENCE implies a sense of sin or misdoing, a feeling of contrition and determination not to sin again: *a humble sense of penitence.* REMORSE implies pangs, qualms of conscience, a sense of guilt, regret, and repentance for sins committed, wrongs done, or duty not performed: *a deep sense of remorse.*

regretful (rĭ grĕt′fәl), *adj.* full of regret; sorrowful because of what is lost, gone, done, etc. **—regret′fully,** *adv.* **—regret′fulness,** *n.*

Regt, 1. regent. **2.** regiment.

regular (rĕg′yŏŏ lә), *adj.* **1.** usual; normal; customary: *to put something in its regular place.* **2.** conforming in form or arrangement; symmetrical: *regular teeth.* **3.** characterized by fixed principle, uniform procedure, etc.: *regular breathing.* **4.** recurring at fixed times; periodic: *regular meals.* **5.** adhering to rule or procedure: *to be regular in one's diet.* **6.** observing fixed times or habits: *regular customer.* **7.** orderly; well-ordered: *a regular life.* **8.** conforming to some accepted rule, discipline, etc. **9.** carried out in accordance with an accepted principle; formally correct. **10.** properly qualified for or engaged in an occupation. **11.** *Colloq.* complete; thorough: *a regular rascal.* **12.** (of a flower) having the members of each of its floral circles or whorls normally alike in form and size. **13.** *Gram.* conforming to the most prevalent pattern of formation, inflection, construction, etc. **14.** *Maths.* governed by one law throughout: *a regular polygon has all its angles and sides equal.* **15.** *Mil.* denoting or belonging to the permanently organized or standing army of a state. **16.** *Eccles.* subject to a religious rule, or belonging to a religious or monastic order (opposed to *secular*): *regular clergy.* **17.** *U.S. Politics.* of, pertaining to, or selected by the recognized agents of a political party: *the regular ticket.* *—n.* **18.** *Eccles.* a member of a duly constituted religious order under a rule. **19.** a soldier in a regular army. **20.** *U.S. Politics.* a party member who faithfully stands by his party. **21.** *Colloq.* a regular customer. [t. L: s. *rēgulāris*; r. ME *reguler*, t. OF] **—reg′ular′ity,** *n.*

regular army, a permanent army maintained in peace as well as in war; standing army.

regularize (rĕg′yŏŏ lә rīz′), *v.t.*, **-rized, -rizing.** to make regular. Also, **regularise.** **—reg′ulariza′tion,** *n.*

regularly (rĕg′yŏŏ lә lĭ), *adv.* **1.** at regular times or intervals. **2.** according to plan, custom, etc.

regulate (rĕg′yŏŏ lāt′), *v.t.*, **-lated, -lating. 1.** to control or direct by rule, principle, method, etc. **2.** to adjust to some standard or requirement, as amount, degree, etc.: *to regulate the temperature.* **3.** to adjust so as to ensure accuracy of operation: *to regulate a watch.* **4.** to put in good order: *to regulate the digestion.* [t. LL: m. s. *rēgulātus*, pp., der. L *rēgula* rule] **—reg′ula′tive, regulatory** (rĕg′yŏŏ lā′tә rĭ), *adj.* **—Syn. 1.** rule, direct, manage, order, adjust, arrange.

regulation (rĕg′yŏŏ lā′shәn), *n.* **1.** a rule or order, as for conduct, prescribed by authority; a governing direction or law. **2.** the act of regulating. **3.** the state of being regulated. *—adj.* **4.** according to or prescribed by regulation: *regulation shoes had to be worn.* **—Syn. 2.** direction, management, control.

regulator (rĕg′yŏŏ lā′tә), *n.* **1.** one who or that which regulates. **2.** *Horol.* **a.** a device in a clock or a watch for causing it to go faster or slower. **b.** a master clock, esp. one of great accuracy, against which other clocks are checked. **3.** *Mach.* **a.** a governor. **b.** a governor employed to control the closing of the port opening for admission of steam to the cylinder of a steam engine. **c.** a reducing valve for regulating steam pressure. **4.** *Elect.* a device which functions to maintain a designated characteristic, as voltage

re′glaze′, *v.t.*, **-glazed, -glazing.**
re′glo′rify′, *v.t.*, **-fied, -fying.**
re′glue′, *v.t.*, **-glued, -gluing.**
re′grade′, *v.t.* **-graded, -grading.**
re′graft′, *v.t.*
re′grant′, *v.t.*
re′grease′, *v.t.*, **-greased, -greasing.**
re′grind′, *v.t.*, **-ground, -grinding.**
re′group′, *v.*
re′grow′, *v.*, **-grew, -grown, -growing.**
re′han′dle, *v.t.*, **-dled, -dling.**
re′hang′, *v.t.*, **-hung, -hanged, -hanging.**
re′har′den, *v.*
re′har′ness, *v.t.*
re′heel′, *v.t.*

or current, at a predetermined value, or to vary it according to a predetermined plan.

regulus (rĕg′yōō ləs), *n.*, *pl.* **-luses, -li** (-lī′). **1.** (*cap.*) *Astron.* a star of the first magnitude in the constellation Leo. **2.** *Metall.* **a.** the metallic mass which forms beneath the slag at the bottom of the crucible or furnace in smelting ores. **b.** an impure intermediate product obtained in smelting ores. [t. L: a little king, dim. of *rex* king; in early chemistry, antimony, so called because it readily combines with gold (the king of metals)]

Regulus (rĕg′yōō ləs), *n.* **Marcus Atilius** (mä′kəs ə tĭl′ĭ əs), died 250? B.C , Roman general.

regulus of antimony, *Metall.* commercially pure metallic antimony.

regur (rĕg′ə, rā′gə), *n.* a rich soil formed from basalt, occurring in tropical regions, notably in the Deccan, in India, its titanium content giving it a dark coloration. Also, **black cotton soil, tropical black earth.** [t. Hind.: m. *regar*]

regurgitate (rĭ gû′jĭ tāt′), *v.*, **-tated, -tating.** —*v.i.* **1.** to surge or rush back, as liquids, gases, undigested food, etc. —*v.t.* **2.** to cause to surge or rush back. [t. ML: m. s. *regurgitātus*, pp.] —**regurgitant** (rĭ gû′jĭ tənt), *n.*, *adj.*

regurgitation (rĭ gû′jĭ tā′shən), *n.* **1.** the act of regurgitating. **2.** *Med.* voluntary or involuntary return of partly digested food from the stomach to the mouth. **3.** *Physiol.* the reflux of blood through leaking heart valves.

rehabilitate (rē′ə bĭl′ĭ tāt′), *v.t.*, **-tated, -tating. 1.** to restore to a good condition; regenerate, or alter to an improved form. **2.** to re-establish in good repute or accepted respectability, as a person or the character, name, etc., after disrepute. **3.** to restore formally to a former capacity or standing, or to rank, rights, or privileges lost or forfeited. [t. ML: m. s. *rehabilitātus*, pp., restored] —**re′habil′ita′tion,** *n.*

rehash (rē′hăsh′), *v.t.* **1.** to work up (old material) in a new form. —*n.* **2.** the act of rehashing. **3.** something rehashed.

rehearsal (rĭ hû′səl), *n.* **1.** a performance beforehand by way of practice or drill. **2.** the act of going through a dramatic, musical, or other performance in private, for practice, before going through it publicly or on some formal occasion. **3.** a repeating or relating: *a rehearsal of grievances.*

rehearse (rĭ hûs′), *v.*, **-hearsed, -hearsing.** —*v.t.* **1.** to perform (a play, part, piece of music, etc.) in private by way of practice, before a public performance. **2.** to drill or train (a person, etc.) by rehearsal, as for some performance or part. **3.** to relate the facts or particulars of; enumerate. —*v.i.* **4.** to rehearse a play, part, etc. [ME *reherce(n)*, t. OF: m. *rehercier*, appar. f. *re-* RE- + *hercier* harrow] —**rehears′er,** *n.* —**Syn. 4.** See **relate.**

reheat (rē′hēt′), *v.t.* **1.** to heat again. —*n.* **2.** Also, **reheating.** *Aeron.* the process of injecting fuel into the jet pipe of a turbojet engine in order to obtain extra thrust by combustion with the unburnt air in the turbine exhaust gases; afterburning.

rehoboam (rē′ə bō′əm, rĭə-), *n.* a very large bottle, esp. of champagne, containing between 5 and 6 gallons. [named after *Rehoboam*, reigned ?922–?915 B.C., first king of Judah; modelled on JEROBOAM]

rehouse (rē′houz′), *v.t.* to provide with a new house or houses. —**re′hous′ing,** *n.*

Reich (rīk; *Ger.* rīKH), *n.* **1.** the Holy Roman Empire, until its dissolution in 1806 (**First Reich**). **2.** the Prussian Empire, 1871–1919 (**Second Reich**). **3.** the German federal republic, 1919–33. **4.** the Nazi state, 1933–45 (**Third Reich**). [G]

Reichsmark (rīks′mäk′; *Ger.* rīKHs′märk), *n.*, *pl.* **-marks, -mark.** the monetary unit of Germany 1924–48. See **Deutsche Mark, Mark.**

Reichsrat (*Ger.* rīKHs′rät), *n.* **1.** *German Hist.* the upper house of the German parliament 1919–45. See **Bundesrat. 2.** *Austrian Hist.* the legislature of Austria in the Austro-Hungarian Empire. Also, **Reichsrath.**

Reichstag (rīks′täg′; *Ger.* rīKHs′täk), *n.* **1.** *German Hist.* the lower house of the German parliament 1919–45. **2.** the building in Berlin where this assembly met 1919–33; destroyed by fire 1933.

Reid (rēd), *n.* **Robert William,** 1851–1939, Scottish anatomist.

Reid's baseline, *Anat.* a line passing through the lower margin of the orbital opening and the auricular point. [named after Robert William REID]

reify (rē′ĭ fī′), *v.t.*, **-fied, -fying.** to convert into or regard as a concrete thing: *to reify an abstract concept.* [f. L *rē(s)* thing + -(I)FY]

Reigate (rī′gĭt), *n.* a town in England, in Surrey. 53,751 (1961).

reign (rān), *n.* **1.** the period or term of ruling, as of a sovereign. **2.** royal rule or sway. **3.** dominating power or influence: *the reign of law.* —*v.i.* **4.** to possess or exercise sovereign power or authority. **5.** to hold the position and name of sovereign without exercising the ruling power. **6.** to have ascendancy; predominate. [ME *reyne*, t. OF: m. *regne*, t. L: m. *regnum*] —**Syn. 2.** dominion, sovereignty.

Reign of Terror, a period of the French Revolution, from about March 1793, to July 1794, during which many people were ruthlessly executed by the ruling faction.

reimburse (rē′ĭm bûs′), *v.t.*, **-bursed, -bursing. 1.** to make repayment to for expense or loss incurred. **2.** to pay back; refund; repay. [f. RE- + *imburse* (t. ML: m. s. *imbursāre*, der. L *in-* IN-[2] + ML *bursa* purse, bag)] —**re′imburse′ment,** *n.*

reimport (rē′ĭm pôt′), *v.t.* to import back into the country of exportation. —**re′im′porta′tion,** *n.*

reimpression (rē′ĭm prĕsh′ən), *n.* **1.** a second or repeated impression. **2.** a reprinting or a reprint.

Reims (rēmz; *Fr.* răNs), *n.* a city in NE France: cathedral; unconditional surrender of Germany, May 7th 1945. 133,914 (1962). Also, **Rheims.**

rein (rān), *n.* **1.** a long, narrow strap or thong, fastened to the bridle or bit, by which a rider or driver restrains and guides a horse or other animal. See illus. under **harness. 2.** any of certain other straps or thongs forming part of a harness, as a bearing rein. **3.** any means of curbing, controlling, or directing; a check; restraint. **4.** complete licence; free scope: *to give free rein to one's imagination.* **5.** (*pl.*) the controlling influence and power. —*v.t.* **6.** to furnish with a rein or reins, as a horse. **7.** to check or guide (a horse, etc.) by pulling at the reins. **8.** to curb; restrain; control. —*v.i.* **9.** to obey the reins: *a horse that reins well.* **10.** to rein a horse (fol. by *in* or *up*). [ME *rene*, t. OF, var. of *resne* (AF *redne*), ult. der. L *retinēre* hold back]

reincarnate (rē ĭn′kä nāt′), *v.t.*, **-nated, -nating.** to give another body to; incarnate again.

reincarnation (rē′ĭn kä nā′shən), *n.* **1.** the belief that the soul, upon death of the body, moves to another body or form. **2.** rebirth of the soul in a new body. **3.** a new incarnation or embodiment, as of a person. —**re′incarna′tionist,** *n.*

reindeer (rān′dĭə′), *n.*, *pl.* **-deer,** (*occasionally*) **-deers.** any of various species of large deer of the genus *Rangifer*, with branched antlers in both males and females, found in northern or arctic regions, and often domesticated. See **caribou.** [ME *raynedere*, t. Scand.; cf. Icel. *hreindȳri*]

European reindeer, *Rangifer tarandus* (Ab. 4½ ft high at the shoulder)

Reindeer Lake, a lake in central Canada, mostly in NE Saskatchewan province. 2436 sq. mi.

reindeer moss, a grey, branched lichen, *Cladonia rangiferina*, widespread in arctic regions, where it is eaten during the winter by reindeer.

reinforce (rē′ĭn fôs′), *v.t.*, **-forced, -forcing. 1.** to strengthen with some added piece, support, or material: *to reinforce a wall.* **2.** to strengthen with additional men or ships for military or naval purposes: *to reinforce a garrison.* **3.** to strengthen; make more forcible or effective: *to reinforce efforts.* **4.** to augment; increase: *to reinforce a supply.* [f. RE- + *inforce*, var. of ENFORCE]

---

re′hem′, *v.t.*, **-hemmed, -hemming.**
re′-ice′, *v.*, **-iced, -icing.**
re′-iden′tify′, *v.t.*, **-fied, -fying.**
re′ignite′, *v.t.*, **-nited, -niting.**
re′illu′minate′, *v.t.*, **-nated, -nating.**
re′implant′, *v.t.*
re′impose′, *v.*, **-posed, -posing.**
re′im′posi′tion, *n.*
re′im′pregnate′, *v.t.*, **-nated, -nating.**
re′impress′, *v.t.*
re′imprint′, *v.t.*
re′impris′on, *v.t.*
re′impris′onment, *n.*
re′inau′gurate′, *v.t.*, **-rated, -rating.**
re′inau′gura′tion, *n.*
re′incite′, *v.t.*, **-cited, -citing.**
re′incor′porate′, *v.t.*, **-rated, -rating.**
re′incur′, *v.t.*, **-curred, -curring.**
re′in′dex, *v.t.*
re′in′dicate′, *v.t.*, **-cated, -cating.**
re′indict′, *v.t.*
re′indoc′trinate′, *v.t.*, **-nated, -nating.**
re′indorse′, *v.t.*, **-dorsed, -dorsing.**
re′indorse′ment, *n.*
re′induce′, *v.t.*, **-duced, -ducing.**
re′indus′trializa′tion, *n.*
re′indus′trialize′, *v.t.*, **-lized, -lizing.**
re′infect′, *v.t.*
re′infec′tion, *n.*
re′in′filtrate′, *v.*, **-trated, -trating.**
re′inflame′, *v.t.*, **-flamed, -flaming.**
re′inflat′able, *adj.*
re′inflate′, *v.t.*, **-flated, -flating.**
re′infla′tion, *n.*

---

reinforced concrete, concrete embodying steel bars to give tensile strength.

reinforcement (rē′ĭn fôs′mənt), *n.* **1.** the act of reinforcing. **2.** the state of being reinforced. **3.** something that reinforces or strengthens. **4.** (*often pl.*) an additional supply of men, ships, etc., for a military or naval force.

Reinhardt (*Ger.* rīn′hårt), *n.* **Max,** 1873–1943, German theatre director, producer, and actor, born in Austria.

reins (rānz), *n.pl. Archaic.* **1.** the kidneys. **2.** the region of the kidneys, or the lower part of the back. **3.** the seat of the feelings or affections, formerly identified with the kidneys (esp. in biblical use). [ME, t. OF; r. ME *reenes,* OE *rēnys,* t. L: m. *rēnēs,* pl. kidneys, loins]

reinstate (rē′ĭn stāt′), *v.t.,* **-stated, -stating.** to put back or establish again, as in a former position or state. **—re′instate′ment,** *n.*

reinsure (rē′ĭn shŏŏə′, -shô′), *v.t.,* **-sured, -suring. 1.** to insure again. **2.** to insure under a contract by which a first insurer relieves himself from a part or from all of the risk and devolves it upon another insurer. **—re′insur′ance,** *n.* **—re′insur′er,** *n.*

reis (*Port.* rəysh), *n.pl., sing.* **real** (*Port.* ryål). a former Portuguese and a Brazilian money of account. [t. Pg., pl. of *rei* king]

reissue (rē′ĭs′yōō, -ĭsh′ōō), *v.t.* **1.** to issue again, especially in a different form, at a different price, etc. *—n.* **2.** that which is reissued.

reiterant (rē ĭt′ə rənt), *adj.* repetitive and constant: *her reiterant chatter was very annoying.*

reiterate (rē ĭt′ə rāt′), *v.t.,* **-rated, -rating.** to repeat; say or do again or repeatedly. [t. L: m. s. *reiterātus,* pp.] **—reit′era′tion,** *n.* **—reiterative** (rē ĭt′ə rə tĭv), *adj.* **—Syn.** See **repeat.**

reject (*v.* rĭ jĕkt′; *n.* rē′jĕkt), *v.t.* **1.** to refuse to have, take, recognize, etc. **2.** to refuse to grant (a demand, etc.). **3.** to refuse to accept (a person); rebuff. **4.** to throw away, discard, or refuse as useless or unsatisfactory. **5.** to cast out or eject; vomit. **6.** to cast out or off. *—n.* **7.** something rejected, as an imperfect article. [t. L: s. *rejectus,* pp., thrown back] **—reject′er,** *n.*

—Syn. 1. See **refuse**[1]. **4.** REJECT, DISCARD imply refusing to take or to keep something as being unsatisfactory or unworthy. To REJECT is to refuse to accept something that is offered or to make a distinction between something acceptable and something not acceptable: *to reject the offer of a position.* To DISCARD is to cast aside as no longer useful something which has served one: *to discard old clothes.* **—Ant. 1.** accept, keep.

rejectamenta (rĭ jĕk′tə mĕn′tə), *n.pl.* **1.** things or matter rejected as useless or worthless. **2.** refuse; excrement. [NL, pl. of *rejectāmentum,* der. L *rejectus,* pp., thrown away. See -MENT]

rejection (rĭ jĕk′shən), *n.* **1.** the act of rejecting. **2.** the state of being rejected. **3.** that which is rejected.

rejig (rē′jĭg′), *v.t.,* **-jigged, -jigging.** *Slang.* to reconstruct, reorganize, etc.

rejoice (rĭ jois′), *v.,* **-joiced, -joicing.** *—v.i.* **1.** to be glad; take delight (*in*). *—v.t.* **2.** to make joyful; gladden. [ME, t. OF: m. *rejoiss-,* stem of *rejoir,* f. *re-* RE- + *joir* joy] **—rejoic′er,** *n.*

rejoicing (rĭ joi′sĭng), *n.* **1.** the act of one who rejoices. **2.** the feeling or the expression of joy. **3.** (*often pl.*) an occasion for expressing joy.

rejoin[1] (rē join′), *v.t.* **1.** to come again into the company of: *to rejoin a party after a brief absence.* **2.** to join together again; reunite. *—v.i.* **3.** to become joined together again. [f. RE- + JOIN]

rejoin[2] (rĭ join′), *v.t.* **1.** to say in answer. *—v.i.* **2.** to answer. **3.** *Law.* to answer the plaintiff's replication. [late ME *rejoyne,* t. AF: m. *rejoyner,* F *rejoindre,* f. *re-* RE- + *joindre* JOIN]

rejoinder (rĭ join′də), *n.* **1.** an answer to a reply; response. **2.** *Law.* the defendant's answer to the plaintiff's replication. Cf. **replication** and **surrejoinder.** [late ME *rejoyner,* t. AF, inf. used as n.; cf. F *rejoindre*]

rejuvenate (rĭ jōō′vĭ nāt′), *v.t.,* **-nated, -nating. 1.** to make young again; restore to youthful vigour, appearance, etc. **2.** *Phys. Geog.* **a.** to renew the activity, erosive power, etc., of (a stream) by the uplifting of the region it drains, or by removal of a barrier in the bed of the stream. **b.** to impress again the characters of youthful topography on (a region) by the action of rejuvenated streams. [f. LL *rejuven(escere)* become young again + -ATE[1]] **—reju′vena′tion,** *n.* **—reju′vena′tor,** *n.*

rejuvenescent (rĭ jōō′vĭ nĕs′ənt), *adj.* **1.** becoming young again. **2.** making young again; rejuvenating. **—reju′venes′cence,** *n.*

rejuvenize (rĭ jōō′vĭ nīz′), *v.t.,* **-nized, -nizing.** to rejuvenate. Also, **rejuvenise.**

-rel, a noun suffix having a diminutive or pejorative force, as in *wastrel.* Also, **-erel.** [ME, t. OF: m. *-erel, -erelle*]

rel., 1. relating. **2.** relative. **3.** relatively. **4.** religion. **5.** religious.

relapse (rĭ lăps′), *v.,* **-lapsed, -lapsing,** *n.* *—v.i.* **1.** to fall or slip back into a former state, practice, etc.: *to relapse into silence.* **2.** to fall back into illness after convalescence or apparent recovery. **3.** to fall back into wrongdoing or error; backslide. *—n.* **4.** the act of relapsing. **5.** a return of a disease or illness after partial recovery. [t. L: m. s. *relapsus,* pp., slipped back] **—relaps′er,** *n.*

relapsing fever, one of a group of fevers characterized by relapses, occurring in many tropical countries, and caused by several species of spirochaetes transmitted by several species of lice and ticks.

relate (rĭ lāt′), *v.,* **-lated, -lating.** *—v.t.* **1.** to tell. **2.** to bring into or establish association, connection, or relation. *—v.i.* **3.** to have reference (*to*). **4.** to have some relation (*to*). [t. L: m. s. *relātus,* pp., reported, carried back] **—relat′er,** *n.*

—Syn. 1. RELATE, RECITE, RECOUNT, REHEARSE mean to tell, report, or describe in some detail an occurrence or circumstance. To RELATE is to give an account of happenings, events, circumstances, etc.: *to relate one's adventures.* To RECITE may mean to give details consecutively, but more often applies to the repetition from memory of something learned with verbal exactness: *to recite a poem.* To RECOUNT is usually to set forth consecutively the details of an occurrence, argument, experience, etc., to give an account in detail: *to recount an unpleasant experience.* REHEARSE implies some formality and exactness in telling, as in repeated practice before final delivery: *to rehearse one's part in a play.*

related (rĭ lā′tĭd), *adj.* **1.** associated; connected. **2.** allied by nature, origin, kinship, marriage, etc. **3.** narrated. **4.** (in diatonic music) of notes belonging to keys which have several notes in common.

relation (rĭ lā′shən), *n.* **1.** an existing connection; a particular way of being related: *the relation between cause and effect.* **2.** (*pl.*) the various connections between peoples, countries, etc.: *commercial or foreign relations.* **3.** (*pl.*) the various connections in which persons are brought together, as by common interests. **4.** the mode or kind of connection between one person and another, between man and God, etc. **5.** connection between persons by blood or marriage. **6.** a relative. **7.** reference; regard; respect: *to plan with relation to the future.* **8.** the action of relating, narrating, or telling; narration. **9.** a narrative; account. **10.** *Maths.* a property which associates two or more quantities or functions. [ME, t. L: s. *relātio* a bringing back, report] **—Syn. 5.** relationship, connection. **9.** recital, report.

relational (rĭ lā′shə nəl), *adj.* **1.** of or pertaining to relations. **2.** indicating or specifying some relation. **3.** *Gram.* serving to indicate relations between other elements in a sentence, as prepositions, conjunctions, etc. Cf. **notional.**

---

re′inform′, *v.t.*
re′infuse′, *v.t.,* **-fused, -fusing.**
re′inhab′it, *v.t.*
re′inject′, *v.t.*
re′-ink′, *v.t.*
re′inoc′ulate′, *v.t.,* **-lated, -lating.**
re′inscribe′, *v.t.,* **-scribed, -scribing.**
re′insert′, *v.t.*
re′inser′tion, *n.*
re′inspect′, *v.t.*
re′inspec′tion, *n.*
re′inspire′, *v.t.,* **-spired, -spiring.**
re′install′, *v.t.*
re′in′stalla′tion, *n.*
re′instal′ment, *n.*
re′in′stitute′, *v.t.,* **-tuted, -tuting.**
re′in′stitu′tion, *n.*
re′instruct′, *v.t.*
re′instruc′tion, *n.*
re′in′tegrate′, *v.,* **-grated, -grating.**
re′in′tegra′tion, *n.*
re′inter′, *v.t.,* **-terred, -terring.**
re′in′terest, *v.t.*
re′inter′ment, *n.*
re′inter′pret, *v.t.*
re′inter′preta′tion, *n.*
re′inter′rogate′, *v.,* **-gated, -gating.**
re′inter′roga′tion, *n.*
re′in′tervene′, *v.i.,* **-vened, -vening.**
re′in′terven′tion, *n.*
re′in′terview′, *v.t.*
re′in′troduce′, *v.t.,* **-duced, -ducing.**
re′in′troduc′tion, *n.*
re′invade′, *v.t.,* **-vaded, -vading.**
re′inva′sion, *n.*
re′invent′, *v.t.*
re′invest′, *v.t.*
re′inves′tigate′, *v.t.,* **-gated, -gating.**
re′inves′tiga′tion, *n.*
re′invest′ment, *n.*
re′invig′orate′, *v.t.,* **-rated, -rating.**
re′invite′, *v.t.,* **-vited, -viting.**
re′invoke′, *v.t.,* **-voked, -voking.**
re′involve′, *v.t.,* **-volved, -volving.**
re′involve′ment, *n.*
re′i′solate′, *v.t.,* **-lated, -lating.**
re′judge′, *v.t.,* **-judged, -judging.**
re′kin′dle, *v.t.,* **-dled, -dling.**
re′knot′, *v.t.,* **-knotted, -knotting.**
re′la′bel, *v.t.,* **-belled, -belling.**
re′lace′, *v.t.,* **-laced, -lacing.**
re′lac′quer, *v.t.*
re′lance′, *v.t.,* **-lanced, -lancing.**

---

relationism (rĭ lā′shə nĭz′əm), *n. Philos.* **1.** the theory that relations exist in their own right. **2.** the theory that knowledge is relative, as opposed to being absolute.

relationship (rĭ lā′shən shĭp′), *n.* **1.** connection; a particular connection. **2.** connection by blood or marriage. **3.** an emotional connection between people.

—**Syn. 2.** RELATIONSHIP, KINSHIP refer to connection with others by blood or by marriage. RELATIONSHIP can be applied to connection either by birth or by marriage: *relationship to a ruling family.* KINSHIP generally denotes common descent, and implies a more intimate connection than relationship: *the obligations of kinship.*

relative (rĕl′ə tĭv), *n.* **1.** one who is connected with another or others by blood or marriage. **2.** something having, or standing in, some relation to something else; esp., in scientific usage, as opposed to *absolute.* **3.** *Gram.* a relative pronoun, adjective, or adverb. —*adj.* **4.** considered in relation to something else; comparative: *the relative merits of a republic and a monarchy.* **5.** existing only by relation to something else; not absolute or independent. **6.** having relation or connection: *relative phenomena.* **7.** having reference or regard; relevant; pertinent (fol. by *to*). **8.** correspondent; proportionate: *value is relative to demand.* **9.** (of a term, name, etc.) depending for significance upon something else: *better is a relative term.* **10.** *Gram.* **a.** designating words which introduce subordinate clauses and refer to some element of the principal clause (the antecedent), as *who* in 'He's the man *who saw you*'. **b.** (of a clause) introduced by such a word. [ME, t. LL: m. s. *relātīvus*, der. L *relātus* carried back] —**rel′ativeness,** *n.*

relative density, *Physics.* **1.** specific gravity. **2.** the ratio of the density of a gas to that of hydrogen under the same conditions.

relative frequency, 1. *Maths.* the ratio of the number of times an event occurs to the number of occasions on which it might occur in the same period. **2.** *Statistics.* the number of items of a certain type divided by the number of all the items considered.

relative humidity. *Meteorol.* See **humidity** (def. 2).

relatively (rĕl′ə tĭv lĭ), *adv.* in a relative manner; comparatively: *a relatively small difference.*

relative major, *Music.* the major key whose tonic is the third degree of a given minor key.

relative minor, *Music.* the minor key whose tonic is the sixth degree of a given major key.

relative pronoun, a pronoun with a relative function. See **relative** (def. 10a).

relativism (rĕl′ə tĭ vĭz′əm), *n.* the theory of knowledge or ethics which holds that criteria of judgement are relative, varying with the individual, time, and circumstance. —**rel′ativist,** *n.*

relativistic (rĕl′ə tĭ vĭs′tĭk), *adj.* **1.** of or pertaining to relativity or relativism. **2.** *Physics.* having, or pertaining to an entity which has a velocity comparable to that of light: *a relativistic particle or mass.*

relativity (rĕl′ə tĭv′ĭ tĭ), *n.* **1.** the state or fact of being relative. **2. principle of relativity,** *Physics.* the principle that there is no absolute motion, or motion with respect to some absolute space filled with ether, but that all motion observable is relative, being that of one portion or manifestation of matter with respect to another portion of matter —a principle which is confirmed by the fact that the velocity of light is constant and is independent of the motion of the source. Among the conclusions resulting from this principle are: that there can be no transmission of energy with a velocity greater than that of light; that the mass of a moving body increases with its velocity, and depends upon its content of internal energy; that time, like motion, is relative and not absolute, so that we cannot speak of the absolute simultaneity of events which occur in different places; that time and space are dependent on each other, time forming with the three dimensions of space a single four-dimensional continuum; that the presence of matter in space is associated with a 'warping' of the continuum in its neighbourhood, so that a freely moving body describes, not a straight line, but a curve (this effect being what is known as gravitation), and that rays of light will be deflected or curved when passing through a gravitational field. When all the velocities considered are very small compared with the velocity of light, the results of this theory are practically indistinguishable from those of previously accepted principles. For velocities approaching that of light, they are very great. The theory was developed by H. A. Lorentz and Albert Einstein in their **special theory of relativity,** dealing with uniform motion, and by Einstein in his **general theory of relativity** (1915), dealing with gravitation. **3.** *Philos.* existence only in relation to a thinking mind.

relativity of knowledge, *Philos.* the doctrine that all human knowledge is relative to the human mind, or that the mind can know concerning things only the effects which they produce upon it and not what the things themselves are.

relator (rĭ lā′tə), *n.* **1.** one who relates or narrates. **2.** *Law.* the person responsible for costs on whose complaint an action is commenced by the attorney general. [t. L. Cf. F *relateur*]

relax (rĭ lăks′), *v.t.* **1.** to make lax, or less tense, rigid, or firm: *to relax the muscles.* **2.** to diminish the force of. **3.** to slacken or abate, as effort, attention, etc. **4.** to make less strict or severe, as rules, discipline, etc. —*v.i.* **5.** to become less tense, rigid, or firm. **6.** to become less strict or severe; grow milder. **7.** to slacken in effort, application, etc.; take relaxation. [ME, t. L: s. *relaxāre*] —**relax′er,** *n.*

relaxation (rē′lăk sā′shən), *n.* **1.** abatement or relief of bodily or mental effort or application. **2.** something affording such relief; a diversion or entertainment. **3.** a loosening or slackening. **4.** diminution or remission of strictness or severity. **5.** *Maths.* a method of solving complex groups of simultaneous equations by successive approximations.

relaxed (rĭ lăkst′), *adj.* **1.** freed from tension; relieved of fatigue, strain, etc. **2.** made less strict and rigid, as rules. **3.** slackened; rendered more pliable.

relaxed throat, a form of sore throat.

relay (rē′lā′, rĭ lā′), *n.* **1.** a set of persons relieving others or taking turns; a shift. **2.** a fresh set of dogs or horses posted in readiness for use in a hunt, on a journey, etc. **3.** *Athletics.* **a.** a relay race. **b.** one of the lengths, or legs, of a relay race. **4.** an automatic device for operating the controls of a larger piece of equipment. **5.** *Elect.* **a.** a device by means of which a change of current or voltage in one circuit can be made to produce a change in the electrical condition of another circuit. **b.** a device that is operative by a variation in the conditions of one electric circuit to effect the operation of other devices in the same or another electric circuit.
—*v.t.* **6.** to carry forward by or as by relays: *to relay a message.* **7.** to provide with or replace by fresh relays. **8.** *Elect.* to retransmit by means of a telegraphic relay, or as such a relay does.
—*v.i.* **9.** *Elect.* to relay a message.
[ME, t. OF: m. *relais*, orig., hounds in reserve along the line of the hunt, der. *relaier* leave behind]

re-lay (rē′lā′), *v.t.* to lay again.

relay race (rē′lā′), a race of two or more teams of contestants, each contestant running part of the distance and being relieved by a team-mate.

relay station, a place from which radio and television programmes, etc., are broadcast, after being received from another station.

release (rĭ lēs′), *v.*, **-leased, -leasing,** *n.* —*v.t.* **1.** to free from confinement, bondage, obligation, pain, etc.; let go. **2.** to free from anything that restrains, fastens, etc. **3.** to allow to become known, be issued or exhibited: *to release an article for publication.* **4.** *Law.* give up, relinquish, or surrender (a right, claim, etc.). —*n.* **5.** a freeing or releasing from confinement, obligation, pain, etc. **6.** liberation from anything that restrains or fastens. **7.** some device for effecting such liberation. **8.** the releasing of something for public exhibition or sale, as a film, record, or the like. **9.** the releasing of an article, statement, etc., to the radio, press, or the like, for publication. **10.** the article so released. **11.** *Law.* **a.** the surrender of a right or the like to another. **b.** a document embodying such a surrender. **12.** *Obs. or Law.* a remission, as of a debt, tax, or tribute. **13.** *Mach.* a control mechanism for starting or stopping a machine, esp. by removing some restrictive apparatus. **14.** *Mach.* **a.** (in a steam-engine) the opening of the exhaust port of the cylinder at or near the end of the working stroke of the piston. **b.** the moment at which the exhaust port is opened. [ME *relesse(n)*, t. OF: m. *relesser*, g. L *relaxāre* relax]

—**Syn. 1.** RELEASE, FREE, DISMISS, DISCHARGE may all mean to set at liberty, let loose, or let go. RELEASE, meaning to set loose, and FREE, when applied to persons, always suggest a helpful action. Both may be used (not always interchangeably) of delivering a person from confinement or obligation: *to free or release prisoners.* FREE (less often, RELEASE) is also used for delivering a person from pain, etc.: *to free someone from fear.* DISMISS, meaning to send away, usually has the meaning of forcing to go unwillingly (*to dismiss a servant*) but may refer to giving permission to go: *the teacher dismissed the class early.* DISCHARGE, meaning originally to relieve of a burden (*to discharge a gun*), has come to refer to that which is sent away and is often a close synonym to DISMISS; it is used in the meaning permit to go, in connection with courts and the army: *the court discharged the man accused of robbery.* **2.** loose, extricate, disengage. **6.** deliverance, emancipation. —**Ant. 1.** bind, restrain.

re′latch′, *v.t.* **re′launch′,** *v.t.* **re′laun′der,** *v.t.* **re′learn′,** *v.*

re-lease (rē′lēs′), *v.t.*, **-leased, -leasing. 1.** to lease again. **2.** *Law.* to make over (land, etc.), as to another.

relegate (rĕl′ĭ gāt′), *v.t.*, **-gated, -gating. 1.** to send or consign to some obscure position, place, or condition. **2.** to consign or commit (a matter, task, etc.), as to a person. **3.** to assign or refer (something) to a particular class or kind. **4.** to send into exile; banish. **5.** *Sport.* to transfer (the lowest scoring team) to a lower division, as a team in a football league. [t. L: s. *relēgātus*, pp., sent back] **—rel′ega′tion,** *n.*

relent (rĭ lĕnt′), *v.i.* **1.** to soften in feeling, temper, or determination; become more mild, compassionate, or forgiving. *—v.t.* **2.** *Obs.* to cause to relent. [ME *relente* melt, appar. t. L: m. *relentescere* grow slack or soft]

relentless (rĭ lĕnt′lĭs), *adj.* that does not relent; unrelenting: *a relentless enemy.* **—relent′lessly,** *adv.* **—relent′lessness,** *n.* **—Syn.** See **inflexible.**

relevant (rĕl′ĭ vənt), *adj.* bearing upon or connected with the matter in hand; to the purpose; pertinent: *a relevant remark.* [t. ML: s. *relevans*, prop. ppr. of L *relevāre* raise up] **—rel′evance, rel′evancy,** *n.* **—rel′evantly,** *adv.* **—Syn.** applicable, germane, apposite, appropriate, suitable, fitting. See **apt.**

reliable (rĭ lī′ə bl), *adj.* that may be relied on; trustworthy: *reliable sources of information.* **—reli′abil′ity, reli′ableness,** *n.* **—reli′ably,** *adv.*

—Syn. trusty, dependable. RELIABLE, INFALLIBLE, TRUSTWORTHY apply to one who or that which can be depended upon with certainty. The person who or that which is RELIABLE can be relied upon; from such a one, satisfactory performance may be expected with complete confidence (it may also have the suggestion of honesty): *a reliable formula.* One who or that which is INFALLIBLE is incapable of making mistakes and is never in error: *an infallible test.* One who or that which is TRUSTWORTHY is worthy of being trusted and believed in, usually because of steadiness and honesty: *trustworthy and accurate reports.* **—Ant.** undependable, questionable, deceitful.

reliant (rĭ lī′ənt), *adj.* **1.** having or showing reliance. **2.** confident; trustful.

relic (rĕl′ĭk), *n.* **1.** a surviving memorial of something past. **2.** an object having interest by reason of its age or its association with the past: *a museum of historic relics.* **3.** a surviving trace of something: *a custom which is a relic of paganism.* **4.** (*pl.*) remaining parts or fragments. **5.** something kept in remembrance. **6.** *Eccles.* (esp. in Roman Catholic and Greek churches) the body, a part of the body, or some personal memorial of a saint, martyr, or other sacred persons, preserved as worthy of veneration. **7.** (*pl.*) the remains of a deceased person. [ME *relik*, OE *relic*, short for *reliquium*, t. L]

relict (rĕl′ĭkt), *n.* **1.** *Ecol.* a plant or animal species living in an environment which has changed from that which is typical for it. **2.** a survivor. **3.** (*pl.*) remains; remnants; residue. **4.** *Archaic or Rare.* a widow. [late ME, t. ML: s. *relicta* widow, prop. fem. of L *relictus*, pp., left behind]

relief (rĭ lēf′), *n.* **1.** deliverance, alleviation, or ease through the removal of pain, distress, oppression, etc. **2.** a means or thing that relieves pain, distress, anxiety, etc. **3.** help or assistance given, as to those in poverty or need. **4.** something affording a pleasing change, as from monotony. **5.** release from a post of duty, as by the coming of a substitute or replacement. **6.** the person or persons thus bringing release. **7.** the deliverance of a besieged town, etc., from an attacking force. **8.** prominence, distinctness, or vividness due to contrast. **9.** the projection of a figure or part from the ground or plane on which it is formed, in sculpture or similar work. **10.** a piece or work in such projection: *high relief.* **11.** an apparent projection of parts in a painting, drawing, etc., giving the appearance of the third dimension. **12.** *Phys. Geog.* the departure of the land surface in any area from that of a level surface. **13.** *Engraving.* any printing process by which the printing ink is transferred to paper, etc., from areas that are higher than the rest of the block. **14.** *Feudal Law.* a fine or composition which the heir of a feudal tenant paid to the lord for the privilege of succeeding to the estate. **15.** a receipt of some state or charitable financial assistance. [ME *relef*, t. OF, der. *relever* RELIEVE; defs 8–13 t. F, t. It.: m. *rilievo*] **—Syn. 1.** mitigation, assuagement, abatement, consolation, comfort. **3.** succour, aid, redress.

Relief (def. 9)

relief map, a map showing the relief of an area, usually by generalized contour lines.

relieve (rĭ lēv′), *v.t.*, **-lieved, -lieving. 1.** to ease or alleviate (pain, distress, anxiety, need, etc.). **2.** to free from anxiety, fear, pain, etc. **3.** to deliver from poverty, need, etc. **4.** to bring efficient aid to (a besieged town, etc.). **5.** to ease (a person) of any burden, wrong, or oppression, as by legal means. **6.** to make less tedious, unpleasant, or monotonous; break or vary the sameness of. **7.** to bring into relief or prominence; heighten the effect of. **8.** to release (one on duty) by coming as or providing a substitute. **9. relieve oneself,** to empty the bowels or bladder. [ME *releve*, t. OF: m. *relever*, g. L *relevāre* raise again, assist] **—reliev′able,** *adj.* **—reliev′er,** *n.* **—Syn. 1.** mitigate, assuage, allay, lighten. See **comfort.**

relievo (rĭ lē′vō), *n., pl.* **-vos, -vi.** relief (defs 9, 10). Also, **rilievo.** [t. It., der. *rilevare* raise, modelled on F *relief*]

relig., religion.

religieuse (*Fr.* rə lē zhyœz′), *n., pl.* **-gieuses** (*Fr.* -zhyœz′). *French.* a woman belonging to a religious order, etc.

religieux (*Fr.* rə lē zhyœ′), *adj., n., pl.* **-gieux** (*Fr.* -zhyœ′). *French. —adj.* **1.** religious; devout; pious. *—n.* **2.** a person bound by monastic vows.

religion (rĭ lĭj′ən), *n.* **1.** the quest for the values of the ideal life, involving three phases: the ideal, the practices for attaining the values of the ideal, and the theology or world view relating the quest to the environing universe. **2.** a particular system in which the quest for the ideal life has been embodied: *the Christian religion.* **3.** recognition on the part of man of a controlling superhuman power entitled to obedience, reverence, and worship. **4.** the feeling or the spiritual attitude of those recognizing such a controlling power. **5.** the manifestation of such feeling in conduct or life. **6.** a point or matter of conscience: *to make a religion of doing something.* **7.** *Obs.* the practice of sacred rites or observances. **8.** (*pl.*) *Obs.* religious rites. [ME, t. L: s. *religio* fear of the gods, religious awe, sacredness, scrupulousness]

religionism (rĭ lĭj′ə nĭz′əm), *n.* **1.** excessive or exaggerated religious zeal. **2.** affected or pretended religious zeal. **—reli′gionist,** *n.*

religiosity (rĭ lĭj′ĭ ŏs′ĭ tĭ), *n.* **1.** the quality of being religious; piety; devoutness. **2.** affected or excessive devotion to religion.

religious (rĭ lĭj′əs), *adj.* **1.** of, pertaining to, or concerned with religion. **2.** imbued with or exhibiting religion; pious; devout; godly. **3.** scrupulously faithful; conscientious: *religious care.* **4.** belonging to a religious order, as persons. **5.** pertaining to or connected with a monastic or religious order. **6.** appropriate to religion or to sacred rites or observances. *—n.* **7.** a member of a religious order, congregation, etc.; a monk, friar, or nun. **8.** (*construed as pl.*) such persons collectively. [ME, t. L: m. s. *religiōsus*] **—reli′giously,** *adv.* **—reli′giousness,** *n.*

—Syn. 2. RELIGIOUS, DEVOUT, PIOUS indicate a spirit of reverence towards God. RELIGIOUS is a general word, applying to whatever pertains to faith or worship: *a religious ceremony.* DEVOUT indicates a fervent spirit, usually genuine and often independent of outward observances: *a deeply devout though unorthodox church member.* PIOUS implies such constant attention to, and extreme conformity with, outward observances as often to suggest sham or hypocrisy: *a pious hypocrite.* **—Ant. 2.** irreligious, scoffing.

relinquish (rĭ lĭng′kwĭsh), *v.t.* **1.** to renounce or surrender (a possession, right, etc.). **2.** to give up; put aside or desist from: *to relinquish a plan.* **3.** to let go: *to relinquish one's hold.* [ME, t. OF: m. *relinquiss-*, s. *relinquir*, g. L *relinquere*] **—relin′quisher,** *n.* **—relin′quishment,** *n.* **—Syn. 2.** yield, cede, waive, forgo, abdicate, leave, quit. See **abandon**[1].

reliquary (rĕl′ĭ kwə rĭ), *n., pl.* **-quaries.** a repository or receptacle for a relic or relics. [t. ML: m. s. *reliquiārium*, der. L *reliquiae*, pl., remains. See RELIC]

relique (rə lēk′, rĕl′ĭk), *n. Archaic.* relic. [F]

reliquiae (rĭ lĭk′wĭ ē′), *n.pl.* remains, as those of fossil organisms. [t. L]

relish (rĕl′ĭsh), *n.* **1.** liking for the taste of something, or enjoyment of something eaten. **2.** pleasurable appreciation of anything; liking: *no relish for such jokes.* **3.** something appetizing or savoury added to a meal, as pickles or olives. **4.** a pleasing or appetizing flavour. **5.** a pleasing or enjoyable quality. **6.** a taste or flavour. **7.** a smack, trace, or touch of something. *—v.t.* **8.** to take pleasure in; like; enjoy. **9.** to make pleasing to the taste. **10.** to like the taste or flavour of. *—v.i.* **11.** to have taste or flavour. **12.** to be agreeable or pleasant. [ME *reles*, t. OF: what is left,

---

re′let′, *v.*, **-let, -letting.**
re′light′, *v.t.*, **-lit** or **-lighted, -lighting.**
re′line′, *v.t.*, **-lined, -lining.**
re′liq′uefy′, *v.*, **-fied, -fying.**
re′liq′uidate′, *v.t.*, **-dated, -dating.**
re′live′, *v.*, **-lived, -living.**
re′load′, *v.t.*
re′loan′, *v.t., n.*
re′locate′, *v.t.*, **-cated, -cating.**
re′loca′tion, *n.*
re′lo′wer, *v.t.*

---

remainder, der. *relaisser* leave behind] —**rel′ishable,** *adj.*

rel. pron., relative pronoun.

relucent (rĭ lo͞o′sənt), *adj.* shining; bright. [t. L: s. *relūcens*, ppr., shining back; r. ME *relusant*, t. OF]

reluct (rĭ lŭkt′), *v.i. Archaic or Rare.* **1.** to struggle against something; resist. **2.** to object; show reluctance. [back-formation from RELUCTANCE, RELUCTANT]

reluctance (rĭ lŭk′təns), *n.* **1.** unwillingness; disinclination: *reluctance to speak.* **2.** *Elect.* the resistance offered to the passage of magnetic lines of force, being numerically equal to the magnetomotive force divided by the magnetic flux. Also, **reluc′tancy.**

reluctant (rĭ lŭk′tənt), *adj.* **1.** unwilling; disinclined. **2.** *Rare.* struggling in opposition. [t. L: s. *reluctans*, ppr., struggling against] —**reluc′tantly,** *adv.*

—**Syn. 1.** hesitant. RELUCTANT, LOATH, AVERSE describe disinclination towards something. RELUCTANT implies some sort of mental struggle, as between disinclination and a sense of duty: *reluctant to expel students.* LOATH describes extreme disinclination: *loath to part from a friend.* (RELUCTANT and LOATH are used with the infinitive.) AVERSE, used with 'to' and a noun or a gerund, describes a long-held dislike or unwillingness, though not a particularly strong feeling: *averse to an idea, averse to getting up early.*

reluctivity (rĕl′ŭk tĭv′ĭ tĭ), *n. Elect.* a specific reluctance, or the magnetic reluctance of a material compared with that of air.

relume (rĭ lyo͞om′), *v.t.*, **-lumed, -luming.** to light or illuminate again. [t. LL: m. s. *relūmināre.* See RE-, ILLUMINE]

rely (rĭ lī′), *v.i.*, **-lied, -lying.** to depend confidently; put trust in (fol. by *on* or *upon*). [ME *relie*, t. OF: m. *relier* bind together, g. L *religāre* bind back]

rem (rĕm), *n.* the quantity of ionizing radiation whose biological effect is equal to that produced by one röntgen of X-rays. [f. *r(oentgen) e(quivalent in) m(an)*]

remain (rĭ mān′), *v.i.* **1.** to continue in the same state; continue to be (as specified): *to remain at peace.* **2.** to stay in a place: *to remain at home.* **3.** to be left after the removal, loss, etc., of another or others. **4.** to be left to be done, told, etc. —*n.* (*always pl.*) **5.** that which remains or is left; a remnant. **6.** miscellaneous, fragmentary, or other writings collected after the author's death. **7.** traces of some quality, condition, etc. **8.** that which remains of a person after death; a dead body. **9.** parts or substances remaining from animal or plant life, occurring in the earth's crust or strata: *fossil remains, organic remains.* [ME *remayn*, t. AF: m. s. *remaindre*, g. L *remanēre*] —**Syn. 1.** stay. See **continue. 2.** wait, tarry. **3.** endure, abide.

remainder (rĭ mān′də), *n.* **1.** that which remains or is left: *the remainder of the day.* **2.** a remaining part. **3.** *Arith.* the quantity that remains after subtraction or division. **4.** *Law.* a future interest so created as to take effect at the end of another estate, as when property is conveyed to A for life and then to B. **5.** (*pl.*) *Philately.* the quantities of stamps on hand after they have been demonetized or otherwise voided for postal use. **6.** a copy of a book remaining in the publisher's stock when the sale has practically ceased, frequently sold at a reduced price. —*adj.* **7.** remaining; left. —*v.t.* **8.** to dispose of or sell as a publisher's remainder. [late ME *remaindre*, t. AF, prop. inf. See REMAIN]

—**Syn. 1.** residuum, remnant, excess, rest. **2.** REMAINDER, BALANCE, RESIDUE, SURPLUS refer to a portion left over. REMAINDER is the general word (*the remainder of one's life*); it may refer in particular to the mathematical process of subtraction: *7 minus 5 leaves a remainder of 2.* BALANCE, originally a bookkeeper's term referring to the amount of money left to one's account, is often used colloquially as a synonym for REMAINDER: *a bank balance.* RESIDUE is used particularly to designate what remains as the result of a process; this is usually a chemical process, but the word may also refer to a legal process concerning inheritance: *a residue of ash left from burning leaves.* SURPLUS suggests that what remains is in excess of what was needed: *a surplus of goods.*

remainderman (rĭ mān′də măn′), *n. Law.* a person entitled to an estate in expectancy.

remake (rē′māk′), *v.t.* **1.** to make again. —*n.* **2.** a remade version of something, esp. a film.

reman (rē′măn′), *v.t.*, **-manned, -manning. 1.** to man again; furnish with a fresh supply of men. **2.** to restore the manliness or courage of.

remand (rĭ mänd′), *v.t.* **1.** to send back, remit, or consign again. **2.** *Law.* (of a court or magistrate) to send back (a prisoner or accused person) into custody, as to await further proceedings. —*n.* **3.** the act of remanding. **4.** the state of being remanded. **5.** a person remanded. [late ME *remaund(en)*, t. LL: m. *remandāre* to send back word, repeat a command]

remand home, a home to which a child may be committed pending his appearance before a juvenile court, or while waiting for a place to be vacant in an approved school.

remanence (rĕm′ə nəns), *n. Elect.* the residual magnetization of a ferromagnetic substance after the magnetizing force has been removed; retentivity.

remanent (rĕm′ə nənt), *adj. Rare.* remaining; left behind. [late ME, t. L: s. *remanens*]

remanet (rĕm′ə nĕt′), *n. Law.* an action which remains to be heard after a sitting. [L: it remains]

remark (rĭ mäk′), *v.t.* **1.** to say casually, as in making a comment. **2.** to note; perceive. **3.** *Obs.* to mark distinctively. —*v.i.* **4.** to make a remark or observation (fol. by *on* or *upon*). —*n.* **5.** the act of remarking; notice. **6.** comment: *to let a thing pass without remark.* **7.** a casual or brief expression of thought or opinion. **8.** *Engraving.* a remarque. [t. F: m. s. *remarquer* note, heed, f. *re-* RE- + *marquer* mark]

—**Syn. 7.** REMARK, COMMENT, NOTE, OBSERVATION imply giving special attention, an opinion, or a judgement. A REMARK is usually a casual and passing expression of opinion: *a remark about a play.* A COMMENT expresses judgement or explains a particular point: *a comment on the author's scholarship.* A NOTE is a memorandum or explanation, as in the margin of a page: *a note explaining a passage.* OBSERVATION suggests a note based on judgement and experience: *an observation on customary usages.*

remarkable (rĭ mä′kə bl), *adj.* **1.** notably or conspicuously unusual, or extraordinary: *a remarkable change.* **2.** worthy of remark or notice. —**remark′ableness,** *n.* —**remark′ably,** *adv.* —**Syn. 2.** notable, noteworthy, striking, extraordinary, wonderful, unusual.

remarque (rĭ mäk′), *n. Engraving.* **1.** a distinguishing mark or peculiarity indicating a particular stage of a plate. **2.** a small sketch engraved on the margin of a plate, and usually removed after a number of early proofs have been printed. **3.** a plate so marked. [t. F]

Remarque (*Ger.* rə märk′), *n.* **Erich Maria** (*Ger.* ĕ′rĭKH mä rē′ä), 1897–1969, U.S. novelist born in Germany.

Rembrandt (rĕm′brănt; *Du.* rĕm′brŏnt), *n.* (*Rembrandt Harmenszoon van Rijn* or *van Ryn*), 1606–69, Dutch painter and etcher.

remediable (rĭ mē′dyə bl), *adj.* capable of being remedied. —**reme′diably,** *adv.*

remedial (rĭ mē′dyəl), *adj.* **1.** affording remedy; tending to remedy something. **2.** of or pertaining to the treatment of physical defects with exercises, etc., rather than by medical or surgical means. **3.** (of teaching) designed to meet the needs of retarded, backward, or maladjusted children. [t. L: s. *remediālis*] —**reme′dially,** *adv.*

remediless (rĕm′ĭ dĭ lĭs), *adj.* not admitting of remedy, as disease, trouble, damage, etc.

remedy (rĕm′ĭ dĭ), *n., pl.* **-dies,** *v.,* **-died, -dying.** —*n.* **1.** something that cures or relieves a disease or bodily disorder; a healing medicine, application, or treatment. **2.** something that corrects or removes an evil of any kind. **3.** *Law.* legal redress; the legal means of enforcing a right or redressing a wrong. **4.** *Coining.* a certain allowance at the mint for deviation from the standard weight and fineness of coins; tolerance. —*v.t.* **5.** to cure or heal. **6.** to put right, or restore to the natural or proper condition: *to remedy a matter.* **7.** to counteract or remove: *to remedy an evil.* [ME, t. L: m. s. *remedium*] —**Syn. 1.** cure, restorative, specific, medicament. **2.** corrective, antidote. **5.** repair, correct, redress. See **cure.**

remember (rĭ mĕm′bə), *v.t.* **1.** to recall to the mind by an act or effort of memory. **2.** to retain in the memory; bear in mind. **3.** to have (something) come into the mind again. **4.** to bear (a person) in mind as deserving a gift, reward, or fee. **5.** to reward; tip. **6.** to mention to another as sending kindly greetings. **7.** *Archaic or Dial.* to remind. —*v.i.* **8.** to possess or exercise the faculty of memory. **9.** *Archaic or Scot.* to have memory or recollection (fol. by *of*). [ME *remembre(n)*, t. OF: m. *remembrer*, g. LL *rememorārī*, f. L: *re-* RE- + *memorāre* call to mind] —**remem′berer,** *n.*

—**Syn. 1.** REMEMBER, RECALL, RECOLLECT refer to bringing back before the conscious mind things which exist in the memory. REMEMBER implies that a thing exists in the memory, though not actually present in the thoughts at the moment, and that it can be called up without effort: *to remember the days of one's childhood.* RECALL, a rather conversational word, implies a voluntary effort, though not a great one: *to recall the words of a song.* RECOLLECT

---

re′lub′ricate′, *v.t.,* **-cated, -cating.**
re′mag′netiza′tion, *n.*
re′mag′netize′, *v.t.,* **-tized, -tizing.**
re′mag′nify′, *v.t.,* **-fied, -fying.**
re′man′ifest′, *v.t.*
re′map′, *v.t.,* **-mapped, -mapping.**
re′mar′riage, *n.*
re′mar′ry, *v.,* **-ried, -rying.**
re′mar′shal, *v.t.,* **-shalled, -shalling.**
re′mas′ter, *v.t.*
re′match′, *v.t.*
re′mate′rialize′, *v.i.,* **-lized, -lizing.**
re′matric′ulate′, *v.i.,* **-lated, -lating.**
re′meas′ure, *v.t.,* **-ured, -uring.**
re′melt′, *v.*

---

implies an earnest voluntary effort to remember some definite, desired fact or thing: *I cannot recollect the exact circumstances.* **—Ant. 1.** forget.

remembrance (rĭ mĕm′brəns), *n.* **1.** a mental impression retained. **2.** the act or fact of remembering. **3.** the power or faculty of remembering. **4.** *Obs.* the length of time over which recollection or memory extends. **5.** the state of being remembered; commemoration. **6.** something that serves to bring to or keep in mind, as a gift. **7.** (*pl.*) greetings. **—Syn. 6.** keepsake, trophy, souvenir.

remembrancer (rĭ mĕm′brən sə), *n.* **1.** one who reminds another of something. **2.** one engaged to do this. **3.** a reminder; memento; souvenir. **4.** See **queen's remembrancer. 5.** an officer of the Corporation of the City of London, whose chief duty is to represent the Corporation before Parliamentary Committees and at Councils and Treasury Boards.

Remembrance Sunday, Armistice Day or the preceding Sunday, commemorating those who fell in the wars 1914–18 and 1939–45. Also, **Remembrance Day.**

remex (rē′mĕks), *n.*, *pl.* **remiges** (rĕm′ĭ jēz′). *Ornith.* a flight feather. [t. L: lit., oarsman (pl. *rēmigēs*), der. *rēmus* oar] **—remigial** (rĭ mĭj′ĭ əl), *adj.*

remind (rĭ mīnd′), *v.t.* to cause (one) to remember. [f. RE- + MIND, v.] **remind′er,** *n.*

remindful (rĭ mīnd′fəl), *adj.* **1.** reviving memory of something; reminiscent. **2.** retaining memory of something; mindful.

reminisce (rĕm′ĭ nĭs′), *v.i.*, **-nisced, -niscing.** to indulge in reminiscence; recall past experiences. [back-formation from REMINISCENCE]

reminiscence (rĕm′ĭ nĭs′əns), *n.* **1.** the act or process of remembering one's past. **2.** a mental impression retained and revived. **3.** (*often pl.*) a recollection narrated or told. **4.** something that recalls or suggests something else. **5.** *Platonic Philos.* the doctrine that, on occasion of perception, the mind can educe from itself universal ideas which are really memories of what it knew in a former state. [t. L: m. *reminiscentia*]

reminiscent (rĕm′ĭ nĭs′ənt), *adj.* **1.** awakening memories of something else; suggestive (fol. by *of*). **2.** characterized by or of the nature of reminiscence or reminiscences. **3.** given to reminiscence, as a person. [t. L: s. *reminiscens*, ppr., remembering] **—rem′inis′cently,** *adv.*

remise[1] (rĭ mīz′), *v.t.*, **-mised, -mising.** *Law.* to give up a claim to; surrender by deed. [t. OF, pp. (fem.) of *remettre* put back, deliver, f. *re-* RE- + *mettre* put (g. L *mittere* send)]

remise[2] (rə mēz′), *n.* *Fencing.* renewal of an attack delivered while on the same lunge. [special use of REMISE[1]]

remiss (rĭ mĭs′), *adj.* **1.** not diligent, careful, or prompt in duty, business, etc. **2.** characterized by negligence or carelessness. **3.** lacking force or energy; languid; sluggish. [ME, t. L: s. *remissus*, pp., lit., sent back]

remissible (rĭ mĭs′ə bl), *adj.* that may be remitted. **—remis′sibil′ity,** *n.*

remission (rĭ mĭsh′ən), *n.* **1.** the act of remitting. **2.** pardon; forgiveness, as of sins or offences. **3.** *Law.* a pardon from the Crown; a release. **4.** abatement or diminution, as of diligence, labour, intensity, etc. **5.** the relinquishment of a payment, obligation, etc. **6.** a temporary decrease or subsidence of manifestations of a disease. **7.** *Obs.* relaxation.

remissness (rĭ mĭs′nĭs), *n.* the state or character of being remiss; slackness. **—Syn.** See **neglect.**

remit (rĭ mĭt′), *v.*, **-mitted, -mitting,** *n.* **—***v.t.* **1.** to transmit or send (money, etc.) to a person or place. **2.** to refrain from inflicting or enforcing, as a punishment, sentence, etc. **3.** to refrain from exacting, as a payment or service. **4.** to pardon or forgive (a sin, offence, etc.). **5.** to slacken; abate: *to remit watchfulness.* **6.** to give back: *to remit a fine.* **7.** *Law.* to send back (a case) to an inferior court for further action. **8.** to put back into a previous position or condition. **9.** to put off; postpone. **10.** *Obs.* to set free; release. **11.** *Obs.* to send back to prison or custody. **12.** *Obs.* to give up; surrender. **—***v.i.* **13.** to transmit money, etc., as in payment. **14.** to abate for a time or at intervals, as a fever. **15.** to slacken; abate. **—***n.* **16.** *Law.* a transfer of the record of an action from one tribunal to another, particularly from an appellate court to the court of original jurisdiction. [ME, t. L: m. *remittere* send back] **—remit′table,** *adj.*

remittal (rĭ mĭt′l), *n.* remission.

remittance (rĭ mĭt′ns), *n.* **1.** the remitting of money, etc., to a recipient at a distance. **2.** money or its equivalent sent from one place to another.

remittent (rĭ mĭt′nt), *adj.* **1.** abating for a time or at intervals: used esp. of a fever in which the symptoms diminish considerably at intervals without disappearing entirely. **—***n.* **2.** a remittent fever. **—remit′tence, remit′tency,** *n.* **—remit′tently,** *adv.*

remitter (rĭ mĭt′ə), *n.* **1.** one who makes a remittance. **2.** *Law.* the principle or operation by which a person who enters on an estate by a defective title, and who previously had an earlier and more valid title to it, is adjudged to hold it by the earlier and more valid one. **3.** *Law.* the act of remitting a case to another court for decision. **4.** restoration, as to a former right or condition.

remnant (rĕm′nənt), *n.* **1.** a part, quantity, or number (usually small) remaining. **2.** a fragment or scrap, esp. an odd piece of cloth, lace, etc., unsold or unused. **3.** a trace; vestige: *remnants of former greatness.* **—***adj.* **4.** remaining. [ME; syncopated var. of ME *remenant*, t. OF, ppr. of *remenoir* remain] **—Syn. 1.** remainder, residue.

remodel (rē′mŏd′l), *v.t.*, **-elled, -elling** or (*U.S.*) **-eled, -eling. 1.** to model again. **2.** to reconstruct; make in an improved form.

remonstrance (rĭ mŏn′strəns), *n.* **1.** the act of remonstrating; expostulation. **2.** a protest: *deaf to remonstrances.* **3. Grand Remonstrance,** a list of grievances presented by Parliament to Charles I in 1641. [late ME, t. ML: m. s. *remonstrantia*]

remonstrant (rĭ mŏn′strənt), *adj.* **1.** remonstrating; expostulatory. **—***n.* **2.** one who remonstrates. **3.** (*cap.*) one of the Dutch Arminians whose doctrinal differences from strict Calvinists were set forth in 1610.

remonstrate (rĕm′ən strāt′), *v.*, **-strated, -strating. —***v.t.* **1.** to say in remonstrance; protest. **2.** *Obs.* to point out; show. **—***v.i.* **3.** to present reasons in complaint; plead in protest. [t. ML: m. s. *remonstrātus*, pp., exhibited] **—remonstration** (rĕm′ən strā′shən), *n.* **—remonstrative** (rĭ mŏn′strə tĭv), *adj.* **—remonstrator** (rĕm′ən strā′tə), *n.*

remontant (rĭ mŏn′tənt), *adj.* **1.** (of certain roses) blooming more than once in a season. **—***n.* **2.** a remontant rose. [t. F, ppr. of *remonter* REMOUNT]

remora (rĕm′ə rə), *n.* **1.** any of various fishes (family *Echeneididae*) having on the top of the head a sucking disc by which they can attach themselves to sharks, turtles, ships, and other moving objects. **2.** *Obs.* or *Archaic.* an obstacle, hindrance, or obstruction. [t. L: name of a fish, lit., delay, hindrance]

Remora,
Echeneis naucrates
(2 to 2½ ft long)

remorse (rĭ môs′), *n.* **1.** deep and painful regret for wrongdoing; compunction. **2.** *Obs.* pity; compassion. [ME *remors*, t. L: s. *remorsus* a biting back] **—Syn. 1.** penitence, contrition. See **regret.**

remorseful (rĭ môs′fəl), *adj.* **1.** full of remorse. **2.** characterized by or due to remorse: *a remorseful mood.* **—remorse′fully,** *adv.* **—remorse′fulness,** *n.*

remorseless (rĭ môs′lĭs), *adj.* without remorse; relentless; pitiless. **—remorse′lessly,** *adv.* **—remorse′lessness,** *n.*

remote (rĭ mōt′), *adj.*, **-moter, -motest. 1.** far apart; far distant in space. **2.** out-of-the-way; retired; secluded: *a remote village.* **3.** distant in time: *remote antiquity.* **4.** distant in relationship or connection: *a remote ancestor.* **5.** far removed; alien: *remote from common experience.* **6.** far off; removed: *principles remote from actions.* **7.** by intervention; not proximate: *remote control.* **8.** slight or faint: *not the remotest idea.* **9.** abstracted; cold and aloof: *she seemed very remote at their first meeting.* [ME, t. L: m. s. *remōtus*, pp., removed] **—remote′ly,** *adv.* **—remote′ness,** *n.*

remote control, *Engineering.* the control of a system by means of electrical, radio, or mechanical signals from a point outside the system.

remotion (rĭ mō′shən), *n.* **1.** the act of removing; removal. **2.** *Obs.* departure.

remoulade (rĕm′ə lād′; *Fr.* rė mōō lȧd′), *n.* a dressing for salads, asparagus, cold fish or meat, etc., made from a highly spiced mayonnaise and hard-boiled egg yolks. [t. F, t. It.: m. *remolata*]

remould (*v.* rē′mōld′; *n.* rē′mōld′), *v.t.* **1.** to recondition (a used motor-vehicle tyre which has a sound fabric

---

re′mem′orize′, *v.t.*, **-rized, -rizing.**
re′merge′, *v.*, **-merged, -merging.**
re′migrate′, *v.i.*, **-grated, -grating.**
re′migra′tion, *n.*
re′mil′itariza′tion, *n.*
re′mil′itarize′, *v.t.*, **-rized, -rizing.**
re′mix′, *v.t.*
re′mo′biliza′tion, *n.*
re′mo′bilize′, *v.*, **-lized, -lizing.**
re′mod′ifica′tion, *n.*
re′mod′ify′, *v.t.*, **-fied, -fying.**
re′mod′ulate′, *v.t.*, **-lated, -lating.**
re′mon′etiza′tion, *n.*
re′mon′etize′, *v.t.*, **-tized, -tizing.**
re′mort′gage, *v.t.*, **-gaged, -gaging.**

---

casing) by moulding on to it new rubber walls and tread. —*n.* **2.** a tyre which has been subjected to this process.

remount (rē mount′), *v.i., v.t.* **1.** to mount again; reascend. —*n.* **2.** a fresh horse, or a supply of fresh horses. [ME, t. OF: m. s. *remonter.* See RE-, MOUNT[1]]

removable (rĭ mo͞o′və bl), *adj.* that may be removed. —**remov′abil′ity, remov′ableness,** *n.* —**remov′ably,** *adv.*

removal (rĭ mo͞o′vəl), *n.* **1.** the act of removing. **2.** a change of residence, position, etc. **3.** dismissal, as from an office.

remove (rĭ mo͞ov′), *v.*, **-moved, -moving,** *n.* —*v.t.* **1.** to move from a place or position; take away; take off: *to remove a book from a desk, remove one's tie.* **2.** to move or shift to another place or position. **3.** to put out; send away: *to remove a tenant.* **4.** to displace from a position or office. **5.** to take, withdraw, or separate (from). **6.** to do away with; put an end to: *to remove a stain.* **7.** to kill; assassinate. —*v.i.* **8.** to move from one place to another, esp. to another locality or residence. **9.** *Poetic.* to go away; depart; disappear. —*n.* **10.** the act of removing. **11.** a removal from one place, as of residence, to another. **12.** the distance by which one person, place, or thing is separated from another. **13.** a step or degree, as in a graded scale. **14.** a degree of relationship: *he is my cousin at two removes.* **15.** (in certain schools) **a.** a form or class intermediate between ordinary yearly stages, as between fourth and fifth form. **b.** a stream of a yearly stage from which pupils may be removed either to a higher or to a lower stage. **16.** *Obs.* a promotion of a pupil to a higher class or form at school. [ME, t. OF: m. *remouvoir*, g. L *removēre*] —**remov′er,** *n.* —**Syn. 2.** transfer, displace.

removed (rĭ mo͞ovd′), *adj.* **1.** remote; separate; not connected with; distinct from. **2.** distant: used in expressing degrees of relationship: *a first cousin twice removed is a cousin's grandchild.*

Remscheid (*Ger.* rĕm′shīt), *n.* a town in West Germany, in central North Rhine-Westphalia. 134,400 (est. 1966).

remunerate (rĭ myo͞o′nə rāt′), *v.t.*, **-rated, -rating. 1.** to pay, recompense, or reward for work, trouble, etc. **2.** to yield a recompense for (work, services, etc.). [t. L: m. s. *remūnerātus*, pp., given back]

remuneration (rĭ myo͞o′nə rā′shən), *n.* **1.** the act of remunerating. **2.** that which remunerates; reward; pay: *little remuneration for his services.*

remunerative (rĭ myo͞o′nə rə tĭv, -nrə tĭv), *adj.* **1.** affording remuneration; profitable: *remunerative work.* **2.** that remunerates. —**remu′neratively,** *adv.*

Remus (rē′məs), *n. Rom. Legend.* the twin brother of **Romulus.**

renaissance (rə nā′səns; *Fr.* rə nĕ säɴs′), *n.* **1.** a new birth; a revival. **2.** (*cap.*) **a.** the activity, spirit, or time of the great revival of art, letters, and learning in Europe during the 14th, 15th, and 16th centuries, marking the transition from the medieval to the modern world. **b.** the forms and treatments in art used during this period. **c.** any similar revival in the world of art and learning. —*adj.* **3.** (*cap.*) of, pertaining to, or denoting the European Renaissance. **4.** (*cap.*) denoting or pertaining to the style of building and decoration succeeding the medieval, originating in Italy in the early 15th century and based upon clarity and mathematical relationship of plan and design, and employing to this end the forms and ornaments of classical Roman art. Also, **renascence.** [t. F, der. *renaître* be born again. See RENASCENT]

Renaix (*Fr.* rə nĕ′), *n.* French name of **Ronse.**

renal (rē′nəl), *adj.* of or pertaining to the kidneys or the surrounding regions. [t. LL: s. *rēnālis*, der. L *rēn* kidney]

Renan (*Fr.* rə näɴ′), *n.* **Ernest** (*Fr.* ĕr nĕst′), 1823–92, French philologist, historian, and critic.

Renard (rĕn′əd), *n.* Reynard.

renascence (rĭ năs′əns), *n.* **1.** rebirth; revival: *a period of moral renascence.* **2.** (*cap.*) the Renaissance.

renascent (rĭ năs′ənt), *adj.* being reborn; springing again into being or vigour: *a renascent interest in Henry James.* [t. L: s. *renascens*, ppr.]

rencounter (rĕn koun′tə), *v.t., v.i.* **1.** to meet hostilely. **2.** to encounter casually. —*n.* Also, **rencontre** (rĕn kŏn′tə; *Fr.* räɴ kôɴ′tr). **3.** a hostile meeting; a battle. **4.** a contest of any kind. **5.** a casual meeting. [t. F: m. *rencontrer*, f. *re-* RE- + *encontrer* ENCOUNTER]

rend (rĕnd), *v.*, **rent, rending.** —*v.t.* **1.** to separate into parts with force or violence: *rent to pieces.* **2.** to tear apart, split, or divide. **3.** to pull or tear violently (fol. by *away, off, up*, etc.). **4.** to tear (one's garments or hair) in grief, rage, etc. **5.** to disturb (the air) sharply with loud noise. **6.** to harrow or distress (the heart, etc.) with painful feelings. —*v.i.* **7.** to render or tear something. **8.** to become rent or torn. [ME *rende(n)*, OE *rendan*, c. OFris. *renda*] —**Syn. 2.** rip, rive, sunder, sever, cleave, chop, fracture. See **tear**[2].

render (rĕn′də), *v.t.* **1.** to make, or cause, to be or become: *to render someone helpless.* **2.** to do; perform: *to render a service.* **3.** to furnish: *to render aid.* **4.** to exhibit or show (obedience, attention, etc.). **5.** to present for consideration, approval, payment, action, etc., as an account. **6.** *Law.* to return; to make a payment in money, kind, or service, as by a tenant to his superior. **7.** to pay as due (a tax, tribute, etc.). **8.** to deliver officially, as judgement. **9.** to reproduce in another language; translate. **10.** to represent; depict, as in painting. **11.** to represent (a perspective view of a projected building) in drawing or painting. **12.** to bring out the meaning of by performance or execution, or interpret, as a part in a drama, a piece of music, a subject in representational art, etc. **13.** to give in return or requital. **14.** to give back; restore (often fol. by *back*). **15.** to give up; surrender. **16.** to cover (brickwork or stone) with a first coat of plaster. **17.** to extract (fat, etc.) from meat trimmings by melting. —*n.* **18.** *Naut.* to slacken or pay out (rope) slowly, as when there is a heavy weight or strain on it. **19.** rendering (def. 3). [ME *rendre(n)*, t. OF, g. Rom. *rendere* give back (b. *prendere*, L *prehendere* take and L *reddere* give back)] —**ren′derable,** *adj.* —**ren′derer,** *n.* —**Syn. 3.** give, supply, contribute.

rendering (rĕn′də rĭng), *n.* **1.** an act or instance of performance, execution, or interpretation of a drama, piece of music, subject, etc. **2.** a translation. **3.** the first coat of plaster applied to brickwork or stone.

rendezvous (rŏn′dĭ vo͞o′; *Fr.* räɴ dė vo͞o′), *n.*, *pl.* **-vous** (-vo͞oz′; *Fr.* -vo͞o′), *v.*, **-voused** (-vo͞od′), **-vousing** (-vo͞o′-ĭng). —*n.* **1.** an appointment or engagement made between two or more persons to meet at a fixed place and time. **2.** a place for meeting or assembling, esp. of troops, ships, or spacecraft. —*v.i., v.t.* **3.** to assemble at a place previously appointed. [t. F, n. use of *rendez vous* present or betake yourself (yourselves)]

rendition (rĕn dĭsh′ən), *n.* **1.** the act of rendering. **2.** translation. **3.** interpretation, as of a role or a piece of music. **4.** *Obs. or Rare.* surrender. [t. obs. F, t. L: m. s. *redditio*, with *-n-* from *rendre* RENDER]

renegade (rĕn′ĭ găd′), *n.* **1.** one who deserts a party or cause for another. **2.** an apostate from a religious faith. —*adj.* **3.** of or like a renegade; traitorous. —*v.i.* **4.** to turn renegade. [t. Sp.: m. *renegado*, der. *renegar* renounce, t. ML: m. *renegāre*, der. L *negāre* deny]

renegado (rĕn′ĭ gä′dō), *n.*, *pl.* **-does.** *Archaic.* a renegade.

renege (rĭ nēg′, rĭ năg′), *v.*, **-neged, -neging,** *n.* —*v.i.* **1.** *Cards.* to revoke. **2.** *Colloq.* to go back on one's word. —*v.t.* **3.** *Archaic.* to deny; disown; renounce. —*n.* **4.** *Cards.* a revoke. Also, **renegue.** [t. ML: m. s. *renegāre*, f. L: *re-* RE- + *negāre* deny] —**reneg′er,** *n.*

renew (rĭ nyo͞o′), *v.t.* **1.** to begin or take up again, as acquaintance, conversation, etc. **2.** to make effective for an additional period: *to renew a lease.* **3.** to restore or replenish: *to renew a stock of goods.* **4.** to make, say, or do again. **5.** to revive; re-establish. **6.** to recover (youth, strength, etc.). **7.** to make new, or as if new, again; restore to a former state. —*v.i.* **8.** to begin again; recommence. **9.** to renew a lease, note, etc. **10.** to become new, or as if new, again. —**renew′able,** *adj.*

—**Syn. 7.** re-create, rejuvenate, regenerate. RENEW, RENOVATE, REPAIR, RESTORE suggest making something the way it formerly was. To RENEW means to bring back to an original condition of freshness and vigour: *to renew one's enthusiasm.* RENOVATE means to make good any dilapidations: *to renovate an old house.* To REPAIR is to put into good or sound condition; to make good any injury, damage, wear and tear, decay, etc.; to mend: *to repair a roof.* To RESTORE is to bring back to its former place or position something which has faded, disappeared, been lost, etc.; to reinstate a person in a rank or position: *to restore a king to his throne.*

renewal (rĭ nyo͞o′əl), *n.* **1.** the act of renewing. **2.** the state of being renewed. **3.** an instance of this.

Renf., Renfrewshire.

Renfrew (rĕn′fro͞o), *n.* **1.** a burgh in Scotland, the county town of Renfrewshire. 17,946 (1961). **2.** Renfrewshire.

Renfrewshire (rĕn′fro͞o shĭə′, -shə), *n.* a county in SW Scotland. 338,815 pop. (1961); 225 sq. mi. *Co. town:* Renfrew. Also, **Renfrew** (rĕn′fro͞o).

Reni (*It.* rĕ′nē), *n.* **Guido** (*It.* gwē′dō), 1575–1642, Italian painter.

Reniform leaf

reniform (rĕn′ĭ fôm′), *adj.* kidney-

re′mul′tiplica′tion, *n.*
re′mul′tiply′, *v.*, **-plied, -plying.**
re′name′, *v.t.*, **-named, -naming.**
re′na′tionalize′, *v.*, **-lized, -lizing.**
re′nav′igate′, *v.t.*, **-gated, -gating.**
re′nego′tiate′, *v.*, **-ated, -ating.**
re′nego′tia′tion, *n.*

shaped: *a reniform leaf, haematite in reniform masses.* [f. *reni-* (comb. form repr. L *rēn* kidney) + -FORM]

renin (rē′nĭn), *n.* an enzyme secreted by the kidneys. [f. L *rēn* kidney + -IN[2]]

renitent (rĭ nī′tənt, rĕn′ĭ-), *adj.* **1.** resisting pressure; resistant. **2.** persistently opposing; recalcitrant. [t. L: s. *renītens,* ppr., struggling, resisting] —**reni′tency,** *n.*

Rennes (*Fr.* rĕn), *n.* a city in NW France: formerly capital of Brittany. 151,948 (1962).

rennet[1] (rĕn′ĭt), *n.* **1.** the lining membrane of the fourth stomach of a calf, or of the stomach of certain other young animals. **2.** *Biochem.* the substance from the stomach of the calf which contains rennin. **3.** a preparation or extract of the rennet membrane, used to curdle milk, as in making cheese, junket, etc. [ME, f. *renne* run + *-et* (OE *-et*), n. suffix]

rennet[2] (rĕn′ĭt), *n.* a sweet kind of apple.

Rennie (rĕn′ĭ), *n.* **John,** 1761–1821, Scottish engineer.

rennin (rĕn′ĭn), *n.* *Biochem.* a coagulating enzyme occurring in the gastric juice of the calf, forming the active principle of rennet, and able to curdle milk.

Reno (rē′nō), *n.* a city in the U.S., in W Nevada: noted for quick and easy divorce. 51,470 (1960).

Renoir (*Fr.* rə nwȧr′), *n.* **1. Jean** (*Fr.* zhäɴ), born 1894, French film director. **2.** his father, **Pierre Auguste** (*Fr.* pyĕr ō gʏst′), 1841–1919, French impressionist painter.

renounce (rĭ nouns′), *v.*, **-nounced, -nouncing,** *n.* —*v.t.* **1.** to give up or put aside voluntarily. **2.** to give up by formal declaration: *to renounce a claim.* **3.** to repudiate; disown. —*v.i.* **4.** *Cards.* **a.** to play a card of a different suit from that led. **b.** to renounce a suit led. —*n.* **5.** *Cards.* an act or instance of renouncing. [ME, t. F: m. s. *renoncer,* g. L *renuntiāre* make known, report] —**renounce′ment,** *n.* —**Syn. 1.** forsake, forgo, relinquish. See **abandon**[1].

renovate (rĕn′ō vāt′), *v.*, **-vated, -vating,** *adj.* —*v.t.* **1.** to make new or as if new again; restore to good condition; repair. **2.** to reinvigorate; refresh; revive. —*adj.* **3.** *Archaic.* renovated. [t. L: m. s. *renovātus,* pp.] —**ren′ova′tion,** *n.* —**ren′ova′tor,** *n.* —**Syn. 1.** See **renew.**

renown (rĭ noun′), *n.* **1.** widespread and high repute; fame. **2.** *Obs.* report or rumour. [ME, t. AF: m. *renoun,* der. OF *renommer* name over again (frequently), der. *nommer* name, g. L *nōmināre*] —**Syn. 1.** celebrity, glory, distinction, note.

renowned (rĭ nound′), *adj.* celebrated; famous.

rensselaerite (rĕn′sə lə rīt′, rĕn′sə lĕə′rīt), *n.* a variety of talc. [named after Stephen Van *Rensselaer,* 1764–1839, U.S. politician]

rent[1] (rĕnt), *n.* **1.** a return or payment made periodically by a tenant to an owner or landlord for the use of land or building. **2.** a similar return or payment for the use of property of any kind. **3.** *Econ.* the excess of the produce or return yielded by a given piece of cultivated land over the cost (labour, capital, etc.) of production; the yield from a piece of land or property. **4.** profit or return derived from any differential advantage in production. **5.** *Obs.* revenue or income. —*v.t.* **6.** to grant the possession and enjoyment of (property) in return for payments to be made at agreed times. **7.** to take and hold (property) in return for payments to be made at agreed times. —*v.i.* **8.** to be leased or let for rent. [ME, t. OF: m. *rente,* g. Rom. *rendita,* g. L *reddita* (*pecūnia*) paid (money), with *-n-* from *pre*(*he*)*ndere* take] —**rent′able,** *adj.* —**Syn. 7.** See **hire.**

rent[2] (rĕnt), *n.* **1.** an opening made by rending or tearing; slit; fissure. **2.** a breach of relations or union. —*v.* **3.** pt. and pp. of **rend.** [n. use of *rent,* v., var. of REND]

rental (rĕn′tl), *n.* **1.** an amount received or paid as rent. **2.** an income arising from rents received. —*adj.* **3.** pertaining to rent. [ME *rentall,* t. AF: m. *rental,* or t. Anglo-L: m. *rentale.* See RENT[1], -AL[2]]

rental library, *U.S.* a circulating library.

rent-collector (rĕnt′kə lĕk′tə), *n.* an agent employed to collect rents from tenants.

rente (*Fr.* räɴt), *n.* *French.* **1.** revenue or income, or the instrument evidencing a right to such periodic receipts. **2.** (*pl.*) perpetual bonds issued by the French government. [see RENT[1]]

renter (rĕn′tə), *n.* **1.** one who rents. **2.** one who holds, or has the use of, property by payment of rent. **3.** a wholesaler in the film trade; a theatre shareholder.

rent-free (rĕnt′frē′), *adv.* **1.** without payment of rent. —*adj.* **2.** not subject to payment of rent: *a rent-free flat.*

rentier (rŏn′tĭ ā′; *Fr.* räɴ tyė′), *n.* one who has a fixed income, as from lands, bonds, etc. [t. F, der. *rente* RENTE]

rent-restriction (rĕnt′rĭ strĭk′shən), *n.* restriction by law of a landlord's right to raise rent.

rent-roll (rĕnt′rōl′), *n.* **1.** a register of the buildings, land, etc., owned by a person, company, or the like, with an account of moneys due and received from them. **2.** the total income from property rented.

rent-seck (rĕnt′sĕk′), *n.* a right to rent in which the renter does not have the usual power of collection by seizure of the tenant's goods. [late ME, t. AF: m. *rente secque,* lit., dry rent]

rent tribunal, an administrative tribunal with power to vary or affirm the rent reserved for premises with a rateable value within prescribed limits.

renunciation (rĭ nŭn′sĭ ā′shən), *n.* **1.** the formal abandoning of a right, title, etc. **2.** a voluntary giving up, esp. as a sacrifice. —**renunciative** (rĭ nŭn′syə tĭv), **renunciatory** (rĭ nŭn′syə tə rĭ, -trĭ), *adj.*

renvoi (rĕn voi′), *n.* *Internat. Law.* the referring of a legal matter to the law of a legal system outside the jurisdiction where it arose.

reopen (rē′ō′pən), *v.t., v.i.* **1.** to open again. **2.** to start again; resume: *to reopen an argument, an attack, etc.*

reorder (rē′ô′də), *v.t.* **1.** to put in order again. **2.** *Com.* to give a reorder for. —*n.* **3.** *Com.* a second or repeated order for the same goods from the same dealer.

reorganization (rē′ô′gə nī zā′shən), *n.* **1.** the act or process of reorganizing. **2.** the state of being reorganized. **3.** *Finance.* a thorough or drastic reconstruction of a business company, including a marked change in capital structure, often following a failure and receivership or bankruptcy trusteeship. Also, **reorganisation.**

reorganize (rē′ô′gə nīz′), *v.t., v.i.*, **-nized, -nizing.** to organize again. Also, **reorganise.** —**re′or′ganiz′er,** *n.*

reorientate (rē ô′rĭ ən tāt′), *v.t.* to orientate afresh or anew. Also, **reorient** (rē ô′rĭ ənt). —**reo′rienta′tion,** *n.*

rep[1] (rĕp), *n.* a transversely corded fabric of wool, silk, rayon, or cotton. Also, **repp.** [t. F: m. *reps*]

rep[2] (rĕp), *n.* *Colloq.* repertory theatre. [shortened form]

rep[3] (rĕp), *n.* *Colloq.* representative (def. 9). [shortened form]

rep[4] (rĕp), *n.* *U.S. Slang.* reputation. [shortened form]

Rep., 1. *U.S.* Representative. **2.** Republic. **3.** *U.S.* Republican.

rep., 1. report. **2.** reported. **3.** reporter.

repaint (rē′pānt′), *v.t.* **1.** to paint again. —*n.* **2.** a part repainted, esp. a part of a picture by a restorer.

repair[1] (rĭ pĕə′), *v.t.* **1.** to restore to a good or sound condition after decay or damage; mend: *to repair a clock.* **2.** to restore or renew by any process of making good, strengthening, etc.: *repair a broken constitution.* **3.** to remedy; make good; make up for: *to repair damage, a loss, a deficiency, etc.* **4.** to make amends for: *repair a wrong done.* —*n.* **5.** the act, process, or work of repairing: *repair of a building.* **6.** (*esp.* pl.) an instance or operation of repairing: *to carry out repairs.* **7.** a part that has been repaired or an addition made in repairing. **8.** the good condition resulting from repairing: *to keep in repair.* **9.** (*usually pl.*) *Accounting.* the cost of making repairs. [ME *repaire*(*n*), t. L: m. *reparāre* put in order] —**repair′able,** *adj.* —**repair′er,** *n.* —**Syn. 1.** remodel, renovate. See **renew.**

repair[2] (rĭ peə′), *v.i.* **1.** to betake oneself or go, as to a place: *he soon repaired in person to London.* **2.** to go frequently or customarily. —*n.* **3.** the act of repairing or going; *to make repair to London.* **4.** *Archaic.* a resort or haunt. [ME *repaire*(*n*), t. OF: m. *repairer* return, g. LL *repatriāre* return to one's country]

repairman (rĭ pĕə′măn′), *n., pl.* **-men.** one whose occupation is repairing things.

repand (rĭ pănd′), *adj.* *Bot.* **1.** having the margin slightly wavy, as a leaf. **2.** slightly wavy. [t. L: s. *repandus* bent back]

Repand leaf

re′nom′inate′, *v.t.*, **-nated, -nating.**
re′nor′malize′, *v.*, **-lized, -lizing.**
re′no′tify′, *v.t.*, **-fied, -fying.**
re′nour′ish, *v.t.*
re′nour′ishment, *n.*
re′num′ber, *v.t.*
re′nu′merate′, *v.t.*, **-rated, -rating.**
re′obtain′, *v.t.*
re′obtain′able, *adj.*
re′oc′cupa′tion, *n.*
re′oc′cupy′, *v.t.*, **-pied, -pying.**
re′op′erate′, *v.*, **-rated, -rating.**
re′oppose′, *v.t.*, **-posed, -posing.**
re′or′chestrate′, *v.*, **-trated, -trating.**
re′or′chestra′tion, *n.*
re′out′line′, *v.t.*, **-lined, -lining.**
re′pac′ify′, *v.t.*, **-fied, -fying.**
re′pack′, *v.*
re′pad′, *v.t.*, **-padded, -padding.**
re′pag′inate′, *v.t.*, **-nated, -nating.**
re′pag′ina′tion, *n.*
re′pan′el, *v.t.*, **-nelled, -nelling.**
re′pa′per, *v.t.*

reparable (rĕp′ə rə bl, rĕp′rə bl), *adj.* capable of being repaired or remedied. Also, **repairable** (rĭ pĕə′rə bl). [t. L: m. s. *reparābilis*] —**rep′arably,** *adv.*

reparation (rĕp′ə rā′shən), *n.* **1.** the making of amends for wrong or injury done: *a wrong which admits of no reparation.* **2.** (*usually pl.*) compensation in money, material, labour, etc., by a defeated nation (as Germany and her allies after World War I) for damage to civilian population and property during war. **3.** restoration to good condition. **4.** repairs. [ME *reparacion,* t. L: m. s. *reparātio*] —**Syn. 1.** See **redress.**

reparative (rĭ pă′rə tĭv), *adj.* **1.** tending to repair. **2.** pertaining to or involving reparation. Also, **reparatory** (rĭ pă′rə tə rĭ, -trĭ).

repartee (rĕp′ä tē′), *n., v.,* **-teed, -teeing. 1.** a ready and witty reply. **2.** speech or talk characterized by quickness and wittiness of reply. **3.** skill in making witty replies. —*v.i.* **4.** *Obs.* to make witty replies. [t. F: m. *repartie* an answering thrust, prop. pp. of *repartir* reply promptly, f. *re-* RE- + *partir* divide (cf. F *jeu parti* question and answer poem or contest)]

repartition (rĕp′ä tĭsh′ən), *n.* **1.** distribution; partition. **2.** redistribution. —*v.t.* **3.** to divide up.

repass (rē′päs′), *v.t., v.i.* to pass back or again. —**repassage** (rē păs′ĭj), *n.*

repast (rĭ päst′), *n.* **1.** a quantity of food taken at or provided for one occasion of eating: *to eat a light repast.* **2.** a taking of food; a meal: *the evening repast.* **3.** *Obs.* food. [ME, t. OF, t. LL: s. *repastus,* prop. pp. of *repascere* feed regularly]

repatriate (*v.* rē păt′rĭ āt′; *n.* rē păt′rĭ ĭt), *v.t.,* **-ated, -ating,** *n.* —*v.t.* **1.** to bring or send back (a person) to his own country, esp. (prisoners of war, refugees, etc.) to the land of citizenship. —*n.* **2.** one who has been repatriated. [t. LL: m. s. *repatriātus,* pp.] —**repat′ria′tion,** *n.*

repay (rĭ pā′), *v.,* **-paid, -paying.** —*v.i.* **1.** to pay back or refund (money, etc.). **2.** to make return for: *repaid with thanks.* **3.** to make return to in any way: *feel repaid for sacrifices made.* **4.** to return: *repay a visit.* —*v.i.* **5.** to make repayment or return. —**repay′able,** *adj.* —**repay′ment,** *n.* —**Syn. 1.** reimburse, indemnify.

repeal (rĭ pēl′), *v.t.* **1.** to revoke or withdraw formally or officially: *to repeal a grant.* **2.** to revoke or annul (a law, tax, duty, etc.) by express legislative enactment; abrogate. —*n.* **3.** the act of repealing; revocation; abrogation. [ME *repele(n),* t. AF: m. *repel(l)er,* f. *re-* RE- + *apeler* APPEAL] —**repeal′able,** *adj.* —**repeal′er,** *n.*

repeat (rĭ pēt′), *v.t.* **1.** to say or utter again (something one has already said): *to repeat a word for emphasis.* **2.** to say or utter in reproducing the words, etc., of another: *repeat a sentence after the teacher.* **3.** to reproduce (utterances, sounds, etc.) as an echo, a gramophone or the like does. **4.** to tell (something heard) to another or others. **5.** to do, make, perform, etc., again: *to repeat an action, a ceremony, a passage of music, etc.* **6.** to go through or undergo again: *to repeat an experience.* —*v.i.* **7.** to do or say something again. **8.** (of food eaten) to rise from the stomach so as to be tasted: *that meat is repeating on me.* **9.** to belch lightly. **10.** (of a firearm) to fire several times without reloading. **11.** (of a watch, clock, etc.) to strike the hour (and sometimes the quarter-hour) last past, when required. **12.** *U.S.* to vote more than once at the same election (a form of fraud). —*n.* **13.** an act of repeating. **14.** something repeated. **15.** an order for goods identical to a previous order. **16.** a radio or television programme that has been broadcast at least once before. **17.** a duplicate or reproduction of something. **18.** *Music.* **a.** a passage to be repeated. **b.** a sign, as a vertical arrangement of dots, calling for the repetition of a passage. [ME *repete(n),* t. L: m. *repetere* do or say again] —**repeat′able,** *adj.*

—**Syn. 1, 5.** REPEAT, RECAPITULATE, REITERATE refer to saying a thing more than once. To REPEAT is to do or say something over again: *to repeat a question, an order.* To RECAPITULATE is to restate in brief form, to summarize, often by repeating the principal points in a discourse: *to recapitulate an argument.* To REITERATE is to do or say something over and over again, to repeat insistently: *to reiterate a refusal, a demand.*

repeated (rĭ pē′tĭd), *adj.* done, made, or said again and again: *repeated attempts.* —**repeat′edly,** *adv.*

repeater (rĭ pē′tə), *n.* **1.** one who or that which repeats. **2.** a repeating firearm. **3.** a watch or clock, esp. a watch, which may be made to strike the hour (and sometimes the quarter-hour, etc.) last past. **4.** *Elect.* an amplifier used in telephone circuits to make good losses of power. **5.** an instrument for automatically retransmitting telegraphic messages. **6.** a recurring decimal. **7.** *U.S. Educ.* a student who repeats a course or group of courses, in which he has previously failed. **8.** *U.S.* one who fraudulently votes more than once at an election.

repeating decimal, *Maths.* a recurring decimal.

repeating rifle or **firearm,** a rifle or firearm capable of discharging a number of shots without reloading.

repechage (rĕp′ĭ shäzh′, rĕp′ĭ shäzh′), *Rowing, etc.* —*n.* **1.** a race in which contestants eliminated in earlier heats contest for a place in the final. —*adj.* **2.** of, pertaining to, or denoting such a race. [t. F: m. *repêchage* lit., act of fishing out again]

repel (rĭ pĕl′), *v.,* **-pelled, -pelling.** —*v.t.* **1.** to drive or force back (an assailant, invader, etc.). **2.** to thrust back or away; reject: *he repelled several useless suggestions.* **3.** to resist effectually (an attack, onslaught): *repel the invader's attack.* **4.** to keep off or out; fail to mix with: *water and oil repel each other.* **5.** to put away from one; refuse to have to do with: *repel temptation.* **6.** to refuse to accept or admit; reject: *to repel a suggestion.* **7.** to discourage the advances of (a person): *he repelled her with his harshness.* **8.** to excite feelings of distaste or aversion: *her slatternly appearance repels me.* **9.** *Mech.* to push back or away by a force, as one body acting upon another (opposed to *attract*). —*v.i.* **10.** to act with a force that drives or keeps away something. **11.** to cause distaste or aversion. [ME *repelle,* t. L: m. *repellere* drive back] —**repel′lence, repel′lency,** *n.* —**repel′ler,** *n.* —**Syn. 1.** repulse, parry, ward off.

repellent (rĭ pĕl′ənt), *adj.* **1.** causing distaste or aversion; repulsive. **2.** repelling; driving back. —*n.* **3.** something that repels. **4.** a medicine that serves to prevent or reduce swellings, tumours, etc. **5.** any of various solutions applied to fabrics to make them water-repellent. —**repel′lently,** *adv.*

repent[1] (rĭ pĕnt′), *v.i.* **1.** to feel self-reproach, compunction, or contrition for past conduct; change one's mind with regard to past action in consequence of dissatisfaction with it or its results (often fol. by *of*). **2.** to feel such sorrow for sin or fault as to be disposed to change one's life for the better; be penitent (often fol. by *of*). —*v.t.* **3.** to remember or regard with self-reproach or contrition: *to repent one's injustice to another.* **4.** to feel sorry for; regret: *to repent one's words.* [ME *repenten,* t. OF: m. *repentir,* f. *re-* RE- + Rom. *penitīre* (r. L *poenitēre*)] —**repent′er,** *n.*

repent[2] (rē′pənt), *adj.* **1.** *Bot.* creeping. **2.** *Zool.* reptant. [t. L: s. *rēpens,* ppr., creeping]

repentance (rĭ pĕn′təns), *n.* **1.** compunction or contrition for wrongdoing or sin. **2.** regret for any past action. —**Syn. 1.** contriteness, penitence, remorse. **2.** sorrow, regret.

repentant (rĭ pĕn′tənt), *adj.* **1.** repenting; experiencing repentance. **2.** characterized by or showing repentance: *a repentant mood.* [ME, t. OF, ppr. of *repentir* REPENT] —**repent′antly,** *adv.*

repeople (rē′pē′pl), *v.t.,* **-pled, -pling. 1.** to furnish again with people. **2.** to restock with animals. [t. OF: m. *repeupler.* See RE-, PEOPLE, v.]

repercussion (rē′pə kŭsh′ən), *n.* **1.** an after-effect, often an indirect result, of some event or action: *the repercussions of the First World War were very widely felt.* **2.** the state of being driven back by a resisting body. **3.** a rebounding or recoil of something after impact. **4.** reverberation; echo. **5.** *Music.* (in a fugue) the point after the development of an episode at which the subject and answer appear again. [ME, t. L: s. *repercussio*]

repercussive (rē′pə kŭs′ĭv), *adj.* **1.** causing repercussion; reverberating. **2.** reflected; reverberated.

repertoire (rĕp′ə twä′), *n.* **1.** the list of dramas, operas, parts, pieces, etc., which a company, actor, singer or the like, is prepared to perform. **2.** all the works of a particular kind considered collectively. [t. F, t. L: m. *repertōrium* inventory, catalogue]

repertory (rĕp′ə tə rĭ, -trĭ), *n., pl.* **-ries. 1.** repertoire. **2.** a type of theatrical company, usually based on a particular theatre, which prepares several plays, operas, or the like, and produces them alternately or in succession, for a limited run only. **3.** a store or stock of things available. **4.** storehouse. [t. L: m. s. *repertōrium*]

repetend (rĕp′ĭ tĕnd′, rĕp′ĭ tĕnd′), *n.* **1.** *Maths.* that part of a recurring decimal repeated indefinitely. **2.** *Music.* a phrase or sound which is repeated. [t. L: s. *repetendum,* neut. ger., (that) which is to be repeated]

répétiteur (rĭ pĕt′ĭ tû′; *Fr.* rė pė tē tœr′), *n. French.* one who rehearses and prompts opera singers.

re′park′, *v.t.*
re′patch′, *v.t.*
re′pave′, *v.t.,* **-paved, -paving.**
re′ped′dle, *v.t.,* **-dled, -dling.**
re′pe′nalize′, *v.t.,* **-lized, -lizing.**

repetition (rĕp′ĭ tĭsh′ən), *n.* **1.** the act of repeating; repeated action, performance, production, or presentation. **2.** repeated utterance; reiteration. **3.** something made by or resulting from repeating. **4.** a reproduction, copy, or replica. **5.** *Civil Law.* an action for recovery of a payment or delivery made by error or upon failure to fulfil a condition. [t. L: s. *repetītio*]

re-petition (rē′pĭ tĭsh′ən), *v.t.* to petition again.

repetitious (rĕp′ĭ tĭsh′əs), *adj.* abounding in repetition; characterized by undue and tedious repetition. —**rep′eti′tiously,** *adv.* —**rep′eti′tiousness,** *n.*

repetitive (rĭ pĕt′ĭ tĭv), *adj.* pertaining to or characterized by repetition.

rephrase (rē′frāz′), *v.t.*, **-phrased, -phrasing.** to phrase again or differently: *he rephrased the statement to give it greater clarity.*

repine (rĭ pīn′), *v.i.*, **-pined, -pining.** to be fretfully discontented; fret; complain. [appar. f. RE- + PINE[2], v.]

replace (rĭ plās′), *v.t.*, **-placed, -placing. 1.** to fill or take the place of; substitute for (a person or thing): *electricity has replaced gas as a means of illumination.* **2.** to provide a substitute or equivalent in the place of: *to replace a broken vase or dish.* **3.** to restore; return; make good: *to replace a sum of money borrowed.* **4.** to restore to a former or the proper place: *the stolen paintings were replaced in the museum.* —**replace′able,** *adj.* —**replac′er,** *n.*

—**Syn. 1.** REPLACE, SUPERSEDE, SUPPLANT refer to putting one thing or person in place of another. To REPLACE is to take the place of, to succeed: *Mr A. will replace Mr B. as chairman.* SUPERSEDE implies that that which is replacing another is an improvement: *the typewriter has superseded the pen.* SUPPLANT implies that which takes the other's place has ousted the former holder, and usurped the position or function esp. by art or fraud: *to supplant a former favourite.* **3.** refund, repay.

replacement (rĭ plās′mənt), *n.* **1.** the act of replacing. **2.** one who or that which replaces another. **3.** *Mil.* a reinforcement. **4.** *Geol.* the process of practically simultaneous removal and deposition by which a new mineral of partly or wholly differing chemical composition grows in the body of an old mineral or mineral aggregate. **5.** *Crystall.* the replacing of an angle or edge by one face or more.

repleader (rē plē′də), *n.* *Law.* **1.** a second pleading. **2.** the right or privilege of pleading again. [f. RE- + PLEAD + -ER[3]. Cf. OF *repledoier*, F *replaider*]

replenish (rĭ plĕn′ĭsh), *v.t.* **1.** to bring back to a state of fullness or completeness, as by supplying what is lacking: *to replenish a stock of goods.* **2.** to supply (a fire, stove, etc.) with fresh fuel. **3.** to fill again or anew. [ME *replenys*, t. OF: m. *repleniss-*, s. *replenir* fill up again, f. *re-* RE- + *plenir* fill, der. *plein* full, g. L *plēnus*] —**replen′isher,** *n.* —**replen′ishment,** *n.*

replete (rĭ plēt′), *adj.* **1.** abundantly supplied or provided (fol. by *with*). **2.** stuffed or gorged with food and drink. [ME, t. L: m. *replētus*, pp., filled] —**replete′ness,** *n.*

repletion (rĭ plē′shən), *n.* **1.** the condition of being replete; fullness. **2.** overfullness resulting from eating or drinking to excess.

replevin (rĭ plĕv′ĭn), *Law.* —*n.* **1. a.** the recovery of goods or chattels wrongfully taken or detained, on security given that the issue shall be tried at law and the goods returned in case of an adverse decision. **b.** the common law action or writ by which goods are replevied. —*v.t.* **2.** to replevy. [late ME, t. AF, der. OF *replevir*; whence also Anglo-L *replevina*]

replevy (rĭ plĕv′ĭ), *v.*, **-plevied, -plevying,** *n.*, *pl.* **-plevies.** *Law.* —*v.t.* **1.** to recover possession of by an action of replevin. —*v.i.* **2.** to take possession of goods or chattels under a replevin order. —*n.* **3.** a seizure in replevin. [late ME, t. OF: m. *replevir*, AF *replever*, f. *re-* RE- + *plevir* PLEDGE]

replica (rĕp′lĭ kə), *n.* **1.** a copy or reproduction of a work of art by the maker of the original. **2.** any copy or reproduction. [t. It., der. *replicare*. See REPLY, v.]

replicate (rĕp′lĭ kĭt), *adj.* folded; bent back on itself. Also, **replicated** (rĕp′lĭ kā′tĭd). [t. L: m. s. *replicātus*, pp.]

replication (rĕp′lĭ kā′shən), *n.* **1.** a reply. **2.** a reply to an answer. **3.** *Law.* the reply of the plaintiff or complainant to the defendant's plea or answer. **4.** *Biol.* the production during the growth of living tissue of exact replicas of complex molecules. **5.** reverberation; echo. **6.** a reproduction, copy, or duplication.

replum (rĕp′ləm), *n.*, *pl.* **-lums, -la** (-lə). *Bot.* a septum formed in a fruit by the ingrowth of the placentas, as in the siliqua of the *Cruciferae.* [t. L: bolt for a door]

reply (rĭ plī′), *v.*, **-plied, -plying,** *n.*, *pl.* **-plies.** —*v.i.* **1.** to make answer in words or writing; answer; respond: *I must reply to his letter at once.* **2.** to respond by some action, performance, etc.: *reply to the enemy's fire.* **3.** to return a sound; echo. **4.** *Law.* to answer a defendant's plea. —*v.t.* **5.** to return as an answer: *he replied that no consideration would induce him to accept.* —*n.* **6.** an answer or response in words or writing. **7.** a response made by some action, performance, etc. **8.** *Music.* answer (def. 8). [ME *replye(n)*, t. OF: m. s. *replier* fold again, turn back, reply, g. L *replicāre* unfold, reply] —**repli′er,** *n.* —**Syn. 6.** See **answer.**

répondez s'il vous plaît (*Fr.* rė pôɴ dė′ sēl vōō plĕ′), *French.* please reply. *Abbrev.*: R.S.V.P.

report (rĭ pôt′), *n.* **1.** an account brought back or presented; a statement submitted in reply to enquiry as the result of investigation, or by a person authorized to examine and bring or send information. **2.** an account of a speech, debate, meeting, etc., esp. as taken down for publication. **3.** a statement or account of a judicial opinion or decision, or of a case argued and determined in a court of justice. **4.** a statement prepared at the end of every term by a school for each pupil to inform his parents of his work and progress. **5.** a statement or announcement. **6.** a statement generally circulated; rumour. **7.** repute; reputation. **8.** a loud noise, as from an explosion. —*v.t.* **9.** to carry and repeat as an answer or message; repeat as what one has heard. **10.** to relate as what has been learned by observation or investigation. **11.** to give or render a formal account or statement of: *to report a deficit.* **12.** to make a formal report on (a bill, etc., officially referred). **13.** to lay a charge against (a person), as to a superior. **14.** to make known the presence or whereabouts of. **15.** to present (oneself) to a person in authority, as in accordance with requirements. **16.** to take down (a speech, etc.) in writing. **17.** to write an account of (an event, situation, etc.), as for publication in a newspaper. **18.** to relate or tell. —*v.i.* **19.** to make a report; draw up or submit a formal report. **20.** to act as a reporter, as for a newspaper. **21.** to present or give an account of oneself, as to one in authority: *to report to one's boss; report sick.* **22.** to present oneself duly, as at a place. [ME *reporte(n)*, t. OF: m. *reporter*, g. L *reportāre*] —**report′able,** *adj.*

reportage (rĭ pô′tĭj), *n.* **1.** the style, manner, or act of reporting news. **2.** journalistic writing in general.

reported speech, *Gram.* the speech or writing of another not quoted verbatim, but modified as to person, tense, etc., so that the hearer or reader is aware that the statements made are at second hand; indirect speech (opposed to *direct speech*).

reporter (rĭ pô′tə), *n.* **1.** one who reports. **2.** one employed to gather and report news for a newspaper, news agency, or broadcasting organization. **3.** one who prepares official reports, as of legal or legislative proceedings.

report stage, *Parl. Proc.* the stage at which a parliamentary bill as amended in committee is reported to the House of Commons or Lords before the third reading.

reposal (rĭ pō′zəl), *n.* the act of reposing.

repose[1] (rĭ pōz′), *n.*, *v.*, **-posed, -posing.** —*n.* **1.** the state of reposing or resting; rest; sleep. **2.** peace or tranquillity. **3.** dignified calmness, as of manner or demeanour. **4.** absence of movement, animation, etc. —*v.i.* **5.** to lie at rest; take rest. **6.** to be at peace or in tranquillity; lie in quiet. **7.** to lie or rest on something. **8.** to lie dead. **9.** to depend or rely on a person or thing. —*v.t.* **10.** to lay to rest; rest; refresh by rest (often used reflexively). [late ME, t. F: m. s. *reposer*, g. L *repausāre*]

repose[2] (rĭ pōz′), *v.t.*, **-posed, -posing. 1.** to put (confidence, trust, etc.) in a person or thing. **2.** *Obs. or Rare.* to deposit. [t. L: m. *repos-* (in *reposui*, *repositus*, forms of *repōnere* replace), modelled on DISPOSE, etc.]

re-pose (rē′pōz′), *v.t.* **-posed, -posing.** to pose again; *he re-posed the question.*

reposeful (rĭ pōz′fəl), *adj.* full of repose; calm; quiet. —**repose′fully,** *adv.* —**repose′fulness,** *n.*

reposit (rĭ pŏz′ĭt), *v.t.* **1.** to put back; replace. **2.** to lay up or store; deposit. [t. L: s. *repositus*, pp., put back in place]

reposition (rē′pə zĭsh′ən, rĕp′ə-), *n.* **1.** the act of depositioning or storing. **2.** replacement, as of a bone.

---

re′pho′tograph′, *v.t.*
re′plan′, *v.t.*, **-planned, -planning.**
re′plant′, *v.t.*
re′plas′ter, *v.t.*
re′plate′, *v.t.*, **-plated, -plating.**
re′play′, *v.t.*
re′play′, *n.*
re′pledge′, *v.t.*, **-pledged, -pledging.**
re′plot′, *v.t.*, **-plotted, -plotting.**
re′plunge′, *v.*, **-plunged, -plunging.**
re′po′lariza′tion, *n.*
re′po′larize′, *v.t.*, **-rized, -rizing.**
re′pol′ish, *v.*
re′pop′ularize′, *v.t.*, **-lized, -lizing.**
re′pop′ulate′, *v.t.*, **-lated, -lating.**
re′pop′ula′tion, *n.*

---

re-position (rē′pə zĭsh′ən), *v.t.* to place in a new position.

repository (rĭ pŏz′ĭ tə rĭ, -trĭ), *n., pl.* **-tories.** **1.** a receptacle or place where things are deposited, stored, or offered for sale, as a warehouse. **2.** a place in which a dead body is deposited. **3.** a person to whom something is entrusted or confided. [t. L: m. s. *repositōrium*]

repossess (rē′pə zĕs′), *v.t.* **1.** to possess again; regain possession of. **2.** to put again in possession of something. —**repossession** (rē′pə zĕsh′ən), *n.*

repoussé (rə pōō′sā; *Fr.* rə pōō sĕ′), *adj.* **1.** (of a design) raised in relief by hammering on the reverse side. **2.** ornamented or made in this kind of raised work. [F, pp. of *repousser*, f. *re-* RE- + *pousser* PUSH, v.]

repp (rĕp), *n.* rep[1].

repr., **1.** represented. **2.** representing. **3.** reprint. **4.** reprinted.

reprehend (rĕp′rĭ hĕnd′), *v.t.* to reprove or find fault with; rebuke; censure; blame. [ME, t. L: s. *reprehendere*]

reprehensible (rĕp′rĭ hĕn′sə bl), *adj.* deserving to be reprehended; blameworthy. —**rep′rehen′sibil′ity, rep′rehen′sibleness,** *n.* —**rep′rehen′sibly,** *adv.* —**Ant.** praiseworthy.

reprehension (rĕp′rĭ hĕn′shən), *n.* the act of reprehending; reproof; censure. —**reprehensive** (rĕp′rĭ hĕn′sĭv), *adj.* —**rep′rehen′sively,** *adv.*

represent (rĕp′rĭ zĕnt′), *v.t.* **1.** to serve to express, designate, stand for, or denote, as a word, symbol, or the like; symbolize. **2.** to express or designate by some term, character, symbol, or the like: *to represent musical sounds by notes.* **3.** to stand or act in the place of, as a substitute, proxy, or agent. **4.** to speak and act for by delegated authority: *to represent one's government in a foreign country.* **5.** to act for (a constituency, etc.) by deputed right in exercising a voice in legislation or government. **6.** to portray, depict, or figure; present the likeness or semblance of, as a picture, image, or the like. **7.** to present to the mind; place clearly before or picture to the mind. **8.** to present in words; set forth; describe; state. **9.** to set forth or describe as having a particular character (fol. by *as, to be,* etc.). **10.** to set forth clearly or earnestly with a view to influencing opinion or action or making protest. **11.** to present, produce, or perform (a play, etc.), as on the stage. **12.** to impersonate (a character, etc.), as in acting. **13.** to serve as an example or specimen of; exemplify: *a genus represented by two species.* **14.** to be the equivalent of; correspond to: *the llama represents the camel in the New World.* [ME *represente(n)*, t. L: m. *repraesentāre*] —**rep′resent′able,** *adj.* —**Syn.** **13.** typify, symbolize.

re-present (rē′prĭ zĕnt′), *v.t.* to present again or anew. —**re′-presenta′tion,** *n.*

representation (rĕp′rĭ zĕn tā′shən), *n.* **1.** the act of representing. **2.** the state of being represented. **3.** the expression or designation by some term, character, symbol, or the like. **4.** speech or action on behalf of a person, body, business house, district, or the like by an agent, deputy, or representative. **5.** the state or fact of being so represented: *to demand representation on a board of directors.* **6.** *Govt.* the state, fact, or right of being represented by delegates having a voice in legislation or government. **7.** the body or number of representatives, as of a constituency. **8.** *Diplomacy.* **a.** the fact or process of speaking and acting for a state. **b.** an utterance on behalf of a state. **9.** presentation to the mind. **10.** a mental image or idea presented to the mind; concept. **11.** the act of portrayal, picturing, or other rendering in visible form. **12.** a picture, figure, statue, etc. **13.** the production, or performance, of a play or the like, as on the stage. **14.** (*often pl.*) a description or statement, as of things true or alleged. **15.** a statement of facts, reasons, etc., made in appealing or protesting; a protest or remonstrance. **16.** *Law.* a statement of fact to which legal liability may attach if material: *a representation of authority.* —**rep′resenta′tional,** *adj.*

representationalism (rĕp′rĭ zĕn tā′shə nə lĭz′əm), *n.* representationism. —**rep′resenta′tionalist,** *n., adj.*

representationism (rĕp′rĭ zĕn tā′shə nĭz′əm), *n. Philos.* a theory of knowledge (one form of which was advocated by Locke) according to which percepts stand for things other than themselves, of which things the mind then obtains knowledge by inference. Cf. **phenomenalism** (def. 2). —**rep′resenta′tionist,** *n., adj*

representative (rĕp′rĭ zĕn′tə tĭv), *adj.* **1.** serving to represent; representing. **2.** standing or acting for another or others. **3.** exemplifying a class; typical: *a representative selection of Elizabethan plays.* **4.** representing a constituency or community or the people generally in legislation or government: *a representative assembly.* **5.** characterized by, founded on, or pertaining to representation of the people in government: *representative of government.* **6.** corresponding to or replacing some other species or the like, as in a different locality. —*n.* **7.** one who or that which represents another or others. **8.** an example or specimen; type; typical embodiment, as of some quality. **9.** a commercial traveller; a travelling salesman. **10.** an agent or deputy: *a legal representative.* **11.** one who represents a constituency or community in a legislative body, esp. a member of the lower house in the U.S. Congress (**House of Representatives**) or in a state legislature. —**rep′resent′atively,** *adv.* —**rep′resent′ativeness,** *n.*

representative peer, one of the number of Scottish and Irish peers chosen by their fellows to sit in the House of Lords.

repress (rĭ prĕs′), *v.t.* **1.** to keep under control, check, or suppress (desires, feelings, action, tears, etc.). **2.** to keep down or suppress (anything objectionable). **3.** to put down or quell (sedition, disorder, etc.). **4.** to reduce (persons) to subjection. **5.** *Psychol.* to reject from consciousness, as thoughts, feelings, memories, or impulses not acceptable to the ego. [ME, t. L: s. *repressus*, pp.] —**repressed** (rĭ prĕst′), *adj.* —**repress′er,** *n.* —**repress′ible,** *adj.* —**Syn.** **1.** See **check.**

re-press (rē′prĕs′), *v.t.* to press again.

repression (rĭ prĕsh′ən), *n.* **1.** the act of repressing. **2.** the state of being repressed. **3.** *Psychol.* the rejection from consciousness of painful or disagreeable ideas, memories, feelings, and impulses.

repressive (rĭ prĕs′ĭv), *adj.* tending or serving to repress. —**repres′sively,** *adv.* —**repres′siveness,** *n.*

reprieve (rĭ prēv′), *v.,* **-prieved, -prieving,** *n.* —*v.t.* **1.** to respite (a person) from impending punishment, esp. to grant a delay of the execution of (a condemned person). **2.** to relieve temporarily from any evil. —*n.* **3.** respite from impending punishment, esp. from execution of a sentence of death. **4.** a warrant authorizing this. **5.** any respite or temporary relief. [ME *repreven* REPROVE, appar. taken in literal sense of test again (involving postponement)]

reprimand (rĕp′rĭ mănd′), *n.* **1.** a severe reproof, esp. a formal one by a person in authority. —*v.t.* **2.** to reprove severely, esp. in a formal way. [t. F: m. *réprimande*, der. *réprimer* repress, reprove] —**Syn.** **1, 2.** See **reproach.**

reprint (*v.* rē′prĭnt′; *n.* rē′prĭnt′), *v.t.* **1.** to print again; print a new impression of. —*n.* **2.** a reproduction in print of matter already printed. **3.** a new impression, without alteration, of any printed work. **4.** *Philately.* an impression from the original plate after issue of the stamps has ceased and their use for postage voided. —**re′print′er,** *n.*

reprisal (rĭ prī′zəl), *n.* **1.** the infliction of similar or greater injury on the enemy in warfare, in retaliation for some injury, as by the punishment or execution of prisoners of war. **2.** an instance of this. **3.** the act or practice of using force, short of war, against another nation, to secure redress of a grievance. **4.** retaliation, or an act of retaliation. **5.** (orig.) the forcible seizing of property or subjects in retaliation. [ME *reprisail*, t. AF: m. *reprisaille*, der. *repris(e)*, pp., taken back] —**Syn.** **1.** See **revenge.**

reprise (rĭ prīz′ *for 1*; rĭ prīz′, rĭ prēz′ *for 2*; rĭ prēz′ *for 3*), *n.* **1.** *Law.* (*usually pl.*) an annual deduction, duty, or payment out of a manor or estate, as an annuity or the like. **2.** *Music.* **a.** a repetition. **b.** a return to the first theme or subject. **3.** *Fencing.* a renewal of action. [ME, t. F, fem. pp. of *reprendre* take back, g. L *reprehendere*]

repro (rē′prō), *n., pl.* **-pros.** *Colloq.* reproduction (def. 3). [shortened form]

reproach (rĭ prōch′), *v.t.* **1.** to find fault with (a person, etc.); blame; censure. **2.** to upbraid (fol. by *with*). **3.** to be a cause of blame or discredit to. —*n.* **4.** blame or censure conveyed by reproaching: *a term of reproach.* **5.** an expression of upbraiding, censure, or reproof. **6.** disgrace, discredit, or blame incurred: *to bring reproach on one's family.* **7.** a cause or occasion of disgrace or discredit. **8.** an object of scorn or contempt. **9.** the **Reproaches,** a series of antiphons sung on Good Friday, in which Christ reproaches His people. [late ME *reproche*, t. F: m. *reprocher*, g. deriv. of L *reprobāre* REPROVE] —**reproach′able,** *adj.* —**reproach′ableness,** *n.* —**reproach′ably,** *adv.* —**reproach′er,** *n.*

—**Syn.** **1.** chide, abuse, reprimand, condemn, criticize. REPROACH, REBUKE, REPRIMAND, SCOLD, REPROVE imply calling one to account for something done or said. REPROACH is censure (often

re′por′tion, *v.t.*
re′postpone′, *v.t.,* **-poned, -poning.**
re′pos′tulate′, *v.t.,* **-lated, -lating.**
re′pour′, *v.t.*
re′prepare′, *v.t.,* **-pared, -paring.**
re′price′, *v.t.,* **-priced, -pricing.**
re′prime′, *v.t.,* **-primed, -priming.**

about personal matters, obligations, and the like) given with an attitude of fault-finding and some intention of shaming: *to reproach one for neglect.* REBUKE suggests sharp or stern reproof given usually formally or officially and approaching REPRIMAND in severity: *he rebuked him strongly for laxness in his accounts.* SCOLD suggests that censure is given at some length, harshly, and more or less abusively; it implies irritation, which may be with or without justification: *to scold a boy for being lazy.* A word of related meaning, but suggesting a milder or more kindly censure, often intended to correct the fault in question, is REPROVE: *to reprove one for inattention.* —**Ant.** 1. praise.

reproachful (rĭ prōch′fəl), *adj.* **1.** full of or expressing reproach or censure; upbraiding: *a reproachful look.* **2.** *Obs.* deserving reproach; shameful. —**reproach′fully,** *adv.* —**reproach′fulness,** *n.*

reproachless (rĭ prōch′lĭs), *adj.* irreproachable.

reprobate (rĕp′rō bāt′), *n., adj., v.,* **-bated, -bating.** —*n.* **1.** an abandoned, unprincipled, or reprehensible person: *a penniless drunken reprobate.* **2.** a person rejected by God or beyond hope of salvation. —*adj.* **3.** morally depraved; unprincipled; bad. **4.** rejected by God; excluded from the number of the elect. —*v.t.* **5.** to disapprove, condemn, or censure. **6.** (of God) to reject (a person), as for sin; exclude from the number of the elect or from salvation. **7.** *Law.* See **approbate** (def. 2). [ME, t. LL: m. s. *reprobātus*, pp., reproved]

reprobation (rĕp′rō bā′shən), *n.* **1.** disapproval, condemnation, or censure. **2.** rejection. **3.** *Theol.* rejection by God, as of persons excluded from the number of the elect or from salvation.

reprobative (rĕp′rə bə tĭv), *adj.* reprobating; expressing reprobation. —**rep′robatively,** *adv.*

reproduce (rē′prə dyōōs′), *v.,* **-duced, -ducing.** —*v.t.* **1.** to make a copy, representation, duplicate, or close imitation of: *to reproduce a picture, voice, etc.* **2.** to produce again or anew by natural process: *to reproduce a broken claw.* **3.** to produce another or more individuals of (some animal or plant kind) by some process of generation or propagation, sexual or asexual. **4.** to cause or foster the reproduction of (animals or plants). **5.** to produce, form, make, or bring about again or anew in any manner. **6.** to call up again before the mind or represent mentally (a past scene, etc.) as by the aid of memory or imagination. **7.** to produce again (a play, etc., produced at an earlier time). —*v.i.* **8.** to reproduce its kind, as an animal or plant; propagate. **9.** to turn out (well, etc.) when copied. —**re′produc′ible,** *adj.* —**Syn.** **3.** generate, beget, propagate. **5.** duplicate, repeat. See **imitate.**

reproducer (rē′prə dyōō′sə), *n.* **1.** one who or that which reproduces. **2.** *Computers.* a machine which duplicates punched cards.

reproduction (rē′prə dŭk′shən), *n.* **1.** the act or process of reproducing. **2.** the state of being reproduced. **3.** that which is made by reproducing; a copy or duplicate, esp. of a picture or the like made by photoengraving or some similar process. **4.** the natural process among animals and plants by which new individuals are generated and the species perpetuated.

reproductive (rē′prə dŭk′tĭv), *adj.* **1.** serving to reproduce. **2.** concerned with or pertaining to reproduction. —**re′produc′tively,** *adv.* —**re′produc′tiveness,** *n.*

reproof (rĭ prōōf′), *n.* **1.** the act of reproving, censuring, or rebuking. **2.** an expression of censure or rebuke.

reprovable (rĭ prōō′və bl), *adj.* deserving of reproof.

reproval (rĭ prōō′vəl), *n.* **1.** the act of reproving. **2.** a reproof.

reprove (rĭ prōōv′), *v.,* **-proved, -proving.** —*v.t.* **1.** to address words of disapproval to (a person, etc.); rebuke; blame. **2.** to express disapproval of (actions, words, etc.). **3.** *Obs.* to disprove or refute. —*v.i.* **4.** to speak in reproof; administer a reproof. [ME, t. OF: m. *reprover*, g. L *reprobāre*] —**reprov′er,** *n.* —**reprov′ingly,** *adv.* —**Syn.** **1.** censure, reprimand, upbraid, chide. See **reproach.**

re-prove (rē′prōōv′), *v.t.* **-proved, -proving.** to prove anew.

rept, report.

reptant (rĕp′tənt), *adj.* **1.** *Zool.* creeping. **2.** *Bot.* repent². [t. L: s. *rēptans*, ppr., creeping]

reptile (rĕp′tīl), *n.* **1.** any of the *Reptilia*, a class of cold-blooded vertebrates, including the lizards, snakes, turtles, alligators, and rhynchocephalians, together with various extinct types. Reptiles are now relatively unimportant, but before the development of birds and mammals they were the dominant class of land animals, appearing as fossils in a great variety of forms. They are distinguished from amphibians chiefly by adaptations to a more completely terrestrial life, without the further elaborations characteristic of the birds and mammals. **2.** any of various creeping or crawling animals, as the lizards, snakes, etc. **3.** a grovelling, mean, or despicable person. —*adj.* **4.** creeping or crawling. **5.** grovelling, mean, or malignant. [ME, t. LL: m. s. *reptilis*, adj.]

reptilian (rĕp tĭl′ĭ ən), *adj.* **1.** belonging or pertaining to the reptiles or *Reptilia.* **2.** reptile-like. **3.** mean; base; malignant. —*n.* **4.** any of the *Reptilia*; a reptile.

Repub., **1.** Republic. **2.** Republican.

republic (rĭ pŭb′lĭk), *n.* **1.** a state in which the supreme power rests in the body of citizens entitled to vote and is exercised by representatives chosen directly or indirectly by them. **2.** any body of persons, etc., viewed as a commonwealth. **3.** a state, especially a democratic state, in which the head of the government is an elected or nominated president, not a hereditary being (distinguished from a state like Great Britain with a *constitutional monarchy*). **4.** (*cap.*) any of the five periods of republican government in France: the **First Republic,** 1792–1804; the **Second Republic,** 1848–52; the **Third Republic,** 1870–1940; the **Fourth Republic,** 1945–58; and the **Fifth Republic,** from 1958. [t. L: m. s. *rēspublica* (abl. *rēpublicā*) state, lit., public matter]

republican (rĭ pŭb′lĭ kən), *adj.* **1.** of, pertaining to, or of the nature of a republic. **2.** favouring a republic. **3.** (*cap.*) of or pertaining to the Republican Party. —*n.* **4.** one who favours a republican form of government. **5.** (*cap.*) a member of the Republican Party.

republicanism (rĭ pŭb′lĭ kə nĭz′əm), *n.* **1.** republican government. **2.** republican principles or adherence to them. **3.** (*cap.*) *U.S. Politics.* the principles or policy of the Republican Party.

republicanize (rĭ pŭb′lĭ kə nīz′), *v.t.,* **-nized, -nizing.** *Chiefly U.S.* to make republican. Also, **republicanise.** —**repub′licaniza′tion,** *n.*

Republican Party, one of the two major political parties of the United States, originated (1854–56) to combat slavery.

republication (rē′pŭb′lĭ kā′shən), *n.* **1.** publication anew. **2.** a book or the like published again.

republic of letters, **1.** the collective body of literary people. **2.** literature.

repudiate (rĭ pyōō′dĭ āt′), *v.t.,* **-ated, -ating.** **1.** to reject as having no authority or binding force, as a claim, etc. **2.** to cast off or disown: *to repudiate a son.* **3.** to reject with disapproval or condemnation, as a doctrine, etc. **4.** to reject with denial, as a charge, etc. **5.** to refuse to acknowledge and pay, as a debt (said specif. of a state, municipality, etc.). [t. LL: m. s. *repudiātus*, pp., rejected, divorced] —**repu′diable,** *adj.* —**repudiative** (rĭ pyōō′dĭ ə tĭv), *adj.* —**repu′dia′tor,** *n.* —**Ant.** **1.** acknowledge.

repudiation (rĭ pyōō′dĭ ā′shən), *n.* **1.** the act of repudiating. **2.** the state of being repudiated. **3.** refusal, as by a state of municipality, to pay a debt lawfully contracted.

repugn (rĭ pyōōn′), *v.t., v.i. Obs.* to resist. [ME *repugne(n)*, t. OF: m. *repugner*, g. L *repugnāre* fight against]

repugnance (rĭ pŭg′nəns), *n.* **1.** the state of being repugnant. **2.** objection, distaste, or aversion. **3.** contradictoriness or inconsistency. Also, **repugnancy.** —**Syn.** **2.** See **dislike.**

repugnant (rĭ pŭg′nənt), *adj.* **1.** distasteful or objectionable. **2.** making opposition; objecting; averse. **3.** opposed or contrary, as in nature or character. [t. L: s. *repugnans*, ppr., fighting against] —**repug′nantly,** *adv.*

repulp (rē pŭlp′), *v.t.* to make into pulp again (something, as paper, which was originally made from pulp).

repulse (rĭ pŭls′), *v.,* **-pulsed, -pulsing,** *n.* —*v.t.* **1.** to drive back, or repel, as an assailant, etc. **2.** to repel with denial, discourtesy, or the like; refuse or reject. —*n.* **3.** the act of repelling. **4.** the act of being repelled, as in hostile encounter. **5.** refusal or rejection. [t. L: m. s. *repulsus*, pp., repelled] —**repuls′er,** *n.*

repulsion (rĭ pŭl′shən), *n.* **1.** the act of repelling or driving back. **2.** the state of being repelled. **3.** the feeling of being repelled; distaste, repugnance, or aversion. **4.** *Physics.* a situation in which bodies are forced apart (opposed to *attraction*).

repulsive (rĭ pŭl′sĭv), *adj.* **1.** causing repugnance or aversion. **2.** tending to repel by denial, discourtesy, or the like. **3.** *Physics.* of the nature of or characterized by physical repulsion; tending to repel or drive back. —**repul′sively,** *adv.* —**repul′siveness,** *n.*

re′pro′cess, *v.t.*
re′proclaim′, *v.t.*
re′pro′gram, *v.t.,* **-grammed, -gramming.**
re′project′, *v.t.*
re′prom′ulgate′, *v.t.,* **-gated, -gating.**
re′prom′ulga′tion, *n.*
re′propose′, *v.,* **-posed, -posing.**
re′provi′sion, *v.t.*
re′pub′lish, *v.t.*
re′punc′tuate′, *v.t.,* **-ated, -ating.**
re′pun′ish, *v.t.*

repurchase (rē/pûr/chəs), *v.*, **-chased, -chasing,** *n.* —*v.t.* **1.** to buy again; regain by purchase. —*n.* **2.** the act of repurchasing. —**re/pur/chaser,** *n.*

reputable (rĕp/yŏŏ tə bl), *adj.* held in good repute; honourable; respectable; estimable. —**rep/utabil/ity,** *n.* —**rep/utably,** *adv.*

reputation (rĕp/yŏŏ tā/shən), *n.* **1.** the estimation in which a person or thing is held, esp. by the community or the public generally; repute: *a man of good reputation.* **2.** favourable repute; good name: *to ruin one's reputation by misconduct.* **3.** a favourable and publicly recognized name or standing for merit, achievement, etc.: *to build up a reputation.* **4.** the estimation or name of being, having, having done, etc., something specified.
—**Syn. 1.** REPUTATION, CHARACTER are often confused. REPUTATION, however, is the word which refers to the position one occupies or the standing that one has in the opinion of others, in respect of attainments, integrity, and the like: *a fine reputation, a reputation for honesty.* CHARACTER is the combination of moral and other traits which make one the kind of person one actually is (as contrasted with what others think of one): *honesty is an outstanding trait of his character.* **2.** fame, distinction, renown. **3.** See **credit.**

repute (rĭ pyŏŏt/), *n.*, *v.*, **-puted, -puting.** —*n.* **1.** estimation in the view of others; reputation: *persons of good repute.* **2.** favourable reputation; good name; credit or note. —*v.t.* **3.** to consider or esteem (a person or thing) to be as specified; account or regard (commonly in the passive): *he was reputed to be a millionaire.* [late ME, t. L: m. s. *reputāre* reckon, think] —**Syn. 2.** See **credit.**

reputed (rĭ pyŏŏ/tĭd), *adj.* accounted or supposed to be such: *the reputed author of a book.* —**reput/edly,** *adv.*

req., 1. required. 2. requisition.

request (rĭ kwĕst/), *n.* **1.** the act of asking for something to be given, or done, esp. as a favour or courtesy; solicitation or petition: *a dying request.* **2.** that which is asked for: *to obtain one's request.* **3.** the state of being much asked for; demand: *to be in great request as an after-dinner speaker.* —*v.t.* **4.** to ask for, solicit (something), esp. politely or formally. **5.** to ask or beg (used with a clause or an infinitive): *to request that he leave, to request to be excused.* **6.** to make request to, ask, or beg (a person, etc.) to do something: *he requested me to go.* [ME *requeste,* t. OF, g. Gallo-Rom. *requaesita,* pp., (things) asked for, der. LL *requaerere* seek, r. L *requirere*] —**Syn. 5.** See **beg.**

requiem (rĕk/wĭ ĕm/), *n.* (*often cap.*) **1.** *Rom. Cath. Ch.* **a.** the mass celebrated for the repose of the souls of the dead. **b.** a celebration of this mass (**Requiem Mass**). **c.** a musical setting of this mass. **2.** any musical service, hymn, or dirge for the repose of the dead. [ME, t. L, acc. of *requies* rest, the first word of the introit of the Latin mass for the dead]

requiescat (rĕk/wĭ ĕs/kăt), *n.* a wish or prayer for the repose of the dead. [L: short for *requiescat in pāce* may he (or she) rest in peace]

requiescat in pace (rĕk/wĭ ĕs/kăt ĭn pä/kā), *Latin.* rest in peace.

require (rĭ kwī/ə), *v.*, **-quired, -quiring.** —*v.t.* **1.** to have need of; need: *he requires medical care.* **2.** to call on authoritatively, order, or enjoin (a person, etc.) to do something: *to require an agent to account for money spent.* **3.** to ask for authoritatively or imperatively; demand. **4.** to impose need or occasion for; make necessary or indipensable: *the work required infinite patience.* **5.** to call for or exact as obligatory: *the law requires annual income-tax returns.* **6.** to place under an obligation or necessity. **7.** to wish to have: *will you require tea at four o'clock?* —*v.i.* **8.** to make demand; impose obligation or need: *to do as the law requires.* [ME, t. L: m. s. *requīrere* search for, require] —**Syn. 2.** See **demand.**

requirement (rĭ kwī/ə mənt), *n.* **1.** that which is required; a thing demanded or obligatory: *a knowledge of Spanish is among the requirements.* **2.** the act or an instance of requiring. **3.** a need: *to meet the requirements of daily life.*
—**Syn. 1.** REQUIREMENT, REQUISITE refer to that which is necessary. A REQUIREMENT is some quality or performance demanded of a person in accordance with certain fixed regulations: *requirements for admission to college.* A REQUISITE is nothing imposed from outside; it is a factor which is judged necessary according to the nature of things, or to the circumstances of the case: *this system combines the two requisites of efficacy and economy.* REQUISITE may also refer to a concrete object judged necessary: *the requisites for perfect grooming.*

requisite (rĕk/wĭ zĭt), *adj.* **1.** required by the nature of things or by circumstances; indispensable: *he has the requisite qualifications.* —*n.* **2.** something requisite; a necessary thing. [late ME, t. L: m. s. *requīsītus,* pp., sought for] —**req/uisitely,** *adv.* —**req/uisiteness,** *n.*
—**Syn. 1.** See **necessary. 2.** See **requirement.**

requisition (rĕk/wĭ zĭsh/ən), *n.* **1.** the act of requiring or demanding. **2.** a demand made. **3.** the demanding authoritatively or formally of something to be done, given, furnished, etc. **4.** an authoritative or official demand. **5.** the form on which such a demand is written. **6.** the state of being required for use or called into service. **7.** a requirement, or essential condition. —*v.t.* **8.** to require or take for use; press into service. **9.** to demand or take, as by authority, for military purposes, public needs, etc.: *to requisition supplies.*

requital (rĭ kwī/tl), *n.* **1.** the act of requiting. **2.** a return or reward for service, kindness, etc. **3.** retaliation for a wrong, injury, etc. **4.** repayment; something given or serving to requite.

requite (rĭ kwīt/), *v.t.*, **-quited, -quiting. 1.** to make repayment or return for (service, benefits, etc.). **2.** to make retaliation for (a wrong, injury, etc.). **3.** to make return to (a person) for service, etc. **4.** to make retaliation on (a person) for a wrong, etc. **5.** to give or do in return. [f. RE- + *quite,* obs. var. of QUIT, v.] —**requit/able,** *adj.* —**requite/ment,** *n.* —**requit/er,** *n.* —**Syn. 1.** repay.

re-radiation (rē/rā dĭ ā/shən), *n.* *Physics.* radiation emitted as a consequence of a previous absorption of radiation.

re-rail (rē rāl/), *v.t.* to replace on the rails.

rerebrace (rĭə/brās/), *n.* a piece of armour for the upper arm; upper cannon. [ME, t. AF: m. (cf. BRACE) *rerebras,* f. *rere* back + *bras* arm]

reredos (rĭə/dŏs), *n.* a screen or a decorated part of the wall behind an altar in a church. [ME, t. AF, aphetic var. of *areredos,* f. *arere* REAR + *dos* back]

re-run (*v.* rē/rŭn/; *n.* rē/rŭn/), *v.*, **-ran, -run, -running,** *n.* —*v.t.* **1.** to run again. —*n.* **2.** the act of re-running. **3.** a reshowing of a cinema film.

res., 1. reserve. 2. residence. 3. resigned.

resail (rē sāl/), *v.i.* to sail back or again.

resale (rē/sāl/, rē sāl/), *n.* the act of reselling. —**resale/able,** *adj.*

resale price maintenance, the establishment of a fixed or minimum retail price for branded products, by agreement between manufacturer and retailer.

rescind (rĭ sĭnd/), *v.t.* **1.** to abrogate; annul, revoke; repeal. **2.** to invalidate (an act, measure, etc.) by a later action or a higher authority. [t. L: s. *rēscindere* cut off, annul] —**rescind/able,** *adj.* —**rescind/er,** *n.*

rescissible (rĭ sĭs/ə bl), *adj.* able to be rescinded.

rescission (rĭ sĭzh/ən), *n.* the act of rescinding.

rescissory (rĭ sĭs/ə rĭ), *adj.* serving to rescind. [t. LL: m. s. *rescissōrius,* der. L *rescissus,* pp., annulled]

rescript (rē/skrĭpt/), *n.* **1.** a written answer, as of a Roman emperor or a pope, to a query or petition in writing. **2.** any edict, decree, or official announcement. **3.** the act, or the product, of rewriting. —*v.t.* **4.** to rewrite (a script). [t. L: s. *rēscriptum,* prop. neut. pp., rescribed, written back. Cf. OF *rescrit*]

rescue (rĕs/kyŏŏ), *v.*, **-cued, -cuing,** *n.* —*v.t.* **1.** to free or deliver from confinement, violence, danger, or evil. **2.** *Law.* to liberate or take by forcible or illegal means from lawful custody. —*n.* **3.** the act of rescuing. [ME *rescoue,* t. OF: m. *rescoure,* der. L *re-* RE- + *excutere* shake out or off] —**res/cuer,** *n.* —**Syn. 1.** liberate, release, save. **3.** liberation, deliverance.

research (rĭ sûch/), *n.* **1.** diligent and systematic enquiry or investigation into a subject in order to discover facts or principles: *research in nuclear physics.* —*v.i.* **2.** to make researches; investigate carefully. —*v.t.* **3.** to investigate carefully: *to research a subject exhaustively.* [t. F (obs.): m. *recerche.* See RE-, SEARCH, v.] —**research/er,** *n.*
—**Syn. 1.** See **investigation.**

research library, a library which concentrates on materials for specialists and scholars in certain fields.

reseat (rē/sēt/), *v.t.* **1.** to provide with a new seat or new seats. **2.** to seat again.

reseau (rĕz/ō; *Fr.* rĕ zō/), *n.*, *pl.* **-seaux** (-zō; *Fr.* -zō/). **1.** a network. **2.** a netted or meshed ground in lace.

---

re/pu/rifica/tion, *n.*
re/pu/rify/, *v.t.,* **-fied, -fying.**
re/pursue/, *v.t.,* **-sued, -suing.**
re/qual/ify/, *v.,* **-fied, -fying.**
re/ques/tion, *v.t.*
re/quick/en, *v.*
re/quote/, *v.t.,* **-quoted, -quoting.**
re/-ra/diate/, *v.,* **-ated, -ating.**
re/-rate/, *v.t.,* **-rated, -rating.**
re/-read/, *v.t.,* **-read, -reading.**
re/-record/, *v.t.*
re/-reel/, *v.*
re/-reg/ister, *v.*
re/-reg/istra/tion, *n.*
re/-reg/ulate/, *v.t.,* **-lated, -lating.**
re/-root/, *v.t.*
re/-route/, *v.t.,* **-routed, -routeing.**
re/sad/dle, *v.,* **-dled, -dling.**
re/salt/, *v.t.*
re/sched/ule, *v.t.,* **-uled, -uling.**
re/scru/tinize/, *v.t.,* **-nized, -nizing.**
re/seal/, *v.t.*
re/secure/, *v.t.,* **-cured, -curing.**

3. *Astron.* a network of fine lines on a glass plate, used in a photographic telescope in order to produce a corresponding network (for measuring purposes) on photographs of the stars. [F, dim. of OF *roiz*, g. L *rēte* net]

resect (rĭ sĕkt′), *v.t.* *Surg.* to cut away or pare off; excise a portion of. [t. L: s. *resectus*, pp., cut back, cut off] —**resec′tion,** *n.*

reseda (rĕs′ĭ də), *n.* **1.** any plant of the genus *Reseda*, esp. *R. odorata*, the garden mignonette. **2.** a greyish green colour. —*adj.* **3.** greyish green, like the flowers of the mignonette plant. [L: plant name; said to be special use of impv. of *resēdāre* heal]

resedaceous (rĕs′ĭ dā′shəs), *adj.* belonging to the *Resedaceae*, or mignonette family of plants.

resemblance (rĭ zĕm′bləns), *n.* **1.** the state or fact of resembling; similarity. **2.** a degree, kind, or point of likeness. **3.** the likeness, appearance, or semblance of something. [ME, t. AF; see RESEMBLE, -ANCE]

—**Syn. 1.** RESEMBLANCE, SIMILARITY imply that there is a likeness between two or more people or things. RESEMBLANCE indicates primarily a likeness in appearance, either a striking one or one which merely serves as a reminder to the beholder: *the boy has a strong resemblance to his father.* SIMILARITY may imply a surface likeness, but usually suggests also a likeness in other characteristics: *there is a similarity in their tastes and behaviour.* —**Ant. 1.** difference.

resemblant (rĭ zĕm′blənt), *adj.* *Archaic.* resembling; similar; having a likeness (*to*).

resemble (rĭ zĕm′bl), *v.t.*, **-bled, -bling. 1.** to be like or similar to. **2.** *Archaic.* to liken or compare. [ME, t. OF: m. *resembler*, f. *re-* RE- + *sembler* be like, g. L *simulāre* simulate, imitate, copy] —**resem′bler,** *n.*

resend (rē′sĕnd′), *v.t.*, **-sent, -sending. 1.** to send again. **2.** to send back.

resent (rĭ zĕnt′), *v.t.* to feel or show displeasure or indignation at, from a sense of injury or insult. [t. F: m. s. *ressentir*, f. *re-* RE- + *sentir*, g. L *sentire* feel]

resentful (rĭ zĕnt′fəl), *adj.* full of, or marked by, resentment. —**resent′fully,** *adv.* —**resent′fulness,** *n.*

resentment (rĭ zĕnt′mənt), *n.* the feeling of displeasure or indignation at something regarded as an injury or insult, or against the author or source of it.

reserpine (rĕs′ə pĭn), *n.* originally, a purified extract from the root of *Rauwolfia serpentina*; now made synthetically: widely used as a tranquillizer and in the treatment of hypertension and various psychogenic illnesses. [t. G: m. *Reserpin*, prob. ult. der. L *serpentīna* (see specific name of the plant)]

reservation (rĕz′ə vā′shən), *n.* **1.** a keeping back, withholding, or setting apart. **2.** the making of some exception or qualification. **3.** an exception or qualification made, expressly or tacitly: *a mental reservation.* **4.** a tract of public land set apart for a special purpose, as (in the U.S.) for the use of an Indian tribe. **5.** the allotting or the securing of accommodation at a hotel, on a train or boat, etc., as for a traveller: *to write for reservations.* **6.** the record or assurance of such an arrangement.

reserve (rĭ zûv′), *v.*, **-served, -serving,** *n.*, *adj.* —*v.t.* **1.** to keep back or save for future use, disposal, treatment, etc. **2.** to retain or secure by express stipulation. **3.** to secure or book, as accommodation. **4.** to set apart for a particular use, purpose, service, etc.: *ground reserved for gardening.* **5.** to keep for some fate, lot, experience, etc. **6.** *Eccles.* to save or set aside (the Eucharistic Hosts) to be administered outside the mass or communion service or at subsequent masses. —*n.* **7.** an amount of capital retained by a company to meet contingencies, or for any other purpose to which the profits of the company may be profitably applied. **8. The Reserve,** that part of the cash in hand which the Bank of England keeps to meet any demand which may be made upon it by its depositors. **9.** something reserved, as for some purpose or contingency; a store or stock. **10.** *Sport.* a player kept in readiness to take the place of a team member who may drop out through injury or the like. **11.** a tract of public land set apart for a special purpose: *a forest reserve.* **12.** a reservation, exception, or qualification. **13.** the act of reserving. **14.** the state of being reserved, as for future use or for some purpose or person: *money in reserve.* **15.** *Mil.* **a.** a fraction of a military force held in readiness to sustain the attack or defence made by the rest of the force. **b.** the part of a country's fighting force not in active service, but used as a further means of defence in case of necessity. **16.** avoidance of familiarity in social relationships; self-restraint in action or speech. **17.** reticence or silence. —*adj.* **18.** kept in reserve; forming a reserve: *a reserve fund or supply.* [ME, t. L: m. *reservāre* keep back] —**Syn. 1.** retain. See **keep.**

re-serve (rē′sûv′), *v.t.* to serve again.

reserve bank, *U.S.* one of the twelve principal banks of the Federal Reserve System.

reserved (rĭ zûvd′), *adj.* **1.** kept in reserve; set apart for a particular use or purpose. **2.** kept by special arrangement for some person or persons: *a reserved seat.* **3.** self-restrained in action or speech; disposed to keep one's feelings, thoughts, or affairs to oneself. **4.** characterized by reserve, as the disposition, manner, etc. **5.** denoting an occupation of national importance which carries exemption from service in the armed forces in times of conscription. —**reservedly** (rĭ zû′vĭd lĭ), *adv.* —**reserv′edness,** *n.*

reserve price, the lowest price at which a person is willing that his property shall be sold at auction.

reservist (rĭ zû′vĭst), *n.* one who belongs to a reserve military force of a country.

reservoir (rĕz′ə vwä′), *n.* **1.** a natural or artificial place where water is collected and stored for use, esp. water for supplying a community, irrigating land, furnishing power, etc. **2.** a receptacle or chamber for holding a liquid or fluid, as oil or gas. **3.** *Biol.* a cavity or part which holds some fluid or secretion. **4.** a place where anything is collected or accumulated in great amount. **5.** a great supply, store, or reserve of something. [t. F, der. *reserver* keep, reserve]

reset (*v.* rē′sĕt′; *n.* rē′sĕt′), *v.*, **-set, -setting,** *n.* —*v.t., v.i.* **1.** to set again. —*n.* **2.** the act of resetting. **3.** that which is reset. **4.** a plant which is replanted.

res gestae (rēz′jĕs′tē), *Latin.* achievements.

reshape (rē′shāp′), *v.t.* **-shaped, -shaping.** to shape again or into different form.

reship (rē′shĭp′), *v.*, **-shipped, -shipping.** —*v.t.* **1.** to ship again. **2.** to transfer from one ship to another. —*v.i.* **3.** to go on a ship again. **4.** (of a member of a ship's crew) to sign up for another voyage. —**re′ship′ment,** *n.*

Resht (*Pers.* răsht), *n.* a city in NW Iran, near the Caspian Sea. 118,634 (est. 1964).

reside (rĭ zīd′), *v.i.*, **-sided, -siding. 1.** to dwell permanently or for a considerable time; have one's abode for a time: *he resided in Swindon.* **2.** (of things, qualities, etc.) to abide, lie, or be present habitually; exist or be inherent (fol. by *in*). **3.** to rest or be vested, as powers, rights, etc. (fol. by *in*). [late ME, t. L: m. s. *residēre*] —**Syn. 1.** live, abide, sojourn, stay, lodge.

residence (rĕz′ĭ dəns), *n.* **1.** the place, esp. the house, in which one resides; dwelling place; dwelling. **2.** a large house. **3.** the act or fact of residing. **4.** living or staying in a place of official or other duty. **5.** the time during which one resides in a place. —**Syn. 1, 2.** See **house.**

residency (rĕz′ĭ dən sĭ), *n.*, *pl.* **-cies. 1.** residence. **2.** (formerly) the official residence in India of a representative of the British governor-general at a native court. **3.** (formerly) an administrative division of the Dutch East Indies.

resident (rĕz′ĭ dənt), *n.* **1.** one who resides in a place. **2.** a diplomatic representative, inferior in rank to an ambassador, residing at a foreign court. **3.** (formerly) a representative of the British governor-general at a native court in India. **4.** the governor of a residency in the former Dutch East Indies. **5.** a bird, animal, etc., that does not migrate. —*adj.* **6.** residing; dwelling in a place. **7.** living or staying at a place in discharge of duty: *resident representative, resident engineer.* **8.** (of qualities) existing; intrinsic. **9.** (of birds, etc.) not migratory. [ME, t. L: s. *residens*]

residential (rĕz′ĭ dĕn′shəl), *adj.* **1.** of or pertaining to residence or residences. **2.** adapted or used for residence: *a residential district.* **3.** (of a hotel, etc.) catering for guests who stay permanently or for extended periods.

residentiary (rĕz′ĭ dĕn′shə rĭ), *adj.*, *n.*, *pl.* **-aries.** —*adj.* **1.** residing; resident. **2.** bound to or involving official residence. —*n.* **3.** a resident. **4.** an ecclesiastic bound to official residence.

residual (rĭ zĭd′yo͞o əl), *adj.* **1.** pertaining to or constituting a residuum; remaining; left over. **2.** *Maths.* formed by the subtraction of one quantity from another: *a residual quantity.* —*n.* **3.** a residual quantity; a remainder.

re′seed′, *v.*
re′seg′regate′, *v.*, **-gated, -gating.**
re′seg′rega′tion, *n.*
re′seize′, *v.t.*, **-seized, -seizing.**
re′sei′zure, *n.*
re′sell′, *v.*, **-sold, -selling.**
re′sep′arate′, *v.*, **-rated, -rating.**
re′sep′ara′tion, *n.*
re′set′tle, *v.*, **-tled, -tling.**
re′set′tlement, *n.*
re′sew′, *v.t.*, **-sewed, -sewn, -sewing.**
re′shar′pen, *v.t.*
re′shine′, *v.*, **-shone, -shining.**
re′shoe′, *v.t.*, **-shoed, -shoeing.**
re′shor′ten, *v.t.*
re′shoul′der, *v.t.*
re′shuf′fle, *v.*, **-fled, -fling.**

4. *Maths.* **a.** the deviation of one of a set of observations or numbers from the mean of the set. **b.** the deviation between an empirical and a theoretical result. [f. RESIDU(E) + -AL[1]] —**resid′ually,** *adv.*

residuary (rĭ zĭd′yo͝o ə rĭ), *adj.* **1.** entitled to the residue of an estate: *a residuary legatee.* **2.** pertaining to or of the nature of a residue, remainder, or residuum. [f. RESIDU(UM) + -ARY]

residue (rĕz′ĭ dyo͞o′), *n.* **1.** that which remains after a part is taken, disposed of, or gone; remainder; rest. **2.** *Chem.* **a.** a quantity of matter remaining after evaporation, combustion, or some other process; a residuum. **b.** an atom or group of atoms considered as a radical or part of a molecule. **c.** that part remaining as a solid on a filter paper after a liquid passes through in the filtration procedure. **3.** *Law.* that which remains of a testator's or intestate's estate when all his liabilities have been discharged [ME, t. F: m. *residu,* t. L: s. *residuum*] —**Syn. 1.** See **remainder.**

residuum (rĭ zĭd′yo͝o əm), *n., pl.* **-sidua** (-zĭd′yo͝o ə). **1.** the residue, remainder, or rest of something. **2.** *Chem.* a quantity or body of matter remaining after evaporation, combustion, distillation, or the like. **3.** any residual product. **4.** *Law.* the residue of an estate. [t. L]

resign (rĭ zīn′), *v.i.* **1.** to give up an office or position (often fol. by *from*). **2.** to submit; yield. —*v.t.* **3.** to give up (an office, position, etc.) formally. **4.** to relinquish, as a right or claim. **5.** to submit (oneself, one's mind, etc.) without resistance. **6.** to hand or sign over; surrender, as to the care or control of another: *to resign a child to foster-parents.* [ME *resignen,* t. OF: m. *resigner,* t. L: m. *resignāre* unseal, annul] —**Syn. 4.** give up, surrender, renounce, abdicate.

re-sign (rē′sīn′), *v.i., v.t.,* to sign again.

resignation (rĕz′ĭg nā′shən), *n.* **1.** the act of resigning. **2.** the formal statement, document, etc., stating that one resigns an office, position, etc. **3.** the state of being submissive; submission; unresisting acquiescence. [ME, t. ML: s. *resignātio*] —**Syn. 3.** meekness, patience.

resigned (rĭ zīnd′), *adj.* **1.** submissive or acquiescent. **2.** characterized by or indicative of resignation. —**resignedly** (rĭ zī′nĭd lĭ), *adv.* —**resign′edness,** *n.*

resile (rĭ zīl′), *v.i.,* **-siled, -siling. 1.** to spring back; rebound; resume the original form or position, as an elastic body. **2.** to shrink back; recoil. [t. L: m. s. *resilire*]

resilience (rĭ zĭl′ĭ əns), *n.* **1.** resilient power; elasticity. **2.** resilient action; rebound; recoil. **3.** power of ready recovery from sickness, depression, or the like; buoyancy; cheerfulness. Also, **resiliency.**

resilient (rĭ zĭl′ĭ ənt), *adj.* **1.** springing back; rebounding. **2.** returning to the original form or position after being bent, compressed, or stretched. **3.** readily recovering, as from sickness, depression, or the like; buoyant; cheerful. [t. L: s. *resiliens,* ppr., rebounding] —**resil′iently,** *adv.*

resin (rĕz′ĭn), *n.* **1.** any of a class of non-volatile, solid or semisolid organic substances (copal, mastic, etc.) obtained directly from certain plants as exudations or prepared by polymerization of simple molecules, and used in medicine and in the making of varnishes and plastics. **2.** (not in scientific usage) a substance of this type obtained from certain pines; rosin. —*v.t.* **3.** to treat or rub with resin. [ME *resyn,* t. L: m. s. *rēsīna,* c. Gk *rhētínē*] —**res′in-like′,** *adj.*

resinate (rĕz′ĭ nāt′), *v.t.,* **-nated, -nating.** to treat with resin, as by impregnation.

resiniferous (rĕz′ĭ nĭf′ə rəs), *adj.* yielding resin.

resinoid (rĕz′ĭ noid′), *adj.* **1.** resin-like. —*n.* **2.** a resinoid substance. **3.** a resinous substance synthetically compounded. **4.** gum resin.

resinous (rĕz′ĭ nəs), *adj.* **1.** full of or containing resin. **2.** of the nature of or resembling resin. **3.** pertaining to or characteristic of resin. Also, **resiny** (rĕz′ĭ nĭ). [t. L: m. s. *rēsīnōsus*]

resist (rĭ zĭst′), *v.t.* **1.** to withstand, strive against, or oppose: *to resist infection.* **2.** to withstand the action or effect of: *gold resists corrosion.* **3.** to refrain or abstain from: *to resist a smile.* —*v.i.* **4.** to make a stand or make efforts in opposition; act in opposition; offer resistance. —*n.* **5.** a substance applied to a surface to enable it to resist corrosion or the like. [ME *resisten,* t. L: m. *resistere* withstand] —**resist′er,** *n.* —**Syn. 1.** See **oppose.** —**Ant. 4.** submit.

resistance (rĭ zĭs′təns), *n.* **1.** the act or power of resisting, opposing, or withstanding. **2.** the opposition offered by one thing, force, etc., to another. **3.** *Elect.* **a.** that property of a conductor by virtue of which the passage of a current is opposed, causing electric energy to be transformed into heat (**true** or **ohmic resistance**). **b.** a conductor or coil offering such opposition; a resistor. **c.** impedance (**apparent resistance**). **4.** (*often cap.*) a secret organization in an enemy-occupied country working to maintain hostilities unofficially after a formal capitulation. [late ME, t. F; r. ME *resistence,* t. OF, t. LL: m. s. *resistentia*]

resistance thermometer, *Physics.* a form of thermometer in which the temperature is deduced from the resistance of a spiral of wire (usually platinum).

resistance welding, a form of welding in which the heat required to fuse the metal surfaces to be welded is produced by a current flowing across the contact resistance between them.

resistant (rĭ zĭs′tənt), *adj.* **1.** resisting. —*n.* **2.** one who or that which resists.

resistible (rĭ zĭs′tə bl), *adj.* that may be resisted. —**resist′ibil′ity,** *n.*

resistive (rĭ zĭs′tĭv), *adj.* resisting; capable of or characterized by resistance.

resistivity (rē′zĭs tĭv′ĭ tĭ), *n.* **1.** the power or property of resistance. **2.** *Elect.* the resistance between opposite faces of a one-centimetre cube of a given material (the reciprocal of *conductivity*).

resistless (rĭ zĭst′lĭs), *adj.* **1.** irresistible. **2.** unresisting. —**resist′lessly,** *adv.* —**resist′lessness,** *n.*

resistor (rĭ zĭs′tə), *n. Elect.* a device, the primary purpose of which is to introduce resistance into an electric circuit.

resit (rē′sĭt′), *v.t., v.i.* to sit (an examination) again after having failed it.

res judicata (rēz′ jo͞o′dĭ kä′tə), *Latin.* a thing adjudicated; a case that has been decided.

resnatron (rĕz′nə trŏn′), *n. Electronics.* a tetrode with the grid connected to form a drift space for the electrons, used to generate large power at very high frequency. [alter. of RESONATOR influenced by words in *-tron,* as DYNATRON]

resole (rē′sōl′), *v.t.,* **-soled, -soling.** to put a new sole on (a shoe, etc.).

resoluble (rĕz′ə lyo͞o bl, rĭ zŏl′yo͝o bl), *adj.* capable of being resolved. [t. LL: m. s. *resolūbilis*] —**reso′lubil′ity,** *n.* —**res′olubleness,** *n.*

re-soluble (rē′sŏl′yo͝o bl), *adj.* capable of being dissolved again.

resolute (rĕz′ə lo͞ot′), *adj.* **1.** firmly resolved or determined; set in purpose or opinion. **2.** characterized by firmness and determination, as the temper, spirit, actions, etc. [ME, t. L: m. s. *resolūtus,* pp., resolved] —**res′olute′ly,** *adv.* —**res′olute′ness,** *n.* —**Syn. 1.** firm, steadfast. See **earnest.**

resolution (rĕz′ə lo͞o′shən), *n.* **1.** a formal determination, or expression of opinion, of a deliberative assembly or other body of persons. **2.** a resolve or determination: *to make a firm resolution to do something.* **3.** the act of resolving or determining as to action, etc. **4.** the mental state or quality of being resolved or resolute; firmness of purpose. **5.** the act or process of resolving or separating into constituent or elementary parts. **6.** the resulting state. **7.** solution or explanation, as of a problem, a doubtful point, etc. **8.** *Music.* **a.** progression of a voice part or of the harmony as a whole from a dissonance to a consonance, or sometimes to another less violent dissonance. **b.** the note or chord to which this is effected. **9.** reduction to a simpler form; conversion. **10.** *Med.* the reduction or disappearance of a swelling or inflammation without suppuration. **11.** *Optics.* **a.** the act or process of distinguishing between the individual parts of an image. **b.** resolving power. [ME *resolucion,* t. L: m. s. *resolūtio*]

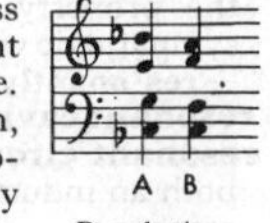

Resolution (def. 8) A, Dissonance; B, Consonance

resolutioner (rĕz′ə lo͞o′shə nə), *n.* one joining in or subscribing to a resolution. Also, **resolutionist.**

resolvable (rĭ zŏl′və bl), *adj.* that may be resolved. —**resolv′abil′ity, resolv′ableness,** *n.*

resolve (rĭ zŏlv′), *v.,* **-solved, -solving,** *n.* —*v.t.* **1.** to fix or settle on by deliberate choice and will; determine (to do something). **2.** to separate into constituent or elementary parts, break up, or disintegrate; separate or break up (fol. by *into*). **3.** to reduce or convert by or as by breaking up or disintegration (fol. by *into* or *to*). **4.** to convert or transform by any process (often reflexive). **5.** to reduce by logical analysis (fol. by *into*). **6.** to settle, determine, or state formally in a vote or

re′sift′, *v.t.*	**re′site′,** *v.t.,*	**re′soak′,** *v.t.*	**re′solic′it,** *v.t.*
re′sight′, *v.t.*	**-sited, -siting.**	**re′sof′ten,** *v.t.*	**re′solid′ify′,** *v.,*
re′sil′ver, *v.t.*	**re′smooth′,** *v.t.*	**re′sol′der,** *v.t.*	**-fied, -fying.**

resolution, as of a deliberative assembly. **7.** to deal with (a question, a matter of uncertainty, etc.) conclusively; explain; solve (a problem). **8.** to clear away or dispel (doubts, etc.), as by explanation. **9.** *Chem.* to separate (a racemic mixture) into its optically active components. **10.** *Music.* to cause (a voice part or the harmony as a whole) to progress from a dissonance to a consonance. **11.** *Optics.* to separate and make visible the individual parts of (an image); to distinguish between. **12.** *Med.* to cause (swellings, inflammation, etc.) to disappear without suppuration.
—*v.i.* **13.** to come to a determination; make up one's mind; determine (often fol. by *on* or *upon*). **14.** to break up or disintegrate. **15.** to be reduced or changed by breaking up or otherwise (fol. by *into* or *to*). **16.** *Music.* to progress from a dissonance to a consonance.
—*n.* **17.** a resolution or determination made, as to follow some course of action. **18.** determination; firmness of purpose.
[ME, t. L: m. *resolvere* loosen, dissolve] —**resolv′er,** *n.*
—**Syn. 1.** See **decide.**

resolved (rĭ zŏlvd′), *adj.* determined; firm in purpose; resolute. —**resolvedly** (rĭ zŏl′vĭd lĭ), *adv.*

resolvent (rĭ zŏl′vənt), *adj.* **1.** resolving; causing solution; solvent. —*n.* **2.** something resolvent. **3.** *Med.* a remedy that causes resolution, as of swellings, etc. [t. L: s. *resolvens*, ppr., resolving]

resolving power, *Optics.* the ability of an optical device to produce separate images of close objects. Also, **resolution.**

resonance (rĕz′ə nəns), *n.* **1.** the state or quality of being resonant. **2.** the prolongation of sound by reflection; reverberation. **3.** the amplification of vocal tone by the bones of the head and upper chest and by the air cavities of the pharynx, mouth, and nasal passages. **4.** *Physics.* **a.** an abnormally large response of a system having a natural frequency to a periodic external stimulus of the same, or nearly the same, frequency. **b.** the increase of intensity of sound by the sympathetic vibration of other bodies. **c.** the prolongation or increase of a wave by the sympathetic vibration of other bodies: used to describe an atom which gives off rays of the same wavelength as it has absorbed. **d.** the phenomenon which occurs in nuclear reactions when the energy of an incident particle or photon is equal, or near to, the value of an appropriate energy level of the struck nucleus. **5.** *Elect.* that condition of a circuit with respect to a given frequency or the like in which the total reactance is zero and the current flow a maximum. **6.** *Chem.* the condition exhibited by a molecule when the actual arrangement of its valency electrons is intermediate between two or more arrangements having nearly the same energy, and the positions of the atomic nuclei are identical. **7.** *Med.* a sound produced when air is present (in percussing for diagnostic purposes).

resonant (rĕz′ə nənt), *adj.* **1.** resounding or re-echoing, as sounds, places, etc. **2.** deep and full of resonance: *a resonant voice.* **3.** pertaining to resonance. **4.** having the property of increasing the intensity of sound by sympathetic vibration. [t. L: s. *resonans*, ppr., resounding] —**res′onantly,** *adv.*

resonant cavity, resonator (def. 4a).

resonant circuit, *Elect.* an electronic circuit containing both an inductance and a capacitance which is capable of resonance.

resonate (rĕz′ə nāt′), *v.i.*, **-nated, -nating. 1.** to resound. **2.** to act as a resonator; exhibit resonance. **3.** *Electronics.* to reinforce oscillations because the natural frequency of the device is the same as the frequency of the source. **4.** to amplify vocal sound by the sympathetic vibration of air in certain cavities and bony structures. —*v.t.* **5.** to cause to resound. [t. L: m. s. *resonātus*, pp., resounded] —**res′ona′tion,** *n.*

resonator (rĕz′ə nā′tə), *n.* **1.** anything that resonates. **2.** an appliance for increasing sound by resonance. **3.** an instrument for detecting the presence of a particular frequency by means of resonance. **4.** *Electronics.* **a.** Also, **cavity resonator.** a hollow enclosure made of conducting material of such dimensions that electromagnetic radiation of a certain frequency will resonate. **b.** any circuit having this frequency characteristic. [t. NL. See RESONATE, -OR[2]]

resorb (rĭ sôb′), *v.t.* to absorb again, as an exudation. [t. L: s. *resorbēre* suck back] —**resorption** (rĭ sôp′shən), *n.* —**resorptive** (rĭ sôp′tĭv), *adj.*

resorcinol (rĭ zô′sĭ nŏl′), *n. Chem.* a colourless crystalline benzene derivative, $C_6H_4(OH)_2$, originally obtained from certain resins, used in medicine and in making dyes. Also, **resorcin.** [f. RES(IN) + ORCINOL]

resort (rĭ zôt′), *v.i.* **1.** to have recourse for use, service, or help: *to resort to war.* **2.** to go, esp. frequently or customarily: *a beach to which many people resort.* —*n.* **3.** a place frequented, esp. by the public generally: *a summer resort.* **4.** a habitual or general going, as to a place or person. **5.** a resorting to some person or thing for aid, service, etc.; recourse: *to have resort to force.* **6.** a person or thing resorted to for aid, service, etc. **7. last resort,** the expedient to which one turns when all others have failed. [ME *resorte(n)*, t. OF: m. *resortir*, f. *re-* RE- + *sortir* issue, go out]

re-sort (rē′sôt′), *v.t.* to sort again.

resound[1] (rĭ zound′), *v.i.* **1.** to re-echo or ring with sound, as a place. **2.** to make an echoing sound, or sound loudly, as a thing. **3.** to be echoed, or ring, as sounds. **4.** to be famed or celebrated. —*v.t.* **5.** to re-echo (a sound). **6.** to proclaim loudly (praises, etc.). **7.** *Rare.* to give forth or utter loudly. [ME *resoun(en)*, f. *re-* RE- + *soun(en)* SOUND[1], after L *resonāre*] —**resound′ingly,** *adv.*

re-sound[2] (rē′sound′), *v.t., v.i.* to sound again. [f. RE- + SOUND[1]]

resounding (rĭ zoun′dĭng), *adj.* **1.** ringing, re-echoing, or reverberating, as a sound or its cause or location. **2.** *Colloq.* thoroughgoing; outstanding; great: *a resounding success.* **3.** *Colloq.* (of actions) firmly executed and often noisy: *a resounding blow.*

resource (rĭ zôs′, rĭ sôs′), *n.* **1.** a source of supply, support, or aid. **2.** (*pl.*) the collective wealth of a country, or its means of producing wealth. **3.** (*often pl.*) money, or any property which can be converted into money; assets. **4.** available means afforded by the mind or the personal capabilities. **5.** an action or measure to which one may have recourse in an emergency; expedient. **6.** capability in dealing with a situation or in meeting difficulties. [t. F: m. *ressource*, der. OF *res(s)sourdre* (f. *re-* RE- + *sourdre*), g. L *resurgere* rise again]

resourceful (rĭ zôs′fəl, rĭ sôs′fəl), *adj.* full of resource; ingenious; skilful in overcoming difficulties. —**resource′fully,** *adv.* —**resource′fulness,** *n.*

resp., 1. respective. **2.** respectively. **3.** respondent.

respect (rĭ spĕkt′), *n.* **1.** a particular, detail, or point (in phrases prec. by *in*): *to be defective in some respect.* **2.** relation or reference (prec. by *in* or *with*): *enquiries with respect to a route.* **3.** esteem or deferential regard felt or shown. **4.** the condition of being esteemed or honoured. **5.** (*pl.*) deferential, respectful, or friendly compliments, as paid by making a call on a person or otherwise: *to pay one's respects.* **6.** consideration or regard, as to something that might influence a choice. **7.** *Archaic.* consideration.
—*v.t.* **8.** to hold in esteem or honour: *to respect one's elders.* **9.** to show esteem, regard, or consideration for: *to respect someone's wishes.* **10.** to treat with consideration; refrain from interfering with: *to respect a person's privacy.* **11.** *Obs.* to relate or have reference to.
[ME, t. L: s. *respectus*, pp., having been regarded] —**respect′er,** *n.*
—**Syn.** 3. RESPECT, ESTEEM, VENERATION imply recognition of personal qualities by approbation, deference, and more or less affection. RESPECT is commonly the result of admiration and approbation, together with deference: *to feel respect for a great scholar.* ESTEEM is deference combined with admiration and often with affection: *to hold a friend in great esteem.* VENERATION is an almost religious attitude of deep respect, reverence, and love, such as we feel for persons or things of outstanding superiority, endeared by long association: *veneration for one's grandparents, for noble traditions.*

respectability (rĭ spĕk′tə bĭl′ĭ tĭ), *n., pl.* **-ties. 1.** the state or quality of being respectable. **2.** respectable social standing, character, or reputation. **3.** respectable people. **4.** (*pl.*) things accepted as respectable.

respectable (rĭ spĕk′tə bl), *adj.* **1.** worthy of respect or esteem; estimable; worthy: *a respectable citizen.* **2.** of good social standing, reputation, etc.: *a respectable neighbourhood.* **3.** pertaining or appropriate to such standing; proper or decent: *respectable language.* **4.** having socially accepted standards of moral behaviour; virtuous: *a respectable girl.* **5.** of presentable appearance; decently clothed. **6.** of moderate excellence; fairly good; fair: *a respectable performance.* **7.** considerable in size, number, or amount: *a respectable navy.* —**respect′ableness,** *n.* —**respect′ably,** *adv.*

respecter of persons, one who is unduly influenced in his dealings by the social standing, importance, etc., of persons.

respectful (rĭ spĕkt′fəl), *adj.* full of, characterized by, or showing respect: *a respectful reply.* —**respect′fully,** *adv.* —**respect′fulness,** *n.* —**Syn.** courteous, polite.

respecting (rĭ spĕk′tĭng), *prep.* regarding; concerning.

respective (rĭ spĕk′tĭv), *adj.* pertaining individually or severally to each of a number of persons, things, etc.; particular: *the respective merits of the candidates.*

respectively (rĭ spĕk′tĭv lĭ), *adv.* with respect to each of

a number in the stated or corresponding order: *labelled respectively A, B, and C.*
respell (rē′spĕl′), *v.t.* to spell again or anew.
Respighi (rĕs pē′gĭ; *It.* rĕs pē′gē), *n.* **Ottorino** (*It.* ōt tō rē′nō), 1879–1936, Italian composer.
respirable (rĕs′pĭ rə bl), *adj.* **1.** capable of being respired. **2.** capable of respiring.
respiration (rĕs′pə rā′shən), *n.* **1.** the act of respiring; inhalation and exhalation of air; breathing. **2.** (in living organisms) the process by which oxygen and carbohydrates are assimilated into the system and the oxidation products (carbon dioxide and water) are given off.
respirator (rĕs′pə rā′tə), *n.* **1.** a device worn over the mouth, or nose and mouth, to prevent the inhalation of noxious substances, etc., as a gasmask. **2.** an apparatus to induce artificial respiration.
respiratory (rĭs pī′ə rə tə rĭ, -trĭ), *adj.* pertaining to or serving for respiration: *the respiratory system of mammals.*
respire (rĭs pī′ə), *v.*, **-spired, -spiring.** *—v.i.* **1.** to inhale and exhale air for the purpose of maintaining life; breathe. **2.** to breathe freely again, after anxiety, trouble, exertion, etc. *—v.t.* **3.** to breathe; inhale and exhale. **4.** *Rare.* to exhale or exude. [ME, t. L: m. *respīrāre*]
respite (rĕs′pĭt, rĕs′pīt), *n.*, *v.*, **-pited, -piting.** *—n.* **1.** a delay or cessation for a time, esp. of anything distressing or trying; an interval of relief: *to toil without respite.* **2.** temporary suspension of the execution of a person condemned to death; a reprieve. *—v.t.* **3.** to relieve temporarily, esp. from anything distressing or trying; give an interval of relief from. **4.** to grant delay in the carrying out of (a punishment, obligation, etc.). [ME *respit*, t. OF, g. LL *respectus* delay, der. L *respectāre* look for, wait for]
resplend (rĭ splĕnd′), *v.i. Rare.* to be resplendent.
resplendence (rĭ splĕn′dəns), *n.* resplendent state; splendour. Also, **resplend′ency.**
resplendent (rĭ splĕn′dənt), *adj.* shining brilliantly; gleaming; splendid: *resplendent in white uniforms.* [t. L: s. *resplendens*, ppr., shining] —**resplend′ently,** *adv.*
respond (rĭ spŏnd′), *v.i.* **1.** to answer; give a reply in words: *to respond briefly to a question.* **2.** to make a return by some action as if in answer: *to respond generously to a charitable appeal.* **3.** *Physiol.* to exhibit some action or effect as if in answer; react: *nerves respond to a stimulus.* **4.** to correspond (fol. by *to*). *—v.t.* **5.** to say in answer; reply. *—n.* **6.** *Archit.* a half-pillar or the like engaged in a wall to support an arch. **7.** *Eccles.* **a.** a short anthem chanted at intervals during the reading of a lection. **b.** responsory. **c.** response. [ME, t. L: s. *respondēre*]
respondence (rĭ spŏn′dəns), *n.* **1.** the act of responding; response: *respondence to a stimulus.* **2.** agreement; correspondence. Also, **respondency.**
respondent (rĭ spŏn′dənt), *n.* **1.** *Law.* a defendant, esp. in appellate and divorce cases. **2.** *Biol.* one who responds or makes reply. *—adj.* **3.** answering; responsive. [t. L: s. *respondens*, ppr., answering]
response (rĭ spŏns′), *n.* **1.** answer or reply, whether in words, in some action, etc. **2.** *Biol.* any behaviour of a living organism which results from stimulation. **3.** *Elect.* the ratio of the output level to the input level of an electrical device or transmission line, at a given frequency. **4.** *Eccles.* **a.** a verse, sentence, phrase, or word said or sung by the choir or congregation in reply to the officiant during public worship. **b.** responsory. [t. L: m. s. *responsum*, neut. of *responsus*, pp., answered; r. ME *respouns(e)*, t. OF: m. *respuns*, *respons* (masc.), *response* (fem.)] **—Syn. 1.** See **answer.**
responsibility (rĭ spŏn′sə bĭl′ĭ tĭ), *n.*, *pl.* **-ties. 1.** the state or fact of being responsible. **2.** an instance of being responsible. **3.** a particular burden of obligation upon one who is responsible: *to feel the responsibilities of one's position.* **4.** something for which one is responsible: *a child is a responsibility to its parents.* **5.** ability to meet debts or payments. **6. on one's own responsibility,** on one's own initiative or authority.
responsible (rĭ spŏn′sə bl), *adj.* **1.** answerable or accountable, as for something within one's power, control, or management (often fol. by *to* or *for*). **2.** involving accountability or responsibility: *a responsible position.* **3.** chargeable with being the author, cause, or occasion of something (fol. by *for*). **4.** having a capacity for moral decisions and therefore accountable; capable of rational thought or action. **5.** able to discharge obligations or pay debts. **6.** reliable in business or other dealings; showing reliability. —**respon′sibleness,** *n.* —**respon′sibly,** *adv.*
responsion (rĭ spŏn′shən), *n.* **1.** (*pl.*) (at Oxford University) formerly the first examination for a B.A. degree, now an alternative examination for otherwise suitable candidates for university places who have not passed O level G.C.E. examination in a required subject. **2.** *Rare.* the act of replying. [late ME, t. L: s. *responsio*]
responsive (rĭ spŏn′sĭv), *adj.* **1.** making answer or reply, esp. responding readily to influences, appeals, efforts, etc. **2.** *Physiol.* acting in response, as to some stimulus. —**respon′sively,** *adv.* —**respon′siveness,** *n.*
responsory (rĭ spŏn′sə rĭ), *n.*, *pl.* **-ries.** *Eccles.* an anthem sung after a lection by a soloist and choir alternately. [ME, t. LL: m. s. *responsoria*, pl.]
respray (*v.* rē′sprā′; *n.* re′sprā′, rē′sprā′), *v.t.*, *n.* *—v.t.* **1.** to spray again. **2.** to paint (a motor vehicle or the like) again by spraying. *—n.* **3.** the act, process, or fact of (a motor vehicle or the like) being or having been repainted in this manner. [RE- + SPRAY[1]]
respring (rē sprĭng′), *v.t.*, **-sprang** or **-sprung, -springing.** to replace the springs of (a mattress, or upholstered piece of furniture).
respublica (rās′po͝ob′lĭ kä′), *n. Latin.* the state; republic; commonwealth.
rest[1] (rĕst), *n.* **1.** the refreshing quiet or repose of sleep: *a good night's rest.* **2.** refreshing ease or inactivity after exertion or labour: *to allow an hour for rest.* **3.** relief or freedom, esp. from anything that wearies, troubles, or disturbs. **4.** mental or spiritual calm; tranquillity: *to set one's mind at rest.* **5.** the repose of death: *to lay the dead to rest.* **6.** cessation or absence of motion: *to bring a machine to rest.* **7.** a pause or interval. **8.** *Music.* **a.** an interval of silence between notes. **b.** a mark or sign indicating this. **9.** *Pros.* a short pause in reading; a caesura. **10.** an establishment for providing shelter or lodging for some class of persons. **11.** a piece or thing for something to rest on: *an elbow rest.* **12.** a support, or supporting device. **13.** *Billiards.* bridge (def. 10). **14. at rest, a.** dead. **b.** quiescent, inactive, or motionless, as something formerly in motion. **c.** tranquil; unworried. **d.** in a state of rest, as asleep. [ME and OE, akin to G *Rast*]

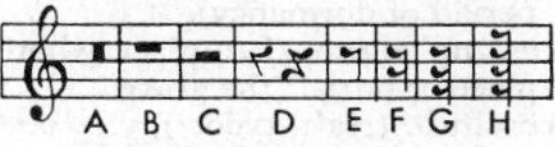

Rests (def. 8b)
A, Breve; B, Semibreve; C, Minim; D, Crotchet; E, Quaver; F, Semiquaver; G, Demisemiquaver; H, Hemidemisemiquaver

—v.i. **15.** to refresh oneself, as by sleeping, lying down, or relaxing. **16.** to relieve weariness by cessation of exertion or labour. **17.** to be at ease; have tranquillity or peace. **18.** to repose in death. **19.** to be quiet or still. **20.** to cease from motion, come to rest, or stop. **21.** to become or remain inactive. **22.** to remain without further action or notice: *to let a matter rest.* **23.** to lie, sit, lean, or be set (fol. by *in, on, against,* etc.): *his arm rested on the table.* **24.** *Agric.* to lie fallow or unworked: *to let land rest.* **25.** to be imposed as a burden or responsibility (fol. by *on* or *upon*). **26.** to rely (fol. by *on* or *upon*). **27.** to be based or founded (fol. by *on* or *upon*). **28.** to be found or be (where specified): *the blame rests with them.* **29.** to be present; dwell; linger (fol. by *on* or *upon*): *the moonlight rests upon the floor.* **30.** to be a responsibility, as something to be done (fol. by *in* or *with*): *it rests with you to complete the job.* **31.** to be fixed or directed on something, as the gaze, eyes, etc. **32.** *Law.* to terminate voluntarily the introduction of evidence in a case. **33.** *Theat. Colloq.* to be unemployed, as an actor. **34. rest on one's laurels,** to allow one's reputation to rely on past achievements, and make no further effort. **35. rest on one's oars, a.** *Rowing.* to stop rowing. **b.** to suspend any activity for a time. *—v.t.* **36.** to give rest to; refresh with rest: *to rest oneself.* **37.** to lay or place for rest, ease, or support: *to rest one's back against a tree.* **38.** to direct (the eyes, etc.): *to rest one's eyes on someone.* **39.** to base, or let depend, as on some ground of reliance. **40.** to bring to rest; halt; stop. **41.** *Law.* to terminate voluntarily the introduction of evidence on: *to rest one's case.* [ME *resten*, OE *restan*, c. OHG *restan*, akin to G *rasten*]
rest[2] (rĕst), *n.* **1.** that which is left or remains; the remainder: *the rest of the money is his.* **2.** the others; those who are left; everyone else: *all the rest are going.* **3.** *Banking.* the reserve fund as shown in the Bank of England return, which has been accumulated from profits which are added from time to time. **4.** the break which a banker makes in the accounts of his customers at the half-yearly balance. [late ME *reste*, t. F, der. *rester*, v. (see below)] *—v.i.* **5.** to continue to be; remain (as specified): *rest assured.* [late ME, t. F: s. *rester*, g. L *restāre* remain]

re′spec′ify′, *v.t.*, **-fied, -fying.**
re′splice′, *v.t.*, **-spliced, -splicing.**
re′spread′, *v.t.*, **-spread, -spreading.**
re′sprin′kle, *v.t.*, **-kled, -kling.**

rest³ (rĕst), *n. Armour.* a lance rest. [ME, aphetic var. of *arest* ARREST, n.]

restate (rē/stāt/), *v.t.*, **-stated, -stating.** to state again or in a new way. —**re/state/ment,** *n.*

restaurant (rĕs/tə rŏnt/, rĕs/trŏnt), *n.* an establishment where meals are served to customers. [t. F, special use of ppr. of *restaurer* RESTORE]

restaurant car, a railway carriage in which meals are served.

restauranteur (rĕs/tə rŏn tû/), *n.* restaurateur. Also, **restauranter** (rĕs/tə rŏn/tə).

restaurateur (rĕs/tŏ rə tû/; *Fr.* rĕs tŏ rȧ tœr/), *n.* the keeper of a restaurant. [F, der. *restaurer* RESTORE]

rest cure, *Med.* a treatment for nervous disorders, consisting of a complete rest, usually combined with systematic diet, massage, etc.

restful (rĕst/fəl), *adj.* **1.** full of, or giving, rest. **2.** being at rest; quiet; tranquil; peaceful. —**rest/fully,** *adv.* —**rest/fulness,** *n.* —**Ant. 1.** disturbing.

rest-harrow (rĕst/hă/rō), *n.* any of several European plants of the leguminous genus *Ononis*, esp. *O. repens* and *O. spinosa*, which have tough stems and roots that hinder the plough. [f. REST¹ + HARROW]

restiform bodies (rĕs/tĭ fôm/), *Anat.* a pair of cordlike bundles of nerve fibres lying one on each side of the medulla oblongata and connecting it with the cerebellum. [*restiform* t. NL: s. *restiformis*, f. L: *resti(s)* rope, cord + *-formis* -FORM]

resting (rĕs/tĭng), *adj.* **1.** that rests. **2.** *Bot.* dormant (applied esp. to spores or seeds which germinate after a period of dormancy).

resting place, 1. a place where a person may rest. **2.** a place of burial; the grave.

restitute (rĕs/tĭ tyōōt/), *v.t., v.i.* to make restitution (of).

restitution (rĕs/tĭ tyōō/shən), *n.* **1.** reparation made by giving an equivalent or compensation for loss, damage, or injury caused; indemnification. **2.** the restoration of property or rights previously taken away, conveyed, or surrendered. **3.** restoration to the former or original state or position. **4.** *Physics.* the return of an elastic material to its original form when released from strain. [ME *restitucion*, t. L: m. s. *restitūtio* a restoring] —**Syn. 1.** See **redress.**

restive (rĕs/tĭv), *adj.* **1.** restless; uneasy; impatient of control, restraint, or delay, as persons. **2.** refractory. **3.** refusing to go forward, as a horse. [f. REST² (def. 5) + -IVE; r. ME *restif* stationary, balking, t. OF: inert] —**res/tively,** *adv.* —**res/tiveness,** *n.*

restless (rĕst/lĭs), *adj.* **1.** characterized by or showing inability to remain at rest: *a restless mood.* **2.** unquiet or uneasy, as a person, the mind, heart, etc. **3.** never at rest, motionless, or still; never ceasing. **4.** without rest; without restful sleep: *a restless night.* **5.** characterized by unceasing activity; averse to quiet or inaction, as persons. —**rest/lessly,** *adv.* —**rest/lessness,** *n.*

rest mass, *Physics.* the mass of a body which is at rest relative to the observer.

restock (rē/stŏk/), *v.t., v.i.* to stock again; replenish.

restoration (rĕs/tə rā/shən), *n.* **1.** the act of restoring; renewal, revival, or re-establishment. **2.** the state or fact of being restored. **3.** a bringing back to a former, original, normal, or unimpaired condition. **4.** restitution of something taken away or lost. **5.** something which is restored. **6.** a representation or reconstruction of an ancient building, extinct animal, or the like, showing it in its original state. **7.** a putting back into a former position, dignity, etc. **8. the Restoration, a.** the re-establishment of the monarchy in England with the return of Charles II in 1660. **b.** the period of the reign of Charles II (1660–85), sometimes extended to include the reign of James II (1685–88). —*adj.* **9.** (*cap.*) denoting, pertaining to, or produced during the period of the Restoration, esp. a form of drama: *Restoration comedy.*

restorative (rĭ stŏ/rə tĭv, -stô/-), *adj.* **1.** serving to restore; pertaining to restoration. **2.** capable of renewing health or strength. —*n.* **3.** a restorative agent. **4.** a means of restoring a person to consciousness.

restore (rĭ stô/), *v.t.*, **-stored, -storing. 1.** to bring back into existence, use, or the like; re-establish: *to restore order.* **2.** to bring back to a former, original, or normal condition, as a building, statue, or painting. **3.** bring back to a state of health, soundness, or vigour. **4.** to put back to a former place, or to a former position, rank, etc. **5.** to give back; make return or restitution of (anything taken away or lost). **6.** to reproduce, reconstruct, or represent (an ancient building, extinct animal, etc.) in the original state. [ME, t. OF: m. s. *restorer*, g. L *restaurāre* restore, repair] —**restor/er,** *n.* —**Syn. 2.** See **renew.**

restrain (rĭ strān/), *v.t.* **1.** to hold back from action; keep in check or under control; keep down; repress. **2.** to deprive of liberty, as a person. [ME *restreyn(en)*, t. OF: m. *restrei(g)n-*, s. *restreindre*, g. L *restringere*] —**restrain/able,** *adj.* —**restrainedly** (rĭ strā/nĭd lĭ), *adv.* —**Syn. 1.** curb, bridle. See **check.**

restrainer (rĭ strā/nə), *n.* **1.** one who or that which restrains. **2.** a chemical, as potassium bromide, added to a photographic developer to retard its action.

restraining order, an injunction made by a court, as one to prevent a husband from visiting his wife during divorce proceedings.

restraint (rĭ strānt/), *n.* **1.** restraining action or influence: *freedom from restraint.* **2.** a means of restraining. **3.** the act of restraining, or holding back, controlling, or checking. **4.** the state or fact of being restrained; deprivation of liberty; confinement. **5.** constraint or reserve in feelings. [ME *restraynte*, t. OF: m. *restraint(e)*, n. use of pp. of *restraindre* restrain] —**Ant. 4.** liberty.

restraint of trade, the restriction of business activity and freedom to compete.

restrict (rĭ strĭkt/), *v.t.* to confine or keep within limits, as of space, action, choice, quantity, etc. [t. L: s. *restrictus*, pp., restrained, restricted] —**restrict/ed,** *adj.* —**restrict/edly,** *adv.* —**Syn.** curb, circumscribe, abridge.

restricted (rĭ strĭk/tĭd), *adj.* **1.** *Mil.* limited to persons authorized to have access, as to information, etc. **2.** *Chiefly U.S.* admitting only members of certain groups, as hotels and the like in segregated localities.

restricted area, 1. an area in which traffic is not permitted to exceed a certain speed. **2.** *Chiefly U.S.* any area from which certain groups or races of people are excluded.

restriction (rĭ strĭk/shən), *n.* **1.** something that restricts; a restrictive condition or regulation; a limitation. **2.** the act of restricting. **3.** the state of being restricted.

restrictive (rĭ strĭk/tĭv), *adj.* **1.** tending or serving to restrict. **2.** of the nature of a restriction. **3.** expressing or implying restriction or limitation of application, as terms, expressions, etc. —**restric/tively,** *adv.*

restrictive clause, *Gram.* a relative clause, usually not set off by commas, which identifies the person or object named by the antecedent (opposed to *descriptive clause*).

restrictive practice, 1. a practice on the part of the members of an association such as a trade union, tending to limit the freedom of choice of their coworkers or employers. **2.** a restrictive trade practice.

restrictive trade practice, a trading agreement contrary to the public interest.

rest-room (rĕst/rŏŏm/, -rōōm/), *n.* **1.** a room set aside for people to rest in, as in an office, factory, etc. **2.** *U.S.* a lavatory, or similar room having washing facilities, etc.

result (rĭ zŭlt/), *n.* **1.** that which results; the outcome, consequence, or effect. **2.** *Maths.* a quantity, value, etc., obtained by calculation. —*v.i.* **3.** to spring, arise, or proceed as a consequence from actions, circumstances, premises, etc.; be the outcome. **4.** to terminate or end in a specified manner or thing. **5.** *Law.* to revert. [late ME, t. L: s. *resultāre* spring back] —**Syn. 1.** See **effect. 3.** See **follow.** —**Ant. 1.** cause.

resultant (rĭ zŭl/tənt), *adj.* **1.** that results; following as a result or consequence. **2.** resulting from the combination of two or more agents: *a resultant force.* —*n.* **3.** *Physics.* a force, velocity, etc., equal in result or effect to two or more other forces, velocities, etc. **4.** that which results.

resultant note, *Acoustics.* an effect in which the vibrations of two notes, fairly close in pitch and sounded simultaneously, give rise to a further set of vibrations which may be heard as a third note. The principle is sometimes used by organ-builders to provide an inexpensive equivalent of a deep register. Also, **resultant tone.**

---

re/sta/bilize/, *v.t.,* **-lized, -lizing.**
re/sta/ble, *v.t.,* **-bled, -bling.**
re/stack/, *v.t.*
re/staff/, *v.t.*
re/stage/, *v.t.,* **-ged, -ging.**
re/stamp/, *v.t.*
re/start/, *v.*
re/sta/tion, *v.t.*
re/ster/ilize/, *v.t.,* **-lized, -lizing.**
re/stim/ulate/, *v.t.,* **-lated, -lating.**
re/stir/, *v.t.,* **-stirred, -stirring.**
re/stitch/, *v.t.*
re/straigh/ten, *v.*
re/streng/then, *v.t.*
re/stress/, *v.t.*
re/strike/, *v.t.* **-struck, -striking.**
re/string/, *v.t.,* **-strung, -stringing.**
re/stud/y, *v.t.,* **-studied, -studying.**
re/stuff/, *v.t.*
re/style/, *v.t.,* **-styled, -styling.**
re/subject/, *v.t.*
re/submerge/, *v.,* **-merged, -merging.**
re/submit/, *v.,* **-mitted, -mitting.**
re/subscribe/, *v.i.,* **-scribed, -scribing.**

---

resume (rĭ zyōōm′), *v.*, **-sumed, -suming.** —*v.t.* **1.** to take up or go on with again after interruption: *to resume a journey.* **2.** to take or occupy again: *to resume one's seat.* **3.** to take, or take on, again: *to resume one's maiden name.* **4.** to take back. —*v.i.* **5.** to go on or continue after interruption. **6.** to begin again. [late ME, t. L: m. s. *resūmere* take up again] —**resum′able,** *adj.* —**resum′er,** *n.*

résumé (rĕz′yōō mā′; *Fr.* rė zʏ mė′), *n.* a summing up; a summary. [t. F, prop. pp. of *résumer* RESUME]

resumption (rĭ zŭmp′shən), *n.* **1.** the act of resuming; a taking back, as of something previously granted. **2.** a taking up or going on with again, as of something interrupted. **3.** a taking, or taking on, again, as of something given up or lost. [late ME, t. L: s. *resumptio*]

resumptive (rĭ zŭmp′tĭv), *adj.* **1.** summarizing. **2.** repeating; repetitive.

resupinate (rĭ syōō′pĭ nĭt), *adj.* **1.** bent backwards. **2.** *Bot.* inverted; appearing as if upside down. [t. L: m. s. *resupinātus,* pp., bent back]

resupination (rĭ syōō′pĭ nā′shən), *n.* *Bot.* resupinate condition.

resupine (rĭ syōō′pīn), *adj.* lying on the back; supine. [t. L: m. s. *resupīnus*]

resurface (rē′sû′fĭs), *v.t.*, **-faced, -facing.** to give a new surface to.

resurgam (rĭ sû′găm), *Latin.* I shall rise again.

resurge (rĭ sûj′), *v.i.*, **-surged, -surging.** to rise again, as from the dead. [t. L: m. s. *resurgere* rise again]

resurgent (rĭ sû′jənt), *adj.* **1.** rising or tending to rise again. —*n.* **2.** one who has risen again. —**resur′gence,** *n.*

resurrect (rĕz′ə rĕkt′), *v.t.* **1.** to raise from the dead; bring to life again. **2.** to bring back into use, practice, etc.: *to resurrect an ancient custom.* —*v.i.* **3.** to rise from the dead. [back-formation from RESURRECTION]

resurrection (rĕz′ə rĕk′shən), *n.* **1.** the act of rising again from the dead. **2.** (*cap.*) the rising again of Christ after His death and burial. **3.** (*cap.*) the rising again of men on the judgement day. **4.** the state of those risen from the dead. **5.** a rising again, as from decay, disuse, etc.; revival. [ME *resur(r)ectioun,* t. LL: m. s. *resurrectio*] —**res′urrec′tional,** *adj.*

resurrectionary (rĕz′ə rĕk′shə nə rĭ), *adj.* **1.** pertaining to or of the nature of resurrection. **2.** pertaining to resurrectionism.

resurrectionism (rĕz′ə rĕk′shə nĭz′əm), *n.* **1.** belief in resurrection. **2.** *Hist.* exhuming and stealing of dead bodies, esp. for dissection; body-snatching.

resurrectionist (rĕz′ə rĕk′shə nĭst), *n.* **1.** one who brings something to life or view again. **2.** a believer in resurrection. **3.** *Rom. Cath. Ch.* a member of the 'Congregation of the Resurrection', founded in 1836. **4.** *Hist.* one who exhumes and steals dead bodies, esp. for dissection; body-snatcher.

resurrection pie, *Colloq.* a pie of reheated meat.

resuscitate (rĭ sŭs′ĭ tāt′), *v.t., v.i.*, **-tated, -tating.** to revive, esp. from apparent death or from unconsciousness. [t. L: m. s. *resuscitātus,* pp., revived] —**resuscitable** (rĭ sŭs′ĭ tə bl), *adj.* —**resus′cita′tion,** *n.* —**resus′citative,** *adj.* —**resus′cita′tor,** *n.*

ret (rĕt), *v.t.*, **retted, retting.** to expose to moisture or soak in water, as flax, in order to soften by partial rotting. [ME *retten, reten,* akin to D *reten.* Cf. also D *roten,* c. d. E *rait,* t. Scand.; cf. Sw. *röta* ret]

ret., **1.** retired. **2.** returned.

retable (rĭ tā′bl), *n.* a decorative structure raised above an altar at the back, often forming a frame for a picture, bas-relief, or the like, and sometimes including a shelf or shelves, as for ornaments. [t. F, f. OF *rere* at the back (g. L *retrō*) + *table* TABLE]

retail (rē′tāl *for 1–4, 6*; rĭ tāl′ *for 5*), *n.* **1.** the sale of commodities to household or ultimate consumers, usually in small quantities (opposed to *wholesale*). —*adj.* **2.** pertaining to, connected with, or engaged in sale at retail: *the retail price.* —*adv.* **3.** at a retail price or in a retail quantity; at retail. —*v.t.* **4.** to sell at retail; to sell directly to the consumer. **5.** to relate or repeat in detail to others: *to retail scandal.* —*v.i.* **6.** to be sold at retail: *it retails at sixpence.* [late ME, t. AF: a cutting, der. *retailler* cut, clip, pare, f. *re-* RE- + *tailler* cut] —**re′tailer,** *n.*

retain (rĭ tān′), *v.t.* **1.** to keep possession of. **2.** to continue to use, practice, etc.: *to retain an old custom.* **3.** to continue to hold or have: *this cloth retains its colour.* **4.** to keep in mind; remember. **5.** to hold in place or position. **6.** to engage, esp. by the payment of a preliminary fee, as a barrister. [ME *reteyne,* t. OF: m. *retenir,* g. Rom. *retenēre,* r. L *retinēre* hold back, keep. Cf. CONTAIN, DETAIN] —**retain′able,** *adj.* —**retain′ment,** *n.* —**Syn. 1.** See **keep.** —**Ant. 1.** relinquish.

retained object, *Gram.* an object in a passive construction identical with the direct or indirect object in the corresponding active construction, as *me* in *the picture was shown me* (corresponding active construction: *they showed me the picture*).

retainer[1] (rĭ tā′nə), *n.* **1.** one who or that which retains. **2.** *Hist.* one attached to a noble household or owing it service. **3.** any servant, esp. a personal or family servant of long standing. **4.** *Mach.* the groove or frame in which roller-bearings operate. [f. RETAIN + -ER[1]]

retainer[2] (rĭ tā′nə), *n.* **1.** the act of retaining in one's service. **2.** the fact of being so retained. **3.** a fee paid to secure services, as of a barrister. **4.** a reduced rent paid during absence for a flat or lodging as an indication of future requirement. [t. F: m. *retenir,* inf. used as n. See RETAIN]

retaining fee, a retainer[2] (def. 3).

retaining wall, **1.** a wall built to hold back a mass of earth, etc. **2.** revetment.

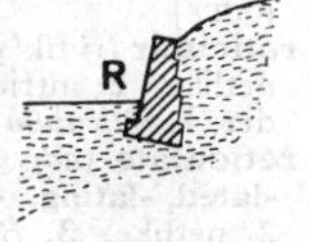

R, Retaining wall

retake (*v.* rē′tāk′; *n.* rē′tāk′), *v.*, **-took, -taken, -taking,** *n.* —*v.t.* **1.** to take again; take back. **2.** to recapture. **3.** *Films.* to film again. —*n.* **4.** a retaking, as of a picture. **5.** a scene, sequence, etc., which is to be or has been filmed again. —**re′tak′er,** *n.*

retaliate (rĭ tăl′ĭ āt′), *v.*, **-ated, -ating.** —*v.i.* **1.** to return like for like, esp. evil for evil or requital (esp. for an injury); take reprisals: *to retaliate for an injury.* —*v.t.* **2.** to make return for or requite (now usually wrong, injury, etc.) [t. LL: m. s. *retāliātus,* pp., requited] —**retaliative** (rĭ tăl′ĭ ə tĭv), **retaliatory** (rĭ tăl′ĭ ə tə rĭ, -trĭ), *adj.*

retaliation (rĭ tăl′ĭ ā′shən), *n.* the act of retaliating; return of like for like; reprisal.

retard (rĭ tăd′), *v.t.* **1.** to make slow; delay the progress of (an action, process, etc.); hinder or impede. **2.** to delay or limit (a person's intellectual or emotional development). —*v.i.* **3.** to be delayed. —*n.* **4.** retardation; delay. **5. in retard,** *Obs.* delayed. [t. L: s. *retardāre*] —**retard′er,** *n.* —**Ant. 1.** accelerate.

retardation (rē′tä dā′shən), *n.* **1.** the act of retarding. **2.** the state of being retarded. **3.** that which retards; a hindrance. **4.** *Physics.* deceleration; rate of decrease of velocity; negative acceleration. **5.** *Music.* a form of suspension which is resolved upwards. Also, **retard′ment.** —**retardative** (rĭ tä′də tĭv), **retardatory** (rĭ tä′də tə rĭ, -trĭ), *adj.*

retarded (rĭ tä′dĭd), *adj.* (of a child) **1.** slow in mental development, having an IQ of 70–85; backward. **2.** seriously delayed in school work, as due to protracted absence through illness; behind.

retarder (rĭ tä′də), *n.* **1.** that which or one who retards. **2.** *Chem.* a substance added to a composition, as paint, plaster, cement, etc., to slow down chemical or physical changes.

retch (rĕch), *v.i.* **1.** to make efforts to vomit. —*n.* **2.** the act or an instance of retching. [OE *hrǣcan* clear the throat (der. *hrāca* clearing of the throat), c. Icel. *hrǣkja* hawk, spit]

retd, **1.** retained. **2.** retired. **3.** returned.

rete (rē′tĭ), *n.*, *pl.* **retia** (rē′shyə, rē′tyə). a network, as of fibres, nerves, or blood vessels. [ME *riet,* t. L: m. *rēte* net]

retene (rē′tēn, rĕt′ēn), *n.* *Chem.* a crystalline hydrocarbon, $C_{18}H_{18}$, obtained from the tar of resinous woods, certain fossil resins, etc. [t. Gk: m. *rhētínē* resin. See -ENE]

retention (rĭ tĕn′shən), *n.* **1.** the act of retaining. **2.** the state of being retained. **3.** power to retain; capacity for retaining. **4.** the act or power of remembering things; memory. [ME, t. L: s. *retentio*]

retentive (rĭ tĕn′tĭv), *adj.* **1.** tending or serving to retain something. **2.** having power or capacity to retain. **3.** having power or ability to remember; having a good memory. —**reten′tiveness,** *n.*

---

re′sum′mon, *v.t.*
re′supply′, *v.t.*, **-plied, -plying.**
re′suppress′, *v.t.*
re′survey′, *v.t.*
re′sur′vey, *n.*
re′suspend′, *v.t.*
re′sweep′, *v.t.*, **-swept, -sweeping.**
re′swee′ten, *v.t.*
re′syn′thesis, *n., pl.* **-ses′.**
re′syn′thesize′, *v.t.*, **-sized, -sizing.**
re′tab′ulate′, *v.t.*, **-lated, -lating.**
re′tack′, *v.t.*
re′tape′, *v.t.*, **-taped, -taping.**
re′tar′, *v.t.*, **-tarred, -tarring.**
re′taste′, *v.t.*, **-tasted, -tasting.**
re′tax′, *v.t.*
re′teach′, *v.t.*, **-taught, -teaching.**
re′tell′, *v.t.*, **-told, -telling.**

---

retentivity (rē′tĕn tĭv′ĭ tĭ), *n.* **1.** power to retain; retentiveness. **2.** remanence.

retepore (rē′tĭ pô′), *n.* any bryozoan of the family *Reteporidae*, which forms colonies with a network-like structure. [t. NL: m. *Rētepora*, the typical genus, f. L *rēte* net + *-pora* (t. Gk: m. *póros* PORE)]

rethink (rē′thĭngk′), *v.*, **-thought, -thinking.** —*v.t.* **1.** to review or alter one's ideas on (a matter), one's plans, etc. —*v.i.* **2.** to think again (about something, etc.). [f. RE- + THINK]

R. et I., **1.** (L *Rex et Imperator*) King and Emperor. **2.** (L *Regina et Imperatrix*) Queen and Empress.

retiarius (rē′tĭ ĕə′rĭ əs, rē′shĭ-), *n.*, *pl.* **-arii** (-ĕə′rĭ ī′). *Rom. Hist.* a gladiator equipped with a net for casting over his opponent. [t. L, der. *rēte* net]

retiary (rē′tyə rĭ, rē′shyə rĭ), *adj.* **1.** using a net or any entangling device. **2.** netlike. **3.** making a net or web, as a spider.

reticent (rĕt′ĭ sənt), *adj.* disposed to be silent; not inclined to speak freely; reserved. [t. L: s. *reticens*, ppr., keeping silent] —**ret′icence,** *n.* —**ret′icently,** *adv.*

reticle (rĕt′ĭ kl), *n.* *Physics.* a network of fine lines, wires, or the like, placed in the focus of the objective of a telescope. [t. L: m. s. *rēticulum*, dim. of *rēte* net. Cf. RETICULE]

reticular (rĭ tĭk′yo͝o lə), *adj.* **1.** having the form of a net; netlike. **2.** intricate or entangled. [t. NL: s. *rēticulāris*, der. L *rēticulum* small net]

reticulate (*adj.* rĭ tĭk′yo͝o lĭt; *v.* rĭ tĭk′yo͝o lāt′), *adj.*, *v.*, **-lated, -lating.** —*adj.* **1.** netted; covered with a network. **2.** netlike. **3.** *Bot.* (of leaves, etc.) having the veins or nerves disposed like the threads of a net. —*v.t.* **4.** to form into a network. **5.** to cover or mark with a network. —*v.i.* **6.** to form a network. [t. L: m. s. *rēticulātus* made like a net]

reticulation (rĭ tĭk′yo͝o lā′shən), *n.* reticulated formation, arrangement, or appearance; a network.

reticule (rĕt′ĭ kyo͞ol′), *n.* **1.** a small purse or bag, orig. of network but later of silk, etc. **2.** *Physics.* reticle. [t. F, t. L: m. s. *rēticulum*, dim. of *rēte* net]

reticulum (rĭ tĭk′yo͝o ləm), *n.*, *pl.* **-la** (-lə). **1.** a network; any reticulated system or structure. **2.** *Anat.* reticular endothelial tissue. **3.** *Zool.* the second stomach of ruminating animals, between the rumen and the omasum. See diag. under **ruminant.** [t. L: little net]

retiform (rē′tĭ fôm′, rĕt′ĭ-), *adj.* netlike; reticulate. [t. NL: *rētiformis*, f. L *rēti-* (comb. form of *rēte* net) + *-formis* -FORM]

retina (rĕt′ĭ nə), *n.*, *pl.* **-nas, -nae** (-nē′). *Anat.* the innermost coat of the posterior part of the eyeball, consisting of a layer of light-sensitive cells connecting with the optic nerve by way of a record layer of nerve cells, and serving to receive the image. See diag. under **eye.** [ME, t. ML, ? der. L *rēte* net] —**ret′inal,** *adj.*

retinene (rĕt′ĭ nēn′), *n.* *Biochem.* the aldehyde of vitamin A, which combines with protein in the substance visual purple. [f. RETIN(A) + -ENE]

retinite (rĕt′ĭ nīt′), *n.* any of various fossil resins, esp. one of those derived from brown coal. [t. F, f. m. s. Gk *rhētínē* resin + *-ite* -ITE[1]]

retinitis (rĕt′ĭ nī′tĭs), *n.* *Pathol.* inflammation of the retina. [NL. See RETINA, -ITIS]

retinol (rĕt′ĭ nŏl′), *n.* a yellowish oil obtained by the distillation of resin, used as a solvent, a mild antiseptic, etc. [f. *retin-* (m. s. Gk *rhētínē* resin) + -OL[2]]

retinoscope (rĕt′ĭ nə skōp′), *n.* *Med.* a skiascope.

retinoscopy (rĕt′ĭ nŏs′kə pĭ), *n.* an objective method of determining the refractive error of an eye. [f. *retino-* (comb. form repr. RETINA) + -SCOPY] —**retinoscopic** (rĕt′ĭ nō skŏp′ĭk), *adj.*

retinue (rĕt′ĭ nyo͞o′), *n.* a body of retainers in attendance upon an important personage; a suite. [ME, t. OF: m. *retenue*, fem. pp. of *retenir* RETAIN]

retire (rĭ tī′ə), *v.*, **-tired, -tiring.** —*v.i.* **1.** to withdraw, or go away or apart, to a place of abode, shelter, or seclusion. **2.** to go to bed. **3.** to withdraw from office, business, or active life: *to retire at the age of sixty.* **4.** to fall back or retreat, as from battle or danger. **5.** to withdraw, go away, or remove oneself. **6.** *Cricket.* to leave the field often because of injury. —*v.t.* **7.** to withdraw from circulation by taking up and paying, as bonds, bills, etc. **8.** to withdraw or lead back (troops, etc.), as from battle or danger; retreat. **9.** to remove from active service or the usual field of activity, as an officer in the army or the navy. [t. F: m. s. *retirer* withdraw, f. *re-* RE- + *tirer* draw] —**Syn. 5.** See **depart.**

retired (rĭ tī′əd), *adj.* **1.** withdrawn from or no longer occupied with one's business or profession: *a retired sea-captain.* **2.** due or given a retired person: *retired pay.* **3.** withdrawn; secluded or sequestered.

retired list, a list of officers who are retired from active service and who may draw a pension.

retirement (rĭ tī′ə mənt), *n.* **1.** the act of retiring. **2.** the state of being retired. **3.** removal or retiring from service, office, or business. **4.** withdrawal into privacy or seclusion. **5.** privacy or seclusion. **6.** a private or secluded place. **7.** retreat of a military force. **8.** repurchase of its own securities by a company.

retiring (rĭ tī′ə rĭng), *adj.* **1.** that retires. **2.** withdrawing from contact with others; reserved; shy.

retorsion (rĭ tô′shən), *n.* *Internat. Law.* retaliation or reprisal by one state identical or similar to an act by an offending state, such as high tariffs or discriminating duties. Also, **retortion.** [t. ML: s. *retorsio*, var. of *retortio* RETORTION]

retort[1] (rĭ tôt′), *v.t.* **1.** to reply in retaliation; make a retort or retorts, often quickly and sharply; reply in kind to. **2.** to return (an accusation, epithet, etc.) upon the person uttering it. **3.** to answer (an argument or the like) by another to the contrary. —*n.* **4.** a severe, incisive, or witty reply, esp. one that counters a first speaker's statement, argument, etc. **5.** the act of retorting. [t. L: s. *retortus*, pp., twisted back] —**Syn. 4.** See **answer.**

retort[2] (rĭ tôt′), *n.* **1.** *Chem.* a vessel, commonly a glass bulb with a long neck bent downwards, used for distilling or decomposing substances by heat. **2.** *Metall.* a vessel, generally cylindrically shaped, within which an ore is heated so that the metal may be removed by distillation or sublimation. **3.** a large autoclave for sterilizing sealed food tins with superheated steam under pressure. [t. ML: s. *retorta*, prop. fem. pp., twisted back. See RETORT[1], v.]

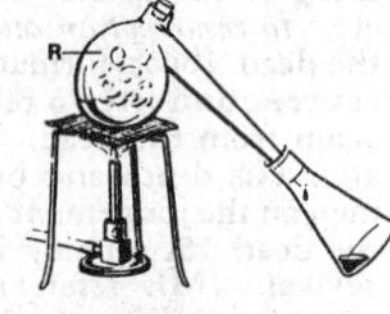
R, Retort[2] (def. 1)

retortion (rĭ tô′shən), *n.* **1.** the act of turning or bending back. **2.** retaliation. **3.** *Internat. Law.* retorsion. [t. ML: s. *retortio*, der. L *retortus*, pp., twisted back]

retouch (rē′tŭch′), *v.t.* **1.** to improve by new touches or the like, as a painting, make-up, etc. **2.** *Photog.* to correct or improve (a negative or print) by the use of a pencil, scraping knife, etc. —*n.* **3.** an added touch to a painting, etc., by way of improvement or alteration. —**re′touch′er,** *n.*

retrace (rĭ trās′), *v.t.*, **-traced, -tracing.** **1.** to trace back; go back over: *to retrace one's steps.* **2.** to go back over with the memory. **3.** to go over again with the sight or attention. [t. F: m. s. *retracer*, f. *re-* RE- + *tracer* TRACE[1]] —**retrace′able,** *adj.*

re-trace (rē′trās′), *v.t.*, **-traced, -tracing.** to trace again, as lines in writing or drawing. [f. RE- + TRACE[1] (defs 18, 19)]

retract[1] (rĭ trăkt′), *v.t.* to draw back or in. [late ME, t. L: s. *retractus*, pp., drawn back]

retract[2] (rĭ trăkt′), *v.t.* **1.** to withdraw (a statement, opinion, etc.) as unjustified. **2.** to withdraw or revoke (a decree, promise, etc.). —*v.i.* **3.** to draw or shrink back. **4.** to withdraw a promise, etc. **5.** to make disavowal of a statement, opinion, etc., or recant. [t. L: s. *retractāre* recall] —**retract′able,** *adj.* —**retractation** (rē′trăk tā′shən), *n.*

retractile (rĭ trăk′tīl), *adj.* *Zool.* capable of being drawn back or in, as the head of a tortoise; exhibiting the power of retraction. —**retractility** (rē′trăk tĭl′ĭ tĭ), *n.*

retraction (rĭ trăk′shən), *n.* **1.** the act of retracting. **2.** the state of being retracted. **3.** withdrawal of a promise, statement, opinion, etc.: *his retraction of the libel came too late.* **4.** retractile power.

retractive (rĭ trăk′tĭv), *adj.* tending or serving to retract.

retractor (rĭ trăk′tə), *n.* **1.** one who or that which retracts. **2.** *Anat.* a muscle that retracts an organ or protruded part, etc. **3.** *Surg.* an instrument or appliance for drawing back an impeding part.

retread (*v.* rē′trĕd′; *n.* rē′trĕd′), *v.*, **-treaded, -treading,** *n.*

---

re′tem′per, *v.t.*
re′test′, *v.t.*
re′test′, *n.*
re′tes′tify′, *v.*, **-fied, -fying.**
retex′ture, *v.t.*, **-tured, -turing.**
re′thatch′, *v.t.*
re′thick′en, *v.*
re′thread′, *v.t.*
re′threat′en, *v.t.*
re′tie′, *v.t.*, **-tied, -tying.**
re′tile′, *v.t.*, **-tiled, -tiling.**
re′time′, *v.t.*, **-timed, -timing.**
re′tint′, *v.t.*
re′ti′tle, *v.t.*, **-tled, -tling.**
re′tool′, *v.*
re′to′tal, *v.t.*, **-talled, -talling.**
re′train′, *v.*
re′transfer′, *v.t.*, **-ferred, -ferring.**
re′translate′, *v.t.*, **-lated, -lating.**
re′transmit′, *v.t.*, **-mitted, -mitting.**
re′transplant′, *v.t.*

—*v.t.* **1.** to recondition (a worn motor-vehicle tyre) by moulding a fresh tread (on to it) and vulcanizing by subjecting to heat and pressure. —*n.* **2.** a retreaded tyre. [f. RE- + TREAD]

re-tread (rē′trĕd′), *v.t.*, *v.i.*, **-trod, -trodden** or **-trod, -treading.** to tread again. [f. RE- + TREAD]

retreat (rĭ trēt′), *n.* **1.** the forced or strategic retirement of an armed force before an enemy, or the withdrawing of a ship or fleet from action. **2.** the act of withdrawing, as into safety or privacy; retirement; seclusion, **3.** a place of refuge, seclusion, or privacy. **4.** an asylum, as for the insane. **5.** a retirement, or a period of retirement, for religious exercises and meditation. **6.** a signal given in the army or navy by drum, bugle, or trumpet, at sunset. [ME *retret*, t. OF, var. of *retrait*, prop. pp. of *retraire* draw back, g. L *retrahere*] —*v.i.* **7.** to withdraw, retire, or draw back, esp. for shelter or seclusion. **8.** to make a retreat, as an army. **9.** *U.S.* to slope backwards; recede: *a retreating chin.* —*v.t.* **10.** to draw or lead back. [ME *retrete(n)*, der. *retret*, n., retreat] —**Syn. 7.** See **depart.** —**Ant. 1.** advance.

retrench (rĭ trĕnch′), *v.t.* **1.** to cut down, reduce, or diminish; curtail (expenses). **2.** to cut off or remove. **3.** *Mil.* to protect by a retrenchment. —*v.i.* **4.** to economize; reduce expenses: *they retrenched by cutting down staff.* [t. F (obs.): s. *retrencher*. See RE-, TRENCH]

retrenchment (rĭ trĕnch′mənt), *n.* **1.** the act of retrenching; a cutting down or off; reduction of expenses. **2.** *Fort.* **a.** an interior work which cuts off a part of a fortification from the rest, and to which a garrison may retreat. **b.** entrenchment.

retribution (rĕt′rĭ byo͞o′shən), *n.* **1.** requital according to merits or deserts, esp. for evil. **2.** something given or inflicted in such requital. **3.** *Theol.* the distribution of rewards and punishments in a future life. [ME, t. L: s. *retribūtio*] —**Syn. 2.** See **revenge.**

retributive (rĭ trĭb′yo͞o tĭv), *adj.* characterized by or involving retribution. Also, **retributory** (rĭ trĭb′yo͞o tə rĭ, -trĭ).

retrieval (rĭ trē′vəl), *n.* **1.** the act of retrieving. **2.** chance of recovery or restoration: *lost beyond retrieval.*

retrieve (rĭ trēv′), *v.*, **-trieved, -trieving,** *n.* —*v.t.* **1.** to recover or regain. **2.** to bring back to a former and better state; restore: *to retrieve one's fortunes.* **3.** to make amends for (an error, etc.). **4.** to make good; repair (a loss, etc.). **5.** *Hunting.* (of dogs) to find and fetch (killed or wounded game). **6.** to rescue or save. —*v.i.* **7.** *Hunting.* to retrieve game. —*n.* **8.** the act of retrieving; recovery. **9.** possibility of recovery. [ME *retreve*, t. OF: m. *retroev-* stressed stem of *retrouver*, f. *re-* RE- + *trouver* find. See TROVER] —**re-triev′able,** *adj.* —**Syn. 1.** See **recover.**

retriever (rĭ trē′və), *n.* **1.** one who or that which retrieves. **2.** any of several breeds of dog for retrieving game, as the golden retriever. **3.** any dog trained to retrieve game.

Labrador retriever (2 ft or more high at the shoulder)

retro-, a prefix meaning 'backwards' in space or time, e.g. *retrogression, retrospect.* [t. L, prefix repr. *retrō*, adv., backward, back, behind]

retroaction (rĕt′rō ăk′shən), *n.* action which is opposed or contrary to the preceding action.

retroactive (rĕt′rō ăk′tĭv), *adj.* operative with respect to past occurrences, as a statute; retrospective. —**ret′roac′tively,** *adv.* —**ret′roactiv′ity,** *n.*

retrobulbar (rĕt′rō bŭl′bə), *adj.* behind the eyeball.

retrocede[1] (rĕt′rō sēd′), *v.i.*, **-ceded, -ceding.** to go back; recede; retire. [t. L: m. *retrōcēdere* yield, go back] —**retrocession** (rĕt′rō sĕsh′ən), *n.*

retrocede[2] (rĕt′rō sēd′), *v.t.*, **-ceded, -ceding.** to cede back (territory, etc.). [f. RETRO- + CEDE] —**retrocession** (rĕt′rō sĕsh′ən), *n.*

retrochoir (rĕt′rō kwī′ə), *n.* that part of a church behind the choir or the high altar. [f. RETRO- + CHOIR, after ML *retrōchorus*]

retroflex (rĕt′rō flĕks′), *adj.* **1.** bent backwards; exhibiting retroflexion. **2.** *Phonet.* with the tip of the tongue raised or tilted upwards: *burn* has a retroflex vowel in a common American pronunciation. [t. L: s. *retrōflexus*, pp., bent back. See FLEX]

retroflexion (rĕt′rō flĕk′shən), *n.* **1.** a bending backwards. **2.** *Pathol.* a bending backwards of the body of the uterus. **3.** *Phonet.* **a.** retroflex articulation. **b.** the acoustic quality resulting from retroflex articulation; r-colour.

retrogradation (rĕt′rō grə dā′shən), *n.* **1.** backward movement. **2.** decline or deterioration.

retrograde (rĕt′rō grād′), *adj.*, *v.*, **-graded, -grading.** —*adj.* **1.** moving backwards; having a backward motion or direction; retiring or retreating. **2.** inverse or reversed, as order. **3.** *Chiefly Biol.* exhibiting degeneration or deterioration. **4.** *Astron.* **a.** denoting an apparent or actual motion in a direction opposite to the order of the signs of the zodiac, or from east to west. **b.** moving in an orbit in the direction opposite to that of the earth in its revolution round the sun. —*v.i.* **5.** to move or go backwards; retire or retreat. **6.** *Chiefly Biol.* to decline to a worse condition; degenerate. **7.** *Astron.* to have a retrograde motion. [ME *retrograd*, t. L: s. *retrōgradus* going backwards]

retrograde rocket, *Aeron.* retro-rocket.

retrogress (rĕt′rō grĕs′), *v.i.* **1.** to go backwards into a worse or earlier condition. **2.** to move backwards.

retrogression (rĕt′rō grĕsh′ən), *n.* **1.** the act of retrogressing; backward movement. **2.** *Biol.* degeneration; retrograde metamorphosis; passing from a more complex to a simpler structure.

retrogressive (rĕt′rō grĕs′ĭv), *adj.* characterized by retrogression; degenerating. —**ret′rogres′sively,** *adv.* —**Ant.** progressive.

retrolental fibroplasia (rĕt′rō lĕn′tl), the formation of fibrous tissue behind the lens of the eye due to the administration of too high concentrations of oxygen to premature babies, causing blindness. [*retrolental* f. RETRO- + *lent-* (s. L *lens* LENS) + -AL[1]]

retro-rocket (rĕt′rō rŏk′ĭt), *n.* *Aero.* **1.** a braking rocket used for slowing down a spacecraft and preparing it for re-entry. **2.** a rocket used to retard one part of a spacecraft from another, as its empty stages. Cf. **posigrade rocket.** Also, **retrograde rocket.**

retrorse (rĭ trôs′), *adj.* turned backwards. [t. L: m. s. *retrōrsus*, contr. of *retrōversus* bent or turned backwards] —**retrorse′ly,** *adv.*

retrospect (rĕt′rō spĕkt′), *n.* **1.** contemplation of the past; a survey of past time, events, etc. **2. in retrospect,** looking backwards in time. —*v.i. Rare.* **3.** to look back in thought. **4.** to refer back (fol. by *to*). —*v.t.* **5.** *Rare.* to look back upon, contemplate, or think of (something past). [back-formation from RETROSPECTION]

retrospection (rĕt′rō spĕk′shən), *n.* action or faculty of looking back on things past; a survey of past events or experiences. [f. s. L *retrōspectus* (pp. of *retrōspicere* look back at) + -ION]

retrospective (rĕt′rō spĕk′tĭv), *adj.* **1.** directed to the past; contemplative of past events, etc. **2.** looking or directed backwards. **3.** retroactive, as a statute. —*n.* **4.** an exhibition of an entire phase or representative examples of an artist's lifework. —**ret′rospec′tively,** *adv.*

retroussé (rə tro͞o′sā; *Fr.* rə tro͞o sĕ′), *adj.* (esp. of the nose) turned up. [t. F, pp. of *retrousser*, f. *re-* RE- + *trousser* TRUSS]

retroversion (rĕt′rō vû′shən), *n.* **1.** a looking or turning back. **2.** the resulting state or condition. **3.** *Pathol.* a tilting or turning backwards of an organ or part: *retroversion of the uterus.* [f. s. L *retrōversus* turned back + -ION]

retsina (rĕt sē′nə, rĕt′sĭ nə), *n.* a white or red Greek wine flavoured with resin from the pine tree while still in the cask. [t. NGk, t. It.: m. *resina* RESIN]

return (rĭ tûn′), *v.i.* **1.** to go or come back, as to a former place, position, state, etc. **2.** to revert to a former owner. **3.** to revert or recur in thought or discourse. **4.** to make reply; retort. —*v.t.* **5.** to put, bring, take, give, or send back: *return a book to its shelf.* **6.** to send or give back in reciprocation, recompense, or requital: *return shot for shot.* **7.** to reciprocate, repay, or requite (something sent, given, done, etc.) with something similar: *return the enemy's fire.* **8.** to answer; retort. **9.** *Law.* to render (a verdict, etc.). **10.** to reflect (light, sound, etc.). **11.** to yield (a profit, revenue, etc.), as in return for labour, expenditure, or investment. **12.** to report or announce officially. **13.** to elect, as to a legislative body. **14.** *Mil.* to put (a weapon) back into its holder. **15.** *Cards.* to respond to (a suit led) by a similar lead. **16.** to turn back or in the reverse direction. **17.** *Chiefly Archit.* to turn away from, or at an angle to, the previous line of direction. —*n.* **18.** the act or fact of returning; a going or coming back; a bringing, sending, or giving back. **19.** a recurrence: *many happy returns of the day.* **20.** reciprocation, repayment, or requital: *profits in return for outlay.* **21.** response or reply. **22.** one who or that which is returned. **23.** a ticket which is returned to a theatre box office by the original purchaser for resale. **24.** the gain realized on an exchange of goods. **25.** (*often pl.*) a yield or profit, as from

re′tri′al, *n.* **re′try′,** *v.t.*, **-tried, -trying.** **re′tune′,** *v.t.* **re′turf′,** *v.t.*

labour, land, business, investment, etc. **26.** a report, esp. a formal or official report: *tax returns; election returns.* **27.** the report or statement of financial condition. **28.** a return ticket. **29.** *Archit.* **a.** the continuation of a moulding, projection, etc., in a different direction. **b.** a side or part which falls away from the front of any straight work. **30.** *Sport.* **a.** the process of returning a ball. **b.** the ball which is returned. **31.** *Econ.* yield per unit as compared to the cost per unit involved in a specific industrial process. **32.** *Law.* **a.** the bringing or sending back of various documents, such as a writ, summons, or subpoena, with a brief written report usually endorsed upon it, by a sheriff, etc., to the court from which it issued. **b.** a certified return by a great variety of officers, such as assessors, collectors, and election officers. **c.** the report or certificate endorsed on such documents. **33.** *Cards.* a lead which responds to a partner's lead. **34. by return,** by the next post. —*adj.* **35.** of or pertaining to return or returning: *a return trip.* **36.** sent, given, or done in return: *a return shot.* **37.** done or occurring again: *a return engagement of the opera.* **38.** (of a game) played so that the loser of a game previous played between the same two players or teams has a chance for revenge. **39.** denoting a person or thing which is returned or returning to a place: *return cargo.* **40.** changing in direction; doubling or returning on itself: *return bend in the road.* [ME *retorne(n)*, t. OF: m. *retorner.* See RE-, TURN, V.]

returnable (rĭ tû′nə bl), *adj.* **1.** that may be returned. **2.** required to be returned.

return crease. See **crease** (def. 3c).

returning officer, an official responsible for the organization of an election, the accuracy of the count, the reading of the results, etc.

return pipe, the pipe in hot-water systems by which the water that has lost heat returns to the boiler.

return ticket, a ticket entitling the holder to travel to a destination and, within a specified period, to return to the point of departure.

retuse (rĭ tyo͞os′), *adj.* (of a leaf, etc.) having an obtuse or rounded apex with a shallow notch. [t. L: m. s. *retūsus*, pp., blunted]

Retuse leaf

Reuben (ro͞o′bĭn), *n.* **1.** the eldest son of Jacob and Leah. Gen. 29, 30, etc. **2.** one of the 12 tribes of Israel. Num. 32. [t. Heb.]

Reuchlin (*Ger.* rŏʏKH′lēn), *n.* **Johann** (*Ger.* yō′hän), 1455–1522, German humanist and scholar.

reunion (rē′yo͞o′nyən), *n.* **1.** the act of uniting again. **2.** the state of being united again. **3.** a gathering of relatives, friends, or associates after separation: *a family reunion.*

Réunion (rē yo͞o′nyən; *Fr.* rè ʏ nyôɴ′), *n.* an island in the Indian Ocean, E of Madagascar: a department of France. 363,000 (est. 1962); 970 sq. mi. *Cap.:* St Denis. See map under **Mauritius.**

reunionist (rē′yo͞o′nyə nĭst), *n.* one who advocates the reunion of the Anglican Church with the Roman Catholic Church. —**re′un′ionism,** *n.* —**re′un′ionis′tic,** *adj.*

reunite (rē′yo͞o nīt′), *v.t., v.i.,* **-nited, -niting.** to unite again, as after separation. —**re′unit′able,** *adj.* —**re′unit′er,** *n.*

Reuters (roi′təz), *n.* a British news agency, founded in London by Baron Paul Julius von Reuter (1816–99).

Reutlingen (*Ger.* rŏʏt′lĭng ən), *n.* a town in West Germany, in central Baden-Württemberg. 74,900 (est. 1966).

rev (rĕv), *n., v.,* **revved, revving.** *Colloq.* —*n.* **1.** a revolution (in an engine or the like). —*v.t.* **2.** to change, esp. to increase the speed of (in a specified way): *to rev a motor up.* —*v.i.* **3.** to undergo revving. [short for REVOLUTION]

Rev., **1.** Revelation. **2.** Revelations. **3.** Reverend.

rev., **1.** revenue. **2.** reverse. **3.** review. **4.** revise. **5.** revised. **6.** revision. **7.** revolution. **8.** revolving.

Reval (*Ger.* rè′väl), *n.* German name of **Tallinn.**

revalue (rē′văl′yo͞o), *v.t.,* **-ued, -uing.** to value again. —**re′val′ua′tion,** *n.*

revamp (rē′vămp′), *v.t.* to vamp afresh; renovate.

reveal (rĭ vēl′), *v.t.* **1.** to make known; disclose; divulge: *to reveal a secret.* **2.** to lay open to view; display; exhibit. —*n.* **3.** a revealing; revelation; disclosure. **4.** *Archit.* **a.** that part of a jamb, or vertical face of an opening for a window or door, included between the face of the wall and that of the frame containing the window or door. **b.** the whole jamb or vertical face of an opening. [ME *revele*, t. L: m. *revēlāre* unveil, reveal] —**reveal′able,** *adj.* —**reveal′er,** *n.*

—**Syn. 1, 2.** REVEAL, DISCLOSE, DIVULGE is to make known something previously concealed or secret. To REVEAL is to uncover as if by drawing away a veil: *the fog lifted and revealed the harbour.* To DISCLOSE is to lay open and thereby invite inspection: *to disclose the plans of an organization.* To DIVULGE is to communicate, sometimes to a large number, what was at first intended to be private, confidential, or secret: *to divulge the terms of a contract.* —**Ant. 2.** conceal, hide.

revealed religion, *Theol.* religion based upon divine revelation in which concepts could not have been reached by man's efforts alone.

revealment (rĭ vēl′mənt), *n.* the act of revealing; revelation.

revegetate (rē′vĕj′ĭ tāt′), *v.i.,* **-tated, -tating. 1.** to grow again, as plants. **2.** to put forth vegetation again, as plants.

reveille (rĭ văl′ĭ, rĭ vĕl′ĭ), *n.* a signal, as of a drum or bugle, sounded at a prescribed hour, to waken soldiers or sailors for the day's duties. [t. F: m. *réveillez*, impv. pl. of *réveiller* awaken, f. *re-* RE- + *veiller*, g. L *vigilāre* keep watch]

revel (rĕv′əl), *v.,* **-elled, -elling** or (*U.S.*) **-eled, -eling,** *n.* —*v.i.* **1.** to take great pleasure or delight (fol. by *in*). **2.** to make merry; indulge in boisterous festivities. —*n.* **3.** boisterous merrymaking or festivity; revelry. **4.** (*often pl.*) an occasion of merrymaking or noisy festivity with dancing, etc. [ME *revel(en)*, t. OF: m. *reveler*, orig., to make noise, rebel, g. L *rebellāre.* See REBEL] —**rev′eller,** *n.*

Revel (*Russ.* rè′vĭly), *n.* Russian name of **Tallinn.**

revelation (rĕv′ĭ lā′shən), *n.* **1.** the act of revealing or disclosing; disclosure. **2.** something revealed or disclosed, esp. a striking disclosure, as of something not before realized. **3.** *Theol.* **a.** God's disclosure of Himself and of His will to His creatures. **b.** an instance of such communication or disclosure. **c.** something thus communicated or disclosed. **d.** that which contains such disclosure, as the Bible. **4. Revelation,** (*often pl.*) the Revelation of St John the Divine. [ME, t. L: s. *revēlātio*]

revelationist (rĕv′ĭ lā′shə nĭst), *n.* one who believes in divine revelation.

Revelation of St John the Divine, The, the last book in the New Testament; the Apocalypse.

revelator (rĕv′ĭ lā′tə), *n.* one who makes a revelation.

revelry (rĕv′əl rĭ), *n., pl.* **-ries.** revelling; boisterous festivity: *the sound of their revelry could be heard across the river.*

revenant (rev′ĭ nənt), *n.* **1.** one who returns. **2.** one who returns as a spirit after death; a ghost. [t. F, prop. ppr. of *revenir* return, f. *re-* RE- + *venir* come, g. L *venīre*]

revenge (rĭ vĕnj′), *n., v.,* **-venged, -venging.** —*n.* **1.** the act of revenging; retaliation for injuries or wrongs; vengeance. **2.** something done in revenging. **3.** the desire to revenge; vindictiveness. **4.** an opportunity of retaliation or satisfaction. —*v.t.* **5.** to take vengeance or exact expiation on behalf of (a person, etc.) or for (a wrong, etc.) esp. in a resentful or vindictive spirit. —*v.i.* **6.** *Obs.* to take revenge. [ME, t. OF: m. s. *revengier*, f. *re-* RE- + *vengier* VENGE] —**reveng′er,** *n.*

—**Syn. 1.** REVENGE, REPRISAL, RETRIBUTION, VENGEANCE suggest a punishment, or injury inflicted in return for one received. REVENGE is the carrying out of a bitter desire to injure another for a wrong done to oneself or to those who seem a part of oneself: *to plot revenge.* REPRISAL, formerly any act of retaliation, is used specifically in warfare for retaliation upon the enemy for his (usually unlawful) actions: *to make a raid in reprisal for one by the enemy.* RETRIBUTION suggests just or deserved punishment, often without personal motives, for some evil done: *a just retribution for wickedness.* VENGEANCE is usually wrathful, vindictive, furious revenge: *implacable vengeance.* **5.** See avenge.

revengeful (rĭ vĕnj′fəl), *adj.* full of revenge; vindictive. —**revenge′fully,** *adv.* —**revenge′fulness,** *n.* —**Syn.** See **spiteful.**

revenue (rĕv′ĭ nyo͞o′), *n.* **1.** the income of a government from taxation, excise duties, customs, or other sources, appropriated to the payment of the public expenses. **2.** the government department charged with the collection of such income. **3.** (*pl.*) the collective items or amounts of income of a person, a state, etc. **4.** the return or yield from any kind of property; income. **5.** an amount of money regularly coming in. **6.** a particular item or source of income. [late ME, t. F, orig. fem. pp. of *revenir* return, f. *re-* RE- + *venir* come]

revenue cutter. See **cutter** (def. 4).

revenue stamp, *U.S.* a stamp showing that a government tax has been paid.

reverberant (rĭ vû′bə rənt), *adj.* reverberating; reechoing.

reverberate (rĭ vû′bə rāt′), *v.,* **-rated, -rating.** —*v.i.*

re′twine′, *v.,* **-twined, -twining.**
re′twist′, *v.*
re′type′, *v.t.,* **-typed, -typing.**
re′u′nifica′tion, *n.*
re′u′nify′, *v.t.,* **-fied, -fying.**
re′uphol′ster, *v.t.*
re′us′able, *adj.*
re′use′, *v.t.,* **-used, -using,** *n.*
re′u′tilize′, *v.t.,* **-lized, -lizing.**
re′vac′cinate′, *v.t.,* **-nated, -nating.**
re′va′porize′, *v.,* **-rized, -rizing.**
re′var′nish, *v.t.*
re′vend′, *v.t.*

1. to re-echo or resound. 2. *Physics.* to be reflected many times, as soundwaves from the walls, etc., of a confined space. 3. to rebound or recoil. 4. to be deflected, as flame in a reverberatory furnace. —*v.t.* 5. to echo back or re-echo (sound). 6. to cast back or reflect (light, etc.). 7. to treat (a substance) in a reverberatory furnace or the like. 8. to deflect (flame or heat) on something, as in a reverberatory furnace. [t. L: m. *reverberātus*, pp., beaten back] —**reverberative** (rĭ vûʹbə rə tĭv), *adj.* —**reverʹberaʹtor,** *n.*

reverberation (rĭ vûʹbə rāʹshən), *n.* 1. a re-echoed sound. 2. the fact of being reverberated or reflected. 3. that which is reverberated. 4. an act or instance of reverberating. 5. *Physics.* multiple reflection of sound in a room, causing a sound to persist after the stopping of the source. 6. the action or process of subjecting something to reflected heat as in a reverberatory furnace. [ME, t. L: s. *reverberātio*]

reverberation time, *Physics.* the time taken, in seconds, for a sound made in a room or auditorium to diminish by 60 decibels. Also, **reverberation period.**

reverberatory (rĭ vûʹbə rə tə rĭ, -trĭ), *adj.*, *n.*, *pl.* **-ries.** —*adj.* 1. characterized or produced by reverberation. 2. denoting a furnace, kiln, or the like, in which the fuel is not in direct contact with the ore, metal, etc., to be heated, but furnishes a flame that plays over the material, esp. by being deflected downwards from the roof. 3. deflected, as flame. —*n.* 4. any device, as a furnace, embodying reverberation.

Section of reverberatory furnace

revere (rĭ vĭəʹ), *v.t.*, **-vered, -vering.** to regard with respect tinged with awe; venerate. [t. L: m. s. *reverērī* feel awe of, fear, revere]

Revere (rĭ vĭəʹ), *n.* **Paul,** 1735–1818, American patriot, famous for his night horseback ride to warn Massachusetts colonists of the coming of British troops.

reverence (rĕvʹə rəns, rĕvʹrəns), *n.*, *v.*, **-renced, -rencing.** —*n.* 1. the feeling or attitude of deep respect tinged with awe; veneration. 2. the outward manifestation of this feeling: *to pay reverence.* 3. a gesture indicative of deep respect; an obeisance, bow, or curtsy. 4. the state of being revered. 5. (*cap.*) a title used in addressing or mentioning a clergyman (prec. by *your* or *his*). —*v.t.* 6. to regard or treat with reverence; venerate. [ME, t. L: m. *reverentia*]

—**Syn.** 1. REVERENCE, WORSHIP imply sentiments of respect and homage. REVERENCE is a strong feeling of deference, respect, and esteem: *reverence shown to the venerable and wise.* WORSHIP, which is associated with an exalted religious feeling of reverence and love, refers primarily not to the feeling itself but to its manifestation in certain practices: *the worship of idols.* Thus, even in such expressions as *worship of beauty*, there is the suggestion of a way of behaviour. —**Ant.** 1. irreverence, contempt.

reverend (rĕvʹə rənd, rĕvʹrənd), *adj.* 1. (*often cap.*) an epithet of respect applied to, or prefixed to the name of, a clergyman. 2. worthy to be revered; entitled to reverence. 3. pertaining to or characteristic of the clergy. —*n.* 4. *Colloq.* a clergyman. [t. L: s. *reverendus*, ger. of *reverērī* revere]

Reverend Mother, the title of respect accorded the abbess or presiding nun of a convent.

reverent (rĕvʹə rənt, rĕvʹrənt), *adj.* feeling, exhibiting, or characterized by reverence; deeply respectful. [t. L: s. *reverens*, ppr., feeling awe of] —**revʹerently,** *adv.*

reverential (rĕvʹə rĕnʹshəl), *adj.* of the nature of or characterized by reverence; reverent: *reverential awe.* —**revʹerenʹtially,** *adv.*

reverie (rĕvʹə rĭ), *n.* 1. a state of dreamy meditation or fanciful musing: *lost in reverie.* 2. a daydream. 3. a fantastic, visionary, or unpractical idea. 4. *Music.* an instrumental composition of a vague and dreamy character. Also, **revery.** [t. F, der. *rêver* to dream]

revers (rĭ vĭəʹ), *n.*, *pl.* **-vers** (-vĭəzʹ). 1. a part of a garment turned back to show the lining or facing, as a lapel. 2. a trimming simulating such a part. 3. the facing used. [t. F. See REVERSE]

reversal (rĭ vûʹsəl), *n.* 1. the act of reversing. 2. an instance of this. 3. the state of being reversed. 4. *Law.* the revocation of a lower court's decision by an appellate court.

reverse (rĭ vûsʹ), *adj.*, *n.*, **-versed, -versing.** —*adj.* 1. opposite or contrary in position, direction, order, or character: *an impression reverse to what was intended.* 2. acting in a manner opposite or contrary to that which is usual, as an appliance or apparatus. 3. with the rear part towards one: *reverse side of a coin.* 4. producing a rearward motion: *reverse gear.* 5. *Motor Vehicles.* of or pertaining to reverse (gear ratio). 6. *Print.* of or pertaining to a type matter which appears white on a solid or screened background. —*n.* 7. the opposite or contrary of something. 8. the back or rear of anything. 9. *Coining.* that side of a coin, medal, etc., which does not bear the principal design (opposed to *obverse*). 10. an adverse change of fortune; a misfortune, check, or defeat: *to meet with an unexpected reverse.* 11. *Motor Vehicles.* a transmission gear ratio driving a car backwards. 12. *Mach.* a reversing mechanism, etc. 13. *Print.* type matter produced in reverse printing. —*v.t.* 14. to turn in an opposite position; transpose. 15. to turn inside out or upside down. 16. to turn in the opposite direction; send on the opposite course. 17. to turn in the opposite order: *to reverse the usual order.* 18. to alter to the opposite in character or tendency, or change completely. 19. to revoke or annul (a decree, judgement, etc.). 20. *Mach.* to cause to revolve or act in an opposite or contrary direction or manner. 21. to drive (a motor vehicle) backwards: *he reversed the car into a parking space.* 22. *Print.* to produce in reverse printing. (often fol. by *out*). 23. **reverse arms,** *Mil.* to carry out a drill manoeuvre in which the rifle is turned muzzle downwards. 24. **reverse stick,** *Hockey.* to hit the ball with the back of the stick, which is a foul. —*v.i.* 25. to turn or move in the opposite or contrary direction, as in dancing. 26. (of an engine) to reverse the action of the mechanism. 27. to drive a vehicle backwards: *he reversed into the garage.* [ME *revers*, t. L: s. *reversus*, pp., turned about] —**reverseʹly,** *adv.* —**reversʹer,** *n.*

—**Syn.** 1. See **opposite.** 14. REVERSE, INVERT agree in meaning to change into a contrary position, order, or relation. To REVERSE is to place or move something so that it is facing in the opposite direction from the one faced previously: *to reverse from right to left; to reverse a decision.* To INVERT is to turn upside down: *to invert a stamp in printing; to invert a bowl over a plate.*

reversible (rĭ vûʹsə bl), *adj.* 1. capable of being reversed or of reversing. 2. capable of re-establishing the original condition after a change by the reversal of that change. 3. (of a fabric, garment, etc.) woven or printed so that either side may be exposed. —*n.* 4. a garment, esp. a coat, that may be worn with either side exposed. —**reversʹibilʹity, reversʹibleness,** *n.* —**reversʹibly,** *adv.*

reversible reaction, *Chem.* a chemical reaction which, under suitable conditions, may be made to proceed in either direction.

reversion (rĭ vûʹshən), *n.* 1. the act of turning something the reverse way. 2. the state of being so turned; reversal. 3. the act of reverting; return to a former practice, belief, condition, etc. 4. *Biol.* **a.** reappearance of ancestral characters that have been absent in intervening generations. **b.** return to an earlier or primitive type; atavism. 5. Also, **reverter.** *Law.* **a.** the returning of an estate to the grantor or his heirs after the interest granted expires. **b.** an estate which so returns. **c.** the right of succeeding to an estate, etc. [ME, t. L: s. *reversio* a turning about]

reversionary (rĭ vûʹshə nə rĭ), *adj.* of, pertaining to, or involving a reversion. Also, **reverʹsional.**

reversioner (rĭ vûʹshə nə), *n.* *Law.* one who possesses a reversion.

reverso (rĭ vûʹsō), *n.* verso.

revert (rĭ vûtʹ), *v.i.* 1. to return to a former habit, practice, belief, condition, etc. 2. to go back in thought or discourse, as to a subject. 3. *Biol.* to return to an earlier or primitive type. 4. *Law.* to go back or to return to the former owner or his heirs. [ME *reverte(n)*, t. OF: m. *revertir*, g. LL *revertire*, r. L *revertere*] —**revertʹible,** *adj.*

reverter (rĭ vûʹtə), *n.* a reversion (def. 5).

revery (rĕvʹə rĭ), *n.*, *pl.* **-eries.** reverie.

revest (rēʹvĕstʹ), *v.t.* 1. to vest (a person, etc.) again, as with ownership or office; reinvest; reinstate. 2. to vest (powers, etc.) again. —*v.i.* 3. to become vested again in a person; go back again to a former owner.

revet (rĭ vĕtʹ), *v.t.*, **-vetted, -vetting.** to face, as an embankment, with masonry or other material. [t. F: m. s. *revêtir*, lit., clothe. See REVEST]

revetment (rĭ vĕtʹmənt), *n.* 1. a facing of masonry or the like, esp. for protecting an embankment. 2. a retaining wall. [t. F: m. *revêtement.* See REVET, -MENT]

review (rĭ vyo͞oʹ), *n.* 1. a critical article or report, as in a periodical, on some literary work, commonly some work of recent appearance; a critique. 2. a periodical publication containing articles on current events or affairs, books, art, etc.: *a literary review.* 3. a viewing again; a second or repeated view of something. 4. *Chiefly U.S.* revision (def. 3). 5. an inspection, or examination by viewing, esp. a formal inspection of any military or naval

reʹverʹifyʹ, *v.t.*, **-fied, -fying.**
reʹveʹto, *v.*, **-toed, -toing.**
reʹvibrateʹ, *v.*, **-brated, -brating.**
reʹvicʹtual, *v.*, **-ualled, -ualling.**

force, parade, or the like. **6.** a viewing of the past; contemplation or consideration of past events, circumstances, or facts. **7.** a general survey of something, esp. in words; a report or account of something. **8.** a judicial re-examination, as by a higher court, of the decision or proceedings in a case. [t. F: m. *revue*, orig. pp. fem. of *revoir* see again, g. L *revidēre*]
—*v.t.* **9.** to view, look at, or look over again. **10.** *Chiefly U.S.* to revise (def. 3). **11.** to inspect, esp. formally or officially. **12.** to look back upon; view retrospectively. **13.** to survey mentally; take a survey of: *to review the situation.* **14.** to present a survey of in speech or writing. **15.** to discuss (a book, etc.) in a critical review; write a critical report upon. **16.** *Law.* to re-examine judicially. —*v.i.* **17.** to write reviews; review books, etc., as for some periodical. [v. use of REVIEW, n.] —**review′able,** *adj.*

—**Syn. 1.** REVIEW, CRITICISM imply carefully examining something, making a judgement, and putting the judgement into (usually) written form. A REVIEW is a survey over a whole subject or division of it; or esp. an article making a critical reconsideration and summary of something written: *a review of the latest book on Chaucer.* A CRITICISM is a judgement, usually in an article, either favourable or unfavourable or both: *a criticism of a proposed plan.*

reviewal (rĭ vyōō′əl), *n.* the act of reviewing.
reviewer (rĭ vyōō′ə), *n.* **1.** one who reviews. **2.** one who writes reviews of new books, films, plays, etc.
revile (rĭ vīl′), *v.*, **-viled, -viling.** —*v.t.* **1.** to assail with contemptuous or opprobrious language; address, or speak of, abusively. —*v.i.* **2.** to speak abusively. [ME *revile(n)*, t. OF: m. *reviler* treat or regard as vile, der. *re-* RE- + *vil* VILE] —**revile′ment,** *n.* —**revil′er,** *n.* —**revil′ingly,** *adv.*
revisal (rĭ vī′zəl), *n.* the act of revising; revision.
revise (rĭ vīz′), *v.*, **-vised, -vising,** *n.* —*v.t.* **1.** to amend or alter: *to revise one's opinion.* **2.** to alter after one or more typings or printings: *to revise a manuscript, proof, or book.* **3.** to go over (a subject, book, etc.) again or study in order to fix it in the memory, as before an examination. —*v.i.* **4.** to go over a subject or the like again to fix it in the memory. —*n.* **5.** a revising. **6.** a revised form of something. **7.** *Print.* a proof sheet taken after alterations have been made, for further examination or correction. [t. F: m. s. *reviser*, t. L: m. *revīsere* go to see again, look back on] —**revis′er,** *n.*
Revised Version of the Bible, a recension of the King James Version of the Bible, prepared by a committee of British and American scholars, the Old Testament being published in 1885, and the New Testament in 1881.
revision (rĭ vĭzh′ən), *n.* **1.** the act or work of revising. **2.** a process of revising. **3.** the process of going over a subject or the like again to fix it in the memory. **4.** a revised form or version, as of a book. [t. LL: s. *revīsio*] —**revi′sional, revi′sionary,** *adj.*
revisionism (rĭ vĭzh′ə nĭz′əm), *n.* the advocacy or act of revising, esp. some political or religious doctrine, practice, or the like.
revisionist (rĭ vĭzh′ə nĭst), *n.* **1.** an advocate of revision, esp. of some political or religious doctrine. **2.** a reviser. —**revi′sionism,** *n.*
revisory (rĭ vī′zə rĭ), *adj.* pertaining to or for the purpose of revision.
revival (rĭ vī′vəl), *n.* **1.** the act of reviving. **2.** the state of being revived. **3.** restoration to life, consciousness, vigour, strength, etc. **4.** restoration to use, acceptance, or currency: *the revival of old customs.* **5.** a renewing of interest in a theory, practice, etc., of the past. **6.** the production anew of an old play. **7.** an awakening, in a church or a community, of interest in and care for matters relating to personal religion. **8.** a service or a series of services for the purpose of effecting a religious awakening: *to hold a revival.* **9.** *Law.* the re-establishment of legal force and effect.
revivalism (rĭ vī′və lĭz′əm), *n.* **1.** the tendency to revive what belongs to the past. **2.** that form of religious activity which manifests itself in revivals.
revivalist (rĭ vī′və lĭst), *n.* **1.** one who revives former customs or methods. **2.** one who promotes or holds religious revivals. —**revi′valis′tic,** *adj.*
Revival of Learning, the Renaissance in its relation to learning.
revive (rĭ vīv′), *v.*, **-vived, -viving.** —*v.t.* **1.** to set going or in activity again: *to revive old feuds.* **2.** to make operative or valid again. **3.** to bring back into notice, use, or currency: *to revive a subject of discussion.* **4.** to produce (an old play) again. **5.** to restore to life or consciousness. **6.** to reanimate or cheer (the spirit, heart, etc., or a person). **7.** to quicken or renew in the mind; bring back: *to revive memories.* **8.** *Chem.* to restore or reduce to its natural or uncombined state, as a metal. —*v.i.* **9.** to return to life, consciousness, vigour, strength, or a flourishing condition. **10.** to recover from depression. **11.** to be quickened, restored, or renewed, as hope, confidence, suspicions, memories, etc. **12.** to return to notice, use, or currency, as a subject, practice, doctrine, etc. **13.** to become operative or valid again. **14.** *Chem.* to recover its natural or uncombined state, as a metal. [ME, t. L: m. *revīvere* live again]
reviver (rĭ vī′və), *n.* **1.** one who or that which revives. **2.** *Colloq.* an intoxicating drink; a stimulant.
revivify (rē vĭv′ĭ fī′), *v.t.*, **-fied, -fying.** to restore to life; give new life to; revive; animate anew. —**revivification** (rē vĭv′ĭ fĭ kā′shən), *n.*
reviviscence (rĕv′ĭ vĭs′əns), *n.* the act or state of being revived; revival; reanimation. Also, **rev′ivis′cency.** —**rev′ivis′cent,** *adj.*
revocable (rĕv′ə kə bl), *adj.* that may be revoked. Also, **revokable** (rĭ vō′kə bl). [late ME, t. L: m. s. *revocābilis*] —**rev′ocabil′ity,** *n.* —**rev′ocably,** *adv.*
revocation (rĕv′ə kā′shən), *n.* **1.** the act of revoking; annulment. **2.** *Law.* nullification or withdrawal, as, for example, of an offer to contract, a will, or a right of agency. [late ME, t. L: s. *revocātio*] —**revocatory** (rĕv′ə kə tə rĭ, -trĭ), *adj.*
revoice (rē′vois′), *v.t.*, **-voiced, -voicing. 1.** to voice again or in return; echo. **2.** to readjust the tone of.
revoke (rĭ vōk′), *v.*, **-voked, -voking,** *n.* —*v.t.* **1.** to take back or withdraw; annul, cancel, or reverse; rescind or repeal: *to revoke a decree.* **2.** *Now Rare.* to recall (what is past). —*v.i.* **3.** *Cards.* to fail to follow suit when one can and should do so; renege. —*n.* **4.** *Cards.* an act or instance of revoking; renege. [ME, t. L: m. *revocāre* call back] —**revok′er,** *n.*
revolt (rĭ vōlt′), *v.i.* **1.** to break away from or rise against constituted authority, as by open rebellion; cast off allegiance or subjection to those in authority; rebel; mutiny. **2.** to turn away in mental rebellion, utter disgust, or abhorrence (fol. by *from*); rebel in feeling (fol. by *against*); feel disgust or horror (fol. by *at*). —*v.t.* **3.** to affect with disgust or abhorrence. —*n.* **4.** the act of revolting; an insurrection or rebellion. **5.** aversion, disgust, or loathing. **6.** the state of those revolting: *to be in revolt.* [t. F: m. *révolte*, t. It.: m. *rivolta* revolt, turning, der. *rivoltare* turn, g. Rom. *revolvitāre*, der. L *revolvere* overturn, revolve] —**revolt′er,** *n.*

—**Syn. 4.** REVOLT, INSURRECTION, REBELLION, REVOLUTION refer to rising in active resistance against civil or governmental authority. A REVOLT is a casting off of allegiance or subjection to rulers or authorities; it is usually a vigorous outbreak, whether brief or prolonged, and may arise from general turbulence or from opposition to tyranny or oppression: *a revolt because of unjust government.* An INSURRECTION may be local or general, and is often unorganized: *a popular insurrection in one province.* A REBELLION is on a larger scale than either of the foregoing, is generally better organized, and has for its object the securing of independence or the overthrow of government: *a widespread rebellion.* A REVOLUTION is a rebellion or any public movement (with or without actual fighting) that succeeds in overthrowing one government or political system and establishing another: *the French Revolution.* Accordingly, it may be used metaphorically of any development that upsets the established order: *the Industrial Revolution.*

revolting (rĭ vōl′tĭng), *adj.* **1.** rebellious. **2.** disgusting; repulsive. —**revolt′ingly,** *adv.*
revolute (rĕv′ə lyōōt′), *adj. Biol.* rolled backwards or downwards; rolled backwards at the tip or margin, as a leaf. [t. L: m. s. *revolūtus*, pp., revolved]
revolution (rĕv′ə lōō′shən), *n.* **1.** a complete overthrow of an established government or political system, as the Glorious Revolution (1688), the French Revolution (1789), the Chinese Revolution (1911), or the Russian Revolution (1917). **2.** a complete or marked change in something. **3.** procedure or course as if in a circuit, as back to a starting point in time. **4.** a single turn of this kind. **5.** *Mech.* **a.** a turning round or rotating, as on an axis. **b.** a moving in a circular or curving course, as about a central point. **c.** a single cycle in such a course. **6.** *Astron.* **a.** (of a heavenly body) the action or fact of going round in an orbit. **b.** a single course of such movement. **c.** an apparent movement round the earth. **7.** round or cycle of events in time, or a recurring period of time. [ME *revolucion*, t. L: m. s. *revolūtio*] —**Syn. 1.** See **revolt.**

A
B
A, Revolute margined leaf; B, Transverse section

revolutionary (rĕv′ə lōō′shə nə rĭ), *adj.*, *n.*, *pl.* **-ries.**

re′vin′dicate′, *v.t.*, **-cated, -cating.**
re′vi′olate′, *v.t.*, **-lated, -lating.**
re′vi′ola′tion, *n.*
re′vis′it, *v.t.*
re′vis′ita′tion, *n.*
re′vi′taliza′tion, *n.*
re′vi′talize′, *v.t.*, **-lized, -lizing.**
re′vote′, *v.*, **-voted, -voting.**
re′warm′, *v.t.*

—*adj.* **1.** pertaining to, characterized by, or of the nature of a revolution, or complete or marked change. **2.** subversive to established procedure, principles, etc. **3.** revolving. —*n.* **4.** one who advocates or takes part in a revolution; revolutionist.

Revolutionary calendar, the calendar of the first French republic.

Revolutionary Wars, a series of wars between France under a revolutionary regime, and England, Austria, Prussia, etc. (1793–1802).

revolution counter, an instrument which indicates the number of revolutions made by a rotating shaft.

revolutionist (rĕv′ə lo͞o′shə nĭst), *n. U.S.* a revolutionary.

revolutionize (rĕv′ə lo͞o′shə nīz′), *v.t.*, **-nized, -nizing.** **1.** to bring about a revolution in; effect a radical change in. **2.** to subject to a political revolution. Also, **revolutionise.**

revolve (rĭ vŏlv′), *v.*, **-volved, -volving.** —*v.i.* **1.** to turn round or rotate, as on an axis. **2.** to move in a circular or curving course, or orbit. **3.** to proceed in a round or cycle. **4.** to come round in the process of time. **5.** to be revolved in the mind. —*v.t.* **6.** to cause to turn round, as on an axis. **7.** to cause to move in a circular or curving course, as about a central point. **8.** to think about; consider. [ME, t. L: m. *revolvere* roll, turn] —**revolv′able,** *adj.* —**Syn. 1.** See **turn.**

revolver (rĭ vŏl′və), *n.* **1.** a pistol having a revolving chambered cylinder for holding a number of cartridges which may be discharged in succession without reloading. **2.** one who or that which revolves.

revolving (rĭ vŏl′vĭng), *adj.* **1.** that revolves. **2.** *Mach.* denoting or pertaining to a radial engine, whose cylinders revolve about a stationary crankshaft, such as a helicopter motor, or the blades of a propeller.

revolving door, a series of doors arranged radially round a pivot, which revolve as people pass through, in order to prevent draughts.

revolving fund, any loan fund intended to be maintained by the repayment of past loans.

revue (rĭ vyo͞o′), *n.* **1.** a form of theatrical entertainment in which recent events, popular fads, etc., are parodied. **2.** any group of skits, dances, and songs. [t. F. See REVIEW, n.]

revulsion (rĭ vŭl′shən), *n.* **1.** a sudden and violent change of feeling or reaction in sentiment. **2.** a violent dislike or aversion for something. **3.** *Med.* the diminution of morbid action in one part of the body by irritation in another. **4.** the act of drawing something back or away. **5.** the fact of being so drawn. [t. L: s. *revulsio* a plucking away]

revulsive (rĭ vŭl′sĭv), *adj.* tending to alter the distribution of blood by causing congestion, esp. in the intestine.

Rev. Ver., Revised Version (of the Bible).

reward (rĭ wôd′), *n.* **1.** something given or received in return or recompense for service, merit, hardship, etc. **2.** a sum of money offered for the detection or capture of a criminal, the recovery of lost or stolen property, etc. —*v.t.* **3.** to recompense or requite (a person, etc.) for service, merit, achievement, etc. **4.** to make return for or requite (service, merit, etc.); recompense. [ME *rewarde*, t. ONF: m. *rewarder*, var. of OF *regarder*. See REGARD] —**reward′er,** *n.*

—**Syn. 1.** REWARD, PRIZE, RECOMPENSE imply something given in return for good. A REWARD is something given or done in return for good (or, more rarely, evil) received; it may refer to something abstract or concrete: *a £50 reward; her devotion was his reward.* PRIZE refers to something concrete offered as a reward of merit, or to be contested for and given to the winner: *to win a prize for an essay.* A RECOMPENSE is something given or done, whether as reward or punishment, for acts performed, services rendered, etc.; or something given in compensation for loss or injury suffered, etc.: *renown was his principal recompense for years of hard work.*

rewarding (rĭ wô′dĭng), *adj.* giving satisfaction that the effort made was worth while: *looking after handicapped children is very rewarding.*

rewire (rē′wī′ə), *v.t.*, **-wired, -wiring.** to provide with new wiring: *to rewire a house, radio, lamp, etc.*

reword (rē′wûd′), *v.t.* **1.** to put into other words. **2.** to repeat.

rewrite (*v.* rē′rīt′; *n.* rē′rīt′), *v.*, **-wrote, -written, -writing,** *n.* —*v.t.* **1.** to write again or in a different form. **2.** *U.S.* to subedit (the news submitted by a reporter). —*n.* **3.** *U.S.* subedited copy.

rex (rĕks), *n.*, *pl.* **reges** (rē′jēz). *Latin.* king.

Reykjavik (rā′kyə vēk′), *n.* a seaport in and the capital of Iceland, in the SW part. 77,220 (1964).

Reymont (*Pol.* rĕy′mŏnt), *n.* **Wladyslaw Stanislaw** (*Pol.* vwȧ dĭs′wȧf stȧ nē′swȧf), (*Ladislas Regmont*), 1868–1925, Polish novelist.

Reynard (rĕn′əd, rĕn′äd), *n.* a name given to the fox, orig. in the medieval beast epic, *Reynard the Fox.* Also, **Renard.**

Reynaud (*Fr.* rĕ nō′), *n.* **Paul** (*Fr.* pŏl), 1878–1966, French public official and statesman; premier of France, 1940.

Reynolds (rĕn′əldz), *n.* **Sir Joshua,** 1723–92, English portrait painter.

Rezaieh (rĕz′ī yā′), *n.* Rizaiyeh.

R.F., Royal Fusiliers.

r.f., radio frequency.

R.F.A., **1.** Royal Field Artillery. **2.** Royal Fleet Auxiliary.

R.F.C., **1.** Royal Flying Corps. **2.** Rugby Football Club.

R.G.S., Royal Geographical Society.

Rh, **1.** *Chem.* rhodium. **2.** See **Rh factor.**

R.H., Royal Highness.

r.h., right hand.

R.H.A., Royal Horse Artillery.

rhabdomancy (răb′də măn′sĭ), *n.* divination by means of a rod or wand, esp. in discovering ores, springs of water, etc. [t. LL: m. s. *rhabdomantīa*, t. Gk: m. *rhabdomanteía*] —**rhab′doman′tist,** *n.*

rhabdomyoma (răb′dō mī ō′mə), *n.*, *pl.* **-mata** (-mə tə), **-mas.** *Pathol.* a tumour made up of striate muscular tissue. Cf. **leiomyoma.** [t. NL, f. Gk *rhábdo(s)* rod + NL *myoma* MYOMA]

rhachis (rā′kĭs), *n.*, *pl.* **rhachises, rhachides** (răk′ĭ dēz′, rā′kĭ-). rachis.

Rhadamanthys (răd′ə măn′thəs), *n.* **1.** *Gk Myth.* a son of Zeus and Europa, rewarded for the justice he exemplified on earth by being made, after his death, a judge in the lower world, where he served with his brothers Minos and Aeacus. **2.** an inflexibly just or severe judge. Also, **Rhadamanthus.** —**Rhadamanthine** (răd′ə măn′thīn), *adj.*

Rhaetia (rē′shyə), *n.* an ancient Roman province in central Europe, comprising what is now E Switzerland and a part of the Tyrol: later extended to the Danube.

Rhaetian (rē′shyən), *adj.* **1.** of or pertaining to Rhaetia. **2.** Rhaeto-Romanic.

Rhaetian Alps, a chain of the Alps in E Switzerland and W Austria. Highest peak, Mt Bernina, 13,295 ft.

Rhaetic (rē′tĭk), *adj. Geol.* pertaining to certain strata, extensively developed in the Rhaetian Alps, having features of the Triassic and Jurassic but generally classed as belonging to the former. Also, **Rhetic.**

Rhaeto-Romanic (rē′tō rō măn′ĭk), *n.* **1.** a group of closely similar Romance languages, comprising Swiss Romansh, Tyrolese Ladino, and Friulian. —*adj.* **2.** denoting or pertaining to these languages.

-rhagia, a word element meaning 'bursting forth'. Also, **-rhage, -rhagy, -rrhagia, -rrhage, -rrhagy.** [t. Gk: (m.) *-rrhagia*]

rhamnaceous (răm nā′shəs), *adj.* belonging to the *Rhamnaceae*, or buckthorn family of plants. [f. s. NL *Rhamnus*, the typical genus (t. Gk: m. *rhámnos* a prickly shrub) + -ACEOUS]

rhapsodical (răp sŏd′ĭ kl), *adj.* **1.** pertaining to, characteristic of, or of the nature of rhapsody. **2.** extravagantly enthusiastic; ecstatic. Also, **rhapsod′ic.** —**rhapsod′ically,** *adv.*

rhapsodist (răp′sə dĭst), *n.* **1.** one who rhapsodizes. **2.** a reciter of epic poetry among the ancient Greeks, esp. a professional reciter of the Homeric poems.

rhapsodize (răp′sə dīz′), *v.*, **-dized, -dizing.** —*v.i.* **1.** to speak or write rhapsodies. **2.** to talk rhapsodically. —*v.t.* **3.** to recite as a rhapsody. Also, **rhapsodise.**

rhapsody (răp′sə dĭ), *n.*, *pl.* **-dies.** **1.** an exalted or exaggerated expression of feeling or enthusiasm. **2.** an epic poem, or a part of such a poem, as a book of the *Iliad*, suitable for recitation at one time. **3.** a similar piece of modern literature. **4.** an unusually intense or irregular poem or piece of prose. **5.** *Music.* an instrumental composition irregular in form and suggestive of improvisation: *Liszt's Hungarian Rhapsodies.* **6.** *Archaic.* a collection of miscellaneous items; medley; jumble. [t. L: m. s. *rhapsōdia*, t. Gk: m. *rhapsōidía* epic recital]

rhatany (răt′ə nĭ), *n.*, *pl.* **-nies.** **1.** a procumbent leguminous shrub, *Krameria triandra*, from Peru, the root of which is used as an astringent and tonic in medicine and also to colour port wine. **2.** some other plant of this genus, esp. *K. argentea.* **3.** the roots of these plants. [t. Pg.: m. *rhatanhia*, or t. Sp.: m. *ratania*; t. Quechua]

rhe (rē), *n. Physics.* a unit of fluidity; the reciprocal of the poise. [abstracted from RHEO-]

Rhea (rīə), *n.* **1.** *Gk Myth.* a daughter of Uranus and Gaea, wife of Cronus, and mother of Zeus and other major deities. She was called 'Mother of the Gods' and identified

re′wash′, *v.t.*
re′wa′ter, *v.t.*
re′weigh′, *v.t.*
re′wind′, *v.t.*, **-wound, -winding.**
re′work′, *v.t.*, **-worked** or **wrought, -working.**
re′wrap′, *v.t.*, **-wrapped, -wrapping.**
re′yoke′, *v.t.*, **-yoked, -yoking.**

with Cybele. **2.** (*l.c.*) a bird of the genus *Rhea*, which consists of South American ratite birds resembling the African ostrich but smaller and having three toes instead of two. [t. L, t. Gk]

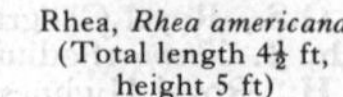

Rhea, *Rhea americana* (Total length 4½ ft, height 5 ft)

-rhea, *Chiefly U.S.* var. of **-rhoea.** Also, **-rrhea.**

Rhea Silvia (rīə′ sĭl′vĭ ə), *Rom. Legend.* a vestal virgin; mother by Mars of Romulus and Remus.

Rhee (rē), *n.* **Syngman** (sĭng′mən), 1875–1965, president of Korea 1948–1960.

Rheims (rēmz; *Fr.* răɴs), *n.* Reims.

Rhein (*Ger.* rīn), *n.* German name of the **Rhine.**

Rheinhausen (*Ger.* rīn hou′zən), *n.* a town in West Germany, in W North Rhine-Westphalia. 73,600 (est. 1966).

Rheinland (*Ger.* rīn′lȧnt), *n.* German name of **Rhineland.**

Rheinland-Pfalz (*Ger.* rīn′lȧnt pfȧlts′), *n.* German name of **Rhineland-Palatinate.**

rhematic (rĭ măt′ĭk), *adj.* **1.** pertaining to the formation of words. **2.** pertaining to or derived from a verb. [t. Gk: m. s. *rhēmatikós* belonging to a verb, a word]

rhenic (rē′nĭk), *adj. Chem.* of or containing rhenium.

Rhenish (rĕn′ĭsh, rē′nĭsh), *adj.* **1.** of the river Rhine or the regions bordering on it. **—***n.* **2.** Rhine wine. [f. L *Rhēn(us)* Rhine + -ISH[1]; r. ME *Rinisch(e)*, t. MHG]

rhenium (rē′nĭ əm), *n. Chem.* a rare metallic element of the manganese subgroup, with a high melting point, used in platinum-rhenium thermocouples. *Symbol:* Re; *at. no.:* 75; *at. wt:* 186·20. [f. s. L *Rhēnus* the Rhine + -IUM]

rheo-, a word element meaning 'something flowing', 'a stream', 'current'. [comb. form repr. Gk *rhéos*]

rheo., rheostat; rheostats.

rheology (rĭ ŏl′ə jĭ), *n.* the study of the deformation and flow of matter. [f. RHEO- + -LOGY]

rheometer (rē ŏm′ĭ tə), *n.* an instrument for measuring the velocity of flow of fluids (e.g., blood flow).

rheoscope (rīə′skōp′), *n.* an instrument which indicates the presence of an electric current. **—rheoscopic** (rīə-skŏp′ĭk), *adj.*

rheostat (rīə′stăt), *n. Elect.* a variable electrical resistor. **—rheostat′ic,** *adj.*

rheotaxis (rīə tăk′sĭs), *n. Biol.* the property in a cell or organism of responding by movement to the stimulus of a current of water.

rheotropism (rē ŏt′rə pĭz′əm), *n.* the effect of a current of water upon the direction of plant growth.

rhesus (rē′səs), *n.* **1.** a macaque monkey, *Macacus rhesus*, common in India, much used in experimental medicine. **2.** (*cap.*) *Gk Myth.* a Thracian ally of Troy whose horses were stolen by Odysseus and Diomedes. An oracle had declared that if his horses drank from the river Xanthus Troy would not fall. [t. L, t. Gk: m. *Rhêsos* (def. 2)]

Rhesus factor (rē′səs), Rh factor.

rhet., **1.** rhetoric. **2.** rhetorical.

Rhetic (rē′tĭk), *adj. Geol.* Rhaetic.

rhetor (rē′tə), *n.* **1.** a master or teacher of rhetoric. **2.** an orator. [t. L, t. Gk; r. ME *rethor*, t. ML]

rhetoric (rĕt′ə rĭk), *n.* **1.** the art or science of all specially literary uses of language in prose or verse, including the figures of speech. **2.** the art of prose in general as opposed to verse. **3.** (in prose or verse) the use of exaggeration or display, in an unfavourable sense. **4.** (orig.) the art of oratory. **5.** (in classical oratory) the art of influencing the thought of one's hearers. [ME *retorik*, t. L: m. s. *rhētorica*, t. Gk: m. *rhētorikḗ* (*téchnē*) the rhetorical (art)]

rhetorical (rĭ tŏ′rĭ kl), *adj.* **1.** belonging to or concerned with mere style or effect. **2.** having the nature of rhetoric. **3.** overelaborate, bombastic in style. **—rhetor′ically,** *adv.*

rhetorical question, a question designed to produce an effect and not to draw an answer.

rhetorician (rĕt′ə rĭsh′ən), *n.* **1.** one versed in the art of rhetoric. **2.** one given to display in language. **3.** a person who teaches rhetoric.

rheum (ro͞om), *n.* **1.** *Pathol.* a thin serous or catarrhal discharge. **2.** catarrh; a cold. [ME *rewme*, t. OF: m. *reume*, t. L: m. *rheuma*, t. Gk: a flow, rheum]

rheumatic (ro͞o măt′ĭk), *adj.* **1.** pertaining to or of the nature of rheumatism. **2.** affected with or subject to rheumatism. **—***n.* **3.** one affected with or subject to rheumatism. **4.** (*pl.*) rheumatic pains. [ME *r(e)umatyk(e)*, t. L: m. s. *rheumaticus*, t. Gk: m. *rheumatikós*]

rheumatic fever, *Pathol.* a serious prevalent disease usually afflicting children and marked by fever, inflammation of the joints, generalized muscle pains, and frequently associated with pathological changes in the heart and the different serous membranes.

rheumaticky (ro͞o măt′ĭ kĭ), *adj.* having aches or pains as those likely to occur in rheumatism.

rheumatism (ro͞o′mə tĭz′əm), *n.* **1.** *Pathol.* a disease commonly affecting the joints and accompanied by constitutional disturbances, now usually thought to be due to a micro-organism; (in a growing child) rheumatic fever. **2.** any of various ailments of the joints or muscles, as certain chronic disabilities of the joints (**chronic rheumatism**) and certain painful affections of the muscles (**muscular rheumatism**). [t. LL: s. *rheumatismus*, t. Gk: m. *rheumatismós* liability to rheum]

rheumatoid (ro͞o′mə toid′), *adj.* **1.** resembling rheumatism. **2.** rheumatic. Also, **rheu′matoi′dal.**

rheumatoid arthritis, *Pathol.* a chronic disease marked by signs and symptoms of inflammation of the joints, frequently accompanied by marked deformities, and ordinarily associated with manifestations of a general or systemic affliction.

Rheydt (*Ger.* rīt), *n.* a town in West Germany, in W North Rhine-Westphalia, adjacent to Mönchen-Gladbach. 99,200 (est. 1966).

Rh factor, *Biochem.* an agglutinogen often present in human blood. Blood containing this factor (**Rh positive**) may cause haemolytic reactions, esp. during pregnancy or after repeated transfusions with blood lacking it (**Rh negative**). In infants it may cause haemolytic anaemias. In full, **Rhesus factor.** [so called because first found in the blood of rhesus monkeys]

R.H.G., Royal Horse Guards.

rhigolene (rĭg′ō lēn′), *n.* an extremely volatile liquid obtained from petroleum: used to produce local anaesthesia by freezing. [f. s. Gk *rhîgos* cold + -OLE[2] + -ENE]

rhin-, var. of **rhino-,** before vowels, as in *rhinencephalon.*

rhinal (rī′nəl), *adj.* of or pertaining to the nose; nasal. [f. RHIN(-) + -AL[1]]

Rhine (rīn), *n.* a river flowing from SE Switzerland through West Germany and the Netherlands into the North Sea: branches off into the **Waal, Lek,** and **IJssel** in its lower course. ab. 820 mi. German, **Rhein.** French, **Rhin** (*Fr.* răɴ). Dutch, **Rijn.**

Rhineland (rīn′lănd′), *n.* that part of West Germany W of the Rhine. German, **Rheinland.**

Rhineland-Palatinate (rīn′lănd pə lăt′ĭ nĭt), *n.* a Land in W West Germany; formerly part of Rhine Province. 3,612,700 pop. (est. 1966); 7655 sq. mi. *Cap.:* Mainz. German, **Rheinland-Pfalz.**

rhinencephalon (rī′nĕn sĕf′ə lŏn′), *n.*, *pl.* **-la** (-lə). *Anat.* the olfactory portion of the brain. [f. RHIN- + ENCEPHALON] **—rhinencephalic** (rī′nĕn sĭ făl′ĭk), *adj.*

Rhine Palatinate, Palatinate (def. 1).

Rhine Province, a former province in W Germany, mostly W of the Rhine; now divided between Rhineland-Palatinate and North Rhine-Westphalia. Also, **Rhineland.** German, **Rheinland.**

rhinestone (rīn′stōn′), *n.* an artificial gem made of paste. [trans. of F *caillou du Rhin* pebble of the Rhine]

Rhine wine, **1.** wine (of many varieties) produced in the valley of the Rhine; hock. **2.** any of a class of white wines, mostly light, still, and dry.

rhinitis (rī nī′tĭs), *n. Pathol.* inflammation of the nose or its mucous membrane.

rhino (rī′nō), *n.*, *pl.* **-nos.** **1.** *Colloq.* a rhinoceros. **2.** *Slang.* money.

rhino-, a word element meaning 'nose'. Also, **rhin-.** [t. Gk, comb. form of *rhîs*]

Indian rhinoceros, *Rhinoceros unicornis* (10 ft long, 5½ to 6½ ft high at the shoulder, horn 1 to 2 ft)

rhinoceros (rī nŏs′ə rəs, rī nŏs′-rəs), *n.*, *pl.* **-roses,** (*esp. collectively*) **-ros.** any of various large, ungainly, thick-skinned, perissodactyl mammals, found in Asia and Africa, family *Rhinocerotidae*, with one or two upright horns on the snout. Five species are still extant. [ME *rinoceros*, t. LL, t. Gk: m. *rhinókerōs*, f. *rhino-* RHINO- + *-kerōs* horned] **—rhinocerotic** (rī′nō sĭ rŏt′ĭk), *adj.*

rhinoceros-beetle (rī nŏs′ə rəs bē′tl), *n.* a large scarab beetle of the tropical species *Oryctes rhinoceros*, the head of which bears a curved horn.

rhinology (rī nŏl′ə jĭ), *n.* the science dealing with the nose and its diseases. **—rhinol′ogist,** *n.*

rhinoplasty (rī′nō plăs′tĭ), *n. Surg.* plastic surgery of the nose. **—rhi′noplas′tic,** *adj.*

rhinoscope (rī′nō skōp′), *n. Med.* an instrument for examining the nasal passages.

rhinoscopy (rī nŏs′kə pĭ), *n. Med.* the investigation of the nasal passages.

R. Hist. S., Royal Historical Society.

rhizanthous (rī zăn′thəs, rĭ zăn′-), *adj. Bot.* producing flowers from the root, or appearing to do so.

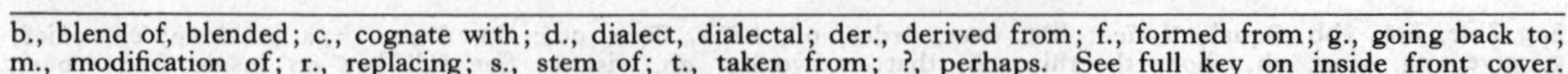

rhizo-, a word element meaning 'root'. [t. Gk, comb. form of *rhíza*]

rhizobium (rī zō′byəm), *n., pl.* **-bia** (-byə). *Bacteriol.* any bacterium of a genus *Rhizobium*, characterized by a rodlike shape, found as nitrogen fixers in nodules on the roots of the bean, clover, etc. [NL, f. *rhizo-* RHIZO- + m. Gk *bíos* life]

rhizocarpous (rī′zō kä′pəs), *adj. Bot.* **1.** bearing subterranean flowers and fruits. **2.** having the root perennial but the stem annual, as perennial herbs.

rhizocephalous (rī′zō sĕf′ə ləs), *adj. Zool.* belonging to the *Rhizocephala*, a group of degenerate hermaphrodite crustaceans which are parasitic chiefly on crabs. [f. s. NL *Rhizocephala*, pl. (f. *rhizo-* RHIZO- + m. Gk *kephalḗ* head) + -OUS]

rhizogenic (rī′zō jĕn′ĭk), *adj. Bot.* producing roots, as certain cells. Also, **rhizogenous** (rī zŏj′ĭ nəs).

rhizoid (rī′zoid), *adj.* **1.** rootlike. —*n.* **2.** (in mosses, etc.) one of the rootlike filaments by which the plant is attached to the substratum. [f. RHIZ(O)- + -OID] —**rhizoi′dal,** *adj.*

rhizome (rī′zōm), *n. Bot.* a rootlike subterranean stem, commonly horizontal in position, which usually produces roots below and sends up shoots progressively from the upper surface. [t. Gk: m. *rhízōma* mass of roots] —**rhizomatous** (rī zŏm′ə təs, -zō′mə-), *adj.*

Forms of rhizome: A, Solomon's-seal, *Polygonatum commutatum*; B, Iris, *Iris versicolor*

rhizomorph (rī′zō môf′), *n. Bot.* a long strandlike structure composed of parallel fungal hyphae, as produced by the honey fungus, *Armillaria mellea.*

rhizomorphous (rī′zō mô′fəs), *adj. Bot.* rootlike in form.

rhizophagous (rī zŏf′ə gəs), *adj.* feeding on roots.

rhizophore (rī′zō fô′), *n.* a branch borne on the aerial stem in the pteridophyte genus *Selaginella* which has no leaves but produces roots when in contact with the soil.

rhizopod (rī′zō pŏd′), *n.* any of the *Rhizopoda*, a class of protozoans having pseudopodia. [t. NL: s. *Rhizopoda*, pl. See RHIZO-, -POD] —**rhizopodan** (rī zŏp′ə dən), *adj., n.* —**rhizop′odous,** *adj.*

rhizopus (rī′zō pəs), *n. Bot.* any fungus of the phycomycetous genus *Rhizopus*, of which the bread mould, *R. nigricans*, is best known. [NL, f. *rhizo-* RHIZO- + m. Gk *poús* foot]

rhizosphere (rī′zō sfĭə′), *n.* the soil in contact with a living root which usually contains more micro-organisms than the rest of the soil.

rhizotomy (rī zŏt′ə mĭ), *n., pl.* **-mies.** *Surg.* the surgical section or cutting of the spinal nerve roots, usually posterior or sensory roots, to eliminate pain or paralysis.

Rh negative. See **Rh factor.**

rho (rō), *n.* the 17th letter (Ρ, ρ) of the Greek alphabet.

Rho., Rhodesia. Also, **Rhod.**

rhod-, var. of **rhodo-,** before vowels, as in *rhodamine.*

rhodamine (rō′də mēn′, -mĭn), *n. Chem.* **1.** a red dye obtained by heating an alkyl aminophenol with phthalic anhydride. **2.** any of various related dyes. [f. RHOD- + AMINE]

Rhode Island (rōd), a state of the NE United States, on the Atlantic coast: a part of New England; the smallest state in the U.S. 859,488 pop. (1960); 1214 sq. mi. *Cap.:* Providence. *Abbrev.:* R.I. —**Rhode Islander.**

Rhode Island Red, one of a variety of the domestic fowl originating in America having dark reddish brown feathers.

Rhodes (rōdz), *n.* **1. Cecil John,** 1853–1902, British colonial capitalist and government administrator in southern Africa. **2.** Greek, **Rhodos.** an island in the Aegean, off the SW coast of Turkey: the largest of the Dodecanese Islands. 61,000 pop. (est. 1961); 542 sq. mi. **3.** Greek, **Rhodos,** a seaport on this island. 27,393 (1961). **4. Colossus of,** a huge bronze statue of Apollo that stood (*c.* 280 B.C.–224 B.C.) at the entrance of Rhodes harbour: one of the Seven Wonders of the World.

Rhodesia (rō dē′zyə), *n.* a country in southern Africa, formerly a self-governing British colony, which in 1965 unilaterally declared itself independent. 4,259,700 pop. (est. 1965); 150,333 sq. mi. *Cap.:* Salisbury. Formerly, **Southern Rhodesia.** —**Rhode′sian,** *adj., n.*

Rhodesia and Nyasaland, Federation of, the former federation of Northern Rhodesia (now Zambia), Southern Rhodesia (now Rhodesia), and Nyasaland (now Malawi); 1953–63. Also, **Central African Federation.**

Rhodesian ridgeback, a hunting dog, over 2 ft high, with a short reddish coat, and a characteristic ridge of hair along the back.

Rhodes scholarship, one of a number of scholarships at Oxford University established by the will of Cecil Rhodes, for selected students (**Rhodes scholars**) from the Commonwealth and the United States.

Rhodian (rō′dyən), *adj.* **1.** of or pertaining to the island, Rhodes. —*n.* **2.** a native or inhabitant of Rhodes.

rhodic (rō′dĭk), *adj. Chem.* of or containing rhodium, esp. in the tetravalent state.

rhodium (rō′dyəm), *n. Chem.* a silvery white metallic element of the platinum family, forming salts which give rose-coloured solutions and used to electroplate microscopes and instrument parts to prevent corrosion. *Symbol:* Rh; *at. wt:* 102·905; *at. no.:* 45; *sp. gr.:* 12·5 at 20°C. [t. NL. See RHOD-, -IUM]

rhodo-, a word element meaning 'rose'. Also, **rhod-.** [t. Gk, comb. form of *rhódon*]

rhodochrosite (rō′dō krō′sīt), *n.* a mineral, manganese carbonate, $MnCO_3$, commonly containing some iron and calcium, and usually rose red in colour; a minor ore of manganese. [t. G: m. *Rhodochrosit*, f. Gk *rhodóchrōs* rose-coloured + *-it* -ITE[1]]

rhododendron (rō′də dĕn′drən), *n. Bot.* any plant of the ericaceous genus *Rhododendron*, comprising evergreen and deciduous shrubs and trees with handsome pink, purple, or white flowers, and oval or oblong leaves, as *R. ponticum*, much cultivated for ornament. [t. NL, t. Gk: lit., rose tree]

rhodolite (rŏd′ə līt′), *n.* a rose red variety of pyrope garnet, sometimes used as a gem.

rhodonite (rŏd′ə nīt′), *n.* a mineral, manganese metasilicate, $MnSiO_3$, occurring usually in rose red masses, sometimes used as an ornamental stone. [t. G: m. *Rhodonit*, f. Gk *rhódon* rose + *-it* -ITE[1]]

Rhodope (rŏd′ə pĭ), *n.* a mountain range in SW Bulgaria. Highest peak, Mus Allah, 9595 ft.

rhodopsin (rō dŏp′sĭn), *n.* visual purple.

rhodora (rō dô′rə), *n.* a low ericaceous shrub, *Rhododendron canadensis*, of North America, with rose-coloured flowers which appear before the leaves. [t. L: kind of plant]

Rhodos (*Gk.* rô′thôs), *n.* See **Rhodes** (defs 2 and 3).

-rhoea, a word element meaning 'flow', 'discharge', as in *gonorrhoea.* Also, **-rrhoea,** *Chiefly U.S.,* **-rhea.** [t. Gk: m. *-(r)rhoia*, der. *rhéein* to flow]

rhomb (rŏm), *n.* rhombus.

rhombencephalon (rŏm′bĕn sĕf′ə lŏn′), *n. Anat.* the part of the brain made up of the cerebellum, the pons, and the medulla oblongata; the hindbrain. [f. RHOMB + ENCEPHALON]

rhombic (rŏm′bĭk), *adj.* **1.** having the form of a rhombus. **2.** having a rhombus as base or cross-section. **3.** bounded by rhombs, as a solid. **4.** *Crystall.* orthorhombic. Also, **rhom′bical.**

rhombohedron (rŏm′bō hē′drən), *n., pl.* **-drons, -dra** (-drə). a solid bounded by six rhombic planes. [f. *rhombo-* (comb. form repr. Gk *rhómbos* rhombus) + -HEDRON] —**rhom′bohe′dral,** *adj.*

rhomboid (rŏm′boid), *n.* **1.** an oblique-angled parallelogram with only the opposite sides equal. —*adj.* **2.** Also, **rhomboi′dal.** having a form like, or approaching that of, a rhombus; shaped like a rhomboid. [t. LL: s. *rhomboides*, t. Gk: m. s. *rhomboeidḗs*]

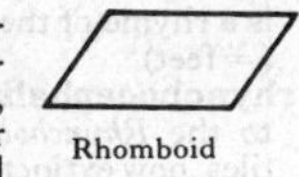
Rhomboid

rhombus (rŏm′bəs), *n., pl.* **-buses, -bi** (-bī). **1.** an oblique-angled equilateral parallelogram. **2.** rhombohedron. [t. L, t. Gk: m. *rhómbos*]

rhonchus (rŏng′kəs), *n., pl.* **-chi** (-kī). *Pathol.* a râle, esp. when produced in the bronchial tubes. [t. L, t. Gk: m. (unrecorded) *rhónchos*, var. of *rhénchos* snoring] —**rhonchal** (rŏng′kl), **rhonchial** (rŏng′kĭ əl), *adj.*

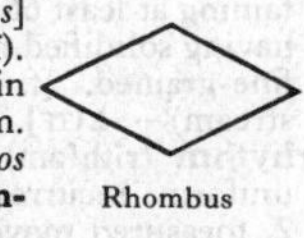
Rhombus

Rhondda (rŏn′də), *n.* a town in Wales, in Glamorganshire. 100,287 (1961).

Rhone (rōn), *n.* a river flowing from the Alps in S Switzerland through Lake Geneva and SE France into the Mediterranean. 504 mi. French, **Rhône** (*Fr.* rōn).

Rhône (*Fr.* rōn), *n.* **1.** the river Rhone. **2.** a department in E central France. 1,116,664 pop. (1962); 1104 sq. mi. *Cap.:* Lyons.

Rhône-Alpes (*Fr.* rōn ălp′), *n.* an administrative region in SE France comprising the departments of Rhône, Loire, Ain, Haute-Savoie, Savoie, Isère, Ardèche, and Drôme. 4,018,598 pop. (1962); 17,220 sq. mi. *Cap.:* Lyons.

rhotacism (rō′tə sĭz′əm), *n. Phonet.* the defective pronunciation of *r*, excessive trilling, or some other pronunciational peculiarity. [t. NL: s. *rhōtacismus*, der. Gk *rhōtakízein* use *rhō* (sound or letter) to excess]

Rh positive. See **Rh factor.**

R.H.S., Royal Horticultural Society.

rhubarb (rōō′bäb), *n.* **1.** any of the herbs constituting the polygonaceous genus *Rheum*, as *R. officinale*, a plant with a medicinal rhizome, and *R. rhaponticum*, a garden plant with edible leafstalks. **2.** the rhizome of any medicinal species of this plant, forming a combined cathartic and astringent. **3.** the edible fleshy leafstalks of any of the garden species, used in making pies, etc. **4.** the word supposedly spoken by actors to simulate noisy conversation in the background. **5.** *Slang.* confused noise, argument, etc., as in a quarrel. **6.** *Slang.* a quarrel or squabble. [ME *rubarbe*, t. OF: m. *reubarbe*, t. ML: m. s. *reubarbarum*, t. Gk: m. *rhéon bárbaron* foreign rhubarb]

Rhum (rŭm), *n.* an island of the Inner Hebrides, Inverness-shire, Scotland.

rhumb (rŭm), *n.* **1.** a rhumb line. **2.** a point of the compass. [t. Sp.: m. *rumbo*, t. L: m. *rhombus* RHOMBUS]

rhumbatron (rŭm′bə trŏn′), *n.* *Electronics.* See **resonator** (def. 4a).

rhumb line, a loxodromic curve; a curve on the surface of a sphere which cuts all meridians at the same angle. It is the path taken by a ship which maintains a constant compass direction.

rhyacolite (rī ăk′ə līt′), *n.* a glassy type of orthoclase found in lava.

Rhyl (rĭl), *n.* a town in Wales, in Flintshire. 21,825 (1961).

rhyme (rīm), *n.*, *v.*, **rhymed, rhyming.** —*n.* **1.** agreement in the terminal sounds of lines of verse, or of words. **2.** a word agreeing with another in terminal sound. **3.** verse or poetry having correspondence in the terminal sounds of the line. **4.** a poem or piece of verse having such correspondence. **5. rhyme or reason,** logic; explanation; meaning: *there was no rhyme or reason for her behaviour.* —*v.t.* **6.** to treat in rhyme, as a subject; turn into rhyme, as something in prose. **7.** to compose (verse, etc.) in metrical form with rhymes. **8.** to use (a word) as a rhyme to another word; use (words) as rhymes. —*v.i.* **9.** to make rhyme or verse; versify. **10.** to use rhyme in writing verse. **11.** to form a rhyme, as one word or line with another. **12.** to be composed in metrical form with rhymes, as verse. Also, **rime.** (The spelling **rime** is strongly preferred by many because it is the etymologically direct form.) [ME *rime*, t. OF, der. *rimer* to rhyme, g. Gallo-Rom. *rimāre* put in a row, der. OHG *rīm* series, row; prob. not connected with L *rhythmus* rhythm] —**rhym′er,** *n.*

rhyme royal, *Pros.* a form of verse introduced into English by Chaucer, consisting of seven-line stanzas of iambic pentameter in which there are three rhymes, the first line rhyming with the third, the second with the fourth and fifth, and the sixth with the seventh.

rhyme scheme, the pattern of rhymes used in a poem, usually marked by letters, as rhyme royal, *ababbcc.*

rhymester (rīm′stə), *n.* a maker of rhyme or verse, esp. of an inferior order; a poetaster. Also, **rimester, rhymist.**

rhyming slang, a form of slang, esp. that originally used among Cockneys, in which the last of two or more words is a rhyme of the word to be represented, as *plates of meat* (= feet).

rhynchocephalian (rĭng′kō sĭ fāl′yən), *adj.* **1.** belonging to the *Rhynchocephalia*, an order of lizard-shaped reptiles, now extinct except for the *Sphenodon* of New Zealand. —*n.* **2.** a rhynchocephalian reptile. [f. s. NL *Rhynchocephalia*, n. pl. (f. Gk: *rhyncho-*, comb. form of *rhýnchos* snout + m. *kephalḗ* head) + -AN]

rhyolite (rī′ə līt′), *n.* a kind of acid volcanic rock containing at least 66 per cent of silica, similar to granite but having solidified rapidly from a larva flow, and as a result fine-grained. [f. *rhyo-* (irreg. comb. form of Gk *rhýax* stream) + -LITE]

rhythm (rĭth′əm), *n.* **1.** movement or procedure with uniform recurrence of a beat, accent, or the like. **2.** measured movement, as in dancing. **3.** *Music.* **a.** the pattern of regular or irregular pulses caused in music by the occurrence of strong and weak melodic and harmonic beats. **b.** a particular form of this: *duple rhythm, triple rhythm.* **4.** the pattern of recurring stress, vowel length, vocalizing, etc., in any utterance in any language. **5.** *Pros.* **a.** a metrical or rhythmical form; metre. **b.** a particular kind of metrical form. **c.** metrical movement. **6.** *Art.* a proper relation and interdependence of parts with reference to one another and to an artistic whole. **7.** procedure marked by the regular recurrence of particular elements, phases, etc. **8.** regular recurrence of elements in a system of motion. **9.** *Physiol.* the regular occurrence of a physiological function. [t. L: s. *rhythmus*, t. Gk: m. *rhythmós*]

rhythm and blues, a commercialized style of popular music in vogue in the early 1960s, using both vocal and instrumental elements, based on the guitar and derived ultimately from the Negro blues style.

rhythm method, a method of avoiding conception by confining sexual intercourse to the infertile phases of the menstrual cycle.

rhythm section, the instruments in a dance band, such as piano, bass, guitar, and percussion, responsible for maintaining a regular beat.

rhythmic (rĭth′mĭk), *adj.* **1.** rhythmical. —*n.* **2.** rhythmics.

rhythmical (rĭth′mĭ kl), *adj.* **1.** periodic, as motion, etc. **2.** having a flowing rhythm. **3.** of or pertaining to rhythm: *an excellent rhythmical sense.* —**rhyth′mically,** *adv.*

rhythmics (rĭth′mĭks), *n.* the science of rhythm and rhythmic forms.

rhythmist (rĭth′mĭst), *n.* **1.** one versed in, or having a fine sense of, rhythm. **2.** one who uses rhythm in a certain way: *a good rhythmist.*

rhyton (rī′tŏn), *n.* an ancient Greek drinking cup or horn. [Gk]

R.I., **1.** (L *Regina et Imperatrix*) Queen and Empress. **2.** (L *Rex et Imperator*) King and Emperor. **3.** Rhode Island.

ria (rīə; *Sp.* ryä), *n.* a wedge-shaped indentation of the sea caused by submergence of the edges of the land where hill ranges and rivers are at right angles to the coastline. [Sp.]

rial (rī′əl), *n.* **1.** the monetary unit of Iran, equivalent to about £0·0055 sterling. **2.** a silver or nickel coin of this value. **3.** riyal. [var. of RIYAL]

rialto (rĭ ăl′tō), *n.*, *pl.* **-tos.** an exchange or mart.

Rialto (rĭ ăl′tō; *It.* rē äl′tô), *n.* **1.** a commercial centre in Venice consisting of an island and the surrounding district. **2.** a bridge, constructed of marble about 1590, spanning the Grand Canal in Venice.

riant (rī′ənt), *adj.* laughing; smiling; cheerful; gay. [t. F, ppr. of *rire*, g. L *rīdēre* laugh] —**ri′antly,** *adv.*

riata (rĭ ä′tə), *n.* *U.S.* a lariat. [t. Sp.: m. *reata*, der. *reatar* tie again, f. *re-* RE- + *atar*, g. L *aptāre* fit, v.]

rib[1] (rĭb), *n.*, *v.*, **ribbed, ribbing.** —*n.* **1.** one of a series of long, slender, curved bones, occurring in pairs, more or less enclosing the thoracic cavity, and articulated with the vertebrae. See diag. under **skeleton.** **2.** a cut of meat, as beef, containing a rib. **3.** some thing or part resembling a rib in form, position, or use, as a supporting or strengthening part. **4.** an arch or arched member, plain or moulded, forming a support of a vault, or a merely decorative feature of like appearance on the surface of a vault or ceiling. **5.** a structural member which supports the shape of something: *an umbrella rib.* **6.** one of the curved timbers or members in a ship's frame which spring upwards and outwards from the keel. **7.** a primary vein of a leaf. **8.** a ridge, as in poplin or rep, caused by heavy yarn. **9.** *Knitting.* a pattern in which plain and purl stitches are alternated. **10.** a wife (in humorous allusion to the creation of Eve. Gen. 2:21–22). **11.** a strip of metal joining the barrel of a double-barrelled shotgun, which acts as a guide to aligning the sights. **12.** *Bookbinding.* **a.** one of the raised lines where the stitching runs across the spine of a book. **b.** such a line used ornamentally. —*v.t.* **13.** to furnish or strengthen with ribs. **14.** to enclose as with ribs. **15.** to mark with riblike ridges or markings. **16.** to knit (an article) in a rib. —*v.i.* **17.** to knit in a rib. [ME and OE, c. G *Rippe*] —**ribbed,** *adj.*

rib[2] (rĭb), *v.t.*, **ribbed, ribbing.** *Slang.* to tease; ridicule; make fun of. [appar. short for *rib-tickle*, v.]

R.I.B.A., Royal Institute of British Architects.

ribald (rĭb′ld), *adj.* **1.** offensive or scurrilous in speech, language, etc.; coarsely mocking or abusive; wantonly irreverent. —*n.* **2.** a ribald person. [ME *ribaut*, t. OF, der. *riber* dissipate, t. MHG: m. *rīben* be on heat, copulate, or der. MD *ribe* whore]

ribaldry (rĭb′l drĭ), *n.* **1.** ribald character, as of language; scurrility. **2.** ribald speech.

riband (rĭb′ənd), *n.* **1.** Also, **ribbon.** *Carp.* a horizontal member fixed to uprights, in strutting, shoring, etc. **2.** *Archaic.* a ribbon. [ME, var. of RIBBON]

ribband (rĭb′ənd), *n.* *Shipbuilding.* a lengthwise timber or the like used to secure a ship's ribs in position while the outside planking or plating is being put on. [appar. f. RIB[1] + BAND]

Ribbentrop (*Ger.* rĭb′ən trŏp), *n.* **Joachim von** (*Ger.* yō′äKH ĭm fŏn), 1893–1946, German Nazi politician: foreign minister 1938–45.

ribbing (rĭb′ĭng), *n.* **1.** ribs collectively. **2.** an assemblage or arrangement of ribs. **3.** *Knitting.* rib (def. 9).

ribbon (rĭb′ən), *n.* **1.** a woven strip or band of fine material, as silk, rayon, etc., finished off at the edges, and varying in width, used for ornament, tying, etc. **2.** material in such strips. **3.** anything resembling or suggesting a ribbon or woven band. **4.** (*pl.*) torn or ragged strips; shreds: *clothes torn to ribbons.* **5.** a long, thin, flexible band of metal, as for a spring, bandsaw, tape measure, etc. **6.** a band of material charged with ink, or supplying ink, for the impression in a typewriter. **7.** *Shipbuilding.* ribband. **8.** a badge of an order of knighthood or other distinction: *the red ribbon of the French Legion of Honour.* **9.** (*pl.*) *Colloq.* reins for driving. —*v.t.* **10.** to adorn with ribbon. **11.** to mark with something suggesting ribbon. **12.** to separate into or reduce to ribbon-like strips. —*v.i.* **13.** to form in ribbon-like strips. [ME *riban*, t. OF, var. of *r(e)uban*, ? t. Gmc; see RUDDY, BAND[2]] —**rib′bon-like′,** *adj.*

ribbon development, the unplanned building of houses, etc., along main roads leading out of large towns.

ribbonfish (rĭb′ən fĭsh′), *n.*, *pl.* **-fishes,** (*esp. collectively*) **-fish.** any of certain marine fishes with a long, compressed ribbon-like body, as the dealfish.

ribbon grass, a tall, perennial variegated grass, *Phalaris arundinacea* var. *variegata.*

ribbonwood (rĭb′ən wo͝od′), *n.* a small evergreen malvaceous tree, *Hoheria populnea*, a native of New Zealand.

ribbon worm, nemertean (def. 1).

Ribera (*Sp.* rē bĕ′rä), *n.* **José** (*Sp.* KHō sĕ′), ('*Lo Spagnoletto*'), 1588–1656, Spanish painter.

riboflavine (rī′bō flā′vĭn), *n. Biochem.* a factor of the vitamin B complex, $C_{17}H_{20}H_4O_6$, found in milk, fresh meat, eggs, fresh vegetables, etc., necessary for growth; lactoflavine; vitamin B_2; vitamin G. Also, **riboflavin.** [f. RIBO(SE) + s. L *flāvus* yellow + -INE[2]]

ribonucleic acid (rī′bō nyo͞o klē′ĭk), *Biochem.* any of a group of compounds of high molecular weight, yielding on hydrolysis purine and pyrimidine bases, ribose, and phosphoric acid, that occur in all living cells, mainly in the cytoplasm. *Abbrev.*: RNA.

ribose (rī′bōs), *n. Chem.* a pentose sugar, $C_5H_{10}O_5$, present in combined form in ribonucleic acid. [f. *rib*(*onic acid*) (ult. irreg. der. ARABINOSE) + (PENT)OSE]

ribosome (rī′bə sōm′), *n. Biol., Biochem.* one of the minute granules present in living cells, containing ribonucleic acid and involved in protein synthesis. —**ri′boso′mal,** *adj.*

ribwort (rĭb′wûrt′), *n.* **1.** a plantain, *Plantago lanceolata*, having narrow leaves with prominent ribs. **2.** any of various similar plantains.

R.I.C., Royal Institute of Chemistry.

Ricardo (rĭ kä′dō), *n.* **David,** 1772–1823, English economist.

Riccio (*It.* rēt′chō), *n.* **David** (*It.* dä′vēd). See **Rizzio.**

rice (rīs), *n., v.,* **riced, ricing.** —*n.* **1.** the starchy seeds or grain of a species of grass, *Oryza sativa*, cultivated in warm climates and constituting an important food. **2.** the plant itself. —*v.t.* **3.** *U.S.* to reduce to a form resembling rice: *to rice potatoes.* [ME *rys*, t. OF: m. *ris*, t. It.: m. *riso*, ult. (through MGk) from Gk *óryza*; of Eastern orig.]

Rice (rīs), *n.* **Elmer,** 1892–1967, U.S. dramatist.

rice paper, 1. a thin, edible paper made from the straw of rice. **2.** a Chinese paper consisting of the pith of certain plants cut and pressed into thin sheets.

rice pudding, a hot or cold sweet dish made with milk and whole or ground rice and sugar.

ricer (rī′sə), *n. U.S.* an implement for ricing potatoes, etc., by pressing them through small holes.

ricercare (*It.* rē chĕr kä′rĕ), *n. Music.* (originally) a piece of contrapuntal music for instruments, using elaborate imitation, later used by composers of elaborate figures. Also, **ricercar** (*It.* rē chĕr kär′). [It.]

rich (rĭch), *adj.* **1.** having wealth or great possessions; abundantly supplied with resources, means, or funds: *a rich man or nation.* **2.** abounding in natural resources: *a rich territory.* **3.** having wealth or valuable resources (fol. by *in*): *a tract rich in minerals.* **4.** abounding (fol. by *in* or *with*): *a country rich in traditions.* **5.** of great value or worth; valuable: *a rich harvest.* **6.** costly; expensively elegant or fine, as dress, jewels, etc. **7.** sumptuous, as a feast. **8.** of valuable materials or elaborate workmanship, as buildings, furniture, etc. **9.** abounding in desirable elements or qualities. **10.** (of food) containing good, nutritious, or choice ingredients, as butter, cream, sugar, etc. **11.** (of wine, gravy, etc.) strong and full flavoured. **12.** (of colour) deep, strong, or vivid. **13.** (of sound, the voice, etc.) full and mellow in tone. **14.** (of smell) strongly scented. **15.** producing or yielding abundantly: *a rich soil.* **16.** abundant, plentiful, or ample: *a rich supply.* **17.** *Colloq.* highly amusing. **18.** *Colloq.* ridiculous, absurd, or preposterous. —*n.* **19.** rich people collectively (usually prec. by *the*). [ME; OE *rīce*, c. G *reich*, of Celtic origin; akin to L *rex* king] —**rich′ly,** *adv.* —**rich′ness,** *n.*

—**Syn. 1.** well-to-do, moneyed. RICH, AFFLUENT, OPULENT, WEALTHY agree in indicating abundance of possessions. RICH is the general word; it may imply that possessions are newly acquired: *a rich oil man.* WEALTHY suggests permanence, stability, and appropriate surroundings: *a wealthy banker.* AFFLUENT and OPULENT both suggest the possession of great wealth; AFFLUENT especially connoting a handsome income and free expenditure of resources; OPULENT suggesting display or luxuriousness: *an affluent family, opulent circumstances.* **15.** fruitful, productive. —**Ant. 1.** poor.

Richard I (rĭch′əd) ('*Richard the Lion-Heart*', '*Richard Coeur de Lion*'), 1157–99, king of England 1189–99.

Richard II, 1367–1400, king of England 1377–99 (successor and grandson of Edward III; son of the Black Prince).

Richard III (*Duke of Gloucester*), 1452–85, king of England 1483–85.

Richardson (rĭch′əd sən), *n.* **1. Henry Handel** (*Henrietta Richardson Robertson*), 1870–1946, Australian novelist. **2. Henry Hobson,** 1838–86, U.S. architect. **3. Sir Owen Williams,** 1879–1959, English physicist. **4. Sir Ralph (David),** born 1902, English actor. **5. Samuel,** 1689–1761, English novelist.

Richelieu (rĭsh′ə lyû′; *Fr.* rē shə lyœ′), *n.* **1. Armand Jean du Plessis** (*Fr.* är mäN zhäN dY plĕ sē′), **Duc de,** 1585–1642, French cardinal and statesman. **2.** a river in SE Canada, in Quebec, flowing from Lake Champlain N to the St Lawrence. ab. 210 mi.

riches (rĭch′ĭz), *n.pl.* abundant and valuable possessions; wealth. [ME, t. OF: m. *richesse* wealth, der. *riche* (of Gmc orig.) RICH]

Richmond (rĭch′mənd), *n.* a city in the U.S., the capital of Virginia, in the E part: port on James river. 219,958 (1960).

Richmond upon Thames, a SW outer London borough. 182,000 (est. 1964).

rich rhyme, complete identity in sound but not in sense, of the rhyming syllables, as *bare, bear* or *mind, undermined.*

Richter (*Ger.* rĭKH′tər *for 1*; *Russ.* rĕKH′tĭr *for 2*), *n.* **1. Jean Paul Friedrich** (*Ger.* zhäN poul frē′drĭKH), ('*Jean Paul*'), 1763–1825, German author. **2. Sviatoslav** (*Russ.* svĭtäs läf′), born 1914, Soviet pianist.

Richthofen (*Ger.* rĭKHt′hō fən), *n.* **Baron Manfred von** (*Ger.* män′frĕt fōn), 1892–1918, German aviator.

ricin (rī′sĭn, rĭs′ĭn), *n. Chem.* a white, toxic protein from the bean of the castor-oil plant. [t. NL: s. *ricinus* a genus of plants, t. L (Pliny)]

ricinoleic acid (rĭs′ĭ nō lē′ĭk, -ĭ nō′lĭ ĭk), *Chem.* an unsaturated hydroxy acid, $C_{17}H_{32}(OH)COOH$, occurring in castor oil in the form of the glyceride. [f. RICIN + -OLE + -IC]

ricinolein (rĭs′ĭ nō′lĭ ĭn), *n. Chem.* the glyceride of ricinoleic acid, the chief constituent of castor oil.

rick[1] (rĭk), *n.* **1.** a stack of hay, straw, or the like, esp. one thatched or covered for protection. —*v.t.* **2.** to pile in ricks. [ME *rek(e)*, OE *hrēac*, c. D *rook*]

rick[2] (rĭk), *v.t.* to sprain or strain as one's neck, back, etc. [var. of WRICK]

rickets (rĭk′ĭts), *n. Pathol.* a disease of childhood, characterized by softening of the bones as a result of malnutrition (ordinarily lack of vitamin D), or insufficient ingestion of calcium, or both, and often resulting in deformities. [orig. uncert.]

rickettsia (rĭ kĕt′sĭ ə), *n.pl.* bacteria-like micro-organisms, apparently members of a single group or genus, which are found living as parasites in arthropods and are the cause of certain human diseases, as Rocky Mountain spotted fever. [named after Howard T. *Ricketts*, 1871–1910, U.S. pathologist] —**rickett′sial,** *adj.*

rickety (rĭk′ĭ tĭ), *adj.* **1.** liable to fall or collapse; shaky: *a rickety chair.* **2.** feeble in the joints; tottering; infirm. **3.** irregular, as motion or action. **4.** affected with or suffering from rickets. **5.** pertaining to or of the nature of rickets. [f. RICKET(S) + -Y[1]]

rickey (rĭk′ĭ), *n., pl.* **-eys.** *U.S.* a drink made principally of spirits (esp. gin), lime juice, and soda water. [named after a Colonel *Rickey*]

rickle (rĭk′l), *Scot. and N Dial.* —*n.* **1.** a loose heap or pile. **2.** a pile of corn, hay, or the like. —*v.t.* **3.** to make or form into a rickle or stack. [? t. Scand.; cf. Norw. *rikl* heap]

Rickman (rĭk′mən), *n.* **Thomas,** 1776–1841, English architect and writer.

Rickmansworth (rĭk′mənz wûth′), *n.* a town in England, in Hertfordshire. 28,442 (1961).

rickrack (rĭk′răk′), *n.* a narrow zigzag braid used to trim clothing, etc. Also, **ricrac.** [dissimilated reduplication of RACK[1]]

Rickshaw

rickshaw (rĭk′shô), *n.* a small two-wheeled hooded vehicle drawn by one or more men, used in Japan and elsewhere; jinrikisha. Also, **ricksha.**

ricochet (rĭk′ə shā′, -shĕt′), *n.*, *v.*, **-cheted, -chetted** (-shād′, -shĕt′ĭd), **-cheting, -chetting** (-shā′ĭng, -shĕt′ĭng). —*n.* **1.** the motion of an object or projectile which rebounds one or more times from a flat surface over which it is passing. —*v.i.* **2.** to move in this way, as a projectile. [t. F; orig. uncert.]

ricotta (rĭ kŏt′ə; *It.* rē kŏt′tä), *n.* a soft Italian cottage cheese.

rictus (rĭk′təs), *n.* **1.** *Zool.* the gape of an animal and particularly of a bird. **2.** *Bot.* the opening of the lipped petals of a flower. [t. L: gape] —**ric′tal,** *adj.*

rid[1] (rĭd), *v.t.*, **rid** or **ridded, ridding. 1.** to clear, disencumber, or free of something objectionable (fol. by *of*). **2.** to disembarrass or relieve (fol. by *of*): *to rid the mind of doubt.* **3.** *Obs. or Archaic.* to deliver, rescue, or save (fol. by *out*, *of*, *from*, etc.). **4. get rid of, a.** to get free, or relieved of. **b.** to get (a thing or person) off one's hands. **c.** to do away with. [ME *rydde*, OE *geryddan* clear (land), c. Icel. *rydhja* clear, empty] —**rid′der,** *n.*

rid[2] (rĭd), *v.* *Archaic.* pt. and pp. of **ride.**

riddance (rĭd′ns), *n.* **1.** a clearing away or out, as of anything undesirable. **2.** a relieving or deliverance from something. **3. good riddance,** a welcome deliverance.

ridden (rĭd′n), *v.* pp. of **ride.**

riddle[1] (rĭd′l), *n.*, *v.*, **-dled, -dling.** —*n.* **1.** a question or statement so framed as to exercise one's ingenuity in answering it or discovering its meaning; conundrum. **2.** a puzzling question, problem, or matter. **3.** a puzzling thing or person. **4.** any enigmatic or dark saying or speech. —*v.i.* **5.** to propound riddles; to speak enigmatically. [ME *redele*, OE *rǣdelle*, var. of *rǣdels(e)* enigma (c. G *Rätsel*), der. *rǣdan* READ[1]] —**Syn. 1.** See **puzzle.**

riddle[2] (rĭd′l), *v.*, **-dled, -dling,** *n.* —*v.t.* **1.** to pierce with many holes suggesting those of a sieve. **2.** to sift through a riddle, as gravel. **3.** to fill with (esp. something undesirable). **4.** to impair or refute completely by persistent verbal attacks: *to riddle a person's reputation.* —*n.* **5.** a coarse sieve, as one for sifting sand in the foundry. [ME *riddil*, OE *hriddel*, dissimilated var. of *hridder*, akin to L *cribrum* sieve]

ride (rīd), *v.*, **rode** or (*Archaic*) **rid; ridden** or (*Archaic*) **rid; riding;** *n.* —*v.i.* **1.** to sit on and manage a horse or other animal in motion; be carried on the back of an animal. **2.** to be carried on something as if on horseback. **3.** to be borne along on or in a vehicle or any kind of conveyance. **4.** to move along in any way; be carried or supported: *distress riding among the people.* **5.** to move or float on the water. **6.** to lie at anchor, as a ship. **7.** to appear to float in space, as a heavenly body. **8.** to turn or rest on something. **9.** to extend or project over something, as the edge of one thing over the edge of another thing. **10.** to work or move (*up*) from the proper position, as a skirt, or the like. **11.** to have a specified character for riding purposes: *the train rides smoothly.* **12. ride for a fall, a.** to ride (a horse) recklessly. **b.** to act in a way which will inevitably bring disaster. —*v.t.* **13.** to sit on and manage (a horse or other animal, or a bicycle or the like) so as to be carried along. **14.** to sit or be mounted on (something) as if on horseback; be carried or borne along on. **15.** to rest on, esp. by overlapping. **16.** to control, dominate, or tyrannize over: *a land that was kingridden.* **17.** *U.S. Slang.* to harass or torment. **18.** to ride over, along or through (a road, boundary, region, etc.). **19.** to execute by riding: *to ride a race.* **20.** *U.S.* to cause to ride. **21.** *Now U.S.* to carry (a person) on something as if riding on a horse: *to ride a person on a rail as punishment.* **22.** to keep (a vessel) at anchor or moored. **23. ride down, a.** to trample under a horse's hooves. **b.** to pursue and catch up with. **24. ride out, a.** to sustain (a gale, etc.) without damage, as while riding at anchor. **b.** to sustain or endure successfully.
—*n.* **25.** a journey or excursion on a horse, etc., or on or in a vehicle. **26.** a way, road, etc., made esp. for riding. **27. take for a ride,** *Colloq.* **a.** to kidnap and murder. **b.** to deceive and wilfully mislead.
[ME *ride(n)*, OE *rīdan*, c. D *rijden*, G *reiten*, Dan. *ride*] —**Syn. 3.** See **drive.**

rideable (rī′də bl), *adj.* **1.** capable of being ridden, as a horse. **2.** capable of being ridden over, through, etc., as a road or a stream. Also, **ridable.**

rident (rī′dnt), *adj.* laughing; smiling; cheerful. [t. L: s. *ridens*, ppr.]

rider (rī′də), *n.* **1.** one who rides a horse or other animal, or a bicycle or the like. **2.** one who or that which rides. **3.** any of various objects or devices straddling, mounted on, or attached to something else. **4.** *Chem.* a small piece of platinum wire used on a chemical balance arm to make the final adjustment. **5.** an additional clause usually unrelated to the main body, attached to a legislative bill in passing it. **6.** an addition or amendment to a document, etc. **7.** *Maths.* a problem arising out of a proposition.

ridge (rĭj), *n.*, *v.*, **ridged, ridging.** —*n.* **1.** a long, narrow elevation of land, or a chain of hills or mountains. **2.** the long and narrow upper part or crest of something, as of an animal's back, a hill, a wave, etc. **3.** *Obs.* the back of an animal. **4.** any raised narrow strip, as on cloth, etc. **5.** the horizontal line in which the tops of the rafters of a roof meet. **6.** *Meteorol.* **a.** a band of relatively high pressure usually joining two anticyclones. **b.** an elongated wedge (def. 3). **7.** the earth thrown up by a plough between furrows. **8.** a strip of arable land, usually between furrows. —*v.t.* **9.** to provide with or form into a ridge or ridges. **10.** to mark with or as with ridges. —*v.i.* **11.** to form ridges. [ME *rigge*, OE *hrycg* spine, crest, ridge, c. D *rug*]

ridgeling (rĭj′lĭng), *n.* *Vet. Sci.* a colt with undescended testicles. Also, **ridgel** (rĭj′əl).

ridgepole (rĭj′pōl′), *n.* **1.** the horizontal timber or member at the top of a roof, to which the upper ends of the rafters are fastened. **2.** the horizontal pole at the top of a tent.

ridge rope, a centre line rope or wire over which a canvas awning is spread.

ridge tile, a special angle tile made to cap the apex of a pitched roof.

ridgeway (rĭj′wā′), *n.* a path or road along a ridge.

ridgy (rĭj′ĭ), *adj.* rising in a ridge or ridges.

ridicule (rĭd′ĭ kyōōl′), *n.*, *v.*, **-culed, -culing.** —*n.* **1.** words or actions intended to excite contemptuous laughter at a person or thing; derision. —*v.t.* **2.** to deride; make fun of. [t. F, t. L: m. *rīdiculum* laughable (thing), prop. neut. adj.] —**rid′icul′er,** *n.*

—**Syn. 1.** mockery, gibes, jeers. **2.** banter, rally, chaff, twit. RIDICULE, DERIDE, MOCK, TAUNT imply making game of a person, usually in an unkind, jeering way. To RIDICULE is to make fun of, either sportively and good-humouredly, or (more often) unkindly with the intention of humiliating: *to ridicule a pretentious person.* To DERIDE is to assail one with scornful laughter: *to deride a statement of belief.* To MOCK is sometimes playfully, sometimes insultingly, to imitate and caricature the appearance or actions of another: *to mock the seriousness of his expression.* To TAUNT is maliciously and exultingly to press upon one's attention (and often on the notice of others) some annoying or humiliating fact: *to taunt a person defeated in a contest.* —**Ant. 1.** praise.

ridiculous (rĭ dĭk′yōō ləs), *adj.* **1.** such as to excite ridicule or derision; absurd, preposterous, or laughable. —*n.* **2.** that which is ridiculous (prec. by *the*). —**ridic′ulously,** *adv.* —**ridic′ulousness,** *n.* —**Syn. 1.** nonsensical, ludicrous, funny. See **absurd.**

riding[1] (rī′dĭng), *n.* **1.** the act of one who or that which rides. —*adj.* **2.** used in travelling or in riding. [f. RIDE + -ING[1]]

riding[2] (rī′dĭng), *n.* **1.** (*cap.*) each of the three administrative divisions into which Yorkshire is divided: *the North Riding, East Riding, and West Riding.* **2.** each of a like group elsewhere. **3.** ride (def. 25). [ME *triding*, t. Scand.; cf. Icel. *thridhjungr* third part; *t-* for *th-* by assimilation to *-t* in *east* and *west*; later *-t t-* simplified to *-t*]

riding boot, a close-fitting knee-high leather boot, worn as part of a riding habit.

riding breeches, calf-length trousers flaring at the sides of the thighs and closely-fitting just below the knee, worn with riding boots.

riding crop, crop (def. 7).

riding light, anchor light.

riding master, a man who teaches horse-riding.

riding school, a place where horse-riding is taught.

riding stables, stables for the housing of saddle horses.

Ridley (rĭd′lĭ), *n.* **Nicholas,** *c.* 1500–55, English bishop, reformer, and Protestant martyr.

ridotto (rĭ dŏt′ō), *n.*, *pl.* **-tos.** a public ball or social gathering, often in masquerade (common in the 18th century). [t. It.: a retreat, resort. See REDOUBT]

Rieka (*Serb.* rē yĕ′kä), *n.* Rijeka.

riel (rē′əl), *n.* **1.** the monetary unit of Cambodia, equal to 100 sen, and equivalent to about £0·119 sterling. **2.** a banknote of this value.

Riemann (*Ger.* rē′män), *n.* **Georg Friedrich Bernhard** (*Ger.* gė ŏrk′ frē′drĭKH bĕrn′härt), 1826–66, German mathematician.

riempie (rĭm′pĭ), *n.* *S African.* a leather thong. [t. Afrikaans]

Rienzi (rĭ ĕn′zĭ; *It.* ryĕn′tsē), *n.* **Cola di** (*It.* kō′lä dē) (*Nicholas Gabrini*), 1313?–54, Roman orator and tribune of the people. Also, **Rienzo** (rĭ ĕn′zō; *It.* ryĕn′tsō).

Riesling (rēs′lĭng), *n.* **1.** a wine grape of Alsace, the Rhine region, and elsewhere. **2.** the wine made from this.

Riet (rēt), *n.* a river in the Republic of South Africa flowing NW through Orange Free State to the Modder. ab. 200 mi.

rietbok (rēt′bŏk′), *n.* *S African.* reedbuck.

Rietveld (*Du.* rēt′vĕlt), *n.* **Gerrit Thomas** (*Du.* KHĕ′rĭt tō′mäs), 1888–1964, Dutch architect.

Rif (rĭf), *n.* **Er** (ĕə), a mountainous coastal region in N Morocco. Also, **Riff.**

rifacimento (rĭ fä′chĭ mĕn′tō), *n.*, *pl.* **-ti** (-tĭ). a recast or adaptation, as of a literary or musical work. [It.: a remaking, der. *rifare* make over, f. *ri-* RE- + *fare* make, g. L *facere*]

rife (rīf), *adj.* **1.** of common or frequent occurrence; prevalent; in widespread existence, activity, or use. **2.** current in speech or report. **3.** abundant, plentiful, or numerous. **4.** abounding (fol. by *with*, formerly *in*). [ME; late OE *rȳfe*, c. MD *rijf*] **—Ant. 3.** scarce.

riff (rĭf), *n. Colloq.* a melodic phrase, constantly repeated, which often serves as the main theme or the background in a piece of jazz. [short for REFRAIN]

Riff (rĭf), *n.* a member of the primitive northern African people of Barbary and the Sahara. —**Riffian** (rĭf′ĭ ən), *adj.*, *n.*

riffle (rĭf′əl), *n.*, *v.*, **-fled, -fling.** —*n.* **1.** *U.S.* **a.** a rapid, as in a stream. **b.** a ripple, as upon the surface of water. **2.** *Mining.* **a.** the lining at the bottom of a sluice or the like, made of blocks or slats of wood, or stones, arranged in such a manner that grooves or openings are left between them for catching and collecting particles of gold. **b.** one of the slats of wood or the like so used. **c.** one of the grooves or openings formed. **3.** the method of riffling cards. —*v.t.*, *v.i.* **4.** to cause or become a riffle. **5.** to flutter and shift, as pages. **6.** to shuffle (cards) by dividing the pack in two, raising the corners slightly, and allowing them to fall alternately together. [b. RIPPLE and RUFFLE[1]]

riffler (rĭf′lə), *n.* a curved file for shaping concave surfaces.

riffraff (rĭf′răf′), *n.* **1.** the worthless or disreputable element of society; the rabble: *the riffraff of the city.* **2.** worthless or low persons. **3.** *Dial.* trash; rubbish. [ME *rif and raf* every particle, things of small value, t. OF: m. *rif et raf*, *rifle rafle*, der. OF *rifler* spoil, *raffler* ravage, snatch away]

rifle[1] (rī′fəl), *n.*, *v.*, **-fled, -fling.** —*n.* **1.** a shoulder firearm with spiral grooves cut in the inner surface of the gun barrel to give the bullet a rotatory motion and thus render its flight more accurate. **2.** one of the grooves. **3.** a cannon with such grooves. **4.** (*pl.*) certain military units or bodies equipped with rifles. —*v.t.* **5.** to cut spiral grooves within (a gun barrel, etc.). [t. LG: m. s. *rifeln* to groove, der. *rive*, *riefe* groove, flute, furrow; akin to OE *rifelede* wrinkled, *rif* violent]

rifle[2] (rī′fəl), *v.t.*, **-fled, -fling. 1.** to ransack and rob (a place, receptacle, etc.). **2.** to search and rob (a person). **3.** to plunder or strip bare of. **4.** to steal or take away. [ME *rifel*, t. OF: s. *rifler* scrape, graze, plunder, t. D: m. *riffelen* scrape, c. RIFLE[1], v.] —**ri′fler,** *n.* **—Syn. 1.** See **rob.**

riflebird (rī′fəl bûd′), *n.* any bird of paradise of the family *Paradisaeidae*, of the genera *Ptilovis* and *Craspedophora*, of New Guinea, etc.

rifle grenade, a hand grenade mounted on a round steel rod which is then fired from the barrel of a rifle.

rifleman (rī′fəl mən), *n.*, *pl.* **-men. 1.** a soldier armed with a rifle. **2.** one skilled in the use of a rifle. **3.** a small New Zealand bush wren, *Acanthisitta chloris.*

rifle range, 1. a target practice ground. **2.** the distance covered by the bullet discharged from a rifle.

rifling (rī′flĭng), *n.* **1.** the act or process of cutting spiral grooves in a gun barrel, etc. **2.** the system of spiral grooves so cut.

rift (rĭft), *n.* **1.** an opening made by riving or splitting; a fissure; a cleft; a chink. **2.** a break in the friendly relations between two people, countries, etc. —*v.i.*, *v.t.* **3.** to burst open; split. [ME, t. Scand.; cf. Dan. *rift* cleft; akin to RIVE, v.]

rift valley, a portion of the earth's crust, bounded on at least two sides by faults, that has been moved downwards in relation to the adjacent portions; graben.

rig (rĭg), *v.*, **rigged, rigging,** *n.* —*v.t.* **1.** *Chiefly Naut.* **a.** to put in proper order for working or use. **b.** to fit (a vessel, a mast, etc.) with the necessary shrouds, stays, etc. **c.** to fit (shrouds, stays, sails, etc.) to the mast, yard, or the like. **2.** *Aeron.* to obtain the correct relative positions of the different components of an aircraft. **3.** to furnish or provide with equipment, etc.; fit (usually fol. by *out* or *up*). **4.** to prepare or put together, esp. as a makeshift (often fol. by *up*). **5.** *Colloq.* to fit or deck with clothes, etc. (often fol. by *out* or *up*). **6.** to manipulate fraudulently: *to rig prices.* —*n.* **7.** the arrangement of the masts, spars, sails, etc., on a boat or ship. **8.** apparatus for some purpose; equipment; outfit. **9.** *U.S. Colloq.* a vehicle with a horse or horses, as for driving. **10.** the equipment used in drilling an oil or gas well. **11.** *Colloq.* costume or dress, esp. when odd or conspicuous. [prob. t. Scand.; cf. d. Sw. *rigga på* to harness] —**rigged,** *adj.*

Riga (rē′gə), *n.* **1.** a seaport in the W Soviet Union, on the Gulf of Riga: capital of the Latvian Republic. 658,000 (est. 1965). **2. Gulf of,** an arm of the Baltic between Latvia and Estonia. ab. 100 mi. long; ab. 60 mi. wide.

rigadoon (rĭg′ə do͞on′), *n.* **1.** a lively dance, formerly popular, for one couple, characterized by a peculiar jumping step, and usually in quick duple rhythm. **2.** a piece of music for this dance, or in its rhythm. [t. F: m. *rigaudon*; named after *Rigaud*, the originator]

rigatoni (rē′gə tō′nĭ; *It.* rē gä tô′nē), *n.pl.* ridged, cut macaroni, sometimes curved. [It.]

Rigel (rī′gl), *n. Astron.* a bluish star, *Beta Orionis*, of the first magnitude in the constellation Orion.

rigger (rĭg′ə), *n.* **1.** one who rigs. **2.** one whose occupation is the fitting of the rigging of ships. **3.** one who works with hoisting tackle, etc. **4.** one of the metal stays which support the rowlock away from the boat's side. **5.** this stay together with the rowlock. **6.** *Aeron.* a mechanic skilled at assembling and repairing aeroplane wings, fuselages, and sometimes control mechanisms.

rigging (rĭg′ĭng), *n.* **1.** the ropes, chains, etc., employed to support and work the masts, yards, sails, etc., on a ship. **2.** a system of wires used to obtain the correct angles of incidence and dihedral, or the relative positions, of different components in an aircraft. **3.** a system of wires by which loads are distributed over the hull of an airship. **4.** tackle in general.

rigging batten, *Naut.* a long narrow strip of wood or metal fastened to a shroud or the like of a ship's rigging as a protection against chafing.

rigging plan, an architectural plan of the rigging of a ship's mast.

Riggs' disease (rĭgz), *Pathol.* pyorrhoea. [named after John M. *Riggs*, 1810–85, U.S. dentist]

right (rīt), *adj.* **1.** in accordance with what is just or good: *right conduct.* **2.** in conformity with fact, reason, or some standard or principle; correct: *the right solution.* **3.** correct in judgement, opinion, or action. **4.** sound or normal, as the mind, etc.; sane, as persons. **5.** in good health or spirits, as persons: *he is all right again.* **6.** in a satisfactory state; in good order: *to put things right.* **7.** principal, front, or upper: *the right side of cloth.* **8.** most convenient, desirable, or favourable. **9.** fitting or appropriate: *to say the right thing.* **10.** genuine; legitimate: *the right owner.* **11.** belonging or pertaining to the side of a person or thing which is turned towards the east when the face is towards the north (opposed to *left*). **12.** belonging or pertaining to the political right. **13.** straight: *a right line.* **14.** formed by, or with reference to, a line or a plane extending to another line or a surface by the shortest course: *a right angle.* **15.** *Geom.* having the axis perpendicular to the base: *a right cone.* **16.** *Colloq.* unquestionable; unmistakeable; true: *he's a right idiot.*
—*n.* **17.** a just claim or title, whether legal, prescriptive, or moral. **18.** that which is due to anyone by just claim: *to give one his right or his rights.* **19.** *Finance.* **a.** the privilege, usually pre-emptive, which accrues to the owners of the stock of a company to subscribe for additional stock or shares at an advantageous price. **b.** (*often pl.*) a privilege of subscribing for a stock or bond. **20.** that which is ethically good and proper and in conformity with the moral law. **21.** that which accords with fact, reason, or propriety. **22.** the right or proper way of thinking: *to be in the right.* **23.** the right side or what is on the right side: *to turn to the right.* **24. the Right,** (*often l.c.*) **a.** that part of a legislative assembly in continental Europe which sits on the right of the president, a position customarily assigned to the conservatives. **b.** a body of persons, political party, etc., holding conservative views. **25. by rights,** in all fairness; rightfully. **26. to rights,** into proper condition: *to set a room to rights.*
—*adv.* **27.** in a right or straight line; straight; directly (fol. by *to, into, through,* etc.): *right to the bottom.* **28.** quite or completely: *his hat was knocked right off.* **29.** immediately: *right after dinner.* **30.** exactly, precisely, or just: *right here.* **31.** uprightly or righteously. **32.** correctly or accurately: *to guess right.* **33.** properly or fittingly: *to behave right, it serves you right.* **34.** advantageously, favourably, or well: *to turn out right.* **35.** towards the right hand; to the right. **36.** *Colloq. or Dial.* extremely: *I was right glad to be there.* **37.** very (used in certain titles): *the right reverend.* **38.** *Slang.* very; really; extraordinarily: *he's right stupid.*
—*v.t.* **39.** to bring or restore to an upright or the proper position. **40.** to set in order or put right. **41.** to bring into conformity with fact, or correct. **42.** to do justice to. **43.** to redress (wrong, etc.).
—*v.i.* **44.** to resume an upright or the proper position.
[ME; OE *reht, riht*, c. D and G *recht*, Icel. *rēttr*, Goth. *raihts*; akin to L *rectus*] **—Syn. 1.** equitable. **2.** accurate, true. **8.** proper, suitable, convenient. **20.** virtue.

rightabout (rīt′ə bout′), *n.* the opposite direction as faced after turning about to the right.

right about turn, *Mil.* a command to turn so as to face in the opposite direction.

right angle, the angle formed by two perpendicular lines intercepting a quarter of a circle drawn about its vertex. See diag. under **angle.** —**right′-an′gled,** *adj.*

right-angled triangle (rīt′ăng′gld), a triangle in which one of the angles is a right angle. Also, **right triangle.**

right ascension, *Astron.* **1.** the rising of a star or point above the horizon on the celestial sphere. **2.** the arc of the celestial equator measured eastwards from the vernal equinox to the foot of the great circle passing through the celestial poles and the point on the celestial sphere in question, and expressed in degrees or time.

right away, directly; immediately: *I'll do it right away.*

right back, *Soccer, Hockey, etc.* the full-back on the right side of the field of play.

right centre, *Rugby Football.* the right of the two middle players in the three-quarter line.

righteous (rī′chəs), *adj.* **1.** characterized by uprightness or morality: *a righteous act.* **2.** morally right or justifiable: *righteous indignation.* **3.** in accordance with right; upright or virtuous: *a righteous and godly man.* —*n.* **4.** righteous people collectively (prec. by *the*). [earlier *rightwos(e), rightwis(e),* OE *rihtwīs,* f. *riht* RIGHT + *wīs* WISE²] —**right′eously,** *adv.* —**right′eousness,** *n.* —**Ant. 3.** evil, wicked.

rightful (rīt′fəl), *adj.* **1.** having a right, or just claim, as to some possession or position: *the rightful owner.* **2.** belonging by right, or just claim: *one's rightful property.* **3.** equitable or just, as actions, etc.: *a rightful cause.* —**right′fully,** *adv.* —**right′fulness,** *n.*

right half, *Soccer, Hockey, etc.* the left of the three players in the half-back line.

right hand, the most efficient help or resource.

right-hand (rīt′hănd′), *adj.* **1.** on or to the right: *right-hand drive.* **2.** of, for, or with the right hand. **3.** most efficient or useful as a helper: *one's right-hand man.*

right-handed (rīt′hăn′dĭd), *adj.* **1.** having the right hand or arm more serviceable than the left; preferring to use the right hand. **2.** adapted to or performed by the right hand. **3.** situated on the side of the right hand. **4.** moving or rotating from left to right, or in the same direction as the hands of a clock. **5.** (of a rope) having the strands forming a spiral to the right. **6. right-handed helix** or **spiral,** one that is turned in this way and runs upwards from left to right when viewed from the side with the axis vertical, as the thread of a right-handed screw.

rightist (rī′tĭst), *n.* **1.** a member of a conservative or reactionary party or a person sympathizing with their views. —*adj.* **2.** having conservative or reactionary political ideas. [f. RIGHT (def. 24) + -IST]

rightly (rīt′lĭ), *adv.* **1.** in accordance with truth or fact; correctly. **2.** in accordance with morality or equity; uprightly. **3.** properly, fitly, or suitably. **4.** *Colloq.* positively, certainly: *I don't rightly know.* [ME; OE *rihtlīce.* See RIGHT, -LY]

right-minded (rīt′mīn′dĭd), *adj.* having right opinions or principles. —**right′-mind′edness,** *n.*

rightness (rīt′nĭs), *n.* **1.** correctness or accuracy. **2.** propriety or fitness. **3.** straightness or directness.

righto (rīt′ō′), *interj. Colloq.* (an expression indicating agreement.)

right of search, *Law.* a privilege of a nation at war to search neutral ships on the high seas for contraband or other matters in violation of neutrality which may subject the ship to seizure.

right of way, 1. a common law or statutory right to proceed ahead of another. **2.** a path or route which may lawfully be used. **3.** a right of passage, as over another's land. **4.** the strip of land acquired for use by a railway for its tracks. **5.** land covered by a public road. **6.** land over which a power line passes.

rights issue, *Stock Exchange.* an issue of stocks or shares offered to members of a company at a preferential price.

right triangle, right-angled triangle.

right turn, *Mil.* a command to face to the right in a prescribed manner while standing.

rightward (rīt′wəd), *adv.* **1.** Also, **rightwards.** towards or on the right. —*adj.* **2.** situated on the right. **3.** directed towards the right.

right whale, any of various large toothless whales, genus *Balaena,* including those hunted commercially.

right wing, 1. the members of a conservative or reactionary political party or section of a party, generally those opposing extensive political reform. **2.** such a group, party, or a group of such parties. **3.** *Sport.* that part of the field of play which forms the right flank of the area being attacked by either team. **4.** *Sport.* a player positioned on the right flank, as the outside right in soccer, the right of the wing-three-quarters in rugby football, etc. —**right′-wing′,** *adj.* —**right′-wing′er,** *n.*

Rigi (rē′gĭ), *n.* a mountain in central Switzerland, near Lake Lucerne. 5906 ft.

rigid (rĭj′ĭd), *adj.* **1.** stiff or unyielding; not pliant or flexible; hard. **2.** firmly fixed, set, or not moving. **3.** inflexible, strict, or severe: *a rigid discipline or disciplinarian.* **4.** rigorously strict regarding opinion or observance. **5.** severely exact; rigorous: *a rigid examination.* **6.** *Aeron.* **a.** (of an airship or dirigible) having its form maintained by a rigid structure contained within the envelope. **b.** pertaining to a helicopter rotor which is fixedly held at its root. [t. L: s. *rigidus*] —**rigid′ity, rig′idness,** *n.* —**rig′idly,** *adv.* —**Syn. 1.** unbending, firm. **3.** rigorous, stringent, austere, stern. See **strict.** —**Ant. 1.** elastic. **3.** lax.

rigmarole (rĭg′mə rōl′), *n.* **1.** a succession of confused or foolish statements; incoherent or rambling discourse. **2.** a long and complicated process. [alter. of obs. *ragman roll* a roll, list, or catalogue, f. *ragman,* in same sense (of obscure orig.) + ROLL]

rigor (rĭg′ə), *n. U.S.* rigour.

rigorism (rĭg′ə rĭz′əm), *n.* **1.** extreme strictness. **2.** *Rom. Cath. Theol.* the theory that in doubtful cases of conscience the strict course is always to be followed. —**rig′orist,** *n.* —**rig′oris′tic,** *adj.*

rigor mortis (rī′gô mô′tĭs, rĭg′ə-), the stiffening of the body after death. [L: lit., stiffness of death]

rigorous (rĭg′ə rəs), *adj.* **1.** characterized by rigour; rigidly severe or harsh, as persons, rules, discipline, etc.: *rigorous laws.* **2.** severely exact or rigidly accurate: *rigorous accuracy.* **3.** severe or sharp, as weather or climate. —**rig′orously,** *adv.* —**rig′orousness,** *n.* —**Syn. 1.** stern, austere. See **strict. 3.** inclement, bitter.

rigour (rĭg′ə), *n.* **1.** strictness, severity, or harshness, as in dealing with persons. **2.** the full or extreme severity of laws, rules, etc.: *the rigour of the law.* **3.** severity of life; hardship. **4.** a severe or harsh act, circumstance, etc. **5.** severity of weather or climate, or an instance of this: *the rigours of winter.* **6.** *Pathol.* a sudden coldness, as that preceding certain fevers; a chill. **7.** stiffness or rigidity. Also, *U.S.,* **rigor.** [ME *rigour,* t. OF, t. L: m. *rigor*]

Rigsdag (*Dan.* rēks′dåg), *n.* formerly, the parliament of Denmark, replaced in 1953 by the Folketing. [cf. RIKSDAG, REICHSTAG]

rigsdaler (rĭgz′dä′lə), *n.* an obsolete Danish silver coin worth sixteen shillings. [see RIX-DOLLAR]

Rig-Veda (rĭg′vā′də), *n. Hinduism.* the Veda of Verses, or Psalms (totalling 1028); the oldest document among the sacred scriptures of the world's living religions, dating not later than the second millennium B.C. See **Veda.** [t. Skt, f. *ric* praise + *veda* knowledge]

R.I.I.A., Royal Institute of International Affairs.

Rijeka (*Serb.* rē yĕ′kȧ), *n.* a seaport in NW Yugoslavia, at the head of the Gulf of Quarnero; seized by d'Annunzio, 1919; a part of Italy 1924–47. 100,989 (1961). Also, **Rieka.** Formerly, **Fiume.** See map under **Dalmatia.**

Rijn (*Du.* rēyn), *n.* Dutch name of the **Rhine.**

Rijswijk (*Du.* rēys′wēyk), *n.* Dutch name of **Ryswick.**

Riksdag (*Sw.* rēks′dåg), *n.* the parliament of Sweden.

Riksmål (*Norw.* rēks′mōl), *n.* a literary and urban language of Norway, based on Danish; Dano-Norwegian. Also, **Bokmål.** Cf. **Landsmål.** [Norw.: state's speech]

rile (rīl), *v.t.,* **riled, riling.** *Colloq.* **1.** to irritate or vex. **2.** *U.S.* to roil (water, etc.). [var. of ROIL]

riley (rī′lĭ), *adj. U.S.* **1.** turbid; muddy. **2.** angry; bad-tempered.

rilievo (rĭl′ĭ ā′vō), *n., pl.* **-vi** (-vē). *Sculpture, Painting, etc.* relief (defs 9, 10). [It.: relief]

Rilke (*Ger.* rĭl′kə), *n.* **Rainer Maria** (*Ger.* rī′nər mȧ rē′ȧ), 1875–1926, German poet and author, born in Prague.

rill¹ (rĭl), *n.* a small rivulet or brook. [cf. D, Fris., and LG *ril,* G *Rille*]

rill² (rĭl), *n. Astron.* any of certain long, narrow trenches or valleys observed on the surface of the moon. Also, **rille.** [t. G. See RILL¹]

rillet (rĭl′ĭt), *n.* a little rill; a streamlet.

rillettes (*Fr.* rē yĕt′), *n. pl. French.* a preparation of small pieces of pork, cooked, cooled and pounded in a mortar.

rim (rĭm), *n., v.,* **rimmed, rimming.** —*n.* **1.** the outer edge, border, or margin, esp. of a circular object. **2.** any edge or margin, often a raised one. **3.** the circular part of a wheel, farthest from the axle. **4.** a circular strip of metal forming the connection between the wheel and tyre of a motor vehicle, and either permanently attached to or removable from the wheel. **5.** *Basketball.* the metal ring in front of the backboard from which the goal net is suspended. —*v.t.* **6.** to furnish with a rim, border, or margin. **7.** (of a ball) to roll round the edge of (a hole). [ME; OE *rima,* c. Icel. *rimi* raised strip of land, ridge]

—**Syn. 1.** RIM, BRIM refer to the boundary of a circular or curved area. A RIM is a line or surface bounding such an area; an edge or border: *the rim of a glass.* BRIM usually means the inside of the rim, at the top of a hollow object (except of a hat); and is used particularly when the object contains something: *the cup was filled to the brim.*

Rimbaud (*Fr.* răɴ bō′), *n.* **(Jean Nicolas) Arthur** (*Fr.* zhäɴ nē kō lȧ ȧr tʏr′), 1854–91, French poet.
rime[1] (rīm), *n., v.t., v.i.,* **rimed, riming.** rhyme.
rime[2] (rīm), *n., v.,* **rimed, riming.** *Meteorol.* —*n.* **1.** a rough, white icy covering deposited on trees, etc., somewhat resembling white frost, but formed only from fog or vapour-bearing air. —*v.t.* **2.** to cover with rime or hoarfrost. [ME; OE *hrīm*, c. D *rijm*]
rimester (rīm′stə), *n.* rhymester.
Rimini (rĭm′ĭ nĭ; *It.* rē′mē nē), *n.* a seaport in Italy, in Emilia, on the Adriatic. 108,374 (1966).
rimose (rī mōs′), *adj.* full of chinks or crevices. [t. L: m. s. *rīmōsus* full of fissures]
Rimsky-Korsakov (rĭm′skĭ kô′sə kŏf′; *Russ.* rēm′skĭy-kôr′sə kəf), *n.* **Nikolai Andreevich** (*Russ.* nĭ kȧ lāy′ ȧn dryĕ′yĭ vĭch), 1844–1908, Russian composer.
rimu (rē′mo͞o), *n.* a tall conifer, *Dacrydium cupressinum*, of New Zealand, having awl-shaped leaves; red pine. [t. Maori]
rimy (rī′mĭ), *adj.,* **rimier, rimiest.** covered with rime.
rind (rīnd), *n.* a thick and firm coat or covering, as of animals, plants, fruits, cheeses, etc. [ME and OE *rind(e)*, c. G *Rinde*]
rinderpest (rĭn′də pĕst′), *n.* *Vet. Sci.* an acute, usually fatal, infectious virus disease of cattle, sheep, etc., characterized by high fever, diarrhoea, lesions of the skin and mucous membranes, etc. [t. G: cattle pest]
ring[1] (rĭng), *n., v.,* **ringed, ringing.** —*n.* **1.** a circular band of metal or other material, esp. one of gold or other precious metal, often set with gems, for wearing on the finger as an ornament, a token of betrothal or marriage, etc. **2.** anything having the form of a circular band. **3.** a circular line or mark. **4.** a circular course: *to dance in a ring.* **5.** the outside edge of a circular body, as a wheel. **6.** a single turn in a spiral or helix or in a spiral course. **7.** *Geom.* the area or space between two concentric circles. **8.** one of the concentric layers of wood produced yearly in the trunks of exogenous trees. **9.** a circle of bark cut from around a tree. **10.** a number of persons or things placed in a circle. **11.** an enclosed circular or other area, as one in which some sport or exhibition takes place: *the ring of a circus.* **12.** an enclosure in which boxing and wrestling matches take place (usually a square area marked off by stakes and ropes). **13.** the sport of boxing. **14.** a space devoted to betting at a racecourse. **15.** competition; contest: *to toss one's hat in the ring.* **16.** a group of persons cooperating for selfish or illegal purposes, as to control a business, monopolize a particular market, etc. **17.** *Chem.* a number of atoms so united that they may be graphically represented in cyclic form. **18. run rings round,** *Colloq.* to be markedly superior to; easily surpass.
—*v.t.* **19.** to surround with a ring; encircle. **20.** to form into a ring. **21.** to put a ring in the nose of (an animal). **22.** to hem in (animals) by riding or circling about them. **23.** to cut away the bark in a ring about (a tree, branch, etc.). **24.** (in ring toss games) to hurl a ring over (a stake or peg).
—*v.i.* **25.** to form a ring or rings. **26.** to move in a ring or a constantly curving course.
[ME; OE *hring*, c. D *ring*, G *Ring*, Icel. *hringr*. Cf. RANK[1]]
—**ring′like′**, *adj.*
—**Syn.** **2.** circlet, circle, hoop. **16.** RING and CLIQUE are terms applied with disapproving connotations to groups of persons. RING suggests a small and intimately related group, combined for selfish and often dishonest purposes: *a gambling ring.* A CLIQUE is a small group which prides itself on its congeniality and exclusiveness: *cliques in a school.*
ring[2] (rĭng), *v.,* **rang, rung, ringing,** *n.* —*v.i.* **1.** to give forth a clear, resonant sound when set in sudden vibration by a blow or otherwise, as a bell, glass, etc. **2.** to seem (true, false, etc.) in the effect produced on the mind: *his words ring true.* **3.** to cause a bell or bells to sound, esp. as a summons: *ring for a messenger.* **4.** to sound loudly; be loud or resonant; resound. **5.** to be filled with sound; re-echo with sound, as a place. **6.** (of the ears) to have the sensation of a continued humming sound.
—*v.t.* **7.** to cause to ring, as a bell, etc. **8.** to produce (sound) by or as if by ringing. **9.** to proclaim, usher in or out, summon, signal, etc., by or as by the sound of a bell: *to ring a person's praises.* **10.** to test (coin, etc.) by the sound produced in striking on something. **11.** to telephone.
—*v.* **12.** Some special verb phrases are:
ring a bell, to arouse a memory; sound familiar.
ring down the curtain, to give a direction to lower a theatre curtain, as at the end of a performance.
ring down the curtain on, to bring to an end.
ring for, to summon by ringing a bell.
ring in, to announce the arrival of by ringing bells.
ring off, to end a telephone conversation.
ring out, 1. to make a loud, resounding noise. **2.** to announce the departure of by ringing.
ring the changes, to vary the manner of performing an action; repeat in varying order.
ring true, to appear to be true, sincere, genuine, etc.
ring up, 1. to telephone. **2.** to record (the cost of an item) on a cash register.
ring up the curtain, to give a direction to raise a theatre curtain, as at the beginning of a performance.
ring up the curtain on, to begin; inaugurate.
—*n.* **13.** a ringing sound, as of a bell, etc.: *the ring of sleighbells.* **14.** a sound or note resembling the ringing of a bell: *there was a ring in his voice.* **15.** any loud sound; sound continued, repeated, or reverberated. **16.** a set or peal of bells. **17.** a telephone call: *give me a ring tomorrow.* **18.** an act of ringing a bell. **19.** a characteristic sound, as of a coin. **20.** a characteristic or inherent quality.
[ME; OE *hringan*, c. Icel. *hringja*, G *ringen*]
ringbolt (rĭng′bōlt′), *n.* a bolt with a ring fitted in an eye at its head.
ringbone (rĭng′bōn′), *n.* *Vet. Sci.* a morbid bony growth on the pastern bones of a horse, often resulting in lameness.
ringdove (rĭng′dŭv′), *n.* **1.** the European woodpigeon, *Columba palumbus*, with two whitish patches on the neck. **2.** Also, **ringed turtledove.** a small Old World pigeon, *Streptopelia risoria*, with a black half-ring around the neck.
ringed (rĭngd), *adj.* **1.** having or wearing a ring or rings. **2.** marked or decorated with a ring or rings. **3.** surrounded by a ring or rings. **4.** formed of or with rings; ringlike or annular.
ringent (rĭn′jənt), *adj.* **1.** gaping. **2.** *Bot.* having widely spread lips, as some corollas. [t. L: s. *ringens*, ppr.]
ringer[1] (rĭng′ə), *n.* **1.** one who or that which rings, encircles, etc. **2.** a quoit or horseshoe so thrown as to encircle a peg. **3.** the throw itself. [f. RING[1] + -ER[1]]
ringer[2] (rĭng′ə), *n.* **1.** one who or that which rings a bell, etc. **2.** *Slang.* an athlete, horse, etc., entered in a competition under false representations as to identity or ability. **3.** *Slang.* a person or thing that closely resembles another. **4.** *Austral. Colloq.* **a.** the fastest shearer of a group. **b.** any person of outstanding competence. [f. RING[2] + -ER[1]]
ring finger, the third finger of the left hand, on which engagement rings, wedding rings, etc., are usually worn.
ringhals (rĭng′hăls), *n.* a poisonous snake of S Africa, *Hemachatus haemachutus*, characterized by the ability to spit its venom at its victim's eyes; spitting snake. Also, **ringhals cobra.**
ringing tone, *Teleph.* a tone indicating to the subscriber that the called number is ringing.
ringleader (rĭng′lē′də), *n.* one who leads others in opposition to authority, law, etc. [der. phrase *to lead the ring* to be first]
ringlet (rĭng′lĭt), *n.* **1.** a small ring or circle. **2.** a curled lock of hair. —**ringleted** (rĭng′lĭ tĭd), *adj.*
ring main, *Elect.* **1.** a method of distributing electricity in which the supply cables form a closed ring, thus localizing supply failure. **2.** a similar system applied to the wiring of a house, factory, etc.
ringmaster (rĭng′mäs′tə), *n.* one in charge of the performances in the ring of a circus.
ringneck (rĭng′nĕk′), *n.* any of various birds having a ring of distinctive colour about the neck, as the ring-necked pheasant, the mallard, etc.
ring-necked pheasant (rĭng′nĕkt′), a gallinaceous Asiatic bird, *Phasianus colchicus*, now acclimatized esp. in Great Britain and the U.S.
ring ouzel, an ouzel cock, *Turdus torquatus*, a partial migrant to N Europe.
ring-road (rĭng′rōd′), *n.* a road skirting a town or town centre, used to relieve traffic congestion.
ringside (rĭng′sīd′), *n.* **1.** the space immediately surrounding an arena, as the first row of seats round a boxing or wrestling ring. **2.** any place providing a close view. —*adj.* **3.** of or pertaining to the area immediately surrounding a ring or arena. **4.** close to the scene of action, or providing a close view.
ringster (rĭng′stə), *n.* *U.S. Colloq.* a member of a ring, esp. a political ring.
ring-streaked (rĭng′strēkt′), *adj.* having streaks or bands of colour round the body.
ringtail (rĭng′tāl′), *n.* **1.** any phalanger of the genus *Pseudocheirus*, related by the structure of the molar teeth to the koala. **2.** *Naut.* a small sail, an extension to the spanker, set abaft it on an extended spanker boom.
ringworm (rĭng′wûm′), *n.* *Pathol.* any of certain contagious skin diseases due to vegetable parasites and characterized by the formation of ring-shaped eruptive patches.
rink (rĭngk), *n.* **1.** a sheet of ice for skating, often one artificially prepared and under cover. **2.** a smooth floor for roller-skating. **3.** a building or enclosure containing a surface prepared for skating. **4.** an area of ice marked off

for the game of curling. **5.** a section of a bowling green where a match can be played. **6.** a set of players on one side in bowling or curling. [orig. Sc.; ME *renk*, appar. t. OF: m. *renc* RANK¹]

rinse (rĭns), *v.*, **rinsed, rinsing,** *n.* —*v.t.* **1.** to wash lightly, as by pouring water into or over or by dipping in water. **2.** to put through clean water, as a final stage in cleansing. **3.** to remove (impurities, etc.) thus. —*n.* **4.** an act or instance of rinsing. **5.** a final application of water to remove impurities, unwanted substances, etc. **6.** the water or the like used. **7.** any liquid preparation used for impermanently tinting the hair. [ME *rynce*, t. OF: m. *reincer*, g. Rom. *recentiāre* make fresh, der. s. L *recens* fresh, recent] —**rins′er,** *n.*

rinsing (rĭn′sĭng), *n.* **1.** the act of one who rinses. **2.** (*chiefly pl.*) the liquid with which anything has been rinsed.

Río Bravo (*Sp.* rē′ō brä′bō), Mexican name of **Rio Grande** (def. 1).

Rio de Janeiro (rē′ō də jə nĭə′rō; *Port.* rē′o͞o dē zhə nāy′-ro͞o), a seaport in and the former capital of Brazil, in the SE part. 3,223,408 (1960). Also, **Rio.**

Río de Oro (*Sp.* rē′ō dĕ ō′rō), **1.** the S part of Spanish Sahara: formerly a Spanish colony; ab. 70,000 sq. mi. **2.** former name of **Spanish Sahara.**

Rio Grande (rē′ō grănd′, grăn′dĭ *for 1*; *Port.* rē′o͞o grən′dē *for 2*), **1.** Mexican, **Río Bravo.** a river flowing from SW Colorado through central New Mexico and along the Texas-Mexico boundary into the Gulf of Mexico. ab. 1800 mi. **2.** a river flowing from SE Brazil W to the Paraná river. ab. 600 mi.

Río Muni (*Sp.* rē′ō mo͞o′nē), a Spanish province in Africa, on the Guinea coast, forming part of Equatorial Guinea. 183,377 pop. (1960); 10,040 sq. mi.

riot (rī′ət), *n.* **1.** any disturbance of the peace by an assembly of persons. **2.** *Law.* the execution of a violent and unlawful purpose by three or more persons acting together, to the terror of the people. **3.** violent or wild disorder or confusion. **4.** loose or wanton living; unrestrained revelry. **5.** an unbridled outbreak, as of emotions, passions, etc. **6.** a brilliant display: *a riot of colour.* **7.** *Colloq.* one who or that which causes great amusement, enthusiasm, etc. **8. run riot, a.** to act without control or restraint; disregard all limits. **b.** to grow luxuriantly or wildly. —*v.i.* **9.** to take part in a riot or disorderly public outbreak. **10.** to live in a loose or wanton manner; indulge in unrestrained revelry. **11.** to indulge unrestrainedly; run riot. **12.** *Hunting.* (of a hound) to follow the scent of an animal other than the intended quarry. —*v.t.* **13.** to spend (money, etc.) or pass (time, etc.) in riotous living (fol. by *away* or *out*). [ME, t. OF: m. *riote* debate, dispute, quarrel, der. *r(u)ihoter* to quarrel, dim. of *ruir* make an uproar, g. L *rugīre* roar] —**ri′oter,** *n.* —**Syn. 1.** outbreak, disorder, brawl.

Riot Act, 1. a statute of 1715 providing that if twelve or more persons assemble unlawfully and riotously, to the disturbance of the public peace, and refuse to disperse upon proclamation (called **reading the Riot Act**), they shall be considered guilty of felony. **2. read the riot act,** *Colloq.* to give a warning to stop unruly or noisy behaviour; censure; reprimand.

riotous (rī′ə təs), *adj.* **1.** characterized by or of the nature of rioting, or disturbance of the peace, as actions. **2.** inciting to or taking part in a riot, as persons. **3.** given to or marked by unrestrained revelry; loose; wanton. **4.** boisterous or uproarious: *riotous laughter.* —**ri′otously,** *adv.* —**ri′otousness,** *n.*

rip¹ (rĭp), *v.*, **ripped, ripping,** *n.* —*v.t.* **1.** to cut or tear apart in a rough or vigorous manner; slash; slit. **2.** to cut or tear away in a rough or vigorous manner. **3.** to saw (wood) in the direction of the grain. —*v.i.* **4.** to become torn apart or split open. **5.** *Colloq.* to move along with violence or great speed.
—*v.* **6.** Some special verb phrases are:
let it rip, to allow an engine, etc., to go as fast as possible by ceasing to check or control its speed.
let rip, 1. to give free rein to anger, passion, etc. **2.** to utter oaths; swear.
rip off, to tear off violently.
rip out, 1. to remove forcibly or violently; wrench. **2.** to utter angrily; shout.
—*n.* **7.** a rent made by ripping; a tear. [late ME; c. Fris. *rippe*, Flem. *rippen* rip; akin to d. E *ripple*, v., scratch] —**Syn. 1.** See **tear².**

rip² (rĭp), *n.* a stretch of rough water at sea or in a river. [see RIP¹, v., RIPPLE¹]

rip³ (rĭp), *n. Colloq.* **1.** a dissolute or worthless person. **2.** a worthless or worn-out horse. **3.** anything of little or no value. [OE *rypa*, var. of *reopa* bundle of corn, sheaf, akin to *rīpan* reap]

R.I.P., (L *requiescat* or *requiescant in pace*) may he or she (or they) rest in peace.

riparian (rī pěə′rĭ ən), *adj.* **1.** of, pertaining to, or situated or dwelling on the bank of a river or other body of water. —*n.* **2.** *Law.* one who owns land on the bank of a natural watercourse or body of water. [f. s. L *rīpārius* belonging to a river bank or shore + -AN]

riparian right, (*usually pl.*) *Law.* a right, as fishing or use of water for irrigation or power, enjoyed by one who owns riparian property.

ripcord (rĭp′kôd′), *n. Aeron.* **1.** a cord or ring which opens a parachute during a descent. **2.** a cord fastened in the bag of a balloon or dirigible so that a sharp pull upon it will rip or open the bag and let the gas escape, thus causing the balloon to descend rapidly.

ripe (rīp), *adj.* **riper, ripest. 1.** ready for reaping or gathering, as grain, fruits, etc.; complete in natural growth or development, as when arrived at the stage most fit for eating or use. **2.** resembling ripe fruit, as in ruddiness and fullness. **3.** fully grown or developed, as animals when ready to be killed and used for food. **4.** advanced to the point of being in the best condition for use, as cheese, beer, etc. **5.** arrived at the highest or a high point of development or excellence; mature. **6.** of mature judgement or knowledge. **7.** characterized by full development of body or mind: *of ripe years.* **8.** advanced in years: *a ripe old age.* **9.** ready for action, execution, etc. **10.** fully prepared or ready to do or undergo something, or for some action, purpose, or end. **11.** ready for some operation or process: *a ripe abscess.* **12.** (of time) fully or sufficiently advanced. [ME and OE; c. D *riip*, G *reif*; akin to OE *rīpan* reap] —**ripe′ly,** *adv.* —**ripe′ness,** *n.*

—**Syn. 1.** RIPE, MATURE, MELLOW refer to that which is no longer in an incomplete stage of development. RIPE implies completed growth beyond which the processes of decay begin: *a ripe harvest.* MATURE means fully grown and developed, of living organisms: *a mature animal or tree.* MELLOW denotes complete absence of sharpness or asperity, with sweetness and richness such as characterize ripeness or age: *mellow fruit or flavour.*

ripen (rī′pən), *v.i.*, *v.t.* **1.** to become or make ripe. **2.** to come or bring to maturity, the proper condition, etc.; mature. [ME *ripe(n)*, OE *rīpian* (c. D *rijpen*), der. *rīpe* RIPE] —**rip′ener,** *n.*

ripieno (rĭ pyĕn′ō), *n. Music.* (in old use) the tutti of an orchestra as opposed to the soloists. [It.: full]

Ripley (rĭp′lĭ), *n.* **1. George,** 1802–80, U.S. literary critic, author, and editor. **2.** a town in England, in Derbyshire. 17,601 (1961).

Ripon (rĭp′ən), *n.* a city in England, in the West Riding of Yorkshire. 10,486 (1961).

riposte (rĭ pŏst′, rĭ pōst′), *n.*, *v.*, **-posted, -posting.** —*n.* **1.** *Fencing.* a quick thrust given after parrying a lunge. **2.** a quick, sharp return in speech or action. —*v.i.* **3.** to make a riposte. **4.** to reply or retaliate. Also, **ripost.** [t. F, t. It.: m. *risposta* response, der. *rispondere* answer, g. L *rēspondēre*]

ripper (rĭp′ə), *n.* **1.** one who or that which rips. **2.** Also, **ripper bill, ripper act.** *U.S.* a legislative bill or act for taking powers of appointment to and removal from office away from the usual holders of these powers and conferring them unrestrictedly on a chief executive, as a governor or a mayor, or on a board of officials.

ripping (rĭp′ĭng), *adj.* **1.** that rips. **2.** *Obs. Slang.* excellent, splendid, or fine.

ripple¹ (rĭp′l), *v.*, **-pled, -pling,** *n.* —*v.i.* **1.** to form small waves or undulations on the surface, as water when agitated by a gentle breeze or by running over a rocky bottom. **2.** to flow with a light ruffling of the surface. **3.** to form or have small undulations. **4.** (of sound) to go on or proceed with an effect like that of water flowing in ripples. —*v.t.* **5.** to form small waves or undulations on; agitate lightly. **6.** to mark as with ripples; give a wavy form to. —*n.* **7.** a small wave or undulation, as on water. **8.** any similar movement or appearance; a small undulation, as in hair. **9.** *U.S.* a small rapid. **10.** a ripple mark. **11.** a sound as of water flowing in ripples: *a ripple of laughter.* [orig. uncert.] —**rip′plingly,** *adv.* —**Syn. 7.** See **wave.**

ripple² (rĭp′l), *n.*, *v.*, **-pled, -pling.** —*n.* **1.** a toothed or comblike device for removing seeds or capsules from flax, etc. —*v.t.* **2.** to remove the seeds or capsules from (flax, etc.) with a ripple. [ME *rypel*; akin to G *Riffel*]

ripple mark, one of the wavy lines or ridges produced on sand, etc., by waves, wind, or the like.

rippler (rĭp′lə), *n.* **1.** one who ripples flax, etc. **2.** an instrument for rippling; ripple.

ripplet (rĭp′lĭt), *n.* a little ripple.

ripply (rĭp′lĭ), *adj.* **1.** characterized by ripples; rippling. **2.** sounding as rippling water.

riprap (rĭp′răp′), *n.*, *v.*, **-rapped, -rapping.** —*n.* **1.** broken stones used for foundations, revetments, etc. **2.** a foundation or wall of stones thrown together irregularly. —*v.t.* **3.** to construct with or strengthen by stones, either loose of fastened with mortar. [varied reduplication of RAP]

rip-roaring (rĭp′rô′rĭng), *adj. Slang.* boisterous; riotous; wild and noisy: *to have a rip-roaring time.*

ripsaw (rĭp′sô′), *n.* a saw used for sawing timber with the grain. [f. RIP[1], v. + SAW[1]]

ripsnorter (rĭp′snô′tə), *n. U.S. Slang.* a very violent or powerful person or thing.

riptide (rĭp′tīd′), *n.* a tide which opposes another or other tides, causing a violent disturbance in the sea.

Ripuarian (rĭp′yo͞o ĕə′rĭ ən), *adj.* **1.** designating or pertaining to the group of Franks who dwelt along the Rhine in the neighbourhood of Cologne during the 4th and 5th centuries A.D. or the code of laws observed by them. —*n.* **2.** a Ripuarian Frank. [f. s. ML *ripuārius* (orig. uncert.) pertaining to the Ripuarian Franks + -AN]

Rip Van Winkle (rĭp′ văn wĭng′kl), (in a story by Washington Irving) a ne'er-do-well who sleeps 20 years and wakes to find everything changed.

rise (rīz), *v.*, **rose, risen, rising,** *n.* —*v.i.* **1.** to get up from a lying, sitting, or kneeling posture; assume a standing position. **2.** to get up from bed: *to rise early.* **3.** to become erect and stiff, as the hair. **4.** to get up after falling or being thrown down. **5.** to become active in opposition or resistance; revolt or rebel. **6.** to be built up, erected, or constructed. **7.** to spring up or grow, as plants. **8.** to become prominent on a surface, as a blister. **9.** to come into existence; appear. **10.** to come into action, as a wind, storm, etc. **11.** to occur: *a quarrel rose between them.* **12.** to originate, issue, or be derived; to have its spring or source. **13.** to move from a lower to a higher position; move upwards; ascend: *a bird rises in the air.* **14.** to come above the horizon, as a heavenly body. **15.** to extend directly upwards: *the tower rises to the height of 60 feet.* **16.** to have an upward slant or curve: *the path rises as it approaches the house.* **17.** *Angling.* (of a fish) to come to the surface of the water to take bait, etc. **18.** to attain higher rank, importance, etc. **19.** to advance to a higher level of action, thought, feeling, expression, etc. **20.** to prove oneself equal to a demand, emergency, etc.: *to rise to the occasion.* **21.** to become animated or cheerful, as the spirits. **22.** to become stirred or roused: *to feel one's temper rising.* **23.** to increase in height, as water: *the river sometimes rose 30 feet in eight hours.* **24.** to swell or puff up, as dough from the action of yeast. **25.** to increase in amount, as prices, etc. **26.** to increase in price or value, as commodities. **27.** to increase in degree, intensity, or force, as colour, fever, etc. **28.** to become louder or of higher pitch, as the voice. **29.** to adjourn, or close a session, as a deliberative body or court. **30.** to return from the dead.
—*v.t.* **31.** to cause to rise. **32.** *Naut.* to cause (something) to rise above the visible horizon by approaching nearer to it; raise.
—*n.* **33.** the act of rising; upward movement or ascent. **34.** appearance above the horizon, as of the sun or moon. **35.** elevation or advance in rank, position, fortune, etc.: *the rise and fall of ancient Rome.* **36.** an increase in height, as of water. **37.** the amount of such increase. **38.** an increase in amount, as of prices. **39.** an increase in price or value, as of commodities. **40.** an increase in amount, as of wages, salary, etc. **41.** the amount of such an increase. **42.** an increase in degree of intensity, as of temperature. **43.** an increase in loudness or in pitch, as of the voice. **44.** the vertical height of any of various things as a stair step, a flight of steps, a roof, an arch, the crown of a road, etc. **45.** origin, source, or beginning: *the rise of a stream in a mountain.* **46.** a coming into existence or notice. **47.** extension upwards. **48.** the amount of this. **49.** upward slope, as of ground or a road. **50.** a piece of rising or high ground. **51.** *Angling.* the movement of a fish to the surface of the water to take a bait. **52. get** or **take a rise out of,** to provoke to anger, annoyance, etc., by banter, mockery, deception, etc. **53. give rise to,** cause, produce.
[ME; OE *risan*, c. D *rijzen*, G *reisen*. Cf. RAISE]

—**Syn. 31.** RISE, RAISE are not synonyms, though the forms of RAISE are commonly and mistakenly used as if they also meant RISE. RISE, the verb with irregular forms, never takes an object: *one rises from a chair.* RAISE, with regular forms (raised, have raised, raising), originally meaning 'to cause something to rise', has to have an object, either a concrete one or an abstract one: *one raises his hat, had raised a question.*

riser (rī′zə), *n.* **1.** one who rises, esp. from bed: *to be an early riser.* **2.** the vertical face of a stair step.

risibility (rĭz′ĭ bĭl′ĭ tĭ), *n.*, *pl.* **-ties. 1.** ability or disposition to laugh. **2.** laughter.

risible (rĭz′ĭ bl), *adj.* **1.** having the faculty or power of laughing; inclined to laughter. **2.** pertaining to or connected with laughing. **3.** capable of exciting laughter; laughable or ludicrous. [t. LL: m. s. *risibilis*, der. L *risus*, pp., laughed at]

rising (rī′zĭng), *adj.* **1.** that rises; advancing, ascending, or mounting. **2.** growing, or advancing to adult years: *the rising generation.* —*adv.* **3.** *U.S. Dial.* somewhat more than; above. **4.** almost; nearly; approaching the age of. —*n.* **5.** the act of one who or that which rises. **6.** an insurrection or revolt. **7.** something that rises; a projection or prominence. **8.** a period of leavening of dough preceding baking. **9.** *Dial.* a morbid swelling, as an abscess, boil, etc.

risk (rĭsk), *n.* **1.** exposure to the chance of injury or loss; a hazard or dangerous chance: *to run risks.* **2.** *Insurance.* **a.** the hazard or chance of loss. **b.** the degree of probability of such loss. **c.** the amount which the insurance company may lose. **d.** a person or thing with reference to the risk involved in insuring him or it. **e.** the type of loss, as life, fire, marine disaster, earthquake, etc., against which insurance policies are drawn. —*v.t.* **3.** to expose to the chance of injury or loss, or hazard: *to risk one's life to save another.* **4.** to venture upon; take or run the risk of: *to risk a fall in climbing; to risk a battle.* [t. F: m. *risque*, t. It.: m. *risc(hi)o*, der. *risicare* to risk, dare, ? der. Gk *rhiza* cliff, root (through meaning of to sail around a cliff)] —**Syn. 1.** venture, peril, jeopardy.

risky (rĭs′kĭ), *adj.*, **riskier, riskiest. 1.** attended with or involving risk; hazardous: *a risky undertaking.* **2.** risqué.

Risorgimento (rĭ sô′jĭ mĕn′tō; *It.* rē sôr jē mĕn′tô), *n.*, *pl.* **-ti** (-tē). the period of and the movement for the liberation and reunification of Italy in the 19th century.

risotto (rĭ zŏt′ō), *n.* an Italian dish of rice flavoured with grated cheese, mushrooms, kidneys, white wine, etc. [It., der. *riso* RICE]

risqué (rĭs′kā; *Fr.* rēs kĕ′), *adj.* daringly close to indelicacy or impropriety: *a risqué story.* [t. F, pp. of *risquer* RISK]

rissole (rĭs′ōl), *n.* a small fried ball, roll, or cake of minced meat or fish mixed with breadcrumbs, egg, etc.; formerly enclosed in a thin envelope of pastry before frying. [t. F, ? ult. der. VL *russeola* (fem. adj.) reddish]

rit., *Music.* ritardando. Also, **ritard.**

ritardando (rĭt′ä dăn′dō; *It.* rē tär dän′dô), *adj. Music.* becoming gradually slower. [It., gerund of *ritardare* RETARD]

rite (rīt), *n.* **1.** a formal or ceremonial act or procedure prescribed or customary in religious or other solemn use: *rites of baptism, sacrificial rites.* **2.** a particular form or system of religious or other ceremonial practice: *the Roman rite, the Scottish rite in freemasonry.* **3.** (*often cap.*) (historically) one of the versions of the Eucharistic service: *the Anglican rite.* **4.** (*often cap.*) liturgy. **5.** (*sometimes cap.*) *Eastern & Western Churches.* a division or differentiation of Churches according to liturgy. **6.** any customary observance or practice. [ME, t. L: m. s. *rītus* ceremony] —**Syn. 1.** See **ceremony.**

ritual (rĭt′yo͞o əl), *n.* **1.** an established or prescribed procedure, code, etc., for a religious or other rite. **2.** a form or system of religious or other rites. **3.** observance of set forms in public worship. **4.** a book of rites or ceremonies. **5.** a book containing the offices to be used by priests in administering the sacraments and for visitation of the sick, burial of the dead, etc. **6.** a ritual proceeding or service: *the ritual of the dead.* **7.** ritual acts or features collectively, as in religious services. **8.** any solemn or customary action, code of behaviour, etc., regulating social conduct. —*adj.* **9.** of the nature of, or practised as, a rite or rites: *a ritual dance.* **10.** of or pertaining to rites: *ritual laws.* [t. L: s. *rituālis*, adj.] —**rit′ually,** *adv.* —**Syn. 1.** See **ceremony.**

ritualism (rĭt′yo͞o ə lĭz′əm), *n.* **1.** adherence to or insistence on ritual. **2.** the study of ritual practices or religious rites. **3.** fondness for ritual.

ritualist (rĭt′yo͞o ə lĭst), *n.* **1.** a student of or authority on ritual practices or religious rites. **2.** one who practises or advocates observance of ritual, as in religious services. —**rit′ualis′tic,** *adj.* —**rit′ualis′tically,** *adv.*

ritualize (rĭt′yo͞o ə līz′), *v.*, **-lized, -lizing.** —*v.i.* **1.** to practise ritualism. —*v.t.* **2.** to convert or make into a ritual. **3.** to convert to ritualism. Also, **ritualise.**

ritzy (rĭt′sĭ), *adj. Slang.* luxurious, elegant. [after the *Ritz* Hotel, London, a luxurious hotel. See -Y[1]]

riv., river.

rivage (rĭv′ĭj), *n. Archaic.* a bank, shore, or coast. [ME, t. OF, der. *rive* bank, g. L *rīpa.* See -AGE]

rival (rī′vəl), *n.*, *adj.*, *v.*, **-valled, -valling** or (*U.S.*) **-valed, -valing.** —*n.* **1.** one who is in pursuit of the same object as another, or strives to equal or outdo another; a competitor. **2.** one who or that which is in a position to dispute preeminence or superiority with another: *a theatre without a rival.* **3.** *Obs.* a companion in duty. —*adj.* **4.** being a rival; competing or standing in rivalry: *rival suitors, rival business houses.* —*v.t.* **5.** to compete with in rivalry: strive to equal or outdo. **6.** to prove to be a worthy rival of: *he soon rivalled the others in skill.* **7.** to equal (something) as if in rivalry. —*v.i.* **8.** *Archaic.* to engage in rivalry;

compete (*with*). [t. L: s. *rīvālis*, orig., one living by or using the same stream as another] **—Syn. 1.** competitor, contestant, emulator, antagonist. See **opponent. —Ant. 1.** partner.

rivalry (rī′vəl rĭ), *n.*, *pl.* **-ries.** the action, position, or relation of a rival or rivals; competition; emulation: *rivalry between Oxford and Cambridge.*

rive (rīv), *v.*, **rived, rived** or **riven, riving.** *—v.t.* **1.** to tear or rend apart. **2.** to strike asunder; split; cleave. **3.** to rend, harrow, or distress (the heart, etc.). *—v.i.* **4.** to become rent or split apart. [ME *rive(n)*, t. Scand.; cf. Icel. *rīfa.* See RIFT]

riven (rĭv′ən), *v.* **1.** pp. of **rive.** *—adj.* **2.** rent or split apart.

river[1] (rĭv′ə), *n.* **1.** a considerable natural stream of water flowing in a definite course or channel or series of diverging and converging channels. **2.** a similar stream of something other than water. **3.** any abundant stream or copious flow: *rivers of lava, blood, etc.* **4. sell down the river,** *Colloq.* to betray; deceive. [ME, t. OF: m. *riv(i)ere*, ult. der. L *rīpa* bank]

river[2] (rī′və), *n.* a person who rives. [f. RIVE + -ER[1]]

Rivera (*Sp.* rē bĕ′rä), *n.* **Diego** (*Sp.* dyĕ′gō), 1886–1957, Mexican painter, esp. of murals.

Rivera y Orbaneja (*Sp.* rē bĕ′rä ē ôr bä nĕ′KHä). See **Primo de Rivera.**

river basin, *Phys. Geog.* the area drained by a river and its branches.

riverbed (rĭv′ə bĕd′), *n.* the channel in which a river flows.

riverhead (rĭv′ə hĕd′), *n.* the spring or source of a river.

river-horse (rĭv′ə hôs′), *n.* hippopotamus.

riverine (rĭv′ə rīn′), *adj.* **1.** of or pertaining to a river. **2.** situated or dwelling beside a river.

Rivers (rĭv′əz), *n.* **William Halse** (hôls), 1865–1922, English physiologist and anthropologist.

riverside (rĭv′ə sīd′), *n.* **1.** the bank of a river. *—adj.* **2.** on the bank of a river.

rivet (rĭv′ĭt), *n.* **1.** a metal pin or bolt for passing through holes in two or more plates or pieces to hold them together, usually made with a head at one end, the other end being hammered into a head after insertion. *—v.t.* **2.** to fasten with a rivet or rivets. **3.** to hammer or spread out the end of (a pin, etc.), in order to form a head and secure something; clinch. **4.** to fasten or fix firmly: *to stand riveted to the spot.* **5.** to hold (the eye, attention, etc.) firmly. [ME *ryvette*, t. OF: m. *rivet*, der. *river* fix, clinch, g. Rom. *rīpāre* make firm, come to shore, der. L *rīpa* shore] —**riv′eter,** *n.*

Riviera (rĭv′ĭ ĕə′rə; *It.* rē vyĕ′rä), *n.* a resort region on the Mediterranean coast extending from Marseilles, in SE France, to La Spezia, in NW Italy.

rivière (rĭv′ĭ ĕə′; *Fr.* rē vyĕr′), *n.* a necklace of diamonds or other gems, esp. in more than one string. [F: lit., river]

rivulet (rĭv′yŏŏ lĭt), *n.* a small stream; a streamlet; a brook. [earlier *rivolet*, t. It.: m. *rivoletto*, dim. of *rivolo*, g. L *rīvulus* small stream]

rix-dollar (rĭks′dŏl′ə), *n.* any of various silver coins of the Netherlands, Denmark, Germany, etc., now mostly disused. See **rigsdaler.** [t. D: m. *rijcksdaler* (now *rijksdaalder*), c. G *Reichstaler* national dollar]

Riyadh (rĭ yäd′), *n.* a city in central Arabia: one of the two capitals of Saudia Arabia. 350,000 (est. 1962). See map under **Saudi Arabia.**

riyal (rĭ yäl′), *n.* **1.** the monetary unit of Yemen, equivalent to about £0·333 sterling. **2.** the monetary unit of Saudi Arabia, equivalent to about £0·0926 sterling. **3. Qatar Dubai riyal,** the monetary unit of Qatar and Dubai, equivalent to about £0·0877 sterling. **4.** a banknote or coin of any of these values. Also, **rial.** [t. Ar., t. Sp.: m. *real* ROYAL (see def. 14)]

Rizaiyeh (rĕz′ĭ yä′), *n.* a town in NW Iran. 91,127 (est. 1964). Also, **Rezaieh.** Formerly, **Urmia.**

Rizal (*Sp.* rē thäl′), *n.* **1. José** (*Sp.* KHō sĕ′), 1861–96, Philippine patriot, novelist, poet, and physician. **2.** Also, **Pasay.** a town in the Philippines, in central Luzon. 132,673 (1960).

Rizzio (*It.* rēt′tsyō), *n.* **David** (*It.* dä′vēd), *c.* 1533–66, Italian musician: secretary and favourite of Mary, Queen of Scots. Also, **Riccio.**

RM, Reichsmark. Also, **r.m.**

rm, *pl.* **rms. 1.** ream. **2.** room.

R.M., 1. Royal Mail. 2. Royal Marines.

R.M.A., Royal Military Academy (Sandhurst).

R.M.S., 1. Royal Mail Service. 2. Royal Mail Steamer.

r.m.s., root mean square.

Rn, *Chem.* radon.

R.N., Royal Navy.

RNA, *Biochem.* ribonucleic acid.

R.N.V.R., Royal Naval Volunteer Reserve.

R.N.Z.A.F., Royal New Zealand Air Force.

R.N.Z.N., Royal New Zealand Navy.

roach[1] (rōch), *n.*, *pl.* **roaches,** (*esp. collectively*) **roach. 1.** a European freshwater fish, *Rutilus rutilus*, of the carp family. **2.** any of various similar fishes, as the **golden shiner,** *Notemigonus crysoleucas*, of eastern North America. **3.** a freshwater sunfish, genus *Lepomis*, of eastern North America. [ME *roche*, t. OF; orig. uncert.]

roach[2] (rōch), *n. Naut.* the curvature at the foot or bottom of a square sail to give a clearance for the fore and aft stay which passes underneath it. [orig. unknown]

road (rōd), *n.* **1.** an open way for passage or travel, usually one wide enough for vehicles, and esp. one between distant points; a highway. **2. a.** *U.S.* a railway. **b.** *Railways.* one of the tracks of a railway: *the train took the wrong road.* **3.** a way or course: *the road to peace.* **4.** (*often pl.*) a protected place near the shore where ships may ride at anchor. **5. one for the road,** *Colloq.* a final alcoholic drink consumed before setting out on a journey, returning home from a public house, etc. **6. on the road, a.** travelling, esp. as a salesman. **b.** on tour, as a theatrical company. **7. take to the road, a.** to begin a journey. **b.** to become a tramp. **c.** *Obs.* to become a highwayman. [ME *rode*, OE *rād* a riding, journey on horseback (akin to *rīdan* ride), c. G *Reede*]

road agent, *U.S.* a highwayman.

roadbed (rōd′bĕd′), *n.* **1.** the bed or foundation structure for the track of a railway. **2.** a layer of ballast directly beneath the sleepers of a railway track. **3.** the material of which a road is composed.

roadblock (rōd′blŏk′), *n.* an obstruction placed across a road by police, soldiers, etc., to halt or slow down traffic for control or inspection, impede the progress of an enemy, etc.

roadbook (rōd′bŏŏk′), *n.* a guide book for motorists, issued by motoring organizations, etc.

road-hog (rōd′hŏg′), *n.* a motorist who drives without consideration for other road users.

roadhouse (rōd′hous′), *n.* an inn, hotel, restaurant, etc., on a main road, esp. in a country district.

roadman (rōd′măn′, -mən), *n.* one who repairs roads. Also, **roadmender** (rōd′mĕn′də).

road metal, broken stone, etc., used for making roads.

road-roller (rōd′rō′lə), *n.* a power-driven roller used for compacting roads.

roadrunner (rōd′rŭn′ə), *n.* a terrestrial cuckoo, *Geococcyx californianus*, of America.

road-sense (rōd′sĕns′), *n.* the ability to use roads safely, as a motorist, pedestrian, dog, etc.

roadside (rōd′sīd′), *n.* **1.** the side or border of the road; the wayside. *—adj.* **2.** on the side of a road.

roadstead (rōd′stĕd′), *n. Naut.* road (def. 4). [f. ROAD + STEAD]

roadster (rōd′stə), *n.* **1.** an open sports car, usually for two persons. **2.** a horse for riding or driving on the road.

roadway (rōd′wā′), *n.* **1.** a way used as a road; a road. **2.** the part of a road used by vehicles, etc.

roadworthy (rōd′wû′thĭ), *adj.* (of a vehicle) fit for use on the roads.

roam (rōm), *v.i.* **1.** to walk, go, or travel about without fixed purpose or direction; ramble; wander; rove. *—v.t.* **2.** to wander over or through: *to roam the countryside.* *—n.* **3.** the act of roaming; a ramble. [ME *romen*; orig. obscure] —**roam′er,** *n.*

—Syn. 1. stray, stroll, prowl. ROAM, RAMBLE, RANGE, ROVE imply wandering about over (usually) a considerable amount of territory. ROAM implies a wandering or travelling over a large area, esp. as prompted by restlessness or curiosity: *to roam through a forest.* RAMBLE implies pleasant, carefree moving about, walking with no specific purpose and for a limited distance: *to ramble through fields near home.* RANGE usually implies wandering over a more or less defined but extensive area in search of something: *cattle range over the plains.* ROVE sometimes implies wandering with specific incentive or aim, as an animal for prey: *bandits rove through these mountains.*

roan (rōn), *adj.* **1.** (chiefly of horses) of a sorrel, chestnut, or bay colour sprinkled with grey or white. **2.** prepared from roan (leather). *—n.* **3.** a roan horse or other animal. **4.** a soft, flexible sheepskin leather, used in bookbinding, often made in imitation of morocco. [ME, t. F, t. Sp.: m. *roano*, ult. der. L *rāvidus* yellow-grey]

Roanne (*Fr.* rwän), *n.* a town in SE central France, in Loire department. 51,723 (1962).

Roanoke (rō′ə nōk′), *n.* a river in the U.S., flowing from western Virginia SE to Albemarle Sound in North Carolina. ab. 380 mi.

Roanoke Island, an island in the U.S., off the NE coast of North Carolina, S of Albemarle Sound: site of Raleigh's unsuccessful attempts at colonization, 1585–87.

roar (rô), *v.i.* **1.** to utter a loud, deep sound, esp. of excitement, distress, or anger. **2.** to laugh loudly or boisterously. **3.** to make a loud noise in breathing, as a horse. **4.** to make a loud noise or din, as thunder, cannon, waves, wind, etc.

5. to function or move with a roar, as a vehicle: *the sports car roared away.* —*v.t.* **6.** to utter or express in a roar. **7.** to bring, put, make, etc. by roaring: *to roar oneself hoarse.* —*n.* **8.** the sound of roaring; a loud, deep sound, as of a person or persons, or of a lion or other large animal. **9.** a loud outburst of laughter. **10.** a loud noise, as of thunder, waves, etc.: *the roar of the surf.* [ME *rore(n)*, OE *rārian*, c. G *röhren*; ult. orig. obscure] —**roar′er,** *n.* —**Syn. 1.** See **cry. 4.** resound, boom, thunder, peal.

roaring (rô′rĭng), *n.* **1.** the act of one who or that which roars. **2.** a loud, deep cry or sound. **3.** *Vet. Sci.* a disease of horses causing them to make a loud noise in breathing under exertion. —*adj.* **4.** that roars, as a person, thunder, etc. **5.** *Colloq.* brisk or highly successful, as trade. **6.** characterized by noisy or boisterous behaviour; riotous.

roaring forties, an area of ocean characterized by stormy seas stretching around the earth south of latitude 40 C, and over which north-west winds, often of gale force, constantly blow.

roast (rōst), *v.t.* **1.** to bake (meat or other food) by dry heat, as in an oven. **2.** to prepare (meat or other food) for eating by direct exposure to dry heat, as on a spit. **3.** to brown by exposure to heat, as coffee. **4.** to embed in hot coals, embers, etc., to cook. **5.** to heat (any material) more or less violently. **6.** to heat (an ore, etc.) with access of air, as to cause oxidation. **7.** to warm (oneself, etc.) at a hot fire. **8.** *Chiefly U.S. Slang.* to ridicule or criticize severely or mercilessly. —*v.i.* **9.** to roast meat, etc. **10.** to undergo the process of becoming roasted. —*n.* **11.** a piece of roasted meat; roasted meat. **12.** a piece of meat for roasting. **13.** something that is roasted. **14.** the act or operation of roasting. **15.** *Chiefly U.S. Slang.* severe criticism. —*adj.* **16.** roasted: *roast beef.* [ME *roste(n)*, t. OF: m. *rostir*, t. Gmc; cf. D *roosten*]

roaster (rōs′tə), *n.* **1.** a contrivance for roasting something. **2.** a pig, chicken, or other animal or article fit for roasting. **3.** one who or that which roasts.

roasting (rōs′tĭng), *adj.* **1.** that roasts. **2.** exceedingly hot; scorching.

rob (rŏb), *v.*, **robbed, robbing.** —*v.t.* **1.** to deprive of something by unlawful force or threat of violence; steal from. **2.** to deprive of something legally belonging or due. **3.** to plunder or rifle (a house, etc.). **4.** to deprive of something unjustly or injuriously: *the shock robbed him of speech.* —*v.i.* **5.** to commit or practise robbery. [ME *robbe(n)*, t. OF: m. *robber*, t. OHG: m. *roubōn*, c. REAVE[1]]
—**Syn. 1.** ROB, RIFLE, SACK refer to seizing possessions which belong to others. ROB is the general word for taking possessions by unlawful force or violence: *to rob a bank, a house, a train.* A term with a more restricted meaning is RIFLE, to make a thorough search for what is valuable or worthwhile, usually within a small space: *to rifle a safe.* On the other hand, SACK is a term for robbery on a huge scale, during war; it suggests destruction accompanying pillage, and often includes the indiscriminate massacre of civilians: *to sack a town or district.* **2.** defraud, cheat.

robalo (rŏb′ə lō′, rō′bə-), *n.*, *pl.* **-los,** (*esp. collectively*) **-lo.** any of the marine fishes constituting the family *Centropomidae*, esp. *Centropomus undecimalis*, a valuable food fish of Florida, the West Indies, etc. [t. Pg., t. Catalan: m. *elobarro*, ult. der. L *lupus* wolf]

roband (rŏb′ənd, rō′bənd), *n.* *Naut.* a short piece of spun yarn or other material, used to secure a sail to a yard, gaff, or the like. Also, **robbin, robin.** [southern form answering to Northern E *raband*, t. D, f. *rā* sailyard + *band* BAND]

Robbe-Grillet (*Fr.* rŏb grē yĕ′), *n.* **Alain** (*Fr.* à lăɴ′), born 1922, French novelist.

robber (rŏb′ə), *n.* one who robs. —**Syn.** See **thief.**

robber baron, *Hist.* a noble who robbed travellers passing through his lands.

robber fly, any of the swift, often large, flies constituting the family *Asilidae*, that prey on other insects.

Robber fly, *Asilus sericeus* (Ab. 1 in. long)

robbery (rŏb′ə rĭ), *n.*, *pl.* **-ries. 1.** the action or practice, or an instance, of robbing. **2.** *Law.* the felonious taking of the property of another from his person or in his immediate presence, against his will, by violence or intimidation. [ME *roberie*, t. OF, der. *rober* ROB]

Robbia (*It.* rŏb′byä), *n.* **Luca della** (*It.* lōō′kä dĕl lä), 1400?–82, Italian artist, esp. in enamelled terracotta.

robbin (rŏb′ĭn), *n.* *Naut.* roband.

robe (rōb), *n.*, *v.*, **robed, robing.** —*n.* **1.** a long, loose or flowing gown or outer garment worn by men or women, esp. for formal occasions; an official vestment, as of a judge. **2.** any long, loose garment: *a bathrobe.* **3.** a woman's gown or dress, esp. of a more elaborate kind. **4.** (*pl.*) apparel in general; dress; costume. **5.** a piece of fur, cloth, knitted work, etc., used as a covering or wrap: *a buffalo robe.* —*v.t.* **6.** to clothe or invest in a robe or robes; dress or apparel. —*v.i.* **7.** to put on a robe. [ME, t. OF: orig., spoil, booty. See ROB]

robe-de-chambre (*Fr.* rŏb də shäɴ′br), *n.* *French.* a dressing gown.

Robert I (rŏb′ət), **1.** See **Bruce** (def. 1). **2.** ('*Robert the Devil*'), died 1035, duke of Normandy (father of William I of England).

Robert Guiscard (*Fr.* rō bĕr gēs kàr′). See **Guiscard.**

Roberts (rŏb′əts), *n.* **Frederick Sleigh** (slā), **Earl,** 1832–1914, British field marshal.

Robertson (rŏb′ət sən), *n.* **1. William,** 1721–93, Scottish historian. **2. Sir William Robert,** 1860–1933, British field marshal.

Robeson (rōb′sən), *n.* **Paul (Le Roy)** (lə roi′), born 1898, U.S. Negro singer and actor.

Robespierre (rōbz′pyēə; *Fr.* rō bĕs pyĕr′), *n.* **Maximilien François Marie Isidore de** (*Fr.* màk sē mē lyăɴ fräɴ swà mà rē ē zē dŏr′ də), 1758–94, French lawyer and revolutionary leader.

robin (rŏb′ĭn), *n.* **1.** any of several small, Old World birds having a red or reddish breast, esp. *Erithacus rubecula*, of Europe. **2.** a large American thrush, *Turdus migratorius*, with a chestnut-red breast and abdomen. **3.** *Naut.* roband. Also, **robin redbreast** for defs 1 and 2. [ME *Robyn*, t. OF: m. *Robin*, dim. of *Robert* Robert]

Robin Goodfellow (gŏŏd′fĕl′ō), the fairy Puck.

Robin Hood, English outlaw of the 12th century, a popular hero in many ballads, who robbed the rich to give to the poor, and who lived chiefly in Sherwood Forest.

Robinson (rŏb′ĭn sən), *n.* **Sir Robert,** born 1886, English chemist.

roble (rō′blā), *n.* **1.** a Californian white oak, *Quercus lobata.* **2.** any of several other trees, esp. of the oak and beech families. [t. Sp. and Pg., g. L *rōbur* oak tree]

roborant (rŏb′ə rənt), *Med.* —*adj.* **1.** strengthening. —*n.* **2.** a tonic. [t. L: s. *rōborans*, ppr., strengthening]

robot (rō′bŏt; *def. 3 also* rō′bō), *n.* **1.** a manufactured or machine-made man. **2.** a merely mechanical being; an automaton. **3.** *S African.* a set of traffic lights. [first used in the play '*R. U. R.*' (by Karel Capek), appar. back-formation from Czech *robotnik* serf] —**ro′botism,** *n.* —**robotistic** (rō′bō tĭs′tĭk), *adj.*

Rob Roy (rŏb′ roi′) (*Robert Macgregor*), 1671–1734, Scottish outlaw.

Robson (rŏb′sən), *n.* **1. Dame Flora,** born 1902, English actress. **2. Mount,** a mountain in SW Canada, in E British Columbia: highest peak in the Canadian Rockies. 12,972 ft.

robust (rə bŭst′), *adj.* **1.** strong and healthy, hardy, or vigorous. **2.** strongly or stoutly built: *his robust frame.* **3.** suited to or requiring bodily strength or endurance. **4.** rough, rude, or boisterous. [t. L: s. *rōbustus*] —**robust′ly,** *adv.* —**robust′ness,** *n.* —**Syn. 1.** sturdy, stalwart. See **strong.** —**Ant. 1.** feeble.

robustious (rə bŭs′tyəs), *adj.* **1.** rough, rude, or boisterous. **2.** robust, strong, or stout. —**robus′tiously,** *adv.*

roc (rŏk), *n.* *Arabian Myth.* a mythological bird of enormous size and strength. [t. Ar.: m. *rukhkh*, prob. t. Pers.]

Roca (rŏk′ə; *Port.* rŏ′kə), *n.* **Cape,** a cape in W Portugal, near Lisbon: the western extremity of the continent of Europe.

rocaille (rŏ kī′; *Fr.* rŏ kày′), *n.* a style of ornamentation based on the forms of shells and rocks characteristic of the rococo period.

rocambole (rŏk′əm bōl′), *n.* a European liliaceous plant, *Allium scorodoprasum*, used like garlic. [t. F, t. G: m. *Rockenbolle*, lit., distaff bulb (from its shape)]

Rochambeau (*Fr.* rō shäɴ bō′), *n.* **Jean Baptiste Donatien de Vimeur** (*Fr.* zhäɴ bà tēst dō nà syăɴ′ də vē mœr′), **Comte de,** 1725–1807, French general, marshal, and commander of the French army in the War of American Independence.

Rochdale (rŏch′dāl′), *n.* a town in England, in Lancashire. 86,180 (est. 1964).

Rochelle (*Fr.* rō shĕl′), *n.* **La** (*Fr.* là). See **La Rochelle.**

Rochelle powder (rō shĕl′), Seidlitz powder.

Rochelle salt, a tartrate of sodium and potassium, used as a laxative. [named after (LA)ROCHELLE]

roche moutonnée (*Fr.* rōsh mōō tō nĕ′), *pl.* **roches moutonnées** (*Fr.* rōsh mōō tō nĕ′), *French.* a knob or rock rounded and smoothed by glacial action.

Rochester (rŏch′ĭs tə), *n.* **1.** a city in the U.S., in W New York State, on the Genesee river. 318,611 (1960). **2.** a town in England, in Kent. 50,143 (1961). **3. John Wilmot** (wĭl′mət), **2nd Earl of,** 1647–80, English satirical court poet and pornographer.

rochet (rŏch′ĭt), *n.* a vestment of linen or lawn, resembling a surplice, worn esp. by bishops and abbots. [ME, t. OF, der. *roc* outer garment, t. Gmc; cf. OE *rocc* outer garment]

rock[1] (rŏk), *n.* **1.** a large mass of stone forming an eminence, cliff, or the like. **2.** *Geol.* **a.** mineral matter of various composition, consolidated or unconsolidated, assembled in masses or considerable quantities in nature, as by the action of heat (**igneous rock**) or of water, air, or ice (**sedimentary rock**), or by the structural alteration of either of these two types by natural agencies of pressure and heat (**metamorphic rock**). **b.** a particular kind of such matter. **3.** stone in the mass. **4.** something resembling or suggesting a rock. **5.** a firm foundation or support: *the Lord is my rock.* **6.** a hard sweet made in various flavours, as peppermint, usually long and cylindrical in shape. **7.** (*usually pl.*) *U.S. Slang.* a piece of money. **8.** (*often cap.*) *Slang.* a jewel, esp. a diamond. **9.** *U.S. Dial or Colloq.* a stone of any size. **10. on the rocks, a.** on rocks, as a shipwrecked vessel. **b.** *Colloq.* into or in a state of disaster or ruin. **c.** (of drinks) with ice-cubes: *Scotch on the rocks.* **11. The Rock,** Gibraltar. [ME *rokk(e)*, OE *-rocc*, t. ML: s. *rocca*] **—rock′-like′,** *adj.*

rock[2] (rŏk), *v.i.* **1.** to move or sway to and fro or from side to side. **2.** to be moved or swayed powerfully with emotion, etc. **3.** *Mining.* to be rocked or panned with a rocker: *this ore rocks slowly.* **4.** to dance to rock'n'roll music. *—v.t.* **5.** to move or sway to and fro or from side to side, esp. gently and soothingly. **6.** to lull in security, hope, etc. **7.** to move or sway powerfully with emotion, etc. **8.** to shake or disturb violently. **9.** *Engraving.* to roughen the surface of (a copperplate) with a rocker preparatory to scraping a mezzotint. **10.** *Mining.* to pan with a cradle: *to rock gravel for gold.* *—n.* **11.** a rocking movement. **12.** rock'n'roll (defs 1, 2). [ME *rocken*, OE *roccian*, c. MD *rocken*; akin to Icel. *rykkja* jerk] **—Syn. 1.** See **swing**[1].

rock-and-roll (rŏk′ ən rōl′), *n.* rock'n'roll.

rockaway (rŏk′ə wā′), *n.* *U.S.* a light four-wheeled carriage with two (or three) seats and a standing top. [appar. named after *Rockaway*, New Jersey]

rock-bass (rŏk′băs′), *n.* an eastern North American freshwater food fish, *Ambloplites rupestris*, of the sunfish family, *Centrarchidae.*

rock bottom, the lowest level: *to touch rock bottom.*

rock-bottom (rŏk′bŏt′əm), *adj.* at the lowest limit; extreme lowest: *rock-bottom prices.*

rock-bound (rŏk′bound′), *adj.* hemmed in by rocks; rocky: *a rock-bound coast.*

rock-brake (rŏk′ brāk′), *n.* a fern of the genus *Pellaea.*

rock-cake (rŏk′kāk′), *n.* a small cake with a rough surface, containing fruit and spice.

rock-cress (rŏk′krĕs′), *n.* any of several small cruciferous herbs of the genus *Arabis*, as. *A. alpina*, the **alpine rock-cress,** a widespread arctic-alpine plant of the Northern Hemisphere.

rock-crystal (rŏk′krĭs′tl), *n.* transparent quartz, esp. of the colourless kind.

rock-dove (rŏk′dŭv′), *n.* a European pigeon, *Columba livia*, from which most domestic pigeons have developed.

Rockefeller (rŏk′ə fĕl′ə), *n.* **1. John Davison** (dā′vĭ sən), 1839–1937, U.S. capitalist and philanthropist. **2.** his son, **John Davison,** 1874–1960, U.S. capitalist and philanthropist. **3.** his grandson, **Nelson Aldrich** (ôl′drĭch), born 1908, U.S. philanthropist; governor of New York State since 1959.

rocker (rŏk′ə), *n.* **1.** one of the curved pieces on which a cradle or a rocking chair rocks. **2.** a rocking chair. **3.** any of various devices that operate with a rocking motion. **4.** *Engraving.* a small steel plate with one curved and toothed edge for roughening a copperplate to make a mezzotint. **5.** *Mining.* a cradle (def. 8). **6.** the curve in an ice-skate blade. **7.** *Colloq.* a young person characterized by rough, unruly behaviour, who usually wears leather clothing and rides a motorcycle. Cf. **mod** (def. 3). **8. off one's rocker,** *Slang.* crazy, mad, demented: *you must be off your rocker to suggest such a thing.*

rocker arm, *Mach.* a lever, usually pivoted near its midpoint, used to transmit motion to a valve stem from a cam.

rockery (rŏk′ə rĭ), *n.*, *pl.* **-ries.** a mound of rocks and earth for growing ferns or other plants.

rocket[1] (rŏk′ĭt), *n.* **1.** *Aeron.* a structure propelled by a rocket engine; used for pyrotechnic effect, signalling, carrying a lifeline, propelling a warhead, launching a spacecraft, etc. **2.** *Colloq.* a severe reprimand; reproof: *I shall get a rocket from the headmaster for breaking the window.* *—v.i.* **3.** to move like a rocket. **4.** (of gamebirds) to fly straight up rapidly when flushed. **5.** to increase rapidly as prices, rents or the like. [t. F: m. *roquet*, or t. It.: m. *rocchetta*, appar. a dim. of *rocca* ROCK[1] with reference to its shape]

rocket[2] (rŏk′ĭt), *n.* any of numerous cruciferous herbs, esp. those belonging to the genera *Barbarea* and *Sisymbrium.* [t. F: m. *roquette*, t. Pr.: m. *rouqueto*, ult. der. L *ērūca* kind of colewort]

rocket base, an area in which military rockets are prepared for firing.

rocket bomb, 1. a bomb equipped with a rocket engine which increases its velocity after it has been dropped from an aircraft. **2.** any rocket-propelled explosive missile, as the V-2.

rocket engine, *Aeron.* a reaction engine containing all the substances necessary for its operation and the combustion of its fuel. Also, **rocket motor.**

rocket gun, any weapon which uses a rocket as a projectile, as a rocket-launcher or bazooka.

rocket-launcher (rŏk′ĭt lôn′chə), *n.* *Mil.* a cylindrical weapon used by infantrymen to fire rockets capable of penetrating several inches of armour-plate.

rocket propulsion, *Aeron.* a type of reaction propulsion in which the thrust is generated by discharging matter contained within the vehicle.

rocket range, an area containing various instruments and equipment, over which rockets are flown for testing.

rocketry (rŏk′ĭ trĭ), *n.* the science of rocket design, development, and flight.

Rock fever, undulant fever. [named after the *Rock* of Gibraltar, where it is prevalent]

rockfish (rŏk′fĭsh′), *n.*, *pl.* **-fishes,** (*esp. collectively*) **-fish. 1.** any of various fishes found about rocks. **2.** the striped bass, *Roccus saxatilis.* **3.** any of the shallow-water marine fish of the genus *Clinus* of South Africa; klipfish. **4.** any of the North Pacific marine fishes of the genus *Sebastodes.* **5.** any fish of the family *Scorpaenidae.*

rock-flour (rŏk′flou′ə), *n.* finely ground rock material produced when a glacier containing rocks abrades its bed. Also, **glacial meal.**

Rockford (rŏk′fəd), *n.* a town in the U.S., in N Illinois. 126,706 (1960).

rock-garden (rŏk′gä′dn), *n.* **1.** a garden on rocky ground or among rocks, for the growing of alpine or other plants. **2.** a garden decorated with rocks of different varieties, colours, shapes, etc.

Rockhampton (rŏk hămp′tən), *n.* a town in NE Australia, in Queensland. 45,000 (est. 1964).

Rockies (rŏk′ĭz), *n.pl.* the Rocky Mountains.

rocking chair, a chair mounted on rockers, or on springs, so as to permit a rocking back and forth.

Rockingham (rŏk′ĭng əm), *n.* **Charles Watson-Wentworth, 2nd Marquess of,** 1730–82, British statesman: prime minister 1765–66; 1782.

rocking horse, a toy horse, as of wood, mounted on rockers, on which children play.

Rocking horse

rock jasmine, any of several alpine, primulaceous plants of the genus *Androsace*, having red, purple, or white flowers.

rockjumper (rŏk′jŭm′pə), *n.* a bird of southern Africa, *Chaetops frenatus*, having black and white plumage, about the size of a thrush, found in rocky areas.

rockling (rŏk′lĭng), *n.* any species of fish of the genus *Mottella*, having barbels on their jaws.

rock'n'roll, 1. a style of popular music with a heavily accented rhythm, related to hillbilly and blues forms. **2.** a dance performed to this music, usually with vigorous, exaggerated movements. **3.** of or pertaining to this music. Also, **rock′-and-roll′, rock-'n-roll.**

rock-oil (rŏk′oil′), *n.* petroleum (def. 1).

rock-plant (rŏk′plänt′), *n.* any plant which grows among rocks, on rockeries, etc.

rockrat (rŏk′răt′), *n.* a small rodent, *Petromys typicus*, of rocky areas of southern Africa.

rockrose (rŏk′rōz′), *n.* **1.** any plant of the genus *Cistus* or some allied genus, as *Helianthemum.* **2.** any cistaceous plant.

rock-salmon (rŏk′săm′ən), *n.* (used by fishmongers, etc.) the dogfish or wolf-fish.

rock-salt (rŏk′sôlt′), *n.* common salt (sodium chloride), occurring in extensive, irregular beds in rocklike masses.

rockshaft (rŏk′shäft′), *n.* *Mach.* a shaft that rocks or oscillates on its journals instead of revolving, as the shaft of a bell or a pendulum, or a shaft operating the valves of a steam-engine.

rock speedwell, a low, woody, scrophulariaceous perennial herb, *Veronica fruticans*, of Europe, having small, blue and red flowers.

rock thrush, 1. a bird of the thrush family, *Monticola saxatilis*, of Europe. **2.** any other member of this genus.

rockweed (rŏk′wēd′), *n.* a fucoid seaweed growing on rocks exposed at low tide.

rock-wool (rŏk′wo͝ol′), *n.* an insulating material consisting of wool-like fibres made from molten rock or slag by forcing a blast of steam through the liquid.

rocky[1] (rŏk′ĭ), *adj.*, **rockier, rockiest. 1.** full of or abounding in rocks. **2.** consisting of rock. **3.** rocklike. **4.** firm as a rock. **5.** (of the heart, etc.) hard or unfeeling. [f. ROCK[1] + -Y[1]] —**rock′iness,** *n.*

rocky[2] (rŏk′ĭ), *adj.*, **rockier, rockiest. 1.** inclined to rock; tottering or shaky. **2.** unpleasantly uncertain. **3.** *Colloq. or Slang.* weak; shaky; dizzy. [f. ROCK[2] + -Y[1]]

Rocky Mountain goat, a long-haired, white, goat-like, bovid ruminant, *Oreamnos montanus,* of the western North American mountains, having short black horns.

Rocky Mountain goat

Rocky Mountains, the chief mountain system in North America, extending from N Mexico to Alaska. Highest peak, Mt McKinley (in Alaska), 20,300 ft; Elbert Peak, 14,431 ft. Also, **Rockies.**

Rocky Mountain spotted fever, *Pathol.* a disease of the typhus-rickettsia group characterized by high fever, pains in joints, bones, and muscles, and a cutaneous eruption, and caused by rickettsia transmitted by ticks. It was first found in the Rocky Mountain area, but is now more widely distributed.

rococo (rə kō′kō; *Fr.* rŏ kȯ kȯ′), *n.* **1.** a style of architecture and decoration, originating in France about 1720, evolved from baroque types and distinguished by its elegant refinement in using different materials (stucco, metal, wood, mirrors, tapestries) for a delicate overall effect and by its ornament of shellwork, foliage, etc. —*adj.* **2.** in the rococo style. **3.** tastelessly or clumsily florid. **4.** antiquated. [t. F, said to be der. *rocaille* rockwork, pebble- or shellwork, der. *roc* ROCK[1]]

rod (rŏd), *n.* **1.** a stick, wand, staff, shaft, or the like, of wood, metal, or other material. **2.** a straight, slender shoot or stem of any woody plant, whether growing upon or cut from the plant. **3.** a pole used in angling or fishing. **4.** a stick used to measure with. **5.** a linear measure of 5½ yards or 16½ feet; a perch or pole. **6.** a square perch or pole (30¼ square yards). **7.** *Bldg Trades.* a standard measure of brickwork, 272 square feet of a standard thickness of 1½ bricks, or 306 cubic feet. **8.** a stick, or a bundle of sticks or switches bound together, used as an instrument of punishment. **9.** punishment or chastisement. **10.** a wand or staff carried as a symbol of office, authority, power, etc. **11.** authority; sway; tyrannical rule. **12.** (in biblical use) an offshoot or branch of a family; a scion; a tribe. **13.** *Anat.* one of the rodlike cells in the retina of the eye which respond to dim light. **14.** *Bacteriol.* any micro-organism which is neither spherical nor spiral, but elongated. See illus. under **bacteria.** [ME and OE *rodd*; appar. akin to Icel. *rudda* kind of club]

rode (rōd), *v.* pt. of **ride.**

rodent (rō′dnt), *adj.* **1.** belonging or pertaining to the *Rodentia,* the order of gnawing or nibbling mammals, that includes the mice, squirrels, beavers, etc. **2.** gnawing. —*n.* **3.** a rodent mammal. [t. L: s. *rōdens,* ppr., gnawing] —**ro′dent-like′,** *adj.*

rodeo (rō dā′ō), *n., pl.* **-deos.** *U.S.* **1.** an exhibition of the skills of cowboys for public entertainment. **2.** a round-up of cattle. [t. Sp.: cattle ring, der. *rodear* go round, der. *rueda* wheel, g. L *rota*]

Rodez (*Fr.* rŏ dĕz′), *n.* a town in S France, the capital of Aveyron department. 24,352 (1962).

Rodin (*Fr.* rŏ dăɴ′), *n.* **Auguste** (*Fr.* ȯ gʏst′), 1840–1917, French sculptor.

Rodney (rŏd′nĭ), *n.* **George Brydges** (brĭj′ĭz), **Baron,** 1719–92, British admiral.

rodomontade (rŏd′ə mŏn tād′, -täd′), *n., adj., v.,* **-taded, -tading.** —*n.* **1.** vainglorious boasting or bragging; pretentious, blustering talk. —*adj.* **2.** bragging. —*v.i.* **3.** to boast; brag; rant. [t. F, t. It.: m. *rodomontata*]

roe[1] (rō), *n.* **1.** the mass of eggs, or spawn, within the ovarian membrane of the female fish (**hard roe**). **2.** the milt or sperm of the male fish (**soft roe**). [ME *row(e),* c. OHG *rogo*]

roe[2] (rō), *n., pl.* **roes,** (*esp. collectively*) **roe.** the roedeer. [ME *roo,* OE *rā,* earlier *rāha,* c. G *Reh*]

Roe (rō), *n.* **Sir A(lliott) V(erdon)** (ăl′ĭ ət vû′dn), 1877–1958, English pioneer aeroplane designer and manufacturer.

roebuck (rō′bŭk′), *n.* a male roedeer.

Roedean (rō′dēn′), *n.* girls' public school in Sussex, near Brighton (founded 1885).

roedeer (rō′dĭə′), *n.* a small, agile deer, *Capreolus capreolus,* the mature male of which has three-pointed antlers. [OE *rāhdēor.* See ROE[2], DEER]

Roentgen (rŏn′tyən; *Ger.* rœnt′gən), *n., adj.* Röntgen.

rogation (rō gā′shən), *n.* **1.** (*usually pl.*) *Eccles.* solemn supplication, esp. as chanted during procession on the three days (**Rogation Days**) before Ascension Day. **2.** *Rom. Hist.* **a.** the proposing by the consuls or tribunes of a law to be passed by the people. **b.** a law so proposed. [ME *rogacio(u)n,* t. L: m. s. *rogātio*]

rogatory (rŏg′ə tə rĭ, -trĭ), *adj.* pertaining to asking or requesting: *a rogatory commission.* [t. ML: m. s. *rogātōrius,* f. L *rogātor* asker, solicitor]

roger (rŏj′ə), *interj.* message received and understood (used in signalling and telecommunications). [*Roger* (personal name) used in telecommunications as a name for *r,* used as an abbreviation for *received*]

Rogers (rŏj′əz), *n.* **Will,** 1879–1935, U.S. actor and humorist.

Roget (rŏzh′ā), *n.* **Peter Mark,** 1779–1869, English physician and lexicographer.

rogue (rōg), *n., v.,* **rogued, roguing.** —*n.* **1.** a dishonest person. **2.** a playfully mischievous person; rascal; scamp. **3.** a vagrant or vagabond. **4.** an elephant or other animal of savage disposition and solitary life. **5.** *Biol.* an individual varying markedly from the normal, usually inferior. —*v.i.* **6.** to live or act like a rogue. —*v.t.* **7.** to cheat. **8.** to uproot or destroy, as plants which do not conform to a desired standard. **9.** to perform this operation upon: *to rogue a field.* [appar. short for obs. *roger* begging vagabond, b. ROAMER and BEGGAR] —**Syn. 1.** See **knave.**

roguery (rō′gə rĭ), *n., pl.* **-gueries. 1.** roguish conduct; rascality. **2.** a rascally act; playful mischief.

rogues' gallery, 1. a collection of portraits of criminals, as at a police station. **2.** *Colloq.* any collection of portraits resembling this.

rogue's march, derisive music played to accompany a person's expulsion from a regiment, community, etc.

roguish (rō′gĭsh), *adj.* **1.** pertaining to, characteristic of, or acting like a rogue; knavish or rascally. **2.** playfully mischievous: *a roguish smile.* —**ro′guishly,** *adv.* —**ro′guishness,** *n.*

roil (roil), *v.t.* **1.** to render (water, etc.) turbid by stirring up sediment. **2.** to disturb or disquiet; irritate; vex. [t. obs. F: m. *ruiler* mix up mortar, der. OF *rieule* mason's formboard, g. L *rēgula* rule]

roily (roi′lĭ), *adj.* turbid; muddy.

roister (rois′tə), *v.i.* **1.** to act in a swaggering, boisterous, or uproarious manner. **2.** to revel noisily or without restraint. [v. use of *roister,* n., t. F: m. *ru(i)stre* ruffian, boor, der. *ru(i)ste* RUSTIC, n.] —**roist′erer,** *n.* —**roist′erous,** *adj.*

Roland (rō′lənd), *n.* Charlemagne's greatest legendary paladin, famous for his prowess and death in the battle of Roncesvalles (A.D. 778), and also for his five days' combat with Oliver, another paladin, in which neither gained the advantage (whence **a Roland for an Oliver** for an equally effective retort or retaliation).

role (rōl), *n.* **1.** the part or character which an actor presents in a play. **2.** proper or customary function: *the teacher's role in society.* Also, **rôle.** [t. F: prop., the roll (as of paper) containing an actor's part]

roll (rōl), *v.i.* **1.** to move along a surface by turning over and over, as a ball or a wheel. **2.** to move or be moved on wheels, as a vehicle or its occupants (often fol. by *along*). **3.** to move onwards or advance in a stream or with an undulating motion, as water, waves, or smoke. **4.** to extend in undulations, as land. **5.** to move (fol. by *on,* etc.) or pass (often fol. by *away,* etc.), as time. **6.** to move (fol. by *round*) as in a cycle, as seasons. **7.** to perform a periodical revolution in an orbit, as a heavenly body. **8.** to continue with or have a deep, prolonged sound, as thunder, etc. **9.** to turn over, or over and over, as a person or animal lying down. **10.** *Colloq.* to luxuriate or abound (in wealth, etc.). **11.** to turn round in different directions, as the eyes in their sockets. **12.** to sway or rock from side to side, as a ship (opposed to *pitch*). **13.** to sail with a rolling motion. **14.** to walk with a rolling or swaying gait. **15.** (of a rocket or guided missile) to rotate about its longitudinal axis in flight. **16.** to form into a roll, or curl up from itself. **17.** to admit of being rolled up, as a material. **18.** to spread out from being rolled up; unroll (fol. by *out,* etc.). **19.** to spread out as under a roller. **20.** *Colloq.* to cast dice. —*v.t.* **21.** to cause to move along a surface by turning over and over, as a cask, a ball, or a hoop. **22.** to move along on wheels or rollers; to convey in a wheeled vehicle. **23.** to drive, impel, or cause to flow onwards with a sweeping motion. **24.** to utter or give forth with a full, flowing, continuous sound. **25.** to trill: *to roll one's r's.* **26.** to cause to turn over, or over and over. **27.** to cause to turn round in different directions, as the eyes. **28.** to cause to sway or rock from side to side, as a ship. **29.** to wrap round an axis, round upon itself, or into a roll, ball, or the like. **30.** to make by forming a roll: *to roll a cigarette.* **31.** to spread out from being rolled up; unroll (fol. by *out,* etc.). **32.** to wrap, enfold, or envelope, as in some covering. **33.** to operate upon with a roller or rollers, as to spread out, level, compact, or the like, with a rolling pin, etc. **34.** to beat (a drum) with rapid, continuous strokes. **35.** to cast (dice). **36.** *Print.* to apply ink to with a roller or series of rollers. **37.** *Slang.* to rob (a drunken or sleeping person). **38. roll up, a.** to form a roll. **b.** *Colloq.* to arrive. **c.** *Colloq.* to gather round. **39. roll in, a.** to arrive. **b.** *Colloq.* to retire to bed. **c.** *Hockey.* to return the ball to play after it has crossed the sideline by rolling it back on to the pitch. —*n.* **40.** a piece of parchment, paper, or the like, as for writing, etc., which is or may be rolled up; a scroll. **41.** a list, register, or catalogue. **42.** a list containing the names of the persons belonging to any company, class, society, etc. **43.** anything rolled up in cylindrical form. **44.** a number of papers or the like rolled up together. **45.** a quantity of cloth, wallpaper, or the like, rolled up in cylindrical form (often forming a definite measure). **46.** a cylindrical or rounded mass of something: *rolls of fat.* **47.** some article of cylindrical or rounded form, as a moulding. **48.** a cylindrical piece upon which something is rolled along to facilitate moving. **49.** a cylinder upon which something is rolled up. **50.** a roller with which something is spread out, levelled, crushed, compacted, or the like. **51.** thin sponge spread with jam, cream, or the like and rolled up. **52.** a small cake of bread, orig. and still often rolled or doubled on itself before baking. **53.** pastry spread with apple, jam, etc., and doubled on itself before baking. **54.** food which is rolled up. **55.** meat rolled up and cooked. **56.** the act or an instance of rolling. **57.** undulation of surface: *the roll of a prairie.* **58.** sonorous or rhythmical flow of words. **59.** a deep, prolonged sound, as of thunder, etc.: *the deep roll of a breaking wave.* **60.** the trill of certain birds. **61.** the continuous sound of a drum rapidly beaten. **62.** a rolling motion, as of a ship. **63.** a rolling or swaying gait. **64.** *Aeron.* a single complete rotation of an aeroplane around the axis of the fuselage with little loss of altitude or change of direction. **65.** the rotation of a rocket or guided missile or the like about its longitudinal axis. **66.** a single throw of dice. **67.** *U.S. Slang.* a wad of paper currency. **68.** *U.S. Slang.* any amount of money. **69.** *Taboo Slang.* the sexual act. [ME *roll(en)*, t. OF: m. *roller*, ult. der. L *rotula*, dim. of *rota* wheel] **—Syn. 42.** See **list**[1]. **—roll′able,** *adj.*

Rolland (*Fr.* rŏ läɴ′), *n.* **Romain** (*Fr.* rŏ mᾰɴ′), 1866–1944, French novelist, music critic, and dramatist.

rollcall (rōl′kôl′), *n.* **1.** the calling of a list of names, as of soldiers or students, to find out who is absent. **2.** a military signal for this, as one given by a drum.

roll-collar (rōl′kŏl′ə), *n.* **1.** a coat collar that rolls over in a continuous fold to the front fastening. **2.** a loose collar on a woman's garment doubled over and fastening at the back. **3.** a soft collar on a man's shirt which forms a roll over the tie instead of lying flat.

rolled gold, metal covered with a thin coating of gold.

rolled steel joist, a steel bar rolled into one of various cross-sections in standard sizes for structural use. *Abbrev.:* R.S.J.

roller (rō′lə), *n.* **1.** one who or that which rolls. **2.** a cylinder, wheel, or the like, upon which something is rolled along. **3.** a cylindrical body, revolving on a fixed axis, esp. one to facilitate the movement of something passed over or around it. **4.** a cylindrical body upon which cloth or other material is rolled up. **5.** a cylinder of plastic, wire, etc., around which hair is rolled to set it. **6.** a cylindrical body for rolling over something to be spread out, levelled, crushed, compacted, impressed, inked, etc. **7.** a device used for applying paint, consisting of a cylinder covered with lamb's wool, felt, or the like, and having a handle. **8.** any of various other revolving cylindrical bodies, as the barrel of a musical box. **9.** a long, swelling wave advancing steadily. **10.** a rolled bandage. **11.** *Ornith.* **a.** a variety of tumbler pigeon. **b.** any of the non-passerine birds constituting the family *Coraciidae*, esp. the **common roller,** *Coracias garrulus.* **c.** a variety of canary, remarkable for rolling or trilling.

roller-bearing (rō′lə bĕə′rĭng), *n.* *Mach.* a bearing in which the shaft or journal turns upon a number of steel rollers running in an annular track.

roller-coaster (rō′lə kōs′tə), *n.* a twining, sloping railway with open cars ridden for the thrills of speed and rapid turns. Also, **switchback, big dipper;** *Chiefly U.S.,* **coaster.**

roller-mill (rō′lə mĭl′), *n.* any mill which pulverizes or otherwise changes material by passing it between rolls.

roller-skate (rō′lə skāt′), *n., v.,* **-skated, -skating.** —*n.* **1.** a form of skate running on small wheels or rollers, for use on a smooth floor, etc. —*v.i.* **2.** to move on roller-skates.

roller-towel (rō′lə toul′), *n.* a long towel sewn together at the ends and hung on a roller.

roll film, *Photog.* a rolled strip of sensitized film for taking successive still pictures.

rollick (rŏl′ĭk), *v.i.* to move or act in a careless, frolicsome manner; behave in a free, hearty, gay, or jovial way. [b. ROMP and FROLIC]

rollicking (rŏl′ĭ kĭng), *adj.* swaggering and jolly: *a pair of rollicking drunken sailors.* Also, **rollicksome** (rŏl′ĭk səm).

roll-in (rōl′ĭn′), *n.* *Hockey.* the act of rolling in.

rolling (rō′lĭng), *n.* **1.** the action, motion, or sound of anything that rolls. —*adj.* **2.** that rolls. **3.** rising and falling in gentle slopes, as land. **4.** moving in undulating billows, as clouds or waves. **5.** rocking or swaying from side to side. **6.** turning or folding over, as a collar. **7.** producing a deep, continuous sound. **8.** *Slang.* drunk.

rolling hitch, a kind of hitch which is made round a spar or the like with the end of a rope, and which jams when the rope is pulled.

rolling mill, 1. a mill or establishment where (heated) iron or other metal is rolled into sheets, bars, or the like. **2.** a machine or set of rollers for rolling out or shaping metal, etc.

rolling pin, a cylinder of wood or other material for rolling out pastry, etc.

rolling stock, the wheeled vehicles of a railway, including engines and carriages.

rolling stone, a wanderer; an itinerant; a person without ties or fixed address.

Rollo (rŏl′ō), *n.* 860?–932?, Scandinavian chieftain: first duke of Normandy. Also, **Hrolf.**

roll-on (rōl′ŏn′), *n.* a woman's elastic foundation garment without fastenings; a girdle.

Rolls (rōlz), *n.* **Charles Stewart,** 1877–1910, English motor-car manufacturer (with Sir F. H. Royce) and pioneer flyer.

roll-top (rōl′tŏp′), *adj.* fitted with a slatted cover that rolls up: *a roll-top desk.*

roll-up (rōl′ŭp′), *n.* *Austral., N.Z.* **1.** an assembly, gathering. **2.** the number of people attending such a meeting.

rollway (rōl′wā′), *n.* *U.S.* **1.** a place on which things are rolled or moved on rollers. **2.** a place where logs are rolled into a stream for transportation. **3.** a pile of logs at the side of a stream awaiting transportation.

roly-poly (rō′lĭ pō′lĭ), *adj., n., pl.* **-lies.** —*adj.* **1.** plump and podgy, as a person, a young animal, etc. —*n.* **2.** a roly-poly person or thing. **3.** a strip of suet-crust pastry spread with jam, fruit, or the like, or sometimes with a savoury mixture, rolled up, wrapped in greaseproof paper, and steamed or boiled as a pudding. **4.** *Austral.* any of several bushy plants, as the tumbleweed, which break loose and roll in the wind. [earlier *rowle powle,* ? var. of *roll ye, poll ye.* See ROLL, v., POLL[1], v. (def. 19)] **—Ant. 1.** scraggy.

Rom. 1. Roman. **2.** Romance. **3.** Romanic. **4.** Romans (New Testament).

rom., roman type.

Roma (*It.* rô′mä), *n.* Italian name of **Rome** (def. 1).

Romagna (rō mä′nyə; *It.* rô mä′nyä), *n.* a former province of the papal states, in NE Italy. *Cap.:* Ravenna.

Romaic (rō mā′ĭk), *n.* **1.** Modern Greek. —*adj.* **2.** of or pertaining to modern Greece, its inhabitants, or their language. [t. Gk: m. s. *Rhōmaïkós* Roman, used of the Eastern empire]

romaine (rō mān′), *n.* a fine woven fabric in plain dyes used as a lining; when printed used for dress goods.

Romains (*Fr.* rŏ mᾰɴ′), *n.* **Jules** (*Fr.* zhʏl), born 1885, French novelist, poet, and dramatist.

roman (*Fr.* rŏ mäɴ′), *n.* *French.* **1.** a metrical narrative, esp. in medieval French literature. **2.** a novel.

Roman (rō′mən), *adj.* **1.** of or pertaining to Rome, ancient or modern, or its inhabitants. **2.** of a kind or character regarded as typical of the ancient Romans. **3.** (*usually l.c.*) designating or pertaining to the upright style of printing types most commonly used in modern books, etc., of which the main text of this dictionary is an example. **4.** denoting or pertaining to the alphabet employed by the Romans for the writing of Latin and since adopted with modifications and additions for writing western European and other languages. **5.** denoting or pertaining to the Roman numerals. **6.** of, pertaining to, or resembling the Roman architecture. **7.** of or pertaining to the Roman Catholic Church. —*n.* **8.** a native, inhabitant, or citizen of ancient or modern Rome. **9.** the dialect of Italian spoken in Rome. **10.** (*usually l.c.*) roman type or letters. **11.** *Colloq.* a member of the Roman Catholic Church. [OE, t. L: s. *Rōmānus*; r. ME *Romain*, t. OF]

roman à clef (*Fr.* rŏ mäɴ ȧ klĕ′), *French.* a novel in which actual persons and events are disguised as fiction. [F: lit., novel with a key]

Roman arch, a semicircular arch.

Roman architecture, the architecture of the ancient Romans, characterized by rational design and planning, the use of vaulting and concrete masonry, and the use of the classical orders only sporadically for purposes of architectural articulation and decoration.

Roman calendar, the ancient Roman calendar, the ancestor of our present calendars.

Roman candle, a kind of firework consisting of a tube which sends out a shower of sparks.

Roman Catholic, **1.** of or pertaining to the Roman Catholic Church. **2.** a member of the Roman Catholic Church.

Roman Catholic Church, the Christian Church of which the pope, or bishop of Rome, is the supreme head.

Roman Catholicism, the faith, practice, membership, and government of the Roman Catholic Church.

romance[1] (*n.* rə măns′, rō′măns; *v.* rə măns′), *n.*, *v.*, **-manced, -mancing,** *adj.* **—***n.* **1.** a tale depicting heroic or marvellous achievements, colourful events or scenes, chivalrous devotion, unusual, even supernatural, experiences, or other matters of a kind to appeal to the imagination. **2.** the world, life, or conditions depicted in such tales. **3.** a medieval tale, orig. one in verse and in some Romance dialect, treating of heroic personages or events: *the Arthurian romances.* **4.** a made-up story; fanciful or extravagant invention or exaggeration. **5.** romantic spirit or sentiment. **6.** romantic character or quality. **7.** a romantic affair or experience; a love affair. **—***v.i.* **8.** to invent or relate romances; indulge in fanciful or extravagant stories. **9.** to think or talk romantically. **—***adj.* **10.** (*cap.*) pertaining to the Romance languages. [ME *romanz*, t. OF, g. VL *Rōmānicē*, adv., in Romance (i.e., in one of the Romance languages), der. L *rōmānicus* Romanic] **—romanc′er,** *n.* **—Syn. 1.** See **novel**[1].

romance[2] (rə măns′), *n.* **1.** *Music.* a short, simple melody, vocal or instrumental, of tender character. **2.** *Spanish Lit.* a short epic narrative poem; historical ballad. [t. F, t. Sp.: kind of poem, ballad, t. OF: m. *romanz.* See ROMANCE[1]]

Romance language, any of the group of languages which have developed out of Latin, in their historical (from 800) or modern forms, principally, Sardinian, Dalmatian (extinct), Rumanian, Italian, Rhaeto-Romanic, French, Provençal, Catalan, Spanish, and Portuguese. [t. OF: from the phrase *langue romance* (now *langue romane*), lit., Romantic language]

Roman cement, a natural cement with hydraulic properties.

Roman Curia, the papal court, as the administrative authority of the Roman Catholic Church.

Roman Empire, **1.** the lands and peoples subject to the authority of ancient Rome. **2.** the form of government established in ancient Rome in 27 B.C., comprising the Principate or Early Empire (27 B.C. to A.D. 284) and the Autocracy or Later Empire (A.D. 284–476). **3.** a later empire, as that of Charlemagne or the Byzantine Empire, regarded as a restoration or continuation of the ancient Roman empire or one of its branches.

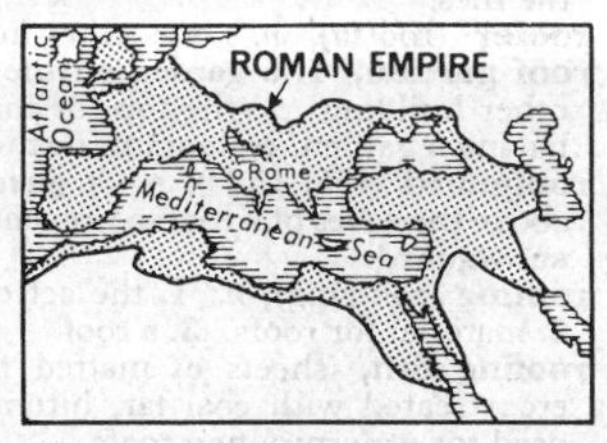

Roman Empire, A.D. 180

Romanesque (rō′mə nĕsk′), *adj.* **1.** denoting or pertaining to the style of architecture which, developing from earlier medieval and Near Eastern types, prevailed in western and southern Europe from the late 10th until the 12th and 13th centuries, characterized by the rich outline of the exterior (towers), the clear organization of the interior (bays), heavy walls, small windows, and the use of open timber roofs and groin, barrel, or rib vaults. **2.** denoting or pertaining to the corresponding styles of sculpture, ornament, and painting. **3.** (*l.c.*) of or pertaining to fanciful or extravagant literature, as romance or fable; fanciful. **—***n.* **4.** the Romanesque style of art or architecture. [f. ROMAN + -ESQUE. Cf. F *romanesque* romantic]

roman-fleuve (*Fr.* rō mäN flœv′), *n.* *French.* See **saga** (def. 2). [F: lit., stream-novel]

România (rō mä′nyə; *Rum.* rō mə nē′ȧ), *n.* Rumanian name of **Rumania.**

Romanic (rō măn′ĭk), *adj.* **1.** derived from the Romans. **2.** pertaining to the Romance languages. **—***n.* **3.** Romance language. [t. L: s. *Rōmānicus* (def. 1)]

Romanism (rō′mə nĭz′əm), *n.* (usually in derogatory use) Roman Catholicism.

Romanist (rō′mə nĭst), *n.* **1.** a member of the Roman Catholic Church. **2.** one versed in Roman institutions, law, etc. **3.** (usually derogatory) a member of a Church, esp. the Church of England, who has a liking for the ritual of the Roman Catholic Church.

Romanize (rō′mə nīz′), *v.*, **-nized, -nizing.** **—***v.t.* **1.** to render Roman Catholic. **2.** to make Roman in character. **—***v.i.* **3.** to conform to Roman Catholic doctrine, etc.; become Roman Catholic. **4.** to follow Roman practices. Also, **Romanise.** **—Ro′maniza′tion,** *n.*

Roman law, the system of jurisprudence elaborated by the ancient Romans, forming the basis of civil law in many countries.

Roman nettle, an annual or biennial urticaceous herb, *Urtica pilulifera*, with minute green female flowers in dense spherical heads.

Roman nose, a nose having a prominent upper part or bridge.

Roman numerals, the numerals in the ancient Roman system of notation, still used for certain limited purposes. The common basic symbols are **I**(= 1), **V**(= 5), **X**(= 10), **L**(= 50), **C**(= 100), **D**(= 500), and **M**(= 1000). Integers are written according to these two rules: If a letter is immediately followed by one of equal or lesser value, the two values are added; thus, XX equals 20, XV equals 15, VI equals 6. If a letter is immediately followed by one of greater value, however, the first is subtracted from the second; thus IV equals 4, XL equals 40, CM equals 900. Examples: XLVII(= 47), CXVI(= 116), MCXX (= 1120), MCMXIV(= 1914). The Roman numerals for one to nine are: I, II, III, IV, V, VI, VII, VIII, IX. Roman numerals are usually written in capital letters, but may be in lower case. A bar over a letter multiplies it by 1000; thus $\overline{X}$ equals 10,000.

Romanov (rō′mə nŏf′; *Russ.* rȧ mȧ′nəf), *n.* **1.** a member of the imperial dynasty which ruled Russia from 1613 to the abdication of Nicholas II in 1917. **2. Mikhail Feodorovich** (*Russ.* mĭ KHȧ ēl′ fĭ ô′də rə vĭch), 1596–1645, tsar of Russia 1613–45. Also, **Romanoff.**

Roman rite, the form in which mass is today most generally said and sung in the Roman Catholic Church, originating in the liturgy of the early Church at Rome.

Romans (rō′mənz), *n.* (in the New Testament) one of the most important doctrinal epistles of Paul, written to the Christian community at Rome.

Romansh (rŏ mănsh′), *n.* **1.** a Rhaeto-Romanic language spoken in the Swiss canton Grisons. It has equal standing with German, French, and Italian as one of the official languages of Switzerland. **2.** Rhaeto-Romanic in general. **—***adj.* **3.** of or pertaining to Romansh. Also, **Romansch.** [t. Rhaetian: ROMANIC]

romantic (rə măn′tĭk), *adj.* **1.** of, pertaining to, or of the nature of romance; characteristic or suggestive of the world of romance: *a romantic adventure.* **2.** proper to romance rather than to real or practical life; fanciful; unpractical; quixotic: *romantic ideas.* **3.** imbued with or dominated by the ideas, spirit, or sentiment prevailing in romance. **4.** displaying or expressing love, emotion, strong affection, etc. **5.** (*sometimes cap.*) of or pertaining to a style of literature, art, and music of the late 18th and the 19th centuries characterized by freedom of treatment, subordination of form to matter, imagination, experimentation with form, picturesqueness, etc. (opposed to *classical*). **6.** imaginary, fictitious, or fabulous. **—***n.* **7.** a romantic person. **8.** a romanticist. **9.** (*pl.*) romantic ideas, ways, etc. **10.** an artist, writer, or musician. [t. F: m. *romantique*, der. *romant* older form of *roman* romance, novel. See ROMANCE[1]] **—roman′tically,** *adv.*

romanticism (rə măn′tĭ sĭz′əm), *n.* **1.** romantic spirit or tendency. **2.** the romantic style or movement in literature and art, or adherence to its principles (as contrasted with *classicism*).

romanticist (rə măn′tĭ sĭst), *n.* an adherent of romanticism in literature or art.

romanticize (rə măn′tĭ sīz′), *v.*, **-cized, -cizing.** **—***v.t.* **1.** to make romantic; invest with a romantic character: *she romanticized her work as an actress.* **—***v.i.* **2.** to have romantic ideas; indulge in romance. Also, **romanticise.**

Romantic Movement, the late 18th- and early 19th-century movement in France, Germany, England, and America to establish romanticism in art and literature.

Romany (rŏm′ə nĭ), *n.*, *pl.* **-nies,** *adj.* **—***n.* **1.** a Gipsy. **2.** Gipsies collectively. **3.** the Indic language of the Gipsies, its various forms differing greatly because of local influences. **—***adj.* **4.** pertaining to Gipsies, their language, or customs. Also, **Rommany.** [t. Gipsy: m. *Romain*, fem. and pl. of *Romano*, adj., der. *Rom* Gipsy, man, husband]

romaunt (rə mônt′), *n.* *Archaic.* a romance, or romantic poem or tale. [t. AF, var. of OF *romant* ROMANCE[1]]

Romberg (rŏm′bûg), *n.* **Sigmund** (sĭg′mənd), 1887–1951, Hungarian composer of light opera, in the U.S.

Rom. Cath., Roman Catholic.

Rom. Cath. Ch., Roman Catholic Church.

Rome (rōm), *n.* **1.** Italian, **Roma.** the capital of Italy, in the central part, on the Tiber: the ancient capital of the Roman Empire; the site of Vatican City, seat of authority of the Roman Catholic Church. 2,563,505 (1966). See map under **San Marino. 2.** the ancient Italian kingdom, republic, and empire whose capital was the city of Rome. **3.** the Roman Catholic Church. **4.** Roman Catholicism.

Romeo (rō′mĭ ō′), *n.* **1.** the romantic hero in Shakespeare's tragedy *Romeo and Juliet.* **2.** any man who behaves amorously or romantically.

Romford (rŏm′fəd), *n.* a town in SE England, in the NE outer London borough of Havering.

Romish (rō′mĭsh), *adj.* (often in derogatory use) of or pertaining to Rome as the centre of the Roman Catholic Church; Roman Catholic.

Rommany (rŏm′ə nĭ), *n., pl.* **-nies,** *adj.* Romany.

Rommel (*Ger.* rŏm′əl), *n.* **Erwin** (*Ger.* ĕr′vēn), 1891–1944, German field marshal; commander of German forces in North Africa in World War II.

Romney (rŏm′nĭ, rŭm′-), *n.* **George,** 1734–1802, English painter.

Romney Marsh (rŏm′nĭ, rŭm′-), **1.** a coastal pasture tract in SE England, in Kent. **2.** a breed of sheep originating in this area.

romp (rŏmp), *v.i.* **1.** to play or frolic in a lively or boisterous manner. **2.** to run or go rapidly and without effort, as in racing. **—*n.* 3.** a romping frolic. **4.** a swift, effortless pace. **5.** a romping person, esp. a girl. [var. of obs. *ramp* rough woman, lit., one who ramps. See RAMP, v.]

rompers (rŏm′pəz), *n.pl.* a one-piece loose outer garment for an infant, combining a bodice and short or long trousers. Also, **crawlers.**

rompish (rŏm′pĭsh), *adj.* given to romping. **—romp′ishness,** *n.*

Romulus (rŏm′yŏŏ ləs), *n. Rom. Legend.* the founder of Rome (753 B.C.) and its first king. The son of Mars by Rhea Silvia, he and his twin brother Remus (whom he eventually killed) were abandoned as infants but suckled by a wolf. The Romans deified him as Quirinus.

Roncesvalles (rŏn′sə vălz′; *Sp.* rón thĕz bä′lyĕs), *n.* a village in N Spain, in the Pyrenees: defeat of part of Charlemagne's army and the death of Roland, A.D. 778. French, **Roncevaux** (*Fr.* rôɴs vō′).

rondavel (rŏn′də vĕl′), *n.* a circular one-roomed building or dwelling, usually having a thatched roof, common in southern Africa. [t. Afrikaans: m. *rondawel*; ult. orig. obscure]

ronde (rŏnd), *n. Print.* a typeface imitative of upright angular handwriting. [t. F: n. use of fem. of *rond* ROUND]

rondeau (rŏn′dō), *n., pl.* **-deaux** (-dō, -dōz). *French Pros.* a short poem of fixed form, consisting of thirteen (or ten) lines on two rhymes and having the opening words or phrase used in two places as an unrhymed refrain. [See RONDEL]

rondel (rŏn′dl), *n. Pros.* a short poem of fixed form, consisting usually of fourteen lines on two rhymes, of which four are made up of the initial couplet repeated in the middle and at the end (the second line of the couplet sometimes being omitted at the end). [ME *rondeal,* t. OF: m. *rondel, rondeau,* dim. of *rond* round]

rondo (rŏn′dō), *n., pl.* **-dos.** *Music.* a work or movement, often the last movement of a sonata, having one principal subject which is stated at least three times in the same key and to which return is made after the introduction of each subordinate theme. [t. It., t. F: m. *rondeau.* See RONDEL]

rondure (rŏn′dyŏŏə), *n. Poetic.* **1.** a circle. **2.** roundness. [t. F: m. *rondeur,* der. *rond* round]

Ronsard (*Fr.* rôɴ sár′), *n.* **Pierre de** (*Fr.* pyĕr′də), 1524–1585, French poet.

Ronse (*Flem.* rôn′sə), *n.* a town in NW central Belgium. 25,500 (est. 1964). French, **Renaix** (*Fr.* rə nĕ′).

Röntgen (rŏn′tyən; *Ger.* rœnt′gən), *n.* **1. Wilhelm Konrad** (*Ger.* vĭl′hĕlm kŏn′rát), 1845–1923, German physicist, discoverer of X-rays. **2.** (*l.c.*) the amount of X- or gamma-radiation that will produce ions in air containing a quantity of positive or negative electricity equal to one electrostatic unit in 0·001293 grams of air. *Abbrev.*: r. **—*adj.* 3.** (*sometimes l.c.*) pertaining to Röntgen rays. **4.** pertaining to Wilhelm Konrad Röntgen. Also, **Roentgen.**

röntgenize (rŏnt′gə nīz′), *v.t.,* **-nized, -nizing.** to subject to the action of Röntgen rays. Also, **röntgenise.**

röntgenogram (rŏnt gĕn′ə grăm′), *n.* a photograph made with Röntgen rays.

röntgenograph (rŏnt gĕn′ə grăf′, -gräf′), *n.* a röntgenogram. **—röntgenography** (rŏnt′gĭ nŏg′rə fĭ), *n.*

röntgenology (rŏnt′gĭ nŏl′ə jĭ), *n.* that branch of medicine concerned with diagnosis and therapeutics through Röntgen rays. **—rönt′genol′ogist,** *n.*

röntgenopaque (rŏnt′gĕ nō pāk′), *adj.* not permitting the passage of Röntgen rays.

röntgenoparent (rŏnt′gĕ nō păr′ənt), *adj.* visible in Röntgen rays.

röntgenotherapy (rŏnt′gĕ nō thĕr′ə pĭ), *n.* treatment of disease by means of Röntgen rays.

Röntgen ray, (*sometimes l.c.*) X-ray.

roo (rōō), *n. Austral. Colloq.* a kangaroo.

rood (rōōd), *n.* **1.** a crucifix, esp. a large one at the entrance to the choir or chancel of a medieval church, often supported on a rood beam or rood screen. **2.** *Archaic.* the cross on which Christ died. **3.** a cross as used in crucifixion. **4.** a unit of length varying locally from $5\frac{1}{2}$ to 8 yards. **5.** a unit of land measure, equal to 40 square rods or $\frac{1}{4}$ acre. **6.** a unit of 1 square rod, or thereabouts. [ME; OE *rōd,* akin to G *Rute.* See ROD]

rood beam, a beam extending across the entrance to the choir or chancel of a church to support the rood, and usually forming the head of a rood screen.

Roodepoort-Maraisburg (rōō′də pōōət′ mə răs′bûg), *n.* a town in the Republic of South Africa in S Transvaal. 95,211 (1960).

rood loft, a loft or gallery over a rood screen.

rood screen, a screen, often of elaborate design, and properly surmounted by a rood, separating the nave from the choir or chancel of a church.

roof (rōōf), *n., pl.* **roofs** (rōōfs, rōōvz). **1.** the external upper covering of a house or other building. **2.** a house. **3.** the highest part or summit. **4.** something which in form or position resembles the roof of a house, as the top of a car, the upper part of the mouth, etc. **5. hit the roof,** *Slang.* become very angry; lose one's temper. **6. raise the roof, a.** to create a loud noise. **b.** to make loud protests or complaints. **—*v.t.* 7.** to provide or cover with a roof. [ME; OE *hrōf,* c. D *roef* cover, cabin]

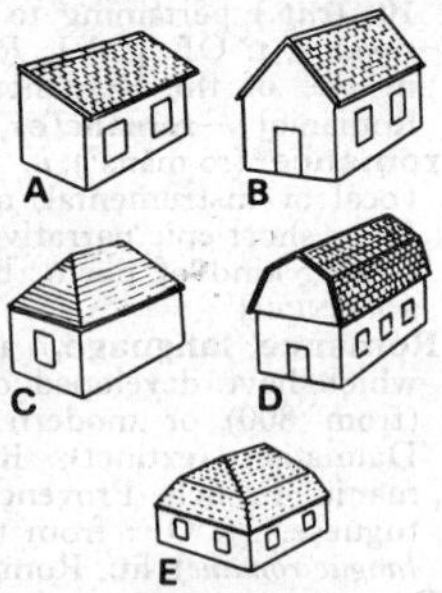

A B C D E

Types of roofs
A, Lean-to;
B, Saddle or ridge;
C, Hip; D, Gambrel; E, Mansard

roofboard (rōōf′bôd′), *n.* a board forming part of a layer sometimes used to cover the rafters of a house under the tiles.

roofer (rōō′fə), *n.* one who makes or repairs roofs.

roof garden, 1. a garden on the flat roof of a house or other building. **2.** the top, or top storey, of a building, having a garden, restaurant, or the like.

roofguard (rōōf′gäd′), *n.* a guard of boards fixed just above the eaves of a roof to prevent snow sliding off. Also, **snowguard.**

roofing (rōō′fĭng), *n.* **1.** the act of covering with a roof. **2.** material for roofs. **3.** a roof.

roofing felt, sheets of matted fibres as asbestos, flax, etc., treated with coal tar, bitumen, or pitch, generally used for waterproofing roofs.

roofless (rōōf′lĭs), *adj.* **1.** having no roof. **2.** without the shelter of a house.

rooftop (rōōf′tŏp′), *n.* the outer part of the roof of a building.

rooftree (rōōf′trē′), *n.* **1.** the ridgepole of a roof. **2.** the roof itself.

rooinek (roi′nĕk′), *n. S African.* (in contemptuous use) an Englishman. [Afrikaans: red neck]

rook[1] (rŏŏk), *n.* **1.** a black European crow, *Corvus frugilegus,* of a gregarious disposition and given to nesting in colonies in trees about buildings. **2.** a sharper, as at cards or dice; a swindler. **—*v.t.* 3.** to cheat; fleece; swindle. [ME *roke,* OE *hrōc,* c. D *roek,* Icel. *hrōkr*]

rook[2] (rŏŏk), *n. Chess.* a piece having the power to move any unobstructed distance in a straight line forwards, backwards, or sideways; a castle. [ME *rok,* t. OF, ult. t. Pers.: m. *rukhkh*]

rookery (rŏŏk′ə rĭ), *n., pl.* **-ries. 1.** a colony of rooks. **2.** a place where rooks congregate to breed. **3.** a breeding place or colony of other birds or animals, as penguins, seals, etc. **4.** *U.S. Colloq.* a crowded tenement house.

rookie (rŏŏk′ĭ), *n. Slang.* a raw recruit, orig. in the army, and hence in any service. Also, **rooky.**

rooky (rŏŏk′ĭ), *adj.* full of or frequented by rooks.

room (rōōm, rŏŏm), *n.* **1.** a portion of space within a building or other structure, separated by walls or partitions from other parts: *a dining room.* **2.** (*pl.*) lodgings or quarters, as in a house or building. **3.** the persons present in a room: *the whole room laughed.* **4.** space, or extent of space, occupied by or available for something: *the desk takes up too much room.* **5.** opportunity or scope for or to do something: *room for improvement or doubt.* —*v.i.* **6.** *U.S.* to occupy a room or rooms; to share a room; lodge. [ME *roume*, OE *rum*, c. D *ruim*, G *Raum*]

roomer (ro͞o′mə, ro͝om′ə), *n.* *U.S.* a lodger.

roomette (ro͝om ĕt′, ro͝om-), *n.* *U.S.* a private sleeping compartment on a train.

roomful (ro͝om′fo͝ol′, ro͝om′-), *n.*, *pl.* **-fuls.** an amount or number sufficient to fill a room.

rooming house, *Chiefly U.S.* a lodging house.

room-mate (ro͝om′māt′, ro͝om′-), *n.* one who shares a room with another or others.

room service, **1.** the serving of food, drinks, etc., to a guest at a hotel, etc., in his room. **2.** the staff at a hotel, etc., which renders this service.

roomy (ro͞o′mĭ, ro͝om′ĭ), *adj.*, **-mier, -miest.** affording ample room; spacious; large. —**room′ily,** *adv.* —**room′iness,** *n.*

roop (ro͞op), *n.* *Vet. Sci.* roup.

roorback (ro͞oə′băk′), *n.* *U.S.* a false and more or less damaging report circulated for political effect. [from *Roorback*, a pretended traveller in whose book of his alleged experiences in the U.S. occurred an account of an incident damaging to the character of James K. Polk]

roose (ro͞oz), *v.t.*, *v.i.*, **roosed, roosing,** *n.* *Chiefly Scot.* praise. [t. Scand.; cf. Icel. *hrōsa* praise]

Roosevelt (rō′zə vĕlt′), *n.* **1.** **(Anna) Eleanor,** 1884–1962, U.S. diplomat and writer (wife of F. D. Roosevelt). **2.** **Franklin Delano** (dĕl′ə nō′), 1882–1945, 32nd president of the U.S., 1933–45. **3.** **Theodore,** 1858–1919, 26th president of the U.S., 1901–09.

roost (ro͞ost), *n.* **1.** a perch upon which domestic fowls rest at night. **2.** a house or place for fowls or birds to roost in. **3.** a place for sitting, resting, or staying. **4.** **rule the roost,** to be in charge; dominate. —*v.i.* **5.** to sit or rest on a roost, perch, etc. **6.** to settle or stay, esp. for the night. **7.** **come home to roost,** to come back upon the originator; recoil. [ME *rooste*, OE *hrōst*, c. MD and Flem. *roest*]

rooster (ro͞os′tə), *n.* a domestic cock. [f. ROOST + -ER[1]]

root[1] (ro͞ot), *n.* **1.** a part of the body of a plant which, typically, develops from the radicle, and grows downwards into the soil, fixing the plant and absorbing nutriment and moisture. **2.** a similar organ developed from some other part of the plant, as one of those by which ivy clings to its support. **3.** any underground part of a plant, as a rhizome. **4.** something resembling or suggesting the root of a plant in position or function. **5.** the embedded or basal portion of a hair, tooth, nail, etc. **6.** the fundamental or essential part: *the root of a matter.* **7.** the source or origin of a thing: *love of money is the root of all evil.* **8.** a person or family as the source of offspring or descendants. **9.** an offshoot or scion. **10.** (*pl.*) **a.** a person's real home and environment: *though he's lived in the city for ten years his roots are still in the country.* **b.** those elements, as personal relationships, a liking for the area, customs, etc., which make a place one's true home: *he lived in London for five years but never established any roots there.* **11.** *Maths.* **a.** a quantity which, when multiplied by itself a certain number of times, produces a given quantity: *2 is the square root of 4, the cube root of 8, and the fourth root of 16.* **b.** a quantity which, when substituted for the unknown quantity in an algebraic equation, satisfies the equation. **12.** *Gram.* **a.** a morpheme which underlies an inflectional paradigm or is used itself as a word or element of a compound. Thus, *dance* is the root of *dancer, dancing.* In German, *seh* is the root of *gesehen.* **b.** such a morpheme as posited for a parent language, such as proto-Indo-European, on the basis of comparison of extant forms in daughter languages. **13.** *Music.* **a.** the fundamental note of a chord or of a series of harmonies. **b.** the lowest note of a chord when arranged as a series of thirds; the fundamental. **14.** *Mach.* that part of a screw thread which connects adjacent flanks at the bottom of the groove. **15.** **root and branch,** entirely; completely: *we destroyed them root and branch.* **16.** **take** (or **strike**) **root, a.** to send out roots and begin to grow. **b.** to become fixed or established. —*v.i.* **17.** to send out roots and begin to grow. **18.** to become fixed or established. —*v.t.* **19.** to fix by, or as if by, roots. **20.** to implant or establish deeply. **21.** to pull, tear, or dig (fol. by *up, out,* etc.) by the roots. **22.** to extirpate; exterminate (with *up, out,* etc.). [ME; OE *rōt*, t. Scand.; cf. Icel. *rōt*] —**root′less,** *adj.*

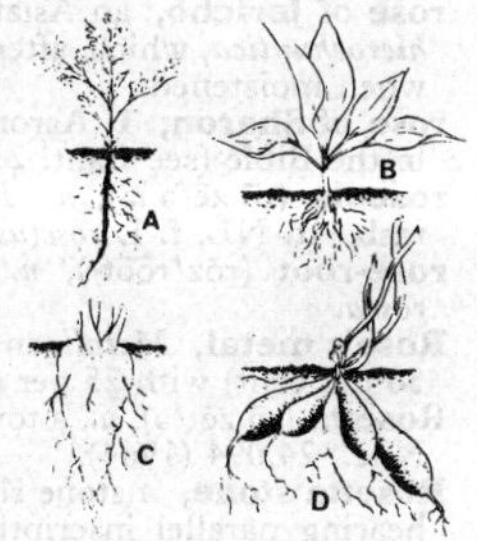

Types of roots
A, Tap (ragweed, *Ambrosia trifida*); B, Fibrous (plantain, *Plantago major*); C, Fleshy (carrot, *Daucus carota*); D, Tuberous (dahlia, *Dahlia rosea*)

root[2] (ro͞ot), *v.i.* **1.** to turn up the soil with the snout, as swine. **2.** to poke, pry, or search, as if to find something. —*v.t.* **3.** to turn over with the snout (often fol. by *up*). **4.** to unearth; bring to light (fol. by *up*, etc.). [var. of obs. *wroot*, OE *wrōtan*, akin to *wrōt* snout] —**root′er,** *n.*

root[3] (ro͞ot), *v.i.* *U.S. Slang.* to give encouragement to, or applaud, a contestant, etc. [? var. of *rout* make a loud noise. Cf. Norw. *ruta*] —**root′er,** *n.*

rootage (ro͞o′tĭj), *n.* **1.** the act of taking root. **2.** firm fixture by means of roots.

root beer, *U.S.* a drink containing the extracted juices of various roots, as of dandelion, sarsaparilla, sassafras, etc.

root cap, *Bot.* a sheath of cells at the end of a root.

root crop, a crop such as beets, carrots, turnips, etc., grown for its edible roots.

root hair, *Bot.* an elongated tubular extension of an epidermal cell of the root serving to absorb water and minerals from the soil.

rootlet (ro͞ot′lĭt), *n.* *Bot.* **1.** a little root. **2.** a small or fine branch of a root. **3.** one of the adventitious roots by which ivy or the like clings to rocks, etc.

root mean square, *Maths.* the square root of the arithmetic mean of the squares of a set of values. *Abbrev.*: r.m.s.

rootrot (ro͞ot′rŏt′), *n.* the damage or decay of roots caused by many plant diseases.

rootstalk (ro͞ot′stôk′), *n.* *Bot.* a rhizome.

rootstock (ro͞ot′stŏk′), *n.* **1.** *Hort.* a root used as a stock in plant propagation. **2.** *Bot.* the basal persistent part of the stems of erect herbacious perennials from which new roots and aerial shoots arise in the next growing season. **3.** a source from which offshoots have originated; ancestral form.

rooty (ro͞o′tĭ), *adj.*, **rootier, rootiest.** abounding in roots. —**root′iness,** *n.*

roove (ro͞ov), *n.*, *v.*, **rooved, rooving.** —*n.* **1.** *Shipbuilding.* a small copper washer used when copper nails are being clinched. —*v.t.* **2.** to secure (a nail) with a roove. [orig. obscure]

rope (rōp), *n.*, *v.*, **roped, roping.** —*n.* **1.** a strong, thick line or cord, commonly one composed of twisted or braided strands of hemp, flax, or the like, or of wire or other material. **2.** (*pl.*) the cords used to enclose a boxing ring or other space. **3.** a hangman's noose. **4.** death by hanging as a punishment. **5.** a quantity of material or a number of things twisted or strung together in the form of a thick cord: *a rope of beads.* **6.** *U.S.* a lasso. **7.** a stringy, viscid, or glutinous formation in a liquid. **8.** (*pl.*) methods; procedure; operations of a business, etc.: *know the ropes; learn the ropes.* **9.** **on the ropes, a.** *Boxing.* driven against the ropes by one's opponent. **b.** in a hopeless position; near to failure. —*v.t.* **10.** to tie, bind, or fasten with a rope. **11.** to enclose or mark off with a rope. **12.** *U.S.* to catch with a lasso. **13.** *Slang.* to draw, entice, or inveigle into something (fol. by *in*). —*v.i.* **14.** to be drawn out into a filament of thread; become ropy. [ME; OE *rāp*, c. D *reep*, G *Reif*]

ropeable (rō′pə bl), *adj.* **1.** capable of being roped. **2.** *Austral., N.Z.* (of animals) wild; intractable. **3.** *Austral., N.Z. Colloq.* angry; bad-tempered. Also, **ropable.**

rope-dance (rōp′däns′), *n.* a performance as of dancing, walking, etc., on a tightrope. —**rope′-dan′cer,** *n.*

rope-ladder (rōp′lăd′ə), *n.* a ladder made of two long pieces of strong rope connected at regular intervals by short pieces of rope, wood, metal, etc.

ropemaking (rōp′mā′kĭng), *n.* the art, act, or process of making rope.

Roper (rō′pə), *n.* a river in N Australia flowing E through Northern Territory to the Gulf of Carpentaria. ab. 250 mi.

ropewalk (rōp′wôk′), *n.* **1.** a long, usually covered, course. **2.** a long, low building, where ropes are made.

rope-walker (rōp′wô′kə), *n.* a tightrope performer.

ropeway (rōp′wā′), *n.* a system of overhead cables, etc., used for transporting goods or passengers.

rope yarn. See **yarn** (def. 2).

ropy (rō′pĭ), *adj.*, **ropier, ropiest.** **1.** resembling a rope or ropes. **2.** forming viscid or glutinous threads, as a liquid. **3.** *Colloq.* worn; deteriorated; below the desired standard. Also, **ropey.** —**rop′iness,** *n.*

roque (rōk), *n.* an American form of croquet. [arbitrary var. of CROQUET]

Roquefort (rŏk′fô; *Fr.* rŏk fôr′), *n.* a strongly flavoured cheese, veined with mould, made from goats' and ewes' milk and ripened in caves at Roquefort, a town in S France.

roquelaure (rŏk′ə lô′), *n.* a cloak reaching to the knees, much worn by men during the 18th century. [t. F, after the Duc de *Roquelaure*, 1656–1738]

roquet (rō′kí), *v.*, **-queted** (-kĭd), **-queting** (-kĭ ĭng), *n.* *Croquet.* —*v.t.* **1.** to cause one's ball to strike (another player's ball). **2.** (of a ball) to strike (another ball). —*v.i.* **3.** to roquet a ball. —*n.* **4.** the act of roqueting. [? alter. of CROQUET]

rorqual (rô′kwəl), *n.* *Zool.* any of the whalebone whales, some being very large, that constitute the genus *Balaenoptera*, having a dorsal fin; a finback. [t. F, t. Norw.: m. *röyrkval* finner-whale]

Common rorqual, *Balaenoptera phipalus* (65 ft long)

Rorschach test (*Ger.* rŏr′shäKH), *Psychol.* a test devised for the analysis of personality, calling for responses to ink blots and drawings. [named after Hermann *Rorschach*, 1884–1922, Swiss psychiatrist]

rort (rôt), *n.* *Austral. Colloq.* **1.** a scheme; trick. **2.** a spree; orgy. [orig. uncert.]

Rosa (*It.* rō′zȧ), *n.* **Monte** (*It.* mōn′tė), a mountain between Switzerland and Italy, in the Pennine Alps: second highest peak of the Alps. 15,217 ft.

rosaceous (rō zā′shəs), *adj.* **1.** belonging to the *Rosaceae*, or rose family of plants, which includes also the blackberry, strawberry, agrimony, spiraea, etc. **2.** having a corolla of five broad petals, like that of a rose. **3.** roselike. **4.** rose-coloured; rosy. [t. L: m. *rosāceus*]

rosaniline (rō zăn′ĭ lĭn, -lēn′, -līn′), *n.* *Chem.* **1.** a red dye, $C_{20}H_{19}N_3$.HCl, derived from aniline and orthotoluidine: a constituent of fuchsine. **2.** the base, $C_{20}H_{21}N_3O$, which with hydrochloric acid forms this dye. [f. ROSE[1] + ANILINE]

rosarian (rō zĕə′rĭ ən), *n.* one who grows roses, for pleasure or profit. [f. ROSE[1] + -ARIAN]

Rosario (*Sp.* rō sä′ryō), *n.* a city in E Argentina: a port on the Paraná river. 671,582 (1960).

rosary (rō′zə rĭ), *n.*, *pl.* **-ries.** **1.** *Rom. Cath. Ch.* **a.** a series of prayers consisting (in the usual form) of fifteen decades of aves, each decade being preceded by a paternoster and followed by a gloria (Gloria Patri), one of the mysteries or events in the life of Christ and of the Virgin Mary being recalled at each decade. **b.** a string of beads used for counting these prayers in reciting them. **2.** (among other religious bodies) a string of beads similarly used in praying. **3.** a rose garden; a bed of roses. [ME, t. L: m. s. *rosārium* rose garden, ML rosary, prop. neut. of *rosārius* of roses]

roscoelite (rŏs′kō līt′), *n.* a greenish brown mineral, similar to muscovite, in which the aluminium is partly replaced by vanadium. [named after Sir Henry *Roscoe*, 1833–1915, English chemist. See -LITE]

Roscommon (rŏs kŏm′ən), *n.* **1.** a county in W Republic of Ireland, in Connaught. 59,217 pop. (1961); 950 sq. mi. **2.** its county town. 1600 (1961).

rose[1] (rōz), *n.*, *v.*, **rosed, rosing.** —*n.* **1.** any of the wild or cultivated, usually prickly-stemmed, showy-flowered shrubs constituting the genus *Rosa*, having in the wild state a corolla of five roundish petals. **2.** any of various related or similar plants. **3.** the flower of any such shrub, usually of a red, pink, white, or yellow colour, and often fragrant. **4.** an ornament shaped like or suggesting a rose; a rosette of ribbon or the like. **5.** the traditional reddish colour of the rose, varying from a purplish red through different shades to a pale pink. **6.** a pinkish red colour in the cheek. **7.** a rose window. **8.** an ornamental plate or socket which surrounds a doorknob on the face of a door, an electric or gas light fitting, on a ceiling, etc. **9.** *Hist.* **a. white rose,** the emblem of the house of York. **b. red rose,** the emblem of the house of Lancaster. **10.** the compass card of the mariners' compass as printed on charts. **11.** a form of cut gem formerly much used with a triangularly faceted top and flat underside: *a rose diamond.* **12.** a perforated cap or plate at the end of a water pipe or the spout of a watering-can, etc., to break a flow of water into a spray. **13. bed of roses,** a situation of luxurious ease; an easy and highly agreeable position. **14. under the rose,** secretly; privately. —*adj.* **15.** of the colour rose. —*v.t.* **16.** to make rose-coloured. **17.** to flush (the cheeks, face, etc.). [ME and OE, t. L: m. *rosa*] —**rose′like′,** *adj.*

rose[2] (rōz), *v.* pt. of **rise.**

rosé (rō′zā; *Fr.* rō zė′), *n.* *French.* a light wine of a translucent pale red colour.

rose acacia, a small tree, *Robinia hispida*, of the southern Allegheny Mountains, in the U.S., having large, dark rose-coloured scentless flowers in racemes.

rose-apple (rōz′ăp′l), *n.* a small, evergreen myrtaceous tree, *Eugenia jambos*, a native of the East Indies, with an edible fruit much used in the tropics in confectionery.

roseate (rō′zĭ ĭt), *adj.* **1.** tinged with rose; rosy. **2.** bright or promising. **3.** optimistic. [f. s. L *roseus* rosy + -ATE[1]] —**ro′seately,** *adv.*

Roseau (rō zō′), *n.* a town in the Windward Islands, the capital of Dominica. 10,417 (1960).

rosebay willowherb (rōz′bā′), a tall perennial herb with handsome spikes of deep pink flowers, *Chamaenerion angustifolium*, widespread in open places throughout N temperate regions.

rose-beetle (rōz′bē′tl), *n.* rose-chafer.

Rosebery (rōz′bə rĭ -brĭ), *n.* **Archibald Philip Primrose, Earl of,** 1847–1929, British statesman and author: prime minister 1894–95.

rosebud (rōz′bŭd′), *n.* the bud of a rose.

rosebush (rōz′bŏŏsh′), *n.* a shrub which bears roses.

rose campion, a frequently cultivated caryophyllaceous herb with red or white flowers, *Lychnis coronaria.*

rose-chafer (rōz′chā′fə), *n.* a scarabaeid beetle of the British Isles, *Cetonia aurata.* Also, **rose-beetle.**

rose cold, a form of hay fever caused by the pollen of roses. Also, **rose fever.**

rose-coloured (rōz′kŭl′əd), *adj.* **1.** of rose colour; rosy; rosaceous. **2.** promising, cheerful, or optimistic.

rose-comb (rōz′kōm′), *n.* a comb, characteristic of some breeds of the domestic fowl, having numerous low, rounded crests not necessarily arranged in line.

rosefish (rōz′fĭsh′), *n.*, *pl.* **-fishes,** (*esp. collectively*) **-fish.** a north Atlantic rockfish, *Sebastes marinus.*

rosella (rō zĕl′ə), *n.* *Austral., N.Z.* **1.** a brilliantly coloured parrot, *Platycercus eximius.* **2.** *Slang.* a sheep that has lost some wool.

rose mallow, **1.** any of various plants of the malvaceous genus *Hibiscus*, bearing rose-coloured flowers. **2.** the hollyhock, *Althaea rosea.*

rosemary (rōz′mə rĭ, -mrĭ), *n.*, *pl.* **-maries.** an evergreen menthaceous shrub, *Rosmarinus officinalis*, native in the Mediterranean region, and yielding a fragrant essential oil. It is a traditional symbol of remembrance. [ME *rose mary*, t. L: m. *rōs maris*, lit., dew of the sea; in E the final *-s* mistaken for pl. sign]

rose-moss (rōz′mŏs′), *n.* a small portulacaceous herb from Brazil, *Portulaca grandiflora*, with many cultivated varieties having colourful flowers.

rose of Heaven, an annual, caryophyllaceous herb with white or red flowers, *Lychnis coeli-rosa*, a native of the Mediterranean region.

rose of Jericho, an Asiatic cruciferous plant, *Anastatica hierochuntica*, which, after drying and curling up, expands when moistened.

rose of Sharon, **1.** Aaron's-beard. **2.** a plant mentioned in the Bible (see Cant. 2:1).

roseola (rō zē′ə lə), *n.* *Pathol.* a kind of rose-coloured rash. [t. NL, f. L *rose(us)* rosy + dim. suffix *-ola*]

rose-root (rōz′rōōt′), *n.* the midsummer-men, *Sedum rosea.*

Rose's metal, *Metall.* an alloy of bismuth (approximately 50 per cent) with 25 per cent each of tin and lead.

Rosetta (rō zĕt′ə), *n.* a town in N Egypt at a mouth of the Nile. 24,094 (1964).

Rosetta stone, a stone slab, found in 1799 near Rosetta, bearing parallel inscriptions in Greek and in Egyptian hieroglyphic and demotic characters, making possible the decipherment of ancient Egyptian hieroglyphics.

rosette (rō zĕt′), *n.* **1.** any arrangement, part, object, or formation more or less resembling a rose. **2.** a rose-shaped arrangement of ribbon or other material, used as an ornament or badge. **3.** an architectural ornament resembling a rose or having a generally circular combination of parts. **4.** *Bot.* a circular cluster of leaves or other organs. [t. F, dim. of *rose* ROSE[1]]

Architectural rosette

rosewater (rōz′wô′tə), *n.* **1.** distilled water tinctured with the essential oil of roses. —*adj.* **2.** having the scent of rosewater. **3.** affectedly delicate, nice, or fine; sentimental.

rose window, a circular window with roselike tracery or radiating mullions.

rosewood (rōz′wŏŏd′), *n.* **1.** any of various reddish cabinet woods (sometimes with a roselike odour) yielded by certain fabaceous tropical trees, esp. of the genus *Dalbergia.* **2.** a tree yielding such wood.

Rosh Hashana (rŏsh′hə shä′nə), the two-day Jewish holiday celebrated at the start of the Jewish New Year, when the shophar is blown. Also, **Rosh Hashona** (hə shō′nə). [t. Heb.: f. *rōsh* head + *hash-shānāh* the year]

Rosicrucian (rō′zĭ kro͞o′shyən), *n.* **1.** one of a number or body of persons (an alleged secret society) prominent in the 17th and 18th centuries, laying claim to various forms of occult knowledge and power and professing esoteric principles of religion. **2.** a member of any of several later or modern bodies or societies professing principles derived from or attributed to the earlier Rosicrucians. —*adj.* **3.** of, pertaining to, or characteristic of the Rosicrucians. [f. *Rosicruc-* (Latinized form of G *Rosenkreuz*, name of supposed founder) + -IAN] —**Ro′si-cru′cianism,** *n.*

rosily (rō′zĭ lĭ), *adv.* **1.** with a rosy colour. **2.** in a rosy manner.

rosin (rŏz′ĭn), *n.* **1.** the hard, brittle resin left after distilling off the oil of turpentine from the crude oleoresin of the pine, used in making varnish, for rubbing on violin bows, etc.; colophony. **2.** (not in scientific usage) resin. —*v.t.* **3.** to cover or rub with rosin. [ME, t. OF: m. *rosine*, var. of *resine* RESIN]

Rosinante (rŏz′ĭ năn′tĭ), *n.* **1.** the old, worn horse of Don Quixote. **2.** (*l.c.*) a broken-down, old horse. [t. Sp.: m. *Rocinante* (ult. der. Rom. *runcīnus* strong low-class horse)]

rosolio (rō zō′lĭ ō′), *n.* a cordial made from raisins and flavoured with rose petals, cloves, cinammon, or the like, popular in southern Europe. Also, **rosoglio.** [t. It., var. of *rosoli*, g. L *rōs sōlis* dew of the sun]

Ross (rŏs), *n.* **1.** Ross and Cromarty. **2. Betsy,** 1752–1836, American woman who designed and made the first U.S. flag. **3. Sir James Clark,** 1800–62, British naval officer and explorer of the Arctic and Antarctic. **4.** his uncle, **Sir John,** 1777–1856, British naval officer and arctic explorer. **5. Sir Ronald,** 1857–1932, British physician.

Ross and Cromarty (krŏm′ə tĭ), a county in NW Scotland. 57,607 pop. (1961); 3089 sq. mi. *Co. town:* Dingwall.

Ross Dependency, a British territory in Antarctica including **Ross Island,** the coasts of the Ross Sea, and adjacent islands: a dependency of New Zealand. ab. 175,000 sq. mi.

Rossetti (rō sĕt′ĭ), *n.* **1. Christina Georgina,** 1830–94, British poet. **2.** her brother, **Dante Gabriel,** 1828–82, British poet and painter.

Ross Ice Shelf, an ice barrier filling the S part of the Ross Sea.

Rossini (rō sē′nĭ; *It.* rōs sē′nē), *n.* **Gioacchino Antonio** (*It.* jō ȧ kē′nō ȧn tō′nyō), 1792–1868, Italian composer.

Ross Sea, an arm of the Antarctic Ocean, S of New Zealand, extending into Antarctica.

Rostand (*Fr.* rōs täN′), *n.* **Edmond** (*Fr.* ĕd mōN′), 1868–1918, French dramatist and poet.

rostellate (rŏs tĕl′ĭt), *adj. Bot.* having a rostellum.

rostellum (rŏs tĕl′əm), *n., pl.* **-la** (-lə). *Bot.* **1.** any small, beaklike process. **2.** a modification of the stigma in many orchids. [t. L, dim. of *rōstrum* beak]

roster (rŏs′tə), *n.* **1.** a list of persons or groups with their turns or periods of duty. **2.** any list, roll, or register. —*v.t.* **3.** to put on a roster; to list. [t. D: m. *rooster* list, orig., gridiron (der. *roosten* roast), from the ruled paper used]

Rostock (*Ger.* rōs′tŏk), *n.* a Baltic seaport in N East Germany. 179,352 (1962).

Rostov (rŏs′tŏv; *Russ.* rȧs tôf′), *n.* a seaport in the S Soviet Union in Europe, on the river Don, near the Sea of Azov. 720,000 (est. 1965). Also, **Rostov-on-Don** (-dŏn′). See map under **Sevastopol.**

rostral (rŏs′trəl), *adj.* of or pertaining to a rostrum. [t. LL: s. *rōstrālis*, f. s. L *rōstrum* beak + *-ālis* -AL[1]]

rostrate (rŏs′trāt), *adj.* furnished with a rostrum or beak.

Rostropovich (*Russ.* rəs trȧ pô′vĭch), *n.* **Mstislav** (*Russ.* mstĭs lȧf′), born 1927, Soviet cellist.

rostrum (rŏs′trəm), *n., pl.* **-trums, -tra** (-trə). **1.** any platform, stage, or the like, for public speaking. **2.** a platform for musicians or their conductor, or the like. **3.** a pulpit. **4.** a beaklike projection from the prow of a ship, esp. one on an ancient warship for ramming an enemy ship. **5.** the platform or elevated place (adorned with the beaks of captured warships) in the ancient Roman forum, from which orations, pleadings, etc., were delivered. **6.** *Biol.* a beaklike process or extension of some part. **7.** *Theat.* a portable platform placed on the stage as part of the scenery. [t. L: beak, in pl., speakers' platform (cf. def. 5)]

rosy (rō′zĭ), *adj.*, **rosier, rosiest. 1.** pink or pinkish red; roseate. **2.** (of persons, the cheeks, lips, etc.) having a fresh, healthy redness. **3.** bright or promising: *a rosy future.* **4.** cheerful or optimistic: *rosy anticipations.* **5.** made or consisting of roses. —**ros′ily,** *adv.* —**ros′iness,** *n.*

—**Syn. 2.** ROSY, RUBICUND, RUDDY are descriptive of a red colour. ROSY suggests a charming warm pink or blooming red: *rosy cheeks, a rosy child.* RUBICUND, today applied only to the complexion, suggests a rich or unnatural red in the face or some part of it, esp. as a result of high living or intemperance in drink: *the rubicund nose of a drunkard.* RUDDY indicates a deep and healthy red such as is associated with life out of doors: *the ruddy face of a woodsman.* —**Ant. 2.** pale.

rosy finch, any finch of the genus *Leucosticte*, of mountain regions, having red or white patches on the back.

rot (rŏt), *v.*, **rotted, rotting,** *n., interj.* —*v.i.* **1.** to undergo decomposition; decay. **2.** to fall or become weak due to decay (fol. by *away, off*, etc.). **3.** to become morally corrupt or offensive. —*v.t.* **4.** to cause to rot. **5.** to ret (flax, etc.). **6.** *Colloq.* to tease or chaff. —*n.* **7.** the process of rotting. **8.** the state of being rotten; decay; putrefaction. **9.** rotting or rotten matter. **10.** *Pathol.* (esp. among laymen) any of various diseases characterized by decomposition. **11.** any of various plant diseases or forms of decay produced by fungi or bacteria. **12.** *Slang.* nonsense. —*interj.* **13.** (an exclamation of dissent, distaste, or disgust. [ME, t. Scand.; cf. Icel. *rot*, n., akin to OE *rotian* to rot] —**Syn. 1.** See **decay.**

rota (rō′tə), *n.* **1.** a round, as of duty. **2.** a roster. **3.** (*cap.*) *Rom. Cath. Ch.* an ecclesiastical tribunal forming a court of final appeal. [t. L: wheel]

rotary (rō′tə rĭ), *adj.* **1.** turning round as on an axis, as an object. **2.** taking place round an axis, as motion. **3.** having a part or parts that rotate, as a machine. **4.** denoting or pertaining to an internal-combustion engine of an aeroplane, having radially arranged cylinders which move about a stationary crankshaft. **5.** *Agric.* denoting various implements having rotating blades, scrapers, or the like: *rotary hoe.* [t. LL: m. s. *rotārius*, der. L *rota* wheel. See -ARY]

Rotary Club, an international organization of businessmen, founded in Chicago in 1905, devoted to service to the community and to the advance of world peace. —**Rotarian** (rō tẽə′rĭ ən), *n.* —**Rotar′ianism,** *n.*

rotary converter, *Elect.* synchronous converter.

rotary hoe, an implement with many finger-like wheels, pulled over the ground for early crop cultivation and destruction of weeds.

rotary plough, a series of swinging knives mounted on a horizontal power-driven shaft which pulverize unploughed soil, for planting, in one operation. Also, **rotary tiller.**

rotary press. See **press**[1] (def. 32b).

rotate[1] (rō tāt′), *v.*, **-tated, -tating.** —*v.t.* **1.** to cause to turn round like a wheel on its axis. **2.** to cause to go through a round of changes; cause to pass or follow in a fixed routine of succession: *to rotate crops.* —*v.i.* **3.** to turn round as on an axis. **4.** to proceed in a fixed routine of succession. [t. L: m. s. *rotātus*, pp., swung round, revolved] —**rotat′able,** *adj.* —**Syn. 1.** See **turn.**

rotate[2] (rō′tāt), *adj. Bot.* wheel-shaped (applied esp. to a gamopetalous short-tubed corolla with a spreading limb). [f. s. L *rota* wheel + -ATE[1]]

Rotate corolla of potato, *Solanum tuberosum*

rotation (rō tā′shən), *n.* **1.** the act of rotating; a turning round as on an axis. **2. a.** the turning of the earth or other celestial body about its own axis. **b.** one complete revolution of such a body. **3.** regularly recurring succession, as of governments. **4.** *Agric.* the process or method of varying, in a definite order, the crops grown on the same ground. —**rota′tional,** *adj.*

rotative (rō′tə tĭv), *adj.* **1.** rotating; pertaining to rotation. **2.** producing rotation. **3.** happening in regular succession.

rotator (rō tā′tə), *n., pl.* **rotators** *for 1*, **rotatores** (rō′tə tô′rēz) *for 2.* **1.** one who or that which rotates. **2.** *Anat.* a muscle serving to rotate a part of the body. [t. L]

rotatory (rō′tə tə rĭ, -trĭ), *adj.* **1.** pertaining to or of the nature of rotation: *rotatory motion.* **2.** rotating, as an object. **3.** passing or following in rotation or succession. **4.** causing rotation, as a muscle, etc.

rote[1] (rōt), *n.* **1.** *Obs.* routine; fixed or mechanical course of procedure. **2. by rote,** in a mechanical way without thought of the meaning. [ME; orig. uncert.]

rote[2] (rōt), *n. Music.* a kind of medieval stringed instrument. [ME, t. OF; of Celtic orig.]

rotenone (rō′tĭ nōn′), *n. Chem.* a crystalline heterocyclic compound, $C_{23}H_{23}O_6$, possessing ketone; olefine, and ether functional groups; the poisonous principle of certain insecticides, derived from the tropical derris plant.

Rotherham (rŏth′ə rəm), *n.* a town in England, in the West Riding of Yorkshire, near Sheffield. 86,780 (est. 1964).

Rothermere (rŏth′ə mĭə′), *n.* **Harold Sidney Harmsworth, 1st Viscount,** 1868–1940, English newspaper proprietor, brother of Viscount Northcliffe.

Rothesay (rŏth′sĭ), *n.* a burgh in Scotland, the county town of Bute. 7656 (1961).

Rothschild (rŏth′chīld′, rŏths′-; *Ger.* rōt′shĭlt), *n.* **1. Lionel Nathan, Baron de,** 1808–79, English banker and politician. **2. Meyer Amschel** (*Ger.* mī′ər äm′shəl), ?1743–1812, German banker: founder of international banking firm (**House of Rothschild**). **3. Nathan Meyer, Baron de,** 1777–1836, son of Meyer Amschel, banker in London. **4. Nathan Meyer, 1st Baron Rothschild,** 1840–1915, son of Lionel Nathan, English banker.

Rothwell (rŏth′wəl), *n.* a town in England, in the West Riding of Yorkshire. 25,360 (1961).

rotifer (rō′tĭ fə), *n.* any of the animalcules constituting the phylum *Rotifera*, found in fresh and salt water, and characterized by a ciliary apparatus on the anterior end; a wheel animalcule. [NL, f. *roti-* (comb. form repr. L *rota* wheel) + *-fer* bearing] —**rotif′eral, rotif′erous,** *adj.*

A rotifer, *Floscularia ringens* (greatly magnified)

rotisserie (rō tĭs′ə rĭ), *n.* **1.** Also, **roasting spit.** a spit, driven by clockwork mechanism or electricity, on which meat, poultry, and game can be cooked. **2.** a restaurant, cafe, etc., where such a spit is used. [t. F: roasting place]

rotl (rŏt′l), *n., pl.* **artal** (ä′tăl), **1.** a unit of weight used in Near- and Middle-Eastern countries, varying widely in value, but approximating to 1 lb. **2.** a varying unit of dry measure, used in these areas. [t. Ar.: m. *raṭl*, ult. from Gk *litra* or L *lībra* pound]

rotogravure (rō′tō grə vyŏŏə′), *n.* **1.** a photo-mechanical intaglio process in which pictures, letters, etc., are printed from an engraved copper cylinder, the ink-bearing lines, etc., which print being depressed (etched in) instead of raised as in ordinary metal type, etc. **2.** a print made by this process. [f. *roto-* (comb. form of L *rota* wheel) + F *gravure* engraving]

rotor (rō′tə), *n.* **1.** *Elect.* the rotating member of a machine (opposed to *stator*). **2.** *Aeron.* a system of rotating aerofoils, usually horizontal, as those of a helicopter. **3.** *Mach.* the rotating assembly of blades in a turbine. **4.** *Naut.* a high, tower-like, cylindrical structure of metal, rising above the deck and rotated by a small motor, which so operates in connection with the wind that it propels the ship (**rotor ship**). [short for ROTATOR]

Rotorua (rō′tə rŏŏ′ə), *n.* a town in New Zealand, on North Island. 23,400 (est. 1965).

rotten (rŏt′n), *adj.* **1.** in a state of decomposition or decay; putrid; tainted, foul, or ill-smelling. **2.** corrupt or offensive morally, politically, or otherwise. **3.** *Slang.* wretchedly bad, unsatisfactory, or unpleasant: *to feel rotten, rotten work.* **4.** contemptible: *a rotten little snob.* **5.** (of soil, rocks, etc.) soft, yielding, or friable as the result of decomposition. [ME *roten*, t. Scand.; cf. Icel. *rotinn*] —**rot′tenly,** *adv.* —**rot′tenness,** *n.* —**Syn. 1.** decomposed, decayed, putrefied, putrescent.

rotten borough, *Hist.* (before the 1832 Reform Bill) any of certain English boroughs which had only a few voters, but still sent members to Parliament.

Rotten Row, a road in London, in Hyde Park, reserved for horse-riding. [? der. F *route du roi* king's road]

rottenstone (rŏt′n stōn′), *n.* a friable stone resulting from the decomposition of a siliceous limestone, used as a powder for polishing metals.

rotter (rŏt′ə), *n. Slang.* a thoroughly bad, worthless, or objectionable person.

Rotterdam (rŏt′ə dăm′; *Du.* rô tər dŏm′), *n.* a seaport in the SW Netherlands. 731,564 (est. 1965). See map under **Hague, The.**

Rottweiler (rŏt′wī′lə), *n.* one of a breed of large, smooth-coated black dogs, originally bred in Germany. [t. G, named after *Rottweil*, town in S Germany]

rotund (rō tŭnd′), *adj.* **1.** rounded; plump. **2.** fulltoned or sonorous: *rotund speeches.* [t. L: s. *rotundus*] —**rotun′dity, rotund′ness,** *n.* —**rotund′ly,** *adv.*

rotunda (rō tŭn′də), *n.* **1.** a round building, esp. one with a dome. **2.** a large and high circular hall or room in a building, esp. one surmounted by a dome. [t. L, fem. of *rotundus* rotund]

roturier (*Fr.* rŏ tʏ ryė′), *n., pl.* **-riers** (*Fr.* -ryė′). *French.* a person of low rank; a plebeian. [F, der. *roture* plebeian tenure, g. L *ruptūra* a breaking]

Rouault (rŏŏ ō′; *Fr.* rwȯ), *n.* **Georges** (*Fr.* zhŏrzh), 1871–1958, French expressionist painter.

Roubaix (*Fr.* rŏŏ bĕ′), *n.* a town in N France, in Nord department. 112,856 (1962).

rouble (rŏŏ′bl), *n.* **1.** the monetary unit of the Soviet Union, equal to 100 kopecks, and equivalent to about £0·463 sterling. **2.** a banknote or coin of this value. Also, **ruble.** [t. Russ.; orig. uncert.]

roué (rŏŏ′ā; *Fr.* rwė), *n.* a debauchee or rake. [t. F, pp. of *rouer* break on the wheel; first applied to the rofligate companions of the Duc d'Orléans (*c.* 1720)]

Rouen (rŏŏ′ŏn; *Fr.* rwäɴ), *n.* a city in N France, capital of Seine-Maritime department, on the Seine: cathedral; execution of Joan of Arc, 1431. 120,851 (1962). See map under **Normandy.**

rouge (rŏŏzh), *n., v.,* **rouged, rouging.** —*n.* **1.** any of various red cosmetics for colouring the cheeks or lips. **2.** a reddish powder, chiefly ferric oxide, used for polishing metal, etc. —*v.t.* **3.** to colour with rouge. —*v.i.* **4.** to use rouge. [t. F: prop. adj., red, g. L *rubeus*]

rouge et noir (*Fr.* rŏŏzh ė nwär′), *French.* a gambling game at cards, played on a table marked with two red and two black diamond-shaped spots on which the players place their stakes; trente et quarante. [F: red and black]

Rouget de Lisle (*Fr.* rŏŏ zhĕ də lēl′), **Claude Joseph** (*Fr.* klōd zhō zĕf′), 1766–1836, French soldier who wrote the *Marseillaise.* Also, **Rouget de l'Isle.**

rough (rŭf), *adj.* **1.** uneven from projections, irregularities, or breaks of surface; not smooth: *rough boards, a rough road.* **2.** (of ground) wild; broken; covered with scrub, boulders, etc. **3.** shaggy: *a dog with a rough coat.* **4.** acting with or characterized by violence. **5.** violently disturbed or agitated, as the sea, water, etc. **6.** violently irregular, as motion. **7.** stormy or tempestuous, as wind, weather, etc. **8.** sharp or harsh: *a rough temper.* **9.** unmannerly or rude. **10.** disorderly or riotous. **11.** *Colloq.* severe, hard, or unpleasant: *to have a rough time of it.* **12.** harsh to the ear, grating, or jarring, as sounds. **13.** harsh to the taste, sharp, or astringent, as wines: *rough cider.* **14.** coarse, as food, cloth, materials, etc. **15.** (of people or their behaviour) lacking culture or refinement. **16.** without refinements, luxuries, or ordinary comforts or conveniences. **17.** requiring exertion or strength rather than intelligence or skill, as work. **18.** unpolished, as language, verse, style, etc.; not elaborated, perfected, or corrected: *a rough draft.* **19.** made or done without any attempt at exactness, completeness, or thoroughness: *a rough guess.* **20.** crude, unwrought, undressed, or unprepared: *a rough diamond, rough rice.* **21.** *Phonet.* with aspiration; having the sound of *h.* **22.** of or pertaining to the back of a racket (from the texture of the strings on that side). **23. cut up rough,** to behave angrily or violently; be upset. **24. rough on, a.** severe towards. **b.** unfortunate for (someone). —*n.* **25.** that which is rough; rough ground. **26.** any piece of work, esp. a work of art, in an unfinished or preliminary condition. **27.** *Golf.* any part of the course bordering the fairway on which the grass, weeds, etc., are not trimmed. **28.** the rough, hard, or unpleasant side or part of anything. **29.** the rough side of a racket. **30.** *Colloq.* a rough person; rowdy. **31. in the rough,** in a rough, crude, unwrought, or unfinished state.
—*adv.* **32.** in a rough manner; roughly.
—*v.t.* **33.** to make rough; roughen. **34.** to treat roughly or harshly. **35.** to subject to some rough preliminary process of working or preparation. (often fol. by *up*). **36.** to cut, shape, or sketch roughly (fol. by *in* or *out*): *to rough out a plan, to rough in the outlines of a face.*
—*v.i.* **37. rough it,** to live without even the ordinary comforts or conveniences: *we roughed it all month long.* [ME; OE *rūh*, c. D *ruig*, G *rauh*] —**rough′ly,** *adv.* —**rough′ness,** *n.* —**Syn. 1.** irregular, rugged, jagged. **4.** disorderly, turbulent, boisterous. —**Ant. 1.** smooth. **4.** gentle.

roughage (rŭf′ĭj), *n.* **1.** rough or coarse material. **2.** the coarser kinds or parts of fodder or food, of less nutritive value, esp. those which assist digestion, as distinguished from those affording more concentrated nutriment.

rough-and-ready (rŭf′ ən rĕd′ĭ), *adj.* **1.** rough, rude, or crude, but good enough for the purpose: *in a rough-and-ready fashion.* **2.** exhibiting or showing rough vigour rather than refinement or delicacy: *a rough-and-ready person.*

rough-and-tumble (rŭf′ən tŭm′bl), *adj.* **1.** characterized by violent, disorganized, unconstrained behaviour: *a rough-and-tumble fight.* **2.** given to such action.

rough book, a book for the preparatory drafts of written compositions, etc.

rough breathing, *Gk Gram.* an aspirate mark (ʽ) placed over initial vowels to indicate a preceding *h* sound. Cf. **smooth breathing.** [trans. of L *spiritus asper*]

roughcast (rŭf′käst′), *n., adj., v.,* **-cast, -casting.** —*n.* **1.** a coarse plaster mixed with gravel, shells, or the like, for outside surfaces, usually thrown against the wall. **2.** a crudely formed pattern or model; a rough. —*adj.* **3.** made of or covered with roughcast; crudely formed. —*v.t.* **4.** to cover or coat with roughcast. **5.** to make, shape, or prepare in a rough form: *to roughcast a story.* —**rough′cast′er,** *n.*

rough diamond, 1. an uncut diamond. **2.** a person without refinement of manner but having an essentially good or likeable personality.

rough-dry (rŭf′drī′), *v.*, **-dried, -drying,** *adj.* —*v.t.* **1.** to dry (clothes, etc.) after washing, without smoothing, ironing, etc. —*adj.* **2.** dry but unironed.

roughen (rŭf′ən), *v.t.*, *v.i.* to make or become rough.

rougher (rŭf′ə), *n.* one who roughs or roughs out.

rough-hew (rŭf′hyōō′), *v.t.*, **-hewed, -hewed** or **-hewn, -hewing. 1.** to hew (timber, stone, etc.) roughly or without smoothing or finishing. **2.** to shape roughly; give crude form to.

rough-house (rŭf′hous′), *n.*, *v.*, **-housed, -housing.** *Slang.* —*n.* **1.** noisy, disorderly behaviour or play; rowdy conduct; a brawl. —*v.i.* **2.** to engage or take part in a rough-house. —*v.t.* **3.** to disturb or harass by a rough-house.

roughish (rŭf′ĭsh), *adj.* rather rough: *a roughish sea.*

roughly (rŭf′lĭ), *adv.* **1.** in a crude, harsh or violent manner. **2.** inexactly; without precision. **3.** approximately; about.

roughneck (rŭf′nĕk′), *n.* *Slang.* **1.** a rough, coarse person. **2.** *Chiefly U.S.* a member of an oil-drilling crew.

rough puff pastry, a rich, flaky pastry used for pies, tarts, etc.; puff pastry; flaky pastry.

roughrider (rŭf′rī′də), *n.* **1.** one who breaks horses to the saddle. **2.** one accustomed to rough or hard riding. **3.** (*also caps.*) *U.S.* an irregular cavalryman.

roughshod (rŭf′shŏd′), *adj.* **1.** shod with horseshoes having projecting nails or points. **2. ride roughshod over,** to override harshly or domineeringly; treat without consideration.

rough-spoken (rŭf′spō′kən), *adj.* having an uncouth or rude manner of speech.

rough stuff, violence, esp. more than the situation seems to require.

roulade (rōō läd′), *n.* a meat roll or galantine. [t. F, der. *rouler* ROLL]

rouleau (rōō′lō), *n.*, *pl.* **-leaux, -leaus** (-lōz). **1.** a cylindrical pile or roll of something. **2.** a number of coins put up in cylindrical form in a paper wrapping. **3.** *Med.* a number of red cells in a cylindrical configuration. [t. F, der. *rôle* roll]

Roulers (rōō lēəz′; *Fr.* rōō lĕrs′), *n.* a town in NW Belgium: battles, 1914, 1918. 35,622 (1962).

roulette (rōō lĕt′), *n.*, *v.*, **-letted, -letting.** —*n.* **1.** a game of chance played at a table, in which an unlimited number of players bet on which of the compartments of a revolving disc or wheel will be the resting-place of a ball circling it in the opposite direction. **2.** the wheel or disc used in this game. **3.** a small wheel, esp. one with sharp teeth, mounted in a handle, for making lines of marks, dots, or perforations: *engravers' roulettes, a roulette for perforating sheets of postage stamps.* **4.** *Philately.* short consecutive cuts in the paper between the individual stamps of the sheet so that they may be readily separated from each other. It differs from perforation in that no paper is removed. —*v.t.* **5.** to mark, impress, or perforate with a roulette. [t. F, dim. of *rouelle* round slice. See ROWEL]

Roulettes (def. 3)

Roumania (rōō mā′nyə), *n.* Rumania. —**Rouma′nian,** *adj.*, *n.*

Roumelia (rōō mē′lyə), *n.* Rumelia.

round (round), *adj.* **1.** circular, as a disc. **2.** ring-shaped, as a hoop. **3.** curved like part of a circle, as an outline. **4.** having a circular cross-section, as a cylinder. **5.** spherical or globular, as a ball. **6.** rounded more or less like a part of a sphere. **7.** free from angularity; curved, as parts of the body. **8.** executed with or involving circular motion: *a round dance.* **9.** completed by passing through a course which finally returns to the place of starting: *a round trip.* **10.** full, complete, or entire: *a round dozen.* **11.** forming, or expressed by, an integer or whole number (with no fraction). **12.** expressed in tens, hundreds, thousands, or the like: *in round numbers.* **13.** roughly correct: *a round guess.* **14.** considerable in amount: *a good round sum of money.* **15.** naturalistically portrayed, as a literary character. **16.** full and sonorous, as sound. **17.** vigorous, brisk, or smart: *a round trot.* **18.** plain, honest, or straightforward. **19.** candid or outspoken. **20.** unmodified, as an oath; positive or unqualified, as an assertion.
—*n.* **21.** something round; a circle, ring, curve, etc.; a circular, ring-shaped, or curved object; a rounded form. **22.** something circular in cross-section, as a rung of a ladder. **23.** a completed course of time, a series of events, operations, etc. **24.** any complete course, series, or succession. **25.** (*sometimes pl.*) a circuit of any place, series of places, etc., covered in a customary or predetermined way: *the postman on his rounds.* **26.** a series (of visits, etc.) **27.** a completed course or spell of activity, commonly one of a series, in some game, sport, competition, or the like. **28.** a recurring period or time, succession of events, duties, etc.: *the daily round.* **29.** a single outburst, as of applause, cheers, etc. **30.** a single discharge of shot by each of a number of guns, rifles, etc., or by a single piece. **31.** a charge of ammunition for a single shot. **32.** a distribution of drink, etc., to all the members of a company. **33.** *Obs.* a dance with the dancers arranged or moving in a circle or ring. **34.** movement in a circle or about an axis. **35.** a form of sculpture in which figures are executed apart from any background (contrasted with *relief*). **36.** the cut of beef below the aitchbone and above the leg. **37. a.** (of bread) a slice. **b.** a sandwich. **38.** *Archery.* a specified number of arrows shot from a specified distance from the target in accordance with the rules. **39.** one of a series of periods (separated by rests) making up a boxing or wrestling match, etc. **40.** *Music.* **a.** a partsong in which the several voices follow one another at equal intervals of time, and at the same pitch as the octave. **b.** (*pl.*) the order followed in ringing a peal of bells in diatonic sequence from the highest to the lowest. **41.** *Golf.* a complete circuit of a prearranged series of holes, usually the whole course of eighteen holes. **42.** *Cards.* a single turn of play by each player. **43. go the rounds, a.** (of people) to make a series of visits. **b.** (of gossip, information, etc.) to become generally known.
—*adv.* **44.** in a circle, ring, or the like, or so as to surround something. **45.** on all sides, or about, whether circularly or otherwise. **46.** in all directions from a centre. **47.** *Chiefly U.S.* in the region about a place: *the country round.* **48.** in circumference: *a tree 40 inches round.* **49.** in a circular or rounded course: *to fly round and round.* **50.** through a round, circuit, or series, as of places or persons: *to show a person round.* **51.** through a round, or recurring period, of time, esp. to the present or a particular time: *when the time rolls round.* **52.** throughout, or from beginning to end of, a recurring period of time: *all the year round.* **53.** by a circuitous or roundabout course. **54.** to a place or point as by a circuit or circuitous course: *to get round into the navigable channel.* **55.** *Chiefly U.S.* in circulation, action, etc.; about. **56.** with a rotating course or movement: *the wheels went round.* **57.** with change to another or opposite direction, course, opinion, etc.: *to sit still without looking round.*
—*prep.* **58.** so as to encircle, surround, or envelop: *to tie paper round a parcel.* **59.** on the circuit, border, or outer part of it. **60.** around; about. **61.** in or from all or various directions from: *to look round one.* **62.** in the vicinity of: *the country round Lincoln.* **63.** in a round, circuit, or course through. **64.** to all or various parts of: *to wander round the country.* **65.** throughout (a period of time): *a resort visited all round the year.* **66.** here and there in: *people standing round a room.* **67.** so as to make a turn or partial circuit about or to the other side of: *to sail round a cape.* **68.** reached by making a turn or partial circuit about (something): *the church round the corner.* **69.** so as to revolve or rotate about (a centre or axis): *the earth's motion round its axis.*
—*v.t.* **70.** to make round. **71.** to free from angularity or flatness; fill out symmetrically; make plump. **72.** to bring to completeness or perfection; finish (often fol. by *off*). **73.** to frame or form neatly, as a sentence, etc. **74.** to end (a sentence, etc.) with something specified. **75.** to encircle or surround. **76.** to make the complete circuit of; pass completely round. **77.** to make a turn or partial circuit about, as to get to the other side of: *to round a cape.* **78.** to cause to move in a circle or turn round. **79.** *Phonet.* to pronounce with the lips forming an approximately oval opening: *'boot' has a rounded vowel.* **80. round on** or **upon,** to attack, usually verbally, with sudden and often unexpected vigour. **81. round up,** to collect (cattle, people, etc.) in a particular place or for a particular purpose.
—*v.i.* **82.** to become round. **83.** to become free from angularity; become plump. **84.** to develop to completeness or perfection. **85.** to take a circular course; make a circuit; go the round, as a guard. **86.** to make a turn or partial circuit about something. **87.** to turn round as on an axis: *to round on one's heels.*
[ME, t. OF: m. *rond*, g. L *rotundus* wheel-shaped] —**round′ish,** *adj.* —**round′ness,** *n.*

roundabout (round′ə bout′), *n.* **1.** a merry-go-round. **2.** a road junction at which the flow of traffic is facilitated by moving in one direction only round a circular arrangement. —*adj.* **3.** circuitous or indirect, as a road, journey, method, statement, person, etc. **4.** *U.S.* cut circularly at the bottom, without tails, as a coat.

round-arm (round′äm′), *adj.*, *adv.* *Cricket.* denoting or employing a manner of bowling in which the arm was held more or less horizontal, now no longer allowed.

round dance, 1. a dance performed by couples and characterized by circular or revolving movement, as the waltz. **2.** (orig.) a dance with the dancers arranged in or moving about in a circle or ring.

rounded (roun′dĭd), *adj.* **1.** curved or convex; reduced to simple curves; made round. **2.** *Phonet.* labialized.

3. Also, **well-rounded.** complete; mature; brought to perfection, as a character in a play, etc.

roundel (roun′dl), *n.* **1.** something round or circular. **2.** a small round pane or window. **3.** a decorative plate, panel, tablet, or the like, round in form. **4.** *Armour.* **a.** a disc of metal which protects the armpit. **b.** a disc of metal on a hafted weapon or a dagger to protect the hand. **5.** *Pros.* **a.** a rondel or rondeau. **b.** a modification of the rondeau consisting of nine lines with two refrains. **6.** a dance in a circle or ring. [ME *roundele,* t. OF: m. *rondel,* der. *rond* ROUND, adj.]

roundelay (roun′dĭ lā′), *n.* **1.** a song in which a phrase, line, or the like is continually repeated. **2.** the music for such a song. **3.** a dance in a circle. [f. ROUNDEL (def. 5) + LAY[4]]

rounder (roun′də), *n.* **1.** one who or that which rounds something. **2.** one who makes a round. **3.** *U.S. Slang.* a habitual drunkard or criminal; an idle frequenter of public resorts. **4.** (*cap.*) a Methodist minister who travels a circuit among his congregations. **5.** (*pl. construed as sing.*) a game played with bat and ball, in which points are scored by running between bases, as in baseball. **6.** a complete run round all the bases in this game.

round game, any game in which each participant plays on his own account.

roundhand (round′hănd′), *n.* **1.** a style of handwriting in which the letters are round, full, and distinct. *—adj.* **2.** denoting or written in this style of handwriting.

Roundhead (round′hĕd′), *n.* a member or adherent of the Parliamentarian or Puritan party during the civil wars of the 17th century (so called in derision by the Cavaliers because they wore their hair cut short).

roundhouse (round′hous′), *n.* **1.** *Naut.* **a.** the captain's accommodation on the quarterdeck in the earlier ships of the East India Company. **b.** the house on the afterdecks of later sailing ships, occupied by apprentices. **c.** the lavatories on the forward top deck in the old ships of the Royal Navy. **2.** a running shed. **3.** *Obs.* a jail.

roundlet (round′lĭt), *n.* a small circle or circular object. [ME *rondlet,* t. OF: m. *rondelet,* dim. of *rondel.* See ROUNDEL]

roundly (round′lĭ), *adv.* in a round manner; vigorously or briskly; outspokenly, severely, or unsparingly.

round robin, **1.** a petition, remonstrance, or other letter or paper, having the signatures arranged in circular form, so as to conceal the order of signing. **2.** any petition, etc., signed by a number of people.

round-shot (round′shŏt′), *n.* a cannonball.

round-shouldered (round′shōl′dəd), *adj.* having the shoulders bent forwards, giving a rounded form to the upper part of the back.

roundsman (roundz′mən), *n., pl.* **-men.** **1.** one who makes rounds, calling on customers to make deliveries, as of milk, bread, etc., or to take orders; a deliveryman. **2.** *U.S.* one who makes rounds of inspection, as, formerly, a police officer who inspects policemen on duty.

round steak, the beef cut directly above the hind leg.

round table, **1.** a number of persons assembled for conference or discussion of some subject, and considered as meeting on equal terms. **2.** (*cap.*) *Arthurian Legend.* **a.** the celebrated table, made round to avoid quarrels as to precedence, about which King Arthur and his knights sat. **b.** King Arthur and his knights as a body.

round-the-clock (round′thə klŏk′), *adj.* (not hyphenated when used predicatively) continuous throughout the day and night: *the police kept up a round-the-clock watch for the suspect.*

round trip, **1.** a circular tour. **2.** *U.S.* a return trip.

round-trip ticket (round′trĭp′), *U.S.* a return ticket.

round-up (round′ŭp′), *n.* **1.** the driving together of cattle, etc., for inspection, branding, or the like, as in the Western U.S. **2.** the men and horses who do this. **3.** the herd so collected. **4.** any similar driving or bringing together, as of people, facts, etc.

roundworm (round′wûm′), *n.* any nematode, esp. *Ascaris lumbricoides,* infesting the human intestine, or other ascarids in other animals.

roup (rōōp), *n.* **1.** *Vet. Sci.* any kind of catarrhal inflammation of the eyes and nasal passages of poultry. **2.** hoarseness or huskiness. Also, **roop.** [orig. uncert.]

roupy (rōō′pĭ), *adj.* **1.** affected with the disease roup. **2.** hoarse or husky.

rouse[1] (rouz), *v.,* **roused, rousing,** *n.* *—v.t.* **1.** to bring out of a state of sleep, unconsciousness, inactivity, fancied security, apathy, depression, etc. **2.** to stir to strong indignation or anger. **3.** to cause (game) to start from a covert or lair. *—v.i.* **4.** to come out of a state of sleep, unconsciousness, inaction, apathy, depression, etc. **5. rouse away,** *Naut.* pull heavily on a rope. *—n.* **6.** a rousing. **7.** *Obs.* a signal for rousing; the reveille. [orig. uncert.] **—rous′er,** *n.* **—Syn. 1.** stir, excite, animate, kindle, stimulate, awaken.

rouse[2] (rouz), *n. Archaic.* a carousal. [? var. of CAROUSE (*drink carouse* being wrongly analysed as *drink a rouse*)]

rouse-about (rous′ə bout′), *n. Austral.* a handyman on a station.

rousing (rou′zĭng), *adj.* **1.** that rouses; stirring: *a rousing song.* **2.** vigorous: *a rousing fire.* **3.** brisk; lively: *a rousing trade.* **4.** *Colloq.* great, extraordinary, or outrageous: *a rousing lie.*

Rousseau (*Fr.* rōō sō′), *n.* **1. Henri** (*Fr.* äN rē′), (*'Le Douanier'*), 1844–1910, French painter. **2. Jean Jacques** (*Fr.* zhäN zhäk′), 1712–78, French philosopher and writer, born in Switzerland. **3. (Pierre Etienne) Théodore** (*Fr.* pyĕr ė tyĕn tĕ ō dŏr′), 1812–1867, French landscape painter.

roustabout (rous′tə bout′), *n. U.S.* **1.** a wharf labourer or deckhand, as on the Mississippi river. **2.** an unskilled labourer who lives by odd jobs. **3.** a rouse-about.

rout[1] (rout), *n.* **1.** a defeat attended with disorderly flight; dispersal of a defeated force in complete disorder: *to put an army to rout.* **2.** a defeated and dispersing army. **3.** a tumultuous or disorderly crowd of persons. **4.** a clamour or fuss. **5.** *Law.* an assembly of three or more persons doing some act towards a violent and unlawful purpose, to the terror of the people. **6.** *Archaic.* a troop, company, or band. **7.** (formerly) a large evening party or social gathering. *—v.t.* **8.** to disperse in defeat and disorderly flight: *to rout an army.* **9.** to defeat utterly. [ME, t. AF: m. *rute,* g. L *rupta,* pp. (fem.), broken]

rout[2] (rout), *v.i.* **1.** to poke, search or rummage. **2.** to root, as swine. *—v.t.* **3.** to turn over or dig up with the snout, as swine. **4.** to bring or get in poking about, searching, etc. (fol. by *out*). **5.** to cause to get from bed (fol. by *up* or *out*). **6.** to force or drive out. **7.** to hollow out or furrow, as with a scoop, gouge, or machine. [see ROOT[2], and cf. MD *ruten* root out]

route (rōōt), *n., v.,* **routed, routeing** or **routing.** *—n.* **1.** a way or road taken or planned for passage or travel. **2.** a customary or regular line of passage or travel. **3.** *Med.* the area of the body through which a curative is introduced: *the digestive route.* *—v.t.* **4.** to fix the route of. **5.** to send or forward by a particular route. [ME, t. F, ult. g. L *rupta* (*via*) broken (road)]

route-march (rōōt′māch′), *n.* a march, often long or arduous, as taken by soldiers in the course of training.

router (rou′tə), *n.* **1.** any of various tools or machines for routing, hollowing out, or furrowing. **2.** a carpentry plane designed for working out the bottom of a rectangular cavity. **3.** a tool or machine for routing out parts of an etched plate, electrotype, etc.

routine (rōō tēn′), *n.* **1.** a customary or regular course of procedure: *the routine of an office.* **2.** regular, unvarying, or mechanical procedure. **3.** *Computers.* a set of orders which cause a digital computer to perform some simple function. **4.** in modern dancing, ballet, etc., a piece of choreography. **5.** a rehearsed or habitual persuasive patter: *a salesman's routine.* *—adj.* **6.** of the nature of, proceeding by, or adhering to routine: *routine duties.* [t. F, der. *route* ROUTE]

routinism (rōō tē′nĭz′əm), *n.* adherence to routine. **—routinist** (rōō tē′nĭst), *n.*

roux (rōō), *n.* a mixture of fat and flour which forms the foundation of most sauces. [t. F: browned, reddish, g. L *russus*]

rove[1] (rōv), *v.,* **roved, roving.** *—v.i.* **1.** to wander about without definite destination; move hither and thither at random, esp. over a wide area. **2.** to wander, as the eyes, mind, etc. *—v.t.* **3.** to wander over or through; traverse: *to rove the woods.* [ME, t. Scand.; cf. Icel. *rāfa*] **—Syn. 1.** See **roam.**

rove[2] (rōv), *v.* a pt. and pp. of **reeve**[2].

rove[3] (rōv), *n., v.,* **roved, roving.** *—n.* **1.** slivers of wool, cotton, etc., formed into slightly twisted strands in a preparatory process of spinning. *—v.t.* **2.** to form (slivers of wool, cotton, etc.) into such roves. [orig. obscure]

rove-beetle (rōv′bē′tl), *n.* any beetle of the family *Staphylinidae,* which comprises numerous insects having long, slender bodies and very short elytra, and which run swiftly.

rove-over (rōv′ō′və), *adj. Pros.* (in sprung rhythm) of or pertaining to the completion of a metrical foot, incomplete at the end of one line, completed with a syllable or syllables from the beginning of the next line.

rover[1] (rō′və), *n.* **1.** one who roves; a wanderer. **2.** *Archery.* **a.** a mark selected at random. **b.** any of a group of set marks at a long distance. **c.** one who starts from a distance. **3.** *Croquet.* a ball that has gone through all the arches and needs only to strike the winning peg to be out of the game. **4.** a senior boy scout, of eighteen years or above. [f. ROVE[1] + -ER[1]]

rover[2] (rō′və), *n. Archaic.* **1.** a sea-robber or pirate. **2.** a pirate ship. [t. MD or MLG, der. *roven* rob]

roving (rō′vĭng), *n.* a strand of loosely assembled fibres, wool, cotton, etc., preparatory to spinning.

row[1] (rō), *n.* **1.** a number of persons or things arranged in a line, esp. a straight line. **2.** a line of adjacent seats facing the same way, as in a theatre. **3.** a street, esp. a narrow one, formed by two continuous lines of buildings. *—v.t.* **4.** *Dial.* to put in a row (often fol. by *up*). [ME *row(e)*, OE *rāw*, akin to Lithuanian *raiwe* stripe]

row[2] (rō), *v.i.* **1.** to use oars or the like for propelling a boat. **2.** to be moved by oars, as a boat. *—v.t.* **3.** to propel (a boat, etc.) by or as by the use of oars. **4.** to convey in a boat, etc., so propelled. **5.** to employ (a number of oars): *the captain's barge rowed twenty oars.* **6.** to use (oars or oarsmen) for rowing. **7.** to perform (a race, etc.) by rowing. **8.** to row against in a race. **9.** to convey or propel (something) in a manner suggestive of rowing. *—n.* **10.** an act of rowing; a turn at the oars. **11.** an excursion in a rowing boat: *to go for a row.* [ME; OE *rōwan*, c. Icel. *rōa*; akin to L *rēmus*, Gk *eretmón*. Cf. RUDDER] **—row′er,** *n.*

row[3] (rou), *n.* **1.** a noisy dispute or quarrel; commotion. **2.** *Colloq.* noise or clamour. *—v.i.* **3.** *Colloq.* to make or engage in a noisy quarrel. *—v.t.* **4.** *Obs. Colloq.* to assail roughly; upbraid severely. [orig. uncert.]

rowan (rō′ən, rou′-), *n.* **1.** the European mountain ash, *Sorbus aucuparia*, a tree with red berries. **2.** either of two American mountain ashes, *S. americana* and *S. sambucifolia.* **3.** the berry of any of these trees. [t. Scand.; cf. Norw. *raun*]

rowboat (rō′bōt′), *n. Chiefly U.S.* a rowing boat.

rowdy (rou′dĭ), *adj.*, **-dier, -diest,** *n.*, *pl.* **-dies.** *—adj.* **1.** of the nature of or characteristic of a rowdy; rough and disorderly. *—n.* **2.** a rough, disorderly person. [orig. obscure] **—row′dily,** *adv.* **—row′diness,** *n.* **—row′dyish,** *adj.*

rowdyism (rou′dĭ ĭz′əm), *n.* rowdy conduct.

rowel (rou′əl), *n.*, *v.*, **-elled, -elling** or (*U.S.*) **-eled, -eling.** **1.** a small wheel with radiating points, forming the extremity of a horseman's spur. **2.** *Vet. Sci.* a piece of leather or the like inserted beneath the skin of a horse or other animal, to cause a discharge. *—v.t.* **3.** to prick, or urge, with a rowel. **4.** *Vet. Sci.* to insert a rowel in. [ME, t. OF: m. *roel*, dim. of *roe, roue*, g. L *rota* wheel]

Spur with rowel

rowen (rou′ən), *n. Dial and U.S.* the second crop of grass or hay in a season; the aftermath. [ME *rewayn*, t. ONF, c. F *regain*]

rowing boat (rō′ĭng), a boat propelled by oars.

Rowlandson (rō′lənd sən), *n.* **Thomas,** 1756–1827, English draughtsman and caricaturist.

Rowley Regis (rō′lĭ rē′jĭs), a town in England, in Staffordshire. 48,146 (1961).

rowlock (rŏl′ək), *n.* a device on or attached by a rigger to a boat's gunwale in or on which the oar rests and swings. Also, *Now Chiefly U.S.*, **oarlock.** [var. of OARLOCK, by assoc. with ROW[2]]

Rowlock

Rox., Roxburgh.

Roxburgh (rŏks′bə rə, -brə), *n.* a county in SE Scotland. 43,171 (1961); 668 sq. mi. *Co. town:* Jedburgh. Also, **Roxburghshire** (rŏks′brə shĭə′, -shə).

royal (roi′əl), *adj.* **1.** of or pertaining to a sovereign, king, queen, or the like, or sovereignty: *royal power, a royal palace, the royal family.* **2.** belonging to the royal family: *a royal prince.* **3.** having the rank of a king or queen. **4.** established or chartered by, or existing under the patronage of, a sovereign: *a royal society.* **5.** proceeding from or performed by a sovereign: *a royal warrant.* **6.** befitting, or appropriate to, a sovereign; kinglike or princely; magnificent; splendid: *royal splendour.* **7.** *Obs. Colloq.* fine, first-rate, or excellent: *in royal spirits.* **8.** having a character befitting a sovereign, as noble, generous, brave, etc. **9.** beyond the common or ordinary in size, quality, etc. **10.** (*usually cap.*) pertaining to the sovereign as civil or military head of state. *—n.* **11.** *Naut.* a sail set on the royal mast, the highest except for the skysail. See illus. under **sail. 12.** a stag having twelve or more points to his antlers. **13.** a size of printing paper, 20 × 25 in., or of writing paper, 19 × 24 in. See **super-royal. 14.** any of various former coins. **15.** *Colloq.* a member of the royal family. [ME, t. OF: m. *roial*, g. L *rēgālis*] **—roy′ally,** *adv.* **—Syn. 1.** regal, majestic. See **kingly.**

Royal Academy, a society founded in 1768 by George III of England to encourage the visual arts by the establishment of a school of design and the holding of an annual exhibition of the works of living artists.

Royal Air Force, the airforce of Great Britain formed in 1918 from the Royal Flying Corps and the Royal Naval Air Service. *Abbrev.:* R.A.F.

Royal assent. See **assent** (def. 3).

Royal Ballet, The, the national ballet company of the United Kingdom.

royal blue, a rich deep blue, often with a faint reddish tinge.

royal fern, a fern, *Osmunda regalis*, with tall fronds.

royal flush, *Poker.* the five highest cards of a suit.

Royal Flying Corps, the precursor (1912–18) of the Royal Air Force. *Abbrev.:* R.F.C.

Royal Horse Guards (*'The Blues'*), a cavalry regiment of the Household Brigade, distinguished by their blue uniform jackets and red plumes on their helmets.

Royal Hospital, a home in Chelsea, London, for deserving retired and invalid soldiers, founded by William III in 1694. See **Chelsea pensioner.**

royal icing, cake icing made from icing sugar and egg-whites, chiefly used for wedding and Christmas cakes, as it hardens and keeps well.

royalist (roi′ə lĭst), *n.* **1.** a supporter or adherent of a king or a royal government, esp. in times of rebellion or civil war. **2.** (*cap.*) an adherent of Charles I during the Civil War. **3.** (*cap.*) *Amer. Hist.* Tory (def. 4). **4.** (*cap.*) an adherent of the house of Bourbon in France. *—adj.* **5.** of or pertaining to royalists. **—roy′alism,** *n.* **—roy′alis′tic,** *adj.*

royal jelly, a substance, secreted from the pharyngeal glands of worker honeybees, and fed to very young larvae and to those selected as queens.

royal mast, *Naut.* the mast next above the topgallant mast.

royal palm, any of various tall decorative feather palms of the genus *Roystones*, including *R. regia* and others.

royal prerogative, the rights of a sovereign, which in theory are unrestricted.

royal purple, a deep bluish purple.

Royal Society, a society founded under the auspices of Charles II in 1662 for the advancement of science; membership is by election.

royal tennis, real tennis.

royalty (roi′əl tĭ), *n.*, *pl.* **-ties. 1.** royal persons collectively. **2.** royal status, dignity, or power; sovereignty. **3.** a prerogative or right belonging to a king or sovereign. **4.** a royal domain; a kingdom; a realm. **5.** character or quality proper to or befitting a sovereign; kingliness; nobility; generosity. **6.** a compensation or portion of proceeds paid to the owner of a right, as a patent, for the use of it. **7.** an agreed portion of the proceeds from his work, paid to an author, composer, etc. **8.** a royal right, as over minerals, granted by a sovereign to a person or company. **9.** any such rights granted by their owner to another. **10.** the payment made for such a right. [ME *roialte*, t. OF. See ROYAL]

Royal Worcester. See **Worcester** (def. 4).

Royce (rois), *n.* **Sir Frederic Henry,** 1863–1933, English motor-car manufacturer (with C. S. Rolls).

Rp., rupiah(s).

R.P., 1. Reformed Presbyterian. **2.** Regimental Police. **3.** Regius Professor.

r.p.m., revolutions per minute.

R.P.S., Royal Photographic Society.

r.p.s., revolutions per second.

rpt, report.

R.Q., respiratory quotient.

R.R., Right Reverend.

-rrhagia, var. of **-rhagia.** Also, **-rrhage, -rrhagy.**

-rrhoea, var. of **-rhoea.** Also, *Chiefly U.S.*, **-rrhea.**

R.S., Royal Society.

RSFSR, Russian Soviet Federated Socialist Republic. Also, **R.S.F.S.R.**

R.S.J., rolled steel joist.

R.S.M., 1. Regimental Sergeant-Major. **2.** Royal Society of Medicine.

R.S.P.C.A., Royal Society for the Prevention of Cruelty to Animals.

R.S.V.P., (French, *répondez s'il vous plaît*) please reply.

rt, right.

R.T., 1. radio-telegraphy or radio-telephony. **2.** radio-transmitter.

Rt Hon., Right Honourable.

Rt Rev., Right Reverend.

Ru, *Chem.* ruthenium.

R.U., Rugby Union.

Ruanda-Urundi (ro͞o ăn′də o͞o ro͞on′dĭ), *n.* a former territory in central Africa, E of the Republic of Congo: formerly part of German East Africa; administered by Belgium as a League of Nations mandate (1918–46) and as a U.N. trust territory (1946–62). Now divided into the independent states of Rwanda and Burundi.

Ruapehu (ro͞o′ə pē′ho͞o), *n.* **Mount,** a volcanic peak in

New Zealand, in North Island; the highest point of North Island. 9175 ft.

rub (rŭb), *v.*, **rubbed, rubbing,** *n.* —*v.t.* **1.** to subject (an object) to pressure and friction, esp. in order to clean, smooth, polish, etc. **2.** to move, spread, or apply (something) with pressure and friction over something else. **3.** to move (things) with pressure and friction over each other (fol. by *together*, etc.). **4.** to force, etc., by rubbing (fol. by *over*, *in*, *into*, etc.). **5.** to remove or erase by rubbing (fol. by *off*, *out*, etc.): *to rub off rust.* **6.** to chafe or abrade. **7. rub down, a.** to rub (the surface of something) as to smooth, reduce, clean, etc. **b.** to massage, dry or clean (an animal, athlete, etc.) by rubbing, as with a towel after exercise, etc. **8. rub out, a.** to erase. **b.** *Slang, Orig. U.S.* to kill. **9. rub shoulders** or **elbows,** to come into social contact. **10. rub (up) the right way,** to please. **11. rub (up) the wrong way,** to annoy. **12. rub up, a.** to polish or smooth. **b.** to refresh or revive one's memory (fol. by *on*). —*v.i.* **13.** to exert pressure and friction on something. **14.** to move with pressure along the surface of something. **15.** to proceed, continue in a course, or keep going, with a little effort or difficulty (fol. by *on*, *along*, *through*, etc.). **16.** to admit of being rubbed (*off*, etc.). —*n.* **17.** the act of rubbing. **18.** something irritating to the feelings; a reproof, gibe, sarcasm, or the like. **19.** an annoying experience or circumstance. **20.** *Bowls.* an obstacle or impediment, as an unevenness of the ground. **21.** a difficulty; source of doubt or difficulty: *there's the rub.* **22.** *Archaic.* any difficulty or obstacle. [ME *rubbe*, c. LG *rubben*, of uncert. orig.]

rub-a-dub (rŭb′ə dŭb′), *n.* the sound of a drum when beaten. [imit.]

Rubáiyát (ro͞o bī′ăt), *n.* **1.** the best-known work of Omar Khayyám, familiar in English through the version by Edward FitzGerald, published in 1859. **2.** (*l.c.*) *Pros.* a quatrain of the kind in the *Rubáiyát.* [t. Pers., t. Ar., fem. pl. of *rubā‘ī* quatrain]

Rub‘ al Khali (ro͞ob′ăl kä′lĭ), the large desert of S Arabia, N of the Hadhramaut and extending from Yemen to Oman.

rubato (ro͞o bä′tō), *adj.*, *n.*, *pl.* **-tos.** *Music.* —*adj.* **1.** having certain notes arbitrarily lengthened while others are correspondingly shortened, or vice versa, as a means of increasing the freedom of expression. —*n.* **2.** a rubato phrase or passage. **3.** rubato performance. [It., for *tempo rubato* stolen time]

rubber[1] (rŭb′ə), *n.* **1.** an elastic material, derived from the latex of *Hevea* and *Ficus* species of the rubber plant; caoutchouc; indiarubber (**natural rubber**). **2.** a class of elastomers made from polymers or copolymers of simple molecules with properties resembling those of natural rubber (**synthetic rubber**). **3.** a piece of indiarubber for erasing pencil marks, etc. **4.** an instrument, tool, etc., used for rubbing something. **5.** a coarse file. **6.** one who rubs, as in order to smooth or polish something. **7.** a cloth, pad or the like, used for polishing, buffing, etc. **8.** one who practises massage, as at a bath. **9.** (*usually pl.*) rubber or rubberized waterproof clothes or shoes; wellington boots; overshoes; a mackintosh. **10.** (*pl.*) *U.S.* galoshes. **11.** *U.S. Slang.* a sheath (def. 6). [f. RUB + -ER[1]]

rubber[2] (rŭb′ə), *n.* **1.** *Bridge, Whist, etc.*, a set of games, usually three or five, a majority of which decides the overall winner. **2.** a series of games on this pattern in various other sports, as cricket, bowls, croquet, etc.

rubber band, a thin, continuous loop of highly elastic rubber, used for holding small objects, etc., together; elastic band.

rubberize (rŭb′ə rīz′), *v.t.*, **-rized, -rizing.** to coat or impregnate with rubber or some preparation of it. Also, **rubberise.**

rubberneck (rŭb′ə nĕk′), *U.S. Slang.* —*n.* **1.** an extremely or excessively curious person. **2.** a tourist. —*adj.* **3.** pertaining to or for such people. —*v.i.* **4.** to look at things in an excessively curious manner.

rubber plant, **1.** a moraceous plant, *Ficus elastica*, with oblong, shining, leathery leaves, growing native as a tall tree in India, the Malay Archipelago, etc., and much cultivated in Europe and America as an ornamental house plant. **2.** any plant yielding caoutchouc.

rubber ring, an inflatable ring-shaped, rubber bladder worn round the waist as an aid to swimming.

rubber stamp, **1.** a device of rubber for printing dates, etc., by hand. **2.** *Colloq.* one who gives approval without consideration.

rubber-stamp (rŭb′ə stămp′), *v.t.* **1.** to imprint with a rubber stamp. **2.** *Colloq.* to give approval without consideration.

rubbery (rŭb′ə rĭ), *adj.* like rubber; elastic; tough.

rubbing (rŭb′ĭng), *n.* **1.** the act of one who or that which rubs. **2.** a reproduction of an incised or sculptured surface made by laying paper or the like upon it and rubbing with some marking substance.

rubbish (rŭb′ĭsh), *n.* **1.** waste or refuse material; debris; litter. **2.** worthless stuff; trash. **3.** nonsense. [ME *robous*, *robys*; orig. obscure. Cf. RUBBLE] —**rub′bishy,** *adj.*

rubble (rŭb′l), *n.* **1.** rough fragments of broken stone, formed by geological action, in quarrying, etc., and sometimes used in masonry. **2.** rough fragments of brick, concrete, or any other building material, esp. when reused for building or foundation. **3.** masonry built of rough fragments of broken stone. **4.** any solid substance, as ice, in irregularly broken pieces. [ME *robyl*, *robel*; orig. obscure. Cf. RUBBISH] —**rub′bly,** *adj.*

rubblework (rŭb′l wûk′), *n.* masonry built of rubble or roughly dressed stones.

rub-down (rŭb′doun′), *n.* massage.

rube (ro͞ob), *n.* *U.S. Slang.* an unsophisticated countryman. [short for *Reuben*, man's name]

rubefacient (ro͞o′bĭ fā′shyənt), *adj.* **1.** producing redness of the skin, as a medicinal application. —*n.* **2.** *Med.* a rubefacient application, as a mustard plaster. [t. L: s. *rubefaciens*, ppr., making red]

rubefaction (ro͞o′bĭ făk′shən), *n.* **1.** a making red, esp. with a rubefacient. **2.** redness of the skin produced by a rubefacient.

rubella (ro͞o bĕl′ə), *n.* German measles. [NL, prop. neut. pl. of L *rubellus* reddish]

rubellite (ro͞o′bĭ līt′), *n.* a deep red variety of tourmaline, used as a gem. [f. s. L *rubellus* reddish + -ITE[1]]

Rubens (ro͞o′bĭnz; *Du.* rʏ′bəns), *n.* **Peter Paul** (*Du.* pē′tər pôwl), 1577–1640, Flemish painter.

rubeola (ro͞o bē′ə lə), *n.* *Pathol.* **1.** measles. **2.** German measles. [NL, dim. (neut. pl.) of L *rubeus* red] —**rube′olar,** *adj.*

rubescent (ro͞o bĕs′ənt), *adj.* becoming red; blushing. [t. L: s. *rubescens*, ppr.] —**rubes′cence,** *n.*

rubiaceous (ro͞o′bĭ ā′shəs), *adj.* belonging to the *Rubiaceae*, or madder family of plants, including also the coffee, cinchona, and ipecacuanha plants, the gardenia, partridgeberry, bedstraw, etc. [f. s. NL *Rubiaceae* (der. L *rubia* madder) + -OUS]

Rubicon (ro͞o′bĭ kən), *n.* **1.** Present name, **Fiumicino.** the river in N Italy forming the southern boundary of Caesar's province of cisalpine Gaul, by crossing which, in 49 B.C., he began a civil war with Pompey. **2.** a boundary or limitation. **3. pass,** or **cross, the Rubicon,** to take a decisive, irrevocable step.

rubicund (ro͞o′bĭ kənd), *adj.* **1.** red or reddish. **2.** of a high colour, as from good living. [t. L: s. *rubicundus*] —**rubicundity** (ro͞o′bĭ kŭn′dĭ tĭ), *n.* —**Syn.** See **rosy.**

rubidium (ro͞o bĭd′ĭ əm), *n.* *Chem.* a silvery white metallic, active element resembling potassium, with no commercial uses. *Symbol:* Rb; *at. wt:* 85·47; *at. no.:* 37; *sp. gr.:* 1·53 at 20°C. [NL, f. s. L *rubidus* red (in allusion to the two red lines in its spectrum) + *-ium* -IUM]

rubiginous (ro͞o bĭj′ĭ nəs), *adj.* rusty; rust-coloured; brownish red. [f. s. L *rūbīgo* rust + -OUS]

Rubinstein (ro͞o′bĭn stīn′; *also Russ.* ro͞o bĭn shtyĕyn′ *for def. 1*), *n.* **1. Anton** (*Russ.* ȧn tôn′), 1829–94, Russian pianist and composer. **2. Artur** (ä′to͞oə), born 1886, U.S. pianist, born in Poland.

rubious (ro͞o′bĭ əs), *adj.* *Rare or Poetic.* ruby-coloured.

ruble (ro͞o′bl), *n.* rouble.

rubric (ro͞o′brĭk), *n.* **1.** a title, heading, direction, or the like, in a manuscript, book, etc., written or printed in red or otherwise distinguished from the rest of the text. **2.** the title or a heading of a statute, etc. (orig. written in red). **3.** a direction for the conduct of divine service or the administration of the sacraments, inserted in liturgical books. **4.** the instructions to the candidate printed at the top of an examination paper. **5.** anything important or worthy of note. [t. L: s. *rubrīca* red earth; r. ME *rubriche*, t. OF]

rubrical (ro͞o′brĭ kl), *adj.* **1.** of, pertaining to, or enjoined by liturgical rubrics. **2.** *Obs.* reddish; marked with red. —**ru′brically,** *adv.*

rubricate (ro͞o′brĭ kāt′), *v.t.*, **-cated, -cating.** **1.** to mark or colour with red. **2.** to furnish with or regulate by rubrics. [t. L: m. s. *rubricātus*, pp.] —**ru′brica′tion,** *n.* —**ru′brica′tor,** *n.*

rubricated (ro͞o′brĭ kā′tĭd), *adj.* (in ancient manuscripts, early printed books, etc.) having titles, catchwords, etc., distinctively coloured.

rubrician (ro͞o brĭsh′ən), *n.* an expert in rubrics.

ruby (ro͞o′bĭ), *n.*, *pl.* **-bies.** **1.** a red variety of corundum, highly prized as a gem (**true ruby** or **oriental ruby**). **2.** a piece of this stone. **3.** any of various similar stones, as the spinel ruby, balas ruby, etc. **4.** deep red; carmine. **5.** a printing type (about 5½ point) of a size between pearl and nonpareil. —*adj.* **6.** ruby-coloured: *ruby lips.* **7.** made from or containing a ruby. [ME, t. OF: m. *rubi(s)*, ult. der. L *rubeus* red]

ruby glass, glass coloured red by colloidal suspensions of elemental gold, copper, or selenium.

ruby silver, **1.** proustite. **2.** pyrargyrite.

ruche (ro͞osh), *n.* a full pleating or frilling of lace, net, muslin, ribbon, etc., used as a trimming or finish. [t. F: lit., beehive, g. LL *rūsca*]

ruching (ro͞o′shĭng), *n.* **1.** material made into a ruche. **2.** ruches collectively.

ruck[1] (rŭk), *n.* **1.** the great mass of undistinguished or inferior persons or things. **2.** a large number or quantity; a crowd or throng. [ME *ruke*, prob. t. Scand.; cf. Norw. *ruka* in same senses; akin to RICK[1], n.]

ruck[2] (rŭk), *n., v.t., v.i.* fold, crease, or wrinkle. [t. Scand.; cf. Icel. *hrukka*]

rucksack (rŭk′săk′), *n.* a kind of knapsack carried by hikers, etc. [t. G: lit., back sack]

ruckus (rŭk′əs), *n. Chiefly U.S. Colloq.* **1.** a commotion; rumpus. **2.** a violent disagreement.

ruction (rŭk′shən), *n. Colloq.* a disturbance, quarrel or row. [cf. obs. *ructation* belching, vomiting, aphetic var. of ERUCTATION]

rudbeckia (rŭd bĕk′ĭ ə), *n.* any of the showy flowered composite herbs constituting the genus *Rudbeckia*, as the tall, frequently cultivated *R. laciniata*, which has a large capitulum with a conical green disc, and golden yellow rays; a coneflower. [NL; named after O. *Rudbeck*, 1630–1702, Swedish botanist]

rudd (rŭd), *n.* a European freshwater fish, *Scardinius erythrophthalmus*, of the carp family. [appar. special use of *rud* (now d.), OE *rudu* redness]

rudder (rŭd′ə), *n.* **1.** a board or plate of wood or metal hinged vertically at the stern of a boat or ship as a means of steering. **2.** a device like a ship's rudder for steering an aeroplane, etc., hinged vertically (for right-and-left steering). [ME *roder, rother*, OE *rōthor*, c. G *Ruder*. See ROW[2]]

R, Rudder (def. 1)

rudderfish (rŭd′ə fĭsh′), *n.* any of various fish reputed to follow ships, as *Kyphosus fuscus* of the Indian and Pacific oceans.

rudderhead (rŭd′ə hĕd′), *n. Naut.* the upper end of the rudderpost which is connected to the quadrant or tiller and controlled by the wheel.

rudderpost (rŭd′ə pōst′), *n. Naut.* **1.** Also, **rudderstock** (rŭd′ə stŏk′). the vertical member at the forward end of a rudder which is hinged to the sternpost and attached to the helm or steering gear. **2.** the vertical member abaft the screw, in single-screw vessels, which holds the rudder.

ruddle (rŭd′l), *n., v.,* **-dled, -dling.** —*n.* **1.** a red variety of ochre, used for marking sheep, colouring, etc. —*v.t.* **2.** to mark or colour with ruddle. [der. *rud*, OE *rudu* a red cosmetic]

ruddock (rŭd′ək), *n. Chiefly Dial.* the European robin, *Erithacus rubecula*. [ME, OE *rudduc*. Cf. d. *rud(d)* red, -OCK]

ruddy (rŭd′ĭ), *adj.,* **-dier, -diest,** *adv.* —*adj.* **1.** of or having a fresh, healthy red colour. **2.** reddish. —*adv.* **3.** *Colloq.* damned; extremely: *I've a ruddy good mind to hit him.* [ME *rudi*, OE *rudig*, der. *rudu* redness] —**rud′diness,** *n.* —**Syn. 1.** See **rosy.**

rude (ro͞od), *adj.,* **ruder, rudest. 1.** discourteous or impolite: *a rude reply.* **2.** without culture, learning, or refinement. **3.** rough in manners or behaviour; unmannerly. **4.** rough, harsh, or ungentle: *rude hands.* **5.** roughly wrought, built, or formed; of a crude make or kind. **6.** unwrought, raw, or crude. **7.** harsh to the ear, as sounds. **8.** without artistic elegance; of a primitive simplicity. **9.** violent or tempestuous, as the waves. **10.** robust, sturdy, or vigorous: *rude strength.* [ME, t. L: m. *rudis*] —**rude′ly,** *adv.* —**rude′ness,** *n.* —**Syn. 1.** uncivil. **2.** rough, unfinished, unrefined. **6.** See **raw.**

ruderal (ro͞o′də rəl), *adj. Bot.* growing near human habitations in waste places.

rudiment (ro͞o′dĭ mənt), *n.* **1.** the elements or first principles of a subject: *the rudiments of grammar.* **2.** (*usually pl.*) a mere beginning, first slight appearance, or undeveloped or imperfect form of something. **3.** *Biol.* an organ or part incompletely developed in size or structure, as one in an embryonic stage, one arrested in growth, or one with no functional activity, as a vestige. [t. L: s. *rudīmentum* beginning]

rudimentary (ro͞o′dĭ mĕn′tə rĭ, -trĭ), *adj.* **1.** pertaining to rudiments or first principles; elementary. **2.** of the nature of a rudiment; undeveloped. **3.** vestigial; abortive. Also, **ru′dimen′tal.** —**ru′dimen′tarily,** *adv.* —**ru′dimen′tariness,** *n.* —**Syn. 1.** See **elementary. 2.** See **imperfect.**

Rudolf (ro͞o′dŏlf), *n.* **Lake,** a lake in E Africa, in N Kenya. ab. 180 mi. long; 3500 sq. mi.

Rudolph I (ro͞o′dŏlf), 1218–91, German king and emperor of the Holy Roman Empire 1273–91: founder of the Habsburg dynasty. Also, **Rudolf.**

rue[1] (ro͞o), *v.,* **rued, ruing,** *n.* —*v.t.* **1.** to feel sorrow over; repent of; regret bitterly. **2.** to wish (that something might never have been done, taken place, etc.): *to rue the day one was born.* —*v.i.* **3.** to feel sorrow; be repentant. **4.** to feel regret. —*n. Archaic.* **5.** sorrow; repentance; regret. **6.** pity or compassion. [ME *rue, rewe*, OE *hrēowan*, c. G *reuen*]

rue[2] (ro͞o), *n.* any of the strongly scented plants constituting the genus *Ruta*, esp. *R. graveolens*, a yellow-flowered herb with decompound leaves formerly much used in medicine. [ME, t. OF and F, g. L *rūta*, t. Gk: m. *rhȳtḗ*]

Rueda (*Sp.* rwĕ′dä), *n.* **Lope de** (*Sp.* lō′pĕ dĕ), *c.* 1510–65, Spanish playwright.

rueful (ro͞o′fəl), *adj.* **1.** such as to cause sorrow or pity; deplorable; pitiable: *a rueful plight.* **2.** feeling, showing, or expressing sorrow or pity; wry; mournful; doleful. —**rue′fully,** *adv.* —**rue′fulness,** *n.*

rufescent (ro͞o fĕs′ənt), *adj. Biol., etc.* somewhat reddish; tinged with red; rufous. [t. L: s. *rūfescens*, ppr., becoming reddish] —**rufes′cence,** *n.*

ruff[1] (rŭf), *n.* **1.** a neckpiece or collar of lace, lawn, etc., gathered or drawn into deep, full, regular folds, much worn in the 16th century by both men and women. **2.** something resembling such a piece in form or position. **3.** a collar, or set of lengthened or specially marked hairs or feathers, on the neck of an animal. **4.** a shorebird, *Philomachus pugnax*, the male of which has an enormous frill of feathers on the neck during the breeding season. The female is called a *reeve.* [? n. use of ROUGH, adj.] —**ruffed,** *adj.*

Ruff, 16th century

ruff[2] (rŭf), *n.* **1.** *Cards.* the act of trumping when one cannot follow suit. **2.** *Obs.* an old game at cards, resembling whist. —*v.t., v.i.* **3.** *Cards.* to trump when unable to follow suit. [prob. t. F: m. *ro(u)ffle*, c. It. *ronfa* a card game]

ruffe (rŭf), *n.* the pope[2], *Acerina cernua.* [ME *ruf, roffe*; ? special use of ROUGH, adj.]

ruffian (rŭf′yən), *n.* **1.** a violent, lawless man; a rough brute. —*adj.* **2.** Also, **ruf′fianly.** pertaining to or characteristic of a ruffian; lawless; brutal. [earlier *rufian*, t. F]

ruffianism (rŭf′yə nĭz′əm), *n.* **1.** conduct befitting a ruffian. **2.** ruffianly character.

ruffle[1] (rŭf′əl), *v.,* **-fled, -fling,** *n.* —*v.t.* **1.** to destroy the smoothness or evenness of: *the wind ruffled the sand.* **2.** to erect (the feathers), as in anger, as a bird. **3.** to annoy, disturb, discompose, or irritate. **4.** to turn over (the pages of a book) rapidly. **5.** to pass (cards) through the fingers rapidly. **6.** to draw up (cloth, lace, etc.) into a ruffle by gathering along one edge. —*v.i.* **7.** to be or become ruffled. —*n.* **8.** a break in the smoothness or evenness of some surface. **9.** a strip of cloth, lace, etc., drawn up by gathering along one edge, and used as a trimming on dress, etc. **10.** some object resembling this, as the ruff of a bird. **11.** a disturbing experience; an annoyance or vexation. **12.** a disturbed state of the mind; perturbation. [ME; c. LG *ruffelen* crumple, rumple; cf. Icel. *hrufla* scratch] —**Syn. 3.** upset, agitate, annoy, vex.

ruffle[2] (rŭf′əl), *n., v.,* **-fled, -fling.** —*n.* **1.** a low, continuous beating of a drum, less loud than a roll. —*v.t.* **2.** to beat (a drum) in this manner. [der. *ruff* in same sense. ? imit.]

rufous (ro͞o′fəs), *adj.* reddish; rufescent; tinged with red; brownish red. [t. L: m. *rūfus* red, reddish]

rug (rŭg), *n.* **1.** a small, often thick, carpet, used as a floor covering or a hanging, and made of woven or tufted wool, cotton, or the like, fur, etc. **2.** a thick, warm blanket used as a coverlet, etc., or wrap, to keep travellers warm. **3. cut a rug,** *U.S. Slang.* to dance, esp. with verve, as to jazz. [t. Scand.; cf. d. Norw. *rugga* coarse covering (for bed or body)]

ruga (ro͞o′gə), *n., pl.* **-gae** (-jē). a wrinkle, fold, or ridge. [t. L]

rugate (ro͞o′gāt, -gĭt), *adj.* wrinkled; rugose.

Rugby (rŭg′bĭ), *n.* **1.** a town in central England, in Warwickshire. 51,698 (1961). **2.** a boys' school there: founded 1567. **3.** Rugby football.

Rugby football, a form of football in which handling and carrying of the ball are permitted. Also, **Rugby, rugger.** Cf. **soccer.** [named after RUGBY (def. 2)]

Rugby League, 1. an organization of Rugby football clubs, operating principally in N England and acting as a law-making body. **2.** one of the two forms of Rugby football, played by teams of thirteen players each, differing from Rugby Union in certain details of the rules and in permitting professionalism.

Rugby Union, 1. an organization of Rugby clubs, controlling most Rugby playing and acting as a law-making body. **2.** one of the two forms of Rugby football, played by teams of fifteen players each, differing from Rugby League in certain details of the rules and restricted to amateurs.

Rugeley (ro͞oj′lĭ), *n.* a town in England, in Staffordshire. 13,012 (1961).

rugged (rŭg′ĭd), *adj.* **1.** roughly broken, rocky, hilly, or otherwise difficult of passage: *rugged ground.* **2.** wrinkled or furrowed: *a rugged face.* **3.** roughly irregular, heavy, or hard in outline or form: *Lincoln's rugged features.* **4.** rough, harsh, or stern, as persons, the nature, etc. **5.** severe, hard, or trying: *a rugged life.* **6.** *Obs.* tempestuous, as weather. **7.** harsh to the ear, as sounds. **8.** rude, uncultivated, or unrefined, but sturdy or strong: *rugged individualism.* **9.** *U.S.* robust or vigorous. **10.** *U.S. Colloq.* uncomfortable; entailing hardship. [ME, t. Scand.; cf. Sw. *rugga* roughen and see RUG] —**rug′gedly,** *adv.* —**rug′gedness,** *n.* —**Ant. 1.** smooth. **4.** mild. **9.** frail.

rugger (rŭg′ə), *n.* Rugby football.

rugose (ro͞o′gōs, ro͞o gōs′), *adj.* **1.** having wrinkles; wrinkled; ridged. **2.** *Bot.* rough and wrinkled (applied to leaves in which the reticulate venation is very prominent beneath with corresponding creases on the upper side). [t. L: m. s. *rūgōsus* wrinkled] —**ru′gosely,** *adv.* —**rugosity** (ro͞o gŏs′ĭ tĭ), *n.*

Ruhmkorff coil (ro͞om′kôf), an induction coil. [named after H. D. *Ruhmkorff*, 1803–77, German physicist]

Ruhr (ro͝oə; *Ger.* ro͞or), *n.* **1.** a river in W West Germany, flowing into the Rhine. 144 mi. **2.** an important mining and industrial region in and around the Ruhr river valley.

ruin (ro͞o′ĭn), *n.* **1.** (*pl.*) the remains of a fallen building, town, etc., or of anything in a state of destruction or decay: *the ruins of an ancient city.* **2.** a ruined building, town, etc. **3.** fallen and wrecked or decayed state; ruinous condition: *a building falls to ruin.* **4.** the downfall, decay, or destruction of anything. **5.** the complete loss of means, position, or the like. **6.** something that causes downfall or destruction. **7.** the downfall of a person. **8.** a person as the wreck of his former self. **9.** the seduction of a woman. —*v.t.* **10.** to reduce to ruin. **11.** to bring (a person, etc.) to financial ruin. **12.** to injure (a thing) irretrievably. **13.** to seduce. —*v.i.* **14.** to fall into ruins. **15.** to come to ruin. [ME *ruine*, t. OF, t. L: m. *ruīna* overthrow, ruin] —**ru′inable,** *adj.* —**ru′ined,** *adj.* —**ru′iner,** *n.*

—**Syn. 3.** dilapidation, decay, ruination, perdition. RUIN, DESTRUCTION, HAVOC imply irrevocable and often widespread damage. DESTRUCTION may be on a large or small scale (*destruction of tissue, of enemy vessels*); it emphasizes particularly the act of destroying, while RUIN and HAVOC emphasize the resultant state. RUIN, from the verb meaning to fall to pieces, suggests a state of decay or disintegration (or an object in that state) which is apt to be more the result of the natural processes of time and change, than of sudden violent activity from without (*the house has fallen in ruins*); only in its figurative application is it apt to suggest the result of destruction from without: *the ruin of her hopes.* HAVOC, originally a cry which served as the signal for pillaging, has changed its reference from that of spoliation to devastation, being used particularly of the destruction following in the wake of natural calamities: *the havoc wrought by flood and pestilence.* Today it is used figuratively to refer to the destruction of hopes and plans: *this sudden turn of events played havoc with her carefully laid designs.* **10.** See **spoil.**

ruination (ro͞o′ĭ nā′shən), *n.* **1.** the act of ruining. **2.** the state of being ruined. **3.** something that ruins.

ruinous (ro͞o′ĭ nəs), *adj.* **1.** bringing or tending to bring ruin; destructive; disastrous: *a ruinous war.* **2.** fallen into ruin; dilapidated. **3.** consisting of ruins. —**ru′inously,** *adv.* —**ru′inousness,** *n.*

Ruisdael (rīz′dāl; *Du.* rœys′dȧl), *n.* **Jacob van** (*Du.* yä′kôp vȧn), 1628?–82, Dutch painter. Also, **Ruysdael.**

Ruiz (*Sp.* rwēth), *n.* **José Martínez** (*Sp.* KHō sĕ′ mȧr tē′nĕth). See **Azorin.**

rule (ro͞ol), *n., v.,* **ruled, ruling.** —*n.* **1.** a principle or regulation governing conduct, action, procedure, arrangement, etc. **2.** the code of regulations observed by a religious order or congregation. **3.** that which customarily or normally occurs or holds good: *the rule rather than the exception.* **4.** control, government, or dominion. **5.** tenure or conduct of reign or office. **6.** a prescribed mathematical method for performing a calculation or solving a problem. **7.** a ruler (def. 2). **8.** *Print.* **a.** a thin, type-high strip of metal, usually brass, for printing a line or lines. **b.** the line printed by this. **9.** *Law.* **a.** a formal order or direction made by a court and limited in application to the case for which it is given (**special rule**). **b.** an order or regulation governing the procedure of a court (**general rule**). **c.** a proposition of law. **10.** (*pl.*) **a.** a fixed area in the neighbourhood of certain prisons, within which certain prisoners were allowed to live on giving security. **b.** the freedom of such an area. **11. as a rule,** usually. **12.** See **work-to-rule.** —*v.t.* **13.** to control or direct; exercise dominating power or influence over. **14.** to exercise authority or dominion over; govern. **15.** to decide or declare judicially or authoritatively; decree. **16.** to mark with lines, esp. parallel straight lines, with the aid of a ruler or the like. **17.** to mark out or form (a line) by this method. **18. rule off,** to mark the end (of something written) by ruling a line beneath. **19. rule out,** to exclude, refuse to admit, declare (something) out of the question. —*v.i.* **20.** to exercise dominating power or influence. **21.** to exercise authority, dominion, or sovereignty. **22.** to make a formal decision or ruling, as on a point at law. **23.** to prevail or be current, as prices. [ME, t. OF: m. *riule*, g. L *rēgula* straight stick, pattern]

—**Syn. 1.** standard, law, canon. See **principle. 14.** RULE, ADMINISTER, COMMAND, GOVERN, MANAGE mean to exercise authoritative guidance or direction. RULE implies the exercise of authority as by a sovereign: *to rule a kingdom.* ADMINISTER places emphasis on the planned and orderly procedures used: *to administer the finances of an institution.* COMMAND suggests military authority and the power to exact obedience; to be in command of: *to command a ship.* To GOVERN is authoritatively to guide or direct persons or things, esp. in the affairs of a large administrative unit: *to govern a state.* To MANAGE is to conduct affairs, i.e., to guide them in a unified way towards a definite goal; or to direct or control people, often by tact, address, or artifice: *to manage a business.*

rule of law, 1. the doctrine that all men are equal before the law, and that the government is subject to the law. **2.** the absence of arbitrary executive power.

rule of the road, a code or custom regulating movement of ships, vehicles, etc., for their mutual convenience and safety.

rule of three, *Maths.* the method of finding the fourth term in a proportion when three terms are given; golden rule.

rule of thumb, 1. a rule based on experience or practice rather than on scientific knowledge. **2.** a rough, practical method of procedure.

ruler (ro͞o′lə), *n.* **1.** one who or that which rules or governs; a sovereign. **2.** a strip of wood, metal, or other material with a straight edge, used in drawing lines, measuring, etc. **3.** one who or that which rules paper, etc. —**rul′ership′,** *n.*

ruling (ro͞o′lĭng), *n.* **1.** an authoritative decision, as by a judge on a point at law. **2.** the act of drawing straight lines with a rule. **3.** ruled lines. —*adj.* **4.** that rules; governing. **5.** predominating. **6.** prevalent.

rum[1] (rŭm), *n.* **1.** an alcoholic spirit distilled from molasses or some other sugar-cane product. **2.** *U.S.* alcoholic drink in general; intoxicating liquor. [? short for obs. *rumbullion.* Cf. F *rebouillir* boil again]

rum[2] (rŭm), *adj. Slang.* **1.** odd, strange, or queer. **2.** *Archaic.* good or fine. Also, **rummy.** [earlier *rome, room* great, of unknown orig.]

Rum (ro͞om), *n.* Arabic name of Rome, once used to designate the Byzantine Empire.

Rum., 1. Rumania. 2. Rumanian.

Rumania (ro͞o mā′nyə), *n.* a republic in SE Europe, bordering on the Black Sea; one of the Balkan States. 18,927,081 pop. (est. 1964); 91,671 sq. mi. *Cap.:* Bucharest. Also, **Roumania.** Rumanian, **România.**

Rumanian (ro͞o mā′nyən), *adj.* **1.** of Rumania, its inhabitants, or their language. —*n.* **2.** a native or inhabitant of Rumania. **3.** the language of Rumania (a Romance language). Also, **Roumanian.**

rumba (rŭm′bə), *n.* **1.** a dance, Cuban in origin and complex in rhythm (in 8/8 time). **2.** an imitation or adaptation of this dance. **3.** the music for this dance or in its rhythm. [t. Sp., prob. of Afr. orig.]

rumble (rŭm′bl), *v.,* **-bled, -bling,** *n.* —*v.i.* **1.** to make a deep, heavy, continuous, resonant sound, as thunder, etc. **2.** to move, travel or be conveyed with such a sound: *the train rumbled on.* **3.** *U.S. Slang.* to take part in a fight, as between gangs. —*v.t.* **4.** to give forth or utter with a rumbling sound. **5.** to cause to make or move with a rumbling sound. **6.** to subject to the action of a rumble or tumbling box, as for the purpose of polishing. **7.** *Slang.* to detect or become suspicious of, as a fraud. —*n.* **8.** a rumbling sound, as of thunder or a heavy vehicle. **9.** *U.S.* a dicky; rumble seat. **10.** a rear part of a carriage containing seating accommodation as for servants or space for baggage. **11.** a tumbling box. **12.** *U.S. Slang.* a fight, esp. between teenage gangs. [ME. Cf. D *rommelen*, prob. of imit. orig.]

rumble seat, *U.S.* a dicky.

rumbly (rŭm′blĭ), *adj.* **1.** rumbling. **2.** attended with, making, or causing a rumbling sound.

rumbustious (rŭm bŭs′tyəs), *adj.* boisterous, noisy. [probably var. of ROBUSTIOUS]

Rumelia (ro͞o mē′lyə), *n.* **1.** the European division of the former Turkish Empire, in the Balkan Peninsula: it included Albania, Macedonia, and Thrace. **2. Eastern Rumelia,** a former autonomous province within this division, which later became S Bulgaria. Also, **Roumelia.**

rumen (roo͞′mĕn), *n.*, *pl.* **-mina** (-mĭ nə). **1.** the first stomach of ruminating animals, lying next to the reticulum. **2.** the cud of a ruminant. [t. L: throat, gullet]

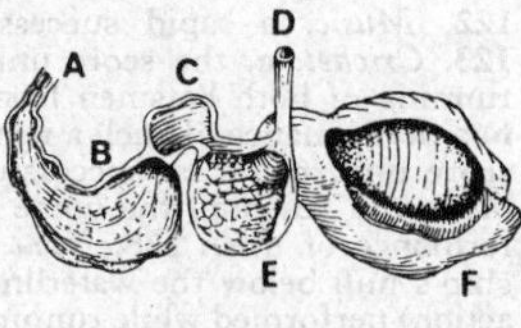

Ruminant stomach
A, Duodenum; B, Abomasum; C, Omasum; D, Oesophagus; E, Reticulum; F, Rumen

Rumford (rŭm′fəd), *n.* **Count.** See **Thompson, Benjamin.**

ruminant (roo͞′mĭ nənt), *n.* **1.** any animal of the artiodactyl suborder or division, *Ruminantia*, which comprises the various 'cloven-hoofed' and cud-chewing quadrupeds: cattle, bison, buffalo, sheep, goats, chamois, deer, antelopes, giraffes, camels, chevrotains, etc. —*adj.* **2.** ruminating; chewing the cud. **3.** given to or characterized by meditation; meditative. [t. L: s. *rūminans*, ppr., ruminating]

ruminate (roo͞′mĭ nāt′), *v.*, **-nated, -nating.** —*v.i.* **1.** to chew the cud, as a ruminant. **2.** to meditate or muse; ponder. —*v.t.* **3.** to chew again. **4.** to meditate on; ponder. [t. L: m. s. *rūminātus*, pp.] —**ru′minat′ingly,** *adv.* —**ru′mina′tion,** *n.* —**ruminative** (roo͞′mĭ nə tĭv), *adj.* —**ru′mina′tor,** *n.*

rummage (rŭm′ĭj), *v.*, **-maged, -maging,** *n.* —*v.t.* **1.** to search thoroughly or actively through (a place, receptacle, etc.), esp. by moving about, turning over, or looking through contents. **2.** to find (fol. by *out* or *up*) by searching. —*v.i.* **3.** to search actively, as in a place or receptacle, or among contents, etc. —*n.* **4.** miscellaneous articles; odds and ends. **5.** a rummaging search. [ult. t. (older) F: m. *arrumage*, n., der. *arrumer* stow goods in hold of ship; orig. uncert.] —**rum′mager,** *n.*

rummage sale, a jumble sale.

rummer (rŭm′ə), *n.* a large drinking glass or cup typically of a heavy goblet shape. [cf. Flem. *rummer*, G *Römer*; orig. uncert.]

rummy[1] (rŭm′ĭ), *n.* a card game in which the object is to match cards into sets and sequences. [orig. uncert.]

rummy[2] (rŭm′ĭ), *n.*, *pl.* **-mies. 1.** *U.S. Slang.* a drunkard. —*adj.* **2.** of or like rum. [f. RUM[1] + -Y[1]]

rummy[3] (rŭm′ĭ), *adj.*, **-mier, -miest.** *Slang.* odd; queer. [f. RUM[2] + -Y[1]]

Rumor (*It.* roo mōr′), *n.* **Mariano** (*It.* mȧ ryȧ′nō), born 1915, Italian statesman: prime minister since 1968.

rumour (roo͞′mə), *n.* **1.** a story or statement in general circulation without confirmation or certainty as to facts. **2.** unconfirmed gossip. —*v.t.* **3.** to circulate, report, or assert by a rumour. Also, *U.S.*, **rumor.** [ME, t. OF, t. L: m. *rūmor*] —**Syn. 1.** talk, gossip, hearsay.

rump (rŭmp), *n.* **1.** the hinder part of the body of an animal. **2.** a cut of beef from this part of the animal, behind the loin and above the round. **3.** the buttocks. **4.** any remnant; the last and unimportant or inferior part; fag-end. **5. the Rump,** the remnant of the Long Parliament established by the expulsion of the Presbyterian members in 1648, dismissed by force in 1653, and restored briefly in 1659–60. [ME *rumpe*, t. Scand.; cf. Dan. *rumpe* rump, c. G *Rumpf* trunk]

Rumpelstiltskin (rŭm′pl stĭlt′skĭn′), *n.* a character in German folklore, who dupes the king's bride into giving up her child and refuses to return it unless she can guess his name; when she succeeds he destroys himself.

rumple (rŭm′pl), *v.*, **-pled, -pling,** *n.* —*v.t.* **1.** to draw or crush into wrinkles; crumple: *a rumpled sheet.* **2.** to ruffle; tousle (often fol. by *up*). —*v.i.* **3.** to become wrinkled or crumpled. —*n.* **4.** a wrinkle or irregular fold; crease. [t. MD: m. *rompel*, n., or t. MLG: m. *rumpel*]

rumpus (rŭm′pəs), *n. Colloq.* **1.** disturbing noise; uproar. **2.** a noisy or violent disturbance or commotion.

rum-runner (rŭm′rŭn′ə), *n. U.S. Colloq.* a person or a ship engaged in smuggling alcoholic drink, esp. spirits.

run (rŭn), *v.*, **ran, run, running,** *n.*, *adj.* —*v.i.* **1.** to move quickly on foot, so as to go more rapidly than in walking (in bipedal locomotion, so that for an instant in each step neither foot is on the ground). **2.** to do this for exercise, as a sport, etc. **3.** to hurry, go quickly. **4.** to move swiftly by other means of locomotion than legs. **5.** to make a quick succession of movements, as with the fingers: *the pianist ran up the scale.* **6.** to move easily or swiftly, as a vehicle, on wheels, a vessel, etc. **7.** to make off quickly, take to flight. **8.** to make a short, quick, or casual journey, as for a visit, etc. (often fol. by *up, over, round*, etc.). **9.** *Racing.* **a.** to take part in a race. **b.** to finish a race in a certain (numerical) position: *he ran second.* **10.** *U.S.* to stand as a candidate for election: *he is running for president.* **11.** *Colloq.* to migrate, as fish: *to run in huge shoals.* **12.** to pass upstream or inshore from deep water to spawn. **13.** to sail or be driven (ashore, into a channel, etc.), as a vessel or those on board. **14.** *Naut.* to sail before the wind. **15.** to ply between places, as a vessel. **16.** to traverse a route, as a public conveyance: *the buses run every hour.* **17.** to roam without restraint (often fol. by *about*): *children running about in the park.* **18.** to have recourse to, as for consolation: *he's always running to his mother.* **19.** to move, revolve, slide, etc., esp. easily, freely, or smoothly: *a rope runs in a pulley.* **20.** to flow, as a liquid or a body of liquid, or as sand, grain, or the like. **21.** to flow along, esp. strongly, as a stream, the sea, etc.: *with a strong tide running.* **22.** to melt and flow, as solder, varnish, etc. **23.** to spread or diffuse when exposed to moisture, as dyestuffs: *the colours in a fabric run.* **24.** to flow, stream, or be wet with a liquid. **25.** to discharge or give passage to a liquid. **26.** to overflow or leak, as a vessel (often fol. by *over*). **27.** to creep, trail, or climb, as vines, etc. **28.** to pass quickly: *a thought ran across his mind.* **29.** to continue in or return to the mind persistently: *a tune running through one's head.* **30.** to recur or be inherent: *madness runs in the family.* **31.** to come undone, as stitches or a fabric; ladder. **32.** to be in operation or continue operating, as a machine. **33.** *Com.* **a.** to accumulate, or become payable in due course, as interest on a debt. **b.** to make many withdrawals in rapid succession. **34.** *Law.* **a.** to have legal force or effect, as a writ. **b.** to continue to operate. **c.** to go along with or accompany: *the easement runs with the land.* **35.** to pass or go by, as time. **36.** to continue to be performed, as a play, over a period. **37.** to be disseminated, spread rapidly, as news. **38.** to spread or pass quickly from point to point: *a shout ran through the crowd.* **39.** to be in a certain form or expression: *so the story runs.* **40.** to extend or stretch. **41.** to have a specified quality, character, form, etc. **42.** to be or tend to be of a specified size or number: *potatoes running large.* **43.** to exist or occur within a specified range of variation. **44.** to pass into a certain state or condition; become: *to run wild.*
—*v.t.* **45.** to cause (an animal, etc.) to move quickly on foot. **46.** to cause (a vehicle, etc.) to move: *I'll just run the car into the garage.* **47.** to traverse (a distance or course) in running: *he ran half a mile.* **48.** to perform by or as by running: *to run a race, run an errand.* **49.** to compete with in a race: *I'll run you to the corner.* **50.** to enter a horse, etc., in a race. **51.** *Chiefly U.S.* to run along: *to run the streets.* **52.** to run or get past or through: *to run a blockade.* **53.** to bring into a certain state by running: *to run oneself out of breath.* **54.** to pursue or hunt (game, etc.). **55.** to drive (livestock), esp. to pasture. **56.** to keep (livestock), as on pasture. **57.** to cause to move, esp. quickly or cursorily: *to run one's fingers through one's hair, to run one's eyes over a letter.* **58.** to cause to ply between places, as a vessel, conveyance, or system of transport: *to run a train service between two cities.* **59.** to convey or transport, as in a vessel or vehicle. **60.** to keep operating or in service, as a machine. **61.** to possess and use, as a car. **62.** to expose oneself to or be exposed to (a risk, etc.). **63.** to sew, esp. with quick, even stitches in a line. **64.** (in some games, as billiards) to complete a series of successful strokes, shots, etc. **65.** to bring, lead, or force into some state, action, etc.: *to run oneself into debt.* **66.** to cause (a liquid) to flow. **67.** to give forth or flow with (a liquid). **68.** to pour forth or discharge. **69.** to cause (a bath, etc.) to contain water; fill. **70.** to cause to move easily, freely, or smoothly: *to run a sail up the mast.* **71.** to drive, force, or thrust. **72.** to extend or build, as in a particular direction: *to run a road through the forest.* **73.** to draw or trace, as a line. **74.** to conduct, administer, or manage, as a business, an experiment, or the like. **75.** (of a newspaper) to publish (a story). **76.** *U.S.* to put up (a candidate) for election. **77.** *Golf.* to hit (a ball) in such a way that it rolls after landing. **78.** to melt, fuse, or smelt, as ore. **79.** to smuggle.
—*v.* **80.** Some special verb phrases are:

cut and run, to take to flight.

run across, to meet or find unexpectedly.

run after, to seek to attract.

run around, 1. to behave promiscuously. **2.** to consort with. **3.** to have a love affair (fol. by *with*).

run away, 1. to take to flight. **2.** to depart: *run away, I'm busy; he ran away to sea.*

run away with, 1. to elope with. **2.** to steal. **3.** to win easily: *he ran away with the election.* **4.** to use up (money, etc.) quickly. **5.** to get out of control, as a horse, a vehicle, one's emotions or ideas, etc. **6.** *Colloq.* to accept (an ideal), esp. erroneously or with insufficient justification: *don't run away with the idea that you can go on behaving so badly.*

run close, to press severely, as a competitor.

run down, 1. to slow up before stopping, as a clock or other mechanism. **2.** to knock down and injure, as a vehicle or driver; run over. **3.** *Naut.* to collide with and cause to sink, as a smaller vessel. **4.** to denigrate; make adverse criticism of. **5.** to reduce, as stocks. **6.** to find, esp. after extensive searching. **7.** to pass quickly over or review: *to run down a list of possibilities.*

run hard, to press severely, as a competitor.

run in, **1.** to cause (new machinery, esp. a motor car) to run at reduced load and speed for an initial period, so that stiffness, etc., is reduced gradually and the machine becomes ready for full operation without damage. **2.** *Colloq.* to arrest. **3.** *Print.* to add (new text matter) without indentation. **4.** *Aeron.* to approach a landing.

run into, **1.** to encounter unexpectedly. **2.** to collide with. **3.** to amount to: *an income running into five figures.*

run off, **1.** to depart or retreat quickly. **2.** to produce, as a duplicator. **3.** to write or otherwise create quickly. **4.** to steal (fol. by *with*). **5.** to elope. **6.** to determine the result of (a tied contest, etc.) by a run-off.

run on, **1.** to have as a topic: *the conversation ran on politics.* **2.** to continue, as talking, at length and without interruption. **3.** (of handwritten lettering) to be linked up. **4.** *Print.* to print as continuous unindented text.

run out, **1.** to depart, as from a room, quickly. **2.** to be completely used up: *the food has run out, time is running out.* **3.** *Cricket.* to put (a batsman) out by hitting the wicket with the ball while neither he nor his bat are touching the ground within the popping crease. **4.** *Naut.* to pass or pay out (a rope). **5.** *U.S.* to drive out; expel.

run out on, to desert; abandon.

run over, **1.** to knock down and injure, as a vehicle or driver. **2.** to exceed (a time-limit or the like). **3.** to review, rehearse, or recapitulate.

run short, to become scarce or nearly used up.

run through, **1.** to rehearse or review. **2.** to exhaust or use up (money, etc.). **3.** to pass a sword or the like through (somebody).

run to, **1.** to be sufficient for: *the money doesn't run to caviar.* **2.** to include: *his books don't run to descriptions.* **3.** to become as specified: *to run to fat.*

run up, **1.** to climb quickly: *a sailor ran up the mast.* **2.** to hoist (a sail, flag, etc.). **3.** to amass or incur, as a bill. **4.** to make, esp. quickly, as something sewn.

run up against, **1.** to meet unexpectedly. **2.** to be impeded by.

run upon, **1.** to have as a topic, as thoughts or a conversation. **2.** (of a ship) to go aground upon.

—n. **81.** an act, instance, or spell of running: *to go for a run.* **82.** a running pace. **83.** an act or instance of escaping, running away, etc. **84.** an act or spell of moving rapidly, as in a boat or vehicle. **85.** the distance covered. **86.** a period or act of travelling, esp. a scheduled journey: *an uneventful run to Paris.* **87.** a quick, short trip. **88.** a spell of driving in a car, riding a horse, etc. **89.** a spell or period of causing something, as a machine, to run or continue operating. **90.** the amount of something produced in any uninterrupted period of operation. **91.** a continuous course of performances, as of a play. **92.** a line or place in knitted or sewn work where a series of stitches have slipped or come undone; a ladder. **93.** the direction of something fixed: *the run of the grain of a piece of timber.* **94.** onward movement, progression, course, etc. **95.** the particular course or tendency of something: *in the normal run of events, the general run of the voting.* **96.** freedom to range over, go through, or use: *the run of the house.* **97.** any rapid or easy course or progress. **98.** a continuous course of some condition of affairs, etc.: *a run of bad luck.* **99.** a continuous extent of something, as a vein of ore. **100.** a continuous series of something. **101.** a set of things in regular order, as a sequence of cards. **102.** any continued or extensive demand, call, or the like. **103.** a spell of being in demand or favour with the public. **104.** a series of sudden and urgent demands for payment, as on a bank. **105.** a spell of causing some liquid to flow. **106.** a flow or rush of water, etc. **107.** *U.S.* a small stream; brook; rivulet. **108.** a kind or class, as of goods. **109.** the ordinary or average kind. **110.** that in or on which something runs or may run. **111.** an enclosure within which domestic animals may range about. **112.** a way, track, or the like, along which something runs or moves. **113.** the habitual track or route taken by certain animals, as mice, rabbits, etc. **114.** a course for a particular purpose or activity, as an inclined course for skiing. **115.** *Austral., N.Z.* a tract of grazing land. **116.** *Mil.* the movement in a straight line up to the point of the launching of a bomb, torpedo, or the like, by an aeroplane, submarine, etc. **117.** *Aeron.* the spell of moving by an aeroplane along the ground or water under its own power preceding take-off and following touchdown. **118.** a trough or pipe through which water, etc., runs. **119.** the movement of a number of fish upstream or inshore from deep water. **120.** large numbers of fish in motion, esp. inshore from deep water or upstream for spawning. **121.** a number of animals moving together. **122.** *Music.* a rapid succession of notes; a roulade. **123.** *Cricket.* **a.** the score unit, made by the successful running of both batsmen from one wicket to the other. **b.** a performance of such a running. **124.** *Baseball.* **a.** the score unit, made by successfully running round all the bases and reaching the home plate. **b.** a successful performance of this. **125.** *Naut.* the curved afterpart of a ship's hull below the waterline. **126.** **at a run,** (of some action) performed while running, or by means of running; without stopping. **127.** **by the run,** *Naut.* without checking, as in letting go a rope in a tackle. **128.** **on the run,** escaped or hiding from pursuit, esp. by the police. **129.** **in the long run,** ultimately. **130.** **in the short run,** ignoring possible future developments; considering only immediate effects, etc.

—adj. **131.** melted or liquefied. **132.** poured in a melted state; run into and cast in a mould.

[ME *rinne(n)*, OE *rinnan*, c. G *rinnen*, Icel. *rinna.* Form *run* orig. pp., later extended to present tense]

runabout (rŭn′ə bout′), *n.* **1.** a light open car, aeroplane, or other vehicle. **2.** one who runs about from place to place.

runagate (rŭn′ə gāt′), *n.* *Archaic.* **1.** a fugitive or runaway. **2.** a vagabond or wanderer. [f. RUN, v. + obs. *agate* away; sense devel. influenced by contam. with obs. *renegate* (ME *renegat*, t. ML: s. *renegātus* RENEGADE)]

run-around (rŭn′ə round′), *n.* *U.S.* **1.** *Slang.* equivocation; evasion. **2.** *Print.* run-round.

runaway (rŭn′ə wā′), *n.* **1.** one who runs away; a fugitive; a deserter. **2.** a horse or vehicle which has broken away from control. **3.** the act of running away. *—adj.* **4.** having run away; escaped; fugitive. **5.** (of a horse, etc.) having escaped from the control of the rider, or driver. **6.** pertaining to or accomplished by running away or eloping: *a runaway marriage.* **7.** easily won, as a race. **8.** *Com.* uncontrolled.

runcible spoon (rŭn′sĭ bl), a utensil with two broad prongs (like a fork) and one sharp, curved prong (like a spoon), or other similar implement. [coined in 1871 by Edward Lear]

runcinate (rŭn′sĭ nĭt, -nāt′), *adj.* *Bot.* (of a leaf, etc.) pinnately incised, with the lobes or teeth curved backwards. [t. NL: m. s. *runcinātus*, der. L *runcina* plane (once thought to mean saw)]

Runcinate leaf

Runcorn (rŭn′kôn′), *n.* a town in England, in Cheshire, on the Mersey estuary. 28,500 (est. 1965).

rundle (rŭn′dl), *n.* **1.** a rung of a ladder. **2.** a wheel or similar rotating object. [var. of ROUNDEL]

rundlet (rŭnd′lĭt), *n.* *Archaic.* **1.** an old British measure of capacity, about 18 wine gallons. **2.** a cask having this capacity. [ME *rondelet*, t. OF, der. *rondelle*, der. *rond* ROUND]

run-down (*adj.* rŭn′doun′; *n.* rŭn′doun′), *adj.* **1.** in a poor or deteriorated state of health; depressed, sick or tired. **2.** fallen into disrepair. **3.** (of a spring-operated watch or clock) not running because not wound. *—n.* **4.** a cursory review or summary of points of information: *this brief run-down of past events will bring you up to date.*

rune[1] (rōōn), *n.* **1.** any of the characters of an alphabet used by the ancient Germanic-speaking peoples, especially the Scandinavians. **2.** something written or inscribed in such characters. [t. Icel.: m. *rūn*]

rune[2] (rōōn), *n.* *Poetic.* a poem, song, or verse. [t. Finnish: m. *runo* poem or canto, t. Scand. See RUNE[1]]

f u þ o r c g w h
n i j ė p x s t b
e ng d l m œ a æ y êa

Runic alphabet, 9th century

rung[1] (rŭng), *v.* pt. and pp. of **ring**[2].

rung[2] (rŭng), *n.* **1.** one of the rounded crosspieces forming the steps of a ladder. **2.** a rounded or shaped piece fixed horizontally, for strengthening purposes, as between the legs of a chair. **3.** a stout stick, rod, or bar, esp. one of rounded section, forming a piece in something framed or constructed: *the rungs of a wheel.* **4.** a stage in a progress or ascent: *the next rung of the ladder to success.* [ME; OE *hrung*, c. G *Runge*]

runic[1] (rōō′nĭk), *adj.* **1.** consisting of or set down in runes: *runic inscriptions.* **2.** (of ornamental knots, figures, etc.) of an interlaced form seen on ancient monuments, metalwork, etc., of the northern European peoples. **3.** mysterious or magical. *—n.* **4.** *Print.* a condensed form of bold typeface. [f. RUNE[1] + -IC]

runic[2] (ro͞o′nĭk), *adj.* of the ancient Scandinavian class or type, as literature, poetry, etc. [f. RUNE[2] + -IC]
run-in (rŭn′ĭn′), *n.* **1.** *Colloq.* disagreement; argument; quarrel. **2.** *Print.* matter that is added to a text, esp. without indenting or making a new paragraph. **3.** the approach to a target by an aeroplane. **4.** the final stretch of a race.
run-in groove, a groove preceding the soundtrack on a gramophone record on which the pick-up is placed.
Runjeet Singh (rŭn′jĭt sĭng′), Ranjit Singh.
runlet[1] (rŭn′lĭt), *n.* a runnel. [f. RUN, n., + -LET]
runlet[2] (rŭn′lĭt), *n.* *Archaic.* rundlet.
runnel (rŭn′əl), *n.* **1.** a small stream or brook, or a rivulet. **2.** a small channel, as for water. [OE *rynel(e)*, var. of *rinelle* dim. of RUN, n.]
runner (rŭn′ə), *n.* **1.** one who or that which runs. **2.** a competitor in a race. **3.** a messenger. **4.** a messenger of a bank, broker, etc. **5.** one acting as collector, agent, or the like for a bank, broker, etc. **6.** one whose business it is to solicit patronage or trade. **7.** something in or on which something else runs or moves, as the strips of wood that guide a drawer, the rails supporting the sliding seat of a rowing boat, etc. **8.** either of the long pieces of wood or metal on which a sledge or the like slides. **9.** the blade of a skate. **10.** a sharp curved blade used to open a furrow for placing seed. **11.** the rotating system of blades driven by the fluid passing through a reaction turbine. **12.** a roller on which something moves along. **13.** an operator or manager, as of a machine. **14.** a long, narrow rug, suitable for a hall or staircase. **15.** a long, narrow strip of linen, embroidery, lace, or the like, for placing across a table. **16.** *Bot.* **a.** a slender, prostrate stem which throws out roots at its nodes or end, thus producing new plants. **b.** a plant that spreads by such stems. **17.** *Foundry.* gate[2] (def. 14). **18.** *Dial.* a smuggler. **19.** a smuggling vessel. **20.** a Bow-Street runner. **21.** a runner bean.

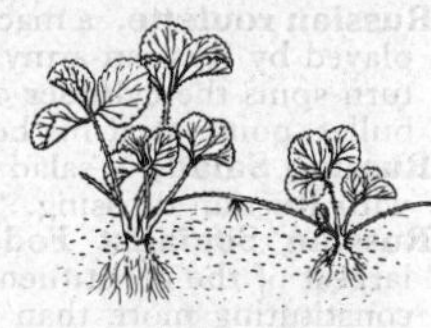
Runner of strawberry

runner bean, a climbing perennial leguminous herb, *Phaseolus multiflorus*, commonly cultivated as an annual for the long green edible pods; string bean; green bean. Also, **scarlet runner.**
runner-up (rŭn′ər ŭp′), *n.* the competitor, player, or team finishing in second place.
running (rŭn′ĭng), *n.* **1.** the act of one who or that which runs. **2.** competition, as in a race: *to be out of the running.* **3.** smuggling: *rum-running.* **4.** managing or directing: *the running of a business.* **5. in the running,** having a chance of success. **6. make the running,** to set the pace, as of a competition. —*adj.* **7.** that runs; moving or passing rapidly. **8.** (of a horse) **a.** going or proceeding rapidly at the gait of a run. **b.** taught to proceed at a run. **9.** creeping or climbing, as plants. **10.** moving or proceeding easily or smoothly. **11.** moving when pulled or hauled, as a rope. **12.** slipping or sliding easily, as a knot or a noose. **13.** operating, as a machine. **14.** (of measurement) linear; straight-line. **15.** cursive, as handwriting. **16.** flowing, as a stream. **17.** liquid or fluid. **18.** current: *the running month.* **19.** prevalent, as a condition, etc. **20.** going or carried on continuously; sustained: *a running commentary.* **21.** extending or repeated continuously, as a pattern. **22.** following in succession (placed after the noun): *for three nights running.* **23.** performed with, by means of, or during a run: *a running jump.* **24.** discharging matter, esp. fluid, as a sore. **25. running battle,** a battle between pursuer and pursued. **26. running fire, a.** sustained discharge of firearms. **b.** anything resembling this.
running board, (esp. formerly) a small ledge, step, or footboard, beneath the doors of a car, to assist passengers entering or leaving.
running gear, the frame, wheels, axles, and power developing and transmitting components of a motor or other self-propelled vehicle, and their attachments and accessories, as distinguished from the body.
running head, *Print.* a descriptive heading repeated at the top of (usually) each page. Also, **running title.**
running knot, a knot made round and so as to slide along a part of the same rope, thus forming a noose (**running noose**) which tightens as the rope is pulled.
running mate, 1. a horse used to establish the pace for another horse in a race. **2.** *U.S.* a candidate for an office linked with another and more important office, as the vice-presidency.
running rigging, *Naut.* the working ropes of a sailing ship used for hauling round the yards and setting or making fast the sails.
running shed, a building for railway engines built over a turntable.
runny (rŭn′ĭ), *adj.* **1.** (of matter) fluid or tending to flow. **2.** tending to flow with or discharge liquid: *a runny nose.*
Runnymede (rŭn′ĭ mēd′), *n.* a meadow on the S bank of the river Thames, W of London in Surrey: the supposed place of the signing of the Magna Carta by King John, 1215.
run-off (rŭn′ŏf′), *n.* **1.** a deciding final contest held after a principal one. **2.** a deciding race held after a dead heat. **3.** *U.S.* something which runs off, as rain which flows off from the land in streams.
run-of-the-mill (rŭn′əv thə mĭl′), *adj.* ordinary; mediocre; commonplace.
run-on (rŭn′ŏn′), *Print.* —*adj.* **1.** designating text which is run on without indentation: *a run-on entry in a dictionary.* —*n.* **2.** text matter which is run on without indentation.
runround (rŭn′round′), *n.* an arrangement of type using a temporarily narrower column around an illustration, etc.
runt (rŭnt), *n.* **1.** an undersized, stunted animal, person, or thing, esp. one that is small as compared with others of its kind. **2.** the smallest in a litter, as of pigs. **3.** a term of opprobrium for a person. [OE **hrunta* (in *Hrunting* name of sword in Beowulf), der. *hrung* RUNG[2]]
run-through (rŭn′thro͞o′), *n.* the performing of a sequence of designated actions, esp. as a trial prior to their official performance; rehearsal.
runty (rŭn′tĭ), *adj.*, **runtier, runtiest.** stunted; dwarfish. —**runt′iness,** *n.*
runway (rŭn′wā′), *n.* **1.** a way along which something runs. **2.** a paved or cleared strip on which aeroplanes land and take off; airstrip. **3.** a private roadway, esp. one having a sloped surface giving access to a garage. **4.** the beaten track of deer or other animals. **5.** a run (def. 111). **6.** *U.S.* the bed of a stream. **7.** *Bowling.* a path over which the bowls are sent back to the bowlers.
Runyon (rŭn′yən), *n.* **(Alfred) Damon** (dā′mən), 1880–1946, U.S. writer and journalist.
rupee (ro͞o pē′), *n.* **1.** the monetary unit of India, equal to 100 paise, and equivalent to about £0·055 sterling. **2.** any of various similar units, the currencies of Pakistan, Ceylon, Mauritius, and Muscat and Oman. **3.** a note or coin of any of these denominations. *Abbrev.:* R, Re. [t. Hind. (Urdu): m. *rupiyah*, g. Skt *rūpya* wrought silver]
Rupert (ro͞o′pət; *Ger.* ro͞o′pĕrt), *n.* **Prince,** 1619–82, German prince who aided his uncle, Charles I of England, in the English Civil War.
rupiah (ro͞o pĭə′), *n.* **1.** the monetary unit of Indonesia, equal to 100 sen, and equivalent to £0·002 sterling. **2.** a coin or banknote of this value. [t. Malay, t. Hind.: m. *rupiyah* RUPEE]
rupture (rŭp′chə), *n.*, *v.*, **-tured, -turing.** —*n.* **1.** the act of breaking or bursting. **2.** the state of being broken or burst. **3.** a breach of harmonious, friendly, or peaceful relations. **4.** *Pathol.* hernia, esp. abdominal hernia. —*v.t.* **5.** to break or burst (a blood vessel, etc.). **6.** to cause a breach of (relations, etc.). **7.** *Pathol.* to affect with hernia. —*v.i.* **8.** to suffer a break or rupture. [t. L: m. *ruptūra*] —**rup′turable,** *adj.*
rupture-wort (rŭp′chə wût′), *n.* any of several small caryophyllaceous herbs of the genus *Herniaria*, as *H. glabra*, the **glabrous rupture-wort.**
rural (ro͝oə′rəl), *adj.* **1.** of, pertaining to, or characteristic of the country (as distinguished from towns or cities), country life, or country people; rustic. **2.** living in the country. **3.** of or pertaining to agriculture: *rural economy.* [ME, t. L: s. *rūrālis*] —**ru′ralism,** *n.* —**ru′ralist,** *n.* —**ru′rally,** *adv.*

—**Syn. 1.** RURAL and RUSTIC are terms which refer to the country. RURAL is the official term: *rural education.* It may be used subjectively, and usually in a favourable sense: *the charm of rural life.* RUSTIC, however, may have either favourable or unfavourable connotations. In a derogatory sense, it means rough, boorish, or crude; in a favourable sense, it may suggest a homelike unsophistication or ruggedness: *rustic simplicity.* —**Ant. 1.** urban.

rural dean, *C. of E.* a cleric ranking below an archdeacon and in charge of a number of parishes.
rural district, an administrative subdivision of a county, usually consisting of several country parishes.
rurality (ro͝oə răl′ĭ tĭ), *n.*, *pl.* **-ties. 1.** rural character. **2.** a rural characteristic, matter, or scene.
ruralize (ro͝oə′rə līz′), *v.*, **-lized, -lizing.** —*v.t.* **1.** to make rural. —*v.i.* **2.** to become rural; rusticate. Also, **ruralise.** —**ru′raliza′tion,** *n.*
ruridecanal (ro͝oə′rĭ dĭ kā′nəl), *adj.* of or pertaining to a rural dean or his office.
Rurik (ro͝oə′rĭk), *n.* died A.D. 879, Scandinavian prince: founder of the Russian monarchy.
ruse (ro͞oz), *n.* a trick, stratagem, or artifice. [ME, n. use of obs. **ruse** to detour, t. F: m. *ruser*. See RUSH[1]]
Ruse (*Bulg.* ro͞o′sĕ), *n.* a town in NE Bulgaria, on the Danube. 126,792 (1964). Also, **Russe.** Formerly, **Rustchuk.**

rush[1] (rŭsh), *v.i.* **1.** to move or go with speed, impetuosity, or violence. **2.** to dash; dash forward for an attack or onslaught. **3.** to go or plunge with headlong or rash haste. **4.** to go, come, pass, etc., rapidly: *tears rushed to her eyes.* —*v.t.* **5.** to send or drive with speed or violence. **6.** to carry or convey with haste: *to rush an injured person to the hospital.* **7.** to perform, complete, or organize (some process or activity) with special haste. **8.** to send, push, force, etc., with unusual speed or undue haste: *to rush a bill through Parliament.* **9.** to attack with a rush. **10.** to overcome or take (a person, force, place, etc.). **11.** *U.S. Slang.* to heap attentions on. **12.** *Rugby Football.* (of a pack of forwards, etc.) to move (the ball) rapidly forwards by short kicks.
—*n.* **13.** the act of rushing; a rapid, impetuous, or headlong onward movement. **14.** a hostile attack. **15. a.** a sudden concerted movement, as in a particular direction. **b.** an eager rushing of numbers of persons to some region to be occupied or exploited, esp. to a new goldfield. **16.** a sudden coming or access: *a rush of blood to his face.* **17.** hurried activity; busy haste: *the rush of city life.* **18.** a hurried state, as from pressure of affairs: *to be in a rush.* **19.** press of work, business, traffic, etc., requiring extraordinary effort or haste. **20.** a period of intense activity: *the Christmas rush.* **21.** a great demand for a commodity, etc. (fol. by *on*): *there was a rush on gold.* **22.** *Rugby Football.* the act by a pack of forwards, etc., of moving the ball rapidly forward by short kicks. **23.** (*pl.*) *Films.* the first prints made after shooting a scene or scenes.
—*adj.* **24.** requiring or performed with haste: *a rush order.* **25.** characterized by rush or press of work, traffic, etc. [ME *rusche(n)*, t. AF: m. *russher, russer*, var. of OF *re(h)usser, re(h)user, ruser*, g. LL *recūsāre* push back, L refuse] —**rush′er,** *n.*
—**Syn. 1.** RUSH, HURRY, DASH, SPEED imply swiftness of movement. RUSH implies haste and sometimes violence in motion through some distance: *to rush to the airport.* HURRY suggests a sense of strain or agitation, a breathless rushing to get to a definite place by a certain time: *to hurry to an appointment.* DASH implies impetuosity or spirited, swift movement for a short distance: *to dash to the shops before they shut.* SPEED means to go fast, usually by means of some type of transportation, and with some smoothness of motion: *to speed along in a limousine.*

rush[2] (rŭsh), *n.* **1.** any plant of the genus *Juncus* (family *Juncaceae*), which comprises grasslike herbs with pithy or hollow stems, found in wet or marshy places. **2.** any plant of the same family. **3.** any of various similar plants. **4.** a stem of such a plant, used for making chair bottoms, mats, baskets, etc. **5.** a former type of floor covering, consisting of such plants scattered on the floor. **6.** something of little or no value: *not worth a rush.* [ME *russhe*, OE *rysc(e)*, c. D *rusch* and G *Rusch*] —**rush′like′,** *adj.*

rush candle, a candle made by dipping a dried and peeled pithy-stemmed rush in tallow. Also, **rush light.**

Rushden (rŭsh′dən), *n.* a town in England, in Northamptonshire. 17,370 (1961).

rush hour, one of the regular periods of particularly heavy traffic in a city, when many people travel between their homes and places of work.

rush line, *American Football.* the forward line of players.

rushy (rŭsh′ĭ), *adj.*, **rushier, rushiest. 1.** abounding with rushes. **2.** covered or strewn with rushes. **3.** consisting or made of rushes. **4.** rushlike.

rus in urbe (rŏŏs′ĭn û′bā), *Latin.* the country in the city.

rusk (rŭsk), *n.* **1.** a type of sweetened tea biscuit. **2.** a piece of bread or cake crisped in the oven. **3.** a similar commercially made product, given esp. to babies when teething, and invalids. [t. Sp. or Pg.: m. *rosca* twist of bread, lit., screw]

Rusk (rŭsk), *n.* **(David) Dean,** born 1909, U.S. statesman: secretary of state 1961–69.

Ruskin (rŭs′kĭn), *n.* **John,** 1819–1900, English author, art critic, and social reformer.

Russ (rŭs), *n.*, *pl.* **Russ,** *adj.* —*n.* **1.** a Russian. —*adj.* **2.** Russian. [t. Russ.: m. *Rusi*]

Russ., 1. Russia. **2.** Russian.

Russell (rŭs′əl), *n.* **1. Bertrand, 3rd Earl,** 1872–1970, English philosopher, mathematician, pacifist, and writer. **2. George William** (*A.E.*), 1867–1935, Irish poet and painter. **3. John Russell, 1st Earl** (*Lord John Russell*), 1792–1878, British statesman; prime minister 1846–52 and 1865–66.

Rüsselsheim (*Ger.* rʏ′səls hīm), *n.* a town in West Germany, in S Hesse. 51,800 (est. 1961).

russet (rŭs′ĭt), *n.* **1.** reddish brown; light brown; yellowish brown. **2.** a coarse reddish brown or brownish homespun cloth formerly in use. **3.** a winter apple with a rough brownish skin. —*adj.* **4.** reddish brown; light brown; yellowish brown. [ME, t. OF: m. *rousset*, dim. of *rous* red, g. L *russus*]

Russia (rŭsh′ə), *n.* **1.** Also, **Russian Empire.** a former empire in E Europe and N and W Asia: overthrown by the Russian Revolution, 1917. *Cap.:* St Petersburg (Leningrad). **2.** the Soviet Union. **3.** the Russian Socialist Federated Soviet Republic.

Russia leather, a fine, smooth leather produced by careful tanning and dyeing, esp. in dark red: orig. prepared in Russia, but imitated elsewhere. Also, **russia.**

Russian (rŭsh′ən), *adj.* **1.** of or pertaining to Russia, its people, or their language. —*n.* **2.** a native or inhabitant of Russia. **3.** a member of the dominant, Slavic race of Russia. **4.** the principal Slavic language, belonging to the East Slavic subgroup, and the predominant language of the Soviet Union. See **Great Russian, Little Russian, White Russian.**

Russian Church, the national Church of Russia (before 1918), a branch of the Orthodox Eastern Church.

Russian dressing, a sharp mayonnaise dressing prepared by the addition of chopped pickles, chili sauce, pimientos, etc.

Russian Empire, Russia (def. 1).

Russianize (rŭsh′ə nīz′), *v.t.*, **-nized, -nizing.** to make Russian; impart Russian characteristics to. Also, **Russianise.**

Russian Orthodox Church, Russian Church.

Russian Revolution, 1. the uprising of March 12th, 1917 (**February Revolution**), by which the tsar's government was abolished and replaced by a constitutional government. **2.** the overthrow of this provisional government by a coup d'état on November 7th, 1917 (**October Revolution**), establishing the Soviet Union.

Russian roulette, a macabre game of chance, as formerly played by Russian army officers, in which each player in turn spins the cylinder of a revolver containing only one bullet, points it at his head, and pulls the trigger.

Russian Salad, a salad of cold cooked vegetables made with Russian dressing.

Russian Socialist Federated Soviet Republic, the largest of the constituent republics of the Soviet Union, constituting more than three-quarters of the total area. 123,400,000 pop. (est. 1963); ab. 6,569,000 sq. mi. *Cap.:* Moscow. *Abbrev.:* RSFSR.

Russian wolfhound, the borzoi.

Russian Zone, that part of Germany administered by the Soviet Union from 1945; reconstituted as the German Democratic Republic in 1949. Cf. **East Germany.**

Russo-, a word element representing Russia, as in *Russophobe, Russophil.*

Russophil (rŭs′ō fĭl), *n.* one who admires or favours Russia or anything Russian. Also, **Russophile** (rŭs′ō fīl′).

Russophobe (rŭs′ō fōb′), *n.* one who fears or hates anything Russian. —**Russophobia** (rŭs′ō fō′byə), *n.*

rust (rŭst), *n.* **1.** the red or orange coating which forms on the surface of iron when exposed to air and moisture, consisting chiefly of ferric hydroxide and ferric oxide. **2.** any film or coating on metal due to oxidation, etc. **3.** a stain resembling iron rust. **4.** any growth, habit, influence, or agency tending to injure the mind, character, abilities, usefulness, etc. **5.** *Bot.* **a.** any of the various plant diseases caused by fungi, esp. members of the *Uredinales*, in which the leaves and stems become spotted and acquire a red to brown colour. **b.** Also, **rust fungus.** a fungus producing such a disease. **6.** rust colour; reddish brown or orange. —*v.i.* **7.** to grow rusty, as iron does; corrode. **8.** to contract rust. **9.** to deteriorate or become impaired, as through inaction or disuse. **10.** to become rust-coloured. —*v.t.* **11.** to affect with rust. **12.** to impair as if with rust. **13.** to make rust-coloured. [ME and OE, c. G *Rost*] —**rust′-able,** *adj.*

Rustchuk (*Bulg.* rŏŏs′chŏŏk), *n.* former name of **Ruse.**

rustic (rŭs′tĭk), *adj.* **1.** of, pertaining to, or living in the country as distinguished from towns or cities; rural. **2.** simple, artless, or unsophisticated. **3.** uncouth, rude, or boorish. **4.** made of roughly dressed limbs or roots of trees, as garden seats, etc. **5.** *Masonry.* having the surface rough or irregular, or the joints deeply sunk or chamfered. —*n.* **6.** a country person. **7.** an unsophisticated country person. [late ME, t. L: s. *rusticus*] —**rus′tically,** *adv.*
—**Syn. 1.** See **rural.**

rusticate (rŭs′tĭ kāt′), *v.*, **-cated, -cating.** —*v.i.* **1.** to go to the country. **2.** to stay or sojourn in the country. —*v.t.* **3.** to send to or domicile in the country. **4.** to make rustic, as persons, manners, etc. **5.** to construct or finish (masonry, etc.) in the rustic manner. **6.** to suspend (a student) from a university as punishment. [t. L: m. s. *rusticātus*, pp., having lived in the country] —**rus′tica′-tion,** *n.* —**rus′tica′tor,** *n.*

rusticity (rŭs tĭs′ĭ tĭ), *n.*, *pl.* **-ties. 1.** the state or quality of being rustic. **2.** rural character or life.

rustle (rŭs′əl), *v.*, **-tled, -tling,** *n.* —*v.i.* **1.** to make a succession of slight, soft sounds, as of parts rubbing gently one on another, as leaves, silks, papers, etc. 2. to cause such sounds by moving or stirring something. 3. *U.S. Slang.* to move, proceed, or work energetically or vigorously. —*v.t.* 4. to move or stir so as to cause a rustling sound. 5. *Western U.S.* to steal (cattle, etc.). 6. *Slang.* to move, bring, get, etc., by energetic action (often fol. by *up*). —*n.* 7. the sound made by anything that rustles. [ME; OE *hrūxlian* make a noise] —**rus′tlingly,** *adv.*

rustler (rŭs′lə), *n.* 1. one who or that which rustles. 2. *Western U.S.* a cattle thief. 3. *U.S. Slang.* an active, energetic person.

rustless (rŭst′lĭs), *adj.* 1. free from rust. 2. rustproof.

rustproof (rŭst′pro͞of′), *adj.* protected from rust; rustless.

rusty[1] (rŭs′tĭ), *adj.*, **-tier, -tiest.** 1. covered or affected with rust. 2. consisting of or produced by rust. 3. of the colour of rust; rust-coloured; tending towards rust. 4. faded or shabby; impaired by time or wear, as clothes, etc. 5. impaired through disuse or neglect: *my Latin is rusty.* 6. having lost agility or alertness; out of practice. 7. (of plants) affected with the rust disease. [ME; OE *rustig*, c. G *rostig*] —**rust′ily,** *adv.* —**rust′iness,** *n.*

rusty[2] (rŭs′tĭ), *adj. Dial.* 1. restive; refractory. 2. ill-tempered; cross. [appar. special use of RUSTY[1] in sense of rough, churlish; but cf. obs. E *resty* RESTIVE]

rut[1] (rŭt), *n., v.,* **rutted, rutting.** —*n.* 1. a furrow or track in the ground, esp. one made by the passage of a vehicle or vehicles. 2. any furrow, groove, etc. 3. a fixed or established way of life: *to get into a rut.* —*v.t.* 4. to make a rut or ruts in; furrow. [orig. uncert.; ? var. of ROUTE]

rut[2] (rŭt), *n., v.,* **rutted, rutting.** —*n.* 1. the periodically recurring sexual excitement of the deer, goat, sheep, etc. —*v.i.* 2. to be in the condition of rut. [ME *rutte*, t. OF: m. *rut*, var. of *ruit*, g. L *rugītus* a roaring]

rutabaga (ro͞o′tə bā′gə, -bĕg′ə), *n. U.S.* the Swedish or yellow turnip, *Brassica napobrassica.* [t. d. Sw.: m. *rotabagge*]

rutaceous (ro͞o tā′shəs), *adj.* 1. of or like rue[2]. 2. belonging to the *Rutaceae*, a family of plants including the rue, dittany, angostura bark tree, orange, lemon, shaddock, kumquat, etc., having pellucid dotted leaves. [t. L: m. *rūtāceus*]

Rutgers University (rŭt′gəz), a men's university in the U.S., at New Brunswick, New Jersey, founded in 1766.

ruth (ro͞oth), *n. Archaic.* 1. pity or compassion. 2. sorrow or grief. [ME *r(e)uthe*, der. *rewe* RUE[1], or *rewe*, n., pity, OE *hrēow*]

Ruth (ro͞oth), *n. Bible.* 1. a Moabite woman who married Boaz in Bethlehem and was an ancestress of David. 2. a book of the Old Testament. [LL, t. Heb.]

Ruthenia (ro͞o thē′nyə), *n.* a former province in E Czechoslovakia. See **Carpatho-Ukraine.**

Ruthenian (ro͞o thē′nyən), *adj.* 1. of or pertaining to the Little Russians, esp. a division of them dwelling in Galicia, Ruthenia, and neighbouring regions. —*n.* 2. one of the Ruthenian people. 3. a Slavic language spoken in Ruthenia, related to Ukrainian.

ruthenic (ro͞o thĕn′ĭk), *adj. Chem.* containing ruthenium in a higher valency state than the corresponding ruthenious compound.

ruthenious (ro͞o thē′nyəs), *adj. Chem.* containing divalent ruthenium.

ruthenium (ro͞o thē′nyəm), *n. Chem.* a steel-grey, rare metallic element, difficult to fuse, belonging to the platinum group of metals, and very little acted on by aqua regia. *Symbol:* Ru; *at. wt:* 101·07; *at. no.:* 44; *sp. gr.:* 12·2 at 20°C. [NL, f. s. ML *Ruthenia* Russia (so named because it was first found in ores from the Ural Mountains) + *-ium* -IUM]

Rutherford (rŭth′ə fəd), *n.* **Ernest Rutherford, 1st Baron,** 1871–1937, British physicist, born in New Zealand.

Rutherglen (rŭth′ə glĕn′), *n.* a burgh in S Scotland, in Lanarkshire. 25,067 (1961).

ruthful (ro͞oth′fəl), *adj. Archaic.* 1. compassionate or sorrowful. 2. such as to excite sorrow or pity. —**ruth′fully,** *adv.* —**ruth′fulness,** *n.*

ruthless (ro͞oth′lĭs), *adj.* without pity or compassion; pitiless; merciless. —**ruth′lessly,** *adv.* —**ruth′lessness,** *n.* —**Syn.** See **cruel.**

rutilant (ro͞o′tĭ lənt), *adj. Rare.* glowing, shining, or glittering with a red or gold light. [t. L: s. *rutilans*, ppr.]

rutile (ro͞o′tĭl, -tīl), *n.* a common mineral, titanium dioxide, TiO_2, having a brilliant metallic-adamantine lustre and usually of a reddish brown colour. It occurs usually in crystals and is used to coat welding rods. [t. F, t. G: m. *Rutil*, t. L: s. *rutilus* red]

Rutland (rŭt′lənd), *n.* a county in central England. 23,956 pop. (est. 1961); 152 sq. mi. *Co. town:* Oakham. Also, **Rut′landshire′.**

ruttish (rŭt′ĭsh), *adj. Obs.* lustful. [f. RUT[2] + -ISH[1]]

rutty (rŭt′ĭ), *adj.*, **-tier, -tiest.** full of or abounding in ruts, as a road. —**rut′tiness,** *n.*

Ruwenzori (ro͞o′wĕn zô′rĭ), *n.* a mountain group in central Africa between Lake Albert and Lake Edward: sometimes identified with Ptolemy's 'Mountains of the Moon'. Highest peak, Mt Stanley, 16,790 ft.

Ruysdael (rīz′däl; *Du.* rœys′dál), *n.* **Jacob van.** See **Ruisdael.**

Ruyter (rī′tə; *Du.* rœy′tər), *n.* **Michel Adriaanszoon de** (*Du.* mē′KHəl á′drē án sôn də), 1607–76, Dutch admiral.

RV, Revised Version (of the Bible).

R.W., 1. Right Worshipful. 2. Right Worthy.

Rwanda (ro͞o ăn′də), *n.* a republic in central Africa, E of the Republic of the Congo: formerly comprising the northern part of the Belgian trust territory of Ruanda-Urundi. 2,634,451 pop. (1962); 10,169 sq. mi. *Cap.:* Kigali.

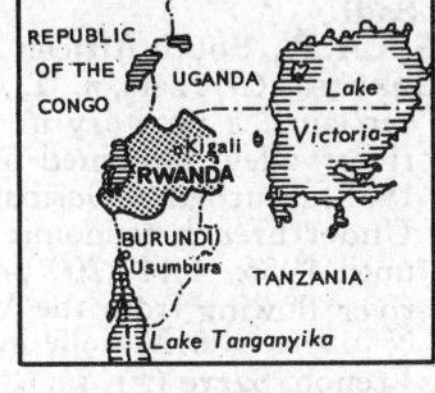

Rwanda

Ry, Railway.

-ry, a suffix of abstract nouns of condition, practice (*heraldry, husbandry, dentistry*), and of collectives (*peasantry, Jewry*). [short form of -ERY]

Ryazan (*Russ.* ryȧ zȧny′), *n.* a town in the central Soviet Union in Europe, on the river Oka. 287,000 (est. 1965).

Rybinsk (*Russ.* rĭ′bĭnsk), *n.* former name of **Shcherbakov.**

Ryde (rīd), *n.* a seaside resort in England, on the Isle of Wight. 19,845 (1961).

rye[1] (rī), *n.* 1. a widely cultivated cereal grass, *Secale cereale*, with one-nerved glumes (differing from wheat which is many-nerved) and two- or three-flowered spikelets. 2. the seeds or grain of this plant, used for making wholemeal flour, for livestock feed, and for a type of whisky in the U.S. 3. an American whisky distilled from a mash containing 51 per cent or more rye grain. 4. *Eastern U.S.* a blended whisky. [ME; OE *ryge*, c. Icel. *rugr*, akin to D *rogge*, G *Roggen*]

rye[2] (rĭ), *n.* a gentleman: *Romany rye.* [t. Gipsy]

rye-bread (rī′brĕd′), *n.* bread made from rye flour.

rye-brome (rī′brōm′), *n.* a weedy grass, *Bromus secalinus.*

rye-grass (rī′gräs′), *n.* a variable perennial grass, *Lolium perenne*, common in waste places throughout north temperate regions and widely grown for fodder.

Ryojunko (rĭ ō′jo͞on kō′), *n.* Japanese name of **Luta.** Also, **Ryojun** (rĭ ō′jo͞on′).

ryot (rī′ət), *n.* (in India) 1. a peasant. 2. one who holds land as a cultivator of the soil. [t. Urdu: m. *raiyat*]

ryotwari (rī′ət wə rĭ), *n.* one of the principal systems of land tenure in India, in which land is held directly from the state by individual peasant proprietors. See **mahalwari, zemindari.** [t. Urdu]

Ryswick (rĭz′wĭk), *n.* a village in SW Netherlands, near The Hague: Treaty of Ryswick, 1697. Dutch, **Rijswijk.**

Ryukyu (rĭ o͞o′kyo͞o′), *n.* a chain of 55 islands in the W Pacific between Japan and Taiwan. Islands S of 28° N lat. under U.S. administration: islands N of 28° returned to Japan. 908,000 pop. (1963); 2046 sq. mi.

S, s (ĕs), *n., pl.* **S's** or **Ss, s's** or **ss.** 1. a consonant, the 19th letter of the English alphabet. 2. something resembling the letter S in shape.

-s[1], a suffix serving to form adverbs, as *always, evenings, needs, unawares.* Cf. **-ways.** [ME and OE *-es*, orig. gen. sing. ending]

-s[2], an ending which marks the third person sing. indicative active of verbs, as in *hits.* [northern ME and OE *-(e)s* (orig. ending of second person, as in L and Gk); r. ME and OE *-(e)th*]

-s[3], 1. an ending which marks the regular plural of nouns, as in *dogs.* 2. a quasi-plural ending occurring in nouns for which there is no proper singular, as *trousers, shorts, scissors.* [ME *-es*, OE *-as*, nom. and acc. pl. of certain classes of strong nouns]

's[1], an ending which marks the possessive sing. of nouns, as in *man's.* [ME and OE *-es*]

's[2], an ending which marks the possessive plur. of nouns, as in *men's.* [pl. use of poss. sing. ending]

's[3], colloquial reduction of: **1.** is: *he's here.* **2.** has: *he's just gone.* **3.** does: *what's he do now?* **4.** us: *let's go.*

S, 1. Saxon. **2.** South. **3.** Southern. **4.** *Chem.* sulphur. **5.** *Physics.* entropy.

S., 1. Sabbath. **2.** Saint. **3.** Saturday. **4.** School. **5.** Sea. **6.** Senate. **7.** September. **8.** *Pharm.* (L *signa*) mark; label. **9.** (*It.*) Signor. **10.** (L *Socius*) Fellow. **11.** South. **12.** Southern. **13.** Sunday.

s., 1. second. **2.** section. **3.** (L *solidus*) shilling; (L *solidi*) shillings. **4.** singular. **5.** son. **6.** south. **7.** southern. **8.** stem. **9.** stem of. **10.** substantive.

Sa, *Chem. Obs.* samarium.

SA, Sturmabteilung.

S.A., 1. Salvation Army. **2.** South Africa. **3.** South America. **4.** South Australia.

s.a., 1. semi-annual. **2.** (L *sine anno*) without year or date. **3.** subject to approval. **4.** sex appeal.

Saadi (sä dē'), *n. c.* 1184–1291?, Persian poet. Also, **Sadi.**

S.A.A.F., South African Air Force.

Saar (sä; *Ger.* zär), *n.* **1.** Also, **Saar Basin; Saarland** (*Ger.* zär'lȧnt). a territory in W West Germany, in the Saar river valley: governed by the League of Nations, 1919–1935; returned to Germany 1935 as a result of a plebiscite. Under French economic control following World War II until 1956. 1,117,200 pop. (est. 1964); 991 sq. mi. **2.** a river flowing from the Vosges mountains in NE France N to the river Moselle in W West Germany. ab. 150 mi. French, **Sarre** (*Fr.* sȧr).

Saarbrücken (sä'brŏŏk'ən; *Ger.* zär brʏk'ən), *n.* a city in West Germany: the chief city of the Saar, in the S part. 134,500 (est. 1966).

Saaremaa (sä'rĭ mä'), *n.* an island in the Baltic at the mouth of the Gulf of Riga, forming part of the Estonian Republic of the Soviet Union. ab. 60,000 pop.; 1144 sq. mi. Also, **Saare** (sä'rĭ), German, **Ösel.**

Saarinen (*Finn.* sä'rē nĕn), *n.* **1. Eero** (*Finn.* ē'rô), 1910–1960, Finnish architect. **2.** his father, **Eliel** (*Finn.* ĕl'ē ĕl), 1873–1950, Finnish architect.

Sab., Sabbath.

Saba (săb'ə), *n.* **1.** an island in the Netherlands Antilles. 1022 pop. (1963); 5 sq. mi. **2.** Sheba.

Sabadell (*Sp.* sȧ bȧ dĕl'), *n.* a town in NE Spain. 128,412 (1965).

sabadilla (săb'ə dĭl'ə), *n.* **1.** a liliaceous plant of Mexico, *Schoenocaulon officinale*, with long grasslike leaves and bitter seeds. **2.** the seeds, which are used medicinally and as a source of veratrine and veratridine. [t. Sp.: m. *cebadilla*, dim. of *cebada* barley]

Sabah (sä'bä), *n.* an independent state of Malaysia in NE Borneo. 506,628 pop. (est. 1964); 29,388 sq. mi. *Cap.*: Jesselton. Formerly, **British North Borneo, North Borneo.**

Sabaoth (sȧ bā'ŏth), *n.pl. Bible, etc.* armies; hosts. [t. L t. Gk, t. Heb.: m. *ç'bhāōth* pl. of *çābhā* army]

Sabatini (săb'ə tē'nĭ; *It.* sȧ bȧ tē'nē), *n.* **Rafael** (răf'ĭ əl), 1875–1950, English writer born in Italy.

sabayon (săb'ī yŏn'; *Fr.* sȧ bȧ yôɴ'), *n.* **1.** a sweet sauce served with a rich sponge or fruit pudding. **2.** French name for **zabaglione.**

sabbat (săb'ăt, săb'ət), *n.* Sabbath (def. 3).

Sabbatarian (săb'ə tĕə'rĭ ən), *n.* **1.** one who observes the seventh day of the week (Saturday) as the Sabbath. **2.** one who adheres to or favours a strict observance of Sunday. [f. obs. *Sabbatary* (t. L: m. s. *sabbatārius* pertaining to the Sabbath) + -AN] **—Sab'batar'ianism,** *n.*

Sabbath (săb'əth), *n.* **1.** the seventh day of the week (Saturday) as the day of rest and religious observance among the Jews and certain Christian sects. See Ex. 20:8–11. **2.** the first day of the week (Sunday), similarly observed by most Christians in commemoration of the resurrection of Christ. **3.** (*l.c.*) Also, **sabbat.** a secret nocturnal meeting of witches. [ME *sabath*, var. of ME and OE *sabat*, t. L: m. s. *sabbatum*, t. Gk: m. *sábbaton*, t. Heb.: m. *shabbāth*] **—Syn. 2.** See **Sunday.**

Sabbath school, 1. a Sunday school. **2.** (among Seventh-Day Adventists) such a school held on Saturday, their holy day.

sabbatic (sə băt'ĭk), *adj.*, *n.* sabbatical. [t. Gk: m. s. *sabbatikós*]

sabbatical (sə băt'ĭ kl), *adj.* **1.** of, pertaining to, or appropriate to the Sabbath. **2.** bringing a period of rest: *sabbatical leave.* **3.** of, denoting, or pertaining to a sabbatical. *—n.* **4.** (in certain universities, etc.) a year, term, or other period, of freedom from teaching granted to a teacher, as for study or travel. [f. SABBATIC + -AL[1]] **—sabbat'ically,** *adv.*

sabbatical year, (among ancient Jews) every seventh year, during which fields were to be left untilled, debtors were to be released, etc.

Sabean (sə bē'ən), *adj.* **1.** of or pertaining to Saba (biblical Sheba). *—n.* **2.** an inhabitant of Saba. Also, **Sabaean.** [f. m. s. L *Sabaeus* (t. Gk: m. *Sabaîos*, der. *Sába*, t. Ar., c. Heb. *Sh'bha*) + -AN]

Sabellian (sə bĕl'ĭ ən), *n.* **1.** one who maintains Sabellianism. *—adj.* **2.** of or pertaining to Sabellianism.

Sabellianism (sə bĕl'ĭ ə nĭz'əm), *n. Theol.* the teaching that the Father, the Son, and the Holy Spirit are not distinct persons within the Godhead (the orthodox doctrine), but only different manifestations under which God has at different times revealed Himself. [named after *Sabellius*, 3rd-century North African theologian]

saber (sā'bə), *n.*, *v.t.*, *U.S.* sabre.

sabin (săb'ĭn, sā'bĭn), *n. Physics.* a unit of acoustic absorption, equal to one square foot of perfectly absorptive surface. [named after W. C. *Sabine*, 1868–1919, U.S. physicist]

Sabine (săb'īn), *adj.* **1.** belonging or pertaining to an ancient people of central Italy who lived chiefly in the Apennines to the north-east of Rome and who were subjugated by the Romans about 290 B.C. *—n.* **2.** one of the Sabine people.

sable (sā'bl), *n.* **1.** a weasel-like mammal, *Mustela zibellina*, of cold regions, valued for its dark brown fur. **2.** a marten, esp. *Mustela americana*. **3.** the fur of the sable. **4.** some similar fur, used as a substitute. **5.** the colour black, often one of the heraldic colours. **6.** (*pl.*) mourning garments. *—adj.* **7.** made of the fur or hair of the sable. **8.** *Poetic.* black; very dark. [ME, t. OF, ult. t. Slavic; cf. Russ. *sobol*]

Sable, *Mustela zibellina* (Total length 28 in., tail 9½ in.)

sable antelope, a large antelope, *Hippotragus niger*, of Africa, with long, sabre-like horns.

sabot (săb'ō; *Fr.* sȧ bō'), *n.* **1.** a wooden shoe made of a single piece of wood hollowed out, worn by peasants in France, Belgium, etc. **2.** a shoe with a thick wooden sole and sides, and top of coarse leather. **3.** *Mil.* a soft metal shoe fitted to the base of a shell before firing in order to increase its muzzle velocity. [t. F, in OF *çabot*, der. *savate* old shoe (ult. t. Ar.: m. *sabbât* sandal), b. with *botte* boot]

sabotage (săb'ə täzh'; *Fr.* sȧ bō tȧzh'), *n.*, *v.*, **-taged, -taging.** *—n.* **1.** malicious injury to work, tools, machinery, etc., or any underhand interference with production or business, by enemy agents during wartime, by employees during a trade dispute, etc. **2.** any malicious attack on or undermining of a cause. *—v.t.* **3.** to injure or attack by sabotage. [t. F, der. *saboter* make a noise with sabots, do work badly, der. *sabot* SABOT]

saboteur (săb'ə tû'; *Fr.* sȧ bō tœr'), *n.* one who commits or practises sabotage. [t. F]

sabre (sā'bə), *n.*, *v.* **-bred, -bring.** *—n.* **1.** a heavy one-edged sword, usually slightly curved, used esp. by cavalry. **2.** a soldier armed with such a sword. **3.** a light sword for fencing and duelling, with a tapering flexible blade and a semicircular guard. *—v.t.* **4.** to strike, wound, or kill with a sabre. Also, *U.S.*, **saber.** [t. F: m. *sabre, sable*, t. G: m. *Sabel* (now *Säbel*), t. Hung.: m. *szablya*] **—sa'bre-like',** *adj.*

sabretache (săb'ə tăsh'), *n.* a case, as of leather, suspended by long straps from the sword-belt of a cavalryman and hanging beside the sabre. [t. F, t. G: m. *Säbeltasche* sabre pocket]

sabre-toothed (sā'bə tōōtht'), *adj.* having sabre-like teeth, as some extinct feline mammals whose long upper canine teeth sometimes extended below the margin of the lower jaw.

sabre-toothed tiger, any of a subfamily, *Machaero-dontinae*, of fossil felines characterized by greatly elongated, sabre-like upper canine teeth, found widely distributed in the Oligocene and into the Pleistocene.

Sabre-toothed tiger, *Smilodon californicus* (6 ft long)

sabulous (săb'yōō ləs), *adj.* sandy; gritty. [t. L: m. s. *sabulōsus*] **—sabulosity** (săb'yōō lŏs'ĭ tĭ), *n.*

sac (săk), *n.* a baglike structure in an animal or plant, as

one containing fluid. [t. L: m. s. *saccus*. See SACK[1]] —**sac′like′**, *adj.*
Sac (săk, sôk), *n.* **1.** (*pl.*) a tribe of Algonquian-speaking Indians, formerly of N Wisconsin and Iowa, now in Iowa and Oklahoma. **2.** a member of this tribe. Also, **Sauk.**
S.A.C., Scottish Automobile Club.
saccate (săk′ĭt, -āt), *adj.* in the form of, or having a sac. [t. ML: m. s. *saccātus*, der. L *saccus*. See SAC]
sacchar-, a word element referring to sugar or saccharine. Also, **saccharo-.** [comb. form repr. Gk *sákchar*, *sákcharon*, etc., sugar]
saccharate (săk′ə rāt′), *n. Chem.* **1.** a salt of saccharic acid. **2.** a compound formed by interaction of sucrose with a metallic oxide, usually lime, and useful in the purification of sugar.
saccharic acid (sə kăr′ĭk), *Chem.* a white crystalline dicarboxylic acid, $COOH(CHOH)_4COOH$, made by the oxidization of glucose.
saccharify (sə kăr′ĭ fī′), *v.t.*, **-fied, -fying.** to convert (starch, etc.) into sugar. —**saccharification** (sə kă′-rĭ fĭ kā′shən), *n.*
saccharimeter (săk′ə rĭm′ĭ tə), *n.* an optical instrument for determining the strength of sugar solutions by measuring polarization of light through them. [t. F: m. *saccharimètre*. See SACCHAR-, -I-, -METER[1]]
saccharimetry (săk′ə rĭm′ĭ trĭ), *n.* the measuring of the amount of sugar in a solution, as with a saccharimeter.
saccharin (săk′ə rĭn), *n. Chem.* a crystalline compound, $C_6H_4SO_2CONH$, obtained from toluene. It is some 400 times as sweet as cane sugar and is used as a sweetening agent in cases of diabetes and obesity.
saccharine (săk′ə rīn′), *adj.* **1.** of a sugary sweetness: *a saccharine smile.* **2.** pertaining to, of the nature of, or containing sugar. —*n.* **3.** saccharin. —**saccharinity** (săk′ə rĭn′ĭ tĭ), *n.*
saccharize (săk′ə rīz′), *v.t.*, **-rized, -rizing. 1.** to convert into sugar; saccharify. **2.** to convert (the starches in grain) to fermentable sugars during mashing. Also, **saccharise.** —**sac′chariza′tion,** *n.*
saccharo-, var. of **sacchar-,** before consonants.
saccharoid (săk′ə roid′), *adj. Geol.* having a granular texture like that of loaf sugar. Also, **sac′charoi′dal.**
saccharolytic (săk′ə rə lĭt′ĭk), *adj.* **1.** *Chem.* of, or causing, the hydrolysis of sugars. **2.** (of bacteria) using simple carbohydrates and starches as a source of energy.
saccharometer (săk′ə rŏm′ĭ tə), *n. Chem.* a type of hydrometer used for determining the concentration of a sugar solution by measuring its specific gravity; usually calibrated to read the percentage of sugar direct.
saccharose (săk′ə rōs′), *n. Chem.* sucrose.
Sacco (săk′ō; *It.* säk′kō), *n.* **Nikola** (*It.* nē kō′lä), 1891–1927, Italian political radical in the U.S., executed for murder together with Bartolomeo Vanzetti after a trial which caused protests from liberals who believed political considerations had influenced the verdict.
sacculate (săk′yŏŏ lĭt, -lāt′), *adj.* formed into or with a sacculate, sac, or saclike dilatations. Also, **sac′culat′ed.** —**sac′cula′tion,** *n.*
saccule (săk′yōōl), *n.* **1.** *Anat.* the smaller of two sacs in the membranous labyrinth of the internal ear. **2.** a little sac. [t. L: m. s. *sacculus*, dim. of *saccus* SAC]
sacculus (săk′yŏŏ ləs), *n.*, *pl.* **-li** (-lī′). saccule. [t. L. See SACCULE]
sacerdotal (săs′ə dō′tl), *adj.* of priests; priestly. [t. L: s. *sacerdōtālis*] —**sac′erdo′tally,** *adv.*
sacerdotalism (săs′ə dō′tə lĭz′əm), *n.* **1.** the system, spirit, or methods of the priesthood. **2.** the belief that the priest has the power to offer sacrifice in offering the Eucharist. **3.** the belief that the priest has supernatural powers of consecration, absolution, etc., vested in him by virtue of his ordination. **4.** (derogatory) priestcraft.
sachem (sā′chəm), *n.* **1.** (among some tribes of American Indians) **a.** the chief. **b.** the chief of a confederation of Indians. **2.** a member of the governing body of the League of the Iroquois. **3.** one of the high officials in the Tammany Society. [t. Algonquian (Narragansett): chief, (Massachusetts Indians) head chief]
sachet (săsh′ā), *n.* **1.** a small sealed bag containing cream, shampoo, or the like. **2.** a small bag, case, pad, etc., containing dry perfume or the like for placing among articles of clothing. **3.** the powder. [t. F, dim. of *sac*, g. L *saccus*. See SACK[1]]
Sachs (*Ger.* zäks), *n.* **Hans** (*Ger.* häns), 1494–1576, Bavarian cobbler and Meistersinger, famous as a writer of poems and plays.
Sachsen (*Ger.* zäk′sən), *n.* German name of **Saxony** (defs 1, 2, and 3).
sack[1] (săk), *n.* **1.** a large bag of stout woven material, as for grain, potatoes, coal, etc. **2.** the amount which a sack will hold, a varying unit of measure. **3.** a woman's loose-fitting, unbelted dress. **4.** Also, **sacque.** a loose-fitting coat or jacket, esp. for women and children. **5.** *Slang.* dismissal or discharge, as from employment. —*v.t.* **6.** to put into a sack or sacks. **7.** *Slang.* to dismiss or discharge, as from employment. [ME *sak*, OE *sacc*, t. L: s. *saccus* bag, sackcloth, t. Gk: m. *sákkos*, t. Heb.: m. *saq*] —**Syn. 1.** See **bag.**
sack[2] (săk), *v.t.* **1.** to pillage or loot after capture; plunder: *to sack a city.* —*n.* **2.** the plundering of a captured place; pillage: *the sack of Troy.* [t. F: m. *sac*, t. It.: m. *sacco*, special use of *sacco* SACK[1]] —**sack′er,** *n.* —**Syn. 1.** See **rob.**
sack[3] (săk), *n.* any of various strong light-coloured wines formerly brought from Spain, the Canary Islands, etc. [t. F: m. (*vin*) *sec* dry (wine), g. L *siccus* dry]
sackbut (săk′bŭt′), *n.* **1.** a medieval form of the trombone. **2.** (in biblical usage) an ancient stringed musical instrument. Dan. 3. [t. F: m. *saquebute*, ONF *saqueboute*, lit., pull-push]
sackcloth (săk′klŏth′), *n.* **1.** sacking. **2.** coarse cloth worn as a sign of mourning or penitence.
sack coat, a man's or woman's loose-fitting coat. Also, **sacque.**
sackful (săk′fŏŏl′), *n.*, *pl.* **-fuls.** the amount that fills a sack.
sacking (săk′ĭng), *n.* stout or coarse woven material of hemp, jute, or the like, used for making sacks, etc.
sackless (săk′lĭs), *adj.* **1.** *Scot.* lacking energy; dispirited. **2.** *Scot.* feeble-minded. **3.** *Archaic.* guiltless. [ME *sak(e)les*, OE *saclēas*. See SAKE[1], -LESS]
sack-race (săk′rās′), *n.* a race in which each competitor jumps forward while his legs are confined in a sack.
Sackville (săk′vĭl), *n.* **Thomas.** See **Dorset, 1st Earl of.**
Sackville-West (săk′vĭl wĕst′), *n.* **Victoria Mary,** 1892–1962, English novelist and poet.
sacque (săk), *n.* a sack coat or jacket.
sacral[1] (sā′krəl), *adj.* of or pertaining to sacred rites or observations. [f. s. L *sacrum* sacred rite (prop. neut. adj.) + -AL[1]]
sacral[2] (sā′krəl), *adj.* of or pertaining to the sacrum. [t. NL: s. *sacrālis*. See SACRUM]
sacrament (săk′rə mənt), *n.* **1.** *Eccles.* a visible sign instituted by Jesus Christ to confer grace or Divine Life on those who worthily receive it. The sacraments of the Protestant Churches are baptism and the Lord's Supper; the sacraments of the Roman Catholic and Greek Orthodox Churches are baptism, confirmation, the Eucharist, matrimony, penance, holy orders, and extreme unction. **2.** (*often cap.*) the Eucharist, or Lord's Supper. **3.** the consecrated elements of the Eucharist, esp. the bread (the **Blessed Sacrament**). **4.** something regarded as possessing a sacred character or a mysterious significance. **5.** a sign, token, or symbol. **6.** an oath; solemn pledge. [ME, t. L: s. *sacrāmentum* oath, solemn engagement]
sacramental (săk′rə mĕn′tl), *adj.* **1.** of, pertaining to, or of the nature of a sacrament, esp. the sacrament of the Eucharist. **2.** peculiarly sacred: *a sacramental obligation.* —*n.* **3.** *Rom. Cath. Ch.* a sacrament-like ritual, object, etc., which the church institutes and uses for obtaining a spiritual effect, such as the sign of the cross, the use of holy water, etc. —**sac′ramen′tally,** *adv.* —**sac′ramental′ity,** *n.*
sacramentalist (săk′rə mĕn′tə lĭst), *n.* one who holds strong convictions about the importance and efficacy of the sacrament.
Sacramentarian (săk′rə mĕn tĕə′rĭ ən), *n.* **1.** one of the Protestant theologians, as Zwingli, maintaining that the bread and wine of the Eucharist can be said to be the body and blood of Christ only in a sacramental (that is, symbolical or metaphorical) sense. —*adj.* **2.** (*l.c.*) pertaining to the sacraments or (*cap.*) to the Sacramentarians.
Sacramento (săk′rə mĕn′tō), *n.* **1.** a city in the U.S., the capital of California, in the central part: a port on the Sacramento river. 191,667 (1960). **2.** a river flowing from N California S to San Francisco Bay. 382 mi.
sacrarium (sə krĕə′rĭ əm), *n.*, *pl.* **-craria** (-krĕə′rĭ ə). **1.** *Eccles.* the sanctuary or chancel. **2.** *Rom. Hist.* a shrine; a sanctuary. [t. L]
sacred (sā′krĭd), *adj.* **1.** appropriated or dedicated to a deity or to some religious purpose; consecrated. **2.** entitled to veneration or religious respect by association with divinity or divine things; holy. **3.** pertaining to or connected with religion (opposed to *profane* and *secular*): *sacred music.* **4.** reverently dedicated to some person or object: *a monument sacred to her memory.* **5.** regarded with reverence: *the sacred memory of a dead hero.* **6.** secured against violation, infringement, etc., by reverence, sense of right, etc.: *sacred oaths, sacred rights.* **7.** properly immune from violence, interference, etc., as a person or

his office. [ME, pp. of *sacren* render holy, t. L: m. *sacrāre*] —**sa′credly,** *adv.* —**sa′credness,** *n.* —**Syn. 2.** See **holy.**

Sacred College, *Rom. Cath. Ch.* the College of Cardinals.

sacred cow, something or somebody that escapes critical examination by virtue of popular esteem, high repute, etc.

sacred fig tree, bo tree.

sacred ibis, an ibis, *Threskiornis aethiopica,* about 2 feet long, with black-and-white plumage: venerated by the ancient Egyptians but now most common S of the Sahara.

sacrifice (săk′rĭ fīs′), *n., v.,* **-ficed, -ficing.** —*n.* **1.** the offering of life (animal, plant, or human) or some material possession, etc., to a deity, as in propitiation or homage. **2.** that which is so offered. **3.** the surrender or destruction of something prized or desirable for the sake of something considered as having a higher or more pressing claim. **4.** the thing so surrendered or devoted. **5.** a loss incurred in selling something below its value. **6.** *Theol.* **a.** Christ's offering of His death to God on behalf of sinful mankind; exemplified in the concept of the Lamb of God taking away the sins of the world. **b.** *Rom. Cath. Ch.* the offering of mass by a priest as a re-representation of the sacrifice of Christ on Calvary. —*v.t.* **7.** to make a sacrifice or offering of. **8.** to surrender or give up, or permit injury or disadvantage to, for the sake of something else. **9.** to dispose of (goods, etc.) regardless of profit. —*v.i.* **10.** to offer or make a sacrifice. [ME, t. F, t. L: m. s. *sacrificium*] —**sac′rific′er,** *n.*

sacrificial (săk′rĭ fĭsh′əl), *adj.* pertaining to or concerned with sacrifice. —**sac′rifi′cially,** *adv.*

sacrilege (săk′rĭ lĭj), *n.* **1.** the violation or profanation of anything sacred or held sacred. **2.** an instance of this. **3.** the stealing of anything consecrated to the service of God. [ME, t. OF, t. L: m. s. *sacrilegium*]

sacrilegious (săk′rĭ lĭj′əs), *adj.* **1.** guilty of sacrilege: *a sacrilegious person.* **2.** involving sacrilege: *sacrilegious practices.* [f. s. L *sacrilegium* sacrilege + -OUS] —**sac′rile′giously,** *adv.* —**sac′rile′giousness,** *n.*

sacring (sā′krĭng), *n. Archaic.* act or ceremony of consecrating, esp. the consecrating of the Eucharistic elements in the mass.

sacring bell, *Rom. Cath. Ch.* a small bell rung during mass at the Elevation.

sacristan (săk′rĭs tən), *n.* **1.** an official in charge of the sacred vessels, vestments, etc., of a church or a religious house. **2.** *Obs. or Archaic.* a sexton. [ME, t. ML: s. *sacristānus*]

sacristy (săk′rĭs tĭ), *n., pl.* **-ties.** an apartment in or a building connected with a church or a religious house, in which the sacred vessels, vestments, etc., are kept. [t. ML: m. s. *sacristia*]

sacro-, a word element: **1.** meaning 'holy'. **2.** referring to the sacrum. [t. L, comb. form of *sacer* (neut. *sacrum*) holy]

sacroiliac (sā′krō ĭl′ĭ ăk′, săk′rō-), *Anat.* —*n.* **1.** the joint where the sacrum and ilium meet. —*adj.* **2.** pertaining to this joint. [f. SACRO- + ILIAC]

sacrosanct (săk′rō săngkt′), *adj.* especially or superlatively sacred or inviolable. [t. L: s. *sacrōsanctus*] —**sac′rosanc′tity,** *n.*

sacrosciatic (sā′krō sī ăt′ĭk, săk′rō-), *adj. Anat.* pertaining to the sacrum and the ischium: *the sacrosciatic ligament.*

sacrum (sā′krəm), *n., pl.* **-cra** (-krə). *Anat.* a bone resulting from the ankylosis of two or more vertebrae between the lumbar and the coccygeal regions, in man composed (usually) of five fused vertebrae and forming the posterior wall of the pelvis. See diag. under **pelvis.** [t. NL, short for L (*os*) *sacrum,* lit., sacred (bone); so called because used in sacrifices]

sad (săd), *adj.,* **sadder, saddest. 1.** sorrowful or mournful: *to feel sad.* **2.** expressive of or characterized by sorrow: *sad looks.* **3.** causing sorrow: *a sad disappointment.* **4.** (of colour) sombre, dark, or dull. **5.** (often humorous) deplorable; shocking: *a sad attempt.* **6.** *Colloq.* (of bread, cake, etc.) soggy, not having risen. **7.** *Archaic.* firm or steadfast. [ME; OE *sæd,* c. G *satt,* Goth. *saths* full, sated; akin to L *sat, satis* enough, *satur* sated, Gk *hádēn* enough] —**sadly** (săd′lĭ), *adv.*

—**Syn. 1.** unhappy, despondent, disconsolate. SAD, DEPRESSED, DEJECTED, MELANCHOLY describe states of low spirits. SAD, the general term, varies in its suggestion from a slight, momentary unhappiness to deep-felt grief, or to a continuous state of combined pensiveness, wistfulness, and resignation: *sorrowful and sad, sad and lonely.* DEPRESSED refers to a temporary lapse in natural buoyancy because of fatigue, unhappiness, a sense of being unable to change unsatisfactory conditions, or the like: *depressed by a visit to the slums.* DEJECTED, though also referring to a temporary state of discouragement caused by some definite event or circumstance, implies lower spirits, being cast down by disappointment, frustration, and the like: *dejected about losing one's position.* MELANCHOLY describes a state caused rather by temperament and a chronically gloomy outlook than by any external reason: *habitually melancholy.*

sadden (săd′n), *v.t., v.i.* to make or become sad.

saddle (săd′l), *n., v.,* **-dled, -dling.** —*n.* **1.** a seat for a rider on the back of a horse or other animal. **2.** a similar seat on a bicycle, machine, etc. **3.** a part of a harness laid across the back of an animal and girded under the belly. **4.** that part of an animal's back on which the saddle is placed. **5.** something resembling a saddle in shape or position. **6.** (of mutton, venison, etc.) a cut including part of the backbone and both loins. **7.** (of poultry) the posterior part of the back. **8.** the saddle of an animal prepared for food. **9.** a ridge connecting two higher elevations. **10.** *Naut.* a hollowed-out piece of wood which provides a resting place for the end of a spar. **11.** the clitellum of an earthworm. **12.** *Ordn.* the support for the trunnion on some guncarriages. **13. in the saddle,** in a position of authority; in control. —*v.t.* **14.** to put a saddle upon (a horse, etc.). **15.** to load or charge, as with a burden. **16.** to impose as a burden or responsibility. —*v.i.* **17.** to put a saddle on a horse (often fol. by *up*). [ME *sadel,* OE *sadol,* c. G *Sattel*] —**sad′dle-like′,** *adj.*

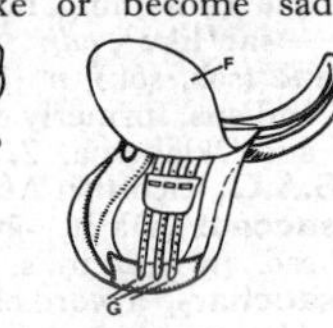

Saddle: A, Pommel; B, Seat; C, Cantle; D, Panel; E, Skirt; F, Flap; G, Girth straps

saddleback (săd′l băk′), *n.* **1.** any of various animals or birds having marks on the back resembling a saddle. **2.** a geometrical shape generated by a parabola passing along the edge of and at right angles to an inverted parabola. —*adj.* **3.** having the shape of a saddleback (def. 2).

saddle-backed (săd′l băkt′), *adj.* **1.** having the back or upper surface curved like a saddle. **2.** having a saddle-like marking on the back, as certain birds.

saddlebag (săd′l băg′), *n.* a large bag, often one of a pair, hung from or laid over a saddle.

saddlebill (săd′l bĭl′), *n.* a tall, handsome stork of tropical Africa, *Ephippiorhynchus senegalensis,* having a saddle-like shield on its large, pointed bill.

saddlebow (săd′l bō′), *n.* the arched front part of a saddle or saddletree.

saddlecloth (săd′l klŏth′), *n.* a cloth placed between a horse's back and the saddle.

saddle graft, *Bot.* a type of graft in which a chisel-shaped projection at the top of the stock is inserted in a groove cut in the base of the scion. See illus. under **graft.**

saddle-horse (săd′l hôs′), *n.* any type of horse which has a strong back and trained gait and is therefore used for riding.

saddler (săd′lə), *n.* one who makes or deals in saddlery.

saddle roof, a roof having two gables. See illus. under **roof.**

saddlery (săd′lə rĭ), *n., pl.* **-dleries. 1.** saddles and other articles pertaining to the equipment of horses, etc. **2.** the work, business, or shop of a saddler.

saddle-soap (săd′l sōp′), *n.* a soap, usually consisting chiefly of Castile, used for cleaning and preserving saddles and other leather articles.

saddle-sore (săd′l sô′), *adj.* **1.** sore after horse-riding. **2.** (of a horse) having sores produced by a saddle.

saddletree (săd′l trē′), *n.* the frame of a saddle.

Saddleworth (săd′l wûth′), *n.* a town in England, in the West Riding of Yorkshire. 17,010 (1961).

Sadducee (săd′yŏŏ sē′), *n.* one of an ancient Jewish sect or party whose views and practices were opposed to those of the Pharisees, and who denied the authority of oral tradition, the resurrection of the dead, the existence of angels, etc. [ME *saduces* (pl.), OE *sadducēas* (pl.), t. LL: m. *Saddūcaeus,* t. LGk: m. *Saddoukaîos,* t. Heb.: m. *Çaddūqī,* der. *Çaddūq* Zadok, name of Hebrew high priest under David] —**Sad′duce′an,** *adj., n.* —**Sad′duceeism,** *n.*

Sade (*Fr.* sȧd), *n.* **Comte Donatien Alphonse François de** (*Fr.* kôɴt dŏ nȧ tyăɴ ȧl fôɴs frăɴ swȧ′ də) (*Marquis de Sade*), 1740–1814, French soldier and novelist, notorious for the mixture of sex and cruelty in his books.

Sadi (sä dē′), *n.* Saadi.

sad-iron (săd′ī′ən), *n.* a solid flatiron. [f. SAD (def. 7) + IRON]

sadism (săd′ĭz′əm, sā′dĭz′əm), *n.* **1.** sexual gratification gained through causing physical pain and humiliation. **2.** any morbid enjoyment in inflicting mental or physical pain. [t. F: m. *sadisme,* from the Marquis de SADE] —**sad′ist,** *n., adj.* —**sadistic** (sə dĭs′tĭk), *adj.* —**sadis′tically,** *adv.*

sadness (săd′nĭs), *n.* **1.** the quality of being sad; unhappiness. **2.** the state of being sad; grief. —**Ant. 1, 2.** joy.

sadomasochism (săd′ō măs′ə kĭz′əm, sā′dō-), *n.* a disturbed condition of the mind marked by the presence of sadistic and masochistic tendencies.

Sadowa (sä′dō ə; *Cz.* sä′dŏ vä), *n.* a village in W Czechoslovakia, in NE Bohemia: Prussian victory over Austrians, 1866.

sad sack, *U.S. Slang.* an ineffective person who always blunders despite good intentions, esp. a soldier.

S.A.E., **1.** Society of Automotive Engineers (in the U.S.). **2.** the standardized scale of gradings of motor oil according to viscosity established by this society.

s.a.e., stamped addressed envelope.

Saenredam (*Du.* sän′rə dŏm), *n.* **Pieter** (*Du.* pē′tər), 1597–1665, Dutch painter.

safari (sə fä′rĭ), *n., pl.* **-ris.** (in eastern Africa) **1.** a journey; an expedition, esp. for hunting. **2.** the persons, animals, etc., forming such an expedition. [t. Swahili, t. Ar.]

Safavi (sə fä′wē), *adj.* of the Persian dynasty which ruled from *c.* 1500 to 1736. Also, **Safavid** (sə fä′wēd).

safe (sāf), *adj.*, **safer, safest,** *n.* **—***adj.* **1.** secure from liability to harm, injury, danger, or risk: *a safe place.* **2.** free from hurt, injury, danger, or risk: *to arrive safe and sound.* **3.** involving no risk of mishap, error, etc.: *a safe estimate.* **4.** dependable or trustworthy: *a safe guide.* **5.** cautious in avoiding danger: *a safe player.* **6.** placed beyond the power of doing harm; in secure custody: *a criminal safe in jail.* **—***n.* **7.** a steel or iron box or repository for money, jewels, papers, etc. **8.** any receptacle or structure for the storage or preservation of articles: *a meat safe.* **—***adv.* **9. play safe,** to act cautiously. [ME *sauf*, t. OF, g. L *salvus* uninjured] **—safe′ly,** *adv.* **—safe′ness,** *n.*

—**Syn. 1.** SAFE, SECURE may both imply that something can be regarded as free from danger. These words are frequently interchangeable. SAFE, however, is rather applied to a person or thing that is out of, or has passed beyond, the reach of danger: *the ship is safe in port.* SECURE is applied to that about which there is no need to fear or worry: *to feel secure about the future, the foundation of the house does not seem very secure.* —**Ant. 3.** unsure, dangerous.

safeblower (sāf′blō′ə), *n.* a burglar who breaks open safes by means of explosives.

safebreaker (sāf′brā′kə), *n.* a burglar who robs safes.

safe-conduct (sāf′kŏn′dŭkt), *n.* **1.** a document securing a safe passage through a region, esp. in time of war. **2.** this privilege. **3.** a conducting in safety.

safe-deposit (sāf′dĭ pŏz′ĭt), *n.* **1.** a building containing safes, strongrooms, etc., where valuables may be stored. **—***adj.* **2.** providing safekeeping for valuables: *a safe-deposit vault or box.*

safeguard (sāf′gäd′), *n.* **1.** something serving as a protection or defence, or ensuring safety. **2.** a permit for safe passage. **3.** a guard or convoy. **4.** a mechanical device for ensuring safety. **—***v.t.* **5.** to guard; protect; secure. [ME *saufegard*, t. OF: m. *sauvegarde*, f. *sauve* (fem. of *sauf*) + *garde*. See SAFE, GUARD]

safekeeping (sāf′kē′pĭng), *n.* protection; care.

safelight (sāf′līt′), *n. Photog.* a light used in a darkroom, fitted with filters which can be adjusted to prevent the passage of light of a frequency which could affect the emulsion and fog the film.

safety (sāf′tĭ), *n., pl.* **-ties. 1.** the state of being safe; freedom from injury or danger. **2.** the quality of insuring against hurt, injury, danger, or risk. **3.** a contrivance or device to prevent injury or avert danger. **4.** the action of keeping safe. **5.** *Obs.* close confinement or custody.

safety belt, **1.** Also, **seat belt.** a belt attached to the frame of a car or seat of an aeroplane, for securing a passenger, driver or pilot against sudden turns, stops, bumps, etc. **2.** a belt or strap fastening a person working at a height to a fixed object, to prevent him from falling.

safety bicycle, a bicycle with two equal-sized wheels.

safety catch, a locking or cut-off device as one that prevents a gun from being fired accidentally.

safety curtain, a fireproof curtain between the stage and the auditorium in a theatre, etc., which must, by law, be lowered during intervals.

safety glass, **1.** glass made by joining two plates or panes with a layer of plastic or artificial resin between them which retains the fragments if the glass is broken; laminated glass. **2.** glass strengthened by heat treatment which tends to make it shatter into small rounded fragments when broken; toughened glass. **3.** glass which is reinforced with a wire mesh within its body; wired glass.

Safety Islands, a group of three French islands off the coast of French Guiana, in South America.

safety lamp, a miner's lamp in which the flame is protected by wire gauze, thus preventing immediate ignition of explosive gases.

safety match, a match designed to ignite only when rubbed on a specially prepared surface.

safety pin, **1.** a pin bent back on itself to form a spring, with a guard to cover the point. **2.** a locking device on grenades, mines, etc., to keep them safe until required for use.

safety razor, a razor provided with a guard or guards to prevent cutting the skin.

safety valve, **1.** a valve in a steam boiler or the like, which, when the pressure becomes abnormal or dangerous, opens and allows the steam or fluid to escape. **2.** a harmless outlet for emotion, nervousness, etc.

safflorite (săf′lə rīt′), *n.* a mineral diarsenide of cobalt which often contains some iron and nickel.

safflower (săf′lou′ə), *n.* **1.** a thistle-like composite herb, *Carthamus tinctorius*, a native of the Old World, bearing large orange-red flower heads. **2.** its dried florets, used medicinally or as a red dyestuff. [t. D: m. *saffloer*, t. OF: m. *saffleur*, t. It.: m. *saffiore*; ult. orig. uncert.]

saffron (săf′rən), *n.* **1.** a crocus, *Crocus sativus*, with handsome purple flowers. **2.** an orange-coloured product consisting of its dried stigmas, used to colour confectionery, for flavouring, etc., in rolls and buns and in chicken rice dishes. **3.** Also, **saffron yellow.** yellow-orange. [ME, t. F: m. *safran*, ult. t. Ar.: m. *za'farān*]

Safi (*Fr.* sȧ fē′), *n.* a fortified seaport in W central Morocco. 100,000 (est. 1965).

Safid Rud (sä fēd′rōōd′), a river flowing from NW Iran into the Caspian Sea. ab. 450 mi.

S Afr., **1.** South Africa. **2.** South African.

safranine (săf′rə nĭn, -nēn′), *n. Chem.* **1.** any of a class of (chiefly red) organic dyes, phenazine derivatives, used for dyeing wool, silk, etc. **2.** a dye, $C_{18}H_{14}N_4$. [var. of *safranin*, t. G, f. *Safran* saffron + *-in* -INE[2]]

S Afr. D., South African Dutch (Afrikaans).

safrole (săf′rōl), *n. Chem.* a colourless or faintly yellow liquid, $C_{10}H_{10}O_2$, obtained from oil of sassafras, etc., and used for flavouring and in perfumery. Also, **safrol** (săf′rŏl). [f. (SAS)SAFR(AS) + -OLE]

sag (săg), *v.*, **sagged, sagging,** *n.* **—***v.i.* **1.** to sink or bend downwards by weight or pressure, esp. in the middle. **2.** to droop; hang loosely: *sagging shoulders.* **3.** to yield through weakness, lack of effort, or the like. **4.** to decline, as in price. **5.** *Naut.* to drift out of the intended course. **—***n.* **6.** the act of sagging. **7.** the degree of sagging. **8.** a place where anything sags; a depression. **9.** moderate decline in prices. **10.** *Naut.* leeway. [ME *sagge*; prob. akin to ND *zakken* subside]

saga (sä′gə), *n.* **1.** a medieval Icelandic or Norse prose narrative of achievements and events in the history of a personage, family, etc. **2.** a form of novel, characteristically French (**roman-fleuve**) but also written in English, in which the members or generations of a family or social group are chronicled in a long and leisurely narrative. **3.** any narrative or legend of heroic exploits. [t. Icel.: story, history; c. SAW[3]]

Saga (sä′gə), *n.* a town in Japan, in NW Kyushu. 134,575 (1965).

sagacious (sə gā′shəs), *adj.* **1.** having acute mental discernment and keen practical sense; shrewd: *a sagacious author.* **2.** *Obs.* keen-scented. [f. SAGACI(TY) + -OUS] **—saga′ciously,** *adv.* **—saga′ciousness,** *n.*

sagacity (sə găs′ĭ tĭ), *n., pl.* **-ties.** acuteness of mental discernment and soundness of judgement. [t. L: m. s. *sagācitas*]

Sagamihara (sä′gə mē′hə rə), *n.* a town in Japan, on SE central Honshu island. 163,381 (1965).

sagamore (săg′ə mô′), *n.* (among the American Indians of New England) a chief or great man. [t. N Amer. Ind. (Abnaki): m. *sāgimo* vanquisher]

Sagan (*Fr.* sȧ gäN′), *n.* **Françoise** (*Fr.* fräN swȧz′), born 1935, French novelist.

sage[1] (sāj), *n., adj.*, **sager, sagest.** **—***n.* **1.** a profoundly wise man; a man famed for wisdom. **2.** a man venerated for his wisdom, judgement, and experience: *the seven sages of ancient Greece.* **—***adj.* **3.** wise, judicious, or prudent: *sage conduct.* **4.** *Obs.* grave or solemn. **—sage′ly,** *adv.* **—sage′ness,** *n.* [ME, t. OF, g. L *-sapius* wise]

sage[2] (sāj), *n.* **1.** a perennial labiate plant, *Salvia officinalis*, whose greyish green leaves are used for seasoning in cookery. **2.** the leaves themselves. **3.** sagebrush. [ME *sauge*, t. OF, g. L *salvia*]

sagebrush (sāj′brŭsh′), *n.* any of various sagelike bushy plants of the composite genus *Artemisia*, common on the dry plains of the western U.S.

sage Derby, a Derby cheese, flavoured with sage; traditionally eaten at Christmas.

sage-green (sāj′grēn′), *n.* **1.** a greyish green colour. **—***adj.* **2.** greyish green.

saggar (săg′ə), *n.* **1.** a box or case made of refractory baked clay in which the finer ceramic wares are enclosed and protected while baking. **—***v.t.* **2.** to place in or upon a saggar. Also, **saggard, sagger, seggar.** [prob. contr. of SAFEGUARD]

Sagitta (sə gĭt′ə), *n.* a northern constellation, near Aquila, the Arrow.

sagittal (săj′ĭ tl), *adj.* **1.** *Anat.* **a.** denoting or pertaining to the suture between the parietal bones of the skull, or to a venous channel within the skull and parallel to this suture. See diag. under **cranium. b.** (in direction or location) from front to back in the median plane, or in a plane parallel to the median. **2.** pertaining to or resembling an arrow or arrowhead. [t. NL: s. *sagittālis*, der. L *sagitta* arrow]

Sagittarius (săj′ĭ tēə′rĭ əs), *n.* **1.** the Archer (a centaur drawing a bow), a zodiacal constellation. **2.** the ninth sign of the zodiac. See diag. under **zodiac.** [t. L]

sagittate (săj′ĭ tāt′), *adj.* shaped like an arrowhead. Also, **sagittiform** (sə jĭt′ĭ fôm′, săj′ĭ tĭ fôm′). [t. NL: m. s. *sagittātus*, der. L *sagitta* arrow]

Sagittate leaf

sago (sā′gō), *n.* a starchy foodstuff derived from the soft interior of the trunk of various palms and cycads, used in making puddings, etc. [t. Malay: m. *sāgū*]

saguaro (sə gwä′rō, sə wä′rō), *n., pl.* **-ros.** an extremely tall cactus, *Carnegiea gigantea*, of Arizona and neighbouring regions, yielding a useful wood and an edible fruit. [t. Sp.; of Amer. Ind. orig.]

Saguenay (săg′ə nā′), *n.* a river in SE Canada, in Quebec province, flowing from Lake St John SE to the St Lawrence: in its lower course it is a fiord ¾–2 mi. wide. 125 mi.

Sagunto (*Sp.* sȧ gōōn′tȯ), *n.* a town in E Spain, N of Valencia: besieged by Hannibal, 219–218 B.C. 27,000 (est. 1967). Ancient, **Saguntum** (sə gŭn′təm).

Sahaptan (sä hăp′tən), *n.* Shahaptian. Also, **Sahaptin** (sä-hăp′tĭn).

Sahara (sə hä′rə), *n.* **1.** a desert in N Africa, extending from the Atlantic to the Nile valley. ab. 3,500,000 sq. mi. **2.** any arid waste.

Saharanpur (sə hä′rən pōōə′), *n.* a city in N India, in Uttar Pradesh. 185,213 (1961).

sahib (sä′ĭb), *n.* (in India) a term of respect applied by natives to a European. [t. Hind., t. Ar.: m. *çāhib* master, lit., friend]

saice (sīs), *n.* syce.

said (sĕd), *v.* **1.** pt. and pp. of **say.** *—adj.* **2.** named or mentioned before: *said witness, said sum.*

Saida (sä′ĭ də), *n.* a seaport in SW Lebanon: the site of ancient Sidon. 22,000 (est. 1963).

saiga (sī′gə), *n.* an antelope, *Saiga tartarica*, of W Asia. [t. Russ.]

Saigon (sī gŏn′), *n.* capital of and seaport in S South Vietnam. 1,500,000 (est. 1963). See map under **Vietnam.**

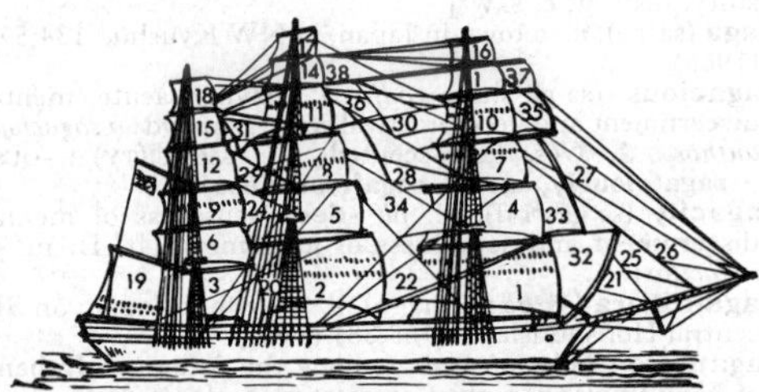

Sails on full-rigged sailing ship

1. Foresail; 2. Mainsail; 3. Crossjack; 4. Fore lower topsail; 5. Main lower topsail; 6. Mizzen lower topsail; 7. Fore upper topsail; 8. Main upper topsail; 9. Mizzen upper topsail; 10. Fore-topgallant sail; 11. Main-topgallant sail; 12. Mizzen-topgallant sail; 13. Fore royal; 14. Main royal; 15. Mizzen royal; 16. Fore skysail; 17. Main skysail; 18. Mizzen skysail; 19. Spanker; 20. Mizzen staysail; 21. Fore-topmast staysail; 22. Main lower topmast staysail; 23. Main upper topmast staysail; 24. Mizzen-topmast staysail; 25. Inner jib; 26. Outer jib; 27. Flying jib; 28. Main-topgallant staysail; 29. Mizzen-topgallant staysail; 30. Main-royal staysail; 31. Mizzen-royal staysail; 32. Lower studdingsail; 33. Fore-topmast studdingsail; 34. Main-topmast studdingsail; 35. Fore-topgallant studdingsail; 36. Main-topgallant studdingsail; 37. Fore-royal studdingsail; 38. Main-royal studdingsail

sail (sāl), *n.* **1.** an expanse of canvas or similar material spread to the wind to make a vessel move through the water. It is called a **square sail** when quadrilateral and extended by a yard, usually at right angles to the masts, and a **fore-and-aft sail** when set on a mast, boom, gaff, or stay, more or less in line with the keel. **2.** some similar piece or apparatus, as the part of an arm of a windmill which catches the wind. **3.** a voyage or excursion, esp. in a sailing vessel. **4.** a sailing vessel or ship. **5.** sailing vessels collectively: *the fleet numbered thirty sail.* **6.** sails for a vessel or vessels, collectively. **7. make sail,** *Naut.* **a.** to set the sail or sails of a boat, or increase the amount of sail already set. **b.** to set out on a voyage. **8. set sail,** to start a voyage. **9. under sail,** with sails set. *—v.i.* **10.** to travel in a vessel conveyed by the action of wind, steam, etc. **11.** to move along or be conveyed by wind, steam, etc.: *steamships sailing to Lisbon.* **12.** to manage a boat, esp. for sport. **13.** to begin a journey by water: *sailing at dawn.* **14.** to move along in a manner suggestive of a sailing vessel: *clouds sailing overhead.* **15.** to travel through the air, as a balloon. **16.** to move along with dignity: *to sail into a room.* **17.** *Colloq.* to go boldly into action (fol. by *in*). *—v.t.* **18.** to sail upon, over, or through: *to sail the seven seas.* **19.** to navigate (a ship, etc.). **20.** to cause to sail (a toy boat or the like). [ME; OE *segl*, c. G *Segel*] **—sail′able,** *adj.* **—sail′less,** *adj.*

sailboat (sāl′bōt′), *n. U.S.* a sailing boat.

sailcloth (sāl′klŏth′), *n.* **1.** a strong canvas or other material such as is used for making sails. **2.** a lightweight canvas material used for making clothing, curtains, etc.

sailer (sā′lə), *n.* **1.** a vessel propelled by a sail or sails. **2.** a vessel with reference to its powers or manner of sailing.

sailfish (sāl′fĭsh′), *n., pl.* **-fishes,** (*esp. collectively*) **-fish.** any of the large marine fishes constituting the genus *Istiophorus*, characterized by a very large dorsal fin likened to a sail, and related to the swordfishes, as *I. americanus*, of the warmer parts of the Atlantic.

Sailfish, *Istiophorus gladius* (9 to 10 ft long)

sailing (sā′lĭng), *n.* **1.** the act of one who or that which sails. **2.** the procedure of solving problems of courses, distances, and positions in navigating a ship, without the use of celestial observations.

sailing boat, a boat propelled by sails.

sailor (sā′lə), *n.* **1.** one whose occupation is sailing or navigation; a mariner; a seaman. **2.** a seaman below the rank of officer. **3.** a person, with reference to freedom from seasickness: *a bad sailor.* **4.** a sailor-hat. [ME *sailer* one who sails]

—Syn. 1. SAILOR, MARINER, SALT, SEAMAN, TAR are terms for one who leads a seafaring life. A SAILOR OR SEAMAN is one whose occupation is on board a ship at sea; one of a ship's crew below the rank of petty officer: *a sailor before the mast, an able-bodied seaman.* MARINER is a term now found only in certain technical expressions: *master mariner* (captain in merchant service), *mariner's compass* (ordinary compass as used on ships); formerly used much as 'sailor' or 'seafaring man' now are, the word seems elevated or quaint: *Rime of the Ancient Mariner.* SALT and TAR are familiar and colloquial terms for old and experienced sailors: *an old salt, a jolly tar.*

sailor-hat (sā′lə hăt′), *n.* **1.** a hat worn by a sailor. **2.** a flat-brimmed straw hat with a low flat crown, worn by women and children.

sailorly (sā′lə lĭ), *adj.* like or befitting a sailor.

sailor's-choice (sā′ləz chois′), *n., pl.* **-choice.** any of several fishes of the Atlantic coast of the U.S., esp. *Lagodon rhomboides*, ranging from Massachusetts to Texas, and *Haemulon parra*, ranging from Florida to Brazil.

sailor suit, a suit in imitation of a sailor's uniform, formerly much worn by children.

sailplane (sāl′plān′), *n.* **1.** a glider designed especially for sustained flight using ascending air currents. *—v.i.* **2.** to soar in a sailplane.

sailyard (sāl′yäd′), *n.* a spar on which sails are extended.

sain (sān), *v.t. Archaic.* **1.** to make the sign of the cross on as to protect against evil influences. **2.** to safeguard by prayer. **3.** to bless. [ME; OE *segnian* (c. G *segnen*), ult. t. L: m. *signāre*]

sainfoin (săn′foin), *n.* a European fabaceous herb, *Onobrychis viciifolia*, cultivated as a forage plant. [t. F, f. *sain* wholesome (or *saint* holy) + *foin* hay, g. L *faenum*]

saint (sānt), *n.* **1.** one of certain persons of exceptional holiness of life formally recognized by the Christian Church as having attained an exalted position in heaven and as being entitled to veneration on earth; a canonized person. **2.** (in certain religious bodies) a designation applied by the members to themselves. **3.** a person of great holiness. **4.** a sanctimonious person. *—v.t.* **5.** to enrol formally among the saints recognized by the church. **6.** to give the name of saint to; reckon as a saint. [ME, t. OF, g. L *sanctus*, pp., consecrated]

Saint. For entries more commonly written in the abbreviated form, see **St.**

Saint Agnes's Eve (ăg′nĭ siz), the night of January 20th, the traditional time for a woman to perform rites to reveal the identity of her future husband.

Saint Andrew's Cross, an X-shaped cross. See illus. under **cross.**

Saint Andrew's Day, November 30th, observed by the

Scottish in honour of St Andrew, the patron saint of Scotland.

Saint Anthony's Cross, a T-shaped cross. See illus. under **cross.**

Saint Barnaby's thistle (bä′nə bĭz), an annual or biennial composite, *Centaurea solstitialis*, a native of SE Europe found as a weed of arable fields elsewhere.

Saint Bernard, one of a breed of large dogs with a massive head, noted for their intelligence: named after the hospice of St Bernard, on the pass of the Great St Bernard in the Alps, where they are kept by the monks for rescuing travellers from the snow.

Saint Bernard
(28 in. high at the shoulder)

Saint-Brieuc (*Fr.* săɴ brē œ′), *n.* a town in NW France, the capital of Côtes-du-Nord department. 47,307 (1968).

Saint Dabeoc's heath (dăb′ĭ ŏks′), a short evergreen ericaceous shrub of W Europe, *Daboecia cantabrica.*

Saint David's Day, March 1st, observed by the Welsh in honour of St David, the patron saint of Wales.

Saint David's Head, a promontory of Pembrokeshire, the most westerly point of Wales.

Saint-Denis (*Fr.* săɴ də nē′), *n.* **1.** a town in N France in Seine-Saint-Denis department. 94,264 (1962). **2.** the capital of Réunion, in the N part. 75,126 (est. 1965).

Sainte-Beuve (*Fr.* săɴt bœv′), *n.* **Charles Augustin** (*Fr.* shȧrl ȯ gʏs tăɴ′), 1804–69, French critic.

sainted (sān′tĭd), *adj.* **1.** enrolled among the saints. **2.** being a saint in heaven. **3.** sacred or hallowed. **4.** saintly.

Saint-Exupéry (*Fr.* săɴ tĕg zʏ pė rē′), *n.* **Antoine de** (*Fr.* äɴ twȧn′də), 1900–45, French author and aviator.

Saint Francis, Cape, a headland in the Republic of South Africa, near the E extremity of the S coast of Cape Province.

Saint-Gaudens (sānt gô′dnz), *n.* **Augustus** (ô gŭs′təs), 1848–1907, U.S. sculptor, born in Ireland.

Saint George's Channel, a sea passage between Ireland and Wales. ab. 100 mi. long; 50–95 mi. wide.

Saint George's cross, the Greek cross as used in the Union Jack. See illus. under **cross.**

Saint George's Day, April 23rd, observed by the English in honour of St George, the patron saint of England.

Saint Helena Bay, an indentation of the Atlantic Ocean in the Republic of South Africa on the W coast of Cape Province.

sainthood (sānt′ho͝od′), *n.* **1.** the character or status of a saint. **2.** saints collectively.

Saint John, 1. a seaport in SE Canada, in New Brunswick, on the Bay of Fundy. 95,563 (1961). **2.** a river forming part of the boundary between Maine and Canada, flowing S and E through New Brunswick to the Bay of Fundy. ab. 450 mi.

Saint-Just (*Fr.* săɴ zhʏst′), *n.* **Louis Antoine Léon de** (*Fr.* lwē äɴ twȧn lė ôɴ′ də), 1767–94, French writer and revolutionary leader.

Saint-Lô (*Fr.* săɴ lō′), *n.* a town in NW France, in Manche department. 17,038 (1964).

Saint-Louis (*Fr.* săɴ lwē′), *n.* a seaport in and the former capital of Senegal, at the mouth of the Senegal river. 47,900 (est. 1962). See map under **Senegal.**

Saint Lucia Bay, an indentation of the Indian Ocean in the Republic of South Africa on the E coast of Natal.

saintly (sānt′lĭ), *adj.*, **-lier, -liest.** like, proper to, or befitting a saint: *saintly lives.* **—saint′liness,** *n.*

Saint-Maur-des-Fossés (*Fr.* săɴ mŏr dė fō sė′), *n.* a town in NE France, in Seine department. 70,397 (1962).

Saint Nicholas, fl. 4th century, bishop of Asia Minor, protector of children; the traditional Father Christmas.

Saint-Ouen (*Fr.* săɴ twăɴ′), *n.* a town in N France, in Seine department. 51,956 (1962).

Saint Patrick's cabbage, a small perennial saxifragaceous herb, *Saxifraga spathularis*, occurring among rocks in mountainous regions of Ireland, NW Spain and N Portugal.

Saint Patrick's Day, March 17th, observed by the Irish in honour of St Patrick, the patron saint of Ireland.

Saint-Pierre (*Fr.* săɴ pyĕr′), *n.* **1. Jacques Henri Bernardin de** (*Fr.* zhȧk äɴ rē bĕr nȧr dăɴ′ də), 1737–1814, French writer. **2.** the capital of Saint Pierre and Miquelon in the S part. 3500 (est. 1967).

Saint Pierre and Miquelon, a French territory consisting of eight small islands in the Atlantic Ocean, S of Newfoundland. 5025 pop. (1962); 93 sq. mi.

Saint-Saëns (*Fr.* săɴ säɴs′), *n.* **Charles Camille** (*Fr.* shȧrl kȧ mēy′), 1835–1921, French composer and pianist.

Saintsbury (sānts′bə rĭ, -brĭ), *n.* **George Edward Bateman,** 1845–1933, English literary critic and historian.

Saint's day, a day in the church calendar set apart for the commemoration of a saint.

saintship (sānt′shĭp), *n.* the qualities of a saint.

Saint-Simon (*Fr.* săɴ sē môɴ′), *n.* **1. Claude Henri** (*Fr.* klōd äɴ rē′), **Count de,** 1760–1825, French socialist and writer. **2. Louis de Rouvroy** (*Fr.* lwē də ro͞o vrwȧ′), 1675–1755, French soldier, diplomat, and author.

Saint Valentine's Day (văl′ən tīnz′), February 14th, when tokens of affection or valentines are given.

Saionji (sī′ŏn jē′), *n.* **Kimmochi** (kēm′mō chē′), 1849–1940, Japanese statesman.

Saipan (sī păn′), *n.* one of the Mariana Islands, in the N Pacific, ab. 1350 mi. S of Japan. 8100 pop. (est. 1960); 71 sq. mi.

Saïs (sā′ĭs), *n.* an ancient city in N Egypt, on the Nile delta: an ancient capital of Lower Egypt.

Saishuto (sī′sho͞o tō′), *n.* Japanese name of **Cheju.** Also, *Korean,* **Saishu** (sī′sho͞o).

saith (sĕth), *v. Archaic or Poetic.* third pers. sing. pres. of **say.**

saithe (sāth), *n.* the coalfish. [Scot., t. Scand.; cf. Icel. *seithr*, Norw. *seid*]

sakabula (săk′ə bo͞o′lə), *n.* a bird of southern Africa, *Euplectes progne*, of the weaver family; long-tailed widow-bird. [t. Zulu: m. *isakabuli*]

Sakai (sä′kī′), *n.* a seaport in S Japan, on S Honshu island, near Osaka. 466,412 (1965).

sake[1] (sāk), *n.* **1.** cause, account, or interest: *for my sake.* **2.** purpose or end: *for the sake of appearances.* [ME; OE *sacu* lawsuit, cause, c. G *Sache*]

sake[2] (sä′kĭ), *n.* a Japanese fermented alcoholic drink made from rice. [t. Jap.]

saker (sā′kə), *n.* an Old World falcon, *Falco sacer cherrug*, used in falconry. [t. F: m. *sacre*, ult. t. Ar.: m. *çaqr*]

Sakhalin (săk′ə lēn′; *Russ.* sə-khȧ lyĕn′), *n.* an island off the SE coast of the Soviet Union in Asia, N of Japan. 640,000 pop. (est. 1966); 28,957 sq. mi.

Sakhalin

Sakhar (sŭk′ə), *n.* See **Sukkur.**

saki (sä′kĭ), *n.* any of several small monkeys of the family *Cebidae*, living in the Amazon basin.

Saki (sä′kĭ), *n.* pen-name of **Hector Hugh Munro.**

Sakti (săk′tĭ; *Skt* shŭk′tĭ), *n. Hinduism.* **1.** the female principle or organ of generative power. **2.** the wife of a Hindu deity, especially of Siva. Also, **Shakti.** [t. Skt: power, force]

Sakyamuni (sä′kyə mo͞o′nĭ), *n.* Buddha.

sal (săl), *n. Chiefly Pharm.* salt. [t. L]

salaam (sə läm′), *n.* **1.** (in the Orient) a salutation meaning 'peace'. **2.** a very low bow or obeisance, esp. with the palm of the right hand placed on the forehead. **—*v.i.* 3.** to salute with a salaam. **4.** to perform a salaam. **—*v.t.* 5.** to salute (someone) with a salaam. [t. Ar.: m. *salām* peace]

salable (sā′lə bl), *adj.* saleable. **—sal′abil′ity,** *n.* **—sal′ably,** *adv.*

salacious (sə lā′shəs), *adj.* **1.** lustful or lecherous. **2.** (of writings, etc.) obscene. [f. *salaci(ty)* (t. L: m. s. *salācitas* lust) + -OUS] **—sala′ciously,** *adv.* **—sala′ciousness, salacity** (sə lăs′ĭ tĭ), *n.*

salad (săl′əd), *n.* **1.** a dish of uncooked green plants or other vegetables, served cold with meat, eggs, cheese, or the like. **2.** any of various raw or cold cooked foods, prepared singly or combined, usually cut up and mixed with a sweet or savoury dressing: *fruit salad, potato salad.* **3.** any herb or plant used for such a dish or eaten raw. **4.** *Dial.* lettuce. [ME *salade*, t. OF, t. OPr.: m. *salada*, der. *salar* to salt, der. L *sal* salt]

salad burnet, a perennial rosaceous herb, *Poterium sanguisorba*, with spherical heads of small flowers some of which are unisexual, occurring in chalk grassland of Europe and W Asia.

salad days, days of youthful inexperience.

salad dressing, a dressing for a salad, as French dressing, mayonnaise, etc.

Saladin (săl′ə dĭn), *n.* (*Salāh-ed-Dīn Yūsuf ibn Ayyūb*), 1137–93, sultan of Egypt and Syria 1175?–93: captor of Jerusalem and opponent of the Crusaders.

Salado (*Sp.* sä lä′dō), *n.* **Río** (*Sp.* rē′ō), a river in N Argentina, flowing SE to the river Paraná. ab. 1000 mi.

Salamanca (săl′ə măng′kə; *Sp.* sä lä män′kä), *n.* a city in W Spain: Wellington's defeat of the French here, 1812. 100,997 (1965).

salamander (săl′ə măn′də), *n.* **1.** any of various tailed amphibians, most of which have an aquatic larval stage but are terrestrial as adults, such as *Salamandra salamandra*, the **European** or **fire salamander** of central and southern Europe. 2. a mythical lizard or other reptile, or a being supposed to be able to live in fire. [ME *salamandre*, t. OF, t. L: m. *salamandra*, t. Gk] —**salamandrine** (săl′ə măn′drĭn), *adj.* —**Syn. 2.** See **sylph.**

Salambria (săl′ăm brē′ə), *n.* a river flowing through Thessaly, Greece, into the Gulf of Salonika. 125 mi. Ancient, **Peneus.**

salami (sə lä′mĭ), *n.* a kind of sausage, originally Italian, often flavoured with garlic. [t. It. (pl.), ult. der. L *salāre* to salt]

Salamis (săl′ə mĭs), *n.* **1.** an island off the SE coast of Greece, in the Gulf of Aegina: the Greeks defeated the Persians near Salamis in a naval battle, 480 B.C. 30,000 pop. (est. 1966); 39 sq. mi. **2.** an ancient city on Cyprus, in the E Mediterranean: the Apostle Paul made his first missionary journey to Salamis. Acts 13:5.

sal ammoniac, ammonium chloride.

salaried (săl′ə rĭd), *adj.* **1.** receiving a salary. **2.** having a salary attached.

salary (săl′ə rĭ), *n., pl.* **-ries.** a fixed periodical payment, usually monthly, paid to a person for regular work or services, esp. work other than that of a manual, mechanical, or menial kind. [ME *salarie*, t. AF, t. L: m. *salārium*, orig., money allowed to soldiers for the purchase of salt]

Salazar (săl′ə zä′; *Port.* sə lə zär′), *n.* **Antonio de Oliveira** (*Port.* ən′tō′nyŏŏ dė ō lē vəy′rə), 1889–1970, prime minister of Portugal 1932–68.

sale (sāl), *n.* **1.** the act of selling. **2.** the quantity sold. **3.** opportunity to sell; demand: *slow sale.* **4.** a special disposal of goods, as at reduced prices. **5.** transfer of property for money or credit. **6. for sale** or **on sale,** offered to be sold; offered to purchasers. [ME; late OE *sala*, c. Icel. and OHG *sala*. See SELL]

Sale (sāl), *n.* a town in England, in Cheshire. 51,336 (1961).

saleable (sā′lə bl), *adj.* subject to or suitable for sale; readily sold. Also, **salable.** —**sale′abil′ity,** *n.* —**sale′ably,** *adv.*

Salem (sā′ləm), *n.* **1.** a seaport in the U.S., in NE Massachusetts: founded 1626; execution of 'witches' 1692. 39,211 (1960). **2.** a town in the U.S., the capital of Oregon, in the NW part. 49,142 (1960). **3.** a city in India, in NE Madras state. 249,145 (1961).

sale of work, a sale of articles made by members of a church society, association, etc., in order to raise funds.

salep (săl′ĕp), *n.* a starchy drug or foodstuff consisting of the dried tubers of certain orchids. [t. Turk., t. d. Ar.: m. *sa'leb*, var. of *tha'leb*, short for *khasyu'th-tha'lab*, lit., fox's testicles]

saleratus (săl′ə rā′təs), *n. U.S.* potassium or sodium bicarbonate, used as an ingredient in baking powder. [t. NL: m. *sal ǣrātus* aerated salt]

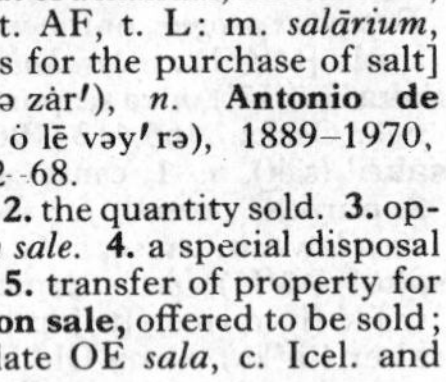

Salerno (sə lû′ nō; *It.* sȧ lĕr′nȯ), *n.* a seaport in SW Italy, in Campania. 139,082 (1966).

Salerno

saleroom (sāl′rŏŏm′, -rŏŏm′), *n.* salesroom.

salesclerk (sālz′klăk′), *n. U.S.* one who sells goods in a shop or store.

salesgirl (sālz′gûl′), *n.* a girl engaged to sell goods, in a shop, store, etc.

saleslady (sālz′lā′dĭ), *n., pl.* **-dies.** a saleswoman.

salesman (sālz′mən), *n., pl.* **-men.** a man engaged in selling.

salesmanship (sālz′mən shĭp′), *n.* **1.** the art of selling. **2.** skill in persuading people to buy by attractive presentation of goods, convincing talk, etc.

sales resistance, opposition or apathy by a prospective customer.

salesroom (sālz′rŏŏm′, -rŏŏm′), *n.* **1.** a room in which goods are sold or displayed. **2.** an auction room.

sales talk, 1. a line of reasoning or argument intended to effect a sale. **2.** any persuasive argument.

sales tax, *U.S.* purchase tax.

saleswoman (sālz′wŏŏm′ən), *n., pl.* **-women.** a woman who sells goods in a shop, store, etc.

Salford (sôl′fəd, sŏl′-), *n.* a city in England, in Lancashire. 148,260 (est. 1965).

Salian (sā′lyən), *adj.* **1.** of or pertaining to the **Salii,** a tribe of Franks who dwelt in the regions of the Rhine near the North Sea. —*n.* **2.** a Salian Frank.

Salic (săl′ĭk, sā′lĭk), *adj.* of or pertaining to the Salian Franks. Also, **Salique.** [t. ML: s. *Salicus*]

salicaceous (săl′ĭ kā′shəs), *adj.* belonging to the *Salicaceae*, a family of trees and shrubs containing the willows and poplars. [f. s. L *salix* willow + -ACEOUS]

salicin (săl′ĭ sĭn), *n.* a colourless, crystalline glucoside, $C_{13}H_{18}O_7$, obtained from the American aspen bark and used as an antipyretic. [t. F: m. *salicine*, f. s. L *salix* willow + *-ine* -INE[2]]

Salic law, 1. a code of laws of the Salian Franks and other Germanic tribes, esp. a provision in this code excluding females from the inheritance of land. **2.** the alleged fundamental law of the French monarchy by which females were excluded from succession to the crown. **3.** any law to the same effect.

salicylate (sə lĭs′ĭ lāt′), *n. Chem.* a salt or ester of salicylic acid. [f. SALIC(IN) + -YL + -ATE[2]]

salicylic acid (săl′ĭ sĭl′ĭk), *Chem.* an acid, $HOC_6H_4CO_2H$, prepared from salicin or from phenol, and used as an antiseptic, in the manufacture of aspirin, and medically as a remedy for rheumatic and gouty affections, usually in the form of a salicylate.

salience (sā′lyəns), *n.* **1.** the state or condition of being salient. **2.** a salient or projecting object, part, or feature.

saliency (sā′lyən sĭ), *n., pl.* **-cies.** salience.

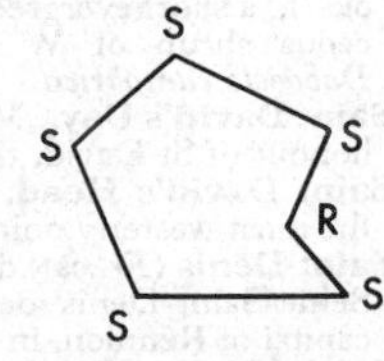

S, Salient angle
R, Re-entering angle

salient (sā′lyənt), *adj.* **1.** prominent or conspicuous: *salient features.* **2.** projecting or pointing outwards, as an angle. **3.** leaping or jumping. —*n.* **4.** a salient angle or part, as the central outward projecting angle of a bastion or an outward projection in a battle line. See diag. under **bastion.** [t. L: s. *saliens*, ppr., leaping forth] —**sa′liently,** *adv.*

salientian (sā′lĭ ĕn′shyən), *adj.* **1.** of or belonging to the salientians; anural. —*n.* **2.** any animal of the amphibian order *Salientia*, of which the toads and frogs are typical. [f. NL *Salienti(a)* (der. L *salīre* leap) + -AN]

saliferous (să lĭf′ə rəs), *adj.* containing or producing salt: *saliferous strata.* [f. L *sal* salt + -(I)FEROUS]

salify (săl′ĭ fī′), *v.t.,* **-fied, -fying. 1.** to form into a salt, as by chemical combination. **2.** to mix or combine with a salt. [t. NL: m. *salificāre*, der. L *sal* salt. See -FY]

salina (sə lī′nə), *n.* **1.** a saline marsh, spring, or the like. **2.** a saltworks. [t. Sp., g. L (found in pl. only)]

saline (sā′līn), *adj.* **1.** salty or saltlike; containing or tasting like common table salt: *a saline solution.* **2.** of or pertaining to a chemical salt, esp. of sodium, potassium, magnesium, etc., as used as a cathartic. —*n.* **3.** a saline medicine. [t. L: m. s. *salīnus* (found only in neut.), der. *sal* salt] —**salinity** (sə lĭn′ĭ tĭ), *n.*

Salinger (săl′ĭn jə), *n.* **J(erome) D(avid),** born 1919, U.S. author.

salinometer (săl′ĭ nŏm′ĭ tə), *n. Chem.* a hydrometer used for determining the concentration of salt solutions.

Salique (săl′ĭk, sā′lĭk), *adj.* Salic.

Salisbury (sôlz′bə rĭ, -brĭ), *n.* **1.** a city in England, the county town of Wiltshire: cathedral. 35,440 (est. 1962). **2.** a city in and the capital of Rhodesia. 313,700 (est. 1964). **3. Robert Arthur Talbot Gascoyne Cecil** (găs′koin), **3rd Marquess of,** 1830–1903, British statesman: prime minister 1885–86; 1886–92; 1895–1902.

Salisbury Plain, an extended elevated region in S England, N of Salisbury: the site of Stonehenge.

Salish (sā′lĭsh), *n.* **1.** (*pl.*) the eponymous tribe of the Salishan speech stock of North American Indians, formerly living in Montana, often called Flatheads by surrounding tribes. **2.** a member of this tribe or the Salishan family of tribes. [t. Amer. Ind. (Salishan): m. *sälst* (Salish) people]

Salishan (sā′lĭ shən, săl′ĭ-), *n.* **1.** an American Indian linguistic stock including Coeur-d'Alene and Flathead and other languages of British Columbia and the northwestern U.S. —*adj.* **2.** of this linguistic family.

saliva (sə lī′və), *n.* a fluid consisting of the secretions produced by glands which discharge into the mouth, containing ptyalin in man and certain other animals; spittle. [ME, t. L] —**salivary** (săl′ĭ və rĭ), *adj.*

salivate (săl′ĭ vāt′), *v.,* **-vated, -vating.** —*v.i.* **1.** *Physiol.* to produce saliva. —*v.t.* **2.** to produce an excessive secretion of saliva in, as by the use of mercury. [t. L: m. s. *salīvātus*, pp., spat out, salivated]

salivation (săl′ĭ vā′shən), *n.* **1.** the act or process of salivating. **2.** an abnormally abundant flow of saliva. **3.** mercurial poisoning.

Salk (sôlk), *n.* **Jonas Edward,** born 1914, U.S. bacteriologist: developed anti-poliomyelitis vaccine (**Salk vaccine**).

Sallal (să lăl′), *n.* **Abdulla** (ăb dŭl′ ə), born 1917, president of Yemen since 1962.

salle à manger (*Fr.* sȧl ȧ mäɴ zhė′), *French.* a dining room.

sallet (săl′ĭt), *n.* a light medieval helmet, usually with a vision slit or a movable visor. [late ME, t. F: m. *salade*, t. It.: m. *celata*, g. L *caelāta*, pp. fem., engraved]

sallow[1] (săl′ō), *adj.* **1.** of a yellowish, sickly hue or complexion: *sallow cheeks.* —*v.t.* **2.** to make sallow. [ME *salowe*, OE *salo*, c. Icel. *sölr* yellow] —**sal′lowish,** *adj.* —**sal′lowness,** *n.*

sallow[2] (săl′ō), *n.* any of several tall shrubby willows with elliptical or ovate leaves, as the common sallow, *Salix cinerea.* [ME; OE *sealh*, c. OHG *salaha*, Icel. *selja*, L *salix*]

sallowy (săl′ō ĭ), *adj.* full of sallows or willows.

Sallust (săl′əst), *n.* (*Caius Sallustius Crispus*), 86–34 B.C., Roman historian.

sally (săl′ĭ), *n., pl.* **-lies,** *v.,* **-lied, -lying.** —*n.* **1.** a sortie of troops from a besieged place upon an enemy. **2.** a sudden rushing forth or activity. **3.** an excursion or expedition. **4.** an outburst or flight of passion, fancy, etc.: *sally of anger.* **5.** a sprightly or brilliant utterance or remark. —*v.i.* **6.** to make a sally, as a body of troops from a besieged place. **7.** to set out on an excursion or expedition. **8.** to set out briskly or energetically. **9.** (of things) to issue forth. —*v.t.* **10.** *Naut.* to force (a ship that is icebound or has run aground) to free herself by making her roll from side to side. [t. F: m. *saillie* issuing forth, outrush, der. *saillir* leap, g. L *salire*]

Sally Lunn (lŭn), a kind of sweet spongy teacake served hot with butter. [named after a woman who sold them in the streets of Bath at the end of the 18th century]

salmagundi (săl′mə gŭn′dĭ), *n.* **1.** a mixed dish consisting of minced meat, anchovies, eggs, onions, oil, etc. **2.** any mixture or miscellany. [t. F: m. *salmigondis*, ult. t. It.: m. *salami conditi* pickled sausages]

salmi (săl′mĭ), *n.* a ragout of roasted game, fowl, or the like, stewed in wine. Also, **salmis** (săl′mĭ; *Fr.* sȧl mē′). [t. F, prob. short for *salmigondis.* See SALMAGUNDI]

salmon (săm′ən), *n., pl.* **-mons,** (*esp. collectively*) **-mon,** *adj.* —*n.* **1.** a marine and freshwater food fish, *Salmo salar* (family *Salmonidae*), with pink flesh, common in the northern Atlantic Ocean near the mouths of large rivers, which it ascends to spawn. **2.** a variety of this species confined to lakes, etc. (**landlocked salmon**). **3.** any of several important food fishes of the North Pacific salmonoid genus *Oncorhynchus*, as the **chinook, king,** or **quinnat, salmon,** *O. tschwaytscha*; the **red, sockeye,** or **blueback, salmon,** *O. nerka*; or the **pink** or **humpback salmon,** *O. gorbuscha.* **4.** light yellowish pink. —*adj.* **5.** of the colour salmon. [ME, t. AF: m. *salmun*, g. s. L *salmo*]

salmon-bass (săm′ən băs′), *n.* kabeljou; the South African food fish, *Otolinthus ruber.*

salmonberry (săm′ən bə rĭ, -brĭ), *n., pl.* **-ries. 1.** the salmon-coloured edible fruit of *Rubus spectabilis*, a raspberry with large red or purple flowers, of the Pacific coast of North America. **2.** the plant.

salmonella (săl′mə nĕl′ə), *n., pl.* **-nellae** (-nĕl′ē). *Bacteriol.* any of several facultatively anaerobic bacteria (genus *Salmonella*), pathogenic for man and warm-blooded animals. [named after Daniel E. *Salmon*, 1850–1914, American pathologist]

salmonoid (săl′mə noid′), *adj.* **1.** resembling a salmon. **2.** belonging or pertaining to the suborder *Salmonoidea*, to which the salmon family belongs. —*n.* **3.** a member of the salmon family, *Salmonidae.* **4.** a salmonoid fish.

salmon pink, salmon (defs 4, 5).

salmon trout, 1. a European trout, *Salmo trutta.* **2.** any large trout.

salol (săl′ŏl), *n.* a white crystalline substance, $C_{13}H_{10}O_3$, prepared by the interaction of salicylic acid and phenol, and used as an antipyretic, antiseptic, etc. [f. *sal*(*icyl*) (see SALICYLATE) + -OL[1]]

Salome (sə lō′mĭ), *n. Bible.* the daughter of Herodias, whose dancing so pleased Herod that he gave her the head of John the Baptist at her request, as dictated by her mother. [t. LL, t. Gk, t. Heb.: m. *shālōm* peace]

salon (săl′ŏn; *Fr.* sȧ lôɴ′), *n., pl.* **-lons** (-lŏnz; *Fr.* -lôɴ′). **1.** a drawing room or reception room in a large house. **2.** an assembly of guests in such a room, esp. such an assembly consisting of leaders in fashion, art, politics, etc. (common during the 17th and 18th centuries). **3.** a hall or place used for the exhibition of works of art. **4.** a fashionable business establishment or shop: *beauty salon, hairdressing salon.* **5.** (*cap.*) (in France) a public showing of works of art by living artists. [t. F, t. It.: m. *salone*, aug. of *sala* hall, t. Gmc; cf. OE *sæl* hall]

Salonika (sə lŏn′ĭ kə), *n.* a seaport in NE Greece, in Macedonia, on the **Gulf of Salonika,** a NW arm of the Aegean. 250,920 (1961). Also, **Salonica** or **Saloniki** (sə lŏn′ĭ kĭ). Official name, **Thessaloniki.** Ancient, **Thessalonica.** See map under **Macedonia.**

saloon (sə lo͞on′), *n.* **1.** a room or place for general use for a specific purpose: *a dining saloon on a ship.* **2.** a large cabin for the common use of passengers on a passenger vessel. **3.** a saloon bar. **4.** *U.S.* any place where alcoholic drinks are sold to be consumed on the premises. **5.** a saloon car or carriage. **6.** *Obs.* a drawing room or reception room. [t. F: m. *salon* SALON]

saloon bar, (in a public house) a division of the bar with higher social status, higher prices, and more comfort than the public bar.

saloon car, a solid-roofed car body seating four or more persons (including the driver) on two full-width seats, both in one compartment.

saloop (sə lo͞op′), *n.* a hot drink prepared from salep, or, later, from sassafras, etc., formerly popular in London. [var. of SALEP]

Salop (săl′əp), *n.* Shropshire. [var. of *Slop*, var. of SHROP(SHIRE)] —**Salopian** (sə lō′pyən), *adj., n.*

Salote Tupou (sə lō′tĭ to͞o′pou), 1900–65, Queen of Tonga 1918–65.

salpa (săl′pə), *n.* any of the pelagic oceanic tunicates constituting the genus *Salpa*, common in warm regions, and having a transparent, more or less fusiform body. [NL, special use of L *salpa* stockfish] —**salpiform** (săl′pĭ fôm′), *adj.*

salpingitis (săl′pĭn jī′tĭs), *n.* inflammation of the uterine or Eustachian tubes.

salpinx (săl′pĭngks), *n., pl.* **salpinges** (săl pĭn′jēz). *Anat.* a trumpet-shaped tube, as the Fallopian (uterine) and Eustachian (auditory) tubes. [NL, t. Gk: trumpet]

salsify (săl′sĭ fĭ), *n.* a purple-flowered plant, *Tragopogon porrifolius*, whose root has an oyster-like flavour and is used as a culinary vegetable; oyster plant. [t. F: m. *salsifis*, t. It.: m. *sassefrica*; ult. orig. uncert.]

sal soda, sodium carbonate.

salt (sôlt), *n.* **1.** a crystalline compound, sodium chloride, NaCl, occurring as a mineral, a constituent of sea water, etc., and used for seasoning food, as a preservative, etc. **2.** *Chem.* a compound which upon dissociation yields cations (positively charged) of a metal, and anions (negatively charged) of an acid radical. **3.** (*pl.*) any of various salts used as purgatives: *Epsom salts.* **4.** a salt-cellar. **5.** a salt marsh. **6.** that which gives liveliness, piquancy, or pungency to anything. **7.** wit; pungency. **8.** *Colloq.* a sailor, esp. an experienced one. **9. salt of the earth,** the best element of people. **10. with a grain of salt,** believe with reservation. **11. worth one's salt,** capable; efficient; deserving one's pay. —*v.t.* **12.** to season with salt. **13.** to cure, preserve, or treat with salt. **14.** to furnish with salt: *to salt cattle.* **15.** *Chem.* **a.** to treat with common salt or with any chemical salt. **b.** to add common salt to (a solution) in order to separate a dissolved substance (usually with *out*). **16.** to introduce rich ore or other valuable matter fraudulently into (a mine, ground, sample, etc.) to create a false impression of value. **17. salt away** or **down, a.** to preserve by adding quantities of salt. **b.** *Colloq.* to lay or store away in reserve: *to salt a lot of money away.* —*adj.* **18.** containing salt; having the taste of salt: *salt water.* **19.** cured or preserved with salt: *salt cod.* **20.** overflowed with or growing in salt water: *salt marsh.* **21.** pungent or sharp: *salt speech.* [ME; OE *sealt*, c. G *Salz*, Icel. and Goth. *salt*; akin to Gk *háls*, L *sal*] —**salt′like′,** *adj.* —**Syn. 8.** See **sailor.**

Salt (sôlt), *n.* a town in Jordan, in the W part. 60,000 (est. 1965).

saltant (săl′tənt), *adj.* dancing; leaping; jumping. [t. L: s. *saltans*, ppr.]

saltarello (săl′tə rĕl′ō; *It.* sȧl tȧ rĕl′lō), *n., pl.* **-relli** (-rĕl′ĭ; *It.* -rĕl′lē). **1.** a lively Italian dance for one person or a couple. **2.** the music for it. [It., ult. der. L *saltāre* dance]

saltation (săl tā′shən), *n.* **1.** dancing; leaping. **2.** an abrupt movement or transition. **3.** movement of particles of sand or the like by wind or water in short intermittent leaps or waves. **4.** *Biol.* a mutation.

saltatorial (săl′tə tô′rĭ əl), *adj.* **1.** pertaining to saltation. **2.** *Zool.* characterized by or adapted for leaping.

saltatory (săl′tə tə rĭ, -trĭ), *adj.* **1.** pertaining to or adapted for saltation. **2.** proceeding by abrupt movements.

saltbush (sôlt′bo͝osh′), *n.* any of several species of drought-resistant fodder plants of the genus *Atriplex*, of Australia.

saltcake (sôlt′kāk′), *n. Chem.* an impure form of sodium sulphate.

saltcellar (sôlt′sĕl′ə), *n.* **1.** a shaker or vessel for salt. **2.** *Colloq.* either of the hollows above the collarbone of thin people. [ME *saltsaler*, f. SALT + (now obs.) *saler* saltceller, t. OF: m. *saliere*, der. *sel* salt, g. L *sal*]

Saltcoats (sôlt′kōts′), *n.* a burgh in Scotland, in Ayrshire, on the Firth of Clyde. 14,187 (1961).

salt dome, in sedimentary rocks, a domelike anticline

having a core of rock-salt which was forced upwards from an underlying bed of salt when in the plastic state under pressure. Also, **salt plug.**

salted (sôl′tĭd), *adj.* **1.** seasoned, cured, or otherwise treated with salt. **2.** *Slang.* experienced in some occupation, etc.

salter (sôl′tə), *n.* **1.** one who makes or deals in salt. **2.** one who salts meat, fish, etc.

saltern (sôl′tən), *n.* **1.** a saltworks. **2.** a plot of land laid out in pools for the evaporation of sea water to produce salt. [OE *sealtærn* saltworks, f. *sealt* SALT + *ærn* house. Cf. BARN[1]]

salt glaze, a glaze formed on stoneware when salt is introduced into the kiln during firing.

saltigrade (săl′tĭ grād′), *adj.* **1.** moving by leaping. **2.** belonging to the *Saltigradae*, a group of saltatorial spiders. [f. *salti-* (comb. form of L *saltus* leap) + -GRADE]

Saltillo (*Sp.* säl tē′lyô), *n.* a city in N Mexico. 117,827 (est. 1965).

saltire (sôl′tī′ə), *n. Her.* an ordinary in the form of a Saint Andrew's Cross. Also, **saltier.** [ME *sawtire*, t. OF: m. *sautoir*, orig., saddle cord for aid in mounting, der. *sauter* leap, g. L *saltāre*]

saltish (sôl′tĭsh), *adj.* somewhat salt; salty.

salt lake, an inland sheet of water with high salinity.

Salt Lake City, a city in the U.S., the capital of Utah, in the N part, near Great Salt Lake. 189,454 (1960).

salt-lick (sôlt′lĭk′), *n.* a place to which wild animals resort to lick salt occurring naturally there.

salt marsh, a marshy tract, wet with salt water or flooded by the sea.

salt mine, **1.** a mine from which salt is excavated. **2.** (*usually pl.*) a place of habitual confinement and drudgery.

Salto (*Sp.* säl′tô; *Port.* säl′to͞o), *n.* a town in NW Uruguay. 60,000 (est. 1964).

Salton Sink (sôl′tən), the lowest part of the Imperial Valley, in S California: submerged by the Colorado river in 1906, forming the **Salton Sea.** 282 ft below sea-level.

saltpan (sôlt′păn′), *n.* a small basin flooded by salt deposits, the remains of an evaporated salt lake which may have entirely disappeared.

saltpetre (sôlt′pē′tə), *n.* **1.** nitre (nitrate of potassium), KNO^3. **2.** Chile saltpetre. Also, *U.S.*, **saltpeter.** [alter. (after SALT) of ME *salpetre*, t. ML: m. *sal petrae* salt of the rock]

saltpit (sôlt′pĭt′), *n.* a pit where salt is obtained.

salt rheum, *U.S.* any of various common cutaneous eruptions, as eczema.

salts of lemon, *Chem.* potassium quadroxalate, $KH_3C_4O_8$. $2H_2O$, a white soluble salt used for removing ink stains.

salt water, water containing a high proportion of salt, esp. sea water.

salt-water (sôlt′wô′tə), *adj.* **1.** of or pertaining to salt water. **2.** inhabiting salt water.

saltworks (sôlt′wûks′), *n.sing. and pl.* a building or place where salt is made.

saltwort (sôlt′wût′), *n.* any of various plants of sea beaches, salt marshes, and alkaline regions, esp. of the chenopodiaceous genus *Salsola*, as *S. kali*, a bushy plant with prickly leaves, or of the chenopodiaceous genus *Salicornia.* See **glasswort.**

salty (sôl′tĭ), *adj.*, **saltier, saltiest. 1.** containing, or tasting of, salt. **2.** piquant; sharp; witty; racy. **—salt′ily,** *adv.* **—salt′iness,** *n.*

salubrious (sə lo͞o′brĭ əs), *adj.* favourable to health; promoting health: now used esp. of air, climate, etc. [f. SALUBRI(TY) (t. L: m. s. *salūbritas* healthfulness) + -OUS] **—salu′briously,** *adv.* **—salu′briousness, salubrity** (sə-lo͞o′brĭ tĭ), *n.*

saluki (sə lo͞o′kĭ), *n.* a smooth silky-coated hunting dog, a member of the greyhound family, about 2 ft high, with long ears, legs, and tail. [t. Ar.: m. *salūqī*, named after *Salūq* ancient city in Arabia]

Salus (sā′ləs), *n.* the Roman goddess of health and prosperity.

salutary (săl′yo͝o tə rĭ, -trĭ), *adj.* **1.** conducive to health; healthful. **2.** promoting or conducive to some beneficial purpose; wholesome. [t. L: m. *salūtāris*] **—sal′utarily,** *adv.* **—sal′utariness,** *n.* **—Syn. 1.** See **healthy.**

salutation (săl′yo͝o tā′shən), *n.* **1.** the act of saluting. **2.** something uttered, written, or done by way of saluting. **3.** the opening of a letter or of a speech as 'Dear Sir', 'Ladies and Gentlemen'.

salutatorian (sə lo͞o′tə tô′rĭ ən), *n.* (in American colleges and schools) the student who delivers the salutatory oration.

salutatory (sə lo͞o′tə tə rĭ, -trĭ), *adj.*, *n.*, *pl.* **-ries. —***adj.* **1.** pertaining to or of the nature of a salutation. **—***n.* **2.** an address of welcome, esp. one given by a member of the graduating class in an American college.

salute (sə lo͞ot′), *v.*, **-luted, -luting,** *n.* **—***v.t.* **1.** to address with expressions of goodwill, respect, etc.; greet. **2.** to make a bow, gesture, or the like to in greeting, farewell, respect, etc. **3.** *Mil.*, *Naval.* to pay respect to or honour by some formal act, as by raising the right hand to the side of the headgear, presenting arms, firing cannon, dipping colours, etc. **—***v.i.* **4.** to perform a salutation. **5.** *Mil.*, *Naval.* to give a salute. **—***n.* **6.** an act of saluting; salutation; greeting. **7.** *Mil.*, *Naval.* **a.** the special act of respect paid in saluting. **b.** the position of the hand or rifle in saluting: *at the salute.* [ME, t. L: m. s. *salūtāre* greet] **—salut′er,** *n.*

salutiferous (săl′yo͝o tĭf′ə rəs), *adj.* salutary.

Salvador (săl′və dô′; *Sp.* säl bä dôr′), *n.* **1.** El Salvador. **2.** Official name of **São Salvador. —Sal′vado′ran, Salvadorian** (săl′və dô′rĭ ən), *adj.*, *n.*

salvage (săl′vĭj), *n.*, *v.*, **-vaged, -vaging. —***n.* **1.** the act of saving a ship or its cargo from perils of the seas. **2.** the property so saved. **3.** compensation given to those who voluntarily save a ship or its cargo. **4.** the saving of anything from fire, danger, etc., or the property so saved. **5.** the value or proceeds upon sale of goods recovered from a shipwreck, fire, danger, or the like. **—***v.t.* **6.** to save from shipwreck, fire, etc. **7.** to recover or save as salvage. [t. ML: m. s. *salvāgium*, der. L *salvāre* save] **—sal′vager,** *n.*

salvarsan (săl′və săn′), *n. Pharm.* **1.** arsphenamine. **2.** (*cap.*) a trademark for this. [f. s. L *salvus* well + ARS(ENIC) + -AN]

salvation (săl vā′shən), *n.* **1.** the act of saving or delivering. **2.** the state of being saved or delivered. **3.** a source, cause, or means of deliverance: *to be the salvation of a friend.* **4.** *Theol.* deliverance from the power and penalty of sin; redemption. [ME, t. LL: s. *salvātio*]

Salvation Army, a quasi-military organization, founded in 1865 by William Booth to revive religion among the masses; renowned for its charitable work among the poor and homeless.

Salvationism (săl vā′shə nĭz′əm), *n.* **1.** religious teaching stressing the salvation of the soul. **2.** the principles of the Salvation Army.

Salvationist (săl vā′shə nĭst), *n.* **1.** a member of the Salvation Army. **2.** a member of any other evangelical movement.

salve[1] (sălv, säv), *n.*, *v.*, **salved, salving. —***n.* **1.** a healing ointment to be applied to wounds and sores for relief or healing. **2.** anything that soothes or mollifies. **—***v.t.* **3.** to soothe as if with salve: *to salve one's conscience.* **4.** *Obs.* to apply salve to. [ME; OE *sealf*, c. G *Salbe*]

salve[2] (sălv), *v.i.*, *v.t.*, **salved, salving.** to save from loss or destruction; to salvage. [back-formation from SALVAGE]

salve[3] (săl′vĭ), *interj.* Hail! [L: be in good health!]

salver (săl′və), *n.* a tray. [f. Sp. *salv(a)* foretasting, hence tray (der. *salvar* protect, save, t. L: m. *salvāre*) + *-er*, modelled on *platter* or the like]

Salvi (*It.* säl′vē), *n.* **Nicola** (*It.* nē kô′lä), 1697–1751, Italian baroque architect.

salvia (săl′vĭ ə), *n.* any of the menthaceous herbs or shrubs constituting the genus *Salvia*, as *S. splendens*, the scarlet salvia, an ornamental garden plant. [t. L]

Salvini (*It.* säl vē′nē), *n.* **Tommaso** (tôm mä′zô), 1829–1916, Italian actor.

salvo[1] (săl′vō), *n.*, *pl.*, **-vos, -voes. 1.** a discharge of artillery or other firearms, in regular succession, often intended as a salute. **2.** a round of cheers, applause, etc. [earlier *salva*, t. It. See SALVE[3]]

salvo[2] (săl′vō), *n.*, *pl.* **-vos.** *Rare.* **1.** an excuse or quibbling evasion. **2.** something to save a person's reputation, feelings, etc. [t. L, abl. of *salvus* safe, used in legal phrases, as *salvō jūre* the right being safe]

sal volatile (săl′və lăt′ĭ lĭ), **1.** ammonium carbonate. **2.** an aromatic alcoholic solution of this salt used as a restorative for fainting, dizziness, etc., by inhalation.

salvor (săl′və), *n.* one who salvages or helps to salvage a ship, cargo, etc.

Salween (săl′wēn), *n.* a river flowing from SW China, S through E Burma to the Bay of Bengal. ab. 1750 mi. See map under **Mandalay.**

Salzburg (sălts′bûg, sôlts′-; *Ger.* zälts′bo͝ork), *n.* **1.** a province in W central Austria. 347,292 pop. (1961); 2762 sq. mi. **2.** the capital of this province: historic city near the German border. 108,114 (1961).

Salzgitter (*Ger.* zälts gĭt′ər), *n.* a town in West Germany, in SE Lower Saxony. 117,900 (est. 1966).

Sam., *Bible.* Samuel.

S Am., 1. South America. **2.** South American.

Samar (sä′mä; *Sp.* sä mär′), *n.* one of the Philippine Islands, in the E part of the group. 969,000 pop. (est. 1963); 5050 sq. mi. See map under **Leyte.**

samara (săm′ə rə), *n. Bot.* an indehiscent, usually one-seeded, winged fruit, as of the elm. [t. NL, special use of L *samara* seed of the elm]

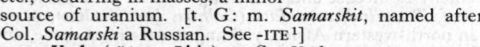

A B C
Samara (cross-sections) A, Ash, *Fraxinus* sp.; B, Elm, *Ulmus* sp.; C, Birch, *Betula* sp.

Samara (*Russ.* sȧ mȧ′rə), *n.* former name of **Kuibyshev.**

Samarang (*Indon.* sə mȧ′räng), *n.* Semarang.

Samaria (sə mĕə′rĭ ə), *n.* **1.** an ancient kingdom in N Palestine between the river Jordan and the Mediterranean: later a province. See map under **Tyre. 2.** the northern kingdom of the ancient Hebrews; Israel. **3.** the ancient capital of this kingdom.

Samaritan (sə mă′rĭ tən), *n.* **1.** an inhabitant of Samaria. **2.** See **good Samaritan. 3.** one who is compassionate and helpful to a fellow being in distress. —*adj.* **4.** pertaining to Samaria, or to Samaritans.

samarium (sə mĕə′rĭ əm), *n. Chem.* a rare-earth metallic element discovered in samarskite. *Symbol:* Sm; *at. wt:* 150 35; *at. no.:* 62. [f. SAMAR(SKITE) + -IUM]

Samarkand (săm′ä kănd′; *Russ.* sə mȧr kȧnt′), *n.* a city in the SW Soviet Union in Asia, N of Afghanistan: taken by Alexander the Great, 329 B.C.; Tamerlane's capital in the 14th century. 233,000 (est. 1965). Also, **Samarcand.**

SAMARKAND SOVIET UNION CHINA IRAN AFGHANISTAN Kabul WEST PAKISTAN KASHMIR
Samarkand

samarskite (sə mä′skīt), *n.* a velvet-black mineral, a complex of columbium and tantalum compounds with uranium, cerium, etc., occurring in masses, a minor source of uranium. [t. G: m. *Samarskit*, named after Col. *Samarski* a Russian. See -ITE[1]]

Sama-Veda (sä′mə vā′də), *n.* See **Veda.**

samba (săm′bə), *n.* a ballroom dance of Brazilian (ultimately African) origin.

sambar (săm′bə), *n.* a medium-to-large deer of the subgenus *Rusa*, having three-pointed antlers, found in south-eastern Asia and many of the Indo-Australian islands. Also, **sambur.** [t. Hind.]

sambo (săm′bō), *n., pl.* **-bos. 1.** the offspring of Negro and Indian (or mulatto) parents. **2.** (*usually cap.*) (offensively) a Negro. [prob. t. Sp.: m. *zambo*]

Sambre (*Fr.* säɴ′br), *n.* a river flowing NE through N France and S Belgium into the Meuse. ab. 100 mi.

Sam Browne belt (săm′broun′), a military belt having a supporting strap over the right shoulder, worn by officers.

sambuca (săm byōō′kə), *n.* an ancient stringed musical instrument used in Greece and the Near East. [t. L, t. Gk: m. *sambýkē*. Cf. Aramaic *sabbeka*]

same (sām), *adj.* **1.** identical with what is about to be or has just been mentioned: *the very same man.* **2.** being one or identical, though having different names, aspects, etc.: *these are one and the same thing.* **3.** agreeing in kind, amount, etc.; corresponding: *two boxes of the same dimensions.* **4.** unchanged in character, condition, etc. —*pron.* **5.** the same person or thing. **6. the same,** with the same manner (used adverbially). **7. all the same, a.** notwithstanding; nevertheless. **b.** immaterial; unimportant. **8. just the same, a.** in the same manner. **b.** nevertheless. [ME and OE, c. Icel. *sami, sama, samr*; in OE used only as adv.]

—**Syn. 1.** similar, like, corresponding, interchangeable, equal. SAME, SIMILAR agree in indicating a correspondence between two or more things. SAME means or pretends to mean alike in kind, degree, quality; that is, identical (with): *to eat the same food every day, at the same price.* SIMILAR means like, resembling, having certain qualities in common, somewhat the same as, of nearly the same kind as: *similar in appearance; because they are similar, toadstools are sometimes thought to be the same as mushrooms.* —**Ant. 1.** different, unlike.

sameness (sām′nĭs), *n.* **1.** the state of being the same; identity; uniformity. **2.** lack of variety; monotony.

S Amer., 1. South America. **2.** South American.

samiel (săm′yĕl), *n.* simoom. [t. Turk.: m. *samyel*, f. *sam* (t. Ar.: m. *samma* to poison) + *yel* wind]

samisen (săm′ĭ sĕn′), *n.* a Japanese guitar-like musical instrument, having an extremely long neck and three strings, played with a plectrum. [t. Jap., t. Chinese: m. *san-hsien* three-stringed (instrument)]

Samisen

samite (săm′īt, sā′mīt), *n.* a heavy silk fabric, sometimes interwoven with gold, worn in the Middle Ages. [ME, t. OF: m. *samit*, t. MGk: m. *hexámiton*, lit., six-threaded]

samlet (săm′lĭt), *n.* a young salmon. [syncopated and dissimilated var. of *salmonet*, f. SALMON + -ET]

Samnium (săm′nĭ əm), *n.* an ancient country in central Italy. —**Samnite** (săm′nīt), *adj., n.*

Samoa (sə mō′ə), *n.* a group of islands in the S Pacific comprising: **Western Samoa** (the former trusteeship of New Zealand), 114,427 pop. (1961); 1133 sq. mi.; and **American Samoa,** 20,051 pop. (1960); 76 sq. mi. Formerly, **Navigators Islands.** See map under **Hawaiian Islands.**

Samoan (sə mō′ən), *adj.* **1.** pertaining to Samoa or its (Polynesian) people. —*n.* **2.** a native or inhabitant of Samoa. **3.** the Polynesian language of Samoa.

Samos (sā′mŏs), *n.* a Greek island in the Aegean, off the W coast of Asia Minor. 52,034 pop. (1961); 194 sq. mi. —**Samian** (sā′myən), *adj., n.*

Samothrace (săm′ō thrās′), *n.* a Greek island in the NE Aegean: the Apostle Paul visited Samothrace on his trip to Macedonia, Acts 16:11. Greek, **Samothrake** (*Gk* sȧ mô thrȧ′kē). —**Samothracian** (săm′ō thrā′shyən), *adj., n.*

samousa (sə mōō′sə), *n.* a savoury pastry with curried meat or vegetable filling, usually triangular in shape. [? t. Malay, g. Swahili *sambusa*]

samovar (săm′ə vä′, săm′ə vä′), *n.* a metal urn, commonly of copper, used in the Soviet Union and elsewhere for heating the water for making tea. [t. Russ.: self-boiler]

Samoyed (săm′oi ĕd′ *for* 1 *and* 2; sə moi′ĕd *for* 3), *n.* **1.** a member of a Ural-Altaic people dwelling in north-western Siberia and along the north-eastern coast of the Soviet Union in Europe. **2.** a family of five closely related Uralian languages scattered over a large area of the north-western Asiatic and north-eastern European Soviet Union. **3.** one of a breed of Russian dogs, medium in size, with a coat of long, dense, white hair. [t. Russ.: self-eater]

Samoyedic (săm′oi ĕd′ĭk), *adj.* of or pertaining to the Samoyeds.

samp (sămp), *n. U.S.* **1.** coarsely ground maize. **2.** a porridge made of it. [t. Algonquian: m. *nasamp*, lit., softened by water]

sampan (săm′păn), *n.* any of various small boats of China, etc., as one propelled by a single scull over the stern, and provided with a roofing of mats. [t. Chinese: m. *san-pan*, lit., three boards]

Sampan

samphire (săm′fī′ə), *n.* **1.** a succulent apiaceous herb, *Crithmum maritimum*, of Europe, growing in clefts of rock near the sea; its fleshy leaves are used in pickles. **2.** the glasswort. [earlier *sampere, sampire*, alter. of F (*herbe de*) *Saint Pierre* St Peter's herb]

sample (säm′pl), *n., adj., v.,* **-pled, -pling.** —*n.* **1.** a small part of anything or one of a number, intended to show the quality, style, etc., of the whole; a specimen. —*adj.* **2.** serving as a specimen: *a sample copy.* —*v.t.* **3.** to take a sample or samples of; test or judge by a sample. [ME, aphetic var. of *essample*, var. of EXAMPLE] —**Syn. 1.** See **example.**

sampler (säm′plə), *n.* **1.** one who samples. **2.** a piece of cloth embroidered with various devices, serving to show a beginner's skill in needlework. [ME *samplere*, t. OF: aphetic m. *essamplaire*, g. LL *exemplārium*, der. L *exemplum* EXAMPLE]

Samson (săm′sən), *n.* **1.** a performer of herculean exploits, the fifteenth of the 'judges' of Israel. Judges 13–16. **2.** any man of extraordinary strength.

Samsun (*Turk.* säm′sōōn), *n.* a seaport in Turkey, on the Black Sea. 87,688 (1960).

Samuel (săm′yōō əl), *n.* **1.** a Hebrew judge and prophet. I Sam. 1–3, 8–15. **2.** either of the two Old Testament books bearing his name.

samurai (săm′ōō rī′), *n., pl.* **-rai.** (in feudal Japan) **1.** a member of the military class. **2.** a retainer of a Japanese feudal noble, holding land or receiving a stipend in rice or money. [t. Jap.]

san (săn), *n. Colloq.* sanatorium.

San (*Pol.* sȧn), *n.* a river flowing from the Carpathian Mountains in the W Soviet Union through SE Poland into the Vistula. ab. 280 mi.

San'a (sä nä′), *n.* a city in the SW Arabian peninsula: the capital of Yemen. 100,000 (est. 1966). Also, **Sanaa.**

San Antonio (săn′ăn tō′nĭ ō′), a city in the U.S. in S Texas: site of the Alamo. 587,718 (1960).

sanative (săn′ə tĭv), *adj.* having the power to heal; curative. [t. ML: m. s. *sānātīvus*]

sanatorium (săn′ə tô′rĭ əm), *n., pl.* **-toriums, -toria** (-tô′rĭ ə). **1.** an establishment for the treatment of invalids, convalescents, etc., esp. in a favourable climate:

a tuberculosis sanatorium. **2.** a health resort. **3.** that part of a boarding school set apart for the treatment or isolation of sick pupils. Also, *U.S.*, **sanitarium.** [t. NL, prop. neut. of LL *sānātōrius* health-giving, der. L *sānātus*, pp., healed] —**Syn. 1.** See **hospital.**

sanatory (săn′ə tə rĭ, -trĭ), *adj.* favourable for health; curative; healing. [t. LL: m. s. *sānātōrius*]

sanbenito (săn′bĕ nē′tō), *n., pl.* **-tos.** (under the Spanish Inquisition) **1.** a yellow garment ornamented with flames, devils, etc., worn by a condemned heretic at an auto-da-fé. **2.** a penitential garment worn by a confessed heretic. [t. Sp., named after *San Benito* St Benedict, from its resemblance to the scapular introduced by him]

San Bernardino (săn′bû′nə dē′nō), a mountain pass in the Alps, in SE Switzerland. 6766 ft high.

San Blas (săn bläs′), **1. Gulf of,** a gulf of the Caribbean on the N coast of Panama. **2. Isthmus of,** the narrowest part of the Isthmus of Panama. 31 mi. wide.

San Carlos (săn kä′ləs; *Sp.* sàn kàr′lòs), a city in the Philippine Islands, on Luzon island. 124,756 (1960).

Sancho Panza (săn′chō păn′zə; *Sp.* sàn′chò pàn′thà), the credulous and amusing squire of Don Quixote.

San Cristóbal (*Sp.* sàn krēs tò′bàl), **1.** a town in S Dominican Republic. 286,094 (1964). **2.** a town in NW Venezuela. 98,777 (1961).

sanctified (săngk′tĭ fīd′), *adj.* **1.** made holy; consecrated: *sanctified wine.* **2.** sanctimonious.

sanctify (săngk′tĭ fī′), *v.t.*, **-fied, -fying. 1.** to make holy; set apart as sacred; consecrate. **2.** to purify or free from sin: *sanctify your hearts.* **3.** to impart religious sanction to; render legitimate or binding: *to sanctify a vow.* **4.** to make productive of or conducive to spiritual blessing. **5.** *Obs.* to entitle to reverence or respect. [t. Eccles. L: m. *sanctificāre* make holy; r. ME *seintefie*, t. OF] —**sanctification** (săngk′tĭ fĭ kā′shən), *n.* —**sanc′tifi′er,** *n.* —**sanc′tifi′able,** *adj.*

sanctimonious (săngk′tĭ mō′nyəs), *adj.* **1.** making a show of holiness; affecting sanctity. **2.** *Obs.* holy; sacred. [f. SANCTIMONY + -OUS] —**sanc′timo′niously,** *adv.* —**sanc′timo′niousness,** *n.*

sanctimony (săngk′tĭ mə nĭ), *n.* **1.** pretended, affected, or hypocritical holiness or devoutness. **2.** *Obs.* sanctity; sacredness. [t. L: m. s. *sanctimōnia*]

sanction (săngk′shən), *n.* **1.** authoritative permission; countenance or support given to an action, etc.; solemn ratification. **2.** something serving to support an action, etc. **3.** binding force given, or something which gives binding force, as to an oath, rule of conduct, etc. **4.** *Law.* **a.** a provision of a law enacting a penalty for disobedience. **b.** the penalty. **5.** *Internat. Law.* action by one or more states towards another state calculated to force it to comply with legal obligations. —*v.t.* **6.** to authorize, countenance, or approve: *sanctioned by usage.* **7.** to ratify or confirm: *to sanction a law.* [t. L: s. *sanctio*]

sanctity (săngk′tĭ tĭ), *n., pl.* **-ties. 1.** holiness, saintliness, or godliness. **2.** sacred or hallowed character: *inviolable sanctity of the temple.* **3.** a sacred thing. [t. L: m. s. *sanctitas*; r. ME *saintite*, t. OF]

sanctuary (săngk′tyŏŏ ə rĭ), *n., pl.* **-ries. 1.** a sacred or holy place. **2.** *Jewish Hist.* **a.** the temple at Jerusalem, particularly the most retired part of it (the **holy of holies**) in which the ark of the covenant was kept. **b.** the tabernacle in the wilderness after the exodus from Egypt. **3.** an especially holy place in a temple or church. **4.** the part of a church about the altar; the chancel. **5.** a church or other sacred place where fugitives were formerly entitled to immunity from arrest; asylum. **6.** immunity afforded by refuge in such a place. **7.** a place protected by law where birds or other animals are left undisturbed. [ME, t. L: m. s. *sanctuārium*] —**Syn. 1.** church, temple, shrine, altar, sanctum, adytum.

sanctum (săngk′təm), *n., pl.* **-tums,** (*Rare*) **-ta** (-tə). **1.** a sacred or holy place. **2.** an especially private place or retreat. [t. L: (neut.) holy]

sanctum sanctorum (săngk′təm săngk tô′rəm), **1.** the holy of holies of the Jewish tabernacle and temple. **2.** any especially private place or retreat. [L (Vulgate), translated from Gk (Septuagint), itself translating Heb. *qōdhesh haqqodhāshīm* holy of holies]

Sanctus (săngk′təs), *n.* **1.** *Liturgy.* the hymn beginning 'Holy, holy, holy, Lord God of hosts', with which the Eucharistic preface culminates. **2.** a musical setting for this hymn. [L: holy, the first word of the hymn]

Sanctus bell, a bell rung during the celebration of mass to give notification of the more solemn portions.

sand (sănd), *n.* **1.** the more or less fine debris of rocks, consisting of small, loose grains, often of quartz. **2.** (*usually pl.*) a tract or region composed principally of sand. **3.** the sand in an hourglass, or a grain of this. **4.** (*pl.*) moments of time or of one's life. **5.** a dull reddish yellow colour. —*v.t.* **6.** to smooth or polish with sand or sandpaper. **7.** to sprinkle with, or as with, sand. **8.** to fill up with sand, as a harbour. **9.** to add sand to: *to sand sugar.* [ME and OE, c. G *Sand*]

Sand (sănd; *Fr.* säNd), *n.* **George** (jôj; *Fr.* zhŏrzh) (*Madame Amandine Lucile Aurore Dudevant*), 1804–76, French novelist.

Sandakan (săn dä′kăn), *n.* a town in Malaysia in NE Sabah. 28,905 (1960).

sandal[1] (săn′dl), *n., v.*, **-dalled, -dalling.** —*n.* **1.** a kind of shoe, consisting of a sole of leather or other material fastened to the foot by thongs or straps. **2.** any of various kinds of low shoes or slippers. **3.** a band for fastening a low shoe or slipper on, by passing over the instep or round the ankle. —*v.t.* **4.** to furnish with sandals. [t. F: m. *sandale*; r. ME *sandalie*, t. L: m. *sandalium*, t. Gk: m. *sandálion*, lit., little sandal] —**san′dalled,** *adj.*

sandal[2] (săn′dl), *n.* sandalwood.

sandalwood (săn′dl wŏŏd′), *n.* **1.** the fragrant heartwood of any of certain Asiatic trees of the genus *Santalum* (family *Santalaceae*), used for ornamental carving and burnt as incense. **2.** any of these trees, esp. *S. album* (**white sandalwood**), an evergreen of India. **3.** any of various related or similar trees or their woods, esp. an East Indian fabaceous tree, *Pterocarpus santalinus* (**red sandalwood**), or its heavy dark red wood, which is used as a dyestuff. [f. *sandal* (t. ML: s. *sandalum*, ult. t. Skt: m. *čandana*) + WOOD]

Sandalwood Island, Sumba.

sandarac (săn′də răk′), *n.* **1.** a brittle, usually pale yellow, more or less transparent, faintly aromatic resin exuding from the bark of the sandarac tree and used chiefly as incense and in making varnish. **2.** a pinaceous tree, *Tetraclinis articulata* (*Callitris quadrivalvis*), native in north-western Africa, yielding the resin sandarac, and having a fragrant, hard, dark-coloured wood much used in building. Also, **sandarach.** [t. L: s. *sandaraca*, t. Gk: m. *sandarákē*]

sandbag (sănd′băg′), *n., v.*, **-bagged, -bagging.** —*n.* **1.** a bag filled with sand, used in fortification, as ballast, etc. **2.** such a bag used as a weapon. —*v.t.* **3.** to furnish with sandbags. **4.** to hit or stun with a sandbag.

sandbank (sănd′băngk′), *n.* a bank of sand in the sea or a river, formed by currents and often exposed at low tide.

sandbar (sănd′bä′), *n.* a bar of sand formed in a river or sea by the action of tides or currents.

sand-binder (sănd′bīn′də), *n.* any plant which can successfully grow in and stabilize loose sand, as the marram grass, *Ammophila arenaria.*

sandblast (sănd′bläst′), *n.* **1.** a blast of air or steam laden with sand, used to clean, grind, cut, or decorate hard surfaces, as of glass, stone, or metal. **2.** the apparatus used to apply such a blast. —*v.t., v.i.* **3.** to clean, smooth, etc., with a sandblast.

sand-blind (sănd′blīnd′), *adj. Archaic.* partially blind; dim-sighted. [ME; for *samblind, f. OE *sām-* half (c. L *sēmi-*) + BLIND]

sandbox (sănd′bŏks′), *n.* a box or receptacle for holding sand, esp. for dropping from a locomotive or a tram on to slippery rails.

sandbox tree, a euphorbiaceous tree, *Hura crepitans*, of tropical America, bearing a furrowed roundish fruit about the size of an orange which when ripe and dry bursts with a sharp report and scatters the seeds.

Sandburg (sănd′bûg, săn′-), *n.* **Carl,** 1878–1967, U.S. poet, biographer, and writer.

sand-cake (sănd′kāk′), *n.* a Madeira-type cake containing cornflour, ground rice, or potato flour.

sand-cast (sănd′käst′), *v.t.*, **-cast, -casting.** to produce (a casting) by pouring molten metal into sand moulds.

sandcastle (sănd′kä′səl), *n.* a model of a castle made by or for children from damp sand.

sand-crack (sănd′krăk′), *n.* **1.** any fine crack or fissure. **2.** a crack or fissure in the hoof of a horse, extending from the coronet downwards towards the sole, occurring on any part of the wall of the hoof, caused by a dryness of horn and liable to cause lameness.

sand-dab (sănd′dăb′), *n.* any of several flatfishes used as food.

sand-dollar (sănd′dŏl′ə), *n.* any of various flat, disclike urchins, esp. *Echinarachnius parma*, which live on sandy bottoms off the coasts of the U.S.

sand-dune (sănd′dyōōn′), *n.* dune.

sand-eel (sănd′ēl′), *n.* an elongate fish of the family *Ammodytidae*, which burrows in sand. Also, **sandlaunce.**

sander (săn′də), *n.* one who or that which sands or sandpapers.

sanderling (săn′də lĭng), *n.* a widespread small shorebird, *Crocethia alba*, found on sandy beaches.

sandflea (sănd′flē′), *n.* **1.** a beach flea. **2.** the chigoe.

sandfly (sănd′flī′), *n.*, *pl.* **-flies.** **1.** a small bloodsucking dipterous fly of the genus *Phlebotomus*, carrier of several human diseases. **2.** a small bloodsucking dipterous fly of the genus *Calicoides*.
sand-glass (sănd′gläs′), *n.* an hourglass.
sand-grouse (sănd′grous′), *n.* any of certain birds inhabiting sandy tracts of the Old World, which constitute the family *Pteroclidae*, structurally allied to the pigeons.
sandhi form (săn′dĭ), the phonetic or phonemic form of a word or phrase occurring in a context of other (preceding and following) forms, when different from the absolute form, e.g., in *Jack's at home* the *'s* is a sandhi form corresponding to the absolute form *is*. [*sandhi*, t. Skt: putting together]
sandhog (sănd′hŏg′), *n.* **1.** a labourer who digs or works in sand. **2.** one who works, usually in a caisson, in tunnelling under water.
sandhopper (sănd′hŏp′ə), *n.* a beach flea.
Sandhurst (sănd′hûst), *n.* a village in England, SE of Reading: Royal Military Academy. 6445 (1961).
Sán Diego (săn′ dĭ ā′gō), a seaport in SW California: naval and marine base. 573,224 (1960).
sand-launce (sănd′lôns′), *n.* sand-eel. Also, **sand-lance** (sănd′läns′).
sand-lizard (sănd′lĭz′əd), *n.* a small lizard, *Lacerta agilis*, which occurs throughout Europe from England (rarely) to western Russia.
sandman (sănd′măn′), *n.* the man who, in the fairytale, makes children sleepy by putting sand in their eyes.
sand-martin (sănd′mä′tĭn), *n.* a small bird, *Riparia riparia*, of the swallow family (*Hirundinidae*), which has a widespread distribution and nests in tunnels in banks of sand.
sandpaper (sănd′pā′pə), *n.* **1.** strong paper coated with a layer of sand or the like, used for smoothing or polishing. —*v.t.* **2.** to smooth or polish with or as with sandpaper.
sandpiper (sănd′pī′pə), *n.* any of numerous shore-inhabiting birds of the family *Scolopacidae*, typically having a piping note and a bill shorter than that of a true snipe, as the **common European sandpiper,** *Actitis hypoleuca*, and the New World **spotted sandpiper,** *Actitis macularia*.

Spotted sandpiper, *Actitis macularia* (8 in. long)

sandpit (sănd′ pĭt′), *n.* a container for holding sand for children to play in.
Sandringham (săn′drĭng əm), *n.* **1.** a village in England, in Norfolk. 557 (1961). **2.** a royal residence and estate near this village.
Sandrocottus (săn′drō kŏt′əs), *n.* Greek name of **Chandragupta.** Also, **Sandracottus** (săn′drə kŏt′əs).
sandshoe (sănd′shōō′), *n.* a light tennis shoe; plimsoll.
sand-spurry (sănd′spŭ′rĭ), *n.* any of several small caryophyllaceous herbs of the genus *Spergularia*, as *S. rubra*, widespread in open sandy places in temperate regions.
sandstone (sănd′stōn′), *n.* a rock formed by the consolidation of sand, the grains being held together by a cement of silica, lime, gypsum, or iron salts.
sandstorm (sănd′stôm′), *n.* a windstorm that bears along clouds of sand.
sand-table (sănd′tā′bl), *n.* *Mil.* a large, shallow wooden tray filled with sand on which can be modelled, in scale, tracts of land, etc., and used for gunnery and tactics.
sandwich (săn′wĭj), *n.* **1.** two slices of bread (or toast), plain or buttered, with a layer of meat, fish, cheese, or the like between. **2.** something formed by a similar combination. —*v.t.* **3.** to put into a sandwich. **4.** to insert between two other things. [named after the 4th Earl of *Sandwich*, 1718–92]
Sandwich (săn′wĭch), *n.* a town in England, in Kent: one of the Cinque Ports. 4370 (est. 1962).
sandwich board, one of the advertising boards carried by a sandwich man.
sandwich course, an educational course combining industrial training and academic studies, as one in which a student spends alternating periods of full-time work in industry, and full-time attendance at a college.
Sandwich Islands (săn′wĭj), former name of the **Hawaiian Islands.**
sandwich man, a man who walks about the streets carrying advertising boards hung before and behind him from straps over the shoulders.
sandwort (sănd′wût′), *n.* any of the plants constituting the caryophyllaceous genus *Arenaria*, many of which grow in sandy soil.
sandy (săn′dĭ), *adj.*, **-dier, -diest.** **1.** of the nature of or consisting of sand; containing or covered with sand. **2.** of a yellowish red colour: *sandy hair*. **3.** having such hair. **4.** shifting or unstable, like sand. —**sand′iness,** *n.*
sandyacht (sănd′yŏt′), *n.* a boatlike structure built on wheels and fitted with sails, used for sailing over large areas of sand.
sane (sān), *adj.*, **saner, sanest.** **1.** free from mental derangement: *a sane person*. **2.** having or showing reason, sound judgement, or good sense: *sane advice*. **3.** *Obs.* sound; healthy. [t. L: m. s. *sānus* sound, healthy] —**sane′ly,** *adv.* —**sane′ness,** *n.*
San Fernando (săn′fû năn′dō), a seaport in the West Indies, in SW Trinidad. 39,830 (1960).
Sanforize (săn′fə rīz′), *v.t.*, **-rized, -rizing.** *Trademark.* to shrink (cotton or linen fabrics) mechanically by a patented process before tailoring. Also, **Sanforise.**
San Francisco (săn′ frən sĭs′kō), a seaport in W. California, on San Francisco Bay: earthquake and fire, 1906. 742,855 (1960).
San Francisco Bay, a large estuary in W California, connected with the Pacific by the Golden Gate. ab. 50 mi. long; 3–12 mi. wide.
sang (săng), *v.* pt. of **sing.**
Sangallo (*It.* sàn gàl′lỏ), *n.* **Antonio da** (*It.* àn tŏ′nyỏ dà), 1485–1546, Italian Renaissance architect.
sangaree (săng′gə rē′), *n.* a drink composed of wine, diluted, sweetened, and spiced. [t. Sp.: m. *sangría*, lit., bleeding (with reference to colour), der. *sangre* blood]
Sanger (săng′ə), *n.* **Margaret,** 1883–1966, U.S. leader in birth-control movement.
sangfroid (sŏng′frwä′; *Fr.* säɴ frwȧ′), *n.* *French.* coolness of mind; calmness; composure. [F: cold blood]
Sangraal (săng grāl′), *n.* the Holy Grail. [ME *sangrayle*, t. OF: m. *Saint Graal*. See SAINT, GRAIL]
sanguiferous (săng gwĭf′ə rəs), *adj.* conveying blood, as a blood vessel. [f. *sangui-* (comb. form repr. L *sanguis* blood) + -FEROUS]
sanguinaria (săng′gwĭ nĕə′rĭ ə), *n.* **1.** the bloodroot. **2.** its medicinal rhizome. [short for L *herba sanguināria* bloody plant (in NL applied to bloodroot)]
sanguinary (săng′gwĭ nə rĭ), *adj.* **1.** attended with or characterized by bloodshed; bloody: *a sanguinary struggle*. **2.** bloodthirsty: *a sanguinary person*. **3.** inflicting the death penalty freely. [t. L: m. s. *sanguinārius*] —**san′guinarily,** *adv.* —**san′guinariness,** *n.*
sanguine (săng′gwĭn), *adj.* **1.** naturally cheerful and hopeful: *a sanguine disposition*. **2.** hopeful or confident: *sanguine expectations*. **3.** ruddy: *a sanguine complexion*. **4.** (in the old physiology) having blood as the predominating humour, and hence ruddy-faced, cheerful, etc. **5.** sanguinary. **6.** blood red; red. —*n.* **7.** a red iron oxide crayon used in making drawings. [ME, t. L: s. *sanguineus*, der. *sanguis* blood (cf. def. 4)] —**san′guinely,** *adv.* —**san′guineness,** *n.*
sanguineous (săng gwĭn′ĭ əs), *adj.* **1.** of, pertaining to, or containing blood. **2.** of the colour of blood. **3.** abounding with blood. **4.** sanguine; confident.
sanguinolent (săng gwĭn′ə lənt), *adj.* **1.** of or pertaining to blood. **2.** containing or tinged with blood; bloody. [t. L: s. *sanguinolentus*]
Sanhedrin (săn′ĭ drĭn), *n.* **1.** the supreme council and highest ecclesiastical and judicial tribunal of the ancient Jewish nation, with seventy-one members. **2.** a similar lower tribunal, with twenty-three members. Also, **Sanhedrim** (săn′ĭ drĭm). [t. LHeb., t. Gk: m. *synédrion*, f. *syn-* SYN- + *hédrion*, der. *hédra* seat]
sanicle (săn′ĭ kl), *n.* any of the umbelliferous herbs constituting the genus *Sanicula*, as *S. europaea*, widespread in woodlands of temperate regions and tropical mountains.
sanidine (săn′ĭ dēn′), *n.* a mineral form of potash felspar, similar to orthoclase, which occurs in lavas.
sanies (sā′nĭ ēz′), *n.* *Pathol.* a thin serous fluid, often greenish, discharged from ulcers, wounds, etc. [t. L]
San Ildefonso (*Sp.* sàn ēl dė fŏn′sỏ), a town in central Spain, near Segovia: termed the 'Spanish Versailles' for its palace (La Granja); treaty, 1800. 3900 (est. 1967).
sanious (sā′nĭ əs), *adj.* characterized by the discharge of a thin fluid, as from an ulcer. [t. L: m. s. *saniōsus* pertaining to or yielding sanies]
sanitarian (săn′ĭ tĕə′rĭ ən), *adj.* **1.** sanitary. —*n.* **2.** one expert or engaged in sanitary work.
sanitarium (săn′ĭ tĕə′rĭ əm), *n.*, *pl.* **-tariums, -taria** (-tĕə′rĭ ə). *U.S.* sanatorium. [f. L *sānit(as)* health + -ARIUM]
sanitary (săn′ĭ tə rĭ, -trĭ), *adj.* **1.** of or pertaining to health or the conditions affecting health, esp. with reference to cleanliness, precautions against disease, etc. **2.** favourable to health; free from dirt, germs, etc. [f. L *sānit(as)* health + -ARY[1]] —**san′itarily,** *adv.* —**san′itariness,** *n.*

—**Syn.** **2.** SANITARY, HYGIENIC agree in being concerned with health. SANITARY refers more especially to conditions affecting health or measures for guarding against infection or disease: *to ensure sanitary conditions in the lavatory.* HYGIENIC is applied more particularly to personal cleanliness and promotion of health: *hygienic standards must be high for those handling food.* —**Ant.** **2.** unclean, unwholesome.

sanitary belt, a narrow elastic belt for holding a sanitary towel in place.

sanitary inspector, an official appointed by a local authority to inspect the condition of sewage and drainage systems, etc.

sanitary towel, a soft, absorbent, disposable pad worn during menstruation to absorb the discharge from the uterus.

sanitation (săn′ĭ tā′shən), *n.* **1.** the study and practical application of sanitary measures. **2.** a drainage system.

sanity (săn′ĭ tĭ), *n.* **1.** the state of being sane; soundness of mind. **2.** soundness of judgement. [t. L: m. s. *sānitas*]

sanjak (săn′jăk), *n.* (in Turkey) one of the administrative districts into which a vilayet is divided. [t. Turk.: m. *sanjāq*, lit., flag, standard]

San Jose (săn′ hō zā′), a city in the U.S., in W California. 204,196 (1960).

San José (*Sp.* sän KHō sĕ′), the capital of Costa Rica, in the central part. 176,219 (1964).

San Jose scale (săn′ hō zā′), a scale insect, *Quadraspidiotus perniciosus*, very injurious to many trees and shrubs throughout the United States, first found at San Jose, California.

San Juan (săn wŏn′; *Sp.* sän KHwän′), a seaport in, and the capital of, Puerto Rico, in the N part. 451,658 (1960).

San Juan Islands, a group of islands between NW Washington and SE Vancouver Island, Canada: a part of Washington.

San Juan Mountains, a range of the Rocky Mountains in SW Colorado and N New Mexico. Highest peak, Uncompahgre Peak, 14,306 ft.

sank (săngk), *v.* pt. of **sink.**

Sankhya (săng′kyə), *n.* one of the six leading systems of Hindu philosophy, stressing the reality and duality of spirit and matter. [t. Skt, var. of *samkhyā* number]

Sankt Moritz (*Ger.* zängkt′ mō′rĭts), German name of **St Moritz.**

San Luis Potosí (*Sp.* sän lwĕs′ pō tō sē′), a city in central Mexico. 180,881 (est. 1965).

San Marino (săn′mə rē′nō; *It.* säm mä rē′nō), a small republic in E Italy: the oldest independent country in Europe. 17,000 pop. (est. 1964); 38 sq. mi. *Cap.*: San Marino.

San Marino

San Martín (*Sp.* sän mär tēn′), **José de** (*Sp.* KHō sĕ′ dĕ), 1778–1850, South American patriot, general and statesman, born in Argentina: won independence from Spain for Chile and Peru.

Sanmicheli (*It.* säm mē kĕ′lē), *n.* **Michele** (*It.* mē kĕ′lĕ), 1484–1559, Italian Mannerist architect.

San Miguel (*Sp.* sän mē gĕl′), a city in E El Salvador. 82,972 (1961).

San Pedro Sula (*Sp.* sän pĕ′ drō sōō′lä), a town in NW Honduras. 84,910 (1965).

San Remo (*It.* sän rĕ′mō), a seaport in NW Italy, on the Riviera: resort. 62,053 (1966).

sans (sănz; *Fr.* säN), *prep.* *Archaic or French.* without. [ME, t. OF, ult. g. L *absentiā*, in the absence of, b. with *sine* without]

San Salvador (săn săl′və dô′; *Sp.* sän säl bä dōr′), **1.** Also, **Watlings Island.** an island in the E Bahamas: first land in the New World seen by Christopher Columbus, 1492. 968 pop. (1963); 60 sq. mi. **2.** the capital of El Salvador. 503,202 (1963).

Sanscrit (săn′skrĭt), *n.* Sanskrit.

sans-culotte (sănz′kyŏŏ lŏt′; *Fr.* säN kY lŏt′), *n.* **1.** (in the French Revolution) a contemptuous nickname for a republican of the poorer class, adopted by the revolutionists as an honourable name, as if synonymous with 'patriot'. **2.** any extreme republican or revolutionary. [t. F: without (knee) breeches] —**sansculottic** (sănz′kyŏŏ lŏt′ĭk), *adj.* —**sans′culot′tism,** *n.* —**sans′culot′tist,** *n.*

sansculottide (sănz′kyŏŏ lŏt′ĭd; *Fr.* säN kY lō tēd′), *n.* (in the calendar of the first French republic) one of the 5 (in leap year 6) complementary days added at the end of the month Fructidor.

San Sebastián (săn′sĭ băs′tyən; *Sp.* sän sĕ bäs tyän′), a seaport in N Spain: resort. 148,644 (1965).

San Severo (*It.* sän sĕ′vĕ rō), a town in Italy in N central Apulia. 51,950 (1966).

sansevieria (săn′sĭ vĭə′rĭ ə), *n.* any plant of the genus *Sansevieria*, grown as a house plant for its stiff sword-shaped leaves. [NL, named after the Prince of *Sanseviero* (18th cent.), a learned Neapolitan]

Sansk., Sanskrit.

Sanskrit (săn′skrĭt), *n.* an extinct Indic language, the ancient classical literary language of India, with a voluminous literature extending over several centuries. It is one of the oldest recorded Indo-European languages. Also, **Sanscrit.** [t. Skt: m. *samskrita* prepared, cultivated] —**Sanskrit′ic,** *adj.* —**San′skritist,** *n.*

Sansovino (*It.* sän sō vē′nō), *n.* **Jacopo** (*It.* yä′kō pō), 1486–1570, Italian sculptor and architect.

sans pareil (*Fr.* säN pä rĕy′), *French.* without equal.

sans peur et sans reproche (*Fr.* säN pœr′ ĕ säN rə prŏsh′), *French.* without fear and without reproach.

sans serif (săn sĕ′rĭf), *Print.* a style of type without serifs.

sans souci (Fr. säN sōō sē′), *French.* carefree.

San Stefano (săn′stĭ fä′nō), a village in Turkey, near Istanbul: treaty between Russia and Turkey, 1878.

Santa Ana (săn′tə ăn′ə; *Sp.* sän′tä ä′nä), **1.** a city in NW El Salvador. 121,095 (1961). **2.** a city in the U.S., in SW California. 100,350 (1960).

Santa Anna (*Sp.* sän′tä ä′nä), **Antonio López de** (*Sp.* än tō′nyō lō′pĕth dĕ), 1795–1876, Mexican general and politician: massacred Alamo defenders. Also, **Santa Ana.**

Santa Barbara (săn′tə bä′bə rə), a town in the U.S., on the SW coast of California: Spanish mission. 58,768 (1960).

Santa Barbara Islands, a group of islands off the SW coast of California.

Santa Clara (*Sp.* sän′tä klä′rä), a city in central Cuba. 142,176 (1960).

Santa Claus (săn′tə klôz′), the patron saint of children, dispenser of gifts on Christmas Eve; Father Christmas; Saint Nicholas. [t. d. D: m. *Sante Klaas* St Nicholas]

Santa Cruz (săn′tə krōōz′; *Sp.* sän′tä krōōth′), **1.** one of the Santa Barbara Islands, off the SW coast of California. **2.** a town in E Bolivia. 83,000 (est. 1965). **3.** St Croix (def. 1).

Santa Cruz de Tenerife (săn′tə krōōz′ də tĕn′ə rĭf′; *Sp.* sän′tä krōōth′ dĕ tĕ nĕ rē′fĕ), a seaport in the Canary Islands on Tenerife island. 150,550 (1965).

Santa Fe (săn′tə fā′), the capital of New Mexico, in the N part: founded *c.* 1605. 34,676 (1960).

Santa Fé (săn′tə fā′; *Sp.* sän′tä fĕ′), a city in E Argentina. 199,179 (est. 1960).

Santa Fe Trail, an important trade route across the U.S., linking Independence, Missouri, and Santa Fe, New Mexico, which flourished from 1822 until about 1880.

Santa Isabel (*Sp.* sän′tä ē sä bĕl′), the capital of Fernando Po, in the NW part. 19,869 (1960).

santal (săn′tl), *n.* sandalwood.

santalaceous (săn′tə lā′shəs), *adj.* belonging to the *Santalaceae*, or sandalwood family of plants. [f. s. NL *Santalāceae* (der. *santalum* sandalwood) + -OUS]

Santa Maria (săn′tə mə rē′ə; *Sp.* sän′tä mä rē′ä), **1.** the flagship of Columbus in his voyage of 1492. **2.** an active volcano in W Guatemala. ab. 12,500 ft.

Santa Marta (*Sp.* sän′tä mär′tä), a seaport on the N coast of Colombia. 104,171 (1964).

Santa Maura (*It.* sän′tä mou′rä), Italian name of **Levkas.**

Santander (săn′tən dĕə′; *Sp.* sän tän dĕr′), *n.* a seaport in N Spain: fine harbour; Altamira prehistoric cave drawings nearby. 128,452 (1965).

Santa Rosa de Copán (*Sp.* sän′tä rō′sä dĕ kō pän′), a town in W Honduras: the site of extensive Mayan ruins. 6417 (1950). Also, **Copán.**

Santayana (săn′tĭ ăn′ə; *Sp.* sän tä yä′nä), *n.* **George,** 1863–1952, U.S. poet, essayist, and philosophical writer, born in Spain.

Sant 'Elia (*It.* sänt ĕ lē′ä), **Antonio** (*It.* än tŏ′nyō), 1888–1916, Italian futurist architect.

Santiago (săn′tĭ ä′gō; *Sp.* sän tyä′gō), *n.* **1.** the capital of Chile, in the central part. 1,169,481 (est. 1960). **2.** Also, **Santiago de Compostela** (*Sp.* dĕ kōm pōs tĕ′lä). a town in NW Spain: pilgrimages; cathedral. 59,200 (est. 1967).

Santiago de Cuba (*Sp.* sän tyä′gō dĕ kōō′bä), a seaport in SE Cuba: naval battle, 1898. 166,384 (1960).

Santiago de los Caballeros (*Sp.* sän tyä′gō dĕ lōs kä bä-lyĕ′rōs), a city in N central Dominican Republic. 329,808 (1964).

Santillana (*Sp.* sän tē lyä′nä), *n.* **Marqués de** (*Íñigo López de Mendoza*), 1398–1458, Spanish poet.

santir (săn′tĭə), *n.* a musical instrument somewhat like a dulcimer, used by the Arabs and Persians. Also, **santur, santour.**

Santo Domingo (săn′tō də mĭng′gō; *Sp.* sän′tô dô mĕn′gô), **1.** the capital of the Dominican Republic on the S coast: the first European settlement in America (1496). 529,396 (1964). **2.** Dominican Republic.

santonica (săn tŏn′ĭ kə), *n.* **1.** a wormwood, *Artemisia cina.* **2.** the dried flower heads of this plant, used as a vermifuge. [t. L, prop. fem. of *Santonicus* pertaining to the Santoni, a tribe of ancient Gaul]

santonin (săn′tə nĭn), *n. Chem.* a crystalline compound, $C_{15}H_{18}O_3$, the active principle of santonica.

Santos (*Port.* sən′to͞os), *n.* a seaport in S Brazil. 265,753 (1960).

Santos-Dumont (*Fr.* säN tōs dʏ mōN′), *n.* **Alberto** (*Fr.* ȧl bĕr′tô), 1873–1932, Brazilian inventor of dirigibles and aeroplanes, in France.

São Francisco (*Port.* səwN frəN sēs′ko͞o), a river flowing through E Brazil into the Atlantic. ab. 1800 mi.

São Luiz (*Port.* səwN lwēs′), a seaport on an island off the NE coast of Brazil. 150,000 (est. 1964).

São Miguel (*Port.* səwN mē gĕl′), the largest island of the Azores. 168,000 pop. (est. 1960); 288 sq. mi.

Saône (*Fr.* sōn), *n.* a river flowing from NE France S to the Rhone at Lyons. ab. 300 mi.

Saône-et-Loire (*Fr.* sōn ė lwȧr′), *n.* a department in E central France. 535,772 pop. (1962); 3330 sq. mi. *Cap.:* Mâcon.

São Paulo (*Port.* səwN päw′lo͞o), a city in S Brazil. 3,825,351 (1960).

São Paulo de Loanda (*Port.* səwN päw′lo͞o də lwən′də), Luanda.

Saorstat Eireann (sĕə′stăt ĕə′rən), *Gaelic.* Irish Free State.

São Salvador (*Port.* səwN sȧl vȧ dôr′), a seaport in E Brazil. 655,735 (1960). Also, **Bahia.** Official name, **Salvador.**

São Tomé (*Port.* səwN to͞o mĕ′), a Portuguese island in the Gulf of Guinea off the W coast of Africa. 63,485 pop. (1960); 323 sq. mi. Also, **São Thomé.**

sap[1] (săp), *n.* **1.** the juice or vital circulating fluid, esp. of a woody plant. **2.** sapwood. **3.** *Slang.* a fool; saphead. [ME; OE *sæp*, c. D *sap*, akin to G *Saft*, Icel. *safi*]

sap[2] (săp), *n., v.,* **sapped, sapping.** —*n.* **1.** *Fort.* a deep narrow trench constructed to approach a besieged place or an enemy's position. —*v.t.* **2.** *Fort.* **a.** to approach (a besieged place, etc.) with deep narrow trenches protected by gabions or parapets. **b.** to dig such trenches in (ground). **3.** to undermine; weaken or destroy insidiously. —*v.i.* **4.** *Fort.* to dig a sap. [earlier *zappe*, t. It.: m. *zappa* spade, hoe]

sapajou (săp′ə jo͞o′), *n.* a capuchin monkey. [t. F; of S Amer. orig.]

sapanwood (săp′ən wo͝od′), *n.* sappanwood.

saphead (săp′hĕd′), *n. Slang.* a simpleton; a fool.

sapheaded (săp′hĕd′ĭd), *adj. Slang.* silly; foolish.

saphena (sȧ fē′nə), *n., pl.* **-nae** (-nē). either of two large superficial veins of the leg, one (**long** or **internal saphena**) on the inner side, and the other (**short, external,** or **posterior saphena**) on the outer and posterior sides. [t. ML, t. Ar.: m. *çāfin*] —**saphe′nous,** *adj.*

sapid (săp′ĭd), *adj.* **1.** having taste or flavour. **2.** palatable. **3.** to one's liking; agreeable. [t. L: s. *sapidus* savoury] —**sapid′ity,** *n.*

sapient (sā′pyənt), *adj.* wise or sage (often used ironically). [late ME, t. L: s. *sapiens*, ppr., being wise] —**sa′pience, sa′piency,** *n.* —**sa′piently,** *adv.*

sapiential (sā′pĭ ĕn′shəl, săp′ĭ-), *adj.* containing, exhibiting, or affording wisdom; characterized by wisdom. [t. LL: s. *sapientiālis*] —**sa′pien′tially,** *adv.*

sapindaceous (săp′ĭn dā′shəs), *adj.* belonging to the *Sapindaceae*, or soapberry family of plants. [f. s. NL *Sapindāceae* (der. *sapindus* soapberry) + -OUS]

sapless (săp′lĭs), *adj.* **1.** destitute of sap; withered: *sapless plants.* **2.** lacking vitality; insipid.

sapling (săp′lĭng), *n.* **1.** a young tree. **2.** a young person.

sapodilla (săp′ə dĭl′ə), *n.* **1.** a large evergreen tree, *Achras zapota*, of tropical America, bearing an edible fruit (**sapodilla plum**) and yielding chicle. **2.** the fruit. [t. Sp.: m. *zapotillo*, dim. of *zapote* SAPOTA]

saponaceous (săp′ō nā′shəs), *adj.* soaplike; soapy. [t. NL: m. *sāpōnāceus*, der. L *sāpo* soap]

saponification number (sə pŏn′ĭ fĭ kā′shən), *Chem.* the number of milligrams of potassium hydroxide required to completely saponify one gram of a fat or oil.

saponify (sə pŏn′ĭ fī′), *v.,* **-fied, -fying.** *Chem.* —*v.t.* **1.** to convert (a fat) into soap by treating with an alkali. **2.** to decompose (any ester), forming the corresponding alcohol and acid or salt. —*v.i.* **3.** to become converted into soap. [t. NL: m. *sāpōnificāre*, f. L: s. *sāpo* soap + *-(i)ficāre* make] —**sapon′ifi′able,** *adj.* —**sapon′ifica′tion,** *n.* —**sapon′ifi′er,** *n.*

saponin (săp′ə nĭn), *n.* any of a group of amorphous glucosidal compounds of steroid structure obtainable from many plants. Their aqueous solutions foam like soap on shaking and are used as detergents. [t. F: m. *saponine*, f. s. L *sāpo* soap + *-ine* -INE[2]]

saponite (săp′ə nīt′), *n.* a soft amorphous mineral found in certain rock cavities consisting of a silicate of magnesium and aluminium.

sapor (sā′pô, -pə), *n.* that quality in a substance which affects the sense of taste; savour; flavour. [t. L] —**saporous** (săp′ə rəs), *adj.*

sapota (sə pō′tə), *n.* **1.** a general term employed in tropical America for widely differing fruits. **2.** the fruit and tree of *Achras sapota.* **3.** the sapodilla. [NL, repr. Sp. and Pg. *zapote*, t. Arahuacan (a Mexican Indian language): m. *zapotl*]

sapotaceous (săp′ə tā′shəs), *adj.* belonging to the *Sapotaceae*, or sapodilla family of plants.

sappanwood (săp′ən wo͝od′), *n.* **1.** a dyewood yielding a red colour, produced by a small East Indian caesalpiniaceous tree, *Caesalpinia sappan.* **2.** the tree itself. Also, **sapanwood.** [f. m. *sapan* (t. Malay: m. *sapang*) + WOOD[1]]

sapper (săp′ə), *n. Colloq.* a private in the Royal Engineers. [f. SAP[2] + -ER[1]]

Sapphic (săf′ĭk), *adj.* **1.** pertaining to Sappho or to certain metres or a form of strophe or stanza used by or named after her. —*n.* **2.** a Sapphic verse. [t. L: s. *sapphicus*, t. Gk: m. *sapphikós*]

Sapphic ode. See **ode** (def. 5).

Sapphira (sə fī′ə rə), *n.* a woman who, with her husband, Ananias, was struck dead for lying. Acts 5.

sapphire (săf′ī′ə), *n.* **1.** a variety of corundum, esp. a transparent blue kind valued as a gem. **2.** a gem of this kind. **3.** the colour of the gem, a deep blue. —*adj.* **4.** resembling sapphire; deep blue: *a sapphire sky.* [t. L: m. s. *sapphīrus*, t. Gk: m. *sáppheiros*; r. ME *saphyr*, t. OF]

sapphirine (săf′ə rīn′, -rĭn), *adj.* **1.** consisting of sapphire; like sapphire, esp. in colour. —*n.* **2.** a pale blue or greenish, usually granular mineral, a silicate of magnesium and aluminium. **3.** a blue variety of spinel.

sapphism (săf′ĭz′əm), *n.* lesbianism. [f. SAPPHO + -ISM]

Sappho (săf′ō), *n.* Greek lyric poetess of Lesbos, lived about 600 B.C.

Sapporo (sä′pô rō′, săp′-), *n.* a city in N Japan, on Hokkaido island. 704,000 (est. 1964).

sappy (săp′ĭ), *adj.* **1.** abounding in sap, as a plant. **2.** full of vitality and energy. **3.** *Slang.* silly or foolish.

sapraemia (să prē′myə), *n. Pathol.* a form of blood-poisoning, esp. that due to the toxins produced by certain micro-organisms. Also, *U.S.*, **sapremia.** [f. SAPR(O)- + -AEMIA] —**saprae′mic,** *adj.*

sapro-, a word element meaning 'rotten', or 'saprophytic', as in *saprolite.* Also, before vowels, **sapr-.** [t. Gk, comb. form of *saprós* putrid]

saprogenic (săp′rō jĕn′ĭk), *adj.* **1.** producing putrefaction or decay, as certain bacteria. **2.** formed by putrefaction. Also, **saprogenous** (să prŏj′ĭ nəs).

saprolegnia (săp′rō lĕg′nĭ ə), *n.* any of a group of aquatic fungi of the genus *Saprolegnia*, which feed on animal matter including diseased fish.

saprolite (săp′rō līt′), *n. Geol.* soft, disintegrated, usually more or less decomposed rock, remaining in its original place.

saprophyte (săp′rō fīt′), *n.* any vegetable organism that lives on dead organic matter, as certain fungi, bacteria, etc. —**saprophytic** (săp′rō fĭt′ĭk), *adj.*

sapsago (săp′sə gō′), *n.* a hard greenish cheese flavoured with melilot, made in Switzerland. [t. G: alter. of *Schabziger*, f. s. *Schaben* grate + *Ziger* a kind of cheese]

sapwood (săp′wo͝od′), *n.* alburnum.

Sar., Sardinia.

saraband (să′rə bănd′), *n.* **1.** a popular and vigorous Spanish castanet dance. **2.** a slow, stately Spanish dance in triple rhythm derived from this. **3.** a piece of music for, or in the rhythm of, this dance, usually forming one of the movements in the classical suite, following the courante. [t. F: m. *sarabande*, t. Sp.: m. *zarabanda*; prob. of oriental orig.]

Saracen (să′rə sən), *n.* **1.** (among the later Romans and Greeks) a member of the nomadic tribes on the Syrian borders of the Roman Empire. **2.** (in later use) an Arab. **3.** any Muslim or Mohammedan, esp. with reference to the Crusades. [mod. E and OE, t. LL: s. *Saracēnus*, t. LGk: m. *Sarakēnós*; r. ME *Sarezin*, t. OF] —**Saracenic** (să′rə sĕn′ĭk), **Sar′acen′ical,** *adj.*

Saragat (să′rə găt′; *It.* sä′rä gät), *n.* **Giuseppe** (*It.* jo͞o zĕp′pė), born 1898, president of Italy since 1964.

Saragossa (să′rə gŏs′ə), *n.* a city in NE Spain, on the river Ebro. 377,412 (1965). Spanish, **Zaragoza.**

Sarah (sĕə′rə), *n.* the wife of Abraham and mother of

Isaac. Earlier, **Sarai** (sĕə′rā ī′). Gen. 17:15–22, etc.

Sarajevo (să′rə yā′vō), *n.* a city in central Yugoslavia, in Bosnia: the assassination of the Austrian archduke Franz Ferdinand here, June 28th, 1914, was the external event that precipitated World War I. 198,914 (1961). Also, **Serajevo.** See map under **Serbia.**

Saranac (să′rə năk′), *n.* any of three lakes in the U.S., in NE New York State, in the Adirondack Mountains: **Upper Saranac, Middle Saranac, Lower Saranac.**

Saratoga (să′rə tō′gə), *n.* a village in the U.S., in E New York State, on the Hudson river: scene of Burgoyne's defeat and surrender in the Battle of Saratoga, 1777. Now called **Schuylerville.**

Saratoga Springs, a town in the U.S., in E New York State: health resort; horseraces. 16,630 (1960).

Saratov (*Russ.* sȧ rȧ′təf), *n.* a city in the E Soviet Union in Europe, on the Volga. 683,000 (est. 1965).

Sarawak (sə rä′wək, -wə), *n.* a former British colony in NW Borneo; now an independent state in the Federation of Malaysia. 818,000 (est. 1964); ab. 50,000 sq. mi. *Cap.:* Kuching.

sarc-, a word element meaning 'flesh', as in *sarcous.* Also, before consonants, **sarco-.** [t. Gk: m. *sark-*, comb. form of *sárx*]

sarcasm (sä′kăz′əm), *n.* **1.** harsh or bitter derision or irony. **2.** an ironical taunt or gibe; a sneering or cutting remark. [t. LL: s. *sarcasmus*, t. LGk: m. *sarkasmós* sneer] **—Syn. 1.** See **irony**[1].

sarcastic (sä kăs′tĭk), *adj.* **1.** characterized by, of the nature of, or pertaining to sarcasm: *a sarcastic reply.* **2.** using, or given to the use of, sarcasm. **—sarcas′tically,** *adv.* **—Syn. 2.** See **cynical.**

sarcenet (säs′nĭt), *n.* a very fine, soft, silk fabric, used esp. for linings. Also, **sarsenet.** [ME, t. AF: m. *sarzinett*, dim. of *Sarzin* Saracen. Cf. OF *drap sarrasinois* Saracen cloth]

sarcocarp (sä′kō käp′), *n. Bot.* **1.** the fleshy mesocarp of certain fruits, as the peach. **2.** any fruit of fleshy consistency.

sarcoma (sä kō′mə), *n., pl.* **-mata** (-mə tə). *Pathol.* any of various malignant tumours originating in the connective tissue, attacking esp. the bones. [NL, t. Gk: m. *sárkōma*] **—sarcomatoid** (sä kō′mə toid′), **sarcomatous** (sä kō′mə təs, -kŏm′ə-), *adj.*

sarcomatosis (sä kō′mə tō′sĭs), *n. Pathol.* a condition marked by the production of an overwhelming number of sarcomata throughout the body. [NL, f. s. Gk *sárkōma* SARCOMA + *-ōsis* -OSIS]

sarcophagus (sä kŏf′ə gəs), *n., pl.* **-gi** (-gī′), **-guses. 1.** a stone coffin, esp. one bearing sculpture or inscriptions, etc., often displayed as a monument. **2.** (among the ancient Greeks) a kind of stone supposed to consume the flesh of corpses, used for coffins. [t. L, t. Gk: m. *sarkophágos*, orig. adj., flesh-eating]

sarcous (sä′kəs), *adj.* consisting of or pertaining to flesh or skeletal muscle. [f. m. s. Gk *sárx* flesh + -OUS]

sard (säd), *n.* a brownish red chalcedony, or a piece of it, used in jewellery, etc. [ME *saarde*, t. L: m. *sarda* SARDIUS]

Sardanapalus (sä′də năp′ə ləs), *n.* Ashurbanipal.

sardine (sä dēn′), *n., pl.* **-dines,** (*esp. collectively*) **-dine. 1.** the young of the common pilchard, often preserved in oil and canned for food. **2.** any of various allied or similar fishes used in this way, esp. the **California sardine,** *Sardinops caeruleus.* [ME *sardyn*, t. It.: m. s. *sardina*, g. L *sardīna*, der. *sarda* kind of fish]

Sardinia (sä dĭn′yə), *n.* **1.** a large island in the Mediterranean, W of Italy: with small nearby islands it comprises a region of Italy. 1,413,289 pop. (1961); 9301 sq. mi. *Cap.:* Cagliari. **2.** a former kingdom (1720–1860), including this island and Savoy, Piedmont, and Genoa (after 1815) in NW Italy; ruled by the House of Savoy. *Cap.:* Turin.

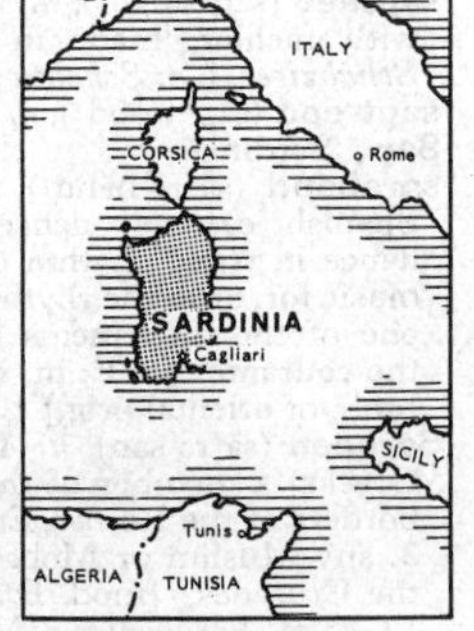

Sardinia (def. 1)

Sardinian (sä dĭn′yən), *adj.* **1.** of or pertaining to Sardinia. *—n.* **2.** a native or inhabitant of Sardinia. **3.** a Romance language spoken in Sardinia.

Sardis (sä′dĭs), *n.* an ancient city in W Asia Minor: the capital of ancient Lydia.

sardius (sä′dĭ əs), *n.* **1.** sard. **2.** the precious stone in the breastplate of the Jewish high priest, thought to have been a ruby. [ME, t. L (Vulgate), t. Gk: m. *sárdios* (stone) of Sardis]

sardonic (sä dŏn′ĭk), *adj.* bitterly ironical; sarcastic; sneering: *a sardonic grin.* [t. F: m. *sardonique*, der. L *Sardonius*, t. Gk: m. *Sardónios* Sardinian, for earlier *sardánios* bitter, scornful, from the notion of a Sardinian plant said to bring on convulsions resembling laughter] **—sardon′ically,** *adv.*

sardonyx (sä′də nĭks), *n.* a kind of onyx containing layers or bands of sard. [ME, t. L, t. Gk. See SARD, ONYX]

Sardou (*Fr.* sȧr dōō′), *n.* **Viktorien** (*Fr.* vēk tō ryăN′), 1831–1908, French dramatist.

sargasso (sä găs′ō), *n.* the gulfweed. [t. Pg.: m. *sargaço*]

Sargasso Sea (sä găs′ō), a relatively calm area in the N Atlantic, NE of the West Indies, where there is an abundance of free-floating plants of the alga *Sargassum.*

sargassum (sä găs′əm), *n.* any seaweed of the genus *Sargassum*, widely distributed in the warmer waters of the globe, as *S. bacciferum*, the common gulfweed. [NL, t. Pg.: m. *sargaço*]

Sargent (sä′jənt), *n.* **1. Sir (Harold) Malcolm (Watts),** 1895–1967, English conductor. **2. John Singer,** 1856–1925, U.S. painter.

Sargon II (sä′gŏn), died 705 B.C., king of Assyria 722–705 B.C.

sari (sä′rĭ), *n., pl.* **-ris.** a long piece of cotton or silk, the principal outer garment of Hindu women, worn round the body with one end over the head or shoulder. [t. Hind.]

sark (säk), *n. Scot. or Archaic.* a shirt or chemise. [ME, t. Scand.; cf. Icel. *serkr*, c. OE *serc*]

Sark (säk), *n.* one of the Channel Islands in the English Channel. 556 pop. (1961); 2 sq. mi.

sarking (sä′kĭng), *n. Scot.* a layer of boarding sometimes used to cover the rafters of a house under the tiles.

sarky (sä′kĭ), *adj. Colloq.* sarcastic.

Sarmatia (sä mā′shyə), *n.* the ancient name used to designate a region, now in Poland and the W Soviet Union, extending from the Vistula to the Volga. **—Sarma′tian,** *adj., n.*

sarmentose (sä mĕn′tōs), *adj. Bot.* having runners. [t. L: m. s. *sarmentōsus*]

Sarmiento (*Sp.* sȧr myĕn′tȯ), *n.* **Domingo Faustino** (*Sp.* dȯ mēn′gȯ fȧws tē′nȯ), 1811–1888, Argentinian poet.

sarong (sə rŏng′), *n.* **1.** the principal garment for both sexes in the Malay Archipelago, etc., consisting of a piece of cloth enveloping the lower part of the body like a skirt. **2.** a kind of cloth for such garments. [t. Malay: m. *sārung.* Cf. Skt *sāranga* variegated]

saros (sā′rŏs), *n. Astron.* the interval between two similar solar eclipses, equal to 18 years, 10–12 days. [t. Gk]

Saros (sä′rŏs), *n.* **Gulf of,** a gulf in the NE part of the Aegean Sea, N of Gallipoli Peninsula.

Saroyan (sə roi′ən), *n.* **William,** born 1908, U.S. author.

Sarpedon (sä pē′dŏn), *n. Gk Legend.* a Lycian prince, son of Zeus, killed by Patroclus in Trojan War.

sarracenia (să′rə sē′nyə), *n.* any plant of the genus *Sarracenia*, comprising American marsh plants with hollow leaves of a pitcher-like form in which insects are trapped and digested, as *S. purpurea*, a common pitcher plant. [NL; named after D. *Sarrazin* of Quebec, who first sent samples of the plant to Europe]

sarraceniaceous (să′rə sē′nĭ ā′shəs), *adj.* belonging to the *Sarraceniaceae*, the American pitcher-plant family.

Sarre (*Fr.* sȧr), *n.* French name of **Saar.**

sarsaparilla (sä′sə pə rĭl′ə), *n.* **1.** any of various climbing or trailing tropical American plants of the genus *Smilax*, having a root which has been much used in medicine as an alterant. **2.** the root. **3.** an extract or other preparation made of it. **4.** *U.S.* a soft drink flavoured with it. [t. Sp.: m. *zarzaparilla*, f. *zarza* bramble + *-parilla* (? dim. of *parsa* vine)]

sarsenet (säs′nĭt), *n.* sarcenet.

Sarthe (*Fr.* sȧrt), *n.* a department in NW France. 443,019 pop. (1962); 2411 sq. mi. *Cap.:* Le Mans.

Sarto (*It.* sȧr′tȯ), *n.* **Andrea Del** (*It.* ȧn drĕ′ȧ dĕl), 1486–1531, Italian painter.

sartorial (sä tô′rĭ əl), *adj.* **1.** of or pertaining to a tailor or his work: *sartorial splendour.* **2.** *Anat.* pertaining to the sartorius. [f. s. L *sartōrius* of a tailor + -AL[1]]

sartorius (sä tô′rĭ əs), *n. Anat.* a flat, narrow muscle, the longest in the human body, running from the hip to the inner side of the shinbone, and crossing the thigh obliquely in front. [NL: lit., pertaining to a tailor]

Sartre (*Fr.* sȧr′tr), *n.* **Jean Paul** (*Fr.* zhäN pōl′), born 1905, French writer and philosopher: exponent of existentialism.

Sarum (sĕə′rəm), *n.* site of an ancient and medieval city in Wiltshire, 2 miles N of Salisbury. Also, **Old Sarum.**

Sarum use, the procedure of service or the general liturgy used in late medieval Salisbury (Sarum).

Sasebo (sä′sē bō′, săs′-), *n.* a seaport in SW Japan, on W Kyushu island. 247,069 (1965).

Saseno (săs′ĭ nō′), *n.* a fortified island at the entrance to Valona Bay, in Albania. 2 sq. mi.

sash[1] (săsh), *n.* a long band or scarf of silk, etc., worn over one shoulder or round the waist, as by military officers as a part of the costume, or by women and children for ornament. [dissimilated var. of *shash*, t. Ar.: turban]

sash[2] (săsh), *n.* **1.** a movable framework in which panes of glass are set, as in a window or the like. **2.** the part of a window which moves. **3.** such frameworks collectively. —*v.t.* **4.** to furnish with sashes or with windows having sashes. [ME; alter. of CHASSIS]

sashcord (săsh′kôd′), *n.* a cord passing over a pulley and attaching a vertically sliding sash to counterweights so that it may be raised or lowered.

sash-window (săsh′wĭn′dō), *n.* a window which opens by sliding sashes up or down.

sasin (săs′ĭn), *n.* the common Indian antelope. [t. Nepalese]

Sask., Saskatchewan.

Saskatchewan (săs kăch′ĭ wən), *n.* **1.** a province in W Canada. 951,000 pop. (est. 1965); 251,700 sq. mi. *Cap.*: Regina. **2.** a river in SW Canada, flowing E to Lake Winnipeg: formed by the junction of the **North Saskatchewan** and **South Saskatchewan.** Length to the source of the South Saskatchewan, ab. 1205 mi.

saskatoon (săs′kə to͞on′), *n.* **1.** any of several shadbushes, esp. the serviceberry, *Amelanchier canadensis.* **2.** the berry of this bush. [t. Cree: m. *misâskwatomin* serviceberry, lit., fruit of *misâskwat* the tree of much wood]

Saskatoon (săs′kə to͞on′), *n.* a city in SW Canada, in Saskatchewan. 112,726 (est. 1965).

sassaby (săs′ə bĭ), *n.*, *pl.* **-bies.** a large, blackish red South African antelope, *Damaliscus lunatus.* [t. Sechwana: m. *tsessébe*]

sassafras (săs′ə frăs′), *n.* **1.** an American lauraceous tree, *Sassafras albidum.* **2.** the aromatic bark of its root, used medicinally and esp. for flavouring beverages, confectionery, etc. [t. Sp.: m. *sasafras*, orig. uncert.]

sassafras oil, a volatile oil derived from the root of the sassafras tree, consisting of camphor, pinene, etc.

Sassanid (săs′ə nĭd), *n.* a member of the Persian dynasty which ruled about A.D. 226–641. Also, **Sassanian** (să sā′nĭ ən).

Sassanidae (să săn′ĭ dē′), *n.pl.* the Sassanids.

Sassari (*It.* sȧs′sȧ rē), *n.* a town in NW Sardinia. 100,028 (1966).

sassatie (sə sä′tĭ), *n.* *Chiefly S African.* sosatie; Cape Malay kebab.

Sassenach (săs′ə năk′), *n.* an Englishman (a name applied by the Scottish inhabitants of the British Isles). [t. Gaelic: m. *Sasunnach* Englishman, f. *Sasunn* Saxon + *-ach* (adj. suffix)]

Sassoon (sə so͞on′), *n.* **Siegfried (Loraine)** (sēg′frēd lô rān′), 1886–1967, British soldier, poet, and writer.

sassy[1] (săs′ĭ), *adj.*, **-sier, -siest,** *Colloq. or Dial.* saucy. [d. var. of SAUCY]

sassy[2] (săs′ĭ), *n.* sassy bark. [t. West African; said to be t. E. See SASSY[1]]

sassy bark, 1. the bark of a large African caesalpiniaceous tree, *Erythrophleum guineense*, used by the natives as a poison in ordeals. **2.** Also, **sassywood** (săs′ĭ wo͝od′). the tree itself. [see SASSY[2]]

sat (săt), *v.* pt. and pp. of **sit.**

Sat., 1. Saturday. **2.** Saturn.

Satan (sā′tn), *n.* the chief evil spirit; the great adversary of man; the devil. Cf. **Lucifer.** [ME and OE, t. L (Vulgate), t. Gk (Septuagint and N.T.), t. Heb.: adversary]

satang (să tăng′), *n.*, *pl.* **-tang.** a Thai bronze coin and money of account equivalent to one hundredth of a baht. Also, **stang.** [t. Siamese: m. *sātān*]

satanic (sə tăn′ĭk), *adj.* **1.** of Satan. **2.** characteristic of or befitting Satan; extremely wicked; diabolical. Also, **satanical.** —**satan′ically,** *adv.*

Satanism (sā′tə nĭz′əm), *n.* **1.** the worship of Satan. **2.** a form of such worship which travesties Christian rites. **3.** satanic disposition or practice. —**Sa′tanist,** *n.*

satchel (săch′əl), *n.* a bag, made of leather, canvas, or the like, usually with a shoulder-strap, used for carrying schoolbooks. [ME, t. OF: m. *sachel*, der. *sac* sack, g. L *saccus.* See SACK[1]]

sate[1] (sāt), *v.t.*, **sated, sating. 1.** to satisfy (any appetite or desire) to the full. **2.** to surfeit; glut. [b. obs. *sade* satiate (OE *sadian*) and L *sat* enough. See SAD]

sate[2] (săt, sāt), *v.* *Archaic.* pt. and pp. of **sit.**

sateen (să tēn′), *n.* a cotton fabric woven in satin weave and resembling satin in gloss. [var. of SATIN, by assoc. with VELVETEEN]

satellite (săt′ə līt′), *n.* **1.** *Astron.* a small body which revolves round a planet; a moon. **2.** an attendant upon a person of importance. **3.** a subservient or obsequious follower. **4.** a country under the domination or influence of another. **5.** a man-made device, usually containing recording and transmitting instruments, for launching into orbit round the earth, another planet, or the sun, for purposes of communication, research, etc. See **communication satellite.** [t. L: m. s. *satelles* attendant, guard]

satellite town, 1. a small town or city dependent on local industry but having economic linkages with a large city from which it is separated by open country. **2.** an extensive collection of commuters' dwellings, physically separate from but associated with a large town.

satiable (sā′shyə bl), *adj.* that can be satiated. —**sa′tiabil′ity, sa′tiableness,** *n.* —**sa′tiably,** *adv.*

satiate (*v.* sā′shĭ āt′; *adj.* sā′shĭ ĭt, -āt′), *v.*, **-ated, -ating,** *adj.* —*v.t.* **1.** to supply with anything to excess, so as to disgust or weary; surfeit; cloy. **2.** *Now Rare.* to satisfy to the full. —*adj.* **3.** *Archaic or Poetic.* satiated. [t. L: m. s. *satiātus*, pp., filled full] —**sa′tia′tion,** *n.*

Satie (*Fr.* sȧ tē′), *n.* **Erik Alfred Leslie** (*Fr.* ĕ rēk ȧl frĕd lĕs lē′), 1866–1925, French composer.

satiety (sə tī′ə tĭ), *n.* the state of being satiated; surfeit. [t. L: m. s. *satietas* abundance]

satin (săt′ĭn), *n.* **1.** a very smooth, glossy fabric made in a warp-face weave, usually rayon or silk. —*adj.* **2.** of or like satin; smooth; glossy. [ME *satine*, t. OF, t. It.: m. **setino*, ult. der. L *sēta* silk] —**sat′in-like′,** *adj.*

satinet (săt′ĭ nĕt′), *n.* **1.** an inferior kind of satin containing cotton. **2.** *Obs.* a thin light satin. Also, **satinette.** [t. F. See SATIN, -ET]

satinpod (săt′ĭn pŏd′), *n.* a European cruciferous biennial plant with purple flowers, *Lunaria annua*, grown for the dried stems and round, flat, satiny replums which are used for interior decoration.

satin stitch, an embroidery stitch in close parallel lines, which gives a satiny finish.

satinwood (săt′ĭn wo͝od′), *n.* **1.** the satiny wood of an East Indian meliaceous tree, *Chloroxylon swietenia*, used for cabinetwork, etc. **2.** the tree itself.

satiny (săt′ĭ nĭ), *adj.* satin-like; smooth; glossy.

satire (săt′ī′ə), *n.* **1.** the use of irony, sarcasm, ridicule, etc., in exposing, denouncing, or deriding vice, folly, etc. **2.** a literary composition, in verse or prose, in which vices, abuses, follies, etc., are held up to scorn, derision, or ridicule. **3.** the species of literature constituted by such composition. [t. L: m. *satira*, var. of *satura* medley, prop. fem. of *satur* full, sated] —**Syn. 1.** See **irony**[1].

satirical (sə tĭ′rĭ kl), *adj.* **1.** of or pertaining to satire; of the nature of satire: *satirical novels.* **2.** indulging in or given to satire: *a satirical poet.* Also, **satir′ic.** —**satir′ically,** *adv.* —**satir′icalness,** *n.* —**Syn. 1.** See **cynical.**

satirist (săt′ə rĭst), *n.* **1.** a writer of satires. **2.** one who indulges in satire.

satirize (săt′ə rīz′), *v.*, **-rized, -rizing.** —*v.t.* **1.** to make the object of satire. —*v.i.* **2.** to write or perform a satire or satires. Also, **satirise.** —**sat′iriz′er,** *n.*

satisfaction (săt′ĭs făk′shən), *n.* **1.** the act of satisfying. **2.** the state of being satisfied. **3.** the cause of being satisfied. **4.** reparation, as of a wrong or injury. **5.** the opportunity of repairing a supposed wrong, as by a duel. **6.** payment, as for debt; discharge, as of obligations. **7.** *Eccles.* the performance by a penitent of the penal acts enjoined by church authority for injury done to another or to God. [ME, t. L: s. *satisfactio*] —**Syn. 2.** gratification, enjoyment, pleasure. **4.** expiation, amends.

satisfactory (săt′ĭs făk′tə rĭ, -trĭ), *adj.* **1.** affording satisfaction; fulfilling all demands or requirements: *a satisfactory answer.* **2.** *Theol.* atoning or expiating. —**sat′isfac′torily,** *adv.* —**sat′isfac′toriness,** *n.*

satisfy (săt′ĭs fī′), *v.*, **-fied, -fying.** —*v.t.* **1.** to fulfil the desires, expectations, needs, or demands of, or content (a person, the mind, etc.); supply fully the needs of (a person, etc.). **2.** to fulfil (a desire, expectation, want, etc.). **3.** to give assurance to; convince: *to satisfy oneself by investigation.* **4.** to answer sufficiently (an objection, etc.); solve (a doubt, etc.). **5.** to discharge fully (a debt, etc.). **6.** to make reparation to (a person, etc.) or for (a wrong, etc.). **7.** to pay (a creditor). **8.** to fulfil the requirements or conditions of: *to satisfy an algebraic equation.* —*v.i.* **9.** to give satisfaction. [ME *satisfye*, t. OF: m. *satisfier*, t. L: m. *satisfacere* do enough] —**sat′isfi′er,** *n.* —**sat′isfy′ingly,** *adv.*

—**Syn. 1.** gratify, appease, pacify. SATISFY, CONTENT refer to meeting one's desires or wishes. TO SATISFY is to meet to the full one's wants, expectations, etc.: *to satisfy a desire to travel.* TO CONTENT is to give enough to keep one from being disposed to find fault or complain: *to content oneself with a moderate meal.*

Sato (sä′tō), *n.* **Eisaku** (ā′sə ko͞o′), born 1901, prime minister of Japan since 1964.

satrap (săt′rəp), *n.* **1.** a governor of a province under the ancient Persian monarchy. **2.** a subordinate ruler, often a despotic one. [ME, t. L: s. *satrapa*, t. Gk: m. *satrápēs*, t. OPers.: lit., country-protector]

satrapy (săt′rə pĭ), *n.*, *pl.* **-trapies.** the province or jurisdiction of a satrap.

Satsuma (săt′so͞o mə), *n.* a former province in SW Japan, on Kyushu island: famous for its porcelain ware.

saturable (săch′ə rə bl), *adj.* that may be saturated. —**sat′urabil′ity,** *n.*

saturate (*v.* săch′ə rāt′; *adj.* săch′ə rĭt, -rāt′), *v.*, **-rated, -rating,** *adj.* —*v.t.* **1.** to cause (a substance) to unite with the greatest possible amount of another substance, through solution, chemical combination, or the like. **2.** to charge to the utmost, as with magnetism. **3.** to soak, impregnate, or imbue thoroughly or completely. **4.** *Mil.* to bomb or shell (an enemy position) so thoroughly that the enemy defences are powerless. **5.** *Mil.* to send so many planes over (a target area) that the enemy electronic tracking equipment is neutralized. —*adj.* **6.** *Chiefly Poetic.* saturated. [t. L: m. s. *saturātus*, pp., satisfied, saturated] —**Syn. 3.** See **wet.**

saturated (săch′ə rā′tĭd), *adj.* **1.** soaked, impregnated, or imbued thoroughly; charged thoroughly or completely; brought to a state of saturation. **2.** (of colours) of maximum chroma or purity; of the highest intensity of hue; free from admixture of white.

saturated compound, *Chem.* **1.** a compound which does not form addition compounds, the molecules of which contain no double or triple bonds. **2.** a compound which has no free valency electrons.

saturated solution, *Chem.* a solution which contains as much solute as can be dissolved under any particular set of conditions.

saturated vapour, *Chem.* a vapour which is sufficiently concentrated to exist in equilibrium with its liquid.

saturation (săch′ə rā′shən), *n.* **1.** the act or process of saturating. **2.** the resulting state. **3.** *Meteorol.* a condition in the atmosphere corresponding to 100 per cent relative humidity. **4.** (of colours) the degree of purity or chroma; degree of freedom from admixture with white.

saturation point, the point at which a substance will receive no more of another substance in solution, chemical combination, etc.

Saturday (săt′ə dĭ), *n.* the seventh day of the week, following Friday. [ME; OE *Sæterdæg*, *Sætern*(*es*)*dæg*, c. D *zaterdag*, LG *Saterdag*, half trans., half adoption of L *Sāturnī dies* day of Saturn (the planet)]

Saturn (săt′ən), *n.* **1.** *Astron.* the second largest planet, the sixth in order from the sun. Its period of revolution is 29·46 years, its mean distance from the sun about 886,700,000 miles, and its diameter 74,130 miles. It has 9 satellites and is remarkable for the thin rings surrounding it, said to be made up of ice crystals. **2.** *Rom. Myth.* the god of agriculture and vegetation, whose reign was characterized by happiness and virtue. **3.** *Alchemy.* the metal lead.

Saturnalia (săt′û nā′lyə), *n.pl.* **1.** (in ancient Rome) the festival of Saturn, celebrated in December, and observed as a time of general feasting and unrestrained merrymaking. **2.** (*l.c.*) any period of unrestrained revelry. [t. L] —**Sat′urna′lian,** *adj.*

Saturnian (să tû′nyən), *adj.* **1.** of or pertaining to the planet Saturn. **2.** of or pertaining to the god Saturn, whose reign is referred to as 'the golden age'. **3.** prosperous, happy, or peaceful: *Saturnian days.*

saturniid (să tû′nĭ ĭd), *n.* **1.** any of the large moths of the family *Saturniidae*, including many of the most strikingly coloured species. —*adj.* **2.** denoting or pertaining to these moths. [t. NL: s. *Sāturniidae*, der. L *Sāturnius* of Saturn]

saturnine (săt′û nīn′), *adj.* **1.** having or showing a sluggish, gloomy temperament; gloomy; taciturn. **2.** suffering from lead poisoning, as a person. **3.** due to absorption of lead, as disorders. [f. SATURN + -INE[1]; the planet being supposed to give a gloomy nature to those born under its sign] —**sat′urnine′ly,** *adv.*

saturnism (săt′ə nĭz′əm), *n.* lead poisoning; plumbism.

Satyagraha (sŭt′yə grŭ′hə), *n.* **1.** (in India) a policy of non-violent resistence to British rule inaugurated by Gandhi in 1919. **2.** any non-violent resistence movement. **3.** the principle of non-violence. [t. Hind., t. Skt: truth-grasping]

satyr (săt′ə), *n.* **1.** *Class. Myth.* one of a class of woodland deities, attendant on Bacchus, represented as part human and part goat, and noted for riot and lasciviousness. **2.** a lascivious man. **3.** a man affected with satyriasis. **4.** any of the rather sombre butterflies that constitute the family *Satyridae.* [ME, t. L: s. *satyrus*, t. Gk: m. *sátyros*] —**satyric** (sə tĭ′rĭk), *adj.*

satyriasis (săt′ĭ rī′ə sĭs), *n.* *Pathol.* morbid and uncontrollable sexual desire in men. [NL, t. Gk]

sauce (sôs), *n.*, *v.*, **sauced, saucing.** —*n.* **1.** any preparation, usually liquid or soft, eaten as a relish or appetizing accompaniment to food. **2.** something that adds piquance. **3.** *Colloq.* impertinence; impudence. **4.** *U.S. Dial.* garden vegetables, etc., eaten with meat. —*v.t.* **5.** to dress or prepare with sauce; season: *meat well sauced.* **6.** to give zest to. **7.** to make agreeable or less harsh. **8.** *Colloq.* to speak impertinently to. [ME, t. OF, g. VL *salsa*, fem. of *salsus* salted]

sauce boat, a low boat-shaped vessel in which sauce is served at table.

saucebox (sôs′bŏks′), *n.* *Colloq.* a saucy person.

saucepan (sôs′pən), *n.* a metal container of moderate depth, usually having a long handle and sometimes a lid, for boiling, stewing, etc.

saucer (sô′sə), *n.* **1.** a small, round, shallow dish to hold a cup. **2.** any similar dish, plate, or the like: any saucer-like thing. [ME, t. OF: m. *saucier*(*e*) vessel for holding sauce, der. *sauce* SAUCE]

saucy (sô′sĭ), *adj.*, **-cier, -ciest.** **1.** impertinent; insolent: *a saucy remark or child.* **2.** piquantly pert; smart: *saucy hat.* —**sau′cily,** *adv.* —**sau′ciness,** *n.*

Saud (soud), *n.* born 1902, king of Saudi Arabia 1953–64.

Saudi Arabia (sô′dĭ), a kingdom in N and central Arabia, including Hejaz, Nejd, and dependencies. 6,000,000 pop. (est. 1963); ab. 800,000 sq. mi. *Capitals:* Mecca and Riyadh.

Saudi Arabia

sauerkraut (sou′ə krout′), *n.* cabbage cut fine, salted, and allowed to ferment until sour. [t. G: f. *sauer* sour + *Kraut* cabbage]

sauger (sô′gə), *n.* a freshwater North American pike-perch, *Stizostedion canadense.*

Sauk (sôk), *n.* Sac.

Saul (sôl), *n.* **1.** the first king of Israel. I Sam. 9. **2.** the original name of the apostle Paul. See Acts 9:1–30, etc.

Saulte Ste Marie (so͞o′sānt′ mə rē′), the rapids of the St Marys river, between NE Michigan and Ontario, Canada.

Sault Ste Marie Canals, two ship canals with locks, N and S of the St Marys river rapids and connecting lakes Superior and Huron: one canal is in Canada and the other in Michigan; heaviest canal traffic in the world. $1\frac{1}{2}$ mi. long. Also, **Soo Canals.**

sauna (sô′nə), *n.* a type of bath originally Finnish, in which the bather is subjected to steam, and then lightly beaten with birch twigs.

saunter (sôn′tə), *v.i.* **1.** to walk with a leisurely gait; stroll. —*n.* **2.** a leisurely walk or ramble; a stroll. **3.** a leisurely gait. [late ME; orig. uncert.] —**saun′terer,** *n.* —**Syn. 1.** See **stroll.**

-saur, a word element meaning 'lizard'. [see SAURO-]

saurel (sô′rəl), *n.* *Chiefly U.S.* scad[2]. [t. F, f. s. L *saurus* lizard (t. Gk: m. *saûros*) + *-el* dim. suffix]

saurian (sô′rĭ ən), *adj.* **1.** belonging or pertaining to the *Sauria*, a group of reptiles orig. including the lizards, crocodiles, etc., but now technically restricted to the lizards or lacertilians. **2.** lizard-like. —*n.* **3.** a saurian animal, as a dinosaur or lizard. [f. s. NL *sauria* an order of reptiles (der. Gk *saûros* lizard) + -AN]

sauro-, a word element meaning 'lizard'. [comb. form of Gk *saûros*]

sauropod (sô′rə pŏd′), *n.* **1.** any of the *Sauropoda*, a group of herbivorous dinosaurs with small head, long neck and tail, and five-toed limbs, the largest known land animals. —*adj.* **2.** belonging or pertaining to the *Sauropoda.* —**sauropodous** (sô rŏp′ə dəs), *adj.*

-saurus, Latinized var. of **-saur.**

saury (sô′rĭ), *n.*, *pl.* **-ries.** **1.** a sharp-snouted fish, *Scomberesox saurus*, of the Atlantic. **2.** any of various related fishes, esp. the **Pacific saury,** *Cololabis saira.* [appar. t. Gk: m. *saûros* sea fish (Aristotle)]

sausage (sŏs′ĭj), *n.* **1.** minced pork, beef, or other meats (often combined), with various added ingredients and seasonings, and packed into a special skin, formerly prepared from the entrails of pigs or ox, but now often made from a synthetic product. **2.** *Aeron.* a sausage-shaped observation balloon, formerly used in warfare. [ME *sausige*, t. ONF: m. *saussiche*, g. LL *salsīcia*, der. L *salsus* salted]

sausage dog, *Colloq.* dachshund.

sausage meat, meat prepared for making sausages.

sausage roll, a roll of baked pastry filled with sausage meat.

sauté (sō′tā; *Fr.* sō tĕ′), *adj.*, *v.*, **-téed, -téeing,** *n.* —*adj.* **1.** cooked or browned in a pan containing a little fat. —*v.t.* **2.** to cook in a small amount of fat; pan-fry. —*n.*

3. a dish of sauté food. [t. F, pp. of *sauter* leap (used in causative sense), g. L *saltāre*]

sauterne (sō tûn′; *Fr.* sō tĕrn′), *n.* a rich sweet white table wine, esp. one produced near Bordeaux, France. Also, **sauternes.** [named after the district *Sauternes*, near Bordeaux, where it is made]

sautoir (*Fr.* sō twȧr′), *n. French.* a long ribbon, chain, beaded band, or the like, worn about the neck.

sauve qui peut (*Fr.* sōv kē pœ′), *French.* a stampede; a general rout. [F: lit., save himself who can]

Sava (sä′və), *n.* a river flowing from NW Yugoslavia E to the Danube at Belgrade. ab. 450 mi. Also, **Save.**

savage (săv′ĭj), *adj.*, *n.*, *v.*, **savaged, savaging.** —*adj.* **1.** wild or rugged, as country or scenery: *savage wilderness.* **2.** uncivilized; barbarous: *savage tribes.* **3.** rude, boorish: *savage manners.* **4.** fierce, ferocious, or cruel; untamed: *savage beasts.* **5.** enraged, or furiously angry, as a person. **6.** *Obs.* uncultivated (as a plant). —*n.* **7.** an uncivilized human being. **8.** a fierce, brutal, or cruel person. **9.** a rude, boorish person. —*v.t.* **10.** to assail violently; maul. [ME *sauvage*, t. OF, g. LL *salvāticus*, of the woods, wild, r. L *silvāticus*] —**sav′agely,** *adv.* —**sav′ageness,** *n.* —**Syn.** 4. See **cruel.**

Savage Island, Niue.

savagery (săv′ĭj rĭ), *n.*, *pl.* **-ries. 1.** uncivilized state or condition; a state of barbarism. **2.** savage nature, disposition, conduct, or act; barbarity.

Savai'i (sä vī′ē), *n.* an island in Western Samoa: the largest of the Samoa group. 31,642 pop. (1961); 703 sq. mi.

savanna (sə văn′ə), *n.* **1.** a plain, characterized by coarse grasses and scattered tree growth, esp. on the margins of the tropics where the rainfall is seasonal, as in the Sudan of Africa. **2.** grassland region with scattered trees, grading into either open plain or woodland, usually in subtropical or tropical regions. Also, **savannah.** [t. Sp.: m. *zavana*, *savana*, t. Carib]

Savannah (sə văn′ə), *n.* **1.** a seaport in the U.S., in E Georgia, near the mouth of the Savannah river. 149,245 (1960). **2.** a river forming most of the boundary between Georgia and South Carolina, flowing SE to the Atlantic. 314 mi.

savant (săv′ənt; *Fr.* sȧ väɴ′), *n.*, *pl.* **savants** (săv′ənts; *Fr.* sȧ väɴ′), a man of learning. [t. F, n. use of (former) ppr. of *savoir*, g. L *sapere* be wise]

savate (sə văt′), *n.* a form of boxing in which the feet, as well as the hands, may be used to deliver blows. [t. F: lit., old shoe]

save[1] (sāv), *n.*, *v.*, **saved, saving.** —*v.t.* **1.** to rescue from danger; preserve from harm, injury, or loss: *to save from drowning.* **2.** to keep safe, intact, or unhurt; safeguard: *God save the King.* **3.** to keep from being lost: *to save the game.* **4.** (in soccer, etc.) to prevent (a goal) being scored by stopping the ball from entering the net. **5.** to avoid the spending, consumption, or waste of: *to save fuel by keeping the fire low.* **6.** to set apart, reserve, or lay by: *to save money.* **7.** to treat carefully in order to reduce wear, fatigue, etc.: *to save one's eyes.* **8.** to prevent the occurrence, use, or necessity of; obviate: *a stitch in time saves nine.* **9.** *Theol.* to deliver from the power and consequences of sin. —*v.i.* **10.** to accumulate or put aside money, etc., as the result of economy (often fol. by *up*): *to save up for a new car.* **11.** to be economical in expenditure. **12.** to preserve something from harm, injury, loss, etc. **13.** (in soccer, etc.) to prevent a goal from being scored by stopping the ball from entering the net. **14.** *Colloq.* to admit of being kept without spoiling, as food. —*n.* **15.** the act or instance of saving, esp. in sports. [ME, t. OF: m. *sauver*, *salver*, g. L *salvāre*] —**sav′able,** *adj.* —**sav′er,** *n.*

save[2] (sāv), *prep.* **1.** except; but. —*conj.* **2.** except; but. **3.** *Archaic.* unless. [ME; var. of SAFE, adj., in obs. sense of reserving, making exception of] —**Syn. 1.** See **except**[1].

Save (sä′vĭ), *n.* Sava.

save-all (sāv′ôl′), *n.* **1.** a means, contrivance, or receptacle for preventing loss or waste. **2.** *Dial.* a miser. **3.** *Dial.* overalls.

saveloy (săv′ĭ loi′), *n.* a highly seasoned, dried sausage. [t. F: alter. of *cervelas* a kind of sausage orig. containing pigs brains, t. It.: m. *cervellata*, der. *cervello* brain, g. L *cerebellum*]

savin (săv′ĭn), *n.* **1.** a juniper, *Juniperus sabina*, whose dried tops are used as a drug. **2.** the drug itself. **3.** the red cedar. Also, **savine.** [ME and OE *savine*, t. VL, g. L (*herba*) *Sabina*, lit., Sabine herb]

saving (sā′vĭng), *adj.* **1.** that saves; rescuing; preserving. **2.** redeeming: *a saving sense of humour.* **3.** economical: *a saving housekeeper.* **4.** making a reservation: *a saving clause.* —*n.* **5.** economy in expenditure, outlay, use, etc. **6.** a reduction or lessening of expenditure or outlay: *a saving of ten per cent.* **7.** that which is saved. **8.** (*pl.*) sums of money saved by economy and laid away. **9.** *Law.* a reservation or exception. —*prep.* **10.** except: *none remains saving these ruins.* **11.** with all due respect to or for: *saving your presence.* —*conj.* **12.** save. [f. SAVE[1] + -ING[2], -ING[1]] —**sav′ingly,** *adv.*

saving grace, a virtue or quality which compensates for faults.

savings account (sā′vĭngz), a bank account on which a preferential rate of interest is allowed in order to encourage savings, usually limited to small amounts.

savings bank, a bank in which money is invested for interest, and in which deposits are safeguarded by law.

savings book, a book for containing entries, savings stamps, etc., recording the amount deposited in a savings bank.

savings stamp, a stamp of small denomination issued by the post office to be purchased and accumulated as a means of saving.

saviour (sā′vyə), *n.* **1.** one who saves, rescues, or delivers: *the saviour of the country.* **2.** (*cap.*) a title of God, esp. of Christ. [ME *sauveour*, t. OF, g. LL *salvātor*. See SAVE[1]]

Savoie (*Fr.* sȧ vwȧ′), *n.* **1.** a department in SE France. 266,678 pop. (1962); 2388 sq. mi. *Cap.:* Chambéry. **2.** French name of **Savoy.**

savoir-faire (săv′wä fēə′; *Fr.* sȧ vwȧr fĕr′), *n.* knowledge of what to do in any situation; tact. [t. F: lit., to know how to act]

savoir-vivre (săv′wä vē′vrə; *Fr.* sȧ vwȧr vē′vr), *n. French.* knowledge of the world and the usages of polite society. [F: lit., to know how to live]

Savona (*It.* sȧ vō′nȧ), *n.* a seaport in Italy, in Liguria. 77,122 (1966).

Savonarola (săv′ə nə rō′lə; *It.* sȧ vō nȧ rŏ′lȧ), *n.* **Girolamo** (*It.* jē rŏ′lȧ mō), 1452–98, Italian monk, reformer, and martyr.

savorous (sā′və rəs), *adj. Chiefly U.S.* having savour; savoury.

savory[1] (sā′və rĭ), *n.*, *pl.* **-vories.** any of the aromatic plants constituting the menthaceous genus *Satureia*, esp. *S. hortensis* (**summer savory**), a European herb used in cookery, or *S. montana* (**winter savory**). [ME *saverey*, OE *sǣtherie*, *saturēge*, t. L: m. *saturēia*]

savory[2] (sā′və rĭ), *adj.*, *n. U.S.* savoury.

savour (sā′və), *n.* **1.** the quality in a substance which affects the sense of taste or of smell. **2.** a particular taste or smell. **3.** distinctive quality or property. **4.** power to excite or interest. **5.** *Archaic.* repute. —*v.i.* **6.** to have savour, taste, or smell. **7.** to exhibit the peculiar characteristics; smack (fol. by *of*). —*v.t.* **8.** to give a savour to; season; flavour. **9.** to perceive by taste or smell, esp. with relish. **10.** to give oneself to the enjoyment of. Also, *U.S.* **savor.** [ME *savour*, t. OF, g. L *sapor* taste, savour] —**sa′vourer,** *n.* —**sa′vourless,** *adj.* —**Syn. 1.** See **taste.**

savoury (sā′və rĭ), *adj.*, *n.*, *pl.* **-vouries.** —*adj.* **1.** having savour; agreeable in taste or smell: *a savoury smell.* **2.** giving a relish; piquant: *savoury dish.* **3.** pleasing or agreeable. —*n.* **4.** an appetizing dish served at the beginning or end of a dinner. Also, *U.S.*, **savory.** [ME *savure*, t. OF: m. *savoure*, pp. See SAVOUR, v.] —**sa′vouriness,** *n.*

savoury mousse, a mousse having as a base a white sauce to which eggs, seasoning, and flavouring are added.

savoy (sə voi′), *n.* a variety of the common cabbage with a compact head and leaves reticulately wrinkled. [named after SAVOY (def. 1)]

Savoy (sə voi′), *n.* **1.** a region in SE France, adjacent to the Swiss-Italian border: formerly a duchy; later a part of the kingdom of Sardinia; ceded to France, 1860. **2. House of,** the rulers of the former duchy of Savoy, and since 1862 comprising the royal house of Italy: prior to the dissolution of the Italian monarchy (1946) it was the oldest reigning dynasty of Europe.

Savoyard (sə voi′äd; *Fr.* sȧ vwȧ yȧr′), *n.* **1.** a native or inhabitant of Savoy. **2.** one enthusiastic about, or connected with, Gilbert and Sullivan operas, so called from the Savoy Theatre in London, where the operas were first given. —*adj.* **3.** of or pertaining to Savoy.

savvy (săv′ĭ), *v.*, **-vied, -vying,** *n.*, *adj.*, **-vier, -viest.** *Slang.* —*v.t.*, *v.i.* **1.** to know; understand. [t. Sp.: alter. of *sabe* (*usted*) do you know] —*n.* **2.** understanding; intelligence; common sense. —*adj.* **3.** well-informed or experienced. [var. of d. Scot. *savie*, t. F: alter. of *savoir* know, g. L *sapere*]

saw[1] (sô), *n.*, *v.*, **sawed, sawn** or **sawed, sawing.** —*n.* **1.** a tool or device for cutting, typically a thin blade of metal with a series of sharp teeth. **2.** any similar tool or device, as a rotating disc in which a sharp continuous edge replaces the teeth. —*v.t.* **3.** to cut or divide with a saw. **4.** to form by cutting with a saw. **5.** to cut as if using a saw: *to saw the air with one's hands.* **6.** to work (something) from side to side like a saw. —*v.t.* 7. to use a saw. 8. to cut with, or as with, a saw. 9. to cut as a saw does. [ME *sawe*, OE *saga*, *sagu*, c. D *zaag*; akin to G *Säge* saw, L *secāre* cut] —**saw′er,** *n.*

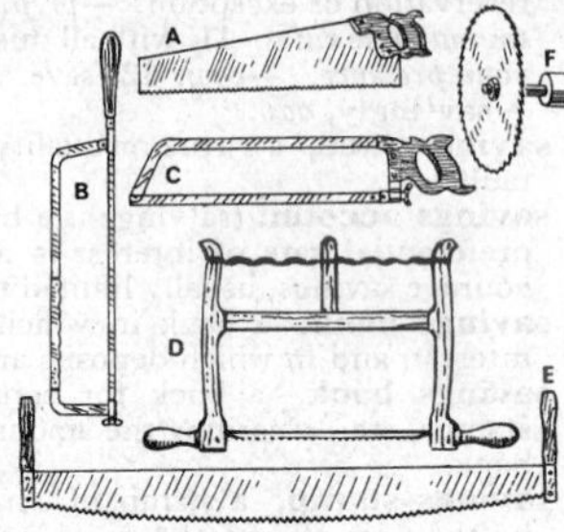

Saws: A, Handsaw; B, Hacksaw; C, Butcher's saw; D, Bowsaw; E, Two-handed crosscut saw; F, Circular saw

saw[2] (sô), *v.* pt. of **see**[1].

saw[3] (sô), *n.* a sententious saying; maxim; proverb: *he could muster an old saw for almost every occasion.* [ME; OE *sagu*, c. G *Sage*, Icel. *saga* SAGA; akin to SAY]

sawbill (sô′bĭl′), *n.* any of the mergansers of the sub-family *Merginae.*

sawbones (sô′bōnz′), *n. Obs. Slang.* a surgeon.

sawbuck (sô′bŭk′), *n. U.S.* 1. a sawhorse. 2. *Slang.* a ten-dollar note. [cf. D *zaagbok*]

sawdust (sô′dŭst′), *n.* small particles of wood produced in sawing.

sawfish (sô′fĭsh′), *n., pl.* **-fishes,** (*esp. collectively*) **-fish.** a large, elongate ray (genus *Pristis*) of tropical coasts and lowland rivers, with a blade-like snout bearing strong teeth on each side.

Sawfish, *Pristis pectinatus* (10 to 20 ft long)

sawfly (sô′flī′), *n., pl.* **-flies.** any of the hymenopterous insects constituting the family *Tenthredinidae*, the females of which are characterized by a pair of sawlike organs for cutting slits in plants to hold their eggs.

sawgrass (sô′gräs′), *n.* any of various cyperaceous plants, esp. of the genus *Cladium*, with the margins of the leaves toothed like a saw.

sawhorse (sô′hôs′), *n.* a movable frame for holding wood that is being sawn.

sawlog (sô′lŏg′), *n.* a log large enough to saw into boards.

sawmill (sô′mĭl′), *n.* an establishment in which timber is sawn into planks, boards, etc., by machinery.

sawpit (sô′pĭt′), *n.* a pit in the ground over which trees are placed for sawing up.

sawset (sô′sĕt′), *n.* an instrument used to bend the point of each alternate tooth of a saw out slightly so that the kerf made by the saw will be wider than its blade.

saw-toothed (sô′to͞otht′), *adj.* having a shape or profile similar to the teeth of a saw.

saw-wort (sô′wût′), *n.* a perennial composite Old World herb with finely toothed leaves, *Serratula tinctoria.*

sawyer (sô′yə), *n.* one who saws, esp. as an occupation. [ME *sawier*, f. SAW[1] + -IER]

sax[1] (săks), *n.* an axelike tool for cutting roofing slate. [ME *sex*, OE *seax* knife]

sax[2] (săks), *n. Colloq.* saxophone.

Sax., 1. Saxon. 2. Saxony.

saxatile (săk′sə tĭl′), *adj.* living or growing on or among rocks. [t. L: m. s. *saxātilis*]

Saxe (*Fr.* sȧks), *n.* **1. Hermann Maurice de** (*Fr.* ĕr mȧn mō rēs′ də), 1696–1750, marshal of France and general. 2. French name of **Saxony.**

Saxe-Altenburg (săks′äl′tən bûg′), *n.* a former duchy in Thuringia, in central Germany.

saxe blue (săks), a shade of greenish light blue.

Saxe-Coburg-Gotha (săks′kō′bûg gō′thə), *n.* 1. a former duchy in central Germany. 2. **House of,** the name of the British royal family from 1902 until 1917, when it became the House of Windsor. 3. **Prince of.** See **Albert** (def. 1).

Saxe-Meiningen (săks′mī′nĭng ən), *n.* a former duchy in Thuringia in central Germany.

Saxe-Weimar-Eisenach (săks′vī′mär ī′zən äKH′), *n.* a former grand duchy in Thuringia in central Germany.

saxhorn (săks′hôn′), *n.* any of a family of brass instruments close to the cornets and tubas. [named after Adolphe *Sax*, 1814–94, a Belgian, who invented the instrument]

Saxhorn

saxicolous (săk sĭk′ə ləs), *adj. Bot., Zool.* living or growing among rocks. Also, **saxicoline** (săk sĭk′ə lĭn′). [f. L *saxi-* (comb. form of *saxum* rock) + s. L *-cola* dweller + -OUS]

saxifragaceous (săk′sĭ frə gā′shəs), *adj.* belonging to the *Saxifragaceae*, or saxifrage family of plants.

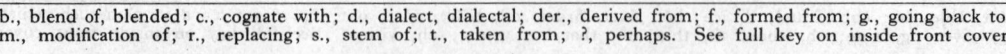

saxifrage (săk′sĭ frĭj), *n.* any of the plants, mostly perennial herbs, constituting the genus *Saxifraga*, many of which grow wild in the clefts of rocks, others being cultivated for their flowers. [ME, t. L: m. *saxifraga* (*herba*), lit., rock-breaking herb]

Saxo Grammaticus (săk′sō grə măt′ĭ kəs), *c.* 1150–*c.* 1206, Danish chronicler.

Saxon (săk′sən), *n.* 1. a person of the English race or of English descent. 2. an Anglo-Saxon. 3. Anglo-Saxon (language). 4. the Old English dialects of the regions settled by the Saxons. 5. the dialect of Old Low German spoken by the Saxons (def. 7). 6. a native or inhabitant of Saxony in modern Germany. 7. a member of a Germanic people anciently dwelling near the mouth of the Elbe, a portion of whom invaded and occupied parts of Britain in the 5th and 6th centuries. —*adj.* 8. English. 9. of or pertaining to the early Saxons (def. 7) or their language. 10. of or pertaining to Saxony in modern Germany. [ME, t. L: s. *Saxo, Saxonēs* (pl.), t. Gmc; r. OE *Seaxan*, pl., g. Gmc]

Saxonism (săk′sə nĭz′əm), *n.* an idiom supposedly peculiarly English and not of foreign (esp. Latin) origin.

Saxony (săk′sə nĭ), *n.* 1. a region and former state in S East Germany. *Cap.:* Dresden. 2. a region and former province in N Germany. *Cap.:* Magdeburg. 3. a medieval and subsequent division of N Germany with varying boundaries: at its height it extended from the Rhine to E of the Elbe. 4. a fine woollen yarn for knitting, etc., or cloth made from it. German, **Sachsen,** French, **Saxe,** for defs 1, 2, 3.

Saxony, 1815

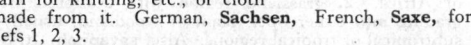

saxophone (săk′sə fōn′), *n.* a musical wind instrument consisting of a conical metal tube (usually brass) with keys or valves, and a clarinet mouthpiece. [f. *sax* (as in SAXHORN) + -O- + -PHONE] —**saxophonist** (săk sŏf′ə nĭst), *n.*

Man playing a saxophone

saxtuba (săks′tyo͞o′bə), *n.* a large (bass) form of saxhorn. [f. *sax* (as in SAXHORN) + TUBA]

say (sā), *v.,* **said, saying,** *n.* —*v.t.* 1. to utter or pronounce; speak. 2. to express in words; state; declare. 3. to state as an opinion, or with assurance: *it is hard to say what is wrong.* 4. to recite or repeat: *to say one's prayers.* 5. to assume as a hypothesis or an estimate: *to learn in, say, ten lessons.* 6. to report or allege; maintain: *people say he will resign.* —*v.i.* 7. to speak; declare; express an opinion. 8. **that is to say,** in other words; otherwise. 9. **I say,** an exclamation to attract attention or to express surprise, protest, joy, etc. —*n.* 10. what a person says or has to say. 11. *Colloq.* the right or opportunity to say, speak or decide. 12. turn to say something: *it is now my say.* 13. **have the last say,** to have the final authority: *the treasurer has the last say on a budget of this size.* [ME; OE *secgan*, c. D *zeggen*, G *sagen*, Icel. *segja*] —**say′er,** *n.* —**Syn.** 1. remark, affirm.

Sayan Mountains (sä yăn′), a range of mountains in the S Soviet Union in Asia. Highest peak, Munku Sardik, 11,447 ft.

sayest (sā′ĭst), *v. Archaic.* 2nd pers. sing. of say. Also, **sayst** (sāst).

saying (sā′ĭng), *n.* 1. something said, esp. a proverb or apophthegm. 2. **go without saying,** to be completely self-evident.

say-so (sā′sō′), *n. Colloq.* 1. one's personal statement or assertion. 2. final authority. 3. a command.

sayyid (sī′ĭd), *n.* (in Mohammedan countries) a person supposed to be descended from Mohammed through his daughter Fatima. [t. Ar.: lord. Cf. CID]

Sb, (L *stibium*) antimony.

sb., substantive.

S-bend (ĕs′bĕnd′), *n.* an S-shaped bend in a pipe, as one forming an air-trap in a water closet.

SBR, styrene-butadiene rubber.

Sc, *Chem.* scandium.

Sc., 1. Science. 2. Scotch. 3. Scotland. 4. Scots. 5. Scottish.

sc., 1. scale. 2. scene. 3. science. 4. scientific. 5. scilicet. 6. screw. 7. scruple.

S.C., 1. Security Council. 2. Signal Corps. 3. South Carolina. 4. Staff Corps. 5. Supreme Court.

s.c., 1. small capitals. 2. supercalendered.

scab (skăb), *n., v.,* **scabbed, scabbing.** —*n.* 1. the encrustation which forms over a sore during healing.

2. *Vet. Sci.* a mangy disease in animals, esp. sheep; scabies. 3. *Plant Pathol.* a hyperplasic plant disease with scablike lesions: *apple scab.* 4. *Slang.* a blackleg. 5. *Slang.* a scoundrel. —*v.i.* 6. to become covered with a scab. 7. to act or work as a scab. 8. *Civ. Eng.* (of a road surface) to loosen aggregate and form potholes. [ME, t. Scand.; cf. Sw. *skabb*, c. d. E *shab*, OE *sceabb.* See SHABBY] —**scab′like′**, *adj.*

scabbard (skăb′əd), *n.* 1. a sheath or cover for the blade of a sword, dagger, or the like. —*v.t.* 2. to put into a scabbard; sheathe. [ME *scauberd*, t. AF: m. *escauberz* (pl.); prob. of Gmc orig.]

scabbard fish, any salt-water fish of the family *Trichiuridae*, with dagger-like teeth and a thin, whip-shaped body; distributed throughout the world.

scabble (skăb′l), *v.t.*, **-led, -ling.** scapple.

scabby (skăb′ĭ), *adj.*, **-bier, -biest.** 1. covered with scabs; blotchy. 2. consisting of scabs. 3. affected with the scab. 4. *Colloq.* mean or contemptible: *that was a scabby trick.*

scabies (skā′bĭ ēz′, -bēz), *n.* any of several infectious skin diseases occurring in sheep and cattle, and in man, caused by parasitic mites; itch. [t. L: roughness, the itch (der. *scabere* scratch, scrape, c. SHAVE)] —**scabietic** (skā′bĭ ĕt′ĭk), *adj.*

scabious[1] (skā′byəs), *adj.* 1. scabby. 2. pertaining to or of the nature of scabies. [t. L: m. *scabiōsus*]

scabious[2] (skā′byəs), *n.* any plant of the composite genus *Scabiosa*, comprising a large number of hairy herbs with flowers in dense heads, as the **small scabious,** *S. colubaria*, of chalk grassland. [ME *scabiose*, t. ML: m. *scabiōsa* (*herba*) scabies-curing herb]

scabland (skăb′lănd′), *n.* rough, barren, badly eroded topography with thin soils and little vegetation.

scabrous (skā′brəs), *adj.* 1. rough with minute points or projections. 2. harsh; full of difficulties. 3. bordering on the indecent; risqué. [t. LL: m. s. *scabrōsus*, der. L *scaber* rough] —**sca′brously,** *adv.* —**sca′brousness,** *n.*

scad[1] (skăd), *n.* (*usually pl.*) *Slang.* a large quantity: *he has scads of money.* [orig. uncert.]

scad[2] (skăd), *n.* a small marine carangoid fish of the genus *Trachurus*; saurel. [? t. Celtic; cf. OIrish *scatān* herring]

Scafell Pike (skô′fĕl′), a mountain peak in NW England, in Cumberland: highest in England. 3210 ft.

scaffold (skăf′əld, -ōld), *n.* 1. a temporary structure for holding workmen and materials during the erection, repair, cleaning, or decoration of a building. 2. an elevated platform on which a criminal is executed. 3. a raised platform or stage for exhibiting spectacles, seating spectators, etc. 4. any raised framework. 5. scaffolding. —*v.t.* 6. to furnish with a scaffold or scaffolding. 7. to support by or place on a scaffold. [ME, t. OF: m. *escafaud*, f. *es-* E- + *cafaud*, ult. g. LL *catafalicum*, f. *cata-* CATA- + s. *fala* tower, gallery + *-icum* -IC] —**scaf′folder,** *n.*

scaffolding (skăf′əl dĭng), *n.* 1. a scaffold or system of scaffolds. 2. materials for scaffolds.

scaglia (skăl′yə), *n.* a reddish Italian limestone.

scagliola (skăl yō′lə), *n.* plasterwork imitating marble, granite, or the like. [t. It.: m. *scagliuola*, dim. of *scaglia* chip of marble, t. Gmc; cf. SCALE[1]]

scalable (skā′lə bl), *adj.* that may be scaled: *the scalable slope of a mountain.*

scalade (skə lād′), *n. Obs. or Archaic.* escalade.

scalage (skā′lĭj), *n. U.S. Forestry.* the amount of timber estimated to be contained in a log being scaled.

scalar (skā′lə), *Maths.* —*adj.* 1. representable by position on a line; having only magnitude: *a scalar variable.* 2. of or pertaining to a scalar, or something utilizing scalars. —*n.* 3. a quantity possessing only magnitude (contrasted with a *vector*). [t. L: s. *scālāris*]

scalare (skə lā′rĭ), *n.* angelfish (def. 2). [t. NL, t. Pg., t. L: neut. of *scālāris* ladder-like (from the markings)]

scalariform (skə lă′rĭ fôm′), *adj. Biol.* ladder-like. [t. NL: s. *scālāriformis*, der. L *scālāris* SCALAR. See -FORM]

scalawag (skăl′ə wăg′), *n.* scallywag.

scald[1] (skôld), *v.t.* 1. to burn or affect painfully with, or as with, hot liquid or steam. 2. to subject to the action of boiling or hot liquid. 3. to heat to a temperature just short of the boiling point: *to scald milk.* —*v.i.* 4. to be or become scalded. —*n.* 5. a burn caused by hot liquid or steam. 6. any similar condition, esp. as the result of too much heat or sunlight. 7. *Plant Pathol.* one of several non-parasitic diseases, especially of the apple, which resemble the effects of too much heat or sunlight. [ME *skalde*(*n*), t. ONF: m. s. *escalder* burn, scald, g. LL *excaldāre* wash in hot water]

scald[2] (skôld), *n.* skald.

scaldfish (skôld′fĭsh′, skäld′-), *n.* a small flat fish, *Arnoglossus laterna*, of British coastal waters.

scalding (skôl′dĭng), *adj.* 1. hot enough to scald. 2. bitter and crushing: *a scalding reply.*

scale[1] (skāl), *n.*, *v.*, **scaled, scaling.** —*n.* 1. one of the thin, flat, horny or hard plates that form the covering of certain animals, as fishes. 2. any thin platelike piece, lamina, or flake such as peels off from a surface. 3. *Bot.* **a.** a small rudimentary body, usually a specialized leaf, covering the leaf buds of deciduous trees in cold climates. **b.** a thin scarious or membranous part of a plant, as a bract of a catkin. **c.** the fleshy food storage structures of a bulb. 4. a scale insect, as the San Jose scale. 5. the protective covering secreted by the scale insect. 6. a coating or encrustation as on the inside of a boiler, formed by the precipitation of salts from the water. 7. (*pl. or sing.*) *Metall.* an oxide, esp. a ferric oxide, forming in blackish scales on iron brought to a high temperature. 8. (*pl.*) something that causes blindness, whether physical or mental. See Acts 9:18. —*v.t.* 9. to remove the scales or scale from: *to scale fish.* 10. to remove in scales or thin layers. 11. to cover with an encrustation or scale. 12. to skip, as a stone over water. —*v.i.* 13. to come off in scales. 14. to shed scales. 15. to become coated with scale, as the inside of a boiler. [ME, t. OF: aphetic m. *escale*; of Gmc orig.] —**scale′like′**, *adj.*

scale[2] (skāl), *n.*, *v.*, **scaled, scaling.** —*n.* 1. the pan, or either of the pans or dishes, of a balance. 2. (*usually pl.*) a balance, or any of various other more or less complicated devices for weighing. 3. **Scales,** *Astron.* the zodiacal constellation or sign Libra; the Balance. 4. **turn the scale(s),** to determine the outcome of something that has been in doubt. 5. **tip the scale(s), a.** to weigh (fol. by *at*). **b.** to influence favourably. —*v.t.* 6. to weigh in or as in scales. 7. to have a weight of. [ME, t. Scand.; cf. Icel. *skālar* (pl.), c. OE *scealu* scale (of a balance)]

scale[3] (skāl), *n.*, *v.*, **scaled, scaling.** —*n.* 1. a succession or progression of steps or degrees; a graduated series. 2. a point on such a scale. 3. a series of marks laid down at determinate distances, as along a line, for purposes of measurement or computation: *the scale of a thermometer.* 4. a graduated line, as on a map, representing proportionate size. 5. a graduated table of prices, wages, etc. 6. an instrument with graduated spaces, for measuring, etc. 7. the proportion which the representation of an object bears to the object: *a model on a scale of one inch to a foot.* 8. the ratio of distances (or, less commonly, of areas) on a map to the corresponding values on the earth. 9. a certain relative or proportionate size or extent: *a residence on a yet more magnificent scale.* 10. a standard of measurement or estimation. 11. *Arith.* a system of numerical notation: *the decimal scale.* 12. *Music.* a succession of notes ascending or descending according to fixed intervals, esp. such a series beginning on a particular note: *the major scale of C.* 13. *Music.* the compass or range of a voice or an instrument. 14. *Educ.*, *Psychol.* a graded series of tests or tasks for measuring intelligence, achievement, adjustment, etc. 15. *Obs.* anything by which one may ascend. 16. *Obs.* a ladder; a flight of stairs. —*v.t.* 17. to climb by, or as by, a ladder; climb up or over. 18. to make according to scale. 19. to reduce in amount according to a fixed scale or proportion (often fol. by *down*): *to scale down wages.* 20. to measure by, or as if by, a scale. 21. *Forestry.* **a.** to measure (logs). **b.** to estimate the amount of (standing timber). —*v.i.* 22. to climb; ascend; mount. 23. to progress in a graduated series. [ME, t. L: m. *scāla* staircase, ladder] —**Syn.** 17. See **climb.**

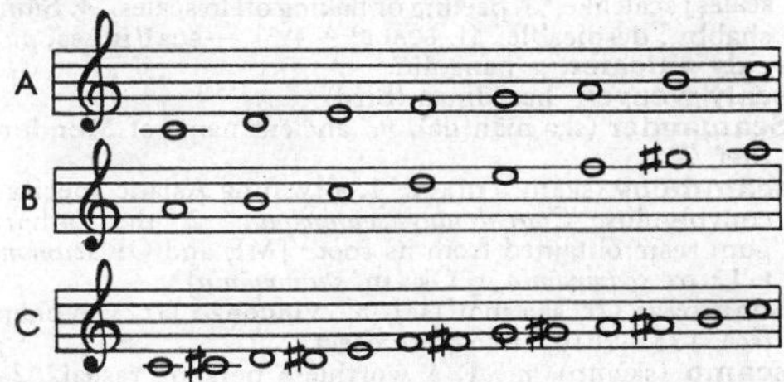

Scales (def. 12): A, Major diatonic; B, Minor diatonic; C, Chromatic

scaleboard (skāl′bôd′, skăb′əd), *n.* 1. a very thin board, as for the back of a picture. 2. *Print.* a thin strip of wood used in justifying. 3. a thin sheet of wood used as veneer, etc. [f. SCALE[2] + BOARD]

scale insect, any of various small plant-destroying insects of the homopterous family *Coccidae*, the females of which mostly have the body and eggs covered by a large scale or shield formed by secretions.

scalene (skā′lēn), *adj.* 1. *Anat.* referring to one of a group of deep muscles in the front and sides of the neck. 2. *Geom.* **a.** (of a cone, etc.) having the axis inclined to the base. **b.** (of a triangle) having three unequal sides. [t. LL: m. s. *scalēnus*, t. Gk: m. *skalēnós* unequal]

scaler (skā′lə), *n. Electronics.* any electronic device which produces an electrical pulse on an output line every time it receives a prescribed number of pulses on an input line.

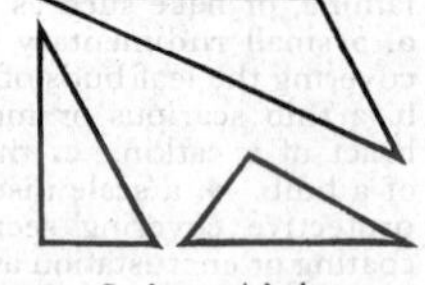
Scalene triangles

Scaliger (skăl′ĭ jə), *n.* **1. Joseph Justus** (jō′zĭf jŭs′təs), 1540–1609, French scholar and critic. **2.** his father, **Julius Caesar** (sē′zə), 1484–1558, Italian scholar, philosopher, and critic, in France.

scallawag (skăl′ə wăg′), *n.* scallywag.

scallion (skăl′yən), *n. Chiefly U.S.* **1.** any onion which does not form a large bulb; spring onion. **2.** shallot. **3.** leek. [ME *scalyon*, t. AF: m. *scal(o)un*, g. L (*caepa*) *Ascalōnia* Ascalonian onion, f. *Ascalon* var. of *Ashkelon* city in Palestine]

scallop (skŏl′əp), *n.* **1.** any of various bivalve molluscs of the genus *Pecten* and allied genera, having fluted shell valves that they clap together to accomplish swimming. **2.** the adductor muscle of certain species of such molluscs, esteemed as an article of food. **3.** one of the shells of such a mollusc, usually having radial ribs and a wavy outer edge. **4.** a scallop shell or a dish in which flaked fish or the like is baked and served. **5.** one of a series of rounded projections along the edge of pastry, a garment, cloth, etc. —*v.t.* **6.** to finish (an edge) with scallops. **7.** to bake (food, usually cut in pieces) in a scallop shell or small container, usually combined with a creamy sauce and topped with breadcrumbs; escallop. Also, **scollop.** [ME *scalop*, t. OF: aphetic m. *escalope* shell; of Gmc orig. Cf. D *schelp* shell] —**scal′loper,** *n.*

scallywag (skăl′ĭ wăg′), *n.* **1.** *Colloq.* a scamp; rascal. **2.** *U.S. Hist.* a native white Southerner of the Reconstruction period, who acted with the Republican Party. Also, **scalawag, scallawag.** [orig. uncert. Cf. WAG (def. 10)]

scalp (skălp), *n.* **1.** the integument of the upper part of the head, usually including the associated subcutaneous structures. **2.** a part of this integument with the accompanying hair, taken by the North American Indians as a trophy of victory. **3.** any token of victory. **4.** the integument on the top of an animal's head, esp. a canine's. **5.** a bed of oysters or mussels. **6.** *Colloq.* a small profit made in quick buying and selling. —*v.t.* **7.** to cut or tear the scalp from. **8.** *Colloq.* to buy and sell so as to make small, quick profits, as stocks. **9.** *Colloq.* to buy (tickets) cheap and sell at other than official rates. —*v.i.* **10.** *Colloq.* to scalp tickets, stocks, etc. [ME (N Dial.), t. Scand.; cf. Icel. *skālpr* leather sheath, d. Dan. *skalp* shell] —**scalp′er,** *n.*

scalpel (skăl′pl), *n.* a small, light, usually straight knife used in surgical and anatomical operations and dissections. [t. L: m. s. *scalpellum*, dim. of *scalprum* knife]

Scalpel

scalp-lock (skălp′lŏk′), *n.* a long lock or tuft of hair left on the scalp by North American Indians as an implied challenge to their enemies.

scaly (skā′lĭ), *adj.*, **-lier, -liest. 1.** covered with or abounding in scales or scale. **2.** characterized by or consisting of scales; scalelike. **3.** peeling or flaking off in scales. **4.** *Slang.* shabby; despicable. [f. SCALE[1] + -Y[1]] —**scal′iness,** *n.*

scaly anteater, a pangolin.

scaly weaver, baardman (bird)

Scamander (skə măn′də), *n.* ancient name of **Menderes** (def. 2).

scammony (skăm′ə nĭ), *n.* **1.** a twining Asiatic species of convolvulus, *Convolvulus scammonia.* **2.** the cathartic gum resin obtained from its root. [ME and OE *scamonie*, t. L: m. *scammōnia*, t. Gk: m. *skammōnía*]

Scamozzi (*It.* skä mŏt′tsē), *n.* **Vincenzo** (*It.* vēn chĕn′tsō), 1552–1616, Italian architect.

scamp (skămp), *n.* **1.** a worthless person; rascal. **2.** a mischievous child. —*v.t.* **3.** to perform (work, etc.) in a hasty or careless manner. [special uses of obs. *scamp*, v., go (on highways), appar. t. D (obs.): m. s. *schampen* flee, t. OF: m. *escamper* DECAMP] —**scamp′er,** *n.* —**scamp′ish,** *adj.*

scamper (skăm′pə), *v.i.* **1.** to run or go hastily or quickly. —*n.* **2.** a scampering; a quick run. [f. obs. *scamp*, v., go + -ER[6]. See SCAMP, n.]

scampi (skăm′pĭ), *n.pl. Cookery.* very large prawns, native to the Adriatic, usually fried in egg and served with hollandaise or tartar sauce. [It., pl. of *scampo*]

scan (skăn), *v.*, **scanned, scanning,** *n.* —*v.t.* **1.** to examine minutely; scrutinize. **2.** to glance at or run through hastily: *to scan a page.* **3.** to analyse (verse) as to its prosodic or metrical structure; read or recite so as to indicate or test the metrical form. **4.** *Television.* to traverse (a surface) with a beam of light or electrons in order to reproduce or transmit a picture. **5.** *Radar.* to sweep a region with a beam from a radar transmitter. —*v.i.* **6.** to examine the metre of verse. **7.** (of verse) to conform to the rules of metre. **8.** *Television.* to scan a surface. —*n.* **9.** the act of scanning; close examination or scrutiny. [ME *scanne*, t. LL: m. *scandere* scan verse, L climb] —**scan′nable,** *adj.* —**scan′ner,** *n.*

Scan., Scandinavia.

Scand., **1.** Scandinavia. **2.** Scandinavian.

scandal (skăn′dl), *n.*, *v.*, **-dalled, -dalling** or (*U.S.*) **-daled, -daling.** —*n.* **1.** a disgraceful or discreditable action, circumstance, etc. **2.** offence caused by faults or misdeeds. **3.** damage to reputation; disgrace. **4.** defamatory talk; malicious gossip. **5.** *Colloq.* gossip in general. **6.** a person whose conduct brings disgrace or offence. —*v.t.* **7.** *Archaic or Dial.* to spread scandal concerning. **8.** *Obs.* to disgrace. **9.** *Obs.* to scandalize. [t. L: s. *scandalum*, orig., trap, t. Gk: m. *skándalon*; r. ME *scandle*, t. ONF] —**Syn. 3.** discredit, dishonour. **4.** slander, calumny. See **gossip.**

scandalize (skăn′də līz′), *v.t.*, **-lized, -lizing.** to shock or horrify by something considered immoral or improper. Also, **scandalise.** —**scan′daliz′er,** *n.*

scandalmonger (skăn′dl mŭng′gə), *n.* one who spreads scandal.

scandalous (skăn′də ləs), *adj.* **1.** disgraceful to reputation; shameful or shocking. **2.** defamatory or libellous, as a speech or writing. —**scan′dalously,** *adv.*

scandent (skăn′dənt), *adj.* climbing, as a plant. [t. L: s. *scandens*, ppr.]

Scanderbeg (skăn′də bĕg′), *n.* (*George Castriota*), 1403?–1468, Albanian chief and hero. Also, **Iskander Bey.**

scandia (skăn′dĭ ə), *n. Chem.* oxide of scandium, Sc_2O_3, a white infusible powder. [special use of L *Scandia* Scandinavia]

scandic (skăn′dĭk), *adj. Chem.* of or pertaining to scandium: *scandic oxide.*

Scandinavia (skăn′dĭ nā′vyə), *n.* **1.** the collective name of Norway, Sweden, Denmark, and sometimes also Finland, Iceland and the Faeroe Islands: the former lands of the Norsemen. **2.** the peninsula consisting of Norway and Sweden. [t. L (Pliny), of Gmc orig.; cf. OE *Scedenig*]

Scandinavian (skăn′dĭ nā′vyən), *adj.* **1.** of or pertaining to Scandinavia, its inhabitants, or their languages. —*n.* **2.** a native or inhabitant of Scandinavia. **3.** the subgroup of Germanic languages that includes the languages of Scandinavia and Iceland in their historical and modern forms; North Germanic.

scandium (skăn′dĭ əm), *n. Chem.* a rare trivalent metallic element present in euxenite. *Symbol:* Sc; *at. wt:* 45·10; *at. no.:* 21. [t. NL. See SCANDIA, -IUM]

scanner (skăn′ə), *n.* **1.** one who or that which scans. **2.** *Radio.* the part of the transmitting aerial by which a beam is made to scan a region. **3.** *Television.* **a.** *Obs.* a device for scanning the object to be transmitted in a television system, consisting of a light source and a rotating perforated disc. **b.** the vehicle in an outside broadcast unit which contains the monitoring screens used by the director.

scansion (skăn′shən), *n. Pros.* the metrical analysis of verse. The usual marks for scansion are ˘ or × for a short or unaccented syllable, ¯ or ´ for a long or accented syllable, ^ for a rest, | for a foot division, and || for a caesura or pause. [t. L: s. *scansio*, lit., a climbing]

scansorial (skăn sô′rĭ əl), *adj. Zool.* **1.** capable of or adapted for climbing, as the feet of certain birds, lizards, etc. **2.** habitually climbing, as a woodpecker. [f. s. L *scansōrius* used for climbing + -AL[1]]

scant (skănt), *adj.* **1.** barely sufficient in amount or quantity; not abundant; inadequate: *to do scant justice.* **2.** limited; not large: *a scant amount.* **3.** barely amounting to as much as indicated: *a scant two hours.* **4.** having an inadequate or limited supply (fol. by *of*): *scant of breath.* —*v.t.* **5.** to make scant; cut down; diminish. **6.** to stint the supply of; withhold. **7.** to treat slightly or inadequately. —*adv.* **8.** *Dial.* scarcely; barely; hardly. [ME, t. Scand.; cf. Icel. *skamt*, neut. of *skammr* short] —**scant′ly,** *adv.* —**scant′ness,** *n.*

scantling (skănt′lĭng), *n.* **1.** a timber of comparatively small cross-section, as a rafter or a purlin. **2.** such timbers collectively. **3.** the size of a timber in width and thickness, or the dimensions of a stone or other building material. **4.** a small quantity or amount. **5.** (*pl.*) *Naut.* the sizes of the component parts of a ship. [late ME *scantilon*, t. OF: aphetic m. *escantillon*, g. ML *scandalium*, der. L *scandere* climb]

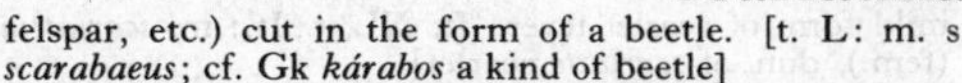

scanty (skănʹtĭ), *adj.*, **scantier, scantiest. 1.** scant in amount, quantity, etc.; barely sufficient. **2.** meagre; not adequate. **3.** lacking amplitude in extent or compass. —**scantʹily,** *adv.* —**scantʹiness,** *n.*
—**Syn. 1.** SCANTY, MEAGRE, SPARSE refer to insufficiency or deficiency in quantity, number, etc. SCANTY denotes smallness or insufficiency of quantity, number, supply, etc.: *a scanty supply of food.* MEAGRE indicates that a person is gaunt and lean (*meagre in appearance*) or, more often, that something is poor, scanty, stinted, inadequate (*meagre fare, a meagre income*). SPARSE applies particularly to that which grows thinly or is thinly strewed or sown, often over a wide area: *sparse vegetation, a sparse population.* —**Ant. 1.** plentiful.

Scapa Flow (skăpʹə), a sound in the Orkney Islands, N of Scotland: British naval base; German warships scuttled, 1919.

scape[1] (skāp), *n.* **1.** *Bot.* a leafless peduncle rising from the ground. **2.** *Zool.* a stemlike part, as the shaft of a feather. **3.** *Archit.* the shaft of a column. [t. L: m. s. *scāpus*, t. Gk (Doric): m. *skâpos* staff, sceptre]

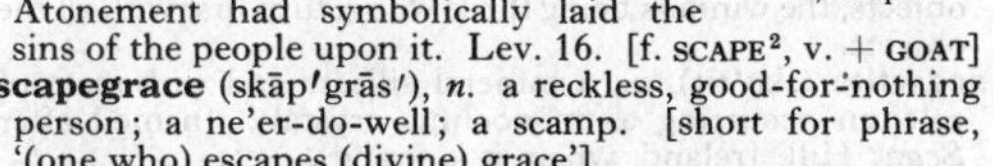

S, Scape

scape[2] (skāp), *n.*, *v.t.*, *v.i.*, **scaped, scaping.** *Archaic.* escape. Also, **'scape.** [ME, aphetic var. of ESCAPE]

scapegoat (skāpʹgōtʹ), *n.* **1.** one who is made to bear the blame for others or to suffer in their place. **2.** (in ancient Jewish ritual) a goat sent into the wilderness after the chief priest on the Day of Atonement had symbolically laid the sins of the people upon it. Lev. 16. [f. SCAPE[2], v. + GOAT]

scapegrace (skāpʹgrāsʹ), *n.* a reckless, good-for-nothing person; a ne'er-do-well; a scamp. [short for phrase, '(one who) escapes (divine) grace']

scapewheel (skāpʹwēlʹ), *n.* *Horol.* See **escape wheel.** [f. SCAPE[2] + WHEEL]

scaphoid (skăfʹoid), *adj.* **1.** boat-shaped. **2.** *Anat.* denoting esp. a bone of the radial side of the carpus, or a bone on the inner side of the tarsus. —*n.* **3.** *Anat.* a scaphoid bone. [t. NL: s. *scaphoīdēs*, t. Gk: m. *skaphoeidḗs*]

scaphopod (skăfʹə pŏdʹ), *n.* a member of the *Scaphopoda*, a class of molluscs with a tubular shell open at both ends. —**scaphopodous** (skă fŏpʹə dəs), *adj.*

scapolite (skăpʹə lītʹ), *n.* any of a group of minerals of variable composition, essentially silicates of aluminium, calcium, and sodium, occurring in crystals and also massive, and usually white or greyish white; wernerite. [t. G: m. *Skapolith.* See SCAPE[1], -LITE]

scapose (skāʹpōs), *adj.* **1.** *Bot.* having scapes; consisting of a scape. **2.** resembling a scape. [f. SCAPE[1] + -OSE[1]]

scapple (skăpʹl), *v.t.*, **-pled, -pling.** to shape or dress (stone) roughly. Also, **scabble.** [t. F: m. *escapeler* dress timber]

s. caps, small capitals.

scapula (skăpʹyŏŏ lə), *n.*, *pl.* **-lae** (-lēʹ). **1.** *Anat.* either of two flat, triangular bones, each forming the back part of a shoulder; a shoulder-blade. See diag. under **shoulder. 2.** *Zool.* a dorsal bone of the pectoral arch. [t. NL: shoulder blade (in L only in pl.)]

scapular (skăpʹyŏŏ lə), *adj.* **1.** of or pertaining to the shoulders or the scapula or scapulae. —*n.* **2.** *Eccles.* a loose, sleeveless monastic garment, hanging from the shoulders. **3.** two small pieces of woollen cloth, joined by strings passing over the shoulders, worn under the ordinary clothing as a badge of affiliation with a religious order, a token of devotion, etc. **4.** *Surg.* a shoulder dressing which keeps the shoulder or another bandage in place. **5.** *Ornith.* a scapular feather. [t. NL: s. *scapulāris*, der. L *scapula* shoulder]

scapulary (skăpʹyŏŏ lə rĭ), *adj.*, *n.*, *pl.* **-laries.** scapular.

scar[1] (skä), *n.*, *v.*, **scarred, scarring.** —*n.* **1.** the mark left by a healed wound, sore, or burn. **2.** any blemish remaining as a trace or result: *scars upon one's good name.* **3.** *Bot.* a mark indicating a former point of attachment, as where a leaf has fallen from a stem. —*v.t.* **4.** to mark with a scar. —*v.i.* **5.** to heal with a resulting scar. [ME, t. OF: aphetic m. *escare*, t. LL: m. *eschara* scab, t. Gk: lit., hearth]

scar[2] (skä), *n.* **1.** a precipitous rocky place; a cliff. **2.** a low or submerged rock in the sea. [ME *skerre*, t. Scand.; cf. Icel. *sker* SKERRY]

scarab (skăʹrəb), *n.* **1.** any scarabaeid beetle, esp. *Scarabaeus sacer*, regarded as sacred by the ancient Egyptians. **2.** a representation or image of a beetle, much used among the ancient Egyptians as a symbol, seal, amulet, or the like. **3.** a gem (as of emerald, green felspar, etc.) cut in the form of a beetle. [t. L: m. s. *scarabaeus*; cf. Gk *kárabos* a kind of beetle]

Scarab (def. 2)
A, Top; B, Bottom

scarabaeid (skăʹrə bēʹĭd), *adj.* **1.** belonging or pertaining to the *Scarabaeidae*, a family of lamellicorn beetles, including the scarabs, June bugs, dung beetles, cockchafers, etc. —*n.* **2.** any scarabaeid beetle. [t. NL: s. *scarabaeidae*, der. L *scarabaeus.* See SCARAB, -ID[2]]

scarabaeoid (skăʹrə bēʹoid), *adj.* Also, **scaraboid** (skăʹrə boidʹ). **1.** resembling a scarab. **2.** of the nature of, or resembling, a scarabaeid. —*n.* **3.** an imitation or counterfeit scarab.

scarabaeus (skăʹrə bēʹəs), *n.*, *pl.* **-baeuses, -baei** (-bēʹī). scarab (defs 2, 3).

Scaramouch (skăʹrə mouchʹ, -mo͞ochʹ), *n.* **1.** a stock character in Italian comedy and farce, a cowardly braggart who is constantly beaten by Harlequin. **2.** (*l.c.*) a rascal or scamp. [t. F: m. *Scaramouche*, t. It.: m. *Scaramuccia*, lit., SKIRMISH]

Scarborough (skäʹbrə), *n.* a seaside resort in England, in the North Riding of Yorkshire. 43,061 (1961).

scarce (skēəs), *adj.*, **scarcer, scarcest,** *adv.* —*adj.* **1.** insufficient for the need or demand; not abundant: *commodities scarce in wartime.* **2.** seldom met with; rare: *a scarce book.* **3. make oneself scarce,** *Colloq.* to make off; keep out of the way. —*adv.* **4.** *Obs.* scarcely. [ME *scars*, t. ONF: scanty, stingy, ult. der. LL *excarpere*, r. L *excerpere* excerpt, pluck] —**scarceʹness,** *n.* —**Syn. 1.** See **rare**[1].

scarcely (skēəsʹlĭ), *adv.* **1.** barely; hardly; not quite. **2.** definitely not. **3.** probably not. —**Syn. 1.** See **hardly.**

scarcement (skēəsʹmənt), *n.* a footing or ledge formed by an offset in a wall.

scarcity (skēəʹsĭ tĭ), *n.*, *pl.* **-ties. 1.** insufficiency or shortness of supply; dearth. **2.** rarity; infrequency.

scare (skēə), *v.*, **scared, scaring,** *n.* —*v.t.* **1.** to strike with sudden fear or terror. **2.** to drive off; frighten away. —*v.i.* **3.** to become frightened: *that horse scares easily.* —*n.* **4.** a sudden fright or alarm, esp. with little or no ground. **5.** a time or state of widespread fear, worry, etc. **6.** *Golf.* the part of a club where the head joins the shaft. [unexplained var. of ME *skerre*, t. Scand.; cf. Icel. *skirra*, der. *skjarr* shy, timid, startled] —**scarʹer,** *n.* —**scarʹingly,** *adv.* —**Syn. 1.** terrify, alarm, startle. See **frighten.**

scarecrow (skēəʹkrōʹ), *n.* **1.** an object, usually a figure of a man in old clothes, set up to frighten crows, etc., away from crops. **2.** a person having a ragged, untidy appearance. **3.** a very thin person. **4.** anything terrifying but not really dangerous.

scaremonger (skēəʹmŭngʹgə), *n.* one who creates or spreads scares.

scarf[1] (skäf), *n.*, *pl.* **scarfs, scarves** (skävz), *v.* —*n.* **1.** a long, broad strip of silk, wool, lace, etc., worn about the neck, shoulders, or head for ornament or protection. **2.** a headscarf. —*v.t.* **3.** to cover or wrap with, or as with, a scarf. **4.** to use in the manner of a scarf. [? t. ONF: m. *escarpe* sash, sling for arm, prob. var. of OF *escharpe* a pilgrim's scrip hung round the neck. Cf. Icel. *skreppa* SCRIP[2]]

scarf[2] (skäf), *n.*, *pl.* **scarfs,** *v.* —*n.* **1.** either of the tapered or specially cut ends of the pieces forming a scarf-joint. **2.** *Whaling.* a strip of skin along the body of the whale. —*v.t.* **3.** to join by a scarf or overlapping joint. **4.** to form a scarf, chamfer, or the like on, for a scarf-joint. **5.** *Whaling.* to make a groove in and remove (the blubber and skin). [t. Scand.; cf. Sw. *skarf* in like senses] —**scarfʹer,** *n.*

scarf-joint (skäfʹjointʹ), *n.* a joint by which the ends of two timbers or the like are fitted with long tapers or laps and glued, nailed, or bolted into a continuous piece.

Scarf-joints

scarfskin (skäfʹskĭnʹ), *n.* the outermost layer of the skin; the epidermis.

scarification (skēəʹrĭ fĭ kāʹshən, skăʹrĭ-), *n.* **1.** the act of scarifying. **2.** the result of scarifying; a scratch or scratches.

scarificator (skēəʹrĭ fĭ kāʹtə), *n.* **1.** one who scarifies. **2.** a surgical instrument for scarifying. [t. NL, der. LL *scarificāre* SCARIFY]

scarify (skēəʹrĭ fīʹ, skăʹrĭ fīʹ), *v.t.*, **-fied, -fying. 1.** to make scratches or superficial incisions in (the skin, a wound, etc.), as in surgery. **2.** to lacerate by severe criticism. **3.** to loosen (the soil) with a type of cultivator. **4.** to hasten the sprouting of (hard-covered seeds) by making incisions in the seedcoats. [late ME, t. LL: m. *scarificāre*, t. Gk: m. *skariphasthai* scratch an outline] —**scarʹifiʹer,** *n.*

scarious (skēəʹrĭ əs), *adj.* *Bot.* thin, dry, and membranous, as certain bracts. [t. NL: m. *scariōsus*, der. L *scaria* thorny shrub]

scarlatina (skäʹlə tēʹnə), *n.* *Pathol.* **1.** scarlet fever. **2.** a mild form of scarlet fever. [t. NL, t. It.: m. *scarlattina* (fem.), dim. of *scarlatto* scarlet]

scarlatinoid (skä'lə tē'noid, skä lăt'ĭ noid'), *adj.* resembling scarlatina or its eruption.

Scarlatti (skä lăt'ĭ; *It.* skär lät'tē), *n.* **1. Alessandro** (*It.* ä lès sän'drô), 1659–1725, Italian composer. **2.** his son, **Domenico** (*It.* dô mè'nē kô), 1685–1757, composer, esp. of harpsichord sonatas.

scarlet (skä'lĭt), *n.* **1.** bright red colour inclining towards orange. **2.** cloth or garments of this colour. *—adj.* **3.** of the colour scarlet. [ME, t. OF: aphetic m. *escarlate,* ? ult. t. Pers.: m. *saqalāt* a rich cloth]

scarlet eggplant, an annual solanaceous herb, *Solanum integrifolium,* a native of Africa with a rounded, yellow or red fruit.

scarlet fever, a contagious febrile disease, now chiefly of children, caused by streptococci and characterized by a scarlet eruption.

scarlet letter, a scarlet letter 'A', formerly worn by one convicted of adultery.

scarlet pimpernel. See **pimpernel.**

scarlet runner, runner bean.

scarlet tanager, an American tanager, *Piranga olivacea.* The male in breeding plumage is bright red with black wings and tail.

scarlet woman, 1. the woman described in Rev. 17, variously explained as symbolizing pagan Rome or (opprobriously) the Church of Rome. **2.** a prostitute or immoral woman.

scarp (skäp), *n.* **1.** a steep face on the side of a hill. **2.** *Fort.* the side of a ditch next to a rampart; an escarp. *—v.t.* **3.** to form or cut into a scarp. [t. It.: m. *scarpa.* See ESCARP]

scarper (skä'pə), *v.i. Slang.* to run away; depart suddenly, esp. leaving behind debts or other commitments. [orig. unknown]

Scarron (*Fr.* skȧ rôɴ'), *n.* **Paul** (*Fr.* pŏl), 1610–60, French novelist, dramatist, and poet.

scarves (skävz), *n.* pl. of **scarf[1].**

scary (skĕə'rĭ), *adj.*, **scarier, scariest.** *Colloq.* **1.** causing fright or alarm. **2.** easily frightened; timid.

scat[1] (skăt), *v.t.*, **scatted, scatting.** *Colloq.* to go off hastily (usually in the imperative). [? f. a hiss + CAT]

scat[2] (skăt), *n., v.*, **scatted, scatting.** *Jazz. —n.* **1.** an improvised form of singing where the vocalist sings nonsense syllables to the tune. **2.** an act or instance of doing this. *—v.i.* **3.** to sing scat. [? imit.]

scathe (skāth), *v.*, **scathed, scathing,** *n.* *—v.t.* **1.** to attack with severe criticism. **2.** *Archaic or Dial.* to hurt, harm, or injure; sear. *—n.* **3.** *Archaic. or Dial.* hurt, harm, or injury. [ME, t. Scand.; cf. Icel. *skathi* harm, damage, c. OE *sc(e)atha* malefactor, injury, G *Schade*] **—scathe'less,** *adj.*

scathing (skā'thĭng), *adj.* **1.** intended to hurt the feelings; scornful; contemptuous, as a remark. **2.** that scathes or sears. **—scath'ingly,** *adv.*

scatology (skă tŏl'ə jĭ), *n.* **1.** *Med.* diagnosis by means of the faeces. **2.** *Palaeon.* the science of fossil excrement. **3.** Also, **coprology.** the study of, or preoccupation with, images of physical filth (excrement) in literature. [f. m. *skato-* (comb. form of Gk *skôr* dung) + -LOGY] **—scatologic** (skăt'ə lŏj'ĭk), **scat'olog'ical,** *adj.*

scatter (skăt'ə), *v.t.* **1.** to throw loosely about; distribute at irregular intervals. **2.** to separate and drive off in various directions; disperse. **3.** *Physics.* **a.** to reflect or diffract electromagnetic radiation, esp. light, so as to diffuse it in many directions. **b.** to deflect irregularly any radiation as a result of its interaction with matter. *—v.i.* **4.** to separate and disperse; go in different directions. *—n.* **5.** the act of scattering. **6.** that which is scattered. [ME *scatere;* orig. uncert.] **—scat'terer,** *n.* **—scat'teringly,** *adv.*

—Syn. 1. See **sprinkle. 2.** SCATTER, DISPEL, DISPERSE, DISSIPATE imply separating and driving something away so that its original form disappears. To SCATTER is to separate something tangible into parts at random, and drive these in different directions: *the wind scattered leaves all over the lawn.* To DISPEL is to drive away or scatter usually intangible things so that they vanish or cease to exist: *photographs of the race dispelled all doubts as to which horse won.* To DISPERSE is to cause (usually) a compact or organized tangible body to separate or scatter in different directions, to be reassembled if desired: *tear gas dispersed the mob.* To DISSIPATE is usually to scatter by dissolving or reducing to small atoms or parts which cannot be brought together again: *he dissipated his money and his energy in useless activities.*

scatterbrain (skăt'ə brān'), *n.* one incapable of serious, connected thought. **—scat'terbrained',** *adj.*

scatter cushion, a small cushion, often brightly coloured, placed at random on a couch, armchairs, etc.

scattergood (skăt'ə go͝od'), *n.* a spendthrift.

scattering (skăt'ə rĭng), *adj.* **1.** distributed or occurring here and there at irregular intervals. **2.** straggling, as an assemblage of parts. **3.** *U.S.* (of votes) cast in small numbers for various candidates. **4.** that scatters. *—n.* **5.** a scattered number or quantity. **6.** *Physics.* the process by which any beam of radiation is deflected or diffused as a result of its interaction with matter.

scatter pin, a woman's small ornamental pin usually worn in groups of two or more on a dress, suit, etc.

scatty (skăt'ĭ), *adj.* scatterbrained; thoughtless; unreliable.

scaup duck (skôp), any of certain diving ducks of the genus *Aythya,* esp. the **greater scaup,** *A. marila,* of Europe and America. [? phonetic var. of *scalp duck*]

scavenge (skăv'ĭnj), *v.*, **-enged, -enging.** *—v.t.* **1.** to search for, and take (anything useable) from discarded material. **2.** to expel or sweep out burnt gases from (the cylinder of an internal-combustion engine). **3.** *Metall.* to clean (molten metal) by the introduction of another substance which will combine chemically with the impurities in it. **4.** to cleanse from filth, as a street. *—v.i.* **5.** to act as a scavenger. **6.** to search amongst refuse or any discarded material for anything useable, as food, clothing, etc. **7.** to become scavenged of burnt gases. [back-formation from SCAVENGER]

scavenger (skăv'ĭn jə), *n.* **1.** one who, or that which scavenges as any of various animals feeding on dead organic matter. **2.** a street cleaner. [alter. of ME *scavager* (cf. *passenger, messenger*), t. AF: m. *scawager,* der. OF *escauver* inspect]

scavenger hunt, a game in which competitors are sent out to accumulate, without purchasing, a number of chosen objects, the winners being those who return first with all the objects.

scawtite (skô'tīt), *n.* a mineral silicate and carbonate of calcium occurring as monoclinic crystals. [named after *Scawt* Hill, Ireland, where it is found]

scena (shā'nə), *n.* an operatic scene; a dramatic recitative, usually followed by an aria.

scenario (sĭ nä'rĭ ō'), *n., pl.* **-narios. 1.** an outline of the plot of a dramatic work, giving particulars as to the scenes, characters, situations, etc. **2.** the outline or manuscript of a film, giving the action in the order in which it takes place, the description of scenes and characters, the printed matter to be shown on the screen, etc. [t. It., t. LL: m. *scēnārius* pertaining to stage scenes, der. L *scēna* scene]

scenarist (sē'nə rĭst), *n.* a writer of scenarios for films.

scend (sĕnd), *Naut. —v.i.* **1.** to be heaved upwards by a swell. *—n.* **2.** this motion. [var. of SEND (def. 15)]

scene (sēn), *n.* **1.** the place where any action occurs. **2.** any view or picture. **3.** an incident or situation in real life. **4.** an exhibition or outbreak of excited or violent feeling before others. **5.** a division of a play or of an act of a play, now commonly representing what passes between certain of the actors in one place. **6.** a unit of dramatic action within a play, in which a single point or effect is made. **7.** the place in which the action of a play or part of a play is supposed to occur. **8.** scenery (def. 2). **9.** an episode, situation, or the like, as described in writing. **10.** the setting of a story or the like. **11.** the stage, esp. of an ancient Greek or Roman theatre. **12.** the world, as of contemporary taste in records, clothing, etc.: *the pop scene.* **13. behind the scenes, a.** out of sight of the audience; offstage. **b.** secretly; privately. **14. on the scene, a.** present: *the first person on the scene was a policeman.* **b.** in fashion. **15. the scene,** the contemporary fashionable world. [t. L: m. *scēna,* t. Gk: m. *skēnḗ* tent, stage] **—Syn. 2.** See **view.**

scene dock, *Theat.* a place for storing scenery, near or beneath the stage. Also, **dock.**

scenery (sē'nə rĭ), *n., pl.* **-neries. 1.** the general appearance of a place; the aggregate of features that give character to a landscape. **2.** hangings, draperies, structures, etc., on the stage to represent some place or furnish decorative background.

scene-shifter (sēn'shĭf'tə), *n.* one employed to change scenery between scenes of a play or the like.

scenic (sē'nĭk), *adj.* **1.** of or pertaining to natural scenery; having fine scenery. **2.** of or pertaining to the stage or to stage scenery; dramatic; theatrical. **3.** representing a scene, action, or the like, as painting or sculpture. Also, **scenical. —sce'nically,** *adv.*

scenic railway, 1. a miniature railway which carries passengers on a tour of a zoo or the like. **2.** a roller-coaster.

scenography (sē nŏg'rə fĭ), *n.* **1.** *Obs.* the representing of objects, as buildings, according to the rules of perspective. **2.** scene painting (used esp. with reference to ancient Greece). [t. L: m. *scēnographia,* t. Gk: m. *skēnographía*] **—scenographic** (sē'nō grăf'ĭk), **sce'nograph'ical,** *adj.*

scent (sĕnt), *n.* **1.** distinctive smell, esp. when agreeable. **2.** a smell left in passing, by means of which an animal or person may be traced. **3.** a track or trail as indicated by such a smell. **4.** the small pieces of paper dropped by the hare in the game of hare and hounds. **5.** a perfume. **6.** the sense of smell. —*v.t.* **7.** to perceive or recognize by the sense of smell. **8.** to perceive or detect in any way: *to scent trouble.* **9.** to impregnate or sprinkle with perfume. —*v.i.* **10.** to hunt by the sense of smell, as a hound. [ME *sent*, t. F: s. *sentir* perceive, g. L *sentīre*] —**scent′less,** *adj.*

scentless mayweed, an annual composite herb, *Tripleurospermum maritimum* esp. *inodorum*, with a yellow disc and white rays, a common weed in Europe and Asia. Also, **scentless camomile.**

sceptic (skĕp′tĭk), *n.* **1.** one who questions the validity or authenticity of something purporting to be knowledge. **2.** one who mistrusts and who maintains a doubting pessimistic attitude towards people, plans, ideas, etc. **3.** one who doubts the truth of the Christian religion or of important elements of it. **4.** (*cap.*) *Philos.* **a.** a member of a philosophical school of ancient Greece, the earliest group of which consisted of Pyrrho and his followers, who maintained that real knowledge of things is impossible. **b.** any later thinker who doubts or questions the possibility of real knowledge of any kind. —*adj.* **5.** pertaining to sceptics, or scepticism; sceptical. **6.** (*cap.*) pertaining to the Sceptics. Also, *U.S.*, **skeptic.** [t. L: m. s. *scepticus* inquiring, reflective, t. Gk: m. *skeptikós*] —**Syn. 3.** See **atheist.**

sceptical (skĕp′tĭ kl), *adj.* **1.** inclined to scepticism; having doubt. **2.** showing doubt: *a sceptical smile.* **3.** denying or questioning the tenets of religion. **4.** of or pertaining to Sceptics or scepticism. —**scep′tically,** *adv.* —**scep′ticalness,** *n.* —**Syn. 1.** See **doubtful.**

scepticism (skĕp′tĭ sĭz′əm), *n.* **1.** sceptical attitude or temper; doubt. **2.** doubt or unbelief with regard to the Christian religion. **3.** the doctrines or opinions of philosophical Sceptics; universal doubt.

sceptre (sĕp′tə), *n.* **1.** a rod or wand borne in the hand as an emblem of regal or imperial power. **2.** royal or imperial power or authority; sovereignty. —*v.t.* **3.** to give a sceptre to; invest with authority. Also, *U.S.*, **scepter.** [ME *sceptre*, t. OF, t. L: m. *scēptrum*, t. Gk: m. *skēptron*] —**scep′tred,** *adj.*

Schadenfreude (shä′dn froi′də), *n. German.* pleasure in others' misfortunes. [G: malicious pleasure, f. *Schade*(*n*) injury + *Freude* joy]

Schaerbeek (*Flem.* sKHär′bėk), *n.* a town in Belgium, a suburb of Brussels. 122,389 (1965).

Schaffhausen (*Ger.* shȧf hou′zən), *n.* **1.** a canton in N Switzerland. 65,981 pop. (1960); 115 sq. mi. **2.** the capital of this canton. 30,904 (1960).

schappe (shăp′ə, shä′pə), *v.*, **schapped** (shăp′əd, shä′pəd), **schapping,** *n.* —*v.t.* **1.** to remove gum from (silk) by fermentation. —*n.* **2.** Also, **schappe silk.** a silk waste used for embroidery and sewing silks, or for combining with other fibres. [t. G (Swiss d.): lit., leavings, der. F *échappement* leakage]

Schaumburg-Lippe (*Ger.* shoum′bŏŏrk lĭp′ə), *n.* a former state in NW Germany.

schedule (shĕd′yōōl), *n.*, *v.*, **-uled, -uling.** —*n.* **1.** a plan of procedure for a specified project with reference to sequence of operations, time allotted for each part, etc.: *the proposed schedule allows four weeks for the completion of the book.* **2.** a list of items to be dealt with during a specified time: *he has a full schedule tomorrow.* **3.** a timetable. **4.** a written or printed statement of details, often in classified or tabular form, esp. one forming an appendix or explanatory addition to another document. **5.** *Obs.* a written paper. —*v.t.* **6.** to make a schedule of; enter in a schedule. **7.** to plan for a certain date: *to schedule publication for June.* [t. LL: m. *scedula*, dim. of L *sceda* leaf of paper, prob. ult. der. L *scindere* split; r. ME *cedule*, t. OF] —**sched′ular,** *adj.* —**Syn. 4.** See **list**[1].

Scheduled Territories, *Banking.* sterling area.

Scheele (shēl; *Sw.* shė′lə), *n.* **Karl Wilhelm** (*Sw.* kärl vĕl′hĕlm), 1742–86, Swedish chemist.

Scheele's green (shēlz), *Chem.* cupric arsenite, $Cu_3(AsO_3)_2.2H_2O$, used as a pigment and insecticide.

scheelite (shē′līt), *n. Mineral.* calcium tungstate, $CaWO_4$, usually occurring in crystals, an important ore of tungsten. [named after K. W. SCHEELE. See -ITE[1]]

Scheffler (*Ger.* shĕf′lər), *n.* **Johannes** (*Ger.* yȯ hȧ′nəs). See **Angelus Silesius.**

Scheldt (skĕlt), *n.* a river flowing from N France through W Belgium and SW Netherlands into the North Sea. ab. 270 mi. Flemish, **Schelde** (*Flem.* sKHĕl′də). French, **Escaut.**

Schelling (*Ger.* shĕl′ĭng), *n.* **Friedrich Wilhelm Joseph von** (*Ger.* frē′drĭKH vĭl′hĕlm yȯ′zĕf fōn), 1775–1854, German philosopher.

schelly (shĕl′ĭ), *n.* a fish, *Coregonus stigmaticus*, very similar to the powan, found in freshwater lakes and rivers in the English Lake District. [var. of N dial. *skelly*, f. *skell* (var. of SCALE) + -Y[1]]

schema (skē′mə), *n.*, *pl.* **-mata** (-mə tə). **1.** a diagram, plan, or scheme. **2.** *Philos.* (in Kantianism) a transcendental product of imagination in accordance with a rule whereby a category of the understanding is made applicable to the manifold of sense. It mediates between the universality of the pure concept (which is opaque to sense) and the particularity of sense (which is opaque to the understanding). [t. Gk: form]

schematic (skĭ măt′ĭk), *adj.* **1.** pertaining to or of the nature of a schema, diagram, or scheme; diagrammatic. —*n.* **2.** a schematic drawing or diagram. —**schemat′ically,** *adv.*

schematism (skē′mə tĭz′əm), *n.* **1.** the particular form or disposition of a thing. **2.** a schematic arrangement. [t. NL: s. *schēmatismus*, t. Gk: m. *schēmatismós* formalization]

schematize (skē′mə tīz′), *v.t.*, **-tized, -tizing.** to reduce to or arrange according to a scheme. Also, **schematise.** [t. Gk: m. s. *schēmatízein*] —**sche′matiza′tion,** *n.* —**sche′matiz′er,** *n.*

scheme (skēm), *n.*, *v.*, **schemed, scheming.** —*n.* **1.** a plan or design to be followed, as for building operations, etc.; a programme of action; a project. **2.** a policy or plan officially adopted by a company, business, etc., as for pensions, loans, etc. **3.** an underhand plot; intrigue. **4.** a visionary or impractical project. **5.** a body or system of related doctrines, theories, etc.: *a scheme of philosophy.* **6.** any system of correlated things, parts, etc., or the manner of its arrangement. **7.** an analytical or tabular statement. **8.** a diagram, map, or the like. **9.** an astrological diagram of the heavens. —*v.t.* **10.** to devise as a scheme; plan; plot; contrive. —*v.i.* **11.** to lay schemes; devise plans; plot. [t. ML: m. *schēma*, t. Gk] —**schem′er,** *n.* —**Syn. 1. 4.** See **plan. 11.** See **plot**[1].

scheming (skē′mĭng), *adj.* given to forming plans, esp. underhand ones; crafty.

scherzando (skĕət săn′dō; *It.* skėr tsȧn′dȯ), *adj.*, *adv.*, *n.*, *pl.* **-dos.** *Music.* —*adj.* **1.** playful; sportive. —*adv.* **2.** playfully; sportively. —*n.* **3.** a passage or movement played in this way.

scherzo (skĕət′sō; *It.* skėr′tsȯ), *n.*, *pl.* **-zos, -zi** (-tsē). *Music.* a movement or passage of lively, playful character, esp. as the second or third division of a sonata or a symphony. [t. It.: sport, jest, t. G: m. *Scherz*]

Scheveningen (*Du.* sKHė′və nĭng ə), *n.* a town in W Netherlands, a suburb of The Hague; seaside resort.

Schiaparelli (*It.* skyȧ pȧ rĕl′lē), *n.* **Giovanni** (*It.* jȯ vȧn′nē), 1835–1910, Italian astronomer.

Schick test (shĭk), *Med.* a diphtheria-immunity test in which diphtheria toxoid is injected cutaneously, nonimmunity being characterized by an inflammation at the injection site. [named after Dr Bela *Schick*, 1877–1967, U.S. paediatrician]

Schiedam (*Du.* sKHē dŏm′), *n.* a town in SW Netherlands, near Rotterdam. 81,956 (1965).

schiller (shĭl′ə), *n.* a peculiar, almost metallic lustre, sometimes with iridescence, occurring on certain minerals. [t. G: play of colours]

Schiller (*Ger.* shĭl′ər), *n.* **Johann Christoph Friedrich von** (*Ger.* yȯ′hȧn krĭs′tŏf frē′drĭKH fōn), 1759–1805, German poet, dramatist, and writer.

schillerize (shĭl′ə rīz′), *v.t.*, **-rized, -rizing.** to give a schiller to (a crystal) by developing microscopic inclusions along certain planes. Also, **schillerise.** —**schillerization** (shĭl′ə rī za′shən), *n.*

schilling (shĭl′ĭng), *n.* **1.** the monetary unit of Austria, equal to 100 groschen, and equivalent to about £0·016 sterling. **2.** a copper coin of this value. **3.** a minor coin formerly used in Germany. [t. G, c. SHILLING]

Schinkel (*Ger.* shĭng′kəl), *n.* **Karl Friedrich,** 1781–1841, German architect.

schipperke (shĭp′ə kĭ), *n.* one of a breed of small black dogs, orig. used as watchdogs on boats in the Netherlands and Belgium. [t. d. D: little boatman]

schism (sĭz′əm), *n.* **1.** division or disunion, esp. into mutually opposed parties. **2.** the parties so formed. **3.** *Eccles.* **a.** a formal division within, or separation from, a church or religious body over some doctrinal difference. **b.** a sect or body formed by such a division. **c.** the offence of causing or seeking to cause such a division. [t. L: m. *schisma*, t. Gk; r. ME *cisme*, t. OF]

schismatic (sĭz măt′ĭk), *adj.* **1.** Also, **schismat′ical.** of, pertaining to, or of the nature of schism; guilty of schism. —*n.* **2.** one who promotes schism; an adherent of a schismatic body.

schist (shĭst), *n.* any of a class of crystalline rocks whose constituent minerals have a more or less parallel or foliated arrangement, due mostly to metamorphic action. [t. F: m. *schiste*, t. L: m. *schistos* fissile, readily splitting, t. Gk: m. *schistós*]

schistose (shĭs′tōs), *adj.* of, resembling, or in the form of schist. **—schistosity** (shĭs tŏs′ĭ tĭ), *n.*

schistosome (shĭs′tə sōm′), *n.* a fluke of long, slender form that inhabits the blood vessels of birds and mammals and is one of the most important and detrimental human parasites in tropical countries.

schizo (skĭt′sō), *Colloq.* **—***n.* **1.** a schizophrenic. **—***adj.* **2.** schizophrenic.

schizo-, a word element referring to cleavage. Also, before vowels, **schiz-**. [t. Gk: parted (cf. *schízein* split), as in *schizópous* with parted toes]

schizocarp (skĭt′sō kärp′), *n. Bot.* a dry fruit which at maturity splits into two or more one-seeded indehiscent carpels. **—schiz′ocar′pous,** *adj.*

schizogenesis (skĭt′sō jĕn′ĭ sĭs), *n. Biol.* reproduction by fission. Also, **schizogomy** (skĭt sŏg′ə mĭ). **—schizogenetic** (skĭt′sō jĭ nĕt′ĭk), *adj.*

schizoid (skĭt′soid), *adj.* **1.** related to, predisposed to, or afflicted with schizophrenia. **—***n.* **2.** one who is afflicted with schizophrenia.

schizomycete (skĭt′sō mī sēt′), *n.* any of the *Schizomycetes*, a class or group of plant organisms comprising the bacteria.

schizomycosis (skĭt′sō mī kō′sĭs), *n. Pathol.* any disease due to schizomycetes.

schizophrenia (skĭt′sō frē′nyə), *n. Psychol.* a mental disorder characterized by apparent splitting of the personality, delusional behaviour, dissociation, and emotional deterioration. **—schizophrene** (skĭt′sō frēn′), *n.* **—schizophrenic** (skĭt′sō frĕn′ĭk), *adj., n.*

schizophyceous (skĭt′sō fĭsh′əs), *adj. Bot.* belonging to the *Schizophyceae*, a class or group of unicellular and multicellular green or bluish green algae, occurring in both salt and fresh water, and often causing pollution of drinking water.

schizophyte (skĭt′sō fīt′), *n.* any of the *Schizophyta*, a group of plants comprising the schizomycetes and the schizophyceous algae, characterized by a simple structure and by reproduction by simple fission or by spores. [t. NL: m. *Schizophyta* (pl.). See SCHIZO-, -PHYTE] **—schizophytic** (skĭt′sō fĭt′ĭk), *adj.*

schizopod (skĭt′sō pŏd′), *n.* **1.** any of the shrimplike crustacean orders *Mysidacea* or *Euphausiacea*, which include the opossum shrimps. **—***adj.* **2.** Also, **schizopodous** (skĭt sŏp′ə dəs). belonging or pertaining to the *Schizopoda*.

schizothymia (skĭt′sō thī′myə), *n. Psychol.* an emotional state or temperament out of keeping with the rational mind. [f. SCHIZO- + Gk *-thymia*, der. *thymós* mind] **—schiz′othy′mic,** *adj.*

Schlegel (*Ger.* shlē′gəl), *n.* **1. August Wilhelm von** (*Ger.* ou′gŏŏst vĭl′hĕlm fŏn), 1767–1845, German critic, translator, and poet. **2.** his brother, **Friedrich von** (*Ger.* frē′drĭKH fŏn), 1772–1829, German poet, critic, and scholar.

Schleiermacher (*Ger.* shlī′ər mȧKH ər), *n.* **Friedrich Ernst Daniel** (*Ger.* frē′drĭKH ĕrnst dȧ′nē ĕl), 1768–1834, German theologian and philosopher.

schlemiel (shlə mēl′), *n. Slang.* an awkward and unlucky person for whom things never turn out right. Also, **schlemihl.** [m. *Schlemihl* surname of title character of book (1814) by Adelbert von Chamisso, 1781–1838; ? surname t. Yiddish, ult. t. Heb.: proper name *Shĕlūmiēl* God is my welfare]

Schlesien (*Ger.* shlē′zĭ ən), *n.* German name of **Silesia.**

Schleswig (shlĕz′wĭg; *Ger.* shlĕs′vĭKH), *n.* **1.** a seaport in N West Germany, on the Baltic. 32,900 (est. 1966). **2.** a former duchy of Denmark: annexed by Prussia, 1864; the N part was returned to Denmark as the result of a plebiscite, 1920. Also, **Sleswick.** Danish, **Slesvig.**

Schleswig-Holstein (*Ger.* shlĕs′vĭKH hŏl′shtīn), *n.* **1.** two duchies of Denmark that were a centre of international tension in the 19th century: annexed by Prussia, 1864 (Schleswig) and 1866 (Holstein). **2.** a state of N West Germany, including the former duchies of Holstein and Lauenburg and part of Schleswig. 2,375,800 pop. (est. 1963); 6055 sq. mi. *Cap.*: Kiel.

Schleswig-Holstein (def. 2)

Schlick (*Ger.* shlĭk), *n.* **Moritz** (*Ger.* mō′rĭts), 1882–1936, German philosopher.

Schliemann (*Ger.* shlē′mȧn), *n.* **Heinrich** (*Ger.* hīn′rĭKH), 1822–90, German archaeologist.

schlieren (shlĭə′rən), *n.pl.* **1.** *Geol.* streaks or irregularly shaped masses in an igneous rock, which differ in texture or composition from the main mass. **2.** *Physics.* areas in a turbulent, transparent fluid which become visible in schlieren photographs because of their different density and refractive index to the bulk of the fluid. [t. G, pl. of *Schliere* streak] **—schlieric** (shlĭə′rĭk), *adj.*

schlieren photography, *Physics.* a method of photographing flow patterns in a turbulent, transparent fluid which depends on differences in density and refractive index within the fluid. **—schlieren photograph.**

schmalz (shmälts), *n. Colloq.* excessive sentimentality, esp. in the arts. Also, **schmaltz.** [t. G: lit., dripping fat]

Schmidt optics (*Ger.* shmĭt), optical systems (used in wide-field cameras and reflecting telescopes) by means of which spherical aberration and coma are reduced to a minimum by specially designed objectives. [named after Bernard *Schmidt*, 1879–1935, German inventor]

Schmitz (*It.* shmēts), *n.* **Ettore** (*It.* ĕt′tō rĕ) ('*Italo Svevo*'), 1861–1928, Italian novelist.

schmo (shmō), *n.* shmo.

schnapper (shnăp′ə, snăp′-), *n.* a food fish *Pagrosomus auratus*, abundant off Australia and New Zealand. [alter. of SNAPPER appar. under German influence]

schnapps (shnăps), *n.* a spirit resembling Hollands gin. Also, **schnaps.** [t. G: dram, nip; akin to *schnappen* snap]

schnauzer (shnou′zə; *Ger.* shnou′tsər), *n.* one of a German breed of terrier with a wiry grey coat. [t. G]

schnitzel (*Ger.* shnĭts′əl), *n. German.* a veal cutlet. [G: lit., a slice]

Schnitzler (*Ger.* shnĭts′lər), *n.* **Arthur** (*Ger.* ȧr′tŏŏr), 1862–1931, Austrian dramatist and novelist.

schnorkle (shnô′kl), *n.* snorkel.

schola cantorum (skō′lə kăn tô′rəm), *Latin.* **1.** a choir school. **2.** the building in which a choir school is held, sometimes integral with the structure of the church or cathedral.

scholar (skŏl′ə), *n.* **1.** a learned or erudite person. **2.** a student; pupil. **3.** a student who, because of merit, etc., is granted money or other aid to pursue his studies. [t. LL: s. *scholāris*; r. ME and OE *scolere*, t. LL (as above)] **—Syn. 2.** See **pupil**[1].

scholarch (skŏl′ärk), *n.* **1.** the head of a school. **2.** the head of an ancient Athenian school of philosophy. [t. Gk: s. *scholárchēs*, f. *schol(ḗ)* school + *-archēs* ruler]

scholarly (skŏl′ə lĭ), *adj.* **1.** of, like, or befitting a scholar: *scholarly habits.* **2.** having the qualities of a scholar: *a scholarly person.* **—***adv.* **3.** like a scholar. **—schol′arliness,** *n.*

scholarship (skŏl′ə shĭp′), *n.* **1.** learning; knowledge acquired by study; the academic attainments of a scholar. **2.** the position of a student who, because of merit, etc., is granted money or other aid to pursue his studies. **3.** the sum of money or other aid granted to a scholar. **4.** a foundation to provide financial assistance to students. **—Syn. 1.** See **learning.**

Scholarship Level, *Educ.* the third grade of the General Certificate of Education, for which public examinations are taken at sixth-form level. Also, **S Level.**

scholastic (skə lăs′tĭk), *adj.* Also, **scholas′tical. 1.** of or pertaining to schools, scholars, or education: *scholastic attainments.* **2.** of or pertaining to the medieval schoolmen. **3.** academic. **4.** pedantic. **—***n.* **5.** (*sometimes cap.*) a schoolman, a disciple of the schoolmen, or an adherent of scholasticism. **6.** a Jesuit student under primary vows, prior to the commencement of training. **7.** the position held by such a student. **8.** a pedantic person. [t. L: s. *scholasticus*, t. Gk: m. *scholastikós* studious, learned] **—scholas′tically,** *adv.*

scholasticism (skə lăs′tĭ sĭz′əm), *n.* **1.** the doctrine of the schoolmen; the system of theological and philosophical teaching predominant in the Middle Ages, based chiefly upon the authority of the Church fathers and of Aristotle and his commentators, and characterized by marked formality in methods. **2.** narrow adherence to traditional teachings, doctrines, or methods.

scholiast (skō′lĭ ăst′), *n.* **1.** an ancient commentator upon the classics. **2.** one who writes scholia. [t. LL: s. *scholiasta*, t. LGk: m. *scholiastḗs*] **—scho′lias′tic,** *adj.*

scholium (skō′lyəm), *n., pl.* **-lia** (-lyə). **1.** (*often pl.*) **a.** an explanatory note or comment. **b.** an ancient annotation upon a passage in a Greek or Latin author. **2.** a note added to illustrate or amplify, as in a mathematical work. [t. ML, t. Gk: m. *schólion* commentary]

Schönberg (shûn′bûg; *Ger.* shœn′bĕrk), *n.* **Arnold** (ä′nəld; *Ger.* ȧr′nōlt), 1874–1951, Austrian composer in the U.S.; originated the twelve-note technique. Also, **Schoenberg.**

Schongauer (*Ger.* shōn′gou ər), *n.* **Martin** (*Ger.* mȧr′tēn), 1445?–91, German painter and engraver.

school[1] (skōōl), *n.* **1.** a place or establishment where instruction is given, esp. one for children. **2.** the body of students or pupils attending a school. **3.** a regular course of meetings of a teacher or teachers and students for instruction: *a school held during the summer months.* **4.** a session of such a course: *no school today.* **5.** a building, room, etc., in a university, set apart for the use of one of the faculties or for some particular purpose. **6.** a particular faculty or department of a modern university having the right to recommend candidates for degrees, etc.: *medical school.* **7.** (*cap., pl.*) *Colloq.* (at Oxford university) the final B.A. examinations. **8.** an instructive place, situation, etc. **9.** a body of scholars, artists, writers, etc., who have been taught by the same master, or who are united by a similarity of method, style, principles, etc.: *the Platonic school of philosophy.* **10.** any body of persons who agree. **11. of the old school,** old-fashioned; high-principled. **12.** *Obs.* the schoolmen. **13.** *U.S. Mil., Naval.* parts of close-order drill applying to the individual (**school of the soldier**), the squad (**school of the squad**), or the like. *—adj.* **14.** of or connected with a school or schools. **15.** *Obs.* of the schoolmen. *—v.t.* **16.** to educate in or as in a school; teach; train. **17.** *Archaic.* to reprimand. [ME *scole*, OE *scōl*, t. L: m. *schola*, t. Gk: m. *scholḗ*, orig., leisure, hence employment of leisure, study]

school² (sko͞ol), *n.* **1.** a large number of fish, porpoises, whales, or the like, feeding or migrating together. *—v.i.* **2.** to form into, or go in, a school, as fish. [ME *schol(e)*, t. D: m. *school* troop, multitude, c. OE *scolu* SHOAL²]

school age, *Educ.* **1.** the age set by law for children to start school attendance. **2.** the period of school attendance required by law.

school board, formerly, a local elected board or committee in charge of education in a parish, town, etc.

schoolbook (sko͞ol′bo͝ok′), *n.* a book for study in schools.

schoolboy (sko͞ol′boi′), *n.* a boy attending a school.

school certificate, formerly, a final secondary school examination in a group of subjects.

schoolfellow (sko͞ol′fĕl′ō), *n.* a schoolmate.

schoolgirl (sko͞ol′gûl′), *n.* a girl attending school.

schoolhouse (sko͞ol′hous′), *n.* **1.** a building in which a school is conducted, esp. a small school in a rural area. **2.** a house attached to a school for the use of the school-teacher.

schooling (sko͞o′lĭng), *n.* **1.** the process of being taught in a school. **2.** education received in a school. **3.** the act of teaching. **4.** *Archaic.* a reprimand.

schoolman (sko͞ol′mən), *n., pl.* **-men. 1.** one versed in scholastic learning or engaged in scholastic pursuits. **2.** (*sometimes cap.*) a master in one of the schools or universities of the Middle Ages; one of the medieval writers who dealt with theology and philosophy after the methods of scholasticism.

schoolmarm (sko͞ol′mäm′), *n. Colloq.* **1.** a schoolmistress, esp. of the old-fashioned type. **2.** any prim woman.

schoolmaster (sko͞ol′mäs′tə), *n.* a man who presides over or teaches in a school.

schoolmate (sko͞ol′māt′), *n.* a companion or associate at school.

schoolmistress (sko͞ol′mĭs′trĭs), *n.* a woman who presides over or teaches in a school.

schoolroom (sko͞ol′ro͞om′, -ro͝om′), *n.* a room in which a school is conducted or pupils are taught.

school ship, training ship.

schoolteacher (sko͞ol′tē′chə), *n.* one who teaches in a school.

schoolyard (sko͞ol′yäd′), *n.* the playground of a school.

school year, *Educ.* the months during a year when a school is open and attendance is required.

schooner (sko͞o′nə), *n.* **1.** a sailing vessel with two or more masts and fore-and-aft rig. **2.** a large glass for sherry. **3.** the amount of liquid contained in such a glass. **4.** *Austral., U.S.* a very tall glass, as for beer. [orig. uncert.; said to be der. New England verb *scoon* skim along (as on water)]

schooner-rigged (sko͞o′nə rĭgd′), *adj.* fore-and-aft-rigged.

Schopenhauer (shō′pən hou′ə; *Ger.* shō′pən hou ər), *n.* **Arthur** (*Ger.* är′to͞or), 1788–1860, German philosopher.

Schopenhauerism (shō′pən hou′ə rĭz′əm), *n.* the pessimistic philosophy of Schopenhauer, who taught that only the cessation of desire could solve the problems arising from the universal impulse of the will to live.

schorl (shôl), *n.* a black tourmaline. [t. G: m. *Schörl*; orig. unknown] —**schorlaceous** (shô lā′shəs), *adj.*

schottische (shŏ tēsh′), *n.* **1.** a round dance resembling the polka. **2.** its music. [t. G: Scottish (dance)]

Schreiner (shrī′nə), *n.* **Olive** (‘*Ralph Iron*’), 1855–1920, British author and feminist.

Schrödinger (*Ger.* shrœ′dĭng ər), *n.* **Erwin** (*Ger.* ĕr′vēn), 1887–1961, Austrian physicist.

Schubert (sho͞o′bət; *Ger.* sho͞o′bĕrt), *n.* **Franz** (*Ger.* fränts), 1797–1828, Austrian composer.

Schumann (sho͞o′mən; *Ger.* sho͞o′män), *n.* **Robert** (*Ger.* rō′bĕrt), 1810–56, German composer.

Schuman Plan, a limited federation of France, West Germany, Belgium, Netherlands, Italy, and Luxembourg (**European Coal and Steel Community**), created in 1952 for pooling coal and steel resources. [proposed by Robert *Schuman*, 1886–1963, French political leader]

Schurz (sho͝oəts), *n.* **Carl,** 1829–1906, U.S. general, statesman, and journalist, born in Germany.

schuss (sho͝os), *n.* **1.** a straight fast run in skiing. *—v.i.* **2.** to execute a schuss. [G: shot]

Schütz (sho͝ots; *Ger.* shʏts), *n.* **Heinrich** (*Ger.* hīn′rĭKH), 1585–1672, German composer.

Schutzstaffel (*Ger.* sho͝ots′shtä fəl), *n. German.* an elite military unit of the Nazi party which served as Hitler's bodyguard and as a special police force. *Abbrev.*: SS. [G: protection squad]

Schuyler (skī′lə), *n.* **Philip John,** 1733–1804, American general in the War of Independence, and statesman.

Schuylerville (skī′lə vĭl), *n.* See **Saratoga.**

schwa (shwä; *Ger.* shvä), *n. Phonet.* **1.** the indeterminate vowel sound, or sounds, of most unstressed syllables of English, however represented; e.g. the sound, or sounds, of *a* in *alone* and *sofa*, *e* in *system*, *i* in *terrible*, *o* in *gallop*, *u* in *circus.* **2.** the phonetic symbol ə. [t. G, t. Heb.: m. *sh'wa*]

Schwaben (*Ger.* shvä′bən), *n.* German name of **Swabia.**

Schwarzwald (*Ger.* shvärts′vält), *n.* German name of the **Black Forest.**

Schweinfurt (*Ger.* shvīn′fo͝ort), *n.* a town in West Germany, in NW Bavaria. 59,200 (est. 1966).

Schweitzer (*Ger.* shvīt′sər), *n.* **Albert,** 1875–1965, musician, doctor, and missionary in Africa, born in Alsace.

Schweiz (*Ger.* shvīts), *n.* German name of **Switzerland.**

Schwerin (*Ger.* shvė rēn′), *n.* a city in N East Germany: former capital of Mecklenburg. 92,356 (1965).

Schwyz (*Ger.* shvēts), *n.* **1.** a canton in central Switzerland, bordering on Lake Lucerne. 78,048 pop. (1960); 350 sq. mi. **2.** its capital. 11,000 (est. 1960).

sci., 1. science. **2.** scientific.

sciaenoid (sī ē′noid), *adj.* **1.** belonging or pertaining to the *Sciaenidae*, a family of carnivorous acanthopterygian fishes including the drumfishes, certain kingfishes, etc. *—n.* **2.** a sciaenoid fish. Also, **sciaenid** (sī ē′nĭd). [f. NL *Sciaen(idae)* (der. L *sciaena*, t. Gk: m. *skíaina* fish name) + -OID]

sciamachy (sī ăm′ə kĭ), *n., pl.* **-chies.** an act or instance of fighting with a shadow or an imaginary enemy. Also, **sciomachy.** [t. Gk: m. s. *skiamachía* shadow fighting]

sciatic (sī ăt′ĭk), *adj.* **1.** of the ischium or back of the hip: *sciatic nerve.* **2.** affecting the hip or the sciatic nerves. [t. ML: s. *sciaticus*, alter. of L *ischiadicus* ISCHIADIC]

sciatica (sī ăt′ĭ kə), *n. Pathol.* **1.** pain and tenderness at some points of the sciatic nerve; sciatic neuralgia. **2.** any painful disorder extending from the hip down the back of the thigh and surrounding area. [late ME, t. ML, prop. fem. of adj. *sciaticus* SCIATIC]

science (sī′əns), *n.* **1. a.** the systematic study of man and his environment based on the deductions and inferences which can be made, and the general laws which can be formulated, from reproducible observations and measurements of events and parameters within the universe. **b.** the knowledge so obtained. **2.** systematized knowledge in general. **3.** a particular branch of knowledge. **4.** skill; proficiency. [ME, t. OF, t. L: m. *scientia* knowledge]

science fiction, a form of fiction which draws imaginatively on scientific knowledge and speculation in its plot, setting, theme, etc.

sciential (sī ĕn′shəl), *adj.* **1.** having knowledge. **2.** of or pertaining to science or knowledge.

scientific (sī′ən tĭf′ĭk), *adj.* **1.** of or pertaining to science or the sciences: *scientific studies.* **2.** occupied or concerned with science: *scientific men.* **3.** regulated by or conforming to the principles of exact science: *a scientific method.* **4.** systematic or accurate of an exact science. [t. LL: s. *scientificus.* See SCIENCE, -FIC] —**sci′entif′ically,** *adv.*

scientist (sī′ən tĭst), *n.* one versed in or devoted to science, esp. physical or natural science.

scientology (sī′ən tŏl′ə jĭ), *n.* an applied philosophy founded in 1950, deriving its allegedly scientific theory of knowledge from an empirical study of life. Its adherents believe that the application of the techniques derived therefrom can bring about desirable changes in the conditions of life. —**sci′entol′ogist,** *n.*

scilla (sĭl′ə), *n.* a plant of the liliaceous genus *Scilla*, bearing bell-shaped flowers in early spring; squill. [t. L, t. Gk: m. *skílla*]

Scilla (sĭl′ə; *It.* shĕl′lä), *n.* modern name of **Scylla.**

Scilly Isles (sĭl′ĭ), a group of about 140 small islands, SW of Land's End. 2274 pop. (1961); 6½ sq. mi. *Cap.:* Hugh Town. Also, **Scilly Islands, Scillies** (sĭl′ĭz). —**Scillonian** (sĭ lō′nyən), *adj.*, *n.*

scimitar (sĭm′ĭ tə), *n.* a curved, single-edged sword of Oriental origin. Also, **scimiter, simitar.** [t. It.: m. *scimitarra*]

scincoid (sĭng′koid), *adj.* **1.** resembling the skinks, as certain lizards. —*n.* **2.** a scincoid lizard. [t. NL: s. *scincoidēs*, der. L *scincus* skink. See -OID]

scintilla (sĭn tĭl′ə), *n.* a spark; a minute particle; a trace: *not a scintilla of recognition.* [t. L: spark]

scintillant (sĭn′tĭ lənt), *adj.* scintillating; sparkling. [t. L: s. *scintillans*, ppr.]

scintillate (sĭn′tĭ lāt′), *v.*, **-lated, -lating.** —*v.i.* **1.** to emit sparks. **2.** *Astron.* to sparkle; flash. **3.** to twinkle, as the stars. —*v.t.* **4.** to emit as sparks; flash forth. **5.** *Physics.* to produce a flash of light in a scintillator. [t. L: m. s. *scintillātus*, pp.]

scintillating (sĭn′tĭ lā′tĭng), *adj.* **1.** sparkling; flashing; twinkling. **2.** witty; amusing: *a scintillating conversation.* **3.** stimulating interest or pleasure: *a scintillating evening.*

scintillation (sĭn′tĭ lā′shən), *n.* **1.** the act of scintillating. **2.** a spark or flash. **3.** *Astron.* the twinkling or tremulous motion of the light of the stars. **4.** *Physics.* a flash of light produced by a scintillator.

scintillation counter, *Physics.* a device for detecting and measuring ionizing radiation by counting the number of flashes it causes in a scintillator.

scintillation spectrometer, *Physics.* a device for determining the energy distribution of a radiation, which consists of a scintillation counter incorporating a suitable electronic circuit.

scintillator (sĭn′tĭ lā′tə), *n.* *Physics.* a phosphor in which the light energy is released only a short time (10^{-10} to 10^{-4} seconds) after excitation.

scintillometer (sĭn′tĭ lŏm′ĭ tə), *n.* *Physics.* an instrument designed to make ionizing radiation observable, esp. from radioactive materials.

sciolism (sī′ə lĭz′əm), *n.* superficial knowledge. [f. s. LL *sciolus* one having little knowledge + -ISM] —**sci′olist,** *n.* —**sci′olis′tic,** *adj.*

sciomachy (sī ŏm′ə kĭ), *n.*, *pl.* **-chies.** sciamachy.

scion (sī′ən), *n.* **1.** a descendant. **2.** a shoot or twig, esp. one cut for grafting or planting; a cutting. [ME, t. OF: m. *cion*, g. s. L *sectio* a cutting, b. with *scier* saw, g. L *secāre* cut]

sciosophy (sī ŏs′ə fĭ), *n.* a system of pretended knowledge usually based on tradition or the like, and not on scientific fact, as astrology.

Scipio (sĭp′ĭ ō′), *n.* **1. Publius Cornelius Scipio Africanus Major** (pŭb′lĭ əs kô nē′lyəs sĭp′ĭ ō′ ăf′rĭ kä′nəs mā′jə) ('*Scipio the Elder*'), 237–183 B.C., Roman general: victor over Hannibal. **2.** his adopted grandson, **Publius Cornelius Scipio Aemilianus Africanus Minor** (ē mĭl′ĭ ä′nəs ăf′rĭ kä′nəs mī′nə) ('*Scipio the Younger*'), *c.* 185–129 B.C., Roman general: besieger and destroyer of Carthage.

scire facias (sī′ə rĭ fā′shĭ ăs′), *Law.* **1.** formerly, a writ requiring the party against whom it is brought to show cause why a judgement, letters patent, etc., should not be executed, vacated, or annulled. **2.** such a proceeding. [L: lit., make (him) to know, after the words in the writ]

scirrhus (sĭ′rəs), *n.*, *pl.* **scirrhi** (sĭ′rī), **scirrhuses.** *Pathol.* a hard, indolent tumour; a hard cancer. [NL, t. Gk: m. *skírrhos*, var. of *skíros* hard covering] —**scirrhous** (sĭ′rəs), **scirrhoid** (sĭ′roid), *adj.*

scissile (sĭs′īl), *adj.* capable of being cut or divided; splitting easily. [t. L: m. s. *scissilis*]

scission (sĭzh′ən), *n.* a cutting, dividing, or splitting; division; separation. [late ME, t. LL: s. *scissio*]

scissor (sĭz′ə), *v.t.* to cut or clip out with scissors.

scissors (sĭz′əz), *n.pl. or sing.* **1.** a cutting instrument consisting of two blades (with handles) so pivoted together that their edges work against each other (often called *a pair of scissors*). **2.** *Gymnastics.* exercises in which the legs execute a scissor-like motion. **3.** *Wrestling.* a hold in which a wrestler encircles the head or body of his opponent with his legs. [ME *sisours*, *cysoures*, t. OF: m. *cisoires* (fem. pl.), g. LL *cisōria* (found only in sing., *cisōrium* cutting instrument), der. L *caesus*, pp., cut, slain; sp. due to confusion with L *scissor* one who cuts]

scissors kick, **1.** *Swimming.* a propelling motion of the legs in which they move somewhat like the blades of a pair of scissors, used in the sidestroke. **2.** *Soccer.* a kick made by jumping, raising one leg, then kicking the ball with the other.

sciurine (sī′yŏŏ rīn, -rīn′), *adj.* of or pertaining to the squirrels and allied rodents of the family *Sciuridae.* [f. s. L *sciūrus* (t. Gk: m. *skíouros* squirrel) + -INE[1]]

sciuroid (sī′yŏŏ roid′, sī yŏŏə′roid), *adj.* **1.** sciurine. **2.** *Bot.* resembling a squirrel tail, as the spikes of certain grasses. [f. s. L *sciūrus* (see SCIURINE) + -OID]

sclaff (sklăf), *Golf.* —*v.t.*, *v.i.* **1.** to scrape (the ground) with the club before hitting the ball. —*n.* **2.** a sclaffing stroke. [spec. use of Scot. *sclaf* shuffle] —**sclaff′er,** *n.*

sclera (sklĭə′rə), *n.* *Anat.* a dense, white, fibrous membrane forming with the cornea the external covering of the eyeball. See diag. under **eye.** [t. NL, t. Gk: m. *sklērá* (fem.) hard]

sclerenchyma (sklĭə rĕng′kĭ mə), *n.* *Bot.* supporting or protective tissue composed of thickened and indurated cells from which the protoplasm has usually disappeared. [f. SCLER(O)- + Gk *énchyma* infusion] —**sclerenchymatous** (sklĭə′rĕng kĭm′ə təs), *adj.*

sclerite (sklĭə′rīt), *n.* *Zool.* any chitinous, calcareous, or similar hard part, plate, spicule, or the like. [f. SCLER(O)- + -ITE[1]] —**scleritic** (sklĭə rĭt′ĭk), *adj.*

scleritis (sklĭə rī′tĭs), *n.* *Pathol.* inflammation of the sclera. Also, **selerotitis.**

sclero-, a word element meaning 'hard'. Also, before vowels, **scler-.** [t. NL, t. Gk: m. *sklēro-*, comb. form of *sklērós*]

scleroderma (sklĭə′rō dû′mə), *n.* *Pathol.* a serious disease in which all the layers of the skin become hardened and rigid. Also, **sclerodermia** (sklĭə′rō dû′mĭ ə). [NL. See SCLERO-, -DERM]

sclerodermatous (sklĭə′rō dû′mə təs), *adj.* *Zool.* covered with a hardened tissue, as scales.

scleroid (sklĭə′roid), *adj.* *Biol.* hard or indurated.

scleroma (sklĭə rō′mə), *n.*, *pl.* **-mata** (-mə tə). *Pathol.* a tumour-like induration of tissue. [NL, t. Gk: m. *sklḗrōma*]

sclerometer (sklĭə rŏm′ĭ tə), *n.* an instrument for determining with precision the degree of hardness of a substance, esp. a mineral.

sclerophyll (sklĭə′rə fĭl), *Bot.* —*n.* **1.** any of various plants, as those found in deserts, which have tough leaves due to the formation of much sclerenchyma. —*adj.* **2.** denoting or pertaining to such a plant.

sclerophylly (sklĭə′rə fĭl′ĭ), *n.* *Bot.* the normal formation of much sclerenchyma in the leaves of a plant, esp. certain plants of desert regions, resulting in thick, tough leaves. —**sclerophyllous** (sklĭə rŏf′ĭ ləs), *adj.*

scleroprotein (sklĭə′rō prō′tēn), *n.* *Biochem.* any of a group of simple proteins characterized by their insolubility.

sclerosed (sklĭə′rōst), *adj.* hardened or indurated, as by sclerosis.

sclerosis (sklĭə rō′sĭs), *n.*, *pl.* **-ses** (-sēz). **1.** *Pathol.* a hardening or induration of a tissue or part; increase of connective tissue or the like at the expense of more active tissue. **2.** *Bot.* a hardening of a tissue or cell wall by thickening or lignification. [t. ML, t. Gk: m. *sklḗrōsis* hardening] —**sclero′sal,** *adj.*

sclerotic (sklĭə rŏt′ĭk), *adj.* **1.** *Anat.* designating or pertaining to sclera. **2.** *Pathol.*, *Bot.* pertaining to or affected with sclerosis. [t. ML: s. *sclērōtica*, t. LGk: m. *sklērōtikḗ*, fem. adj., pertaining to hardening]

sclerotitis (sklĭə′rō tī′tĭs), *n.* *Pathol.* scleritis. —**sclerotitic** (sklĭə′rō tĭt′ĭk), *adj.*

sclerotium (sklĭə rō′shyəm), *n.*, *pl.* **-tia** (-shyə). *Bot.* a vegetative, resting, food-storage body in certain higher fungi, composed of a compact mass of indurated mycelia. [NL, f. *sclerot-* (t. Gk: m. s. *sklērṓtēs* hardness) + *-ium* -IUM] —**sclerotial** (sklĭə rō′shyəl), *adj.*

sclerotomy (sklĭə rŏt′ə mĭ), *n.*, *pl.* **-mies.** *Surg.* incision into the sclera, as to extract foreign bodies.

sclerous (sklĭə′rəs), *adj.* hard; firm; bony. [t. Gk: m. *sklērós* hard]

S.C.M., State Certified Midwife.

scoff[1] (skŏf), *n.* **1.** an expression of mockery, derision, or derisive scorn; a jeer. **2.** an object of mockery or derision. —*v.i.* **3.** to speak derisively; mock; jeer (often fol. by *at*). —*v.t.* **4.** *Obs.* to deride. [ME *scof*, t. Scand.; cf. obs. Dan. *skof* mockery] —**scoff′er,** *n.* —**scoff′ingly,** *adv.*

—**Syn. 3.** SCOFF, JEER, SNEER imply behaving with scornful disapproval towards someone or about something. To SCOFF is to express insolent doubt or derision, openly and emphatically: *to scoff at a new invention.* To JEER is to shout in disapproval and scorn more coarsely and unintelligently than in scoffing: *you may jeer, but can you do any better?* To SNEER is to show by facial expression or tone of voice ill-natured contempt or disparagement: *he sneered unpleasantly in referring to his opponent's misfortunes.*

scoff[2] (skŏf), *Slang.* —*v.t.*, *v.i.* **1.** to eat greedily and quickly. —*n.* **2.** food. [t. Afrikaans: m. *schoft* meal, D quarter (of the day)]

scold (skōld), *v.t.* **1.** to find fault with; chide. —*v.i.* **2.** to find fault; reprove. **3.** to use abusive language. —*n.* **4.** a person, esp. a woman, addicted to abusive speech. [ME, var. of *scald*, t. Scand.; cf. Icel. *skāld* poet]

—**scold′er,** *n.* —**scold′ing,** *adj., n.* —**scold′ingly,** *adv.* —**Syn. 1.** See **reproach.**

scolecite (skŏl′ĭ sīt′, skō′lĭ-), *n.* a zeolite mineral, a hydrous calcium aluminium silicate, $CaAl_2Si_3O_{10}.3H_2O$, occurring in masses and (usually) needle-shaped crystals, commonly white. [f. m. s. Gk *skṓlēx* worm + -ITE[1]]

scolex (skō′lĕks), *n., pl.* **scoleces** (skō lē′sēz). *Zool.* the anterior segment or head of a tapeworm, provided with organs of attachment. It develops singly or in multiples in the larval stage; when it reaches the final host it gives rise to the chain of segments by growth from its posterior end or neck. [NL, t. Gk: m. *skṓlēx* worm]

scoliosis (skŏl′ĭ ō′sĭs), *n. Pathol.* lateral curvature of the spine. [NL, t. Gk: m. *skolíōsis* a bending]

scollop (skŏl′əp), *n., v.t.* scallop.

scolopendrid (skŏl′ə pĕn′drĭd), *n.* any of the *Scolopendrida*, an order of myriapods including many large and poisonous centipedes. [t. NL: s. *Scolopendridae* (pl.), der. *scolopendra*, t. Gk: m. *skolópendra* kind of multiped. See -ID[2]] —**scolopendrine** (skŏl′ə pĕn′drīn, -drĭn), *adj.*

scombroid (skŏm′broid), *adj.* **1.** resembling the mackerel. **2.** belonging or pertaining to the mackerel family (*Scombridae*) or the superfamily (*Scombroidea*) containing the mackerel family. —*n.* **3.** a mackerel or related scombroid fish. Also, **scombrid** (skŏm′brĭd). [f. m. s. Gk *skómbros* mackerel + -OID]

sconce[1] (skŏns), *n.* a wall bracket for holding one or more candles or other lights. [ME, t. monastic L: m. *sconsa*, der. *absconsa*, fem. pp., hidden]

sconce[2] (skŏns), *n., v.,* **sconced, sconcing.** —*n.* **1.** *Fort.* a small detached fort or earthwork, as for defence of a pass or ford. **2.** *Obs. or Rare.* a shelter, screen, or protection. —*v.t.* **3.** *Fort.* to protect with a sconce. **4.** *Obs. or Rare.* to fortify; shelter. [t. D: m. *schans*]

sconce[3] (skŏns), *v.,* **sconced, sconcing,** *n.* —*v.t.* **1.** to exact a penalty or fine, as in some universities from undergraduates for a breach of etiquette. —*n.* **2.** such a fine, or a penalty, as the drinking of a large quantity of beer, often within a specified time. **3.** a drinking mug which holds this quantity of beer. [orig. obscure]

sconce[4] (skŏns), *n. Colloq.* **1.** the head or skull. **2.** sense or wit. [? special use of SCONCE[1] or SCONCE[2]]

scone (skŏn, skōn), *n.* a light plain cake, quickly made, containing very little fat, either baked in a very hot oven or cooked on a griddle (**drop scone**); usually eaten split open and spread with butter, etc. [t. MD: m. *schoon* (*brōt*) fine bread. See SHEEN, BREAD]

Scone (sko͞on), *n.* **The Stone of,** a famous stone, formerly at Scone, Scotland, upon which the Scottish kings sat at coronation, now beneath the coronation chair in Westminster Abbey.

scoop (sko͞op), *n.* **1.** a ladle or ladle-like utensil, esp. a small, deep shovel with a short handle, for taking up flour, sugar, etc. **2.** the bucket of a dredge, steam-shovel, etc. **3.** *Surg.* a spoonlike apparatus used to remove substances or foreign objects. **4.** a place scooped out; a hollow. **5.** act of scooping; a movement as of scooping. **6.** the quantity taken up. **7.** *Colloq.* a big haul, as of money. **8.** an item of news, etc., published or broadcast in advance of, or to the exclusion of, rival newspapers, broadcasting organizations, etc. —*v.t.* **9.** to take up or out with, or as with a scoop. **10.** to gather together or appropriate with the arms or hands (often fol. by *up*): *he scooped up the jewels and put them into his pocket.* **11.** to empty with a scoop. **12.** to form a hollow or hollows in. **13.** to form with or as with a scoop. **14.** *Journalism Slang.* to get the better of (a rival newspaper, broadcasting organization, etc.) by publishing or broadcasting an item of news, etc., first. **15.** *Hockey.* to hit under the ball so that it rises into the air. —*v.i.* **16.** to remove or gather something with, or as with, a scoop. [ME *scope*, t. MLG or MD: vessel used for drawing or bailing water] —**scoop′er,** *n.*

scoop neck, a low rounded neckline on a woman's dress, blouse, etc. Also, **scoop neckline.**

scoot (sko͞ot), *Colloq.* —*v.i.* **1.** to dart; go swiftly or hastily. —*v.t.* **2.** to send or impel at high speed. —*n.* **3.** a swift, darting movement or course. [of Scand. orig.; akin to SHOOT]

scooter (sko͞o′tə), *n.* **1.** a low vehicle with two wheels, one in front of the other, and a tread or footboard between them, and sometimes with a saddle or seat. It is steered by a handlebar and propelled by pushing against the ground with one foot. **2.** motor scooter. —*v.i.* **3.** to go, or travel in or on a scooter.

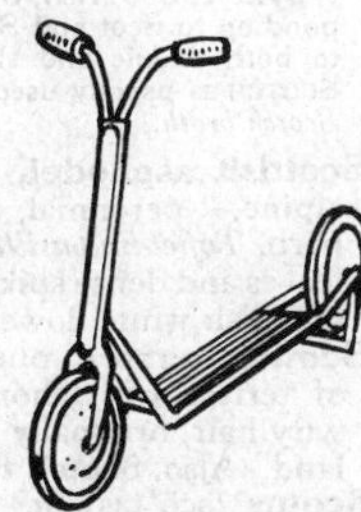
Scooter (def. 1)

scop (skŏp), *n.* an Old English bard or poet. [OE, c. Icel. *skop* mockery. See SCOFF, SCOLD]

scopa (skŏp′ə), *n., pl.* **-as, -ae** (-əz, -ē). *Entomol.* a bunch of hairs on an insect's legs or abdomen for collecting pollen. [t. L] —**scop′ate,** *adj.*

scope (skōp), *n.* **1.** extent or range of view, outlook, application, operation, effectiveness, etc.: *an investigation of wide scope.* **2.** space for movement or activity; opportunity for operation: *to give one's fancy full scope.* **3.** extent in space; a tract or area. **4.** length, or a length. **5.** *Naut.* the length of cable at which a vessel rides when at anchor. **6.** *Rare.* aim; purpose. **7.** short form of *microscope, periscope, radarscope,* etc. [t. It.: m. *scopo*, t. Gk: m. *skopós* mark, aim] —**Syn. 1.** See **range.**

-scope, a word element referring to instruments for viewing, as in *telescope.* [t. NL: m. s. *-scopium*, t. Gk: m. *-skópion* or *-skopeîon*, der. *skopeîn* look at]

scopolamine (skō pŏl′ə mēn′, -mĭn, skō′pə lăm′ēn, -ĭn), *n. Chem., Pharm.* a crystalline alkaloid, $C_{17}H_{21}NO_4$, obtained from the rhizome of certain solanaceous plants, used as a depressant and mydriatic, and in producing the so-called twilight sleep. [f. s. NL *Scopola* (genus of plants named after G.A. *Scopoli*, 1723–88, Italian botanist) + AMINE]

scopoline (skō′pə lēn′, -lĭn), *n. Pharm.* a crystalline glucoside, $C_8H_{13}NO_2$, a derivative of scopolamine, used as a narcotic.

scopula (skŏp′yo͝o lə), *n., pl.* **-las, -lae** (-ləz, -lē′). *Entomol.* a small tuft of hairs, as on the feet of some spiders. [t. LL: der. L *scōp*(*a*) broom + *-ula* -ULE]

scopulate (skŏp′yo͝o lāt′, -lĭt), *adj. Zool.* broom-shaped; brushlike.

-scopy, a word element for forming abstract action nouns related to *-scope*, as in *telescopy.* [t. Gk: m. s. *-skopía*, lit., watching. See -SCOPE]

scorbutic (skô byo͞o′tĭk), *adj.* pertaining to, of the nature of, or affected with scurvy. Also, **scorbu′tical.** [t. NL: s. *scorbūticus*, der. ML *scorbūtus* scurvy, appar. t. D: m. *scheurbot* (now *scheurbuik*)]

scorch (skôch), *v.t.* **1.** to affect in colour, taste, etc., by burning slightly. **2.** to parch or shrivel with heat. **3.** to criticize severely. —*v.i.* **4.** to be or become scorched. **5.** *Colloq.* to ride at high speed. —*n.* **6.** a superficial burn. [b. unrecorded *scorp* shrivel (t. Scand.; cf. Icel. *skorpinn* shrivelled) and PARCH] —**Syn. 1.** See **burn**[1].

scorched earth, a condition or policy in which all things useful to an invading army are destroyed, as by fire.

scorcher (skô′chə), *n.* **1.** one who or that which scorches. **2.** *Colloq.* a very hot day. **3.** anything caustic or severe. **4.** *Obs. Colloq.* an excessively fast driver.

scorching (skô′chĭng), *adj.* **1.** burning; very hot. **2.** caustic or scathing. —**scorch′ingly,** *adv.*

scordatura (skô′də to͞oə′rə), *n. Music.* the tuning of a stringed instrument to notes other than the normal in order to produce special effects. [It., der. *scordato*, pp., played out of tune]

score (skô), *n., v.,* **scored, scoring.** —*n.* **1.** the record of points made by the competitors in a game or match. **2.** the aggregate of points made by a side or individual. **3.** the scoring of a point or points. **4.** *U.S. Educ.* the performance of an individual, or sometimes of a group, in an examination or test, expressed by a letter, number, or other symbol. **5.** a notch or scratch; a stroke or line. **6.** a notch or mark for keeping an account or record. **7.** a reckoning or account so kept. **8.** any account showing indebtedness. **9.** an amount recorded as due. **10.** a line drawn as a boundary, the beginning of a race, etc. **11.** a group or set of twenty: *about a score of years ago.* **12.** (*pl.*) a great many. **13.** account, reason, or ground: *to complain on the score of low pay.* **14.** a successful move, remark, etc. **15.** *Music.* **a.** a written or printed piece of music with all the vocal and instrumental parts arranged on staves, one under the other. **b.** the background music to a film, play, etc. **16.** *Colloq.* latest news or state of progress: *what's the score on the new space rocket?* **17. pay off** or **settle a score, a.** to avenge a wrong. **b.** to fulfil an obligation.
—*v.t.* **18.** to gain for addition to one's score in a game. **19.** to make a score of. **20.** to be worth (as points): *four aces score one hundred.* **21.** *U.S. Educ.* to evaluate the responses a person has made on (a test or an examination). **22.** *Music.* **a.** to orchestrate. **b.** to write out in score. **c.** to compose the music for (a film, play, etc.). **23.** *Cookery.* to cut with shallow slashes, as meat. **24.** to make notches, cuts, or lines in or on. **25.** to record by notches, marks, etc.; to reckon (often fol. by *up*). **26.** to write down as a debt. **27.** to record as a debtor. **28.** to gain or win: *a comedy scoring a great success.* **29.** *U.S.* to censure severely: *newspapers scored him severely for the announcement.* **30. score off,** gain an advantage over.

—*v.i.* **31.** to make a point or points in a game or contest. **32.** to keep score, as of a game. **33.** to achieve an advantage or a success. **34.** to make notches, cuts, lines, etc. [ME; late OE *scoru*, t. Scand.; cf. Icel. *skor* notch] —**scor′er,** *n.*

scoreboard (skô′bôd′), *n.* a board on which the score of a game, match, etc., is exhibited, as at a cricket ground.

scorebook (skô′bo͝ok′), *n.* a book in which scores, as of cricket matches, are kept.

scorecard (skô′käd′), *n.* a card on which a score is kept.

scoresheet (skô′shēt′), *n.* a sheet of paper on which a score is kept.

scoria (skô′rĭ ə), *n., pl.* **scoriae** (skô′rĭ ē′). **1.** the refuse, dross, or slag left after smelting or melting metals. **2.** a clinker-like cellular lava. [t. L, t. Gk: m. *skōría* slag] —**scoriaceous** (skô′rĭ ā′shəs), *adj.*

scorification (skô′rĭ fĭ kā′shən), *n.* *Metall.* the process of separating a precious metal from its ore by heating it to a high temperature in the presence of lead and borax in a scorifier.

scorifier (skô′rĭ fī′ə), *n.* *Metall.* a refractory crucible used in the process of scorification.

scorify (skô′rĭ fī′), *v.t.*, **-fied, -fying.** to reduce to scoria. [f. SCORI(A) + -FY]

scorn (skôn), *n.* **1.** open or unqualified contempt; disdain. **2.** mockery or derision. **3.** an object of derision or contempt. **4.** *Archaic.* a derisive or contemptuous action or speech. —*v.t.* **5.** to treat or regard with scorn. **6.** to reject or refuse with scorn. —*v.i.* **7.** to mock; jeer. [ME; var. of *skarn*, t. OF: aphetic m. *escarn* mockery, derision; of Gmc orig.] —**scorn′er,** *n.* —**Syn. 1.** See **contempt.** —**Ant. 2.** praise.

scornful (skôn′fəl), *adj.* full of scorn; derisive; contemptuous: *he smiled in a scornful way.* —**scorn′fully,** *adv.* —**scorn′fulness,** *n.*

scorpaenoid (skô pē′noid), *adj.* **1.** of the scorpaenids. —*n.* **2.** a scorpaenid. [f. s. L *scorpaena* (t. Gk: m. *skórpaina* prickly fish) + -OID]

Scorpio (skô′pĭ ō′), *n.* **1.** *Astron.* the Scorpion, a zodiacal constellation, containing the star Antares. **2.** the eighth sign of the zodiac. Also, **Scorpius.** See diag. under **zodiac.** [ME, t. L. See SCORPION]

scorpioid (skô′pĭ oid′), *adj.* **1.** resembling a scorpion. **2.** belonging to the *Scorpionida*, the order of arachnids comprising the scorpions. **3.** curved (at the end) like the tail of a scorpion. **4.** *Bot.* of or pertaining to a type of cymous inflorescence in which the axis is coiled like the tail of a scorpion. [t. Gk: m. s. *skorpioeidés*]

scorpion (skô′pyən), *n.* **1.** any of numerous arachnids belonging to the order *Scorpiones* (*Scorpionida*) from the warmer parts of the world, having a long narrow tail terminating in a venomous sting. **2.** (*cap.*) *Astron.* Scorpio. **3.** an insect which stings or which superficially resembles a true scorpion. **4.** a (supposed) whip or scourge armed with spikes. I Kings: 12; 11. [ME, t. L: s. *scorpio* (der. *scorpius*, t. Gk: m. *skorpíos*)]

Scorpion, *Buthus carolinus* (Ab. 3 in. long)

scorpion-fish (skô′pyən fĭsh′), *n.* a rockfish, esp. of the genus *Scorpaena*, which has poisonous dorsal spines.

scorpion-fly (skô′pyən flī′), *n.* any of the harmless insects of the order *Mecoptera*, in which the male has an abdominal structure resembling a scorpion sting.

scorpion-grass (skô′pyən gräs′), *n.* any plant of the genus *Myosotis*; a forget-me-not.

scorpion senna, a deciduous leguminous shrub of central and S Europe, *Coronilla emerus*, with yellow flowers.

Scorpius (skô′pyəs), *n.* *Astron.* Scorpio.

scot (skŏt), *n.* *Hist.* **1.** a payment or charge; one's share of a payment. **2.** an assessment or tax. [ME, t. Scand.; cf. Icel. *skot*, c. OE *gescot* payment]

Scot (skŏt), *n.* **1.** a native or inhabitant of Scotland; a Scotsman. **2.** one of an ancient Gaelic people who came from northern Ireland about the 6th century and settled in the north-western part of Great Britain, and after whom Scotland was named. [ME; OE *Scottas* (pl.), t. LL: m. *Scottī* the Irish; of unknown orig.]

Scot., 1. Scotland. 2. Scottish. 3. Scotch.

scot and lot, **1.** *Hist.* a municipal tax assessed proportionately upon the members of a community. **2. pay scot and lot,** to pay in full; settle.

scotch (skŏch), *v.t.* **1.** to injure so as to make harmless. **2.** to cut, gash, or score. **3.** to put an end to; stamp out; suppress: *the spokesman soon scotched the rumours about a strike.* **4.** to block or prop with a scotch. —*n.* **5.** a cut, gash, or score. **6.** a block or wedge put under a wheel, barrel, etc., to prevent slipping. [b. SCORE and NOTCH]

Scotch (skŏch), *adj.* **1.** Scottish. —*n.* **2.** the Scottish people. **3.** Scotch whisky. **4.** Scottish (def. 3). [var. of SCOTS] —**Syn. 1.** See **Scottish.**

Scotch blackface, one of a variety of black-faced domestic sheep popular in Scotland.

Scotch bluebell, the harebell.

Scotch broth, a thick soup made from beef stock and pearl barley.

Scotch collops, a savoury dish made of minced meat.

Scotch egg, a hard-boiled egg enclosed in sausage meat, coated with egg and breadcrumbs and deep fried.

Scotch fir, Scots pine.

Scotchman (skŏch′mən), *n., pl.* **-men. 1.** a Scotsman. **2.** *Naut.* a length of timber or metal fitted on half the circumference of a shroud or backstay to prevent chafing.

Scotch mist, a fine light drizzle, common in the Scottish Highlands.

Scotch rose, burnet rose.

Scotch Tape, *Trademark.* an adhesive tape, made of cellulose and usually transparent.

Scotch terrier, Scottish terrier.

Scotch thistle, a large biennial thistle, *Onopordum acanthium*, widespread in Europe and W Asia but rare and doubtfully native in Scotland.

Scotch whisky, barley-malt whisky distilled in Scotland.

Scotch woodcock, scrambled eggs and anchovies on toast.

scoter (skō′tə), *n.* any of the large diving ducks constituting the genus *Melanitta*, found in northern parts of the Northern Hemisphere.

scot-free (skŏt′frē′), *adj.* **1.** free from penalty or payment; unhurt: *to get off scot-free.* **2.** free from payment of scot.

scotia (skō′shə), *n.* *Archit.* a concave moulding, as at the base of a column. [t. L, t. Gk: m. *skotía*, lit., darkness]

Scotia (skō′shə), *n.* *Poetic.* Scotland. [t. ML, der. LL *Scōtus* SCOT]

Scotism (skō′tĭz′əm), *n.* the doctrines of Duns Scotus, fundamental of which were that distinctions which the mind inevitably draws, though non-existent apart from their relations to mind, are to be considered as real. —**Sco′tist,** *n.*

Scotland (skŏt′lənd), *n.* a division of the United Kingdom in the N part of Great Britain. 5,178,490 pop. (1961); 29,796 sq. mi. *Cap.:* Edinburgh.

Scotland Yard, **1.** a short street in London, formerly the site of the London police headquarters. **2.** the London police, esp. the branch engaged in criminal investigation.

scotoma (skŏ tō′mə), *n., pl.* **-mata** (-mə tə). *Pathol.* loss of vision in a part of the visual field; a blind spot. [t. LL, t. Gk: m. *skótōma* dizziness]

Scots (skŏts), *n.* **1.** the Scottish dialect of English. —*adj.* **2.** Scottish or Scotch. [ME *Scottis*, northern var. of SCOTTISH] —**Syn. 2.** See **Scotch.**

Scotsman (skŏts′mən), *n., pl.* **-men.** a native of Scotland. Also, **Scotchman.**

Scots pine, a tall coniferous tree of Europe and temperate Asia, *Pinus sylvestris*, grown for its valuable timber. Also, **Scotch fir.**

Scott (skŏt), *n.* **1. Sir George Gilbert,** 1811–78, English architect. **2. Robert Falcon,** 1868–1912, British naval officer and antarctic explorer. **3. Sir Walter,** 1771–1832, Scottish novelist and poet.

Scotticism (skŏt′ĭ sĭz′əm), *n.* a Scottish idiom.

Scottie (skŏt′ĭ), *n.* *Colloq.* **1.** a Scotsman. **2.** a Scottish terrier. Also, **Scotty.**

Scottish (skŏt′ish), *adj.* **1.** of or pertaining to the Scots, their country, the dialect of English spoken there, or their literature. —*n.* **2.** the people of Scotland collectively. **3.** the dialects of English spoken in Scotland; Scottish English; Scots; Scotch.

—**Syn.** 1. SCOTTISH, SCOTS, SCOTCH are proper adjectives corresponding to Scot and Scotland. SCOTTISH and SCOTS are applied to both people and things: *Scots soldiers; Scottish Highlands.* SCOTCH is usually used with objects not people: *Scotch whisky; Scotch broth.*

Scottish asphodel, an arctic-alpine, perennial, liliaceous herb, *Tofieldia pusilla*, with stiff leaves and dense spikes of small, greenish white flowers.

Scottish terrier (10 in. high at the shoulder)

Scottish terrier, one of a breed of terrier with short legs and wiry hair, originally from Scotland. Also, **Scotch terrier.**

Scotus (scō′təs), *n.* See **Duns Scotus.**

scoundrel (skoun′drəl), *n.* **1.** an

unprincipled, dishonourable man; a villain. —*adj.* **2.** *Rare.* scoundrelly. [orig. uncert.] —**Syn. 1.** See **knave.**

scoundrelly (skoun′drə lĭ), *adj.* **1.** having the character of a scoundrel. **2.** of or like a scoundrel.

scour[1] (skou′ə), *v.t.* **1.** to cleanse or polish by hard rubbing: *to scour pots and pans.* **2.** to remove (dirt, grease, etc.) from something by hard rubbing. **3.** to clear out (a channel, drain, etc.). **4.** to purge thoroughly, as an animal. **5.** to clear or rid of what is undesirable. **6.** to remove by, or as by, cleansing; get rid of. —*v.i.* **7.** to rub a surface in order to cleanse or polish it. **8.** to remove dirt, grease, etc. **9.** to become clean and shining by rubbing. **10.** to be capable of being cleaned by rubbing. **11.** (of animals, esp. cattle) to have diarrhoea. —*n.* **12.** act of scouring. **13.** the place scoured. **14.** an apparatus or a material used in scouring. **15.** persistent diarrhoea in animals, esp. cattle. [ME, prob. t. MD or MLG: m. *schūren*, prob. t. OF: m. *escurer*, g. L *ex-* EX-[1] and *cūrāre* care for, clean]

scour[2] (skou′ə), *v.i.* **1.** to move rapidly or energetically. **2.** to range about, as in search of something. —*v.t.* **3.** to run or pass quickly over or along. **4.** to range over, as in search. [ME *scoure.* Cf. Norw. *skura* rush]

scourer[1] (skou′ə rə), *n.* one who or that which scours or cleanses. [f. SCOUR[1] + -ER[1]]

scourer[2] (skou′ə rə), *n.* **1.** one who scours or ranges about. **2.** (in the 17th and 18th centuries) a prankster who roamed the streets at night. [f. SCOUR[2] + -ER[1]]

scourge (skûj), *n., v.,* **scourged, scourging.** —*n.* **1.** a whip or lash, esp. for the infliction of punishment or torture. **2.** any means of punishment. **3.** a cause of affliction or calamity. —*v.t.* **4.** to whip with a scourge; lash. **5.** to punish or chastise severely; afflict; torment. [ME, t. AF: m. *escorge*, ult. der. LL *excoriāre* strip off the hide] —**scourg′er,** *n.*

scouring (skou′ə rĭng), *n.* **1.** diarrhoea in animals, esp. cattle. **2.** the act of one who or that which scours. **3.** (*pl.*) that which is removed by scouring.

scouring rush, any of certain horsetails, esp. *Equisetum hyemale*, formerly used for scouring and polishing.

scouse (skous), *n.* **1.** *Naut.* a baked food served to sailors, as **bread scouse** which contains no meat. See **lobscouse.** **2.** (*cap.*) a person who lives in Liverpool. **3.** (*cap.*) the dialect of English spoken in Liverpool. [shortened form of LOBSCOUSE]

scout[1] (skout), *n.* **1.** a soldier, warship, aeroplane, or the like, employed in reconnoitring. **2.** a person sent out to obtain information. **3.** *Sport.* **a.** a person detailed to observe and report on the techniques, players, etc., of opposing teams. **b.** a person detailed to seek and recommend new players for recruitment to a club. **4.** a talent scout. **5.** the act of scouting. **6.** boy scout. **7.** *Colloq.* a fellow: *a good scout.* **8.** a college servant, as at Oxford University. —*v.i.* **9.** to act as a scout; reconnoitre. —*v.t.* **10.** to examine, inspect, or observe for the purpose of obtaining information; reconnoitre: *to scout the enemy's defences.* **11.** *Colloq.* to seek; search for (usually fol. by *out* or *up*): *try and scout out an entertainer for Saturday night.* [ME *scowte*, t. OF: m. *escoute* (fem.) action of listening, der. *escouter* listen, g. L *auscultāre*]

scout[2] (skout), *v.t., v.i.* to reject with scorn; flout. [t. Scand.; cf. Icel. *skūta* scold]

scouter (skou′tə), *n.* **1.** one who or that which scouts. **2.** an officer in a company of boy scouts.

scouting (skou′tĭng), *n.* **1.** the act or an instance of reconnoitring, gaining information, etc. **2.** the activities of a scout or scouts.

scoutmaster (skout′mäs′tə), *n.* **1.** the leader or officer in charge of a band of scouts. **2.** the adult leader of a troop of boy scouts.

scow (skou), *n.* a large, flat-bottomed, unpowered vessel used chiefly for freight, as mud or coal; a low-grade lighter or barge. [t. D: m. *schouw* ferryboat]

scowl (skoul), *v.i.* **1.** to draw down or contract the brows in a sullen or angry manner. **2.** to have a gloomy or threatening look. —*v.t.* **3.** to affect or express with a scowl. —*n.* **4.** a scowling expression, look, or aspect. [ME *skoul*, t. Scand.; cf. Dan. *skule*] —**scowl′er,** *n.* —**scowl′ingly,** *adv.*

scr., scruple (defs 3, 4).

scrabble (skrăb′l), *v.,* **-bled, -bling,** *n.* —*v.i.* **1.** to scratch or scrape, as with the claws or hands. **2.** to scrawl; scribble. **3.** to struggle to gain possession of something. **4.** to scratch or grope about clumsily or blindly. —*v.t.* **5.** to scratch at. **6.** to write hurriedly; scribble. —*n.* **7.** a scrabbling or scramble. **8.** a scrawled character, writing, etc. **9.** (*cap.*) *Trademark.* a game similar to anagrams and crossword puzzles in which 2 to 4 players use counters of varying point values to form words on a playing board. [t. D: m. s. *schrabbelen*, freq. of *schrabben* scratch]

scrag (skrăg), *n., v.,* **scragged, scragging.** —*n.* **1.** a lean person or animal. **2.** the lean end of a neck of mutton, etc. **3.** *Slang.* the neck of a human being. —*v.t.* **4.** *Slang.* to wring the neck of; hang; garrotte. [prob. akin to CRAG[2]]

scraggly (skrăg′lĭ), *adj.,* **-glier, -gliest.** irregular; ragged; straggling.

scraggy (skrăg′ĭ), *adj.,* **-gier, -giest. 1.** lean or thin. **2.** meagre. **3.** irregular; jagged. —**scrag′gily,** *adv.* —**scrag′giness,** *n.*

scram (skrăm), *v.i.,* **scrammed, scramming.** *Slang.* to get out quickly; go away. [alter. of SCRAMBLE]

scramble (skrăm′bl), *v.,* **-bled, -bling,** *n.* —*v.i.* **1.** to make one's way hurriedly by use of the hands and feet, as over rough ground. **2.** to struggle with others for possession; strive rudely with others. **3.** to ride in a scramble. **4.** *Mil., Naval, etc.* (of the crew of an aircraft, submarine, etc., or the craft itself) to prepare for immediate action, as in intercepting the enemy. —*v.t.* **5.** to collect in a hurried or disorderly manner (fol. by *up*, etc.). **6.** to mix together confusedly. **7.** to cook (eggs) in a pan, mixing whites and yolks with butter, milk, etc. **8.** *Electronics.* to transmit (a radio signal) in a garbled form, so that it can be decoded only by a special receiver, and not by a normal instrument. —*n.* **9.** a climb or progression over rough, irregular ground, or the like. **10.** a form of motorcycle race in which competitors must race over very rough, uneven ground. **11.** a struggle for possession. **12.** any disorderly struggle or proceeding. **13.** *Mil., Naval, etc.* an emergency preparation for action. [nasalized var. of SCRABBLE] —**scram′bler,** *n.*

scrannel (skrăn′əl), *adj.* *Archaic.* **1.** thin or slight. **2.** squeaky or unmelodious. [cf. Norw. *skran* lean]

Scranton (skrăn′tən), *n.* a city in the U.S., in NE Pennsylvania. 111,443 (1960).

scrap[1] (skrăp), *n., adj., v.,* **scrapped, scrapping.** —*n.* **1.** a small piece or portion; a fragment: *scraps of paper.* **2.** (*pl.*) fragments of food, as those left over after a meal. **3.** a detached piece of something written or printed: *scraps of poetry.* **4.** (*pl.*) the remains of animal fat after the oil has been extracted. **5.** scrap metal. **6.** anything discarded as useless, unwanted or worn-out. —*adj.* **7.** consisting of scraps or fragments: *scrap heap.* **8.** in the form of fragments or remnants of use only for reworking, as metal. **9.** discarded or left over. —*v.t.* **10.** to make into scraps or scrap; break up. **11.** to discard as useless or worthless. [ME *scrappe*, t. Scand.; cf. Icel. *skrap* scraps, trifles, lit., scrapings]

scrap[2] (skrăp), *n., v.i.,* **scrapped, scrapping.** *Slang.* fight or quarrel. [var. of SCRAPE (cf. defs 5, 6, 10)]

scrapbook (skrăp′bo͝ok′), *n.* a blank book in which photographs, newspaper cuttings, etc., are pasted.

scrape (skrāp), *v.,* **scraped, scraping,** *n.* —*v.t.* **1.** to deprive of or free from an outer layer, adhering matter, etc., by drawing or rubbing something, esp. a sharp or rough instrument, over the surface. **2.** to remove (an outer layer, adhering matter, etc.) in this way. **3.** to scratch; produce as by scratching. **4.** to collect by or as by scraping, or laboriously, or with difficulty (fol. by *up* or *together*). **5.** to rub harshly on or across (something). **6.** to draw or rub (a thing) roughly across something. **7.** to level (an unpaved road) with a grader. **8.** **scrape through,** to succeed in by a narrow margin: *he just scraped through his final examinations.* —*v.i.* **9.** to scrape something. **10.** to rub against something gratingly. **11.** to produce a grating and unmusical tone from a string instrument. **12.** to draw back the foot in making a bow. **13.** to practise laborious economy or saving. **14. scrape an acquaintance with somebody,** force one's attentions upon somebody in order to get acquainted with him. **15. bow and scrape,** to behave with exaggerated respect; be servile. **16. scrape through,** to manage to get by with difficulty; succeed by a narrow margin: *it was difficult having no money, but somehow we managed to scrape through.* —*n.* **17.** the act of scraping. **18.** a drawing back of the foot in making a bow. **19.** a scraping sound. **20.** a scraped place. **21.** an embarrassing situation. **22.** a fight; struggle; scrap. [ME, t. Scand.; cf. Icel. *skrapa*]

scraper (skrā′pə), *n.* **1.** one who or that which scrapes. **2.** any of various implements for scraping.

scraperboard (skrā′pə bôd′), *n.* *Art.* a china clay coated cardboard covered with Indian ink, which is scratched to form a design in white against a black background.

scraping (skrā′pĭng), *n.* **1.** the act of one who or that which scrapes. **2.** the sound. **3.** (*usually pl.*) that which is scraped off, up, or together.

scrap iron, old iron used for remelting or reworking.

scrap merchant, 1. a dealer in scrap metal. **2.** a rag-and-bone man.

scrap metal, pieces of old metal that can be reworked, esp. scrap iron.

scrapple (skrăp′l), *n.* *U.S.* a sausage-like preparation of minced pork, herbs, meal, etc., fried in slices. [der. SCRAP[1]]

scrappy (skrăp′ĭ), *adj.*, **-pier, -piest.** **1.** made up of scraps or of odds and ends; fragmentary; disconnected. **2.** *Slang.* given to fighting. —**scrap′pily,** *adv.* —**scrap′piness,** *n.*

scratch (skrăch), *v.t.* **1.** to break or mark slightly by rubbing, scraping, or tearing with something sharp or rough. **2.** to dig, scrape, or to tear (*out, off*, etc.) with the claws, the nails, etc. **3.** to rub or scrape lightly with the fingernails, etc., as to relieve itching. **4.** to rub gratingly, as a match, on something. **5.** to erase or strike out (writing, a name, etc.). **6.** to withdraw (a horse, etc.) from the list of entries in a race or competition. **7.** to write or draw by scraping or cutting into a surface.
—*v.i.* **8.** to use the nails, claws, etc., for tearing, digging, etc. **9.** to relieve itching by rubbing with the nails, etc. **10.** to make a slight grating noise, as a pen. **11.** to manage with difficulty: *scratch along on very little money.* **12.** to withdraw from a contest. **13.** *Billiards.* to commit a scratch.
—*n.* **14.** a mark produced by scratching, such as one on the skin. **15.** a rough mark of a pen, etc.; a scrawl. **16.** an act of scratching. **17.** the sound produced by scratching. **18.** the starting place, starting time, or status of a competitor in a handicap who has no allowance and no penalty. **19.** *Billiards.* **a.** a shot resulting in a penalty. **b.** a fluke. **20.** **from scratch,** from the beginning or from nothing. **21.** **up to scratch,** conforming to a certain standard; satisfactory.
—*adj.* **22.** starting from scratch, or without allowance or penalty, as a competitor. **23.** *Colloq.* done by or dependent on chance: *a scratch shot.* **24.** *Colloq.* gathered hastily and indiscriminately: *a scratch crew.*
[b. obs. *scrat* and *cratch*, both meaning scratch] —**scratch′er,** *n.*

scratches (skrăch′ĭz), *n.pl.* (*construed as sing.*) *Vet. Sci.* a disease of horses, in which dry rifts or chaps appear on the skin near the fetlock, behind the knee or in front of the hock.

scratchy (skrăch′ĭ), *adj.*, **-ier, -iest.** **1.** that scratches: *a scratchy pen.* **2.** consisting of mere scratches. **3.** uneven; haphazard. **4.** suffering from scratches. —**scratch′ily,** *adv.* —**scratch′iness,** *n.*

scrawl (skrôl), *v.t., v.i.* **1.** to write or draw in a sprawling awkward manner. —*n.* **2.** something scrawled, as a letter or a note. **3.** awkward or careless handwriting: *his scrawl is difficult to read.* [special use of obs. *scrawl* sprawl, influenced by SCRIBBLE, etc.] —**scrawl′er,** *n.* —**scrawl′y,** *adj.*

scrawny (skrô′nĭ), *adj.*, **-nier, -niest.** lean; thin; scraggy: *a long scrawny neck.* [var. of *scranny*, var. of SCRANNEL] —**scraw′niness,** *n.* —**Ant.** robust.

screak (skrēk), *v.i.* *U.S. and Dial.* **1.** to screech. **2.** to creak. —*n.* **3.** a screech. [t. Scand.; cf. Icel. *skrǣkja*]

scream (skrēm), *v.i.* **1.** to utter a loud, sharp, piercing cry. **2.** to emit a shrill, piercing sound, as a whistle, etc. **3.** to laugh immoderately. **4.** to make something known by violent, startling words. **5.** to be startlingly conspicuous, used esp. of colours. **6.** **scream for,** to want something desperately. —*v.t.* **7.** to utter with a scream or screams. **8.** to make by screaming: *to scream oneself hoarse.* —*n.* **9.** a loud, sharp, piercing cry. **10.** a shrill, piercing sound. **11.** *Colloq.* someone or something that is very funny. [ME *screme*; orig. uncert.]
—**Syn.** **1.** SCREAM, SHRIEK, SCREECH apply to crying out in a loud, piercing way. To SCREAM is to utter a loud, piercing cry, esp. of pain or fear: *to scream with terror.* The word is used also for a little, barely audible cry given by one who is startled. SHRIEK usually refers to a sharper and briefer cry than SCREAM; when due to fear or pain, it is indicative of more terror or distress; SHRIEK is also used for the loud, shrill, excited cries of women or girls: *to shriek with laughter.* SCREECH emphasizes the disagreeable shrillness and harshness of an outcry; the connotation is lack of dignity: *to screech like an old crone.*

screamer (skrē′mə), *n.* **1.** one who or that which screams. **2.** *Slang.* someone or something causing screams of astonishment, mirth, etc. **3.** *Print. Slang.* an exclamation mark. **4.** any of the long-toed South and Central American birds which constitute the family *Anhimidae*, including *Anhima cornuta* (**horned screamer**) and *Chauna chavaria* and *C. torquata* (both known as **crested screamer**).

screaming (skrē′mĭng), *adj.* **1.** that screams. **2.** startling in effect: *screaming colours.* **3.** causing screams of mirth: *a screaming farce.* —*n.* **4.** the act or sound of one who or that which screams. —**scream′ingly,** *adv.*

scree (skrē), *n.* a steep mass of detritus on the side of a mountain. [t. Scand.; cf. Icel. *skridha* landslip and OE *scrīthan* go, glide]

screech (skrēch), *v.i.* **1.** to utter a harsh, shrill cry. —*v.t.* **2.** to utter with a screech. —*n.* **3.** a harsh, shrill cry. [var. of archaic *scritch*; prob. imit.] —**screech′er,** *n.* —**screech′y,** *adj.* —**Syn.** **1.** See **scream.**

screech owl, any owl with a harsh cry, esp. the barn owl, *Tyto alba.*

screed (skrēd), *n.* **1.** a long speech or piece of writing; harangue. **2.** *Plastering.* **a.** a strip of plaster or wood of the proper thickness, applied to a wall as a guide or gauge for the rest of the work. **b.** the plaster, etc., laid to level off. [ME *screde*, doublet of *shrede*, OE *scrēade* SHRED]

screen (skrēn), *n.* **1.** a covered frame or the like, movable or fixed, serving as a shelter, partition, etc.: *a firescreen.* **2.** an ornamental partition of wood, stone, etc., as in a church. **3.** something affording a surface for displaying films, slides, etc. **4.** films collectively. **5.** (in a television set) the end of a cathode-ray tube on which the visible image is formed. **6.** a sightscreen. **7.** anything that shelters, protects, or conceals: *a screen of secrecy.* **8.** wire mesh serving as protection: *window screens.* **9.** a sieve or riddle, as for grain, sand, etc. **10.** *Mil.* a body of men sent out to cover the movement of an army. **11.** *Naval.* a protective formation of small vessels, as destroyers. **12.** *Physics.* a shield designed to prevent interference between various effects: *electric screens.* **13.** *Photoengraving.* **a.** a transparent plate containing two sets of the fine parallel lines, one crossing the other, used in the halftone process. **b.** a plastic sheet containing a special optical pattern for converting a continuous tone original into a series of dots of differing size.
—*v.t.* **14.** to shelter, protect, or conceal with, or as with, a screen. **15.** to sift by passing through a screen. **16.** to project (pictures, etc.) on a screen. **17.** to photograph with a film camera. **18.** to provide with a screen or screens. **19.** to adapt (a story, play, etc.) for presentation, as a film. **20.** to check the loyalty, character, ability, etc., of applicants, employees, or the like. **21.** **screen off,** to conceal, shut off, behind a screen.
—*v.i.* **22.** to be projected, or suitable for projection, on a screen.
[ME *scren(e)*, t. OF: aphetic m. *escren*, var. of *escrime*, t. OHG: m. *skirm* (G *Schirm*)] —**screen′able,** *adj.* —**screen′er,** *n.* —**Syn.** **7.** See **cover.**

screening (skrē′nĭng), *n.* **1.** the act or work of one who screens. **2.** fluoroscopy. **3.** (*pl.*) matter separated out with a screen.

screenplay (skrēn′plā′), *n.* the script of a film, including details of camera positions and movement, action, dialogue, lighting, etc.

screw (skroo͞), *n.* **1.** a metal device resembling and serving as a nail, having a slotted head and a tapering spiral thread, and driven into wood, etc., with the aid of a screwdriver (**woodscrew**). **2.** a mechanical device consisting of a cylinder having a helical ridge winding round it (**external** or **male screw**). **3.** a corresponding part into which such a device fits when turned, consisting of a cylindrical socket in whose wall is cut a helical groove (**internal** or **female screw**). **4.** something having a spiral form. **5.** a propeller. **6.** *Slang.* pressure; force: *to put the screw on a debtor.* **7.** a little tobacco, salt, etc., in a twisted paper. **8.** a twisting movement; a turn of a screw. **9.** *Slang.* a hard bargainer; a miser. **10.** *Slang.* a broken-down horse. **11.** *Slang.* wages. **12.** *Slang.* a prison warder. **13.** *Taboo. Slang.* sexual intercourse. **14.** **have a screw loose,** *Slang.* to be slightly eccentric; have crazy ideas.
—*v.t.* **15.** to force, press, hold fast, stretch tight, etc., by or as by means of a screw. **16.** to operate or adjust by a screw, as a press. **17.** to attach with a screw or screws: *to screw a bracket to a wall.* **18.** to work (a screw, etc.) by turning. **19.** to twist; contort; distort. **20.** to force: *screw up one's courage.* **21.** to put compulsion on; force (a seller) to lower a price (often fol. by *down*). **22.** *Slang.* to extract or extort. **23.** *Taboo Slang.* (of a man) to have sexual intercourse with.
—*v.i.* **24.** to turn as or like a screw. **25.** to be adapted for being connected or taken apart by means of a screw or screws (fol. by *on, together, off*, etc.). **26.** to turn with a twisting motion. **27.** *Slang.* to practise extortion.
[ME; cf. OF *escro(ue)* nut, MD *schrūve* screw]

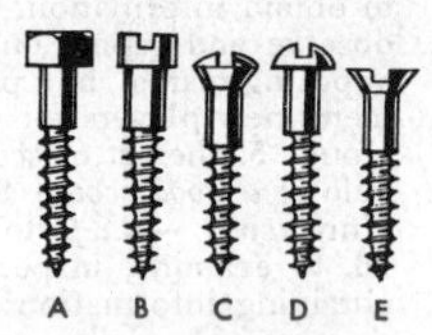

Screws: A, Square-head setscrew; B, Cheese-head setscrew; C, Oval-head woodscrew; D, Round-head woodscrew; E, Flat-head woodscrew

screw axis, *Crystall.* an axis of symmetry about which the atoms in a crystal lattice are arranged.

screwball (skroo͞′bôl′), *U.S. Slang.* —*n.* **1.** an erratic, eccentric, or unconventional person. —*adj.* **2.** erratic, eccentric, or unconventional.

screwdriver (skroo͞′drī′və), *n.* a tool fitting into the slotted head of a screw for driving in or withdrawing it by turning.

screwed (skroo͞d), *adj.* **1.** fastened with a screw or screws. **2.** having grooves like a screw. **3.** twisted; awry. **4.** *Colloq.* drunk; intoxicated.

screw-eye (skroo͞′ī′), *n.* a screw having a ring-shaped head.

screw-jack (skroo͞′jăk′), *n.* a jack which obtains its lifting power by means of a screw. Also, **jackscrew.**

screw-nail (skroo͞′nāl′), *n.* *Chiefly Scot.* a woodscrew.

screw pile, *Civ. Eng.* a bearing pile with a screw tip, turned into the ground with a capstan, used in soft mud or the like, for the foundation of bridges and other constructions.

screw-pine (skroo͞′pīn′), *n.* a pandanus (plant): so called from its leaves, which have a spiral arrangement.

screw-propeller (skroo͞′prə pĕl′ə), *n.* a device consisting of a number of specially shaped blades radiating from a central hub, used to propel a vehicle, as a ship.

screws (scroo͞z), *n. pl.* *Colloq.* rheumatism.

screw thread, **1.** the helical ridge of a screw. **2.** a full turn of the spiral ridge of a screw.

screw-top (skroo͞′tŏp′), *n.* **1.** a type of lid of a jar, bottle, or the like, designed to fit on by screwing. —*adj.* **2.** having a screw-top.

screw-worm (skroo͞′wûm′), *n.* the larva of a dipteran insect, *Callitroga macellaria*, widespread in America, which feeds upon the skin of living domestic animals, occasionally man.

screwy (skroo͞′ĭ), *adj.*, **-ier, -iest.** *Slang.* **1.** eccentric; crazy. **2.** strange; peculiar.

Scriabin (skrĭə′bĭn; *Russ.* skryä′bĭn), *n.* **Aleksandr Nikolaievich** (*Russ.* ə lĭk sän′dər nĭ kä lä′yĭ vĭch), 1872–1915, Russian composer and pianist.

scribal (skrī′bl), *adj.* of, pertaining to, or denoting a scribe.

scribble[1] (skrĭb′l), *v.*, **-bled, -bling,** *n.* —*v.t.* **1.** to write hastily or carelessly: *to scribble a letter.* **2.** to cover with meaningless writing or marks (often fol. by *over*). —*v.i.* **3.** to write literary matter in a hasty, careless way. **4.** to make meaningless marks. —*n.* **5.** a hasty or careless piece of writing or drawing. [ME *scribyl, scrible,* t. ML: m. s. *scrībillāre.* Cf. L *conscrībillāre* scribble]

scribble[2] (skrĭb′l), *v.t.*, **-bled, -bling.** (of wool, cotton, etc.) to card; pass through a scribbler. [t. Flem.: m. *schribbelen,* akin to SCRUB[1]]

scribbler[1] (skrĭb′lə), *n.* **1.** an unimportant writer or author. **2.** one who scribbles.

scribbler[2] (skrĭb′lə), *n.* **1.** a carding machine, as for wool. **2.** one who runs or looks after such a machine.

scribbling block, a block or pad of paper for writing down notes, memoranda, casual thoughts or the like. Also, **scribbling pad.**

scribe[1] (skrīb), *n.*, *v.*, **scribed, scribing.** —*n.* **1.** a penman or copyist, as one who, formerly, made copies of manuscripts, etc. **2.** any of various officials of ancient or former times who performed clerical duties. **3.** *Jewish Hist.* one of a class of teachers who interpreted the Jewish law to the people. **4.** a writer or author. —*v.t.* **5.** *Rare.* to write or write down. [ME, t. L: m. *scrība* writer]

scribe[2] (skrīb), *v.*, **scribed, scribing,** *n.* —*v.t.* **1.** to mark or score (wood, etc.) with a pointed instrument. —*n.* **2.** a pointed instrument for so marking (wood, etc.); scriber. [? aphetic var. of DESCRIBE]

Scribe (*Fr.* skrēb), *n.* **Augustin Eugène** (*Fr.* ō gүs tăN œ-zhĕn′), 1791–1861, French dramatist.

scriber (skrī′bə), *n.* a tool for scribing wood, etc.

scrim (skrĭm), *n.* **1.** a cotton or linen fabric of open weave, used for curtains, etc. **2.** such a fabric, used for cleaning, polishing, etc. **3.** *Theat.* a piece of such fabric, used as a drop to give the effect of opacity, hazy translucency, etc. [orig. uncert.]

scrimmage (skrĭm′ĭj), *n.*, *v.*, **-maged, -maging.** —*n.* **1.** a rough or vigorous struggle. **2. a.** *Rugby.* a scrum. **b.** *Soccer.* any disorganized mix-up. **c.** *American Football.* the action between contesting lines of players when the ball is put in play. —*v.i.*, *v.t.* **3.** to engage in a scrimmage. [var. of *scrimish,* var. of SKIRMISH] —**scrim′mager,** *n.*

scrimp (skrĭmp), *v.t.* **1.** to be sparing of or in; stint. **2.** to keep on short allowance, as of food. —*v.i.* **3.** to use severe economy: *they scrimped on butter as best they could.* —*adj.* **4.** scant. [orig. obscure; ? akin to SHRIMP]

scrimpy (skrĭm′pĭ), *adj.*, **-pier, -piest.** scanty; meagre. —**scrimp′ily,** *adv.* —**scrimp′iness,** *n.*

scrimshank (skrĭm′shăngk′), *v.i.* *Colloq.* to avoid one's work or obligations; shirk.

scrimshaw (skrĭm′shô′), *n.* **1.** carved or scratched work or articles of bone, ivory, steel, wood, etc., made by sailors in leisure times. —*v.t.* **2.** to make (scrimshaw). —*v.i.* **3.** to make scrimshaw. [orig. obscure]

scrip[1] (skrĭp), *n.* **1.** a writing, esp. a receipt or certificate. **2.** a scrap of paper. **3.** *Finance.* shares or stock issued to existing shareholders in a scrip issue. **4.** *Finance.* a certificate that part of the issue price of a debenture, bond, or share has been paid, and setting out the amounts and dates when further sums are due. **5.** *U.S. Colloq.* **a.** paper currency in denominations of less than one dollar, formerly issued in the United States. **b.** such currency as a whole. [var. of SCRIPT]

scrip[2] (skrĭp), *n.* *Archaic.* a bag or wallet carried by wayfarers. [ME *scrippe,* t. Scand.; cf. Icel. *skreppa*]

scrip issue, an issue of stock, etc., where the purchase price is payable by instalments according to the terms of the prospectus.

scripsit (skrĭp′sĭt), *v.* *Latin.* he (she) wrote (it, this).

script (skrĭpt), *n.* **1.** handwriting; handwritten letters or lettering; the characters used in handwriting. **2.** the working text, manuscript, or the like, of a play, film, television programme, etc., or the contents of such a document. **3.** a manuscript or document. **4.** the written work submitted by an examination candidate. **5.** *Law.* **a.** an original document. **b.** a draft of a will or codicil, or written instructions for it. **6.** *Print.* a typeface imitating handwriting. [t. L: s. *scriptum,* neut. pp., (something) written, r. ME *scrit,* t. OF: aphetic m. *escrit*]

Script., **1.** Scriptural. **2.** Scripture.

scriptorium (skrĭp tô′rĭ əm), *n.*, *pl.* **-toriums, -toria** (-tô′rĭ ə). a room in a monastery set apart for the writing or copying of manuscripts. [t. ML, prop. neut. of L *scriptōrius* of writing]

scriptural (skrĭp′chə rəl), *adj.* of, pertaining to, or in accordance with the Scriptures. Also, **Scriptural.** —**scrip′turally,** *adv.*

Scripture (skrip′chə), *n.* **1.** the sacred writings of the Old and the New Testaments or of either of them (often called **Holy Scripture** or **the Scriptures**); Holy Writ; the Bible. **2.** (*l.c.*) any writing or book, esp. of a sacred nature. [ME *scriptur,* t. L: s. *scriptūra* writing]

scrivener (skrĭv′nə), *n.* *Archaic.* **1.** a professional or public writer; a clerk. **2.** a notary. [ME, f. obs. *scriveyn* (t. OF) + -ER[1]]

scrobiculate (skrō bĭk′yo͝o lĭt, -lāt′), *adj.* *Bot., Zool.* furrowed or pitted. [f. s. LL *scrobiculus* (dim. of *scrobis* ditch, trench) + -ATE[1]]

scrod (skrŏd), *n.* *U.S.* a young codfish, esp. one that is split for cooking. [? akin to SHRED]

scrofula (skrŏf′yo͝o lə), *n.* *Pathol.* a constitutional disorder of a tuberculous nature, characterized chiefly by swelling and degeneration of the lymphatic glands, esp. of the neck, and by inflammation of the joints, etc.; king's evil. [t. ML, sing. of L *scrōfulae* glandular swelling]

scrofulous (skrŏf′yo͝o ləs), *adj.* **1.** pertaining to, of the nature of, or affected with scrofula. **2.** morally corrupt. —**scrof′ulously,** *adv.* —**scrof′ulousness,** *n.*

scroll (skrōl), *n.* **1.** a roll of parchment or paper, esp. one with writing on it. **2.** something, esp. an ornament, resembling a partly unrolled sheet of paper or having a spiral or coiled form. **3.** the ornamental carving, resembling this, at the head of a violin or similar instrument. **4.** a piece of writing; a list or schedule. —*v.t.* **5.** to cut into scrolls, as wooden ornamentation. **6.** to write, as in a scroll. —*v.i.* **7.** formed into, as, or like a scroll. [ME *scrowle,* var. of *scrowe,* t. AF: m. *escrowe*; of Gmc orig. and akin to SHRED]

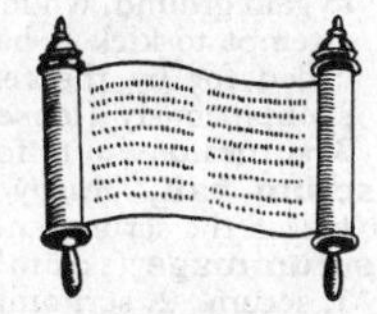
Scroll (def. 1)

scroll-saw (skrōl′sô′), *n.* **1.** a narrow saw mounted vertically in a frame and operated with an up-and-down motion, used for cutting curved ornamental designs. **2.** such a saw mounted in a power-driven machine.

scrollwork (skrōl′wûk′), *n.* **1.** decorative work in which scroll forms are important. **2.** ornamental work cut out with a scroll-saw.

Scrooge (skroo͞j), *n.* a miserly, ill-tempered person. [after Ebenezer *Scrooge,* a character in Dickens's '*Christmas Carol*']

scroop (skroo͞p), *v.i.* **1.** to emit a harsh, grating sound. —*n.* **2.** a scrooping sound. [imit.]

scrophulariaceous (skrŏf′yo͝o lĕə′rĭ ā′shəs), *adj.* belonging to the *Scrophulariaceae,* or figwort family of plants, including the snapdragon, foxglove, toadflax, mullein, eyebright, etc. [f. s. NL *Scrophulāria* the typical genus (reputed remedy for scrofula) + -ACEOUS]

scrotum (skrō′təm), *n.*, *pl.* **-ta** (-tə). *Anat.* the pouch of skin that contains the testicles and their coverings. [t. L] —**scro′tal,** *adj.*

scrouge (skrouj, skroo͞j), *v.t.*, *v.i.*, **scrouged, scrouging.** *Colloq. or Dial.* to squeeze; crowd.

scrounge (skrounj), *v.*, **scrounged, scrounging.** *Slang.* —*v.i.* **1.** to borrow, sponge, or pilfer. **2.** to gather, as by foraging; search out (often fol. by *around*). —*v.t.* **3.** to obtain by borrowing, scrounging, or pilfering. [var. of d. *scringe* to glean. ? akin to SCRIMP] —**scroung′er,** *n.*

scrub[1] (skrŭb), *v.*, **scrubbed, scrubbing,** *n.* —*v.t.* **1.** to rub hard with a brush, cloth, etc., or against a rough surface, in washing. **2.** to cleanse (a gas). **3.** *Slang.* to cancel. —*v.i.* **4.** to cleanse things by hard rubbing. **5.** *Horseracing Slang.* (of a jockey) to move the whip or arms rhythmically to and fro, to encourage the horse during the final stretch of the race. —*n.* **6.** the act of scrubbing. [ME *scrobbe*, appar. t. MD: m. *schrubben, schrobben* scratch, rub, scrub]

scrub[2] (skrŭb), *n.* **1.** low trees or shrubs, collectively. **2.** a large area covered with scrub, as the Australian bush, or American sagebrush. **3.** an animal of common or inferior breeding. **4.** a mean, insignificant person. **5.** anything undersized or inferior. **6.** *U.S. Sport.* a scrub team, etc., or a member of it. —*adj.* **7.** stunted or undersized; inferior. **8.** *U.S. Sport.* composed of substitute or untrained players or members, as a team, etc.; scratch. **9.** belonging or pertaining to such a team, etc. **10.** participated in by such teams, as a game. [var. of SHRUB[1]]

scrubber[1] (skrŭb′ə), *n.* **1.** one who or that which scrubs. **2.** an apparatus for purifying gases. **3.** *Slang.* a promiscuous or mercenary girl; a girl of loose morals (used as a term of abuse).

scrubber[2] (skrŭb′ə), *n.* *Austral.* a beast which has taken to the bush or scrub and run wild.

scrubbing-board (skrŭb′ĭng bôd′), *n.* a board having a corrugated surface on which to scrub clothes. Also, **scrub-board.**

scrubbing-brush (skrŭb′ĭng brŭsh′), *n.* a brush used for scrubbing, esp. floors, clothes, or very dirty hands. Also, **scrub-brush.**

scrub-bird (skrŭb′bûd′), *n.* either of two Australian species of birds of the genus *Atrichornis* akin to the lyrebird.

scrubby (skrŭb′ĭ), *adj.*, **-bier, -biest.** **1.** low or stunted, as trees. **2.** consisting of or covered with stunted trees, etc., or scrub. **3.** undersized or inferior, as animals. **4.** wretched; shabby. —**scrub′biness,** *n.*

scruff[1] (skrŭf), *n.* the nape or back of the neck. [var. of d. *scuft*, t. D: m. *schoft* horse's withers]

scruff[2] (skrŭf), *n.* **1.** *Metall.* dross formed during tin-plating. **2.** *Colloq.* a scruffy person. [metathetic var. of SCURF]

scruffy (skrŭf′ĭ), *adj.* *Colloq.* unkempt or dirty; shabby.

scrum (skrŭm), *n.*, *v.*, **scrummed, scrummed.** *Rugby Football.* —*n.* **1.** a method of restarting play after a rule infringement, in which the opposing forwards pack together and push in formation, heads down, in an attempt to gain ground, while the ball is thrown in and the hookers attempt to kick it back to their team-mates. It may be called for by the referee (**set scrum**), or it may form spontaneously (**loose scrum**). **2.** the formation. —*v.t.* **3. scrum down,** to form a scrum. [short for SCRUMMAGE]

scrum half, *Rugby Football.* the player who puts the ball in the scrum, and tries to catch it as it emerges.

scrummage (skrŭm′ĭj), *n.*, *v.t.*, *v.i.*, **-maged, -maging.** **1.** scrum. **2.** scrimmage. —**scrum′mager,** *n.*

scrump (skrŭmp), *v.i.*, *v.t.* to pilfer (apples); rob (orchards). [d. var. of SCRIMP]

scrumptious (skrŭmp′shəs), *adj.* *Colloq.* deliciously tasty; superlatively fine or nice; splendid: *to have a scrumptious time.* [orig. d., meaning 'stingy', ult. der. SCRIMP]

scrumpy (skrŭm′pĭ), *n.* *Dial.* rough, dry farm cider, a speciality of SW England. [der. SCRUMP, SCRIMP in obs. adj. sense 'withered', the apples used in making such cider being withered]

scrunch (skrŭnch), *v.t.*, *v.i.* **1.** to crunch; crush. —*n.* **2.** the act or sound of scrunching. [var. of CRUNCH]

scruple (skrōō′pl), *n.*, *v.*, **-pled, -pling.** —*n.* **1.** hesitation or reluctance from conscientious or other restraining reasons. **2.** a very small portion or amount. **3.** a unit of weight equal to 20 grains or $\frac{1}{3}$ of a drachm, apothecaries' weight. **4.** an ancient Roman unit of weight equivalent to $\frac{1}{24}$ of an ounce or $\frac{1}{288}$ of an as or pound. —*v.i.* **5.** to have scruples. —*v.t.* **6.** *Obs.* to have scruples about; hesitate at. [t. L: m. s. *scrūpulus*, lit., small stone, fig., anxiety, doubt, scruple (dim. of *scrūpus* sharp stone)]

scrupulous (skrōō′pyōō ləs), *adj.* **1.** having scruples; having or showing a strict regard for what is right. **2.** punctiliously or minutely careful, precise, or exact. —**scrupulosity** (skrōō′pyōō lŏs′ĭ tĭ), **scru′pulousness,** *n.* —**scru′pulously,** *adv.*

—**Syn.** 2. SCRUPULOUS, PUNCTILIOUS imply abiding exactly by rules. SCRUPULOUS implies conscientious carefulness in attending to details: *scrupulous attention to details.* PUNCTILIOUS suggests strictness, preciseness, and rigidity, esp. in observance of social conventions. —**Ant.** 2. careless.

scrutable (skrōō′tə bl), *adj.* that may be penetrated or understood by investigation.

scrutator (skrōō tā′tə), *n.* one who investigates.

scrutineer (skrōō′tĭ nĭə′), *n.* an official examiner, esp. of votes at an election.

scrutinize (skrōō′tĭ nīz′), *v.t.*, **-nized, -nizing.** to examine closely or critically. Also, **scrutinise.** —**scru′tiniz′er,** *n.* —**scru′tiniz′ingly,** *adv.*

scrutiny (skrōō′tĭ nĭ), *n.*, *pl.* **-nies.** **1.** searching examination or investigation; minute inquiry. **2.** a searching look. [t. LL: m. s. *scrūtinium*] —**Syn.** 1. See **examination.**

scry (skrī), *v.*, **scried, scrying.** *Archaic.* —*v.t.* **1.** to perceive, esp. by crystal-gazing. —*v.i.* **2.** to practise crystal-gazing. [var. of DESCRY]

scuba (skyōō′bə), *n.* a portable breathing device for free-swimming divers, consisting of a mouthpiece joined by hoses to one or two tanks of compressed air which are strapped on the back. [f. *s(elf-) c(ontained) u(nderwater) b(reathing) a(pparatus)*]

scud (skŭd), *v.*, **scudded, scudding,** *n.* —*v.i.* **1.** to run or move quickly or hurriedly. **2.** *Naut.* to run before a gale with little or no sail set. —*n.* **3.** the act of scudding. **4.** clouds, spray, or the like, driven by the wind; a driving shower; a gust of wind. **5.** low drifting clouds appearing beneath a cloud from which precipitation is falling. [t. Scand.; cf. Norw. *skudda* push]

Scudéry (*Fr.* skʏ dė rē′), *n.* **Magdeleine de** (*Fr.* măg də-lĕn′ də), 1607–1701, French novelist.

scudo (skōō′dō), *n.*, *pl.* **-di** (-dē). any of various former gold and silver coins of Italian states. [t. It., g. L *scūtum* shield]

scuff (skŭf), *v.t.* **1.** to scrape with the feet. **2.** to mar by scraping or hard use, as shoes, furniture, etc. —*v.i.* **3.** to walk without raising the feet; shuffle. —*n.* **4.** the act or sound of scuffing. **5.** a type of slipper that does not have a quarter or a counter. [? short for SCUFFLE]

scuffle (skŭf′əl), *v.*, **-fled, -fling,** *n.* —*v.i.* **1.** to struggle or fight in a scrambling, confused manner. **2.** to go or move in hurried confusion. **3.** to move at a shuffle; scuff. —*n.* **4.** a confused struggle or fight. **5.** a shuffling: *a scuffle of feet.* **6.** *U.S. and Dial.* a spadelike hoe which is pushed instead of pulled. [? of Scand. orig.; cf. Sw. *skuffa* push] —**scuf′fler,** *n.*

scull (skŭl), *n.* **1. a.** an oar worked from side to side over the stern of a boat as a means of propulsion. **b.** one of a pair of oars operated, one on each side, by one person. **2.** a boat propelled by a scull or sculls, esp. a light racing boat propelled by one rower with a pair of oars. **3.** (*pl.*) a sculling race. **4.** an act of sculling. —*v.t.* **5.** to propel or convey by means of a scull or sculls. —*v.i.* **6.** to propel a boat with a scull or sculls. [ME; orig. unknown] —**scull′er,** *n.*

scullery (skŭl′ə rĭ), *n.*, *pl.* **-leries.** **1.** a small room where the rough, dirty work of a kitchen is done. **2.** the place in which kitchen utensils are cleaned and kept. [ME *squillerye*, t. OF: m. *escuelerie*, ult. der. *escuele* dish, g. L *scutella* salver]

scullion (skŭl′yən), *n.* *Archaic.* **1.** a kitchen servant who does menial work. **2.** a low or contemptible person. [ME *sculyon*, ? t. OF: m. *escouillon* dishcloth]

sculp (skŭlp), *v.t.*, *v.i.* to sculpt. [t. L: s. *sculpere* carve]

sculpin (skŭl′pĭn), *n.* **1.** a small freshwater fish of the genus *Cottus* (family *Cottidae*), with a large head armed on each side with one or more spines; bullhead. **2.** any marine fish of the same family. [? t. NL: m. s. *scorpæna*. See SCORPAENOID]

sculpsit (skŭlp′sĭt), *v.* *Latin.* (he or she) engraved, carved, or sculptured (it).

sculpt (skŭlpt), *v.t.* **1.** to make (a sculpture). **2.** to make a sculpture of (some person or thing). —*v.i.* **3.** to make a sculpture. **4.** to practise sculpture. [t. F: s. *sculpter*, t. L: m. s. *sculptus* (pp. of *sculpere*). See SCULP]

sculptor (skŭlp′tə), *n.* one who practises the art of sculpture. [t. L] —**sculptress** (skŭlp′trĭs), *n. fem.*

sculpture (skŭlp′chə), *n.*, *v.*, **-tured, -turing.** —*n.* **1.** the fine art of forming figures or designs in relief, in intaglio, or in the round by cutting marble, wood, granite, etc., by fashioning plastic materials, by modelling in clay, or by making moulds for casting in bronze or other metal. **2.** such work collectively. **3.** a piece of such work. —*v.t.* **4.** to carve, make, or execute by sculpture, as a figure, design, etc.; represent in sculpture. **5.** *Phys. Geog.* to change the form of (the land surface) by erosion. [ME, t. L: m. *sculptūra*] —**sculp′tural,** *adj.* —**sculp′turally,** *adv.*

sculpturesque (skŭlp′chə rĕsk′), *adj.* in the manner of, or suggesting, sculpture: *sculpturesque beauty.* —**sculp′turesque′ly,** *adv.* —**sculp′turesque′ness,** *n.*

scum (skŭm), *n.*, *v.*, **scummed, scumming.** —*n.* **1.** a film of foul or extraneous matter on a liquid. **2.** refuse or offscourings: *scum of the earth.* **3.** low, worthless persons. **4.** the scoria of molten metals. —*v.t.* **5.** to remove the scum from. **6.** to remove as scum. —*v.i.* **7.** to form scum; become covered with scum. [ME, t. MD: m. *schūme*, c. G *Schaum* foam]

scumble (skŭm′bl), *v.*, **-bled, -bling,** *n. Painting and Drawing.* —*v.t.*, *v.i.* **1.** to modify the effect of (a painting) by overlaying parts of it with a thin application of opaque or semi-opaque colour. —*n.* **2.** application of such colour. **3.** the colour used. **4.** the effect produced by this technique. [der. SCUM]

scummy (skŭm′ĭ), *adj.*, **-mier, -miest. 1.** consisting of or having scum. **2.** *Colloq.* worthless; despicable.

Scunthorpe (skŭn′thôp), *n.* a town in England, in Lincolnshire. 67,324 (1961).

scupper (skŭp′ə), *n.* **1.** *Naut.* an opening in the side of a ship at or just below the level of the deck, to allow water to run off. —*v.t.* **2.** to sink (a ship) deliberately. **3.** *Slang.* to overwhelm; surprise and massacre. **4.** *Slang.* to deprive of any chance of success. [orig. uncert.]

scurf (skûf), *n.* **1.** the scales or small shreds of epidermis that are continually exfoliated from the skin; dandruff. **2.** any scaly matter or incrustation on a surface. [ME and OE, t. Scand.; cf. Dan. *skurv*, c. OE *sceorf*] —**scurf′y,** *adj.*

scurrile (skŭ′rīl), *adj.* scurrilous. Also, **scurril** (skŭ′rĭl). [t. L: m. s. *scurrīlis*]

scurrility (skŭ rĭl′ĭ tĭ), *n.*, *pl.* **-ties. 1.** scurrilous quality. **2.** a scurrilous remark or attack.

scurrilous (skŭ′rĭ ləs), *adj.* **1.** grossly or indecently abusive: *a scurrilous attack.* **2.** characterized by or using low buffoonery; coarsely jocular or derisive: *a scurrilous jest.* [see SCURRILE, -OUS] —**scur′rilously,** *adv.* —**scur′rilousness,** *n.*

scurry (skŭ′rĭ), *v.*, **-ried, -rying,** *n.*, *pl.* **-ries.** —*v.i.* **1.** to go or move quickly or in haste. —*v.t.* **2.** to send hurrying along. —*n.* **3.** a scurrying rush: *we heard the scurry of little feet down the stairs.* **4.** a flurry or flittering passage, as of snow, leaves, birds, etc. **5.** a fairly short run or race. [abstracted from HURRY-SCURRY]

scurvy (skû′vĭ), *n.*, *adj.*, **-vier, -viest.** —*n.* **1.** *Pathol.* a disease marked by swollen and bleeding gums, livid spots on the skin, prostration, etc., due to a diet lacking in vitamin C. —*adj.* **2.** low, mean, or contemptible: *a scurvy trick.* [orig. adj., f. SCURF + -Y[1]] —**scur′vily,** *adv.* —**scur′viness,** *n.*

scurvy grass, a cruciferous plant, *Cochlearia officinalis*, purported to be a remedy for scurvy.

scut (skŭt), *n.* a short tail, esp. that of a hare, rabbit, or deer. [t. Scand.; cf. Icel. *skott* tail]

scutage (skyo͞o′tĭj), *n.* (in the feudal system) a payment or tax levied on a fee-holding knight, esp. one exacted in lieu of military service. [late ME, t. ML: m. s. *scūtāgium*, der. L *scūtum* shield]

Scutari (sko͞o′tə rĭ, sko͞o tä′rĭ), *n.* **1.** Also, **Skutari.** Turkish, **Usküdar.** a section of Istanbul, Turkey, on the Asiatic shore of the Bosporus. 116,195 (1965). **2.** Albanian, **Shkodër.** a town in NW Albania, on Lake Scutari: a former capital of Albania. 45,925 (est. 1964). **3. Lake,** a lake between NW Albania and Yugoslavia. ab. 135 sq. mi.

scutate (skyo͞o′tāt), *adj.* **1.** *Bot.* formed like a round buckler. **2.** *Zool.* having scutes, shields, or large scales. [t. L: m. s. *scūtātus* having a shield] —**scuta′tion,** *n.*

scutch[1] (skŭch), *v.t.* **1.** to dress (flax) by beating. **2.** to thresh. —*n.* Also, **scutch′er** (for defs 3, 4, 5). **3.** a device for scutching flax fibre. **4.** one who scutches flax fibres. **5.** a thresher. **6.** a flat double-edged cutting head with a handle set perpendicularly to the cutting edges, used in trimming brick. [cf. OF *escousser* shake]

scutch[2] (skŭch), *n.* the couch-grass, *Agropyron refens.*

scutcheon (skŭch′ən), *n.* **1.** an escutcheon. **2.** *Zool.* a scute.

scute (skyo͞ot), *n. Zool.* **1.** a dermal plate, as on an armadillo, turtle, etc. **2.** a large scale. [t. L: m. s. *scūtum* shield]

scutellate (skyo͞o′tĭ lāt′, -lĭt), *adj. Zool.* **1.** having scutes. **2.** formed into a scutellum. Also, **scu′tellat′ed.** [t. NL: m. s. *scūtellātus.* See SCUTELLUM, -ATE[1]]

scutellation (skyo͞o′tĭ lā′shən), *n. Zool.* **1.** scutellate state or formation; a scaly covering, as on a bird's leg. **2.** arrangement of scutella or scales.

scutellum (skyo͞o tĕl′əm), *n.*, *pl.* **-tella** (-tĕl′ə). *Zool.*, *Bot.* a small plate, scutum, or other shieldlike part. [t. NL, irreg. dim. of L *scūtum* shield]

scutiform (skyo͞o′tĭ fôm′), *adj.* shield-shaped. [t. NL: s. *scūtiformis*, f. L *scūti-* shield + *-formis* -FORM]

scutter (skŭt′ə), *v.i.*, *n.* *Chiefly Dial.* scurry. [var. of SCUTTLE[2]]

scuttle[1] (skŭt′l), *n.* **1.** a coalscuttle; a coal hod. **2.** a large basket. [ME and OE *scutel*, orig., a dish or platter, t. L: m. s. *scutella*]

scuttle[2] (skŭt′l), *v.*, **-tled, -tling,** *n.* —*v.i.* **1.** to run with quick, hasty steps; hurry (often fol. by *off*, *away*, etc.). —*n.* **2.** a quick pace; a short, hurried run. [? var. of *scuddle*, freq. of SCUD]

scuttle[3] (skŭt′l), *n.*, *v.*, **-tled, -tling.** —*n.* **1.** a small rectangular opening in a ship's deck, with a movable lid or cover. **2.** a similar opening in a ship's side. **3.** the part of a motor vehicle between the bonnet and the body. —*v.t.* **4.** to cut a hole or holes through the bottom, sides, or deck of (a ship or boat) for any purpose, esp. through the bottom or sides for the purpose of sinking it. **5.** to sink (a vessel) by cutting a hole below the waterline or opening the seacocks. [late ME *skottell* hatchway lid, appar. der. D *schutten* to shut. Cf. F *écoutille*, Sp. *escotilla* hatchway]

scuttlebutt (skŭt′l bŭt′), *n.* **1.** *Naut.* a cask having a hole cut in it for the introduction of a cup or dipper, and used to hold drinking water. **2.** *U.S. Slang.* rumour; gossip.

scutum (skyo͞o′təm), *n.*, *pl.* **-ta** (-tə). **1.** *Zool.* scute (def. 1). **2.** *Rom. Hist.* a large, oblong shield, as of heavy-armed legionaries. [t. L: shield]

Scylla (sĭl′ə), *n.* **1.** Italian, **Scilla** (*It.* shĕl′lȧ). a dangerous rock on the Italian side of the Strait of Messina, facing Charybdis, a whirlpool on the Sicilian side, both personified in classical mythology as female monsters. **2. between Scylla and Charybdis,** between two equal evils or dangers, either one of which can be safely avoided only by risking the other.

scyphiform (sī′fĭ fôm′), *adj. Bot.* shaped like a cup or goblet.

scyphistoma (sī fĭs′tə mə), *n.* the polyp stage of a jellyfish.

scyphozoan (sī′fə zō′ən), *n.* one of the *Scyphozoa*, a class of coelenterates comprising the larger medusae or jellyfishes. [t. NL: f. *Scyphozo(a)* (f. m. Gk *skypho-*, comb. form of *skýphos* cup, can + *-zoa* -ZOA) + -AN]

scyphus (sī′fəs), *n.*, *pl.* **-phi** (-fī). a large ancient Greek drinking cup. [NL, special use of L *scyphus* goblet, t. Gk: m. *skýphos* can, cup]

scythe (sīth), *n.*, *v.*, **scythed, scything.** —*n.* **1.** an agricultural implement consisting of a long, curved blade fastened at an angle to a handle, for mowing grass, etc., by hand. —*v.t.*, *v.i.* **2.** to cut or mow with a scythe. [ME *sith*, OE *sīthe*, c. Icel. *sigdh*; spelling *sc* by pseudo-etymological assoc. with L *scindere* cut]

Scythia (sĭth′ĭ ə), *n.* the ancient name of an undefined region in SE Europe and Asia, lying N and E of the Black and Caspian seas: now part of the Soviet Union.

Scythian (sĭth′ĭ ən), *adj.* **1.** pertaining to Scythia, its people, or their language. —*n.* **2.** a native or inhabitant of Scythia. **3.** an extinct Iranian language.

sd, sound.

s.d., sine die.

S.D., **1.** Senior Deacon. **2.** South Dakota.

S. Dak., South Dakota.

'sdeath (zdĕth), *interj. Archaic.* (a reduced form of *God's death*, used as an oath.)

se-, a prefix applied mainly to stems not used as words, having a general meaning of setting apart or taking away, as in *seclude, seduce.* [t. L]

Se, *Chem.* selenium.

SE, **1.** South-east. **2.** South-eastern. Also, **S.E.**

sea (sē), *n.* **1.** the salt waters that cover the greater part of the earth's surface. **2.** a division of these waters, of considerable extent, more or less definitely marked off by land boundaries: *the North Sea.* **3.** one of the seven seas. **4.** a large lake or landlocked body of water. **5.** the turbulence of the ocean or other body of water as caused by the wind; the waves. **6.** a large, heavy wave or swell: *heavy seas rocked the boat.* **7.** one of various more or less clearly defined areas on the surface of the moon, formerly thought to be areas of water. **8.** a widely extended, copious, or overwhelming quantity: *a sea of faces, a sea of troubles.* **9.** Some special noun phrases are:
at sea, **1.** out on the ocean. **2.** in a state of perplexity.
by sea, on a ship.
follow the sea, to follow a nautical career.
go to sea, **1.** to set out upon a voyage. **2.** to take up a nautical career.
half seas over, drunk.
the high seas, the sea away from land, esp. outside territorial waters.
put to sea, to set out from port.
—*adj.* **10.** of, pertaining to, or adapted for the sea.
[ME *see*, OE *sǣ*, c. D *zee*, G *See*, Icel. *sǣr*, Goth. *saiws*]

sea air, the air or atmosphere of the sea or seacoast, considered to be beneficial to the health.

sea-anchor (sē′ăng′kə), *n.* a floating anchor used at sea to prevent a ship from drifting or to keep its head to the wind: commonly consisting of a framed cone of canvas dragged along with its large open base towards the ship.

sea-anemone (sē′ə nĕm′ə nĭ), *n.* any of the common marine animals of the phylum *Coelenterata*, class *Anthozoa*, of sedentary habits, having a columnar body topped by a disc bearing one or more circles of tentacles.

sea area, any one of the 28 meteorological divisions designating areas of the coastal waters of the British Isles; used in weather forecasts for shipping.

sea-aster (sē′ăs′tə), *n.* a perennial composite herb with yellow discs and purple rays, *Aster tripolium*, common in saline situations of the coast and inland of Europe and Asia.

seabag (sē′băg′), *n.* a bag, usually of canvas, closed at the top by a string, used by sailors and others for stowing kit; a nautical kitbag.

sea-bank (sē′băngk′), *n.* **1.** an embankment to keep back the sea. **2.** the seashore.

sea-bass (sē′băs′), *n.* any of a number of marine serranoid fishes, as *Morone labrax* of the N Atlantic and Mediterranean.

sea-bean (sē′bēn′), *n.* **1.** any of various beans or seeds washed up by the sea, often after being carried for great distances. **2.** the operculum of any of various molluscs.

seabed (sē′bĕd′), *n.* the ground under the sea or an area of sea.

Seabee (sē′bē′), *n.* *U.S.* a member of the construction battalions of the U.S. Navy, established in Dec. 1941, to build landing facilities, airfields, etc., in combat areas. [alter. of *C.B.*, abbreviation for *Construction Battalion.*]

seabird (sē′bûd′), *n.* a bird frequenting the sea or coast.

sea-biscuit (sē′bĭs′kĭt), *n.* ship's biscuit; hardtack.

seablite (sē′blīt′), *n.* any of several plants belonging to the chenopodiaceous genus *Suaeda*, as *S. maritima*, an annual herb widespread in salt marshes.

seaboard (sē′bôd′), *Chiefly U.S.* —*n.* **1.** the line where land and sea meet; the seashore. —*adj.* **2.** bordering on or adjoining the sea.

seaborn (sē′bôn′), *adj.* born in or of the sea; produced in or by the sea.

seaborne (sē′bôn′), *adj.* conveyed by sea; carried on the sea.

sea-bread (sē′brĕd′), *n.* ship's biscuit; hardtack.

sea-bream (sē′brēm′), *n.* **1.** any of a number of British, South African, or Australian marine sparoid food fishes, as the **common sea-bream,** *Pagellus centrodontus*, of Europe. **2.** any sparoid fish.

sea-breeze (sē′brēz′), *n.* a thermally produced wind blowing during the day from the cool ocean surface on to the adjoining warm land.

sea-buckthorn (sē′bŭk′thôn′), *n.* an elaeagnaceous shrub with narrow silvery leaves, *Hippophaë rhamnoides*, widespread in coastal regions of Europe and temperate Asia.

sea-butterfly (sē′bŭt′ə flī′), *n.* a pteropod mollusc, having feet with flat lateral lobes resembling the wings of a butterfly.

sea-campion (sē′kăm′pyən), *n.* a perennial caryophyllaceous herb with white flowers, *Silene maritima*, which occurs on the coast and inland on mountains of W Europe.

sea-canary (sē′kə nĕə′rĭ), *n.* the white whale, *Delphinapterus leucas*, which has a trilling voice.

sea-captain (sē′kăp′tĭn), *n.* the master of a ship, esp. a merchantman.

sea change, 1. a complete or radical transformation. **2.** a change brought about by the sea.

sea-chest (sē′chĕst′), *n.* a chest used, esp. formerly, by sailors to store kit.

sea-coal (sē′kōl′), *n.* **1.** *Obs.* coal brought by sea (distinguished from *charcoal*). **2.** coal washed up by the sea.

seacoast (sē′kōst′), *n.* the land immediately adjacent to the sea.

sea-cock (sē′kŏk′), *n.* **1.** a valve in the hull of a ship for admitting water, as to a ballast tank. **2.** a gurnard.

sea-cow (sē′kou′), *n.* **1.** any sirenian, as the manatee, dugong, etc. **2.** *Obs.* the hippopotamus.

sea-crayfish (sē′krā′fĭsh′), *n.* the spiny lobster.

sea-cucumber (sē′kyōō′kŭm′bə), *n.* a holothurian.

sea-dog (sē′dŏg′), *n.* **1.** a sailor, esp. one of long experience. **2.** the harbour seal.

sea-dragon (sē′drăg′ən), *n.* **1.** the dragonet. **2.** any of various pipefish, esp. the *Phycidurus eques* of Australian shores.

sea-duck (sē′dŭk′), *n.* any diving duck of the subfamily *Aythyinae*, including the scaups, goldeneyes, scoters, eiders, etc., found principally on salt water.

sea-eagle (sē′ē′gl), *n.* any of various eagles of the genus *Haliaetus* which feed on fish, esp. the **grey sea-eagle,** *H. albicilla*, of the Old World and Greenland.

sea-ear (sē′ĭə′), *n.* abalone.

sea-elephant (sē′ĕl′ĭ fənt), *n.* the elephant seal.

sea-fan (sē′făn′), *n.* any of certain anthozoans, esp. *Gorgonia flabellum* of the West Indies, in which the colony assumes a fanlike form.

seafarer (sē′fĕə′rə), *n.* **1.** a sailor. **2.** a traveller on the sea.

seafaring (sē′fĕə′rĭng), *adj.* **1.** that travels by sea. **2.** following the sea as a calling. —*n.* **3.** the business or calling of a sailor. **4.** travelling by sea.

sea-feather (sē′fĕth′ə), *n.* any of various alcyonarians having a plume-like branched skeleton.

sea-fight (sē′fīt′), *n.* a fight between ships at sea.

sea-floor (sē′flô′), *n.* the seabed.

sea-foam (sē′fōm′), *n.* **1.** the foam of the sea. **2.** meerschaum.

sea-fog (sē′fŏg′), *n.* a thick fog common along coastlines, caused by a difference between land and sea temperatures.

sea-food (sē′fōōd′), *n.* any saltwater fish or shellfish which is used for food.

seafowl (sē′foul′), *n.* a seabird.

sea-fox (sē′fŏks′), *n.* the thresher shark.

seafront (sē′frŭnt′), *n.* **1.** the side or edge of land and buildings bordering on the sea. **2.** a road or promenade at a seaside town, running along the edge of the sea.

seagirt (sē′gût′), *adj.* surrounded by the sea.

sea-god (sē′gŏd′), *n.* a god, as the Roman Neptune, having power over the sea or a part of the sea. —**sea′-god′dess,** *n. fem.*

seagoing (sē′gō′ĭng), *adj.* **1.** designed or fit for going to sea, as a vessel. **2.** going to sea; seafaring.

sea-gooseberry (sē′gōōz′bə rĭ, -brĭ), *n.* a rounded pelagic ctenophore, esp. of the genera *Pleurobrachia* and *Hormiphora*, of British coastal waters.

sea green, a clear, light bluish green (the colour of the sea on a clear day). —**sea-green′,** *adj.*

seagull (sē′gŭl′), *n.* a gull, esp. any of the marine species.

Seaham (sē′əm), *n.* a seaport in England, in Durham. 26,048 (1961).

sea hard-grass (häd′gräs′), a small annual grass, *Parapholis strigosa*, of coastal salt marshes in W Europe.

sea-hawk (sē′hôk′), *n.* the skua.

sea-heath (sē′hēth′), *n.* a small tough perennial with minute leaves and pink flowers, *Frankenia laevis*, occurring on salt marshes in Europe and W Asia.

sea-hedgehog (sē′hĕj′hŏg′), *n.* **1.** a sea-urchin. **2.** a globefish.

sea-holly (sē′hŏl′ĭ), *n.* the eryngo (plant), *Eryngium maritimum.*

seahorse (sē′hôs′), *n.* **1.** a fish (genus *Hippocampus*) of the pipefish family, with a prehensile tail and a beaked head that is turned at right angles to the body. **2.** a fabled marine animal with the foreparts of a horse and the hinder parts of a fish. **3.** a walrus.

Seahorse, *Hippocampus hippocampus* (Ab. 5 in. long)

sea-hound (sē′hound′), *n.* a dogfish.

sea-island (sē′ī′lənd), *adj.* **1.** of a group of islands (**Sea Islands**) off South Carolina and Georgia. **2.** denoting a long-staple variety of cotton grown on these islands and elsewhere, or the plant producing it.

sea-kale (sē′kāl′), *n.* a broad-leaved, maritime, cruciferous plant, *Crambe maritima*, of Europe, used as a potherb.

sea-king (sē′kĭng′), *n.* one of the piratical Scandinavian chiefs who ravaged the coasts of medieval Europe. [trans. of Icel. *sǣkonungr*. Cf. OE *sǣcyning*]

seal[1] (sēl), *n.* **1.** a device impressed on a piece of wax or the like, or an impression, wafer, etc., affixed to a document as evidence of authenticity or attestation. **2.** a stamp engraved with such a device. **3.** an impression made with such a stamp. **4.** *Law.* a mark or symbol attached to a legal document and imparting a formal quality to it, originally defined as wax with an impression. **5.** a piece of wax or similar substance, affixed to a document, an envelope, a door, etc., which cannot be opened without breaking this. **6.** anything that effectively closes a thing. **7.** something for keeping a thing close or secret. **8.** a decorative stamp: *a Christmas seal.* **9.** a mark or the like serving as visible evidence of something. **10.** *Plumbing.* **a.** a small amount of water left standing in a trap to prevent the escape of foul air from below. **b.** the depth of the water between the dip and the overflow of a trap. **11. set one's seal on** or to, to approve or endorse. **12. the seals,** the tokens or signs of public office.
—*v.t.* **13.** to affix a seal to in authorization, confirmation, etc. **14.** to approve, authorize, or confirm: *to seal an agreement.* **15.** to impress a seal upon as an evidence of legal or standard exactness, measure, quality, etc. **16.** to fasten with a seal. **17.** to close by any form of fastening

that must be broken before access can be had. **18.** to fasten or close as if by a seal. **19.** to decide irrevocably: *to seal someone's fate.* **20.** to grant under one's seal or authority, as a pardon. **21.** *Mormon Ch.* to make for ever binding, to give in marriage, or to join in family ties, according to the principle of marriage for eternity. **22.** *Elect.* to bring (a plug and jack or socket, etc.) into locked or fully aligned position. [ME *seel*, t. OF, g. LL *sigellum*, r. L *sigillum*] **—seal′able,** *adv.*

seal² (sēl), *n., pl.* **seals,** *(esp. collectively for 1)* **seal,** *v.* **—***n.* **1.** any of the marine carnivores of the suborder *Pinnipedia*, including the eared or fur seals, as the sea-lion and fur seal of commerce, and the earless or hair seals, of which the **harbour seal,** *Phoca vitulina*, is best known. **2.** the skin of the seal. **3.** leather made from it. **4.** the fur of the fur seal; sealskin. **5.** a fur used as a substitute for sealskin. **—***v.i.* **6.** to hunt or take seals. [ME *sele*, OE *seolh*, c. Icel. *selr*]

Harbour seal, *Phoca vitulina* (Up to 6½ ft long)

sealant (sē′lənt), *n.* **1.** a substance used for sealing documents, etc., as sealing wax. **2.** any of various fluids, chemical preparations, etc., used to give a tough watertight coating to a surface, as on timber, concrete, or the like.

sea-lark (sē′läk′), *n.* the name given to any of various shore birds, as the sandpiper, sanderling, etc.

sea-lavender (sē′lăv′ĭn də), *n.* any plant of the plumbaginaceous genus *Limonium*, as *L. vulgare*, a perennial herb with bluish purple flowers which occurs on coastal salt marshes in N temperate regions.

sea-lawyer (sē′lô′yə), *n. Colloq.* an argumentative or querulous sailor.

seal brown, rich, dark brown suggestive of dressed and dyed sealskin.

sea-leather (sē′lĕth′ə), *n.* the skin of sharks, porpoises, dogfishes, etc., prepared for the same purposes as ordinary leather.

sealed book, something beyond the possibility of understanding.

sealed orders, sealed written orders, not to be opened until after leaving port, given to the commander of a vessel to instruct him where to proceed on a voyage.

sea-legs (sē′lĕgz′), *n.pl. Colloq.* **1.** the ability to walk with steadiness or ease on a rolling ship. **2.** the ability to resist seasickness.

sea-lemon (sē′lĕm′ən), *n.* a large yellowish nudibranch mollusc, *Archidoris britannica*, common on coasts of Europe, including Britain.

sea-leopard (sē′lĕp′əd), *n.* the wolf-fish.

sealer¹ (sē′lə), *n.* **1.** one who or a device which affixes or impresses seals. **2.** *Obs. except U.S.* an officer appointed to examine and test weights and measures, and to set a stamp upon such as are true to the standard. [f. SEAL¹ + -ER¹]

sealer² (sē′lə), *n.* a person or vessel engaged in hunting seals. [f. SEAL² + -ER¹]

sealery (sē′lə rĭ), *n., pl.* **-ries.** *Archaic or Rare.* **1.** the occupation of hunting or taking seals. **2.** a place where seals are caught.

sea-letter (sē′lĕt′ə), *n.* a ship's passport carried in wartime by a neutral vessel describing its cargo, crew, destination, etc.

sea-lettuce (sē′lĕt′ĭs), *n.* any seaweed of the genus *Ulva*, a green alga with large leaf-like blades.

sea-level (sē′lĕv′əl), *n.* the horizontal plane or level corresponding to the surface of the sea when halfway between mean high and low water.

sea-lily (sē′lĭl′ĭ), *n.* a crinoid.

sealing wax, a resinous preparation, soft when heated, used for sealing letters, etc.

sea-lion (sē′lī′ən), *n.* any of various eared seals of large size, as *Eumetopias jubata* of the northern Pacific, and *Zalophus californianus* of the Pacific coast of North America.

sea loch, loch (def. 2).

Sea Lord, one of two (First and Second) senior executives who are also serving naval officers on the admiralty board of the Ministry of Defence.

seal ring, a finger ring bearing a seal; a signet ring.

sealskin (sēl′skĭn′), *n.* **1.** the skin of the seal. **2.** the skin or fur of the fur seal, dressed for use. **3.** a garment or article made of this fur. **—***adj.* **4.** made of or resembling sealskin.

sea-lungwort (sē′lŭng′wût), *n.* a boraginaceous herb, *Mertensia maritima*, with blue flowers, growing on northern seacoasts.

Sealyham (sē′lĭ əm), *n.* a terrier of Welsh origin having short legs, square jaws, and a shaggy white coat with markings on the head and ears. [named after *Sealyham*, a village in Pembrokeshire, Wales, where it was first bred]

Sealyham terrier (10 in. high at the shoulder)

seam (sēm), *n.* **1.** the line formed by sewing together pieces of cloth, leather, or the like. **2.** any line between abutting edges; a crack or fissure; a groove. **3.** any linear indentation or mark, as a wrinkle or a scar. **4.** *Knitting.* a line of stitches formed by purling. **5.** *Geol.* a comparatively thin stratum; a bed, as of coal. **—***v.t.* **6.** to join with a seam; sew the seams of. **7.** to furrow; mark with wrinkles, scars, etc. **—***v.i.* **8.** to become cracked, fissured, or furrowed. [ME *seme*, OE *sēam*, c. G *Saum*; akin to SEW] **—seam′er,** *n.* **—seam′less,** *adj.*

seamaid (sē′mād′), *n. Poetic.* **1.** a mermaid. **2.** a goddess or nymph of the sea.

seaman (sē′mən), *n., pl.* **-men. 1.** one whose occupation it is to assist in the navigation of a ship; a sailor, specif. one below the rank of officer. **2.** *Naval.* a rating, esp. one who works on deck. **—Syn. 1.** See **sailor.**

seamanlike (sē′mən līk′), *adj.* like or befitting a seaman; showing good seamanship.

seamanship (sē′mən shĭp′), *n.* the knowledge of and skill in all things pertaining to the operation, management, safety, and maintenance of ships and vessels other than in the engineering department.

seamark (sē′mäk′), *n.* a conspicuous object on land, visible from the sea, serving as a guide, warning of danger, etc., to ships.

seam bowling, *Cricket.* bowling in which the seam of the ball is used to make it swerve in flight and on bouncing. **—seam bowler.**

sea-mew (sē′myōō′), *n.* a seagull, esp. a common European species, *Larus canus.*

sea mile, mile (def. 1b).

sea-milkwort (sē′mĭlk′wût), *n.* a small, primulaceous, perennial herb with fleshy leaves, *Glaux maritima*, which occurs in N temperate coastal regions.

sea-monster (sē′mŏn′stə), *n.* a monster inhabiting or thought to inhabit the sea.

sea-moss (sē′mŏs′), *n.* a bryozoan.

sea-mouse (sē′mous′), *n.* any of various large marine annelids of the genus *Aphrodite* and allied genera, of a somewhat mouselike appearance, due to a covering of long, fine, hairlike setae.

seam-set (sēm′sĕt′), *n.* a metalworker's tool for flattening seams.

seamstress (sĕm′strĭs), *n.* a woman whose occupation is sewing. Also, **sempstress.**

seam-welding (sēm′wĕl′dĭng), *n.* a process for joining sheets of thermoplastic material by softening, using direct or dielectric heating, and pressing the parts together along a prescribed line.

seamy (sē′mĭ), *adj.,* **-mier, -miest. 1.** not pleasing or favourable; bad; sordid: *the seamy side of life.* **2.** having or showing seams; of the nature of a seam. **—seam′iness,** *n.*

Seanad Éireann (săn′ăd ĕə′rən), the Senate of the Republic of Ireland. See **Oireachtas.**

seance (sā′ŏns), *n.* **1.** a meeting of spiritualists seeking to receive communications from spirits. **2.** session. Also, *French,* **séance** (*Fr.* sĕ äNs′). [t. F: a sitting, der. OF *seoir* (g. L *sedēre*) sit]

sea-onion (sē′ŭn′yən), *n.* a liliaceous plant, *Urginea maritima*, of Mediterranean regions, yielding medicinal squill. Also, **sea-squill.**

sea-otter (sē′ŏt′ə), *n.* a marine otter, *Enhydra lutris*, of the shores of the northern Pacific, with a very valuable fur.

Sea-otter, *Enhydra lutris* (Total length ab. 4 ft, tail ab. 1 ft)

sea-pen (sē′pĕn′), *n.* a coelenterate consisting of a central fleshy axis bearing fleshy lateral leaves provided with small polyps, exemplified by *Pennatula* and related forms.

sea-perch (sē′pûch′), *n.* any fish of the viviparous, almost exclusively marine family *Embiotocidae.*

sea-pink (sē′pĭngk′), *n.* an Old World, maritime, plumbaginaceous, perennial herb, *Armeria maritima*, which has narrow tufted leaves and dense heads of pink or white flowers; thrift.

seaplane (sē′plăn′), *n.* **1.** an aeroplane that can land on water, provided with floats instead of landing wheels. **2.** *U.S.* a hydroplane.

seaport (sē′pôt′), *n.* **1.** a port or harbour providing accommodation for seagoing vessels. **2.** a town or city at such a place.

sea-power (sē′pou′ə), *n.* **1.** a nation having an important navy or great influence on the sea. **2.** naval strength.

sea-purse (sē′pûs′), *n.* the horny egg case of certain rays and sharks.

sea-purslane (sē′pûs′lĭn), *n.* a small chenopodiaceous shrub, *Halimione portulacoides*, common on the edges of salt marsh channels in temperate regions.

seaquake (sē′kwāk′), *n.* an agitation of the sea due to a submarine eruption or earthquake.

sear[1] (sĭə), *v.t.* **1.** to burn or char the surface of. **2.** to mark with a branding iron. **3.** to burn or scorch injuriously or painfully. **4.** to harden, or make callous or unfeeling. **5.** to dry up or wither. **6.** to brown the surface of (meat) by a brief application of high heat. —*v.i.* **7.** to become dry or withered, as vegetation. —*n.* **8.** a mark or the like made by searing. —*adj.* **9.** *Chiefly Poetic.* sere. [ME *sere* (adj.), OE *sēar*, c. D *zoor*] —**Syn. 1.** See **burn**[1].

sear[2] (sĭə), *n.* a pivoted piece in the firing mechanism of small arms which holds the hammer at full cock or half-cock. [t. OF: m. *serre* lock, grasp, der. *serrer* to grasp, hold, ult. g. LL *serāre* to bar, bolt (der. L *sera* bar), b. with *serrāre* to saw (der. *serra* saw)]

sea-ranger (sē′rān′jə), *n.* a senior girl guide or ranger receiving special training in seamanship, etc.

sea-raven (sē′rā′vən), *n.* a large marine fish of the genus *Hemitripterus*, as *H. americanus*, common on the northern Atlantic coast of America.

search (sûch), *v.t.* **1.** to go or look through carefully in seeking to find something. **2.** to examine (a person) for concealed objects by going through his pockets or the like. **3.** to scrutinize or question: *to search one's feelings, search someone's face.* **4.** to probe (a wound, etc.). **5.** (of wind, cold, gunfire, etc.) to pierce or penetrate. **6.** *Mil.* to fire artillery over (an area) with successive changes in elevation. **7.** to bring or find (*out*) by a search: *to search out all the facts.* **8. search me,** *Slang.* I don't know. —*v.i.* **9.** to seek; make examination or investigation. —*n.* **10.** the act of searching; careful examination or investigation. **11.** the search of a neutral vessel, or the examining of its papers, cargo, etc., as at sea, by officers of a belligerent state, in order to verify its nationality and ascertain whether it carries contraband, etc. [ME *serch(en)*, t. OF: m. *cerchier*, g. LL *circāre*, der. L *circus* circle] —**search′able,** *adj.* —**search′er,** *n.*

searching (sû′chĭng), *adj.* **1.** examining carefully or thoroughly. **2.** penetrating, as the eyes, gaze, etc. **3.** piercing or sharp, as the wind, etc. —**search′ingly,** *adv.*

searchlight (sûch′līt′), *n.* **1.** a device, usually consisting of a light and reflector, for throwing a beam of light in any direction. **2.** a beam of light so thrown.

search-party (sûch′pä′tĭ), *n.* a group of people organized to search for someone or something missing.

search-warrant (sûch′wŏ′rənt), *n.* *Law.* a court order authorizing the searching of a house, etc., as for stolen goods.

Searle (sûl), *n.* **Humphrey,** born 1915, English composer.

sea-robber (sē′rŏb′ə), *n.* pirate.

sea-robin (sē′rŏb′ĭn), *n.* any of various gurnards (fishes), esp. certain American species of the genus *Prionotus.*

sea-rocket (sē′rŏk′ĭt), *n.* an annual, succulent, cruciferous herb, *Cakile maritima*, which occurs on coastal sand in Europe and W Asia.

sea room, space at sea free from obstruction in which a ship can be easily manoeuvred or navigated.

sea-rover (sē′rō′və), *n.* **1.** a pirate. **2.** a pirate ship.

seascape (sē′skāp′), *n.* a view or picture of the sea.

sea-scorpion (sē′skô′pyən), *n.* a small, shore-living fish, *Cottus bubalis*, of Atlantic coasts.

sea-scout (sē′skout′), *n.* a boy scout receiving training in seamanship, etc.

sea-serpent (sē′sû′pənt), *n.* **1.** an enormous imaginary snakelike or dragon-like marine animal. **2.** (*caps.*) the southern constellation Hydrus.

sea-shell (sē′shĕl′), *n.* the shell of any marine mollusc.

seashore (sē′shô′), *n.* **1.** land along the sea or ocean. **2.** *Law.* the ground between the ordinary high-water and low-water marks.

seasick (sē′sĭk′), *adj.* affected with seasickness.

seasickness (sē′sĭk′nĭs), *n.* nausea or other physical derangement caused by the motion of a vessel at sea.

seaside (sē′sīd′), *n.* **1.** the seashore; the seacoast. —*adj.* **2.** situated at, or pertaining to, the seaside.

sea-snail (sē′snāl′), *n.* a small, scaleless, littoral fish of the family *Liparidae*, esp. *Liparis liparis* of N Atlantic coasts.

sea-snake (sē′snāk′), *n.* any of the venomous marine snakes with a finlike tail, constituting the family *Hydrophiidae* of tropical seas.

sea-snipe (sē′snīp′), *n.* the name given to any of various shore birds, as the sandpiper.

season (sē′zən), *n.* **1.** one of the four periods of the year (spring, summer, autumn, and winter), astronomically beginning each at an equinox or solstice, but geographically at different dates in different climates. **2.** a period of the year characterized by particular conditions of weather, temperature, etc. **3.** the period of the year when something is best or available: *the oyster season.* **4.** a period of the year marked by certain conditions, festivities, activities, etc.: *the cricket season, a dull season in trade.* **5.** any period or time. **6.** a suitable, proper, fitting, or right time. **7.** a season ticket. **8. in good season,** sufficiently early. **9. in season, a.** in the time or state for use, eating, hunting, etc. **b.** at the right time; opportunely. **10. out of season, a.** not in the time or state for use, eating, hunting, etc. **b.** not at the right time. —*v.t.* **11.** to heighten or improve the flavour of (food) by adding condiments, spices, herbs, or the like. **12.** to give relish or a certain character to: *conversation seasoned with wit.* **13.** to mature, ripen, or condition by exposure to suitable conditions or treatment. **14.** to dry and harden (timber) by due process. **15.** to accustom or harden: *troops seasoned by battle.* **16.** to moderate, alleviate, or temper: *to season one's admiration.* —*v.i.* **17.** to become seasoned, matured, hardened, or the like. [ME *seson(e)*, t. OF: m. *seson*, g. s. L *satio* (time of) sowing] —**sea′soner,** *n.*

seasonable (sē′zə nə bl), *adj.* **1.** suitable to the season: *seasonable weather.* **2.** timely; opportune. **3.** early. —**sea′sonableness,** *n.* —**sea′sonably,** *adv.* —**Syn. 2.** See **opportune.**

seasonal (sē′zə nəl), *adj.* pertaining to or dependent on the seasons of the year or some particular season; periodical: *seasonal work.* —**sea′sonally,** *adv.*

seasoning (sē′zə nĭng), *n.* something that seasons, esp. salt, spices, herbs, or other condiments.

season ticket, a ticket valid any number of times for a specified period, usually at a reduced rate.

sea-spider (sē′spī′də), *n.* a slender, carnivorous, marine, eight-legged arthropod, as *Pycnogonum littorale* of N African coasts.

sea-squill (sē′skwĭl′), *n.* sea-onion.

sea-squirt (sē′skwût′), *n.* an ascidian; tunicate.

sea-swallow (sē′swŏl′ō), *n.* **1.** tern[1]. **2.** a stormy petrel.

seat (sēt), *n.* **1.** something for sitting on, as a chair or bench; the place on or in which one sits. **2.** the part of a chair or the like on which one sits. **3.** the part of the body on which one sits; the buttocks. **4.** the part of the garment covering it. **5.** manner of sitting, as on horseback. **6.** that on which the base of anything rests. **7.** the base itself. **8.** *Carp.* any surface of intended contact, as the prepared bearing of a beam. **9.** a place in which something prevails or is established: *a seat of learning.* **10.** an established place or centre, as of government. **11.** a part of the body considered as the place in which a function or emotion is situated: *the head is the seat of the intellect.* **12.** site, location, or locality. **13.** abode or residence, esp. a country mansion with parkland. **14.** the throne or authority of a king, bishop, etc. **15.** a place for a spectator in a theatre or the like. **16.** right of admittance to such a place, esp. as indicated by ticket. **17.** a right to sit as a member in a legislative or similar body, as the House of Commons. **18.** a right to the privileges of membership in a stock exchange or the like. **19.** a parliamentary constituency. **20.** a directorship of a limited company. **21. take a seat,** to sit down. —*v.t.* **22.** to place on a seat or seats; cause to sit down. **23.** to find seats for; accommodate with seats: *a hall that seats a thousand persons.* **24.** to put a seat on or into (a chair, a garment, etc.). **25.** to fix firmly or accurately in a particular place. **26.** to put in a position of authority or in a legislative body. [ME *sete*, t. Scand.; cf. Icel. *sǣti*, c. OE *sǣt* position for ambush G *Gesäss*] —**seat′er,** *n.*

sea-tangle (sē′tăng′gl), *n.* any of various seaweeds, esp. of the genus *Laminaria.*

seat belt, safety belt (def. 1).

seating (sē′tĭng), *n.* **1.** the act of furnishing with seats. **2.** the arrangement of the seats in a building, etc. **3.** material for seats, esp. upholstery. **4.** manner of sitting, as on horseback. **5.** *Civ. Eng.* a supporting surface, as for a heavy load.

SEATO (sē′tō), *n.* South-East Asia Treaty Organization.

sea-trout (sē′trout′), *n.* **1.** any of various species of trout found in salt water, as the salmon trout, *Salmo trutta.* **2.** any of several fishes of the genus *Cynoscion.*

seat-stick (sēt′stĭk′), *n.* a shooting stick.

Seattle (sĭ ăt′l), *n.* a seaport in the U.S., in W Washington. 557,087 (1960). See map under **Vancouver.**

sea-unicorn (sē′yōō′nĭ kôn′), *n.* the narwhal.

sea-urchin (sē′û′chĭn), *n.* any echinoderm of the class *Echinoidea,* comprising marine animals having a more or less globular or discoid form, and a spine-bearing shell composed of many calcareous plates.

seawall (sē′wôl′), *n.* a strong wall or embankment to prevent the advance of the sea, act as a breakwater, etc.

seawan (sē′wən), *n.* beads, usually unstrung, made from shells, used by North American Indians as money. Also, **sewan.** [t. Algonquian (Narragansett): m. *siwān* scattered, der. *siwen* he scatters]

seaward (sē′wəd), *adj.* **1.** facing or tending towards the sea: *their seaward course.* **2.** coming from the sea, as a wind. —*n.* **3.** the direction towards the sea or away from the land. —*adv.* **4.** seawards.

seawards (sē′wədz), *adv.* towards the sea. Also, **seaward.**

seaware (sē′wĕə′), *n.* seaweed, esp. coarse, large seaweed, used for manure, etc.

sea water, the water which comprises the seas of the earth, consisting of about 96·4 per cent water, 2·8 per cent common salt, 0·4 per cent magnesium chloride, 0·2 per cent magnesium sulphate, 0·1 per cent each of calcium sulphate and potassium chloride (average composition excluding inland seas).

seawater (sē′wô′tə), *adj.* of, pertaining to, denoting, or existing in sea water.

seaway (sē′wā′), *n.* **1.** a way over the sea. **2.** the open sea. **3.** the progress of a ship through the waves. **4.** a rough sea. **5.** an inland channel, canal, or waterway, navigable by ocean-going ships.

seaweed (sē′wēd′), *n.* **1.** any plant or plants growing in the ocean. **2.** a marine alga.

sea-whip (sē′wĭp′), *n.* a gorgonian coral with a flexible axis.

sea-wife (sē′wīf′), *n.* a wrasse.

sea-wolf (sē′wŏŏlf′), *n.* any of several marine fishes, as the wolf-fish.

seaworthy (sē′wû′thĭ), *adj.* (of a ship) adequately and safely constructed and equipped to sail at sea. —**sea′-wor′thiness,** *n.*

sea-wrack (sē′răk′), *n.* seaweed, esp. of the larger kinds cast up on the shore.

sebaceous (sĭ bā′shəs), *adj.* *Physiol.* **1.** pertaining to, of the nature of, or resembling tallow or fat; fatty; greasy. **2.** secreting a fatty substance. [t. NL: m. *sēbāceus,* der. L *sēbum* tallow]

sebaceous glands, any of the cutaneous glands which secrete oily matter for lubricating hair and skin. See diag. under **hair.**

sebacic acid (sĭ băs′ĭk, -bā′sĭk), *Chem.* a white crystalline dibasic acid, $(CH_2)_8(COOH)_2$. [alteration of earlier SEBACEOUS (*acid*), r. *-eous* with *-ic*]

Sebastian (sĭ băs′tyən), *n.* **Saint,** died A.D. 288?, Christian martyr.

Sebastopol (sĭ băs′tə pl), *n.* Sevastopol.

sebiferous (sĭ bĭf′ə rəs), *adj.* *Bot.* producing vegetable wax or tallow. [f. *sebi-* (comb. form repr. L *sēbum* tallow, grease) + -FEROUS]

seborrhoea (sĕb′ə rĭə′), *n.* *Pathol.* an excessive and morbid discharge from the sebaceous glands. Also, *Chiefly U.S.,* **seborrhea.** [NL: f. *sēbo-* (comb. form repr. L *sēbum* grease) + -(R)RHOEA]

sebum (sē′bəm), *n.* *Physiol.* the fatty secretion of the sebaceous glands. [t. L: tallow, grease]

sec[1] (sĕk), *adj.* *French.* (of wines) dry; not sweet.

sec[2] (sĕk), *n.* *Colloq.* a second: *wait just a sec, please.*

sec, secant.

sec., **1.** second. **2.** secondary. **3.** secretary. **4.** section. **5.** sector. **6.** secundum.

secant (sē′kənt), *Maths.* —*n.* **1.** a straight line which cuts a circle or other curve. **2. a.** the ratio of the hypotenuse to the base in a right-angled triangle; the reciprocal of the cosine of an angle. **b.** (orig.) a line from the centre of a circle through one extremity of an arc to the tangent from the other extremity. **c.** the ratio of the length of this line to that of the radius of the circle. —*adj.* **3.** cutting or intersecting, as one line or surface in relation to another. [t. L: s. *secans,* ppr., cutting]

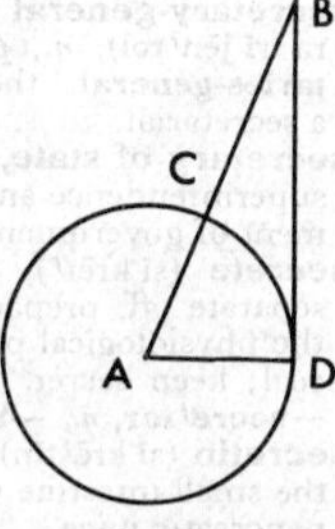

Secant
Ratio of AB to AD, secant of angle A; AB, secant of arc CD

secateurs (sĕk′ə təz, sĕk′ə tûz′), *n.pl.* a scissor-like cutting instrument for pruning shrubs, etc., typically having a pair of crossed, short, curved blades, and a spring for returning them to the open position; pruning shears. [t. F, ult. der. L *secāre* cut]

secco (sĕk′ō; *It.* sĕk′kȯ), *adj.* *Italian.* **1.** *Music.* unaccompanied: *recitativo secco.* **2.** *Painting.* executed on dry plaster: *fresco secco.* [It.: dry]

secede (sĭ sēd′), *v.i.,* **-ceded, -ceding.** to withdraw formally from an alliance or association, as from a political or religious organization. [t. L: m. s. *sēcēdere* go back, withdraw] —**seced′er,** *n.*

secern (sĭ sûn′), *v.t.* to distinguish; discriminate.

secernent (sĭ sû′nənt), *adj.* *Physiol.* secreting. [t. L: s. *sēcernens,* ppr., separating]

secession (sĭ sĕsh′ən), *n.* **1.** the act of seceding. **2.** (*often cap.*) *U.S. Hist.* the attempted withdrawal from the Union of eleven Southern states in 1860–61, which brought on the Civil War. [t. L: s. *sēcessio*] —**seces′sional,** *adj.*

secessionist (sĭ sĕsh′ə nĭst), *n.* one who secedes or who favours secession. —**seces′sionism,** *n.*

sech (sĕsh), *n.* *Maths.* hyperbolic secant. See **hyperbolic functions.**

seclude (sĭ klōōd′), *v.t.,* **-cluded, -cluding.** to shut off or keep apart; place in or withdraw into solitude. [t. L: m. s. *sēclūdere*]

secluded (sĭ klōō′dĭd), *adj.* shut off or separated from others: *a secluded place.* —**seclud′edly,** *adv.* —**seclud′edness,** *n.*

seclusion (sĭ klōō′zhən), *n.* **1.** the act of secluding. **2.** the state of being secluded; retirement; solitude: *he sought seclusion in the attic so that he could study undisturbed.* **3.** a secluded place.

seclusionist (sĭ klōō′zhə nĭst), *n.* one who favours seclusion or lives a secluded life.

seclusive (sĭ klōō′sĭv), *adj.* **1.** tending to seclude. **2.** causing or providing seclusion. —**seclu′sively,** *adv.* —**seclu′siveness,** *n.*

second[1] (sĕk′ənd), *adj.* **1.** next after the first in order, place, time, rank, value, quality, etc.; the ordinal of two. **2.** alternate: *every second Monday.* **3.** *Music.* the lower of two parts for the same instrument or voice: *second alto, second trombone.* **4.** additional; further: *to get a second chance.* **5.** repeating, closely resembling, or imitating a historical person or event: *she's a second Cleopatra.* —*n.* **6.** one who or that which comes next to or after the first, in order, quality, rank, etc.: *King Charles the Second.* **7.** the next to highest class of honours in a university degree examination. **8.** (*pl.*) *Colloq.* (at a meal) **a.** a second helping. **b.** a second course. **9.** *Motor Vehicles.* second gear. **10.** *Music.* **a.** a note on the next degree up from a given note. **b.** the interval between such notes. **c.** the harmonic combination of such notes. **d.** the lower of two parts in a piece of concerted music. **e.** a voice or instrument rendering such a part. **f.** an alto. **11.** *Boxing, Wrestling, etc.* one who assists a contestant in his corner between rounds. **12.** one who acts as representative of and an aid to a principal in a duel. **13.** one who aids or supports another; an assistant; a backer. **14.** (*sometimes pl.*) *Com.* a product or material that is below the normal or required standard, though not unuseable, and is sold at a reduced price. —*v.t.* **15.** to support, back up, or assist. **16.** to further or advance, as aims. **17.** to express support of (a motion, etc.) as a necessary preliminary to further discussion of the motion or to a vote on it. **18.** to act as second to (a duellist, etc.). —*adv.* **19.** in the second place, group, etc. [ME *seconde,* t. F, t. L: m. *secundus*] —**sec′onder,** *n.* —**sec′ondly,** *adv.*

second[2] (sĕk′ənd), *n.* **1.** a sixtieth part of a minute of time; the basic SI unit of time, formally defined in 1960 as the fraction 1/31, 556,925·9747 of the tropical year for 1900 January 0 at 12 hours ephemeris time. **2.** *Geom., etc.* the sixtieth part of a minute of a degree (often represented by the sign ″; thus, 12° 10′30″ means 12 degrees, 10 minutes, and 30 seconds). **3.** a moment or instant. [ME *seconde,* t. F, t. ML: m. *secunda* (*minūta*), i.e., the result of the second sexagesimal division of the hour]

second[3] (sĭ kŏnd′), *v.t.* to transfer (a military officer or other) temporarily to another post, organization, or responsibility. [Cf. F *en second* in the second rank] —**second′ment,** *n.*

Second Advent. See **advent** (def. 4). —**Second Adventist.**

secondary (sĕk′ən də rĭ, -drĭ), *adj., n., pl.* **-aries.** —*adj.* **1.** next after the first in order, place, time, importance, etc. **2.** belonging or pertaining to a second order, division, stage, period, rank, or the like. **3.** derived or derivative; not primary or original. **4.** of minor importance; subordinate; auxiliary. **5.** *Educ.* denoting or pertaining to secondary education. 6. *Chem.* **a.** involving, or obtained from replacement of, two atoms or radicals. **b.** denoting or containing a carbon atom united to two other carbon atoms in a chain or ring molecule. **7.** *Elect.* denoting or pertaining to the induced circuit, coil, or current in an induction coil or the like. **8.** *Geol.* **a.** denoting or pertaining to a clastic rock derived from older rocks. **b.** denoting or pertaining to a mineral produced from another mineral by decay, alteration, or the like. **c.** denoting or pertaining to a soil-formed rock material which has been transported. **9.** *Gram.* **a.** (of derivation) with an underlying element which is itself further analysable, as *likeably* composed of *likeable* + *ly*, but the first element *likeable* is further analysable into *like* + *able*. **b.** (of Latin, Greek, Sanskrit tenses) having reference to past time only. **10.** *Ornith.* pertaining to any of a set of flight feathers on the second segment (that corresponding to the forearm in higher vertebrates) of a bird's wing. —*n.* **11.** one who or that which is secondary. **12.** a subordinate; a delegate or deputy. **13.** *Elect.* a secondary circuit or coil. **14.** *Ornith.* a secondary feather. [ME, t. L: m. s. *secundārius*] —**sec′ondarily,** *adv.*

secondary accent, *Phonet.* a stress accent weaker than primary accent but stronger than lack of stress. Also, **secondary stress.**

secondary cell, *Elect.* a voltaic cell which can be charged by passing a current through it in the opposite direction to the electromotive force, and which can therefore be used as a convenient device for storing electrical energy.

secondary colour, a colour produced by mixing two or more primary colours, as orange, green, or violet.

secondary education, education immediately following primary education, for children over the age of 11, sometimes leading to further education.

secondary emission, *Physics.* the emission of electrons (**secondary electrons**) from a metal which is struck by a beam of fast-moving electrons (**primary electrons**) or ions from another source.

secondary group, *Sociol.* a group of people with whom one's contacts are detached and impersonal.

secondary modern school, a school providing secondary education, esp. in subjects which are intended to be primarily practical rather than academic, for children who fail the eleven-plus examination, or who are otherwise selected for this type of education.

secondary school, a school, esp. a grammar school, secondary modern school, or comprehensive school, providing post-primary education.

second ballot, a ballot held at certain kinds of election to ensure an absolute majority for the victor, when no candidate has secured one in a first ballot; the least successful candidate or candidates in the first ballot are excluded from the second, and all electors are entitled to vote again.

second-best (sĕk′ənd bĕst′), *adj.* **1.** next after the best in quality, performance, etc. **2. come off second best,** to be defeated in a contest. Also (esp. in predicative use), **second best.**

second childhood, senility; dotage.

second class, 1. a class of accommodation on a train, boat, etc., less luxurious and less expensive than first class. **2.** the standard of comfort of such accommodation. **3.** the next to highest class in a university degree examination.

second-class (sĕk′ənd kläs′), *adj.* **1.** of or belonging to the second class. **2.** second-rate; inferior. **3.** treated as if inferior: *women are second-class citizens.*

Second Coming, Second Advent.

seconde (sĭ kŏnd′; *Fr.* sə gôɴd′), *n. Fencing.* the second of eight defensive positions. [t. F, fem. of *second* SECOND[1]]

Second Empire. See **Empire** (def. 5).

second fiddle, 1. a minor or secondary part: *to play second fiddle.* **2.** one who plays such a part.

second floor, 1. the third storey of a building, counting upwards from ground level; the floor two above the ground floor. **2.** *Chiefly U.S.* the second storey, in Britain called the first floor.

second growth, the growth that follows the destruction of virgin forest.

second-hand (sĕk′ənd hănd′), *adj.* **1.** obtained from another; not original: *second-hand knowledge.* **2.** previously used or owned: *second-hand clothes.* **3.** dealing in previously used goods: *a second-hand bookseller.* —*adv.* **4.** after having been owned by another person: *to buy goods second-hand.*

Second International. See **international** (def. 6).

second lieutenant, *Mil.* the lowest commissioned rank in the Army and Royal Marines.

second mortgage, a mortgage taken out in addition to an existing mortgage.

second nature, habit, tendency, etc., so long practised that it is inalterably fixed in one's character: *correcting the English of others is second nature to him.*

secondo (sĕ kŏn′dō), *n., pl.* **-di** (-dē). *Music.* **1.** the second or lower part in a duet, esp. in piano duets. **2.** its performer. [It., g. L *secundus*]

second person, *Gram.* See **person** (def. 11a).

second-rate (sĕk′ənd rāt′), *adj.* **1.** of the second rate or class, as to size, quality, etc. **2.** inferior; mediocre: *a second-rate person.* —**sec′ond-rat′er,** *n.*

Second Reich. See **Reich** (def. 2).

Second Republic. See **Republic** (def. 4).

second sight, a supposed faculty of seeing distant objects and future events; clairvoyance.

second string, an alternative resort or recourse, intended to achieve one's aims upon the failure of an initial course of action.

second-string (sĕk′ənd strĭng′), *adj.* of or pertaining to an alternative plan, course of action, etc.

second thigh, (of a horse) the gaskin.

second thoughts, a revised opinion; reconsideration.

second wind, the feeling of relief coming after an initial period of great effort.

Second World War. See **World War II.**

secrecy (sē′krĭ sĭ), *n., pl.* **-cies. 1.** the state of being secret or concealed: *a meeting in strict secrecy.* **2.** privacy; retirement; seclusion. **3.** ability to keep a secret. **4.** secretive habits; lack of openness. [f. obs. *secre(e)* SECRET + -CY; r. ME *secretee,* f. *secre* secret + *-tee* -TY[2]]

secret (sē′krĭt), *adj.* **1.** done, made, or conducted without the knowledge of others: *secret negotiations.* **2.** kept from the knowledge of any but the initiated: *a secret sign.* **3.** faithful or cautious in keeping secrets; close-mouthed; reticent. **4.** designed to escape observation or knowledge: *a secret drawer.* **5.** retired or secluded, as a place. **6.** beyond ordinary human understanding. —*n.* **7.** something secret, hidden, or concealed. **8.** a mystery: *the secrets of nature.* **9.** the reason or explanation, not immediately or generally apparent: *the secret of his success.* **10.** a method or art known only to the initiated or the few: *the secret of happiness.* **11.** (*cap.*) *Liturgy.* a variable prayer in the Roman and other Western liturgies, said inaudibly by the celebrant after the offertory, etc., and immediately before the preface. **12. in secret,** secretly. [ME *secrete,* t. F, t. L: m. *sēcrētus* (adj.), orig. pp., divided off] —**se′cretly,** *adv.*

secret agent, a spy.

secretaire (sĕk′rə tĕə′), *n.* a writing desk with drawers, etc., for papers, books, or the like. [t. F: m. *secrétaire* SECRETARY]

secretariat (sĕk′rə tĕə′rĭ ət), *n.* **1.** the officials or office entrusted with maintaining records and performing secretarial duties, esp. for an international organization. **2.** a group or department of secretaries. **3.** the place where a secretary transacts business, preserves records, etc. [t. F, t. ML: s. *sēcrētāriātus* the office of a secretary. See SECRETARY]

secretary (sĕk′rə trĭ), *n., pl.* **-taries. 1.** a person who conducts correspondence, keeps records, etc., for an individual or an organization. **2.** a private secretary. **3.** a secretary of state. **4.** a writing desk; secretaire. **5.** a former style of handwriting. [t. ML: m. s. *sēcrētārius* confidential officer, der. L *sēcrētum* (something) secret. See SECRET] —**secretarial** (sĕk′rə tĕə′rĭ əl), *adj.* —**sec′retaryship′,** *n.*

secretary bird, a large, long-legged raptorial bird, *Sagittarius serpentarius,* of Africa, which feeds on reptiles (so called from its crest, which suggests pens stuck over the ear).

Secretary bird, *Sagittarius serpentarius* (Up to 4 ft long)

secretary-general (sĕk′rə trĭ jĕn′rəl), *n., pl.* **secretaries-general.** the head of a secretariat.

secretary of state, an officer of state charged with the superintendence and management of a particular department of government.

secrete (sĭ krēt′), *v.t.,* **-creted, -creting. 1.** *Biol.* to separate off, prepare, or elaborate from the blood, as in the physiological process of secretion. **2.** to hide or conceal; keep secret. [t. L: m. s. *sēcrētus,* pp., put apart] —**secre′tor,** *n.* —**Syn. 2.** See **hide**[1].

secretin (sĭ krē′tĭn), *n. Biochem.* a hormone produced in the small intestine which activates the pancreas to secrete pancreatic juice.

secretion (sĭ krē′shən), *n.* **1.** the process or function of an animal body, executed in the glands, by which various substances, as bile, milk, etc., are separated and elaborated from the blood. **2.** the product secreted. [t. L: s. *sēcrētio*] **—secretionary** (sĭ krēʹshə nə rĭ), *adj.*

secretive (sĭ krēʹtĭv), *adj.* **1.** having or showing a disposition to secrecy; reticent: *he seemed secretive about his new job.* **2.** secretory. **—secreʹtively,** *adv.* **—secreʹtiveness,** *n.*

secretory (sĭ krēʹtə rĭ), *adj., n., pl.* **-ries.** **—***adj.* **1.** pertaining to secretion. **2.** performing the office of secretion. **—***n.* **3.** a secretory organ, vessel, or the like.

secret service, 1. a department of government concerned with national security, particularly with espionage and counterespionage, esp. (*caps.*) in Britain, an investigatory body attached to the Home Office. **2.** official service of a secret nature; espionage.

secret society, a society whose members use secret oaths, passwords, rites, etc., and conceal their activities from outsiders.

sect (sĕkt), *n.* **1.** a body of persons adhering to a particular religious faith; a religious denomination. **2.** a group regarded as deviating from the general religious tradition or as heretical. **3.** (in the sociology of religion) a Christian denomination characterized by insistence on strict qualifications for membership, as distinguished from the more inclusive groups called churches. [ME *secte,* t. L: m. *secta* following]

-sect, a word element meaning 'cut', as in *intersect.* [t. L: s. *sectus,* pp.]

sect., section.

sectarian (sĕk tēəʹrĭ ən), *adj.* **1.** of or pertaining to sectaries or sects. **2.** confined or devoted to a particular sect, esp. narrowly or excessively. **—***n.* **3.** a member of a sect. **4.** a bigoted adherent of a sect. [f. SECTARY + -AN]

sectarianism (sĕk tēəʹrĭ ə nĭzʹəm), *n.* the spirit or tendencies of sectarians; adherence or excessive devotion to a particular sect, esp. in religion.

sectarianize (sĕk tēəʹrĭ ə nīzʹ), *v.t.,* **-nized, -nizing.** to make sectarian. Also, **sectarianise.**

sectary (sĕkʹtə rĭ), *n., pl.* **-ries.** a member of, or one zealously devoted to, a particular sect. [t. ML: m. s. *sectārius,* der. L *secta* sect]

sectile (sĕkʹtĭl), *adj.* capable of being cut smoothly by a knife. [t. L: m. s. *sectilis*] **—sectility** (sĕk tĭlʹĭ tĭ), *n.*

section (sĕkʹshən), *n.* **1.** a part cut off or separated. **2.** a distinct portion of a book, writing, newspaper, or the like; a subdivision, as of a chapter; a division of a legal code. **3.** one of a number of parts that can be fitted together to make a whole: *sections of a fishing rod.* **4.** a distinct part of a country, community, class, or the like. **5.** the act of cutting; separation by cutting. **6.** a thin slice of a tissue, mineral, or the like, as for microscopic examination. **7.** a representation of an object as it would appear if cut by a plane, showing the internal structure; cross-section. **8.** *Mil.* **a.** a small unit, which may consist of two or more squads. **b. staff section,** one of the subdivisions of any staff. **9.** one of the administrative parts into which a subdivision of a police force is organized. **10.** *Surg.* any of various operations involving an incision, esp. a caesarian section. **11.** *Railways.* a length of track between two signal boxes, into which no train may enter or leave without authority. **12.** a subdivision of a chapter in a book, etc. **13.** Also, **section mark.** a mark (§) used to denote a section of a book, chapter, or the like, or as a mark of reference to a footnote or the like. **14.** a division of an orchestra or band composed of all the instruments of one class: *the brass section.* **—***v.t.* **15.** to cut or divide into sections. **16.** to cut through so as to present a section. [t. L: s. *sectio* a cutting]

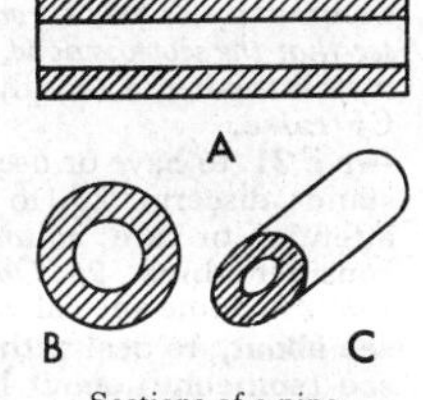

Sections of a pipe
A, Longitudinal;
B, Cross or transverse;
C, Oblique

sectional (sĕkʹshə nəl), *adj.* **1.** pertaining to a particular section; local; partial or partisan: *full of sectional pride.* **2.** composed of several independent sections. **—secʹtionally,** *adv.*

sectionalism (sĕkʹshə nə lĭzʹəm), *n.* excessive regard for sectional or local interests; sectional spirit, prejudice, etc.

sectionalize (sĕkʹshə nə līzʹ), *v.t.,* **-lized, -lizing. 1.** to render sectional. **2.** to divide into sections, esp. geographical sections. Also, **sectionalise. —secʹtionalizaʹtion,** *n.*

section gang, *U.S.* a group of workmen who maintain a section of railway track.

section house, a hostel providing accommodation for unmarried police officers.

sector (sĕkʹtə), *n.* **1.** *Geom.* a plane figure bounded by two radii and the included arc of a circle, ellipse, or the like. **2.** a mathematical instrument consisting of two flat rulers hinged together at one end and bearing various scales. **3.** *Mil.* one of the sections of a forward fighting area as divided for military operations, etc. **4.** any field or division of a field of activity. **—***v.t.* **5.** to divide into sectors. [t. LL, special use of L *sector* cutter] **—secʹtoral,** *adj.*

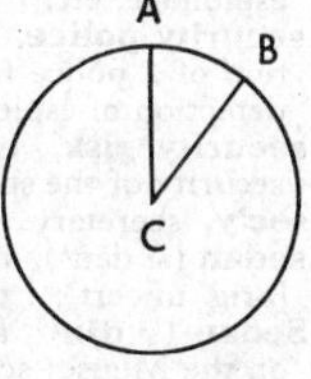

ACB, Sector of a circle

sectorial (sĕk tôʹrĭ əl), *adj.* **1.** sectoral. **2.** *Zool.* adapted for cutting, as teeth.

secular (sĕkʹyŏŏ lə), *adj.* **1.** of or pertaining to the world, or to things not religious, sacred, or spiritual; temporal; worldly. **2.** not pertaining to or connected with religion, as literature, music, etc. **3.** dealing with non-religious subjects, or, esp., excluding religious instruction, as education, etc. **4.** (of members of the clergy) not belonging to a religious order (opposed to *regular*). **5.** occurring or celebrated once in an age or century: *the secular games of Rome.* **6.** going on from age to age; continuing through long ages. **—***n.* **7.** a layman. **8.** one of the secular clergy. [t. L: m. s. *saeculāris* belonging to an age, LL worldly; r. ME *seculer,* t. OF] **—secʹularly,** *adv.*

secularism (sĕkʹyŏŏ lə rĭzʹəm), *n.* **1.** secular spirit or tendencies, esp. a system of political or social philosophy which rejects all forms of religious faith and worship. **2.** the view that public education and other matters of civil policy should be conducted without the introduction of a religious element. **—secʹularist,** *n.* **—secʹularisʹtic,** *adj.*

secularity (sĕkʹyŏŏ lăʹrĭ tĭ), *n., pl.* **-ties. 1.** secularism. **2.** worldliness. **3.** a secular matter.

secularize (sĕkʹyŏŏ lə rīzʹ), *v.t.,* **-rized, -rizing. 1.** to make secular; separate from religious or spiritual connection or influences; make worldly or unspiritual; imbue with secularism. **2.** to change (clergy) from regular to secular. **3.** to transfer (property) from ecclesiastical to civil possession or use. Also, **secularise. —secʹularizaʹtion,** *n.* **—secʹularizʹer,** *n.*

secund (sĭ kŭndʹ), *adj. Bot., Zool.* arranged on one side only; unilateral. [t. L: s. *secundus* following]

Secunderabad (sĭ kŭnʹdə rə bădʹ), *n.* a town and former military cantonment in central India, adjacent to Hyderabad; now a suburb of that city. Also, **Sikandarabad.**

secundine (sĕkʹən dīnʹ, -dĭn), *n. Obs. Bot.* the inner integument of an ovule. [t. L: m. *secundīnae* (pl.) afterbirth]

secundum (sĭ kŭnʹdəm), *prep. Latin.* according to.

secure (sĭ kyŏŏəʹ), *adj., v.,* **-cured, -curing. —***adj.* **1.** free from or not exposed to danger; safe. **2.** not liable to fall, yield, become displaced, etc., as a support or a fastening. **3.** affording safety, as a place. **4.** in safe custody or keeping. **5.** free from care; without anxiety. **6.** sure; certain: *to be secure of victory.* **7.** that can be counted on: *victory is secure.* **8.** *Obs.* overconfident. **—***v.t.* **9.** to get hold or possession of; obtain. **10.** to make secure from danger or harm; make safe. **11.** to make secure or certain; ensure. **12.** to make firm or fast. **13.** to confine or pinion. **14.** to make impregnable, or nearly so, as a military position. **15.** to assure a creditor of payment by the pledge or mortgaging of property. **—***v.i.* **16.** to be safe; get security: *to secure against danger.* [t. L: m. s. *sēcūrus* free from care] **—secureʹly,** *adv.* **—secureʹness,** *n.* **—securʹer,** *n.* **—Syn. 1.** See **safe. 9.** See **get.**

security (sĭ kyŏŏəʹrĭ tĭ), *n., pl.* **-ties. 1.** freedom from danger, risk, etc.; safety. **2.** freedom from care, apprehension, or doubt; confidence. **3.** something that secures or makes safe; a protection; a defence. **4.** protection from or measures taken against espionage, theft, infiltration, sabotage, or the like. **5.** an assurance; guarantee. **6.** *Law.* **a.** something given or deposited as surety for the fulfilment of a promise or an obligation, the payment of a debt, etc. **b.** one who becomes surety for another. **c.** an evidence of debt or of property, as a bond or a certificate of stock. **7.** (*usually pl.*) stocks and shares, etc. [ME, t. L: m. s. *sēcūritas*]

Security Council, the organ of the United Nations principally responsible for the maintenance of international peace and security, consisting of five permanent members with the right of veto (Nationalist China, France, Great Britain, the United States, and the Soviet Union) and ten elected members serving for two years.

Security Force, a body of troops sent by the United Nations Security Council to encourage peaceful settlements in cases of international dispute. Official name, **United Nations Peacekeeping Force.**

security guard, one whose occupation is to guard money or valuables, esp. while in transit.

security officer, one whose occupation is to guard a business, factory, or the like against damage, industrial espionage, etc.

security police, **1.** a force of security guards. **2.** a section of a police force having mainly secret duties, as the detection of espionage, protection of political leaders, etc.

security risk, one who is considered a threat to the security of the state or some other organization.

sec'y, secretary.

sedan (sĭ dăn'), *n.* **1.** *U.S.* a saloon car. **2.** a sedan chair. [orig. uncert.; ? t. It., ult. der. L *sēdes* seat]

Sedan (sĭ dăn'; *Fr.* sə däN'), *n.* a town in NE France, on the Meuse: scene of the disastrous defeat of Napoleon III in the Franco-Prussian War, 1870. 21,766 (1962).

sedan chair, a portable wheelless vehicle for one person, borne on poles by two men, one before and one behind, much used during the 17th and 18th centuries.

Sedan chair

sedate (sĭ dāt'), *adj., v.,* **-dated, -dating.** —*adj.* **1.** calm, quiet, or composed; sober; undisturbed by passion or excitement. —*v.t.* **2.** to calm or put to sleep by means of sedatives. [t. L: m. s. *sēdātus*, pp., calmed] —**sedate'ly,** *adv.* —**sedate'ness,** *n.* —**Syn. 1.** See **staid.** —**Ant. 1.** frivolous.

sedation (sĭ dā'shən), *n.* **1.** the state of being tranquillized or in an induced condition of reduced pain. **2.** the act or fact of soothing or allaying irritability or pain.

sedative (sĕd'ə tĭv), *adj.* **1.** tending to calm or soothe. **2.** *Med.* allaying irritability or excitement; assuaging pain; lowering functional activity. —*n.* **3.** a sedative agent or remedy.

se defendendo (sē'dē'fĕn dĕn'dō), *Law.* defending himself (a plea in a murder or manslaughter trial). [L]

sedentary (sĕd'n tə rĭ, -trĭ), *adj.* **1.** characterized by or requiring a sitting posture: *a sedentary occupation.* **2.** accustomed to sit much or take little exercise. **3.** *Chiefly Zool.* **a.** abiding in one place; not migratory. **b.** referring to animals that move about but little or are permanently attached. **4.** *Geol.* denoting or pertaining to a soil formed directly from the solid rocks under it. [t. L: m. s. *sedentārius*] —**sed'entarily,** *adv.* —**sed'entariness,** *n.*

Seder (sā'də), *n. Judaism.* a ceremonial dinner which is held on the first night (or first two nights) of the Passover. [t. Heb.: m. *sēdher* order]

sedge (sĕj), *n.* **1.** any of various rushlike or grasslike plants constituting the cyperaceous genus *Carex*, growing in wet places. **2.** the cyperaceous plant, *Carex mariscus*, having tough leaves which are used for thatching. **3.** any cyperaceous plant. [ME *segge*, OE *secg*; akin to SAW[1]; appar. so named because of its sawlike edges]

sedged (sĕjd), *adj.* **1.** made of sedge. **2.** abounding or bordered with sedge: *sedged brooks.*

Sedgemoor (sĕj'mōōə'), *n.* a broad plain in SW England: Monmouth's final defeat, 1685.

sedge warbler, a small warbler, *Acrocephalus schoenobaenus*, inhabiting marshy places in Europe and western Asia.

sedgy (sĕj'ĭ), *adj.* **1.** abounding, covered, or bordered with sedge. **2.** of or like sedge.

sedile (sē dī'lĭ), *n., pl.* **sedilia** (sē dĭl'yə). *Eccles.* one of the seats (usually three) on the south side of the chancel, often recessed, for the use of the officiating clergy. [t. L: seat]

sediment (sĕd'ĭ mənt), *n.* **1.** matter which settles to the bottom of a liquid; lees; dregs. **2.** *Geol.* mineral or organic matter deposited by water, air, or ice. [t. F, t. L: s. *sedimentum* a setting]

sedimentary (sĕd'ĭ mĕn'tə rĭ), *adj.* **1.** of, pertaining to, or of the nature of sediment. **2.** *Geol.* formed by deposition of sediment, as rocks. Also, **sedimental.** —**sed'imen'tarily,** *adv.*

sedimentation (sĕd'ĭ mĕn tā'shən), *n.* the deposition or accumulation of sediment.

sedition (sĭ dĭsh'ən), *n.* **1.** incitement of discontent or rebellion against the government; action or language promoting such discontent or rebellion. **2.** *Archaic.* rebellious disorder. [ME *sedicion*, t. L: m. s. *sēditio*, lit., a going apart] —**Syn. 1.** See **treason.**

seditionary (sĭ dĭsh'ə nə rĭ), *adj., n., pl.* **-aries.** —*adj.* **1.** seditious. —*n.* **2.** one guilty of sedition.

seditious (sĭ dĭsh'əs), *adj.* **1.** of, pertaining to, or of the nature of sedition. **2.** given to or guilty of sedition. —**sedi'tiously,** *adv.* —**sedi'tiousness,** *n.*

seduce (sĭ dyōōs'), *v.t.,* **-duced, -ducing. 1.** to induce to have sexual intercourse. **2.** to lead astray; entice away from duty or rectitude; corrupt. **3.** to lead or draw away, as from principles, faith, or allegiance. **4.** to win over; entice. [late ME, t. L: m. s. *sēdūcere* lead aside] —**seduc'er,** *n.* —**seduc'ible,** *adj.* —**Syn. 1.** beguile, inveigle. See **tempt.**

seduction (sĭ dŭk'shən), *n.* **1.** the act or an instance of seducing. **2.** condition of being seduced. **3.** a means of seducing; an enticement. Also, **seduce'ment.**

seductive (sĭ dŭk'tĭv), *adj.* tending to seduce; enticing; captivating: *a seductive smile.* —**seduc'tively,** *adv.* —**seduc'tiveness,** *n.*

seductress (sĭ dŭk'trĭs), *n.* a woman who seduces, entices, or leads astray; a female seducer. [t. L: m. *sēductrix*]

sedulity (sĭ dyōō'lĭ tĭ), *n.* sedulous quality.

sedulous (sĕd'yōō ləs), *adj.* **1.** diligent in application or attention; persevering. **2.** persistently or carefully maintained: *sedulous flattery.* [t. L: m. *sēdulus* busy, careful] —**sed'ulously,** *adv.* —**sed'ulousness,** *n.*

sedum (sē'dəm), *n.* any plant of the crassulaceous genus *Sedum*, which comprises fleshy, chiefly perennial, herbs with (usually) yellow, white, or pink flowers. Cf. **stonecrop.** [NL, special use of L *sedum* houseleek]

see[1] (sē), *v.,* **saw, seen, seeing.** —*v.t.* **1.** to observe, be aware of, or perceive, with the eyes. **2.** to look at; make an effort to observe in this way. **3.** to imagine, remember, or retain a mental picture of: *I see the house as it used to be.* **4.** to perceive or be aware of with any or all of the senses: *I hate to see a good man turn to crime.* **5.** to have experience or knowledge of: *to see life, to see a bit of variety.* **6.** to view, or visit or attend as a spectator: *have you seen the old part of town?* **7.** to discern with the intelligence; perceive mentally; understand: *do you see where you went wrong?* **8.** to be willing that; to allow: *I'll see you dead first, I can't see an animal suffer.* **9.** to recognize; appreciate: *I don't see the use of that.* **10.** to interpret; regard; consider: *I see the problem quite differently.* **11.** to accept as reasonable or likely; be able to conceive or believe without difficulty: *I just don't see him as Prime Minister.* **12.** to predict; foresee. **13.** to ascertain, find out, or learn, as by enquiry: *see who is knocking.* **14.** to meet socially; visit. **15.** to visit formally; consult: *to see a doctor.* **16.** to receive as a visitor or the like: *the Minister will see you now.* **17.** to spend time in the company of, esp. romantically. **18.** to accompany or escort: *may I see you home?* **19.** to ensure: *see that the work is done.* **20.** *Poker, etc.* to match (a bet) or match the bet of (another better) by making an equal bet. Cf. **raise.**

—*v.i.* **21.** to have or use the power of sight. **22.** to understand; discern. **23.** to enquire or find out. **24.** to give attention or care: *go and see to it now.* **25.** to deliberate; consider; think. **26.** *Obs. or Dial.* to look.

—*n.* **27.** Some special verb phrases are:

see about, to deal with or attend to.

see (someone) about his business, to send away, esp. forcibly.

see into, to investigate: *the manager must see into the circumstances of the dismissal of these workers.*

see off, 1. to attend the departure of, esp. as a courtesy; send off. **2.** to turn away, esp. forcibly; cause to leave.

see out, 1. to see off. **2.** to continue in (an undertaking) until it is finished. **3.** to live until the end of or outlive (a person or period).

see over, to inspect.

see through, 1. to penetrate or detect: *to see through a disguise, see through an imposture.* **2.** to remain until the completion of; work to ensure the successful outcome of: *to see a project through.* **3.** to help or support in the achievement or completion of: *his family saw him through university.*

[ME; OE *sēon*, c. D *zien*, G *sehen*, Icel. *sjá*, Goth. *saihwan*] —**Syn. 1.** See **watch.**

see[2] (sē), *n. Eccles.* the seat, centre of authority, office, or jurisdiction of a bishop. [ME *se*, t. OF, var. (influenced by L) of *sie*, *sied*, ult. g. L *sēdes*]

Seebeck effect (sē'bĕk; *Ger.* zē'bĕk), *Physics.* the production of an electric current in a circuit consisting of two wires of different metals, the two junctions of which are maintained at different temperatures. Also, **thermoelectric effect.** [named after T. J. *Seebeck*, 1770–1831, German physicist]

seed (sēd), *n., pl.* **seeds, seed,** *v.* —*n.* **1.** the propagative part of a plant, esp. as preserved for growing a new crop, including ovules, tubers, bulbs, etc. **2.** such parts collectively. **3.** *Bot.* a structure containing an embryo plant, and food reserves formed from an

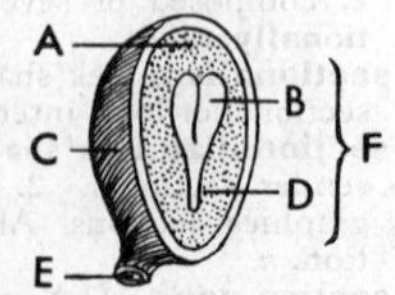

Cross-section of violet seed: A, Endosperm; B, Cotyledon; C, Testa; D, Radicle; E, Hilium; F, Embryo

ovule after it has been fertilized. **4.** any small, seedlike part or fruit, as a grain of wheat. **5.** the germ or beginning of anything: *the seeds of discord.* **6.** offspring; progeny. **7.** birth: *not of mortal seed.* **8.** semen or sperm. **9.** the ovum or ova of certain animals, as the lobster and the silkworm moth. **10.** seed oyster. **11.** a small bubble in glass. **12.** a player who has been seeded: *Jones is number three seed this year.* **13. go** or **run to seed, a.** to pass to the stage of yielding seed. **b.** to approach the end of vigour, usefulness, prosperity, etc. —*v.t.* **14.** to sow (land) with seed. **15.** to sow or scatter (seed). **16.** *Chem.* to add a small crystal to (a super-saturated solution, or a super-cooled liquid), in order to initiate crystallization. **17.** to sow or scatter (clouds) with crystals or particles of silver iodide, solid carbon dioxide, etc., to induce precipitation. **18.** to remove the seeds from (fruit). **19.** to modify (the ordinary drawing of lots for position in a tournament, as at tennis) by distributing certain outstanding players so that they will not meet in the early rounds of play. **20.** to distribute (outstanding players) in this manner: *Jones was seeded fifth last year.* —*v.i.* **21.** to sow seed. **22.** to produce or shed seed. [ME; OE *sēd* (Anglian), *sǣd*, c. G *Saat*] —**seed′less,** *adj.* —**seed′like′,** *adj.*

seedbed (sēd′bĕd′), *n.* an area of soil specially prepared for the germination of seeds.

seedcake (sēd′kāk′), *n.* a sweet cake containing aromatic seeds, esp. carraway.

seed capsule, *Bot.* the ripened walls of the ovary; pericarp. Also, **seedcase** (sēd′kās′).

seedcoat (sēd′kōt′), *n.* *Bot.* the outer integument of a seed.

seed corn, ears or kernels of maize set apart as seed.

seed crystal, **1.** *Chem.* a small crystal added to a solution to initiate crystallization. **2.** one of a large number of crystals scattered into clouds to induce precipitation.

seed drill. See **drill**² (def. 2).

seed-eater (sēd′ē′tə), *n.* any of various tropical American and African finches, many of which resemble canaries.

seeder (sē′də), *n.* **1.** one who or that which seeds. **2.** an apparatus for sowing seeds in the ground.

seed leaf, *Bot.* a cotyledon.

seedling (sēd′lĭng), *n.* a young plant developed from the embryo after germination of a seed.

seed oysters, spat of oysters; very young oysters.

seed pearl, a very small pearl (less than ¼ grain).

seed plant, a seed-bearing plant; a spermatophyte.

seed potato, a potato tuber kept for planting the following season.

seedsman (sēdz′mən), *n., pl.* **-men. 1.** a dealer in seed. **2.** a sower of seed.

seedtime (sēd′tīm′), *n.* the season for sowing seed.

seed vessel, *Bot.* a seed capsule.

seedy (sē′dĭ), *adj.,* **-dier, -diest. 1.** abounding in seed. **2.** gone to seed. **3.** rather disreputable or shabby. **4.** wearing shabby clothes. **5.** *Colloq.* out of sorts physically. —**seed′ily,** *adv.* —**seed′iness,** *n.*

seeing (sē′ĭng), *conj.* in view of the fact (that); considering; inasmuch as.

seek (sēk), *v.,* **sought, seeking.** —*v.t.* **1.** to go in search or quest of: *to seek a new home.* **2.** to try to find by searching or endeavour: *to seek a solution.* **3.** to try to obtain: *to seek fame.* **4.** to try or attempt (fol. by an infinitive): *to seek to convince a person.* **5.** to ask for; request: *to seek advice.* **6.** *Obs.* to search or explore. **7. be sought after,** to be desired or in demand. —*v.i.* **8.** to make search or inquiry. [ME *seke*, OE *sēcan*, c. G *suchen*] —**seek′er,** *n.*

seel (sēl), *v.t.* **1.** *Falconry.* to close (the eyes of a hawk), esp. by sewing up the lids, in order to make it responsive to training. **2.** *Archaic.* to blind. **3.** *Archaic.* to deceive. [ME *sille(n)*, t. MF: m. *siller*, der. *cil* eyelash]

Seeland (sē′lənd), *n.* Zealand.

seem (sēm), *v.i.* **1.** to appear to be; appear (to be, feel, do, etc.). **2.** to appear to oneself (to be, do, etc.): *I seem to hear someone calling.* **3.** to appear to exist: *there seems no need to go now.* **4.** to appear to be true or the case: *it seems likely to rain.* [ME *seme*, t. Scand.; cf. Icel. *sæma* (impers.) beseem, befit] —**seem′er,** *n.*

—**Syn. 4.** SEEM, APPEAR, LOOK refer to an outward aspect which may or may not be contrary to reality. SEEM is applied to that which has an aspect of truth and probability: *it seems warmer today.* APPEAR suggests the giving of an impression which may be superficial or illusory: *the house appears to be deserted.* LOOK more vividly suggests the use of the eye (literally or figuratively) or the aspect as perceived by the eye: *she looked very frightened.*

seeming (sē′mĭng), *adj.* **1.** apparent; appearing to be such (whether truly or falsely): *a seeming advantage.* —*n.* **2.** appearance, esp. outward or deceptive appearance. —**seem′ingly,** *adv.*

seemly (sēm′lĭ), *adj.,* **-lier, -liest,** *adv.* —*adj.* **1.** fitting or becoming with respect to propriety or good taste; decent; decorous. **2.** of pleasing appearance; handsome. **3.** *Archaic.* suitable. —*adv.* **4.** in a seemly manner; fittingly; becomingly. [ME *semeli*, t. Scand.; cf. Icel. *sǣmilegr* becoming] —**seem′liness,** *n.*

seen (sēn), *v.* pp. of **see**¹.

seep (sēp), *v.i.* **1.** to pass gradually, as liquid, through a porous substance; ooze. **2.** to enter or infiltrate gradually, as ideas. —*n.* **3.** moisture that seeps out. **4.** *U.S.* a small spring, or soakage of ground water at the surface. [? var. of d. *sipe*, OE *sīpian*, c. MLG *sīpen*]

seepage (sē′pĭj), *n.* **1.** that which seeps or leaks out. **2.** the act or process of seeping; leakage.

seer¹ (sĭə), *n.* **1.** one who foretells future events; a prophet. **2.** a magician, clairvoyant, or other person claiming to have occult powers; a palmist, crystal-gazer, or the like. **3.** *Rare.* one who sees; an observer. [f. SEE¹ + -ER¹] —**seeress** (sĭə′rĭs), *n. fem.*

seer² (sĭə), *n.* a unit of weight in India varying in amount but usually equal to nearly 2 lbs 1 oz. avoirdupois. Also, **ser.** [t. Hind.]

seersucker (sĭə′sŭk′ə), *n.* a fabric, usually striped cotton with alternate stripes crinkled in the weaving. [t. Hind., t. Pers.: alter. of *shīr o shakkar*, lit., milk and sugar]

seesaw (sē′sô′), *n.* **1.** a plank or beam balanced at the middle so that its ends may rise and fall alternately. **2.** a children's game in which participants ride up and down on the ends of such a plank. **3.** moving up and down or back and forth. **4.** an up-and-down or a back-and-forth movement or procedure. **5.** *Whist.* a crossruff. —*v.i., v.t.* **6.** to move, or cause to move, in the manner of a seesaw. —*adj.* **7.** moving alternately in opposite directions. [varied reduplication suggested by SAW¹]

seethe (sēth), *v.,* **seethed** or (*Obs.*) **sod; seethed** or (*Obs.*) **sodden** or **sod; seething;** *n.* —*v.i.* **1.** to surge or foam, as a boiling liquid. **2.** to be in a state of physical or mental agitation; to be excited, discontented, or agitated. **3.** to boil or stew, as meat. —*v.t.* **4.** to boil; prepare, cook, or extract the essence of by boiling, stewing, etc. **5.** *Obs.* to soak or steep. —*n.* **6.** an instance, state or act of seething; commotion or turmoil. [ME; OE *sēothan*, c. G *sieden*] —**seeth′ingly,** *adv.* —**Syn. 2.** See **boil**¹.

Seger cone (sē′gə; *Ger.* zē′gər), a cone of clay and various oxides so compounded that it will soften and bend over at a specific temperature, used to indicate the temperature within a furnace; a pyrometric cone. [named after H. A. *Seger*, died 1893, German ceramist]

segment (*n.* sĕg′mənt; *v.* sĕg-mĕnt′), *n.* **1.** one of the parts into which anything naturally separates or is naturally divided; a division or section. **2.** *Geom.* **a.** a part cut off from a figure (esp. a circular or a spherical one) by a line or a plane, as a part of a circular area contained by an arc and its chord, or by two parallel lines or planes. **b.** a finite section of a line. **3.** *Zool.* any one of the rings that compose the body of an arthropod, or any other animal with a comparable structure, or one of the sections of a limb between the joints. **4.** *Elect.* one of the insulated elements which form a commutator. —*v.t., v.i.* **5.** to separate or divide into segments. [t. L: s. *segmentum*] —**segmental** (sĕg-mĕn′tl), **segmentary** (sĕg′mən tə rĭ, -trĭ), *adj.* —**segmen′tally,** *adv.*

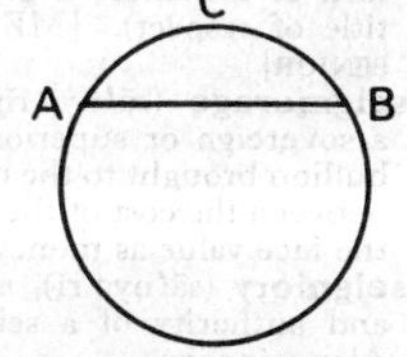

ACB, Segment of a circle

segmentation (sĕg′mĕn tā′shən), *n.* **1.** division into segments. **2.** *Biol.* **a.** the subdivision of an organism or of an organ into more or less equivalent parts. **b.** cell-division. Cf. **cleavage.**

segmentation cavity, *Embryol.* a blastocoel; the hollow of a blastula.

segno (sĕn′yō), *n., pl.* **-gni** (-nyē). *Music.* **1.** a sign. **2.** a sign or mark at the beginning or end of a repetition. [It., g. L *signum*]

Segovia (sĭ gō′vyə; *Sp.* sĕ gō′byä), *n.* **1. Andrés** (*Sp.* än drĕs′), born 1893, Spanish guitarist. **2.** a city in central Spain: Roman aqueduct. 33,360 (1960).

segregate (*v.* sĕg′rĭ gāt′; *adj.* sĕg′rĭ gĭt), *v.,* **-gated, -gating,** *adj.* —*v.t.* **1.** to separate or set apart from the others or from the main body; isolate. **2.** to impose a policy of segregation on (a specific racial, religious or other group). **3.** to impose a policy of segregation on (a place, community, or state). —*v.i.* **4.** to separate or go apart; separate from the main body and collect in one place; become segregated. **5.** to practise, enforce, or adopt a policy of segregation. **6.** *Biol.* (of allelomorphic characters) to separate according to Mendel's laws. —*adj.* **7.** segregated; set apart. [ME, t. L: m. s. *sēgregātus*, pp., separated from the flock] —**seg′rega′tive,** *adj.* —**seg′rega′tor,** *n.*

segregated (sĕg′rĭ gā′tĭd), *adj.* **1.** subject to a policy of, practising, or characterized by segregation. **2.** restricted to a single racial or other group. **3.** providing separate facilities for members of different racial or other groups. **4.** discriminating against a particular racial or other group.

segregation (sĕg′rĭ gā′shən), *n.* **1.** the act of segregating. **2.** the state of being segregated. **3.** something segregated. **4.** the policy or practice of providing separate facilities for racial groups living in the same area, and as far as possible preventing contact between them. **5.** a set of laws implementing this, as by restricting members of such races to certain residential areas, institutions, or facilities. **6.** *Biol.* the separation of genes in paternal chromosomes from those in maternal chromosomes at the reduction division, and the consequent separation of their hereditary characters as observed in the progeny of hybrids.

segregationist (sĕg′rĭ gā′shə nĭst), *n.* an advocate, adherent, or practitioner of racial segregation.

seguidilla (sĕg′ĭ dē′lyə), *n.* **1.** *Pros.* a stanza of four to seven lines with a distinctive rhythm. **2.** a Spanish dance in triple rhythm for two persons. **3.** the music for it. [t. Sp., der. *seguida* following, sequence]

seicento (*It.* sĕy chĕn′tō), *n.* the 17th century, with reference to the Italian art or literature of that period. [It., short for *mille seicento* one thousand six hundred]

seiche (sāsh), *n.* an occasional rhythmical movement from side to side of the water of a lake, with fluctuation of the water-level. [t. Swiss F]

Seidlitz powder (sĕd′lĭts), an aperient consisting of two powders, one tartaric acid and the other a mixture of sodium bicarbonate and Rochelle salt: dissolved separately, mixed, and drunk while effervescing. [named after *Seidlitz*, village in Bohemia]

seif-dune (sāf′dyo͞on′), *n.* (in deserts, esp. the Sahara) a ridge of blown sand, sometimes several miles long, stretching across the desert in the direction of the prevailing wind. [*seif* t. Ar.: sword]

seignant (sā′nyŏng; *Fr.* sĕ nyäɴ′), *adj.*, *Cookery, French.* underdone; rare.

seigneur (sĕ nyû′; *Fr.* sĕ nyœr′), *n.* a feudal lord. [t. F, g. L *senior.* See SENIOR] —**seigneu′rial,** *adj.*

seigneury (sā′nyə rĭ), *n.* the domain, house, or status of a seigneur. Also, **seigneurie.**

seignior (sā′nyə), *n.* *Archaic.* **1.** a lord; a ruler. **2.** the lord of a manor; a gentleman (also formerly used as a title of respect). [ME *segnour*, t. AF, g. L *senior.* See SENIOR]

seigniorage (sā′nyə rĭj), *n.* **1.** something claimed by a sovereign or superior as a prerogative, as a charge on bullion brought to the mint to be coined. **2.** the difference between the cost of the bullion plus minting expenses and the face value as money of the pieces coined.

seigniory (sā′nyə rĭ), *n.*, *pl.* **-ries.** **1.** the rights, power, and authority of a seignior. **2.** *Hist.* a lord's domain. Also, **signory.**

seignorial (sā nyô′rĭ əl), *adj.* of or pertaining to a seignior. Also, **seignioral** (sā′nyə rəl).

seine (sān), *n.*, *v.*, **seined, seining.** —*n.* **1.** a fishing net which hangs vertically in the water, having floats at the upper edge and sinkers at the lower. —*v.t.* **2.** to fish for or catch with a seine. **3.** to use a seine in (water). —*v.i.* **4.** to fish with a seine. [ME *seyn(e)*, OE *segne*, ult. t. L: m. *sagēna*, t. Gk: m. *sagḗnē* fishing net] —**sein′er,** *n.*

Seine (sān; *Fr.* sĕn), *n.* **1.** a river flowing from E France NW through Paris to the English Channel. ab. 480 mi. See map under **Compiègne.** **2.** a former department in N France, now divided into four departments (Hauts-de-Seine, Paris, Seine-Saint-Denis, and Val-de-Marne). 185 sq. mi. *Cap.:* Paris.

Seine-et-Marne (*Fr.* sĕn ė màrn′), *n.* a department in N France. 524,486 pop. (1962): 2275 sq. mi. *Cap.:* Melun.

Seine-et-Oise (*Fr.* sĕn ė wàz′), *n.* a former department in N France divided in 1964 between Essone, Val d'Oise, and Yvelines.

Seine-Maritime (*Fr.* sĕn mà rē tēm′), *n.* a department in N France. 1,035,844 pop. (1962); 2448 sq. mi. *Cap.:* Rouen.

Seine-Saint-Denis (*Fr.* sĕn săɴ də nē′), *n.* a department in N France, NE of Paris. 1,225,000 pop. (est. 1962); 91 sq. mi.

seise (sēz), *v.t.* **seised, seising.** to put in seisin or legal possession of. Also, **seize.**

seisin (sē′zĭn), *n.* *Law.* **1.** (orig.) possession of either land or chattel. **2.** the kind of possession, or right to possession, characteristic of estates of freehold. Also, **seizin.** [ME *saisine*, t. OF, der. *saisir* SEIZE]

seism (sī′zəm), *n.* an earthquake. [t. Gk: s. *seismós*]

seismic (sīz′mĭk), *adj.* pertaining to, of the nature of, or caused by an earthquake. Also, **seis′mal, seis′mical.** [f. s. Gk *seismós* earthquake + -IC]

seismic focus, a point within the earth's crust at which an earthquake originates.

seismic prospecting, a method of exploring the underlying strata of the earth, in which small explosive charges are fired, the resulting vibrations providing geological information.

seismo-, a word element meaning 'seismic', as in *seismology.* [t. Gk, comb. form of *seismós* earthquake]

seismogram (sīz′mə grăm′), *n.* a record made by a seismograph.

seismograph (sīz′mə grăf′, -gräf′), *n.* an instrument for recording the phenomena of earthquakes. —**seismographic** (sīz′mə grăf′ĭk), *adj.*

seismography (sīz mŏg′rə fĭ), *n.* **1.** the scientific description of earthquake phenomena. **2.** the science of the use of the seismograph.

seismology (sīz mŏl′ə jĭ), *n.* the science or study of earthquakes and their phenomena. —**seismologic** (sīz′mə lŏj′ĭk), **seis′molog′ical,** *adj.* —**seis′molog′ically,** *adv.* —**seismol′ogist,** *n.*

seismometer (sīz mŏm′ĭ tə), *n.* an instrument for measuring the direction, intensity, and duration of earthquakes. —**seismometric** (sīz′mə mĕt′rĭk), **seis′momet′rical,** *adj.*

sei whale (sā), a cetacean, *Balaenoptera borealis*, of the rorqual family (family *Balaenopteridae*) up to 60 ft long, with a worldwide distribution. [part. trans. of Norw. *seihval*, lit., coalfish-whale]

seize (sēz), *v.*, **seized, seizing.** —*v.t.* **1.** to lay hold of suddenly or forcibly; grasp: *to seize a weapon.* **2.** to grasp with the mind: *to seize an idea.* **3.** to take posession of by force or at will: *to seize enemy ships.* **4.** to take possession or control of as if by suddenly laying hold: *panic seized the crowd.* **5.** to take possession of by legal authority; confiscate: *to seize smuggled goods.* **6.** seise. **7.** to capture; take into custody. **8.** to take advantage of promptly: *to seize an opportunity.* **9.** *Naut.* to bind, lash, or fasten together with several turns of light rope, cord, or the like. —*v.i.* **10.** to lay hold suddenly or forcibly: *to seize on a rope.* **11. seize up,** to become jammed or stuck solid, as an engine through excessive heat. [ME *sayse*, t. OF: m. *saisir*, g. VL *sacire* set, put (in possession), t. Gmc; cf. Goth. *satjan* SET] —**seiz′er;** *Law,* **seizor** (sē′zə, -zô), *n.* —**Syn. 7.** apprehend, arrest. **7, 8.** See **catch.** —**Ant. 7.** release.

seizin (sē′zĭn), *n.* *Law.* seisin.

seizing (sē′zĭng), *n.* **1.** the act of seizing. **2.** *Naut.* a binding or lashing, consisting of several turns of light line, marline, wire, or the like, holding two ropes, etc., together.

Nautical seizings

seizure (sē′zhə), *n.* **1.** the act of seizing. **2.** a taking possession, legally or by force. **3.** a sudden attack, as of disease.

sejant (sē′jənt), *adj.* *Her.* in a sitting posture. [also *seiant*, t. OF: m. *seant*, ppr. of *seoir* sit, g. L *sedēre*]

selachian (sĭ lā′kĭ ən), *adj.* **1.** belonging to the *Selachii*, a large group of fishes comprising the sharks, skates, and rays. —*n.* **2.** a selachian fish, as a shark. [f. s. NL *selachiī*, pl. (r. *selachē*, t. Gk: sharks) + -AN]

selaginella (sĕl′ə jĭ nĕl′ə), *n.* *Bot.* any of a genus of heterosporous vascular cryptogams, typical of the *Selaginellacae*, including species cultivated in conservatories. [NL, dim. of L *Selago* a genus of plant]

selah (sē′lə), *n.* a word occurring frequently in the Psalms, supposed to be a liturgical or musical direction, probably a direction by the leader to raise the voice, or perhaps indicating a pause. [t. Heb.]

selamlik (sĭ läm′lĭk), *n.* the portion of a Turkish palace or house reserved for men. [t. Turk.]

Selangor (sə lăng′ə), *n.* a state in W Malaysia. 1,221,661 pop. (est. 1962); 3160 sq. mi. *Cap.:* Kuala Lumpur.

Selden (sĕl′dən), *n.* **John,** 1584–1654, English historian and antiquary.

seldom (sĕl′dəm), *adv.* **1.** rarely; infrequently; not often. —*adj.* **2.** *Obs.* rare; infrequent. [ME; OE *seldum*, var. of *seldan*, c. G *selten*]

select (sĭ lĕkt′), *v.t.* **1.** to choose in preference to another or others; pick out. —*adj.* **2.** selected; chosen in preference to others. **3.** choice; of special value or excellence. **4.** carefully or fastidiously chosen; exclusive: *a select party.* [t. L: s. *sēlectus*, pp., chosen] —**select′ness,** *n.* —**selec′tor,** *n.* —**Syn. 1.** See **choose.**

selectee (sĭ lĕk′tē′), *n.* *U.S.* one selected by draft for military or naval service.

selection (sĭ lĕk′shən), *n.* **1.** the act of selecting or the fact of being selected; choice. **2.** a thing or a number of things selected. **3.** a range of things from which selection may be made: *a shop with a wide selection of hats.* **4.** a horse, etc., picked out as likely to win a race. **5.** *Austral.* a block

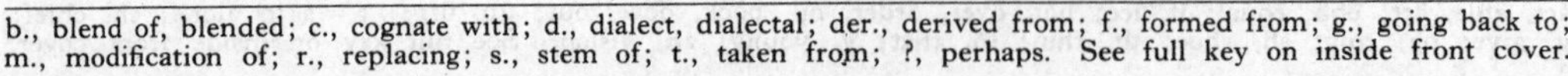

of land acquired under the system of free selection; Crown land, the freehold of which is acquired by annual payments. 6. *Biol.* the singling out of certain forms of animal and vegetable life for reproduction and perpetuation, either by the operation of natural causes (cf. **natural selection**) which result in the survival of the fittest, or by man's agency (**artificial selection**) as in breeding animals and in cultivating fruits, vegetables, etc. 7. *Linguistics.* **a.** the choice of one form instead of another in a position where both can occur, e.g., of *ask* instead of *tell* or *with* in the phrase *ask John.* **b.** the choice of one form class in a construction, to the exclusion of others which do not occur there, e.g., of a noun like *John* as direct object of *ask*, to the exclusion of adjectives and adverbs. **c.** the feature of a construction resulting from such a choice. The phrases *ask John, tell John,* and *with John* differ in selection; no adjective or adverb occurs as direct object of a verb in English. **—Ant. 1.** rejection.

selective (sĭ lĕk′tĭv), *adj.* **1.** having the function or power of selecting; making selection. **2.** fastidious; discriminating. **3.** characterized by selection. **4.** *Radio.* having good selectivity.

selective employment tax, a tax levied on businesses according to the number of their employees not directly concerned with manufacturing. *Abbrev.:* S.E.T.

selective service, compulsory military service on a selective basis.

selective transmission, *Mach.* a motor vehicle gearbox in which the available forward and reverse speeds may be engaged in any order, without passing progressively through the different changes of gear.

selectivity (sĭ lĕk′tĭv′ĭ tĭ), *n.* **1.** the state or quality of being selective. **2.** *Elect.* the property of a circuit, instrument, or the like, by virtue of which it responds to electric oscillations of a particular frequency. **3.** *Radio.* (of a receiving set) the ability to receive any one of a band of frequencies or waves to the exclusion of others.

selectman (sĭ lĕkt′mən), *n., pl.* **-men.** *U.S.* (in New England) one of a board of town officers chosen to manage certain public affairs.

selector (sĭ lĕk′tə), *n.* **1.** one who or a device which selects. **2.** one who chooses the members of a team or the like. **3.** *Elect.* a mechanism which can be set to one of several positions, thus closing one of several circuits. **4.** *Austral.* one who farms a selection.

selenate (sĕl′ĭ nāt′), *n. Chem.* a salt of selenic acid.

Selene (sĭ lē′nĭ), *n. Gk Myth.* the goddess of the moon. Cf. **Luna.** [t. Gk, personification of *selḗnē* moon]

selenic (sĭ lē′nĭk, -lĕn′ĭk), *adj. Chem.* of or containing selenium, esp. in the hexavalent state.

selenic acid, *Chem.* a strong, corrosive, dibasic acid, H_2SeO_4, resembling sulphuric acid.

selenious (sĭ lē′nyəs), *adj. Chem.* of or containing tetravalent or divalent selenium.

selenite (sĕl′ĭ nīt′), *n.* **1.** a variety of gypsum, found in transparent crystals and foliated masses. **2.** *Chem.* a salt of selenious acid. [t. L: m. *selēnītēs,* t. Gk: lit., (stone) of the moon]

selenium (sĭ lē′nyəm), *n. Chem.* a non-metallic element chemically resembling sulphur and tellurium, occurring in several allotropic forms (crystalline, amorphous, etc.), and having an electrical resistance which varies under the influence of light. *Symbol:* Se; *at. wt:* 78·86; *at. no.:* 34; *sp. gr.:* (grey) 4·80 at 25°C, (red) 4·50 at 25°C. [NL, f. s. Gk *selḗnē* moon + *-ium* -IUM]

selenium cell, *Elect.* a photoelectric cell which depends upon the influence of light on the conductivity of a strip of selenium supported between two metal electrodes.

selenium rectifier, *Elect.* a rectifier which consists of alternate layers of iron and selenium in contact.

seleno-, 1. a word element meaning 'moon', as in *selenology.* **2.** *Chem.* a combining form of *selenium.* [comb. form of Gk *selḗnē* moon]

selenography (sē′lĭ nŏg′rə fĭ), *n.* the science dealing with the moon, esp. with reference to its physical features. [See SELENE, -GRAPHY] **—se′lenog′rapher,** *n.* **—selenographic** (sĭ lē′nō grăf′ĭk), *adj.*

selenology (sē′lĭ nŏl′ə jĭ), *n.* that branch of astronomy dealing with the moon. **—se′lenol′ogist,** *n.*

selenotropism (sē′lĭ nŏt′rə pĭz′əm), *adj.* the movement of parts of plants caused by moonlight. **—sele′notrop′ic,** *adj.*

Seleucia (sĭ lyōō′shyə), *n.* **1.** an ancient city of Babylonia, on the Tigris, N of Babylon. **2.** an ancient coastal city in NW ancient Syria, near the mouth of the river Orontes: the port of Antioch.

Seleucid (sĭ lyōō′sĭd), *n., pl.* **-cids, -cidae** (-sĭ dē′), *adj.* —*n.* **1.** a member of a dynasty founded in Asia about 312 B.C. by Seleucus I, and at one time ruling over Bactria, Persia, Babylon, and Syria. It lasted until about 64 B.C. —*adj.* **2.** of or pertaining to the Seleucids. **—Seleucidan** (sĭ lyōō′sĭ dən), *adj.*

Seleucus I (sĭ lyōō′kəs), **Nicator** (nī kā′tô), *c.* 358–281? B.C., Macedonian general of Alexander the Great, and ruler and conqueror in Babylonia, Syria, etc.

self (sĕlf), *n., pl.* **selves,** *adj., pron., pl.* **selves.** *—n.* **1.** a person or thing referred to with respect to individuality; one's own person: *one's own self.* **2.** one's nature, character, etc.: *one's better self.* **3.** personal interest; selfishness. **4.** *Philos.* the ego as opposed to the non-ego; the unifying condition of all one's knowing, feeling, and willing, as opposed to what one knows, feels, and wills. **5.** an emphatic form, as used addressing someone: *your good self.* *—adj.* **6.** being the same throughout, as a colour; uniform. **7.** being of one piece or material with the rest. **8.** *Archaic.* same. *—pron.* **9.** myself, himself, etc.: *to make a cheque payable to self.* [ME and OE, c. D *zelf,* G *Selb*]

self-, prefixal use of *self,* appearing in various parts of speech, expressing principally reflexive action, e.g., subject identical with direct object, as in *self-control, self-government, self-help;* with indirect-object or adverbial-type relations, as in *self-conscious, self-centred, self-evident.*

self-abasement (sĕlf′ə bās′mənt), *n.* abasement or humiliation of oneself, esp. as a penance or punishment administered from guilt or shame.

self-abnegation (sĕlf′ăb′nĭ gā′shən), *n.* self-denial.

self-absorbed (sĕlf′əb sôbd′), *adj.* particularly preoccupied with one's own thoughts, interests, etc., esp. to the exclusion of others.

self-absorption (sĕlf′əb sôp′shən), *n.* **1.** preoccupation with oneself, esp. to the exclusion of other interests. **2.** *Physics.* absorption of part of the radiation emitted by a radioactive material by the material itself.

self-abuse (sĕlf′ə byōōs′), *n.* **1.** masturbation. **2.** criticism, deprecation, or disparagement of oneself.

self-accusing (sĕlf′ə kyōō′zĭng), *adj.* penitent; accepting or assuming blame.

self-acting (sĕlf′ăk′tĭng), *adj.* automatic.

self-addressed (sĕlf′ə drĕst′), *adj.* addressed to oneself.

self-adjusting (sĕlf′ə jŭs′tĭng), *adj.* capable of adjusting itself, or automatically returning to an original position, as a machine.

self-aggrandizement (sĕlf′ə grăn′dĭz mənt), *n.* increase of one's own power, wealth, etc., usually aggressively. Also, **self-aggrandisement.**

self-annealing (sĕlf′ə nē′lĭng), *adj. Metall.* denoting or pertaining to certain metals, as lead, tin and zinc, which recrystallize at air temperatures so that they may be cold-worked without strain-hardening.

self-appointed (sĕlf′ə poin′tĭd), *adj.* acting or speaking as if having authority, without being authorized or requested to do so.

self-assertion (sĕlf′ə sû′shən), *n.* insistence on or expression of one's own importance, claims, wishes, opinions, etc. **—self′-asser′tive,** *adj.*

self-assurance (sĕlf′ə shŏŏə′rəns, -shô′rəns), *n.* self-confidence.

self-assured (sĕlf′ə shŏŏəd′, -shôd′), *adj.* self-confident.

self-aware (sĕlf′ə wĕə′), *adj.* **1.** conscious of or knowing one's character, abilities, and weaknesses, etc. **2.** excessively aware of or obsessed with oneself. **—self′-aware′ness,** *n.*

self-binder (sĕlf′bīn′də), *n.* a combine harvester which binds (corn, etc.) automatically.

self-centred (sĕlf′sĕn′təd), *adj.* **1.** engrossed in self; selfish. **2.** centred in oneself or itself. **3.** being itself fixed as a centre.

self-centring (sĕlf′sĕn′tə rĭng), *adj.* **1.** automatically returning to a central position after displacement. **2.** (of a

self′-ac′cusa′tion, *n.*
self′-accu′satory, *adj.*
self′-accused′, *adj.*
self′-adhe′sive, *adj.*
self′-admin′istered, *adj.*
self′-admin′istering, *adj.*
self′-ad′mira′tion, *n.*
self′-admir′ing, *adj.*
self′-admir′ingly, *adv.*
self′-adorn′ment, *n.*
self′-ad′ula′tion, *n.*
self′-advance′ment, *n.*
self′-adver′tisement, *n.*
self′-ad′vertis′ing, *adj.*
self′-align′ing, *adj.*
self′-align′ment, *n.*
self′-amuse′ment, *n.*
self′-anal′ysis, *n.*
self′-applaud′ing, *adj.*
self′-applause′, *n.*
self′-appre′ciat′ing, *adj.*
self′-appre′cia′tion, *n.*
self′-appro′val, *n.*
self′-au′thoriz′ing, *adj.*
self′-ban′ishment, *n.*
self′-ben′efiting, *adj.*
self′-betray′al, *n.*
self′-can′celled, *adj.*
self′-can′celling, *adj.*
self′-cas′tigat′ing, *adj.*
self′-cas′tiga′tion, *n.*
self′-chas′tisement, *n.*
self′-clean′ing, *adj.*
self′-clos′ing, *adj.*
self′-cock′ing, *adj.*
self′-cogni′tion, *n.*

lathe chuck) containing a mechanism which ensures that the jaws are always concentric.

self-coloured (sĕlf′kŭl′ərd), *adj.* **1.** of one uniform colour. **2.** of the natural colour.

self-command (sĕlf′kə mänd′), *n.* self-control.

self-complacent (sĕlf′kəm plā′sənt), *adj.* pleased with oneself; self-satisfied. —**self′-compla′cently,** *adv.*

self-composed (sĕlf′kəm pōzd′), *adj.* calm within oneself; composed. —**self′-compo′sedly,** *adv.*

self-conceit (sĕlf′kən sēt′), *n.* an excessively good opinion of oneself, one's abilities, etc. —**self′-conceit′ed,** *adj.*

self-confessed (sĕlf′kən fĕst′), *adj.* known to be such on one's own testimony: *a self-confessed murderer.*

self-confidence (sĕlf′kŏn′fĭ dəns), *n.* confidence in one's own judgement, ability, power, etc., sometimes to an excessive degree. —**self′-con′fident,** *adj.* —**self′-con′fidently,** *adj.*

self-congratulation (sĕlf′kən grăt′yo͝o lā′shən), *n.* approval, esp. uncritical, of one's achievements, qualities, abilities, etc. —**self′-congrat′ulatory,** *adj.*

self-conscious (sĕlf′kŏn′shəs), *adj.* **1.** excessively conscious of oneself as an object of observation to others. **2.** conscious of oneself or one's own thoughts, etc. —**self′-con′sciously,** *adv.* —**self′-con′sciousness,** *n.*

self-consistent (sĕlf′kən sĭs′tənt), *adj.* **1.** consistent with oneself or itself. **2.** consistent with one's stated principles.

self-contained (sĕlf′kən tānd′), *adj.* **1.** containing in oneself or itself all that is necessary; independent. **2.** (of a flat or house) having its own kitchen, bathroom, and lavatory; not necessitating sharing. **3.** reserved or uncommunicative. **4.** self-possessed; calm. **5.** (of a machine) complete in itself.

self-content (sĕlf′kən tĕnt′), *n.* satisfaction with oneself; self-complacency. Also, **self′-content′ment.**

self-contradiction (sĕlf′kŏn′trə dĭk′shən), *n.* **1.** the act or fact of contradicting oneself or itself. **2.** a statement containing contradictory elements. —**self′-con′tradic′tory,** *adj.*

self-control (sĕlf′kən trōl′), *n.* control of oneself or one's actions, feelings, etc.

self-critical (sĕlf′krĭt′ĭ kl), *adj.* **1.** finding fault, esp. to an excessive degree, with one's own actions or motives. **2.** assessing one's actions, motives, or achievements impartially. —**self′-crit′ically,** *adv.* —**self′-crit′icism.** *n.*

self-deception (sĕlf′dĭ sĕp′shən), *n.* the act or fact of deceiving oneself. Also, **self-deceit** (sĕlf′dĭ sēt′). —**self′-decep′tive,** *adj.*

self-defeating (sĕlf′dĭ fē′tĭng), *adj.* (of an action, plan, argument, or the like) having inherent defects or contradictions which serve to frustrate or nullify the original purpose.

self-defence (sĕlf′dĭ fĕns′), *n.* **1.** the act of defending one's own person, reputation, etc. **2.** *Law.* the use of reasonable force against an attacker, constituting a defence in criminal law and tort. —**self′-defen′sive,** *adj.*

self-denial (sĕlf′dĭ nī′əl), *n.* the sacrifice of one's own desires; unselfishness. —**self′-deny′ing,** *adj.* —**self′-deny′ingly,** *adv.*

self-deprecating (sĕlf′dĕp′rə kā′tĭng), *adj.* modest; understating one's worth. —**self′-dep′recat′ingly,** *adv.* —**self′-dep′reca′tion,** *n.*

self-destruction (sĕlf′dĭ strŭk′shən), *n.* the destruction of oneself or itself; suicide.

self-determination (sĕlf′dĭ tû′mĭ nā′shən), *n.* **1.** determination by oneself or itself, without outside influence. **2.** the determining by a people or nationality of the form of government it shall have, without reference to the wishes of any other nation. —**self′-deter′mined,** *adj.* —**self′-deter′mining,** *adj., n.*

self-devotion (sĕlf′dĭ vō′shən), *n.* devotion of oneself; self-sacrifice. —**self′-devo′tional,** *adj.*

self-discipline (sĕlf′dĭs′ĭ plĭn), *n.* discipline and training of oneself, usually for improvement.

self-distrust (sĕlf′dĭs trŭst′), *n.* lack of confidence in oneself, one's abilities, etc.

self-educated (sĕlf′ĕd′yo͝o kā′tĭd), *adj.* educated by one's own efforts, without formal instruction, or without financial assistance. —**self′-ed′uca′tion,** *n.*

self-effacement (sĕlf′ĭ fās′mənt), *n.* the act or fact of keeping oneself in the background, as in humility. —**self′-effac′ing,** *adj.*

self-employed (sĕlf′ĭm ploid′), *adj.* deriving one's income directly from one's own work, profession, or business, and not as a salary from an employer.

self-esteem (sĕlf′ĭs tēm′), *n.* favourable opinion of oneself; conceit. —**Syn.** See **pride.** —**Ant.** diffidence.

self-evident (sĕlf′ĕv′ĭ dənt), *adj.* evident in itself without proof; axiomatic. —**self′-ev′idence,** *n.* —**self-ev′idently,** *adv.*

self-examination (sĕlf′ĭg zăm′ĭ nā′shən), *n.* examination into one's own state, conduct, motives, etc.

self-excited (sĕlf′ĭk sī′tĭd), *adj. Elect.* denoting or pertaining to an electrical machine in which the magnetic field system is supplied by current from the machine itself, or an auxiliary machine attached to it.

self-executing (sĕlf′ĕk′sĭ kyo͞o′tĭng), *adj.* providing for its own execution, and needing no legislation to enforce it: *a self-executing treaty.*

self-existent (sĕlf′ĭg zĭs′tənt), *adj.* **1.** existing independently of any cause, as God. **2.** having an independent existence. —**self′-exist′ence,** *n.*

self-explanatory (sĕlf′ĭk splăn′ə tə rĭ, -trĭ), *adj.* needing no explanation; obvious. Also, **self′-explain′ing.**

self-expression (sĕlf′ĭk sprĕsh′ən), *n.* the expression or assertion of one's personality by poetry, music, etc., or by one's behaviour, esp. unhampered by limitations imposed by an outside authority.

self-feeder (sĕlf′fē′də), *n. Chiefly U.S.* **1.** a machine that fuels itself, or feeds itself with raw materials or the like. **2.** a device attached to a machine that supplies it with fuel or raw materials or the like. **3.** *Agric.* an automatic machine for feeding livestock.

self-fertilization (sĕlf′fû′tĭ lĭ zā′shən), *n. Bot.* the fertilization of a flower by its own pollen (opposed to *cross-fertilization*). Also, **self-fertilisation.**

self-forgetful (sĕlf′fə gĕt′fəl), *adj.* forgetful, or not thinking, of one's own advantage, interest, etc.

self-governed (sĕlf′gŭv′ənd), *adj.* governed by itself, or having self-government, as a state or community; independent. —**self′-gov′erning,** *adj.*

self-government (sĕlf′gŭv′ən mənt), *n.* **1.** government of a state, community, or other body or persons by its members jointly; democratic government. **2.** political independence of a country, people, region, etc. **3.** the condition of being self-governed. **4.** self-control.

self-hardening (sĕlf′hä′dn ĭng), *adj. Metall.* denoting or pertaining to any of certain steels which harden without the usual quenching, etc., necessary for ordinary steel. —**self′-hard′ened,** *adj.*

selfheal (sĕlf′hēl′), *n.* **1.** a small, perennial, labiate herb, *Prunella vulgaris,* once accredited with great remedial virtues. **2.** any of various other plants similarly credited.

self-help (sĕlf′hĕlp′), *n.* the state or an act of achieving one's ends unaided by others.

selfhood (sĕlf′ho͝od), *n.* **1.** the state of being an individual person. **2.** one's personality. **3.** selfishness.

self-identity (sĕlf′ī dĕn′tĭ tĭ), *n.* the identity, or consciousness of identity, of a thing with itself.

self-important (sĕlf′ĭm pô′tnt), *adj.* having or showing an exaggerated opinion of one's own importance; conceited or pompous. —**self′-impor′tance,** *n.* —**self′-impor′tantly,** *adv.*

---

self′-com′menda′tion, *n.*
self′-com′prehen′ding, *adj.*
self′-com′prehen′sion, *n.*
self′-con′demna′tion, *n.*
self′-condem′natory, *adj.*
self′-condemned′, *adj.*
self′-confine′ment, *n.*
self′-confin′ing, *adj.*
self′-consol′ing, *adj.*
self′-consum′ing, *adj.*
self′-contempt′, *n.*
self′-correc′ting, *adj.*
self′-creat′ed, *adj.*
self′-damna′tion, *n.*
self′-debase′ment, *n.*
self′-deceived′, *adj.*
self′-defin′ing, *adj.*
self′-def′ini′tion, *n.*
self′-deg′rada′tion, *n.*
self′-delu′sion, *n.*
self′-depre′cia′tion, *n.*
self′-dep′riva′tion, *n.*
self′-destroyed′, *adj.*
self′-destruc′tive, *adj.*
self′-devel′opment, *n.*
self′-direc′ted, *adj.*
self′-direc′ting, *adj.*
self′-dis′appro′val, *n.*
self′-discov′ery, *n.*
self′-dis′engage′ment,
self′-disgust′, *n.*
self′-dispa′ragement, *n.*
self′-dispa′raging, *adj.*
self′-display′, *n.*
self′-dissat′isfac′tion, *n.*
self′-dissat′isfied′, *adj.*
self′-dis′solu′tion, *n.*
self′-doubt′, *n.*
self′-dram′atiza′tion, *n.*
self′-driv′en, *adj.*
self′-elec′ted, *adj.*
self′-elec′tion, *n.*
self′-emp′tying, *adj.*
self′-enam′oured, *adj.*
self′-engrossed′, *adj.*
self′-enrich′ment, *n.*
self′-eval′ua′tion, *n.*
self′-ex′ulta′tion, *n.*
self′-ex′culpa′tion, *n.*
self′-excus′ing, *adj.*
self′-ex′ile, *n.*
self′-ex′iled, *adj.*
self′-expo′sure, *n.*
self′-exter′mina′tion, *n.*
self′-fil′ling, *adj.*
self′-flag′ella′tion, *n.*
self′-flat′tery, *n.*
self′-fo′cusing, *adj.*
self′-fulfil′ment, *n.*
self′-gen′erat′ed, *adj.*
self′-giv′ing, *adj.*
self′-glo′rify′ing, *adj.*
self′-grat′ifica′tion, *n.*
self′-hat′red, *n.*
self′-heal′ing, *adj.*
self′-hum′bling, *adj.*
self′-humil′ia′tion, *n.*
self′-hypno′sis, *n.*
self′-ig′norant, *adj.*
self′-im′mola′tion, *n.*

---

self-imposed (sĕlf′ĭm pōzd′), *adj.* imposed on one by oneself: *a self-imposed task.*

self-improvement (sĕlf′ĭm pro͞ov′mənt), *n.* improvement of one's mind, education, status, etc., by one's own efforts.

self-induced (sĕlf′ĭn dyo͞ost′), *adj.* **1.** induced by oneself or itself. **2.** produced by self-induction.

self-inductance (sĕlf′ĭn dŭk′təns), *n. Elect.* **1.** the property of a circuit in which self-induction occurs. **2.** a measure of this property equal to the rate of change of flux linkages in a circuit accompanying a rate of change of one unit of current per second in that circuit; coefficient of self-induction.

self-induction (sĕlf′ĭn dŭk′shən), *n. Elect.* the production of an induced electromotive force in a circuit by a varying current in that circuit.

self-indulgent (sĕlf′ĭn dŭl′jənt), *adj.* **1.** indulging one's own desires, passions, etc., esp. at the expense of other considerations. **2.** characterized by such indulgence. **—self′-indul′gence,** *n.* **—self′-indul′gently,** *adv.*

self-inflicted (sĕlf′ĭn flĭk′tĭd), *adj.* inflicted on one by oneself: *a self-inflicted wound.*

self-insurance (sĕlf′ĭn sho͞oə′rəns, -shô′rəns), *n.* **1.** the insuring of one's property, etc., through oneself, as by setting aside a fund for the purpose. **2.** the amount by which the actual value of one's property exceeds the cover provided by an insurance policy.

self-interest (sĕlf′ĭn′trĭst), *n.* **1.** regard for one's own interest or advantage, esp. with disregard of others. **2.** personal interest or advantage.

selfish (sĕl′fĭsh), *adj.* **1.** devoted to or caring only for oneself, one's welfare, interests, etc. **2.** characterized by caring only for oneself: *selfish motives.* **—self′ishly,** *adv.* **—self′ishness,** *n.* **—Syn. 1.** self-interested, self-seeking, egoistic.

self-justification (sĕlf′jŭs′tĭ fĭ kā′shən), *n.* **1.** the act or fact of explaining or explaining away one's actions, motives, etc. **2.** a justification or raison d'être which is inherent in a thing. **3.** *Print.* the automatic adjustment of lines being typeset.

self-justifying (sĕlf′jŭs′tĭ fī′ĭng), *adj.* **1.** excusing or explaining one's actions, etc., as to avoid blame, esp. excessively. **2.** containing in itself its justification or raison d'être. **3.** *Print.* automatically adjusting the length of lines being typeset.

self-knowledge (sĕlf′nŏl′ĭj), *n.* knowledge of oneself, one's character, abilities, etc.

selfless (sĕlf′lĭs), *adj.* unselfish.

self-liquidating (sĕlf′lĭk′wĭ dā′tĭng), *adj.* assured of being sold and converted into cash within a short period of time or before the date on which the supplier, etc., must be paid: *a self-liquidating loan.*

self-loading (sĕlf′lō′dĭng), *adj.* reloading automatically, as a firearm.

self-locking (sĕlf′lŏk′ĭng), *adj.* **1.** locking automatically when closed, as a door or lid. **2.** having a self-locking lid, door, or device.

self-love (sĕlf′lŭv′), *n.* **1.** egotism; selfishness, narcissism, **2.** the instinct by which man's actions are directed to the promotion of his own welfare. **3.** *Philos.* the self-respect that constitutes a man's proper relation with himself. **—self′-lov′ing,** *adj.*

self-made (sĕlf′mād′), *adj.* **1.** having succeeded in life unaided: *a self-made man.* **2.** made by oneself.

self-mastery (sĕlf′mäs′tə rĭ), *n.* self-control.

self-mate (sĕlf′māt′), *n. Chess.* **1.** a move or series of moves which lead inevitably to the mating of a player's own king. **2.** a problem in which this is the object. Also, **suimate, sui.**

self-moving (sĕlf′mo͞o′vĭng), *adj.* moving of itself, without external agency.

self-murder (sĕlf′mû′də), *n.* suicide. **—self′-mur′derer,** *n.*

self-opinion (sĕlf′ə pĭn′yən), *n.* **1.** opinion, esp. exaggerated opinion, of oneself. **2.** obstinacy in one's views.

self-opinionated (sĕlf′ə pĭn′yə nā′tĭd), *adj.* **1.** conceited. **2.** obstinate in one's own opinion.

self-pity (sĕlf′pĭt′ĭ), *n.* exaggerated or self-indulgent pity for oneself, or exaggeration of one's misfortunes. **—self′-pit′ying,** *adj.*

self-pollinated (sĕlf′pŏl′ĭ nā′tĭd), *adj. Bot.* having the pollen transferred from the anthers to the stigmas of the same flower. **—self′-pol′lina′tion,** *n.*

self-portrait (sĕlf′pô′trĭt), *n.* a portrait of an artist, photographer, or the like, by himself.

self-possessed (sĕlf′pə zĕst′), *adj.* having or showing control of one's feelings, behaviour, etc. **—self′-posses′sion,** *n.*

self-preservation (sĕlf′prĕz′ə vā′shən), *n.* preservation of oneself from harm or destruction.

self-propelled (sĕlf′prə pĕld′), *adj.* **1.** propelled by itself. **2.** (of a vehicle, etc.) propelled by its own engine, motor, or the like, rather than drawn or pushed by a horse, locomotive, etc. **—self′-propel′ling,** *adj.*

self-protection (sĕlf′prə tĕk′shən), *n.* protection of oneself or itself.

self-raising (sĕlf′rā′zĭng), *adj.* denoting flour that contains a raising agent, as sodium bicarbonate. Also, **self-rising.**

self-realization (sĕlf′rĭə′lĭ zā′shən), *n.* the fulfilment of one's potential capacities. Also, **self-realisation.**

self-recording (sĕlf′rĭ kô′dĭng), *adj.* recording automatically, as an instrument.

self-regard (sĕlf′rĭ gäd′), *n.* **1.** consideration for oneself or one's own interests. **2.** self-respect. **—self′-regar′ding,** *adj.*

self-registering (sĕlf′rĕj′ĭs tə rĭng), *adj.* registering automatically, as an instrument; self-recording.

self-reliance (sĕlf′rĭ lī′əns), *n.* reliance on oneself or one's own powers; confidence; independence. **—self′-reli′ant,** *adj.*

self-renunciation (sĕlf′rĭ nŭn′sĭ ā′shən), *n.* renunciation of one's own will, interests, etc.; self-sacrifice. **—self′-renun′ciatory,** *adj.*

self-reproach (sĕlf′rĭ prōch′), *n.* blame or censure by one's own conscience.

self-respect (sĕlf′rĭ spĕkt′), *n.* proper esteem or regard for the dignity of one's character.

self-respecting (sĕlf′rĭ spĕk′tĭng), *adj.* having or showing self-respect.

self-restraint (sĕlf′rĭ strānt′), *n.* restraint imposed on one by oneself; self-control.

self-righteous (sĕlf′rī′chəs), *adj.* righteous in one's own esteem; pharisaic. **—self′-right′eously,** *adv.* **—self′-right′eousness,** *n.*

self-righting (sĕlf′rī′tĭng), *adj.* denoting something, as a boat, which is built in such a way that it automatically rights itself after being upset.

self-rising (sĕlf′rī′zĭng), *adj.* self-raising.

self-sacrifice (sĕlf′săk′rĭ fīs′), *n.* sacrifice of one's interests, desires, etc., as for duty or the good of another. **—self′-sac′rific′ing,** *adj.*

selfsame (sĕlf′sām′), *adj.* (the) very same; identical. **—self′same′ness,** *n.*

self-satisfaction (sĕlf′săt′ĭs făk′shən), *n.* satisfaction with oneself, one's achievements, etc.; smugness.

self-satisfied (sĕlf′săt′ĭs fīd′), *adj.* feeling or showing satisfaction with oneself; complacent.

self-sealing (sĕlf′sē′lĭng), *adj.* denoting or pertaining to a device, container, etc., which seals itself: *a self-sealing envelope.*

self-seeker (sĕlf′sē′kə), *n.* one who seeks his own interest or selfish ends.

self-seeking (sĕlf′sē′kĭng), *n.* **1.** the seeking of one's own interest or selfish ends. *—adj.* **2.** given to or characterized by self-seeking; selfish.

self-service (sĕlf′sû′vĭs), *adj.* **1.** (of a restaurant, lift or other service) operating on the principle that the custom-

self′-incrim′inat′ing, *adj.*
self′-incrim′ina′tion, *n.*
self′-incurred′, *adj.*
self′-inflat′ing, *adj.*
self′-infla′tion, *n.*
self′-inter′roga′tion, *n.*
self′-in′troduc′tion, *n.*
self′-invit′ed, *adj.*
self′-judge′ment, *n.*
self′-la′cera′tion, *n.*
self′-laud′atory, *adj.*
self′-lev′elling, *adj.*
self′-locat′ing, *adj.*
self′-lub′ricat′ing, *adj.*
self′-maintained′, *adj.*
self′-maintain′ing, *adj.*
self′-main′tenance, *n.*
self′-mor′tifica′tion, *n.*
self′-mul′tiply′ing, *adj.*
self′-mu′tila′tion, *n.*
self′-neglect′, *n.*
self′-obsessed′, *adj.*
self′-percep′tion, *n.*
self′-perfec′ting, *adj.*
self′-perpet′uat′ing, *adj.*
self′-perpet′ua′tion, *n.*
self′-persua′sion, *n.*
self′-polic′ing, *adj.*
self′-pow′ered, *adj.*
self′-praise′, *n.*
self′-preoc′cupa′tion, *n.*
self′-preoc′cupied′, *adj.*
self′-prep′ara′tion, *n.*
self′-pres′enta′tion, *n.*
self′-proclaimed′, *adj.*
self′-prop′agat′ing, *adj.*
self′-propul′sion, *n.*
self′-prov′ing, *adj.*
self′-pun′ishing, *adj.*
self′-pun′ishment, *n.*
self′-pu′rify′ing, *adj.*
self′-quota′tion, *n.*
self′-re′construc′tion, *n.*
self′-ref′orma′tion, *n.*
self′-refut′ing, *adj.*
self′-reg′ulating, *adj.*
self′-reg′ula′tion, *n.*
self′-rep′resenta′tion, *n.*
self′-repres′sion, *n.*
self′-reproof′, *n.*
self′-revealed′, *adj.*
self′-reveal′ing, *adj.*
self′-rev′ela′tion, *n.*
self′-rev′erence, *n.*
self′-rule′, *n.*
self′-sat′isfy′ing, *adj.*
self′-schooled′, *adj.*
self′-scru′tiny, *n.*
self′-search′ing, *adj.*
self′-serv′ing, *adj.*
self′-sin′king, *adj.*
self′-slain′, *adj.*
self′-sold′, *adj.*

ers, passengers, etc., perform part or all of the service themselves. —*n.* 2. a restaurant or section of a restaurant operating on this principle. 3. the act of serving oneself.

self-sown (sĕlf′sōn′), *adj.* 1. sown by itself, or without human or animal agency. 2. sown by any agency other than man, as by birds, the wind, etc.

self-starter (sĕlf′stä′tə), *n.* a device which starts an internal-combustion engine without cranking by hand, as an electric motor, a spring, gas pressure, etc.

self-styled (sĕlf′stīld′), *adj.* (of a title or characterization), applied to himself by the person so called, esp. undeservedly: *a self-styled genius.*

self-sufficient (sĕlf′sə fĭsh′ənt), *adj.* 1. able to supply one's own needs. 2. having undue confidence in one's own resources, powers, etc. Also, **self-sufficing** (sĕlf′-sə fī′sĭng). —**self′-suffi′ciency,** *n.*

self-support (sĕlf′sə pôt′), *n.* the act or fact of supporting or maintaining oneself unaided. —**self′-support′ed,** *adj.*

self-supporting (sĕlf′sə pô′tĭng), *adj.* 1. having an income great enough to cover all outgoings. 2. requiring no props or other supports; independent: *a self-supporting wall.*

self-surrender (sĕlf′sə rĕn′də), *n.* the surrender or yielding up of oneself, one's will, affections, etc., as to another person, an influence, etc.

self-sustaining (sĕlf′sə stā′nĭng), *adj.* self-supporting.

self-tapping screw (sĕlf′tăp′ĭng), a screw which is capable of cutting a female thread in the hole into which it is screwed.

self-taught (sĕlf′tôt′), *adj.* taught by oneself without aid from others.

self-will (sĕlf′wĭl′), *n.* 1. wilfulness. 2. obstinacy.

self-willed (sĕlf′wĭld′), *adj.* obstinately or perversely insistent on one's own desires or opinions.

self-winding (sĕlf′wīn′dĭng), *adj.* (of a clock or watch) winding itself automatically by a motor, by its wearer's movements, or the like.

Seljuk (sĕl jo͞ok′), *adj.* 1. denoting or pertaining to certain Turkish dynasties which ruled over large parts of Asia from the 11th to the 13th century. —*n.* 2. a member of a Seljuk dynasty or of a tribe ruled by them. Also, **Seljukian** (sĕl jo͞o′kĭ ən).

Selk., Selkirkshire.

Selkirk (sĕl′kûk), *n.* 1. **Alexander** (orig. *Alexander Selcraig*), 1676–1721, Scottish sailor marooned on a Pacific island: supposed prototype of Robinson Crusoe. 2. a burgh in Scotland, the county town of Selkirkshire. 5635 (1961). 3. Selkirkshire.

Selkirkshire (sĕl′kûk shĭə′, -shə), *n.* a county in SE Scotland. 21,055 pop. (1961); 268 sq. mi. *Co. town:* Selkirk. Also, **Selkirk.**

sell (sĕl), *v.*, **sold, selling,** *n.* —*v.t.* 1. to give up or make over for a consideration; dispose of to a purchaser for a price. 2. to deal in; keep for sale. 3. to act as a dealer in or seller of: *he sells insurance.* 4. to facilitate or induce the sale of: *the package sells the product.* 5. to induce or attempt to induce purchasers for: *he used to be a good actor, but now he is selling soap on television.* 6. to cause to be accepted: *to sell an idea to the public.* 7. *Slang.* to cheat or hoax. —*v.i.* 8. to sell something; engage in selling. 9. to be on sale; find purchasers. 10. to win acceptance, approval, or adoption.
—*v.* 11. Some special verb phrases are:
be sold on, *Slang.* to approve of or accept, esp. uncritically.
sell dearly, to part with after great and protracted resistance: *to sell one's life dearly.*
sell down the river, *Slang.* to betray.
sell off, to sell at reduced prices, or with some other inducement for quick sale.
sell out, 1. to dispose of (goods or a particular product) entirely by selling; have none left (of). 2. to betray.
sell up, 1. to liquidate by selling the assets (of). 2. to sell a business.
—*n.* 12. *Colloq.* an act of selling or salesmanship. Cf. **hard sell, soft sell.** 13. *Slang.* a hoax or deception. 14. *Slang.* a disappointment.
[ME *selle(n)*, OE *sellan*, c. LG *sellen*] —**Syn.** 1. See **trade.**

seller (sĕl′ə), *n.* 1. one who sells; a vendor. 2. an article, as a book, considered with reference to its sale: *one of the worst sellers in its price range.* 3. a selling-plate.

seller's market, a market in which the seller is at an advantage because of scarcity of supply.

selling-plate (sĕl′ĭng plāt′), *n.* a horserace whose winner must be offered for sale at auction. Also, **selling-race.**

selling-plater (sĕl′ĭng plā′tə), *n.* 1. a horse that competes in a selling-plate. 2. something or someone second-rate.

Sellotape (sĕl′ə tāp′), *n. Trademark.* an adhesive tape made of cellulose and usually transparent.

sell-out (sĕl′out′), *n.* 1. a betrayal. 2. *Colloq.* a play, show, etc., for which all seats are sold.

Seltzer (sĕlt′sə), *n.* 1. a natural effervescent mineral water containing common salt and small quantities of sodium, calcium, and magnesium carbonates. 2. (*also l.c.*) an artificial water of similar composition. Also, **Seltzer water.** [t. G: m. *Selterser*, der. *Selters*, a village near Wiesbaden]

selva (sĕl′və), *n.*, *pl.* **-vas** (sĕl′vəz; *Port.* sĕl′vás). a tract of dense, tropical rainforest in the Amazon basin.

selvage (sĕl′vĭj), *n.* 1. the edge of woven fabric finished to prevent fraying, often in a narrow tape effect, different from the body of the fabric. 2. any similar strip or part of surplus material, as at the side of wallpaper. Also, **selvedge.** [late ME, f. SELF + EDGE. Cf. D *zelfegge*]

selves (sĕlvz), *n.* pl. of **self.**

Sem., 1. Seminary. 2. Semitic.

semantic (sĭ măn′tĭk), *adj.* 1. pertaining to signification or meaning. 2. *Linguistics.* concerning the meaning of words and other linguistic forms. [t. Gk: m. s. *sēmantikós* significant]

semantics (sĭ măn′tĭks), *n.* 1. *Linguistics.* the systematic study of the meanings of words and changes thereof. 2. *Logic.* that branch of modern logic which studies the relations between signs and what they denote or signify.

semaphore (sĕm′ə fô′), *n.*, *v.*, **-phored, -phoring.** —*n.* 1. an apparatus for conveying information by means of signals, esp. a device consisting of a pivoted arm used on railways. 2. a system of signalling by hand, in which a flag is held in each hand at arm's length in various positions. —*v.t.*, *v.i.* 3. to signal by semaphore. [f. Gk *sêma* sign + -PHORE] —**semaphoric** (sĕm′ə fŏ′-rĭk), *adj.*

Semaphore signal
A, Clear; B, Stop

Semarang (*Indon.* sə mä′ràng), *n.* a seaport in Indonesia, in N Java. 503,153 (1961). Also, **Samarang.**

semasiology (sĭ mā′sĭ ŏl′ə jĭ), *n.* semantics, esp. the study of semantic change. [f. s. Gk *sēmasía* signification + -(O)LOGY] —**semasiological** (sĭ-mā′sĭ ə lŏj′ĭ kl), *adj.* —**sema′siol′ogist,** *n.*

sematic (sĭ măt′ĭk), *adj. Biol.* serving as a sign or warning of danger, as the conspicuous colours or markings of certain poisonous animals. [f. s. Gk *sêma* sign + -IC]

semblable (sĕm′blə bl), *Archaic.* —*adj.* 1. like or similar. 2. seeming or apparent. —*n.* 3. likeness; resemblance. [ME, t. OF, der. *sembler* appear. See SEMBLANCE] —**sem′-blably,** *adv.*

semblance (sĕm′bləns), *n.* 1. an outward aspect or appearance. 2. an assumed or unreal appearance; a mere show. 3. a likeness, image, or copy. [ME, t. OF, der. *sembler* be like, seem, g. L *similāre*, for *simulāre*]

semé (sĕm′ā; *Fr.* sə mė′), *adj. Her.* strewn or covered with small figures of the same kind, as stars or flowers. Also, **semée.** [t. F, pp. of *semer* sow, strew, g. L *sēmināre*]

semeiology (sē′mĭ ŏl′ə jĭ), *n.* 1. the science of signs. 2. sign language. 3. the branch of medical science dealing with symptoms. Also, **semiology.** [f. m. Gk *sēmeîo(n)* sign + -LOGY]

semeiotic (sē′mĭ ŏt′ĭk), *adj.* 1. *Med.* pertaining to symptoms; symptomatic. 2. *Obs.* pertaining to signs. Also, **semeiotical, semiotic, semiotical.** [f. m. s. Gk *sēmeîon* sign + -OTIC]

Semele (sĕm′ĭ lĭ), *n. Gk Myth.* the daughter of Cadmus, and mother by Zeus of Dionysus. Zeus destroyed her by lightning when she asked to see him in his true form.

semen (sē′mĕn), *n.* the impregnating fluid produced by male reproductive organs; seed; sperm. [t. L: seed]

semester (sĭ mĕs′tə), *n.* 1. (in many U.S. educational institutions) one of either two or three divisions of the academic year, consisting of between 15 and 18 weeks. See **term.** 2. (in German universities) a session, lasting about six months, inclusive of periods of recess. [t. G, t. L: m. *sēme(n)stris*, f. *sē-* (comb. form of *sex* six) + *menstris* monthly] —**semes′tral,** *adj.*

---

self′-sta′biliz′ing, *adj.*
self′-stim′ulat′ed, *adj.*
self′-stim′ulat′ing, *adj.*
self′-stim′ula′tion, *n.*
self′-suppres′sion, *n.*
self′-tap′ping, *adj.*
self′-teach′ing, *adj.*
self′-ter′minat′ing, *adj.*
self′-tes′ting, *adj.*
self′-thread′ing, *adj.*
self′-tigh′tening, *adj.*
self′-tip′ping, *adj.*
self′-tor′ment, *n.*
self′-tor′ture, *n.*
self′-tor′turing, *adj.*
self′-trained′, *adj.*
self′-trans′forma′tion, *n.*
self′-tui′tion, *n.*
self′-unload′ing, *adj.*
self′-val′ua′tion, *n.*
self′-val′uing, *adj.*
self′-var′ying, *adj.*
self′-vin′dicat′ing, *adj.*
self′-wor′ship, *n.*

---

semi (sĕm′ĭ), *n. Colloq.* a semidetached house.

semi-, a prefix modifying the latter element of the word, meaning 'half' in its precise and less precise meanings, as in *semicircle, semiannual, semidetached, semiaquatic.* [t. L, c. Gk *hēmi-*, OE *sām-, sōm-* half]

semiannual (sĕm′ĭ ăn′yo͞o əl), *adj.* **1.** occurring every half-year. **2.** lasting for half a year. —**sem′ian′nually,** *adv.*

semiaquatic (sĕm′ĭ ə kwăt′ĭk), *adj. Bot., Zool.* partly aquatic; growing or living close to water, and sometimes found in or entering water.

semiautomatic (sĕm′ĭ ô′tə măt′ĭk), *adj.* **1.** partly automatic. **2.** (of a firearm) self-loading, but requiring a separate pull of the trigger at each shot. —*n.* **3.** a self-loading rifle or other firearm.

semibreve (sĕm′ĭ brēv′), *n. Music.* a note having half the length of a breve, being the longest note in common use. See illus. under **note.**

semicentennial (sĕm′ĭ sĕn tĕn′yəl), *Chiefly U.S.* —*adj.* **1.** occurring at, or celebrating, the completion of fifty years (half a century). —*n.* **2.** a semicentennial celebration.

semicircle (sĕm′ĭ sû′kl), *n.* **1.** the half of a circle. **2.** anything having, or arranged in, the form of a half of a circle. —**semicircular** (sĕm′ĭ sû′kyo͝o lə), *adj.*

semicircular canal, *Anat.* any of three curved tubular canals in the labyrinth of the ear, concerned with equilibrium. See diag. under **ear.**

semicivilized (sĕm′ĭ sĭv′ĭ līzd′), *adj.* half or partly civilized. Also, **semicivilised.**

semicoke (sĕm′ĭ kōk′), *n.* Coalite.

semicolon (sĕm′ĭ kō′lən), *n.* a mark of punctuation (;) used to indicate a more distinct separation between parts of a sentence than that indicated by a comma.

semiconductor (sĕm′ĭ kən dŭk′tə), *n. Elect.* **1.** a substance whose conductivity at normal temperatures is intermediate between that of a metal and an insulator, and whose conductivity increases with a rise in temperature over a certain range, as germanium and silicon. **2.** a device, as a transistor, which is based on the electronic properties of such substances.

semiconscious (sĕm′ĭ kŏn′shəs), *adj.* half-conscious; not fully conscious.

semicylinder (sĕm′ĭ sĭl′ĭn də), *n.* one of the halves of a cylinder which has been dissected lengthways. —**semicylindrical** (sĕm′ĭ sĭ lĭn′drĭ kl), *adj.*

semidetached (sĕm′ĭ dĭ tăcht′), *adj.* partly detached (used esp. of a pair of houses joined by a common wall but detached from other buildings).

semidiameter (sĕm′ĭ dī ăm′ĭ tə), *n.* **1.** the half of a diameter; a radius. **2.** half the angular diameter of a celestial body.

semidiurnal (sĕm′ĭ dī û′nəl), *adj.* **1.** pertaining to, consisting of, or accomplished in half a day. **2.** occurring every twelve hours.

semidivine (sĕm′ĭ dĭ vīn′), *adj.* partly divine.

semidocumentary (sĕm′ĭ dŏk′yo͞o mĕn′tə rĭ), *adj.* **1.** (of a film) having both documentary and imaginary elements, as a fictional story with an actual background. —*n.* **2.** a semidocumentary film.

semidome (sĕm′ĭ dōm′), *n.* half a dome, esp. as formed by a vertical section, as over a semicircular apse.

semielliptical (sĕm′ĭ ĭ lĭp′tĭ kl), *adj.* shaped like the half of an ellipse, esp. one whose base is the major axis of the ellipse.

semifinal (sĕm′ĭ fī′nəl), *Sport.* —*adj.* **1.** designating a round, contest, match, etc., which immediately precedes the final and decisive one. **2.** pertaining to such a round, contest, etc. —*n.* **3.** a semifinal round, contest, etc.

semifinalist (sĕm′ĭ fī′nə lĭst), *n. Sport.* any player who competes in the semifinals.

semifluid (sĕm′ĭ flo͞o′ĭd), *adj.* **1.** imperfectly fluid, having both fluid and solid characteristics. —*n.* **2.** a semifluid substance. Also, **semiliquid** (sĕm′ĭ lĭk′wĭd).

semilunar (sĕm′ĭ lo͞o′nə), *adj.* shaped like a half-moon; crescent.

semilunar bone, *Anat.* the second bone from the thumb side of the proximal row of the carpus.

semilunar cartilage, *Anat.* one of two cartilages inside the knee joint.

semilunar valve, *Anat.* **1.** a crescent-shaped valve consisting of three flaps, in the orifice of the aorta, which prevents blood from flowing back into the left ventricle. **2.** a similar valve in the pulmonary artery, which prevents blood from flowing back into the right ventricle.

semimonthly (sĕm′ĭ mŭnth′lĭ), *adj., n., pl.* **-lies,** *adv.* —*adj.* **1.** occurring every half month. —*n.* **2.** a thing occurring every half month. **3.** a semimonthly publication. —*adv.* **4.** every half month.

seminal (sĕm′ĭ nəl), *adj.* **1.** of, pertaining to, or of the nature of semen. **2.** *Bot.* of or pertaining to seed. **3.** highly original and influential. **4.** having possibilities of future, development. **5.** rudimentary; embryonic. [ME, f. s. L *sēmen* seed + -AL[1]] —**sem′inally,** *adv.*

seminar (sĕm′ĭ nä′), *n.* **1.** a small group of students, as in a university, engaged in advanced study and original research under a professor or the like. **2.** the gathering place of such a group. **3.** a course or subject of study for advanced graduate students. **4.** a meeting of students, usually at an advanced level, for discussion of and instruction in a specified topic, usually chaired by a teacher. [t. G, t. L: m. s. *sēminārium* (neut.) of or for seed]

seminarist (sĕm′ĭ nə rĭst), *n.* **1.** one who attends a seminary, as in training for the priesthood. **2.** one who teaches in a seminary. **3.** (formerly) a priest trained overseas for the mission to England. —**seminarian** (sĕm′ĭ nĕə′rĭ ən), *adj.*

seminary (sĕm′ĭ nə rĭ), *n., pl.* **-naries. 1.** *Rom. Cath. Ch.* a college for the education of men for the priesthood or ministry. **2.** a school, esp. one of higher level. **3.** (formerly) a school for young ladies. **4.** *U.S.* a seminar. **5.** a place of origin and development. [late ME, t. L: m. s. *sēminārium* nursery]

semination (sĕm′ĭ nā′shən), *n.* dissemination.

seminiferous (sĕm′ĭ nĭf′ə rəs), *adj.* **1.** *Anat.* conveying or containing semen. **2.** *Bot.* bearing or producing seed. [f. *semini-* (t. NL, comb. form. repr. L *sēmen* seed) + -FEROUS]

Seminole (sĕm′ĭ nōl′), *n., pl.* **-nole, -noles** (-nōlz′), *adj.* —*n.* **1.** a member of a Muskhogean tribe of American Indians, an offshoot of the Creeks, resident in Florida, and now also in Oklahoma. **2.** their language. —*adj.* **3.** of or pertaining to this tribe. [t. Creek: m. *Sim-a-nó-le,* or *Isti siminóla* separatist, runaway]

semiofficial (sĕm′ĭ ə fĭsh′əl), *adj.* having some degree of official authority. —**sem′ioffi′cially,** *adv.*

semiology (sē′mĭ ŏl′ə jĭ), *n.* semeiology.

semiotic (sē′mĭ ŏt′ĭk), *adj.* semeiotic.

Semipalatinsk (*Russ.* sĭ mĭ pä lä′tĭnsk), *n.* a city in the S Soviet Union in Asia, on the river Irtish. 188,000 (est. 1963).

semipalmate (sĕm′ĭ păl′mĭt), *adj.* partially or imperfectly palmate, as a bird's foot; half-webbed. Also, **sem′ipal′mated.**

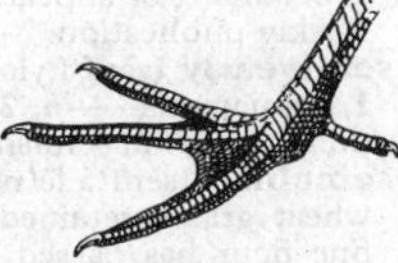
Semipalmate foot

semiparasitic (sĕm′ĭ pă′rə sĭt′ĭk), *adj.* **1.** *Biol.* commonly parasitic but capable of living on dead or decaying animal

sem′iabsor′bent, *adj.*
sem′iab′stract, *adj.*
sem′iac′adem′ic, *adj.*
sem′iac′tive, *adj.*
sem′iac′tively, *adv.*
sem′iac′tiveness, *n.*
sem′iadhe′sive, *adj.*
sem′iadhe′sively, *adv.*
sem′iadhe′siveness, *n.*
sem′iag′ricul′tural, *adj.*
sem′ian′archis′tic, *adj.*
sem′ian′imate, *adj.*
sem′iarch′, *n.*
sem′iar′id, *adj.*
sem′iarid′ity, *n.*
sem′iartic′ulate, *adj.*
sem′iauton′omous, *adj.*
sem′ibi′ograph′ical, *adj.*
sem′ibi′ograph′ically, *adv.*
sem′icap′italist, *adj.*
sem′icar′tilag′inous, *adj.*
sem′ichaot′ic, *adj.*
sem′iclas′sical, *adj.*
sem′iclas′sically, *adv.*
sem′icler′ical, *adj.*
sem′icollo′quial, *adj.*
sem′icolo′nial, *adj.*
sem′icontin′uous, *adj.*
sem′icrys′talline′, *adj.*
sem′icul′tivat′ed, *adj.*
sem′icul′tured, *adj.*
sem′ides′ert, *n.*
sem′idiaph′anous, *adj.*
sem′idomes′ticat′ed, *adj.*
sem′idor′mant, *adj.*
sem′iduc′tile, *adj.*
sem′idur′able, *adj., n.*
sem′ierect′, *adj.*
sem′iexper′imen′tal, *adj.*
sem′iexper′imen′tally, *adv.*
sem′ific′tional, *adj.*
sem′ifig′urative, *adj.*
sem′ifig′uratively, *adv.*
sem′ifin′ished, *adj.*
sem′ifit′ted, *adj.*
sem′ifor′mal, *adj.*
sem′iheret′ical, *adj.*
sem′ihyster′ical, *adj.*
sem′i-indus′trialized′, *adj.*
sem′i-instinc′tive, *adj.*
sem′i-instinc′tively, *adv.*
sem′i-in′tellec′tual, *adj., n.*
sem′i-intox′icat′ed, *adj.*
sem′i-iron′ic, *adj.*
sem′i-iron′ical, *adj.*
sem′i-iron′ically, *adv.*
sem′i-i′solat′ed, *adj.*
sem′iliq′uid, *adj., n.*
sem′ilit′erate, *adj.*
sem′imat′, *adj.*
sem′imo′bile, *adj.*
sem′imonar′chical, *adj.*
sem′imonop′olis′tic, *adj.*
sem′inar′rative, *adj.*
sem′ina′tionalis′tic, *adj.*
sem′inoctur′nal, *adj.*
sem′inomad′ic, *adj.*
sem′inude′, *adj.*
sem′inu′dity, *n.*
sem′iobjec′tive, *adj.*
sem′ipa′ralysed′, *adj.*

matter. 2. *Bot.* partly parasitic and partly photosynthetic.
semipermanent (sĕm′ĭ pû′mə nənt), *adj.* intended to last for some time but not for ever, as a position subject to review, or a dye that will wash out after frequent washing or special treatment.
semipermeable (sĕm′ĭ pû′myə bl), *adj.* permeable to some substances more than to others: *a semipermeable membrane.*
semiplastic (sĕm′ĭ plăs′tĭk), *adj.* imperfectly plastic.
semipolar bond (sĕm′ĭ pō′lə), *Chem.* a valency bond in which two electrons are donated by one atom to another atom which requires both of them to complete its octet.
semiporcelain (sĕm′ĭ pôs′lĭn), *n.* a partly vitrified, somewhat porous and non-translucent pottery ware, inferior to porcelain.
semiprecious (sĕm′ĭ prĕsh′əs), *adj.* (of a gem) having value, but not classified as precious, as the amethyst, garnet, etc.
semipublic (sĕm′ĭ pŭb′lĭk), *adj.* partly or to some degree public.
semiquaver (sĕm′ĭ kwā′və), *n. Music.* a note equivalent to one-sixteenth of a semibreve; half a quaver.
Semiramis (sĕ mĭ′rə mĭs), *n. Gk Legend.* an Assyrian queen of surpassing greatness, wisdom, and beauty: the founder of Babylon. See **Ninus.**
semirigid (sĕm′ĭ rĭj′ĭd), *adj. Aeron.* designating a type of airship whose shape is maintained by means of a rigid keel-like structure and by internal gas pressure.
semiskilled (sĕm′ĭ skĭld′), *adj.* partly skilled or trained.
semisolid (sĕm′ĭ sŏl′ĭd), *adj.* **1.** not completely solid; very viscous. *—n.* **2.** a semisolid substance.
Semite (sē′mīt), *n.* **1.** a member of a speech family comprising the Hebrews, Arabs, Assyrians, etc., supposedly descended from Shem. Gen. 10. **2.** a Jew. [t. NL: m. *Sēmīta,* der. L *Sēm* Shem, t. Gk. See -ITE[1]]
Semitic (sĭ mĭt′ĭk), *n.* **1.** an important family of languages, including Akkadian, Hebrew, Aramaic, Arabic, and Amharic. *—adj.* **2.** of or pertaining to the Semites or their languages. **3.** Jewish.
Semitics (sĭ mĭt′ĭks), *n.* the study of the Semitic languages, literature, etc.
Semitism (sĕm′ĭ tĭz′əm), *n.* **1.** Semitic characteristics, esp. the ways, ideas, influence, etc., of the Jewish people. **2.** a Semitic word or idiom.
Semitist (sĕm′ĭ tĭst), *n.* an authority on Semitics.
semitone (sĕm′ĭ tōn′), *n. Music.* the smallest interval in the chromatic scale of Western music. Also, *U.S.,* **half-tone.**
semitranslucent (sĕm′ĭ trănz lo͞o′sənt), *adj.* imperfectly translucent.
semitransparent (sĕm′ĭ trănz pă′rənt), *adj.* imperfectly transparent.
semitropical (sĕm′ĭ trŏp′ĭ kl), *adj.* subtropical.
semivitreous (sĕm′ĭ vĭt′rĭ əs), *adj.* partially vitreous, as mineral constituents of volcanic rocks.
semivowel (sĕm′ĭ vou′əl), *n. Phonet.* a speech sound of vowel quality used as a consonant, such as *w* in *wet* or *y* in *yet.*
semiweekly (sĕm′ĭ wē′klĭ), *adj., n., pl.* **-lies,** *adv.* *—adj.* **1.** occurring or appearing every half week. *—n.* **2.** a semiweekly publication. *—adv.* **3.** every half week.
semiyearly (sĕm′ĭ yĭə′lĭ), *adj., n., pl.* **-lies,** *adv.* *—adj.* **1.** semiannual. *—n.* **2.** a semiannual thing, as a publication. *—adv.* **3.** semiannually.
semolina (sĕm′ə lē′nə), *n.* the large, hard parts of wheat grains retained in the bolting machine after the fine flour has passed through it: used for making puddings, etc. [t. It.: m. *semolino,* dim. of *semola* bran, g. L *simila* fine flour]
Sempach (*Ger.* zĕm′päKH), *n.* a village in central Switzerland, in Lucerne canton: Austrian defeat by the Swiss (1386). 1345 (1960).
semper fidelis (sĕm′pə fĭ dā′lĭs), *Latin.* always faithful.
semper paratus (sĕm′pə pə rä′təs), *Latin.* always ready.
sempiternal (sĕm′pĭ tû′nəl), *adj. Archaic or Literary.* everlasting; eternal. [ME, t. LL: s. *sempiternālis,* der. L *sempiternus* everlasting] —**sempiternity** (sĕm′pĭ tû′nĭ-tĭ), *n.*
semplice (sĕm′plĭ chĭ; *It.* sĕm′plĕ chĕ), *adj. Music.* plain and simple. [It.]
sempre (sĕm′prĭ; *It.* sĕm′prĕ), *adv. Music.* throughout. [It.]
sempstress (sĕmp′strĭs, sĕm′strĭs), *n.* seamstress.

sen[1] (sĕn), *n.* a former Japanese monetary unit and copper or bronze coin, equal to the hundredth part of a yen.
sen[2] (sĕn), *n.* a Cambodian monetary unit and coin, equal to the hundredth part of a riel.
sen[3] (sĕn), *n.* a coin of Indonesia equal to a hundredth part of a rupiah.
Sen., **1.** Senate. **2.** Senator. **3.** Senior.
Senanayake (sĕn′ə nī′ə kə), *n.* **Dudley** (dŭd′lĭ), born 1911, prime minister of Ceylon 1952–53, 1960, and from 1965 to 1970.
Sénancour (*Fr.* sĕ näN ko͞or′), *n.* **Étienne Pivert de** (*Fr.* ĕ tyĕn pē vĕr′ də), 1770–1846, French writer.
senarmontite (sĕn′ä mŏn′tīt), *n.* a mineral trioxide of antimony which crystallizes in the cubic system. [named after Henri de *Sénarmont,* died 1862, French mineralogist]
senary (sē′nə rĭ), *adj.* of or pertaining to the number six. [t. L: m. s. *sēnārius*]
senate (sĕn′ĭt), *n.* **1.** an assembly or council of citizens having the highest deliberative functions in the government; a legislative assembly of a state or nation. **2.** (*cap.*) the upper house of the legislature of certain countries, as the United States, France, Italy, Canada, Ireland, Republic of South Africa, Australia, and some Latin-American countries. **3.** the supreme council of state in ancient Rome, whose membership and functions varied at different periods. **4.** a governing, advisory, or disciplinary body, as in certain universities. [ME *senat,* t. L: s. *senātus*]
senator (sĕn′ə tə), *n.* a member of a senate. [ME *senatour,* t. L: m. *senātor*] —**sen′atorship′,** *n.*
senatorial (sĕn′ə tô′rĭ əl), *adj.* **1.** of or pertaining to a senator or senators; characteristic of or befitting a senator. **2.** consisting of senators. **3.** *U.S.* entitled to elect a senator: *a senatorial district.*
senatus consultum (sə nā′təs kən sŭl′təm), *pl.* **senatus consulta** (kən sŭl′tə). *Latin.* a decree of the senate of ancient Rome.
send (sĕnd), *v.,* **sent, sending,** *n.* *—v.t.* **1.** to cause to go; direct or order to go: *to send a messenger.* **2.** to cause to be conveyed or transmitted to a destination: *to send a letter.* **3.** to compel, order, or force to go: *to send someone away.* **4.** to impel, or throw: *he sent down a fast ball.* **5.** to cause to become: *to send somebody mad.* **6.** to give (fol. by *forth, out,* etc.), as light, smell, or sound. **7.** *Elect.* **a.** to transmit. **b.** to transmit (an electromagnetic wave, etc.) in the form of pulses. **8.** *Colloq.* to excite or inspire. (as a jazz musician, listener, or other person). **9. send down, a.** to expel from a university, esp. from Oxford or Cambridge. **b.** to imprison; sentence to a term of imprisonment. **10. send in,** to submit, as an application, request, competition entry, etc. **11. send off, a.** to cause to depart. **b.** to be present at a departure, as of a friend. **12. send on,** to dispatch in advance, as luggage. **13. send up,** *Colloq.* **a.** to mock or ridicule; satirize. **b.** to imprison. *—v.i.* **14.** to dispatch a message, messenger, etc. **15.** *Naut.* **a.** to lurch forward from the force of a wave. **b.** to scend. **16. send for,** to summon: *send for a doctor.* *—n.* **17.** *Naut.* **a.** the driving impulse of a wave or waves upon a ship. **b.** the act of sending; a sudden plunge of a vessel. [ME *sende(n),* OE *sendan,* c. G *senden*]
Sendai (sĕn′dī′), *n.* a city in central Japan, on N Honshu island. 480,000 (est. 1964).
sendal (sĕn′dl), *n.* a silk fabric in use during the Middle Ages, or a piece or garment of it. [ME, t. OF: m. *cendal,* prob. ult. t. Gk: m. *sindṓn* fine linen]
sender (sĕn′də), *n.* **1.** one who or that which sends. **2.** a transmitter of electrical pulses, as in telegraphy.
send-off (sĕnd′ŏf′), *n. Colloq.* **1.** a friendly demonstration for a person, etc., setting out on a journey, career, etc. **2.** a start given to a person or thing.
send-up (sĕnd′ŭp′), *n. Colloq.* a satire or parody.
Seneca (sĕn′ĭ kə), *n.* **Lucius Annaeus** (lo͞o′syəs ə nē′əs), *c.* 4 B.C. – A.D. 65, Roman philosopher, statesman, and tragedian.
Seneca (sĕn′ĭ kə), *n.* **1.** (*pl.*) the largest tribe of the Five Nations of North American Indians, in western New York State and conspicuous in the wars south and west of Lake Erie. **2.** a member of this tribe. [Anglicization of Dutch pron. of Mohegan rendering of Iroquoian *oneniute′ a′ka* Oneida, with different suffix *oneniute′ ron′ non,* lit., people of the standing or projecting rock or stone]
senega (sĕn′ĭ gə), *n.* **1.** the root of a milkwort, *Polygala*

sem′iper′vious, *adj.*
sem′ipolit′ical, *adj.*
sem′ireac′tionary, *adj., n.*
sem′ire′alis′tic, *adj.*
sem′ire′alis′tically, *adv.*
sem′irefined′, *adj.*
sem′irespec′tabil′ity, *n.*
sem′irespec′table, *adj., n.*
sem′iretir′ed, *adj.*
sem′iretire′ment, *n.*
sem′irhyth′mic, *adj.*
sem′iround′, *adj.*
sem′iru′ral, *adj.*
sem′iso′cialist, *adj., n.*
sem′isoft′, *adj.*
sem′isub′terra′nean, *adj.*
sem′isweet′, *adj.*
sem′itradi′tional, *adj.*
sem′iur′ban, *adj.*
sem′iwild′, *adj.*

senega, of the eastern U.S., dried and used as an expectorant. 2. the plant. [var. of SENECA, from its use by this people]

Senegal (sĕn′ĭ gôl′), *n.* **1.** a republic in W Africa: independent member of the French Community; formerly part of French West Africa. 3,489,852 pop. (est. 1965); 76,084 sq. mi. *Cap.*: Dakar. **2.** a river in W Africa, rising in E Mali, flowing NW to the Atlantic at St Louis. ab. 1000 mi. French, **Sénégal** (*Fr.* sėnė̇gȧl′).

Senegal

Senegalese (sĕn′ĭ gə lēz′), *adj., n., pl.* **-lese.** —*adj.* **1.** of or pertaining to Senegal (def. 1). —*n.* **2.** a native or inhabitant of Senegal.

Senegambia (sĕn′ĭ găm′bĭ ə), *n.* a region in W Africa between the rivers Senegal and Gambia, now mostly in Senegal.

senescent (sĭ nĕs′ənt), *adj.* growing old; ageing. [t. L: s. *senescens*, ppr., growing old] —**senes′cence,** *n.*

seneschal (sĕn′ĭ shəl), *n.* an officer in the household of a medieval prince or dignitary, who had full charge of domestic arrangements, ceremonies, the administration of justice, etc.; a steward. [ME, t. OF, t. ML: m. *seniscalcus*, t. Gmc; cf. OHG *siniscalh*, lit., old servant]

Senghor (*Fr.* säN gŏr′), *n.* **Léopold Sédar** (*Fr.* lė ŏ pōl sė dȧr′), born 1906, president of Senegal since 1960.

senhor (sĕ nyô′; *Port.* sĭ nyȯr), *n., pl.* **senhors,** *Port.* **senhores** (*Port.* sĭ nyȯ′rĭsh). *Portuguese.* **1.** a gentleman. **2.** (as a form of address) sir; Mr. [Pg., g. L *senior*. See SENIOR]

senhora (sĕ nyô′rə; *Port.* sĭ nyȯ′rə), *n., pl.* **senhoras** (*Port.* sĭ nyȯ′rash). *Portuguese.* **1.** a lady; gentlewoman. **2.** madame; Mrs.

senhorita (sĕn′yō rē′tə; *Port.* sĭ nyȯ rē′tə), *n., pl.* **-tas** (*Port.* -təsh). *Portuguese.* **1.** a young lady. **2.** Miss.

senile (sē′nīl), *adj.* **1.** of, pertaining to, or characteristic of old age. **2.** mentally or physically infirm due to old age. **3.** *Phys. Geog.* (of topographical features) having advanced in reduction by erosion, etc., to a featureless plain that stands everywhere at base level. [t. L, neut. of *senīlis*]

senility (sĭ nĭl′ĭ tĭ), *n.* senile state; old age; the weakness or mental infirmity of old age.

senior (sē′nyə), *adj.* **1.** older or elder (often used after the name of the older of two persons bearing the same name). *Abbrev.*: Sr *or* Sen. **2.** of higher rank or standing, esp. by virtue of longer service. **3.** (in British educational institutions) pertaining to secondary education. **4.** (in American universities, colleges, and schools) denoting or pertaining to the highest class or the last year of the course. —*n.* **5.** a person who is older than another. **6.** one of higher rank or standing, esp. by virtue of longer service. **7.** an older and often more privileged pupil in a British grammar or public school. **8.** *U.S.* a member of the senior class in a university, college, or school. **9.** *Rowing.* an oarsman who has won a top-class event. [ME, t. L, compar. of *senex* old]

senior citizen, (in euphemistic use) an old person.

seniority (sē′nĭ ŏ′rĭ tĭ), *n., pl.* **-ties.** **1.** the state or fact of being senior; priority of birth; superior age. **2.** priority or precedence in age or service.

senior pupil, (in British schools) a pupil between the ages of 11 and 19.

senior school, **1.** a division of some British public schools for older pupils, usually those over the age of fourteen. **2.** *Obs.* a former type of British school for pupils between the ages of eleven and fourteen.

senior secondary school, (in Scotland) a school for pupils between the ages of twelve and eighteen.

senior service, (*sometimes cap.*) *Colloq.* the Royal Navy (contrasted with the Army and Royal Air Force).

Senlac (sĕn′lăk), *n.* a hill in SE England, in Sussex: site of the Battle of Hastings, 1066. See **Hastings** (def. 2).

senna (sĕn′ə), *n.* **1.** a cathartic drug consisting of the dried leaflets of various plants of the caesalpiniaceous genus *Cassia*, as **Alexandrian senna** from *C. acutifolia*, or **Arabian senna** from *C. angustifolia*. **2.** any plant yielding this drug. **3.** any of various similar plants, as *Cassia marylandica*. [t. NL, t. Ar.: m. *sanā*]

Sennacherib (sĕ năk′ə rĭb), *n.* died 681 B.C., king of Assyria 705–681 B.C.

Sennar (sĕn′ä, sĕ nä′), *n.* a region in E Sudan between the White and Blue Nile rivers, S of Khartoum: a former kingdom.

sennet (sĕn′ĭt), *n.* a call on a trumpet or the like to announce the entrance or exit of actors in Elizabethan drama. [var. of SIGNET]

sennight (sĕn′īt), *n. Archaic.* a week. Also, **se'nnight.** [ME *sennyght*, *sevenyght*, OE *seofan nihta* seven nights. See SEVEN, NIGHT. Cf. FORTNIGHT]

sennit (sĕn′ĭt), *n.* a kind of flat braided cordage used on shipboard, formed by plaiting strands of rope yarn or other fibre. Also, **sinnet.** [earlier *sinnet*; ? f. SEVEN + KNIT]

señor (sĕ nyô′; *Sp.* sė nyȯr′), *n., pl.* **-ñores** (-nyô′rĭz; *Sp.* -nyȯ′rės). *Spanish.* **1.** a gentleman. **2.** (as a term of address) sir. **3.** (as a title) Mr. [Sp., g. L *senior*. See SENIOR]

señora (sĕ nyô′rə; *Sp.* sė nyȯ′rȧ), *n. Spanish.* **1.** Mrs; madame. **2.** lady; gentlewoman.

señorita (sĕn′yō rē′tə; *Sp.* sė nyȯ rē′tȧ), *n. Spanish.* **1.** Miss. **2.** young lady.

sensate (sĕn′sāt), *adj.* **1.** perceived by the senses. **2.** endowed with the faculty of sensation. [t. LL: m. s. *sensātus*, pp. See SENSE, -ATE[1]]

sensation (sĕn sā′shən), *n.* **1.** the operation or function of the senses; perception through the senses. **2.** a mental condition produced through an organ of sense or resulting from a particular condition of some part of the body; a physical feeling, as of cold, dizziness, etc. **3.** *Physiol.* the faculty of perception of stimuli. **4.** *Psychol.* an experience arising directly from stimulation of sense organs. **5.** a mental feeling, esp. a state of excited feeling. **6.** a mental impression or feeling of seeming to perceive: *he had the sensation that he was being watched.* **7. a.** a state of excited feeling or interest caused among a number of persons or throughout a community by some occurrence, etc. **b.** an expression of such a feeling, as sound or movement of a crowd. **8.** a cause of such feeling or interest. [t. ML: s. *sensātio*, der. LL *sensātus* having sense] —**Syn.** **2.** See **sense.**

sensational (sĕn sā′shə nəl), *adj.* **1.** such as to produce a startling impression, esp. of an erotic, sadistic, or horrific kind: *a sensational novel.* **2.** aiming at such impressions, as a writer, etc. **3.** of or pertaining to sensation or the senses. **4.** *Colloq.* extremely pleasing or exciting; especially or extraordinarily good or excellent. **5.** causing a sensation (def. 7). —**sensa′tionally,** *adv.*

sensationalism (sĕn sā′shə nə lĭz′əm), *n.* **1.** matter, language, or style producing or designed to produce startling or thrilling impressions, or to excite and please vulgar taste. **2.** the exploitation of cheap emotional excitement by popular newspapers, novels, etc. **3.** the tendency of a writer, artist, etc., to be obsessed with a desire to thrill. **4.** *Ethics.* the doctrine that the good is to be judged only by the gratification of the senses; sensualism. **5.** *Philos.* the doctrine that sensation is the sole origin of knowledge; sensuism. —**sensa′tionalist,** *n.*

sensationism (sĕn sā′shə nĭz′əm), *n. Psychol.* a school of psychology which holds that mental life is constituted solely of sensations. —**sensa′tionist,** *n.*

sensation-monger (sĕn sā′shən mŭng′gə), *n.* one who busies himself with or purveys sensationalism, esp. for financial gain.

sense (sĕns), *n., v.,* **sensed, sensing.** —*n.* **1.** each of the special faculties connected with bodily organs by which man and other animals perceive external objects and their own bodily changes (commonly reckoned as sight, hearing, smell, taste, and touch). **2.** these faculties collectively. **3.** their operation or function; sensation. **4.** a feeling or perception produced through the organs of touch, taste, etc., or resulting from a particular condition of some part of the body: *to have a sense of cold.* **5.** a faculty or function of the mind analogous to sensation: *the moral sense.* **6.** any special capacity for perception, estimation, appreciation, etc.: *a sense of humour.* **7.** (*usually pl.*) clear or sound mental faculties; sanity. **8.** any more or less vague perception or impression: *a sense of security.* **9.** a mental discernment, realization, or recognition: *a just sense of the worth of a thing.* **10.** the recognition of something as incumbent or fitting: *a sense of duty.* **11.** sound practical intelligence; common sense: *he has no sense.* **12.** what is sensible or reasonable: *to talk sense.* **13.** the meaning, or one of the meanings, of a word, statement, or a passage. **14.** interpretation; understanding. **15.** the approximate, or the general overall meaning of a speech, book, essay, etc. **16.** an opinion or judgement formed or held, now esp. by an assemblage or body of persons: *the sense of a meeting.* **17.** *Maths.* one of two opposite directions in which a vector may point. **18. in a sense,** according to one interpretation; in a way; in one but not every way. **19. make sense, a.** to be intelligible or acceptable. **b.** to understand. —*v.t.* **20.** to perceive by or as by the senses; become aware of. **21.** to perceive without certainty; be aware of dimly, vaguely or without positive sensory confirmation. **22.** to comprehend or understand, esp. instinctively rather than by rational means. [ME, t. L: m. s. *sensus*]

—**Syn.** 4. SENSE, SENSATION refer to consciousness of stimulus or of a perception with an interpretation as pleasant or unpleasant. A SENSE is an awareness or recognition of something; the stimulus may be subjective, and the entire process may be mental or intellectual: *a sense of failure.* A SENSATION is an impression derived from an objective (external) stimulus through any of the sense organs: *a sensation of heat.* The feeling is also applied to a general, indefinite bodily feeling: *a sensation of weariness.* 13. See **meaning.**

sense datum, *Psychol.* any experiential factor that results from the action of a stimulus on a sense organ.

senseless (sĕns′lĭs), *adj.* 1. unconscious. 2. destitute or deprived of sensation; insentient. 3. destitute of mental perception or appreciation. 4. stupid or foolish, as persons or actions. 5. *Rare.* nonsensical or meaningless, as words: *this letter is either ingenious code or senseless.* —**sense′lessly,** *adv.* —**sense′lessness,** *n.*

sense organ, a specialized structure which receives impressions, such as one of the tastebuds or tactile corpuscles.

sensibility (sĕn′sĭ bĭl′ĭ tĭ), *n., pl.* **-ties.** 1. capacity for sensation or feeling; responsiveness to sensory stimuli. 2. mental susceptibility or responsiveness; quickness and acuteness of apprehension or feeling. 3. keen consciousness or appreciation. 4. (*pl.*) emotional capacities. 5. (*sing. or pl.*) liability to feel hurt or offended; sensitive feelings. 6. capacity for the higher or more refined feelings; delicate sensitiveness of taste. 7. the property, as in plants or instruments, of being readily affected by external influences.

—**Syn.** 2. SENSIBILITY, SUSCEPTIBILITY, SENSITIVENESS, SENSITIVITY mean capacity to respond to, or be affected by, something. SUSCEPTIBILITY is the state or quality of being impressionable and responsive, esp. to emotional stimuli; in the plural much the same as SENSIBILITY: *a person of keen susceptibilities.* SENSIBILITY is, particularly, capacity to respond to aesthetic and emotional stimuli; delicacy of emotional or intellectual perception: *the sensibility of the artist.* SENSITIVENESS is the state or quality of being sensitive, having a capacity of sensation and of responding to external stimuli: *sensitiveness to light.* SENSITIVITY is esp. capability of being sensitive to physiological, chemical action: *the sensitivity of a nerve.* —**Ant.** 1. apathy.

sensible (sĕn′sə bl), *adj.* 1. having, using, or showing good sense or sound judgement. 2. cognizant; keenly aware (usually fol. by *of*): *sensible of his fault.* 3. appreciable; considerable: *a sensible reduction.* 4. capable of being perceived by the senses: *the sensible universe.* 5. capable of feeling or perceiving, as organs or parts of the body. 6. perceptible to the mind. 7. conscious: *speechless but still sensible.* 8. *Obs.* sensitive. [ME, t. LL: m. *sensibilis*] —**sen′sibleness,** *n.* —**sen′sibly,** *adv.* —**Syn.** 1. See **practical.**

sensillum (sĕn sĭl′əm), *n. Zool.* a very small, simple sense organ.

sensitive (sĕn′sĭ tĭv), *adj.* 1. endowed with sensation. 2. readily affected by external agencies or influences. 3. having acute mental or emotional sensibility; easily affected, pained, annoyed, etc. 4. pertaining to or connected with the senses or sensation. 5. *Physiol.* having a low threshold of sensation or feeling. 6. responding to stimulation, as leaves which move when touched. 7. highly susceptible to certain agents, as photographic plates, films, or paper to light. 8. constructed to indicate, measure, or be affected by small amounts or changes, as a balance or thermometer. 9. *Radio.* easily affected by external influences, esp. by radio waves. [ME, t. ML: m. *sensitīvus,* der. L *sensus* sense] —**sen′sitively,** *adv.* —**sen′sitiveness,** *n.*

sensitive plant, 1. a tropical American plant, *Mimosa pudica,* cultivated in greenhouses, with bipinnate leaves whose leaflets fold together when touched. 2. any of various other plants sensitive to touch.

sensitivity (sĕn′sĭ tĭv′ĭ tĭ), *n., pl.* **-ties.** 1. the state or quality of being sensitive. 2. *Physiol.* **a.** the ability of an organism or part of an organism to react to stimuli; irritability. **b.** degree of susceptibility to stimulation. 3. *Radio.* the ability to react to incoming radio waves. 4. *Elect.* the change in deflection of an electrical instrument per unit of applied torque. —**Syn.** 1. See **sensibility.**

sensitize (sĕn′sĭ tīz′), *v.t.,* **-tized, -tizing.** 1. to render sensitive. 2. *Photog.* to render (a plate, film, etc.) sensitive to light or other forms of radiant energy. Also, **sensitise.** —**sen′sitiza′tion,** *n.* —**sen′sitiz′er,** *n.*

sensitometer (sĕn′sĭ tŏm′ĭ tə), *n. Photog.* an instrument for making a series of accurately known exposures on photographic surfaces, used to determine sensitivity and other properties.

sensor (sĕn′sə), *n.* 1. an electronic device in a spacesuit or the like which detects a change in some function of the wearer, esp. a physiological change, and converts it into a signal for measuring, recording, or for the taking of some action. 2. any similar device which detects a variable quantity and converts it into a signal.

sensorimotor (sĕn′sə rĭ mō′tə), *adj.* 1. *Physiol.* of or pertaining to sensation and motor activity. 2. *Psychol.* of or pertaining to motor activity triggered by sensory stimuli.

sensorium (sĕn sô′rĭ əm), *n., pl.* **-soria** (-sô′rĭ ə), **-soriums.** *Anat.* the supposed seat of sensation in the brain, usually taken as the cortex or grey matter. [t. LL, der. L *sensus,* pp., felt]

sensory (sĕn′sə rĭ), *adj.* 1. pertaining to sensation. 2. *Physiol.* denoting a structure that conveys an impulse which results or tends to result in sensation, as a nerve. Also, **sensorial** (sĕn sô′rĭ əl).

sensual (sĕn′syōō əl), *adj.* 1. excessively inclined to the gratification of the senses; voluptuous. 2. lewd or unchaste. 3. pertaining to or given to the gratification of the senses or the indulgence of appetite. 4. of or pertaining to the senses or physical sensation. 5. pertaining to the doctrine of sensationalism. [late ME, t. LL: s. *sensuālis.* See SENSE, -AL[1]] —**sen′sually,** *adv.*

—**Syn.** 1. SENSUAL, SENSUOUS, VOLUPTUOUS refer to experience through the senses. SENSUAL refers, usually unfavourably, to the enjoyments derived from physical sensations, generally implying grossness or lewdness: *a sensual delight in eating, sensual excesses.* SENSUOUS refers, favourably or literally, to what is experienced through the senses: *sensuous enjoyment in the feel of rich silks, sensuous poetry.* VOLUPTUOUS implies the luxurious gratification of sensuous or sensual desires: *voluptuous joys, voluptuous beauty.* —**Ant.** 1. ascetic.

sensualism (sĕn′syōō ə lĭz′əm), *n.* 1. subjection to sensual appetites; sensuality. 2. *Ethics.* the theory that the highest good consists in sensual gratification. 3. *Philos.* the doctrine of sensationalism. 4. *Aesthetics.* emphasis on objective sensuality, or on the quality of the sensual as the most important in the beautiful.

sensualist (sĕn′syōō ə lĭst), *n.* 1. one given to the indulgence of the senses or appetites. 2. one who holds the doctrine of sensationalism. —**sen′sualis′tic,** *adj.*

sensuality (sĕn′syōō ăl′ĭ tĭ), *n., pl.* **-ties.** 1. sensual nature. 2. excessive indulgence in sensual pleasures. 3. lewdness; unchastity. Also, **sen′sualness.**

sensualize (sĕn′syōō ə līz′), *v.t.,* **-lized, -lizing.** to render sensual. Also, **sensualise.** —**sen′sualiza′tion,** *n.*

sensuism (sĕn′syōō ĭz′əm), *n. Philos.* sensationalism.

sensuous (sĕn′syōō əs), *adj.* 1. of or pertaining to the senses. 2. perceived by or affecting the senses: *the sensuous qualities of music.* 3. readily affected through the senses: *a sensuous temperament.* —**sen′suously,** *adv.* —**sen′suousness,** *n.* —**Syn.** 1. See **sensual.**

sent (sĕnt), *v.* pt. and pp. of **send.**

sentence (sĕn′təns), *n., v.,* **-tenced, -tencing.** —*n.* 1. a linguistic form (a word or a sequence of words arranged in a grammatical construction) which is not part of any larger construction, typically expressing an independent statement, inquiry, command, or the like, e.g., *Fire!* or *Summer is here* or *Who's there?* 2. *Law.* **a.** an authoritative decision; a judicial judgement or decree, esp. the judicial determination of the punishment to be inflicted on a convicted criminal. **b.** the punishment itself. 3. *Music.* a period. 4. *Obs.* a saying, apophthegm, or maxim. 5. *Obs.* an opinion pronounced on some particular question. —*v.t.* 6. to pronounce sentence upon; condemn to punishment. [ME, t. F, t. L: m. *sententia* opinion] —**sen′tencer,** *n.*

sentential (sĕn tĕn′shəl), *adj.* pertaining to or of the nature of a sentence.

sentential calculus, *Logic.* any symbolic systematic set of rules for joining or dividing sentences to form other sentences.

sentential connective, *Logic.* a symbol, such as 'not', 'or', 'implies', used to combine two or more sentences to form a new sentence.

sententious (sĕn tĕn′shəs), *adj.* 1. abounding in pithy sayings or maxims: *sententious style.* 2. affectedly judicial in utterance; moralizing; self-righteous. 3. given to or using pithy sayings or maxims. 4. of the nature of a maxim; pithy. [late ME, t. L: m. s. *sententiōsus*] —**senten′tiously,** *adv.* —**senten′tiousness,** *n.*

sentience (sĕn′shəns), *n.* sentient condition or character; capacity for sensation or feeling. Also, **sentiency.**

sentient (sĕn′shənt), *adj.* 1. that feels; having the power of perception by the senses. 2. characterized by sensation. —*n.* 3. one who or that which is sentient. 4. the mind. [t. L: s. *sentiens,* ppr., feeling] —**sen′tiently,** *adv.*

sentiment (sĕn′tĭ mənt), *n.* 1. mental attitude with regard to something; opinion. 2. a mental feeling; emotion: *a sentiment of pity.* 3. refined or tender emotion; manifestation of the higher or more refined feelings. 4. exhibition or manifestation of feeling or sensibility, or appeal to the tender emotions, in literature, art, or music. 5. a thought influenced by or proceeding from feeling or emotion. 6. the thought or feeling intended to be conveyed by words as distinguished from the words themselves. [t. LL: s. *sentīmentum*, der. L *sentīre* feel; r. ME *sentement*, t. OF]

—**Syn. 1.** See **opinion. 2.** See **feeling. 3.** SENTIMENT, SENTIMENTALITY are terms for sensitiveness to emotional feelings. SENTIMENT is a sincere and refined sensibility, a tendency to be influenced by emotion rather than by reason or fact: *to appeal to sentiment.* SENTIMENTALITY implies affected, excessive, sometimes mawkish sentiment: *weak sentimentality.* —**Ant. 2.** realism, logic.

sentimental (sĕn′tĭ mĕn′tl), *adj.* **1.** expressive of or appealing to sentiment or the tender emotions: *a sentimental song.* **2.** pertaining to or dependent on sentiment: *sentimental reasons.* **3.** weakly emotional; mawkishly susceptible or tender: *a sentimental schoolgirl.* **4.** characterized by or showing sentiment or refined feeling. —**sen′timen′tally,** *adv.*

sentimentalism (sĕn′tĭ mĕn′tə lĭz′əm), *n.* **1.** sentimental tendency or character; predominance of sentiment over reason. **2.** weak emotionalism; excessive indulgence in sentiment. **3.** a display of sentimentality.

sentimentalist (sĕn′tĭ mĕn′tə lĭst), *n.* one given to sentiment or sentimentality.

sentimentality (sĕn′tĭ mĕn tăl′ĭ tĭ), *n., pl.* **-ties.** sentimental quality, disposition, behaviour, etc. —**Syn.** See **sentiment.**

sentimentalize (sĕn′tĭ mĕn′tə līz′), *v.,* **-lized, -lizing.** —*v.i.* **1.** to indulge in sentiment. —*v.t.* **2.** to render sentimental, as a person, etc. **3.** to be sentimental over; turn into an object of sentiment. Also, **sentimentalise.**

sentinel (sĕn′tĭ nəl), *n., v.,* **-nelled, -nelling** or (*U.S.*) **-neled, -neling.** —*n.* **1.** one who or that which watches, or stands as if watching. **2.** a soldier stationed as a guard to challenge all comers and prevent a surprise attack: *to stand sentinel.* —*v.t.* **3.** to watch over or guard as a sentinel. [t. F: m. *sentinelle*, t. It.: m. *sentinella*, der. LL **sentīnāre* avoid danger, der. *sentīre* perceive]

sentry (sĕn′trĭ), *n., pl.* **-tries. 1.** a soldier stationed at a place to keep guard and prevent the passage of unauthorized persons, watch for fires, etc.; a sentinel. **2.** a member of a guard or watch. [? short for obs. *centrinel*, var. of SENTINEL]

sentry-box (sĕn′trĭ bŏks′), *n.* a small structure for sheltering a sentry from bad weather.

sentry-go (sĕn′trĭ gō′), *n.* the duty performed by a sentry pacing his beat while on guard duty, etc.

Senusi (sĕ nōō′sĭ), *n., pl.* **-sis.** a member of a fanatical and belligerent North African Muslim sect. Also, **Senussi.** —**Senu′sian,** *adj.*

Seoul (sōl), *n.* the capital of South Korea, in the W part. 3,376,030 (1963). Japanese, **Keijo.** See map under **Korea.**

Sep., 1. September. **2.** Septuagint.

sepal (sĕp′l), *n. Bot.* each of the individual leaves or parts of the calyx of a flower. See diag. under **epigynous flower.** [t. NL: s. *sepalum*, b. *sep-* (irreg. f. Gk *sképē* covering) and L (*pet*)*alum*) petal]

S, Sepal

-sepalous, a word element meaning 'having sepals', as in *polysepalous.* [f. SEPAL + -OUS]

separable (sĕp′ə rə bl, sĕp′rə bl), *adj.* capable of being separated. —**sep′arabil′ity, sep′arableness,** *n.* —**sep′arably,** *adv.*

separate (*v.* sĕp′ə rāt′; *adj., n.* sĕp′rĭt), *v.,* **-rated, -rating,** *adj., n.* —*v.t.* **1.** to keep apart or divide, as by an intervening barrier, space, etc. **2.** to put apart; part: *to separate persons fighting.* **3.** to disconnect; disunite: *to separate Church and state.* **4.** to remove from personal association, as a married person. **5.** to part or divide (an assemblage, mass, compound, etc.) into individuals, components, or elements. **6.** to take (fol. by *from* or *out*) by such parting or dividing: *separate metal from ore.* —*v.i.* **7.** to part company; withdraw from personal association (often fol. by *from*). **8.** to draw or come apart; become disconnected or disengaged. **9.** to become parted from a mass or compound, as crystals. **10.** (of a married couple) to stop living together but without becoming divorced. —*adj.* **11.** separated, disconnected, or disjoined. **12.** unconnected or distinct: *two separate questions.* **13.** being or standing apart; cut off from access: *separate houses.* **14.** existing or maintained independently: *separate organizations.* **15.** individual or particular: *each separate item.* —*n.* **16.** (*pl.*) articles of women's clothing that can be worn in combination with a variety of others, as matching or contrasting blouses, skirts, jumpers, etc. [ME, t. L: m. s. *sēparātus*, pp.] —**sep′arately,** *adv.* —**sep′arateness,** *n.*

—**Syn. 1.** SEPARATE, DIVIDE imply a putting apart or keeping apart of things from each other. To SEPARATE is to remove from each 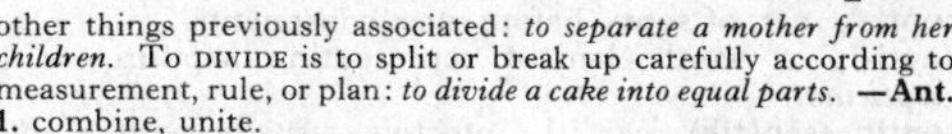 other things previously associated: *to separate a mother from her children.* To DIVIDE is to split or break up carefully according to measurement, rule, or plan: *to divide a cake into equal parts.* —**Ant. 1.** combine, unite.

separation (sĕp′ə rā′shən), *n.* **1.** the act of separating. **2.** the state of being separated. **3.** a place, line, or point of parting. **4.** *Law.* **a.** a judicial decree absolving the parties from the duty of cohabitation. **b.** cessation of conjugal cohabitation, as by mutual consent.

separation allowance, an allowance made by a soldier to his wife and augmented by the state.

separation energy, *Physics.* the energy required to remove a particle from an atomic nucleus.

separatist (sĕp′ə rə tĭst, sĕp′rə-), *n.* **1.** one who separates, withdraws, or secedes, as from an established Church. **2.** an advocate of separation, esp. ecclesiastical or political separation. —**separatism** (sĕp′ə rə tĭz′əm, sĕp′rə-), *n.*

separative (sĕp′ə rə tĭv, sĕp′rə tĭv), *adj.* tending to separate; causing separation.

separator (sĕp′ə rā′tə), *n.* **1.** one who or that which separates. **2.** an apparatus for separating one thing from another, as cream from milk, steam from water, wheat from chaff, valuable minerals from one another, etc. **3.** *Elect.* a thin, perforated insulator used to separate the plates in a secondary cell. —**se′paratory,** *adj.*

Sephardim (sĭ fä′dĭm), *n.pl.* Spanish-Portuguese Jews and their descendants. Cf. **Ashkenazim.** [t. Heb., der. *s'phārādh*, country mentioned in Obad. 20] —**Sephar′dic,** *adj.*

sepia (sē′pyə), *n.* **1.** a brown pigment obtained from the inklike secretion of various cuttlefish, and used with brush or pen in drawing. **2.** a drawing made with sepia. **3.** a dark brown. **4.** *Photog.* a brown-coloured image, supposed to duplicate sepia ink. **5.** a cuttlefish of the genus *Sepia* or some allied genus. —*adj.* **6.** of a brown similar to that from sepia ink. [t. L, t. Gk]

sepiolite (sē′pyə līt′), *n.* meerschaum. [t. G: m. *Sepiolith*, f. Gk *sēpio(n)* cuttlebone + *-lith* -LITE]

sepoy (sē′poi), *n.* (in India) a native soldier in the military service of Europeans, esp. of the British. [t. Pg.: m. *sipae*, t. Hind. and Pers.: m. *sipāhī* horseman, der. *sipāh* army]

Sepoy Rebellion, Indian Mutiny.

sepsis (sĕp′sĭs), *n. Pathol.* local or generalized bacterial invasion of the body, especially by pyogenic organisms: *dental sepsis, wound sepsis.* [NL, t. Gk]

sept (sĕpt), *n.* **1.** a clan (orig. with reference to tribes or families in Ireland). **2.** *Anthropol.* a group believing itself derived from a common ancestor. [special use of *sept* enclosure, fold (t. L: s. *sēptum*), by assoc. with obs. *sect* clan (Irish)]

sept-, a prefix meaning 'seven', as in *septet.* Also, **septem-, septe-, septi-**[1]. [t. L, comb. form of *septem*]

Sept., 1. September. **2.** Septuagint.

septa (sĕp′tə), *n.* pl. of **septum.**

septal (sĕp′tl), *adj.* of or pertaining to a septum.

septarium (sĕp tēə′rĭ əm), *n., pl.* **-taria** (-tēə′rĭ ə). *Geol.* a concretionary nodule or mass, usually of calcium carbonate or of argillaceous carbonate of iron, traversed within by a network of cracks filled with calcite and other minerals. [NL, der. L *sēptum* enclosure] —**septar′ian,** *adj.*

septate (sĕp′tāt), *adj.* divided by a septum or septa. [t. NL: m. s. *sēptātus.* See SEPTUM, -ATE[1]]

septavalent (sĕp′tə vā′lənt), *adj.* heptavalent.

September (sĕp tĕm′bə), *n.* the ninth month of the year, containing 30 days. [OE, t. L, the seventh month in the early Roman calendar]

Septembrist (sĕp tĕm′brĭst), *n.* (in the French Revolution) one of those who instigated or took part in the massacre of royalist and other inmates of the prisons of Paris, September 2nd–6th, 1792.

septempartite (sĕp′tĕm pä′tīt), *adj.* separated into seven sections.

septenary (sĕp′tĭ nə rĭ), *adj., n., pl.* **-naries.** —*adj.* **1.** of or pertaining to the number seven; forming a group of seven. **2.** septennial. —*n.* **3.** a group or set of seven. **4.** a period of seven years. **5.** the number seven. **6.** *Pros.* a line with seven feet. [t. L: m. s. *septēnārius*]

septennial (sĕp tĕn′yəl), *adj.* **1.** occurring every seven years. **2.** of or for seven years. [f. s. L *septennium* seven years + -AL[1]] —**septen′nially,** *adv.*

septentrional (sĕp tĕn′trĭ ə nəl), *adj. Archaic.* northern. [ME, t. L: s. *septentriōnālis*, equiv. to *septem triōnēs* seven oxen (i.e. the seven stars of the constellation the Great Bear) + *-ālis* -AL[1]]

septet (sĕp tĕt′), *n.* **1.** any group of seven persons or things. **2.** a company of seven singers or players. **3.** a musical composition for seven voices or instruments. Also, **septette.** [t. G. See SEPT-, -ET]

septi-[1], var. of **sept-**, before most consonants.

septi-[2], a word element representing **septum,** as in *septicidal*.

septic (sĕp′tĭk), *adj.* **1.** infective, usually with a pus-forming microbe. **2.** pertaining to or of the nature of sepsis; infected. *—n.* **3.** an agent which causes sepsis. [t. L: s. *sēpticus*, t. Gk: m. *sēptikós*] **—septicity** (sĕp tĭs′ĭ tĭ), *n.*

septicaemia (sĕp′tĭ sē′myə), *n. Pathol.* the invasion and persistence of pathogenic bacteria in the bloodstream. Also, **septicemia.** [NL, f. Gk. See SEPTIC, -AEMIA] **—sep′ticae′mic,** *adj.*

septicidal (sĕp′tĭ sī′dl), *adj. Bot.* characterized by splitting through the septa or dissepiments, as a mode of dehiscence. [f. SEPTI-[2] + s. L *-cīdere* cut + -AL[1]]

Septicidal dehiscence A, Valves; B, Dissepiments; C, Axis

septic sore throat, *Pathol.* an acute, toxic, streptococcus infection of the throat producing fever, tonsillitis, and other serious effects.

septic tank, a tank in which solid organic sewage is decomposed and purified by anaerobic bacteria.

septifragal (sĕp tĭf′rə gl), *adj. Bot.* characterized by the breaking away of the valves from the septa or dissepiments, in dehiscence. [f. SEPTI-[2] + L *frag-* break + -AL[1]]

septillion (sĕp tĭl′yən), *n.* **1.** (usually with *one* or *a*) a cardinal number represented (in Britain and Germany) by one followed by 42 zeros, and (in the U.S. and France) by one followed by 24 zeros. *—adj.* **2.** (usually with *one* or *a*) amounting to one septillion in number. [t. F, f. L *sept(em)* + *(m)illion* MILLION] **—septil′lionth,** *n., adj.*

septime (sĕp′tēm), *n. Fencing.* the seventh of eight defensive positions. [t. L: m. s. *septimus*]

septivalent (sĕp′tĭ vā′lənt), *adj. Chem.* heptavalent. Also, **septavalent** (sĕp′tə vā′lənt).

septuagenarian (sĕp′tyōō ə jĭ nĕə′rĭ ən), *adj.* **1.** of the age of 70 years, or between 70 and 80 years old. *—n.* **2.** a septuagenarian person.

septuagenary (sĕp′tyōō ə jē′nə rĭ), *adj., n., pl.* **-naries.** septuagenarian. [t. L m. s. *septuāgēnārius*]

Septuagesima (sĕp′tyōō ə jĕs′ĭ mə), *n.* the third Sunday before Lent (more fully, **Septuagesima Sunday**). [t. L: *septuāgēsima* (*dies*) seventieth day]

Septuagint (sĕp′tyōō ə jĭnt′), *n.* the Greek version of the Old Testament traditionally said to have been made at the request of Ptolemy II, king of Egypt (309–247? B.C.), by 72 Jewish scholars, in 72 days. [t. L: s. *septuāginta* seventy]

septum (sĕp′təm), *n., pl.* **-ta** (-tə). **1.** *Biol.* a dividing wall, membrane, or the like in a plant or animal structure; a dissepiment. **2.** an osmotic membrane. [t. L: enclosure]

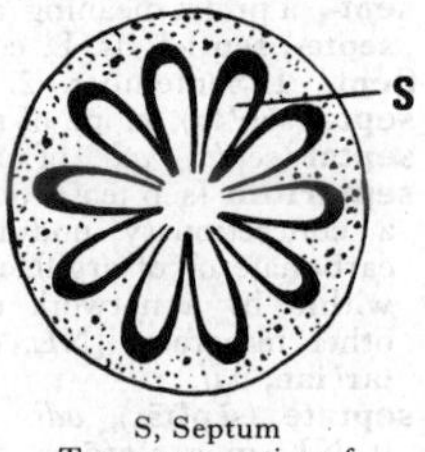

S, Septum Transverse section of the ovary of flax

septuple (sĕp′tyōō pl), *adj., v.,* **-pled, -pling.** *—adj.* **1.** sevenfold; seven times as great. *—v.t., v.i.* **2.** to make or become seven times as great. [t. LL: m. s. *septuplus*]

septuplet (sĕp′tyōō plĭt, sĕptyōō′plĭt), *n.* **1.** any group or combination of seven related items. **2.** one of seven offspring born at one birth. **3.** *Music.* a group of seven notes to be played in the time of four or six.

sepulcher (sĕp′l kə), *n., v.t. U.S.* sepulchre.

sepulchral (sĭ pŭl′krəl), *adj.* **1.** of, pertaining to, or serving as a tomb. **2.** of or pertaining to burial. **3.** proper to or suggestive of a tomb; funereal or dismal. **4.** hollow and deep: *sepulchral tone.* **—sepul′chrally,** *adv.*

sepulchre (sĕp′l kə), *n., v.,* **-chred, -chring.** *—n.* **1.** a tomb, grave, or burial place. **2.** *Eccles.* a structure or a recess in some churches of the Middle Ages in which the sacred elements, the cross, etc., were deposited with due ceremonies on Good Friday to be taken out at Easter, in commemoration of Christ's entombment and resurrection (often called **Easter sepulchre**). *—v.t.* **3.** to place in a sepulchre; bury. Also, *U.S.,* **sepulcher.** [ME *sepulcre,* t. OF, t. L: m. *sepulcrum*]

sepulture (sĕp′l chə), *n.* **1.** the act of placing in a sepulchre or tomb; burial. **2.** *Archaic.* sepulchre; tomb. [ME *sepulture,* t. OF, t. L: m. *sepultūra*]

seq., **1.** sequel. **2.** (L *sequens*) the following (one).

seqq., (L *sequentia*) the following (ones).

sequacious (sĭ kwā′shəs), *adj.* **1.** *Archaic.* following another person, esp. unreasoningly. **2.** following with smooth regularity, as musical notes, thoughts, etc. [f. SEQUACI(TY) (t. L: m. s. *sequācitas* facility in following) + -OUS] **—sequa′ciously,** *adv.* **—sequacity** (sĭ kwăs′ĭ tĭ), *n.*

sequel (sē′kwəl), *n.* **1.** a literary work, complete in itself, but continuing a preceding work. **2.** an event or circumstance following something; subsequent course of affairs. **3.** a result, consequence, or inference. [ME *sequele,* t. L: m. *sequēla*]

sequela (sĭ kwē′lə), *n., pl.* **-lae** (-lē). *Pathol.* a morbid affection resulting from a previous disease. [t. L]

sequence (sē′kwəns), *n.* **1.** the following of one thing after another; succession. **2.** order of succession: *a list of books in alphabetical sequence.* **3.** a continuous or connected series: *a sonnet sequence.* **4.** something that follows; a subsequent event; result; consequence. **5.** *Music.* a melodic or harmonic pattern repeated at different pitches, with or without modulation. **6.** *Rom. Cath. Ch.* a hymn sometimes sung after the gradual and before the gospel; a prose. **7.** *Films.* a portion of a film story set in the same place and time, and without interruptions or breaks of any kind. **8.** *Cards.* a set of three or more cards following one another in order of value. **9.** *Maths.* a set of numbers in which each member is derived, either directly or indirectly, from the preceding member or members. [ME, t. LL: m. *sequentia,* der. L *sequens,* ppr., following] **—Syn. 1.** See **series.**

sequencer (sē′kwən sə), *n. Aerospace, Electronics.* an electronic device which arranges for a number of actions to take place in a predetermined order.

sequent (sē′kwənt), *adj.* **1.** following; successive. **2.** following logically or naturally; consequent. **3.** characterized by continuous succession; consecutive. *—n.* **4.** that which follows in order or as a result. [t. L: s. *sequens,* ppr., following]

sequential (sĭ kwĕn′shəl), *adj.* **1.** characterized by regular sequence of parts. **2.** following; subsequent; consequent. **—sequen′tially,** *adv.*

sequester (sĭ kwĕs′tə), *v.t.* **1.** to remove or withdraw into solitude or retirement; seclude. **2.** to remove or separate. **3.** *Law.* to remove (property) temporarily from the possession of the owner; seize and hold, as the property and income of a debtor, until legal claims are satisfied. **4.** *Internat. Law.* to requisition, hold, and control (enemy property). [ME *sequestre,* t. LL: m. *sequestrāre* separate, der. L *sequester* depositary, trustee]

sequestered (sĭ kwĕs′təd), *adj.* secluded or out-of-the-way: *a sequestered village.*

sequestrate (sĭ kwĕs′trāt), *v.t.,* **-trated, -trating. 1.** *Law.* **a.** to sequester (property). **b.** to confiscate. **c.** to make bankrupt. **2.** *Archaic.* to separate; seclude. **—sequestrator** (sē′kwĕs trā′tə, sĭ kwĕs′trā′tə), *n.*

sequestration (sē′kwĕs trā′shən), *n.* **1.** removal or separation; banishment or exile. **2.** withdrawal, retirement, or seclusion. **3.** *Law.* **a.** the sequestering of property. **b.** confiscation or seizure.

sequestrectomy (sē′kwĕs trĕk′tə mĭ), *n., pl.* **-mies.** *Surg.* the removal of dead spicules or portions, esp. of bone.

sequestrum (sĭ kwĕs′trəm), *n., pl.* **-tra** (-trə). *Pathol.* a dead portion of bone separated from the living bone. [NL, special use of L *sequestrum* something detached, prop. neut of *sequester* mediating]

sequin (sē′kwĭn), *n.* **1.** a small shining disc or spangle used to ornament a dress, etc. **2.** Also, **zecchino, zechin.** a former Italian and Turkish gold coin, first minted in Venice about 1280. [t. F, t. It.: m. *zecchino,* a Venetian coin, der. *zecca* mint, t. Ar.: m. *sikka* a die for coins] **—se′quined,** *adj.*

sequoia (sĭ kwoi′ə), *n.* either of two related, extremely large coniferous trees in California, the big tree, *Sequoiadendron,* and the redwood, *Sequoia,* both formerly included in the genus *Sequoia.* [t. NL, named after *Sikwâyi,* died 1843, a Cherokee Indian, inventor of a syllabary for writing Cherokee]

sequoiadendron (sĭ kwoi′ə dĕn′drən), *n.* the coniferous big tree of the western slopes of the Sierra Nevada mountains in California, *Sequoiadendron giganteum,* or *Sequoia gigantea.*

Sequoia National Park, a national park in the U.S., in central California: giant sequoia trees. 604 sq. mi.

ser (sĭə), *n.* seer[2].

ser., **1.** series. **2.** sermon.

serac (sĕ′răk), *n.* a large block or pinnacle-like mass of ice on a glacier, formed by melting or movement of the ice. [t. Swiss F, orig. the name of a white cheese]

seraglio (sĕ rä′lĭ ō′), *n., pl.* **-raglios. 1.** the part of a Muslim house or palace in which the wives and concubines are secluded; a harem. **2.** a Turkish palace, esp. of the Sultan. [t. It.: m. *serraglio* (rendering Turk. *serāī* SERAI), ult. der. L *serāre* lock up]

serai (sĕ rī′), *n., pl.* **-rais.** (in Eastern countries) a caravanserai. [t. Turk., t. Pers.: lodging, palace]

Seraing (*Fr.* sə răN′), *n.* a town in E Belgium. 40,949 (est. 1964).

Serajevo (sĕ′rə yä′vō), *n.* Sarajevo.

serang (sə răng′), *n.* a boatswain, foreman, or other person having authority over work, esp. in southern Africa among Malays. [t. Pers., equiv. to *sar* chief + *hang* power]

serape (sĕ rä′pĭ), *n.* a kind of shawl or blanket, often of gay colours, worn by Spanish-Americans. [t. Mex. Sp.]

seraph (sĕ′rəf), *n., pl.* **-aphs, -aphim** (-ə fĭm). **1.** one of the celestial beings hovering above God's throne in Isaiah's vision. Isa. 6. **2.** a member of the highest order of angels, often represented as a child's head with wings above, below, and on each side. [back-formation from *seraphim* (pl.), ME *serafin*, t. LL: m. *seraphim*, t. Heb.]

seraphic (sĭ răf′ĭk), *adj.* of, like, or befitting a seraph. Also, **seraph′ical.** —**seraph′ically,** *adv.*

seraphim (sĕ′rə fĭm), *n.* a pl. of **seraph.**

Serapis (sĕ′rə pĭs), *n.* a deity of Egyptian origin who was worshipped as the dead Apis under the attributes of Osiris. His cult was started under the Ptolemies and introduced into Greece and Rome.

Serb (sûb), *n.* **1.** a Serbian. **2.** Serbo-Croat (language). **3.** Serbian (language). —*adj.* **4.** Serbian. [t. Serbian]

Serbia (sû′byə), *n.* a former kingdom in S Europe: now (with revised boundaries) a constituent republic of Yugoslavia, in the SE part. 7,642,227 pop. (1961); ab. 35,000 sq. mi. *Cap.:* Belgrade. Formerly, **Servia.**

Serbia in the 19th century

Serbian (sû′byən), *adj.* **1.** of Serbia, its inhabitants, or their language. —*n.* **2.** a native or inhabitant of Serbia, esp. one of the Slavic race inhabiting it. **3.** Serbo-Croat, esp. as spoken in Serbia.

Serbo-, a word element representing **Serb.**

Serbo-Croat (sû′bō krō′ăt), *n.* the principal Slavic language of Yugoslavia, usually written with Cyrillic letters in Serbia but with Roman letters in Croatia. Also, **Serbo-Croatian** (sû′bō krō ā′shən).

Serbonian (sû bō′nyən), *adj.* of or designating a large marshy tract in ancient northern Egypt, in which entire armies are said to have been swallowed up. [f. *Serboni(s)* (t. Gk: name of the marsh) + -AN]

Serbs, Croats, and Slovenes, Kingdom of the. See **Yugoslavia.**

sere[1] (sĭə), *adj.* dry; withered. [var. of SEAR[1]]

sere[2] (sĭə), *n.* the series of stages in an ecological succession. [back-formation from SERIES]

serein (sĕ răn′), *n. Meteorol.* a very fine rain falling from a clear sky after sunset. [F: evening damp, OF *serain* nightfall, der. L *sērum* evening, *sērus* late]

Seremban (sə rĕm′bən), *n.* a town in Malaysia, the capital of Negri Sembilan. 52,091 (1957).

serenade (sĕ′rĭ nād′), *n., v.,* **-naded, -nading.** —*n.* **1.** a complimentary performance of vocal or instrumental music in the open air at night, as by a lover under the window of his lady. **2.** a piece of music suitable for such performance. —*v.t., v.i.* **3.** to entertain with or perform a serenade. [t. F, t. It.: m. *serenata.* See SERENATA] —**ser′enad′er,** *n.*

serenata (sĕ′rĭ nä′tə), *n., pl.* **-tas, -te** (-tĭ). *Music.* **1.** a form of pastoral cantata, often of a dramatic or imaginative character. **2.** an instrumental composition in several movements, intermediate between the suite and the symphony. [t. It.: an evening song, der. *sereno* the open air, n. use of adj. *sereno* serene (g. L *serēnus*), influenced by L *sērum* evening]

Serendip (sĕ′rĕn dĭp′), *n.* former name of **Ceylon.**

serendipity (sĕ′rən dĭp′ĭ tĭ), *n.* the faculty of making desirable but unsought-for discoveries by accident. [f. ('*The Three Princes of*) SERENDIP' (who had this faculty) by H. Walpole + -ITY]

serene (sĭ rēn′), *adj.* **1.** calm; peaceful; tranquil: *serene sea, a serene old age.* **2.** clear; fair: *serene weather.* **3.** (*often cap.*) an epithet used in titles of princes, etc.: *his Serene Highness.* —*n.* **4.** *Archaic.* a clear or tranquil expanse of sky, sea, etc. [t. L: m. s. *serēnus*] —**serene′ly,** *adv.* —**serene′ness,** *n.* —**Syn. 1.** unruffled, undisturbed. See **peaceful.** —**Ant. 1.** agitated.

serenity (sĭ rĕn′ĭ tĭ), *n., pl.* **-ties. 1.** the state or quality of being serene; calmness; tranquillity. **2.** clearness, as of the sky, air, etc. **3.** (*usually cap.*, with **his, your,** etc.) a title of honour given to certain reigning princes, etc.

Serenity (sĭ rĕn′ĭ tĭ), *n.* **Sea of,** a dark plain, *Mare Serenitatis,* in the first quadrant of the face of the moon.

Sereth (*Ger.* zē′rĕt), *n.* German name of **Siret.**

serf (sûf), *n.* **1.** a person in a condition of servitude, required to render services to his lord, and commonly attached to the lord's land and transferred with it from one owner to another. **2.** *Obs.* a slave. [late ME, t. F, g. L *servus* slave] —**serfdom** (sûf′dəm), **serf′hood′,** *n.*

serge (sûj), *n.* **1.** a twilled worsted or woollen fabric used esp. for clothing. **2.** cotton, rayon, or silk in a twill weave. [t. F; r. ME *sarge,* t. OF, g. var. of L *sērica* silken]

sergeant (sä′jənt), *n.* **1.** a non-commissioned army officer of rank above that of corporal. **2.** a police officer ranking between constable and inspector. **3.** *Obs.* a tenant by military service, below the rank of knight. [ME *sergeaunte,* t. OF: m. *sergent,* g. s. L *serviens,* ppr., serving] —**sergeancy** (sä′jən sĭ), **ser′geantship′,** *n.*

sergeant major, *Mil.* a non-commissioned officer of the highest rank; a warrant officer.

Sergt, Sergeant.

serial (sĭə′rĭ əl), *n.* **1.** anything published, broadcast, etc., in instalments at regular intervals, as a novel appearing in successive issues of a magazine. —*adj.* **2.** published in instalments or successive parts: *a serial story.* **3.** pertaining to such publication. **4.** of, pertaining to, or arranged in a series. **5.** *Telecom., Computers.* of or pertaining to a system in which information is transmitted along a path digit by digit. [t. NL: s. *seriālis,* der. L *series* series] —**se′rially,** *adv.*

serialize (sĭə′rĭ ə līz′), *v.t.,* **-lized, -lizing.** to publish, broadcast, televise, etc., in serial form. Also, **serialise.** —**se′rializa′tion,** *n.*

serial number, an individual number given to a particular person, article, etc., for identification.

serial technique, *Music.* a method of composition in which not only the notes may be ordered in a strictly defined manner, as in twelve-note music, but also their durations, timbres, etc.

seriate (sĭə′rĭ ĭt), *adj.* arranged or occurring in one or more series. —**se′riately,** *adv.*

seriatim (sĭə′rĭ ā′tĭm, sĕ′rĭ-), *adv.* in a series; one after another. [t. ML, der. L *series* series; modelled on *literatim, verbatim,* etc.]

sericeous (sĭ rĭsh′əs), *adj.* **1.** silky. **2.** covered with silky down, as a leaf. [t. L: m. *sēriceus*]

sericin (sĕ′rĭ sĭn), *n. Chem.* a gelatinous organic compound obtained from silk.

sericite (sĕ′rĭ sīt′), *n.* a mineral, similar in composition to muscovite, occurring as a decomposition product of orthoclase. [t. G: m. *Sericit,* f. *seric-* (repr. L *sēricum* silk) + *-it* -ITE[1]]

sericulture (sĕ′rĭ kŭl′chə), *n.* the rearing and keeping of silkworms, for the production of raw silk. Also, **sericiculture.** [t. F: (m.) *sériciculture,* f. *sérici-* (repr. L *sēricum* silk) + *culture* CULTURE] —**ser′icul′tural,** *adj.* —**ser′icul′turist,** *n.*

seriema (sĕ′rĭ ē′mə), *n.* **1.** a large bird, *Cariama cristata,* with long legs and a crested head, native in southern Brazil, etc. **2.** a smaller allied bird, *Chunga burmeisteri,* native to Argentina. [t. NL, t. Tupi: m. *siriema,* crested]

series (sĭə′rēz, -rĭz), *n., pl.* **-ries,** *adj.* —*n.* **1.** a number of things, events, etc., ranged or occurring in spatial, temporal, or other succession; a sequence. **2.** a set, as of coins, stamps, etc. **3.** a set of volumes, as of a periodical, or as issued in like form with similarity of subject or purpose. **4.** *Maths.* a sequence of numbers or expressions so related that the *n*th term can be written in a general form. **5.** *Rhet.* a succession of coordinate sentence elements. **6.** *Music.* an arrangement of twelve notes in a particular order taken as the basis of a composition. **7.** *Geol.* a division of a system of rocks, marked by sedimentary deposits formed during a geological epoch. **8.** *Elect.* an arrangement of conductors or cells such that the same current flows through each. The components are said to be **in series** (opp. to *in parallel*). —*adj.* **9.** *Elect.* consisting of, or having, components in series. [t. L]

—**Syn. 1.** SERIES, SEQUENCE, SUCCESSION are terms for an orderly following of things one after another. SERIES is applied to a number of things of the same kind, usually related to each other, arranged or happening in order: *a series of football matches.* SEQUENCE stresses the continuity in time, thought, cause and effect, etc.: *the scenes came in a definite sequence.* SUCCESSION implies that one thing is followed by another (or others in turn), usually though not necessarily with a relation or connection between them: *succession to a throne, a succession of calamities.*

series-wound (sĭə′rĭz wound′), *adj. Elect.* denoting a commutator motor in which the field circuit and armature circuit are connected in series.

serif (sĕ′rĭf), *n. Print.* a smaller line used to finish off a main stroke of a letter, as at the top and bottom of M.

See diag. under **type.** Also, **seriph.** [prob. t. D: m. *schreef* stroke, line, der. *schrijwen* write]
serin (sĕr′ĭn), *n.* a small finch, *Serinus serinus,* of Europe, north-west Africa, etc., from which the common canary has been developed. [t. F; orig. uncert.]
serine (sĕr′ēn, sĭə′rēn, -rĭn), *n. Biochem.* an amino acid, $CH_2OH.CH(NH_2).COOH$, occurring in proteins and obtained by the hydrolysis of sericin, the protein constituting silk gum. [f. SER(UM) + -INE²]
seringa (sĭ rĭng′gə), *n.* **1.** any of several Brazilian trees of the genus *Hevea,* yielding rubber. **2.** a graceful deciduous tree, *Kirkia acuminata,* of southern Africa. [t. Pg.]
Seringapatam (sə rĭng′gə pə tăm′), *n.* a town in S India: the former capital of Mysore state; taken by the British, 1799.
seriocomic (sĭə′rĭ ō kŏm′ĭk), *adj.* partly serious and partly comic. Also, **seriocomical.**
serious (sĭə′rĭ əs), *adj.* **1.** of grave or solemn disposition or character; thoughtful. **2.** of grave aspect. **3.** being in earnest; not trifling. **4.** demanding earnest thought or application: *serious reading.* **5.** weighty or important: *a serious matter.* **6.** giving cause for apprehension; critical: *a serious illness.* [ME, t. LL: m. s. *sēriōsus,* der. L *sērius*] —**se′riously,** *adv.* —**se′riousness,** *n.* —**Syn. 1.** See **earnest.**
serjeant (sä′jənt), *n.* **1.** a serjeant-at-arms. **2.** Also, **serjeant-at-law.** (formerly) a member of a superior order of barristers.
serjeant-at-arms (sä′jənt ət ämz′), *n.* an executive officer of a legislative or other body, whose duty it is to enforce the commands of the body, preserve order, and arrest individuals of distinction, e.g. the two who attend on the Houses of Parliament.
Serlio (*It.* sĕr′lyō), *n.* **Sebastiano** (*It.* sĕ bäs tyä′nō), 1475–1554, Italian painter and architect.
sermon (sû′mən), *n.* **1.** a discourse for the purpose of religious instruction or exhortation, esp. one based on a text of Scripture and delivered from a pulpit. **2.** any similar serious discourse or exhortation. **3.** a long, tedious speech. [ME, t. L: s. *sermo* discourse, ML sermon]
sermonic (sû mŏn′ĭk), *adj.* pertaining to, of the nature of, or resembling a sermon. Also, **sermonical.**
sermonize (sû′mə nīz′), *v.,* **-nized, -nizing.** —*v.i.* **1.** to deliver or compose a sermon; preach. —*v.t.* **2.** to give serious exhortation to; lecture. Also, **sermonise.** —**ser′moniz′er,** *n.*
Sermon on the Mount, the discourse delivered by Jesus, recorded in Matt. 5–7 and Luke 6:20–49.
sero-, a word element representing **serum,** as in *serology.*
serology (sĭ rŏl′ə jĭ), *n.* the scientific study of the properties and action of the serum of the blood.
seromucous (sĭə′rō myōō′kəs), *adj. Med.* both serous and mucous.
serosa (sĭ rō′sə), *n.* a serous membrane.
serotine¹ (sĕr′ə tīn′), *adj. Rare.* late. Also, **serotinous** (sĭ rŏt′ĭ nəs). [t. F, t. L: m. *sērōtinus* late]
serotine² (sĕr′ə tīn′), *n.* a small European bat, *Vespertilio* (*Vesperugo*) *serotinus.* [t. F, t. L: m. *sērōtina* (fem.) late, i.e. flying late in the evening]
serotonin (sĕ′rə tō′nĭn), *n.* a hormone which induces muscular contraction: found in the brain, intestines, and platelets. [f. SERO- + TON(E) + -IN²]
serous (sĭə′rəs), *adj.* **1.** of a watery nature, or resembling serum. **2.** containing serum; secreting serum. **3.** pertaining to or characterized by serum. [t. L: m. s. *sērōsus*] —**serosity** (sĭ rŏs′ĭ tĭ), *n.*
serous fluid, any of various animal liquids resembling blood serum, as the fluids of the serous membranes.
serous membrane, *Anat., Zool.* any of various thin membranes, as the peritoneum, which line certain cavities of the body and exude a serous fluid.
serow (sĕr′ō), *n.* a goat antelope, genus *Capricornis,* of eastern Asia, related to the goral. [t. Sikkimese: m. *saro*]
Serowe (sĕ rō′wĭ), *n.* a town in E Botswana. 34,182 (1964).
serpent (sû′pənt), *n.* **1.** a snake. **2.** a wily, treacherous, or malicious person. **3.** Satan. Gen. 3:1–5. **4.** a kind of firework which burns with serpentine motion or flame. **5.** an old wooden musical wind instrument of serpentine form and deep tone. [ME, t. L: s. *serpens* creeping thing, prop. ppr. of *serpere* creep, c. Gk *hérpein*]

Man playing a serpent, 18th century

serpentine¹ (sû′pən tīn′), *adj.* **1.** of or pertaining to a serpent. **2.** moving in a winding course or having a winding form; tortuous; winding. **3.** having the qualities of a serpent; subtle, artful, or cunning. [ME, t. L: m. *serpentīnus*]
serpentine² (sû′pən tīn′), *n.* a common mineral, hydrous magnesium silicate, $H_4Mg_3Si_2$, usually oily green and sometimes spotted, occurring in many varieties: used for architectural and decorative purposes. [ME, t. ML: m. *serpentīnum,* prop. neut. of L *serpentīnus*]
serpigo (sû pī′gō), *n. Pathol.* a creeping or spreading skin disease, as ringworm. [ME, t. ML, der. L *serpere* creep] —**serpiginous** (sû pĭj′ĭ nəs), *adj.*
serranoid (sĕ′rə noid′), *adj.* **1.** belonging to the *Serranidae,* a numerous family of fishes including the sea-basses, groupers, jewfishes, etc. —*n.* **2.** a serranoid fish, as the red grouper. [f. s. NL *Serrānus,* genus of fishes (der. L *serra* saw, sawfish) + -OID]
serrate (sĕ′rĭt *for 1–3*; sĕ rāt′ *for 4*), *adj., v.,* **-rated, -rating.** —*adj.* **1.** having notches or teeth along the edge like a saw: *a serrate leaf*; *a serrate blade.* **2.** having a grooved edge, as certain coins. **3.** having notches or teeth along the edge. —*v.t.* **4.** to make serrate or serrated. [t. L: m. s. *serrātus* saw-shaped]
serrated (sĕ rā′tĭd), *adj.* serrate; having a notched or grooved edge.
serration (sĕ rā′shən), *n.* **1.** serrated condition or form. **2.** a serrated edge or formation. **3.** one of the notches or teeth of such an edge or formation. Also, **serrature** (sĕ′rə chə).

Serrate leaf

serriform (sĕ′rĭ fôm′), *adj.* resembling the notched edge of a saw; serrate. [f. *serri-* (t. NL, comb. form repr. L *serra* saw) + -FORM]
serrulate (sĕ′rōō lāt′, -lĭt), *adj.* finely or minutely serrate, as a leaf. Also, **ser′rulat′ed.** [t. NL: m. s. *serrulātus,* der. L *serrula,* dim. of *serra* saw]
serrulation (sĕ′rōō lā′shən), *n.* **1.** serrulate condition or form. **2.** a fine or minute serration.
serry (sĕ′rĭ), *v.i., v.t.,* **-ried, -rying.** to crowd closely together. [appar. t. F: m. *serré,* pp. of *serrer* press close, ult. g. L *serāre* bar, bolt, der. L *sera* bar] —**ser′ried,** *adj.*
Sertorius (sû tô′rĭ əs), *n.* **Quintus** (kwĭn′təs), died 72 B.C., Roman general and statesman.
sertularian (sû′tyōō lĕə′rĭ ən), *n. Zool.* a type of hydroid that forms stiff feathery colonies in which the cups holding the zooids are sessile. [f. s. NL *Sertulāria,* genus name (der. L *sertula,* dim. of *serta* garland) + -AN]
serum (sĭə′rəm), *n., pl.* **sera** (sĭə′rə), **serums. 1.** the clear, pale yellow liquid which separates from the clot in the coagulation of blood; blood serum. **2.** a fluid of this kind obtained from the blood of an animal which has been rendered immune to some disease by inoculation, used as an antitoxic or therapeutic agent. **3.** any watery animal fluid. **4.** (of milk). **a.** that portion left after butterfat, casein, and albumin have been removed. **b.** that portion left after the manufacture of cheese. [t. L: whey]
serval (sû′vəl), *n.* a long-limbed African cat, *Felis serval,* having a tawny coat spotted with black. [t. NL, t. Pg.: m. (*lobo*) *cerval* lynx, der. L (*lupus*) *cervus* (wolf) deer]

Serval, *Felis serval* (Total length ab. 4 ft, tail 1 ft)

servant (sû′vənt), *n.* **1.** a person employed in domestic duties. **2.** a person in the service of another. **3.** a person employed by the government: *a public servant.* [ME, t. OF, prop. ppr. of *servir* SERVE]

—**Syn. 1.** SERVANT, EMPLOYEE refer to persons who work for others for pay. SERVANT, with the exception of such traditional expressions as *public servant* or *civil servant,* is now restricted largely to one who works in domestic service: *a faithful old servant.* EMPLOYEE may refer to anyone who is employed, especially by the government or by a business or industrial concern: *government employees, factory employees.*

serve (sûv), *v.,* **served, serving,** *n.* —*v.i.* **1.** to act as a servant. **2.** to wait at table; hand food to guests. **3.** to render assistance; help. **4.** to go through a term of service; do duty as a soldier, sailor, councillor, juror, etc. **5.** to have definite use; be of use. **6.** to answer the purpose: *that will serve to explain my actions.* **7.** to be favourable, suitable, or convenient, as weather, time, etc. **8.** *Tennis, etc.* to put the ball in play. **9.** *Eccles.* to act as server. —*v.t.* **10.** to be in the service of; work for. **11.** to render service to; help. **12.** to go through (a term of service, imprisonment, etc.). **13.** to render active service to (a king, commander, etc.). **14.** to render obedience or homage to (God, a sovereign, etc.). **15.** to perform the duties of (an office, etc.): *to serve his mayoralty.* **16.** to be useful or of service to. **17.** to answer the requirements of; suffice. **18.** to contribute to; promote. **19.** to wait upon; set food before. **20.** to set (food) on a table. **21.** to act as a host or hostess in offering (someone) food or drink: *may I serve you some sherry?* **22.** to act as a host or hostess in offering (food or drink) to someone: *she served cocktails to her guests.* **23.** to provide with a regular or continuous supply of something. **24.** to treat in a specified manner: *his car served him well.* **25.** to gratify (desire, etc.). **26.** (of a male animal) to mate with. **27.** *Tennis, etc.* to put (the ball) in play. **28.** *Law.* **a.** to make legal delivery of (a process or writ). **b.** to present (a person) with a writ. **29.** to operate or work (a gun, etc.). **30.** *Naut., etc.* to bind or wind (a rope, etc.) with small cord or the like, as to strengthen or protect it. **31. serve out,** to distribute. —*n.* **32.** the act, manner, or right of serving, as in tennis. [ME *serven*, t. OF: m. *servir*, g. L *servīre*]

server (sûr′ vər), *n.* **1.** one who serves. **2.** that which serves or is used in serving as a salver. **3.** *Eccles.* an attendant on the priest at mass, who arranges the altar, makes the responses, etc. **4.** *Tennis, etc.* the player who puts the ball in play.

Servetus (sûr vē′təs), *n.* **Michael,** 1511–53, Spanish physician and theologian, accused of heresey and burnt at the stake. Spanish, **Miguel Serveto** (*Sp.* mē gĕl′ sĕr bĕ′tō).

Servia (sûr′ vyə), *n.* former name of **Serbia.** —**Ser′vian,** *adj., n.*

service (sûr′ vĭs), *n., adj., v.,* **-viced, -vicing.** —*n.* **1.** an act of helpful activity. **2.** the supplying or supplier of any articles, commodities, activities, etc., required or demanded. **3.** the providing or a provider of some accommodation required by the public, as messengers, telegraphs, telephones, or conveyance. **4.** the organized system of apparatus, appliances, employees, etc., for supplying some accommodation required by the public. **5.** the supplying or a supplier of water, gas, or the like to the public. **6.** the performance of duties as a servant; occupation or employment as a servant. **7.** employment in any duties or work for another, a government, etc. **8.** a department of public employment, or the body of public servants in it: *the diplomatic service.* **9.** the duty or work of public servants. **10.** the serving of a sovereign, state, or government in some official capacity. **11.** *Mil.* **a.** (*pl.*) the armed forces: *in the services.* **b.** period or duration of active service. **c.** a branch of the armed forces, as the army or navy. **12.** (*often pl.*) the performance of any duties or work for another; helpful activity: *medical services.* **13.** the act of servicing a piece of machinery, esp. a motor vehicle. **14.** public religious worship according to prescribed form and order: *divine service.* **15.** a ritual or form prescribed for public worship or for some particular occasion: *the marriage service.* **16.** the serving of God by obedience, piety, etc. **17.** a musical setting of the sung portions of a liturgy. **18.** a set of dishes, utensils, etc., for a particular use: *a dinner service.* **19.** *Law.* the the serving of a process or writ upon a person. **20.** *Naut., etc.* a small cord or the like wound about a rope, etc., as for strengthening or protection. **21.** *Tennis, etc.* **a.** the act or manner of putting the ball in play. **b.** the ball as put in play. **22.** the mating of a female animal by the male. **23. at someone's service,** ready to help; at one's disposal: *my chauffeur will be at your service during your stay here.* **24. be of service,** to be helpful or useful: *If I can be of service to you please call me.* —*adj.* **25.** of service; useful. **26.** of, pertaining to, or used by, servants, tradesmen, etc.: *service stairs.* **27.** of or pertaining to the armed forces. —*v.t.* **28.** to make fit for service; restore to condition for service: *to service a car.* **29.** (of a male animal) to mate with (a female animal). **30.** to meet interest and other payments on, as a government debt: *to service a debt.* [ME; OE *serfise*, t. OF: m. *servise*, g. L *servitium*]

Service (sûr′ vĭs), *n.* **Robert William,** 1874–1958, Canadian writer, born in England.

serviceable (sûr′ vĭ sə bl), *adj.* **1.** being of service; useful. **2.** capable of doing good service. **3.** wearing well; durable: *serviceable cloth.* **4.** *Archaic.* diligent or attentive in serving. —**serv′iceabil′ity, serv′iceableness,** *n.* —**serv′iceably,** *adv.*

serviceberry (sûr′ vĭs bĕ′rĭ), *n., pl.* **-ries. 1.** a North American rosaceous shrub or small tree (*Amelanchier canadensis*) with a berry-like fruit; shadbush or Juneberry. **2.** any of various other species of *Amelanchier.*

service book, a book containing the order of a religious service.

service charge, a proportion of a bill, as at a restaurant, hotel, etc., added on to the total to pay for service.

service court, *Tennis, etc.* that area of a court into which a served ball must fall.

service dress, the ordinary dress for members of the armed forces, as opposed to full dress, battledress, etc.

service flat, a flat in which certain services, as cleaning, meals, etc., are provided.

service hatch, an opening in a wall through which food can be passed from the kitchen to the dining room. Also, **serving hatch.**

service lift, a goods lift.

service line, *Tennis, etc.* the boundary line of a court behind which the server must stand when serving.

serviceman (sûr′ vĭs măn′, -mən), *n., pl.* **-men.** a member of the armed forces. —**ser′vicewom′an,** *n. fem.*

service pipe, a pipe connecting a building with a gas or water main.

service road, a minor road running parallel to a main road and serving local traffic.

service station, a filling station equipped for repairing and servicing motor vehicles.

service tree, either of two European trees, *Sorbus domestica*, bearing a small, acid fruit that is edible when overripe, or *S. torminalis* (**wild service tree**), with similar fruit.

servient tenement (sûr′ vĭ ənt). See **dominant tenement.**

serviette (sûr′ vĭ ĕt′), *n.* a napkin. [t. F, der. *servir* serve]

servile (sûr′ vīl), *adj.* **1.** obsequious: *servile flatterers.* **2.** of or pertaining to slaves; proper to or customary for slaves; characteristic of a slave; abject: *servile obedience.* **3.** yielding slavishly, or truckling (fol. by *to*). **4.** slavishly exact; without originality. **5.** being in slavery; oppressed. —*n.* **6.** a servile person. [ME, t. L: m. s. *servīlis*] —**ser′vilely,** *adv.* —**servility** (sûr vĭl′ĭ tĭ), **ser′vileness,** *n.*

—**Syn. 1, 2.** SERVILE, MENIAL, OBSEQUIOUS, SLAVISH characterize one who behaves like a slave or an inferior. SERVILE means cringing, fawning, abjectly submissive, *servile behaviour.* MENIAL applies to that which is considered an undesirable kind of drudgery: *the most menial tasks.* OBSEQUIOUS implies the ostentatious subordination of oneself to the wishes of another, either from fear or from hope of gain: *an obsequious waiter.* SLAVISH stresses the dependence and laborious toil of one who follows or obeys with abject submission: *slavish attentiveness to orders.* —**Ant. 1.** domineering.

serving (sûr′ vĭng), *n.* **1.** the act of one who, or that which serves. **2.** a portion of food or drink; a helping. —*adj.* **3.** used for dishing out and distributing food at the table: *serving spoon.*

serving hatch, service hatch.

Servite (sûr′ vīt), *n. Rom. Cath. Ch.* a member of an order of mendicant friars, founded in 1233 in Florence.

servitor (sûr′ vĭ tə), *n.* one who is in or at the service of another; an attendant. [ME, t. OF, t. LL]

servitude (sûr′ vĭ tyōōd′), *n.* **1.** slavery; bondage: *political or intellectual servitude.* **2.** compulsory service or labour as a punishment for criminals: *penal servitude.* **3.** *Law.* a right possessed by one person with respect to some other person's property, and consisting either of a right to use such property, or of power to prevent certain uses of the other property. [late ME, t. L: m. *servitūdo*] —**Syn. 1.** See **slavery.** —**Ant. 1.** liberty.

servo (sûr′ vō), *n.* servomechanism.

servocontrol (sûr′ vō kən trōl′), *n., v.* **-trolled, -trolling.** —*n.* **1.** a servomechanism used as a control. **2.** *Aeron.* **a.** a servo tab. **b.** a control system operated by the pilot of an aircraft which is powered, or power-assisted. —*v.t.* **3.** to control by means of a servomechanism.

servomechanism (sûr′ vō mĕk′ə nĭz′əm, sûr′ vō mĕk′-), *n.* a mechanism which is used to convert a low-powered mechanical motion into one which requires considerably greater power. The output power is usually proportional to the input power and the device is often electronically controlled. —**servomechanical** (sûr′ vō mĭ kăn′ĭ kl), *adj.* [f. SERV(E) + -O- + MECHANISM]

servomotor (sûr′ vō mō′ tə), *n.* any motor which provides the power for a servomechanism.

servo tab, *Aeron.* a control-surface tab which is operated by the control stick, the movement from which operates the control surface to which it is attached.

sesame (sĕs′ə mĭ), *n.* **1.** a tropical herbaceous plant, *Sesamum indicum*, whose small oval seeds are edible and yield an oil. **2.** the seeds themselves. **3.** See **open sesame.** [t. Gk; r. late ME *sysane*, ult. t. Gk: m. *sēsámē*]

sesamoid (sĕs′ə moid′), *adj. Anat.* shaped like a sesame seed, as certain small nodular bones and cartilages. [t. L: s. *sēsamoīdēs*, t. Gk: m. *sēsamoeidḗs*]

sesqui-, 1. a word element meaning 'one and a half', as in *sesquicentennial.* **2.** a prefix applied to compounds where the ratio of radicals is 2:3: *iron sesquichloride* (Fe_2Cl_3). [t. L, contr. of *sēmis* a half + *-que* besides]

sesquicentenary (sĕs′kwĭ sĕn tē′nə rĭ), *adj., n., pl.* **-ries.** —*adj.* **1.** of or pertaining to a 150th anniversary. —*n.* **2.** a 150th anniversary. **3.** its celebration.

sesquicentennial (sĕs′kwĭ sĕn tĕn′ yəl), *adj.* **1.** consisting of or marking the completion of a period of a century and a half, or 150 years. **2.** consisting of or recurring every 150 years. —*n.* **3.** *U.S.* a sesquicentenary.

sesquioxide (sĕs′kwĭ ŏk′sīd), *n. Chem.* an oxide containing three atoms or equivalents of oxygen to two of the other element or of some radical.

sesquipedalian (sĕs′kwĭ pĭ dā′lyən), *adj.* **1.** measuring a foot and a half. **2.** given to using long words. **3.** (of words or expressions) very long. —*n.* **4.** a sesquipedalian word. [f. *sesquipedal* (t. L: s. *sesquipedālis*) + -IAN]

sessile (sĕs′ĭl), *adj. Biol.* **1.** attached by the base, or without any distinct projecting support, as a leaf issuing directly from the stem. **2.** permanently attached. [t. L, neut. of *sessilis* sitting down]

A, Sessile flower; B, Sessile leaves

session (sĕsh′ən), *n.* **1.** the sitting together of a court, council, legislature, or the like, for conference or the transaction of business: *Parliament is now in session.* **2.** a single continuous sitting, or period of sitting, of persons so assembled. **3.** a continuous series of sittings or meetings of a court, legislature, or the like. **4.** the period or term during which such a series is held. **5.** (*pl.*) the sittings or a sitting of justices in court, to execute the powers confided to them by commission, charter, or statute. **6.** a single continuous course or period of lessons, study, etc., in the work of a day at school: *two afternoon sessions a week.* **7.** a portion of the year into which instruction is organized at a college or other educational institution. **8.** a period of time during which a person or group of persons performs an activity: *a dancing session; a cards session.* [ME, t. L: s. *sessio*] —**ses′sional,** *adj.*

sesterce (sĕs′tûs), *n.* an ancient Roman coin equal to a quarter of a denarius. [t. L: m. *sestertius*, prop. adj., two and a half]

sestertium (sĕs tû′tyəm), *n., pl.* **-tia** (-tyə). an ancient Roman money of account equal to a thousand sesterces. [L]

sestet (sĕs tĕt′), *n.* **1.** the last six lines of a sonnet. **2.** sextet (def. 2). [t. It.: m. *sestetto*, dim. of *sesto* sixth, g. L *sextus*]

sestina (sĕs tē′nə), *n. Pros.* a poem of six six-line stanzas and a three-line envoy, orig. without rhyme, in which each stanza repeats the end words of the lines of the first stanza, but in different order, the envoy using the six words again, three in the middle of the lines and three at the end. Also, **sextain.** [t. It., der. *sesto* sixth. See SESTET]

Sestos (sĕs′tŏs), *n.* an ancient Thracian town on the Hellespont opposite Abydos: Xerxes crossed the Hellespont here when he began his invasion of Greece. See **Hero and Leander.**

Sesto San Giovanni (*It.* sĕs′tō sän jō vän′nē), a town in N Italy, in Lombardy; a suburb of Milan. 81,968 (1966).

set (sĕt), *v.*, **set, setting,** *n., adj.* —*v.t.* **1.** to put in a particular place or position: *to set a vase on a table.* **2.** to put into some condition or relation: *to set a house on fire.* **3.** to apply: *to set fire to a house.* **4.** to cause to begin: *to set someone thinking.* **5.** to put (a price or value) upon something. **6.** to fix the value of at a certain amount or rate. **7.** to put (*much, little store*, etc.) as a measure of esteem. **8.** to post, station, or appoint for the purpose of performing some duty: *to set spies on a person.* **9.** to incite or urge to attack: *to set the dogs on an intruder.* **10.** to fix, appoint, or ordain: *to set a limit.* **11.** to place in thought or estimation: *to set an early date.* **12.** to present or fix for others to follow: *to set an example.* **13.** to prescribe or assign, as a task. **14.** to prescribe for study for examination: *the examiners have set 'King Lear' this year.* **15.** to compile and prescribe (an examination, etc.). **16.** to put in the proper position, order, or condition for use; adjust or arrange. **17.** to cover with a cloth or cloths and arrange cutlery, crockery, etc., on; lay: *to set the table.* **18.** to adjust according to a standard: *to set a clock.* **19.** to fix or mount (a gem, etc.) in gold or the like; place in a frame or setting. **20.** to adorn with, or as with, precious stones. **21.** to fix at a given point or calibration: *to set a micrometer.* **22.** to sharpen as by honing: *to set a razor.* **23.** to bend out the points of alternate teeth of (a saw) in opposite directions. **24.** to cause to sit; seat. **25.** to put (a hen) on eggs to hatch them. **26.** to place (eggs) under a hen or in an incubator. **27.** to put into a fixed, rigid, or settled state, as the countenance, the muscles, or the mind. **28.** to cause (something, as mortar) to become firm or hard. **29.** *U.S.* to prove (dough). **30.** to change into a curd. **31.** to cause (hair, etc.) to assume a desired shape, style, or form, as by inserting clips, rollers, etc. when it is wet. **32.** to cause to take a particular direction. **33.** *Surg.* to put (a broken or dislocated bone) back in position. **34.** (of a hunting dog) to indicate the position of (game) by standing stiffly and pointing with the muzzle. **35.** to pitch, as a tune. **36.** *Music.* **a.** to fit, as words to music. **b.** to arrange for musical performance. **c.** to arrange (music) for certain voices or instruments. **37.** to put on (stage) the scenery and properties for an act or scene. **38.** to spread (a sail) so as to catch the wind. **39.** *Print.* **a.** to arrange (type) in the order required for printing. **b.** to put together types corresponding to (copy): *to set an article.* **40.** to begin to form (fruit, etc.). **41.** to sink (a nail head) with a nail set. **42.** *Scot. and N Dial.* to be fitting, suitable, or becoming.
—*v.i.* **43.** to pass below the horizon; sink: *the sun sets every evening.* **44.** to decline; wane. **45.** to assume a fixed or rigid state, as the countenance, the muscles, etc. **46.** to become firm or solid, as mortar. **47.** *U.S.* (of dough) to prove. **48.** to become a curd. **49.** (of hair) to assume a desired shape, style, form, etc., by the insertion of clips, rollers, etc., when it is wet. **50.** to sit on eggs, as a hen. **51.** to hang or fit, as clothes. **52.** (of the ovary of a flower) to develop into fruit. **53.** (of a hunting dog) to indicate the position of game. **54.** to have a certain direction or course, as a wind, current, etc. **55.** (of a sail) to fill and take shape. **56.** *Dancing.* to face in a certain direction while moving backwards and forwards or in opposite directions, esp. in country-dancing and square-dancing: *set to your partners.* **57.** *Print.* to occupy a certain width: *this copy should be set to fifty ems.*
—*v.* **58.** Some special verb phrases are:
set about, 1. to begin; start. **2.** to attack.
set against, to cause to be hostile or antagonistic to.
set aside, 1. to put to one side. **2.** to discard from use. **3.** to dismiss from the mind. **4.** to annul or quash: *to set aside a verdict.*
set back, to hinder; stop or delay.
set down, 1. to put down in writing or print. **2.** to consider: *to set someone down as a fool.* **3.** to rebuke or snub. **4.** to ascribe or attribute. **5.** to allow (passengers) to alight from a bus, etc.
set eyes on, to see.
set forth, 1. to give an account of; expound. **2.** to start.
set in, 1. to begin: *darkness set in.* **2.** (of wind, tide, or the like) to blow or flow towards the shore.
set off, 1. to explode. **2.** to cause to explode. **3.** to begin; start, as on a journey. **4.** to intensify or improve by contrast. **5.** *Banking.* to hold a credit balance on (one account) against a debit balance on another account held by the same person, company, etc.
set on, 1. to attack: *three men suddenly set on him.* **2.** to urge or persuade.
set out, 1. to arrange. **2.** to state or explain methodically. **3.** to start, as on a journey. **4.** to have an intention or goal: *to set out to become prime minister.*
set to, 1. to apply oneself; start, as to work. **2.** to start to fight.
set sail, to start a voyage.
set up, 1. to erect. **2.** to start a business, etc. **3.** to provide (with): *his parents set him up with books for university.* **4.** to claim to be: *to set up as an expert.* **5.** to raise (a cry, etc.).
set upon, to attack, esp. suddenly.
—*n.* **59.** the act or state of setting. **60.** a number of things customarily used together or forming a complete assortment, outfit, or collection: *a set of dishes.* **61.** a series of volumes by one author, about one subject, or the like. **62.** a number or group of persons associating or classed together: *the smart set.* **63.** the fit or hang of an article of clothing: *the set of his coat.* **64.** fixed direction or bent, as of the mind, etc. **65.** bearing or carriage: *the set of one's shoulders.* **66.** the indication by a hunting dog of the position of game. **67.** a permanent deformation or change in shape, as to a piece of machinery. **68.** the assumption of a fixed, rigid or hard state, as by mortar, etc. **69.** a radio or television receiving apparatus. **70.** *Philately.* a group of stamps which form a complete series. **71.** *Tennis, etc.* a group of six or, until either player is two games ahead, more games counting as one of the units of a match. **72.** a construction representing a place in which action takes place in a film, television production, or the like. **73.** a number of pieces of stage scenery arranged together. **74.** *Mach.* the bending out of the points of alternate teeth of a saw in opposite directions. **75.** *Hort.* a young plant, or a slip, tuber, or the like, suitable for setting out or planting. **76.** *Dancing, etc.* **a.** the number of couples required to execute a quadrille or the like. **b.** a series of movements or figures that make up a quadrille or the like. **77.** the direction of a wind, current, etc. **78.** *Naut.* the fit and shape of sails. **79.** *Psychol.* readiness to respond in a specific way. **80.** *Maths.* a collection of numbers, elements, or objects which have some factor in common, so that they belong to the same class. **81.** a nail set.

82. sett (in any sense). **83. a dead set,** *Colloq.* a determined attempt, as by a girl to win a man's attention.
—*adj.* **84.** fixed beforehand: *a set time.* **85.** prescribed beforehand: *set rules.* **86.** deliberately composed; customary: *set phrases.* **87.** fixed; rigid: *a set smile.* **88.** resolved or determined; habitually or stubbornly fixed: *to be set in one's opinions.* **89.** formed, built, or made (as specified): *stockily set.*
[ME *sette(n)*, OE *settan*, c. G *setzen*]
—Syn. 1. See **put. 62.** See **circle.**

Set (sĕt), *n. Egypt. Myth.* the god of evil, brother or son and deadly opponent of Osiris, and represented with a beast's head and snout: called by the Greeks Typhon. Also, **Seth.** [t. Gk: m. *Seth*, t. Egypt.: m. *Setesh*]

S.E.T., selective employment tax.

seta (sē′tə), *n., pl.* **-tae** (-tē). *Zool., Bot.* a stiff hair; a bristle-like part. [t. L: bristle]

setaceous (sĭ tā′shəs), *adj.* **1.** bristle-like; bristle-shaped. **2.** furnished with bristles. [t. NL: m. *sētāceus*]

setback (sĕt′băk′), *n.* **1.** a check to progress; reverse. **2.** *Archit.* **a.** a flat, plain offset in a wall. **b.** such a setting back at a particular height in a tall building, or one of a number of such recessions at different heights, for allowing better light and ventilation in the street.

set chisel, a cold chisel.

set-down (sĕt′doun′), *n.* a rebuke or snub.

Seth (sĕth), *n.* the third son of Adam. Gen. 4:25. [t. L (Vulgate), t. Gk (Septuagint), t. Heb.: m. *Shēth*]

seti-, a word element meaning 'bristle'. [comb. form repr. L *sēta*]

Sétif (*Fr.* sė tēf′), *n.* a town in NE Algeria. 94,000 (1960).

setiform (sē′tĭ fôm′), *adj.* bristle-shaped; setaceous.

setigerous (sĭ tĭj′ə rəs), *adj.* having setae or bristles. Also, **setiferous** (sĭ tĭf′ə rəs). [f. L *sētiger* having bristles + -OUS]

set-in (sĕt′ĭn′), *adj.* (of a sleeve) joined to the body of a garment by a seam at the shoulder. Cf. **raglan.**

set-off (sĕt′ŏf′), *n.* **1.** anything that counterbalances or makes up for something else. **2.** a counterbalancing debt or claim. **3.** *Archit.* an offset. **4.** *Print.* a faulty transfer of superabundant or undried ink on a printed sheet to any opposed surface, as the opposite page.

seton (sē′tn), *n. Surg.* **1.** a thread or the like inserted beneath the skin in order to maintain an artificial passage or issue. **2.** the issue itself. [t. F, t. It.: m. *setone*, der. *seta* silk]

Seton (sē′tn), *n.* **Ernest Thompson,** 1860–1946, English writer and illustrator in the U.S.

setose (sē′tōs), *adj.* covered with setae or bristles; bristly. [t. L: m. s. *sētōsus*]

set piece, 1. a piece of theatrical scenery used as part of a stage set. **2.** an arrangement of fireworks on a scaffolding forming a design or picture when lighted. **3.** a work of art, literature, music, or the like, conforming to a conventional structure, style, etc.

set point, *Tennis.* the point needed to win a set.

setscrew (sĕt′skro͞o′), *n.* a screw holding firmly together two machine parts, one being otherwise subject to movement along the other. Also, **grubscrew.**

set square, a flat piece of wood, plastic, or the like, in the shape of a right-angled triangle, used in mechanical drawing.

sett (sĕt), *n.* **1.** a small rectangular paving block of stone or wood. **2.** any of various tools for shaping, as a hammer-shaped chisel for paring or cutting metal. **3.** the adjustment of a weaver's reed, determining the pattern. **4.** a square or pattern of a tartan. **5.** the home or burrow of a badger. Also, **set.** [var. of SET]

settee¹ (sė tē′), *n.* a seat for two or more persons, with a back and usually arms, and usually upholstered. [? dim. of SEAT]

settee² (sė tē′), *n. Hist.* **1.** a decked vessel used until the 19th century, in the Mediterranean. **2. settee sail,** a type of lateen sail used in such vessels.

setter (sĕt′ə), *n.* **1.** one who or that which sets. **2.** one of a breed of long-haired hunting dogs which originally had the habit of crouching when game was scented, but which are now trained to stand stiffly and point the muzzle towards the scented game, the breed being made up of three distinct groups: Irish setters, English setters, and Gordon setters.

set theory, the branch of mathematics that deals with the properties of sets (def. 80).

setting (sĕt′ĭng), *n.* **1.** the act of one who or that which sets. **2.** the surroundings or environment of anything. **3.** that in which something, as a jewel, is set or mounted. **4.** a group of all the combined articles, as of cutlery, china, etc., required for setting a table, or a single place at a table. **5.** the period or locale in which the action of a play, film, etc., takes place. **6.** the scenery, costumes, etc., of a play. **7.** *Music.* **a.** a piece of music composed for certain words. **b.** a piece of music composed for a particular medium, or arranged for a medium other than the original.

setting coat, *Bldg Trades.* the finishing coat in plastering; skimming coat.

settle¹ (sĕt′l), *v.*, **-tled, -tling.** —*v.t.* **1.** to appoint or fix definitely; agree upon (a time, price, conditions, etc.). **2.** to place in a desired position or in order. **3.** to pay (a bill, account due, or the like). **4.** to close (an account) by payment. **5.** to take up residence in (a country, place, house, etc.). **6.** to cause to take up residence. **7.** to furnish (a place) with inhabitants or settlers. **8.** to establish in a way of life, a business, etc. **9.** to bring to rest; quiet (the nerves, stomach, etc.). **10.** *Colloq.* to cause to cease from opposition or annoyance. **11.** to make stable; place on a permanent basis. **12.** to cause (a liquid) to deposit dregs. **13.** to cause (dregs, etc.) to sink. **14.** to cause to sink down gradually; make firm or compact. **15.** to close up; dispose of finally: *to settle an estate.* **16.** *Law.* **a.** to secure (property, title, etc.) on or to a person by formal or legal process. **b.** to terminate (legal proceedings) by mutual consent of the parties.
—*v.i.* **17.** to decide; arrange (often fol. by *on* or *upon*): *to settle on a plan of action.* **18.** to make a financial arrangement; pay (often fol. by *up*). **19.** to take up residence in a new country or place. **20.** to come to rest, as from flight: *a bird settled on a bough.* **21.** to come to rest in a particular place: *a cold settles in one's head.* **22.** to sink down gradually; subside. **23.** to become clear, by the sinking of particles, as a liquid. **24.** to sink to the bottom as sediment. **25.** to become firm or compact, as the ground. **26. settle down, a.** to come to a rest; become calm or composed. **b.** to apply oneself to serious work. **c.** to set oneself to a regular way of life, esp. upon marrying. **27. settle in,** to move into a new home and adapt oneself to new surroundings. **28. settle with, a.** to pay one's debts to. **b.** to come to an agreement with.
[ME; OE *setlan* (c. D *zetelen* place, settle), der. *setl* SETTLE²]

settle² (sĕt′l), *n.* a long seat or bench, usually wooden and with arms and high back. [ME; OE *setl*, c. G *Sessel.* See SIT, v.]

settlement (sĕt′l mənt), *n.* **1.** the act of settling. **2.** the state of being settled. **3.** the act of making stable or putting on a permanent basis. **4.** the resulting state. **5.** arrangement; adjustment. **6.** the establishment of a person in an employment, office, or charge. **7.** the settling of persons in a new country or place. **8.** a colony, esp. in its early stages. **9.** a small village or collection of houses, esp. in a sparsely populated area. **10.** the satisfying of a claim or demand; a coming to terms. **11.** *Law.* **a.** final disposition of an estate or the like. **b.** the settling of property, title, etc., upon a person. **c.** the property so settled. **12.** legal residence in a particular place, or the right to maintenance, if a pauper. **13.** *Sociol.* a welfare establishment in an underprivileged area providing social, cultural, and educational facilities for the people in the area, including personnel to assist them. **14.** a subsidence or sinking of a structure or part of one.

settlement worker, one who devotes time to a settlement (def. 13).

settler (sĕt′lə), *n.* **1.** one who or that which settles. **2.** one who settles in a new country. **3.** *Law.* one who disposes of property by creating a succession of interests in it.

settler's clock, *n. Austral.* the kookaburra.

settling (sĕt′lĭng), *n.* **1.** the act of one who or that which settles. **2.** (*usually pl.*) sediment.

settling day, a day fixed for the settling of accounts and completion of transactions, esp. on the Stock Exchange.

set-to (sĕt′to͞o′), *n., pl.* **-tos.** a fight; argument. [f. SET + TO]

Setúbal (*Port.* sə to͞o′bál), *n.* a seaport in Portugal, near Lisbon. 44,435 (1960).

setula (sĕt′yo͝o lə), *n., pl.* **-lae** (-lē′). *Zool., Bot.* a short blunt seta or bristle-like part. Also, **setule** (sĕt′yo͝ol). [t. NL, dim. of *seta* SETA]

setulose (sĕt′yo͝o lōs′), *adj. Zool., Bot.* having or covered with setulae. Also, **setulous** (sĕt′yo͝o ləs).

set-up (sĕt′ŭp′), *n.* **1.** organization; arrangement; general state of affairs. **2.** *Surveying.* a station or point at which a surveying instrument is set up for taking a number of readings. **3.** *U.S.* carriage, as of the body. **4.** *U.S.* ice, soda-water, etc., for mixing. **5.** *U.S. Slang.* a contest or undertaking which presents no real challenge or problems, as a fixed boxing match; a foregone conclusion.

set width, the width of the lower-case alphabet of a given face and size of type, used to assess the amount of type matter that can be set in a given area.

Seurat (*Fr.* sœ rá′), *n.* **Georges** (*Fr.* zhôrzh), 1859–91, French painter.

Sevastopol (sĭ văs′ tə pl; *Russ.* sĭ vás tô′ pəly), *n.* a fortified seaport in the SW Soviet Union in Europe: famous for its heroic resistance during sieges of 349 days in 1854–55, and 245 days in 1941–42. 169,000 (est. 1963). Also, **Sebastopol.**

Sevastopol

seven (sĕv′ən), *n.* **1.** a cardinal number, six plus one. **2.** a symbol for this number, as 7 or VII. **3.** a set of seven persons or things. **4.** a playing card with seven pips. **5.** *(pl.) Cards.* a game in which the players lay down their cards to form sequences in the same suits, the winner being the player who gets rid of his cards first. **6. the Seven,** *Colloq.* the European Free Trade Area. *—adj.* **7,** amounting to seven in number. [ME; OE *seofon*, c. G *sieben*]

Seven against Thebes, *Gk Legend.* the seven heroes (Adrastus, Amphiaraus, Capaneus, Hippomedon, Parthenopaeus, Polynices, and Tydeus) who made an expedition against Thebes to seat Polynices on the throne. They were defeated, but ten years later the descendants of the Seven (the Epigoni) attacked Thebes successfully.

seven deadly sins. See **deadly sins.**

sevenfold (sĕv′ən fōld′), *adj.* **1.** comprising seven parts or members; seven times as great or as much. *—adv.* **2.** in sevenfold measure.

Seven Hills of Rome, the seven hills (the Aventine, Caelian, Capitoline, Esquiline, Palatine, Quirinal, and Viminal) on and about which the ancient city of Rome was built.

Sevenoaks (sĕv′ən ōks′), *n.* a town in England, in Kent. 17,604 (1961).

sevenpence (sĕv′ən pəns), *n.* seven pennies.

sevenpenny (sĕv′ən pə nĭ), *adj.* **1.** of the amount or value of sevenpence. *—n.* **2.** something purchased for sevenpence.

seven seas, the navigable waters of the world.

seventeen (sĕv′ən tēn′), *n.* **1.** a cardinal number, ten plus seven. **2.** a symbol for this number, as 17 or XVII. **3.** a set of this many persons or things. *—adj.* **4.** amounting to seventeen in number. [ME *seventene*, OE *seofontene*, c. D *zeventien*]

seventeenth (sĕv′ən tēnth′), *adj.* **1.** next after the sixteenth. **2.** being one of seventeen equal parts. *—n.* **3.** a seventeenth part, esp. of one ($\frac{1}{17}$). **4.** the seventeenth member of a series.

seventh (sĕv′ənth), *adj.* **1.** next after the sixth. **2.** being one of seven equal parts. *—n.* **3.** a seventh part, esp. of one ($\frac{1}{7}$). **4.** the seventh member of a series. **5.** *Music.* **a.** a note on the seventh degree from a given note (counted as the first). **b.** the interval between such notes. **c.** the harmonic combination of such notes.

seventh chord, *Music.* a chord formed by the superposition of three thirds.

seventh-day (sĕv′ənth dā′), *adj.* *(often cap.)* designating certain Christian sects who make Saturday their chief day of rest and religious observance: *Seventh-Day Adventists.*

seventh heaven, **1.** (in Talmudic literature) the highest heaven, where God and the most exalted angels dwell. **2.** a state of extreme happiness: *she was in the seventh heaven with her new washing machine.*

seventy (sĕv′ən tĭ), *n., pl.* **-ties,** *adj.* *—n.* **1.** a cardinal number, ten times seven. **2.** a symbol for this number, as 70 or LXX. **3. the Seventy,** the body of (seventy-two) scholars who, according to tradition, made the Septuagint. **4.** *(pl.)* the numbers from 70 to 79 of a series, esp. with reference to the years of a person's age, or the years of a century, esp. the twentieth. *—adj.* **5.** amounting to seventy in number. [ME; OE *seofontig*, c. G *siebzig*] **—seventieth** (sĕv′ən tĭ ĭth), *adj., n.*

seventy-eight (sĕv′ən tĭ āt′), *n.* *Colloq.* a gramophone record designed to turn at seventy-eight revolutions per minute, standard before the introduction of microgroove records.

seventy-five (sĕv′ən tĭ fīv′), *n.* *Mil.* a gun with a 75 mm. calibre.

seventy-four (sĕv′ən tĭ fô′), *n.* a large edible fish of South African waters, *Polysteganus undulosus*, related to the sea-breams.

seven-up (sĕv′ən ŭp′), *n.* *Cards.* all fours.

Seven Wonders of the World, the seven most remarkable structures of ancient times: the Egyptian pyramids, the Mausoleum erected by Artemisia at Halicarnassus, the Temple of Artemis at Ephesus, the walls and Hanging Gardens of Babylon, the Colossus of Rhodes, the statue of Zeus by Phidias at Olympia, and the Pharos or lighthouse at Alexandria.

seven-year itch, *Colloq.* marital boredom or discontent considered to develop after about seven years of marriage.

Seven Years War, the war (1756–63) over Silesia in which England and Prussia defeated France, Austria, Russia, Sweden, and Saxony.

sever (sĕv′ə), *v.t.* **1.** to put apart; separate. **2.** to divide into parts, esp. forcibly; cut; cleave. **3.** to break off or dissolve (ties, relations, etc.). *—v.i.* **4.** to separate or part, from each other or one from another; to become divided into parts. **5.** to make a separation or division, as between things. [ME *severe(n)*, t. AF: m. *severer*, g. LL *sēperāre*, r. L *sēparāre*] **—Ant. 1.** unite.

severable (sĕv′ə rə bl), *adj.* **1.** capable of being severed. **2.** *Law.* separable or capable of being treated as separate from a whole legal right or obligation: *a severable contract obligation.*

several (sĕv′rəl), *adj.* **1.** being more than two or three, but not many. **2.** respective; individual: *they went their several ways.* **3.** separate; different: *three several occasions.* **4.** single; particular. **5.** divers; various: *the several steps in a process.* **6.** *Law.* binding two or more persons who may be sued separately on a common obligation. *—n.* **7.** several persons or things; a few; some. [ME, t. AF, g. L *sēpar* distinct + *-ālis* -AL[1]]

severally (sĕv′rə lĭ), *adv.* **1.** separately; singly. **2.** respectively.

severalty (sĕv′ə rəl tĭ, sĕv′rəl tĭ), *n., pl.* **-ties. 1.** the state of being separate. **2.** the condition, as of land, of being held or owned by separate or individual right.

severance (sĕv′ə rəns), *n.* **1.** the act of severing. **2.** the state of being severed. **3.** *Law.* a dividing into parts, as in a contract. **4.** a breaking off, as of relations. [ME, t. AF. See SEVER, -ANCE]

severance pay, money paid by a firm to employees or directors in compensation for loss of employment.

severe (sĭ vĭə′), *adj.,* **-verer, -verest. 1.** harsh; harshly extreme: *severe criticism or laws.* **2.** serious; stern: *a severe face.* **3.** grave: *a severe illness.* **4.** rigidly restrained in style or taste; simple; plain. **5.** causing discomfort or distress by extreme character or conditions, as weather, cold, heat, etc.; unpleasantly violent, as rain or wind, a blow or shock, etc. **6.** hard to endure, perform, fulfil, etc.: *a severe test.* **7.** rigidly exact, accurate, or methodical: *severe conformity to standards.* [t. L: m. s. *sevērus*] **—severe′ly,** *adv.* **—severe′ness,** *n.* **—Syn. 2.** See **stern**[1]. **—Ant. 1.** lenient. **2.** gentle.

Severini (*It.* sĕ vĕ rē′ nē), *n.* **Gino** (*It.* jē′ nō), 1883–1966, Italian futurist painter.

severity (sĭ vĕ′ rĭ tĭ), *n., pl.* **-ties. 1.** harshness, sternness, or rigour. **2.** austere simplicity, as of style or taste. **3.** violence or sharpness, as of cold, pain, etc. **4.** grievousness; hard or trying character or effect. **5.** gravity; austerity. **6.** rigid exactness or accuracy.

Severn (sĕv′ən), *n.* a river flowing from central Wales, through Shropshire, Worcestershire, and Gloucestershire into the Bristol Channel: the longest river in Great Britain. 220 mi.

Severus (sĭ vĭə′ rəs), *n.* **Lucius Septimius** (lo͞o′ syəs sĕp tĭm′ ĭ əs), A.D. 146–211, Roman emperor A.D. 193–211.

Sévigné (*Fr.* sė vē nyė′), *n.* **Marie de** (*Fr.* mȧ rē′ də) (*Marie de Rabutin-Chantal*), 1626–96, French letter-writer.

Seville (sə vĭl′), *n.* a port in SW Spain on the river Guadalquivir: site of the Alcazar; cathedral. 531,571 (1965). Spanish, **Sevilla** (*Sp.* sė bē′ lyȧ).

Seville orange. See **orange** (def. 2).

Sèvres (*Fr.* sĕ′ vr), *n.* **1.** a suburb of Paris in N France. 20,292 (1962). **2.** a kind of porcelain made there.

sew (sō), *v.,* **sewed, sewn** or **sewed, sewing.** *—v.t.* **1.** to join or attach by a thread or the like, as with a needle. **2.** to make, repair, etc., (a garment) by such means. **3.** to fasten or secure with stitches: *to sew flour in bags.* **4.** to close (a hole, wound, etc.) by means of stitches (usually fol. by *up*). **5. sew up,** *Colloq.* to complete or conclude (arrangements, discussions, etc.) successfully or satisfactorily. *—v.i.* **6.** to work with a needle and thread, or with a sewing machine. [ME *sewe(n)*, OE *siw(i)an*; akin to L *suere*]

sewage (syo͞o′ ĭj), *n.* the waste matter which passes through sewers.

sewage ejector, a device for lifting sewage from one level to another.

sewage farm, a place where sewage is rendered harmless, by turning it in rotation over a large area of land.

sewan (sē′ wən), *n.* seawan.

Seward (sē′ wəd, syo͞o′ əd), *n.* **William Henry,** 1801–72, U.S. statesman.

Seward Peninsula, a peninsula in W Alaska, on Bering Strait.

sewer[1] (syōō′ə), *n.* an artificial conduit, usually underground, for carrying off waste water and refuse, as from a town or city. [ME, t. OF: m. *sewiere* channel from a fishpond, g. L *ex* out of + *aquāria*, fem., of water]

sewer[2] (sō′ə), *n.* one who or that which sews. [f. SEW + -ER[1]]

sewer[3] (syōō′ə), *n.* (formerly) a household officer or head servant in charge of the service of the table. [ME, t. AF: aphetic m. *asseour* seater, g. L *assidēre* sit at]

sewerage (syōō′ə′rĭj), *n.* **1.** the removal of waste water and refuse by means of sewers. **2.** a system of sewers. **3.** sewage.

sewer gas, the contaminated air of sewers, containing methane and carbon dioxide. Also, **sewage gas.**

sewer rat, any rat inhabiting sewers, as the brown rat, *Rattus norvegicus.*

sewing (sō′ĭng), *n.* **1.** the act or work of one who sews. **2.** something sewn or to be sewn.

sewing circle, a group of women who meet regularly to sew for the benefit of charity or the like.

sewing machine, any of various hand-operated, foot-operated or electric machines used for sewing, embroidery, etc.

sewn (sōn), *v.* a pp. of **sew.**

sex (sĕks), *n.* **1.** the character of being either male or female: *persons of different sexes.* **2.** the sum of the anatomical and physiological differences with reference to which the male and the female are distinguished, or the phenomena depending on these differences. **3.** the instinct or attraction drawing one sex towards another, or its manifestation in life and conduct. **4.** men collectively, or women collectively: *the fair sex.* **5. to have sex,** *Colloq.* to have sexual intercourse. —*v.t.* **6.** to ascertain the sex of. [ME, t. L: s. *sexus* sex, ? orig., division]

sex-, a word element meaning 'six', as in *sexcentenary.* [t. L, comb. form of *sex*]

sexagenarian (sĕk′sə jĭ nĕə′rĭ ən), *adj.* **1.** of the age of 60 years, or between 60 and 70 years old. —*n.* **2.** a sexagenarian person.

sexagenary (sĕk săj′ĭ nə rĭ), *adj., n., pl.* **-ries.** —*adj.* **1.** of or pertaining to the number 60. **2.** composed of or proceeding by sixties. **3.** sexagenarian. —*n.* **4.** a sexagenarian. [t. L: m. s. *sexāgēnārius*]

Sexagesima (sĕk′sə jĕs′ĭ mə), *n.* the second Sunday before Lent (more fully, **Sexagesima Sunday**). [t. L: *sexāgēsima (dies)* sixtieth day]

sexagesimal (sĕk′sə jĕs′ĭ məl), *adj.* **1.** pertaining to or based upon the number 60. —*n.* **2.** a fraction whose denominator is 60 or a power of 60. [t. ML: s. *sexāgēsimālis*, der. L *sexāgēsimus* sixtieth]

sex appeal, the quality of attracting the opposite sex.

sexcentenary (sĕks′sĕn tē′nə rĭ), *adj., n., pl.* **-ries.** —*adj.* **1.** pertaining to six hundred or a period of six hundred years; marking the completion of six hundred years. —*n.* **2.** a six-hundredth anniversary, or its celebration.

sex chromosome, *Biol.* any chromosome carrying sex-determining factors, esp. such chromosomes that differ morphologically from the ordinary autosomes, called X and Y, W and Z chromosomes.

sexed (sĕkst), *adj.* having sexuality to a specified degree: *she was highly sexed.*

sexennial (sĕks ĕn′yəl), *adj.* **1.** of or for six years. **2.** occurring every six years. —*n.* **3.** *U.S.* a sexcentenary. [f. s. L *sexennium* + -AL[1]] —**sexen′nially,** *adv.*

sex hygiene, a branch of hygiene which concerns itself with sex and sexual behaviour as it relates to the well-being of the individual and the community.

sexivalent (sĕk′sĭ vā′lənt), *adj. Chem.* hexavalent. Also, **sexavalent.**

sex kitten, *Colloq.* a sexually attractive and provocative young woman.

sexless (sĕks′lĭs), *adj.* **1.** having or seeming to have no sex. **2.** having or seeming to have no sexual desires. **3.** having no sex appeal. —**sex′lessly,** *adv.* —**sex′lessness,** *n.*

sex-linkage (sĕks′lĭng′kĭj), *n. Genetics.* inheritance in which both parents do not contribute equally to their progeny because the genes involved are borne on the sex chromosomes in which the parents differ.

sexology (sĕk sŏl′ə jĭ), *n.* the study of the sexual behaviour of human beings.

sexpartite (sĕks pä′tīt), *adj.* divided into or consisting of six parts, as a vault, etc. [f. SEX- + PARTITE]

sext (sĕkst), *n. Eccles.* the third of the seven canonical hours, or the service for it, orig. fixed for the sixth hour of the day (or noon). [ME, t. L: s. *sexta* (*hōra*) sixth (hour)]

sextain (sĕks′tān), *n.* sestina.

sextan (sĕks′tən), *adj.* **1.** (of a fever, etc.) characterized by paroxysms which recur every sixth day. —*n.* **2.** a sextan fever or ague. [t. NL: s. *sextāna* (der. L *sextus* sixth), short for *sextāna febris*]

Sextans (sĕks′tənz), *n., gen.* **Sextantis** (sĕks tăn′tĭs). *Astron.* an equatorial constellation between Hydra and Leo. [t. L. See SEXTANT]

sextant (sĕks′tənt), *n.* **1.** an astronomical instrument used in measuring angular distances, esp. the altitudes of sun, moon, and stars at sea in determining latitude and longitude. **2.** (*cap.*) *Astron.* Sextans. [t. L: s. *sextans* sixth part]

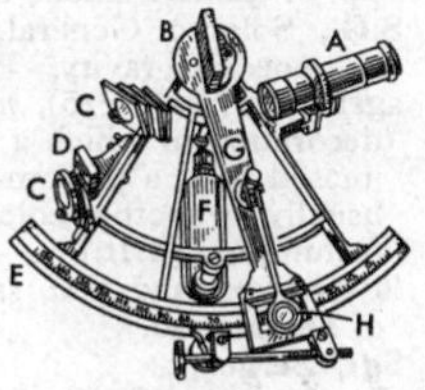

Sextant
A, Telescope; B, Mirror; C, Coloured glass filters; D, Half-mirror, half-glass; E, Graduated arc; F, Handle; G, Movable index arm; H, Magnifying glass

sextet (sĕks tĕt′), *n.* **1.** any group or set of six. **2.** Also, **sestet. a.** a company of six singers or players. **b.** a musical composition for six voices or instruments. Also, **sextette.** [alter. of SESTET, ult. der. L *sex* six]

sextile (sĕks′tĭl), *Astron.* —*adj.* **1.** denoting or pertaining to the aspect or position of two heavenly bodies when 60° distant from each other. —*n.* **2.** a sextile position or aspect. [t. L: m. s. *sextīlis* sixth]

sextillion (sĕks tĭl′yən), *n.* **1.** (usually with *one* or *a*) a cardinal number represented (in Britain and Germany) by one followed by 36 zeros, or (in the U.S. and France) by one followed by 21 zeros. —*adj.* **2.** (usually with *one* or *a*) amounting to one sextillion in number. [t. F: f. s. L *sextus* sixth (power of) + (*m*)*illion* MILLION] —**sextil′lionth,** *adj., n.*

sexto (sĕks′tō), *n. Print.* a page with an area which is one sixth of the whole printing sheet. [t. L, abl. sing. of *sextus* sixth]

sextodecimo (sĕks′tō dĕs′ĭ mō′), *n., pl.* **-mos,** *adj. Bookbinding.* —*n.* **1.** a volume printed from sheets folded to form 16 leaves or 32 pages, approximately 4 × 6 inches. *Abbrev.*: 16mo. or 16°. —*adj.* **2.** in sextodecimo. Also, **sixteenmo.** [t. L, abl. sing. of *sextusdecimus* sixteenth]

sexton (sĕks′tən), *n.* a church officer and guardian who is charged with taking care of the church, its contents, and the graveyard, ringing the bell, gravedigging, etc. [ME *segerstone*, t. AF: m. *segrestaine*, t. ML: m. *sacristānus* sacristan]

sextuple (sĕks′tyōō pl), *adj., v.,* **-pled, -pling.** —*adj.* **1.** sixfold; consisting of six parts; six times as great. —*v.t., v.i.* **2.** to make or become six times as great. [f. s. L *sextus* sixth + *-uple*, as in QUINTUPLE]

sextuplet (sĕks′tyōō plĭt), *n.* **1.** one of the six children born at one birth. **2.** a group or combination of six things.

sexual (sĕk′syōō əl), *adj.* **1.** of or pertaining to sex. **2.** occurring between or involving the two sexes. **3.** having sex or sexual organs, or reproducing by processes involving both sexes, as animals or plants. [t. LL: s. *sexuālis*] —**sex′ually,** *adv.*

sexual intercourse, the insertion of the penis into the vagina followed by ejaculation; coitus; copulation.

sexuality (sĕk′syōō ăl′ĭ tĭ), *n.* **1.** sexual character; possession of sex. **2.** the recognition or emphasizing of sexual matters.

sexual selection, the theory, first propounded by Darwin, that the selection by some animals of attractive mates has resulted in the evolution of features which are in other respects disadvantageous.

sexy (sĕk′sĭ), *adj.* **-ier, -iest. 1.** having or involving a predominant or excessive concern with sex: *a sexy novel.* **2.** sexually interesting or exciting; having sex appeal. —**sex′ily,** *adv.* —**sex′iness,** *n.*

Seychelles (sā shĕl′, -shĕlz′), *n.pl.* a group of 92 islands in the Indian Ocean, NE of Madagascar: a British colony. 46,472 pop. (1964); 156 sq. mi. *Cap.*: Victoria.

Seymour (sē′mô), *n.* **Jane,** *c.* 1510–37, third wife of Henry VIII of England, and mother of Edward VI.

sf, science fiction.

sf., *Music.* sforzando. Also, **sfz.**

Sfax (sfăks), *n.* a seaport in N Africa, in E Tunisia. 70,000 (est. 1961).

Sforza (*It.* sfôr′tsä), *n.* **1. Count Carlo** (*It.* kär′lô), 1873–1952, Italian statesman: anti-Fascist leader. **2. Francesco** (*It.* frän chĕs′kô), 1401–66, Italian condottiere, and duke of Milan 1450–66. **3.** his father, **Giacomuzzo** or **Muzio** (*It.* jä kô mōōt′tsô *or* mōōt′tsyô) **Attendolo** (*It.* ät tĕn′dô lô), 1369–1424, Italian condottiere. **4. Lodovico** (*It.* lô dô vē′kô) ('*the Moor*'), 1451–1508, duke of Milan 1494–1500: son of Francesco Sforza.

sforzando (sfôt săn′dō; *It.* sfôr tsän′dô), *adj., adv. Music.* with force (used as a direction, to indicate that a note or chord is to be rendered with special emphasis). Also, **forzando, sforzato** (sfôt säʹtō; *It.* sfôr tsäʹtō). *Abbrev.*: sf., sfz. [It., ger. of *sforzare* force]

sfumato (sfo͞o mäʹtō), *n. Art.* the transition of tone or colour from light to dark by imperceptible stages. [It., pp. of *sfumare* smoke out, fade; c. FUME]

S.G., Solicitor General.

s.g., specific gravity.

sgraffito (sgrä fēʹtō), *n., pl.* **-ti** (-tē). **1.** a technique of decoration in which a top layer of plaster, paint, etc., is incised with a pattern partially to reveal a second layer usually of another colour. **2.** an object decorated by this technique [t. It.]

's Gravenhage (*Du.* sKHrä vən häʹKHə), *n.* Dutch name of **The Hague.**

Sgt, Sergeant.

sh., **1.** sheep. **2.** *Bookbinding.* sheet. **3.** shilling.

sh (sh), *interj.* an exclamation requesting or demanding silence.

shabby (shăbʹĭ), *adj.,* **-bier, -biest. 1.** having the appearance impaired by wear, use, etc.: *shabby clothes.* **2.** wearing worn clothes; seedy. **3.** making a poor appearance. **4.** meanly ungenerous or unfair; contemptible, as persons, actions, etc. [f. *shab* (ME; OE *sceabb* scab) + -Y[1]] —**shabʹbily,** *adv.* —**shabʹbiness,** *n.*

shabby-genteel (shăbʹĭ jĕn tēlʹ), *adj.* trying to appear genteel and dignified despite shabbiness.

Shabuoth (shä vo͞oʹōth, shə vo͞oʹəs), *n.pl.* the Jewish holiday Feast of Weeks, or Pentecost.

shack (shăk), *n.* **1.** a rough cabin; shanty. —*v.i.* **2. shack up,** to live at a place; reside: *you can come and shack up with us till your house is ready.* [short for *shackle* in same sense, itself short for RAMSHACKLE]

shackle (shăkʹl), *n., v.,* **-led, -ling.** —*n.* **1.** a ring or fastening of iron or the like for securing the wrist, ankle, etc.; a fetter. **2.** a hobble or fetter for a horse or other animal. **3.** any of various fastening or coupling devices, as the curved bar of a padlock which passes through the staple. **4.** anything that serves to prevent freedom of procedure, thought, etc. —*v.t.* **5.** to put a shackle or shackles on; confine or restrain. **6.** to fasten or couple with a shackle. **7.** to restrain in action, thought, etc. [ME *shackle,* OE *sceacel* fetter, c. LG *schakel* hobble (for a horse)] —**shackʹler,** *n.*

Shackleton (shăkʹl tən), *n.* **Sir Ernest Henry,** 1874–1922, British antarctic explorer.

shad (shăd), *n., pl.* **shad,** (*for different species*) **shads. 1.** a deep-bodied herring of North America, *Alosa sapidissima,* that runs up streams to spawn, and is valued as a food fish. **2.** any other species of *Alosa* or of related genera. **3.** any of several unrelated fishes. [OE *sceadd*; cf. LG *schade*]

shadberry (shădʹbə rĭ, -brĭ), *n., pl.* **-ries. 1.** the fruit of the shadbush. **2.** the shadbush itself.

shadbush (shădʹbo͝osh'), *n.* **1.** the North American serviceberry, *Amelanchier canadensis,* a shrub or small tree with racemose white flowers and a berry-like fruit. **2.** any of various other species of *Amelanchier.* Also, **shadblow** (shădʹblō'). [f. *shad* (? d. var. of SHADE) + BUSH[1]]

shaddock (shădʹək), *n.* **1.** the large roundish or pear-shaped, usually pale yellow, orange-like edible fruit of the rutaceous tree, *Citrus decumana,* grown extensively in the Orient; pomelo. **2.** the tree itself. [named after Captain *Shaddock,* 17th-cent. English sea-captain, who brought the seed from the East Indies to Jamaica]

shade (shād), *n., v.,* **shaded, shading.** —*n.* **1.** the comparative darkness caused by the interception of rays of light. **2.** an area of comparative darkness; a shady place. **3.** (*pl.*) darkness gathering at the close of day. **4.** (*chiefly pl.*) a retired or obscure place. **5.** comparative obscurity. **6.** a spectre or ghost. **7.** a lampshade. **8.** anything used for protection against excessive light, heat, etc. **9.** (*pl.*) *Slang.* sunglasses. **10.** *Class. Myth.* **a.** an inhabitant of Hades. **b.** (*pl.*) the spirits of the dead collectively. **c.** the world or abode of the dead; Hades. **11.** a shadow. **12.** degree of darkening of a colour by adding black or by decreasing the illumination. **13.** comparative darkness as represented pictorially; the dark part, or a dark part, of a picture. **14.** a slight variation, amount, or degree: *there is not a shade of difference between them.* **15. cast** or **put in the shade,** to surpass; render insignificant by comparison. —*v.t.* **16.** to produce shade in or on. **17.** to obscure, dim, or darken. **18.** to screen or hide from view. **19.** to protect (something) from light, heat, etc., as by a screen; to cover or screen (a light, candle, etc.). **20.** to introduce degrees of darkness into (a drawing or painting) for effects of light and shade or different colours. **21.** to render the values of light and dark in (a painting or drawing). **22.** to change by imperceptible degrees into something else. —*v.i.* **23.** to pass or change by slight graduations, as one colour or one thing into another. [ME; OE *sceadu.* See SHADOW] —**shadeʹless,** *adj.*

—**Syn. 1.** SHADE, SHADOW imply partial darkness or something less bright than the surroundings. SHADE indicates the lesser brightness and heat of an area where the direct rays of light do not fall: *the shade of a tree.* It differs from SHADOW in that it implies no particular form or definite limit, while a SHADOW often represents in form or outline the object which intercepts the light: *the shadow of a dog.* **8.** See **curtain.** —**Ant. 1.** light, glare.

shade tree, *U.S.* a tree planted or valued for its shade.

shading (shāʹdĭng), *n.* **1.** a slight variation or difference of colour, character, etc. **2.** the act of one who or that which shades. **3.** the representation of the different values in a painting or drawing.

shadoof (shə do͞ofʹ), *n.* a contrivance used in Egypt and other Middle Eastern countries for raising water, esp. for irrigation, consisting of a long suspended rod with a bucket at one end and a weight at the other. Also, **shaduf.** [t. Egypt. Ar.: m. *shādūf*]

Shadoofs

shadow (shădʹō), *n.* **1.** a dark figure or image cast on the ground or some surface by a body intercepting light. **2.** shade or comparative darkness; an instance or area of comparative darkness. **3.** (*pl.*) darkness coming after sunset. **4.** shelter; protection. **5.** a slight suggestion; a trace: *not a shadow of a doubt.* **6.** a spectre or ghost: *pursued by shadows.* **7.** a shadowy or faint image: *shadows of things to come.* **8.** a mere semblance: *the shadow of power.* **9.** a reflected image. **10.** the dark part, or shade, or a dark part, of a picture. **11.** a cloud, as on friendship or reputation. **12.** a constant or dominant threat, influence, etc.: *under the shadow of the atomic bomb.* **13.** an inseparable companion. **14.** one who follows a person in order to keep watch upon him, as a spy or detective. —*v.t.* **15.** to overspread with shadow; shade. **16.** to cast a gloom over; cloud. **17.** to screen or protect from light, heat, etc. **18.** to follow (a person) about secretly, in order to keep watch over his movements. **19.** to represent faintly, prophetically, etc. (often fol. by *forth*). **20.** *Archaic.* to shelter or protect. **21.** *Obs.* to shade in painting, drawing, etc. [ME; OE *scead(u)we,* oblique case of *sceadu* SHADE c. D *schaduw*; akin to G *Schatten*] —**shadʹower,** *n.* —**shadʹowless,** *adj.* —**Syn. 1.** See **shade.**

shadow bands, *Astron.* parallel bands of light and shade which can sometimes be seen to sweep across the ground just before totality in a solar eclipse; they are caused by irregular refraction of light from the thin crescent formed by the earth's atmosphere.

shadow-boxing (shădʹō bŏkʹsĭng), *n.* boxing carried on with an imaginary opponent, as for exercise.

shadow cabinet, *Politics.* the group of members of the chief opposition party who act as party spokesmen on major issues, and who would, if in power, be members of the cabinet. See **cabinet.**

shadowgraph (shădʹō grăfʹ, -gräfʹ), *n.* **1.** a picture produced by throwing a shadow, as of the hands, on a lighted screen. **2.** a radiograph. **3.** *Aerospace.* an image which shows the density gradients in the flow about a body which is itself presented in silhouette.

shadow play, theatrical entertainment consisting of the shadows of puppets, live actors, etc., projected on to a screen illuminated from behind.

shadowy (shădʹō ĭ), *adj.* **1.** resembling a shadow in faintness, slightness, etc.: *shadowy outlines.* **2.** unsubstantial, unreal, or illusory. **3.** abounding in shadow; shady: *a shadowy path.* **4.** enveloped in shadow. **5.** casting a shadow.

Shadrach (shāʹdrăk), *n.* a companion of Daniel: one of the three (Shadrach, Meshach, Abednego) thrown into the fiery furnace of Nebuchadnezzar. Dan. 3:12–30.

shaduf (shə do͞ofʹ), *n.* shadoof.

Shadwell (shădʹwəl), *n.* **Thomas,** 1642?–92, English dramatist: poet laureate 1688–92.

shady (shāʹdĭ), *adj.,* **-dier, -diest. 1.** abounding in shade; shaded: *shady paths.* **2.** giving shade. **3.** shadowy; indistinct; spectral. **4.** *Colloq.* uncertain; questionable; of dubious character or reputation. **5. keep shade,** *U.S. Slang.* to keep out of sight, or in hiding. **6. on the shady side of,** *U.S. Colloq.* beyond in age: *on the shady side of forty.* —**shadʹily,** *adv.* —**shadʹiness,** *n.*

SHAEF (shāf), *n.* Supreme Headquarters Allied Expeditionary Forces.

shaft (shäft), *n.* **1.** a long pole or rod forming the body of various weapons, as a spear, lance, or arrow. **2.** something directed as in sharp attack: *shafts of sarcasm.* **3.** a ray or beam: *shaft of sunlight.* **4.** the handle of a hammer, axe, golf club, or other long implement. **5.** a revolving bar serving to transmit motion, as from an engine to various machines. **6.** a flagpole. **7.** the body of a column or pillar between the base and the capital; a column. See diag. under **column. 8.** a monument in the form of a column, obelisk, or the like. **9.** either of the parallel bars of wood between which the animal drawing a vehicle is placed. **10.** any well-like passage or vertical enclosed space, as in a building: *a lift shaft.* **11.** an inclined (sloping) or vertical passageway into a mine. **12.** *Bot.* the trunk of a tree. **13.** *Zool.* the main stem of a feather distal to the superior umbilicus. **14.** that part of a candlestick which supports its branches. [ME; OE *sceaft*, c. G *Schaft*]

Shaftesbury (shäfts′bə rĭ, -brĭ), *n.* **1. Anthony Ashley Cooper, 1st Earl of,** 1621–83, English statesman. **2. Anthony Ashley Cooper, 7th Earl of,** 1801–85, English philanthropist.

shafting (shäf′tĭng), *n. Mach.* **1.** shafts for communicating motion. **2.** a system of such shafts. **3.** material for such shafts.

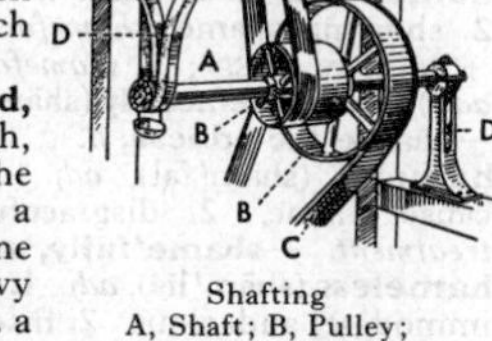

Shafting
A, Shaft; B, Pulley; C, Belt; D, Support

shag[1] (shăg), *n., v.,* **shagged, shagging.** —*n.* **1.** rough, matted hair, wool, or the like. **2.** a mass of this. **3.** a cloth with a nap, at times one of silk but commonly a heavy or rough woollen fabric. **4.** a coarse tobacco cut into fine shreds. —*v.t.* **5.** to make rough or shaggy, esp. with vegetation. **6.** to make rough or sharp. [OE *sceacga* wool, etc., c. Icel. *skegg* beard, der. *skaga* stick out]

shag[2] (shăg), *n.* a small cormorant, *Phalacrocorax aristotelis*, with dark green plumage, found in rocky coastal areas of Europe and northern Africa.

shag[3] (shăg), *v.,* **shagged, shagging,** *n. Taboo.* —*v.t.* **1.** to have sexual intercourse with. **2.** to tire; exhaust. **3.** to chase; run after. —*v.i.* **4.** to masturbate. —*n.* **5.** an act or instance of sexual intercourse, esp. group sexual activity. [orig. unknown]

shagbark (shăg′bäk′), *n. U.S.* **1.** a species of hickory, *Carya ovata*, with rough bark, yielding light-coloured, ellipsoidal, slightly angular nuts, but most valued for its wood. **2.** the wood. **3.** the nut of this tree. Also, **shagbark hickory** (for defs 1, 2).

shagged (shăgd), *adj. Slang.* tired out; exhausted.

shaggy (shăg′ĭ), *adj.,* **-gier, -giest. 1.** covered with or having long, rough hair. **2.** unkempt. **3.** rough and matted; forming a bushy mass, as the hair, mane, etc. **4.** having a rough nap, as cloth. —**shag′gily,** *adv.* —**shag′giness,** *n.*

shaggy dog story, a generally long and involved funny story whose humour lies in the pointlessness or irrelevance of its conclusion.

shagreen (shă grēn′), *n.* **1.** a kind of untanned leather with a granular surface, prepared from the skin of the horse, shark, seal, etc. **2.** the rough skin of certain sharks, used as an abrasive. —*adj.* **3.** Also, **shagreened′.** consisting of or covered with shagreen. [formerly *chagrin*, t. F, t. Turk.: m. *çāghrī*, lit., the rump of a horse]

shagroon (shə grōōn′), *n. N.Z. Colloq.* an Australian stockman settled in New Zealand. [t. Irish: m. *Shaughraun* Saxon]

shah (shä), *n.* king: esp. used (*usually cap.*) as a title of the ruler of Iran. Cf. **Padishah.** [t. Pers.]

Shahaptian (shä hăp′ tĭ ən), *n.* **1.** an American Indian linguistic stock of central Idaho and adjoining parts of Oregon and Washington, including Nez Percé. —*adj.* **2.** of or pertaining to the Shahaptian Indian tribes. Also, **Sahaptan, Sahaptin.** [t. Amer. Ind. (Salishan): m. *sáptini*, in pl. *Saháptini*]

Shah Jahan (shä′ jə hän′), 1592?–1666, Mogul emperor in India, 1628?–58: built the Taj Mahal.

Shahjahanpur (shä′jə hän′pōō′), *n.* a town in India, in central Uttar Pradesh. 110,432 (1961).

Shairp (shäp; *Scot.* shĕrp), *n.* **John Campbell** (′*Principal Shairp*′), 1819–85, Scottish poet and critic.

Shaitan (shī tän′), *n.* **1.** (in Muslim usage) Satan; the devil. **2.** (*l.c.*) a person of evil disposition; a vicious animal. [t. Ar., t. Heb.: alter. of *sātān* Satan]

shake (shāk), *v.,* **shook, shaken, shaking,** *n.* —*v.i.* **1.** to move or sway with short, quick, irregular vibratory movements. **2.** to tremble with emotion, cold, etc. **3.** to fall (fol. by *down*, *off*, etc.) by such motion: *sand shakes off readily.* **4.** to totter; become unsteady. **5.** to clasp a person's hand in greeting, agreement, etc. **6.** *Music.* to execute a trill. **7. shake down, a.** to settle in or retire to a bed, esp. a makeshift or temporary one. **b.** to settle comfortably in or adapt oneself to new surroundings, etc.
—*v.t.* **8.** to move to and fro with short, quick, forcible movements. **9.** to brandish or flourish. **10.** to bring, throw, force, rouse, etc., by or as by some vigorous movement to and fro; cause to quiver or tremble: *leaves shaken by the breeze.* **11.** to cause to totter or waver: *to shake the very foundations of society.* **12.** to agitate or disturb profoundly in feeling. **13.** to unsettle; weaken: *to shake one's faith.* **14.** *Music.* to trill (a note, etc.). **15.** to mix (dice) before they are cast. **16.** *U.S. Slang.* to get rid of; escape from; elude. **17. shake down, a.** to bring down. **b.** to cause to settle. **c.** to condition: *to shake down a vessel by a first voyage.* **d.** *U.S. Slang.* to extort money from. **e.** *U.S. Slang.* to search (someone); frisk. **18. shake hands,** to clasp hands in greeting, congratulation, agreement, etc. **19. shake off, a.** to get rid of; free oneself from. **b.** to get away from; elude. **20. shake one's head,** to turn the head from side to side to indicate reluctance, disapproval, etc. **21. shake the dust from one's feet,** to make one's departure, esp. with a determination not to return. **22. shake up, a.** to shake in order to mix, loosen, etc. **b.** to upset. **c.** to disturb or agitate mentally or physically.
—*n.* **23.** the act of shaking. **24.** tremulous motion. **25.** a tremor. **26.** a disturbing blow; shock. **27.** something resulting from shaking. **28.** *Colloq.* an earthquake. **29.** a fissure in the earth. **30.** a crack or fissure in timber, produced during growth by wind, sudden change of temperature, or the like. **31.** *Music.* a trill. **32.** a drink made by shaking ingredients together: *a milk shake.* **33.** (*pl.*) *Colloq.* a state of trembling, esp. that induced by alcoholism. **34.** a dance in which the body is moved rhythmically in time to music. **35.** *Slang.* an instant. **36. a brace of shakes,** a very short time; an instant. **37. no great shakes,** *Colloq.* of no particular importance; unimpressive. [ME; OE *sceacan*, c. LG *schacken*]
—**Syn. 1.** SHAKE, QUIVER, TREMBLE, VIBRATE refer to an agitated movement which, in living things, is often involuntary. To SHAKE is to agitate more or less quickly, abruptly, and often unevenly so as to disturb the poise, stability, or equilibrium of a person or thing: *a pole shaking under his weight.* To QUIVER is to exhibit a slight vibratory motion such as that resulting from disturbed or irregular (surface) tension: *the surface of the pool quivered in the breeze.* To TREMBLE (used more often of a person) is to be agitated by intermittent, involuntary movements of the muscles, much like shivering and caused by fear, cold, weakness, great emotion, etc.: *even stout hearts tremble with dismay.* To VIBRATE is to exhibit a rapid, incessant rhythmical motion: *a violin string vibrates when a bow is drawn across it.*

shakedown (shāk′doun′), *n.* **1.** a bed of straw, blankets, or other bedding spread on the floor. **2.** any makeshift bed. **3.** the process of shaking down. **4.** *U.S. Slang.* extortion, esp. by blackmail or threatened violence. **5.** *U.S. Slang.* a thorough search. —*adj.* **6.** (of a course, flight, etc.) intended to test a new ship, aircraft, etc., under normal operating conditions.

shake hole, a sinkhole or swallow-hole, esp. in the Pennines.

shake-out (shāk′out′), *n.* **1.** *Stock Exchange.* a sharp drop in certain share values. **2.** *Com.* the elimination of companies, products, etc., owing to increased competition in a declining market or rising standards of quality.

shaker (shā′kə), *n.* **1.** one who or that which shakes. **2.** that with which or from which something is shaken: *a cocktail shaker; flour shaker.* **3.** (*cap.*) one of an American communistic celibate religious sect so called, popularly, from the movements of the body which form part of their ceremonial. —**Shak′erism,** *n.*

Shakespeare (shāk′spĭə′), *n.* **William,** 1564–1616, English poet and dramatist. Also, **Shakspere, Shakspeare.**

Shakespearian (shāk spĭə′rĭ ən), *adj.* **1.** of, pertaining to, or suggestive of Shakespeare or his works. —*n.* **2.** a Shakespearian scholar; a specialist in the study of the works of Shakespeare. Also, **Shakespearean, Shaksperian.** —**Shakespear′ianism,** *n.*

shake-up (shāk′ŭp′), *n.* a thorough change in a business, department, or the like, as by dismissals, demotions, etc.

Shakhty (*Russ.* shäKH′tĭ), *n.* a town in the S Soviet Union in Europe, in the Donets Basin. 213,000 (est. 1965).

shaking (shā′kĭng), *n.* **1.** the act of one who or that which shakes. **2.** ague, with or without chill and fever.

shaking palsy, a disease of the brain, characterized by tremors, esp. of fingers and hands, rigidity of muscles, slowness of movements and speech, and a masklike, expressionless face; Parkinson's disease.

shakings (shā′kĭngz), *n. Naut.* a collection or tangle, as of ropes, canvas, etc.

shako (shăk′ō), *n.*, *pl.* **-os.** a military cap in the form of a cylinder or truncated cone, with a peak and a plume or pompon. [t. Magyar: m. *csákó* peaked (cap)]

Shako

Shakspere (shāk′spĭə′), *n.* **William.** See **Shakespeare.** Also, **Shak′speare′.** —**Shaksper′ian,** *adj.*, *n.*

Shakti (shŭk′tĭ), *n. Hinduism.* Sakti.

shaky (shā′kĭ), *adj.*, **-kier, -kiest.** **1.** shaking. **2.** trembling; tremulous. **3.** liable to break down or give way; insecure; not to be depended upon. **4.** wavering, as in allegiance. —**shak′ily,** *adv.* —**shak′iness,** *n.*

shale (shāl), *n.* a rock of fissile or laminated structure formed by the consolidation of clay or argillaceous material. [special use of obs. *shale* scale (of a fish, etc.), OE *scealu* shell, husk. See SCALE[1]]

shale oil, oil obtained by the distillation of various forms of shale.

shall (shăl; *unstressed* shəl), *aux. v.*, *pres. sing.* 1 **shall;** 2 **shall** or (*Archaic*) **shalt;** 3 **shall;** *pl.* **shall;** *pt.* 1 **should;** 2 **should** or (*Archaic*) **shouldst** or **shouldest;** *pl.* **should;** imperative, inf., and participles lacking. **1.** (used, generally, in the first person to indicate simple future time): *I shall go today.* **2.** (used, generally in the second and third persons, to indicate promise or determination): *you shall do it.* **3.** (used interrogatively, in questions that admit of *shall* in the answer): *Shall he be told? He shall.* **4.** (used conditionally in all persons to indicate future time): *if he shall come.* [ME *shal*, OE *sceal*, c. Icel. *skal*; akin to G *soll*]

—**Syn.** SHALL, WILL are two distinct and separate verbs but the confusion between them is of such long standing that certain arbitrary rules for usage were established. According to those, SHALL is used in the first person (both singular and plural) to indicate futurity, and simply foretells or declares what is about to take place: *I shall go to town tomorrow.* Used with the second or third persons, SHALL implies authority, command, threat, promise, determination, or inevitability: *thou shalt not steal.* With the first person, WILL denotes consent, promise, determination, or resolution: *we will meet you at noon.* WILL in the second and third persons (sing. or pl.) indicates simple futurity: *they will come by train.* Interrogatively, WILL is used to ask about what will happen in the future: *will there be any room?* (i.e. *is there going to be any room?*); SHALL is used in the first person to ask the hearer to decide what should happen: *Shall I open the window? Yes, do. Where shall we meet? At the station.*

shalloon (shă lo͞on′), *n.* a light, twilled woollen fabric used chiefly for linings. [ME *chalon* coverlet, appar. t. F: m. *chalon*, from *Châlons-sur-Marne*]

shallop (shăl′əp), *n.* (formerly) a small, light boat. [t. F: m. *chaloupe*, t. D: m. *sloep*]

shallot (shə lŏt′), *n.* **1.** a plant of the lily family, *Allium ascalonicum*, whose bulb forms bulblets which are used for flavouring in cookery and as a vegetable. **2.** the bulb or bulblet. [aphetic var. of *eschalot*, t. F: m. *eschalotte*, alter. of OF *eschaloigne*. See SCALLION]

shallow (shăl′ō), *adj.* **1.** of little depth; not deep: *shallow water, a shallow dish.* **2.** lacking depth; superficial: *a shallow mind.* —*n.* **3.** (*usually pl.*) a shallow part of a body of water; a shoal. —*v.t.*, *v.i.* **4.** to make or become shallow. [ME *schalowe*. Cf. OE *sceald* shallow] —**shal′lowly,** *adv.* —**shal′lowness,** *n.*

shalt (shălt), *v. Archaic.* 2nd pers. sing. of **shall.**

shaly (shā′lĭ), *adj.* of, like, or containing shale.

sham (shăm), *n.*, *adj.*, *v.*, **shammed, shamming.** —*n.* **1.** something that is not what it purports to be; a spurious imitation. **2.** *Chiefly U.S.* a cover or the like for giving a thing a different outward appearance. **3.** *Obs.* hoax. —*adj.* **4.** pretended; counterfeit: *sham attacks.* **5.** designed or used as a sham. —*v.t.* **6.** to produce an imitation of; pretend to be. **7.** to assume the appearance of: *to sham illness.* —*v.i.* **8.** to make a false pretence; pretend. [special use of *sham*, northern var. of SHAME] —**Syn. 4.** spurious, make-believe, simulated. See **false.** —**Ant. 4.** genuine.

shaman (shăm′ən), *n.* a medicine man and priest who works with the supernatural. [t. G: m. *Schamane*, t. Russ.: m. *shaman*, t. Tungusic: m. *samân*] —**shamanic** (shə măn′ĭk), *adj.*

shamanism (shăm′ə nĭz′əm), *n.* **1.** the primitive religion of northern Asia embracing a belief in controlling spirits who can be influenced only by shamans. **2.** any similar religion. —**sham′anist,** *n.*, *adj.* —**sham′anis′tic,** *adj.*

Shamash (shä′mäsh), *n.* the Assyro-Babylonian sun-god.

shamble[1] (shăm′bl), *n.* **1.** (*pl. often construed as sing.*) **a.** a slaughterhouse. **b.** any place of carnage. **c.** any place or thing in confusion or disorder. **2.** *Dial.* a table or stall for the sale of meat. [ME *shamel*, OE *sc(e)amel* stool, table, ult. t. L: m. s. *scamellum*, dim. of *scamnum* bench]

shamble[2] (shăm′bl), *v.*, **-bled, -bling,** *n.* —*v.i.* **1.** to walk or go awkwardly; shuffle. —*n.* **2.** a shambling gait. [v. use of *shamble*, adj., awkward, itself attributive use of SHAMBLE[1]]

shame (shām), *n.*, *v.*, **shamed, shaming.** —*n.* **1.** the painful feeling arising from the consciousness of something dishonourable, improper, ridiculous, etc., done by oneself or another. **2.** susceptibility to this feeling: *to be without shame.* **3.** disgrace; ignominy. **4.** a fact or circumstances bringing disgrace or regret. **5. for shame!** *Archaic.* you should feel shame! **6. put to shame, a.** to disgrace. **b.** to outdo or surpass. —*v.t.* **7.** to cause to feel shame; make ashamed. **8.** to drive, force, etc., through shame. **9.** to cover with ignominy or reproach; disgrace. —*interj.* **10.** *S African.* (an exclamation of surprise, approval, or the like): *Oh, shame! What a lovely baby.* [ME; OE *sc(e)amu*, c. G *Scham*]

—**Syn. 1.** SHAME, HUMILIATION imply painful feelings caused by lowering of one's pride or self-respect. SHAME is a painful feeling caused by the consciousness or exposure of unworthy or indecent conduct or circumstances: *one feels shame at being caught in a lie.* HUMILIATION is mortification or chagrin at being humbled in the estimation of others: *being ignored gives one a sense of humiliation.* —**Ant. 1.** pride, self-esteem, self-respect.

shamefaced (shām′fāst′), *adj.* **1.** modest or bashful. **2.** showing shame: *shamefaced apologies.* [f. SHAME, n., + FACE, n. + -ED[3]; r. *shamefast*, OE *sceamfæst* (see FAST[1], *adj.*)] —**shamefacedly** (shām′fā′sĭd lĭ, shām′fāst′lĭ), *adv.* —**shame′fac′edness,** *n.*

shameful (shām′fəl), *adj.* **1.** that causes or ought to cause shame. **2.** disgraceful or scandalous: *shameful treatment.* —**shame′fully,** *adv.* —**shame′fulness,** *n.*

shameless (shām′lĭs), *adj.* **1.** completely lacking in shame; immodest; audacious. **2.** insensible to disgrace. **3.** showing no shame: *shameless conduct.* —**shame′lessly,** *adv.* —**shame′lessness,** *n.* —**Syn. 1.** unblushing, brazen, indecent.

shammer (shăm′ə), *n.* one who shams.

shammy (shăm′ĭ), *n.*, *pl.* **-mies.** chamois (def. 2). [respelling of CHAMOIS to indicate pronunciation]

Shamo (shä′mō′), *n.* Chinese name of the **Gobi.**

shampoo (shăm po͞o′), *v.*, **-pooed, -pooing.** *n.* —*v.t.* **1.** to wash (the head or hair), esp. with a cleaning preparation. **2.** to clean (upholstery, carpets, etc.), with a special preparation. **3.** *Archaic.* to massage. —*n.* **4.** the act of shampooing. **5.** a preparation used for shampooing. [t. Hind.: m. *chāmpo*, impv. of *chāmpnā* to shampoo, lit., to press, squeeze] —**shampoo′er,** *n.*

shamrock (shăm′rŏk′), *n.* a plant with trifoliate leaflets believed to have been used by St Patrick to symbolize the Trinity, esp. wood sorrel, *Oxalis acetosella*, white clover, *Trifolium repens*, or lesser yellow trefoil, *T. dubium.* [t. Irish: m. *seamróg*, dim. of *seamar* clover]

Shamrock

Shan (shän), *n.* **1.** a group of Mongoloid tribes in the hills of Burma. **2.** a northern Thai language, spoken in the Shan States.

shandrydan (shăn′drĭ dăn′), *n.* a rickety, old-fashioned vehicle.

shandy (shăn′dĭ), *n.* a mixed drink of beer with ginger beer or lemonade. [shortened form of obs. *shandygaff*, of obscure orig.]

shanghai[1] (shăng′hī, shăng hī′), *v.t.*, **-haied, -haiing.** *Naut.* to obtain (a man) for the crew of a ship by unscrupulous means, as by force, drugs, or fraud. [appar. short for 'to ship to SHANGHAI']

shanghai[2] (shăng′hī), *n.*, *v.*, **-haied, -haiing.** *Austral.*, *N.Z.* —*n.* **1.** a child's catapult; sling. —*v.t.* **2.** to shoot with a catapult.

Shanghai (shăng′hī′), *n.* **1.** a seaport and industrial city in E China, near the mouth of the Yangtze. 10,000,000 (est. 1965). See map under **Shantung.** **2.** one of a long-legged breed of domestic fowls supposedly introduced from Shanghai.

Shangrila (shăng′grĭ lä′), *n.* a paradise on earth. [named after a hidden paradise in James Hilton's '*Lost Horizon*']

shank (shăngk), *n.* **1.** that part of the leg in man between the knee and the ankle. **2.** a part in certain animals corresponding or analogous to the human shank. See illus. under **horse.** **3.** the whole leg. **4.** a cut of meat from the top part of the front (**fore shank**) or back (**hind shank**) leg. **5.** that portion of an instrument, tool, etc., connecting the acting part with the handle or any like part. **6.** the long, straight, middle part of an anchor. **7.** *Music.* crook[1] (def. 7). **8.** the latter end or part of anything. **9.** the narrow part of a woman's shoe connecting the broad part of the sole with the heel. **10.** the piece of metal or fibre used to give it form. **11.** *Print.* the body of a type, between the shoulder and the foot. —*v.i.* **12.** (of a leaf, flower, fruit, etc.) to decay as a result of disease. **13.**

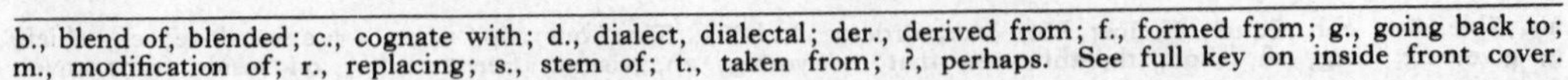

Chiefly Scot. and Dial. to travel on foot. [ME; OE *sc(e)anca*, c. LG *schanke* leg, thigh]

shanks's pony, *Colloq.* one's own legs, esp. as a means of travelling, as opposed to riding on horseback or in a conveyance. Also, **shanks's mare.**

Shannon (shăn′ən), *n.* **1.** the largest river in Ireland, rising in Co. Cavan and flowing SW to the Atlantic and forming the border of Connaught with Leinster and Munster. 240 mi. **2.** an international airport in W Ireland, near Limerick.

shanny (shăn′ĭ), *n.* a small blenny, *Blennius pholis*, with no scales, the most common of the blennies of the British Isles.

Shansi (shăn′se′), *n.* a province in N China. 15,960,000 pop. (1957); 60,394 sq. mi. *Cap.:* Taiyüan.

Shan States (shän), two groups of native states (Northern and Southern) in E Burma, along the river Salween. 2,000,000 pop. (est. 1956); ab. 56,000 sq. mi.

shan't (shänt), *Colloq.* contraction of *shall not.*

Shantung (shăn′tŭng′), *n.* **1.** a maritime province in NE China. 54,030,000 pop. (est. 1957); 56,447 sq. mi. *Cap.:* Tsinan. **2.** a peninsula in the E part of this province, extending into the Yellow Sea. **3.** (*l.c.*) a silk fabric, a heavy variety of pongee made of rough, spun wild silk. **4.** (*l.c.*) a fabric imitating this made of rayon or cotton.

Shantung (def. 1)

shanty[1] (shăn′tĭ), *n., pl.* **-ties.** a roughly built hut, cabin, or house. [probably t. Canadian F: alter. of *chantier* log hut, F shed, g. L *canthērius* framework]

shanty[2] (shăn′tĭ), *n., pl.* **-ties.** a sailors' song, esp. one sung in rhythm to work. Also, **chanty, chantey.** [alter. of F *chanter* sing. See CHANT]

shanty[3] (shăn′tĭ), *n.* *Austral.* a public house, usually unlicensed.

shantytown (shăn′tĭ toun′), *n.* a town or section of a town consisting of roughly built, dilapidated huts, shacks, etc.

shape (shāp), *n., v.,* **shaped, shaping.** *—n.* **1.** the quality of a thing depending on its outline or external surface. **2.** the form of a particular thing, person, or being. **3.** something seen indistinctly, as in outline or silhouette. **4.** an imaginary form; phantom. **5.** an assumed appearance; guise. **6.** a particular or definite form or nature: *things taking shape.* **7.** proper form; orderly arrangement. **8.** condition: *affairs in bad shape.* **9.** something used to give form, as a mould or a pattern. **10. take shape,** to assume a definite or concrete form. [ME, n. use of SHAPE, v.; r. ME *shap*, OE (*ge*)*sceap* form, creature, c. Icel. *skap* state, mood] *—v.t.* **11.** to give definite form, shape, or character to; fashion or form. **12.** to couch or express in words: *to shape a statement.* **13.** to adjust; adapt. **14.** to direct (one's course). **15.** *Obs.* to appoint; decree. *—v.i.* **16.** to develop; take place in a specified manner; assume a definite form or character (sometimes fol. by *up*). [ME; r. ME *schippe*, OE *scieppan* create, shape (pp. *scapen*, whence current present form), c. Goth. *gaskapjan* create] **—shap′er,** *n.* **—Syn. 1.** See **form.**

SHAPE (shāp), *n.* Supreme Headquarters Allied Powers in Europe.

shapeless (shāp′lĭs), *adj.* **1.** having no definite or regular shape or form. **2.** lacking beauty or elegance of form. **—shape′lessly,** *adv.* **—shape′lessness,** *n.*

shapely (shāp′lĭ), *adj.,* **-lier, -liest.** having a pleasing shape; well-formed. **—shape′liness,** *n.*

shard (shäd), *n.* **1.** a fragment, esp. of broken earthenware. **2.** *Zool.* **a.** a scale. **b.** a shell, as of an egg or snail. **3.** *Entomol.* the elytron of a beetle. Also, **sherd.** [ME; OE *sceard*, c. LG *schaard*]

share[1] (shĕə), *n., v.,* **shared, sharing.** *—n.* **1.** the portion or part allotted or belonging to, or contributed or owed by, an individual or group. **2.** one of the equal fractional parts into which the capital stock of a limited company is divided. *—v.t.* **3.** to divide and distribute in shares; apportion. **4.** to use, participate in, enjoy, etc., jointly. *—v.i.* **5.** to have a share or part; take part (often fol. by *in*). [ME; OE *scearu* cutting, division, c. G *Schar* troop. See SHEAR, v.] **—shar′er,** *n.*

—Syn. 5. SHARE, PARTAKE, PARTICIPATE mean to join with others or to receive in common with others. To SHARE is to give or receive a part of something, or to enjoy or assume something in common: *to share another's experiences.* To PARTAKE is to take for one's own personal use a portion of something; it is found mainly in formal language: *to partake of food.* To PARTICIPATE is esp. to join with others in some thought, feeling, or particularly, some action: *to participate in a race, in a conversation.*

share[2] (shĕə), *n.* a ploughshare. [ME; OE *scear*, c. G *Schar*; akin to SHARE[1], SHEAR]

share certificate, a document showing the entitlement of its owner to a number of shares in a company.

sharecropper (shĕə′krŏp′ə), *n.* *U.S.* a tenant farmer who pays as rent a share of the crop.

shareholder (shĕə′hōl′də), *n.* one who holds or owns a share or shares, as in a company.

share-out (shĕər′out′), *n.* a distribution, as of profits, etc.

share-pusher (shĕə′po͝osh′ə), *n.* a dealer in stocks and shares who uses means, often fraudulent, to induce the public to buy them.

Shari (shä′rĭ), *n.* a river flowing NW from the Central African Republic into Lake Chad. ab. 1400 mi.

Sharjah (shä′jä), *n.* See **Trucial States.**

shark[1] (shäk), *n.* any of a group of elongate elasmobranch (mostly marine) fishes, certain species of which are large and ferocious, and destructive to other fishes and sometimes dangerous to man. [orig. obscure] **—shark′like′,** *adj.*

Basking shark, *Cetorhinus maximus* (Up to 40 ft in length)

shark[2] (shäk), *n.* **1.** a person who preys greedily on others, as by swindling, usury, etc. **2.** *U.S. Slang.* one who has unusual ability in a particular field. *—v.t.* **3.** to obtain by trickery or fraud; steal. *—v.i.* **4.** *U.S.* to live by shifts and stratagems. [t. G: m. *Schork*, var. of *Schurke* rascal]

sharkskin (shäk′skĭn′), *n.* a heavy rayon suiting with a dull or chalklike appearance.

Sharon (shĕə′rŏn), *n.* a fertile coastal plain in ancient Palestine.

sharp (shäp), *adj.* **1.** having a thin cutting edge or a fine point; well adapted for cutting or piercing. **2.** terminating in an edge or point; not blunt or rounded. **3.** having sudden change of direction, as a turn. **4.** abrupt, as an ascent. **5.** composed of hard, angular lines, as a person's features. **6.** clearly outlined; distinct. **7.** marked, as a contrast. **8.** pungent or biting in taste. **9.** piercing or shrill in sound. **10.** keenly cold, as weather, etc. **11.** intensely painful; distressing: *sharp pain.* **12.** harsh; merciless: *sharp words.* **13.** fierce or violent: *a sharp struggle.* **14.** keen or eager: *sharp desire.* **15.** quick or brisk. **16.** vigilant: *a sharp watch.* **17.** mentally acute: *a sharp mind.* **18.** shrewd or astute: *sharp at making a bargain.* **19.** shrewd to the point of dishonesty: *sharp practice.* **20.** *Music.* **a.** above an intended pitch, as a note; too high. **b.** (of a note) raised a semitone in pitch: *F sharp.* **21.** *Phonet.* fortis; voiceless. **22.** stylish or elegant, esp. in an ostentatious manner.
—v.t. **23.** *Music.* to raise in pitch, esp. one semitone.
—v.i. **24.** *Music.* to sound above the true pitch.
—adv. **25.** keenly or acutely. **26.** abruptly or suddenly: *to pull a horse up sharp.* **27.** punctually: *at one o'clock sharp.* **28.** vigilantly: *look sharp!* **29.** briskly; quickly. **30.** *Music.* above the true pitch.
—n. **31.** something sharp. **32.** a needle with a very sharp point. **33.** a sharper. **34.** *Colloq.* an expert. **35.** *Music.* **a.** a note one semitone above a given note. **b.** (in musical notation) the symbol (♯) indicating this.
[ME; OE *scearp*, c. G *scharf*] **—sharp′ly,** *adv.* **—sharp′ness,** *n.*

—Syn. 1. SHARP, KEEN refer to the edge or point of an instrument, tool, and the like. SHARP applies, in general, to a cutting edge or a point capable of piercing: *a sharp knife, razor.* KEEN is esp. applied to long edges, as of a sabre: *a keen sword blade.* **17.** SHARP, KEEN, INTELLIGENT, QUICK may be applied figuratively to mental qualities. SHARP implies an acute, sensitive, alert, penetrating quality: *a sharp mind.* KEEN implies observant, incisive, and vigorous: *a keen intellect.* INTELLIGENT means not only acute, alert, and active, but also able to reason and understand: *an intelligent reader.* QUICK suggests lively and rapid comprehension, prompt response to instruction, and the like: *quick at figures.* **—Ant. 1.** blunt. **17.** dull; stupid.

Sharp (shäp), *n.* **William** (*Fiona Macleod*), 1855?–1905, Scottish poet and critic.

sharp-cut (shäp′kŭt′), *adj.* clearly defined; having distinct outlines.

sharp-edged (shäp′ĕjd′), *adj.* having a sharp edge or edges.

sharpen (shä′pən), *v.t., v.i.* to make or become sharp or sharper. **—sharp′ener,** *n.*

sharper (shäʹpə), *n.* **1.** a shrewd swindler. **2.** a professional gamester: *a card sharper.*
sharp-eyed (shäpʹīdʹ), *adj.* having keen sight.
sharpie (shäʹpĭ), *n.* a kind of long, flat-bottomed boat with one or (commonly) two masts, each rigged with a triangular sail, formerly in use along the N Atlantic coast of the U.S.
sharp-set (shäpʹsĕtʹ), *adj.* **1.** very hungry. **2.** keen or eager. **3.** set to present a sharply angled edge.
sharpshooter (shäpʹshōōʹtə), *n.* one skilled in shooting, esp. with a rifle; marksman; sniper. —**sharpʹshootʹing,** *n.*
sharp-sighted (shäpʹsīʹtĭd), *adj.* **1.** having keen sight. **2.** having or showing mental acuteness. —**sharpʹsightʹedness,** *n.*
sharp-tongued (shäpʹtŭngdʹ), *adj.* characterized by harshness or bitterness in speech.
sharp-witted (shäpʹwĭtʹĭd), *adj.* having or showing a keen intelligence; acute. —**sharpʹ-witʹtedness,** *n.*
Shashtri (shăsʹtrĭ), *n.* **Lal Bahadur** (lălʹbäʹhə dōōʹ), 1904–66, Indian statesman: prime minister 1964–66.
Shasta (shăsʹtə), *n.* **Mount,** a volcanic peak in N California, in the Cascade Range. 14,161 ft.
Shatt-al-Arab (shătʹăl ăʹrəb), a river in SE Iraq, formed by the junction of the Tigris and Euphrates rivers, flowing SE to the Persian Gulf. 123 mi.
shatter (shătʹə), *v.t.* **1.** to break in pieces, as by a blow. **2.** to damage, as by breaking or crushing: *ships shattered by storms.* **3.** to impair; weaken; destroy (health, nerves, etc.). —*v.i.* **4.** to break suddenly into fragments. —*n.* **5.** (*pl.*) *Chiefly Dial.* fragments resulting from shattering. [ME *schater(en).* Cf. SCATTER] —**Syn. 1.** See **break.**
shave (shāv), *v.*, **shaved, shaved** or **shaven, shaving,** *n.* —*v.i.* **1.** to remove a growth of beard with a razor. —*v.t.* **2.** to remove hair from (the face, legs, etc.) by cutting it close to the skin. **3.** to cut off (hair, esp. the beard) close to the skin (often fol. by *off* or *away*). **4.** to cut or scrape away the surface of with a sharp-edged tool: *to shave hides in preparing leather.* **5.** to reduce to shavings or thin slices: *to shave wood.* **6.** to cut or trim closely: *to shave a lawn.* **7.** to scrape or graze; come very near to: *to shave a corner.* **8.** *U.S.* to purchase (a note) at the rate of discount greater than is legal or customary. —*n.* **9.** the act or process of shaving. **10.** a thin slice; a shaving. **11.** a narrow miss or escape: *a close shave.* **12.** any of various tools for shaving, scraping, removing thin slices, etc. [ME; OE *sceafan,* c. D, LG *schaven,* G *schaben*]
shaveling (shāvʹlĭng), *n.* *Archaic.* **1.** a shaven-headed clergyman. **2.** young fellow; youngster.
shaver (shāʹvə), *n.* **1.** one who or that which shaves. **2.** *Colloq.* a youngster; fellow. **3.** one who makes close bargains or is extortionate.
shavetail (shāvʹtālʹ), *n.* *U.S. Army Slang.* a second lieutenant.
Shavian (shāʹvyən), *adj.* **1.** of, pertaining to, or characteristic of George Bernard Shaw: *Shavian wit.* —*n.* **2.** an admirer of George Bernard Shaw or of his works.
shaving (shāʹvĭng), *n.* **1.** (*often pl.*) a very thin piece or slice, esp. of wood. **2.** the act of one who or that which shaves.
Shaw (shô), *n.* **1. George Bernard,** 1856–1950, Irish dramatist, critic, and novelist. **2. Henry Wheeler.** See **Billings,** Josh. **3. Richard Norman,** 1831–1912, British architect. **4. Thomas Edward.** See **Lawrence,** Thomas Edward.
shawl (shôl), *n.* a piece of material, worn as a covering for the shoulders, head, etc., chiefly by women, in place of coat or hat. [t. Pers.: m. *shāl*]
shawm (shôm), *n.* an early woodwind instrument with a double reed, forerunner of the modern oboe. [ME *schallemelle,* t. OF: m. *chalemel,* g. L *calamellus* little pipe, der. L *calamus* reed]
Shawnee (shô nēʹ), *n.*, *pl.* **-nees,** (*esp. collectively*) **-nee. 1.** a member of an Algonquian-speaking tribe formerly in the east-central U.S., now in Oklahoma. **2.** the Algonquian language of the Shawnee tribe. [t. Fox and other Algonquian dialects; cf. *shawun* south, *shawunoki* southerners]
shay (shā), *n.* *Colloq.* a chaise. [back-formation from CHAISE, taken as pl.]
Shays (shāz), *n.* **Daniel,** 1747–1825, leader of a popular insurgent movement (**Shays' Rebellion,** 1786–87) in Massachusetts.
Shazar (shə zäʹ), *n.* **Zalman** (zälʹmən), born 1889, Israeli statesman: president of Israel since 1963.
Shcherbakov (*Russ.* shchər bə kôfʹ), *n.* a town in the central Soviet Union in Europe, on the Volga. 208,000 (est. 1965).
she (shē; *unstressed* shĭ), *pron.*, *poss.* **her,** *obj.* **her,** *pl.* **they;** *n.*, *pl.* **shes. 1.** the female in question or last mentioned. —*n.* **2.** any woman or any female person or animal (correlative to *he*). —*adj.* **3.** female or feminine, esp. of animals. [ME, sandhi var. of ME *ghe,* OE *hēo.* See HE]
shea (shĭə), *n.* an African sapotaceous tree, *Butyrospermum parkii,* the seeds of which yield a butter-like fat (**shea butter**), used as food, in making soap, etc. [t. Mandingo: m. *sye*]
sheading (shēʹdĭng), *n.* any of the six administrative subdivisions of the Isle of Man. [var. of *shedding,* verbal n. of SHED[2]]
sheaf (shēf), *n.*, *pl.* **sheaves,** *v.* —*n.* **1.** one of the bundles in which cereal plants, as wheat, rye, etc., are bound after reaping. **2.** any bundle, cluster, or collection: *a sheaf of papers.* —*v.t.* **3.** to bind into a sheaf or sheaves. [ME *shefe,* OE *scēaf,* c. D *schoof,* G *Schaub* wisp of straw]
shear (shĭə), *v.*, **sheared** or (*Archaic*) **shore; sheared** or **shorn; shearing;** *n.* —*v.t.* **1.** to remove by or as by cutting with a sharp instrument: *to shear wool from sheep.* **2.** to cut the hair, fleece, wool, etc., from. **3.** to strip or deprive (fol. by *of*): *shorn of its legislative powers.* **4.** *Dial.* to reap with a sickle. **5.** *Archaic.* to cut with a sharp instrument (usually fol. by *through*). —*v.i.* **6.** *Mech., etc.* to become fractured by a shear or shears. **7.** *Dial.* to reap grain, etc., with a sickle. —*n.* **8.** (*pl.*) scissors of large size (usually called a **pair of shears**). **9.** (*pl.*) any of various other cutting implements or machines resembling or suggesting scissors. **10.** one blade of a pair of shears. **11.** the act or process of shearing. **12.** a shearing of sheep (used in stating the age of sheep): *a sheep of one shear* (*one year old*). **13.** a quantity of wool, grass, etc., cut off at one shearing. **14.** any machine using an adaption of the shearing principle, esp. to cut metal sheets. **15.** *Mech.* the tendency produced by loads to deform or fracture a member by sliding one section against another. **16.** (*pl.*) shearlegs. [ME *shere(n),* OE *sceran,* c. D and G *scheren,* Icel. *skera*] —**shearʹer,** *n.*
shear-hog (shĭəʹhŏgʹ), *n.* a sheep after its first shearing.
shearlegs (shĭəʹlĕgzʹ), *n.* an apparatus for hoisting heavy weights, consisting of two or more spars fastened together near the top with their lower ends separated and a tackle suspended from the top and steadying guys. Also, **shears, sheerlegs.**
shearling (shĭəʹlĭng), *n.* a shear-hog.
shear strain, *Mech.* the lateral deformation produced in a body by a shearing force, usually expressed as the ratio of the lateral displacement between two points lying in parallel planes to the vertical distance between them.
shear stress, *Mech.* the magnitude of a shearing force per unit area of cross-section.
shearwater (shĭəʹwôʹtə), *n.* any of various long-winged seabirds, esp. of the genus *Puffinus,* allied to the petrels, appearing, when flying low, to cleave the water with their wings. [f. SHEAR, v. + WATER, n.]
sheatfish (shētʹfĭshʹ), *n.*, *pl.* **-fishes,** (*esp. collectively*) **-fish.** a large freshwater fish, *Silurus glanis,* the great catfish of central and eastern Europe, sometimes reaching 400 lbs. [f. *sheat* (var. of SHEATH, mistranslation of G *Scheide*) + FISH]
sheath (shēth), *n.*, *pl.* **sheaths** (shēthz), *v.* —*n.* **1.** a case or covering for the blade of a sword, dagger, or the like. **2.** any similar covering. **3.** *Biol.* a closely enveloping part or structure, as in an animal or plant organism. **4.** *Bot.* the leaf base when it forms a vertical coating surrounding the stem. **5.** *Elect.* the metal covering of a cable. **6.** a thin covering, usually of rubber, worn over the penis during sexual intercourse to prevent conception or venereal infection. —*v.t.* **7.** to sheathe. [ME *sheth(e),* OE *scēath,* c. G *Scheide*]
sheathbill (shēthʹbĭlʹ), *n.* either of two seabirds with white plumage, *Chionis alba* and *C. minor,* of the colder parts of the Southern Hemisphere: so called from the horny case which partly sheathes the bill.
sheathe (shēth), *v.t.*, **sheathed, sheathing. 1.** to put (a sword, etc.) into a sheath. **2.** to plunge (a sword, etc.) in something as if in a sheath. **3.** to enclose in or as in a casing or covering. **4.** to cover or provide with a protective layer or sheathing: *to sheathe a roof with copper.* [ME *shethe,* der. SHEATH] —**sheathʹer,** *n.*
sheathing (shēʹthĭng), *n.* **1.** the act of one who sheathes. **2.** that which sheathes; a covering or outer layer of metal, wood, or other material, as one of the metal plates on a ship's bottom, the first covering of boards on a house, etc. **3.** material for forming any such covering.
sheath-knife (shēthʹnīfʹ), *n.* a knife carried in a sheath.
sheave[1] (shēv), *v.t.*, **sheaved, sheaving.** to gather, collect, or bind into a sheaf or sheaves. [der. SHEAF]
sheave[2] (shēv), *n.* **1.** a grooved wheel forming a pulley. **2.** any of various other wheels or discs with a grooved rim. [ME *sheeve;* akin to G *Scheibe* disc]
sheave-block (shēvʹblŏkʹ), *n.* *Naut.* an iron or wooden

shell containing a revolving sheave or sheaves through which a rope runs.

sheaves (shēvz), *n.* **1.** pl. of **sheaf. 2.** pl. of **sheave.**

Sheba (shē′bə), *n.* **1. Queen of,** the queen who visited Solomon to verify what she had heard of his wisdom. I Kings 10:1–13. **2.** the biblical name of an ancient country in S Arabia, noted for its extensive trade in spices, gems, etc. Also, **Saba.**

shebang (shĭ băng′), *n. Slang.* **1.** thing; affair; business. **2.** a hut; shanty; shack.

Shebat (shĭ bät′), *n.* (in the Jewish calendar) the fifth month of the year. [t. Heb.: m. *sh'bhat*]

shebeen (shĭ bēn′), *n.* **1.** *Irish and Scot.* a place where alcoholic drinks are sold illegally. **2.** *S African.* such an illegal tavern for Africans. **3.** any cheap or sordid tavern. [t. Irish: m. *sībín* small mug, small beer]

Shechem (shē′kĕm), *n.* a town of ancient Palestine, near the city of Samaria; now in Israeli-occupied NW Jordan. Modern, **Nablus.**

shed¹ (shĕd), *n.* **1.** a slight or rough structure built for shelter, storage, etc. **2.** a large, strongly built structure, often open at the sides or end. **3.** an outhouse. [ME *shadde*, OE *scead, sced* shelter, SHADE]

shed² (shĕd), *v.*, **shed, shedding,** *n.* —*v.t.* **1.** to pour forth (water, etc.) as a fountain. **2.** to emit and let fall (tears). **3.** to cast; give or send forth (light, sound, fragrance, etc.). **4.** to throw off readily: *cloth that sheds water.* **5.** to cast off or let fall by natural process (leaves, hair, feathers, skin, shell, etc.). **6. shed blood, a.** to cause blood to flow. **b.** to kill by violence. —*v.i.* **7.** to fall off, as leaves, etc.; drop out, as seed, grain, etc. **8.** to cast off hair, feathers, skin, or other covering or parts by natural process. —*n.* **9.** a watershed. **10.** *Textiles.* an opening in the warp threads made by the heddles through which the shuttle passes. [ME; OE *scēadan*, earlier *sc(e)ādan*, c. D and G *scheiden*]

she'd (shēd; *unstressed* shĭd), contraction of: **1.** she had. **2.** she would.

shedder (shĕd′ə), *n.* **1.** one who or that which sheds. **2.** a lobster, crab, etc., just before it moults.

sheen (shēn), *n.* **1.** lustre; brightness; radiance. **2.** *Poetic.* gleaming attire. —*adj. Archaic.* **3.** shining. **4.** beautiful. —*v.i.* **5.** *Scot. and N Dial.* to be bright, shine. [ME *sheene*, d. OE *scēne* beautiful, bright, c. G *schön*] —**Syn. 1.** See **polish.**

sheeny¹ (shē′nĭ), *adj.* shining; lustrous.

sheeny² (shē′nĭ), *n.* (used offensively) a Jew.

sheep (shēp), *n.*, *pl.* **sheep. 1.** any of the ruminant mammals constituting the genus *Ovis* (family *Bovidae*), closely allied to the goats, esp. *O. aries*, which has many domesticated varieties or breeds, valuable for their flesh, fleece, etc. **2.** leather made from the skin of these animals. **3.** a meek, timid, or stupid person. **4.** (in collocations with *goats*) good, worthy, or superior people or things. [ME; OE *scēp* (Anglian), *scēap*, c. G *Schaf*] —**sheep′like′,** *adj.*

Sheep, Southdown variety, *Ovis aries* (2 ft high at the shoulder)

sheepberry (shēp′bə rĭ, -brĭ), *n.*, *pl.* **-ries.** a caprifoliaceous shrub or small tree, *Viburnum lentago*, of North America, bearing cymes of small white flowers, and edible, berry-like black drupes.

sheepcote (shēp′kōt′), *n.* a pen or covered structure for sheltering sheep.

sheep dip, 1. a lotion or wash applied to the fleece or skin of sheep to kill vermin. **2.** a deep trough containing such a liquid through which sheep are driven.

sheepdog (shēp′dŏg′), *n.* a dog trained to watch and tend sheep.

sheepfold (shēp′fōld′), *n.* an enclosure for sheep.

sheepish (shē′pĭsh), *adj.* **1.** awkwardly bashful or embarrassed. **2.** like sheep, as in meekness, timidity, etc. —**sheep′ishly,** *adv.* —**sheep′ishness,** *n.*

sheep's bit, a campanulaceous biennial herb with dense heads of small blue flowers, *Jasione montana*, occurring in grassland in Europe.

sheep's eyes, amorous or flirtatious glances.

sheep's fescue, a variable perennial grass, *Festuca ovina.*

sheepshank (shēp′shăngk′), *n.* a kind of knot, hitch, or bend made on a rope to shorten it temporarily.

sheepshead (shēps′hĕd′), *n.* **1.** a deep-bodied, black-banded food fish, *Archosargus probatocephalus*, of the Atlantic coast of the U.S. **2.** a freshwater fish, *Aplodinotus grunniens*, of E North America. **3.** a labroid food fish, *Pimelometopon pulchrum*, common in southern California. **4.** a foolish or stupid person.

sheepshearing (shēp′shiə′rĭng), *n.* **1.** the act of shearing sheep. **2.** the time or season of shearing sheep, or a feast held then. —**sheep′shear′er,** *n.*

sheepskin (shēp′skĭn′), *n.* **1.** the skin of a sheep, esp. such a skin dressed with the wool on, as for a garment. **2.** leather, parchment, or the like made from the skin of sheep. **3.** *U.S. Colloq.* a diploma. —*adj.* **4.** made from the skin of a sheep.

sheep's sorrel, a slender polygonaceous herb, *Rumex acetosella*, with hastate leaves of an acid taste, abounding in poor, dry soils of temperate regions.

sheep tick, a parasitic, wingless fly, *Melophagus ovinus*, of the dipterous family *Hippoboscidae*, which afflicts sheep.

sheepwalk (shēp′wôk′), *n.* a tract of land on which sheep are pastured.

sheer¹ (shiə), *adj.* **1.** transparently thin; diaphanous, as fabrics, etc. **2.** unmixed with anything else: *sheer rock.* **3.** unqualified; utter: *a sheer waste of time.* **4.** extending down or up very steeply: *a sheer descent of rock.* **5.** *Obs.* bright; shining. —*adv.* **6.** clear; completely; quite. **7.** down or up very steeply. —*n.* **8.** thin, diaphanous material, as chiffon or voile. [ME *schere*, c. Icel. *skærr* clear, bright, pure; akin to OE *scīr*] —**sheer′ly,** *adv.* —**sheer′ness,** *n.* —**Syn. 3.** absolute, downright. **4.** abrupt, precipitous, perpendicular.

sheer² (shiə), *v.i.* **1.** to deviate from a course, as a ship; swerve. —*v.t.* **2.** to cause to sheer. —*n.* **3.** a deviation or divergence, as of a ship from her course; a swerve. **4.** the upward longitudinal curve of a ship's deck or bulwarks. **5.** the position in which a ship at anchor is placed to keep her clear of the anchor. [special use of SHEAR, v. Cf. D and G *scheren* depart]

sheerlegs, shearlegs.

Sheerness (shiə′nĕs′), *n.* a seaport in England, in Kent, at the mouth of the Thames: government dockyards. 14,123 (1961).

sheet¹ (shēt), *n.* **1.** a large rectangular piece of linen, cotton, or other material, used as an article of bedding, commonly one of a pair spread immediately above and below the sleeper. **2.** a broad, thin mass, layer, or covering. **3.** a broad, relatively thin piece of iron, glass, etc. **4.** an oblong or square piece of paper or parchment, esp. one on which to write or print. **5.** a newspaper. **6.** *Printing and Bookbinding.* a piece of paper printed and folded so as to form pages of the required size. **7.** *Philately.* the impression from a plate, etc., on a single piece of paper, before the individual stamps have been separated. **8.** an extent, stretch, or expanse, as of lightning, water, etc.: *sheets of flame.* **9.** *Geol.* a more or less horizontal mass of rock, esp. eruptive rock intruded between strata or spread over a surface. —*v.t.* **10.** to furnish with sheets. **11.** to wrap in a sheet. **12.** to cover with a sheet or layer of something: *sheeted with ice.* [ME *shete*, OE *scēte* (Anglican), *sciete*, der. *scēat* lap, c. G *Schoss*, Icel. *skaut* skirt]

sheet² (shēt), *n.* **1.** *Naut.* a rope or chain fastened: **a.** to a lower aftercorner of a sail, or to the boom of a fore-and-aft sail, to control its trim. **b.** to both lower corners of a square sail to extend them to the yardarms below. **2.** (*pl.*) the spaces beyond the thwarts in the forward or the after end of an open boat. **3. three sheets in** (or **to**) **the wind,** *Colloq.* intoxicated. —*v.t.* **4.** *Naut.* to trim, extend, or secure by means of a sheet or sheets. **5. sheet (sails) home,** to extend (sails) to the utmost by hauling on the sheets. [ME *schete*, OE *scēata* rope tied to lower corner of a sail, c. LG *schote*; in some senses akin to SHOOT]

sheet anchor, 1. a large anchor used only in cases of emergency. **2.** a final reliance or resource. [late ME *shute anker*; orig. uncert.]

sheet bend, *Naut.* a knot used to bend the end of a line on to a bight or eye of another line, used esp. with large lines.

sheeting (shē′tĭng), *n.* **1.** the act of covering with or forming into sheets. **2.** material used for making sheets, as cotton, linen, etc.

sheet iron, iron in sheets or thin plates.

sheet lightning, lightning appearing merely as a general illumination over a broad surface, usually due to the reflection of the lightning of a distant thunderstorm.

sheet metal, metal in sheets or thin plates.

sheet music, musical compositions printed on unbound sheets.

Sheffield (shĕf′ēld), *n.* a city in central England, in the West Riding of Yorkshire. 494,344 (1961).

sheikh (shāk), *n.* (in Arab and other Muslim use) **1.** chief or head; the headman of a village or tribe. **2.** the head of a religious body. Also, **sheik.** [t. Ar.: m. *shaikh* old man]

sheikhdom (shāk′dəm), *n.* the land or territory under the control of a sheikh. Also, **sheikdom.**

sheila (shē′lə), *n.* *Austral.*, *N.Z.*, *S African*, *Colloq.* a girl.

shekel (shĕk′l), *n.* **1.** an ancient, orig. Babylonian, unit of weight, of varying value (taken as equal to the fiftieth or the sixtieth part of a mina, and to about half an ounce). **2.** a coin of this weight, esp. the chief silver coin of the Hebrews. **3.** (*pl.*) *Slang.* money. [t. Heb.: m. *sheqel*, akin to *shāqal* weigh]

Obverse Reverse
Hebrew shekel

Shekinah (shĕ kī′nə), *n. Judaism.* the divine presence, or a radiance forming the visible manifestation of the divine presence. [t. L Heb.: lit., dwelling]

Shelburne (shĕl′bən), *n.* **William Petty, 2nd Earl of,** 1737–1805, British statesman: prime minister 1782–83.

sheldrake (shĕl′drāk′), *n., pl.* **-drakes,** (*esp. collectively*) **-drake. 1.** any of the Old World ducks constituting the genera *Tadorna* and *Casarca*, certain of which are highly variegated in colour. **2.** any of various other ducks, esp. the goosander or merganser. [ME *sheldedrake*; prob. f. *sheld* particoloured (now obs.) + DRAKE[1]]

Sheldrake, *Tadorna tadorna* (26 in. long)

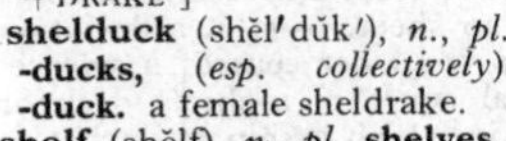

shelduck (shĕl′dŭk′), *n., pl.* **-ducks,** (*esp. collectively*) **-duck.** a female sheldrake.

shelf (shĕlf), *n., pl.* **shelves. 1.** a thin slab of wood or other material fixed horizontally to a wall, or in a frame, for supporting objects. **2.** the contents of such a shelf. **3.** a shelf-like surface or projection; a ledge. **4.** a sandbank or submerged extent of rock in the sea or a river. **5.** *Mining, etc.* bedrock, as under alluvial deposits. **6.** *Archery.* the upper portion of the hand, as it grasps the bow, on which the arrow rests. **7. on the shelf,** (of a woman) unmarried and without prospects of marriage. [ME. Cf. LG *schelf*; akin to OE *scylfe*] —**shelf′-like′**, *adj.*

shelf mark, a symbol on the spine of a book indicating the place where it belongs in a library.

shell (shĕl), *n., pl.* **shells** or (for 7–10) **shell. 1.** a hard outer covering of an animal, as the hard case of a mollusc, or either half of the case of a bivalve mollusc. **2.** any of various objects resembling a shell, as in shape, or in being more or less concave or hollow. **3.** the material constituting any of various kinds of shells. **4.** the hard exterior of an egg. **5.** a more or less hard outer covering of a seed, fruit, or the like, as the hard outside portion of a nut, the pod of peas, etc. **6.** an enclosing case or cover suggesting a shell. **7.** a hollow projectile for a cannon, etc., filled with an explosive charge arranged to explode during flight or upon impact or after penetration. **8.** a metallic cartridge used in small arms and small artillery pieces. **9.** a cartridge. **10.** a cartridge-like pyrotechnic device which explodes in the air. **11.** *Cookery.* a flan-case. **12.** *Physics.* a class of electron orbits in an atom, all of which have the same energy. **13.** *Rowing.* a light racing boat having a very thin, carvel-built hull; best boat; fine boat. **14.** tortoiseshell. **15.** a mollusc. **16.** the walls, external structure, etc., of an unfinished building, ship, etc., or of one whose interior has been destroyed: *after the fire only the shell of the factory remained.* **17.** *Bldg Trades.* a roof whose surface is used as a structural membrane. **18.** an attitude of reserve or shyness, esp. one that conceals emotions, thoughts, etc. **19.** (in some schools) a form or class in the junior or middle school.
—*v.t.* **20.** to take out of the shell, pod, etc. **21.** to remove the shell of. **22.** to separate (maize etc.) from the ear or cob. **23.** to throw shells or explosive projectiles into, upon, or among; bombard. **24. shell out,** *Slang.* to hand over; pay up.
—*v.i.* **25.** to fall or come out of the shell, husk, etc. **26.** to come away or fall off, as a shell or outer coat.
[ME; OE *scell* (Anglian), *sciell*, c. D *schel.* See SCALE[1]] —**shell′-like′**, *adj.*

she'll (shēl; *unstressed* shĭl), contraction of: **1.** she will. **2.** she shall.

shellac (shə lăk′), *n., v.,* **-lacked, -lacking.** —*n.* **1.** lac which has been purified and formed into thin plates, used for making varnish, polish, and sealing wax, and in electrical insulation. **2.** a varnish (**shellac varnish**) made by dissolving this material in alcohol or a similar solvent. —*v.t.* **3.** to coat or treat with shellac. [f. SHELL + LAC[1], trans. of F *laque en écailles* lac in thin plates] —**shellack′er,** *n.*

shellback (shĕl′băk′), *n.* an experienced sailor, esp. an old one.

shellbark (shĕl′bärk′), *n.* shagbark.

shell bean, *U.S.* **1.** any of the various kinds of bean (plant) which are cultivated for their edible seeds. **2.** the seed itself.

Shelley (shĕl′ĭ), *n.* **1. Mary Wollstonecraft (Godwin)** (wo͝ol′stən krăft′), 1797–1851, English author: wife of Percy Bysshe Shelley. **2. Percy Bysshe** (bĭsh), 1791–1822, English poet.

shellfire (shĕl′fī′ə), *n. Mil.* the firing of explosive shells or projectiles.

shellfish (shĕl′fĭsh′), *n., pl.* **-fishes,** (*esp. collectively*) **-fish.** an aquatic animal (not a fish in the ordinary sense) having a shell, as the oyster and other molluscs and the lobster and other crustaceans. [ME *shelfish*, OE *scilfisc*, c. Icel. *skelfiskr.* See SHELL, FISH]

Shellharbour (shĕl′hä′bə), *n.* a town in Australia, in SE New South Wales. 19,000 (est. 1965).

shell jacket, *Mil.* **1.** mess jacket. **2.** a full dress jacket worn by the Royal Horse Artillery.

shellproof (shĕl′pro͞of′), *adj.* protected against the explosive effect of shells or bombs.

shell shock, *Psychiatry.* nervous or mental disorder in various forms, characterized by loss of self-command, memory, speech, sight, or other powers, at first supposed to be brought on by the explosion of shells in battle, but now explained as the result of the cumulative strain of modern warfare. —**shell′-shocked′**, *adj.*

shelly (shĕl′ĭ), *adj.*, **-lier, -liest. 1.** abounding in shells. **2.** consisting of a shell or shells. **3.** like a shell or shells.

Shelta (shĕl′tə), *n.* a tinkers' jargon of Ireland and parts of Great Britain, based on deliberately altered Gaelic. [orig. obscure]

shelter (shĕl′tə), *n.* **1.** something which affords protection or refuge, as from bad weather, bombing, etc.; a place of refuge or safety. **2.** protection afforded; refuge. —*v.t.* **3.** to be a shelter for; afford shelter to. **4.** to provide with a shelter; place under cover. **5.** to protect as by shelter; take under one's protection. —*v.i.* **6.** to take shelter; find a refuge. [orig. uncert.] —**shel′terer,** *n.* —**shel′terless,** *adj.* —**Syn. 1.** See **cover.**

shelve[1] (shĕlv), *v.t.*, **shelved, shelving. 1.** to place on a shelf or shelves. **2.** to lay or put aside from consideration: *to shelve the question.* **3.** to remove from active service; cease to employ; dismiss. **4.** to furnish with shelves. [der. *shelves*, pl. of SHELF]

shelve[2] (shĕlv), *v.i.*, **shelved, shelving.** to slope gradually. [orig. disputed; cf. OE *sceolh* squinting, awry, Icel. *skelgja* make squint]

shelving (shĕl′vĭng), *n.* **1.** material for shelves. **2.** shelves collectively.

Shem (shĕm), *n.* the eldest of the three sons of Noah. Gen. 10:21.

shemozzle (shĭ mŏz′əl), *n. Colloq.* an uproar; row. [t. Yiddish: m. *schlemozzel*, der. Heb. *shellōmazzāl* bad luck]

Shenandoah (shĕn′ən dō′ə), *n.* **1.** a river in the U.S. flowing through N Virginia NE to the Potomac at Harpers Ferry, West Virginia. ab. 200 mi. **2.** a valley along a part of the course of this river, between the Blue Ridge and the Allegheny Mountains.

shenanigan (shĭ năn′ĭ gən), *n.* (*often pl.*) *Colloq.* nonsense; deceit; trickery. [orig. uncert.]

Shensi (shĕn′sē′), *n.* a province in N China. 18,130,000 pop. (est. 1957); 72,919 sq. mi. *Cap.:* Sian.

Shenyang (shĕn′yăng′), *n.* a town in NE China, the capital of Liaoning province. 2,423,000 (est. 1958). Also, **Mukden.**

she-oak (shē′ōk′), *n.* any Australian tree of the genus *Casuarina* which has slender, grooved, green branches bearing whorls of scale leaves, and hard durable wood.

Sheol (shē′ōl, shē′ŏl), *n.* **1.** the abode of the dead or of departed spirits. **2.** (*l.c.*) hell. [t. Heb.]

shepherd (shĕp′əd), *n.* **1.** a man who herds, tends, and guards sheep. **2.** one who watches over or protects a group of people. **3.** a clergyman. **4. the Shepherd,** Jesus Christ. **5.** *Austral.* a miner who retains a claim without working it. —*v.t.* **6.** to tend or guard as a shepherd. **7.** to watch over carefully. **8.** *Austral.* (of a miner) to retain (a claim) without working it. [ME *shepherde*, OE *scēphyrde.* See SHEEP, HERD[2]] —**shepherdess** (shĕp′ə dĭs), *n. fem.*

shepherd dog, a sheepdog.

shepherd's cress, a small annual, cruciferous herb, *Teesdalia nudicaulis*, of sandy places in Europe and N Africa.

shepherd's needle, an annual umbelliferous herb with long narrow fruits, *Scandix pecten-veneris*, a widespread weed of cultivated land in temperate regions.

shepherd's pie, a cooked dish of seasoned mince, topped with a crust of browned mashed potato; cottage pie.

shepherd's plaid, *Textiles.* a woollen shawl-like material, made in a checked pattern.

shepherd's-purse (shĕp′ədz pûs′), *n.* a cruciferous weed,

Capsella bursa-pastoris, with white flowers and purselike pods.

shepherd's weather-glass, the scarlet pimpernel, *Anagallis arvensis.*

Sheppard's adjustment (shĕp′ədz), *Statistics.* a method of correcting the bias in standard deviations and higher moments of distributions due to grouping values of the variable. [named after William *Sheppard,* 20th-cent. English statistician]

sherardize (shĕ′rə dīz′), *v.t.,* **-dized, -dizing.** *Metall.* to plate iron or steel with zinc by heating the metal in contact with zinc powder to a temperature slightly below the melting point of zinc. Also, **sherardise.** [named after *Sherard* Cowper-Coles, d. 1936, English inventor]

Sheraton (shĕ′rə tən), *n.* **1. Thomas,** 1751–1806, English cabinet-maker and furniture designer. *—adj.* **2.** pertaining to, or in the style of, Thomas Sheraton.

sherbet (shû′bət), *n.* **1.** a powdered confection eaten dry or used to make effervescent drinks. **2.** a frozen fruit-flavoured mixture, made with egg whites, gelatine etc. [t. Turk. and Pers., der. Ar. *sharbah,* lit., a drink]

Sherbrooke (shû′bro͝ok′), *n.* a town in Canada, in SW Quebec province. 66,554 (1961).

sherd (shûd), *n.* shard.

Sheridan (shĕ′rĭ dən), *n.* **1. Philip Henry,** 1831–88, U.S. general. **2. Richard Brinsley** (brĭnz′lĭ), 1751–1816, Irish dramatist and political leader.

sherif (shĕ rēf′), *n.* **1.** the governor of Mecca, traditionally a descendant of the Prophet Mohammed. **2.** an Arab prince or ruler. **3.** emir (def. 2). Also, **shereef′.** [t. Ar.: m. *sharīf* noble, glorious, der. *sharafa* be exalted]

sheriff (shĕ′rĭf), *n.* **1.** the chief officer of the Crown in a county, appointed annually, who acts as presiding officer at parliamentary elections and discharges a number of other, mainly ceremonial duties. **2.** *U.S.* the law enforcement officer of a county or other civil subdivision of a state. [ME *sher(r)ef,* OE *scirgerēfa.* See SHIRE, REEVE[1]]

Sherman (shû′mən), *n.* **William Tecumseh** (tĭ kŭm′sə), 1820–91, U.S. general.

Sherpa (shû′pə), *n.* one of a tribe of people of Mongolian stock living in the Solo Khumbu valley of Nepal: they often serve as guides in mountain climbing.

Sherrington (shĕ′rĭng tən), *n.* **Sir Charles Scott,** 1861–1952, English physiologist.

sherry (shĕ′rĭ), *n., pl.* **-ries.** a fortified and blended wine of southern Spain, or a similar wine made elsewhere. [earlier *sherris,* taken as pl., t. Sp.: m. *(vino de) Xeres* (wine of) Xeres, now JEREZ in southern Spain]

sherry cobbler, a cobbler (drink) made with sherry, sliced fruits, sugar and ice.

's Hertogenbosch (*Du.* s hĕr tō KHən bôs′), *n.* a town in the S Netherlands. 76,263 (1965). French, **Bois-le-Duc.**

Sherwood (shû′wo͝od′), *n.* **Robert Emmet,** 1896–1955, U.S. dramatist.

Sherwood Forest, an ancient royal forest in central England, chiefly in Nottinghamshire: the traditional haunt of Robin Hood.

Shetland Islands (shĕt′lənd), an island group NE of the Orkney Islands, comprising a county of Scotland. 17,809 pop. (1961); 550 sq. mi. *Co. town:* Lerwick. Also, **Shetland** or **Zetland.**

Shetland pony, a pony of a small, sturdy, rough-coated breed, orig. from the Shetland Islands.

Shetland sheep, a sheep of a breed from the Shetland Islands, providing a light fleece of very fine wool and good quality mutton.

Shetland wool, 1. the wool of Shetland sheep. **2.** thin, loosely twisted, wool yarn for knitting or weaving.

Shetland pony (Up to 3 ft high at the shoulder)

shew (shō), *v.t., v.i.,* **shewed, shewn, shewing,** *n. Chiefly Archaic.* show.

shewbread (shō′brĕd′), *n.* (among the ancient Jews) the bread placed every Sabbath before Jehovah, on the table beside the altar of incense, and eaten at the end of the week by the priests alone. Ex. 25:30; Lev. 24:5–9. Also, **showbread.** [trans. of G *Schaubrot,* L (Vulgate) *pānes prōpositionis,* Gk (Septuagint) *ártoi enōpioi,* rendering Heb. *lechem pānīm*]

SHF, *Radio.* super high frequency.

Shiah (shē′ə), *n.* **1.** one of the two great religious divisions of Islam, which regards Ali (the son-in-law of Mohammed) as the latter's legitimate successor and rejects the first three caliphs together with the Sunnite books. **2.** a Shiite. [t. Ar.: m. *shī'ah* sect]

shibboleth (shĭb′ə lĕth′), *n.* **1.** a peculiarity of pronunciation, or a habit, mode of dress, etc., which distinguishes a particular class or set of persons. **2.** a test word or pet phrase of a party, sect, etc. **3.** a Hebrew word used by Jephthah as a test word by which to distinguish the fleeing Ephraimites (who could not pronounce the *sh*) from his own men, the Gileadites. Judges 12:4–6. [t. Heb.: stream in flood]

shicer (shī′sə), *n. Austral. Slang.* **1.** an unproductive gold mine. **2.** a swindler.

shickered (shĭk′əd), *adj. Austral., N.Z. Colloq.* drunk.

shied (shīd), *v.* pt. and pp. of **shy.**

shield (shēld), *n.* **1.** a piece of defensive armour of various shapes, carried on the left arm or in the hand to protect the body in battle. **2.** something shaped like a shield. **3.** anything used or serving to protect. **4.** *Ordn.* a steel screen attached to a gun to protect its gunners, mechanism, etc. **5.** *Mining.* a movable framework for protecting a miner at the place at which he is working. **6.** *Physics.* a mass of material used to prevent the passage of radiation from one place to another, esp. to prevent the escape of radiation from a reactor. **7.** *Zool.* a protective plate or the like on the body of an animal, as a scute, enlarged scale, etc. **8.** *Geol.* a large, exposed mass of pre-Cambrian rocks forming a stable part of the earth's crust. **9.** *Her.* a shield-shaped escutcheon on which armorial bearings are displayed. *—v.t.* **10.** to protect with or as with a shield. **11.** to serve as a protection for. **12.** *Obs.* to avert; forbid. *—v.i.* **13.** to act or serve as a shield. [ME *shelde,* OE *sceld,* c. D *schild,* G *Schild*] —**shield′er,** *n.* —**shield′like′,** *adj.*

Ancient Roman shield

shield-fern (shēld′fûn′), *n.* any fern of the genus *Polystichum,* which have peltate indusia, as *P. setiferum,* the soft shield-fern of temperate woods.

shift (shĭft), *v.i.* **1.** to move from one place, position, etc., to another. **2.** to manage to get along or succeed. **3.** to get along by indirect methods; employ shifts or evasions. **4.** to change gear in driving a motor vehicle. **5.** *Archaic or Dial.* to change one's clothes. *—v.t.* **6.** to put by and replace by another or others; change. **7.** to transfer from one place, position, person, etc., to another: *to shift the blame on someone else.* **8.** *Linguistics.* to undergo a systematic phonetic change. *—n.* **9.** a shifting from one place, position, person, etc., to another; a transfer. **10.** the portion of the day scheduled as a day's work when a factory, etc., operates continuously during the 24 hours, or works both day and night: *night shift.* **11.** a group of workmen so employed. **12.** *Mining.* a fault, or the dislocation of a seam or stratum. **13.** *Music.* (in playing the violin or a similar instrument) any change in position of the left hand on the fingerboard. **14.** *Linguistics.* a change, or system of parallel changes, which seriously affects the phonetic or phonemic structure of the language, as the change in English vowels from Middle English to Modern English. **15.** an expedient; ingenious device. **16.** an evasion, artifice, or trick. **17.** change or substitution. **18. a.** a woman's loose-fitting dress. **b.** *Archaic or Dial.* a woman's chemise or undergarment. **19.** *Motor Vehicles.* a gearlever. **20.** change or substitution. **21. make shift, a.** to manage to get along or succeed. **b.** to manage with effort or difficulty. **c.** to do one's best (fol. by *with*). [ME; OE *sciftan,* c. G *schichten* arrange] —**shift′er,** *n.*

shift key, a device on a typewriter for adjusting the position of the keys or carriage to type capital letters.

shiftless (shĭft′lĭs), *adj.* lacking in resource or ambition; inefficient; lazy. —**shift′lessly,** *adv.* —**shift′lessness,** *n.*

shifty (shĭf′tĭ), *adj.,* **-tier, -tiest. 1.** given to or full of evasions; deceitful; furtive. **2.** resourceful; fertile in expedients. —**shift′ily,** *adv.* —**shift′iness,** *n.*

Shihchiachuang (shē′chä chwăng′), *n.* a city in NE China, in Hopeh province. 623,000 (est. 1958).

Shiite (shē′īt), *n.* a member of the Shiah sect. [f. m. SHIAH + -ITE[1]] —**Shi′ism,** *n.* —**Shiitic** (shē ĭt′ĭk), *adj.*

shikar (shĭ kä′), *n.* (in India) hunting, as of game. [t. Urdu, t. Pers.]

shikari (shĭ kä′rĭ), *n., pl.* **-ris.** (in India) a hunter or guide. Also, **shikaree.** [t. Urdu, der. *shikār* shikar, t. Pers.]

Shikoku (shē′kō ko͞o′), *n.* an island in SW Japan, S of Honshu island: the smallest of the main islands of Japan. 3,941,800 pop. (1967); 7249 sq. mi. See map under **Hiroshima.**

Shildon (shĭl′dən), *n.* a town in England, in Durham. 14,372 (1961).
shill (shĭl), *n. U.S. Slang.* the accomplice of a street pedlar, gambler, etc., esp. one who poses as a customer to encourage others.
shillelagh (shə lā′lə, -lĭ), *n.* (in Ireland) a cudgel of blackthorn or oak. Also, **shillalah, shillala, shillelah.** [from the name of a barony and village in County Wicklow]
shilling (shĭl′ĭng), *n.* **1.** (until 1971) a cupronickel or silver coin of the United Kingdom equal to $\frac{1}{20}$ of a pound or five new pence. **2.** any similar coin or banknote of certain other countries. **3.** the monetary unit of certain countries, as Kenya, Uganda, Somali Republic. **4.** schilling. —*adj.* **5.** of the price or value of a shilling. *Abbrev.*: s., sh. [ME; OE *scilling*, c. D *schelling*, G *Schilling*, Icel. *skillingr*]
Shillong (shĭ lŏng′), *n.* a town in S India, the capital of Assam, in the W central part: resort. 102,398 (1961).
shillyshally (shĭl′ĭ shăl′ĭ), *v.*, **-lied, -lying,** *n.*, *pl.* **-lies,** *adj.*, *adv.* —*v.i.* **1.** to be irresolute; vacillate. —*n.* **2.** irresolution; indecision; vacillation. —*adj.* **3.** irresolute; undecided; vacillating. —*adv.* **4.** irresolutely. [dissimilated var. of repeated question *Shall I? Shall I?* Cf. DILLYDALLY]
Shiloh (shī′lō), *n.* an ancient town in Palestine, now in Israeli-occupied Jordan.
shily (shī′lĭ), *adv.* shyly.
shim (shĭm), *n.*, *v.*, **shimmed, shimming.** —*n.* **1.** a thin strip of metal, wood, or the like, for filling in, as for bringing one part in line with another. —*v.t.* **2.** to fill out or bring to a level by inserting a shim or shims. [orig. uncert.]
shimiaan (shĭm′ĭ än′), *n. S African.* an alcoholic drink made by the natives from treacle and water left to ferment in the sun. [t. Zulu: *isishimeyana*]
Shimizu (shē′mĭ zōō′), *n.* a town in Japan, in central Honshu island. 218,559 (1965).
shimmer (shĭm′ə), *v.i.* **1.** to shine with a subdued, tremulous light; gleam faintly. —*n.* **2.** a subdued, tremulous light or gleam. [ME *schimere*, late OE *scimerian*, appar. freq. of *scīmian* shine. Cf. G *schimmern*] —**Syn. 1.** See **glisten.**
shimmery (shĭm′ə rĭ), *adj.* shimmering; shining softly.
shimmy (shĭm′ĭ), *n.*, *pl.* **-mies,** *v.*, **-mied, -mying.** —*n.* **1.** an American ragtime dance, marked by shaking of the hips or shoulders. **2.** excessive wobbling in the front wheels of a motor vehicle. **3.** *Colloq. or Dial.* a chemise. —*v.i.* **4.** to dance the shimmy. **5.** to vibrate; shake. [alter. of CHEMISE]
Shimonoseki (shĭm′ə nō sĕk′ĭ), *n.* a seaport in Japan, on SW Honshu island: the treaty ending the Chino-Japanese War was signed there, 1895. 254,376 (1965).
shin (shĭn), *n.*, *v.*, **shinned, shinning.** —*n.* **1.** the front part of the leg from the knee to the ankle. **2.** the lower part of the foreleg in cattle; the metacarpal bone. **3.** the shinbone or tibia, esp. its sharp edge or front portion. **4.** a cut of beef, usually used for stewing. —*v.t.*, *v.i.* **5.** to climb by holding fast with the hands or arms and legs and drawing oneself up. [ME *s(c)hine*, OE *scinu*, c. D *scheen*, G *Schienbein*]
Shinar (shī′nə), *n.* the biblical name of Babylonia, or the southern part known as Sumer.
shinbone (shĭn′bōn′), *n.* the tibia.
shindig (shĭn′dĭg′), *n. Slang.* **1.** a dance, party, or other festivity, esp. a noisy one. **2.** a disturbance; quarrel; row. [orig. obscure; ? f. SHIN + DIG a dig on the shin]
shindy (shĭn′dĭ), *n.*, *pl.* **-dies.** *Slang.* **1.** a row; rumpus. **2.** a merrymaking; party. [? for SHINTY]
shine (shīn), *v.*, **shone** or (*esp. for def. 8*) **shined, shining,** *n.* —*v.i.* **1.** to give forth, or glow with, light; shed or cast light. **2.** to be bright with reflected light; glisten; sparkle. **3.** to be unusually bright, as the eyes or face. **4.** to appear with brightness or clearness, as feelings. **5.** to excel; be conspicuous: *to shine at sports.* —*v.t.* **6.** to cause to shine. **7.** to direct the light of (a lamp, etc.): *shine the torch over here.* **8.** to put a gloss or polish on (shoes, etc.). —*n.* **9.** radiance; light. **10.** lustre; polish. **11.** sunshine; fair weather: *come rain or shine.* **12.** a polish given to shoes. **13.** a giving of such a polish. **14.** *U.S. Colloq.* a caper; prank. **15.** *U.S. Colloq.* a liking; fancy: *to take a shine to.* **16. take the shine out of, a.** to remove or spoil the lustre or brilliance of. **b.** to surpass; excel; get the better of; humiliate. [ME; OE *scīnan*, c. G *scheinen*]
—**Syn. 1.** SHINE, BEAM, GLARE refer to the emitting or reflecting of light. SHINE refers to a steady glowing or reflecting of light: *to shine in the sun.* That which BEAMS gives forth a ray of bright light: *to beam like a star.* GLARE refers to the shining of a light which is not only bright but so strong as to be unpleasant and dazzling: *to glare like a headlight.*
shiner (shī′nə), *n.* **1.** one who or that which shines. **2.** *Slang.* a black eye. **3.** any of various small American freshwater fishes, mostly minnows, with glistening scales, as the **golden shiner,** *Notemigonus crysoleucas*, and the numerous species of *Notropis.*
shingle[1] (shĭng′gl), *n.*, *v.*, **-gled, -gling.** —*n.* **1.** a thin piece of wood, asbestos, etc., usually oblong and with one end thicker than the other, used in overlapping rows to cover the roofs and sides of houses. **2.** a woman's close-cropped haircut. **3.** *U.S. Colloq.* a small signboard, esp. that of a professional man. —*v.t.* **4.** to cover (a roof, etc.) with shingles. **5.** to cut (hair) close to the head. [ME; var. of *shindle*, ult. t. L: m. *scindula*] —**shin′gler,** *n.*
shingle[2] (shĭng′gl), *n.* **1.** small, water-worn stones or pebbles such as lie in loose banks or layers on the seashore. **2.** an extent of small, loose stones or pebbles. [earlier *chingle*; ? of imit. orig.]
shingles (shĭng′glz), *n. sing. or pl. Pathol.* a cutaneous disease characterized by vesicles which sometimes form a girdle about the body; herpes zoster. [ME *schingles*, t. ML: m. *cingulus* (var. of *cingulum* girdle) used to translate Gk *zōnē* or *zōstēr*, name of the disease]
shingly (shĭng′glĭ), *adj.* consisting of or covered with shingle, or small, loose stones or pebbles.
shining (shī′nĭng), *adj.* **1.** radiant; gleaming; bright. **2.** resplendent; brilliant: *shining talents.* **3.** conspicuously fine: *a shining example.* —**shin′ingly,** *adv.* —**Syn. 1.** See **bright.**
shinny[1] (shĭn′ĭ), *n.*, *pl.* **-nies,** *v.i.*, **-nied, -nying.** shinty.
shinny[2] (shĭn′ĭ), *v.i.*, **-nied, -nying.** *U.S. Colloq.* to climb using the shins. [der. SHIN, n.]
Shinto (shĭn′tō), *n.* the native religion of Japan, primarily a system of nature and ancestor worship. Also, **Shin′toism.** [t. Jap., t. Chinese: m. *shin tao* way of the gods] —**Shin′toist,** *n.*, *adj.*
shinty (shĭn′tĭ), *n.*, *pl.* **-ties,** *v.*, **-tied, -tying.** **1.** a simple variety of hockey, played with a ball or the like and clubs curved at one end. **2.** the club used. —*v.i.* **3.** to play shinty. **4.** to drive the ball at shinty. Also, **shinny.** [? var. of *shin ye*, cry used in the game]
shiny (shī′nĭ), *adj.*, **-nier, -niest.** **1.** bright; glossy. **2.** worn to a glossy smoothness, as clothes. —**shin′iness,** *n.*
ship (shĭp), *n.*, *v.*, **shipped, shipping.** —*n.* **1.** any vessel intended or used for navigating the water, esp. one of large size and not propelled by oars, paddles, or the like. **2.** *Naut.* a vessel with a bowsprit and three or more masts (foremast, mainmast, and mizzenmast), each consisting of a lower mast, a topmast, and topgallant mast. **3.** the crew of a vessel. **4.** an airship or aeroplane. **5. take ship,** to embark. **6. when one's ship comes in or home,** when one has become prosperous or acquired a fortune. —*v.t.* **7.** to put or take on board a ship or the like, for transportation; to send or transport by ship, rail, etc. **8.** *Naut.* to take in (water) over the side, as a vessel does when waves break over it. **9.** to bring (an object) into a ship or boat. **10.** to engage for service on a ship. **11.** to fix (oars, etc.) in a ship or boat in the proper place for use. **12.** *Colloq.* to send away or get rid of. —*v.i.* **13.** to go on board a ship; embark. **14.** to engage to serve on a ship. [ME; OE *scip*, c. D *schip*, G *Schiff*]
-ship, a suffix of nouns denoting condition, character, office, skill, etc., as in *kingship, friendship, statesmanship.* [ME; OE *-scipe*, c. West Fris. and West Flem. *-schip*; akin to G *-schaft*]
shipboard (shĭp′bôd′), *n.* **1.** a ship, or its deck or interior. **2. on shipboard,** on or in a ship.
ship-breaker (shĭp′brā′kə), *n.* a contractor who buys and breaks up old ships.
ship-broker (shĭp′brō′kə), *n.* an agent who transacts business for shipowners, as procuring cargoes and arranging insurance, etc.
shipbuilder (shĭp′bĭl′də), *n.* one whose occupation is the construction of ships. —**ship′build′ing,** *n.*, *adj.*
ship canal, a canal navigable by ships.
ship chandler, one who deals in cordage, canvas, and other supplies for ships.
Shipka Pass (shĭp′kə), a mountain pass over the Balkan Mountains, in central Bulgaria. 4376 ft high.
Shipley (shĭp′lĭ), *n.* a town in England, in the West Riding of Yorkshire. 29,762 (1961).
shipload (shĭp′lōd′), *n.* **1.** a full load for a ship. **2.** the amount of cargo or passengers carried by a ship.
shipman (shĭp′mən), *n.*, *pl.* **-men.** *Archaic or Poetic.* **1.** a sailor. **2.** the master of a ship.
shipmaster (shĭp′mäs′tə), *n.* the master, commander, or captain of a ship.
shipmate (shĭp′māt′), *n.* one who serves with another on the same vessel.
shipment (shĭp′mənt), *n.* **1.** the act of shipping goods, etc.; the delivery of goods, etc., for transporting. **2.** the quantity of goods shipped. **3.** that which is shipped.

ship money, (formerly) a tax levied in time of war on ports, maritime towns, etc., to provide ships.

ship of the line, (formerly) a ship with heavy enough armour and gunpowder to be in the line of battle; a battleship.

shipowner (shĭp′ō′nə), *n.* an owner of a ship or ships.

shippen (shĭp′ən), *n. Dial.* shippon.

shipper (shĭp′ə), *n.* one who ships goods, or makes shipments.

shipping (shĭp′ĭng), *n.* **1.** the act of one who ships goods, etc. **2.** the action or business of sending or transporting goods, etc., by ship, rail, etc. **3.** ships collectively, or their aggregate tonnage. **4.** *Obs.* a voyage.

shipping agent, the representative of a shipowner, who transacts business on his behalf.

shipping clerk, a clerk who attends to shipments.

shipping master, an official who supervises the engagement and discharge of seamen.

shipping office, 1. the office of a shipping agent. **2.** an office where seamen are engaged.

shipping room, a place in a business concern where goods are packed and shipped.

shippon (shĭp′ən), *n. Dial.* a cowshed. Also, **shippen.** [ME *shepon*, OE *scypen*; c. G *Schuppen*]

ship-rigged (shĭp′rĭgd′), *adj. Naut.* rigged with three or more masts, with square sails on all masts.

ship's articles, the terms on which seamen serve on a ship.

ship's biscuit, a kind of coarse, hard biscuit.

shipshape (shĭp′shāp′), *adj.* **1.** in good order; well arranged; neat; tidy. *—adv.* **2.** in a shipshape manner.

ship's husband, a person appointed as an agent or manager of a ship by the owner.

ship's papers, paper (def. 8).

shipway (shĭp′wā′), *n.* **1.** the structure which supports a ship being built. **2.** ship canal.

shipworm (shĭp′wûm′), *n.* any of various marine bivalve molluscs which burrow into the timbers of ships, etc.

shipwreck (shĭp′rĕk′), *n.* **1.** the destruction or loss of a ship, as by sinking. **2.** the remains of a ship. **3.** destruction or ruin: *the shipwreck of one's hopes.* *—v.t.* **4.** to cause to suffer shipwreck. **5.** to destroy; ruin. *—v.i.* **6.** to suffer shipwreck.

shipwright (shĭp′rīt′), *n.* one employed in the construction or repair of ships.

shipyard (shĭp′yäd′), *n.* a yard or enclosure near the water, in which ships are built or repaired.

shiralee (shĭ′rə lē′), *n. Austral.* swag[2] (def. 2).

Shiraz (shĭə räz′), *n.* a city in SW Iran. 317,086 (est. 1966).

shire (shī′ə), *n.* **1.** one of the counties of Great Britain. **2. the Shires,** the counties in the Midlands in which hunting is especially popular. [ME; OE *scīr*, c. OHG *scīra* care, official charge]

Shiré (shĭə′rā), *n.* a river in SE Africa, flowing from Lake Malawi S to the Zambezi river. ab. 370 mi.

shire horse (shī′ə), one of a breed of large, strong draught horses.

shirk (shûk), *v.t.* **1.** to evade (work, duty, etc.). *—v.i.* **2.** to evade work, duty, etc. *—n.* **3.** Also, **shirker.** one who seeks to avoid work, duty, etc. [? t. G: m. *Schurke* parasite, sharper. Cf. SHARK[2]]

Shirley (shû′lĭ), *n.* **James,** 1596–1666, English dramatist.

shirr (shû), *v.t.* **1.** to draw up or gather (cloth) on parallel threads. **2.** to bake (food, usually eggs) in a small shallow container or ramekin dish. *—n.* **3.** Also, **shirring.** a shirred arrangement of cloth, etc. [orig. uncert.]

shirt (shût), *n.* **1.** a garment for the upper part of a man's body, usually with buttons down the front, a collar and short sleeves, or long sleeves with cuffs. **2.** *U.S.* an undershirt; vest; singlet. **3.** a nightshirt. **4. in one's shirt sleeves,** not wearing a jacket. **5. keep one's shirt on,** to refrain from losing one's temper or becoming impatient. **6. put one's shirt on,** to bet heavily or all one has on (a horse, etc.). [ME *schirte*, OE *scyrte*; akin to G *Schürze* apron. Cf. SKIRT]

shirt-band (shût′bănd′), *n.* the neckband of a shirt.

shirt-front (shût′frŭnt′), *n.* the starched front of a white dress shirt; dicky.

shirting (shû′tĭng), *n.* a fabric for men's shirts.

shirt-tail (shût′tāl′), *n.* that part of a shirt below the waist.

shirtwaister (shût′wās′tə), *n.* a woman's loose-fitting dress buttoned down the front to the waist.

shirty (shû′tĭ), *adj. Colloq.* bad-tempered; annoyed.

shish kebab (shēsh′kĭ băb′), kebab.

shit (shĭt), *v.,* **shitted** or (*Obs.*) **shit; shitted** or (*Obs.*) **shitten; shitting;** *n., interj. Taboo.* *—v.i.* **1.** to defecate. *—n.* **2.** faeces; dung; excrement. **3.** the act of defecating. **4.** *Slang.* a contemptible or despicable person. **5.** *Slang.* nonsense; rubbish; lies. **6.** (*pl.*) *Slang.* a state of extreme fear or terror. *—interj.* **7.** (an exclamation expressing anger, disgust, disappointment, disbelief, etc.) Also, **shite.** [ME *shiten*, OE *scītan* (n. *scite* dung); c. MLG *schīten*, D *schijten*, G *scheissen*]

shittim wood (shĭt′ĭm), the wood of which the ark of the covenant and various parts of the Jewish tabernacle were made. Ex. 25–27. Also, **shittim.**

shiv (shĭv), *n. Slang.* a knife. [alter. of *chiv* blade, t. Gipsy]

Shiva (shē′və, shĭv′ə), *n. Hinduism.* one of the three chief divinities, the third member of the Hindu trinity: known also as 'the Destroyer'. Also, **Siva.** [t. Hind., t. Skt: m. *çiva* propitious] **—Shi′vaism,** *n.* **—Shi′vaist,** *n.* **—Shi′vais′tic,** *adj.*

shivaree (shĭv′ə rē′), *n., v.,* **-reed, -reeing.** *U.S.* *—n.* **1.** a mock serenade with kettles, pans, horns, etc. **2.** a noisy celebration. *—v.t.* **3.** to serenade with kettles, etc. [alter. of CHARIVARI]

shiver[1] (shĭv′ə), *v.i.* **1.** to shake or tremble with cold, fear, excitement, etc. *—v.i.* **2.** (of a sail) to shake when too close to the wind. *—n.* **3.** a tremulous motion; a tremble or quiver. **4. the shivers,** a fit or attack of shivering. [ME *chivere*; orig. uncert.]

—Syn. 1. SHIVER, QUAKE, SHUDDER refer to a vibratory muscular movement, a trembling, usually involuntary. We SHIVER with cold, or a sensation such as that of cold: *to shiver in thin clothing on a frosty day, to shiver with pleasant anticipation.* We QUAKE esp. with fear: *to quake with fright.* We SHUDDER with horror or abhorrence; the agitation is more powerful and deep-seated than shivering or trembling: *to shudder at pictures of a concentration camp.*

shiver[2] (shĭv′ə), *v.t., v.i.* **1.** to break or split into fragments. *—n.* **2.** a fragment; a splinter. [ME *schivere*, n., splinter; akin to G *Schiefer* slate]

shivery[1] (shĭv′ə rĭ), *adj.* **1.** shivering; quivering; tremulous. **2.** inclined to shiver or shake. **3.** causing shivering. [f. SHIVER[1] + -Y[1]]

shivery[2] (shĭv′ə rĭ), *adj.* readily breaking into shivers or fragments; brittle. [f. SHIVER[2] + -Y[1]]

shivoo (shī vo͞o′), *n. Austral. Colloq.* a party; celebration; spree.

Shizuoka (shē′zo͞o ō′kə), *n.* a seaport in central Japan, on S Honshu island. 367,705 (1965).

Shkodër (*Alb.* shkȯ′dər), *n.* Albanian name of **Scutari** (def. 2). Also, **Shkodra** (*Alb.* shkȯ′drȧ).

S.H.M., *Maths.* simple harmonic motion.

shmo (shmō), *n. Slang.* a foolish, boring or stupid person. Also, **schmo.** [t. Yiddish]

Shoa (shō′ə), *n.* a former kingdom in E Africa: now a province of Ethiopia. 25,290 sq. mi.

shoal[1] (shōl), *n.* **1.** a place where a body of water is shallow. **2.** a sandbank or sandbar in the bed of a body of water, esp. one which shows at low water. *—adj.* **3.** of little depth, as water; shallow. *—v.i.* **4.** to become shallow or more shallow. *—v.t.* **5.** to cause to become shallow. **6.** *Naut.* to proceed from a greater to a less depth of (water). [ME *schold, schald*, OE *sceald* shallow]

shoal[2] (shōl), *n.* **1.** any large number of persons or things. **2.** a group of fish crowded fairly close together. *—v.i.* **3.** to collect in a shoal; throng. [OE *scolu* shoal (of fishes), multitude, troop, c. D *school.* See SCHOOL[2]]

shoaly (shō′lĭ), *adj.* full of shoals or shallows.

shoat (shōt), *n.* a young weaned pig. Also, **shote.** [ME. Cf. Flem. *schote* young pig]

shock[1] (shŏk), *n.* **1.** a sudden and violent blow, or impact, collision, or encounter. **2.** a sudden disturbance or commotion. **3.** something that shocks mentally, emotionally, etc. **4.** *Pathol.* a sudden collapse of the nervous mechanism caused by violent physical or psychic factors, such as severe injuries or a strong emotional disturbance. **5.** the physiological effect produced by the passage of an electric current through the body. *—v.t.* **6.** to strike with intense surprise, horror, disgust, etc. **7.** to strike against violently. **8.** to give an electric shock to. *—v.i.* **9.** to come into violent contact; collide. [appar. t. F: m. *choc*, der. *choquer* strike against, shock, t. MD: m. *schokken*] **—shock′able,** *adj.*

—Syn. 6. SHOCK, STARTLE, PARALYSE, STUN suggest a sudden, sharp surprise which affects one somewhat like a blow. SHOCK suggests a strong blow, as it were, to one's nerves, sentiments, sense of decency, etc.: *the onlookers were shocked by the accident.* STARTLE implies the sharp surprise of sudden fright: *to be startled by a loud noise.* PARALYSE implies such a complete shock as to render one temporarily helpless: *paralysed with fear.* STUN implies such a shock as bewilders or stupefies: *stunned by the realization of an unpleasant truth.*

shock[2] (shŏk), *n.* **1.** a group of sheaves of grain placed on end and supporting one another in the field. *—v.t.* **2.** to make into shocks. [ME; c. LG *schok* shock of grain, group of sixty, G *Schock* sixty]

shock[3] (shŏk), *n.* **1.** a thick, bushy mass, as of hair. *—adj.* **2.** shaggy, as hair. [? var. of SHAG[1]]

shock absorber, 1. *Mach.* a device for deadening shock or concussion, esp. one on a motor vehicle for checking sudden or excessive movements of the suspension. **2.** *Aeron.* the part of an aircraft undercarriage which absorbs the impact on landing.

shocker (shŏk′ə), *n.* **1.** one who or that which shocks. **2.** *Colloq.* a sensational work of fiction. **3.** *Colloq.* an unpleasant or disagreeable person.

shockheaded (shŏk′hĕd′ĭd), *adj.* having a shock or thick mass of hair on the head.

shocking (shŏk′ĭng), *adj.* **1.** causing intense surprise, disgust, horror, etc. **2.** *Colloq.* very bad: *shocking manners.* —**shock′ingly,** *adv.*

shockproof (shŏk′pro͞of′), *adj.* protected against damage likely to result from shocks.

shock tactics, *Mil.* a method of attack by mobile units in which the suddenness, violence, and massed weight of the first impact produce the main effect.

shock treatment, *Psychiatry.* a method of treating certain mental disorders, as schizophrenia, by shocks induced either by drugs or by electroconvulsive therapy. Also, **shock therapy.**

shock troops, *Mil.* troops especially selected, trained, and equipped for engaging in assault.

shock wave, a region of abrupt change of pressure and density moving in a gas or liquid at or above the velocity of sound.

shod (shŏd), *v.* pt. and pp. of **shoe.**

shoddy (shŏd′ĭ), *n., pl.* **-dies,** *adj.,* **-dier, -diest.** —*n.* **1.** a fibrous material obtained by shredding woollen rags or waste. **2.** anything inferior made to resemble what is of superior quality; anything inferior but pretentious. **3.** pretence, as in art, manufacture, etc. —*adj.* **4.** pretending to a superiority not possessed; sham. **5.** of poor quality or badly made: *shoddy workmanship, shoddy goods.* **6.** made of or containing shoddy. [orig. uncert.] —**shod′dily,** *adv.* —**shod′diness,** *n.*

shoe (sho͞o), *n., pl.* **shoes,** (*Archaic*) **shoon;** *v.,* **shod, shoeing.** —*n.* **1.** an external covering, usually of leather, for the human foot, consisting of a more or less stiff or heavy sole and a lighter upper part. **2.** *U.S.* a boot (def. 1). **3.** some thing or part resembling a shoe in form, position, or use. **4.** a horseshoe, or a similar plate for the hoof of some other animal. **5.** a ferrule or the like, as of iron, for protecting the end of a staff, pole, etc. **6.** the part of a brake mechanism fitting into the drum and expanded outwardly to apply the friction lining to the drum rim for stopping or slowing a car, etc. **7.** the outer casing of a pneumatic tyre. **8.** a drag or skid for a wheel of a vehicle. **9.** a part having a larger area than the end of an object on which it fits, serving to disperse or apply its thrust. **10.** the sliding contact by which an electric locomotive takes its current from the conductor rail. **11.** *Bldg Trades.* the bearing surface or area of contact of a roof truss, girder, etc. **12.** a band of iron on the bottom of the runner of a sledge. **13. in someone's shoes,** in the position or situation of another: *I shouldn't like to be in his shoes.* **14. know where the shoe pinches,** to know the cause or real meaning of trouble, misfortune, sorrow, etc., esp. from personal experience. —*v.t.* **15.** to provide or fit with a shoe or shoes. **16.** to protect or arm at the point, edge, or face with a ferrule, metal plate, or the like. [ME *shoo,* OE *scōh,* c. G *Schuh*]

shoebill (sho͞o′bĭl′), *n.* a large African wading bird, *Balaeniceps rex,* with a broad bill shaped somewhat like a shoe, found esp. on the White Nile.

Shoebill, *Balaeniceps rex* (Ab. 5 ft high, total length 3½ ft)

shoeblack (sho͞o′blăk′), *n.* a bootblack.

shoehorn (sho͞o′hôn′), *n.* a shaped piece of horn, metal, or the like, inserted in a shoe at the heel to make it slip on more easily.

shoelace (sho͞o′lās′), *n.* a string or lace for fastening a shoe.

shoemaker (sho͞o′mā′kə), *n.* one who makes or mends shoes.

shoer (sho͞o′ə), *n.* one who shoes horses, etc.

shoeshine (sho͞o′shīn′), *n.* **1.** the polished surface of a shoe. **2.** the act or instance of cleaning or polishing a shoe or shoes.

shoestring (sho͞o′strĭng′), *n.* **1.** a shoelace. **2. on a shoestring,** with a very small amount of money.

shoetree (sho͞o′trē′), *n.* a device, usually of metal or wood, placed in shoes when they are not being worn, to maintain the shape.

shofar (shō′fä), *n.* shophar.

shogun (shō′go͞on), *n.* (in Japan) **1.** a title originating in the 8th century, in the wars against the Ainus, equivalent to commander-in-chief. **2.** (in later history) a member of a quasi-dynasty, holding real power while the imperial dynasty remained theoretically and ceremonially supreme. [t. Jap., t. Chinese: m. *chiang chün* lead army (i.e., general)]

shogunate (shō′go͞o nĭt, -nāt′), *n.* the office or rule of a shogun.

Sholapur (shō′lə po͞oə′), *n.* a town in India, in S Maharashtra. 337,583 (1961).

Sholokhov (*Russ.* shô′lə KHəf), *n.* **Mikhail Aleksandrovich** (*Russ.* mĭ KHä ĕl′ ə lĭk sän′drə vĭch), born 1905, Soviet novelist.

shone (shŏn), *v.* pt. and pp. of **shine.**

shoo (sho͞o), *interj., v.,* **shooed, shooing.** —*interj.* **1.** (an exclamation used to scare or drive away poultry, birds, etc.) —*v.t.* **2.** to drive away by calling 'shoo'. **3.** to ask or compel (a person) to leave. —*v.i.* **4.** to call out 'shoo'. [cf. G *schu*]

shook[1] (sho͝ok), *n.* **1.** a set of staves and headings sufficient for one hogshead, barrel, or the like. **2.** a set of the parts of a box, piece of furniture, or the like, ready to be put together. **3.** *U.S.* a shock of sheaves or the like. [? var. of SHOCK[2], n.]

shook[2] (sho͝ok), *v.* pt. of **shake.**

shoon (sho͞on), *n. Archaic.* pl. of **shoe.**

shoot (sho͞ot), *v.,* **shot, shooting,** *n.* —*v.t.* **1.** to hit, wound, or kill with a missile discharged from a weapon. **2.** to execute or put to death with a bullet. **3.** to send forth (arrows, bullets, etc.) from a bow, firearm, or the like. **4.** to discharge (a weapon): *to shoot a gun.* **5.** to send forth like an arrow or bullet: *to shoot questions at someone.* **6.** to fling; throw; propel; direct. **7.** to send swiftly along. **8.** to go over (country) in shooting game. **9.** to pass rapidly through, over, down, etc.: *to shoot a rapid.* **10.** to emit (rays, etc.) swiftly. **11.** to variegate by threads, streaks, etc., of another colour. **12.** to cause to extend or project. **13.** to discharge or empty; send down a chute. **14.** *Football, Hockey, etc.* to kick or drive (the ball, etc.), as at the goal. **15.** to accomplish by kicking or driving the ball, etc.: *to shoot a goal.* **16.** to propel (a marble or the like) from the thumb and forefinger. **17.** *Dice.* to toss (the dice). **18.** *Photog.* to photograph or film. **19.** to put forth (buds, branches, etc.), as a plant. **20.** to slide (a bolt, etc.) into or out of its fastening. **21.** to take the altitude of (a heavenly body): *to shoot the sun.* **22.** *Mining.* to detonate. **23. shoot a line,** *Colloq.* to boast. **24. shoot down, a.** to kill or cause to fall by hitting with a shot. **b.** to bring down (an aircraft) by gunfire. **c.** to defeat decisively (an argument or person putting forward an argument). **25. shoot off one's mouth,** *Orig. U.S. Slang.* **a.** to talk indiscreetly, esp. to reveal secrets, etc.; talk wildly or tactlessly. **b.** to exaggerate; boast. **26. shoot one's bolt,** to do one's utmost. **27. shoot up,** *Colloq.* to cause damage, confusion, etc., by reckless or haphazard shooting. —*v.i.* **28.** to send forth missiles, from a bow, firearm, or the like. **29.** to send forth missiles, or be discharged, as a firearm. **30.** to move, start to move, or pass suddenly or swiftly; dart; be propelled (fol. by *ahead, away, into, off,* etc.). **31.** to come forth from the ground, as a stem, etc. **32.** to put forth buds or shoots, as a plant; germinate. **33.** to grow, esp. rapidly (often fol. by *up*). **34.** *Photog.* to photograph or film. **35.** *Films.* to begin to film a scene. **36.** to extend; jut: *a cape shooting out into the sea.* **37.** to propel a ball, etc., in a particular direction or way, as in games. **38.** to cause sharp, darting pains in a part of the body: *pain shot through his arm.* **39.** to kill game with a gun for sport. **40.** *Colloq.* to begin, esp. to begin to talk. —*n.* **41.** an act of shooting with a bow, firearm, etc. **42.** an expedition for shooting game. **43.** a match or contest at shooting. **44.** a growing or sprouting, as of a plant. **45.** a new or young growth which shoots off from some portion of a plant. **46.** the amount of such growth. **47.** a young branch, stem, twig, or the like. **48.** a sprout which is not three feet high. **49.** *Rowing.* the interval between strokes. [ME *shote,* var. of *shete,* OE *scēotan,* c. G *schiessen,* Icel. *skjōta*]

shooter (sho͞o′tə), *n.* **1.** one who shoots. **2.** *Colloq.* something that shoots; a gun, pistol, or the like. **3.** *Cricket.* a ball which moves along the ground without rising on being pitched.

shooting box, a small house or lodge for the accommodation of a sportsman or sportsmen during the shooting season. Also, **shooting lodge.**

shooting brake, **1.** an estate car. **2.** (formerly) a horse-drawn open carriage used on shooting expeditions, to carry equipment, etc.

shooting gallery, a place, usually indoors, equipped with targets, used to practise shooting.

shooting iron, *U.S. Slang.* a firearm, esp. a pistol or revolver.

shooting star, **1.** a falling star; a meteor. **2.** the American cowslip, *Dodecatheon meadia,* having bright nodding flowers and reflexed lobes of the corolla.

shooting stick, a walking stick with a spike at one end and a small, folding seat at the other, used by spectators at sporting events, etc.; seat-stick.

shooting war, open war between countries involving actual conflict between armies, etc.

shop (shŏp), *n.*, *v.*, **shopped, shopping.** —*n.* **1.** a building where goods are sold retail. **2.** a place for doing certain work; a workshop. **3. all over the shop,** all over the place; in confusion. **4. set up shop,** to set oneself up in business. **5. shut up shop,** to close a business either temporarily or permanently. **6. talk shop,** to discuss one's trade, profession, or business. —*v.i.* **7.** to visit shops for purchasing or examining goods. —*v.t.* **8.** to inform against, betray, to the police. [ME *shoppe*, OE *sceoppa* booth, c. G *Schopf* lean-to; akin to SHIPPON]

shop assistant, one who sells goods in a retail shop.

shopfitter (shŏp′ fĭt′ə), *n.* a person employed to decorate and build and sometimes design the interiors and facades of shops, showrooms and the like.

shop floor, 1. that part of a factory where the machines, etc., are situated. **2.** workers collectively, esp. factory workers. —**shop′floor′**, *adj.*

shopgirl (shŏp′ gûl′), *n.* a girl employed as a shop assistant.

shophar (shō′fä), *n.* an ancient Jewish musical instrument of the trumpet kind, usually made of the curved horn of a ram, still used in Jewish religious services, as on Rosh Hashana. Also, **shofar.** [t. Heb.]

shopkeeper (shŏp′kē′pə), *n.* one who owns or runs a shop.

shoplifter (shŏp′lĭf′tə), *n.* one who steals goods from a shop, as while ostensibly making purchases. [f. obs. *shoplift* shoplifter (f. SHOP + LIFT) + -ER[1]] —**shop′lift′ing,** *n.*

shopman (shŏp′mən), *n.*, *pl.* **-men. 1.** one employed to sell goods in a shop. **2.** *Rare.* a shopkeeper.

shopper (shŏp′ə), *n.* one who shops.

shopping (shŏp′ĭng), *n.* **1.** the act of one who shops. **2.** the articles bought.

shopping centre, a group of shops, stores, etc., within a single architectural plan, supplying most of the basic shopping needs, esp. in suburban areas.

shopsoiled (shŏp′soild′), *adj.* worn, dirtied, faded, etc., as goods handled and displayed in a shop or store. Also **shopworn.**

shop steward, a trade-union official representing workers in a factory, workshop, etc.

shopwalker (shŏp′wô′kə), *n.* a person employed in a large shop or store to direct customers, supervise assistants, etc.

shopwindow (shŏp′wĭn′dō), *n.* a window used for display of merchandise.

shopworn (shŏp′wôn′), *adj.* shopsoiled.

shore[1] (shô), *n.* **1.** land along the edge of a sea, lake, large river, etc. **2.** some particular country: *my native shore.* **3.** land: *marines serving on shore.* **4.** *Law.* the space between the ordinary high-water mark and low-water mark. —*adj.* **5.** of, pertaining to, or situated on land. [ME *schore*, prob. t. MLG, c. D *schoor* sea marsh]

—**Syn. 1.** SHORE, BANK, BEACH, COAST refer to an edge of land abutting on an ocean, lake, or other large body of water. SHORE is the general word: *the ship reached shore.* BANK denotes the land along a river or other watercourse, sometimes steep but often not: *the river flows between its banks.* BEACH refers to sandy or pebbly margins along a shore, esp. those made wider at ebb tide: *a private beach for bathers.* COAST applies only to land along an ocean: *the Pacific coast.*

shore[2] (shô), *n.*, *v.*, **shored, shoring.** —*n.* **1.** a supporting post or beam and auxiliary members, esp. one placed obliquely against the side of a building, a ship in dock, or the like; a prop; a strut. —*v.t.* **2.** to support by a shore or shores; prop (usually fol. by *up*). [ME, prob. t. MLG: m. *schore*, c. D *schoor* prop]

shore[3] (shô), *v.* *Archaic.* pt. of **shear.**

Shore (shô), *n.* **Jane,** 1445?–1527, mistress of Edward IV of England.

shorebird (shô′bûd′), *n.* a limicoline bird, as one which frequents the seashore, estuaries, etc., esp. the snipes, sandpipers, plovers, turnstones, etc., constituting the families *Charadriidae* and *Scolopacidae.*

Shoreditch (shô′dĭch′), *n.* a district in the NE London borough of Hackney.

shore leave, *Naval.* **1.** permission to spend time ashore. **2.** the time spent ashore.

shoreless (shô′lĭs), *adj.* **1.** boundless. **2.** without a shore for landing on: *a shoreless island.*

shoreline (shô′līn′), *n.* the line where shore and water meet.

shoreward (shô′wəd), —*adj.* **1.** situated near, directed towards, or facing the shore. —*adv.* **2.** shorewards.

shorewards (shô′wədz), *adv.* towards the shore or land. Also, **shoreward.**

shore-weed (shô′wēd′), *n.* a small aquatic, perennial herb, *Littorella uniflora*, which occurs submerged in shallow water of lakes in N and central Europe.

shoring (shô′rĭng), *n.* **1.** shores or props for supporting a building, a ship, etc. **2.** the act of setting up shores.

shorn (shôn), *v.* pp. of **shear.**

short (shôt), *adj.* **1.** having little length; not long. **2.** having little height; not tall; low. **3.** extending or reaching only a little way. **4.** brief; not extensive: *a short speech.* **5.** concise, as writing. **6.** rudely brief; curt; hurting: *short temper, he was short with her.* **7.** low in amount; scanty: *short rations.* **8.** not reaching a mark or the like, as a throw or a missile. **9.** below the standard in extent, quantity, duration, etc.: *short measure.* **10.** less than; inferior to (fol. by *of*): *little short of the best.* **11.** having a scanty or insufficient amount of (money, food, etc.): *we are short of bread.* **12.** breaking or crumbling readily, as pastry that contains a large proportion of butter or other shortening. **13.** (of metals) deficient in tenacity; friable; brittle. **14.** (of the head or skull) of less than ordinary length from front to back. **15.** *Com.* **a.** not possessing at the time of sale commodities or stocks that one sells. **b.** denoting or pertaining to sales of commodities or stocks which the seller does not possess; depending for profit on a decline in prices. **16.** *Phonet.* **a.** lasting a relatively short time: *bit* has a shorter vowel than *bid* or *bead.* **b.** belonging to a class of sounds considered as usually shorter in duration than another class, such as the vowel of *hot* as compared to *bought*; conventionally, the vowels of *bat, bet, bit, hot, good,* and *but.* **17.** (of an alcoholic drink) small, usually with a comparatively high alcoholic content. **18. make short work of,** to finish or dispose of quickly. **19. nothing short of,** nothing less than. **20. short for,** being a shorter form of: *'phone' is short for 'telephone'.* —*adv.* **21.** abruptly or suddenly: *to stop short.* **22.** briefly; curtly. **23.** on the nearer side of an intended or particular point: *to fall short.* **24.** without going to the length (fol. by *of*): *to stop short of actual crime.* **25.** *Com.* without possessing at the time the stocks, etc., sold: *to sell short.* **26. be taken short,** *Colloq.* to have a sudden and urgent need to urinate or defecate. **27. cut short,** to end abruptly; curtail; interrupt.
—*n.* **28.** something that is short. **29.** what is deficient or lacking. **30.** (*pl.*) short trousers, reaching to the knee or shorter, worn by boys and for sports, leisure, etc. **31.** *Mil.* a shot which strikes or bursts short of the target. **32.** *Elect.* a short circuit. **33.** *Com.* one who has sold short. **34.** *Pros.* a short sound or syllable. **35.** *Films.* a short film. **36. for short,** by way of abbreviation. **37. in short,** in a few words; in brief; briefly.
—*v.t.*, *v.i.* **38.** to short-circuit.
[ME; OE *sc(e)ort*] —**short′ness,** *n.*

—**Syn. 4.** SHORT, BRIEF are opposed to long, and indicate slight extent or duration. SHORT may imply duration but is also applied to physical distance and certain purely spatial relations: *a short journey.* BRIEF refers esp. to duration of time: *brief intervals.* —**Ant. 4.** long.

short account, *Banking.* **1.** a short seller's account. **2.** the total short sales in a market, or the total short sales of a particular commodity.

shortage (shô′tĭj), *n.* **1.** deficiency in quantity. **2.** an amount deficient.

shortbread (shôt′brĕd′), *n.* a type of thick, crisp biscuit.

shortcake (shôt′kāk′), *n.* **1.** shortbread. **2.** *Chiefly U.S.* a rich type of scone, with a filling of fruit and cream.

short-change (shôt′chānj′), *v.t.*, **-changed, -changing.** *Colloq.* **1.** to give less than proper change to. **2.** to cheat. —**short′-chang′er,** *n.*

short circuit, *Elect.* an abnormal connection of relatively low resistance, whether made accidentally or intentionally, between two points of different potential in a circuit.

short-circuit (shôt′sû′kĭt), *Elect.* —*v.t.* **1.** to establish a short circuit in. **2.** to carry (a current) as a short circuit. **3.** to cut off by a short circuit. —*v.i.* **4.** to form a short circuit.

shortcoming (shôt′kŭm′ĭng), *n.* a failure or defect in conduct, condition, etc.

short covering, *Finance.* purchases made to provide for sales already made without possessing the commodities or stocks sold.

shortcrust (shôt′krŭst′), *adj.* short (def. 12).

short cut, a shorter or quicker way.

short-dated (shôt′dā′tĭd), *adj.* having little time to run.

short division, *Maths.* division in which all working out is done mentally and not written down.

shorten (shô′tn), *v.t.* **1.** to make shorter; curtail. **2.** to take in; reduce: *to shorten sail.* **3.** to make (pastry, etc.) short, as with butter or other fat. —*v.i.* **4.** to become shorter. **5.** (of odds) to decrease. —**short′ener,** *n.*

—**Syn. 1.** condense, lessen, limit, restrict. SHORTEN, ABBREVIATE, ABRIDGE, CURTAIL mean to make shorter or briefer. SHORTEN is a general word meaning to make less in extent or duration: *to shorten a dress, a prisoner's sentence.* The other three words suggest methods of shortening. To ABBREVIATE is to make shorter by omission or contraction: *to abbreviate a word.* To ABRIDGE is to reduce in length or size by condensing, summarizing, and the like: *to abridge a document.* CURTAIL suggests deprivation and lack of completeness because of cutting off some part: *to curtail an explanation.* **—Ant.** 1. lengthen.

shortening (shôt′nĭng), *n.* butter, lard, or other fat, used to make pastry, etc., short.

Shorter Catechism, one of the two catechisms established by the Westminster Assembly in 1647, used in Presbyterian, and, formerly, in Congregational churches.

shorthand (shôt′hănd′), *n.* **1.** a method of rapid handwriting using extremely simple strokes in place of letters, often with other abbreviating devices. *—adj.* **2.** using shorthand. **3.** written in shorthand.

shorthanded (shôt′hăn′dĭd), *adj.* not having the necessary number of workmen, helpers, etc.

shorthead (shôt′hĕd′), *n.* **1.** a brachycephalic person. **2.** a head with a cephalic index of 81 and over. **—short′-head′ed,** *adj.*

shorthorn (shôt′hôn′), *n.* one of a breed of dairy or beef cattle, with white, red, or roan markings, having short horns.

shortie (shô′tĭ), *adj.* of or denoting a garment designed to be of short length, as a nightdress.

shortish (shô′tĭsh), *adj.* rather short.

short leg, *Cricket.* **1.** the on side fielding position close to and almost level with the batsman. **2.** a fielder in this position.

short list, a list of especially favoured candidates for a position, promotion, etc., who have been selected from a larger group of applicants.

short-list (shôt′lĭst′), *v.t.* to put (someone) on a short list.

short-lived (shôt′lĭvd′), *adj.* living or lasting only a little while.

shortly (shôt′lĭ), *adv.* **1.** in a short time; soon. **2.** briefly; concisely. **3.** curtly; abruptly.

short-range (shôt′rānj′), *adj.* having a limited extent in distance or time.

short score, *Music.* a condensation of a full score for piano rehearsals with the instrumentation indicated.

short shrift, 1. short shriving or time for shriving, or confession and absolution, given to a condemned person before execution. **2.** little consideration or attention in dealing with a person, a matter, etc.

short-sighted (shôt′sī′tĭd), *adj.* **1.** unable to see far; near-sighted; myopic. **2.** lacking in foresight. **—short′-sight′edly,** *adv.* **—short′-sight′edness,** *n.*

short-spoken (shôt′spō′kən), *adj.* speaking in a short, brief, or curt manner.

shortstop (shôt′stŏp′), *n. Baseball.* **1.** the position of the player who covers the infield between second and third base. **2.** the fielder in this position.

short story, a piece of prose fiction, usually under 10,000 words.

short-tempered (shôt′tĕm′pəd), *adj.* having a hasty temper.

short-term (shôt′tûm′), *adj.* **1.** covering a comparatively short period of time. **2.** having a maturity within a comparatively short time: *a short-term loan.*

short ton, 2000 lbs.

short-waisted (shôt′wās′tĭd), *adj.* of less than average length from the shoulders to the waist.

short wave, *Radio.* an electromagnetic wave 60 metres or less in length. **—short′-wave′,** *adj.*

short-winded (shôt′wĭn′dĭd), *adj.* short of breath; liable to difficulty in breathing.

Shoshone (shō shō′nĭ), *n.* **1.** a river in the U.S., in NW Wyoming, flowing into the Big Horn river. 120 mi. **2.** a dam on this river. 328 ft high. **3.** an American Indian language of the Shoshonean group.

Shoshonean (shō shō′nĭ ən, shō′shə nē′ən), *adj.* **1.** belonging to or constituting a linguistic group of North American Indians of the western U.S., including the Shoshone, Comanche, Ute, Paiute, Hopi, etc.; a subdivision of the great Uto-Aztecan speech family. *—n.* **2.** the Shoshonean languages collectively.

Shostakovich (shŏs′tə kō′vĭch; *Russ.* shə stȧ kô′vĭch), *n.* **Dimitri Dimitrievich** (*Russ.* dĭ mē′trĭy dĭ mē′trĭ yĭ vĭch), born 1906, Soviet composer.

shot[1] (shŏt), *n., pl.* **shots** or (for 5, 7) **shot**; *v.,* **shotted, shotting.** *—n.* **1.** the discharge or a discharge of a firearm, bow, etc. **2.** the range of the discharge, or the distance covered by the missile in its flight. **3.** an attempt to hit with a projectile discharged from a gun or the like. **4.** the act of shooting. **5.** a small ball or pellet of lead, of which a number are used for one charge of a sportsman's gun. **6.** such pellets collectively: *a charge of shot.* **7.** a projectile for discharge from a firearm or cannon. **8.** such projectiles collectively. **9.** a person who shoots: *he was a good shot.* **10.** anything like a shot. **11.** a heavy metal ball which competitors cast as far as possible in shot-putting contests. **12.** an aimed stroke, throw, or the like, as in games, etc. **13.** an attempt or try. **14.** a remark aimed at some person or thing. **15.** a guess at something. **16.** *Colloq.* an injection of a drug, vaccine, etc. **17.** *U.S.* a small quantity of something, esp. of liquor. **18.** *Photog., Films.* **a.** the making of a photograph. **b.** a photograph. **c.** a length of cinefilm taken without stopping or cutting. **19.** *Mining, etc.* an explosive charge in place for detonation. **20.** *Banking Colloq.* loose coin collectively. **21. big shot,** *Colloq.* an important person. **22. like a shot,** instantly; very quickly. **23. shot in the arm,** *Colloq.* something that gives renewed confidence, vigour, etc. **24. shot in the dark,** a wild or random guess. *—v.t.* **25.** to load or supply with shot. **26.** to weight with shot. **27. to be** or **get shot of,** *Colloq. or Dial.* to be rid of. [ME; OE *sc(e)ot, gesceot,* c. G *Schoss, Geschoss*; akin to SHOOT]

shot[2] (shŏt), *v.* **1.** pt. and pp. of **shoot.** *—adj.* **2.** woven so as to present a play of colours, as silk. **3.** spread or streaked with colour.

shote (shōt), *n.* shoat.

shotgun (shŏt′gŭn′), *n.* **1.** a smoothbore gun for firing small shot to kill birds and small quadrupeds, though often used with buckshot to kill larger animals. *—adj.* **2.** of, pertaining to, or used in a shotgun.

shotgun wedding, a wedding hastened or forced by the pregnancy of the bride.

shot noise, *Electronics.* fluctuation in a circuit due to the random motion of electrons.

shot-put (shŏt′po͝ot′), *n.* **1.** the athletic exercise of putting the shot. See **shot**[1] (def. 11). **2.** one throw of the shot in this exercise.

shot-putter (shŏt′po͝ot′ə), *n.* one who takes part in the shot-put.

shott (shŏt), *n.* **1.** a shallow, temporary salt lake or salt marsh in the deserts of N Africa. **2.** a hollow or depression containing such a salt lake or marshy area. [t. Ar.]

shotten (shŏt′n), *adj.* **1.** (of fish, esp. herring) that has recently spawned. **2.** *Pathol.* dislocated. [old pp. of SHOOT]

shot tower, a tower in which shot is made by pouring molten lead through a sieve and then letting it drop into a tank of water.

should (sho͝od), *v.* **1.** pt. of **shall. 2.** (specially used) **a.** to denote duty, propriety, or expediency: *you should not do that.* **b.** to make a statement less direct or blunt: *I should hardly say that.* **c.** to emphasize the uncertainty in conditional and hypothetical clauses: *if it should be true.* [ME *sholde,* OE *sc(e)olde.* See SHALL] **—Syn. 2a.** See **must**[1].

shoulder (shōl′də), *n.* **1.** either of two corresponding parts of the human body, situated at the top of the trunk and extending respectively from the right side and left side of the neck to the upper joint of the corresponding arm. **2.** (*pl.*) these two parts together with the portion of the back joining them, forming a place where burdens are sometimes carried. **3.** a corresponding part in animals. See illus. under **horse. 4.** the upper foreleg and adjoining parts of a sheep, etc. **5.** the joint connecting the arm of the foreleg with the trunk. **6.** a shoulder-like part or projection. **7.** a cut of meat including the upper joint of the foreleg. **8.** *Fort.* the angle of a bastion between the face and the flank. **9.** *Print.* the flat surface on a type body extending beyond the base of the letter or character. See diag. under **type. 10.** that part of a garment which covers, or fits over the shoulder. **11.** *Leather Mfg.* that part of the hide anterior to the butt. **12.** either of two strips of land bordering a road, esp. that part on which vehicles can be parked in an emergency. Cf. **hard shoulder. 13. give the cold shoulder to,** to treat coldly; ignore; snub. **14. have broad shoulders,** to be able to accept responsibility. **15. put one's shoulder to the wheel,** to work hard. **16. rub shoulders with,** to associate with; come into contact with. **17. shoulder to shoulder,** with united action and support. **18. straight from the shoulder,** without evasion. *—v.t.* **19.** to push, as with the shoulder, esp. roughly. **20.** to take upon or support with the shoulder. **21.** to assume as a burden, or responsibility: *to shoulder the expense.* *—v.i.* **22.** to push with the shoulder. [ME *sholder,* OE *sculdor,* c. G *Schulter*]

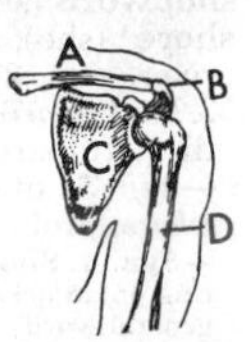

Diagram of left shoulder (front view) • A, Clavicle; B, Acromion; C, Scapula; D, Humerus

shoulder arms, *Mil.* **1.** the order given in arms drill when the rifle is brought into a vertical position, muzzle pointing upwards, on the right side of the body, and held by the right hand at the trigger guard. **2.** to carry out this movement.

shoulder-blade (shōl′də blād′), *n.* the scapula.
shoulder-flash (shōl′də flăsh′), *n. Mil.* a cloth emblem worn on the shoulder to signify regiment or special duties.
shoulder knot, a knot of ribbon or lace worn on the shoulder, as by men of fashion in the 17th and 18th centuries, by servants in livery, or by women or children.
shoulder-strap (shōl′də străp′), *n.* a strap worn over the shoulder as to support a garment.
shouldn't (shŏŏd′nt), contraction of *should not.*
shouldst (shŏŏdst), *v. Archaic.* 2nd pers. sing. of **should.** Also, **shouldest** (shŏŏd′ĭst).
shout (shout), *v.i.* **1.** to call or cry out loudly and vigorously. **2.** to speak or laugh noisily or unrestrainedly. *—v.t.* **3.** to express by a shout or shouts. **4.** *Austral., N.Z. Colloq.* to stand (a person) a round of drinks; treat. **5. shout down,** to drown (another's words) by shouting or talking loudly. *—n.* **6.** a loud call or cry. **7.** a loud burst, as of laughter. **8.** *Austral., N.Z. Colloq.* the act of standing a round of drinks. [ME; c. Icel. *skūta* scold, chide] **—shout′er,** *n.* **—Syn. 1.** See **cry.**
shove (shŭv), *v.,* **shoved, shoving,** *n.* *—v.t.* **1.** to move along by force from behind. **2.** to push roughly or rudely; jostle. *—v.i.* **3.** to push. **4. shove off, a.** to push a boat off. **b.** *Slang.* to leave; start. *—n.* **5.** an act of shoving. [ME *showve,* OE *scūfan,* c. G *schauben* (obs.)] **—shov′er,** *n.* **—Syn. 1.** See **push.**
shovel (shŭv′əl), *n., v.,* **-elled, -elling,** or (*U.S.*) **-eled, -eling.** *—n.* **1.** an implement consisting of a broad blade or scoop attached to a handle, used for taking up and removing loose matter, as earth, snow, coal, etc. **2.** a contrivance or machine for shovelling, removing matter, etc. **3.** a shovelful. **4.** *Colloq.* a shovel hat. *—v.t.* **5.** to take up and cast or remove with a shovel. **6.** to gather or put in quantities or carelessly: *to shovel food into one's mouth.* **7.** to dig or clear with a shovel: *to shovel a path.* *—v.i.* **8.** to work with a shovel. [ME *schovel,* OE *scofl*; akin to G *Schaufel*]
shovelboard (shŭv′əl bôd′), *n.* shuffleboard.
shoveler (shŭv′ə lə), *n.* **1.** Also, **shovelbill** (shŭv′əl bĭl′). a widely distributed freshwater duck, *Anas clypeata,* with a broad, flat bill; spoonbill. **2.** *U.S.* shoveller.
shovelful (shŭv′əl fŭl), *n.* as much as a shovel will hold.
shovel hat, a hat with a broad brim turned up at the sides and projecting with a shovel-like curve in front and behind; worn by some ecclesiastics.
shoveller (shŭv′ə lə), *n.* **1.** Also, *U.S.,* **shoveler.** one who or that which shovels. **2.** shoveler.
show (shō), *v.,* **showed, shown** or **showed, showing,** *n.* *—v.t.* **1.** to cause or allow to be seen; exhibit; display; present. **2.** to point out: *to show the way.* **3.** to guide; escort: *he showed me to my room.* **4.** to make clear; make known; explain. **5.** to prove; demonstrate. **6.** to indicate; register: *the thermometer showed ten degrees below zero.* **7.** to allege, as in a legal document; plead, as a reason or cause. **8.** to produce, as facts in an affidavit or at a hearing. **9.** to make evident by appearance, behaviour, etc.: *to show one's feelings.* **10.** to accord or grant (favour, etc.). **11. show off,** to exhibit for approval or admiration, or ostentatiously: *she was showing off her new dress.* **12. show up, a.** to expose (faults, etc.); reveal. **b.** to appear superior to (another); outdo. *—v.i.* **13.** to be seen; be or become visible. **14.** to look or appear: *to show to advantage.* **15.** *Colloq.* to give an exhibition, display, or performance. **16.** *U.S.* to finish in third place in a horse race, etc. **17. show off,** to display one's abilities, cleverness, etc., with the object of gaining attention. **18. show up, a.** to stand out in a certain way; appear: *blue shows up well against that background.* **b.** to turn up; appear at a certain place. *—n.* **19.** a display: *a show of freedom.* **20.** ostentatious display. **21.** any kind of public exhibition. **22.** the act of showing. **23.** appearance: *to make a sorry show.* **24.** an unreal or deceptive appearance. **25.** an indication; trace. **26.** *Pathol.* (in pregnancy) a discharge of blood and mucosal tissue, indicating the onset of labour. **27.** *Colloq.* a theatrical performance or company. **28.** *U.S. Colloq.* a chance: *to get a fair show.* **29.** a sight or spectacle. **30.** any undertaking, organization, etc.; affair. **31.** a public collection of things on display; a competitive exhibition of farm produce, livestock, etc. **32. give the show away,** to reveal all the details of a plan, scheme, etc. **33. run the show,** to control or manage a business, etc. **34. steal the show,** to attract most attention; be the most popular person or item, in a theatrical performance, etc. **35. stop the show,** (in a theatrical performance, etc.) to be applauded so enthusiastically as to cause the performance to be temporarily interrupted. [ME *showen,* var. of *shewan* look at, show, OE *scēawian* look at, c. D *schowen,* G *schauen* look at] **—show′er,** *n.*
—Syn. 19. SHOW, DISPLAY, OSTENTATION, POMP suggest the presentation of a more or less elaborate, often pretentious, appearance for the public to see. SHOW often indicates an external appearance which may or may not accord with actual facts: *a show of modesty.* DISPLAY applies to an intentionally conspicuous show: *a great display of wealth.* OSTENTATION is vain, ambitious, pretentious, or offensive display: *tasteless and vulgar ostentation.* POMP suggests such a show of dignity and authority as characterizes a ceremony of state: *the coronation was carried out with pomp and ceremonial.*
showbill (shō′bĭl′), *n.* a poster advertising a show.
show biz (bĭz), *Slang.* show business.
showboat (shō′bōt′), *n.* a boat, esp. a paddlewheel steamer, used as a travelling theatre.
showbread (shō′brĕd′), *n.* shewbread.
show business, the entertainment industry, esp. that part concerned with variety.
showcase (shō′kās′), *n.* **1.** a glass case for the display and protection of articles in shops, museums, etc. **2.** a setting or display for exhibiting something at its best, or on a trial basis.
showdown (shō′doun′), *n.* **1.** the laying down of one's cards, face upwards, in a card game, esp. poker. **2.** a confrontation of parties for the final settlement of a contested issue.
shower (shou′ə), *n.* **1.** a brief fall of rain, or hail, sleet, or sometimes, snow. **2.** a similar fall, as of tears, sparks, or bullets. **3.** a large supply or quantity: *a shower of questions.* **4.** *Chiefly U.S.* a bestowal of presents on a prospective bride: *a linen shower.* **5.** a shower-bath. **6.** *Physics.* a group of high-energy particles which originate from one fast particle, from cosmic radiation, or an accelerator. *—v.t.* **7.** to wet as with a shower. **8.** to pour down in a shower. **9.** to bestow liberally or lavishly. *—v.i.* **10.** to rain in a shower. **11.** to take a shower-bath. [ME *shour,* OE *scūr,* c. G *Schauer*] **—show′ery,** *adj.*
shower-bath (shou′ə bäth′), *n.* **1.** a bath in which water is showered upon the body from above. **2.** the apparatus for this.
shower party, *Chiefly U.S.* a party given for a prospective bride, to which guests bring gifts for her new home.
showerproof (shou′ə prōōf′), *adj.* (of clothing) treated so as to resist rain.
showgirl (shō′gûl′), *n.* a girl who sings, dances, etc., usually in a chorus, in a variety show, nightclub, or the like.
showing (shō′ĭng), *n.* **1.** an exhibition; show. **2.** a setting forth or presentation, as of facts or conditions.
show-jumping (shō′jŭm′pĭng), *n.* the riding of horses in competitions in order to display skill in riding over and between obstacles. **—show′-jum′per,** *n*
showman (shō′mən), *n., pl.* **-men. 1.** one who exhibits a show. **2.** one who presents things well. **—show′manship′,** *n.*
shown (shōn), *v.* pp. of **show.**
show-off (shō′ŏf′), *n.* one given to pretentious display or exhibitionism.
showpiece (shō′pēs′), *n.* **1.** an article to be displayed in an exhibition, show, etc. **2.** an article worthy of exhibition as an excellent example of its kind.
showplace (shō′plās′), *n.* **1.** a castle, stately home, or the like, renowned for its beauty, historical interest, etc., and open to the public. **2.** any building renowned for its beauty, design, etc.: *the director's home is a real showplace.*
showroom (shō′rōōm′, -rŏŏm′), *n.* a room used for the display of goods or merchandise.
show stopper, a song, act, performance, etc., that temporarily interrupts a show because of the enthusiastic applause of the audience.
show window, a display window in a store.
showy (shō′ĭ), *adj.,* **showier, showiest. 1.** making an imposing display: *showy flowers.* **2.** ostentatious; gaudy. **—show′ily,** *adv.* **—show′iness,** *n.* **—Syn. 2.** See **gaudy**[1].
shrank (shrăngk), *v.* pt. of **shrink.**
shrapnel (shrăp′nəl), *n.* **1.** *Mil.* **a.** a hollow projectile containing bullets or the like and a bursting charge, designed to explode before reaching its target, and to set free a shower of missiles. **b.** such projectiles collectively. **2.** shell fragments. [named after the inventor, H. *Shrapnel,* 1761–1842, officer in the British army]
shred (shrĕd), *n., v.,* **shredded** or **shred, shredding.** *—n.* **1.** a piece cut or torn off, esp. in a narrow strip. **2.** a bit; scrap. *—v.t.* **3.** to cut or tear into small pieces, esp. small strips; reduce to shreds. *—v.i.* **4.** to tear; be reduced to shreds. [ME *schrede,* OE *scrēade,* c. G *Schrot* chips] **—shred′der,** *n.*
Shreveport (shrēv′pôt′), *n.* a city in the U.S., in NW Louisiana, on the Red River. 164,372 (1960).

Common shrew, *Sorex araneus* (Total length 4½ in., tail 1½ in.)

shrew (shrōō), *n.* **1.** any of various small, insectivore mammals of the genus *Sorex* and allied genera, having a long, sharp snout and a mouselike form, as the **watershrew,** *Neomys fodiens,* of Europe and the British Isles. **2.** a woman of violent temper and speech; a termagant. [OE *scrēawa*; of unknown origin]

shrewd (shro͞od), *adj.* **1.** astute or sharp in practical matters: *a shrewd politician.* **2.** *Archaic.* keen; piercing. **3.** *Archaic.* malicious. **4.** *Obs.* bad. **5.** *Obs.* shrewish. **6.** *Obs.* artful. [ME *shrewed,* pp. of *shrew* curse (now obs.), v. use of SHREW, n.] —**shrewd′ly,** *adv.* —**shrewd′ness,** *n.* —**Syn. 1.** See **acute.**

shrewish (shro͞o′ĭsh), *adj.* having the disposition of a shrew. —**shrew′ishly,** *adv.* —**shrew′ishness,** *n.*

shrewmouse (shro͞o′mous′), *n., pl.* **-mice.** a shrew, esp. *Sorex araneus,* the common shrew of Europe.

Shrewsbury (shrōz′bə rĭ, shro͞oz′-, -brĭ), *n.* a town in England, the county town of Shropshire. 50,120 (est. 1962).

shriek (shrēk), *n.* **1.** a loud, sharp, shrill cry. **2.** a loud, high sound of laughter. **3.** any loud, shrill sound, as of a whistle. —*v.i.* **4.** to utter a loud, sharp, shrill cry, as birds. **5.** to cry out sharply in a high voice: *to shriek with pain.* **6.** to utter loud, high-pitched sounds in laughing. **7.** (of a musical instrument, a whistle, the wind, etc.) to give forth a loud, shrill sound. —*v.t.* **8.** to cry in a shriek: *to shriek defiance.* [earlier *shrick,* northern var. of *shritch* (now d.), ME *schriche*] —**shriek′er,** *n.* —**Syn. 5.** See **scream.**

shrieve[1] (shrēv), *n. Obs.* sheriff.

shrieve[2] (shrēv), *v.t., v.i.,* **shrieved, shrieving.** *Archaic.* shrive.

shrift (shrĭft), *n. Archaic.* **1.** the imposition of penance by a priest on a penitent after confession. **2.** absolution or remission of sins granted after confession and penance. **3.** confession to a priest. **4.** the act of shriving. **5. short shrift, a.** little consideration in dealing with someone or something; summary treatment. **b.** *Obs.* a brief space of time for confession allowed to a condemned criminal before his execution. [ME; OE *scrift* (c. D *schrift* and G *Schrift* writing), der. SHRIVE]

shrike (shrīk), *n.* any of numerous predacious oscine birds of the family *Laniidae,* with a strong hooked and toothed bill, which feed on insects and sometimes on small birds and other animals, as the butcher-birds of the genus *Lanius,* and the thick-headed shrikes of the genus *Pachycephala,* of the Australian region. [OE *scrīc*]

shrill (shrĭl), *adj.* **1.** high-pitched and piercing: *a shrill cry.* **2.** producing such sound. **3.** full of such sound. **4.** *Poetic.* keen; piercing. —*v.t., v.i.* **5.** to cry shrilly. —*n.* **6.** a shrill sound. —*adv.* **7.** shrilly. [ME *shrille,* c. G *schrill* (of LG orig.); akin to OE *scrallettan* sound loudly] —**shrill′ness,** *n.* —**shril′ly,** *adv.*

shrimp (shrĭmp), *n.* **1.** any of various small, long-tailed, chiefly marine, decapod crustaceans of the genus *Crangon* and allied genera (suborder *Macrura*), as the European *C. vulgaris,* esteemed as a table delicacy. **2.** *Colloq.* a diminutive or insignificant person. —*v.i.* **3.** to catch or attempt to catch shrimps. [ME *shrimpe.* Cf. G *shrumpfen* shrink up, and OE *scrimman* shrink] —**shrimp′er,** *n.*

Shrimp, *Crangon vulgaris* (2 in. long)

shrine (shrīn), *n., v.,* **shrined, shrining.** —*n.* **1.** a receptacle for sacred relics; a reliquary. **2.** an erection, often of a stately or sumptuous character, enclosing the remains or relics of a saint or other holy objects and forming an object of religious veneration and pilgrimage. **3.** any structure or place consecrated or devoted to some saint or deity, as an altar, chapel, church, or temple. **4.** any place or object hallowed by its history or associations. —*v.t.* **5.** to enshrine. [ME *schrine,* OE *scrīn* (c. G *Schrein*), t. L: m. s. *scrinium* case for books and papers]

shrink (shrĭngk), *v.,* **shrank** or **shrunk, shrunk** or **shrunken, shrinking,** *n.* —*v.i.* **1.** to draw back, as in retreat or avoidance. **2.** to contract with heat, cold, moisture, etc. **3.** to become reduced in extent or compass. —*v.t.* **4.** to cause to shrink or contract. **5.** *Textiles.* to cause to shrink in order to prevent future shrinkage. —*n.* **6.** a shrinking. **7.** a shrinking movement. [ME *schrinke(n),* OE *scrincan,* c. MD *schrinken*; akin to Sw. *skrynka* wrinkle] —**shrink′able,** *adj.* —**shrink′er,** *n.* —**shrink′ingly,** *adv.* —**Syn. 3.** See **decrease.** —**Ant. 3.** expand.

shrinkage (shrĭng′kĭj), *n.* **1.** the act or fact of shrinking. **2.** the amount or degree of shrinking. **3.** reduction or depreciation in quantity, value, etc. **4.** contraction of a fabric in finishing or washing. **5.** the difference between the original weight of livestock and that after it has been prepared for marketing.

shrive (shrīv), *v.,* **shrove** or **shrived, shriven** or **shrived, shriving.** —*v.t.* **1.** to impose penance on for sin. **2.** to grant absolution to (a penitent). **3.** to confess to a priest, for the purpose of obtaining absolution. **4.** to hear the confession of. —*v.i.* **5.** to hear confessions. **6.** to go to or make confession. Also, *Archaic,* **shrieve.** [ME; OE *scrīfan* (c. G *schreiben* write), ult. t. L: m. *scrībere* write]

shrivel (shrĭv′əl), *v.t., v.i.,* **-elled, -elling** or (*U.S.*) **-eled, -eling. 1.** to contract and wrinkle, as from great heat or cold. **2.** to wither; make or become impotent. [orig. unknown] —**Syn. 1.** See **wither.**

shroff (shrŏf), *n.* **1.** (in India) a banker or moneychanger. **2.** (in China, etc.) a native expert employed to test coins and separate the base from the genuine. —*v.t.* **3.** to test (coins) in order to separate the base from the genuine. —*v.i.* **4.** to act as a shroff. [earlier *sharoffe,* t. Pg.: m. *xarrafo,* t. Hind.: m. *çairāf* money-changer]

Shrops., Shropshire.

Shropshire (shrŏp′shĭə, -shə), *n.* **1.** a county in W England. 297,313 pop. (1961); 134 sq. mi. *Co. town:* Shrewsbury. *Abbrev.:* Salop. **2.** a hornless breed of mutton sheep having dark brown or black face and legs, and fleece of a white wool.

shroud (shroud), *n.* **1.** a white cloth or sheet in which a corpse is wrapped for burial. **2.** something which covers or conceals like a garment: *a shroud of rain.* **3.** (*usually pl.*) *Naut.* one of a set of strong ropes extended from the mastheads to the sides of a ship to help support the masts. See illus. under **ratline. 4.** *Mech.* **a.** circular webs used to stiffen the sides of gear teeth, esp. nonmetallic gears. **b.** a strip used to strengthen turbine blades. **c.** a deflecting wall close to the inlet part of an internal-combustion engine used to promote turbulence of the incoming air. **5.** *Aeron.* the rearward extension of the skin of a fixed aerofoil surface to cover all or part of the leading edge of a control surface. —*v.t.* **6.** to wrap or clothe for burial. **7.** to cover; hide from view. **8.** to veil, as in obscurity or mystery. **9.** *Obs.* to shelter. —*v.i.* **10.** *Archaic.* to take shelter. [ME; OE *scrūd,* c. Icel. *skrūdh*; akin to SHRED] —**shroud′less,** *adj.*

shroud-laid (shroud′lād′), *adj.* (of a rope) made with four strands and (usually) a central core or heart.

shrove (shrōv), *v.* pt. of **shrive.**

Shrove Sunday, the Sunday before Ash Wednesday.

Shrovetide (shrōv′tīd′), *n.* the three days before Ash Wednesday, once a time of confession and absolution.

Shrove Tuesday, the last day of Shrovetide, long observed as a season of merrymaking before Lent; Pancake Day.

shrub[1] (shrŭb), *n.* a woody perennial plant smaller than a tree, usually having permanent stems branching from or near the ground. [ME *shrubbe,* OE *scrybb* brushwood, c. d. Dan. *skrub*] —**shrub′like′,** *adj.*

shrub[2] (shrŭb), *n.* a cordial made of different fruits, spirits, and sugar, formerly popular. [t. Ar., metathetic var. of *shurb* drink]

shrubbery (shrŭb′ə rĭ), *n., pl.* **-beries. 1.** shrubs collectively. **2.** a plantation or plot of shrubs.

shrubby (shrŭb′ĭ), *adj.,* **-bier, -biest. 1.** shrublike. **2.** abounding in shrubs. **3.** consisting of shrubs. —**shrub′biness,** *n.*

shrug (shrŭg), *v.,* **shrugged, shrugging,** *n.* —*v.t.* **1.** to raise and lower (the shoulders), expressing indifference, disdain, etc. **2. shrug off,** to disregard; take no notice of: *to shrug off an insult.* —*v.i.* **3.** to raise and lower the shoulders, expressing indifference, disdain, etc. —*n.* **4.** this movement. [ME]

shrunk (shrŭngk), *v.* pp. and a pt. of **shrink.**

shrunken (shrŭng′kən), *v.* a pp. of **shrink.**

shuck (shŭk), *U.S.* —*n.* **1.** a husk, shell, or pod, as the outer covering of maize, hickory nuts, chestnuts, etc. **2.** (*pl.*) *Colloq.* something useless: *not worth shucks.* **3.** the shell of an oyster or clam. —*v.t.* **4.** to remove the shucks from: *she sat there placidly shucking the peas.* **5.** to remove as or like shucks. [orig. unknown] —**shuck′er,** *n.*

shucks (shŭks), *interj. U.S. Colloq.* (an exclamation of disgust or regret.)

shudder (shŭd′ə), *v.i.* **1.** to tremble with a sudden convulsive movement, as from horror, fear, or cold. —*n.* **2.** a convulsive movement of the body, as from horror, fear, or cold. [ME *shodder, shuder* (c. G *schaudern*), freq. of OE *scūdan* move, shake] —**shud′deringly,** *adv.* —**Syn. 1.** See **shiver**[1].

shuffle (shŭf′əl), *v.,* **-fled, -fling,** *n.* —*v.i.* **1.** to walk without lifting the feet or with clumsy steps and a shambling gait. **2.** to scrape the feet over the floor in dancing. **3.** to get (*into,* etc.) in a clumsy manner: *to shuffle into one's clothes.* **4.** to get (*in, out of,* etc.) in an underhand or evasive manner: *to shuffle out of responsibilities.* **5.** to act in a shifty or evasive manner; employ deceitful pretences; equivocate. **6.** to mix cards in a pack so as to change their relative position. —*v.t.* **7.** to move (the feet, etc.) along the ground or floor without lifting them. **8.** to perform (a dance, etc.) with such movements. **9.** to move this way and that. **10.** to put, thrust, or bring (*in*, *out*, etc.) trickily, evasively, or haphazardly. **11.** to mix (cards in a pack) so as to change their relative position. **12.** to jumble together; mix in a disorderly heap. **13.** **shuffle off, a.** to thrust aside or get rid of. **b.** to go off with a shuffling gait. —*n.* **14.** a scraping movement; a dragging gait. **15.** an evasive trick; evasion. **16.** the act of shuffling. **17.** a shuffling of cards in a pack. **18.** right or turn to shuffle in card-playing. **19.** a dance in which the feet are shuffled along the floor. [t. LG: m. *schuffeln* walk clumsily or with dragging feet. See SHOVE] —**shuf′fler,** *n.*

shuffleboard (shŭf′əl bōd′), *n.* **1.** a game in which coins or discs are driven along a smooth board, table, or other surface, towards certain lines, etc., on it. **2.** the board, table, or the like. **3.** a similar game played as on board a ship's deck with large discs pushed with a cue. Also, **shovelboard.**

shufty (shŭf′tĭ), *n., pl.* **-ties.** *Slang.* a look; glance or view.

Shulamite (shōō′lə mīt′), *n.* epithet of the bride in the Song of Solomon 6:13.

Shumen (*Bulg.* shōō′mĕn), *n.* former name of **Kolarovgrad.**

shun (shŭn), *v.t.*, **shunned, shunning.** to keep away from (a place, person, etc.), from dislike, caution, etc.; take pains to avoid. [ME *shunen*, OE *scunian*; orig. obscure] —**shun′ner,** *n.*

shunt (shŭnt), *v.t.* **1.** to move or turn aside or out of the way. **2.** to sidetrack; get rid of. **3.** *Elect.* to divert (a part of a current) by connecting a circuit element in parallel with another; to place on or furnish with a shunt. **4.** to move (a train, or part of it) from one line of rails to another or from the main track to a siding. —*v.i.* **5.** to move or turn aside or out of the way. **6.** (of a train) to move from one railway track to another, or from one point to another; to move railway trucks about as in a goods yard. —*n.* **7.** the act of shunting; a move. **8.** *Elect.* a conducting element bridged across a circuit or a portion of a circuit, establishing a current path auxiliary to the main circuit. **9.** a railway siding. [ME; orig. obscure, ? der. SHUN] —**shunt′er,** *n.*

shush (shōōsh), *interj.* **1.** hush (a command to be quiet or silent). —*v.t., v.i.* **2.** to make or become silent.

Shushan (shōō′shăn), *n.* biblical name of **Susa.**

shut (shŭt), *v.*, **shut, shutting,** *adj., n.* —*v.t.* **1.** to put (a door, cover, etc.) in position to close or obstruct. **2.** to close the doors of (often fol. by *up*): *shut up the shop.* **3.** to close by bringing together or folding: *to shut one's eyes.* **4.** to confine; enclose: *to shut a bird into a cage.* **5.** to bar; exclude: *to shut a person from one's house.* **6.** to close down; cease normal operations: *they decided to shut the office during redecoration.* **7.** *Obs.* to bolt; bar. —*v.i.* **8.** to become shut or closed; close. —*v.* **9.** Some special verb phrases are:

keep one's mouth shut, **1.** to remain silent. **2.** to keep a secret.

shut away, to hide or confine.

shut down, **1.** to close by lowering, as a lid. **2.** to cover or envelop, as fog. **3.** to close down, esp. for a time, as a factory. **4.** *Colloq.* to put a stop or check to (fol. by *on* or *upon*). **5.** to stop (a machine, engine, etc.).

shut in, to imprison; confine; enclose.

shut off, **1.** to stop the flow of (water, electricity, etc.). **2.** to keep separate; isolate.

shut one's eyes to, to refuse to notice; ignore.

shut out, to exclude; keep out.

shut up, **1.** to imprison; confine; hide from view. **2.** *Colloq.* to stop talking; become silent. **3.** *Colloq.* to stop (someone) from talking; silence.

—*adj.* **10.** closed; fastened up. **11.** *Dial. or Colloq.* free or rid (fol. by *of*).

—*n.* **12.** the act or time of shutting or closing. **13.** the line where two pieces of welded metal are united.

[ME *schutte*, OE *scyttan* bolt (a door); akin to SHOOT]

—**Syn. 1.** See **close.**

shutdown (shŭt′doun′), *n.* a shutting down; a closing of a factory or the like.

Shute (shōōt), *n.* **Nevil** (*Nevil Shute Norway*), 1899–1960, English novelist.

shut-eye (shŭt′ī′), *n. Slang.* sleep.

shut-in (shŭt′ĭn′), *adj.* **1.** *U.S.* confined to the house, hospital, etc. **2.** *Psychol.* disposed to desire solitude. —*n.* **3.** *U.S.* a person confined by infirmity or disease to the house, hospital, etc.

shut-off (shŭt′ŏf′), *n. U.S.* cut-out.

shut-out (shŭt′out′), *n.* **1.** the act of shutting out. **2.** the state of being shut out.

shutter (shŭt′ə), *n.* **1.** a hinged or otherwise movable cover for a window. **2.** a movable cover, slide, etc., for an opening. **3.** one who or that which shuts. **4.** *Photog.* a mechanical device for opening and closing the aperture of a camera lens to expose a plate or film. —*v.t.* **5.** to close or provide with shutters. —**Syn. 1.** See **curtain.**

shuttle (shŭt′l), *n., v.*, **-tled, -tling.** —*n.* **1.** a device in a loom for passing or shooting the weft thread through the shed from one side of the web to the other, usually consisting of a boat-shaped piece of wood containing a bobbin on which the weft thread is wound. **2.** the sliding container that carries the lower thread in a sewing machine. —*v.t., v.i.* **3.** to move quickly to and fro like a shuttle. [ME *schutylle*, *shittle*, OE *scytel* dart, arrow, c. Icel. *skutill* harpoon; akin to SHUT, SHOOT]

shuttlecock (shŭt′l kŏk′), *n.* **1.** a piece of cork, or similar light material, with feathers stuck in one end, intended to be struck to and fro, as with a racket in the game of badminton or with a battledore in the game of battledore. **2.** the game of battledore. —*v.t.* **3.** to send, or bandy to and fro, like a shuttlecock. —*v.i.* **4.** to move to and fro like a shuttlecock.

Shuttlecock

shuttle service, a transport service, usually running over a short route, esp. an emergency service when normal services have been disrupted.

Shvernik (*Russ.* shvĕr′nĭk), *n.* **Nikolai** (*Russ.* nĭ kȧ lăy′), born 1888, president of the Soviet Union 1946–53.

shy[1] (shī), *adj.*, **shyer, shyest** or **shier, shiest,** *v.*, **shied, shying,** *n., pl.* **shies.** —*adj.* **1.** bashful; retiring. **2.** easily frightened away; timid. **3.** suspicious; distrustful. **4.** reluctant; wary. **5.** *U.S.* short: *shy of funds.* **6.** *U.S. Slang.* short in amount, degree, etc. **7.** *Colloq.* failing to pay something due, as one's ante in poker. **8.** not bearing or breeding freely, as plants or animals. **9.** **fight shy of,** to avoid; keep away from. —*v.i.* **10.** to start back or aside, as in fear, esp. a horse. **11.** to draw back; recoil. —*n.* **12.** a sudden start aside, as in fear. [ME *schey*, OE *scēoh*, c. MHG *schiech*; akin to G *scheu*] —**shy′er,** *n.* —**shy′ly,** *adv.* —**shy′ness,** *n.*

—**Syn. 1.** SHY, BASHFUL, DIFFIDENT imply a manner which shows discomfort or lack of confidence in association with others. SHY implies a constitutional shrinking from contact or close association with others, together with a wish to escape notice: *shy and retiring.* BASHFUL suggests timidity about meeting others, and trepidation and awkward behaviour when brought into prominence or notice: *a bashful child.* DIFFIDENT emphasizes self-distrust, fear of censure, failure, etc., and a hesitant, tentative manner as a consequence: *a diffident approach to a subject.* —**Ant. 1.** bold, confident.

shy[2] (shī), *v.*, **shied, shying,** *n., pl.* **shies.** —*v.i., v.t.* **1.** to throw with a sudden swift movement: *to shy a stone.* —*n.* **2.** a sudden swift throw. **3.** a cockshy. **4.** *Colloq.* a gibe or sneer. **5.** *Colloq.* a try; an attempt. [orig. uncert.]

Shylock (shī′lŏk′), *n.* **1.** an extortionate usurer. **2.** any mean person. [after *Shylock*, character in Shakespeare's '*Merchant of Venice*']

shyster (shī′stə), *n. Slang, Chiefly U.S.* **1.** one who gets along by petty, sharp practices. **2.** a lawyer who uses unprofessional or questionable methods. [appar. f. SHY in slang sense of shady, disreputable + -STER]

si (sē), *n. Music.* the syllable used for the seventh note of a scale and sometimes for the note B. [see GAMUT]

Si (sē), *n.* a river in S China, flowing from Yünnan province E to the South China Sea near Canton. ab. 1250 mi. Also, **Si-kiang.**

Si, *Chem.* silicon.

SI, Système International (d'Unités).

sial (sī′əl), *n.* the lighter granitic layer of the lithosphere which forms the continents, overlying the sima, and composed largely of silica and alumina. [b. SI(LICA) + AL(UMINA)]

sialagogic (sī′ə lə gŏj′ĭk), *Med.* —*adj.* **1.** encouraging salivary flow. —*n.* **2.** sialagogue.

sialagogue (sī′ə lə gŏg′, sī ăl′ə gŏg′), *Med.* —*adj.* **1.** promoting the flow or secretion of saliva. —*n.* **2.** a sialagogue agent or medicine. [t. NL: m. s. *sialagōgus*, f. Gk: s. *síalon* saliva + m. *agōgós* leading, drawing forth]

Sialkot (sĭ ăl′kŏt), *n.* a city in Pakistan, in W Punjab: military station. 164,346 (1961).

sialoid (sī′ə loid′), *adj.* resembling saliva. [f. s. Gk *síalon* saliva + -OID]

Siam (sī ăm′, sī′ăm), *n.* **1.** former name of a kingdom in SE Asia. Official name (1939–45 and since 1949), **Thailand. 2. Gulf of,** an arm of the South China Sea, S of Thailand.

siamang (sī′ə măng′), *n.* a large black gibbon, *Hylobates syndactylus*, of Sumatra and the Malay Peninsula, with very long arms and having the second and third digits united. [t. Malay, der. *āmang* black]

Siamese (sī′ə mēz′), *adj., n., pl.* **-mese.** —*adj.* **1.** of or pertaining to Siam, its people, or their language. **2.** (in allusion to the Siamese twins) inseparable, closely connected, similar. *—n.* **3.** a native of Siam. **4.** the official language of Thailand, and the most important Thai language.

Siamese cat, one of a breed of slender, short-haired cats, originating in Siam, having blue eyes, a small head, and a fawn or grey colour with extremities of a darker shading.

Siamese fighting fish, a bony fish, *Betta splendens*, originating in Thailand, which has become highly coloured as a result of selective breeding, and the males of which are very pugnacious.

Siamese twins, **1.** two Siamese men, Chang and Eng (1811–74), who were born joined to each other by a short, tubular, cartilaginous band. **2.** any twins who are born joined together in any manner.

Sian (sē′ăn′, shē′-), *n.* a city in and the capital of Shensi province in central China. 1,368,000 (est. 1958). Also, **Singan.**

Siangtan (syăng′tăn′, shyăng′-), *n.* a city in S China, in Hunan province. 247,000 (est. 1958).

sib[1] (sĭb), *adj.* **1.** related by blood; akin. *—n.* **2.** a kinsman; relative. **3.** one's kin or kindred. [ME *(i)sib*, OE *(ge)sibb* related (as n., a relation); cf. Icel. *sifi* kinsman]

sib[2] (sĭb), *n. Colloq.* a sibling.

Sibelius (sĭ bā′lyəs; *Fin.* sē′bĕ lē o͞os), *n.* **Jean Julius Christian** (*Fin.* zhän yo͞o′lyo͞os krēs′tyän), 1865–1957, Finnish composer.

Siberia (sī bĭə′rĭ ə), *n.* a part of the Soviet Union, in N Asia, extending from the Ural Mountains to the Pacific. Russian, **Sibir** (*Russ.* sĭ bēry′). See map under **date line.** **—Sibe′rian,** *adj., n.*

Siberian crab-apple, a small rosaceous tree of NE Asia, *Malus prunifolia* frequently cultivated for its clusters of yellow fruits.

Siberian wallflower, a cultivated cruciferous perennial with orange flowers, called *Cheiranthus allionii* by gardeners but probably a hybrid of the genus *Erysimum.*

sibilant (sĭb′ĭ lənt), *adj.* **1.** hissing. **2.** *Phonet.* characterized by a hissing sound; denoting sounds like those spelt with *s* in *this, rose, pressure, pleasure.* *—n.* **3.** *Phonet.* a sibilant sound. [t. L: s. *sibilans*, ppr.] **—sib′ilance, sib′ilancy,** *n.* **—sib′ilantly,** *adv.*

sibilate (sĭb′ĭ lāt′), *v.,* **-lated, -lating.** *—v.i.* **1.** to hiss. *—v.t.* **2.** to utter or pronounce with a hissing sound. **—sib′ila′tion,** *n.*

Sibiu (*Rum.* sē bēw′), *n.* a town in central Rumania. 109;546 (1966).

sibling (sĭb′lĭng), *n.* a brother or sister. [OE]

Sibu (sē bo͞o′), *n.* a town in Malaysia, in Sarawak. 29,630 (1960).

sibyl (sĭb′ĭl), *n.* **1.** any of certain women of antiquity reputed to possess powers of prophecy or divination. **2.** a prophetess or witch. [ME *sibil*, t. ML: m. s. *Sibilla*, L *Sibylla*, t. Gk] **—sibyl′ic, sibylline** (sĭb′ĭ līn′, sĭ bĭl′īn), *adj.*

Sibylline Books, *Rom. Hist.* a collection of oracular utterances, in Greek hexameters, concerning religious worship and Roman policy. They were reputedly bought by Tarquinius Superbus from the Cumaean sibyl.

sic[1] (sĭk), *adv. Latin.* so; thus (often used parenthetically to show that something has been copied exactly from the original).

sic[2] (sĭk), *v.t.,* **sicked, sicking.** **1.** to attack (esp. of a dog). **2.** to incite to attack. [var. of SEEK]

Sic., **1.** Sicilian. **2.** Sicily.

Sicanian (sĭ kā′nyən), *adj.* Sicilian.

siccative (sĭk′ə tĭv), *adj.* **1.** causing or promoting absorption of moisture; drying. *—n.* **2.** a siccative substance, esp. in paint. [t. LL: m. s. *siccātīvus*, der. *siccāre* to dry]

sice (sīs), *n.* syce.

Sicilian Vespers (sĭ sĭl′yən), a general massacre of the French in Sicily by the natives, begun at the sound of the vesper bell on Easter Monday, 1282.

Sicilies (sĭs′ĭ lĭz), *n.pl.* **The Two,** a former kingdom in Sicily and S Italy: it existed intermittently from 1130 to 1861.

Sicily (sĭs′ĭ lĭ), *n.* the largest island in the Mediterranean, comprising a region of Italy: separated from the SW tip of the Italian mainland by the Strait of Messina. 4,711,783 pop. (1961); 9924 sq. mi. *Cap.:* Palermo. Italian, **Sicilia** (*It.* sē chē′lyä). See map under **Malta.** **—Sicilian** (sĭ sĭl′yən); *adj., n.*

sick (sĭk), *adj.* **1.** affected with nausea; inclined to vomit, or vomiting. **2.** affected with any disorder of health; ill, unwell, or ailing. **3.** of or attended with sickness. **4.** of or appropriate to sick persons: *on sick leave.* **5.** deeply affected with some feeling comparable to physical disorder, as sorrow, longing, repugnance, weariness, etc.: *sick at heart.* **6.** morbid; macabre: *sick humour; a sick joke.* **7.** *Colloq.* disgusted; chagrined. **8.** pale; wan. **9.** not in proper condition; impaired. **10.** *Agric.* **a.** failing to sustain adequate harvests of some crop, usually specified: *a lucerne-sick soil.* **b.** containing harmful micro-organisms: *a sick field.* *—n.* **11.** sick people. **12.** vomit. *—v.t., v.i.* **13. sick up,** to vomit. [ME *sik, sek*, OE *sēoc*, c. G *siech*]
—Syn. 1. SICK, AILING, INDISPOSED refer to any departure from a state of health. SICK refers to a condition presumably temporary, however severe. AILING implies a somewhat unhealthy condition, usually extending over some time. INDISPOSED applies to a slight, temporary illness. See also **ill.** **—Ant. 1.** well, healthy.

sick bay, a hospital or infirmary, as on board a ship.

sickbed (sĭk′bĕd′), *n.* a bed used by a sick person.

sicken (sĭk′ən), *v.i., v.t.* to become or make sick.

sickening (sĭk′ə nĭng), *adj.* making sick; causing nausea, disgust, or loathing: *a sickening display of bad temper.* **—sick′eningly,** *adv.*

Sickert (sĭk′ət), *n.* **Walter Richard,** 1860–1942, British impressionist painter.

sick headache, headache accompanied by nausea; migraine.

sickish (sĭk′ĭsh), *adj.* **1.** somewhat sickening or nauseating. **2.** somewhat sick or ill. **—sick′ishly,** *adv.* **—sick′ishness,** *n.*

sickle (sĭk′l), *n.* **1.** an implement for cutting grain, grass, etc., consisting of a curved, hooklike blade mounted in a short handle. **2.** (*cap.*) *Astron.* a group of stars in the constellation Leo, likened to this implement. [ME *sikel*, OE *sicol* (c. G *Sichel*), t. L: m. s. *secula*]

Sickle

sick leave, leave of absence granted because of illness.

sicklebill (sĭk′l bĭl′), *n.* **1.** any of various birds with a curved bill, esp. the white ibis, *Threskioris molucca*, of Australia. *—adj.* **2.** of or pertaining to any such bird.

sickle cell, a cell containing a mutant gene which affects the blood of humans, usually Negroes: thought to offer resistance to malaria. **—sick′le-cell′,** *adj.*

sickle-cell anaemia, a hereditary disease characterized by the crystallization of sickle cells within erythrocytes, distorting them and clogging blood vessels.

sickle feather, one of the paired, elongated, sickle-shaped, middle feathers of the tail of the cock.

sick list, **1.** a list of persons who are ill. **2. on the sick list,** *Colloq.* not well; ill: *he has been on the sick list for a week now.*

sickly (sĭk′lĭ), *adj.,* **-lier, -liest,** *adv., v.,* **-lied, -lying.** *—adj.* **1.** not strong; unhealthy; ailing. **2.** of, connected with, or arising from ill health: *a sickly complexion.* **3.** marked by the prevalence of ill health, as a region. **4.** causing sickness. **5.** (of food) rich; too sweet. **6.** nauseating. **7.** weak; mawkish: *sickly sentimentality.* **8.** faint or feeble, as light, colour, etc. *—adv.* **9.** *Obs.* in a sick or sickly manner. *—v.t.* **10.** *Obs.* to cover with a sickly hue. **—sick′liness,** *n.* **—Syn. 1.** unwell, frail, weak, puny.

sickness (sĭk′nĭs), *n.* **1.** a particular disease or malady. **2.** state of being sick; illness. **3.** nausea.

sickness benefit, money paid by the state to somebody who is out of work because of illness.

sick parade, *Mil., etc.* a special parade held for those personnel who require medical attention.

sick pay, a wage or salary or a proportion of one paid to an employee absent from work owing to illness.

sick room, a room in which a sick person is confined.

sic passim (sĭk′păs′ĭm), *Latin.* the same wherever found (as in a book or notes).

sic transit gloria mundi (sĭk′ trăn′sĭt glô′rĭ ä′ mo͞on′dē), *Latin.* thus passes away the glory of this world (or worldly glory).

Sicyon (sĭsh′ĭ ən), *n.* an ancient city in S Greece, near Corinth.

Sidcup (sĭd′kəp), *n.* an urban district of London in the SE outer boroughs of Bromley and Bexley.

Siddhartha (sĭ dä′tə), *n.* Buddha.

Siddons (sĭd′nz), *n.* **Sarah** (nee *Kemble*), 1755–1831, English actress.

siddur (sĭd′o͝oə), *n., pl.* **-durim, -durs.** *Judaism.* the book containing daily, Sabbath and festival prayers. [t. Heb.: order]

side (sīd), *n., adj., v.,* **sided, siding.** *—n.* **1.** one of the surfaces or lines bounding a thing. **2.** either of the two surfaces of paper, cloth, etc. **3.** one of the two surfaces of an object other than the front, back, top, and bottom. **4.** either of the two lateral (right and left) parts of a thing. **5.** either lateral half of the body of a person or an animal, esp. of the trunk. **6.** the space immediately beside someone or something: *the girl stood at his side.*

7. an aspect; phase: *all sides of a question.* **8.** region, direction, or position with reference to a central line, space, or point: *the east side of a city.* **9.** a department or division, as of teaching in a school: *the science side, the arts side.* **10.** a slope, as of a hill. **11.** one of two or more parties concerned in a case, contest, etc. **12.** line of descent through either the father or the mother: *his maternal side.* **13.** *Slang.* pretentious airs: *to put on a side.* **14.** either of two lateral parts of the framework of a ship. **15.** *Billiards.* a spinning motion imparted to a ball by a quick stroke on one side of its centre. **16. on the side, a.** separate from the main subject. **b.** *Colloq.* as a sideline; secretly. **17. on the . . . side,** tending towards the quality or condition specified: *this coffee is a little on the weak side.* **18. put on one side,** to leave for later consideration; shelve. **19. side by side,** next to one another; together; in close proximity. **20. take sides,** to support or show favour for one person or party in a dispute, contest, or the like. *—adj.* **21.** being at or on one side: *the side aisles of a theatre.* **22.** coming from one side: *side glance.* **23.** directed towards one side: *side blow.* **24.** subordinate: *a side issue.* *—v.i.* **25. side with** or **against,** to place oneself with or against a side or party to support or oppose an issue. [ME and OE; c. G *Seite*]

side-arms (sīd′ämz′), *n.pl. Mil.* weapons (as pistol, sword, etc.) carried at the side or in the belt.

side band, *Radio.* the band of frequencies lying on either side of a modulated carrier wave.

sideboard (sīd′bôd′), *n.* **1.** a piece of furniture, as in a dining room, often with shelves, drawers, etc., for holding articles of table service. **2.** (*pl.*) short whiskers extending from the hairline to below the ears and worn with an unbearded chin.

sideburns (sīd′bûnz′), *n.pl. Chiefly U.S.* sideboards. [alter. of BURNSIDES]

sidecar (sīd′kä′), *n.* a small car attached on one side to a motorcycle and supported on the other by a wheel of its own: used for a passenger, parcels, etc.

side card, *Cards.* **1.** *Poker.* the highest card in a hand that is not part of a scoring combination, determining the ranking of two otherwise equal hands by its denomination. **2.** any card other than a trump.

side chain, *Chem.* a group of atoms which is attached to an atom, forming part of a larger chain or a cyclic compound, esp. such a group of atoms which has replaced an atom of hydrogen.

sided (sī′dĭd), *adj.* denoting the width of a frame in ship construction.

side-dish (sīd′dĭsh′), *n.* a dish served in addition to the principal dish of a course.

side-dress (sīd′drĕs′), *v.t.* to give (plants etc.) fertilizer by working it into the side along the side of a row.

side-drum (sīd′drŭm′), *n.* a small double-headed drum carried at the side, having snares across the lower head to produce a rattling or reverberating effect.

Side-drum

side effect, any effect produced, as of a drug, other than those originally intended, esp. an unpleasant or harmful effect.

sidehead (sīd′hĕd′), *n.* a heading or subheading which appears in the margin of printed matter. Also, **side′head′ing.**

sidekick (sīd′kĭk′), *n. U.S. Slang.* a close friend or assistant.

sidelight (sīd′līt′), *n.* **1.** light coming from the side. **2.** incidental information. **3.** either of the two small lights at the front of a vehicle used at night for indicating the width of the vehicle to other road-users, and for parking. **4.** either of two lights carried by a vessel under way at night, a red one on the port side and a green on the starboard. **5.** a window or other aperture for light, in the side of a building, ship, etc. **6.** a window at the side of a door or another window.

sideline (sīd′līn′), *n.* **1.** a line at the side of something. **2.** an additional or auxiliary line of goods or of business. **3.** *Sport.* **a.** a line or mark defining the limit of play on the side of the field in football, etc. **b.** (*pl.*) the area immediately beyond any of the sidelines. **c.** the place occupied by those not playing in the contest.

sidelong (sīd′lŏng′), *adj.* **1.** directed to one side. *—adv.* **2.** towards the side; obliquely.

sideman (sīd′mən), *n., pl.* **-men** (-mən). *U.S.* an instrumentalist in a band or orchestra, esp. one supporting a soloist.

sidenote (sīd′nōt′), *n.* a note made in the margin of a page.

sidepiece (sīd′pēs′), *n.* a piece forming a side or a part of a side, or fixed by the side, of something.

sidereal (sī dĭə′rĭ əl), *adj.* **1.** determined by the stars: *sidereal time.* **2.** of or pertaining to the stars. [f. s. L *sīdereus* pertaining to the stars + -AL[1]]

sidereal day, the interval between two successive passages of the vernal equinox over the meridian, being about 4 minutes shorter than a mean solar day.

sidereal hour, one 24th part of a sidereal day.

sidereal period, (of a planet) the time taken to complete one revolution of the sun with reference to the fixed stars.

sidereal year. See **year** (def. 6).

siderite (sī′də rīt′), *n.* **1.** Also, **chalybite.** a common mineral, iron carbonate, $FeCO_3$, usually occurring in yellowish to deep brown cleavable masses: a minor ore of iron. **2.** a meteorite consisting almost entirely of metallic minerals. [t. L: m. *sidērites*, t. Gk; in later use f. SIDER(O)- + -ITE[1]] **—sideritic** (sī′də rĭt′ĭk), *adj.*

sidero-, a word element meaning 'iron', 'steel', as in *siderolite.* Also, before vowels, **sider-.** [t. Gk, comb. form of *sidēros* iron]

side road, a minor road, turning off a main road; a byroad.

siderolite (sī′də rə līt′), *n.* a meteorite of roughly equal proportions of metallic iron and stony matter.

siderosis (sī′də rō′sĭs), *n. Pathol.* a disease of the lungs due to inhaling iron or other metallic particles. **—siderotic** (sĭd′ə rŏt′ĭk), *adj.*

siderostat (sĭd′ə rō stăt′), *n. Astron.* a device attached to an astronomical telescope which, by rotating the reflecting surface to correct for the earth's rotation, enables the instrument to reflect a portion of the sky in a fixed direction. **—siderostatic** (sĭd′ə rō stăt′ĭk), *adj.*

side-saddle (sīd′săd′l), *n.* **1.** a saddle on which the rider sits with both feet on the same (usually the left) side of the horse: used chiefly by women. *—adv.* **2.** seated on or as on a side-saddle.

sideshow (sīd′shō′), *n.* **1.** a minor show or exhibition in connection with a principal one as at a fair, circus, or the like. **2.** any subordinate event or matter.

sideslip (sīd′slĭp′), *v.,* **-slipped, -slipping,** *n.* *—v.i.* **1.** to slip to one side. **2.** (of an aeroplane when banked excessively) to slide sideways in a downward direction, towards the centre of the curve executed in turning. *—n.* **3.** the act of sideslipping.

sidesman (sīdz′mən), *n., pl.* **-men.** *C. of E.* a person elected to assist the churchwardens of a parish, esp. in the collection of alms.

side-splitting (sīd′splĭt′ĭng), *adj.* convulsively uproarious: *side-splitting farce.* **—side′-split′tingly,** *adv.*

sidestep (sīd′stĕp′), *v.,* **-stepped, -stepping,** *n.* *—v.i.* **1.** to step to one side, as in avoidance. **2.** to be evasive in reaching a decision, solving a problem, etc. *—v.t.* **3.** to avoid by stepping to one side. **4.** to evade (a decision, problem, etc.). *—n.* **5.** an act or instance of sidestepping. **—side′step′per,** *n.*

sidestick (sīd′stĭk′), *n. Printing.* a strip of wood on metal which is placed beside type either in galley or in a printing forme in order to hold the type in position.

side street, a separate, private, or obscure street; a bystreet.

sidestroke (sīd′strōk′), *n.* a swimming stroke in which the body is turned sideways in the water, the hands pull alternately, and the legs perform a scissors kick.

sideswipe (sīd′swīp′), *v.,* **-swiped, -swiping,** *n.* *—v.t.* **1.** to strike with a sweeping stroke or blow with or along the side. *—n.* **2.** such a stroke or blow.

sidetrack (sīd′trăk′), *v.t., v.i.* **1.** to move or distract from the main subject or course. *—n.* **2.** *U.S.* a railway siding. **3.** an act of sidetracking; a diversion; distraction.

side-valve engine (sīd′vălv′), a type of internal-combustion engine in which the valves are housed in the cylinder block and are operated from below.

sidewalk (sīd′wôk′), *n. U.S.* a pavement.

sidewall (sīd′wôl′), *n.* the part of a pneumatic tyre between the edge of the tread and the rim of the wheel.

sideward (sīd′wəd), *adj.* **1.** directed or moving towards one side. *—adv.* **2.** sidewards.

sidewards (sīd′wədz), *adv.* towards one side.

sideway (sīd′wā′), *n.* **1.** a byway. **2.** a passage, as at the side of a house. *—adj., adv.* **3.** *U.S.* sideways.

sideways (sīd′wāz′), *adv., adj.* **1.** with the side foremost. **2.** facing to the side. **3.** towards or from one side. Also, **sidewise** (sīd′wīz′).

side-wheel (sīd′wēl′), *adj.* having a paddle-wheel on each side, as a steamer. **—side′-wheel′er,** *n.*

side-whiskers (sīd′wĭs′kəz), *n.* sideboards. **—side′-whis′kered,** *adj.*

sidewinder (sīd′wīn′də), *n.* **1.** *U.S. Slang.* a disabling swinging blow from the side. **2.** the small species of rattlesnake, *Crotalus cerastes*, that moves in loose sand by throwing loops of the body forward.

Sidi-bel-Abbès (*Fr.* sē dē bĕl à bĕs′), *n.* a town in NW Algeria. 105,000 (1960).

Sidi Ifni (*Sp.* sē dē ēf′nē), a town in and the capital of Ifni. 13,770 (1963).

siding (sī′dĭng), *n.* **1.** a short branch off a railway track, often connected at both ends of the main-line track, and used for shunting or for loading, unloading, and storing goods trucks. **2.** *U.S.* the boarding, metal, or composition forming the sides of a timber building.

sidle (sī′dl), *v.*, **-dled, -dling,** *n.* —*v.i.* **1.** to move sideways or obliquely. **2.** to edge along furtively. —*n.* **3.** a sidling movement. [back-formation from *sideling* SIDELONG]

Sidney (sĭd′nĭ), *n.* **Sir Philip,** 1554–86, English poet, writer, statesman, and soldier. Also, **Sydney.**

Sidon (sī′dn), *n.* a city of ancient Phoenicia. Modern, **Saida.** See map under **Tyre.** —**Sidonian** (sī dō′nyən), *adj.*, *n.*

Sidra (sĭd′rə), *n.* **Gulf of,** a large, open gulf of the Mediterranean, on the N coast of Libya.

siècle (*Fr.* syĕ′kl), *n.* *French.* an age; a century; a generation. [F (in OF *secle*), t. L: m. *saeculum* generation]

siege (sēj), *n.*, *v.*, **sieged, sieging.** —*n.* **1.** the operation of reducing and capturing a fortified place by surrounding it, cutting off supplies, undermining, bringing guns to bear, bombing, and other offensive operations. **2.** any prolonged or persistent endeavour to overcome resistance. **3.** *Obs.* a seat. **4.** *Obs.* rank. **5.** *Obs.* a throne. **6. lay siege to,** to besiege. —*v.t.* **7.** to lay siege to; besiege. [ME, t. OF: m. *sege, siege,* ult. der. L *sedēre* sit]

—**Syn. 1.** SIEGE, BLOCKADE are terms for prevention of free movement to or from a place during wartime. SIEGE implies surrounding a city and cutting off its communications, and usually includes direct assaults on its defences. BLOCKADE is applied more often to operations by ships, which block all commerce and especially thereby cut off food and other supplies to defenders.

Siege Perilous, *Arthurian Legend.* a vacant seat at the Round Table, which could be filled only by the predestined finder of the Holy Grail, and was fatal to pretenders. [f. SIEGE (def. 3) + PERILOUS]

Siegfried (sēg′frēd; *Ger.* zēk′frēt), *n.* *German Legend.* the hero of the Nibelungenlied, a prince of a region on the lower Rhine. He captures the treasure of the Nibelungs, slays a dragon, and wins Brunhild for King Gunther. The hero of a cycle of operas by Wagner.

Siegfried line, a zone of fortifications in W Germany facing the Maginot line, constructed in the years preceding the invasion of France, 1940.

Siemens (sē′mənz; *Ger.* zē′məns), *n.* **1. Werner von** (*Ger.* vĕrn′ər fōn), 1816–92, German inventor. **2.** his brother, **Sir William** (*Karl Wilhelm Siemens*), 1823–83, British inventor, born in Germany.

Siena (sĭ ĕn′ə; *It.* syĕ′nȧ), *n.* a town in central Italy, in Tuscany: cathedral. 65,114 (1966). —**Sienese** (sĭə nēz′), *adj.*, *n.*

Sienkiewicz (*Pol.* shĕng kyĕ′vĭch), *n.* **Henryk** (*Pol.* hĕn′rĭk), 1846–1916, Polish novelist.

sienna (sĭ ĕn′ə), *n.* **1.** a ferruginous earth used as a yellowish brown pigment (**raw sienna**) or, after roasting in a furnace, as a reddish brown pigment (**burnt sienna**). **2.** the colour of such a pigment. [short for It. *terra di Sien(n)a* earth of Siena]

sierra (sĭ ĕ′rə), *n.* a chain of hills or mountains the peaks of which suggest the teeth of a saw. [t. Sp.: lit., saw, g. L *serra*]

Sierra Leone (sĭ ĕ′rə lĭ ōn′), an independent country in W Africa: member of the Commonwealth of Nations; formerly a British colony and protectorate. 2,183,000 pop. (1963); 27,925 sq. mi. *Cap.:* Freetown.

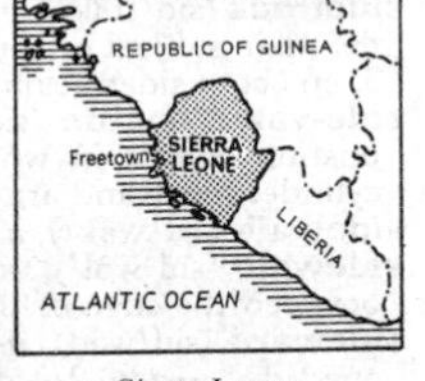

Sierra Leone

Sierra Madre (sĭ ĕ′rə mä′drĭ; *Sp.* syĕr′rȧ mȧ′drė), two parallel mountain chains in Mexico, bordering the central plateau on the E and W.

Sierra Nevada (sĭ ĕ′rə nə vä′də *for* 1; *Sp.* syĕr′rȧ nė bȧ′dȧ *for* 2), **1.** a mountain range in the U.S., in E California. Highest peak, Mt Whitney, 14,495 ft. **2.** a mountain range in S Spain. Highest peak, Mulhacén, 11,420 ft.

siesta (sĭ ĕs′tə), *n.* a midday or afternoon rest or nap, esp. as taken in Spain and other hot countries. [t. Sp., g. L *sexta* sixth (hour), midday]

sieur (*Fr.* syœr), *n.* an old French title of rank or respect for a man, now chiefly in French legal use.

sieve (sĭv), *n.*, *v.*, **sieved, sieving.** —*n.* **1.** an instrument, with a meshed or perforated bottom, used for separating coarse from fine parts of loose matter, for straining liquids, etc., esp. one with a circular frame and fine meshes or perforations. **2.** *Colloq.* one who cannot keep a secret. **3. have a head like a sieve,** to be very forgetful. —*v.t.* **4.** to put or force through a sieve; sift. [ME *sive,* OE *sife,* c. G *Sieb*]

sieve cell, *Bot.* an elongated, nucleated, food-conducting cell of the phloem of pteridophytes and gymnosperms with perforations in the walls (**sieve pores**) arranged in circumscribed areas (**sieve areas**) which afford cytoplasmic communication with similar adjacent cells.

sieve tube, *Bot.* a longitudinal, food-conducting, tube-like structure present in the phloem of angiosperms composed of **sieve tube elements** (cells containing cytoplasm but not nuclei) placed end to end with perforations (**sieve pores**) confined mostly to their ends (**sieve plates**) where they are in contact with each other.

sift (sĭft), *v.t.* **1.** to separate the coarse parts of (flour, ashes, etc.) with a sieve. **2.** to scatter by means of a sieve: *to sift sugar on to cake.* **3.** to separate by or as by a sieve. **4.** to examine closely. **5.** to question closely. —*v.i.* **6.** to use a sieve; sift something. **7.** to pass through, or as through a sieve. [ME *siften,* OE *siftan* (der. *sife* SIEVE), c. G *sichten*] —**sift′er,** *n.*

sig., **1.** signature. **2.** signor.

sigh (sī), *v.i.* **1.** to let out one's breath audibly, as from sorrow, weariness, relief, etc. **2.** to yearn or long. **3.** to make a sound suggesting a sigh: *sighing wind.* —*v.t.* **4.** to express with a sigh. **5.** to lament with sighing. —*n.* **6.** the act or sound of sighing. [ME *sighe(n),* back-formation from *sihte* sighed, past tense of ME *siken, sichen,* OE *sīcan,* of unknown orig.] —**sigh′er,** *n.*

sight (sīt), *n.* **1.** the power or faculty of seeing; vision. **2.** the act or fact of seeing. **3.** range of vision: *in sight of land.* **4.** a view; glimpse. **5.** mental view or regard. **6.** something seen or to be seen; spectacle: *the sights of the town.* **7.** *Colloq.* something that looks odd or unsightly: *she looks a sight in her new hat; after falling in the mud his clothes were a sight.* **8.** *Colloq.* a great display or number. **9.** *Colloq.* a great deal: *it's a sight better here than at the last hotel.* **10.** an observation taken with a surveying or other instrument. **11.** a device on or used with a surveying instrument, a firearm, etc., serving to guide the eye. **12.** *Obs.* insight. **13. at sight, a.** as soon as one sees a thing. **b.** *Com.* on presentation: *a bill of exchange payable at sight.* **14. catch sight of,** to glimpse; see, esp. briefly or momentarily. **15. know by sight,** to recognize (somebody or something) seen previously. **16. not by a long sight,** on no account; definitely not. —*v.t.* **17.** to get sight of: *to sight a ship.* **18.** to take a sight or observation of, esp. with an instrument. **19.** to direct by a sight or sights, as a firearm. **20.** to provide with sights, or adjust the sights of, as a gun. —*v.i.* **21.** to take a sight, as in shooting. [ME; OE *gesiht* (c. G *Gesicht*), *sihth,* der. *sēon* SEE[1]]

sight bill, a bill of exchange payable on presentation, without any days of grace. Also, *Chiefly U.S.,* **sight draft.**

sightless (sīt′lĭs), *adj.* **1.** blind. **2.** invisible.

sightly (sīt′lĭ), *adj.*, **-lier, -liest. 1.** pleasing to the sight. **2.** *U.S.* affording a fine view. —**sight′liness,** *n.*

sight-read (sīt′rēd′), *v.t.*, *v.i.*, **-read, -reading.** to play, read, or sing (music) from a written or printed score without previous rehearsal or study. —**sight′-read′er,** *n.*

sightscreen (sīt′skrēn′), *n.* *Cricket.* a white screen set on the boundary behind the wicket, as an aid to the batsman in sighting the ball.

sightseeing (sīt′sē′ĭng), *n.* the act of seeing objects or places of interest. —**sight′se′er,** *n.*

sigil (sĭj′ĭl), *n.* a seal; signet. [t. LL: m. s. *sigillum,* dim. of *signum* mark] —**sigillary** (sĭj′ĭ lə rĭ), *adj.*

Sigismund (sĭg′ĭs mənd; *Ger.* zē′gĭs mo͝ont), *n.* 1368–1437, Holy Roman emperor 1411–37.

sigma (sĭg′mə), *n.* the eighteenth letter (Σ, σ, ς = English S, s) of the Greek alphabet.

sigma pile, *Physics.* an assembly consisting of a neutron source and a moderator without any fissile material, used to study the properties of moderators.

sigmate (sĭg′mĭt, -māt), *adj.* having the form of the Greek sigma or the letter S.

sigmoid (sĭg′moid), *adj.* **1.** having the form of the letter C. **2.** having the form of the letter S. **3.** pertaining to the sigmoid flexure: *the sigmoid artery* (which supplies this flexure). Also, **sigmoi′dal.** [t. Gk: m. s. *sigmoeidés.* See -OID]

sigmoid flexure, **1.** *Zool.* an S-shaped curve consisting of several parts. **2.** *Anat.* the last curve of the large intestine before terminating in the rectum.

sign (sīn), *n.* **1.** a token; indication. **2.** a conventional mark, figure, or symbol used technically instead of the word or words which it represents, as an abbreviation. **3.** *Music.* a signature. **4.** *Maths.* the plus or minus sign. **5.** a motion or gesture intended to express or convey an idea. **6.** an inscribed board, space, etc., serving for information, advertisement, warning, etc., on a building,

along a street, or the like. 7. *Med.* the objective indications of a disease. 8. a trace; vestige. 9. an omen; portent. 10. *Astron.* any of the twelve divisions of the zodiac, each denoted by the name of a constellation or its symbol, and each (because of the precession of the equinoxes) now containing the constellation west of the one from which it took its name.
—*v.t.* **11.** to affix a signature to. **12.** to write as a signature: *to sign one's name.* **13.** to engage by written agreement: *to sign a new player.* **14.** to indicate; betoken. **15.** to communicate by a sign. **16.** to mark with a sign, esp. the sign of the cross. **17.** *Obs.* to direct or appoint by a sign. —*v.i.* **18.** to write one's signature, as a token of agreement, obligation, receipt, etc. **19.** to make a sign or signal. —*v.* **20.** Some special verb phrases are:
sign away, to dispose of by affixing one's signature to a document.
sign off, 1. to cease broadcasting a radio or television programme, as at the end of the day. 2. to withdraw from some responsibility, project, etc.
sign on, 1. to employ; hire. 2. to commit oneself to employment, as by signing a contract.
sign up, to enlist, as for the armed services.
[ME, t. OF: m. *signe,* t. L: m. *signum* mark, signal]
—**Syn.** 9. indication, hint. SIGN, OMEN, PORTENT name that which gives evidence of a future event. SIGN is a general word for whatever gives evidence of an event, past, present, or future: *dark clouds are a sign of rain or snow.* An OMEN is an augury or warning of things to come; formerly depending upon religious practices or beliefs, it is used only of the future, in general, as good or bad: *birds of evil omen.* PORTENT, limited, like OMEN, to prophecy of the future, may be used of a specific event, usually a misfortune: *portents of war.*

Signac (*Fr.* sē nyȧk′), *n.* **Paul** (*Fr.* pŏl), 1863–1935, French neo-impressionist painter.

signal (sĭg′nəl), *n., adj., v.,* **-nalled, -nalling** or (*U.S.*) **-naled, -naling.** —*n.* **1.** a gesture, act, light, etc., serving to warn, direct, command, or the like. **2.** anything agreed upon or understood as the occasion for concerted action. **3.** an act, event, or the like, which precipitates an action: *the signal for revolt.* **4.** a token; indication. **5.** *Radio, etc.* **a.** the impulses, waves, sounds, etc., transmitted or received. **b.** the wave which modulates the carrier wave. **6.** *Cards.* a play which reveals to one's partner a wish that he continue or discontinue the suit led. —*adj.* **7.** serving as a sign: *a signal flag.* **8.** conspicuous or notable: *a signal exploit.* —*v.t.* **9.** to make a signal to. **10.** to make known by a signal. —*v.i.* **11.** to make communication by a signal or signals. [ME, t. ML: s. *signāle,* prop. neut. adj., der. L *signum* SIGN] —**sig′naller,** *n.*

signal box, a raised cabin above a railway line, from which railway signals, points, etc., are worked.

signal generator, *Electronics.* a device which generates artificial signals to test electronic equipment.

signalize (sĭg′nə līz′), *v.t.,* **-lized, -lizing. 1.** to make notable. **2.** to point out particularly. Also, **signalise.**

signally (sĭg′nə lĭ), *adv.* conspicuously; notably.

signalman (sĭg′nəl mən), *n., pl.* **-men. 1.** a man employed to operate railway signals. **2.** a serving soldier of the Royal Corps of Signals whose duty is to operate communications instruments, lay lines of communications, etc.

signatory (sĭg′nə tə rĭ, -trĭ), *adj., n., pl.* **-ries.** —*adj.* **1.** that has signed, or has joined in signing, a document: *the signatory powers to a treaty.* —*n.* **2.** a signer, or one of the signers, of a document, as a treaty.

signature (sĭg′nĭ chə), *n.* **1.** a person's name, or a mark representing it, as signed or written by himself or by deputy, as in subscribing a letter or other document. **2.** the act of signing a document. **3.** *Music.* a sign or set of signs at the beginning of a stave to indicate the key or the time of a piece. **4.** a signature tune. **5.** *Pharm.* that part of a prescription which gives the directions to be marked on the container of the medicine. **6.** *Print.* **a.** a letter or other symbol generally placed by the printer at the foot of the first page of every section to guide the binder in arranging the sections in sequence. **b.** a sheet thus marked. **c.** a printed sheet folded to form a section of a book. [t. ML: m. s. *signātūra*]

signature tune, *Television, Radio, etc.* a song or musical arrangement which regularly identifies a programme, entertainer, etc.

signboard (sīn′bôd′), *n.* a board bearing an inscription, advertisement, or the like.

sign digit, *Computers.* a zero or figure one preceding a number stored in a computer to show whether the number is positive or negative.

signer (sī′nə), *n.* **1.** one who signs. **2.** one who writes his name, as in token of agreement, etc.

signet (sĭg′nĭt), *n.* **1.** a small seal, as in a finger ring. **2.** a small official seal. **3.** an impression made by or as if by a signet. —*v.t.* **4.** to stamp or mark with a signet. [ME, t. ML: s. *signētum,* der. L *signum* SIGN]

signet ring, a finger ring containing a small seal, one's initials, or the like.

significance (sĭg nĭf′ĭ kəns), *n.* **1.** importance; consequence. **2.** meaning; import. **3.** the quality of being significant or having a meaning. Also, **signif′icancy.** —**Syn. 2.** See **meaning.**

significant (sĭg nĭf′ĭ kənt), *adj.* **1.** important; of consequence. **2.** expressing a meaning; indicative. **3.** having a special or covert meaning; suggestive. —*n.* **4.** *Archaic.* something significant; a sign. [t. L: s. *significans,* ppr., signifying] —**signif′icantly,** *adv.* —**Syn. 2.** See **expressive.**

significant figures, *Maths.* the digits in a number excluding the zeros after an integral number or before a decimal fraction (except those added to signify accuracy): in 0·0352 and in 35,200 the significant figures are 352.

signification (sĭg′nĭ fĭ kā′shən), *n.* **1.** meaning; import; sense. **2.** the act or fact of signifying; indication.

significative (sĭg nĭf′ĭ kə tĭv), *adj.* **1.** serving to signify. **2.** significant; suggestive.

signify (sĭg′nĭ fī′), *v.,* **-fied, -fying.** —*v.t.* **1.** to make known by signs, speech, or action. **2.** to be a sign of; mean; portend. —*v.i.* **3.** to be of importance or consequence. [ME *signefie(n),* t. L: m. *significāre* show by signs] —**sig′nifi′er,** *n.* —**Syn. 2.** represent, indicate, denote.

sign language, a substitute for speech using gestures, as the methods used by deaf-mutes, between speakers of different languages, etc.

sign manual, *pl.* **signs manual.** a signature, esp. that of a sovereign or official on a public document.

signor (sē′nyô; *It.* sēn nyȯr′), *n., pl.* **-nori** (*It.* -rē). *Italian.* **1.** Mr; sir. **2.** a gentleman; an aristocrat.

signora (sē nyô′rə; *It.* sēn nyȯ′rȧ), *n., pl.* **-re** (*It.* -rė). *Italian.* **1.** Mrs; Madam. **2.** lady; gentlewoman. [It., fem., der. *signore.* See SIGNORE]

signore (sē nyô′rĭ; *It.* sēn nyȯ′rė), *n., pl.* **-ri** (*It.* -rē). *Italian.* **1.** gentleman. **2.** Mr; sir. [It., g. L *senior* SENIOR]

signorina (sē′nyô rē′nə; *It.* sēn nyȯ rē′nȧ), *n., pl.* **-ne** (*It.* -nė). *Italian.* **1.** Miss. **2.** young lady. [It., dim. of *signora* SIGNORA]

signorino (sē′nyô rē′nō; *It.* sēn nyȯ rē′nȯ), *n., pl.* **-ni** (*It.* -nē). *Italian.* young sir or master (used as a title of respect). [It., dim. of *signore* SIGNOR]

signory (sē′nyə rĭ), *n., pl.* **-ries.** seigniory.

signpost (sīn′pōst′), *n.* a post by the roadside or at an intersection bearing a sign for the guidance of travellers.

sign-writer (sīn′rī′tə), *n.* one who designs and produces signs, as for shops, public houses, etc. —**sign′-writ′ing,** *n.*

Sigurd (sĭg′ōōəd; *Ger.* zē′gōōrt), *n.* (in the Poetic Edda and the Volsunga Saga) the Scandinavian counterpart of the Siegfried of the Nibelungenlied.

Sikandarabad (sĭ kŭn′də rə băd′), *n.* Secunderabad.

Sikang (shē′kăng′), *n.* a province in W China; now part of Szechwan.

Sikh (sēk), *n.* **1.** a member of a religious sect founded near Lahore in NW India by a Hindu reformer. —*adj.* **2.** of or pertaining to the Sikhs or Sikhism. [t. Hind.: lit., disciple]

Sikhism (sē′kĭz′əm), *n.* the religious system and practices of the Sikhs. Starting in the 16th century as an attempt to effect a peaceful harmony of Hinduism and Islam in India, Sikhism has branched off into a new independent religion.

Si-kiang (sē′kyăng′, shē′-), *n.* Si.

Sikkim (sĭk′ĭm), *n.* a state in the Himalayas, a protectorate of the Indian government, between Nepal and Bhutan. 162,189 pop. (1961); 2818 sq. mi. *Cap.:* Gangtok. —**Sikkimese** (sĭk′ĭm ēz′), *adj., n.*

Sikorsky (sĭ kô′skĭ), *n.* **Igor** (ē′gô), born 1889, U.S. aeronautical engineer, born in Russia.

silage (sī′lĭj), *n.* fodder preserved in a silo; ensilage. [f. SILO + -AGE modelled on ENSILAGE]

silane (sĭl′ān), *n.* *Chem.* any one of a group of silicon hydrides with the general formula, Si_nH_{2n+2}.

sild (sĭld), *n.* a young herring. [t. Norw.]

silenaceous (sī′lĭ nā′shəs), *adj.* caryophyllaceous.

silence (sī′ləns), *n., v.,* **-lenced, -lencing,** *interj.* —*n.* **1.** absence of any sound or noise; stillness. **2.** the state or fact of being silent; muteness. **3.** omission of mention: *to pass over a matter in silence.* **4.** oblivion. **5.** secrecy. —*v.t.* **6.** to put or bring to silence; still. **7.** to put to rest (doubts, etc.); quiet. **8.** *Mil.* to still (enemy guns, etc.), as by a more effective fire. —*interj.* **9.** be silent! [ME, t. OF, t. L: m. s. *silentium*]

silencer (sī′lən sə), *n.* **1.** one who or that which silences. **2.** an expansion chamber fitted to the exhaust pipe of an internal-combustion engine to reduce the noise made by the exhaust gases. **3.** a device for deadening the report of a firearm.

silent (sī′lənt), *adj.* **1.** making no sound; quiet; still. **2.** refraining from speech. **3.** speechless; mute. **4.** taciturn; reticent. **5.** characterized by absence of speech or sound: *a silent prayer; a silent film.* **6.** tacit: *a silent assent.* **7.** omitting mention of something, as in a narrative. **8.** inactive or quiescent, as a volcano. **9.** not sounded or pronounced: *a silent letter*, such as 'b' in 'doubt'. [t. L: s. *silens*, ppr., being silent] **—si′lently,** *adv.* **—si′lentness,** *n.* **—Syn. 1.** See **still**[1]. **—Ant. 1.** noisy. **2.** talkative, loquacious.

silent partner, *Chiefly U.S.* a sleeping partner.

Silenus (sī lē′nəs), *n., pl.* **-ni** (-nī) *for 2. Gk Myth.* **1.** the foster father of Dionysus, and leader of the satyrs. **2.** (*l.c.*) a satyr.

silesia (sī lē′shyə), *n.* a lightweight, smooth-finished, twilled, cotton fabric, used for linings, originally made in Silesia.

Silesia (sī lē′shyə), *n.* a region in central Europe: formerly divided between Germany (the largest portion), Poland, and Czechoslovakia; by provision of the Potsdam agreement (1945) the greater part of German Silesia is now in Poland; rich deposits of coal, iron, and other minerals. German, **Schlesien.** Polish, **Śląsk.** Czech, **Slezsko.** **—Sile′sian,** *adj., n.*

silhouette (sĭl′o͞o ĕt′), *n., v.,* **-etted, -etting.** **—***n.* **1.** an outline drawing, uniformly filled in with black, like a shadow. **2.** a dark image outlined against a lighter background. **—***v.t.* **3.** to show in, or as in, a silhouette. [named after Etienne de *Silhouette*, 1709–67, French author and politician]

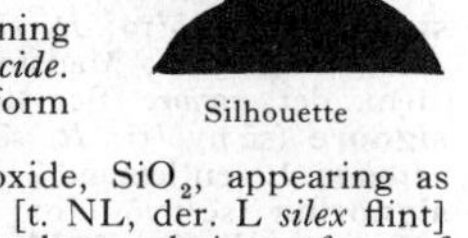
Silhouette

silic-, a word element meaning 'flint', 'silica', 'silicon', as in *silicide.* Also, **silici-, silico-.** [comb. form repr. L *silex* flint]

silica (sĭl′ĭ kə), *n.* silicon dioxide, SiO_2, appearing as quartz, sand, flint, and agate. [t. NL, der. L *silex* flint]

silica gel, *Chem.* a highly absorbent gelatinous form of silica, used as a drying agent and catalyst support.

silica glass, a vitreous material consisting almost entirely of silica. Also, **quartz glass, vitreous silica, fused silica.**

silicane (sĭl′ĭ kān′), *n. Chem.* a gas formed by the action of hydrochloric acid on magnesium silicide, SiH_4; silicomethane.

silicate (sĭl′ĭ kĭt, -kāt′), *n. Chem.* any salt derived from the silicic acids or from silica.

siliceous (sĭ lĭsh′əs), *adj.* **1.** containing, consisting of, or resembling silica. **2.** growing in soil rich in silica. Also, **silicious.** [t. L: m. *siliceus* of flint or limestone]

silicic (sĭ lĭs′ĭk), *adj. Chem.* **1.** containing silicon. **2.** of or pertaining to silica or acids derived from it.

silicic acid, any of certain acids formed when alkaline silicates are treated with acids. Amorphous gelatinous masses, they dissociate readily into silica and water.

silicide (sĭl′ĭ sīd′), *n. Chem.* a compound, usually of two elements only, one of which is silicon.

silicified wood (sĭ lĭs′ĭ fīd′), wood which has been changed into quartz by a replacement of the cellular structure of the wood by siliceous waters.

silicify (sĭ lĭs′ĭ fī′), *v.t., v.i.,* **-fied, -fying.** to convert or be converted into silica. **—silic′ifica′tion,** *n.*

silicium (sĭ lĭs′ĭ əm), *n. Chem., Obs.* silicon. [NL, f. *silic-* SILIC- + *-ium* -IUM]

silico-, var. of **silic-,** before consonants.

silicon (sĭl′ĭ kən), *n. Chem.* a non-metallic element, having amorphous and crystalline forms, occurring in the combined state in minerals and rocks and constituting more than one fourth of the earth's crust; used in steel-making, etc. *Symbol:* Si; *at. wt:* 28·086; *at. no.:* 14; *sp. gr.:* 2·4 at 20°C. [f. SILIC- + *-on*, modelled on BORON, CARBON]

silicon carbide, *Chem.* a very hard crystalline compound, SiC, made by fusing carbon and sand, used as an abrasive, refractory, and an electrical resistance; carbon silicide.

silicone (sĭl′ĭ kōn′), *n. Chem.* any of a number of compounds made by substituting silicon for carbon in an organic substance, and characterized by greater stability and resistance to extremes of temperature than the parent substance. Among the silicones are oils, greases, resins, and a group of synthetic rubbers. [f. SILIC- + -ONE]

silicosis (sĭl′ĭ kō′sĭs), *n. Pathol.* a disease of the lungs due to inhaling siliceous particles, as by stonecutters. [f. SILIC- + -OSIS]

silicule (sĭl′ĭ kyo͞ol′), *n. Bot.* a short siliqua. Also, **silicle** (sĭl′ĭ kl). [t. L: m. *silicula*, dim. of *siliqua* pod]

siliculose (sĭ lĭk′yo͝o lōs′), *adj. Bot.* **1.** bearing silicules. **2.** having the form or appearance of a silicule.

siliqua (sĭ lē′kwə, sĭl′ĭ kwə), *n., pl.* **-quae** (-kwē), **-quas.** *Bot.* the characteristic, elongated, dry dehiscent fruit of cruciferous plants in which the loculus is divided by a false septum or replum. Also, **silique** (sĭ lēk′, sĭl′ĭk). [t. L: pod]

Siliquae A, Charlock, *Sinapis arvensis;* B, Black mustard, *Brassica nigra*

siliquose (sĭl′ĭ kwōs′), *adj.* **1.** bearing siliquae. **2.** resembling a siliqua or silicule. Also, **siliquous** (sĭl′ĭ kwəs).

silk (sĭlk), *n.* **1.** the fine, soft, lustrous fibre obtained from the cocoon of the silkworm. **2.** thread made of this fibre. **3.** cloth made of this fibre. **4.** a garment of this cloth. **5.** the gown of such material, worn distinctively by a Queen's or King's Counsel at the bar. **6.** any fibre or filamentous matter resembling silk. **7.** the hair-like styles on an ear of maize. **8.** *Colloq.* a Queen's or King's Counsel. **9. to take silk,** to become a Queen's or King's Counsel. **—***adj.* **10.** made of silk. **11.** resembling silk; silky. **12.** of or pertaining to silk. **—***v.i.* **13.** *U.S.* (of corn) to be in the course of forming silk. **—***v.t.* **14.** to clothe or cover with silk. [ME; OE *sioloc, seoloc* (c. Icel. *silki*), t. Baltic or Slavic. Cf. Prussian *silkas*, Russian *sheolk*]

silk cotton, the silky covering of the seeds of certain tropical trees of the family *Bombacaceae*, used for stuffing cushions, etc. See **kapok.**

silk-cotton tree, any of several trees of the family *Bombacaceae*, having seeds surrounded by silk cotton, esp. *Ceiba pentandra*, from which kapok is obtained.

silken (sĭl′kən), *adj.* **1.** made of silk. **2.** like silk. **3.** smooth; soft. **4.** clad in silk. **5.** elegant; luxurious.

silks (sĭlks), *n.pl.* the shirt and cap of a jockey worn in a race.

silk-screen (sĭlk′skrēn′), *n.* a stencil process using fine cloths that have been painted with an impermeable coating except in areas where colour is to be forced through on to paper, etc.

silk-stocking (sĭlk′stŏk′ĭng), *adj.* **1.** luxurious; aristocratic. **—***n.* **2.** a person of the luxurious class; an aristocrat.

silkweed (sĭlk′wēd′), *n.* any milkweed of the family *Asclepiadaceae*, so called from the silky down in the pod.

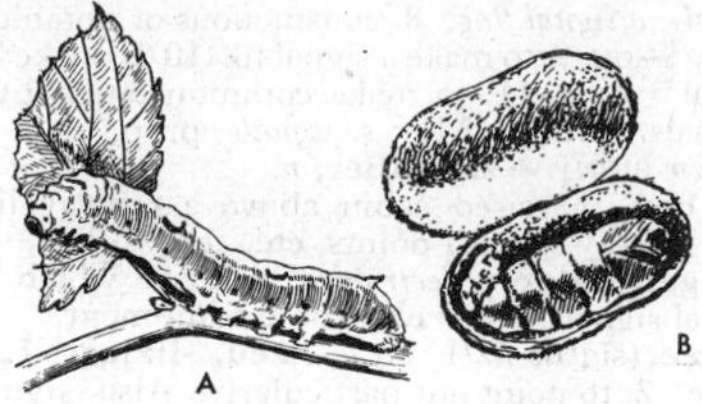

A, Silkworm, *Bombyx mori;* B, Section of cocoon showing pupa

silkworm (sĭlk′wûm′), *n.* the caterpillar of any moth of the families *Bombycidae* and *Saturniidae*, which spins a fine, soft filament (silk) to form a cocoon, in which it is enclosed while in the pupal stage, esp. the **Chinese silkworm,** *Bombyx mori.* [ME *sylkewyrme*, OE *seolcwyrm.* See SILK, WORM]

silky (sĭl′kĭ), *adj.,* **-kier, -kiest.** **1.** of or like silk; lustrous; smooth. **2.** *Bot.* covered with fine, soft, closely set hairs, as a leaf. **—silk′ily,** *adv.* **—silk′iness,** *n.*

silky oak, any of several Australian trees of the genus *Grevillea*, esp. *G. robusta*, having bright orange, red, or white flowers.

sill (sĭl), *n.* **1.** a horizontal timber, block, or the like, serving as a foundation of a wall, house, etc. **2.** the horizontal piece or member beneath a window, door, or other opening. **3.** *Geol.* a tabular body of intrusive igneous rock, ordinarily between beds of sedimentary rocks or layers of volcanic ejecta. [ME *sille*, OE *syl, syll(e)*, c. LG *süll*; akin to G *Schwelle*]

sillabub (sĭl′ə bŭb′), *n.* a dish made of milk or cream poured over wine, cider, or ale, sweetened and flavoured with spices, lemon rind, etc. Also, **syllabub.**

Sillanpaa (*Fin.* sĕl′läm pä), *n.* **Frans Eemil** (*Fin.* fränts-ĕ′mĕl), 1888–1964, Finnish author.

siller (sĭl′ə), *n. Scot.* silver.

sillimanite (sĭl′ĭ mə nīt′), *n.* fibrolite. [named after Benjamin *Silliman*, died 1864, U.S. geologist. See -ITE[1]]

silly (sĭl′ĭ), *adj.,* **-lier, -liest,** *n., pl.* **-lies.** **—***adj.* **1.** lacking good sense; foolish; stupid. **2.** absurd or ridiculous. **3.** *Colloq.* stunned. **4.** *Cricket.* (of a fielding position) close in to the batsman's wicket: *silly mid-off.* **5.** *Archaic.* simple-minded. **6.** *Obs.* simple; homely. **7.** *Obs.* weak; helpless. **—***n.* **8.** *Colloq.* a silly person. [var. of earlier *seely* happy, helpless, silly, ME *seli*, OE *sēlig* (Anglian), *sælig* (c. G *selig*), f. *sēl*, *sæl* happiness + *-ig* -Y[1]] —**sil′lily,** *adv.* —**sil′liness,** *n.* —**Syn. 1.** See **foolish.** —**Ant. 1.** sensible.

silo (sī′lō), *n., pl.* **-los,** *v.,* **-loed, -loing.** —*n.* **1.** an airproof tower-like structure in which fermenting green fodder is preserved for future use as silage. **2.** a pit or underground watertight space for storing grain, green feeds, etc. **3.** an underground launching site for a ballistic missile. —*v.t.* **4.** to put into or preserve in a silo. [t. Sp., g. L *sirus*, t. Gk: m. *sirós* pit to keep grain in]

Siloam (sī lō′əm, sī-), *n. Bible.* a pool at Jerusalem. John 9:7.

Silone (sĭ lō′nĭ; *It.* sē lô′nè), *n.* **Ignazio** (ĭg nät′sĭ ō′; *It.* ēn nyȧt′tsyò), born 1900, Italian writer.

siloxane (sĭ lŏk′sān), *n. Chem.* any of a group of compounds with the general formula R_2SiO.

silt (sĭlt), *n.* **1.** earthy matter, fine sand, or the like, carried by moving or running water and deposited as a sediment. —*v.i.* **2.** to become filled or choked up with silt. —*v.t.* **3.** to fill or choke up with silt. [ME *silte.* Cf. OE *unsylt* unsalted, G *Sülze* saltpan] —**silt′y,** *adj.*

siltstone (sĭlt′stōn′), *n. Geol.* a consolidated silt; a fine sandstone.

silundum (sĭ lŭn′dəm), *n. U.S.* silicon carbide. [b. SILICON and CARBORUNDUM]

Silures (sī lyŏŏə′rēz), *n.pl.* an ancient British people who lived chiefly in south-eastern Wales at the time of the Roman conquest and were in active resistance to it about A.D. 48.

Silurian (sī lyŏŏə′rĭ ən), *adj.* **1.** of or pertaining to the Silures or their country. **2.** *Geol.* pertaining to an early Palaeozoic geological period or system of rocks. —*n.* **3.** *Geol.* the Silurian period or system of rocks.

silurid (sī lyŏŏə′rĭd), *n.* **1.** any of the *Siluridae*, or catfish family, comprising chiefly freshwater fishes with long barbels and without true scales, and including many species used for food. —*adj.* **2.** belonging to or pertaining to the *Siluridae.* Also, **siluroid** (sī lyŏŏə′roid). [t. NL: s. *Silūridae*, der. L *silūrus* a river-fish, t. Gk: m. *sílouros*]

silvan (sĭl′vən), *adj., n.* sylvan. [t. L: s. *silvānus*, der. *silva* wood. See -AN]

Silvanus (sĭl vā′nəs), *n.* a Roman god of forests and fields.

silver (sĭl′və), *n.* **1.** *Chem.* a white ductile metallic element, used for making mirrors, coins, ornaments, table utensils, etc. *Symbol:* Ag (for argentum); *at. wt:* 107·87; *at. no.:* 47; *sp. gr.:* 10·5 at 20°C. **2.** coin made of silver or of a metal resembling silver; money. **3.** silverware; table articles made of or plated with silver. **4.** something resembling this metal in colour, lustre, etc. **5.** a lustrous greyish white or whitish grey; colour of metallic silver. —*adj.* **6.** consisting or made of silver; plated with silver. **7.** of or pertaining to silver. **8.** (of coins) made of a metal or alloy resembling silver, as cupronickel. **9.** producing or yielding silver. **10.** resembling silver: *the silver waves.* **11.** having the colour silver, or tinted with silver: *a silver dress; silver blue.* **12.** clear and soft: *silver sounds.* **13.** eloquent; persuasive: *a silver tongue.* **14.** indicating the 25th event of a series, as a wedding anniversary. —*v.t.* **15.** to coat with silver or some silver-like substance. **16.** to give a silvery colour to. —*v.i.* **17.** to become a silver colour. [ME; OE *siolfor*, c. G *Silber*] —**sil′verer,** *n.* —**sil′ver-like′,** *adj.*

silver age, (in Greek and Roman mythology) the second of the ages of mankind, inferior to the first or golden age, and a period of luxury and impiety.

silverbell (sĭl′və bĕl′), *n.* any of the handsome North American shrubs or small trees, with white bell-shaped flowers, constituting the styracaceous genus *Halesia.* Also, **silverbell tree.**

silver birch, 1. a widespread, Old World, betulaceous tree, *Betula pendula*, having a whitish papery bark. **2.** any other member of the genus *Betula* with a similar bark.

silver bromide, *Chem.* a light-sensitive compound, AgBr, which is of basic importance in photography. It is obtained from the reaction of a bromide with a silver salt.

silver chloride, *Chem.* a light-sensitive compound, AgCl, used in sensitizing photographic paper.

silver fir, a pinaceous tree with leaves whitish beneath, *Abies alba*, a native of S and central Europe widely planted for ornament.

silverfish (sĭl′və fĭsh′), *n., pl.* **-fishes,** (*esp. collectively*) **-fish. 1.** a white or silvery goldfish, *Carassius auratus.* **2.** any of various other silvery fishes, as the tarpon, or shiner. **3.** a food fish of southern African coasts, *Polysteganus argyrozona*, of the bream family. **4.** any of certain small, wingless, thysanuran insects (genus *Lepisma*) damaging to books, wallpaper, etc.

silver fluoride, *Chem.* a brownish water-soluble solid, AgF, used as a disinfectant.

silver foil, silver paper.

silver fox, the common red fox of North America, *Vulpes fulva*, in a melanistic variation; in which the pelage is black, overlaid with silvery grey ends of the longer hairs.

silver frost, glaze ice.

silver glance, argentite.

silvering (sĭl′və rĭng), *n.* **1.** the act or process of coating with silver or a substance resembling silver. **2.** the coating thus applied.

silver iodide, *Chem.* a light-sensitive compound, AgI, used in photography and medicine.

silverly (sĭl′və lĭ), *adv.* with a silvery appearance or sound.

silver maple, a large North American tree, *Acer saccharinum*, frequently cultivated for its attractive foliage.

silvern (sĭl′vən), *adj. Archaic.* of or like silver.

silver nitrate, *Chem.* a salt, $AgNO_3$, obtained by treating silver with nitric acid, and appearing in commerce as colourless crystals or white fused or moulded masses, used in photography, medicine, etc.

silver paper, a thin sheet of silver, or silver-like metal (esp. aluminium), used for wrapping foods, tobaccos, and other domestic articles. Also, **silver foil.**

silver plate, 1. a thin silver coating deposited on the surface of another metal, usually by electrolysis. **2.** silver-plated tableware.

silver-plate (sĭl′və plāt′), *v.t.,* **-plated, -plating.** to deposit a layer of silver on another (baser) metal, usually by electrolysis.

silverside (sĭl′və sīd′), *n.* a cut of beef from the topside, below the aitchbone and above the leg, usually boiled or pickled.

silversmith (sĭl′və smĭth′), *n.* one who makes and repairs articles of silver.

silver standard, a monetary system with silver of specified weight and fineness as the unit of value.

silver-tongued (sĭl′və tŭngd′), *adj.* eloquent; persuasive.

silver tree, a small proteaceous tree, *Leucadendron argenteum*, having hairy leaves with a silvery sheen, indigenous to the Cape peninsula in the Republic of South Africa.

silverware (sĭl′və wĕə′), *n.* articles, esp. for table use, made of silver.

silver wedding, the 25th anniversary of a wedding.

silverweed (sĭl′və wēd′), *n.* a rosaceous plant, *Potentilla anserina*, with pinnate leaves having on the underside a silvery pubescence.

silvery (sĭl′və rĭ), *adj.* **1.** resembling silver; of a lustrous greyish white colour. **2.** having a clear, ringing sound like that of silver. **3.** containing or covered with silver. —**sil′veriness,** *n.*

silviculture (sĭl′vĭ kŭl′chə), *n.* the cultivation of forest trees; forestry. Also, **sylviculture.** [f. L *silvi-* (comb. form of *silva* wood) + CULTURE] —**sil′vicul′tural,** *adj.* —**sil′vicul′turist,** *n.*

s'il vous plaît (*Fr.* sēl vōō plĕ′), *French.* please.

sima (sī′mə), *n.* the denser layer of the lithosphere underlying the sial; it forms the floor of much of the oceans and is composed largely of silica and magnesia. [b. SI(LICA) + MA(GNESIA)]

simar (sĭ mä′), *n.* cymar. [t. F: m. *simarre*, t. It.: m. *zimarra* robe, cassock, t. Sp.: m. *zamarra* sheepskin, t. Basque: m. *zamar*]

simarouba (sĭm′ə rōō′bə), *n.* **1.** any of the trees of the simaroubaceous genus *Simaruba*, of tropical America, with pinnate leaves, a drupaceous fruit, and a root whose bark contains a tonic principle. **2.** the bark. Also, **simaruba.** [t. Carib]

simaroubaceous (sĭm′ə rōō bā′shəs), *adj.* belonging to the *Simarubaceae*, a family of trees and shrubs, mostly tropical, which includes the ailanthus, quassia, etc. Also, **simarubaceous.**

Simenon (*Fr.* sĕm nôɴ′), *n.* **Georges** (*Fr.* zhôrzh), born 1903, Belgian novelist.

Simeon (sĭm′ĭ ən), *n.* a devout man of Jerusalem who, recognizing the infant Jesus as the Christ, spoke the Nunc Dimittis. Luke 2:25–35.

Simferopol (*Russ.* sĭm fĭ rô′pəly), *n.* a city in the SW Soviet Union. 213,000 (est. 1965).

Simhath Torah (sĭm KHäth′ tô rä′; sĭm′KHäs tô′rä), the Jewish holiday of Rejoicing over the Law, on the ninth day of Tabernacles. Also, **Simchas′ Torah′.**

simian (sĭm′ĭ ən), *adj.* **1.** of or pertaining to an ape or monkey. **2.** characteristic of apes or monkeys. —*n.* **3.** an ape or monkey. [f. s. L *sīmia* ape + -AN]

similar (sĭm′ĭ lə), *adj.* **1.** having likeness or resemblance, esp. in a general way. **2.** *Geom.* (of figures) having the same shape; having corresponding sides proportional and corresponding angles equal. [f. s. L *similis* like + -AR[1]] —**sim′ilarly,** *adv.* —**Syn. 1.** See **same.**

similarity (sĭm′ĭ lă′rĭ tĭ), *n., pl.* **-ties. 1.** state of being similar; likeness. **2.** a point of resemblance. —**Syn. 1.** See **resemblance.**

simile (sĭm′ĭ lĭ), *n.* **1.** a figure of speech directly expressing a resemblance, in one or more points, of one thing to another, as *a man like an ox.* **2.** an instance of this figure, or a use of words exemplifying it. [ME, t. L, neut. of *similis* like]

similitude (sĭ mĭl′ĭ tyo͞od′), *n.* **1.** likeness; resemblance. **2.** a person or thing that is the like, match, or counterpart of another. **3.** semblance; image. **4.** a likening or comparison; a parable or allegory. [ME, t. L: m. *similitūdo*]

simious (sĭm′ĭ əs), *adj.* simian.

simitar (sĭm′ĭ tə), *n.* scimitar.

Simla (sĭm′lə), *n.* a town in N India, capital of Himachal Pradesh: the summer capital of India. 42,600 (1961).

simmer (sĭm′ə), *v.i.* **1.** (of food) to cook in a liquid just below the boiling point. **2.** to make a gentle murmuring sound, as liquids just below the boiling point. **3.** to be in a state of subdued activity, excitement, etc. **4. simmer down,** *Colloq.* to become calm or calmer. —*v.t.* **5.** to cook (food) in a liquid just below the boiling point. —*n.* **6.** state or process of simmering. [earlier *simber,* ME *simper*; orig. unknown] —**Syn. 3.** See **boil**[1].

simnel cake (sĭm′nəl), a rich fruit cake topped with a layer of almond paste. [*simnel* ME, t. OF: m. *simenel,* ult. der. L *simila.* See SEMOLINA]

Simon (sī′mən), *n.* **1.** Also, **Simon Peter.** the original name of Peter the apostle. Mark 3:16. **2.** a brother or relative of Jesus. Mark 6:3. **3.** a tanner of Joppa at whose house St Peter resided. Acts 10:6. **4.** (*Simon Magus*) a sorcerer of Samaria. Acts 8:9–24.

Simon (sī′mən), *n.* **Viscount John (Allsebrook),** 1873–1954, British statesman and lawyer.

simoniac (sĭ mō′nĭ ăk′), *n.* one who practises simony. —**simoniacal** (sī′mə nī′ə kl), *adj.* —**si′moni′acally,** *adv.*

Simonides (sī mŏn′ĭ dēz′), *n.* 556?–468? B.C., Greek lyric poet. Also, **Simonides of Ceos** (sā′ŏs).

Simon Legree (sī′mən lĭ grē′), **1.** the brutal slave dealer in *Uncle Tom's Cabin* by Harriet Beecher Stowe. **2.** any harsh, merciless master.

Simonov (*Russ.* sē′mə nəf), *n.* **Konstantin Mikhailovich** (*Russ.* kən stȧn tēn′ mĭ KHȧy′lə vĭch), born 1915, Soviet writer.

Simon-Pure (sī′mən pyo͞oə′), *adj.* real; genuine. [from *Simon Pure,* a Quaker in Mrs Centlivre's comedy, '*A Bold Stroke for a Wife*' (1718), who is impersonated by one of the other characters]

Simonstown (sī′mənz toun′), *n.* a town in the Republic of South Africa, in W Cape Province: naval base. 15,340 (est. 1963).

simony (sī′mə nĭ), *n.* **1.** making profit out of sacred things. **2.** the sin of buying or selling ecclesiastical preferments, benefices, etc. Also, **si′monism.** [ME *symonie,* t. ML: m. *simōnia,* der. SIMON (def. 4). See Acts 8:18–19] —**si′monist,** *n.*

simoom (sĭ mo͞om′), *n.* a hot, suffocating sand-laden wind of the deserts of Arabia, Syria, Africa, etc. Also, **simoon** (sĭ mo͞on′). [t. Ar.: m. *semūm,* der. *samm* poison]

simp (sĭmp), *n. Slang.* a fool. [for SIMPLETON]

simper (sĭm′pə), *v.i.* **1.** to smile in a silly, self-conscious way. —*v.t.* **2.** to say with a simper. —*n.* **3.** a silly, self-conscious smile. [orig. uncert. Cf. G *zimper* affected] —**sim′perer,** *n.* —**sim′peringly,** *adv.*

simple (sĭm′pl), *adj.,* **-pler, -plest,** *n.* —*adj.* **1.** easy to understand, deal with, use, etc.: *a simple matter, simple tools.* **2.** not elaborate or artificial: *a simple style.* **3.** not ornate or luxurious. **4.** unaffected; unassuming. **5.** not complex or complicated: *a simple design.* **6.** occurring or considered alone; mere; bare: *the simple truth or fact.* **7.** sincere; innocent. **8.** common or ordinary: *a simple soldier.* **9.** plain; unpretentious. **10.** humble or lowly. **11.** unimportant or insignificant. **12.** unlearned; ignorant. **13.** lacking mental acuteness or sense. **14.** *Chem.* **a.** composed of one substance or element: *a simple substance.* **b.** not mixed. **15.** *Bot.* not divided into parts: *a simple leaf* (one having only a single blade), *a simple stem* (one that does not branch). **16.** *Zool.* not compound: *a simple ascidian.* **17.** *Music.* single; uncompounded or without overtones: *simple note.* —*n.* **18.** an ignorant or foolish person. **19.** something simple, unmixed, or uncompounded. **20.** *Archaic.* a herb or plant used for medicinal purposes. **21.** *Archaic.* a person of humble condition. [ME, t. OF, t. L: m. *simplus* or *simplex*] —**sim′pleness,** *n.*

—**Syn. 9.** SIMPLE, HOMELY, PLAIN imply absence of adornment or embellishment. That which is SIMPLE is not elaborate or complex: *a simple type of dress.* HOMELY suggests a wholesome simplicity without artificial refinement or elegance, since it characterizes that which is comfortable and attractive: *a homely cottage.* That which is PLAIN has little or no adornment: *expensive but plain clothing.*

simple fraction, a ratio of two whole numbers.

simple fruit, a fruit formed from one pistil.

simple harmonic motion, *Maths.* a form of vibratory motion which may be represented by projecting on to the diameter of a circle the uniform motion of a point round its circumference. *Abbrev.*: S.H.M.

simple-hearted (sĭm′pl hä′tĭd), *adj.* sincere; open; frank.

simple interest, interest which is not compounded, that is, payable only on the principal amount of a debt.

simple machine, one of the six (sometimes more) elementary mechanisms: the lever, wheel and axle, pulley, screw, inclined plane, and wedge.

simple majority, majority (def. 3).

simple-minded (sĭm′pl mīn′dĭd), *adj.* **1.** artless; unsophisticated. **2.** lacking in mental acuteness or sense. **3.** mentally deficient. —**sim′ple-mind′edly,** *adv.* —**sim′ple-mind′edness,** *n.*

simple sentence, a sentence with only one clause.

simple time, *Music.* rhythm characterized by a metrical unit divisible by two.

simpleton (sĭm′pl tən), *n.* a foolish, ignorant, or half-witted person; fool. [f. SIMPLE + -TON]

simple vow. See **vow** (def. 4).

simplex (sĭm′plĕks), *adj.* simple; consisting of or characterized by a single element, action, or the like: *a simplex circuit* (in which one telephone call and one telegraph message are transmitted simultaneously over a single pair of wires). [t. L]

simplicidentate (sĭm′plĭ sĭ dĕn′tāt), *adj.* belonging or pertaining to the *Simplicidentata,* in which there is only one pair of upper incisor teeth, formerly regarded as a suborder or division of rodents (including all except the hares, rabbits, and pikas), but now regarded as a separate order, the *Lesomorpha.* [f. *simplici-* (comb. form of L *simplex* simple) + DENTATE]

simplicity (sĭm plĭs′ĭ tĭ), *n., pl.* **-ties. 1.** state or quality of being simple. **2.** freedom from complexity, intricacy, or division into parts. **3.** absence of luxury, pretentiousness, ornament, etc.; plainness. **4.** naturalness; sincerity; artlessness. **5.** lack of acuteness or shrewdness. [ME *symplicite,* t. L: m. s. *simplicitas*]

simplify (sĭm′plĭ fī′), *v.t.,* **-fied, -fying.** to make less complex or complicated; make plainer or easier. [t. F: m. s. *simplifier,* t. ML: m. *simplificāre.* See -FY] —**sim′plifica′tion,** *n.* —**sim′plifi′er,** *n.*

Simplon (sĭm′plŏn; *Fr.* săN plôN′), *n.* **1.** a mountain pass in S Switzerland, in the Lepontine Alps: crossed by a road constructed by Napoleon. 6592 ft high. **2.** a tunnel between Switzerland and Italy, NE of Simplon Pass. 12¼ mi. long.

simply (sĭm′plĭ), *adv.* **1.** in a simple manner. **2.** plainly; unaffectedly. **3.** artlessly. **4.** merely; only. **5.** unwisely; foolishly. **6.** absolutely: *simply irresistible.* [ME *simpleliche,* f. SIMPLE + *-liche* -LY]

Simpson Desert (sĭmp′sən), an area of arid country in central Australia. ab. 30,000 sq. mi.

simulacrum (sĭm′yo͞o lā′krəm), *n., pl.* **-cra** (-krə). **1.** a mere, faint, or unreal semblance. **2.** a representation. [t. L]

simulant (sĭm′yo͞o lənt), *adj.* **1.** simulating; imitating. **2.** *Biol.* similar in form or position (usually fol. by *of*). —*n.* **3.** one who or that which simulates.

simular (sĭm′yo͞o lə), *n.* **1.** one who or that which simulates. —*adj.* **2.** simulated; false. **3.** simulative (fol. by *of*). [f. SIMUL(ATE) + -AR[3]]

simulate (*v.* sĭm′yo͞o lāt′; *adj.* sĭm′yo͞o lĭt, -lāt′), *v.,* **-lated, -lating,** *adj.* —*v.t.* **1.** to make a pretence of. **2.** to assume or have the appearance of. **3.** *Maths.* to set up an analogue of (a system) in order to study its properties. —*adj.* **4.** *Archaic.* simulated. [t. L: m. s. *simulātus,* pp., made like] —**simulative** (sĭm′yo͞o lə tĭv), *adj.* —**sim′ulatively,** *adv.*

simulation (sĭm′yo͞o lā′shən), *n.* **1.** pretending; feigning. **2.** assumption of a particular appearance or form. **3.** *Maths.* the use of an analogue in order to study the properties of a system. **4.** *Psychiatry.* the conscious attempt to imitate some mental or physical disorder to escape punishment or to gain some desirable objective.

simulator (sĭm′yo͞o lā′tə), *n.* **1.** one who or that which simulates. **2.** a training or experimental device that simulates movement, flight, or some other condition.

simultaneous (sĭm′əl tā′nyəs), *adj.* existing, occurring, or operating at the same time: *simultaneous movements.* [t. ML: m. *simultāneus* simulated; meaning altered by assoc. with L *momentāneus* and L *simul* at the same time as] —**sim′ulta′neously,** *adv.* —**sim′ulta′neousness, simultaneity** (sĭm′əl tə nĭə′tĭ), *n.*

simultaneous equations, *Alg.* equations which must be satisfied by the same values of the unknowns.

sin[1] (sĭn), *n.*, *v.*, **sinned, sinning.** —*n.* **1.** transgression of divine law. **2.** an act regarded as such transgression, or any violation, esp. a wilful or deliberate one of some religious or moral principle. **3.** any serious transgression or offence. —*v.i.* **4.** to do a sinful act. **5.** to offend against a principle, standard, etc. —*v.t.* **6.** to do or perform sinfully. **7.** to bring, drive, etc., by sinning. [ME; OE *syn(n)*, akin to D *zonde*, G *Sünde* sin, L *sons* guilty] —**Syn. 3.** See **crime.**

sin[2] (sīn), *n. Maths.* sine[1].

Sinai (sī′nī ī′), *n.* **1.** Also, **Sinai Peninsula.** a peninsula in NE Egypt at the N end of the Red Sea between the Gulfs of Suez and Aqaba. ab. 230 mi. long. **2. Mount,** the mountain, of uncertain identity, from which the law was given to Moses. Ex. 19. —**Sinaitic** (sī′nĭ ĭt′ĭk), *adj.*

Sinatra (sĭ nä′trə), *n.* **Frank** (*Francis Albert*), born 1917, U.S. singer and actor.

since (sĭns), *adv.* **1.** from then till now (often preceded by *ever*). **2.** between a particular past time and the present; subsequently: *he at first refused, but has since consented.* **3.** ago; before now: *long since.* —*prep.* **4.** continuously from or counting from: *since noon.* **5.** between (a past time or event) and the present: *changes since the war.* —*conj.* **6.** in the period following the time when: *he has written once since he left.* **7.** continuously from or counting from the time when: *busy since he came.* **8.** because; inasmuch as. [ME *syns, synnes,* f. *syn, sine* (contracted var. of *sithen,* OE *siththan* then) + adv. suffix *-es*] —**Syn. 8.** See **because.**

sincere (sĭn sēə′), *adj.*, **-cerer, -cerest. 1.** free from any element of deceit, dissimulation, or duplicity. **2.** *Archaic.* pure; unmixed. **3.** *Obs.* sound; unimpaired. [t. L: m. s. *sincērus*] —**sincere′ly,** *adv.* —**sincere′ness,** *n.* —**Syn. 1.** candid, honest. See **earnest.**

sincerity (sĭn sĕ′rĭ tĭ), *n.*, *pl.* **-ties.** freedom from deceit, dissimulation, or duplicity; honesty. [t. L: m. s. *sincēritas*] —**Syn.** See **honour.**

sinciput (sĭn′sĭ pŭt′), *n. Anat.* the forepart of the skull. Cf. **occiput.** [t. L: half a head] —**sincipital** (sĭn sĭp′ĭ tl), *adj.*

Sinclair (sĭng klēə′, sĭng′klēə), *n.* **Upton Beall** (bĕl), 1878–1968, U.S. novelist, socialist, and reformer.

Sind (sĭnd), *n.* a former province in Pakistan, in the lower Indus valley; now part of West Pakistan. 48,136 sq. mi. *Cap.:* Karachi.

sine[1] (sīn), *n. Maths.* **1.** (of an angle) a trigonometric function equal to the ratio of the ordinate of the end point of the arc to the radius vector of this end point, the origin being at the centre of the circle on which the arc lies and the initial point of the arc being on the x-axis. *Abbrev.:* sin. **2.** (orig.) a perpendicular line drawn from one extremity of an arc of a circle to the diameter which passes through its other extremity. [t. L: m. *sinus* curve, used to translate Ar. *jaib* chord of an arc]

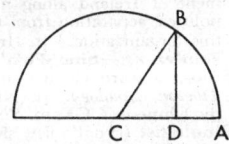

BD, Sine of arc AB; ratio of BD to CB, sine of angle ACB

sine[2] (sī′nĭ), *prep. Latin.* without.

sinecure (sī′nĭ kyo͝oə′), *n.* **1.** an office requiring little or no work, esp. one yielding profitable returns. **2.** an ecclesiastical benefice without cure of souls. [short for L phrase (*beneficium*) *sine cūrā,* with E *cure* substituted for *cūrā*] —**si′necur′ist,** *n.*

sine die (sī′nĭ dī′ē), *Latin.* without a day; without fixing a day for future action or meeting.

sine qua non (sī′nĭ kwā nŏn′), *Latin.* something essential; an indispensable condition. [L: lit., without which not]

sinew (sĭn′yo͞o), *n.* **1.** a tendon. **2.** that which supplies strength. **3.** strength; vigour. —*v.i.* **4.** to furnish with sinews; strengthen as by sinews. [ME; OE *sinu* (nom.), *sinuwe* (gen.), c. G *Sehne,* Icel. *sin*] —**sin′ewless,** *adj.*

sine wave, *Physics.* a periodic oscillation which can be represented geometrically by a curve having an equation of the form $y = a \sin x$.

sinewy (sĭn′yo͞o ĭ), *adj.* **1.** having strong sinews; strong. **2.** vigorous; forcible, as language, style, etc. **3.** like a sinew; tough; stringy. **4.** from or characteristic of strong sinews.

sinfonia (sĭn′fə nĭə′; *It.* sēn fô nē′ä), *n.*, *pl.* **-nie** (*It.* -nē′ĕ). *Music.* a symphony. [It.]

sinful (sĭn′fəl), *adj.* full of sin; wicked. —**sin′fully,** *adv.* —**sin′fulness,** *n.* —**Syn.** iniquitous, depraved, evil.

sing (sĭng), *v.*, **sang** or **sung, sung, singing,** *n.* —*v.i.* **1.** to utter words or sounds in succession with musical modulations of the voice. **2.** to execute a song or voice composition, as a professional singer. **3.** to produce melodious sounds, as certain birds, insects, etc. **4.** to compose verse; tell of something in verse. **5.** to admit of being sung, as verses. **6.** to give out a continuous ringing, whistling, murmuring, or other sound of musical quality, as a kettle coming to the boil, a brook, etc. **7.** to make a short ringing, whistling, or whizzing sound: *the bullet sang past his ear.* **8.** to have the sensation of a ringing or humming sound, as the ears. **9. sing out,** *Colloq.* to call out in a loud voice; shout. —*v.t.* **10.** to utter with musical modulations of the voice, as a song. **11.** to escort or accompany with singing. **12.** to proclaim enthusiastically: *to sing a person's praises.* **13.** to bring, send, put, etc., with or by singing: *to sing a child to sleep.* **14.** to chant or intone. —*n.* **15.** the act or performance of singing. **16.** a singing, ringing, or whistling sound, as of a bullet. [ME; OE *singan,* c. G *singen*] —**sing′able,** *adj.*

sing., singular.

Singan (sĕn′găn′), *n.* Sian.

Singapore (sĭng′gə pô′, sĭng′ə-), *n.* **1.** an island state in SE Asia, at the S end of the Malay Peninsula: an independent member of the Commonwealth of Nations, formerly part of the Malaysia federation. 1,844,200 pop. (est. 1964); 220 sq. mi. **2.** a seaport in this state: naval base. 1,079,400 (est. 1962).

Singapore

singe (sĭnj), *v.*, **singed, singeing,** *n.* —*v.t.* **1.** to burn superficially. **2.** to burn the ends or projections of (hair, etc.). **3.** to subject to flame in order to remove hair, etc. —*v.i.* **4.** to burn slightly; scorch. —*n.* **5.** a superficial burn. **6.** the act of singeing. [ME *senge,* OE *sencgan,* c. G *sengen*; akin to Icel. *sangr* singed, burnt] —**Syn. 1.** See **burn**[1].

singer (sĭng′ə), *n.* **1.** one who sings, esp. a trained or professional vocalist. **2.** a poet. **3.** a singing bird.

Singer (sĭng′ə), *n.* **Isaac Merrit,** 1811–75, U.S. sewing-machine inventor.

Singhalese (sĭng′gə lēz′), *adj.*, *n.*, *pl.* **-lese.** Sinhalese.

single (sĭng′gl), *adj.*, *v.*, **-gled, -gling,** *n.* —*adj.* **1.** one only; separate; individual. **2.** of or pertaining to one person, family, etc.: *a single room.* **3.** alone; solitary. **4.** unmarried. **5.** pertaining to the unmarried state. **6.** of one against one, as combat or fight. **7.** consisting of one part, element, or member. **8.** sincere; honest: *single devotion.* **9.** having but one set of petals, as a flower. **10.** *Archaic.* of only moderate strength or body, as ale, etc. **11.** (of the eye) seeing rightly. —*v.t.* **12.** to pick or choose out from others (usually fol. by *out*): *to single out a fact for special mention.* —*n.* **13.** something single or separate; a single one. **14.** a ticket for a train, bus, etc., valid for a one-way journey only. **15.** a gramophone record which contains only one short musical piece on each side. **16.** (*pl.*) *Tennis, etc.* a game or match played with one person on each side. **17.** *Golf.* a contest between two golfers (as differentiated from a *foursome*). **18.** *Cricket.* a hit for which one run is scored. [ME *sengle,* t. OF, g. L *singulus*] —**Syn. 1.** See **only.**

single-acting (sĭng′gl ăk′tĭng), *adj.* (of any reciprocating machine or implement) acting effectively in only one direction (distinguished from *double-acting*).

single-action (sĭng′gl ăk′shən), *adj.* (of a firearm) requiring cocking of the hammer before firing: *a single-action rifle.*

single-breasted (sĭng′gl brĕs′tĭd), *adj.* (of a coat, jacket, or the like) having a single row of buttons in the front for fastening. See **double-breasted.**

single cream, a thin cream containing a minimum of 18 per cent butterfat.

single-cross (sĭng′gl krŏs′), *n. Genetics.* the first-generation hybrid between two inbred lines.

single-decker (sĭng′gl dĕk′ə), *n.* a bus, tram, or the like without an upper deck. Cf. **double-decker.**

single entry, *Bookkeeping.* a simple accounting system in which each transaction is noted by only one entry.

single file, a line of persons or things arranged one behind the other; Indian file.

single-foot (sĭng′gl fo͝ot′), *n. U.S.* **1.** a gait of a horse; the rack. —*v.i.* **2.** (of a horse) to go at such a gait.

single-handed (sĭng′gl hăn′dĭd), *adj.* **1.** acting or working alone or unaided. **2.** performed or accomplished by one person alone. **3.** having, using, or requiring the use of but one hand or one person. —**sin′gle-hand′edly,** *adv.*

single-hearted (sĭng′gl hä′tĭd), *adj.* sincere in feeling or spirit; without duplicity. —**sin′gle-heart′edly,** *adv.*

single-minded (sĭng′gl mīn′dĭd), *adj.* **1.** having or showing undivided purpose. **2.** having or showing a sincere mind; steadfast. —**sin′gle-mind′edly,** *adv.* —**sin′gle-mind′edness,** *n.*

singleness (sĭng′gl nĭs), *n.* the state or quality of being single.

single-phase (sĭng′gl fāz′), *adj. Elect.* denoting or pertaining to a circuit having an alternating current of one phase.

singlestick (sĭng′gl stĭk′), *n.* **1.** a stick requiring the use of but one hand, used in fencing, etc. **2.** fencing, etc., with such a stick. **3.** any short, heavy stick.

singlet (sĭng′glĭt), *n.* **1.** a man's vest. **2.** a short, sleeveless garment worn with shorts, by athletes, boxers, etc. **3.** *Chem.* a chemical bond consisting of one shared electron.

singleton (sĭng′gl tən), *n.* **1.** something occurring singly. **2.** *Cards.* a card which is the only one of a suit in a hand. [f. SINGLE + -TON]

singly (sĭng′glĭ), *adv.* **1.** apart from others; separately. **2.** one at a time; as single units. **3.** single-handed. [ME *senglely.* See SINGLE, -LY]

Sing Sing (sĭng′ sĭng′), a prison in the U.S., in New York State. [orig. name of *Ossining,* town in New York State]

singsong (sĭng′sŏng′), *n.* **1.** verse, or a piece of verse, of a jingling or monotonous character. **2.** monotonous rhythmical cadence, tone, or sound. **3.** an informal gathering at which the company sing; community singing. —*adj.* **4.** characterized by a regular rising and falling intonation. **5.** monotonous in rhythm.

singular (sĭng′gyo͝o lə), *adj.* **1.** extraordinary; remarkable: *singular success.* **2.** unusual or strange; odd; eccentric. **3.** being the only one of the kind; unique. **4.** separate; individual. **5.** *Gram.* designating the number category that normally implies one person, thing, or collection, as English *man, thing, he, goes.* **6.** *Logic.* of or pertaining to a proposition that concerns one specified member of a class: *'Croesus was wealthy' is a singular proposition.* Cf. **particular** (def. 8); **universal** (def. 9). **7.** *Obs.* pertaining to an individual. **8.** *Obs.* private. —*n.* **9.** *Gram.* the singular number, or a form therein. [ME, t. L: s. *singulāris*] —**sin′gularly,** *adv.* —**sin′gularness,** *n.*

singularity (sĭng′gyo͝o lă′rĭ tĭ), *n., pl.* **-ties. 1.** the state, fact, or quality of being singular. **2.** something singular; a peculiarity.

singularize (sĭng′gyo͝o lə rīz′), *v.t.,* **-rized, -rizing.** to make singular. Also, **singularise.**

sinh (shĭn, sĭnsh), *n. Maths.* hyperbolic sine. See **hyperbolic functions.**

Sinhalese (sĭn′hə lēz′), *adj., n., pl.* **-lese.** —*adj.* **1.** pertaining to Ceylon, certain natives of Ceylon, or their language. —*n.* **2.** a member of the Sinhalese people or the Sinhalese people collectively. **3.** the Indic language spoken by the Sinhalese; the leading language of Ceylon. Also, **Singhalese.** [f. m. Skt *Sinhala* Ceylon + -ESE]

sinhalite (sĭn′ə līt′, sĭn′hə-), *n.* a mineral, magnesium aluminium borate, used as a gem. [f. SINHAL(ESE) + -ITE[1]]

Sinicism (sĭ′nĭ sĭz′əm, sĭn′ĭ-), *n.* Chinese methods or customs; a Chinese usage. [f. *Sinic* Chinese (t. ML: s. *Sinicus,* t. MGk: m. *Sinikós*) + -ISM]

Sining (sē′nĭng′), *n.* a city in NW China, the capital of Chinghai province. 150,000 (est. 1958).

sinister (sĭn′ĭs tə), *adj.* **1.** threatening or portending evil; ominous. **2.** bad; evil; base. **3.** unfortunate; disastrous; unfavourable. **4.** of or on the left side; left. **5.** *Her.* on the shield at the left of the bearer. See diag. under **escutcheon.** [ME, t. L; orig. referring to omens observed on the left (the unlucky) side] —**sin′isterly,** *adv.* —**sin′isterness,** *n.* —**sin′isterwise′,** *adv.*

sinistral (sĭn′ĭs trəl), *adj.* of or pertaining to the left side; left (opposed to *dextral*). —**sin′istrally,** *adv.*

sinistrorse (sĭn′ĭs trôs′, sĭn′ĭs trôs′), *adj.* rising spirally from right to left (from a point of view at the centre of the spiral), as a stem. [t. L: m. s. *sinistrorsus* towards the left] —**sin′istror′sal,** *adj.*

sinistrous (sĭn′ĭs trəs), *adj.* **1.** ill-omened; unlucky; disastrous. **2.** sinistral.

sink (sĭngk), *v.,* **sank** or **sunk, sunk** or **sunken, sinking,** *n.* —*v.i.* **1.** to descend gradually to a lower level, as water, flames, etc. **2.** to go down towards or below the horizon. **3.** to slope downwards, as ground. **4.** to go under or to the bottom; become submerged. **5.** to settle or fall gradually, as a heavy structure. **6.** to fall slowly from weakness, fatigue, etc. **7.** to pass gradually (into slumber, silence, oblivion, etc.). **8.** to pass or fall into some lower state, as of fortune, estimation, etc. **9.** to degenerate; decline. **10.** to fail in physical strength. **11.** to decrease in amount, extent, degree, etc., as value, prices, rates, etc. **12.** to become lower in tone or pitch, as sound. **13.** to enter or permeate the mind; become understood (fol. by *in, into,* etc.). **14.** to fall in; become hollow, as the cheeks. **15.** to be or become deeply absorbed in a mental state (usually fol. by *in* or *into*): *he sank into a state of deep depression.* **16.** to drop or fall (on to a seat, bed, etc.) through weariness or fatigue: *she put down her shopping and sank thankfully into the nearest armchair.* **17.** to sit or lie down in a slow, luxurious manner: *she sank back into the soft cushions and dreamed.* —*v.t.* **18.** to cause to fall or descend. **19.** to cause to sink or become submerged. **20.** to depress (a part, area, etc.), as by excavating. **21.** to put down or lay (a pipe, post, etc.), as into the ground. **22.** *Golf, Billiards, etc.* to cause (the ball) to run into a hole. **23.** to bring to a worse state; lower. **24.** to bring to ruin or perdition. **25.** to reduce in amount, extent, etc., as value or prices. **26.** to lower (the voice, etc.). **27.** to suppress; ignore; omit. **28.** to invest (money), now esp. unprofitably. **29.** to lose (money) in an unfortunate investment, etc. **30.** to make (a hole, shaft, well, etc.) by excavating or boring downwards; hollow out (any cavity). —*n.* **31.** a basin or receptacle, esp. in a kitchen, for receiving and carrying off dirty water. **32.** a low-lying area where waters collect or where they disappear by sinking down into the ground or by evaporation. **33.** a place of vice or corruption. **34.** a drain or sewer. **35.** *Physics.* any device, place, or part of a system in which energy is consumed or drained from the system. **36.** *Rare.* a cesspool. [ME; OE *sincan,* c. G *sinken*] —**sink′able,** *adj.*

sinkage (sĭng′kĭj), *n.* the act, process, or amount of sinking.

sinker (sĭng′kə), *n.* **1.** one who or that which sinks. **2.** one employed in sinking, as one who sinks shafts. **3.** a weight of lead, etc., for sinking a fishing line, fishing net, or the like in the water. **4.** *U.S. Slang.* a doughnut.

sinkhole (sĭngk′hōl′), *n.* **1.** Also, **pothole, swallow-hole.** a hole formed in soluble rock by the action of water, serving to conduct surface water to an underground passage. **2.** a low-lying area where waters collect; sink (def. 32).

Sinkiang (sĭn′kyăng′), *n.* an autonomous region in NW China, formerly a province. 5,640,000 pop. (est. 1953); 705,961 sq. mi. *Cap.:* Urumchi. Official name, **Sinkiang Uighur.**

sinking fund, a fund created to wipe out a debt by degrees, or to provide for the expiry of a lease.

sinless (sĭn′lĭs), *adj.* free from or without sin. —**sin′lessly,** *adv.* —**sin′lessness,** *n.*

sinner (sĭn′ə), *n.* one who sins; a transgressor.

sinnet (sĭn′ĭt), *n.* sennit.

Sinn Fein (shĭn′ fān′), **1.** a political organization in Ireland, founded about 1905, advocating the advancement of Ireland along national lines and its complete political separation from Great Britain. **2.** a member of this organization. [t. Irish: we ourselves] —**Sinn′-Fein′er,** *n.* —**Sinn′-Fein′ism,** *n.*

Sino-, a word element meaning 'Chinese', as in *Sino-Tibetan, Sinology.* [t. NL, comb. form repr. L *Sīnae* the Chinese (t. Gk: m. *Sînai*)]

Sinologist (sĭ nŏl′ə jĭst, sĭ-), *n.* one versed in Sinology. Also, **Sinologue** (sĭ′nə lŏg′, sĭn′ə-).

Sinology (sĭ nŏl′ə jĭ, sĭ-), *n.* the study of the language, literature, history, customs, etc., of China. —**Sinological** (sĭ′nə lŏj′ĭ kl, sĭn′ə-), *adj.*

Sino-Tibetan (sĭ′nō tĭ bĕt′n, sĭn′ō-), *n.* **1.** a linguistic family, including languages spoken from Tibet to the coast, from north China to Thailand: Tibeto-Burman, Chinese, and Thai. —*adj.* **2.** denoting or pertaining to this linguistic group.

sinter (sĭn′tə), *n.* **1.** siliceous or calcareous matter deposited by springs, as that formed around the vent of a geyser. **2.** *Metall.* the product of a sintering operation. —*v.t.* **3.** *Metall.* to bring about the agglomeration of particles of a metal (or other substance as glass or carbides) by heating, usually under pressure, to just below the melting point of the substance, or in the case of a mixture, to the melting point of the lowest melting constituent. [t. G: dross. See CINDER]

Sint Maarten (*Du.* sĭnt mär′tə), Dutch name of **St Martin.**

sinuate (sĭn′yo͞o ĭt, -āt′), *adj.* **1.** bent in and out; winding; sinuous. **2.** *Bot.* having the margin strongly or distinctly wavy, as a leaf. Also, **sin′uat′ed.** [t. L: m. s. *sinuātus,* pp., bent, wound] —**sin′uately,** *adv.*

Sinuate leaf

sinuation (sĭn′yo͞o ā′shən), *n.* a winding; a sinuosity.

Sinuiju (sĭ no͞o′ĭ jo͞o′), *n.* a city in W North Korea, the capital of North Pyongan province. 118,414 (1944).

sinuosity (sĭn′yo͞o ŏs′ĭ tĭ), *n., pl.* **-ties. 1.** (*often pl.*) a curve, bend, or turn. **2.** sinuous form or character.

sinuous (sĭn′yo͞o əs), *adj.* **1.** having many curves, bends, or turns; winding. **2.** indirect; devious.

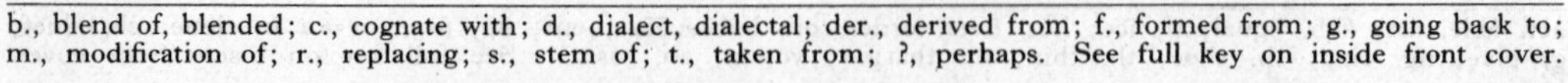

3. *Bot.* sinuate, as a leaf. [t. L: m. s. *sinuōsus*] —**sin'uousness,** *n.* —**sin'uously,** *adv.*

sinus (sī'nəs), *n., pl.* **-nuses.** **1.** a curve; bend. **2.** a curving part or recess. **3.** *Anat.* **a.** any of various cavities, recesses, or passages, as a hollow in a bone, or a reservoir or channel for venous blood. **b.** one of the hollow cavities in the skull connecting with the nasal cavities. **c.** an expanded area in a canal or tube. **4.** *Pathol.* a narrow, elongated abscess with a small orifice; a narrow passage leading to an abscess or the like. **5.** *Bot.* a small, rounded depression between two projecting lobes, as of a leaf. [t. L]

sinusitis (sī'nə sī'tĭs), *n. Pathol.* inflammation of a sinus or sinuses.

sinusoid (sī'nə soid'), *n.* **1.** *Maths.* a curve having an equation of the form $y = a \sin x$. **2.** *Zool.* a thin-walled, irregularly shaped space, usually containing venous blood, found in some vertebrates.

sinusoidal (sī'nə soi'dl), *adj.* **1.** of or pertaining to a sinusoid. **2.** *Physics.* having a characteristic which can be represented geometrically by a sine wave, as a *sinusoidal current.*

Sion (sī'ən), *n.* Zion.

-sion, a suffix having the same function as **-tion,** as in *compulsion.* [t. L: s. *-sio,* f. *-s,* final surd in pp. stem + *-io,* noun suffix. Cf. -TION]

Siouan (sōō'ən), *n.* **1.** a North American Indian linguistic family formerly widespread from Saskatchewan to the lower Mississippi and in the Virginia and Carolina piedmont, including Iowa, Osage, Dakota, Winnebago, Crow, and Catawba. —*adj.* **2.** denoting or pertaining to this linguistic group.

Sioux (sōō), *n., pl.* **Sioux** (sōō, sōōz), *adj.* —*n.* **1.** (*pl.*) the Dakota tribe proper of the Siouan linguistic family as distinguished from the Assiniboin tribe of the Dakota division of Siouan-speaking North American Indians. —*adj.* **2.** of or pertaining to this tribe.

sip (sĭp), *v.,* **sipped, sipping,** *n.* —*v.t.* **1.** to drink a little at a time. **2.** to drink from by sips. **3.** to take in; absorb. —*v.i.* **4.** to drink by sips. —*n.* **5.** an act of sipping. **6.** a small quantity taken by sipping. [ME *sippe,* OE *sypian* drink in] —**sip'per,** *n.* —**Syn. 1.** See **drink.**

siphon (sī'fən), *n.* **1.** a tube or conduit in the form of an inverted U through which liquid flows over the wall of a tank or reservoir to a lower elevation by atmospheric pressure. **2.** a soda siphon. **3.** a projecting tubular part of some animals, through which water enters or leaves the body. —*v.t., v.i.* **4.** to convey or pass through a siphon. Also, **syphon.** [t. L: s. *sīpho,* t. Gk: m. *sīphōn* pipe, tube] —**si'phonal, siphonic** (sī fŏn'ĭk), *adj.*

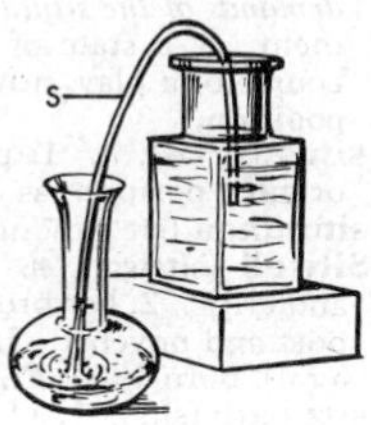

S, Siphon

siphonage (sī'fə nĭj), *n.* the action of a siphon.

siphono-, combining form meaning 'siphon', 'tube', as in *siphonostele.* [t. Gk, comb. form of *sīphōn*]

siphonophore (sī'fə nə fô', sī fŏn'ə fô'), *n.* any of the *Siphonophora,* an order of pelagic hydrozoans occurring in many diverse forms but consisting typically of a hollow stem or stock, budding into a number of polyps and bells. [t. NL: m. *sīphōnophora* (pl.), t. Gk: m. *sīphōnophóros* tube-carrying. See SIPHONO-, -PHORE]

siphonostele (sī'fə nə stē'lĭ, -stēl'), *n. Bot.* a hollow tube of vascular tissue enclosing a pith and embedded in ground tissue.

Siple (sī'pl), *n.* **Mount,** a mountain on the Marie Byrd Land coast of Antarctica, S of Amundsen Sea. ab. 15,000 ft.

sippet (sĭp'ĭt), *n.* a small bit; a fragment. [f. SIP + -ET]

sipunculid (sī pŭng'kyōō lĭd), *n.* any of a group of annelid worms of the family *Sipunculidae.*

Siqueiros (*Sp.* sē kĕy'rōs), *n.* **David Alfaro** (*Sp.* dä bēd' äl fä'rō), born 1896, Mexican mural painter.

sir (sû), *n.* **1.** a respectful or formal term of address used to a man. **2.** (*cap.*) the distinctive title of a knight or baronet: *Sir Walter Scott.* **3.** (*cap.*) a title of respect for some notable personage of ancient times: *Sir Pandarus of Troy.* **4.** a lord; gentleman. **5.** an ironic or humorous title of respect: *sir critic.* **6.** *Archaic.* a title of respect prefixed to a noun designating profession, rank, etc.: *sir priest.* [weak var. of SIRE]

Siracusa (*It.* sē rä kōō'zä), *n.* Italian name of **Syracuse** (def. 2).

Siraj-ud-daula (sĭ rä'jōōd dou'lə), *n.* 1728?–57, the nawab of Bengal who resisted British colonization in India: ordered the Black Hole of Calcutta; defeated by Clive in 1757. Also, **Surajah Dowlah** (sə rä'jə dou'lə).

sirdar (sû'dä), *n.* **1.** (in India, Pakistan, etc.) a military chief or leader. **2.** (formerly) the British commander of the Egyptian army. [t. Hind., t. Pers.: m. *sardār,* lit., head-possessing one (i.e. commander)]

sire (sī'ə), *n., v.,* **sired, siring.** —*n.* **1.** the male parent of a quadruped. **2.** a respectful term of address, now used only to a sovereign. **3.** *Poetic.* a father or forefather. **4.** *Obs.* a lord; person of importance. —*v.t.* **5.** to beget. [ME, t. OF, g. L *senior* SENIOR]

siren (sī'ə rən), *n.* **1.** *Class. Myth.* one of several sea nymphs, part woman and part bird, supposed to lure mariners to destruction by their seductive singing. **2.** any alluring or seductive woman. **3.** an acoustic instrument for producing sounds, consisting essentially of a disc pierced with holes arranged equidistantly in a circle, rotated over a jet or stream of compressed air, steam, or the like, so that the stream is alternately interrupted and allowed to pass. **4.** a device of this kind used as a whistle, fog signal, warning sound on an ambulance, fire-engine, or the like, etc. **5.** any of certain eel-like salamanders of the family *Sirenidae* with small forelimbs and no hind ones, and permanent external gills. —*adj.* **6.** of or like a siren. **7.** dangerously alluring. [ME, t. L, t. Gk: m. *seirḗn* sea nymph]

sirenian (sī rē'nyən), *n.* any of the *Sirenia,* an order of aquatic herbivorous mammals that includes the manatee, dugong, etc. [f. s. NL *Sīrēnia* (der. L *sīrēn* SIREN) + -AN]

siren suit, 1. a one-piece trousered garment made of a tough fabric, worn by men doing dirty or rough work. **2.** a similar garment of wool, nylon, or the like, worn by babies.

Siret (*Russ.* sĭ rĕt'), *n.* a river flowing from the Carpathian Mountains in the SW Soviet Union SE through E Rumania to the Danube. ab. 270 mi. German, **Sereth.**

Sir Gawain and the Green Knight. See **Gawain and the Green Knight.**

Sirius (sĭ'rĭ əs), *n.* the Dog Star, in Canis Major: the brightest star in the heavens. [t. L, t. Gk: m. *Seírios*]

sirloin (sû'loin'), *n.* the portion of the loin of beef in front of the rump. [earlier *surloyn.* Cf. OF *surlonge,* f. *sur* over, above + *longe* loin]

sirocco (sĭ rŏk'ō), *n., pl.* **-cos. 1.** a hot, dry, dust-laden wind blowing from northern Africa and affecting parts of southern Europe; the chili. **2.** a warm, sultry south or south-east wind accompanied by rain, occurring in the same regions. **3.** any hot, oppressive wind, esp. one in the warm sector of a cyclone. [t. F: m. *siroco,* t. It.: m. *scirocco,* ult. t. Ar.: m. *shoruq,* der. *sharq* east]

sirrah (sĭ'rə), *n. Archaic.* a term of address used to inferiors in impatience, contempt, etc. [unexplained var. of SIR]

sir-reverence (sû'rĕv'ə rəns, -rĕv'rəns), *n. Obs.* an expression used apologetically, as before unseemly or indelicate words. [mistaken spelling of *sa'reverence,* reduced form of *save reverence* saving (your or his) reverence]

Sir Roger de Coverley, an English country dance performed by two facing rows of dancers. [named after Sir Roger de COVERLEY]

sirup (sĭ'rəp), *n. U.S.* syrup.

sisal (sī'səl), *n.* **1.** Also, **sisal hemp.** a fibre yielded by *Agave sisalana* of Yucatan, used for making ropes, etc. **2.** a plant yielding such fibre. [named after *Sisal,* a port in Yucatán]

siskin (sĭs'kĭn), *n.* a small fringilline bird, esp. *Carduelis spinus* of Europe. [earlier *syskin,* t. Flem., var. of *sijsken* (now *sijsje*). Cf. MLG *sisek,* appar. t. Pol.: m. *czyzik*]

Sisley (*Fr.* sē slĕ'), *n.* **Alfred** (*Fr.* äl frĕd'), 1833–99, French impressionist painter.

Sismondi (sĭs mŏn'dĭ; *Fr.* sēs mōɴ dē'), *n.* **Jean Charles Léonard Simonde de** (*Fr.* zhäɴ shärl lĕ ō när sē mōɴd' də), 1773–1842, Swiss historian and economist.

sissy (sĭs'ĭ), *n., pl.* **-sies.** cissy.

Sistan (sĭs tän'), *n.* an inland drainage basin on the borders of Iran, Afghanistan and Pakistan, surrounding a lake into which the river Helmand drains.

sister (sĭs'tə), *n.* **1.** a daughter of the same parents (**full sister** or **sister-german**). **2.** a daughter of only one of one's parents. **3.** member of the same kinship group, nationality, profession, etc.; a female associate, a female. **4.** a thing regarded as feminine and associated as if by kinship with something else. **5.** a female member of a religious community, which observes the simple vows of poverty, chastity, and obedience: *a Sister of Charity.* **6.** a senior nurse, esp. one in charge of a hospital ward. —*adj.* **7.** being a sister; related by, or as by, sisterhood: *sister ships.* [ME, t. Scand.; cf. Icel. *systir,* c. OE *sweostor,* G *Schwester,* Goth. *swistar;* akin to Russ. *sestra,* L *soror*]

sisterhood (sĭs'tə hōōd'), *n.* **1.** state of being a sister. **2.** a group of sisters, esp. of women bound by religious vows or similarly devoted. **3.** any organization of women with a common aim or interest.

sister-in-law (sĭs'tər ĭn lô'), *n., pl.* **sisters-in-law. 1.** a husband's or wife's sister. **2.** a brother's wife. **3.** a husband's or wife's brother's wife.

sisterly (sĭs′tə lĭ), *adj.* of, like, or befitting a sister.

Sistine (sĭs′tīn), *adj.* of or pertaining to any pope named Sixtus. [t. It.: m. *Sistino*]

Sistine Chapel, the chapel of the pope in the Vatican at Rome, built for Pope Sixtus IV, and decorated with frescoes by Michelangelo and others.

sistroid (sĭs′troid), *adj.* *Geom.* included between the convex sides of two intersecting curves (opposed to *cissoid*): *a sistroid angle.* [orig. unknown]

sistrum (sĭs′trəm), *n., pl.* **-tra** (-trə). an ancient Egyptian musical instrument, a form of metal rattle, used esp. in the worship of Isis. [t. L, t. Gk: m. *seîstron*]

Sistrum

Sisyphean (sĭs′ĭ fē′ən), *adj.* **1.** of or pertaining to Sisyphus. **2.** endless and unavailing, as labour or a task.

Sisyphus (sĭs′ĭ fəs), *n.* *Gk Myth.* a king of Corinth, condemned in Hades to roll a heavy stone up a steep hill, only to have it always roll down again when he approached the top.

sit (sĭt), *v.*, **sat** or (*Archaic*) **sate, sitting.** —*v.i.* **1.** to rest on the lower part of the body; be seated. **2.** to be situated; dwell. **3.** to rest or lie. **4.** to place oneself in position for an artist, photographer, etc.: *to sit for a portrait.* **5.** to act as a model. **6.** to remain quiet or inactive. **7.** (of a bird) to perch or roost. **8.** to cover eggs to hatch them. **9.** to fit or be adjusted, as a garment. **10.** to occupy a seat in an official capacity, as a judge or bishop. **11.** to have a seat, be an elected representative, as in parliament. **12.** to be convened or in session, as an assembly. **13.** to act as a babysitter. **14.** to be a candidate for an examination; take an examination. —*v.t.* **15.** to cause to sit; seat (often with *down*). **16.** to sit upon (a horse, etc.). **17.** to provide seating room for; seat: *a table which sits eight people.* —*v.* **18.** Some special verb phrases are:

be sitting pretty, *Colloq.* to be comfortably established; be at an advantage.

sit down, to take a seat; be seated.

sit in for, to take the place of temporarily: *he'll be out for an hour so I'll sit in for him.*

sit in on, take part in as a spectator, observer, or visitor: *we were allowed to sit in on the debate.*

sit on or **upon, 1.** to have a place (on a committee, etc.): *he has sat on several committees during the past few years.* **2.** *Colloq.* to check; rebuke; repress.

sit out, 1. to stay till the end of: *though the film was boring we sat it out.* **2.** to take no part in; keep one's seat during (a dance, etc.): *she sat out the last few dances because she was tired.*

sit tight, to take no action; bide one's time: *I'll sit tight till I know what the decision is.*

sit up, 1. to raise oneself from a lying to a sitting position. **2.** to stay up later than usual; not go to bed. **3.** to sit upright or erect. **4.** to be startled; become interested or alert: *the speaker's next announcement made us sit up.* [ME *sitte(n)*, OE *sittan*, c. D *zitten*, G *sitzen*, Icel. *sitja*; akin to L *sedēre*]

sitar (sĭ tä′), *n.* a guitar-like instrument of India, having a long neck and usually three strings. Also, **sittar.** [t. Hind.]

sitatunga (sĭt′ə tŏŏng′gə), *n.* a spiral-horned antelope, *Tragelaphus spekei*, of central Africa. Also, **situtunga.** [t. Tonga or Lozi]

sit-down (sĭt′doun′), *n.* **1.** a sit-down strike. **2.** a period or instance of sitting for relaxation, talk, etc.: *they had a pleasant half-hour's sit-down together.* **3.** an organized passive protest in which demonstrators sit down in a public place in order to draw attention to their cause.

sit-down strike (sĭt′doun′), a strike during which workers refuse either to leave their place of employment or to work or to allow others to work until the strike is settled. Also, **sit-down.**

site (sīt), *n., v.*, **sited, siting.** —*n.* **1.** the position of a town, building, etc., esp. as to its environment. **2.** the area on which anything, as a building, is, has been or is to be situated. —*v.t.* **3.** to locate; place; provide with a site: *to site a gun.* [t. L: m. *situs* position]

sith (sĭth), *adv., conj., prep.* *Archaic.* since.

Sithole (sĭ tō′lĭ), *n.* **Ndabaningi** (ən dä′bə nĭng′gĭ), born 1920, Rhodesian political leader, in confinement since 1963.

sit-in (sĭt′ĭn′), *n.* an organized passive protest in which the demonstrators occupy seats normally prohibited to them, as in a restaurant, and refuse to move.

Sitka (sĭt′kə), *n.* a town in SE Alaska, on an island in the Alexander Archipelago: the capital of former Russian America. 3237 (1960).

sito-, a word element referring to food. [t. Gk, comb. form of *sîtos* food made from grain]

sitomania (sī′tō mā′nyə), *n.* *Pathol.* morbid craving for food.

sitophobia (sī′tō fō′byə), *n.* *Pathol.* morbid aversion to food.

sitosterol (sī tŏs′tə rōl′), *n.* *Chem.* a sterol, $C_{29}H_{49}OH$, derived from wheat, corn, Calabar beans, etc. [f. SITO- + (CHOLE)STEROL]

sits vac., situations vacant.

sittar (sĭ tä′), *n.* sitar.

sitter (sĭt′ə), *n.* **1.** one who sits, as for a portrait. **2.** a brooding bird. **3.** a baby-sitter. **4.** *Colloq.* something easily accomplished, as a catch in cricket, a mark to be shot at, etc.

sitting (sĭt′ĭng), *n.* **1.** the act of one who or that which sits. **2.** a period of remaining seated, as for a portrait. **3.** an uninterrupted period of sitting, as to read a book. **4.** a brooding, as of a hen upon eggs, or the number of eggs on which a bird sits during one hatching. **5.** a session, as of a court or legislature. **6.** an occasion of serving a meal to a company, in a restaurant, etc.

Sittingbourne (sĭt′ĭng bôn′), *n.* a town in England, in Kent. with Milton, 23,616 (1961).

Sitting Bull, a noted Sioux Indian warrior, tribal leader, and sacred dreamer of Hunkpapa Teton division of the Sioux: born in South Dakota, 1834; died 1890.

sitting duck, 1. any particularly easy mark to shoot at. **2.** *Colloq.* one who is easily duped or defeated.

sitting room, a room for sitting in, as by a family communally; living room; drawing room.

situate (*v.* sĭt′yŏŏ āt′; *adj.* sĭt′yŏŏ āt′, -ĭt), *v.*, **-ated, -ating,** *adj.* —*v.i.* **1.** to give a site to; locate. —*adj.* **2.** *Archaic.* located; placed. [t. LL: m. s. *situātus*, pp., der. L *situs* site]

situated (sĭt′yŏŏ ā′tĭd), *adj.* **1.** located; placed. **2.** in certain circumstances: *well situated financially.*

situation (sĭt′yŏŏ ā′shən), *n.* **1.** manner of being situated; a location or position with reference to environment. **2.** a place or locality. **3.** condition; case; plight. **4.** the state of affairs; combination of circumstances: *to meet the demands of the situation.* **5.** a position or post of employment. **6.** a state of affairs of special significance in the course of a play, novel, etc. —**Syn. 4.** See **state. 5.** See **position.**

situs (sī′təs), *n.* **1.** position; situation. **2.** the proper or original position, as of a part or organ. [t. L]

situtunga (sĭt′ə tŏŏng′gə), *n.* sitatunga.

Sitwell (sĭt′wəl), *n.* **1. Edith,** 1887–1964, English poet and critic. **2.** her brother, **Sir Osbert,** 1892–1969, English poet and novelist. **3.** her brother, **Sacheverell** (sə shĕv′ə rəl), born 1900, English poet and novelist.

sitz bath (sĭts), **1.** a bathtub in which the thighs and trunk of the body to the waistline are immersed in warm water. **2.** the bath so taken. [half adoption, half trans. of G *Sitzbad*, f. *Sitz* seat and *Bad* bath]

SI unit, a unit of the Système International d'Unités.

Siva (sē′və, sĭv′ə), *n.* *Hinduism.* Shiva. —**Si′vaism,** *n.* —**Si′vaist,** *n.* —**Si′vais′tic,** *adj.*

Sivan (sē vän′), *n.* (in the Jewish calendar) the ninth month of the civil and third of the ecclesiastical year. [t. Heb.]

Sivas (sĭ′väs), *n.* a town in central Turkey. 93,370 (1960).

six (sĭks), *n.* **1.** a cardinal number, five plus one. **2.** a symbol for this number, as 6 or VI. **3.** a set of this many persons or things. **4.** a playing card, die face, etc., with six pips. **5.** *Cricket.* a hit scoring six runs, the ball reaching the boundary without touching the ground. **6. at sixes and sevens,** in disorder or confusion. —*adj.* **7.** amounting to six in number. [ME and OE, c. D *zes*, LG *ses*, G *sechs*, Icel. *sex*, L *sex*]

Six (sĭks), *n.* **the, 1.** *Colloq.* the European Economic Community. **2.** Also, *French*, **les six** (*Fr.* lĕ sēs′). a group of French composers, associated in the 1920s.

sixer (sĭk′sə), *n.* *Slang.* **1.** *Cricket.* a six (def. 5). **2.** any group of six things, as sixpence. **3.** a patrol leader in the wolf cubs.

sixfold (sĭks′fōld′), *adj.* **1.** comprising six parts or members. **2.** six times as great or as much. —*adv.* **3.** in sixfold measure.

six-footer (sĭks′fŏŏt′ə), *n.* *Colloq.* **1.** one who is six feet tall or over. **2.** that which is six feet long.

Six Nations, the Five Nations (which see) of the Iroquois confederacy and the Tuscaroras.

sixpence (sĭks′pəns), *n.* **1.** six pennies. **2.** (until 1971 in Great Britain) a cupronickel coin of this value.

sixpenny (sĭks′pə nĭ), *adj.* **1.** of the amount or value of sixpence; costing sixpence. **2.** of trifling value; cheap; paltry. —*n.* **3.** something purchased for sixpence, esp. a journey by public transport.

six-shooter (sĭks′sho͞o′tə), *n. Slang.* a revolver with which six shots can be fired without reloading.

sixte (sĭkst), *n. Fencing.* the sixth of eight defensive positions; part of the target. [F]

sixteen (sĭks′tēn′), *n.* **1.** a cardinal number, ten plus six. **2.** a symbol for this number, as 16 or XVI. —*adj.* **3.** amounting to sixteen in number. [ME *sixtene*, OE *sixtēne*, c. D *zestien*, G *sechzehn*, Icel. *sextān*]

sixteenmo (sĭks′tēn′mō), *n.*, *pl.* **-mos,** *adj. Bookbinding.* sextodecimo.

sixteenth (sĭks′tēnth′), *adj.* **1.** next after the fifteenth. **2.** being one of sixteen equal parts. —*n.* **3.** a sixteenth part, esp. of one ($\frac{1}{16}$). **4.** the sixteenth member of a series. **5.** *Music.* See **sixteenth note.**

sixteenth note, *U.S. Music.* a semiquaver.

sixth (sĭksth), *adj.* **1.** next after the fifth. **2.** being one of six equal parts. —*n.* **3.** a sixth part, esp. of one ($\frac{1}{6}$). **4.** the sixth member of a series. **5.** sixth form. **6.** *Music.* **a.** a note on the sixth degree from a given note (counted as the first). **b.** the interval between such notes. **c.** the harmonic combination of such notes. —**sixth′ly,** *adv.*

sixth chord, *Music.* an inversion of a triad in which the second note (next above the root) is in the bass.

sixth form, *Educ.* the highest classes in a grammar or public school for pupils over 16.

sixth-former (sĭksth′fô′mə), *n.* a member of a sixth form.

sixth sense, a power of perception beyond the five senses; intuition.

sixtieth (sĭks′tĭ ĭth), *adj.* **1.** next after the fifty-ninth. **2.** being one of sixty equal parts. —*n.* **3.** a sixtieth part, esp. of one ($\frac{1}{60}$). **4.** the sixtieth member of a series.

Sixtus (sĭks′təs), *n.* the name of five popes.

sixty (sĭks′tĭ), *n.*, *pl.* **-ties,** *adj.* —*n.* **1.** a cardinal number, ten times six. **2.** a symbol for this number, as 60 or LX. **3.** (*pl.*) the numbers from 60 to 69 of a series, esp. with reference to the years of a person's age, or the years of a century, esp. the twentieth. —*adj.* **4.** amounting to sixty in number. [ME; OE *sixtig*, c. D *zestig*, G *sechzig*, Icel. *sextigir*]

sixty-fourth note (sĭks′tĭ fôth′), *U.S. Music.* hemidemisemiquaver.

sixty-four-thousand-dollar question (sĭks′tĭ fô thou′zənd dŏl′ə), the crucial, decisive, or fundamental issue of a matter. Also, **sixty-four-dollar question.** [named after the final prize of a popular U.S. television quiz programme]

sixty-nine (sĭks′tĭ nīn′), *n.* See **soixante-neuf.**

sizable (sī′zə bl), *adj.* sizeable. —**siz′ableness,** *n.* —**siz′ably,** *adv.*

sizar (sī′zə), *n.* formerly (at Cambridge and Dublin) an undergraduate who received aid from the college for maintenance in return for the performance of certain duties. [der. SIZE (see def. 6)]

size[1] (sīz), *n.*, *v.*, **sized, sizing.** —*n.* **1.** the dimensions, proportions, or magnitude of anything: *the size of a city.* **2.** considerable or great magnitude: *to seek size rather than quality.* **3.** one of a series of graduated measures for articles of manufacture or trade: *children's sizes of shoes.* **4.** extent; amount; range. **5.** *Colloq.* actual condition, circumstances, etc. **6.** *Obs.* a fixed standard, as for food or drink. —*v.t.* **7.** to separate or sort according to size. **8.** to make of a certain size. **9. to size up,** to form an estimate of; to come up to a certain standard. **10.** *Obs.* to regulate according to a standard. [ME *syse*, t. OF: m. *sise*, aphetic var. of *assize* ASSIZE; later meanings arose from def. 10]

—**Syn. 1.** SIZE, VOLUME, MASS, BULK are terms referring to extent or dimensions of that which has magnitude and occupies space. SIZE is the general word: *of great size, small in size.* VOLUME often applies to something which has no fixed shape: *smoke has volume.* MASS, too, does not suggest shape, but suggests the weight of a quantity of matter in a solid body: *a mass of concrete.* BULK suggests weight, and often a recognizable, though perhaps unwieldy, shape: *the huge bulk of an elephant.*

size[2] (sīz), *n.*, *v.*, **sized, sizing.** —*n.* **1.** any of various gelatinous or glutinous preparations made from glue, starch, etc., used for glazing or coating paper, cloth, etc. —*v.t.* **2.** to coat or treat with size. [ME *syse*; ? special use of SIZE[1]]

sizeable (sī′zə bl), *adj.* **1.** of considerable size; fairly large: *he inherited a sizeable fortune.* **2.** *Obs.* of convenient size. Also, **sizable.** —**size′ableness,** *n.* —**size′ably,** *adv.*

sized (sīzd), *adj.* having size as specified: *middle-sized.*

sizing (sī′zĭng), *n.* **1.** the act or process of applying size or preparing with size. **2.** size, as for glazing paper.

sizy (sī′zĭ), *adj.* thick; viscous. [f. SIZE[2] + -Y[1]]

sizzle (sĭz′əl), *v.*, **-zled, -zling,** *n.* —*v.i.* **1.** to make a hissing sound, as in frying or burning. **2.** *Colloq.* to be very hot. —*n.* **3.** a sizzling sound. [imit.] —**siz′zler,** *n.*

S.J., Society of Jesus (Jesuit).

Sjælland (*Dan.* syĕ′lån), *n.* Danish name of **Zealand.**

sjambok (shăm′bŏk), *n. Chiefly S African.* **1.** a heavy whip of rhinoceros or other hide. —*v.t.* **2.** to strike with or as with such a whip. [t. Afrikaans, der. Hindi *chābuk* CHABOUK]

skaapsteker (skäp′stĭk′ə), *n.* any of various harmless colubrine African snakes, as the **spotted skaapsteker,** *Trimerorhinus rhombeatus.* [t. Afrikaans, f. *skaap* SHEEP + *stek* prick, STICK + *-er* -ER]

Skagen (skä′gən), *n.* See **Skaw, The.**

Skagerrak (skăg′ə răk′), *n.* an arm of the North Sea between Denmark and Norway. ab. 140 mi. long; ab. 75 mi. wide.

Skagway (skăg′wā′), *n.* a town in SE Alaska, near the famous White and Chilkoot passes to the Klondike gold fields: railway terminus. 659 (1960).

skald (skôld), *n.* an ancient Scandinavian poet. Also, **scald.** [t. Icel.: poet]

skat (skăt), *n.* a card game in which there are three active players, 32 cards being used. [t. G, t. It.: m. *scarto* a discard, der. *scartare* to discard]

skate[1] (skāt), *n.*, *v.*, **skated, skating.** —*n.* **1.** a steel blade attached to the bottom of a shoe, enabling a person to glide on ice. **2.** a shoe with such a blade attached. **3.** a roller-skate, **4.** *Elect.* the sliding contact which collects current in an electric traction system. —*v.i.* **5.** to glide over ice, the ground, etc., on skates. **6.** to glide or slide smoothly along. **7.** to avoid, as in conversation (fol. by *round* or *over*). **8. skate on thin ice,** to place oneself in a delicate situation; touch on a contentious topic. [t. D: m. *schaats*, MD *schaetse*, t. ONF: m. *escache* stilt]

skate[2] (skāt), *n.*, *pl.* **skates,** (*esp. collectively*) **skate.** any of certain rays (genus *Raja*), usually having a pointed snout and spines down the back, but no serrated spine on the tail, as the common skate, *R. batis*, of European coastal waters. [ME *scate*, t. Scand.; cf. Icel. *skata*]

skate[3] (skāt), *n. Slang.* a term of contempt for a person, a horse, or the like. [? special use of SKATE[2]]

skateboard (skāt′bôd′), *n.* a short plank on roller-skate wheels, ridden, usually standing up, as a recreation.

skater (skā′tə), *n.* **1.** one who skates. **2.** a water-strider.

Common skate, *Raja batis* (Up to 7 ft in length)

Skaw (skô), *n.* **The,** a cape at the N tip of Denmark. Also, **Skagen.**

skean (skēn), *n.* a kind of knife or dagger formerly used in Ireland and among the Scottish Highlanders. [t. Irish and Gaelic: m. *sgian*]

Skeat (skēt), *n.* **Walter William,** 1835–1912, English philologist and lexicographer.

skedaddle (skĭ dăd′l), *v.*, **-dled, -dling,** *n. Orig. U.S. Slang.* —*v.i.* **1.** to run away; disperse in flight. —*n.* **2.** a hasty flight. [orig. obscure]

skee (skē), *n.*, *pl.* **skees, skee,** *v.i.*, **skeed, skeeing.** ski.

skeet (skēt), *n.* a form of clay-pigeon shooting, in which clay targets are thrown from two traps forty yards apart and the shooter moves to different stations, thus firing from various angles as in real game shooting. [? special use of d. *skeet* scatter, var. of SCOOT]

skeg (skĕg), *n.* **1.** the afterpart of a ship's keel. **2.** a projection abaft a ship's keel for the support of a rudder. [t. D: m. *scheg*, t. Scand.; cf. Icel. *skegg* beard]

Skegness (skĕg′nĕs′), *n.* a town in England, on the E coast of Lincolnshire: resort. 12,843 (1961).

skein (skān), *n.* **1.** a length of thread or yarn wound in a coil. **2.** anything resembling this, as a flight of geese, coil of hair, or the like. [ME *skayne*, t. OF: m. *escaigne*]

skeletal (skĕl′ĭ tl), *adj.* **1.** of or pertaining to a skeleton. **2.** like a skeleton.

skeleton (skĕl′ĭ tən), *n.* **1.** the bones of a human or other animal body considered together, or assembled or fitted together as a framework; the

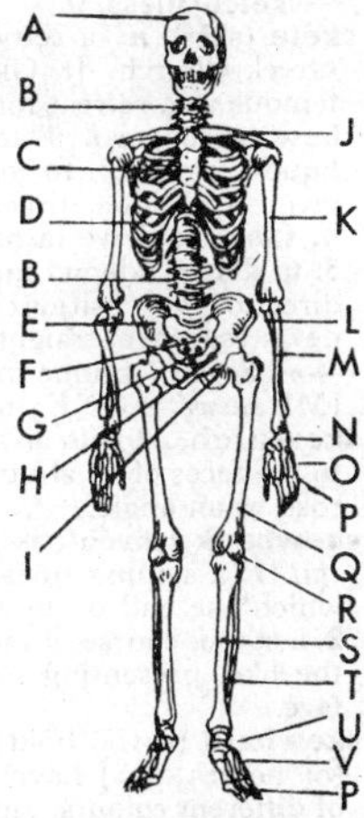

Human skeleton
A, Cranium; B, Vertebrae; C, Sternum; D, Ribs; E, Ilium; F, Sacrum; G, Coccyx; H, Pubis; I, Ischium; J, Clavicle; K, Humerus; L, Ulna; M, Radius; N, Carpus; O, Metacarpus; P, Phalanx; Q, Femur; R, Patella; S, Tibia; T, Fibula; U, Tarsus; V, Metatarsus

bony or cartilaginous framework of a vertebrate animal. **2.** *Colloq.* a very lean person or animal. **3.** a supporting framework, as of a leaf, building, or ship. **4.** mere lifeless, dry, or meagre remains. **5.** an outline, as of a literary work; basic essentials. **6. skeleton in the cupboard,** some fact in the history or lives of a family which is kept secret as a cause of shame. *—adj.* **7.** of or pertaining to a skeleton. **8.** like a skeleton or mere framework. **9.** reduced to the essential minimum: *skeleton staff.* [t. NL, t. Gk, neut. of *skeletós* dried up]

skeletonize (skĕl′ĭ tə nīz′), *v.t.*, **-ized, -izing. 1.** to reduce to a skeleton. **2.** to construct in outline. Also, **skeletonise.**

skeleton key, a key with nearly the whole substance of the bit filed away, so that it may open various locks. Also, **master key, pass key.**

skellum (skĕl′əm), *n. Archaic or Dial.* a rascal. [t. D: m. *schelm,* t. G]

skelm (skĕlm), *n. S African.* a rogue. [t. Afrikaans, t. D: m. *schelm,* r. SKELLUM]

skelp (skĕlp), *Scot. and N Dial. or Colloq.* *—v.t.* **1.** to slap or spank. *—n.* **2.** a slap. [ME; orig. uncert.]

Skelton (skĕl′tən), *n.* **John,** *c.* 1460–1529, English poet.

skep (skĕp), *n.* **1.** a basket or hamper, as of wicker. **2.** a specific quantity such as would be contained by such a basket. **3.** a beehive, esp. one made of wicker or straw. [ME *skeppe,* t. Scand.; cf. Icel. *skeppa* half-bushel]

skeptic (skĕp′tĭk), *n., adj. U.S.* sceptic. **—skep′tical,** *adj.* **—skep′ticism,** *n.*

skerm (skûm), *n. S African.* a thick hedge made to keep out wild animals. [t. Afrikaans: fence]

skerrick (skĕ′rĭk), *n. Austral., N.Z.* a very small quantity; a scrap: *not a skerrick left.* [orig. Brit. d.; ult. orig. obscure]

skerry (skĕ′rĭ), *n., pl.* **-ries.** *Chiefly Scot.* **1.** a small, rocky island. **2.** a coastline with a series of such islands offshore. [Orkney word, t. Scand.; cf. Icel. *sker* reef]

sketch (skĕch), *n.* **1.** a simply or hastily executed drawing or painting, esp. a preliminary one, giving the essential features without the details. **2.** a rough design, plan, or draft, as of a literary work. **3.** a brief or hasty outline of facts, occurrences, etc. **4.** a short play, usually of a comic or musical nature, or slight dramatic performance, as one forming part of a revue. *—v.t.* **5.** to make a sketch of. **6.** to set forth in a brief or general account. *—v.i.* **7.** to make a sketch or sketches. [t. D: m. *schets,* t. It.: m. *schizzo,* g. L *schedium* extemporaneous poem, t. Gk: m. *schédios* extempore] **—sketch′er,** *n.* **—Syn. 5.** See **depict.**

sketchable (skĕch′ə bl), *adj.* suitable for being sketched.

sketchbook (skĕch′bo͝ok′), *n.* **1.** a book for making sketches in. **2.** a book of literary or other sketches. Also, **sketchblock, sketchpad.**

sketchy (skĕch′ĭ), *adj.*, **sketchier, sketchiest. 1.** like a sketch; giving only outlines. **2.** slight; imperfect; incomplete; superficial: *a sketchy meal.* **—sketch′ily,** *adv.* **—sketch′iness,** *n.*

skete (skēt), *n.* a settlement of monks or ascetics of the Greek Church. [t. Gk: *skḗtē,* after *skētís* desert in Egypt famous as a retreat for hermits]

skew (skyo͞o), *v.i.* **1.** to turn aside or swerve; take an oblique course. **2.** to look obliquely; squint. *—v.t.* **3.** to give an oblique direction to; shape or form obliquely. **4.** *Carp.* to drive (a nail) obliquely; to drive a skewnail. **5.** to distort; depict unfairly. *—adj.* **6.** having an oblique direction or position; slanting. **7.** having a part which deviates from a straight line, right angle, etc.: *skew gearing.* *—n.* **8.** an oblique movement, direction, or position. [ME *skewe,* t. ONF: m. s. *eskiu(w)er* escape. See ESCHEW]

skew arch, *Archit.* an arch whose axis is not perpendicular to the faces of its abutments, as where a railway crosses a road at an angle.

skewback (skyo͞o′băk′), *n. Archit.* **1.** a sloping surface against which the end of an arch rests. **2.** a stone, course of masonry, or the like, presenting such a surface.

S, Skewback

skewbald (skyo͞o′bôld′), *adj.* **1.** (of horses, etc.) having patches of different colours, esp. of white and brown. *—n.* **2.** a skewbald horse or pony. Cf. **piebald.** [cf. obs. E *skewed* skewbald (orig. uncert.)]

skewer (skyo͞oə), *n.* **1.** a long pin of wood or metal for putting through meat to hold it together or in place while being cooked. **2.** any similar pin for some other purpose. *—v.t.* **3.** to fasten with, or as with, skewers. [earlier *skiver,* of unknown orig.]

skewnail (skyo͞o′nāl′), *n. Carp.* a nail driven obliquely.

skew-whiff (skyo͞o′wĭf′), *adv. Colloq.* askew.

ski (skē; *Norw.* shē), *n., pl.* **skis, ski,** *v.*, **ski'd** or **skied, skiing.** *—n.* **1.** one of a pair of long, slender pieces of hard wood, metal, or plastic, one fastened to each shoe, used for travelling or gliding over snow, and often (esp. as a sport) down slopes. **2.** a water ski. *—v.i.* **3.** to travel on or use skis. **4.** to water ski. Also, **skee.** [t. Norw., var. of *skid,* c. Icel. *skīdh,* OE *scid* thin slip of wood, G *Scheit* thin board]

skiascope (skī′ə skōp′), *n. Med.* an apparatus which determines the refractive power of the eye by observing the lights and shadows on the pupil when a mirror illumines the retina; retinoscope. [f. Gk *skía* shadow + -SCOPE] **—skiascopy** (skī ăs′kə pĭ), *n.*

skibob (skē′bŏb′), *n.* **1.** a vehicle used for gliding down snow slopes, consisting of a low seat and steering handle supported by two short skis; the rider wears small skis for balance. *—v.i.* **2.** to ride such a vehicle. [f. SKI + BOB(SLEIGH)]

skid (skĭd), *n., v.,* **skidded, skidding.** *—n.* **1.** a plank, bar, log, or the like, esp. one of a pair, on which something heavy may be slid or rolled along. **2.** *U.S.* one of a number of such logs or planks forming a skidway. **3.** a plank or the like, esp. one of a number, on or by which something is supported. **4.** *Naut.* **a.** (*pl.*) a skidboard. **b.** (*usually pl.*) a framework above the main deck on which ships' boats are carried. **5.** a shoe or some other device for preventing the wheel of a vehicle from rotating, as when descending a hill. **6.** a runner on the underpart of some aeroplanes, enabling the machine to slide along the ground when alighting. **7.** an act of skidding: *the car went into a skid on the icy road.* *—v.t.* **8.** to place on or slide along a skid or skids. **9.** to check with a skid, as a wheel. *—v.i.* **10.** to slide along without rotating, as a wheel to which a brake has been applied. **11.** to slip or slide sideways relative to direction of wheel rotation, as a car in turning a corner rapidly. **12.** to slide forward under its own momentum, as a car when the wheels have been braked. **13.** (of an aeroplane when not banked sufficiently) to slide sideways, away from the centre of the curve executed in turning. [orig. uncert.; ? irreg. t. Scand.; cf. Icel. *skīdh,* akin to SKI]

skidboard (skĭd′bôd′), *n. Naut.* a large wooden framework on a quay used to slide cargo up and down when loading a ship. Also, **skids.**

Skiddaw (skĭd′ô, skĭ dô′), *n.* a mountain in England, in the Lake District. 3054 ft.

skiddoo (skĭ do͞o′), *interj. U.S. Slang.* get out; go away.

skid fin, *Aeron.* an auxiliary aerofoil over the upper main wing in some early aeroplanes.

skidlid (skĭd′lĭd′), *n. Slang.* a motorcyclist's crash-helmet.

skidpan (skĭd′păn′), *n.* a place where motorists or the like may learn and practise the control of skidding vehicles on a prepared slippery surface.

skidway (skĭd′wā), *n.* **1.** a platform, often sloping, on which logs are piled ready for sawing. **2.** a path or way made of logs along which objects are rolled along.

Skien (*Norw.* shē′ən), *n.* a town in S Norway. 45,440 (1965).

skier (skē′ə), *n.* one who skis.

skiey (skī′ĭ), *adj.* skyey.

skiff (skĭf), *n.* any of various types of boats small enough for sailing or rowing by one person. [t. F: m. *esquif,* t. It.: m. *schifo,* t. OHG: m. *scif* SHIP]

skiffle (skĭf′əl), *n.* a style of music popular during the 1950s based on American folksongs and played on an arbitrary mixture of guitars and improvised instruments, esp. the washboard.

skiing (skē′ĭng), *n.* the use of skis, for travelling, or sport.

skijoring (skē jô′rĭng), *n.* a sport in which a skier is pulled over snow or ice, generally by a horse. [t. Norw.: m. *skikjøring* ski-driving] **—skijor′er,** *n.*

ski-jump (skē′jŭmp′), *n.* **1.** a jump made by a skier. **2.** the runway designed for such a jump consisting of a ramp overhanging a slope. **—ski′jump′er,** *n.*

skilful (skĭl′fəl), *adj.* **1.** having or exercising skill. **2.** showing or involving skill: *a skilful display of fancy diving.* **3.** *Obs.* reasonable. Also, *U.S.,* **skillful.** **—skil′fully,** *adv.* **—skil′fulness,** *n.*

—Syn. 1. SKILFUL, SKILLED, EXPERT refer to readiness and adroitness in an occupation, craft, or art. SKILFUL suggests esp. adroitness and dexterity: *a skilful watchmaker.* SKILLED implies having had training and long experience and thus having acquired a high degree of proficiency: *not an amateur but a skilled workman.* EXPERT means having the highest degree of proficiency; it may mean much the same as skilful or skilled, or both: *expert workmanship.* **—Ant. 1.** awkward, clumsy, amateurish.

ski-lift (skē′lĭft′), *n.* a device for carrying skiers up a slope, typically consisting of chairs suspended from an endless cable; cable lift.

skill[1] (skĭl), *n.* **1.** the ability that comes from knowledge, practice, aptitude, etc., to do something well. **2.** competent excellence in performance; expertness; dexterity. **3.** *Obs.* understanding. **4.** *Obs.* a reason; cause. [ME, t. Scand.; cf. Icel. *skil* distinction]

skill[2] (skĭl), *v.i. Archaic.* **1.** to matter. **2.** to help. [t. Scand.; cf. Icel. *skilja* distinguish]

skilled (skĭld), *adj.* **1.** having skill; trained or experienced. **2.** showing, involving, or requiring skill, as work. **3.** of or pertaining to workers performing a specific operation requiring apprenticeship or other special training or experience. **—Syn. 1.** See **skilful.**

skillet (skĭl′ĭt), *n.* a frying pan. [orig. obscure]

skillful (skĭl′fəl), *adj. U.S.* skilful.

skillion (skĭl′yən), *n. Austral., N.Z.* a lean-to or outhouse.

skilly (skĭl′ĭ), *n.* a thin soup, broth, or gruel, formerly used in prisons and workhouses. [shortened form of obs. *skilligalee*; ult. orig. unknown]

skim (skĭm), *v.*, **skimmed, skimming,** *n.* **—***v.t.* **1.** to take up or remove (floating matter) from a liquid with a spoon, ladle, etc.: *to skim cream.* **2.** to clear (liquid) thus: *to skim milk.* **3.** to move or glide lightly over or along the surface of (the ground, water, etc.). **4.** to cause (a thing) to fly over or near a surface, or in a smooth course: *to skim stones.* **5.** to go over in reading, treatment, etc., in a superficial manner. **6.** to cover (liquid, etc.) with a thin layer. **—***v.i.* **7.** to pass or glide lightly along over or near a surface. **8.** to go, pass, glance, etc. over something in a superficial way (usually fol. by *over*). **9.** to become covered with a thin layer. **—***n.* **10.** the act of skimming. **11.** that which is skimmed off as skimmed milk. **12.** *Obs.* scum. [d. var. of obs. *scum*, v., skim. See SCUM]

skimble-scamble (skĭm′bl skăm′bl), *adj. Archaic.* rambling; confused; nonsensical.

skimmed milk, milk from which the cream has been skimmed. Also, **skim milk.**

skimmer (skĭm′ə), *n.* **1.** one who or that which skims. **2.** a shallow utensil, usually perforated, used in skimming liquids. **3.** any of various gull-like birds of the family *Rynchopidae*, which skim the water with the elongated lower mandible touching the water in obtaining food.

skimming (skĭm′ĭng), *n.* **1.** (*usually pl.*) that which is removed by skimming. **2.** (*pl.*) *Metall.* dross.

skimming coat, *Bldg Trades.* setting coat.

skimp (skĭmp), *v.t., v.i.* **1.** to scrimp. **2.** to scamp; make or do hastily or inattentively. **—***adj.* **3.** skimpy. [orig. obscure]

skimpy (skĭm′pĭ), *adj.*, **skimpier, skimpiest. 1.** lacking in size, fullness, etc.; scanty: *a skimpy hem.* **2.** too thrifty; stingy: *a skimpy housewife.* **—skimp′ily,** *adv.* **—skimp′iness,** *n.*

skin (skĭn), *n.*, *v.*, **skinned, skinning. —***n.* **1.** the external covering or integument of an animal body, esp. when soft and flexible. **2.** such an integument stripped from the body of an animal; pelt. **3.** any integumentary covering, outer coating, or surface layer, as an investing membrane, the rind or peel of fruit, or a film on liquid. **4.** a single nacreous layer in a pearl, the outermost at any time. **5.** the planking or iron plating which covers the ribs of a ship. **6.** a container made of animal skin, used for holding liquids. **7.** one's resistance or sensitivity to criticism, censure, etc.: *a thick skin, a thin skin.* **8. jump out of one's skin,** to be very frightened, surprised, or the like. **9. save one's skin,** to escape harm. **10. by the skin of one's teeth,** scarcely; just; barely. **11. get under one's skin, a.** to irritate one. **b.** to fascinate or attract one. **—***v.t.* **12.** to strip or deprive of skin; flay; peel. **13.** to strip off, as or like skin. **14.** to cover with or as with skin. **15.** *Slang.* to strip of money or belongings; fleece, as in gambling. **—***v.i.* **16.** *U.S. Slang.* to slip off hastily. [ME, t. Scand.; cf. Icel. *skinn*, c. d. G *Schind*, *Schinde* skin of fruit]

—Syn. 2. SKIN, HIDE, PELT are names for the outer covering of animals, including man. SKIN is the general word: *an abrasion of the skin, the skin of a muskrat.* HIDE applies to the skin of large animals, such as cattle: horses, elephants: *a buffalo hide.* PELT applies to the untanned skin of smaller animals: *a mink pelt.* HIDE usually refers to leathery skin, and PELT to fur.

skin and bones, 1. an extremely emaciated physique. **2.** a person having such a physique.

skinbound (skĭn′bound′), *adj.* having the skin drawn tightly over the flesh, as in scleroderma.

skin-deep (skĭn′dēp′), *adj.* **1.** superficial; slight. **—***adv.* **2.** slightly; superficially.

skin-diving (skĭn′dī′vĭng), *n.* an underwater activity in which the diver, equipped with a lightweight mask, an aqualung or snorkel, and foot fins, can move about quickly and easily. **—skin′-dive′,** *v.i.* **—skin′-div′er,** *n.*

skin effect, *Elect.* the effect which causes an alternating current, esp. of radio frequencies, to concentrate near the surface of a conductor, so increasing its effective resistance.

skinflint (skĭn′flĭnt′), *n.* a mean, niggardly person.

skin friction drag, aerodynamic resistance due to the tangential forces of moving air on the surface of a body.

skinful (skĭn′fo͝ol′), *n. Slang.* a large quantity of alcoholic drink consumed: *that drunk's had a skinful.*

skin game, *Slang.* **1.** a dishonest activity, business, etc. **2.** a swindle. [SKIN (def. 15) + GAME]

skin grafting, *Surg.* the transplanting of healthy skin from the patient's or another's body to a wound or burn, to form new skin.

skinhead (skĭn′hĕd′), *n. Colloq.* a member of any group of young men identified by close-cropped hair and sometimes indulging in aggressive activities.

skink (skĭngk), *n.* any of the harmless, generally smooth-scaled, lizards constituting the family *Scincidae*, as *Scincus scincus*, of North Africa, formerly much used (dried) for medicinal purposes. [t. L: m. s. *scincus*, t. Gk: m. *skinkos*]

Skink, *Eumeces fasciatus* (Ab. 2 to 3 in. long)

skinned (skĭnd), *adj.* **1.** having a skin, esp. as specified: *thick-skinned, light-skinned.* **2. keep one's eyes skinned,** to be extremely vigilant.

skinner (skĭn′ə), *n.* **1.** one who skins. **2.** one who prepares, or deals in, skins.

Skinner (skĭn′ə), *n.* **1. Otis,** 1858–1942, U.S. actor. **2.** his daughter, **Cornelia Otis,** born 1901, U.S. actress and author.

skinnery (skĭn′ə rĭ), *n.*, *pl.* **-neries.** a place where skins are prepared, as for the market.

skinny (skĭn′ĭ), *adj.*, **-nier, -niest. 1.** lean; emaciated. **2.** of or like skin. **—skin′niness,** *n.*

skint (skĭnt), *adj. Slang.* penniless. [? var. of *skinned*. See SKIN (def. 15)]

skin-tight (skĭn′tīt′), *adj.* fitting as tightly as skin.

skip[1] (skĭp), *v.*, **skipped, skipping,** *n.* **—***v.i.* **1.** to spring, jump, or leap lightly; gambol. **2.** to pass from one point, thing, subject, etc., to another, disregarding or omitting what intervenes. **3.** *Colloq.* to go away hastily; abscond. **4.** *Educ., Chiefly U.S.* to be advanced more than one class. **5.** to ricochet, as a missile passing with rebounds along a surface. **6.** to use a skipping-rope. **—***v.t.* **7.** to jump lightly over. **8.** to miss out, as part of a continuum or one of a series. **9.** to pass over without reading, notice, mention, action, etc. **10.** to send (a missile) ricocheting along a surface. **11.** *Colloq.* to leave hastily, or flee from, as a place. **—***n.* **12.** a skipping movement; a light jump. **13.** a gait marked by such jumps. **14.** a passing from one point or thing to another, with disregard of what intervenes. **15.** *U.S. Music.* a leap. [ME. Cf. MSw. *skuppa* skip]

—Syn. 1. SKIP, BOUND refer to an elastic, springing movement. To SKIP is to give a series of light, quick leaps alternating the feet: *to skip about.* BOUND suggests a series of long, rather vigorous leaps; it is also applied to a springing or leaping type of walking or running rapidly and actively: *a dog came bounding up to meet him.*

skip[2] (skĭp), *n.* the captain of a team or side at curling or bowling. [short for SKIPPER[1]]

skip[3] (skĭp), *n.* **1.** a container attached to a crane or cable for transporting materials or refuse in building operations. **2.** a metal box for raising coal or minerals up a mine shaft. **3.** skep. [var. of SKEP]

skip distance, *Electronics.* the minimum distance from a transmitter at which waves reflected from the ionosphere can be detected.

skipjack (skĭp′jăk′), *n.*, *pl.* **-jacks,** (*esp. collectively*) **-jack. 1.** any of various fishes that leap from the water. **2.** an important tuna, *Katsuwonus pelamis*, of tropical waters.

ski-plane (skē′plān′), *n.* an aircraft fitted with skis, able to land on snow.

skipper[1] (skĭp′ə), *n.* **1.** the master or captain of a ship, esp. of a small trading or fishing vessel. **2.** a captain or leader, as of a team. **—***v.t.* **3.** to act as skipper of. [ME, t. MD: m. *schipper*, der. *schip* SHIP]

skipper[2] (skĭp′ə), *n.* **1.** one who or that which skips. **2.** any of various insects that hop or fly with jerky motions. **3.** any of the quick-flying lepidopterous insects constituting the family *Hesperiidae*, closely related to the true butterflies. **4.** the saury. [f. SKIP[1] + -ER[1]]

skippet (skĭp′ĭt), *n.* a small round box for protecting a seal as attached by a ribbon or cord to a document. [orig. uncert.; ? f. SKIP[3] + -ET]

skipping-rope (skĭp′ĭng rōp′), *n.* a rope, usually having handles at the ends, which is swung in a loop round one who leaps to let it pass between him and the ground.

skirl (skûl), *Scot. and N Dial.* **—***v.i., v.t.* **1.** to sound loudly and shrilly (used esp. of the bagpipe). **2.** to shriek. **—***n.* **3.** the sound of the bagpipe. **4.** a shrill sound. [metathetic var. of ME *scrille*, t. Scand.; cf. d. Norw. *skrylla*]

skirmish (skû′mĭsh), *n.* **1.** *Mil.* a fight between small bodies of troops, esp. advanced or outlying detachments of opposing armies. **2.** any brisk encounter. **—***v.i.* **3.** to engage in a skirmish. [ME *skirmysshe*, t. OF: m. *eskirmiss-*, s. *eskirmir*, t. OHG: m. *skirman* defend, der. *skirm* shield. See SCREEN] **—skir′misher,** *n.* **—Syn. 1.** See **battle**[1].

skirr (skû), *v.i.* **1.** to go rapidly; fly; scurry. **2.** to go rapidly over. —*n.* **3.** a grating or whirring sound. [imit.]

skirret (skĭr′rĭt), *n.* an umbelliferous plant, *Sium sisarum*, cultivated in Europe for its edible tuberous root. [ME *skirwhit(e)*, f. *skire* pure (t. Scand.; cf. Icel. *skīrr*) + WHITE]

skirt (skût), *n.* **1.** the lower part of a gown, coat, or the like, hanging from the waist. **2.** a separate garment (outer or under) worn by women and girls, extending from the waist downwards. **3.** some part resembling or suggesting the skirt of a garment. **4.** one of the flaps hanging from the sides of a saddle. See illus. under **saddle. 5.** a skirting board or bordering finish in building. **6.** (*usually pl.*) the bordering, marginal, or outlying part of a place, group, etc. **7.** a cut of beef from the flank. **8.** *Slang.* a woman or girl. —*v.t.* **9.** to lie on or along the border of. **10.** to border or edge with something. **11.** to pass along or around the border or edge of: *to skirt a town.* **12.** *Austral., N.Z.* to remove skirtings from fleece. —*v.i.* **13.** to be, lie, live, etc., on or along the edge of something. **14.** to pass or go around the border of something. [ME, t. Scand.; cf. Icel. *skyrta* SHIRT]

skirting (skû′tĭng), *n.* **1.** material for making skirts. **2.** a skirting board. **3.** (*pl.*) *Austral., N.Z.* the trimmings or inferior parts of fleece.

skirting board, a line of boarding protecting an interior wall next to the floor.

ski-stick (skē′stĭk′), *n.* one of two slender poles, metal-tipped and having a disc near the lower end to prevent it sinking into the snow, used by a skier for balance and to increase speed.

skit (skĭt), *n.* **1.** a slight parody, satire, or caricature, esp. dramatic or literary. **2.** a short satirical play. **3.** *Scot. and N Dial.* a good-humoured joke. [ME: harlot; cf. d. *skite* move fast. See SKITTER]

skite (skīt), *v.i.* **1.** *Austral., N.Z. Colloq.* to boast; brag. —*n.* **2.** a boast; brag.

skitter (skĭt′ə), *v.i.* **1.** to go, run, or glide lightly or rapidly. **2.** to skim along a surface. **3.** *Angling.* to draw a spoon or a baited hook over the water with a skipping motion. —*v.t.* **4.** to cause to skitter. [freq. of d. *skite* move fast, ? t. Scand.; cf. Icel. *skeyti* dart]

skittish (skĭt′ĭsh), *adj.* **1.** apt to start or shy. **2.** restlessly or excessively lively. **3.** fickle; uncertain. **4.** coy. [akin to SKITTER] —**skit′tishly,** *adv.* —**skit′tishness,** *n.*

skittle (skĭt′l), *n.* **1.** (*pl.*) ninepins. **2.** one of the pins. —*v.t.* **3.** to knock over or send flying, in the manner of skittles. [t. Scand.; cf. Dan. *skyttel* kind of ball (child's plaything)]

skive[1] (skīv), *v.t.*, **skived, skiving.** to split or cut (leather, etc.) into layers or slices; shave (hides, etc.). [t. Scand.; cf. Icel. *skīfa*, v., n., slice, c. ME *schive* slice (of bread)]

skive[2] (skīv), *v.i.*, **skived, skiving.** *Slang.* to shirk one's work or duty. [orig. obscure] —**skiv′er,** *n.*

skiver (skī′və), *n.* **1.** one who or that which skives. **2.** a thin sheepskin used for bookbinding, gloves, etc.

skivvy (skĭv′ĭ), *n., pl.* **skivvies.** *Slang.* (in contemptuous use) a female servant, esp. doing rough work. Also, **skivy.**

skoal (skōl), *n.* a word used in drinking someone's health. [t. Scand.; cf. Dan. *skaal* bowl, toast]

skokiaan (skŏk′ĭ än′), *n. S African.* an alcoholic drink, formerly prohibited, brewed at home mainly by urban Africans. [Johannesburg d.]

skolly (skŏl′ĭ), *n. S African.* (esp. among Cape Coloured people) a gangster. [Capetown d.]

Skopje (*Serb.* skôp′yĕ), *n.* a city in SE Yugoslavia: earthquake, 1963. 171,893 (1961).

Skt, Sanskrit. Also, **Skr.**

skua (skyoo͞′ə), *n.* a predatory gull or jaeger. [t. Faeroese: m. *skūgvur*, c. Icel. *skūfr*; orig. uncert.]

Great skua, *Catharacta skua* (2 ft long)

skulduggery (skŭl dŭg′ə rĭ), *n.* dishonourable proceedings; mean dishonesty or trickery. [var. of d. *sculduddery*; orig. obscure]

skulk (skŭlk), *v.i.* **1.** to lie or keep in hiding, as for some evil or cowardly reason. **2.** to shirk duty; malinger. **3.** to move or go in a mean, stealthy manner; sneak; slink. —*n.* **4.** one who skulks. **5.** an act of skulking. [ME, t. Scand.; cf. Dan. *skulke*] —**skulk′er,** *n.* —**Syn. 1.** See **lurk.**

skull (skŭl), *n.* **1.** the bony framework of the head, enclosing the brain and supporting the face; the skeleton of the head. **2.** (usually in disparaging use) the head as the seat of intelligence or knowledge. **3.** a death's-head. [ME *scolle*, t. Scand.; cf. d. Norw. *skol, skul* shell (of an egg or a nut)]

skull and crossbones, a representation of a front view of a human skull above two crossed bones, orig. used on pirate's flags, and now used as a warning sign, as in designating poisons.

skullcap (skŭl′kăp′), *n.* **1.** a brimless cap of silk, velvet, or the like, fitting closely to the head. **2.** any of various labiate herbs (genus *Scutellaria*) in which the calyx suggests a helmet, esp. *S. galericulata*, a common plant in wet places.

skunk (skŭngk), *n.* **1.** a small, striped, fur-bearing, bushy-tailed, North American mammal, *Mephitis mephitis*, of the weasel family, *Mustelidae*, which ejects a fetid fluid when attacked. **2.** its fur, used in garments. **3.** any of various allied or similar animals, as a spotted variety (genus *Spilogale*) or the members of the genus *Conepatus*. **4.** *Colloq.* a thoroughly contemptible person. —*v.t.* **5.** *U.S. Slang.* (in games) to beat so completely as to keep from scoring. [t. Amer. Ind. (Algonquian): m. *segankw* or *segongw* (Abnaki); c. Cree *sikâk*, Chippewa *shikag*, etc.]

Skunk, *Mephitis mephitis* (Total length 2 ft, tail 6½ to 7 in.)

skunk cabbage, 1. a low, fetid, broad-leaved, araceous plant, *Symplocarpus foetidus*, of North America, growing in moist ground. **2.** a similar araceous plant, *Lysichitum americanum*, found on the western coast of North America and in Siberia, Japan, etc. Also, **skunkweed** (skŭngk′wēd′).

Skutari (skoo͞′tə rĭ, skoo͞ tä′rĭ), *n.* Scutari (def. 1).

skutterudite (skŭt′ə rə dīt′), *n.* a mineral arsenide of cobalt and nickel occurring in greyish-white cubic crystals; used as a source of cobalt and nickel. [named after *Skutterud* in Norway]

sky (skī), *n., pl.* **skies,** *v.*, **skied** or **skyed, skying.** —*n.* **1.** (*often pl.*) the region of the clouds or the upper air. **2.** (*often pl.*) the heavens or firmament, appearing as a great arch or vault. **3.** the supernal or celestial heaven. **4.** climate. **5.** *Obs.* a cloud. **6. to the skies,** highly; extravagantly. —*v.t.* **7.** *Colloq.* to raise aloft; strike (a ball) high into the air. **8.** *Colloq.* to hang (a picture, etc.) high on the wall of a gallery. **9.** *Rowing.* to lift (the blade of an oar) too high above the water before a stroke. —*v.i.* **10.** *Rowing.* to sky a blade. [ME, t. Scand.; cf. Icel. *skȳ* cloud, c. OE *scēo* cloud] —**sky′like′,** *adj.*

sky blue, the colour of the unclouded sky in daytime; azure. —**sky′-blue′,** *adj.*

sky-diving (skī′dī′vĭng), *n.* parachute-jumping as a sport. —**sky′-di′ver,** *n.*

Skye (skī), *n.* an island in the Inner Hebrides, in Inverness-shire, Scotland. 7765 pop. (1961); 670 sq. mi.

Skye terrier, a small short-legged, very shaggy terrier.

Skye terrier (Ab. 9 in. high at the shoulder)

skyey (skī′ĭ), *adj. Chiefly Poetic.* **1.** of or from the sky. **2.** in the sky; lofty. **3.** skylike; sky blue. Also, **skiey.**

sky-high (skī′hī′), *adv., adj.*, very high.

skylark[1] (skī′läk′), *n.* a European lark, *Alauda arvensis*, noted for its singing in flight.

skylark[2] (skī′läk′), *v.i.* **1.** to frolic, sport or play about, esp. boisterously or in high spirits; play tricks. —*v.t.* **2.** to trick or play a trick on. [f. SKY + LARK[2], assoc. with LARK[1]]

Skylark, *Alauda arvensis* (7 in. long)

skylight (skī′līt′), *n.* **1.** an opening in a roof or ceiling, fitted with glass, for admitting daylight. **2.** the frame set with glass fitted to such an opening.

skyline (skī′līn′), *n.* **1.** the boundary line between earth and sky; the apparent horizon. **2.** the outline of something seen against the sky.

skyman (skī′mən), *n., pl.* **-men.** *Colloq.* an aviator.

sky pilot, 1. *Slang.* a clergyman. **2.** *U.S. Slang.* an aviator.

skyrocket (skī′rŏk′ĭt), *n.* **1.** a rocket (firework) that ascends into the air and explodes at a height. —*v.i.* **2.** *Colloq.* to move like a skyrocket; rise suddenly.

Skyros (skē′rŏs), *n.* a Greek island of the Northern Sporades group, in the W Aegean. 3193 pop. (1951); 81 sq. mi.

skysail (skī′sāl′; *Naut.* -səl), *n. Naut.* (in a square-rigged vessel) a light square sail next above the royal. See illus. under **sail.**

skyscraper (skī′skrā′pə), *n.* a relatively tall building of many storeys, esp. one for office or commercial use.

skyward (skī′wəd), *adj.* **1.** directed or tending towards the sky. —*adv.* **2.** skywards.

skywards (skī′wədz), *adv.* towards the sky. Also, **skyward.**

sky wave, *Radio.* a radio wave reflected by the ionosphere (opposed to *ground wave*).

skywriting (skī′rī′tĭng), *n.* **1.** the act or practice of writing against the sky with chemically produced smoke released from an aeroplane. **2.** the words, etc., traced.

s.l., (L *sine loco*) without place.

S.L., **1.** solicitor-at-law. **2.** south latitude.

slab[1] (slăb), *n., v.,* **slabbed, slabbing.** —*n.* **1.** a broad, flat, somewhat thick piece of stone, wood, or other solid material. **2.** a thick slice of anything: *a slab of bread.* **3.** a rough outside piece cut from a log, as in sawing it into boards. **4.** *Slang.* a mortuary table. **5.** *Print.* ink table. —*v.t.* **6.** to make into a slab or slabs. **7.** to cover or lay with slabs. **8.** to cut the slabs or outside pieces from (a log, etc.). [ME *slabbe, sclabbe*; orig. uncert.]

slab[2] (slăb), *adj.* *Archaic.* thick in consistency. [cf. Dan. *slab* mire, Icel. *slabb* slush]

slabber (slăb′ə), *v.i., v.t., n.* *U.S. and Dial.* slobber.

slab-sided (slăb′sī′dĭd), *adj.* *U.S. Colloq.* **1.** having the sides long and flat, like slabs. **2.** tall and lank.

slack[1] (slăk), *adj.* **1.** not tense or taut; loose: *slack rope.* **2.** indolent; negligent; remiss. **3.** slow; sluggish. **4.** lacking in activity; dull; not brisk: *slack times for business.* **5.** sluggish, as the water, tide, or wind.
—*adv.* **6.** in a slack manner; slackly.
—*n.* **7.** a slack condition, interval, or part. **8.** part of a rope, sail, or the like, that hangs loose, without strain upon it. **9.** a decrease in activity, as in business, work, etc. **10.** a period of decreased activity. **11.** *Geog.* a cessation in a strong flow, as of a tide at its turn. **12.** an act or period of lazing or idling. **13.** *Scot. and N Dial.* **a.** a depression between hills, in a hillside, or in the surface of ground. **b.** a boggy or wet hollow, or a morass. **14.** *Pros.* (in sprung rhythm) the unaccented syllable or syllables.
—*v.t.* **15.** to be remiss in respect to (some matter, duty, right, etc.); shirk; leave undone. **16.** to make or allow to become less active, vigorous, intense, etc.; relax or abate (efforts, labour, speed, etc.). **17.** to moderate. **18.** to make loose, or less tense or taut, as a rope; loosen. **19.** to slake (lime).
—*v.i.* **20.** to be remiss; shirk one's duty or part. **21.** to become less active, vigorous, rapid, etc. **22.** to moderate; slacken. **23.** to become less tense or taut, as a rope; to ease off. **24.** to become slaked, as lime.
[ME *slac,* OE *sleac, slæc,* c. Icel. *slakr*] —**slack′ly,** *adv.* —**slack′ness,** *n.*

slack[2] (slăk), *n.* the fine screenings of coal; small or refuse coal. [ME *slac,* t. MLG or MD: m. *schlacke* dross, splinterings. See SLAG]

slacken (slăk′ən), *v.i., v.t.* **1.** to make or become less active, vigorous, intense, etc. **2.** to make or become looser or less taut.

slacker (slăk′ə), *n.* one who avoids work, effort, etc.

slacks (slăks), *n.pl.* a kind of trousers, esp. those worn by either men or women as informal or sports wear.

slack water, the period of still water between tides.

slag (slăg), *n., v.,* **slagged, slagging.** —*n.* **1.** the more or less completely fused and vitrified matter separated during the reduction of a metal from its ore. **2.** the scoria from a volcano. —*v.t.* **3.** to convert into slag. —*v.i.* **4.** to form slag; become a slaglike mass. [t. MLG: m. *slagge,* c. G *Schlacke* dross, slag] —**slag′gy,** *adj.*

slagheap (slăg′hēp′), *n.* a pile or small hill, formed of waste matter from coal-mining, smelting, or some other process.

slain (slān), *v.* pp. of **slay.**

slake (slāk), *v.,* **slaked, slaking.** —*v.t.* **1.** to allay (thirst, desire, wrath, etc.) by satisfying. **2.** to cool or refresh. **3.** to disintegrate or treat (lime) with water or moist air, causing it to change into calcium hydroxide (**slaked lime**). **4.** to make less active, vigorous, intense, etc.; refresh. **5.** *Obs.* to make loose or less tense. —*v.i.* **6.** (of lime) to become slaked. **7.** *Rare.* to become less active, vigorous, etc. [ME; OE *slacian,* der. *slæc* slack]

slalom (slä′ləm), *n.* **1.** a downhill skiing race over a winding course defined by artificial obstacles. **2.** a similar race for canoes. [t. Norw.]

slam[1] (slăm), *v.,* **slammed, slamming,** *n.* —*v.t., v.i.* **1.** to shut with force and noise. **2.** to dash, strike, etc., with violent and noisy impact. **3.** *Slang.* to criticize severely. —*n.* **4.** a violent and noisy closing, dashing, or impact. **5.** the noise made. **6.** *Slang.* a severe criticism. [orig. uncert.]

slam[2] (slăm), *n.* *Cards.* **1.** the winning of all the tricks in one deal, as at whist (in bridge, called **grand slam**), or of all but one (in bridge, called **little slam**). **2.** an old type of card game associated with ruff. [orig. obscure]

slamse mense (slăm′sə mĕn′sə), *pl.* *S African.* the Malays of Cape Province. [Afrikaans: m. ISLAM + *mense* men]

slander (slăn′də), *n.* **1.** defamation; calumny. **2.** a malicious, false, and defamatory statement or report. **3.** *Law.* defamation in a transient form, as speech. —*v.t.* **4.** to utter slander concerning; defame. —*v.i.* **5.** to utter or circulate slander. [ME *sclandre,* t. AF: m. *esclaundre,* t. L: m. *scandalum.* See SCANDAL] —**slan′derer,** *n.* —**slan′derous,** *adj.* —**slan′derously,** *adv.* —**slan′derousness,** *n.*

slang (slăng), *n.* **1.** language differing from standard or written speech in vocabulary and construction, involving extensive metaphor, ellipsis, humorous usage, etc., less conservative and more informal than standard speech, and sometimes regarded as being in some way inferior. **2.** vulgar or abusive language. **3.** the jargon of a particular class, profession, etc. **4.** back slang. **5.** rhyming slang. —*v.i.* **6.** to use slang or abusive language. —*v.t.* **7.** to assail with abusive language. [orig. uncert.]

slanging match, a quarrelsome exchange, esp. of abuse.

slangkop (slăng′kŏp), *n.* a southern African plant, *Ornithoglossom glaucum,* poisonous to cattle. [t. Afrikaans: snake head]

slangy (slăng′ĭ), *adj.,* **slangier, slangiest.** **1.** pertaining to or of the nature of slang. **2.** using much slang. —**slang′ily,** *adv.* —**slang′iness,** *n.*

slank (slăngk), *v.* *Archaic.* pt. of **slink.**

slant (slănt), *v.i.* **1.** to slope; be directed or lie obliquely. —*v.t.* **2.** to slope; direct or turn so as to make (something) oblique. **3.** *Chiefly U.S.* **a.** to distort or give partisan emphasis to (a newspaper story, article, etc.) in order to present a point of view, esp. a critical one. **b.** to present (a publication, piece of writing, etc.) so as to attract a specified class of people. —*n.* **4.** slanting or oblique direction; slope: *the slant of a roof.* **5.** a slanting line, surface, etc. **6.** a mental leaning or tendency, esp. unusual or unfair; bias. **7.** an attitude, approach, or way of treating subjects, as the mood of a piece of writing, a mental tendency, etc. [defs 1–3 var. of *slent* (t. Scand.; cf. Norw. *slenta*), with vowel of ASLANT. Defs 4–7 aphetic var. of ASLANT] —**slant′ing,** *adj.* —**slant′ingly, slant′ly,** *adv.* —**Syn.** **1.** See **slope**[1]. **4.** incline, inclination, pitch, obliquity, obliqueness. **7.** angle.

slantwise (slănt′wīz′), *adv.* **1.** aslant; obliquely. —*adj.* **2.** slanting; oblique. Also, **slantways** (slănt′wāz′).

slap (slăp), *n., v.,* **slapped, slapping,** *adv.* —*n.* **1.** a smart blow, esp. with the open hand or with something flat. **2.** the sound of such a blow. **3.** a sarcastic or censuring hit or rebuke. —*v.t.* **4.** to strike smartly, esp. with the open hand or with something flat. **5.** to bring (the hands, etc.) against with a smart blow. **6. a.** to put or apply vigorously, haphazardly or in large quantities. **b.** to dash or cast forcibly. **7.** **slap down, a.** to put down forcibly. **b.** to rebuke or suppress the enthusiasm of. —*adv.* **8.** smartly; suddenly. **9.** *Colloq.* directly; straight. [t. LG: m. *slapp, slappe*; imit.]

slap-bang (slăp′băng′), *adv.* *Colloq.* violently; suddenly.

slapdash (slăp′dăsh′), *adv., adj.* **1.** in a hasty, haphazard manner. **2.** carelessly hasty or offhand. —*n.* **3.** roughcast.

slaphappy (slăp′hăp′ĭ), *adj.* *Colloq.* **1.** cheerful. **2.** irresponsible. **3.** punch-drunk.

slapjack (slăp′jăk′), *n.* **1.** a simple card game. **2.** *U.S.* a pancake.

slapstick (slăp′stĭk′), *n.* **1.** broad comedy in which rough play and knockabout methods prevail. **2.** a stick or lath used by harlequins, clowns, etc., as in pantomime, for striking other performers, often a combination of laths which make a loud, clapping noise without hurting a person struck. —*adj.* **3.** marked by the use of slapstick.

slap-up (slăp′ŭp′), *adj.* *Colloq.* first-rate; excellent.

slash (slăsh), *v.t.* **1.** to cut with a violent sweep or by striking violently and at random. **2.** to lash. **3.** to cut, reduce, or alter, esp. drastically. **4.** to make slits in (a garment) to show an underlying fabric. —*v.i.* **5.** to lay about one with sharp strokes; make one's way by cutting. **6.** to make a sweeping, cutting stroke. —*n.* **7.** a sweeping stroke. **8.** a cut or wound made with such a stroke; a gash. **9.** an ornamental slit in a garment showing an underlying fabric. **10.** *U.S.* (in forest land) **a.** an open area strewn with debris of trees from felling or from wind or fire. **b.** the debris itself. **11.** (*often pl.*) *U.S.* a tract of wet or swampy ground overgrown with bushes or trees. **12.** *Taboo Slang.* **have a slash,** to urinate. [ME *slasch(en),* ? t. OF: m. *eslachier* break] —**slash′er,** *n.*

slashing (slăsh′ĭng), *n.* **1.** slash. —*adj.* **2.** sweeping; cutting. **3.** violent; severe. **4.** severely critical or sarcastic. **5.** dashing; impetuous. **6.** *Colloq.* very large or fine: *a slashing fortune.* —**slash′ingly,** *adv.*

Śląsk (*Pol.* shlôNsk), *n.* Polish name of **Silesia.**

slat[1] (slăt), *n.*, *v.*, **slatted, slatting.** —*n.* **1.** a long, thin, narrow strip of wood, metal, etc., used as a support for a bed, as one of the horizontal laths of a venetian blind, etc. **2.** *Aeron.* an auxiliary aerofoil constituting the forward part of a slotted aerofoil. —*v.t.* **3.** to furnish or make with slats. [ME *slatt*, var. of *sclat*, t. OF: m. *esclat* piece broken or split off, akin to *escalater* burst]

slat[2] (slăt), *v.*, **slatted, slatting,** *n. Dial.* —*v.t.* **1.** to throw or dash with force. —*v.i.* **2.** to flap violently, as sails. —*n.* **3.** a slap; a sharp blow. [orig. obscure]

slate[1] (slāt), *n.*, *v.*, **slated, slating.** —*n.* **1.** a fine-grained rock formed by the compression of mudstone, that tends to split along parallel cleavage planes, usually at an angle to the planes of stratification. **2.** a thin piece or plate of this rock or a similar material, used esp. for roofing, or (when framed) for writing on. **3.** a dull, dark bluish grey. **4.** *U.S.* a tentative list of candidates, officers, etc., for acceptance by a nominating convention or the like. **5. clean slate,** a good record. **6. put on the slate,** to record a debt, as on a slate; give credit for. —*v.i.* **7.** to cover with or as with slate. **8.** *U.S.* to write or set down for nomination or appointment. [ME *sclate*, t. OF: m. *esclate* (fem.). See SLAT[1]]

slate[2] (slāt), *v.t.* **1.** to censure or reprimand severely. **2.** *Colloq.* to criticize or review adversely. [app. special use of SLATE[1]]

slate club, *Colloq.* **1.** a society whose members pay regular, usually small instalments towards the ultimate acquisition of goods, as at Christmas. **2.** a friendly society. **3.** a provident club.

slating (slā′tĭng), *n.* **1.** the operation of covering with slates. **2.** slates collectively. **3.** the material for slating.

slattern (slăt′ən), *n.* a slovenly, untidy woman or girl; a slut.

slatternly (slăt′ən lĭ), *adj.* **1.** having the appearance or ways of a slattern. **2.** characteristic or suggestive of a slattern. —*adv.* **3.** in the manner of a slattern.

slaty (slā′tĭ), *adj.*, **slatier, slatiest. 1.** consisting of, resembling, or pertaining to slate. **2.** slate-coloured.

slaughter (slô′tə), *n.* **1.** the killing or butchering of cattle, sheep, etc., esp. for food. **2.** the brutal or violent killing of a person. **3.** the killing by violence of great numbers of persons; carnage; massacre. —*v.t.* **4.** to kill or butcher (animals), esp. for food. **5.** to kill in a brutal or violent manner. **6.** to slay in great numbers; massacre. **7.** *Colloq.* to defeat thoroughly. [ME *slaghter*, t. Scand.; cf. Icel. *slātr* butcher's meat, *slātra* kill; akin to SLAY] —**slaugh′terer,** *n.*

—**Syn. 4–6.** SLAUGHTER, BUTCHER, MASSACRE all imply violent and bloody methods of killing. SLAUGHTER and BUTCHER, primarily referring to the killing of animals for food, are used also of the brutal or indiscriminate killing of human beings: *to slaughter cattle, to butcher a pig.* MASSACRE indicates a general slaughtering of helpless or unresisting victims: *to massacre the peasants of a region.*

slaughterhouse (slô′tə hous′), *n.* a building or place where animals are butchered for food; an abattoir.

slaughterous (slô′tə rəs), *adj.* murderous; destructive.

Slav (släv), *n.* **1.** one of a race of peoples widely spread over eastern, south-eastern, and central Europe, including the Russians and Ruthenians (**Eastern Slavs**), the Bulgars, Serbs, Croats, Slavonians, Slovenes, etc. (**Southern Slavs**), and the Poles, Czechs, Moravians, Slovaks, etc. (**Western Slavs**). **2.** Slavic. —*adj.* **3.** of, pertaining to, or characteristic of, the Slavs; Slavic. [t. ML: s. *Slavus*; r. ME *Sclave*, t. ML: m. s. *Sclavus*]

Slav., Slavic.

slave (slāv), *n.*, *v.*, **slaved, slaving.** —*n.* **1.** one who is the property of and wholly subject to, another; a bondservant. **2.** one who works for and is the prisoner of another; one who works under duress and without payment. **3.** one entirely under the domination of some influence: *a slave to cigarettes.* **4.** a drudge. —*v.i.* **5.** to work like a slave; drudge. —*v.t.* **6.** to enslave. [ME *sclave*, t. OF: m. *esclave*, t. ML: m. *sclavus* slave, SLAV; from the fact that many Slavs were reduced to slavery]

slave-ant (slāv′ănt′), *n.* an ant, as *Formica fusca,* held in captivity by any other species, as *Formica sanguinea* (called **slave-making ants**).

Slave Coast, the coast of W equatorial Africa, N of the Gulf of Guinea and between the Benin and Volta rivers: a centre of slave traffic, 16th–19th centuries.

slavedriver (slāv′drī′və), *n.* **1.** an overseer of slaves. **2.** a hard taskmaster.

slaveholder (slāv′hōl′də), *n.* one who owns slaves.

slave-labour (slāv′lā′bə), *n.* **1.** work performed by slaves. **2.** persons working under duress considered collectively, as prisoners in concentration camps or labour camps. **3.** *Colloq.* work considered as very badly paid.

slaver[1] (slā′və), *n.* **1.** a dealer in or an owner of slaves. **2.** a vessel engaged in the traffic in slaves. [f. SLAVE + -ER[1]]

slaver[2] (slăv′ə), *v.i.* **1.** to let saliva run from the mouth; slobber. **2.** to fawn. **3.** to express great desire by or as by slavering. —*v.t.* **4.** to wet or smear with saliva. —*n.* **5.** saliva coming from the mouth. **6.** drivel; twaddle. [ME, appar. t. Scand.; cf. Icel. *slafra*]

slavery (slā′və rĭ), *n.* **1.** the condition of a slave; bondage. **2.** the keeping of slaves as a practice or institution. **3.** a state of subjection like that of a slave. **4.** severe toil; drudgery.

—**Syn. 1.** SLAVERY, BONDAGE, SERVITUDE refer to involuntary subjection to another or others. SLAVERY emphasizes the idea of complete ownership and control by a master: *the institution of slavery.* BONDAGE indicates a state of subjugation or captivity often involving burdensome and degrading labour: *in bondage to a cruel master.* SERVITUDE is compulsory service, often such as is required by a legal penalty: *penal servitude.* —**Ant. 1.** liberty.

slave state, any of the states of the southern U.S. in which domestic slavery was practised and advocated up to the Civil War.

slave trade, 1. (*also caps.*) the transport of Negroes from Africa to America during the 17th–19th centuries. **2.** any commercial trading in slaves. —**slave′-trad′er,** *n.* —**slave′-trad′ing,** *n.*

slave traffic, slave trade.

slavey (slā′vĭ), *n.*, *pl.* **-veys.** *Colloq.* a female domestic servant; maid of all work.

Slavic (släv′ĭk), *n.* **1.** one of the principal groups of Indo-European languages, usually divided into **West Slavic** (Polish, Czech, Slovak, Serbian), **East Slavic** (Russian, Ukrainian, Ruthenian), and **South Slavic** (Old Church Slavonic, Bulgarian, Serbo-Croat, and Slovene). —*adj.* **2.** of or pertaining to the Slavs, or their languages.

slavish (slā′vĭsh), *adj.* **1.** of or befitting a slave: *slavish submission.* **2.** being or resembling a slave; abjectly submissive. **3.** base; mean; ignoble: *slavish fears.* **4.** painstakingly faithful, as a copy; lacking originality: *a slavish reproduction.* —**slav′ishly,** *adv.* —**slav′ishness,** *n.* —**Syn. 2.** See **servile.** —**Ant. 2.** independent.

Slavism (slä′vĭz′əm), *n.* the racial character, spirit, or tendencies of the Slavs.

Slavo-, form of **Slav** used in combination, as in *Slavo-Germanic.*

slavocracy (slā vŏk′rə sĭ), *n.*, *pl.* **-cies. 1.** the rule or domination of slaveholders. **2.** a dominating body of slaveholders. [f. SLAV(E) + -O- + -CRACY]

Slavonia (slə vō′nyə), *n.* a region in N Yugoslavia.

Slavonian (slə vō′nyən), *adj.* **1.** of or pertaining to Slavonia or its inhabitants. **2.** Slavic. —*n.* **3.** a native or inhabitant of Slavonia. **4.** a Slav.

Slavonic (slə vŏn′ĭk), *adj.* **1.** Slavonian. **2.** Slavic.

Slavophil (slä′vō fĭl′), *n.* **1.** a friend or admirer of the Slavs. —*adj.* **2.** friendly to or admiring the Slavs; favouring the Slavic interests, aims, etc. Also, **Slavophile** (slä′vō fīl′). —**Slavophilism** (slə vŏf′ĭ lĭz′əm, slä′vō fĭ lĭz′əm), *n.*

Slavophobe (slä′vō fōb′), *n.* one who fears the Slavs, or their influence or ascendancy.

slaw (slô), *n.* sliced or chopped cabbage served uncooked or cooked (cold or hot) with seasoning or dressing; coleslaw. [t. D: m. *sla*, short for *salade* SALAD]

slay (slā), *v.t.*, **slew, slain, slaying.** *Archaic.* **1.** to kill by violence. **2.** to destroy; extinguish. **3.** *Obs.* to strike; smite. [ME; OE *slēan*, c. G *schlagen*] —**slay′er,** *n.*

sleave (slēv), *v.*, **sleaved, sleaving,** *n.* —*v.t.* **1.** to divide or separate into filaments, as silk. —*n.* **2.** a filament of silk obtained by separating a thicker thread. **3.** a silk in the form of such filaments. **4.** *Poetic, Lit.* anything matted or ravelled. [OE *slǣfan*, akin to *slīfan* split]

sleazy (slē′zĭ), *adj.*, **-zier, -ziest. 1.** shabby, shoddy, untidy, or grubby. **2.** thin or poor in texture, as a fabric; flimsy. [orig. uncert.] —**slea′zily,** *adv.* —**slea′ziness,** *n.*

sled (slĕd), *n.*, *v.*, **sledded, sledding.** —*n.* **1.** a vehicle mounted on runners for conveying loads over snow, ice, rough ground, etc. **2.** a sledge, esp. a small one. **3.** a small vehicle of this kind used in tobogganing, etc.; a toboggan. —*v.i.* **4.** to ride or be carried on a sled. —*v.t.* **5.** to convey on a sled. [ME *sledde*, t. MFlem. or MLG; akin to G *Schlitten* sled]

sledder (slĕd′ə), *n.* **1.** one who rides on a sled. **2.** a horse or other animal that draws a sled.

sledding (slĕd′ĭng), *n.* **1.** the state of the ground permitting use of a sled. **2.** the going, or kind of travel, for sleds, as determined by the ground, etc.: *rough sledding.* **3.** the act of conveying or riding on a sled.

sledge[1] (slĕj), *n.*, *v.*, **sledged, sledging.** —*n.* **1.** any of various vehicles mounted on runners for travelling or conveying loads over snow, ice, rough ground, etc. **2.** a vehicle mounted on runners, and of various forms, used for travelling over snow and ice, as in northern countries;

a sleigh. 3. a sled, esp. a large one. 4. a toboggan. —*v.t.*, *v.i.* 5. to convey or travel by sledge. [t. MD: m. *sleedse*]

sledge² (slĕj), *n.*, *v.*, **sledged, sledging.** —*n.* 1. a sledge-hammer. —*v.i.*, *v.t.* 2. to strike, beat with or strike down with or as with a sledge-hammer. [ME *slegge*, OE *slecg*, c. D *slegge*]

sledge-hammer (slĕj′hăm′ə), *n.* 1. a large heavy hammer, often held with both hands, as used by blacksmiths, etc.; sledge. —*adj.* 2. like a sledge-hammer; powerful or ruthless. —*v.t.* 3. to strike or fell with, or as with, a sledge-hammer.

sleek¹ (slēk), *adj.* 1. smooth; glossy, as hair, an animal, etc. 2. well-fed or well-groomed. 3. smooth of manners, speech, etc. 4. suave; insinuating. [var. of SLICK¹] —**sleek′ly,** *adv.* —**sleek′ness,** *n.*

sleek² (slēk), *v.t.* to make sleek; smooth. [var. of SLICK²] —**sleek′er,** *n.*

sleeky (slē′kĭ), *adj.* 1. sleek; smooth. 2. artful; sly. Also, *Scot.*, **sleekit** (slē′kĭt).

sleep (slēp), *v.*, **slept, sleeping,** *n.* —*v.i.* 1. to take the repose or rest afforded by a suspension of the voluntary exercise of the bodily functions and the natural suspension, complete or partial, of consciousness. 2. to be dormant, quiescent, or inactive, as faculties. 3. to be unalert or inattentive. 4. to lie in death. 5. **sleep around,** to be sexually promiscuous. 6. **sleep in,** to sleep at the place of one's work. 7. **sleep out, a.** to sleep away from the place of one's work. **b.** to sleep in the open air. 8. **sleep on,** to postpone (a decision, etc.) overnight. 9. **sleep with,** to have sexual intercourse with. —*v.t.* 10. to take rest in (sleep). 11. to have beds or sleeping accommodation for: *a caravan that sleeps four.* 12. to spend or pass (time, etc.) in sleep (fol. by *away* or *out*). 13. to get rid of (a headache, etc.) by sleeping (fol. by *off* or *away*). —*n.* 14. the state of a person, animal, or plant that sleeps. 15. a period of sleeping: *a brief sleep.* 16. dormancy or inactivity. 17. the repose of death. [ME *slepe*, OE *slēpan*, *slāpan*, c. G *schlafen*]

sleeper (slē′pə), *n.* 1. one who or that which sleeps. 2. a timber, concrete, or steel beam forming part of a railway track, serving as a foundation or support for the rails. 3. a bed, place, or compartment in a sleeping-car. 4. a sleeping-car. 5. a ring worn in the ear lobe after piercing to prevent the hole from closing.

sleeping (slē′pĭng), *n.* 1. condition of being asleep. —*adj.* 2. that sleeps. 3. used for sleeping.

sleeping-bag (slē′pĭng băg′), *n.* a large bag, usually waterproof and warmly lined, for sleeping in, esp. for use out of doors.

sleeping-car (slē′pĭng kä′), *n.* a railway coach fitted with berths, compartments, etc., for passengers who wish to sleep during the journey.

sleeping-draught (slē′pĭng dräft′), *n.* a drink containing a drug which induces sleep.

sleeping partner, 1. a partner taking no active part in the conduct of a business, or not openly announced as a partner. 2. a person with whom one sleeps.

sleeping-pill (slē′pĭng pĭl′), *n.* a tablet, capsule, or pill, containing a soporific drug.

sleeping sickness, *Pathol.* 1. African sleeping sickness. 2. a form of inflammation of the brain marked by extreme weakness, drowsiness, or sleepiness, usually associated with paralysis, of some cerebral nerves.

sleepless (slēp′lĭs), *adj.* 1. without sleep: *a sleepless night.* 2. alert. 3. always active: *the sleepless ocean.* —**sleep′lessly,** *adv.* —**sleep′lessness,** *n.*

sleep-movement (slēp′mo͞ov′mənt), *n.* *Bot.* one of the movements of leaves and flowers or their parts, when they close at night.

sleepwalking (slēp′wô′kĭng), *n.* 1. the state or act of walking or performing other activities while asleep. —*adj.* 2. of or pertaining to the state of walking while asleep. —**sleep′walk′er,** *n.*

sleepy (slē′pĭ), *adj.*, **sleepier, sleepiest.** 1. ready or inclined to sleep; drowsy. 2. of or showing drowsiness. 3. languid; languorous. 4. lethargic; sluggish. 5. quiet: *a sleepy village.* 6. inducing sleep. 7. over-ripe, as fruit. —**sleep′ily,** *adv.* —**sleep′iness,** *n.*

sleepyhead (slē′pĭ hĕd′), *n.* *Colloq.* a sleepy or lazy person.

sleet (slēt), *n.* 1. snow or hail and rain falling together. 2. *Chiefly U.S.* the frozen coating on trees, wires, and other bodies that sometimes forms when rain or sleet falls at a low temperature. 3. *U.S.* frozen or partly frozen rain. —*v.i.* 4. to send down sleet. 5. to fall as or like sleet. [ME *slete*, akin to LG *slote*, G *Schlossen* hail] —**sleet′y,** *adj.*

sleeve (slēv), *n.*, *v.*, **sleeved, sleeving.** —*n.* 1. the part of a garment that covers the arm, varying in form and length but commonly tubular. 2. *Mach.* a tubular piece, as of metal, fitting over a rod or the like. 3. a cover or container for a gramophone record. 4. **laugh up one's sleeve,** to be secretly or inwardly amused. 5. **up one's sleeve,** secretly ready or at hand. 6. **wear one's heart on one's sleeve,** to display one's emotions openly. —*v.t.* 7. to furnish with sleeves. 8. *Mech.* to fit with a sleeve; join or fasten by means of a sleeve. [ME *sleve*, OE *slēfe* (Anglian), c. D *sloof* apron] —**sleeve′less,** *adj.*

sleeve valve, *Mech.* a thin metal sleeve with ports cut in it which is made to rotate and reciprocate between the cylinder and the piston of an internal-combustion engine so that it acts either as an inlet or exhaust valve.

sleigh (slā), *n.* 1. a vehicle on runners, drawn by horses, dogs, etc., and used for transport on snow or ice. 2. a toboggan. —*v.i.* 3. to travel or ride in a sleigh. [t. D: m. *slee*, short for *slede* SLED] —**sleigh′er,** *n.*

sleighbell (slā′bĕl′), *n.* a small bell attached to a sleigh or its harness.

sleight (slīt), *n.* 1. skill; dexterity. 2. *Rare.* an artifice; stratagem. 3. *Obs.* cunning; craft. [ME, var. of *slegthe*, t. Scand.; cf. Icel. *slǣgdh*, der. *slægr* SLY]

sleight of hand, 1. skill in feats of jugglery or legerdemain. 2. the performance of such feats. 3. a feat of jugglery or legerdemain.

slender (slĕn′də), *adj.* 1. small in circumference in proportion to height or length. 2. small in size, amount, extent, etc.: *a slender income.* 3. having little value, force or justification: *slender prospects.* 4. thin or weak, as sound. [ME *slendre*, *sclendre*; orig. uncert.] —**slen′derly,** *adv.* —**slen′derness,** *n.*

—**Syn.** 1. SLENDER, SLIGHT, SLIM imply a tendency towards thinness. As applied to the human body, SLENDER implies a generally attractive and pleasing thinness: *slender hands.* SLIGHT often adds the idea of frailness to that of thinness: *a slight figure almost fragile in appearance.* SLIM implies a lithe or delicate thinness: *a slim and athletic figure.* —**Ant.** 1. fat, stocky.

slenderize (slĕn′də rīz′), *v.t.*, **-rized, -rizing.** 1. to make slender or more slender. 2. *U.S.* to cause to appear slender: *dresses that slenderize the figure.* Also, **slenderise.**

slept (slĕpt), *v.* pt. and pp. of **sleep.**

Slesvig (*Dan.* slĕs′vĭ), *n.* Danish name of **Schleswig.**

Sleswick (slĕs′wĭk), *n.* Schleswig.

sleuth (slo͞oth), *n.* 1. *Colloq.* a detective. 2. a sleuthhound or bloodhound. —*v.t.*, *v.i.* 3. to track or trail as a detective does. [ME *sloth*, t. Scand.; cf. Icel. *slōdh* track, trail]

sleuthhound (slo͞oth′hound′), *n.* 1. a bloodhound. 2. a detective.

S Level, *Educ.* Scholarship Level.

slew¹ (slo͞o), *v.* pt. of **slay.**

slew² (slo͞o), *v.t.* 1. to turn or twist (something), esp. upon its own axis or without moving it from its place. 2. to cause to swing round. —*v.i.* 3. to swerve awkwardly; swing round; twist. —*n.* 4. such a movement. 5. the position reached by slewing. [orig. uncert.]

slew³ (slo͞o), *n.* *U.S. and Can.* a marshy pool or inlet. [var. of SLOUGH¹]

Slezsko (*Cz.* slĕs′kŏ), *n.* Czech name of **Silesia.**

slice (slīs), *n.*, *v.*, **sliced, slicing.** —*n.* 1. a thin, broad, flat piece cut from something: *a slice of bread.* 2. a part; portion. 3. any of various implements with a thin, broad blade or part, as for turning food in a frying pan, for serving fish at table, for taking up printing ink, etc. 4. *Sport.* a slicing stroke, kick, hit, etc. —*v.t.* 5. to cut into slices; divide into parts. 6. to cut through or cleave like a knife: *the ship sliced the sea.* 7. to cut (*off, away, from,* etc.) as or like a slice. 8. to remove by means of a slice (implement), slice bar, or the like. 9. *Sport.* **a.** (in cricket, golf, soccer, etc.) to hit or kick the ball with the striking surface oblique, deliberately or accidentally, so that it does not travel along the line of force of the stroke. **b.** (in rowing) to put the blade slantwise into the water instead of square to the surface, so that it goes too deep. —*v.i.* 10. *Sport.* to slice the ball. [ME, t. OF: m. *esclice*, *esclisse* splinter, sliver of wood, ult. t. Gmc; cf. OHG *slitz* slit] —**slice′able,** *adj.* —**slic′er,** *n.*

slice bar, a long-handled instrument with a blade at the end, for clearing away or breaking up clinkers, etc., in a furnace.

slick¹ (slĭk), *adj.* 1. sleek; glossy. 2. smooth of manners, speech, etc. 3. sly; shrewdly adroit. 4. ingenious; cleverly devised. 5. slippery, as though covered with oil. —*n.* 6. a smooth place or spot, as an oil-covered area on the sea. 7. a patch or film of oil or the like, as on the sea. 8. *U.S. Slang.* a magazine in which the paper is finished to have a more or less glossy surface, implying a high-grade content, but sometimes regarded as intellectually shallow. —*adv.* 9. smoothly; cleverly. [ME *slike*, adj., c. Flem. *sleek* even, smooth] —**slick′ly,** *adv.* —**slick′ness,** *n.*

slick² (slĭk), *v.t.* 1. to make sleek or smooth. 2. *U.S. Colloq.* to make smart or fine (fol. by *up*). [ME *slike(n)*, v., OE *-slician*; akin to Icel. *slīkja* give a gloss to]

slickenside (slĭk′ən sīd′), *n.* *Geol.* a rock surface which has become more or less polished and striated from the sliding or grinding motion of an adjacent mass of rock. [f. *slicken* (d. var. of SLICK[1]) + SIDE]

slicker (slĭk′ə), *n. U.S.* **1.** a long, loose oilskin or waterproof outer coat. **2.** *Colloq.* a swindler; a sly cheat. **3.** *Foundry.* a small trowel used for smoothing the surface of the mould.

slide (slīd), *v.*, **slid, slid** or **slidden, sliding,** *n.* —*v.i.* **1.** to move along in continuous contact with a smooth or slippery surface: *to slide down a snow-covered hill.* **2.** to slip, as one losing foothold or as a vehicle skidding. **3.** to glide or pass smoothly onwards. **4.** to slip easily, quietly, or unobtrusively (fol. by *in, out, away,* etc.). **5.** to go unregarded: *to let things slide.* **6.** to pass or fall gradually into a specified state, character, practice, etc.
—*v.t.* **7.** to cause to slide, as over a surface or with a smooth, gliding motion. **8.** to slip (something) easily or quietly (fol. by *in, into,* etc.).
—*n.* **9.** the act of sliding. **10.** a smooth surface for sliding on. **11.** *Geol.* **a.** a landslide or the like. **b.** the mass of matter sliding down. **12.** a single image for projection in a projector; transparency (def. 4b). **13.** a plate of glass or other material on which objects are placed for microscopic examination. **14.** Also, **hair slide.** a clip for holding a woman's hair in place. **15.** that which slides, as part of a machine. **16.** *Music.* **a.** an embellishment or grace-note consisting of an upward or downward series of three or more notes, the last of which is the principal note. **b.** a portamento. **c.** (in instruments of the trumpet class, esp. the trombone) a section of the tube, usually U-shaped, which can be pushed in or out to alter the length of the air column and thus the pitch of the notes. **17.** *Rowing.* a sliding seat or its runners. **18.** a construction bearing an inclined smooth slope for children to slide down for amusement.
[ME; OE *slīdan*, c. MLG *slīden*] —**slid′er,** *n.*
—**Syn. 1.** SLIDE, GLIDE, SLIP suggest movement over a smooth surface. SLIDE suggests a rather brief movement of one surface over another in contact with it: *to slide downhill.* GLIDE suggests a continuous, smooth, easy, and (usually) noiseless motion: *a skater glides over the ice.* To SLIP is to slide smoothly, often in a sudden or accidental way: *to slip on the ice and fall.*

slide bars, guide bars.

slide fastener, a zip (def. 1).

Slide Mountain, a mountain in the U.S., in SE New York State: highest peak of the Catskill Mountains. 4204 ft.

slide rule, a device for rapid calculation, consisting essentially of a rule having a sliding piece moving along it, both marked with graduated logarithmic scales.

slide valve, 1. *Mach.* a valve that slides (without lifting) to open or close an aperture, as the valves of the ports in the cylinders of certain steam-engines. **2.** *Music.* a perforated slide used to cut off the air supply to a rank of organ pipes when a key is depressed.

sliding scale, 1. a variable scale, esp. of industrial costs, as wages, raw materials, etc., which may be adapted to demand. **2.** a wage scale varying with the selling price of goods produced, the cost of living, or profits.

sliding seat, *Rowing.* a seat on runners which moves forward and back with the rower's movement to lengthen his stroke.

Sliema (slē′mə), *n.* a town in E Malta. 23,399 (1957).

Slieve Donard (slēv′dŏn′äd), the highest peak of Northern Ireland, in Co. Down. 2796 ft.

slight (slīt), *adj.* **1.** small in amount, degree, etc.: *a slight increase, a slight smell.* **2.** of little weight, or importance; trifling. **3.** slender; slim. **4.** frail; flimsy. **5.** lacking in solid or substantial qualities. —*v.t.* **6.** to treat as of slight importance. **7.** to treat with indifference; ignore. **8.** to snub; ignore pointedly. —*n.* **9.** slighting indifference or treatment. **10.** an instance of slighting treatment. **11.** a pointed and contemptuous ignoring; an affront. [ME; OE *sliht* smooth (in *earthslihtes* close to earth), c. Icel. *slēttr* smooth, G *schlicht* smooth, *schlecht* bad, Goth. *slaihts* smooth] —**slight′ly,** *adv.* —**slight′ness,** *n.*
—**Syn. 3.** See **slender. 6.** SLIGHT, DISREGARD, NEGLECT, OVERLOOK mean to pay no attention or too little attention to someone or something. To SLIGHT is irresponsibly to give only superficial attention to something important: *to slight someone's work.* To DISREGARD is to pay no attention to a person or thing: *to disregard the rules*; in some circumstances, to DISREGARD may be admirable: *to disregard a handicap.* To NEGLECT is to shirk paying sufficient attention to a person or thing: *to neglect one's correspondence.* To OVERLOOK is to fail to see someone or something (possibly because of carelessness): *to overlook a bill which is due.* **11.** See **insult.** —**Ant. 6.** notice.

slighting (slī′tĭng), *adj.* derogatory; disparaging. —**slight′ingly,** *adv.*

Sligo (slī′gō), *n.* **1.** a county in Northern Ireland in Connaught province. 53,561 pop. (1961); 694 sq. mi. **2.** its county town: a seaport. 13,145 (1961).

slim (slĭm), *adj.*, **slimmer, slimmest,** *v.*, **slimmed, slimming.** —*adj.* **1.** slender, as in girth or form; slight in build or structure. **2.** poor; insufficient; meagre: *a slim chance, a slim excuse.* **3.** small, inconsiderable, or scanty: *a slim income.* **4.** *Obs.* crafty. —*v.t.* **5.** to make slim. —*v.i.* **6.** to make oneself slim, as by dieting, exercise, etc. **7.** to become slim. [t. D or LG; c. G *schlimm* bad] —**slim′ly,** *adv.* —**slim′ness,** *n.* —**Syn. 1.** See **slender.**

Slim (slĭm), *n.* **William Joseph, 1st Viscount,** 1891–1970, British field marshal.

slime (slīm), *n.*, *v.*, **slimed, sliming.** —*n.* **1.** thin, glutinous mud. **2.** any ropy or viscous liquid matter, esp. of a foul or offensive kind. **3.** a viscous secretion of animal or vegetable origin. **4.** *Colloq.* servility; quality of being ingratiating. —*v.t.* **5.** to cover or smear with, or as with, slime. **6.** to remove slime from, as fish for canning. [ME *slyme*, OE *slīm*, c. G *Schleim*]

slime mould, a group of primitive organisms having a motile amoeboid stage and a non-motile spore-producing stage, thus showing characteristics of both the animal and plant kingdoms.

slimmer (slĭm′ə), *n.* one who makes himself, or tries to make himself, slimmer or lighter by dieting, etc.

slimsy (slĭm′zĭ), *adj. U.S.* flimsy; frail.

slimy (slī′mĭ), *adj.*, **slimier, slimiest. 1.** of or like slime. **2.** abounding in or covered with slime. **3.** foul; vile. **4.** *Colloq.* servile; unpleasantly ingratiating. —**slim′ily,** *adv.* —**slim′iness,** *n.*

sling[1] (slĭng), *n.*, *v.*, **slung, slinging.** —*n.* **1.** an instrument for hurling stones, etc., by hand, consisting of a strap or piece for holding the missile, with two strings attached, the ends of which are held in the hand (or attached to a staff), the whole being whirled rapidly before discharging the missile. **2.** a catapult. **3.** a rope or chain used in hoisting cargo in and out of a ship. **4.** a bandage used to suspend an injured part of the body, as an arm or hand, by looping round the neck. **5.** a strap, band, or the like forming a loop by which something is suspended or carried, as a strap attached to a rifle and passed over the shoulder. **6.** the act of slinging. **7.** (*usually pl.*) *Naut.* **a.** a rope or chain supporting a yard. **b.** a rope, wire, or chain forming a loop, used for hoisting cargo, etc. —*v.t.* **8.** to throw, cast, or hurl; fling, as from the hand. **9.** to place in or secure with a sling to raise or lower. **10.** to raise, lower, etc., by such means. **11.** to hang in a sling or so as to swing loosely: *to sling a rifle over one's shoulder.* **12.** to suspend. [ME *slynge(n)*, t. Scand.; cf. Icel. *slyngva*] —**sling′er,** *n.*

sling[2] (slĭng), *n.* an iced alcoholic drink, containing gin or the like, water, sugar, and lemon or lime juice. [cf. G *schlingen* swallow]

slingshot (slĭng′shŏt′), *n. U.S.* **1.** a catapult (def. 1). **2.** a sling (def. 1).

slink (slĭngk), *v.*, **slunk** or (*Archaic*) **slank; slunk; slinking;** *n.*, *adj.* —*v.i.* **1.** to go in a furtive, abject manner, as from fear, cowardice, or shame. **2.** to move stealthily, as to evade notice. —*v.t.* **3.** (of cows, etc.) to bring forth (young) prematurely. —*n.* **4.** a prematurely born calf or other animal. —*adj.* **5.** born prematurely: *a slink calf.* [ME *slynke*, OE *slincan* creep, crawl, c. LG *slinken*, G *schlinken*] —**slink′ingly,** *adv.*

slinky (slĭng′kĭ), *adj. Colloq.* **1.** sinuous; gliding; slender and flowing. **2.** stealthy; sinister, or menacing, esp. in movement.

slip[1] (slĭp), *v.*, **slipped** or (*Archaic*) **slipt; slipped; slipping;** *n.* —*v.i.* **1.** to pass or go smoothly or easily; glide; slide (fol. by *along, away, down, off, over, through,* etc.): *water slips off a smooth surface.* **2.** to slide suddenly and involuntarily, as on a smooth surface; to lose one's foothold. **3.** to move, slide, or start from place, position, fastenings, the hold, etc. **4.** to get away, escape, or be lost: *to let an opportunity slip.* **5.** to go, come, get, etc., easily or quickly: *to slip into a dress.* **6.** to pass insensibly, as from the mind or memory; pass quickly or imperceptibly (fol. by *away, by,* etc.), as time. **7.** to go quietly; steal. **8.** to move quickly and lightly. **9.** to pass superficially, carelessly, or without attention, as over a matter. **10.** to make a slip, mistake, or error (often fol. by *up*). **11.** *Colloq.* to become somewhat reduced in quantity or quality: *the market slipped today.* **12. let slip,** to say unintentionally: *to let slip the truth.*
—*v.t.* **13.** to cause to slip, pass, put, draw, etc., with a smooth, easy, or sliding motion: *to slip one's hand into a drawer.* **14.** to put or draw quickly or stealthily: *to slip a letter into a person's hand.* **15.** to put (*on*) or take (*off*) easily or quickly, as a garment. **16.** to let slip from fastenings, the hold, etc. **17.** to release from a leash or the like, as a hound or a hawk. **18.** to untie or undo (a knot). **19.** *Naut.* to let go entirely, as an anchor cable or an anchor. **20.** to let pass unheeded; neglect or miss. **21.** to pass over or omit, as in speaking or writing. **22.** to slip away from, escape from or elude, as a pursuer. **23.** to release oneself

from (restraint, etc.). **24.** to escape (one's memory, notice, knowledge, etc.). **25.** (of animals) to bring forth (offspring) prematurely. **26.** *Motor Vehicles.* to operate (the clutch) gradually so that the drive to the wheels increases speed smoothly. **27. be slipping,** to be losing one's acuteness, abilities, or the like. **28. let slip,** to say or reveal unintentionally.
—*n.* **29.** the act of slipping. **30.** a slipping of the feet, as on slippery ground. **31.** a mishap. **32.** a mistake, often inadvertent, as in speaking or writing: *a slip of the tongue.* **33.** an error in conduct; an indiscretion. **34.** the eluding of a pursuer, guard, or other person: *to give someone the slip.* **35.** something easily slipped on or off. **36.** a kind of dog's lead. **37.** a woman's sleeveless underdress. **38.** a pillowcase. **39.** a slipway. **40.** *Naut.* the difference between the theoretical speed at which a screw propeller or paddle-wheel would move if it were working against a solid and the actual speed at which it advances through the water. **41.** *U.S.* a space between two wharves or in a dock, for vessels to lie in. **42.** (in pumps) the difference between the actual volume of water or other liquid delivered by a pump during one complete stroke, and the theoretical volume as determined by calculation of the displacement. **43.** *Elect.* the fraction by which the rotor speed of an induction motor is less than the speed of rotation of the stator field. **44.** *Cricket.* **a.** the position of a fielder who stands behind and to the offside of the wicket-keeper. **b.** the fielder himself. **45.** *Geol.* **a.** the relative displacement of formerly adjacent points on opposite sides of a fault, measured along the fault plane. **b.** a small fault. **46.** *Metall.* the deformation of a metallic crystal caused by one part gliding over another part along a plane (**slip plane**). **47.** (*pl.*) *Theatre.* **a.** the space on either side of the stage. **b.** similar parts of the auditorium.
[ME *slyppe*, prob. t. MLG: m. *slippen*, c. d. G *schlippen*, akin to OE *slipor* slippery] **—Syn. 2.** See **slide. 32.** See **mistake.**

slip[2] (slĭp), *n.*, *v.*, **slipped, slipping.** —*n.* **1.** a piece suitable for propagation cut from a plant; a scion or cutting. **2.** any long, narrow piece or strip, as of wood, paper, land, etc. **3.** a young person, esp. one of slender form. **4.** a small paper form on which information is noted: *a withdrawal slip.* **5.** a galley proof. **6.** a small whetstone with a wedge-shaped cross-section in which one or two sides are rounded. **7.** *U.S.* a long seat or narrow pew, as in a church. —*v.t.* **8.** to take slips or cuttings from (a plant); take (a part), as a slip from a plant. [late ME, t. MD or MLG: m. *slippe* cut, slit, strip, etc.]

slip[3] (slĭp), *n.* *Ceramics.* potter's clay made semifluid with water, used for coating or decorating pottery. [ME and OE *slype*; orig. uncert. Cf. Norw. *slip* slime]

slip-coach (slĭp′kōch′), *n.* a coach at the end of a train which can be detached without stopping the train. Also, **slip-carriage.**

slip cover, *U.S.* a loose cover.

slipknot (slĭp′nŏt′), *n.* a knot which slips easily along the cord or line round which it is made. See illus. under **knot.**

slipnoose (slĭp′no͞os′), *n.* a noose with a knot that slides along the rope, thus forming a noose that tightens as the rope is pulled.

slip-on (slĭp′ŏn′), *adj.* **1.** designed to be slipped on easily, as a loose blouse. **2.** slipover. —*n.* **3.** a slip-on garment or article of dress.

slipover (slĭp′ō′və), *adj.* designed for slipping over the head, as a blouse or sweater; a pullover.

slippage (slĭp′ĭj), *n.* **1.** the act of slipping. **2.** the amount or extent of slipping. **3.** *Mach.* the amount of work dissipated by slipping of parts, excess play, etc.

slipped disc, a protrusion of an intervertebral disc, often responsible for pain in the back radiating down the back of the leg.

slipper (slĭp′ə), *n.* **1.** a light shoe into which the foot may be easily slipped for indoor wear. **2.** any similar shoe, as a woman's shoe for dancing. —*v.t.* **3.** to beat with a slipper. [f. SLIP[1], v. + -ER[1]] —**slip′pered,** *adj.* —**slip′per-like′,** *adj.*

slippering (slĭp′ə rĭng), *n.* a beating with a slipper.

slipperless (slĭp′ə lĭs), *adj.* without slippers.

slipper satin, fine satin with a dull finish.

slippery (slĭp′ə rĭ, slĭp′rĭ), *adj.*, **-perier, -periest. 1.** tending to cause slipping or sliding, as ground, surfaces, things, etc. **2.** tending to slip from the hold or grasp or from position: *a slippery rope.* **3.** likely to slip away or escape. **4.** not to be depended on; fickle; shifty, tricky, or deceitful. **5.** unstable or insecure, as conditions, etc. [f. obs. *slipper* slippery (ME *sliper*, OE *slipor*) + -Y[1]] —**slip′periness,** *n.*

slippery elm, 1. a species of elm, *Ulmus fulva*, of eastern North America, with a mucilaginous inner bark. **2.** the bark, used as a demulcent.

slip plane, *Metall.* See **slip**[1] (def. 46).

slippy (slĭp′ĭ), *adj.* *Now Colloq. or Dial.* **1.** slippery. **2.** nimble, quick, or sharp. —**slip′piness,** *n.*

sliprail (slĭp′rāl′), *n.* *Austral.* part of a fence which can serve as a gate.

slipring (slĭp′rĭng′), *n.* *Elect.* a metal ring, usually of copper or cast iron, mounted so that current may be conducted through stationary brushes into or out of a rotating member.

slip-road (slĭp′rōd′), *n.* a road for entering or leaving a motorway.

slipsheet (slĭp′shēt′), *U.S.* —*v.t.*, *v.i.* **1.** to interleaf. —*n.* **2.** an interleafed sheet.

slipshod (slĭp′shŏd′), *adj.* **1.** untidy, or slovenly; careless or negligent. **2.** wearing slippers or loose shoes, esp. ones down at the heel.

slipslop (slĭp′slŏp′), *n.* *Colloq.* **1.** a sloppy food or drink. **2.** meaningless, loose, or trifling talk or writing. [varied redupl. of SLOP[1]]

slipstream (slĭp′strēm′), *n.* **1.** *Aeron.* the air current forced back by an aircraft propeller or jet at speeds greater than the surrounding air. **2.** any similar air current behind any moving object.

slipt (slĭpt), *v.* *Archaic.* pt. of **slip**[1].

slip-up (slĭp′ŭp′), *n.* *Colloq.* a mistake or blunder: *several minor slip-ups in spelling.*

slipway (slĭp′wā′), *n.* an inclined plane or ramp, esp. one sloping to the water, serving as a landing place or a site on which vessels are built or repaired.

slit (slĭt), *v.*, **slit, slitting,** *n.* —*v.t.* **1.** to cut apart or open along a line; make a long cut, fissure, or opening in. **2.** to cut or rend into strips; split. —*n.* **3.** a straight, narrow cut, opening, or aperture. [ME *slitte*, OE *-slittan* (N dial.), c. OHG *slizzan* (G *schlitzen*) split, slit. See SLICE] —**slit′ter,** *n.*

slither (slĭth′ə), *v.i.* **1.** to slide down or along a surface, esp. unsteadily or with more or less friction or noise. **2.** to go or walk with a sliding motion. —*v.t.* **3.** to cause to slither or slide. —*n.* **4.** a slithering movement; a slide. [ME; var. of d. *slidder* (c. LG *slidderan*), OE *slidrian*, freq. of *slīdan* SLIDE]

slit trench, 1. *Mil.* a narrow trench for one or more persons for protection against enemy fire and shrapnel. **2.** a foxhole. **3.** any narrow trench.

Sliven (*Bulg.* slĕ′vĕn), *n.* a town in E central Bulgaria. 67,491 (1964).

sliver (slĭv′ə), *n.* **1.** a slender piece, as of wood, split, broken, or cut off, usually lengthwise or with the grain; splinter. **2.** a continuous strand or band of loose, untwisted wool, cotton, etc., ready for roving or slubbing. —*v.t.* **3.** to split or cut off, as a sliver; split or cut into slivers. **4.** to form (wool, cotton, etc.) into slivers. —*v.i.* **5.** to split. [ME *slivere*, der. *slyve*, OE *slīfan* split]

slivovitz (slĭv′ə vĭts, slē′və-), *n.* a colourless plum brandy, common in south-eastern Europe. [t. Serbo-Croat: m. *sljivovica*]

Sloane (slōn), *n.* **Sir Hans,** 1660–1753, British physician and naturalist.

slob (slŏb), *n.* **1.** *Irish.* mud or ooze, or a stretch of mud, esp. along a shore. **2.** *Slang.* a stupid, clumsy, uncouth, or slovenly person. [t. Irish: m. *slab* mud, t. E. See SLAB[2]]

slobber (slŏb′ə), *v.i.* **1.** to let saliva, etc., run from the mouth; slaver; dribble. **2.** to indulge in mawkish sentimentality. —*v.t.* **3.** to wet or make foul by slobbering. **4.** to utter with slobbering. —*n.* **5.** saliva or liquid dribbling from the mouth; slaver. **6.** mawkishly sentimental speech or actions. Also, **slabber.** [var. of *slabber*, der. SLAB[2]] —**slob′berer,** *n.*

slobbery (slŏb′ə rĭ), *adj.* **1.** characterized by slobbering. **2.** disagreeably wet; sloppy.

sloe (slō), *n.* **1.** the small, sour, blackish fruit (drupe) of the blackthorn, *Prunus spinosa.* **2.** the shrub itself. [ME *slo*, OE *slā(h)*, c. G *Schlehe*]

sloe-eyed (slō′īd′), *adj.* having eyes like sloes; dark-eyed or having attractively narrow eyes.

sloe gin, a cordial or liqueur flavoured with sloe.

slog (slŏg), *v.*, **slogged, slogging,** *n.* *Slang.* —*v.t.* **1.** to hit hard, as in boxing, cricket, etc. **2.** to drive with blows. —*v.i.* **3.** to deal heavy blows. **4.** to walk steadily and firmly; plod heavily. **5.** to toil. —*n.* **6.** a strong blow with little finesse. **7.** a spell of hard work or walking. [var. of SLUG[2], v.] —**slog′ger,** *n.*

slogan (slō′gən), *n.* **1.** a distinctive cry or phrase of any party, class, body, or person; a catchword. **2.** a war cry or gathering cry, as formerly used among the Scottish clans. [t. Gaelic: m. *sluagh-ghairm* army cry]

sloop (slo͞op), *n.* a single-masted sailing vessel carrying fore-and-aft sails consisting of jibs, foresail, and mainsail and gaff-topsail. [t. D: m. *sloep*, c. G *Schlup*; akin to OE *slūpan* glide]

sloop-of-war (slo͞op′ə wô′), *n. Obs.* a relatively small sailing or steam vessel, mounting guns or cannons on only one deck.

slop[1] (slŏp), *v.*, **slopped, slopping,** *n.* —*v.t.* **1.** to spill or splash (liquid). **2.** to spill liquid upon. —*v.i.* **3.** to spill or splash liquid (sometimes fol. by *about*). **4.** (of liquid) to run (over) in spilling. **5.** *Colloq.* (of persons, etc.) to be unduly effusive; gush (fol. by *over*). **6.** to walk or go through mud, slush, or water. —*n.* **7.** a quantity of liquid carelessly spilled or splashed about. **8.** (*often pl.*) weak or unappetizing liquid or semiliquid food. **9.** (*often pl.*) the dirty water, liquid refuse, etc., of a household or the like. **10.** swill, or the refuse of the kitchen, etc., often used as food for pigs or the like. **11.** liquid mud. **12.** (*pl.*) *Distilling.* the mash remaining after distilling. [ME *sloppe* mudhole, OE *-sloppe* (in *cusloppe* cowslip, lit., cow slime); akin to SLIP[3]]

slop[2] (slŏp), *n.* (*often pl.*) **1.** clothing, bedding, tobacco, etc., supplied or sold to seamen from the ship's stores. **2.** a loose outer garment, as a jacket, tunic, or smock. **3.** cheap ready-made clothing in general. **4.** *Archaic.* wide knickerbockers. [ME *sloppe*, OE *-slop* (in *oferslop* overgarment), c. Icel. *sloppr* gown]

slop-basin (slŏp′bā′sən), *n.* a small bowl for the reception of teacup dregs at table. Also, **slop′-bowl′.**

slop chest, a store of seamen's clothing, tobacco, and other personal articles kept on board a ship for sale to the crew during a voyage.

slope (slōp), *v.*, **sloped, sloping,** *n.* —*v.i.* **1.** to take or have an inclined or slanting direction, esp. downwards or upwards from the horizontal. **2.** to descend or ascend at a slant. —*v.t.* **3.** to direct at a slope or inclination; incline from the horizontal. **4.** to form with a slope or slant. —*n.* **5.** inclination or slant, esp. downwards or upwards. **6.** deviation from the horizontal. **7.** an inclined surface. **8.** (*often pl.*) an area of sloping ground. **9.** *Mil.* the position of standing with the rifle resting at a slope on the shoulder. [aphetically der. *aslope*, adv., on a slant] —**slop′er,** *n.* —**slop′ing,** *adj.* —**slop′ingly,** *adv.* —**slop′ingness,** *n.*

—**Syn. 1.** SLOPE, SLANT mean to incline away from some surface or line used as a reference. To SLOPE is to incline in an oblique direction from a perpendicular line: *the ground slopes sharply here.* To SLANT is to fall to one side, to lie obliquely to some line whether horizontal or perpendicular: *the road slants off to the right.*

slope[2] (slōp), *v.i.*, **sloped, sloping.** *Slang.* **1.** to move or go. **2. slope off,** to go away, esp. furtively.

slop-pail (slŏp′pāl′), *n.* a pail for removing slops.

sloppy (slŏp′ĭ), *adj.*, **-pier, -piest. 1.** muddy, slushy, or very wet, as ground, walking, weather, etc. **2.** splashed or soiled with liquid. **3.** of the nature of slops, as food; watery and unappetizing. **4.** *Colloq.* weak, silly, or maudlin: *sloppy sentiment.* **5.** *Colloq.* loose, careless, or slovenly: *to use sloppy English.* **6.** *Colloq.* untidy, as dress. —**slop′pily,** *adv.* —**slop′piness,** *n.*

sloppy joe, a loose, thick sweater.

slopshop (slŏp′shŏp′), *n.* a cheap clothing shop.

slopwork (slŏp′wûk′), *n.* **1.** the manufacture of cheap clothing. **2.** clothing of this kind. **3.** any work done cheaply or poorly. —**slop′work′er,** *n.*

slosh (slŏsh), *n.* **1.** slush. **2.** *Colloq.* watery or weak drink. **3.** *Colloq.* a heavy blow. —*v.i.* **4.** to splash in slush, mud, or water. —*v.t.* **5.** to stir in some fluid: *to slosh the mop in the pail.* **6.** to pour, stir, spread, etc., a liquid or similar (often fol. by *in, on, round,* etc.). [b. SLOP[1] and SLUSH] —**slosh′y,** *adj.*

sloshed (slŏsht), *adj. Slang.* drunk.

slot[1] (slŏt), *n.*, *v.*, **slotted, slotting.** —*n.* **1.** a narrow, elongated depression or aperture, esp. one to receive or admit something. **2.** *Aeron.* an air passage in an aerofoil directing the air from the lower to the upper surface. —*v.t.* **3.** to provide with a slot or slots; make a slot in. **4.** to insert into a slot (usually fol. by *in*). [ME, t. OF: m. *esclot* hollow between breasts] —**slot′ter,** *n.*

slot[2] (slŏt), *n.* **1.** the track or trail of a deer or other animal, as shown by the marks of the feet. **2.** the track, trace, or trail of anything. [t. AF and OF: m. *esclot* hoofprint of a horse; prob. akin to SLEUTH]

sloth (slōth), *n.* **1.** habitual disinclination to exertion; indolence; laziness. **2.** either of two genera of sluggish arboreal edentates of the family *Bradypodidae* of tropical America: the **two-toed sloth,** *Choloepus,* having two toes on the front foot, and the **three-toed sloth,** *Bradypus,* having three toes on the front foot. [ME *slowth* (f. SLOW + -TH[1]), r. OE *slǣwth* (der. *slǣw*, var. of *slaw* SLOW)]

Two-toed sloth
Choloepus hoffmanni
(2 ft long)

sloth-bear (slōth′bĕə′), *n.* a coarse-haired, long-snouted bear, *Melursus ursinus,* of SE Asia.

Sloth-bear,
Melursus ursinus
(2½ ft high at the shoulder, total length ab. 5 ft)

slothful (slōth′fəl), *adj.* sluggardly; indolent; lazy. —**sloth′fully,** *adv.* —**sloth′fulness,** *n.* —**Syn.** See **idle.**

slot-machine (slŏt′ məshēn′), *n.* a machine for vending small articles, weighing, gambling, etc., operated by dropping a coin in a slot.

slouch (slouch), *v.i.* **1.** to sit or stand in an awkward, drooping posture. **2.** to move or walk with loosely drooping body and careless gait. **3.** to have a droop or downward bend, as a hat. —*v.t.* **4.** to cause to droop or bend down, as the shoulders or a hat. —*n.* **5.** a drooping or bending forward of the head and shoulders; an awkward, drooping carriage of a person. **6.** a drooping or hanging down of the brim of a hat, etc. **7.** an awkward, ungainly, or slovenly person. **8.** *U.S. Slang.* an inefficient or inferior person or thing (esp. with a negative). [orig. uncert.; first occurs as n.] —**slouch′y,** *adj.* —**slouch′ily,** *adv.* —**slouch′iness,** *n.*

slouch hat, a soft hat, esp. one with a broad, flexible brim.

slough[1] (slou *for 1, 3*; slo͞o *for 2*), *n.* **1.** a piece of soft, muddy ground; a hole full of mire, as in a road; marsh; swamp. **2.** *U.S., Can.* a marshy or reedy pool, pond, inlet, or the like. **3.** a condition of degradation, embarrassment, or helplessness. [ME; OE *slōh*, c. MLG *slōch*, MHG *sluoche* ditch] —**slough′y,** *adj.*

slough[2] (slŭf), *n.* **1.** the skin of a snake, esp. the outer skin which is shed periodically. **2.** *Pathol.* a mass or layer of dead tissue which separates from the surrounding or underlying tissue. **3.** *Bridge.* a discard. —*v.i.* **4.** to be shed or cast off, as the slough of a snake. **5.** to cast off a slough. **6.** *Pathol.* to separate from the sound flesh, as a slough. —*v.t.* **7.** to cast (fol. by *off*). **8.** to shed as or like a slough. **9.** *Bridge.* to dispose of (a losing card). [ME *slugh(e)*, *slouh*, c. G *Schlauch* skin, bag] —**slough′y,** *adj.*

Slough (slou), *n.* a town in SE England, in Buckinghamshire. 84,900 (est. 1964).

Slovak (slō′văk), *n.* **1.** one of a Slavic people dwelling in Slovakia. **2.** the language of Slovakia, a Slavic language very similar to Czech. —*adj.* **3.** of or pertaining to the Slovaks, their language, etc. [t. Czech, c. Polish *Slowak.* Cf. SLOVENE]

Slovakia (slō văk′ĭ ə), *n.* an independently administered region of E Czechoslovakia. 4,350,533 pop. (est. 1965); 18,921 sq. mi. *Cap.*: Bratislava. Czech, **Slovensko** (*Cz.* slŏ′vĕn skŏ). —**Slovakian** (slō văk′ĭ ən), *adj.*, *n.*

sloven (slŭv′ən), *n.* **1.** one who is habitually negligent of neatness or cleanliness in dress, appearance, etc. **2.** one who works, or does anything, in a negligent, slipshod manner. [ME *sloveyn.* Cf. D *slof* careless, negligent]

Slovene (slō′vēn), *n.* **1.** one of a Slavic people dwelling in Slovenia. **2.** a South Slavic language spoken in Slovenia. —*adj.* **3.** of or pertaining to the Slovenes, their language, etc. [t. G, t. Slovenian, g. OSlavonic *Slovĕne.* Cf. SLAV, SLOVAK]

Slovenia (slō vē′nyə), *n.* a constituent republic of Yugoslavia, in the NW part. 1,591,523 pop. (1961); 6265 sq. mi. *Cap.*: Ljubljana. —**Slove′nian,** *adj.*, *n.*

slovenly (slŭv′ən lĭ), *adj.*, **-lier, -liest,** *adv.* —*adj.* **1.** having the habits of a sloven; untidy. **2.** characteristic of a sloven; slipshod. —*adv.* **3.** in a slovenly manner. —**slov′enliness,** *n.* —**Ant. 1.** neat.

slow (slō), *adj.* **1.** taking or requiring a comparatively long time for moving, going, acting, occurring, etc.; not fast, rapid or swift. **2.** leisurely; gradual, as change, growth, etc. **3.** sluggish in nature, disposition, or function. **4.** dull of perception or understanding, as a person, the mind, etc. **5.** not prompt, readily disposed, or in haste (fol. by *to* or an infinitive): *slow to take offence.* **6.** burning or heating with little speed or intensity, as a fire or an oven. **7.** slack, as trade. **8.** showing a time earlier than the correct time, as a clock. **9.** passing heavily, or dragging, as time. **10.** not progressive; behind the times. **11.** dull, humdrum, uninteresting or tedious. **12.** *Photog.* (of film) requiring a long exposure. **13.** *Sport.* (of a pitch, track, court, etc., or its surface) tending to slow down movement, as of a ball. —*adv.* **14.** in a slow manner; slowly. —*v.t.* **15.** to make slow or slower. **16.** to retard; reduce the speed of (often fol. by *up, down,* etc.). —*v.i.* **17.** to become slow or slower; slacken in speed (often fol. by *up, down,* etc.). [ME; OE *slāw* sluggish, dull, c. D *sleeuw.* Cf. SLOTH] —**slow′ly,** *adv.* —**slow′ness,** *n.*

—**Syn. 1.** SLOW, DELIBERATE, GRADUAL, LEISURELY mean unhurried and not happening rapidly. That which is SLOW acts or moves without haste or rapidity: *a slow procession of cars.* DELIBERATE implies the slowness which marks careful consideration before and while acting: *a deliberate and calculating manner.* GRADUAL suggests the slowness of that which advances one step at a time: *a gradual improvement in service.* That which is LEISURELY moves with the slowness allowed by ample time or the absence of pressure: *an unhurried and leisurely stroll.* **4.** See **dull.** **—Ant.** **1.** fast, hasty, sudden, hurried.

slowcoach (slō′kōch′), *n. Colloq.* a slow or dull person.

slowdown (slō′doun′), *n.* **1.** *U.S.* a go-slow. **2.** a slowing down.

slow handclap, clapping by an audience, slow, and often in unison, usually to express displeasure, impatience at delay, or the like.

slow march, a march in slow time.

slow match, a slow-burning match or fuse, often consisting of a rope or cord soaked in a solution of saltpetre.

slow-motion (slō′mō′shən), *adj. Films.* denoting or pertaining to films in which the images move more slowly than their originals, due to having been photographed at a greater number of frames per second than normal, or being projected more slowly than normal.

slow neutron, *Physics.* a neutron whose kinetic energy is less than ten electron volts.

slow time, the pace used in marching on certain ceremonial parades, as burials, usually 65 paces to the minute.

slow-witted (slō′wĭt′ĭd), *adj.* slow of wit or intelligence; dull of understanding.

slow-worm (slō′wûm′), *n.* a European species of limbless lizard, *Anguis fragilis*; blindworm.

sloyd (sloid), *n.* a system of manual training in woodworking, etc., orig. developed in Sweden. [t. Sw.: m. *slöjd* craft, industrial art, woodworking, c. SLEIGHT]

slub (slŭb), *v.*, **slubbed, slubbing,** *n.* **—***v.t.* **1.** to draw out and twist slightly after carding or slivering, as wool or cotton. **—***n.* **2.** the partially twisted wool or the like produced by slubbing. **3.** yarn made with bunches of untwisted fibres at intervals. [orig. uncert.]

sludge (slŭj), *n.* **1.** mud, mire, or ooze; slush. **2.** a deposit of ooze at the bottom of bodies of water. **3.** any of various more or less mudlike deposits or mixtures. **4.** the sediment in a steam boiler or water tank. **5.** a later stage of sea freezing than frazil, in which the ice particles coagulate to form a thick, soupy surface layer having a mat appearance. **6.** a mixture of some finely powdered substance and water. **7.** sediment deposited during the treatment of sewage. **8.** a fine, mudlike powder produced by a mining drill. [ME *slich* slime; ? imit.] **—sludg′y,** *adj.*

slue (slōō), *v.*, **slued, sluing,** *n.* slew².

slug¹ (slŭg), *n.* **1.** any of various slimy, elongated terrestrial gastropods related to the terrestrial snails, but having no shell or only a rudimentary one. **2.** a slow-moving animal, vehicle, or the like. **3.** any heavy piece of crude metal. **4.** a piece of lead or other metal for firing from a gun. **5.** a metal disc used as a coin, generally counterfeit. **6.** *Print.* **a.** a thick strip of type metal less than type-high. **b.** such a strip containing a type-high number, etc., for temporary use. **c.** a line of type in one piece, as produced by a linotype machine. **7.** *Mech.* a unit of mass, equal to about 32·2 pounds, which, if acted upon by a force of one pound, will have an acceleration of one foot per second. [ME *slugge*, t. Scand.; cf. d. Norw. *sluggje* heavy, slow person]

Common garden slug, *Arion hortensis* (1½ in. long)

slug² (slŭg), *v.*, **slugged, slugging,** *n. U.S. Colloq.* **—***v.t.* **1.** to strike heavily; hit hard, esp. with the fist; to slog. **—***n.* **2.** a heavy blow, esp. with the fist. [? orig., hit with a slug (piece of lead)]

slugabed (slŭg′ə bĕd′), *n. Archaic.* one given to lying long in bed, as from laziness.

sluggard (slŭg′əd), *n.* **1.** one who is habitually inactive or slothful. **—***adj.* **2.** sluggardly. [ME *slogard(e)*, f. obs. *sluggy* sluggish + -ARD]

sluggardly (slŭg′əd lĭ), *adj.* like or befitting a sluggard; slothful; lazy.

slugger (slŭg′ə), *n. Chiefly U.S. Colloq.* **1.** one who strikes hard, esp. with the fists or a baseball bat. **2.** a prizefighter. **3.** a slogger.

sluggish (slŭg′ĭsh), *adj.* **1.** indisposed to action or exertion, esp. by nature; inactive, slow, or of little energy or vigour. **2.** not acting or working with full vigour, as bodily organs. **3.** moving slowly, or having little motion, as a stream. **4.** slow, as motion. **—slug′gishly,** *adv.* **—slug′gishness,** *n.* **—Syn. 1.** See **inactive.**

sluice (slōōs), *n.*, *v.*, **sluiced, sluicing.** **—***n.* **1.** an artificial channel for conducting water, fitted with a sluicegate. **2.** the body of water held back or controlled by a sluicegate. **3.** any contrivance for regulating a flow from or into a receptacle. **4.** a channel, esp. one carrying off surplus water; a drain. **5.** a stream of surplus water. **6.** an artificial channel of water for moving solid matter on or in: *a lumbering sluice.* **7.** *Mining.* **a.** a long, sloping trough or the like, with grooves in its bottom, into which water is directed to separate gold from gravel or sand. **b.** a long inclined trough to wash ores in. **8.** *Colloq.* a brief wash, esp. in running water. **—***v.t.* **9.** to let out (water, etc.) or draw off the contents of (a pond, etc.) by, as or by, the opening of a sluice. **10.** to open a sluice upon. **11.** to flush or cleanse with a rush of water. **12.** *Mining.* to wash in a sluice. **13.** to send (logs, etc.) down a sluiceway. **—***v.i.* **14.** to flow or pour through or as through a sluice. **15.** *Colloq.* to wash briefly, esp. in running water. [ME *scluse*, t. OF: m. *escluse*, g. LL *exclūsa*, fem. pp., shut out]

sluicegate (slōōs′gāt′), *n.* a gate at the upper end of a sluice for regulating the flow.

sluiceway (slōōs′wā′), *n.* **1.** a channel controlled by a sluicegate. **2.** any artificial channel for water.

slum (slŭm), *n.*, *v.*, **slummed, slumming.** **—***n.* **1.** (*often pl.*) an overpopulated, squalid part of a city, inhabited by the poorest people. **2.** a squalid street, place, dwelling, or the like. **—***v.i.* **3.** to visit slums, esp. from curiosity. **4.** to live in squalid or disorganized circumstances (often fol. by *it*). [first occurs as slang word for room; orig. obscure] **—slum′mer,** *n.* **—slum′my,** *adj.*

slumber (slŭm′bə), *v.i.* **1.** (often literary) to sleep, esp. deeply. **2.** to sleep lightly; doze; drowse. **3.** to be in a state of inactivity, negligence, quiescence, or calm. **—***v.t.* **4.** to spend (time) in slumbering (fol. by *away*, etc.). **5.** to drive (away) by slumbering. **—***n.* **6.** (*often pl.*) sleep, esp. deep sleep. **7.** light sleep. **8.** a period of sleep. **9.** a state of inactivity, quiescence, etc. [ME *slumeren*, freq. of *slumen* slumber, doze, der. OE *slūma*, n. Cf. G *schlummern*] **—slum′berer,** *n.*

slumberous (slŭm′bə rəs, -brəs), *adj.* **1.** inclined to slumber; sleepy; heavy with drowsiness, as the eyelids. **2.** causing or inducing sleep. **3.** pertaining to, characterized by, or suggestive of slumber. **4.** inactive or sluggish; calm or quiet. Also, **slum′bery, slum′brous.**

slump (slŭmp), *v.i.* **1.** to drop heavily and limply. **2.** to sink into a bog, muddy place, etc., or through ice or snow. **3.** to fall suddenly and markedly, as prices, the market, etc. **4.** to have a decided falling off in progress, as an enterprise, a competitor, etc. **5.** to sink heavily, as the spirits, the posture, etc. **—***n.* **6.** the act of slumping. **7.** a considerable decline in the economy, a market, etc. **8.** a decline in prices or sales. **9.** a decided falling off in progress, as in an undertaking. [v. use of d. *slump* bog, c. LG *schlump*]

slung (slŭng), *v.* pt. and pp. of **sling.**

slung shot, *U.S.* a piece of metal, a stone, etc., fastened to a short strap, chain, or the like, used as a weapon.

slunk (slŭngk), *v.* pt. and pp. of **slink.**

slur (slû), *v.*, **slurred, slurring,** *n.* **—***v.t.* **1.** to pass over lightly, or without due mention or consideration (often fol. by *over*). **2.** to pronounce (a syllable, word, etc.) indistinctly, as in hurried or careless utterance. **3.** *Music.* **a.** to sing in a single breath, or play without a break (two or more notes of different pitch). **b.** to mark with a slur. **4.** to calumniate, disparage, or depreciate. **5.** *Obs.* to smirch or sully. **—***v.i.* **6.** to go through anything hurriedly and carelessly. **—***n.* **7.** a slurred utterance or sound. **8.** *Music.* **a.** the combination of two or more notes of different pitch, sung to a single syllable or played without a break. **b.** a curved mark indicating this. **9.** a disparaging remark; a slight. **10.** a blot or stain, as upon reputation; discredit. **11.** *Print.* a spot which is blurred or unclear. [der. d. *slur* fluid mud, ? akin to Icel. *slor* offal (of fish)]

Slur (def. 8)

slurry (slŭ′rĭ), *n.* **1.** a suspension of a solid in a liquid, esp. a thin paste containing cement. **2.** a semifluid mixture of clay or the like and water.

slush (slŭsh), *n.* **1.** snow in a partly melted state. **2.** liquid mud; watery mire. **3.** refuse fat, grease, etc., from the galley of a ship. **4.** *Colloq. or U.S.* a mixture of grease and other materials for lubricating. **5.** *Colloq.* silly, sentimental, or weakly emotional writing, talk, etc. **—***v.t.* **6.** to splash with slush. **7.** to wash with much water, as by dashing it on. **8.** *Colloq. or U.S.* to grease, polish, or cover with slush. **9.** *U.S.* to flush. [appar. c. Norw. *slusk* slops] **—slush′y,** *adj.*

slush fund, *U.S.* **1.** a fund for use in campaign propaganda or the like, esp. secretly or illicitly, as in bribery. **2.** a fund from the sale of slush, refuse fat, etc., aboard ship, spent for any small luxuries.

slut (slŭt), *n.* **1.** a dirty, slovenly woman. **2.** an immoral woman. **3.** a female dog. [ME; cf. d. E *slut* mud, d. Norw. *slutr* sleet, impure liquid] **—slut′tish,** *adj.*

sly (slī), *adj.*, **slyer, slyest** or **slier, sliest.** **1.** cunning or wily, as persons or animals, or their actions, ways, etc. **2.** stealthy, insidious, or secret. **3.** playfully artful, mischievous, or roguish: *sly humour.* **4. on the sly,** secretly. [ME *sly, sley,* t. Scand.; cf. Icel. *slœgr* sly, cunning, Sw. *slög* dexterous] —**sly'ly,** *adv.* —**sly'ness,** *n.* —**Syn. 2.** surreptitious, underhand, furtive.

sly grog, *Austral., N.Z.* illegally sold liquor.

slype (slīp), *n. Archit.* a covered passage, esp. one from the transept of a cathedral to the chapterhouse. [cf. West Flem. *slijpe* secret path]

Sm, *Chem.* samarium.

S.M., 1. (F *Sa Majesté*) His (Her) Majesty. **2.** (L *Scientiae Magister*) Master of Science. **3.** sergeant major.

smack[1] (smăk), *n.* **1.** a taste or flavour, esp. a slight flavour distinctive or suggestive of something. **2.** a trace, touch, or suggestion of something. **3.** a taste, mouthful, or small quantity. —*v.i.* **4.** to have a taste, flavour, trace, or suggestion (often fol. by *of*). [ME *smacke,* OE *smæc,* c. MLG *smak,* G (*Ge*)*schmack* taste]

smack[2] (smăk), *v.t.* **1.** to strike smartly, esp. with the open hand or anything flat. **2.** to bring, put, throw, send, etc., with a sharp, resounding blow or a smart stroke. **3.** to separate (the lips) smartly so as to produce a sharp sound, often as a sign of relish, as in eating. —*v.i.* **4.** to smack together, as the lips. **5.** to come or strike smartly or forcibly, as against something. **6.** to make a sharp sound as of striking against something. —*n.* **7.** a smart, resounding blow, esp. with something flat. **8.** a resounding or loud kiss. **9.** a smacking of the lips, as in relish. **10. have a smack at,** to attempt. **11. smack in the eye,** *Colloq.* **a.** a snub. **b.** a setback or disappointment. —*adv.* **12.** *Colloq.* with a smack; suddenly and sharply. **13.** *Colloq.* directly; straight. [cf. D and LG *smakken,* d. G *schmacken*; of imit. orig.]

smack[3] (smăk), *n.* **1.** a sailing vessel, usually sloop-rigged, used esp. in coasting and fishing. **2.** a fishing vessel with a well to keep fish alive. [t. D: m. *smak*]

smacker (smăk'ə), *n.* **1.** one who or that which smacks. **2.** smack[2] (def. 7). **3.** smack[2] (def. 8). **4.** *Slang.* a pound (money).

smacking (smăk'ĭng), *adj.* **1.** smart, brisk, or strong, as a breeze. **2.** unusually big or large.

small (smôl), *adj.* **1.** of limited size; of comparatively restricted dimensions; not big; little. **2.** slender, thin, or narrow. **3.** not large, as compared with other things of the same kind. **4.** not great in amount, degree, extent, duration, value, etc. **5.** not great numerically. **6.** of low numerical value; denoted by a low number. **7.** having only little land, capital, etc., or carrying on business on a limited scale: *a small businessman.* **8.** of minor importance, moment, weight, or consequence. **9.** (of a letter) lower-case. **10.** humble, modest, or unpretentious. **11.** characterized by or indicative of littleness of mind or character; mean-spirited; ungenerous. **12.** ashamed or mortified: *to feel small.* **13.** of little strength or force. **14.** (of sound or the voice) gentle, soft, or low. **15.** (of a child) young. **16.** weak; diluted. —*adv.* **17.** in a small manner. **18.** into small pieces: *to slice small.* **19.** in low tones; softly. **20. sing small,** to become humble; behave humbly. —*n.* **21.** that which is small. **22.** persons or things which are small considered collectively. **23.** the lower central part of the back. **24.** (*pl.*) *Colloq.* small items of personal laundry; underclothes. [ME *smal(e),* OE *smæl,* c. D *smal,* G *schmal*] —**small'ness,** *n.*

—**Syn. 1.** See **little. 3.** SMALLER, LESS indicate a diminution, or not so large a size or quantity in some respect. SMALLER, as applied to concrete objects, is used with reference to size: *smaller apples.* LESS is used of material in bulk, with reference to amount, and in cases where attributes such as value and degree are in question: *a penny is less than sixpence.* As an abstraction, amount may be either SMALLER or LESS, though SMALLER is usually used when the idea of size is suggested: *a smaller opportunity.* LESS is used when the idea of quantity is present: *less courage.* **8.** trifling, trivial, petty. —**Ant. 3.** larger, more.

small ad, one of a number of short advertisements in small type in a newspaper, magazine, etc., usually concerned with individual needs.

smallage (smô'lĭj), *n. Obs.* celery, *Apium graveolens,* esp. in its wild state. [ME *smalege, smalache,* f. *smal* small + *ache* parsley (t. OF, g. L *apium*)]

small arms, firearms collectively which are small enough to be carried by a man, as rifles, revolvers, etc. —**small'-arms',** *adj.*

small beer, 1. weak beer. **2.** *Colloq.* matters or persons of little or no importance.

small calorie. See **calorie** (def. 1a).

small capitals, small capital letters; letters having the form of regular upper-case letters of a particular printing type, but being about the same height as the lower-case letters. Also, **small caps.** *Abbrev.:* s.c.

small change, 1. metallic money of small denomination. **2.** that which is trifling, ordinary, or common.

small circle, a circle on a sphere, whose plane does not pass through the centre of the sphere.

smallclothes (smôl'klōz', -klōthz'), *n.pl. Archaic.* knee breeches, esp. those worn in the 18th and 19th century.

small end, the end of a connecting rod in an engine which is connected to the piston or the piston rod.

small fry, 1. small or young fish. **2.** young or unimportant persons or objects.

small hail, *Meteorol.* hail in pellets comprising soft-hail nuclei with outer coverings of clear ice.

smallholding (smôl'hōl'dĭng), *n.* **1.** a holding of agricultural land smaller than an ordinary farm. **2.** *Law.* a holding of land of between one and fifty acres, or exceeding fifty acres but having an annual value of less than £100. —**small'hol'der,** *n.*

small hours, the early hours of the morning; the hours following midnight.

smallish (smô'lĭsh), *adj.* rather small.

small letter, a lower-case letter.

small-minded (smôl'mīn'dĭd), *adj.* selfish or narrow in attitude. —**small'-mind'edness,** *n.*

small pica, a printing type (11 point) of a size between long primer and pica.

smallpox (smôl'pŏks'), *n.* an acute, highly contagious, febrile disease characterized by a pustular eruption which often leaves permanent pits or scars.

smallreed (smôl'rēd'), *n.* any of several species of grasses of the genus *Calamagrostis,* as the **purple smallreed,** *C. canescens.*

small-scale (smôl'skāl'), *adj.* **1.** relatively small and showing little detail, as a map, model, etc. **2.** unambitious, or of small extent, as an enterprise.

smallsword (smôl'sôd'), *n.* a light, tapering sword for thrusting, used esp. in fencing during the 16th–18th centuries.

small talk, light, unimportant talk; chitchat.

small-time (smôl'tīm'), *adj. Colloq.* of insignificant or petty style, or importance.

smalt (smôlt), *n.* **1.** a deep blue pigment prepared by powdering a glass coloured with cobalt. **2.** a glass made by fusing cobalt oxide and silica. [t. F, t. It.: m. *smalto,* t. G: m. *Schmalte*; akin to SMELT[1]]

smaltite (smôl'tīt), *n.* a mineral diarsenide of cobalt which often also contains a diarsenide of nickel. Also, **smaltine** (smôl'tīn).

smarm (smäm), *v.t., v.i. Colloq.* **1.** (often fol. by *down*) to smooth or stick down, esp. with grease or the like, as hair. **2.** to fawn ingratiatingly; flatter; be servile. —*n.* **3.** flattery; unctiousness; fulsomeness. [dial. *smarm,* var. of *smalm*; orig. uncert.]

smarmy (smä'mĭ), *adj.* ingratiating, falsely charming, or flattering.

smart (smät), *v.i.* **1.** to be a source of sharp local and, usually, superficial pain, as a wound. **2.** to cause a sharp pain, as an irritating application, a blow, etc. **3.** to wound the feelings, as with words. **4.** to feel a sharp pain, as in a wounded surface. **5.** to suffer keenly from wounded feelings. **6.** to suffer in punishment or in return for something. —*v.t.* **7.** to cause a sharp pain to or in.
—*adj.* **8.** sharp or keen, as pain. **9.** sharply severe, as blows, strokes, etc. **10.** sharply brisk, vigorous, or active. **11.** quick or prompt in action, as persons. **12.** having or showing quick intelligence or ready capability; clever. **13.** shrewd or sharp, as a person in dealing with others, or as dealings, bargains, etc. **14.** cleverly ready or effective, as a speaker or a speech, rejoinder, etc. **15.** dashingly or effectively neat or trim in appearance, as persons, dress, etc. **16.** socially elegant, or fashionable. **17.** *U.S. Colloq. or Dial.* considerable, or fairly large.
—*adv.* **18.** in a smart manner; smartly.
—*n.* **19.** sharp local pain, usually superficial, as from a wound or sting. **20.** keen mental suffering, as from wounded feelings, affliction, grievous loss, etc.
[ME *smerten,* OE *smeortan,* c. G *schmerzen* smart; prob. akin to L *mordēre* bite] —**smart'ly,** *adv.* —**smart'ness,** *n.* —**Ant. 12.** dull.

smart aleck (ăl'ĭk), an obnoxiously conceited and cocky person or one who claims to be very well-informed; a know-all. Also, **smart alec.**

smarten (smä'tn), *v.t.* (sometimes fol. by *up*) **1.** to make more trim or spruce; improve in appearance. **2.** to make brisker, as a pace.

smart set, collectively, sophisticated, fashionable people.

smash (smăsh), *v.t.* **1.** to break to pieces with violence and often with a crashing sound, as by striking, letting fall, or dashing against something; shatter; crush. **2.** to defeat utterly, as a person; overthrow or destroy, as a thing. **3.** to ruin financially. **4.** *Tennis.* to strike (the ball) hard and fast with an overhand stroke. —*v.i.* **5.** to break to pieces from a violent blow or collision. **6.** to dash with a shattering or crushing force or with great violence; crash (fol. by *against, into, through,* etc.). **7.** to become financially ruined or bankrupt (often fol. by *up*). —*n.* **8.** a smashing or shattering, or the sound of it. **9.** a destructive collision. **10.** smashed or shattered condition. **11.** a process or state of collapse, ruin, or destruction. **12.** financial failure or ruin. **13.** a drink made of brandy, or other spirits, with sugar, water, mint, and ice. **14.** a smash-hit. **15.** *Tennis.* a forceful overhead stroke. [? b. SMACK² and MASH] —**smash′er,** *n.* —**Syn. 1.** See **break.**

smash-and-grab (smăsh′ən grăb′), *n.* a robbery performed at top speed by breaking a shopwindow, as of a jeweller's, snatching the goods, and running away.

smasher (smăsh′ə), *n.* **1.** *Slang.* an extremely attractive person. **2.** one who or that which smashes. **3.** a smash.

smash-hit (smăsh′hĭt′), *n.* *Colloq.* an immediately and extremely successful play, film, record, or the like.

smashing (smăsh′ĭng), *adj.* *Slang.* extremely fine; first-rate.

smash-up (smăsh′ŭp′), *n.* a complete smash; a violent collision.

smatter (smăt′ə), *v.t.* **1.** *Obs.* to speak (a language, words, etc.) with superficial knowledge or understanding. **2.** to dabble in. —*n.* **3.** slight or superficial knowledge; a smattering. [ME, t. Scand.; cf. Sw. *smattra* patter, rattle] —**smat′terer,** *n.*

smattering (smăt′ə rĭng), *n.* a slight or superficial knowledge of something. —**smat′teringly,** *adv.*

smear (smĭə), *v.t.* **1.** to rub or spread with oil, grease, paint, dirt, etc.; daub with anything. **2.** to spread or daub (oil, grease, etc.) on or over something. **3.** to rub or draw (something) over a thing so as to produce a smear. **4.** to rub something over (a thing) so as to cause a smear, sully, or blur. **5.** to soil or sully, as one's reputation. —*n.* **6.** a mark or stain made by, or as by, smearing. **7.** something smeared, or to be smeared, on a thing, as a glaze for pottery. **8.** a small quantity of something smeared on a slide for microscopic examination. **9.** an act of defamation; slur. [ME *smere,* OE *smeoru,* c. G *Schmer* grease]

smear campaign, an organized effort to ruin a person by vilification, as by means of newspaper articles.

smear-word (smĭə′wûd′), *n.* a slanderous or defaming term or epithet.

smeary (smĭə′rĭ), *adj.*, **smearier, smeariest. 1.** showing smears; smeared; bedaubed. **2.** tending to smear or soil. —**smear′iness,** *adj.*

smectic (smĕk′tĭk), *adj.* *Physics.* denoting or pertaining to a mesomorphous substance the atoms or molecules of which lie in parallel planes.

smell (smĕl), *v.*, **smelled** or **smelt, smelling,** *n.* —*v.t.* **1.** to perceive through the nose, by means of the olfactory nerves; inhale the odour of. **2.** to test by the sense of smell. **3.** to perceive, detect, or discover by shrewdness or sagacity. **4.** to search or find as if by smell (fol. by *out*). —*v.i.* **5.** to have the sense of smell. **6.** to search or investigate (usually fol. by *around*). **7.** to give out an odour, esp. as specified: *to smell sweet.* **8.** to give out an offensive odour. **9.** to have the odour (fol. by *of*). **10.** to have a trace or suggestion (fol. by *of*). **11.** to seem or be unpleasant or bad. —*n.* **12.** the faculty or sense of smelling. **13.** that quality of a thing which is or may be smelled; odour. **14.** a trace or suggestion. **15.** the act of smelling. [ME *smellen, smullen*; orig. uncert.]

smeller (smĕl′ə), *n.* **1.** one who smells. **2.** one who tests by smelling. **3.** *Slang.* the nose.

smelling bottle, a small bottle or the like to hold smelling salts or some similar preparation.

smelling salts, a preparation for sniffing, consisting essentially of ammonium carbonate with some agreeable scent, used as a restorative in cases of faintness, headache, etc.

smelly (smĕl′ĭ), *adj.*, **smellier, smelliest.** emitting a strong or offensive smell.

smelt¹ (smĕlt), *v.t.* **1.** to fuse or melt (ore) in order to separate the metal contained. **2.** to obtain or refine (metal) in this way. [prob. t. MD or MLG: s. *smelten,* c. G *schmelzen* melt, smelt. See MELT]

smelt² (smĕlt), *n.*, *pl.* **smelts,** (*esp. collectively*) **smelt.** a small silvery food fish, *Osmerus eperlanus,* of Europe. [ME and OE. Cf. Norw. *smelta* whiting]

smelt³ (smĕlt), *v.* pt. and pp. of **smell.**

smelter (smĕl′tə), *n.* **1.** one who or that which smelts. **2.** the owner of, or a workman in, a smeltery. **3.** a place or establishment where ores are smelted.

smeltery (smĕl′tə rĭ), *n.*, *pl.* **-ries.** smelter (def. 3).

Smetana (smĕt′ə nə; *Cz.* smĕ′tä nä), *n.* **Bedřich** (*Cz.* bĕ′dər zhĕKH), 1824–84, Czech composer.

Smethwick (smĕth′ĭk), *n.* a town in central England, in Staffordshire, near Birmingham. 67,800 (est. 1964).

smew (smyo͞o), *n.* a small saw-billed duck or merganser, *Mergus albellus,* of northerly parts of the eastern hemisphere, the adult male of which is white, marked with black and grey, and, on the crested head, with green. [orig. uncert.; ? var. of MEW²]

smilacaceous (smī′lə kā′shəs), *adj.* belonging to the *Smilacaceae,* the smilax or prickly ivy family of plants. [f. s. L *smilax* SMILAX + -ACEOUS]

smilax (smī′lăks), *n.* **1.** any plant of the genus *Smilax,* of the tropical and temperate zones, consisting mostly of vines with woody stems. **2.** a delicate, twining liliaceous plant, *Asparagus asparagoides,* with glossy, bright green leaves, cultivated by florists. [t. L, t. Gk]

smile (smīl), *v.*, **smiled, smiling,** *n.* —*v.i.* **1.** to assume a facial expression, characterized esp. by a widening of the mouth, indicative of pleasure, favour, kindliness, amusement, derision, scorn, etc. **2.** to look with such an expression, esp. (fol. by *at, on,* or *upon*) in a pleasant or kindly way, or (fol. by *at*) in amusement. **3.** to have a pleasant or agreeable aspect, as natural scenes, objects, etc. —*v.t.* **4.** to assume or give (a smile). **5.** to express by a smile: *to smile approval.* **6.** to bring, put, drive, etc., by smiling: *to smile one's tears away.* **7.** to look with favour, or support (fol. by *on* or *upon*). —*n.* **8.** the act of smiling; a smiling expression of the face. **9.** favouring look or regard: *fortune's smile.* **10.** pleasant or agreeable look or aspect. [ME, c. OHG *smilan,* Dan. *smile*] —**smil′er,** *n.* —**smil′ingly,** *adv.* —**Syn. 8.** See **laugh.** —**Ant. 8.** frown.

smirch (smûch), *v.t.* **1.** to discolour or soil with some substance, as soot, dust, dirt, etc., or as the substance does. **2.** to sully or tarnish, as with disgrace. —*n.* **3.** a dirty mark or smear. **4.** a stain or blot, as on reputation. [ME *smorch*; b. SMEAR and SMUTCH]

smirk (smûk), *v.i.* **1.** to smile in an affected, would-be agreeable, or offensively familiar way. —*v.t.* **2.** to utter with a smirk. —*n.* **3.** the smile or the facial expression of one who smirks. [ME; OE *sme(a)rcian*] —**smirk′er,** *n.* —**smirk′ingly,** *adv.*

smite (smīt), *v.*, **smote** or (*Obs.*) **smit; smitten** or **smit; smiting.** —*v.t.* **1.** to strike or hit hard, as with the hand, a stick or weapon, etc., or as the hand or a weapon does. **2.** to deal (a blow, etc.) by striking hard. **3.** to render by, or as by, a blow: *to smite a person dead.* **4.** to strike down or slay. **5.** to afflict, chasten, or punish in a grievous manner. **6.** to fall upon or attack with deadly or disastrous effect, as lightning, blight, pestilence, etc., do. **7.** to affect mentally with a sudden pang: *his conscience smote him.* **8.** to affect suddenly and strongly with a specified feeling: *smitten with terror.* **9.** to impress favourably; charm; enamour. —*v.i.* **10.** to strike; deal a blow or blows. **11.** to come, fall, etc., with or as with the force of a blow. [ME; OE *smītan,* c. G *schmeissen* strike] —**smit′er,** *n.*

smith (smĭth), *n.* **1.** a worker in metal. **2.** a blacksmith. —*v.t.* **3.** to make by forging. [ME and OE, c. G *Schmied*]

Smith (smĭth), *n.* **1. Adam,** 1723–90, Scottish political economist. **2. Alfred Emanuel,** 1873–1944, U.S. political leader. **3. Ian Douglas,** born 1919, Rhodesian political leader: prime minister since 1964; declared independence unilaterally, 11th November 1965. **4. Captain John,** 1580–1631, English adventurer, colonist in Virginia (1607). **5. Joseph,** 1805–44, U.S. religious leader who founded the Mormon Church. **6. Logan Pearsall** (lō′gən pĭə′sôl), 1865–1946, U.S. essayist, in England. **7. Sydney,** 1771–1845, English clergyman and writer. **8. William,** 1769–1839, English geologist.

Smith College, a women's college in the U.S., in Massachusetts, founded 1871.

smithereens (smĭth′ə rēnz′), *n.pl.* *Colloq.* small fragments. [der. *smithers* (orig. unknown), with Irish dim. suffix *-een*]

smithery (smĭth′ə rĭ), *n.*, *pl.* **-eries. 1.** the work or craft of a smith. **2.** a smithy.

Smithfield (smĭth′fēld′), *n.* a district in the city of London, famous for its meat and other markets.

smithing (smĭth′ĭng, smĭth′-), *n.* the art or process of forging iron or steel.

Smith's cress, a cruciferous perennial herb, *Lepidium heterophyllum,* a widespread weed of temperate regions.

Smithson (smĭth′sən), *n.* **James** (until 1800: *James Lewis Macie*), 1765–1829, English chemist and mineralogist: founded Smithsonian Institution.

Smithsonian Institution (smĭth sō′nyən), an institution in Washington, D.C., founded 1846 with a grant left by James Smithson, for the increase and diffusion of knowledge.

smithsonite (smĭth′sə nīt′), *n.* **1.** Also, **calamine.** a native carbonate of zinc, $ZnCO_3$; an important ore of zinc. **2.** *Obs.* the zinc silicate, hemimorphite. [named after James SMITHSON]

smithy (smĭth′ĭ), *n.*, *pl.* **smithies. 1.** the workshop of a smith, esp. a blacksmith. **2.** a forge.

smitten (smĭt′n), *adj.* **1.** struck, as with a hard blow. **2.** stricken with affliction, etc. **3.** *Colloq.* very much in love. —*v.* **4.** pp. of **smite.**

smock (smŏk), *n.* **1.** any loose overgarment, esp. one worn to protect the clothing while at work: *an artist's smock.* —*v.t.* **2.** to clothe in a smock. **3.** to draw (a fabric) by needlework into a honeycomb pattern with diamond-shaped recesses. [ME; OE *smocc,* c. OHG *smoccho;* orig. name of garment with a hole for the head. Cf. Icel. *smjūga* to put on (a garment) over the head]

smock frock, a loose overgarment of linen or cotton formerly worn by farm labourers, etc.

smocking (smŏk′ĭng), *n.* **1.** smocked needlework. **2.** embroidery stitches used to hold gathered cloth in a pattern of even folds.

smog (smŏg), *n.* a mixture of smoke and fog. —**smog′gy,** *adj.*

smoke (smōk), *n., v.,* **smoked, smoking.** —*n.* **1.** the visible exhalation given off by a burning or smouldering substance, esp. the grey, brown, or blackish mixture of gases and suspended carbon particles resulting from the combustion of wood, peat, coal, or other organic matter. **2.** something resembling this, as vapour or mist, flying particles, etc. **3.** something unsubstantial, evanescent, or without result. **4.** obscuring conditions. **5.** an act or spell of smoking tobacco, or the like. **6.** that which is smoked, as a cigar or cigarette. **7.** *Phys. Chem.* a dispersed system of solid particles in a gaseous medium. **8. go** or **end up in smoke, a.** to be burnt up completely. **b.** to have no solid result; end or disappear without coming to anything. —*v.i.* **9.** to give off or emit smoke. **10.** to give out smoke offensively or improperly, as a stove. **11.** to send forth steam or vapour, dust, or the like. **12.** to draw into the mouth and puff out the smoke of tobacco or the like, as from a pipe, cigar, or cigarette. **13.** *U.S.* to ride or travel (along) with great speed. —*v.t.* **14.** to draw into the mouth and puff out (the smoke of tobacco, etc.). **15.** to use (a pipe, cigarette, etc.) in this process. **16.** to expose to smoke. **17.** to fumigate (rooms, etc.). **18.** to cure (meat, fish, etc.) by exposure to smoke. **19.** to colour or darken by smoke. **20.** to drive by means of smoke, as an animal from its hole or a person from a hiding place (fol. by *out,* etc.). **21.** to force into public view or knowledge (fol. by *out*). [ME; OE *smoca;* akin to Scot. *smeek* (OE *smēocan*) emit smoke]

smokebomb (smōk′bŏm′), *n.* a bomb which, when set off, emits a large quantity of smoke, as used for military purposes, in theatricals, etc.

smokehouse (smōk′hous′), *n.* a building or place in which meat, fish, etc., are treated with smoke.

smokejack (smōk′jăk′), *n.* (formerly) an apparatus for turning a roasting spit, set in motion by the current of ascending gases in a chimney.

smokeless (smōk′lĭs), *adj.* emitting, producing, or having no (or little) smoke.

smokeless powder, any of various substitutes for ordinary gunpowder which give off little or no smoke, esp. one composed wholly or mostly of guncotton.

smokeless zone, an urban area where only smokeless fuels are permitted.

smoke-oh (smō′kō), *n. Austral., N.Z. Colloq.* a rest from work; tea-break.

smoker (smō′kə), *n.* **1.** one who or that which smokes. **2.** a railway carriage or compartment in which passengers are permitted to smoke. **3.** an informal concert of light entertainment, esp. one in which members of the audience are the performers. **4.** Also, **smoking concert.** (formerly) an informal gathering of men, usually at a club or the like, for light entertainment.

smokeroom (smōk′ro͞om′, -ro͝om′), *n.* a room set apart for smoking, as in a hotel, ship, clubhouse, etc.

smokescreen (smōk′skrēn′), *n.* **1.** a mass of dense smoke produced to conceal an area, vessel, or aeroplane from the enemy. **2.** any device or artifice used for concealment of the truth, as a mass of verbiage.

smokestack (smōk′stăk′), *n.* a pipe for the escape of the smoke or gases of combustion, as on a steamship, locomotive, or building.

smoke tree, 1. an anacardiaceous treelike shrub, *Cotinus coggygria,* native in southern Europe and Asia Minor, bearing small flowers in large panicles, that develop a light, feathery appearance suggestive of smoke. **2.** a related American species, *Cotinus americanus.*

smoking concert, smoker (def. 4).

smoking-jacket (smō′kĭng jăk′ĭt), *n.* a loose, comfortable jacket, usually of a soft decorative fabric as velvet, worn by men for informal use at home.

smoking room, smokeroom.

smoky (smō′kĭ), *adj.,* **smokier, smokiest. 1.** emitting smoke, or much smoke, as a fire, a torch, etc. **2.** hazy; darkened or begrimed with smoke. **3.** having the character or appearance of smoke. **4.** pertaining to or suggestive of smoke. **5.** of a dull or brownish grey; cloudy. —**smok′ily,** *adv.* —**smok′iness,** *n.*

Smoky Mountains. See **Great Smoky Mountains.**

smolder (smōl′də), *v.i., n. U.S.* smoulder.

Smolensk (smō lĕnsk; *Russ.* smä lyĕnsk′), *n.* a town in the W Soviet Union: Napoleon defeated the Russians here, 1812. 170,000 (est. 1963).

Smollett (smŏl′ĭt), *n.* **Tobias George** (tō bī′əs), 1721–71, English novelist.

smolt (smōlt), *n.* a young, silvery salmon going down to the sea. [akin to SMELT[2]]

smooch (smo͞och), *Colloq.* —*v.i.* **1.** to kiss; cuddle; behave amorously. —*n.* **2.** the act of smooching. [orig. unknown]

smoodge (smo͞oj), *v.i. Austral., N.Z.* **1.** to kiss; caress. **2.** to flatter; curry favour. —**smoodg′er,** *n.*

smooth (smo͞oth), *adj.* **1.** free from projections or irregularities of surface such as would be perceived in touching or stroking. **2.** free from hairs or a hairy growth. **3.** free from inequalities of surface, ridges or hollows, obstructions, etc. **4.** generally flat or unruffled, as a calm sea. **5.** of uniform consistency; free from lumps, as a batter, a sauce, etc. **6.** free from or proceeding without breaks, abrupt bends, etc. **7.** free from unevenness or roughness: *smooth driving.* **8.** easy and uniform, as an outline, motion, the working of a machine, etc. **9.** having projections worn away: *a tyre worn smooth.* **10.** free from hindrances or difficulties. **11.** undisturbed, tranquil, or equable, as the feelings, temper, etc. **12.** easy, flowing, elegant, or polished, as speech, a speaker, etc. **13.** pleasant, agreeable, or ingratiatingly polite, as manner, persons, etc.; bland or suave. **14.** free from harshness or sharpness of taste, as wine. **15.** not harsh to the ear, as sound. **16.** *Phonet.* without aspiration. **17.** *Tennis.* of or pertaining to the back of a racket (from the texture of the strings on that side). —*adv.* **18.** in a smooth manner; smoothly. —*v.t.* **19.** to make smooth of surface, as by scraping, planing, pressing, stroking, etc. (sometimes fol. by *down*). **20.** to remove (projections, etc.) in making something smooth (often fol. by *away* or *out*). **21.** to tranquillize, calm, or soothe, as the feelings. **22.** to gloss over or palliate, as something unpleasant or wrong (usually fol. by *over*). **23.** *Obs.* to make more polished, elegant, agreeable, or plausible, as wording, verse, manners, the person, etc. —*n.* **24.** the act of smoothing. **25.** that which is smooth; a smooth part or place. **26.** the smooth side of a racket. [ME *smothe,* OE *smōth.* Cf. OE *smēthe* smooth, c. OS *smōthi*] —**smooth′er,** *n.* —**smooth′ly,** *adv.* —**smooth′ness,** *n.* —**Syn. 1.** See **level.** —**Ant. 1.** rough.

smoothbore (smo͞oth′bō′), *adj.* **1.** (of firearms) having a smooth bore; not rifled. —*n.* **2.** such a firearm.

smooth breathing, *Gk Gram.* a symbol (ʼ) indicating non-aspiration of the initial vowel. Cf. **rough breathing.** [trans. of L *spiritus lenis*]

smoothen (smo͞o′thən), *v.t., v.i.* to make or become smooth.

smooth-faced (smo͞oth′făst′), *adj.* **1.** beardless or clean-shaven. **2.** having a smooth surface, as cloth. **3.** deceitfully ingratiating.

smoothing-iron (smo͞o′thĭng ī′ən), *n.* **1.** iron (def. 4). **2.** a tool resembling this, used in the process of smoothing hot asphalt.

smoothing plane, *Carp.* a small plane used for finishing wooden surfaces.

smooth-spoken (smo͞oth′spō′kən), *adj.* **1.** speaking easily and well. **2.** polished in speech and manner. **3.** smooth-tongued.

smooth-tongued (smo͞oth′tŭngd′), *adj.* **1.** Also, **smooth-spoken.** plausible. **2.** flattering; glib.

smorgasbord (smô′gəs bôd′, smŭ′-), *n.* a buffet meal of various hot and cold hors d'oeuvres, salads, meat dishes, etc., popular in Scandinavia. Also, **smörgåsbord** (*Sw.* smœr′gōs bōd). [t. Sw.: *smörgåsbord,* equiv. to *smörgås* sandwich + *bord* table]

smørrebrod (*Dan.* smœ′rə brœth), *n.* smorgasbord. [t. Dan., equiv. to *smørre* butter + *brod* bread]

smote (smōt), *v.* pt. of **smite.**

smother (smŭth′ə), *v.t.* **1.** to stifle or suffocate, esp. by smoke or by depriving of the air necessary for life. **2.** to extinguish or deaden (fire, etc.) by covering so as to exclude air. **3.** to cover closely or thickly (often fol. by *up*); envelop (in). **4.** to suppress: *to smother a scandal.* **5.** to repress, as feelings impulses, etc. —*v.i.* **6.** to become stifled or suffocated; be prevented from breathing freely by smoke or otherwise. **7.** to be stifled; be suppressed or concealed. —*n.* **8.** dense, stifling smoke. **9.** a smoking or smouldering state, as of burning matter; a smouldering fire. **10.** dust, fog, spray, etc., in a dense or enveloping cloud. **11.** an overspreading profusion of anything. [ME *smorther,* der. OE *smorian* suffocate] —**smoth′ery,** *adj.*

smoulder (smōl′də), *v.i.* **1.** to burn or smoke without flame. **2.** to exist or continue in a suppressed state or without outward demonstration. **3.** to display repressed feelings, esp. of indignation: *his eyes smouldered.* —*n.* **4.** dense smoke resulting from slow or suppressed combustion. **5.** a smouldering fire. Also, *U.S.*, **smolder.** [ME *smoulder(en)*, der. *smoulder* smoky vapour, dissimilated var. of earlier *smorther* SMOTHER, n.]

smouse (smous), *n. S African.* a hawker, esp. in rural areas. [orig. uncert.]

smudge (smŭj), *n.*, *v.*, **smudged, smudging.** —*n.* **1.** a dirty mark or smear. **2.** a smeary state. **3.** a blurred mass: *the house was a smudge on the horizon.* **4.** a stifling smoke. **5.** *U.S.* a smoky fire, esp. one made for the purpose of driving away mosquitoes, etc. —*v.t.* **6.** to mark with dirty streaks or smears. **7.** *U.S.* to fill with smoke from a smudge, as to drive away insects. —*v.i.* **8.** to form a smudge on something. **9.** to be or become smudged. [ME *smoge*; orig. uncert.]

smudgy (smŭj′ĭ), *adj.*, **smudgier, smudgiest.** **1.** marked with smudges; smeared; smeary. **2.** emitting a stifling smoke; smoky. **3.** *Dial.* close or sultry, as air. —**smudg′ily,** *adv.* —**smudg′iness,** *n.*

smug (smŭg), *adj.*, **smugger, smuggest.** **1.** complacently proper, righteous, clever, etc.; self-satisfied. **2.** trim; spruce; smooth; sleek. [? t. D: m. *smuk* neat] —**smug′ly,** *adv.* —**smug′ness,** *n.*

smuggle (smŭg′l), *v.*, **-gled, -gling.** —*v.t.* **1.** to import or export (goods) secretly, without payment of legal duty or in violation of law. **2.** to bring, take, put, etc., surreptitiously: *she smuggled the gun into the jail inside a cake.* —*v.i.* **3.** to smuggle goods. [t. LG: m. s. *smuggeln*, c. G *schmuggeln*] —**smug′gler,** *n.*

smut (smŭt), *n.*, *v.*, **smutted, smutting.** —*n.* **1.** a particle of soot; sooty matter. **2.** a black or dirty mark; a smudge. **3.** indecent talk or writing; obscenity. **4.** a fungous disease of plants, esp. cereals, in which the affected parts are converted into a black powdery mass of spores, caused by fungi of the order *Ustilaginales.* **5.** the fungus itself. —*v.t.* **6.** to soil or smudge. —*v.i.* **7.** to become affected with smut, as a plant. [alter. of earlier *smit* (OE *smitte*) by association with SMUDGE, SMUTCH]

smutch (smŭch), *v.t.* **1.** to smudge or soil. —*n.* **2.** a smudge or stain. **3.** dirt, grime, or smut. [? t. MHG: m. *smutzen* smear] —**smutch′y,** *adj.*

Smuts (smŭts), *n.* **Jan Christiaan** (yăn′ krĭs′tyən), 1870–1950, South African statesman and general: prime minister, 1919–24 and 1939–48.

smutty (smŭt′ĭ), *adj.*, **-tier, -tiest.** **1.** soiled with smut, soot, or the like; grimy; dirty. **2.** indecent or obscene, as talk, writing, etc.: *a smutty novel.* **3.** given to such talk, etc., as a person. **4.** (of plants) affected with the smut disease. —**smut′tily,** *adv.* —**smut′tiness,** *n.*

Smyrna (smû′nə), *n.* former name of **Izmir.**

Sn, (L *stannum*) *Chem.* tin.

snack (snăk), *n.* **1.** a small portion of food or drink; a light meal. **2.** a share or portion. [n. use of *snack*, v., snap. Cf. MD *snacken* snap]

snack-bar (snăk′bä′), *n.* a cafe where snacks are served.

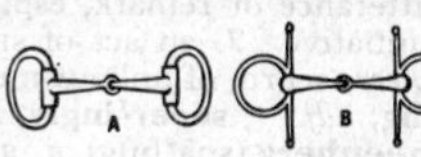

snaffle[1] (snăf′əl), *n.*, *v.*, **-fled, -fling.** —*n.* **1.** a slender, jointed bit used on a bridle. —*v.t.* **2.** to put a snaffle on (a horse, etc.); control by or as by a snaffle. [cf. D *snavel*, G *Schnabel* beak, mouth]

A, Snaffle; B, Cheek snaffle

snaffle[2] (snăf′əl), *v.t.*, **-fled, -fling.** *Colloq.* **1.** to steal. **2.** to take away quickly before anyone else: *early shoppers snaffled up the sales bargains.*

snafu (snă fo͞o′), *n.*, *adj.*, *v.*, **-fued, -fuing.** *U.S. Orig. Mil. Slang.* —*n.* **1.** chaos; a muddled situation. —*adj.* **2.** in disorder; out of control; chaotic. —*v.t.* **3.** to throw into disorder; muddle. [from the initial letters of *s(ituation) n(ormal) : a(ll) f(ouled) u(p)*]

snag (snăg), *n.*, *v.*, **snagged, snagging.** —*n.* **1.** a short, projecting stump, as of a branch broken or cut off. **2.** any sharp or rough projection. **3.** *Chiefly U.S.* a tree or part of a tree held fast in the bottom of a river or other water and forming an impediment or danger to navigation. **4.** a stump of a tooth; a projecting tooth. **5.** any obstacle or impediment: *to strike a snag in carrying out plans.* **6.** a small hole or ladder caused by catching a stocking, or the like, on a sharp object. —*v.t.* **7.** to ladder; catch upon, or damage by, a snag. **8.** *Chiefly U.S.* to obstruct or impede, as a snag does. **9.** to clear of snags. [cf. d. Norw. *snag* stump, etc., Icel. *snagi* clothes peg] —**snag′like′,** *adj.*

snaggy (snăg′ĭ), *adj.*, **-gier, -giest.** **1.** having snags or sharp projections, as a tree. **2.** abounding in snags or obstructions, as a river. **3.** snaglike; projecting sharply or roughly.

snail (snāl), *n.* **1.** a mollusc of the class *Gastropoda* having a single, usually spirally coiled shell. **2.** a slow or lazy person; a sluggard. [ME; OE *snegel*, c. G *Schnägel*] —**snail′-like′,** *adj.*

Common garden snail, *Helix aspersa* (Up to 1½ in. high, 1¾ in. wide)

snail-paced (snāl′pāst′), *adj.* slow of pace or motion, like a snail; sluggish.

snake (snāk), *n.*, *v.*, **snaked, snaking.** —*n.* **1.** a scaly, limbless, usually slender reptile, occurring in venomous and non-venomous forms, widely distributed in numerous genera and species and constituting the order (or suborder) *Serpentes.* **2.** a treacherous person; an insidious enemy. **3.** something resembling a snake in form or manner. **4.** any of various flexible coil springs used for clearing drains, threading wires, etc., through tubes, or the like. **5. snake in the grass,** a very deceitful or treacherous person; a hidden enemy. —*v.i.* **6.** to move, twist, or wind in the manner of a snake: *the path snakes through the field.* —*v.t.* **7.** to follow (a course) in the shape of a snake: *he snaked his way through the jungle.* **8.** *U.S.* to drag or haul, esp. by a chain or rope fastened around one end of the object, as a log. **9.** *U.S.* to jerk (fol. by *out*, etc.). [ME; OE *snaca*, c. MLG *snake.* Cf. Icel. *snākr*] —**snake′like′,** *adj.*

snakebird (snāk′bûd′), *n.* any of various totipalmate swimming birds of the family *Anhingidae*, having a long, snaky neck.

snakebite (snāk′bīt′), *n.* a bite from a snake, esp. a poisonous one.

snake-charmer (snāk′chä′mə), *n.* one who pretends to hypnotize snakes, making them move, rise up, etc., as entertainment.

snake dance, a ceremonial dance of the American Indians, in which snakes or their images are held or symbolically imitated.

snake fence, *Chiefly U.S.* a fence of zigzag outline made of rails laid horizontally with the ends resting one across another at an angle; a worm fence.

Snake River, a river in the U.S., flowing from NW Wyoming through S Idaho and N along the Oregon-Idaho boundary into the Columbia river in SE Washington. 1038 mi.

snakeroot (snāk′ro͞ot′), *n.* **1.** any of various plants whose roots have been regarded as a remedy for snakebites, as *Aristolochia serpentaria* (**Virginia snakeroot**), a herb with medicinal rhizome and rootlets. **2.** the root or rhizome of such a plant.

snake's-head (snāks′hĕd′), *n.* the fritillary, *Fritillaria meleagris.*

snakeskin (snāk′skĭn′), *n.* the skin of a snake, esp. as used for leather.

snakeweed (snāk′wēd′), *n.* bistort (def. 1).

snaky (snā′kĭ), *adj.*, **snakier, snakiest.** **1.** of or pertaining to a snake or snakes. **2.** abounding in snakes, as a place. **3.** snakelike; twisting, winding, or sinuous. **4.** venomous; treacherous or insidious. **5.** consisting of, entwined with, or bearing snakes or serpents.

snap (snăp), *v.*, **snapped, snapping,** *n.*, *adj.*, *adv.* —*v.i.* **1.** to make a sudden, sharp sound; crackle. **2.** to click, as a mechanism. **3.** to move, strike, shut, catch, etc., with a sharp sound, as a lid. **4.** to break suddenly, esp. with a sharp, cracking sound, as something slender and brittle. **5.** to flash, as the eyes. **6.** to act or move with quick, neat motions of the body: *to snap to attention.* **7.** *Photog.* to take snapshots. **8.** to make a quick or sudden bite or snatch. **9.** to utter a quick, sharp speech, reproof, retort, etc. **10. snap out of it,** to recover quickly from a mood, as anger, unhappiness, etc.
—*v.t.* **11.** to seize with, or as with, a quick bite or snatch (usually fol. by *up* or *off*). **12.** to secure hastily, as a decision not subjected to due deliberation. **13.** to cause to make a sudden, sharp sound: *to snap one's fingers.* **14.** *U.S.* to crack (a whip). **15.** to bring, strike, shut, open, operate, etc., with a sharp sound or movement: *to snap a lid down.* **16.** to utter or say in a quick, sharp manner (sometimes fol. by *out*). **17.** to break suddenly, esp. with a crackling sound. **18.** *Photog.* to take a snapshot of. **19.** to fire (a pistol, or the like) quickly and spontaneously. **20. snap one's fingers at,** to disregard; scorn. **21. snap (someone's) head off,** to speak angrily and sharply to.
—*n.* **22.** a sharp, crackling or clicking sound, or a movement or action causing such a sound: *a snap of the fingers.* **23.** a catch or the like operating with such a sound. **24.** a sudden breaking, as of something brittle or tense, or a sharp, crackling sound caused by it. **25.** a small, thin, brittle or crisp biscuit. **26.** crispness, smartness, or liveliness, as of

writings or style. 27. *Colloq.* briskness, vigour, or energy, as of persons or actions. 28. a quick, sharp speech, or manner of speaking. 29. a quick or sudden bite or snatch, as at something. 30. something obtained by or as by biting or snatching. 31. short spell, as of cold weather. 32. *Photog.* a snapshot. 33. a simple card game in which cards are thrown in turn on to a pile. When a card of equal value to the preceding card is laid, the first player to call 'snap' wins the pile. 34. *U.S. Slang.* an easy and profitable or agreeable position, piece of work, or the like. 35. *Dial.* a snack, esp. a packed lunch.
—*adj.* 36. denoting devices closing by pressure on a spring catch, or articles using such devices. 37. made, done, taken, etc., suddenly or offhand: *a snap judgement.*
—*adv.* 38. in a brisk, sudden manner.
—*interj.* 39. (used in the game of snap to take cards from an opponent.) [t. D or LG: m. s. *snappen*]

snapbean (snăp′bēn′), *n. U.S.* 1. any of various kinds of beans (plant) whose unripe pods are used as foods. 2. the pod itself.

snapdragon (snăp′drăg′ən), *n.* 1. a plant of the scrophulariaceous genus *Antirrhinum*, esp. *A. majus*, a plant long cultivated for its spikes of showy flowers, of various colours, with a corolla that is supposed to look like the mouth of a dragon. 2. the game of flapdragon.

snap fastener, press-stud.

snapper (snăp′ə), *n.* 1. any of various large marine fishes of the family *Lutianidae* of warm seas, as the **red snapper,** *Lutianus blackfordii*, a food fish of the Gulf of Mexico. 2. any of various other fishes, as the bluefish, *Pomatomus saltratix*. 3. the snapping turtle.

snapping beetle, a click beetle.

Snapping turtle, *Chelydra serpentina* (20 to 30 in. long)

snapping turtle, a large and savage turtle, *Chelydra serpentina*, of American rivers, having powerful jaws with which it lunges and snaps at an enemy.

snappish (snăp′ĭsh), *adj.* 1. apt to snap or bite, as a dog. 2. disposed to speak or reply quickly and sharply, as a person. 3. impatiently or irritably sharp; curt. —**snap′pishly,** *adv.* —**snap′pishness,** *n.*

snappy (snăp′ĭ), *adj.*, **-pier, -piest.** 1. snappish, as a dog, a person, the speech, etc. 2. snapping or crackling in sound, as a fire. 3. quick or sudden in action or performance. 4. *Colloq.* crisp, smart, lively, brisk, etc. 5. **make it snappy,** *Colloq.* to hurry up. —**snap′pily,** *adv.* —**snap′piness,** *n.*

snap-roll (snăp′rōl′), *n. Aeron.* a rapidly executed roll. Also, **flick-roll.**

snapshot (snăp′shŏt′), *n.* 1. a photograph taken quickly without any formal arrangement of the subject, mechanical adjustment of the camera, etc. 2. a quick shot taken without deliberate aim.

snare[1] (snĕə), *n., v.,* **snared, snaring.** —*n.* 1. a device, usually consisting of a noose, for capturing birds or small animals. 2. anything serving to entrap, entangle, or catch unawares; a trap. 3. *Surg.* a noose which removes tumours, etc., by the roots or the base. —*v.t.* 4. to catch with a snare; entrap; entangle. 5. to catch or involve by trickery or wile. [ME, t. Scand. (cf. Icel. *snara*); r. OE *snearh*, c. OHG *snarahha*] —**snar′er,** *n.* —**Syn.** 1. See **trap**[1].

snare[2] (snĕə), *n.* one of the strings of gut stretched across the skin of a side-drum. [t. LG: string]

snare-drum (snĕə′drŭm′), *n.* side-drum.

snark (snäk), *n.* a mysterious, imaginary animal. [b. SNAKE and SHARK; coined by Lewis Carroll]

snarl[1] (snäl), *v.i.* 1. to growl angrily or viciously, as a dog. 2. to speak in a savagely sharp, angry, or quarrelsome manner. —*v.t.* 3. to utter or say with a snarl. —*n.* 4. the act of snarling. 5. a snarling sound or utterance. [freq. of obs. *snar* snarl, c. D and LG *snarren*, G *schnarren*] —**snarl′er,** *n.* —**snarl′ingly,** *adv.* —**snarl′y,** *adj.*

snarl[2] (snäl), *n.* 1. a tangle, as of thread or hair. 2. a complicated or confused condition or matter. 3. a knot in wood. —*v.t.* 4. to bring into a tangled condition, as thread, hair, etc.; tangle. 5. to render complicated or confused. 6. to raise or emboss, as parts of a thin metal vessel, by hammering on a tool (**snarling iron**) held against the inner surface of the vessel. —*v.i.* 7. to become tangled; get into a tangle. [ME *snarle* snare, t. Scand.; cf. O Swed. *snarel* noose, der. *snara* SNARE[1]]

snash (snăsh), *Scot. and N Dial.* —*n.* 1. abuse; insolence. —*v.i.* 2. to use abusive language. [orig. obscure]

snatch (snăch), *v.i.* 1. to make a sudden effort to seize something, as with the hand (usually fol. by *at*). —*v.t.* 2. to seize by a sudden or hasty grasp (often fol. by *up, from, out of, away,* etc.). 3. to take, get, secure, etc., suddenly or hastily. 4. to rescue or save by prompt action. —*n.* 5. the act of snatching. 6. a sudden motion to seize something. 7. *Colloq.* a robbery by a quick seizing of goods. 8. a bit, scrap, or fragment of something: *snatches of conversation.* 9. a brief spell of effort, activity, or any experience: *to work in snatches.* 10. a brief period of time. [ME *snacchen*, var. of earlier *snecchen*; orig. uncert.] —**snatch′er,** *n.*

snatch block, *Naut.* a block with a hinged piece that is lifted to admit the rope and then secured.

snatchy (snăch′ĭ), *adj.* consisting of, occurring in, or characterized by snatches; spasmodic; irregular.

snath (snăth), *n.* the shaft or handle of a scythe. Also, **snathe** (snāth). [unexplained var. of *snead*, ME *snede*, OE *snǣd*; orig. uncert.]

snazzy (snăz′ĭ), *adj. Colloq.* 1. (of clothes) very smart; strikingly fashionable; stylish. 2. (of a person) very well-dressed. 3. brightly patterned; having gay designs.

sneak (snēk), *v.i.* 1. to go in a stealthy or furtive manner; slink; skulk (fol. by *about, along, in, off, out,* etc.). 2. to act in a furtive, underhand, or mean way. 3. to let out secrets, esp. deceitfully; tell tales. 4. *Colloq.* to leave quickly and quietly (fol. by *out, off, away,* etc.). —*v.t.* 5. to move, put, pass, etc., in a stealthy or furtive manner. 6. *Colloq.* to take surreptitiously, or steal. —*n.* 7. one who sneaks; a sneaking, underhand, or contemptible person. 8. a telltale. 9. *Colloq.* an act of sneaking; a quiet departure. [akin to OE *snīcan* sneak along] —**Syn.** 1. See **lurk.**

sneaker (snē′kə), *n.* 1. *U.S. Colloq.* a shoe with a rubber or other soft sole used esp. in gymnasiums. 2. one who sneaks; a sneak.

sneaking (snē′kĭng), *adj.* 1. acting in a furtive or underhand way. 2. deceitfully underhand, as actions, etc.; contemptible. 3. secret; not generally avowed, as a feeling, notion, suspicion, etc. —**sneak′ingly,** *adv.*

sneakthief (snēk′thēf′), *n.* a burglar who steals by sneaking into houses through open doors, etc.

sneaky (snē′kĭ), *adj.*, **sneakier, sneakiest.** like or suggestive of a sneak; sneaking. —**sneak′ily,** *adv.* —**sneak′iness,** *n.*

sneck[1] (snĕk), *Chiefly Scot. and N Dial.* —*n.* 1. the latch of a door or gate, or the lever which raises the bar of this. —*v.t.* 2. to latch (a door or gate). —*v.i.* 3. (of a door, etc.) to shut; latch. [ME (N dial.) *snekken*; akin to SNATCH]

sneck[2] (snĕk), *n. Bldg Trades.* a small piece, esp. of stone.

snecked (snĕkt), *adj. Bldg Trades.* furnished with snecks.

snecked masonry, any of various kinds of stone walling, ranging from rubblework to ashlar, in which small pieces of stone are inserted between larger ones.

sned (snĕd), *v.t.*, **snedded, snedding.** *Scot. and N Dial.* to cut off (a branch); prune (a tree). [ME **sneden*, OE *snǣdan* to cut; c. G *schneiden* cut]

sneer (snĭə), *v.i.* 1. to smile or curl the lip in a manner that shows scorn, contempt, etc. 2. to speak or write in a manner expressive of derision, scorn, or contempt. —*v.t.* 3. to utter or say in a sneering manner. 4. to bring, put, force, etc., by sneering. —*n.* 5. a look or expression suggestive of derision, scorn, or contempt. 6. a derisive or scornful utterance or remark, esp. one more or less covert or insinuative. 7. an act of sneering. [ME *snere*, c. N Fris. *sneere* scorn, of unknown orig.] —**sneer′er,** *n.* —**sneer′ing,** *adj.* —**sneer′ingly,** *adv.* —**Syn.** 2. See **scoff**[1].

Sneeuberg (snā′bûg), *n.* a mountain range in the Republic of South Africa, in central Cape Province. Highest point, 8209 ft.

sneeze (snēz), *v.*, **sneezed, sneezing,** *n.* —*v.i.* 1. to emit air or breath suddenly, forcibly, and audibly through the nose and mouth by involuntary, spasmodic action. 2. *Colloq.* to show contempt for, or treat with contempt (fol. by *at*). —*n.* 3. an act or sound of sneezing. [late ME *snese*, earlier *fnese*, OE *fnēosan*, c. MHG *fnūsen*] —**sneez′er,** *n.* —**sneez′y,** *adj.*

sneezewood (snēz′wŏŏd′), *n.* a small meliaceous tree, *Ptaeoxylon obliquum*, producing durable timber, a native of S and tropical Africa.

sneezewort (snēz′wût′), *n.* an asteraceous plant, *Achillea ptarmica*, a native of Europe, the powdered leaves of which cause sneezing.

snell (snĕl), *n.* a short piece of gut or the like by which a fishhook is attached to a longer line. [orig. unknown]

Snell's law (snĕlz), *Optics.* the law that for a ray of light refracted at a surface separating two media, the ratio of the sine of the angle of incidence to the sine of the angle of refraction is a constant. [named after Willebrod *Snell* van Royen, died 1626, Dutch mathematician]

snick (snĭk), *v.t.* 1. to cut, snip, or nick. 2. to strike sharply. 3. to snap (a gun, etc.). 4. *Cricket.* to hit (the ball), esp. accidentally, with the edge of the bat. —*v.i.* 5. to click. —*n.* 6. a small cut; a nick. 7. a click. 8. *Cricket.* a. a glancing blow given to the ball. b. the ball so hit. [orig. uncert. Cf. Scot. *sneck* cut (off), Icel. *snikka* whittle]

snicker (snĭk′ə), *v.i.* **1.** (of a horse) to make a low snorting neigh. **2.** *Chiefly U.S.* to snigger. —*v.t.* **3.** *Chiefly U.S.* to snigger. —*n.* **4.** *Chiefly U.S.* a snigger.

nickersnee (snĭk′ə snē′), *n.* a knife, esp. one used as a weapon. [var. (by alliterative assimilation) of earlier *stick or snee* thrust or cut, t. D: m. *steken* stick and *snijen* cut]

snide (snīd), *adj.* **1.** derogatory in a nasty, insinuating manner: *snide remarks about the Mayor.* **2.** counterfeit; bogus.

sniff (snĭf), *v.i.* **1.** to draw air through the nose in short, audible inhalation. **2.** to clear the nose by so doing; sniffle, as with emotion. **3.** to smell by short inhalations. **4.** to show disdain, contempt, etc., by a sniff (often fol. by *at*). —*v.t.* **5.** to draw in or up through the nose by sniffing, as air, smells, liquid, powder, etc.; inhale. **6.** to perceive by, or as if by, smelling. —*n.* **7.** an act of sniffing; a single short, audible inhalation. **8.** the sound made. **9.** a scent or smell perceived. [ME; back-formation from SNIVEL] —**snif′fer,** *n.*

sniffle (snĭf′əl), *v.,* **-fled, -fling,** *n.* —*v.i.* **1.** to sniff repeatedly, as from a cold in the head or in repressing tearful emotion. —*n.* **2.** an act or sound of sniffling. **3. the sniffles,** a condition marked by sniffling. [freq. of SNIFF]

sniffy (snĭf′ĭ), *adj.,* **sniffier, sniffiest.** *Colloq.* inclined to sniff, as in disdain; disdainful; supercilious.

snifter (snĭf′tə), *n.* **1.** *Slang.* a small drink of an alcoholic beverage. **2.** *Chiefly U.S.* a balloon glass.

snigger (snĭg′ə), *v.i.* **1.** to laugh in a half-suppressed, often indecorous or disrespectful, manner. —*v.t.* **2.** to utter with a snigger. —*n.* **3.** a sniggering laugh. Also, *Chiefly U.S.,* **snicker.** [imit.]

sniggle (snĭg′l), *v.,* **-gled, -gling,** *n.* —*v.i.* **1.** to fish for eels by thrusting a baited hook into their lurking places. —*v.t.* **2.** to take by sniggling. —*n.* **3.** the baited hook used in sniggling. [der. *snig* eel, ME *snigge*]

snip (snĭp), *v.,* **snipped, snipping,** *n.* —*v.t.* **1.** to cut with a small, quick stroke, or a succession of such strokes, with scissors or the like. **2.** to take off by, or as by, cutting thus. —*v.i.* **3.** to cut with small, quick strokes. —*n.* **4.** the act of snipping, as with scissors. **5.** a small cut, notch, slit, etc., made by snipping. **6.** the sound made by snipping. **7.** a small piece snipped off. **8.** a small piece, bit, or amount of anything. **9.** *Colloq.* a small or insignificant person. **10.** a bargain; a certainty of success. **11.** a light mark, patch, or the like on the nose or lip of a horse. **12.** (*pl.*) small, stout hand shears for the use of sheet metal workers. [cf. D and LG *snippen* snip, snatch, clip]

snipe (snīp), *n., v.,* **sniped, sniping.** —*n.* **1.** any of several long-billed limicoline birds constituting the genera *Capella* and *Lymnocryptes*, frequenting marshes and much sought by sportsmen, as the **common snipe,** *C. gallinago*, the European **great snipe,** *C. media,* and the European **jacksnipe,** *Lymnocryptes minima.* **2.** any of several related shorebirds, as the **red-breasted snipe,** *Limnodromus griseus.* **3.** a shot, usually from a hidden position. —*v.i.* **4.** to shoot or hunt snipe. **5.** to shoot at individual soldiers, etc., as opportunity offers from a concealed or long-range position. —*v.t.* **6.** to shoot at, esp. from a concealed or long-range position. [ME *snype*, t. Scand.; cf. Icel. *snipa*] —**snip′er,** *n.* —**snipe′like′,** *adj.*

Common snipe, *Capella gallinago* (11 in. long)

snippet (snĭp′ĭt), *n.* **1.** a small piece snipped off; a small bit, scrap, or fragment. **2.** *U.S. Colloq.* a small or insignificant person.

snippy (snĭp′ĭ), *adj.,* **-pier, -piest. 1.** *Colloq.* sharp or curt, esp. in a supercilious way. **2.** scrappy or fragmentary. Also, **snippety** (snĭp′ĭ tĭ). —**snip′piness,** *n.*

snitch[1] (snĭch), *v.t. Slang.* to snatch or steal. [? var. of SNATCH]

snitch[2] (snĭch), *Slang.* —*v.i.* **1.** to turn informer. —*n.* **2.** an informer. [orig. uncert.] —**snitch′er,** *n.*

snitchy (snĭch′ĭ), *adj. Austral., N.Z. Slang.* bad-tempered.

snivel (snĭv′əl), *v.,* **-elled, -elling** or (*U.S.*) **-eled, -eling,** *n.* —*v.i.* **1.** to weep or cry with sniffing. **2.** to affect a tearful state; whine. **3.** to run at the nose. **4.** to draw up mucus audibly through the nose. —*v.t.* **5.** to utter with snivelling or sniffing. —*n.* **6.** weak or pretended weeping. **7.** a light sniff, as in weeping. **8.** a hypocritical show of feeling. **9.** mucus running from the nose. [ME *snyvele.* Cf. OE *snyflung*, der. *snofl* mucus] —**sniv′eller,** *n.* —**sniv′elly,** *adj.*

snob (snŏb), *n.* **1.** one who admires, imitates, or cultivates those with social rank, wealth, etc., and is condescending or overbearing to others. **2.** one who affects social importance and exclusiveness. **3.** one who has, or assumes, knowledge of a subject or subjects, and scorns anyone without this. [orig. nickname for cobbler or cobbler's apprentice; orig. uncert.]

snobbery (snŏb′ə rĭ), *n., pl.* **-beries.** snobbish character, conduct, trait, or act.

snobbish (snŏb′ĭsh), *adj.* **1.** of, pertaining to, or characteristic of a snob. **2.** having the character of a snob. Also, *Colloq.,* **snob′by.** —**snob′bishly,** *adv.* —**snob′bishness, snob′bism,** *n.*

snoek (snōōk), *n. S African.* the barracuda. [t. Afrikaans]

snoep (snōōp), *n. S African.* mean; miserly. [t. Afrikaans]

snog (snŏg), *Slang.* —*v.i.* **1.** to kiss; cuddle; behave amorously. —*n.* **2.** the act of snogging. [orig. uncert.]

snood (snōōd), *n.* **1.** the distinctive headband formerly worn by young unmarried women in Scotland and northern England. **2.** a band or fillet for the hair. **3.** a netlike hat or part of a hat, or material worn over the back of a woman's hair. —*v.t.* **4.** to bind or confine (the hair) with a snood. [OE *snōd*; orig. uncert.]

snook[1] (snōōk), *v.i. Chiefly Scot.* to lurk; lie in ambush; pry about. [ME *snoke*, t. Scand.; cf. d. Norw. *snoka* snuff, smell]

snook[2] (snōōk), *n.* a gesture of defiance, putting the thumb to the nose. [orig. unknown]

snooker (snōō′kə), *n.* **1.** a game played on a billiard table with fifteen red balls and six balls of other colours, the object being to pocket them. —*v.t.* **2.** *Colloq.* to obstruct or hinder (someone), esp. from reaching some object, aim, etc. [orig. unknown]

snoop (snōōp), *Colloq.* —*v.i.* **1.** to prowl or pry; go about in a sneaking, prying way; pry in a mean, sly manner. —*n.* **2.** an act or instance of snooping. **3.** one who snoops. [t. D: m. *snoepen* take and eat (food or drink) on the sly] —**snoop′er,** *n.* —**snoop′y,** *adj.*

snoot (snōōt), *n. Slang.* the nose. [d. or colloq. var. of SNOUT]

snooty (snōō′tĭ), *adj.,* **snootier, snootiest. 1.** *Colloq.* snobbish. **2.** haughty; supercilious.

snooze (snōōz), *v.i.,* **snoozed, snoozing.** *Colloq.* to sleep; slumber; doze; nap. [orig. uncert.]

snore (snô), *v.,* **snored, snoring,** *n.* —*v.i.* **1.** to breathe during sleep with hoarse or harsh sounds. —*v.t.* **2.** to spend or pass (time) in snoring (fol. by *away* or *out*). —*n.* **3.** an act of snoring, or the sound made. [ME; ? b. SNIFF and ROAR] —**snor′er,** *n.*

snorkel (snô′kl), *n.* **1.** a device on a submarine consisting of two vertical tubes for the intake and exhaust of air for diesel engines and general ventilation, thus permitting cruising at periscope depth for very long periods. **2.** a tube enabling a person swimming face downwards in the water to breathe, consisting of a tube, one end of which is put in the mouth while the other projects above the surface. —*v.i.* **3.** to swim using such a device, usually in order to look at the seabed, rocks, etc. Also, **schnorkle.** [t. G: m. *Schnorchel*]

Snorri Sturluson (snŏ′rĭ stû′lə sən), 1179–1241, Icelandic historian and poet.

snort (snôt), *v.i.* **1.** to force the breath violently through the nostrils with a loud, harsh sound, as a horse, etc. **2.** to express contempt, indignation, etc., by such a sound. **3.** *Colloq.* to laugh outright or boisterously. —*v.t.* **4.** to utter with a snort. **5.** to expel by or as by snorting. —*n.* **6.** the act or sound of snorting. [ME; ? b. SNORE and ME *route* snore (OE *hrūtan*)]

snorter (snô′tə), *n.* **1.** one who or that which snorts. **2.** *Colloq.* anything unusually strong, large, difficult, dangerous, as a fast ball in cricket, a gale, etc. **3.** *Slang.* an alcoholic drink.

snot (snŏt), *n.* **1.** mucus from the nose. **2.** *Slang.* a contemptible person. [OE *gesnot*]

snotty (snŏt′ĭ), *adj.* **1.** of or pertaining to snot. **2.** *Colloq.* (esp. of a child) dirty. **3.** *Colloq.* snobbish; arrogant.

snout (snout), *n.* **1.** the part of an animal's head projecting forward and containing the nose and jaws; the muzzle. **2.** *Entomol.* a prolongation of the head bearing the feeding organs, as in scorpion-flies and snout-beetles. **3.** anything that resembles or suggests an animal's snout in shape, function, etc. **4.** a nozzle or spout. **5.** *Slang.* a person's nose, esp. when large or prominent. **6.** *Slang.* tobacco. [ME, c. D *snuit*, G *Schnauze*]

snout-beetle (snout′bē′tl), *n.* a weevil (def. 1) having a protruding snout or rostrum.

snow[1] (snō), *n.* **1.** the aqueous vapour of the atmosphere precipitated in partially frozen crystalline form and falling to the earth in white flakes. **2.** these flakes as forming a layer on the ground, etc. **3.** the fall of these flakes. **4.** something resembling snow. **5.** the white hair of age. **6.** *Poetic.* white blossoms. **7.** *Poetic.* the white colour of snow. **8.** *Chem.* carbon dioxide snow. **9.** *Slang.* cocaine or heroin. **10.** white spots on a television screen caused by a weak signal. —*v.i.* **11.** to send down snow; fall as snow. **12.** to descend like snow. **13. be snowed under,** to be overcome by something, as work. —*v.t.* **14.** to let fall as or like snow. **15.** to cover, obstruct, isolate, etc., with snow (fol. by *over, under, up,* etc.). [ME; OE *snāw,* c. D *sneeuw,* G *Schnee*] —**snow′like′,** *adj.*

snow² (snō), *n. Naut.* a 17th–18th century brig with a try-sail mast abaft the main lower mast. [t. D: m. *snaauw*]

Snow (snō), *n.* **Sir Charles (Percy),** born 1905, English teacher, administrator, and novelist.

snowball (snō′bôl′), *n.* **1.** a ball of snow pressed or rolled together. **2.** Also, **snowball tree.** any of certain shrubs, varieties of the genus *Viburnum,* esp. the sterile cultivated variety of the guelder rose, *Vibernum opulus,* with white flowers borne in large snowball-like clusters. **3.** a dance begun by one couple who, after a few minutes, take different partners who in turn do likewise until all the members of the company are dancing. —*v.t.* **4.** to throw snowballs at. —*v.i.* **5.** to grow larger at an accelerating rate.

snowberry (snō′bə rĭ, -brĭ), *n., pl.* **-ries.** a caprifoliaceous shrub, *Symphoricarpos albus,* native in North America, cultivated for its ornamental white berries.

snowbird (snō′bûd′), *n. U.S. Slang.* a cocaine or heroin addict.

snow blindness, temporary blindness caused by reflection of strong light on snow, over a period of time. —**snow′-blind′,** *adj.*

snowblink (snō′blĭngk′), *n.* the peculiar reflection that arises from fields of snow or ice.

snowbound (snō′bound′), *adj.* shut in and prevented from travelling by snow.

snowbroth (snō′brŏth′), *n.* melting or melted snow.

snow-bunting (snō′bŭn′tĭng), *n.* a fringilline bird, *Plectrophenax nivalis,* inhabiting cold parts of the Northern Hemisphere, including Britain, where it is a winter migrant.

snow cap, a cap of snow on the top of a mountain, over a polar region, etc. —**snow-capped** (snō′kăpt′), *adj.*

snow-clad (snō′klăd′), *adj.* covered with snow.

Snowdon (snō′dn), *n.* a mountain in NW Wales, part of the Snowdonia massif: the highest in Wales and England, 3560 ft: a national park.

Snowdonia (snō dō′nyə), *n.* a mountainous area in NW Wales including Snowdon.

snowdrift (snō′drĭft′), *n.* **1.** a mass or bank of snow driven together by wind. **2.** snow driven before wind.

snowdrop (snō′drŏp′), *n.* **1.** a low spring-blooming amaryllidaceous herb, *Galanthus nivalis,* bearing drooping white flowers. **2.** its bulbous root or flower.

snowdrop tree, any tree or shrub of the styracaceous genus *Halesia,* as *H. carolina,* with attractive, white, bell-shaped flowers; silverbell.

snowfall (snō′fôl′), *n.* **1.** a fall of snow. **2.** the amount of snow at a particular place or in a given time.

snowfield (snō′fēld′), *n.* an area of permanent snow found in a hollow high in altitude or latitude.

snowflake (snō′flāk′), *n.* **1.** one of the small feathery masses or flakes in which snow falls. **2.** any of certain European amaryllidaceous plants (genus *Leucojum*) resembling the snowdrop.

snow gauge, an instrument for measuring the depth of a snowfall.

snow goose, a large white bird of the family *Anatidae, Anser caerulescens* widespread in the Northern Hemisphere including (occasionally) Britain.

snowguard (snō′găd′), *n.* a roofguard.

snow-in-summer (snō′ĭn sŭm′ə), *n.* dusty miller.

snow leopard, the ounce.

snowline (snō′līn′), *n.* the line, as on mountains, above which there is perpetual snow.

snowman (snō′măn′), *n., pl.* **-men** (-mĕn′). a figure, resembling that of a man, made out of packed snow.

snowplough (snō′plou′), *n.* **1.** a contrivance for clearing away snow from roads, railways, etc. **2.** *Skiing.* a technique in which a skier moves with the skis turned inwards. Also, *Chiefly U.S.,* **snowplow.**

snow pudding, a light pudding, prepared by folding whipped eggwhites into a lemon gelatine mixture.

snowshed (snō′shĕd′), *n. U.S.* a structure, as over an extent of railway on a mountainside, for protection against snow.

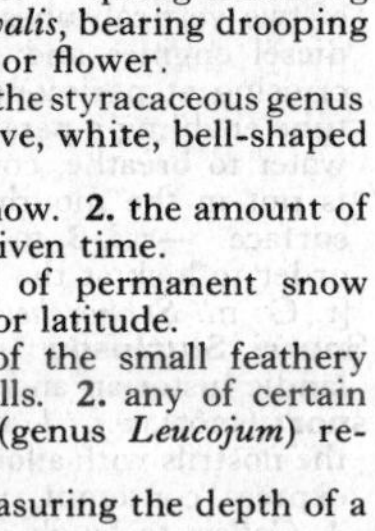

snowshoe (snō′shōō′), *n., v.,* **-shoed, -shoeing.** —*n.* **1.** a contrivance attached to the foot to enable the wearer to walk on deep snow without sinking in, as a ski, or esp., a light racket-shaped frame across which is stretched a network of rawhide. —*v.i.* **2.** to walk or travel on snowshoes. —**snow′sho′er,** *n.*

Snowshoes

snowslip (snō′slĭp′), *n.* the sliding down of a mass of snow on a slope. Also, **snowslide.**

snowstorm (snō′stôm′), *n.* a storm accompanied by a heavy fall of snow.

snow-white (snō′wīt′), *adj.* white as snow.

snowy (snō′ĭ), *adj.,* **snowier, snowiest. 1.** abounding in or covered with snow. **2.** characterized by snow, as weather, etc. **3.** consisting of snow; pertaining to or resembling snow. **4.** snow-white. **5.** immaculate; unsullied; stainless. —**snow′ily,** *adv.* —**snow′iness,** *n.*

Snowy (snō′ĭ), *n.* **1. Mountains,** a group of mountains in the Australian Alps, in New South Wales and Victoria; highest point, Mt Kosciusko, 7316 ft. **2. River,** a river in Australia, rising in SE New South Wales and flowing S to the Tasman Sea. 265 mi.

snowy owl, a large owl, *Nyctea scandiaca,* of N Europe, Asia, and North America.

snub (snŭb), *v.,* **snubbed, snubbing,** *n., adj.* —*v.t.* **1.** to treat with disdain or contempt. **2.** to put, force, etc., by doing this: *to snub one into silence.* **3.** to check or rebuke sharply. **4.** to check or stop suddenly (a rope or cable running out). **5.** *Naut.* to stop or bring up (a boat, or the like) by means of a rope or line made fast to a buoy, anchor, etc. **6.** *U.S.* to check (an animal, or the like) in a similar way. **7.** to pull up thus. —*n.* **8.** an act of snubbing; a sharp rebuke. **9.** a disdainful affront or slight. **10.** a sudden check given to a rope or cable running out of a moving boat, or the like. **11.** a snub nose. —*adj.* **12.** (of the nose) short, and turned up at the tip. [ME, t. Scand.; cf. Icel. *snubba* rebuke] —**snub′ber,** *n.*

snubby (snŭb′ĭ), *adj.,* **-bier, -biest. 1.** somewhat snub, as the nose. **2.** tending to snub people.

snuff¹ (snŭf), *v.t.* **1.** to draw in through the nose by inhaling. **2.** to perceive by or as by smelling. **3.** to examine by smelling, as an animal does. —*v.i.* **4.** to draw air, etc., into the nostrils by inhaling, as in order to smell something. **5.** to inhale powdered tobacco; take snuff. **6.** *Obs.* to express disdain, contempt, displeasure, etc., by sniffing (often fol. by *at*). —*n.* **7.** an act of snuffing; an inhalation; a sniff. **8.** smell or scent. **9.** a preparation of powdered tobacco, usually taken into the nostrils by inhalation. **10.** a pinch of such tobacco. **11. up to snuff,** *Colloq.* **a.** good enough; up to a satisfactory standard. **b.** shrewd; not easily tricked. [t. MD: s. *snuffen* snuffle]

snuff² (snŭf), *n.* **1.** the charred or partly consumed portion of a candlewick or the like. **2.** a thing of little or no value, esp. if left over. —*v.t.* **3.** to cut off or remove the snuff of (a candle, etc.). **4.** to extinguish (fol. by *out*). —*v.i.* **5. snuff it,** *Colloq.* to die. [ME *snoffe*; orig. uncert.]

snuffbox (snŭf′bŏks′), *n.* a box for holding snuff, esp. one small enough to be carried in the pocket.

snuffer¹ (snŭf′ə), *n.* **1.** one who snuffs or sniffs. **2.** one who takes snuff. [f. SNUFF¹ + -ER¹]

snuffer² (snŭf′ə), *n.* **1.** (*usually pl.*) an instrument for snuffing out candles, etc. **2.** one who snuffs candles. [f. SNUFF² + -ER¹]

Snuffers, 18th century

snuffle (snŭf′əl), *v.,* **-fled, -fling,** *n.* —*v.i.* **1.** to draw air into the nose for the purpose of smelling something. **2.** to draw the breath or mucus through the nostrils in an audible or noisy manner. **3.** to speak through the nose or with a nasal twang (often implying canting or hypocritical speech). **4.** to sniff; snivel. —*v.t.* **5.** to utter in a snuffling or nasal tone. —*n.* **6.** an act of snuffling. **7.** a nasal tone of voice. **8. the snuffles,** *Colloq.* a condition of the nose, as from a cold, causing snuffling. [t. D or Flem.: m. s. *snuffelen,* freq. of *snuffen.* See SNUFF¹, v.] —**snuf′fler,** *n.*

snuffy (snŭf′ĭ), *adj.,* **snuffier, snuffiest. 1.** resembling snuff. **2.** soiled with snuff. **3.** given to the use of snuff. **4.** easily displeased; huffy. —**snuff′iness,** *n.*

snug (snŭg), *adj.,* **snugger, snuggest,** *v.,* **snugged, snugging,** *adv., n.* —*adj.* **1.** comfortable or cosy, as a place, living quarters, etc. **2.** trim, neat, or compactly arranged, as a ship or its parts. **3.** fitting closely, but comfortably, as a garment. **4.** more or less compact or limited in size, and sheltered or warm. **5.** *U.S. and Dial.* comfortably situated, as persons, etc. **6.** pleasant or agreeable, esp. in a small, exclusive way. **7.** enabling one to live in comfort: *a snug fortune.* **8.** in hiding: *to lie snug.* **9.** *Obs.* secret. —*v.i.* **10.** to lie closely or comfortably; nestle. —*v.t.* **11.** to make snug. **12.** *Naut.* to prepare (a ship) for a storm by taking in sail, lashing deck gear, etc. (usually fol. by *down*). —*adv.* **13.** in a snug manner. —*n.* **14.** the private bar in a public house. [t. MD: m. *snuggher* smart, shipshape] —**snug′ly,** *adv.* —**snug′ness,** *n.*

snuggery (snŭg′ə rĭ), *n., pl.* **-geries. 1.** a snug place or position. **2.** a comfortable or cosy room. **3.** snug (def. 14).

snuggle (snŭg′l), *v.,* **-gled, -gling.** —*v.i.* **1.** to lie or press closely, as for comfort or from affection; nestle; cuddle. —*v.t.* **2.** to draw or press closely, as for comfort or from affection. [freq. of SNUG, v.]

sny (snī), *n. Shipbuilding.* the upward curving of a plank, esp. a boat's outer planking. [orig. unknown]

so[1] (sō), *adv.* **1.** in the way or manner indicated, described, or implied: *do it so.* **2.** in that or this manner or fashion; thus. **3.** as stated or reported: *is that so?* **4.** in the aforesaid state or condition: *it is broken, and has long been so.* **5.** to that extent; in that degree: *do not walk so fast.* **6.** very or extremely: *you are so kind.* **7.** very greatly: *my head aches so!* **8.** (used as the antecedent in the correlation *so . . . as*, expressing comparison) to such a degree or extent: *so far as I know.* **9.** having the purpose of. **10.** for a given reason; hence; therefore. **11.** because of; for the reason that. **12.** in such manner as to follow or result from. **13.** in the way that follows; in this way. **14.** in such way as to end it. **15. and so, a.** (a continuative used to confirm or emphasize a previous statement): *I said I would come, and so I will.* **b.** likewise or correspondingly: *he is going, and so am I.* **c.** consequently or accordingly: *she is ill, and so cannot come.* **d.** thereupon or thereafter: *and so they were married.* **16. and so forth, a.** continuing in the same way. **b.** etcetera. **17. and so on,** et cetera. **18. just so,** in perfect order; carefully arranged: *her room was just so.* **19. or so,** about thus, or about that amount or number: *a day or so ago.* **20. quite so,** exactly as you have just stated. **21. so as, a.** with the result or purpose (followed by an infinitive). **b.** provided that. **22. so called, a.** called or designated thus. **b.** incorrectly called or styled thus. **23. so much,** an unspecified amount. **24. so much for,** there is no more to be said or done about: *so much for your childhood ideals.* **25. so that, a.** with the effect or result that. **b.** in order that: *he wrote so that they might expect him.* **c.** provided that. **26. so to speak** (or **say**), to use such manner of speaking. **27. so what!,** *Colloq.* what does that matter.
—*conj.* **28.** *Colloq.* consequently; with the result that. **29.** under the condition that (often fol. by *that*).
—*pron.* **30.** such as has been stated: *to be good and stay so.* **31.** more or less: *at three o'clock or so.*
—*interj.* **32.** how can that be! **33.** that will do! stop! [ME; OE *swā*, c. D *zoo*, G *so*] —**Syn. 10.** See **therefore.**

so[2] (sō), *n. Music.* soh. [See GAMUT]

So., 1. South. **2.** southern.

soak (sōk), *v.i.* **1.** to lie in and become saturated or permeated with water or some other liquid. **2.** to pass, as a liquid, through pores or interstices (usually fol. by *in, through, out,* etc.). **3.** to be thoroughly wet. **4.** to become known slowly to: *the facts soaked into his mind.* **5.** *Colloq.* to drink immoderately. —*v.t.* **6.** to place and keep in liquid in order to saturate thoroughly; steep. **7.** to wet thoroughly, or drench. **8.** to permeate thoroughly, as liquid or moisture. **9.** *Slang.* to intoxicate with alcohol. **10.** *Colloq.* to drink, esp. to excess. **11.** to take in or up by absorption (often fol. by *up*): *blotting paper soaks up ink.* **12.** to draw (*out*) by or as by soaking. **13.** *Colloq.* to charge excessively. **14.** *Slang.* to put in pawn. **15.** *U.S. Colloq.* to beat hard; punish severely. —*n.* **16.** the act of soaking. **17.** the state of being soaked. **18.** the liquid in which anything is soaked. **19.** *Slang.* a heavy drinker. **20.** *Slang.* a prolonged drinking bout. [ME *soke*, OE *socian*; akin to SUCK, v.] —**soak′er,** *n.* —**Syn. 7.** See **wet.**

soakage (sō′kij), *n.* **1.** the act of soaking. **2.** liquid which has oozed out or been absorbed.

soakaway (sōk′ə wā′), *n.* a pit filled with rubble, etc., into which rainwater, or waste water, is sometimes drained.

so-and-so (sō′ən sō′), *n., pl.* **-sos. 1.** someone or something not definitely named: *Mr So-and-so.* **2.** *Colloq.* a very mean, unkind person: *she really is a so-and-so.*

Soane (sōn), *n.* **Sir John,** 1753–1837, English architect.

soap (sōp), *n.* **1.** a substance used for washing and cleansing purposes, usually made by treating a fat with an alkali (as sodium or potassium hydroxide), and consisting chiefly of the sodium or potassium salts of the acids contained in the fat. **2.** any metallic salt of an acid derived from a fat. **3.** *Colloq.* flattery. **4.** *U.S. Slang.* money, esp. as used for bribery in politics. —*v.t.* **5.** to rub, cover or treat with soap. **6.** to flatter (often fol. by *up*). [ME *sope*, OE *sāpe*, c. G *Seife*]

soapbark (sōp′bärk′), *n.* **1.** a rosaceous Chilean tree, *Quillaja saponaria*, bearing undivided evergreen leaves and small white flowers: the inner bark is used as a substitute for soap. **2.** the inner bark of this tree, used as a substitute for soap; quillai bark.

soapberry (sōp′bĕ′rĭ), *n., pl.* **-ries. 1.** any of certain tropical and subtropical trees of the genus *Sapindus*, esp. *S. saponaria*, used as a substitute for soap. **2.** a tree bearing such fruit, as *S. drummondii*, of the southwestern U.S., which yields a useful wood.

soapbox (sōp′bŏks′), *n.* **1.** a box, usually wooden, in which soap has been packed, esp. one used as a temporary platform by orators addressing people in the streets. **2.** any place, means, or the like, used by a person to make a speech, voice opinions, etc.

soap flakes, soap manufactured into flakes and sold esp. for washing clothes, etc.

soap opera, *Colloq.* a radio or television play presented serially in short regular programmes, dealing usually with domestic problems, esp. in a highly emotional manner. [so called because originally sponsored on U.S. radio networks by soap manufacturers]

soap powder, 1. soap in a powdered form, esp. as sold for washing clothes. **2.** detergent in powder form.

soapstone (sōp′stōn′), *n.* a massive variety of talc with a soapy or greasy feel, used for hearths, tabletops, carved ornaments, etc.; steatite.

soapsuds (sōp′sŭdz′), *n.pl.* suds made with water and soap.

soapwort (sōp′wûrt′), *n.* a caryophyllaceous herb, *Saponaria officinalis*, whose leaves were formerly used for cleansing.

soapy (sō′pĭ), *adj.,* **soapier, soapiest. 1.** containing, or impregnated with, soap: *soapy water.* **2.** covered with soap or lather. **3.** of the nature of soap; resembling soap. **4.** pertaining to or characteristic of soap. **5.** *Colloq.* flattering; given to using smooth words. —**soap′ily,** *adv.* —**soap′iness,** *n.*

soar (sô), *v.i.* **1.** to fly upwards, as a bird. **2.** to fly at a great height, without visible movements of the pinions, as a bird. **3.** *Aeron.* to fly without engine power, esp. in a sailplane, using ascending air currents. **4.** to rise or ascend to a height, as a mountain. **5.** to rise or aspire to a higher or more exalted level. —*n.* **6.** the act of soaring. **7.** the height attained in soaring. [ME *sore*, t. OF: m. *essorer* fly up, soar, g. LL *exaurāre*, der. *ex-* out of + *aura* air] —**soar′er,** *n.* —**Syn. 1.** See **fly**[1].

sob (sŏb), *v.,* **sobbed, sobbing,** *n.* —*v.i.* **1.** to weep with a sound caused by a convulsive catching of the breath. **2.** to make a sound resembling this. —*v.t.* **3.** to utter with sobs. **4.** to put, send, etc., by sobbing or with sobs: *to sob oneself to sleep.* —*n.* **5.** the act of sobbing; a convulsive catching of the breath in weeping. **6.** any sound suggesting this. [ME *sobbe(n)*; appar. imit.] —**sob′bingly,** *adv.*

sobeit (sō bē′ĭt), *conj. Archaic.* if it be so that; provided.

sober (sō′bə), *adj.* **1.** not intoxicated or drunk. **2.** habitually temperate, esp. with alcoholic drink. **3.** quiet or sedate in demeanour, as persons. **4.** marked by seriousness, gravity, solemnity, etc., as demeanour, speech, etc. **5.** subdued in tone, as colour; not gay or showy, as clothes. **6.** free from excess, extravagance, or exaggeration: *sober facts.* **7.** showing self-control. **8.** sane or rational. —*v.i., v.t.* **9.** to make or become sober. [ME, t. OF: m. *sobre*, t. L: m. s. *sōbrius*] —**so′berly,** *adv.* —**so′berness,** *n.* —**Syn. 4.** See **grave**[2]. **5.** sombre, dull. —**Ant. 4.** gay.

soberminded (sō′bə mīn′dĭd), *adj.* self-controlled; sensible. —**so′ber-mind′edness,** *n.*

sobersides (sō′bə sīdz′), *n. Colloq.* a serious person.

Sobieski (sō′bĭ ĕs′kĭ), *n.* **John,** 1624–96, Polish general who, as John III, was king of Poland (1674–96).

sobosobo (sō′bō sō′bō), *n.* an African variety of black nightshade, *Solanum nigrum* var. *guineense*, the fruit of which is used for making jams, pies, etc. [t. Zulu: m. *umsobosobo*]

Sobranje (sō brä′nyĭ), *n.* the national assembly of Bulgaria, consisting of a single chamber of elected deputies. [t. Bulgarian: assembly]

sobriety (sō brī′ə tĭ), *n.* **1.** the state or quality of being sober. **2.** temperance or moderation, esp. in the use of strong drink. **3.** seriousness, gravity, or solemnity. [ME *sobrietie*, t. L: m. *sōbrietas*]

sobriquet (sō′brĭ kā′), *n.* a nickname. Also, **soubriquet.** [t. F; orig. uncert.]

sob-sister (sŏb′sĭs′tə), *n. Chiefly U.S.* a woman journalist who writes a newspaper or magazine feature in a sentimental style.

sob-story (sŏb′stô′rĭ), *n. Colloq.* **1.** a story full of sentiment and pathos. **2.** an excuse: *she arrived very late and gave them a sob-story about a broken clock.*

sob-stuff (sŏb′stŭf′), *n. Colloq.* sentimental matter as in literature, in the cinema, a story of bad luck, etc., designed to arouse the emotions.

soc (sŏk), *n. Early Eng. Law.* soke. [OE *socn*]

Soc., 1. socialist. **2.** society.

socage (sŏk′ĭj), *n. Medieval Eng. Law.* the system of non-military land tenure, usually free as distinguished from servile, by which land was commonly held in England. [ME, t. AF: f. *soc* SOKE + *-age* -AGE] —**soc′ager,** *n.*

so-called (sō′kôld′), *adj.* **1.** called or designated thus. **2.** incorrectly called or styled thus.

soccer (sŏk′ə), *n.* association football. [f. (AS)SOC(IATION) + -ER[1]]

Sochi (*Russ.* sôʹchĭ), *n.* a seaport in the S Soviet Union in Europe. 179,000 (est. 1965).

sociability (sōˈshə bĭlʹĭ tĭ), *n.*, *pl.* **-ties.** sociable disposition; inclination for the society of others.

sociable (sōʹshə bl), *adj.* **1.** inclined to associate with or be in the company of others. **2.** friendly or agreeable in company; companionable. **3.** characterized by or pertaining to companionship with others. *—n.* **4.** *U.S.* an informal social gathering, esp. of members of a church. [t. L: m. s. *sociābilis*] —**soʹciableness,** *n.* —**soʹciably,** *adv.* —**Syn. 1.** See **social.**

social (sōʹshəl), *adj.* **1.** pertaining to, devoted to, or characterized by friendly companionship or relations: *a social club.* **2.** friendly or sociable, as persons or the disposition, spirit, etc. **3.** pertaining to, connected with, or suited to polite or fashionable society: *a social function.* **4.** living, or disposed to live, in companionship with others or in a community, rather than in isolation. **5.** of or pertaining to human society, esp. as a body divided into classes according to worldly status: *social rank.* **6.** of or pertaining to the life and relation of human beings in a community: *social problems.* **7.** denoting or pertaining to activities designed to remedy or alleviate certain unfavourable conditions of life in a community, esp. among the poor: *social work.* **8.** pertaining to or advocating socialism. **9.** (of animals) living together in communities, as bees, ants, etc. (opposed to *solitary*). **10.** *Bot.* growing in patches or clumps. *—n.* **11.** a social gathering or party. [t. L: s. *sociālis*] —**soʹcially,** *adv.* —**soʹcialness,** *n.*

—**Syn. 1.** SOCIAL, SOCIABLE agree in being concerned with the mutual relations of mankind living in an organized society. SOCIAL is a general word: *social laws, equals, advancement.* SOCIABLE means fond of company and society, companionable, genial, and affable, good at 'mixing': *a friendly and sociable sort of person.* A SOCIAL evening is one spent in company with others at a more or less formal event; a SOCIABLE evening is one spent companionably with perhaps only one person or a few. —**Ant. 4.** individual, introverted.

social class, 1. a group which is part of the hierarchical structure of a society, usually classified by occupation, and having common economic, cultural or political status. **2.** the phenomenon of horizontal stratification in society in terms of economic, cultural, or political status.

social climber, one who tries to move up into a higher social class, esp. by associating with people from that class. —**social climbing.**

social control, *Sociol.* **1.** the enforcement of conformity by society upon its members, either by law or by attitudes. **2.** the influence of any element in social life working to maintain the pattern of such life.

social credit, *Econ.* the doctrine that the state should control retail prices, and profits should be distributed among consumers.

Social Democrat, a member of any of certain political parties with socialist principles, as in West Germany and elsewhere.

social development, *Sociol.* the formation and transformation of social life, customs, institutions, etc. Also, **social evolution.**

social differentiation, *Sociol.* the state or process by which elements in society possess or develop distinct characteristics, as in the specialization resulting from division of labour.

social disorganization, *Sociol.* **1.** the breaking-up of the structure of a social organization. **2.** the non-existence of a social organization.

social distance, *Sociol.* the extent to which individuals or groups are removed from or excluded from participating in each other's life.

social environment, *Sociol.* culture factor.

social evolution, *Sociol.* social development.

social heritage, *Sociol.* the entire inherited pattern of cultural activity present in a society.

social interaction, *Sociol.* the reciprocal stimulation and response taking place between individuals and between groups, with particular reference to cultural activity.

socialise (sōʹshə līzˈ), *v.t.*, **-lised, -lising.** socialize.

socialism (sōʹshə lĭzˈəm), *n.* **1.** a theory or system of social organization which advocates the vesting of the ownership and control of the means of production, capital, land, etc., in the community as a whole. **2.** procedure or practice in accordance with this theory.

social isolation, *Sociol,* a state or process in which persons, groups, or cultures lose or do not have communication or cooperation with one another. Social isolation often develops into open conflict.

socialist (sōʹshə lĭst), *n.* **1.** an advocate of socialism. **2.** (*often cap.*) a person who belongs to the Labour Party in Great Britain or any similar party elsewhere. *—adj.* **3.** pertaining to socialists or socialism.

socialistic (sōˈshə lĭsʹtĭk), *adj.* **1.** *Chiefly U.S.* socialist. **2.** tending towards or sympathizing with socialism.

socialistically (sōˈshə lĭsʹtĭ kə lĭ, -klĭ), *adv.* in a socialist or socialistic manner or direction.

Socialist Party, 1. any of various parties professing socialist principles. **2.** *U.S.* a political party advocating socialism formed about 1900 by members of the **Social Democratic Party** and the **Socialist Labour Party.** **3.** *Colloq.* the British or any other Labour Party.

socialite (sōʹshə līt'), *n.* a member of the social elite, or one who aspires to be such.

sociality (sōˈshĭ ălʹĭ tĭ), *n.*, *pl.* **-ties. 1.** social nature or tendencies as shown in the assembling of individuals in communities. **2.** the action on the part of individuals of associating together in communities. **3.** the state or quality of being social.

socialize (sōʹshə līzˈ), *v.*, **-lized, -lizing.** *—v.t.* **1.** to make social; make fit for life in companionship with others. **2.** to make socialistic; establish or regulate according to the theories of socialism. **3.** *Educ.* to turn from an individual activity into one involving all or a group of pupils. *—v.i.* **4.** to go into society; frequent social functions. **5.** to be sociable and mix freely, as at a social gathering. Also, **socialise.** —**soˈcializaʹtion,** *n.*

socialized medicine, *U.S.* any of various systems to provide the entire population, esp. the lower-income groups, with medical care through federal subsidization of medical and health services, general regulation of these services, etc.

social organization, *Sociol.* the structure of relations inside a group, usually the relations of subgroups and of institutions.

social process, *Sociol.* the means by which culture and social organization change or are preserved.

social science, social studies.

social security, the provision by the state for the economic and social welfare of the public by means of old-age pensions, sickness and unemployment benefits.

social service, organized welfare efforts carried on under professional rules by a trained personnel.

social settlement. See **settlement** (def. 13).

social studies, a broad group of subjects, as economics, social history, sociology, etc., relating to man's function as a social being. Also, **social science.**

Social War, 1. *Gk Hist.* the war between Athens and its confederates in 357–355 B.C. **2.** *Rom. Hist.* the war between Rome and its Italian allies in 90–88 B.C.

social welfare, a system of services set up by a state for the benefit of the community.

social work, organized work directed towards the betterment of social conditions in the community, as by seeking to improve the condition of the poor, to promote the welfare of children, etc. —**social worker.**

societal (sə sīʹə tl), *adj.* social (def. 6).

society (sə sīʹə tĭ), *n.*, *pl.* **-ties. 1.** an organization of persons associated together for religious, benevolent, literary, scientific, political, patriotic, or other purposes. **2.** a body of individuals living as members of a community: *a society of human beings.* **3.** the body of human beings generally, associated or viewed as members of a community: *the evolution of human society.* **4.** human beings collectively regarded as a body divided into classes according to worldly status: *the lower classes of society.* **5.** a body of persons associated by their calling, interests, etc.: *diplomatic society.* **6.** those with whom one has companionship. **7.** companionship or company: *to enjoy one's society.* **8.** the social relations, activities, or life of the polite or fashionable world. **9.** the body of those associated in the polite or fashionable world; the rich upper class. **10.** the condition of those living in companionship with others, or in a community, rather than in isolation. **11.** any community. **12.** *Ecol.* a closely integrated grouping of organisms of the same species held together by mutual dependence and showing division of labour. **13.** *U.S. Eccles.* an ecclesiastical society. *—adj.* **14.** of or pertaining to polite society: *a society party.* [t. L: m. *societas*] —**Syn. 1.** See **circle.**

Society Islands, a group of islands in the S Pacific: a part of French Polynesia; largest island, Tahiti. (Excluding minor islands) 61,607 pop. (1962); 453 sq. mi. *Cap.:* Papeete. See map under **Hawaiian Islands.**

Society of Friends, the Christian sect founded by George Fox about 1650, opposed to the taking of oaths and all war; commonly called Quakers.

Society of Jesus. See **Jesuit.**

Socinian (sō sĭnʹĭ ən), *n.* **1.** a follower of Socinus who denied Christ's divinity, although holding that he was miraculously begotten and entitled to adoration. *—adj.* **2.** of or pertaining to the Socinians or their doctrines. —**Socinʹianism,** *n.*

Socinus (sō sīʹnəs), *n.* **Faustus** (fôsʹtəs) (*Fausto Sozzini*), 1539–1605, and his uncle, **Laelius** (lēʹlĭ əs) (*Lelio Sozzini*),

1525–62, Italian Protestant theologians and reformers.
socio-, a word element representing 'social', 'sociological', as in *sociometry*. [comb. form repr. L *socius* companion]
sociol., **1.** sociological. **2.** sociology.
sociology (sō′sĭ ŏl′ə jĭ), *n.* the science or study of the origin, development, organization, and functioning of human society; the science of the fundamental laws of social relations, institutions, etc. —**so′ciolog′ical,** *adj.* —**so′ciol′ogist,** *n.*
sociometry (sō′sĭ ŏm′ĭ trĭ), *n.* the measurement of attitudes of social acceptance or rejection through expressed preferences among members of a social grouping.
sock[1] (sŏk), *n.* **1.** a short stocking reaching about halfway to the knee, or only above the ankle. **2.** a light shoe worn by ancient Greek and Roman comic actors, sometimes taken as a symbol of comedy. **3. pull one's socks up,** *Colloq.* to make more effort. See **buskin.** [ME *sokke*, OE *socc*, t. L: s. *soccus* (def. 2)]
sock[2] (sŏk), *Slang.* —*v.t.* **1.** to strike or hit hard. —*n.* **2.** a hard blow. [orig. uncert.]
sockdolager (sŏk dŏl′ə jə), *n. U.S. Slang.* **1.** something unusually large, heavy, etc. **2.** a decisive reply, argument, etc. **3.** a heavy, finishing blow. [slang coinage based on SOCK[2] + DOXOLOGY (in slang sense of finish) + -ER[1]]
socket (sŏk′ĭt), *n.* **1.** a hollow part or piece for receiving and holding some part or thing. **2.** one of a set of different-sized circular heads with flanges on the inner circumference, for use with a ratchet spanner. **3.** *Elect.* a connecting device to which the wires of a circuit may be attached and which is arranged for the insertion of a plug. **4.** *Anat.* **a.** a hollow in one part, which receives another part: *the socket of the eye.* **b.** the concavity of a joint: *the socket of the hip.* **5.** the shank of a golf club. —*v.t.* **6.** to place in or fit with a socket. **7.** *Golf.* to hit (the ball) with the shank of the club. [ME *socket*, t. AF, dim. of *soc* ploughshare; of Celtic orig.]
socket outlet, *Elect.* a socket (def. 3).
sockeye (sŏk′ī′), *n.* the red salmon, *Oncorhynchus nerka*, most highly valued of the Pacific salmons. [t. Amer. Ind. (Salishan): alter. of *sukkegh* Fraser river salmon, blueback, etc.]
socle (sō′kl), *n. Archit.* a low, plain member supporting a wall, pedestal, or the like. [t. F, t. It.: m. *zoccolo*, g. L *socculus*, dim. of *soccus* SOCK[1]]
Socotra (sə kō′trə), *n.* an island in the Indian Ocean, S of Arabia: a part of South Yemen. ab. 9000 pop.; 1382 sq. mi. *Cap.*: Tamarida. Also, **Sokotra.**
Socrates (sŏk′rə tēz′), *n.* 469?–399 B.C., Athenian philosopher.
Socratic (sŏ krăt′ĭk), *adj.* **1.** of or pertaining to Socrates or his philosophy, followers, etc. —*n.* **2.** a follower of Socrates. **3.** one of the Greek philosophers stimulated by Socrates. —**Socrat′ically,** *adv.*
Socratic irony. See **irony**[1] (def. 3).
Socratic method, the use of questions as employed by Socrates to develop a latent idea, as in the mind of a pupil, or to elicit admissions, as from an opponent, tending to establish or to confute some proposition.
sod[1] (sŏd), *n.*, *v.*, **sodded, sodding.** —*n.* **1.** a piece (usually square or oblong) cut or torn from the surface of grassland, containing the roots of grass, etc. **2.** the surface of the ground, esp. when covered with grass; turf; sward. —*v.t.* **3.** to cover with sods. [ME, t. MD or MLG: m. *sode* turf]
sod[2] (sŏd), *v. Obs.* pt. and pp. of **seethe.**
sod[3] (sŏd), *n. Taboo Slang.* **1.** sodomite. **2.** a disagreeable person.
soda (sō′də), *n.* **1.** sodium hydroxide, NaOH; caustic soda. **2.** the oxide of sodium, Na_2O. **3.** sodium (in phrases): *carbonate of soda.* **4.** soda-water. **5.** a drink made with soda-water, served with fruit or other syrups, ice-cream, etc. **6.** (in faro) the turned-up card in the dealing box before one begins to play. [t. ML, t. It., ? back-formation from ML *sodānum* glasswort, t. Ar.: m. *suwwād* or m. *sudā* headache (for which the plant was used as a remedy)]
soda ash. See **sodium carbonate.**
soda biscuit, a biscuit using soda and sour milk or buttermilk as leavening agents.
soda bread, a yeastless bread, risen by the addition of bicarbonate of soda and cream of tartar.
soda fountain, **1.** a counter at which sodas, ice-cream, snacks, etc., are served. **2.** a container from which soda-water is drawn by taps.
soda lime, a mixture of sodium hydroxide and calcium hydroxide.
sodalite (sō′də līt′), *n.* a mineral, sodium aluminium silicate with sodium chloride, $3NaAlSiO_4.NaCl$, occurring in crystals and in massive form, white, grey, or blue in colour: found in certain alkali-rich igneous rocks.
sodality (sō dăl′ĭ tĭ), *n.*, *pl.* **-ties.** **1.** fellowship. **2.** an association or society. **3.** *Rom. Cath. Ch.* a society with religious or charitable objects. [t. L: m. *sodālitas*]
soda nitre, impure naturally occurring sodium nitrate; caliche; Chile saltpetre.
soda siphon, a bottle filled with carbonated water, fitted with a bent tube through the neck, the soda-water being forced out, when a valve is opened, by the pressure on its surface by the gas accumulating within the bottle.
soda-water (sō′də wô′tə), *n.* **1.** an effervescent beverage consisting of water charged with carbon dioxide. **2.** (orig.) a beverage made with sodium bicarbonate.
sodden (sŏd′n), *adj.* **1.** soaked with liquid or moisture. **2.** heavy, doughy, or soggy, as food. **3.** having the appearance of having been soaked. **4.** bloated, as the face. **5.** expressionless, dull, or stupid. **6.** *Rare.* boiled. —*v.t.*, *v.i.* **7.** to make or become sodden. [ME *sothen*, pp. of SEETHE] —**sod′denly,** *adv.* —**sod′denness,** *n.*
Soddy (sŏd′ĭ), *n.* **Frederick** (frĕd′rĭk), 1877–1956, English chemist who worked on radioactivity.
sodium (sō′dyəm), *n. Chem.* a soft, silver-white metallic element which oxidizes rapidly in moist air, occurring in nature only in the combined state. The metal is used in the synthesis of sodium peroxide, sodium cyanide, and lead tetraethyl. *Symbol*: Na (for *natrium*); *at. wt*: 22·9898; *at. no.*: 11; *sp. gr.*: 0·97 at 20°C. [f. SOD(A) + -IUM]
sodium bicarbonate, *Chem.* a white, crystalline compound, $NaHCO_3$, used in cooking, medicine, etc. Also, **sodium hydrogen carbonate.**
sodium carbonate, *Chem.* a compound of sodium, Na_2CO_3, occurring in an anhydrous form as a white powder, called **soda ash,** and as a hydrate, $Na_2CO_3.10H_2O$, known as **washing soda.**
sodium chlorate, *Chem.* a sodium salt, $NaClO_3$, used in explosives, as an antiseptic in toothpastes, etc.
sodium chloride, *Chem.* common salt, NaCl.
sodium dichromate, *Chem.* a red, water-soluble, crystalline salt, $Na_2Cr_2O_7.2H_2O$; used as an oxidizing agent, in electroplating, and in the manufacture of inks and dyes. Also, **sodium bichromate.**
sodium glycocholate (sō′dyəm glī′kə kō′lāt), *Biochem.* sodium salt of glycocholic acid, found in bile.
sodium hydroxide, *Chem.* a white caustic solid, NaOH, used in making soap, etc.; caustic soda.
sodium nitrate, *Chem.* a crystalline water-soluble compound, $NaNO_3$, which occurs naturally as Chile saltpetre, used in fertilizers, explosives, and glass.
sodium pentothal, a barbiturate, injected intravenously as a general anaesthetic. Also, **Pentothal sodium, thiopental sodium, thiopentone sodium.**
sodium peroxide, *Chem.* a yellow, water-soluble compound, Na_2O_2, formed when sodium burns in air; used as an oxidizing agent and in bleaching.
sodium silicate, *Chem.* a white, water-soluble compound, Na_2SiO_3, used in dyeing, printing, fireproofing, and preserving; waterglass.
sodium sulphate, *Chem.* a white, water-soluble compound, $Na_2SO_4.10H_2O$, used in the manufacture of dyes, soaps, detergents, etc.; Glauber salt.
sodium taurocholate (sō′dyəm tô′rə kō′lāt), *Biochem.* sodium salt of taurocholic acid, found in bile.
sodium thiosulphate, *Chem.* a water-soluble crystalline salt, $Na_2S_2O_3.5H_2O$, sometimes called **sodium hyposulphite** (the 'hypo' of photographers, used as a fixing bath).
sodium-vapour lamp (sō′dyəm vā′pə), *Elect.* an electric lamp in which sodium vapour is activated by current passing between two electrodes, producing a yellow, glareless light which is widely used for street lighting.
Sodom (sŏd′əm), *n.* **1.** an ancient city near the Dead Sea, which, according to the Bible, was destroyed by fire from heaven because of the wickedness of its inhabitants. Gen. 18–19. **2.** any very wicked place.
Sodoma, Il (*It.* sō′dō mä, ēl), *n.* **Giovanni Antonio de' Bazzi** (*It.* jō vän′nē än tō′nyō dē bät′tsē), 1477–1549, Italian painter.
Sodomite (sŏd′ə mīt′), *n.* **1.** an inhabitant of Sodom. **2.** (*l.c.*) one who practises sodomy.
sodomy (sŏd′əm ĭ), *n.* **1.** sexual intercourse using the anal orifice, esp. of one man with another. **2.** bestiality. **3.** any sexual practice regarded as unnatural or perverted. [ME, t. OF: m. *sodomie*. See SODOM, -Y]
Soekarno (sōō kä′nō), *n.* See **Sukarno.**
Soemba (sōōm′bə), *n.* Dutch name of **Sumba.**
Soembawa (sōōm bä′wə), *n.* Dutch name of **Sumbawa.**
Soerabaja (sōōə′rə bī′ə), *n.* Dutch name of **Surabaya.**
soever (sō ĕv′ə), *adv.* at all; in any case; of any kind; in any way (used with generalizing force after *who*, *what*, *when*, *where*, *how*, *any*, *all*, etc., sometimes separated by intervening words, often in composition): *choose what person soever you please.*

-soever, a suffix making intensive and generalized forms of interrogatives, as in *whatsoever.*

sofa (sō′fə), *n.* a long upholstered seat, or couch, with a back, and two arms or raised ends. [t. Ar.: m. *soffeh* part of floor made higher for use as a seat]

soffit (sŏf′ĭt), *n. Archit.* the under surface of an architrave, arch, beam, or the like. [earlier *soffita, -o,* t. It., f. *so-* (g. L *sub*) under + *-fita, -fito,* pp. of *figgere* (g. L *figere*) fix]

soffritto (*It.* sŏ frēt′tō), *Italian Cookery.* —*adj.* **1.** underdone; slightly cooked. —*n.* **2.** a vegetable mixture used as a base for soups, meat dishes, etc.

Sofia (sō′fyə; *Bulg.* sō′fē yȧ), *n.* the capital of Bulgaria, in the W part. 747,272 (1964). Also, **Sofiya.** See map under **Iron Gate.**

soft (sŏft), *adj.* **1.** yielding readily to touch or pressure; easily penetrated, divided, or altered in shape; not hard or stiff. **2.** relatively deficient in hardness, as metal. **3.** smooth and agreeable to the touch; not rough or coarse. **4.** producing agreeable sensations; pleasant, easeful, or comfortable: *soft slumber.* **5.** low or subdued in sound; gentle and melodious. **6.** not harsh or unpleasant to the eye; not glaring, as light or colour. **7.** not hard or sharp, as outlines. **8.** gentle or mild, as wind, rain, etc.; genial or balmy, as climate, air, etc. **9.** gentle, mild, lenient, or compassionate. **10.** smooth, soothing, or ingratiating, as words. **11.** not harsh or severe, as terms. **12.** yielding readily to the tender emotions, as persons; impressionable. **13.** sentimental, as language. **14.** not strong or robust; delicate; incapable of great endurance or exertion. **15.** *Colloq.* not hard, trying, or severe; involving little effort: *a soft job.* **16.** (of water) relatively free from mineral salts that interfere with the action of soap. **17.** *Photog.* having delicate gradations of tone (opposed to *contrasty*): **18.** *Physics.* (of radiation) having a relatively long wavelength and low penetrating power. **19.** *Metall.* **a.** (of solder) having a relatively low melting point, usually below 700°F. **b.** (of iron) containing little carbon; being incapable of retaining magnetic properties when the magnetizing field is removed. **20.** *Astronautics.* (of a landing of a space vehicle) gentle, not harmful to the vehicle or its contents, usually implying an impact velocity of less than 20 m.p.h. **21.** *Phonet.* **a.** (of consonants) lenis, esp. lenis and voiced. **b.** (of *c* and *g*) pronounced as in *cent* and *gem.* **c.** (of consonants in Slavic languages) palatalized. **22.** *Colloq.* easily influenced or swayed, as a person, the mind, etc.; easily imposed upon. **23.** *Colloq.* foolish; feeble; weak. **24. be soft on someone,** *Colloq.* to be sentimentally inclined towards someone, esp. without showing it openly. **25. have a soft spot for someone** or **something,** to be fond of someone or something. —*n.* **26.** that which is soft or yielding; the soft part; softness. —*adv.* **27.** in a soft manner. —*interj. Archaic.* **28.** be quiet! hush! **29.** not so fast! stop! [ME *softe,* OE *sōfte,* c. G *sanft*] —**soft′ly,** *adv.* —**soft′ness,** *n.*

softa (sŏf′tə), *n. Islam.* a Muslim student of theology and sacred law. [t. Turk., t. Pers.: m. *sūhtah,* lit., fired (by love of learning)]

softball (sŏft′bôl′), *n.* **1.** a form of baseball played with a larger and softer ball. **2.** the ball itself.

soft-boiled (sŏft′boild′), *adj.* (of an egg) lightly boiled so that the yoke remains unset.

soft breathing, *Gk Gram.* smooth breathing.

soft coal, bituminous coal.

soft drink, a drink which is not alcoholic or intoxicating, as ginger beer, lemonade, etc.

soften (sŏf′ən), *v.t., v.i.* to make or become soft or softer. —**sof′tener,** *n.*

softening of the brain, *Pathol.* **1.** a softening of the cerebral tissues, which are transformed into a mushy, fatlike substance. **2.** *Obs.* dementia associated with general paresis.

soft-finned (sŏft′fĭnd′), *adj. Ichthyol.* having fins supported by articulated rays rather than by spines, as a malacopterygian (contrasted with *spiny-finned*).

soft furnishings, materials used for interior decoration, as for curtains and chair covers.

soft goods, merchandise as textiles, furnishings, etc.

soft hail, *Meteorol.* hail comprising easily compressible, crisp, opaque pellets of ice; graupel.

soft-headed (sŏft′hĕd′ĭd), *adj.* foolish; stupid. —**soft′-head′edness,** *n.*

soft-hearted (sŏft′hä′tĭd), *adj.* very generous or sympathetic. —**soft′-heart′edness,** *n.*

soft pedal, a pedal, as on a piano, for lessening the volume.

soft-pedal (sŏft′pĕd′l), *v.*, **-alled, -alling** or (*U.S.*) **-aled, -aling.** —*v.i.* **1.** to use the soft pedal. —*v.t.* **2.** to soften the sound of by means of the soft pedal. **3.** *Colloq.* to tone down; make less strong, uncompromising, noticeable, or the like.

soft rot, *Bot.* any plant disease caused by bacteria or fungi resulting in a marked softening of the tissue, esp. that due to a bacterium *Erwinia carotovora.*

soft sell, a method of advertising or selling which is quietly persuasive, subtle, and indirect. See **hard sell.**

soft-shelled crab (sŏft′shĕld′), the common edible crab, *Cancer pagurus,* recently moulted and therefore in a suitable state to be cooked and eaten in its entirety. Also, **soft′shell′.**

soft-shelled turtle, a turtle with a leathery shell overlying the bony carapace and plastron, instead of the usual one of horny plates. The many species constitute the family *Trionychidae.* See **leatherback.**

soft shower, cascade shower.

soft soap, 1. the semifluid soap produced when potassium hydroxide is used in the saponification of a fat or an oil. **2.** *Colloq.* smooth words; flattery.

soft-soap (sŏft′sōp′), *v.t.* **1.** to apply soft soap to. **2.** to ply with smooth words; cajole; flatter. —*v.i.* **3.** to use soft soap in washing. —**soft′-soap′er,** *n.*

soft-spoken (sŏft′spō′kən), *adj.* **1.** (of persons) speaking with a soft or gentle voice; mild. **2.** (of words) softly or mildly spoken; persuasive.

software (sŏft′wĕə′), *n. Computers.* a collection of computer programs which is normally provided with a computer, enabling it to be used efficiently.

softwood (sŏft′wŏŏd′), *n.* **1.** any wood which is relatively soft or easily cut. **2.** a tree yielding such a wood. **3.** *Forestry.* a coniferous tree or its wood.

softy (sŏf′tĭ), *n., pl.* **-ties.** *Colloq.* **1.** one who is easily imposed upon. **2.** an effeminate or unmanly person. **3.** a soft, silly, or weak-minded person.

SOGAT (sō′găt), *n.* Society of Graphical and Allied Trades.

Sogdian (sŏg′dĭ ən), *n.* **1.** an individual belonging to the ancient peoples of Iran who lived in Sogdiana. **2.** the extinct Iranian language of Sogdiana.

Sogdiana (sŏg′dĭ ä′nə), *n.* a province of the ancient Persian Empire between the Oxus and Jaxartes rivers: now in the SW Soviet Union in Asia. *Cap.:* Samarkand.

soggy (sŏg′ĭ), *adj.*, **-gier, -giest. 1.** soaked; thoroughly wet. **2.** damp and heavy, as ill-baked bread. **3.** spiritless, dull, or stupid. [der. *sog* bog (now d.). Cf. d. Norw. *soggjast* get soaked] —**sog′gily,** *adv.* —**sog′giness,** *n.*

Sogne (*Norw.* sŏng′nə), *n.* a fiord in SW Norway. 115 mi. long.

soh (sō), *n.* sol[1].

Soho (sō′hō), *n.* a district in London, noted for its restaurants, nightclubs, etc.

soi-disant (*Fr.* swȧ dē zäɴ′), *adj. French.* **1.** calling oneself thus; self-styled: *a soi-disant marquess.* **2.** so-called or pretended: *a soi-disant science.*

soigné (*Fr.* swȧ nyė′), *adj. masc. French.* **1.** carefully done. **2.** well groomed. —**soignée,** *adj. fem.*

soil[1] (soil), *n.* **1.** that portion of the earth's surface in which plants grow; a well-developed system of inorganic and organic material and of living organisms. **2.** a particular kind of earth: *sandy soil.* **3.** the ground as producing vegetation or cultivated for its crops: *fertile soil.* **4.** a country, land, or region: *on foreign soil.* **5.** the ground or earth. [ME *soyle,* t. AF: m. *soyl,* g. L *solium* seat, confused with *solum* ground]

soil[2] (soil), *v.t.* **1.** to make dirty or foul, esp. on the surface: *to soil one's clothes.* **2.** to smirch, smudge, or stain. **3.** to sully or tarnish, as with disgrace; defile morally, as with sin. —*v.i.* **4.** to become soiled. —*n.* **5.** the act of soiling. **6.** the fact or state of being soiled. **7.** a spot, mark, or stain due to soiling. **8.** dirty or foul matter; filth; sewage. **9.** ordure; manure or compost. [ME *soilen,* t. OF: m. *suill(i)er, soill(i)er,* der. *souille* pigsty, ult. der. L *sus* pig]

soil[3] (soil), *v.t.* **1.** to feed (cattle, etc.) on freshly cut green fodder, for fattening. **2.** to feed (horses, cattle, etc.) on green food, for purging. [orig. uncert.]

soilage (soi′lĭj), *n.* grass or leafy plants raised as feed for livestock.

soil creep, slow, almost imperceptible, down-slope movement of soil under the influence of gravity.

soil mechanics, the science of the study of soils and their behaviour.

soil pipe, *Plumbing.* a pipe carrying liquid wastes from all fixtures, including water closets. Cf. **waste pipe.**

soilure (soi′lyə), *n. Archaic.* a stain.

soiree (swä′rā), *n.* an evening party or social gathering, often for a particular purpose: *a musical soiree.* Also, *French,* **soirée** (*Fr.* swȧ rė′). [t. F, der. *soir* evening, g. L *sērō* late, adv., der. *sērus* late]

Soissons (*Fr.* swȧ sôɴ′), *n.* a town in N France, on the river Aisne: battles, A.D. 486, 1918, 1944. 24,360 (1962).

soixante-neuf (swăs′ŏnt nûf′; *Fr.* swȧ säɴt nœf′), *n.*

Colloq. simultaneous fellation and cunnilinctus. [F: sixty-nine, from the position of two people engaged in this practice, resembling the figures 69. The French term is *six-à-neuf*]

sojourn (sŏj′ûn, sŭj′ûn, -ən), *v.i.* **1.** to dwell for a time in a place; make a temporary stay. —*n.* **2.** a temporary stay. [ME *sojurne*, t. OF: m. *sojorner*, der. *so-* (g. L *sub-* SUB-) + *jorn* day (g. L *diurnum* daily)] —**so′journer,** *n.*

soke (sōk), *n. Early Eng. Law.* **1.** the privilege of holding court, usually connected with the feudal rights of lordship. **2.** a district over which local jurisdiction was exercised. [late ME, t. ML: m. *soca*, t. OE: m. *sōcn* seeking, enquiry, jurisdiction; akin to SEEK]

Soke (sōk), *n.* a former administrative division in Huntingdonshire. 74,758 (1961). Also, **Soke of Peterborough.**

sokeman (sōk′mən), *n., pl.* **-men.** a feudal tenant or vassal, usually holding in socage.

Sokoto (sō′kə tō′), *n.* a sultanate and province in NW Nigeria: in the 19th century it was the centre of a Fulani empire. 4,394,771 pop. (1965); 36,338 sq. mi.

Sokotra (sə kō′trə), *n.* Socotra.

sol[1] (sōl), *n. Music.* the syllable used for the fifth note of a scale, and sometimes for the note G. Also, **so, soh.** See **solfa.** [ME, t. L. See GAMUT]

sol[2] (sōl), *n.* an old French coin and money of account, equal to the twentieth part of a livre. [t. F, g. L *solidus* (*nummus*) solid (coin)]

sol[3] (sōl; *Sp.* sól), *n., pl.* **soles** (*Sp.* só′lės). **1.** the monetary unit of Peru, equal to 100 centavos, and equivalent to about £0·0109 sterling. **2.** a note or coin of this value. **3.** Also, **libra.** a former gold coin of Peru. [t. Sp.: sun, g. L *sōl*]

sol[4] (sōl), *n. Chem.* a colloidal suspension of a solid in a liquid. [abstracted from (HYDRO)SOL]

Sol (sōl), *n.* **1.** the sun, personified by the Romans as a god. **2.** *Obs.* gold. [t. L]

Sol., **1.** Solicitor. **2.** Solomon.

sol., **1.** soluble. **2.** solution.

sola[1] (sō′lə), *adj.* fem. of **solus.**

sola[2] (sō′lə), *n.* **1.** an Indian pithy-stemmed plant, *Aeschynomene aspera.* **2.** its pith, used for making topees.

solace (sŏl′ĭs), *n., v.,* **-aced, -acing.** —*n.* **1.** comfort in sorrow or trouble; alleviation of distress or discomfort. **2.** something that gives comfort, consolation, or relief. —*v.t.* **3.** to comfort, console, or cheer (a person, oneself, the heart, etc.). **4.** to alleviate or relieve (sorrow, distress, etc.). [ME *solas*, t. OF, g. L *solācium*] —**sol′acement,** *n.* —**sol′acer,** *n.* —**Syn. 1.** consolation, relief, cheer. **4.** soothe.

solan (sō′lən), *n.* the gannet. Also, **solan goose.** [ME *soland*, f. Scand.; cf. Icel. *sūla* gannet, Dan. *and* duck]

solanaceous (sŏl′ə nā′shəs), *adj.* belonging to the *Solanaceae*, or nightshade family of plants, which includes, besides the many species of *Solanum*, the belladonna, henbane, thorn-apple, tobacco, capsicum pepper, tomato, petunia, etc. [f. s. NL *Sōlānāceae* (pl.) (der. L *sōlānum* nightshade) + -OUS]

solander (sō lăn′də), *n.* a box, esp. one for botanical specimens, made in the form of a book, the front cover being the lid. [named after its inventor, D. C. *Solander*, 1736–82, Swedish botanist]

solanum (sō lā′nəm), *n.* any plant of the genus *Solanum*, which comprises gamopetalous herbs, shrubs, and small trees, including the nightshades, aubergine, common potato, etc. [t. L: nightshade]

solar (sō′lə), *adj.* **1.** of or pertaining to the sun: *solar phenomena.* **2.** determined by the sun: *solar hour.* **3.** proceeding from the sun, as light or heat. **4.** operating by the light or heat of the sun, as a mechanism. **5.** indicating time by means of or with reference to the sun: *a solar chronometer.* **6.** *Astrol.* subject to the influence of the sun. —*n.* **7.** any room, esp. a large room or one on an upper storey, for family use in a large house or castle. [t. L: s. *sōlāris*]

solar apex, *Astron.* the point on the celestial sphere towards which the solar system is moving, relative to the stars.

solar battery, *Electronics.* a battery containing solar cells, usually mounted in panels. Also, **solar paddle.**

solar cell, a photovoltaic cell that converts sunlight directly into electrical energy.

solar constant, *Astron.* the average rate at which energy from the sun would be received by one sq. cm. of the earth's surface in the absence of the atmosphere, assuming that the incident radiation is normal to the surface and that the earth is at its mean distance from the sun; equal to approximately 2 calories per minute per sq. cm.

solar day. See **day** (def. 3c).

solar flare, *Astron.* a short-lived, high-temperature outburst, seen as a bright area in the sun's atmosphere.

solar furnace, a furnace using sunlight as the direct source of heat.

solarism (sō′lə rĭz′əm), *n.* the interpretation of myths by reference to the sun, esp. such interpretation carried to an extreme. —**so′larist,** *n.*

solarium (sō lĕə′rĭ əm), *n., pl.* **-laria** (-lĕə′rĭ ə). a room, gallery, or the like, exposed to the sun's rays, as at a seaside hotel or for convalescents in a hospital. [t. L]

solarize (sō′lə rīz′), *v.,* **-rized, -rizing.** —*v.t.* **1.** *Photog.* to produce partial reversal in, as from a negative to a positive image, by exposure to light during development. **2.** to affect by sunlight. —*v.i.* **3.** *Photog.* to become injured by overexposure. Also, **solarise.** —**so′lariza′tion,** *n.*

solar month. See **month** (def. 1).

solar parallax, *Astron.* the angle subtended by the mean equatorial radius of the earth at a distance of one astronomical unit.

solar plexus, **1.** *Anat.* a network of nerves situated at the upper part of the abdomen, behind the stomach and in front of the aorta. **2.** *Colloq.* a point on the stomach wall, just below the sternum, where a blow will affect this nerve centre.

solar system, the sun together with all the planets, satellites, asteroids, etc., revolving around it.

solar wind, *Astron.* the streams of ionized atoms (esp. hydrogen) constantly emanating from the sun.

solar year. See **year** (def. 5).

sold (sōld), *v.* pt. and pp. of **sell.**

soldan (sŏl′dən, sōl′dən), *n.* a Muslim ruler of the Middle Ages, esp. the sultan of Egypt.

solder (sŏl′də), *n.* **1.** any of various fusible alloys, some (**soft solders**) fusing readily, and others (**hard solders**) fusing only at red heat, applied in a melted state to metal surfaces, joints, etc., to unite them. **2.** anything that joins or unites. —*v.t.* **3.** to unite with solder or some other substance or device. **4.** to join closely and intimately. **5.** to mend; repair; patch up. —*v.i.* **6.** to unite things with solder. **7.** to become soldered or become united; grow together. [ME *soudur*, t. OF: m. *soldure*, der. *solder* to solder, g. L *solidāre* make firm] —**sol′derer,** *n.*

soldering-iron (sŏl′də rĭng ī′ən), *n.* a tool used for soldering.

soldier (sōl′jə), *n.* **1.** one who serves in an army for pay; one engaged in military service. **2.** one of the rank and file in such service, sometimes including non-commissioned officers. **3.** a man of military skill or experience. **4.** one who contends or serves in any cause. **5.** *Zool.* (in certain ants and termites) an individual with powerful jaws or other device for protecting the colony. **6.** *Bldg Trades, Colloq.* anything straight or upright, as a brick on end or a vertical batten. —*v.i.* **7.** to act or serve as a soldier. **8.** *Colloq.* to make a mere show of working; feign illness; malinger. [ME *souldeour*, t. OF, der. *soulde* pay, der. L *solidus.* See SOL[2]] —**sol′diership′,** *n.*

soldierlike (sōl′jə līk′), *adj.* **1.** having the character, appearance, etc., of a soldier. **2.** soldierly.

soldierly (sōl′jə lĭ), *adj.* of, like, or befitting a soldier.

soldier of fortune, a military adventurer, ready to serve anywhere for pay, etc.

soldier orchid, an orchid with greyish violet flowers, *Orchis militaris*, which occurs on chalk grassland in Europe.

soldiery (sōl′jə rĭ), *n., pl.* **-ries.** **1.** soldiers collectively. **2.** a body of soldiers. **3.** military training.

soldo (sŏl′dō; *It.* sŏl′dô), *n., pl.* **-di** (-dē). a former Italian copper coin, the twentieth part of a lira (or 5 centesimi). [t. It., g. L *solidus.* See SOL[2]]

sole[1] (sōl), *adj.* **1.** being the only one or ones; only. **2.** being the only one of the kind; unique. **3.** belonging or pertaining to one individual or group to the exclusion of all others; exclusive: *the sole right to a thing.* **4.** functioning automatically or with independent power. **5.** *Chiefly Law.* unmarried. **6.** *Archaic.* alone. [t. L: m. s. *sōlus* alone; r. ME *soul(e)*, t. OF] —**Syn. 1.** See **only.**

sole[2] (sōl), *n., v.,* **soled, soling.** —*n.* **1.** the bottom or under surface of the foot. **2.** the corresponding under part of a shoe, boot, or the like, or this part exclusive of the heel. **3.** a separate, shaped piece of material fitted into a shoe at the bottom. **4.** the bottom, under surface, or lower part of anything. **5.** *Golf.* the under surface or part of a golf club which rests on the ground. —*v.t.* **6.** to furnish with a sole, as a shoe. **7.** *Golf.* to place the sole of (a club) on the ground, to make a stroke. [ME and OE, t. L: s. *solea* sandal, shoe] —**soled,** *adj.*

sole[3] (sōl), *n., pl.* **soles,** (*esp. collectively*) **sole.** **1.** any flatfish of the families *Soleidae* and *Cynoglossidae*, with a hooklike snout. **2.** any of several other flatfishes used as food, especially when filleted. [ME, t. F, g. L *solea.* See SOLE[2]]

solecism (sŏl′ĭ sĭz′əm), *n.* **1.** a substandard intrusion into standard speech, as 'they was'. **2.** a breach of good manners or etiquette. **3.** any error, impropriety, or inconsistency. [t. L: m. s. *soloecismus*, t. Gk: m. *soloikismós* incorrectness of speech] —**sol′ecis′tic,** *adj.*

solely (sōl′lĭ), *adv.* **1.** as the only one or ones: *solely responsible.* **2.** exclusively or only: *plants found solely in the tropics.* **3.** wholly; merely.

solemn (sŏl′əm), *adj.* **1.** grave, sober, or mirthless, as a person, the face, speech, tone, mood, etc. **2.** gravely or sombrely impressive; such as to cause serious thoughts or a grave mood: *solemn music.* **3.** serious or earnest: *solemn assurances.* **4.** characterized by dignified or serious formality, as proceedings; of a formal or ceremonious character. **5.** made in due legal or other express form, as a declaration, agreement, etc. **6.** marked or observed with religious rites; having a religious character. **7.** made according to religious forms. [ME *solempne*, t. L: m. *sōlempnis*] —**sol′emnly,** *adv.* —**sol′emness,** *n.* —**Syn. 1.** See **grave**[2].

solemnity (sə lĕm′nĭ tĭ), *n., pl.* **-ties. 1.** the state or character of being solemn; earnestness; gravity; impressiveness. **2.** (*often pl.*) a solemn observance, ceremonial proceeding, or special formality. **3.** observance of rites or ceremonies, esp. a formal, solemn, ecclesiastical observance, as of a feast day. [ME *solempnete*, t. L: m. s. *sōlempnitas*]

solemnize (sŏl′əm nīz′), *v.t.,* **-nized, -nizing. 1.** to observe or commemorate with rites or ceremonies. **2.** to hold or perform (ceremonies, etc.) in due manner. **3.** to perform the ceremony of (marriage). **4.** to go through with ceremony or formality. **5.** to render solemn, serious or grave. Also, **solemnise.** —**sol′emniza′tion,** *n.* —**sol′emniz′er,** *n.*

solemn vow, a vow made with great sincerity or formality.

solenette (sō′lĭ nĕt′), *n.* the smallest of the British soles, *Solea lutea.*

solenodon (sə lĕn′ə dən), *n.* a rare insectivore, *Atopogale cubana*, about the size of a rat, now confined to Cuba and Haiti. [t. NL, f. Gk: *sōlḗn* pipe + *odṓn* (Ionic) tooth]

solenoid (sō′lĭ noid′), *n.* an electrical conductor wound as a helix with a small pitch, or as two or more coaxial helices, current through which establishes a magnetic field. [f. Gk *sōlḗn* channel, pipe, shellfish + -OID] —**so′lenoi′dal,** *adj.* —**so′lenoi′dally,** *adv.*

A, Solenoid with both ends returned to the middle; B, Diagram of A

Solent (sō′lənt), *n.* **The,** a channel between the Isle of Wight and the mainland of S England. 2–5 mi. wide.

Soleure (*Fr.* sô lœr′), *n.* French name of **Solothurn.**

solfa (sŏl′fä′), *n., v.,* **-faed, -faing.** —*n.* **1.** *Music.* the set of syllables, *do* or *ut, re, mi, fa, sol, la,* and *si* or *te* (all but *do* and *si* or *te* are attributed to Guido d'Arezzo), sung to the respective notes of the scale. **2.** the system of singing notes to these syllables. —*v.i.* **3.** to use the solfa syllables in singing, or to sing these syllables. —*v.t.* **4.** to sing to the solfa syllables, as a tune. [f. SOL + FA. See GAMUT] —**sol′fa′ist,** *n.*

solfatara (sŏl′fə tä′rə), *n.* a volcanic vent or area which gives off only sulphurous gases, steam, and the like. [t. It. (Neapolitan), der. *solfo*, g. L *sulfur* SULPHUR] —**sol′fata′ric,** *adj.*

solfeggio (sŏl fĕj′ĭ ō′), *n., pl.* **-feggi** (fĕj′ē), **-feggios.** *Music.* **1.** an exercise for the voice in which the solfa syllables are used. **2.** the use of the solfa syllables to name or represent the notes of a melody or voice part, or the notes of the scale, or of a particular series, as the scale of C; solmization. [t. It., der. *sol, fa.* See SOLFA]

Solferino (sŏl′fə rē′nō; *It.* sôl fĕ rē′nô), *n.* **1.** a village in N Italy, in Lombardy: battle, 1859. 2929 (1951). **2.** (*l.c.*) a dye obtained from rosaniline. **3.** (*l.c.*) vivid purplish pink.

soli-[1], a word element meaning 'alone', 'solitary', as in *solifidian.* [t. L, comb. form of *solus*]

soli-[2], a word element meaning 'sun'. [t. L, comb. form of *sōl*]

solicit (sə lĭs′ĭt), *v.t.* **1.** to seek for by entreaty, earnest or respectful request, formal application, etc.: *to solicit contributions.* **2.** to entreat or petition (a person, etc.) for something or to do something; urge; importune. **3.** to seek to influence or incite to action, esp. unlawful or wrong action. **4.** to accost (another) with immoral intention, as a prostitute. —*v.i.* **5.** to make petition or request, as for something desired. **6.** to accost another with immoral intention. **7.** to endeavour to obtain orders or trade, as for a business house. [ME, t. L: s. *sōlicitāre* disturb, incite]

solicitation (sə lĭs′ĭ tā′shən), *n.* **1.** the act of soliciting. **2.** entreaty, urging, or importunity; a petition or request. **3.** enticement or allurement. **4.** *Law.* **a.** the crime of asking another to commit or to aid in a crime. **b.** loitering and importuning passers-by for the purpose of prostitution.

solicitor (sə lĭs′ĭ tə), *n.* **1.** one who solicits. **2.** a member of that branch of the legal profession whose services consist of advising clients, representing them before the lower courts, and preparing cases for barristers to try in the higher courts. **3.** *U.S.* an officer having charge of the legal business of a city, town, etc. **4.** See **Official Solicitor. 5.** *U.S.* one whose business is to solicit business, trade, etc.

solicitor general, *pl.* **solicitors general. 1.** the second law officer of the crown, ranking after the attorney general. **2.** the chief law officer in some states of the U.S.

solicitous (sə lĭs′ĭ təs), *adj.* **1.** anxious or concerned over something (fol. by *about, for,* etc., or a clause): *solicitous about a person's health.* **2.** anxiously desirous: *solicitous of the esteem of others.* **3.** eager (fol. by infinitive): *to be solicitous to please.* **4.** careful or particular. [t. L: m. *sōlicitus*] —**solic′itously,** *adv.* —**solic′itousness,** *n.*

solicitude (sə lĭs′ĭ tyōōd′), *n.* **1.** the state of being solicitous; anxiety or concern; anxious desire or care. **2.** (*pl.*) causes of anxiety or care. **3.** excessive anxiety or assistance. [t. L: m. *sōlicitūdo*]

solid (sŏl′ĭd), *adj.* **1.** having three dimensions (length, breadth, and thickness), as a geometrical body or figure. **2.** of or pertaining to bodies or figures of three dimensions: *solid geometry.* **3.** having the interior completely filled up, free from cavities, or not hollow: *a solid ball of matter.* **4.** without openings or breaks: *a solid wall.* **5.** firm, hard, or compact in substance: *solid ground.* **6.** having relative firmness, coherence of particles, or persistence of form, as matter that is not liquid or gaseous: *solid particles floating in a liquid.* **7.** pertaining to such matter: *ice is water in a solid state.* **8.** dense, thick, or heavy in nature or appearance: *solid masses of cloud.* **9.** substantial, or not flimsy, slight, or light, as buildings, furniture, fabrics, food, etc. **10.** of a substantial character; not superficial, trifling, or frivolous: *solid learning.* **11.** undivided or continuous: *a solid row of buildings.* **12.** whole or entire: *one solid hour.* **13.** forming the whole; being the only substance or material: *solid gold.* **14.** uniform in tone or shade, as a colour. **15.** real or genuine: *solid comfort.* **16.** sound or good, as reasons, arguments, etc. **17.** sober-minded or sensible. **18.** financially sound or strong. **19.** cubic: *a solid foot contains 1728 solid inches.* **20.** having the lines not separated by leads, or having few open spaces, as type or printing. **21.** thorough, vigorous, great, big, etc. (with emphatic force, often after *good*): *a good solid blow.* **22.** firmly united or consolidated: *a solid combination.* **23.** united in opinion, policy, etc., or unanimous. **24.** *U.S. Colloq.* on a friendly, favourable, or advantageous footing. **25.** *U.S. Slang.* (of dance music, rhythm, etc.) excellent. —*n.* **26.** a body or magnitude having three dimensions (length, breadth, and thickness). **27.** a solid substance or body; a substance exhibiting rigidity. **28.** (*pl.*) food that is not in liquid form. [ME, t. L: s. *solidus*] —**sol′idly,** *adv.* —**sol′idness,** *n.* —**Syn. 5.** See **firm**[1]. —**Ant. 6.** fluid.

solidago (sŏl′ĭ dā′gō), *n., pl.* **-gos.** any plant of the composite genus *Solidago*, mostly native to North America; a goldenrod. [t. NL, special use of ML *solidago* comfrey, der. L *solidus* SOLID]

solid angle, *Geom.* an angle formed by three or more planes intersecting in a common point or at the vertex of a cone.

solidarity (sŏl′ĭ dăr′ĭ tĭ), *n., pl.* **-ties. 1.** solidary character or relation. **2.** union or fellowship arising from common responsibilities and interests, as between members of a group or between classes, peoples, etc. **3.** community of interests, feelings, purposes, etc. [t. F: m. *solidarité*, der. *solidaire*, ult. der. L *solidus* solid]

solidary (sŏl′ĭ də rĭ, -drĭ), *adj.* characterized by or involving community of responsibilities and interests.

solid geology, the geological features of a district without the drift.

solid geometry, the geometry of solid figures; geometry of three dimensions.

solidify (sə lĭd′ĭ fī′), *v.,* **-fied, -fying.** —*v.t.* **1.** to make solid; make into a hard or compact mass; change from a liquid or gaseous to a solid form. **2.** to unite firmly or consolidate. **3.** to form into crystals. —*v.i.* **4.** to become solid. **5.** to form into crystals. [see SOLID, -(I)FY] —**solid′ifica′tion,** *n.*

solidity (sə lĭd′ĭ tĭ), *n., pl.* **-ties. 1.** the state, property, or quality of being solid. **2.** substantialness. **3.** strength of mind, character, finances, etc. **4.** *Geom.* the amount of space occupied by a solid body; volume.

solid propellant, *Aeron.* a rocket propellant in solid form, usually a mixture of fuel and oxidant.

solid solution, 1. a solid homogeneous mixture of two or more substances, as some alloys, glasses, etc. **2.** *Chem.* a mixed crystal of two or more isomorphous substances.

solid-state (sŏl′ĭd stāt′), *adj. Physics.* of or pertaining to electronic devices which are composed entirely of components in the solid state (as semiconductors, transistors, etc.).

solid-state physics, the branch of physics that deals with the structure and properties of solids, esp. the structure and properties of semiconductors.

solidus (sŏl′ĭ dəs), *n., pl.* **-di** (-dī′). **1.** a Roman gold coin introduced by Constantine, which continued under the Byzantine Empire and received in western Europe the name bezant. Cf. **bezant** (def. 1). **2.** (in medieval Europe) a money of account valued at 12 denarii. **3.** the shilling mark, a sloping line (/) representing the old long form of the letter s (abbreviation of solidus), as used to separate shillings from pence (as in 2/6 for 2 shillings and 6 pence), and generally as a dividing line, as in dates, fractions, etc. [t. LL. See SOL[2]]

solifidian (sŏl′ĭ fĭd′ĭ ən), *n. Theol.* one who maintains that faith alone, without works, is all that is necessary for justification. [f. SOLI-[1] + L *fid(es)* faith + -IAN]

solifluxion (sŏl′ĭ flŭk′shən), *n.* **1.** slow, downward, movement of rock debris or soil saturated with meltwater over permanently frozen subsoil in tundra regions. **2.** soil creep. **3.** down-slope movement of soil, faster than soil creep. Also, **solifluction.**

Solihull (sō′lĭ hŭl′), *n.* a town in England, in Warwickshire. 95,977 (1961).

soliloquize (sə lĭl′ə kwīz′), *v.,* **-quized, -quizing.** *—v.i.* **1.** to utter a soliloquy; talk to oneself. *—v.t.* **2.** to utter in a soliloquy; say to oneself. Also, **soliloquise.** —**soliloquist** (sə lĭl′ə kwĭst), **solil′oquiz′er,** *n.* —**solil′oquiz′ingly,** *adv.*

soliloquy (sə lĭl′ə kwĭ), *n., pl.* **-quies.** the act of talking when alone or as if alone; an utterance or discourse by one who is talking to himself or is regardless of any hearers present. [t. LL: m. s. *sōliloquium*]

Soliman (sŏl′ĭ mən), *n.* Suleiman.

Solimões (*Port.* sŏ lē məwNzh′), *n.* Brazilian name of a part of the Amazon, from its junction with the Río Negro to the Peruvian border.

Solingen (*Ger.* zō′lĭng ən), *n.* an industrial city in NW West Germany, in central North Rhine-Westphalia. 175,100 (est. 1966).

solipsism (sŏl′ĭp sĭz′əm), *n. Metaphys.* the theory that the self is the only object of verifiable knowledge, or that nothing but the self exists. [f. SOL(I)-[1] + L *ips(e)* self + -ISM] —**sol′ipsist,** *n.*

solitaire (sŏl′ĭ tĕə′, sŏl′ĭ tĕə′), *n.* **1.** a game played by one person alone, as a game played with marbles or pegs on a board having hollows or holes. **2.** *U.S.* patience (def. 4). **3.** a precious stone, esp. a diamond, set by itself, as in a ring. [t. F, t. L: m. *sōlitārius* alone]

solitary (sŏl′ĭ tə rĭ, -trĭ), *adj., n., pl.* **-ries.** *—adj.* **1.** quite alone; without companions; unattended. **2.** living alone; avoiding the society of others. **3.** alone by itself. **4.** characterized by the absence of companions: *solitary confinement.* **5.** done without assistance or accompaniment; done in solitude. **6.** being the only one or ones: *a solitary exception.* **7.** characterized by solitude, as a place; unfrequented, secluded, or lonely. **8.** *Zool.* not social, as certain wasps. *—n.* **9.** one who lives alone or in solitude, or avoids the society of others. **10.** one who lives in solitude from religious motives. **11.** *Colloq.* solitary confinement. [ME, t. L: m. s. *sōlitārius*] —**sol′itarily,** *adv.* —**sol′itariness,** *n.*

solitude (sŏl′ĭ tyōōd′), *n.* **1.** the state of being or living alone; seclusion. **2.** remoteness from habitations, as of a place; absence of human life or activity. **3.** a lonely, unfrequented place. [ME, t. L: m. *sōlitūdo*]

—**Syn. 1.** SOLITUDE, ISOLATION refer to a state of being or living alone. SOLITUDE emphasizes the quality of being or feeling lonely and deserted: *to live in solitude.* ISOLATION may mean merely a detachment and separation from others: *in isolation because of having an infectious disease.*

solleret (sŏl′ə rĕt′), *n.* flexible armour for the foot, made of overlapping plates. See illus. under **armour.** [t. OF: m. *soleret*, dim. of *soler* shoe, ult. der. LL *subtel* arch of foot]

solmization (sŏl′mĭ zā′shən), *n. Music.* the act, process, or system of using certain syllables, esp. the solfa syllables, to represent the notes of the scale. Also, **solmisation.** [t. F: m. *solmisation*, der. *solmiser*, der. *sol* SOL[1] + *mi* MI]

Solna (*Sw.* sŏl′nȧ), *n.* a town in Sweden N of Stockholm. 54,715 (1964).

solo (sō′lō), *n., pl.,* **-los, -li** (-lē). *adj., adv. —n.* **1.** a musical composition performed by or intended for one singer or player, with or without accompaniment. **2.** any performance, as a dance, by one person. **3.** a flight in an aeroplane during which the aviator is unaccompanied by an instructor or other person. **4.** *Cards.* any of certain games in which one person plays alone against others. **5.** a motorcycle without a sidecar. *—adj.* **6.** *Music.* performing alone, as an instrument or its player. **7.** performed alone; not combined with other parts of equal importance; not concerted. **8.** alone; without a companion or partner: *a solo flight in an aeroplane. —adv.* **9.** alone: *he made his first flight solo.* [t. It., g. L *sōlus* alone]

Solo (sō′lō), *n.* former name of **Surakarta.**

soloist (sō′lō ĭst), *n.* one who performs a solo or solos.

Solomon (sŏl′ə mən), *n.* **1.** a 10th century B.C. king of Israel, famous for his wisdom. He was the son of David. **2.** an extraordinarily wise man; a sage. [t. L, t. Gk, t. Heb.: m. *Sh'lōmōh*]

Solomon Islands, an archipelago in the W Pacific, E of New Guinea: the larger, SE part forms a British protectorate. 139,730 pop. (1965); 11,458 sq. mi.; the NW islands (formerly a German colony), principally Bougainville and Buka, are part of the Australian trusteeship Territory of New Guinea. 64,080 pop. (est. 1964); ab. 4100 sq. mi. See map under **Coral Sea.**

Solomon's-seal (sŏl′ə mənz sēl′), *n.* any of various plants of the liliaceous genus *Polygonatum*, with a thick rootstock bearing seal-like scars.

Solomon's seal, Star of David.

Solon (sō′lŏn), *n.* **1.** *c.* 638–*c.* 558 B.C., Athenian statesman: noted for his political reforms and his wisdom. **2.** a wise lawgiver.

so long, *Colloq.* goodbye.

Solothurn (*Ger.* zō′lō tōōrn), *n.* **1.** a canton in NW Switzerland. 200,816 pop. (1960); 306 sq. mi. **2.** the capital of this canton 17,500 pop. (est. 1966). French, **Soleure.**

Soloviev (*Russ.* sə lȧv yôf′), *n.* **Vladimir Sergeevich** (*Russ.* vlȧ dē′mĭr sĭr gyė′yĭ vĭch), 1853–1900, Russian philosopher, critic, and poet.

solstice (sŏl′stĭs), *n.* **1.** *Astron.* either of the two times in the year when the sun is at its greatest distance from the celestial equator and apparently does not move either north or south, about June 21st, when it enters the sign of Cancer, and about December 22nd, when it enters the sign of Capricorn (called respectively, in the Northern Hemisphere, **summer solstice** and **winter solstice**). **2.** either of the two points in the ecliptic farthest from the equator. **3.** a farthest or culminating point; a turning point. [ME, t. OF, t. L: m. *sōlstitium*]

solstitial (sŏl stĭsh′əl), *adj.* **1.** of or pertaining to a solstice or the solstices: *a solstitial point.* **2.** occurring at or about the time of a solstice. **3.** characteristic of the summer solstice. [t. L: s. *sōlstitiālis*]

Solti (shŏl′tĭ; *Hung.* shŏl′tē), *n.* **Georg** (*Hung.* gė′ôrk), born 1912, German conductor born in Hungary.

solubility (sŏl′yōō bĭl′ĭ tĭ), *n., pl.* **-ties.** the quality or property of being capable of being dissolved; relative capability of being dissolved. The extent to which a solute will dissolve in a solvent, usually expressed in grams of solute per 100 grams of solvent, at a specified temperature.

soluble (sŏl′yōō bl), *adj.* **1.** capable of being dissolved or liquefied. **2.** capable of being solved or explained. [ME, t. L: m. s. *solūbilis*] —**sol′ubleness,** *n.* —**sol′ubly,** *adv.*

soluble glass, waterglass (def. 5).

solus (sō′ləs), *adj. masc.* alone; by oneself: used esp. in stage directions. [t. L] —**sola** (sō′lə), *adj. fem.*

solute (sŏ lyōōt′), *n.* **1.** the substance dissolved in a given solution. *—adj.* **2.** dissolved; in solution. **3.** *Bot.* not adhering; free. [t. L: m. s. *solūtus*, pp.]

solution (sə lōō′shən), *n.* **1.** the act of solving a problem, etc., or state of being solved. **2.** a particular instance or method of solving; an explanation or answer. **3.** *Maths.* **a.** the act of determining the answer to a problem. **b.** the answer. **4.** the act by which a gas, liquid, or solid is dispersed homogeneously in a gas, liquid, or solid without chemical change. **5.** the fact of being dissolved; dissolved state: *salt in solution.* **6.** a homogeneous molecular mixture of two or more substances. **7.** *Med.* **a.** the termination of a disease. **b. solution of continuity,** a breach or break in anything, esp. one in parts of the body normally continuous, as from fracture or laceration. [ME *solucion*, t. L: m. s. *solūtio*]

solvable (sŏl′və bl), *adj.* **1.** capable of being solved, as a problem. **2.** capable of being dissolved. —**solv′abil′ity, solv′ableness,** *n.*

solvate (sŏl′vāt), *n.*, *v.*, **-vated, -vating.** *Chem.* —*n.* **1.** a substance formed by solvation. —*v.t.* **2.** to convert into a solvate.

solvation (sŏl vā′shən), *n. Chem.* the process of association or combination between solvent molecules and molecules or ions of the solute being dissolved.

Solvay process (sŏl′vā), a process for manufacturing soda from sodium chloride (common salt). It consists essentially of saturating a concentrated solution of sodium chloride with ammonia, and passing carbon dioxide through it; the product of this reaction (sodium bicarbonate) is then calcined, and yields soda. [named after Ernest *Solvay*, 1838–1922, Belgian chemist]

solve (sŏlv), *v.t.*, **solved, solving. 1.** to clear up or explain; find the answer to. **2.** to work out the answer or solution to (a mathematical problem). [ME, t. L: m. s. *solvere* loosen, dissolve] —**solv′er,** *n.*

solvency (sŏl′vən sĭ), *n.*, *pl.* **-cies.** solvent condition; ability to pay all just debts.

solvent (sŏl′vənt), *adj.* **1.** able to pay all just debts. **2.** having the power of dissolving; causing solution. —*n.* **3.** the component of a solution which dissolves the other component: *water is a solvent for sugar.* **4.** something that solves or explains. [t. L: s. *solvens*, ppr., dissolving]

Solway Firth (sŏl′wā′), an arm of the Irish Sea between SW Scotland and NW England. 38 mi. long.

Solyman (sŏl′ĭ mən), *n.* Suleiman.

Som., Somerset.

soma (sō′mə), *n.*, *pl.* **-mata** (-mə tə). *Biol.* the body of an organism as contrasted with its germ cells. [NL, t. Gk: body]

Somali (sō mä′lĭ), *n.*, *pl.* **-li, -lis. 1.** a member of a Hamitic race dwelling in Somaliland and adjacent regions. **2.** a modern Cushitic language.

Somaliland (sō mä′lĭ lănd′), *n.* a coastal region in E Africa, including French Somaliland, the Somali Republic, and part of Ethiopia.

Somali Republic, an independent republic on the E coast of Africa, formed from former British Somaliland and the former Italian trust territory of Somalia. 1,950,000 pop. (1959); 246,155 sq. mi. *Cap.:* Mogadiscio. Also, **Somalia** (sō mä′lĭ ə).

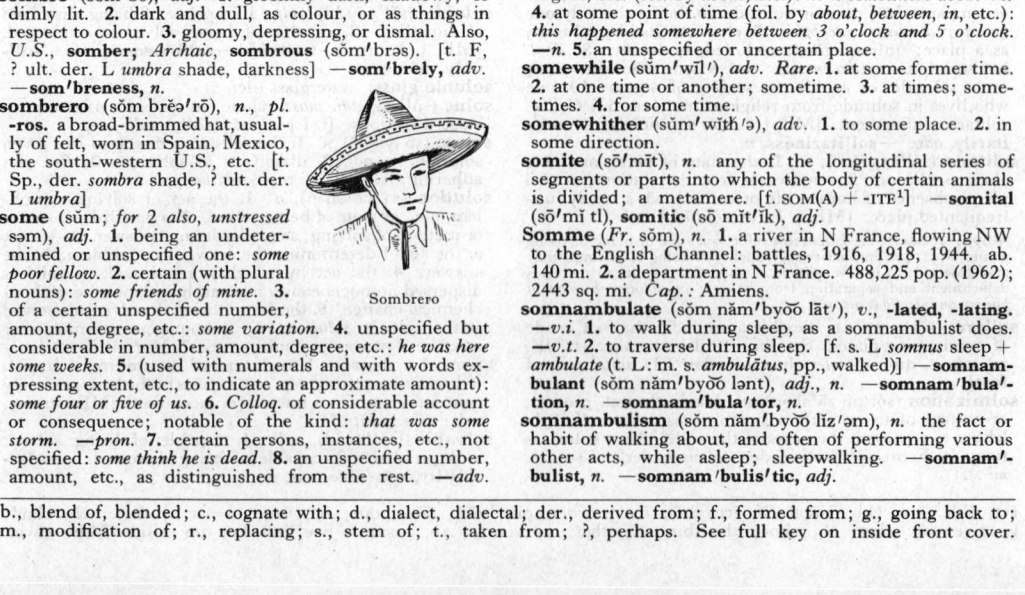

Somali Republic

somatic (sō măt′ĭk), *adj.* **1.** *Anat.*, *Zool.* pertaining to the cavity of the body of an animal, or, more especially, to its walls. **2.** *Biol.* pertaining to the soma. **3.** of the body; bodily; physical. [t. Gk: m. s. *sōmatikós*]

somatic cell, *Biol.* one of the cells which take part in the formation of the body, becoming differentiated into the various tissues, organs, etc.

somatology (sō′mə tŏl′ə jĭ), *n.* that branch of anthropology which deals with man's physical characteristics. [f. *somato-* (comb. form repr. Gk *sôma* body) + -LOGY] —**somatologic** (sō′mə tə lŏj′ĭk), **so′matolog′ical,** *adj.* —**so′matol′ogist,** *n.*

somatopleure (sō′mə tə plŏŏə′, -plû′), *n. Embryol.* the outer of the two layers into which the mesoderm of vertebrates splits, and which forms the body wall.

sombre (sŏm′bə), *adj.* **1.** gloomily dark, shadowy, or dimly lit. **2.** dark and dull, as colour, or as things in respect to colour. **3.** gloomy, depressing, or dismal. Also, *U.S.*, **somber;** *Archaic*, **sombrous** (sŏm′brəs). [t. F, ? ult. der. L *umbra* shade, darkness] —**som′brely,** *adv.* —**som′breness,** *n.*

sombrero (sŏm brēə′rō), *n.*, *pl.* **-ros.** a broad-brimmed hat, usually of felt, worn in Spain, Mexico, the south-western U.S., etc. [t. Sp., der. *sombra* shade, ? ult. der. L *umbra*]

Sombrero

some (sŭm; *for 2 also, unstressed* səm), *adj.* **1.** being an undetermined or unspecified one: *some poor fellow.* **2.** certain (with plural nouns): *some friends of mine.* **3.** of a certain unspecified number, amount, degree, etc.: *some variation.* **4.** unspecified but considerable in number, amount, degree, etc.: *he was here some weeks.* **5.** (used with numerals and with words expressing extent, etc., to indicate an approximate amount): *some four or five of us.* **6.** *Colloq.* of considerable account or consequence; notable of the kind: *that was some storm.* —*pron.* **7.** certain persons, instances, etc., not specified: *some think he is dead.* **8.** an unspecified number, amount, etc., as distinguished from the rest. —*adv.* **9.** *Slang.* to some degree or extent; somewhat. **10.** *U.S. Colloq.* to a great degree or extent; considerably: *that's going some!* [ME; OE *sum*, c. MLG and MHG *sum*, Icel. *sumr*, Goth. *sums*]

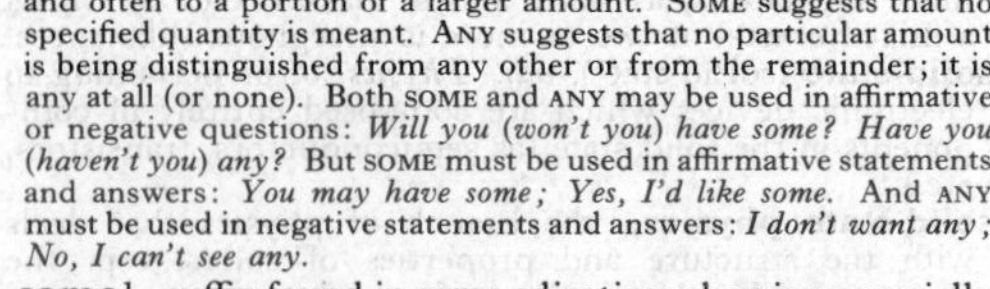
—**Syn. 8.** SOME, ANY refer to an appreciable amount or number, and often to a portion of a larger amount. SOME suggests that no specified quantity is meant. ANY suggests that no particular amount is being distinguished from any other or from the remainder; it is any at all (or none). Both SOME and ANY may be used in affirmative or negative questions: *Will you (won't you) have some? Have you (haven't you) any?* But SOME must be used in affirmative statements and answers: *You may have some; Yes, I'd like some.* And ANY must be used in negative statements and answers: *I don't want any; No, I can't see any.*

-some¹, suffix found in some adjectives showing especially a tendency, as in *quarrelsome, burdensome.* [ME; OE *-sum*, akin to G *-sam*]

-some², collective suffix used with numerals, as in *twosome, threesome, foursome.* [special use of SOME]

-some³, a word element meaning 'body', as in *chromosome.* [see SOMA]

somebody (sŭm′bə dĭ), *pron.*, *n.*, *pl.* **-bodies.** —*pron.* **1.** some person. —*n.* **2.** a person of some note or importance.

some day, at an indefinite future time.

somedeal (sŭm′dēl′), *adv. Archaic or Dial.* somewhat.

somehow (sŭm′hou′), *adv.* **1.** in some way not specified, apparent, or known. **2. somehow or other,** in a way not as yet determined.

someone (sŭm′wŭn′, -wən), *pron.*, *n.* somebody.

somersault (sŭm′ə sôlt′), *n.* **1.** an acrobatic movement of the body in which it describes a complete revolution, heels over head. **2.** a complete overturn or reversal, as of opinion. —*v.i.* **3.** to perform a somersault. [t. OF: m. *sombresaut*, t. Pr.: m. *sobresaut*, f. *sobre* (g. L *suprā*) above + *saut* (g. L *saltus*) leap]

Somerset (sŭm′ə sĭt), *n.* a county in SW England. 598,556 pop. (1961); 1616 sq. mi. *Co. town:* Taunton. Also, **Somersetshire** (sŭm′ə sĭt shĭə′, -shə).

Somerset House, a government building in the Strand, London, in which are housed the offices of the Registrar-General of births, marriages, and deaths for England and Wales, the registrars of wills and probates, the commissioners of inland revenue, etc.

something (sŭm′thĭng′), *pron.* **1.** some thing; a certain undetermined or unspecified thing. —*n.* **2.** a thing or person of some value or consequence. —*adv.* **3.** in some degree; to some extent; somewhat.

sometime (sŭm′tīm′), *adv.* **1.** at some indefinite or indeterminate point of time: *he will arrive sometime next week.* **2.** at an indefinite future time: *come over sometime.* **3.** *Rare.* sometimes; on some occasions. **4.** at one time; formerly. **5.** *Obs.* on a certain occasion in the past. —*adj.* **6.** having been formerly; former: *sometime professor of history at Oxford.*

sometimes (sŭm′tīmz′), *adv.* **1.** on some occasions; at times; now and then. **2.** *Obs.* once; formerly.

someway (sŭm′wā′), *adv.* in some way; somehow.

somewhat (sŭm′wŏt′), *adv.* **1.** in some measure or degree; to some extent. —*n.* **2.** some part, portion, amount, etc.

somewhere (sŭm′wēə′), *adv.* **1.** in or at some place not specified, determined, or known. **2.** to some place not specified or known. **3.** at or to some point in amount, degree, etc. (fol. by *about*, etc.): *he is somewhere about 60.* **4.** at some point of time (fol. by *about, between, in*, etc.): *this happened somewhere between 3 o'clock and 5 o'clock.* —*n.* **5.** an unspecified or uncertain place.

somewhile (sŭm′wīl′), *adv. Rare.* **1.** at some former time. **2.** at one time or another; sometime. **3.** at times; sometimes. **4.** for some time.

somewhither (sŭm′wĭth′ə), *adv.* **1.** to some place. **2.** in some direction.

somite (sō′mīt), *n.* any of the longitudinal series of segments or parts into which the body of certain animals is divided; a metamere. [f. SOM(A) + -ITE¹] —**somital** (sō′mĭ tl), **somitic** (sō mĭt′ĭk), *adj.*

Somme (*Fr.* sŏm), *n.* **1.** a river in N France, flowing NW to the English Channel: battles, 1916, 1918, 1944. ab. 140 mi. **2.** a department in N France. 488,225 pop. (1962); 2443 sq. mi. *Cap.:* Amiens.

somnambulate (sŏm năm′byŏŏ lāt′), *v.*, **-lated, -lating.** —*v.i.* **1.** to walk during sleep, as a somnambulist does. —*v.t.* **2.** to traverse during sleep. [f. s. L *somnus* sleep + *ambulate* (t. L: m. s. *ambulātus*, pp., walked)] —**somnambulant** (sŏm năm′byŏŏ lənt), *adj.*, *n.* —**somnam′bula′tion,** *n.* —**somnam′bula′tor,** *n.*

somnambulism (sŏm năm′byŏŏ lĭz′əm), *n.* the fact or habit of walking about, and often of performing various other acts, while asleep; sleepwalking. —**somnam′bulist,** *n.* —**somnam′bulis′tic,** *adj.*

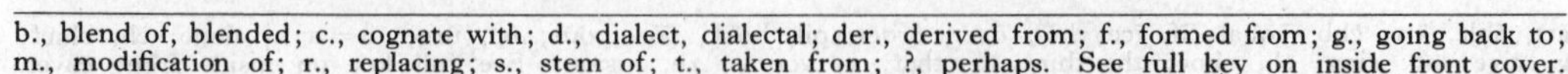

somniferous (sŏm nĭf′ə rəs), *adj.* inducing sleep, as drugs, etc. [f. L *somnifer* sleep-bearing + -OUS]

somnific (sŏm nĭf′ĭk), *adj.* causing sleep; soporific; somniferous. [t. L: s. *somnificus*]

somniloquy (sŏm nĭl′ə kwĭ), *n.* the act or habit of talking while asleep. —**somnil′oquist,** *n.*

somnolent (sŏm′nə lənt), *adj.* **1.** sleepy; drowsy. **2.** tending to cause sleep. [late ME, t. L: s. *somnolentus*] —**som′nolence, som′nolency,** *n.* —**som′nolently,** *adv.*

son (sŭn), *n.* **1.** a male child or person in relation to his parents. **2.** one adopted as a son; one in the legal position of a son. **3.** any male descendant. **4.** a son-in-law. **5.** one related as if by ties of sonship. **6.** a male person looked upon as the product or result of particular agencies, forces, influences, etc.: *sons of liberty.* **7.** a familiar term of address to a man or boy from an older person, an ecclesiastic, etc. **8. the Son,** the second person of the Trinity; Jesus Christ. [ME *sone,* OE *sunu,* c. D *zoon,* G *Sohn,* Icel. *sunr, sonr,* Goth. *sunus*]

sonance (sō′nəns), *n.* **1.** the condition or quality of being sonant. **2.** *Obs.* a sound; a tune.

sonant (sō′nənt), *adj.* **1.** sounding; having sound. **2.** *Phonet.* voiced. —*n.* **3.** *Phonet.* **a.** a speech sound which by itself makes a syllable or subordinates to itself the other sounds in the syllable; a syllabic sound (opposed to *consonant*). **b.** a voiced sound. **c.** (in Indo-European) a sonorant. [t. L: s. *sonans,* ppr., sounding] —**sonantal** (sō năn′tl), *adj.*

sonar (sō′nä), *n.* **1.** any device or method of echo ranging or echolocation involving underwater sonics. **2.** an echo sounder. [*so*(*und*) *n*(*avigation*) *a*(*nd*) *r*(*anging*)]

sonata (sə nä′tə), *n.* *Music.* an extended instrumental composition usually in several (commonly three or four) movements in contrasted moods and keys, each movement being developed with a balanced form in mind. [t. It., fem. pp. of *sonare* sound; orig. a sounded (i.e. instrumental) composition as opposed to one sung]

sonata form, *Music.* the formal exposition and development of contrasting themes in the first movement and sometimes later movements of a sonata or symphony.

sonatina (sŏn′ə tē′nə; *It.* sô nä tē′nä), *n., pl.* **-nas, -ne** (*It.* -nĕ). *Music.* a short or simplified sonata. [t. It., dim. of *sonata* SONATA]

sonde (sŏnd), *n.* *Aerospace.* a rocket, balloon, or the like carrying equipment at a high altitude or in space. [t. F: plumbline t. Gmc: cf. SOUND[3]]

son et lumière (sŏn′ā lyōō′mĭ ĕə′; *Fr.* sôɴ nĕ lʏ myĕr′), a dramatic presentation staged at night in a building of historical interest, as a palace, castle, etc., and portraying by means of actors, music, and lighting effects, episodes in the history of the building and important events associated with it. [F: sound and light]

song (sŏng), *n.* **1.** a short metrical composition combining words and music; a ballad; a lyric. **2.** a piece adapted for singing or simulating a piece to be sung: *Mendelssohn's 'Songs without Words'.* **3.** poetical composition; poetry. **4.** the act or art of singing; vocal music. **5.** that which is sung. **6.** the musical or tuneful sounds produced by certain birds, insects, etc. **7. for a song,** at a very low price. **8. make a song (and dance) about,** *Colloq.* to make a fuss about. [ME and OE, c. G *Sang,* Icel. *söngr*]

songbird (sŏng′bûd′), *n.* **1.** a bird that sings. **2.** any of the passerine birds of the suborder *Oscines,* which contains those with the most highly developed vocal organs. **3.** a woman who sings.

song cycle, a series of songs unified by their subject or musical content.

songful (sŏng′fəl), *adj.* abounding in song; melodious.

songless (sŏng′lĭs), *adj.* devoid of song; lacking the power of song, as a bird.

Song of Solomon, The, a book of the Old Testament; Canticles. Also, **The Song of Songs.**

songster (sŏng′stə), *n.* **1.** one who sings; a singer. **2.** a writer of songs or poems; a poet. **3.** a songbird. [ME; OE *sangestre,* c. D *zangster.* See SONG, -STER] —**songstress** (sŏng′strĭs), *n.fem.*

song thrush, a common European songbird, *Turdus philomelos.*

songwriter (sŏng′rī′tə), *n.* one who writes the words or music, or both, for popular songs.

sonhood (sŭn′hŏŏd), *n.* sonship.

sonic (sŏn′ĭk), *adj.* **1.** of or pertaining to sound. **2.** denoting a speed approximating that of the propagation of sound.

sonic boom, *Aeron.* a sudden loud sound caused by the shock waves generated by an aircraft, or other object, travelling at or above the speed of sound.

soniferous (sō nĭf′ə rəs), *adj.* conveying or producing sound. [f. *soni-* (t. L, comb. form of *sonus* sound) + -FEROUS]

son-in-law (sŭn′ĭn lô′), *n., pl.* **sons-in-law.** the husband of one's daughter.

sonnet (sŏn′ĭt), *n.* **1.** *Pros.* a poem, properly expressive of a single complete thought, idea, or sentiment, of 14 lines (usually in 5-foot iambic metre) with rhymes arranged according to one of certain definite schemes, being in the strict or Italian form divided into a major group of 8 lines (the octave) followed by a minor group of 6 lines (the sestet), and in a common English form into 3 quatrains followed by a couplet. —*v.i.* **2.** to compose sonnets. —*v.t.* **3.** to celebrate in a sonnet or sonnets. [t. F, t. It.: m. *sonetto,* t. O Pr.: m. *sonet,* der. *son* sound, g. L *sonus*]

sonneteer (sŏn′ĭ tĭə′), *n.* **1.** a composer of sonnets. —*v.i.* **2.** to compose sonnets.

sonny (sŭn′ĭ), *n., pl.* **-nies.** little son (often used as a familiar term of address to a boy).

sonorant (sŏn′ə rənt), *n.* *Phonet.* a voiced sound less sonorous than a vowel but more sonorous than a stop or fricative, as *l, r, m, n, y, w*: such a sound may be now a sonant, now a consonant, as in modern English; thus, *y* is a sonant in *any,* a consonant in *yet.*

sonority (sə nŏ′rĭ tĭ), *n., pl.* **-ties.** the condition or quality of being resonant or sonorous.

sonorous (sə nô′rəs, sŏn′ə rəs), *adj.* **1.** giving out, or capable of giving out, a sound, esp. a deep resonant sound, as a thing or a place. **2.** loud, deep, or resonant, as a sound. **3.** rich and full in sound, as language, verse, etc. **4.** highflown; grandiloquent: *a sonorous address.* [t. L: m. *sonōrus*] —**sono′rously,** *adv.* —**sono′rousness,** *n.*

-sonous, a word element used in adjectives to refer to sounds, as in *unisonous.* [t. L: m. *-sonus*]

sonship (sŭn′shĭp), *n.* the state, fact, or relation of being a son.

sonsy (sŏn′sĭ), *adj.,* **-sier, -siest.** *Scot., Irish, and N Dial.* buxom or comely. [f. d. *sonse* prosperity (t. Gaelic: m. *sonas*) + -Y[1]]

Soo Canals (sōō), Sault Ste Marie Canals.

Soochow (sōō′chou′), *n.* former name of **Wuhsien.**

sook (sŏŏk), *n.* *Austral., N.Z.* (usually of children) a coward.

sool (sōōl, sŏŏl), *v.t.* *Austral., N.Z.* to incite (a dog) to attack or chase an animal or person.

soon (sōōn), *adv.* **1.** within a short period after this (or that) time, event, etc.: *we shall soon know.* **2.** before long; in the near future; at an early date. **3.** promptly or quickly: *no sooner said than done.* **4.** readily or willingly: *I would as soon walk as ride.* **5.** *Dial.* early in a period of time. **6.** *Obs.* immediately, or at once. [ME; OE *sōna* at once, c. OHG *sān,* akin to Goth. *suns*]

sooner (sōō′nə), *n.* *U.S.* **1.** one who settles on government land before it is legally opened to settlers in order to gain the choice of site. **2.** one who gains an unfair advantage by getting ahead of others.

Soong (sŏŏng), *n.* **1. Ching-ling** (chĭng′lĭng′), born 1890, widow of Sun Yat-sen. **2. Mei-ling** (mā′lĭng′), born 1898, wife of Chiang Kai-shek.

soot (sŏŏt), *n.* **1.** a black carbonaceous substance produced during the imperfect combustion of coal, wood, oil, etc., rising in fine particles and adhering to the sides of the chimney or pipe conveying the smoke. —*v.t.* **2.** to mark, cover, or treat with soot. [ME; OE *sōt,* c. d. D *zoet*]

sooth (sōōth), *n.* **1.** *Archaic.* truth, reality, or fact. [ME; OE *sōth,* c. OS *sōth.* See SOOTH, adj.]
—*adj.* **2.** *Poetic.* soothing, soft, or delicious. **3.** *Archaic.* true or real. [ME; OE *sōth,* c. OS *sōth,* Icel. *sannr,* akin to Goth. *sunjis* true] —**sooth′ly,** *adv.*

soothe (sōōth), *v.,* **soothed, soothing.** —*v.t.* **1.** to tranquillize or calm, as a person, the feelings, etc.; relieve, comfort, or refresh. **2.** to mitigate, assuage, or allay, as pain, sorrow, doubt, etc. —*v.i.* **3.** to exert a soothing influence; bring tranquillity, calm, ease, or comfort. [ME *sothe,* OE *sōthian,* der. *sōth* SOOTH, adj.] —**sooth′er,** *n.* —**sooth′ing,** *adj.* —**sooth′ingly,** *adv.* —**Syn. 1.** See **comfort. 2.** See **allay.**

soothsay (sōōth′sā′), *v.i.,* **-said, -saying.** to foretell events; predict.

soothsayer (sōōth′sā′ə), *n.* one who professes to foretell events. [ME *sothseyere;* f. SOOTH, adj. or n., + SAY, v., + -ER[1]]

soothsaying (sōōth′sā′ĭng), *n.* **1.** the practice or art of foretelling events. **2.** a prediction or prophecy.

sooty (sŏŏt′ĭ), *adj.,* **-ier, -iest. 1.** covered, blackened, or smirched with soot. **2.** consisting of or resembling soot. **3.** of a black, blackish, or dusky colour. —**soot′ily,** *adv.* —**soot′iness,** *n.*

sop (sŏp), *n., v.,* **sopped, sopping.** —*n.* **1.** a piece of bread or the like dipped, or for dipping, in liquid food. **2.** anything thoroughly soaked. **3.** something given to pacify or quiet, or as a bribe. **4.** *Colloq.* a weak or cowardly person. —*v.t.* **5.** to dip or soak (bread, etc.) in some

liquid. 6. to drench. 7. to take up (water, etc.) by absorption (usually fol. by *up*). —*v.i.* 8. to become or be soaking wet. 9. (of a liquid) to soak (*in*, etc.). [ME; OE *sopp*]
sop., soprano.
Soper (sō′pə), *n.* **Donald Oliver, Baron,** born 1903, English Methodist preacher.
soph., a sophomore.
sophism (sŏf′ĭz′əm), *n.* 1. a specious but fallacious argument, used to display ingenuity in reasoning or to deceive someone. 2. any false argument; a fallacy. [t. L: m. *sophisma*, t. Gk: clever device, argument; r. ME *sophime*, t. OF]
sophist (sŏf′ĭst), *n.* 1. (*often cap.*) a. any of a class of professional teachers in ancient Greece who gave instruction in various fields, as in general culture, rhetoric, politics, or disputation. b. any member of a portion of this class at a later period who, while professing to teach skill in reasoning, concerned himself with ingenuity and specious effectiveness rather than soundness of argument. 2. one who reasons adroitly and speciously rather than soundly. 3. a man of learning. [t. L: s. *sophista*, t. Gk: m. *sophistḗs*]
sophister (sŏf′ĭs tə), *n.* *Chiefly Hist.* 1. (in certain universities) a student after the completion of his first year, esp. one in his second or third year (**junior** or **senior sophister**). 2. a specious but unsound reasoner. 3. *Obs.* an ancient Greek sophist.
sophistic (sə fĭs′tĭk), *adj.* 1. of the nature of sophistry; fallacious. 2. characteristic or suggestive of sophistry. 3. given to the use of sophistry. 4. of or pertaining to sophists or sophistry. Also, **sophis′tical.** —**sophis′tically,** *adv.* —**sophis′ticalness,** *n.*
sophisticate (*v.* sə fĭs′tĭ kāt′; *n.* sə fĭs′tĭ kāt′, -kĭt), *v.*, **-cated, -cating,** *n.* —*v.t.* 1. to make less natural, simple, or ingenuous; to make worldly-wise. 2. to mislead or pervert. —*v.i.* 3. to use sophistry; quibble. —*n.* 4. a sophisticated person. [t. ML: m. s. *sophisticātus*, pp., der. L *sophisticus* sophistical. See SOPHIST]
sophisticated (sə fĭs′tĭ kā′tĭd), *adj.* 1. (of a person, the ideas, tastes, manners, etc.) altered by education, experience, etc., to be worldly-wise; changed from the natural character or simplicity; refined; artificial. 2. adapted to the tastes of sophisticates: *sophisticated music.* 3. deceptive; misleading. 4. (of machinery, etc.) complex; intricate. —**Ant.** 1. naive.
sophistication (sə fĭs′tĭ kā′shən), *n.* 1. sophisticated character, ideas, tastes, or ways as the result of education, worldly experience, etc. 2. change from the natural character or simplicity, or the resulting condition. 3. impairment or debasement, as of purity or genuineness. 4. the use of sophistry; a sophism or quibble.
sophistry (sŏf′ĭs trĭ), *n.*, *pl.* **-ries.** 1. a subtle, tricky, specious, but generally fallacious method of reasoning. 2. a false argument; sophism.
Sophocles (sŏf′ə klēz′), *n.* 495?–406? B.C., Greek dramatist. —**Sophoclean** (sŏf′ə klē′ən), *adj.*
sophomore (sŏf′ə mō′), *n.* *Chiefly U.S.* a student in the second year of the course at a university, college, or school. [f. *sophom* (var. of SOPHISM, def. 1, with reference to the fact that such arguments were used as school exercises) + m. -OR [2]] —**soph′omor′ic, soph′omor′ical,** *adj.*
Sophy (sō′fĭ), *n.*, *pl.* **-phies.** *Hist.* a Western title for one of the Persian Safavi dynasty. [t. Pers.: m. *çafī*, surname of the dynasty]
-sophy, a word element referring to systems of thought, as in *theosophy.* [t. Gk: m. s., *-sophía*, comb. form of *sophía* skill, wisdom]
sopor (sō′pə), *n.* *Pathol.* a deep, unnatural sleep; lethargy. [t. L]
soporiferous (sŏp′ə rĭf′ə rəs), *adj.* bringing sleep; soporific. [f. L *sopōrifer* sleep-bringing + -OUS] —**sop′orif′erously,** *adv.* —**sop′orif′erousness,** *n.*
soporific (sŏp′ə rĭf′ĭk), *adj.* 1. causing or tending to cause sleep. 2. pertaining to or characterized by sleep or sleepiness; sleepy; drowsy. —*n.* 3. something causing sleep, as a drug or medicine. [f. SOPOR + -(I)FIC]
sopping (sŏp′ĭng), *adj.* soaked; drenched: *sopping wet.*
soppy (sŏp′ĭ), *adj.*, **-pier, -piest.** 1. soaked, drenched, or very wet, as ground. 2. rainy, as weather. 3. *Colloq.* excessively sentimental; mawkish; silly. —**sop′pily,** *adv.* —**sop′piness,** *n.*
soprano (sə prä′nō), *n.*, *pl.* **-pranos, -prani** (-prä′nē), *adj.* *Music.* —*n.* 1. the uppermost part or voice. 2. the highest singing voice in women and boys. 3. a part for such a voice. 4. a singer with such a voice. —*adj.* 5. of or pertaining to soprano; having the compass of a soprano. [t. It., der. *sopra* above, g. L *suprā*]
soprano clef, *Music.* a sign locating middle C on the bottom line of the stave.
Sorata (*Sp.* sō rä′tä), *n.* **Mount,** a mountain in W Bolivia, in the Andes, near Lake Titicaca, with two peaks: Ancohuma, 21,490 ft, and Illampu, 21,276 ft.
sorb (sôb), *n.* 1. a European service tree, *Sorbus domestica.* 2. its fruit (**sorb apple**). [t. L: s. *sorbum* serviceberry, or *sorbus* service tree]
Sorb (sôb), *n.* a Wend. [t. G: m. *Sorbe.* See SERB]
sorbet (sô′bət), *n.* 1. an iced dessert made with fruit and liqueurs or heavy wines; served between meals to clear the palate. 2. a water-ice. 3. sherbet (def. 2). [t. F: water-ice, t. Turk. and Pers. See SHERBET]
Sorbian (sô′byən), *adj.* 1. of or pertaining to the Wends or their language. —*n.* 2. a Slavic language spoken by an isolated group in Prussia and Saxony; Wendish; Lusatian. 3. a Wend.
sorbite (sô′bīt), *n.* *Metall.* 1. a steel microstructure consisting of ferrite and finely divided cementite, which is produced when martensite is tempered above 450°C. 2. a constituent of steel produced by the decomposition of austenite when the rate of cooling is too slow to yield a troostitic structure, and too rapid to produce a pearlitic structure. [named after H. C. *Sorby*, 1829–1908, English metallurgist. See -ITE [1]] —**sorbit′ic,** *adj.*
sorbitol (sô′bĭ tŏl′), *n.* *Chem.* a white crystalline powder, $CH_2OH(CHOH)_4CH_2OH$, which occurs in certain fruits and which is isomeric with mannitol. Used in the manufacture of resins and varnishes and as a substitute for sugar. Also, **sorbit, sorbol.**
Sorbonist (sô′bə nĭst), *n.* a student or a graduate of the Sorbonne. [t. NL: s. *Sorbonista*, or t. F: m. *Sorboniste.* See SORBONNE
Sorbonne (sô bŏn′; *Fr.* sŏr bŏn′), *n.* 1. the seat of the faculties of letters, arts, and science of the University of Paris. 2. a theological college founded in Paris in 1257 by Robert de Sorbon, suppressed in 1792, and ceasing to exist about 1850. [F, named after Robert de *Sorbon*]
sorbose (sô′bōs), *n.* *Biochem.* a ketohexose, $C_6H_{12}O_6$, derived from the mountain ash, and obtainable industrially by bacterial oxidization, used in the synthesis of vitamin C. [f. SORB(ITOL) + -OSE [2]]
sorcerer (sô′sə rə), *n.* one supposed to exercise supernatural powers through evil spirits; a magician or enchanter. [f. SORCER(Y) + -ER [2]; r. ME *sorser*, t. OF: m. *sorcier*, g. VL **sortiārius*] —**sorceress** (sô′sə rĭs), *n. fem.*
sorcerous (sô′sə rəs), *adj.* 1. of the nature of or involving sorcery. 2. using sorcery.
sorcery (sô′sə rĭ), *n.*, *pl.* **-ceries.** the art, practices, or spells of a sorcerer; magic, esp. black magic in which supernatural powers are exercised through the aid of evil spirits; witchcraft. [ME, t. ML: m. s. *sorceria*, ult. der. L *sors* lot] —**Syn.** See **magic.**
sordid (sô′dĭd), *adj.* 1. dirty or filthy; squalid. 2. morally mean or ignoble: *sordid gains.* 3. meanly selfish, self-seeking, or mercenary. [t. L: s. *sordidus* dirty, base] —**sor′didly,** *adv.* —**sor′didness,** *n.* —**Syn.** 1. foul, squalid. 2. degraded, low, base. See **mean** [2].
sordino (sô dē′nō), *n.*, *pl.* **-ni** (-nē). *Music.* a mute (def. 11). Also, **sourdine.** [t. It., ult. der. L *surdus* deaf, mute]
sore (sô), *adj.*, **sorer, sorest,** *n.*, *adv.* —*adj.* 1. physically painful or sensitive, as a wound, hurt, diseased part, etc. 2. suffering bodily pain from wounds, bruises, etc., as a person. 3. suffering mental pain; grieved, distressed, or sorrowful: *to be sore at heart.* 4. causing great mental pain, distress, or sorrow: *a sore bereavement.* 5. causing very great suffering, misery, hardship, etc.: *sore need.* 6. *Colloq., Chiefly U.S.* irritated, offended, or feeling aggrieved: *What are you sore about?* 7. being an occasion of annoyance or irritation: *a sore subject.* —*n.* 8. a sore spot or place on the body. 9. a source or cause of grief, distress, irritation, etc. —*adv.* 10. *Archaic or Poetic.* sorely. [ME; OE *sār*, c. D *zeer*, G *sehr* very] —**sore′ly,** *adv.* —**sore′ness,** *n.*
sorehead (sô′hĕd′), *n.* *U.S. Slang.* a disgruntled or vindictive person, esp. an unsportsmanlike loser.
sore mouth, *Vet. Sci.* ecthyma of sheep.
sorghum (sô′gəm), *n.* 1. a cereal grass, *Sorghum vulgare*, of many varieties, which may be divided into four groups, the **sweet sorghums** (used especially for making molasses or syrup and for forage), the **grain sorghums** (used for forage and as a food for man), the **grass sorghums** (used principally for producing hay), and the **broomcorns** (used for making brooms and brushes). 2. the syrup made from the sweet or saccharine sorghums. [t. NL, der. It. *sorgo*, g. L *syricum* Syrian]
sorgo (sô′gō), *n.*, *pl.* **-gos.** any of the sweet sorghums. Also, **sorgho.** [t. It. See SORGHUM]
soricine (sŏ′rĭ sīn′), *adj.* of or resembling the shrews. See **shrew** (def. 1). [t. L: m. s. *sōricīnus*]
sorites (sŏ rī′tēz), *n.* *Logic.* a form of argument having several premises and one conclusion, and resolvable into

a number of syllogisms, the conclusion of each of which is a premise of the next. [t. L, t. Gk: m. *sōreítēs*, lit., heaped] —**soritical** (sō rĭt′ĭ kl), *adj.*

Sorolla y Bastida (*Sp.* sō rō′lyä ē bäs tē′dä), **Joaquín** (*Sp.* KHwä kēn′), 1863–1923, Spanish painter.

soroptimist (sō rŏp′tĭ mĭst), *n. Chiefly U.S.* a member of an association of professional and business women, devoted mainly to charity work. [irreg. f. L *sor(ōr)* sister + OPTIMIST]

sororate (sŏ′rə rāt′), *n.* marriage with a wife's sister.

sororicide (sə rŏ′rĭ sīd′), *n.* **1.** one who kills his or her sister. **2.** the act of killing one's sister. [t. L: m. s. *sorōricīda* (def. 1), *sorōricīdium* (def. 2). See -CIDE] —**soror′icid′al,** *adj.*

sorority (sə rŏ′rĭ tĭ), *n., pl.* **-ties.** *U.S.* a society or club of women or girls, as in a college. [t. ML: m. s. *sorōritas*]

sorosis[1] (sə rō′sĭs), *n., pl.* **-ses** (-sēz). *Bot.* a fleshy multiple fruit composed of many flowers, seed capsules, and receptacles consolidated, as in the pineapple and mulberry. [t. NL, f. s. Gk *sōrós* heap + *-ōsis* -OSIS]

sorosis[2] (sə rō′sĭs), *n., pl.* **-ses** (sēz), **-sises.** *U.S.* a women's society or club. [name of a women's club founded in 1868: der. SORORITY, influenced by SOROSIS[1]]

sorption (sôp′shən), *n. Phys. Chem.* the binding of one substance by another by any mechanism, such as absorption, adsorption, or persorption. [abstracted from ABSORPTION, etc.]

sorrel[1] (sŏ′rəl), *n.* **1.** light reddish brown. **2.** a horse of this colour. —*adj.* **3.** having the colour sorrel. [ME *sorel*, t. OF, der. *sore* yellowish brown, t. Gmc; cf. MLG *sōr* sere]

sorrel[2] (sŏ′rəl), *n.* **1.** any of various plants of the genus *Rumex*, having succulent acid leaves used in salads, sauces, etc. **2.** any of various sour-juiced plants of the genus *Oxalis*; wood sorrel. **3.** any of various similar plants. [ME *sorell*, t. OF: m. *surele*, der. *sur*, adj., t. Gmc: SOUR]

sorrel tree, a North American ericaceous tree, *Oxydendrum arboreum*, having leaves with an acid flavour and racemes of white flowers.

Sorrento (sə rĕn′tō; *It.* sōr rĕn′tō), *n.* a seaport in Italy, on the Bay of Naples: resort; cathedral; ancient ruins. 7600 (est. 1960).

sorrow (sŏ′rō), *n.* **1.** distress caused by loss, affliction, disappointment, etc.; grief, sadness, or regret. **2.** a cause or occasion of grief or regret. **3.** an affliction, misfortune, or trouble. —*v.i.* **4.** to feel sorrow; grieve. [ME; OE *sorg*, c. G *Sorge*] —**sor′rower,** *n.*

—**Syn.** 1. SORROW, DISTRESS, GRIEF, MISERY, WOE imply bitter suffering, especially as caused by loss or misfortune. SORROW is the most general term. GRIEF is keen suffering, esp. for a particular reason. DISTRESS implies anxiety, anguish, or acute suffering caused by the pressure of trouble or adversity. MISERY suggests such great and unremitting pain or wretchedness of body or mind as crushes the spirit. WOE is deep or inconsolable grief or misery. —**Ant.** 1. joy.

sorrowful (sŏ′rə fəl), *adj.* **1.** full of or feeling sorrow; grieved; sad. **2.** indicative or expressive of sorrow; mournful; plaintive. **3.** involving or causing sorrow; distressing. —**sor′rowfully,** *adv.* —**sor′rowfulness,** *n.*

sorry (sŏ′rĭ), *adj.*, **-rier, -riest. 1.** feeling regret, compunction, sympathy, pity, etc.: *to be sorry for a remark.* **2.** of a deplorable, pitiable, or miserable kind: *to come to a sorry end.* **3.** sorrowful, grieved, or sad. **4.** associated with sorrow; suggestive of grief or suffering; melancholy; dismal. **5.** wretched, poor, mean, or pitiful: *a sorry horse.* [ME; OE *sārig* (c. LG *sērig*, OHG *sērag*), der. *sār* SORE] —**sor′rily,** *adv.* —**sor′riness,** *n.* —**Syn. 5.** See **wretched.**

sort (sôt), *n.* **1.** a particular kind, species, variety, class, group, or description, as distinguished by the character or nature: *to discover a new sort of mineral.* **2.** character, quality, or nature. **3.** a more or less adequate or inadequate example of something. **4.** manner, fashion, or way. **5.** (*usually pl.*) *Print.* one of the kinds of characters of a fount of type. **6. a good sort,** *Colloq.* one who is likeable or possesses admirable qualities. **7. of sorts, a.** of a mediocre or poor kind. **b.** of one sort or another; of an indefinite kind. **8. out of sorts, a.** not in a normal condition of good health, spirits, or temper. **b.** *Print.* short of certain characters of a fount of type. **9. sort of,** *Colloq.* to a certain extent; in some way; as it were. —*v.t.* **10.** to arrange according to sort, kind, or class; separate into sorts; classify. **11.** to separate or take (*out*) from other sorts, or from others. **12.** to assign to a particular class, group, or place (fol. by *with, together*, etc.). —*v.i.* **13.** *Archaic.* to agree; accord. **14.** *Scot. and Dial.* to associate. [ME, t. OF: m. *sorte*, g. L *sors* lot, condition, LL class, order] —**sort′able,** *adj.*

sorter (sô′tə), *n.* **1.** one who or that which sorts. **2.** a post-office employee who sorts letters.

sortie (sô′tĭ), *n., v.*, **-tied, -tieing.** —*n.* **1.** a sally of troops from a besieged place to attack the besiegers. **2.** a body of troops making such a sally. **3.** the flying of a military aircraft on a mission, as a bombing raid. —*v.i.* **4.** to go out on a sortie. [t. F: a going out, der. *sortir* go out]

sortilege (sô′tĭ lĭj), *n.* **1.** the drawing of lots for divination; divination by lot. **2.** sorcery; magic. [ME, t. ML: m. s. *sortilegium*, der. L *sortilegus* diviner]

sorus (sô′rəs), *n., pl.* **sori** (sô′rī). *Bot.* one of the clusters of sporangia on the back of the fronds of ferns. [NL, t. Gk: m. *sōrós* heap]

SOS (ĕs′ō ĕs′), **1.** the letters represented by the radio telegraphic signal used, as by ships in distress, to call for help. **2.** *Colloq.* any call for help. [said to stand for *Save Our Souls*]

sosatie (sə sä′tĭ), *n. Chiefly S African.* a Cape Malay dish, consisting of curried mutton or pork, roasted in small pieces on a skewer over a wood fire. Also, **sassatie.** [t. Malay: m. *sisate* mincemeat]

Sosnowiec (*Pol.* sŏs nŏ′vyĕts), *n.* a town in S Poland. 138,000 (est. 1964).

so-so (sō′sō′), *adj.* **1.** indifferent; neither very good nor very bad. —*adv.* **2.** in an indifferent or passable manner; indifferently; tolerably.

sostenuto (sŏs′tə nōō′tō), *adj., n., pl.* **-tos, -ti** (-tē). *Music.* —*adj.* **1.** sustained or prolonged in the time value of the notes. —*n.* **2.** a movement or passage played in this manner. [It., pp. of *sostenere* sustain]

sot (sŏt), *n.* **1.** a confirmed drunkard. **2.** one befuddled by drink. [ME *sotte*, OE *sott*, t. VL: s. *sottus*; orig. uncert.]

soteriology (sō tĭə′rĭ ŏl′ə jĭ), *n. Theol.* the doctrine of salvation through Jesus Christ. [f. Gk *sōtērio(s)* saving + -LOGY] —**soteriologic** (sō tĭə′rĭ ə lŏj′ĭk), **sote′riolog′ical,** *adj.*

Sothic (sō′thĭk, sŏth′ĭk), *adj.* of Sirius, the Dog Star. [f. s. Gk *Sôthis*, Egyptian name for Sirius + -IC]

Sothic cycle, (in the ancient Egyptian calendar) a period of 1460 Sothic years. Also, **Sothic period.**

Sothic year, the fixed year of the ancient Egyptians, determined by the heliacal rising of Sirius, and equivalent to 365¼ days.

Sotho (sō′tō), *n.* **1.** the principal Bantu language of Lesotho. **2.** a member of the people speaking this language.

sottish (sŏt′ĭsh), *adj.* **1.** stupefied, as with drink. **2.** given to excessive drinking. **3.** pertaining to or befitting a sot. —**sot′tishly,** *adv.* —**sot′tishness,** *n.*

sotto voce (sŏt′ō vō′chĭ; *It.* sōt′tō vō′chĕ), in a low tone intended not to be overheard. [t. It.: under (normal) voice (level)]

sou (sōō), *n.* **1.** (formerly) a French bronze coin equal to either 5 or 10 centimes. **2.** (loosely) a 5-centime piece. [t. F, in OF *sol* SOL[2]]

sou., 1. south. 2. southern.

sou' (sou), *n., adj., adv. Chiefly Naut.* south.

souari nut (sōō ä′rĭ), the large, edible, oily nut of a tall tree, *Caryocar nuciferum*, of tropical South America; butternut. [t. Galibi: m. *saouari*]

soubise (sōō bēz′), *n.* a strained white onion sauce for meats, etc. [named after Charles de Rohan, Prince de *Soubise*, 1715–87, marshal of France]

soubrette (sōō brĕt′), *n.* **1.** a maidservant or lady's maid in a play or opera, esp. one displaying coquetry, pertness, and intrigue. **2.** an actress playing such a role. **3.** any lively or pert young woman character. [t. F, t. Pr.: m. *soubreto*, fem. of *soubret* coy, reserved, der. *soubra* to set aside, (earlier) be left over, g. L *superāre* be above] —**soubret′tish,** *adj.*

soubriquet (sōō′brĭ kā′), *n.* sobriquet.

soucar (sou kä′), *n.* a Hindu banker. Also, **sowcar.** [t. Hind.: m. *sāhūkār* great merchant]

souchong (sōō′shŏng′, -chŏng′), *n.* a variety of black tea grown in India and Ceylon. [t. Chinese: m. Cantonese *siu-chung* small sort]

Soudan (*Fr.* sōō däN′), *n.* French name of **Sudan.**

souffle (sōō′fəl), *n. Pathol.* a murmuring or blowing sound. [t. F, der. *souffler* blow. See SOUFFLÉ]

soufflé (sōō′flā), *n.* **1.** a light baked dish made fluffy with beaten eggwhites combined with egg yolks, white sauce, and fish, cheese, or other ingredients. **2.** a similar sweet or savoury cold dish like a mousse. —*adj.* **3.** puffed-up; made light, as by beating and cooking. [t. F, pp. of *souffler* blow, puff, g. L *sufflāre* blow up]

Soufflot (*Fr.* sōō flō′), *n.*, **Jacques Germain** (*Fr.* zhäk zhĕr măN′), 1713–80, French architect.

Soufrière (*Fr.* sōō fryĕr′), *n.* **1.** a volcano in the West Indies on St Vincent island. 4048 ft. **2.** a volcano in the West Indies on Guadeloupe. 4869 ft.

sough (sou), *v.i.* **1.** to make a rushing, rustling, or murmuring sound. —*n.* **2.** such a sound. [ME *swoghe*, OE *swōgan* make a noise, c. OS *swōgan* and akin to OE *swēgan* make a noise (c. Goth *-swōgjan*)]

sought (sôt), *v.* pt. and pp. of **seek.**

soul (sōl), *n.* **1.** the principle of life, feeling, thought, and action in man, regarded as a distinct entity separate from the body, and commonly held to be separable in existence from the body; the spiritual part of man as distinct from the physical. **2.** the spiritual part of man regarded in its moral aspect, or as believed to survive death and be subject to happiness or misery in a life to come. **3.** the emotional part of man's nature, or the seat of the feelings or sentiments. **4.** high-mindedness; noble warmth of feeling, spirit or courage, etc. **5.** the animating principle or essential element or part of something. **6.** the inspirer or moving spirit of some action, movement, etc. **7.** the embodiment of some quality. **8.** a disembodied spirit of a deceased person. **9.** a human being; person. [ME; OE *sāwl*, c. Goth. *saiwala*, akin to D *ziel*, G *Seele*, Icel. *sāl*]

soulful (sōl′fəl), *adj.* of, or expressive of, deep feeling or emotion: *soulful eyes.* **—soul′fully,** *adv.* **—soul′fulness,** *n.*

soulless (sōl′lĭs), *adj.* **1.** without a soul. **2.** lacking in nobility of soul, as persons; without spirit or courage. **—soul′lessly,** *adv.* **—soul′lessness,** *n.*

Soult (*Fr.* sōōlt), *n.* **Nicolas Jean de Dieu** (nē kŏ lȧ zhäɴ də dyœ′) (*Duke of Dalmatia*), 1769–1851, French marshal.

Soumak rug (sōō mäk′), Kashmir rug.

sound[1] (sound), n. **1.** the sensation produced in the organs of hearing when certain vibrations (**soundwaves**) are caused in the surrounding air or other elastic medium, as by a vibrating body. **2.** the vibrations in the air, or vibrational energy, producing this sensation: longitudinal vibrations propagated at about 1100 feet per second. **3.** the particular auditory effect produced by a given cause: *the sound of music.* **4.** any auditory effect, or vibrational disturbance such as to be heard. **5.** a noise, vocal utterance, musical note, or the like. **6.** *Phonet.* a segment of speech corresponding to a single articulation or to a combination of articulations constantly associated in the language; a phone. **7.** the quality of an event, letter, etc., as it affects a person: *this report has a bad sound.* **8.** the distance within which the noise of something may be heard. **9.** mere noise, without meaning. **10.** *Obs.* a report; news; tidings. [ME *soun*, t. AF: var. of OF *son*, g. L *sonus*] *—v.i.* **11.** to make or emit a sound. **12.** to give forth a sound as a call or summons. **13.** to be heard, as a sound. **14.** to convey a certain impression when heard or read: *to sound strange.* **15.** to give a specific sound: *to sound loud.* **16.** to give the appearance of being: *to sound true.* **17.** *Law.* to have as its basis or the import of (usually fol. by *in*): *his action sounds in contract.* **18. sound off,** *Colloq.* **a.** to speak or complain frankly. **b.** to speak angrily; lose one's temper. **c.** to boast; exaggerate. **d.** *U.S.* to call one's name, sequence, number, etc. *—v.t.* **19.** to cause (an instrument, etc.) to make or emit a sound. **20.** to give forth (a sound). **21.** to announce, order, or direct by a sound as of a trumpet: *to sound a retreat.* **22.** to utter audibly, pronounce, or express: *to sound each letter.* **23.** to examine by percussion or auscultation. *—adj.* **24.** of, pertaining to, or by the medium of radio broadcasting (as opposed to television broadcasting). [ME *soune(n)*, t. OF: m. *soner*, g. L *sonāre*]

—**Syn. 1.** SOUND, NOISE, TONE refer to something heard. SOUND and NOISE are often used interchangeably for anything perceived by means of hearing. SOUND, however, is more general in application, being used for anything within earshot: *the sound of running water.* NOISE, caused by irregular vibrations, is more properly applied to a loud, discordant, or unpleasant sound: *the noise of shouting.* TONE is applied to a musical sound; one conceived of as possessing a certain quality, resonance, pitch, to express emotion, etc.

sound[2] (sound), *adj.* **1.** free from injury, damage, decay, defect, disease, etc.; in good condition; healthy; robust: *a sound heart.* **2.** financially strong, secure, or reliable: *a sound business.* **3.** solidly good or reliable: *sound judgement.* **4.** without defect as to truth, justice, or reason: *sound advice.* **5.** of substantial or enduring character: *sound value.* **6.** without logical defect, as reasoning. **7.** without legal defect, as a title. **8.** theologically correct or orthodox, as doctrines or a theologian. **9.** free from moral defect or weakness; upright, honest, or good; honourable; loyal. **10.** unbroken and deep, as sleep. **11.** vigorous, hearty, or thorough, as a beating. **12. sound as a bell,** in perfect health or condition. *—adv.* **13.** in a sound manner. [ME *sund*, OE *gesund*, c. D *gezond*, G *gesund*] **—sound′ly,** *adv.* **—sound′ness,** *n.*

sound[3] (sound), *v.t.* **1.** to measure or try the depth of (water, a deep hole, etc.) by letting down a lead or plummet at the end of a line, or by some equivalent means. **2.** to measure (depth) in such a manner, as at sea. **3.** to examine or test (the bottom of water, etc.) with a lead that brings up adhering bits of matter. **4.** to examine or investigate; seek to fathom or ascertain: *to sound a person's views.* **5.** to seek to elicit the views or sentiments of (a person) by indirect inquiries, suggestive allusions, etc. (often fol. by *out*). **6.** *Surg.* to examine, as the urinary bladder, with a sound (def. 11). *—v.i.* **7.** to use the lead and line (or some other device) for measuring depth, etc., as at sea. **8.** to go down or touch bottom, as a lead. **9.** to plunge downwards or dive, as a whale. **10.** to make investigation; seek information, esp. by indirect inquiries, etc. *—n.* **11.** *Surg.* a long, solid, slender instrument for sounding or exploring body cavities or canals. [ME; OE *sund* channel (in *sundgyrd* sounding pole, lit., channel pole), t. Scand.; cf. Icel. *sund* channel, c. OE *sund* sea; akin to SWIM]

sound[4] (sound), *n.* **1.** a relatively narrow passage of water, not a stream, between larger bodies or between the mainland and an island: *Long Island Sound.* **2.** an inlet, arm, or recessed portion of the sea: *Puget Sound.* **3.** the air-bladder of a fish. [ME; OE *sund* swimming, channel, sea. See SOUND[3]]

Sound (sound), *n.* **The,** a strait between SW Sweden and the Danish island of Zealand, connecting the Kattegat and the Baltic. ab. 75 mi. long; 3–30 mi. wide. Swedish and Danish, **Öresund.**

sound barrier, (in popular usage) the sudden large increase in drag which occurs when an aircraft reaches the speed of sound.

soundboard (sound′bôd′), *n.* sounding-board.

soundbox (sound′bŏks′), *n.* **1.** a chamber in a musical instrument, as the body of a violin, for increasing the sonority of its tone. **2.** the part of an acoustic gramophone pick-up in which the mechanical movements of the needle are converted into acoustic impulses, usually based upon a diaphragm vibrated by the needle.

sound effect, any sound other than speech or music forming part of a radio or television programme or a film and used to create an effect, as the noise of a train, storm, gunfire, etc.

sounder[1] (soun′də), *n.* **1.** one who or that which makes a sound or noise, or sounds something. **2.** *Teleg.* a receiving instrument by the sounds of which a telegraphic message may be read. [f. SOUND[1] + -ER[1]]

sounder[2] (soun′də), *n.* one who or that which sounds the depth of water, etc. [f. SOUND[3] + -ER[1]]

sound hole, a hole, usually in the shape of an *f*, cut in the sounding-board of a violin or similar stringed instrument, with the object of increasing vibration.

sounding[1] (soun′dĭng), *adj.* **1.** emitting or producing a sound or sounds. **2.** resounding or sonorous. **3.** having an imposing sound; high-sounding; pompous. [f. SOUND[1] + -ING[2]] **—sound′ingly,** *adv.*

sounding[2] (soun′dĭng), *n.* **1.** (*often pl.*) the act or process of measuring depth, examining the bottom of water, etc., with or as with a lead and line. **2.** the act or process of making measurements of remote atmospheric characteristics, by such means as balloon or rocket, esp. for meteorological purposes. **3.** (*pl.*) depths of water ascertained by means of a lead and line, or sonar apparatus, as at sea. **4.** (*pl.*) parts of the water in which the ordinary sounding lead will reach bottom. [f. SOUND[3] + -ING[1]]

sounding balloon, *Meteorol.* a small free balloon used to obtain meteorological information from the upper atmosphere.

sounding-board (soun′dĭng bôd′), *n.* **1.** a thin, resonant plate of wood forming part of a musical stringed instrument, and so placed as to enhance the power and quality of the tone. **2.** a structure over, or behind and above, a speaker, orchestra, etc., to reflect the sound towards the audience. **3.** a board used in the deadening of floors, partitions, etc. **4.** one whose reactions to new methods, ideas, etc., serve as a test of their general acceptability or effectiveness. **5.** one who propagates opinions or ideas.

sounding line, a line weighted with a lead or plummet (**sounding lead**) and bearing marks to show the length paid out, used for sounding, as at sea.

sounding rocket, **1.** *Meteorol.* a research rocket used to obtain meteorological information from the upper atmosphere. **2.** *Aerospace.* a rocket used to explore regions up to 4000 mi. above the surface of the earth.

soundless[1] (sound′lĭs), *adj.* without sound. [f. SOUND[1] + -LESS] **—sound′lessly,** *adv.*

soundless[2] (sound′lĭs), *adj.* unfathomable. [f. SOUND[3] + -LESS]

soundpost (sound′pōst′), *n.* *Music.* a small wooden post separating the belly and back of stringed instruments, and used both to support the structure and to act as a focus for the vibrations.

soundproof (sound′prōōf′), *adj.* **1.** impervious to sound. *—v.t.* **2.** to cause to be soundproof.

sound ranging, the location of a sound source by microphonic detection of the sound signals.

soundtrack (sound′trăk′), *n.* **1.** a strip at the side of a cinema film which carries the sound recording. **2.** such a recording, esp. when transferred on to a gramophone record.

soundwave (sound′wāv′), *n. Physics.* a longitudinal vibration in an elastic medium by which sound is propagated.

soup (so͞op), *n.* **1.** a liquid food made from meat, fish, or vegetables, with various added ingredients, by boiling or simmering. **2. in the soup,** *Colloq.* in trouble. *—v.t.* **3. soup up,** *Slang.* to modify (an engine, esp. of a motor car) in order to increase its power. [t. F: m. *soupe* sop, broth, of Gmc orig.; cf. OE *sūpan* sip, *sopp* SOP]

soupçon (so͞op′sŏng; *Fr.* so͞op sôN′), *n.* **1.** a suspicion; a slight trace or flavour. **2.** a very small amount. [t. F, g. LL *suspectio,* r. L *suspicio* suspicion]

soup kitchen, **1.** a place where food, usually soup, is served free or at little charge to the poor. **2.** *Mil.* a mobile kitchen.

soup plate, a deep plate used for serving soup.

soup-spoon (so͞op′spo͞on′), *n.* a large spoon, usually with a rounded bowl, used for eating soup.

sour (sou′ə), *adj.* **1.** having an acid taste, such as that of vinegar, lemon juice, etc.; tart. **2.** rendered acid or affected by fermentation; fermented. **3.** characteristic of what is so affected: *a sour smell.* **4.** distasteful or disagreeable; unpleasant. **5.** harsh in spirit or temper; austere; morose; embittered; peevish. **6.** *Agric.* (of soil) having excessive acidity. **7.** (of substances such as petrol) contaminated by sulphur compounds. *—n.* **8.** that which is sour; something sour. **9.** *U.S.* a drink, as whisky or gin with lemon juice, sugar, etc. *—v.i., v.t.* **10.** to become or make sour. [ME; OE *sūr,* c. G *sauer*] **—sour′ish,** *adj.* **—sour′ly,** *adv.* **—sour′ness,** *n.*

source (sôs), *n.* **1.** any thing or place from which something comes, arises, or is obtained; origin. **2.** a spring of water from the earth, etc., or the place of issue; a fountain; the beginning or place of origin of a stream or river. **3.** a book, statement, person, etc., supplying information. **4.** *U.S.* the person or business making interest or divided payments. [ME, t. OF, n. use of pp. of *sourdre* rise, spring up, g. L *surgere* rise]

source book, a book, collection of documents, etc., serving as an authoritative basis for the historical study of a subject.

source material, original authoritative materials used in research, as diaries, manuscripts, records, etc.

sourdine (so͞oə dēn′), *n. Music.* **1.** sordino. **2.** kit². **3.** *Hist.* an obsolete member of the oboe family. [t. F, der. *sourd* deaf, g. L *surdus*]

sourdough (sou′ə dō′), *n.* **1.** *Western U.S. and Can., Alaska, and Dial.* leaven, esp. fermented dough kept from one baking to start the next instead of beginning each time with fresh yeast. **2.** a prospector or pioneer, esp. in Alaska or Canada. *—adj.* **3.** *Western U.S. and Can., Alaska.* leavened with sourdough.

sour fig, any of various plants of the family *Aizoaceae,* esp. *Mesembryanthemum edule,* of arid land in southern Africa, having brilliant white, yellow or pink flowers, and a sour-tasting fruit used for making jam and in the preparation of medicine; Hottentot fig.

sour gourd, **1.** the acid fruit of a bombacaceous tree, *Adansonia gregorii,* of northern Australia. **2.** the tree. **3.** the fruit of the baobab, *A. digitata,* of Africa.

sour grapes, the act of pretending to despise something, only because one cannot have it. [after the fox (in a fable by Aesop) who pretended that the grapes he could not reach were sour]

sour gum, the tupelo, *Nyssa sylvatica.*

sourpuss (sou′ə po͝os′), *n. Colloq.* one having a sour or gloomy disposition; an embittered person.

soursop (sou′ə sŏp′), *n.* **1.** the large, slightly acid, pulpy fruit of a small tree, *Annona muricata,* native in the West Indies. **2.** the tree.

Sousa (so͞o′zə), *n.* **John Philip,** 1854–1932, U.S. composer of marches.

sousaphone (so͞o′zə fōn′), *n.* a form of bass tuba, similar to the helicon, used in brass bands. [f. SOUSA + -PHONE. Cf. SAXOPHONE]

souse¹ (sous), *v.,* **soused, sousing,** *n. —v.t.* **1.** to plunge into water or other liquid. **2.** to drench with water, etc. **3.** to dash or pour, as water. **4.** to steep in pickling liquid; pickle. **5.** *Slang.* to intoxicate. *—v.i.* **6.** to plunge into water, etc.; fall with a splash. **7.** to be soaked or drenched. **8.** to be steeping or soaking in something. **9.** *Slang.* to drink to intoxication. *—n.* **10.** an act of sousing. **11.** something kept or steeped in pickle, esp. the head, ears, and feet of a pig. **12.** a liquid used as a pickle. **13.** *Slang.* a drunkard. [ME *sows,* t. OF: m. *souce,* t. OHG: m. *sulza* brine; akin to SALT]

souse² (sous), *v.,* **soused, sousing,** *n. Archaic. —v.i.* **1.** to swoop. *—v.t.* **2.** to swoop or pounce on. *—n.* **3.** *Falconry.* **a.** a rising while in flight. **b.** a swooping or pouncing. [var. of SOURCE in (now obs.) sense 'rise']

Sousse (*Fr.* so͞os), *n.* a seaport in NE Tunisia. 48,172 (1956). Also, **Susa.**

soutache (so͞o tăsh′; *Fr.* so͞o tȧsh′), *n.* a narrow braid, commonly of mohair, silk, or rayon, used for trimming. [t. F, t. Hung.: m. *sujtas* trimming]

soutane (so͞o tăn′; *Fr.* so͞o tȧn′), *n. Eccles.* a cassock. [t. F, t. It.: m. *sottana,* der. *sotto* under, g. L *subtus*]

souter (so͞o′tə), *n. Scot. and N Dial.* a shoemaker; cobbler. [ME; OE *sūtere,* t. L: m. *sūtor,* der. *suere* to sew]

south (south), *n.* **1.** a cardinal point of the compass directly opposite to the north. **2.** the direction in which this point lies. **3.** (*l.c. or cap.*) a quarter or territory situated in this direction. **4.** (*cap.*) that part of England lying south of an imaginary line drawn between the Wash and the Severn, esp. the urban areas. **5.** (*cap.*) the general area south of Pennsylvania and the Ohio river and east of the Mississippi, consisting mainly of those states which formed the Confederacy during the American Civil War. **6.** *Chiefly Poetic.* the south wind. *—adj.* **7.** lying towards or situated in the south. **8.** directed or proceeding towards the south. **9.** coming from the south, as a wind. **10.** (*cap.*) designating the southern part of a region, nation, country, etc.: *South Atlantic.* *—adv.* **11.** towards or in the south. **12.** from the south. Also, *esp. Naut.,* **sou'** (sou). [ME; OE *sūth,* c. OHG *sund-*; akin to G *Süd*]

South Africa, Republic of, an independent republic in southern Africa. 17,474,000 pop. (est. 1964); 471,445 sq. mi. *Capitals:* Pretoria and Cape Town. Formerly, **Union of South Africa.**

Republic of South Africa

South African, **1.** of southern Africa. **2.** of the Republic of South Africa. **3.** a native or inhabitant of the Republic of South Africa, esp. one of European descent.

South African Dutch, **1.** Afrikaans. **2.** the Boers.

South African Republic, **1.** the Republic of South Africa. **2.** the name of Transvaal when it was a Boer state.

Southall (sou′thôl), *n.* a district in the W outer London borough of Ealing.

Southam (sou′t͟həm), *n.* a town in England, in Warwickshire. 15,457 (1961).

South America, a continent in the S part of the Western Hemisphere. 170,000,000 (est. 1965); ab. 6,900,000 sq. mi. **—South American.**

Southampton (south ămp′tən, -hămp′-), *n.* a seaport in England, in Hampshire. 204,822 (1961).

South Arabia, **1. Federation of,** a federation in S Arabia, lasting from 1959–68, comprising 16 states of the Protectorate of South Arabia and the state (former colony) of Aden. **2. Protectorate of,** a former British protectorate in S Arabia, comprising various states and tribal units and including the island of Socotra. See **South Yemen.**

South Australia, a state in southern Australia. 1,054,237 pop. (est. 1965); 380,070 sq. mi. *Cap.:* Adelaide.

South Bend, a town in the U.S., in N Indiana. 132,445 (1960).

southbound (south′bound′), *adj.* travelling towards the south.

south by east, *Navig., Survey.* 11° 15′ (one point) east of south. *Abbrev.:* S by E. Also, *esp. Naut.,* **sou' by east.**

south by west, *Navig., Survey.* 11° 15′ (one point) west of south. *Abbrev.:* S by W. Also, *esp. Naut.,* **sou' by west.**

South Carolina, a state in the SE United States, on the Atlantic coast. 2,382,594 pop. (1960); 31,055 sq. mi. *Cap.:* Columbia. *Abbrev.:* S.C. **—South Carolinian.**

South Caucasian, **1.** a family of languages of southern Caucasia, including Georgian. **2.** of or pertaining to South Caucasian.

South China Sea, a part of the Pacific, partially enclosed by SE China, Vietnam, the Malay Peninsula, Borneo, and the Philippines.

South Dakota (də kō′tə), a state in the N central United States: a part of the Middle West. 680,514 pop. (1960); 77,047 sq. mi. *Cap.:* Pierre. *Abbrev.:* S Dak. **—South′ Dako′tan.**

Southdown (south′doun′), *n.* one of a breed of short-woolled sheep, yielding high-quality mutton, orig. reared on the South Downs.

South Downs, a range of low hills in S England extending from Dorset to Sussex.

South Dum Dum (south′dŭm′dŭm′), a town in SE West Bengal, India. 111,284 (1961).

south-east (south′ēst′), *n.* **1.** the point or direction midway between south and east. **2.** a region in this direction. —*adj.* **3.** lying towards or situated in the south-east. **4.** directed or proceeding towards the south-east. **5.** coming from the south-east, as a wind. —*adv.* **6.** towards or in the south-east. **7.** from the south-east. Also, *esp. Naut.*, **sou'-east.** —**south′-eas′terner,** *n.*

South-East Asia Treaty Organization, the group of nations that signed the **South-East Asia Collective Defence Treaty** in 1954: Australia, France, Great Britain, New Zealand, Pakistan, the Philippines, Thailand, and the United States. *Abbrev.*: SEATO

south-east by east, *Navig., Survey.* 11° 15′ (one point) east of south-east; 123° 45′ from due north. *Abbrev.*: SE by E. Also, *esp. Naut.*, **sou'-east by east.**

south-east by south, *Navig., Survey.* 11° 15′ (one point) south of south-east; 146° 15′ from due north. *Abbrev.*: SE by S. Also, *esp. Naut.*, **sou'-east by sou'.**

south-easter (south′ē′stə), *n.* a wind, gale, or storm from the south-east. Also, *esp. Naut.*, **sou'-easter** (sou′ē′stə).

south-easterly (south′ē′stə lĭ), *adj.* **1.** of or situated in the south-east. **2.** towards or from the south-east. —*adv.* **3.** towards or from the south-east. Also, *esp. Naut.*, **sou'-easterly** (sou′ē′stə lĭ).

south-eastern (south′ē′stən), *adj.* situated in, proceeding towards, or coming from the south-east. Also, *esp. Naut.*, **sou'-eastern** (sou′ē′stən).

south-eastward (south′ēst′wəd), *adj.*, *adv.* **1.** Also, **south-eastwardly;** *esp. Naut.*, **sou'-eastwardly.** towards the south-east. —*n.* **2.** the south-east. Also, *esp. Naut.*, **sou'-eastward** (sou′ēst′wəd).

south-eastwards (south′ēst′wədz), *adv.* south-eastward. Also, *esp. Naut.*, **sou'-eastwards** (sou′ēst′wədz).

Southend-on-Sea (south′ĕnd ŏn sē′), *n.* a town in England, in Essex, on the Thames estuary: resort. 165,093 (1961). Also, **Southend.**

souther (sou′thə), *n.* a wind or storm from the south.

southerly (sŭth′ə lĭ), *adj.* **1.** moving, directed, or situated towards the south. **2.** coming from the south, as a wind. —*adv.* **3.** towards the south. **4.** from the south. —**south′-erliness,** *n.*

southern (sŭth′ən), *adj.* **1.** lying towards, or situated in the south. **2.** directed or proceeding southwards. **3.** (*cap.*) coming from the south, as wind. **4.** of or pertaining to the south. **5.** *Astron.* south of the celestial equator or of the zodiac. [ME; OE *sūtherne.* See SOUTH, -ERN]

Southern Alps, a mountain range in New Zealand, on South Island. Highest peak, Mt Cook, 12,349 ft.

Southern Coalsack. See **coalsack** (defs 2, 3).

Southern Cross, *Astron.* the southern constellation Crux: its four chief stars are in the form of a cross.

Southern Crown, *Astron.* the Corona Australis.

Southerner (sŭth′ə nə), *n.* (*sometimes l.c.*) a native or inhabitant of a southern country or region, esp. southern England or the southern states of the U.S.

Southern Fish, *Astron.* the constellation Piscis Austrinus.

Southern Hemisphere, the half of the earth between the South Pole and the equator.

southernly (sŭth′ən lĭ), *adj.*, *adv.* southerly.

southernmost (sŭth′ən mōst′), *adj.* farthest south.

Southern Rhodesia, former name of **Rhodesia.**

Southern Uplands, a series of hill ranges in S Scotland from Kirkcudbrightshire to E Lothian, including the Lowther, Moorfoot, and Lammermuir hills. Highest point, Merrick, NW Kirkcudbrightshire, 1765 ft.

southernwood (sŭth′ən wŏŏd′), *n.* a woody-stemmed wormwood, *Artemisia abrotanum*, of southern Europe, having aromatic, finely dissected leaves.

Southey (sou′thĭ, sŭth′ĭ), *n.* **Robert,** 1774–1843, English poet and prose writer: poet laureate 1813–43.

Southgate (south′gĭt), *n.* a district in the N outer London borough of Enfield.

South Georgia, a British island in the S Atlantic, ab. 800 mi. SE of the Falkland Islands. 800 pop. (est. 1965); ab. 1000 sq. mi.

South Holland, a province in SW Netherlands. 2,847,175 (est. 1964); 1212 sq. mi. *Cap.*: The Hague. Dutch, **Zuid Holland.**

southing (sou′thĭng), *n.* **1.** *Astron.* **a.** the transit of a heavenly body across the celestial meridian. **b.** south declination. **2.** movement or deviation towards the south. **3.** distance due south made by a ship.

South Island, the largest island of New Zealand. 785,520 pop. (est. 1965); 58,093 sq. mi. See map under **New Zealand.**

South Korea, a country in E Asia: formed in 1948 after the division of Korea at 38°N. 27,132,176 pop. (1963); 38,452 sq. mi. *Cap.*: Seoul. Official name, **Republic of Korea.**

southland (south′lănd′), *n.* **1.** a land lying in or towards the south. **2.** the southern part of a country.

southmost (south′mōst′), *adj.* southernmost.

southpaw (south′pô′), *Colloq.* —*n.* **1.** a person who is left-handed. **2.** *Boxing.* a boxer who stands with his right arm and right leg forward. —*adj.* **3.** left-handed.

South Pole, **1.** that end of the earth's axis of rotation marking the southernmost point of the earth. **2.** *Astron.* the zenith of the earth's south pole; the point at which the earth's axis produced cuts the southern half of the celestial sphere.

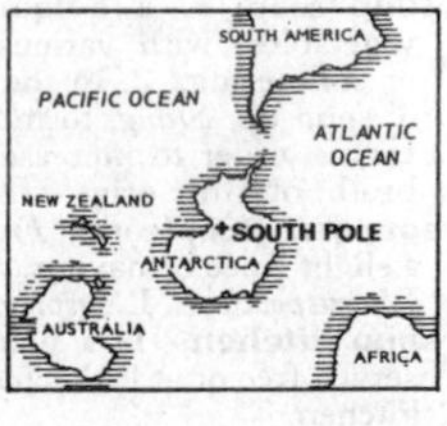

South Pole

Southport (south′pôt′), *n.* a town in England, in Lancashire: seaside resort. 72,004 (1961).

southron (sŭth′rən), *n.* **1.** a southerner. **2.** (*usually cap.*) *Scot.* an Englishman. [ME; alter. of earlier *southren* (var. of SOUTHERN) on model of *Saxon*, etc.]

South Sea Bubble, a financial and political scandal in Great Britain, resulting from the collapse in 1720 of the South Sea Company, sponsored by the king and government, after it had taken over the national debt.

South Sea Islands, the islands in the S Pacific Ocean. See **Oceania.**

South Seas, the seas south of the equator.

South Shields, a town in England, in Co. Durham. 109,521 (1961).

south-south-east (south′south′ēst′), *Navig., Survey.* —*n.* **1.** the point of the compass midway between south and south-east; 157° 30′ from north. —*adj.* **2.** lying or situated in this direction. —*adv.* **3.** to, in, or from this direction. *Abbrev.*: SSE. Also, *esp. Naut.*, **sou'-sou'-east** (sou′sou′-ēst′).

south-south-west (south′south′wĕst′), *Navig., Survey.* —*n.* **1.** the point of the compass midway between south and south-west; 202° 30′ from north. —*adj.* **2.** lying or situated in this direction. —*adv.* **3.** to, in, or from this direction. *Abbrev.*: SSW. Also, *esp. Naut.*, **sou'-sou'-west** (sou′sou′wĕst′).

South Suburban (south′ sə bû′bən), a town in India, in West Bengal: a suburb of Calcutta. 185,811 (1961).

South Vietnam, a country in SE Asia, formed by the provisional division in 1954 of Vietnam at about 17°N. 14,200,000 pop. (est. 1962); 66,263 sq. mi. *Cap.*: Saigon. Official name, **Republic of Vietnam.** See map under **Vietnam.**

southward (south′wəd; *Naut.* sŭth′əd), —*adj.* **1.** moving, bearing, facing, or situated towards the south. —*n.* **2.** the southward part, direction, or point. —*adv.* **3.** southwards. —**south′wardly,** *adj.*, *adv.*

southwards (south′wədz), *adv.* towards the south. Also, **southward.**

Southwark (sŭth′ək), *n.* a S inner borough of London. 310,600 (est. 1965).

south-west (south′wĕst′), *n.* **1.** the point or direction midway between south and west. **2.** a region in this direction. —*adj.* **3.** lying towards or situated in the south-west. **4.** directed or proceeding towards the south-west. **5.** coming from the south-west, as a wind. —*adv.* **6.** in the direction of a point midway between south and west. **7.** from this direction. Also, *esp. Naut.*, **sou'-west** (sou′wĕst′).

South-West Africa, a territory in SW Africa: a mandate of the Republic of South Africa. 526,004 pop. (1965); 317,725 sq. mi. *Cap.*: Windhoek. Formerly, **German South-West Africa.**

south-west by south, *Navig., Survey.* 11°15′ (one point) south of south-west; 213° 45′ from due north. *Abbrev.*: SW by S. Also, *esp. Naut.*, **sou'-west by sou'.**

south-west by west, *Navig., Survey.* 11°15′ (one point) west of south-west; 236° 15′ from due north. *Abbrev.*: SW by W. Also, *esp. Naut.*, **sou'-west by west.**

south-wester (south′wĕs′tə), *n.* a wind, gale, or storm from the south-west. Also, *esp. Naut.*, **sou'-wester** (sou′wĕs′tə).

south-westerly (south′wĕst′tə lĭ), *adj.*, *adv.* towards or from the south-west. Also, *esp. Naut.*, **sou'-westerly** (sou′wĕs′tə lĭ).

south-western (south′wĕs′tən), *adj.* situated in, proceeding towards, or coming from the south-west. Also, *esp. Naut.*, **sou'-western** (sou′wĕs′tən).

south-westward (south′wĕst′wəd), *adv.*, *adj.* **1.** Also, **south-westwardly;** *esp. Naut.*, **sou'-westwardly.** towards the south-west. —*n.* **2.** the south-west. Also, *esp. Naut.*, **sou'-westward** (sou'wĕst'wəd).

south-westwards; (south'wĕst'wədz), *adv.* south-westward. Also, *esp. Naut.*, **sou'-westwards** (sou'wĕst'wədz).

South Yemen, an independent state in S Arabia formed in 1968 from the former Federation of South Arabia. 800,000 pop. (est. 1968); ab. 112,000 sq. mi. *Cap.*: Medina al Shaab. Official name, **People's Republic of South Yemen.**

Souvanna Phouma (sōō văn'ə pōō'mə), **Prince,** born 1901, prime minister of Laos since 1962.

souvenir (sōō'və nĭə', sōō'və nĭə'), *n.* **1.** something given or kept for remembrance; a memento. **2.** a memory. [t. F: n. use of *souvenir* (reflex.) to remember, t. L: m. *subvenīre* come to mind]

sou'wester (sou'wĕs'tə), *n.* **1.** a waterproof hat, usually of oilskin, having the brim very broad behind, worn esp. by seamen. **2.** south-wester.

sovereign (sŏv'rĭn), *n.* **1.** a monarch; a king or queen. **2.** one who has sovereign power or authority. **3.** a group or body of persons or a state possessing sovereign authority. **4.** a British gold coin, generally equivalent to £1 until withdrawn from circulation in 1914; latterly minted for the gold reserve and for use abroad. —*adj.* **5.** belonging to or characteristic of a sovereign or sovereignty. **6.** having supreme rank, power, or authority. **7.** supreme, as power, authority, etc. **8.** greatest in degree; utmost or extreme. **9.** being above all others in character, importance, excellence, etc. **10.** efficacious or potent, as a remedy. [ME, t. OF: m. *soverain*, ult. der. L *super* above] —**sov'ereignly,** *adv.*

sovereignty (sŏv'rən tĭ), *n.*, *pl.* **-ties.** **1.** the quality or state of being sovereign. **2.** the status, dominion, power, or authority of a sovereign. **3.** supreme and independent power or authority in government as possessed or claimed by a state or community. **4.** a sovereign state, community, or political unit.

Sovetsk (*Russ.* sȧ vyĕtsk'), *n.* a town in the W Soviet Union in Europe on the river Memel; formerly in East Prussia. 85,900 (1959). Formerly, **Tilsit.**

soviet (sō'vĭ ət), *n.* **1.** (in the Soviet Union) **a.** (before the revolution) a council of any kind, presumably elected by all. **b.** (after the revolution) a local council, orig. elected only by manual workers, with certain powers of local administration. **c.** (after the revolution) a higher local council elected by a local council, part of a pyramid of soviets, culminating in the **Supreme Soviet.** **2.** any similar assembly connected with a socialist governmental system elsewhere. —*adj.* **3.** of a soviet. **4.** (*cap.*) of the Soviet Union: *a Soviet statesman.* [t. Russ.: m. *sovyet* council]

sovietism (sō'vĭ ə tĭz'əm), *n.* the soviet system of government. —**so'vietist,** *n.*, *adj.*

sovietize (sō'vĭ ə tīz'), *v.t.*, **-tized, -tizing.** to bring under the influence or domination of the Soviet Union. Also, **sovietise.** —**sovietization** (sō'vĭ ə tī zā'shən), *n.*

Soviet Russia, 1. a conventional name of the Soviet Union. **2.** Russian Socialist Federated Soviet Republic.

Soviet Union, a federal union of fifteen constituent republics, in E Europe and W and N Asia, comprising the larger part of the former Russian Empire. 232,000,000 pop. (est. 1966); 8,649,489 sq. mi. *Cap.*: Moscow. Official name, **Union of Soviet Socialist Republics.**

sovran (sŏv'rən), *n.*, *adj. Poetic.* sovereign.

sow¹ (sō), *v.*, **sowed, sown** or **sowed, sowing.** —*v.t.* **1.** to scatter (seed) over land, earth, etc., for growth; plant (seed, and hence a crop). **2.** to scatter seed over (land, earth, etc.) for the purpose of growth. **3.** to introduce for development; seek to propagate or extend; disseminate: *to sow distrust or dissension.* **4.** to strew or sprinkle with anything. —*v.i.* **5.** to sow seed, as for the production of a crop. [ME *sowen*, OE *sāwan*, c. G *säen*; akin to L *serere*] —**sow'er,** *n.*

sow² (sou), *n.* **1.** an adult female pig. **2.** the adult female of various other animals. **3.** *Metall.* **a.** a large oblong mass of iron which has solidified in the common channel through which the molten metal flows to the smaller channels in which the pigs solidify. **b.** the common channel itself. [ME; OE *sū*, c. G *Sau*]

sowar (sō wä', -wô'), *n. India.* a mounted soldier, policeman, etc. [t. Urdu, t. Pers.: m. *sawār* horseman]

sowbane (sou'bān'), *n.* a chenopodiaceous herb, *Chenopodium hybridum*, of Europe; commonly found on waste ground.

sowbread (sou'brĕd'), *n.* a primulaceous perennial herb, *Cyclamen hederifolium*, a native of S Europe, widely cultivated in England and Wales.

sowbug (sou'bŭg'), *n.* any of various small terrestrial isopods, esp. of the genus *Oniscus*; woodlouse.

sowcar (sou kä'), *n.* soucar.

Sowerby Bridge (sou'ə bĭ brĭj'), a town in England, in the West Riding of Yorkshire. 16,224 (1961).

sown (sōn), *v.* pp. of **sow**¹.

sow-thistle (sou'thĭs'əl), *n.* any plant of the composite genus *Sonchus*, esp. *S. oleraceus*, a common weed having thistle-like leaves, yellow flowers, and a milky juice.

Soxhlet apparatus (sŏks'lĭt; *Ger.* zōks'lĕt), *Chem.* a laboratory apparatus for extracting the soluble portion of any substance by continuously circulating a boiling solvent through it. [named after Franz von *Soxhlet*, 1848–1926, German agricultural chemist]

soya (soi'ə), *n.* **1.** a salty, fermented sauce much used on fish and other dishes in the Orient, prepared from soya beans. **2.** the soya bean. Also, **soy** (soi). [t. Jap., var. of *shoy*, short for *shō-yu*, t. Chinese: m. *shi-yu* (f. *shi* kind of bean + *yu* oil)]

soya bean, 1. a bushy, leguminous plant, *Glycine soja*, of SE Asia. **2.** the seed of this plant used as food, a livestock feed, and for a number of commercial purposes, and yielding an oil used as a food and in the manufacture of soap, candles, etc.

Sozzini (*It.* sōt tsē'nē), *n.* Italian name of **Socinus.**

sozzled (sŏz'əld), *adj. Slang.* drunk. [f. obs. *sozzle* drunken stupor (akin to SOUSE¹) + -ED³]

Sp., 1. Spain. **2.** Spaniard. **3.** Spanish.

sp., 1. special. **2.** species. **3.** specific. **4.** specimen. **5.** spelling. **6.** spirit.

s.p., (L *sine prole*) without issue.

spa (spä), *n.* a mineral spring, or a locality in which such springs exist. [special use of SPA]

Spa (spä; *Fr.* spȧ), *n.* a town in E Belgium, SE of Liège: famous mineral springs. 9391 (1965).

Spaak (späk; *Fr.* spȧk), *n.* **Paul Henri** (*Fr.* pōl äɴ rē'), born 1899, Belgian statesman: prime minister 1961–65.

spaanspek (spän'spĕk'), *n. S African.* a sweet melon, *Melo hispanicus*, a variety of cantaloup, of Cape Province. [t. Afrikaans: Spanish bacon, from the colour of the flesh]

space (spās), *n.*, *v.*, **spaced, spacing.** —*n.* **1.** the unlimited or indefinitely great general receptacle of things, commonly conceived as an expanse extending in all directions (or having three dimensions), in which, or occupying portions of which, all material objects are located. **2.** the portion or extent of this in a given instance; extent or room in three dimensions: *the space occupied by a body.* **3.** that part of the universe which lies outside the earth's atmosphere in which the density of matter is very low; outer space. **4.** extent or area; a particular extent of surface: *to fill in blank spaces in a document.* **5.** a seat, berth, or room on a train, aeroplane, etc. **6.** linear distance; a particular distance: *trees set at equal spaces apart.* **7.** extent, or a particular extent, of time: *a space of two hours.* **8.** an interval of time; a while: *after a space he continued his story.* **9.** *Music.* one of the degrees or intervals between the lines of the stave. **10.** *Print.* one of the blank pieces of metal used to separate words, etc. **11.** *Teleg.* a period of time having a fixed relation to dots and dashes, during which no signal is transmitted in morse or similar systems. —*v.t.* **12.** to fix the space or spaces of; divide into spaces. **13.** to set some distance apart. **14.** *Print., etc.* **a.** to separate (words, letters, or lines) by spaces. **b.** to extend by inserting more space or spaces (usually fol. by *out*). [ME, t. OF: m. *espace*, t. L: m. *spatium*] —**spac'er,** *n.*

space-bar (spās'bä'), *n.* a horizontal bar on a typewriter which is depressed in order to move the carriage one space to the left.

space capsule, a container for instruments or astronauts which is capable of being sent into space and which can be recovered on its return.

spacecraft (spās'kräft'), *n.* a vehicle capable of travelling in space.

space heater, a domestic or industrial heater used for heating an enclosed area, as a room or workshop.

space lattice, lattice (def. 3).

spaceless (spās'lĭs), *adj.* **1.** independent of space; infinite. **2.** occupying no space.

spaceman (spās'măn'), *n.* a traveller in outer space. —**space'wom'an,** *n. fem.*

spaceport (spās'pôt'), *n.* a place where rockets are launched, esp. rockets carrying manned spacecraft.

space probe, a rocket-propelled missile capable of travelling in space and of radioing back to earth information concerning its environment.

spaceship (spās'shĭp'), *n.* a manned spacecraft.

space station, a manned artificial satellite in orbit around the earth.

spacesuit (spās'syōōt'), *n.* a pressure suit.

space-time (spās'tīm'), *n.* **1.** a four-dimensional continuum in which the coordinates are the three spatial coordinates and time. The events and objects of any spatial and temporal region may be conceived as part of this continuum. *—adj.* **2.** of or pertaining to any system with three spatial and one temporal coordinates. **3.** of or pertaining to both space and time.

space travel, flight in space in a manned spacecraft.

spacing (spā′sĭng), *n.* **1.** the act of one who or that which spaces. **2.** the fixing or arranging of spaces.

spacious (spā′shəs), *adj.* **1.** containing much space, as a house, room, court, street, etc.; amply large. **2.** occupying much space; vast. **3.** of a great extent or area; broad; large; great. **4.** broad in scope, range, inclusiveness, etc. [ME, t. L: m. s. *spatiōsus*] **—spa′ciously,** *adv.* **—spa′ciousness,** *n.* **—Syn. 1.** roomy, capacious.

spade[1] (spād), *n.*, *v.*, **spaded, spading.** *—n.* **1.** a tool for digging, having an iron blade adapted for pressing into the ground with the foot, and a long handle commonly with a grip or crosspiece at the top. **2.** some implement, piece, or part resembling this. **3.** a sharp projection on a guncarriage embedded in the ground to restrict backward movement of the carriage during recoil. **4.** a cutting tool used to strip the blubber or skin, as from a whale. **5. call a spade a spade,** to call a thing by its real name; speak plainly or bluntly. *—v.t.* **6.** to dig, cut, or remove with a spade. [ME; OE *spadu*, c. G *Spaten*] **—spadeful** (spād′fŏŏl′), *n.*

spade[2] (spād), *n.* **1.** a black figure shaped like an inverted heart with a short stem at the cusp opposite the point, used on playing cards. **2.** a card of the suit bearing such figures. **3.** (*pl.*) the suit of cards bearing this figure. **4.** *Slang.* (used offensively) a Negro. [t. It., pl. of *spada*, orig., sword, later mark on cards, g. L *spatha*, t. Gk: m. *spáthē* wooden blade]

spadefoot (spād′fŏŏt′), *n.* any of several toads of the family *Pelobatidae*, widely distributed in Europe and Asia, usually in sandy areas, where they burrow into the earth for concealment.

spadework (spād′wûk′), *n.* preliminary or initial work, esp. of a laborious or tedious nature.

spadiceous (spā dĭsh′əs), *adj.* **1.** *Bot.* **a.** of the nature of a spadix. **b.** bearing a spadix. **2.** of a bright brown colour. [t. NL: m. *spādīceus*, der. L *spādix* SPADIX]

spadix (spā′dĭks), *n.*, *pl.* **spadices** (spādī′sēz). *Bot.* an inflorescence consisting of a spike with a fleshy or thickened axis, usually enclosed in a spathe. [t. L, t. Gk: torn-off palm bough, as adj., brown, palm-coloured]

A, Spadix
B, Spathe

spado (spā′dō), *n.*, *pl.* **spadones** (spə dō′nēz). an impotent or castrated man. [t. L, t. Gk: m. *spádōn* eunuch]

spae (spā), *v.t.*, *v.i.*, **spaed, spaeing.** *Scot. and N Dial.* to prophesy; predict. [ME *spa(n)*, t. Scand.; cf. Icel. *spá*]

spaghetti (spə gĕt′ĭ), *n.* a kind of pasta of Italian origin, usually made from durum wheat in the form of long, slender, cordlike pieces. [t. It., pl. of *spaghetto*, dim. of *spago* cord]

spagyric (spə jĭ′rĭk), *Rare.* *—adj.* **1.** pertaining to alchemy. *—n.* **2.** an alchemist. [t. NL: m. s. *spagiricus*, prob. coined by Paracelsus] **—spagyrist** (spăj′ĭ rĭst), *n.*

spahi (spä′hē, spä′ē), *n.*, *pl.* **-his. 1.** (formerly) one of a body of native Algerian cavalry in the French service. **2.** (formerly) a cavalryman in the Turkish army. Also, **spahee.** [t. Turk.: m. *sipāhī*, t. Pers.]

Spain (spān), *n.* a country in SW Europe. (Including the Balearic and Canary Islands) 30,903,137 pop. (1960); 194,883 sq. mi. *Cap.:* Madrid. Spanish, **España.** See map under **Barbary Coast.**

spake (spāk), *v. Archaic.* pt. of **speak.**

Spalato (*It.* spä′lä tō), *n.* Italian name of **Split.**

Spalding (spôl′dĭng), *n.* a town in England, in Lincolnshire. 14,821 (1961).

spall (spôl), *n.* **1.** a chip or splinter, as of stone or ore. *—v.t.* **2.** to break into smaller pieces, as ore; split or chip. *—v.i.* **3.** to break or split off in chips or bits. [ME *spalle* chip. Cf. E d. *spale* chip and *spald*, v., split, c. G *spalten*]

spallation (spə lā′shən), *n. Physics.* a nuclear reaction in which a high-energy incident particle, or photon, causes the struck nucleus to emit several particles or fragments.

spam (spăm), *n.* **1.** a kind of canned luncheon meat. **2.** (*cap.*) a trademark for this.

span[1] (spăn), *n.*, *v.*, **spanned, spanning.** *—n.* **1.** the distance between the tip of the thumb and the tip of the little finger when the hand is fully extended. **2.** a unit of length corresponding to this distance, commonly taken as 9 inches. **3.** a distance, amount, piece, etc., of this length or of some small extent. **4.** the distance or space between two supports of a bridge, beam, or similar structure. **5.** the full extent, stretch, or reach of anything: *the span of memory.* **6.** *Aeron.* the distance between the wingtips of an aeroplane. **7.** a short space of time, as the term or period of living. **8.** (*pl.*) *S African Colloq.* lots; great numbers; crowds: *spans and spans of people.* *—v.t.* **9.** to measure by, or as by, the hand with the thumb and little finger extended. **10.** to encircle with the hand or hands, as the waist. **11.** to extend over or across (a space, a river, etc.). **12.** to provide with something that extends over: *to span a river with a bridge.* **13.** to extend, reach, or pass over (space or time). [ME and OE, c. G *Spanne*]

span[2] (spăn), *n.* a pair of horses or other animals harnessed and driven together. [t. Flem., D, or LG, der. *spannen* fasten, unite] **—Syn.** See **pair.**

span[3] (spăn), *v. Archaic.* pt. of **spin.**

Span., Spanish.

Spandau (*Ger.* shpän′dou), *n.* a suburb of West Berlin: prison.

spandrel (spăn′drəl), *n. Archit.* **1.** the triangular space between either half of the extrados of an arch and a rectangular moulding or part enclosing the arch. **2.** the space included between the extradoses of two adjacent arches and a horizontal moulding or part above. [ME *spaundrell*, appar. dim. of AF *spaundre*; orig. uncert.]

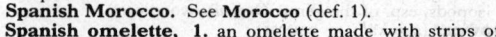

A, Spandrel (def. 1)
B, Spandrel (def. 2)

spangle (spăng′gl), *n.*, *v.*, **-gled, -gling.** *—n.* **1.** a small, thin, often circular piece of glittering material, as metal, for decorating garments, etc. **2.** any small, bright drop, object, spot, or the like. *—v.t.* **3.** to decorate with spangles. **4.** to sprinkle or stud with small, bright pieces, objects, spots, etc. *—v.i.* **5.** to glitter with, or like spangles. [ME *spangele*, f. *spange* spangle (t. MD) + *-le*, dim. suffix]

Spaniard (spăn′yəd), *n.* a native or inhabitant of Spain. [ME, t. OF: m. *Espaniard.* See -ARD]

spaniel (spăn′yəl), *n.* **1.** a dog of any of various breeds of small or medium size, usually with a long, silky coat and drooping ears; used in hunting and as pets. **2.** a submissive, fawning, or cringing person. [ME *spaynel*, t. OF: m. *espaigneul* Spanish (dog), g. L *Hispāniolus*]

Spanish (spăn′ĭsh), *adj.* **1.** of or pertaining to Spain, its people, or their language. *—n.* **2.** the Spanish people collectively. **3.** a Romance language, the language of Spain, standard also in Latin America (except Brazil).

Spanish America, the Spanish-speaking countries south of the United States: Mexico, Central America (except British Honduras), South America (except Brazil and the Guianas), and most of the West Indies.

Spanish-American (spăn′ĭsh ə mĕ′rĭ kən), *adj.* **1.** denoting or pertaining to the parts of America where Spanish is the prevailing language. **2.** pertaining to Spain and America, sometimes to Spain and the United States: *the Spanish-American War of 1898.* *—n.* **3.** a native or inhabitant of a Spanish-American country, esp. a person of Spanish descent.

Spanish Armada, Armada (def. 1).

Spanish bayonet, any of certain plants of the liliaceous genus *Yucca*, with narrow, spine-tipped leaves.

Spanish broom, a papilionaceous shrub with long rushlike stems and yellow flowers, *Spartium junceum*, a frequently cultivated native of S Europe.

Spanish chestnut, 1. a large, deciduous fagaceous tree, *Castanea sativa*, a native of S Europe and Asia Minor but frequently cultivated elsewhere for its edible nut and valuable timber. **2.** the nut itself. Also, **sweet chestnut.**

Spanish Civil War, the civil war in Spain, lasting from 1936–39 in which the republican government (supported by the Comintern and other left-wing and anarchist groups) was overthrown by the army led by General Franco (aided by fascist and other right-wing groups).

Spanish fly, a blister beetle, *Lytta vesicatoria*, which is dried and powdered to yield cantharides.

Spanish fly, *Lytta vesicatoria* (Ab. ¾ in. long)

Spanish Guinea, former name of **Equatorial Guinea.**

Spanish mackerel, any of various scombroid marine food fishes, as *Pneumatophorus colias* of the British Isles.

Spanish Main, 1. (formerly) the mainland of America adjacent to the Caribbean Sea, esp. between the mouth of the river Orinoco and the Isthmus of Panama. **2.** the Caribbean Sea: the route of the Spanish treasure galleons; a former haunt of pirates.

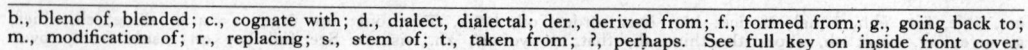

Spanish Morocco. See **Morocco** (def. 1).

Spanish omelette, 1. an omelette made with strips of

pimiento, garlic, and tomatoes and cooked like a pancake. 2. (in Spain) an omelette made with sauté potatoes.

Spanish onion, a large sized, mild, succulent onion.

Spanish rice, rice cooked with onions, herbs, and spices; served as a side-dish.

Spanish Sahara, a Spanish province in NW Africa. 23,793 pop. (1960); 102,680 sq. mi. *Cap.*: El Aiún. Formerly, **Río de Oro.**

Spanish Town, a town in SE Jamaica. 14,439 (1960).

spank[1] (spăngk), *v.t.* **1.** to strike (a person, usually a child) with the open hand, a slipper, etc., esp. on the buttocks, as in punishment. *—n.* **2.** a blow given in spanking; a smart or resounding slap. [imit.]

spank[2] (spăngk), *v.i.* to move quickly, vigorously, or smartly. [back-formation from SPANKING[1]]

spanker (spăng′kə), *n.* **1.** *Naut.* **a.** the lower fore-and-aft sail on the aftermost mast of a ship or barque. See illus. under **sail. b.** (on a schooner-rigged vessel having more than three masts) the fourth mast and sail counting aft from the bow. **2.** *Colloq.* a smartly moving animal, esp. a fast horse. **3.** *Dial.* anything exceptionally large, fine, or of superior quality. [f. SPANK[2] + -ER[1]]

spanking[1] (spăng′kĭng), *adj.* **1.** moving rapidly and smartly. **2.** quick and vigorous, as the pace. **3.** blowing briskly, as a breeze. **4.** *Colloq.* unusually fine, great, large, etc. *—adv.* **5.** remarkably; very. [cf. Dan. *spanke* strut]

spanking[2] (spăng′kĭng), *n.* **1.** the act of one who spanks. **2.** this act administered as a punishment.

span-loading (spăn′ lō′dĭng), *n. Aeron.* See **loading** (def. 4).

spanner (spăn′ə), *n.* **1.** one who or that which spans. **2.** a tool for catching upon or gripping and turning or twisting the head of a bolt, a nut, a pipe, or the like, commonly consisting of a bar of metal with fixed or adjustable jaws. **3. spanner in the works,** *Colloq.* any cause of confusion or impediment. [t. G]

span roof, *Bldg Trades.* a roof having two equally inclined sloping sides.

spar[1] (spä), *n.*, *v.*, **sparred, sparring.** *—n.* **1.** *Naut.* a stout pole such as those used for masts, etc.; a mast, yard, boom, gaff, or the like. **2.** *Aeron.* a principal lateral member of the framework of a wing of an aeroplane. *—v.t.* **3.** to provide or make with spars. [ME *sparre.* Cf. G *sparren,* Icel. *sperra* rafter]

spar[2] (spä), *v.*, **sparred, sparring,** *n.* *—v.i.* **1.** *Boxing.* **a.** to make the motions of attack and defence with the arms and fists; practise boxing. **b.** to box with light blows, esp. while seeking an opening in an opponent's defence. **2.** to strike or fight with the feet or spurs, as cocks, etc. **3.** to bandy words; dispute. *—n.* **4.** a motion of sparring. **5.** a boxing match. **6.** a dispute. [ME; orig. meaning thrust (n. and v.); orig. uncert.]

spar[3] (spä), *n.* any of various more or less lustrous crystalline minerals, as fluorspar. [back-formation from *sparstone* spar, OE *spærstan* gypsum. Cf. MLG *spar*]

sparable (spă′rə bl), *n.* a small, headless nail used by shoemakers. [var. of *sparrow bill*]

spar buoy, *Naut.* a buoy shaped like a log or spar, anchored vertically. See illus. under **buoy.**

spar deck, *Naut.* the upper deck of a vessel, extending from stem to stern. See diag. under **forecastle.**

spare (spēə), *v.*, **spared, sparing,** *adj.*, **sparer, sparest,** *n.* *—v.t.* **1.** to refrain from harming or destroying; leave uninjured; forbear to punish: *to spare a fallen adversary.* **2.** to deal gently or leniently with; show consideration for: *to spare a person's feelings.* **3.** to save from strain, discomfort, annoyance, or the like, or from a particular cause of it: *to spare oneself trouble.* **4.** to refrain from, forbear, omit, or withhold, as action or speech. **5.** to refrain from employing, as some instrument, means, aid, etc.: *to spare the rod.* **6.** to set aside for a particular purpose: *to spare land for a garden.* **7.** to part with or let go, as from a supply, esp. without inconvenience or loss: *to spare a few coppers.* **8.** to dispense with or do without. **9.** to use economically or frugally; refrain from using up or wasting. **10.** to have left over or unused: *we have food for ten and to spare.* *—v.i.* **11.** to use economy; be frugal. **12.** to refrain from action; forbear. **13.** to refrain from inflicting injury or punishment; exercise lenience or mercy. *—adj.* **14.** kept in reserve, as for possible use: *a spare tyre.* **15.** being in excess of present need; free for other use: *spare time.* **16.** frugally restricted; meagre, as living, diet, etc. **17.** lean or thin, as a person. **18.** scanty or scant, as in amount, fullness, etc. **19.** sparing, economical, or temperate, as persons. *—n.* **20.** a spare thing, part, etc., as an extra tyre for emergency use. **21.** *Tenpin Bowling.* **a.** the knocking down of all the pins in two consecutive bowls. **b.** the score made by bowling a spare. [ME; OE *sparian,* c. D and G *sparen*] **—spare′ly,** *adv.* **—spare′ness,** *n.* **—spar′er,** *n.* **—Syn. 17.** See **thin.**

sparerib (spēə′rĭb′), *n.* a cut of pork containing ribs from the upper or fore end of the row, where there is little meat adhering. [transposed var. of *ribspare,* t. MHG: m. *ribbespēr* rib cut. Cf. E *spare,* n., cut, slit]

sparge (späj), *v.t.*, *v.i.*, **sparged, sparging.** to scatter or sprinkle. [t. L: m. s. *spargere* sprinkle] **—sparg′er,** *n.*

sparing (spēə′rĭng), *adj.* **1.** that spares. **2.** economical (*in*); chary (*of*). **3.** lenient or merciful. **4.** frugally restricted. **5.** scanty; limited. **—spar′ingly,** *adv.*

spark[1] (späk), *n.* **1.** an ignited or fiery particle such as is thrown off by burning wood, etc., or produced by one hard body striking against another. **2.** *Elect.* **a.** the light produced by a sudden discontinuous discharge of electricity through air or another dielectric. **b.** the discharge itself. **c.** any electric arc of relatively small energy content. **d.** such a spark in the sparking plug of an internal-combustion engine. **e.** the arrangement of devices producing and governing this spark. **3.** a small amount or trace of something. **4.** a trace of life or vitality. *—v.i.* **5.** to emit or produce sparks. **6.** to issue as or like sparks. **7.** to send forth gleams or flashes. **8.** (of the ignition in an internal-combustion engine) to function correctly in forming the sparks. *—v.t.* **9.** *Colloq.* to kindle or stimulate (interest, activity, etc.). **10. spark off,** to bring about; cause; precipitate. [ME; OE *spearca,* c. MD and MLG *sparke*]

spark[2] (späk), *n.* **1.** a gay, elegant, or showily dressed young man. **2.** a beau, lover, or suitor. *—v.t.* **3.** *U.S. Colloq.* to pay attentions to (a woman); court. *—v.i.* **4.** *U.S. Colloq.* to engage in courtship; be the beau or suitor. [either fig. use of SPARK[1]; or metathetic var. of *sprack* lively, t. Scand.; cf. Icel. *sprækr* sprightly] **—spark′-ish,** *adj.*

Spark (späk), *n.* **Muriel Sarah,** born 1918, Scottish novelist.

spark coil, *Elect.* a coil of many turns of insulated wire on an iron core, used for producing sparks.

sparker (spä′kə), *n.* **1.** something that produces sparks. **2.** an apparatus used to test insulation on wires.

spark gap, *Elect.* a space between two electrodes across which a discharge of electricity may take place.

spark generator, an alternating current power source with a capacitor discharging across a spark gap.

sparking plug, a device inserted in the cylinder of an internal-combustion engine, containing two terminals between which passes the electric spark for igniting the explosive gases. Also, **spark plug.**

sparking potential, *Elect.* the difference in potential required to make a spark pass across a given gap. Also, **sparking voltage.**

sparkle (spä′kl), *v.*, **-kled, -kling,** *n.* *—v.i.* **1.** to issue in or as in little sparks, as fire, light, etc. **2.** to emit little sparks, as burning matter. **3.** to shine with little gleams of light, as a brilliant gem; glisten brightly; glitter. **4.** to effervesce, as wine. **5.** to be brilliant, lively, or vivacious. *—v.t.* **6.** to cause to sparkle. *—n.* **7.** a little spark or fiery particle. **8.** a sparkling appearance, lustre, or play of light: *the sparkle of a diamond.* **9.** brilliance; liveliness or vivacity. [freq. of SPARK[1]] **—Syn. 3.** See **glisten.**

sparkler (spä′klə), *n.* **1.** one who or that which sparkles. **2.** a firework that emits little sparks. **3.** a sparkling gem. **4.** *Colloq.* a bright eye.

spark photography, photography using a spark as a source of illumination when a very brief exposure is required, as for photographing fast-moving objects, etc.

sparks (späks), *n. Slang.* a radio operator or electrician.

spark transmitter, *Radio.* a transmitting set which generates electromagnetic waves because of the characteristic of a spark gap and a tuned circuit through which energy can surge.

sparling (spä′lĭng), *n.* the European smelt, *Osmerus eperlanus.* [ME *sperlyng(e),* t. OF: m. *esperlinge,* of Gmc orig.]

sparoid (spă′roid), *adj.* **1.** resembling a sea-bream. **2.** belonging or pertaining to the *Sparidae,* a family of deep-bodied fishes including the sea-breams. *—n.* **3.** a sparoid fish. [t. NL: s. *sparoīdēs,* der. L *sparus,* t. Gk: m. *spáros* kind of fish. See -OID]

sparrow (spă′rō), *n.* **1.** a small, hardy, pugnacious weaverbird, *Passer domesticus,* of Europe, introduced into Australia, America, etc., as a destroyer of insects, but now commonly regarded as a pest; house sparrow. **2.** any of various weaverbirds (family *Ploceidae*) of the Old World. **3.** any of numerous American finches (family *Fringillidae*), as the **chipping sparrow** (*Spizella passerina*). [ME *sparowe,* OE *spearwa,* c. Goth. *sparwa,* Icel. *spörr*]

sparrowgrass (spă′rō gräs′), *n. Colloq.* asparagus.

sparrowhawk (spă′rō hôk′), *n.* **1.** a small, short-winged European hawk, *Accipiter nisus,* which preys extensively on birds. **2.** a small American falcon, *Falco sparverius,* which preys especially on grasshoppers, small mammals, etc.

sparry (spä′rĭ), *adj.* of or pertaining to mineral spar.

sparse (späs), *adj.*, **sparser, sparsest. 1.** thinly scattered or distributed: *a sparse population.* **2.** thin; not thick or dense: *sparse hair.* **3.** scanty; meagre. [t. L: m. s. *sparsus*, pp., scattered] —**sparse′ly,** *adv.* —**sparse′ness, sparsity** (spä′sĭ tĭ), *n.* —**Syn. 1.** See **scanty.**

Sparta (spä′tə), *n.* an ancient city in S Greece: the capital of Laconia and the chief city of the Peloponnesus; at one time the dominant city of Greece; famous for strict discipline and training of soldiers. Also, **Lacedaemon.**

Sparta

Spartacus (spä′tə kəs), *n.* died 71 B.C., a Thracian who became a slave and gladiator in Italy, and leader of an insurrection of slaves.

Spartan (spä′tn), *adj.* **1.** of or pertaining to Sparta or its people. **2.** suggestive of the ancient Spartans; rigorously simple, frugal, or austere; sternly disciplined; brave. —*n.* **3.** a native or inhabitant of Sparta. **4.** a person of Spartan characteristics. —**Spar′tanism,** *n.*

sparteine (spä′tĭ ēn′, -ĭn), *n.* a bitter, poisonous, liquid alkaloid, $C_{15}H_{26}N_2$, obtained from the common broom, *Cytisus scoparius*, used in medicine. [f. m. s. NL *spartium* genus of broom (der. Gk *spártos* broom) + -INE [2]]

spasm (spăz′əm), *n.* **1.** *Pathol.* a sudden, abnormal, involuntary muscular contraction; an affection consisting of a continued muscular contraction (**tonic spasm**), or of a series of alternating muscular contractions and relaxations (**clonic spasm**). **2.** any sudden, brief spell of great energy, activity, feeling, etc. [ME *spasme*, t. L: m. *spasmus* or *spasma*, t. Gk: m. *spasmós* or *spásma*]

spasmodic (spăz mŏd′ĭk), *adj.* **1.** pertaining to or of the nature of a spasm; characterized by spasms. **2.** resembling a spasm or spasms; sudden and violent, but brief; intermittent: *spasmodic efforts.* **3.** given to or characterized by bursts of excitement. Also, **spasmod′ical.** [t. ML: s. *spasmodicus*, der. Gk *spasmṓdēs*] —**spasmod′ically,** *adv.*

spastic (spăs′tĭk), *Pathol.* —*adj.* **1.** pertaining to, of the nature of, or characterized by spasm, esp. tonic spasm. —*n.* **2.** a person exhibiting such spasms, esp. one who has cerebral palsy. [t. L: s. *spasticus*, t. Gk: m. *spastikós*] —**spas′tically,** *adv.*

spat[1] (spăt), *n.*, *v.*, **spatted, spatting.** —*n.* **1.** a light blow; a slap; a smack. **2.** *U.S.* a petty quarrel. —*v.i.* **3.** to slap. **4.** *U.S.* to engage in a petty quarrel or dispute. **5.** to splash; spatter. —*v.t.* **6.** to strike lightly; slap. [prob. imit.]

spat[2] (spăt), *v.* pt. and pp. of **spit.**

spat[3] (spăt), *n.* (*usually pl.*) a short gaiter worn over the instep, usually fastened under the foot with a strap. [short for SPATTERDASH]

spat[4] (spăt), *n.* **1.** the spawn of an oyster or similar shellfish. **2.** young oysters collectively. **3.** a young oyster. [orig. uncert.; ? akin to SPIT [1], v.]

spate (spāt), *n.* **1.** a sudden, almost overwhelming, outpouring: *a spate of words.* **2.** a flood or inundation; a state of flood. **3.** a sudden heavy downpour of rain. [ME; orig. obscure]

spathaceous (spə thā′shəs), *adj.* *Bot.* **1.** of the nature of or resembling a spathe. **2.** having a spathe.

spathe (spāth), *n.* *Bot.* a bract or pair of bracts, often large and coloured, subtending or enclosing a spadix or flower cluster. See **spadix.** [t. Gk: sword blade] —**spathed,** *adj.* —**spathose** (spā′thōs, spăth′ōs), *adj.*

spathic (spăth′ĭk), *adj.* *Mineral.* like spar. Also, **spathose** (spăth′ōs). [f. G *Spath* spar + -IC]

spatial (spā′shəl), *adj.* **1.** of or pertaining to space. **2.** existing or occurring in space; having extension in space. [f. s. L *spatium* SPACE + -AL [1]] —**spatiality** (spā′shĭ ăl′ĭ tĭ), *n.* —**spa′tially,** *adv.*

spatio-, a word element meaning space. [f. s. L *spatium* SPACE + -O-]

spatter (spăt′ə), *v.t.* **1.** to scatter or dash in small particles or drops: *to spatter mud.* **2.** to splash with something in small particles: *to spatter the ground with water.* **3.** to sprinkle or spot with something that soils or stains. —*v.i.* **4.** to send out small particles or drops, as boiling matter. **5.** to strike as in a shower, as bullets. —*n.* **6.** the act or the sound of spattering: *the spatter of rain on a roof.* **7.** a splash or spot of something spattered. [appar. a freq. of D and LG *spatten* burst, spout] —**spat′teringly,** *adv.*

spatterdash (spăt′ə dăsh′), *n.* **1.** (*usually pl.*) a kind of long gaiter worn to protect the trousers or stockings from mud, etc., as in riding. **2.** *Bldg Trades.* a cement and sand mixture thrown on to a wall as a primer for a first coat of plaster. [f. SPATTER + DASH]

spatterdock (spăt′ə dŏk′), *n.* **1.** a coarse yellow-flowered pond lily, *Nuphar advena*, common in stagnant waters. **2.** any pond lily of genera *Nymphaea* and *Nuphar*, esp. one with yellow flowers.

spatula (spăt′yo͞o lə), *n.* an implement with a broad, flat, flexible blade, used for blending foods, mixing drugs, spreading plasters and paints, etc. [t. L, var. of *spathula*, dim. of *spatha.* See SPADE [2]] —**spat′ular,** *adj.*

spatulate (spăt′yo͞o lĭt), *adj.* **1.** shaped like a spatula; rounded more or less like a spoon. **2.** *Bot.* having a broad, rounded end and a narrow, attenuate base, as a leaf.

Spatulate leaf

spavin (spăv′ĭn), *n.* *Vet. Sci.* **1.** any disease of the hock joint of horses in which enlargements occur, after causing lameness. The enlargement may be due to collection of fluids (**bog spavin**) or to bony growth (**bone spavin**). **2.** an excrescence or enlargement so formed. [ME *spaveyne*, t. OF: m. *espavain*; orig. obscure] —**spav′ined,** *adj.*

spawn (spôn), *n.* **1.** *Zool.* the mass of sex cells of fishes, amphibians, molluscs, crustaceans, etc., after being emitted. **2.** *Bot.* the mycelium of mushrooms, esp. of the species grown for the market. **3.** (usually disparaging) **a.** a swarming brood or numerous progeny. **b.** any person or thing regarded as the offspring of some stock, idea, etc. —*v.i.* **4.** to shed the sex cells, esp. as applied to animals that shed eggs and sperm directly into water. —*v.t.* **5.** to produce (spawn). **6.** to give birth to; give rise to. **7.** (usually disparaging) to produce in large numbers, or with excessive fecundity. **8.** to plant with mycelium. [ME, t. AF: m. *espaundre* spill, g. L *expandere* expand] —**spawn′er,** *n.*

spay (spā), *v.t.* to remove the ovaries of (a female animal). [ME, t. AF: m. s. *espeier* cut with a sword, der. *espee* sword. See ÉPÉE]

speak (spēk), *v.*, **spoke** or (*Archaic*) **spake; spoken** or (*Archaic*) **spoke; speaking.** —*v.i.* **1.** to utter words or articulate sounds with the ordinary (talking) voice. **2.** to make oral communication or mention: *to speak to a person of various matters.* **3.** to converse. **4.** to deliver an address, discourse, etc. **5.** to make a statement in written or printed words. **6.** to make communication or disclosure by any means; convey significance. **7.** to emit a sound, as a musical instrument; make a noise or report. **8.** (of hunting dogs) to give tongue; bay. —*v.t.* **9.** to utter orally and articulately: *to speak words of praise.* **10.** to express or make known with the voice: *to speak the truth.* **11.** to declare in writing or printing, or by any means of communication. **12.** to make known, indicate, or reveal. **13.** to use, or be able to use, in oral utterance, as a language: *to speak French.* **14.** *Naut.* to communicate with (a passing vessel, etc.) at sea, as by voice or signal. **15.** *Archaic.* to speak to or with. —*v.* **16.** Some special verb phrases are:

so to speak, to use a certain way of speaking; as one might say.

speak for, 1. to recommend; intercede for; to act as spokesman for. **2.** to reserve; bespeak: *this dress is already spoken for.*

speak for oneself, to express only one's own views.

speak for yourself, (an expression of disagreement.)

speak of, worth mentioning: *he has no money to speak of.*

speak out, to express one's views openly and without reserve.

speak up, to speak loudly and clearly.

speak well for, to be favourable evidence for.

[ME *spek(en)*, OE *specan*, unexplained var. of *sprecan*, c. G *sprechen*] —**speak′able,** *adj.*

—**Syn. 1.** SPEAK, CONVERSE, TALK mean to make vocal sounds, usually for purposes of communication. To SPEAK is to utter one or more words, not necessarily connected; it usually implies conveying intelligence, and may apply to anything from a few informal words to delivering a formal address before an audience: *to speak sharply.* To CONVERSE is to exchange ideas with someone by speaking: *to converse with a friend.* To TALK is to utter intelligible sounds without regard to content: *the child is learning to talk.*

speak-easy (spēk′ē′zĭ), *n.*, *pl.* **-easies.** *U.S.* a place where alcoholic drinks are illegally sold, esp. between 1919 and 1933 when prohibition was in force.

speaker (spē′kə), *n.* **1.** one who speaks. **2.** one who speaks formally before an audience; an orator. **3.** (*usually cap.*) the presiding officer of the House of Commons, of the U.S. House of Representatives, or some other similar assembly. **4.** a loudspeaker. **5.** *U.S.* a book of selections for practice in declamation. —**speak′ership′,** *n.*

speaking (spē′kĭng), *n.* **1.** the act, utterance, or discourse of one who speaks. —*adj.* **2.** that speaks; giving information as if by speech: *a speaking proof of a thing.* **3.** highly expressive. **4.** lifelike: *a speaking likeness.* **5.** used in, suited to, or involving speaking or talking: *the speaking voice.* **6.** permitting of speaking, as in greeting or conversation: *they are no longer on speaking terms.* **7.** of or pertaining to declamation.

speaking trumpet, 1. a trumpet-shaped device for amplifying sounds, held to the ear by a deaf person to enable him to hear better. **2.** a megaphone.

speaking tube, a tube for conveying the voice to a distance, as from one part of a building to another.

spear[1] (spĭə), *n.* **1.** a weapon for thrusting or throwing, consisting of a long wooden staff to which a sharp head, as of iron or steel, is fixed. **2.** a soldier or other person armed with such a weapon. **3.** some similar weapon or instrument, as one for spearing fish. **4.** the act of spearing. —*v.t.* **5.** to pierce with or as with a spear. —*v.i.* **6.** to go or penetrate like a spear. [ME and OE *spere,* c. D *speer,* G *Speer*] —**spear′er,** *n.*

spear[2] (spĭə), *n.* **1.** a sprout or shoot of a plant; an acrospire of grain; a blade of grass, etc. —*v.i.* **2.** to sprout; shoot; send up or rise in a spear or spears. [var. of SPIRE[1], ? influenced by SPEAR[1]]

spearfish (spĭə′fĭsh′), *n., pl.* **-fishes,** *(esp. collectively)* **-fish.** a marlin.

spear-grass (spĭə′gräs′), *n.* **1.** a perennial umbelliferous plant of New Zealand, *Aciphylla squarrosa,* having a large basal rosette of stiff, narrow leaves about 2 ft long and inflorescences up to 9 ft high. **2.** any of various other grasses, esp. couch-grass, *Agropyron repens.*

spearhead (spĭə′hĕd′), *n.* **1.** the sharp-pointed head which forms the piercing end of a spear. **2.** any person or thing that leads an attack, undertaking, etc. —*v.t.* **3.** to act as a spearhead for.

spearman (spĭə′mən), *n., pl.* **-men.** one who is armed with or uses a spear.

spearmint (spĭə′mĭnt′), *n.* the common garden mint, *Mentha spicata,* an aromatic herb much used for flavouring. [f. SPEAR[1] + MINT[1]]

spear side, the male side, or line of descent, of a family (opposed to *distaff side*).

spearwort (spĭə′wût′), *n.* any of certain ranunculaceous herbs of wet places with long narrow leaves as the **lesser spearwort,** *Ranunculus flammula,* and the **greater spearwort,** *R. lingua.*

spec (spĕk), *n. Colloq.* **1.** speculation. **2. on spec,** as a guess, risk, or gamble: *to buy shares on spec.*

spec., 1. special. 2. specially. 3. specification.

special (spĕsh′əl), *adj.* **1.** of a distinct or particular kind or character: *a special kind of key.* **2.** being a particular one; particular, individual, or certain: *a special day.* **3.** pertaining or peculiar to a particular person, thing, instance, etc.: *the special features of a plan.* **4.** having a particular function, purpose, application, etc.: *a special messenger.* **5.** dealing with particulars, or specific, as a statement. **6.** distinguished or different from what is ordinary or usual: *a special occasion.* **7.** extraordinary; exceptional; exceptional in amount or degree; especial: *special importance.* **8.** great; being such in an exceptional degree: *a special friend.* —*n.* **9.** a special person or thing. **10.** a special train. **11.** a special edition of a newspaper. **12.** a special constable. [ME, t. L: s. *speciālis*] —**spec′ially,** *adv.*

—**Syn. 6.** SPECIAL, PARTICULAR, SPECIFIC refer to something pointed out for attention and consideration. SPECIAL means given unusual treatment because of being uncommon: *a special sense of a word.* PARTICULAR implies something selected from the others of its kind and set off from them for attention: *a particular variety of orchid.* SPECIFIC implies plain and unambiguous indication of a particular instance, example, etc.: *a specific instance of cowardice.* —**Ant. 1.** general.

special constable, a man temporarily or periodically serving as a policeman, in time of emergency, for extra duties, etc.

special delivery, a delivery of mail outside normal hours, on payment of an extra fee.

specialism (spĕsh′ə lĭz′əm), *n.* devotion or restriction to a special branch of study, etc.

specialist (spĕch′ə lĭst), *n.* **1.** one who devotes himself to one subject, or to one particular branch of a subject or pursuit. **2.** a medical practitioner who devotes his attention to a particular class of diseases, etc. **3.** *U.S. Army.* a soldier with special technical qualifications ranking below a corporal. —**spec′ialis′tic,** *adj.*

speciality (spĕsh′ĭ ăl′ĭ tĭ), *n., pl.* **-ties. 1.** special or particular character. **2.** a special or distinctive quality or characteristic; a peculiarity. **3.** a special point or item; a particular; detail. **4.** a special subject of study, line of work, or the like. **5.** an article particularly dealt in, manufactured, etc., or one to which the dealer or manufacturer professes to devote special care. **6.** an article of unusual or superior design or quality. **7.** a novelty; a new article. **8.** an article with such strong consumer demand that it is at least partially removed from price competition. Also, **specialty.** [ME *specialite,* t. OF: m. (*e*)*specialite, t.* LL: m. s. *speciālitas*]

specialize (spĕsh′ə līz′), *v.,* **-lized, -lizing.** —*v.i.* **1.** to pursue some special line of study, work, etc.; make a speciality. **2.** *Biol.* to become specialized. —*v.t.* **3.** to render special or specific; invest with a special character, function, etc. **4.** to adapt to special conditions; restrict to specific limits. **5.** to restrict payment of (a negotiable instrument) by endorsing over to a specific payee. **6.** *Biol.* to modify or differentiate (an organism or one of its organs) to adapt it to a special function or environment. **7.** to specify; particularize. Also, **specialise.** —**spec′ializa′tion,** *n.*

special licence, a licence granted by the Archbishop of Canterbury authorizing a marriage at any time or place.

special partner, *U.S.* a limited partner.

special pleading, 1. *Law.* pleading that alleges special or new matter in avoidance of the allegations made by the opposite side. **2.** pleading or arguing that ignores unfavourable features of a case.

special school, a school providing education for children suffering from some physical or mental disability.

special sort, *Print.* a printing character not normally found in a type fount, as an accented letter, etc.; a peculiar; an arbitrary.

special theory of relativity, *Physics.* that part of the theory of relativity which applies to observers in uniform motion.

specialty (spĕsh′əl tĭ), *n., pl.* **-ties. 1.** *Law.* **a.** a special agreement, contract, etc., expressed in an instrument under seal. **b.** a negotiable instrument not under seal. **2.** speciality. [ME *specialte,* t. OF: m. (*e*)*specialte,* var. of (*e*)*specialite* SPECIALITY]

specie (spē′shē), *n.* **1.** coin; coined money. **2. in specie, a.** in kind. **b.** (of money) in actual coin. [t. L, abl. sing. of *species* SPECIES]

species (spē′shēz; *Lat.* spē′shĭ ēz′), *n., pl.* **-cies. 1.** a group of individuals having some common characteristics or qualities; distinct sort or kind. **2.** the basic category of biological classification, intended to designate a single kind of animal or plant, any variations existing among the individuals being regarded as not affecting the essential sameness which distinguishes them from all other organisms. **3.** *Logic.* **a.** any group contained in a next larger group (the genus). **b.** the sum of those qualities of such a contained group that are common to all members of the group and are sufficient to identify it, i.e. to specify its members. **4.** *Eccles.* **a.** the external form or appearance of the bread or the wine in the Eucharist. **b.** either of the Eucharistic elements. **5.** *Obs.* specie. [t. L: appearance, sort]

specif., 1. specific. 2. specifically.

specifiable (spĕs′ĭ fī′ə bl), *adj.* that may be specified.

specific (spĭ sĭf′ĭk), *adj.* **1.** having a special application, bearing, or reference; specifying, explicit, or definite: *specific mention.* **2.** specified, precise, or particular: *a specific sum of money.* **3.** peculiar or proper to something, as qualities, characteristics, effects, etc. **4.** of a special or particular kind. **5.** *Zool., Bot.* of or pertaining to a species: *specific characters.* **6.** *Med.* **a.** (of a disease) produced by a special cause or infection. **b.** (of a remedy) having special effect in the prevention or cure of a certain disease. **7.** *Com.* denoting customs or duties levied in fixed amounts per unit (number, volume, weight, etc.). —*n.* **8.** something specific, as a statement, quality, etc. **9.** *Med.* a specific remedy. [t. ML: s. *specificus,* der. L *species*] —**specif′ically,** *adv.* —**specificity** (spĕs′ĭ fĭs′ĭ tĭ), *n.*

—**Syn. 1.** See **special.** —**Ant. 2.** vague.

specific activity, *Physics.* **1.** the activity per unit mass of a pure radioactive isotope. **2.** the activity of a radioactive isotope in a material per unit mass of that material.

specification (spĕs′ĭ fĭ kā′shən), *n.* **1.** the act of specifying. **2.** a statement of particulars; a detailed description setting forth the dimensions, materials, etc., for a proposed building, engineering work, or the like. **3.** something specified, as in a bill of particulars; a specified particular, item, or article. **4.** the act of making specific. **5.** the state of having a specific character.

specific charge, *Physics.* the charge to mass ratio of an elementary particle.

specific gravity, *Physics.* the ratio of the mass of a given volume of any substance to that of the same volume of some other substance taken as a standard, water being the standard for solids and liquids, and hydrogen or air for gases; relative density.

specific heat, *Physics.* **1.** the heat required to raise unit mass of a substance through one degree of temperature, expressed in joules per kilogram per kelvin, calories per gram per degree C, or B.T.U.s per pound per degree F. **2.** (orig.) the ratio of the heat capacity of a substance to that of some standard material.

specific impulse, *Aeron.* a measure of the efficiency of a rocket propellant equal to the ratio of the thrust produced (in pounds) to the rate of consumption (in pounds per second); the length of time one pound of propellant would last if expended at a rate which would produce a continuous and uniform thrust of one pound.

specific thermal conductivity. See **thermal conductivity.**

specific volume, *Physics.* the volume occupied by one gram of a substance at a specified temperature and pressure; the reciprocal of density.

specify (spĕs′ĭ fī′), *v.*, **-fied, -fying.** —*v.t.* **1.** to mention or name specifically or definitely; state in detail. **2.** to give a specific character to. **3.** to name or state as a condition. —*v.i.* **4.** to make a specific mention or statement. [ME, t. ML: m. *specificāre,* der. *specificus* specific, der. L *species* sort, kind]

specimen (spĕs′ĭ mĭn), *n.* **1.** a part or an individual taken as exemplifying a whole mass or number; a typical animal, plant, mineral, part, etc. **2.** *Med.* a sample of a substance to be examined or tested for a specific purpose. **3.** *Colloq.* a person as a specified kind, or in some respect a peculiar kind, of human being. [t. L] —**Syn. 1.** See **example.**

speciosity (spē′shĭ ŏs′ĭ tĭ), *n.*, *pl.* **-ties. 1.** the state of being specious or plausible. **2.** something pleasing to the eye but deceptive. **3.** *Obs.* the state of being beautiful.

specious (spē′shəs), *adj.* **1.** apparently good or right but without real merit; superficially pleasing: *specious arguments.* **2.** pleasing to the eye, but deceptive. **3.** *Obs.* pleasing to the eye; fair. [ME, t. L: m. s. *speciōsus* fair, fair-seeming, der. *species* sort, kind] —**spe′ciously,** *adv.* —**spe′ciousness,** *n.* —**Syn. 1.** See **plausible.** —**Ant. 1.** genuine.

speck (spĕk), *n.* **1.** a small spot differing in colour or substance from that of the surface or material upon which it appears. **2.** a very little bit or particle. **3.** something appearing small by comparison or by distance. —*v.t.* **4.** to mark with, or as with, a speck or specks. [ME *specke,* OE *specca*]

speckle (spĕk′l), *n.*, *v.*, **-led, -ling.** —*n.* **1.** a small speck, spot, or mark, as on skin. **2.** speckled colouring or marking. —*v.t.* **3.** to mark with, or as with, speckles. [f. SPECK + *-le,* dim. and freq. suffix]

specs (spĕks), *n.pl. Colloq.* spectacles; glasses.

spectacle (spĕk′tə kl), *n.* **1.** anything presented to the sight or view, esp. something of a striking kind. **2.** a public show or display, esp. on a large scale. **3.** (*pl.*) a device to aid defective vision or to protect the eyes from light, dust, etc., consisting usually of two glass lenses set in a frame which rests on the nose and is held in place by pieces passing over or around the ears (often called **a pair of spectacles**). **4.** (*often pl.*) something resembling spectacles in shape or function. **5.** (*often pl.*) any of various devices suggesting spectacles, as one attached to a semaphore to display lights of different colours by coloured glass. **6. make a spectacle of oneself,** to draw attention to oneself by unseemly behaviour. [ME, t. L: m. *spectāculum*]

spectacled (spĕk′tə kld), *adj.* **1.** provided with or wearing spectacles. **2.** *Zool.* having a marking resembling a pair of spectacles.

spectacular (spĕk tăk′yŏŏ lə), *adj.* **1.** pertaining to or of the nature of a spectacle; marked by or given to great display. **2.** dramatic; thrilling. —*n.* **3.** a lavishly produced film, television show, etc. —**spectac′ularly,** *adv.*

spectator (spĕk tā′tə), *n.* **1.** one who looks on; an onlooker. **2.** one who is present at and views a spectacle or the like. [t. L]

spectra (spĕk′trə), *n.* pl. of **spectrum.**

spectral (spĕk′trəl), *adj.* **1.** pertaining to or characteristic of a spectre; of the nature of a spectre. **2.** resembling or suggesting a spectre. **3.** of, pertaining to, or produced by a spectrum or spectra. —**spectrality** (spĕk trăl′ĭ tĭ), *n.* —**spec′trally,** *adv.*

spectral classification, *Astron.* a method of classifying stars, according to their emission spectra, into ten major classes.

spectral series, *Physics.* a series of lines in the emission spectrum of a substance, each line representing a particular energy level of an atom of an element.

spectre (spĕk′tə), *n.* **1.** a visible incorporeal spirit, esp. one of a terrifying nature; ghost; phantom; apparition. **2.** some object or source of terror or dread. Also, *U.S.,* **specter.** [t. L: m. s. *spectrum* apparition] —**Syn. 1.** See **ghost.**

spectro-, a word element representing **spectrum.**

spectrobolometer (spĕk′trō bō lŏm′ĭ tə), *n. Physics.* a combined spectroscope and bolometer, for determining the distribution of radiant heat or energy in a spectrum.

spectrogram (spĕk′trō grăm′), *n. Physics.* a representation or photograph of a spectrum.

spectrograph (spĕk′trō grăf′, -gräf′), *n. Physics.* **1.** a spectrogram. **2.** an apparatus for making a spectrogram.

spectroheliogram (spĕk′trō hē′lĭ ə grăm′), *n. Astron.* a photograph of the sun made with a spectroheliograph.

spectroheliograph (spĕk′trō hē′lĭ ə grăf′, -gräf′), *n. Astron.* an apparatus for making photographs of the sun with monochromatic light, to show the details of the sun's surface and surroundings as they would appear if only that one kind of light were emitted.

spectrometer (spĕk trŏm′ĭ tə), *n. Physics.* any of certain optical instruments for observing a spectrum and measuring the deviation of refracted rays, used for determining wavelengths, angles between faces of a prism, etc.

spectrophotometer (spĕk′trō fō tŏm′ĭ tə), *n. Physics.* an instrument for making photometric comparisons between parts of spectra. —**spec′trophotom′etry,** *n.*

spectroscope (spĕk′trə skōp′), *n. Physics.* an optical instrument for producing and examining the spectrum of the light or radiation from any source. —**spectroscopic** (spĕk′trə skŏp′ĭk), **spec′troscop′ical,** *adj.* —**spec′troscop′ically,** *adv.*

spectroscopy (spĕk trŏs′kə pĭ), *n. Physics.* the science dealing with the use of the spectroscope and with spectrum analysis. —**spectroscopist** (spĕk trŏs′kə pĭst), *n.*

spectrum (spĕk′trəm), *n.*, *pl.* **-tra** (-trə), **-trums.** *Physics.* **1.** the band of colours, or the coloured lines or bands, formed when a beam of light from a luminous body or incandescent gas undergoes dispersion by being passed through a prism or reflected from a diffraction grating; the series of colours, passing by insensible degrees from red to violet (ordinarily described as red, orange, yellow, green, blue, indigo and violet), produced when white light (as sunlight) is passed through a prism, the white light being dispersed into rays of different colour and wavelength, the rays of longest wavelength producing the colour red, and the rays of shortest wavelength producing the colour violet. **2.** this band or series of colours together with extensions at the ends which are not visible to the eye, but which are studied by means of photography, heat effects, etc., and which are produced by the dispersion of radiant energy other than ordinary light rays. **3.** any wide range of interrelated ideas, objects, beliefs, etc. [t. L: appearance, form]

spectrum analysis, *Physics.* the determination of the constitution or condition of bodies and substances by means of the spectra they produce. Also, **spectrographic analysis.**

specular (spĕk′yŏŏ lə), *adj.* **1.** pertaining to, or having the properties of, a mirror. **2.** pertaining to a speculum. [t. L: s. *speculāris* of or like a mirror]

speculate (spĕk′yŏŏ lāt′), *v.i.*, **-lated, -lating. 1.** to engage in thought or reflection, or meditate (often fol. by *on, upon,* or a clause). **2.** to indulge in conjectural thought. **3.** *Com.* to buy and sell commodities, shares, etc., in the expectation of profit through a change in their market value; engage in any business transaction involving considerable risk, or the chance of large gains. [t. L: m. s. *speculātus,* pp., observed, examined]

speculation (spĕk′yŏŏ lā′shən), *n.* **1.** the contemplation or consideration of some subject. **2.** a single instance or process of consideration. **3.** a conclusion or opinion reached thereby. **4.** conjectural consideration of a matter; conjecture or surmise. **5.** trading in commodities, shares, etc., in the hope of profit from changes in the market price; engagement in business transactions involving considerable risk but offering the chance of large gains. **6.** a speculative commercial venture or undertaking.

speculative (spĕk′yŏŏ lə tĭv), *adj.* **1.** pertaining to, of the nature of, or characterized by speculation, contemplation, conjecture, or abstract reasoning. **2.** theoretical, rather than practical. **3.** given to speculation, as persons, the mind, etc. **4.** of the nature of or involving commercial or financial speculation. **5.** engaging in or given to such speculation. —**spec′ulatively,** *adv.* —**spec′ulativeness,** *n.*

speculative philosophy, any philosophy in which the thinker's own intuition provides a part of the data that is subjected to rational criticism. In Kant, criticism directed upon theoretical, as opposed to practical, reason.

speculator (spĕk′yŏŏ lā′tə), *n.* **1.** one engaged in commercial or financial speculation. **2.** one devoted to mental speculation. [t. L: scout, explorer]

speculum (spĕk′yŏŏ ləm), *n.*, *pl.* **-la** (-lə), **-lums. 1.** a mirror or reflector, esp. one of polished metal, as on a reflecting telescope. 2. *Surg.* an instrument for rendering a part accessible to observation, as by enlarging an orifice. 3. *Zool.* a lustrous or specially coloured area on the wing of certain birds. [t. L]

speculum metal, *Metall.* any of several copper and tin alloys used for mirrors and reflectors.

sped (spĕd), *v.* pt. and pp. of **speed.**

Spee (*Ger.* shpė), *n.* **Maximilian von** (*Ger.* mäk sĭ mē′lĭ än fōn), 1861–1914, German admiral.

speech (spēch), *n.* **1.** the faculty or power of speaking; oral communication; expression of human thought and emotions by speech sounds and gesture. **2.** that which is spoken; an utterance, remark, or declaration: *an eloquent speech.* **3.** a form of communication in spoken language, made by a speaker before an audience for a given purpose. **4.** any single utterance of an actor in the course of a play, etc. **5.** the form of utterance characteristic of a particular people or region; a language or dialect. **6.** manner of speaking, as of a person. **7.** a field of study devoted to the theory and practice of oral communication. **8.** *Archaic.* rumour. [ME *speche*, OE *spǣc*, unexplained var. of *sprǣc*, c. G *Sprache*]

—Syn. 1. SPEECH, LANGUAGE refer to the means of communication used by people. SPEECH is the expression of ideas and thoughts by means of articulate vocal sounds, or the faculty of thus expressing ideas and thoughts. LANGUAGE is a set of conventional signs, used conventionally and not necessarily articulate or even vocal (any set of signs, signals, or symbols, which convey meaning, including written words, may be called language): *a spoken language.* Thus, LANGUAGE is the set of conventions, and SPEECH is the action of putting these to use: *he couldn't understand the speech of the natives because it was in a foreign language.* **3.** SPEECH, ADDRESS, ORATION, HARANGUE are terms for a communication to an audience. SPEECH is the general word, with no implication of kind or length, or whether planned or not. An ADDRESS is a rather formal, planned speech, appropriate to a particular subject or occasion. An ORATION is a polished, rhetorical address, given usually on a notable occasion, that employs eloquence and studied methods of delivery. A HARANGUE is a violent, informal speech, often addressed to a casual audience, and intended to arouse strong feeling (sometimes to lead to mob action).

speech community, 1. the aggregate of all the people who use a given language or dialect. **2.** a group of people geographically distributed so that there is no break in intelligibility from place to place.

speech-day (spēch′dā′), *n.* an annual ceremony at a school, attended by parents, when speeches are made and prizes distributed.

speechify (spē′chĭ fī′), *v.i.*, **-fied, -fying.** to make a speech or speeches.

speechless (spēch′lĭs), *adj.* **1.** temporarily deprived of speech by strong emotion, physical weakness, exhaustion, etc.: *speechless with horror.* **2.** characterized by absence or loss of speech: *speechless astonishment.* **3.** lacking the faculty of speech; dumb. **4.** not expressed in speech or words. **5.** refraining from speech. **—speech′lessly,** *adv.* **—speech′lessness,** *n.* **—Syn. 1.** See **dumb.**

speech sound, any vocal or articulated sound used in human oral communication.

speech-therapy (spēch′thĕ′rə pĭ), *n.* the correction of defects of articulation resulting from psychological or physical disorders.

speed (spēd), *n.*, *v.*, **sped** or **speeded, speeding.** *—n.* **1.** rapidity in moving, going, travelling, or any proceeding or performance; swiftness; celerity. **2.** the ratio of the distance covered by a moving body to the time taken. **3.** *Motor Vehicles.* a transmission gear-ratio. **4.** *Photog.* a measure of the exposure required by an emulsion. **5.** *Archaic.* success or prosperity. **6. at full speed,** as fast as possible. *—v.t.* **7.** to promote the success of (an affair, undertaking, etc.); further, forward, or expedite. **8.** to direct (the steps, course, way, etc.) with speed. **9.** to increase the rate of speed of (usually fol. by *up*): *to speed up industrial production.* **10.** to bring to a particular speed, as a machine. **11.** to cause to move, go, or proceed, with speed. **12.** to expedite the going of: *to speed the parting guest.* **13.** *Archaic.* to cause (a person, etc.) to succeed or prosper. *—v.i.* **14.** to move, go, pass, or proceed with speed or rapidity. **15.** to drive a vehicle at a rate exceeding the maximum permitted by law. **16.** to increase the rate of speed or progress (fol. by *up*). **17.** to get on or fare in a specified or particular manner. **18.** *Archaic.* to succeed or prosper. [ME *spede*, OE *spēd* (c. D *spoed*). Cf. OE *spōwan* prosper, succeed] **—speed′er,** *n.* **—speed′ster,** *n.*

—Syn. 1. SPEED, VELOCITY agree in meaning rapidity of motion, esp. in relation to time. SPEED (orig. prosperity or success) is now, except in such archaic expressions as *to wish one good speed*, applied to relative rapidity of motion: *the speed of light, a speed of thirty miles per hour.* VELOCITY, the more learned or technical form, is sometimes interchangeable with SPEED (*the velocity of light*); it is commonly used to refer to high rates of speed, linear or circular: *velocity of a projectile.* **14.** See **rush** . **—Ant. 1.** slowness.

speedboat (spēd′bōt′), *n.* a motor boat so constructed that it will move rapidly through the water.

speed-cop (spēd′kŏp′), *n.* *Slang.* a policeman, often a motorcyclist, who enforces the observation of speed-limits.

speed-limit (spēd′lĭm′ĭt), *n.* **1.** the maximum speed at which a vehicle is legally permitted to travel, as on a particular road in certain conditions. **2.** the regulation prescribing this.

speed-merchant (spēd′mû′chənt), *n.* *Slang.* one who drives a motor vehicle extremely fast.

speedometer (spĭ dŏm′ĭ tə), *n.* a device attached to a motor vehicle or the like to record the distance covered in miles and the rate of travel in miles per hour.

speed-trap (spēd′trăp′), *n.* **1.** any of various devices used by the police, as radar, etc., to verify the speed of motor vehicles. **2.** a place on a road where such a device is set up.

speed-up (spēd′ŭp′), *n.* an increasing of speed.

speedway (spēd′wā′), *n.* **1.** a racing track for motor vehicles, esp. motorcycles. **2.** *Chiefly U.S.* a road or course for fast driving, motoring, or the like, or on which more than ordinary speed is allowed.

speedwell (spēd′wĕl′), *n.* any of various herbs of the scrophulariaceous genus *Veronica*, as *V. officinalis* **(common speedwell)** with pale blue flowers, or *V. chamaedrys* **(germander speedwell)** with bright blue flowers. [so called because its period of flowering is speedily over]

speedy (spē′dĭ), *adj.*, **-dier, -diest. 1.** characterized by speed; rapid; swift; fast. **2.** coming, given, or arrived at, quickly or soon; prompt; not delayed: *a speedy recovery.* **—speed′ily,** *adv.* **—speed′iness,** *n.*

speiss (spīs), *n.* a product consisting chiefly of one or more metallic arsenides (as of iron, nickel, etc.), obtained in smelting certain ores. [t. G: m. *Speise*, lit., food]

spelaean (spĭ lē′ən), *adj.* of, pertaining to, or inhabiting caves. Also, **spelean.** [f. s. NL *spēlaeus* (der. L *spēlaeum* cave, t. Gk: m. *spḗlaion*) + -AN]

speleology (spē′lĭ ŏl′ə jĭ), *n.* the exploration and study of caves. Also, **spelaeology. —speleological** (spē′lĭ ə lŏj′ĭ kl), *adj.* **—spe′leol′ogist,** *n.*

spell[1] (spĕl), *v.*, **spelt** or **spelled, spelling.** *—v.t.* **1.** to name, write, or otherwise give (as by signals), in order, the letters of (a word, syllable, etc.). **2.** (of letters) to form (a word, syllable, etc.). **3.** to read letter by letter or with difficulty (often fol. by *out*). **4.** to discern or find, as if by reading or study (often fol. by *out*). **5.** to signify; amount to: *this delay spells disaster for us.* *—v.i.* **6.** to name, write, or give the letters of words, etc. **7.** to express words by letters, esp. correctly. [ME, t. OF: m. s. *espeller*, of Gmc orig.; akin to SPELL[2]]

spell[2] (spĕl), *n.* **1.** a form of words supposed to possess magic power; a charm, incantation, or enchantment. **2.** any dominating or irresistible influence; fascination. [ME and OE *spell* discourse. Cf. SPIEL]

spell[3] (spĕl), *n.* **1.** a continuous course or period of work or other activity: *to take a spell at the wheel.* **2.** a turn of work so taken. **3.** a turn, bout, fit, or period of anything experienced or occurring: *a spell of coughing.* **4.** *Colloq.* an interval or space of time, usually indefinite or short. **5.** a period of weather of a specified kind: *a hot spell.* **6.** *Austral.* an interval or period of rest. **7.** *Rare.* a person or set of persons taking a turn of work to relieve another. [OE *gespelia*, n., substitute. Cf. OE *spala* in same sense] *—v.t.* **8.** *Chiefly U.S.* to take the place of or relieve (a person, etc.) for a time. **9.** *Chiefly Austral.* to give an interval of rest to. *—v.i.* **10.** *Austral.* to take an interval of rest. [var. of d. *spele*, OE *spelian* represent]

spellbind (spĕl′bīnd′), *v.t.*, **-bound, -binding.** to render spellbound; bind or hold as by a spell.

spellbinder (spĕl′bīn′də), *n.* *Colloq.* a speaker, esp. a politician, who holds his audience spellbound.

spellbound (spĕl′bound′), *adj.* bound by, or as by, a spell; enchanted, entranced, or fascinated: *a spellbound audience.* [f. SPELL[2] + BOUND[1]]

speller (spĕl′ə), *n.* **1.** one who spells words, etc. **2.** a spelling book.

spelling (spĕl′ĭng), *n.* **1.** the manner in which words are spelt; orthography. **2.** a group of letters representing a word. **3.** the act of a speller. **4.** the ability to spell or degree of proficiency in spelling.

spelling book, a textbook to teach spelling.

spelling pronunciation, a pronunciation based on the spelling, usually a variant of the traditional pronunciation.

Spellman (spĕl′mən), *n.* **Francis Joseph,** 1889–1968, U.S. Roman Catholic clergyman: cardinal 1946–68.

spelt[1] (spĕlt), *v.* pt. and pp. of **spell**[1].

spelt[2] (spĕlt), *n.* a kind of wheat, *Triticum spelta* (or a race of *T. sativum*), anciently much cultivated, used in developing improved varieties of wheat. [OE (c. G *Spelz, Spelt*), t. LL: s. *spelta*]

spelter (spĕl′tə), *n.* zinc, esp. in the form of ingots. [orig. obscure; akin to MD *speauter* and PEWTER]

spelunker (spĭ lŭng′kə), *n. Obs.* one who explores caves. [f. m. s. L *spēlunca* + -ER[1]]

Spenborough (spĕn′bə rə, -brə), *n.* a town in England, in the West Riding of Yorkshire. 36,417 (1961).

Spence (spĕns), *n.* **Sir Basil (Urwin)** (û′wĭn), born 1907, English architect.

spencer[1] (spĕn′sə), *n.* **1.** a short coat or jacket, formerly worn by men. **2.** a jacket or bodice, formerly worn by women. **3.** a kind of woman's vest, worn for extra warmth. [named after George John *Spencer*, 1758–1834, 2nd Earl Spencer]

spencer[2] (spĕn′sə), *n.* a kind of wig worn in the 18th century. [named after Charles *Spencer*, 1674–1722, 3rd Earl of Sunderland]

spencer[3] (spĕn′sə), *n. Naut.* a type of spanker sail, set on a gaff from the after mast of a square-rigged ship.

Spencer (spĕn′sə), *n.* **Herbert,** 1820–1903, English philosopher.

Spencer Gulf, an inlet of the Great Australian Bight on the coast of South Australia, between the Eyre and Yorke peninsulas. ab. 200 mi. long and 50 mi. wide at the entrance.

Spencerian (spĕn sĭə′rĭ ən), *adj.* **1.** of or pertaining to Herbert Spencer or his philosophy. —*n.* **2.** a follower of Herbert Spencer.

Spencerianism (spĕn sĭə′rĭ ə nĭz′əm), *n.* the philosophy of Herbert Spencer, who attempted, through the concept of evolution, to make a systematic unity of all knowledge.

spend (spĕnd), *v.*, **spent, spending.** —*v.t.* **1.** to pay out, disburse, or expend; dispose of (money, wealth, resources, etc.). **2.** to employ (labour, thought, words, time, etc.) on some object, in some proceeding, etc. **3.** to pass (time) in a particular manner, place, etc. **4.** to use up, consume, or exhaust: *the storm had spent its fury.* **5.** to give (one's blood, life, etc.) for some cause. —*v.i.* **6.** to spend money, etc. **7.** *Obs.* to be used up. [ME *spende*, OE *spendan* (c. G *spenden*), ult. t. L: m. *expendere* EXPEND] —**spend′able,** *adj.* —**spend′er,** *n.*

—**Syn. 1.** SPEND, DISBURSE, EXPEND, SQUANDER refer to paying out money. SPEND is the general word: *we spend more on living expenses now.* DISBURSE implies expending from a specific source or sum to meet specific obligations, or paying in definite allotments: *the treasurer has authority to disburse funds.* EXPEND is more formal, and implies spending for some definite and (usually) sensible or worthy object: *to expend most of one's salary on necessities.* SQUANDER suggests lavish, wasteful, or foolish expenditure: *to squander a legacy.* —**Ant. 1.** save, keep.

Spender (spĕn′də), *n.* **Stephen,** born 1909, English poet and critic.

spending money, money for small personal expenses; pocket-money.

spendthrift (spĕnd′thrĭft′), *n.* **1.** one who spends his possessions or money extravagantly or wastefully; a prodigal. —*adj.* **2.** wastefully extravagant; prodigal.

Spengler (spĕng′glə; *Ger.* shpĕng′lər), *n.* **Oswald** (*Ger.* ŏs′vălt), 1880–1936, German philosophical writer.

Spenser (spĕn′sə), *n.* **Edmund,** *c.* 1552–99, English poet.

Spenserian (spĕn sĭə′rĭ ən), *adj.* **1.** of or characteristic of Spenser or his work. —*n.* **2.** an imitator of Spenser. **3.** a Spenserian stanza. **4.** verse in Spenserian stanzas.

Spenserian stanza, the stanza used by Spenser in his *Faerie Queene* and employed since by other poets, consisting of eight iambic pentameter lines and a final Alexandrine, with a rhyme scheme of ababbcbcc.

Spenser Mountains, a range of mountains in South Island, New Zealand; the northern extension of the Southern Alps. Highest peak, Mount Travers, 7666 ft.

spent (spĕnt), *v. v.* **1.** pt. and pp. of **spend.** —*adj.* **2.** used up, consumed, or exhausted.

sperm[1] (spûm), *n.* **1.** spermatic fluid. **2.** a male reproductive cell; a spermatozoon. [ME *sperme*, t. L: m. *sperma*, t. Gk]

sperm[2] (spûm), *n.* **1.** spermaceti. **2.** sperm whale. **3.** sperm oil. [abbrev. of defs above]

sperm-, a word element representing **sperm**[1]. Also, **spermo-.**

-sperm, a terminal combining form of **sperm**[1], as in *angiosperm.*

spermaceti (spû′mə sĕt′ĭ, -sē′tĭ), *n.* a whitish, waxy substance obtained from the oil in the head of the sperm whale, used in making ointments, cosmetics, etc. [t. ML: orig. phrase *sperma cētī* sperm of whale]

-spermal, a word element used to form adjectives related to **sperm**[1]. [f. -SPERM + -AL[1]]

spermary (spû′mə rĭ), *n.*, *pl.* **-ries.** a sperm gland; an organ in which spermatozoa are generated; testis.

spermatic (spû măt′ĭk), *adj.* **1.** of, pertaining to, or of the nature of sperm; seminal; generative. **2.** pertaining to a spermary.

spermatic cord, *Anat.* the solid neck of the spermatic sac by which the testicle is suspended within the scrotum; it contains the vas deferens, the blood vessels and nerves of the testicles, etc.

spermatic fluid, the male generative fluid; semen.

spermatic sac, *Anat.* the hollow portion of the inguinal bursa which contains the testis and is lined by peritoneum.

spermatium (spû mā′tyəm), *n.*, *pl.* **-tia** (-tyə). *Bot.* **1.** the non-motile male gamete of the red algae. **2.** a minute, colourless cell (conjectured to be a male reproductive body) developed within spermogonia. [NL, t. Gk: m. *spermátion*, dim. of *spérma* SPERM[1]]

spermato-, var. of **sperm-.** Also, **spermat-.** [t. Gk, comb. form of *spérma* SPERM[1]]

spermatocyte (spû′mə tō sīt′), *n. Biol.* a male germ cell at the maturation stage, giving rise to spermatozoids and spermatozoa.

spermatogenesis (spû′mə tō jĕn′ĭ sĭs), *n. Biol.* the genesis or origin and development of spermatozoa. Also, **spermatogeny** (spû′mə tŏj′ĭ nĭ). —**spermatogenetic** (spû′mə tō-jĭ nĕt′ĭk), *adj.*

spermatogonium (spû′mə tō gō′nĭ əm), *n.*, *pl.* **-nia** (-nĭ ə). *Biol.* one of the primitive germ cells giving rise to spermatocytes. [NL. See SPERMATO-, -GONIUM] —**sper′matogo′nial,** *adj.*

spermatoid (spû′mə toid′), *adj.* resembling sperm.

spermatophore (spû′mə tō fô′), *n. Zool.* a special case or capsule containing a number of spermatozoa, produced by the male of certain insects, molluscs, annelids, etc., and some vertebrates. —**spermatophoral** (spû′mə tŏf′ə rəl), *adj.*

spermatophyte (spû′mə tō fīt′), *n.* any of the *Spermatophyta*, a primary division or group of plants embracing those that bear seeds. —**spermatophytic** (spû′mə tō fĭt′-ĭk), *adj.*

spermatorrhoea (spû′mə tō rĭə′), *n. Pathol.* abnormally frequent involuntary emission of semen. Also, *U.S.*, **spermatorrhea.**

spermatozoid (spû′mə tō zō′ĭd), *n. Bot.* a motile male gamete produced in an antheridium. [f. SPERMATO-ZO(ON) + -ID]

spermatozoon (spû′mə tō zō′ŏn), *n.*, *pl.* **-zoa** (-zō′ə). *Biol.* one of the minute, usually actively motile, gametes in semen, which serve to fertilize the ovum; a mature male reproductive cell. —**sper′matozo′al, sper′matozo′an, sper′matozo′ic,** *adj.*

spermic (spû′mĭk), *adj.* spermatic.

spermo-, var. of **sperm-,** before consonants.

spermogonium (spû′mə gō′nĭ əm), *n.*, *pl.* **-nia** (-nĭ ə). *Bot.* one of the cup-shaped or flask-shaped receptacles in which the spermatia of certain fungi are produced. [NL. See SPERMO-, -GONIUM]

sperm oil, an oil from the sperm whale.

spermophile (spû′mō fīl′), *n.* any of various American terrestrial rodents of the squirrel family, esp. of the genus *Citellus* (or *Spermophilus*), sometimes sufficiently numerous to do much damage to crops, as the ground squirrels, susliks, etc.

spermophyte (spû′-mō fīt′), *n. Bot.* spermatophyte.

spermous (spû′məs), *adj.* of the nature of or pertaining to sperm.

sperm whale, a large, square-headed whale, *Physeter macrocephalus*, valuable for oil and spermaceti; cachalot.

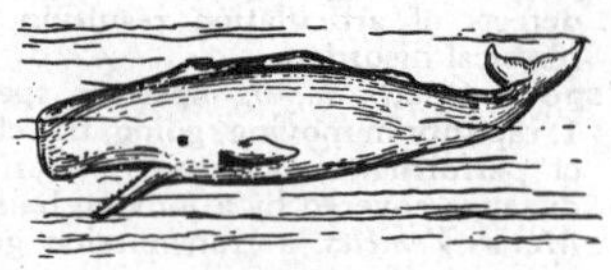

Sperm whale, *Physeter macrocephalus* (Male 75 to 85 ft long; female 23 to 30 ft long)

Sperrin Mountains (spĕ′rĭn), a range of low mountains in Northern Ireland on the border of counties Londonderry and Tyrone. Highest point, Mullaghclogha, 2088 ft.

sperrylite (spĕ′rĭ līt′), *n.* a mineral, platinum arsenide, $PtAs_2$, occurring in minute tin-white crystals, usually cubes: a minor ore of platinum. [named after F. L. *Sperry*, of Sudbury, Ontario, Canada, where it was found. See -LITE]

spew (spyoo), *v.i.* **1.** to discharge the contents of the stomach through the mouth; vomit. —*v.t.* **2.** to eject from the stomach through the mouth; vomit. **3.** to thrust forth or discharge violently. —*n.* **4.** that which is spewed; vomit. Also, **spue** (for 1, 2). [ME; OE *spīwan*, c. G *speien*. Cf. L *spuere*] —**spew′er,** *n.*

Spey (spā), *n.* a river in N Scotland flowing from S Inverness-shire to the Moray Firth, forming the border of Moray with Banffshire: 107 mi.

Speyer (*Ger.* shpī′ər), *n.* a town in SW West Germany, on the Rhine. 42,000 (est. 1966). Also, **Spires.**

Spezia (*It.* spĕtʹtsyȧ), *n.* See **La Spezia.**
sp. gr., specific gravity.
sphacelate (sfăsʹĭ lātʹ), *v.t., v.i.,* **-lated, -lating.** *Pathol.* to affect or be affected with sphacelus; mortify. —**sphacʹ-elaʹtion,** *n.*
sphacelus (sfăsʹĭ ləs), *n. Pathol.* a gangrenous or mortified mass of tissue; necrosis. [t. L, t. Gk: m. *sphákelos*]
sphagnous (sfăgʹnəs), *adj.* pertaining to, abounding in, or consisting of sphagnum.
sphagnum (sfăgʹnəm), *n.* any of the bog mosses constituting the genus *Sphagnum,* found chiefly in temperate regions of high rainfall and low insolation, where they may build up deep layers of peat; used in the mass by gardeners in potting and packing plants, and (formerly) in surgery for dressing wounds, etc. [NL, t. Gk: m. *sphágnos* a moss]
sphalerite (sfălʹə rītʹ, sfāʹlə-), *n.* a very common mineral, zinc sulphide, ZnS, usually containing some iron and a little cadmium, occurring in yellow, brown, or black crystals or cleavable masses with resinous lustre: the principal ore of zinc and cadmium; blende; blackjack. [f. s. Gk *sphalerós* deceptive, uncertain + -ITE[1]]
sphene (sfēn), *n.* a mineral, calcium titanium silicate, $CaTiSiO_5$, occurring in many rocks, usually in wedge-shaped crystals; titanite. [t. Gk: m. *sphḗn* wedge; with reference to the shape of its crystals]
sphenic (sfēʹnĭk), *adj.* wedge-shaped. [f. Gk *sphḗn* wedge + -IC]
sphenogram (sfēʹnə grămʹ), *n.* a cuneiform character. [f. *spheno-* (t. Gk, comb. form of *sphḗn* wedge) + -GRAM]
sphenoid (sfēʹnoid), *adj.* Also, **sphenoiʹdal. 1.** wedge-shaped. **2.** *Anat.* denoting or pertaining to the compound bone of the base of the skull, at the roof of the pharynx. —*n.* **3.** *Anat.* the sphenoid bone. [t. NL: s. *sphēnoīdes,* t. Gk: m. *sphēnoeidḗs* wedgelike]
spheral (sfĭəʹrəl), *adj.* **1.** of or pertaining to a sphere. **2.** spherical. **3.** symmetrical; perfect in form.
sphere (sfĭə), *n., v.,* **sphered, sphering.** —*n.* **1.** a solid geometrical figure generated by the revolution of a semicircle about its diameter; a round body whose surface is at all points equidistant from the centre. **2.** any rounded body approximately of this form; a globular mass, shell, etc. **3.** a heavenly body; a planet or star. **4.** celestial sphere. **5.** *Ancient Astron.* any of the transparent, concentric, spherical shells, or 'heavens', in which the planets, fixed stars, etc., were supposed to be set. **6.** the place or environment within which a person or thing exists; a field of activity or operation: *to be out of one's sphere.* **7.** a particular social world, stratum of society, or walk of life. **8.** a field of something specified: *a sphere of influence.* —*v.t.* **9.** to enclose in, or as in, a sphere. **10.** to form into a sphere. **11.** *Poetic.* to place among the heavenly spheres. [ME, t. LL: m. *sphēra,* L *sphaera,* t. Gk: m. *sphaîra*] —**sphereʹlikeʹ,** *adj.* —**Syn. 2.** See **ball**[1].
-sphere, a word element representing **sphere,** as in *planisphere;* having a special use in the names of the layers of gases, etc., surrounding the earth and other celestial bodies, as in *ionosphere.*
spherical (sfĕʹrĭ kl), *adj.* **1.** having the form of a sphere; globular. **2.** formed in or on a sphere, as a figure. **3.** of or pertaining to a sphere or spheres: *spherical trigonometry.* **4.** pertaining to the heavenly bodies, or to their supposed revolving spheres or shells. **5.** pertaining to the heavenly bodies regarded astrologically as exerting influence on mankind and events. Also, **spheric.** —**sphericality** (sfĕʹrĭ kălʹĭ tĭ), *n.* —**spherʹically,** *adv.*
spherical aberration, variation in focal length of a lens from centre to edge, due to its spherical shape.
spherical angle, *Geom.* an angle formed by arcs of great circles of a sphere.
spherical triangle, *Geom.* a triangle formed by arcs of great circles of a sphere.
sphericity (sfĕ rĭsʹĭ tĭ), *n., pl.* **-ties.** spherical state or form.
spherics[1] (sfĕʹrĭks), *n. Maths.* the geometry and trigonometry of figures formed on the surface of a sphere. [pl. of SPHERIC(AL). See -ICS]
spherics[2] (sfĕʹrĭks), *n.* a branch of meteorology in which weather forecasting and atmospheric conditions are studied by means of electronic devices. [f. (ATMO)SPHERIC + *-s.* See -ICS]
spheroid (sfĭəʹroid), *Geom.* —*n.* **1.** a solid revolution obtained by rotating an ellipse about one of its two axes. See diag. under **prolate.** —*adj.* **2.** spheroidal.
spheroidal (sfĭə roiʹdl), *adj.* **1.** pertaining to a spheroid or spheroids. **2.** shaped like a spheroid; approximately spherical. Also, **spheroiʹdic.** —**spheroiʹdally,** *adv.*
spheroidicity (sfĭəʹroi dĭsʹĭ tĭ), *n.* spheroidal state or form. Also, **spheroidity** (sfĭə roiʹdĭ tĭ).
spherometer (sfĭə rŏmʹĭ tə), *n.* an instrument for measuring the curvature of spheres and curved surfaces.
spherule (sfĕʹrōōl), *n.* a small sphere or spherical body. [t. L: m. *sphaerula,* dim. of *sphaera* SPHERE] —**spheʹrular,** *adj.*
spherulite (sfĕʹrōō lītʹ), *n.* a rounded aggregate of radiating crystals formed in certain igneous rocks. —**spherulitic** (sfĕʹrōō lĭtʹĭk), *adj.*
sphery (sfĭəʹrĭ), *adj. Rare.* **1.** having the form of a sphere; spherelike. **2.** pertaining to the heavenly bodies, or to their supposed revolving spheres or shells. **3.** resembling a heavenly body; starlike.
sphincter (sfĭngkʹtə), *n. Anat.* a circular band of voluntary or involuntary muscle which encircles an orifice of the body or one of its hollow organs. [t. L, t. Gk: m. *sphinktḗr* band] —**sphincʹteral,** *adj.*
sphingomyelin (sfĭngʹgō mīʹĭ lĭn), *n. Biochem.* any of a group of closely related phosphatides occurring in the brain and other tissues.
sphinx (sfĭngks), *n., pl.* **sphinxes, sphinges** (sfĭnʹjēz). **1.** *Egypt. Antiq.* **a.** a figure of an imaginary creature having the head of a man or an animal and the body of a lion. **b.** (*usually cap.*) the colossal recumbent stone figure of this kind near the pyramids of El Giza. **2.** (*cap.*) *Gk Myth.* a monster of Greek mythology, variously represented, commonly with the head and breast of a woman, the body of a lion or a dog, and wings, which proposed a riddle to passers-by near Thebes, killing those unable to guess it. Oedipus solved it and the Sphinx killed herself. **3.** some similar monster. **4.** a sphinxlike person or thing, as one given to enigmatic or inscrutable behaviour. [t. L, t. Gk]

Sphinx at El Giza

sphinx-moth (sfĭngksʹmŏthʹ), *n.* a hawkmoth.
sphragistic (sfrə jĭsʹtĭk), *adj.* of or pertaining to seals or signet rings. [t. Gk: m. s. *sphrāgistikós*]
sphragistics (sfrə jĭsʹtĭks), *n.* the scientific study of seals or signet rings.
sp. ht, specific heat.
sphygmic (sfĭgʹmĭk), *adj. Physiol., etc.* of or pertaining to the pulse. [t. Gk: m. s. *sphygmikós*]
sphygmo-, a word element meaning 'pulse'. Also, before vowels, **sphygm-.** [t. Gk, comb. form of *sphygmós*]
sphygmogram (sfĭgʹmō grămʹ), *n.* a tracing or diagram produced by a sphygmograph.
sphygmograph (sfĭgʹmō grăfʹ, -gräfʹ), *n.* an instrument for recording the rapidity, strength, and uniformity of the arterial pulse. —**sphygmographic** (sfĭgʹmō grăfʹĭk), *adj.* —**sphygmography** (sfĭg mŏgʹrə fĭ), *n.*
sphygmoid (sfĭgʹmoid), *adj. Physiol., etc.* resembling the pulse; pulselike.
sphygmomanometer (sfĭgʹmō mə nŏmʹĭ tə), *n. Physiol.* an instrument for measuring the pressure of the blood in an artery. [f. SPHYGMO- + MANOMETER]
sphygmometer (sfĭg mŏmʹĭ tə), *n.* an instrument for measuring the strength of the pulse.
sphygmus (sfĭgʹməs), *n. Physiol.* the pulse. [NL, t. Gk: m. *sphygmós* pulsation]
spica (spīʹkə), *n., pl.* **-cae** (-sē). **1.** *Archaeol.* an ear of grain. **2.** a type of bandage extending from an extremity to the trunk by means of successive turns and crosses. **3.** *Bot.* a spike, as of a flower. **4.** (*cap.*) Alpha Virginis, a blue-white star of the first magnitude in the constellation Virgo. [t. L]
spicate (spīʹkāt), *adj. Bot.* **1.** having spikes, as a plant. **2.** arranged in spikes, as flowers. **3.** in the form of a spike, as in inflorescence. [t. L: m. s. *spicātus,* pp., furnished with spikes]
spiccato (spĭ käʹtō; *It.* spēk kȧʹtô), *adj., adv. Music.* detached; (in violin playing) denoting distinct notes produced by short, abrupt, rebounding motions of the bow. [It., pp. of *spiccare* detach, separate]
spice (spīs), *n., v.,* **spiced, spicing.** —*n.* **1.** any of a class of pungent or aromatic substances of vegetable origin, as pepper, cinnamon, cloves, and the like, used as seasoning, preservatives, etc. **2.** such substances as material or collectively. **3.** *Poetic.* a spicy or aromatic smell or fragrance. **4.** something that gives interest; a piquant element or quality. **5.** piquancy, or interest. **6.** a trace, flavour, or suggestion: *a spice of humour in conversation.* —*v.t.* **7.** to prepare or season with a spice or spices. **8.** to give flavour, piquancy, or interest to by something added. [ME, t. OF: m. *espice,* t. L: m. *species* SPECIES]
spicebush (spīsʹbŏŏshʹ), *n.* a yellow-flowered lauraceous shrub, *Lindera benzoin,* of North America, whose bark and leaves have a spicy smell.
Spice Islands, Moluccas.
spicery (spīʹsə rĭ), *n., pl.* **-eries. 1.** spices. **2.** spicy

flavour or fragrance. **3.** *Obs.* a storeroom or place for spices. [ME, t. OF: m. *espicerie*, der. *espice* SPICE]

spick-and-span (spĭk′ən spăn′), *adj.* **1.** neat and clean. **2.** perfectly new; fresh. Also, **spick and span.** [short for *spick-and-span-new*, var. of *span-new*, t. Scand.; cf. Icel. *spānnýr*, lit., chip-new]

spicula (spĭk′yŏŏ lə), *n.*, *pl.* **-lae** (-lē′). a spicule. [NL, dim. of L *spīca* SPIKE[2]. Cf. SPICULUM]

spiculate (spĭk′yŏŏ lāt′, -lĭt), *adj.* **1.** having the form of a spicule. **2.** covered with or having spicules; consisting of spicules. Also, **spicular** (spĭk′yŏŏ lə). [t. L: m. s. *spīculātus*, pp., pointed]

spicule (spĭk′yōōl, spī′kyōōl), *n.* **1.** a small or minute, slender, sharp-pointed body or part; a small, needle-like crystal, process, or the like. **2.** *Zool.* one of the small, hard, calcareous or siliceous bodies which serve as the skeletal elements of various animals. [t. L. See SPICULA]

spiculum (spĭk′yŏŏ ləm), *n.*, *pl.* **-la** (-lə). *Zool.* a small, needle-like body, part, process, or the like. [t. L, dim. of *spīca* SPIKE[2]]

spicy (spī′sĭ), *adj.*, **spicier, spiciest. 1.** seasoned with or containing spice. **2.** characteristic or suggestive of spice. **3.** of the nature of or resembling spice. **4.** abounding in or yielding spices. **5.** aromatic or fragrant. **6.** piquant or pungent: *spicy criticism.* **7.** of a somewhat improper, scandalous, or sensational nature. **8.** *Slang.* full of spirit. —**spi′cily,** *adv.* —**spi′ciness,** *n.*

spider (spī′də), *n.* **1.** *Zool.* any of the eight-legged, wingless, predatory, insect-like arachnids which constitute the order *Araneida*, most of which spin webs that serve as nests and as traps for prey. **2.** any of various other arachnids resembling or suggesting these. **3.** any of various things resembling or suggesting a spider. **4.** a device consisting of several elastic cables held together at a central point, used to strap down a load; octopus. **5.** *U.S.* a frying pan, orig. one with legs or feet. **6.** a trivet or tripod, as for supporting a pot or pan on a hearth. **7.** a lightly built cart, phaeton, or wagon with a high body and large slender wheels. **8.** a person who entraps others, or lures them by his wiles. **9.** *Agric.* a pulverizing instrument used with a cultivator. [ME *spithre*, OE *spīthra*, c. Dan. *spinder*, lit., spinner]

Black widow spider, *Latrodectus lugubris* (½ in. long)

spider crab, any of various crabs with long, slender legs and comparatively small triangular body.

spiderman (spī′də măn′), *n.* **1.** one who works on high buildings, esp. as an erector of the steel framework. **2.** a steeplejack.

spider monkey, any of various acrobatic monkeys of tropical America, genera *Ateles*, with a slender body, long slender limbs, and a long prehensile tail.

spider orchid, any of several species of orchids of the genus *Ophrys*, as *O. sphegodes* of chalk grassland in Europe.

spiderwort (spī′də wût′), *n.* **1.** any plant of the genus *Tradescantia*, comprising perennial herbs with blue-, purple-, or rose-coloured flowers. **2.** any plant of the same family (*Commelinaceae*).

Spider monkey, *Ateles geoffroyi* (Total length up to 5 ft, tail 3 ft)

spidery (spī′də rĭ), *adj.* **1.** like a spider or a spider's web; very thin and attenuated. **2.** full of spiders.

spiegeleisen (spē′gl ī′zən), *n.* *Metall.* a lustrous, crystalline pig-iron containing a large amount of manganese, sometimes 15 per cent or more, used in making steel. Also, **spiegel.** [t. G: lit., mirror-iron]

spiel (shpēl), *Slang.* —*n.* **1.** glib or plausible talk, esp. for the purpose of persuasion, swindling, seduction, etc. **2.** a salesman's, conjurer's, or swindler's patter. **3.** any talk or speech. —*v.i.* **4.** to talk plausibly; deliver a patter or sales talk. —*v.t.* **5.** to attempt to lure, persuade, or deceive (someone) by glib talk. [t. G: play]

spieler (shpē′lə), *n.* *Slang.* **1.** one who delivers or is proficient at, delivering a spiel, a glib talker. **2.** a salesman, barker, etc. **3.** a swindler; cardsharp. [f. SPIEL + -ER[1]]

spier (spī′ə), *n.* one who spies, watches, or discovers. Also, **spyer.**

spiffing (spĭf′ĭng), *adj.* *Slang.* first-rate; excellent. [orig. uncert.; ? akin to SPIFFY]

spiffy (spĭf′ĭ), *adj.*, **spiffier, spiffiest.** *Slang.* spruce; smart; fine. [f. d. *spiff* smartness + -Y[1]]

spiflicate (spĭf′lĭ kāt′), *v.t.*, **-cated, -cating.** *Slang.* (now often jocular) to destroy utterly; hurt, punish, or damage; destroy or kill. Also, **spifflicate.** [orig. uncert.]

spiflicated (spĭf′lĭ kā′tĭd), *Slang.* —*v.* **1.** pp. of **spiflicate.** —*adj.* **2.** drunk. Also, **spifflicated.**

spignel (spĭg′nəl), *n.* a small, umbelliferous, perennial herb, *Meum athamanticum*, occurring among grass in mountains in Europe. [ME *spigurnel*, t. ML: m. s. *spigurnella*, of obscure orig.]

spigot (spĭg′ət), *n.* **1.** a small peg or plug for stopping the vent of a cask, etc. **2.** a small peg which stops the passage in the tap of a cask, etc. **3.** *U.S.* a tap or cock for controlling the flow of liquid from a pipe or the like. **4.** the end of a pipe which enters the enlarged end of another pipe to form a joint. [ME, var. of *spicket*, der. SPIKE[1]]

spike[1] (spīk), *n.*, *v.*, **spiked, spiking.** —*n.* **1.** a large, strong nail or pin, esp. of iron. **2.** such a nail used for fastening rails to sleepers, used extensively in the U.S. and elsewhere. **3.** a stiff, sharp-pointed piece or part. **4.** a sharp-pointed piece of metal, etc., fastened in something, with the point outwards, as for defence. **5.** a sharp metal projection on the sole of a shoe, as of a golf player, to prevent slipping. **6.** (*pl.*) Also, **track shoes.** running shoes having such projections. **7.** the antler of a young deer, when straight and without branches. —*v.t.* **8.** to fasten or secure with a spike or spikes. **9.** *Elect.* a very short pulse of large amplitude. **10.** to provide or set with a spike or spikes. **11.** to pierce with or impale on a spike. **12.** to set or stud with something suggesting spikes. **13.** to render (a muzzle-loading gun) useless by driving a spike into the touch-hole. **14.** to make ineffective, or frustrate the action or purpose of: *to spike a rumour.* **15.** *Slang.* (of a newspaper editor) to reject (a story). **16.** *U.S. Slang.* to add alcoholic liquor to (a drink or beverage, in itself usually non-alcoholic). **17. spike someone's guns,** to frustrate (someone's) plans. [ME, t. Scand.; cf. Norw. *spik* nail, c. OE *spic-* in *spicing* nail] —**spike′like′,** *adj.*

spike[2] (spīk), *n.* **1.** an ear, as of wheat or other grain. **2.** *Bot.* an inflorescence in which the flowers are sessile (or apparently so) along an elongated, unbranched axis. [ME *spik*, t. L: m. s. *spīca* ear of grain]

Spikes[2] A, Plantain, *Plantago maior*; B, Barley, genus *Hordeum*

spike heel, *Chiefly U.S.* a stiletto heel.

spike lavender, a species of lavender, *Lavandula latifolia*, having spikes of pale purple flowers, and yielding an oil **(oil of spike)** used in painting, etc.

spikelet (spīk′lĭt), *n.* *Bot.* a small or secondary spike in grasses; one of the flower clusters, the unit of inflorescence (consisting of two or more flowers and subtended by one or more glumes disposed around one axis).

spikenard (spīk′näd), *n.* **1.** an aromatic East Indian valerianaceous plant, *Nardostachys jatamansi*, supposedly the same as the ancient nard. **2.** an aromatic substance used by the ancients, supposed to be obtained from this plant. **3.** any of various similar or related plants. [ME, t. ML: m. *spīca nardi* spike of nard]

spike-rush (spīk′rŭsh′), *n.* any plant of the cyperaceous genus *Eleocharis*, as the **common spike-rush,** *E. palustris*, a rhizomatous perennial with narrow leaves, common on the edges of ponds.

spiky (spī′kĭ), *adj.* **1.** having a spike or spikes. **2.** having the form of a spike; spikelike. **3.** (of a person or one's temperament) short-tempered; easily irritated; difficult to deal with, or unyielding.

spile (spīl), *n.*, *v.*, **spiled, spiling.** —*n.* **1.** a peg or plug of wood, esp. one used as a spigot. **2.** *U.S. and Dial.* a spout for conducting sap from the sugar maple. **3.** a heavy stake or beam driven into the ground, etc., as a support; a pile. —*v.t.* **4.** to stop up (a hole) with a spile or peg. **5.** to furnish with a spigot or spout, as for drawing off a liquid. **6.** to tap by means of a spile. **7.** to furnish, strengthen, or support with spiles or piles. [t. MD or MLG, c. G *Speil*]

spilikin (spĭl′ĭ kĭn), *n.* *Obs.* spillikin.

spiling (spī′lĭng), *n.* **1.** piles; spiles. **2.** the dimensions of the curve of a ship's timbers.

spill[1] (spĭl), *v.*, **spilt** or **spilled, spilling,** *n.* —*v.t.* **1.** to cause or allow (liquid, or any matter in grains or loose pieces) to run or fall from a container, esp. accidentally or wastefully. **2.** to shed (blood), as in killing or wounding. **3.** to scatter. **4.** *Naut.* to let the wind out of (a sail). **5.** to cause to fall from a horse, vehicle, or the like. **6.** *Slang.* to divulge, disclose, or tell. —*v.i.* **7.** (of a liquid, loose particles, etc.) to run or escape from a container, esp. by accident or in careless handling. —*n.* **8.** a spilling, as of liquid. **9.** a quantity spilt. **10.** the mark made. **11.** a throw or fall from a horse, vehicle, or the like. [ME; OE *spillan*, c. MLG *spillen*]

spill[2] (spĭl), *n.* **1.** a splinter. **2.** a slender piece of wood or twisted paper, for lighting candles, lamps, etc. **3.** a peg made of metal. **4.** a small pin for stopping a cask; spile. [ME *spille*; akin to SPILE]

spillikin (spĭl′ĭ kĭn), *n. Obs.* **1.** a thin strip or rod of wood, paper, bone, or the like; a jackstraw. **2.** (*pl. construed as sing.*) a game in which such rods must be withdrawn singly from a pile without disturbing the others; jackstraws. Also, **spilikin.** [dim. of SPILL[2]]

spillway (spĭl′wā′), *n.* a passageway through which surplus water escapes from a reservoir.

spilt (spĭlt), *v.* pt. and pp. of **spill**[1].

spin (spĭn), *v.*, **spun** or (*Archaic*) **span; spun; spinning;** *n.* —*v.t.* **1.** to make (yarn) by drawing out, twisting, and winding fibres. **2.** to form (any material) into thread. **3.** (of spiders, silkworms, etc.) to produce (a thread, cobweb, gossamer, silk, etc.) by extruding from the body a long, slender filament of a natural viscous matter that hardens in the air. **4.** to cause to turn round rapidly, as on an axis; twirl; whirl: *to spin a coin on a table.* **5.** (in sheet metalwork) to shape into hollow, rounded form, during rotation on a lathe or wheel, by pressure with a suitable tool. **6.** to produce, fabricate, or evolve in a manner suggestive of spinning thread, as a story. **7. a.** *Cricket.* of a bowler, to cause (the ball) to revolve on its axis so that on bouncing it changes direction or speed. **b.** *Tennis, etc.* to hit (the ball) so that it behaves thus. **8. spin a yarn, a.** to tell a tale. **b.** to tell a false or improbable story or version of an event. **9. spin out, a.** to draw out, protract, or prolong: *to spin out a story tediously.* **b.** to spend (time, one's life, etc.). **c.** to make last, as money; eke out. —*v.i.* **10.** to turn round rapidly, as on an axis, as the earth, a top, etc. **11.** to produce a thread from the body, as spiders, silkworms, etc. **12.** to move, go, run, ride, or travel rapidly. **13.** to be affected with a sensation of whirling, as the head. **14.** to fish with a spinning or revolving bait. —*n.* **15.** the act of causing a spinning or whirling motion. **16.** a spinning motion given to a ball or the like when thrown or struck. **17.** a moving or going rapidly along. **18.** a rapid run, ride, drive, or the like, as for exercise or enjoyment. **19.** *Colloq.* a state of confusion or excitement. **20.** *Aeron.* a manoeuvre in which an aircraft makes a continuous spiral descent with the mean angle of incidence above the stalling angle. **21.** *Physics.* the angular momentum of a molecule, atom, or particle, when it has no velocity of translation. [ME *spinne(n)*, OE *spinnan*, c. D and G *spinnen*] —**Syn. 10.** See **turn.**

spina bifida (spī′nə bĭf′ĭ də), *Pathol.* a congenital defect in the development of the vertebral column giving rise to a hernial protrusion of the meninges.

spinach (spĭn′ĭj), *n.* **1.** a chenopodiaceous annual herb, *Spinacia oleracea*, cultivated for its succulent leaves, which are eaten boiled. **2.** the leaves. [t. OF: m. *(e)spinache, espinage*, t. ML: m. *spinachia*, t. Sp.: m. *espinaca*, t. Ar.: m. *isfināj*, b. with L *spīna* thorn]

spinal (spī′nəl), *adj.* of, pertaining, or belonging to any spine or thornlike structure, esp. to the backbone. [t. LL: s. *spīnālis*]

spinal canal, the tube formed by the vertebrae in which the spinal cord and its membranes are located.

spinal column, (in a vertebrate animal) the bones of vertebrae forming the axis of the skeleton and protecting the spinal cord; the spine; the backbone.

spinal cord, the cord of nervous tissue extending through the spinal column.

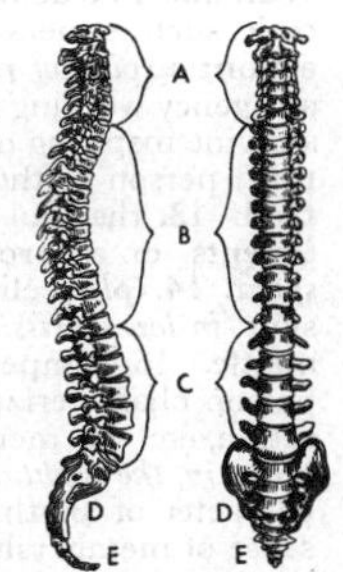

Human spinal column (side and front view) A, Seven cervical vertebrae; B, Twelve dorsal vertebrae; C, Five lumbar vertebrae; D, Five sacral vertebrae; E, Four caudal or coccygeal vertebrae, forming a coccyx

spindle (spĭn′dl), *n.*, *adj.*, *v.*, **-dled, -dling.** —*n.* **1.** a rounded rod, usually of wood, tapering towards each end, used in spinning by hand to twist into thread the fibres drawn from the mass on the distaff, and to wind the thread on as it is spun. **2.** the rod on a spinning wheel by which the thread is twisted and on which it is wound. **3.** one of the rods of a spinning machine which bear the bobbins on which the thread is wound as it is spun. **4.** any rod or pin suggestive of a spindle used in spinning, as one which turns round or on which something turns; an axle, axis, or shaft. **5.** either of the two shaftlike parts in a lathe which support the work to be turned, one (**live spindle**) rotating and imparting motion to the work, and the other (**dead spindle**) not rotating. **6.** a small axis, arbor, or mandrel. **7.** a measure of yarn, varying according to the material (15,120 yards for cotton; 14,400 yards for linen). **8.** a hydrometer. **9.** *Biol.* the fine threads of achromatic material arranged within the cell, during mitosis, in a fusiform manner. **10.** a short turned or circular ornament, as in a baluster or stair rail. **11.** *U.S. Naut.* a staff or marker, as for a reef, rock, wreck, or the like. —*adj.* **12.** of or resembling spindles. **13.** *U.S.* denoting the maternal line of descent; distaff: *the spindle side of the house.* —*v.t.* **14.** to fit with a spindle or spindles. **15.** to give the form of a spindle to. —*v.i. Obs. or U.S.* **16.** to shoot up, or grow, into a long, slender stalk or stem, as a plant. **17.** to grow tall and slender, often disproportionately so. [ME *spindel*, OE *spinel* (c. D *spindel*, G *Spindel*), der. *spinnan* SPIN]

spindlelegs (spĭn′dl lĕgz′), *n.pl.* spindleshanks. —**spindle-legged** (spĭn′dl lĕgd′, -lĕg′ĭd), *adj.*

spindleshanks (spĭn′dl shăngks′), *n.pl. Colloq.* **1.** long, thin legs. **2.** (*construed as sing.*) a tall, thin person with such legs. —**spindle-shanked** (spĭn′dl shăngkt′), *adj.*

spindle tree, 1. a shrub or small tree of Europe and W Asia, *Euonymus europaeus* (family *Celastraceae*), with a hard wood formerly much used for making spindles. **2.** any of various allied plants.

spindling (spĭnd′lĭng), *adj.* **1.** long or tall and slender, often disproportionately so. **2.** growing into a long, slender stalk or stem, often a too slender or weakly one. —*n.* **3.** *Rare.* a spindling person or thing.

spindly (spĭnd′lĭ), *adj.*, **-dlier, -dliest.** long or tall and slender; attenuated; slender and fragile.

spin-drier (spĭn′drī′ə), *n.* a machine for spin-drying laundry, often forming part of an automatic washing machine. Also, **spin-dryer.**

spindrift (spĭn′drĭft′), *n.* spray swept by a violent wind along the surface of the sea. Also, **spoondrift.**

spin-dry (spĭn′drī′), *v.t.*, **-dried, -drying.** to dry (laundry) by spinning it in a tub so that the moisture is extracted by centrifugal force.

spine (spīn), *n.* **1.** the vertebral or spinal column; the backbone. **2.** any backbone-like part. **3.** a pointed process or projection, as of a bone. **4.** a stiff, pointed process or appendage on an animal, as a quill of a porcupine, or a sharp, bony ray in a fish's fin. **5.** a ridge, as of ground, rock, etc. **6.** a sharp-pointed, hard or woody outgrowth on a plant; a thorn. **7.** *Bookbinding.* the part of a book's cover that holds the front and back together, and which usually indicates the title and author. [ME, t. L: m. *spīna*] —**spined,** *adj.* —**spine′like′,** *adj.*

spinel (spĭ nĕl′), *n.* **1.** any of a group of minerals composed principally of oxides of magnesium, aluminium, iron, manganese, chromium, etc., characterized by their hardness and octahedral crystals. **2.** a mineral of this group, essentially magnesium aluminate, $MgAl_2O_4$, and having varieties used as ornamental stones in jewellery. [t. F: m. *(e)spinelle*, t. It.: m. *spinella*, dim. of *spina* thorn, g. L]

spineless (spīn′lĭs), *adj.* **1.** without spines. **2.** having no spine. **3.** having a weak spine; limp. **4.** without moral force, resolution, or courage; feeble. —**spine′lessly,** *adv.* —**spine′lessness,** *n.* —**Ant. 4.** resolute.

spinescent (spī nĕs′ənt), *adj.* **1.** *Bot.* **a.** becoming spine-like. **b.** ending in a spine. **c.** bearing spines. **2.** *Zool.* somewhat spinelike; coarse, as hair. [t. LL: s. *spīnescens*, ppr., growing thorny]

spinet (spĭ nĕt′), *n.* **1.** a small keyboard instrument resembling the harpsichord. **2.** an early small square piano. **3.** *U.S.* a commercial name for a modern small upright piano. [t. F: m. *espinette*, ? named after Giovanni *Spinetti*, fl. 1500, Venetian inventor]

spiniferous (spī nĭf′ə rəs), *adj.* spiny.

spinifex (spĭn′ĭ fĕks′), *n.* any of the spiny grasses of the genus *Spinifex*, chiefly of Australia, often useful as binding sand on the seashore. [NL: f. m. *spīna* spine + *-fex* maker]

spinnaker (spĭn′ə kə), *n. Naut.* a large triangular sail with a light boom (**spinnaker boom**), carried by yachts on the side opposite the mainsail when running before the wind, or with the wind abaft the beam. [supposedly der. *Sphinx* (mispronounced *spinks*), name of yacht on which this sail was first regularly used]

spinner (spĭn′ə), *n.* **1.** one who or that which spins. **2.** a revolving bait used in trolling or casting for fish. **3.** a spider. **4.** *Cricket.* a ball bowled with spin.

spinneret (spĭn′ə rĕt′), *n.* **1.** an organ or part by means of which a spider, insect larva, or the like spins a silky thread for its web or cocoon. **2.** a finely perforated tube or plate through which a viscous liquid passes into the solidifying medium during the course of manufacture of man-made fibres. [dim. of SPINNER]

spinney (spĭn′ĭ), *n.*, *pl.* **-neys. 1.** a thicket or copse. **2.** a small plantation or group of trees. [ME *spenne*, t. OF: m. *espinei* thorny place, der. *espine* SPINE]

spinning (spĭn′ĭng), *n.* **1.** the technique or act of changing fibrous substances into yarn or thread. **2.** *Angling.* the technique or act of casting and drawing back the bait, often a revolving device, in such a way as to simulate the motion of a live fish.

spinning jenny, an early spinning machine having more than one spindle, whereby one person could spin a number of yarns simultaneously.

spinning wheel, an old-fashioned device for spinning wool, flax, etc., into yarn or thread consisting essentially of a single spindle driven by a large wheel operated by hand or foot.

Spinning wheel

spinode (spī′nōd), *n.* a cusp (def. 3). [irreg. f. L *spī(na)* spine + NODE]

spin-off (spĭn′ ŏf′), *n.* a by-product, esp. of space research: *the non-stick frying pan is a commercially valuable spin-off of space research.*

spinose (spī′nōs), *adj.* *Chiefly Biol.* full of spines; spiniferous; spinous. [t. L: m. s. *spīnōsus*] —**spi′nosely,** *adv.* —**spinosity** (spī nŏs′ĭ tĭ), *n.*

spinous (spī′nəs), *adj.* **1.** covered with or having spines; thorny, as a plant. **2.** armed with or bearing sharp-pointed processes, as an animal; spiniferous. **3.** spinelike.

Spinoza (spĭ nō′zə), *n.* **Baruch** or **Benedict de** (bä′ro͝ok *or* bĕn′ĭ dĭkt də), 1632–77, Dutch philosopher of Portuguese Jewish origin.

Spinozism (spĭ nō′zĭz′əm), *n.* the pantheistic philosophy of Spinoza, teaching that extension and thought are each an attribute of the one substance. —**Spino′zist,** *n.*

spin stabilization, *Aerospace.* stabilization of a spacecraft, etc., by spinning, so that the craft remains pointing in a given direction. —**spin′-sta′bilized′,** *adj.*

spinster (spĭn′stə), *n.* **1.** a woman still unmarried beyond the usual age of marrying; an old maid. **2.** *Chiefly Law.* a woman who has never married. **3.** *Obs.* a woman (sometimes, any person) who spins, esp. as a regular occupation. [ME, f. SPIN + -STER] —**spin′sterhood′,** *n.* —**spin′sterish,** *adj.*

spinthariscope (spĭn thă′rĭ skōp′), *n.* *Physics.* an apparatus for observing the scintillations produced in a prepared screen, as of zinc sulphide, by the action of radioactive rays. [f. Gk *spinthari(s)* spark + -SCOPE]

spinule (spī′nyo͞ol), *n.* a small spine. [t. L: m. s. *spīnula,* dim. of *spīna* SPINE] —**spinulose** (spī′nyo͞o lōs′), *adj.*

spiny (spī′nĭ), *adj.,* **spinier, spiniest. 1.** abounding in or having spines; thorny, as a plant. **2.** covered with or having sharp-pointed processes, as an animal. **3.** in the form of a spine; resembling a spine; spinelike. **4.** perplexing or troublesome, as a problem; thorny. —**spin′iness,** *n.*

spiny anteater, an echidna.

spiny-finned (spī′nĭ fĭnd′), *adj.* having fins with sharp bony rays, as an acanthopterygian.

spiny lobster, any of the crustaceans of the family *Palinuridae.*

spiracle (spī′ə rə kl, spī′rə kl), *n.* **1.** a breathing hole; an opening by which a confined space has communication with the outer air; an airhole. **2.** *Zool.* **a.** an aperture or orifice through which air or water passes in the act of respiration, as the blowhole of a cetacean. **b.** an opening in the head of sharks and rays through which water is drawn and passed over gills. **c.** one of the external orifices of a tracheal respiratory system, usually on the sides of the body. See diag. under **insect.** [ME, t. L: m. s. *spīrāculum*] —**spiracular** (spĭ răk′yo͞o lə), *adj.* —**spirac′ulate,** *adj.*

spiraea (spī rĭə′), *n.* any of the herbs or shrubs constituting the rosaceous genus *Spiraea,* with racemes, cymes, panicles, or corymbs of small white or pink flowers, certain species of which are much cultivated for ornament, esp. the **Japanese spiraea,** *S. japonica.* Also, **spirea.** [t. L, t. Gk: m. *speiraía* meadowsweet]

spiral[1] (spī′ə rəl), *n., adj., v.,* **-ralled, -ralling** or (*U.S.*) **-raled, -raling.** —*n.* **1.** a plane curve traced by a point which runs continuously round and round a fixed point or centre while constantly receding from or approaching it. **2.** a single circle or ring of a spiral or helical curve or object. **3.** a spiral or helical object, formation, or form. **4.** a helix. **5.** *Aeron.* a manoeuvre in which an aeroplane descends in a helix of small pitch and large radius, with the angle of incidence within that of the normal flight range. **6.** *Econ.* a reciprocal interaction of price and cost changes forming an overall economic change upwards (**inflationary spiral**) or downwards (**deflationary spiral**). —*adj.* **7.** resembling or arranged in a spiral or spirals. **8.** (of a curve) like a spiral. **9.** helical. —*v.i.* **10.** to take a spiral form or course. **11.** *Aeron.* to move an aeroplane through a spiral course. —*v.t.* **12.** to cause to take a spiral form or course. [t. ML: s. *spīrālis*] —**spi′rally,** *adv.*

Spirals (def. 3)

spiral[2] (spī′ə rəl), *adj.* pertaining to or of the nature of a spire; spirelike; tall and tapering. [f. SPIR(E)[1] + -AL]

spiral galaxy, *Astron.* one of the extragalactic stellar systems which shows spiral structure. Also, **spiral nebula.**

spirant (spī′ə rənt), *n., adj.* *Phonet. Obsolesc.* fricative. [t. L: s. *spīrans,* ppr., breathing]

spire[1] (spī′ə), *n., v.,* **spired, spiring.** —*n.* **1.** a tall, tapering structure, generally an elongated, upright cone or pyramid, erected on a tower, roof, etc. **2.** such a structure forming the upper part of the steeple, or the whole steeple. See illus. under **steeple. 3.** a tapering, pointed part of something; a tall, sharp-pointed summit, peak, or the like. **4.** the highest point or summit of something. **5.** a sprout or shoot of a plant; an acrospire of grain; a blade or spear of grass, etc. —*v.i.* **6.** to shoot or rise into spirelike form; rise or extend to a height in the manner of a spire. [ME; OE *spīr,* c. D *spier,* G *Spier*] —**spire′like′,** *adj.*

spire[2] (spī′ə), *n.* **1.** a coil or spiral. **2.** one of the series of convolutions of a coil or spiral. **3.** *Zool.* the upper, convoluted part of a spiral shell, above the aperture. [t. L: m. *spīra,* t. Gk: m. *speîra* coil, winding] —**spire′like′,** *adj.*

spirea (spī rĭə′), *n.* spiraea.

spired (spī′əd), *adj.* having a spire.

spireme (spī′ə rēm′), *n.* *Biol.* the chromatin of a cell nucleus, when in a continuous or segmented threadlike form, during mitosis. [t. Gk: m. *speirēma* coil]

Spires (spī′əz), *n.* Speyer.

spiriferous (spī′ə rĭf′ə rəs), *adj.* **1.** having a spire, or spiral upper part, as a univalve shell. **2.** having spiral appendages, as a brachiopod.

spirillum (spī rĭl′əm), *n., pl.* **-rilla** (-rĭl′ə). **1.** any of the bacteria constituting the genus *Spirillum,* characterized by spirally twisted, rigid forms and having a bundle of 5 to 20 flagella. See illus. under **bacteria. 2.** any of various similar micro-organisms. [NL, dim. of L *spīra* SPIRE[2]]

spirit (spĭ′rĭt), *n.* **1.** the principle of conscious life, orig. identified with the breath; the vital principle in man, animating the body or mediating between body and soul. **2.** the incorporeal part of man: *present in spirit though absent in body.* **3.** the soul as separable from the body at death. **4.** conscious, incorporeal being, as opposed to matter: *the world of spirit.* **5.** a supernatural, incorporeal being, esp. one inhabiting a place or thing or having a particular character: *evil spirits.* **6.** a fairy, sprite, or elf. **7.** an angel or demon. **8.** an inspiring or animating principle such as pervades and tempers thought, feeling, or action: *a spirit of reform.* **9.** (*cap.*) the divine influence as an agency working in the heart of man. **10.** (in biblical use) a divine inspiring or animating being or influence. **11.** the third person of the Trinity; Holy Spirit. **12. the Spirit,** God. **13.** the soul or heart as the seat of feelings or sentiments, or as prompting to action: *to break a person's spirit.* **14.** (*pl.*) feelings with respect to exaltation or depression: *in low spirits.* **15.** fine or brave vigour or liveliness; mettle. **16.** temper or disposition: *meek in spirit.* **17.** a person characterized according to character, disposition, action, etc. **18.** mental or moral attitude; mood: *take something in the right spirit.* **19.** the dominant tendency or character of anything: *the spirit of the age.* **20.** vigorous sense of membership in a group: *team spirit.* **21.** the true or general meaning or intent of a statement, etc. (opposed to *letter*). **22.** *Chem.* **a.** an aqueous solution of ethyl alcohol, esp. one obtained by distillation. **b.** the essence or active principle of a substance as extracted in liquid form, esp. by distillation. **23.** (*often pl.*) a strong distilled alcoholic liquor. **24.** *Pharm.* a solution in alcohol of an essential or volatile principle. **25.** any of certain subtle fluids formerly supposed to permeate the body.
—*adj.* **26.** pertaining to something which works by burning alcoholic spirits. **27.** of or pertaining to spiritualist bodies or activities.
—*v.t.* **28.** to animate with fresh ardour or courage; inspirit. **29.** to encourage; urge (*on*) or stir (*up*), as to action. **30.** to carry (*away, off,* etc.) mysteriously or secretly.
[ME, t. L: s. *spīritus* breathing]
—**Syn. 2.** life, mind, consciousness. **5.** See **ghost.**

spirited (spĭ′rĭ tĭd), *adj.* **1.** having a spirit, or having spirits, as specified: *low-spirited.* **2.** having or showing mettle, courage, vigour, liveliness, etc. —**spir′itedly,** *adv.* —**spir′itedness,** *n.*

spirit gum, a spirit-soluble, fast-drying preparation, as used for attaching false hair to an actor's skin.

spiritism (spĭ′rĭ tĭz′əm), *n.* the doctrine or practices of spiritualism. —**spir′itist,** *n.* —**spir′itis′tic,** *adj.*

spiritless (spĭr′ĭt lĭs), *adj.* **1.** without spirit. **2.** without ardour, vigour, animation, etc. —**spir′itlessly,** *adv.* —**spir′itlessness,** *n.*

spirit level, a device for testing horizontality, consisting of a glass tube containing an oil or spirit, as alcohol, with a movable bubble which is only in the centre of the tube if the device is horizontal.

spiritoso (spĭ′rĭ tō′sō), *adj. Music.* spirited; lively. [It.]

spiritous (spĭ′rĭ təs), *adj. Obs.* **1.** of the nature of spirit; immaterial, ethereal, or refined. **2.** high-spirited. **3.** spirituous.

spirit-rapping (spĭ′rĭt răp′ĭng), *n.* supposed communication between the living and the dead by rapping out messages on a table or the like. —**spir′it-rap′per,** *n.*

spirits of hartshorn, an aqueous solution of ammonia. Cf. **hartshorn** (def. 2).

spirits of salt, a solution of hydrochloric acid in water.

spirits of turpentine, oil of turpentine.

spirits of wine, alcohol.

spiritual (spĭ′rĭ tyo͝o əl), *adj.* **1.** of, pertaining to, or consisting of spirit or incorporeal being. **2.** of or pertaining to the spirit or soul as distinguished from the physical nature. **3.** standing in a relationship of the spirit; nonmaterial: *a spiritual attitude, a spiritual father.* **4.** characterized by or suggesting predominance of the spirit; ethereal or delicately refined. **5.** of or pertaining to the spirit as the seat of the moral or religious nature. **6.** of or pertaining to sacred things; pertaining or belonging to the church; ecclesiastical; religious; devotional; sacred. **7.** of or relating to the conscious thoughts and emotions. —*n.* **8.** a traditional religious song, esp. of American Negroes. **9.** (*pl.*) affairs of the church. **10.** a spiritual thing or matter. [t. L: s. *spīrituālis*] —**spir′itually,** *adv.* —**spir′itualness,** *n.*

spiritualism (spĭ′rĭ tyo͝o ə lĭz′əm), *n.* **1.** the belief or doctrine that the spirits of the dead, surviving after the mortal life, can and do communicate with the living, esp. through a person (a medium) particularly susceptible to their influence. **2.** the practices or the phenomena associated with this belief. **3.** the belief that all or some reality is immaterial and therefore spiritual. **4.** *Metaphys.* any doctrine that asserts the separate but related existence of God, human (or other rational) beings, and physical nature. **5.** spiritual quality or tendency. **6.** insistence on the spiritual side of things, as in philosophy or religion.

spiritualist (spĭ′rĭ tyo͝o ə lĭst), *n.* **1.** an adherent of spiritualism. **2.** one who concerns himself with or insists on the spiritual side of things. —*adj.* **3.** Also, **spir′itualis′tic.** of or pertaining to spiritualists or spiritualism.

spirituality (spĭ′rĭ tyo͝o ăl′ĭ tĭ), *n., pl.* **-ties. 1.** the quality or fact of being spiritual. **2.** incorporeal or immaterial nature. **3.** predominantly spiritual character, as shown in thought, life, etc.; spiritual tendency or tone. **4.** (*often pl.*) property or revenue of the church or of an ecclesiastic in his official capacity.

spiritualize (spĭ′rĭ tyo͝o ə līz′), *v.t.,* **-lized, -lizing. 1.** to make spiritual. **2.** to invest with a spiritual meaning. Also, **spiritualise.** —**spir′itualiza′tion,** *n.*

spiritualty (spĭ′rĭ tyo͝o əl tĭ), *n., pl.* **-ties.** *Obs. or Hist.* **1.** (*often pl.*) ecclesiastical property or revenue. **2.** the body of ecclesiastics; the clergy.

spirituel (spĭ′rĭ tyo͝o ĕl′; *Fr.* spē rē tʏ ĕl′), *adj.* **1.** showing a refined and graceful mind or wit. **2.** light and airy in movement; ethereal. [t. F. See SPIRITUAL] —**spir′ituelle′,** *adj., fem.*

spirituous (spĭ′rĭ tyo͝o əs), *adj.* **1.** containing, of the nature of, or pertaining to alcohol; alcoholic. **2.** (of liquors) distilled, as opposed to fermented. —**spir′ituousness,** *n.*

spiritus asper (spĭ′rĭ təs ăs′pə), *Gram.* the rough breathing. [L]

spiritus lenis (spĭ′rĭ təs lē′nĭs), *Gram.* the smooth breathing. [L]

spirit varnish, a varnish consisting of a solution of resin, or resins, in industrial methylated spirits.

spirket (spû′kĭt), *n. Shipbuilding.* a space between the floor timbers of a wooden ship. [orig. uncert.; ? akin to OE *spircing* scattering]

spirketting (spû′kĭ tĭng), *n. Naut. Obs.* the planks of the deck nearest the sides of a wooden ship. Also, *U.S.*, **spirketing.**

spiro-[1], a word element referring to 'respiration', as in *spirograph.* [comb. form repr. L *spīrāre* breathe]

spiro-[2], a word element meaning 'coil', 'spiral', as in *spirochaete.* [t. Gk: m. *speiro-*, comb. form of *speîra*]

spirochaete (spī′ə rō kēt′), *n.* slender, corkscrew-like bacterial micro-organisms constituting the genus *Spirochaeta*, and found on man, animals, and plants, and in soil and water. Some cause disease, as the *Spirochaeta pallida* or *Treponema pallidum* (the causative agent of syphilis); most, however, are saprophytic. Also, *Chiefly U.S.*, **spi′rochete′.** [t. NL: m. *Spirochaeta*, f. Gk: m. *speiro-* SPIRO-[2] + m. *chaítē* hair]

spirochaetosis (spī′ə rō kĭ tō′sĭs), *n. Vet. Sci.* a specific, infectious, usually fatal blood disease of chickens caused by a spirochaete, *Borrelia anserina.* Also, *Chiefly U.S.*, **spirochetosis.**

spirograph (spī′ə rə grăf′, -gräf′), *n.* an instrument for recording respiratory movements.

spirogyra (spī′ə rə jī′ə rə), *n. Bot.* a widely distributed freshwater green alga (genus *Spirogyra*) having peripheral, spiral chromatophores. [NL, f. Gk: m. *speiro-* SPIRO-[2] + m. *gŷros* circle, ring]

spiroid (spī′ə roid′), *adj.* more or less spiral; resembling a spiral. [t. NL: s. *spiroīdes.* See SPIRO-[2], -OID]

spirometer (spī′ə rŏm′ĭ tə), *n.* an instrument for determining the capacity of the lungs. [f. SPIRO-[1] + -METER[1]] —**spirometric** (spī′ə rə mĕt′rĭk), *adj.* —**spirom′etry,** *n.*

spirt (spût), *v.i., v.t., n.* spurt.

spirula (spī′ə ro͞o lə), *n., pl.* **-lae** (-lē′). any of the small decapod dibranchiate cephalopods of the genus *Spirula*, having in the hinder part of the body, but not completely internal, a shell in the form of a flat spiral with separated whorls, which is divided by partitions into a series of chambers. [NL, dim. of L *spira* SPIRE[2]]

Spirula, *Spirula spirula* (2 in. long)

spiry[1] (spī′ə rĭ), *adj.* **1.** having the form of a spire, slender shoot, or tapering pointed body; tapering up to a point like a spire. **2.** abounding in spires or steeples. [f. SPIRE[1] + -Y[1]]

spiry[2] (spī′ə rĭ), *adj.* spiral; coiled; curling. [f. SPIRE[2] + -Y[1]]

spit[1] (spĭt), *v.,* **spat** or **spit, spitting,** *n.* —*v.i.* **1.** to eject saliva from the mouth; expectorate. **2.** to do this at or on a person, etc., to express hatred, contempt, etc. **3.** to sputter. **4.** to fall in scattered drops or flakes, as rain or snow. **5.** to make a noise as of spitting. —*v.t.* **6.** to eject (saliva, etc.) from the mouth. **7.** to throw out or emit, esp. violently. **8.** to utter vehemently. **9. spit it out,** *Colloq.* speak. —*n.* **10.** saliva, esp. when ejected. **11.** the act of spitting. **12.** a frothy or spitlike secretion exuded by various insects; spittle[1] (def. 2). **13.** a light fall of rain or snow. **14.** Also, **spitting image.** *Colloq.* the image, likeness, or counterpart of a person, etc. [ME; OE *spittan*, c. d. G *spitzen*, akin to OE *spǣtan* spit] —**spit′like′,** *adj.* —**spit′ter,** *n.*

spit[2] (spĭt), *n., v.,* **spitted, spitting.** —*n.* **1.** a sharply pointed, slender rod or bar for thrusting into or through and holding meat to be roasted at a fire or grilled. **2.** any of various rods, pins, or the like used for particular purposes. **3.** a device for roasting meat, etc., comprising such a rod, together with a mechanism for revolving it, and a source of heat; a rotisserie. **4.** a narrow point of land projecting into the water. **5.** a long, narrow shoal extending from the shore. —*v.t.* **6.** to pierce, stab, or transfix, as with a spit; impale on something sharp. **7.** to thrust a spit into or through. [ME; OE *spitu*, c. D and LG *spit*]

spital (spĭt′l), *n. Obs.* **1.** a hospital, esp. one for the poor. **2.** a shelter on a highway. [short for HOSPITAL; r. earlier *spittle*, ME *spitel*, c. G *Spital.* Cf. d. It. *spitale*]

spit and polish, assiduous attention to smartness, esp. of soldiers; excessive concern with discipline.

spitchcock (spĭch′kŏk′), *n.* **1.** an eel split, cut into pieces, and broiled or fried. —*v.t.* **2.** to split, cut up, and broil or fry (an eel, fowl, etc.). **3.** to treat severely. [orig. uncert.]

spite (spīt), *n., v.,* **spited, spiting.** —*n.* **1.** a keen, ill-natured desire to humiliate, annoy, or injure another; venomous ill will. **2.** a particular instance of such ill will; a grudge. **3.** *Archaic.* vexation or chagrin. **4. in spite of,** in disregard or defiance of; notwithstanding. —*v.t.* **5.** to wreak one's spite or malice on. **6.** to annoy or thwart, out of spite. **7.** *Archaic.* to fill with spite; vex; offend. [ME; aphetic var. of DESPITE, n.] —**Syn. 1.** See **grudge. 4.** See **notwithstanding.**

spiteful (spīt′fəl), *adj.* full of spite or malice; showing spite; malicious; malevolent; venomous: *she was a spiteful and jealous old woman.* —**spite′fully,** *adv.* —**spite′fulness,** *n.*

—**Syn.** SPITEFUL, REVENGEFUL, VINDICTIVE refer to a desire to inflict a wrong or injury on someone, usually in return for one received. SPITEFUL implies a mean or malicious desire for (often petty) revenge: *a spiteful attitude towards a former friend.* REVENGEFUL is a strong word, implying a deep, powerful, and continued intent to repay a wrong: *a fierce and revengeful spirit.* VINDICTIVE does not imply action necessarily, but stresses the unforgiving nature of the avenger: *a vindictive look.*

spitfire (spĭt′fī′ə), *n.* **1.** a person of fiery temper, easily provoked to outbursts, esp. a girl or woman. **2.** (*cap.*) a British single-engined fighter aircraft much used in World War II.

Spithead (spĭt′hĕd′), *n.* a navigation channel off the S coast of England between Portsmouth and the Isle of Wight.

Spitsbergen (spĭts′bû′gən), *n.* a group of islands in the Arctic Ocean, N of and belonging to Norway. 2961 rotating pop. (est. 1961); 24,293 sq. mi. Also, **Spitzbergen** Norwegian, **Svalbard.**

Spitsbergen

spitting image, spit[1] (def. 14).

spitting snake, the ringhals.

spittle[1] (spĭt′l), *n.* **1.** saliva; spit. **2.** the frothy protective secretion exuded by spittle insects. [alter. (conformed to SPIT[1]) of obs. or d. *spattle,* ME *spatel,* OE *spātl,* akin to *spǣtan* spit]

spittle[2] (spĭt′l), *n. Archaic.* spital.

spittle insect, a froghopper.

spittoon (spĭ to͞on′), *n.* a bowl, etc., for spitting into.

spitz (spĭts), *n.* any of a number of small or medium-sized breeds of dog having dense hair, pointed muzzle, and erect ears, as the elkhound. [G: pointed, with ref. to the muzzle]

spitzkoppie (spĭts′kŏp′ĭ), *n. S African.* kopje.

spiv (spĭv), *n. Colloq.* one who lives by his wits, without working or by dubious business activity, and, usually affecting ostentatious dress and tastes. [back-formation from d. *spiving* smart. See SPIFFY] **—spiv′vy,** *adj.*

splanchnic (splăngk′nĭk), *adj.* of or pertaining to the viscera or entrails; visceral. [t. NL: s. *splanchnicus,* t. Gk: m. *splanchnikós*]

splash (splăsh), *v.t.* **1.** to wet or soil by dashing masses or particles of water, mud, or the like; spatter. **2.** to fall upon (something) in scattered masses or particles, as a liquid does. **3.** to cause to appear spattered. **4.** to dash (water etc.) about in scattered masses or particles. **5.** to make (one's way) with splashing. **6.** *Colloq.* to display or print very noticeably, as a newspaper. **7.** *Colloq.* to spend (money) freely. *—v.i.* **8.** to dash a liquid or semiliquid substance about. **9.** to fall, move, or go with a splash or splashes. **10.** (of liquid) to dash or fall in scattered masses or particles. **11.** (of a bullet) to disintegrate on impact. **12.** *Colloq.* to spend money freely (often fol. by *out*). *—n.* **13.** the act of splashing. **14.** the sound of splashing. **15.** a quantity of some liquid or semiliquid substance splashed upon or in a thing. **16.** a spot caused by something splashed. **17.** a patch, as of colour or light. **18.** a striking show, or an ostentatious display; sensation or excitement. **19. make a splash,** to be noticed; make an impression on people. [alter. of PLASH[1]]

splashback (splăsh′băk′), *n.* a screen of glass, etc., protecting the wall above a washbasin.

splashboard (splăsh′bôd′), *n.* **1.** a board, guard, or screen to protect from splashing, as a dashboard of a vehicle or a guard placed over a wheel to intercept water, dirt, etc. **2.** a screen to prevent water or spray from coming on the deck of a boat.

splasher (splăsh′ə), *n.* **1.** one who or that which splashes. **2.** something that protects from splashes.

splashy (splăsh′ĭ), *adj.*, **splashier, splashiest. 1.** making a splash or splashes. **2.** making the sound of splashing. **3.** full of or marked by splashes, or irregular spots, spotty. **4.** wet, soft, or muddy. **5.** *Colloq.* making a show or display.

splat (splăt), *n.* a broad, flat piece of wood, as the central upright part of the back of a chair. [cf. OE *splātan* split]

splatter (splăt′ə), *v.i., v.t.* to splash.

splay (splā), *v.t.* **1.** to spread out, expand, or extend. **2.** to form with an oblique angle; make slanting; bevel. **3.** to make with a splay or splays. **4.** to disjoin; dislocate. *—v.i.* **5.** to have an oblique or slanting direction. **6.** to spread or flare. *—n.* **7.** *Archit.* Also, **reveal.** a surface which makes an oblique angle with another, as where the opening through a wall for a window or door widens from the window or door proper towards the face of the wall. *—adj.* **8.** spread out; wide and flat; turned outwards. **9.** oblique or awry. [aphetic var. of DISPLAY]

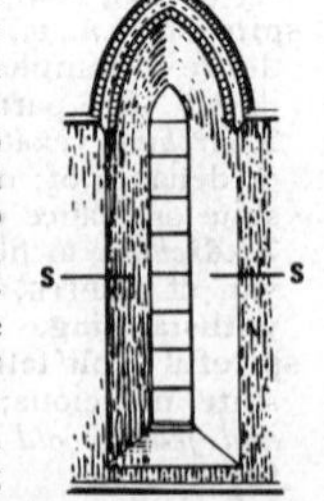

S, Splay

splayfoot (splā′fo͝ot′), *n.* a broad, flat foot, esp. one turned outwards. **—splay′-foot′ed,** *adj.*

spleen (splēn), *n.* **1.** a highly vascular, glandlike but ductless organ, situated in man near the cardiac end of the stomach, in which the blood undergoes certain corpuscular changes. **2.** *Obs.* this organ as supposed (variously) to be the seat of mirth, spirit or courage, ill humour, melancholy, etc. **3.** ill humour, peevish temper, or spite: *venting his spleen on his unfortunate wife.* **4.** *Archaic.* melancholy. **5.** *Obs.* caprice. [ME, t. L: m. *splēn,* t. Gk] **—spleen′ish, spleen′y,** *adj.*

spleenful (splēn′fəl), *adj.* **1.** full of or displaying spleen. **2.** ill-humoured; irritable or peevish; spiteful.

spleenwort (splēn′wût′), *n.* any of various ferns of the genus *Asplenium,* having linear or oblong sori on the undersurface of the leaf along the acropetal side of an oblique veinlet, as the **black spleenwort,** *A. adiantum-nigrum.*

splendent (splĕn′dənt), *adj.* **1.** shining or radiant, as the sun; gleaming or lustrous, as metal, marble, etc. **2.** brilliant in appearance, colour, etc.; gorgeous; magnificent; splendid. **3.** very conspicuous; illustrious. [late ME, t. L: s. *splendens,* ppr., shining]

splendid (splĕn′dĭd), *adj.* **1.** gorgeous; magnificent; sumptuous. **2.** grand; superb, as beauty. **3.** glorious, as a name, reputation, victory, etc. **4.** strikingly admirable or fine: *splendid talents.* **5.** excellent, fine, or very good: *to have a splendid time.* **6.** *Rare.* brilliant in appearance, colour, etc. [t. L: s. *splendidus*] **—splen′didly,** *adv.* **—splen′didness,** *n.* **—Syn. 1.** See **magnificent.**

splendiferous (splĕn dĭf′ə rəs), *adj. Colloq.* splendid; magnificent; fine. [f. ML *splendifer* (r. LL *splendōrifer*) splendour-bearing + -OUS]

splendour (splĕn′də), *n.* **1.** brilliant or gorgeous appearance, colouring, etc.; magnificence, grandeur, or pomp, or display of it: *the splendour and pomp of his coronation.* **2.** brilliant distinction; glory: *the splendour of ancient Roman architecture.* **3.** great brightness; brilliant light or lustre. **4. sun in splendour,** *Her.* the sun depicted with its rays, and a human face. Also, *U.S.*, **splen′dor.** [late ME, t. L] **—splen′dorous,** *adj.*

splenectomy (splĭ nĕk′tə mĭ), *n., pl.* **-mies.** *Surg.* excision or removal of the spleen.

splenetic (splĭ nĕt′ĭk), *adj.* Also, **splenet′ical. 1.** of the spleen; splenic. **2.** irritable, peevish; spiteful. **3.** *Obs.* melancholy. *—n.* **4.** a splenetic person. [t. LL: s. *splēnēticus*] **—splenet′ically,** *adv.*

splenic (splĕn′ĭk, splē′nĭk), *adj.* of or pertaining to, connected with, or affecting the spleen: *splenic nerves.* [t. L: s. *splēnicus,* t. Gk: m. *splēnikós*]

splenitis (splĭ nī′tĭs), *n. Pathol.* inflammation of the spleen.

splenius (splē′nĭ əs), *n., pl.* **-nii** (-nĭ ī′). *Anat.* one of a pair of bandage-shaped muscles which run obliquely upwards on the back and sides of the neck. [NL, t. Gk: m. *splēnion* bandage] **—sple′nial,** *adj.*

splenomegaly (splē′nō mĕg′ə lĭ), *n. Pathol.* an enlargement of the spleen. [f. Gk: s. *splḗn* SPLEEN + m. *megálē* fem. of *mégas* great]

splice (splīs), *v.,* **spliced, splicing,** *n. —v.t.* **1.** to join together or unite, as two ropes or parts of a rope, by the interweaving of strands. **2.** to unite, as two pieces of timber, etc., by overlapping. **3.** to join or unite. **4.** *Slang.* to join in marriage. **5. splice the mainbrace,** *Naut.* to issue an extra allowance of drink, esp. rum. *—n.* **6.** a joining of two ropes or parts of a rope by splicing. **7.** the union so effected. **8.** a joining or junction of two pieces of timber, etc., by overlapping and fastening the ends. **9.** the wedge-shaped extension of the handle of a cricket bat or the like that fits into the blade. [t. MD: m. *splissen*; ? akin to SPLIT] **—splic′er,** *n.*

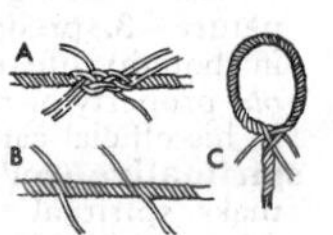

Rope splices
A, Short splice;
B, Long splice;
C, Eye splice

splice graft, *Hort.* a type of graft in which a V-shaped cut is made in the stock.

spline (splīn), *n., v.,* **splined, splining.** *—n.* **1.** a long, narrow, relatively thin strip of wood, metal, etc.; a slat. **2.** a long, flexible strip of wood or the like used in drawing curves. **3.** *Mach.* one of a number of uniformly spaced keys cut into a shaft parallel to its axis. *—v.t. Mach.* **4.** to fit with a spline or key. **5.** to provide with a groove for a spline or key. [orig. E Anglian dial.; ? akin to SPLINTER]

splint (splĭnt), *n.* **1.** a thin piece of wood or other rigid material used to immobilize a fractured or dislocated bone, or to maintain any part of the body in a fixed position. **2.** one of a number of thin strips of wood woven together to make a chair seat, basket, etc. **3.** *Vet. Sci.* an exostosis or bony enlargement of a splint-bone of a horse or a related animal. **4.** one of a number of overlapping bands or strips of metal in armour for protecting the body and limbs. **5.** *Dial.* a splinter. *—v.t.* **6.** to secure, hold in position, or support by means of a splint or splints, as a fractured bone. **7.** to support as if with splints. [ME *splente,* t. MLG: metal plate or pin; akin to SPLINTER] **—splint′like′,** *adj.*

splint-bone (splĭnt′bōn′), *n.* one of the rudimentary, splintlike metacarpal or metatarsal bones of the horse or some allied animal, closely applied one on each side of the back of each cannon bone.

splinter (splĭn′tə), *n.* **1.** a rough piece of wood, bone, etc., usually comparatively long, thin, and sharp, split or broken off from a main body. **2.** *Obs.* a splint. **3.** a fragment of metal resulting from the explosion of a bomb or shell. —*v.t.* **4.** to split or break into splinters. **5.** to break off in splinters. **6.** *Obs.* to secure or support by a splint or splints, as a broken limb. —*v.i.* **7.** to be split or broken into splinters. **8.** to break off in splinters. [ME, t. MD or MLG. See SPLINT] —**splin′tery,** *adj.*

splinter-bone (splĭn′tə bōn′), *n. Colloq.* the fibula.

splinter group, a group of members of an organization, party, or the like, who set up independently, as after disagreement with the parent body on some matter of principle.

split (splĭt), *v.*, **split, splitting,** *n.*, *adj.* —*v.t.* **1.** to rend or cleave lengthwise; separate or part from end to end or between layers, often forcibly or by cutting. **2.** to separate off by rending or cleaving lengthwise: *to split a piece from a block.* **3.** to tear or break asunder; rend or burst. **4.** to divide into distinct parts or portions. **5.** to separate (a part) by such division. **6.** to divide (persons) into different groups, factions, parties, etc., as by discord. **7.** to separate off (a group, etc.) by such division. **8.** to divide between two or more persons, etc.: *to split a bottle of wine.* **9.** to separate into parts by interposing something: *to split an infinitive.* **10.** *Chem.* to divide (molecules or atoms) by cleavage into smaller parts. **11.** to make (a vote) less effective by offering more than one candidate with a similar policy: *Liberal intervention split the anti-Conservative vote and lost Labour the seat.* **12. split one's sides,** to laugh heartily. **13. split the difference,** to reach a compromise by which each side concedes an equal amount. —*v.i.* **14.** to break or part lengthways, or suffer longitudinal division. **15.** to part, divide, or separate in any way. **16.** to break asunder; part by striking on a rock, by the violence of a storm, etc., as a ship. **17.** to become separated off by such a division, as a piece or part from a whole. **18.** to break up or separate through disagreement, etc. **19.** *Colloq.* to divide something with another or others. **20.** *Slang.* to commit a betrayal by divulging information. **21.** *Slang.* to leave hurriedly. **22. split on,** *Slang.* to betray, denounce, or divulge secrets concerning. **23. split up,** *Colloq.* to part; leave each other; become separated. —*n.* **24.** the act of splitting. **25.** a crack, rent, or fissure caused by splitting. **26.** a piece or part separated by or as by splitting. **27.** a strip split from an osier, used in basketmaking. **28.** a breach or rupture in a party, etc., or between persons. **29.** a faction, party, etc., formed by a rupture or schism. **30.** *Colloq.* something combining different elements, as a drink composed of half spirits, half soda-water. **31.** *Colloq.* a dish made from sliced fruit (usually banana) and ice-cream, and covered with syrup and nuts. **32.** *Colloq.* a drink containing only half the usual quantity. **33.** a half-sized bottle, as one of soda-water. **34.** (*usually pl.*) the feat of separating the legs while sinking to the floor, until they extend at right angles to the body, as in stage performances. **35.** *Tenpin Bowling.* the arrangement of the remaining pins after the first bowl so that a spare is practically impossible. **36.** one of the thicknesses of leather into which a skin is cut. **37.** *Colloq.* an act or arrangement of splitting, as of a sum of money. —*adj.* **38.** that has undergone splitting; parted lengthwise; cleft. **39.** divided. [t. MD: m. s. *splitten*, akin to G *spleissen*] —**split′ter,** *n.*

Split (splĭt; *Serb.* splēt), *n.* a seaport in W Yugoslavia: Roman ruins. 93,386 (1961). Italian, **Spalato.**

split infinitive, a simple infinitive with a word between the *to* and the verb, as *to readily understand.*

split-level (splĭt′lĕv′əl), *adj.* denoting or pertaining to a building having certain floors at other than main storey level, or a room with a floor at more than one level.

split pea, a pea dried and split, used for soups and as a vegetable.

split personality, *Colloq.* **1.** schizophrenia. **2.** any apparent alternation by someone between two dissociated modes of behaviour, temperaments, or the like.

split-phase (splĭt′fāz′), *adj. Elect.* pertaining to a current from a single-phase source which has been split into two separate phases in two branches of a circuit.

split pin, cotter pin.

split ring, a ring, as a key ring, having a split by means of which things may be attached and removed.

split second, a very short period of time.

split-second (splĭt′sĕk′ənd), *adj.* **1.** performed with great precision. **2.** achieved or arrived at immediately.

splitting (splĭt′ĭng), *adj.* **1.** that splits. **2.** overpoweringly noisy, as if to split the ears. **3.** violent or severe, as a headache. **4.** very fast or rapid.

splotch (splŏch), *n.* **1.** a large, irregular spot; blot; stain. —*v.t.* **2.** to mark with splotches. Also, **splodge** (splŏj). [? b. OE *splott* spot and PATCH] —**splotch′y,** *adj.*

splurge (splûj), *n.*, *v.*, **splurged, splurging.** *Colloq.* —*n.* **1.** an ostentatious display, esp. of wealth. —*v.t.* **2.** to spend (money) extravagantly. —*v.i.* **3.** to be extravagant: *we splurged and bought new hats.* [? b. SPLASH and SURGE]

splutter (splŭt′ə), *v.i.* **1.** to talk hastily and confusedly or incoherently, as in excitement or embarrassment. **2.** to make a spluttering sound, or emit particles of something explosively, as something frying or a pen scattering ink. **3.** to fly or fall in particles or drops; spatter, as a liquid. —*v.t.* **4.** to utter hastily and confusedly or incoherently; sputter. **5.** to spatter (a liquid, etc.). **6.** to bespatter (a person, etc.). —*n.* **7.** spluttering utterance or talk; a dispute; a noise or fuss. **8.** a sputtering or spattering of liquid, etc. [b. SPLASH and SPUTTER] —**splut′terer,** *n.*

Spock (spŏk), *n.* **Benjamin,** born 1903, U.S. paediatrician.

Spode (spōd), *n.* **1. Josiah,** 1754–1827, English potter. **2.** china or porcelain made by him. **3.** the firm founded by him. —*adj.* **4.** pertaining to, made, or originated by Josiah Spode.

spodumene (spŏd′yo͝o mēn′), *n.* a mineral, lithium aluminium silicate, $LiAlSi_2O_6$, occurring in prismatic crystals, transparent varieties being used as gems: an ore of lithium. Cf. **kunzite.** [t. Gk: m. *spodoúmenos*, ppr., burning to ashes]

spoil (spoil), *v.*, **spoiled** or **spoilt, spoiling,** *n.* —*v.t.* **1.** to damage or impair (a thing) irreparably as to excellence, value, usefulness, etc.: *to spoil a sheet of paper.* **2.** to impair in character or disposition by unwise treatment, benefits, etc., esp. by excessive indulgence. **3.** *Archaic or Rare.* to strip (persons, places, etc.) of goods, valuables, etc.; plunder, pillage, or rob. **4.** *Archaic.* to take by force, or carry off as booty. —*v.i.* **5.** to become spoiled, bad, or unfit for use, as food or other perishable substances; become tainted or putrid. **6.** to plunder, pillage, or rob. **7. be spoiling for,** eager for (a fight, action, etc.) —*n.* **8.** (*often pl.*) booty, loot, or plunder taken in war or robbery. **9.** (*usually pl.*) *Chiefly U.S.* public offices with their emoluments and advantages viewed as won by a victorious political party: *the spoils of office.* **10.** treasures won or accumulated. **11.** waste materials, as those cast up in mining, excavating, quarrying, etc. [ME, t. OF: m. s. *espoillier*, g. L *spoliāre*; ? also an aphetic var. of DESPOIL] —**spoil′er,** *n.*

—**Syn. 1.** SPOIL, RUIN, WRECK agree in meaning to impair the value, quality, usefulness, etc., of anything. SPOIL is the general term: *to spoil a delicate fabric.* RUIN implies doing completely destructive or irreparable injury: *to ruin one's health.* WRECK implies a violent breaking up or demolition: *to wreck one's career with drink.*

spoilage (spoi′lĭj), *n.* **1.** an act or instance of spoiling. **2.** that which is spoiled: *spoilage of fruit on the way to market.*

spoilfive (spoil′fīv′), *n. Cards.* a game played by from three to ten persons having five cards each.

spoil ground, *Naut.* a charted area designated for the deposit of dredgings.

spoilsman (spoilz′mən), *n.*, *pl.* **-men.** *U.S.* one who seeks or receives a share in political spoils; an advocate of the spoils system in politics.

spoilsport (spoil′spôt′), *n.* one who interferes with the pleasure of others.

spoils system, *U.S.* the system or practice in which public offices with the emoluments and advantages are at the disposal of the victorious party for its own purposes and in its own (rather than the public) interest.

spoilt (spoilt), *v.* **1.** a pt. and pp. of **spoil.** —*adj.* **2.** selfish; used to getting one's own way.

Spokane (spō kăn′), *n.* a town in the U.S., in E Washington state. 181,608 (1960).

spoke[1] (spōk), *v.* pt. and archaic pp. of **speak.**

spoke[2] (spōk), *n.*, *v.*, **spoked, spoking.** —*n.* **1.** one of the bars, rods, or rungs radiating from the hub or nave of a wheel and supporting the rim or felloe. See diag. under **felloe. 2.** one of a number of pins or handles projecting from a cylinder or wheel, or joining hub and rim, esp. on a steering wheel. **3.** a rung of a ladder. **4. put a spoke in one's wheel,** to interfere with one's plans. —*v.t.* **5.** to fit or furnish with or as with spokes. [ME; OE *spāca*, c. D *speek*, G *Speiche*]

spoken (spō′kən), *v.* **1.** pp. of **speak.** —*adj.* **2.** uttered or expressed by speaking; oral (opposed to *written*). **3.** (in compounds) speaking, or using speech, as specified: *fair-spoken, plain-spoken.*

spokeshave (spōk′shāv′), *n.* a cutting tool having a blade set between two handles, orig. for shaping spokes, but now in general use for dressing curved edges of wood and in forming round bars and shapes.

spokesman (spōks′mən), *n.*, *pl.* **-men. 1.** one who speaks for another or others. **2.** the principal advocate or practitioner (of a movement, organization, etc.), considered as speaking on its behalf. **3.** a public speaker. —**spokes′-wom′an,** *n. fem.*

spoliate (spō′lĭ āt′), *v.t., v.i.,* **-ated, -ating.** to despoil; plunder.

spoliation (spō′lĭ ā′shən), *n.* the act of spoiling, plundering, or despoiling. [ME *spoliacio(u)n,* t. L: m. s. *spoliātio*] —**spoliative** (spō′lĭ ə tĭv), *adj.* —**spo′lia′tor,** *n.*

spondaic (spŏn dā′ĭk), *adj.* **1.** of or pertaining to a spondee. **2.** constituting a spondee. **3.** consisting of spondees; characterized by a spondee or spondees. Also, **spon-da′ical.** [t. L: s. *spondaicus*]

spondee (spŏn′dē), *n. Pros.* a foot consisting of two long syllables or two heavy beats. [ME, t. L: m. s. *spondēus,* t. Gk: m. *spondeîos*]

spondulicks (spŏn doo′lĭks), *n.pl., construed as sing. Chiefly U.S. Slang.* money. Also, **spondulix.** [orig. unknown]

spondylitis (spŏn′dĭ lī′tĭs), *n. Pathol.* a generalized affection of the vertebrae. [NL, f. s. L *spondylus* (t. Gk: m. *sphóndylos* vertebra) + *-ītis* -ITIS]

spondylolisthesis (spŏn′dĭ lō lĭs thē′sĭs), *n. Pathol.* forward displacement of a vertebra over a lower segment.

sponge (spŭnj), *n., v.,* **sponged, sponging.** —*n.* **1.** any of a group of aquatic (mostly marine) animals (phylum *Porifera*) which are characterized by a porous structure and (usually) a horny, siliceous, or calcareous skeleton or framework, and which, except in the larval state, are fixed, occurring in large, complex, often plantlike colonies. **2.** the light, yielding, porous, fibrous skeleton or framework of certain animals or colonies of this group, from which the living matter has been removed, characterized by readily absorbing water, and becoming soft when wet while retaining toughness: used in bathing, in wiping or cleansing surfaces, in removing marks (as from a slate), and for other purposes. **3.** any of various other spongelike substances. **4.** a sponge-down. **5.** one who or that which absorbs something freely, as a sponge does water. **6.** one who persistently lives at the expense of others; a parasite. **7.** a metal, as platinum, when obtained as a porous or spongy mass consisting of fine, loosely cohering particles. **8.** *Cookery.* **a.** dough raised with yeast, esp. before kneading, as for bread. **b.** a light sweet pudding of spongy texture, made with gelatine, eggs, fruit juice or other flavouring material, etc. **c.** sponge cake. **9. throw in (up) the sponge,** *Colloq.* to give up; abandon hope or one's efforts. —*v.t.* **10.** to wipe or rub with a wet sponge, as in order to clean or moisten. **11.** to remove with a wet sponge (fol. by *off, away,* etc.). **12.** to wipe out or efface with or as with a sponge (often fol. by *out*). **13.** to take up or absorb with a sponge or the like (often fol. by *up*): *to sponge up water.* **14.** to get from another or at another's expense by indirect exactions, trading on generosity, etc.: *to sponge a dinner.* —*v.i.* **15.** to take in liquid by absorption. **16.** to gather sponges. **17.** *Colloq.* to live at the expense of others. **18. sponge on,** to live as a parasite of. [ME and OE, t. L: m. *spongia,* t. Gk] —**sponge′like′,** *adj.*

sponge bag, a waterproof bag for holding toilet articles, as used when travelling.

sponge cake, a very light kind of sweet cake, made with a comparatively large proportion of eggs but no shortening.

sponge-down (spŭnj′doun′), *n.* a wash in a small amount of water, esp. with a sponge or flannel, rather than by immersion.

sponge finger, a small sponge cake, approximately finger-shaped, and often coated with a hard layer of crystallized sugar.

sponger (spŭn′jə), *n.* **1.** one who or that which sponges. **2.** a person who sponges on others. **3.** a person or a vessel engaged in gathering sponges.

sponge rubber, foam rubber.

spongy (spŭn′jĭ), *adj.,* **-gier, -giest. 1.** of the nature of or resembling a sponge; light, yielding, and porous; without firmness and readily compressible, as pith, flesh, etc. **2.** absorbing or holding water or the like, as a sponge does, or yielding it as when pressed. **3.** pertaining to a sponge. **4.** porous but hard, as bone. —**spon′giness,** *n.*

sponsion (spŏn′shən), *n.* **1.** an engagement or promise, esp. one made on behalf of another. **2.** the act of becoming surety for another. [t. L: s. *sponsio*]

sponson (spŏn′sən), *n.* **1.** a structure projecting from the side of a ship, as a gun platform, or a platform for handling gear. **2.** a buoyant appendage at the gunwale of a canoe to resist capsizing. **3.** the projection which covers and protects the paddlewheels of a paddle-steamer. **4.** a protuberance at the side of a flying-boat hull designed to increase lateral stability in the water. [var. of EXPANSION]

sponsor (spŏn′sə), *n.* **1.** one who vouches or is responsible for a person or thing. **2.** one who makes an engagement or promise on behalf of another; a surety. **3.** one who answers for an infant at baptism, making the required professions and promises; a godfather or godmother. **4.** *Chiefly U.S.* a person, firm, or other organization that finances a radio or television programme in return for advertisement of a commercial product, a political party, etc. —*v.t.* **5.** to act as sponsor for; promise, vouch, or answer for. [t. L] —**sponsorial** (spŏn sô′rĭ əl), *adj.* —**spon′sorship′,** *n.*

spontaneity (spŏn′tə nē′ĭ tĭ), *n., pl.* **-ties. 1.** the state, quality, or fact of being spontaneous. **2.** spontaneous activity. **3.** (*pl.*) spontaneous impulses, movements, or actions.

spontaneous (spŏn tā′nyəs), *adj.* **1.** proceeding from a natural personal impulse, without effort or premeditation; natural and unconstrained: *a spontaneous action or remark.* **2.** (of impulses, motion, activity, natural processes, etc.) arising from internal forces or causes, or independent of external agencies. **3.** growing naturally or without cultivation, as plants, fruits, etc. **4.** produced by natural process. [t. L: m. *spontāneus*] —**sponta′neously,** *adv.* —**sponta′neousness,** *n.* —**Syn. 1.** See **voluntary.**

spontaneous combustion, the ignition of a substance or body from the rapid oxidation of its own constituents, without heat from any external source.

spontaneous generation, *Biol.* abiogenesis.

spontoon (spŏn to͞on′), *n. Mil.* a shafted weapon with broad blade and basal crossbar used in the 18th and 19th centuries. [t. F: m. *sponton,* t. It.: m. *spuntone,* der. *puntone* point, der. *punto,* g. L *punctum*]

spoof (spo͞of), *n., v.t., v.i., adj. Slang.* parody; hoax. [coined by Arthur Roberts, 1852–1933, British comedian] —**spoof′er,** *n.*

spook (spo͝ok), *n. Colloq.* a ghost; a spectre. [t. D, c. G *Spuk*]

spooky (spo͞o′kĭ), *adj.,* **spookier, spookiest.** *Colloq.* like or befitting a spook or ghost; suggestive of spooks; eerie. Also, **spook′ish.**

spool (spo͞ol), *n.* **1.** any cylindrical piece or appliance on which something is wound. **2.** such a device for holding film, magnetic tape, or the like, which is stopped from slipping off by a disc on each side. **3.** a small cylindrical piece of wood or other material on which yarn is wound in spinning, for use in weaving; a bobbin. **4.** *Chiefly U.S.* reel[1] (def. 3). —*v.t.* **5.** to wind on a spool. [ME *spole,* t. MD or MLG; c. G *Spule*]

spoom (spo͞om), *v.i. Obs. or Archaic.* to run or scud, as a ship before the wind. [var. of obs. *spoon* in same sense]

spoon (spo͞on), *n.* **1.** a utensil consisting of a bowl or concave part and a handle, for taking up or stirring liquid or other food, or other matter. **2.** any of various implements, objects, or parts resembling or suggesting this. **3.** Also, **spoonbait.** *Angling.* a lure used in casting or trolling for fish, consisting of a bright spoon-shaped piece of metal or the like, swivelled above one or more fishhooks and revolved as it is drawn through the water. **4.** *Golf.* a club (No. 3 wood) with a wooden head whose face is more lofted than that of the brassy, and with a shorter shaft. **5.** a curved piece projecting from the top of a torpedo tube to guide the torpedo in a horizontal direction and prevent it from striking the side of the ship. **6. be born with a silver spoon in one's mouth,** to inherit social or financial advantages and privileges. —*v.t.* **7.** to take up or transfer in or as in a spoon. **8.** to hollow out or shape like a spoon. **9.** *Sport.* **a.** to push or shove (the ball) with a lifting motion instead of striking it soundly, as in croquet or golf. **b.** to hit (the ball) up in the air as in cricket. **10.** *Colloq.* to show affection towards, esp. in an openly sentimental manner. —*v.i.* **11.** *Sport.* to spoon the ball. **12.** to fish with a spoon. **13.** *Colloq.* to show affection, esp. in an openly sentimental manner. **14.** *Angling.* to rise a spoon. [ME and OE *spōn,* c. LG *spon,* Icel. *spōnn*; akin to G *Span*]

spoonbill (spo͞on′bĭl′), *n.* **1.** any of the wading birds of the genera *Platalea* and *Ajaia,* closely related to the ibises, and having a long, flat bill with spoonlike tip. **2.** any of various birds having a similar bill, as the shoveler (*Anas clypeata*). **3.** the paddlefish.

spoondrift (spo͞on′drĭft′), *n.* spindrift. [f. *spoon* scud, run before the wind (orig. uncert.) + DRIFT]

spoonerism (spo͞o′nə rĭz′əm), *n.* a slip of the tongue whereby initial or other sounds of words are transposed, as in 'our queer old dean' for 'our dear old queen'. [named after Rev. W. A. *Spooner,* 1844–1930, of New College, Oxford, noted for such slips]

spooney (spo͞o′nĭ), *adj.,* **spoonier, spooniest,** *n., pl.* **spoonies.** *Colloq.* spoony.

spoon-fed (spo͞on′fĕd′), *v.t.,* **-fed, -feeding. 1.** to give food by means of a spoon. **2.** to treat with excessive solicitude. **3.** to deprive of a chance to act or think for oneself.

spoonful (spo͞on′fo͝ol′), *n., pl.* **-fuls. 1.** as much as a spoon can hold. **2.** a small quantity.

spoony (spōō′nĭ), *adj.*, **spoonier, spooniest,** *n., pl.* **spoonies.** *Colloq.* —*adj.* **1.** foolishly or sentimentally amorous. **2.** foolish; silly. —*n.* **3.** one who is foolishly or sentimentally amorous. **4.** a simple or foolish person.

spoor (spŏŏə, spô), *n.* **1.** a track or trail, esp. that of a wild animal pursued as game. —*v.t., v.i.* **2.** to track by or follow a spoor. [t. Afrikaans, t. D; c. OE and Icel. *spor*, akin to G *Spur*] —**spoor′er,** *n.*

spor-, var. of **sporo-,** before vowels, as in *sporangium.*

Sporades (spŏ′rə dēz′), *n.pl.* two groups of Greek islands in the Aegean: the **Northern Sporades,** off the E coast of Greece, and the **Southern Sporades** (including the Dodecanese), off the SW coast of Asia Minor.

sporadic (spə răd′ĭk), *adj.* **1.** appearing or happening at intervals in time; occasional: *sporadic outbreaks.* **2.** appearing in scattered or isolated instances, as a disease. **3.** occuring singly, or widely apart, in locality: *sporadic genera of plants.* Also, **sporad′ical.** [t. ML: s. *sporadicus*, t. Gk: m. *sporadikós*] —**sporad′ically,** *adv.* —**sporad′icalness,** *n.*

sporadic cholera. See **cholera.**

sporangium (spə răn′jĭ əm), *n., pl.* **-gia** (-jĭ ə). *Bot.* the case or sac within which spores (asexual reproductive cells) are produced. Also, **spore case.** [t. NL, f. *spor-* SPOR- + m. Gk *angeîon* vessel] —**sporan′gial,** *adj.*

spore (spô), *n., v.,* **spored, sporing.** —*n.* **1.** *Biol.* a walled body that contains or produces one or more uninucleate organisms that develop into an adult individual, esp.: **a.** a reproductive body (**asexual spore**) produced asexually and capable of growth into a new individual, such individuals often, as in ferns, etc., being one (a gametophyte) unlike that which produced the spore. **b.** a walled reproductive body (**sexual spore**) produced sexually (by the union of two gametes). **2.** a germ, germ cell, seed, or the like. —*v.i.* **3.** to bear or produce spores. [t. NL: m. *spora*, t. Gk: seed]

spore case, sporangium.

sporiferous (spô rĭf′ə rəs, spŏ-), *adj.* bearing spores.

sporo-, a word element meaning 'seed'. Also, **spor-.** [comb. form repr. Gk *sporá* seed]

sporocarp (spô′rō käp′, spŏ′-), *n. Bot.* (in higher fungi, lichens, and red algae) a multicellular body developed for the formation of spores.

sporocyst (spô′rō sĭst′, spŏ′-), *n. Zool.* **1.** a walled body resulting from the multiple division of a sporozoan, which produces one or more sporozoites. **2.** a stage in development of trematodes which gives rise, non-sexually, to daughter cercaria.

sporogenesis (spô′rō jĕn′ĭ sĭs, spŏ′-), *n. Biol.* **1.** the production of spores; sporogony. **2.** reproduction by means of spores. —**sporogenous** (spô rŏj′ĭ nəs, spŏ-), *adj.*

sporogony (spô rŏg′ə nĭ, spŏ-), *n.* the process of multiplication in the sexual phase of parasitic protozoans of the class *Sporozoa*, giving rise to sporozoites.

sporophore (spô′rō fô′, spŏ′-), *n. Bot.* **1.** a simple or branched fungal hypha specialized to bear spores. **2.** the whole spore-producing structure of a gill-bearing fungus; a toadstool.

sporophyll (spô′rō fĭl, spŏ′-), *n. Bot.* a more or less modified leaf which bears sporangia. Also, **spo′rophyl.**

sporophyte (spô′rō fīt′, spŏ′-), *n. Bot.* the asexual form of a plant in the alternation of generations (opposed to *gametophyte*).

sporotrichosis (spô′rō trĭ kō′sĭs, spŏ′-), *n.* an infectious fungus disease of horses and man, marked by ulceration of superficial lymphatic vessels of the skin.

sporozoan (spô′rə zō′ŏn, spŏ′-), *n.* **1.** one of the *Sporozoa*, a class of the phylum *Protozoa*, consisting of parasites that multiply by sporogenesis, i.e. by dividing into reproductive bodies. —*adj.* **2.** belonging or pertaining to the *Sporozoa.*

sporozoite (spô′rə zō′īt, spŏ′-), *n. Zool.* one of the minute active bodies into which the spore of certain sporozoans divides, each developing into an adult individual.

sporran (spŏ′rən), *n.* (in Scottish Highland costume) a large pouch, commonly of fur, worn hanging from the belt in front. [t. Gaelic: m. *sporan*, c. Irish *sparān*]

S, Sporran

sport (spôt), *n.* **1.** an activity pursued for exercise or pleasure, usually requiring some degree of physical prowess, as hunting, fishing, racing, baseball, tennis, golf, bowling, wrestling, boxing, etc. **2.** a particular form of pastime. **3.** (*pl.*) a meeting for athletic competition. **4.** the pastime of hunting, shooting, or fishing with reference to the pleasure achieved: *we had good sport today.* **5.** diversion; recreation; pleasant pastime. **6.** playful trifling, jesting, or mirth: *to do or say a thing in sport.* **7.** derisive jesting; ridicule. **8.** an object of derision; a laughing-stock. **9.** something sported with or tossed about like a plaything: *to be the sport of circumstances.* **10.** *U.S.* a sportsman. **11.** a person of sportsmanlike or admirable qualities; one who exhibits boldness or good humour in the face of risk or ridicule: *be a good sport.* **12.** *U.S. Colloq.* one who is interested in pursuits involving betting or gambling. **13.** *U.S. Colloq.* a flashy person; any person who affects fine clothes, smart manners or pastimes, etc. **14.** *Biol.* an animal or a plant, or a part of a plant, that shows an unusual or singular deviation from the normal or parent type; a mutation. **15.** *Obs.* amorous dalliance.
—*adj.* **16.** *U.S.* sports.
—*v.i.* **17.** to amuse oneself with some pleasant pastime or recreation. **18.** to play, frolic, or gambol, as a child or an animal. **19.** to engage in some open-air or athletic pastime or sport. **20.** to deal lightly; trifle. **21.** to ridicule. **22.** *Bot.* to mutate. **23.** *Archaic.* to trifle playfully.
—*v.t.* **24.** to have or wear, esp. ostentatiously, proudly, etc. **25.** *Colloq.* to display freely or with ostentation: *to sport a roll of money.* **26.** to pass (time) in amusement or sport. **27.** to spend or squander recklessly or lightly (often fol. by *away*). **28.** *Obs.* to amuse (esp. oneself).
[ME *sporte*; aphetic var. of DISPORT] —**sport′er,** *n.* —**sport′ful,** *adj.* —**sport′fully,** *adv.* —**sport′fulness,** *n.*
—**Syn. 1.** game. **5.** amusement. See **play. 6.** fun, frolic.

sporting (spô′tĭng), *adj.* **1.** engaging in, given to, or interested in open-air or athletic sport. **2.** concerned with or suitable for such sport. **3.** sportsmanlike. **4.** interested in or connected with sport or pursuits involving betting or gambling. **5.** willing to take a chance. **6.** even or fair; involving reasonable odds, as a gamble: *a sporting chance.* —**sport′ingly,** *adv.*

sportive (spô′tĭv), *adj.* **1.** playful or frolicsome; jesting, jocose, or merry. **2.** done in sport, rather than in earnest. **3.** pertaining to or of the nature of sport or sports. **4.** *Biol.* mutative. **5.** *Obs.* amorous. —**sport′ively,** *adv.* —**sport′iveness,** *n.*

sports (spôts), *adj.* **1.** of, pertaining to, or devoted to a sport or sports: *the sports department of a store.* **2.** concerned with sport: *the sports editor of a newspaper.* **3.** (of garments, etc.) suitable for use in open-air sports, or for outdoor or informal use.

sports car, a high-powered car with low, rakish lines, usually for two persons.

sports day, a day when a school or the like holds athletic contests.

sports jacket, a man's jacket for informal wear, typically made of tweed or checked cloth. Also, **sports coat.**

sportsman (spôts′mən), *n., pl.* **-men. 1.** a man who engages in sport, esp. in some open-air sport such as hunting, fishing, racing, etc. **2.** one who exhibits qualities especially esteemed in those who engage in sports, such as fairness, good humour when losing, willingness to take risks, etc. —**sports′manlike′, sports′manly,** *adj.* —**sports′wom′an,** *n. fem.*

sportsmanship (spôts′mən shĭp′), *n.* **1.** sportsmanlike conduct. **2.** the character, practice, or skill of a sportsman.

sportswear (spôts′wĕə′), *n.* **1.** clothing for wear while engaged in some sport. **2.** clothing for outdoor or other leisure use.

sporty (spô′tĭ), *adj.*, **sportier, sportiest.** *Colloq.* **1.** flashy; vulgarly showy. **2.** stylish. **3.** like or befitting a sportsman. —**sport′iness,** *n.*

sporulate (spŏ′rŏŏ lāt′), *v.i.*, **-lated, -lating.** *Biol.* to undergo multiple division resulting in the production of spores. —**spor′ula′tion,** *n.*

sporule (spŏ′rōōl), *n. Biol.* a spore, esp. a small spore. [t. NL: m. s. *sporula*, dim. of *spora* SPORE]

spot (spŏt), *n., v.,* **spotted, spotting,** *adj.* —*n.* **1.** a mark made by foreign matter, as mud, blood, paint, ink, etc.; a stain, blot, or speck, as on a surface. **2.** a blemish of the skin, as a pimple. **3.** a relatively small, usually roundish, part of a surface differing from the rest in appearance or character. **4.** a moral blemish, as on character or reputation; stain or flaw. **5.** a place or locality: *a monument marks the spot.* **6.** a position or period of time in a programme of entertainment assigned to a particular performer. **7.** a short period of advertising time on radio or television: *they booked ten twenty-second spots per week.* **8.** a spotlight. **9.** *Billiards.* **a.** any of several marked points on a billiard table. **b.** the spot-ball. **10.** *Colloq.* a small quantity of something: *a spot of tea.* **11.** *Colloq.* a predicament: *he was in a bit of a spot when the crash came.* **12. change one's spots,** to alter one's fundamental character. **13. knock spots off,** *Colloq.* to outdo without difficulty or by a large margin. **14. on the spot, a.** instantly. **b.** at the place in question. **c.** obliged to deal with a situation.

d. in trouble, embarrassment, or danger. **e.** without change of location. **15. soft spot,** a special sympathy or affection: *she has a soft spot for small animals.* **16. tight spot,** a serious predicament. **17. weak spot,** an aspect of a person's character which is sensitive to criticism or opposition. —*v.t.* **18.** to stain with spots. **19.** to sully; blemish. **20.** to mark or diversify with spots, as of colour. **21.** to see or perceive, esp. suddenly, by chance, or when it is difficult to do so. **22.** *Colloq.* to detect or recognize. **23.** to scatter in various spots. **24.** *Billiards.* to place (a ball) on a particular spot. **25.** *U.S. Mil.* to pinpoint. —*v.i.* **26.** to make a spot; cause a stain. **27.** to become or tend to become spotted, as some fabrics when spattered with water. —*adj.* **28.** *Com.* made, paid, delivered, etc., at once: *a spot sale.*
[ME *spotte,* c. MD and LG *spot* speck, Icel. *spotti* bit, small piece]

spot-ball (spŏt′bôl′), *n. Billiards.* one of the white balls, distinguished from the other by being marked with a small black spot. Also, **spot.**

spot cash, payment for goods immediately on their delivery.

spot check, 1. an inspection made without warning, as of motor vehicles, etc. **2.** a check made on a random sample, as of manufactured articles.

spot kick, *Soccer Colloq.* penalty kick.

spotless (spŏt′lĭs), *adj.* **1.** free from spot, stain, blemish, marks, etc. **2.** immaculate; well-dressed. —**spot′lessly,** *adv.* —**spot′lessness,** *n.*

spotlight (spŏt′līt′), *n.* **1.** (in theatrical use) a strong light with a narrow beam thrown upon a particular spot on the stage in order to render some object, person, or group especially conspicuous. **2.** the lamp producing such light. **3.** a similar lamp attached to a car, usually not able to be swivelled. **4.** conspicuous public attention. —*v.t.* **5.** to direct a spotlight at.

spot-on (spŏt′ŏn′), *adj. Colloq.* absolutely right or accurate.

spotted (spŏt′ĭd), *adj.* **1.** marked with or characterized by a spot or spots. **2.** sullied; blemished.

spotted crake, a small, short-billed rail, *Porzana porzana,* of Europe and W Asia; water-crake.

spotted dick, a steamed or boiled suet pudding containing currants, etc. Also, **spotted dog.**

spotted dog, 1. *Colloq.* the Dalmatian (def. 4). **2.** spotted dick.

spotted fever, *Pathol.* **1.** any of several fevers characterized by spots on the skin, esp. as in cerebrospinal meningitis or typhus. **2.** tick fever.

spotted hyena. See **hyena.**

spotted laurel, laurel (def. 5).

spotter (spŏt′ə), *n.* **1.** *Mil.* the person who determines for the gunner the fall of shots in relation to the target. **2.** Also, **spotter plane.** a light aircraft that determines targets for artillery. **3.** one who watches for enemy aircraft, as in civil defence. **4.** one whose pastime is to spot and note the numbers or types of buses, trains, etc. **5.** *U.S. Colloq.* one employed to keep watch on others, esp. on employees as for evidence of dishonesty.

spotty (spŏt′ĭ), *adj.*, **-tier, -tiest. 1.** full of or having spots; occurring in spots: *a spotty face.* **2.** irregular or uneven in quality or character. —**spot′tily,** *adv.* —**spot′tiness,** *n.*

spot-weld (spŏt′wĕld′), *v.t., v.i.* **1.** to weld (two pieces of metal) together by compressing them between two electrodes through which a heavy current passes for a short time. **2.** to join (thermoplastic materials) together at a number of spots by using dielectric heating. —*n.* **3.** the welded joint so formed.

spousal (spou′zəl), *n.* **1.** (*often pl.*) the ceremony of marriage; nuptials. —*adj.* **2.** nuptial; matrimonial.

spouse (spouz), *n., v.,* **spoused, spousing.** —*n.* **1.** either member of a married pair in relation to the other; one's husband or wife. —*v.t.* **2.** *Obs.* to join, give, or take in marriage. [ME, t. OF: m. *spus* (masc.), *spuse* (fem.), g. L *sponsus,* pp., betrothed]

spout (spout), *v.t.* **1.** to discharge or emit (a liquid, etc.) in a stream with some force. **2.** *Colloq.* to utter or declaim in an oratorical manner. —*v.i.* **3.** to discharge a liquid, etc., in a jet or continuous stream. **4.** to issue with force, as liquid through a narrow orifice. **5.** *Colloq.* to talk or speak at some length or in an oratorical manner. —*n.* **6.** a pipe or tube, or a tubular or liplike projection, by which a liquid is discharged or poured. **7.** a trough or chute for discharging or conveying grain, flour, etc. **8.** a waterspout. **9.** a continuous stream of liquid, etc., discharged from, or as if from, a spout, upwards under pressure or falling from a higher to a lower level. **10.** a chute or shaft formerly common in pawnbrokers' shops, up which articles pawned were sent for storage. **11.** *Slang.* a pawnbroker's shop. **12. up the spout,** *Slang.* **a.** ruined; lost. **b.** pawned. [ME *spoute(n),* c. D *spuiten;* akin to Icel. *spȳta* SPIT[1]] —**spout′er,** *n.* —**spout′less,** *adj.* —**Syn. 3.** See **flow. 5.** declaim, rant, harangue.

spp., species (pl. of **specie**).

S.P.Q.R., (L *Senatus Populusque Romanus*) the Senate and People of Rome.

sprag (sprăg), *n.* **1.** a chock or pointed steel bar hinged to the rear axle of a vehicle and let down to arrest backward movement on gradients; dogstick. **2.** a spoke of a wheel. **3.** a post or support used in mining. [special use of d. *sprag* twig, OE *spræc* shoot]

sprain (sprān), *v.t.* **1.** to overstrain or wrench (the ankle, wrist, or other part of the body at a joint) so as to injure without fracture or dislocation. —*n.* **2.** a violent straining or wrenching of the parts around a joint, without dislocation. **3.** the condition of being sprained. [orig. uncert.] —**Syn. 1.** See **strain[1].**

sprang (sprăng), *v.* pt. of **spring.**

sprat (sprăt), *n.* **1.** a small, herring-like marine fish, *Clupea sprattus,* of European waters; brisling. **2. a sprat to catch a mackerel,** something given in expectation of a larger return. [var. of earlier *sprot,* ME and OE *sprott,* c. G *Sprote*]

sprawl (sprôl), *v.i.* **1.** to be stretched out in irregular or ungraceful movements, as the limbs. **2.** to lie or sit with the limbs stretched out in a careless or ungraceful posture. **3.** to fall in such a manner. **4.** to work one's way awkwardly along with the aid of all the limbs; scramble. **5.** to spread out in a straggling or irregular manner, as vines, buildings, handwriting, etc. —*v.t.* **6.** to stretch out (the limbs) as in sprawling. **7.** to spread out or distribute in a straggling manner. —*n.* **8.** the act of sprawling; a sprawling posture. **9.** a straggling array of something. [ME *spraule(n),* OE *sprēawlian,* c. North Fris. *spraweli*] —**sprawl′er,** *n.*

sprawly (sprô′lĭ), *adj.* tending to sprawl; straggly.

spray[1] (sprā), *n.* **1.** water or other liquid broken up into small particles and blown or falling through the air. **2.** a jet of fine particles of liquid discharged from an atomizer or other appliance, as for medicinal treatment, etc. **3.** a liquid to be discharged in such a jet. **4.** an appliance for discharging it. **5.** a quantity of small objects, flying or discharged through the air: *a spray of bullets.* —*v.t.* **6.** to scatter in the form of fine particles. **7.** to apply as a spray: *to spray insecticide upon plants.* **8.** to sprinkle or treat with a spray: *to spray plants with insecticide.* **9.** to direct a spray of particles, missiles, etc., upon. —*v.i.* **10.** to scatter spray; discharge a spray. **11.** to issue as spray. [cf. MD *sprayen* sprinkle] —**spray′er,** *n.*

spray[2] (sprā), *n.* **1.** a single slender shoot, twig, or branch with its leaves, flowers, or berries, growing or detached. **2.** an ornament, decorative figure, etc., with a similar form. [ME; orig. uncert.]

spray-gun (sprā′gŭn′), *n.* a device for forcing paint, etc., through a small nozzle so that it issues in a fine, even spray.

spread (sprĕd), *v.*, **spread, spreading,** *n.* —*v.t.* **1.** to draw or stretch out to the full width, as a cloth, a rolled or folded map, folded wings, etc. (often fol. by *out*). **2.** to extend over a greater or a relatively great area, space, or period (often fol. by *out*): *to spread out handwriting.* **3.** to force apart, as walls, rails, etc., under pressure. **4.** to flatten out: *to spread the end of a rivet by hammering.* **5.** to display the full extent of; set forth in full. **6.** to dispose or distribute in a sheet or layer: *to spread hay to dry.* **7.** to apply in a thin layer or coating. **8.** to extend or distribute over a region, place, etc. **9.** to overlay, cover, or coat with something. **10.** to set or prepare (a table, etc.), as for a meal. **11.** to send out in various directions, as light, sound, mist, etc. **12.** to shed or scatter abroad; diffuse or disseminate, as knowledge, news, disease, etc. **13.** *Phonet.* to spread (the lips), as for the vowel ē of *me.* **14.** *Colloq.* to exert (oneself) to an unusual extent to produce a good effect or fine impression.
—*v.i.* **15.** to become stretched out or extended, as a flag in the wind; expand, as in growth. **16.** to extend over a greater or a considerable area or period. **17.** to be or lie outspread or fully extended or displayed, as a landscape or scene. **18.** to admit of being spread or applied in a thin layer, as a soft substance. **19.** to become extended or distributed over a region, as population, animals, plants, etc. **20.** to become diffused abroad, or disseminated, as light, influences, rumours, ideas, infection, etc. **21.** to be forced apart, as rails; go out of gauge.
—*n.* **22.** expansion; extension; diffusion. **23.** the extent of spreading: *to measure the spread of branches.* **24.** capacity for spreading: *the spread of an elastic material.* **25.** widening of girth: *middle-age spread.* **26.** a stretch, expanse, or extent of something. **27.** a cloth covering for a bed, table, or the like, esp. a bedspread. **28.** *Colloq.* a meal set out, esp. a feast. **29.** *Colloq.* a pretentious display made. **30.** any food preparation for spreading on bread, etc., as fruit,

jam, or peanut butter. **31.** *Aeron.* the wingspan. **32.** *Stock Exchange.* **a.** the difference between the highest and the lowest prices at which business has been done during one day. **b.** the difference between the prices quoted by a stockjobber for buying and selling. **33.** a pair of facing pages of a book, magazine, or the like, or any part of them. Cf. **double-page spread.**
—*adj.* **34.** extended, esp. fully. **35.** *Jewellery.* (of a gem) flat and shallow. **36.** *Phonet.* (of the lips) forming a long, narrow opening, as for the vowel ē in *me.*
[ME *sprede(n),* OE *sprǣdan,* c. G *spreiten*] —**spread′er,** *n.*
—**Syn. 1.** unfold, unroll, unfurl, open, expand. **12.** disperse, scatter, circulate.

spread eagle, 1. a representation of an eagle with outspread wings (used as an emblem of the U.S.). **2.** *U.S. Colloq.* a boastful person. **3.** an ice-skating movement, in which the skater describes a circular figure.

spread-eagle (sprĕd′ē′gl), *adj., v.,* **-gled, -gling.** —*adj.* **1.** having or suggesting the form of a spread eagle. **2.** *U.S. Colloq.* boastful or bombastic, esp. in the display of patriotism or national vanity. —*v.t.* **3.** to stretch out in the manner of a spread eagle. **4.** *Slang.* to knock (a person) out. —*v.i.* **5.** to perform the spread eagle in skating. **6.** *Slang.* to form a shape or take a position resembling a spread eagle.

spread-eagleism (sprĕd′ē′gə lĭz′əm), *n. U.S. Colloq.* boastfulness or bombast, esp. in the display of patriotism or national vanity.

Sprechgesang (*Ger.* shprĕKH′gə zäng), *n. German.* (in music) a type of vocalizing between speech and song, originated by Schönberg. [G: lit., speech song]

Sprechstimme (*Ger.* shprĕKH′stĭm ə), *n. German.* (in music) a vocal part employing Sprechgesang. [G: lit., speech voice]

spree (sprē), *n.* **1.** a lively frolic. **2.** a bout or spell of drinking to intoxication. **3.** a session or period of indulgence: *a spending spree.* [orig. uncert.]

Spree (*Ger.* shprė), *n.* a river in East Germany, flowing through Berlin into the river Havel. ab. 220 mi.

sprig (sprĭg), *n., v.,* **sprigged, sprigging.** —*n.* **1.** a small spray of some plant with its leaves, flowers, etc. **2.** a shoot, twig, or small branch. **3.** an ornament or a decorative figure having the form of such a spray. **4.** *Humorous.* a person as a scion or offshoot of a family or class. **5.** a youth or young fellow. **6.** a small wedge-shaped piece of tin for holding glass in a sash. **7.** a headless brad. —*v.t.* **8.** to decorate (fabrics, pottery, etc.) with a design of sprigs. **9.** to fasten with brads. **10.** to remove a sprig or sprigs from (plants or trees). [ME *sprigge,* orig. uncert.] —**sprig′gy,** *adj.*

sprightly (sprīt′lĭ), *adj.,* **-lier, -liest,** *adv.* —*adj.* **1.** animated, vivacious, or gay; lively. —*adv.* **2.** in a sprightly manner. [f. *spright,* var. of SPRITE + -LY] —**spright′liness,** *n.*

spring (sprĭng), *v.,* **sprang** or **sprung, sprung, springing,** *n., adj.* —*v.i.* **1.** to rise or move suddenly and lightly as by some inherent power: *to spring into the air, a tiger about to spring.* **2.** to go or come suddenly as if with a leap: *blood springs to the face.* **3.** to fly back or away in escaping from a forced position, as by resilient or elastic force or from the action of a spring: *a trap springs.* **4.** to start or work out of place, as parts of a mechanism, structure, etc. **5.** to issue suddenly, as water, blood, sparks, fire, etc. (often fol. by *forth, out,* or *up*). **6.** to come into being, rise, or arise (often fol. by *up*): *industries spring up.* **7.** to arise by growth, as from a seed or germ, bulb, root, etc.; grow, as plants. **8.** to proceed or originate, as from a source or cause. **9.** to have one's birth, or be descended, as from a family, person, stock, etc. **10.** to rise or extend upwards, as a spire. **11.** to take an upward course or curve from a point of support, as an arch. **12.** to start or rise from cover, as partridges, pheasants, etc. **13.** to become bent or warped, as boards. **14.** to explode, as a mine. **15.** (of a cricket bat or the like) to lose its resilience, as by perishing of the rubber springs. **16.** *Archaic.* to begin to appear, as day, light, etc.
—*v.t.* **17.** to cause to spring. **18.** to cause to fly back, move, or act by elastic force, a spring, etc.: *to spring a lock.* **19.** to cause to start out of place or work loose. **20.** to split or crack. **21.** to come to have by cracking, etc.: *to spring a leak.* **22.** to bend by force, or force (*in*) by bending, as a slat or bar. **23.** to explode (a mine). **24.** to bring out, disclose, produce, make, etc., suddenly: *to spring a joke.* **25.** to equip or fit with springs. **26.** to cause (a cricket bat or the like) to lose its resilience. **27.** to leap over. **28.** *Slang.* to cause or enable (someone) to escape from prison.
—*n.* **29.** a leap, jump, or bound. **30.** a springing or starting from place. **31.** a flying back from a forced position. **32.** an elastic or springy movement. **33.** elasticity or springiness. **34.** a split or crack, as in a mast; a bend or warp, as in a board. **35.** an issue of water from the earth, flowing away as a small stream or standing as a pool or small lake, or the place of such an issue: *mineral springs.* **36.** a source of something; a beginning or cause of origin. **37.** the rise of an arch, or the point or line at which an arch springs from its support. **38.** the first season of the year, between winter and summer. **39.** the first and freshest period: *the spring of life.* **40.** an elastic contrivance or body, as a strip or wire of steel coiled spirally, which recovers its shape after being compressed, bent, etc. **41.** any device or contrivance designed to impart resilience or elasticity, as one of a set of rubber strips running down the inside of the handle of a cricket bat. **42.** *Archaic.* the dawn, as of day, light, etc.
—*adj.* **43.** of, pertaining to, characteristic of, or suitable for the season of spring: *spring flowers.* **44.** sown in the spring, as a cereal forming a second crop. **45.** young: *spring chicken.* **46.** resting on or containing springs: *a spring bed; spring mattress.*
[ME; OE *springan,* c. D and G *springen,* Icel. *springa*] —**spring′less,** *adj.* —**Syn. 1.** leap, jump, bound. **5.** shoot, dart, fly. **8.** emerge, emanate, issue, flow. **33.** resiliency, buoyancy, vigour. **36.** origin.

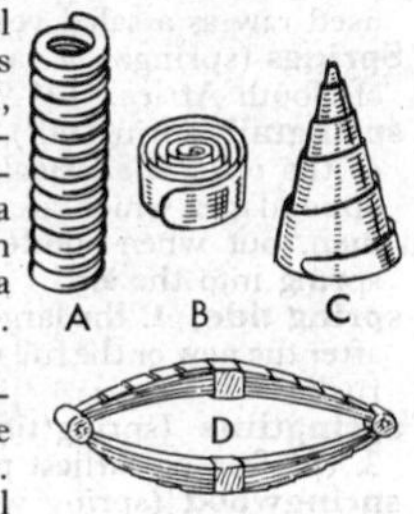

Springs (def. 40)
A, Spiral; B, Coil; C, Volute; D, Leaf

springal[1] (sprĭng′l), *n. Archaic.* an ancient military engine for throwing stones or other missiles. [ME, t. OF: m. *espringale,* der. *espringuer* spring; of Gmc orig.]

springal[2] (sprĭng′l), *n.* springald[1].

springald[1] (sprĭng′ld), *n. Archaic.* a youth; a young fellow. [ME *springold,* f. SPRING (def. 39) + *-old* (of obscure origin)]

springald[2] (sprĭng′ld), *n.* springal[1].

spring balance, a balance in which weight is determined by the extent to which a coiled spring is extended.

springboard (sprĭng′bôd′), *n.* **1.** a projecting semiflexible board from which persons dive. **2.** a flexible board used as a take-off in vaulting, tumbling, etc., to increase the height of leaps. **3.** anything serving to assist departure, initiation of a project, or the like.

springbok (sprĭng′bŏk′), *n., pl.* **-boks,** (*esp. collectively*) **-bok.** a South African gazelle, *Antidorcas marsupialis,* which has a habit of springing upwards in play or when alarmed. Also, **springbuck** (sprĭng′bŭk′). [t. Afrikaans: f. *spring(en)* SPRING + *bok* goat, antelope]

Springbok, *Antidorcas marsupialis* ($2\frac{1}{2}$ ft high at the shoulder, total length ab. 5 ft)

spring-clean (sprĭng′klēn′), *v.t., v.i.* to clean thoroughly and completely, as traditionally done to homes in the spring of each year. —**spring′-clean′er,** *n.* —**spring′-clean′ing,** *n.*

springe (sprĭnj), *n., v.,* **springed, springing.** —*n.* **1.** a snare for catching small game. —*v.t.* **2.** to catch in a springe. —*v.i.* **3.** to set springes. [ME *sprengen,* akin to obs. *sprenge,* v., cause to spring, OE *sprengean*]

springer (sprĭng′ə), *n.* **1.** one who or that which springs. **2.** a springer spaniel. **3.** *Archit.* the impost of an arch, or the bottom stone of an arch resting upon the impost. See diag. under **arch. 4.** a sea fish, *Mugil cephalus*; harder.

springer spaniel, either of two breeds of short-haired spaniel, used to flush game. See **English springer spaniel** and **Welsh springer spaniel.**

Springer spaniel (Ab. 20 in. high)

spring fever, a listless or restless feeling felt by some people at the beginning of spring weather.

Springfield (sprĭng′fēld′), *n.* **1.** a city in S Massachusetts, on the Connecticut river. 174,463 (1960). **2.** the capital of Illinois, in the central part. 83,271 (1960).

springhaas (sprĭng′häs′), *n., pl.* **-haas, -hase** (-hä′zə) or **-haases.** a kangaroo-like rodent, *Pedetes capensis,* of southern Africa, having very short forelimbs and large hind feet. There is only one species in the family. [t. Afrikaans: lit., jumping hare]

springhalt (sprĭng′hôlt′), *n.* stringhalt.

springhead (sprĭng′hĕd′), *n.* **1.** the spring or fountainhead from which a stream flows. **2.** the source of something.

springhouse (sprĭng′hous′), *n. Chiefly U.S.* a shed or outhouse built over a spring, for cool or moist storage.

springlet (sprĭngʹlĭt), *n.* a little spring (of water).

spring-loaded (sprĭngʹlōʹdĭd), *adj.* (of a machine part) held in or returned to position by means of a spring. —**springʹ-loadʹing,** *n., adj.*

springlock (sprĭngʹlŏkʹ), *n.* a lock which fastens automatically by a spring.

spring onion, a type of onion having a small bulb, chiefly used raw as a salad vegetable.

Springs (sprĭngz), *n.* a city in Transvaal, in the Republic of South Africa. 141,943 (1960).

springtail (sprĭngʹtālʹ), *n.* any of various wingless insects of the order *Collembola,* having a pair of elastic tail-like appendages which are ordinarily folded under the abdomen, but when suddenly extended enable the insect to spring into the air.

spring tide, 1. the large rise and fall of the tide at or soon after the new or the full moon. **2.** any great flood or swelling rush.

springtime (sprĭngʹtīmʹ), *n.* **1.** the season of spring. **2.** the first or earliest period. Also, **springʹtideʹ.**

springwood (sprĭngʹwŏŏdʹ), *n.* that part of an annual ring of wood which grows in the spring and early summer, characterized by larger, thinner-walled cells (distinguished from *summerwood*).

springy (sprĭngʹĭ), *adj.,* **springier, springiest. 1.** characterized by spring or elasticity; elastic; resilient: *a springy step.* **2.** abounding in or having springs (of water), as land. —**springʹily,** *adv.* —**springʹiness,** *n.*

sprinkle (sprĭngʹkl), *v.,* **-kled, -kling,** *n.* —*v.t.* **1.** to scatter, as a liquid or a powder, in drops or particles. **2.** to disperse or distribute here and there. **3.** to overspread with drops or particles of water, powder, or the like. **4.** to diversify or intersperse with objects scattered here and there. —*v.i.* **5.** to scatter or disperse a liquid, powder, or the like in drops or particles. **6.** to be sprinkled. **7.** to rain slightly. —*n.* **8.** the act of sprinkling. **9.** that which is sprinkled. **10.** a light rain. **11.** a small quantity or number. [ME *sprenkle,* c. G *sprenkeln*]

—**Syn. 1.** SPRINKLE, SCATTER, STREW mean to fling, spread, or disperse. To SPRINKLE is to fling about small drops or particles: *to sprinkle water on clothes, powder on plants.* To SCATTER is to disperse or spread widely: *to scatter seeds.* To STREW is to scatter, esp. in such a way as to cover or partially cover a surface: *to strew flowers on a grave.* —**Ant. 1.** concentrate.

sprinkler (sprĭngʹklə), *n.* **1.** any device which sprinkles, esp. a small stand or the like with a rose or perforated hose for watering with a fine, even spray. **2.** one who sprinkles.

sprinkler system, a system of ceiling pipes in a building, with valves which open automatically at certain temperatures, used for extinguishing fires.

sprinkling (sprĭngʹklĭng), *n.* **1.** a small quantity or number scattered here and there. **2.** a small quantity sprinkled.

sprint (sprĭnt), *v.i.* **1.** to race at full speed, esp. for a short distance, as in running, rowing, etc. —*v.t.* **2.** to cover by sprinting: *to sprint a hundred yards.* —*n.* **3.** a short race at full speed. **4.** a spell of running at full speed, as to the finish of a long race. **5.** a brief spell of great activity. [t. Scand.; cf. Icel. *spretta* (where *tt* is for early *nt*)] —**sprintʹer,** *n.*

sprit (sprĭt), *n. Naut.* a small pole or spar crossing a fore-and-aft sail diagonally from the mast to the upper aftermost corner, thus serving to extend the sail. [ME *spret,* OE *sprēot,* c. D *spriet,* G *Spriet*]

S, Sprit

sprite (sprīt), *n.* an elf, fairy, or goblin. [ME, t. OF: m. *esprit,* or similarly reduced from *esperit(e),* AF *spirit(e)* SPIRIT] —**Syn.** See **fairy.**

spritsail (sprĭtʹsālʹ; *Naut.* -səl), *n. Naut.* a sail extended by a sprit.

sprocket (sprŏkʹĭt), *n.* **1.** *Mach.* one of a set of projections on the rim of a wheel which engage the links of a chain. **2.** *Mach.* a sprocket wheel. **3.** *Carp.* a wedge-shaped piece fitted to the bottom of a rafter to flatten the slope at the eaves. [f. *sprock* (of obscure orig.; ? akin to SPUR + -ET]

sprocket wheel, *Mach.* a wheel having sprockets.

sprog (sprŏg), *n. Slang.* **1.** a child or youngster. **2.** a new recruit, as in an airforce. [orig. obscure]

sprout (sprout), *v.i.* **1.** to begin to grow; shoot forth, as a bud from a seed or stock. **2.** (of a seed, plant, the earth, etc.) to put forth buds or shoots. **3.** to develop or grow quickly. —*v.t.* **4.** to cause to sprout. **5.** to remove sprouts from. —*n.* **6.** a shoot of a plant. **7.** a new growth from a germinating seed, or from a rootstock, tuber, bud, or the like. **8.** something resembling or suggesting a sprout, as in growth. **9.** a scion or descendant. **10.** Brussels sprout. [ME *spruten,* OE *sprūtan,* c. G *spriessen*]

spruce[1] (sprōōs), *n.* **1.** any member of the coniferous genus *Picea,* consisting of evergreen trees with short angular needle-shaped leaves attached singly around twigs, as *P. abies* (**Norway spruce**), *P. glauca* (**white spruce** or **Canadian spruce**), and *P. mariana* (**black spruce**). **2.** any of various allied trees, as the Douglas fir and the hemlock spruce. **3.** the wood of any such tree. —*adj.* **4.** made of or containing such trees or such wood. [ME, sandhi var. of *Pruce* Prussia, t. OF, t. ML: m. *Prussia*]

spruce[2] (sprōōs), *adj.,* **sprucer, sprucest,** *v.,* **spruced, sprucing.** —*adj.* **1.** smart in dress or appearance; trim; neat; dapper. —*v.t.* **2.** to make spruce or smart (often fol. by *up*). —*v.i.* **3.** to make oneself spruce (usually fol. by *up*). [? special use of SPRUCE[1] through (obs.) *Spruce leather,* a leather from Prussia used in jerkins, etc.] —**spruceʹly,** *adv.* —**spruceʹness,** *n.*

spruce beer, a fermented beverage made with spruce leaves and twigs, or an extract from them.

spruce grouse. See **grouse**[1].

sprue[1] (sprōō), *n. Foundry.* **1.** an opening through which molten metal is poured into a mould. **2.** the waste piece of metal cast in this opening. [orig. obscure]

sprue[2] (sprōō), *n. Pathol.* a chronic disease, occurring chiefly in the tropics, characterized by diarrhoea, ulceration of the mucous membrane of the digestive tract, and a smooth, shining tongue; psilosis. [t. D: m. *spruw*]

spruik (sprŏŏk), *v.i. Austral. Slang.* to harangue or address a meeting. [orig. uncert.: ? der. D *spreken* speak]

spruiker (sprŏŏʹkə), *n. Austral. Slang.* a showman or public speaker, esp. a demagogue.

spruit (sprāt; *Du.* sprœyt), *n. S African.* a small, fast-flowing river or watercourse, esp. one that is dry except during and after rain. [t. Afrikaans, t. D (obs.): m. *sprute* SPROUT]

sprung (sprŭng), *v.* pt. and pp. of **spring.**

sprung rhythm, a system of prosody with the accent always on the first syllable of every foot followed by a varying number of unaccented syllables, all feet being given equal time length.

spry (sprī), *adj.,* **spryer, spryest** or **sprier, spriest.** active; nimble; brisk. [orig. obscure] —**spryʹly,** *adv.* —**spryʹness,** *n.*

spud (spŭd), *n., v.,* **spudded, spudding.** —*n.* **1.** a spadelike instrument, esp. one with a narrow blade, as for digging up or cutting the roots of weeds. **2.** a chisel-like tool for removing bark. **3.** *Surg.* a blunt-ended instrument used to remove wax from ears, and foreign bodies from eyes. **4.** *Colloq.* a potato. **5.** *Slang.* a person (esp. used as a term of address). —*v.t.* **6.** to remove with a spud. —*v.i.* **7.** to dig with a spud. [ME *spudde* kind of knife]

spud-bashing (spŭdʹbăshʹĭng), *n. Slang.* the act of peeling potatoes.

spudder (spŭdʹə), *n. Colloq.* **1.** an employee at an oil well. **2.** a rig or oil rig, esp. one used to begin a well.

spue (spyōō), *v.i., v.t.,* **spued, spuing.** spew.

spume (spyōōm), *n., v.,* **spumed, spuming.** —*n.* **1.** foam; froth; scum. —*v.i.* **2.** to foam; froth. —*v.t.* **3.** to send forth as or like foam or froth. [ME, t. L: m. *spūma*] —**spuʹmous, spuʹmy,** *adj.*

spumescent (spyōō mĕsʹənt), *adj.* foamy; foamlike; frothy. —**spumesʹcence,** *n.*

spumone (spōō mōʹnĭ; *It.* spōō mòʹnė), *n.* Italian ice-cream of a very fine and smooth texture, usually containing chopped fruit or nuts. Also, **spumoʹni.** [t. It.]

spun (spŭn), *v.* **1.** pt. and pp. of **spin.** —*adj.* **2.** formed by or as by spinning: *spun rayon, spun silk.*

spun glass, fibreglass.

spunk (spŭngk), *n.* **1.** *Colloq.* pluck; spirit; mettle. **2.** *Taboo Slang.* semen. **3.** touchwood or tinder. [b. SPARK[1] and obs. *funk* spark, touchwood (c. D *vonk,* G *Funke* spark)]

spunky (spŭngʹkĭ), *adj.,* **spunkier, spunkiest.** *Colloq.* plucky; spirited. —**spunkʹily,** *adv.* —**spunkʹiness,** *n.*

spun sugar, candy floss.

spun yarn, *Naut.* cord formed of rope yarns loosely twisted together, for serving ropes, bending sails, etc.

spur (spû), *n., v.,* **spurred, spurring.** —*n.* **1.** a pointed device attached to a horseman's boot heel, for goading a horse onwards, etc. **2.** anything that goads, impels, or urges to action or speed. **3.** something projecting, and resembling or suggesting a spur. **4.** a sharp piercing or cutting instrument fastened on the leg of a gamecock, for use in fighting. **5.** a stiff, usually sharp, horny process on the leg of various birds, esp. the domestic cock. **6.** a short or stunted branch or shoot, as of a tree. **7.** one of the principal lateral roots of a tree. **8.** a slender, usually hollow, projection from some part of a flower, as from the calyx of the larkspur or the corolla of the violet. **9.** *Phys. Geog.*

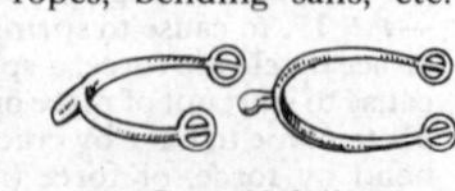
Spurs (def. 1)

a ridge or line of elevation projecting from or subordinate to the main body of a mountain or mountain range. **10.** a structure built to protect a river bank from a fast current; a river groyne. **11.** griff. **12.** *Archit.* **a.** a short wooden brace, usually temporary, for strengthening a post or some other part. **b.** any offset from a wall, etc., as a buttress. **13.** *Railways.* a siding. **14. on the spur of the moment,** suddenly; without premeditation. **15. win one's spurs,** to achieve one's first distinction or success.
—*v.t.* **16.** to prick with, or as with, spurs or a spur, as in order to urge on. **17.** to strike or wound with the spur, as a gamecock. **18.** to furnish with spurs or a spur.
—*v.i.* **19.** to prick one's horse with the spur; ride quickly. **20.** to proceed hurriedly; press forward. [ME; OE *spura*, c. G *Sporn*] —**spur′like′,** *adj.* —**spur′rer,** *n.*

spurge (spûj), *n.* any plant of the genus *Euphorbia*, some species of which have purgative properties. [ME, t. OF: m. *espurge*, der. *espurgier* purge, g. L *expurgāre*]

spur gear, *Mach.* a gear in which spur wheels are employed. Also, **spur gearing.** See illus. under **gear.**

spurge laurel, a laurel-like shrub, *Daphne laureola*, of southern and western Europe and western Asia, with evergreen leaves and green axillary flowers.

Spurgeon (spû′jən), *n.* **Charles Haddon,** 1834–92, English Baptist preacher.

spurious (spyo͞o′rĭ əs), *adj.* **1.** not genuine or true; counterfeit; not from the reputed, pretended, or right source; not authentic. **2.** of illegitimate birth; bastard. **3.** *Bot.* bearing superficial resemblances but having morphological differences. [t. L: m. *spurius* false] —**spu′riously,** *adv.* —**spu′riousness,** *n.*

spurn (spûn), *v.t.* **1.** to reject with disdain; treat with contempt; scorn; despise. **2.** *Obs.* to kick. —*v.i.* **3.** to show disdain or contempt. **4.** *Obs.* to kick (often fol. by *against*). —*n.* **5.** disdainful rejection; contemptuous treatment. **6.** a kick. [ME; OE *spurnan*, akin to OHG *spurnan*] —**spurn′er,** *n.* —**Syn. 1.** See **refuse[1].**

spurred (spûd), *adj.* **1.** having spurs or a spur. **2.** bearing spurs or spurlike spines. **3.** having the form of a spur. **4.** urged or encouraged.

spurrey (spŭ′rĭ), *n., pl.* **-ries.** spurry.

spurrier (spŭ′rĭ ə), *n.* a maker of spurs.

spurry (spŭ′rĭ), *n., pl.* **-ries. 1.** any of various herbs of the caryophyllaceous genus *Spergula*, esp. a white-flowered species, *S. arvensis*, with numerous whorled linear leaves. **2.** any of various allied or similar plants. [t. MD: m. *spurie*. Cf. ML *spergula*]

spurt (spût), *v.i.* **1.** to gush or issue suddenly in a stream or jet, as a liquid. **2.** to show marked activity or energy for a short period. —*v.t.* **3.** to throw or force out suddenly in a stream or jet, as a liquid. —*n.* **4.** a forcible gush of water, etc., as from a confined place. **5.** a sudden outburst, as of feeling. **6.** a marked increase of effort for a short period or distance, as in running, rowing, etc. Also, **spirt.** [var. of *spirt*, metathetic var. of *sprit*, ME *sprutten*, OE *spryttan* come forth; akin to SPROUT] —**Syn. 1.** See **flow.**

spurtle (spû′tl), *n.* *Scot. and N Dial.* **1.** a flat implement, as for stirring porridge. **2.** a sword. [orig. obscure]

spur wheel, *Mach.* a wheel with projecting teeth on the periphery, which are placed radially about and parallel to the axis; cogwheel.

Spur wheel

sputnik (spo͝ot′nĭk; *Russ.* spo͞ot′nĭk), *n.* an artificial satellite, esp. an early Soviet one. [Russ.: companion]

sputter (spŭt′ə), *v.i.* **1.** to emit particles of anything in an explosive manner, as a candle does in burning. **2.** to eject particles of saliva, food, etc., from the mouth in a similar manner. **3.** to utter words or sounds in an explosive, incoherent manner. —*v.t.* **4.** to emit (anything) in small particles, as if by spitting. **5.** to eject (saliva, food, etc.) in small particles explosively and involuntarily, as in excitement. **6.** to utter explosively and incoherently. **7.** to deposit (a thin film of a metal) on a surface by making a disc of the metal the cathode of a low-pressure discharge system and introducing the surface between this cathode and a high-voltage anode. —*n.* **8.** the act, process, or sound of sputtering. **9.** explosive, incoherent utterance. **10.** matter ejected in sputtering. [freq. of SPOUT, c. D *sputteren*] —**sput′terer,** *n.*

sputum (spyo͞o′təm), *n., pl.* **-ta** (-tə). **1.** spittle mixed with mucus, purulent matter, or the like. **2.** that which is expectorated; spittle. [t. L]

spy (spī), *n., pl.* **spies,** *v.,* **spied, spying.** —*n.* **1.** one who keeps secret watch on the actions of others. **2.** one employed by a government to obtain secret information or intelligence, esp. with reference to military or naval affairs of other countries. **3.** the act of spying; a careful view. —*v.i.* **4.** to make secret observations. **5.** to be on the lookout; keep watch. **6.** to examine or search closely or carefully. —*v.t.* **7.** to make secret observations in (a place) with hostile intent (now usually fol. by *out*). **8.** to inspect or examine closely or carefully. **9.** to find (*out*) by observation or scrutiny. **10.** to catch sight of; descry; see. [ME *spien*, t. OF: m. *espier* ESPY]

spyer (spī′ə), *n.* spier.

spyglass (spī′gläs′), *n.* a small telescope.

spy-hole (spī′hōl′), *n.* a peephole, esp. one in a front door, as of a flat, through which those inside may examine callers before opening the door.

Sq., Square (in place-names).

sq., 1. sequence. **2.** (L *sequens*) the following (one). **3.** (L *sequentia*) the following (ones). **4.** squadron. **5.** square.

sq. cm., square centimetre or square centimetres.

sq. ft, square foot or square feet.

sq. in., square inch or square inches.

sq. km., square kilometre or square kilometres.

sq. mi., square mile or square miles.

sq. mm., square millimetre or square millimetres.

Sqn Ldr, squadron leader.

sqq., *pl.* (L *sequentia*) the following ones.

squab (skwŏb), *n.* **1.** a nestling pigeon, marketed when fully grown but still unfledged. **2.** a short, stout person. **3.** a thickly stuffed, soft cushion. —*adj.* **4.** short and thick or broad. **5.** (of birds) unfledged or lately hatched. [appar. t. Scand.; cf. d. Sw. *sqvabb* loose fat flesh, d. Norw. *skvabb* soft wet mass]

squabble (skwŏb′l), *v.,* **-bled, -bling,** *n.* —*v.i.* **1.** to engage in a petty quarrel. —*v.t.* **2.** *Print. Obs.* pie[3] (def. 2). —*n.* **3.** a petty quarrel. [? imit.; cf. d. Sw. *sqvabbel*] —**squab′bler,** *n.*

squabby (skwŏb′ĭ), *adj.,* **-bier, -biest.** short and stout; squat. —**squab′bily,** *adv.*

squad (skwŏd), *n., v.,* **squadded, squadding.** —*n.* **1.** a small number of soldiers (commonly ten men, a sergeant, and a corporal); the smallest military unit. **2.** any small group or party of persons engaged in a common enterprise, etc. —*v.t.* *U.S.* **3.** to form into squads. **4.** to assign to a squad. [t. F: m. *escouade*, var. of *esquadre* squadron, t. It.: m. *squadra* SQUARE]

squad car, a patrol-car.

squadron (skwŏd′rən), *n.* **1.** a portion of a naval fleet, or a detachment of warships employed on a particular service; a subdivision of a fleet. **2.** an armoured cavalry or cavalry unit consisting of two or more troops (companies), a headquarters, and certain supporting units. **3.** the basic administrative and tactical unit of an airforce, smaller than a group and composed of two or more flights. **4.** a number of persons grouped or united together for some purpose; a group or body in general. —*v.t.* **5.** to form into a squadron or squadrons; marshal or array in or as in squadrons. [t. It.: m. *squadrone*, der. *squadra* SQUARE]

squadron leader, 1. a commissioned officer in the Royal Air Force ranking above a flight lieutenant and below a wing-commander. **2.** an officer of equivalent rank in any of various other airforces.

squail (skwāl), *v.i., v.t.* *Chiefly Dial.* to throw a stick, esp. a loaded stick (at).

squalid (skwŏl′ĭd), *adj.* **1.** foul and repulsive, as from the want of care or cleanliness; dirty; filthy. **2.** wretched; miserable; degraded. [t. L: s. *squālidus*] —**squal′idly,** *adv.* —**squalidity** (skwŏ lĭd′ĭ tĭ), **squal′idness,** *n.* —**Syn. 1.** See **dirty.**

squall[1] (skwôl), *n.* **1.** *Meteorol.* a sudden strong wind which dies away rapidly after lasting only a few minutes, often associated with a temporary change of wind direction. **2.** *Colloq.* a disturbance or commotion. —*v.i.* **3.** to blow in a squall. [? akin to SQUALL[2]]

squall[2] (skwôl), *v.i.* **1.** to cry out loudly; scream violently. —*v.t.* **2.** to utter in a screaming tone. —*n.* **3.** the act or sound of squalling. [imit.] —**squall′er,** *n.*

squally (skwô′lĭ), *adj.,* **squallier, squalliest. 1.** characterized by squalls. **2.** *Colloq.* threatening.

squalor (skwŏl′ə), *n.* filth and misery. [t. L]

squama (skwā′mə), *n., pl.* **-mae** (-mē). a scale or scale-like part, as of epidermis or bone. [t. L]

squamate (skwā′māt), *adj.* provided or covered with squamae or scales; scaly. [t. L: m. s. *squāmātus*]

squamation (skwā mā′shən), *n.* **1.** the state of being squamate. **2.** the arrangement of the squamae or scales of an animal.

squamosal (skwə mō′səl), *adj.* **1.** *Anat.* pertaining to the thin scalelike bone (an element of the temporal bone) in the side of the skull above and behind the ear. **2.** *Zool.* pertaining to a corresponding bone in other vertebrates. **3.** squamous. —*n.* **4.** a squamosal bone.

squamose (skwā′mōs), *adj.* squamous. —**squa′mosely,** *adv.* —**squa′moseness,** *n.*

squamous (skwā′məs), *adj.* covered with or formed of

squamae or scales; scalelike. [t. L: m. s. *squāmōsus*] —**squa′mously,** *adv.* —**squa′mousness,** *n.*
squamulose (skwăm′yo͝o lōs′, skwā′myo͝o-), *adj.* furnished or covered with small scales.
squander (skwŏn′də), *v.t.* **1.** to spend (money, time, etc.) extravagantly or wastefully (often fol. by *away*). **2.** *Dial.* to scatter. —*n.* **3.** extravagant or wasteful expenditure. [orig. obscure] —**squan′derer,** *n.* —**Syn. 1.** waste, dissipate. See **spend.**
square (skwēə), *n., v.,* **squared, squaring,** *adj.,* **squarer, squarest,** *adv.* —*n.* **1.** a four-sided plane figure having all its sides equal and all its angles right angles. **2.** anything having this form or a form approximating it. **3.** one of the rectangular or otherwise shaped divisions of a game board, as a chess or draughts board. **4.** an open area in a city or town, as at the intersection of streets, often planted with grass, trees, etc. **5.** *U.S.* a block of buildings in a town marked off by neighbouring and intersecting streets along each side. **6.** an L-shaped or T-shaped instrument for determining or testing right angles, and for other purposes. **7.** *Maths.* the second power of a number or quantity: *the square of 4 is 4 × 4, or 16.* **8.** *Bldg Trades.* a unit of surface measurement equalling 100 square feet. **9.** *Mil.* (formerly) a body of troops drawn up in quadrilateral form. **10.** *Slang.* one who is ignorant of or uninterested in the latest fads. **11.** *Rowing.* the position of the blade of an oar at right angles to the water before it is dropped in to begin a stroke. **12.** *Obs.* a true standard. **13. on the square,** fair; fairly. **14. out of square,** not at right angles.
—*v.t.* **15.** to reduce to square, rectangular, or cubic form. **16.** to mark out in squares or rectangles. **17.** to test for deviation from a right angle, straight line, or plane surface. **18.** *Maths.* **a.** to find the equivalent of in square measure. **b.** to multiply (a number or quantity) by itself. **c.** to describe or find a square which is equivalent to: *to square a circle.* **19.** to bring to the form of a right angle or right angles; set at right angles to something else. **20.** to make the score of (a contest, etc.) even. **21.** to set (the shoulders, arms, etc.) so as to present an approximately rectangular outline. **22.** to make straight, level, or even. **23.** to regulate, as by a standard. **24.** to adjust harmoniously or satisfactorily; balance; settle: *to square a debt.* **25.** *Rowing.* to turn (the blade of an oar) from the feather to a right angle to the surface before dropping it to begin a stroke. **26.** *Slang.* to bribe.
—*v.i.* **27.** to accord or agree (often fol. by *with*): *his theory does not square with the facts.* **28. square away,** *Naut.* to arrange the yards so that they are at right angles to the fore-and-aft line of the ship. **29. square off,** to assume a posture of offence or defence, as in boxing. **30. square the circle,** to attempt the impossible. **31. square up,** to pay or settle a bill, debt, etc. **32. square up to,** to face, esp. courageously; prepare to contest or resist.
—*adj.* **33.** of the form of a right angle; having some part or parts rectangular: *a square corner.* **34.** having four sides and four right angles, but not equilateral; cubical or approximately so; rectangular and of three dimensions: *a square box.* **35.** at right angles, or perpendicular: *one line square to another.* **36.** *Naut.* at right angles to the mast and the keel, as a yard. **37.** designating a unit representing an area in the form of a square: *a square mile.* **38.** pertaining to such units, or to surface measurement: *square measure.* **39.** *Maths.* **a.** See **square number. b.** See **square root. 40.** of a specified length on each side of a square: *an area 2 feet square.* **41.** having a square section, or one that is merely rectangular: *a square file.* **42.** having a solid, sturdy form with rectilinear and angular outlines. **43.** straight, level, or even, as a surface or surfaces. **44.** leaving no balance of debt on either side; having all accounts settled: *to make accounts square.* **45.** just, fair, or honest. **46.** straightforward, direct, or unequivocal. **47.** *Colloq.* substantial or satisfying: *a square meal.* **48.** *Slang.* ignorant of or uninterested in the latest fashions; conventional.
—*adv.* **49.** so as to be square; in square or rectangular form. **50.** at right angles. **51.** *Colloq.* solidly or directly: *to hit a nail square on the head.* **52.** *Colloq.* fairly, honestly, or uprightly. [ME, t. OF: m. *esquarrer*, ult. der. L *ex-* EX[1] + *quadrāre* to square, QUADRATE] —**square′ly,** *adv.* —**square′ness,** *n.* —**squar′er,** *n.*
square bracket, *Print.* either of the two parenthetical marks: [ ].
square dance, a dance, as a quadrille, by couples arranged in a square or in some set form.
square-dance (skwēə′däns′), *v.i.,* **-danced, -dancing.** to perform or take part in a square dance. —**square′-dan′cer,** *n.*
square deal, *Colloq.* **1.** a mutually fair and honest arrangement or attitude. **2.** a distribution of cards according to the rules of a game, without cheating.
squared ring (skwēəd), *Colloq.* the boxing ring. Also, **squared circle.**
squarehead (skwēə′hĕd′), *n. Slang.* (derogatory) **1.** a German or a Dutchman. **2.** a Scandinavian.
square knot, *U.S.* a reef knot.
square-law detector (skwēə′lô′), *Electronics.* an electronic circuit which produces an output proportional to the square of its input voltage.
square leg, *Cricket.* a fielding position on the leg side at right angles to the pitch opposite the batsman's wicket.
square measure, a system of units for the measurement of surfaces or areas.
square number, a number which is the square of some integer number, as 1, 4, 9, 16, 25, etc., with respect to 1, 2, 3, 4, 5, etc.
square piano. See **piano**[1] (def. 4).
square-rigged (skwēə′rĭgd′), *adj. Naut.* having square sails as the principal sails.
square root, *Maths.* the quantity of which a given quantity is the square: *4 is the square root of 16.*
square sail, *Naut.* See **sail** (def. 1).
square-shooter (skwēə′sho͞o′tə), *n. U.S. Colloq.* an honest, fair person.
square-shouldered (skwēə′shōl′dəd), *adj.* having shoulders set so as to present an approximately rectangular outline.
square thread, *Mech.* a screw thread with a deep pitch in which the thread profile is U-shaped instead of V-shaped, used for transmitting thrust.
square-toed (skwēə′tōd′), *adj.* **1.** having a broad, square toe, as a shoe. **2.** *Colloq.* old-fashioned and unpretentious in habits, ideas, etc.
square-toes (skwēə′tōz′), *n., construed as sing. Colloq.* an old-fashioned person.
square wave, *Physics.* a wave form which alternates between two fixed values for equal lengths of time, the time of transition between the two values being very short.
squarish (skwēə′rĭsh), *adj.* approximately square.
squarrose (skwā′rōs, skwŏ′rōs), *adj. Biol.* denoting any rough or ragged surface. [t. L: m. s. *squarrōsus*]
squash[1] (skwŏsh), *v.t.* **1.** to press into a flat mass or pulp; crush. **2.** to suppress or put down; quash. **3.** *Colloq.* to silence, as with a crushing retort. —*v.i.* **4.** to be pressed into a flat mass or pulp. **5.** (of a soft, heavy body) to fall heavily. **6.** to make a splashing sound; splash. —*n.* **7.** the act or sound of squashing. **8.** the fact of being squashed. **9.** something squashed or crushed. **10.** something soft and easily crushed. **11.** a great number of people in a comparatively small space. **12.** Also, **squash rackets, squash racquets.** a game like rackets but played with a rubber ball on a smaller court and with a shorter racket. **13.** Also, **squash tennis.** *U.S.* a game resembling squash rackets, played with a larger ball and racket. **14.** a small indiarubber ball used in squash rackets. **15.** a beverage based upon a fruit juice, often diluted. [t. OF: m. s. *esquasser.* See QUASH; ? partly imit.] —**squash′er,** *n.*
squash[2] (skwŏsh), *n. U.S.* any of various vegetables of the genus *Cucurbita*, resembling a marrow, pumpkin, or the like. [t. Narragansett (Massachusetts) abbrev. of *askútasquash*, lit., vegetables eaten green]
squashed fly biscuit, *Colloq.* garibaldi biscuit.
squashy (skwŏsh′ĭ), *adj.,* **squashier, squashiest. 1.** easily squashed; pulpy. **2.** soft and wet, as ground, etc. **3.** having a squashed appearance. —**squash′ily,** *adv.* —**squash′iness,** *n.*
squat (skwŏt), *v.,* **squatted** or **squat, squatting,** *adj., n.* —*v.i.* **1.** to sit down in a low or crouching position with the legs drawn up closely beneath or in front of the body. **2.** to crouch or cower down, as an animal. **3.** to adopt a low position, as a heavily laden ship. **4.** to settle on land or occupy a building without any title or right. **5.** *Chiefly Austral., U.S., etc.* to settle on public land under government regulation, as to acquire title. —*v.t.* **6.** to cause (a person, oneself, etc.) to squat. —*adj.* **7.** short and thickset or thick, as persons, animals, the body, etc. **8.** low and thick or broad. **9.** seated or being in a squatting position; crouching. —*n.* **10.** the act or fact of squatting. **11.** a squatting position or posture. [ME, t. OF: m. s. *esquatir*, f. *es-* (g. L *ex-* EX-[1]) out + *quatir* press down (der. L *coactus*, pp., driven together)] —**squat′ly,** *adv.* —**squat′ness,** *n.*
squatter (skwŏt′ə), *n.* **1.** one who or that which squats. **2.** one who settles on land or occupies a building without title or right. **3.** *Chiefly Austral., U.S., etc.* one who settles on land under government regulation, as to acquire title.
squattocracy (skwŏ tŏk′rə sĭ), *n. Austral. Slang.* squatters collectively.
squatty (skwŏt′ĭ), *adj.,* **-tier, -tiest.** short and thick; low and broad.
squaw (skwô), *n.* a North American Indian woman or wife. [t. Narragansett: m. *eskaw* woman]

squawk (skwôk), *v.i.* **1.** to utter a loud, harsh cry, as a duck or other fowl when frightened. **2.** *Slang.* to complain loudly and vehemently. —*v.t.* **3.** to give forth with a squawk. —*n.* **4.** a loud, harsh cry or sound. **5.** *Slang.* a loud, vehement complaint. [b. SQUALL² and CROAK] —**squawk′er,** *n.*

squaw man, a white or other non-Indian man married to an Indian squaw.

squeak (skwēk), *n.* **1.** a short, sharp, shrill cry; a sharp, high-pitched sound. **2.** *Colloq.* a bare chance. **3.** *Colloq.* a narrow escape. —*v.i.* **4.** to utter or emit a squeak or squeaky sound. **5.** *Slang.* to confess or turn informer. —*v.t.* **6.** to utter or produce with a squeak or squeaks. [ME *squeke,* appar. t. Scand.; cf. Sw. *sqväka* croak] —**squeak′er,** *n.*

squeaky (skwē′kĭ), *adj.,* **squeakier, squeakiest.** squeaking; tending to squeak: *his squeaky shoes could be heard along the corridor.* —**squeak′ily,** *adv.* —**squeak′iness,** *n.*

squeal (skwēl), *n.* **1.** a more or less prolonged, sharp, shrill cry, as of pain, fear, etc. **2.** *Slang.* a protest or complaint. —*v.i.* **3.** to utter or emit a squeal or squealing sound. **4.** *Slang.* to turn informer. **5.** *Slang.* to protest or complain. —*v.t.* **6.** to utter or produce with a squeal. **7.** *Slang.* to disclose or reveal, as something secret. [imit.] —**squeal′er,** *n.*

squeamish (skwē′mĭsh), *adj.* **1.** easily nauseated or sickened; qualmish. **2.** easily shocked by anything slightly immodest; prudish. **3.** excessively particular or scrupulous as to the moral aspect of things. **4.** fastidious or dainty. [late ME *squaymysch,* r. ME *squaymous,* earlier *scoymous,* t. AF: m. *escoymous*; orig. unknown] —**squeam′ishly,** *adv.* —**squeam′ishness,** *n.*

squeegee (skwē′jē′), *n., v.,* **-geed, -geeing.** —*n.* **1.** an implement edged with rubber or the like, for removing water from windows after washing, sweeping water from wet decks, etc. **2.** *Photog.* a device for removing surplus water from negatives or prints. —*v.t.* **3.** to sweep, scrape, or press with a squeegee. Also, **squilgee.** [? der. *squeege,* var. of SQUEEZE]

squeeze (skwēz), *v.,* **squeezed, squeezing,** *n.* —*v.t.* **1.** to press forcibly together; compress. **2.** to apply pressure to in order to extract something: *to squeeze a lemon.* **3.** to thrust forcibly; force by pressure; cram: *to squeeze three suits into a small suitcase.* **4.** to force out, extract, or procure by pressure (usually fol. by *out* or *from*): *to squeeze juice from an orange.* **5.** to embrace; hug. **6.** to press (someone's hand, arm, etc.) as an expression of affection, sympathy, etc. **7.** to harass or oppress (a person, etc.) by exactions. **8.** *Colloq.* to put pressure upon (a person or persons) to act in a given way, esp. by blackmail. **9.** to obtain a facsimile impression of.

—*v.i.* **10.** to exert a compressing force. **11.** to force a way through some narrow or crowded place (fol. by *through, in, out,* etc.).

—*n.* **12.** the act of squeezing. **13.** the fact of being squeezed. **14.** a tight pressure of another's hand within one's own, as in friendliness. **15.** a hug or close embrace. **16.** *Colloq.* a situation from which extrication is difficult: *in a tight squeeze.* **17.** a crowded gathering or assembly. **18.** a restriction, demand, or pressure, as imposed by a government: *a credit squeeze.* **19.** a small quantity or amount of anything obtained by squeezing. **20.** a facsimile impression of an inscription or the like, obtained by pressing some plastic substance over or around it. **21.** *Colloq.* the act of blackmailing.

[var. of obs. *squize* squeeze, OE *cwȳsan* (with *s-* by false division of words in sandhi)] —**squeez′er,** *n.*

squelch (skwĕlch), *v.t.* **1.** to strike or press with crushing force; crush down; squash. **2.** *Colloq.* to put down or suppress completely; silence, as with a crushing retort. —*v.i.* **3.** to make a splashing sound. **4.** to tread heavily in water, mud, wet shoes, etc., with such a sound. —*n.* **5.** a squelched or crushed mass of anything. **6.** a squelching sound. **7.** *Electronics.* a circuit which cuts off the output of a radio receiver until a signal begins. **8.** *Colloq.* a crushing argument or retort. [var. of *quelch* (b. QUELL and CRUSH), with *s-* by false division of words in sandhi] —**squelch′er,** *n.*

squeteague (skwĭ tēg′), *n.* any of several fishes of the genus *Cynoscion,* of the North American Atlantic coast, esp. *C. regalis,* an important food fish. [t. Narragansett: m. *pesukwiteag,* lit., they give glue]

squib (skwĭb), *n., v.,* **squibbed, squibbing.** —*n.* **1.** a short witty or sarcastic saying or writing. **2.** a firework consisting of a tube or ball filled with powder, which burns with a hissing noise terminated usually by a slight explosion. **3.** any firework. **4.** a pyrotechnic device used to fire the igniter in a rocket. **5.** *Obs.* a mean or paltry fellow. —*v.i.* **6.** to write squibs. **7.** to shoot a squib. **8.** to go off with a small, sharp sound. **9.** to move swiftly and irregularly. —*v.t.* **10.** to assail in squibs or lampoons. **11.** to toss, shoot, or utilize as a squib. [orig. uncert.]

squid (skwĭd), *n., pl.* **squids,** (*esp. collectively*) **squid.** any of various decapod dibranchiate cephalopods, esp. any of certain small species (as of *Loligo* and *Ommastrephes*) having slender bodies and caudal fins and much used for bait. [orig. obscure]

Squid, *Loligo vulgaris* (Up to 20 in. long)

squiffy (skwĭf′ĭ), *adj.* *Slang.* slightly intoxicated; tipsy. [orig. obscure]

squiggle (skwĭg′l), *n., v.,* **-gled, -gling.** —*n.* **1.** a short twist or curve, as in drawing or writing. —*v.i.* **2.** to twist or curve; appear as squiggles. —*v.t.* **3.** to form squiggles; scribble. [b. SQUIRM and WRIGGLE —**squig′gly,** *adj.*

squilgee (skwĭl′jē′), *n., v.t.,* **-geed, -geeing.** squeegee.

squill (skwĭl), *n.* **1.** the bulb of the sea-onion, *Urginea maritima,* cut into thin slices and dried, and used in medicine chiefly as an expectorant. **2.** the plant itself. **3.** any of the plants of the liliaceous genus *Scilla.* [ME, t. L: s. *squilla,* var. of *scilla,* t. Gk: m. *skilla*]

squilla (skwĭl′ə), *n., pl.* **squillas, squillae** (skwĭl′ē). a mantis crab. [t. L. See SQUILL]

squinancy (skwĭn′ən sĭ), *n.* a small, rubiaceous, perennial herb, *Asperula cynanchica,* common on dry, calcareous soils. Also, **squinancy wort.** [ME, t. ML: m. s. *(s)quinansia* QUINSY]

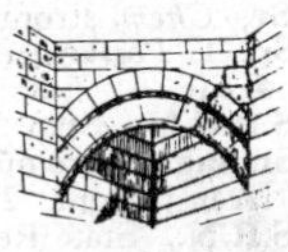
Squinch

squinch (skwĭnch), *n.* *Archit.* a small arch, corbelling, or the like, built across the interior angle between two walls, as in a square tower for supporting the side of a superimposed octagonal spire. [var. of obs. or d. *scunch* for *scuncheon,* ME *sconchon,* t. OF: m. *escoinson,* appar. der. *es-* (g. L *ex-* EX-¹) out + *coin* angle (g. L *cuneus* wedge)]

squint (skwĭnt), *v.i.* **1.** to look with the eyes partly closed. **2.** to be affected with strabismus; be cross-eyed. **3.** to look or glance obliquely or sideways; look askance. **4.** to make or have an indirect reference; tend or incline (fol. by *towards,* etc.). —*v.t.* **5.** to close (the eyes) partly in looking. **6.** to cause to squint; cause to look obliquely. —*n.* **7.** *Pathol.* an affection of the eye consisting in non-coincidence of the optic axes; strabismus. **8.** *Colloq.* a furtive glance. **9.** a looking obliquely or askance. **10.** an indirect reference; inclination. **11.** an oblique or perverse tendency. **12.** Also, **hagioscope.** a small opening in a church wall giving a view of the altar. **13.** *Bldg Trades.* (in brickwork) a special component consisting of a brick with splayed ends. —*adj.* **14.** looking obliquely; looking with a side glance; looking askance. **15.** affected with strabismus, as the eyes. [aphetic var. of ASQUINT, adv. (used as adj.)] —**squint′er,** *n.*

squint-eyed (skwĭnt′īd′), *adj.* **1.** affected with or characterized by strabismus. **2.** looking obliquely or askance.

squire (skwī′ə), *n., v.,* **squired, squiring.** —*n.* **1.** (in England) a country gentleman, esp. the chief landed proprietor in a district. **2.** *U.S.* a justice of the peace, local judge, or other local dignitary (chiefly used as a title) in country districts and small towns. **3.** a young man of gentle birth who, as an aspirant to knighthood, attended upon a knight; an esquire. **4.** a personal attendant, as of a person of rank. **5.** a man who attends or escorts a lady in public. —*v.t.* **6.** to attend as or in the manner of a squire. [ME *squier,* t. OF: m. *esquier.* See ESQUIRE]

squirearchy (skwī′ə rä′kĭ), *n., pl.* **-archies.** **1.** the class of squires collectively. **2.** rule or government by a squire or squires. Also, **squirarchy.** [f. SQUIRE + -ARCHY]

squireling (skwī′ə lĭng), *n.* a petty squire.

squirm (skwûm), *v.i.* **1.** to wriggle or writhe. **2.** to feel or display discomfort or disgust as from reproof, embarrassment, or repulsion. —*n.* **3.** a squirming or wriggling movement. [b. SKEW and WORM, v.] —**squirm′y,** *adj.*

Grey squirrel, *Sciurus carolinensis* (Total length 1½ ft, tail 8½ in.)

squirrel (skwĭ′rəl), *n.* **1.** any of the arboreal, bushy-tailed rodents constituting the genus *Sciurus* (family *Sciuridae*), as the **red squirrel** of Europe (including Britain) and Asia, *S. vulgaris,* and the **grey squirrel,** *S. carolinensis,* of North America and (by introduction) Britain. **2.** any of various other members of the family *Sciuridae,* as the chipmunks, flying squirrels, woodchucks, etc. **3.** the pelt or fur of such an animal. **4.** *Colloq.*

a person who hoards objects of little value. [ME *squirel*, t. AF: m. *esquirel*, dim. der. LL *sciūrus*, t. Gk: m. *skíouros*, der. *skiá* shadow + *ourá* tail] —**squir′rel-like′**, *adj.*

squirrel cage, a cage containing a cylindrical framework that is rotated by a squirrel or the like running around inside it.

squirrel-cage motor (skwĭ′rəl kāj′), *Elect.* a type of induction motor in which the rotor consists of a number of copper bags parallel to the axis of the motor, resembling a squirrel cage.

squirrelfish (skwĭ′rəl fĭsh′), *n.* any fish of the tropical marine highly-coloured family *Holocentridae*, or of the related family *Melamplaidae*.

squirrel-tail grass (skwĭ′rəl tāl′), a small annual grass, *Hordeum marinum*, which occurs in dry coastal regions of S and W Europe.

squirt (skwût), *v.i.* **1.** to eject liquid in a jet from a narrow orifice. **2.** to issue in a jetlike stream. —*v.t.* **3.** to cause (liquid) to issue in a jet from a narrow orifice. **4.** to wet or bespatter with a liquid so ejected. —*n.* **5.** the act of squirting. **6.** a jet, as of water. **7.** an instrument for squirting, as a syringe. **8.** a small quantity of liquid squirted. **9.** *Colloq.* **a.** an insignificant, self-assertive fellow. **b.** a short person. [orig. obscure] —**squirt′er,** *n.*

squirting cucumber, a cucurbitaceous plant, *Ecballium elaterium*, native in the Mediterranean region, whose ripened fruit forcibly ejects the seeds and juice.

squish (skwĭsh), *Colloq.* —*v.t.* **1.** to squeeze or squash. —*v.i.* **2.** (of water, soft mud, etc.) to make a gushing sound. —*n.* **3.** a noise made by squishing. —**squish′y,** *adj.*

sq. yd, square yard; square yards.

sr, *Maths.* steradian.

Sr, *Chem.* strontium.

Sr, **1.** *Portuguese.* Senhor. **2.** Senior. **3.** *Spanish.* Señor. **4.** Sir.

S.R.C.N., State Registered Children's Nurse.

Srinagar (srē nŭg′ə), *n.* the capital of Kashmir, on the river Jhelum. 285,257 (1961).

S.R.N., State Registered Nurse.

SS, **1.** (L *Sancti*) Saints. **2.** Schutzstaffel.

ss, sections.

S.S., **1.** steamship. **2.** Sunday School.

SS.D., (L *Sanctissimus Dominus*) Most Holy Lord (a title of the pope).

SSE, south-south-east. Also, **S.S.E.**

ssp., subspecies.

SSR, Soviet Socialist Republic. Also, **S.S.R.**

SSW, south-south-west. Also, **S.S.W.**

St, **1.** Saint. **2.** Strait. **3.** Street.

st, **1.** stet. **2.** strait. **3.** street.

st., **1.** stanza. **2.** statute. **3.** stone (weight).

s.t., short ton.

sta., **1.** station. **2.** stationary.

stab (stăb), *v.*, **stabbed, stabbing,** *n.* —*v.t.* **1.** to pierce or wound with, or as with, a pointed weapon. **2.** to thrust or plunge (a knife, etc.) into something. **3.** to penetrate sharply, like a knife. **4.** to make a thrusting or plunging motion at or in. **5.** to roughen the surface of (brickwork) so that it will hold plaster. **6. stab (someone) in the back,** *Colloq.* to do harm to (somebody), esp. somebody defenceless or unsuspecting, as by making a treacherous attack upon his reputation. —*v.i.* **7.** to thrust with or as with a knife or other pointed weapon: *to stab at an adversary.* **8.** to deliver a wound, as with a pointed weapon. —*n.* **9.** the act of stabbing. **10.** a thrust or blow with, or as with, a pointed weapon. **11.** a wound made by stabbing. **12.** a sudden, usually painful sensation. **13.** *Colloq.* an attempt, try. [ME, var. of d. *stob* in same sense, ? v. use of ME *stob* stick] —**stab′ber,** *n.*

Stabat Mater (stä′băt mä′tə), **1.** a celebrated 13th-century Latin hymn on the Virgin Mary at the Cross. **2.** a musical setting for this. [L: the mother was standing]

stabile (stā′bĭl), *adj.* **1.** fixed in position; stable. **2.** *Med.* **a.** resistant to moderate degrees of heat. **b.** denoting or pertaining to a mode of application of electricity in which the active electrode is kept stationary over the part to be acted upon (opposed to *labile*). [t. L: m. s. *stabilis* STABLE²]

stability (stə bĭl′ĭ tĭ), *n.*, *pl.* **-ties.** **1.** firmness in position. **2.** continuance without change; permanence. **3.** steadfastness, as of character or purpose. **4.** resistance to change, esp. adverse change. **5.** the ability of a ship or aircraft to return to its original position when accidentally displaced. **6.** *Rom. Cath. Ch.* a vow taken by a Benedictine monk, binding him to remain a member of the same community and house.

stabilize (stā′bĭ līz′), *v.*, **-lized, -lizing.** —*v.t.* **1.** to make stable. **2.** to maintain at a given or unfluctuating level or quantity. **3.** *Aeron.* to put or keep (an aircraft) in stable equilibrium, as by some special device. —*v.i.* **4.** to become stable. Also, **stabilise.** —**sta′biliza′tion,** *n.*

stabilizer (stā′bĭ lī′zə), *n.* **1.** one who or that which stabilizes. **2.** one of a pair of retractable horizontal planes fitted to a ship below the waterline to stabilize it. **3.** *Chem.* any substance which is added to explosives, plastics, paints, foods, chemicals, etc., in order to retard any undesirable spontaneous chemical or physical changes; an inhibitor. **4.** *U.S. Aeron.* tailplane. Also, **stabiliser.**

stable¹ (stā′bl), *n.*, *v.*, **-bled, -bling.** —*n.* **1.** a building for the lodging and feeding of horses, cattle, etc. **2.** such a building with stalls. **3.** a collection of animals belonging in such a building. **4.** *Racing.* **a.** an establishment where racehorses are kept and trained. **b.** the horses belonging to, or the persons connected with, such an establishment. —*v.t.* **5.** to put or lodge in or as in a stable. —*v.i.* **6.** to live in or as in a stable. [ME, t. OF: m. *estable*, g. L *stabulum*]

stable² (stā′bl), *adj.* **1.** not likely to fall or give way, as a structure, support, foundation, etc.; firm; steady. **2.** able or likely to continue or last; enduring or permanent: *a stable government.* **3.** steadfast; not wavering or changeable, as a person, the mind, etc. **4.** *Physics.* having or showing an ability or tendency to maintain or re-establish position, form, etc.: *stable equilibrium.* **5.** *Chem.* not readily decomposing, as a compound; resisting molecular or chemical change. [ME, t. F, g. L *stabilis*] —**sta′bleness,** *n.* —**sta′bly,** *adv.*

stableboy (stā′bl boi′), *n.* one who works in a stable. Also, **stableman** (stā′bl măn′, -mən).

stable equilibrium, a state of a body such that after any displacement the body will return to its original position.

stabling (stā′blĭng), *n.* **1.** the act of putting into a stable. **2.** accommodation for horses, etc., in a stable or stables. **3.** stables collectively.

stablish (stăb′lĭsh), *v.t. Archaic.* establish.

stacc., *Music.* staccato.

staccato (stə kä′tō; *It.* stàk kà′tò), *Music.* —*adj.* **1.** detached, disconnected, or abrupt. **2.** with breaks between the successive notes. —*adv.* **3.** in a staccato manner. Cf. **legato.** [t. It., pp. of *staccare*, short for *distaccare* DETACH]

Written Played

Staccato phrase

stack (stăk), *n.* **1.** a large, usually circular or rectangular pile of hay, straw, or the like. **2.** any more or less orderly pile or heap. **3.** a number of chimneys or flues grouped together. **4.** a single chimney or funnel for smoke, or a vertical pipe inside or outside a building for passing waste products down, circulating heat, or expelling exhaust gases. **5.** *Geol.* a column or pillar of rock, isolated from the shore by the erosive action of waves. **6.** *Colloq.* a great quantity or number. **7.** a number of muskets or rifles hooked together to stand on the ground in a conical group. **8.** a measure for coal and wood, equal to 108 cubic feet. **9.** *Aeron.* a number of aircraft circling at different altitudes above an aerodrome awaiting their signal to land. —*v.t.* **10.** to pile or arrange in a stack: *to stack hay.* **11.** to place (rifles, etc.) in a stack. **12.** to cover or load with something in stacks or piles. **13.** to arrange (playing cards in the pack) in an unfair manner. **14.** *Aeron.* to control the aircraft waiting to land at an airport, so that they form a stack. [ME *stak*, t. Scand.; cf. Icel. *stakkr* haystack; akin to Russ. *stog* haystack] —**stack′er,** *n.*

stacte (stăk′tē), *n.* *Bible.* one of the sweet spices which composed the holy incense of the ancient Jews. Ex. 30:34. [t. L, t. Gk: m. *staktḗ*, fem. of *staktós* distilling in drops; r. ME *stacten*, t. L, acc. of *stactē*]

staddle (stăd′l), *n.* **1.** the lower part of a stack of corn, hay, etc. **2.** a supporting frame for a stack; a platform upon which a stack or rick is placed. **3.** any supporting base or framework. [ME *stathel*, OE *stathol*, Icel. *stödhull* milking place]

stadholder (stăd′hōl′də), *n.* stadtholder.

stadia¹ (stā′dyə), *Civ. Eng.* —*n.* **1.** a method of surveying in which distances are read by noting the interval on a graduated rod (**stadia rod**) intercepted by two parallel crosshairs (**stadia hairs** or **wires**) mounted in the telescope of a surveyor's level, the rod being placed at one end of the distance to be measured and the theodolite at the other. —*adj.* **2.** pertaining to stadia surveying. [orig. uncert.; prob. special use of STADIA²]

stadia² (stā′dyə), *n.* pl. of **stadium.**

stadiometer (stā′dĭ ŏm′ĭ tə), *n.* an instrument for measuring the lengths of curves, dashed lines, etc., by running a toothed wheel over them. [f. *stadio-* (comb. form of STADIUM) + -METER¹]

stadium (stā′dyəm), *n.*, *pl.* **-dia** (-dyə), **-diums.** **1.** a sports arena, usually oval, with tiers of seats for spectators. **2.** an ancient Greek course for races, typically semicircular, with tiers of seats for spectators. **3.** an ancient Greek unit of length, equal at Athens to about 607 feet. **4.** a stage of development in a process, disease, etc. [t. L, t. Gk: m. *stádion*]

stadtholder (stăd′hōl′də), *n.* **1.** the chief magistrate of the former republic of the United Provinces of the Netherlands. **2.** (formerly, in the Netherlands) the viceroy or governor of a province. Also, **stadholder.** [t. D: m. *stadhouder*, f. *stad* place, city + *houder* holder]

Staël-Holstein (*Fr.* stål ōls tĕn′), *n.* **Anne Louise Germaine Necker** (*Fr.* ȧn lwēz zhĕr mĕn nĕ kĕr′), **Baronne de** (*Madame de Staël*), 1766–1817, French writer.

staff[1] (stäf), *n., pl.* **staffs, staves** (stāvz), *adj., v.* —*n.* **1.** a stick, pole, rod, or wand for aid in walking or climbing, for use as a weapon, etc. **2.** a rod or wand serving as an ensign of office or authority, as a crozier, baton, truncheon, or mace. **3.** a pole on which a flag is hung or displayed. **4.** something which serves to support or sustain: *bread is the staff of life.* **5.** a body of assistants to a manager, superintendent, or executive head. **6.** a body of persons charged with carrying out the work of an establishment or executing some undertaking. **7.** the teaching personnel of a school, college, or the like. **8.** *Mil., Naval.* **a.** a body of officers without command authority, appointed to assist a commanding officer. **b.** the parts of any army concerned with administrative matters, planning, etc., instead of with actual participation in combat. **9.** *Music.* stave (def. 5). **10.** *Archaic or Dial.* a stick or pole forming part of something, as the shaft of a spear, a rung of a ladder, etc. —*adj.* **11.** of, or being a member of, a military or naval staff or unit: *staff officer.* —*v.t.* **12.** to provide with a staff. [ME; OE *stæf*, c. D *staf*, G *Stab*, Icel. *stafr*]

staff[2] (stäf), *n.* a kind of plaster combined with fibrous material, used for temporary ornamental buildings, etc. [orig. unknown]

Staffa (stăf′ə), *n.* See **Fingal's Cave.**

staff notation, musical notation in which a stave is used. Cf. **tonic sol-fa.**

staff officer, *Mil.* a commissioned officer attached to the general staff.

Stafford (stăf′əd), *n.* **1.** a town in central England: the county town of Staffordshire. 48,280 (est. 1962). **2.** Staffordshire.

Staffordshire (stăf′əd shĭə′, -shə), *n.* a county in central England. 1,733,887 pop. (1961); 1154 sq. mi. *Co. town:* Stafford. *Abbrev.:* Staffs. Also, **Stafford.**

Staffordshire terrier, one of a breed of stocky dogs having a short, glossy coat of various colours.

staffroom (stäf′ro͝om′, -ro͞om′), *n.* a common room for the staff of a school, college, etc.

Staffs, Staffordshire.

staff sergeant, a non-commissioned officer, with the rank of sergeant, acting in a specialized capacity.

stag (stăg), *n., v.,* **stagged, stagging,** *adj.* —*n.* **1.** an adult male deer. **2.** the male of various other animals. **3.** *Colloq.* a man, esp. one at a social gathering exclusively for men. **4.** a swine castrated after maturation of the sex organs. **5.** *Stock Exchange.* one who applies for shares of a new issue in the hope of a quick sale at a profit. —*v.i.* **6.** *Colloq.* to go to a social function without a woman partner. —*adj.* **7.** *Colloq.* for or of men only: *a stag party.* [ME *stagge*, OE (unrecorded) *stagga*, akin to Icel. *steggr* male fox, tomcat]

Stag of red deer, *Cervus elaphus* (4 ft high at the shoulder, antlers 3 ft long)

stag-beetle (stăg′bē′tl), *n.* any of the lamellicorn beetles constituting the family *Lucanidae.* The males have mandibles resembling a stag's antlers.

stage (stāj), *n., v.,* **staged, staging.** —*n.* **1.** a single step or degree in a process; a particular period in a process of development. **2.** a raised platform or floor, as for speakers, performers, etc. **3.** *Theat.* **a.** the platform in a theatre on which the actors perform. **b.** this platform with all the parts of the theatre, and all the apparatus behind the proscenium. **4.** the theatre, the drama, or the dramatic profession. **5.** the scene of any action. **6.** a stagecoach. **7.** (formerly) a place of rest on a journey; a regular stopping place of a stagecoach or the like, for the change of horses, etc. **8.** one of the divisions of a bus route, etc., for which a fare is fixed; fare stage. **9.** the distance between two places of rest on a journey; each of the portions of a journey. **10.** a portion or period of a course of action, of life, etc. **11.** *Zool.* **a.** any one of the major time periods in the development of an insect, as the embryonic, larval, pupal, and imaginal stages. **b.** any one of the periods of larval growth between moults. **12.** *Econ., Sociol.* a major phase of the economic or sociological life of man or society: *the matriarchal stage.* **13.** *Geol.* a division of stratified rocks next in rank to series, representing deposits formed during the fraction of an epoch that is called an age. **14.** the small platform of a microscope on which the object is examined. See diag. under **microscope. 15.** *Radio.* a part of a complex circuit, as a transistor and its associated passive elements in an amplifier having several transistors. **16.** a powered section of a rocket which can be jettisoned after firing. **17. by easy stages,** without rushing; working or travelling with many stops. **18. go on the stage,** to take up acting as a career. **19. hold the stage,** to be the centre of attention. —*v.t.* **20.** to put, represent, or exhibit on or as on a stage. **21.** to furnish with a stage or staging. **22.** to write, direct, or produce (a play) as if the action were taking place in a specific place or period of time. **23.** to plan, organize, or carry out (an action) in which each participant has a specific task to perform. —*v.i.* **24.** to be suitable for presentation on the stage. **25.** to travel by stages, or by stagecoach. [ME, t. OF: m. *estage*, ult. der. L *stāre* stand]

stagecoach (stāj′kōch′), *n.* a coach that runs regularly over a fixed route with passengers, parcels, etc.

Stagecoach

stagecraft (stāj′kräft′), *n.* skill in or the art of writing, adapting, or staging plays.

stage direction, an instruction written into the script of a play, indicating actions or movements of the performers, or requirements for the settings, costumes, etc.

stage door, a door at the back or side of a theatre, used by performers and other authorized theatre personnel.

stage effect, an effect, as of noise, music, lighting, used in producing a play, etc.

stage fright, nervousness experienced on facing an audience, esp. for the first time.

stagehand (stāj′hănd′), *n.* a person employed to move properties, regulate lighting, etc., in a dramatic production.

stage left, the part of a theatre stage that is left of the centre as an actor faces the audience.

stage-manager (stāj′măn′ĭ jə), *n.* one who superintends the performance of a play and regulates the stage arrangements. —**stage′-man′agement,** *n.*

stage-name (stāj′nām′), *n.* a name, other than the real one, assumed by an actor or actress.

stager (stā′jə), *n.* **1.** a person of experience in some profession, way of life, etc.; an old hand. **2.** *Archaic.* an actor. **3.** See **old stager.**

stage right, the part of a theatre stage which is right of the centre as an actor faces the audience.

stagestruck (stāj′strŭk′), *adj.* obsessed with the desire to go on the stage.

stage whisper, **1.** a loud whisper on a stage, meant to be heard by the audience. **2.** a whisper meant to be heard by others than the person addressed.

stagger (stăg′ə), *v.i.* **1.** to walk, move, or stand unsteadily; sway. **2.** to begin to doubt or waver, as in opinion; hesitate. —*v.t.* **3.** to cause to reel, totter, or become unsteady. **4.** to shock; render helpless with amazement or the like. **5.** to cause to waver or falter. **6.** to arrange in a zigzag order or manner, as spokes in the hub of a wheel. **7.** *Aeron.* to arrange (the planes of a biplane, etc.) so that the entering edge of an upper plane is either in advance of or behind that of a corresponding lower plane. **8.** to arrange in some other order or manner than the regular, uniform, or usual one, esp. at such intervals that there is a continuous overlapping: *to stagger lunch hours so that the cafeteria is not overcrowded.*
—*n.* **9.** the act of staggering; a reeling or tottering movement or motion. **10.** a staggered order or arrangement. **11.** *Aeron.* **a.** a staggered arrangement of planes. **b.** the amount of staggering. **12.** (*pl. construed as sing.*). Also, **blind staggers.** *Vet. Sci.* any of various forms of cerebral and spinal disease in horses, cattle, and other animals, characterized by blindness, a staggering gait, sudden falling, etc.
[var. of obs. or d. *stacker*, ME *staker*(*en*), t. Scand.; cf. Icel. *stakra*] —**stag′gerer,** *n.* —**stag′geringly,** *adv.*

—**Syn. 1.** STAGGER, REEL, TOTTER suggest an unsteady manner of walking. To STAGGER is successively to lose and regain one's equilibrium and the ability to maintain one's direction: *to stagger with exhaustion, a heavy load, or intoxication.* To REEL is to sway dizzily and be in imminent danger of falling: *to reel when faint with hunger.* TOTTER suggests the immediate likelihood of falling from weakness or feebleness, and is used particularly as of infants or the very aged, who walk with shaky, uncertain, faltering steps: *an old man tottered along with a cane.*

staggerbush (stăg′ə bo͝osh′), *n.* an American ericaceous shrub, *Pieris mariana*, with a foliage poisonous to animals.

staghound (stăg′hound′), *n.* a hound used for hunting stags, etc., resembling the foxhound, but larger.

staging (stā′jĭng), *n.* **1.** the act or process of putting a play on the stage. **2.** a temporary platform or structure of posts and boards for support, as in buildings; scaffolding. **3.** the business of running stagecoaches. **4.** the act of travelling by stages or by stagecoach.

staging area, a predetermined place of assembly for troops to form up prior to an action, embarkation, etc.

Stagirite (stăj′ĭ rīt′), *n.* **1.** a native or inhabitant of **Stagira,** a city of ancient Macedonia. **2. the Stagirite,** Aristotle, who was born there.

stagnant (stăg′nənt), *adj.* **1.** not running or flowing, as water, air, etc. **2.** foul from standing, as a pool of water. **3.** inactive, sluggish, or dull. **4.** making no progress; not developing. [t. L: s. *stagnans*, ppr.] —**stag′nancy,** *n.* —**stag′nantly,** *adv.*

stagnate (stăg′nāt, stăg nāt′), *v.i.*, **-nated, -nating. 1.** to cease to run or flow, as water, air, etc. **2.** to become foul from standing, as a pool of water. **3.** to become inactive, sluggish, or dull. **4.** to make no progress; stop developing. [t. L: m. s. *stagnātus*, pp.] —**stagna′tion,** *n.*

stag party, a party exclusively for men, esp. one held for a bachelor just before his marriage (opposed to *hen party*).

stag's horn fern (stăgz′hôn′), a fern of the tropical epiphytic genus *Platycerium*, having large fertile leaves resembling a stag's horn. Also, **elkhorn fern.**

stag's-horn moss (stăgz′hôn′), a small club moss, *Lycopodium clavatum*, a homosporous pteridophyte of hills and mountains.

stagy (stā′jĭ), *adj.*, **stagier, stagiest.** of, pertaining to, or suggestive of the stage; theatrical. —**sta′gily,** *adv.*

Stahlhelm (*Ger.* shtäl′hĕlm), *n.* a monarchist, nationalist military organization founded by former soldiers in Germany after World War I. [t. G: steel helmet]

staid (stād), *adj.* **1.** of settled or sedate character; not flighty or capricious. **2.** *Rare.* fixed, settled, or permanent. —*v.* **3.** a pt. and pp. of **stay**[1]. [var. of *stayed*, pp. of STAY[1]] —**staid′ly,** *adv.* —**staid′ness,** *n.*

—**Syn. 1.** STAID, SEDATE, SETTLED indicate a sober and composed type of conduct. STAID indicates an ingrained seriousness and propriety which shows itself in complete decorum; a colourless kind of correctness is indicated: *a staid and uninteresting old maid.* SEDATE applies to one who is noticeably quiet, composed, and sober in conduct: *a sedate and dignified young woman.* One who is SETTLED has become fixed, esp. in a sober or determined way, in his manner, judgements, or mode of life: *he is young to seem so settled in his ways.* —**Ant. 1.** flighty, frivolous, unstable.

stain (stān), *n.* **1.** a discoloration produced by foreign matter; a spot. **2.** a natural spot or patch of different colour, as on the body of an animal. **3.** a cause of reproach; blemish: *a stain on one's reputation.* **4.** a solution or suspension of colouring matter in water, spirit, or oil, designed to colour a surface (esp. wooden) by penetration without hiding it. **5.** a dye made into a solution and used to colour textiles, etc. **6.** a reagent or dye used in staining microscopic specimens. —*v.t.* **7.** to discolour with spots or streaks of foreign matter. **8.** to bring reproach upon; blemish. **9.** to sully with guilt or infamy; corrupt. **10.** to colour in a particular way. **11.** to colour with something which penetrates the substance. **12.** to treat (a microscopic specimen) with some reagent or dye in order to colour the whole or parts and so give distinctness, contrast of tissues, etc. —*v.i.* **13.** to produce a stain. **14.** to become stained; take a stain. [ME *steyne*, t. Scand. (cf. Icel. *steina* to paint); in some senses, aphetic var. of DISTAIN] —**stain′able,** *adj.* —**stain′er,** *n.* —**stain′less,** *adj.* —**stain′lessly,** *adv.*

stained glass, coloured, enamelled, or painted glass, as used in church windows. —**stained′-glass′,** *adj.*

stainer (stā′nə), *n.* **1.** one who or that which stains. **2.** a coloured pigment which is added in small quantity to a prepared paint in order to modify its colour.

Staines (stānz), *n.* a town in England, in Surrey (formerly in Middlesex), on the Thames. 49,838 (1961).

stainless steel, a hard steel alloyed with a high percentage of chromium, from 8 to approximately 25 per cent, proof against rust and many corrosive agents.

stair (stĕə), *n.* **1.** one of a series or flight of steps forming a means of passage from one storey or level to another, as in a building. **2.** (*pl.*) such steps collectively, esp. as forming a flight or a series of flights. **3.** a series or flight of steps; a stairway: *a winding stair.* **4. below stairs,** in the servants' quarters. [ME *steire*, OE *stǣger*, c. D and LG *steiger* landing stage]

stair-carpet (stĕə′kä′pĭt), *n.* a long, narrow carpet used for covering stairs.

staircase (stĕə′kās′), *n.* a flight of stairs with its framework, bannisters, etc., or a series of such flights.

stairfoot (stĕə′fo͝ot′), *n.* the bottom of a staircase.

stairhead (stĕə′hĕd′), *n.* the top of a staircase.

stair-rod (stĕə′rŏd′), *n.* one of a series of rods fixed into the angle of a flight of stairs for holding the stair-carpet in place.

stairway (stĕə′wā′), *n.* a way up and down by a series of stairs; a staircase.

stairwell (stĕə′wĕl′), *n.* the vertical shaft or opening containing a stairway.

staithe (stāth), *n. Naut.* a riverside berth or pier at which ships can load coal by gravity into their holds. [ME, t. Scand.; cf. Icel. *stöth*, c. OE *stæth* shore]

stake[1] (stāk), *n.*, *v.*, **staked, staking.** —*n.* **1.** a stick or post pointed at one end for driving into the ground as a boundary mark, a part of a fence, a support for a plant, etc. **2.** a post, esp. one to which a person is bound for execution, usually by burning. **3.** one of a number of vertical posts fitting into sockets or staples on the edge of the platform of a vehicle, as to retain the load. **4. pull up stakes,** *Colloq.* to leave one's job, home, etc., and move away. **5. the stake,** the punishment of death by burning. —*v.t.* **6.** to mark with stakes (often fol. by *off* or *out*). **7.** to possess, lay claim to or reserve a share of (land, profit, etc.) (usually fol. by *out* or *off*). **8.** to protect, separate, or close off by a barrier of stakes. **9.** to support with a stake or stakes, as a plant. **10.** to tether or secure to a stake, as an animal. **11.** to fasten with a stake or stakes. [ME; OE *staca*, c. D *staak*, G *Stake*; akin to STICK[1]]

stake[2] (stāk), *n.*, *v.*, **staked, staking.** —*n.* **1.** that which is wagered in a game, race, or contest. **2.** an interest held in something. **3.** *Colloq.* personal concern, interest, involvement, etc. **4.** the funds with which a gambler operates. **5.** (*often pl.*) a prize in a race or contest. **6.** (*pl. construed as sing.*) a race in which equal amounts are contributed by all the owners of the competing horses for prize money. **7.** *U.S. Colloq.* a grubstake. **8. at stake,** involved; in a state of being staked or at hazard. —*v.t.* **9.** to put at hazard upon the result of a game, the event of a contingency, etc.; wager; venture or hazard. **10.** to furnish with necessaries or resources, often by way of a business venture with a view to a possible return. [cf. D *staken* fix, place]

stakeboat (stāk′bōt′), *n. Rowing.* a moored boat from which the stern of a competing boat is held before starting a race.

Staked Plain (stākt), Llano Estacado.

stakeholder (stāk′hōl′də), *n.* the holder of the stakes of a wager, etc.

Stakhanovism (stă kăn′ə vĭz′əm), *n.* a method developed (1935) in the Soviet Union to increase production by rewarding individual initiative. [named after A. G. *Stakhanov*, born 1905, Russian coal-miner. See -ISM] —**Stakhan′ovite′,** *adj.*, *n.*

stalactite (stăl′ək tīt′), *n.* a deposit, usually of calcium carbonate, shaped like an icicle, hanging from the roof of a cave or the like, and formed by the dripping of percolating calcareous water. [t. NL: m. *stalactītēs*, f. *stalact-* (t. Gk: m. s. *stalaktós* dripping) + *-ītēs* -ITE[1]] —**stalactitic** (stăl′ək tĭt′ĭk), **stal′actit′ical,** *adj.*

A, Stalactite; B, Stalagmite

stalag (stăl′ăg; *Ger.* shtä′läk), *n.* a German camp for prisoners of war. [G: *Sta*(*mm*)*lag*(*er*) group camp]

stalagmite (stăl′əg mīt′), *n.* a deposit, usually of calcium carbonate, more or less resembling an inverted stalactite, formed on the floor of a cave or the like by the dripping of percolating calcareous water. [t. NL: m. *stalagmītēs*, f. *stalagm-* (t. Gk: s. *stalagmós* dropping) + *-ītēs* -ITE[1]] —**stalagmitic** (stăl′əg mĭt′ĭk), **stal′agmit′ical,** *adj.*

stalagmometry (stăl′əg mŏm′ĭ trĭ), *n. Chem.* the measurement of surface tension by determining the weight or volume of liquid drops.

St Albans (ôl′bənz), a city in SE England, in Hertfordshire: Norman cathedral; site of two battles in the Wars of the Roses, 1455, 1461. 50,293 (1961). Ancient, **Verulamium.**

stale[1] (stāl), *adj.*, **staler, stalest,** *v.*, **staled, staling.** —*adj.* **1.** not fresh; vapid or flat, as beverages; dry or hardened, as bread. **2.** having lost novelty or interest; hackneyed; trite: *a stale joke.* **3.** having lost fresh vigour, quick intelligence, initiative, or the like, as from overstrain, boredom, etc. **4.** *Law.* having lost force or effectiveness through absence of action, as a claim. —*v.t.*, *v.i.* **5.** to make or become stale. [ME, ? t. AF: m. **estale* (F *étale* still (water)), der. *estaler* stop] —**stale′ly,** *adv.* —**stale′ness,** *n.*

stale[2] (stāl), *n.*, *v.*, **staled, staling.** —*n.* **1.** urine, esp. of horses and cattle. —*v.i.* **2.** (of livestock, esp. horses and cattle) to urinate. [ME; special use of STALE[1]]

stalemate (stāl′māt′), *n.*, *v.*, **-mated, -mating.** —*n.* **1.** *Chess.* a position of the pieces when no move can be made by a player without putting his own king in check, the result being a draw. **2.** any position in which no action can be taken; a deadlock. —*v.t.* **3.** to subject to a stalemate. **4.** to bring to a standstill. [f. *stale* a standstill (special use of STALE[1]) + MATE[2]]

Stalin (stä′lĭn), *n.* **1. Joseph** (*Iosif Vissarionovich Dzugashvili*), 1879–1953, Soviet marshal and statesman: general secretary of the Soviet Communist Party 1922–53; premier of the U.S.S.R. 1941–53. **2.** Stalino. **3.** former name (1949–57) of **Varna. 4.** former name (1950–60) of **Braşov.**

Stalinabad (*Russ.* stə lĭ nȧ bȧt′), *n.* former name (1929–61) of **Dyushambe.**

Stalingrad (stä′lĭn grăd′; *Russ.* stə lĭn grȧt′), *n.* former name (1925–61) of **Volgograd.**

Stalinism (stä′lĭ nĭz′əm), *n.* the policy or practices of Communism associated with Stalin, esp. government by oppressive dictatorship and the liquidation of opposition and potential opposition. —**Sta′linist,** *adj., n.*

Stalino (*Russ.* stȧ′lĭ nə), *n.* former name (1935–62) of **Donetsk.** Also, **Stalin.**

Stalinsk (*Russ.* stȧ′lĭnsk), *n.* former name (1932–61) of **Novokuznetsk.**

stalk[1] (stôk), *n.* **1.** the stem or main axis of a plant. **2.** any slender supporting or connecting part of a plant, as the petiole of a leaf, the peduncle of a flower, or the funicle of an ovule. **3.** a similar structural part of an animal. **4.** a stem, shaft, or slender supporting part of anything. [ME *stalke,* f. OE *stæla* stalk + *-k* suffix] —**stalk′like′,** *adj.*

stalk[2] (stôk), *v.i.* **1.** to pursue or approach game, etc., stealthily. **2.** to walk with slow, stiff, or haughty strides. **3.** to proceed with slow, implacable and often sinister movement: *famine stalked through the land.* **4.** *Obs.* to walk or go stealthily along. —*v.t.* **5.** to pursue (game, a person, etc.) stealthily. **6.** to stalk over or through. —*n.* **7.** an act or course of stalking game or the like. **8.** a slow, stiff stride or gait. [ME *stalke,* OE *-stealcian* move stealthily, appar. der. (with *-k* suffix) OE *stalian* go stealthily. See STEAL] —**stalk′er,** *n.*

stalking-horse (stô′kĭng hôs′), *n.* **1.** a horse, or a figure of a horse, behind which a hunter conceals himself in stalking game. **2.** anything put forward to mask plans or efforts; a pretext. **3.** *Politics, Chiefly U.S.* a candidate used to screen a more important candidate or to draw votes from a rival and hence cause his defeat.

stalkless (stôk′lĭs), *adj.* **1.** having no stalk. **2.** *Bot.* sessile.

stalky (stô′kĭ), *adj.* **1.** abounding in stalks. **2.** stalklike; long and slender. —**stalk′ily,** *adv.* —**stalk′iness,** *n.*

stall[1] (stôl), *n.* **1.** a compartment in a stable or shed, for the accommodation of one animal. **2.** a stable or shed for horses or cattle. **3.** a booth, bench, table, or stand on which merchandise is displayed or exposed for sale. **4.** a carrel. **5.** one of a number of fixed enclosed seats in the choir or chancel of a church for the use of the clergy. **6.** a chairlike seat in a theatre, separated from others by armrests. **7.** (*pl.*) the front part of the auditorium on the ground floor of a theatre. **8.** a small compartment or chamber for any of various purposes. **9.** a working area in a mine. **10.** a sheath or cover for a finger or toe. **11.** the fact or an instance of an engine or a vehicle stopping, as through inadequate fuel supply or overloading. **12.** *Aeron.* the fact or an instance of causing an aeroplane to fly at an angle of incidence greater than the angle of maximum lift, causing loss of control and downward spin. —*v.t.* **13.** to put or keep in a stall or stalls, as animals. **14.** to confine in a stall for fattening, as cattle. **15.** to bring to a standstill; check the progress or motion of, esp. of a vehicle or an engine by unintentionally overloading it or giving an inadequate fuel supply. **16.** *Aeron.* to fly (an aeroplane) at an angle of incidence greater than the angle of maximum lift, causing loss of control and downward spin. **17.** to cause to stick fast, as in mire or snow. —*v.i.* **18.** to come to a standstill; be brought to a stop, esp. unintentionally. **19.** to stick fast, as in mire. **20.** *Aeron.* **a.** (of an aeroplane) to become stalled. **b.** (of an aviator) to stall an aeroplane. **21.** to occupy a stall, as an animal. [ME; OE *steall,* c. G *Stall*]

stall[2] (stôl), *Slang.* —*n.* **1.** anything used as a pretext, pretence, or trick. —*v.i.* **2.** to act evasively or deceptively. **3.** *Sport.* to play below one's best in order to deceive for any reason. —*v.t.* **4.** to put off, evade, or deceive (often fol. by *off*). [var. of late ME *stale* decoy bird, t. AF: m. *estale,* t. OE: m. *stæl* (in *stælhrān* decoy reindeer), akin to G *Stell* (in *Stellvogel* decoy bird)]

stallage (stô′lĭj), *n.* rent for the right to erect a stall in a marketplace, on a fairground, or elsewhere.

stall-feed (stôl′fēd′), *v.t.,* **-fed, -feeding. 1.** to keep and feed (an animal) in a stall. **2.** to fatten by this process, as an animal for killing.

stalling angle, *Aeron.* the angle of attack providing maximum lift: below this angle the airflow becomes turbulent, leading to an abrupt loss of lift.

stallion (stăl′yən), *n.* a male horse not castrated, esp. one kept for breeding. [ME *stalun,* t. OF: m. *estalon*; of Gmc orig.]

Stalloy (stăl′oi), *n. Metall.* a tradename for a steel containing up to 3½ per cent silicon, widely used in electrical machines owing to its low energy loss due to hysteresis.

stalwart (stôl′wət), *adj.* **1.** strongly and stoutly built; well-developed and robust. **2.** strong and brave; valiant. **3.** firm, steadfast, or uncompromising. —*n.* **4.** a physically stalwart person. **5.** a steadfast or uncompromising partisan. [ME; Scot. var. of *stalward,* earlier *stalwurthe,* OE *stǣlwierthe* serviceable, f. *stǣl* (contr. of *stathol* foundation) + *wierthe* WORTH] —**stal′wartly,** *adv.* —**stal′wartness,** *n.* —**Syn. 1.** See **strong.**

Stalybridge (stā′lĭ brĭj′), *n.* a town in England, in Cheshire. 21,947 (1961).

Stambul (stăm bo͞ol′), *n.* **1.** the oldest part and principal Turkish residential section of Istanbul, S of the Golden Horn. **2.** Istanbul. Also, **Stamboul** (stăm bo͞ol′; *Fr.* stäɴ bo͞ol′).

stamen (stā′mĕn), *n., pl.* **stamens, stamina** (stăm′ĭ nə). *Bot.* the pollen-bearing organ of a flower, consisting of the filament and the anther. See diag. under **epigynous flower.** [t. L: thread, warp in the upright loom]

stamin (stăm′ĭn), *n.* a coarse woollen fabric. [ME, t. MF: m. (*e*)*stamine,* t. L: m. *staminea,* adj., consisting of threads; akin to STAMEN]

stamina[1] (stăm′ĭ nə), *n.* **1.** strength of physical constitution; power to endure disease, fatigue, privation, etc. **2.** *Obs.* germinal elements; rudiments. [t. L, pl. of *stāmen* thread (specifically, those spun by the Fates determining length of life)]

stamina[2] (stăm′ĭ nə), *n.* a pl. of **stamen.**

staminal (stăm′ĭ nəl), *adj.* **1.** of or pertaining to stamina. **2.** *Bot.* of or pertaining to stamens.

staminate (stăm′ĭ nĭt, -nāt′), *adj. Bot.* **1.** having a stamen or stamens. **2.** having stamens but no pistils. See illus. under **amentum.**

staminiferous (stăm′ĭ nĭf′ə rəs), *adj. Bot.* bearing or having a stamen or stamens.

staminodium (stăm′ĭ nō′dĭ əm), *n., pl.* **-dia** (-dĭ ə). *Bot.* **1.** a sterile or abortive stamen. **2.** a part resembling such a stamen. Also, **staminode** (stăm′ĭ nōd′). [t. NL. See STAMEN, -ODE[1], -IUM]

staminody (stăm′ĭ nō′dĭ), *n. Bot.* the metamorphosis of any of various flower organs (as a sepal or a petal) into a stamen.

stammel (stăm′əl), *Obs.* —*n.* **1.** a coarse woollen cloth, usually dyed red. **2.** the colour red. —*adj.* **3.** red. [ME, t. MF: m. (*e*)*stamel;* akin to STAMEN]

stammer (stăm′ə), *v.i.* **1.** to speak with involuntary breaks and pauses or with spasmodic repetitions of syllables or sounds. —*v.t.* **2.** to say with a stammer (often fol. by *out*). —*n.* **3.** a stammering mode of utterance. **4.** a stammered utterance. [ME; OE *stamerian,* akin to G *stammeln*] —**stam′merer,** *n.* —**stam′meringly,** *adv.*

—**Syn. 2.** STAMMER, STUTTER agree in referring to a speech difficulty. STAMMER indicates difficulty or a block in uttering a word or syllable, which results in broken or inarticulate sounds that seem to stick in the mouth, and sometimes in complete stoppage of speech; it may be caused by sudden excitement, confusion, embarrassment, or other emotion, or by lack of muscular control: *to stammer an apology for a tactless remark.* STUTTER indicates rapid, involuntary, spasmodic repetition of an (especially initial) sound or syllable of a word; stuttering, though accentuated by excitement, is more likely than stammering to be an inherent speech defect: *to stutter more noticeably when called upon to speak in public.*

stamp (stămp), *v.t.* **1.** to strike or beat with a forcible downward thrust of the foot. **2.** to bring (the foot) down forcibly or smartly on the ground, floor, etc. **3.** to trample, force, drive, etc., by or as by beating down with the foot (usually fol. by *out* or *on*): *to stamp out a fire or a rebellion.* **4.** to crush or pound with or as with a pestle. **5.** to impress with a particular mark or device, as to indicate genuineness, approval, ownership, etc. **6.** to impress with an official mark. **7.** to mark or impress with any characters, words, designs, etc. **8.** to impress (a design, figure, words, etc.) on something; imprint deeply or permanently on anything. **9.** to affix an adhesive paper stamp to (a letter, etc.). **10.** to characterize, distinguish, or reveal.

—*v.i.* **11.** to bring the foot down forcibly or smartly, as in crushing something, expressing rage, etc. **12.** to walk with forcible or heavy, resounding steps: *to stamp out of a room in anger.*

—*n.* **13.** the act or an instance of stamping. **14.** a die, engraved block, or the like, for impressing a design, characters, words, or marks. **15.** an impression, design, characters, words, etc., made with or as with a stamp. **16.** an official mark indicating genuineness, validity, etc., or payment of a duty or charge. **17.** the impression of a public seal required for revenue purposes, to be obtained from a government office, for a fee, on the paper or parchment

on which deeds, bills, receipts, etc., are written. **18.** a peculiar or distinctive impress or mark: *a story which bears the stamp of truth.* **19.** character, kind, or type. **20.** a small adhesive piece of paper printed with a distinctive design, issued by a government for a fixed sum, for attaching to documents, goods subject to duty, letters, etc., to show that a charge has been paid: *an excise stamp, a postage stamp.* **21.** a similar piece of paper issued by a private organization to show that the charges for postage have been paid: *a local stamp.* **22.** a similar piece of paper issued privately for various purposes: *a trading stamp.* **23.** an instrument for stamping, crushing, or pounding. **24.** a heavy piece of iron or the like, as in a stamp mill, for dropping on and crushing ore or other material.
[early ME *stampen*, c. G *stampfen*] **—Syn. 3.** See **abolish.**

stamp-collector (stămp′kə lĕk′tə), *n.* a philatelist.

stamp duty, a tax imposed on certain legal documents, as cheques, receipts, conveyances, etc., on which a stamp is impressed or affixed.

stampede (stăm pēd′), *n., v.,* **-peded, -peding.** —*n.* **1.** a sudden scattering or headlong flight of a body of cattle or horses in fright. **2.** any headlong general flight or rush. —*v.i.* **3.** to scatter or flee in a stampede. **4.** to make an unconcerted general rush. —*v.t.* **5.** to cause to stampede. [t. Mex. Sp.: m. *estampida*, der. *estampar* press, of Gmc orig. See STAMP] —**stamped′er,** *n.*

stamper (stăm′pə), *n.* **1.** one who or that which stamps. **2.** *U.S.* one who applies postmarks and cancels postage stamps in a post office. **3.** an instrument for stamping. **4.** a pestle, esp. one in a stamp mill. **5.** the final negative metal mould used in manufacturing gramophone records.

stamping ground, *Colloq.* the habitual place of resort of an animal or person.

stamp mill, *Metall.* a mill or machine in which ore is crushed to powder by means of heavy stamps or pestles.

stamp note, a certificate issued by a customs officer permitting freight to be loaded, as after settlement of any duties payable.

stamp office, an office at which stamp duties are received and stamps issued.

stance (stăns), *n.* **1.** the position or bearing of the body while standing: *a boxer's stance.* **2.** emotional or intellectual attitude to something: *a hostile stance towards modern poetry.* **3.** *Cricket, Golf, etc.* the relative position of a player's feet when making a stroke. **4.** *Mountaineering.* **a.** the position of a climber when belaying another. **b.** a ledge where a belay can be made. [t. F, t. It.: m. *stanza* station, stopping place, room, ult. der. L *stans*, ppr., standing]

stanch[1] (stänch), *v.t.* **1.** to stop the flow of (a liquid, esp. blood). **2.** to stop the flow of blood from (a wound). **3.** *Archaic or Dial.* to check, appease, allay, or assuage. —*v.i.* **4.** to stop flowing, as blood; be stanched. —*n.* **5.** *Civ. Eng.* a device on primitive river navigation systems in which changes of level are overcome by sending boats down in a rush of water. Also, **staunch.** [ME, t. OF: m. s. *estanchier*] —**stanch′er,** *n.*

stanch[2] (stänch, stônch), *adj.* staunch[2]. —**stanch′ly,** *adv.* —**stanch′ness,** *n.*

stanchion (stän′shən), *n.* **1.** an upright bar, beam, post, or support, as in a window, stall, ship, etc. —*v.t.* **2.** to furnish with stanchions. **3.** to secure by or to a stanchion or stanchions. [ME *stanchon*, t. OF: m. *estanchon*, der. *estance* STANCE]

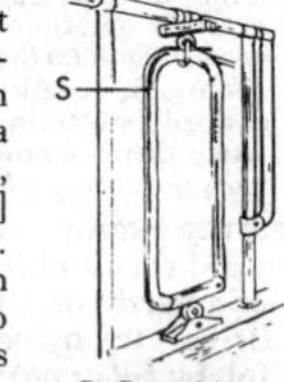

S, Stanchion of a cattle stall

stand (stănd), *v.,* **stood, standing,** *n.* —*v.i.* **1.** to take or keep an upright position on the feet (opposed to *sit, lie,* etc.). **2.** to have a specified height when in this position: *he stands six feet in his socks.* **3.** to remain motionless or steady on the feet. **4.** to cease moving; halt; stop: *stand and deliver!; to stand and fight.* **5.** to take a position or stand as indicated: *to stand aside.* **6.** to remain firm or steadfast, as in a cause. **7.** to take up or maintain a position or attitude with respect to a person, question, or the like: *to stand sponsor for a person.* **8.** to adopt a certain course or attitude, as of adherence, support, opposition, or resistance. **9.** (of things) to be in an upright position (opposed to *lie*); be set on end; rest on or as on a support; be set, placed, or fixed. **10.** to be located or situated. **11.** to be at a certain degree: *the temperature stands at 80°.* **12.** (of an account, score, etc.) to show a specified position of the parties concerned: *the account stands in my favour.* **13.** to remain erect and entire; resist change, decay, or destruction. **14.** to continue in force or remain valid. **15.** to become or remain still or stationary. **16.** to be or become stagnant, as water. **17.** (of persons or things) to be or remain in a specified state, condition, relation, etc.: *he stood alone in his opinion.* **18.** to be likely or in a position as specified: *to stand to lose.* **19.** to become or be a candidate, as for parliament. **20.** *Naut.* **a.** to take or hold a particular course at sea. **b.** to move in a certain direction: *to stand offshore.* **21.** (of a stallion) to be at stud.
—*v.t.* **22.** to cause to stand; set upright; set. **23.** to face or encounter: *to stand an assault.* **24.** to endure, undergo, or submit to: *to stand trial.* **25.** to endure or undergo without hurt or damage, or without giving way: *he cannot stand the sun.* **26.** to tolerate. **27.** *Colloq.* to bear the expense of; pay for.
—*v.* **28.** Some special verb phrases are:

stand a chance, to have a chance or possibility, esp. of winning, surviving, or the like.

stand back, to get out of the way, as by moving backwards.

stand by, 1. to wait in a state of readiness: *stand by for further instructions.* **2.** to aid, uphold, or sustain. **3.** to adhere to (an agreement, promise, etc.); abide by.

stand down, 1. to go off duty. **2.** to withdraw, as from a contest. **3.** *Law.* to leave the witness box.

stand for, 1. to endure or tolerate: *I won't stand for any nonsense.* **2.** to represent: *the symbol x stands for an unknown quantity.* **3.** to be an advocate of: *he stands for racial equality.* **4.** to be a candidate for: *to stand for parliament.*

stand in, 1. to act as a substitute or representative. **2.** to join in; take a part in.

stand in good stead, to be of use or advantage to: *his knowledge of Czech stood him in good stead in Prague.*

stand off, 1. to keep at a distance. **2.** to suspend from employment, esp. temporarily: *owing to the drop in sales, the factory is standing men off.*

stand on, 1. to rest or depend on. **2.** to be punctilious about (ceremony, etc.); claim respect for (one's rights, dignity, etc.). **3.** *Naut.* to continue on the same course or tack.

stand one's ground, to be unyielding; remain steadfast in the face of opposition or attack.

stand out, 1. to project or protrude. **2.** to be prominent or conspicuous. **3.** to hold aloof. **4.** to persist in opposition or resistance.

stand to, *Naval.* to assemble or take up assigned posts in readiness, as for inspection or awaiting orders.

stand to reason, to be in accordance with reason.

stand up, 1. to assume a standing position, esp. from sitting. **2.** *Slang.* to fail to keep an appointment with, esp. with a member of the opposite sex.

stand up for, to defend the cause of; support.

stand up to, 1. to remain in good condition despite: *to stand up well to wear.* **2.** to resist or oppose, esp. bravely.

stand with, to ally oneself with.

—*n.* **29.** the act of standing; an assuming of or a remaining in an upright position. **30.** a coming to a position of rest; a halt or stop. **31.** a halt to give battle or repel an attack. **32.** a determined opposition to or support for some cause, circumstance, or the like. **33.** *Cricket.* a period of batting and scoring, usually of some length, during which neither batsman is out: *a ninth wicket stand of 44.* **34.** the place where a person or thing stands; station. **35.** *U.S.* a witness box. **36.** a raised platform or other structure, as for spectators at a racecourse or a sports field, or along the route of a ceremonial parade, or for a band or the like. **37.** a place, usually under cover, from which a hunter or sportsman shoots game. **38.** a framework on or in which articles are placed for support, exhibition, etc. **39.** a piece of furniture of various forms, on or in which to put articles. **40.** *Chiefly U.S.* a stall where articles are displayed for sale or for some other purpose. **41.** *U.S.* a site or place for business. **42.** a place or station occupied by vehicles available for hire. **43.** *U.S.* the growing trees, or those of a particular species, on a given area. **44.** *U.S.* a standing growth, as of grass, wheat, etc. **45.** a halt of a theatrical company on tour, to give a performance or performances: *one-night stands.* **46.** the town at which a theatrical company gives a performance. **47.** *Archaic.* the arms and accoutrements for one soldier. [ME; OE *standan*, c. MD *standen*, OHG *stantan*, Icel. *standa*, Goth. *standan*] **—Syn. 25.** See **bear**[1].

standard (stăn′dəd), *n.* **1.** anything taken by general consent as a basis of comparison; an approved model. **2.** the authorized exemplar of a unit of weight or measure. **3.** a certain commodity in which the basic monetary unit is stated, historically usually either gold or silver (**gold standard, silver standard,** or **single standard**), or both gold and silver in a fixed proportion to each other (**bimetallic standard**). **4.** the legal rate of intrinsic value for coins. **5.** the prescribed degree of fineness for gold or silver. **6.** a grade or level of excellence, achievement, or advancement: *a high standard of living.* **7.** a level of quality which is regarded as normal, adequate, or acceptable. **8.** a fitting or size, as for clothes, which is regarded as normal or average. **9.** (*usually pl.*) behaviour, beliefs, etc., regarded as

socially desirable or acceptable. **10.** a class in certain schools. **11.** a flag, emblematic figure, or other object raised on a pole to indicate the rallying point of an army, fleet, etc. **12.** a flag indicating the presence of a sovereign. **13.** *Mil.* **a.** any of various military or naval flags. **b.** the colours of a mounted unit. **14.** *Her.* a long tapering flag or ensign, as of a king or a nation. **15.** something which stands or is placed upright. **16.** an upright support or supporting part. **17.** an upright timber, bar, or rod. **18.** *Hort.* a tree, shrub, or other plant having a tall, erect stem, and not grown in bush form or trained upon a trellis or other support. **19.** *Bot.* a vexillum. **20.** a piece of music or the like of lasting popularity, esp. one often revived with new arrangements.
—*adj.* **21.** serving as a basis of weight, measure, value, comparison, or judgement. **22.** of recognized excellence or established authority: *a standard author.* **23.** normal, adequate, acceptable, or average: *standard goods; a standard fitting.* **24.** (of a variety of a given language, or of usage in the language) characterized by preferred pronunciations, expressions, grammatical constructions, etc., the use of which is considered essential to social or other prestige, failure to conform to them tending to bring the speaker into disfavour. [ME, t. OF: aphetic m. *estandard,* t. Gmc (cf. G *Standort* standing-place), conformed to suffix *-ard* -ARD]

—**Syn.** **1.** STANDARD, CRITERION mean a measure or test. A STANDARD is an authoritative model or measure, a pattern for guidance, by comparison with which the quantity, excellence, correctness, etc., of other things may be determined: *standards of liquid measure.* A CRITERION is a test which is used to judge value, suitability, probability, etc., of something already existing: *wealth is no criterion of a man's worth.*

standard atmosphere, **1.** *Meteorol.* any hypothetical atmosphere the physical properties of which are given arbitrary values, approximating to mean conditions, for such purposes as comparing the performance of aircraft, ballistic calculations, etc. **2.** *Physics.* a standard unit of atmospheric pressure equal to 760 millimetres of mercury.

standard-bearer (stăn′dəd bĕə′rə), *n.* **1.** an officer or soldier of an army or military unit who bears a standard. **2.** a conspicuous leader of a movement, political party, etc.

standard-bred (stăn′dəd brĕd′), *adj.* *U.S.* of or pertaining to a breed of trotting and pacing horses used chiefly for harness racing.

standard candle. See **candle** (def. 3b).

standard cell, normal element.

standard deviation, *Statistics.* the square root of the average of the squares of a set of deviations about an arithmetic mean; the root mean square of the deviations of a set of values.

standard gauge. See **gauge** (def. 14).

standardize (stăn′də dīz′), *v.t.,* **-dized, -dizing.** **1.** to bring to or make of an established standard size, weight, quality, strength, or the like: *to standardize manufactured parts.* **2.** to compare with or test by a standard. Also, **standardise.** —**stand′ardiza′tion,** *n.* —**stand′ardiz′er,** *n.*

standard-lamp (stăn′dəd lămp′), *n.* a lamp having a tall support, standing on the floor of a room.

standard of living, a grade or level of subsistence and comforts in everyday life enjoyed by a community, a class in a community, or an individual: *widespread unemployment will depress the nation's standard of living.*

standard solution, *Chem.* a solution of known concentration, as a normal solution.

standard time, the civil time officially adopted for a country or region, usually the civil time of some specific meridian lying within the region.

stand-by (stănd′bī′), *n., pl.* **-bys.** **1.** a staunch supporter or adherent; one who can be relied upon. **2.** something upon which one can rely; a chief support. **3.** something kept in a state of readiness for use, as for an emergency.

standee (stăn dē′), *n.* **1.** *Chiefly U.S.* one who stands, as at a theatrical performance, on a bus, etc., where no seats are vacant. **2.** a standee bus, train, or the like. —*adj.* **3.** denoting or pertaining to public service vehicles designed to carry large numbers of standing passengers.

stand-in (stănd′ĭn′), *n.* **1.** a substitute for a film actor or actress during the preparation of lighting, cameras, etc., or in dangerous scenes. **2.** any substitute.

standing (stăn′dĭng), *n.* **1.** position or status, as to rank, credit, reputation, etc.: *men of good standing.* **2.** good position, financial viability, or credit. **3.** length of existence, continuance, residence, membership, experience, etc. **4.** the act of one who or that which stands. **5.** the period during which a person or thing stands. **6.** a place where a person or thing stands. —*adj.* **7.** that stands erect or upright. **8.** performed in or from an erect position: *a standing jump.* **9.** still; not flowing or stagnant, as water; stationary. **10.** continuing without cessation or change; lasting or permanent. **11.** continuing in operation, force, use, etc.: *a standing rule.* **12.** out of use; idle: *a standing engine.* —**Syn.** **2.** See **credit.**

standing army, a permanently organized military force kept up by a nation.

standing order, **1.** any of the rules ensuring continuity of procedure during the meetings of an assembly, esp. the rules governing the conduct or business in parliament. **2.** *Mil.* (formerly) a general order that is always in force in a command and that establishes uniform procedures for it.

standing rigging, *Naut.* the stays, shrouds, etc., which secure the masts.

standing room, **1.** room or space in which to stand. **2.** accommodation for standing only, as in a theatre where all the seats have been taken.

standing start, a start to a race from a stationary position (opposed to *flying start*).

standing stone, *Archaeol.* a menhir.

standing wave, **1.** Also, **stationary wave.** *Physics.* a distribution of wave displacements, such that the distribution in space is periodic, with fixed maximum and minimum points, with the maxima occurring everywhere at the same time, as in vibrations of strings, electric potentials, acoustic pressures, etc. **2.** *Meteorol.* an ascending or descending current of air associated in certain circumstances with wind flow over mountains or hills.

standish (stăn′dĭsh), *n.* *Archaic.* a stand for ink, pens, and other writing materials. [prob. f. STAND + DISH]

Standish (stăn′dĭsh), *n.* **Myles** or **Miles** (mīlz), *c.* 1584–1656, English settler at Plymouth, Massachusetts, in 1620: military captain of the colony.

stand-off (stănd′ŏf′), *n.* **1.** *U.S.* a standing off or apart; aloofness. **2.** *U.S.* something that counterbalances. **3.** stand-off half. —*adj.* **4.** standing off or apart; aloof; reserved.

stand-off half, *Rugby Football.* one of the two half-backs, acting chiefly as a link between the scrum half and the three-quarters. Also, **fly half.**

stand-offish (stănd′ŏf′ĭsh), *adj.* aloof; reserved; unfriendly. —**stand′-off′ishly,** *adv.* —**stand′-off′ishness,** *n.*

stand oil, a thick oil used in paints, etc., made by heating linseed oil to temperatures of 315°C, and higher.

standout (stănd′out′), *n.* *U.S. Colloq.* one who persists in opposition or resistance.

standpat (stănd′păt′), *U.S. Colloq.* —*n.* **1.** Also, **stand′pat′ter.** one who holds to an existing order of things, policy, etc., refusing to consider proposals of change. —*adj.* **2.** characterized by standing pat.

standpipe (stănd′pīp′), *n.* a vertical pipe or tower into which water is pumped to obtain a required head.

standpoint (stănd′point′), *n.* **1.** the point at which one stands to view something. **2.** the mental position from which one views and judges things.

St Andrews (ăn′dro͞oz), a seaport in E Scotland, in Fife county; resort; golf courses. 9888 (1961).

standstill (stănd′stĭl′), *n.* a standing still; a state of cessation of movement or action; a halt; a pause; a stop.

stand-to (stănd′to͞o′), *n.* an assembly or taking up of posts, as for inspection or to await orders.

stand-up (stănd′ŭp′), *adj.* **1.** standing erect; upright, as a collar. **2.** performed, taken, etc., while one stands: *a stand-up meal.* **3.** (of a fight) characterized by hard and frequent blows rather than defensive skill or evasiveness.

stane (stān), *n., adj., v.* *Scot. and N Dial.* stone.

stang[1] (stăng), *v.* *Obs.* pt. of **sting.**

stang[2] (stăng), *n.* *Scot. and N Dial.* a stake or pole. [ME, t. Scand.; cf. Icel. *stong*; c. OE *stæng,* Dan. *stang*]

stang[3] (stăng), *n.* satang.

stanhope (stăn′əp), *n.* a kind of light, two-wheeled, open, one-seat carriage hung on four springs. [named after Fitzroy *Stanhope,* 1787–1864]

Stanislavov (*Russ.* stə nĭs lȧ′vəf), *n.* a city in the SW Soviet Union, in the Ukrainian Republic: formerly in Poland. 66,000 (est. 1959). German, **Stanislau.** Polish, **Stanislawów** (*Pol.* stȧ nē swȧ′vo͞of).

Stanislavsky (stăn′ĭs lăv′skĭ; *Russ.* stə nĭs lȧf′skĭy), *n.* **Konstantin** (*Russ.* kən stȧn tēn′), 1863–1938, Russian producer and actor.

stank[1] (stăngk), *v.* a pt. of **stink.**

stank[2] (stăngk), *n.* **1.** *Scot. and N Dial.* a pond, pool, moat, or the like. **2.** *Civ. Eng.* a small timber cofferdam made watertight with clay. —*v.t.* **3.** to make watertight, esp. with clay, as the banks of a stream. [ME, t. OF: m. *estanc* STAUNCH[2]]

Stanley (stăn′lĭ), *n.* **1. Arthur Penrhyn** (pĕn′rĭn) (*Dean Stanley*), 1815–81, English clergyman and author. **2. Sir Henry Morton** (orig. *John Rowlands*), 1841–1904, English explorer in Africa. **3.** the capital of the Falkland Islands, on East Falkland. 1074 (1964). **4. Mount,** a mountain with two summits in central Africa between Uganda and the Congo: highest peak in the Ruwenzori group. 16,790 ft.

Stanley Falls, seven cataracts of the river Congo, on the equator in N Democratic Republic of the Congo.

Stanley Pool, a lake on the boundary between W Democratic Republic of the Congo and the Republic of Congo (former Middle Congo), formed by the widening of the river Congo ab. 330 mi. from its mouth: ab. 20 mi. long and 15 mi. wide.

Stanleyville (stăn′lĭ vĭl), *n.* former name of **Kisangani.**

stannary (stăn′ə rĭ), *n., pl.* **-ries. 1.** a tin-mining region or district. **2.** a place where tin is mined or smelted. [t. ML: m. s. *stannāria*, der. LL *stannum* tin]

stannate (stăn′āt), *n. Chem.* a salt of stannic acid.

stannic (stăn′ĭk), *adj. Chem.* of or containing tin, esp. in the tetravalent state. [f. s. LL *stannum* tin + -IC]

stannic acid, *Chem.* any of a series of amorphous powders with the general formula $SnO_2.XH_2O$; **alpha-stannic acid** is formed by the action of alkalis on stannic chloride and **beta-stannic acid** by the action of nitric acid on metallic tin.

stannic oxide, *Chem.* a white, amorphous, insoluble powder, SnO_2, used in polishing powders, etc.; tin ash.

stannic sulphide, a yellowish compound, SnS_2, used in making gilding preparations; mosaic gold.

stanniferous (stă nĭf′ə rəs), *adj.* bearing tin.

stannite (stăn′īt), *n.* **1.** a mineral, iron-black to steel-grey in colour, with a metallic lustre, copper iron tin sulphide, Cu_2FeSnS_4: an ore of tin; tin pyrites. **2.** *Chem.* a salt of stannous acid.

stannous (stăn′əs), *adj. Chem.* containing divalent tin.

stannum (stăn′əm), *n.* tin. *Symbol.:* Sn [t. LL: tin (in L, alloy of silver and lead)]

Stanovoi (*Russ.* stə nȧ vôy′), *n.* a mountain system in the E Soviet Union in Asia: a watershed between the Pacific and Arctic oceans. Highest peak, 8143 ft.

stanza (stăn′zə), *n. Pros.* a group of lines of verse, commonly four or more in number, arranged and repeated according to a fixed plan as regards the number of lines, the metre, and the rhyme, and forming a regularly repeated metrical division of a poem. [t. It., ult. der. L *stans*, ppr., standing] —**stanzaic** (stăn zā′ĭk), *adj.* —**Syn.** See **verse.**

stapelia (stə pē′lyə), *n.* any of the plants constituting the asclepiadaceous genus *Stapelia*, native in South Africa, with short, fleshy, leafless stems, and flowers which are often oddly coloured or mottled and in most species emit a fetid, carrion-like smell. [named after J. B. *Stapel*, died 1636, Dutch botanist]

stapes (stā′pēz), *n. Anat.* the innermost of three small bones in the middle ear of man and other mammals, having a stirrup-like shape. See diag. under **ear.** [t. NL, special use of ML *stapes* stirrup] —**stapedial** (stă pē′dyəl), *adj.*

staphylo-, 1. a word element referring to **staphylococcus. 2.** a word element referring to the uvula. [comb. form repr. Gk *staphylḗ* bunch of grapes]

staphylococcus (stăf′ĭ lō kŏk′əs), *n., pl.* **-cocci** (-kŏk′sī). *Bacteriol.* any of certain species of micrococcus in which the individual organisms form irregular clusters, as *Micrococcus* (or *Staphylococcus*) *pyogenes*, which causes pus formation. [f. STAPHYLO- + COCCUS] —**staphylococcal** (stăf′ĭ lō kŏk′l), **staphylococcic** (stăf′ĭ lō kŏk′sĭk), *adj.*

staphyloma (stăf′ĭ lō′mə), *n., pl.* **-mata** (-mə tə). *Pathol.* any of various local bulgings of the eyeball.

staphyloplasty (stăf′ĭ lō plăs′tĭ), *n.* the remedying of defects of the soft palate by plastic surgery.

staphylorrhaphy (stăf′ĭ lŏr′rə fĭ), *n.* the uniting of a cleft palate by plastic surgery. [f. STAPHYLO- + *-rrhaphy* (t. Gk: m. s. *-rhaphia*, der. *rhaphḗ* suture)]

staple[1] (stā′pl), *n., v.,* **-pled, -pling.** —*n.* **1.** a bent piece of wire used to bind papers, sections of a book, etc., together. **2.** a U-shaped or other piece of metal with pointed ends for driving into a surface to hold a hasp, hook, pin, bolt, or the like. —*v.t.* **3.** to secure or fasten by a staple or staples: *to staple three sheets together.* [ME; OE *stapol* support, c. G *Stapel*]

staple[2] (stā′pl), *n., adj., v.,* **-pled, -pling.** —*n.* **1.** a principal commodity grown or manufactured in a locality. **2.** a principal commodity in a mercantile field; goods in steady demand; goods of known or recognized quality. **3.** a principal item, thing, feature, element, or part. **4.** the fibre of wool, cotton, flax, rayon, etc., considered with reference to length and fineness. **5.** a particular length and degree of fineness of the fibre of wool, cotton, etc. **6.** *Hist.* a town or place appointed by royal authority as the seat of a body of merchants having the exclusive right of purchase of certain classes of goods for export. —*adj.* **7.** chief or prominent among the products exported or produced by a country or district; chiefly or largely dealt in or consumed. **8.** chief or principal, as industries. **9.** principally used: *staple subjects of conversation.* —*v.t.* **10.** to sort or classify according to the staple or fibre, as wool. [late ME *stapull*, *staple* (def. 6), t. MD (directly or through AF): m. *stapel* mart, orig. support. See STAPLE[1]]

stapler[1] (stā′plə), *n.* **1.** a stapling machine. **2.** one who operates a stapling machine or who staples by hand. [f. STAPLE[1] + -ER[1]]

stapler[2] (stā′plə), *n.* **1.** one who sorts according to the staple or fibre. **2.** *Hist.* a merchant of the staple. [f. STAPLE[2] + -ER[2]]

stapling machine, a wire-stitching machine, esp. one used in bookbinding.

star (stä), *n., adj., v.,* **starred, starring.** —*n.* **1.** any of the heavenly bodies appearing as apparently fixed luminous points in the sky at night. **2.** *Astron.* any of the self-luminous bodies outside the solar system, as distinguished from planets, comets, and meteors. The sun is classed with the stars and appears to be a typical member of the galaxy. **3.** any heavenly body. **4.** *Astrol.* **a.** a heavenly body, esp. a planet that is considered as influencing mankind and events. **b.** (*pl.*) a horoscope, esp. one in a magazine, etc. **5.** one's destiny, fortune, or luck, esp. as regarded as influenced by the heavenly bodies. **6.** a conventional figure having rays (commonly five or six) proceeding from, or angular points disposed in a regular outline about, a central point, and considered as representing a star of the sky. **7.** *Jewellery.* a brilliant having six, not eight, triangular facets just below the table. **8.** a white mark on the forehead of an animal, esp. a horse; a blaze. **9.** *Print., etc.* an asterisk. **10.** a person who is pre-eminent or distinguished in some art, profession, or other field. **11.** a prominent actor, singer, or the like, esp. one who plays the leading role in a performance. **12.** a starfish. **13. see stars,** to seem to see bright flashes of light, as after a heavy blow on the head.
—*adj.* **14.** brilliant, prominent, or distinguished; chief.
—*v.t.* **15.** to set with, or as with, stars; spangle. **16.** to present or feature (an actor, etc.) as a star. **17.** to mark with a star or asterisk, as for special notice.
—*v.i.* **18.** to shine as a star; be brilliant or prominent. **19.** (of an actor, etc.) to appear as a star.
[ME *sterre*, OE *steorra*, c. D *ster*, MHG *sterre*, akin to L *stella*, Gk *astḗr*]

star-anise (stär′ăn′ĭs), *n.* an aromatic, evergreen magnoliaceous shrub or small tree, *Illicium anisatum*, a native of Japan.

star-apple (stär′ăp′l), *n.* **1.** the edible fruit of a West Indian sapotaceous tree, *Chrysophyllum cainito*, of the size of an apple, and when cut across presenting a star-shaped figure within. **2.** the tree.

Stara Zagora (*Bulg.* stȧ′rȧ zȧ gŏ′rȧ), a town in central Bulgaria. 88,951 (1964).

starboard (stä′bəd, -bôd′), *Naut.* —*n.* **1.** the side of a ship to the right of a person looking towards the bow (opposed to *larboard* and *port*). See illus. under **aft.** —*adj.* **2.** pertaining to the starboard; on the right side. —*adv.* **3.** towards the right side. —*v.t., v.i.* **4.** to turn (the helm) to starboard. [ME *sterbord*, OE *stēorbord*, f. *stēor* steering + *bord* side (of a ship). See STEER[1], v., BOARD, n.]

starch (stäch), *n.* **1.** a white, tasteless solid, chemically a carbohydrate, $(C_6H_{10}O_5)_n$, occurring in the form of minute grains in the seeds, tubers, and other parts of plants, and forming an important constituent of rice, corn, wheat, beans, potatoes, and many other vegetable foods; amylum. Starch is separable into amylose and amylopectin fractions. **2.** a commercial preparation of this substance used (dissolved in water) to stiffen linen, etc., in laundering, and employed also for many industrial purposes. **3.** (*pl.*) foods rich in starch. **4.** stiffness or formality, as of manner. **5.** *U.S. Slang.* zest; stamina. —*v.t.* **6.** to stiffen or treat with starch. **7.** to make stiff or rigidly formal (sometimes fol. by *up*). [ME *sterce*, v., OE *stercean* make stiff or resolute (in *stercedferhth* made resolute in mind), der. *stearc* STARK] —**starch′er,** *n.* —**starch′less,** *adj.*

A B

Starch grains
A, Cells of potato, *Solanum tuberosum*, containing grains; B, Grains (all greatly magnified)

Star Chamber, 1. a former court of inquisitorial and criminal jurisdiction in England, which sat in secret without a jury, and was noted for its arbitrary methods and severe punishments (abolished 1641). **2.** any tribunal, committee, or the like, which proceeds by arbitrary or unfair methods.

starch-gum (stäch′gŭm′), *n.* dextrin.

starch-reduced (stäch′rĭ dyo͞ost′), *adj.* (of foodstuffs, esp. bread) prepared so as to contain less starch than normal, in order to aid slimming.

starchy (stä′chĭ), *adj.*, **starchier, starchiest.** **1.** pertaining to, or of the nature of, starch. **2.** containing starch. **3.** stiffened with starch. **4.** stiff and formal, as in manner. —**starch′ily,** *adv.* —**starch′iness,** *n.*

star-crossed (stä′krŏst′), *adj.* characterized by consistent ill fortune; having much bad luck, as if brought about by the influence of the stars: *Romeo and Juliet were star-crossed lovers.*

stardom (stä′dəm), *n.* **1.** the world or class of professional stars, as in films. **2.** the status of a star.

star drift, *Astron.* a very slow motion common to a number of fixed stars in the same part of the heavens.

stardust (stä′dŭst′), *n.* **1.** a mass of distant stars seen as dust. **2.** a dreamy romantic quality.

stare (stêə), *v.*, **stared, staring,** *n.* —*v.i.* **1.** to gaze fixedly, esp. with the eyes wide open. **2.** to stand out boldly or obtrusively to view. **3.** (of hair, feathers, etc.) to stand on end; bristle. —*v.t.* **4.** to stare at. **5.** to put, bring, etc., by staring: *to stare one out of countenance.* **6. stare out,** to gaze fixedly at (someone) until he looks away. **7. stare one in the face, a.** to be inescapably obvious. **b.** to be impending and require immediate action. —*n.* **8.** a staring gaze; a fixed look with the eyes wide open: *the banker greeted him with a glassy stare.* [ME; OE *starian,* c. D *staren,* Icel. *stara*] —**star′er,** *n.*

starfish (stä′fĭsh′), *n., pl.* **-fishes,** (*esp. collectively*) **-fish.** any echinoderm of the class *Asteroidea,* comprising marine animals having the body radially arranged, usually in the form of a star, with five or more rays or arms radiating from a central disc; an asteroid.

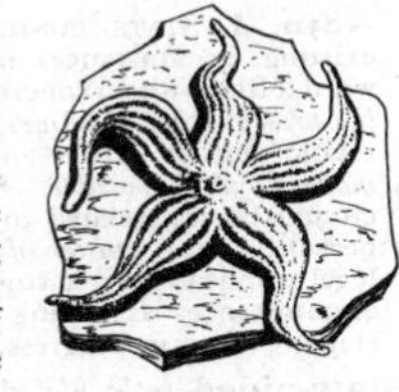
Starfish, *Asterias rubens* (3½ in. long)

starflower (stä′flou′ə), *n.* any of various plants with starlike flowers, as the star-of-Bethlehem or a plant of the primulaceous genus *Trientalis.*

stargaze (stä′gāz′), *v.i.*, **-gazed, -gazing.** **1.** to gaze at or observe the stars. **2.** to daydream. —**star′gaz′ing,** *n.*

stargazer (stä′gā′zə), *n.* **1.** one who gazes at the stars; an astrologer or an astronomer. **2.** a dreamy, vacant, abstracted person. **3.** any of the fishes constituting the family *Uranoscopidae,* having eyes directed upwards.

stark (stäk), *adj.* **1.** sheer, utter, downright, or arrant: *stark madness.* **2.** absolutely naked. **3.** stiff or rigid in substance, muscles, etc. **4.** rigid in death. **5.** harsh, grim, or desolate to the view, as places, etc. **6.** *Archaic.* hard, stern, or severe. —*adv.* **7.** utterly, absolutely, or quite: *stark mad.* **8.** *Dial.* in a stark manner; stoutly or vigorously. [ME; OE *stearc* stiff, c. G *stark* strong] —**stark′ly,** *adv.*

Starker (stä′kə), *n.* **Janos** (yä′nŏs; *Hung.* yå′nôsh), born 1924, U.S. cellist born in Hungary.

starkers (stä′kəz), *adj. Slang.* **1.** stark-naked. **2.** absolutely mad; insane.

stark-naked (stäk′nā′kĭd), *adj.* completely naked. [f. STARK + NAKED; r. ME *start-naked*: *start,* OE *steort* tail]

starless (stä′lĭs), *adj.* having no stars visible: *a starless night.*

starlet (stä′lĭt), *n.* **1.** a small star. **2.** a young actress who plays small and usually sexy parts, esp. in films, and who receives publicity as a potential star.

starlight (stä′līt′), *n.* **1.** the light proceeding from the stars. —*adj.* **2.** of or pertaining to starlight. **3.** starlit.

starlike (stä′līk′), *adj.* **1.** star-shaped. **2.** shining like a star.

starling[1] (stä′lĭng), *n.* any of numerous passerine birds constituting the family *Sturnidae,* esp. the common European species, *Sturnus vulgaris.* [ME; OE *stærling,* der. *stær* starling, c. G *Star.* See -LING[1]]

Starling, *Sturnus vulgaris* (8½ in. long)

starling[2] (stä′lĭng), *n.* a set of piles driven into a riverbed upstream of a bridge pier to protect it from floating debris, the force of the current, etc. [? alter. of obs. *staddling,* akin to STADDLE]

starlit (stä′lĭt′), *adj.* lit by the stars, or by the stars only.

star-nosed (stä′nōzd′), *adj.* having a starlike ring of small, fleshy radiating processes about the end of the snout, as an American mole, *Condylura cristata.*

star-of-Bethlehem (stä′rəv bĕth′lĭ əm, -hĕm′), *n.* a liliaceous plant of Europe and Asia, *Ornithogalum umbellatum,* with star-shaped flowers.

Star of Bethlehem, the star which guided the three Magi ('wise men') from the East to the manger of the infant Jesus in Bethlehem. Matt. 2:2, 9, 10.

Star of David, a figure resembling a six-pointed star, formed of two equilateral triangles interlaced, one being inverted; used as a symbol of Judaism.

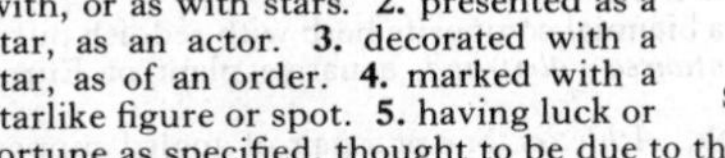
Star of David

Starr (stä), *n.* **Ringo** (rĭng′gō). See **Beatles.**

starred (städ), *adj.* **1.** set or studded with, or as with stars. **2.** presented as a star, as an actor. **3.** decorated with a star, as of an order. **4.** marked with a starlike figure or spot. **5.** having luck or fortune as specified, thought to be due to the influence of the stars. **6.** having ill fortune.

starred first, (at Cambridge and some other universities) a first-class honours degree with a distinction.

starry (stä′rĭ), *adj.*, **-rier, -riest.** **1.** abounding with or lit by stars: *a starry sky.* **2.** of, pertaining to, or proceeding from the stars. **3.** of the nature of or consisting of stars: *starry worlds.* **4.** resembling a star; star-shaped or stellate. **5.** shining like stars: *starry eyes.* **6.** studded with starlike figures or markings. —**star′rily,** *adv.* —**star′riness,** *n.*

starry-eyed (stä′rĭ īd′), *adj.* **1.** having brightly shining eyes, as with emotion. **2.** excessively optimistic or romantic.

Stars and Bars, the flag adopted by the Confederate States of America, consisting of two broad horizontal bars of red separated by one of white, with a blue union marked with as many white stars, arranged in a circle, as the number of Confederate States.

Stars and Stripes, the national flag of the United States, consisting of thirteen horizontal stripes, alternately red and white, equal to the number of the original states, with a blue union marked with white stars equal in number to the whole number of states.

star sapphire, a sapphire which exhibits by reflected light a star composed of three bright rays, resulting from the crystalline structure of the gem.

star shell, a shell which bursts in the air and produces a bright light: used to illuminate enemy positions.

star-spangled (stä′spăng′gld), *adj.* spangled with stars.

Star-Spangled Banner, The, **1.** the national flag of the United States. **2.** the national anthem of the United States, composed in 1814 by Francis Scott Key.

star stone, any precious stone exhibiting asterism.

star-studded (stä′stŭd′ĭd), *adj.* **1.** having many stars visible: *a clear, star-studded night.* **2.** marked by the presence of many notable or famous persons, esp. actors.

start (stät), *v.i.* **1.** to begin to move, go, or act; set out, as on a journey. **2.** to begin any course of action or procedure, as one's career, life, etc. **3.** (of a process or performance) to begin. **4.** to come suddenly into activity, life, view, etc.; come, rise, or issue suddenly. **5.** to spring or move suddenly from a position or place: *to start from one's seat.* **6.** to move with a sudden, involuntary jerk or twitch, as from a shock of surprise, alarm, or pain. **7.** to protrude: *eyes starting from their sockets.* **8.** to spring, slip, or work loose from place or fastenings, as timbers or other structural parts. **9.** to be among the starters in a race, contest, or the like. —*v.t.* **10.** to set moving, going, or acting: *to start an engine, a fire, etc.* **11.** to set in operation; establish: *to start a newspaper.* **12.** to enter upon or begin: *to start a letter.* **13.** to cause or enable (a person, etc.) to set out on a journey, a course of action, a career, or the like: *to start one's son in business.* **14.** to cause (timbers, structural parts, etc.) to start from place or fastenings. **15.** to rouse (game) from its lair or resting place; flush. **16.** to draw or discharge (liquid or other contents) from a vessel or container, or empty (a container). **17.** to force (a screw, nail, or the like) into a surface a little way to give it a hold before driving. **18.** *Archaic or Dial.* to cause to start involuntarily; startle.

—*n.* **19.** a beginning to move, go, or act; the beginning or outset of anything; a setting in motion. **20.** an impulse to move or proceed; a signal to start, as on a course or in a race. **21.** the place or point from which competitors in a race, travellers, or the like set out: *thirty athletes assembled at the start; Edinburgh was the start to our tour of Scotland.* **22.** the first part of anything: *the start of his article was good, but later it became unreadable.* **23.** a sudden, springing movement from a position. **24.** a sudden, involuntary jerking movement of the body: *to awake with a start.* **25.** a lead or advance of specified amount, as over competitors or pursuers. **26.** the position or advantage of one who starts first; the lead: *she has got the start on the rest of us.* **27.** a chance or opportunity given to one of starting on a course or career. **28.** a spurt of activity: *to work by fits and starts.* **29.** a starting of parts from their place or fastenings in a structure. **30.** the resulting condition. **31.** *Archaic.* a burst, outburst, or sally, as of emotion, wit, or fancy.

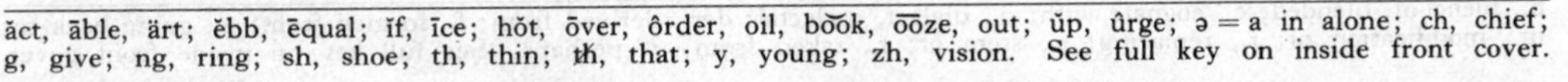

[ME; akin to STARTLE and OE *styrtan* start, c. G *stürzen* fall, rush, make fall] **—Syn. 12.** See **begin.**

starter (stä′tə), *n.* **1.** one who or that which starts. **2.** a person who gives the signal for starting, as in a race. **3.** a self-starter. **4.** any competitor who begins a race, contest, or the like. **5.** a bacterial culture used to start fermentation, as in the manufacture of cheese or the like. **6.** the first course of a meal.

star thistle, a biennial composite herb with reddish purple capitula, *Centaurea calcitrapa*, a native plant of Europe and W Asia.

starting block, *Athletics.* one of a pair of angled supports for the feet, nailed to the track, to increase the power of a sprinter from a crouching start.

starting gate, a device to start a race of horses, greyhounds, or the like, typically a set of stalls having barriers which are lifted simultaneously at the moment of starting.

starting grid, *Motor-Racing.* the starting area, usually marked with bays on which the cars are positioned according to speeds in practice.

starting handle, a handle used to crank an internal-combustion engine to start it.

starting price, *Horseracing, Greyhound-Racing, etc.* the betting odds on an animal at the time when a race begins.

startle (stä′tl), *v.*, **-tled, -tling,** *n.* **—***v.t.* **1.** to disturb or agitate suddenly by a shock of surprise, alarm, or the like. **2.** to cause to start involuntarily, as under a sudden shock. **—***v.i.* **3.** to start involuntarily, as from a shock of surprise or alarm. **—***n.* **4.** a sudden shock of surprise, alarm, or the like. **5.** something that startles. [ME *stertle* rush, caper, OE *steartlian* kick, struggle. See START, v.] **—star′tler,** *n.* **—star′tling,** *adj.* **—star′tlingly,** *adv.* **—Syn. 1.** See **shock**[1].

starvation (stä vā′shən), *n.* **1.** the condition of being starved. **2.** the process of starving.

starvation diet, a diet containing so little nutriment as to cause or be likely to cause slow starvation.

starvation wages, wages insufficient to support the earner and his dependants, if any, above subsistence level.

starve (stäv), *v.*, **starved, starving. —***v.i.* **1.** to die or perish from hunger. **2.** to be in process of perishing, or to suffer severely, from hunger. **3.** *Colloq.* to be hungry. **4.** to suffer from extreme poverty and need. **5.** to pine or suffer for lack of something specified (fol. by *for*). **6.** *Dial.* to perish or suffer extremely from cold. **7.** *Obs.* to die. **—***v.t.* **8.** to cause to starve; weaken or reduce by lack of food. **9.** to subdue, or force to some condition or action, by hunger: *to starve a besieged garrison into surrender.* **10.** to cause to suffer for lack of something needed or craved. **11.** *Dial.* to cause to perish, or to suffer extremely, from cold. [ME *sterve(n)*, OE *steorfan* die, c. G *sterben*] **—Syn. 1, 2.** See **hungry.**

starveling (stäv′lĭng), *adj.* **1.** starving; suffering from lack of nourishment; pining with want; poverty-stricken. **2.** poor in condition or quality. **3.** such as to entail or suggest starvation. **—***n.* **4.** a person, animal, or plant that is starving.

starwort (stä′wût′), *n.* any plant belonging to the genus *Callitriche*, small aquatics with star-shaped rosettes of floating leaves.

stash (stăsh), *v.t.*, *v.i.* *Slang.* to put away, as for safekeeping or in a prepared place. [b. STOW and CACHE]

stasis (stā′sĭs), *n.* *Pathol.* stagnation in the flow of any of the fluids of the body, as of the blood in an inflamed area, the intestinal contents proximal to an obstruction, etc. [t. NL, t. Gk]

stassfurtite (stăs′fə tīt′), *n.* a massive variety of boracite resembling fine-grained white marble. [named after *Stassfurt*, town in Germany]

-stat, a word element meaning 'standing', 'stationary', as in *thermostat.* [t. Gk: m. *-statēs* that stands]

stat., **1.** statuary. **2.** statue. **3.** statute (miles).

state (stāt), *n.*, *adj.*, *v.*, **stated, stating. —***n.* **1.** the condition of a person or thing, as with respect to circumstances or attributes: *a state of disrepair.* **2.** condition with respect to constitution, structure, form, phase, or the like: *a liquid state, the larval state.* **3.** a mode or form of existence: *the future state.* **4.** a person's condition or position in life, or estate, station, or rank. **5.** the style of living befitting a person of high rank and great wealth; sumptuous, imposing, or ceremonious display of dignity; pomp: *a hall used on occasions of state.* **6.** a particular condition of mind or feeling: *to be in an excited state.* **7.** a particularly tense, nervous, or excited condition: *to be in quite a state over a matter.* **8.** a body of people occupying a definite territory and organized under one government, esp. a sovereign government. **9.** the territory, or one of the territories, of a government. **10.** (*sometimes cap.*) any of the commonwealths or bodies politic, each more or less independent as regards internal affairs, which together make up a federal union, as in the United States of America or the Commonwealth of Australia. **11.** the domain or the authority of a state. **12.** (*often cap.*) the body politic as organized for civil rule and government (often contrasted with the Church). **13.** the operations or activities of supreme civil government, or the sphere of supreme civil authority and administration: *affairs of state.* **14.** *Obs. except. Mil.* a statement or report, esp. one giving details of numbers, casualties, etc. **15. lie in state,** (of a body) to be publicly displayed in honour before burial. **16. the States,** *Colloq.* the United States of America. **—***adj.* **17.** of or pertaining to the supreme civil government or authority. **18.** of or pertaining to one of the commonwealths which make up a federal union, as any of the states of the U.S. **19.** characterized by, attended with, or involving ceremony: *a state dinner.* **20.** used on or reserved for occasions of ceremony. **—***v.t.* **21.** to declare definitely or specifically: *to state one's views.* **22.** to set forth formally in speech or writing: *to state a case.* **23.** to set forth in proper or definite form: *to state a problem.* **24.** to say. **25.** to fix or settle, as by authority. [ME; partly var. of ESTATE; partly t. L: m. *status* condition; in defs. 8–13 a devel. from L *status rērum* state of things, or *status reī publicae* state of the republic] **—stat′able, state′able,** *adj.*

—Syn. 1. STATE, CONDITION, SITUATION, STATUS are terms for existing circumstances or surroundings. STATE is the general word, often with no concrete implications or material relationships: *the present state of affairs.* CONDITION carries an implication of a relationship to causes and circumstances: *the weather conditions made flying impossible.* SITUATION suggests an arrangement of circumstances, related to one another and to the character of a person: *he was master of the situation.* STATUS carries official or legal implications; it suggests a complete picture of interrelated circumstances as having to do with rank, position, standing, a stage reached in progress, etc.: *the status of negotiations.*

state-aided (stāt′ā′dĭd), *adj.* receiving financial support from the state, as a school.

statecraft (stāt′kräft′), *n.* **1.** the art of government and diplomacy. **2.** *Archaic.* crafty statesmanship.

stated (stā′tĭd), *adj.* **1.** fixed or settled: *for a stated fee.* **2.** explicitly set forth; declared as fact. **3.** recognized or official. **—stat′edly,** *adv.*

statehood (stāt′hŏŏd′), *n.* the condition or status of a state, esp. a state of the U.S.

statehouse (stāt′hous′), *n.* *U.S.* the building in which the legislature of a state sits.

stateless (stāt′lĭs), *adj.* without nationality. **—state′lessness,** *n.*

stately (stāt′lĭ), *adj.*, **-lier, -liest,** *adv.* **—***adj.* **1.** dignified or majestic; imposing in magnificence, elegance, etc.: *a stately palace.* **—***adv.* **2.** in a stately manner. **—state′liness,** *n.*

statement (stāt′mənt), *n.* **1.** something stated. **2.** a communication or declaration in speech or writing setting forth facts, particulars, etc. **3.** *Com.* an abstract of an account, as one rendered to show the balance due. **4.** the occurrence of a theme, subject, or motif in a piece of music. **5.** the act or manner of stating something.

Staten Island (stăt′n), an island in the U.S., facing New York Bay, comprising Richmond borough of New York City. 221,991 pop. (1960); 64½ sq. mi.

state paper, an official document relating to affairs of state.

state prison, *U.S.* a prison maintained by a state for the confinement of felons.

state prisoner, **1.** a prisoner held by a state for offences against the body politic or views thought to be inimical to the state, rather than for crimes against the law. **2.** *U.S.* an inmate of a state prison.

stater (stā′tə), *n.* any of various gold or silver or electrum coin units or coins of the ancient Greek states or cities. [t. L, t. Gk: standard of weight or money]

state-registered nurse (stāt′rĕj′ĭs təd), a fully qualified nurse. *Abbrev.:* S.R.N.

state religion, the official religion of a country, as established by law.

state rights, states' rights.

stateroom (stāt′rŏŏm′, -rōōm′), *n.* **1.** a private room or cabin on a ship. **2.** *U.S.* a private sleeping compartment on a train. **3.** any magnificent room for use on state occasions.

state's attorney, *U.S.* (in judicial proceedings) the legal representative of the state, equivalent to the British public prosecutor.

state scholarship, formerly, a scholarship financed by the state for university or other further education.

state school, any school financed by the state or local authority, in which compulsory education is given free. See **comprehensive school, grammar school, secondary modern school, primary school.**

state's evidence, *U.S.* evidence given by an accomplice in a crime against the other defendants. Cf. **queen's evidence.**

States-General (stāts′jĕn′rəl), *n.* **1.** the parliament of the present kingdom of the Netherlands. **2.** the legislative body in France before the French Revolution.

stateside (stāt′sīd′), *U.S.* —*adj.* **1.** of, in, or towards the United States. —*adv.* **2.** in or towards the United States.

statesman (stāts′mən), *n., pl.* **-men. 1.** a man who is versed in the management of affairs of state. **2.** one who exhibits ability of the highest kind in directing the affairs of a government or in dealing with important public issues. **3.** *Dial.* a small landowner. [f. *state's*, gen. of STATE + MAN, after F *homme d'état*] —**states′manlike′, states′manly,** *adj.* —**stateswoman** (stāts′wo͝om′ən), *n. fem.* —**Syn. 2.** See **politician.**

statesmanship (stāts′mən shĭp′), *n.* the character or procedure of a statesman; skill in the management of public affairs.

States of the Church, Papal States.

states' rights, *U.S.* the rights belonging to the separate states of the United States (used esp. with reference to the strict construction of the Constitution, by which all rights not delegated by the Constitution to the federal government are regarded as belonging to the states). Also, **state rights.**

state trial, a trial for offences against the state.

state trooper, *U.S.* a member of a paramilitary force having jurisdiction only within the boundaries of a state.

state university, *U.S.* a university maintained by the government of a state as the highest public educational institution.

static (stăt′ĭk), *adj.* Also, **stat′ical. 1.** pertaining to or characterized by a fixed or stationary condition. **2.** *Elect.* denoting or pertaining to electricity at rest, as that produced by friction, or the production of such electricity. **3.** denoting or pertaining to atmospheric electricity interfering with the sending and receiving of wireless messages, etc. **4.** *Physics.* acting by mere weight without producing motion: *static pressure.* **5.** *Sociol.* denoting or pertaining to a condition of social life in which no changes are taking place. **6.** *Econ.* pertaining to fixed relations, or different combinations of fixed quantities: *static population.* —*n.* *Elect.* **7.** static or atmospheric electricity. **8.** interference due to such electricity. [t. NL: s. *staticus*, t. Gk: m. *statikós*] —**stat′ically,** *adv.*

statice (stăt′ĭ sĭ), *n.* any of several plumbaginaceous plants of the genus *Limonium*, as *L. latifolium* of E Europe, frequently cultivated for their inflorescences which are dried and used for indoor decoration. [t. NL, t. Gk: m. *statikḗ*, fem., astringent, STATIC]

static firing, *Aeron.* the firing of a rocket, held down on a special test stand, to measure thrust, etc.

static machine, *Physics.* a Wimshurst machine.

static-pressure tube (stăt′ĭk prĕsh′ə), an open-ended tube used to measure the static pressure of a fluid by positioning it so that the pressure recorded is unaffected by movements of the fluid itself or of a body (as an aircraft) passing through it.

statics (stăt′ĭks), *n.* (*pl. construed as sing.*) that branch of mechanics which deals with bodies at rest or forces in equilibrium. [see STATIC, -ICS]

static water, water collected and stored in tanks, reservoirs, etc., esp. for emergency use.

station (stā′shən), *n.* **1.** a position assigned for standing or remaining in; the place in which anything stands. **2.** the place at which something stops; a regular stopping place, as on a railway. **3.** the building or buildings at a railway stopping place or terminal. **4.** a terminal for buses or coaches. **5.** a police station. **6.** a fire station. **7.** a place equipped for some particular kind of work, service, or the like: *a power station.* **8.** standing, as of persons or things, in a scale of estimation, rank, or dignity. **9.** *Mil.* **a.** a military place of duty. **b.** a semipermanent army post. **10.** *Naval.* **a.** a place or region to which a warship or fleet is assigned for duty. **b.** a position assigned to a member of the crew of a warship during action. **11.** (in India) formerly, a place where the British officials of a district or the officers of a garrison reside. **12.** a radio station. **13.** the wavelength on which a radio or television programme is broadcast; a frequency or channel: *tune in to another station.* **14.** *Biol.* a particular place or the kind of place where a given animal or plant is found. **15.** *Chiefly Austral. and N.Z.* an establishment with its buildings, lands, etc., for raising sheep or cattle. **16.** *Survey.* **a.** a point where an observation is taken. **b.** a length of 100 feet along a survey line. **17.** a position, office, rank, calling, or the like. **18.** *Eccles.* one of the stations of the cross. **19.** *Archaic.* the fact or condition of standing still. —*adj.* **20.** of or pertaining to a station: *station buildings.* **21.** in charge of a station: *a station sergeant in the police force.* —*v.t.* **22.** to assign a station to; place or post in a station or position. [ME, t. L: s. *statio*]

station agent, *U.S.* a stationmaster.

stationary (stā′shə nə rĭ), *adj., n., pl.* **-aries.** —*adj.* **1.** standing still; not moving. **2.** having a fixed position; not movable. **3.** established in one place; not itinerant or migratory. **4.** remaining in the same condition or state; not changing. —*n.* **5.** one who or that which is stationary. [ME, t. L: m. s. *statiōnārius*] —**sta′tionarily,** *adv.* —**sta′tionariness,** *n.*

stationary engine, a steam engine or other heat engine which remains in a fixed place.

stationary orbit, *Aeron.* synchronous orbit.

stationary state, *Physics.* an energy state of a system, as an atom or molecule, when it is not emitting electromagnetic radiation.

stationary wave, standing wave (def. 1).

stationer (stā′shə nə), *n.* **1.** one who sells the materials used in writing, as paper, pens, pencils, ink, etc. **2.** *Obs.* a bookseller. **3.** *Obs.* a publisher. [ME, t. L: m. s. *statiōnārius* stationary, in ML applied to a tradesman who had a shop, as contrasted with a vendor]

Stationers' Company, a company or guild of the City of London, incorporated in 1556, comprising booksellers, printers, bookbinders, and dealers in writing materials, etc.

Stationers' Hall, the hall in London of the Stationers' Company, at which books were registered for copyright before the passing of the Copyright Act in 1842.

stationery (stā′shə nə rĭ), *n.* **1.** writing paper. **2.** writing materials, as pens, pencils, paper, etc.

Stationery Office, a government department which publishes and distributes government pamphlets, etc.

station house, a house or building at or serving as a station, esp. a police station or railway station.

stationmaster (stā′shən mäs′tə), *n.* a person in charge of a railway station.

stations of the cross, *Eccles.* a series of fourteen representations of successive incidents from the Passion of Christ, each with a wooden cross, or a series of wooden crosses alone, set up in a church (or sometimes in the open air) and visited in order, for prayer and meditation.

station wagon, estate car.

statism (stā′tĭz′əm), *n.* **1.** the principle or policy of concentrating extensive economic, political, and related controls in the state at the cost of individual liberty. **2.** support of or belief in the sovereignty of a state, usually a republic. **3.** *Obs. or Rare.* statecraft; politics.

statist[1] (stā′tĭst), *n.* **1.** a supporter of statism. **2.** *Obs.* a statesman. —*adj.* **3.** of or pertaining to statism or statists. [f. STAT(E) + -IST]

statist[2] (stā′tĭst), *n.* statistician. [shortened form]

statistical (stə tĭs′tĭ kl), *adj.* of or pertaining to statistics; consisting of or based on statistics. Also, **statis′tic.** —**statis′tically,** *adv.*

statistical independence, *Statistics.* a condition on the two-way probability distribution of two variables such that the conditional probability distribution of one variable for a given value of a second variable is identical with that for any other given value of the second variable.

statistician (stăt′ĭs tĭsh′ən), *n.* an expert in, or compiler of, statistics. Also, **statist.**

statistics (stə tĭs′tĭks), *n.* **1.** (*construed as sing.*) the science which deals with the collection, classification, and use of numerical facts or data, bearing on a subject or matter. **2.** (*construed as pl.*) the numerical facts or data themselves. [pl. of *statistic*, t. G: m. *Statistik*, t. NL: m. s. *statisticus*, orig., pertaining to a statist]

Statius (stā′shyəs), *n.* **Publius Papinius** (pŭb′lĭ əs pə pĭn′ĭ əs), A.D. *c.* 45–*c.* 96, Roman poet.

statocyst (stăt′ō sĭst′), *n. Zool.* a type of sense organ consisting of a sac enclosing sensory hairs and particles of sand, lime, etc., that has an equilibrating function serving to indicate position in space. [f. Gk *statό(s)* standing + -CYST]

stator (stā′tə), *n.* **1.** *Elect.* the fixed part of an electrical machine (motor or generator) which contains the stationary magnetic circuits. **2.** *Aeron.* the system of fixed radial aerofoils in an axial compressor or turbine.

statoscope (stăt′ə skōp′), *n.* **1.** *Physics.* a form of aneroid barometer for registering minute variations of atmospheric pressure. **2.** *Aeron.* an instrument for detecting a small rate of rise or fall of an aircraft. [f. Gk *statό(s)* standing + -SCOPE]

statuary (stăt′yo͞o ə rĭ), *n., pl.* **-aries,** *adj.* —*n.* **1.** statues collectively. —*adj.* **2.** of, pertaining to, or suitable for statues. [t. L: m. s. *statuārius* of statues]

statue (stăt′yo͞o), *n.* a representation of a person or an animal carved in stone or wood, moulded in a plastic material, or cast in bronze or the like, esp. one of some size, in the round. [ME, t. F, t. L: m. *statua*]

Statue of Liberty, a giant statue, on Liberty Island, New York harbour, of a woman with a torch in one upraised hand and a tablet in the other, given to the U.S. by France.

statuesque (stăt′yo͞o ĕsk′), *adj.* like or suggesting a statue, as in formal dignity, grace, immobility, proportions, or beauty. —**stat′uesque′ly,** *adv.* —**stat′uesque′ness,** *n.*

statuette (stăt′yo͞o ĕt′), *n.* a small statue. [t. F, dim. of *statue* STATUE]

stature (stăch′ə), *n.* **1.** the height of an animal body, esp. of man. **2.** the height of any object. **3.** degree of development or achievement attained. **4.** impressive achievement; moral greatness. [ME, t. OF, t. L: m. *statūra*]

status (stā′təs), *n.* **1.** condition, position, or standing socially, professionally, or otherwise. **2.** the relative rank or social position of an individual or group. **3.** the relative standing, position, or condition of anything. **4.** the state or condition of affairs. **5.** *Law.* the standing of a person before the law. [t. L] —**Syn. 4.** See **state.**

status quo (kwō), *Latin.* the existing or previously existing state or condition. Also, **status in quo.** [L: state in which]

status symbol, a possession which is considered to be proof of the owner's prestige, wealth, social position, etc.

statutable (stăt′yo͞o tə bl), *adj.* **1.** (of an offence) recognized by statute; legally punishable. **2.** prescribed, authorized, or permitted by statute.

statute (stăt′yo͞ot), *n.* **1.** *Law.* **a.** an enactment made by a legislature and expressed in a formal document. **b.** the document in which such an enactment is expressed. **2.** *Internat. Law.* an instrument annexed or subsidiary to an international agreement, as a treaty. **3.** a permanent rule established by an institution, corporation, etc., for the conduct of its internal affairs. [ME, t. F: m. *statut,* t. LL: s. *statūtum,* prop. neut. of L *statūtus,* pp., decreed, set up]

statute book, a register of statutes enacted by a legislature.

statute law, law established by legislative enactments.

statute mile. See **mile** (def. 1a).

statute of limitations, *Law.* a statute defining the period within which a claim may be prosecuted.

Statute of Westminster, a statute passed in 1931 which formally ratified the independent status of the dominions within the British Empire and Commonwealth.

statutory (stăt′yo͞o tə rĭ, -trĭ), *adj.* **1.** of, pertaining to, or of the nature of a statute. **2.** prescribed or authorized by statute. **3.** conforming to statute. **4.** (of an offence) recognized by statute; legally punishable.

statutory declaration, a declaration in accordance with a given act of Parliament, made in the presence of a magistrate or commissioner for oaths.

statutory instrument, a statutory rule or order, often required to be laid before Parliament.

St Augustine (ô′gəs tēn′), a seacoast town in the U.S., in NE Florida: founded by the Spanish, 1565; oldest city in the U.S.; resort. 14,734 (1960).

staunch[1] (stônch), *v.t., v.i., n.* stanch[1]. —**staunch′er,** *n.*

staunch[2] (stônch), *adj.* **1.** firm or steadfast in principle, adherence, loyalty, etc., as a person. **2.** characterized by firmness or steadfastness. **3.** strong; substantial. **4.** impervious to water or other liquids; watertight. Also, **stanch.** [late ME *sta(u)nch,* t. OF: m. *estanche,* fem. of *estanc;* akin to STANCH[1]] —**staunch′ly,** *adv.* —**staunch′ness,** *n.* —**Syn. 1.** See **steadfast.**

staurolite (stô′rə līt′), *n.* a mineral, basic iron aluminium silicate, $HFeAl_5Si_2O_{13}$, occurring in brown to black prismatic crystals, which are often twinned in the form of a cross. [t. F, f. Gk *stauró(s)* cross + *-lite* -LITE] —**staurolitic** (stô′rə lĭt′ĭk), *adj.*

stauroscope (stô′rə skōp′), *n.* an optical instrument for determining the position of the planes of light vibration in sections of crystals.

St Austell (sənt ôs′tl), a town in England, in Cornwall. 25,027 (1961).

Stavanger (stə văng′ə; *Norw.* stä väng′ər), *n.* a seaport in SW Norway. 78,435 (1965).

stave (stāv), *n., v.,* **staved** or **stove, staving.** —*n.* **1.** one of the thin, narrow, shaped pieces of wood which form the sides of a cask, tub, or similar vessel. **2.** a stick, rod, pole, or the like. **3.** a rung of a ladder, chair, etc. **4.** *Pros.* **a.** a verse or stanza of a poem or song. **b.** the alliterating sound in a line of verse; thus, *w* is the stave in *the way of the wind.* **5.** Also, **staff.** *Music.* a set of horizontal lines, now five in number, with the corresponding four spaces between them, music being written on both the lines and spaces. —*v.t.* **6.** to break in a stave or staves of. **7.** to break a hole in; crush inwards (often fol. by *in*). **8.** to break (a hole) in a boat, etc. **9.** to break to pieces, splinters, etc. **10.** to furnish with a stave or staves. **11.** to beat with a stave or staff. **12. stave off,** to put, ward, or keep off, as by force or evasion. —*v.i.* **13.** to become staved in, as a boat; break in or up. [ME; back-formation from STAVES, pl. of STAFF[1]] —**Syn. 4.** See **verse.**

Staveley (stāv′lĭ), *n.* a town in England, in Derbyshire. 18,071 (1961).

staves (stāvz), *n.* **1.** a pl. of **staff**[1]. **2.** pl. of **stave.**

stavesacre (stāvz′ā′kə), *n.* **1.** a larkspur, *Delphinium staphisagria,* native in Europe and Asia Minor, having violently emetic and cathartic poisonous seeds. **2.** the seeds. [ME *staphisagrie,* t. L: m. *staphisagria* wild raisin, t. Gk]

Stavropol (*Russ.* stäv′rə pəly), *n.* a city in the S Soviet Union in Europe. 165,000 (est. 1965). Formerly, **Voroshilovsk.**

stay[1] (stā), *v.,* **stayed** or **staid, staying,** *n.* —*v.i.* **1.** to remain in a place, situation, company, etc.; dwell or reside: *we cannot stay at home.* **2.** to continue to be (as specified), as to condition, etc.: *to stay clean.* **3.** to hold out or endure, as in a contest. **4.** to keep up, as with a competitor in a race (usually fol. by *with*). **5.** *Poker.* to continue in a hand by meeting a bet, ante, or raise. **6.** to stop or halt. **7.** to pause or wait, as for a moment, before proceeding or continuing; linger or tarry. **8.** *Archaic.* to cease or desist. **9.** *Archaic.* to stand firm. **10. stay put,** to remain where placed; not to move from a position. —*v.t.* **11.** to stop or halt. **12.** to hold back, detain, or restrain, as from going further. **13.** to suspend or delay (proceedings, etc.). **14.** to suppress or quell (violence, strife, etc.). **15.** to appease or satisfy temporarily the cravings of (the stomach, appetite, etc.). **16.** to remain through or during (a period of time, etc.). **17.** to remain to the end of; last out; endure. **18.** *Archaic.* to await. —*n.* **19.** an act of stopping. **20.** a stop, halt, or pause; a standstill. **21.** a sojourn or temporary residence. **22.** *Law.* a stoppage or arrest of action; a suspension of a judicial proceeding. **23.** *Colloq. U.S.* staying power; endurance. **24.** *Obs.* a cause of stoppage or restraint.
[late ME, prob. t. OF: m. *estai-,* s. *ester* stand, g. L *stāre*]

stay[2] (stā), *n., v.,* **stayed, staying.** —*n.* **1.** something used or serving to support or steady a thing; a prop; a brace. **2.** a flat strip of steel, plastic, etc., for stiffening corsets, etc. **3.** (*pl.*) a corset. —*v.t.* **4.** to support, prop, or hold up (sometimes fol. by *up*). **5.** to rest for support. **6.** to sustain or strengthen mentally or spiritually. **7.** to fix or rest in dependence or reliance. [appar. same as STAY[3]. Cf. F *étayer,* of Gmc orig.]

stay[3] (stā), *n., v.,* **stayed, staying.** *Chiefly Naut.* —*n.* **1.** a strong rope, now commonly of wire, used to support a mast. **2.** any rope similarly used; a guy. **3. in stays,** heading into the wind while going about from one tack to the other. —*v.t.* **4.** to support or secure with a stay or stays: *to stay a mast.* **5.** to put (a ship) on the other tack. —*v.i.* **6.** (of a ship) to change to the other tack. [ME *stey(e),* OE *stæg,* c. D *stag,* G *Stag*]

stay-at-home (stā′ət hōm′, -ə tōm′), *adj.* **1.** unadventurous; not inclined to travel. —*n.* **2.** a stay-at-home person.

staying power, ability or strength to last or endure; stamina.

staysail (stā′sāl′; *Naut.* -səl), *n. Naut.* any sail hoisted on a stay, as a triangular sail between two masts. See illus. under **sail.**

S.T.B., **1.** (L *Sacrae Theologiae Baccalaureus*) Bachelor of Sacred Theology. **2.** (L *Scientiae Theologicae Baccalaureus*) Bachelor of Theology.

St Bernard (sənt bû′nəd; *Fr.* săɴ bĕr när′), **1. Great,** a mountain pass between SW Switzerland and NW Italy, in the Pennine Alps: Napoleon led his army over it, 1800; hospice. 8108 ft high. **2. Little,** a mountain pass between SE France and NW Italy, in the Alps, S of Mont Blanc. 7177 ft high. **3.** Saint Bernard (dog).

St Christopher (krĭs′tə fə), St Kitts.

St Clair (klĕə), **1.** a river forming part of the boundary between Michigan and Canada, flowing from Lake Huron S to Lake St Clair. 41 mi. **2. Lake,** a lake between SE Michigan and Ontario province, Canada. ab. 30 mi. long; ab. 450 sq. mi.

St-Cloud (*Fr.* săɴ klo͞o′), *n.* a suburb of Paris in N France, on the Seine: former royal palace. 26,746 (1962).

St Croix (sənt kroi′), **1.** Also, **Santa Cruz.** the largest of the Virgin Islands, in the U.S. part of the group. 14,973 pop. (1960); 82 sq. mi. **2.** a river flowing from NW Wisconsin along the Wisconsin-Minnesota boundary into the Mississippi. 164 mi. **3.** a river forming a part of the boundary between Maine and New Brunswick, Canada, flowing into Passamaquoddy Bay. 75 mi.

St-Cyr-l'Ecole (*Fr.* săɴ sēr lĕ kōl′), *n.* a town in N France, W of Versailles: military academy. 10,000 (est. 1966).

STD, subscriber trunk dialling.

S.T.D., (L *Sacrae Theologiae Doctor*) Doctor of Sacred Theology.

St-Denis (*Fr.* săɴ də nē′), *n.* **1.** a suburb of Paris in N France: famous abbey, the burial place of many French kings. 94,264 (1962). **2.** a seaport in and the capital of Réunion island, in the N part. 75,126 (1965).

Ste, (F *Sainte*) Saint (female).

stead (stĕd), *n.* **1.** the place of a person or thing as occupied by a successor or substitute: *since he could not come, his brother came in his stead.* **2.** *Archaic.* a place or locality. **3. stand in good stead,** to be useful or advantageous to. *—v.t.* **4.** *Archaic.* to be of service, advantage, or avail to. [ME and OE *stede,* c. G *statt*]

steadfast (stĕd′fəst, -făst′), *adj.* **1.** fixed in direction; steadily directed: *a steadfast gaze.* **2.** firm in purpose, resolution, faith, attachment, etc., as a person. **3.** unwavering, as resolution, faith, adherence, etc. **4.** firmly established, as an institution or a state of affairs. **5.** firmly fixed in place or position. Also, **stedfast.** [ME *stedefast,* OE *stedefæst,* f. *stede* STEAD + *fæst* FAST[1]] **—stead′fastly,** *adv.* **—stead′fastness,** *n.*

—Syn. 2. STEADFAST, STAUNCH, STEADY imply a sureness and continuousness that may be depended upon. STEADFAST literally means fixed in place, but is chiefly used figuratively to indicate undeviating constancy or resolution: *steadfast in one's faith.* STAUNCH literally means watertight, as of a vessel, and therefore strong and firm; fig., it is used of loyal support that will endure strain: *a staunch advocate of free trade.* Literally, STEADY is applied to that which is relatively firm in position or continuous in movement or duration; fig., it implies sober regularity or persistence: *to run at a steady pace.* **—Ant. 2.** capricious, variable.

steady (stĕd′ĭ), *adj.,* **steadier, steadiest,** *interj., n., pl.* **steadies,** *v.,* **steadied, steadying,** *adv.* *—adj.* **1.** firmly placed or fixed; stable in position or equilibrium; even or regular in movement: *a steady ladder.* **2.** free from change, variation, or interruption; uniform; continuous: *a steady wind.* **3.** constant, regular, or habitual: *steady drinkers.* **4.** free from excitement or agitation: *steady nerves.* **5.** firm, unwavering, or steadfast, as persons or their principles, policy, etc. **6.** settled, staid, or sober, as a person, habits, etc. **7.** *Naut.* (of a vessel) keeping nearly upright, as in a heavy sea. *—interj.* **8.** be calm! control yourself! **9.** *Naut.* (a helm order to keep a vessel on a certain course.) *—n.* **10.** *Colloq.* a regular boyfriend or girlfriend. *—v.t.* **11.** to make steady, as in position, movement, action, character, etc. *—v.i.* **12.** to become steady. *—adv.* **13.** in a firm or steady manner. **14. go steady,** *Colloq.* to go about regularly with the same boyfriend or girlfriend. [f. STEAD + -Y[1]] **—stead′ier,** *n.* **—stead′ily,** *adv.* **—stead′iness,** *n.* **—Syn. 2.** undeviating, invariable, regular, constant. **5.** See **steadfast.**

steady state theory, *Astron.* the cosmological theory that the universe has always existed in a steady state and that the expansion of the universe is compensated by the continuous creation of matter as a property of space itself. Cf. **big bang theory.**

steak (stāk), *n.* **1.** a tender slice of meat, usually beef or fish, for grilling, frying, etc. **2.** chopped meat prepared in the same manner as a steak. [ME *steike,* t. Scand.; cf. Icel. *steik*]

steak tartare (tä tä′, tä′tə), raw minced steak, served with tartar sauce. Also, **steak tartar, tartar steak.**

steal (stēl), *v.,* **stole, stolen, stealing,** *n.* *—v.t.* **1.** to take or take away dishonestly or wrongfully, esp. secretly. **2.** to appropriate (ideas, credit, words, etc.) without right or acknowledgement. **3.** to take, get, or win by insidious, surreptitious, or subtle means: *to steal a nap during a sermon.* **4.** to move, bring, convey, or put secretly or quietly (fol. by *away, from, in, into,* etc.). **5.** (in various games) to gain (a point, etc.) by strategy, by chance, or by luck. **6.** to obtain more than one's share; appropriate entirely to oneself: *the new baby stole everybody's attention.* **7. steal a march on,** to obtain an advantage over, esp. by surreptitious means. **8. steal someone's thunder,** to appropriate or use another's idea, plan, etc. **9. steal the show,** to achieve great success, as an actor in a play, etc. *—v.i.* **10.** to commit or practise theft. **11.** to move, go, or come secretly, quietly, or unobserved. **12.** to pass, come, spread, etc., imperceptibly, gently, or gradually: *the years steal by.* *—n.* **13.** *Colloq.* the act of stealing; a theft. **14.** *U.S. Colloq.* the thing stolen. **15.** *U.S. Colloq.* something acquired at very little cost or at a cost well below its true value. [ME *stele(n),* OE *stelan,* c. D *stelen,* G *stehlen,* Icel. *stela*] **—steal′er,** *n.*

stealing (stē′lĭng), *n.* **1.** the act of one who steals. **2.** (*chiefly pl.*) *U.S.* something stolen. *—adj.* **3.** that steals.

stealth (stĕlth), *n.* **1.** secret, clandestine, or surreptitious procedure. **2.** *Obs.* a secret departure. **3.** *Obs.* **a.** the act of stealing; theft. **b.** the thing stolen. [ME *stelthe.* See STEAL, V., -TH[1]]

stealthy (stĕl′thĭ), *adj.,* **stealthier, stealthiest.** done, characterized, or acting by stealth; furtive: *stealthy footsteps.* **—stealth′ily,** *adv.* **—stealth′iness,** *n.*

steam (stēm), *n.* **1.** water in the form of an invisible gas or vapour. **2.** water changed to this form by boiling, extensively used for the generation of mechanical power, for heating purposes, etc. **3.** the mist formed when the gas or vapour from boiling water condenses in the air. **4.** an exhalation. **5.** *Colloq.* power or energy. **6. let off steam,** *Colloq.* to release repressed emotions, by behaving in an unrestrained manner. *—v.i.* **7.** to emit or give off steam or vapour. **8.** to rise or pass off in the form of steam, as vapour. **9.** to become covered with condensed steam, as a surface. **10.** to generate or produce steam, as in a boiler. **11.** to move or travel by the agency of steam. *—v.t.* **12.** to expose to or treat with steam, as in order to heat, cook, soften, renovate, or the like. **13.** to emit or exhale (steam or vapour); send out in the form of steam. **14.** to convey by the agency of steam, as in a steamship. *—adj.* **15.** heated by or heating with steam: *steam radiator.* **16.** propelled by or propelling with a steam-engine: *a steam train.* **17.** operated by steam. **18.** conducting steam: *a steampipe.* **19.** bathed with, or affected by, steam. **20.** *Colloq.* (jocularly) antiquated; old-fashioned; belonging to the age of steam: *steam radio.* [ME *steme,* OE *stēam,* c. D *stoom*]

steamboat (stēm′bōt′), *n.* a steamship, esp. a small one.

steam-boiler (stēm′boi′lə), *n.* a receptacle in which water is boiled to generate steam.

steam-chest (stēm′chĕst′), *n.* (in a steam-engine) the chamber from which the steam enters the cylinder. Also, **steam box.**

steamed-up (stēmd′ŭp′), *adj.* *Colloq.* excited or angry.

steam-engine (stēm′ĕn′jĭn), *n.* an engine worked by steam, typically one in which a sliding piston in a cylinder is moved by the expansive action of the steam generated in a boiler.

steamer (stē′mə), *n.* **1.** something propelled or operated by steam, as a steamship. **2.** one who or that which steams. **3.** a device or container in which something is steamed.

steam hammer, a heavy, steam-operated, mechanical hammer, used in forges.

steam heat, heat obtained by the condensation of steam in pipes, radiators, etc.

steam-jacket (stēm′jăk′ĭt), *n.* a hollow casing round a cylinder, which is filled with steam in order to heat the cylinder.

steampipe (stēm′pīp′), *n.* a pipe for conveying steam from a boiler.

steam point, *Physics.* the temperature at which the maximum vapour pressure of water is equal to one standard atmosphere, equal to 100°C or 212°F.

steamroller (stēm′rō′lə), *n.* **1.** a heavy locomotive, orig. steam-powered, having a roller or rollers, for crushing or levelling materials in road-making. **2.** an overpowering force, esp. one that crushes opposition with ruthless disregard of rights. *—v.t.* **3.** to go over or crush as with a steamroller or an overpowering force. *—adj.* **4.** suggestive of a steamroller: *steamroller tactics.*

steamship (stēm′shĭp′), *n.* a commercial ship propelled by a steam-driven engine.

steam-shovel (stēm′shŭv′əl), *n.* a machine for digging or excavating, operated by its own engine and boiler.

steam turbine. See **turbine** (def. 2).

steamy (stē′mĭ), *adj.,* **steamier, steamiest. 1.** consisting of or resembling steam. **2.** full of or abounding in steam; emitting steam. **3.** covered with or as if with condensed steam. **—steam′ily,** *adv.* **—steam′iness,** *n.*

Ste Anne de Beaupré (sənt ăn′ də bō prā′; *Fr.* săN tȧn də bō prē′), a village in SE Canada, on the St Lawrence, NE of Quebec: Roman Catholic shrine.

steapsin (stĭ ăp′sĭn), *n.* *Biochem.* the lipase of the pancreatic juice. [b. STEA(RIN) and (PE)PSIN]

stearate (stĭə′rāt), *n.* *Chem.* a salt or ester of stearic acid.

stearic (stĭ ă′rĭk), *adj.* **1.** of or pertaining to suet or fat. **2.** *Chem.* of or derived from stearic acid.

stearic acid, *Chem.* a monobasic organic acid, $C_{17}H_{35}$-COOH, the glycerides of which are the principal components of animal fats. See **stearin.**

stearin (stĭə′rĭn), *n.* **1.** *Chem.* any of the three glyceryl esters of stearic acid, esp. $C_3H_5(C_{18}H_{35}O_2)_3$, a soft, white, odourless solid found in many natural fats; tristearin. **2.** a crude mixture of stearic and palmitic acids used for making candles. Also, **stearine** (stĭə′rĭn). [t. F: m. *stéarine,* f. Gk *stéar* fat + *-ine* -IN[2]]

stearoptene (stĭə rŏp′tēn), *n.* *Chem.* the oxygenated solid part of an essential oil (opposed to *eleoptene,* the liquid part). [f. *stearo-* (repr. Gk *stéar* tallow, fat, suet) + *-ptene* (t. Gk: m. s. *ptēnós* winged, volatile)]

steatite (stĭə′tīt), *n.* *Geol.* soapstone. [t. L: m. *steatītis,* t. Gk: doughlike (stone)] **—steatitic** (stĭə tĭt′ĭk), *adj.*

steatopygia (stĭə′tō pĭj′ĭ ə, -pī′jĭ ə), *n.* abnormal accumulation of fat on and about the buttocks, as among the Hottentots, Bushmen, and other South African peoples, esp. the women. Also, **steatopyga** (stĭə′tō pī′gə). [NL, f. *steato-* (repr. Gk *stéar* fat) + *-pȳgia* (der. Gk *pȳgḗ* rump)]

—**steatopygic** (stĭə′tō pĭj′ĭk), **steatopygous** (stĭə tŏp′ĭ gəs), *adj.*

steatorrhoea (stĭə′tə rĭə′), *n. Pathol.* a condition in which an excess of fat is excreted causing frothy, foul-smelling faeces.

stedfast (stĕd′fəst, -fäst′), *adj.* steadfast.

steed (stēd), *n.* **1.** a horse, esp. one for riding. **2.** a high-spirited horse. [ME *stēde*, OE *stēda* stallion, der. *stōd* STUD[2]; cf. Icel. *stedda* mare]

steel (stēl), *n.* **1.** iron in a modified form, artificially produced, containing a certain amount of carbon (more than in wrought iron and less than in cast iron) and other constituents, and possessing a hardness, elasticity, strength, etc., which vary with the composition and the heat treatment: commonly made by removing a certain amount of the carbon from pig-iron, and used in making tools, girders, etc. **2. high** or **hard steel,** steel with a comparatively high percentage of carbon. **3. low, mild,** or **soft steel,** steel with a comparatively low percentage of carbon. **4. medium steel,** a tough-tempering steel having a medium carbon content. **5.** something made of steel, as a knife-sharpener, for striking sparks from flints, etc. **6.** a sword; instrument or tool of this metal. **7.** a flat strip of steel for stiffening corsets, etc. **8.** *Stock Exchange.* **a.** the market quotation of a steel concern. **b.** stocks, shares, etc., of steel companies. —*adj.* **9.** pertaining to or made of steel. **10.** like steel in colour, hardness, or strength. —*v.t.* **11.** to fit with steel, as by pointing, edging, or overlaying. **12.** to cause to resemble steel in some way. **13.** to render insensible, inflexible, unyielding, determined, etc. [ME and d. OE *stēle*, c. D *staal*, G *Stahl*, Icel. *stāl*]

steel band, a band originating in the Caribbean islands using instruments made from petrol drums, usually tuned to a specific pitch.

steel blue, dark bluish grey.

Steele (stēl), *n.* **Sir Richard,** 1672–1729, English essayist and dramatist.

steel engraving, *Print.* **1.** a method of incising (letters, designs, etc.) on steel. **2.** the imprint, as on paper, from a plate of engraved steel.

steel grey, dark metallic grey with a bluish tinge.

steelhead (stēl′hĕd′), *n., pl.* **-heads,** (*esp. collectively*) **-head.** a large, silvery trout, *Salmo gairdnerii*, of the Pacific coast from California northwards, now generally regarded as the sea-run form of the rainbow trout, highly prized as a game fish.

steel wool, fine shavings of steel, usually in a tangled mass, and used for scouring, polishing, etc.

steelwork (stēl′wûk′), *n.* steel parts or articles.

steelworker (stēl′wû′kə), *n.* one employed in the manufacturing of steel.

steelworks (stēl′wûks′), *n.pl. or sing.* an establishment where steel is made and often manufactured into girders, rails, etc.

steely (stē′lĭ), *adj.,* **steelier, steeliest. 1.** consisting or made of steel. **2.** resembling or suggesting steel; hard or strong like steel. **3.** unfeeling or merciless. —**steel′iness,** *n.*

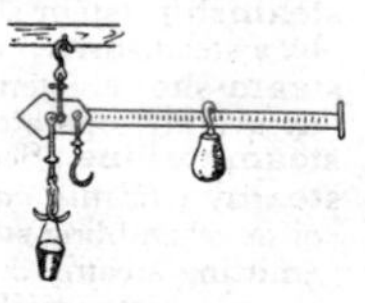
Steelyard

steelyard (stĭl′yäd′), *n.* a portable balance with two unequal arms, the longer one having a movable counterpoise, and the shorter one bearing a hook or the like for holding the object to be weighed. [t. G: mistaken translation of *Stahlhof* sample (court) yard]

Steen (*Du.* stėn), *n.* **Jan** (*Du.* yŏn), 1626–79), Dutch painter.

steenbok (stēn′bŏk′), *n.* a small South African antelope, *Raphicerus campestris*, frequenting rocky places, and lacking dewclaws. Also, **steinbok.** [t. Afrikaans: lit., stonebuck]

Steenbok, *Raphicerus campestris* (Ab. 2 ft high at the shoulder, ab. 3 ft long)

steep[1] (stēp), *adj.* **1.** having an almost perpendicular slope or pitch, or a relatively high gradient, as a hill, an ascent, stairs, etc. **2.** *Colloq.* unduly high, or exorbitant, as a price or amount. **3.** *Colloq.* extreme or extravagant, as a statement. **4.** *Obs.* high or lofty. —*n.* **5.** a steep place; a declivity, as of a hill. [ME *stepe*, OE *stēap*; akin to STOOP[1]] —**steep′ly,** *adv.* —**steep′ness,** *n.*

steep[2] (stēp), *v.t.* **1.** to soak in water or other liquid, as for the purpose of softening, cleansing, or the like, or of extracting some constituent. **2.** to wet thoroughly in or with any liquid, or as a liquid does; drench, saturate, or imbue. **3.** to immerse in some pervading, absorbing, or stupefying influence or agency: *a mind steeped in romance.* —*v.i.* **4.** to lie soaking in a liquid. —*n.* **5.** the act or process of steeping. **6.** the state of being steeped. **7.** a liquid in which something is steeped. [ME *stepe*, c. Sw. *stöpa*] —**steep′er,** *n.*

steepen (stē′pən), *v.t., v.i.* to make or become steeper.

steeple (stē′pl), *n.* **1.** a lofty tower attached to a church, temple, or the like, and often containing bells. **2.** such a tower with a spire or other superstructure surmounting it. **3.** a spire on the top of the tower or roof of a church or the like. [ME *stepyl*, OE *stēpel*, der. *stēap* high, steep]

A, Steeple; B, Spire

steeplebush (stē′pl bŏŏsh′), *n.* the hardhack.

steeplechase (stē′pl chās′), *n.* **1.** a horserace over a course furnished with artificial ditches, hedges, and other obstacles. **2.** a horserace across country; point-to-point. **3.** a race run on foot by persons across country or over a course having obstacles, as ditches, hurdles, etc. —*v.i.* **4.** to ride or run in a steeplechase. —**stee′plechas′er,** *n.*

steeplejack (stē′pl jăk′), *n.* a man who climbs steeples, tall chimneys, etc., to make repairs. Also, **spiderman.**

steer[1] (stĭə), *v.t.* **1.** to guide the course of (anything in motion) by a rudder, helm, wheel, etc.: *to steer a ship.* **2.** to follow or pursue (a particular course). **3.** *Colloq.* to direct the course of. —*v.i.* **4.** to direct the course of a vessel, vehicle, aeroplane, or the like by the use of a rudder or other means. **5.** to direct the course, or pursue a course (as specified). **6.** (of a vessel, etc.) to admit of being steered; be steered or guided in a particular direction. **7. steer clear of,** to avoid. —*n.* **8.** *U.S. Slang.* a suggestion on what to do: *a good steer.* [ME *stere*, OE *stēoran*, c. D *sturen*, G *steuern*, Icel. *stýra*] —**steer′able,** *adj.* —**steer′er,** *n.*

steer[2] (stĭə), *n.* a castrated male bovine, esp. one raised for beef; ox; bullock. [ME; OE *steor*, c. D *stier*, G *Stier*]

steerage (stĭə′rĭj), *n.* **1.** a part or division of a ship, orig. that containing the steering apparatus, later varying in use. **2.** (in a passenger ship) the part allotted to the passengers who travel at the cheapest rate.

steerageway (stĭə′rĭj wā′), *n.* sufficient forward movement to permit a ship to be manoeuvred.

steering committee, a committee, esp. one of a legislative body, entrusted with the preparation of the agenda of a conference, session, etc.

steering gear, the apparatus or mechanism for steering a ship, motor vehicle, bicycle, aeroplane, etc.

steering wheel, a wheel turned by the driver, pilot, etc., in steering a motor vehicle, ship, etc.

steersman (stĭəz′mən), *n., pl.* **-men. 1.** one who steers a ship; helmsman. **2.** one who drives a machine.

steeve[1] (stēv), *v.,* **steeved, steeving,** *n.* —*v.t.* **1.** to pack tightly, as cotton or other cargo in a ship's hold. —*n.* **2.** a long derrick or spar, with a block at one end, used in stowing cargo. [late ME, t. F: m. *estiver*, or t. Pr.: m. *estibar*, g. L *stīpāre* pack]

steeve[2] (stēv), *v.,* **steeved, steeving,** *n. Naut.* —*v.i.* **1.** (of a bowsprit, etc.) to incline upwards at an angle instead of extending horizontally. —*v.t.* **2.** to set (a bowsprit, etc.) at an upward inclination. —*n.* **3.** the angle that a bowsprit or the like makes with the horizontal. [cf. OE *stīfig* steep]

Stefan's law (stĕf′ənz), *Physics.* the law which states that the total energy emitted by a black body in the form of radiant heat, per unit of surface area per unit time, is proportional to the fourth power of its absolute temperature. Also, **Stefan-Boltzman law** (*Ger.* shtĕ′fȧn bōlts′mȧn). [named after Josef *Stefan*, 1835–93, Austrian physicist]

Stefansson (stĕf′ən sən), *n.* **Vilhjalmur** (vĭl′hyoul′mə), 1879–1962, U.S. arctic explorer, born in Canada.

Steffens (stĕf′ənz), *n.* **(Joseph) Lincoln,** 1866–1936, U.S. author, journalist, and editor.

stego-, a word element meaning 'cover', as in *stegosaur.* [comb. form repr. Gk *stégos*, var. of *stégē* roof]

stegomyia (stĕg′ə mī′ə), *n.* former name of the mosquito, *Aëdes aegypti*, which transmits yellow fever.

stegosaur (stĕg′ə sô′), *n.* any of the herbivorous dinosaurs constituting the genus *Stegosaurus*, reptiles of great size (sometimes nearly 40 feet long) with a heavy bony armour.

Stegosaur, *Stegosaurus stenops* (18 ft long)

Steiermark (*Ger.* shtī′ər-märk), *n.* German name of **Styria.**

stein (stīn), *n.* **1.** an earthenware mug, esp. for beer. **2.** the quantity of beer held by this. [t. G: lit., stone]

---

b., blend of, blended; c., cognate with; d., dialect, dialectal; der., derived from; f., formed from; g., going back to; m., modification of; r., replacing; s., stem of; t., taken from; ?, perhaps. See full key on inside front cover.

Stein (stīn *for 1*; *Ger.* shtīn *for 2*), *n.* **1. Gertrude,** 1874–1946, U.S. author in France. **2. Heinrich Friedrich Karl** (*Ger.* hīn′rĭKH frē′drĭKH kȧrl), **Baron vom und zum** (*Ger.* fôm o͝ont tso͞om), 1757–1831, German statesman.

Steinamanger (*Ger.* shtī nä mäng′ər), *n.* German name of **Szombathely.**

Steinbeck (stīn′bĕk), *n.* **John (Ernst)** (ûrnst), 1902–68, U.S. novelist.

steinbok (stīn′bŏk′), *n.* **1.** the steenbok. **2.** an ibex.

Steiner (stī′nə; *Ger.* shtī′nər), *n.* **Rudolf** (ro͞o′dŏlf), 1861–1925, Austrian philosopher, founder of anthroposophy.

Steinmetz (stīn′mĕts), *n.* **Charles Proteus** (prō′tĭ əs), 1865–1923, U.S. electrical engineer, born in Germany.

stela (stē′lə), *n., pl.* **stelae** (stē′lē). stele (defs 1–3).

stele (stē′lĭ), *n., pl.* **-lae** (-lē), **-les** (-lēz). **1.** *Archaeol.* an upright slab or pillar of stone bearing an inscription, sculptural design, or the like. **2.** *Archit.* a prepared surface on the face of a building, a rock, etc., bearing an inscription or the like. **3.** (in ancient Greece and Rome) a burial stone. **4.** *Bot.* the central cylinder of vascular tissue, etc., in the stem or root of a plant. Also, **stela** (for defs 1–3). [t. Gk: standing block (of stone)]

St Elias (ĭ lī′əs), **Mount,** a mountain between SE Alaska and SW Yukon territory, Canada. 18,008 ft.

stellar (stĕl′ə), *adj.* **1.** of or pertaining to the stars; consisting of stars. **2.** starlike. **3.** pertaining to a leading actor, etc. [t. LL: s. *stellāris*, der. L *stella* star]

stellarator (stĕl′ə rā′tə), *n.* *Physics.* an experimental apparatus for research in thermonuclear reactions, consisting of a toroid containing magnetically controlled plasma.

stellar evolution, *Astron.* the process by which stars evolve during the course of their histories.

stellate (stĕl′ĭt, -āt), *adj.* being or arranged in the form of a conventional star; star-shaped. Also, **stel′lated.** [t. L: m. s. *stellātus*] **—stel′lately,** *adv.*

stelliferous (stĕ lĭf′ə rəs), *adj.* *Obs.* having or abounding with stars. [f. L *stellifer* star-bearing + -OUS]

stelliform (stĕl′ĭ fôm′), *adj.* star-shaped. [t. NL: s. *stelliformis*]

Stellite (stĕl′īt), *n.* *Metall. Trademark.* a hard noncorroding alloy of cobalt, chromium, tungsten, molybdenum, and iron; used for surgical instruments, etc.

stellular (stĕl′yo͞o lə), *adj.* **1.** having the form of a small star or small stars. **2.** spotted with star-shaped specks of colour. [f. s. LL *stellula* small star + -AR¹]

St Elmo's fire (ĕl′mōz), a corposant.

stem¹ (stĕm), *n., v.,* **stemmed, stemming.** *—n.* **1.** the ascending axis of a plant, whether above or below ground, which ordinarily grows in an opposite direction to the root or descending axis. **2.** the stalk which supports a leaf, flower, or fruit. **3.** the main body of that portion of a tree, shrub, or other plant which is above ground; a trunk; a stalk. **4.** a petiole; a peduncle; a pedicel. **5.** a stalk of bananas. **6.** something resembling or suggesting the stem of a plant, flower, etc. **7.** a long, slender part: *the stem of a tobacco pipe.* **8.** the slender, upright part of a goblet, wineglass, etc. **9.** the cylindrical projection on a watch, having a knob at the end for winding. **10.** the circular rod of some locks about which the key fits and rotates. **11.** the stock, or line of descent, of a family; ancestry or pedigree. **12.** *Gram.* the element common to all the forms of an inflectional paradigm, or to some subset thereof, usually more than a root. Thus *ten-* or *tan-* would be the root of Latin *tendere* and *tend-* would be the stem. **13.** *Music.* the vertical line forming part of a note. **14.** the main or relatively thick stroke of a letter in printing, etc. See diag. under **type.** *—v.t.* **15.** to remove the stem from (a fruit, etc.). *—v.i.* **16.** to originate (usually fol. by *from*). [ME; OE *stemn*, akin to G *Stamm*] **—stem′less,** *adj.*

stem² (stĕm), *v.t.,* **stemmed, stemming. 1.** to stop or check. **2.** to dam up (a stream, etc.). **3.** to tamp, plug, or make tight, as a hole or a joint. **4.** *Scot.* to stanch (bleeding, etc.). *—v.i.* **5.** *Skiing.* to perform a stem turn. [ME, t. Scand.; cf. Icel. *stemma*, c. G *stemmen*] **—stem′less,** *adj.*

stem³ (stĕm), *v.t.,* **stemmed, stemming. 1.** to make headway against (a tide, current, gale, etc.). **2.** to make progress against (any opposition). [v. use of STEM⁴]

stem⁴ (stĕm), *n.* *Naut.* **1.** an upright at the bow of a ship into which the side timbers or plates are jointed. **2.** the forward part of a ship: *from stem to stern.* [OE *stefn, stemn* prow, stern (special used of STEM¹)]

stemmer¹ (stĕm′ə), *n.* **1.** one who stems (tobacco, etc.). **2.** a device for stemming (grapes, etc.).

stemmer² (stĕm′ə), *n.* an implement for stemming or tamping.

stemson (stĕm′sən), *n.* *Naut.* a curved timber in the bow, having its lower end scarfed into the keelson. [der. STEM⁴, modelled after KEELSON]

stem turn, *Skiing.* a turn in which the ski heel is pushed outwards so that the ski slides over the snow at an angle to the direction of movement.

stem-winder (stĕm′wīn′də), *n.* a watch wound by turning a knob at the stem.

stem-winding (stĕm′wīn′dĭng), *adj.* wound, as a watch, by turning a knob at the stem.

stench (stĕnch), *n.* **1.** an offensive smell; stink. **2.** ill-smelling quality. [ME; OE *stenc*, c. D *stank*, G *Stank*]

stench trap, trap¹ (def. 5).

stencil (stĕn′səl), *n., v.,* **-cilled, -cilling** or (*U.S.*) **-ciled, -ciling.** *—n.* **1.** a thin sheet of cardboard or metal cut through so as to reproduce a design when colour is rubbed through it. **2.** the letters, designs, etc., produced. *—v.t.* **3.** to mark or paint (a surface) or produce (letters, etc.) by means of a stencil. [earlier *stanesile*, appar. der. ME *stansel(en)* adorn with a variety of colours, t. OF: m. *estanceler*, der. *estencele*, g. L *scintilla* spark]

Stendhal (*Fr.* stăN dȧl′), *n.* (*Marie Henri Beyle*) 1783–1842, French novelist and critic.

sten gun, a light submachine gun. [*sten* f. *S*(*hephard and*) *T*(*urpin*) + EN(FIELD) the inventors and the place of manufacture]

steno-, a word element meaning 'little', 'narrow', referring especially to shorthand, as in *stenography.* [comb. form repr. Gk *stenós* narrow, close]

stenograph (stĕn′ə grăf′, -gräf′), *n.* **1.** a character written in shorthand. **2.** any of various keyboard instruments, somewhat resembling a typewriter, used for writing in shorthand, as by means of phonetic or arbitrary symbols. *—v.t.* **3.** to write in shorthand.

stenographer (stĕ nŏg′rə fə), *n.* a person who specializes in taking dictation in shorthand. Also, **stenog′raphist.**

stenography (stĕ nŏg′rə fĭ), *n.* the art of writing in shorthand. **—stenographic** (stĕn′ə grăf′ĭk), **sten′ograph′ical,** *adj.* **—sten′ograph′ically,** *adv.*

stenopetalous (stĕn′ō pĕt′ə ləs), *adj.* having narrow petals.

stenophyllous (stĕn′ō fĭl′əs), *adj.* having narrow leaves.

stenosis (stĭ nō′sĭs), *n., pl.* **-ses** (-sēz). *Pathol.* narrowing of a passage or vessel. [NL, t. Gk]

stenotype (stĕn′ə tīp′), *n.* **1.** a keyboard instrument resembling a typewriter, used in a system of phonetic shorthand. **2.** (*cap.*) a trademark for this machine. **3.** the symbols typed in one stroke on a stenotype machine.

stenotypy (stĕn′ə tī′pĭ), *n.* shorthand in which alphabetic letters or types are used to produce shortened forms of words or groups of words.

Stentor (stĕn′tô), *n.* **1.** (in the *Iliad*) a Greek herald with a loud voice. **2.** (*l.c.*) a person having a very loud or powerful voice.

stentorian (stĕn tô′rĭ ən), *adj.* very loud or powerful in sound: *a stentorian voice.*

step (stĕp), *n., v.,* **stepped, stepping.** *—n.* **1.** a movement made by lifting the foot and setting it down again in a new position, as in walking, running, marching, or dancing. **2.** the space passed over or measured by one movement of the foot in stepping: *to move a step nearer.* **3.** the sound made by the foot in stepping. **4.** a mark or impression made by the foot on the ground; footprint. **5.** the manner of walking; gait. **6.** pace uniform with that of another or others, or in time with music: *to that step.* **7.** (*pl.*) movements or course in stepping or walking: *to retrace one's steps.* **8.** a move or proceeding, as towards some end or in the general course of action: *the first step towards peace.* **9.** a degree on a scale. **10.** a support for the foot in ascending or descending: *a step of a ladder, stair, etc.* **11.** a very short distance; a distance easily walked. **12.** a repeated pattern or unit of movement in a dance formed by a combination of foot and body motions. **13.** *Music.* **a.** a degree of the scale. **b.** the interval between two adjacent scale degrees; a second. **14.** (*pl.*) a stepladder. **15.** *Mech., etc.* a part or offset resembling a step of a stair. **16.** *Naut.* a socket, frame, or platform for supporting the lower end of a mast. **17.** *Quarrying.* a flat-topped ledge on the face of a quarry. **18. break step,** to stop marching or walking in step. **19 in step, a.** moving at the same pace as others. **b.** in harmony or conformity. **20. out of step, a.** not moving at the same pace as others. **b.** not in harmony or conformity. **21. step by step,** by degrees; gradually. **22. take steps,** to initiate a course of action. **23. watch one's step,** to go, behave, etc., with caution. *—v.i.* **24.** to move, go, etc., by lifting the foot and setting it down again in a new position, or by using the feet alternately in this manner: *to step forward.* **25.** to walk, or go on foot, esp. for a few steps or a short distance: *please step this way.* **26.** to move with measured steps, as in a dance. **27.** to go briskly or fast, as a horse. **28.** to come easily as if by a step of the foot: *to step into a fortune.* **29.** to put the foot down, as on the ground, a support, etc.; tread (*on* or

upon), by intention or accident: *to step on a worm.* **30.** to press with the foot, as on a lever, spring, or the like, in order to operate some mechanism.
—*v.t.* **31.** to take (a step, pace, stride, etc.). **32.** to go through or perform the steps of (a dance). **33.** to move or set (the foot) in taking a step. **34.** to measure (a distance, ground, etc.) by steps (sometimes fol. by *off* or *out*). **35.** to make or arrange in the manner of a series of steps. **36.** *Naut.* to fix (a mast) in its step.
—*v.* **37.** Some special verb phrases are:
step down, 1. to decrease. **2.** to resign; relinquish a position, etc.
step in, to intervene; become involved.
step on it, *Colloq.* to hasten; hurry.
step out, 1. to leave a place, esp. for a short time. **2.** to walk briskly. **3.** *U.S.* to go out to a social gathering, etc.; walk out.
step up, to increase.
[ME; d. OE *steppe*, var. of OE *stepe*, *stæpe*, c. D and LG *stap*] —**step′like′,** *adj.* —**step′per,** *n.*

step-, a prefix indicating connection between members of a family by the remarriage of a parent, and not by blood. [ME; OE *stēop-*, c. G *Stief-*, Icel. *stjūp* bereaved, orphaned]

stepbrother (stĕp′brŭth′ə), *n.* one's stepfather's or stepmother's son by a former marriage.

stepchild (stĕp′chīld′), *n.*, *pl.* **-children.** a child of one's husband or wife by a former marriage.

step-cut (stĕp′kŭt′), *adj.* *Jewellery.* (of the facets) cut in sloping steps; trap-cut.

stepdame (stĕp′dām′), *n.* *Archaic.* a stepmother.

stepdaughter (stĕp′dô′tə), *n.* a daughter of one's husband or wife by a former marriage.

step-down (stĕp′doun′), *adj.* *Elect.* converting from a higher to a lower voltage: *a step-down transformer.*

stepfather (stĕp′fä′thə), *n.* a man who occupies one's father's place by marriage to one's mother.

step function, *Maths.* a function whose graph resembles a step.

stephanite (stĕf′ə nīt′), *n.* a mineral, silver antimony sulphide, Ag_5SbS_4: an ore of silver.

stephanotis (stĕf′ə nō′tĭs), *n.* a climbing shrub of the asclepiadaceous genus *Stephanotis*, widespread in the tropics and subtropics having large white flowers.

Stephen (stē′vən), *n.* **1. Saint,** *c.* 975–1038, first king of Hungary, 997–1038. **2.** (*Stephen of Blois*) 1097?–1154, king of England 1135–54 (successor and nephew of Henry I). **3. Sir Leslie,** 1832–1904, English biographer, critic, and editor.

Stephens (stē′vənz), *n.* **James,** 1882–1950, Irish poet and novelist.

Stephenson (stē′vən sən), *n.* **1. George,** 1781–1848, English inventor and engineer. **2.** his son, **Robert,** 1803–1859, English engineer.

step-in (stĕp′ĭn′), *adj.* **1.** (of garments, shoes, etc.) put on by being stepped into. —*n.* **2.** (*pl.*) a step-in garment.

stepladder (stĕp′lăd′ə), *n.* a ladder having flat steps or treads in place of rungs and a hinged support to keep it upright.

stepmother (stĕp′mŭth′ə), *n.* a woman who occupies one's mother's place by marriage to one's father.

Stepney (stĕp′nĭ), *n.* a district in the E inner London borough of Tower Hamlets.

step-parent (stĕp′pĕə′rənt), *n.* a stepfather or stepmother.

steppe (stĕp), *n.* **1.** an extensive plain, esp. one without trees. **2. The Steppes, a.** the vast Russian grasslands, esp. those in the S and E European and W and SW Asiatic parts of the Soviet Union. **b.** Kirghiz Steppe. [t. Russ.: m. *step*]

stepping stone, 1. a stone, or one of a line of stones, in shallow water, a marshy place, or the like, used for stepping on in crossing. **2.** a stone for use in mounting or ascending. **3.** any means of advancing or rising.

stepping switch, *Elect.* a rotating device which closes each of a set of electric circuits in turn.

step rocket, *Aeron.* a multistage rocket.

stepsister (stĕp′sĭs′tə), *n.* one's stepfather's or stepmother's daughter by a former marriage.

stepson (stĕp′sŭn′), *n.* a son of one's husband or wife by a former marriage.

step-up (stĕp′ŭp′), *adj.* *Elect.* converting from a lower to a higher voltage: *a step-up transformer.*

stepwise (stĕp′wīz′), *adv.* in a steplike arrangement.

-ster, a suffix of personal nouns, often derogatory, referring especially to occupation or habit, as in *songster*, *gamester*, *trickster*, also having less apparent connotations, as in *youngster*, *roadster*. [ME; OE *-estre*, *-istre*, c. D *-ster*, MLG *-(e)ster*]

steradian (stə rā′dyən), *n.* *Geom.* a unit of solid angle equal to the angle at the centre of a sphere which encloses an area on its surface equal to the square of its radius. *Symbol:* sr

stercoraceous (stû′kə rā′shəs), *adj.* *Physiol.* consisting of, resembling, or pertaining to dung or faeces. Also, **stercorous** (stû′kə rəs). [t. L: m. *stercorāceus*]

sterculiaceous (stû kyōō′lĭ ā′shəs), *adj.* belonging to the *Sterculiaceae*, a family of trees and shrubs, mostly tropical, including the cacao and cola nut trees. [f. s. NL *Sterculiāceae*, der. *Sterculia*, name of the typical genus (der. L *Sterculius* god of manuring) + -OUS]

stere (stĭə; *Fr.* stĕr), *n.* a cubic metre, equivalent to 35·31477 cu. ft or 1·307954 cu. yds. [t. F, t. Gk: m. *stereós* solid]

stereo-, a word element referring to hardness, solidity, three-dimensionality, as in *stereogram*, *stereoscope*. Also, before some vowels, **stere-.** [comb. form repr. Gk. *stereós* solid]

stereo (stĭə′rĭ ō′, stĕ′-), *n.*, *pl.* **stereos,** *adj.* —*n.* **1.** stereophonic sound reproduction. **2.** any system, equipment, etc., for reproducing stereophonic sound. **3.** a stereoscopic photograph. **4.** stereoscopic photography. **5.** *Print.* stereotype. —*adj.* **6.** pertaining to stereoscopic sound, stereoscopic photography, etc.

stereobate (stĭə′rĭ ə bāt′, stĕ′-), *n.* *Archit.* **1.** the foundation or base upon which a building or the like is erected. **2.** the solid platform or structure (including the stylobate) upon which the columns of a classical building rest. [t. L: s. *stereobata*, f. Gk: *stereo-* STEREO- + m. *-bátēs* stepping, going. Cf. STYLOBATE] —**stereobatic** (stĭə′rĭ ə băt′ĭk, stĕ′-), *adj.*

stereochemistry (stĭə′rĭ ō kĕm′ĭs trĭ, stĕ′-), *n.* that branch of chemistry which deals with the relative arrangement in space of the atoms or groups of atoms constituting a molecule.

stereochrome (stĭə′rĭ ə krōm′, stĕ′-), *n.*, *v.* **-chromed, -chroming.** —*n.* **1.** a picture produced by a process in which waterglass is used as a vehicle or as a preservative coating. —*v.t.*, *v.i.* **2.** to produce (a picture) by stereochromy. —**ster′eochro′mic,** *adj.* —**ster′eochro′mically,** *adv.*

stereochromy (stĭə′rĭ ə krō′mĭ, stĕ′-), *n.* the stereochrome process. [t. G: m. *Stereochromie*. See STEREOCHROME, -Y[3]]

stereogram (stĭə′rĭ ə grăm′, stĕ′-), *n.* **1.** a diagram or picture representing objects in a way to give the impression of solidity. **2.** a stereograph. **3.** a stereo gramophone.

stereograph (stĭə′rĭ ə grăf′, -gräf′, stĕ′-), *n.* a single or double picture for a stereoscope.

stereography (stĭə′rĭ ŏg′rə fĭ, stĕ′-), *n.* the art of delineating the forms of solid bodies on a plane; a branch of solid geometry dealing with the construction of regularly defined solids. —**stereographic** (stĭə′rĭ ə grăf′ĭk, stĕ′-), **ster′eograph′ical,** *adj.* —**ster′eograph′ically,** *adv.*

stereo-isomer (stĭə′rĭ ō ī′sə mə, stĕ′-), *n.* *Chem.* a compound which is stereo-isomeric with one or more other compounds.

stereo-isomerism (stĭə′rĭ ō ī sŏm′ə rĭz′əm, stĕ′-), *n.* *Chem.* the isomerism ascribed to different relative positions of the atoms or groups of atoms in the molecules of optically active compounds. —**ster′eo-i′somer′ic,** *adj.*

stereometry (stĭə′rĭ ŏm′ĭ trĭ, stĕ′-), *n.* the measurement of volumes. —**stereometric** (stĭə′rĭ ə mĕt′rĭk, stĕ′-), **ster′eomet′rical,** *adj.*

stereophonic (stĭə′rĭ ə fŏn′ĭk, stĕ′-), *adj.* of or denoting a system of reproducing sound by simultaneously transmitting or recording separate signals from more than one position, as in a studio, for receiving through the same number of similarly arranged loudspeakers to give a spatial effect and thus greater realism. [f. STEREO- + PHONIC]

stereophotography (stĭə′rĭ ō fə tŏg′rə fĭ, stĕ′-), *n.* photography which produces stereoscopic images. —**stereophotograph** (stĭə′rĭ ō fō′tə grăf′, -gräf′, stĕ′-), *n.* —**stereophotographic** (stĭə′rĭ ō fō′tə grăf′ĭk, stĕ′-), *adj.*

stereopsis (stĭə′rĭ ŏp′sĭs, stĕ′-), *n.* stereoscopic vision. [NL. See STEREO-, -OPSIS]

stereopticon (stĭə′rĭ ŏp′tĭ kən, stĕ′-), *n.* an improved form of projector usually consisting of two complete lanterns arranged so that one picture appears to dissolve while another is forming. [t. NL, f. Gk: *stere-* STERE(O)- + m. Gk *optikón* OPTIC]

stereo-regular rubber (stĭə′rĭ ō rĕg′yōō lə, stĕ′-), any of a group of synthetic elastomers manufactured by the process of solution polymerization using specific catalysts capable of controlling the stereo-isomerism of the products, thus enabling the structure and properties of natural rubber to be substantially copied.

stereoscope (stĭə′rĭ ə skōp′, stĕ′-), *n.* an optical instrument through which two pictures of the same object, taken from slightly different points of view, are viewed, one by each eye, producing the effect of a single picture of the object, with the appearance of depth or relief.

stereoscopy (stĭə'rĭ ŏs'kə pĭ, stĕ'-), *n.* **1.** the study of the stereoscope and its techniques. **2.** three-dimensional vision. —**stereoscopic** (stĭə'rĭ ə skŏp'ĭk, stĕ'-), **ster'eoscop'ical,** adj. —**ster'eoscop'ically,** *adv.* —**ster'eos'copist,** *n.*

stereotaxis (stĭə'rĭ ə tăk'sĭs, stĕ'-), *n.* a movement of an organism in response to contact with a solid.

stereotropism (stĭə'rĭ ŏt'rə pĭz'əm, stĕ'-), *n.* a tropism determined by contact with a solid.

stereotype (stĭə'rĭ ə tīp', stĕ'-), *n., v.,* **-typed, -typing.** —*n.* **1.** a process of making metal plates to use in printing by taking a mould of composed type or the like in papier-mâché or other material and then taking from this mould a cast (plate) in type metal. **2.** a plate made by this process. **3.** a set form; convention; standardized idea or concept. —*v.t.* **4.** to make a stereotype of. **5.** to give a fixed form to. —**ster'eotyp'er,** *n.* —**stereotypic** (stĭə'rĭ ə tĭp'ĭk, stĕ'-), **ster'eotyp'ical,** *adj.*

stereotyped (stĭə'rĭ ə tīpt', stĕ'-), *adj.* **1.** reproduced in stereotype plates. **2.** fixed or settled in form; hackneyed; conventional. —**Syn. 2.** See **commonplace.**

stereotypy (stĭə'rĭ ə tī'pĭ, stĕ'-), *n.* the stereotype process.

steric (stĭə'rĭk, stĕ'rĭk), *adj. Chem.* pertaining to the spatial relationship of atoms in the molecule. Also, **ster'ical.** [f. STER(EO)- + -IC]

sterile (stĕ'rĭl), *adj.* **1.** free from living germs or micro-organisms: *sterile bandage.* **2.** incapable of producing, or not producing, offspring. **3.** barren; unproductive of vegetation, as soil. **4.** *Bot.* **a.** denoting a plant in which reproductive structures fail to develop. **b.** bearing no stamens or pistils. **5.** unproductive of results; fruitless. [t. L: m. s. *sterilis* barren] —**ster'ilely,** *adv.* —**sterility** (stĕ rĭl'ĭ tĭ), *n.* —**Ant. 2, 3.** fertile.

sterilization (stĕ'rĭ lī zā'shən), *n.* **1.** the act of sterilizing. **2.** the condition of being sterilized. **3.** the destruction of all living micro-organisms, as pathogenic or saprophytic bacteria, vegetative forms, and spores. Also, **sterilisation.**

sterilize (stĕ'rĭ līz'), *v.t.,* **-lized, -lizing. 1.** to destroy micro-organisms in, usually by bringing to a high temperature with steam, dry heat, or boiling liquid. **2.** to destroy (one's) ability to reproduce by removing sex organs or inhibiting their functions. Also, **sterilise.** —**ster'iliz'er,** *n.*

sterling (stû'lĭng), *adj.* **1.** consisting of or pertaining to British money. **2.** (of silver) being of standard quality, 92½ per cent pure silver. **3.** made of sterling silver: *sterling cutlery.* **4.** thoroughly excellent: *a man of sterling worth.* **5.** *Austral.* born in Great Britain or Ireland. —*n.* **6.** the standard of fineness of legal coin in Britain: **a.** for silver (**sterling silver**), before 1920, 0·925; now, 0·500. **b.** for gold at one time, 0·995 but now, 0·91666. **7.** silver having the sterling fineness of 0·925, used esp. in manufacture. **8.** manufactured goods of sterling silver. **9.** *Austral.* one born in Great Britain or Ireland. [ME, name of a silver coin, ? f. *ster* STAR + -LING[1] (with reference to the little star on some of the coins)]

sterling area, an association of countries including the United Kingdom and its dependencies and all other Commonwealth countries (except Canada), the Republic of Ireland, Iceland, Jordan, and Kuwait, which hold their currency reserves in London and use sterling in international trade.

stern[1] (stûn), *adj.* **1.** firm, strict, or uncompromising: *stern discipline.* **2.** hard, harsh, or severe: *a stern warning.* **3.** rigorous or austere; of an unpleasantly serious character: *stern times.* **4.** grim or forbidding in aspect: *a stern face.* [ME; OE *styrne*; akin to G *starr* stiff, Gk *stereós* hard, solid] —**stern'ly,** *adv.* —**stern'ness,** *n.*

—**Syn. 1, 2.** STERN, SEVERE, HARSH agree in referring to methods, aspects, manners, or facial expressions. STERN implies uncompromising, inflexible firmness, and sometimes a hard, forbidding, or 'withdrawn' aspect or nature: *a stern parent.* SEVERE implies strictness, lack of sympathy, and a tendency to impose a hard discipline on others: *a severe judge.* HARSH suggests a great severity and roughness, and cruel, unfeeling treatment of others: *a harsh critic.* —**Ant. 1.** mild.

stern[2] (stûn), *n.* **1.** the hinder part of a ship or boat (often opposed to *stem*). **2.** the hinder part of anything. [ME, ? t. Scand.; cf. Icel. *stjörn* steering (see def. of STERNPOST)]

Stern (stûn), *n.* **Isaac,** born 1920, U.S. violinist born in Russia.

sternal (stû'nəl), *adj.* of or pertaining to the sternum.

stern chase, *Naut.* a chase in which the pursuing vessel follows in the wake of the other or astern of it.

stern-chaser (stûn'chā'sə), *n.* a cannon mounted in the stern of a sailing ship.

Sterne (stûn), *n.* **Laurence,** 1713–68, English clergyman and novelist.

sternmost (stûn'mōst'), *adj.* **1.** farthest astern or in the rear. **2.** nearest the stern.

sternpost (stûn'pōst'), *n. Naut.* the principal piece of timber or iron in the stern of a vessel, having its lower end fastened to the keel, and usually serving as a support for the rudder. See diag. under **transom.**

stern sheets, *Naut.* the afterpart of an open boat, occupied by the person in command and by passengers.

sternum (stû'nəm), *n., pl.* **-na** (-nə), **-nums.** *Anat., Zool.* a bone or series of bones extending along the middle line of the ventral portion of the body of most vertebrates, consisting in man of a flat, narrow bone connected with the clavicles and the true ribs; the breastbone. See diag. under **skeleton.** [NL, t. Gk: m. *stérnon* chest, breast]

sternutation (stû'nyo͞o tā'shən), *n.* the act of sneezing. [t. L: s. *sternūtātio*]

sternutator (stû'nyo͞o tā'tə), *n. Chem. Warfare.* a chemical agent causing nose irritation, coughing, etc.

sternutatory (stû nyo͞o'tə tə rĭ, -trĭ), *adj., n., pl.* **-ries.** —*adj.* **1.** Also, **sternu'tative.** causing or tending to cause sneezing. —*n.* **2.** a sternutatory substance.

sternwards (stûn'wədz), *adv.* towards the stern; astern.

sternway (stûn'wā'), *n. Naut.* the movement of a ship backwards, or stern foremost.

stern-wheel (stûn'wēl'), *adj.* propelled by a paddle-wheel at the stern. —**stern'-wheel'er,** *n.*

steroid (stĕ'roid), *n. Biochem.* any of a large group of certain fat-soluble compounds, most of which have specific physiological action. Among them are the sterols, bile acids, and many hormones.

sterol (stĕ'rŏl), *n. Biochem.* any of a group of steroid alcohols derived from plants or animals, as cholesterol and ergosterol. [abstracted from (CHOLE)STEROL, (ERGO)-STEROL]

stertor (stû'tə), *n. Pathol.* a heavy snoring sound accompanying respiration in certain diseases. [NL, der. L *stertere* snore]

stertorous (stû'tə rəs), *adj.* **1.** characterized by stertor or heavy snoring. **2.** breathing in this manner. —**ster'torously,** *adv.* —**ster'torousness,** *n.*

stet (stĕt), *v.,* **stetted, stetting.** —*v.i.* **1.** let it stand: a direction on a printer's proof, a manuscript, or the like to retain cancelled matter (usually accompanied by a row of dots under or beside the matter). —*v.t.* **2.** to mark with the word 'stet' or with dots. [t. L: let it stand]

stetho-, a word element meaning 'chest'. Also, before vowels, **steth-.** [comb. form repr. Gk *stêthos*]

stethometer (stĕ thŏm'ĭ tə), *n. Med.* an instrument for measuring the respiratory movements of the walls of the chest and abdomen.

stethoscope (stĕth'ə skōp'), *n. Med.* an instrument used in auscultation to convey sounds in the chest or other parts of the body to the ear of the examiner. —**stethoscopy** (stĕ thŏs'kə pĭ), *n.*

stethoscopic (stĕth'ə skŏp'ĭk), *adj.* **1.** pertaining to the stethoscope or to stethoscopy. **2.** made or obtained by the stethoscope. Also, **steth'oscop'ical.** —**steth'oscop'ically,** *adv.*

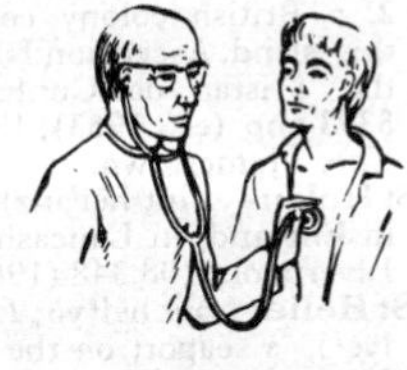
Stethoscope

St-Étienne (*Fr.* săɴ tė tyĕn'), *n.* a town in SE central France, the capital of Loire department. 201,242 (1962).

stetson (stĕt'sən), *n.* a man's hat having a broad brim and a wide crown, formerly common in the western U.S. [named after the original maker, *c.* 1865]

Stettin (*Ger.* shtĕ tēn'), *n.* a seaport in NW Poland: formerly in Germany. 303,000 (est. 1964). Polish, **Szczecin.**

St Eustatius (sənt yo͞o stā'shəs), an island in the Netherlands Antilles. 1103 pop. (1963); 7 sq. mi.

stevedore (stē'vĭ dô'), *n., v.,* **-dored, -doring.** —*n.* **1.** a firm or individual engaged in the loading or unloading of a vessel. —*v.t.* **2.** to load or unload the cargo of (a ship). —*v.i.* **3.** to load or unload a vessel. [t. Sp: m. *estivador,* der. *estivar* pack, stow, g. L *stīpāre* press]

stevedore's knot, a knot which forms a lump in a line to prevent it from passing through a hole, etc.

Stevenage (stē'və nĭj), *n.* a new town in England, in Hertfordshire. 54,149 (est. 1965).

Stevenson (stē'vən sən), *n.* **1. Adlai** (ăd'lā), 1900–65, U.S. statesman. **2. Robert Louis (Balfour)** (băl'fô, -fə), 1850–94, Scottish novelist, essayist, and poet.

stew (styo͞o), *v.t.* **1.** to cook (food) by simmering or slow boiling. —*v.i.* **2.** to undergo cooking by simmering or slow boiling. **3.** *Colloq.* to fret, worry, or fuss. **4. stew in one's own juice,** to suffer one's own misfortunes or the consequences of one's own actions without help. —*n.* **5.** a preparation of meat, fish, or other food cooked by stewing. **6.** *Colloq.* a state of uneasiness, agitation, or worry. **7.** *Obs.* a vessel for boiling or stewing. **8.** (*usually pl.*) *Archaic.* a brothel. [ME, t. OF: m. s. *estuver,* g. VL *extūfāre* perspire, der. *tūfus* vapour, t. Gk: m. *tŷphos*]

steward (styōō͝əd), *n.* **1.** one who manages another's property or financial affairs; one who administers anything as the agent of another or others. **2.** one who has charge of the household of another, providing for the table, directing the servants, etc. **3.** an employee who has charge of the table, the servants, etc., in a club or other establishment. **4.** any attendant on a ship or aircraft who waits on passengers. **5.** one responsible for arranging the details and conduct of a public meeting, race meeting, public entertainment, etc. **6.** *U.S. Navy.* a petty officer in charge of officers' quarters and mess. —*v.t.* **7.** to act as steward of; manage. —*v.i.* **8.** to act or serve as steward. [ME; OE *stīweard, stigweard,* f. *stig* hall + *weard* keeper, WARD] —**steward′ship′,** *n.*

stewardess (styōō͝ə′dĭs, styōō͝ə dĕs′), *n.* a woman attendant on board an aircraft or ship who waits on passengers.

Stewart (styōō͝ət), *n.* **1.** See **Darnley, Lord Henry. 2. Dugald** (dōō′gld), 1753–1828, Scottish philosopher. **3.** Stuart (def. 1).

Stewart Island, one of the islands of New Zealand, S of South Island. 540 pop. (est. 1965); 670 sq. mi.

stewed (styōōd), *adj.* **1.** cooked by simmering or slow boiling, as food. **2.** (of tea) made disagreeably strong by being infused too long. **3.** *Slang.* intoxicated or drunk.

Steyr (*Ger.* shtī′ər), *n.* a town in Austria, in W Upper Austria. 38,306 (1961).

St Gallen (sənt găl′ən; *Ger.* zàngkt gà′lən), **1.** a canton in NE Switzerland. 339,489 pop. (1960); 777 sq. mi. **2.** the capital of this canton. 76,279 (1960). French, **St Gall** (*Fr.* săN gȧl′).

St George's (sənt jô′jĭz), a seaport in and the capital of Grenada, in the SW part. 7305 (1960).

St George's Channel, a channel between Wales and Ireland, connecting the Irish Sea and the Atlantic. Least width, 43 mi. See map under **Ulster.**

St-Germain-en-Laye (*Fr.* săN zhĕr măN äN lĕ′), *n.* a town in N France, in Yvelines department, near Paris: royal chateau and forest; treaties 1570, 1632, 1679, 1919. 40,000 (est. 1964).

St Gotthard (sənt gŏt′əd; *Fr.* săN gō tȧr′), **1.** a range of the Alps in S Switzerland. Highest peak, 10,490 ft. **2.** a mountain pass over this range. 6935 ft high. **3.** a railway tunnel under this pass. 9¼ mi.

St Helena (sĕn′tĭ lē′nə), **1.** a British island in the S Atlantic: Napoleon's place of exile, 1815–1821. 4634 pop. (1964); 47 sq. mi. **2.** a British colony comprising this island, Ascension Island, and the Tristan da Cunha group. 5393 pop. (est. 1963); 126 sq. mi. *Cap.:* Jamestown.

St Helena (def. 1)

St Helens (sənt hĕl′ĭnz), a town in England, in Lancashire, near Liverpool. 108,348 (1961).

St Helier (sənt hĕl′yə; *Fr.* săN tĕ-lyė′), a seaport on the island of Jersey in the English Channel: resort. 26,484 (1964).

′sthenia (sthĭ nī′ə, sthē′nĭ ə), *n. Pathol.* strength; excessive vital force. Cf. **asthenia.** [NL, abstracted from *asthenia* ASTHENIA]

sthenic (sthĕn′ĭk), *adj.* sturdy; heavily and strongly built. [abstracted from ASTHENIC]

Stheno (sthē′nō, sthĕn′ō), *n. Gk Legend.* one of the three Gorgons.

stibine (stĭb′īn), *n. Chem.* antimonous hydride, SbH_3, a colourless poisonous gas. [f. STIB(IUM) + -INE[2]]

stibium (stĭb′ĭ əm), *n.* antimony. [t. L] —**stib′ial,** *adj.*

stibnite (stĭb′nīt), *n.* a mineral, antimony sulphide, Sb_2S_3, lead grey in colour with a metallic lustre, occurring in crystals, often acicular, or in bladed masses: the most important ore of antimony. [f. STIB(I)N(E) + -ITE[1]]

stich (stĭk), *n.* a verse or line of poetry. [t. Gk: s. *stíchos* row, line, verse]

stichic (stĭk′ĭk), *adj.* **1.** pertaining to or consisting of stichs. **2.** composed of lines of the same metrical form throughout. [t. Gk: m. s. *stichikós*]

stichometry (stĭ kŏm′ĭ trĭ), *n.* the practice of writing a prose text in lines of lengths corresponding to divisions in the sense and indicating phrasal rhythms. [t. LGk: m. *stichometría*] —**stichometric** (stĭk′ō mĕt′rĭk), **stich′-omet′rical,** *adj.*

stichomythia (stĭk′ō mĭth′ĭ ə), *n.* dramatic practice of dialogue in which each speaker uses exactly one line of the verse. Also, **stichomythy** (stĭ kŏm′ĭ thĭ). [t. Gk] —**stich′omyth′ic,** *adj.*

-stichous, *Bot., Zool.* a word element referring to rows, as in *distichous.* [t. Gk: m. *-stichos* (adj. suffix) having stichs]

stick[1] (stĭk), *n., v.,* **sticked, sticking.** —*n.* **1.** a branch or shoot of a tree or shrub cut or broken off. **2.** a relatively long and slender piece of wood. **3.** an elongated piece of wood for burning, for carpentry, or for any special purpose. **4.** a rod or wand; a baton. **5.** a walking stick or cane. **6.** a club or cudgel. **7.** an elongated, sticklike piece of some material: *a stick of rock.* **8.** *Sport.* the stick used in hockey or lacrosse. **9.** *Aeron.* a lever, usually with a handle, by which the longitudinal and lateral motions of an aeroplane are controlled; joystick. **10.** *Naut.* a mast, or a part of a mast. **11.** *Print.* a composing stick. **12.** *Mil.* **a.** a group of bombs so arranged as to be released in a row across a target. **b.** the bombload. **13.** (*pl.*) *Colloq.* the backwoods, or any region distant from cities or towns. **14.** *U.S. Colloq.* a portion of liquor, as brandy, added to a beverage, etc. **15.** (*usually pl.*) a piece of furniture. **16.** *Colloq.* a dull or uninteresting person. **17.** *U.S. Colloq.* a marijuana cigarette. **18. in a cleft stick,** in a dilemma, awkward position, etc. **19. wrong end of the stick,** a complete misunderstanding of facts, a situation, etc. —*v.t.* **20.** to furnish with a stick or sticks in order to support or prop, as a plant. **21.** *Print.* to set (type) in a composing stick. [ME *stikke,* OE *sticca,* akin to G *stecken*]

stick[2] (stĭk), *v.,* **stuck, sticking,** *n.* —*v.t.* **1.** to pierce or puncture with a pointed instrument, as a dagger, spear, or pin; stab. **2.** to kill by this means: *to stick a pig.* **3.** to thrust (something pointed) in, into, through, etc.: *to stick a pin into a balloon.* **4.** to fasten in position by thrusting the point or end into something: *to stick a nail in a wall.* **5.** to fasten in position by, or as by, something thrust through: *to stick a badge on one's coat.* **6.** to fix or impale upon something pointed: *to stick a potato on a fork.* **7.** to set with things piercing the surface: *to stick a cushion full of pins.* **8.** to furnish or adorn with things attached or set here and there. **9.** to place upon a stick or pin for exhibit: *to stick butterflies.* **10.** to thrust or poke into a place or position indicated: *to stick one's head out of the window.* **11.** to place in a specified position: *stick your books on the table.* **12.** to fasten or attach by causing to adhere: *to stick a stamp on a letter.* **13.** to bring to a standstill; render unable to proceed or go back: *to be stuck in the mud.* **14.** to endure; tolerate. **15.** to confuse; perplex; puzzle. **16.** to impose an unpleasant task upon. **17.** *U.S. Slang.* to cheat. —*v.i.* **18.** to have the point piercing, or embedded in something. **19.** to remain attached by adhesion: *the mud sticks to one's shoes.* **20.** to hold, cleave, or cling: *to stick to a horse's back.* **21.** to remain persistently or permanently: *a fact that sticks in the mind.* **22.** to remain firm in resolution, opinion, statement, attachment, etc.; hold faithfully, as to a promise or bargain. **23.** to keep steadily or unremittingly at a task, undertaking, or the like (fol. by *at* or *to*): *to stick at a job.* **24.** to become fastened, hindered, checked, or stationary by some obstruction. **25.** to be at a standstill, as from difficulties. **26.** to hesitate or scruple (usually fol. by *at*). **27.** to be thrust, or extend, project, or protrude (fol. by *through, from, out, up,* etc.). **28.** to remain or stay, usually for a considerable time: *I can't bear to stick indoors all day.*

—*v.* **29.** Some special verb phrases are:

stick around, *Slang.* to stay nearby; linger.

stick by or **to,** to remain loyal or faithful to.

stick in one's throat, to be hard to accept.

stick out, 1. to protrude; thrust out. **2.** to be obvious, conspicuous, etc. **3.** to endure; stand one's ground.

stick out for, to continue to ask for; be persistent in demanding.

stick (something) out, to endure; put up with until the very end: *they were bored by the film but stuck it out for two hours.*

stick together, to remain' friendly, loyal, etc., to one another.

stick up, 1. to project or protrude upwards. **2.** *Slang.* to rob, esp. at gunpoint.

stick up for, to speak or act in favour of; defend; support.

stick up to, to confront boldly; resist strongly.

stick with, to remain loyal to.

—*n.* **30.** a thrust with a pointed instrument; a stab. **31.** the quality of adhering or of causing things to adhere. **32.** something causing adhesion. **33.** *Obs.* a stoppage or standstill. **34.** *Obs.* something causing delay or difficulty. [ME *stike(n),* OE *stician,* akin to (M)LG *stikken*]

—**Syn. 19.** STICK, ADHERE, COHERE mean to cling to or be tightly attached to something. ADHERE implies that one kind of material clings tenaciously to another; COHERE adds the idea that a thing is attracted to and held by something like itself: *particles of sealing wax cohere and form a mass which will adhere to tin.* STICK, more colloquial, often used as the general term, is used particularly when a third kind of material is involved: *a gummed label will stick to a parcel.*

sticker (stĭk′ə), *n.* **1.** one who or that which sticks. **2.** an adhesive label. **3.** a persistent, diligent person. **4.** *Colloq.*

something that nonplusses or puzzles one. **5.** a bur, thorn, or the like. **6.** a weapon used for piercing or stabbing.

stickful (stĭk′fŏŏl′), *n.*, *pl.* **-fuls.** *Print.* as much set type as a composing stick will hold.

sticking place, the place in an animal's neck where the knife is thrust in slaughtering. Also, **sticking point.**

sticking plaster, an adhesive cloth or other material for covering and closing superficial wounds, etc.

sticking point, 1. a point at which further progress is impeded or becomes impossible. **2.** sticking place.

stick insect, any of certain orthopterous insects of the family *Phasmidae*, with long, slender, twiglike bodies.

Stick insect, *Diapheromera femorata* (3 in. long)

stick-in-the-mud (stĭk′ĭn *th*ə mŭd′), *n.* one who is unadventurous, lacking initiative, or opposed to new ideas, progress, novelty, etc.

stickjaw (stĭk′jô′), *n.* *Colloq.* any glutinous toffee, chewing gum, pudding, etc.

stickle (stĭk′l), *v.i.*, **-led, -ling. 1.** to argue or haggle insistently, esp. on trivial matters. **2.** to raise objections; scruple; demur. [ME *stightle* set in order, freq. of obs. *stight*, OE *stihtan*, c. G *stiften*]

stickleback (stĭk′l băk′), *n.* any of the small, pugnacious, spiny-backed fishes of the family *Gasterosteidae*, of fresh waters and sea inlets, esp. *Gasterosteus aculeatus*, **the three-spined stickleback,** and *G. spinachia*, **the fifteen-spined stickleback,** a saltwater species. [ME *stykylbak*, f. OE *sticol* scaly + *bæc* back]

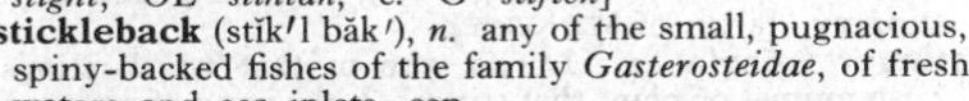

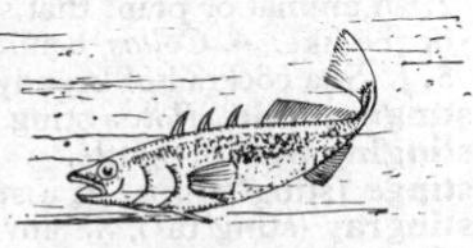

Three-spined stickleback, *Gasterosteus aculeatus* (2 to 3 in. long)

stickler (stĭk′lə), *n.* **1.** a person who insists on something unyieldingly (fol. by *for*): *a stickler for ceremony.* **2.** any puzzling or difficult problem.

stickpin (stĭk′pĭn′), *n.* *U.S.* a tiepin.

sticktight (stĭk′tīt′), *n.* a composite herb, *Bidens frondosa*, having flat, barbed achenes which adhere to clothing, etc.

stick-up (stĭk′ŭp′), *n.* *Slang.* a hold-up or robbery.

stickweed (stĭk′wēd′), *n.* the ragweed.

sticky (stĭk′ĭ), *adj.*, **stickier, stickiest. 1.** having the property of adhering, as glue; adhesive. **2.** covered with adhesive matter: *sticky hands.* **3.** (of the weather, etc.) humid: *an unbearably sticky day.* **4.** *Colloq.* difficult to deal with; awkward; troublesome. **5.** *Colloq.* disagreeable; painful. **—stick′ily,** *adv.* **—stick′iness,** *n.*

stickybeak (stĭk′ĭ bēk′), *Austral., N.Z.* **—***v.t.* **1.** to pry; meddle. **—***n.* **2.** one who pries.

sticky tape, *Colloq.* adhesive tape.

sticky willie, cleavers.

stiff (stĭf), *adj.* **1.** rigid or firm in substance; not flexible, pliant, or easily bent: *a stiff collar.* **2.** not moving or working easily: *a stiff hinge.* **3.** (of a person, etc.) moving only with difficulty, as from cold, age, exhaustion, etc. **4.** blowing violently, strongly, or with steady force: *stiff winds.* **5.** strong, as alcoholic beverages. **6.** firm in purpose or resolution; unyielding; stubborn. **7.** stubbornly maintained, as a struggle, etc. **8.** firm against any lowering action, as prices, etc. **9.** rigidly formal, as persons, manners, proceedings, etc. **10.** lacking ease and grace; awkward: *a stiff style of writing.* **11.** excessively regular, as a design; not graceful in form or arrangement. **12.** laborious or difficult, as a task. **13.** severe, as a penalty. **14.** excessive; unusually high or great, as a price, demand, etc. **15.** firm from tension; taut: *to keep a stiff rein.* **16.** relatively firm in consistency, as semisolid matter: *a stiff jelly.* **17.** dense, compact, or tenacious: *stiff soil.* **18.** *Naut.* (of a ship) resistant to rolling; stable. **19.** *Scot. and N Dial.* sturdy, stout, or strongly built. **20.** *Slang.* drunk. **—***n.* *Slang.* **21.** a dead body; corpse. **22.** (abusively) a person. **23.** a drunk. **24.** a racehorse that is certain to lose. **—***adv.* **25.** in a rigid state: *the clothes were frozen stiff.* **26.** completely; extremely: *we were all scared stiff.* [ME; OE *stīf*, c. G *steif*; akin to L *stīpāre* crowd, pack] **—stiff′ish,** *adj.* **—stiff′ly,** *adv.* **—stiff′ness,** *n.* **—Syn. 1.** See **firm**[1].

stiffen (stĭf′ən), *v.t.* **1.** to make stiff. **—***v.i.* **2.** to become stiff or tense. **—stiff′ener,** *n.*

stiff-necked (stĭf′nĕkt′), *adj.* **1.** having a stiff neck. **2.** stubborn; perversely obstinate; refractory.

stifle[1] (stī′fəl), *v.*, **-fled, -fling. —***v.t.* **1.** to kill by impeding respiration; smother. **2.** to keep back or repress: *to stifle a yawn.* **3.** to suppress, crush, or stop: *to stifle a revolt.* **—***v.i.* **4.** to become stifled or suffocated. **5.** to suffer from difficulty in breathing, as in a close atmosphere. [t. Scand.; cf. Icel. *stífla* stop up] **—sti′fler,** *n.*

stifle[2] (stī′fəl), *n.* the joint of the hind leg of a horse, dog, etc., between the femur and the tibia. Also, **stifle joint.** See illus. under **horse.** [ME; orig. uncert.]

stifling (stī′flĭng), *adj.* suffocating; oppressively close: *a stifling atmosphere.* **—sti′flingly,** *adv*

stigma (stĭg′mə), *n.*, *pl.* **stigmata** (stĭg′mə tə), **stigmas** (*esp. defs 4 and 5*). **1.** a mark of disgrace; a stain, as on one's reputation. **2.** a characteristic mark or sign of defect, degeneration, disease, etc. **3.** *Pathol.* a spot or mark on the skin; esp. a place or point on the skin which bleeds during certain mental states, as in hysteria. **4.** *Zool.* a small mark, spot, pore, or the like, on an animal or organ, as: **a.** the eyespot, usually red, of a protozoan. **b.** (in insects) an entrance into the respiratory system. **5.** *Bot.* that part of a pistil which receives the pollen. See diag. under **epigynous flower. 6.** *Rom. Cath. Ch.* marks said to have been supernaturally impressed upon certain persons in the semblance of the wounds on the crucified body of Christ. **7.** *Archaic.* a mark made by a branding iron on the skin of a criminal or slave. [t. L, t. Gk]

stigmatic (stĭg măt′ĭk), *adj.* **1.** pertaining to a stigma, mark, spot, or the like. **2.** *Bot.* pertaining to or having the character of a stigma (part of the pistil). **3.** *Optics.* converging to a point; anastigmatic. **—***n.* **4.** *Rom. Cath. Ch.* one marked with stigmata.

stigmatism (stĭg′mə tĭz′əm), *n.* **1.** *Optics.* a condition in which there is no astigmatism. **2.** *Pathol.* the condition in which stigmata are present.

stigmatize (stĭg′mə tīz′), *v.t.*, **-tized, -tizing. 1.** to mark with a stigma or brand. **2.** to set some mark of disgrace or infamy upon. **3.** to produce stigmata, marks, spots, or the like on. Also, **stigmatise. —stig′matiza′tion,** *n.* **—stig′matiz′er,** *n.*

Stijl (*Du.* stĕyl′), *n.* **De** (*Du.* də), a Dutch modern art movement, initiated in 1917 and concerned with geometrical abstraction. [D, lit., the style, title of a periodical founded by Van Doesburg in 1917]

stilbene (stĭl′bēn), *n.* *Chem.* a colourless, crystalline insoluble substance, $C_6H_5{\cdot}CH{:}CH{\cdot}C_6H_5$, used in the dyestuffs industry.

stilbite (stĭl′bīt), *n.* a white to brown or red zeolite mineral, a hydrous silicate of calcium and aluminium, occurring in sheaf-like aggregates of crystals and in radiated masses. [f. s. Gk *stilbein* glitter + -ITE[2]]

stilboestrol (stĭl bē′strəl), *n.* *Biochem.* a synthetic hormone, $C_{18}H_{20}O_2$, the parent substance of a group of oestrogenic agents, some of which are more active than those of the human body. Also, *U.S.*, **stilbestrol.**

stile[1] (stīl), *n.* **1.** a series of steps or the like for ascending and descending in getting over a fence, etc., which remains closed to cattle. **2.** a turnstile. [ME; OE *stigel*, der. *stīgan*, c. G *steigen* ascend, go]

stile[2] (stīl), *n.* *Carp.* a vertical member in a wainscot, panelled door, or other piece of framing. [prob. t. D: m. *stijl* pillar, doorpost, prop]

stiletto (stĭ lĕt′ō), *n.*, *pl.* **-tos,** *v.*, **-toed, -toing. —***n.* **1.** a dagger having a narrow blade, thick in proportion to its width. **2.** a small sharp-pointed instrument for making eyelet holes in needlework. **—***v.t.* **3.** to stab or kill with a stiletto. [t. It., dim. of *stilo* dagger, t. L: m. *stilus* pointed instrument]

stiletto heel, a high heel on a woman's shoe that tapers to an extremely small base.

Stilicho (stĭl′ĭ kō′), *n.* **Flavius** (flā′vyəs), 359?–408, Roman general and statesman.

still[1] (stĭl), *adj.* **1.** remaining in place or at rest; motionless; stationary: *to stand still.* **2.** free from sound or noise, as a place, time, etc.; silent. **3.** subdued or low in sound; hushed: *a still small voice.* **4.** free from commotion of any kind; quiet; tranquil; calm. **5.** without waves or perceptible current, as water. **6.** not effervescent or sparkling, as wine. **7.** *Photog.* denoting or pertaining to a still (photograph).
—*n.* **8.** *Poetic.* stillness or silence. **9.** a single photographic picture, esp. a print of one of the frames of a film.
—*adv.* **10.** at this or that time; as previously: *is she still here?* **11.** up to this or that time: *points still unsettled.* **12.** in the future as in the past: *objections will still be made.* **13.** even or yet (with comparatives or the like): *still more complaints.* **14.** even then; yet; nevertheless: *to be rich and still crave for more.* **15.** without sound or movement. **16.** *Poetic or Dial.* steadily; constantly; always.
—*conj.* **17.** and yet; but yet; nevertheless: *it was futile, still they fought.*
—*v.t.* **18.** to silence or hush (sounds, etc.). **19.** to calm,

appease, or allay. **20.** to quiet (waves, winds, commotion, tumult, passion, pain, etc.). *—v.i.* **21.** to become still or quiet. [ME and OE *stille*, c. G *Still*]
—Syn. 2. STILL, QUIET, HUSHED, NOISELESS, SILENT indicate the absence of noise and of excitement or activity accompanied by sound. STILL indicates the absence of sound or movement: *the house was still.* QUIET implies relative freedom from noise, activity, or excitement: *a quiet engine, a quiet holiday.* HUSHED implies the suppression of sound or noise: *a hushed whisper.* NOISELESS and SILENT characterize that which does not reveal its presence or movement by any sound: *a noiseless footstep, a room silent and deserted.* **17.** See **but**[1]. **—Ant. 2.** noisy. **4.** moving.

still[2] (stĭl), *n.* **1.** a distilling apparatus, consisting of a vessel in which the substance is heated and vaporized and a cooling device or coil for condensing the vapour. **2.** a distillery. *—v.t., v.i.* **3.** *Rare or Obs.* to distil. [aphetic var. of DISTIL(L)]

stillbirth (stĭl′bûth′), *n.* **1.** the birth of a dead child or organism. **2.** a foetus dead at birth.

stillborn (stĭl′bôn′), *adj.* dead when born.

stiller (stĭl′ə), *n. Rare or Obs.* a distiller.

still hunt, *U.S.* **1.** a hunt for game carried on stealthily, as by stalking or under cover. **2.** *Colloq.* a quiet or secret pursuit of any object.

still-hunt (stĭl′hŭnt′), *U.S.* *—v.t.* **1.** to pursue by a still hunt. *—v.i.* **2.** to carry on a still hunt.

stilliform (stĭl′ĭ fôm′), *adj.* drop-shaped. [f. *stilli-* (comb. form of L *stilla* drop) + -FORM]

still life, *pl.* **still lifes.** a picture representing inanimate objects, such as fruit, flowers, etc. **—still′-life′,** *adj.*

stillness (stĭl′nĭs), *n.* **1.** absence of motion. **2.** quiet; silence; hush.

stillroom (stĭl′ro͝om′, -ro͞om′), *n.* **1.** (in a hotel) a room in which tea, coffee, etc., are prepared. **2.** (in a large house) a room in which preserves, etc., are kept and tea, coffee, etc., prepared.

Stillson wrench (stĭl′sən), **1.** a monkey-wrench with a pivoted adjustable jaw that grips pipes, etc., more tightly when pressure is exerted on the handle. **2.** a trademark for such a wrench.

Stillson wrench

stilly (*adv.* stĭl′lĭ; *adj.* stĭl′ĭ), *adv.* **1.** quietly; silently. *—adj.* **2.** *Poetic.* still; quiet.

stilt (stĭlt), *n.* **1.** one of two poles, each with a support for the foot at some distance above the ground. **2.** one of several high posts underneath any structure built above land or over water. **3.** any of various limicoline birds, esp. of the genus *Himantopus*, with very long legs, long neck, and slender bill, and living esp. in marshes. *—v.t.* **4.** to raise on or as on stilts. [ME *stilte*, c. LG *stilte*, Norw. *stilta* pole]

stilted (stĭl′tĭd), *adj.* **1.** stiffly dignified or formal, as speech, literary style, etc.; pompous. **2.** *Archit.* raised on or as on stilts: a stilted arch. **—stil′tedly,** *adv.* **—stil′tedness,** *n.*

Stilted arch

Stilton (stĭl′tən), *n.* a rich, waxy, white cheese, veined with mould. [after *Stilton* in Huntingdonshire]

Stilwell (stĭl′wəl), *n.* **Joseph W.,** 1883–1946, U.S. general.

Stimson (stĭm′sən), *n.* **Henry Lewis,** 1867–1950, U.S. statesman: secretary of war 1911–13, 1940–45; secretary of state 1929–33.

stimulant (stĭm′yo͞o lənt), *n.* **1.** *Physiol., Med.* something that temporarily quickens some vital process or the functional activity of some organ or part. **2.** any beverage or food that stimulates. **3.** *Rare.* a stimulus or incentive. *—adj.* **4.** *Physiol., Med.* temporarily quickening some vital process or functional activity. **5.** stimulating. [t. L: s. *stimulans*, ppr., stimulating, inciting]

stimulate (stĭm′yo͞o lāt′), *v.,* **-lated, -lating.** *—v.t.* **1.** to rouse to action or effort, as by pricking or goading; spur on; incite: *to stimulate production.* **2.** *Physiol., Med., etc.* to excite (an organ, etc.) to its functional activity. **3.** to invigorate by an alcoholic or other stimulant. *—v.i.* **4.** to act as a stimulus or stimulant. [t. L: m. s. *stimulātus*, pp., goaded on] **—stim′ula′tor,** *n.* **—stim′ula′tion,** *n.* **—Syn. 1.** See **animate.**

stimulated emission, *Physics.* the process by which a photon is emitted by an atom in an excited quantum state, as the result of the impact from outside of a photon of exactly equal energy: it is on this principle that masers and lasers work.

stimulative (stĭm′yo͞o lə tĭv), *adj.* **1.** serving to stimulate. *—n.* **2.** a stimulating agency.

stimulus (stĭm′yo͞o ləs), *n., pl.* **-li** (-lī′), **-luses. 1.** something that incites to action or exertion, or quickens action, feeling, thought, etc.; an incentive. **2.** *Physiol., etc.* something that excites an organism or part to functionable activity. [NL, special use of L *stimulus* goad, sting]

sting (stĭng), *v.,* **stung, stinging,** *n.* *—v.t.* **1.** to prick or wound with some sharp-pointed, often venom-bearing, organ, with which certain animals are furnished: *to be stung by a bee.* **2.** to affect painfully or irritatingly, esp. as a result of contact with certain plants: *to be stung by nettles.* **3.** to cause mental or moral suffering: *to be stung with remorse.* **4.** to goad or drive as by sharp irritation. **5.** *Slang.* to obtain money from, esp. by overcharging. *—v.i.* **6.** to use or have a sting, as bees. **7.** to cause a sharp, smarting pain, as some plants, an acrid liquid or gas, etc. **8.** to cause acute mental pain or irritation, as annoying thoughts, etc. **9.** to feel acute mental pain or irritation. **10.** to feel a smarting pain, as from the sting of an insect or from a blow.
—n. **11.** the act of stinging. **12.** a wound, pain, or smart caused by stinging. **13.** any sharp or smarting wound, hurt, or pain (physical or mental). **14.** anything, or an element in anything, that wounds, pains, or irritates: *to feel the sting of defeat.* **15.** capacity to wound or pain. **16.** a sharp stimulus or incitement: *driven by the sting of jealousy.* **17.** *Bot.* a glandular hair on certain plants, as nettles, which emits an irritating fluid. **18.** *Zool.* any of various sharp-pointed, often venom-bearing, organs of insects and other animals, capable of inflicting painful or dangerous wounds.
[ME; OE *stingan*, c. Icel. *stinga*]

stingaree (stĭng′ə rē′, stĭng′ə rē′), *n.* *U.S., Austral.* a stingray. [alter. of STINGRAY]

stinger (stĭng′ə), *n.* **1.** one who or that which stings. **2.** an animal or plant that stings. **3.** the sting of an insect or the like. **4.** *Colloq.* a stinging blow, remark, or the like. **5.** *U.S.* a cocktail of brandy and a liqueur.

stinging hair, *Bot.* a sting.

stinging nettle, nettle.

stingo (stĭng′gō), *n.* **1.** a strong beer. **2.** energy; vigour.

stingray (stĭng′rā′), *n.* any of the rays, esp. of the family *Dasyatidae*, having a long, flexible tail armed near the base with a strong, serrated bony spine, with which they can inflict severe and very painful wounds.

Stingray, *Dasyatis pastinaca* (Up to ab. 8 ft long)

stingy[1] (stĭn′jĭ), *adj.,* **-gier, -giest. 1.** reluctant to give or spend; niggardly; penurious. **2.** scanty or meagre. [orig. meaning 'having a sting', 'bad-tempered', der. d. *stinge* sting, OE *steng*] **—stin′gily,** *adv.* **—stin′giness,** *n.*

stingy[2] (stĭng′ĭ), *adj.* having a sting. [f. STING + -Y[1]]

stink (stĭngk), *v.,* **stank** or **stunk, stunk, stinking,** *n.* *—v.i.* **1.** to emit a strong offensive smell. **2.** to be in extremely bad repute or disfavour. **3.** *Slang.* to be very inferior in quality. **4.** *Slang.* to have a large quantity of something, esp. money (usually fol. by *of* or *with*). *—v.t.* **5. stink out, a.** to cause to stink. **b.** to repel, drive out, etc., by an offensive smell. *—n.* **6.** a strong offensive smell; stench. **7.** *Colloq.* a commotion; fuss; scandal. **8.** (*pl.*) *Schoolboy Slang.* chemistry. [ME; OE *stincan*, c. D and LG *stinken.* Cf. STENCH] **—stink′ing,** *adj.* **—stink′ingly,** *adv.*

stink bomb, a small bomb which emits a foul smell when it explodes.

stinker (stĭng′kə), *n.* **1.** one who or that which stinks. **2.** *Slang.* a dishonourable, disgusting, or objectionable person. **3.** any device emitting a stink, as a bomb, pot, etc. **4.** any of several large petrels. **5.** *Slang.* something difficult, as a task, problem, etc.

stinkhorn (stĭngk′hôn′), *n.* any of various ill-smelling fungi of the basidiomycetous genus *Phallus*, esp. *P. impudicus.*

stinking (stĭng′kĭng), *adj.* **1.** foul-smelling. **2.** *Slang.* disgusting; disgraceful. **3.** *Slang.* drunk. **4.** *Slang.* very rich.

stinking iris, gladdon.

stinking smut, a type of smut on wheat; bunt.

stinkpot (stĭngk′pŏt′), *n.* **1.** a jar containing combustibles, etc., which generate offensive and suffocating vapours; formerly used in warfare. **2.** *Slang.* one who or that which stinks.

stinkstone (stĭngk′stōn′), *n.* any of various stones which emit a fetid smell on being struck or rubbed, as from embedded decomposed organic matter.

stink trap, trap[1] (def. 5).

stinkweed (stĭngk′wēd′), *n.* any of various ill-smelling plants, as the jimson weed.

stinkwood (stĭngk′wo͝od′), *n.* **1.** one of several trees or shrubs with fetid wood, esp. *Ocotea bullata* of southern

Africa, used for furniture. **2.** the wood of any of these trees or shrubs.

stint[1] (stĭnt), *v.t.* **1.** to limit to a certain amount, number, share, or allowance, often unduly; set limits to; restrict. **2.** *Archaic.* to discontinue, cease, or bring to an end. —*v.i.* **3.** to be sparing or frugal; get along on a scanty allowance. **4.** *Archaic and Dial.* to cease action; desist. —*n.* **5.** limitation or restriction, esp. as to amount: *to give without stint.* **6.** a limited or prescribed quantity, share, rate, etc.: *to exceed one's stint.* **7.** an allotted amount or piece of work: to do one's daily stint. **8.** *Obs.* a stop; halt. [ME; OE *styntan* make blunt, dull, c. Icel. *stytta* shorten. Cf. STUNT, v.] —**stint′er,** *n.* —**stint′ingly,** *adv.*

stint[2] (stĭnt), *n.* any of various small shorebirds, esp. the **little stint,** *Erolia minuta,* of Europe. [orig. obscure]

stipe (stīp), *n.* **1.** *Bot.* a stalk or slender support, as the petiole of a fern frond, the stem supporting the pileus of a mushroom, or a stalklike elongation of the receptacle of a flower. **2.** *Zool.* a stemlike part, as a footstalk; a stalk. [t. F, t. L: m. *stīpes* log, post]

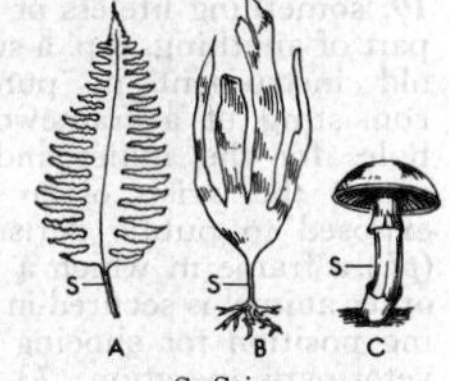

S, Stipe
A, Fern; B, Kelp; C, Mushroom

stipel (stī′pl), *n. Bot.* a secondary stipule situated at the base of a leaflet of a compound leaf. [t. NL: m. s. *stipella,* dim. of L *stipula.* See STIPULE] —**stipellate** (stī pĕl′ĭt, -āt), *adj.*

stipend (stī′pĕnd), *n.* fixed or regular pay; periodic payment; salary. [ME *stipendy,* t. L: m. s. *stipendium*]

stipendiary (stī pĕn′dyə rĭ), *adj., n., pl.* **-ries.** —*adj.* **1.** receiving a stipend; performing services for regular pay. **2.** paid for by a stipend, as services. **3.** pertaining to or of the nature of a stipend. —*n.* **4.** one who receives a stipend.

stipendiary magistrate, a legally qualified paid magistrate who may do alone all acts authorized to be done by two justices of the peace.

stipes (stī′pēz), *n., pl.* **stipites** (stĭp′ĭ tēz′). **1.** *Zool.* the second joint in a maxilla of crustaceans and insects. **2.** *Bot.* a stipe. [t. L: log, post]

stipitate (stĭp′ĭ tāt′), *adj.* having, or supported by, a stipe: *a stipitate ovary.* [t. NL: m. s. *stīpitātus,* f. s. *stīpes* STIPE + *-ātus* -ATE[1]]

stipitiform (stĭp′ĭ tĭ fôm′), *adj.* having the form of a stipe.

stipple (stĭp′l), *v.,* **-pled, -pling,** *n.* —*v.t.* **1.** to paint, engrave, or draw by means of dots or small touches. —*n.* Also, **stip′pling. 2.** the method of painting, engraving, etc., by stippling. **3.** stippled work; a painting, engraving, or the like, executed by means of dots or small spots. [t. D: m. s. *stippelen,* freq. of *stippen* dot, speckle] —**stip′pler,** *n.*

stipulate[1] (stĭp′yo͝o lāt′), *v.,* **-lated, -lating.** —*v.i.* **1.** to make an express demand or arrangement (*for*), as a condition of agreement. —*v.t.* **2.** to arrange expressly or specify in terms of agreement: *to stipulate a price.* **3.** to require as an essential condition in making an agreement. **4.** to promise, in making an agreement. [t. L: m. s. *stipulātus,* pp.] —**stip′ula′tor,** *n.* —**stipulatory** (stĭp′yo͝o lə tə rĭ, -trĭ), *adj.*

stipulate[2] (stĭp′yo͝o lĭt, -lāt′), *adj.* having stipules. [f. STIPULE + -ATE[1]]

stipulation (stĭp′yo͝o lā′shən), *n.* **1.** the act of stipulating. **2.** something stipulated; a condition in an agreement or contract.

stipule (stĭp′yo͞ol), *n. Bot.* one of a pair of lateral appendages, often leaf-like, at the base of a leaf petiole in many plants. [t. L: m. *stipula,* dim. of *stīpes.* See STIPE] —**stip′ular,** *adj.*

S, Stipule
A, Smilax; B, Dog rose; C, Pea; D, False acacia

stir[1] (stû), *v.,* **stirred, stirring,** *n.* —*v.t.* **1.** to move or agitate (a liquid, or any matter in separate particles or pieces) so as to change the relative position of component parts, as by passing an implement continuously or repeatedly through: *to stir one's coffee with a spoon.* **2.** to move, esp. in some slight way: *he would not stir a finger to help them.* **3.** to set in tremulous, fluttering, or irregular motion; shake: *leaves stirred by the wind.* **4.** to move briskly; bestir: *to stir oneself.* **5.** to rouse from inactivity, quiet, contentment, indifference, etc. (often fol. by *up*). **6.** to incite, instigate, or prompt (often fol. by *up*): *to stir up a people to rebellion.* **7.** to affect strongly; excite: *to stir pity, the heart, etc.* **8.** *Rare.* to bring up for notice or discussion. **9.** *Dial.* to disturb. —*v.i.* **10.** to move, esp. slightly or lightly: *not a leaf stirred.* **11.** to move about, esp. briskly. **12.** to be in circulation, current, or afoot: *is there any news stirring?* **13.** to become active, as from some rousing or quickening impulse. **14.** to be emotionally moved or strongly affected. —*n.* **15.** the act of stirring or moving, or the sound made. **16.** movement; brisk or busy movement. **17.** a state or occasion of general excitement; a commotion. **18.** a mental impulse, sensation, or feeling. **19.** a jog or thrust. [ME; OE *styrian,* akin to G *stören* disturb. Cf. STORM] —**Syn. 17.** fuss. See **ado.** —**Ant. 17.** quiet.

stir[2] (stû), *n. Slang.* a prison. [orig. unknown]

Stir., Stirlingshire.

stirabout (stû′rə bout′), *n.* a kind of porridge.

Stirling (stû′lĭng), *n.* **1.** a burgh in Scotland, the county town of Stirlingshire: a port on the river Forth. 27,553 (1961). **2.** Stirlingshire.

Stirling Range, a low mountain range in S Western Australia; highest point, Bluff Knoll, 3640 ft.

Stirlingshire (stû′lĭng shĭə′, -shə), *n.* a county in central Scotland. 194,858 pop. (1961); 466 sq. mi. *Co. town:* Stirling. Also, **Stirling.**

stirpiculture (stû′pĭ kŭl′chə), *n.* the production of special stocks or strains by careful breeding. [f. *stirpi-* (comb. form of STIRPS) + CULTURE] —**stir′picul′tural,** *adj.* —**stir′picul′turist,** *n.*

stirps (stûps), *n., pl.* **stirpes** (stû′pēz). **1.** a stock; a family, or a branch of a family; a line of descent. **2.** *Law.* one from whom a family is descended. **3.** *Bot. Obs.* a race or permanent variety. [t. L: stem, root, stock]

stirrer (stû′rə), *n.* **1.** one who or that which stirs. **2.** an implement or device for stirring something.

stirring (stû′rĭng), *adj.* **1.** that stirs; moving, active, bustling, or lively. **2.** rousing, exciting, or thrilling: *a stirring speech.* —**stir′ringly,** *adv.*

stirrup (stĭ′rəp), *n.* **1.** a loop, ring, or other contrivance of metal, wood, leather, etc., suspended from the saddle of a horse to support the rider's foot. **2.** any of various similar supports, or any of various clamps, etc., used for special purposes. **3.** *Naut.* a short rope with an eye at the end, hung from a yard to support a footrope, the footrope being rove through the eye. **4.** one of a series of vertical steel loops used in a reinforced concrete beam to resist shear. [ME; OE *stigrāp* (f. *stige* ascent + *rāp* ROPE), c. G *Stegreif*]

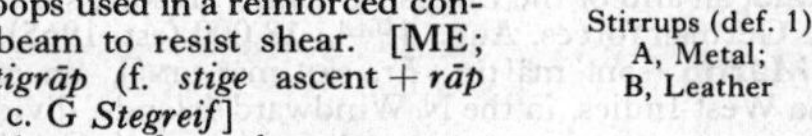

Stirrups (def. 1)
A, Metal; B, Leather

stirrup bone, *Anat.* the stapes.

stirrup cup, a farewell drink, esp. one offered to a rider already mounted for departure.

stirrup leather, the strap which holds the stirrup of a saddle.

stirrup pump, a small hand pump held steady by a foot bracket and used in fire fighting.

stitch[1] (stĭch), *n.* **1.** one complete movement of a threaded needle through a fabric or material such as to leave behind it a single loop or portion of thread, as in sewing, embroidery, surgical closing of wounds, etc. **2.** a loop or portion of thread disposed in place by one movement in sewing: *to rip out stitches.* **3.** a particular mode of disposing the thread in sewing, or the style of work produced. **4.** one complete movement of the needle or other implement used in knitting crocheting, netting, tatting, etc. **5.** the portion of work produced. **6.** a thread or bit of any fabric or of clothing, etc.: *every stitch of clothing.* **7.** a sudden, sharp pain, esp. in the intercostal muscles. —*v.t.* **8.** to work upon, join, or fasten with stitches; sew; ornament with stitches. **9.** to put staples through for fastening. —*v.i.* **10.** to make stitches; sew (by hand or machine). [ME *stiche,* OE *stice,* c. G *Stich* prick] —**stitch′er,** *n.*

stitch[2] (stĭch), *n. Dial.* a distance, as in walking. [OE *stycce* piece, short time, c. G *Stück*]

stitchwort (stĭch′wût′), *n.* any of certain herbs of the genus *Stellaria* (or *Alsine*), as *S. holostea,* an Old World white-flowered species. [f. STITCH[1] + WORT]

stithy (stĭth′ĭ), *n., pl.* **stithies,** *v.,* **stithied, stithying.** —*n.* **1.** an anvil. **2.** a forge or smithy. —*v.t.* **3.** *Archaic.* to forge. [ME *stithie,* var. of *stethie,* t. Scand.; cf. Icel. *stedhja* (acc.)]

stiver (stī′və), *n.* **1.** a former coin of the Netherlands of low value. **2.** a small amount of anything. [t. D: m. *stuiver*]

St James's Palace, 1. a palace in London: the royal residence from the time of Henry VIII until the accession of Victoria. **2.** the royal court of the United Kingdom. Also, **St James's.**

St John, 1. **Henry.** See **Bolingbroke, 1st Viscount.** 2. an island of the Virgin Islands, in the U.S. part of the group. 925 pop. (1960); ab. 20 sq. mi. 3. **Lake,** a lake in SE Canada, in Quebec province, draining into the Saguenay river. 365 mi. See also **Saint John.**

St Johns, a river in the U.S., flowing through NE Florida into the Atlantic. 276 mi.

St John's, 1. a seaport in and the capital of Newfoundland, in the SE part of the island. 90,838 (1961). 2. a seaport in the West Indies, the capital of Antigua, in the N part of the island. 21,637 (1961). Also, **St John.**

St-John's-wort (sənt jŏnz′ wûtʹ), *n.* any of various herbs or shrubs of the genus *Hypericum,* having yellow flowers and pellucid-dotted leaves.

St Joseph, a town in the U.S., in NW Missouri, on the Missouri river. 79,673 (1960).

St Kitts (sənt kĭts′), an island in the West Indies, in the N Windward Islands. 38,113 pop. (1960); 68 sq. mi. Also, **St Christopher.**

St Kitts-Nevis-Anguilla (sənt kĭts′nē′vĭs ăng gwĭl′ə), a British colony in the West Indies, in the Leeward Islands, comprising St Kitts, Nevis, Anguilla, and the islet of Sombrero. 56,693 pop. (1960); 155 sq. mi.

St Laurent (*Fr.* săN lō räN′), 1. **Louis Stephen,** born 1882, prime minister of Canada, 1948–57. 2. **Yves Mathieu,** (*Fr.* ēv mȧ tyœ′), born 1936, French couturier.

St Lawrence, 1. a river in SE Canada, flowing NE from Lake Ontario, draining the five Great Lakes into the Gulf of St Lawrence. ab. 760 mi. 2. **Gulf of,** an arm of the Atlantic between SE Canada and Newfoundland.

St Lawrence Seaway, a waterway system developed jointly by the U.S. and Canada to permit the passage of large ships from the Atlantic Ocean up the St Lawrence river through a series of canals and locks.

St Leger (sənt lĕj′ə), a horserace, founded 1776, run annually at Doncaster.

St Lô (*Fr.* săN lō′), a town in NW France, the capital of Manche department: World War II battle June-July 1944. 16,500 (est. 1966).

St Louis (sənt lo͞o′ĭ, -lo͞o′ĭs), a city in the U.S., in E Missouri: a port on the Mississippi. 750,026 (1960).

St Lucia (sənt lo͞o′shə), an island and British colony in the West Indies, in the central Windward Islands. 94,718 pop. (1960); 233 sq. mi. *Cap.:* Castries.

St Malo (*Fr.* săN mȧ lō′), a fortified seaport in NW France, in Ille-et-Vilame department, on the **Gulf of St Malo,** an arm of the English Channel: resort; surrendered by German forces, Aug., 1944. 18,000 (est. 1965).

St Martin (sənt mä′tĭn; *Fr.* săN mȧr tăN′), an island in the West Indies, in the N Windward Islands, divided into two parts: the N part is a dependency of Guadeloupe. 4502 pop. (1963); 20 sq. mi.; the S part belongs to the Netherlands Antilles. 3643 pop. (1963); 17 sq. mi. Dutch, **Sint Maarten.**

St Marylebone (sənt mĕə′rĭ lə bōn′, sənt mă′rə lə bən), a district of central London.

St Marys (sənt mĕə′rĭz), a river in N central U.S. and S Canada forming the boundary between NE Michigan and Ontario, flowing SE from Lake Superior into Lake Huron. ab. 60 mi. See **Sault Ste Marie Canals.**

St Michael and St George, an order of knighthood, founded 1818.

St Moritz (sənt mō′rĭts), a resort in SE Switzerland: a popular centre for winter sports. 3000 (est. 1964); 6037 ft high. German, **Sankt Moritz.**

St Nazaire (*Fr.* săN nȧ zĕr′), a seaport in W France, in Loire-Atlantique department, on the Loire estuary. 58,286 (1962).

St Niklaas (*Flem.* sĭnt nē klȧs′), a town in E Belgium, in N East Flanders province. 48,430 (est. 1964). French, **St Nicolas** (*Fr.* săN nē kō lȧ′).

stoa (stō′ə), *n., pl.* **stoae** (stō′ē), **stoas.** *Gk Archit.* a portico, usually a detached portico of considerable length, that is used as a promenade or meeting place. [t. Gk]

stoat (stōt), *n.* the ermine, *Mustela erminea,* of Europe, Asia and North America, esp. when in brown summer pelage. [ME *stote;* orig. unknown]

stochastic (stō kăs′tĭk), *adj. Statistics.* based on one item in the probability distribution of an ordered set of observations; conjectural. [t. Gk: m. s. *stochastikós,* der. *stóchos* mark, aim]

stock (stŏk), *n.* 1. an aggregate of goods kept on hand by a merchant, business firm, manufacturer, etc., for the supply of customers. 2. a quantity of something accumulated, as for future use: *a stock of provisions.* 3. livestock. 4. *Hort.* **a.** a stem, tree, or plant that furnishes slips or cuttings; a stock plant. **b.** a stem in which a graft is inserted and which is its support. 5. the trunk or main stem of a tree or other plant, as distinguished from roots and branches. 6. a rootstock. 7. the type from which a group of animals or plants has been derived. 8. a race or other related group of animals or plants. 9. the person from whom a given line of descent is derived; the original progenitor. 10. a line of descent; a tribe, race, or ethnic group. 11. *Ethnol.* a major division of mankind, as Caucasoid, Mongoloid, Negroid. 12. a group of languages having certain features in common and considered to be ultimately related. 13. *Zool.* a compound organism. 14. the handle of a whip, etc. 15. *Firearms.* **a.** the wooden or metal piece to which the barrel and mechanism of a rifle or like firearm are attached. **b.** a part of an automatic weapon, as a machine-gun, similar in position or function. 16. the stump of a tree left standing. 17. a log or block of wood. 18. a dull or stupid person. 19. something lifeless or senseless. 20. the main upright part of anything, esp. a supporting structure. 21. (*pl.*) an old instrument of punishment consisting of a framework with holes for the ankles and (sometimes) the wrists of an offender exposed to public derision. 22. (*pl.*) a frame in which a horse or other animal is secured in a standing position for shoeing or for a veterinary operation. 23. (*pl.*) the frame on which a boat rests while under construction. 24. a tool for holding dies used in cutting screw-threads on a rod. 25. the piece of metal or wood which constitutes the body of a carpenter's plane. 26. the raw material from which anything is made: *paper stock.* 27. *Cookery.* the liquor or broth prepared by boiling meat, fish, etc., with or without vegetables, etc., and used esp. as a foundation for soups, sauces, etc. 28. any of various widely cultivated cruciferous plants of the genus *Matthiola,* esp. *M. incana* and the **night-scented stock,** *M. bicornis.* 29. a collar or a neckcloth fitting like a band about the neck. 30. *Cards.* that portion of a pack of cards which, in certain games, is not dealt out to the players, but is left on the table, to be drawn from as occasion requires. 31. *Theat.* the repertoire of pieces produced by a stock company. 32. *Finance.* **a.** the capital of a company converted from fully paid shares. **b.** the shares of a particular company. **c.** capital stock. 33. a stocking. 34. repute; standing. 35. *Obs.* the part of a plough to which the irons, handles, etc., are attached. 36. **in stock,** available for use or sale. 37. **on the stocks,** under construction; in preparation. 38. **out of stock,** not available for use or sale. 39. **take stock, a.** to make an inventory of stock on hand. **b.** to make an appraisal of resources, prospects, etc. 40. **take** or **put stock in,** *U.S.* to put confidence in; trust; believe.

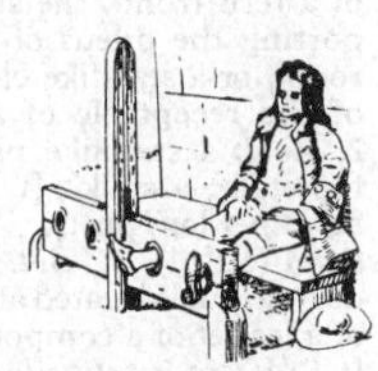
Stocks (def. 21)

—*adj.* 41. kept regularly on hand, as for use or sale; staple; standard: *stock articles.* 42. having as one's job the care of a concern's goods: *a stock clerk.* 43. of the common or ordinary type; in common use: *a stock argument.* 44. commonplace: *a stock remark.* 45. designating or pertaining to livestock raising: *stock farming.* 46. *Com.* of or pertaining to the stock of a company. 47. *Theat.* **a.** pertaining to repertory plays or pieces, or to a stock company. **b.** appearing together in a repertoire, as a company. **c.** forming part of a repertoire, as a play.

—*v.t.* 48. to furnish with a stock or supply. 49. to furnish with stock, as a farm with horses, cattle, etc. 50. to lay up in store, as for future use. 51. to fasten to or provide with a stock, as a rifle, plough, bell, anchor, etc. 52. *Obs.* to put in the stocks as a punishment.

—*v.i.* 53. to lay in a stock of something (often fol. by *up*). [ME; OE *stoc(c),* c. G *Stock*]

stockade (stō kād′), *n., v.,* **-aded, -ading.** —*n.* 1. *Fort.* a defensive barrier consisting of strong posts or timbers fixed upright in the ground. 2. an enclosure or pen made with posts and stakes. 3. *U.S.* a prison for military personnel. —*v.t.* 4. to protect, fortify, or encompass with a stockade. [t. F (obs.): m. *estocade,* ult. der. OPr. *estaca* stake, of Gmc orig. See STAKE[1]]

stock agent, *Austral., N.Z.* 1. a buyer and seller of stock. 2. a firm which supplies provisions to a stock station.

stock book, *Com.* a ledger for recording amounts of goods bought and sold.

stockbreeder (stŏk′brē′də), *n.* one who breeds and raises livestock.

stockbroker (stŏk′brō′kə), *n.* a broker who buys and sells stocks and shares for customers for a commission. —**stockbrokerage** (stŏk′brō′kə rĭj), **stock′brok′ing,** *n.*

stock car, 1. a car, esp. an old one, adapted for stock-car racing. 2. *U.S.* a cattle truck. —**stock′-car′,** *adj.*

stock-car racing (stŏk′kä′), a type of motor racing using stock cars, characterized by frequent collisions.

stock certificate, a certificate evidencing ownership of one or more shares of a company's stock.
stock company, 1. *U.S.* joint-stock company. 2. *U.S.* a repertory company.
stock dove, a wild pigeon of Europe, *Columba oenas.*
stock exchange, 1. (*often cap.*) a building or place where stocks and shares are bought and sold. 2. an association of brokers, jobbers, and dealers in stocks and bonds, who meet to transact business according to fixed rules.
stock farm, a farm devoted to breeding livestock. —**stock farmer.** —**stock farming.**
stockfish (stŏk′fĭsh′), *n., pl.* **-fishes,** (*esp. collectively*) **fish.** fish, as the cod or haddock, cured by splitting and drying in the air without salt.
Stockhausen (*Ger.* shtŏk′hou zən), *n.* **Karlheinz** (*Ger.* kärl′hīnts′), born 1928, German composer.
stockholder (stŏk′hōl′də), *n.* 1. *Chiefly U.S.* a shareholder. 2. *Austral.* an owner of livestock.
Stockholm (stŏk′hōm; *Sw.* stŏk′hŏlm), *n.* the capital and chief seaport of Sweden, in the SE part. 793,714 (1964).
stockhorse (stŏk′hôs′), *n. Austral.* a horse trained in the handling of stock.
stockinet (stŏk′ĭ nĕt′), *n.* an elastic machine-knitted fabric used in making undergarments, etc. [alter. of *stockinget,* f. STOCKING + -ET]
stocking (stŏk′ĭng), *n.* 1. a close-fitting covering, usually knitted (by hand or machine) and of wool, cotton, nylon, silk, etc., for the foot and leg. 2. something resembling such a covering. 3. **in one's stocking feet,** wearing socks or stockings but without shoes. [f. STOCK, n. (def. 33) + -ING[1]] —**stock′inged,** *adj.* —**stock′ingless,** *adj.*
stock-in-trade (stŏk′ĭn trād′), *n.* 1. goods, assets, etc., necessary for carrying on a business. 2. the abilities, resources, etc., characteristic of or belonging to a particular group: *eloquence is part of a salesman's stock in trade.*
stockish (stŏk′ĭsh), *adj.* like a block of wood; stupid.
stockist (stŏk′ĭst), *n.* one who keeps goods in stock.
stockjobber (stŏk′jŏb′ə), *n.* 1. a stock exchange dealer who acts as an intermediary between brokers and buyers but does not deal directly with the public. 2. *U.S.* a seller of stock, esp. of worthless securities. —**stock′job′bery, stock′job′bing,** *n.*
stockman (stŏk′mən), *n., pl.* **-men.** 1. *U.S., Austral.* a man who raises livestock. 2. a man employed on a stock farm. 3. *U.S.* a man in charge of a stock of goods.
stock market, a market where stocks and shares are bought and sold; a stock exchange.
stockpile (stŏk′pīl′), *n., v.* **-piled, -piling.** —*n.* 1. a supply of material, as a pile of gravel in road maintenance. 2. a large supply of essential materials, held in reserve for use during a period of shortage, etc. 3. a supply of munitions, weapons, etc., accumulated for possible future use. —*v.t.* 4. to accumulate for future use. —*v.i.* 5. to accumulate in a stockpile. —**stock′pil′er,** *n.*
Stockport (stŏk′pôt′), *n.* a town in England, in Cheshire. 142,543 (1961).
stockpot (stŏk′pŏt′), *n.* a pot in which stock for soup, etc., is made and kept.
stock raising, the breeding and rearing of different kinds of livestock. —**stock raiser.**
stockrider (stŏk′rī′də), *n. Austral.* a man employed to look after stock.
stockroom (stŏk′ro͞om′, -ro͝om′), *n.* a room in which a stock of materials or goods is kept for use or sale.
stock-route (stŏk′ro͞ot′), *n. Austral., N.Z.* a right of way for travelling cattle, sheep, etc.
stock-still (stŏk′stĭl′), *adj.* motionless.
stocktaking (stŏk′tā′kĭng), *n.* 1. the examination and listing of goods, assets, etc., in a shop, business, etc. 2. a reappraisal or reassessment of one's position, progress, prospects, etc.
Stockton-on-Tees (stŏk′tən ŏn tēz′), *n.* an industrial town in England, in Durham. 81,274 (1961).
stockwhip (stŏk′wĭp′), *n., v.,* **-whipped, -whipping,** *Austral., N.Z.* —*n.* 1. a long, bullock-hide whip used in handling stock. —*v.t.* 2. to control (cattle, etc.) with a stockwhip.
stocky (stŏk′ĭ), *adj.,* **-ier, -iest.** 1. of solid and sturdy form or build; thickset (and often short). 2. having a strong, stout stem, as a plant. —**stock′ily,** *adv.* —**stock′iness,** *n.*
stockyard (stŏk′yäd′), *n.* 1. an enclosure with pens, sheds, etc., connected with a slaughterhouse, railway, market, etc., for the temporary keeping of cattle, sheep, swine, or horses. 2. a yard for livestock.
stodge (stŏj), *n., v.,* **stodged, stodging.** *Colloq.* —*n.* 1. heavy, indigestible, and unappetizing food. 2. uninteresting or difficult reading matter. —*v.t.* 3. to stuff full with food, etc. —*v.i.* 4. to stuff oneself full of food. [b. STUFF and GORGE]
stodgy (stŏj′ĭ), *adj.,* **-ier, -iest.** 1. heavy, dull, or uninteresting; tediously commonplace. 2. of a thick, semisolid consistency; heavy, as food. 3. stocky; thickset. —**stodg′ily,** *adv.* —**stodg′iness,** *n.*
stoechiology (stē′kĭ ŏl′ə jĭ), *n.* stoichiology. —**stoechiological** (stē′kĭ ə lŏj′ĭ kl), *adj.*
stoechiometry (stē′kĭ ŏm′ĭ trĭ), *n.* stoichiometry.
stoep (sto͞op), *n.* (in South Africa) a raised platform or veranda at the front (and sometimes at the side) of a house. [t. Afrikaans]
stogey (stō′gĭ), *n., pl.* **-gies.** stogy.
stogy (stō′gĭ), *n., pl.* **-gies.** *U.S.* 1. a long, slender, roughly made, inexpensive cigar. 2. a coarse, heavy boot or shoe. Also, **stogie.** [earlier *stoga,* short for *Conestoga,* name of a Pennsylvania town]
Stoic (stō′ĭk), *adj.* 1. of or pertaining to the school of philosophy founded by Zeno, who taught that men should be free from passion, unmoved by joy or grief, and submit without complaint to unavoidable necessity. 2. (*l.c.*) stoical. —*n.* 3. a member or adherent of the Stoic school of philosophy. 4. (*l.c.*) one who maintains or affects a mental attitude of austere fortitude. [ME, t. L: s. *stōicus,* t. Gk: m. *stōïkós,* der. *stoá* a porch, specifically the porch in Athens where Zeno lectured]
Stoica (*Rum.* stoy′kȧ), *n.* **Chivu** (kē vo͞o′), born 1908, Rumanian statesman: president of the Rumanian State Council 1965–67.
stoical (stō′ĭ kl), *adj.* 1. impassive; characterized by calm or austere fortitude, suggesting, or befitting the Stoics, as in repression of emotion: *a stoical sufferer.* 2. (*cap.*) of or pertaining to the Stoics. —**sto′ically,** *adv.* —**sto′icalness,** *n.*
stoicheiology (stoi′kĭ ŏl′ə jĭ), *n.* stoichiology. —**stoicheiological** (stoi′kĭ ə lŏj′ĭ kl), *adj.*
stoicheiometry (stoi′kĭ ŏm′ĭ trĭ), *n.* stoichiometry.
stoichiology (stoi′kĭ ŏl′ə jĭ), *n.* a physiological study of the cellular components of tissues. Also, **stoechiology.** —**stoichiological** (stoi′kĭ ə lŏj′ĭ kl), *adj.*
stoichiometric (stoi′kĭ ə mĕt′rĭk), *adj. Chem.* 1. of or pertaining to stoichiometry. 2. (of a compound) containing its component elements in the exact proportions represented by its formula. 3. (of a mixture) yielding on complete reaction a stoichiometric compound. Also, **stoichiometrical.**
stoichiometry (stoi′kĭ ŏm′ĭ trĭ), *n. Chem.* 1. the calculation of the quantities of chemical elements or compounds involved in chemical reactions. 2. the branch of chemistry dealing with relationships of combining elements, esp. quantitatively. Also, **stoechiometry.** [f. m. Gk *stoicheio-* (comb. form of *stoicheîon* component) + -METRY]
Stoicism (stō′ĭ sĭz′əm), *n.* 1. the philosophy of the Stoics. 2. (*l.c.*) conduct conforming to the precepts of the Stoics; repression of emotion; indifference to pleasure or pain. —**Syn.** 2. See **patience.**
stoke[1] (stōk), *v.,* **stoked, stoking.** —*v.t.* 1. to poke, stir up, and feed (a fire). 2. to tend the fire of (a furnace, esp. one used with a boiler to generate steam for an engine); supply with fuel. —*v.i.* 3. to shake up the coals of a fire. 4. to tend a fire or furnace; act as a stoker: *to make a living by stoking.* [back-formation from STOKER]
stoke[2] (stōk), *n. Physics.* a unit of viscosity equal to the viscosity of a fluid in poises divided by its density in grams per cubic centimetre. [named after Sir George *Stokes,* 1819–1903, British physicist]
stokehold (stōk′hōld′), *n. Naut.* the space or compartment containing the furnaces, boilers, etc., of a ship.
stokehole (stōk′hōl′), *n.* 1. a compartment where furnace fires are worked, as in a steamship. 2. a hole through which a furnace is stoked.
Stoke Newington, a district of the NE inner London borough of Hackney.
Stoke-on-Trent (stōk′ŏn trĕnt′), *n.* a town in England, in Staffordshire: pottery. 265,306 (1961).
Stoke Poges (stōk′pō′jĭs), a village in England, in Buckinghamshire: the churchyard here is probably the scene of Gray's *Elegy.*
stoker (stō′kə), *n.* 1. one who or that which stokes. 2. one employed to tend a furnace used in generating steam, as on a locomotive or a steamship. 3. a mechanical device for supplying solid fuel to a furnace. [t. D, der. *stoken* feed a fire]
Stokes' law (stōks), *Physics.* the law which states that a small sphere falling under the action of gravity through a viscous medium reaches a constant velocity which is proportional to the square of the diameter of the sphere, and the difference between the density of the sphere and the medium through which it is falling: it is inversely proportional to the viscosity of the viscous medium. [see STOKE[2]]
Stokowski (stə kŏf′skĭ), *n.* **Leopold Antoni Stanislaw**

(lĭə′pōld ăn′tə nĭ stăn′ĭ slăv′), born 1882, U.S. orchestral conductor, born in England.

STOL (stŏl), *n. Aeron.* an aircraft capable of taking off and landing within a relatively short distance. [*S(hort) T(ake)-O(ff and) L(anding)*]

stole¹ (stōl), *v.* pt. of **steal.**

stole² (stōl), *n.* **1.** an ecclesiastical vestment, a narrow strip of silk or other material worn over the shoulders (by deacons, over the left shoulder only) and hanging down in front to the knee or below. **2.** a collar of fur, marabou, or the like, extending downwards in front, worn by women. **3.** *Archaic.* a long robe, esp. one worn by Roman matrons. [ME and OE, t. L: m. *stola*, t. Gk: m. *stolḗ* clothing, robe]

stolen (stō′lən), *v.* pp. of **steal.**

stolid (stŏl′ĭd), *adj.* not easily moved or stirred mentally; impassive; unemotional. [t. L: s. *stolidus*] —**stolidity** (stŏ lĭd′ĭ tĭ), **stol′idness,** *n.* —**stol′idly,** *adv.*

stolon (stō′lŏn), *n.* **1.** *Bot.* **a.** a slender branch or shoot, usually a runner or prostrate stem, which takes root at the tip and eventually develops into a new plant. **b.** a rhizome, as of some grasses, used for vegetative reproduction. **2.** *Zool.* a rootlike extension in a compound organism, usually giving rise to new zooids by budding. [t. L: s. *stolo*]

S, Stolon (def. 1a) of wild strawberry, *Fragaria vesca*

stoloniferous (stō′lō nĭf′ərəs), *adj. Bot., Zool.* producing stolons.

stoma (stō′mə), *n., pl.* **stomata** (stō′mə tə, stŏm′ə tə). **1.** *Bot.* any of various small apertures, esp. one of the minute orifices or slits in the epidermis of leaves, etc. **2.** *Zool.* a mouth or ingestive opening, esp. when in the form of a small or simple aperture. [NL, t. Gk: mouth]

stomach (stŭm′ək), *n.* **1.** (in man and other vertebrates) **a.** a saclike enlargement of the alimentary canal, forming an organ of storage, dilution, and digestion. **b.** such an organ, or an analogous portion of the alimentary canal, when divided into two or more sections or parts, or any one of these sections. **2.** any analogous digestive cavity or tract in invertebrates. **3.** the part of the body containing the stomach; the belly or abdomen. **4.** appetite for food. **5.** desire, inclination, or liking. **6.** *Obs.* spirit or courage. **7.** *Obs.* pride. **8.** *Obs.* resentment or anger. —*v.t.* **9.** to take into or retain in the stomach. **10.** to endure or tolerate. **11.** *Obs.* to be offended at or resent. [ME *stomak*, t. OF: m. *estomac*, t. L: m. *stomachus*, t. Gk: m. *stómachos* throat, gullet, stomach]

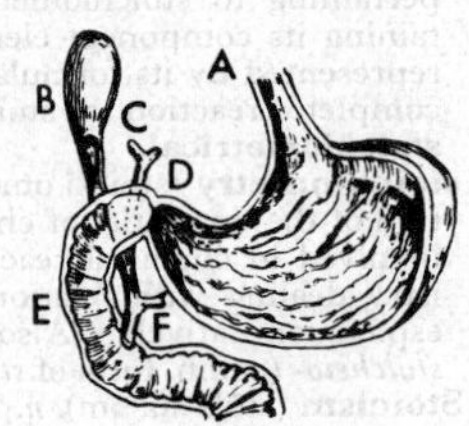

Human stomach (def. 1a) A, Oesophagus; B, Gall Bladder; C, Biliary duct; D, Pylorus; E, Duodenum; F, Pancreatic duct

stomach-ache (stŭm′ək āk′), *n.* a pain in the stomach or abdomen; gastralgia; colic.

stomacher (stŭm′ə kə), *n.* an ornamented article of dress for covering the stomach and chest, formerly worn by both men and women; esp. one worn by women under a bodice.

Stomacher

stomachic (stə măk′ĭk), *adj.* Also, **stomach′ical. 1.** of or pertaining to the stomach; gastric. **2.** beneficial to the stomach; stimulating gastric digestion; sharpening the appetite. —*n.* **3.** a stomachic agent or drug.

stomach pump, a small pump or syringe used for withdrawing the contents of the stomach, or for injecting into the stomach.

stomach worm, a nematode worm of the family *Trichostrongylidae, Haemonchus contortus*, parasitic in sheep and related animals; wireworm.

stomachy (stŭm′ə kĭ), *adj. Dial.* **1.** easily angered or offended. **2.** having a large stomach.

stomata (stō′mə tə, stŏm′ə tə), *n.* pl. of **stoma.**

stomatal (stō′mə tl, stŏm′ə tl), *adj.* **1.** of, pertaining to, or of the nature of a stoma. **2.** having stomata.

stomatic (stō măt′ĭk), *adj.* **1.** pertaining to the mouth. **2.** acting as a remedy for diseases of the mouth, as a drug. **3.** stomatal.

stomatitis (stō′mə tī′tĭs, stŏm′ə-), *n. Pathol.* inflammation of the mouth. [NL, f. Gk: s. *stóma* mouth + *-ītis* -ITIS]

stomato-, a word element referring to the mouth, as in *stomatoplasty.* Also, before vowels, **stomat-.** [t. Gk, comb. form of *stóma* mouth]

stomatology (stō′mə tŏl′ə jĭ, stŏm′ə-), *n.* the science dealing with the mouth and its diseases.

stomatoplasty (stŏm′ə tə plăs′tĭ, stō′mə-), *n.* plastic surgery of the mouth.

stomatopod (stŏm′ə tə pŏd′, stō′mə-), *n.* any of the *Stomatopoda*, an order of crustaceans having some of the legs close to the mouth and having the gills borne on the abdominal segments.

stomatous (stŏm′ə təs, stō′mə-), *adj.* stomatal.

-stome, a word element referring to the mouth, as in *cyclostome.* [comb. form repr. (1) Gk *stóma* mouth, (2) Gk *stómion* little mouth]

stomodaeum (stō′mə dē′əm, stŏm′ə-), *n., pl.* **-daea** (-dē′ə). *Embryol.* the part of the primary oral cavity which begins as an invagination of the ectoderm. Also, **stomodeum.** [NL: f. *stom-* (see -STOME) + *odaeum* (t. Gk: m. *hodaîon*, neut., on the way)] —**sto′modae′al,** *adj.*

-stomous, an adjectival suffix corresponding to **-stome,** as in *monostomous.*

stomp (stŏmp), *n.* **1.** *U.S., Dial., or Colloq.* stamp. **2.** a kind of jazz music. **3.** a dance, usually characterized by stamping of the feet, done to such music. —*v.i.* **4.** *U.S., Dial., or Colloq.* to stamp. **5.** to perform the stomp. —*v.t.* **6.** *U.S., Dial., or Colloq.* to stamp.

-stomy, a combining form used in names of surgical operations for making an artificial opening. [t. Gk: m. s. *-stomia*, der. *stóma* mouth]

stone (stōn), *n., pl.* **stones** (*except* **stone** for def. 6), *adj., v.,* **stoned, stoning.** —*n.* **1.** the hard substance of which rocks consist. **2.** a particular kind of rock. **3.** a piece of rock of definite size, shape, etc., for a particular purpose. **4.** a piece of rock of small or moderate size. **5.** precious stone. **6.** a British unit of weight of varying values, the principal being the avoirdupois stone of 14 lbs. **7.** something resembling a small stone or pebble. **8.** any hard, stone-like seed. **9.** *Bot.* the hard endocarp of a drupe. **10.** *Med.* a calculous concretion in the body, as in the kidney, gall bladder, or urinary bladder. **11.** a gravestone or tombstone. **12.** a grindstone. **13.** a millstone. **14.** a hailstone. **15.** a polished granite stone used in curling. **16.** a light grey or beige colour. **17.** *Print.* a table with a smooth surface used for composing page formes, formerly made of stone. **18.** a piece in the game of dominoes, backgammon, etc. **19.** (*pl.*) *Obs.* testicles. —*adj.* **20.** made of or pertaining to stone. **21.** made of stoneware: *a stone jug or bottle.* —*v.t.* **22.** to throw stones at; drive by pelting with stones. **23.** to put to death by pelting with stones. **24.** to provide or fit with stones, as by paving, lining, facing, etc. **25.** to rub with or on a stone, as to sharpen, polish, smooth, etc. **26.** to free from stones, as fruit. **27.** *Obs.* to turn into stone; petrify. [ME; OE *stān*, c. G *Stein*] —**stone′less,** *adj.* —**ston′er,** *n.*

Stone Age, the time during which early man lived and made implements of stone, chiefly of flint; it corresponds to the Pleistocene and Holocene epochs up to the beginning of the Bronze Age.

stone-bass (stōn′băs′), *n.* a deep-water sea-perch, *Polyprion cernium*, up to 6 feet long, found chiefly in the Mediterranean Sea and S Atlantic Ocean.

stone-blind (stōn′blīnd′), *adj.* completely blind. —**Syn.** See **blind.**

stone-bramble (stōn′brăm′bl), *n.* a rosaceous herb, *Rubus saxatilis*, widespread in stony places on hills in N temperate regions.

stone-broke (stōn′brōk′), *adj. U.S. Slang.* stony-broke.

stonechat (stōn′chăt′), *n.* any of various small, Old World, passerine birds, esp. of the genus *Saxicola*, as *S. torquata.* [f. STONE + *chat*, small bird so called because of its chattering cry]

stone-cold (stōn′kōld′), *adj.* as cold as stone; very cold; lifeless.

stonecrop (stōn′krŏp′), *n.* **1.** any plant of the genus *Sedum*, esp. a mosslike herb, *Sedum acre*, with small, fleshy leaves and yellow flowers, frequently growing on rocks and walls. **2.** any of various plants of related genera. [ME *stooncroppe*, OE *stāncrop.* See STONE, CROP]

stone curlew, any of various birds of the family *Burhinidae*, esp. *Burhinus oedicnemus* of Europe, Asia, and W Africa.

stonecutter (stōn′kŭt′ə), *n.* **1.** Also, **stone-dresser** (stōn′drĕs′ə). one who cuts or carves stone in preparation for building. **2.** a machine for cutting or dressing stone.

stoned (stōnd), *adj. Colloq.* completely drunk.

---

b., blend of, blended; c., cognate with; d., dialect, dialectal; der., derived from; f., formed from; g., going back to; m., modification of; r., replacing; s., stem of; t., taken from; ?, perhaps. See full key on inside front cover.

stone-dead (stōn′dĕd′), *adj.* completely lifeless; utterly dead.

stone-deaf (stōn′dĕf′), *adj.* completely deaf.

stonefish (stōn′fĭsh′), *n.* a highly venomous tropical fish, *Synanceja verrucosa,* resembling a piece of stone or coral.

stonefly (stōn′flī′), *n.* any of the insects constituting the order *Plecoptera,* whose larvae abound under stones in streams.

stone fruit, a fruit with a stone or hard endocarp, as a peach or a plum; a drupe.

stonehand (stōn′hănd′), *n. Print.* the printing craftsman responsible for imposing type prior to printing.

Stonehaven (stōn′hā′vən), *n.* a burgh in Scotland, the county town of Kincardine. 4500 (1961).

Stonehenge (stōn′hĕnj′), *n.* a prehistoric monument in S England, in Wiltshire, N of Salisbury, consisting of a large circle of megalithic posts and lintels.

stone-lily (stōn′lĭl′ĭ), *n.* a fossil crinoid.

stone-marten (stōn′mä′tĭn), *n.* a marten, *Mustela foina,* of Europe, Asia, and N Africa, having a white mark on the throat and breast.

stonemason (stōn′mā′sən), *n.* a dresser of or builder in stone. **—stone′ma′sonry,** *n.*

stone parsley, a biennial, umbelliferous herb, *Sison amomum,* a roadside plant of W Europe and the Mediterranean region.

stone's-throw (stōnz′thrō′), *n.* the distance a stone may be thrown; a short distance.

stonewall (stōn′wôl′), *v.i.* **1.** *Cricket.* (of a batsman) to play a defensive game only. *—v.t.* **2.** to obstruct, hinder, as the passage of a parliamentary bill. **—stone′wall′er,** *n.*

stoneware (stōn′wēə′), *n.* a more or less vitrified pottery ware, usually made from a single clay.

stonework (stōn′wûk′), *n.* **1.** work in stone; stone masonry. **2.** (*usually pl.*) an establishment where stone is prepared for building, etc. **—stone′work′er,** *n.*

stonewort (stōn′wût′), *n.* a green alga of the class *Charophyceae,* having a jointed plant body frequently encrusted with lime and usually growing in fresh water.

stonk (stŏngk), *n. Mil. Slang.* heavy shelling; a severe bombardment.

stonkered (stŏng′kəd), *adj. Austral., N.Z. Slang.* **1.** defeated; destroyed; overthrown. **2.** exhausted.

stony (stō′nĭ), *adj.*, **stonier, stoniest.** **1.** full of or abounding in stones or rock. **2.** pertaining to or characteristic of stone. **3.** resembling or suggesting stone, esp. hard like stone. **4.** unfeeling; merciless; obdurate. **5.** motionless or rigid; without expression, as the eyes or look. **6.** petrifying: *stony fear.* **7.** having a stone or stones, as a fruit. **8.** *Slang.* stony-broke. **—ston′ily,** *adv.* **—ston′iness,** *n.*

stony-broke (stō′nĭ brōk′), *adj. Slang.* having no money whatever.

stony coral, a true coral or madrepore consisting of numerous anthozoan polyps embedded in the calcareous material that they secrete.

stony-hearted (stō′nĭ hä′tĭd), *adj.* hard-hearted.

stood (stŏŏd), *v.* pt. and pp. of **stand.**

stooge (stōōj), *n., v.,* **stooged, stooging.** *—n.* **1.** *Colloq.* an entertainer who feeds lines to a comedian and is often the object of his ridicule. **2.** *Slang.* one who acts on behalf of another, esp. in obsequious or secretive fashion. *—v.i.* **3.** *Slang.* to act as a stooge. [orig. uncert.]

stook (stŏŏk), *n., v.t.* shock². [ME *stouk;* c. MLG *stūke,* G *Stauche* muff]

stool (stōōl), *n.* **1.** a seat, either low or high, without arms or a back, usually for a single person. **2.** a short, low support for resting the feet on, kneeling on, sitting on, etc. **3.** *Archaic.* a chair, seat, or position of authority. **4.** the stump, base, or root of a tree or other plant which has been cut down, from which new shoots or stems appear annually. **5.** the base of plants which annually produce new stems, etc. **6.** a cluster of shoots or stems springing up from a stool or from any root, or a single shoot or layer. **7.** *U.S.* a bird fastened as a decoy. **8.** *U.S.* a decoy duck or similar decoy. **9.** a privy. **10.** the mass of matter evacuated at each movement of the bowels. **11.** *U.S.* the sill of a window. **12. fall between two stools,** to fail to select either of two alternatives, as through indecision or hesitation. *—v.i.* **13.** to throw up shoots from the base or root, as a plant; form a stool. [ME; OE *stōl,* c. G *Stuhl*]

stool ball, a game similar to cricket, often played by women.

stool pigeon, **1.** a pigeon used as a decoy. **2.** *Chiefly U.S.* nark (def. 1). **3.** *Chiefly U.S. Slang.* a person employed as a decoy or secret confederate, as by gamblers.

stoop¹ (stōōp), *v.i.* **1.** to bend the head and shoulders, or the body generally, forwards and downwards from an erect position: *to stoop over a desk.* **2.** to carry the head and shoulders habitually bowed forwards: *to stoop from age.* **3.** to bend, bow, or lean (said of trees, precipices, etc.). **4.** to descend from one's level of dignity; condescend; deign. **5.** to lower oneself by undignified or unworthy behaviour. **6.** to swoop down, as a hawk at prey. **7.** *Rare.* to submit; yield. **8.** *Obs.* to come down from a height. *—v.t.* **9.** to bend (oneself, one's head, etc.) forwards and downwards. **10.** *Archaic.* to abase, humble, or subdue. *—n.* **11.** the act of stooping; a stooping movement. **12.** a stooping position or carriage of body. **13.** a descent from dignity or superiority; a condescension. **14.** a downward swoop, as of a hawk. [ME *stoupe,* OE *stūpian;* akin to STEEP¹]

stoop² (stōōp), *n.* stoep.

stoop³ (stōōp), *n. Archaic and Dial.* a post or pillar; support; prop.

stop (stŏp), *v.,* **stopped** or (*Poetic*) **stopt, stopping,** *n.* *—v.t.* **1.** to cease from, leave off, or discontinue: *to stop running.* **2.** to cause to cease; put an end to: *to stop noise in the street.* **3.** to interrupt, arrest, or check (a course, proceeding, process, etc.). **4.** to cut off, intercept, or withhold: *to stop supplies.* **5.** to restrain, hinder, or prevent (fol. by *from*): *to stop a person from doing something.* **6.** to prevent from proceeding, acting, operating, continuing, etc.: *to stop a speaker, a car, etc.* **7.** to block, obstruct, or close (a passageway, channel, opening, duct, etc.) (often fol. by *up*). **8.** to fill the hole or holes in (a wall, a decayed tooth, etc.). **9.** to close (a container, tube, etc.) with a cork, plug, bung, or the like. **10.** to close the external orifice of (the ears, nose, mouth, etc.). **11.** *Fencing, Boxing, etc.* **a.** to check (a stroke, blow, etc.); parry; ward off. **b.** to defeat by a knockout or the like. **12.** *Banking.* to notify a banker not to honour (a cheque) on presentation. **13.** *Bridge.* to have an honour card and a sufficient number of protecting cards to keep an opponent from continuing to win in (a suit). **14.** *Music.* **a.** to close (a fingerhole, etc.) in order to produce a particular note from a wind instrument. **b.** to press down (a string of a violin, etc.) in order to alter the pitch of the note produced from it. **c.** to insert the hand in (the bell of a horn) in order to alter the pitch and quality of the note. **d.** to produce (a particular note) by so doing. **15.** *Colloq.* to stay: *I stopped there for dinner.* *—v.i.* **16.** to come to a stand, as in a course or journey; halt. **17.** to cease moving, proceeding, speaking, acting, operating, etc.; to pause; desist. **18.** to cease; come to an end. *—v.* **19.** Some special verb phrases are:

stop by, to call somewhere briefly on the way to another destination.

stop down, *Photog.* to reduce the aperture size of (a camera).

stop off, to halt for a brief stay in a place before leaving for another destination.

stop over, *U.S.* to make a stopover.

—n. **20.** the act of stopping. **21.** a cessation or arrest of movement, action, operation, etc.; end. **22.** a stay or sojourn made at a place, as in the course of a journey. **23.** a place where buses or other vehicles halt. **24.** a closing or filling up, as of a hole. **25.** a blocking or obstructing, as of a passage or way. **26.** *Fencing.* the action of a fencer who stands still instead of parrying a blow and then thrusting, allowing his opponent to run on his sword. **27.** a plug or other stopper for an opening. **28.** an obstacle, impediment, or hindrance. **29.** any piece or device that serves to check or control movement or action in a mechanism. **30.** *Banking.* stop order. **31.** *Music.* **a.** the act of closing a finger hole, etc., or of pressing down a string, of an instrument, in order to produce a particular note. **b.** a device or contrivance, as on an instrument, for accomplishing this. **c.** (in an organ) a graduated set of pipes of the same kind and giving tones of the same quality. **d.** a knob or handle which is drawn out or pushed back to permit or prevent the sounding of such a set of pipes or to control some other part of the organ. **e.** a similar group of reeds on a reed organ. **32.** *Zool.* the angle between the forehead and the nose or the face of a mammal, esp. that of a dog. **33.** *Naut.* a piece of small line used to lash or fasten something, as a furled sail. **34.** *Phonet.* **a.** an articulation which interrupts the flow of air from the lungs. **b.** a consonant sound resulting from stop articulation: *p, b, t, d, k,* and *g* are the English stops. **35.** *Photog.* the aperture size of a lens, esp. as indicated by an f number. **36.** a full stop. **37.** the word 'stop' spelt out, and used instead of a full stop in telegraphic and cable messages. **38.** (*pl.*) a family of games in which a player continues to play cards in a certain sequence until he is stopped, and can no longer play. **39.** *Cards.* **a.** a card which interrupts the run of a sequence. **b.** *Bridge.* an honour card covered by a sufficient number of lesser cards to prevent an opponent from continuing to win a suit. [ME *stoppe,* OE *stoppian,* c. D and LG *stoppen,* G *stopfen,* all ult. t. VL. Cf. It. *stoppare* plug (with tow), der. *stoppa,* g. L *stuppa* tow, t. Gk: m. *stýppē*]

—Syn. 3. STOP, ARREST, CHECK, HALT imply causing a cessation of movement or progress (literal or figurative). STOP is the general term for the idea: *to stop a clock.* ARREST usually refers to stopping by imposing a sudden and complete restraint: *to arrest development.* CHECK implies bringing about an abrupt, partial, or temporary stop: *to check a trotting horse.* To HALT means to make a temporary stop, esp. one resulting from a command: *to halt a company of soldiers.* **17.** STOP, CEASE, PAUSE imply bringing movement, action, progress, or conditions to an end. STOP is used in speaking of objects in motion or action: *the clock stopped.* CEASE, a more literary and formal word, suggests the coming to an end of that which has had considerable duration: *a storm ceases.* PAUSE implies the prospect of resumption after a short interval: *one pauses in speaking.* —**Ant.** 3, 17. start, begin.

stopcock (stŏp′kŏk′), *n.* a valve, with a tapered plug operated by a handle, used to control the flow of a liquid or gas from a receptacle or through a pipe.

stopcylinder press (stŏp′sĭl′ĭn də), *Print.* a press in which the cylinder revolves only during the printing of the sheet and is stationary whilst the forme returns to print the next sheet.

stope (stōp), *n., v.,* **stoped, stoping.** —*n.* **1.** any excavation made in a mine to remove the ore which has been rendered accessible by the shafts and drifts. —*v.t., v.i.* **2.** to mine or work by stopes. [appar. akin to STEP, n.]

stoper (stō′pə), *n.* a rock drill, orig. one used for making stopes.

Stopes (stōps), *n.* **Marie Carmichael,** 1880–1958, English pioneer of birth control.

stopgap (stŏp′găp′), *n.* **1.** something that fills the place of something lacking; a temporary substitute; a makeshift. —*adj.* **2.** makeshift.

stop-go (stŏp′gō′), *Colloq.* —*n.* **1.** a period of successive inflation and deflation. —*adj.* **2.** of or pertaining to such a period: *stop-go policies.*

Stoph (*Ger.* shtōf), *n.* **Willi** (*Ger.* vĭl′ē), born 1914, chairman of the Council of Ministers of the German Democratic Republic since 1964.

stoping (stō′pĭng), *n. Geol.* the breaking off and assimilation of blocks of rock by an intruding magma, a process by which magmas move upwards through the earth's crust. Also, **magmatic stoping.** [pres. part. of STOPE]

stoplight (stŏp′līt′), *n.* brakelight.

stop order, *Banking.* an order, as by the drawer of a cheque, etc., not to make payment.

stopover (stŏp′ō′və), *n. U.S.* any brief stop in the course of a journey, esp. one with the privilege of proceeding later on the ticket originally issued.

stoppage (stŏp′ĭj), *n.* **1.** the act of stopping; cessation of activity, etc. **2.** the state of being stopped. **3.** the amount of anything stopped.

stop payment, an order by the drawer of a cheque to his bank not to pay a specified cheque.

stopped (stŏpt), *adj.* **1.** halted or checked. **2.** closed, filled up, or obstructed. **3.** *Music.* **a.** having the upper end plugged or closed, as an organ pipe. **b.** acted upon by stopping, as a string. **c.** produced by the stopping of a string, etc. **d.** having the bell stopped by the inserted hand, as in a French horn, to lower the pitch or to muffle the sound. **4.** *Phonet.* involving stop articulation.

stopper (stŏp′ə), *n.* **1.** one who or that which stops. **2.** a plug or piece for closing a bottle, tube, or the like. **3.** *Naut.* a short length of small or medium-sized Manila rope or light chain secured to a ringbolt or the like, used to hold a larger rope while it is being made fast permanently. —*v.t.* **4.** to close, secure, or fit with a stopper.

stopping (stŏp′ĭng), *n.* **1.** the action of one who or that which stops. **2.** *Mining.* a barrier erected to stop the passage of air, gas, fire, or an explosion. **3.** *Colloq.* a tooth filling.

stopping power, *Physics.* a measure of the ability of substance to reduce the kinetic energy of a charged particle passing through it. The **linear stopping power** is the energy lost per unit distance. The **mass stoppage power** is the linear stopping power divided by the density of the substance.

stopple (stŏp′l), *n., v.,* **-pled, -pling.** —*n.* **1.** a stopper for a bottle or the like. —*v.t.* **2.** to close or fit with a stopple.

stop press, **1.** news inserted in a newspaper after printing has begun. **2.** the space for this.

stopwatch (stŏp′wŏch′), *n.* a watch with a hand or hands that can be stopped or started at any instant, and which is adapted for indicating fractions of a second (used for timing races, etc.).

storage (stô′rĭj), *n.* **1.** the act of storing. **2.** the state or fact of being stored. **3.** capacity or space for storing. **4.** *Computers.* the capacity of a device to hold information. **5.** a place where something is stored. **6.** the price charged for storing goods.

storage battery, *Elect.* a battery of secondary cells used for storing electricity; an accumulator.

storage cell, *Elect.* a cell in a storage battery.

storage device, *Computers.* the memory of a computer.

storage heater, an appliance in which heat is stored when cheap or easily obtainable, and given out when expensive or unobtainable. Also, **heat reservoir.**

storax (stô′răks), *n.* **1.** any shrub or tree of the genus *Styrax*, having attractive white flowers. **2.** a solid resin with a vanilla-like scent obtained from a small styracaceous tree, *Styrax officinalis*, formerly much used in medicine and perfumery. **3.** a liquid balsam (**liquid storax**) obtained from species of liquidambar, esp. from the wood and inner bark of *Liquidambar orientalis* (**Levant storax**), a tree of Asia Minor, etc., and used in medicine, perfumery, etc. [t. L, t. Gk: m. *stýrax*]

store (stô), *n., v.,* **stored, storing.** —*n.* **1.** a large shop with many departments or branches. **2.** a supply or stock (of something), esp. one for future use. **3.** (*pl.*) supplies of food, clothing, or other requisites, as for a household or other establishment, a ship, naval or military forces, or the like. **4.** the state of being stored up, on hand, or in reserve: *to keep a thing in store.* **5.** *Chiefly U.S.* a shop. **6.** a storehouse or warehouse. **7.** measure of esteem or regard: *to set little store by a thing.* **8.** quantity, esp. great quantity; abundance, or plenty. **9.** a computer memory. **10. in store, a.** kept in readiness for future use. **b.** coming in the future: *she did not know what was in store for her.* **c.** deposited in a warehouse until needed.
—*v.t.* **11.** to supply or stock with something, as for future use. **12.** to lay up or put away, as a supply for future use (often with *up* or *away*). **13.** to deposit in a storehouse, warehouse, or other place, for keeping. [ME, aphetic var. of *astore*, t. OF: m. *estorer* build, furnish, stock, g. L *instaurāre* renew, restore, make] —**stor′able,** *adj.*

storehouse (stô′hous′), *n.* **1.** a house or building in which things are stored. **2.** any repository or source of abundant supplies, as of facts or knowledge.

storekeeper (stô′kē′pə), *n.* **1.** one who has charge of a store or stores. **2.** *Chiefly U.S.* a shopkeeper.

storeroom (stô′ro͞om′, -ro͝om′), *n.* **1.** a room in which stores are kept. **2.** room or space for storage.

storey (stô′rĭ), *n., pl.* **-reys.** **1.** a complete horizontal section of a building, having one continuous or approximately continuous floor. **2.** the set of rooms on the same floor or level of a building. **3.** each of the stages separated by floors, one above another, of which a building consists. Also, *Chiefly U.S.*, **story.** [ME, der. OF *estorer* build. See STORE]

storeyed (stô′rĭd), *adj.* having storeys or floors: *a two-storeyed house.* Also, *Chiefly U.S.*, **storied.** [f. STOREY + -ED[3]]

storied[1] (stô′rĭd), *adj.* **1.** recorded or celebrated in history or story. **2.** ornamented with designs representing historical, legendary or similar subjects. [f. STORY[1] + -ED[3]]

storied[2] (stô′rĭd), *adj. Chiefly U.S.* storeyed.

storiette (stô′rĭ ĕt′), *n. Chiefly U.S.* a very short story. Also, **storyette.** [dim. of STORY[1]. See -ETTE]

White stork, *Ciconia ciconia* (3 ft or more high, total length 3 ft)

stork (stôk), *n.* one of the long-legged, long-necked, long-billed wading birds, allied to the ibises and herons, which constitute the family *Ciconiidae*, esp. *Ciconia ciconia* (**white stork**) of Europe. [ME; OE *storc*, c. G *Storch*]

stork's-bill (stôks′bĭl′), *n.* any herbaceous plant of the geraniaceous genus *Erodium*, as *E. cicutarium*, the **common stork's-bill,** so called from the long-beaked fruit.

storm (stôm), *n.* **1.** a disturbance of the normal condition of the atmosphere, manifesting itself by winds of unusual force or direction, often accompanied by rain, snow, hail, thunder and lightning, or flying sand or dust. **2.** a heavy fall of rain, snow, or hail, or a violent outbreak of thunder, and lightning, unaccompanied by strong wind. **3.** *Meteorol.* a wind of Beaufort scale force 11, i.e., one about 68 miles per hour. **4.** a violent assault on a fortified place, strong position, or the like. **5.** a heavy descent or discharge of missiles, blows, or the like. **6.** a violent disturbance of affairs, as a civil, political, social, or domestic commotion. **7.** a violent outburst or outbreak: *a storm of applause.* **8. storm in a teacup,** a great deal of fuss arising out of a very unimportant matter. **9. take by storm, a.** to take by military assault. **b.** to captivate and overwhelm completely. —*v.i.* **10.** *Chiefly U.S.* to blow with unusual force, or to rain, snow, hail, etc., esp. with violence (used impersonally): *it stormed all day.* **11.** to rage or complain with violence or fury. **12.** to deliver a violent attack or fire, as with artillery. **13.** to rush to an assault or attack. **14.** to rush with angry violence: *to storm out of a room.* —*v.t.* **15.** to subject to or as to a storm. **16.** to utter or say with angry vehemence. **17.** to assault (a fortified place). [ME and OE, c. D *storm*, G *Sturm*]

Storm (*Ger.* shtŏrm), *n.* **Theodor Woldsen** (*Ger.* tė′ō dōr-vŏlt′sən), 1817–88, German poet and novelist.
Stormberg (stôm′bûg), *n.* a mountain range in the Republic of South Africa in the E of Cape Province. Highest peak, 7114 ft.
stormbound (stôm′bound′), *adj.* confined or detained by storms.
storm canvas, *Naut.* a set of storm sails.
storm cellar, *U.S.* a cellar or underground chamber for refuge during violent storms.
storm centre, **1.** the centre of a cyclonic storm, the area of lowest pressure and of comparative calm. **2.** a centre of disturbance, tumult, trouble, or the like.
storm-cloud (stôm′kloud′), *n.* a large black cloud, usually signifying that a storm is imminent.
storm-cock (stôm′kŏk′), *n.* the missel thrush.
storm door, *U.S.* an outer or additional door for protection against inclement weather, as during the winter.
stormer (stô′mə), *n.* one who storms.
storm jib, *Naut.* a small jib made of very strong canvas.
storm-lantern (stôm′lăn′tən), *n.* a lantern made so that the flame is protected against wind, rain, etc.
stormless (stôm′lĭs), *adj.* without storms.
stormproof (stôm′pro͞of′), *adj.* proof against storms or storming.
Storms (stômz), *n.* **Ocean of,** a large dark plain, *Oceanus Procellarum,* in the second and third quadrants of the face of the moon.
storm sail, *Naut.* a sail of very strong and heavy canvas of smaller dimensions than usual, set in gales and storms.
storm sewer, a channel providing additional drainage for times of heavy rain or flooding.
storm signals, *Naut.* signals in the form of flags, shapes, or lights exhibited at points round the coast to warn vessels of the approach of bad weather.
storm-trooper (stôm′tro͞o′pə), *n.* **1.** a member of a body of storm troops or shock troops. **2.** *German Hist.* a member of the Sturmabteilung; Brownshirt.
storm troops, shock troops.
storm window, a glass covering over a window, providing extra insulation and protection from cold and wind.
stormy (stô′mĭ), *adj.*, **stormier, stormiest. 1.** affected or characterized by, or subject to, storms; tempestuous: *a stormy sea.* **2.** characterized by violent commotion, actions, speech, passions, etc.: *a stormy debate.* **—storm′ily,** *adv.* **—storm′iness,** *n.*
stormy petrel, 1. Also, **storm petrel.** a small black-and-white bird, *Hydrobates pelagicus,* of the deep seas. **2.** a person whose coming is supposed to portend trouble.
Stornoway (stô′nə wā′), *n.* a town in N Scotland, in the Hebrides, on the island of Lewis. 5221 (1961).
Storting (stô′tĭng), *n.* the parliament of Norway, composed of the Lagting and the Odelsting. Also, **Storthing.** [t. Norw.: f. *stor* great + *ting* assembly]
story¹ (stô′rĭ), *n., pl.* **-ries,** *v.*, **-ried, -rying.** **—*n.* 1.** a narrative, either true or fictitious, in prose or verse, designed to interest or amuse the hearer or reader; a tale. **2.** a fictitious tale, shorter and less elaborate than a novel. **3.** such narratives or tales as a branch of literature. **4.** the plot, or succession of incidents of a novel, poem, drama, etc. **5.** a narration of a series of events, or a series of events that are or may be narrated. **6.** a narration of the events in the life of a person or the existence of a thing, or such events as a subject for narration. **7.** a report or account of a matter; a statement. **8.** *Journalism.* an account of some event, situation, etc., in a newspaper. **9.** *Colloq.* a lie; a fib. **10.** *Obs.* history. **—*v.t.* 11.** to ornament with pictured scenes, as from history or legend. **12.** *Rare.* to tell the history or story of; tell as a story. [ME, t. AF: m. *estorie,* g. L *historia*]
story² (stô′rĭ), *n., pl.* **-ries.** *Chiefly U.S.* storey.
storybook (stô′rĭ bo͝ok′), *n.* **1.** a book containing a story or stories, fiction or non-fiction, esp. for children. **—*adj.* 2.** of or pertaining to childish fiction: *he lives in a storybook world.*
storyette (stô′rĭ ĕt′), *n.* storiette.
storyteller (stô′rĭ tĕl′ə), *n.* **1.** one who tells stories. **2.** *Colloq.* one who tells fibs.
Storyville (stô′rĭ vĭl), *n.* a district of New Orleans, formerly a red-light area, well-known as the centre of jazz development at the beginning of the 20th century.
stoss (stŏs; *Ger.* shtōs), *adj. Geol.* denoting the end or side, as of a hill, drumlin, etc., that receives, or has received, the thrust of a glacier. [t. G: thrust, push]
stotinka (stō tĭng′kə), *n., pl.* **-ki** (-kĭ). a minor Bulgarian coin, the hundredth part of a lev. [t. Bulg.]
St-Ouen (*Fr.* săɴ twăɴ′), *n.* a town in France, N of Paris. 52,103 (1962).
stound¹ (stound), *Dial.* **—*n.* 1.** a state of amazement. **—*v.t.* 2.** to bewilder, shock, or stupefy. [ME; aphetic var. of ASTOUND]
stound² (stound), *n. Obs. except Dial.* **1.** a short time; a moment. **2.** a pang. [ME *stund,* OE; c. G *Stunde* hour]
stoup (sto͞op), *n.* **1.** a basin for holy water, as at the entrance of a church. **2.** *Scot.* a pail or bucket. **3.** *Archaic, Scot., and N Dial.* **a.** a drinking vessel of various sizes, as a cup or tankard. **b.** the amount it holds. [ME *stowpe,* t. Scand.; cf. Icel. *staup,* c. OE *stēap*]

Stoup (def. 1)

stour (stou′ə), *n.* **1.** *Scot. and N Dial.* **a.** a tumult or uproar. **b.** a storm; flying dust. **2.** *Obs.* an armed conflict; battle.
Stourbridge (stou′ə brĭj′), *n.* a town in England, in Worcestershire. 42,631 (1961).
stoush (stoush), *Austral. Slang.* **—*n.* 1.** a fight. **2. the big stoush,** World War I. **—*v.t.* 3.** to fight (someone or something). [var. of STASH]
stout (stout), *adj.* **1.** bulky in figure, solidly built, or thickset; corpulent or fat. **2.** bold, hardy, or dauntless: *a stout heart.* **3.** a firm; stubborn: *stout resistance.* **4.** strong of body, stalwart, or sturdy: *stout fellows.* **5.** having endurance or staying power, as a horse. **6.** strong in substance or construction. **7.** strong and thick or heavy. **—*n.* 8.** any of various beers darker and heavier than ales. [ME, t. OF: m. *estout* brave, proud, t. Gmc; cf. MLG *stolt*] **—stout′ly,** *adv.* **—stout′ness,** *n.*
—Syn. 1. STOUT, FAT, PLUMP imply corpulence of body. STOUT describes a heavily built but usually strong and healthy body: *a handsome stout lady.* FAT, an informal word with unpleasant connotations, suggests an unbecoming fleshy stoutness; it may, however, apply also to a hearty fun-loving type of stout person: *a fat old man, fat and jolly.* PLUMP connotes a pleasing roundness and is often used as a complimentary or euphemistic equivalent for stout, fleshy, etc.: *a plump figure attractively dressed.* **—Ant. 1.** thin, lean.
stout-hearted (stout′hä′tĭd), *adj.* brave and resolute; dauntless. **—stout′-heart′edly,** *adv.*
stove¹ (stōv), *n., v.,* **stoved, stoving.** **—*n.* 1.** an apparatus, portable or fixed, and in many forms, for furnishing heat, as for comfort, cooking, or mechanical purposes, commonly using coal, oil, gas, or electricity. **2.** a heated chamber or box for some special purpose, as a drying room, or a kiln for firing pottery. **—*v.t.* 3.** to apply heat to (metalware, etc.) in a kiln to fuse paint to its surface. [ME; OE *stofa* hot air bathroom, c. G *Stube* sitting room]
stove² (stōv), *v.* a pt. and pp. of **stave.**
stovepipe (stōv′pīp′), *n.* **1.** a pipe, as of sheet metal, serving as a stove chimney or to connect a stove with a chimney flue. **2.** *Colloq.* a stovepipe hat.
stovepipe hat, *Colloq.* a tall silk hat.
stover (stō′və), *n.* **1.** coarse roughage used as feed for livestock. **2.** *Chiefly U.S.* stalks and leaves, not including grain, of such forages as corn and sorghum. **3.** *Dial.* fodder minus the grain portion of the plant. [ME, t. OF: m. *estover* necessaries, ESTOVERS]
stow (stō), *v.t.* **1.** *Naut.* to place (cargo, etc.) in the hold or some other part of a ship. **2.** to put in a place or receptacle as for storage or reserve; pack. **3.** to fill (a place or receptacle) by packing. **4.** (of a place or receptacle) to afford room for; hold. **5.** *Slang.* to desist from. **6. stow it,** *Slang.* be quiet. **7.** *Obs.* to lodge or quarter. **8.** to put away, as in a safe or convenient place (fol. by *away*). **—*v.i.* 9. stow away,** to conceal oneself aboard a ship or other conveyance in order to get a free trip. [ME, der. *stowe* place, OE *stōw,* c. Icel. *-stō* (in *eldstō* fireplace)]
stowage (stō′ĭj), *n.* **1.** the act or operation of stowing. **2.** the state or manner of being stowed. **3.** room or accommodation for stowing something. **4.** a place in which something is or may be stowed. **5.** that which is stowed or to be stowed. **6.** a charge for stowing something.
stowaway (stō′ə wā′), *n.* one who conceals himself aboard a ship or other conveyance, as to get a free trip.
Stowe (stō), *n.* **Harriet Elizabeth Beecher,** 1811–96, U.S. writer: author of *Uncle Tom's Cabin.*
S.T.P., *Chem.* standard temperature and pressure; a temperature of 0°C and a pressure of 760 mm. of mercury. Also, **N.T.P.**
St Pancras (sənt păng′krəs), a district of the inner London borough of Camden.
St Paul, a city in the U.S., the capital of Minnesota, in the SE part: a port on the Mississippi. 313,411 (1960).
St Paul's, a cathedral in London, begun 1675, after the designs of Wren, in place of an earlier cathedral destroyed in 1666.
St Peter Port, a town in and the capital of Guernsey. 15,707 (1964).
St Peter's, the great metropolitan church of the see of Rome, one of the finest examples of Renaissance architecture, and especially noted for the structure of its pedimented dome.

St Petersburg (sənt pē′təz bûg′), **1.** the capital of Russia under the tsars: renamed **Petrograd** in 1914, and **Leningrad** in 1924. **2.** a seaport in W Florida, on Tampa Bay: winter resort. 181,298 (1960).

St Pierre (sənt pyĕə′; *Fr.* säN pyĕr′), **1.** a town in Réunion, in the Indian Ocean. 35,000 (est. 1968). **2.** a former city on Martinique, in the French West Indies: destroyed (with the entire population of 26,000) by an eruption of the volcano Mt Pelée, 1902.

St Pierre and Miquelon (mĭk′ə lŏn′; *Fr.* mē klôN′), two small groups of islands off the S coast of Newfoundland: France's only colony in North America; important base for fishing. 5134 (1960); 93 sq. mi. *Cap.*: St Pierre.

St Quentin (sənt kwĕn′tĭn; *Fr.* säN käN täN′), a town in N France, on the Somme: retaken from the Germans, 1918. 61,071 (1962).

str., **1.** steamer. **2.** strait. **3.** *Music.* **a.** string. **b.** strings.

strabismus (strə bĭz′məs), *n. Pathol.* a disorder of vision due to the turning of one eye or both eyes from the normal position so that both cannot be directed at the same point or object at the same time; squint; cross-eye. [NL, t. Gk: m. *strabismós*] —**strabis′mal, strabis′mic, strabis′mical,** *adj.*

Strabo (strā′bō), *n. c.* 63 B.C.–A.D. 21 ?, Greek geographer and historian.

strabotomy (strə bŏt′ə mĭ), *n., pl.* **-mies.** *Surg.* the operation of dividing one or more of the muscles of the eye for the cure of strabismus.

Strachey (strā′chĭ), *n.* **(Giles) Lytton** (jīlz′ lĭt′n), 1880–1932, English writer and biographer.

straddle (străd′l), *v.,* **-dled, -dling,** *n.* —*v.i.* **1.** to walk, stand, or sit with the legs wide apart; stand or sit astride. **2.** to stand wide apart, as the legs. **3.** *U.S. Colloq.* to take an equivocal position in regard to something; appear to favour both sides. —*v.t.* **4.** to walk, stand, or sit with one leg on each side of; stand or sit astride of. **5.** to spread (the legs) wide apart. **6.** *U.S. Colloq.* to take an equivocal position in regard to; appear to favour both sides of. **7.** *Mil.* to cover (an area) with bombs. **8.** *Gunnery.* to fire (shots) beyond and short of (a target) in order to fix range. —*n.* **9.** the act of straddling. **10.** the distance straddled over. **11.** *U.S. Colloq.* a taking of an equivocal or non-committal position. **12.** *U.S. Finance.* a double option. [appar. northern var. of *stroddle*, akin to *striddle*, freq. of STRIDE] —**strad′dler,** *n.* —**strad′dlingly,** *adv.*

Stradivari (străd′ĭ vä′rĭ; *It.* strä dē vä′rĕ), *n.* **Antonio** (*It.* än tô′nyô) (*Antonius Stradivarius*), *c.* 1644–1737, Italian violin-maker of Cremona.

Stradivarius (străd′ĭ vä′rĭ əs), *n.* a violin or other instrument made by Stradivari or his family.

strafe (străf), *v.t.,* **strafed, strafing.** **1.** to attack (ground troops or installations) by aircraft with machine-gun fire. **2.** to bombard heavily. **3.** *Slang.* to punish. —*n.* **4.** an attack or assault. [t. G: from the phrase *Gott strafe England* God punish England] —**straf′er,** *n.*

Strafford (străf′əd), *n.* **Thomas Wentworth, 1st Earl of,** 1593–1641, English statesman.

straggle (străg′l), *v.i.,* **-gled, -gling.** **1.** to stray from the road, course, or line of march. **2.** to wander about in a scattered fashion; ramble. **3.** to go, come, or spread in a scattered, irregular fashion. [ME; b. STRAY and DRAGGLE] —**strag′gler,** *n.*

straggly (străg′lĭ), *adj.* straggling; rambling.

straight (strāt), *adj.* **1.** without a bend, crook, or curve; not curved; direct: a straight path. **2.** flat; horizontal. **3.** (of a line) lying evenly between its points; generated by a point moving constantly in the same direction. **4.** evenly formed or set: *straight shoulders.* **5.** delivered with the arm extended straight from the shoulder, as a blow: *straight left.* **6.** without circumlocution; candid: *a straight answer.* **7.** honest, honourable, or upright, as conduct, dealings, methods, persons, etc. **8.** *Colloq.* reliable, as reports, information, etc. **9.** right or correct, as reasoning, thinking, a thinker, etc. **10.** continuous or unbroken: *in straight succession.* **11.** *U.S.* thoroughgoing or unreserved: *a straight comedy.* **13.** undiluted, as an alcoholic beverage; neat. **14.** *Theat.* (of a play, acting style, etc.) serious; without music or dancing and not primarily comic in intent. **15.** *Cards.* made up of cards in consecutive denomination, as the two, three, four, five, and six. —*adv.* **16.** in a straight line: *to walk straight.* **17.** in an even form or position: *pictures hung straight.* **18.** directly: *to go straight to a place.* **19.** without circumlocution (often fol. by *out*). **20.** honestly, honourably, or virtuously: *to live straight.* **21.** in a continuous course: *to keep straight on.* **22.** at once; immediately; without delay: *I'll come straight over.* **23.** in the proper order or condition, as a room: *he set the room straight after the meeting.* **24.** correctly; on a right or honourable course: *she soon set him straight after his mistake.* **25.** *U.S.* without discount regardless of the quantity bought: *candy bars are ten cents straight.* **26. go straight,** to lead an honest life, esp. after a prison sentence. —*n.* **27.** the condition of being straight. **28. the straight and narrow,** a way of life governed by strict moral principles. **29.** a straight form or position. **30.** a straight line. **31.** a straight part, as of a racecourse. **32.** *Poker.* a sequence of five cards of various suits. Cf. **sequence.** [ME, orig. pp. of STRETCH] —**straight′ly,** *adv.* —**straight′ness,** *n.*

straight angle, an angle of 180°. See diag. under **obtuse angle.**

straightaway (strāt′ə wā′), *adv.* **1.** immediately; at once; right away. —*adj.* **2.** *U.S.* straight onwards, without turn or curve, as a racecourse. —*n.* **3.** *U.S.* a straightaway course or part.

straightedge (strāt′ĕj′), *n.* a bar or strip of wood or metal, of various sizes, having at least one edge of sufficiently reliable straightness, for use in obtaining or testing straight lines, plane surfaces, etc.

straighten (strā′tn), *v.t., v.i.* to make or become straight in direction, form, position, character, conduct, condition, etc. —**straight′ener,** *n.*

straight face, a deliberately serious expression, esp. in an attempt to suppress laughter: *she managed to keep a straight face despite their antics.* —**straight′-faced′,** *adj.*

straight fight, a contest, as at an election, between two candidates only.

straight flush, *Poker.* a sequence of five cards of the same suit.

straightforward (strāt′fô′wəd), *adj.* **1.** going or directed straight forward: *a straightforward glance.* **2.** proceeding without circuity; direct. **3.** free from crookedness or deceit; honest: *straightforward in one's dealings.* **4.** without difficulty; uncomplicated: *the subject set was very straightforward.* —*adv.* **5.** *Chiefly U.S.* Also, **straightforwards.** straight ahead; directly or continuously forward. —**straight′for′wardly,** *adv.* —**straight′for′wardness,** *n.* —**Ant.** **1.** devious.

straight joint, *Bldg Trades.* a fault in brick or stone masonry, by which one vertical joint is situated immediately above another.

straight-line (strāt′līn′), *adj. Mach.* **1.** indicating a linear arrangement of the working parts of a machine, as in some compressors. **2.** denoting an apparatus copying or initiating motion along a straight line.

straight-line motion, *Mach.* a device, as a linkage, initiating motion in a straight line, or transferring motion from a curved line to a straight.

straight man, *Theat.* an entertainer who plays his part straight, usually as a foil for a comedian.

straight-out (strāt′out′), *adj. U.S. Colloq.* **1.** thoroughgoing: *a straight-out Democrat.* **2.** frank; aboveboard.

straightway (strāt′wā′), *adv. Archaic.* immediately; at once.

strain[1] (strān), *v.t.* **1.** to draw tight or taut; stretch, esp. to the utmost tension: *to strain a rope.* **2.** to exert to the utmost: *to strain one's ears to catch a sound.* **3.** to impair, injure, or weaken by stretching or overexertion, as a muscle. **4.** to cause mechanical deformation in (a body or structure) as the result of stress. **5.** to stretch beyond the proper point or limit: *to strain the meaning of a word.* **6.** to make excessive demands upon: *to strain one's resources, credit, etc.* **7.** to pass (liquid matter) through a filter, sieve, or the like, in order to hold back the denser or solid constituents. **8.** to draw off (clear liquid) or hold back (solid particles, etc.) from liquid matter by using a filter, sieve, or the like. **9.** to clasp tightly in the arms, the hand, etc. **10.** *Obs.* to constrain, as to a course of action. —*v.i.* **11.** to pull forcibly: *a dog straining at a leash.* **12.** to stretch one's muscles, nerves, etc., to the utmost. **13.** to make violent physical efforts; strive hard. **14.** to be subjected to tension or stress; suffer strain. **15.** to filter, percolate, or ooze. **16.** to trickle or flow. —*n.* **17.** any force or pressure tending to alter shape, cause fracture, etc. **18.** strong muscular or physical effort; great or excessive effort of any kind. **19.** an injury to a muscle, tendon, etc., due to excessive tension or use; a sprain. **20. a.** an injury to or deformation of any body or structure resulting from stress. **b.** the extent of such deformation expressed as the ratio of the dimensional change to the original unstrained dimension (length, area, or volume). **21.** the condition of being strained or stretched. **22.** extreme or excessive striving after some object or effect. **23.** severe, trying, or wearing pressure or effect: *the strain of hard work.* **24.** a severe demand on resources, feelings, a person, etc.: *a strain on one's hospitality.* **25.** *Obs.* a flow or burst of language, eloquence, etc. **26.** (*sing. or pl., often collective pl.*) a passage of music or song as rendered or heard: *the strains of a violin.* **27.** *Music.* a section of a piece of music more or less complete in itself. **28.** a passage or piece of poetry. **29.** tone, style, or spirit in expression: *a humorous strain.* **30.** *Rare.* a particular degree, height, or pitch attained. [ME *streyne,* t. OF: m. *estrein-,* s. *estreindre* bind tightly, clasp, squeeze, g. L *stringere* draw tight]

—**Syn. 3.** STRAIN, SPRAIN imply a wrenching, twisting, and stretching of muscles and tendons. To STRAIN is to stretch tightly, make taut, wrench, tear, cause injury to, by long-continued or sudden and too violent effort or movement: *to strain one's heart by over-exertion, one's eyes by reading small print.* To SPRAIN is to strain excessively (but without dislocation) by a sudden twist or wrench, the tendons and muscles connected with a joint, esp. those of the ankle or wrist: *to sprain an ankle.*

strain² (strān), *n.* **1.** the body of descendants of a common ancestor, as a family or stock. **2.** any of the different lines of ancestry united in a family or an individual. **3.** a group of plants distinguished from other plants of the variety to which it belongs by some intrinsic quality, such as a tendency to yield heavily. **4.** an artificial variety of a species of domestic animal or cultivated plant. **5.** a variety, esp. of micro-organisms. **6.** ancestry or descent. **7.** hereditary or natural character, tendency, or trait: *a strain of insanity in a family.* **8.** a streak or trace. **9.** *Rare.* a kind or sort. [ME *straine,* unexplained var. of *strene,* OE *gestrēon* acquisition, c. OHG *gistriuni*]

strained (strānd), *adj.* affected or produced by effort; forced; not natural or spontaneous.

strainer (strā′nə), *n.* **1.** one who or that which strains. **2.** a filter, sieve, or the like for straining liquids. **3.** a stretcher or tightener.

strain gauge, *Physics, Mach.* a grid of fine wires attached to a surface under stress so that any change in the dimensions of the surface is imparted to the wires causing a change in their electrical resistance. This change in resistance is proportional to the strain produced by the stress.

strain-hardening (strān′häd′nĭng), *n. Metall.* an increase in the hardness of a metal resulting from the permanent change to its crystalline structure caused by cold working. Also, **work-hardening.** —**strain′-hard′ened,** *adj.*

straining beam, (in a queen-post roof) a horizontal beam uniting the tops of the two queen posts, and resisting the thrust of the roof. Also, **straining piece.** See diag. under **queen post.**

strait (strāt), *n.* **1.** (*often pl. with sing. sense*) a narrow passage of water connecting two large bodies of water. **2.** (*often pl.*) a position of difficulty, distress, or need. **3.** *Archaic.* a narrow passage, space, or area. **4.** *Rare.* an isthmus. —*adj.* **5.** *Archaic.* narrow. **6.** *Archaic or Lit.* affording little room, as a place, bounds, etc. **7.** *Archaic.* strict in requirements, principles, etc. [ME, t. OF: m. *estreit* tight, narrow, g. L *strictus,* pp., bound] —**strait′ly,** *adv.* —**strait′ness,** *n.* —**Syn. 2.** See **emergency.**

straiten (strā′tn), *v.t.* **1.** to put into difficulties, esp. financial ones: *in straitened circumstances.* **2.** to restrict in range, extent, amount, pecuniary means, etc. **3.** *Archaic or Lit.* to make narrow. **4.** *Archaic.* to confine within narrow limits.

straightjacket (strāt′jăk′ĭt), *n.* a kind of coat for confining the arms of violently insane persons, etc.

straitlaced (strāt′lāst′), *adj.* **1.** excessively strict in conduct or morality; puritanical; prudish. **2.** *Archaic.* tightly laced, or wearing tightly laced garments.

Straits dollar (strāts), a former denomination of currency circulating in the Straits Settlements.

Straits Settlements, a former British crown colony in SE Asia, which included the settlements of Singapore, Penang, Malacca, and Labuan.

strake (strāk), *n.* **1.** *Naut.* one continuous longitudinal line or breadth of planking or plates on the side or bottom of a vessel. **2.** *Mech.* any one section of the metal tyre on a wooden wheel. **3.** *Mech.* a metal plate let into a rubber tyre. [ME; appar. akin to STRETCH]

Stralsund (*Ger.* shträl′zo͝ont), *n.* a seaport in N East Germany: a member of the medieval Hanseatic League; besieged by Wallenstein, 1628. 68,925 (1965).

stramineous (strə mĭn′ĭ əs), *adj.* **1.** of straw; strawlike. **2.** straw-coloured; yellowish. [t. L: m. *strāmineus*]

stramonium (strə mō′nyəm), *n.* **1.** the jimson weed. **2.** the dried leaves of this plant, used in medicine as an analgesic, antispasmodic, etc. [NL; orig. uncert.]

strand¹ (strănd), *v.t.* **1.** to drive aground on a shore, esp. of the sea, as a ship, a fish, etc. **2.** (usually in the passive) to bring into a helpless position. **3.** to leave without means of transport. —*v.i.* **4.** to be driven or run ashore, as a ship, etc.; run aground. —*n.* **5.** *Poetic.* the land bordering the sea or ocean, or, formerly, a river; the shore. **6. The Strand,** a well-known street in central London. [ME and OE, c. D and G *Strand*]

strand² (strănd), *n.* **1.** each of a number of strings or yarns which are twisted together to form a rope, cord, or the like. **2.** a similar part of a wire rope. **3.** a fibre or filament, as in animal or plant tissue. **4.** a thread of the texture of anything, as cloth. **5.** a tress of hair. **6.** a string of pearls, beads, etc. —*v.t.* **7.** to form (a rope, etc.) by twisting strands. **8.** to break one or more strands of (a rope). [ME *strond;* orig. uncert.]

strandline (strănd′līn′), *n.* a shoreline, esp. one from which the sea or a lake has receded.

strange (strānj), *adj.,* **stranger, strangest,** *adv.* —*adj.* **1.** unusual, extraordinary, or curious; odd; queer: *a strange remark to make.* **2.** out of one's natural environment: *to feel strange in a place.* **3.** situated, belonging, or coming from outside one's own or a particular locality: *to move to a strange place.* **4.** outside one's previous experience; hitherto unknown; unfamiliar: *the writing is strange to me.* **5.** unacquainted; unaccustomed (*to*) or inexperienced (*at*). **6.** distant or reserved. **7.** *Archaic.* foreign. —*adv.* **8.** *Colloq.* in a strange manner. [ME, t. OF: m. *estrange,* g. L *extrāneus* external, foreign] —**strange′ly,** *adv.* —**strange′ness,** *n.*

—**Syn. 1.** STRANGE, PECULIAR, ODD, QUEER refer to that which is out of the ordinary. STRANGE implies that the thing or its cause is unknown or unexplained, it is unfamiliar and unusual: *a strange expression.* That which is PECULIAR mystifies, or exhibits qualities not shared by others: *peculiar behaviour.* That which is ODD is irregular or unconventional, and sometimes approaches the bizarre: *an odd custom.* QUEER sometimes adds to ODD the suggestion of something abnormal and eccentric: *queer in the head.* —**Ant. 1.** familiar.

strangeness (strānj′nĭs), *n.* **1.** the fact or quality of being strange. **2.** *Physics.* a quantum number used to account for the slowness with which certain transformations between elementary particles happen.

stranger (strān′jə), *n.* **1.** a person with whom one has, or has hitherto had, no personal acquaintance. **2.** an outsider. **3.** a visitor or guest. **4.** a newcomer in a place or locality. **5.** a person or thing that is unaccustomed or new (fol. by *to*): *he is no stranger to poverty.* **6.** *Law.* one not privy or party to an act, proceeding, etc. **7.** *Archaic.* a foreigner or alien.

—**Syn. 1, 2.** STRANGER, ALIEN, FOREIGNER all refer to someone regarded as outside or distinct from a particular group. STRANGER may apply to one who does not belong to some group—social, professional, national, etc.—or may apply to a person with whom one is not acquainted. ALIEN emphasizes a difference in political allegiance and citizenship from that of the country in which one is living. FOREIGNER emphasizes a difference in language, customs, and background.

strangle (străng′gl), *v.,* **-gled, -gling,** *n.* —*v.t.* **1.** to kill by compression of the windpipe, as by a cord around the neck. **2.** to kill by stopping the breath in any manner; choke; stifle; suffocate. **3.** to prevent the continuance, growth, rise, or action of; suppress. —*v.i.* **4.** to be choked, stifled, or suffocated. —*n.* **5.** (*pl. construed as sing.*) an infectious febrile disease of equine animals, characterized by catarrh of the upper air passages and suppuration of the submaxillary and other lymphatic glands; distemper. [ME, t. OF: m. *estrangler,* g. L *strangulāre,* t. Gk: m. *strangalân*] —**stran′gler,** *n.*

stranglehold (străng′gl hōld′), *n.* **1.** *Wrestling.* a hold by which the adversary's breathing is stopped. **2.** anything which prevents motion or development of a person or group.

strangulate (străng′gyo͞o lāt′), *v.t.,* **-lated, -lating.** **1.** *Pathol., Surg.* to compress or constrict (a duct, intestine, vessel, etc.) so as to prevent circulation or suppress function. **2.** to strangle. [t. L: m. s. *strangulātus,* pp., strangled] —**stran′gula′tion,** *n.*

strangury (străng′gyo͞o rĭ), *n. Pathol.* a condition of the urinary organs in which the urine is painfully emitted, drop by drop. [ME, t. L: m. s. *strangūria,* t. Gk: m. *strangouria*]

strap (străp), *n., v.,* **strapped, strapping.** —*n.* **1.** a narrow strip of flexible material, esp. leather, for fastening or holding things together, etc. **2.** a looped band of leather, strong material, etc., for lifting, holding, pulling, or attaching. **3.** *Obs. except Dial.* a strop for a razor. **4.** a long, narrow piece or object; strip; band. **5.** a straplike ornament, as a watch-strap. **6.** See **shoulder-strap. 7.** *Elect.* a short thick conductor connecting two points in a circuit. —*v.t.* **8.** to fasten or secure with a strap or straps. **9.** *Obs.* to sharpen on a strap or strop. **10.** to beat or flog with a strap. [var. of STROP] —**strap′like′,** *adj.*

straphanger (străp′hăng′ə), *n. Colloq.* a passenger in an overfull bus, train, or the like who has to stand holding on to a strap suspended from above. —**strap′hang′ing,** *n.*

strapless (străp′lĭs), *adj.* **1.** having no straps. **2.** designed to have no shoulder-straps, leaving the shoulders bare, as a woman's evening gown.

strappado (strə pā′dō, -pä′do), *n., pl.* **-does. 1.** a form of punishment or torture in which the victim, tied to a rope, was raised to a height and suddenly let fall almost to the ground. 2. the instrument used for this purpose. [t. It.: m. *strappata*, der. *strappare* drag, pull]

strapper (străp′ə), *n.* **1.** one who or that which straps. **2.** *Colloq.* a tall, robust person.

strapping (străp′ĭng), *adj.* *Colloq.* **1.** tall, robust, and strongly built. **2.** very large of its kind; whopping. **3.** a thrashing. —*n.* **4.** straps collectively.

strapwork (străp′wûk′), *n.* *Archit.* a form of decoration which originated *c.* 1540 in the Netherlands, consisting of interlaced raised bands.

strapwort (străp′wût′), *n.* a small caryophyllaceous annual herb with narrow leaves, *Corrigiola littoralis*, found in wet sandy places of SW Europe, W Asia and N Africa.

Strasbourg (străz′bûg; *Fr.* stràz bo͞or′), *n.* a fortress city in NE France, near the Rhine: cathedral. 228,971 (1962). German, **Strassburg** (*Ger.* shtràs′bo͝ork).

strass[1] (străs), *n.* paste (def. 7). [t. G, t. F: m. *stras*, prob. named after Josef *Strasser*, 18th-cent. German jeweller, the inventor]

strass[2] (străs), *n.* silk waste resulting from the making of skeins. [t. F: m. *strasse*, t. It.; m. *straccio*]

strata (strä′tə), *n.* a pl. of **stratum.**

stratagem (străt′ĭ jəm), *n.* **1.** a plan, scheme, or trick for deceiving the enemy. **2.** any artifice, ruse, or trick. [t. F: m. *stratagème*, t. L: m. *stratēgēma*, t. Gk]

stratal (strä′tl), *adj.* of a stratum or strata.

strategic (strə tē′jĭk), *adj.* **1.** pertaining to, characterized by, or of the nature of strategy: *strategic movements.* **2.** important in strategy: *a strategic point.* **3.** important; highly crucial to one's position. Also, **strate′gical.** —**strate′gically,** *adv.*

strategist (străt′ĭ jĭst), *n.* one versed in strategy: *a great military strategist.*

strategy (străt′ĭ jĭ), *n.*, *pl.* **-gies.** **1.** Also, *Chiefly U.S.*, **strategics** (strə tē′jĭks). generalship; the science or art of combining and employing the means of war in planning and directing large military movements and operations. **2.** the use, or a particular use, of this science or art. **3.** skilful management in getting the better of an adversary or attaining an end. **4.** the method of conducting operations, esp. by the aid of manoeuvring or stratagem. [t. Gk: m. s. *stratēgía* generalship]

—**Syn. 1.** A distinction is made between STRATEGY and TACTICS in military use, STRATEGY dealing with the planning and directing of projects, which involve the movements of forces, etc., and TACTICS rather with the actual processes of moving or handling forces.

Stratford de Redcliffe (də rĕd′klĭf), **Stratford Canning, Viscount,** 1786–1880, British diplomat.

Stratford-on-Avon (străt′fəd ŏn ā′vən), *n.* a town in central England, on the river Avon, in Warwickshire: Shakespeare's birthplace. 16,859 (1961). Also, **Stratford-upon-Avon.**

strath (străth), *n.* *Scot.* a wide valley. [t. Gaelic: m. *srath*]

Strathmore (străth′mô′), *n.* a wide valley in Scotland, running from NE to SW through Angus and Perthshire.

strathspey (străth′spā′), *n.* **1.** a Scottish dance, similar to a reel, but slower. **2.** the music for this. [named after *Strath Spey*, a district and valley in Inverness-shire]

strati-, a word element representing **stratum,** as in *stratify.*

stratification (străt′ĭ fĭ kā′shən), *n.* **1.** the act of stratifying. **2.** stratified state or appearance: *the stratification of medieval society.* **3.** *Geol.* **a.** formation of strata; deposition or occurrence in strata. **b.** a stratum (def. 3).

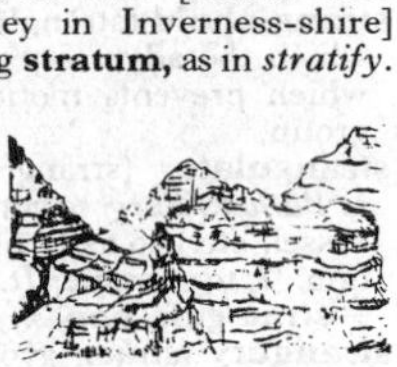

Stratification

stratiform (străt′ĭ fôm′), *adj.* **1.** *Geol.* occurring as a bed or beds; arranged in strata. **2.** *Anat.* noting a cartilage occurring in thin layers in bones. **3.** *Meteorol.* having the appearance or character of a stratus.

stratify (străt′ĭ fī′), *v.*, **-fied, -fying.** —*v.t.* **1.** to form in strata or layers. **2.** to preserve or germinate (seeds) by placing them between layers of earth. —*v.i.* **3.** to form strata. **4.** *Geol.* to lie in beds or layers. **5.** *Sociol.* to develop horizontal status groups in society. [t. NL: m. *strātificāre*. See STRATI-, -FY]

stratig., stratigraphy.

stratigraphy (strə tĭg′rə fĭ), *n.* a branch of geology dealing with the classification, nomenclature, correlation, and interpretation of stratified rocks. —**stratigrapher** (strə-tĭg′rə fə), **stratigraphist** (strə tĭg′rə fĭst), *n.* —**stratigraphic** (străt′ĭ grăf′ĭk), **strat′igraph′ical,** *adj.*

strato-, a word element meaning 'low and horizontal', as in *stratosphere.* [t. NL, comb. form repr. L *strātus*, a spreading out]

stratocracy (strə tŏk′rə sĭ), *n.* government by the army. —**stratocrat** (străt′ə krăt′), *n.* —**stratocratic** (străt′ə-krăt′ĭk), *adj.*

stratocruiser (străt′ō kro͞o′zə), *n.* **1.** a passenger or transport aeroplane designed to fly at stratospheric altitudes. **2.** (*cap.*) a trademark for such an aeroplane.

stratocumulus (strā′tō kyo͞o′myo͞o ləs), *n.*, *pl.* **-li** (-lī′). *Meteorol.* a low cloud or cloud layer consisting of large, dark, rounded masses, in groups, lines, or waves, the individual elements being larger than in an altocumulus.

stratosphere (străt′ə sfĭə′), *n.* *Meteorol.* **1.** the region of the atmosphere outside the troposphere but within the ionosphere, characterized by relatively uniform temperature over considerable differences in altitude or by a markedly different lapse rate from that of the troposphere below. **2.** *Obs.* all of the earth's atmosphere lying outside the troposphere. —**stratospheric** (străt′ə sfĕ′rĭk), *adj.*

stratum (strä′təm), *n.*, *pl.* **strata** (strä′tə), **stratums. 1.** a layer of material, formed either naturally or artificially, often one of a number of parallel layers placed one upon another. **2.** one of a number of portions likened to layers or levels. **3.** *Geol.* a single bed of sedimentary rock, generally consisting of one kind of matter representing continuous deposition. **4.** *Biol.* a layer of tissue; a lamella. **5.** a layer of the ocean or the atmosphere distinguished by natural or arbitrary limits. **6.** *Sociol.* a level or grade of a people or population with reference to social position or education: *the lowest stratum of society.* [NL; in L something spread out]

stratus (strā′təs), *n.*, *pl.* **-ti** (-tī). *Meteorol.* a continuous horizontal sheet of cloud, resembling fog but not resting on the ground, usually of uniform thickness and comparatively low altitude.

stratus fractus (frăk′təs), *Meteorol.* a stratus cloud broken up into irregular, ragged fragments.

Straus (strous; *Ger.* shtrous), *n.* **Oscar** (ŏs′kə; *Ger.* ŏs′kàr), 1870–1954, Austrian composer.

Strauss (strous; *Ger.* shtrous), *n.* **1. David Friedrich** (*Ger.* dä′vēt frē′drĭKH), 1808–74, German theologian and author. **2. Johann** (*Ger.* yō′hàn), 1804–49, Austrian composer. **3.** his son, **Johann,** 1825–99, Austrian composer, esp. of waltzes. **4. Richard** (rĭch′əd; *Ger.* rĭKH′àrt), 1864–1949, German composer and conductor.

Stravinsky (strə vĭn′skĭ; *Russ.* strà vēn′skĭy), *n.* **Igor Feodorovich** (*Russ.* ē′gəry fyô′də rə vĭch), born 1882, Russian composer living in the U.S. Also, **Stravinski.**

straw (strô), *n.* **1.** a single stalk or stem, esp. of certain species of grain, chiefly wheat, rye, oats, and barley. **2.** a mass of such stalks, esp. after drying and threshing, used as fodder, as material for hats, etc. **3.** a hollow paper tube, plant stem, etc., used in drinking some beverages, etc. **4.** anything of trifling value or consequence: *not to care a straw.* **5.** a desperate and insubstantial expedient: *to clutch at a straw.* **6. man of straw, a.** a person having little or no position, financial or moral resources, or the like. **b.** an imaginary person, as one set up to represent a point of view. **7. the last straw,** the final fact, circumstance, etc., which makes a situation unbearable. —*adj.* **8.** of, pertaining to, or made of straw. **9.** *Chiefly U.S.* of little value or consequence; worthless. **10.** *Chiefly U.S.* sham; fictitious. [ME; OE *strēaw*]

strawberry (strô′bə rĭ, -brĭ), *n.*, *pl.* **-ries. 1.** the fruit of any of the stemless herbs constituting the rosaceous genus *Fragaria*, consisting of an enlarged fleshy receptacle bearing achenes on its exterior. **2.** the plant bearing it. —*adj.* **3.** of the colour of a strawberry; reddish: *strawberry blonde.*

strawberry bush, the wahoo[1] (def. 1).

strawberry mark, a reddish birthmark.

strawberry shrub, any of various species of the genus *Calycanthus* (or *Butneria*), shrubs with dark brown or purplish red flowers of distinctive fragrance.

strawberry tomato, 1. the small, edible, tomato-like fruit of the solanaceous plant *Physalis pruinosa.* **2.** the plant bearing it.

strawberry tree, an evergreen ericaceous shrub or tree, *Arbutus unedo*, a native of southern Europe, bearing a scarlet, strawberry-like fruit.

strawboard (strô′bôd′), *n.* coarse, yellow paper board made of straw pulp, used in packing, and for making boxes, etc.

straw boss, *U.S. Colloq.* a subordinate boss.

straw colour, a pale yellow similar to the colour of straw. —**straw′-col′oured,** *adj.*

straw vote, *Chiefly U.S.* an unofficial vote taken, as at a casual gathering or in a particular district, to obtain some indication of the general drift of opinion. Also, **straw poll.**

straw wine, *U.S.* wine (usually sweet and rich) from grapes that have been dried in the sun on a bed of straw.

strawy (strô′ĭ), *adj.* **1.** of, containing, or resembling straw. **2.** strewed or thatched with straw.

stray (strā), *v.i.* **1.** to go from the proper course or place or beyond the proper limits, esp. without settled course or purpose; ramble; roam. **2.** to wander (fol. by *away, off, from, into, to,* etc.). **3.** to deviate, as from the set or right course; go astray; get lost. **4.** to digress. —*n.* **5.** a domestic animal found wandering at large or without an owner. **6.** any homeless or friendless creature or person; a thing that has strayed. **7.** (*pl.*) *Radio.* static. —*adj.* **8.** straying, or having strayed, as a domestic animal. **9.** found or occurring apart from others, or as an isolated or casual instance. **10.** *Radio.* undesired: *stray capacitance.* [aphetic var. of ME *astray,* t. OF: m. s. *estraier,* ult. g. L *extrā vagārī* wander outside] —**stray′er,** *n.*

strayline (strā′līn′), *n. Naut.* a section of the logline between the logchip and the mark on the line which indicates the precise point at which the computation of the speed of the vessel shall begin. The strayline is not counted in this computation.

streak (strēk), *n.* **1.** a long, narrow mark, smear, band of colour, or the like: *streaks of mud, a streak of lightning.* **2.** a portion or layer of something, distinguished by colour or nature from the rest; a vein or stratum: *streaks of fat in meat.* **3.** a vein, strain, or admixture of anything: *a streak of humour.* **4.** *U.S. Colloq.* a run (of luck): *to have a streak of bad luck.* **5.** *Mineral.* the line of powder obtained by scratching a mineral or rubbing it upon a hard, rough white surface, often differing in colour from the mineral in the mass, and forming an important distinguishing character. **6.** *Bacteriol.* the inoculation of a medium with a loop which contains the material to be inoculated, by passing the loop in a direct or zigzag line over the medium, without scratching the surface. —*v.t.* **7.** to mark with a streak or streaks. **8.** to dispose in the form of a streak or streaks. —*v.i.* **9.** to become streaked. **10.** to flash or go rapidly, like a streak of lightning. [ME *streke,* OE *strica;* akin to STRIKE]

streaky (strē′kĭ), *adj.,* **streakier, streakiest. 1.** occurring in streaks or a streak. **2.** marked with or characterized by streaks. **3.** *Colloq.* varying or uneven in quality, etc. —**streak′ily,** *adv.* —**streak′iness,** *n.*

stream (strēm), *n.* **1.** a body of water flowing in a channel or bed, as a river, rivulet, or brook. **2.** a steady current in water, as in a river or the ocean: *to row against the stream.* **3.** any flow of water or other liquid or fluid: *streams of blood.* **4.** a current of air, gas, or the like; a beam or trail of light. **5.** a continuous flow or succession of anything: *a stream of words.* **6.** prevailing direction; drift: *the stream of opinion, a stream of cars.* **7.** *Educ.* a division of children in a school to bring together those of similar age and ability in one class. —*v.i.* **8.** to flow, pass, or issue in a stream, as water, tears, blood, etc. **9.** to send forth or throw off a stream; run or flow (fol. by *with*): *eyes streaming with tears.* **10.** to extend in a beam or trail, as light. **11.** to move or proceed continuously like a flowing stream, as a procession. **12.** to wave or float outwards, as a flag in the wind. **13.** to hang in a loose, flowing manner, as long hair. —*v.t.* **14.** to send forth or discharge in a stream. **15.** to cause to stream or float outwards, as a flag. **16.** to overspread or suffuse with a stream or streams. **17.** *Educ.* to divide into streams. [ME; OE *strēam,* c. G *Strom*]

—**Syn. 1.** STREAM, CURRENT refer to a steady flow. In this use they are interchangeable. In the sense of running water, however, a STREAM is a flow which may be as small as a brook or as large as a river: *a number of streams have their sources in mountains.* CURRENT refers to the most rapidly moving part of the stream: *this river has a swift current.*

streamer (strē′mə), *n.* **1.** something that streams. **2.** a long, narrow flag or pennant. **3.** a long, flowing ribbon, feather, or the like, used for ornament, as in dress. **4.** a long, narrow strip of paper, usually brightly coloured, thrown in festivities, or used for decorating rooms or the like. **5.** any long, narrow piece or thing, as a spray of a plant or a strip of cloud. **6.** a stream of light, esp. one appearing in some forms of the aurora borealis. **7.** the headline which extends across the width of the newspaper, usually at the top of the first page, and often sensational.

streamlet (strēm′lĭt), *n.* a small stream; a rivulet.

streamline (strēm′līn′), *n., v.,* **-lined, -lining.** —*n.* **1.** a teardrop line of contour, as of a motor car. **2.** *Physics.* a line of motion in a fluid; the actual path of a particle in a flowing fluid mass whose motion is steady. —*v.t.* **3.** to make streamlined.

streamlined (strēm′līnd′), *adj.* **1.** denoting, pertaining to, or having a shape designed to offer the least possible resistance in passing through the air, etc., allowing an uninterrupted flow of the fluid about it: *a streamlined motor car.* **2.** designed to make more efficient, often by simplifying methods, organization, etc.

streamline flow, *Physics.* a type of fluid flow in which the motion of the fluid is such that continuous streamlines can be drawn through the whole length of its course at any instant.

stream of consciousness, *Psychol.* thought regarded as a succession of states constantly moving onwards in time.

stream-of-consciousness novel (strēm′əv kŏn′shəs nĭs), a novel in which the action is reported through, or together with, the thoughts of one or several characters.

streamy (strē′mĭ), *adj.* **1.** abounding in streams or watercourses. **2.** flowing in a stream; streaming.

streek (strēk), *Scot. and N Dial.* —*v.t.* **1.** to stretch or extend (one's limbs). **2.** to stretch out (an arm, hand, etc.) to touch or take hold of something. **3.** to lay out (a corpse). —*v.i.* **4.** to lie down; stretch out. [var. of STRETCH]

street (strēt), *n.* **1.** a public way or road, paved or unpaved, in a village, town, or city, usually including a pavement or pavements, and having houses, shops, or the like, on one side or both sides. **2.** such a way or road together with the adjacent buildings. **3.** a main way or thoroughfare, as distinct from a lane, alley, or the like. **4.** the inhabitants of or the people in a street. **5. on the streets,** earning one's living as a prostitute. **6. the man in the street,** the average person; a typical citizen. **7. the street,** *U.S.* the principal business or financial section of a city, esp. Wall Street in New York City. **8. up one's street,** in the sphere that one knows or likes best. [ME; d. OE *strēt,* OE *strǣt,* c. D *straat,* G *Strasse,* all ult. t. L: m. (*via*) *strāta* paved (road)]

—**Syn. 1.** STREET, ALLEY, AVENUE, BOULEVARD all refer to public ways or roads in municipal areas. A STREET is a road in a village, town, or city, esp. a road lined with houses. An ALLEY is a narrow path or footway, esp. between, or behind a row of buildings. An AVENUE is properly a prominent street, often bordered by fine residences and impressive buildings, or with trees on each side. A BOULEVARD is a beautiful, broad street, lined with rows of stately trees, esp. used as a promenade.

Street (strēt), *n.* **George Edmund,** 1824–81, English architect.

street Arab, a child having no home and making his way by begging, stealing, etc. Also, **street urchin.**

streetcar (strēt′kä′), *n. U.S.* a tram.

street furniture, the conventional equipment of urban streets, as bus-shelters, streetlights, litter bins, etc.

streetlight (strēt′līt′), *n.* a light of electricity or gas for illuminating streets, roads, etc., often supported by a column.

streetwalker (strēt′wô′kə), *n.* one who walks the streets, esp. a soliciting prostitute. —**street′ walk′ing,** *n.*

strength (strĕngth), *n.* **1.** the quality or state of being strong; bodily or muscular power; vigour, as in robust health. **2.** mental power, force, or vigour. **3.** moral power, firmness, or courage. **4.** power by reason of influence, authority, resources, numbers, etc. **5.** number, as of men or ships in a force or body: *a regiment of a strength of three thousand.* **6.** effective force, potency, or cogency, as of inducements or arguments. **7.** power of resisting force, strain, wear, etc. **8.** vigour of action, language, feeling, etc. **9.** large proportion of the effective or essential properties of a beverage, chemical, or the like. **10.** a particular proportion of these properties; intensity, as of light, colour, sound, flavour, or smell. **11.** something that makes strong; a support or stay. **12.** *Finance.* a commodity or price which is either firm or rising. **13. on the strength of,** relying on; on the basis of. [ME; OE *strength(u),* der. STRONG]

—**Syn. 4.** STRENGTH, POWER, FORCE, MIGHT suggest capacity to do something. STRENGTH is inherent capacity to manifest energy, to endure, and to resist. POWER is capacity to do work and to act. FORCE is the exercise of power: *one has the power to do something; he exerts force when he does it; and he has sufficient strength to complete it.* MIGHT is power or strength in a great or overwhelming degree: *the might of an army.* —**Ant. 4.** weakness.

strengthen (strĕng′thən), *v.t.* **1.** to make stronger; give strength to. —*v.i.* **2.** to gain strength; grow stronger. —**strength′ener,** *n.*

strenuous (strĕn′yo͞o əs), *adj.* **1.** vigorous, energetic, or zealously active, as a person, etc. **2.** characterized by vigorous exertion, as action, efforts, life, etc.: *a strenuous opposition.* [t. L: m. *strēnuus;* akin to Gk *strēnḗs* strong] —**stren′uously,** *adv.* —**stren′uousness, strenuosity** (strĕn′yo͞o ŏs′ĭ tĭ), *n.* —**Syn. 1.** See **active.**

strepitous (strĕp′ĭ təs), *adj.* noisy. [f. s. L *strepitus* noise + -OUS]

strepsipterous (strĕp sĭp′tə rəs), *adj.* belonging or pertaining to the *Strepsiptera,* an order of minute insects with reduced fore wings and large hind wings, the females of which are usually degenerate wormlike parasites.

strepto-, a word element meaning 'curved', as in *streptococcus.* [t. Gk, comb. form of *streptós*]

streptococcus (strĕp′tō kŏk′əs), *n., pl.* **-cocci** (-kŏk′sī). *Bacteriol.* one of a group of organisms (genus *Streptococcus*) which divide in one plane only, and remain attached to one another, forming long, short, or conglomerated chains. Some cause very important diseases such as scarlet fever, erysipelas, puerperal sepsis, sepsis, etc.

—streptococcic (strĕp′tō kŏk′sĭk), **streptococcal** (strĕp′-tō kŏk′l), *adj.*

streptomycin (strĕp′tō mī′sĭn), *n. Med.* an antibiotic effective against diseases caused by bacteria, including several against which penicillin is ineffective, as tuberculosis.

streptothricin (strĕp′tō thrī′sĭn), *n.* an antibacterial substance derived from the soil fungus, *Actinomyces lavendulae.* Also, **streptothrysin.**

Stresemann (*Ger.* shtrė′zə mȧn), *n.* **Gustav** (*Ger.* go͝os′-tȧf), 1878–1929, German statesman.

stress (strĕs), *v.t.* **1.** to lay stress or emphasis on; emphasize. **2.** *Phonet.* to pronounce strongly or with a stress accent. **3.** to subject to stress or strain. **4.** *Mech.* to subject to mechanical stress. [v. use of STRESS, n.; r. ME *stress*, prob. t. OF: m. s. *estrecier*, ult. der. L *strictus*, pp., drawn tight, compressed]
—*n.* **5.** importance or significance attached to a thing; emphasis: *to lay stress upon successive incidents.* **6.** *Phonet.* relative loudness resulting from special effort or emphasis in utterance. **7.** accent or emphasis on a syllable or syllables in speech, esp. so as to form a metrical pattern. **8.** the syllable accented. **9.** emphasis in music, rhythm, etc. **10.** the physical pressure, pull, or other force exerted on one thing by another. **11.** *Mech.* **a.** the action on a body of any system of balanced forces whereby strain or deformation results. **b.** the amount of stress, usually measured in number of pounds per square inch. **c.** a load, force, or system of forces producing a strain. **d.** the internal resistance or reaction of an elastic body to the external forces applied to it. **12.** *Rare.* strong or straining exertion. [aphetic var. of DISTRESS]

-stress, a feminine equivalent of **-ster,** as in *seamstress, songstress.* [f. *-str* (syncopated var. of -STER) + -ESS]

stressed skin, *Aeron.* monocoque.

stretch (strĕch), *v.t.* **1.** to draw out or extend (oneself, the body, limbs, wings, etc.) to the full length or extent (often fol. by *out*): *to stretch oneself out on the ground.* **2.** to hold out, reach forth, or extend (the hand or something held, the head, etc.). **3.** to extend, spread, or place so as to reach from one point or place to another: *to stretch a rope across a road.* **4.** to draw tight or taut: *to stretch the strings of a violin.* **5.** to lengthen, widen, distend, or enlarge by tension: *to stretch a rubber band.* **6.** to draw out, extend, or enlarge unduly: *a sweater stretched at the elbows.* **7.** to extend or force beyond the natural or proper limits; strain: *to stretch the facts.* **8. stretch a point,** to go beyond the usual limits; make concessions. **9. stretch one's legs,** to take a walk.
—*v.i.* **10.** to recline at full length (usually fol. by *out*): *to stretch out on a couch.* **11.** to extend the hand, or reach, as for something. **12.** to extend over a distance, area, period of time, or in a particular direction: *the forest stretches for miles.* **13.** to stretch oneself by extending the limbs, straining the muscles, etc. **14.** to become stretched, or admit of being stretched, to greater length, width, etc., as any elastic material.
—*n.* **15.** the act of stretching. **16.** the state of being stretched. **17.** capacity for being stretched. **18.** a continuous length, distance, tract, or expanse: *a stretch of meadow.* **19.** one of the two straight sides of a racecourse, as distinguished from the bend or curve at each end, esp. that part of the course (**home stretch**) between the last turn and the winning post. **20.** an extent in time or duration: *a stretch of ten years.* **21.** *Slang.* a term of imprisonment.
—*adj.* **22.** made to stretch in order to fit different shapes and sizes, as clothing: *stretch stockings.*
[ME; OE *streccan*, c. G *strecken*] —**stretch′able,** *adj.*
—**Syn. 5.** See **lengthen.**

stretcher (strĕch′ə), *n.* **1.** a kind of litter, usually of canvas stretched on a frame, esp. for carrying the sick, wounded, or dead. **2.** one who or that which stretches. **3.** any of various instruments for extending, widening, distending, etc. **4.** a bar, beam, or fabricated material, serving as a tie or brace. **5.** a narrow crosspiece in a boat, for a rower to push his feet against. **6.** a brick or stone laid horizontally with its length in the direction of the face of a wall, usually planned to give added strength to the structure. **7.** a simple wooden framework on which the canvas of an oil painting is stretched.

stretcher-bearer (strĕch′ə bēə′rə), *n.* a man, esp. a serviceman, who helps to carry a stretcher, as in removing the wounded from a battlefield.

stretch-out (strĕch′out′), *n. U.S.* **1.** deliberate extension of time for meeting a production quota. **2.** a method of factory management by which employees do additional work without commensurate increase in wages.

stretchy (strĕch′ĭ), *adj.* **1.** capable of being stretched; elastic. **2.** liable to stretch unduly.

Stretford (strĕt′fəd), *n.* a town in England, a suburb of Manchester, in SE Lancashire. 60,364 (1961).

stretta (strĕt′ə; *It.* strėt′tȧ), *n.*, *pl.* **-te** (*It.* -tė), **-tas.** *Music.* **1.** a concluding passage taken at an accelerated speed. **2.** stretto.

stretto (strĕt′ō; *It.* strėt′tȯ), *n.*, *pl.* **-ti** (*It.* -tē), **-tos.** *Music.* (in a fugue) the close overlapping of voices so that each succeeding one enters before the preceding one has completed its statement of the subject, often in the final section. [t. It.: narrow, g. L *strictus*, pp., drawn tight]

strew (stro͞o), *v.t.*, **strewed, strewed** or **strewn, strewing.** **1.** to let fall in separate pieces or particles over a surface; scatter or sprinkle: *to strew seed in a garden bed.* **2.** to cover or overspread (a surface, place, etc.) with something scattered or sprinkled: *to strew a floor with rushes.* **3.** to be scattered or sprinkled over (a surface, etc.). [ME *strewe*, OE *strēowian*, c. G *streuen*] —**Syn. 1.** See **sprinkle.**

stria (strī′ə), *n.*, *pl.* **striae** (strī′ē). **1.** a slight furrow or ridge; a narrow stripe or streak, esp. one of a number in parallel arrangement. **2.** (*pl.*) *Geol.* scratches or tiny grooves on the surface of a rock, resulting from the action of moving ice, as of a glacier. **3.** (*pl.*) *Mineral.* parallel lines or tiny grooves on the surface of a crystal, or on a cleavage face of a crystal, due to its molecular organization. **4.** *Pathol.* a linear mark on the abdomen which may appear in pregnancy or obesity or in some endocrine abnormalities. **5.** Also, **strix.** *Archit.* a fillet between the flutes of a column. [t. L: furrow, channel]

striate (*v.* strī′āt; *adj.* strī′ĭt), *v.*, **-ated, -ating.** *adj.* —*v.t.* **1.** to mark with striae; furrow; stripe; streak. —*adj.* **2.** Also, **striat′ed.** marked with striae; furrowed; striped.

striation (strī ā′shən), *n.* **1.** striated condition or appearance. **2.** a stria; one of many parallel striae.

stricken (strĭk′ən), *adj.* **1.** struck; hit or wounded by a weapon, missile, or the like. **2.** smitten or afflicted, as with disease, trouble, or sorrow. **3.** deeply affected, as with horror, fear, or other emotions. **4.** characterized by or showing the effects of affliction, trouble, misfortune, a mental blow, etc.

strickle (strĭk′l), *n.*, *v.*, **-led, -ling.** —*n.* **1.** a straightedge used to sweep off heaped-up grain or the like to a level with the rim of a measure. **2.** *Foundry.* a shaped board used for forming a mould. **3.** a piece of wood covered with grease and sand, emery, etc., to sharpen scythes. —*v.t.* **4.** to sweep or remove with a strickle. [ME *strikylle*, OE *stricel*; akin to STRIKE]

strict (strĭkt), *adj.* **1.** characterized by or acting in close conformity to requirements or principles: *strict observance.* **2.** stringent or exacting in requirements, obligations, etc.: *strict laws, a strict judge.* **3.** closely or rigorously enforced or maintained. **4.** exact or precise: *a strict statement of facts.* **5.** narrowly or carefully limited: *a strict construction of the constitution.* **6.** close, careful, or minute: *a strict search.* **7.** absolute, perfect, or complete: *told in strict confidence.* **8.** *Obs.* drawn tight or close. [t. L: *strictus*, pp., drawn together, tight, severe] —**strict′ly,** *adv.* —**strict′ness,** *n.*
—**Syn. 1.** STRICT, RIGID, RIGOROUS, STRINGENT imply inflexibility, severity, and an exacting quality. STRICT 'drawn close or tight' implies great exactness, esp. in the observance or enforcement of rules: *strict discipline.* RIGID, literally stiff or unbending, applies to that which is (often unnecessarily or narrowly) inflexible: *rigid rules.* RIGOROUS, with the same literal meaning, applies to that which is severe, exacting, and uncompromising, esp. in action or application: *rigorous self-denial.* STRINGENT applies to that which is vigorously exacting and severe: *stringent measures to suppress disorder.* —**Ant. 1.** lax.

striction (strĭk′shən), *n.* the act of drawing tight, constricting, or straining. [t. L: s. *strictio*]

stricture (strĭk′chə), *n.* **1.** a remark or comment, esp. an adverse criticism. **2.** a morbid contraction of any passage or duct of the body. **3.** *Rare.* a drawing or binding tightly, or something that binds tightly. **4.** *Obs.* strictness. [ME, t. L: m. *strictūra*]

stride (strīd), *v.*, **strode, stridden, striding,** *n.* —*v.i.* **1.** to walk with long steps, as with vigour, haste, impatience, or arrogance. **2.** to take a long step. **3.** to straddle. —*v.t.* **4.** to walk with long steps along, on, through, over, etc.: *to stride the deck.* **5.** to pass over or across by one stride: *to stride a ditch.* **6.** to straddle. —*n.* **7.** a striding or a striding gait. **8.** a long step in walking. **9.** (in animal locomotion) act of progressive movement, completed when all the feet are returned to the same relative position as at the beginning. **10.** the distance covered by such a movement. **11.** a regular or steady course, pace, etc.: *to take it in one's stride.* **12.** a step forward in development or progress: *rapid strides in mastering algebra.* [ME; OE *strīdan*, c. LG *strīden.* Cf. also G *streiten* quarrel] —**strid′er,** *n.*

strident (strī′dnt), *adj.* making or having a harsh sound; grating; creaking. [t. L: s. *stridens*, ppr., creaking] —**stri′dence, stri′dency,** *n.* —**stri′dently,** *adv.*

stridor (strī′dô), *n.* **1.** a harsh, grating, or creaking sound. **2.** *Pathol.* a harsh respiratory sound due to any of various forms of obstruction. [t. L]

stridulate (strĭd′yo͝o lāt′), *v.i.*, **-lated, -lating.** to produce a shrill grating sound, as a cricket, by rubbing together certain parts of the body; shrill. —**strid′ula′tion, strid′ula′tor,** *n.* —**stridulatory** (strĭd′yo͝o lā′tə rĭ), *adj.*

stridulous (strĭd′yo͝o ləs), *adj.* **1.** making or having a harsh or grating sound. **2.** *Pathol.* pertaining to or characterized by stridor. [t. L: m. *strīdulus*] —**strid′ulously,** *adv.* —**strid′ulousness,** *n.*

strife (strīf), *n.* **1.** conflict, discord, or variance: *to be at strife.* **2.** a quarrel, struggle, or clash. **3.** *Obs. or Rare.* strenuous effort. **4.** *Obs. or Rare.* competition or rivalry. [ME, t. OF: aphetic m. *estrif.* See STRIVE] —**strife′ful, strife′less,** *adj.*

striges (strī′jēz), *n.* pl. of **strix.**

strigiform (strĭj′ĭ fôm′), *adj.* belonging or pertaining to the *Strigiformes*, the order of birds which includes the owls.

strigil (strĭj′ĭl), *n.* **1.** an instrument with a curved blade, used by the ancient Greeks and Romans for scraping the skin at the bath and in the gymnasium. **2.** *Archit.* one of a series of decorative S-shaped flutings, esp. in Roman architecture. [t. L: s. *strigilis*]

strigose (strī′gōs), *adj.* **1.** *Bot.* set with stiff bristles or hairs; hispid. **2.** *Zool.* marked with fine ridges or grooves. [t. NL: m. s. *strigōsus*, der. L *striga* row of bristles]

Strijdom (*Afrik.* strĕy′dəm), *n.* **Johannes Gerhardus** (*Afrik.* yȯ hŏ′nəs KHė rŏr′dəs), 1893–1958, South African statesman; prime minister of the Union of South Africa, 1954–8.

strike (strīk), *v.*, **struck, struck** or (esp. for 29–32) **stricken, striking,** *n.* —*v.t.* **1.** to deliver a blow, stroke, or thrust with (the hand, a weapon, etc.). **2.** to deal a blow or stroke to (a person or thing), as with the fist, a weapon, or a hammer; hit. **3.** to deal or inflict (a blow, stroke, etc.). **4.** to drive or thrust forcibly: *to strike the hands together.* **5.** to produce (fire, sparks, light, etc.) by percussion, friction, etc.; cause (a match) to ignite by friction. **6.** to smite or blast with some natural or supernatural agency: *struck by lightning.* **7.** to come into forcible contact or collision with: *the ship struck a rock.* **8.** to fall upon (something), as light or sound. **9.** to enter the mind of; occur to: *a happy thought struck him.* **10.** to catch or arrest (the eyes, etc.): *the first object that strikes one's sight.* **11.** to impress strongly: *a picture which strikes one's fancy.* **12.** to impress in a particular manner: *how does it strike you?* **13.** to come across, meet with, or encounter suddenly or unexpectedly: *to strike the name of a friend in a newspaper.* **14.** to come upon or find (ore, oil, etc.) in prospecting, boring, or the like. **15.** to send down or put forth (a root, etc.), as a plant, cutting, etc. **16.** to balance (a ledger, etc.). **17.** to remove from the stage (the scenery and properties of an act or scene). **18.** *Naut.* **a.** to lower or take down (a sail, mast, etc.). **b.** to lower (a sail, flag, etc.) as a salute or as a sign of surrender. **c.** to lower (something) into the hold of a vessel by means of a rope and tackle. **19.** to hook (a fish) by a jerk or sudden movement of the tackle. **20.** to harpoon, spear, as in hunting. **21.** (in various technical uses) to make level or smooth. **22.** to make level or even, as a measure of grain, salt, etc., by drawing a strickle across the top, or, as potatoes, by making the projections equal to the depressions. **23.** to efface or cancel with, or as with, the stroke of a pen (fol. by *off, out,* etc.). **24.** to forbid (someone) to continue practising his profession because of unprofessional conduct, or the like (fol. by *off*): *the doctor was struck off for advertising.* **25.** to stamp (a coin, medal, etc.) or impress (a device), by a stroke. **26.** to remove or separate with a cut (usually fol. by *off*). **27.** *Rowing.* to make (a specified number of strokes) in a given time: *Oxford struck forty in the first minute.* **28.** to indicate (the hour of day) by a stroke or strokes, as a clock: *to strike twelve.* **29.** to afflict suddenly, as with disease, suffering, or death. **30.** to affect deeply or overwhelm, as with terror, fear, etc. **31.** to render (blind, dumb, etc.) suddenly, as if by a blow. **32.** to cause (a feeling) to enter suddenly: *to strike terror into a person,* **33.** to induce a favourable reaction in: *he was struck by her beauty.* **34.** to start suddenly into (vigorous movement): *the horse struck a gallop.* **35.** to assume (an attitude or posture). **36.** to cause (chill, warmth, etc.) to pass or penetrate quickly. **37.** to come upon or reach in travelling or in a course of procedure. **38.** to make, conclude, or ratify (an agreement, treaty, etc.). **39.** to reach by agreement, as a compromise. **40.** to enter upon or form (an acquaintance, etc.) (usually fol. by *up*). **41.** to estimate or determine (a mean or average). **42.** to break (camp). **43.** to leave off (work), as a coercive measure, or as at the close of the day. **44.** (of an orchestra) to begin to play (a tune).

—*v.i.* **45.** to deal or aim a blow or stroke, as with the fist, a weapon, or a hammer; make an attack. **46.** to knock, rap, or tap. **47.** to hit or dash on or against something, as a moving body; come into forcible contact. **48.** to run upon a bank, rock, or other obstacle, as a ship. **49.** to fall, as light or sound (fol. by *on* or *upon*). **50.** to make an impression on the mind, senses, etc., as something seen or heard. **51.** to come suddenly or unexpectedly (fol. by *on* or *upon*): *to strike on a new way of doing a thing.* **52.** to sound by percussion: *the clock strikes.* **53.** to be indicated by such sounding: *the hour has struck.* **54.** to be ignited by friction, as a match. **55.** to make a stroke, as with the arms or legs in swimming or with an oar in rowing. **56.** to produce a sound, music, etc., by touching a string or playing upon an instrument. **57.** (of an orchestra) to begin to play. **58.** to take root, as a slip of a plant. **59.** to go, proceed, or advance, esp. in a new direction. **60.** (of an employee or employees) to engage in a strike. **61.** *Naut.* **a.** to lower the flag or colours, esp. as a salute or as a sign of surrender. **b.** to run up the white flag of surrender. **62.** *Angling.* to swallow or grasp the bait (applied to fish). **63. strike out, a.** to direct one's course boldly. **b.** *Baseball.* (of a batter) to make three strikes and be declared 'out'.

—*n.* **64.** an act of striking. **65.** a concerted stopping of work or withdrawal of workers' services in order to compel an employer to accede to demands or in protest against terms or conditions imposed by employer. **66.** *Baseball.* an unsuccessful attempt on the part of the batter to hit a pitched ball, or anything ruled to be equivalent to this. **67.** *Tenpin Bowling.* **a.** the knocking down of all the pins with the first bowl. **b.** the score made by bowling a strike. **68.** *Brewing.* the critical temperature of the water during mashing. **69.** *Angling.* the process of grabbing at the bait. **70.** *Geol.* **a.** the direction of the line formed by the intersection of the bedding plane of a bed or stratum of sedimentary rock with a horizontal plane. **b.** the direction or trend of a structural feature, as an anticlinal axis or the lineation resulting from metamorphism. **71.** the discovery of a rich vein of ore in mining, of oil in drilling, etc. [ME; OE *strīcan*, c. G *streichen.* Cf. STREAK, STROKE[1]]

—**Syn.** **2.** STRIKE, HIT, KNOCK imply suddenly bringing one body in contact with another. STRIKE suggests such an action in a general way: *to strike a child.* HIT is less formal than STRIKE, and often implies giving a single blow, but usually a strong one and definitely aimed: *to hit a cricket ball.* To KNOCK is to strike, often with a tendency to displace the object struck; it also means to strike repeatedly: *to knock someone down, to knock at a door.* See **beat.** —**Ant. 1.** miss.

strikebound (strīk′bound′), *adj.* unable to function because of a strike.

strikebreaker (strīk′brā′kə), *n.* one who takes part in breaking up a strike of workers, either by working or by furnishing workers for the employer.

strikebreaking (strīk′brā′kĭng), *n.* action directed at breaking up a strike of workers.

strike fault, *Geol.* a fault the trend of which is parallel to the strike of the affected rocks.

strike pay, an allowance paid by a trade union to members on strike. Also, **strike benefit.**

striker (strī′kə), *n.* **1.** one who or that which strikes. **2.** a worker who is on strike. **3.** the clapper in a clock that strikes the hours or rings an alarm. **4.** *Cricket.* the batsman who is facing the bowling. **5.** one who strikes fish, etc., with a spear or harpoon. **6.** *Whaling.* the harpoon.

striking (strī′kĭng), *adj.* **1.** that strikes. **2.** attractive; impressive. **3.** being on strike, as workmen. —**strik′-ingly,** *adv.*

striking circle, *Hockey.* circle (def. 9).

Strindberg (strĭnd′bûg; *Sw.* strĕn′bĕry), *n.* **Johan August** (*Sw.* yo͞o′hȧn ȧw′go͞ost), 1849–1912, Swedish novelist, dramatist, and essayist.

string (strĭng), *n.*, *v.*, **strung; strung** or (*Rare*) **stringed; stringing.** —*n.* **1.** a line, cord, or thread, used for tying parcels, etc. **2.** a narrow strip of cloth, leather, etc., for tying parts together: *strings of a bonnet.* **3.** something resembling a string or thread. **4.** a number of objects, as beads or pearls, threaded or arranged on a cord. **5.** any series of things arranged or connected in a line or following closely one after another: *a string of islands or of vehicles; to ask a string of questions.* **6.** a set or number, as of animals: *a string of racehorses.* **7.** (in musical instruments) a tightly stretched cord or wire which produces a note when caused to vibrate, as by plucking, striking, or friction of a bow. **8.** (*pl.*) **a.** stringed musical instruments, esp. such as are played with a bow. **b.** players on such instruments in an orchestra or band. **9. two strings to one's bow.** See **second string. 10.** a cord or fibre in a plant. **11.** the tough piece uniting the two parts of a pod: *the strings of beans.* **12.** *Archit.* **a.** a string-course. **b.** one of the sloping sides of a stair, supporting the treads and risers. **13.** *Billiards.* a stroke made by each player from the head of the table to the opposite cushion and back, to determine, by means

of the resultant positions of the balls, who shall open the game. **14.** *Colloq.* limitations on any proposal: *a proposal with no strings attached.* **15.** *Obs.* a ligament, tendon, nerve, or the like, in an animal body. **16. keep on a string,** to have someone under one's control, esp. emotionally: *she kept him on a string and then agreed to marry him.* **17. pull strings,** *Colloq.* to seek one's own advancement by using social contacts and other means not directly connected with one's ability or suitability.
—*v.t.* **18.** to furnish with or as with a string or strings. **19.** to extend or stretch (a cord, etc.) from one point to another. **20.** to thread on, or as on, a string: *to string beads.* **21.** to connect in, or as in, a line; arrange in a series or succession. **22.** to adjust the string of (a bow); tighten the strings of (a musical instrument) to the required pitch. **23.** to provide or adorn with something suspended or slung: *a room strung with festoons.* **24.** to deprive of a string or strings; strip the strings from: *to string beans.* **25.** to make tense, as the sinews, nerves, mind, etc. **26.** to kill by hanging (usually fol. by *up*).
—*v.i.* **27.** to form into or move in a string or series. **28.** to form into a string or strings, as glutinous substances do when pulled. —*v.* **29.** Some special verb phrases are:
highly strung, very nervous; tense by nature.
string along or **on,** *Colloq.* to fool or hoax.
string along with, *Colloq.* to go along with; accompany; cooperate with; agree with.
string out, a. to extend or spread out at intervals. **b.** to extend over a period of time; prolong.
[ME; OE *streng*, c. D *streng*; akin to G *strang*, L *stringere* bind, Gk *strangálē* halter] —**string′like′,** *adj.*
string bag, a loosely woven bag, originally made of string, now often made of plastic, or the like.
string band, a band of stringed instruments.
string bass, double bass (def. 1).
string bean, 1. any of various kinds of bean (plant) the unripe pods of which are used as food, usually after stripping off the fibrous thread along the side. **2.** the pod itself.
stringboard (strĭng′bôd′), *n.* a board or the like covering the ends of the steps in a staircase.
string-course (strĭng′kôs′), *n.* a horizontal band or course of stone, etc., projecting beyond or flush with the face of a building, often moulded and sometimes richly carved.

S, String-course

stringed (strĭngd), *adj.* **1.** (of a musical instrument) having a string or strings. **2.** pertaining to such instruments: *stringed music.*
stringency (strĭn′jən sĭ), *n., pl.* **-cies. 1.** stringent character or condition. **2.** strictness; closeness; rigour. **3.** tightness; straitness: *stringency in the money market.*
stringendo (strĭn jĕn′dō; *It.* strĕn-jĕn′dô), *adj., adv. Music.* progressively quickening the tempo. [It., ppr. of *stringere* compress, draw tight, g. L]
stringent (strĭn′jənt), *adj.* **1.** narrowly binding; rigorously exacting; strict; severe: *stringent laws.* **2.** compelling, constraining, or urgent: *stringent necessity.* **3.** convincing or forcible, as arguments, etc. **4.** (of the money market) tight; characterized by a shortage of loan money. [t. L: s. *stringens*, ppr., drawing tight] —**strin′gently,** *adv.* —**Syn. 1.** See **strict.**
stringer (strĭng′ə), *n.* **1.** one who or that which strings. **2.** *Bldg Trades.* **a.** a long horizontal timber connecting upright posts, supporting a floor, or the like. **b.** a cross-member keeping horizontal timbers in position. **3.** *U.S. Archit.* the string of a stair. **4.** *Chiefly U.S.* a longitudinal timber spanning a bent of a railway trestle or bridge. **5.** *Naut.* a narrow, flat steel plate, extending the whole length of a ship, and forming part of the skeleton construction which strengthens and supports the hull of the ship. **6.** *Journalism.* a freelance or part-time correspondent of a newspaper, usually paid a retaining fee.
stringhalt (strĭng′hôlt′), *n.* a nervous disorder in horses, causing exaggerated flexing movements of the hind legs in walking. Also, **springhalt.**
string line, *Billiards.* baulk line.
stringline (strĭng′līn′), *n. Bldg Trades.* a length of string or cord stretched between two points to indicate a level, as in bricklaying.
string orchestra, an orchestra which normally consists of violins, violas, cellos, and double-basses.
stringpiece (strĭng′pēs′), *n. Building, etc.* a long piece of timber or the like (esp. a horizontal one) in a framework or structure, as for strengthening the structure or connecting or supporting parts.
string-pulling (strĭng′po͝ol′ĭng), *n. Colloq.* the act or fact of seeking one's own advancement by using social contacts and other means not directly connected with one's ability or suitability. —**string′-pul′ler,** *n.*
string quartet, a quartet, usually consisting of two violins, a viola, and a cello.
stringy (strĭng′ĭ), *adj.*, **stringier, stringiest. 1.** resembling a string; consisting of strings or stringlike pieces. **2.** coarsely or toughly fibrous, as meat. **3.** sinewy or wiry, as a person. **4.** ropy, as a glutinous liquid. —**string′iness,** *n.*
stringy-bark (strĭng′ĭ băk′), *n. Austral.* any of several eucalypts with a tough, fibrous bark.
strip[1] (strĭp), *v.*, **stripped** or (*Rare*) **stript, stripping.** —*v.t.* **1.** to deprive of covering: *to strip a fruit of its rind.* **2.** to deprive of clothing; make bare or naked. **3.** to take away or remove: *to strip pictures from a wall.* **4.** to deprive or divest: *to strip a tree of its fruit.* **5.** to clear out or empty: *to strip a house of its contents.* **6.** to deprive of equipment; dismantle: *to strip a ship of rigging.* **7.** to rob, plunder, or dispossess: *to strip a man of his possessions.* **8.** to separate the leaves from the stalks of (tobacco). **9.** to remove the midrib, etc., from (tobacco leaves). **10.** *Mach.* to tear off the thread of (a screw, bolt, etc.) or the teeth of (a gear, etc.), as by applying too much force. **11.** to remove old paint, distemper, etc., from a surface prior to redecorating. **12.** *Chem.* to remove the most volatile components from a mixture by distillation or evaporation. **13.** to draw the last milk from (a cow), esp. by a stroking and compressing movement. **14.** to draw out (milk) thus. **15.** (in filmsetting) to make up a composite sheet of film using individual pieces (often fol. by *in*). —*v.i.* **16.** to strip something; esp., to strip oneself of clothes. **17.** to perform a striptease. **18.** to become stripped. [ME *stripe*, OE *-strȳpan*, c. D *stroopen*]
—**Syn. 7.** STRIP, DEPRIVE, DISPOSSESS, DIVEST imply more or less forcibly taking something away from someone. To STRIP is to take something completely (often violently), from a person or thing so as to leave in a destitute or powerless state: *to strip a man of all his property, the bark from a tree.* To DEPRIVE is to take away forcibly or coercively what one has, or to withhold what one might have: *to deprive one of his income.* To DISPOSSESS is to deprive of the holding or use of something: *to dispossess the tenants of a house.* DIVEST usually means depriving of rights, privileges, powers, or the like: *to divest a king of authority.* —**Ant. 4.** supply, furnish.
strip[2] (strĭp), *n., v.*, **stripped, stripping.** —*n.* **1.** a narrow piece, comparatively long and usually of uniform width: *a strip of cloth, metal, land, etc.* **2.** a continuous series of pictures, as in a newspaper, illustrating incidents, conversation, etc. See **comic strip. 3.** *Philately.* three or more stamps joined either in a horizontal or vertical row. —*v.t.* **4.** to cut into strips. [late ME, ? t. MLG: m. *strippe* strap; akin to STRIPE[1]]
strip cartoon. See **comic strip.**
strip club, a place of entertainment where striptease is performed.
stripe[1] (strīp), *n., v.*, **striped, striping.** —*n.* **1.** a relatively long, narrow band of a different colour, appearance, weave, material, or nature from the rest of a surface or thing: *the stripes of a zebra.* **2.** a striped fabric or material. **3.** a strip of braid or the like. **4.** (*pl.*) a number or combination of such strips, worn on a military, naval, or other uniform as a badge of rank, service, good conduct, wounds, etc. **5.** a strip, or long, narrow piece of anything. **6.** a streak or layer of a different nature within a substance. **7.** *Chiefly U.S.* style, variety, sort, or kind: *a man of quite a different stripe.* —*v.t.* **8.** to mark or furnish with a stripe or stripes. [t. MD]
stripe[2] (strīp), *n.* a stroke with a whip, rod, etc., as in punishment. [late ME; ? special use of STRIPE[1]]
striped (strīpt), *adj.* having stripes or bands. Also, **stri′py.**
striped hyena, a scavenging carnivorous mammal, *Hyaena hyaena*, of SW Asia and Africa.
striper (strī′pə), *n. Slang.* a naval officer who wears stripes on the sleeve of his uniform: *a three-striper* (*a naval commander*).
stripe rust, a fungal disease of cereals caused by *Puccinia striiformis*, a member of the order *Uredinales.*
stripe smut, any of several diseases of grasses caused by fungi of the order *Ustilaginales*, as *Urocystis agropyri* on wheat.
strip lighting, lighting by long cylindrical glass strips which are either fluorescent tubes or which contain long filaments.
stripling (strĭp′lĭng), *n.* a youth just passing from boyhood to manhood. [f. STRIP[2] + -LING[1]]
stripper (strĭp′ə), *n.* **1.** one who strips. **2.** a striptease dancer. **3.** that which strips, as an appliance, machine or solvent for stripping.
striptease (strĭp′tēz′), *n.* **1.** an act in which a woman disrobes garment by garment, usually to the accompaniment

of music before an audience. —*adj.* **2.** of or pertaining to such an act.

strive (strīv), *v.i.*, **strove, striven, striving. 1.** to exert oneself vigorously; try hard. **2.** to make strenuous efforts towards any end: *to strive for success.* **3.** to contend in opposition, battle, or any conflict. **4.** to struggle vigorously, as in opposition or resistance: *to strive against fate.* **5.** *Archaic.* to contend in rivalry; vie. [ME, t. OF: m. *estriver* quarrel, contend; of Gmc orig.] —**striv′er,** *n.* —**Syn. 1.** See **try.**

strix (strĭks), *n., pl.* **striges.** *Archit.* a channel or groove in a fluted column. Also, **stria.**

strobe (strōb), *n. Colloq., Photog.* a high-intensity flash device used in stroboscopic photography or an analogous electronic system. [short for STROBOSCOPE]

strobila (strə bī′lə), *n. Zool.* a segmented structure produced by transverse fission, such as the entire body of a tapeworm, or in jellyfish a body in the process of division so as to produce other jellyfish. [NL, t. Gk: m. *strobílē* plug of lint twisted into the shape of a fir cone]

strobilus (strō′bĭ ləs), *n., pl.* **-luses, -li** (-lī′). *Bot.* a compact reproductive structure consisting of a central axis bearing either simple sporophylls, as in club-mosses and male cones of conifers, or compound scales bearing ovules as in female cones of conifers. Also, **strobile** (strō′bīl).

stroboscope (strō′bə skōp′), *n.* an instrument used in studying the motion of a body (esp. one in rapid revolution or vibration) by rendering it visible at frequent intervals, as by illuminating it with an electric spark or the like, or by viewing it through openings in a revolving disc. [f. *strobo-* (comb. form repr. Gk *stróbos* a twisting) + -SCOPE] —**stroboscopic** (strō′bə skŏp′ĭk), *adj.*

strode (strōd), *v.* pt. of **stride.**

Stroessner (strûs′nə), *n.* **Alfredo** (äl frā′dō), born 1912, president of Paraguay since 1954.

stroganoff (strŏg′ə nŏf′), *n.* a dish of meat cooked in a sauce of sour cream, mushrooms, etc. [named after Count Paul *Stroganoff*, 19th-century Russian diplomat]

Stroheim (*Ger.* shtrō′hīm), *n.* **Erich von** (*Ger.* ĕ′rĭKH fōn), born 1885, German film director and actor in the U.S.

stroke[1] (strōk), *n., v.,* **stroked, stroking.** —*n.* **1.** an act of striking, as with the fist, a weapon, a hammer, etc.; a blow. **2.** a hitting of or upon anything. **3.** a striking of a clapper or hammer, as on a bell, or the sound produced by this. **4.** a throb or pulsation, as of the heart. **5.** something likened to a blow in its effect, as in causing pain, injury, or death, as an attack of apoplexy or paralysis. **6.** a destructive discharge of electricity. **7.** a piece of luck, fortune, etc., befalling one: *a stroke of good luck.* **8.** a vigorous movement, as if in dealing a blow. **9.** a single complete movement, esp. one continuously repeated in some process. **10.** *Mech.* **a.** one of a series of alternating continuous movements of something back and forth over or through the same line. **b.** the complete movement of a moving part (esp. a reciprocating part) in one direction. **c.** the distance traversed. **d.** a halfway revolution of an engine during which the piston travels from one extreme of its range to the other. **11.** each of the succession of movements of the arms and legs in swimming. **12.** a type or method of swimming: *the crawl is a rapid stroke.* **13.** a vigorous attempt to attain some object: *a bold stroke for liberty.* **14.** a measure adopted for a particular purpose. **15.** a feat or achievement: *a stroke of genius.* **16.** an act, piece, or amount of work, etc.: *not to do a stroke of work.* **17.** a distinctive or effective touch in a literary composition. **18.** a movement of a pen, pencil, brush, graver, or the like. **19.** a mark traced by or as if by a pen, pencil, brush, or the like. **20.** (in some games) a hitting of the ball in a certain manner: *an overhand stroke.* **21.** *Rowing.* **a.** a single pull of the oar. **b.** manner or style of moving the oars. **c.** the oarsman nearest to the stern of the boat, to whose strokes those of the other oarsmen must conform. **d.** the position in the boat occupied by this oarsman.
—*v.t.* **22.** to mark with a stroke or strokes, as of a pen; cancel, as by a stroke of a pen. **23.** to row as stroke oarsman of (a boat or crew); row as stroke in (a race). [ME, c. G *Streich*; akin to STRIKE] —**Syn. 1.** See **blow**[1].

stroke[2] (strōk), *v.,* **stroked, stroking,** *n.* —*v.t.* **1.** to pass the hand or an instrument over (something) lightly or with little pressure; rub gently, as in soothing or caressing. —*n.* **2.** the act or an instance of stroking; a stroking movement. [ME; OE *strācian*, c. G *streichen*; akin to STRIKE]

stroke play, *Golf.* medal play.

stroll (strōl), *v.i.* **1.** to walk leisurely as inclination directs; ramble; saunter; take a walk. **2.** to wander or rove from place to place; roam: *strolling minstrels.* —*v.t.* **3.** *Obs. except U.S.* to saunter along or through. —*n.* **4.** a leisurely walk; a ramble; a saunter: *a short stroll before supper.* [orig. uncert.]
—**Syn. 1.** STROLL, MEANDER, SAUNTER refer to carefree and leisurely walking for pleasure. To STROLL is to walk in a leisurely way as fancy leads, often for the mere pleasure of being out of doors: *to stroll down the street.* To MEANDER is to pursue an indefinite and wandering course: *to meander about the countryside.* To SAUNTER is to go along idly at a slow, easy gait: *to saunter aimlessly.* —**Ant. 1.** hasten.

stroller (strō′lə), *n.* **1.** a saunterer. **2.** a wanderer; vagrant. **3.** an itinerant performer. **4.** *U.S.* a pushchair.

stroma (strō′mə), *n., pl.* **-mata** (-mə tə). **1.** the colourless, spongelike framework of a red blood corpuscle or other cell. **2.** the connective tissue forming the framework of an organ (contrasted with *parenchyma*). **3.** *Bot.* a dense mass of hyphae in which a fungus may develop. [NL; in LL bed covering, t. Gk: a spread] —**stromatic** (strō măt′ĭk), **stro′matous,** *adj.*

Stromboli (strŏm′bə lĭ; *It.* strôm′bô lē), *n.* **1.** an island in the Lipari group, N of Sicily. **2.** an active volcano on this island. 3040 ft.

strong (strŏng), *adj.* **1.** having, showing, or involving great bodily or muscular power; physically vigorous or robust. **2.** mentally powerful or vigorous: *a strong mind.* **3.** especially powerful, able, or competent in a specified field or respect: *strong in mathematics.* **4.** of great moral power, firmness, or courage: *strong under temptation.* **5.** powerful in influence, authority, resources, or means of prevailing or succeeding: *a strong nation.* **6.** clear and firm; loud: *a strong voice.* **7.** well-supplied or rich in something specified: *a strong hand at cards.* **8.** of great force, effectiveness, potency, or cogency: *strong arguments.* **9.** able to resist force or stand strain, wear, etc.: *strong walls, cloth, etc.* **10.** firm or unfaltering under trial: *strong faith.* **11.** moving or acting with force or vigour: *strong wind.* **12.** containing alcohol, or much alcohol: *strong drink.* **13.** intense, as light or colour. **14.** distinct, as marks or impressions; marked, as a resemblance or contrast. **15.** strenuous or energetic; forceful or vigorous: *strong efforts.* **16.** hearty, fervent, or thoroughgoing: *strong prejudice.* **17.** having a large proportion of the effective or essential properties or ingredients: *strong tea.* **18.** having a high degree of flavour or smell: *strong perfume.* **19.** of an unpleasant or offensive flavour or smell: *strong butter.* **20.** *Com.* characterized by steady or advancing prices. **21.** *Gram.* **a.** (of Germanic verbs) indicating differentiation in tense by internal vowel change rather than by the addition of a common inflectional ending, as *sing, sang, sung*; *ride, rode, ridden.* **b.** (of Germanic nouns and adjectives) inflected with endings generally distinctive of case, number, and gender, as Ger. *alter Mann* 'old man'. —*adv.* **22.** in a strong manner; powerfully; forcibly; vigorously. **23.** in number: *the army was twenty thousand strong.* **24. going strong,** continuing vigorously, in good health: *he is very old but still going strong.* [ME and OE, c. MD *stranc*; akin to D and G *streng* severe, strict] —**strong′ly,** *adv.*
—**Syn. 1.** STRONG, HALE, ROBUST, STALWART, STURDY imply having health and vitality. STRONG is the general term and denotes the power of enduring strain, resisting disease, or exerting great muscular force: *strong enough to lift a piano.* HALE indicates a condition of sound or vigorous health, esp. in later life: *hale in spite of his age.* ROBUST suggests oaken strength, combining toughness of body with perfect health: *robust enough to meet all the storms of life.* STALWART suggests tallness or largeness combined with great strength or solidity: *he looks stalwart and uncompromising.* STURDY suggests stockiness and solidity, or well-knit strength that is hard to shake or overcome: *not tall but sturdy.* —**Ant. 1.** weak.

strongarm (strŏng′ärm′), *Colloq.* —*adj.* **1.** having, using, or involving the use of muscular or physical force: *strong-arm methods.* —*v.t. U.S.* **2.** to employ violent methods upon. **3.** to steal from by force.

strongbox (strŏng′bŏks′), *n.* a strongly made chest for preserving money, jewels, etc.

strong breeze, *Meteorol.* a wind of Beaufort scale force 6, i.e. one about 28 miles per hour.

stronger sex, men.

strong gale, *Meteorol.* a wind of Beaufort scale force 9, i.e. one about 50 miles per hour.

stronghold (strŏng′hōld′), *n.* **1.** a strong or well-fortified place; a fortress. **2.** a place where anything, as an ideology, opinion, etc., is strong.

strong language, forcible words and expressions, esp. those used in swearing.

strong man, 1. a man who performs feats of strength for entertainment, as in a circus. **2.** the most powerful person in an organization, state, or the like.

strong-minded (strŏng′mīn′dĭd), *adj.* **1.** having or showing a strong mind or vigorous mental powers. **2.** (of women) claiming mental and legal equality with men. —**strong′-mind′edly,** *adv.* —**strong′-mind′edness,** *n.*

strong nuclear interaction, *Physics.* the strongest form of interaction known in nature, being some 100 times stronger than electromagnetic interactions; it occurs between nucleons, hyperons, and some mesons, when they are in extremely close proximity, and accounts for the stability of the atomic nucleus.

strong point, a person's special quality or talent.

strongroom (strŏng′ro͝om′, -ro͝om′), *n.* a room for valuables in a bank or the like, built so as to resist fire and theft.

strong-willed (strŏng′wĭld′), *adj.* **1.** having a powerful will; resolute. **2.** stubborn.

strongyle (strŏn′jĭl), *n.* any of the nematode worms constituting the family *Strongylidae*, parasitic as adults in the intestine principally of horses; in the larval stage they burrow into the mucosa, and some enter the circulatory system, giving rise to serious pathological conditions. [t. NL: m. *Strongylus* (name of typical genus), t. Gk: m. *strongýlos* round]

strontia (strŏn′tyə), *n.* *Chem.* **1.** strontium oxide, SrO, a white amorphous powder resembling lime in its general character. **2.** strontium hydroxide, $Sr(OH)_2$. [NL, der. *Strontian*, parish in Argyllshire, where discovered]

strontian (strŏn′tyən), *n.* **1.** strontianite. **2.** strontia. **3.** strontium.

strontianite (strŏn′tyə nīt′), *n.* a mineral, strontium carbonate, $SrCO_3$, occurring in radiating, fibrous, or granular aggregates and crystals, varying from white to yellow and pale green: a minor ore of strontium. [f. *Strontian* (see STRONTIA) + -ITE[1]]

strontium (strŏn′tyəm), *n.* *Chem.* a bivalent metallic element whose compounds resemble those of calcium: found in nature only in the combined state, as in strontianite. The radioactive isotope **strontium-90** is produced in certain nuclear reactions and is sometimes present in fall-out, it is extremely dangerous to mammals as it tends to be assimilated in bones in place of calcium which it resembles chemically. *Symbol:* Sr; *at. wt:* 87·62; *at. no.:* 38; *sp. gr.:* 2·6. —**strontic** (strŏn′tĭk), *adj.*

strontium unit, *Physics.* a measure of the concentration of **strontium-90** in an organic medium, as milk, bone, soil, etc., relative to the concentration of calcium in the same medium. One strontium unit is equivalent to 10^{-12} curies of strontium-90 per gram of calcium. *Abbrev.:* S.U.

strop (strŏp), *n., v.,* **stropped, stropping.** —*n.* **1.** a strip of leather or other flexible material, or a long, narrow piece of wood having its faces covered with leather or an abrasive, or some similar device, used for sharpening razors. **2.** *Naut.* **a.** a ring of rope fitted round a block or spar, with an eye used for connecting. **b.** a large ring of rope used as a sling. —*v.t.* **3.** to sharpen on, or as on, a strop. [ME *stroppe*, OE *strop*, c. D and LG *strop*, prob. t. L: m. s. *stroppus* strap]

strophanthin (strō făn′thĭn), *n.* a bitter, poisonous glycoside obtained from the ripe seeds of various species of strophanthus, esp. *Strophanthus rombe:* used in medicine as a cardiac stimulant. [f. STROPHANTH(US) + -IN[2]]

strophanthus (strō făn′thəs), *n.* **1.** any of the shrubs or small trees of the apocynaceous genus *Strophanthus*, mostly natives of tropical Africa. **2.** the seed. [NL, f. Gk: s. *stróphos* twisted band + m. *ánthos* flower]

strophe (strō′fĭ), *n.* **1.** the part of an ancient Greek choral ode sung by the chorus when moving from right to left. **2.** the first of two metrically corresponding series of lines forming divisions of a lyric poem (the second being the antistrophe), or in a longer poem, the first section of such a metrical pattern whenever it is repeated. **3.** (in modern poetry) any separate or extended section in a poem, opposed to the stanza, a group of lines which necessarily repeats a metrical pattern. [t. Gk: a turning] —**strophic** (strŏf′ĭk), *adj.* —**Syn. 3.** See **verse.**

strophulus (strŏf′yo͞o ləs), *n.* *Pathol.* a papular eruption of the skin in infants, occurring in several forms and usually harmless. [NL: alter. of ML *scrophulus* red gum, itself alter. of L *scrōfulae* SCROFULA]

stroppy (strŏp′ĭ), *adj. Slang.* rebellious and difficult to control; awkward; complaining. [alter. of OBSTREPEROUS]

Stroud (stroud), *n.* a town in England, in Gloucestershire. 17,461 (1961).

Štrougal (stro͞o′gl; *Cz.* strôw′gål), *n.* **Lubomir** (*Cz.* lo͞o′bō mēr), born 1924, prime minister of Czechoslovakia since 1970.

strove (strōv), *v.* pt. of **strive.**

strow (strō), *v.,* **strowed, strown** or **strowed, strowing.** *Archaic.* strew.

struck (strŭk), *v.* **1.** pt. and a pp. of **strike. 2. struck on,** *Slang.* in love or infatuated with.

struck jury, *U.S. Law.* a jury obtained by a special agreement between the opposing attorneys, each striking out members of an empanelled group until twelve remain.

struck measure, a measure, esp. of grain, even with the top of a receptacle.

structural (strŭk′chə rəl), *adj.* **1.** of or pertaining to structure; pertaining or essential to a structure. **2.** *Biol.* pertaining to organic structure; morphological. **3.** *Geol.* pertaining to the structure of rock, etc. **4.** *Chem.* pertaining to or showing the arrangement or mode of attachment of the atoms which constitute the molecule of a substance. **5.** resulting from, or pertaining to, political or economic structure. —**struc′turally,** *adv.*

structural formula. See **formula** (def. 4).

structure (strŭk′chə), *n.* **1.** mode of building, construction, or organization; arrangement of parts, elements, or constituents. **2.** something built or constructed; a building, bridge, dam, framework, etc. **3.** a complex system considered from the point of view of the whole rather than of any single part: *the structure of modern science.* **4.** anything composed of parts arranged together in some way; an organization. **5.** *Biol.* mode of organization; construction and arrangement of tissues, parts, or organs. **6.** *Geol.* **a.** the attitude of a bed or stratum, or of beds or strata, of sedimentary rocks, as indicated by the dip and strike. **b.** coarser features of rocks as contrasted with their texture. **7.** the manner by which atoms in a molecule are joined to each other, especially in organic chemistry where it is represented by a diagram of the molecular arrangement. [t. L: m. *structūra*] —**Syn. 2.** See **building.**

strudel (stro͞o′dl; *Ger.* shtro͞o′dəl), *n.* any of a variety of pastries, usually with fruits, cheeses, etc., rolled in a paper-thin blanket of dough. [t. G]

struggle (strŭg′l), *v.,* **-gled, -gling,** *n.* —*v.i.* **1.** to contend with an adversary or opposing force. **2.** to contend resolutely with a task, problem, etc.; strive: *to struggle for existence.* **3.** to advance with violent effort: *to struggle through the snow.* —*v.t.* **4.** *Chiefly U.S.* to bring, put, etc., by struggling. **5.** to make (one's way) with violent effort. —*n.* **6.** the act or process of struggling. **7.** a strong effort, or series of efforts, against any adverse agencies or conditions. **8.** a fight, usually on a small scale involving only a few people. [ME; ? f. *strug-* (b. STRIVE and TUG) + *-le*, freq. suffix] —**strug′gler,** *n.*

—**Syn. 6.** STRUGGLE, BRUSH, CLASH, refer to a hostile meeting of opposing persons, parties, or forces. STRUGGLE implies vigorous bodily effort or violent exertion: *a hand-to-hand struggle.* A BRUSH is a brief, but smart, and often casual combat: *a brush between patrols.* CLASH implies a direct and sharp collision between opposing parties, efforts, interests, etc.: *a clash of opinions.*

struggle for existence, *Biol.* the ability of an organism to adapt to changes in environment, pressure of populations, means of subsistence, esp. as a factor in evolution.

strum (strŭm), *v.,* **strummed, strumming,** *n.* —*v.t.* **1.** to play on (a stringed musical instrument) unskilfully or carelessly. **2.** to produce (notes, etc.) by such playing: *to strum a tune.* **3.** to play (chords, etc.) as a simple accompaniment. —*v.i.* **4.** to play chords on a stringed instrument unskilfully or as a simple accompaniment. —*n.* **5.** the act of strumming. [b. STRING and THUMB] —**strum′mer,** *n.*

struma (stro͞o′mə), *n., pl.* **-mae** (-mē). **1.** *Pathol.* **a.** scrofula. **b.** goitre. **2.** *Bot.* a cushion-like swelling on an organ, as that at one side of the base of the capsule in many mosses. [NL, special use of L: scrofulous tumour]

Struma (*Bulg.* stro͞o′må), *n.* a river flowing through SW Bulgaria and NE Greece into the Aegean. ab. 225 mi.

strumose (stro͞o′mōs), *adj. Bot.* having a struma or strumae.

strumous (stro͞o′məs), *adj. Pathol.* **1.** affected with struma. **2.** characteristic of or of the nature of struma.

strumpet (strŭm′pĭt), *n.* a prostitute; a harlot. [f. *strump-* (cf. G *strumpf* stump) + -ET]

strung (strŭng), *v.* pt. and pp. of **string.**

strut[1] (strŭt), *v.,* **strutted, strutting,** *n.* —*v.i.* **1.** to walk with a vain, pompous bearing, as with head erect and chest thrown out, as if expecting to impress observers. —*n.* **2.** the act of strutting; a strutting walk or gait. [ME *stroute*, OE *strūtian* stand stiffly; akin to STRUT[2]] —**strut′ter,** *n.*

—**Syn. 1.** STRUT and SWAGGER refer especially to carriage in walking. STRUT implies swelling pride or pompousness; to walk with a stiff, pompous, affected, self-conscious gait: *a turkey struts about the farmyard.* SWAGGER implies a domineering, sometimes jaunty, superiority or challenge, and a self-important manner: *to swagger down the street.*

strut[2] (strŭt), *n., v.,* **strutted, strutting.** —*n.* **1.** a piece of wood or iron, or some other member of a structure, designed for the reception of pressure or weight in the direction of its length. —*v.t.* **2.** to brace or support by a strut or struts. [cf. LG *strutt* stiff; akin to STRUT[1]]

struthious (stro͞o′thĭ əs), *adj.* related to or resembling the ostrich. [f. LL *strūthi(o)* ostrich (t. Gk: m. *strouthíon*) + -OUS]

strutting (strŭt′ĭng), *adj.* that struts; walking pompously; pompous. —**strut′tingly,** *adv.*

strychnic (strĭk′nĭk), *adj.* of or obtained from strychnine.

strychnine (strĭk′nēn), *n.* a colourless crystalline poison, $C_{21}H_{22}N_2O_2$, derived from the nux vomica: has a powerful stimulating effect on the central nervous system and can be used in small quantities to stimulate the appetite. Also, *Archaic.* **strychnia** (strĭk′nĭ ə). [t. F, f. s. L *strychnos* (t. Gk: kind of nightshade) + *-ine* -INE²]

strychninism (strĭk′nē nĭz′əm), *n. Pathol. Obs.* a morbid condition induced by an overdose, or by excessive use, of strychnine.

St Swithin's Day (sənt swĭth′ĭnz), July 15th; the legend is that if it rains on this day it will rain for 40 days thereafter, but if it is fine 40 days of fine weather will follow. [named after *St Swithin*, 800?–862, bishop of Winchester 842–862]

St Thomas, **1.** one of the Virgin Islands, in the U.S. part of the group. 16,201 pop. (1960); 32 sq. mi. **2.** former name of **Charlotte Amalie. 3.** São Tomé.

St Tropez (*Fr.* săɴ trō pĕ′), a fishing port in SE France, in Var department: holiday resort.

Stuart (styōōət), *n.* **1.** Also, **Stewart.** the royal house which reigned in Scotland from Robert II to James VI (1371–1603) and in England and Scotland from James I (previously James VI of Scotland) to Anne (1603–1714). **2. Mary.** See **Mary Stuart** of Scotland.

stub (stŭb), *n., v.,* **stubbed, stubbing.** —*n.* **1.** a short projecting part. **2.** the end of a fallen tree, shrub, or plant left fixed in the ground; a stump. **3.** a short remaining piece, as of a pencil, a candle, a cigar, etc. **4.** something unusually short, as a short, thick nail or a short-pointed, blunt pen. **5.** a worn horseshoe nail. **6.** the counterfoil of a chequebook, etc. —*v.t.* **7.** to strike, as one's toe, against something projecting from a surface. **8.** to clear of stubs, as land. **9.** to dig up by the roots; grub up (roots). **10. stub out,** to extinguish (a cigarette) by pressing the lighted end against a hard surface. [ME and OE, c. MLG and MD *stubbe*]

stub axle, *Motor Vehicles.* a short axle which carries a wheel used for steering a vehicle, and which is capable of restricted angular movement about a kingpin.

stubbed (stŭbd), *adj.* **1.** reduced to or resembling a stub; short and thick; stumpy. **2.** abounding in or rough with stubs. —**stub′bedness,** *n.*

stubble (stŭb′l), *n.* **1.** (*usually pl.*) the stump of a grain stalk or the like, left in the ground when the crop is cut. **2.** such stumps collectively. **3.** any short, rough growth, as of beard. [ME, t. OF: m. *stuble,* g. LL *stupula.* See STIPULE] —**stub′bled, stub′bly,** *adj.*

stubborn (stŭb′ən), *adj.* **1.** unreasonably obstinate; obstinately perverse. **2.** fixed or set in purpose or opinion; resolute. **3.** obstinately maintained, as a course of action: *a stubborn resistance.* **4.** hard to deal with or manage. **5.** hard, tough, or stiff, as stone or wood. [ME *stiborn(e)*, appar. der. OE *stybb* STUB] —**stub′bornly,** *adv.* —**stub′bornness,** *n.*

—**Syn. 2.** STUBBORN, DOGGED, OBSTINATE, PERSISTENT imply fixity of purpose or condition, and resistance to change. STUBBORN and OBSTINATE both imply resistance to advice, entreaty, remonstrance, or force; but STUBBORN implies more of innate quality and is the more frequently used when referring to inanimate things: *stubborn disposition, stubborn difficulties.* DOGGED implies pertinacity and grimness in doing something, esp. in the face of discouragements: *dogged determination.* PERSISTENT implies having staying or lasting qualities, resoluteness, and perseverance: *persistent questioning.* —**Ant. 2.** complaisant, obedient, manageable.

Stubbs (stŭbz), *n.* **1. George,** 1724–1806, English painter. **2. William,** 1825–1901, English bishop and historian.

stubby (stŭb′ĭ), *adj.,* **-bier, -biest. 1.** of the nature of or resembling a stub. **2.** short and thick or broad; thickset. **3.** consisting of or abounding in stubs. **4.** bristly, as the hair or beard. —**stub′biness,** *n.*

stub nail, 1. a short, thick nail. **2.** an old or worn horseshoe nail.

stucco (stŭk′ō), *n., pl.* **-coes, -cos,** *v.,* **-coed, -coing.** —*n.* **1.** a plaster (as of slaked lime, chalk, and pulverized white marble, or of plaster of Paris and glue) used for cornices and mouldings of rooms and for other decorations. **2.** a cement or concrete imitating stone, for coating exterior walls of houses, etc. **3.** any of various plasters, cements, etc. **4.** work made of such materials. —*v.t.* **5.** to cover or ornament with stucco. [t. It., t. Gmc; cf. OHG *stukki* crust] —**stuc′coer,** *n.*

stuccowork (stŭk′ō wûk′), *n.* work made of stucco.

stuck (stŭk), *v.* **1.** pt. and pp. of **stick². 2. stuck on,** *Chiefly U.S. Slang.* struck on; infatuated with.

stuck-up (stŭk′ŭp′), *adj. Colloq.* conceited; haughty.

stud¹ (stŭd), *n., v.,* **studded, studding.** —*n.* **1.** a boss, knob, nailhead, or other protuberance projecting from a surface or part, esp. as an ornament. **2.** a post or upright prop, as in the wall of a building. **3.** any of various projecting pins, lugs, or the like on machines, etc. **4.** a short rod, threaded on both ends, screwed in and projecting from something, used to fasten parts together or used as a short journal as in the change gears on a screw-cutting lathe. **5.** a kind of small button or fastener, commonly of metal, bone, or the like, in the form of a small knob and a disc connected by a stem, used (when passed through small buttonholes or the like) for holding together parts of clothing (as detachable collars to shirts) or for ornament. **6.** See **stud poker.** —*v.t.* **7.** to set with or as with studs, bosses, or the like. **8.** to scatter over with things set at intervals. **9.** (of things) to be scattered over the surface of. **10.** to set or scatter (objects) at intervals over a surface. **11.** to furnish with or support by studs or upright props. [ME *stude,* OE *studu,* c. MHG *stud;* akin to G *Stütze*]

stud² (stŭd), *n.* **1.** a number of horses, as for racing or hunting, belonging to one owner. **2.** an establishment in which horses are kept for breeding. **3.** *U.S.* a studhorse or stallion. —*adj.* **4.** of, associated with, or pertaining to a studhorse. **5.** retained for breeding purposes. [ME and OE *stōd,* c. Icel. *stōdh*]

studbook (stŭd′bo͝ok′), *n.* a genealogical register of a stud; a book giving the pedigree of horses.

studding (stŭd′ĭng), *n.* **1.** studs of a wall, partition, or the like, collectively. **2.** material for such studs.

studdingsail (stŭd′ĭng sāl′; *Naut.* stŭn′səl), *n. Naut.* a light sail sometimes set outboard of either of the leeches of a square sail, and extended by booms. See illus. under **sail.**

student (styo͞o′dnt), *n.* **1.** one who is engaged in a course of study and instruction, as at a college, university, or professional or technical school. **2.** one who studies a subject systematically or in detail. [ME, t. L: s. *studens,* ppr., being eager, studying; r. ME *studiant,* t. OF] —**Syn. 1.** See **pupil¹.**

studentship (styo͞o′dnt shĭp′), *n.* **1.** the state or condition of being a student. **2.** a grant of money for a student; scholarship.

stud-farm (stŭd′fām′), *n.* a place where horses are bred.

studhorse (stŭd′hôs′), *n.* a stallion kept for breeding.

studied (stŭd′ĭd), *adj.* **1.** marked by or suggestive of effort, rather than spontaneous or natural: *studied simplicity.* **2.** carefully considered. **3.** *Rare.* learned. —**stud′iedly,** *adv.* —**stud′iedness,** *n.* —**Syn. 1.** See **elaborate.**

studio (styo͞o′dĭ ō′), *n., pl.* **-dios. 1.** the workroom or atelier of an artist, as a painter or sculptor. **2.** a room or place in which some form of art is pursued: *a music studio.* **3.** a room or set of rooms specially equipped for broadcasting radio or television programmes or making recordings. **4.** (*often pl.*) all the buildings occupied by a company engaged in making films. [t. It., t. L: m. *studium* zeal, study, LL a place for study]

studio couch, a kind of divan used as both a couch and a bed.

studious (styo͞o′dyəs), *adj.* **1.** disposed or given to study: *a studious boy.* **2.** concerned with, characterized by, or pertaining to study: *studious tastes.* **3.** zealous, assiduous, or painstaking: *studious care.* **4.** studied or carefully maintained. **5.** *Poetic.* (of places) used or frequented for purposes of study. [ME, t. L: m. s. *studiōsus*] —**stu′diously,** *adv.* —**stu′diousness,** *n.*

stud poker, a variety of poker in which some rounds of cards are dealt face up.

studwork (stŭd′wûk′), *n.* **1.** construction with studs or upright scantlings. **2.** work containing or supported by studs.

study (stŭd′ĭ), *n., pl.* **studies,** *v.,* **studied, studying.** —*n.* **1.** application of the mind to the acquisition of knowledge, as by reading, investigation, or reflection. **2.** the cultivation of a particular branch of learning, science, or art: *the study of law.* **3.** a particular course of effort to acquire knowledge: *to pursue special medical studies.* **4.** something studied or to be studied. **5.** a thorough examination and analysis of a particular subject. **6.** a written account of this. **7.** zealous endeavour or assiduous effort. **8.** the object of the endeavour or effort. **9.** deep thought, reverie, or a state of abstraction: *to be in a brown study.* **10.** a room, in a house or other building, set apart for private study, reading, writing, or the like. **11.** *Music.* a composition, usually instrumental, combining the instructive purpose of an exercise with a certain amount of artistic value; an étude. **12.** *Lit.* **a.** a composition, executed for exercise or as an experiment in a particular method of treatment. **b.** such a composition dealing in detail with a particular subject. **13.** *Art.* something produced as an educational exercise, or as a memorandum or record of observations or effects, or as a guide for a finished production. —*v.i.* **14.** to apply oneself to the acquisition of knowledge, as by reading, investigation, practice, etc. **15.** to apply oneself, or endeavour. **16.** to think deeply, reflect, or consider. —*v.t.* **17.** to apply oneself to acquiring a knowledge of (a branch of learning, science, or art, or a subject), esp. systematically. **18.** to examine or investigate carefully and

in detail: *to study the political situation.* **19.** to observe attentively; scrutinize: *to study a person's face.* **20.** to read (a book, document, etc.) with careful effort. **21.** to seek to learn or memorize, as a part in a play. **22.** to give careful consideration to. **23.** to aim at; seek to acquire.
[ME *studie*, t. L: m. *studium* zeal, application, study, LL a place for study]

—Syn. 18. STUDY, CONSIDER, REFLECT, WEIGH imply fixing the mind upon something generally with a view to some decision or action. STUDY implies an attempt to obtain a grasp of something by methodical or exhaustive thought: *to study a problem.* To CONSIDER is to fix the thought upon something and give it close attention before making a decision concerning it, or beginning an action connected with it: *consider ways and means.* REFLECT implies looking back quietly over past experience and giving it consideration: *reflect on similar cases in the past.* WEIGH implies a deliberate and judicial estimate, as by a balance: *weigh a decision.*

stuff (stŭf), *n.* **1.** the material of which anything is made. **2.** material to be worked upon, or to be used in making something. **3.** matter or material indefinitely: *cushions filled with some soft stuff.* **4.** woven material or fabric. **5.** *Colloq.* property, as personal belongings, equipment, etc. **6.** something to be swallowed, as food, drink, or medicine. **7.** inward character, qualities, or capabilities. **8.** *Slang.* actions, performances, talk, etc.: *to cut out the rough stuff.* **9.** worthless matter or things. **10.** worthless or foolish ideas, talk, or writing. **11.** *Colloq.* literary, artistic, or musical material, productions, compositions, etc. **12.** *Colloq.* one's own trade, profession, occupation, etc.: *to know one's stuff.* **13. do one's stuff,** *Colloq.* to do what is expected of one; show what one can do. **14. that's the stuff,** *Colloq.* that is what is needed, right, proper, etc.
—v.t. **15.** to fill (a receptacle), esp. by packing the contents closely together; cram full. **16.** to fill (an aperture, cavity, etc.) by forcing something into it. **17.** to fill or line with some kind of material as a padding or packing. **18.** to fill or cram (oneself, one's stomach, etc.) with food. **19.** to fill (a chicken, turkey, piece of meat, etc.) with seasoned breadcrumbs or other savoury matter. **20.** to fill the skin of (a dead animal) with material, preserving the natural form and appearance. **21.** *U.S.* to put fraudulent votes into (a ballot box). **22.** to thrust or cram (something) tightly into a receptacle, cavity, or the like. **23.** to pack tightly in a confined place; crowd together. **24.** to crowd (a vehicle, room, etc.) with persons. **25.** to fill (the mind) with details, facts, etc. **26.** *Leather Mfg.* to treat (a skin, etc.) with a composition of tallow and other ingredients. **27.** to stop up or plug; block or choke (usually fol. by *up*). **28.** *Taboo Slang.* (of males) to have sexual intercourse with. *—v.i.* **30.** to cram oneself with food; feed gluttonously. **31.** *Taboo Slang.* **get stuffed,** (used offensively) to go away, leave (one) alone. [ME, t. OF: m. *estoffe* material, provision, der. *estoffer* provide, t. Gmc (cf. MHG *stopfen*), t. LL: m. *stuppāre*, der. *stuppa* tow. Cf. STOP]
—Syn. 1–3. See **matter. 9.** rubbish, trash. **10.** nonsense, twaddle, balderdash. **15.** cram, pack, fill.

stuffed shirt (stŭft), *Slang.* a pompous, pretentious person.

stuffing (stŭf′ĭng), *n.* **1.** the act of one who or that which stuffs. **2.** that with which anything is or may be stuffed. **3.** seasoned breadcrumbs or other filling used to stuff a chicken, turkey, etc., before cooking. **4. knock** or **beat the stuffing out of,** *Colloq.* to destroy the self-confidence of or defeat utterly.

stuffing box, *Mach.* a contrivance for securing a steam-tight, airtight, or watertight joint at the place or hole where a movable rod (as a piston rod) enters a vessel, consisting typically of a cylindrical box or chamber through the middle of which the rod passes, the rest of the space being filled with packing held in by a cover or adjustable member at one end of the box.

stuffing nut, the nut on a stuffing box that serves to condense the packing and so to tighten the seal.

stuffy (stŭf′ĭ), *adj.*, **stuffier, stuffiest. 1.** close or ill-ventilated, as a room; oppressive from lack of freshness, as the air, etc. **2.** lacking in interest, as writing or discourse. **3.** affected with a sensation of obstruction in the respiratory passages, as a person. **4.** dull; boring; tedious. **5.** conceited; self-important. **6.** straitlaced; prim; easily shocked. **7.** old-fashioned; immune to new ideas. **—stuff′ily,** *adv.* **—stuff′iness,** *n.*

stull (stŭl), *n. Mining.* **1.** a timber prop. **2.** one piece of timber set for a mine support, usually the top piece. [cf. G *Stollen* prop]

stultify (stŭl′tĭ fī′), *v.t.*, **-fied, -fying. 1.** to make, or cause to appear, foolish or ridiculous. **2.** to render absurdly or wholly futile or ineffectual, as efforts. **3.** *Law.* to allege or prove to be of unsound mind; allege (oneself) to be insane. [t. LL: m. s. *stultificāre*, der. L *stultus* foolish. See -FY] **—stultification** (stŭl′tĭ fĭ kā′shən), *n.* **—stul′tifi′er,** *n.*

stumble (stŭm′bl), *v.*, **-bled, -bling,** *n.* *—v.i.* **1.** to strike the foot against something in walking, running, etc., so as to stagger or fall; trip. **2.** to walk or go unsteadily. **3.** to make a slip, mistake, or blunder, esp. a verbal one. **4.** to proceed in a hesitating or blundering manner, as in action or speech. **5.** to come accidentally or unexpectedly (fol. by *on, upon, across,* etc.). **6.** to falter or hesitate, as at an obstacle to progress or belief. *—v.t.* **7.** to cause to stumble; trip. **8.** to give pause to; puzzle or perplex. *—n.* **9.** the act of stumbling. **10.** a moral lapse or error. **11.** a slip or blunder. [ME, c. Norw. *stumla*; akin to STAMMER] **—stum′bler,** *n.* **—stum′blingly,** *adv.*

stumbling block, an obstacle or hindrance to progress, belief, etc.

stumer (styo͞o′mə), *n. Slang.* **1.** a worthless or forged cheque. **2.** anything counterfeit or bogus. [orig. unknown]

stump (stŭmp), *n.* **1.** the lower end of a tree or plant left after the main part falls or is cut off; a standing tree trunk from which the utter part and the branches have been removed. **2.** the part of a limb of the body remaining after the rest has been cut off. **3.** a part of a broken or decayed tooth left in the gum. **4.** a short remnant of a pencil, candle, cigar, etc. **5.** any basal part remaining after the main or more important part has been removed. **6.** a wooden or artificial leg. **7.** (*usually pl.*) *Colloq.* a leg: *to stir one's stumps.* **8.** a short, stumpy person. **9.** a heavy step or gait, as of a wooden-legged or lame person. **10.** *Chiefly U.S.* the platform or place of political speech-making: *to go on the stump.* **11.** an instrument consisting of a short, thick, roll of paper or soft leather, or a bar of indiarubber or other soft material, usually cut to a blunt point at each end, used for rubbing the lights and shades in crayon drawing or charcoal drawing, or for otherwise altering the effect. **12.** *Cricket.* each of the three upright sticks which, with the two bails laid on the top of them, form a wicket. **13. draw stumps,** *Cricket.* to cease play.
—v.t. **14.** to reduce to a stump; truncate; lop. **15.** to clear of stumps, as land. **16.** *U.S. Colloq.* to stub, as one's toe. **17.** to nonplus, embarrass, or render completely at a loss. **18.** *Chiefly U.S. Colloq.* to make political speeches in or to. **20.** *Cricket.* (of the wicket-keeper) to put (a batsman) out by knocking down a stump or by dislodging a bail with the ball held in the hand, at a moment when the batsman is out of his ground. **21.** to tone or modify (crayon drawings, etc.) by means of a stump.
—v.i. **22.** to walk heavily or clumsily, as if with a wooden leg: *the sailor stumped across the deck.* **23.** *Chiefly U.S. Colloq.* to make speeches in an election campaign. **24. stump up,** *Colloq.* to pay up or hand over money required.
[ME *stomp*, c. G *Stumpf*]

stumpage (stŭm′pĭj), *n. U.S.* **1.** standing timber with reference to its value. **2.** the right to cut such timber on the owner's land. **3.** the value of such timber.

stumper (stŭm′pə), *n.* **1.** one who or that which stumps. **2.** a puzzling question; poser; problem.

stump-jump plough (stŭmp′jŭmp′), *Austral.* a plough designed to avoid roots and stumps in newly cleared ground.

stumpnose (stŭmp′nōz′), *n.* either of two South African sea fish, the edible **red stumpnose,** *Chrysoblephus gibbiceps*, and the **white stumpnose,** *Austrospanus globiceps.*

stump orator, *U.S.* one who travels around making political speeches; a demagogue; rabble rouser. **—stump oratory.**

stumptail (stŭmp′tāl′), *n.* the krombek (bird), *Sylvietta rufescens*, of Africa.

stumpy (stŭm′pĭ), *adj.*, **stumpier, stumpiest. 1.** of the nature of or resembling a stump. **2.** short and thick; stubby; stocky. **3.** abounding in stumps. **—stump′ily,** *adv.* **—stump′iness,** *n.*

stun (stŭn), *v.*, **stunned, stunning,** *n.* *—v.t.* **1.** to deprive of consciousness or strength by or as by a blow, fall, etc. **2.** to strike with astonishment; astound; amaze. **3.** to daze or bewilder by distracting noise. *—n.* **4.** the act of stunning. **5.** the condition of being stunned. [ME; OE *stunian* resound, crash. Cf. OF *estoner* resound, stun]
—Syn. 1. See **shock**[1].

stung (stŭng), *v.* pt. and pp. of **sting.**

stunk (stŭngk), *v.* a pt. and the pp. of **stink.**

stunner (stŭn′ə), *n.* **1.** one who or that which stuns. **2.** *Colloq.* a person or thing of striking excellence, beauty, attractiveness, etc.

stunning (stŭn′ĭng), *adj.* **1.** that stuns. **2.** *Colloq.* of striking excellence, beauty, etc. **—stun′ningly,** *adv.*

stunsail (stŭn′səl), *n.* studdingsail.

stunt[1] (stŭnt), *v.t.* **1.** to check the growth or development of; dwarf; hinder the increase or progress of. *—n.* **2.** a check in growth or development. **3.** arrested development. **4.** a creature hindered from attaining its proper growth. [v. use of *stunt*, adj. (now d.), dwarfed, stubborn (in ME and OE foolish), c. MHG *stunz*, Icel. *stuttr* short]

stunt[2] (stŭnt), *n.* **1.** a performance serving as a display of strength, activity, skill, or the like, as in athletics, etc.; a feat. **2.** anything done to attract publicity. *—v.i.* **3.** to do a stunt or stunts. [orig. uncert.]

stunted (stŭn′tĭd), *adj.* having failed to reach full growth; dwarfish; underdeveloped.

stunt man, one who is paid to perform hazardous or acrobatic feats, esp. one who replaces a film actor in scenes requiring such feats.

stupa (stōō′pə), *n.* a monumental pile of earth or other material, either dome-shaped or pyramidal, in memory of Buddha or a Buddhist saint, and commemorating some event or marking a sacred spot. [t. Skt]

stupe (styōōp), *n.* two or more layers of flannel or other cloth soaked in hot water, applied to the skin as a counterirritant. [ME, t. L: m. *stūpa* tow]

stupefacient (styōō′pĭ fā′shyənt), *adj.* **1.** stupefying; producing stupor. *—n.* **2.** a drug or agent that produces stupor. [t. L: s. *stupefaciens*, ppr., stupefying]

stupefaction (styōō′pĭ făk′shən), *n.* **1.** the act of stupefying. **2.** the state of being stupefied; stupor; numbness of the faculties. **3.** overwhelming amazement.

stupefactive (styōō′pĭ făk′tĭv), *adj.* serving to stupefy.

stupefy (styōō′pĭ fī′), *v.t.*, **-fied, -fying. 1.** to put into a state of stupor; dull the faculties of. **2.** to stun as with a narcotic, a shock, strong emotion, etc. **3.** to overwhelm with amazement; astound. [t. L: m. s. *stupefacere*] **—stu′-pefi′er,** *n.*

stupendous (styōō pĕn′dəs), *adj.* **1.** such as to cause amazement; astounding; marvellous. **2.** amazingly large or great; immense: *a stupendous mass of information.* [t. L: m. *stupendus*, ger., to be wondered at] **—stupen′-dously,** *adv.* **—stupen′dousness,** *n.*

stupid (styōō′pĭd), *adj.* **1.** lacking ordinary activity and keenness of mind; dull. **2.** characterized by, indicative of, or proceeding from mental dullness: *a stupid act.* **3.** tediously dull or uninteresting: *a stupid book.* **4.** in a state of stupor; stupefied. *—n.* **5.** *Colloq.* a stupid person. [t. L: s. *stupidus*] **—stu′pidly,** *adv.* **—stu′pidness,** *n.* **—Syn. 1.** See **dull. 2.** See **foolish.**

stupidity (styōō pĭd′ĭ tĭ), *n.*, *pl.* **-ties. 1.** the state, quality, or fact of being stupid. **2.** a stupid act, notion, speech, etc.

stupor (styōō′pə), *n.* **1.** suspension or great diminution of sensibility, as in disease or as caused by narcotics, intoxicants, etc. **2.** a state of suspended or deadened sensibility. **3.** mental torpor, or apathy; stupefaction. [ME, t. L] **—stu′porous,** *adj.*

sturdy[1] (stû′dĭ), *adj.*, **-dier, -diest. 1.** strongly built, stalwart, or robust. **2.** strong, as in substance, construction, texture, etc.: *sturdy walls.* **3.** firm, stout, or indomitable: *sturdy defenders.* **4.** of strong or hardy growth, as a plant. [ME, t. OF: m. *estourdi* dazed, reckless, pp. of *estourdir* stun, LL *exturdīre* deafen (with chatter), der. *turdus* turtledove] **—stur′dily,** *adv.* **—stur′diness,** *n.* **—Syn. 1.** hardy, muscular, brawny. See **strong. 3.** resolute, vigorous.

sturdy[2] (stû′dĭ), *n.* *Vet. Sci.* gid. [ME adj. meaning 'giddy', t. OF. See STURDY[1]] **—stur′died,** *adj.*

sturgeon (stû′jən), *n.* any of various large ganoid fishes of the family *Acipenseridae*, found in fresh and salt waters of the North Temperate Zone, and valued for their flesh and as a source of caviar and isinglass. [ME, t. AF, var. of OF *sturg(i)un*, g. VL *sturio*, t. Gmc; cf. OHG *sturio*]

Sturmabteilung (*Ger.* shtōōrm′ăp′tī lōōng),′ *n.* a Nazi Party militia, the Brownshirts, formed in the early 1920s, notorious for its violence and terrorism before 1934, and thereafter an instrument of physical training and political education. *Abbrev.:* SA. [G: lit., storm section]

Sturm und Drang (*Ger.* shtōōrm′ōōnt drăng′), a period in German literature (about 1770–90) noted for the impetuosity of thought and style of the younger writers and an insistence on the claims of feeling and intuition as against the prevailing rationalism. [G: storm and stress]

Sturt (stût), *n.* **Charles,** 1795–1869, English explorer in Australia.

Sturt Desert, an arid area in central Australia on the borders of South Australia and Queensland.

Sturt's desert pea (stûts), an Australian plant, *Clianthus formosus*, with brilliant scarlet and purple flowers, found in inland desert country.

stutter (stŭt′ə), *v.t.*, *v.i.* **1.** to utter (sounds) in which the rhythm is interrupted by blocks or spasms, repetitions, or prolongation of sounds or syllables, sometimes accompanied by facial contortions. *—n.* **2.** unrhythmical and distorted speech characterized principally by blocks or spasms interrupting the rhythm. [freq. of d. *stut*, ME *stutte(n)*, akin to D *stotteren*] **—stut′terer,** *n.* **—stut′-teringly,** *adv.* **—Syn. 1.** See **stammer.**

Stuttgart (stōōt′gät; *Ger.* shtōōt′gärt), *n.* a city in West Germany, capital of Baden-Württemberg, in the N central part. 630,500 (est. 1966).

St Valentine's Day (sənt văl′ən tīnz′), February 14th, traditionally the day on which valentines are given.

St Vincent (sənt vĭn′sənt), **1.** a British colony (including the N part of the Grenadines) in the West Indies, in the S Windward Islands. 80,042 pop. (1960); 150 sq. mi. *Cap.:* Kingstown. **2. Cape,** the SW tip of Portugal: naval battle, 1797. **3. Gulf,** an indentation of the Great Australian Bight on the coast of South Australia E of the Yorke Peninsula. ab. 100 mi. long and 40 mi. wide.

St Vitus's dance (sənt vī′tə sĭz), *Pathol.* chorea (def. 1). Also, **St Vitus dance.**

sty[1] (stī), *n.*, *pl.* **sties,** *v.*, **stied, stying.** *—n.* **1.** a pen or enclosure for pigs. **2.** any filthy abode. **3.** a place of bestial debauchery. *—v.t.* **4.** to keep or lodge in or as in a sty. *—v.i.* **5.** to live in or as in a sty. [ME; OE *stig*, c. Icel. *stī*; akin to D *stijg*]

sty[2] (stī), *n.*, *pl.* **sties.** *Pathol.* a circumscribed inflammatory swelling, like a small boil, on the edge of the eyelid. Also, **stye.** [back-formation from ME *styanye*, f. *styan* (OE *stīgend* sty, lit., rising) + *ye* EYE, but taken to mean sty on eye]

stygian (stĭj′ĭ ən), *adj.* **1.** of or pertaining to the river Styx or the lower world. **2.** dark or gloomy. **3.** infernal; hellish. [f. s. L *Stygius* (t. Gk: m. *Stýgios*) + -AN]

styl-, var. of **stylo-,** before vowels, as in *stylar.*

stylar (stī′lə), *adj.* having the shape of a style (def. 11); resembling a pen, pin, or peg.

style (stīl), *n.*, *v.*, **styled, styling.** *—n.* **1.** a particular kind, sort, or type, as with reference to form, appearance, or character. **2.** a particular, distinctive, or characteristic mode of action. **3.** a mode of living, as with respect to expense or display. **4.** elegant or fashionable mode of living. **5.** a mode of fashion, as in dress; esp. good or approved fashion; elegance; smartness. **6.** characteristic mode of writing or speaking, as determined by period, literary form, personality, etc.: *the style of Johnson.* **7.** the features of a literary composition belonging to the form of expression other than the content. **8.** a manner or tone adopted in speaking to others. **9.** a particular, distinctive, or characteristic mode or form of construction or execution in any art or work. **10.** a descriptive or distinguishing appellation; esp., a legal, official, or recognized title: *a firm trading under the style of Smith, Jones & Co.* **11.** Also, **stylus.** an instrument of metal, bone, or the like, used by the ancients for writing on a waxed tablet, having one end pointed for incising the letters, and the other end blunt for rubbing out writing and smoothing the tablet. **12.** something resembling or suggesting such an instrument. **13.** a pointed instrument for drawing, etching, or writing. **14.** the gnomon of a sundial. **15.** a mode of reckoning time. **16. Old Style** or **New Style,** the reckoning of time according to the Julian calendar (which see) or the Gregorian calendar (which see) respectively, the dates in the former calendar being replaced in the latter calendar by dates 10 days later from 1582 to 1700, 11 days later from 1700 to 1800, 12 days later from 1800 to 1900, and 13 days later since 1900, so that now Sept. 3rd, Old Style, is the same as Sept. 16th, New Style. **17.** *Bot.* a narrow, usually cylindrical and more or less filiform extension of the ovary, which, when present, bears the stigma at its apex. **18.** *Zool.* a small, slender, pointed process or part. **19.** the rules of spelling, punctuation, capitalization, etc., observed by a publishing house, newspaper, etc. *—v.t.* **20.** to call by a particular style or appellation (as specified); to denominate; name; call. **21.** to design in accordance with a given or new style: *to style an evening dress.* **22.** to make conform to a specific style. *—v.i.* **23.** to do decorative work with a style or stylus. [ME, t. OF, t. L: m. s. *stilus* (incorrectly *stylus*); orig. def. 11, whence 9, whence 1, etc. In defs 14 and 17, confused with derivs of Gk *stŷlos* pillar] **—styl′er,** *n.* **—Syn. 5.** See **fashion.**

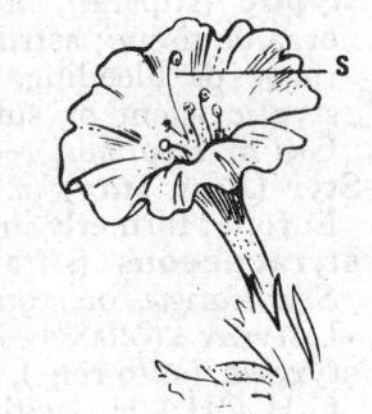

S, Style (def. 17)

stylebook (stīl′bŏŏk′), *n.* **1.** a book containing rules of usage in typography, punctuation, etc., employed by printers, editors, and writers. **2.** a book featuring styles, fashions, or the rules of styles.

stylet (stī′lĭt), *n.* **1.** a stiletto or dagger. **2.** some similar sharp-pointed instrument. **3.** *Med.* **a.** a probe. **b.** a wire run through the length of a catheter, cannula, or needle to make it rigid or to clear it. **4.** *Zool.* style (def. 18). [t. F, t. It.: m. *stiletto* STILETTO]

styliform (stī′lĭ fôm′), *adj.* having the shape of a style (def. 11); stylar.

stylish (stī′lĭsh), *adj.* characterized by style, or by conforming to the fashionable standard; modishly elegant; smart. —**styl′ishly,** *adv.* —**styl′ishness,** *n.*

stylist (stī′lĭst), *n.* **1.** a writer or speaker who is skilled in or who cultivates a literary style. **2.** one who designs clothing, interior decorations, etc. **3.** one who cultivates any particular style.

stylistic (stī lĭs′tĭk), *adj.* of or pertaining to style. —**stylis′tically,** *adv.*

stylite (stī′līt), *n. Eccles. Hist.* one of a class of solitary ascetics who lived on the top of high pillars or columns. [t. Eccl. Gk: m. *stȳlítēs*, der. Gk *stŷlos* pillar]

stylize (stī′līz), *v.t.*, **-lized, -lizing.** to conform to a particular style, as of representation or treatment in art; conventionalize. Also, **stylise.** —**styl′iza′tion,** *n.* —**styl′izer,** *n.*

stylo-, a combining form, frequent in scientific terminology, representing (1) **style,** (2) **styloid.**

stylobate (stī′lə bāt′), *n. Archit.* a continuous base supporting a row of columns; that part of a stereobate immediately beneath the columns. [t. L: m. s. *stylobata*, t. Gk: m. *stȳlobátēs*]

stylograph (stī′lə grăf′, -gräf′), *n.* a fountain pen in which the writing point is a fine, hollow tube instead of a nib.

stylographic (stī′lə grăf′ĭk), *adj.* **1.** of or pertaining to a stylograph. **2.** of or pertaining to stylography. Also, **stylographical.** —**sty′lograph′ically,** *adv.*

stylography (stī lŏg′rə fĭ), *n.* the art of writing, tracing, drawing, etc., with a stylus. [f. *stylo-* (comb. form repr. STYLUS) + -GRAPHY]

styloid (stī′loid), *adj. Anat.* **1.** resembling a style; slender and pointed. **2.** denoting several bony processes on the temporal bone, radius, ulna, etc. [t. NL: s. *stȳloīdēs*, t. Gk: m. *stȳloeidḗs*]

stylolite (stī′lə līt′), *adj.* **1.** of or pertaining to a column-like structure found in certain limestones, the columns having grooved sides and being composed of limestone and generally at right angles or highly inclined to the bedding planes. —*n.* **2.** a stylolite structure. [f. Gk *stŷlo(s)* pillar + -LITE]

stylopodium (stī′lə pō′dyəm), *n., pl.* **-dia** (-dyə). *Bot.* a glandular disc or expansion surmounting the ovary in umbelliferous plants and supporting the styles.

stylus (stī′ləs), *n.* **1.** a pointed instrument for writing on wax or other suitable surfaces. **2.** a cutting tool, often needle-shaped, used to cut grooves in making gramophone records. **3.** a needle tipped with diamond, sapphire, etc., for reproducing the sound of a gramophone record. **4.** any of various pointed instruments used in drawing, tracing, stencilling, etc. [t. L, var. of *stilus*]

stymie (stī′mĭ), *n., v.*, **-mied, -mieing.** —*n.* **1.** *Golf.* a position in which an opponent's ball is lying directly between the player's ball and the hole for which he is playing. **2.** any problem which is difficult to resolve. —*v.t.* **3.** to hinder or block, as with a stymie; thwart; frustrate.

stymy (stī′mĭ), *n., pl.* **-mies,** *v.t.*, **-mied, -mying.** stymie.

stypsis (stĭp′sĭs), *n.* the employment or application of styptics. [t. LL, t. Gk]

styptic (stĭp′tĭk), *adj.* Also, **styp′tical. 1.** contracting organic tissue; astringent; binding. **2.** checking haemorrhage or bleeding, as a drug; haemostatic. —*n.* **3.** a styptic agent or substance. [ME; t. L: s. *stypticus*, t. Gk: m. *styptikós*] —**stypticity** (stĭp tĭs′ĭ tĭ), *n.*

Styr (*Russ.* stĭry), *n.* a river in the W Soviet Union in Europe: formerly in Poland. ab. 300 mi.

styracaceous (stī′ə rə kā′shəs), *adj.* belonging to the *Styracaceae*, or storax family of shrubs and trees. [f. s. L *styrax* STORAX + -ACEOUS]

styrene (stī′ə rēn′), *n.* a colourless liquid hydrocarbon $C_6H_5CH{:}CH_2$, with a fragrant, aromatic smell, used in making synthetic rubber. [f. L *styr(ax)* STORAX + -ENE]

styrene-butadiene rubber, a widely used, general-purpose, synthetic rubber consisting of a copolymer of butadiene and about 35 per cent styrene. *Abbrev.*: SBR.

styrene resin, the transparent plastic formed by the polymerization of styrene and characterized by its thermoplastic properties.

Styria (stĭ′rĭ ə), *n.* a province in SE Austria: formerly a duchy. 1,137,865 pop. (1961); 6327 sq. mi. *Cap.*: Graz. German, **Steiermark.**

Styx (stĭks), *n. Gk Myth.* a river of the lower world, over which the souls of the dead were ferried by Charon, and by which the gods swore their most solemn oaths.

S.U., *Physics.* strontium unit.

su-, var. of **sub-** before *sp.*

suable (syōō′ə bl), *adj.* capable of being sued; liable to be sued. —**su′abil′ity,** *n.*

Suakin (sōō ä′kĭn), *n.* a seaport in NE Sudan, on the Red Sea. 5000 (est. 1967).

Suárez (*Sp.* swȧ′rèth), *n.* **Francisco** (*Sp.* frȧn thēs′kō), 1548–1617, Spanish theologian and philosopher.

suasion (swā′zhən), *n.* **1.** the act of advising or urging, or attempting to persuade. **2.** an instance of this; a persuasive effort. [ME, t. L: s. *suāsio*] —**suasive** (swā′sĭv), **suasory** (swā′sə rĭ), *adj.*

suave (swäv), *adj.* (of persons or their manner, speech, etc.) smoothly agreeable or polite; agreeably or blandly urbane. [t. L: m. *suāvis* gentle; r. *suaif*, t. F] —**suave′ly,** *adv.* —**Ant.** blunt.

suavity (swä′vĭ tĭ), *n., pl.* **-ties. 1.** suave or smoothly agreeable quality (of persons, manner, etc.). **2.** (*pl.*) suave or courteous actions or manners; amenities. Also, **suaveness.**

sub (sŭb), *n., adj., v.*, **subbed, subbing.** —*n.* **1.** subaltern. **2.** subeditor. **3.** submarine. **4.** subordinate. **5.** subscription. **6.** substitute. **7.** an advance against wages, etc. —*adj.* **8.** substandard. —*v.i.* **9.** to act as a substitute for another. **10.** to pay or receive an advance against wages, etc. —*v.t.* **11.** to pay or receive (an advance against wages, etc.). **12.** to subedit.

sub-, **1.** a prefix meaning 'under', 'not quite', or 'somewhat', freely used as a formative (*subarctic, subcortex, substandard, subacid*), also attached to stems not used independently, with various extensions of meaning (*subject, subtract, subvert*). **2.** *Chem.* **a.** a prefix indicating a basic compound, as in *subacetate, subcarbonate, subnitrate.* **b.** a prefix indicating that the element is present in a relatively small proportion, i.e. in a low oxidation state, as in *subchloride, suboxide.* Also, **su-, suc-, suf-, sug-, sum-, sup-.** [t. L, repr. *sub*, prep., under, close to; akin to HYPO-]

subacid (sŭb′ăs′ĭd), *adj.* **1.** slightly or moderately acid or sour: *a subacid fruit.* **2.** (of speech, temper, etc., or a person) somewhat tart or sharp. —**subacidity** (sŭb′ə sĭd′ĭ tĭ), **sub′ac′idness,** *n.*

subacute (sŭb′ə kyōōt′), *adj.* somewhat or moderately acute.

subadar (sōō′bə dä′), *n. India.* **1.** a provincial governor of the Mogul empire. **2.** the chief native officer of a company of native troops in the British Indian service. Also, **subahda.** [t. Urdu]

subagent (sŭb′ā′jənt), *n.* **1.** one to whom agency duties are assigned by an agent. **2.** one who works for or under the supervision of an agent.

subalpine (sŭb′ăl′pīn), *adj.* **1.** pertaining to the regions at the foot of the Alps. **2.** *Bot.* growing on mountains below the limit of tree growth, and above the foothill, or montane, zone.

subaltern (sŭb′l tən), *adj.* **1.** having an inferior or subordinate position or rank; subordinate. **2.** *Mil.* of or pertaining to a commissioned officer below the rank of captain. **3.** *Logic.* denoting the relation of one proposition to another when the first is implied by the second but not conversely. In Aristotelian logic, a particular proposition stands in this relation to the universal proposition having the same subject, predicate, and quality as the particular. —*n.* **4.** one who has a subordinate position. **5.** *Mil.* a commissioned officer below the rank of captain. **6.** *Logic.* a subaltern proposition. [t. LL: s. *subalternus*, f. L *sub* under + *alternus* one after the other, alternate]

subalternate (sŭb′ôl tû′nĭt), *adj. Bot.* placed singly along an axis, but tending to become grouped oppositely. —**subalternation** (sŭb′ôl′tə nā′shən), *n.*

subantarctic (sŭb′ănt äk′tĭk), *adj.* of, or pertaining to, or similar to the region lying immediately to the north of the Antarctic Circle.

subapostolic (sŭb′ăp′əs tŏl′ĭk), *adj.* of or pertaining to the period of time immediately after the apostles.

subaquatic (sŭb′ə kwăt′ĭk), *adj.* living or growing partly on land, partly in water.

subaqueous (sŭb′ā′kwĭ əs), *adj.* **1.** existing or situated under water. **2.** occurring or performed under water. **3.** used under water.

subarctic (sŭb′äk′tĭk), *adj.* of, pertaining to, or similar to the region immediately south of the Arctic Circle.

subarid (sŭb′ă′rĭd), *adj.* moderately arid.

subassembly (sŭb′ə sĕm′blĭ), *n.* an assembly, as of machine parts, forming part of a larger assembly but capable of being treated as a separate unit for certain purposes.

subastringent (sŭb′ə strĭn′jənt), *adj.* slightly astringent.

subatomic (sŭb′ə tŏm′ĭk), *adj. Physics.* **1.** denoting or pertaining to a particle which is smaller than an atom. **2.** denoting or pertaining to any process which occurs within an atom.

subaudition (sŭb′ô dĭsh′ən), *n.* **1.** the act of understanding or mentally supplying something not expressed. **2.** something mentally supplied; understood or implied meaning. [t. L: s. *subaudītio*]

subauricular (sŭb/ô rĭk′yo͝o lə), *adj. Anat.* situated below the ear.

subaxillary (sŭb/ăk′sĭ lə rĭ), *adj. Bot.* situated or placed beneath an axil.

sub-base (sŭb′bās/), *n. Archit.* the lowest part of a base (as of a column) which consists of two or more horizontal members. —**sub′-ba′sal,** *adj.*

sub-basement (sŭb′bās/mənt), *n.* a basement, or one of a series of basements, below the main basement of a building.

sub-bass (sŭb′bās/), *n. Music.* a pedal stop producing the lowest notes of an organ.

subcalibre (sŭb/kăl′ĭ bə), *adj. Mil.* **1.** (of a projectile) having a diameter less than the calibre of the gun from which it is fired, the projectile being fitted with a disc large enough to fill the bore, or being fired from a tube attached to the inside or the outside of the gun. **2.** used in firing such a projectile: *a subcalibre gun.*

subcartilaginous (sŭb/kä/tĭ lăj′ĭ nəs), *adj. Anat., Zool.* **1.** partially or incompletely cartilaginous. **2.** situated below or beneath cartilage.

subcategory (sŭb/kăt′ĭ gə rĭ), *n.* a subordinate category.

subcelestial (sŭb/sĭ lĕs′tyəl), *adj.* **1.** being beneath the heavens; mundane. —*n.* **2.** a subcelestial being.

subcellar (sŭb′sĕl/ə), *n.* a cellar beneath another cellar.

subclass (sŭb′kläs/), *n.* **1.** a primary division of a class. **2.** a category of related orders within a class. —*v.t.* **3.** to place in a subclass.

subclavian (sŭb/klā′vyən), *Anat.* —*adj.* **1.** situated or extending beneath the clavicle, as certain arteries, veins, etc. **2.** pertaining to such an artery, vein, or the like. —*n.* **3.** a subclavian artery, vein, or the like. [f. s. NL *subclāvius* (der. L *sub-* SUB- + *clāvis* key) + -AN]

subclavian groove, *Anat.* either of two shallow depressions on the first rib, one for the subclavian artery and the other for the subclavian vein.

subclimax (sŭb/klī′măks), *n. Ecol.* the imperfect development of a climax community because of some factor (such as repeated fires in a forest) which arrests the normal succession.

subclinical (sŭb/klĭn′ĭ kl), *adj. Med.* of or pertaining to a disease whose symptoms are so mild that they remain undetected in usual clinical examinations.

subcommittee (sŭb′kə mĭt/ĭ), *n.* a secondary committee appointed out of a main committee.

subconscious (sŭb/kŏn′shəs), *adj.* **1.** existing or operating beneath or beyond consciousness: *the subconscious self.* **2.** imperfectly or not wholly conscious. —*n.* **3.** the totality of mental processes of which the individual is not aware; unreportable mental activities. —**sub/con′sciously,** *adv.* —**sub/con′sciousness,** *n.*

subcontinent (sŭb/kŏn′tĭ nənt), *n.* a large land mass, smaller than a continent.

subcontract (*n.* sŭb/kŏn′trăkt; *v.* sŭb/kən trăkt′), *Law.* —*n.* **1.** a contract by which one agrees to render services or to provide materials necessary for the performance of another contract. —*v.t.* **2.** to make a subcontract for. —*v.i.* **3.** to make a subcontract.

subcontractor (sŭb/kən trăk′tə), *n.* one who contracts to render some performance for another which the latter requires for the performance of his own contract.

subcontrary (sŭb/kŏn′trə rĭ), *Logic.* —*adj.* **1.** pertaining to the relation between any two propositions, both of which may be true, but only one of which can be false. —*n.* **2.** any such proposition.

subcortex (sŭb/kô′tĕks), *n., pl.* **-tices** (-tĭ sēz/). *Anat.* the portions of the brain situated beneath the cerebral cortex.

subcortical (sŭb/kô′tĭ kl), *adj. Anat.* situated beneath the cerebral cortex.

subcritical (sŭb/krĭt′ĭ kl), *adj. Physics.* denoting or pertaining to a nuclear reaction or a nuclear reactor in which the chain-reaction is not self-sustaining. See **supercritical.**

subculture (sŭb kŭl′chə), *v.,* **-tured, -turing,** *n.* —*v.t.* **1.** *Bacteriol.* to cultivate (a bacterial strain) again on a new medium. —*n.* **2.** *Bacteriol.* a culture derived in this way. **3.** *Sociol.* a distinct network of behaviour, beliefs and attitudes existing within a larger culture.

subcutaneous (sŭb/kyo͞o tā′nyəs), *adj.* **1.** situated or lying under the skin, as tissue. **2.** performed or introduced under the skin, as an injection by a syringe. **3.** living below the several layers of the skin, as certain parasites. —**sub/cuta′neously,** *adv.*

subdeacon (sŭb/dē′kən), *n.* a member of the clerical order next below that of deacon. —**subdeaconate** (sŭb/-dē′kə nĭt), *n.*

subdean (sŭb′dēn′), *n.* an assistant dean. —**sub/dean′-ery,** *n.*

subdelirium (sŭb/dĭ lĭ′rĭ əm), *n., pl.* **-liriums, -liria** (-lĭ′rĭ ə). *Med.* a mild or intermittent delirium.

subdiaconal (sŭb/dĭ ăk′ə nəl), *adj.* of or pertaining to a subdeacon.

subdiaconate (sŭb/dĭ ăk′ə nĭt), *n.* **1.** the office or dignity of a subdeacon. **2.** a body of subdeacons.

subdistrict (sŭb′dĭs/trĭkt), *n.* a division of a district.

subdivide (sŭb/dĭ vīd′), *v.,* **-vided, -viding.** —*v.t.* **1.** to divide (a part, or an already divided whole) into smaller parts; divide anew after a first division. **2.** to divide into parts. —*v.i.* **3.** to become separated into subdivisions.

subdivision (sŭb′dĭ vĭzh/ən), *n.* **1.** the act or process of subdividing, or the fact of being subdivided. **2.** an instance of this. **3.** one of the parts into which something is subdivided.

subdominant (sŭb/dŏm′ĭ nənt), *n. Music.* the fourth note of a scale, next below the dominant.

subdual (səb dyo͞o′əl), *n.* **1.** the act of subduing. **2.** the state of being subdued.

subduct (səb dŭkt′), *v.t. Rare.* to take away or withdraw; deduct. —**subduc′tion,** *n.*

subdue (səb dyo͞o′), *v.t.,* **-dued, -duing.** **1.** to conquer and bring into subjection. **2.** to overpower by superior force; overcome. **3.** to bring into mental subjection, as by persuasion or by inspiring awe or fear; render submissive. **4.** to repress (feelings, impulses, etc.). **5.** to bring (land) under cultivation. **6.** to reduce the intensity, force, or vividness of (sound, light, colour, etc.); tone down; soften. **7.** to allay (inflammation, etc.). [ME, through AF, t. OF: m. *so(u)duire* seduce, g. L *subdūcere* remove by stealth; sense development in AF affected by L *subdere* (subdue)] —**subdu′able,** *adj.* —**subdued′ly,** *adv.* —**subdued′ness, subdu′er,** *n.* —**Syn. 1.** See **defeat.** —**Ant. 4.** awaken, arouse. **6.** intensify.

subdued (səb dyo͞od′), *adj.* **1.** quiet; gentle; cowed; inhibited. **2.** (of colours, etc.) not harsh; reduced in intensity; muted.

subedit (sŭb′ĕd′ĭt), *v.t., v.i. Journalism.* to edit and correct (material written by others).

subeditor (sŭb′ĕd′ĭ tə), *n.* **1.** *Journalism.* one who edits and corrects material written by others. **2.** an assistant or subordinate editor. —**subeditorial** (sŭb/ĕd′ĭ tô′rĭ əl), *adj.* —**sub′ed′itorship/,** *n.*

subereous (syo͞o bĭə′rĭ əs), *adj.* of the nature of or resembling cork; suberose. [t. L: m. *sūbereus*]

suberic (syo͞o bĕ′rĭk), *adj.* of or pertaining to cork. [t. F: m. *subérique,* f. L *sūber* cork + *-ique* -IC]

suberic acid, *Chem.* a crystalline dibasic acid, $(CH_2)_6(COOH)_2$, derived from cork.

suberin (syo͞o′bə rĭn), *n. Bot., Biochem.* a substance contained in and characteristic of cork tissue.

suberization (syo͞o′bə rī zā′shən), *n.* . *Bot., Biochem.* the impregnation of cell walls with suberin, causing the formation of cork. Also, **suberisation.**

suberize (syo͞o′bə rīz/), *v.t.,* **-rized, -rizing.** *Bot.* to change into cork tissue. Also, **suberise.** [f. L *sūber* cork + -IZE]

suberose (syo͞o′bə rōs/), *adj.* of the nature of cork; cork-like; corky. Also, **suberous** (syo͞o′bə rəs).

subfamily (sŭb′făm′ĭ lĭ), *n., pl.* **-lies. 1.** *Biol.* a category of related genera within a family. **2.** *Linguistics.* (in the classification of languages) a category of a lower order than a family.

subfebrile (sŭb/fē′brīl), *adj. Med.* of or denoting a condition in which the temperature is slightly above normal.

subfusc (sŭb′fŭsk), *adj.* **1.** of sombre hue; dusky; somewhat dark. —*n.* **2.** clothes of a dark or drab colour. **3.** (at Oxford University) formal academic dress. [t. L: s. *subfuscus,* equiv. to *sub-* SUB- + *fuscus* dark]

subgenus (sŭb/jē′nəs), *n., pl.* **-genera** (-jĕn′ə rə), **-genuses.** a subordinate genus; a subdivision of a genus. —**subgeneric** (sŭb/jĭ nĕ′rĭk), *adj.*

subglacial (sŭb/glā′syəl), *adj.* **1.** beneath a glacier: *a subglacial stream.* **2.** formerly beneath a glacier: *a subglacial deposit.* —**sub/gla′cially,** *adv.*

subgroup (sŭb′gro͞op/), *n.* **1.** a subordinate group; a division of a group. **2.** *Chem.* a vertical division of a group in the periodic table; family.

subheading (sŭb′hĕd/ĭng), *n.* **1.** a title or heading of a subdivision or subsection in a chapter, treatise, essay, newspaper article, etc. **2.** a subordinate division of a heading or title. Also, **sub′head/.**

subhuman (sŭb/hyo͞o′mən), *adj.* **1.** below the human race or type; less than or not quite human. **2.** almost human.

subincision (sŭb/ĭn sĭzh′ən), *n.* the making of an incision of the urethra through the underside of the penis, a custom performed by some primitive tribes, esp. the Australian aborigines.

subindex (sŭb/ĭn′dĕks), *n., pl.* **-dices** (-dĭ sēz/), **-dexes.** *Maths., etc.* a specifying or distinguishing figure or letter following and slightly below a figure, letter, or symbol: *2 is the subindex in* b_2.

subinfeudate (sŭb′ĭn fyōō′dāt), *v.t.*, *v.i.*, **-dated, -dating.** to grant subinfeudation (to).

subinfeudation (sŭb′ĭn′fyōō dā′shən), *n. Feudal Law.* **1.** secondary infeudation; the granting of a portion of an estate by a feudal tenant to a subtenant, held of the tenant on terms similar to those of the grant to him. **2.** the tenure established. **3.** the estate or fief so created.

subinfeudatory (sŭb′ĭn fyōō′də tə rĭ, -trĭ), *n.*, *pl.* **-ries.** one who holds by subinfeudation.

subirrigate (sŭb′ĭ′rĭ gāt′), *v.t.*, **-gated, -gating.** to irrigate beneath the surface of the ground, as with water passing through a system of underground pipes or transmitted through the subsoil from ditches, etc. —**sub′ir′riga′tion,** *n.*

subito (sōō′bĭ tō′; *It.* sōō′bē tô), *adv. Music.* suddenly; abruptly: *f. subito, p. subito.* [It., t. L, abl. of *subitus* sudden]

subj., **1.** subject. **2.** subjective. **3.** subjectively. **4.** subjunctive.

subjacent (sŭb jā′sənt), *adj.* **1.** situated or occurring underneath or below; underlying. **2.** forming a basis. **3.** being in a lower situation, though not directly beneath. [t. L: s. *subjacens,* ppr., lying under] —**subja′cency,** *n.*

subject (*n.*, *adj.* sŭb′jĭkt; *v.* səb jĕkt′), *n.* **1.** something that forms a matter of thought, discourse, investigation, etc.: *a subject of conversation.* **2.** a branch of knowledge organized into a system so as to form a suitable course of study. **3.** a ground, motive, or cause: *a subject for complaint.* **4.** the theme of a sermon, book, story, etc. **5.** a theme or melodic phrase on which a musical work or movement is based. **6.** an object, scene, incident, or the like, chosen by an artist for representation, or as represented in art. **7.** one who is under the dominion or rule of a sovereign. **8.** one who owes allegiance to a government and lives under its protection: *a Swedish subject.* **9.** such people collectively. **10.** *Gram.* (in English and many other languages) the word or words of a sentence which represent the person or object performing the action expressed in the predicate, e.g., *he* in *he has a hat.* **11.** one who or that which undergoes, or may undergo, some action. **12.** one who or that which is under the control or influence of another. **13.** a person as an object of medical, surgical, or psychological treatment or experiment. **14.** a dead body as used for dissection. **15.** *Logic.* that part of a proposition of which the predicate is asserted or denied. **16.** *Philos.* **a.** the substance in which attributes inhere. **b.** substance; external reality as distinguished from its appearance; that which is the object of reference in predication. **c.** the self or ego to which all experiences or mental operations are attributed.
—*adj.* **17.** being under domination, control, or influence (often fol. by *to*). **18.** being under dominion, rule, or authority, as of a sovereign or a state, or some governing power; owing allegiance or obedience (*to*). **19.** open or exposed (fol. by *to*): *subject to ridicule.* **20.** being dependent or conditional upon something (fol. by *to*): *his consent is subject to your approval.* **21.** being under the necessity of undergoing something (fol. by *to*): *all men are subject to death.* **22.** liable, as to something (esp. something undesirable) that may or often does befall (fol. by *to*): *subject to headaches.*
—*v.t.* **23.** to bring under domination, control, or influence (usually fol. by *to*). **24.** to bring under dominion, rule, or authority, as of a conqueror or a governing power (usually fol. by *to*). **25.** to cause to undergo or experience something (fol. by *to*): *to subject metal to a white heat.* **26.** to make liable, lay open, or expose (fol. by *to*): *to subject oneself to ridicule.* **27.** *Obs.* to place beneath something or make subjacent.
[t. L: s. *subjectus,* pp., placed under; r. ME *suget,* t. OF]
—**Syn. 1.** SUBJECT, THEME, TOPIC are often interchangeable to express the material being considered in a speech or written composition. SUBJECT is a broad word for whatever is treated of in writing, speech, art, etc.: *the subject for discussion.* THEME and TOPIC are usually narrower and apply to some limited or specific part of a general subject. A THEME is often the underlying conception of a discourse or composition, perhaps not put into words but easily recognizable: *the theme of a need for reform runs throughout his work.* A TOPIC is the statement of what is to be treated in a section of a composition: *the topic is treated fully in this section.*

subject catalogue, (in libraries) a catalogue with entries listed by subject only.

subjectify (səb jĕk′tĭ fī′), *v.t.* **-fied, -fying. 1.** to make subjective. **2.** to identify with (a subject); interpret in a subjective manner. —**subjectification** (səb jĕk′tĭ fĭ kā′shən), *n.*

subjection (səb jĕk′shən), *n.* **1.** the act of subjecting. **2.** the state or fact of being subjected.

subjective (səb jĕk′tĭv), *adj.* **1.** existing in the mind; belonging to the thinking subject rather than to the object of thought (opposed to *objective*). **2.** pertaining to or characteristic of an individual thinking subject; personal; individual: *subjective poetry.* **3.** belonging to the thinking subject rather than to the object of thought. **4.** introspective. **5.** relating to or of the nature of a subject as it is known in the mind as distinct from a thing in itself. **6.** relating to properties or specific conditions of the mind as distinct from general or universal experience. **7.** pertaining to the subject or substance in which attributes inhere; essential. **8.** *Gram.* **a.** pertaining to or constituting the subject of a sentence. **b.** (in English and some other languages) denoting a case specialized for that use: in *he hit the ball, he* is in the subjective case. **c.** similar to such a case in meaning. **9.** *Philos.* **a.** of or pertaining to thought, as opposed to an object of thought. **b.** descriptive of a philosophy that regards thought as real and substantial. **10.** *Obs.* pertaining to or befitting one who is subject to dominion, rule, or control. —**subjec′tively,** *adv.* —**subjectivity** (sŭb′jĕk tĭv′ĭ tĭ), **subjec′tiveness,** *n.*

subjectivism (səb jĕk′tĭ vĭz′əm), *n.* **1.** the philosophical theory that one mind can know nothing but itself and its characteristics. (See **idealism,** def. 5a.) **2.** any epistemological theory that attaches preponderating importance to the subjective factor of knowledge. **3.** the ethical theory that the rightness or wrongness of an action depends upon the mental state of a particular person. **4.** any theological theory that attaches preponderating importance to religious experience as opposed to revelation or historical evidence. **5.** subjectivity. —**subjec′tivist,** *n.* —**subjec′tivis′tic,** *adj.*

subject matter, 1. the substance of a discourse, book, writing, or the like, as distinguished from its form or style. **2.** the matter which is subject to some action or operation. **3.** the matter out of which a thing is formed.

subjoin (sŭb′join′), *v.t.* **1.** to add at the end, as of something said or written; append. **2.** to place in sequence or juxtaposition to something else.

sub judice (sŭb′ jōō′dĭ sĭ), *Latin.* before a judge or court of law; under judicial consideration.

subjugate (sŭb′jōō gāt′), *v.t.*, **-gated, -gating. 1.** to bring under complete control or into subjection; subdue; conquer. **2.** to make submissive or subservient. [t. L: m. s. *subjugātus,* pp., brought under the yoke] —**sub′juga′tion,** *n.* —**sub′juga′tor,** *n.*

subjunction (sŭb jŭngk′shən), *n.* **1.** the act of subjoining. **2.** the state of being subjoined. **3.** something subjoined.

subjunctive (səb jŭngk′tĭv), *Gram.* —*adj.* **1.** (in many languages) designating or pertaining to a verb mood having among its functions use in various subordinate clauses. —*n.* **2.** the subjunctive mood. **3.** a verb in it, as *be* in *if it be true.* [t. LL: m. s. *subjunctīvus,* der. L *subjunctus,* pp., subjoined]

subkingdom (sŭb′kĭng′dəm), *n.* a phylum.

sublapsarianism (sŭb′lăp sĕə′rĭ ən), *n.* infralapsarianism. [f. s. NL *sublapsārius* (f. L: *sub-* SUB- + s. *lapsus* fall + *-ārius,* adj. suffix) + -AN + -ISM]

sublate (sŭb lāt′), *v.t.* **-lated, -lating.** (in Hegelian philosophy) to set aside but not wholly to dispense with; to supersede while retaining something of the nature of what is superseded. [f. L: *sub-* SUB- + m. s. *latus,* pp., borne; trans. of G *aufheben* as used by Hegel]

sublease (*n.* sŭb′lēs′; *v.* sŭb′lēs′), *n.*, *v.*, **-leased, -leasing.** —*n.* **1.** a lease granted by one who is himself a lessee of the property. —*v.t.* **2.** to sublet. —**sublessee** (sŭb′lĕ sē′), *n.* —**sublessor** (sŭb′lĕ sô′), *n.*

sublet (sŭb′lĕt′), *v.t.*, **-let, -letting. 1.** to let to another person, the party letting being himself a lessee. **2.** to let (work, etc.) under a subcontract.

sublethal (sŭb′lē′thəl), *adj.* almost lethal or fatal.

sublieutenant (sŭb′lĕ tĕn′ənt), *n.* a naval officer ranking below a lieutenant. —**sub′lieuten′ancy,** *n.*

sublimate (*v.* sŭb′lĭ māt′; *n.*, *adj.* sŭb′lĭ mĭt), *v.*, **-mated, -mating,** *n.*, *adj.* —*v.t.* **1.** *Psychol.* to deflect (sexual or other biological energies) into socially constructive or creative channels. **2.** *Chem., etc.* **a.** to sublime (a solid substance); extract by this process. **b.** to refine or purify (a substance). **3.** to make nobler or purer. —*v.i.* **4.** to become sublimated; undergo sublimation. —*n.* **5.** *Chem.* the crystals, deposit, or material obtained when a substance is sublimated; esp. corrosive sublimate. —*adj.* **6.** sublimated. [t. L: m. s. *sublīmātus,* pp., elevated] —**sub′lima′tion,** *n.*

sublime (sə blīm′), *adj.*, *n.*, *v.*, **-limed, -liming.** —*adj.* **1.** elevated or lofty in thought, language, etc.: *sublime poetry.* **2.** impressing the mind with a sense of grandeur or power; inspiring awe, veneration, etc.: *sublime scenery.* **3.** supreme or perfect: *a sublime moment.* **4.** *Poetic.* of lofty bearing. **5.** *Poetic.* haughty or proud. **6.** *Archaic.* raised aloft. —*n.* **7.** that which is sublime: *the sublime in art.* **8.** the highest degree or example (fol. by *of*). —*v.t.*

9. to make higher, nobler, or purer. 10. *Chem., etc.* to convert (a solid substance) by heat into a vapour, which on cooling condenses again to solid form, without apparent liquefaction. 11. *Chem., etc.* to cause to be given off by this or some analogous process. —*v.i.* 12. *Chem., etc.* to volatilize from the solid state to a gas, and then condense again as a solid without passing through the liquid state. [ME, t. L: m. s. *sublīmāre* elevate, der. *sublīmis*, adj., lofty] —**sublime′ly,** *adv.* —**sublime′ness,** *n.*

Sublime Porte (pôt). See **Porte.**

subliminal (sŭb′lĭm′ĭ nəl), *adj. Psychol.* (of stimuli, etc.) being or operating below the threshold of consciousness or perception; subconscious: *subliminal advertising.* —**sub′lim′inally,** *adv.*

sublimity (sə blĭm′ĭ tĭ), *n., pl.* **-ties. 1.** the state or quality of being sublime. **2.** a sublime person or thing.

sublingual (sŭb′lĭng′gwəl), *Anat.* —*adj.* **1.** situated under the tongue, or on the underside of the tongue. —*n.* **2.** a sublingual gland, artery, or the like.

sublunary (sŭb′lo͞o′nə rĭ), *adj.* **1.** situated beneath the moon. **2.** of, on, or being the earth; terrestrial. **3.** mundane or worldly. Also, **sublunar** (sŭb′lo͞o′nə).

submachine gun (sŭb′mə shēn′), a lightweight automatic or semiautomatic gun, fired from the shoulder or hip.

subman (sŭb′măn′), *n., pl.* **-men.** a man of very low mental or physical capacity.

submarginal (sŭb′mä′jĭ nəl), *adj.* **1.** *Biol.* near the margin. **2.** below the margin. **3.** not worth cultivating, as land; unproductive. —**sub′mar′ginally,** *adv.*

submarine (sŭb′mə rēn′, sŭb′mə rēn′), *n.* **1.** a type of vessel that can be submerged and navigated under water, esp. one used in warfare for the discharge of torpedoes, guided missiles, etc. **2.** something submarine, as a plant, animal, etc. —*adj.* **3.** situated, occurring, operating, or living under the surface of the sea. **4.** of, pertaining to, or carried on by submarine ships: *submarine warfare.* —**sub′ma′riner,** *n.*

submaxilla (sŭb′măk sĭl′ə), *n., pl.* **-maxillae** (-măksĭl′ē). *Anat., Zool.* the lower jaw or lower jawbone.

submaxillary (sŭb′măk sĭl′ə rĭ), *adj.* of or pertaining to the lower jaw or lower jawbone.

submaxillary gland, either of two saliva-producing glands beneath the lower jaw, one on each side.

submediant (sŭb′mē′dĭ ənt), *n. Music.* the sixth note of a scale, being midway between the subdominant and the upper tonic.

submerge (səb mûj′), *v.,* **-merged, -merging.** —*v.t.* **1.** to put under water; plunge below the surface of water or any enveloping medium. **2.** to cover with or as water; immerse. —*v.i.* **3.** to sink or plunge under water, or beneath the surface of any enveloping medium. [t. L: m. s. *submergere*] —**submer′gence,** *n.* —**Syn. 1.** See **dip.**

submerged (səb mûjd′), *adj.* **1.** under the surface of water or any other enveloping medium. **2.** hidden or obscured. **3.** overwhelmed by circumstances, etc.

submergible (səb mû′jĭ bl), *adj., n.* submersible. —**submer′gibil′ity,** *n.*

submerse (səb mûs′), *v.t.,* **-mersed, -mersing.** to submerge. [t. L: m. s. *submersus*, pp., submerged] —**submersion** (səb mû′shən), *n.*

submersed (səb mûst′), *adj.* **1.** submerged. **2.** *Bot.* growing under water.

submersible (səb mû′sə bl), *adj.* **1.** that may be submersed. —*n.* **2.** (formerly) a submarine.

submicroscopic (sŭb′mī′krə skŏp′ĭk), *adj.* smaller than can be seen through a microscope.

submission (səb mĭsh′ən), *n.* **1.** the act of submitting. **2.** the condition of having submitted. **3.** submissive conduct or attitude. **4.** that which is submitted. **5.** *Law.* an agreement to abide by a decision or obey an authority in some matter referred to arbitration. **6.** *Wrestling.* inability to stand an opponent's hold: in professional wrestling the first contestant to win the best of three pinfalls or submissions is declared the winner. [ME, t. L: s. *submissio*]

submissive (səb mĭs′ĭv), *adj.* **1.** inclined or ready to submit; unresistingly or humbly obedient. **2.** marked by or indicating submission: *a submissive reply.* —**submis′sively,** *adv.* —**submis′siveness,** *n.*

submit (səb mĭt′), *v.,* **-mitted, -mitting.** —*v.t.* **1.** to yield in surrender, compliance, or obedience. **2.** to subject (esp. oneself) to conditions imposed, treatment, etc. **3.** to refer to the decision or judgement of another or others. **4.** to state or urge with deference (usually fol. by a clause): *I submit that full proof should be required.* —*v.i.* **5.** to yield in surrender, compliance, or obedience: *to submit to a conqueror.* **6.** to allow oneself to be subjected to something imposed or to be undergone: *to submit to punishment.* **7.** to defer to the opinion, judgement, etc., of another. [ME *submitte*, t. L: m. *submittere* lower, put under] —**submit′table, submissible** (səb mĭs′ə bl), *adj.* —**submit′tal,** *n.* —**submit′ter,** *n.* —**Syn. 1.** comply, bow. See **yield.** —**Ant. 1.** resist.

submontane (sŭb′mŏn′tān), *adj.* **1.** under or beneath a mountain or mountains. **2.** at or near the foot of mountains. **3.** pertaining to the lower slopes of mountains. —**sub′mon′tanely,** *adv.*

submultiple (sŭb′mŭl′tĭ pl), *n.* **1.** a number which is contained within another an exact number of times without a remainder. —*adj.* **2.** pertaining to or denoting a number that is a submultiple.

subnormal (sŭb′nô′məl), *adj.* **1.** below the normal; less than or inferior to the normal. **2.** lacking in one or more important psychological traits, as intelligence, personality, etc. —*n.* **3.** a subnormal person. —**subnormality** (sŭb′nô măl′ĭ tĭ), *n.*

suboceanic (sŭb′ō′shĭ ăn′ĭk), *adj.* beneath the ocean.

suborbital (sŭb′ô′bĭ tl), *adj.* **1.** *Anat.* lying below the orbit of the eye. **2.** (of a spacecraft, etc.) not in orbit.

suborder (sŭb′ô′də), *n.* a category of related families within an order.

subordinal (sŭb′ô′dĭ nəl), *adj.* of, pertaining to, or ranked as a suborder.

subordinate (*adj., n.* sə bô′dĭ nĭt; *v.* sə bô′dĭ nāt′), *adj., n., v.,* **-nated, -nating.** —*adj.* **1.** placed in or belonging to a lower order or rank. **2.** of lesser importance; secondary. **3.** subject to or under the authority of a superior. **4.** subservient. **5.** dependent. **6.** *Gram.* **a.** denoting or pertaining to a subordinate clause or other dependent phrase. **b.** denoting or pertaining to a subordinating conjunction. **7.** *Obs.* submissive. —*n.* **8.** a subordinate person or thing. —*v.t.* **9.** to place in a lower order or rank. **10.** to make secondary (fol. by *to*). **11.** to make subject, subservient, or dependent (fol. by *to*). [late ME, t. ML: m. s. *subordinātus*, pp., subordinated] —**subor′dina′tion,** *n.* —**subor′dinately,** *adv.* —**subor′dinative,** *adj.*

subordinate clause, *Gram.* a clause that modifies and is dependent upon a main clause, as '*When I came*' in the sentence '*They were glad when I came*'.

subordinating conjunction, *Gram.* a conjunction introducing a subordinate clause, as '*when*' in '*They were glad when I came*'.

subordinationism (sə bô′dĭ nā′shə nĭz′əm), *n. Theol.* the doctrine that the first person of the Holy Trinity is superior to the second and the third. —**subor′dina′tionist,** *adj.*

suborn (sŭ bôn′), *v.t.* to bribe or procure (a person) to commit some unlawful or wrongful act, usually perjury. [t. L: s. *subornāre* equip secretly] —**subornation** (sŭb′ô nā′shən), *n.* —**subornative** (sŭ bô′nə tĭv), *adj.* —**suborn′er,** *n.*

Subotica (*Serb.* so͞o′bô tē tsȧ), *n.* a town in NE Yugoslavia. 75,036 (1961). Hungarian, **Szabadka.**

suboxide (sŭb′ŏk′sīd), *n. Chem.* the oxide of an element containing the smallest proportion of oxygen.

subphylum (sŭb′fī′ləm), *n., pl.* **-la** (-lə). *Biol.* a category ranking below a phylum.

subplot (sŭb′plŏt′), *n.* a secondary plot in a play, novel, etc., as distinct from the main plot.

subpoena (səb pē′nə), *n., v.,* **-naed, -naing.** *Law.* —*n.* **1.** the usual writ process for the summoning of witnesses. —*v.t.* **2.** to serve with a subpoena. [ME, t. L: m. *sub poenā* under penalty, the first words of the writ]

subpolar (sŭb′pō′lə), *adj.* **1.** subantarctic. **2.** subarctic.

subprincipal (sŭb′prĭn′sĭ pl), *n.* **1.** an assistant or deputy principal. **2.** *Carp.* an auxiliary rafter or additional supporting member. **3.** *Music.* (in an organ) a sub-bass of the open diapason class.

subregion (sŭb′rē′jən), *n.* a division or subdivision of a region, esp. a division of a zoogeographical region. —**sub′re′gional,** *adj.*

subreption (səb rĕp′shən), *n.* **1.** the act of obtaining something, as an ecclesiastical dispensation, by suppression or fraudulent concealment of facts. **2.** a fallacious representation, or an inference from it. [t. L: s. *subreptio* theft] —**subreptitious** (sŭb′rĕp tĭsh′əs), *adj.*

subrogate (sŭb′rə gāt′), *v.t.,* **-gated, -gating. 1.** to put into the place of another; substitute for another. **2.** *Civ. Law.* to substitute a claim against one person for a claim against another person, or transfer a lien originally imposed on one piece of property to another piece of property. [t. L: m. s. *subrogātus*, pp., put in another's place] —**sub′roga′tion,** *n.*

sub rosa (sŭb′ rō′zə), confidentially; privately. [t. L: under the rose; the rose being the symbol of the Egyptian god Horus, identified by the Greeks with Harpocrates, god of silence]

subroutine (sŭb′roo̅ tēn′), *n. Computers.* a routine used by a computer program to perform some function necessary to carry out the program.
subscapular (sŭb′skăp′yo̅o̅ lə), *Anat.* —*adj.* **1.** beneath, or on the deep surface of, the scapula, as a muscle, artery, etc. —*n.* **2.** a subscapular muscle, artery, etc.
subscribe (səb skrīb′), *v.*, **-scribed, -scribing.** —*v.t.* **1.** to promise, as by signing an agreement, to give or pay (a sum of money) as a contribution, payment, share, etc. **2.** to give or pay in fulfilment of such a promise. **3.** to express assent or adhesion to (a contract, etc.) by signing one's name; attest by signing, as a statement or a will. **4.** to write or inscribe (something) beneath or at the end of a thing; sign (one's name) to a document, etc. —*v.i.* **5.** to undertake, as by signing an agreement, to give or pay money for some special purpose. **6.** to obtain a subscription to a magazine, newspaper, etc. **7.** to give or pay money as a contribution, payment, etc. **8.** to sign one's name to something. **9.** to assent by, or as by, signing one's name. **10.** to give consent or sanction. [ME, t. L: m. s. *subscrībere*]
subscriber (səb skrī′bə), *n.* **1.** one who subscribes, esp. to a magazine. **2.** one who rents telephone equipment for use through an exchange.
subscriber trunk dialling, *Teleph.* a system for making trunk calls in which the subscriber dials the required number himself. *Abbrev.:* STD.
subscript (sŭb′skrĭpt′), *adj.* **1.** written below (distinguished from *adscript*). **2.** placed low on the line, as the '2' in 'H_2O'. —*n.* **3.** something written below. [t. L: s. *subscriptus*, pp.]
subscription (səb skrĭp′shən), *n.* **1.** a monetary contribution towards some object or a payment for shares, a book, a periodical, etc. **2.** the right to receive a periodical for a sum subscribed. **3.** the dues paid by a member of a club, society, etc. **4.** a fund raised through sums of money subscribed. **5.** a sum subscribed. **6.** the act of subscribing; the signing of one's name, as to a document. **7.** something written beneath or at the end of a thing. **8.** a signature attached to a paper. **9.** assent, agreement, or approval expressed by, or as by, signing one's name. **10.** *Eccles.* assent to or acceptance of a body of principles or doctrines, the purpose of which is to establish uniformity. **11.** *C. of E.* formal acceptance of the Thirty-nine Articles of 1563 and the Book of Common Prayer. [late ME, t. L: s. *subscriptio*] —**subscriptive** (səb skrĭp′tĭv), *adj.* —**subscrip′tively,** *adv.*
subscription library, a circulating library.
subsection (sŭb′sĕk′shən), *n.* a part or division of a section.
subsequence (sŭb′sĭ kwəns), *n.* **1.** the state or fact of being subsequent. **2.** that which is subsequent; sequel.
subsequent (sŭb′sĭ kwənt), *adj.* **1.** occurring or coming later or after: *subsequent events.* **2.** following in order or succession: *a subsequent section in a treaty.* [late ME, t. L: s. *subsequens*, ppr.] —**sub′sequently,** *adv.*
subserve (səb sûv′), *v.t.*, **-served, -serving.** **1.** to be useful or instrumental in promoting (a purpose, action, etc.). **2.** *Obs.* to serve under. [t. L: m. s. *subservīre*]
subservient (səb sû′vyənt), *adj.* **1.** serving or acting in a subordinate capacity; subordinate. **2.** (of persons, their conduct, etc.) servile; excessively submissive; obsequious. **3.** of use as a means to promote a purpose or end. [t. L: s. *subserviens*, ppr.] —**subser′vience, subser′viency,** *n.* —**subser′viently,** *adv.*
subset (sŭb′sĕt′), *n.* a subordinate set.
subside (səb sīd′), *v.i.*, **-sided, -siding.** **1.** to sink to a low or lower level. **2.** to become quiet, less violent, or less active; abate; *the laughter subsided.* **3.** to sink or fall to the bottom; settle, as lees; precipitate. [t. L: m. s. *subsīdere* settle down] —**subsidence** (səb sī′dns, sŭb′sĭ dəns), *n.* —**subsid′er,** *n.*
subsidiary (səb sĭd′yə rĭ), *adj.*, *n.*, *pl.* **-ries.** —*adj.* **1.** serving to assist or supplement; auxiliary; supplementary; tributary, as a stream. **2.** subordinate or secondary. —*n.* **3.** a subsidiary thing or person. **4.** *Music.* a subordinate theme or subject. [t. L: m. s. *subsidiārius* belonging to a reserve] —**subsid′iarily,** *adv.*
subsidiary company, a company the controlling interest in which is owned by another company.
subsidize (sŭb′sĭ dīz′), *v.t.*, **-dized, -dizing.** **1.** to furnish or aid with a subsidy. **2.** to purchase the assistance of by the payment of a subsidy. **3.** to secure the cooperation of by bribery; buy over. Also, **subsidise.** [f. SUBSID(Y) + -IZE] —**sub′sidiza′tion,** *n.* —**sub′sidiz′er,** *n.*
subsidy (sŭb′sĭ dĭ), *n.*, *pl.* **-dies.** **1.** a direct pecuniary aid furnished by a government to a private industrial undertaking, a cultural organization, or the like. **2.** a sum paid, often in accordance with a treaty, by one government to another, to secure some service in return. **3.** a grant or contribution of money. **4.** money formerly granted by Parliament to the Crown for special needs. [ME, t. L: m. s. *subsidium* assistance]
—**Syn.** **1.** SUBSIDY, SUBVENTION are both grants of money, especially governmental, to aid private undertakings. A SUBSIDY is usually given to promote commercial enterprise: *a subsidy to farmers during a war.* A SUBVENTION is usually a grant to stimulate enterprises connected with science and the arts: *a subvention to a research chemist by one of the major industrial companies.*
subsist (səb sĭst′), *v.i.* **1.** to exist, or continue in existence. **2.** to continue alive; live, as on food, resources, etc. **3.** to have existence in, or by reason of, something. **4.** to reside, lie, or consist (fol. by *in*). **5.** *Philos.* **a.** to have existence of some kind or other. **b.** to possess the quality of truth and of amenability to thought and to logical construction. —*v.t.* **6.** to provide sustenance or support for; maintain. [t. L: s. *subsistere* stand firm, be adequate to]
subsistence (səb sĭs′təns), *n.* **1.** the state or fact of subsisting; continuance. **2.** the state or fact of existing. **3.** the providing of sustenance or support. **4.** means of supporting life; a living or livelihood. **5.** *Philos.* **a.** the process of substance assuming individualization; a single autonomous human being with certain rights. **b.** the rank of something possessing the quality of truth and the ability of being construed logically.
subsistence allowance, **1.** money paid in advance to an employee to enable him to supply his immediate needs, until his regular payday. **2.** money paid to an employee in addition to his salary to cover incidental expenses. **3.** money paid to members of the armed forces in lieu of meals; an allowance for food. Also, **subsistence money.**
subsistence farming, farming in which the produce is consumed by the farmer and his family leaving little or no surplus for marketing. Also, **subsistence agriculture.**
subsistence level, a standard of living just sufficient to maintain life.
subsoil (sŭb′soil′), *n.* **1.** the bed or stratum of earth or earthy material immediately under the surface soil. —*v.t., v.i.* **2.** to plough so as to break up part of the subsoil.
subsolar (sŭb′sō′lə), *adj.* **1.** directly beneath the sun. **2.** between the tropics.
subsonic (sŭb′sŏn′ĭk), *adj.* **1.** (of sound frequencies) below the audible limit. **2.** (of velocities) below the velocity of sound in the medium.
subspecies (sŭb′spē′shēz), *n.*, *pl.* **-cies.** a subdivision of a species, esp. a geographical or ecological subdivision. —**subspecific** (sŭb′spĭ sĭf′ĭk), *adj.*
subst., **1.** substantive. **2.** substantively. **3.** substitute.
substance (sŭb′stəns), *n.* **1.** that of which a thing consists; matter or material. **2.** a species of matter of definite chemical composition. **3.** the matter with which thought, discourse, study, or the like, is occupied; subject matter. **4.** the actual matter of a thing, as opposed to the appearance or shadow; reality. **5.** substantial or solid character or quality: *claims lacking in substance.* **6.** body: *soup without much substance.* **7.** the meaning or gist, as of speech or writing. **8.** something that has separate or independent existence. **9.** *Philos.* **a.** that which exists by itself, and in which accidents or attributes inhere; that which receives modifications, and is not itself a mode; that which is causally active; that which is more than an event. **b.** the essential part, or essence, of a thing. **c.** the thing as a continuing whole. **10.** possessions, means, or wealth: *to squander one's substance.* **11.** **in substance,** **a.** substantially. **b.** actually; really. [ME, t. OF, g. L *substantia*] —**Syn.** **1.** See **matter.**
substandard (sŭb′stăn′dəd), *adj.* **1.** below standard; inadequate; inferior. **2.** denoting or pertaining to a dialect or a feature of usage differing from the standard language in such a way that the use is often considered uneducated or socially inferior.
substantial (səb stăn′shəl), *adj.* **1.** of a corporeal or material nature; real or actual. **2.** of ample or considerable amount, quantity, size, etc.: *a substantial sum of money.* **3.** of solid character or quality; firm, stout, or strong. **4.** being such with respect to essentials: *two stories in substantial agreement.* **5.** wealthy or influential: *one of the substantial men of the town.* **6.** of real worth or value: *substantial reasons.* **7.** pertaining to the substance, matter, or material of a thing. **8.** of or pertaining to the essence of a thing; essential, material, or important. **9.** being a substance; having independent existence. **10.** *Philos.* pertaining to or of the nature of substance rather than accidents. —*n.* **11.** something substantial. [ME *substancial*, t. LL: m. s. *substantiālis*] —**substantiality** (səb stăn′shĭ ăl′ĭ tĭ), **substan′tialness,** *n.* —**substan′tially,** *adv.* —**Ant.** **1.** ethereal.
substantialism (səb stăn′shə lĭz′əm), *n. Philos.* the doctrine that there are substantial realities behind phenomena. —**substan′tialist,** *n.*
substantiate (səb stăn′shĭ āt′), *v.t.*, **-ated, -ating.** **1.** to

establish by proof or competent evidence: *to substantiate a charge.* **2.** to give substantial existence to. **3.** to present as having substance. —**substan′tia′tion,** *n.* —**substantiative** (səb stăn′shĭ ə tĭv), *adj.*

substantive (sŭb′stən tĭv), *n.* **1.** *Gram.* **a.** a noun. **b.** a noun, pronoun, or other word or phrase having nominal function in sentences or inflected like a noun. **c.** (in Latin and other languages where adjectives are inflected like nouns) a noun or adjective, as Latin *puella* 'girl' and *bona* 'good' in *puella bona est* 'the girl is good'. —*adj.* **2.** *Gram.* **a.** pertaining to substantives. **b.** used in a sentence like a noun: *a substantive adjective.* **c.** expressing existence: '*to be*' *is a substantive verb.* **3.** having independent existence; independent. **4.** belonging to the real nature or essential part of a thing; essential. **5.** real or actual. **6.** of considerable amount or quantity. **7.** *Law.* pertaining to the rules of right which courts are called on to apply, as distinguished from rules of procedure (opposed to *adjective*). **8.** *Dyeing.* (of colours) attaching directly to the material without the aid of a mordant or the like (opposed to *adjective*). [ME, t. LL: m. s. *substantivus* standing by itself, der. L *substantia* substance] —**substantival** (sŭb′stən tī′vəl), *adj.* —**sub′stantively,** *adv.* —**sub′stantiveness,** *n.*

substantive rank (səb stăn′tĭv), *Mil.* a permanent rank in the forces, attained after a suitable length of service and usually after successfully taking certain qualifying examinations.

substation (sŭb′stā′shən), *n.* **1.** a subsidiary station. **2.** *Elect.* an installation in an electrical distribution system, between the generating station and the low-tension network, in which transformation, conversion, or switching takes place.

substituent (sŭb stĭt′yŏŏ ənt), *n.* *Chem.* an atom or atomic group which takes the place of another atom or group present in the molecule of the original compound. [t. L: s. *substituens*, ppr., substituting]

substitute (sŭb′stĭ tyōōt′), *n.*, *v.*, **-tuted, -tuting.** —*n.* **1.** a person or thing acting or serving in place of another. **2.** (formerly) one who, for a consideration, served in an army or navy in the place of a conscript. **3.** *Gram.* a word which under given conditions replaces any of a class of other words or constructions, as English *do* replacing verbs (I *know* but he *doesn't*). —*v.t.* **4.** to put (one person or thing) in the place of another. **5.** to take the place of; replace. —*v.i.* **6.** to act as substitute. **7.** *Chem.* to replace one or more elements or radicals in a compound by other elements or radicals. [ME, t. L: m. s. *substitūtus*, pp.] —**sub′stitu′tion,** *n.* —**sub′stitu′tional, substitutionary** (sŭb′stĭ tyōō′shə nə rĭ), *adj.* —**sub′stitu′tionally,** *adv.*

substitutive (sŭb′stĭ tyōō′tĭv), *adj.* **1.** serving as, or capable of serving as, a substitute. **2.** pertaining to or involving substitution.

substrate (sŭb′strāt), *n.* **1.** a substratum. **2.** *Biochem.* the substance acted upon by an enzyme or ferment.

substratum (sŭb′strä′təm), *n.*, *pl.* **-strata** (-strä′tə). **1.** that which is spread or laid under something else; a stratum or layer lying under another. **2.** something which underlies, or serves as a basis or foundation. **3.** *Agric.* the subsoil. **4.** *Biol.* the base or material on which an organism lives. **5.** *Metaphys.* that which is regarded as supporting accidents or attributes; substance, as that in which qualities inhere. [NL: (neut. pp.) spread underneath] —**sub′stra′tive,** *adj.*

substruction (sŭb strŭk′shən), *n.* a foundation or substructure. [t. L: s. *substructio*] —**substruc′tional,** *adj.*

substructure (sŭb′strŭk′chə), *n.* **1.** a structure forming the foundation of a building or the like. **2.** the foundations, piers, abutments, and other parts of a bridge upon which the superstructure rests. —**substruc′tural,** *adj.*

subsume (səb syōōm′), *v.t.*, **-sumed, -suming.** **1.** to consider (an idea, term, proposition, etc.) as part of a more comprehensive one. **2.** bring (a case, instance, etc.) under a rule. **3.** to take up into or include in a larger or higher class or a more inclusive classification. [t. NL: m. s. *subsūmere*, f. L *sub-* SUB- + *sūmere* take]

subsumption (səb sŭmp′shən), *n.* **1.** the act of subsuming. **2.** the state of being subsumed. **3.** that which is subsumed. **4.** a proposition subsumed under another. —**subsumptive** (səb sŭmp′tĭv), *adj.*

subtangent (sŭb′tăn′jənt), *n.* *Geom.* the part of the x-axis cut off between the ordinate of a given point of a curve and the tangent at the point.

subteen (sŭb′tēn′), *n.* *Colloq.* a young person approaching adolescence.

subtemperate (sŭb′tĕm′pə rĭt, -prĭt), *adj.* pertaining to or occurring in the colder parts of the Temperate Zone.

subtenant (sŭb′tĕn′ənt), *n.* one who rents land, a house, or the like from a tenant. —**sub′ten′ancy,** *n.*

subtend (səb tĕnd′), *v.t.* **1.** *Geom., etc.* to extend under; be opposite to: *a chord subtending an arc.* **2.** *Bot.* (of a leaf, bract, etc.) to enclose or embrace in its axil. [t. L: s. *subtendere* stretch under]

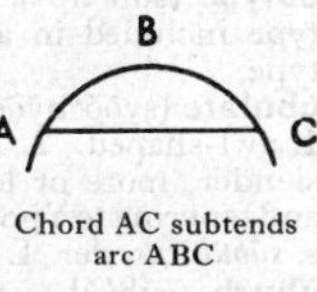

Chord AC subtends arc ABC

subter-, a prefix meaning 'position underneath', with figurative applications, as in *subterfuge.* [t. L, comb. form of *subter*, prep. and adv.]

subterfuge (sŭb′tə fyōōj′), *n.* an artifice or expedient employed to escape the force of an argument, to evade unfavourable consequences, hide something etc. [t. LL: m. s. *subterfugium*, der. L *subterfugere* flee secretly]

subternatural (sŭb′tə năch′ə rəl, -năch′rəl), *adj.* below what is natural; less than natural.

subterranean (sŭb′tə rā′nyən), *adj.* **1.** existing, situated, or operating below the surface of the earth; underground. **2.** existing or operating out of sight or secretly; hidden or secret. Also, **sub′terra′neous.** [f. s. L *subterrāneus* below the earth + -AN]

subtile (sŭt′l), *adj.* subtle. —**sub′tilely,** *adv.* —**sub′tileness, subtility** (sŭb tĭl′ĭ tĭ), **sub′tilty,** *n.*

subtilize (sŭt′ĭ līz′), *v.*, **-lized, -lizing.** —*v.t.* **1.** to elevate in character; sublimate. **2.** to render (the mind, senses, etc.) acute or keen. **3.** to introduce subtleties into; argue subtly about. **4.** to make thin, rare, or more fluid or volatile; refine. —*v.i.* **5.** to make subtle distinctions; argue subtly. Also, **subtilise.** —**sub′tiliza′tion,** *n.*

subtitle (sŭb′tī′tl), *n.* **1.** a secondary or subordinate title of a literary work, usually of explanatory character. **2.** a repetition of the leading words in the full title of a book at the head of the first page of text. **3.** *Films.* **a.** one of a series of captions projected on to the lower part of the screen which translate and summarize the dialogue of foreign language films. **b.** (in silent films) a title or caption usually giving an explanation to a following scene. —*v.t.* **4.** to give a subtitle to.

subtle (sŭt′l), *adj.* **1.** thin, tenuous, or rarefied, as a fluid, scent, etc. **2.** fine or delicate, often when likely to elude perception or understanding: *subtle irony.* **3.** delicate or faint and mysterious: *a subtle smile.* **4.** requiring mental acuteness, penetration, or discernment: *a subtle point.* **5.** characterized by mental acuteness or penetration: *a subtle understanding.* **6.** cunning, wily, or crafty. **7.** insidious in operation, as poison, etc. **8.** skilful, clever, or ingenious. [ME *sutell*, t. OF: m. *soutil*, g. L *subtilis* fine, delicate] —**sub′tleness,** *n.* —**subtly** (sŭt′lĭ), *adv.*

subtlety (sŭt′l tĭ), *n.*, *pl.* **-ties.** **1.** the state or quality of being subtle. **2.** delicacy or nicety of character or meaning; acuteness or penetration of mind; delicacy of discrimination. **3.** a fine-drawn distinction. **4.** something subtle.

subtonic (sŭb′tŏn′ĭk), *n.* *Music.* the seventh note of a scale, being the next below the upper tonic.

subtopia (sŭb tō′pyə), *n.* a partially built-up country area in which the use of standardized materials in building, street furniture, etc., has created the impression of a suburb and blurred the distinction between town and country. [f. SUB(URBAN) + (U)TOPIA]

subtract (səb trăkt′), *v.t.* **1.** to withdraw or take away, as a part from a whole. **2.** *Maths.* to take (one number or quantity) from another; deduct. —*v.i.* **3.** to take away something or a part, as from a whole. [t. L: s. *subtractus*, pp., carried away] —**subtract′er,** *n.*

—**Syn.** 1, 3. SUBTRACT, DEDUCT express diminution in sum or quantity. To SUBTRACT suggests taking a part from a whole or a smaller from a larger: *to subtract expenses from winnings to find the overall profit.* To DEDUCT is to take away an amount or quantity from an aggregate or total so as to lessen or lower it: *to deduct a discount.* SUBTRACT is both transitive and intransitive, and has general or figurative uses; DEDUCT is always transitive and usually concrete and practical in application. —**Ant.** 1. add.

subtraction (səb trăk′shən), *n.* **1.** the act of subtracting. **2.** *Maths.* the operation of finding the difference between two numbers or quantities (denoted by the symbol —).

subtractive (səb trăk′tĭv), *adj.* **1.** tending to subtract; having power to subtract. **2.** *Maths.* (of a quantity) that is to be subtracted; having the minus sign (—).

subtractive colour, *Photog.* any of the three colours magenta, blue-green, and yellow which form the basis of the subtractive process of colour photography.

subtractive process, *Photog.* a process of colour photography in which the colours are formed by combinations of the subtractive colours.

subtrahend (sŭb′trə hĕnd′), *n.* *Maths.* the number or quantity to be taken from another (the minuend) in subtraction. [t. L: s. *subtrahendus*, ger., to be subtracted]

subtropical (sŭb′trŏp′ĭ kl), *adj.* **1.** bordering on the tropics; nearly tropical. **2.** pertaining to or occurring in a region intermediate between tropical and temperate.

subtropics (sŭb′trŏp′ĭks), *n.pl.* subtropical regions.

subtype (sŭb′tīp′), *n.* **1.** a subordinate type. **2.** a special type included in a more general type.

subulate (syōō′byōō lĭt, -lāt′), *adj.* **1.** awl-shaped. **2.** *Bot., Zool., etc.* slender, more or less cylindrical, and tapering to a point. [t. NL: m. s. *sūbulātus*, der. L *sūbula* awl]

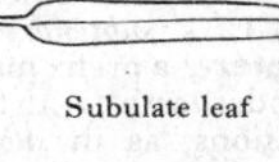
Subulate leaf

suburb (sŭb′ûb), *n.* **1.** a district, usually a residential one, lying immediately outside a city or town. **2.** an outlying part. [ME *suburbe*, t. L: m. s. *suburbium*]

suburban (sə bû′bən), *adj.* **1.** pertaining to, inhabiting, or being in a suburb or the suburbs of a city or town. **2.** characteristic of a suburb or suburbs. **3.** narrow-minded; conventional in outlook. —*n.* **4.** a suburbanite.

suburbanite (sə bû′bə nīt′), *n.* one who lives in the suburbs of a city or town.

suburbanize (sə bû′bə nīz′), *v.t.*, **-nized, -nizing.** to make into a suburb; give suburban characteristics to. Also, **suburbanise.** —**subur′baniza′tion,** *n.*

suburbia (sə bû′bĭ ə), *n.* **1.** suburbs collectively. **2.** suburban inhabitants collectively. **3.** the characteristic life of people in suburbs.

suburbicarian (sə bû′bĭ kēə′rĭ ən), *adj.* **1.** being near the city (of Rome). **2.** denoting or pertaining to any of the dioceses surrounding Rome, each of which is under the jurisdiction of a cardinal bishop. [f. s. LL *suburbicārius* suburban + -AN]

subvention (səb vĕn′shən), *n.* **1.** a grant of pecuniary aid, esp. by a government or some other authority, in aid or support of some object, institution, or undertaking. **2.** the furnishing of aid or relief. [t. L: s. *subventio*, der. *subvenīre* come to the aid of] —**subventionary** (səb vĕn′shə nə rĭ), *adj.* —**Syn. 1.** See **subsidy.**

sub verbo (sŭb′ vû′bō), *Latin.* (used as a direction to a reference) under the word or heading. Also, **sub voce** (sŭb′ vō′sĭ).

subversion (səb vû′shən), *n.* **1.** the act of subverting; overthrow. **2.** the state of being subverted; destruction. **3.** that which subverts or overthrows. Also, **subversal** (səb vû′səl). [ME, t. LL: s. *subversio*]

subversive (səb vû′sĭv), *adj.* **1.** tending to subvert; such as to cause subversion. —*n.* **2.** one who adopts subversive principles or policies.

subvert (səb vût′), *v.t.* **1.** to overthrow (something established or existing). **2.** to cause the downfall, ruin, or destruction of. **3.** *Rare.* to undermine the principles of; corrupt. [ME, t. L: s. *subvertere*] —**subvert′er,** *n.*

subway (sŭb′wā′), *n.* **1.** an underground passage or tunnel enabling pedestrians to cross beneath a street, railway line, etc. **2.** *U.S.* an underground railway.

suc-, var. of **sub-** (by assimilation) before *c.*

succedaneum (sŭk′sĭ dā′nyəm), *n.*, *pl.* **-nea** (-nyə). a substitute. [NL, neut. sing. of L *succēdāneus* taking the place of something] —**suc′ceda′neous,** *adj.*

succeed (sək sēd′), *v.i.* **1.** to turn out or terminate according to desire; turn out successfully; have the desired result. **2.** to have (good or ill) success: *I have succeeded very badly.* **3.** to accomplish what is attempted or intended. **4.** to achieve success in a particular field; prosper. **5.** to follow or replace another by descent, election, appointment, etc. (often fol. by *to*). **6.** to come next after something else in an order or series. —*v.t.* **7.** to come after and take the place of, as in an office or estate. **8.** to come next after in an order or series, or in the course of events; follow. [ME *succede*, t. L: m. *succēdere* go up, be successful] —**succeed′er,** *n.*

—**Syn. 1.** SUCCEED, FLOURISH, PROSPER, THRIVE mean to do well. To SUCCEED is to turn out well, to attain a goal: *it is everyone's wish to succeed in life.* To FLOURISH is to give evidence of success or a ripe development of power, reputation, etc.: *culture flourishes among free people.* To PROSPER is to achieve and enjoy material success: *he prospered but was still discontented.* THRIVE suggests vigorous growth and development such as results from natural vitality or favourable conditions: *the children thrived in the sunshine.* **5.** See **follow.** —**Ant. 1.** fail.

succentor (sək sĕn′tə), *n.* *Eccles.* a precentor's deputy. [t. LL, der. L *succinere* accompany, sing to]

succès de scandale (*Fr.* sYk sĕ də skäɴ dăl′), *French.* a success due to notoriety or scandal rather than intrinsic merit.

succès d'estime (*Fr.* sYk sĕ dĕs tēm′), *French.* a success consisting of honour or respect (rather than of popularity or profit).

succès fou (*Fr.* sYk sĕ fōō′), *French.* a huge success.

success (sək sĕs′), *n.* **1.** the favourable or prosperous termination of attempts or endeavours. **2.** the gaining of wealth, position, or the like. **3.** a successful performance or achievement. **4.** a thing or a person that is successful. **5.** *Obs.* outcome. [t. L: s. *successus*]

successful (sək sĕs′fəl), *adj.* **1.** achieving or having achieved success. **2.** having succeeded in obtaining wealth, position, or the like. **3.** resulting in or attended with success. —**success′fully,** *adv.*

succession (sək sĕsh′ən), *n.* **1.** the coming of one after another in order, sequence, or the course of events; sequence. **2.** a number of persons or things following one another in order or sequence. **3.** the right, act or process, by which one person succeeds to the office, rank, estate or the like, of another. **4.** the order or line of those entitled to succeed. **5.** the descent or transmission, or the principle or mode of transmission, of a throne, dignity, estate, or the like. **6.** *Ecol.* the progressive replacement of one community by another in development towards climax vegetation. [ME, t. L: s. *successio*] —**succes′sional,** *adj.* —**succes′sionally,** *adv.* —**Syn. 2.** See **series.**

successive (sək sĕs′ĭv), *adj.* **1.** following in order or in uninterrupted course: *three successive days.* **2.** following another in a regular sequence: *the second successive day.* **3.** characterized by or involving succession. —**succes′sively,** *adv.* —**succes′siveness,** *n.*

—**Syn. 1.** SUCCESSIVE, CONSECUTIVE apply to things which follow one upon another. SUCCESSIVE refers merely to the position of one with reference to another: *discouraged by successive misfortune.* CONSECUTIVE denotes a close and uninterrupted sequence, sometimes with the implication of an established order: *the army was finally routed by defeats on three consecutive days.*

successor (sək sĕs′ə), *n.* **1.** one who or that which succeeds or follows. **2.** one who succeeds another in an office, position, or the like. [t. L; r. ME *successour*, t. AF]

succinct (sək sĭngkt′), *adj.* **1.** expressed in few words; concise; terse. **2.** characterized by conciseness or verbal brevity. **3.** compressed into a small area or compass. **4.** *Archaic.* encircled, as by a girdle. [ME, t. L: s. *succinctus*, pp., girded up] —**succinct′ly,** *adv.* —**succinct′ness,** *n.*

succinic (sŭk sĭn′ĭk), *adj.* **1.** pertaining to or obtained from amber. **2.** *Chem.* of or derived from succinic acid. [t. F: m. *succinique*, f. s. L *succinum* amber + *-ique* -IC]

succinic acid, *Chem.* a white crystalline soluble acid, $(CH_2)_2(COOH)_2$, which occurs naturally in amber and is manufactured synthetically; used in dyes, perfumes and lacquers.

succory (sŭk′ə rĭ), *n.*, *pl.* **-ries.** chicory.

succotash (sŭk′ə tăsh′), *n.* a dish of North American Indian origin, consisting of green maize and beans. [t. Narragansett: m. *msiquatash*]

succour (sŭk′ə), *n.* **1.** help; relief; aid; assistance. **2.** one who or that which gives help, relief, aid, etc. —*v.t.* **3.** to help or relieve in difficulty, need, or distress; aid; assist. Also, *U.S.*, **succor.** [ME *sucurs*, t. AF, OF, der. *secourir* to help, g. L *succurrere*] —**suc′courer,** *n.* —**Syn. 1.** See **help.**

succuba (sŭk′yōō bə), *n.*, *pl.* **-bae** (-bē′). a succubus.

succubus (sŭk′yōō bəs), *n.*, *pl.* **-bi** (-bī′). **1.** a demon in female form fabled to have sexual intercourse with men in their sleep. **2.** any demon or evil spirit. Cf. **incubus.** [ME, t. ML: masc. form of *succuba* strumpet]

succulent (sŭk′yōō lənt), *adj.* **1.** full of juice; juicy. **2.** rich in desirable qualities. **3.** affording mental nourishment; not dry. **4.** (of plants, etc.) having fleshy and juicy tissues. [t. L: s. *succulentus*] —**suc′culence, suc′culency,** *n.* —**suc′culently,** *adv.*

succumb (sə kŭm′), *v.i.* **1.** to give way to superior force; yield. **2.** to yield to disease, wounds, old age, etc.; die. [late ME, t. L: s. *succumbere*]

succursal (sŭ kû′səl), *adj.* subsidiary; esp. denoting a religious establishment which is dependent upon a principal one. [t. F, der. L *succursus* SUCCOUR]

succuss (sŭ kŭs′), *v.t.* **1.** to shake up; shake. **2.** *Med.* to shake (a patient) in order to determine if a fluid is present in the thorax or elsewhere. [t. L: s. *succussus*, pp., tossed up]

succussion (sŭ kŭsh′ən), *n.* the act or an instance of succussing. [t. L: s. *succussio*] —**succussive** (sŭ kŭs′ĭv), *adj.*

such (sŭch), *adj.* **1.** of the kind, character, degree, extent, etc., of that or those indicated or implied: *such a man is dangerous.* **2.** of that particular kind or character: *the food, such as it was, was plentiful.* **3.** like or similar: *tea, coffee, and such commodities.* **4.** (preceding an adjective used attributively) so, or in such a manner or degree: *such terrible deeds.* **5.** (with omission of an indication of comparison) of so extreme a kind; so great, good, bad, etc.: *he is such a liar.* **6.** being as stated or indicated: *such is the case.* **7.** being the person or thing, or the persons or things, indicated: *if any member be behind in his payments, such member shall be suspended.* **8.** Also, **such and such.** being definite or particular, but not named or specified: *it happened at such a time in such* *a town.* —*pron.* **9.** such a person or thing, or such persons or things. **10.** the person or thing, or the persons or things, indicated: *he claims to be a friend but is not such.* **11. as such, a.** as being what is indicated; in that capacity: *the leader, as such, is entitled to respect.* **b.** in itself or themselves: *wealth, as such, does not appeal to him.* **12. such as, a.** of the kind specified: *people such as these are not to be trusted.* **b.** for example: *he likes outdoor sports such as tennis and football.* [ME; OE *swulc*, var. of *swylc*, c. G *solch*]

suchlike (sŭch′līk′), *adj.* **1.** of any such kind; similar. —*pron.* **2.** persons or things of such a kind.

Suchow (so͞o′chou′), *n.* a city in China, in NW Kiangsu province. 710,000 (est. 1958).

suck (sŭk), *v.t.* **1.** to draw into the mouth by action of the lips and tongue which produces a partial vacuum: *to suck lemonade through a straw.* **2.** to draw (water, moisture, air, etc.) by any process resembling this: *plants suck up moisture from the earth.* **3.** to apply the lips or mouth to, and draw upon by producing a partial vacuum, esp. for extracting fluid contents: *to suck an orange.* **4.** to apply the mouth to, or take into the mouth, and draw upon similarly, for some other purpose: *to suck one's thumb.* **5.** to take into the mouth and absorb by action of the tongue, etc.: *to suck a piece of toffee.* **6.** to render or bring (as specified) by or as by sucking. —*v.i.* **7.** to draw something in by producing a partial vacuum in the mouth, esp. to draw milk from the breast. **8.** to draw or be drawn by, or as by, suction. **9.** (of a pump) to draw air instead of water, as when the water is low or a valve is defective. **10. suck in,** *Slang.* to cheat; swindle; deceive; defraud. **11. suck up to,** *Slang.* to flatter; toady; fawn upon. —*n.* **12.** the act or instance of sucking with the mouth or otherwise. **13.** a sucking force. **14.** the sound produced by sucking. **15.** that which is sucked; nourishment drawn from the breast. **16.** *Colloq.* a small draught of liquid. [ME *soke, souke(n)*, OE *sūcan*, c. L *sūgere*; akin to OE *sūgan*, G *saugen*]

sucker (sŭk′ə), *n.* **1.** one who or that which sucks. **2.** an infant or a young animal that is suckled, esp. a suckling pig. **3.** a part or organ of an animal adapted for sucking nourishment, or for adhering to an object as by suction. **4.** any member of the cyprinoid family *Catostomidae*, comprising freshwater fishes which are mostly North American and often used as food. **5.** the piston of a pump which works by suction, or the valve of such a piston. **6.** a pipe or tube through which anything is drawn. **7.** *Slang.* a person easily deceived or imposed upon; dupe. **8.** *Bot.* a shoot rising from a subterranean stem or a root. **9.** *U.S. Colloq.* a lollipop. —*v.t.* **10.** to strip off suckers or shoots from (a plant); remove superfluous shoots from (tobacco, etc.). —*v.i.* **11.** to send out suckers or shoots, as a plant.

suckerfish (sŭk′ə fĭsh′), *n., pl.* **-fishes,** (*esp. collectively*) **-fish.** a remora (def. 1).

sucking-pig (sŭk′ĭng pĭg′), *n.* a newborn or very young pig, esp. one suitable for roasting.

suckle (sŭk′l), *v.,* **-led, -ling.** —*v.t.* **1.** to nurse at the breast. **2.** to nourish or bring up. **3.** to put to suck. —*v.i.* **4.** to suck at the breast. [freq. of SUCK]

suckling (sŭk′lĭng), *n.* an infant or a young animal that is not yet weaned.

Suckling (sŭk′lĭng), *n.* **Sir John,** 1609–42, English poet.

sucrase (syo͞o′krās), *n. Chem.* invertase.

Sucre (*Sp.* so͞o′krĕ), *n.* **1. Antonio José de** (*Sp.* än tō′nyō KHō sĕ′ dĕ), 1795–1830, Venezuelan general and South American liberator: first president of Bolivia, 1826–28. **2.** a city in S Bolivia: the nominal capital (La Paz is the seat of the government). 54,000 (est. 1965). **3.** (*l.c.*) the monetary unit of Ecuador equal to 100 centavos, and equivalent to about £0·0208 sterling.

sucroclastic (syo͞o′krō klăs′tĭk), *adj. Biochem.* (of enzymes) capable of hydrolysing complex carbohydrates.

sucrose (syo͞o′krōs), *n. Chem.* a crystalline disaccharide, $C_{12}H_{22}O_{11}$, the sugar obtained from the sugar cane, the sugar beet, and sorghum, and forming the greater part of maple sugar. Also, **saccharose.** [f. F *sucr(e)* SUGAR + -OSE²]

suction (sŭk′shən), *n.* **1.** the act, process, or condition of sucking. **2.** the tendency to suck a substance into an interior space when the atmospheric pressure is reduced in the space. **3.** the reduction of pressure in order to cause such a sucking. **4.** the act or process of sucking a gas or liquid by such means. [t. L: s. *suctio*]

suction pump, a pump for raising water or the like by suction, consisting essentially of a vertical cylinder in which a piston works up and down, both with valves.

suction stop, *Phonet.* click (def. 3).

suctorial (sŭk tô′rĭ əl), *adj.* **1.** adapted for sucking or suction, as an organ; functioning as a sucker, whether for imbibing or for adhering. **2.** having sucking organs; imbibing or adhering by suckers. **3.** pertaining to or characterized by suction.

Sudan (so͞o dăn′), *n.* **1.** Formerly, **Anglo-Egyptian Sudan.** a republic in NE Africa, south of Egypt and bordering the Red Sea. 13,011,000 pop. (est. 1964); 967,500 sq. mi. *Cap.*: Khartoum. **2.** French, **Soudan.** a region in N Africa, S of the Sahara and Libyan deserts, extending from the Atlantic to the Red Sea. **3.** See **Mali.**

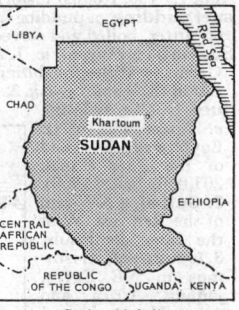

Sudan (def. 1)

Sudanese (so͞o′də nēz′), *n., pl.* **-nese,** *adj.* —*n.* **1.** a native of Sudan. —*adj.* **2.** of or pertaining to Sudan or its people.

sudarium (syo͞o dĕə′rĭ əm), *n., pl.* **-daria** (-dĕə′rĭ ə). **1.** a cloth for wiping the face; a handkerchief. **2.** veronica (def. 2). [t. L]

sudatorium (syo͞o′də tô′rĭ əm), *n., pl.* **-toria** (-tô′rĭ ə). a hot-air bath for inducing sweating. [t. L, prop. neut. of *sūdātōrius* sweat-producing]

sudatory (syo͞o′də tə rĭ, -trĭ), *adj.* **1.** pertaining to or causing sweating. **2.** pertaining to a sudatorium. —*n.* **3.** a sudatorium. [see SUDATORIUM]

Sudbury (sŭd′bə rĭ, -brĭ), *n.* a town in Canada, in SE Ontario. 78,061 (est. 1964).

sudd (sŭd), *n.* (in the White Nile) floating vegetable matter which often obstructs navigation. [t. Ar.]

sudden (sŭd′n), *adj.* **1.** happening, coming, made, or done quickly, without warning or unexpectedly: *a sudden attack.* **2.** sharp; abrupt: *a sudden turn.* **3.** *Archaic.* unpremeditated, as actions. **4.** *Archaic.* quickly made, prepared, provided, etc. —*adv.* **5.** *Poetic.* suddenly. —*n.* **6.** an unexpected occasion or occurrence. **7. all of a sudden,** suddenly; without warning; quite unexpectedly. [ME *soden*, t. AF: m. *sodein*, g. m. L *subitāneus*] —**sud′denly,** *adv.* —**sud′denness,** *n.*

—**Syn. 2.** SUDDEN, UNEXPECTED, ABRUPT describe acts, events, or conditions for which there has been no preparation or gradual approach. SUDDEN refers to the quickness of an occurrence, though the event may have been expected: *a sudden change in the weather.* UNEXPECTED emphasizes the lack of preparedness for what occurs or appears: *an unexpected crisis.* ABRUPT characterizes something involving a swift adjustment; the effect is often unpleasant, unfavourable, or the cause of dismay: *an abrupt change in manner.*

Sudermann (*Ger.* zo͞o′dər män), *n.* **Hermann** (*Ger.* hĕr′män), 1857–1928, German dramatist and novelist.

Sudeten (so͞o dā′tn; *Ger.* zo͞o dĕ′tən), *n.* **1.** Also, **Sudetes** (so͞o dē′tēz). a mountain range extending along the N boundary of Czechoslovakia between the Oder and Neisse rivers. See map under **Moravian Gate. 2.** a native or inhabitant of the Sudetenland. **3.** Sudetenland.

Sudetenland (so͞o dā′tn lănd′; *Ger.* zo͞o dĕ′tən länt), *n.* a mountainous region in N and NW Czechoslovakia, including the Sudeten and the Erz Gebirge: annexed by Germany 1938; returned to Czechoslovakia 1945. Also, **Sudeten.**

sudor (syo͞o′dô), *n.* sweat; perspiration. [t. L] —**sudoral** (syo͞o′də rəl), *adj.*

sudoriferous (syo͞o′də rĭf′ə rəs), *adj.* bearing or secreting sweat. [f. LL *sūdōrifer* sweat-bringing + -OUS]

sudorific (syo͞o′də rĭf′ĭk), *adj.* **1.** causing sweat; diaphoretic. **2.** sudoriparous. —*n.* **3.** a sudorific agent. [t. NL: s. *sūdōrificus*, der. L *sūdor* sweat]

sudoriparous (syo͞o′də rĭp′ə rəs), *adj.* producing or secreting sweat. [t. NL: m. *sūdōriparus*]

Sudra (syo͞o′drə), *n.* a Hindu of the lowest caste. [t. Skt]

suds (sŭdz), *n.pl.* **1.** soapy water. **2.** foam; lather. **3.** *Slang.* beer. [? t. MD: m. *sudse* marsh] —**sud′sy,** *adj.*

sue (syo͞o), *v.,* **sued, suing.** —*v.t.* **1.** to institute process in law against, or bring a civil action against. **2.** to make petition or appeal to. **3.** *Archaic.* to woo or court. —*v.i.* **4.** to institute legal proceedings, or bring suit. **5.** to make petition or appeal. **6.** *Archaic.* to be suitor to a woman. [ME, t. AF: m. *suer*, var. of OF *sivre*, g. VL *sequere*, r. L *sequi* follow] —**suer** (syo͞o′ə), *n.*

Sue (so͞o; *Fr.* sʏ), *n.* **Eugène** (*Fr.* œ zhĕn′) (*Marie Joseph Sue*), 1804–57, French novelist.

suede (swād), *n.* **1.** kid or other leather finished on the flesh side with a soft, napped surface, or on the outer side after removal of a thin outer layer. **2.** a napped fabric suggesting this. Also, **suède.** [t. F: lit., Sweden]

suet (syo͞o′ĭt), *n.* the hard fatty tissue about the loins and kidneys of cattle, sheep, etc., used in cookery, etc., and prepared as tallow. [ME, f. AF *su(e)* (g. L *sēbum* tallow, suet) + -ET] —**su′ety,** *adj.*

Suetonius (swē tō′nyəs), *n.* (*Gaius Suetonius Tranquillus*), A.D. 75–150, Roman historian.

suet pudding, a pudding mixture with suet added in place of butter, boiled and served with a sweet sauce.

Suevian (swē′vyən), *n.* **1.** a member of a group of ancient Germanic tribes inhabiting a large area of central Europe east of the Rhine. —*adj.* **2.** of or pertaining to the Suevians.

Suez (so͞o′ĭz, syo͞o′ĭz), *n.* **1.** a seaport in NE Egypt, near the S end of the Suez Canal. 203,000 (est. 1960). **2. Gulf of,** a NW arm of the Red Sea, W of the Sinai Peninsula. **3. Isthmus of,** an isthmus in NE Egypt, joining Africa and Asia. 72 mi. wide.

Suez Canal

Suez Canal, a canal across the Isthmus of Suez, connecting the Mediterranean and the Red Sea. ab. 100 mi. long.

suf-, var. of **sub-** (by assimilation) before *f.*

suf., suffix. Also, **suff.**

Suff., Suffragan. Also, **Suffr.**

suffer (sŭf′ə), *v.i.* **1.** to undergo or feel pain or distress. **2.** to sustain injury, disadvantage or loss. **3.** to undergo a penalty, esp. of death. **4.** to be the object of some action. **5.** *Obs.* to endure patiently or bravely. —*v.t.* **6.** to undergo, experience, or be subjected to (pain, distress, injury, loss, or anything unpleasant). **7.** to undergo (any action, process, etc.): *to suffer change.* **8.** to tolerate or allow. **9.** to allow or permit (to do or be as stated). [t. L: s. *sufferre*; r. ME *suffre(n)*, t. AF: m. *suffrir*, g. LL *sufferīre*] —**suf′ferable,** *adj.* —**suf′ferableness,** *n.* —**suf′ferably,** *adv.* —**suf′ferer,** *n.*

sufferance (sŭf′ə rəns), *n.* **1.** tolerance, as of a person or thing; tacit permission. **2.** capacity to endure pain, hardship, etc. **3.** *Archaic.* the suffering of pain, distress, injury, etc. **4.** *Archaic.* patient endurance. **5. on sufferance,** reluctantly tolerated.

suffering (sŭf′ə rĭng, sŭf′rĭng), *n.* **1.** the act of one who suffers. **2.** a particular instance of this.

suffice (sə fīs′), *v.*, **-ficed, -ficing.** —*v.i.* **1.** to be enough or adequate, as for needs, purposes, etc. —*v.t.* **2.** to be enough or adequate for; satisfy. [t. L: m. s. *sufficere*; r. ME *suffyse*, t. OF] —**suffic′er,** *n.*

sufficiency (sə fĭsh′ən sĭ), *n.*, *pl.* **-cies. 1.** the state or fact of being sufficient; adequacy. **2.** a sufficient number or amount; enough. **3.** adequate provision or supply, esp. of wealth.

sufficient (sə fĭsh′ənt), *adj.* **1.** that suffices; enough or adequate: *sufficient proof or protection.* **2.** *Archaic.* competent or capable, as a person. [ME, t. L: s. *sufficiens*, ppr., sufficing] —**suffi′ciently,** *adv.*

suffix (sŭf′ĭks), *n.* **1.** *Gram.* an affix which follows the element to which it is added, as *-ly* in *kindly.* **2.** something suffixed. —*v.t.* **3.** *Gram.* to add as a suffix. **4.** to affix at the end of something: *to suffix a syllable to a word.* **5.** to fix or put under. —*v.i.* **6.** *Gram.* (of a linguistic form) to admit a suffix. [t. NL: s. *suffixum*, prop. neut. pp., fastened on] —**suffixal** (sŭf′ĭk səl), *adj.* —**suffixion** (sŭ fĭk′shən), *n.*

sufflate (sŭ flāt′), *v.t.*, **-flated, -flating.** *Obs.* to blow up; inflate. [t. L: m. s. *sufflātus*, pp.] —**suffla′tion,** *n.*

suffocate (sŭf′ə kāt′), *v.*, **-cated, -cating.** —*v.t.* **1.** to kill by preventing the access of air to the blood through the lungs or analogous organs, as gills. **2.** to impede the respiration of **3.** to cause discomfort to through lack of cool or fresh air. **4.** to overcome or extinguish; suppress. —*v.i.* **5.** to become suffocated; stifle; smother. **6.** to feel discomfort through lack of cool or fresh air. [t. L: m. s. *suffōcātus*, pp., choked] —**suf′focat′ingly,** *adv.* —**suf′foca′tion,** *n.* —**suf′foca′tive,** *adj.*

Suffolk (sŭf′ək), *n.* **1.** a county in E England, divided for administrative purposes into **East Suffolk** and **West Suffolk.** 471,614 pop. (1961); 1482 sq. mi. *Co. town:* Ipswich. **2.** one of a breed of sheep noted for mutton of high quality. **3.** Also, **Suffolk Punch.** one of a breed of heavy draught horses of chestnut colour. **4.** one of a breed of small, black pigs.

suffragan (sŭf′rə gən), *adj.* **1.** assisting or assistant, applied: **a.** to any bishop in relation to the archbishop or metropolitan who is his superior. **b.** to an assistant or subsidiary bishop who performs episcopal functions in a diocese, but has no ordinary jurisdiction, as, in the Church of England, a bishop consecrated to assist the ordinary bishop of a see in part of his diocese. **2.** (of a see or diocese) subordinate to an archiepiscopal or metropolitan see. —*n.* **3.** a suffragan bishop. [ME *suffragane*, t. ML: s. *suffrāgāneus* assistant, der. L *suffrāgor* I support (vote for). See SUFFRAGE]

suffrage (sŭf′rĭj), *n.* **1.** the right of voting, esp. in political elections. **2.** a vote given in favour of a proposed measure, a candidate, or the like. **3.** *Eccles.* a prayer, esp. a short intercessory prayer or petition. [ME, t. L: m. s. *suffrāgium*]

suffragette (sŭf′rə jĕt′), *n.* a woman who advocates female suffrage. —**suf′fraget′tism,** *n.*

suffragist (sŭf′rə jĭst), *n.* an advocate of the grant or extension of political suffrage, esp. to women.

suffumigate (sə fyo͞o′mĭ gāt′), *v.t.*, **-gated, -gating.** to fumigate from below; apply fumes or smoke to. [t. L: m. s. *suffūmigātus*, pp.] —**suffu′miga′tion,** *n.*

suffuse (sə fyo͞oz′), *v.t.*, **-fused, -fusing.** to overspread with or as with a liquid, colour, etc. [t. L: m. s. *suffūsus*, pp., overspread] —**suffusion** (sə fyo͞o′zhən), *n.* —**suffusive** (sə fyo͞o′sĭv), *adj.*

Sufi (so͞o′fĭ), *n.*, *pl.* **-fis.** a member of an ascetic and mystical Muslim sect. [t. Ar.: m. *çūfī* man of wool, prob. with reference to the woollen garments worn]

Sufism (so͞o′fĭz′əm), *n.* the ascetic and mystical system of the Sufis. Also, **Sufiism** (so͞o′fĭ ĭz′əm). —**Sufis′tic,** *adj.*

sug-, var. of **sub-** (by assimilation) before *g.*

sugar (sho͝og′ə), *n.* **1.** a sweet crystalline substance, sucrose, cane sugar, or beet sugar, $C_{12}H_{22}O_{11}$, obtained chiefly from the juice of the sugar cane or sugar beet, but present in sorghum, maple sap, etc., and extensively used for food purposes. **2.** a member of the same class of carbohydrates. **3.** *Slang.* money. —*v.t.* **4.** to cover, sprinkle, mix, or sweeten with sugar. **5.** to make agreeable. —*v.i.* **6.** to form sugar. **7.** to make maple sugar. **8.** (in making maple sugar) to complete the boiling down of the syrup in preparation for granulation (fol. by *off*). [ME *sugure, zugure*, t. ML: m. *zugurum*, t. Ar.: m. *sukkar*; r. ME *sucure, zucur*, t. OF: m. *sukere, zuchre*, ult. t. Ar.]

sugar basin, a small basin for serving sugar at table. Also, **sugar bowl.**

sugar beet, a variety of beet, *Beta vulgaris*, with a white root, cultivated for the sugar it yields.

sugarbird (sho͝og′ə bûd′), *n.* a sunbird.

sugar bush, a large proteaceous shrub of southern Africa, *Protea mellifera*, with large heads of whitish flowers. Also, *S African*, **suikerbos.**

sugarbush (sho͝og′ə bo͝osh′), *n.* *U.S., Can.* a small plantation, orchard, or grove of sugar maples.

sugar candy, a confection made by suspending strings in a strong sugar solution, which is left standing in a cool place until the candy is deposited on the string.

sugar cane, a tall grass, *Saccharum officinarum*, of tropical and warm regions, having a stout, jointed stalk, and constituting the chief source of sugar.

sugar-coated (sho͝og′ə kō′tĭd), *adj.* **1.** covered with sugar. **2.** (of something unpleasant) disguised so as to appear agreeable, pleasant, or acceptable.

sugar corn, sweet corn (def. 1).

sugar daddy, *Slang.* a rich middle-aged or old man who lavishes money and gifts on a young woman.

sugared (sho͝og′əd), *adj.* **1.** covered, mixed, or sweetened with sugar. **2.** sweetened as if with sugar; made agreeable; honeyed, as words, speech, etc.

sugar loaf, 1. a large, approximately conical loaf or mass of hard refined sugar. **2.** anything resembling this in shape. —**sug′ar-loaf′,** *adj.*

sugar maple, any of several maples having a sweet sap, esp. *Acer saccharum*, of eastern North America, which yields a timber used in making furniture and is the chief source of maple sugar.

sugar of lead, lead acetate.

sugar pine, a tall pine, *Pinus lambertiana*, of California, Oregon, etc., having cones 20 in. long.

sugarplum (sho͝og′ə plŭm′), *n.* a small sweetmeat made of sugar with various flavouring and colouring ingredients; a bonbon.

sugar soap, a substance with the appearance of brown sugar, which when dissolved in water gives an alkaline solution; used for cleaning surfaces to be painted.

sugar tongs, small tongs used for serving cubes of sugar at table.

sugary (sho͝og′ə rĭ), *adj.* **1.** of, containing, or resembling sugar. **2.** sweet; excessively sweet. **3.** dulcet: honeyed; cloying; deceitfully agreeable: *her sugary words of greetings sounded insincere.* —**sug′ariness,** *n.*

Suger (*Fr.* SY zhĕ′), *n.* 1081–1151, French cleric and statesman.

suggest (sə jĕst′), *v.t.* **1.** to place or bring (an idea, proposition, plan, etc.) before a person's mind for consideration or possible action. **2.** to propose (a person or thing) as suitable or possible. **3.** (of things) to prompt the consideration, making, doing, etc., of. **4.** to bring before a person's mind indirectly or without plain expression. **5.** (of a thing) to call up in the mind (another thing) through association or natural connection of ideas. [t. L: s. *suggestus*, pp., placed under, added, furnished] **—suggest′er,** *n.* **—Syn. 4.** See **hint.**

suggestible (sə jĕs′tə bl), *adj.* **1.** capable of being influenced by suggestion. **2.** that may be suggested. **—suggest′ibil′ity,** *n.*

suggestion (sə jĕs′chən), *n.* **1.** the act of suggesting. **2.** the state of being suggested. **3.** something suggested, as a proposal, plan, etc. **4.** a slight trace: *he speaks English with just a suggestion of a foreign accent.* **5.** the calling up in the mind of one idea by another by virtue of some association or of some natural connection between the ideas. **6.** the idea thus called up. **7.** *Psychol.* **a.** the process of accepting a proposition for belief or action in the absence of the intervening and critical thought that would normally occur. **b.** a proposition for belief or action accepted in this way. **c.** the offering of a stimulus in such a way as to produce an uncritical response. [ME, t. L: s. *suggestio*]

suggestive (sə jĕs′tĭv), *adj.* **1.** that suggests; tending to suggest thoughts, ideas, etc. **2.** pertaining to hypnotic suggestion. **3.** such as to suggest something improper or indecent. **—sugges′tively,** *adv.* **—sugges′tiveness,** *n.* **—Syn. 1.** See **expressive.**

Suharto (sōō hä′tō), *n.* **General,** born 1921, Indonesian statesman: president since 1967. Also, **Soeharto.**

sui (syōō′ĭ, syōō′ī), *n. Chess, Colloq.* suimate.

suicidal (syōō′ĭ sī′dl), *adj.* **1.** pertaining to, involving, or suggesting suicide; tending or leading to suicide. **2.** dangerously rash or foolish. **—su′icid′ally,** *adv.*

suicide (syōō′ĭ sīd′), *n.* **1.** one who intentionally takes his own life. **2.** the intentional taking of one's own life. **3.** deliberate destruction of one's own interests or prospects. **4. commit suicide,** to kill oneself intentionally. [t. NL: m. s. *suicidium.* See -CIDE]

sui generis (sōō′ī jĕn′ə rĭs), *Latin.* of his, her, its, or their own kind; unique.

sui juris (jŏŏə′rĭs), *Law.* one capable of managing his affairs and assuming legal responsibility for his acts, as distinguished from others, as lunatics and infants, whose legal capacity is limited. [L: of one's own right]

suikerbos (sā′kə bŏs′, sōō′-), *n. S African.* sugar bush. [t. Afrikaans]

suimate (syōō′ĭ māt′, syōō′ī māt′), *n. Chess.* self-mate. [f. L *sui-* of oneself + MATE[2]]

suint (sōō′ĭnt, swĭnt), *n.* the natural grease of the wool of sheep, consisting of a mixture of fatty matter and potassium salts, used as a source of potash and in the preparation of ointments. [t. F, der. *suer* sweat]

Suir (shŏŏə), *n.* a river in SE Ireland flowing from Co. Tipperary to the Atlantic at Waterford. 85 mi.

Suisse (*Fr.* swēs), *n.* French name of **Switzerland.**

suit (syōōt), *n.* **1.** a set of garments, vestments, or armour, intended to be worn together. **2.** a set of outer garments of the same material, worn by men, normally consisting of trousers, jacket, and sometimes a waistcoat. **3.** a set of outer garments worn by women, usually consisting of skirt and jacket, and sometimes a blouse. **4.** the act or process of suing in a court of law; legal prosecution. **5.** *Cards.* **a.** one of the sets or classes (usually four: spades, clubs, hearts, and diamonds) into which playing cards are divided. **b.** the aggregate of cards belonging to one of these sets held in a player's hand at one time. **6.** a number of things of this kind or purpose forming a series or set. **7.** the wooing or courting of a woman. **8.** the act of making petition or appeal. **9.** a petition, as to a person of exalted station. **10. follow suit, a.** to play a card of the suit led. **b.** to follow another's example. **11. strong suit,** something one is very good at; one's forte. *—v.t.* **12.** to provide with a suit of clothes; clothe; array. **13.** to make appropriate, adapt, or accommodate, as one thing to another. **14.** to be appropriate or becoming to. **15.** to be or prove satisfactory, agreeable, or acceptable to; satisfy or please. **16. suit oneself,** to do what one chooses, regardless of the interests or advice of others. *—v.i.* **17.** to be appropriate or suitable; accord. **18.** to be satisfactory, agreeable, or acceptable. [ME, t. AF: m. *suite,* var. of OF *sieute,* der. *s(u)ivre* follow. See SUE]

suitable (syōō′tə bl), *adj.* such as to suit; appropriate; fitting; becoming. **—suit′abil′ity, suit′ableness,** *n.* **—suit′ably,** *adv.*

suitcase (syōōt′kās′), *n.* a portable rectangular travelling bag, usually with stiffened frame, for carrying clothes, etc.

suite (swēt), *n.* **1.** a company of followers or attendants; a train or retinue. **2.** a number of things forming a series or set. **3.** a connected series of rooms to be used together by one person or a number of persons. **4.** a set of furniture of similar design and complementary in function: *a three-piece suite consists of a settee and two armchairs.* **5.** *Music.* **a.** an ordered series of instrumental dances, in the same or related keys, commonly preceded by a prelude. **b.** an ordered series of instrumental movements of any character. **6.** a course in a meal following a main course, usually consisting of a light, sweet dish, fruit, or the like; sweet. [t. F, der. *suivre.* See SUIT]

suiting (syōō′tĭng), *n.* a fabric for making suits.

suitor (syōō′tə), *n.* **1.** one who courts or woos a woman. **2.** *Law.* a petitioner or plaintiff. **3.** one who sues or petitions for anything.

Suiyüan (soi′ywän′, swā′yōō än′), *n.* a part of the Inner Mongolian Autonomous Region, in N China; formerly a province. *Cap.:* Huhehot. 127,413 sq. mi.

Sukarno (sōō kä′nō), *n.* **Achmed** (äk′mĕd, äKH′mĕd), 1901–70, Indonesian statesman: president 1949–67. Also, **Soekarno.**

sukiyaki (sōō′kĭ yä′kĭ), *n.* a Japanese dish containing fried meat, vegetables, onions, etc., usually cooked with soya sauce, often at the table. [t. Jap.]

Sukkoth (sŏŏk′ōt, -ōth), *n.pl.* the Jewish holiday of the Feast of Tabernacles (Lev. 23:34–43), beginning on the eve of the 15th of Tishri and lasting originally eight days, and in later Judaism nine days. [t. Heb.]

Sukkur (sŭk′ə), *n.* a town in S West Pakistan, on the river Indus. 103,216 (1961). Also, **Sakhar.**

Sulawesi (sōō′lə wā′sĭ), *n.* Indonesian name of **Celebes.**

sulcate (sŭl′kāt), *adj.* having long, narrow grooves or channels, as a stem; furrowed; cleft, as a hoof. Also, **sul′cated.** [t. L: m. s. *sulcātus,* pp., furrowed] **—sulca′tion,** *n.*

Sulcate stalk of valerian, *Valeriana officinalis*

sulcus (sŭl′kəs), *n., pl.* **-ci** (-sī). **1.** a furrow or groove. **2.** *Anat.* a fissure between two convolutions of the brain. [t. L]

Suleiman (sōō′lĭ män′), *n.* (′*The Magnificent*′) 1495?–1566, sultan of the Turkish Empire 1520–66. Also, **Soliman, Solyman.**

sulf-, *U.S.* var. of **sulph.**

sulfur (sŭl′fə), *n.* *U.S.* sulphur.

sulfuret (*n.* sŭl′fyōō rĭt; *v.* sŭl′fyōō rĕt′), *n., v.t.,* (*U.S.*) **-reted, -reting.** *U.S.* sulphuret.

sulk (sŭlk), *v.i.* **1.** to hold aloof in a sullen, morose, ill-humoured, or offended mood. *—n.* **2.** a state or fit of sulking. **3.** (*pl.*) ill humour shown by sulking: *to have the sulks.* **4.** Also, **sulk′er.** one who sulks. [back-formation from SULKY]

sulky (sŭl′kĭ), *adj.,* **sulkier, sulkiest,** *n., pl.* **sulkies.** *—adj.* **1.** sullenly ill-humoured or resentful; marked by ill-humoured aloofness. **2.** (of weather, etc.) gloomy. *—n.* **3.** a light two-wheeled one-horse carriage for one person. [? der. OE *-solcen* slothful, remiss; cf. N Fris. *sulkig* sulky; in def. 3, so called as holding only one person] **—sulk′ily,** *adv.* **—sulk′iness,** *n.*

Sulla (sŭl′ə), *n.* **Lucius Cornelius** (lōō′syəs kô nē′lyəs) (′*Felix*′), 138–78 B.C. Roman general and dictator.

sullage (sŭl′ĭj), *n.* **1.** refuse, scum, or filth. **2.** scoria. **3.** silt. [cf. OE *sol* mire]

sullen (sŭl′ən), *adj.* **1.** showing ill humour by a gloomy silence or reserve. **2.** silently and persistently ill-humoured; morose. **3.** indicative of gloomy ill humour: *sullen silence.* **4.** gloomy or dismal, as weather, sounds, etc. **5.** sluggish, as a stream. **6.** *Obs.* malignant, as planets, influences, etc. [ME *solein,* t. AF, der. *sol* SOLE[1]] **—sul′lenly,** *adv.* **—sul′lenness,** *n.* **—Syn. 1.** See **cross.**

Sullivan (sŭl′ĭ vən), *n.* **1. Sir Arthur Seymour,** 1842–1900, English composer; collaborator with Sir W. S. Gilbert. **2. Louis Henri,** U.S. architect, 1856–1924, early advocate of functionalism in architecture.

sully (sŭl′ĭ), *v.,* **-lied, -lying,** *n., pl.* **-lies.** *—v.t.* **1.** to soil, stain, or tarnish. **2.** to mar the purity or lustre of; defile. *—v.i.* **3.** to become sullied, soiled, or tarnished. *—n. Obs.* **4.** the act of sullying. **5.** a stain. [ME *solien,* OE (*ā*)*solian* become dirty, der. *sol* dirty]

Sully (sŭl′ĭ; *Fr.* sʏ lē′), *n.* **Maximilien de Béthune** (*Fr.* mȧk sē mēl yăN′ də bė tʏn′), **Duc de,** 1560–1641, French statesman.

Sully-Prudhomme (*Fr.* sʏ lē prʏ dŏm′), *n.* **René François Armand** (*Fr.* rə nė fräN swȧ ȧr mäN′), 1839–1907, French poet.

sulph-, *Chem.* a prefix indicating a compound in which sulphur has been substituted for oxygen, as *sodium sulphantimonate* (Na_3SbS_4) compared with sodium antimonate (Na_3SbO_4). Thus, formulas such as *sulphantimonite, sulpharsenate,* etc., can be deduced from the formulas of the corresponding antimonite, arsenate, etc. Also, before consonants, **sulpho-**; *U.S.*, **sulf-, sulfo-.** [comb. form repr. SULPHUR]

sulphadiazine (sŭl′fə dī′ə zēn′), *n. Pharm.* a sulphanilamide derivative, $C_{10}H_{10}N_4O_2S$, particularly effective against staphylococcal and gonococcal infections. Also, *U.S.*, **sulfadiazine.**

sulpha drugs (sŭl′fə), a group of compounds containing the radical SO_2NH_2, used as antibacterials in treatment of various diseases, wounds, burns, etc. Also, **sulphas** (sŭl′fəz); *U.S.*, **sulfa drugs, sulfas.**

sulphaguanidine (sŭl′fə gwä′nĭ dēn′), *n. Pharm.* a sulphanilamide derivative, $C_7H_{10}N_4O_2S$, effective against bacterial dysentery. Also, *U.S.*, **sulfaguanidine.**

sulphanilamide (sŭl′fə nĭl′ə mīd′), *n. Pharm.* a white crystalline amide of sulphanilic acid, $NH_2C_6H_4SO_2NH_2$, effective against infections caused by haemolytic streptococci, the gonococci, etc. Also, *U.S.*, **sulfanilamide.**

sulphapyridine (sŭl′fə pĭ′rĭ dīn′, -dēn′), *n. Pharm.* a sulphanilamide derivative, $C_{11}H_{11}N_3O_2S$, more toxic than sulphanilamide but somewhat more effective against infections caused by pneumococci. Also, *U.S.*, **sulfapyridine.**

sulpharsphenamine (sŭlf′äs′fĕn ə mēn′, -fĭ năm′ĭn), *n. Pharm.* a compound having the same characteristics as arsphenamine but less efficient and not so irritating to the body. Also, *U.S.*, **sulfarsphenamine.**

sulphate (sŭl′fāt), *n.*, *v.*, **-phated, -phating.** —*n.* **1.** *Chem.* a salt of sulphuric acid. —*v.t.* **2.** to combine, treat, or impregnate with sulphuric acid, or with a sulphate or sulphates. **3.** to convert into a sulphate. **4.** *Elect.* to deposit lead sulphate on during sulphation. —*v.i.* **5.** to become sulphated. Also, *U.S.*, **sulfate.** [t. NL: m. s. *sulphātum*, f. L *sulph(ur)* SULPHUR + *-ātum* -ATE[2]] —**sulphatic** (sŭl făt′ĭk), *adj.*

sulphathiazole (sŭl′fə thī′ə zōl′), *n. Pharm.* a sulphanilamide derivative, $C_9H_9N_3O_2S_2$, effective in the treatment of pneumonia and staphylococcus infections. Also, *U.S.*, **sulfathiazole.**

sulphation (sŭl fā′shən), *n. Elect.* the process of forming a deposit of lead sulphate on the lead plates of an accumulator. Also, *U.S.*, **sulfation.**

sulphatize (sŭl′fə tīz′), *v.t.*, **-tized, -tizing.** to convert into a sulphate as by the roasting of ores. Also, **sulphatise;** *U.S.*, **sulfatize.**

sulphide (sŭl′fīd), *n. Chem.* a compound of sulphur with a more electropositive element or, less often, a radical. Also, **sulphid** (sŭl′fĭd); *U.S.*, **sulfide, sulfid.**

sulphite (sŭl′fīt), *n. Chem.* a salt of sulphurous acid. Also, *U.S.*, **sulfite.**

sulpho-, var. of **sulph-** before a consonant. Also, *U.S.*, **sulfo-.**

sulphonamide (sŭl fŏn′ə mīd′), *n.* **1.** *Chem.* an amide of a sulphonic acid, containing the radical SO_2NH_2. **2.** *Pharm.* any of a group of sulphonamide compounds possessing antibacterial activity, as sulphanilamide. Also, *U.S.*, **sulfonamide.**

sulphonate (sŭl′fə nāt′), *n.*, *v.*, **-nated, -nating.** *Chem.* —*n.* **1.** an ester or salt derived from a sulphonic acid. —*v.t.* **2.** to make into a sulphonic acid, as by treating an aromatic hydrocarbon with concentrated sulphuric acid. Also, *U.S.*, **sulfonate.**

sulphonation (sŭl′fə nā′shən), *n. Chem.* the process of attaching the sulphonic acid radical, $-SO_3H$, directly to carbon in an organic compound. Also, *U.S.*, **sulfonation.**

sulphone (sŭl′fōn), *n. Chem.* any of a class of organic compounds containing the bivalent SO_2 group united with two hydrocarbon radicals. Also, *U.S.*, **sulfone.**

sulphonic (sŭl fŏn′ĭk), *adj. Chem.* **1.** denoting or pertaining to the group SO_2OH. **2.** denoting or pertaining to any of the acids, mostly organic, containing the SO_3H group. Also, *U.S.*, **sulfonic.**

sulphonic acid, *Chem.* any of a large group of organic compounds containing the sulphonic radical. They are strong acids, giving neutral sodium salts and used in the synthesis of phenols, dyes, and other substances. Also, *U.S.*, **sulfonic acid.**

sulphonium (sŭl fō′nyəm), *n. Chem.* the ion obtained by adding a proton to hydrogen sulphide, as $(H_3S)^+$. Also, *U.S.*, **sulfonium.**

sulphonyl (sŭl′fə nĭl), *n.* sulphuryl. Also, *U.S.*, **sulfonyl.**

sulphonyl chloride, *Chem.* denoting the radical $-SO_2Cl$. Also, *U.S.*, **sulfonyl chloride.**

sulphur (sŭl′fə), *n.* **1.** *Chem.* a non-metallic element which exists in several forms, the ordinary one being a yellow rhombic crystalline solid, and which burns with a blue flame and a suffocating smell: used esp. in making gunpowder and matches, in vulcanizing rubber, in medicine, etc. *Symbol:* S; *at. wt:* 32·064; *at. no.:* 16; *sp. gr.:* 2·07 at 20°C. **2.** a pale yellow with a greenish tinge. **3.** any of various yellow or orange butterflies of the family *Pieridae.* —*v.t.* **4.** to treat or fumigate with sulphur. Also, *U.S.*, **sulfur.** [ME, t. L] —**sul′phury,** *adj.*

sulphurate (sŭl′fyŏŏ rāt′), *v.t.*, **-rated, -rating.** to combine, treat, or impregnate with sulphur, the fumes of burning sulphur, or the like. Also, *U.S.*, **sulfurate.** —**sul′phura′tion,** *n.* —**sul′phura′tor,** *n.*

sulphur-bottom (sŭl′fə bŏt′əm), *n.* the blue whale, *Sibbaldus musculus*, of arctic seas, with yellowish underparts: the largest mammal that has ever lived.

sulphur dioxide, *Chem.* a colourless suffocating gas, SO_2, formed when sulphur burns. Also, *U.S.*, **sulfur dioxide.**

sulphureous (sŭl fyŏŏə′rĭ əs), *adj.* consisting of, containing, pertaining to, or resembling sulphur; sulphur-coloured. Also, *U.S.*, **sulfureous.** —**sulphu′reously,** *adv.* —**sulphu′reousness,** *n.*

sulphuret (*n.* sŭl′fyŏŏ rĭt; *v.* sŭl′fyŏŏ rĕt′), *n.*, *v.*, **-retted, -retting.** *Chem.* —*n.* **1.** a sulphide. —*v.t.* **2.** to treat or combine with sulphur. Also, *U.S.*, **sulfuret.** [t. NL: s. *sulphurētum.* See SULPHUR, -URET]

sulphuretted hydrogen, *Chem.* hydrogen sulphide.

sulphuric (sŭl fyŏŏə′rĭk), *adj. Chem.* of, pertaining to, or containing sulphur, esp. in the hexavalent stage. Also, *U.S.*, **sulfuric.**

sulphuric acid, *Chem.* the dibasic acid of sulphur. H_2SO_4, a colourless oily liquid, made from sulphur trioxide and used in many industrial processes: formerly called oil of vitriol. Also, *U.S.*, **sulfuric acid.**

sulphuric ether, *Chem.* ether (def. 1a). Also, *U.S.*, **sulfuric ether.**

sulphurize (sŭl′fyŏŏ rīz′), *v.t.*, **-rized, -rizing. 1.** to combine, treat, or impregnate with sulphur. **2.** to fumigate with sulphur dioxide. Also, **sulphurise;** *U.S.*, **sulfurize.** —**sul′phuriza′tion,** *n.*

sulphurous (sŭl′fə rəs), *adj.* **1.** *Chem.* relating to sulphur. **2.** of the yellow colour of sulphur. **3.** *Chem.* containing tetravalent sulphur. **4.** pertaining to the fires of hell; hellish. **5.** fiery or heated. **6.** thundery. Also, *U.S.*, **sulfurous.**

sulphurous acid, *Chem.* an acid, H_2SO_3, formed by dissolving sulphur dioxide in water, known mainly by its salts (sulphites). Also, *U.S.*, **sulfurous acid.**

sulphur point, *Chem.* the temperature at which liquid sulphur is in equilibrium with its vapour at one standard atmosphere; equal to 444·6°C. Also, *U.S.*, **sulfur point.**

sulphur trioxide, *Chem.* an irritant, corrosive, low-melting solid, SO_3, prepared by oxidation of sulphur dioxide; an intermediate in the manufacture of sulphuric acid. Also, *U.S.*, **sulfur trioxide.**

sulphurweed (sŭl′fə wēd′), *n.* hog's-fennel. Also, **sulphur-root, sulphurwort.**

sulphuryl (sŭl′fyŏŏ rĭl, -fə rĭl), *n. Chem.* the bivalent radical of sulphuric acid, $-SO_2-$. Also, *U.S.*, **sulfuryl.**

sulphuryl chloride, *Chem.* a colourless fluid, SO_2Cl_2, with a very pungent smell, used as a chlorinating agent, etc. Also, *U.S.*, **sulfuryl chloride.**

Sulpician (sŭl pĭsh′ən), *n. Rom. Cath. Ch.* a member of a college of secular priests, founded in Paris in 1642 to train ordinands. [t. F: m. *sulpicien*, named after St *Sulpice*, the parish in which this college was founded]

sultan (sŭl′tən), *n.* **1.** the sovereign of a Muslim country. **2.** (*cap.*) any of the former sovereigns of Turkey. [t. ML: s. *sultānus*, t. Ar.: m. *sulṭān* king, ruler, power] —**sultanic** (sŭl tăn′ĭk), *adj.* —**sul′tanship′,** *n.*

sultana (sŭl tä′nə), *n.* **1.** a wife or a concubine of a sultan. **2.** any close female relative of a sultan. **3.** a kind of small seedless raisin. [t. It., fem. of *sultano* SULTAN]

sultanate (sŭl′tə nĭt), *n.* **1.** the office or rule of a sultan. **2.** the territory ruled over by a sultan.

sultry (sŭl′trĭ), *adj.*, **-trier, -triest. 1.** oppressively hot and close or moist; sweltering. **2.** oppressively hot, as the weather, etc. **3.** characterized by or associated with sweltering heat. **4.** characterized by or arousing temper or passion. [f. *sulter* (var. of SWELTER) + -Y[1]] —**sul′trily,** *adv.* —**sul′triness,** *n.*

Sulu (sōō′lōō), *n.* a member of the most numerous and most highly cultivated tribe of Moros, or Muslim Malays of the south-western Philippine Islands, found chiefly in the Sulu Archipelago. [t. Malay]

Sulu Archipelago, an island group in the SW Philippine Islands, separating the Celebes Sea from the **Sulu Sea,** an arm of the Pacific NE of Borneo. 390,000 pop. (est. 1965); 1086 sq. mi. *Cap.:* Jolo.

sum (sŭm), *n.*, *v.*, **summed, summing.** —*n.* **1.** the aggregate of two or more numbers, magnitudes, quantities, or particulars as determined by mathematical process: *the sum of 5 and 7 is 12.* **2.** a particular aggregate or total, esp. with reference to money: *the expenses came to an enormous sum.* **3.** a quantity or amount, esp. of money: *to lend small sums.* **4.** a series of numbers or quantities to be added up. **5.** an arithmetical problem to be solved, or such a problem worked out and having the various steps shown. **6.** the total amount, or the whole. **7.** the substance or gist of a matter, comprehensively viewed or expressed: *the letter contains the sum and substance of his opinions.* **8.** concise or brief form: *in sum.* **9.** a summary. *—v.t.* **10.** to combine into an aggregate or total (often fol. by *up*). **11.** to ascertain the sum of, as by addition. **12.** to bring into or contain in a small compass (often fol. by *up*). **13. sum up, a.** to reckon: *to sum up advantages and disadvantages.* **b.** to bring into or contain in a brief and comprehensive statement: *the article sums up the work of the year.* **c.** to form a quick estimate of: *to sum someone up.* **d.** to give a brief and comprehensive statement or summary. *—adj.* **14.** denoting or pertaining to a sum: *sum total.* [t. L: m. s. *summa*, prop. fem. of *summus* highest; r. ME *somme*, t. OF] **—Syn. 1.** See **number.**

sum-, occasional var. of **sub-** (by assimilation) before *m.*

sumach (so͞o′măk, sho͞o′măk), *n.* **1.** any of the plants of the anacardiaceous genus *Rhus*, as *R. coriaria* of southern Europe. **2.** a preparation of dried and powdered leaves of certain species of *Rhus*, used in dyeing, tanning, etc. **3.** the wood of any of these plants. Also, (esp. def. 2) **sumac.** [ME, t. OF, t. Ar.: m. *summāq*]

Sumatra (so͞o mä′trə), *n.* a large island in the W part of Indonesia. 15,700,000 pop. (est. 1961); 164,147 sq. mi. See map under **Singapore.** —**Suma′tran,** *adj., n.*

Sumba (so͞om′bə), *n.* one of the Lesser Sunda Islands, in Indonesia. 251,126 pop. (1961); 4306 sq. mi. Also, **Sandalwood Island.** Dutch, **Soemba.**

Sumbawa (so͞om bä′wə), *n.* one of the Lesser Sunda Islands, in Indonesia: destructive eruption of Mt Tambora, 1815. 195,554 pop. (1961); 5965 sq. mi. Dutch, **Soembawa.**

Sumer (so͞o′mə), *n.* a region in S Mesopotamia, containing the sites of many ancient cities and a civilization which flourished perhaps as early as 5000 B.C. See map under **Chaldea.**

Sumerian (so͞o mĭə′rĭ ən), *adj.* **1.** of or pertaining to Sumer, its inhabitants, their civilization, or language. *—n.* **2.** one of the Sumerian people. **3.** the language of the Sumerians, of unknown relationship, preserved in very ancient cuneiform inscriptions.

summa (sŭm′ə), *n., pl.* **summae** (sŭm′ē). a treatise giving a summary or synthesis of a whole subject, esp. a detailed exposition of religious doctrine. [L]

summa cum laude (so͞om′ä ko͞om lou′dā), *Latin.* with the highest honour or praise (used chiefly in American universities to grant the highest of three special honours for above-average academic performance).

summand (sŭm′ănd′, sŭm′ănd′), *n. Arith.* a part or item of a sum.

summarize (sŭm′ə rīz′), *v.t.,* **-rized, -rizing. 1.** to make a summary of; state or express in a concise form. **2.** to constitute a summary of. Also, **summarise.** —**sum′mariza′tion,** *n.* —**sum′mariz′er, sum′marist,** *n.*

summary (sŭm′ə rĭ), *n., pl.* **-ries,** *adj. —n.* **1.** a brief and comprehensive presentation of facts or statements; an abstract, compendium, or epitome. *—adj.* **2.** brief and comprehensive; concise. **3.** direct and prompt; unceremoniously fast. **4.** (of legal proceedings, jurisdiction, etc.) conducted without or exempt from the various steps and delays of full proceedings. [ME, t. ML: m. s. *summārius*, der. L *summa* sum] —**summarily** (sŭm′ə rĭ lĭ), *adv.* —**sum′mariness,** *n.*

—**Syn. 1.** SUMMARY, BRIEF, DIGEST, SYNOPSIS are terms for a short version of a longer work. A SUMMARY is a brief statement or restatement of main points, esp. as a conclusion to a work: *the summary of a chapter.* A BRIEF is detailed outline, by headings and subheadings, of a discourse (usually legal) to be completed: *a brief for an argument.* A DIGEST is an abridgement of an article, book, etc., or an organized arrangement of material under headings and titles: *a magazine consisting of digests, a digest of Roman law.* A SYNOPSIS is usually a compressed statement of the plot of a novel, play, etc.: *a synopsis of Hamlet.*

summat (sŭm′ət), *adv., pron., n. Colloq. or Dial.* somewhat or something. [spelling var. of SOMEWHAT]

summation (sŭ mā′shən), *n.* **1.** the process of summing. **2.** the result of this; an aggregate or total. **3.** *U.S. Law.* the final arguments of opposing counsel before a case goes to the jury.

summer[1] (sŭm′ə), *n.* **1.** the second and the warmest season of the year, between spring and autumn. **2.** a period of warm, sunny weather associated with this season. **3.** a whole year as represented by this season: *a child of eight summers.* **4.** the period of finest development, perfection, or beauty previous to any decline: *the summer of life.* *—adj.* **5.** of, pertaining to, or characteristic of summer; *summer resorts.* **6.** suitable for use or wear in summer. **7.** having the weather or warmth of summer. *—v.i.* **8.** to spend or pass the summer. *—v.t.* **9.** to keep, feed, or manage during the summer. **10.** to make summer-like. [ME *sumer*, OE *sumor*, c. G *Sommer*] —**sum′mer-like′,** *adj.*

summer[2] (sŭm′ə), *n.* **1.** a principal timber or beam, as in a floor or any spanning structure. **2.** a stone at the top of a pier, column, or the like, as to support an arch. **3.** a lintel. [ME, t. AF: m. *sumer* beam, packhorse, ult. der. LL *sagma* packsaddle, t. Gk]

summer chrysanthemum, an annual composite garden plant, *Chrysanthemum coronarium*, having numerous yellowish white flower heads; crown daisy.

summerhouse (sŭm′ə hous′), *n.* a simple, often rustic structure in a park or garden, intended to provide a shady, cool place in the summer.

summer lightning, *Colloq.* lightning which can be seen but is too far away for the resulting thunder to be heard.

summer pudding, a cold sweet sponge cake, the centre of which is filled with stewed fruit, as redcurrants.

summersault (sŭm′ə sôlt′), *n., v.i.* somersault.

summer school, a course of teaching at a university which takes place during the summer vacation for groups other than regular students.

summer solstice. *Astron.* See **solstice** (def. 1).

summertime (sŭm′ə tīm′), *n.* **1.** the season of summer. **2.** any daylight-saving time, as the former British Summer Time.

summerwood (sŭm′ə wo͝od′), *n.* that part of an annual ring of a tree which grows in summer and the later part of the season, characterized by thick-walled cells (distinguished from *springwood*).

summery (sŭm′ə rĭ), *adj.* of, like, or befitting summer.

summing-up (sŭm′ĭng ŭp′), *n.* **1.** a recapitulation or review of the leading points of an argument or the like. **2.** the survey of the evidence given by a judge to a jury before it withdraws to consider its verdict.

summist (sŭm′ĭst), *n.* one who writes a summa, esp. St Thomas Aquinas as the author of *Summa Theologica.*

summit (sŭm′ĭt), *n.* **1.** the highest point or part, as of a hill, a line of travel, or any object; the top; the apex. **2.** the highest point of attainment or aspiration. **3.** the highest state or degree. **4.** a meeting or conference between heads of state or the heads of any other organization. **5.** diplomacy at the highest level. *—adj.* **6.** (in diplomacy) between heads of state: *summit conference.* [late ME *sommet*, t. F, der. L *summum*, prop. neut. of *summus* highest]

summon (sŭm′ən), *v.t.* **1.** to call as with authority to some duty, task, or performance; call upon (to do something). **2.** to call for the presence of, as by command, message, or signal; call (fol. by *to, away, from,* etc.). **3.** to call or notify to appear at a specified place, esp. before a court: *to summon a defendant.* **4.** to call together (an assembly, council, or other body) by authority, as for deliberation or action: *to summon a parliament.* **5.** to call into action; rouse; call forth (often fol. by *up*): *to summon up all one's courage.* **6.** to call upon to surrender. [t. L: s. *summonēre* suggest, ML summon; r. ME *somonen*, t. OF] —**sum′monable,** *adj.* —**sum′moner,** *n.* **—Syn. 3.** See **call.**

summons (sŭm′ənz), *n., pl.* **-monses,** *v. —n.* **1.** an authoritative command, message, or signal by which one is summoned. **2.** a call to do something: *a summons to surrender.* **3.** *Law.* a call or citation by authority to appear before a court, or the writ by which the call is made. **4.** an authoritative call or notice to appear at a specified place, as for a particular purpose or duty. **5.** a call issued for the meeting of an assembly or parliament. *—v.t.* **6.** to serve with a summons; summon. [ME *somonse*, t. AF, OF, der. *somondre* SUMMON]

summum bonum (so͞om′o͝om bŏn′o͝om), *Latin.* the highest or chief good.

sumo (syo͞o′mō), *n.* a style of wrestling in Japan, in which the object is to force the opponent out of the ring or to make any part of his body other than the feet touch the ground. [t. Jap.]

sump (sŭmp), *n.* **1.** a pit, well, or the like in which water or other liquid is collected. **2.** *Mach.* a container situated at the lowest point in a circulating system, esp. the crankcase of an internal-combustion engine, which acts as an oil reservoir. **3.** *Mining.* **a.** a space at the bottom of a shaft or below a passageway where water is allowed to collect. **b.** a pilot shaft or tunnel pushed out in front of a main bore. **4.** *Dial.* a swamp, bog, or muddy pool. [ME *sompe*, t. MLG or MD: m. *sump*, c. G *Sumpf*]

sumpter (sŭmp′tə), *n. Archaic.* a packhorse or any animal for carrying baggage, etc. [ME, t. OF: m. *som(m)etier*, ult. der. LL *sagma* packsaddle, t. Gk. Cf. SUMMER[2]]

sumptuary (sŭmp′tyo͞o ə rĭ), *adj.* pertaining to, dealing with, or regulating expense or expenditure. [t. L: m. s. *sumptuārius*]

sumptuary law, a law regulating personal habits which offend the moral or religious conscience of the community.

sumptuous (sŭmp′tyo͞o əs), *adj.* **1.** entailing great expense, as from fine workmanship, choice materials, etc.; costly: *a sumptuous residence.* **2.** luxuriously fine; splendid or superb. [late ME, t. L: m. s. *sumptuōsus* expensive] —**sump′tuously,** *adv.* —**sump′tuousness,** *n.*

Sumter (sŭm′tə, sŭmp′-), *n.* **Fort,** a fort in the harbour of Charleston, South Carolina: its bombardment by the Confederates opened the American Civil War, April 12th, 1861.

Sumy (*Russ.* so͞o′mĭ), *n.* a city in NE Ukraine, in the S Soviet Union in Europe. 123,000 (est. 1964).

sun (sŭn), *n., v.,* **sunned, sunning.** —*n.* **1.** the star which is the central body of the solar system and around which the planets revolve, and from which they receive light and heat. Its mean distance from the earth is about 92,900,000 miles, its diameter about 864,100 miles, and its mass about 332,958 times that of the earth. Its period of surface rotation is about 26 days at its equator but longer in greater latitudes. **2.** the sun considered with reference to its position in the sky, its visibility, the season of the year, the time at which or the place where it is seen, etc. **3.** a self-luminous heavenly body. **4.** sunshine: *to be exposed to the sun.* **5.** a figure or representation of the sun, as a heraldic bearing usually surrounded with rays and charged with the features of a human face. **6.** something likened to the sun in brightness, splendour, etc. **7.** *Archaic.* a day. **8.** *Archaic.* a year. **9.** *Archaic.* sunrise or sunset. **10. a place in the sun,** a pleasant or advantageous situation. **11. under the sun,** anywhere on earth: *the most beautiful girl under the sun.* —*v.t.* **12.** to expose to the sun's rays. **13.** to warm, dry, etc., in the sunshine. **14.** to put, bring, make, etc. (as specified), by exposure to the sun's rays. —*v.i.* **15.** to expose oneself to the sun's rays. [ME and OE *sunne,* c. G *Sonne*]

Sun., Sunday.

sun-and-planet (sŭn′ən plăn′ĭt), *adj.* denoting a system of toothed gearing in which a small wheel moves round a larger wheel.

sun animalcule, a heliozoan.

Sunay (*Turk.* so͞o nāy′), *n.* **Cevdet** (*Turk.* chĕv dĕt′), born 1900, president of Turkey since 1966.

sunbaked (sŭn′bākt′), *adj.* baked or dried and hardened by the heat of the sun.

sunbath (sŭn′băth′), *n.* an exposure of the body directly to the rays of the sun.

sunbathe (sŭn′bāth′), *v.i.* **-bathed, -bathing.** to expose one's body to the sun in order to acquire a suntan or as a relaxation. —**sun′bath′er,** *n.*

sunbeam (sŭn′bēm′), *n.* a beam or ray of sunlight.

sunbird (sŭn′bûd′), *n.* any of various small, brilliantly coloured Old World birds of the family *Nectariniidae.*

sun-bittern (sŭn′bĭt′ən), *n.* a South American bird, *Eurypyga helias,* with variegated plumage, allied to the rails.

sunblind (sŭn′blīnd′), *n.* a shade, as a venetian blind or an awning, on a window to afford protection from the sun.

sunbonnet (sŭn′bŏn′ĭt), *n.* a large bonnet of cotton or other light material shading the face and projecting down over the neck, worn by women and girls.

sunbow (sŭn′bō′), *n.* a bow or arc of prismatic colours like a rainbow, appearing in the spray of cataracts, etc.

sunbreak (sŭn′brāk′), *n.* a brise-soleil. [trans. of F BRISE-SOLEIL, modelled on WINDBREAK]

sunburn (sŭn′bûn′), *n., v.,* **-burnt** or **-burned, -burning.** —*n.* **1.** superficial inflammation of the skin, caused by excessive or too sudden exposure to the sun's rays. —*v.t., v.i.* **2.** to affect or be affected with sunburn.

sunburst (sŭn′bûst′), *n.* **1.** a burst of sunlight; a sudden shining of the sun through rifted clouds. **2.** a firework, a piece of jewellery, an ornament, or the like, resembling the sun with rays issuing in all directions.

sun-cured (sŭn′kyo͝oəd′), *adj.* cured or preserved by exposure to the sun.

sundae (sŭn′dā), *n.* a portion of ice-cream with fruit or other syrup poured over it, and often whipped cream, chopped nuts, or other additions. [orig. uncert.]

Sunda Islands (sŭn′də; *Du.* so͞on′dä), an island chain in the Malay Archipelago, including Sumatra, Java, and the **Lesser Sunda Islands,** those smaller islands extending from Java E to Timor.

sun-dance (sŭn′däns′), *n.* a religious ceremony associated with the sun, practised by North American Indians of the Plains, consisting of dancing attended with various symbolic rites, commonly including self-torture.

Sunda Strait, a strait separating Sumatra from Java. Least width, ab. 16 mi.

Sunday (sŭn′dĭ), *n.* **1.** the first day of the week, the Sabbath of most Christian sects, observed in commemoration of the resurrection of Christ. **2. a month of Sundays,** an extremely long time. —*adj.* **3.** of, pertaining to, occurring on, or suitable for Sunday. [ME; OE *sunnandæg,* c. G *Sonntag*; trans. of L *dies sōlis,* Gk *hēméra hēlíou*]

—**Syn. 1.** SUNDAY, SABBATH are not properly synonyms. SUNDAY, kept as a day of special worship and rest from business, is the first day of the week: *Palm Sunday.* The SABBATH, the day on which the fourth Commandment enjoins abstention from work of all kinds, is the seventh day of the Jewish week; the name has been applied to Sunday by some Protestant religious bodies: *to observe the Sabbath.*

Sunday best, one's best clothes.

Sunday-go-to-meeting (sŭn′dĭ gō′tə mē′tĭng), *adj. U.S. Colloq.* most dressed-up; most presentable; best: *Sunday-go-to-meeting shoes.*

Sunday school, 1. a school, now usually in connection with a church, for religious (and formerly also secular) instruction on Sunday. **2.** the members of such a school. Also, **Sabbath school.**

Sundays River (sŭn′dāz), a river in the Republic of South Africa flowing SE through S Cape Province to the Indian Ocean. 250 mi.

sundeck (sŭn′dĕk′), *n.* **1.** a deck of a passenger ship exposed to the sun. **2.** *U.S.* a sunroof.

sunder (sŭn′də), *v.t.* **1.** to separate; part; divide; sever. —*v.i.* **2.** to become separated; part. [ME; late OE *sundrian,* c. G *sondern*] —**sun′derer,** *n.*

sunderance (sŭn′də rəns, -drəns), *n.* separation.

Sunderland (sŭn′də lənd), *n.* a seaport in NE England, in Durham: shipbuilding. 189,629 (1961).

sundew (sŭn′dyo͞o′), *n.* any of a group of small bog plants, species of the genus *Drosera,* with sticky hairs that capture insects.

sundial (sŭn′dī′əl), *n.* an instrument for indicating the time of day by the position of a shadow (as of a gnomon) cast by the sun on a graduated plate or surface.

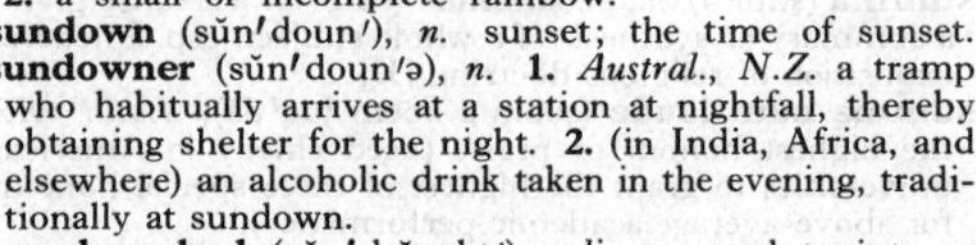

Sundial

sun-disc (sŭn′dĭsk′), *n.* **1.** the disc of the sun. **2.** a figure or representation of this, esp. in religious symbolism.

sundog (sŭn′dŏg′), *n.* **1.** a parhelion. **2.** a small or incomplete rainbow.

sundown (sŭn′doun′), *n.* sunset; the time of sunset.

sundowner (sŭn′doun′ə), *n.* **1.** *Austral., N.Z.* a tramp who habitually arrives at a station at nightfall, thereby obtaining shelter for the night. **2.** (in India, Africa, and elsewhere) an alcoholic drink taken in the evening, traditionally at sundown.

sun-drenched (sŭn′drĕncht′), *adj.* exposed to intense light and heat from the sun: *the sun-drenched shores of the Mediterranean.*

sundress (sŭn′drĕs′), *n.* a low-cut, light summer dress, as worn for sunbathing.

sun-dried (sŭn′drīd′), *adj.* **1.** dried in the sun, as bricks, raisins, etc. **2.** dried up or withered by the sun.

sundries (sŭn′drĭz), *n.pl.* sundry things or items.

sundry (sŭn′drĭ), *adj.* **1.** various or divers: *sundry persons.* —*pron.* **2. all and sundry,** everyone collectively and individually. [ME; OE *syndrig* private, separate, der. *sundor* apart. See -Y[1]]

Sundsvall (*Sw.* so͞onds′väl), *n.* a seaport in E Sweden, on the Gulf of Bothnia. 58,174 (1964).

sunfast (sŭn′făst′), *adj.* not subject to fading in sunlight.

sunfish (sŭn′fĭsh′), *n., pl.* **-fishes,** (*esp. collectively*) **-fish. 1.** a huge fish, the **ocean sunfish,** *Mola mola,* having a deep body abbreviated behind, seeming to consist of little more than the head. **2.** any fish of the same family, *Molidae.* **3.** any of the small freshwater fishes of the family *Centrarchidae,* of North America, closely related to the perch.

sunflower (sŭn′flou′ə), *n.* any plant of the composite genus *Helianthus,* characterized by yellow-rayed flowers, as *H. annuus,* the common species of North America, a tall plant grown for its showy flowers, and for its seeds which are valued as food for poultry and as the source of an oil.

sung (sŭng), *v.* pt. and pp. of **sing.**

Sung (so͝ong), *n.* a Chinese dynasty, A.D. 960–1279, under which culture, esp. art and Confucian philosophy, flourished in the Yangtze region, until overthrown by the Mongols.

Sungari (so͝ong′gə rĭ), *n.* a river in NE China, flowing into the river Amur on the Siberian frontier. ab. 800 mi.

Sungkiang (so͝ong′kyăng′), *n.* a former province in NE China, now a part of Inner Mongolian Autonomous Region. 79,151 sq. mi.

sunglass (sŭn′gläs′), *n.* a burning-glass.

sunglasses (sŭn′glä′sĭz), *n.pl.* spectacles having tinted or darkened lenses to protect the eyes from the glare of the sun.

sunglow (sŭn′glō′), *n.* a diffused hazy light seen round the sun, due to particles of foreign matter in the atmosphere.
sun-god (sŭn′gŏd′), *n.* **1.** the sun considered or personified as a deity. **2.** a god identified or associated with the sun.
sunhat (sŭn′hăt′), *n.* **1.** a soft, usually light-coloured hat with a shady brim. **2.** a sunbonnet.
sun-helmet (sŭn′hĕl′mĭt), *n.* a topee.
suni (sōō′nĭ), *n.* either of two very small African antelopes of the genus *Nesotragus*, very shy and of nocturnal habits. [t. a Bantu language of Southern Africa]
sunk (sŭngk), *v.* a pt. and pp. of **sink.**
sunken (sŭng′kən), *v.* **1.** a pp. of **sink.** —*adj.* **2.** having sunk or having been sunk beneath the surface; submerged. **3.** having settled down to a lower level, as walls. **4.** depressed or lying below the general level, as a garden. **5.** hollow: *sunken cheeks.*
sunken garden, a garden or part of a garden lying below the level of the surrounding ground.
sunk fence. See **ha-ha.**
sunlamp (sŭn′lămp′), *n.* **1.** a lamp which generates ultraviolet rays, used as a therapeutic device, to induce artificial suntan, etc. **2.** a source of light used in cinema photography, consisting essentially of a bright lamp whose light is intensified and directed by an arrangement of parabolic mirrors.
sunless (sŭn′lĭs), *adj.* **1.** characterized by lack of sunlight; dark: *a sunless room.* **2.** overcast: *a sunless day.* **3.** gloomy; dismal; depressing: *a sunless attitude to life.* —**sun′lessly,** *adv.* —**sun′lessness,** *n.*
sunlight (sŭn′līt′), *n.* the light of the sun.
sunlit (sŭn′lĭt′), *adj.* lit by the sun.
sun-lounge (sŭn′lounj′), *n.* a room having extensive windows positioned so as to admit much sunlight. Also, **sun-parlour** (sŭn′pä′lə); *U.S.*, **sun-parlor.**
sunn (sŭn), *n.* **1.** a tall East Indian fabaceous shrub, *Crotalaria juncea*, with slender branches and yellow flowers, and an inner bark which yields a hemplike fibre used for making ropes, sacking, etc. **2.** the fibre. Also, **sunn hemp.** [t. Hind.: m. *san*]
Sunna (sŭn′ə), *n.* the traditional part of Muslim law, claimed to be based on the words and acts of Mohammed, although not attributed verbatim to him. [t. Ar.: form, way, path]
Sunnite (sŭn′īt), *n.* one of the so-called orthodox Muslims, who accepts the Sunna as of almost equal importance with the Koran. Also, **Sunni** (sŭn′ĭ). Cf. **Shiite.** [der. SUNNA]
sunny (sŭn′ĭ), *adj.*, **-nier, -niest. 1.** abounding in sunshine: *a sunny day.* **2.** exposed to, lit or warmed by the direct rays of the sun: *a sunny room.* **3.** pertaining to or proceeding from the sun; solar. **4.** resembling the sun. **5.** cheery, cheerful, or joyous: *a sunny disposition.* —**sun′nily,** *adv.* —**sun′niness,** *n.*
sunny side, 1. the side exposed to most sunlight, as the south-facing side of a house. **2.** a comparatively cheerful or optimistic point of view.
sun-porch (sŭn′pôch′), *n.* a porch or veranda, sometimes partially enclosed with glass, positioned so as to catch much sunlight.
sun-power (sŭn′pou′ə), *n.* power obtained from concentrated heat of the sun's rays.
sunproof (sŭn′prōōf′), *adj.* impervious to damage by the rays of the sun.
sunray (sŭn′rā′), *n.* **1.** a ray of the sun. **2.** (*pl.*) ultraviolet rays, as from a sunlamp. —*adj.* **3.** sending forth ultraviolet rays: *a sunray lamp.*
sunrise (sŭn′rīz′), *n.* **1.** the rise or ascent of the sun above the horizon in the morning. **2.** the atmospheric phenomena accompanying this. **3.** the time when the sun rises.
sunroof (sŭn′rōōf′), *n.* **1.** a flat roof or a raised platform adjoining a house, hotel, etc., used for sunbathing. **2.** a sunshine roof.
sunroom (sŭn′rōōm′, -rŏŏm′), *n.* a sun-lounge.
sunset (sŭn′sĕt′), *n.* **1.** the setting or descent of the sun below the horizon in the evening. **2.** the atmospheric phenomena accompanying this. **3.** the time when the sun sets. **4.** the close or final stage of any period.
sunshade (sŭn′shād′), *n.* **1.** something used as a protection from the rays of the sun. **2.** a parasol. **3.** *Chiefly U.S.* a sunblind, esp. one over a shopwindow.
sunshine (sŭn′shīn′), *n.* **1.** the shining of the sun; the direct light of the sun. **2.** brightness or radiance; cheerfulness, happiness, or prosperity. **3.** a source of cheer or happiness. **4.** the effect of the sun in lighting and heating a place. **5.** a place where the direct rays of the sun fall. —*adj.* **6.** bright, cheerful, or prosperous. —**sun′shin′y,** *adj.*
sunshine roof, a part of a car roof which can be slid open to admit sunlight.
sunspot (sŭn′spŏt′), *n.* *Astron.* one of the relatively dark patches which appear periodically on the surface of the sun, and which have a certain effect on terrestrial magnetism and other terrestrial phenomena. Their appearance is spasmodic but their number reaches a maximum approximately every eleven years (the **sunspot cycle**).
sun spurge, a small euphorbiaceous annual herb, *Euphorbia helioscopia*, with a flat inflorescence which is turned towards the sun, a common weed of Europe.
sunstone (sŭn′stōn′), *n.* aventurine felspar.
sunstroke (sŭn′strōk′), *n.* a condition caused by excessive exposure to the sun, marked by prostration, which may lead to convulsions, coma, and death.
sunstruck (sŭn′strŭk′), *adj.* affected with sunstroke.
sunsuit (sŭn′syōōt′), *n.* a playsuit, as worn for sunbathing, on the beach, etc.
suntan (sŭn′tăn′), *n.* brownness of the skin induced by exposure to the sun, cultivated by some as a mark of health or beauty. Also, **tan.** —**sun′-tanned′,** *adj.*
suntrap (sŭn′trăp′), *n.* any place which is built or situated so that it receives a large amount of sun.
sun-up (sŭn′ŭp′), *n.* sunrise.
sunward (sŭn′wəd), *adj.* **1.** directed towards the sun. —*adv.* **2.** sunwards.
sunwards (sŭn′wədz), *adv.* towards the sun. Also, **sunward.**
sunwise (sŭn′wīz′), *adv.* **1.** in the direction of the sun's apparent daily motion. **2.** clockwise.
sun-worship (sŭn′wû′shĭp), *n.* the practice of giving reverence to the sun as a deity. —**sun′-wor′shipper,** *n.*
Sun Yat-sen (sōōn′yăt′sĕn′), 1867–1925, Chinese political leader.
suo jure (sōō′ō jōōə′rĭ), *Latin.* in his (her, its, one's) own right.
suo loco (lŏk′ō), *Latin.* in one's own or rightful place.
Suomi (*Finn.* sōō′ô mē), *n.* Finnish name of **Finland.**
sup[1] (sŭp), *v.*, **supped, supping.** —*v.i.* **1.** to eat the evening meal; take supper. —*v.t.* **2.** to provide with or entertain at supper. [ME *sope*, t. OF: m. *soper*]
sup[2] (sŭp), *v.*, **supped, supping,** *n.* —*v.t.* **1.** to take (liquid food, or any liquid) into the mouth in small quantities, as from a spoon or a cup. —*v.i.* **2.** to take liquid into the mouth in small quantities, as by spoonfuls or sips. —*n.* **3.** a mouthful or small portion of liquid food or of drink. [ME *suppe*, OE *suppa*, akin to OE *sūpan*, c. G *saufen* drink. Cf. SIP, SOP, SUP[1], SOUP]
sup-, var. of **sub-** (by assimilation) before *p.*
sup., 1. superior. **2.** superlative. **3.** supine. **4.** supplement. **5.** supplementary. **6.** supra.
super (syōō′pə), *n.* *Colloq.* **1.** superintendent. **2.** supernumerary. —*adj.* **3.** supervisor. **4.** goods of a superior quality, grade, size, etc. **5.** superficial. **6.** superfine. **7.** *Colloq.* extremely fine, great, pleasing, etc. —*v.i.* **8.** to supervise.
super-, 1. a prefix meaning 'superior to' or 'over-', applied variously, as of quality (*superman*), size (*superdreadnought*), degree (*superheat, supersensitive*), space (*superstructure*), and other meanings (*supersede, supernatural*). **2.** *Chem.* a prefix having the same sense as 'per-'. [t. L, comb. form of *super*, adv. and prep., above, beyond, in addition]
superable (syōō′pə rə bl, -prə bl), *adj.* capable of being overcome; surmountable. [t. L: m. s. *superābilis*] —**sup′erably,** *adv.*
superabound (syōō′pə rə bound′), *v.i.* **1.** to abound beyond something else. **2.** to be very abundant or too abundant (fol. by *in* or *with*).
superabundant (syōō′pə rə bŭn′dənt), *adj.* exceedingly or excessively abundant; being more than sufficient. —**su′perabun′dance,** *n.* —**su′perabun′dantly,** *adv.*
superacute (syōō′pə rə kyōōt′), *adj.* extremely acute.
superadd (syōō′pər ăd′), *v.t.* to add over and above; join as a further addition; add besides. [t. L: s. *superaddere*] —**superaddition** (syōō′pə rə dĭsh′ən), *n.*
superannuate (syōō′pə răn′yōō āt′), *v.t.*, **-ated, -ating. 1.** to allow to retire from service or office on a pension, on account of age or infirmity. **2.** to set aside as out of date; remove as too old. [t. ML: m. s. *superannātus* over a year old (said of cattle); for *-u-* see ANNUAL]
superannuated (syōō′pə răn′yōō ā′tĭd), *adj.* **1.** retired on account of age or infirmity. **2.** too old for use, work, service, or a position. **3.** antiquated or obsolete.
superannuation (syōō′pə răn′yōō ā′shən), *n.* **1.** the act of superannuating. **2.** the state of being superannuated. **3.** a pension or allowance to a superannuated person.
superb (syōō pûb′), *adj.* **1.** stately, majestic, or grand: *superb jewels.* **2.** admirably fine or excellent: *a superb performance.* **3.** of a proudly imposing appearance or kind: *superb beauty.* [t. L: s. *superbus* proud, distinguished] —**superb′ly,** *adv.* —**superb′ness,** *n.* —**Syn. 1.** See **magnificent.**

supercalender (syōō′pə kăl′ən də), *v.t.* **1.** to give a high-gloss finish to by pressing in a calender. —*n.* **2.** a calender for doing this.

supercalendered paper, paper with a surface glazed by repeated runs through highly polished copper or zinc rollers.

supercargo (syōō′pə kä′gō), *n., pl.* **-goes.** an officer on a merchant ship who is in charge of the cargo and the commercial concerns of the voyage. [earlier *supracargo*, t. Sp.: m. *sobrecargo*]

supercharge (syōō′pə chäj′), *v.t.*, **-charged, -charging.** **1.** to supply air to (an internal-combustion engine) at greater than atmospheric pressure; boost. **2.** to charge with an excessive amount of emotion, tension, energy, or the like. **3.** to pressurize (a gas or liquid).

supercharger (syōō′pə chä′jə), *n.* a mechanism attached to an internal-combustion engine to deliver to the cylinders a volume of air greater than that from the suction of the pistons alone, used to increase power; booster.

superciliary (syōō′pə sĭl′ĭ ə rĭ), *adj.* **1.** situated over the eye. **2.** *Anat., Zool.* **a.** of or pertaining to the eyebrow. **b.** having a conspicuous line or marking over the eye, as certain birds. **3.** on the frontal bone at the level of the eyebrow. —*n.* **4.** a superciliary ridge or mark. [t. NL: m. *superciliāris*, der. L *supercilium* eyebrow]

supercilious (syōō′pə sĭl′ĭ əs), *adj.* haughtily disdainful or contemptuous, as persons, their expression, bearing, etc. [t. L: m. s. *superciliōsus*] —**su′percil′iously,** *adv.* —**su′percil′iousness,** *n.*

superclass (syōō′pə kläs′), *n. Biol.* a group or category of related classes within a phylum or subphylum.

superconductivity (syōō′pə kŏn′dŭk tĭv′ĭ tĭ), *n. Physics.* the phenomenon of greatly increased electrical conductivity shown by certain substances at temperatures approaching absolute zero. —**superconductor** (syōō′pə kən dŭk′tə), *n.* —**su′perconduct′ing,** *adj.*

supercool (syōō′pə kōōl′), *v.t.* **1.** to cool (a liquid) below its freezing point without producing solidification. —*v.i.* **2.** to become supercooled.

supercritical (syōō′pə krĭt′ĭ kl), *adj. Physics.* denoting or pertaining to a nuclear reaction or a nuclear reactor in which a chain-reaction is self-sustaining. Cf. **subcritical.**

superdense (syōō′pə dĕns′), *adj.* extremely dense or compressed. —**su′perden′sity,** *n.*

superdense theory, *Astron.* the cosmological theory that the universe has evolved from one superdense agglomeration of matter which suffered an explosion; the observed expansion of the universe is regarded as a result of this explosion, the galaxies flying apart like fragments from an exploding bomb.

superdreadnought (syōō′pə drĕd′nôt′), *n.* a battleship of the general type of the dreadnought, but much larger and with superior armament.

super-duper (sōō′pə dōō′pə), *adj. Slang.* extremely fine, great, pleasing, etc. [dissimilated redupl. of SUPER (def. 7)]

superego (syōō′pər ē′gō), *n. Psychol.* that part of the psychic apparatus which mediates between ego drives and social ideals, acting as a conscience which may be partly conscious and partly unconscious.

superelevated (syōō′pər ĕl′ĭ vā′tĭd), *adj.* (of a curve in a road or railway track) having superelevation; banked.

superelevation (syōō′pər ĕl′ĭ vā′shən), *n.* **1.** an elevation at a curve of the outer rail of a railway track or outer side of a road above the inner, to counteract centrifugal force of vehicles; cant. **2.** the vertical difference between the inner and outer rails of a track, or sides of road, at a curve.

supereminent (syōō′pər ĕm′ĭ nənt), *adj.* of superior eminence, rank, or dignity; distinguished, conspicuous, or noteworthy above others. [t. L: s. *supereminens*] —**su′perem′inence,** *n.* —**su′perem′inently,** *adv.*

supererogate (syōō′pər ĕ′rə gāt′), *v.i.*, **-gated, -gating.** to do more than duty requires. [t. LL: m. s. *superērogātus*, pp., f. L *super* above + *ērogātus*, pp., paid out] —**su′perer′oga′tion,** *n.*

supererogatory (syōō′pə re rŏg′ə tə rĭ, -trĭ), *adj.* **1.** going beyond the requirements of duty. **2.** superfluous.

superfamily (syōō′pə făm′ĭ lĭ), *n., pl.* **-lies.** *Biol.* a group or category ranking above a family.

superfecundation (syōō′pə fē′kən dā′shən), *n. Physiol.* the fertilization of two ova during the same menstrual cycle by two different acts of coition.

superfetate (syōō′pə fē′tāt), *v.i.*, **-tated, -tating.** *Physiol.* to fertilize an ovum after a prior conception but before the first one has run its course. [t. LL: m. s. *superfētātus*, pp.] —**su′perfeta′tion,** *n.*

superficial (syōō′pə fĭsh′əl), *adj.* **1.** of or pertaining to the surface: *superficial measurement.* **2.** being at, on, or near the surface: *a superficial wound.* **3.** external or outward: *a superficial resemblance.* **4.** concerned with or comprehending only what is on the surface or obvious: *a superficial observer.* **5.** shallow; not profound or thorough: *a superficial writer.* **6.** apparent, rather than real: *superficial piety.* [ME, t. LL: s. *superficiālis*, der. L *superficies* SUPERFICIES] —**superficiality** (syōō′pə fĭsh′ĭ ăl′ĭ tĭ), **su′perfi′cialness,** *n.* —**su′perfi′cially,** *adv.*

superficies (syōō′pə fĭsh′ēz), *n., pl.* **-cies.** **1.** the surface, outer face, or outside of a thing. **2.** the outward appearance, esp. as distinguished from the inner nature. [t. L]

superfine (syōō′pə fīn′), *adj.* **1.** extra fine; unusually fine. **2.** excessively fine, refined, or nice.

superfluidity (syōō′pə flōō ĭd′ĭ tĭ), *n. Physics.* the property of a fluid in which internal friction is negligible and thermal conductivity very high: exhibited by helium below 2·186°K.

superfluity (syōō′pə flōō′ĭ tĭ), *n., pl.* **1.** the state of being superfluous. **2.** superabundant or excessive amount. **3.** something superfluous, as a luxury.

superfluous (syōō pû′flōō əs), *adj.* **1.** being over and above what is sufficient or required. **2.** unnecessary or needless. **3.** *Obs.* lavish or extravagant. [ME, t. L: m. *superfluus* overflowing] —**super′fluously,** *adv.* —**super′fluousness,** *n.*

superflux (syōō′pə flŭks′), *n.* a superfluity.

superfuse (syōō′pə fyōōz′), *v.t.* **-fused, -fusing.** *Obs.* **1.** to pour (a liquid, etc.) over or on something. **2.** to sprinkle or cover (something) with a liquid or the like. [t. L: m. s. *superfūsus*, pp.] —**superfusion** (syōō′pə fyōō′zhən), *n.*

supergiant (syōō′pə jī′ənt), *n. Astron.* any of a number of very large, highly luminous, low-density stars, as Betelgeuse or Antares.

superglacial (syōō′pə glā′syəl), *adj.* **1.** on the surface of a glacier. **2.** believed to have been formerly on the surface of a glacier: *superglacial debris.*

superheat (*n.* syōō′pə hēt′, *v.* syōō′pə hēt′), *n.* **1.** the state of being superheated. **2.** the amount of superheating. —*v.t.* **3.** to heat to an extreme degree or to a very high temperature. **4.** to heat (a liquid) above its boiling point without the formation of bubbles of vapour. **5.** to heat (a gas, as steam not in contact with water) to such a degree that its temperature may be lowered or its pressure increased without the conversion of any of the gas into liquid. —**su′perheat′er,** *n.*

superheterodyne (syōō′pə hĕt′ə rə dīn′), *Radio.* —*adj.* **1.** denoting or pertaining to a method of receiving radio signals by which the incoming modulated wave is changed by the heterodyne process to a lower frequency (the intermediate frequency, which is inaudible) and then submitted to stages of radiofrequency amplification with subsequent detection and audio-frequency amplification. —*n.* **2.** a superheterodyne receiver.

super high frequency, *Radio.* a radio frequency of between 3000 and 30,000 megahertz. *Abbrev.:* SHF.

superhighway (syōō′pə hī′wā′), *n. U.S.* a motorway.

superhuman (syōō′pə hyōō′mən), *adj.* **1.** above or beyond what is human; having a higher nature or greater powers than man. **2.** exceeding ordinary human power, achievement, experience, etc.: *a superhuman effort.* —**superhumanity** (syōō′pə hyōō măn′ĭ tĭ), *n.* —**su′perhu′manly,** *adv.*

superimpose (syōō′pə rĭm pōz′), *v.t.*, **-posed, -posing.** **1.** to impose, place, or set on something else. **2.** to put or join as an addition (fol. by *on* or *upon*). —**superimposition** (syōō′pə rĭm′pə zĭsh′ən), *n.*

superincumbent (syōō′pə rĭn kŭm′bənt), *adj.* **1.** lying or resting on something else. **2.** situated above; overhanging. **3.** exerted from above, as pressure. —**su′perincum′bence, su′perincum′bency,** *n.*

superinduce (syōō′pə rĭn dyōōs′), *v.t.*, **-duced, -ducing.** to bring in or induce as an added feature, circumstance, etc.; superimpose. [t. LL: m. s. *superindūcere*] —**su′perinduce′ment,** *n.* —**superinduction** (syōō′pə rĭn dŭk′shən), *n.*

superintend (syōō′pə rĭn tĕnd′, syōō′prĭn-), *v.t., v.i.* to oversee and direct (work, processes, affairs, etc.); exercise supervision over (an institution, place, etc.). [t. LL: s. *superintendere*] —**su′perintend′ence,** *n.*

superintendency (syōō′pə rĭn tĕn′dən sĭ, syōō′prĭn-), *n., pl.* **-cies.** **1.** a district under a superintendent. **2.** the position or work of a superintendent.

superintendent (syōō′pə rĭn tĕn′dənt, syōō′prĭn-), *n.* **1.** one who has the oversight or direction of some work, enterprise, establishment, institution, house, etc. **2.** a police officer ranking above chief inspector and below chief superintendent. **3.** the rank. —*adj.* **4.** superintending. —**su′perinten′dentship′,** *n.*

superior (syōō pĭə′rĭ ə), *adj.* **1.** higher in station, rank,

su′perceles′tial, *adj.* **su′perexalta′tion,** *n.* **su′perex′cellence,** *n.* **su′perex′cellent,** *adj.*

degree, or grade: *a superior officer.* **2.** above the average in excellence, merit, intelligence, etc. **3.** of higher grade or quality. **4.** greater in quantity or amount: *superior numbers.* **5.** showing a consciousness or feeling of being above others in such respects: *superior airs.* **6.** not yielding or susceptible (fol. by *to*): *to be superior to temptation.* **7.** *Bot.* **a.** situated above some other organ. **b.** (of a calyx) seeming to originate from the top of the ovary. **c.** (of an ovary) free from the calyx. **8.** *Print.* higher than the main line of type, as algebraic exponents, reference figures, etc.; superscript. **9.** *Astron.* **a.** (of a planet) having an orbit outside that of the earth. **b.** (of a conjunction of an inferior planet) denoting a conjunction in which the sun is between the earth and the planet. *—n.* **10.** one superior to another or others. **11.** *Print.* a superior letter or figure. **12.** *Eccles.* the head of a monastery, convent, or the like. [ME, t. L, compar. of *superus* above] **—supe′riorly,** *adv.*

Superior (syōō pĭə′rĭ ə), *n.* **Lake,** the northernmost of the Great Lakes, between the United States and Canada: the largest body of fresh water in the world. ab. 400 mi. long; ab. 31,810 sq. mi.; greatest depth, 1290 ft; 602 ft above sea-level.

superior court, 1. in England, the Court of Appeal and the High Court of Justice. **2.** in many states of the U.S., the court of general jurisdiction.

superiority (syōō pĭə′rĭ ŏ′rĭ tĭ), *n.* the quality or fact of being superior.

superiority complex, *Colloq.* an exaggerated estimation of one's own worth. [modelled on INFERIORITY COMPLEX]

superjacent (syōō′pə jā′ sənt), *adj.* lying above or upon something else. [t. LL: s. *superjacens,* ppr.]

superl., superlative.

superlative (syōō pû′lə tĭv), *adj.* **1.** of the highest kind or order; surpassing all other or others; supreme; extreme: *superlative wisdom.* **2.** being more than is proper or normal; exaggerated in language or style. **3.** *Gram.* **a.** denoting the highest degree of the comparison of adjectives and adverbs, as English *smoothest* in contrast to *smooth* and *smoother.* **b.** having or pertaining to the function or meaning of this degree of comparison. *—n.* **4.** something superlative; a superlative example. **5.** the utmost degree. **6.** *Gram.* the superlative degree, or a form therein. [ME, t. LL: m. s. *superlātīvus,* der. L *superlātus,* pp., carried beyond] **—super′latively,** *adv.* **—super′lativeness,** *n.*

superlunary (syōō′pə lōō′nə rĭ), *adj.* **1.** situated above or beyond the moon. **2.** celestial, rather than earthly. Also, **su′perlu′nar.**

superman (syōō′pə măn′), *n., pl.* **-men. 1.** a man of more than human powers. **2.** an ideal superior being conceived by Nietzsche as the product of human evolution, being in effect a ruthless egoist of superior strength, cunning, and force of will. **3.** a man who prevails by virtue of such characteristics. [trans. of G *Übermensch*]

supermarket (syōō′pə mä′kĭt), *n.* a large, usually self-service retail store or market selling food and other domestic goods.

supermedial (syōō′pə mē′dyəl), *adj.* above the middle or centre.

supermundane (syōō′pə mŭn′dān), *adj.* above earthly or worldly things.

supernal (syōō pû′nəl), *adj.* **1.** being in or belonging to the heaven of divine beings; heavenly, celestial, or divine. **2.** lofty; of more than earthly or human excellence, powers, etc. **3.** being on high or in the sky or visible heavens. [late ME, f. s. L *supernus* being above, on high + -AL[1]] **—super′nally,** *adv.*

supernatant (syōō′pə nā′tnt), *adj.* floating above, or on the surface. [t. L: s. *supernatans,* ppr.]

supernational (syōō′pə năsh′nəl), *adj.* **1.** supranational. **2.** extremely or fanatically patriotic. **—su′pernat′ionally,** *adv.* **—su′pernat′ionalism,** *n.* **—su′pernat′ionalist,** *n.*

supernatural (syōō′pə năch′rəl, -năch′ə rəl), *adj.* **1.** being above or beyond what is natural; not explicable in terms of natural laws or phenomena. **2.** of or pertaining to supernatural beings, as ghosts, spirits, etc. **3.** abnormal; extraordinary; unprecedented: *a man of supernatural intelligence.* *—n.* **4.** supernatural forces, effects, and beings collectively. **5.** the action of the supernatural as it intervenes in the natural order. **6.** a supernatural being. **—su′pernat′urally,** *adv.*

supernaturalism (syōō′pə năch′rə lĭz′əm, -năch′ə rə-), *n.* **1.** supernatural character or agency. **2.** belief in the doctrine of supernatural (divine) agency as manifested in the world, in human events, religious revelation, etc. **—su′pernat′uralist,** *n., adj.* **—su′pernat′uralis′tic,** *adj.*

supernaturalize (syōō′pə năch′rə līz′), *v.t.* **-lized, -lizing.** to make supernatural or attribute supernatural qualities. Also, **supernaturalise.**

supernormal (syōō′pə nô′məl), *adj.* **1.** beyond that which is normal. **2.** in greater number, amount, concentration, or the like than normal. **—supernormality** (syōō′pə nômăl′ĭ tĭ), *n.* **—su′pernor′mally,** *adv.*

supernova (syōō′pə nō′ və), *n.* *Astron.* an extremely bright nova which can become up to 10^8 times brighter than the sun during its explosive process; only two have been observed in the Milky Way, but they occur fairly frequently in other galaxies.

supernumerary (syōō′pə nyōō′mə rə rĭ, -nyōōm′rə rĭ), *adj., n., pl.* **-aries.** *—adj.* **1.** being in excess of the usual, proper, or prescribed number; additional; extra. **2.** associated with a regular body or staff as an assistant or substitute in case of necessity. *—n.* **3.** a supernumerary or extra person or thing. **4.** a supernumerary official or employee. **5.** *Theat.* one not belonging to the regular company, who appears on the stage but has no lines to speak. [t. LL: m. s. *supernumerārius* in excess, der. L phrase *super numerum* beyond the number]

superorder (syōō′pər ô′də), *n.* *Biol.* a group or category of related orders within a class or subclass.

superordinate (*adj., n.* syōō′pər ô′dĭ nĭt; *v.* syōō′pər ô′dĭ nāt′), *adj., n., v.* **-nated, -nating.** *—adj.* **1.** higher in rank, degree, etc. **2.** *Logic.* of superior order or generality, as genus to species or as universal to particular. *—n.* **3.** one who or something which is superordinate. **4.** *Logic.* a proposition or a class of higher generality than another. *—v.t.* **5.** to place in a superordinate position or relation.

superordination (syōō′pər ô′dĭ nā′shən), *n.* *Logic.* the act of making a proposition or a class superordinate to another.

superorganic (syōō′pə rô găn′ĭk), *adj.* **1.** above or beyond what is organic. **2.** *Sociol.* of or pertaining to elements of a society or culture conceived as independent of the individual members of the society.

superoxide (syōō′pər ŏk′sīd), *n.* *Chem.* a higher oxide of a metal which yields hydrogen peroxide on treatment with a dilute acid.

superphosphate (syōō′pə fŏs′fāt), *n.* **1.** an artificial fertilizer consisting of a mixture of calcium sulphate and calcium dihydrogen phosphate, $Ca(H_2PO_4)_2$, made by treating bone ash and basic slag (calcium phosphate) with sulphuric acid. **2.** any fertilizer containing this mixture.

superphysical (syōō′pə fĭz′ĭ kl), *adj.* above or beyond what is physical; hyperphysical.

superpose (syōō′pə pōz′), *v.t.,* **-posed, -posing. 1.** to place above or upon something else, or one upon another. **2.** *Geom.* to place (one figure) ideally in the space occupied by another, so that the two figures coincide throughout their whole extent. [t. F: m. s. *superposer,* f. *super-* SUPER- + *poser* POSE[1], after L *superpōnere*] **—su′peros′able,** *adj.*

superposition (syōō′pə pə zĭsh′ən), *n.* **1.** the act or fact of superposing. **2.** *Geol.* the principle that in sedimentary rocks an upper stratum is younger than a lower one, unless earth movements have reversed the order of strata.

superpower (syōō′pə pou′ə), *n.* **1.** power, esp. mechanical or electric power, on an extraordinary scale secured by the linking together of a number of separate power systems, with a view to more efficient and economical generation and distribution. **2.** an extremely powerful and influential nation.

super-royal (syōō′pə roi′əl), *n.* a size of printing paper, 20½ × 27½ inches, or of writing paper, 19½ × 27½ inches.

supersaturate (syōō′pə săch′ə rāt′), *v.t.,* **-rated, -rating.** *Chem.* to increase the concentration of (a solution) beyond saturation; saturate abnormally. **—su′persat′ura′tion,** *n.*

superscribe (syōō′pə skrīb′), *v.t.,* **-scribed, -scribing. 1.** to write (words, letters, one's name, etc.) above or on something. **2.** to inscribe or mark (something) with writing at the top or on the outside or surface; put an inscription above or on. [t. LL: m. s. *superscrībere*]

superscript (syōō′pə skrĭpt′), *adj.* **1.** written above, as a diacritical mark or a correction of a word. **2.** higher than the main line of type; superior. *—n.* **3.** a superscript or superior letter, figure, etc. **4.** *Obs.* a superscription, as of a letter.

superscription (syōō′pə skrĭp′shən), *n.* **1.** the act of superscribing. **2.** that which is superscribed. **3.** an address on a letter or the like. **4.** *Pharm.* the Latin word *recipe* (take), or the symbol ℞ in a prescription.

supersede (syōō′pə sēd′), *v.t.,* **-seded, -seding. 1.** to replace in power, authority, effectiveness, acceptance, use, etc., as by another person or thing. **2.** to set aside, as void, useless, or obsolete, now usually in favour of something mentioned. **3.** to displace in office or promotion by another. **4.** to succeed to the position, function, office, etc., of; supplant. [t. L: m. s. *supersedēre* sit above] **—su′persed′er,** *n.* **—Syn. 1.** See **replace.**

su′peror′dinary, *adj.* **su′perra′tional,** *adj.* **su′perra′tionally,** *adv.* **su′persales′man,** *n.*

supersedeas (syo͞o′pə sē′dĭ ăs′), *n. Law.* (formerly) a writ showing good cause to stay proceedings.
supersedure (syo͞o′pə sē′jə), *n.* **1.** the act of superseding. **2.** the state of being superseded. Also, **supersession** (syo͞o′pə sĕsh′ən).
supersensible (syo͞o′pə sĕn′sə bl), *adj.* beyond the reach of the senses. —**su′persen′sibly,** *adv.*
supersensitive (syo͞o′pə sĕn′sĭ tĭv), *adj.* hypersensitive. —**su′persen′sitiveness,** *n.*
supersensitize (syo͞o′pə sĕn′sĭ tīz′), *v.t.* **-tized, -tizing.** to make supersensitive. Also, **supersensitise.** —**su′persen′sitiza′tion,** *n.* —**su′persen′sitiz′er,** *n.*
supersensory (syo͞o′pə sĕn′sə rĭ), *adj.* beyond, or independent of, the organs of sense.
supersensual (syo͞o′pə sĕn′syo͞o əl), *adj.* **1.** beyond the range of the senses. **2.** spiritual. **3.** very sensual.
superserviceable (syo͞o′pə sû′vĭ sə bl), *adj.* too disposed to be of service; officious.
supersession (syo͞o′pə sĕsh′ən), *n.* **1.** the state of being superseded. **2.** supersedure.
supersonic (syo͞o′pə sŏn′ĭk), *adj.* **1.** (of sound frequencies) above the audible limit; ultrasonic. **2.** (of velocities) above the velosity of sound in the medium.
supersonics (syo͞o′pə sŏn′ĭks), *n.pl.* (*construed as sing.*) ultrasonics.
superstate (syo͞o′pə stāt′), *n.* a state or a governing power presiding over states subordinated to it.
superstition (syo͞o′pə stĭsh′ən), *n.* **1.** a belief or notion entertained, regardless of reason or knowledge, of the ominous significance of a particular thing, circumstance, occurrence, proceeding, or the like. **2.** any blindly accepted belief or notion. **3.** a system or collection of superstitious beliefs and customs. **4.** irrational fear of what is unknown or mysterious, esp. in connection with religion. **5.** (used pejoratively) belief in a religion or sect other than one's own. [ME, t. L: s. *superstitio*, lit., a standing over, as in wonder or awe]
superstitious (syo͞o′pə stĭsh′əs), *adj.* **1.** of the nature of, characterized by, or proceeding from superstition: *superstitious fears.* **2.** pertaining to or connected with superstition: *superstitious legends.* **3.** full of or addicted to superstition. —**su′persti′tiously,** *adv.* —**su′persti′tiousness,** *n.*
superstratum (syo͞o′pə strä′təm), *n., pl.* **-ta** (-tə), **-tums.** an overlying stratum or layer.
superstructure (syo͞o′pə strŭk′chə), *n.* **1.** all of an edifice above the basement or foundation. **2.** any structure built on something else. **3.** *Naut.* the parts of a vessel, as a warship, built above the main deck. **4.** that part of a bridge which rests on the piers and abutments. **5.** anything erected on a foundation or basis.
supersubtle (syo͞o′pə sŭt′l), *adj.* extremely or excessively subtle; oversubtle. —**su′persub′tlety,** *n.*
supertanker (syo͞o′pə tăng′kə), *n.* a very large tanker (ship).
supertax (syo͞o′pə tăks′), *n.* **1.** a tax in addition to a normal tax, as one upon income above a certain amount. **2.** a surtax.
superterrestrial (syo͞o′pə tĭ rĕs′trĭ əl), *adj.* above the earth or earthly things; celestial.
supertonic (syo͞o′pə tŏn′ĭk), *n. Music.* the second note of a scale, being the next above the tonic.
supervene (syo͞o′pə vēn′), *v.i.,* **-vened, -vening.** **1.** to come as something additional or extraneous (sometimes fol. by *on* or *upon*). **2.** to ensue. [t. L: m. s. *supervenīre* follow] —**supervenience** (syo͞o′pə vē′nyəns), **supervention** (syo͞o′pə vĕn′shən), *n.* —**supervenient** (syo͞o′pə vē′nyənt), *adj.*
supervise (syo͞o′pə vīz′), *v.t.,* **-vised, -vising.** to oversee (a process, work, workers, etc.) during execution or performance; superintend; have the oversight and direction of. [t. ML: m. s. *supervīsus*, pp.]
supervision (syo͞o′pə vĭzh′ən), *n.* the act or function of supervising; oversight; superintendence.
supervisor (syo͞o′pə vī′zə), *n.* **1.** one who supervises; a superintendent. **2.** (at some universities) a tutor who supervises the work of a student, esp. a research student or one studying for a higher degree. **3.** *U.S. Educ.* an official responsible for assisting the teachers in the preparation of syllabuses, in devising teaching methods, etc. **4.** *U.S.* an elected administrative officer in some states, often a member of a board governing a county. —**su′pervi′sorship′,** *n.*
supervisory (syo͞o′pə vī′zə rĭ), *adj.* pertaining to or having supervision.
supinate (syo͞o′pĭ nāt′), *v.,* **-nated, -nating.** *Physiol.* —*v.t.* **1.** to render supine; rotate or place (the hand or forelimb) so that the palmar surface is upwards when the limb is stretched forwards horizontally. —*v.i.* **2.** to become supinated. [t. L: m. s. *supīnātus*, pp., bent backwards, laid on the back]
supination (syo͞o′pĭ nā′shən), *n. Physiol.* **1.** a turning of the hand so that the palm is facing upwards and the bones of the forearm are parallel (opposed to *pronation*). **2.** a comparable motion of the foot, consisting of adduction followed by inversion. **3.** the result of this rotation; the position so assumed.
supinator (syo͞o′pĭ nā′tə), *n. Anat.* a muscle which causes supination. [NL. See SUPINATE, -OR[2]]
supine (*adj.* syo͞o pīn′, syo͞o′pīn; *n.* syo͞o′pīn), *adj.* **1.** lying on the back, or with the face or front upwards. **2.** having the palm upwards, as the hand. **3.** inactive; passive; inert; esp., inactive or passive from indolence or indifference. —*n.* **4.** (in Latin) a noun form derived from verbs, appearing only in the accusative and the dative-ablative, as *dictū* in *mirābile dictū* 'wonderful to say'. **5.** an analogous form in some other language. [t. L: m. s. *supīnus*] —**supine′ly,** *adv.*—**supine′ness,** *n.*
supp., supplement. Also, **suppl.**
supper (sŭp′ə), *n.* **1.** the evening meal; the last meal of the day, taken in the evening. **2.** any evening repast, often one forming part of a social entertainment. [ME, t. OF: m. *so(u)per*, n. use of *souper* SUP[1]]—**sup′perless,** *adj.*
suppertime (sŭp′ə tīm′), *n.* **1.** the time in the late evening when supper is eaten. —*adj.* **2.** denoting, pertaining to, or taking place at this time.
supplant (sə plänt′), *v.t.* **1.** to displace or supersede, as one thing does another. **2.** to take the place of (another), as in office or favour, through scheming, strategy, or the like. **3.** to replace (one thing) by something else. [ME *supplante(n)*, t. L: m. *supplantāre* trip up, overthrow] —**supplantation** (sŭp′län tā′shən), *n.* —**supplant′er,** *n.* —**Syn. 2.** See **replace.**
supple (sŭp′l), *adj.,* **-pler, -plest,** *v.,* **-pled, -pling.** —*adj.* **1.** bending readily without breaking or deformation; pliant; flexible: *a supple rod.* **2.** characterized by ease in bending; limber; lithe: *supple movements.* **3.** characterized by ease and adaptability in mental action. **4.** compliant or yielding. **5.** obsequious; servile. —*v.t., v.i.* **6.** to make or become supple. [ME *souple*, t. OF, g. L *supplex* bending under] —**sup′pleness,** *n.* —**Ant. 1.** rigid.
supplejack (sŭp′l jăk′), *n.* **1.** a strong, pliant cane or walking stick. **2.** any of various climbing shrubs with strong stems suitable for making walking sticks.
supplement (*n.* sŭp′lĭ mənt; *v.* sŭp′lĭ mĕnt′), *n.* **1.** something added to complete a thing, supply a deficiency, or reinforce or extend a whole. **2.** a part added to a book, document, or the like to supply deficiencies or correct errors. **3.** a part, usually of special character, issued as an additional feature of a newspaper or other periodical. **4.** *Maths.* the quantity by which an angle or an arc falls short of 180° or a semicircle. —*v.t.* **5.** to complete, add to, or extend by a supplement; form a supplement or addition to. **6.** to supply (a deficiency). [ME, t. L: s. *supplēmentum*] —**sup′plementa′tion,** *n.* —**sup′plement′er,** *n.* —**Syn. 2.** See **appendix. 5.** See **complement.**

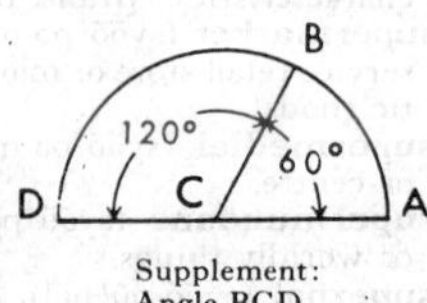

Supplement: Angle BCD, supplement of angle BCA

supplemental (sŭp′lĭ mĕn′tl), *adj.* **1.** supplementary. **2.** *Law.* additional. —**sup′plemen′tally,** *adv.*
supplementary (sŭp′lĭ mĕn′tə rĭ, -trĭ), *adj.* **1.** Also, **sup′plemen′tal.** of the nature of or forming a supplement; additional. —*n.* **2.** one who or that which is supplementary. —**sup′plemen′tarily,** *adv.*
supplementary angle, *Maths.* either of two angles whose sum is 180°.
supplementary benefits. See **national assistance.**
suppletion (sə plē′shən), *n. Gram.* **1.** the presence of one or more suppletive forms in a paradigm. **2.** the use of suppletive forms, or an instance of such use.
suppletive (sə plē′tĭv, sŭp′lĭ tĭv), *adj. Gram.* **1.** (of a linguistic form) serving as an inflected form of a word with a totally different stem, e.g., *went* as the preterite of *go.* **2.** (of a paradigm) including one or more suppletive forms. **3.** (of inflection) characterized by the use of suppletive forms.
suppletory (sŭp′lĭ tə rĭ, -trĭ), *adj.* supplying a deficiency. [t. LL: m. s. *supplētorius*, der. L *supplētus*, pp., filled up]
suppliance[1] (sə plī′əns), *n.* the act of supplying. Also, **supplial** (sə plī′əl).
suppliance[2] (sŭp′lĭ əns), *n.* the act of supplicating; entreaty; supplication.

su′persales′manship′, *n.* **su′persubstan′tial,** *adj.* **su′persuper′lative,** *n.* **su′pertem′poral,** *adj.*

suppliant (sŭp′lĭ ənt), *n.* **1.** one who supplicates; a humble petitioner. —*adj.* **2.** supplicating. **3.** expressive of supplication, as words, actions, etc. [ME, t. F, ppr. of *supplier*, OF *souplier*, g. L *supplicāre* supplicate] —**sup′pliantly,** *adv.* —**sup′pliantness, sup′pliance,** *n.*

supplicant (sŭp′lĭ kənt), *adj.* **1.** supplicating. —*n.* **2.** a suppliant. [t. L: s. *supplicans*, ppr.]

supplicate (sŭp′lĭ kāt′), *v.*, **-cated, -cating.** —*v.i.* **1.** to pray humbly; make humble and earnest entreaty or petition. —*v.t.* **2.** to pray humbly to; entreat or petition humbly. **3.** to seek by humble entreaty. [late ME, t. L: m. s. *supplicātus*, pp., begged] —**Syn. 3.** See **appeal.**

supplication (sŭp′lĭ kā′shən), *n.* the act of supplicating; humble prayer, entreaty, or petition.

supplicatory (sŭp′lĭ kə tə rĭ, -trĭ), *adj.* making or expressing supplication.

supply[1] (sə plī′), *v.*, **-plied, -plying,** *n.*, *pl.* **-plies.** —*v.t.* **1.** to furnish (a person, establishment, place, etc.) with what is lacking or requisite. **2.** to furnish or provide (something wanting or requisite): *to supply electricity to a community.* **3.** to make up (a deficiency); make up for (a loss, lack, absence, etc.); satisfy (a need, demand, etc.). **4.** to fill (a place, vacancy, etc.); occupy as a substitute. —*v.i.* **5.** to fill the place of another, esp. a schoolteacher, as a substitute or temporarily. —*n.* **6.** the act of supplying, furnishing, providing, satisfying, etc. **7.** that which is supplied. **8.** a quantity of something provided or on hand, as for use; a stock or store. **9.** (*usually pl.*) a provision, stock, or store of food or other things necessary for maintenance. **10.** a parliamentary grant or provision of money for the expenses of government. **11.** *Econ.* the quantity of a commodity, etc., that is in the market and available for purchase, or that is available for purchase at a particular price. **12.** *Elect.* a source of electrical energy. **13.** (*pl.*) *Mil.* **a.** articles and materials used by an army or navy of types rapidly used up, such as food, clothing, soap, and fuel. **b.** the furnishing of supplies, and the management of supply units and installations. **14.** one who supplies a vacancy or takes the place of another, esp. temporarily. **15.** *Obs.* reinforcements. **16.** *Obs.* aid. —*adj.* **17.** *Elect.* denoting or pertaining to a source of electrical energy or its characteristics. [ME *supplye*, t. OF: m. *so(u)pl(e)ier*, g. L *supplēre* fill up] —**suppli′er,** *n.*

supply[2] (sŭp′lĭ), *adv.* in a supple manner. Also, **supplely** (sŭp′l lĭ). [f. SUPP(LE) + -LY]

supply day, a day on which a legislative body is asked to approve the estimates of government expenditure.

supply teacher, a schoolteacher who teaches temporarily in the place of regular teachers who are ill or absent.

support (sə pôt′), *v.t.* **1.** to bear or hold up (a load, mass, structure, part, etc.). **2.** to sustain or withstand (weight, etc.) without giving way. **3.** to undergo or endure, esp. with patience or submission; tolerate. **4.** to sustain (a person, the mind, spirits, courage, etc.) under trial or affliction. **5.** to maintain (a person, family, establishment, institution, etc.) by supplying with things necessary to existence; provide for. **6.** to uphold (a person, cause, policy, etc.) by aid or countenance; back; second (efforts, aims, etc.). **7.** to maintain or advocate (a theory, etc.). **8.** to corroborate (a statement, etc.). **9.** to sustain or act (a part, role, or character). **10.** to act with or second (a leading actor), as on a stage; assist in any performance. **11.** to form a secondary part of a programme with: *the main film will be supported by two short documentaries.* —*n.* **12.** the act of supporting. **13.** the state of being supported. **14.** maintenance, as of a person, family, etc., with necessities, means, or funds. **15.** a thing or a person that supports. **16.** a prop or stay for carrying part of the weight of a structure. **17.** a thing or a person that gives aid or assistance. **18.** an actor, actress, or company playing secondary or subordinate roles. **19.** the material, as canvas or wood, on which a picture is painted. [ME, t. OF: s. *supporter* bear, g. L *supportāre* convey]

—**Syn. 1, 6.** SUPPORT, MAINTAIN, SUSTAIN, UPHOLD all mean to hold up and to preserve. To SUPPORT is to hold up or add strength to, literally or figuratively: *the columns support the roof.* To MAINTAIN is to support so as to preserve intact: *to maintain an attitude of defiance.* To SUSTAIN, a rather elevated word, suggests completeness and adequacy in supporting: *the court sustained his claim.* UPHOLD applies esp. to supporting or backing another, as in a statement, opinion, or belief: *to uphold the rights of a minority.* **14.** See **living.**

supportable (sə pô′tə bl), *adj.* capable of being supported; endurable; maintainable. —**support′abil′ity, support′ableness,** *n.* —**support′ably,** *adv.*

supporter (sə pô′tə), *n.* **1.** one who or that which supports. **2.** a device, usually elastic cotton webbing, for holding up some part of the body, esp. one used by male athletes to support the genitals. **3.** one who supports a sporting team, esp. by attending matches to shout encouragement. **4.** an upholder, backer, or advocate. **5.** *Her.* a figure as of an animal or a man, holding up an escutcheon or standing beside it.

supposal (sə pō′zəl), *n.* supposition.

suppose (sə pōz′), *v.*, **-posed, -posing.** —*v.t.* **1.** to assume (something), without reference to its being true or false, for the sake of argument or for the purpose of tracing the consequences: *suppose the distance to be one mile.* **2.** to consider as a possibility suggested or an idea or plan proposed (used in the imperative): *suppose we wait till tomorrow.* **3.** to assume as true, or believe, in the absence of positive knowledge or of evidence to the contrary: *it is supposed that the occurrence was an accident.* **4.** to take for granted, assume, or presume, without especial thought of possible error: *I supposed that you had gone.* **5.** to think, with reference to mere opinion: *what do you suppose he will do?* **6.** (of a proposition, theory, etc.) to make or involve the assumption of: *this theory supposes the existence of life on Mars.* **7.** (of facts, circumstances, etc.) to require logically; imply; presuppose. **8.** *Obs.* to expect. —*v.i.* **9.** to assume something; presume; think. [ME, t. OF: m. *sup(p)oser*, f. *sup-* SUB- + *poser* POSE[1], after L *suppōnere*] —**suppos′able,** *adj.* —**suppos′ably,** *adv.* —**suppos′er,** *n.* —**Syn. 3.** See **think**[1].

supposed (sə pōzd′), *adj.* **1.** assumed as true, regardless of fact; hypothetical: *a supposed case.* **2.** accepted or received as true, without positive knowledge and perhaps erroneously: *the supposed site of an ancient temple.* **3.** merely thought to be such: *to sacrifice real for supposed gains.* —**supposedly** (sə pō′zĭd lĭ), *adv.*

supposing (sə pō′zĭng), *conj.* on the supposition or premise that.

supposition (sŭp′ə zĭsh′ən), *n.* **1.** the act of supposing. **2.** that which is supposed; an assumption; a hypothesis. [late ME, t. ML: s. *suppositio* (in L a putting under) used as trans. of Gk *hypóthesis* HYPOTHESIS] —**sup′posi′tional,** *adj.* —**sup′posi′tionally,** *adv.*

suppositious (sŭp′ə zĭsh′əs), *adj.* **1.** supposititious. **2.** suppositional.

supposititious (sə pŏz′ĭ tĭsh′əs), *adj.* **1.** fraudulently substituted or pretended; spurious; not genuine. **2.** hypothetical. [t. L: m. *suppositītius*] —**suppos′iti′tiously,** *adv.* —**suppos′iti′tiousness,** *n.*

suppositive (sə pŏz′ĭ tĭv), *adj.* **1.** of the nature of or involving supposition; suppositional. **2.** supposititious or false. **3.** *Gram.* expressing supposition, as the words *if*, *granting*, or *provided.* —*n.* **4.** *Gram.* a suppositive word. —**suppos′itively,** *adv.*

suppository (sə pŏz′ĭ tə rĭ, -trĭ), *n.*, *pl.* **-ries.** a solid conical mass of medicinal substance inserted into the rectum or vagina to be dissolved therein. [t. LL: m. s. *suppositōrium* (thing) placed under, der. L *suppositus*, pp., placed under]

suppress (sə prĕs′), *v.t.* **1.** to put an end to the activities of (a person, body of persons, etc.). **2.** to do away with by or as by authority; abolish; stop (a practice, etc.). **3.** to keep in or repress (a feeling, smile, groan, etc.). **4.** to withhold from disclosure or publication (truth, evidence, a book, names, etc.). **5.** to arrest (a flow, haemorrhage, etc.). **6.** to quell; crush; vanquish or subdue (a revolt, rebel, etc.). **7.** *Elect.* **a.** to reduce or eliminate any unwanted oscillations in a circuit. **b.** to reduce current surges in the high-tension circuit of a motor-car engine to eliminate interference with the car radio. [ME, t. L: s. *suppressus*, pp., put down] —**suppres′sible,** *adj.* —**suppres′sive,** *adj.*

suppression (sə prĕsh′ən), *n.* **1.** the act of suppressing or state of being suppressed. **2.** *Psychol.* conscious inhibition of an impulse. **3.** *Elect.* the reduction or elimination of unwanted oscillations in a circuit. **4.** *Radio, etc.* the elimination of a frequency or group of frequencies from a signal. **5.** *Bot.* the elimination of parts of a plant by the action of frost, disease, insects, etc.

suppressor (sə prĕs′ə), *n.* **1.** Also, **suppresser.** one who or that which suppresses. **2.** *Elect.* **a.** a circuit which reduces or eliminates unwanted oscillations in an electrical system. **b.** a device which reduces current surges in the high-tension circuit of a motor-car engine.

suppurate (sŭp′yo͝o rāt′), *v.i.*, **-rated, -rating.** to produce or discharge pus, as a wound; maturate. [t. L: m. s. *suppūrātus*, pp., caused to secrete pus]

suppuration (sŭp′yo͝o rā′shən), *n.* **1.** the process of suppurating. **2.** the matter produced by suppuration.

suppurative (sŭp′yo͝o rə tĭv), *adj.* **1.** suppurating, or characterized by suppuration. **2.** promoting suppuration. —*n.* **3.** a medicine that promotes suppuration.

supra (syo͞o′prə), *adv.* above: esp. used in making reference to parts of a text. [L: above, beyond]

---

su′pra-axil′lary, *adj.** **su′pracil′iary,** *adj.* **su′praclavic′ular,** *adj.* **su′pracos′tal,** *adj.*

supra-, a prefix meaning 'above', equivalent to **super-,** but emphasizing situation or position, as in *supraorbital, suprarenal.* [t. L, repr. *suprā,* adv. and prep.]

supralapsarian (syo͞o′prə lăp sēə′rĭ ən), *n.* one who believes in supralapsarianism. [f. s. NL *supralapsārius* (der. L *suprā-* SUPRA- + *lapsus* fall, lapse) + -AN]

supralapsarianism (syo͞o′prə lăp sēə′rĭ ə nĭz′əm), *n. Theol.* the doctrine that the decree of election and reprobation, expressing the ultimate purpose of God, preceded the means by which this purpose was to be accomplished, namely the decree of man's creation and the decree which permitted his fall (opposed to *infra-* or *sublapsarianism*).

supraliminal (syo͞o′prə lĭm′ĭ nəl), *adj. Psychol.* above the limen or threshold of consciousness; of or in consciousness.

supramolecular (syo͞o′prə mə lĕk′yo͝o lə), *adj.* **1.** above the molecule; of greater complexity than a molecule. **2.** composed of an aggregation of molecules.

supranational (syo͞o′prə năsh′nəl), *adj.* overriding national sovereignty; outside the authority of a single national government. —**su′pranat′ionalism,** *n.* —**su′pranat′ionally,** *adv.*

supraorbital (syo͞o′prə ô′bĭ tl), *adj. Anat.* situated above the eye socket.

supra protest, *Law.* upon or after protest (a phrase used with reference to an acceptance or a payment of a bill by a third person for the honour of the drawer after protest for non-acceptance or non-payment by the drawee). [t. It.: m. *sopra protesto* upon protest]

suprarenal (syo͞o′prə rē′nəl), *Anat.* —*adj.* **1.** situated above or on the kidney. **2.** pertaining to or connected with a suprarenal. —*n.* **3.** a suprarenal body, capsule, or gland.

suprarenal gland, *Anat., Physiol., Zool.* either of a pair of ductless glands, located in man at the upper end, and in most vertebrates at the anterior end, of the kidneys, which secrete adrenaline and a number of steroid hormones; adrenal gland. See diag. under **kidney.**

supremacist (syo͞o prĕm′ə sĭst), *n.* **1.** a believer in the supremacy of one particular group, esp. a racial group: *white supremacist.* —*adj.* **2.** advocating or believing in such supremacy. —**suprem′atism,** *n.*

supremacy (syo͞o prĕm′ə sĭ), *n.* **1.** the state of being supreme. **2.** supreme authority or power. Also, **supremity.**

suprematism (syo͞o prĕm′ə tĭz′əm), *n.* a modern art movement, originating in Russia about 1913, concerned with geometrical abstraction. —**suprem′atist,** *n., adj.*

supreme (syo͞o prēm′), *adj.* **1.** highest in rank or authority; paramount; sovereign; chief. **2.** of the highest quality, character, importance, etc.: *supreme courage.* **3.** greatest, utmost, or extreme: *supreme disgust.* **4.** last (with reference to the end of life): *the supreme moment.* [t. L: m. s. *suprēmus,* superl. of *superus* that is above] —**supreme′ly,** *adv.* —**supreme′ness,** *n.*

suprême (syo͞o prēm′), *n. Cookery.* **1.** the breast and wings of poultry and game, esp. when served with a rich cream sauce. **2.** the best cut of any meat. [t. F]

Supreme Being, the sovereign of the universe; God.

supreme commander, *U.S.* the military, naval, or air officer commanding all allied forces in a theatre of war.

Supreme Court, *U.S.* **1.** the highest court of the nation. **2.** (in most states) the highest court of the state.

Supreme Court of Judicature, (in Great Britain) a court having two divisions, the High Court of Justice and the Court of Appeal.

supreme sacrifice, the sacrifice of one's own life.

Supreme Soviet, the supreme legislative body of the Soviet Union, consisting of two houses, one house representative on the basis of population, the other assuring every nationality, however small, some representation.

supremo (syo͞o prē′mō), *n.* a supreme ruler; dictator, esp. a military dictator. [t. Sp.: short for *generalissimo supremo* supreme general]

Supt, superintendent. Also, **supt.**

sur-[1], a prefix corresponding to **super-** but mainly attached to stems not used as words and having figurative applications (*survive, surname*), used especially in legal terms (*surrebuttal*). [late ME, t. F, g. L *super-* SUPER-]

sur-[2], occasional var. of **sub-** (by assimilation) before *r.*

sura (so͞o′rə), *n.* one of the 114 chapters of the Koran. Also, **surah.** [t. Ar.: m. *sūrah* row, step, degree]

Surabaya (so͞oə′rə bĭ′ə), *n.* a seaport in NE Java: second largest city of Indonesia. 1,007,945 (1961).

surah[1] (syo͞oə′rə), *n.* a soft twilled silk or rayon fabric. [appar. named after SURAT]

surah[2] (so͞oə′rə), *n.* sura.

Surajah Dowlah (sə rä′jə dou′lə). See **Siraj-ud-daula.**

Surakarta (so͞oə′rə kä′tə), *n.* a city in central Java, in Indonesia. 367,626 (1961). Formerly, **Solo.**

sural (syo͞oə′rəl), *adj. Anat.* of or pertaining to the calf of the leg. [t. NL: s. *sūrālis,* der. L *sūra* calf of the leg]

Surat (so͞oə′rət), *n.* a seaport in W India, in Gujarat state: the first British settlement in India, 1612. 288,026 (1961).

surbase (sû′bās′), *n. Archit.* a moulding above a base, as that immediately above a skirting board, the crowning moulding of a pedestal, etc. —**surbase′ment,** *n.*

surbased (sû′bāst′), *adj. Archit.* **1.** having a surbase. **2.** depressed; flattened. **3.** (of an arch) having a rise of less than half the span. [Anglicization of F *surbaissé,* f. *sur-* (intensive) + *baissé* lowered. See BASE[2]]

Surbiton (sû′bĭ tən), *n.* a suburban district of the SW outer London borough of Kingston upon Thames.

surcease (sû sēs′), *v.,* **-ceased, -ceasing,** *n. Archaic.* —*v.i.* **1.** to cease from some action; desist. **2.** to come to an end. —*v.t.* **3.** to cease from; leave off. —*n.* **4.** cessation; end. [ME *sursese,* t. OF: m. *sursis,* pp. of *surseoir* refrain, suspend, g. L *supersedēre* desist, conformed to CEASE]

surcharge (*n.* sû′chäj′; *v.* sû chäj′), *n., v.,* **-charged, -charging.** —*n.* **1.** an additional or excessive charge for payment, tax, etc. **2.** an excessive sum or price charged. **3.** *Philately.* an overprint which alters or restates the face value or denomination of a stamp to which it has been applied. **4.** *Law.* the act of surcharging. **5.** an additional or excessive load or burden. —*v.t.* **6.** to subject to an additional or extra charge (for payment). **7.** to overcharge. **8.** to show an omission in (an account) of something that operates as a charge against the accounting party. **9.** *Philately.* to print a surcharge on. **10.** to put an additional or excessive burden upon; overload. [ME, t. OF. See SUR-[1], CHARGE, v.] —**surcharg′er,** *n.*

surcingle (sû′sĭng′gl), *n.* **1.** a girth for a horse or other animal, esp. a large girth passing over and keeping in place a blanket, pack, or the like. **2.** a girdle with which a garment, esp. a cassock, is fastened. [ME *sursengle,* t. OF: m. *surcengle,* f. *sur-* SUR-[1] + *cengle* (g. L *cingula* girdle)]

surcoat (sû′kōt′), *n.* **1.** a garment worn over medieval armour, often embroidered with heraldic arms. **2.** an outer coat or garment. [ME *surcote,* t. OF. See SUR-[1], COAT]

Surcoat, 13th century

surculose (sû′kyo͝o lōs′), *adj. Bot.* producing suckers. [t. L: s. *surculōsus*]

surd (sûd), *adj.* **1.** *Maths.* (of a quantity) not capable of being expressed in rational numbers; irrational. **2.** *Phonet.* voiceless. —*n.* **3.** *Maths.* a surd quantity. **4.** *Phonet.* a voiceless consonant. [t. L: s. *surdus* deaf, indistinct]

sure (sho͞oə, shô), *adj.,* **surer, surest,** *adv.* —*adj.* **1.** free from apprehension or doubt as to the reliability, character, action, etc., of something (often fol. by *of*): *to be sure of one's data.* **2.** confident, as of something expected: *sure of ultimate success.* **3.** convinced, fully persuaded, or positive, as of something firmly believed: *sure of a person's guilt.* **4.** assured or certain beyond question: *man is sure of death.* **5.** worthy of confidence; reliable: *a sure messenger.* **6.** firm or stable: *to stand on sure ground.* **7.** unfailing; never disappointing expectations: *a sure cure.* **8.** unerring; never missing, slipping, etc.: *a sure aim.* **9.** admitting of no doubt or question: *sure proof.* **10.** inevitable: *death is sure.* **11.** destined; bound inevitably; certain: *he is sure to come.* **12.** *Archaic.* secure or safe. **13. be sure,** be certain or careful (to do or be as specified): *be sure to close the windows.* **14. for sure,** as a certainty; surely. **15. make sure, a.** to be certain (that something is done). **b.** to be confident in the support or possession (*of*). **16. to be sure,** surely; certainly; without doubt. —*adv.* **17.** *Colloq.* surely, undoubtedly, or certainly. **18.** *U.S. Colloq.* inevitably or without fail. [ME, t. OF, g. L *sēcūrus* secure] —**sure′ness,** *n.*

—**Syn. 1.** SURE, CERTAIN, CONFIDENT, POSITIVE indicate full belief and trust that something is true. SURE, CERTAIN, and POSITIVE are often used interchangeably. SURE, the simplest and most general, denotes mere absence of doubt. CERTAIN suggests that there are definite reasons which have freed one from doubt. CONFIDENT emphasizes the strength of the belief or the certainty of expectation felt. POSITIVE implies emphatic certainty, which may even become overconfidence or dogmatism. —**Ant. 1.** doubtful.

sure enough (sho͞oə′rĭ nŭf′, shô′-), *Colloq.* as expected; in actual fact: *he was expected to win, and sure enough he did.*

sure-enough (sho͞oə′rĭ nŭf′, shô′-), *adj. U.S. Dial. or Colloq.* real; genuine.

sure-fire (sho͞oə′fī′ə, shô′-), *adj. Colloq.* certain to succeed; assured: *a sure-fire winner for tomorrow's race.*

---

su′pralu′nar, *adj.* **su′pramaxil′lary,** *adj.* **su′pramun′dane,** *adj.* **su′pranor′mal,** *adj.* **su′prara′tional,** *adj.* **su′prasen′sible,** *adj.* **su′prasen′sory,** *adj.* **su′pratem′poral,** *adj.*

---

sure-footed (sho͝oəʹfo͝otʹĭd, shôʹ-), *adj.* **1.** not liable to stumble, slip, or fall. **2.** proceeding surely; unerring. —**sure′-foot′edly,** *adv.* —**sure′foot′edness,** *n.*

surely (sho͝oəʹlĭ, shôʹlĭ), *adv.* **1.** firmly; unerringly; without missing, slipping, etc. **2.** undoubtedly, assuredly, or certainly: *the results are surely encouraging.* **3.** (in emphatic utterances that are not necessarily sustained by fact) assuredly: *surely you are mistaken.* **4.** inevitably or without fail: *slowly but surely the end approached.*

Sûreté (*Fr.* sʏʀ tě′), *n.* the French criminal investigation department.

sure thing, **1.** a certainty; something assured beyond doubt. **2.** *Chiefly U.S.* assuredly; certainly.

surety (sho͝oəʹtĭ, sho͝oəʹrĭ tĭ), *n., pl.* **1.** security against loss or damage; security for the fulfilment of an obligation, the payment of a debt, etc.; a pledge, guaranty, or bond. **2.** one who has made himself responsible for another. **3.** the state or quality of being sure. **4.** certainty. **5.** that which makes sure; ground of confidence or safety. **6.** one who is legally answerable for the debt, default, or miscarriage of another. **7.** the quality of being sure; assurance or sureness. [ME *seurte*, t. OF, g. s. L *sēcūritas*]

suretyship (sho͝oəʹtĭ shĭp′, sho͝oəʹrĭ tĭ shĭp′), *n. Law.* the relationship between the surety, the principal debtor, and the creditor.

surf (sûf), *n.* **1.** the swell of the sea which breaks upon a shore or upon shoals. **2.** the mass or line of foamy water caused by the breaking of the sea upon a shore, etc. —*v.i.* **3.** to bathe in and ride on surf, as with a surfboard. [earlier *suff*, ? var. of SOUGH] —**Syn. 1.** See **wave.**

surface (sûʹfĭs), *n., adj., v.,* **-faced, -facing.** —*n.* **1.** the outer face, or outside, of a thing. **2.** any face of a body or thing: *the six surfaces of a cube.* **3.** extent or area of outer face; superficial area. **4.** the outward appearance, esp. as distinguished from the inner nature: *to look below the surface of a matter.* **5.** *Geom.* any figure having only two dimensions; part or all of the boundary of a solid. **6.** *Aeron.* an aerofoil. —*adj.* **7.** of, on, or pertaining to the surface. **8.** superficial; external; apparent, rather than real. **9.** of, on, or pertaining to land and/or sea: *surface travel.* —*v.t.* **10.** to finish as to surface; give a particular kind of surface to; make even or smooth. —*v.i.* **11.** to rise to the surface. **12.** to resume something, as an earlier or habitual mode of life after a period of devotion to a particular activity: *we look forward to surfacing after finishing this work.* **13.** *Mining.* **a.** to wash surface deposits of ore. **b.** to mine at or near the surface. **14.** to work on or at the surface. [t. F, f. *sur-* SUR-[1] + *face* FACE. Cf. SUPERFICIES] —**sur′facer,** *n.*

surface-active agent (sûʹfĭs ăkʹtĭv), *Chem.* any substance which when added to a liquid reduces its surface tension and thus increases its spreading or wetting properties. Also, **surfactant.**

surface dressing, **1.** a method of repairing roads by spreading chippings or gravel over a coat of hot tar. **2.** the dressing applied.

surface mail, mail carried on the earth's surface (opposed to *airmail*).

surface plate, *Mach.* a flat plate used by mechanics for testing surfaces which are to be made perfectly flat.

surface tension, *Physics.* a property of liquid or solid matter due to unbalanced molecular forces near a surface, and the measure thereof; an apparent tension in an actually non-existent surface film associated with capillary phenomena, cohesion, and adhesion.

surfacing (sûʹfĭ sĭng), *n.* **1.** the act or process of giving a surface to anything. **2.** the material for a surface layer: *surfacing for a road.* **3.** the act of rising to the surface. **4.** *Mining.* the act or process of washing surface deposits.

surfactant (sû făkʹtənt), *n. Chem.* a surface-active agent. [f. SURF(ACE)-ACT(IVE) A(GE)NT]

surfboard (sûfʹbôd′), *n.* a narrow board about five feet long used as a kind of a float in a sport consisting of riding the crest of a wave towards the shore.

surfboat (sûfʹbōt′), *n.* a strong, buoyant rowing boat with high ends, adapted for passing through surf.

surf duck, a scoter, esp. the surf scoter.

surfeit (sûʹfĭt), *n.* **1.** excess; an excessive amount. **2.** excess in eating or drinking. **3.** oppression or disorder of the system due to excessive eating or drinking. **4.** general disgust caused by excess or satiety. —*v.t.* **5.** to bring to a state of surfeit by excess of food or drink. **6.** to supply with anything to excess or satiety; satiate. —*v.i.* **7.** to eat or drink to excess. **8.** to suffer from the effects of overfeeding. **9.** to indulge to excess in anything. [ME *sorfait*, t. OF: excess, prop. pp. of *sorfaire* overdo, f. *sor-* SUR-[1] + *faire* do (g. L *facere*)] —**sur′feiter,** *n.*

surf scoter, a large North American diving duck occasionally seen in Britain, *Melanitta perspicillata*, the adult male being black except for two white patches on the head.

surfy (sûʹfĭ), *adj.,* **surfier, surfiest.** abounding with surf; forming or resembling surf.

surg., **1.** surgeon. **2.** surgery. **3.** surgical.

surge (sûj), *n., v.,* **surged, surging.** —*n.* **1.** a strong forward or upward movement, rush, or sweep, like that of swelling or rolling waves: *the onward surge of an angry mob.* **2.** a strong, wavelike volume or body of something: *a surge of smoke.* **3.** the rolling swell of the sea. **4.** the swelling and rolling sea; *the surge was seething free.* **5.** a swelling wave; billow. **6.** a large swelling or abrupt wave, the change in depth or pressure generally being maintained after passage. **7.** *Elect.* a sudden rush of current, a violent oscillatory disturbance, or the like. **8.** *Mach.* an unevenness or irregularity in motion or action in an engine. **9.** *Naut.* a surging, or slipping back, as of a rope. —*v.i.* **10.** to rise and fall, or move along, on the waves, as a ship: *to surge at anchor.* **11.** to rise or roll in waves, or like waves: *a crowd surges about a spot.* **12.** to rise as if by a heaving or swelling force: *blood surges to the face.* **13.** *Elect.* to increase suddenly, as a current; oscillate violently. **14.** *Naut.* **a.** to slack off or loosen a rope or cable around a capstan or windlass. **b.** to slip back, as a rope. —*v.t.* **15.** to cause to surge or roll in or as in waves. **16.** to heave or sway with a waving motion. **17.** *Naut.* to slacken (a rope). [orig. uncert. Cf. F *surgeon* spring]

surgeon (sûʹjən), *n.* **1.** one who treats injuries, deformities, and diseases by manual operation or instrumental appliances. **2.** a medical practitioner or physician qualified to practise surgery. **3.** an army or naval medical officer. **4.** a surgeonfish. [ME *surgien*, t. AF, contr. of OF *serurgien*. See CHIRURGEON]

surgeoncy (sûʹjən sĭ), *n., pl.* **-cies.** the office or position of a surgeon, as in the army or navy. Also, **sur′geonship′.**

surgeonfish (sûʹjən fĭsh′), *n., pl.* **-fishes,** (*esp. collectively*) **-fish.** any tropical coral-reef fish of the family *Acanthuridae*, with one or more spines near the base of the tail fin.

surgeon general, *pl.* **surgeons general.** **1.** the chief of medical service in the army or navy. **2.** *U.S.* the chief of public health.

surgeon's knot, a knot resembling a reef knot but with a double turn in the first part, used by surgeons for tying ligatures, etc.

surgery (sûʹjə rĭ), *n., pl.* **-geries.** **1.** the art, practice, or work of treating diseases, injuries, or deformities by manual operation or instrumental appliances. **2.** the branch of medicine concerned with such treatment. **3.** treatment, operations, etc., performed by a surgeon. **4.** a room or place for surgical operations. **5.** the consulting room of a medical practitioner, dentist, or the like. [ME, t. OF: m. *surgerie*]

surgical (sûʹjĭ kl), *adj.* **1.** pertaining to or involving surgery. **2.** used in surgery. —**sur′gically,** *adv.*

surgical appliance, any device designed to be worn to support a damaged or deformed part of the body.

surgical boot, a specially constructed boot or shoe designed to support or correct a deformed foot or leg.

surgical spirit, *Chem.* ethyl alcohol usually containing oil of wintergreen and castor oil, used for cleansing the skin of a patient before an operation, etc.

surgy (sûʹjĭ), *adj.,* **surgier, surgiest.** billowy; surging or swelling.

suricate (syo͞oəʹrĭ kāt′), *n.* the meerkat, *Suricata suricatta.* [earlier *surikate*, t. F, t. D: m. *surikat* macaque]

Surinam (so͞oəʹrĭ năm′), *n.* a possession of the Netherlands on the NE coast of South America, considered an integral part of the Dutch realm. 330,000 pop. (est. 1962); 60,230 sq. mi. *Cap.:* Paramaribo. Also, **Dutch Guiana.** See map under **Guiana.**

Surinam toad, the pipa.

surloin (sûʹloin′), *n.* sirloin.

surly (sûʹlĭ), *adj.,* **-lier, -liest.** **1.** churlishly rude or ill-humoured, as a person or the manner, tone, expression, etc. **2.** (of an animal) ill-tempered and unfriendly. **3.** *Obs.* lordly; arrogant. [var. of obs. *sirly* (f. SIR + -LY) lordly] —**sur′lily,** *adv.* —**sur′liness,** *n.*

surmise (*v.* sû mīz′; *n.* sû mīz′, sûʹmīz), *v.,* **-mised, -mising,** *n.* —*v.t.* **1.** to think or infer without certain or strong evidence; conjecture; guess. —*v.i.* **2.** to conjecture or guess. —*n.* Also, **surmisal. 3.** a matter of conjecture. **4.** an idea or thought of something as being possible or likely, although without any certain or strong evidence. **5.** conjecture or surmising. [ME, t. OF, pp. of *surmettre* accuse] —**surmis′able,** *adj.* —**surmis′er,** *n.* —**Syn. 1.** See **guess.**

surmount (sû mount′), *v.t.* **1.** to mount upon; get on the top of; mount upon and cross over: *to surmount a hill.* **2.** to get over or across (barriers, obstacles, etc.). **3.** to prevail over. **4.** to be on top of or above: *a statue surmounting a pillar.* **5.** to furnish with something placed on top or above: *to surmount a tower with a spire.* **6.** *Obs.* to surpass or excel; exceed in amount. [ME *surmounte(n)*, t. OF: m. *surmonter.* See SUR-[1], MOUNT[1]] —**surmount′able,** *adj.* —**surmount′er,** *n.*

surmullet (sû mŭl′ĭt), *n.* a goatfish.

surname (sû′nām′), *n., v.,* **-named, -naming.** —*n.* **1.** the name which a person has in common with the other members of his family, as distinguished from his Christian or first name; a family name. **2.** a name added to a person's name or names, as from birth or abode or from some characteristic or achievement. —*v.t.* **3.** to give a surname to; call by a surname. [ME; half adoption, half trans. of F *surnom*]

surpass (sû päs′), *v.t.* **1.** to go beyond in amount, extent, or degree; be greater than; exceed. **2.** to go beyond in excellence or achievement; be superior to; excel. **3.** to be beyond the range or capacity of; transcend: *misery that surpasses description.* [t. F: s. *surpasser*, f. *sur-* (intensive) + *passer* PASS] —**surpass′able,** *adj.* —**Syn. 2.** See **excel.**

surpassing (sû pä′sĭng), *adj.* **1.** that surpasses, exceeds, or excels; extraordinary: *structures of surpassing magnificence.* —*adv.* **2.** *Obs. exc. Poetic.* surpassingly. —**surpass′ingly,** *adv.* —**surpass′ingness,** *n.*

surplice (sû′plĭs), *n.* **1.** a loose-fitting, broad-sleeved white vestment properly of linen, worn over the cassock by clergymen and choristers. **2.** a garment in which the fronts cross each other diagonally. [ME, t. AF: m. *surpliz*, syncopated var. of OF *sourpeliz* over-fur (garment)] —**sur′pliced,** *adj.*

Surplice

surplus (sû′pləs), *n.* **1.** that which remains above what is used or needed. **2.** an amount of assets in excess of what is requisite to meet liabilities. **3.** *Accounting.* the excess of assets over liabilities accumulated throughout the existence of a business, excepting assets against which stock certificates have been issued. —*adj.* **4.** being a surplus; being in excess of what is required: *the surplus wheat of America.* [ME, t. OF. Cf. ML *superplus.* See PLUS] —**Syn. 1.** See **remainder.**

surplusage (sû′plə sĭj), *n.* **1.** surplus; excess. **2.** an excess of words.

surprint (sû′prĭnt′), *v.t.* **1.** to print over with additional marks or matter; overprint. **2.** to print (additional marks, etc.) over something already printed. —*n.* **3.** something surprinted.

surprisal (sə prī′zəl), *n.* **1.** the act of surprising. **2.** the state of being surprised. **3.** a surprise.

surprise (sə prīz′), *v.,* **-prised, -prising,** *n.* —*v.t.* **1.** to come upon suddenly and unexpectedly; catch (a person, etc.) in the act of doing something; discover (a thing) suddenly. **2.** to assail, attack, or capture suddenly or without warning, as an army, fort, or person that is unprepared. **3.** to strike with a sudden feeling of wonder that arrests the thoughts, as at something unexpected or extraordinary. **4.** to bring out, esp. by a surprise: *to surprise the facts from the witness.* **5.** to lead or bring (a person, etc.) unawares, as into doing something not intended. —*n.* **6.** an act of surprising. **7.** a sudden assault, attack, or capture. **8.** a sudden and unexpected event, action, or the like. **9.** the state or feeling of being surprised as by something unexpected. **10.** something that excites this feeling, as an unexpected or extraordinary occurrence. **11. take by surprise, a.** to come upon unawares or without visible preparation. **b.** to catch unprepared. **c.** to amaze; astonish. —*adj.* **12.** sudden and unexpected: *a surprise attack.* [late ME, t. F, pp. of *surprendre* surprise, f. *sur-* SUR-[1] + *prendre* take] —**surpris′er,** *n.*

—**Syn. 3.** SURPRISE, ASTONISH, AMAZE, ASTOUND mean to strike with wonder because of unexpectedness, strangeness, unusualness, etc. To SURPRISE is to take unawares or to affect with wonder: *surprised by his sudden change of front.* To ASTONISH is to strike with wonder by something unlooked for, startling, or seemingly inexplicable: *astonished at his strange behaviour.* To AMAZE is to astonish so greatly as to disconcert or bewilder: *amazed at his complete loss of self-control.* To ASTOUND is to overwhelm with surprise that one is unable to think or act: *astounded by his utter callousness.*

surprising (sə prī′zĭng), *adj.* that surprises. —**surpris′ingly,** *adv.* —**surpris′ingness,** *n.*

surra (sōō′rə), *n. Vet. Sci.* a severe infectious disease of horses, camels, elephants, and dogs caused by a blood-infecting protozoan parasite, *Trypanosoma evansi.* [t. Marathi: m. *sūra* air breathed through the nostrils]

surrealism (sə rĭə′lĭz′əm), *n.* a movement in literature and art from about 1919, based on the expression of imagination uncontrolled by reason, and seeking to suggest the activities of the subconscious mind. [t. F: m. *surréalisme.* See SUR-[1], REALISM] —**surreal′ist,** *n., adj.* —**surrea′lis′tic,** *adj.* —**surrea′lis′tically,** *adv.*

surrebuttal (sû′rĭ bŭt′l), *n. Law.* the giving of evidence to meet a defendant's rebuttal.

surrebutter (sû′rĭ bŭt′ə), *n. Law.* a plaintiff's reply to a defendant's rebutter.

surrejoinder (sû′rĭ join′də), *n. Law.* a plaintiff's reply to a defendant's rejoinder.

surrender (sə rĕn′də), *v.t.* **1.** to yield (something) to the possession or power of another; deliver up possession of (something) upon demand or compulsion: *to surrender a fort.* **2.** to give (oneself) up, esp. as a prisoner or to some emotion, course of action, or the like. **3.** to give up, abandon, or relinquish (comfort, hope, etc.). **4.** to yield or resign (an office, privilege, etc.) in favour of another. **5.** *Obs.* to return: *to surrender thanks.* —*v.i.* **6.** to give oneself up, as into the power of another or of an emotion, course of action, etc.; submit or yield. —*n.* **7.** the act of surrendering. **8.** *Insurance.* the abandonment of a policy by the party insured, for a consideration, the amount receivable (**surrender value**) depending on the number of years elapsed from the commencement of the risk. **9.** the deed by which a legal surrendering is made. [late ME, t. AF, f. *sur-* SUR-[1] + *rendre* RENDER] —**Syn. 1.** See **yield. 4.** relinquish, waive, cede, resign, abandon. **6.** capitulate.

surreptitious (sŭ′rəp tĭsh′əs), *adj.* **1.** obtained, done, made, etc., by stealth; secret and unauthorized; clandestine: *a surreptitious glance.* **2.** acting in a stealthy way. **3.** obtained by subreption; subreptitious. [late ME, t. L: m. *surreptītius*, der. *subreptus*, pp., snatched away secretly] —**sur′repti′tiously,** *adv.* —**sur′repti′tiousness,** *n.*

surrey (sŭ′rĭ), *n., pl.* **-reys.** *U.S.* a light, four-wheeled, two-seat carriage, with or without a top, for four persons.

Surrey

Surrey (sŭ′rĭ), *n.* **1.** a county in SE England. 1,733,036 pop. (1961); 722 sq. mi. *Co. town:* Guildford. **2. Henry Howard, Earl of,** 1517?–47, English poet.

surrogate (*n.* sŭ′rə gĭt; *v.* sŭ′rə gāt′), *n., v.,* **-gated, -gating. 1.** one appointed to act for another; a deputy. **2.** the deputy of an ecclesiastical judge, esp. of a bishop or his chancellor. **3.** a substitute. **4.** *U.S.* a judicial officer having jurisdiction over the probate of wills, the administration of estates, etc. —*v.t.* **5.** to put into the place of another as a successor, substitute, or deputy; substitute for another. **6.** to subrogate. [t. L: m. s. *surrogātus*, pp., put in another's place] —**sur′rogateship′,** *n.* —**sur′roga′tion,** *n.*

surround (sə round′), *v.t.* **1.** to enclose on all sides, or encompass. **2.** to form an enclosure round; encircle. **3.** to enclose (a body of troops, fortification, or the like) so as to cut off communication or retreat. —*n.* **4.** a border which surrounds, as of uncovered floor around a carpet. **5.** (*pl.*) surroundings. **6.** *Hunting.* **a.** a method of catching wild beasts by encircling them and driving them to a chosen spot. **b.** the area surrounded. [late ME *suround*, t. AF: s. *surounder*, g. LL *superundāre* overflow; conformed to SUR-[1] + ROUND]

surrounding (sə roun′dĭng), *n.* **1.** that which surrounds. **2.** (*pl.*) environing circumstances, conditions, etc.; environment. **3.** the act of encircling or enclosing. —*adj.* **4.** that encloses or encircles. **5.** neighbouring; nearby; in the environment of.

sursum corda (sû′səm kô′də), *Latin.* **1.** lift up your hearts (a versicle in the Latin mass, answered by the people or choir *Habemus ad Dominum* 'We lift them up unto the Lord'). **2.** an encouraging exhortation.

surtax (sû′tăks′), *n.* **1.** one of a graded series of additional taxes levied on incomes exceeding a certain amount. **2.** an additional or extra tax on something already taxed. —*v.t.* **3.** to put an additional or extra tax on; charge with a surtax.

surtout (sû′tōō; *Fr.* sʏr tōō′), *n. Obs.* an overcoat. [t. F, f. *sur* SUR-[1] + *tout* (g. L *tōtus*) everything]

surv., **1.** surveying. **2.** surveyor.

surveillance (sû vā′ləns), *n.* **1.** watch kept over a person, etc., esp. over a suspect, a prisoner, or the like. **2.** supervision or superintendence. [t. F, der. *surveiller.* See SURVEILLANT]

surveillant (sû vā′lənt), *adj.* **1.** exercising surveillance. —*n.* **2.** one who exercises surveillance. [t. F, prop. ppr. of *surveiller*, f. *sur-* SUR-[1] + *veiller* (g. L *vigilāre*) watch over]

survey (*v.* sû vā′, sû′vā; *n.* sû′vā), *v., n., pl.* **-veys.** —*v.t.* **1.** to take a general or comprehensive view of. **2.** to view in detail, esp. to inspect or examine formally or officially in order to ascertain condition, value, etc. **3.** to determine the form, boundaries, position, extent, etc., of, as a part of the earth's surface, by linear and angular measurements and the application of the principles of geometry and trigonometry. **4.** to collect sample opinions, facts, figures or the like in order to estimate the total overall situation. —*v.i.* **5.** to survey land, etc.; practise surveying. —*n.* **6.** the act of surveying; a comprehensive view. **7.** a formal or official examination of the particulars of something made in order to ascertain condition, character, etc. **8.** a statement or description embodying the result of this. **9.** a determining of form, boundaries, position, extent, etc., as of a part of the earth's surface, by linear and angular measurements, etc. **10.** an organization or body of persons engaged in such an operation. **11.** the plan or description resulting from such an operation. **12.** a partial poll or gathering of sample opinions, facts or figures in order to estimate the total or overall situation. [ME *surveie(n)*, t. OF: m. *surveier*, ult. f. L *super-* SUPER- + *vidēre* see] —**sur·vey′able,** *adj.*

survey., surveying.

surveying (sû vā′ĭng), *n.* **1.** the process, occupation, or art of making surveys of land, etc. **2.** the act of one who surveys.

surveyor (sû vā′ə), *n.* **1.** one whose business it is to survey land, etc. **2.** an overseer or supervisor. **3.** one who inspects something officially for the purpose of ascertaining condition, value, etc. **4.** *Law.* an inspector of taxes. **5.** *U.S.* a customs officer whose duty it is to ascertain the quantity and value of imported merchandise. —**survey′orship′,** *n.*

surveyor's chain. See **chain** (def. 9).

surveyor's level. See **level** (defs 8, 9).

surveyor's measure, a system of units of length used in surveying land, based on the surveyor's chain of 66 feet.

survival (sə vī′vəl), *n.* **1.** the act or fact of surviving. **2.** one who or that which survives, esp. a surviving custom, observance, belief, or the like.

survival of the fittest, *Biol.* the fact or the principle of the survival of the forms of animal and vegetable life best fitted for existing conditions, while related but less fit forms become extinct. See **natural selection.**

survive (sə vīv′), *v.*, **-vived, -viving.** —*v.i.* **1.** to remain alive after the death of someone or after the cessation of something or the occurrence of some event; continue to live. **2.** to remain in existence after some person, thing, or event; continue to exist. **3.** *Colloq.* to remain unaffected or nearly so: *she doesn't love me, but I'll survive.* —*v.t.* **4.** to continue to live or exist after the death, cessation, or occurrence of; outlive. **5.** *Colloq.* to remain unaffected or nearly unaffected by. [late ME, t. AF: m. s. *survivre*, f. *sur-* SUR-[1] + *vivre* live, g. L *vīvere*] —**surviv′ing,** *adj.*

—**Syn.** 4. SURVIVE, OUTLIVE refer to remaining alive longer than someone else or after some event. SURVIVE usually means to succeed in keeping alive against odds, to live after some event which has threatened one: *to survive a motor-car accident.* It is also used of living longer than another person (usually a relative), but, today, mainly in the passive, as in the fixed phrase: *the deceased is survived by his wife and children.* OUTLIVE stresses capacity for endurance, the time element, and sometimes a sense of competition: *he outlived all his enemies.* It is also used, however, of one who has lived too long: *he has outlived his usefulness.*

survivor (sə vī′və), *n.* **1.** one who or that which survives. **2.** *Law.* that one of two or more designated persons, as joint tenants or others having a joint interest, who outlives the other or others. —**survi′vorship′,** *n.*

Susa[1] (sōō′sə), *n.* a ruined city in W Iran: the capital of ancient Elam; palaces of Darius I and Artaxerxes I. Biblical name, **Shushan.**

Susa[2] (*It.* sōō′zà), *n.* Sousse.

susceptance (sə sĕp′təns), *n.* *Elect.* the ratio of the reactance to the square of the impedance in an alternating-current circuit.

susceptibility (sə sĕp′tə bĭl′ĭ tĭ), *n.*, *pl.* **-ties.** **1.** the state or character of being susceptible: *susceptibility to disease.* **2.** capability of being affected, esp. easily; capacity for receiving mental or moral impressions; tendency to be emotionally affected. **3.** (*pl.*) capacities for emotion; sensitive feelings. **4.** *Elect.* the ratio of the magnetization produced in a substance to the magnetizing force. —**Syn.** 2. See **sensibility.**

susceptible (sə sĕp′tə bl), *adj.* **1.** capable of receiving, admitting, undergoing, or being affected by, something (fol. by *of* or *to*): *susceptible of a high polish, of various interpretations, etc.* **2.** accessible or especially liable: *susceptible to a disease, flattery.* **3.** capable of being affected, esp. easily; readily impressed; impressionable. [t. ML: m. s. *susceptibilis*, der. L *susceptus*, pp., taken up] —**suscep′tibleness,** *n.* —**suscep′tibly,** *adv.*

susceptive (sə sĕp′tĭv), *adj.* **1.** receptive. **2.** susceptible. —**susceptivity** (sŭs′ĕp tĭv′ĭ tĭ), **suscep′tiveness,** *n.*

suslik (sŭs′lĭk), *n.* **1.** a common ground squirrel or spermophile, *Citellus* (or *Spermophilus*) *citellus*, of Europe and Asia. **2.** the fur of this animal. [t. Russ.]

suspect (*v.* sə spĕkt′; *n.*, *adj.* sŭs′pĕkt), *v.t.* **1.** to imagine to be guilty, false, counterfeit, undesirable, defective, bad, etc., with insufficient proof or with no proof. **2.** to imagine or believe to be rightly chargeable with something stated, usually something wrong or something considered as undesirable, on little or no evidence: *to suspect a person of murder.* **3.** to imagine to be the case or to be likely; surmise: *I suspect his knowledge did not amount to much.* —*v.i.* **4.** to imagine something, esp. something evil, wrong, or undesirable, to be the case; have suspicion. —*n.* **5.** one suspected; a person suspected of a crime, offence, or the like. —*adj.* **6.** suspected; open to suspicion. [ME, t. L: s. *suspectus*, pp.] —**suspect′er,** *n.*

suspend (sə spĕnd′), *v.t.* **1.** to hang by attachment to something above. **2.** to attach so as to allow free movement, as on a hinge. **3.** to keep from falling or sinking, as if by hanging: *solid particles suspended in a liquid.* **4.** to hold or keep undetermined; refrain from forming or concluding definitely: *to suspend one's judgement.* **5.** to defer or postpone, as sentence on a convicted person. **6.** to cause to cease, or bring to a stop or stay, usually for a time: *to suspend payment.* **7.** to cause to cease for a time from operation or effect, as a law, rule, privilege, or the like. **8.** to debar, usually for a time, from the exercise of an office or function or the enjoyment of a privilege: *a student may be suspended for a breach of discipline.* **9.** to put or hold in a state of suspense. —*v.i.* **10.** to come to a stop, usually temporarily; cease from operation for a time. **11.** to stop payment; be unable to meet financial obligations. [ME *suspende(n)*, t. L: m. *suspendere*] —**Syn.** 6. intermit, discontinue, defer. See **interrupt.**

suspended animation, temporary cessation of the vital functions, as due to asphyxia.

suspender (sə spĕn′də), *n.* **1.** a strap with fastenings to support women's stockings, attached to a corset or belt. **2.** a similar device attached to a garter below the knee to support men's socks. **3.** (*pl.*) *U.S.* braces. **4.** (in a suspension bridge) one of the cables or chains which support the deck from the main suspension cables. **5.** one who or that which suspends.

suspender belt, a narrow belt or wide band of fabric or elastic, having suspenders attached to support women's stockings. Also, *U.S.*, **garter belt.**

suspense (sə spĕns′), *n.* **1.** a state of mental uncertainty, as in awaiting a decision or outcome, usually with more or less apprehension or anxiety. **2.** a state of mental indecision. **3.** undecided or doubtful condition, as of affairs: *for a few days matters hung in suspense.* **4.** the state or condition of being suspended; suspension. [ME, t. AF: m. *suspens*, in phrase *en suspens* in suspense, g. L *suspensus*, pp., suspended] —**suspense′ful,** *adj.*

suspense account, an account in which items are entered which, for some reason, cannot at once be placed in the account to which they are intended to go.

suspensible (sə spĕn′sə bl), *adj.* capable of being suspended. —**suspen′sibil′ity,** *n.*

suspension (sə spĕn′shən), *n.* **1.** the act of suspending. **2.** the state of being suspended. **3.** temporary abrogation, as of a law or privilege. **4.** stoppage of payment of debts, etc., through financial inability, or insolvency. **5.** *Phys. Chem.* the state in which particles of a solid are mixed with a fluid but are undissolved. **6.** *Phys. Chem.* a substance in such a state. **7.** *Phys. Chem.* a system consisting of small particles kept dispersed by agitation (in **mechanical suspension**), or by the molecular motion in the surrounding medium (in **colloidal suspension**). **8.** something on or by which something else is hung. **9.** the arrangement of springs, shock absorbers, hangers, etc., in a motor vehicle, railway carriage, etc., connecting the wheel-suspension units or axles to the chassis frame. **10.** *Elect.* a wire or filament by which the moving part of an instrument or device is suspended. **11.** *Music.* **a.** the prolongation of a note in one chord into the following chord, usually producing a temporary dissonance. **b.** the note so prolonged. **c.** the dissonance produced. [t. LL: s. *suspensio*]

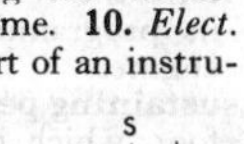

S, Suspension (def. 11a)

suspension bridge, a bridge in which the roadway or deck is suspended from cables, usually hung between towers of masonry or steel, and fastened at the extremities.

suspension point, *Chiefly U.S.* one of a group of dots or full stops which indicates ellipsis.

suspensive (sə spĕn′sĭv), *adj.* **1.** pertaining to or characterized by suspension. **2.** undecided in mind. **3.** pertaining to or characterized by suspense. **4.** (of words, phrases, etc.) keeping one in suspense. **5.** having the effect of suspending the operation of something. —**suspen′sively,** *adv.* —**suspen′siveness,** *n.*

suspensoid (sə spĕn′soid), *n.* *Chem.* a sol in which the disperse phase is solid. [b. SUSPENS(ION) + (COLL)OID]

suspensor (sə spĕn′sə), *n.* **1.** a suspensory ligament, bandage, etc. **2.** *Bot.* a row of cells formed by divisions of the zygote which push the embryo into the endosperm during the early development of a seed. [t. ML, der. L *suspensus,* pp., suspended]

suspensory (sə spĕn′sə rĭ), *adj., n., pl.* **-ries.** —*adj.* **1.** serving or fitted to suspend or hold up, as a ligament, muscle, bandage, etc. **2.** suspending the operation of something. —*n.* **3.** a suspensory bandage, ligament, muscle, or the like.

sus. per coll., *Law.* the note formerly made by a judge against the name of one convicted of a capital crime. [L *suspendātur per collum* let him be hanged by the neck]

suspicion (sə spĭsh′ən), *n.* **1.** the act of suspecting; imagination of the existence of guilt, fault, falsity, defect, or the like, on slight evidence or without evidence. **2.** the state of mind or feeling of one who suspects. **3.** the state of being suspected. **4.** an instance of suspecting something. **5.** imagination of anything to be the case or to be likely; a vague notion of something. **6.** a slight trace: *a suspicion of a smile.* —*v.t.* **7.** *Dial. and U.S. Colloq.* to suspect. [late ME, t. L: s. *suspicio*; r. ME *suspecioun,* t. AF, g. L *suspectio*]

—**Syn.** 2. doubt, mistrust, misgiving. SUSPICION, DISTRUST are terms for a feeling that appearances are not reliable. SUSPICION is the positive tendency to doubt the trustworthiness of appearances and therefore to believe that one has detected possibilities of something unreliable, unfavourable, menacing, or the like: *to feel suspicion about the honesty of a cashier.* DISTRUST is a passive want of trust, faith, or reliance in a person or thing: *to feel distrust of one's own ability.*

suspicional (sə spĭsh′ə nəl), *adj.* of or pertaining to suspicion, esp. morbid or insane suspicions.

suspicious (sə spĭsh′əs), *adj.* **1.** liable to cause or excite suspicion; questionable. **2.** inclined to suspect; esp., inclined to suspect evil; distrustful. **3.** full of or feeling suspicion. **4.** expressing or indicating suspicion. —**suspi′ciously,** *adv.* —**suspi′ciousness,** *n.*

suspiration (sŭs′pĭ rā′shən), *n.* a long, deep sigh.

suspire (sə spīr′), *v.i.,* **-spired, -spiring.** *Archaic.* **1.** to sigh. **2.** to breathe. [t. L: m. s. *suspīrāre* sigh]

Susquehanna (sŭs′kwĭ hăn′ə), *n.* a river in the U.S. flowing from central New York State through E Pennsylvania and NE Maryland into Chesapeake Bay. 444 mi.

Sussex (sŭs′ĭks), *n.* **1.** a county in SE England, now divided for administrative purposes into **East Sussex** and **West Sussex.** 1,075,893 pop. (1961); 1457 sq. mi. *Co. town:* Lewes. **2.** one of an English breed of chickens having white plumage with black markings. **3.** one of a breed of English red beef cattle.

Sussex spaniel, one of a breed of spaniels having short legs and a golden-liver coat.

sustain (sə stān′), *v.t.* **1.** to hold or bear up from below; bear the weight of; be the support of, as in a structure. **2.** to bear (a burden, charge, etc.). **3.** to undergo, experience, or suffer (injury, loss, etc.); endure without giving way or yielding. **4.** to keep (a person, the mind, the spirits, etc.) from giving way, as under trial or affliction. **5.** to keep up or keep going, as an action or process: *to sustain a conversation.* **6.** to supply with food and drink, or the necessities of life, as persons. **7.** to provide for by furnishing means or funds, as an institution. **8.** to support by aid or countenance, as a person or cause. **9.** to uphold as valid, just, or correct, as a claim or the person making it. **10.** to confirm or corroborate, as a statement. [ME *susteine,* t. OF: m. *sustenir,* g. L *sustinēre*] —**sustain′able,** *adj.* —**sustain′ment,** *n.* —**Syn. 1.** See **support.**

sustainer (sə stā′nə), *n. Aerospace.* an engine that maintains the velocity of a rocket vehicle, once it has achieved its programmed velocity through the use of a booster engine.

sustaining pedal, a pedal on a piano operated by the right foot, which holds the dampers off the strings and thus prolongs the note. Also, **loud pedal.**

sustaining program, *U.S.* a radio or television programme without a commercial sponsor.

sustenance (sŭs′tĭ nəns), *n.* **1.** means of sustaining life; nourishment. **2.** means of livelihood. **3.** the process of sustaining. **4.** the state of being sustained.

sustentacular (sŭs′tĕn tăk′yŏŏ lə), *adj. Anat.* supporting. [f. s. L *sustentāculum* a support + -AR[1]]

sustentation (sŭs′tĕn tā′shən), *n.* **1.** maintenance in being or activity; the sustaining of life through vital processes. **2.** provision with means or funds for upkeep. **3.** means of sustaining life; sustenance. [ME, t. L: s. *sustentātio*] —**sustentative** (sŭs′tĕn tā′tĭv, sə stĕn′tətĭv), *adj.*

sustention (sə stĕn′shən), *n.* **1.** the act of sustaining. **2.** the state or quality of being sustained. [coinage on model of DETENTION] —**sustentive** (sə stĕn′tĭv), *adj.*

susurrant (syōō sŭ′rənt), *adj.* softly murmuring; whispering. [t. L: s. *susurrans,* ppr.]

susurration (syōō′sə rā′shən), *n.* a soft murmur; whisper.

susurrus (syōō sŭ′rəs), *n.* a soft murmuring sound; whisper. [t. L]

Suth., Sutherland.

Sutherland (sŭth′ə lənd), *n.* **1. Graham (Vivian),** born 1903, English painter. **2. Joan,** born 1926, Australian soprano. **3.** a county in N Scotland. 13,442 pop. (1961); 2028 sq. mi. *Co. town:* Dornoch.

Sutherland Falls, a waterfall in New Zealand, in SW South Island. 1904 ft.

Sutlej (sŭt′lĭj), *n.* a river flowing from SW Tibet through NW India into the river Indus in West Pakistan. ab. 900 mi.

sutler (sŭt′lə), *n.* a person who follows an army and sells provisions, etc., to the soldiers. [t. early mod. D: m. *soeteler,* der. *soetelen* have a humble occupation]

sutra (sōō′trə), *n.* **1.** (*also cap.*) *Sanskrit Lit.* one of a body of aphoristic rules forming a link between the Vedic and the later Sanskrit literature. **2.** concise rules or teachings, chiefly in Hindu or Buddhist literature. Also, **sutta** (sŏŏt′ə). [t. Skt: thread, rule]

suttee (sŭ tē′, sŭt′ē), *n.* **1.** a former Hindu practice in which a widow immolated herself on the funeral pyre of her husband. **2.** a Hindu widow who immolated herself in this manner. [t. Skt: m. *satī* faithful wife] —**suttee′ism,** *n.*

Sutter's Mill (sŭt′əz), the place in central California, NE of Sacramento, near which gold was discovered (1848), precipitating the gold rush of 1849.

Sutton (sŭt′n), *n.* a S outer London borough. 169,019 (est. 1964).

Sutton Coldfield (sŭt′n kōld′fēld′), a town in England, in Warwickshire, near Birmingham. 72,165 (1961).

Sutton Hoo (sŭt′n hōō′), an archaeological site in Suffolk: an Anglo-Saxon ship and various precious ornaments, etc., discovered here, were possibly buried in honour of a king of East Anglia about A.D. 650.

Sutton-in-Ashfield (sŭt′n ĭn ăsh′fēld′), *n.* a town in England, in Nottinghamshire. 40,438 (1961).

suture (sōō′chə), *n., v.,* **-tured, -turing.** —*n.* **1.** *Surg.* **a.** a joining of the lips or edges of a wound or the like by stitching or some similar process. **b.** a particular method of doing this. **c.** one of the stitches or fastenings employed. **2.** *Anat.* **a.** the line of junction of two bones, esp. of the skull, in an immovable articulation. **b.** the articulation itself. **3.** *Zool., Bot.* the line of junction, or the junction, of contiguous parts, as the line of closure between the valves of a bivalve shell, a seam where carpels of a pericarp join, etc. **4.** a seam as formed in sewing; a line of junction between two parts. **5.** a sewing together, or a joining as by sewing. —*v.t.* **6.** to unite by or as by a suture. [t. L: m. *sūtūra*] —**su′tural,** *adj.* —**su′turally,** *adv.*

suum cuique (sōō′ŏŏm kwē′kwā), *Latin.* his own to each; to each what rightfully belongs to him.

Suva (sōō′və), *n.* a seaport in and the capital of Fiji, on Viti Levu island. 54,160 (1966).

Suvla Bay (sōōv′lə), a bay on the W coast of Gallipoli Peninsula in European Turkey: landing of Anzacs and battle, Aug. 1915.

Suvorov (*Russ.* sōō vô′rəf), *n.* **Aleksandr Vasilevich** (*Russ.* ə lĭk sän′dər vä sē′lyĭ vĭch) (*Count Suvorov Rumnikski, Prince Italiski*), 1729–1800, Russian field marshal.

Suwannee (sōō wŏn′ĭ), *n.* a river in the U.S., in SE Georgia and N Florida, flowing SW to the Gulf of Mexico. ab. 240 mi. Also, **Swanee.**

suzerain (sōō′zə rān′), *n.* **1.** a sovereign or a state exercising political control over a dependent state. **2.** *Hist.* a feudal overlord. —*adj.* **3.** characteristic of, or being, a suzerain. [t. F, der. *sus* above (g. L *su(r)sum* upwards), modelled on *souverain* sovereign]

suzerainty (sōō′zə rən tĭ), *n., pl.* **-ties.** the position or authority of a suzerain.

Suzuka (sōō′zōō kə, sōō zōō′kə), *n.* a town in Japan, in S central Honshu island. 100,594 (1965).

S.V., **1.** (L *Sancta Virgo*) Holy Virgin. **2.** (L *Sanctitas Vestra*) Your Holiness.

s.v., **1.** sailing vessel. **2.** sub verbo. **3.** sub voce.

Svalbard (*Nor.* sväl′bär), *n.* Norwegian name of **Spitsbergen.**

svarabhakti (svŭ′rə bŭk′tĭ), *n. Linguistics.* the insertion of a vowel between *r* or *l* and a following consonant, as the pronunciation of *film* as (fĭl′əm) in some British English dialects. [t. Skt: f. *svara* vowel + *bhakti* apportionment]

svelte (svĕlt), *adj.* slender, esp. gracefully slender in figure; lithe. [t. F, t. It.: m. *svelto,* lit., plucked]

Svengali (svĕng gä′lĭ), *n.* a person who moulds or creates another. [after a character in George Du Maurier's novel, '*Trilby*']

Sverdlovsk (*Russ.* svĭr dlôfsk′), *n.* a city in the W Soviet

Union in Asia, on the E slope of the Ural Mountains: execution of Tsar Nicholas II and his family, 1918. 919,000 (est. 1965). Formerly, **Ekaterinburg.**

Sverige (*Sw.* svĕ′ryə), *n.* Swedish name of **Sweden.**

Svevo (*It.* zvĕ′vô), *n.* **Italo** (*It.* ē′tä lô) (*Ettore Schmitz*), 1861–1928, Italian novelist.

Svizzera (*It.* zvēt′tsĕ rä), *n.* Italian name of **Switzerland.**

Svoboda (*Cz.* svŏ′bŏ dä), *n.* **General Ludvik** (*Cz.* lōōd′vĕk), born 1895, Czechoslovak statesman: president since 1968.

SW, 1. south-west. **2.** south-western.

Sw., 1. Sweden. **2.** Swedish.

S.W., 1. South Wales. **2.** south-west. **3.** south-western.

swab (swŏb), *n., v.,* **swabbed, swabbing.** —*n.* **1.** a large mop used on shipboard for cleaning decks, etc. **2.** *Med.* a piece of sponge, cloth, cottonwool, or the like, often mounted on a stick, for cleansing the mouth of a sick person, or for applying medicaments, taking specimens of discharges and secretions, etc. **3.** the material collected with a swab. **4.** a cleaner for the bore of a firearm. **5.** *Slang.* a contemptible or useless person. —*v.t.* **6.** to clean with or as with a swab. **7.** to take up, or apply, as moisture, with or as with a swab. **8.** to pass (a swab, etc.) over a surface. Also, **swob.** [back-formation from SWABBER]

swabber (swŏb′ə), *n.* one who uses a swab. [t. D: m. *zwabber*, der. *zwabben* slop about]

Swabia (swā′bĭ ə), *n.* **1.** a medieval duchy in SW Germany: it comprised the area now included in Baden-Württemberg and Bavaria. **2.** a district in S West Germany, in SW Bavaria. ab. 3900 sq. mi. *Cap.:* Augsburg. German, **Schwaben.** —**Swa′bian,** *adj., n.*

swaddle (swŏd′l), *v.,* **-dled, -dling,** *n.* —*v.t.* **1.** to bind (an infant, esp. a newborn infant) with long, narrow strips of cloth to prevent free movement; wrap tightly with clothes. **2.** to wrap (anything) round with bandages. —*n.* **3.** a long, narrow strip of cloth used for swaddling or bandaging. [ME *swathel*, OE *swæthel* swaddling band, akin to SWATHE[1], v.]

swaddling clothes, 1. clothes consisting of long, narrow strips of cloth for swaddling an infant. **2.** long clothes for an infant. **3.** the earliest period of existence of a person or thing; a period of infancy, immaturity, etc. **4.** a constricting influence; rigid supervision of actions, movement, etc.

swaddy (swŏd′ĭ), *n.* *Slang.* a soldier. [orig. uncert. Cf. d. *swad* lout]

Swadeshi (swə dā′shĭ), *n.* (formerly in India) **1.** the encouragement of domestic production and the boycott of foreign, esp. British, goods as a step towards home rule. —*adj.* **2.** made in India. [t. Bengali: native products]

Swadlincote (swŏd′lĭng kōt′), *n.* a town in England, in Derbyshire. 19,222 (1961).

swag[1] (swăg), *n., v.,* **swagged, swagging.** —*n.* **1.** a wreath of flowers, fruit, etc., fastened up at both ends and hanging down in the middle, used as an ornament. **2.** a swaying or lurching movement. —*v.i.* **3.** to move heavily or unsteadily or up and down; sway. **4.** to hang loosely and heavily; sink down. —*v.t.* **5.** to cause to sway, sink, or sag. [prob. t. Scand.; cf. Norw. *svagga* sway]

swag[2] (swăg), *n., v.,* **swagged, swagging.** —*n.* **1.** *Slang.* plundered property; booty. **2.** *Austral.* a bundle or roll carried across the shoulders or otherwise, and containing the personal belongings of a traveller through the bush, a miner, etc.; shiralee; bluey. —*v.i.* **3.** *Austral.* to travel about carrying one's bundle of personal belongings. [special use of SWAG[1]]

swage (swāj), *n., v.,* **swaged, swaging.** —*n.* **1.** a tool for bending cold metal to a required shape. **2.** a tool, die, or stamp for giving a particular shape to metal on an anvil, in a stamping press, etc. **3.** swage block. —*v.t.* **4.** to bend or shape by means of a swage. [ME, t. OF: m. *souage*]

A B C

Swages (def. 1)
A, Collar swage;
B, Spring swage;
C, Guide swage

swage block, an iron block containing holes and grooves of various sizes, used for heading bolts and shaping objects not easily worked on an anvil.

swagger (swăg′ə), *v.i.* **1.** to walk or strut with a defiant or insolent air. **2.** to boast or brag noisily. —*v.t.* **3.** to bring, drive, force, etc., by blustering. —*n.* **4.** swaggering gait, bearing, or air; arrogant show of affected superiority. [freq. of SWAG[1]] —**swag′gerer,** *n.* —**swag′geringly,** *adv.* —**Syn. 1.** See **strut**[1].

swagger stick, a short stick or cane sometimes carried by army officers, soldiers, etc.

swaggie (swăg′ĭ), *n.* *Austral. Colloq.* a swagman.

swagman (swăg′măn′), *n.* *Austral.* **1.** a tramp. **2.** one who carries a swag.

Swahili (swä hē′lĭ), *n., pl.* **-lis,** (*esp. collectively*) **-li. 1.** a member of a Bantu people with a large infusion of Arab blood, who inhabit Zanzibar and the neighbouring coast of Africa. **2.** their language, a lingua franca in E and central Africa. [t. Ar.: coastal] —**Swahi′lian,** *adj.*

swain (swān), *n.* *Chiefly Poetic.* **1.** a country lad. **2.** a country gallant. **3.** a lover. [early ME *swein* servant, t. Scand.; cf. Icel. *sveinn* boy] —**swain′ish,** *adj.* —**swain′ishness,** *n.*

swale (swāl), *n.* a low place in a tract of land, usually moister and often having a ranker vegetation than the adjacent higher land. [orig. cool spot. Cf. Icel. *svalr* cool]

swallow[1] (swŏl′ō), *v.t.* **1.** to take into the stomach through the throat or gullet (oesophagus), as food, drink, or other substances. **2.** to take in so as to envelop; withdraw from sight; assimilate; consume (often fol. by *up*). **3.** *Colloq.* to accept without question or suspicion. **4.** to accept without opposition; put up with: *to swallow an insult.* **5.** to suppress (emotion, a laugh, sob, etc.) as if by drawing it down one's throat. **6.** to take back or retract (one's words, etc.). —*v.i.* **7.** to perform the act of swallowing. —*n.* **8.** the act of swallowing. **9.** a quantity swallowed at one time; a mouthful. **10.** capacity for swallowing. **11.** *Naut.* the space in a block between the groove of the sheave and the shell, through which the rope runs. [ME *swolwe*, var. of *swelwe*, OE *swelgan*, c. G *schwelgen*] —**swal′lowable,** *adj.* —**swal′lower,** *n.*

swallow[2] (swŏl′ō), *n.* **1.** any of numerous small, long-winged passerine birds constituting the family *Hirundinidae*, notable for their swift, graceful flight and for the extent and regularity of their migrations, as the common swallow, *Hirundo rustica*, of both Old and New Worlds. **2.** a swallow-like bird not of this family, as, in America, the chimney swallow, *Chaetura pelagica.* [ME *swalwe*, OE *swealwe*, akin to G *Schwalbe*] —**swal′low-like′,** *adj.*

swallow dive, a dive in which the diver while in the air assumes a position with arms outstretched to the side, legs straight and together.

swallow-hole (swŏl′ō hōl′), *n.* a sinkhole.

swallowtail (swŏl′ō tāl′), *n.* **1.** a swallow's tail, or a deeply forked tail like that of a swallow. **2.** any of various butterflies of the family *Papilionidae*, having the hind wings prolonged so as to suggest the tail of a swallow as *Papilio machaon* of Europe, North Africa, Asia, and North America. **3.** a swallow-tailed coat.

Swallowtail butterfly, *Papilio machaon* (¾ in. long, wingspan 3 in.)

swallow-tailed (swŏl′ō tāld′), *adj.* **1.** having a deeply forked tail like that of a swallow, as various birds. **2.** having an end or part suggesting a swallow's tail.

swallow-tailed coat, a man's dress coat having the lower part cut away over the hips and descending in a pair of tapering skirts behind.

swallow-wort (swŏl′ō wûrt′), *n.* **1.** the greater celandine, *Chelidonium majus.* **2.** any of various asclepiadaceous plants, esp. a herb, *Vincetoxicum officinale* (or *Cynanchum vincetoxicum*) of Europe, with an emetic root formerly esteemed as a counterpoison.

swam (swăm), *v.* pt. of **swim.**

swami (swä′mĭ), *n., pl.* **-mis.** a title for a Hindu religious teacher. [t. Hind.: master, t. Skt: m. *svāmin*]

swamp (swŏmp), *n.* **1.** a piece or tract of wet, spongy land; marshy ground. **2.** a tract of soft, wet ground having a growth of certain kinds of trees, but unfit for cultivation. —*v.t.* **3.** to flood or drench with water or the like. **4.** *Naut.* to sink or fill (a boat) with water. **5.** to plunge or sink in or as in a swamp. **6.** to overwhelm. **7.** to render helpless. —*v.i.* **8.** to fill with water and sink, as a boat. **9.** to sink or stick in or as in a swamp. **10.** to be plunged into or overwhelmed with difficulties, etc. [akin to SUMP] —**swamp′ish,** *adj.* —**swamp′less,** *adj.*

swamphen (swŏmp′hĕn′), *n.* any of the Old World and Australasian aquatic birds of the genus *Porphyrio*, of the rail family, as the **purple swamphen,** *Porphyrio porphyrio.*

swampland (swŏmp′lănd′), *n.* land covered with swamps.

swampy (swŏm′pĭ), *adj.,* **-pier, -piest. 1.** of the nature of, resembling, or abounding in swamps. **2.** found in swamps.

swan[1] (swŏn), *n.* **1.** any large, stately swimming bird of the subfamily *Cygninae*, having a

Mute swan, *Cygnus olor* (5 ft long)

long, slender neck, such as the **mute swan** (*Cygnus olor*) of Europe, Asia, and North Africa. **2.** a person or thing of unusual beauty, excellence, purity, or the like. **3.** a sweet singer or poet. **4.** *Astron.* (*cap.*) the northern constellation Cygnus. [ME and OE, c. G *Schwan*] **—swan′like′,** *adj.*

swan² (swŏn), *v.i.* *U.S. Dial.* to swear (used chiefly as an exclamation of surprise): *I swan!* [prob. alter. of d. (North.) *Is' wan* I shall warrant]

Swan (swŏn), *n.* a river in SW Western Australia flowing NW then W to the Indian Ocean. The upper course or Avon river (220 mi.) is connected to the **Lower Swan** (40 mi.) by 20 mi. of rapids.

Swanee (swŏn′ĭ), *n.* Suwannee.

swanee whistle, *Music.* a simple woodwind instrument worked by a plunger, used esp. in traditional jazz recordings.

swang (swăng), *v.* *Archaic and Dial.* pt. of **swing**¹.

swanherd (swŏn′hûd′), *n.* one who tends swans.

swank (swăngk), *n.* **1.** *Colloq.* dashing smartness, as in bearing, appearance, etc.; style. **2.** swagger. **—*adj.*** **3.** *Colloq.* pretentiously stylish. **—*v.i.*** **4.** to swagger in behaviour; show off. [? akin to MLG *swank* supple, MHG *swanken* sway]

swanky (swăng′kĭ), *adj.*, **-kier, -kiest.** *Colloq.* **1.** conceited; boastful. **2.** expensive; smart; luxurious. **—swank′ily,** *adv.* **—swank′iness,** *n.*

swan maiden, one of a class of fabled maidens, in many Indo-European and Asiatic tales, capable of transforming themselves into swans, as by a robe or shift of swan's feathers or a magic ring or chain.

swan neck, a curve in a tube, pipe, handrail, etc., shaped like the neck of a swan; an S-shaped bend.

swannery (swŏn′ə rĭ), *n.*, *pl.* **-ries.** a place where swans are kept and reared.

swan's-down (swŏnz′doun′), *n.* **1.** the down or under plumage of a swan, used for trimming, powder puffs, etc. **2.** a fine, soft, thick woollen cloth. Also, **swansdown.**

Swansea (swŏn′zĭ), *n.* a seaport in Wales, in Glamorganshire. 167,322 (1961). See map under **Wales.**

swanskin (swŏn′skĭn′), *n.* **1.** the skin of a swan, with the feathers on. **2.** a kind of fine twilled flannel.

swan song, 1. the fabled song of the dying swan. **2.** the last work, utterance, or achievement of a poet, a composer, or other person, before his death or retirement.

swan-upping (swŏn′ŭp′ĭng), *n.* **1.** the taking up of young swans to mark them with nicks on the beak as a sign of being owned by the Crown or some corporation. **2.** an annual expedition for this purpose on the Thames. [f. SWAN¹ + *upping*, der. UP, v.]

swap (swŏp), *v.*, **swapped, swapping,** *n.* **—*v.t.*** **1.** to exchange, barter, or trade, as one thing for another. **—*v.i.*** **2.** to make an exchange. **—*n.*** **3.** an exchange. Also, **swop.** [ME *swappe* strike, strike hands (in bargaining), c. d. G *schwappen* box (the ear)] **—swap′per,** *n.*

swaraj (swə räj′), *n.* (in India) **1.** self-government. **2.** (*cap.*) (formerly in British India) the political party supporting this principle. [t. Hind.: m. *svarāj*, f. Skt: *sva* own + *rāj* rule] **—swaraj′ism,** *n.* **—swaraj′ist,** *n.*, *adj.*

sward (swôd), *n.* **1.** the grassy surface of land; turf. **2.** a stretch of turf; a growth of grass. **—*v.t.*** **3.** to cover with sward or turf. **—*v.i.*** **4.** to become covered with sward. [ME; OE *sweard* skin, c. G *Schwarte* rind]

sware (swĕə), *v.* *Archaic.* pt. of **swear.**

swarf (swôf, swäf), *n.* chips of metal, plastic, etc., removed by a cutting tool during machining or grinding. [ME, OE (*ge*)*swearf*; c. Icel. *svarf*]

swarm¹ (swôm), *n.* **1.** a body of honeybees which emigrate from a hive and fly off together under the direction of a queen, to start a new colony. **2.** a body of bees settled together, as in a hive. **3.** a great number of things or persons, esp. in motion. **4.** *Biol.* a group or aggregation of free-floating or free-swimming cells or organisms. **—*v.i.*** **5.** to fly off together in a body from a hive to start a new colony, as bees. **6.** to move about, along, forth, etc., in great numbers, as things or persons. **7.** to congregate or occur in swarms or multitudes; be exceedingly numerous, as in a place or area. **8.** (of a place) to be thronged or overrun; abound or teem (fol. by *with*). **9.** *Biol.* to move or swim about in a swarm. **—*v.t.*** **10.** to swarm about, over, or in; throng; overrun. **11.** to produce a swarm of. [ME; OE *swearm*, c. G *Schwarm*, Icel. *svarmr* tumult] **—Syn. 3.** multitude, throng. See **crowd.**

swarm² (swôm), *v.i.*, *v.t.* to climb (a tree, pole, or the like) by clasping it with the hands or arms and legs and drawing oneself up; shin (usually fol. by *up*). [special use of SWARM¹]

swarmer (swô′mə), *n.* **1.** one of a number that swarm; one of a swarm. **2.** *Biol.* a swarm spore.

swarm spore, *Biol.* any minute, motile, naked reproductive body produced in great numbers or occurring in groups or aggregations.

swart (swôt), *adj.* *Literary or Dial.* swarthy. Also, *Archaic or Dial.*, **swarth.** [ME; OE *sweart*, c. G *schwarz*] **—swart′ness,** *n.*

Swart (swôt), *n.* **Charles Robberts** (rŏb′əts), born 1894, South African statesman: president 1961–68.

Swartberg (swät′bûg′, swôt′-; *Afrik.* swŏrt′bĕrKH), *n.* Zwartberg.

swarthy (swô′thĭ), *adj.*, **-thier, -thiest.** dark-coloured, now esp. as the skin, complexion, etc., of a person. [var. of *swarty*, f. SWART + -Y¹] **—swarth′ily,** *adv.* **—swarth′iness,** *n.* **—Syn.** See **dusky.**

swash (swŏsh), *v.i.* **1.** to splash as things in water, or as water does. **2.** to dash about, as things in violent motion. **3.** to swagger. **—*v.t.*** **4.** to dash or cast violently, esp. to dash (water, etc.) about, down, etc. **—*n.*** **5.** a swashing blow, stroke, or movement, or the sound of it. **6.** the dashing of water, waves, etc. **7.** the sound made by such a dashing. **8.** the ground over which water washes. **9.** a channel of water through or behind a sandbank. [prob. imit.] **—swash′ingly,** *adv.*

swashbuckler (swŏsh′bŭk′lə), *n.* a swaggering swordsman or bully. Also, **swash′er.** [f. SWASH (i.e., strike swords against shields) + BUCKLER] **—swash′buck′ling,** *adj.*, *n.*

swash letter, *Print.* a decorative letter available in addition to normal ones, in certain founts of type.

swastika (swŏs′tĭ kə), *n.* **1.** a figure used as a symbol or an ornament in the Old World and in America since prehistoric times, consisting of a cross with arms of equal length, each arm having a continuation at right angles, and all four continuations turning the same way. **2.** this figure with clockwise arms as the official emblem of the Nazi Party and the Third Reich. [t. Skt: m. *svastika*, der. *svasti* well-being]

Nazi swastika

swat¹ (swŏt), *v.*, **swatted, swatting,** *n.* *Colloq.* **—*v.t.*** **1.** to hit with a smart or violent blow. **—*n.*** **2.** a smart or violent blow. Also, *U.S.*, **swot.** [orig. var. of SQUAT] **—swat′ter,** *n.*

swat² (swŏt), *v.*, **swatted, swatting,** *n.* swot².

Swat (swŏt), *n.* a former state in NW India, now forming part of West Pakistan.

swatch (swŏch), *n.* a sample of cloth or other material.

swath (swôth), *n.* **1.** the space covered by the stroke of a scythe or the cut of a mowing machine. **2.** the piece or strip so cut. **3.** a line or ridge of grass, grain, or the like, cut and thrown together by a scythe or mowing machine. **4.** a strip, belt, or long and relatively narrow extent of anything. Also, **swathe.** [ME; OE *swæth*, c. G *Schwade*]

swathe¹ (swāth), *v.*, **swathed, swathing,** *n.* **—*v.t.*** **1.** to wrap, bind, or swaddle with bands of some material; wrap up closely or fully. **2.** to enfold or envelop, as wrappings do. **3.** to wrap (cloth, a bandage, etc.) round something. **—*n.*** **4.** a band of linen or the like in which something is wrapped; a wrapping; a bandage. [ME; late OE *swathian*, der. *swath-* (in *swathum* bandages)] **—swath′er,** *n.*

swathe² (swāth), *n.* swath.

Swatow (swŏt′ou, swŏ tou′), *n.* a seaport in China, in Kwangtung province. 215,000 (est. 1954).

swatter (swŏt′ə), *n.* one who or that which swats.

sway (swā), *v.i.* **1.** to move to and fro, as something fixed at one end or resting on a support; swing to and fro. **2.** to move or incline to one side or in a particular direction. **3.** to incline in opinion, sympathy, tendency, etc. **4.** to fluctuate or vacillate, as in opinion. **5.** to wield power; exercise rule. **—*v.t.*** **6.** to cause to move to and fro; cause to incline from side to side. **7.** to cause to move to one side or in a particular direction. **8.** *Naut.* to hoist or raise, as a yard or topmast (usually fol. by *up*). **9.** to cause to fluctuate or vacillate. **10.** to cause (the mind, etc., or the person) to incline or turn in a specified way. **11.** to cause to swerve, as from a purpose or a course of action. **12.** to dominate; direct. **13. a.** *Archaic or Poetic.* to wield (a weapon or instrument, esp. the sceptre). **b.** to exercise rule or sovereignty over. **—*n.*** **14.** the act of swaying; swaying movement. **15.** rule; dominion. **16.** dominating power or influence. [ME, t. Scand.; cf. Icel. *sveigja* sway] **—sway′er,** *n.* **—sway′ingly,** *adv.* **—Syn. 1.** See **swing**¹.

sway-back (swā′băk′), *n.* an excessive downward curvature of the spinal column in the dorsal region, esp. of horses.

sway-backed (swā′băkt′), *adj.* having the back sagged to an unusual degree; having a sway-back.

Swazi (swä′zĭ), *n.*, *pl.* **-zis,** (*esp. collectively*) **-zi.** **1.** a member of a Bantu tribe of southern Africa, related to the Zulu. **2.** the Bantu language spoken by this people.

Swaziland (swä′zĭ lănd′), *n.* a British-protected state in

S Africa between S Mozambique and SE Transvaal in the Republic of South Africa. 280,300 pop. (est. 1962); 6704 sq. mi. *Cap.:* Mbabane.
sweal (swēl), *v.t., v.i. Dial.* **1.** to burn. **2.** to melt, as a candle; waste away. [ME *swelen,* OE *swǣlan* to burn; c. G *schwälen,* Icel. *svæla* burn out]
swear (swĕə), *v.,* **swore** or (*Archaic.*) **sware; sworn; swearing.** —*v.i.* **1.** to make a solemn declaration with an appeal to God or some superhuman being in confirmation of what is declared; make affirmation in a solemn manner by some sacred being or object, as the deity or the Bible. **2.** to engage or promise on oath or in a solemn manner; vow; bind oneself by oath (usually fol. by *to*). **3.** to give evidence or make any statement on oath or by solemn declaration (usually fol. by *to*). **4.** to use profane or taboo oaths or language, as in imprecation or anger or for mere emphasis.
—*v.t.* **5.** to declare or affirm by swearing by a deity, some sacred object, etc. **6.** to affirm or say with solemn earnestness or great emphasis. **7.** to promise or undertake on oath or in a solemn manner; vow. **8.** to testify or state on oath or by solemn declaration; make oath to (something stated or alleged). **9.** to take (an oath), as in order to give solemnity or force to a declaration, promise, etc. **10.** to administer an oath to; bind by an oath (usually fol. by *to*): *to swear someone to secrecy.*
—*v.* **11.** Some special verb phrases are:
swear at, to speak to with curses or blasphemies; abuse.
swear by, 1. to name (some sacred being or thing, etc.) as one's witness or guarantee in swearing. **2.** to rely on; have confidence in.
swear in, to admit to office or service by administering an oath.
swear off, *Colloq.* to promise to give up something, esp. intoxicating drink.
swear out, *U.S.* to secure (a warrant for arrest) by making an accusation under oath.
—*n.* **12.** *Colloq.* the act of swearing or cursing.
[ME *swere(n),* OE *swerian,* c. G *schwören*] —**swear′er,** *n.*
—**Syn. 4.** See **curse.**
swearword (swĕə′wûd′), *n.* a word used in swearing or cursing; an obscene or blasphemous word.
sweat (swĕt), *v.,* **sweat** or **sweated, sweating,** *n.* —*v.i.* **1.** to excrete watery fluid through the pores of the skin, as from heat, exertion, etc.; perspire, esp. freely or profusely. **2.** to exude moisture, as green plants piled in a heap. **3.** to gather moisture from the surrounding air by condensation. **4.** (of tobacco) to ferment. **5.** *Colloq.* to exert oneself strenuously; work hard. **6.** *Colloq.* to feel distress, as from anxiety, impatience, vexation, etc. —*v.t.* **7.** to emit (watery fluid, etc.) through the pores of the skin. **8.** to exude (moisture, etc.) in drops or small particles. **9.** to send forth or get rid of with or like perspiration (often fol. by *out* or *off*). **10.** to wet or stain with perspiration. **11.** to cause (a person, a horse, etc.) to sweat. **12.** to cause (substances, etc.) to exude moisture, esp. as a step in some industrial process of treating or preparing. **13.** to cause (persons, etc.) to work hard. **14.** to employ (workers) at low wages, for long hours or under other unfavourable conditions. **15.** *U.S. Slang.* to deprive (a person) of money, etc., as by exaction. **16.** *U.S. Slang.* to subject (a person) to severe questioning in order to extract information. **17.** *Metall.* **a.** to heat (metal) to partial fusion in order to remove an easily fusible constituent. **b.** to heat (solder or the like) until it melts; join (metal parts) by heating, esp. after applying solder. **18.** to remove part of the metal from (coins, esp. gold) by friction, as by shaking them in a bag. **19.** to cause (tobacco) to ferment. **20. sweat blood,** *Slang.* to be under a strain; be anxious; worry. **21. sweat it out,** *Slang.* to hold out; endure until the end. **22. sweat out,** to get rid of by sweating.
—*n.* **23.** the process of sweating or perspiring, as from heat, exertion, perturbation, disease, etc. **24.** the secretions of sweat glands; the product of sweating. **25.** a state or period of sweating. **26.** a process of inducing sweating or perspiration, or of being sweated, as in medical or other special treatment. **27.** moisture or liquid matter exuded from something or gathered on a surface in drops or small particles. **28.** an exuding of moisture by a substance, etc., or an inducing of such exudation, as in some industrial process. **29.** a run given to a horse for exercise, as before a race. **30.** *Colloq.* a state of perturbation, anxiety, or impatience. **31.** *Colloq.* hard work. [ME *swete(n),* OE *swǣtan,* c. D *zweeten,* G *schweissen*] —**sweat′less,** *adj.* —**Syn. 24.** See **perspiration.**
sweatband (swĕt′bănd′), *n.* a band in a hat or cap to protect it against sweat from the head.
sweatbox (swĕt′bŏks′), *n.* **1.** a device for sweating tobacco leaves, figs, etc. **2.** any confined space in which a person is made to sweat, esp. a cell in which a prisoner is confined.
sweated (swĕt′ĭd), *adj.* **1.** made by underpaid workers. **2.** underpaid and overworked. **3.** having poor working conditions.
sweater (swĕt′ə), *n.* **1.** a knitted jersey, usually of thick wool, worn by athletes during exercise, or for warmth, casual wear, etc. **2.** one who or that which sweats. **3.** an employer who underpays and overworks employees.
sweater girl, *Colloq.* a young woman with a well-developed bust, esp. one who wears tight sweaters to emphasize this.
sweat gland, *Anat.* one of the minute, coiled, tubular glands of the skin that secrete sweat; a sudoriferous gland.
sweating sickness, a febrile epidemic disease which appeared in the 15th and 16th centuries, characterized by profuse sweating, and frequently fatal in a few hours.
sweating system, the practice of employing workers in sweatshops.
sweatshirt (swĕt′shût′), *n.* a loose pullover worn esp. by athletes to prevent chill or to induce sweating.
sweatshop (swĕt′shŏp′), *n.* a workshop, or the like, employing workers at low wages during overlong hours, under insanitary or otherwise unfavourable conditions.
sweaty (swĕt′ĭ), *adj.,* **-ier, -iest. 1.** covered, moist, or stained with sweat. **2.** causing sweat. **3.** laborious. —**sweat′ily,** *adv.* —**sweat′iness,** *n.*
Swed., 1. Sweden. 2. Swedish.
Swede (swēd), *n.* **1.** a native or inhabitant of Sweden. **2.** (*l.c.*) a cultivated variety of a cruciferous plant, *Brassica napus,* frequently grown for its edible, swollen taproot. **3.** the root itself. [t. MLG or MD]
Sweden (swē′dn), *n.* a kingdom in N Europe, in the E part of the Scandinavian peninsula. 7,695,200 pop. (est. 1964); 173,394 sq. mi. *Cap.:* Stockholm. Swedish, **Sverige.** See map under **Baltic.**
Swedenborg (swē′dn bôg′; *Sw.* svė′dən bŏry), *n.* **Emanuel** (*Sw.* ė mȧ′nōō ĕl) (orig. *Emanuel Swedberg*), 1688–1772, Swedish scientist, philosopher, theologian, and mystic.
Swedenborgian (swē′dn bô′jyən), *adj.* **1.** pertaining to Emanuel Swedenborg, or to his religious doctrines, or to the body of followers adhering to these doctrines and constituting the Church of the New Jerusalem, or New Church. —*n.* **2.** a believer in the religious doctrines of Swedenborg. —**Swe′denbor′gianism,** *n.*
Swedish (swē′dĭsh), *adj.* **1.** of or pertaining to Sweden, its inhabitants, or their language. —*n.* **2.** a Germanic language, the language of Sweden and parts of Finland, closely related to Danish and Norwegian. **3.** the people of Sweden collectively.
Swedish massage, a massage utilizing Swedish movements.
Swedish movements, a system of muscular exercises for hygienic or therapeutic purposes.
sweeny (swē′nĭ), *n. Vet. Sci.* atrophy of the shoulder muscles in horses. [cf. d. G *Schweine* atrophy]
sweep (swēp), *v.,* **swept, sweeping,** *n.* —*v.t.* **1.** to move, drive, or bring, by passing a broom, brush, or the like over the surface occupied, or as the broom or other object does: *to sweep dust away.* **2.** to move, bring, take, etc., by or as by a steady, driving stroke or with continuous, forcible actions: *the wind sweeps the snow into drifts.* **3.** to pass or draw (something) over a surface, or about, along, etc., with a steady, continuous stroke or movement: *to sweep a brush over a table.* **4.** to clear or clean (a floor, room, chimney, etc.) of dirt, litter, etc., by means of a broom or the like. **5.** to make (a path, etc.) by clearing a space with a broom or the like. **6.** to clear (a surface, place, etc.) of something on or in it: *to sweep the sea of enemy ships.* **7.** to pass over (a surface, region, etc.) with a steady, driving movement or unimpeded course, as winds, floods, etc. **8.** to direct the gaze over (a region, etc.) with the unaided eye or with a telescope or the like; survey with a continuous view over the whole extent. **9.** to win an overwhelming victory, as in an election: *the Labour Party swept the polls in the 1965 election.* **10.** *Music.* **a.** to pass the fingers or bow over (a musical instrument, its strings or keys, etc.) as in playing. **b.** to bring forth (music) thus.
—*v.i.* **11.** to sweep a floor, room, etc., as with a broom, or as a broom does: *a new broom sweeps clean.* **12.** to move steadily and strongly or swiftly (fol. by *along, by, down over,* etc.). **13.** to pass in a swift but stately manner, as a person, a procession, etc. **14.** to walk in long, trailing garments. **15.** to trail, as garments, etc. **16.** to move or pass in a continuous course, esp. a wide curve or circuit: *his glance swept about the room.* **17.** to extend in a continuous or curving stretch, as a road, a shore, fields, etc. **18.** to conduct an underwater search by towing a drag under the surface of the water, as for mines, a lost anchor, or the like.

—*n.* **19.** the act of sweeping, esp. a moving, removing, clearing, etc., by or as by the use of a broom: *to abolish all class distinctions at one sweep.* **20.** the steady, driving motion or swift onward course of something moving with force or unimpeded: *the sweep of the wind or waves.* **21.** a trailing movement, as of garments. **22.** a swinging or curving movement or stroke, as of the arm or a weapon, oar, etc. **23.** reach, range, or compass, as of something sweeping about: *the sweep of a road about a marsh.* **24.** a continuous extent or stretch: *a broad sweep of sand.* **25.** a curving, esp. widely or gently curving, line, form, part, or mass. **26.** matter removed or gathered by sweeping. **27.** a lever-like device for raising or lowering a bucket in a well, consisting essentially of a long pole pivoted on an upright post. **28.** a large oar used in small vessels, sometimes to assist the rudder in turning the vessel but usually to propel the craft. **29.** one who sweeps, esp. a chimney-sweep. **30.** *Cards.* **a.** (in whist) the winning of all the tricks in a hand. Cf. **slam**² (def. 1). **b.** (in cassino) a pairing or combining, and hence taking, of all the cards on the board. **31.** *Physics.* **a.** an irreversible process tending towards thermal equilibrium. **b.** the motion of the spot across the screen of a cathode-ray tube. **32.** a sweepstake. **33.** *Colloq.* a disreputable person; scoundrel. **34. make a clean sweep,** to get rid of completely.
[ME *swepe*; cf. OE *geswēpa* sweepings, akin to *swāpan* sweep, c. G *schweifen*] —**sweep′er,** *n.*

sweepback (swēp′băk′), *n. Aeron.* the shape of, or the angle formed by, an aeroplane wing whose leading or trailing edges slope backwards. —**swept′back′,** *adj.*

sweeping (swē′pĭng), *adj.* **1.** of wide range or scope; far-reaching. **2.** moving or passing about over a wide area: *a sweeping glance.* **3.** moving, driving, or passing steadily or forcibly on. **4.** without limitations; indiscriminate; disregarding details: *a sweeping statement.* **5.** decisive; overwhelming: *a sweeping victory.* —*n.* **6.** the act of one that sweeps. **7.** (*pl.*) matter swept out or up, as dust, refuse, etc.: *put the sweepings in this box.* —**sweep′ingly,** *adv.* —**sweep′ingness,** *n.*

sweep's brush, a common woodrush, *Luzula campestris.*

sweepstake (swēp′stāk′), *n.* **1.** a race or other contest in which the prize consists of the stakes contributed by the various competitors. **2.** the prize itself. **3.** a method of gambling, as on the outcome of a horserace, in which each participant contributes a stake, usually by buying a numbered ticket entitling him to draw the name of a competitor, the winnings being provided from the stake money. Also, **sweep′stakes′.** [f. SWEEP + STAKE²]

sweet (swēt), *adj.* **1.** pleasing to the taste, esp. having the pleasant taste or flavour characteristic of sugar, honey, etc. **2.** not rancid, or stale; fresh. **3.** fresh as opposed to salt, as water. **4.** pleasing to the ear; making a pleasant or agreeable sound; musical. **5.** pleasing to the smell; fragrant; perfumed. **6.** pleasing or agreeable; yielding pleasure or enjoyment; delightful. **7.** pleasant in disposition or manners; amiable; kind or gracious, as a person, action, etc. **8.** dear; beloved; precious. **9.** easily managed; done or effected without effort. **10.** (of wine) sweet-tasting (opposed to *dry*). **11.** free from sourness or acidity, as soil. **12.** *Chem.* **a.** devoid of corrosive or acidic substances. **b.** (of substances such as petrol) containing no sulphur compounds. **13.** *Jazz.* performed with a regular beat, moderate tempo, and with melodic harmony. **14. sweet on,** *Colloq.* in love with; fond of.
—*adv.* **15.** in a sweet manner; sweetly.
—*n.* **16.** sweet taste or flavour; sweet smell; sweetness. **17.** that which is sweet. **18.** any of various small confections made wholly or partly from sugar crystallized by boiling. **19.** any sweet dish, as a pudding, tart, fruit, etc., served at the end of a meal; suite. **20.** something pleasant to the mind or feelings. **21.** a beloved person; darling; sweetheart.
[ME and OE *swēte*, c. D *zoet*, G *süss*, Icel. *sǣtr*, akin to Goth. *suts*, L *suāvis*] —**sweet′ly,** *adv.* —**sweet′ness,** *n.*
—**Syn. 1.** sugary, honeyed. **4.** melodious, mellifluous, harmonious. **7.** winning, lovable, charming.

Sweet (swēt), *n.* **Henry,** 1845–1912, English philologist and linguist.

sweet alyssum, a cruciferous garden plant, *Lobularia maritima,* with small white or violet flowers.

sweet-and-sour (swēt′n sou′ə), *adj.* (of a sauce) flavoured with sugar and vinegar and used with meat, esp. pork, fish, etc., as in oriental cookery.

sweet basil, a plant of the mint family, *Ocimum basilicum,* whose leaves are used in cookery.

sweet bay, laurel (def. 1).

sweetbread (swēt′brĕd′), *n* **1.** the pancreas (**stomach sweetbread**) of an animal, esp. a calf or a lamb, used for food. **2.** the thymus gland (**neck sweetbread** or **throat sweetbread**), likewise so used.

sweetbrier (swēt′brī′ə), *n.* a rose, *Rosa rubiginosa,* a native of Europe and central Asia, with a tall stem, stout-hooked prickles often mixed with bristles, and single pink flowers; the eglantine. Also, **sweetbriar.**

sweet cherry, any of several cultivated forms of the rosaceous tree, *Prunus avium,* having sweet fruit.

sweet chestnut, Spanish chestnut.

sweet cicely, any of several umbelliferous plants nearly allied to chervil, as an English species, *Myrrhis odorata,* sometimes used as a potherb, or some species of the North American genus *Osmorhiza.*

sweet cider, cider which has not fermented.

sweet clover, melilot.

sweet corn, **1.** any maize of a sweetish flavour and suitable for eating, esp. a particularly sweet variety, *Zea mays* v. *saccharata.* **2.** the unripe and tender ears of maize, esp. when used as a table vegetable and when the kernels have been removed from the cob; green corn.

sweeten (swē′tn), *v.t.* **1.** to make sweet. **2.** to make mild or kind; soften. **3.** to make (the breath, air, etc.) sweet or fresh, as with a mouthwash, spray, etc. **4.** to alleviate; make less disagreeable. **5.** *Slang.* to bribe. **6.** *Slang.* (in poker) to increase (a pot) by adding stakes before opening. —*v.i.* **7.** to become sweet.

sweetener (swēt′nə), *n.* **1.** one who or that which sweetens. **2.** *Slang.* a bribe.

sweetening (swēt′nĭng), *n.* **1.** something that sweetens food, etc. **2.** the process of causing something to be sweet.

sweet fern, a small North American shrub, *Comptonia peregrina* (*Myrica asplenifolia*), with aromatic fernlike leaves.

sweet flag, an araceous plant, *Acorus calamus,* with long, sword-shaped leaves and a pungent, aromatic rootstock; calamus.

sweet gale, gale²; bog myrtle.

sweet gum, the American liquidambar, *Liquidambar styraciflua.* or the balsamic liquid exuded by it.

sweetheart (swēt′hät′), *n.* **1.** one of a pair of lovers with relation to the other, sometimes esp. the girl or woman. **2.** a beloved person (often used in affectionate address).

sweetie (swē′tĭ), *n. Colloq.* **1.** a sweetheart (often used as a term of endearment). **2.** a sweet; confection.

sweeting (swē′tĭng), *n.* **1.** a sweet variety of apple. **2.** *Archaic.* a beloved person; darling; sweetheart.

sweetish (swē′tĭsh), *adj.* somewhat sweet. —**sweet′ishly,** *adv.* —**sweet′ishness,** *n.*

sweet marjoram, marjoram.

sweetmeat (swēt′mēt′), *n.* **1.** a sweet delicacy, prepared with sugar, honey, or the like, as preserves, sweets, or (formerly) cakes or pastry. **2.** (*usually pl.*) any sweet delicacy of the confectionery kind, as crystallized fruit, sugar-covered nuts, sweets, bonbons, etc.

sweet oil, olive oil.

sweet pea, an annual climbing plant, *Lathyrus odoratus,* bearing sweet-scented flowers.

sweet pepper, any of the mild-flavoured peppers, *Capsicum frutescens* v. *grossum,* used for stuffing, pickling, or as a vegetable.

sweet potato, **1.** a convolvulaceous plant of central America, *Ipomaea batatas,* widely cultivated in the tropics for its edible root. **2.** the root.

sweet-scented (swēt′sĕn′tĭd), *adj.* having a pleasantly sweet smell; fragrant.

sweetshop (swēt′shŏp′), *n.* a shop that sells sweets.

sweet spirit of nitre, *Pharm.* an alcoholic solution of ethyl nitrite, $C_2H_5NO_2$, employed medicinally as a diaphoretic, diuretic, and antispasmodic.

sweet-tempered (swēt′tĕm′pəd), *adj.* having a kind and gentle disposition.

sweet tooth, *Colloq.* a strong liking for sweets, sweet dishes, etc.

sweet vernal grass, a perennial grass with a strong smell of new-mown hay, *Anthoxanthum odoratum,* widespread in N temperate regions.

sweet william, a kind of pink, *Dianthus barbatus,* bearing small flowers of various colours in dense clusters.

swell (swĕl), *v.,* **swelled, swollen** or **swelled, swelling,** *n., adj.* —*v.i.* **1.** to grow in bulk, as by absorption of moisture, by inflation or distention, by addition of material in the process of growth, or the like. **2.** to rise in waves, as the sea. **3.** to well up, as a spring or as tears. **4.** to bulge out or be protuberant, as a sail, a cask in the middle. **5.** to grow in amount, degree, force, or the like. **6.** to increase gradually in volume or intensity, as sound. **7.** to arise and grow within one, as a feeling or emotion. **8.** to become puffed up with pride; behave or talk arrogantly or pretentiously.
—*v.t.* **9.** to cause to grow in bulk. **10.** to increase gradually in loudness, as a musical note. **11.** to cause (a thing) to bulge out or be protuberant. **12.** to increase in amount,

degree, force, etc. **13.** to affect with swelling emotion. **14.** to puff up with pride.
—*n.* **15.** the act of swelling. **16.** condition of being swollen. **17.** increase in bulk; inflation or distention. **18.** a part that bulges out, or a protuberant part. **19.** a wave, esp. when long and unbroken, or such waves collectively. **20.** a gradually rising elevation of the land. **21.** increase in amount, degree, force, etc. **22.** gradual increase in loudness of sound. **23.** *Music.* **a.** a gradual increase (crescendo) followed by a gradual decrease (diminuendo) in loudness or force of musical sound. **b.** the sign (< >) for indicating this. **c.** a contrivance, as in an organ, by which the loudness of notes may be varied. **24.** a swelling of emotion within one. **25.** *Slang.* **a.** a fashionably dressed person. **b.** a person of high social standing.
—*adj. Slang.* **26.** (of things) stylish; elegant; grand: *a swell hotel.* **27.** (of persons) fashionably dressed; of high standing, esp. socially. **28.** first-rate; excellent.
[ME; OE *swellan*, c. G *schwellen*] —**Ant. 1.** contract.

swell box, *Music.* a box or chamber containing a set of pipes in a pipe organ or of reeds in a reed organ, and having movable slats or shutters which can be opened or closed to increase or diminish the loudness of the notes.

swelled head, *Colloq.* an excessively high opinion of oneself; conceit.

swellfish (swĕl′fĭsh′), *n., pl.* **-fishes,** (*esp. collectively*) **-fish.** puffer (def. 2).

swelling (swĕl′ĭng), *n.* **1.** the act of one that swells. **2.** the condition of being swollen. **3.** a swollen part; a protuberance or prominence. **4.** *Pathol.* an abnormal enlargement or protuberance.

swell organ, *Music.* **1.** the section of an organ which is fitted with a swell box. **2.** the stops which control it.

swelter (swĕl′tə), *v.i.* **1.** to suffer or languish with oppressive heat; perspire profusely from heat. —*v.t.* **2.** to oppress, or cause to languish, with heat. **3.** *Archaic.* to exude like sweat, as venom. —*n.* **4.** a sweltering condition. [ME *sweltre*, freq. of *swelt* die, swoon, OE *sweltan*, c. Icel. *svelta*]

sweltering (swĕl′tə rĭng), *adj.* **1.** suffering or languishing with oppressive heat. **2.** characterized by oppressive heat, as a place, the weather, etc.; sultry. —**swel′teringly,** *adv.*

swempi (swĕm′pĭ), *n.* the light-winged partridge or francolin, *Francolinus coqui.* [t. Zulu: *inswempe*]

swept (swĕpt), *v.* pt. and pp. of **sweep.**

sweptback (swĕpt′băk′), *adj. Aeron.* (of the wing of an aircraft) having its leading and trailing edges slanted backwards relative to its longitudinal axis.

sweptwing (swĕpt′wĭng′), *adj. Aeron.* (of an aircraft, etc.) having sweptback wings.

swerve (swûv), *v.,* **swerved, swerving,** *n.* —*v.i.* **1.** to turn aside abruptly in movement or direction; deviate suddenly or sharply from the straight or direct course. —*v.t.* **2.** to cause to turn aside. —*n.* **3.** the act of swerving; a turning aside; a deviation. **4.** that which swerves. [ME; OE *sweorfan* rub, file, c. D *zwerven* rove] —**swerv′er,** *n.* —**Syn. 1.** See **deviate.**

swift (swĭft), *adj.* **1.** moving with great speed or velocity; fleet; rapid: *a swift ship.* **2.** coming, happening, or performed quickly or without delay. **3.** quick or prompt to act, etc.: *swift to act.* —*adv.* **4.** swiftly. —*n.* **5.** any of the rapidly flying birds of the families *Apodidae* and *Hemiprocnidae*, such as *Apus apus*, the common swift of Europe and Asia. **6.** any of various small lizards, esp. of the genus *Sceloporus*, which run with great swiftness. **7.** an adjustable device upon which a hank of yarn is placed in order to wind off skeins or balls. [ME and OE; akin to SWEEP] —**swift′ly,** *adv.* —**swift′ness,** *n.* —**Syn. 1.** speedy, fast. See **quick.** —**Ant. 1.** slow.

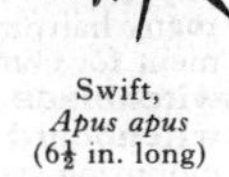

Swift, *Apus apus* (6½ in. long)

Swift (swĭft), *n.* **Jonathan** (*Dean Swift*), 1667–1745, English satirist and cleric, born in Ireland.

swifter (swĭf′tə), *n. Naut.* **1.** a small line joining the outer ends of the bars of a capstan to confine them to their sockets while the capstan is being turned. **2.** the forward shroud of the lower rigging on either side of a mast. **3.** *Obs.* a rope used to encircle a boat lengthways in order to strengthen and defend its sides. [der. *swift*, v., tie fast; cf. Icel. *svipta* to reef (sails)]

swift-footed (swĭft′fo͝ot′ĭd), *adj.* swift in running.

swig (swĭg), *n., v.,* **swigged, swigging.** *Colloq.* —*n.* **1.** a large or deep drink, esp. of alcoholic liquor, taken in one swallow; draught. —*v.t., v.i.* **2.** to drink heartily or greedily. —**swig′ger,** *n.*

swill (swĭl), *n.* **1.** liquid or partly liquid food for animals, esp. kitchen refuse given to pigs; pigswill. **2.** kitchen refuse in general; rubbish. **3.** any liquid matter; slops. **4.** a deep draught of alcoholic drink, esp. beer. —*v.i.* **5.** to drink greedily or excessively. —*v.t.* **6.** to drink (something) greedily or to excess; guzzle. **7.** to wash or cleanse by flooding with water. [ME *swile(n)*, OE *swilian*, var. of *swillan*; orig. unknown] —**swil′ler,** *n.*

swim (swĭm), *v.,* **swam, swum, swimming,** *n.* —*v.i.* **1.** to move along or in water by movements of the limbs, fins, tail, etc.; move on or in water or other liquid in any way, esp. on the surface. **2.** to float on the surface of water or other liquid. **3.** to move, rest, or be suspended in air or the like, as if swimming in water. **4.** to move, glide, or go smoothly over a surface. **5.** to be immersed or steeped in, or overflowed or flooded with, a liquid. **6.** to be dizzy or giddy; have a whirling sensation; seem to whirl. —*v.t.* **7.** to move along on or in by swimming; float on or in; cross by swimming, as a stream. **8.** to cause to swim; cause to float, as on a stream. **9.** to furnish with sufficient water to swim or float. **10.** to perform (a particular stroke) in swimming. —*n.* **11.** an act, instance, or period of swimming. **12.** a motion as of swimming; a smooth gliding movement. **13. in the swim,** actively engaged in current affairs, social activities, etc. [ME *swimme(n)*, OE *swimman*, c. G *schwimmen*] —**swim′mer,** *n.*

swim bladder, an air-bladder (def. 2).

swimmeret (swĭm′ə rĕt′), *n.* (in many crustaceans) one of a number of abdominal limbs or appendages, usually adapted for swimming, and for carrying eggs, and thus distinguished from other limbs adapted for walking or seizing.

swimming (swĭm′ĭng), *n.* **1.** the act or technique of swimming. **2.** vertigo; dizziness. —*adj.* **3.** capable of, adapted for, or used in swimming. **4.** immersed in or overflowing with, or as with, water. **5.** having a sensation of dizziness, vertigo, etc.

swimming bath, a swimming pool, esp. an indoor one.

swimming costume, a close fitting garment or garments worn when swimming.

swimmingly (swĭm′ĭng lĭ), *adv.* without difficulty; with great success.

swimming pool, an artificial pool, esp. one in the open air, for swimming in.

swimming trunks, a pair of trunks worn by men when swimming.

swimsuit (swĭm′syo͞ot′), *n.* swimming costume.

Swinburne (swĭn′bûn′), *n.* **Algernon Charles** (ăl′jə nən), 1837–1909, English poet and critic.

swindle (swĭn′dl), *v.,* **-dled, -dling,** *n.* —*v.t.* **1.** to cheat (a person) out of money, etc. **2.** to obtain by fraud or deceit. —*v.i.* **3.** to put forward plausible schemes or use unscrupulous artifice to defraud others; cheat; defraud. —*n.* **4.** the act of swindling; a fraudulent transaction or scheme. **5.** anything deceptive; a fraud. [back-formation from *swindler*, t. G: m. *Schwindler*, der. *schwindeln* be giddy, swindle] —**swin′dler,** *n.*

Swindon (swĭn′dən), *n.* a town in England, in Wiltshire: railway works. 91,739 (1961).

swine (swīn), *n., pl.* **swine. 1.** the domestic pig. **2.** any animal of the same family, *Suidae*, of the artiodactyl suborder *Suina*, as the European wild boar, *Sus scrofa*, or of the closely related peccary family of the New World, *Tayassuidae*. **3.** a coarse, gross, or brutishly sensual person. **4.** a contemptible person. [ME; OE *swīn*, c. G *Schwein*; akin to SOW²]

swinecress (swīn′krĕs′), *n.* any of the small cruciferous herbs of the genus *Coronopus*, as *C. squamatus*, a widespread plant of waste places which can withstand considerable treading.

swine fever, a specific, acute, usually fatal, highly contagious disease of swine caused by a filterable virus. Also, *U.S.*, **hog cholera.**

swineherd (swīn′hûd′), *n.* one who herds or tends swine.

swine pox, 1. a variety of chickenpox. **2.** *Vet. Sci.* a mild pox disease of swine, caused by a virus related to that of cowpox and characterized by the appearance of pustules in the skin, esp. of the abdomen.

swing¹ (swĭng), *v.,* **swung** or (*Archaic and Dial.*) **swang; swung; swinging,** *n.* —*v.t.* **1.** to cause to move to and fro, sway, or oscillate, as something suspended from above: *ladies swinging their parasols.* **2.** to cause to move in alternate directions, or in either direction, about a fixed point or line of support, as a door on its hinges. **3.** to move (something held or grasped) with an oscillating or rotary movement: *swing a club about one's head.* **4.** to cause to move in a curve as if about a central point. **5.** to suspend so as to hang freely, as a hammock or a door. **6.** to sway, influence, or manage as desired: *to swing the voting in an election.*

—*v.i.* **7.** to move to and fro, as something suspended from above, as a pendulum. **8.** to move to and fro on a swing, as for amusement. **9.** to move in alternate directions, or in either direction, about a point or line of support, as a gate on its hinges. **10.** to move in a curve as if about a central point, as around a corner. **11.** to move with a free, swaying motion, as soldiers on the march. **12.** to be suspended so as to hang freely, as a bell, etc. **13.** *Colloq.* to suffer death by hanging. **14.** to change or shift one's attention, opinion, interest, etc.; fluctuate. **15.** to aim at or hit something with a sweeping movement of the arm. **16.** *Slang.* **a.** to be characterized by a lively, modern, or knowledgeable attitude to life. **b.** (of two people) to be in mental or spiritual harmony; be in accord in outlook or feeling. **c.** (of a place) to have a lively atmosphere.
—*n.* **17.** the act or the manner of swinging; movement in alternate directions, or in a particular direction. **18.** the amount of such movement. **19.** a curving movement or course. **20.** a moving of the body with a free, swaying motion, as in walking. **21.** a steady, marked rhythm or movement, as of verse or music. **22.** *U.S. Colloq.* a shift or period of work. **23.** *U.S.* freedom of action: *have free swing.* **24.** active operation: *to get into the swing of things.* **25.** something that is swung or that swings. **26.** a seat suspended from above as in a loop of rope or between ropes or rods, in which one may sit and swing to and fro for amusement. **27.** a steady rhythm or movement, as in a piece of poetry, music, etc. **28. in full swing,** *Colloq.* fully active; operating at maximum speed or with maximum efficiency.
[ME; OE *swingan*, c. G *schwingen.* Cf. OE *swinge* blow]
—**Syn. 7.** SWING, SWAY, OSCILLATE, ROCK suggest a movement back and forth. SWING expresses the comparatively regular motion to and fro of a body supported from the end or ends, esp. from above: *a lamp swings from the ceiling.* To SWAY is to swing gently: *the lantern sways in the breeze.* OSCILLATE refers to the smooth, regular, alternating movement of a body within certain limits between two fixed points: *a pendulum oscillates.* ROCK indicates the slow and regular movement back and forth of a body as on curved supports: *a cradle rocks.*

swing[2] (swĭng), *n., adj., v.,* **swung, swinging.** —*n.* **1.** Also, **swing music.** a smooth, orchestral type of jazz popular in the 1930s; often arranged for big bands. **2.** the rhythmic element that excites dancers and listeners to move in time to jazz music. —*adj.* **3.** of, pertaining to, or characteristic of, swing music. —*v.t.* **4.** to play (a piece of music) in the style of swing. [special use of SWING[1]]

swing boat, a boat-shaped carriage suspended from a frame for swinging in at a fairground.

swing bridge, a bridge which is pivoted at its centre and opens horizontally to allow ships to pass; pivot bridge.

swing door, a door that opens on being pushed or pulled from either side and swings shut by itself.

swinge (swĭnj), *v.t.,* **swinged, swinging.** *Archaic.* to whip; punish. [ME *swenge* shake, smite, OE *swengan*, causative of *swingan* SWING] —**swinger** (swĭn′ jə), *n.*

swingeing (swĭn′jĭng), *adj. Colloq.* **1.** forcible; strong. **2.** great; large.

swinger (swĭng′ə), *n.* **1.** one who or that which swings. **2.** *Slang.* an active, lively, or modern person.

swinging (swĭng′ĭng), *adj.* **1.** characterized by or capable of swinging or being swung. **2.** *Slang.* fine; excellent. **3.** *Slang.* lively, active, vigorous, and modern. —**swing′-ingly,** *adv.*

swinging post, the post from which a door or gate hangs.

swingle (swĭng′gl), *n., v.,* **-gled, -gling.** —*n.* **1.** a wooden instrument shaped like a large knife, for beating flax or hemp and scraping from it the woody or coarse portions. —*v.t.* **2.** to clean (flax or hemp) by beating and scraping with a swingle. [ME *swyngel*, t. MD: m. *swinghel*, c. OE *swingell* rod]

swingletree (swĭng′gl trē′), *n.* whippletree.

swing shift, *U.S. Colloq.* **1.** a work shift in industry, from mid-afternoon (usually 3 p.m.) until 12 midnight. **2.** a group of workers on this shift.

swing-wing (swĭng′wĭng′), *adj. Aeron.* **1.** denoting or pertaining to an aircraft wing which can be swung from one position to another in flight in order to provide the best characteristics both for take-off and low speeds as well as for supersonic flight. —*n.* **2.** an aircraft fitted with such wings.

swinish (swī′nĭsh), *adj.* like or befitting swine; brutishly gross or sensual. —**swin′ishly,** *adv.* —**swin′ishness,** *n.*

swink (swĭngk), *v.i.* **swank** or **swonk, swonken, swinking,** *n. Archaic.* labour; toil. [ME; OE *swincan*, akin to SWING[1]] —**swink′er,** *n.*

Swinton (swĭn′tən), *n.* **1.** a town in England, in Lancashire. (with Pendlebury) 40,470 (1961). **2.** a town in England, in the West Riding of Yorkshire. 13,420 (1961).

swipe (swīp), *n., v.,* **swiped, swiping.** —*n.* **1.** *Colloq.* a sweeping stroke; a stroke with full swing of the arms, as in cricket or golf. **2.** a lever-like device for raising or lowering a weight, esp. a bucket in a well; a sweep. —*v.t.* **3.** *Colloq.* to strike with a sweeping blow. **4.** *Slang.* to steal. —*v.i.* **5.** *Colloq.* to make a sweeping stroke. [akin to SWEEP]

swipes (swīps), *n.pl.* **1.** poor, washy beer; small beer. **2.** malt liquor in general. [? der. *swipe*, v., drink at a gulp, special use of SWIPE]

swipple (swĭp′l), *n.* the freely swinging part of a flail, which falls upon the grain in threshing; a swingle. Also, **swiple.** [ME *swepelles* broom, OE *swǣpels(e)* robe; akin to SWEEP]

swirl (swûl), *v.i.* **1.** to move about or along with a whirling motion; whirl; eddy. **2.** to be dizzy or giddy, or swim, as the head. —*v.t.* **3.** to cause to swirl or whirl; twist. —*n.* **4.** a swirling movement; a whirl; an eddy. **5.** a twist, as of hair about the head or of trimming on a hat. [? imit.; ? akin to d. Norw. *svirla*, D *zwirrelen* whirl, d. G *schwirrlen* totter]

swirly (swû′lĭ), *adj.* swirling, whirling, or twisted.

swish (swĭsh), *v.i.* **1.** to move with or make a sibilant sound, as a slender rod cutting sharply through the air, or as small waves washing on the shore. **2.** to rustle, as silk. —*v.t.* **3.** to flourish, whisk, etc., with a swishing movement or sound: *to swish a cane.* **4.** to bring, take, etc., with or as with such a movement or sound: *to swish off the tops of plants with a cane.* **5.** to flog or whip. —*n.* **6.** a swishing movement or sound. **7.** a stock or rod for flogging, or a stroke with this. **8.** *U.S. Slang.* a male homosexual. —*adj.* **9.** *Slang.* smart. [imit.]

Swiss (swĭs), *adj.* **1.** of, pertaining to, associated with or characteristic of Switzerland or its inhabitants. —*n.* **2.** a native or inhabitant of Switzerland. **3.** Also, **Swiss muslin.** a thin crisp fabric, often with woven or printed dots or figures. [t. F: m. *Suisse*, t. MHG: m. *Swiz*]

Swiss chard, chard (def. 3).

Swiss cheese, Emmenthaler.

Swiss Guard, a member of a corps of bodyguards protecting the pope, membership of which is restricted to natives of Switzerland.

swiss roll, a rolled sponge cake filled with jam or cream.

Swit., Switzerland. Also, **Switz., Swtz.**

switch (swĭch), *n.* **1.** a slender, flexible shoot, rod, etc., used esp. in whipping, beating, etc. **2.** the act of switching; a stroke, lash, or whisking movement. **3.** a slender growing shoot, as of a plant. **4.** a separate bunch or tress of long hair (or some substitute) fastened together at one end, worn by women to supplement their hair. **5.** *Elect.* a device for turning on or off or directing an electric current, or making or breaking a circuit. **6.** *Chiefly U.S.* point (def. 41). **7.** a turning, shifting, or changing: *a switch of votes to another candidate.* **8.** *Bridge.* a change to a suit other than the one played or bid previously. **9.** a tuft of hair at the end of the tail of some animals.
—*v.t.* **10.** to whip or beat with a switch or the like; lash: *he switched the lad with a cane.* **11.** to move, swing, or whisk (a cane, a fishing line, etc.) like a switch, or with a swift, lashing stroke. **12.** to exchange; shift. **13.** to turn, shift, or divert: *to switch conversation from a painful subject.* **14.** *Elect.* to connect, disconnect, or redirect an electric circuit by operating a switch: *he switched on a light.* **15.** *Chiefly U.S.* shunt (def. 4).
—*v.i.* **16.** to strike with or as with a switch. **17.** to change direction or course; turn, shift, or change. **18.** to be shifted, turned, etc. by means of a switch. [cf. LG *swutsche*] —**switch′er,** *n.* —**switch′like′,** *adj.*

switchback (swĭch′băk′), *n.* **1.** a mountain road having many hairpin bends. **2.** *Railways.* a zigzag track arrangement for climbing a steep gradient. **3.** a roller-coaster.

switchblade (swĭch′blād′), *n.* a flick-knife.

switchboard (swĭch′bôd′), *n. Elect.* **1.** a structural unit mounting switches, instruments, and/or meters necessary for the control of electrical energy. **2.** an arrangement of switches, plugs, and jacks mounted on a board or frame enabling an operator to make temporary connections between telephone users.

switchbox (swĭch′bŏks′), *n. Elect.* a box housing one or more electrical switches.

switchgear (swĭch′gĭə′), *n. Elect.* any form of electrical switch, esp. for high voltages.

switchman (swĭch′mən), *n., pl.* **-men.** *U.S.* pointsman (def. 1).

switch-over (swĭch′ō′və), *n.* a changeover.

Switz., Switzerland.

Switzer (swĭt′sə), *n.* a Swiss. [t. MHG]

Switzerland (swĭt′sə lənd), *n.* a republic in central Europe. 5,429,061 pop. (1960); 15,944 sq. mi. *Cap.:* Bern. French, **Suisse.** German, **Schweiz.** Italian, **Svizzera.** See map under **Lombardy.**

swive (swīv), *v.t., v.i.,* **swived, swiving.** *Taboo, Archaic.*

to copulate (with). [ME *swyve(n)*, OE *swīfan* revolve. Cf. SWIVEL]

swivel (swĭv′əl), *n.*, *v.*, **-elled, -elling** or (*U.S.*) **-eled, -eling.** —*n.* **1.** a fastening device which allows the thing fastened to turn round freely upon it. **2.** such a device consisting of two parts, each of which turns round independently, as a compound link of a chain one part of which turns freely in the other by means of a headed pin or the like. **3.** a pivoted support for allowing a gun to turn round in a horizontal plane. **4.** a swivel gun. —*v.t.* **5.** to turn on or as on a swivel. **6.** to fasten by a swivel; furnish with a swivel. —*v.i.* **7.** to turn on a swivel, pivot, or the like. [ME *swyvel*, t. Scand.; cf. Icel. *sweifla* swing, akin to OE *swīfan* revolve] —**swiv′el-like′,** *adj.*

swivel chair, a chair whose seat revolves on a swivel.

swivel gun, a gun mounted on a pedestal so that it can be turned from side to side or up and down.

swivel pin, kingpin (def. 1).

swiz (swĭz), *n.* *Colloq.* **1.** a disappointment. **2.** a fraud; swindle.

swizzle (swĭz′əl), *n.* **1.** a drink composed of rum, crushed ice, lemon or lime juice, bitters and sugar. **2.** *Colloq.* a swindle. [orig. unknown]

swizzle stick, *Colloq.* a small rod for stirring drinks.

swob (swŏb), *n.*, *v.t.*, **swobbed, swobbing.** swab.

swollen (swō′lən), *v.* **1.** pp. of **swell.** —*adj.* **2.** Also, *Archaic,* **swoln** (swōln). swelled; enlarged by or as by swelling; puffed up; tumid. **3.** turgid or bombastic. —**swol′lenly,** *adv.* —**swol′lenness,** *n.*

swollen-headed (swō′lən hĕd′ĭd), *adj.* inordinately proud of oneself; conceited; vain.

swoon (swo͞on), *v.i.* **1.** to faint; lose consciousness. **2.** to become enraptured; enter a state of ecstasy. —*n.* **3.** a faint or fainting fit; syncope. [ME *swo(w)ne*, OE *geswōgen* in a swoon] —**swoon′ingly,** *adv.*

swoop (swo͞op), *v.i.* **1.** to sweep through the air, as a bird or a bat, esp. down upon prey. **2.** to come down in a sudden swift attack (often fol. by *down* or *on* or *upon*): *the enemy troops swooped down on the town.* —*v.t.* **3.** to take, lift, or remove, with, or as with, a sweeping motion (often fol. by *up*). —*n.* **4.** the act of swooping; a sudden, swift descent. **5. at one fell swoop,** all at once. [var. of ME *swope*, OE *swāpan* sweep]

swop (swŏp), *v.t.*, *v.i.*, **swopped, swopping,** *n.* swap.

sword (sôd), *n.* **1.** a weapon having various forms but consisting typically of a long, straight or slightly curved blade, sharp-edged on one side or both sides, with one end pointed and the other fixed in a hilt or handle. **2.** this weapon as the symbol of military power, punitive justice, authority, etc. **3.** a cause of death or destruction. **4.** war, combat, or slaughter; military force or power. **5. cross swords, a.** to join in combat. **b.** to argue; disagree violently. **6. put to the sword,** to massacre; slaughter. [ME; OE *sweord*, c. G *Schwert*] —**sword′less,** *adj.* —**sword′like′,** *adj.*

sword bayonet, a kind of short sword for attaching to the muzzle of a gun, to be used as a bayonet.

sword-bearer (sôd′bĕə′rə), *n.* an official who carries a sword on certain ceremonial occasions.

sword-belt (sôd′bĕlt′), *n.* a belt from which a sword is hung.

swordbill (sôd′bĭl′), *n.* a hummingbird, *Ensifera ensifera*, of South America, whose slender bill is longer than its body.

sword cane, a swordstick.

swordcraft (sôd′kräft′), *n.* **1.** knowledge of, or skill with, the sword. **2.** military skill or power.

sword dance, any of various dances performed with a sword in the hand or in which swords are laid on the ground and danced around.

swordfish (sôd′fĭsh′), *n.*, *pl.* **-fishes,** (*esp. collectively*) **-fish.** **1.** a large marine food fish, *Xiphias gladius*, with the upper jaw elongated into a swordlike weapon. **2.** (*cap.*) *Astron.* the southern constellation Dorado.

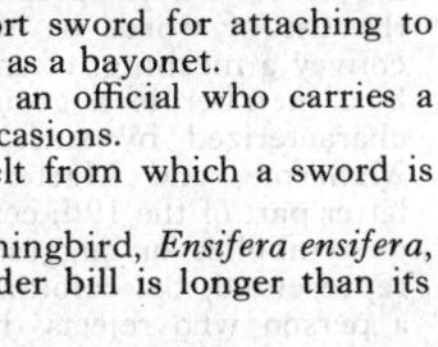

Swordfish, *Xiphias gladius* (Up to 14 ft long)

sword grass, any of various grasses or plants with swordlike or sharp leaves, as the sword lily.

sword knot, a looped strap, ribbon, or the like, attached to the hilt of a sword, as a support or ornament.

sword lily, a gladiolus.

swordplay (sôd′plā′), *n.* the action, practice, or art of wielding a sword; fencing.

swordsman (sôdz′mən), *n.*, *pl.* **-men.** **1.** one who uses, or is skilled in the use of, a sword. **2.** a fencer. **3.** a soldier. Also, **swordman.** —**swords′manship′,** *n.*

swordstick (sôd′stĭk′), *n.* a cane walking stick or the like, having a hollow shaft which serves as a sheath for a sword.

swordtail (sôd′tāl′), *n.* any of several small, viviparous, Mexican cyprinodont fishes of the genus *Xiphophorus*, commonly cultivated in home aquariums.

swore (swô), *v.* pt. of **swear.**

sworn (swôn), *v.* **1.** pp. of **swear.** —*adj.* **2.** having taken an oath; bound by or as by an oath. **3.** confirmed; inveterate; avowed.

swot[1] (swŏt), *v.t.*, **swotted, swotting,** *n.* *U.S.* swat[1].

swot[2] (swŏt), *v.*, **swotted, swotting,** *n.* *Slang.* —*v.i.* **1.** to study hard. —*v.t.* **2.** to study (a subject) hard. **3. swot up,** to make great efforts to learn, memorize, or completely familiarize oneself with. —*n.* **4.** Also, **swot′ter.** one who studies hard. [d. var. of SWEAT]

swound (swound), *n.*, *v.i.* *Archaic or Dial.* swoon.

'swounds (zwoundz, zoundz), *interj.* *Obs.* zounds.

Swtz., Switzerland.

swum (swŭm), *v.* pp. of **swim.**

swung (swŭng), *v.* pt. and pp. of **swing.**

sy-, var. of **syn-,** before *s* followed by a consonant, and before *z*, as in *systaltic.*

S.Y., steam yacht.

Sybaris (sĭb′ə rĭs), *n.* an ancient Greek city in S Italy: noted for its wealth and luxury; destroyed 510 B.C.

sybarite (sĭb′ə rīt′), *n.* **1.** (*cap.*) an inhabitant of Sybaris. **2.** one devoted to luxury and pleasure; an effeminate voluptuary. —**sybaritic** (sĭb′ə rĭt′ĭk), *adj.* —**syb′arit′ically,** *adv.*

sycamine (sĭk′ə mīn′), *n.* a mulberry (tree), probably the black mulberry. See Luke 17:6. [t. L: m. s. *sȳcamīnus*, t. Gk: *sȳkáminos*, t. Aram.: m. *shiqmīn* (pl.)]

sycamore (sĭk′ə mô′), *n.* **1.** (in Europe) a maple, *Acer pseudoplatanus*, grown as a shady ornamental tree and for its wood. **2.** (in the U.S.) the plane tree or buttonwood, *Platanus occidentalis.* **3.** a tree, *Ficus sycomorus*, of the Near East, allied to the common fig and bearing an edible fruit. [ME *sycomore*, t. LL: m. *sȳcomorus*, t. Gk: m. *sȳkómoros*]

syce (sīs), *n.* (in India) a groom. Also, **syce.** [t. Hind., t. Ar.: m. *sā'is*]

sycee (sī sē′), *n.* fine uncoined silver in lumps of various sizes usually bearing a banker's or assayer's stamp or mark, used in China as a medium of exchange. Also, **sycee silver.** [t. Chinese: m. *sai sz'*, Cantonese var. of Mandarin *si sz'* fine silk, so called because when pure it may be drawn out into fine threads]

syconium (sī kō′nyəm), *n.*, *pl.* **-nia** (-nyə). *Bot.* a multiple fruit developed from a hollow fleshy receptacle containing numerous flowers, as in the fig. [NL, f. m. Gk *sŷkon* fig + *-ium* -IUM]

sycophancy (sĭk′ə fən sī), *n.*, *pl.* **-cies.** **1.** self-seeking or servile flattery. **2.** the character or conduct of a sycophant.

sycophant (sĭk′ə fənt), *n.* a self-seeking flatterer; a fawning, servile parasite. [t. L: s. *sȳcophanta*, t. Gk: m. *sȳkophántēs* slanderer, false accuser] —**sycophantic** (sĭk′ə făn′tĭk), **syc′ophan′tical,** *adj.* —**syc′ophan′tically,** *adv.*

sycosis (sī kō′sĭs), *n.* *Pathol.* an inflammatory disease of the hair follicles, marked by a pustular eruption. [NL, t. Gk: m. *sȳkōsis*]

Sydney (sĭd′nĭ), *n.* **1. Sir Philip.** See **Sidney.** **2.** a seaport in Australia, the capital of New South Wales, in the E part. 2,300,100 (est. 1964). See map under **Canberra.** **3.** a seaport in Canada, in Nova Scotia, on NE Cape Breton Island. 33,617 (1961).

Syene (sī ē′nĭ), *n.* ancient name of **Aswan** (def. 1).

syenite (sī′ĭ nīt′), *n.* a granular igneous rock consisting typically of felspar (orthoclase) and hornblende. [t. L: m. s. *Syēnītēs* (*lapis*) (stone) of SYENE] —**syenitic** (sī′ĭ nĭt′ĭk), *adj.*

syl-, var. of **syn-** (by assimilation) before *l*, as in *syllepsis.*

syll., **1.** syllable. **2.** syllabus.

syllabary (sĭl′ə bə rĭ), *n.*, *pl.* **-baries.** **1.** a list or catalogue of syllables. **2.** a set of written symbols, each of which represents a syllable of the language to be written.

syllabi (sĭl′ə bī′), *n.* a pl. of **syllabus.**

syllabic (sĭ lăb′ĭk), *adj.* **1.** of, pertaining to, or consisting of a syllable or syllables. **2.** pronounced with careful distinction of syllables. **3.** of or pertaining to poetry based on the number of syllables as distinct from poetry depending on stresses or quantities. **4.** (of chanting, etc.) having each syllable sung to one note only. **5.** *Phonet.* syllable-forming or syllable-dominating; sonantal. —*n.* **6.** *Phonet.* a syllabic sound. See **sonant** (def. 3a). —**syllab′ically,** *adv.*

syllabicate (sĭ lăb′ĭ kāt′), *v.t.*, **-cated, -cating.** to syllabify. —**syllab′ica′tion,** *n.*

syllabify (sĭ lăb′ĭ fī′), *v.t.*, **-fied, -fying.** to form or divide into syllables. —**syllabification** (sĭ lăb′ĭ fĭ kā′-shən), *n.*

syllabism (sĭl′ə bĭz′əm), *n.* **1.** the use of syllabic characters, as in writing. **2.** division into syllables.

syllabize (sĭl′ə bīz′), *v.t.*, **-bized, -bizing.** to syllabify. Also, **syllabise.**

syllable (sĭl′ə bl), *n.*, *v.*, **-bled, -bling.** —*n.* **1.** *Phonet.* a segment of speech uttered with a single impulse of air-pressure from the lungs, and consisting of one sound of relatively great sonority (see **sonant,** def. 3a), with or without one or more subordinated sounds of relatively small sonority (see **consonant,** def. 1). **2.** (in writing systems) a character or a set of characters representing (more or less exactly) such an element of speech. **3.** the least portion or amount of speech or writing; the least mention: *do not breathe a syllable of all this.* —*v.t.* **4.** to utter in syllables; articulate. **5.** to represent by syllables. —*v.i.* **6.** to utter syllables; speak. [ME *sillable,* t. AF, var. of OF *sillabre,* t. L: m. *syllaba,* t. Gk: m. *syllabḗ*]

syllabub (sĭl′ə bŭb′), *n.* sillabub.

syllabus (sĭl′ə bəs), *n.*, *pl.* **-buses, -bi** (-bī′). **1.** an outline or summary of a course of studies, lectures, etc. **2.** subjects to be studied on a particular course, as at a school, university, etc. [t. NL: mistake for L *sittyba* title-slip on a book, t. Gk]

syllepsis (sĭ lĕp′sĭs), *n.*, *pl.* **-ses** (-sēz). *Gram.*, *Rhet.* the use of one word for two syntactical functions, as *are* in *neither he nor we are willing,* or in two senses, as *fought* in *he fought with desperation and his trusty sword.* [t. LL, t. Gk: a taking together] —**sylleptic** (sĭ lĕp′tĭk), *adj.* —**syllep′tically,** *adv.*

syllogism (sĭl′ə jĭz′əm), *n.* **1.** *Logic.* an argument with two premises and a conclusion. Both the premises of a **categorical syllogism** are categorical propositions, containing just three distinct terms between them, e.g. *all men are mortal* (major premise), *Socrates is a man* (minor premise), therefore *Socrates is mortal* (conclusion); at least one premise in a **hypothetical syllogism** is a hypothetical proposition, e.g. *if Smith is eligible to vote he is a citizen* (major premise), *Smith is eligible to vote* (minor premise), *therefore Smith is a citizen* (conclusion); at least one premise in a **disjunctive syllogism** is a disjunctive proposition, e.g. *either Smith is out of town or he is ill* (major premise). *Smith is not ill* (minor premise), *therefore he is out of town* (conclusion). **2.** deductive reasoning. [t. L: s. *syllogismus,* t. Gk: m. *syllogismós*; r. ME *silogime,* t. F]

syllogistic (sĭl′ə jĭs′tĭk), *adj.* Also, **syllogistical. 1.** of or pertaining to a syllogism. **2.** like or consisting of syllogisms. —*n.* **3.** that part of logic which deals with syllogisms. **4.** syllogistic reasoning. —**syl′logis′tically,** *adv.*

syllogize (sĭl′ə jīz′), *v.i.*, *v.t.*, **-gized, -gizing.** to argue or reason by syllogisms. Also, **syllogise.** —**syl′logiza′tion,** *n.* —**syl′logiz′er,** *n.*

sylph (sĭlf), *n.* **1.** a slender, graceful, lightly moving woman or girl. **2.** one of a race of imaginary beings supposed (orig. in the system of Paracelsus) to inhabit the air. [t. NL: s. *sylphes* (pl.) coined by Paracelsus] —**sylph′like′, sylph′ish, sylph′y,** *adj.*

—**Syn. 2.** SYLPH, SALAMANDER, UNDINE (NYMPH), GNOME were imaginary beings inhabiting the four elements once believed to make up the physical world. All except the GNOMES were feminine. SYLPHS dwelt in the air and were light, dainty, and airy beings. SALAMANDERS dwelt in fire: *'a salamander that . . . lives in the midst of flames'* (Addison). UNDINES were water spirits: *by marrying a man, an undine could acquire a mortal soul.* (They were also called NYMPHS, though nymphs were ordinarily minor nature divinities who dwelt in woods, hills, and meadows as well as in waters.) GNOMES were little old men or dwarfs, dwelling in the earth: *'ugly enough to be king of the gnomes'* (Hawthorne).

sylphid (sĭl′fĭd), *n.* **1.** a little or young sylph. **2.** a female sylph. [t. F: m. *sylphide,* der. *sylphe* SYLPH]

Sylva (sĭl′və), *n.* **Carmen** (kä′mĕn), 1843–1916, pen-name of Elizabeth, Queen of Rumania.

sylvan (sĭl′vən), *adj.* **1.** of, pertaining to, or inhabiting the woods. **2.** consisting of or abounding in woods or trees; wooded; woody. —*n.* **3.** a person dwelling in a woodland region. **4.** a fabled deity or spirit of the woods. Also, **silvan.** [t. L: m. s. *silvānus, sylvānus,* der. *silva* forest]

sylvanite (sĭl′və nīt′), *n.* a mineral, gold silver telluride, $(AuAg)Te_2$, silver-white with metallic lustre, often occurring in crystals so arranged as to resemble written characters: an ore of gold. [f. (TRAN)SYLVAN(IA), where it was first found, + -ITE[1]]

sylviculture (sĭl′vĭ kŭl′chə), *n.* silviculture.

sylvinite (sĭl′vĭ nīt′), *n.* a mineral consisting of a mixture of sylvite and halite.

sylvite (sĭl′vīt), *n.* a common mineral, potassium chloride, KCl, colourless to milky white or red, occurring in crystals, usually cubes, and masses with cubic cleavage; bitter in taste: the most important source of potassium. Also, **sylvin, sylvine** (sĭl′vĭn). [f. *Sylv-* (in NL *sal Sylvii* salt of *Sylvius* (trans. of name of Jacques *Dubois,* died 1555, French physician)) + -ITE[1]]

sym-, var. of **syn-,** before *b, p,* and *m,* as in *symphony.*

sym., 1. symbol. **2.** *Chem.* symmetrical. **3.** symphony. **4.** symptom.

symbiont (sĭm′bĭ ŏnt′), *n.* *Biol.* an organism living in a state of symbiosis. [t. Gk: s. *symbiôn,* ppr., living together] —**sym′bion′tic,** *adj.* —**sym′bion′tically,** *adv.*

symbiosis (sĭm′bĭ ō′sĭs), *n.* *Biol.* the living together of two species of organisms: a term usually restricted to cases in which the union of the two animals or plants is advantageous or necessary to both, as the case of the fungus and alga which together make up the lichen; mutualism. [t. NL, t. Gk] —**symbiotic** (sĭm′bĭ ŏt′ĭk), **sym′biot′ical,** *adj.* —**sym′biot′ically,** *adv.*

symbol (sĭm′bl), *n.*, *v.*, **-bolled, -bolling** or (*U.S.*) **-boled, -boling.** —*n.* **1.** something used or regarded as standing for or representing something else; a material object representing something immaterial; an emblem, token, or sign. **2.** a letter, figure, or other character or mark, or a combination of letters or the like, used to represent something: *the algebraic symbol, x; the chemical symbol, Au.* —*v.t.* **3.** to symbolize. [t. LL: s. *symbolum,* t. Gk: m. *sýmbolon* mark, token, ticket]

symbolic (sĭm bŏl′ĭk), *adj.* **1.** serving as a symbol of something (often fol. by *of*). **2.** of, pertaining to, or expressed by a symbol. **3.** characterized by or involving the use of symbols: *symbolic language.* Also, **symbolical.** —**symbol′ically,** *adv.* —**symbol′icalness,** *n.*

symbolical books, *Eccles.* the books of a religion containing the creeds, beliefs, etc.

symbolic logic, *Maths.*, *Computers.* a system of logic that has been reduced to a set of precise rules, used in mathematical proofs and also in constructing digital computers.

symbolics (sĭm bŏl′ĭks), *n.* the study and comparison of the expression of the creed of different churches and sects.

symbolism (sĭm′bə lĭz′əm), *n.* **1.** the practice of representing things by symbols, or of investing things with a symbolic meaning or character. **2.** a set or system of symbols. **3.** symbolic meaning or character. **4.** the principles and practice of symbolists in art or literature. **5.** (*cap.*) a movement of the late 19th century in French literature. **6.** the belief that in the Eucharist the bread and wine undergo no change of any kind, but represent the body and blood of Christ in a purely figurative way.

symbolist (sĭm′bə lĭst), *n.* **1.** one who uses symbols or symbolism. **2.** one versed in the study or interpretation of symbols. **3.** *Literature.* **a.** a writer who seeks to express or suggest ideas, emotions, etc., by emphasizing the symbolic value of language as a means of communicating otherwise inexpressible experiences of reality, as by the use of words or even word-sounds (as vowels) to convey a meaning, often with a mystical or vague effect. **b.** a member of a group of French and Belgian poets characterized by such procedure (including Verlaine, Mallarmé, and Maeterlinck), which arose during the latter part of the 19th century. **4.** *Art.* an artist who seeks to symbolize or suggest particular ideas by the objects represented, the colours used, etc. **5.** (*often cap.*) *Eccles.* a person who rejects the doctrine of transubstantiation and views the Eucharist symbolically. **6.** a person who favours the use of symbols in religious services. —*adj.* **7.** Also, **sym′bolis′tic.** of or pertaining to symbolists or symbolism.

symbolize (sĭm′bə līz′), *v.*, **-lized, -lizing.** —*v.t.* **1.** to be a symbol of; stand for, or represent, as a symbol does. **2.** to represent by a symbol or symbols. **3.** to regard or treat as symbolic. —*v.i.* **4.** to use symbols. Also, **symbolise.** —**sym′boliza′tion,** *n.*

symbology (sĭm bŏl′ə jĭ), *n.* **1.** the study of symbols. **2.** the use of symbols; symbolism. [t. NL: m. *symbologia,* f. (by haplology) *symbolo-* (see SYMBOL) + *-logia* -LOGY]

symmetallism (sĭ mĕt′ə lĭz′əm), *n.* the use of two (or more) metals, as gold and silver, combined in assigned proportions as a monetary standard.

symmetrical (sĭ mĕt′rĭ kl), *adj.* **1.** characterized by or exhibiting symmetry; well proportioned, as a body or whole; regular in form or arrangement of corresponding parts. **2.** *Logic, Maths.* denoting a relation, such that if it is valid between *a* and *b* it is valid between *b* and *a*: as, $a = b$ implies $b = a$. **3.** *Bot.* **a.** divisible into two similar parts by more than one plane passing through the centre; actinomorphic. **b.** (of a flower) having the same number of parts in each whorl. **4.** *Chem.* **a.** having a structure which exhibits a regular repeated pattern of the component parts. **b.** denoting a benzene derivative in which three substitutions have occurred at alternate carbon atoms. **5.** *Pathol.* affecting corresponding parts simultaneously, as certain diseases. Also, **symmet′ric.** —**symmet′rically,** *adv.* —**symmet′ricalness,** *n.*

symmetrize (sĭm′ĭ trīz′), *v.t.*, **-trized, -trizing.** to reduce to symmetry; make symmetrical. Also, **symmetrise.** —**sym′metriza′tion,** *n.*

symmetry (sĭm′ĭ trĭ), *n.*, *pl.* **-tries. 1.** the correspondence, in size, form, and arrangement, of parts on opposite sides of a plane, line, or point; regularity of form or arrangement with reference to corresponding parts. **2.** the proper or due proportion of the parts of a body or whole to one another with regard to size and form; excellence of proportion. [t. LL: m. s. *symmetria*, t. Gk]

Symonds (sĭm′ənz), *n.* **John Addington,** 1840–1893, English critic and poet.

Symons (sī′mənz), *n.* **Arthur,** 1865–1945, English poet and critic.

sympathetic (sĭm′pə thĕt′ĭk), *adj.* **1.** characterized by, proceeding from, exhibiting, or feeling sympathy; sympathizing; compassionate. **2.** acting or affected by, of the nature of, or pertaining to a special natural sympathy or affinity; congenial. **3.** looking with favour or liking upon (often fol. by *to* or *towards*): *he is sympathetic to the project.* **4.** *Anat., Physiol.* **a.** pertaining to that portion of the autonomic nervous system which is made up of a system of nerves and ganglia which arise from the thoracic and lumbar regions of the spinal cord, and which supply the walls of the vascular system and the various viscera and glands where they function in opposition to the parasympathetic system, as in dilating the pupil of the eye, etc. **b.** *Obs.* designating the autonomic nervous system in its entirety. **5.** *Physics.* (of vibrations, sounds, etc.) produced by vibrations conveyed through the air (or other medium) from a body already in vibration. Cf. **resonance** (def. 4). —**sym′pathet′ically,** *adv.*

sympathetic ink, a fluid for producing writing that is invisible until brought out by heat, chemicals, etc.

sympathetic magic, magic depending upon the belief that an object or event can affect another at a distance because of a supposed sympathetic connection between them.

sympathetic string, a thin wire string used in various musical instruments, and not played upon, but set into vibration by the plucked or bowed strings, to reinforce the sound.

sympathize (sĭm′pə thīz′), *v.i.*, **-thized, -thizing. 1.** to be in sympathy, or agreement of feeling; share in a feeling or feelings (often fol. by *with*). **2.** to feel a compassionate sympathy, as for suffering or trouble (often fol. by *with*). **3.** to express sympathy or condole (often fol. by *with*). **4.** to be in approving accord, as with a person, cause, etc.: *sympathize with a person's aims.* **5.** to agree, correspond, or accord. Also, **sympathise.** [t. F: m. s. *sympathiser*, der. *sympathie* SYMPATHY. See -IZE] —**sym′pathiz′er,** *n.* —**sym′pathiz′ingly,** *adv.*

sympathy (sĭm′pə thĭ), *n.*, *pl.* **-thies. 1.** community of or agreement in feeling, as between persons or on the part of one person with respect to another. **2.** the community of feeling naturally existing between persons of like tastes or opinion or of congenial dispositions. **3.** the fact or the power of entering into the feelings of another, esp. in sorrow or trouble; fellow feeling, compassion, or commiseration. **4.** (*pl.*) feelings or impulses of compassion. **5.** favourable or approving accord; favour or approval. **6.** agreement, consonance, or accord. **7.** *Psychol.* a relation between persons whereby the condition of one induces a responsive condition in another. **8.** *Physiol., Pathol.* the relation between parts or organs whereby a condition, affection, or disorder of one part induces some effect in another. [t. L: m. s. *sympathīa*, t. Gk: m. *sympátheia*, lit., feeling with another]

sympathy strike, a strike by a body of workers, not because of grievances against their own employer, but by way of endorsing and aiding another body of workers who are on strike or have been locked out.

sympetalous (sĭm pĕt′ə ləs), *adj. Bot.* gamopetalous.

symphonic (sĭm fŏn′ĭk), *adj.* **1.** *Music.* of, pertaining to, or having the character of a symphony. **2.** of or pertaining to symphony, or harmony of sounds. **3.** characterized by similarity of sound, as words.

symphonic poem, *Music.* a form of tone poem scored for a symphony orchestra, originated by Liszt in the mid 19th century and developed esp. by Richard Strauss, in which a literary or pictorial 'plot' is treated with considerable programme detail.

symphonious (sĭm fō′nyəs), *adj.* harmonious; in harmonious agreement or accord. —**sympho′niously,** *adv.*

symphonist (sĭm′fə nĭst), *n.* one who performs or composes symphonies.

symphony (sĭm′fə nĭ), *n.*, *pl.* **-nies. 1.** *Music.* **a.** an elaborate instrumental composition in three or more movements, similar in form to a sonata but written for an orchestra, and usually of far grander proportions and more varied elements. **b.** an instrumental passage occurring in a vocal composition, or between vocal movements in a composition. **c.** an instrumental piece, often in several movements, forming the overture to an opera or the like. **2.** anything characterized by a harmonious combination of elements and esp. an effective combination of colours. **3.** *Archaic or Poetic.* harmony of sounds. **4.** *Archaic or Poetic.* harmony in general. [ME *symphonie*, t. L: m. *symphōnia*, t. Gk: lit., a sounding together]

symphony orchestra, a large orchestra composed of wind, string, and percussion instruments and designed to perform symphonic compositions.

symphysial (sĭm fĭz′ĭ əl), *adj.* referring to a symphysis. Also, **symphys′eal.**

symphysiotomy (sĭm′fĭ zĭ ŏt′ə mĭ), *n. Obstetrics.* the operation of dividing the pubic symphysis in order to facilitate the delivery of a baby. Also, **symphyseotomy.**

symphysis (sĭm′fĭ sĭs), *n.*, *pl.* **-ses** (-sēz′). **1.** *Anat., Zool.* **a.** the growing together, or the fixed or nearly fixed union, of bones, as that of the two halves of the lower jaw in man, or of the pubic bones in the anterior part of the pelvic girdle. **b.** a line of junction or articulation so formed. **2.** *Bot.* a coalescence or growing together of parts. [NL, t. Gk] —**symphystic** (sĭm fĭs′tĭk), *adj.*

sympodium (sĭm pō′dyəm), *n.*, *pl.* **-dia** (-dyə). *Bot.* an axis or stem which simulates a simple stem but is made up of the bases of a number of axes which arise successively as branches one from another, as in the grapevine; a pseudaxis. Cf. **monopodium.** [NL. See SYM-, PODIUM]

Sympodium

symposiac (sĭm pō′zĭ ăk′), *adj.* **1.** of, pertaining to, or suitable for a symposium. —*n.* **2.** a symposium.

symposiarch (sĭm pō′zĭ äk′), *n.* **1.** the president, director, or master of a symposium. **2.** the toastmaster. [t. Gk: s. *symposiarchos*]

symposium (sĭm pō′zyəm), *n.*, *pl.* **-siums, -sia** (-zyə). **1.** a meeting or conference for discussion of some subject. **2.** a collection of opinions expressed, or articles contributed, by several persons on a given subject or topic. **3.** an account of such a meeting or of the conversation at it. **4.** (among the ancient Greeks) a convivial meeting, usually following a dinner, for drinking, conversation, and intellectual discussion. [t. L, t. Gk: m. *sympósion* (def. 4)]

symptom (sĭmp′təm), *n.* **1.** any phenomenon or circumstance accompanying something and serving as evidence for it. **2.** a sign or indication of something. **3.** *Pathol.* a phenomenon which arises from and accompanies a particular disease or disorder and serves as an indication of it. [t. LL: m. *symptōma*, t. Gk] —**symp′tomless,** *adj.*

symptomatic (sĭmp′tə măt′ĭk), *adj.* **1.** pertaining to a symptom or symptoms. **2.** of the nature of or constituting a symptom; indicative (often fol. by *of*). **3.** according to symptoms: *a symptomatic classification of disease.* Also, **symptomatical.** —**symp′tomat′ically,** *adv.*

symptomatology (sĭmp′tə mə tŏl′ə jĭ), *n.* that branch of medical science which deals with symptoms. [t. NL: m. s. *symptōmatologia.* See SYMPTOM, -LOGY]

syn-, a prefix in learned words having the same function as **co-** (def. 1), as in *synthesis, synoptic.* Also, **sy-, syl-, sym-, sys-.** [t. Gk, comb. form of *sýn*, prep., with, and adv., together]

syn., 1. synonym. **2.** synonymous. **3.** synonymy.

synaeresis (sĭ nĭə′rə sĭs), *n. Gram.* **1.** the contraction of two syllables or two vowels into one; esp. the contraction of two vowels so as to form a diphthong (opposed to *diaeresis*). **2.** synizesis. Also, *U.S.* **syneresis.** [t. LL, t. Gk: m. *synaíresis*, lit., a taking together]

synaesthesia (sĭn′ēs thē′zyə), *n.* a sensation produced in one physical sense when a stimulus is applied to another sense, as when the hearing of a certain sound induces the visualization of a certain colour. Also, *U.S.*, **synesthesia.**

synagogue (sĭn′ə gŏg′), *n.* **1.** a Jewish house of worship, usually also providing religious instruction. **2.** an assembly or congregation of the Jews for the purposes of worship. [ME *sinagoge*, t. LL: m. *synagōga*, t. Gk: m. *synagōgē* meeting, assembly] —**synagogical** (sĭn′ə gŏj′ĭ kl), **synagogal** (sĭn′ə gŏg′l), *adj.*

synaloepha (sĭn′ə lē′fə), *n.* the blending of two successive vowels into one. Also, **synalepha, synalephe** (sĭn′ə lē′fĭ). [t. L, t. Gk: m. *synaloiphḗ*]

synapse (sĭ′năps), *n. Physiol.* the region of contact between processes of two or more nerve cells, across which an impulse passes. [t. Gk: m. *sýnapsis* connection]

synapsis (sĭ năp′sĭs), *n., pl.* **-ses** (-sēz). **1.** *Biol.* the conjugation of homologous chromosomes, one from each parent, during early meiosis. **2.** *Physiol.* synapse. [NL, t. Gk] —**synaptic** (sĭ năp′tĭk), *adj.*

synarthrodia (sĭn′ä thrō′dĭ ə), *n., pl.* **-diae** (-dĭ ē′). synarthrosis. [NL] —**syn′arthro′dial,** *adj.*

synarthrosis (sĭn′ä thrō′sĭs), *n., pl.* **-ses** (-sēz). *Anat.* immovable articulation; a fixed or immovable joint; a suture. [NL, t. Gk]

sync (sĭngk), *Cinema, Computers, etc., Colloq.* —*n.* **1.** synchronization. —*v.i., v.t.* **2.** to synchronize.

syncarp (sĭn′käp), *n. Bot.* **1.** an aggregate fruit. **2.** a collective fruit. [t. NL: m. s. *syncarpium*, f. Gk: *syn-* SYN- + m. *karpíon*, dim. of *karpós* fruit]

syncarpous (sĭn kä′pəs), *adj. Bot.* **1.** of the nature of or pertaining to a syncarp. **2.** composed of or having united carpels.

synchro-cyclotron (sĭng′krō sī′klə trŏn′), *n. Physics.* a type of cyclotron which enables relativistic energies to be achieved by modulating the frequency of the accelerating electric field.

synchroflash (sĭng′krō flăsh′), *adj.* of or pertaining to photography which synchronizes the operation of the flashgun with the opening of the shutter.

synchromesh (sĭng′krō mĕsh′), *Motor Vehicles.* —*adj.* **1.** of, pertaining to or fitted with a system consisting of small friction clutches, by means of which the speeds of the driven and driving gears in a gearbox are automatically synchronized before they engage, to assist gear changing and reduce wear. —*n.* **2.** such a system. [f. SYNCHRO(NOUS) + MESH]

synchronal (sĭng′krə nəl), *adj.* synchronous. Also, **synchronic** (sĭng krŏn′ĭk), **synchron′ical.**

synchronism (sĭng′krə nĭz′əm), *n.* **1.** coincidence in time; contemporaneousness; simultaneousness. **2.** the arrangement or treatment of synchronous things or events in conjunction, as in a history. **3.** a tabular arrangement of historical events or personages, grouped together according to their dates. **4.** *Physics., Elect., etc.* the state of being synchronous. —**syn′chronis′tic, syn′chronis′tical,** *adj.* —**syn′chronis′tically,** *adv.*

synchronize (sĭng′krə nīz′), *v.,* **-nized, -nizing.** —*v.i.* **1.** to occur at the same time, or coincide or agree in time. **2.** to go on at the same rate and exactly together; recur together. —*v.t.* **3.** to cause to indicate the same time, as one clock with another. **4.** to cause to go on at the same rate and exactly together. **5.** to cause to agree in time of occurrence; assign to the same time or period, as in a history. Also, **synchronise.** [t. Gk: m. s. *synchronízein* be contemporary with] —**syn′chroniza′tion,** *n.* —**syn′chroniz′er,** *n.*

synchronoscope (sĭng krŏn′ə skōp′), *n.* synchroscope.

synchronous (sĭng′krə nəs), *adj.* **1.** occurring at the same time; coinciding in time; contemporaneous; simultaneous. **2.** going on at the same rate and exactly together; recurring together. **3.** *Physics, Elect., etc.* having the same frequency and no phase difference. [t. LL: m. *synchronus*, t. Gk: m. *sýnchronos*] —**syn′chronously,** *adv.* —**syn′chronousness,** *n.*

synchronous computer, a computer whose operation is controlled by an electronic clock.

synchronous converter, *Elect.* a synchronous machine for converting alternating current to direct current, or vice versa, in which armature winding is connected to collector rings and to a commutator; rotary converter.

synchronous machine, *Elect.* an alternating-current machine in which the average speed of normal operation is exactly proportional to the frequency of the system to which it is connected.

synchronous orbit, *Aeron.* a circular orbit in which a satellite moves around the earth once while the earth rotates once on its axis and thus remains fixed above a particular point above the equator; geostationary orbit; stationary orbit.

synchronous speed, *Elect.* the speed at which an alternating-current machine must operate to generate electromotive force at a given frequency.

synchroscope (sĭng′krə skōp′), *n. Elect.* an instrument for indicating synchronism between two related motions, as two aircraft engines or two electrical machines. Also, **synchronoscope.**

synchrotron (sĭng′krə trŏn′), *n. Physics.* an accelerator of the cyclotron type in which the magnetic field is modulated but the electric field is maintained at a constant frequency.

synchrotron radiation, *Astron.* the emission of radio-frequency electromagnetic radiation by insterstellar gas clouds in radio galaxies, believed to be analogous to the light emitted by high-energy electrons in a synchrotron.

synchro unit (sĭng′krō), *Elect.* a type of alternating-current motor designed to maintain continuously, at some remote place, the same rotational angle that may be imposed by force upon the electrically connected rotating element of a similar motor.

synclastic (sĭng klăs′tĭk), *adj. Maths.* denoting or pertaining to a point of a surface (such as a sphere) at which the two principal curvatures have the same sign (opp. to *anticlastic*). [f. SYN + m. s. Gk *klastós* broken + -IC]

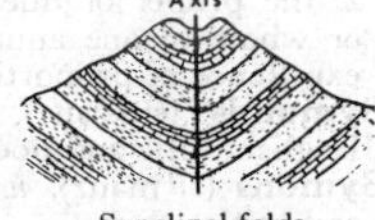

Synclinal folds

synclinal (sĭng klī′nəl), *adj.* **1.** sloping downwards in opposite directions so as to meet in a common point or line. **2.** *Geol.* **a.** inclining upwards on both sides from a median line or axis, as a downward fold of rock strata. **b.** pertaining to such a fold. [f. m. s. Gk *synklī́nein* lean together + -AL[1]]

syncline (sĭng′klīn), *n. Geol.* a synclinal fold.

Syncopation

syncopate (sĭng′kə pāt′), *v.t.,* **-pated, -pating. 1.** *Music.* **a.** to place (the accents) on beats which are normally unaccented. **b.** to employ notes so affected in (a passage, piece, etc.). **2.** *Gram.* to contract (a word) by omitting one or more sounds from the middle, as in reducing *Gloucester* to *Gloster.* [t. LL: m. s. *syncopātus*, pp., cut short, der. *syncopē* SYNCOPE] —**syn′copa′tor,** *n.*

syncopation (sĭng′kə pā′shən), *n.* **1.** *Music.* a shifting of the normal accent, usually by stressing normally unaccented beats. **2.** *Gram.* a syncope.

syncope (sĭng′kə pĭ), *n.* **1.** *Gram.* the contraction of a word by omitting one or more sounds from the middle, as in the reduction of *never* to *ne'er.* **2.** *Pathol.* brief loss of consciousness associated with transient cerebral anaemia, as in heart block, sudden lowering of the blood pressure, etc.; fainting. [ME, t. L, t. Gk: m. *synkopḗ* a cutting up] —**syncopic** (sĭng kŏp′ĭk), *adj.*

syncretism (sĭng′krĭ tĭz′əm), *n.* **1.** the attempted reconciliation or union of different or opposing principles, practices, or parties, as in philosophy or religion. **2.** (in linguistic change) the merging into one of two or more former categories, as the substandard English usage of *was* in '*We was, you was, they was*' as well as in '*I was, he was*'. [t. NL: s. *syncrētismus*, t. Gk: m. *synkrētismós*] —**syncretic** (sĭng krĕt′ĭk), **syncretistic** (sĭng′krĭ tĭs′tĭk), **syn′cretis′tical,** *adj.*

syncretize (sĭng′krĭ tīz′), *v.t., v.i.,* **-tized, -tizing.** to attempt to combine or unite, as different or opposing principles, parties, etc. Also, **syncretise.** [t. NL: m. s. *syncrētizāre*, t. Gk: m. *synkrētízein* der. *Krḗtē* CRETE, whose inhabitants were notorious for their factious quarrels]

syncytium (sĭn sĭt′ĭ əm), *n., pl.* **-cytia** (-sĭt′ĭ ə). *Zool.* animal tissue with many nuclei but without cell walls. [t. NL. See SYN-, CYTO, -IUM]

Syndactyl foot of kingfisher

syndactyl (sĭn dăk′tĭl), *adj.* **1.** having certain digits joined together. —*n.* **2.** a syndactyl animal. Also, **syndactyle.** [f. SYN- + m. s. Gk *dáktylos* finger, toed] —**syndactylism** (sĭn dăk′tĭ lĭz′əm), *n.*

syndesmosis (sĭn′dĕs mō′sĭs), *n., pl.* **-ses** (-sēz). *Anat.* a connection of bones by ligaments, fasciae, or membranes other than in a joint. [NL, f. Gk: s. *sýndesmos* ligament + *-ōsis* -OSIS] —**syndesmotic** (sĭn′dĕs mŏt′ĭk), *adj.*

syndetic (sĭn dĕt′ĭk), *adj.* **1.** serving to unite or connect; connective; copulative. **2.** conjunctive (def. 3c). Also, **syndet′ical.** [t. Gk: m. s. *syndetikós*] —**syndet′ically,** *adv.*

syndic (sĭn′dĭk), *n.* **1.** a person chosen to represent and transact business for a society, corporation or the like. **2.** a magistrate having different powers in different countries. [t. LL: s. *syndicus* advocate, delegate, t. Gk: m. *sýndikos* defendant's advocate]

syndical (sĭn′dĭ kl), *adj.* **1.** denoting or pertaining to a union of persons engaged in a particular trade. **2.** of or pertaining to syndicalism.

syndicalism (sĭn′dĭ kə lĭz′əm), *n.* a form or development of trade unionism, originating in France, which aims at the possession of the means of production and distribution, and ultimately at the control of society, by the federated bodies of industrial workers, and which seeks to realize its purposes through general strikes, terrorism, sabotage, or other means. —**syn′dicalist,** *adj.*, *n.* —**syn′dicalis′tic,** *adj.*

syndicate (*n.* sĭn′dĭ kĭt; *v.* sĭn′dĭ kāt′), *n.*, *v.*, **-cated, -cating.** —*n.* **1.** a combination of persons, as business associates, commercial firms, etc., formed for the purpose of carrying out some project, esp. one requiring large resources of capital. **2.** any agency which buys and supplies articles, stories, etc., for simultaneous publication in a number of newspapers or other periodicals in different places. **3.** a council or body of syndics. **4.** (formerly) a local organization of employers or employees in Italy under the fascist regime. —*v.t.* **5.** to combine into a syndicate. **6.** to publish simultaneously, or supply for simultaneous publication, in a number of newspapers or other periodicals in different places. [t. F: m. *syndicat*, der. *syndic* SYNDIC] —**syn′dica′tion,** *n.*

syndrome (sĭn′drōm), *n.* *Pathol.*, *Psychol.* the pattern of symptoms in a disease or the like; a number of characteristic symptoms occurring together. [t. NL, t. Gk: a running together] —**syndromic** (sĭn drŏm′ĭk), *adj.*

syne (sĭn), *adv.*, *prep.*, *conj.* *Scot.* since.

synecdoche (sĭ nĕk′də kĭ), *n.* *Rhet.* a figure of speech by which a part is put for the whole or the whole for a part, the special for the general or the general for the special, as in 'a fleet of ten *sail*' (for *ships*), or 'a *Croesus*' (for a *rich man*). [t. LL, t. Gk m. *synekdochē*; r. ME *synodoche*, t. ML] —**synecdochic** (sĭn′ĕk dŏk′ĭk), **syn′ecdoch′ical,** *adj.*

synecious (sĭ nē′shəs), *adj.* synoicous.

synecology (sĭn′ĭ kŏl′ə jĭ), *n.* *Ecol.* that branch of autecology which deals with the relation between the species or group and its environment. Cf. **autecology.**

syneresis (sĭ nĭə′rə sĭs), *n.* **1.** synaeresis. **2.** *Chem.* the separation of liquid from a gel.

synergetic (sĭn′ə jĕt′ĭk), *adj.* working together; cooperative.

synergic curve, *Aeron.* the optimum path that a rocket should follow to put a satellite in orbit with the least expenditure of energy.

synergism (sĭn′ə jĭz′əm, sĭ nû′-), *n.* **1.** *Theol.* the doctrine that the human will cooperates with the Holy Ghost in the work of regeneration. **2.** the joint action of two substances, as drugs, which increase each other's effectiveness when taken together.

synergist (sĭn′ə jĭst, sĭ nû′jĭst), *n.* **1.** *Physiol.*, *Med.* a bodily organ, a medicine, etc., that cooperates with another or others; an adjuvant. **2.** *Theol.* one who holds the doctrine of synergism. **3.** *Chem.* any substance which increases the effect of some other substance.

synergistic (sĭn′ə jĭs′tĭk), *adj.* working together; synergetic.

synergy (sĭn′ə jĭ), *n.*, *pl.* **-gies.** **1.** combined action. **2.** the cooperative action of two or more bodily organs or the like. **3.** the cooperative action of two or more stimuli or drugs. [t. NL: m. s. *synergia*, t. Gk] —**synergic** (sĭ nû′jĭk), *adj.*

synesis (sĭn′ĭ sĭs), *n.* *Gram.* a construction having a feature which is syntactically extraordinary, as the replacement of an expected singular verb by a plural verb to agree with the sense rather than the syntax of a subject, e.g. '*a number of men are going*'. [NL, t. Gk: comprehension]

synesthesia (sĭn′ēs thē′zyə), *n.* synaesthesia.

syngamy (sĭng′gə mĭ), *n.* *Biol.* union of gametes, as in fertilization or conjugation; sexual reproduction. —**syngamic** (sĭng găm′ĭk), **syngamous** (sĭng′gə məs), *adj.*

Synge (sĭng), *n.* **John Millington,** 1871–1909, Irish dramatist.

syngenesis (sĭn jĕn′ĭ sĭs), *n.* **1.** *Biol.* sexual reproduction. **2.** *Geol.* the formation of ores at the same time as the enclosing rock. Cf. **epigenesis.**

syngenetic (sĭn′jĭ nĕt′ĭk), *adj.* **1.** *Biol.* of or pertaining to sexual reproduction. **2.** *Geol.* of or pertaining to ores which were formed at the same time as the enclosing rock.

synizesis (sĭn′ĭ zē′sĭs), *n.* *Phonet.* the combination into one syllable of two vowels (or of a vowel and a diphthong) that do not form a diphthong. [t. LL, t. Gk]

synod (sĭn′əd), *n.* **1.** an assembly of ecclesiastics or other church delegates duly convoked, pursuant to the law of the church, for the discussion and decision of ecclesiastical affairs; an ecclesiastical council. **2.** any council. [ME, t. LL: s. *synodus*, t. Gk: m. *sýnodos* assembly] —**syn′odal,** *adj.*

synodic (sĭ nŏd′ĭk), *adj.* *Astron.* pertaining to a conjunction, or to two successive conjunctions of the same bodies: *synodic month.* Also, **synodical.** —**synod′ically,** *adv.*

synoicous (sĭ noi′kəs), *adj.* *Bot.* having male and female flowers on one head, as in many composite plants. Also, **synecious, synoecious** (sĭ nē′shəs). [f. m. s. Gk *synoikia* a living together + -OUS]

synonym (sĭn′ə nĭm), *n.* **1.** a word having the same, or nearly the same, meaning as another in the language, e.g., *joyful, elated, glad.* **2.** a word or expression accepted as another name for something, e.g., *Arcadia* for *pastoral simplicity.* **3.** *Bot.*, *Zool.* a rejected scientific name, other than a homonym. [ME, t. LL: s. *synōnymum*, t. Gk: m. *synṓnymon*, prop. neut. of *synṓnymos* synonymous] —**syn′onym′ic, syn′onym′ical,** *adj.* —**synonymity** (sĭn′ə nĭm′ĭ tĭ), *n.*

synonymize (sĭ nŏn′ĭ mīz′), *v.t.*, **-mized, -mizing.** to give synonyms for (a word, name, etc.); furnish with synonyms. Also, **synonymise.**

synonymous (sĭ nŏn′ĭ məs), *adj.* having the character of synonyms or a synonym; equivalent in meaning; expressing or implying the same idea. [t. ML: m. *synōnymus*, t. Gk: m. *synṓnymos*] —**synon′ymously,** *adv.* —**synon′ymousness,** *n.*

synonymy (sĭ nŏn′ĭ mĭ), *n.*, *pl.* **-mies.** **1.** the character of being synonymous; equivalence in meaning. **2.** the study of synonyms. **3.** a set, list, or system of synonyms. **4.** *Bot.*, *Zool.* **a.** a list of the scientific names for a particular species or other group, or for various species, etc., with discriminations or explanatory matter. **b.** these names collectively, whether listed or not. [t. LL: m. s. *synōnymia*, t. Gk]

synop., synopsis.

synopsis (sĭ nŏp′sĭs), *n.*, *pl.* **-ses** (-sēz). **1.** a brief or condensed statement giving a general view of some subject. **2.** a compendium of headings or short paragraphs giving a view of the whole. **3.** the outline of the plot of a novel, play, film, etc. [t. LL, t. Gk: general view] —**Syn.** See **summary.**

synoptic (sĭ nŏp′tĭk), *adj.* **1.** pertaining to or constituting a synopsis; affording or taking a general view of the whole or of the principal parts of a subject. **2.** (*often cap.*) taking a common view (applied to the first three Gospels, Matthew, Mark, and Luke, from their similarity in contents, order, and statement). **3.** (*often cap.*) pertaining to the synoptic Gospels. —*n.* **4.** one of the synoptic Gospels. **5.** one of their authors. [t. NL: s. *synopticus*, t. Gk: m. *synoptikós*] —**synop′tically,** *adv.*

synoptic chart, a chart showing distribution of meteorological conditions over a region at a given moment.

synoptic meteorology, a branch of meteorology analysing data taken simultaneously over a large area, for the purpose of weather forecasting.

synovia (sĭ nō′vyə, sī-), *n.* *Physiol.* a lubricating liquid resembling the white of an egg, secreted by certain membranes, as those of the joints. [NL; coined by Paracelsus] —**syno′vial,** *adj.*

synovitis (sī′nō vī′tĭs, sĭn′ō-), *n.* *Pathol.* inflammation of a synovial membrane. [f. SYNOV(IA) + -ITIS]

synsepalous (sĭn sĕp′ə ləs), *adj.* *Bot.* gamosepalous.

syntactical (sĭn tăk′tĭ kl), *adj.* of or pertaining to syntax. Also, **syntactic.** —**syntac′tically,** *adv.*

syntactic construction, *Gram.* a construction composed wholly of independent words, without bound forms.

syntax (sĭn′tăks), *n.* **1.** *Gram.* **a.** the patterns of formation of sentences and phrases from words in a particular language. **b.** the study and description thereof. **2.** *Logic.* **a.** that branch of modern logic which studies the various kinds of signs that occur in a system and the possible arrangements of those signs, complete abstraction being made of the meaning of the signs. **b.** the outcome of such a study when directed upon a specified language. **3.** *Obs.* a system. [t. LL: m. *syntaxis*, t. Gk: arrangement]

synthesis (sĭn′thĭ sĭs), *n.*, *pl.* **-ses** (-sēz′). **1.** the combination of parts or elements, as material substances or objects of thought, into a complex whole (opposed to *analysis*). **2.** a complex whole made up of parts or elements combined. **3.** *Chem.* the forming or building up of a more complex substance or compound by the union of elements or the combination of simpler compounds or radicals. **4. a.** reasoning from the universal or general to the particular, or from a principle to its exemplification. **b.** (in Kant) the unification, by the understanding, of one concept with another not contained in it. **c.** (in Fichte) the union of thesis and antithesis. **d.** a forerunner of the Hegelian dialectic, which claims to unite contradictory judgements in a higher truth. [t. L, t. Gk: lit., a taking together] —**syn′thesist,** *n.*

synthesize (sĭn′thĭ sīz′), *v.t.*, **-sized, -sizing.** **1.** to make up by combining parts or elements. **2.** to combine into a complex whole. **3.** to treat synthetically. **4.** *Chem.* to manufacture (a complex product, esp. a product resembling one of natural origin) by combining simple substances. Also, **synthesise.** —**syn′thesiza′tion,** *n.* —**syn′thesiz′er,** *n.*

synthetic (sĭn thĕtʹĭk), *adj.* **1.** of, pertaining to, proceeding by, or involving synthesis (opposed to *analytic*). **2.** denoting or pertaining to chemical compounds, resins, rubbers, etc., formed by chemical reaction in a laboratory or chemical plant, as opposed to those of natural origin. **3.** (of languages) characterized by the use of affixes (bound forms) to express relationships between words, as in Latin; as opposed to *analytic*, as in English. Also, **synthetical.** **—*n.* 4.** something made by a synthetic (chemical) process. [t. NL: s. *syntheticus*, t. Gk: m. *synthetikós*] **—synthetʹically,** *adv.*

synthetic geometry, elementary geometry as distinct from analytic geometry.

synthetize (sĭnʹthĭ tīzʹ), *v.t.*, **-tized, -tizing.** synthesize. Also, **synthetise.** **—synʹthetizaʹtion,** *n.* **—synʹthetizʹer,** *n.*

syntonic (sĭn tŏnʹĭk), *adj. Elect.* adjusted to oscillations of the same or a particular frequency. Also, **syntonʹical.** **—syntonʹically,** *adv.*

syntonize (sĭnʹtə nīzʹ), *v.t.*, **-nized, -nizing.** to render syntonic; to tune to the same frequency. Also, **syntonise.** [f. SYNTON(Y) + -IZE] **—synʹtonizaʹtion,** *n.*

syntony (sĭnʹtə nĭ), *n. Elect.* the state or condition of being syntonic. [t. Gk: m. s. *syntonía* tension]

syphilis (sĭfʹĭ lĭs), *n. Pathol.* a chronic, infectious venereal disease, caused by the micro-organism *Spirochaeta pallida*, or *Treponema pallidum* (see **spirochaete**), and communicated by contact or heredity, usually having three stages, the first **(primary syphilis)**, in which a hard chancre forms at the point of inoculation, the second **(secondary syphilis)**, characterized by skin affections and constitutional disturbances, and the third **(tertiary syphilis)**, characterized by affections of the bones, muscles, viscera, nervous system, etc. [t. NL, der. *Syphilus*, name of shepherd suffering from the disease in L poem of 16th century by G. *Fracastoro*]

syphilitic (sĭfʹĭ lĭtʹĭk), *adj.* **1.** pertaining to or affected with syphilis. **—*n.* 2.** one affected with syphilis.

syphiloid (sĭfʹĭ loidʹ), *adj.* resembling syphilis.

syphilology (sĭfʹĭ lŏlʹə jĭ), *n.* the study or science of syphilis. **—syphʹilolʹogist,** *n.*

syphon (sīʹfən), *n., v.t., v.i.* siphon.

Syr., 1. Syria. **2.** Syriac. **3.** Syrian.

syr., *Pharm.* syrup.

Syracuse (sĭʹrə kyōōsʹ *for 1*; sĭʹə rə kyōōzʹ *for 2*), *n.* **1.** a town in the U.S., in central New York State. 216,038 (1960). **2.** Italian, **Siracusa.** a seaport in Italy, in SE Sicily: the ancient city here was founded by the Carthaginians, 734 B.C.; battles, 413 B.C., 212 B.C. 98,294 (1966). **—Syrʹacusʹan,** *adj., n.*

Syr Darya (*Russ.* sĭr dáry yáʹ), a river in the SW Soviet Union in Asia, flowing from the Tien Shan Mountains NW to the Aral Sea. ab. 1300 mi. Ancient, **Jaxartes.**

Syrette (sĭ rĕtʹ), *n. Trademark.* a collapsible tube with an attached hypodermic needle for the subcutaneous administration of medication. [f. SYR(INGE) + -ETTE]

Syria (sĭʹrĭ ə), *n.* **1.** a republic in SW Asia at the E end of the Mediterranean. 5,500,000 pop. (est. 1962); 71,227 sq. mi. *Cap.:* Damascus. **2.** a territory mandated to France in 1922, including the present republics of Syria and Lebanon (Latakia and Djebel Druze were incorporated into Syria, 1942): the French mandatory powers were nominally terminated as of January 1st, 1944. **3.** an ancient country in SW Asia, including what is now Syria, Lebanon, Israel, and adjacent areas: a part of the Roman Empire, 64 B.C.–A.D. 636. **—Syrʹian,** *adj., n.*

Syriac (sĭʹrĭ ăkʹ), *n.* an Aramaic language. [t. L: s. *Syriacus*, t. Gk: m. *Syriakós*]

syringa (sĭ rĭngʹgə), *n.* **1.** any of the shrubs constituting the genus *Philadelphus*, including species cultivated for ornament, esp. *P. coronarius*, a familiar cultivated species with fragrant white flowers. **2.** a lilac (genus *Syringa*). [t. NL, t. Gk: m. *sŷrinx* pipe]

syringe (sĭʹrĭnj, sĭ rĭnjʹ), *n., v.*, **-ringed, -ringing.** **—*n.* 1.** *Med.* a small device consisting of a glass, metal, rubber, or plastic tube, narrowed at its outlet, and fitted with either a piston or a rubber bulb for drawing in a quantity of fluid and ejecting it in a stream, used for cleaning wounds, injecting fluids into the body, etc. **2.** any similar device for pumping and spraying liquids through a small aperture. **—*v.t.* 3.** to cleanse, wash, inject, etc., by means of a syringe. [back-formation from *syringes*, t. Gk, pl. of *sŷrinx* pipe; r. late ME *siryng*, t. ML]

synringeal (sĭ rĭnʹjĭ əl), *adj. Ornith.* of, pertaining to, or connected with the syrinx.

syringomyelia (sĭ rĭngʹgō mī ēʹlĭ ə), *n. Pathol.* a disease of the spinal cord in which the nerve tissue is replaced by a cavity filled with fluid. [NL, f. *syringo-* (comb. form of Gk *sŷrinx* pipe) + s. Gk *myelós* marrow (of the spinal cord) + *-ia* -IA]

syrinx (sĭʹrĭngks), *n., pl.* **syringes** (sĭ rĭnʹjēz), **syrinxes.** **1.** *Anat.* the Eustachian tube. **2.** *Ornith.* the vocal organ of birds, situated at or near the bifurcation of the trachea into the bronchi. **3.** (*cap.*) *Gk Myth.* a nymph who was pursued by Pan and, to escape him, was turned into a reed, of which he made the panpipe. **4.** panpipe. [t. L, t. Gk]

Syrinx of raven A, Modified tracheal and bronchial rings forming syrinx; B, Trachea; C, Right and left bronchi

syrphid (sûʹfĭd), *n.* any of the *Syrphidae*, or hoverflies, a family of dipterous insects or flies, some of which are beneficial, their larvae feeding on plant lice. Also, **syrphian** (sûʹfĭ ən). [f. s. Gk *sýrphos* gnat + -ID²]

syrup (sĭʹrəp), *n.* **1.** any of various sweet, more or less viscid liquids, consisting of fruit, juices, water, etc., boiled with sugar. **2.** molasses. **3.** any of various solutions of sugar used in pharmacy. **4.** any of various thick sweet liquids for use in cooking, prepared from molasses, glucose, etc., water, and often with a flavouring agent. **5.** *Colloq.* excessive or cloying sweetness or sentimentality. **—*v.t.* 6.** to bring to the form or consistency of syrup. **7.** to cover, fill, or sweeten with syrup. Also, *U.S.*, **sirup.** [ME *syrope*, t. OF: m. *sirop*, ult. t. Ar.: m. *sharāb* beverage] **—syrʹuplikeʹ,** *adj.*

syrupy (sĭʹrə pĭ), *adj.* **1.** resembling syrup in appearance or quality. **2.** *Colloq.* excessively sentimental; cloying: *syrupy music.*

sys-, var. of **syn-,** before *s*, as in *syssarcosis.*

syssarcosis (sĭsʹä kōʹsĭs), *n. Anat.* the union of bones by muscle. [NL, t. Gk]

syst., system.

systaltic (sĭs tălʹtĭk), *adj. Physiol.* **1.** rhythmically contracting. **2.** of the nature of contraction. **3.** characterized by alternate contraction (systole) and dilatation (diastole), as the action of the heart. [t. LL: s. *systalticus*, t. Gk: m. *systaltikós* contractile]

system (sĭsʹtĭm), *n.* **1.** an assemblage or combination of things or parts forming a complex or unitary whole: *a mountain system, a railway system.* **2.** any assemblage or set of correlated members: *a system of currency, a system of shorthand characters.* **3.** an ordered and comprehensive assemblage of facts, principles, doctrines, or the like in a particular field of knowledge or thought: *a system of philosophy.* **4.** a coordinated body of methods, or a complex scheme or plan of procedure: *a system of government, a penal system.* **5.** any formulated, regular, or special method or plan of procedure: *a system of marking, numbering, or measuring.* **6.** due method, or orderly manner of arrangement or procedure: *have system in one's work.* **7.** a number of heavenly bodies associated and acting together according to certain natural laws: *the solar system.* **8.** the world or universe. **9.** *Astron.* a hypothesis or theory of the disposition and arrangements of the heavenly bodies by which their phenomena, motions, changes, etc., are explained: *the Ptolemaic system, the Copernican system.* **10.** *Biol.* **a.** an assemblage of parts of organs of the same or similar tissues, or concerned with the same function: *the nervous system, the digestive system.* **b.** the entire human or animal body: *to expel poison from the system.* **11.** a method or scheme of classification: *the Linnean system of plants.* **12.** *Geol.* a major division of rocks comprising sedimentary deposits and igneous masses formed during a geological period. **13.** *Phys. Chem.* **a.** any substance or group of substances considered apart from the surroundings. **b.** a sample of matter consisting of one or more components in equilibrium in one or more phases: a system is called binary if containing two components, ternary, if containing three, etc. [t. LL: m. *systēma*, t. Gk: organized whole] **—sysʹtemless,** *adj.*

systematic (sĭsʹtĭ mătʹĭk), *adj.* **1.** having, showing, or involving a system, method, or plan: *a systematic course of reading, systematic efforts.* **2.** characterized by system or method; methodical: *a systematic person, systematic habits.* **3.** arranged in or comprising an ordered system: *systematic theology.* **4.** concerned with classification: *systematic botany.* **5.** pertaining to, based on, or in accordance with a system of classification: *the systematic names of plants.* Also, **systematical.** **—sysʹtematʹically,** *adv.* **—Syn. 2.** See **orderly.**

systematics (sĭsʹtĭ mătʹĭks), *n.* the study of systems, or of classification.

systematism (sĭsʹtĭ mə tĭzʹəm), *n.* **1.** the practice of systematizing. **2.** adherence to system.

systematist (sĭsʹtĭ mə tĭst), *n.* **1.** one who constructs a system. **2.** a naturalist engaged in classification. **3.** one who adheres to system.

systematize (sĭs′tĭ mə tīz′), *v.t.*, **-tized, -tizing.** to arrange in or according to a system; reduce to a system; make systematic. Also, **systematise.** —**sys′tematiza′tion,** *n.* —**sys′tematiz′er,** *n.*

systematology (sĭs′tĭ mə tŏl′ə jĭ), *n.* the science of systems or their formation.

Système International d'Unités (*Fr.* sēs tĕm ăɴ tĕr-nä syō näl′ dʏ nē tē′), an international system of units derived from the MKS system, in which the six basic units are the metre, kilogram, second, ampere, degree Kelvin, and the candela. The unit of energy in all forms is the joule.

systemic (sĭs tĕm′ĭk, sĭs tē′mĭk), *adj.* **1.** of or pertaining to a system. **2.** *Physiol. and Pathol.* **a.** pertaining to or affecting the entire bodily system, or the body as a whole. **b.** pertaining to a particular system of parts or organs of the body. —**system′ically,** *adv.*

systemize (sĭs′tĭ mīz′), *v.t.*, **-mized, -mizing.** to systematize. Also, **systemise.** —**sys′temiza′tion,** *n.* —**sys′temiz′er,** *n.*

systole (sĭs′tə lĭ), *n.* **1.** *Physiol.* the normal rhythmical contraction of the heart, esp. that of the ventricles, which drives the blood into the aorta and the pulmonary artery. Cf. **diastole.** **2.** *Class. Pros.* the shortening of a syllable regularly long. [t. NL, t. Gk: contraction] —**systolic** (sĭs tŏl′ĭk), *adj.*

Syzran (*Russ.* sĭz′rəny), *n.* a town in the E Soviet Union in Europe, on the Volga. 165,000 (est. 1965).

syzygy (sĭz′ĭ jĭ), *n.*, *pl.* **-gies. 1.** *Astron.* the conjunction or opposition of two heavenly bodies; a point in the orbit of a body, as the moon, at which it is in conjunction with or in opposition to the sun. **2.** *Class. Pros.* a group or combination of two feet (by some restricted to a combination of two feet of different kinds). [t. LL: m. s. *syzygia*, t. Gk: conjunction] —**syzygial** (sĭ sĭj′ĭ əl), **syzygetic** (sĭz′-ĭ jĕt′ĭk), *adj.* —**syz′yget′ically,** *adv.*

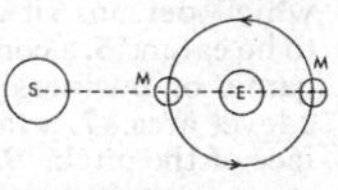

M, M, Syzygies of moon; S, Sun; E, Earth

Szabadka (*Hung.* sŏ′bŏt kŏ), *n.* Hungarian name of **Subotica.**

Szczecin (*Pol.* shchĕt′shĕn), *n.* Polish name of **Stettin.**

Szechwan (sä′chwän′), *n.* a province in central China. 72,160,000 pop. (1957); 220,000 sq. mi. *Cap.:* Chengtu. Also, **Szechuan.**

Szeged (*Hung.* sĕ′gĕd), *n.* a town in S Hungary, on the Tisza river. 105,000 (est. 1962). German, **Szegedin** (*Ger.* sĕ′gĕ dĕn).

Székesfehérvár (*Hung.* sĕ′kĕsh fĕ hĕr vär), *n.* a town in W central Hungary. 60,000 (est. 1962).

Szell (zĕl; *Hung.* sĕl), *n.* **George,** born 1897, U.S. conductor, born in Hungary.

Szolnok (*Hung.* sōl′nōk), *n.* a town in E central Hungary. 50,000 (est. 1962).

Szombathely (*Hung.* sôm′bŏt hĕy), *n.* a town in W Hungary: founded A.D. 48. 57,000 (est. 1962). German, **Steinamanger.**

T

T, t (tē), *n.*, *pl.* **T's** or **Ts, t's** or **ts. 1.** a consonant, the 20th letter of the English alphabet. **2.** something shaped like the letter T. **3. to a T,** exactly: *to suit or fit to a T.*

T, 1. absolute temperature. **2.** (surface) tension. **3.** *Physics.* tesla.

t, *Statistics.* distribution.

't, a shortened form of *it*, before or after a verb, as in *'twas, 'tis, do't, see't.*

t-, *Chem.* **1.** tertiary (def. 2a). **2.** trans- (def. 2).

-t, a suffix forming the past tense or past participle of certain verbs; an equivalent of **-ed.** [(1) pp., ME and OE *-t, -(e)d*, OE *-od*; (2) past tense, ME and OE *-te, -(e)de*, OE *-ode*]

T., 1. Territory. **2.** Tuesday.

t., 1. taken from. **2.** tare. **3.** teaspoon. **4.** temperature. **5.** (L *tempore*) in the time of. **6.** tenor. **7.** *Gram.* tense. **8.** territory. **9.** time. **10.** tome. **11.** ton. **12.** transitive.

Ta, *Chem.* tantalum.

ta (tä), *interj. Slang.* thankyou. [shortened and altered form of *thank you*]

T.A., Territorial Army.

Taal (täl), *n.* Afrikaans (usually prec. by *the*). [t. D: speech]

T.A.B., Typhoid A and B (bacilli); a vaccine made from dead typhoid-paratyphoid A and B bacilli.

tab[1] (tăb), *n.*, *v.*, **tabbed, tabbing.** —*n.* **1.** a small flap, strap, loop, or similar appendage, as on a garment, etc. **2.** a tag or label. **3.** *Aeron.* a hinged portion at the trailing edge of an aileron, elevator, or other control surface on an aircraft. **4.** a stiffened projecting piece from a file, paper, or the like, for ready identification; tag. —*v.t.* **5. keep tabs on,** *Colloq.* to keep account of or a check on: *keep tabs on your expenses.* **6.** to furnish or ornament with a tab or tabs. [orig. uncert.]

tab[2] (tăb), *n. Colloq.* tabulator.

tabanid (tăb′ə nĭd), *n.* **1.** a large bloodsucking dipterous fly of the family *Tabanidae*, esp. a horsefly. —*adj.* **2.** belonging or pertaining to the *Tabanidae.*

tabard (tăb′əd), *n.* **1.** a loose outer garment, with short sleeves or without sleeves, worn by knights over their armour and usually emblazoned with the arms of the wearer. **2.** an official garment of a herald, emblazoned with the arms of his sovereign or ruler. **3.** a coarse, heavy, short coat with or without sleeves, formerly used as an outdoor garment. [ME, t. OF]

T, Tabard (def. 2)

tabaret (tăb′ə rĭt), *n.* a durable upholstery fabric made of satin and watered silk stripes. [? der. TABBY (def. 6)]

tabasco (tə băs′kō), *n.* **1.** a pungent sauce used as a condiment, prepared from the fruit of a variety of capsicum. **2.** (*cap.*) a trademark for this. [named after *Tabasco*, state of Mexico]

tabbinet (tăb′ĭ nĕt′), *n.* a fabric resembling poplin, made of silk and wool. Also, **tabinet.** [obs. *tabine* (? f. TABB(Y) + -INE[2]) + -ET]

tabby (tăb′ĭ), *n.*, *pl.* **-bies,** *adj.*, *v.*, **-bied, -bying.** —*n.* **1.** a cat with a striped or brindled coat. **2.** a female cat. **3.** an old maid; a spinster. **4.** any spiteful female gossip or tattler. **5.** plain weave. **6.** a watered silk fabric, or any other watered material, as moreen. —*adj.* **7.** striped or brindled. **8.** made of or resembling tabby. —*v.t.* **9.** to give a wavy or watered appearance to (silk, etc.). [aphetic var. of ME *attaby*, t. OF: m. *atabis*, t. Ar.: m. *'attābī* rich watered silk, der. *'Attābīya* quarter of Baghdad where first made]

taberdar (tăb′ə dä′, -də), *n.* (at Queen's College, Oxford) a student for an advanced degree who receives a scholarship from the college. [f. *taberd*, var. of TABARD + -AR[3]] —**tab′erdarship′,** *n.*

tabernacle (tăb′ə năk′l), *n.*, *v.*, **-nacled, -nacling. 1.** the tent used by the Jews as a portable sanctuary before their final settlement in Palestine. **2.** any place of worship, esp. one designed for a large congregation. **3.** a canopied niche or recess, as for an image. **4.** *Eccles.* an ornamental receptacle for the reserved Eucharist, now generally found on the altar. **5.** the human body as the temporary abode of the soul. **6.** *Archaic.* a temporary habitation, as a tent or hut. **7.** *Archaic.* a dwelling place. **8.** *Naut.* an upright support to house the foot of a mast which can be raised and lowered. —*v.i.*, *v.t.* **9.** to dwell or place in or as in a tabernacle. [ME, t. L: m. *tabernāculum* tent, booth, der. L *taberna* hut, booth] —**tabernacular** (tăb′ə năk′yŏŏ lə), *adj.*

tabes (tā′bēz), *n. Pathol.* **1.** syphilis of the spinal cord and its appendages, characterized by shooting pains and other sensory disturbances, and in the later stages by locomotor ataxia and paralysis. **2.** a gradually progressive emaciation; consumption. [t. L: a decay]

tabescent (tə bĕs′ənt), *adj.* wasting away. [t. L: s. *tābescens*, ppr.] —**tabes′cence,** *n.*

tabes dorsalis (tā′bēz dô sä′lĭs), *Pathol.* locomotor ataxia. [NL: tabes of the back]

tabetic (tə bĕt′ĭk), *adj.* **1.** Also **tabid** (tăb′ĭd). pertaining to or affected with tabes. —*n.* **2.** one affected with tabes.

tabinet (tăb′ĭ nĕt′), *n.* tabbinet.

tablature (tăb′lə chə), *n.* **1.** a tabular space, surface, or structure. **2.** *Music.* any of various former systems of notation using symbols, as letters or numbers, indicating the strings or frets to be played. [t. F, t. It.: m. *tavolatura*, der. *tavola*, g. L *tabula* table]

table (tā′bl), *n.*, *v.*, **-bled, -bling.** —*n.* **1.** an article of furniture consisting of a flat top resting on legs or on a pillar. **2.** such an article of furniture designed for the play of any various games: *a billiard table.* **3.** the board at or round which persons sit at meals. **4.** the food placed on a table to be eaten. **5.** a company of persons at a table, as for a meal, game, or business transaction. **6.** a flat or plane surface; a level area. **7.** a tableland or plateau. **8.** *Cricket.* the surface of the pitch. **9.** a flat and relatively thin piece of wood, stone, metal, or other hard substance, esp. one artificially shaped for a particular purpose. **10.** anything resembling a table, as a horizontal gravestone supported on pillars. **11.** *Print.* ink table. **12.** *Archit.* a flat, vertical, usually rectangular surface forming a distinct feature in a wall, and often ornamental. **13.** a smooth, flat board or slab on which inscriptions, etc., may be put. **14.** (*pl.*) **a.** the tablets on which certain collections of laws were anciently inscribed, used most often of the Twelve Tables. **b.** the laws themselves. **15.** an arrangement of words, numbers, or signs, or combinations of them, as the multiplication tables, to exhibit a set of facts or relations in a definite, compact, and comprehensive form; a synopsis or scheme. **16.** *Anat.* the inner or outer hard layer or any of the flat bones of the skull. **17.** *Music.* the sounding-board of a violin or similar stringed instrument. **18.** *Jewellery.* **a.** the upper horizontal surface of a faceted gem. **b.** a gem with such a surface. **19. keep a good table,** to provide plentiful, high-quality food. **20. on the table,** *Parl. Proc.* **a.** under discussion; put forward for discussion. **b.** *U.S.* postponed. **21. turn the tables,** to cause a complete reversal of circumstances. **22. under the table, a.** drunk to the extent of being incapable. **b.** given as a bribe. —*v.t.* **23.** to enter in or form into a table or list. **24.** to place or lay on a table. **25.** *Parl. Proc.* **a.** to place (a proposal, resolution, etc.) on the table of an assembly for discussion. **b.** *U.S.* to shelve or postpone. [ME; OE *tablu,* var. of *tabule,* t. L: m. *tabula* board] —**ta′bleless,** *adj.*

tableau (tăb′lō), *n., pl.* **-leaux, -leaus. 1.** a picture, as of a scene. **2.** a picturesque grouping of persons or objects; a striking scene. **3.** a tableau vivant. [t. F: a table, picture, der. *table* TABLE]

tableau vivant (*Fr.* tȧ blō vē väN′), *pl.* **tableaux vivants** (*Fr.* tȧ blō vē väN′). *French.* a representation of a picture, statue, scene, etc., by one or more persons suitably costumed and posed. [F: living picture]

table-book (tā′bl bŏŏk′), *n.* a notebook or notepad.

tablecloth (tā′bl klŏth′), *n.* a cloth for covering the top of a table, esp. during a meal.

table-cut (tā′bl kŭt′), *adj. Jewellery.* cut with a very large table joined to the girdle with a bevel.

table d'hôte (tä′bl dōt′; *Fr.* tȧ blə dōt′), *pl.* **tables d'hôte** (tä′blz dōt′; *Fr.* tȧ blə dōt′). a meal of prearranged courses served at a fixed time and price, for guests at a hotel or restaurant. Cf. **à la carte.** [t. F: the host's table]

tableland (tā′bl lănd′), *n.* an elevated and generally level region of considerable extent; a plateau.

table-lifting (tā′bl lĭf′tĭng), *n.* **1.** the supposed lifting of tables by supernatural rather than physical forces. **2.** spiritualism.

table linen, tablecloths, napkins, etc., for use at meals.

tablemat (tā′bl măt′), *n.* a mat, usually bearing an ornamental design, made of some heat-absorbing material, placed under hot dishes on a table.

Table Mountain, a mountain in the Republic of South Africa, near Cape Town. 3550 ft.

table skittles, a game in which a ball suspended on a string is swung to knock down pins standing on a board.

tablespoon (tā′bl spōōn′), *n.* **1.** a spoon larger than a teaspoon and a dessertspoon, used in the service of the table and as a standard measuring unit in recipes. **2.** a unit of capacity, equal to ½ fluid ounce, or 3 household teaspoons. **3.** a tablespoonful.

tablespoonful (tā′bl spōōn fŏŏl′), *n., pl.* **-fuls.** the quantity a tablespoon holds, equal to about four teaspoonfuls.

tablet (tăb′lĭt), *n.* **1.** a number of sheets of writing paper or the like fastened together at the edge; a pad. **2.** a small, flat slab or surface, esp. one bearing or intended to bear an inscription, carving, or the like. **3.** a leaf or sheet of some inflexible material for writing or marking on, esp. one of a pair or set hinged or otherwise fastened together. **4.** (*pl.*) the set as a whole. **5.** a small, flat or flattish cake or piece of some solid or solidified substance, as a drug, chemical, or the like. **6.** a cake, as of soap. [ME *tablette,* t. F, der. *table* TABLE]

table talk, informal conversation at meals.

table tennis, a miniature tennis game usually played indoors, on a table with small bats and a hollow celluloid or plastic ball; ping-pong.

tabletop (tā′bl tŏp′), *n.* **1.** the top of a table. **2.** a flat surface resembling this.

table-turning (tā′bl tû′nĭng), *n.* **1.** the movement of a table supposedly due to supernatural forces. **2.** spiritualism.

tableware (tā′bl wâr′), *n.* dishes, utensils, etc., used at table or meals.

tabloid (tăb′loid), *n.* **1.** a newspaper, about one half the ordinary page size, emphasizing pictures and concise writing. **2.** a compressed portion of various drugs, chemicals, etc. **3.** anything short or condensed, as a play. —*adj.* **4.** compressed in or as in a tabloid: *a tabloid newspaper.* [f. TABL(ET) + -OID]

taboo (tə bōō′), *adj., n., pl.* **-boos,** *v.,* **-booed, -booing.** —*adj.* **1.** forbidden to general use; placed under a prohibition or ban. **2.** (among the Polynesians and other peoples of the southern Pacific) separated or set apart as sacred or unclean. —*n.* **3.** a prohibition or interdiction of anything; exclusion from use or practice. **4.** (among the Polynesians, etc.) **a.** the system or practice, or an act, whereby things are set apart as sacred, forbidden to general use, or placed under a prohibition or interdiction. **b.** the fact of being so set apart, forbidden, or placed. **5.** exclusion from social relations; ostracism. —*v.t.* **6.** to put under a taboo; prohibit or forbid. **7.** to ostracize, as a person. Also, **tabu.** [t. Tongan: m. *tabu*] —**Syn. 6.** See **forbid.**

tabor (tā′bə), *n.* **1.** a kind of small drum formerly in use, esp. as an accompaniment to a pipe or fife. —*v.i.* **2.** to play upon, or as upon, a tabor; drum. —*v.t.* **3.** to strike or beat, as a tabor. Also, **tabour.** [ME *tabour,* t. OF; of oriental orig.; cf. Pers. *tabūrāk* drum] —**ta′borer,** *n.*

taboret (tăb′ə rĭt), *n.* **1.** a low seat without back or arms, for one person; a stool. **2.** a frame for embroidery. **3.** a small tabor. Also, **tabouret.** [ME *taberett,* f. *taber* TABOR + *-ett* -ET]

taborin (tăb′ə rĭn), *n.* a small tabor. Also, **tabourin.**

tabret (tăb′rĭt), *n.* a small tabor.

Tabriz (tä brēz′), *n.* a city in NW Iran: the capital of Azerbaijan province. 387,803 (est. 1964).

tabu (tə bōō′), *adj., n., v.t.* taboo.

tabular (tăb′yōō lə), *adj.* **1.** pertaining to or of the nature of a table or tabulated arrangement. **2.** ascertained from or computed by the use of tables. **3.** having the form of a table, tablet, or tablature. **4.** flat and expansive. [t. L: s. *tabulāris* relating to a board or plate] —**tab′ularly,** *adv.*

tabula rasa (tăb′yōō lə rä′sə), a mind as yet free from impressions. [t. L: scraped tablet]

tabularize (tăb′yōō lə rīz′), *v.t.* to tabulate. Also, **tabularise.** —**tab′ulariza′tion,** *n.*

tabulate (*v.* tăb′yōō lāt′, *adj.* tăb′yōō lĭt, -lāt′), *v.,* **-lated, -lating,** *adj.* —*v.t.* **1.** to put or form into a table, scheme, or synopsis; formulate tabularly. —*v.i.* **2.** to operate or set the tabulator on a typewriter. —*adj.* **3.** shaped like a table or tablet; tabular. **4.** having transverse dissepiments, as certain corals. [t. L: m. s. *tabulātus,* pp., boarded, planked] —**tab′ula′tion,** *n.*

tabulator (tăb′yōō lā′tə), *n.* **1.** one who or that which tabulates. **2.** an attachment to a typewriter for moving the carriage a set number of spaces along each time it is pressed, used for setting out matter in tabular form, as accounts. **3.** a machine which reads punched cards, performs certain simple calculations and prints the results.

tacamahac (tăk′ə mə hăk′), *n.* **1.** any of certain resinous substances used in incenses, ointments, etc. **2.** any tree yielding such a product. **3.** (in North America) the balsam poplar, *Populus tacamahaca.* Also, **tacamahaca** (tăk′ə mə hăk′ə). [t. Sp.: m. *tacama(ha)ca,* t. Nahuatl: m. *tecomah(a)ca* scented copal]

tacet (tā′sĕt), *Music.* an indication that an instrument or voice is to be silent for a time. [L: (it) is silent]

tache (tăsh, täsh), *n. Archaic.* a buckle; clasp. Also, **tach.** [late ME, t. F. See TACK[1]]

tacheometer (tăk′ĭ ŏm′ĭ tə), *n.* **1.** an instrument for determining the speed of blood in the vessels. **2.** an instrument used in surveying to measure the distance from the point of observation to another point at which a staff is held. The length of the staff seen between two reference hairs in the telescope of the instrument is multiplied by a factor to give the distance. **3.** any of various other instruments for measuring speed. Also, **tachometer, tachymeter.** [t. F: m. *tachéomètre,* f. *taché-* (m. Gk *tácheos,* gen. sing. of *táchos* speed) + *-mètre* -METER[1]] —**tacheometric** (tăk′ĭ ə mĕt′rĭk), **tacheometrical** (tăk′ĭ ə mĕt′rĭ kl), *adj.* **tacheometrically** (tăk′ĭ ə mĕt′rĭ kəlĭ, -klĭ), *adv.* —**tach′eom′etry,** *n.*

Tachikawa (tä chē′kə wə′, tăch′ĭ kä′wə), *n.* a town in Japan, in SE central Honshu island. 100,719 (1965).

tachina fly (tăk′ĭ nə), any of the dipterous insects of the family *Tachinidae,* the larvae of which are parasitic on other insects such as caterpillars, beetles, etc. [f. NL *tachina* (t. Gk, fem. of *tachinós* swift) + FLY]

tachisme (tä′shĭz′əm; *Fr.* tȧ shēzm′), *n.* (*sometimes cap.*) a style of action painting, originating in France in the 20th century. [t. F, der. *tache* blot, stain]

tachistoscope (tə kĭs′tə skōp′), *n.* an apparatus used in experimental psychology which exposes to view an object, group of objects, letters, words, etc., for a selected brief period of time. [f. Gk *táchisto(s)* swiftest + -SCOPE] —**tachistoscopic** (tə kĭs′tə skŏp′ĭk), *adj.*

tacho-, a word element meaning 'swift'. [t. Gk, comb. form of *táchos* speed, akin to *tachýs.* See TACHY-]

tachogram (tăk′ə grăm′), *n.* the record produced by the action of a tachometer.

tachograph (tăk′ə grăf′, -gräf′), *n.* **1.** a recording tachometer. **2.** a record made by such an instrument. [f. TACHO- + -GRAPH]

tachometer (tă kŏm′ĭ tə), *n.* **1.** an instrument for measuring the number of revolutions per minute made by a revolving shaft. **2.** a tacheometer. [f. TACHO- + -METER[1]] —**tachometric** (tăk′ə mĕt′rĭk), **tachometrical** (tăk′ə mĕt′rĭ kl), *adj.* —**tachometrically** (tăk′ə mĕt′rĭ kəlĭ, -klĭ), *adv.* —**tachom′etry,** *n.*

tachy-, a word element meaning 'swift', as in *tachygraphy.* [t. Gk, comb. form of *tachýs*]

tachycardia (tăk′ĭ kä′dĭ ə), *n. Med.* an abnormally fast heartbeat. —**tachycardiac** (tăk′ĭ kä′dĭ ăk′), *adj.*

tachygraph (tăk′ĭ grăf′, -gräf′), *n.* **1.** tachygraphic writing. **2.** a tachygraphic writer.

tachygraphy (tă kĭg′rə fĭ), *n.* the Greek and Roman handwriting used for rapid stenography and writing. —**tachyg′rapher, tachyg′raphist,** *n.* —**tachygraphic** (tăk′ĭ grăf′ĭk), **tach′igraph′ical,** *adj.*

tachylyte (tăk′ĭ līt′), *n.* a black, glassy form of basalt, readily fusible and of a high lustre. Also, **tachylite.** [t. G: m. *Tachylit,* f. Gk: *tachy-* TACHY- + s. *lytós* soluble] —**tachylytic** (tăk′ĭ lĭt′ĭk), *adj.*

tachymeter (tă kĭm′ĭ tə), *n.* a tacheometer. [f. TACHY- + -METER[1]] —**tachymetric** (tăk′ĭ mĕt′rĭk), **tachymetrical** (tăk′ĭ mĕt′rĭ kl), *adj.* —**tachymetrically** (tăk′ĭ mĕt′rĭ kəlĭ, -klĭ), *adv.* —**tachym′etry,** *n.*

tachypnoea (tăk′ĭp nē′ə), *n. Med.* abnormally rapid breathing. Also, *U.S.,* **tachypnea.** [f. TACHY- + *-pnoea* (t. Gk: m. *-pnoia,* Doric d. for *pnoē̂* breath)]

tacit (tăs′ĭt), *adj.* **1.** silent; saying nothing. **2.** not openly expressed, but implied; understood or inferred. **3.** unspoken: *tacit consent.* [t. L: s. *tacitus,* pp.] —**tac′itly,** *adv.* —**tac′itness,** *n.*

taciturn (tăs′ĭ tûn′), *adj.* inclined to silence, or reserved in speech; not inclined to conversation. [t. L: s. *taciturnus*] —**taciturnity** (tăs′ĭ tû′nĭ tĭ), *n.* —**tac′iturn′ly,** *adv.*

Tacitus (tăs′ĭ təs), *n.* **Publius Cornelius** (pŭb′lĭ əs kô nē′lyəs), A.D. *c.* 55–*c.* 120, Roman historian, noted for his concise style. —**Tacitean** (tăs′ĭ tē′ən), *adj.*

tack[1] (tăk), *n.* **1.** a short, sharp-pointed nail or pin, usually with a flat and comparatively large head. **2.** a stitch, esp. a long stitch used in fastening seams, etc., preparatory to a more thorough sewing. **3.** a fastening, esp. in a temporary manner. **4.** the quality of being tacky; stickiness. **5.** *Naut.* **a.** a rope which confines the foremost lower corner of a course on a square-rigged ship. **b.** the part of a sail to which such a rope is fastened. **c.** the lower forward corner of a fore-and-aft sail. **d.** a line secured to the lower outboard corner of a studdingsail to haul it to the end of the boom. **6.** *Naut.* **a.** the direction or course of a ship in relation to the position of her sails: *the starboard tack* (when close-hauled with the wind on the starboard side); *the port tack* (when close-hauled with the wind on the port side). **b.** a course obliquely against the wind. **c.** one of the series of straight runs which make up the zigzag course of a ship proceeding to windward. **7.** a course of action or conduct, esp. one differing from some preceding or other course. **8.** one of the movements of a zigzag course on land. **9.** the equipment collectively which pertains to the saddling and harnessing of horses; saddlery. **10. on the wrong tack,** following a false line of reasoning; under a wrong impression. —*v.t.* **11.** to fasten by a tack or tacks: *to tack a rug.* **12.** to secure by some slight or temporary fastening. **13.** to join together; unite or combine. **14.** to attach as something supplementary; append or annex (usually fol. by *on* or *on to*). **15.** *Naut.* **a.** to change the course of (a ship) to the opposite tack. **b.** navigate (a ship) by a series of tacks. —*v.i.* **16.** *Naut.* **a.** to change the course of a ship by bringing her head into the wind and then causing it to fall off on the other side: *he ordered us to tack at once.* **b.** to change its course in this way, as a ship. **c.** to proceed to windward by a series of courses as close to the wind as the vessel will sail, the wind being alternately on one bow and then on the other. **17.** to follow a zigzag course or route. **18.** to change one's course of action or conduct. [ME, t. AF: m. *taque* a fastening, clasp, nail, ult. t. Gmc; cf. G *Zacken* prong, D *tak* twig] —**tack′er,** *n.* —**tack′less,** *adj.*

tack[2] (tăk), *n.* food; fare. [orig. obscure]

tack[3] (tăk), *n. Scot. and N Dial.* **1.** tenure or tenancy of land, etc. **2.** a catch of fish. [ME *tak,* t. Scand., cf. Icel. *tak* chattels; c. TAKE]

tacket (tăk′ĭt), *n. Dial.* a nail, esp. a hobnail. [ME *taket,* f. TACK[1] + -ET]

tackle (tăk′l), *n., v.,* **-led, -ling.** —*n.* **1.** equipment, apparatus, or gear, esp. for fishing. **2.** a mechanism or apparatus, as a rope and block or a combination of ropes and blocks, for hoisting, lowering, and shifting objects or materials. **3.** any system of leverage using several pulleys. **4.** *Naut.* **a.** the gear and rigging used in handling a ship, esp. that used in working the sails, etc. **b.** a purchase consisting of a rope running over two or more sheaves or pulleys. **c.** an arrangement of rope and blocks or sheaves for multiplying power. **5.** an act of tackling, as in football. —*v.t.* **6.** to undertake to deal with, master, solve, etc. **7.** *Colloq.* to lay hold upon, attack, or encounter. **8.** *Soccer, Hockey, etc.* to get or attempt to get the ball from (an opponent). **9.** *Rugby Football, etc.* to seize and pull down (an opponent having the ball). **10.** to harness (a horse). —*v.i.* **11.** *Football, Hockey, etc.* to tackle an opponent. [ME *takel* gear, t. MLG, der. *taken* seize, c. TAKE, v.] —**tack′ler,** *n.*

tackling (tăk′lĭng), *n.* gear; tackle.

tacky[1] (tăk′ĭ), *adj.* adhesive; sticky, as a paint, varnish, or the like, when partly dry. [f. TACK[1] + -Y[1]]

tacky[2] (tăk′ĭ), *adj.,* **-ier, -iest.** *U.S. Colloq.* shabby; dowdy. [orig. obscure]

Tacna-Arica (*Sp.* täk′nä ä rē′kä), *n.* a maritime region in W South America, long in dispute between Chile and Peru: annexed by Chile, 1883; divided as a result of arbitration into Tacna department, Peru, and Arica department, Chile, 1929.

tacnode (tăk′nōd), *n. Geom.* a point of contact between two parts of the same curve. [irreg. f. L *tac(tus)* touch + NODE]

Tacoma (tə kō′mə), *n.* **1.** a seaport in the U.S., in W Washington, on Puget Sound. 147,979 (1960). **2. Mount.** See **Rainier, Mount.**

Taconic (tă kō′nĭk), *adj.* of or pertaining to the major mountain-building episode which occurred at the end of the Ordovician period in North America. [name of a mountain range forming part of the Appalachian Mountains]

taconite (tăk′ə nīt′), *n. U.S.* a low-grade iron ore found in the region of Lake Superior as a hard rock formation: it contains about 51 per cent silica and 27 per cent iron.

tact (tăkt), *n.* **1.** a keen sense of what to say or do to avoid giving offence; skill in dealing with difficult or delicate situations. **2.** touch; the sense of touch. [t. L: s. *tactus* sense of touch]

tactful (tăkt′fəl), *adj.* having or manifesting tact: *a tactful person, a tactful reply.* —**tact′fully,** *adv.* —**tact′fulness,** *n.* —**Syn.** See **diplomatic.**

tactic (tăk′tĭk), *n.* **1.** tactics. **2.** a system or a detail of tactics. **3.** a plan or procedure for achieving a desired end. —*adj.* **4.** of or pertaining to arrangement or order; tactical. [t. NL: s. *tactica,* t. Gk: m. *taktikḗ,* fem. of *taktikós,* der. *taktós* ordered]

tactical (tăk′tĭ kl), *adj.* **1.** of or pertaining to tactics, esp. military or naval tactics. **2.** characterized by skilful tactics or adroit manoeuvring or procedure: *tactical movements.* —**tac′tically,** *adv.*

tactical unit, *Mil.* a group organized to operate independently in action and sharing a specific objective.

tactician (tăk tĭsh′ən), *n.* one versed in tactics.

tactics (tăk′tĭks), *n.* **1.** the art or science of disposing military or naval forces for battle and manoeuvring them in battle. **2.** (*construed as pl.*) the manoeuvres themselves. **3.** (*construed as pl.*) mode of procedure for gaining advantage or success. [pl. of TACTIC. See -ICS] —**Syn. 1.** See **strategy.**

tactile (tăk′tīl), *adj.* **1.** of or pertaining to the organs or sense of touch; endowed with the sense of touch. **2.** perceptible to the touch; tangible. [t. L: m. s. *tactilis* tangible] —**tactility** (tăk tĭl′ĭ tĭ), *n.*

taction (tăk′shən), *n. Obs.* touch; contact.

tactless (tăkt′lĭs), *adj.* without tact; showing no tact: *a tactless person.* —**tact′lessly,** *adv.* —**tact′lessness,** *n.*

tactual (tăk′tyŏŏ əl), *adj.* **1.** of or pertaining to touch. **2.** communicating or imparting the sensation of contact; arising from or due to touch. [f. L *tactu(s)* touch + -AL[1]] —**tac′tually,** *adv.*

tad (tăd), *n. U.S.* a small child, esp. a boy. [short for TADPOLE]

Tadema (tăd′ĭ mə), *n.* **Sir Lawrence Alma-.** See **Alma-Tadema.**

Tadjik (*Russ.* tȧd zhĭk′), *n., pl.* **-jik.** Tajik (person).

Tadmor (tăd′mô), *n.* biblical name of **Palmyra.**

tadpole (tăd′pōl′), *n.* the aquatic larva or immature form of frogs, toads, etc., esp. after the enclosure of the gills and before the appearance of the forelimbs and the resorption of the tail. [ME *taddepol*, f. *tadde* TOAD + *pol* POLL (head)]

Tadpole, showing early stages of growth

Tadzhikistan (*Russ.* təd zhĭ kyĭ-stån′), *n.* a constituent republic of the Soviet Union in Asia, N of Afghanistan. 2,267,000 pop. (1963); 54,900 sq. mi. *Cap.*: Dyushambe. Also, **Tajikistan.** Official name, **Tadzhik Soviet Socialist Republic.**

taedium vitae (tē′dyəm vī′tē), *Latin.* a feeling that life is unbearably wearisome. Also, **tedium vitae.** [L: wearisome of life]

Taegu (tĕ gōō′), *n.* a city in S South Korea. 716,684 (1963). Japanese, **Taikyu.**

Taejon (tĕ jŏn′), *n.* a city in W South Korea. 303,377 (1964). Japanese, **Taiden.**

tael (tāl), *n.* **1.** liang. **2.** any of various other similar units of weight in the Far East. **3.** a Chinese money of account, being the value of this weight of standard silver. [t. Pg., t. Malay: m. *tahil* weight]

ta'en (tān), *v. Poetic.* taken.

taenia (tē′nĭ ə), *n., pl.* **-niae** (-nĭ ē′). **1.** *Archaeol.* a headband or fillet. **2.** *Archit.* the fillet or band on the Doric architrave, which separates it from the frieze. See diag. under **column. 3.** *Anat.* a ribbon-like structure, as certain bands of white nerve fibres in the brain. **4.** *Zool.* tapeworm. Also, *U.S.*, **tenia.** [t. L, t. Gk: m. *tainía*]

taeniacide (tē′nĭ ə sīd′), *n. Med.* an agent that destroys tapeworms. Also, *U.S.*, **teniacide.** —**tae′niacid′al,** *adj.*

taeniafuge (tē′nĭ ə fyōōj′), *Med.* —*adj.* **1.** expelling tapeworms, as a medicine. —*n.* **2.** an agent or medicine to expel tapeworms from the body.

taeniasis (tĭ nī′ə sĭs), *n. Pathol.* a diseased condition due to the presence of taeniae or tapeworms.

T.A.F., Tactical Air Force.

Tafawa Balewa (tə fä′wə bə lā′wə), **Alhaji Sir Abubakar** (ăl hăj′ĭ sər ăb′ōō bä′kə), 1912–66, Nigerian statesman: prime minister 1957–66.

tafelberg (tä′fəl bûg′), *n. S African.* a mesa. [t. Afrikaans, f. *tafel* table + *berg* mountain]

tafelkop (tä′fəl kŏp′), *n. S African.* a butte. [t. Afrikaans, f. *tafel* table + *kop* head]

taffarel (tăf′ə rəl, -rĕl′), *n. Obs.* taffrail. Also, **tafferel.**

taffeta (tăf′ĭ tə), *n.* **1.** a lustrous silk or rayon fabric of plain weave. **2.** any of various other fabrics of silk, linen, wool, etc., in use at different periods. —*adj.* **3.** of or resembling taffeta. [ME *taffata*, t. ML, ult. t. Pers.: m. *tāftah* silken or linen cloth]

taffrail (tăf′rāl′), *n. Naut.* **1.** the upper part of the stern of a vessel. **2.** the rail across the stern. [earlier *tafferel*, t. D: m. *tafereel* panel (dim. of *tafel* TABLE)]

taffy (tăf′ĭ), *n. U.S.* toffee. [var. of TOFFEE]

Taffy (tăf′ĭ), *n. Colloq.* a Welshman. [Welsh form of *Davy*, shortened form of *David*, proper name and name of patron saint of Wales]

tafia (tăf′ĭ ə), *n.* a kind of rum made from the lower grades of molasses, refuse sugar, etc., in Haiti. [orig. uncert.]

Tafilelt (tă fē′lĕlt), *n.* a former oasis region in SE Morocco; ab. 500 sq. mi. Also, **Tafilalet** (tăf′ĭ lä′lĕt).

Taft (tăft), *n.* **William Howard,** 1857–1930, 27th president of the U.S. (1909–13) and chief justice of the Supreme Court (1921–30).

tag[1] (tăg), *n., adj., v.,* **tagged, tagging.** —*n.* **1.** a piece or strip of strong paper, leather, or the like, for attaching by one end to something as a mark or label. **2.** any small hanging or loosely attached part or piece; tatter. **3.** a loop of material sewn on a garment so that it can be hung up. **4.** a point or binding of metal, plastic, or other hard substance at the end of a cord, lace, or the like. **5.** *Angling.* a small piece made of tinsel or the like, tied to the shank of a hook at the body of an artificial fly. **6.** a tag end. **7.** the refrain of a song or poem. **8.** the last words of a speech in a play, etc., as a curtain line or cue. **9.** an addition to a speech or writing, as the moral of a fable. **10.** a trite quotation or cliché, esp. one in Latin. **11.** a word or phrase applied as characteristic of a person or group. **12.** a curlicue in writing. **13.** a lock of hair. **14.** a matted lock of wool on a sheep. **15.** the tip of the tail of a fox. **16.** *Obs.* the rabble. —*v.t.* **17.** to furnish with a tag or tags; attach a tag to. **18.** to append as a tag to something else. **19.** to apply as characteristic a word or phrase to (a person or group). **20.** to remove tags of wool from (a sheep). **21.** *Colloq.* to follow closely. —*v.i.* **22.** to follow closely; go along or about as a follower (usually fol. by *along*). [ME; b. TATTER and RAG[1]] —**tag′like′,** *adj.*

tag[2] (tăg), *n., v.,* **tagged, tagging.** —*n.* **1.** a children's game in which one player chases the others till he touches one of them, who then takes his place as pursuer. **2.** *Wrestling.* an act of touching hands over the top rope by two team-mates in tag wrestling. —*adj.* **3.** denoting or pertaining to a form of professional wrestling in which two teams of two compete one at a time. The wrestler outside the ring must hold a tagrope, and the two may change places at any time by touching hands over the top rope. —*v.t.* **4.** to touch in or as in the game of tag. Also, **tig.** [? special use of TAG[1]]

Tagalog (tə gä′lŏg), *n.* **1.** a member of a Malayan people native in the Philippines. **2.** the principal Indonesian language of the Philippines.

Taganrog (*Russ.* tə gån rôk′), *n.* a seaport in the S Soviet Union in Europe, on the **Gulf of Taganrog,** a NE arm of the Sea of Azov. 234,000 (est. 1965).

tag day, *U.S.* a flag day.

tag end, the tail end or concluding part, as of a proceeding; fag end.

tagger (tăg′ə), *n.* **1.** one who or that which tags. **2.** (*pl.*) iron in very thin sheets, either uncoated or coated with tin.

tagliatelle (tăl′yə tĕl′ĭ; *It.* tȧl yȧ tĕl′lĕ), *n.* a kind of pasta made with egg and shaped into long, flat pieces. [t. It., f. s. *tagliato* (pp. of *tagliare* to cut) + *-elle* fem. pl. dim. suffix]

Tagore (tə gô′), *n.* **Sir Rabindranath** (rə bĭn′drə nät′), 1861–1941, Indian poet, writing in Bengali and English.

tagrag (tăg′răg′), *n.* **1.** riffraff; rabble. **2.** a tatter.

tagrope (tăg′rōp′), *n. Wrestling.* a short rope attached to a corner of the ring, which a tag wrestler outside the ring must be holding when he touches hands to change places with his team-mate in the ring.

taguan (tăg′wən), *n.* the largest of the flying squirrels, *Petaurista philippensis*, of India and south-east Asia.

Tagus (tā′gəs), *n.* a river flowing generally W through central Spain and Portugal to the Atlantic near Lisbon. 566 mi. Spanish, **Tajo.** Portuguese, **Tejo.**

taha (tä′hä), *n.* a sparrow-like passerine weaverbird, *Euplectes afra*, with yellow and brown plumage, widespread in Africa.

Tahiti (tä hē′tĭ), *n.* the principal island of the Society Islands, in the S Pacific. 52,068 pop. (1962); 402 sq. mi. *Cap.*: Papeete. See map under **Hawaiian Islands.**

Tahitian (tä hē′tĭ ən, tä hē′shyən), *adj.* **1.** of or pertaining to Tahiti, its inhabitants, or their language. —*n.* **2.** a native or inhabitant of Tahiti. **3.** the language of Tahiti, a Polynesian language.

tahr (tä), *n.* any of various wild goats of the genus *Hemitragus*, of S Asia, as the **Himalayan tahr,** *H. jemlahicus*; mountain ibex. Also, **thar.** [t. Nepalese]

tahsildar (tə sēl′dä′), *n.* (in India) a collector for, or official of, the revenue department. Also, **tahsceldar.** [t. Urdu, f. Pers.: *tahsil* collection + *-dar*, agent suffix]

Tai (tī), *n., adj.* Thai.

Taichung (tī′chōōng′), *n.* a city in W central Taiwan. 207,000 (est. 1964). Japanese, **Taichu** (tī′chōō′).

Taiden (tī′dĕn′), *n.* Japanese name of **Taejon.**

Taieri (tī′yə rĭ), *n.* a river in S South Island, New Zealand, flowing SE to the Pacific Ocean. 175 mi.

taiga (tī′gä), *n.* the coniferous, evergreen forests of subarctic lands, covering vast areas of northern North America and Eurasia. [t. Russ.]

Taihoku (tī′hō′kōō), *n.* Japanese name of **Taipeh.**

Taikyu (tī′kyōō′), *n.* Japanese name of **Taegu.**

tail[1] (tāl), *n.* **1.** the hindmost part of an animal, esp. when forming a distinct flexible appendage to the trunk. **2.** something resembling or suggesting this in shape or position: *the tail of a kite.* **3.** the hinder, bottom, or concluding part of anything; the rear. **4.** the final or concluding part of anything. **5.** the inferior or refuse part of anything. **6.** a long braid or tress of hair. **7.** *Astron.* the luminous train extending from the head of a comet. **8.** *Colloq.* (*pl.*) the reverse of a coin. **9.** an arrangement of objects or persons extending as or as if a tail. **10.** a downward stroke, as of a printed or written letter, the stem of a musical note, etc. **11.** a retinue. **12.** *Aeron.* the stabilizing and control surfaces at the after end of an aircraft. **13.** (*pl.*) **a.** the skirts of certain coats, as a swallow-tailed coat. **b.** a swallow-tailed coat. **c.** full-dress attire. **14.** the lower part of a pool or section of a stream. **15.** *Colloq.* the buttocks. **16.** *Taboo Slang.* **a.** the vagina. **b.** a woman considered as an object of coitus. **17.** *Colloq.* a person who follows another, esp. one who is employed to do so in order to observe or hinder escape. **18. turn tail, a.** to turn the back, as in aversion or fright. **b.** to run away; flee. **19. with one's tail between one's legs,** in a state of utter defeat or humiliation; abjectly.

—*adj.* **20.** coming from behind: *a tail wind.* **21.** being at the back or rear: *a tail-light.*
—*v.t.* **22.** to form or furnish with a tail. **23.** to form or constitute the tail or end of (a procession, etc.). **24.** to terminate; follow like a tail. **25.** to join or attach (one thing) at the tail or end of another. **26.** *Bldg Trades.* to fasten (a beam, etc.) by one of its ends (fol. by *in, into,* etc.). **27.** *Austral.* to tend or herd (sheep or cattle). **28.** to dock the tail of: *tailed lambs.* **29.** to remove the stalk of. **30.** to seize by the tail: *to tail an otter.* **31.** *Slang.* to follow in order to hinder escape or to observe: *to tail a suspect.*
—*v.i.* **32.** to form or move in a line or continuation suggestive of a tail: *hikers tailing up a narrow path.* **33.** (of a boat, etc.) to have or take a position with the stern in a particular direction. **34.** *Colloq.* to follow close behind. **35.** *Bldg Trades.* (of a beam, etc.) to be fastened by the end (fol. by *in, into,* etc.). **36. tail away** or **off,** to decrease gradually; decline.
[ME; OE *tægel,* c. Icel. *tagl*] —**tail′less,** *adj.* —**tail′-like′,** *adj.*

tail² (tāl), *n.* **1.** *Law.* the limitation of an estate to a person and the heirs of his body, or some particular class of such heirs. **2.** *Print., Bookbinding.* the bottom of a page or book. —*adj.* **3.** *Law.* limited to a specified line of heirs; being in tail. [ME, t. OF: m. *taille* cutting, tax, der. *taillier,* v., cut] —**tail′less,** *adj.*

tail-block (tāl′blŏk′), *n.* *Naut.* a sheave-block with a small length of rope spliced round it for making fast in any position.

tailboard (tāl′bôd′), *n.* the board at the back of a truck, wagon, etc., which can be removed or let down for convenience in loading and unloading. Also, *Chiefly U.S.,* **tailgate.**

tail coat, a man's evening coat with a pair of divided tapering skirts behind; a swallow-tailed coat.

tail end, **1.** the rear part of anything. **2.** the tag end; the final part.

tailgate (tāl′gāt′), *n.* **1.** *U.S.* a tailboard. **2.** *Jazz.* the flamboyant style of trombone-playing characteristic of traditional New Orleans jazz, so called because in processions the trombonist sat at the rear of a lorry. —*adj.* **3.** *Jazz.* denoting, pertaining to, or of this style of trombone-playing.

tailgater (tāl′gā′tə), *n.* a tailgate trombone-player.

tailing (tā′lĭng), *n.* **1.** the part of a projecting stone or brick tailed or inserted in a wall. **2.** (*pl.*) the residue of any product, as in mining; leavings.

taille (tī; *Fr.* tȧy), *n., pl.* **tailles** (tī, tīz; *Fr.* tȧy). *French Hist.* a tax formerly levied by a French king or overlord on land or on his subjects.

tail-light (tāl′līt′), *n.* a light, usually red, at the rear of a motor vehicle, train, etc. Also, **tail-lamp** (tāl′lămp′).

tailor (tā′lə), *n.* **1.** one whose business it is to make or mend outer garments, especially for men. —*v.i.* **2.** to do the work of a tailor. —*v.t.* **3.** to make by tailor's work. **4.** to fit or furnish with clothing. [ME, t. OF: m. *tailleor* cutter, der. *taillier* cut] —**tai′lorless,** *adj.*

tailorbird (tā′lə bûd′), *n.* any of various small Asiatic passerine birds of the genus *Orthotomus* and its near relatives, which stitch leaves together to form and hide their nests.

tailoring (tā′lə rĭng), *n.* **1.** the business or work of a tailor. **2.** the skill or craft of a tailor.

tailor-made (tā′lə mād′), *adj.* **1.** made by or as by a tailor (applied esp. to women's garments made of more substantial fabrics or with plainness of cut and finish). **2.** made by a tailor to a particular order for an individual customer. **3.** designed for a particular need or taste.

tailor's chalk, pipeclay.

tailpiece (tāl′pēs′), *n.* **1.** a piece added at the end; an end piece or appendage. **2.** *Print.* a small decorative design at the end of a chapter or at the bottom of a page. **3.** (in musical instruments of the violin family) a triangular piece of wood, usually of ebony, to which the lower ends of the strings are fastened.

tailplane (tāl′plān′), *n.* *Aeron.* a horizontal surface at the rear end of an aircraft providing longitudinal stability. Also, *Chiefly U.S.,* **horizontal stabilizer.**

tailrace (tāl′rās′), *n.* **1.** the race, flume, or channel leading away from a waterwheel or the like. **2.** *Mining.* the channel for conducting tailings or refuse away in water.

tail skid, *Aeron.* a runner under the tail of an aeroplane.

tail spin, **1.** *Aeron.* spin (def. 20). **2.** *Colloq.* a sudden collapse into a state of utter confusion; flat spin.

tailstock (tāl′stŏk′), *n.* (on a lathe or grinder) the movable or sliding frame supporting the dead spindle.

tail wind, a favourable wind blowing from behind an aircraft or vessel, etc., thus increasing its speed.

Taimyr (*Russ.* tȧy mĭr′), *n.* a large peninsula in the N Soviet Union in Asia between the Kara and Laptev seas. Also, **Taimir.**

Tainan (tī′năn′), *n.* a city in SW Taiwan. 375,101 (1965).

Taine (tān; *Fr.* tĕn), *n.* **Hippolyte Adolphe** (*Fr.* ē pô-lēt ȧ dôlf′), 1828–93, French literary critic and historian.

Taino (tī′nō), *n., pl.* **-nos.** **1.** a member of an extinct Arawakan Indian tribe of the West Indies. **2.** their language.

taint (tānt), *n.* **1.** a touch of something offensive or deleterious; a latent or incipient defect or corruption. **2.** a trace of infection, contamination, or the like. **3.** a trace of dishonour or discredit. **4.** *Obs.* colour or tinge. —*v.t.* **5.** to modify as by a touch of something offensive or deleterious. **6.** to infect, contaminate, or corrupt. **7.** to sully or tarnish. **8.** *Obs.* to colour or tinge. —*v.i.* **9.** to become tainted. [ME *taynte,* b. OF *teint* (pp. of *teindre* colour, t. L: m. *tingere*) and aphetic var. of ATTAINT] —**taint′less,** *adj.*

tainture (tān′chə), *n.* *Obs.* taint.

taipan (tī′păn), *n.* a venomous snake, *Oxyuranus scutellatus,* of New Guinea and N Australia, about 10 feet long.

Taipeh (tī′pā′), *n.* the capital of Taiwan, in the N part of the island. 1,076,649 (1965). Also, **Taipei.** Japanese, **Taihoku.** See map under **Taiwan.**

Taiping (tī′pĭng′), *n.* a town in and the capital of Perak state, Malaysia. 48,206 (1957).

Taiping (tī′pĭng′), *n.* a supporter of or participant in an unsuccessful revolution in China (the **Taiping Rebellion,** 1850–64), led by Hung Hsiu-chüan, who attempted to overthrow the Manchu dynasty and introduce agrarian reforms. [t. Chinese, f. *tai* great + *ping* peace]

Taisho (tī′shō′), *n.* *Jap. Hist.* the artistic style associated with the reign of the Japanese emperor Yoshihito, 1912–26.

Taiwan (tī′wän′), *n.* a Chinese island separated from SE China by **Taiwan Strait:** a possession of Japan, 1895–1945; part of China 1945–49; homeland of Nationalist Chinese since 1949. See **Nationalist China.** 11,375,085 pop. (1962); 13,890 sq. mi. *Cap.:* Taipeh. Also, **Formosa.** —**Tai′wanese′,** *adj., n.*

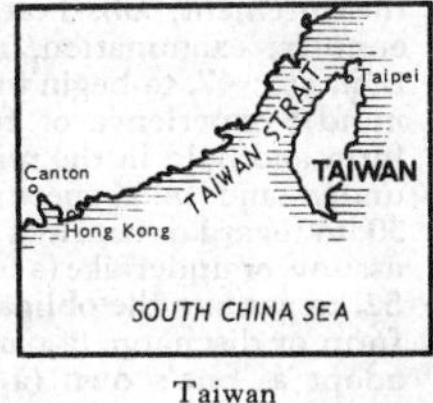

Taiwan

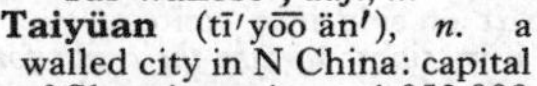

Taiyüan (tī′yōō än′), *n.* a walled city in N China: capital of Shansi province. 1,053,000 (est. 1958). Also, **Yangkü.**

Ta'iz (tī ēz′), *n.* a town in SW Yemen. 30,000 (est. 1961). Also, **Ta'izz.**

taj (täj), *n., pl.* **tajes** (tä′jĭz). a tall, conical cap worn in Muslim countries. [t. Ar.]

Tajik (*Russ.* tȧd zhĭk′), *n., pl.* **-jik.** **1.** a person of Iranian descent living in the Tadzhik Republic and vicinity. **2.** Tadzhikistan. Also, **Tadjik.**

Tajikistan (*Russ.* tȧd zhĭ kĭ stän′), *n.* Tadzhikistan.

Taj Mahal (täj′ mə häl′, täzh′-), a white marble mausoleum built at Agra, India, by the Mogul emperor Shah Jahan (fl. 1628–58) for his favourite wife. [t. Urdu, t. Pers.: crown of buildings]

Tajo (*Sp.* tä′KHō), *n.* Spanish name of **Tagus.**

takahe (tä′kə hē′), *n.* a large, flightless bird of New Zealand, *Notornis mantelli.* [t. Maori]

Takamatsu (täk′ə măt′sōō), *n.* a seaport in SW Japan, on Shikoku island. 243,444 (1965).

Takao (tä kou′), *n.* former name of **Kaohsiung.**

Takaoka (tä kä′ō kä′), *n.* a town in Japan, in W central Honshu island. 139,502 (1965).

Takapuna (tŭk′ə pōō′nə), *n.* a N suburb of Auckland, in New Zealand. 22,600 (est. 1965).

Takatsuki (tə kät′sōō kĭ, tä′kət sōō′kĭ), *n.* a town in Japan, in S Honshu island. 130,735 (1965).

take (tāk), *v.,* **took, taken, taking,** *n.* —*v.t.* **1.** to get into one's hands or possession by force or artifice. **2.** to seize, catch, or capture. **3.** to grasp, grip or hold. **4.** to get into one's hold, possession, control, etc., by one's own action but without force or artifice. **5.** to select; pick out from a number: *take a chocolate from a box.* **6.** to receive or accept willingly. **7.** to receive by way of payment or charge. **8.** to obtain by making payment: *to take a house in central London.* **9.** to get or obtain from a source; derive. **10.** to receive into the body or system, as by swallowing or inhaling: *to take food.* **11.** to eat or use habitually, as a foodstuff, flavouring, etc.: *to take sugar in tea.* **12.** to quote, esp. without acknowledgement: *this writer has taken whole pages from Forster.* **13.** to carry off or remove (fol. by *away,* etc.). **14.** to remove by death. **15.** to subtract or deduct: *to take 2 from 5.* **16.** to carry or convey: *take your lunch with you.* **17.** to convey or transport: *we took the children to the seaside by car.* **18.** to have recourse to (a vehicle, etc.) as a means of progression or travel: *to take a bus to the top of the hill.* **19.** to effect a change in the position or condition of: *his ability took him to the top.* **20.** to conduct or lead: *where will this road take me?* **21.** to attempt to get over, through, round, etc. (something that presents itself), or succeed in doing this: *the horse took the hedge with an easy jump.* **22.** (of a disease, illness, or the like) to attack or affect: *to be taken with a fit.* **23.** to become affected by: *a stone which will take a high polish.* **24.** to absorb or become impregnated with (a colour, etc.). **25.** to surprise; detect; come upon: *to take a thief in the act of stealing.* **26.** to receive or adopt (a person) into some specified or implied relation: *to take a woman in marriage.* **27.** to have sexual intercourse with: *to take a woman by force.* **28.** to secure regularly by payment: *to take a magazine.* **29.** to adopt and enter upon (a way, course, etc.); proceed to deal with in some manner: *to take a matter under consideration.* **30.** to proceed to occupy: *to take a seat.* **31.** to receive in a specified manner: *to take a thing kindly.* **32.** to avail oneself of (an opportunity, etc.). **33.** to obtain or exact (satisfaction or reparation). **34.** to receive, or be the recipient of (something bestowed, administered, etc.): *to take first prize.* **35.** to have, undergo, enjoy, etc., as for one's benefit: *to take a bath, take a rest.* **36.** to occupy, use up, or consume (space, material, time, etc.). **37.** to attract and hold: *a well-dressed shop window takes one's eye.* **38.** to captivate or charm: *a pretty ring takes one's fancy.* **39.** to assume or adopt (a symbol, badge, or the like): *to take the veil.* **40.** to make, put forth, etc.: *to take exception.* **41.** to write down (notes, a copy, etc.); take a record of (a speech, etc.). **42.** to go into or enter: *to take the field.* **43.** to make (a reproduction, picture, or photograph of something). **44.** to make a figure or picture, esp. a photograph, of (a person or thing). **45.** to make or perform (a measurement, observation, etc.). **46.** to ascertain by enquiry, examination, measurement, scientific observation, etc. **47.** to begin to have (a certain feeling or state of mind); experience or feel (delight, pride, etc.). **48.** to form and hold in the mind: *to take a gloomy view.* **49.** to understand in a specified way: *how do you take this?* **50.** to regard or consider: *he was taken to be wealthy.* **51.** to assume or undertake (a function, duty, responsibility, etc.). **52.** to assume the obligation of (a vow, pledge, etc.); perform or discharge (a part, service, etc.). **53.** to assume or adopt as one's own (a part or side in a contest, etc.); assume or appropriate as if by right: *to take the credit for something, to take a liberty.* **54.** to grasp or apprehend, understand, or comprehend. **55.** to do, perform, execute, etc.: *to take a walk.* **56.** to accept and comply with (advice, etc.). **57.** to suffer or undergo: *to take insults.* **58.** to enter into the enjoyment of (recreation, a holiday, etc.). **59.** to employ for some specified or implied purpose: *to take measures to check an evil.* **60.** to require: *it takes courage to do that.* **61.** *Cards, Chess, etc.* to capture or win (a trick, piece, etc.). **62.** *Gram.* to have by usage, either as part of itself or with it in construction (a particular form, accent, etc., or a case, mode, etc.), as a word or the like.

—*v.i.* **63.** to catch or engage, as a mechanical device. **64.** to strike root, or begin to grow, as a plant. **65.** to adhere, as ink, etc. **66.** to win favour or acceptance, as a play. **67.** to have the intended result or effect, as a medicine, inoculation, etc. **68.** to enter into possession, as of an estate. **69.** to apply or devote oneself. **70.** to make one's way; proceed; go. **71.** to become (sick or ill). **72.** to admit of being photographed (well, badly, etc.). **73.** to admit of being taken (out, apart, etc.). **74.** *Angling.* (of a fish) to bite.

—*v.* **75.** Some special verb phrases are:

take aback, to surprise; disconcert; startle.

take after, **1.** to resemble (a parent, etc.). **2.** *U.S.* to pursue.

take back, **1.** to retrieve; regain possession of. **2.** to retract or withdraw. **3.** to allow to return: *to take back one's erring husband.* **4.** to return for exchange, etc.: *to take a faulty radio back to the shop.*

take care, to act or think cautiously.

take care of, to look after; protect.

take down, **1.** to pull down. **2.** to remove by pulling apart or taking apart. **3.** to write down. **4.** to lower in power, strength, pride, arrogance, etc.: *I'll take him down a peg or two.*

take for, to believe or assume to be, esp. mistakenly: *I took him for the postman.*

take for granted, **1.** to accept or assume without question. **2.** to fail to ascribe credit, merit, worth, or the like to: *it is very upsetting to have one's work taken for granted.*

take from, to detract from or reduce: *he may behave foolishly, but that does not take from the value of his work.*

take in, **1.** to receive and accommodate; provide lodging for. **2.** to alter (a garment or garments) in order to make smaller; reduce the size or measurement of. **3.** to include; encompass. **4.** to comprehend; understand; grasp the meaning of. **5.** to deceive, trick, or cheat.

take it, **1.** *Colloq.* to endure pain, misfortune or the like with fortitude. **2.** to react in a manner specified: *when I broke the news, he took it very badly.* **3.** to assume: *I take it from your silence that this is true.*

take it out of, to exhaust; sap one's strength or energy.

take it out on, to vent wrath, anger, or the like, on.

take off, **1.** to remove. **2.** to lead off or away. **3.** to set off; take one's departure. **4.** to leave the ground, as an aeroplane. **5.** to withdraw, as from service. **6.** to remove by death. **7.** *Colloq.* to imitate or mimic.

take on, **1.** to hire. **2.** to undertake to handle. **3.** to acquire: *to take on a new aspect.* **4.** *Colloq.* to start a quarrel or fight with: *take on someone your own size.* **5.** *Colloq.* to show great excitement, grief, or other emotion.

take out, **1.** to extract: *to take out a tooth.* **2.** to escort or accompany (a woman). **3.** to obtain; apply for and get; *to take out an insurance policy.* **4.** to vent: *to take out one's rage on the dog.* **5.** to destroy; eliminate; render harmless: *to take out a military installation by bombing.*

take over, to assume or acquire control of.

take place, to happen; occur.

take to, **1.** to apply, devote, or addict oneself to: *to take to drink.* **2.** to respond kindly or favourably to. **3.** to go to: *to take to one's bed.* **4.** to resort to; have recourse to: *to take to one's heels.*

take up, **1.** to lift; pick up. **2.** to occupy oneself with; adopt the practice or study of: *to take up Greek.* **3.** to occupy (time, space, or the like). **4.** to resume or continue: *to take up where one left off.*

take upon oneself, to assume the responsibility for.

take up with, to associate with.

—*n.* **76.** an act or instance of taking. **77.** that which is taken. **78.** the quantity of fish, etc., taken at one time. **79.** money taken; gross profit; takings. **80.** *Journalism.* a portion of copy assigned to a keyboard operator or compositor, usually part of a story or article. **81.** *Films, etc.* **a.** a scene or a portion of a scene photographed at one time without any interruption or break. **b.** an instance of such continuous operation of the camera. **82.** *Recording.* a single uninterrupted sequence of recorded sound. **83.** *Med.* a successful inoculation, vaccination, or the like. [ME; late OE *tacan*, t. Scand.; cf. Icel. *taka*, c. MD *taken* grasp, seize; akin to Goth. *tēkan* touch] —**tak′er,** *n.*

take-down (tāk′doun′), *n.* *Colloq.* the state of being humbled.

take-home pay (tāk′hōm′), salary remaining after all deductions, esp. tax deductions, have been made.

take-in (tāk′ĭn′), *n.* *Colloq.* a deception, fraud, or imposition.

take-off (tāk′ŏf′), *n.* **1.** a taking or setting off; the leaving of the ground in leaping or in beginning a flight in an aeroplane. **2.** the place or point at which one takes off. **3.** *Colloq.* an imitating or mimicking; caricature.

take-over (tāk′ō′və), *n.* **1.** acquisition of control, esp. of a business company by the purchase of the majority of its shares. —*adj.* **2.** denoting or pertaining to such acquisition: *a take-over bid.*

take-up (tāk′ŭp′), *n.* **1.** the act of taking up. **2.** *Mach.* any device for taking up slack or lost motion.

take-up spool, (in a tape-recorder, cine-projector, etc.) a spool which receives the tape or film after it has been played or projected.

taking (tā′kĭng), *n.* **1.** the act of one who or that which takes. **2.** the state of being taken. **3.** that which is taken. **4.** (*pl.*) receipts. **5.** *Colloq. or Dial.* state of agitation or distress. —*adj.* **6.** captivating, winning, or pleasing. **7.** *Colloq.* infectious or contagious. —**tak′ingly,** *adv.* —**tak′ingness,** *n.*

taking-off (tā′kĭng ŏf′), *n.* assassination; murder; killing.

Takla Makan (tä′klə mə kän′), an uninhabited desert of sand-dunes in the Tarim Basin of central Asia.

Takoradi (tăk′ə rä′dĭ), *n.* a seaport in SW Ghana. 41,000 (est. 1960).

talapoin (tăl′ə poin′), *n.* a small, yellowish monkey, *Cercopithecus talapoin*, of West Africa, the smallest of the guenons. [ult. t. Talaing (Old Penguan): m. *tala pôi* my lord, applied originally to Buddhist monks]

talaria (tə lēə′rĭ ə), *n.pl.* *Class. Myth.* the winged sandals, or small wings fastened to the ankles, of Hermes (or Mercury).

Talavera de la Reina (*Sp.* tä lä be′rä de lä rey′nä), a town in central Spain, on the river Tagus: British and Spanish defeat of the French, 1809. 21,728 (est. 1960).

talayot (tə lä′yŏt), *n.* a prehistoric round or square stone tower found in the Balearic Islands. [t. Catalan Sp.: m. *talaiot*]

talc (tălk), *n.*, *v.*, **talcked, talcking** or **talced** (tălkt), **talcing** (tăl′king). —*n.* **1.** Also, **talcum** (tăl′kəm). a soft greenish grey mineral, hydrous magnesium silicate, $H_2Mg_3(SiO_3)_4$, unctuous to the touch, and occurring usually in foliated masses or compact, used in making lubricants, talcum powder, electrical insulation, etc. —*v.t.* **2.** to treat or rub with talc. [t. ML: s. *talcum*, t. Ar.: m. *ṭalq*]

Talcahuano (*Sp.* täl kä wä′nō), *n.* a seaport in central Chile. 102,323 (est. 1963).

talcose (tăl′kōs), *adj.* containing, or composed largely of, talc. Also, **talcous** (tăl′kəs).

talcum powder, powdered talc or soapstone, usually perfumed for toilet use.

tale (tāl), *n.* **1.** a narrative purporting to relate the facts about some real or imaginary event, incident, or case; a story. **2.** a literary compositi‹.. having the form of such a narrative: *Chaucer's 'Canterbury Tales'.* **3.** a falsehood; lie. **4.** a rumour or piece of gossip, esp. when malicious. **5.** *Archaic.* the full number or amount. **6.** *Archaic.* enumeration, numbering, or counting. **7.** *Obs.* talk or discourse. [ME; OE *talu* reckoning, speech, c. D *taal* speech, language, G *Zahl* number]

tale-bearer (tāl′bĕə′rə), *n.* one who carries tales or gossip likely to breed mischief. —**tale′-bear′ing,** *adj.*, *n.*

talent (tăl′ənt), *n.* **1.** a special natural ability or aptitude: *a talent for drawing.* **2.** a capacity for achievement or success; natural ability: *young men of talent.* **3.** persons of ability. **4.** a power of mind or body considered as committed to one for use and improvement (from the parable in Matt. 25: 14–30). **5.** an ancient unit of weight, varying with time and place, the later Attic talent being estimated at about 58 lbs avoirdupois, and the Hebrew talent about double this. **6.** this weight of gold, silver, or the like as a monetary unit. **7.** *Obs.* inclination or disposition. [ME and OE *talente*, t. L: m. *talenta*, pl. of *talentum*, t. Gk: m. *tálanton* (defs. 5, 6); def. 7 from OF *talent*] —**Syn. 1.** See **ability.**

talented (tăl′ən tĭd), *adj.* having talent; gifted.

talent scout, a person whose business is to discern and engage people with potential talent, esp. in the entertainment business.

taler (tä′lə), *n.*, *pl.* **-ler.** thaler.

tales (tā′lēz), *n. Law.* **1.** (*orig. as pl.*) persons chosen from among the bystanders or those present in court to serve on the jury when the original panel has become deficient in number. **2.** the order or writ summoning them. [t. ML: *tālēs* (*dē circumstantibus*) such (of the bystanders)]

talesman (tā′lēz mən), *n.*, *pl.* **-men.** a person summoned as one of the tales.

taleteller (tāl′tĕl′ə), *n.* a tale-bearer. —**tale′tell′ing,** *adj.*, *n.*

tali-, a word element meaning 'ankle', as in *taligrade.* [comb. form repr. L *tālus*]

Talien (tä′lyĕn′), *n.* Chinese name of **Dairen.**

Taliesin (tăl′ĭ ĕs′ĭn), *n.* fl. A.D. 6th century, Welsh bard to whom a collection of medieval poetry is ascribed.

taligrade (tăl′ĭ grād′), *adj. Zool.* walking on the outer side of the foot.

talion (tăl′ĭ ən), *n.* retaliation as authorized by law, esp. when the punishment inflicted corresponds in kind and degree to the injury, as 'eye for eye' (Lev. 24:20). [ME, t. L: s. *tālio*]

taliped (tăl′ĭ pĕd′), *adj. Pathol.* **1.** (of a foot) twisted or distorted out of shape or position. **2.** (of a person) club-footed. —*n.* **3.** a taliped person or animal.

talipes (tăl′ĭ pēz′), *n. Pathol.* **1.** club foot. **2.** the condition of being club-footed. [f. TALI- + L *pēs* foot]

talipot (tăl′ĭ pŏt′), *n.* a tall palm, *Corypha umbraculifera* of southern India and Ceylon, whose large leaves are much used for making fans and umbrellas, for covering houses, and in place of writing paper. [t. Malayalam: m. *tālipat*, t. Hind.: m. *tālpat*, g. Skt *tālapattra* leaf of the fan palm]

talisman (tăl′ĭz mən), *n.*, *pl.* **-mans. 1.** a stone, ring, or other object, engraved with figures or characters under certain superstitious observances of the heavens, which is supposed to possess occult powers, and is worn as an amulet or charm. **2.** any amulet or charm. **3.** anything of almost magic power. [t. Ar.: m. *tilsaman*, pl. of *tilsam*, t. LGk: m. *télesma* talisman, (earlier) religious rite, performance, completion] —**talismanic** (tăl′ĭz măn′ĭk), **tal′isman′ical,** *adj.*

talk (tôk), *v.i.* **1.** to speak or converse; perform the act of speaking. **2.** to make known or interchange ideas, information, etc., by means of spoken words. **3.** to consult or confer. **4.** to gossip. **5.** to chatter or prate. **6.** to reveal information: *to make a spy talk.* **7.** to communicate ideas by other means than speech, as by writing, signs, or signals. **8.** to make sounds imitative or suggestive of human speech. —*v.t.* **9.** to express in words; utter: *to talk sense.* **10.** to use as a spoken language; speak: *he can talk three languages.* **11.** to discuss: *to talk politics.* **12.** to persuade, bring, put, influence, etc., by talk: *to talk a person into buying something.* —*v.* **13.** Some special verb phrases are:

talk big, *Colloq.* to speak boastfully.

talk (someone or **something) down, 1.** to override in argument by speaking in a loud, persistent manner. **2.** *Aeron.* to radio landing instructions to (an aircraft or pilot) when landing is difficult.

talk down to, to speak condescendingly to.

talk into, to persuade someone to take some course, esp. against his original intention.

talk out, 1. to resolve (differences) by discussion: *unions and management usually attempt to talk out their differences before resorting to industrial action.* **2.** *Parl. Proc.* to thwart (the passage of a piece of legislation) by prolonging discussion until the adjournment.

talk over, to discuss.

talk round, 1. to discuss generally and discursively, without coming to the essential point. **2.** to persuade; bring round to one's own way of thinking.

—*n.* **14.** the act of talking; speech; conversation, esp. of a familiar or informal kind. **15.** a lecture or informal speech. **16.** a conference. **17.** report or rumour; gossip. **18.** a subject or occasion of talking, esp. of gossip. **19.** mere empty speech. **20.** a way of talking: *baby talk.* **21.** language, dialect, or lingo. **22.** sound imitative or suggestive of human speech: *the talk of monkeys.* [ME, c. East Fris. *talken*; akin to TALE, n., TELL, v.] —**talk′able,** *adj.* —**talk′er,** *n.* —**Syn. 1.** See **speak.**

talkative (tô′kə tĭv), *adj.* inclined to talk a great deal. —**talk′atively,** *adv.* —**talk′ativeness,** *n.*

—**Syn.** TALKATIVE, GARRULOUS, LOQUACIOUS agree in referring to one who talks a great deal. TALKATIVE is a mildly unfavourable word applied to one who is in the habit of talking a great deal and often without significance: *a talkative child.* The GARRULOUS person talks with wearisome persistence about personal and trivial things: *a garrulous old woman.* A LOQUACIOUS person, intending to be sociable, talks continuously and at length: *a loquacious hostess.* —**Ant.** taciturn.

talkback (tôk′băk′), *n. Television, Radio, etc.* a communications system enabling spoken directions from the control room to be conveyed to cameramen, directors, etc., in the studio.

talkdown (tôk′doun′), *n. Aeron.* the operation of radioing instructions to an aircraft to enable it to land in fog or other difficult circumstances.

talkie (tô′kĭ), *n. Obs. Colloq.* a cinema film having a soundtrack.

talking picture, *Obs.* a film with a soundtrack.

talking point, a subject for discussion or dispute.

talking-to (tô′kĭng to͞o′), *n.*, *pl.* **-tos.** *Colloq.* a scolding.

tall (tôl), *adj.* **1.** having a relatively great stature; of more than average height: *tall grass.* **2.** having stature or height as specified: *a man six feet tall.* **3.** *Colloq.* high, great, or large in amount: *a tall price.* **4.** *Colloq.* extravagant; difficult to believe: *a tall story.* **5.** *Colloq.* difficult to accomplish: *a tall order.* **6.** *Colloq.* high-flown or grandiloquent. **7.** *Obs.* proper. **8.** *Obs.* handsome. **9.** *Obs.* excellent. **10.** *Obs.* valiant. [ME *tal*, OE *getæl* prompt; c. OHG *gizal* swift, OS *gital* quick] —**tall′ish,** *adj.* —**tall′ness,** *n.* —**Syn. 1.** See **high.** —**Ant. 1.** low, short.

tallage (tăl′ĭj), *n.* **1.** a tax imposed upon the tenants of a manor by the lord. **2.** a compulsory tax levied by the Norman and early Angevin kings of England upon the demesne lands of the Crown and upon all royal towns. [ME, t. OF: m. *taillage*, der. *taillier* cut, limit, tax]

Tallahassee (tăl′ə hăs′ĭ), *n.* a town in the U.S., the capital of Florida, in the N part. 48,174 (1960).

tallboy (tôl′boi′), *n.* **1.** a tall chest of drawers supported on a low stand. **2.** a tall chimneypot. **3.** a tall-stemmed glass for wine, etc.

Talleyrand-Périgord (tăl′ĭ rănd′; *Fr.* tȧ lĕ räɴ pĕ rĕ-gôr′), *n.* **Charles Maurice de** (*Fr.* shȧrl mō rēs′ də), 1754–1838, French statesman, noted for his craftiness.

tall hat, a top-hat.

Tallinn (tăl′ĭn), *n.* a seaport in the NW Soviet Union, on the Gulf of Finland: capital of Estonia. 330,000 (est. 1965). Russian, **Revel.** German, **Reval.**

Tallis (tăl′ĭs), *n.* **Thomas,** 1505–85, English composer and organist.

tallith (tăl′ĭth), *n.* a mantle or a scarf-like garment with fringes at the four corners, worn over the shoulders by male Jews at prayer. [t. Heb., der. *tālal* cover]

tall oil (täl), a resinous secondary product resulting from the manufacture of chemical wood pulp: used in making soaps, etc. [t. Sw.: m. *tallöl* pine beer]

tallow (tăl′ō), *n.* **1.** the fatty tissue or suet of animals. **2.** the harder fat of sheep, cattle, etc., separated by melting from the fibrous and membranous matter naturally mixed with it, and used to make candles, soap, etc. **3.** any of various similar fatty substances: *vegetable tallow.* —*v.t.* **4.** to smear with tallow. —*v.i.* **5.** to produce tallow. [ME *talgh*, c. G *Talg*] —**tal′low-like′**, *adj.* —**tal′lowy,** *adj.*

tally (tăl′ĭ), *n., pl.* **-lies,** *v.,* **-lied, -lying.** —*n.* **1.** a stick of wood with notches cut to indicate the amount of a debt or payment, often split lengthwise across the notches, the debtor retaining one piece and the creditor the other. **2.** anything on which a score or account is kept. **3.** a notch or mark made on or in a tally. **4.** an account or reckoning; a record of debit and credit, of the score of a game, or the like. **5.** a number or group of objects recorded. **6.** a mark made to register a certain number of objects, in keeping account, as, for instance, a group of five. **7.** a number of objects serving as a unit of computation. **8.** a ticket, label, or mark used as a means of identification, etc. **9.** anything corresponding to another thing as a counterpart. **10. live tally,** *Now Chiefly N Dial.* to cohabit outside marriage. —*v.t.* **11.** to mark or enter on a tally; register; record. **12.** to count or reckon up. **13.** to furnish with a tally or identifying label. **14.** to cause to correspond or agree. —*v.i.* **15.** to correspond, as one part of a tally with the other; accord or agree: *Does his story tally with John's?* [ME *taly*, t. AF: m. *tallie*, ult. t. L: m. *tālea* rod. See TAIL [2]] —**tal′lier,** *n.*

tallyclerk (tăl′ĭ kläk′), *n.* a clerk employed to check ship's cargoes against a list.

tally-ho (tăl′ĭ hō′), *n., pl.* **-hos,** *interj., v.,* **-hoed** or **-ho'd, -hoing.** —*n.* **1.** a mail coach or a four-in-hand pleasure coach. **2.** a cry of 'tally-ho'. —*interj.* **3.** (a huntsman's cry on catching sight of the fox.) —*v.t.* **4.** to arouse (hounds in hunting, etc.) by crying 'tally-ho'. —*v.i.* **5.** to utter a cry of 'tally-ho'. [t. F: m. *taiaut*]

tallyman (tăl′ĭ mən), *n., pl.* **-men.** *Now Chiefly N Dial.* **1.** one who sells goods, esp. cheap and shoddy goods, and collects payment by instalments. **2.** a man who lives with a woman outside marriage. —**tal′lywom′an,** *n.fem.*

tallyshop (tăl′ĭ shŏp′), *n.* *Now Chiefly N Dial.* a shop where goods are sold to be paid for by instalments.

Talman (tôl′mən), *n.* **William,** 1650–1720, English architect.

Talmud (tăl′mŏŏd), *n.* **1.** the two commentaries on the Mishnah, one produced in Palestine (at about A.D. 375) and the other in Babylonia (at about A.D. 500); Gemara. **2.** the Mishnah and the commentary on it. [t. Heb.: study, instruction] —**Talmud′ic, Talmud′ical,** *adj.*

Talmudist (tăl′mŏŏ dĭst), *n.* **1.** one of the writers or compilers of the Talmud. **2.** one who accepts the doctrines of the Talmud. **3.** one versed in the Talmud.

talon (tăl′ən), *n.* **1.** a claw, esp. of a bird of prey. **2.** *Colloq.* a finger or fingernail, esp. when regarded as grasping or attacking. **3.** (in a lock) the shoulder on the bolt against which the key presses in shooting the bolt. **4.** *Cards.* the cards left over after the deal; the stock. [ME, t. OF: heel, g. s. LL *tālo* talon, r. L *tālus* ankle, heel] —**tal′oned,** *adj.*

Talos (tā′lŏs), *n.* *Gk Myth.* **1.** the inventive nephew of Daedalus, by whom he was jealously slain. **2.** a man of brass made by Hephaestus for Minos, to guard Crete.

taluk (tä′lŏŏk, tä lŏŏk′), *n.* (in India) **1.** a hereditary estate. **2.** a subdivision of a revenue district. [t. Urdu, t. Ar.: m. *ta'alluq* estate]

talus[1] (tā′ləs), *n., pl.* **-li** (-lī). *Anat.* the astragalus. [t. L]

talus[2] (tā′ləs), *n.* **1.** a slope. **2.** *Geol.* a sloping mass of rocky fragments at the base of a cliff. **3.** *Fort.* the sloping side or face of a wall. [t. F, t. L: ankle]

talweg (täl′vĕg), *n.* *Geog.* a longitudinal section along the bed of a river. Also, **thalweg.** [G: valley way]

tam (tăm), *n.* tam-o'-shanter.

tamable (tā′mə bl), *adj.* tameable.

tamale (tə mä′lĭ), *n.* a Mexican dish made of crushed maize and minced meat, seasoned with red peppers, etc., wrapped in maize husks, and steamed. Also, **tamal.** [back-formation from *tamales*, t. Mex. Sp.: pl. of *tamal*, t. Aztec: m. *tamalli*]

Tamale (tă mä′lĭ), *n.* a town in N Ghana. 40,327 (1960).

tamandua (tăm′ən dŏŏə′), *n.* the four-toed anteater, *Tamandua tetradactyla*, a prehensile-tailed, arboreal edentate of the forests of tropical America. Also, **tamandu** (tăm′ən dōō′). [t. Pg., t. Tupi, f. *taa* ant + m. *munden* trap]

tamara (tə mä′rə), *n.* *Cookery.* a mixture of spices, esp. cinnamon and cloves, used in Italian cooking.

tamarack (tăm′ə răk′), *n.* **1.** an American larch, *Larix laricina*, yielding a useful timber. **2.** any of several very similar related trees. **3.** the wood of these trees. [t. N Amer. Ind. (Algonquian)]

tamarau (tăm′ə rou′), *n.* a small, sturdy wild buffalo, *Bubalus mindorensis*, of Mindoro, in the Philippines, having thick brown hair and short, massive horns. [t. Tagalog]

tamarin (tăm′ə rĭn), *n.* any of various South American primates of the genus *Callithrix*, allied to the marmosets, lacking ear tufts and tail rings. [t. F, t. Carib d. of Cayenne]

tamarind (tăm′ə rĭnd), *n.* **1.** the fruit of a large caesalpiniaceous tropical tree, *Tamarindus indica*, a pod containing seeds enclosed in a juicy acid pulp that is used in beverages and food. **2.** the tree, cultivated throughout the tropics for its fruit, fragrant flowers, shade, and timber. [t. ML: s. *tamarindus*, t. Ar.: m. *tamrhindī* date of India]

tamarisk (tăm′ə rĭsk), *n.* a plant of the Old World tropical genus *Tamarix*, esp. *T. gallica*, native in the Mediterranean region, an ornamental shrub or small tree with slender, feathery branches. [ME *tamariscus*, t. LL. Cf. L *tamarix*]

tamasha (tə mä′shə), *n.* (in the East Indies) a spectacle; entertainment. [t. Urdu, t. Ar.: a short walk]

Tamatave (*Fr.* tȧ mȧ tȧv′), *n.* a seaport on the E coast of Madagascar. 50,500 (1964).

Tambora (tăm′bə rä′), *n.* a volcano in Indonesia, on N Sumbawa island: eruption 1815. 9042 ft.

tambour (tăm′bŏŏə), *n.* **1.** a drum. **2.** a drummer. **3.** a circular frame consisting of two hoops, one fitting within the other, in which cloth is stretched for embroidering. **4.** embroidery done on this. **5.** a vestibule in a church porch. **6.** *Real Tennis.* a sloping buttress in the court. —*adj.* **7.** shaped like a drum, as the rolling mechanism of a roll-top desk. —*v.t., v.i.* **8.** to embroider on a tambour. [late ME, t. F. See TABOR]

tambourin (tăm′bōō rĭn; *Fr.* täɴ bōō răɴ′), *n.* **1.** a Provençal dance in 2/4 time, with a drone bass. **2.** the tune or rhythm for this dance.

tambourine (tăm′bə rēn′), *n.* a small drum consisting of a circular wooden frame with a skin stretched over it and several pairs of jingles (metal discs) inserted into the frame, played by striking with the knuckles, shaking, etc. [t. F: m. *tambourin*, dim. of *tambour* TAMBOUR] —**tam′bourin′ist,** *n.*

Tambourine

Tambov (*Russ.* tȧm bôf′), *n.* a city in the central Soviet Union in Europe. 203,000 (est. 1965).

Tamburlaine (tăm′bə lān′), *n.* Tamerlane.

tame (tām), *adj.,* **tamer, tamest,** *v.,* **tamed, taming.** —*adj.* **1.** changed from the wild or savage state; domesticated: *a tame bear.* **2.** gentle, fearless, or without shyness, as if domesticated, as an animal. **3.** tractable, docile, or submissive, as a person, the disposition, etc. **4.** lacking in animation; dull; insipid: *a tame existence.* **5.** spiritless or pusillanimous. **6.** cultivated, or improved by cultivation, as a plant, its fruit, etc. **7.** local: *a tame genius.* **8.** rendered manageable for human or domestic use: *a tame water supply.* —*v.t.* **9.** to make tame; domesticate; make tractable; subdue. **10.** to deprive of courage, ardour, or interest. **11.** to soften; tone down. **12.** to bring under control or render manageable, as for domestic or human use: *to tame the natural resources of a country.* [ME; OE *tam*, c. G *zahm*; akin to Goth. *tamjan*, v., L *domāre*] —**tame′abil′ity, tam′abil′ity, tame′ableness, tam′ableness,** *n.* —**tame′able, tam′able,** *adj.* —**tame′ly,** *adv.* —**tame′ness,** *n.* —**tam′er,** *n.*

tameable (tā′mə bl), *adj.* that may be tamed. Also, **tamable.**

tameless (tām′lĭs), *adj.* untamed or untameable. —**tame′lessness,** *n.*

Tamerlane (tăm′ə lān′), *n.* (*Timour* or *Timur*), 1336?–1405, Mongol conqueror of most of southern and western Asia; ruler of Samarkand 1369–1405. Also, **Tamburlaine.**

Tamil (tăm′ĭl), *n.* **1.** a member of a people of Dravidian stock of southern India and Ceylon. **2.** their language, spoken chiefly to the south of Madras. —*adj.* **3.** of or pertaining to the Tamils or their language.

tamis (tăm′ĭ, -ĭs), *n., pl.* **tamises** (tăm′ĭz, tăm′ĭ sĭz). a cloth sieve or strainer. Also, **tammy.** [t. F: sieve; r. OE *temes*]

Tammany Hall (tăm′ə nĭ), **1.** a powerful Democratic political organization in New York City, founded in 1789 as a fraternal benevolent society **(Tammany Society)**, and noted for its unscrupulous political methods. **2.** the building in which the Tammany organization had its headquarters. [t. Amer. Ind.: m. *taminy*, var. form of name of an Indian chief in 17th-cent. Pennsylvania]

Tammerfors (tăm′ə fôz′; *Sw.* tȧ mər fôrs′), *n.* Swedish name of **Tampere.**

Tammuz (tăm′o͞oz, -ŭz), *n.* **1.** (in the Jewish calendar) the tenth month of the civil and fourth of the ecclesiastical year. **2.** a Babylonian god of the springtime and of vegetation, whose return to life from the underworld symbolized the rebirth of earth at spring. Also, **Thammuz.** [t. Heb.]

tammy[1] (tăm′ĭ), *n.* a fabric of glazed woollen or mixed fibres, used for linings, underwear, etc. [orig. unknown]

tammy[2] (tăm′ĭ), *n., pl.* **-mies.** tamis.

tammy[3] (tăm′ĭ), *n., pl.* **-mies.** tam-o'-shanter.

tam-o'-shanter (tăm′ə shăn′tə), *n.* a cap, of Scottish origin, with a flat crown larger in diameter than the headband; tam. [named after the hero of a poem by Burns]

tamp (tămp), *v.t.* **1.** to force in or down by repeated, somewhat light strokes. **2.** (in blasting) to fill (the hole made by the drill) with earth, etc., after the powder or explosive has been introduced. [appar. akin to TAMPION]

Tampa (tăm′pə), *n.* a seaport in W Florida, on **Tampa Bay,** an inlet of the Gulf of Mexico: fishing resort. 274,970 (1960).

tamper[1] (tăm′pə), *v.i.* **1.** to meddle, esp. for the purpose of altering, damaging, misusing, etc. (fol. by *with*): *to tamper with a lock.* **2.** to engage secretly or improperly in something. **3.** to undertake underhand or corrupt dealings, as in order to influence improperly (fol. by *with*): *to tamper with a witness.* [var. of TEMPER, v.] —**tam′perer,** *n.*

tamper[2] (tăm′pə), *n.* one who or that which tamps. [f. TAMP + -ER[1]]

Tampere (*Finn.* täm′pĕ rĕ), *n.* a city in SW Finland. 139,416 (1965). Swedish, **Tammerfors.**

Tampico (tăm pē′kō; *Sp.* täm pē′kô), *n.* a seaport in E Mexico. 139,867 (1965).

tampion (tăm′pĭ ən), *n.* a wooden plug or stopper placed in the muzzle of a piece of ordnance when not in use, to keep out dampness and dust. Also, **tompion.** [t. F: m. *tampon,* var. of *tapon,* der. *tape* plug]

tampon (tăm′pŏn), *Surg.* —*n.* **1.** a plug of cotton or the like inserted into an orifice, wound, etc., as to stop haemorrhage. **2.** a similar device used internally to absorb menstrual flow. —*v.t.* **3.** to fill or plug with a tampon. [t. F. See TAMPION]

tamponade (tăm′pə nād′), *n.* **1.** *Surg.* the use of a tampon, as to stop haemorrhage. **2.** *Pathol.* a condition in which the action of the heart is impaired because of pressure created by fluid collecting in the pericardium.

tam-tam (tăm′tăm′), *n.* **1.** a gong with indefinite pitch. **2.** tom-tom. [var. of TOM-TOM]

Tamworth (tăm′wəth), *n.* **1.** a town in England, in Staffordshire. 13,646 (1961). **2.** a town in Australia, in NE New South Wales. 20,500 (1965). **3.** one of a breed of red pigs, chiefly used for bacon, orig. bred in Staffordshire.

tan[1] (tăn), *v.,* **tanned, tanning,** *n., adj.* —*v.t.* **1.** to convert (a hide) into leather, esp. by soaking or steeping in a bath prepared from oak or hemlock bark or synthetically. **2.** to make brown by exposure to ultraviolet rays, as of the sun. **3.** *Colloq.* to beat or thrash. —*v.i.* **4.** to become tanned. —*n.* **5.** the brown colour imparted to the skin by exposure to the sun or open air; suntan. **6.** yellowish or tawny brown. **7.** the bark of the oak, hemlock, etc., bruised and broken by a mill, and used for tanning hides. —*adj.* **8.** of the colour of tan; tawny or yellowish brown. **9.** used in or relating to tanning processes, materials, etc. [ME *tanne,* late OE *tannian,* t. ML: m. *tannāre,* der. *tannum,* n.] —**tan′nable,** *adj.*

tan[2] (tăn), *n. Trig.* tangent.

tana (tä′nə), *n.* a large tree shrew (family *Tupaiidae*) *Tupaia tana,* of Sumatra and Borneo. [t. Malay: m. (*tupai*) *tanah* ground (shrew)]

Tana (tä′nə), *n.* **1.** a river in E Africa, in Kenya, flowing SE to the Indian Ocean. ab. 500 mi. **2. Lake.** Also, **Lake Tsana.** a lake in NW Ethiopia: the source of the Blue Nile. ab. 1150 sq. mi.

tanager (tăn′ə jə), *n.* any of numerous small, usually brightly coloured oscinine birds constituting the New World family *Thraupidae,* most of which inhabit the warmer parts of South America. [t. NL: m. *tanagra,* t. Tupi: m. *tangara*]

Tanagra (tăn′ə grə), *n.* a town in ancient Greece, in Boeotia; terracotta figurines: Spartan victory over the Athenians 457 B.C.

tanagrine (tăn′ə grĭn), *adj.* of or pertaining to the tanagers; belonging to the tanager family.

Tanana (tə nä′nə), *n.* a river flowing from E Alaska NW to the Yukon river. ab. 700 mi. long.

Tananarive (*Fr.* tȧ nȧ nȧ rēv′), *n.* the capital of the Malagasy Republic, in the central part. 298,813 (1964). Also, **Antananarivo.**

tanbark (tăn′bäk′), *n.* bark used in tanning; tan.

Tancred (tăng′krĕd), *n.* died 1112, Norman soldier; a leader of the first Crusade.

tandem (tăn′dəm), *adv.* **1.** one behind another; in single file: *to drive horses tandem.* —*adj.* **2.** having animals, seats, parts, etc., arranged tandem, or one behind another: *a tandem bicycle.* —*n.* **3.** a bicycle for two riders, having twin seats, pedals, etc. **4.** a team of horses harnessed in tandem. **5.** a two-wheeled carriage, with a high driver's seat, drawn by two or more horses. **6.** any mechanism having a tandem arrangement. **7. in tandem,** one behind the other. [t. L: at length (in time), prob. at first humorously used]

Tandem

tandem generator, *Physics.* an accelerator consisting of two electrostatic generators in tandem.

tang[1] (tăng), *n.* **1.** a strong taste or flavour. **2.** the distinctive flavour or quality of a thing. **3.** a pungent or distinctive smell. **4.** a smack, touch, or suggestion of something. **5.** a long and slender projecting strip, tongue, or prong forming part of an object, as a chisel, file, knife, etc., and serving as a means of attachment for another part, as a handle or stock. **6.** surgeonfish. —*v.t.* **7.** to furnish with a tang. [ME *tange,* t. Scand.; cf. Icel. *tangi* pointed object, akin to TONGS]

tang[2] (tăng), *n., v.t., v.i.* ring; clang; twang. [imit.]

Tang (tăng), *n.* a Chinese dynasty, A.D. 618–907, noted for territorial expansion (esp. cultural contact with central Asia), first development of printing, the political as well as religious importance of Buddhism, and the highest development of Chinese poetry.

Tanganyika (tăng′gə nyē′kə), *n.* **1. Lake,** a lake in central Africa between the Republic of Congo and Tanzania: the longest freshwater lake in the world. ab. 450 mi. long; 30–45 mi. wide; ab. 12,700 sq. mi. **2.** a former state in Africa, now forming the mainland part of **Tanzania.** —**Tan′ganyi′kan,** *n.*

Tange (tŭng′ĭ), *n.* **Kenzo** (kĕn′zō), born 1913, Japanese architect.

tangelo (tăn′jĭ lō′), *n., pl.* **-los. 1.** a hybrid between the tangerine orange and the pomelo or grapefruit trees. **2.** its fruit. [b. TANG(ERINE) and (POM)ELO]

tangency (tăn′jən sĭ), *n.* the state of being tangent.

tangent (tăn′jənt), *adj.* **1.** touching. **2.** *Geom.* touching, as a straight line in relation to a curve or surface; passing through two (or more) consecutive points of a curve or surface. **3.** in contact along a single line or element, as a plane with a cylinder. —*n.* **4.** *Geom.* a tangent line or plane. **5.** *Trig.* **a.** the ratio of the perpendicular side to the base in a right-angled triangle. **b.** (of an angle) a trigonometric function equal to the ratio of the ordinate of the end point of the arc to the abscissa of this end point, the origin being at the centre of the circle on which the arc lies and the initial point of the arc being on the x-axis. *Abbrev.:* tan. **c.** (orig.) a straight line perpendicular to the radius of a circle at one end of an arc and extending from this point to the produced radius which cuts off the arc at its other end. **6.** *Survey.* the straight portion of a survey line between curves, as on railway or road alignment. **7.** the metal pin that strikes the strings on a clavichord, causing it to sound. **8.** a sudden divergence from one course, thought, etc., to another: *to fly off at a tangent.* [t. L: s. *tangens,* ppr., touching]

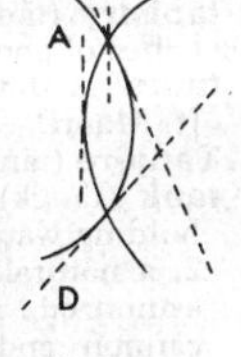

Tangents A, Ordinary; B, Inflectional; C, Cuspidal; D, Nodal

tangent galvanometer, *Elect.* a galvanometer consisting of a coil of wire held in a vertical plane parallel to the earth's magnetic field with a small magnetic needle pivoted at the centre of the coil; the current passing through the coil is proportional to the tangent of the angle of deflection of the needle.

tangential (tăn jĕn′shəl), *adj.* **1.** pertaining to or of the nature of a tangent; being or moving in the direction of a tangent. **2.** merely touching; slightly connected. **3.** divergent or digressive. Also, **tangental** (tăn jĕn′tl). —**tangen′tially,** *adv.*

tangerine (tăn′jə rēn′), *n.* **1.** a small, loose-skinned variety of mandarin orange. See **mandarin** (def. 5). **2.** deep orange; reddish orange. —*adj.* **3.** of a deep orange colour. [f. TANG(I)ER + -INE[1]]

tangi (tăng′ē), *n. N.Z.* a Maori funeral or wake. [t. Maori]

tangible (tăn′jə bl), *adj.* **1.** capable of being touched; discernible by the touch; material or substantial. **2.** real or actual, rather than imaginary or visionary. **3.** definite;

not vague or elusive: *no tangible grounds for suspicion.* **4.** (of an asset) capable of being possessed or realized; having the form of real property or chattels. **—*n.* 5.** (*usually pl.*) something capable of being possessed or realized. [t. L: m. s. *tangibilis*] **—tan′gibil′ity, tan′gibleness,** *n.* **—tan′gibly,** *adv.*

Tangier (tăn′jĭə′), *n.* a seaport in N Morocco near the Strait of Gibraltar; formerly capital of the internationalized **Tangier Zone** which became part of Morocco in 1956. 142,000 (est. 1963). Also, **Tangiers.**

Tangier

tangle (tăng′gl), *v.*, **-gled, -gling,** *n.* **—*v.t.* 1.** to bring together into a mass of confusedly interlaced or intertwisted threads, strands, or other like parts; snarl. **2.** to involve in something that hampers, obstructs, or overgrows: *bushes tangled with vines.* **3.** to catch and hold in, or as in, a net or snare. **—*v.i.* 4.** to be or become tangled. **5.** *Colloq.* to conflict, quarrel, or argue (usually fol. by *with*). **—*n.* 6.** a tangled condition. **7.** a tangled or confused mass or assemblage of something. **8.** a confused jumble: *a tangle of contradictory statements.* **9.** *Colloq.* a conflict, quarrel, or disagreement. [ME *tangil,* nasalized var. of *tagil* entangle, t. Scand.; cf. d. Sw. *taggla* disarrange] **—tan′gler,** *n.* **—tan′gly,** *adj.*

tango (tăng′gō), *n., pl.* **-gos,** *v.,* **-goed, -going. —*n.* 1.** a dance of Spanish-American origin, danced by couples, and having many varied steps, figures, and poses. **2.** music for this dance. **—*v.i.* 3.** to dance the tango. [t. Amer. Sp.] **—tan′goist,** *n.*

tangram (tăng′grăm), *n.* a Chinese puzzle consisting of a square cut into five triangles, a square, and a rhomboid, which can be combined so as to form a great variety of other figures.

Tangshan (tăng′shăn′), *n.* a city in Hopeh province in NE China. 812,000 (est. 1958).

Tanguy (*Fr.* tăɴ gē′), *n.* **Yves** (*Fr.* ēv), 1900–55, French surrealist painter, in the U.S. after 1939.

tangy (tăng′ĭ), *adj.,* **tangier, tangiest.** having a tang.

tanh (thăn, tănsh), *n. Maths.* hyperbolic tangent. See **hyperbolic functions.**

Tanis (tā′nĭs), *n.* an ancient city of Lower Egypt, in the Nile delta: ancient capital of Egypt. Biblical, **Zoan.**

tanist (tăn′ĭst), *n. Hist.* the successor apparent to a Celtic chief, usually the oldest or worthiest of his kin, chosen by election among the tribe during the chief's lifetime. [t. Irish, Gaelic: m. *tānaiste* immediate heir to estate]

tanistry (tăn′ĭs trĭ), *n.* the system among various Celtic tribes of choosing a tanist.

taniwha (tăn′ĭ wä′), *n. N.Z.* a mythical water monster. [t. Maori]

Tanjore (tăn jô′), *n.* former name of **Thanjavur.**

tank (tăngk), *n.* **1.** a large receptacle or structure for holding water or other liquid or a gas: *tanks for storing oil.* **2.** a natural or artificial pool, pond, or lake. **3.** *Mil.* an armoured, self-propelled combat vehicle, armed with cannon and machine-guns and moving on caterpillar tracks. **—*v.t.* 4.** to put or store in a tank. **5.** a tank engine. **—*v.i.* 6.** *Colloq.* to move like a tank: *a footballer tanking down the wing.* **7. tank up,** to fill the tank of a motor vehicle with fuel. [t. Gujarati: m. *tānkh* pool; r. ME *stank,* t. OF: m. *estanc* pool. See STANCH[1]] **—tank′less,** *adj.* **—tank′like′,** *adj.*

tankage (tăng′kĭj), *n.* **1.** the capacity of a tank or tanks. **2.** the act or process of storing liquid in a tank. **3.** the price charged for this. **4.** the residue from tanks in which carcasses and other offal have been steamed and the fat has been rendered, used as a fertilizer.

tankard (tăng′kəd), *n.* a large drinking cup, now usually with a handle and (sometimes) a hinged cover. [ME; cf. MD *tanckaert*]

Tankard

tanked up, *Colloq.* intoxicated, esp. with beer.

tank engine, a steam locomotive that carries its own water and coal, and does not have a tender.

tanker (tăng′kə), *n.* a ship, aircraft, road or rail vehicle designed to carry oil or other liquid in bulk.

tank farming, hydroponics.

tank furnace, a furnace in which glass is melted in a bath constructed from refractory blocks.

tank glass, glass melted in a tank furnace rather than in a pot.

tank wagon, a railway wagon for carrying oil or other liquid in a large tank. Also, **tank car.**

tan-liquor (tăn′lĭk′ə), *n.* an aqueous extract of tanbark. Also, **tan-ooze, tan-pickle.**

tannage (tăn′ĭj), *n.* **1.** tanning. **2.** that which has been tanned; the product of tanning.

tannate (tăn′āt), *n. Chem.* a salt of tannic acid.

Tannenberg (tăn′ən bûg′; *Ger.* tä′nən bĕrk), *n.* a village in N Poland, formerly in East Prussia: the scene of a decisive German victory over the Russians 1914.

tanner[1] (tăn′ə) *n.* one whose occupation it is to tan hides. [ME and OE *tannere.* See TAN[1]]

tanner[2] (tăn′ə), *n. Slang.* sixpence.

tannery (tăn′ə rĭ), *n., pl.* **-neries.** a place where tanning is carried on.

Tannhäuser (tăn′hoi′zə; *Ger.* tän′hŏʏ zər), *n.* a Middle High German lyric poet of the 13th century. A legend tells of his stay with Venus in the Venusberg and his later repentance.

tannic (tăn′ĭk), *adj. Chem.* pertaining to, derived from, or related to tan or its tanning principle.

tannin (tăn′ĭn), *n. Chem.* any of a group of astringent vegetable principles or compounds, as the reddish compound which gives the tanning properties to oak bark or the whitish compound (the **common tannin,** or **tannic acid**) which occurs in large quantities in nut-galls. [f. s. ML *tannum* TAN[1], n., + -IN[2], on model of F *tanin*]

tanning (tăn′ĭng), *n.* **1.** the process or art of converting hides or skins into leather. **2.** a making brown, as by exposure to the sun. **3.** *Colloq.* a thrashing.

Tannoy (tăn′oi), *n. Trademark.* a public-address system.

Tanoan (tä′nō ən), *n.* **1.** an American Indian linguistic stock, which includes three surviving languages spoken in pueblos in northern New Mexico, including Taos. **—*adj.* 2.** of or pertaining to this stock.

tanrec (tăn′rĕk), *n.* tenrec.

tansy (tăn′zĭ), *n., pl.* **-sies. 1.** any plant of the composite genus *Tanacetum* of Europe and Asia, esp. *T. vulgare,* a coarse, strong-scented herb with toothed pinnate leaves and corymbs of yellow flowers. **2.** any of various plants resembling this. [ME, t. OF: m. *tanesie,* var. of *athanasie,* t. ML: m. *athanasia,* t. Gk: immortality]

Tanta (tăn′tə), *n.* a city in N Egypt, in the Nile delta. 184,000 (1960).

tantalate (tăn′tə lāt′), *n. Chem.* a salt of any tantalic acid.

tantalic (tăn tăl′ĭk), *adj. Chem.* of or pertaining to tantalum, esp. in the pentavalent state.

tantalic acid, *Chem.* an acid, $HTaO_3$, which forms complex salts (tantalates).

tantalite (tăn′tə līt′), *n.* a mineral, iron tantalate, $FeTa_2O_6$, usually containing manganese and columbium, occurring in heavy (sp. gr. 6·0–7·4) black crystals: the principal ore of tantalum.

tantalize (tăn′tə līz′), *v.t.,* **-lized, -lizing.** to torment with, or as with, the sight of something desired but out of reach; tease by arousing expectations that are repeatedly disappointed. Also, **tantalise.** [f. TANTAL(US) + -IZE] **—tan′taliza′tion,** *n.* **—tan′taliz′er,** *n.* **—tan′taliz′ingly,** *adv.*

tantalous (tăn′tə ləs), *adj. Chem.* containing trivalent tantalum.

tantalum (tăn′tə ləm), *n. Chem.* a rare element usually associated with columbium. On account of its resistance to strong acids, it is used for handling such reactive acids as hydrochloric. *Symbol:* Ta; *at. wt:* 180·948; *at. no.:* 73; *sp. gr.:* 16·6. [t. NL; der. TANTALUS, from its incapacity to absorb acid]

Tantalus (tăn′tə ləs), *n.* **1.** *Gk Myth.* a son of Zeus and the nymph Pluto: father of Pelops and Niobe. For revealing secrets of the gods, he was condemned to stand, hungry and thirsty, in water up to his chin, under a tree laden with fruit. **2.** (*l.c.*) a stand containing visible decanters, secured by a lock.

tantamount (tăn′tə mount′), *adj.* equivalent, as in value, force, effect, or signification. [appar. f. F *tant* (g. L *tantum* so much) + AMOUNT] **—Syn.** See **equal.**

tantara (tăn′tə rə, tăn tä′rə), *n.* **1.** a blast of a trumpet or horn. **2.** any similar sound. [imit.]

tantivy (tăn tĭv′ĭ), *adv., adj., n., pl.* **-tivies,** *interj.* **—*adv.* 1.** at full gallop or speed: *to ride tantivy.* **—*adj.* 2.** swift; rapid. **—*n.* 3.** a gallop; a rush. **4.** a hunting cry; a cry of 'tantivy'. **—*interj.* 5.** (a hunting cry when the chase is at full speed.) [? imit.]

tant mieux (*Fr.* täɴ myœ′), *French.* so much the better.

tanto (tăn′tō; *It.* tän′tō), *adv. Music.* too much; so much. [t. It., g. L *tantum* so much]

tant pis (*Fr.* täɴ pē′), *French.* so much the worse.

Tantra (tăn′trə, tŭn′-), *n.* **1.** *Hinduism.* one of several books in dialogue form setting out the requirements of ritual, discipline, etc. **2.** one of a similar series of Buddhist devotional books. **3.** Tantrism. [t. Skt: lit., loom]

Tantrism (tăn′trĭst, tŭn′-), *n. Hinduism, etc.* the doctrine of the books of Tantra, teaching that the visible world presents an unending dance of the believers with the

Divine, in which unity of the worshipper with the worshipped is ultimately achieved.

tantrum (tăn′trəm), *n.* a sudden burst of ill humour; a fit of ill temper or passion. [orig. uncert.]

Tanzania

Tanzania (tăn′zə nĭə′), *n.* a republic in E Africa comprising the former country Tanganyika, the islands of Zanzibar and Pemba, and adjacent small islands. 9,542,000 pop. (est. 1960); 362,820 sq. mi. *Cap.:* Dar-es-Salaam.

Tao (tä′ō), *n.* **1.** the concept of the Taoist philosophy, that all existence has been only in relation to an external absolute. **2.** the ideal striven for by Taoists. **3.** (in Taoist belief) the course of life and its foundation in relation to eternal truth. [t. Chinese: path or way (i.e. way of belief)]

Taoism (tä′ō ĭz′əm), *n.* **1.** a philosophical system developed by Lao-tse advocating a discipline of non-intervention with the course of nature and of absolute sincerity and honesty, whereby the disciple can attain a state of harmony with Tao. **2.** a system of religious belief founded upon the teachings of Lao-tse but incorporating in its present form elements drawn from several more primitive and animistic sources, including sorcery and pantheism. It is one of the principal religions of China. Also, **Hsuan Chiao.** —**Ta′oist,** *n., adj.* —**Ta′ois′tic,** *adj.*

Taos (tous), *n.* **1.** an American Indian language of the Tanoan family. **2.** a member of an American Indian people occupying pueblos in New Mexico.

tap[1] (tăp), *v.,* **tapped, tapping,** *n.* —*v.t.* **1.** to strike lightly but audibly; strike with slight blows. **2.** to make, put, etc., by tapping. **3.** to strike (the hand, foot, etc.) lightly upon or against something. **4.** to add a thickness of leather to the sole or heel of (a boot or shoe), as in repairing. —*v.i.* **5.** to strike lightly but audibly, as to attract attention. **6.** to strike light blows. —*n.* **7.** a light but audible blow. **8.** the sound made by this. **9.** (*pl.*) *U.S. Mil.* last post. **10.** a thickness of leather added to the sole or heel of a boot or shoe, as in repairing. **11.** a piece of metal attached to the toe or heel of a shoe to make the tapping of a dancer more audible. [ME *tappen,* t. F: m. s. *taper* strike, slap; of Gmc orig.] —**tap′pable,** *adj.*

tap[2] (tăp), *n., v.,* **tapped, tapping.** —*n.* **1.** any device for controlling the flow of liquid from a pipe or the like by opening or closing an orifice; a cock. **2.** a cylindrical stick, long plug, or stopper for closing an opening through which liquid is drawn, as in a cask; a spigot. **3.** the liquid, esp. beer, drawn through a particular tap. **4.** *Surg.* withdrawal of fluid: *bloody tap.* **5.** a taphouse or taproom. **6.** an instrument for cutting the thread of a female screw. **7.** a hole made in tapping, as one in a pipe to furnish connection for a branch pipe. **8.** *Elect.* a connection brought out of a winding at some point between its extremities. **9.** *Archaic.* a particular kind or quality of drink. **10. on tap, a.** ready to be drawn off and served, as drink, esp. beer, in a cask. **b.** furnished with a tap or cock, as a barrel containing drink, esp. beer. **c.** ready for immediate use. —*v.t.* **11.** to draw off (liquid) by drawing out or opening a tap, or by piercing the container; draw liquid from (any vessel or reservoir). **12.** to draw the tap or plug from, or pierce (a cask, etc.). **13.** to penetrate, reach, etc., for the purpose of drawing something off: *to tap one's resources.* **14.** *Slang.* to extract money from, esp. in a crafty manner. **15.** to gain or effect secret access to: *to tap telephone wires to hear conversations.* **16.** to furnish (a cask, etc.) with a tap. **17.** to cut a female screw thread in (a hole, etc.). **18.** to open outlets from (power lines, roads, pipes, etc.). [ME; OE *tæppa,* c. G *zapfen*] —**tap′pable,** *adj.*

tapa (tä′pə), *n.* **1.** an unwoven cloth of the Pacific islands, made by steeping and beating the inner bark of the paper-mulberry tree, *Broussonetia papyrifera.* **2.** the bark. **3.** the tree. Also, **tappa.** [t. Polynesian]

Tapajós (*Port.* tä pä zhôs′), *n.* a river flowing NE through central Brazil to the Amazon. ab. 1100 mi.

tap-bolt (tăp′bōlt′), *n.* stud[1] (def. 4).

tap-cinder (tăp′sĭn′də), *n.* slag produced in iron founding.

tap dance, a dance in which the rhythm or rhythmical variation is audibly tapped out by the toe or heel.

tap-dance (tăp′däns′), *v.i.,* **-danced, -dancing.** to perform a tap dance. —**tap′-dan′cer,** *n.*

tape (tāp), *n., v.,* **taped, taping.** —*n.* **1.** a long narrow strip of linen, cotton, or the like, used for tying garments, etc. **2.** a long narrow strip of paper, metal, etc. **3.** a tape measure. **4.** a magnetic tape. **5.** a string or the like stretched across the finishing line in a race and broken by the winning contestant. **6.** the ribbon of white paper on which a ticker prints quotations or news. —*v.t.* **7.** to furnish with a tape or tapes. **8.** to tie up or bind with tape. **9.** to measure with, or as if with a tape measure. **10.** to tape-record. **11. have (someone) taped,** *Colloq.* to understand thoroughly, esp. a person's weaknesses or guile. **12. have (something) taped,** *Colloq.* to be in complete control of or be easily able to do (something). [ME, unexplained var. of ME *tappe,* OE *tæppe* strip (of cloth)] —**tap′er,** *n.* —**tape′less,** *adj.* —**tape′like′,** *adj.*

tape deck, 1. the basic equipment of a tape-recorder, excluding the amplifier, microphone and loudspeaker. **2.** *Computers.* a tape unit.

tape-grass (tāp′gräs′), *n.* a submerged aquatic plant with narrow leaves, *Vallisneria spiralis,* family *Hydrocharitaceae,* of warm temperate regions and frequently grown in aquariums.

tape machine, a telegraphic instrument which automatically prints share prices, market reports, etc., on a tape (**ticker tape**). Also, *U.S.,* **ticker.**

tape measure, a long strip or ribbon, as of linen or steel, marked with subdivisions of the foot or metre for measuring. Also, *Chiefly U.S.,* **tapeline** (tāp′līn′).

tape punch, *Computers.* a machine which punches information on to paper tape.

taper (tā′pə), *v.i.* **1.** to become gradually slenderer towards one end. **2.** to grow gradually lean. —*v.t.* **3.** to make gradually smaller towards one end. **4.** to reduce gradually. —*n.* **5.** gradual diminution of width or thickness in an elongated object. **6.** gradual decrease of force, capacity, etc. **7.** a spire or slender pyramid; anything having a tapering form. **8.** a candle, esp. a very slender one. **9.** a long wick coated with wax, tallow, or the like, as for use in lighting candles or gas. **10.** a feeble light. [ME *tapere* candle, OE *tapor*; orig. uncert.] —**ta′perer,** *n.* —**ta′peringly,** *adv.*

tape-reader (tāp′rē′də), *n.* *Computers.* a machine that converts information on punched paper tape into electrical impulses as the tape is drawn through the machine.

tape-record (tāp′rĭ kôd′), *v.t.* to transcribe on to magnetic tape.

tape-recorder (tāp′rĭ kô′də), *n.* a device for recording an electrical signal, esp. one produced by sound, in which a magnetic tape moves past an inductance coil which magnetizes the tape in relation to the input signal. The signal is recovered from the magnetized tape by a play-back circuit and can be erased by demagnetizing the tape.

tape-recording (tāp′rĭ kô′dĭng), *n.* **1.** a magnetic tape on which speech, music, etc., has been recorded. **2.** the act of recording on magnetic tape.

tapestry (tăp′ĭs trĭ), *n., pl.* **-tries,** *v.,* **-tried, -trying.** —*n.* **1.** a fabric consisting of a warp upon which coloured threads are woven by hand to produce a design, often pictorial, and used for wall hangings, furniture coverings, etc. **2.** a machine-woven reproduction of true tapestry. —*v.t.* **3.** to furnish, cover, or adorn with tapestry. [ME *tapestrye,* t. F: m. *tapisserie,* der. *tapissier* maker of tapestry, der. *tapis* TAPIS] —**tap′estry-like′,** *adj.*

tapetum (tə pē′təm), *n., pl.* **-ta** (-tə). **1.** *Bot.* a layer of cells often investing the archespore in a developing sporangium and absorbed as the spores mature. **2.** *Anat., Zool.* any of certain membranous layers or the like, as in the choroid or retina. [t. LL, r. L *tapēte* carpet] —**tape′tal,** *adj.*

tape unit, *Computers.* a machine that handles magnetic tape in a computer system.

tapeworm (tāp′wûm′), *n.* any of various flat or tapelike worms of the class *Cestoda,* lacking any alimentary canal, and parasitic when adult in the alimentary canal of man and other vertebrates: usually characterized by having the larval and adult stages in different hosts.

taphole (tăp′hōl′), *n.* *Metall.* a hole in a blast furnace or the like through which molten metal or slag is drawn off.

taphouse (tăp′hous′), *n., pl.* **-houses.** a house where alcoholic drink is kept on tap for sale; a tavern.

tapioca (tăp′ĭ ō′kə), *n.* a granular farinaceous food substance prepared from cassava starch by drying while moist on heated plates, used for making puddings, thickening soups, etc. [t. Pg., t. Brazilian (Tupi-Guarani): m. *tipioca,* f. *tipi* residue + *og, ók* squeeze out]

tapiolite (tăp′ĭ ə līt′), *n.* a mineral, niobate and tantalate of iron and manganese, which crystallizes in the tetragonal system: an ore of tantalum. [t. Sw.: m. *tapiolit,* f. *Tapio* Finnish forest spirit + *-lit* -LITE]

South American tapir, *Tapirus terrestris* (Ab. 3 ft high at the shoulder, 6 ft long)

tapir (tā′pə), *n.* any of various slate-coloured stout-bodied perissodactyl ungulates (family *Tapiridae*) of the genus *Tapirus* of tropical America and south-east Asia, somewhat resembling swine and having a flexible snout. [t. Brazilian (Tupi); m. *tapira*]

tapis (tăp′ē, tăp′ĭ; *Fr.* tȧ pē′), *n.*, *pl.* **tapis.** **1.** a carpet, tapestry, or other covering. **2. on the tapis,** under consideration or discussion. [t. F, g. LL *tapētium*, t. Gk: m. *tapḗtion*, dim. of *tápēs* cloth wrought with figures]

tappa (tăp′ə), *n.* tapa.

tapper[1] (tăp′ə), *n.* one who or that which taps or strikes lightly. [f. TAP[1] + -ER[1]]

tapper[2] (tăp′ə), *n.* **1.** one who or that which taps, as trees for the sap or juice. **2.** one who cuts screw threads in a hole. [f. TAP[2] + -ER[1]]

tappet (tăp′ĭt), *n.* *Mach.* (in a machine or engine) a projecting part, arm, or the like which intermittently comes in contact with another part to which it communicates or from which it receives an intermittent motion. [f. TAP[1] + -ET]

tapping[1] (tăp′ĭng), *n.* **1.** the act of one who or that which taps or strikes lightly. **2.** the sound so made. [f. TAP[1] + -ING[1]]

tapping[2] (tăp′ĭng), *n.* **1.** the act of one who or that which taps casks, etc. **2.** that which is drawn by tapping. **3.** the operation of cutting a screw thread in a hole. [f. TAP[2] + -ING[1]]

taproom (tăp′rōōm′, -rŏŏm′), *n.* a room, as in a tavern, in which alcoholic drink is sold; bar.

taproot (tăp′rōōt′), *n.* *Bot.* a main root descending downwards from the radicle and giving off small lateral roots.

tapster (tăp′stə), *n.* *Archaic.* a bartender or barmaid. [ME; OE *tæppestre.* See TAP[2], n., -STER] —**tapstress** (tăp′strĭs), *n. fem.*

tap-water (tăp′wô′tə), *n.* water from a household tap; domestic water.

tar[1] (tä), *n.*, *v.*, **tarred, tarring.** —*n.* **1.** any of various dark-coloured viscid products obtained by the destructive distillation of certain organic substances, such as coal, wood, etc. **2.** coal-tar pitch. —*adj.* **3.** made of or covered with tar. —*v.t.* **4.** to smear or cover with, or as with, tar. **5. tarred with the same brush,** having similar faults. [ME *terre*, OE *terw-* (s. *teru*), c. D *teer*, G *Teer*; akin to TREE]

tar[2] (tä), *n.* *Colloq.* a sailor. [said to be short for TARPAULIN] —**Syn.** See **sailor.**

tara (tä′rə), *n.* a variety of bracken, *Pteridium aquilinum*, with edible rhizomes, of New Zealand and Tasmania. [t. Maori]

Tara (tă′rə, tä′rə), *n.* a village in Ireland, near Dublin: the **Hill of Tara** was the home of the ancient Irish kings.

taradiddle (tă′rə dĭd′l), *n.* tarradiddle.

taranaki (tă′rə năk′ĭ), *adj.* *N.Z. Colloq.* made of wires and battens, as a gate. [t. Maori]

tarantass (tă′rən tăs′), *n.* a large four-wheeled Russian carriage mounted without springs on two parallel longitudinal wooden bars. Also, **tarantas.** [t. Russ.: m. *tarantas*]

tarantella (tă′rən tĕl′ə), *n.* **1.** a rapid, whirling southern Italian dance in very quick sextuple (orig. quadruple) rhythm, usually performed by a single couple, and formerly supposed to be a remedy for tarantism. **2.** a popular dance derived from it. **3.** a piece of music for either dance or in its rhythm. [t. It., der. TARANTO, g. L *Tarentum*]

tarantism (tă′rən tĭz′əm), *n.* a nervous affection characterized by an uncontrollable impulse to dance; esp. as prevalent in southern Italy from the 15th to the 17th century and popularly attributed to the bite of the tarantula (def. 1). [f. It. TARANT(O) + -ISM. See TARANTELLA, TARANTULA]

Taranto (tə răn′tō; *It.* tä′rän tô), *n.* a fortified seaport in SE Italy, on the **Gulf of Taranto,** an arm of the Mediterranean: founded by the Greeks in the 8th century B.C.; naval base. 211,760 (1966). Ancient, **Tarentum.**

tarantula (tə răn′työŏ lə), *n.*, *pl.* **-las, -lae** (-lē′). **1.** a large spider of southern Europe, *Lycosa tarantula*, whose bite was formerly supposed to cause tarantism. **2.** any large spider, esp. one of the family *Theraphosidae* of America. **3.** a name given to several animals which are thought to be venomous, as certain snakes and lizards. [t. ML, t. It.: m. *tarantola*, der. TARANTO]

Texas tarantula, *Eurypelma hentzi* (Body ab. 2 in. long)

taraxacum (tə răk′sə kəm), *n.* **1.** any of the composite plants, mostly stemless herbs, constituting the genus *Taraxacum*, as the dandelion. **2.** the root of the dandelion, used in medicine as a tonic, diuretic, and aperient. [t. ML, t. Ar.: m. *tarakhshaqōq*, t. Pers.: m. *talkh chakōk* bitter herb]

Tarbes (*Fr.* tȧrb), *n.* a town in SW France, capital of Hautes-Pyrénées. 50,715 (1962).

tarboosh (tä bōōsh′), *n.* a cap of cloth or felt (nearly always red) with a tassel, worn by Muslim men either by itself or as the inner part of the turban. Also, **tarbush, tarbouche.** [t. Ar.: m. *tarbūsh*]

Tarboosh

tarbrush (tä′brŭsh′), *n.* **1.** a brush for applying tar. **2. a touch of the tarbrush,** (used offensively) Negro or other coloured ancestry or appearance.

tarbuttite (tä′bə tīt′), *n.* a mineral basic zinc phosphate which occurs in sheaf-like aggregates. [named after Percy *Tarbutt*, Australian mining engineer]

Tardenoisian (tä′də noi′zĭ ən, -nwä′zĭ-), *adj.* *Archaeol.* belonging to a stage of culture transitional between Palaeolithic and Neolithic. [named after *Tardenois*, village in France, site of finds]

Tardieu (*Fr.* tȧr dyœ′), *n.* **André Pierre Gabriel Amédée** (*Fr.* äN drĕ pyĕr gȧ brē ĕl ȧ mĕ dĕ′), 1876–1945, French statesman.

tardigrade (tä′dĭ grād′), *adj.* **1.** slow in pace or movement. **2.** of or pertaining to the *Tardigrada*, a class or subclass of minute herbivorous arthropods, lacking well-developed circulatory or respiratory systems. —*n.* **3.** a tardigrade animal. [t. L: m. *tardigradus*]

tardo (tä′dō; *It.* tȧr′dô), *adj.* *Music.* slow. [t. It., g. L *tardus*]

tardy (tä′dĭ), *adj.*, **-dier, -diest.** **1.** moving or acting slowly; slow; sluggish. **2.** late or behindhand. **3.** delaying through reluctance. [ME *tardive*, t. F, g. LL *tardīvus*, der. L *tardus* slow] —**tar′dily,** *adv.* —**tar′diness,** *n.* —**Ant. 2.** prompt.

tare[1] (tĕə), *n.* **1.** any of various vetches, esp. *Vicia sativa.* **2.** the seed of a vetch. **3.** (in biblical use) some injurious weed, possibly the darnel. [ME; cf. MD *tarwe* wheat]

tare[2] (tĕə), *n.*, *v.*, **tared, taring.** —*n.* **1.** the weight of the wrapping, receptacle, or conveyance containing goods. **2.** a deduction from the gross weight to allow for this. **3.** the weight of a vehicle without cargo, passengers, etc. **4.** *Chem.* a counterweight used to balance the weight of a container. —*v.t.* **5.** to ascertain, note, or allow for, the tare of. [late ME, t. ML: m. *tara*, t. Ar.: m. *tarha* deduction]

Tarentum (tə rĕn′təm), *n.* ancient name of **Taranto.**

targe (täj), *n.* *Archaic.* a round shield. [ME, t. OF; r. OE *targa*, t. Scand.; cf. Icel. *targa* shield, c. OHG *zarga* frame]

target (tä′gĭt), *n.* **1.** a device, usually marked with concentric circles, to be aimed at in shooting practice or contests. **2.** any object used for this purpose. **3.** anything fired at or aimed at. **4.** a goal to be reached. **5.** *Fencing.* the portion of a fencer's body on which a touch may be scored. **6.** an object of abuse, scorn, derision, etc.; a butt. **7.** *Survey.* **a.** the sliding sight on a levelling rod. **b.** any marker on which sights are taken. **8.** *Hist.* a small round shield or buckler. [late ME, t. F: m. *targuete.* See TARGE] —**tar′getless,** *adj.*

target-practice (tä′gĭt prăk′tĭs), *n.* the act of shooting at targets for practice in accuracy in aiming.

Targum (tä′gəm), *n.*, *pl.* **Targums, Targumim** (tä′gōō-mēm′). a translation or paraphrase of the various divisions of the Hebrew Old Testament in Aramaic. [t. Aram.: interpretation] —**Targumic** (tä gōō′mĭk), *adj.* —**Tar′gumist,** *n.*

tariff (tă′rĭf), *n.* **1.** an official list or table showing the duties or customs imposed by a government on exports or, esp., imports. **2.** the system of duties so imposed. **3.** any duty in such a list or system. **4.** any table of charges, as of a transport undertaking. **5.** a bill of fare. —*v.t.* **6.** to subject to a tariff. **7.** to put a valuation on according to a tariff. [t. It.: s. *tariffa*, t. Ar.: m. *tarif* notification, information] —**tar′iffless,** *adj.*

tariff reform, an early 20th-century movement pressing for economic protection for British goods by the imposition of tariffs on imports (opposed to *free trade*). —**tar′iff-reform′er,** *n.*

Tarim (tä′rēm′), *n.* a river in NW China, in Sinkiang, flowing through the vast **Tarim Basin,** cradled between the Kunlun and Tien Shan mountain systems, and ending in a number of small lakes in a desert region. ab. 1000 mi.

Tarim Basin

Tarkington (tä′kĭng tən), *n.* **(Newton) Booth,** 1869–1946, U.S. novelist and playwright.

tarlatan (tä′lə tən), *n.* a thin, open, stiff cotton fabric, not washable. [t. F: m. *tarlatane*; orig. uncert.]

tarmac (tä′măk), *n., adj., v.,* **-macked, -macking.** —*n.* **1.** (*cap.*) *Trademark.* tarmacadam. **2.** a road or airport runway made of tarmacadam. —*adj.* **3.** made of or surfaced with tarmacadam. —*v.t.* **4.** to surface (a road, runway or the like) with tarmacadam.

tarmacadam (tä′mə kăd′əm), *n.* **1.** a road-surfacing mixture consisting of small stones or gravel bound together with tar or a mixture of tar and bitumen. —*adj.* **2.** made of or having a surface of such a mixture. [f. TAR[1] + MACADAM]

tarn (tän), *n.* a small mountain lake or pool. [ME *terne,* t. Scand.; cf. Icel. *tjörn*]

Tarn (*Fr.* tàrn), a department in S France. 319,560 pop. (1962); 2231 sq. mi. *Cap.:* Albi.

tarnation (tä nā′shən), *Colloq. or Dial.* —*interj.* **1.** damnation. —*n.* **2.** an act or instance of saying 'tarnation'. **3.** eternal damnation. —*adj.* **4.** damned: *I can't get the tarnation car to start.* [f. '*tarn*(*al*) d. var. of ETERNAL + (DAMN)ATION]

Tarn-et-Garonne (*Fr.* tàrn ė gà rŏn′), *n.* a department in S France. 175,847 pop. (1962); 1440 sq. mi. *Cap.:* Montauban.

tarnish (tä′nĭsh), *v.t.* **1.** to dull or alter the lustre of (esp. a metallic surface by oxidation, etc.); discolour. **2.** to diminish or destroy the purity of; stain; sully. —*v.i.* **3.** to grow dull or discoloured; lose lustre. **4.** to become sullied. —*n.* **5.** a tarnished coating. **6.** tarnished condition; discoloration; alteration of the lustre. **7.** stain or blemish. [t. F: m. *terniss-,* s. *ternir,* der. *terne* dull, dark, prob. of Gmc orig.; cf. MHG *ternen* darken, OE *derne* obscure] —**tar′nishable,** *adj.* —**tar′nisher,** *n.*

Tarnopol (*Russ.* tàr nô′pəly), *n.* Ternopol.

Tarnów (*Pol.* tàr′no͞of), *n.* a town in SE Poland, in Galicia. 71,000 (est. 1960).

taro (tä′rō), *n., pl.* **-ros. 1.** a tuberous araceous herb *Colocasia esculenta,* cultivated in the tropics for the root which, though poisonous, is made edible by boiling. **2.** the root. [t. Polynesian]

tarogato (tă′rə gä′tō), *n.* a Hungarian clarinet-like musical instrument.

tarot (tă′rō), *n.* **1.** one of a pack of 78 cards, made up of four suits of 14 cards each, with 22 triumph cards. **2.** a triumph card in such a pack, bearing a symbolic or mythological character, now chiefly used in cartomancy. **3.** (*pl.*) *Obs.* a game played with these cards. —*adj.* **4.** of or pertaining to the tarots, esp. the triumph cards. [t. F, t. It.: m. *tarocco*]

tarpan (tä′păn), *n.* a variety of wild horse, *Equus caballus gomelini,* widespread in Europe in prehistoric times, but now extinct. [t. Russ., t. Kirghiz]

tarpaulin (tä pô′lĭn), *n.* **1.** a protective covering of canvas or other material waterproofed with tar, paint, or wax. **2.** a hat, esp. a sailor's, made of or covered with such material. **3.** *Rare.* a sailor. [earlier *tarpauling,* f. TAR[1] + PALL[1] + -ING[1]]

Tarpeia (tä pē′ə), *n. Rom. Legend.* a vestal virgin who betrayed Rome to the Sabines and was crushed by their shields when she asked for reward.

Tarpeian (tä pē′ən), *adj.* of or denoting a rock on the Capitoline Hill at Rome from which traitors were hurled.

tarpon (tä′pŏn), *n.* a large fish, *Tarpon atlanticus,* of the warmer waters of the Atlantic, with compressed body and huge silvery scales. [orig. uncert.; cf. D *tarpoen*]

Tarquin (tä′kwĭn), *n.* **1.** one of a famous family of kings of early Rome. **2.** (*Lucius Tarquinius Superbus, 'the Proud'*) died after 510 B.C. last Roman king (*c.* 534–510 B.C.) of this family.

tarradiddle (tă′rə dĭd′l), *n.* **1.** a lie about a small matter; fib. **2.** nonsense; rubbish. Also, **taradiddle.**

tarragon (tă′rə gən), *n.* **1.** an Old World composite plant, *Artemisia dracunculus,* whose aromatic leaves are used for flavouring. **2.** the leaves themselves. Also, **estragon.** [t. Sp.: m. *taragona,* t. Ar.: m. *tarkhūn,* prob. t. Gk: m. *drákōn* dragon, or *drakóntion* type of arum]

Tarrasa (*Sp.* tä rä′sä), *n.* a town in NE Spain, near Barcelona. 116,692 (1965).

tarriance (tă′rĭ əns), *Archaic.* **1.** delay; tarrying; waiting. **2.** sojourn.

tarry[1] (tă′rĭ), *v.,* **-ried, -rying,** *n., pl.* **-ries.** —*v.i.* **1.** to remain or stay, as in a place; sojourn. **2.** to delay or be tardy in acting, starting, coming, etc.; linger or loiter. **3.** to wait. —*v.t.* **4.** *Archaic.* to wait for. —*n.* **5.** *Archaic.* a stay; sojourn. [ME; orig. uncert.] —**tar′rier,** *n.* —**Syn. 3.** See **wait.**

tarry[2] (tä′rĭ), *adj.* of or like tar; smeared with tar. [f. TAR[1] + -Y[1]] —**tar′riness,** *n.*

tarsal (tä′səl), *adj.* **1.** of or pertaining to the tarsus of the foot or leg. **2.** pertaining to the tarsi of the eyelids. —*n.* **3.** a tarsal bone, joint, or the like.

Tarshish (tä′shĭsh), *n.* an ancient country, said to have been in S Spain: sea trade in silver and gold. I Kings 10:22.

tarsia (tä′sĭ ə), *n.* inlay or marquetry in wood; intarsia. [t. It.]

Tarsier, *Tarsius carbonarius* (Total length 14 in.)

tarsier (tä′sĭ ə), *n.* a small arboreal primate, genus *Tarsius,* with enormous eyes, sole representative of a suborder, *Tarsiodea*: found in Indonesia and parts of the Philippines. [t. F, der. *tarse* TARSUS]

tarsometatarsus (tä′sō mĕt′ə tä′səs), *n., pl.* **-si** (-sī). the large bone in the lower leg of a bird with which the toe bones articulate: the third segment from the body in the leg of a bird. [f. *tarso-* (comb. form of TARSUS) + METATARSUS] —**tar′somet′atar′sal,** *adj.*

tarsus (tä′səs), *n., pl.* **-si** (-sī). *Anat., Zool.* **1.** the proximal segment of the foot; the collection of bones between the tibia and the metatarsus, entering into the construction of the ankle joint and into the instep of man. See diag. under **skeleton. 2.** the small plate of connective tissue along the border of an eyelid. **3.** tarsometatarsus. **4.** the fifth segment of an insect's leg. See diag. under **coxa.** [NL, t. Gk: m. *tarsós* flat of the foot]

Tarsus (tä′səs), *n.* a city in S Turkey, near the Mediterranean: an important seaport of ancient Cilicia, on the river Cydnus; birthplace of St Paul. 51,184 (1960).

tart[1] (tät), *adj.* **1.** sharp to the taste; sour or acid: *tart apples.* **2.** sharp in character, spirit, or expression; cutting; caustic: *a tart remark.* [ME; OE *teart* sharp, rough. Cf. G *trotz*] —**tart′ish,** *adj.* —**tart′ishly,** *adv.* —**tart′ly,** *adv.* —**tart′ness,** *n.*

tart[2] (tät), *n.* **1.** a small and saucer-shaped shell of pastry, filled with cooked fruit or other sweetened preparation, and having no top crust. **2.** pie covered with a top crust containing fruit or the like. **3.** *Slang.* a girl or woman, esp. of low character. **4.** *Slang.* a prostitute. —*v.t.* **5. tart up,** *Slang.* to adorn; make attractive, esp. with cheap ornaments and cosmetics. [ME *tarte,* t. OF: (m.) *tart(r)e,* g. L *tortula* (der. *torta,* pp., twisted) or ? b. L *tortula* and *tartarum* baked crust]

Tartan

tartan[1] (tä′tn), *n.* **1.** a woollen or worsted cloth woven with stripes of different colours and widths crossing at right angles, worn chiefly by the Scottish Highlanders, each clan having its distinctive pattern. **2.** a design of such a plaid known by name of the clan wearing it. **3.** any plaid. —*adj.* **4.** of, pertaining to, or resembling tartan. **5.** made of tartan. [appar. t. F: m. *tiretaine* linsey-woolsey]

tartan[2] (tä′tn), *n.* a single-masted vessel with a lateen sail and a jib, used in the Mediterranean. [t. F: m. *tartane,* t. It.: m. *tartana,* t. Ar.: m. *tartaneh*]

tartar (tä′tə), *n.* **1.** a hard substance deposited on the teeth by the saliva, consisting of calcium phosphate, mucus, etc. **2.** the deposit from wines, potassium bitartrate. **3.** the partially purified product midway between the crude form (argol) and the further purified form (cream of tartar). [t. ML: s. *tartarum,* t. Gk: m. *tártaron* (of Ar. orig.); r. ME *tartre,* t. F]

Tartar (tä′tə), *n.* **1.** a member of any of a mingled host of Mongolian, Turkish, and other tribes, who, under the leadership of Genghis Khan, overran Asia and eastern Europe during the Middle Ages. **2.** a member of the descendants of this people variously intermingled with other races and tribes, now inhabiting parts of the European and W and central Asiatic Soviet Union. **3.** any of several Turkic languages of W central Asia, particularly Uzbek. **4.** (*also l.c.*) a savage, intractable person. **5.** (*l.c.*) a shrew or vixen. **6. catch a Tartar,** to catch or have dealings with something that or someone who proves unexpectedly troublesome or powerful. —*adj.* **7.** pertaining to a Tartar or Tartars, or to their language. Also, **Tatar.** [ME, t. ML: s. *Tartarus,* t. Pers.: m. *Tatar,* by association with TARTARUS]

tartare (tä tä′, tä′tə). See **steak tartare.** Also, **tartar.**

Tartarean (tä tēə′rĭ ən, -tä′rĭ-), *adj.* of or pertaining to Tartarus; infernal.

tartar emetic, potassium antimonyl tartrate, $K(SbO)C_4H_4O_6 . \frac{1}{2}H_2O$, a poisonous salt with a sweetish metallic taste, occurring in white crystals or as a white granular powder, used in medicine, dyeing, etc.

Tartarian (tä tä′rĭ ən), *adj.* of or pertaining to Tartars.

tartaric (tä tă′rĭk), *adj.* pertaining to or derived from tartar.

tartaric acid, *Chem.* an organic acid, $(CHOHCOOH)_2$,

existing in four isomeric modifications, the common or dextrorotatory form being a colourless crystalline compound obtained from grapes, etc.

tartarize (tä′tə rīz′), *v.t.*, **-rized, -rizing.** *Chem.* to impregnate, combine, or treat with tartar, or potassium bitartrate. Also, **tartarise.** —**tar′tariza′tion,** *n.*

tartarous (tä′tə rəs), *adj.* of or containing tartar.

tartar sauce (tä′tə), a mayonnaise dressing usually with chopped pickles, onions, olives, capers, and green herbs added. [t. F: m. *sauce tartare*]

tartar steak, steak tartar.

Tartarus (tä′tə rəs), *n. Class. Myth.* **1.** a sunless abyss below Hades, in which Zeus imprisoned the Titans. **2.** (later) a place of punishment for the wicked. **3.** Hades, or the lower world in general.

Tartary (tä′tə rĭ), *n.* the historical name used to designate an indefinite region in E Europe and Asia, sometimes extending to the Sea of Japan. Also, **Tatary.**

tartlet (tät′lĭt), *n.* a small tart.

tartrate (tä′trāt), *n. Chem.* a salt or ester of tartaric acid. [t. F, der. *tartre* TARTAR]

tartrated (tä′trā tĭd), *adj. Chem.* formed into a tartrate: combined with tartaric acid.

tartrazine (tä′trə zēn′), *n. Chem.* a type of yellow dye used in food materials. [f. *tartro-* (comb. form repr. TARTAR) + AZ(O)- + -INE[2]]

Tartu (*Russ.* tär′to͞o), *n.* a town in the W Soviet Union, in Estonia. 77,000 (est. 1962). German, **Dorpat.** Russian, **urev.**

Tartuffe (tä′tyo͞of; *Fr.* tȧr tʏf′), *n.* a hypocritical pretender to piety. [name of the hero of a comedy (1667) by Molière] —**Tartuf′fian,** *adj.*

Tarzan (tä′zən), *n. Colloq.* a person of superior strength and agility. [name of the hero of a series of jungle stories by Edgar Rice Burroughs, 1875–1950, U.S. writer]

Tashkent (tăsh kĕnt′; *Russ.* tȧsh kyĕnt′), *n.* a city in the SW Soviet Union in Asia: the capital of Uzbekistan. 1,106,000 (est. 1965).

task (täsk), *n.* **1.** a definite piece of work assigned or falling to a person; a duty. **2.** any piece of work. **3.** a matter of considerable labour or difficulty. **4. take to task,** to call to account, as for fault; blame or censure. **5.** *Obs.* a tax or impost. —*v.t.* **6.** to subject to severe or excessive labour or exertion; put a strain upon (powers, resources, etc.). **7.** to impose a task on. **8.** *Obs.* to tax. [ME, t. ML: m. s. *tasca*, metathetic var. of *taxa* TAX] —**task′er,** *n.* —**task′less,** *adj.*

task force, *Mil.* a temporary grouping of units under one commander, formed for the purpose of carrying out a specific operation or mission.

taskmaster (täsk′mäs′tə), *n.* one whose function it is to assign tasks to others, esp. burdensome tasks. —**task′-mis′tress,** *n. fem.*

taskwork (täsk′wûk′), *n.* **1.** work imposed or done as a task, esp. unpleasant work. **2.** work done or paid for by the job, rather than by the time it takes.

Tasm., Tasmania.

Tasman (tăz′mən; *Du.* tŏs′mŏn), *n.* **1. Abel Janszoon** (*Du.* ŏ′bəl yŏn′sŏn), 1602?–59, Dutch navigator, discoverer of Tasmania, New Zealand, and other islands in the S Pacific. **2. Mount,** a peak in the Southern Alps, South Island, New Zealand. 11,475 ft.

Tasmania

Tasman Bay, an indentation of the Tasman Sea in the N coast of South Island, New Zealand.

Tasmania (tăz mā′nyə), *n.* an island S of Australia: one of the states of the Commonwealth of Australia. 364,566 pop. (1964); 26,215 sq. mi. *Cap.:* Hobart. Formerly, **Van Diemen's Land.** —**Tasma′-nian,** *adj.*, *n.*

Tasmanian devil, a ferocious carnivorous marsupial, *Sarcophilus harrisii*, of Tasmania having a black coat with white markings; ursine dasyure.

Tasmanian devil, *Sarcophilus harrisii* (Total length 3 ft, tail 1 ft)

Tasmanian wolf, the thylacine. Also, **Tasmanian tiger.**

Tasman Sea (tăz′-mən), a part of the Pacific between SE Australia and New Zealand.

tass (tăs), *n. Scot., Irish, and N Dial.* **1.** a cup or small goblet. **2.** a small drink or draught, esp. an alcoholic one. Also, **tassie.** [late ME *tasse*, t. MF]

Tass (tăs), *n.* a news-gathering agency of the Soviet Union. [t. Russ., f. *T(elegrafnoye) A(genstvo) S(ovyetskovo) S(oyuza)* Telegraphic Agency of the Soviet Union]

tasse (tăs), *n. Armour.* a tasset.

tassel[1] (tăs′əl), *n.*, *v.*, **-selled, -selling** or (*U.S.*) **-seled, -seling.** —*n.* **1.** a pendent ornament, orig. a clasp consisting commonly of a bunch of threads, small cords, or strand hanging from a roundish knob or head. **2.** something resembling this, as the inflorescence of certain plants, esp. that at the summit of a stalk of maize. —*v.t.* **3.** to furnish or adorn with tassels. **4.** to form into a tassel or tassels. **5.** to remove the tassel from (growing maize), as in order to improve the crop. —*v.i.* **6.** (of maize, etc.) to put forth tassels. [ME, t. OF: fastening for a cloak] —**tas′selly,** *adj.*

tassel[2] (tăs′əl), *n. Obs.* tercel.

tasset (tăs′ĭt), *n. Armour.* one of a pair of defences for the upper thighs suspended from the waist plates by straps. Also, **tasse.** See illus. under **armour.**

tassie (tăs′ĭ), *n. Scot., Irish, and N Dial.* tass.

Tasso (tăs′ō; *It.* täs′sō), *n.* **Torquato** (*It.* tōr kwä′tō), 1544–95, Italian poet.

taste (tāst), *v.*, **tasted, tasting,** *n.* —*v.t.* **1.** to try the flavour or quality of (something) by taking some into the mouth: *to taste food.* **2.** to eat or drink a little of: *he hadn't tasted food for three days.* **3.** to perceive or distinguish the flavour of: *to taste the wine in a sauce.* **4.** to have or get experience, esp. a slight experience. **5.** *Archaic.* to perceive in any way, esp. by smell. **6.** *Archaic.* to enjoy or appreciate. **7.** *Obs.* to touch, feel, or handle; test or try. —*v.i.* **8.** to try the flavour or quality of something. **9.** to eat or drink a little (usually fol. by *of*): *Susan tasted slyly of the cake.* **10.** to perceive or distinguish the flavour of anything. **11.** to have experience, or make trial in experience, of something. **12.** to have a particular flavour: *the milk tastes sour.* **13.** to smack or savour (usually fol. by *of*).

—*n.* **14.** the act of tasting food, drink, or the like. **15.** the sense by which the flavour or savour of things is perceived when they are brought into contact with special organs of the tongue. **16.** sensation, flavour, or quality as perceived by these organs. **17.** a small quantity tasted; a morsel, bit, or sip. **18.** a relish, liking, or predilection for something: *a taste for music.* **19.** the sense of what is fitting, harmonious, or beautiful; the perception and enjoyment of what constitutes excellence in the fine arts, literature, etc. **20.** manner, style, or general character as showing perception, or lack of perception, of what is fitting or beautiful; characteristic or prevailing style. **21.** a slight experience or a sample of something. **22.** *Obs.* test or trial. **23. to one's taste,** agreeable or pleasing to one: *he couldn't find a tie to his taste.*

[ME, t. OF: m. *taster* try by touching, ult. g. b. L *tangere* touch and *gustāre* taste] —**tast′able,** *adj.*

—**Syn. 16.** TASTE, FLAVOUR, SAVOUR refer to a quality that is perceived when a substance is placed upon the tongue. TASTE is the general word: *the taste of roast beef.* FLAVOUR is a characteristic taste, usually of a pleasing kind, and as of some ingredient put into the food: *lemon flavour.* SAVOUR implies pleasing scent as well as taste or flavour, and connotes enjoyment in tasting: *the sauce has an excellent savour.* —**Ant. 18.** antipathy.

tastebud (tāst′bŭd′), *n.* any of a number of small, flask-shaped bodies in the epithelium of the tongue, etc., the special organs of taste.

tasteful (tāst′fəl), *adj.* having, displaying, or in accordance with, good taste. —**taste′fully,** *adv.* —**taste′fulness,** *n.*

tasteless (tāst′lĭs), *adj.* **1.** having no taste or flavour; insipid. **2.** dull; uninteresting. **3.** lacking in good taste; showing lack of good taste. **4.** *Rare.* lacking the sense of taste. —**taste′lessly,** *adv.* —**taste′lessness,** *n.*

taster (tās′tə), *n.* **1.** one who tastes, esp. one skilled in distinguishing the qualities of wine, tea, etc., by the taste. **2.** *Colloq.* one who samples and reports on manuscripts for a publisher. **3.** a container for taking samples or tasting. **4.** a wide shallow vessel, usually metal, in which wine is tested. **5.** a pipette.

tasty (tās′tĭ), *adj.*, **tastier, tastiest. 1.** pleasing to the taste; savoury; appetizing. **2.** *Colloq.* having or showing good taste. —**tast′ily,** *adv.* —**tast′iness,** *n.*

tat[1] (tăt), *v.i.*, *v.t.*, **tatted, tatting.** to do, or make by, tatting. [orig. unknown]

tat[2] (tăt), *n.* See **tit for tat.**

ta-ta (tă′tä′), *interj. Colloq.* goodbye.

Tatabánya (*Hung.* tŏ′tŏ bä nyŏ), *n.* a town in N Hungary. 56,000 (est. 1962).

Tatar (tä′tə), *n.*, *adj.* Tartar. —**Tatarian** (tä tĕə′rĭ ən, -tä′rĭ-), **Tataric** (tä tä′rĭk), *adj.*

Tatary (tä′tə rĭ), *n.* Tartary.

Tate (tāt), *n.* **1. Sir Henry,** 1819–99, English sugar refiner and philanthropist: founder of the **Tate Gallery. 2. (John Orley) Allen,** born 1899, U.S. poet, critic, and editor. **3. Nahum** (nā′əm), 1652–1715, English poet and dramatist, born in Ireland: poet laureate 1692–1715.

tater (tā′tə), *n. Dial.* a potato. Also, **tatie** (tăt′ĭ).

tatouay (tăt′o͞o ā′, tä′to͞o ī′), *n.* an armadillo, *Tatoua unicintus,* of tropical South America. [t. Pg. (Brazilian) *tatuay,* t. Guarani, der. *tatu* armadillo + *ay* valueless (i.e. as food; inedible)]

Tatra Mountains (tä′trə), a group of mountains in N Czechoslovakia and S Poland: a part of the central Carpathian Mountains. Highest peak, Gerlachovka, 8737 ft. Also, **High Tatra.** See map under **Moravian Gate.**

tatter[1] (tăt′ə), *n.* **1.** a torn piece hanging loose from the main part, as of a garment, etc. **2.** a separate torn piece. **3.** (*pl.*) torn or ragged clothing. [ME *tater,* t. Scand.; cf. Icel. *tötturr* rag] *—v.t.* **4.** to tear or wear to tatters. *—v.i.* **5.** to become ragged. [back-formation from TATTERED]

tatter[2] (tăt′ə), *n.* one who makes tatting. [f. TAT[1] + -ER[1]]

tatterdemalion (tăt′ə də māl′yən), *n.* a person in tattered clothing; a ragged fellow. [f. TATTER[1]; + second element of uncert. orig.]

tattered (tăt′əd), *adj.* **1.** torn to tatters; ragged. **2.** wearing ragged clothing. [f. TATTER[1], n. + -ED[3]]

tattersall (tăt′ə sôl′), *n.* **1.** a fabric with brightly coloured crossbars in a plaid pattern. *—adj.* **2.** made of this fabric: a *tattersall vest.* [from *Tattersall's,* London horse market, where brightly coloured blankets were used]

tatting (tăt′ĭng), *n.* **1.** the process or work of making a kind of knotted lace of cotton or linen thread with a shuttle. **2.** such lace. [orig. unknown]

tattle (tăt′l), *v.,* **-tled, -tling,** *n. —v.i.* **1.** to let out secrets. **2.** to chatter, prate, or gossip. *—v.t.* **3.** to utter idly; disclose by gossiping. *—n.* **4.** the act of tattling. **5.** idle talk; chatter; gossip. [ME *tatle,* appar. t. M Flem.: m. *tatelen,* c. LG *tateln* gabble] —**tat′tlingly,** *adv.*

tattler (tăt′lə), *n.* one who tattles; a telltale.

tattletale (tăt′l tāl′), *n. Chiefly U.S.* **1.** tale-bearer. *—adj.* **2.** telltale; revealing.

tattoo[1] (tə to͞o′), *n., pl.* **-toos. 1.** a signal on a drum, bugle, or trumpet at night, for soldiers or sailors to retire to their quarters. **2.** any similar beating or pulsation. **3.** an outdoor military pageant or display. [t. D: m. *taptoe,* lit., the tap (is) to, i.e. the taproom is shut]

tattoo[2] (tə to͞o′), *n., pl.* **-toos,** *v.,* **-tooed, -tooing.** *—n.* **1.** the act or practice of marking the skin with indelible patterns, pictures, legends, etc., by making punctures in it and inserting pigments. **2.** a pattern, picture, legend, etc., so made. *—v.t.* **3.** to mark with tattoos. **4.** to put pictures, legends, etc., on the skin. [earlier *tattow,* t. Polynesian: m. *tatau*] —**tattoo′er,** *n.*

tatty (tăt′ĭ), *adj.* untidy; shabby; tawdry.

tau (tô, tou), *n.* the nineteenth letter (Τ, τ) of the Greek alphabet.

Tauber (tou′bə), *n.* **Richard,** 1892–1948, British tenor, born in Austria.

tau cross, a T-shaped cross. See illus. under **cross.**

taught (tôt), *v.* pt. and pp. of **teach.**

taunt (tônt), *v.t.* **1.** to reproach in a sarcastic or insulting manner. **2.** to provoke by taunts; mock. *—n.* **3.** an insulting gibe or sarcasm; scornful reproach or challenge. **4.** *Obs.* an object of insulting gibes or scornful reproaches. [orig. uncert.] —**taunt′er,** *n.* —**taunt′ingly,** *adv.* **—Syn. 2.** See **ridicule.**

Taunton (tôn′tən), *n.* a town of England, the county town of Somerset. 35,192 (1961).

taupe (tōp), *n.* dark grey usually slightly tinged with brown, purple, yellow, or green. [t. F, g. L *talpa* mole]

Taupo (tou′pō), *n.* **Lake,** a lake in New Zealand, in central North Island. 239 sq. mi.

Tauranga (tou′rŏng′ə), *n.* a town in New Zealand, in N North Island. 22,300 (est. 1965).

taurine[1] (tô′rīn), *adj.* **1.** of, pertaining to, or resembling a bull. **2.** pertaining to the zodiacal sign Taurus. [t. L: m. s. *taurīnus* pertaining to a bull]

taurine[2] (tô′rēn, tô′rĭn), *n. Chem.* a neutral crystalline substance, $H_2NCH_2CH_2SO_3H$, obtained from the bile of oxen and other animals, from muscles, lung tissue, etc., and as a decomposition product of taurocholic acid. [f. TAURO(CHOLIC) + -INE[2]]

taurobolium (tô′rə bō′lyəm), *n., pl.* **-lia** (-lyə). a ceremony forming part of certain ancient Mediterranean cults in which the worshippers were baptized with the blood of a sacrificed bull. Also, **tauroboly** (tô rŏb′ə lĭ).

taurocholic acid (tô′rə kŏl′ĭk), *Chem.* an acid, $C_{26}H_{45}NO_7S$, occurring as a sodium salt in the bile of oxen, etc., which on hydrolysis yields taurine and cholic acid. [f. *tauro-* (comb. form of Gk *taûros* bull, ox) + CHOLIC ACID]

tauromachy (tô rŏm′ə kĭ), *n.* the art or practice of bullfighting.

Taurus (tô′rəs), *n., gen.* **Tauri** (tô′rī). **1.** the Bull, a zodiacal constellation. **2.** the second sign of the zodiac. See diag. under **zodiac.** [t. L: bull]

Taurus (tô′rəs), *n.* a mountain range in S Turkey. Highest peak, ab. 13,000 ft.

taut (tôt), *adj.* **1.** tightly drawn; tense; not slack. **2.** in good order or condition; tidy; neat. [ME *toght,* appar. b. *towen* (OE *togen* drawn) and TIGHT] —**taut′ly,** *adv.* —**taut′ness,** *n.*

tauten (tô′tn), *v.t., v.i.* to make or become taut.

tauto-, a word element meaning 'same', as in *tautonym.* [t. Gk, comb. form of *tautó,* contr. of *tò autó* the same]

tautog (tô′tŏg), *n.* a black labroid fish, *Tautoga onitis,* of the N Atlantic coast of the U.S. [t. Narragansett: m. *tautauog* (sheepsheads, pl. of *tau, tautau*]

tautologize (tô tŏl′ə jīz′), *v.i.,* **-gized, -gizing.** to use tautology. Also, **tautologise.**

tautology (tô tŏl′ə jĭ), *n., pl.* **-gies. 1.** needless repetition of an idea, esp. in other words in the immediate context, without imparting additional force or clearness, as *to descend down.* **2.** an instance of this. **3.** *Logic.* **a.** a law that can be shown on the basis of certain rules to exclude no logical possibilities. **b.** an instance of such a law, e.g., *either Smith owns a car or he doesn't own a car.* [t. LL: m. s. *tautologia,* t. Gk] —**tautological** (tô′tə lŏj′ĭ kl), *adj.* —**tau′tolog′ically,** *adv.* —**tautol′ogist,** *n.*

tautomer (tô′tə mə), *n. Chem.* a compound which is tautomeric with one or more other compounds. [back-formation from TAUTOMERISM]

tautomerism (tô tŏm′ə rĭz′əm), *n. Chem.* the ability of certain organic compounds to react in isomeric structures which differ from each other in the position of a hydrogen atom and a double bond. The individual tautomers are in equilibrium and some pairs of tautomeric isomers have been isolated. [f. TAUTO- + s. Gk *méros* part + -ISM] —**tautomeric** (tô′tə mĕ′rĭk), *adj.*

tautomerization (tô tŏm′ə rī zā′shən), *n. Chem.* conversion into a tautomeric structure. Also, **tautomerisation.**

tautonym (tô′tə nĭm), *n. Bot., Zool.* a scientific name in which the generic and the specific name are the same, as *Chloris chloris* (the greenfinch). [t. Gk: s. *tautṓnymos* of same name] —**tau′tonym′ic,** *adj.*

tavern (tăv′ən), *n.* a public house; inn. [ME *taverne,* t. OF, g. L *taberna* hut, booth, inn] —**tav′ernless,** *adj.* **—Syn.** See **hotel.**

taverner (tăv′ə nə), *n.* **1.** *Archaic.* the owner of a tavern. **2.** *Obs.* a frequenter of taverns. [ME, t. OF: m. *tavernier*]

Taverner (tăv′ə nə), *n.* **John,** *c.* 1495–1548?, English composer and organist.

taw[1] (tô), *n.* **1.** a choice or fancy marble with which to shoot. **2.** a game of marbles. **3.** the line from which the players shoot. [? t. Scand.; cf. Icel. *taug* string, rope (whence E line)]

taw[2] (tô), *v.t.* **1.** to prepare or dress (some raw material) for use or further manipulation. **2.** *Obs. or Dial.* to beat; flog. [ME *tawe,* OE *tawian,* c. D *touwen*] —**taw′er,** *n.*

tawdry (tô′drĭ), *adj.,* **-drier, -driest.** (of finery, etc.) gaudy; showy and cheap. [short for (*Sain*)*t Audrey lace,* i.e. lace bought at her fair in Ely] —**taw′drily,** *adv.* —**taw′driness,** *n.*

tawney (tô′nĭ), *adj.,* **-nier, -niest,** *n.* tawny.

Tawney (tô′nĭ), *n.* **Richard Henry,** 1880–1962, British historian, born in India.

tawny (tô′nĭ), *adj.* **-nier, -niest,** *n. —adj.* **1.** of a dark yellowish or yellowish brown colour. *—n.* **2.** a shade of brown tinged with yellow; dull yellowish brown. [ME, t. OF: m. *tane,* pp., TANNED] —**taw′niness,** *n.*

tawse (tôz), *n. Chiefly Scot.* a leather strap divided at the end into narrow strips used for inflicting corporal punishment. Also, **taws.** [pl. of *taw* thong, n. use of TAW[2]]

tax (tăks), *n.* **1.** a compulsory monetary contribution demanded by a government for its support and levied on incomes, property, goods purchased, etc. **2.** a burdensome charge, obligation, duty, or demand. *—v.t.* **3.** to impose tax on. **4.** to lay a burden on; make serious demands. **5.** to take to task; censure; reprove; accuse. **6.** *U.S. Colloq.* to charge. [ME, t. L: s. *taxāre* reprove, appraise, ML impose a tax] —**tax′abil′ity, tax′ableness,** *n.* —**tax′ably,** *adv.* —**tax′er,** *n.* —**tax′less,** *adj.*

taxable (tăk′sə bl), *adj.* **1.** capable of being taxed; subject to tax. *—n.* **2.** (*usually pl.*) *U.S.* persons, property, etc., subject to tax.

taxaceous (tăk sā′shəs), *adj.* belonging to the *Taxaceae,* or yew family of trees and shrubs. [f. s. NL *Taxāceae* (der. L *taxus* yew) + -OUS]

taxation (tăk sā′shən), *n.* **1.** the act of taxing. **2.** the fact of being taxed. **3.** a tax imposed. **4.** the revenue raised by taxes.

tax avoidance, the taking of lawful measures to minimize one's tax liabilities.

tax collector, an official who collects taxes.

taxeme (tăk'sēm), *n. Linguistics.* a feature of the arrangement of elements in a construction, as selection, order, modification, or modulation. [der. TAX(IS), modelled after PHONEME]

tax evasion, the taking of illegal steps to deprive the revenue of fiscal dues.

tax-free (tăks'frē'), *adj.* free from taxation.

taxi (tăk'sĭ), *n., pl.* **taxis,** *v.,* **taxied, taxiing** or **taxying.** 1. Also, **taxicab.** a motor car for public hire, esp. one fitted with a taximeter. —*v.i.* 2. to ride or travel in a taxi. 3. (of an aeroplane) to move over the surface of the ground or water under its own power, except when preparing to take off or just after landing. —*v.t.* 4. to cause (an aeroplane) to taxi. [short for TAXICAB]

taxicab (tăk'sĭ kăb'), *n.* a taxi. [short for *taximeter cab.* See TAXIMETER]

taxi dancer, *U.S.* a girl or woman employed in a dance hall, etc., to dance with patrons, who pay a stipulated amount for each dance.

taxidermy (tăk'sĭ dû'mĭ), *n.* the art of preparing and preserving the skins of animals, and stuffing and mounting them in lifelike form. [f. *taxi-* (comb. form of Gk *táxis* arrangement) + *-dermy* (m. s. Gk *-dermia,* der. *dérma* skin)] —**tax'ider'mal, tax'ider'mic,** *adj.* —**tax'ider'mist,** *n.*

taximeter (tăk'sĭ mē'tə), *n.* a device fitted to a taxi or other vehicle, for automatically computing and indicating the fare due. [t. F: m. *taximètre,* der. *taxe* charge. See -METER[1]]

taxiplane (tăk'sĭ plān'), *n. U.S.* an aeroplane available for chartered or unscheduled trips.

taxi rank, a cab rank.

taxis (tăk'sĭs), *n.* 1. arrangement, order, as in one of the physical sciences. 2. *Biol.* the movement of an organism in a particular direction in response to an external stimulus. 3. *Surg.* the replacing of a displaced part, or the reducing of a hernial tumour or the like, by manipulation without cutting. [t. NL. t. Gk: arrangement]

-taxis, a word element meaning 'arrangement', as in *chemotaxis.* [t. Gk]

taxite (tăk'sīt), *n. Geol.* a lava appearing to be formed from fragments, because of its parts having different colours, textures, etc. [f. TAX(IS) + -ITE[1]] —**taxitic** (tăk-sĭt'ĭk), *adj.*

taxonomy (tăk sŏn'ə mĭ), *n.* 1. classification, esp. in relation to its principles or laws. 2. that department of science, or of a particular science, which deals with classification. [t. F: m. *taxonomie,* f. Gk: m. *táxis* arrangement + m. *nomía* distribution] —**taxonomic** (tăk'sə nŏm'ĭk), **tax'onom'ical,** *adj.* —**tax'onom'ically,** *adv.* —**taxon'omist, taxon'omer,** *n.*

taxpayer (tăks'pā'ə), *n.* one who pays a tax or is subject to taxation.

-taxy, var. of **-taxis,** as in *heterotaxy.*

Tay (tā), *n.* the longest river of Scotland, flowing from Perthshire through central Scotland into the **Firth of Tay** (25 mi. long), an estuary of the North Sea. 117 mi.

Tay Bridge, a bridge over the Firth of Tay at Dundee; a previous bridge on this site destroyed 1879.

Taylor (tā'lə), *n.* 1. **A(lan) J(ohn) P(ercivale),** born 1906, English historian. 2. **Brook,** 1685–1731, English mathematician. 3. **Jeremy,** 1613–67, English cleric and writer. 4. **Tom,** 1817–80, English dramatist. 5. **Zachary,** 1784–1850, U.S. statesman and general: 12th president of the U.S., 1849–50.

tayra (tī'rə), *n.* a mammal, *Eira barbara,* related to the martens, found in the forests of Central and South America.

tazza (tăt'sə), *n.* a shallow, saucer-like ornamental bowl, usually on a high base or foot. [t. It.]

Tb, *Chem.* terbium.

T.B., tuberculosis.

t.b., 1. trial balance. 2. tuberculosis.

T-bar (tē'bä'), *n.* a metal bar having a T-shaped cross-section.

Tbilisi (*Russ.* dbĭ lē'sĭ), *n.* official name of **Tiflis.**

tbs., tablespoon; tablespoons. Also, **tbsp.**

Tc, *Chem.* technetium.

Tchaikovsky (chī kŏf'skĭ; *Russ.* chĭy kôf'skĭy), *n.* **Peotr Ilyich** (*Russ.* pyôtr ĭl yēch'), 1840–93, Russian composer.

Tchekhoff (chĕk'ŏf; *Russ.* chĕ'KHəf), *n.* Chekhov.

T.D., Territorial Decoration.

te[1] (tē), *n. Music.* the seventh degree of the scale in tonic sol-fa. Also, **ti.** [substituted for SI to avoid confusion with the sharp of SOL. See GAMUT]

te[2] (tē), *n.* ti[1].

Te, *Chem.* tellurium.

tea (tē), *n.* 1. the dried and prepared leaves of the shrub, *Thea sinensis,* from which a somewhat bitter, aromatic beverage is made by infusion in boiling water. 2. the shrub itself, which is extensively cultivated in China, Japan, India, etc., and has fragrant white flowers. 3. the beverage so prepared, served hot or iced. 4. any kind of leaves, flowers, etc., so used, or any plant yielding them. 5. any of various infusions prepared from the leaves, flowers, etc., of other plants, and used as beverages or medicines. 6. beef tea. 7. a light meal taken in the late afternoon. 8. high tea. 9. *Slang.* marijuana. [t. Chinese: m. *t'e,* d. var. of Mandarin and Cantonese *ch'a*] —**tea'less,** *adj.*

tea bag, a small container of paper or cloth filled with tea-leaves; infused in boiling water for making tea.

tea ball, *U.S.* a perforated metal ball in which tea-leaves are placed to be immersed in boiling water to make tea.

teaberry (tē'bə rĭ, -brĭ), *n., pl.* **-ries.** the spicy red fruit of the American wintergreen, *Gaultheria procumbens.*

tea biscuit, a small, round, soft biscuit, usually made with shortening and sugar.

tea-break (tē'brāk'), *n.* a pause from work, usually in the middle of the morning or afternoon, for tea, coffee, etc.

tea caddy, a small box, tin, etc., for holding tea.

teacake (tē'kāk'), *n.* a flat, round cake made with a yeast dough, and often toasted and served with butter.

teacart (tē'kät'), *n. U.S.* a tea-trolley.

teach (tēch), *v.,* **taught, teaching.** —*v.t.* 1. to impart knowledge of or skill in; give instruction in: *he teaches mathematics.* 2. to impart knowledge or skill to; give instruction to: *he teaches a large class.* —*v.i.* 3. to impart knowledge or skill; give instruction. [ME *teche(n),* OE *tǣcan*; akin to TOKEN]

Teach (tēch), *n.* **Edward** ('*Blackbeard*'), died 1718, English pirate.

teachable (tē'chə bl), *adj.* 1. capable of being instructed, as a person; docile. 2. capable of being taught, as a subject. —**teach'abil'ity, teach'ableness,** *n.* —**teach'ably,** *adv.*

teacher (tē'chə), *n.* one who teaches or instructs, esp. as a profession; instructor. —**teach'erless,** *adj.*

tea-chest (tē'chĕst'), *n.* a large wooden box or crate in which tea is packed.

teach-in (tēch'ĭn'), *n., pl.* **teach-ins.** a prolonged public debate about a subject of topical interest conducted by persons having a special knowledge of the subject.

teaching (tē'chĭng), *n.* 1. the act of one who or that which teaches; the work or profession of a teacher. 2. that which is taught; a doctrine or precept.

teaching aid, any material, device, etc., used by a teacher in addition to standard classroom instruction to stimulate the interest of pupils.

teaching hospital, a hospital associated with a medical school and providing students, etc., with facilities in various branches of medical study.

teaching machine, a mechanical teaching device, operated by the user, which presents him with items of information in a planned sequence, allowing him to pass to the next item only when he has answered correctly questions about the previous one.

teacloth (tē'klŏth'), *n.* a cloth for drying crockery, etc., after it has been washed; a tea-towel.

tea-cosy (tē'kō'zĭ), *n.* a covering for a teapot to keep the tea hot.

teacup (tē'kŭp'), *n.* 1. a cup in which tea is served, usually of small or moderate size. 2. a teacupful.

teacupful (tē'kŭp fo͝ol'), *n., pl.* **-fuls.** as much as a teacup will hold; about four fluid ounces.

tea-dance (tē'däns'), *n.* an afternoon dance during which tea and light refreshment is served. Also, **thé dansant.**

tea-garden (tē'gä'dn), *n.* 1. an open-air cafe, restaurant, etc., in which tea and other refreshments are served. 2. a tea plantation.

tea-gown (tē'goun'), *n.* (formerly) a loose gown worn by women at afternoon tea.

tea-house (tē'hous'), *n.* a restaurant where tea is served, esp. in Japan and China.

teak (tēk), *n.* 1. a large East Indian verbenaceous tree, *Tectona grandis,* with a hard, durable, yellowish brown, resinous wood, used for shipbuilding, making furniture, etc. 2. the wood. 3. any of various similar trees or woods. [earlier *teke,* t. Pg.: m. *teca,* t. Malayalam: m. *tēkka*]

teakettle (tē'kĕt'l), *n.* kettle (def. 1).

teal (tēl), *n., pl.* **teals,** (*esp. collectively*) **teal.** any of various small freshwater ducks, as the European **green-winged teal,** *Anas crecca,* and the American **blue-winged teal,** *A. discors.* [ME *tele.* Cf. D *teling*]

tea-leaf (tē'lēf'), *n., pl.* **-leaves** (-lēvz'). a fragment of the leaf of the tea plant, esp. when remaining in the teapot or cup after the tea has been infused.

team (tēm), *n.* 1. a number of persons associated in some joint action, esp. one of the sides in a match: *a team of football players.* **2.** two or more horses, oxen, or other animals harnessed together to draw a vehicle, plough or the like. **3.** two or more draught animals, or one such animal, together with the harness and the vehicle drawn. **4.** *Dial.* a family or brood of young animals. **5.** *Obs.* offspring or progeny; race or lineage. —*v.t.* **6.** to join together in a team. **7.** *U.S.* to convey or transport by means of a team. —*v.i.* **8.** *U.S.* to drive a team. **9. team up with,** to work together with; collaborate with. [ME *teme,* OE *tēam,* c. G *Zaum,* Icel. *taumr* bridle, rein]

team-mate (tēm′māt′), *n.* a member of the same team.

teamster (tēm′stə), *n.* **1.** one who drives a team, esp. as an occupation. **2.** *U.S.* one who drives a lorry, esp. as an occupation.

teamwork (tēm′wûk′), *n.* **1.** the work of a team with reference to coordination of effort and to collective efficiency. **2.** work done with a team.

Te Anau (tē ä′nou), **Lake.** a lake in New Zealand, in S South Island. 133 sq. mi.

tea-party (tē′pä′tĭ), *n.* an afternoon social gathering at which tea and other refreshments are served.

tea-planter (tē′plän′tə), *n.* one who cultivates tea plants for a living.

teapot (tē′pŏt′), *n.* a container with a lid, spout, and handle, in which tea is made and from which it is poured.

teapoy (tē′poi), *n.* **1.** a small three-legged table or stand. **2.** a small table for use in serving tea. [f. *ti* three (t. Hind.: m. *tīn*) + *poy* foot (t. Pers.: m. *pāi*)]

tear[1] (tĭə), *n.* **1.** a drop of the limpid fluid secreted by the lachrymal gland, appearing in or flowing from the eye, chiefly as the result of emotion, esp. of grief. **2.** something resembling or suggesting a tear, as a drop of a liquid or a tearlike mass of a solid substance. **3.** (*pl.*) grief; sorrow. **4. in tears,** weeping. [ME *tere,* OE *tēar* (c. Icel. *tār*), Vernerian var. of *teagor,* c. Goth. *tagr*; akin to Gk *dákry,* Cornish *dagr*] —**tear′less,** *adj.*

tear[2] (tēə), *v.,* **tore, torn, tearing,** *n.* —*v.t.* **1.** to pull apart or in pieces by force, esp. so as to leave ragged or irregular edges. **2.** to pull or pluck violently or with force. **3.** to distress greatly: *a heart torn with anguish.* **4.** to rend or divide: *a country torn by civil war.* **5.** to wound or injure by, or as by, rending; lacerate. **6.** to produce or effect by rending: *to tear a hole in one's coat.* **7.** to remove by force: to be unable to tear oneself away from a place. —*v.i.* **8.** to become torn. **9.** to make a tear or rent. **10.** *Colloq.* to move or go with violence or great haste. —*v.* **11.** Some special verb phrases are:

tear at, to pluck violently at; attempt to tear.

tear down, to pull down; destroy; demolish.

tear into, to attack violently, either physically or verbally.

tear off, a. to pull or pluck violently. **b.** *Colloq.* to perform or do, esp. rapidly or casually.

tear up, a. to tear into small pieces. **b.** to cancel; annul.

torn between, unable to choose between conflicting desires, duties, etc.

—*n.* **12.** the act of tearing. **13.** a rent or fissure. **14.** a rage or passion; violent flurry or outburst. **15.** *U.S. Slang.* a spree. [ME *tere,* OE *teran,* c. D *teren,* G *zehren* destroy, consume, Goth. *gatairan* destroy; akin to Gk *dérein* flay]

—**Syn. 1.** TEAR, REND, RIP mean to pull apart. To TEAR is to split the fibres of something by pulling apart, usually so as to leave ragged or irregular edges: *to tear open a letter.* REND implies force or violence in tearing apart or in pieces: *to rend one's clothes in grief.* RIP implies vigorous tearing asunder, esp. along a seam or line: *to rip the sleeves out of a coat.*

tearaway (tēə′rə wā′), *n.* *Colloq.* an impetuous or unruly person.

teardrop (tĭə′drŏp′), *n.* a tear[1].

tearful (tĭə′fəl), *adj.* **1.** full of tears; weeping. **2.** causing tears. —**tear′fully,** *adv.* —**tear′fulness,** *n.*

tear gas (tĭə), a gas used in warfare or in riots, which makes the eyes smart and water, thus producing a temporary blindness; lachrymator.

tear-jerker (tĭə′jû′kə), *n.* *Colloq.* an excessively sentimental novel, film, or the like.

tearoom (tē′ro͞om′, -ro͝om′), *n.* a room or restaurant where tea and other refreshments are served to customers.

tea-rose (tē′rōz′), *n.* any of several varieties of cultivated roses having a scent supposed to resemble that of tea.

tear sheet (tēə), a sheet or page in a magazine, journal, etc., perforated or cut so that it may be torn out easily if required.

teary (tĭə′rĭ), *adj.* **1.** of or like tears. **2.** tearful.

Teasdale (tēz′dāl′), *n.* **Sara,** 1884–1933, U.S. poet.

tease (tēz), *v.,* **teased, teasing,** *n.* —*v.t.* **1.** to worry or irritate by persistent petty requests, trifling raillery, or other annoyance, often in sport. **2.** to pull apart or separate the adhering fibres of, as in combing or carding wool; comb or card (wool, etc.); shred. **3.** to raise a nap on (cloth) with teasels; teasel. **4.** *Chiefly U.S.* to backcomb. —*v.i.* **5.** to worry or disturb a person, etc., by importunity or persistent petty annoyance. —*n.* **6.** the act of teasing. **7.** the state of being teased. **8.** one who or that which teases or annoys. [ME *tese,* OE *tǣsan* tear up, c. D *teezen* pull] —**teas′er,** *n.* —**teas′ingly,** *adv.*

teasel (tē′zəl), *n., v.,* **-selled, -selling** or (*U.S.*) **-seled, -seling.** —*n.* **1.** any of the herbs with prickly leaves and flower heads constituting the dipsacaceous genus *Dipsacus.* **2.** the dried flower head or bur of *D. fullonum,* used for teasing or teaselling cloth. **3.** any mechanical contrivance used for teaselling. —*v.t.* **4.** to raise a nap on (cloth) with teasels; dress by means of teasels. Also, **teazel, teazle.** [ME *tesel,* OE *tǣsel*; akin to TEASE, v.] —**tea′seller,** *n.*

tea-set (tē′sĕt′), *n.* a number of cups, saucers, plates, etc., with a teapot, usually of the same pattern, used in serving tea. Also, **tea-service** (tē′sû′vĭs).

teashop (tē′shŏp′), *n.* a small restaurant where tea and other light refreshments are served.

teaspoon (tē′spo͞on′), *n.* **1.** the small spoon commonly used to stir tea, coffee, etc. **2.** a teaspoonful.

teaspoonful (tē′spo͞on fo͝ol′), *n., pl.* **-fuls.** as much as a teaspoon can hold, about one fluid drachm.

tea-strainer (tē′strā′nə), *n.* a device for holding back tealeaves when pouring out tea.

teat (tēt), *n.* **1.** the protuberance on the breast or udder in female mammals (except the monotremes), where the milk ducts discharge; a nipple or mamilla. **2.** something resembling a teat. [ME *tete,* t. OF. See TIT[2]]

tea-table (tē′tā′bl), *n.* a table at which tea is served.

tea-taster (tē′tās′tə), *n.* one whose occupation is to test and grade samples of tea by tasting them. —**tea′-tas′-ting,** *n.*

teatime (tē′tīm′), *n.* the time of day at which tea is served.

tea-towel (tē′tou′əl), *n.* teacloth.

tea-tray (tē′trā′), *n.* a tray on which articles used in serving tea are carried.

tea-tree (tē′trē′), *n.* any of several trees or shrubs of the genus *Leptospermum,* of Australia and New Zealand.

tea-trolley (tē′trŏl′ĭ), *n.* a small table on wheels for carrying articles for use in serving tea.

tea-urn (tē′ûn′), *n.* an urn in which tea is made in large quantities.

tea-wagon (tē′wăg′ən), *n.* *U.S.* a tea-trolley.

teazel (tē′zəl), *n., v.t.,* **-zelled, -zelling** or (*U.S.*) **-zeled, -zeling.** teasel.

teazle (tē′zəl), *n., v.t.,* **-zled, -zling.** teasel.

Tebaldi (*It.* tĕ bäl′dē), *n.* **Renata** (*It.* rĕ nä′tä), born 1922, Italian operatic soprano.

Tebet (tā′vāth, tā′vĕs), *n.* (in the Jewish calendar) the fourth month of the year. Also, **Tebeth** (tĕb′ĕth).

tec (tĕk), *n.* *Slang.* a detective.

tech (tĕk), *n.* *Colloq.* a technical college.

tech., **1.** technical. **2.** technology.

technetium (tĕk nē′shyəm), *n.* *Chem.* an element of the manganese family which does not occur in nature but is present in the fission products of uranium. *Symbol:* Tc; *at. no.:* 43. The most stable isotope has *at. wt:* 99. The first element to be made artificially. Also, *Obs.,* **masurium.** [f. s. Gk *technētós* artificial + -IUM]

technic (tĕk′nĭk), *n.* **1.** technique. **2.** a technicality. **3.** technics (def. 2). —*adj.* **4.** technical. [t. Gk: m. s. *technikós* pertaining to art, skilful, technical]

technical (tĕk′nĭ kl), *adj.* **1.** belonging or pertaining to an art, science, or the like: *technical skill.* **2.** peculiar to or characteristic of a particular art, science, profession, trade, etc.; *technical details.* **3.** using terms or treating a subject in a manner peculiar to a particular field, as a writer or a book. **4.** skilled in, or familiar in a practical way with, a particular art, trade, etc., as a person. **5.** pertaining to or connected with the mechanical or industrial arts and the applied sciences: *a technical school.* **6.** so considered from a strictly legal point of view or a rigid interpretation of the rules: *a military engagement ending in a technical defeat.* —**tech′nically,** *adv.* —**tech′nicalness,** *n.*

technical college, an institution for further education which provides courses in technology, agriculture, commerce, art, social studies, etc.

technicality (tĕk′nĭ kăl′ĭ tĭ), *n., pl.* **-ties. 1.** technical character. **2.** the use of technical methods or terms. **3.** something that is technical; a technical point, detail, or expression.

technical sergeant, *U.S.* (in the Air Force and Marine Corps) a non-commissioned officer ranking below a master sergeant and above a staff sergeant.

technician (tĕk nĭsh′ən), *n.* **1.** one versed in the technicalities of a subject. **2.** one skilled in the technique of an art, as music or painting.

Technicolor (tĕk′nĭ kŭl′ə), *n.* *Trademark.* a process of making cinema films in colour by means of superimposing

the three primary colours to produce a final coloured print.
technics (těk′nĭks), *n.* **1.** technique. **2.** the study or science of an art or of arts in general, esp. of the mechanical or industrial arts.
technique (těk nēk′), *n.* **1.** method of performance; way of accomplishing. **2.** technical skill, esp. in artistic work. [t. F. See TECHNIC]
techno-, a word element referring to 'technic', 'technology'. [t. Gk, comb. form of *téchnē* art, skill]
technocracy (těk nŏk′rə sĭ), *n.* **1.** a theory and movement (prominent about 1932) advocating control of industrial resources and reorganization of the social system, based on the findings of technologists and engineers. **2.** a system of government which applies this theory. **—technocrat** (těk′nə krăt′), *n.* **—tech′nocrat′ic,** *adj.*
technography (těk nŏg′rə fĭ), *n.* description of the arts.
technol., technology.
technological (těk′nə lŏj′ĭ kl), *adj.* of or pertaining to technology; relating to science and industry. Also, **tech′nolog′ic. —tech′nolog′ically,** *adv.*
technology (těk nŏl′ə jĭ), *n.* **1.** the branch of knowledge that deals with science and engineering, or its practice, as applied to industry; applied science. **2.** the terminology of an art, science, etc.; technical nomenclature. [t. Gk: m. s. *technologia* systematic treatment] **—technol′ogist,** *n.*
techy (těch′ĭ), *adj.*, **-ier, -iest.** tetchy. **—tech′ily,** *adv.* **—tech′iness,** *n.*
tectonic (těk tŏn′ĭk), *adj.* **1.** of or pertaining to building or construction; constructive; architectural. **2.** *Geol.* **a.** pertaining to the structure of the earth's crust. **b.** referring to the forces or conditions within the earth that cause movements of the crust such as earthquakes, folds, faults and the like. **c.** designating the results of such movements: *tectonic valleys.* [t. LL: s. *tectonicus*, t. Gk: m. *tektonikós* (def. 1)] **—tecton′ically,** *adv.*
tectonics (těk tŏn′ĭks), *n.* **1.** the science or art of assembling, shaping, or ornamenting materials in construction; the constructive arts in general. **2.** structural geology.
ted[1] (těd), *v.t.*, **tedded, tedding.** to spread out for drying, as newly mown hay. [ME, c. d. G *zetten* scatter]
ted[2] (těd), *n.* *Slang.* a teddy boy.
tedder (těd′ə), *n.* **1.** one who teds. **2.** an implement that spreads and turns newly mown grass or hay from the swath for the purpose of drying.
Tedder (těd′ə), *n.* **Arthur William, 1st Baron,** 1890–1967, Royal Air Force officer: deputy supreme commander of Allied Expeditionary Forces 1943–45.
teddy bear, a stuffed toy bear. [said to be named after *Theodore* Roosevelt]
teddy boy, *Colloq.* (in the mid-1950s) a boy in his teens or early twenties who dressed in a fashion resembling that of the Edwardian era and identified himself with others affecting a similar style of dress.
Te Deum (tē′dē′əm), *n.* **1.** an ancient Latin hymn of praise, in the form of a psalm, sung regularly at matins in the Roman Catholic Church and (in an English translation) at morning prayer in the Anglican Church, as well as on special occasions as a service of thanksgiving. **2.** a musical setting of the hymn. **3.** a service of thanksgiving in which this hymn forms a prominent part. [L, first two words of the hymn]
tedious (tē′dyəs), *adj.* **1.** marked by tedium; long and tiresome: *tedious tasks, journeys, etc.* **2.** prolix so as to cause weariness, as a speaker. [ME, t. LL: m. s. *taediōsus*] **—te′diously,** *adv.* **—te′diousness,** *n.* **—Syn. 1.** wearisome, tiresome, wearing, tiring, monotonous, irksome. **—Ant. 1.** interesting, absorbing.
tedium (tē′dyəm), *n.* the state of being wearisome; irksomeness; tediousness. [t. L: m. *taedium*]
tee[1] (tē), *n.* **1.** the letter T, t. **2.** something shaped like a T, as a three-way joint used in fitting pipes together. **3.** the mark aimed at in various games, as curling. **—*adj.*** **4.** having a crosspiece at the top; shaped like a T.
tee[2] (tē), *n.*, *v.*, **teed, teeing.** *Golf.* **—*n.*** **1.** Also, **teeing ground.** the starting place, usually a hard mound of earth, at the beginning of play for each hole. **2.** a small heap of sand, or a rubber, plastic, or wooden object, from which the ball is driven at the beginning of a hole. **—*v.t.*** **3.** to place (the ball) on a tee. **—*v.i.*** **4.** to strike the ball from a tee (fol. by *off*). [orig. uncert.]
teem[1] (tēm), *v.i.* **1.** to abound or swarm; be prolific or fertile (fol. by *with*). **2.** *Obs.* to be or become pregnant; bring forth young. **—*v.t.*** **3.** *Obs.* to produce (offspring). [ME *teme(n)*, OE *tēman, tieman* produce (offspring), der. *tēam* child-bearing, offspring] **—teem′er,** *n.*
teem[2] (tēm), *v.i.*, *v.t.* to empty or pour out; discharge. [ME *teme(n)*, t. Scand.; cf. Icel. *tœma*, der. *tōmr*, adj.]
teeming (tē′mĭng), *adj.* **1.** abounding or swarming with something, as with people. **2.** prolific or fertile.
teen (tēn), *adj.* *Colloq.* teenage.
-teen, a termination forming the cardinal numerals from 13 to 19. [ME and OE *-tēne*, comb. form of TEN, c. G *-zehn*]
teenage (tēn′āj′), *adj.* of, pertaining to, or characteristic of a teenager.
teenager (tēn′ā′jə), *n.* a person in his or her teens.
teens (tēnz), *n. pl.* the period of one's life between the ages of 12 and 20.
teeny (tē′nĭ), *adj.*, **-nier, -niest.** *Colloq. or Dial.* tiny.
teepee (tē′pē), *n.* tepee.
Tees (tēz), *n.* a river in N England, flowing E along the boundary between Durham and Yorkshire to the North Sea. ab. 70 mi.
tee-shirt (tē′shûrt′), *n.* T-shirt.
Teesside (tēz′sīd′), *n.* a county borough in NE England, including Billingham, Eston, Middlesborough, Redcar, Stockton and Thornaby-on-Tees. 370,000 (est. 1968). Also, **Tees-side.**
teeter (tē′tə), *Chiefly U.S.* **—*v.i.*** **1.** to seesaw. **2.** to move unsteadily. **—*v.t.*** **3.** to move (anything) with a seesaw motion. **—*n.*** **4.** a seesaw. **5.** a seesaw motion. [var. of *titter*, t. Scand.; cf. Icel. *titra*, c. G *zittern* tremble, quiver]
teeth (tēth), *n.* pl. of **tooth.**
teethe (tēth), *v.i.*, **teethed, teething.** to grow teeth; cut one's teeth.
teething (tē′thĭng), *n.* **1.** the first growth of teeth. **2.** the phenomena associated with this.
teething ring, a circular disc, usually of plastic, ivory, bone, etc., on which a teething baby may bite.
teething troubles, difficulties, usually temporary ones, which occur at the initial stages of an enterprise.
teethridge (tēth′rĭj′), *n.* *Phonet.* alveolar ridge.
teetotal (tē tō′tl), *adj.* **1.** of or pertaining to, advocating, or pledged to total abstinence from intoxicating drink. **2.** *U.S. Colloq.* absolute; complete. [der. TOTAL, with redupl. of initial *t-* for emphasis] **—teeto′tally,** *adv.*
teetotalism (tē tō′tə lĭz′əm), *n.* the principle or practice of total abstinence from intoxicating drink.
teetotaller (tē tōt′lə), *n.* one who abstains totally from intoxicating drink. Also, *U.S.*, **teetotaler.**
teetotum (tē′tō tŭm′), *n.* **1.** any small top spun with the fingers. **2.** a kind of die having four sides, each marked with a different initial letter, spun with the fingers in an old game of chance. [earlier *T totum*, f. *T.* (abbr. for *tōtum*, used on toy) + *tōtum* (neut. of L *tōtus* all)]
teg (těg), *n.* a sheep that is one or two years old. [orig. uncert.]
tegmen (těg′mĭn), *n.*, *pl.* **-mina** (mĭ nə). **1.** a cover, covering, or integument. **2.** *Bot.* the delicate inner integument or coat of a seed. **3.** (in certain orthopterous insects) one of a pair of leathery fore wings serving as a protective covering for the hind wings in certain insects. [t. L: covering] **—tegminal** (těg′mĭ nəl), *adj.*
Tegucigalpa (*Sp.* tė gōō thē gäl′pä), *n.* the capital of Honduras, in the S part. 167,992 (1965).
tegular (těg′yōō lə), *adj.* **1.** pertaining to or resembling a tile. **2.** consisting of or arranged like tiles. [f. s. L *tēgula* tile + -AR[1]] **—teg′ularly,** *adv.*
tegument (těg′yōō mənt), *n.* a covering or investment; an integument. [t. L: s. *tegumentum*] **—tegumental** (těg′yōō měn′tl), **tegumentary** (těg′yōō měn′tə rĭ), *adj.*
tehee (tē hē′), *interj.*, *n.*, *v.*, **-heed, -heeing.** **—*interj.*** **1.** (the sound of a tittering laugh.) **—*n.*** **2.** a titter; a snigger. **—*v.i.*** **3.** titter; snigger. [ME; imit.]
Teheran (tėə rän′; *Pers.* tėh rän′), *n.* the capital of Iran, in the N part: wartime conference of Roosevelt, Churchill, and Stalin, 1943. 2,213,116 (est. 1964). Also, **Tehran.**
Tehuantepec (*Sp.* tė wän tė-pĕk′), *n.* **Isthmus of,** an isthmus in S Mexico between the **Gulf of Tehuantepec,** an open bay of the Pacific, and the **Gulf of Campeche.** 125 mi. wide.

Isthmus of Tehuantepec

Tehuelche (*Sp.* tė wĕl′chė), *n.* a member of an Indian people of Patagonia. [t. Patagonian: south-east]
Teide (*Sp.* tėy′dė), *n.* **Pico de** (*Sp.* pē′kō dė), a volcanic peak in the Canary Islands, on Tenerife. 12,190 ft. Also, **Pico de Tenerife.**
te igitur (tā′ ĭg′ĭ tōōə′), *Eccles.* the first paragraph of the canon in the Roman and some other Latin liturgies. [L: thee therefore]
Teilhard de Chardin (*Fr.* tĕ yär də shär dăN′), **Pierre** (*Fr.* pyĕr), 1881–1955, French philosopher.
Tejo (*Port.* tə′zhōō), *n.* Portuguese name of **Tagus.**
tektite (tĕk′tīt), *n.* a small glasslike body, whose chemical composition is unrelated to the geological formation in

which it is found; believed to be of meteoric origin. **Carbonaceous tektites** contain traces of carbon compounds. [f. s. Gk *tēktós* molten + -ITE¹]

tel-¹, var. of **tele-¹**, as in *telaesthesia.* Properly, this form should occur wherever the following word or word element begins with a vowel. However, **teleo-** is more frequently found.

tel-², var. of **tele-²**, as in *telencephalon.* For form, see **tel-¹**.

tel., **1.** telegram. **2.** telegraph. **3.** telephone.

telaesthesia (tĕl′ēs thē′zyə), *n.* sensation or perception received at a distance without the normal operation of the recognized organs. Also, *U.S.*, **telesthesia.** [t. NL. See TEL-¹, AESTHESIA]

telamon (tĕl′ə mən), *n.*, *pl.* **telamones** (tĕl′ə mō′nēz). *Archit.* a figure of a man used like a supporting column; an atlas (def. 6). [t. L, t. Gk: name of mythological hero]

Telamon (tĕl′ə mən), *n. Gk Legend.* the father of Ajax and Teucer.

telangiectasis (tĭ lăn′jĭ ĕk′tə sĭs), *n.*, *pl.* **-ses** (-sēz′). *Pathol.* chronic dilatation of the capillaries and other small blood vessels, as seen in the faces of alcoholics, those exposed to raw, cold climates, and certain congenital sufferers. [NL, f. Gk: s. *télos* end + m. s. *angeîon* receptacle + m. *éktasis* extension] —**telangiectatic** (tĭlăn′jĭ ĕk tăt′ĭk), *adj.*

Telautograph (tĕl ô′tə grăf′, -gräf′), *n. Trademark.* a form of telegraph for reproducing handwriting, drawings, etc., the movements of a pen or pencil at one end of the line being reproduced in a pen or pencil at the other end by a system of electromagnets. —**telautographic** (tĕl ô′-tə grăf′ĭk), *adj.* —**telautography** (tĕl′ô tŏg′rə fĭ), *n.*

Tel-Aviv (tĕl′ə vēv′), *n.* a city in W Israel. 394,000 (with Jaffa; est. 1964).

tele-¹, a word element meaning 'distant', especially 'transmission over a distance', as in *telegraph.* Also, **tel-¹**, **telo-¹**. [comb. form repr. Gk *têle* far]

tele-², a word element referring to the end, as in *teleological.* Also, **tel-²**, **teleo-**, **telo-²**. [comb. form repr. Gk *télos* end, *téleos* complete]

telecast (tĕl′ə käst′), *v.*, **-cast** or **-casted**, **-casting**, *n.* —*v.i., v.t.* **1.** to broadcast by television. —*n.* **2.** a television broadcast.

telecommunications (tĕl′ĭ kə myōō′nĭ kā′shənz), *n.* the science or technology of telegraphic or telephonic communications by line or radio transmission.

teledu (tĕl′ĭ dōō′), *n.* a small badger-like mammal, *Mydaus javanensis*, of the mountains of Java, Sumatra, and Borneo, which (like the skunk) ejects a fetid secretion, and which is coloured like the skunk but has a short tail. [t. Malay]

telefacsimile (tĕl′ĭ făk sĭm′ĭ lĭ), *n.* a system for transmitting and reproducing printed matter by telephone.

teleferic (tĕl′ĭ fĕ′rĭk), *n.* **1.** a cableway. —*adj.* **2.** of or denoting a cableway. [t. F: m. *téléphérique*]

teleg., **1.** telegram. **2.** telegraph. **3.** telegraphy.

telega (tĕ lā′gə), *n.* a crude Russian cart having four wheels and no springs. [t. Russ.]

telegony (tĭ lĕg′ə nĭ), *n. Genetics.* the supposed influence of a previous sire upon the progeny subsequently borne by the same mother to other sires. —**telegonic** (tĕl′-ĭ gŏn′ĭk), *adj.*

telegram (tĕl′ĭ grăm′), *n.* a communication sent by telegraph; a telegraphic message. —**tel′egram′mic, telegrammatic** (tĕl′ĭ grə măt′ĭk), *adj.*

telegraph (tĕl′ĭ grăf′, -gräf′), *n.* **1.** an apparatus, system, or process for transmitting messages or signals to a distance, esp. by means of an electrical device consisting essentially of a transmitting or sending instrument and a distant receiving instrument connected by a conducting wire, or other communications channel, the making and breaking of the circuit at the sending end causing a corresponding effect, as on a sounder, at the receiving end. **2.** a telegraphic message. —*v.t.* **3.** to transmit or send (a message, etc.) by telegraph. **4.** to send a message to (a person) by telegraph. —*v.i.* **5.** to send a message by telegraph. —**telegrapher** (tĭ lĕg′-rə fə), **teleg′raphist**, *n.* —**telegraphic** (tĕl′ĭ grăf′ĭk), **tel′egraph′ical**, *adj.* —**tel′egraph′ically**, *adv.*

telegraphese (tĕl′ĭ grə fēz′), *n.* a manner of writing or speaking characterized by the concise and elliptical style in which telegrams are worded.

telegraphoscope (tĕl′ĭ grăf′ə skōp′), *n.* a telegraphic device by means of which a picture may be reproduced at a distance.

telegraph plant, an East Indian plant, *Desmodium gyrans*, remarkable for the spontaneous, jerking signal-like motions of its leaflets.

telegraph pole, a pole for supporting telegraph wires.

telegraphy (tĭ lĕg′rə fĭ), *n.* the art or practice of constructing or operating telegraphs.

telekinesis (tĕl′ĭ kĭ nē′sĭs), *n.* the production of motion in a body, apparently without the application of material force, a power long claimed by spiritualist mediums. [f. TELE-¹ + Gk *kinēsis* movement]

Telemachus (tĭ lĕm′ə kəs), *n. Gk Legend.* the son of Odysseus and Penelope. With his father he slew the suitors of Penelope.

Telemann (*Ger.* tĕ′lə män), *n.* **Georg Philipp** (*Ger.* gė ŏrk′ fē′lĭp), 1681–1767, German composer.

telemark (tĕl′ĭ mäk′), *n. Skiing.* a turn made by placing one ski well in front of the other and gradually turning the tip of the forward ski in the direction to be turned. [named after *Telemark*, a county in Norway]

telemeter (tĭ lĕm′ĭ tə), *n.* **1.** any of certain devices or attachments for determining distances by measuring the angle subtending a known distance. **2.** *Elect.* the complete measuring, transmitting, and receiving apparatus for indicating, recording, or integrating at a distance, by electrical translating means, the value of a quantity. **3.** *Photog.* a small rangefinder. —**telemetric** (tĕl′ĭ mĕt′-rĭk), *adj.*

telemetry (tĭ lĕm′ĭ trĭ), *n. Elect.* the collection of information by telemeter.

telemotor (tĕl′ĭ mō′tə), *n.* a mechanical, electrical or hydraulic system, by which power is applied at and controlled from a distant point, esp. such a system actuating a ship's rudder.

telencephalon (tĕl′ĕn sĕf′ə lŏn′), *n. Anat.* the anterior end of the embryonic nervous system which forms the cerebral hemisphere in the adult vertebrate. —**telencephalic** (tĕl′ĕn sĭ făl′ĭk), *adj.*

teleo-, var. of **tele-²**, as in *teleology.*

teleological argument, *Metaphys.* the argument for the existence of God based on the assumption that order in the universe implies an orderer and cannot be a natural feature of the universe.

teleology (tĕl′ĭ ŏl′ə jĭ), *n.* **1.** the doctrine of final causes or purposes. **2.** the study of the evidences of design or purpose in nature. **3.** such design or purpose. **4.** the belief that purpose and design are a part of, or are apparent in, nature. **5.** the doctrine in vitalism that phenomena are guided not only by mechanical forces but also by the ends towards which they move. Cf. **final causes.** [t. NL: m. *teleologia*, f. Gk. See TELEO-, -LOGY] —**teleological** (tĕl′ĭ ə lŏj′ĭ kl), *adj.* —**tel′eolog′ically,** *adv.* —**teleologist** (tĕl′ĭ ŏl′ə jĭst), *n.*

teleost (tĕl′ĭ ŏst′), *adj.* **1.** belonging or pertaining to the *Teleostei*, the group of fishes that have a skeleton composed at least in part of bone rather than of cartilage, including the large majority of living species. —*n.* **2.** a teleost fish. [t. NL: back-formation from *teleostei*, pl. (f. Gk: *tele-* TELE-² + m. *ostéon* bone), by false analysis of pl. form] —**tel′eos′tean,** *adj.*, *n.*

telepathist (tĭ lĕp′ə thĭst), **1.** a student of or believer in telepathy. **2.** one having telegraphic power.

telepathy (tĭ lĕp′ə thĭ), *n.* communication of one mind with another by some means other than the normal use of the senses. —**telepathic** (tĕl′ĭ păth′ĭk), *adj.* —**tel′epath′ically,** *adv.*

teleph., telephony.

telephone (tĕl′ĭ fōn′), *n.*, *v.*, **-phoned, -phoning.** —*n.* **1.** an apparatus, system, or process for transmission of sound or speech to a distant point, esp. by an electrical device. —*v.t.* **2.** to speak to or summon (a person) by telephone. **3.** to send (a message, etc.) by telephone. —*v.i.* **4.** to send a message by telephone. —**tel′ephon′er,** *n.* —**telephonic** (tĕl′ĭ fŏn′ĭk), *adj.* —**tel′ephon′ically,** *adv.*

telephone box, a callbox. Also, **telephone kiosk.**

telephonist (tĭ lĕf′ə nĭst), *n.* one who operates a telephone or a telephone switchboard.

telephony (tĭ lĕf′ə nĭ), *n.* the art or practice of constructing or operating telephones.

telephoto (tĕl′ĭ fō′tō), *adj.* **1.** denoting or pertaining to telephotography. **2.** denoting or pertaining to a form of photographic lens used in telephotography (def. 1) which produces magnified images.

telephotograph (tĕl′ĭ fō′tə grăf′, -gräf′), *n.* **1.** a picture made with a telephoto lens. **2.** a picture transmitted by wire or radio.

telephotography (tĕl′ĭ fə tŏg′rə fĭ), *n.* **1.** the art of photographing objects too distant for the ordinary camera, by the use of telephoto lenses. **2.** the art of electrically reproducing photographs or facsimiles over a communications channel. —**telephotographic** (tĕl′ĭ fō′-tə grăf′ĭk), *adj.*

teleprinter (tĕl′ĭ prĭn′tə), *n.* an instrument having a typewriter keyboard which transmits and receives messages by telegraph transmission.

Teleprompter (tĕl′ĭ prŏmp′tə), *n. Trademark.* an electronic prompting device used esp. by television performers, speakers, etc., on which the magnified text of the script is unrolled at a pace suitable to the speaker's speed of delivery.

teleran (těl′ĭ răn′), *n. Electronics.* a system of aircraft navigation using radar to map the sky above an airfield, which, together with the map of the airfield itself and other pertinent data, is transmitted by television to the aeroplane approaching the field. [short for *Tele(vision) R(adar) A(ir) N(avigation)*]

telerecord (těl′ĭ rĭ kôd′), *v.t.* to record (a programme, etc.) for showing on television.

telerecording (těl′ĭ rĭ kô′dĭng), *n.* a recorded television programme.

telescope (těl′ĭ skōp′), *n., adj., v.,* **-scoped, -scoping.** —*n.* **1.** an optical instrument for making distant objects appear nearer and larger. There are two principal forms, one (**refracting telescope**) consisting essentially of a lens or object glass for forming an image of the object and an eyepiece or combination of lenses for magnifying this image, and the other (**reflecting telescope**) having a similar arrangement but containing a concave mirror or speculum instead of an object glass. **Astronomical telescopes** are used for viewing objects outside the earth; **terrestrial telescopes** are used for viewing distant objects on the earth's surface. —*adj.* **2.** consisting of parts which fit and slide one within another. —*v.t.* **3.** to force together, one into another, or force into something else, in the manner of the sliding tubes of a jointed telescope. **4.** to condense; shorten. —*v.i.* **5.** to slide together, or into something else in the manner of the tubes of a jointed telescope. **6.** to be driven one into another, as railway carriages in a collision. [t. NL: m. s. *telescopium,* f. m. s. Gk *teleskópos* far-seeing + *-ium* -IUM]

telescopic (těl′ĭ skŏp′ĭk), *adj.* **1.** of, pertaining to, or of the nature of a telescope. **2.** obtained by means of a telescope: *a telescopic view of the moon.* **3.** seen by a telescope; visible only through a telescope. **4.** far-seeing: *a telescopic eye.* **5.** consisting of parts which slide one within another like the tubes of a jointed telescope, and thus capable of being extended or shortened. Also, **tel′escop′ical.** —**tel′escop′ically,** *adv.*

telescopy (tĭ lĕs′kə pĭ), *n.* **1.** the use of the telescope. **2.** telescopic investigation. —**telescopist** (tĭ lĕs′kə pĭst), *n.*

telesis (těl′ĭ sĭs), *n. Sociol.* deliberate, purposeful utilization of the processes of nature and society to obtain particular goals. [t. Gk: completion]

telespectroscope (těl′ĭ spěk′trə skōp′), *n. Astron.* an instrument for analysing the spectra of astronomical bodies, consisting of a telescope attached to a spectroscope.

telestereoscope (těl′ĭ stĭə′rĭ ə skōp′, -stě′rĭ-), *n.* a binocular optical instrument used for stereoscopic viewing of distant objects; a small rangefinder.

telesthesia (těl′ēs thē′zyə), *n. U.S.* telaesthesia.

telethermometer (těl′ĭ thə mŏm′ĭ tə), *n.* any of various thermometers that indicate or record temperatures at a distance, as by means of an electric current. —**tel′ethermom′etry,** *n.*

Teletype (těl′ĭ tīp′), *n. U.S. Trademark.* a teleprinter.

teletypewriter (těl′ĭ tīp′rī′tə), *n. U.S.* a teleprinter.

teleview (těl′ĭ vyōō′), *v.t., v.i.* to view with a television receiver; watch television. —**tel′eview′er,** *n.*

televise (těl′ĭ vīz′), *v.t.,* **-vised, -vising.** to send or receive by television.

television (těl′ĭ vĭzh′ən), *n.* **1.** the broadcasting of a still or moving image via radio waves to receivers which project it on a picture tube for viewing at a distance from the point of origin. **2.** the process employed. **3.** the field of broadcasting by television. **4.** a television receiver. —**televisional** (těl′ĭ vĭzh′ə nəl), **televisionary** (těl′ĭ vĭzh′ə nə rĭ), *adj.*

telex (těl′ěks), *n.* **1.** an international service provided by postal authorities in which teleprinters are loaned to subscribers. **2.** a teleprinter. **3.** a message received or sent by teleprinter.

telfer (těl′fə), *n., adj., v.t.* telpher. —**tel′ferage,** *n.*

Telford (těl′fəd), *n.* **Thomas,** 1757–1834, Scottish civil engineer.

telic (těl′ĭk), *adj.* **1.** *Gram.* expressing end or purpose, as a clause. **2.** tending to a definite end. [t. Gk: m. s. *telikós* final]

teliospore (tē′lĭ ə spô′, těl′ĭ-), *n. Bot.* a spore of certain rust fungi which carries the fungus through the winter and which, on germination, produces the promycelium.

telium (tē′lĭ əm, těl′ĭ-), *n. Bot.* the sorus of the rust fungi bearing teliospores.

tell (těl), *v.* **told, telling.** —*v.t.* **1.** to give an account or narrative of; narrate; relate (a story, tale, etc.): *to tell one's life story.* **2.** to make known by speech or writing (a fact, news, information, etc.); communicate. **3.** to announce or proclaim. **4.** to utter (the truth, a lie, etc.). **5.** to express in words (thoughts, feelings, etc.). **6.** to reveal or divulge (something secret or private). **7.** to say plainly or positively: *I cannot tell just what was done.* **8.** to discern (a distant person or thing) so as to be able to identify or describe: *can you tell who that is over there?* **9.** to recognize or distinguish: *you could hardly tell the difference between them.* **10.** to inform or apprise (a person, etc.) of something. **11.** to assure emphatically: *I won't, I tell you!* **12.** to bid, order, or command: *tell him to stop.* **13. tell off, a.** to mention one after another, as in enumerating; count or set one by one or in exact amount: *to tell off five yards.* **b.** to separate from the whole, a group, etc., and assign to a particular task. **c.** *Colloq.* to scold; rebuke severely. —*v.i.* **14.** to give an account or report: *he told about his experience.* **15.** to give evidence or be an indication (fol. by *of*): *to tell of wonders.* **16.** to disclose something secret or private; play the informer (usually fol. by *on*). **17.** to know; be certain: *how can we tell if there is a life after death?* **18.** to have force or effect; operate effectively: *a contest in which every stroke tells.* **19.** to produce a marked or severe effect: *the strain was telling on his health.* **20.** *Dial.* to talk or chat.
[ME *telle,* OE *tellan,* c. D *tellen* reckon, count, Icel. *telja* tell, count, akin to TALE] —**tell′able,** *adj.*

Tell (těl), *n.* **William** or (*Ger.*) **Wilhelm** (vĭl′hělm), (? fl. 1307) a legendary Swiss patriot said to have been forced by the Austrian governor to shoot an apple off his son's head with a bow and arrow.

teller (těl′ə), *n.* **1.** one who or that which tells, relates, or communicates; a narrator. **2.** *Chiefly U.S.* one employed in a bank to receive or pay out money over the counter. **3.** one who tells, counts, or enumerates, as one appointed to count votes. —**tell′ership′,** *n.*

Téllez (*Sp.* tě′lyěth), *n.* **Gabriel** (*Sp.* gä bryěl′). See **Tirso de Molina.**

telling (těl′ĭng), *adj.* **1.** having force or effect; effective; striking: *a telling blow.* **2.** indicative of one's feelings; revealing: *a telling blush.* —**tell′ingly,** *adv.*

telltale (těl′tāl′), *n.* **1.** one who heedlessly or maliciously reveals private or confidential matters; a tattler; a tale-bearer. **2.** a thing serving to reveal or disclose something. **3.** any of various indicating or registering devices, as a time clock. **4.** *Music.* a gauge on an organ for indicating the air pressure. **5.** an indicator showing the position of a ship's rudder. —*adj.* **6.** that reveals or betrays what is not intended to be known: *a telltale blush.* **7.** giving notice or warning of something, as a mechanical device.

tellur-, *Chem.* a prefix indicating the presence of tellurium, as in *tellurite.*

tellurate (těl′yōō rāt′), *n. Chem.* a salt of telluric acid, of the type H_2TeO_4.

tellurian[1] (tě lyŏŏə′rĭ ən), *adj.* **1.** of or characteristic of the earth or an inhabitant of the earth. —*n.* **2.** an inhabitant of the earth. [f. s. L *tellūs* earth + -IAN]

tellurian[2] (tě lyŏŏə′rĭ ən), *n.* tellurion.

telluric[1] (tě lyŏŏə′rĭk), *adj.* **1.** of or pertaining to the earth; terrestrial. **2.** of or proceeding from the earth or soil. [f. s. L *tellūs* earth + -IC]

telluric[2] (tě lyŏŏə′rĭk), *adj. Chem.* **1.** of or containing tellurium, especially in the hexavalent state. **2.** containing tellurium in a higher valency state than the corresponding tellurous compound. [f. TELLUR- + -IC]

telluride (těl′yōō rīd′), *n. Chem.* a compound of tellurium with an electropositive element or, less often, a radical.

tellurion (tě lyŏŏə′rĭ ən), *n.* an apparatus for showing how the diurnal rotation and annual revolution of the earth and the obliquity of its axis produce the alternation of day and night and the changes of the seasons. Also, **tellurian**[2]. [var. of TELLURIUM]

tellurite (těl′yōō rīt′), *n. Chem.* **1.** a salt of tellurous acid, of the type H_2TeO_3. **2.** a mineral, tellurium dioxide, TeO_2.

tellurium (tě lyŏŏə′rĭ əm), *n. Chem.* a rare silver-white element resembling sulphur in its chemical properties, and usually occurring in nature combined with gold, silver, or other metals of high atomic weight. Used in alloys and the electrolytic refining of zinc. *Symbol:* Te; *at. wt:* 127·60; *at. no.:* 52. [t. NL, f. s. L *tellūs* earth + *-ium* -IUM]

tellurize (těl′yōō rīz′), *v.t.,* **-rized, -rizing.** *Chem.* to mix or cause to combine with tellurium. Also, **tellurise.**

tellurous (těl′yōō rəs, tě lyŏŏə′rəs), *adj. Chem.* containing tetravalent tellurium.

Tellus (těl′əs), *n. Rom. Myth.* an ancient Italian deity of the Earth, goddess of marriage and fertility.

telly (těl′ĭ), *n. Colloq.* television.

telo-[1], var. of **tele-**[1], as in *telodynamic.*

telo-[2], var. of **tele-**[2], as in *telophase.*

telodynamic (tĕl′ō dī năm′ĭk), *adj.* pertaining to the transmission of power over considerable distances, as by means of endless wire ropes on pulleys.

telophase (tĕl′ə fāz′), *n. Biol.* the final stage of mitotic cell division, in which new nuclei are formed.

telpher (tĕl′fə), *n.* **1.** a travelling unit, car, or carrier in a telpherage. **2.** telpherage. —*adj.* **3.** of or pertaining to a system of telpherage. —*v.t.* **4.** to transport by means of a telpherage. Also, **telfer.** [var. of *telephore*, f. TELE-[1] + PHORE]

telpherage (tĕl′fə rĭj), *n.* a transport system in which cars or carriers are suspended from or run on wire cables or the like, esp. one in which the cars are individually operated by electricity. Also **telferage.**

telson (tĕl′sən), *n.* the last segment, or an appendage of the last segment, of certain crustaceans and arachnids, as the middle flipper of a lobster's tail. [t. Gk: boundary, limit]

Telstar (tĕl′stä′), *n.* one of a series of active communication satellites (1962) used for transmitting television programmes across the Atlantic, and for scientific purposes.

Telugu (tĕl′ə gōō′), *n., pl.* **-gu, -gus,** *adj.* —*n.* **1.** a Dravidian language spoken in India in the region north of Madras. **2.** one of the people speaking this language. —*adj.* **3.** of Telugu or the Telugu.

temblor (tĕm′blô), *n., pl.* **-blors, -blores** (tĕm blô′rēz). *Chiefly U.S.* a tremor; an earthquake. [t. Sp., der. *temblar* tremble, g. Rom. *tremulāre*, der. L *tremulus* trembling]

temerarious (tĕm′ə rēə′rĭ əs), *adj. Rare.* reckless; rash. [t. L: m. *temerārius*] —**tem′erar′iously,** *adv.* —**tem′erar′iousness,** *n.*

temerity (tĭ mĕ′rĭ tĭ), *n.* reckless boldness; rashness. [late ME *temeryte*, t. L: m. s. *temeritas*]

Temesvár (*Hung.* tĕ′mĕsh vár), *n.* Hungarian name of **Timisoara.**

temp (tĕmp), *n. Colloq.* a temporary member of an office staff, esp. a secretary.

temp., 1. temperate. **2.** temporary. **3.** (L *tempore*) in the time of.

Tempe (tĕm′pĭ), *n.* **Vale of,** a valley in E Greece, in Thessaly, between Mounts Olympus and Ossa.

Tempelhof (tĕm′pl hŏf′; *Ger.* tĕm′pəl hóf), *n.* a district of S West Berlin: international airport.

temper (tĕm′pə), *n.* **1.** a particular state of mind or feelings. **2.** habit of mind, esp. with respect to irritability or patience, outbursts of anger, or the like. **3.** heat of mind or passion, shown in outbursts of anger, resentment, etc. **4.** calm disposition or state of mind. **5.** a substance added to something to modify its properties or qualities. **6.** the particular degree of hardness and elasticity imparted to steel, etc., by tempering. **7.** *Archaic.* a middle course; compromise. **8.** *Obs.* the constitution or character of a substance. **9. keep one's temper,** to remain calm or patient, esp. despite provocation. **10. lose one's temper,** to become suddenly angry or enraged. —*v.t.* **11.** to moderate or mitigate. **12.** to soften or tone down. **13.** to bring to a proper, suitable, or desirable state by, or as by, blending or admixture. **14.** to moisten, mix, and work up into proper consistency, as clay or mortar. **15.** to heat and cool or quench (metal) to bring to the proper degree of hardness, elasticity, etc. **16.** to produce internal stresses in (glass) by sudden cooling from low red heat; toughen. **17.** to tune (a keyboard instrument, as a piano, organ, etc.) so as to make the notes available in different keys or tonalities. **18.** *Archaic.* to combine or blend in due proportions. **19.** *Obs.* to pacify. —*v.i.* **20.** to be or become tempered. [ME; OE *temprian*, t. L: m. *temperāre* divide or proportion duly, temper] —**tem′perable,** *adj.* —**tem′perabil′ity,** *n.* —**tem′perer,** *n.* —**Syn. 2.** See **disposition. 12.** See **modify.**

tempera (tĕm′pə rə), *n. Painting.* paint made from pigment ground in water and mixed with an emulsion of egg yolk or some similar substance. [t. It., in phrase *pingere a tempera* paint in distemper, der. *temp(e)rare* temper, g. L]

temperament (tĕm′pə rə mənt, -prə mənt), *n.* **1.** the individual peculiarity of physical organization by which the manner of thinking, feeling, and acting of every person is permanently affected; natural disposition. **2.** unusual personal make-up manifested by peculiarities of feeling, temper, action, etc., with disinclination to submit to ordinary rules or restraints. **3.** the combination of the four cardinal humours, the relative proportions of which were supposed to determine physical and mental constitution. **4.** *Music.* **a.** the tuning of a keyboard instrument as the piano, organ, etc., so that it can be played in all keys. **b.** a particular system of doing this. **5.** *Obs.* the act of tempering or moderating. **6.** *Obs.* climate. **7.** *Obs.* temperature. [late ME, t. L: s. *temperāmentum* due mixture] —**Syn. 1.** See **disposition.**

temperamental (tĕm′pə rə mĕn′tl, -prə mĕn′tl), *adj.* **1.** having or exhibiting a strongly marked individual temperament. **2.** moody, irritable or sensitive. **3.** liable to behave erratically; unstable; unreliable. **4.** of or pertaining to temperament; constitutional. —**tem′peramen′tally,** *adv.*

temperance (tĕm′pə rəns), *n.* **1.** moderation or self-restraint in action, statement, etc.; self-control. **2.** habitual moderation in the indulgence of a natural appetite or passion, esp. in the consumption of alcoholic drink. **3.** total abstinence from alcoholic drink. [ME, t. AF: m. *temperaunce*, t. L: m. *temperantia* moderation]

temperate (tĕm′pə rĭt, tĕm′prĭt), *adj.* **1.** moderate or self-restrained; not extreme in opinion, etc. **2.** moderate as regards indulgence of appetite or passion, esp. in the consumption of alcoholic drink. **3.** not excessive in degree, as things, qualities, etc. **4.** moderate in respect of temperature. [ME, t. L: m. s. *temperātus*, pp.] —**tem′perately,** *adv.* —**tem′perateness,** *n.*

Temperate Zone, *Geog.* the parts of the earth's surface lying between each of the tropics and the polar circles nearest to it. Also, **Variable Zone.**

temperature (tĕm′prĭ chə), *n.* **1.** a measure of the degree of hotness or coldness of a body or substance which determines the rate at which heat will be transferred to or from it. As this is related to the kinetic energies of the constituent atoms, ions, or molecules of the substance, which cannot be directly ascertained, temperature has to be measured with respect to an arbitrary scale. See **thermometer. 2.** *Physiol., Pathol.* **a.** the degree of heat of a living body, esp. the human body. **b.** the excess of this above the normal (which, in the adult human being is about 98·4°F, or about 37°C). **3.** *Obs.* mildness, as of the weather. **4.** *Obs.* temperament. [t. L: m. s. *temperātūra*]

temperature gradient, *Meteorol.* rate of change of temperature with distance.

temperature inversion, *Meteorol.* an anomalous increase of temperature with height in the troposphere.

tempered (tĕm′pəd), *adj.* **1.** having a temper or disposition (as specified): *good-tempered.* **2.** *Music.* tuned in accordance with some other temperament than just or pure temperament; specif., tuned in equal temperament. **3.** made less intense or violent, esp. by the influence of something added. **4.** (of metal, glass, etc.) having had internal stresses altered by heat treatment.

tempest (tĕm′pĭst), *n.* **1.** an extensive current of wind rushing with great velocity and violence, esp. one attended with rain, hail, or snow; a violent storm. **2.** a violent commotion, disturbance, or tumult. —*v.t.* **3.** to affect by or as by a tempest; disturb violently. [ME *tempeste*, t. OF, g. Rom. *tempesta* time, storm, der. L *tempestas* season]

tempestuous (tĕm pĕs′tyōō əs), *adj.* **1.** characterized by or subject to tempests: *the tempestuous ocean.* **2.** of the nature of or resembling a tempest: *a tempestuous wind.* **3.** tumultuous; turbulent: *a tempestuous period.* [late ME, t. LL: m. s. *tempestuōsus*] —**tempes′tuously,** *adv.* —**tempes′tuousness,** *n.*

Templar (tĕm′plə), *n.* **1.** a member of a military order founded by Crusaders in Jerusalem about 1118 and suppressed in 1312. **2.** a lawyer or other person living in the Temple, London. **3.** a member of an order of Freemasons in the U.S. Also, **Knight Templar** for 1 and 3. [t. ML: apocopated s. *templārius*, der *templum* TEMPLE[1]; r. ME *templer*, t. OF: m. *templier*]

template (tĕm′plĭt), *n.* **1.** a pattern, mould, or the like, usually consisting of a thin plate of wood or metal, serving as a gauge or guide in mechanical work. **2.** *Bldg Trades.* a horizontal piece of timber, stone, or the like, in a wall, to receive and distribute the pressure of a girder, beam, etc. **3.** *Shipbuilding.* either of two wedges in each of the temporary blocks forming the support for the keel of a ship while building. Also, **templet.** [orig. uncert.; ? t. F: (m.) *templet* stretcher, der. L *templum* small timber, purlin]

temple[1] (tĕm′pl), *n.* **1.** an edifice or place dedicated to the service or worship of a deity or deities. **2.** (*usually cap.*) any of the three successive buildings, or groups of buildings, in ancient Jerusalem which were devoted to the worship of Jehovah. **3.** *U.S.* a synagogue. **4.** an edifice erected as a place of worship; a church, esp. a large or imposing one. **5.** any place or object regarded as occupied by the Divine Presence, as the body of a Christian (I Cor. 6:19). **6.** (in France) a Protestant church. **7.** a Mormon church. **8.** a building, usually large or pretentious, devoted to some public use: *a temple of music.* **9.** (*cap.*) either of two establishments of the medieval Templars, one in London and the other in Paris. **10.** (*cap.*) either of two groups of buildings (**Inner Temple** and **Middle Temple**) on the site of the Templars' former establishment in London, occupied by two of the Inns of Court. **11.** (in the U.S.) a building used by the masonic Templars.

[ME *tempel*, OE *templ*, t. L: s. *templum*] —**tem′ple-like′,** *adj.*

temple² (tĕm′pl), *n.* **1.** the flattened region on either side of the human forehead. **2.** a corresponding region in lower animals. **3.** *U.S.* either sidepiece of a pair of spectacles, extending back above the ears. [ME, t. OF, g. Rom. *tempula*, r. L *tempora*, pl., temples]

temple³ (tĕm′pl), *n.* (in a loom) a device for keeping the cloth stretched to the proper width during the weaving. [late ME *tempylle*, t. F: m. *temple* TEMPLATE]

Temple (tĕm′pl), *n.* **1. Sir William,** 1628–99, English statesman, diplomat, and author. **2. William,** 1881–1944, English prelate: archbishop of Canterbury, 1942–44.

Temple of Artemis, the large and imposing temple at Ephesus, dedicated to Artemis (Diana). See **Seven Wonders of the World.**

templet (tĕm′plĭt), *n.* template.

Templewood (tĕm′pl wo͝od′), *n.* **Samuel John Gurney Hoare** (gû′nĭ hô′), **1st Viscount,** 1880–1959, British statesman.

tempo (tĕm′pō), *n.*, *pl.* **-pos, -pi** (-pē). **1.** *Music.* relative rapidity or rate of movement (usually indicated by such terms as adagio, allegro, etc., or by reference to the metronome). **2.** characteristic rate, rhythm, or pattern of work or activity: *the tempo of city life.* [t. It., g. L *tempus* time]

temporal¹ (tĕm′pə rəl, tĕm′prəl), *adj.* **1.** of or pertaining to time. **2.** pertaining to or concerned with the present life or this world; worldly. **3.** enduring for a time only; temporary; transitory. **4.** *Gram.* **a.** of, pertaining to, or expressing time: *a temporal adverb.* **b.** of or pertaining to the tenses of a verb. **5.** secular, lay, or civil (as opposed to *spiritual* or *ecclesiastical*). —*n.* **6.** (*chiefly pl.*) a temporal possession, estate, or the like; a temporality. **7.** (*chiefly pl.*) that which is temporal; a temporal matter or affair. [ME, t. L: s. *temporālis* pertaining to or enduring for a time] —**tem′porally,** *adv.*

temporal² (tĕm′pə rəl, tĕm′prəl), *Anat.* —*adj.* **1.** of, pertaining to, or situated near the temple or a temporal bone. —*n.* **2.** any of several parts in the temporal region, esp. the temporal bone. [t. L: m. *temporālis*]

temporal bone, *Anat.* either of a pair of complex bones forming part of the sides and base of the skull.

temporality (tĕm′pə răl′ĭ tĭ), *n.*, *pl.* **-ties. 1.** temporal character or nature; temporariness. **2.** something temporal. **3.** (*chiefly pl.*) a temporal possession, revenue, or the like, as of the church or clergy.

temporary (tĕm′pə rə rĭ, tĕm′prə rĭ), *adj.* lasting, existing, serving, or effective for a time only; not permanent: *a temporary need.* [t. L: m. s. *temporārius*] —**tem′porarily,** *adv.* —**tem′porariness,** *n.*

—**Syn.** TEMPORARY, TRANSIENT, TRANSITORY agree in referring to that which is not lasting or permanent. TEMPORARY implies an arrangement established with no thought of continuance but with the idea of being changed soon: *a temporary structure.* TRANSIENT describes that which is in the process of passing by, and which will therefore last or stay only a short time: *a transient condition.* TRANSITORY describes an innate characteristic by which a thing, by its very nature, lasts only a short time: *life is transitory.*

temporize (tĕm′pə rīz′), *v.i.*, **-rized, -rizing. 1.** to act indecisively or evasively to gain time or delay matters. **2.** to comply with the time or occasion; yield temporarily or ostensibly to the current of opinion or circumstances. **3.** to treat or parley so as to gain time (fol. by *with*). **4.** to come to terms (usually fol. by *with*). **5.** to effect a compromise (usually fol. by *between*). Also, **temporise.** [t. ML: m. *temporizāre*, der. *temporāre* delay] —**tem′poriza′tion,** *n.* —**tem′poriz′er,** *n.* —**tem′poriz′ingly,** *adv.*

tempt (tĕmpt), *v.t.* **1.** to induce or persuade by enticement or allurement. **2.** to allure, appeal strongly to, or invite: *the offer tempts me.* **3.** to render strongly disposed (to do something). **4.** to try to dispose or incite; assail with enticements, esp. to evil. **5.** to put to the test in a venturesome way; risk provoking; provoke: *to tempt one's fate.* **6.** *Obs.* to try or test. [ME, t. L: s. *temptāre* handle, touch, try, test] —**tempt′able,** *adj.*

—**Syn. 1.** TEMPT, SEDUCE may both mean to allure or entice to something unwise or wicked. To TEMPT is to attract by holding out the probability of gratification or advantage, often in the direction of that which is wrong or unwise: *to tempt a man with a bribe.* To SEDUCE is literally to lead astray, sometimes from that which absorbs one or demands attention, but more often, in a moral sense, from rectitude, chastity, etc.: *to seduce a person away from loyalty.* —**Ant. 1.** dissuade.

temptation (tĕmp tā′shən), *n.* **1.** the act of tempting; enticement or allurement. **2.** something that tempts, entices, or allures. **3.** the fact or state of being tempted, esp. to evil. **4.** an instance of it. [ME *temptacion*, t. L: m. s. *temptātio*]

tempter (tĕmp′tə), *n.* **1.** one who or that which tempts, esp. to evil. **2. the Tempter,** the devil. —**temptress** (tĕmp′trĭs), *n. fem.*

tempting (tĕmp′tĭng), *adj.* that tempts; enticing or inviting. —**tempt′ingly,** *adv.* —**tempt′ingness,** *n.*

tempus fugit (tĕm′pəs fyo͞o′jĭt), *Latin.* time flies.

Temuco (*Sp.* tĕ mo͞o′kô), *n.* a town in S Chile. 111,980 (1960).

ten (tĕn), *n.* **1.** a cardinal number, nine plus one. **2.** a symbol for this number, as 10 or X. **3.** a set of this many persons or things. **4.** a playing card with ten pips. —*adj.* **5.** amounting to ten in number. [ME; OE *tēn*, c. G *zehn*, Goth. *taihun*, L *decem*, Gk *déka*]

ten., 1. tenor. **2.** *Music.* tenuto.

tenable (tĕn′ə bl), *adj.* capable of being held, maintained, or defended, as against attack or objection: *a tenable theory.* [t. F, der. *tenir*, g. L *tenēre* hold, keep] —**ten′abil′ity, ten′ableness,** *n.* —**ten′ably,** *adv.*

tenace (tĕn′ās), *n.* *Whist, Bridge.* a combination of the best and third best cards of a suit (**major tenace**), or of the second and fourth best cards (**minor tenace**). [t. Sp.: m. *tenaza* pincers (referring to cards)]

tenacious (tĭ nā′shəs), *adj.* **1.** holding fast; characterized by keeping a firm hold (often fol. by *of*). **2.** highly retentive: *a tenacious memory.* **3.** pertinacious, persistent, stubborn, or obstinate. **4.** adhesive or sticky; viscous or glutinous. **5.** holding together; cohesive; not easily pulled asunder; tough. [f. TENACI(TY) + -OUS] —**tena′ciously,** *adv.* —**tena′ciousness,** *n.*

tenacity (tĭ năs′ĭ tĭ), *n.* **1.** the quality or property of being tenacious. **2.** *Engineering.* ultimate stress. [t. L: m. s. *tenācitas*] —**Syn. 1.** See **perseverence.**

tenaculum (tĭ năk′yo͞o ləm), *n.*, *pl.* **-la** (-lə). *Surg.* a small sharp-pointed hook set in a handle, used for seizing and picking up parts, etc., in operations and dissections. [t. LL: instrument for holding, der. L *tenēre* hold]

tenaille (tĭ nāl′), *n.* *Fort.* an outwork containing one or two re-entering angles, raised in the main ditch immediately in front of a curtain, between two bastions. Also, **tenail.** [t. F: forceps, pl. See TENACULUM]

tenancy (tĕn′ən sĭ), *n.*, *pl.* **-cies. 1.** a holding, as of lands, by any kind of title; tenure; occupancy of land, a house, or the like, under a lease or on payment of rent. **2.** the period of a tenant's occupancy. **3.** occupation of or residence in any place, position, etc. **4.** *Obs.* a holding, or piece of land held by a tenant.

tenant (tĕn′ənt), *n.* **1.** one who holds land, a house, or the like, of another (the landlord) for a period of time, as a lessee or occupant for rent. **2.** *Law.* **a.** a person or body of persons holding land under a landlord in leasehold tenure. **b.** any holder of land. **3.** an occupant or inhabitant of any place. —*v.t.* **4.** to hold or occupy as a tenant; dwell in; inhabit. —*v.i.* **5.** to dwell or live (fol. by *in*). [ME *tenaunt*, t. F: m. *tenant*, ppr. of *tenir* hold, g. L *tenēre*] —**ten′antable,** *adj.* —**ten′antless,** *adj.*

tenant farmer, one who farms land which he has rented from another.

tenantry (tĕn′ən trĭ), *n.*, *pl.* **-tries. 1.** tenants collectively; the body of tenants on an estate. **2.** the state or condition of being a tenant.

tench (tĕnch), *n.*, *pl.* **tenches,** (*esp. collectively*) **tench.** a freshwater cyprinoid fish, *Tinca tinca*, of Europe. [ME *tenche*, t. OF, g. LL *tinca*]

Ten Commandments, the precepts spoken by God to Israel, delivered to Moses on Mount Sinai; the Decalogue. Ex. 20:24; 12:34, and Deut. 5.

tend¹ (tĕnd), *v.i.* **1.** to be disposed or inclined in action, operation, or effect (to do something): *the particles tend to unite.* **2.** to be disposed towards a state of mind, emotion, quality, etc. **3.** to incline in operation or effect; lead or conduce, as to some result or resulting condition: *measures tending to improved working conditions, governments are tending towards democracy.* **4.** to be directed or lead, as a journey, course, road, etc. (usually fol. by *to*, *towards*, etc.). [ME, t. F: s. *tendre*, g. L *tendere* stretch, go, strive; akin to Gk *teínein*, Skt *tan* stretch]

tend² (tĕnd), *v.t.* **1.** to attend to by work or services, care, etc.: *to tend a fire.* **2.** to look after; watch over and care for; minister to or wait on with service. **3.** *Naut.* to handle or watch (a line, etc.). —*v.i.* **4.** to attend by action, care, etc. (usually fol. by *to*). **5.** *Obs.* to attend or wait upon; serve: (usually fol. by *on* or *upon*). [ME *tende*; aphetic var. of ATTEND]

tendance (tĕn′dəns), *n.* **1.** attention; care; ministration, as to the sick. **2.** *Archaic.* attendants collectively.

tendencious (tĕn dĕn′shəs), *adj.* tendentious.

tendency (tĕn′dən sĭ), *n.*, *pl.* **-cies. 1.** natural or prevailing disposition to move, proceed, or act in some direction or towards some point, end, or result: *the tendency of falling bodies towards the earth.* **2.** an inclination, bent, or predisposition to something. **3.** special and definite purpose in a novel or other literary work. [t. ML: m. *tendentia*, der. L *tendere* TEND¹]

—**Syn.** 1. TENDENCY, DIRECTION, TREND refer to inclination or line of action. A TENDENCY is an inclination towards a certain line of action (whether or not the action follows), and is often the result of inherent qualities, nature, or habit: *a tendency to procrastinate.* DIRECTION is the line along which an object or course of action moves, often towards some set point or intended goal: *the change is in the direction of improvement.* TREND emphasizes movement in a certain direction, although neither the course nor the goal may be very definite: *there was no evidence of a trend in the stock market.*

tendentious (tĕn dĕn′shəs), *adj.* having or showing a definite tendency, bias, or purpose; described or written so as to influence in a desired direction or present a particular point of view: *a tendentious novel.* Also, **tendencious.** —**tenden′tiously,** *adv.* —**tenden′tiousness,** *n.*

tender[1] (tĕn′də), *adj.* **1.** soft or delicate in substance; not hard or tough: *a tender steak.* **2.** weak or delicate in constitution; not strong or hardy. **3.** young or immature: *children of tender age.* **4.** delicate or soft in quality: *tender blue.* **5.** delicate, soft, or gentle: *the tender touch of her hand.* **6.** soft-hearted; easily touched; sympathetic; compassionate. **7.** affectionate or loving; sentimental or amatory. **8.** considerate or careful; chary or reluctant (usually fol. by *of*). **9.** acutely or painfully sensitive. **10.** readily made uneasy, as the conscience. **11.** yielding readily to force or pressure; easily broken; fragile. **12.** of a delicate or ticklish nature; requiring careful or tactful handling: *a tender subject.* **13.** (of a ship) apt to lean over easily; crank. —*v.t.* **14.** to make tender. **15.** *Archaic or Dial.* to regard or treat with tenderness. [ME, t. F: m. *tendre*, g. L *tener* soft, delicate, tender] —**ten′derly,** *adv.* —**ten′derness,** *n.*

tender[2] (tĕn′də), *v.t.* **1.** to present formally for acceptance; make formal offer of: *to tender one's resignation.* **2.** to offer or proffer. **3.** *Law.* to offer, as money or goods, in payment of a debt or other obligation, esp. in exact accordance with the terms of the law and of the obligation. —*n.* **4.** the act of tendering; an offer of something for acceptance. **5.** that which is tendered or offered, esp. money in payment of something. **6.** *Com.* an offer made in writing by one party to another to execute certain work, supply certain commodities, etc., at a given cost. **7.** *Law.* an offer, as of money or goods, in payment or satisfaction of a debt or other obligation. [t. AF, g. L *tendere*] —**ten′derer,** *n.* —**Syn. 1.** See **offer.**

tender[3] (tĕn′də), *n.* **1.** one who tends; one who attends to or takes charge of something. **2.** an auxiliary vessel employed to attend one or more other vessels, as for supplying provisions. **3.** a small rowing boat or motor boat carried or towed by a yacht. **4.** a wagon attached to a steam locomotive, for carrying coal, water, etc. [late ME; aphetic var. of ATTENDER]

tenderfoot (tĕn′də fo͝ot′), *n., pl.* **-foots, -feet** (-fēt′). *Colloq.* **1.** a raw, inexperienced person; a novice. **2. a.** formerly, the initial membership award in the boy scout movement. **b.** a holder of this award. **3.** *U.S.* a newcomer to the ranching and mining regions of the western U.S., unused to hardships.

tender-hearted (tĕn′də hä′tĭd), *adj.* soft-hearted; sympathetic. —**ten′der-heart′edness,** *n.*

tenderize (tĕn′də rīz′), *v.t.* **-rized, -rizing.** *Cookery.* to make (meat) tender by beating, marinading, etc. Also, **tenderise.**

tenderloin (tĕn′də loin′), *n.* **1.** a strip of tender meat forming part of the loin of beef, pork, etc., lying under the short ribs and consisting of the psoas muscle. **2.** a cut of beef lying between the sirloin and ribs. **3.** *U.S.* (*cap.*) a district in a city (orig. New York City) noted for vice and police corruption. [def. 3 so called from its furnishing the 'best cut' of graft]

tendinous (tĕn′dĭ nəs), *adj.* **1.** of the nature of or resembling a tendon. **2.** consisting of tendons. [t. ML: m. s. *tendinōsus* full of tendons]

tendon (tĕn′dən), *n.* *Anat.* a cord or band of dense, tough, inelastic, white fibrous tissue, serving to connect a muscle with a bone or part; a sinew. [t. ML: s. *tendō*, t. Gk: m. *ténōn* sinew (by assoc. with L *tendere* stretch)]

tendril (tĕn′drĭl), *n.* *Bot.* a filiform leafless organ climbing plants, often growing in spiral form, which attaches itself to or twines round some other body, so as to support the plant. [t. F: m. *tendrillon* tender shoot, der. *tendron* tender part, OF *tendrun*, g. LL *tenerumen*, der. *tener* tender] —**ten′drillar, ten′drilous,** *adj.*

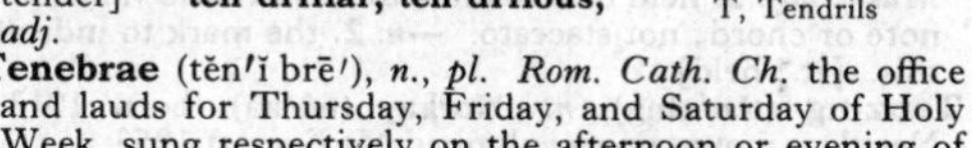

T, Tendrils

Tenebrae (tĕn′ĭ brē′), *n., pl.* *Rom. Cath. Ch.* the office and lauds for Thursday, Friday, and Saturday of Holy Week, sung respectively on the afternoon or evening of Wednesday, Thursday, and Friday of that week, at which candles are gradually extinguished. [t. L: lit., darkness]

tenebrific (tĕn′ĭ brĭf′ĭk), *adj.* producing darkness. [f. s. L *tenebrae*, pl., darkness + -(I)FIC]

tenebrism (tĕn′ĭ brĭz′əm), *n.* a method of painting using highly directional lighting to produce sharp contrasts of light and shadow, as used by Caravaggio in the early 17th century and by his followers.

tenebrous (tĕn′ĭ brəs), *adj.* dark; gloomy; obscure. [late ME, t. L: m. s. *tenebrōsus* dark]

Tenedos (tĕn′ĭ dŏs′), *n.* a small Turkish island in the Aegean, near the entrance to the Dardanelles. Turkish, **Bozcaada.**

tenement (tĕn′ĭ mənt), *n.* **1.** any house or building; dwelling house. **2.** a portion of a house or building occupied by a tenant as a separate dwelling. **3.** a tenement house. **4.** any habitation, abode, or dwelling place. **5.** any species of permanent property, as lands, houses, rents, an office, a franchise, etc., that may be held of another. **6.** (*pl.*) freehold interests in things immovable considered as subjects of property. [ME, t. OF, der. *tenir* hold, g. L *tenēre*] —**tenemental** (tĕn′ĭ mĕn′tl), **tenementary** (tĕn′ĭ mĕn′tə rĭ), *adj.*

tenement house, a house divided into flats, esp. one in the poorer, crowded parts of a large city.

Tenerife (tĕn′ə rēf′; *Sp.* tĕ nĕ rē′fĕ), *n.* **1.** the largest of the Canary Islands, off the NW coast of Africa. 394,466 pop. (est. 1962); 794 sq. mi. *Cap.:* Santa Cruz de Tenerife. **2. Pico de** (*Sp.* pē′kō dĕ). See **Teide, Pico de.** Also, **Teneriffe.**

tenesmus (tĭ nĕz′məs), *n.* *Pathol.* the urgent desire to urinate or defecate, without the ability to do so. [t. ML, g. L *tenesmos*, t. Gk: straining]

tenet (tĕn′ĭt, tē′nĭt), *n.* any opinion, principle, doctrine, dogma, or the like, held as true. [t. L: he holds]

tenfold (tĕn′fōld′), *adj.* **1.** comprising ten parts or members. **2.** ten times as great or as much. —*adv.* **3.** in tenfold measure.

ten-gallon hat (tĕn′găl′ən), a cowboy's broad-brimmed hat with a high, soft crown.

Tengri Khan (tĕng′grĭ kän′), the highest peak of the Tien Shan mountains, in central Asia. ab. 23,950 ft.

Tengri Nor (tĕng′grĭ nô′), a salt lake in E Tibet, NW of Lhasa. ab. 700 sq. mi.; 15,186 ft above sea-level.

tenia (tē′nĭ ə), *n., pl.* **-niae** (-nĭ ē′). *U.S.* taenia.

teniacide (tē′nĭ ə sīd′), *n.* *U.S.* taeniacide.

Teniers (tĕn′ĭ əz; *Fl.* tə nērs′; *Fr.* tĕ nyĕ′), *n.* **1. David,** 1582–1649, Flemish painter. **2.** his son, **David,** 1610–90, Flemish painter.

ten lost tribes, lost tribes.

Tenn., Tennessee.

tennantite (tĕn′ən tīt′), *n.* a mineral, copper arsenic sulphide, approx. Cu_3AsS_3, usually containing some antimony and grading into tetrahedrite: an ore of copper. [named after Smithson *Tennant*, 1761–1815, English chemist. See -ITE[1]]

tenner (tĕn′ə), *n.* *Colloq.* **1.** a ten-pound note. **2.** ten pounds. **3.** *Austral., U.S.* a ten-dollar note.

Tennessee (tĕn′ĭ sē′), *n.* **1.** a state in the SE United States. 3,567,089 pop. (1960); 42,246 sq. mi. *Cap.:* Nashville. *Abbrev.:* Tenn. **2.** a river flowing from E Tennessee through N Alabama, W Tennessee, and SW Kentucky into the Ohio river. 652 mi. —**Ten′nesse′an,** *adj., n.*

Tennessee Valley Authority, an organization set up by the U.S. government in 1933 to harness the Tennessee river for cheap electric power, irrigation, flood control, increased navigation, etc. *Abbrev.:* TVA.

Tenniel (tĕn′yəl), *n.* **Sir John,** 1820–1914, English caricaturist and illustrator.

tennis (tĕn′ĭs), *n.* **1.** a game, played on a tennis court, in which two players, or two pairs of players, hit a tennis ball backwards and forwards with rackets over a centrally placed net. When a player commits a fault, points are awarded to the other side. **2.** real tennis. [ME *tenetz*, *teneys*, t. AF: m. *tenetz*, impv., hold, take]

tennis ball, a hollow rubber ball covered with white cloth, used in tennis.

tennis court. See **court** (def. 6).

tennis elbow, a painful condition of the elbow accompanied by inflammation, caused by undue exertion while playing tennis or other games.

tennis racket. See **racket**[2] (def. 1).

Tennyson (tĕn′ĭ sən), *n.* **Alfred, 1st Baron,** 1809–92, English poet: poet laureate 1850–92.

Tennysonian (tĕn′ĭ sō′nyən), *adj.* **1.** of, pertaining to, or characteristic of Tennyson or his writings. —*n.* **2.** an admirer or imitator of Tennyson.

teno-, a word element meaning 'tendon', as in *tenotomy.* [comb. form repr. Gk *ténōn*]

tenon (tĕn′ən), *n.* **1.** a projection shaped on an end of a piece of wood, etc., for insertion in a corresponding cavity (mortise) in another piece, so as to form a joint. See diag. under **mortise.** —*v.t.* **2.** to provide with a tenon. **3.** to shape so as to fit into a mortise. **4.** to join securely. [ME, t. OF, der. *tenir* hold, g. L *tenēre*]

tenonitis (tĕn′ə nī′tĭs), *n. Pathol.* inflammation of a tendon.

tenon saw, a saw consisting of a thin, parallel-sided blade, whose upper edge is reinforced, and whose lower (cutting) edge has some 10–14 teeth per inch.

tenor (tĕn′ə), *n.* **1.** the course of thought or meaning which runs through something written or spoken; purport, drift. **2.** continuous course, progress, or movement. **3.** *Music.* **a.** the highest natural male voice. **b.** a part sung by or written for such a voice, esp. the next to the lowest part in four-part harmony. **c.** a singer with such a voice. **d.** an instrument corresponding in compass to this voice, esp. the viola. **e.** the lowest-toned bell of a peal. **4.** *Obs.* quality, character, or condition. —*adj.* **5.** *Music.* of, pertaining to, or having the compass of, a tenor. [ME, t. (M)L: course, etc.] —**ten′orless,** *adj.*

tenor clef, *Music.* a sign placing middle C on the next to the top line of the stave.

tenorite (tĕn′ə rīt′), *n.* a mineral, copper oxide, which occurs as small black scales in volcanic regions or in copper veins. [named after G. *Tenore*, died 1861, Italian botanist. See -ITE[1]]

tenorrhaphy (tĭ nŏ′rə fĭ), *n., pl.* **-phies.** *Surg.* suture of a tendon. [f. TENO- + m. s. Gk -*(r)rhaphia*]

tenosynovitis (tĕn′ō sĭ′nə vī′tĭs), *n. Pathol.* inflammation of the tendon sheath.

tenotomy (tĭ nŏt′ə mĭ), *n., pl.* **-mies.** *Surg.* the cutting or division of a tendon.

tenpence (tĕn′pəns), *n.* a sum of money equal to ten pennies.

tenpenny (tĕn′pə nĭ), *adj.* **1.** of the amount or value of tenpence. —*n.* **2.** something purchased for tenpence, esp. a journey by public transport.

tenpin (tĕn′pĭn′), *n.* one of the pins used in tenpin bowling.

tenpin bowling, a form of bowling played with ten wooden pins at which a ball is bowled to knock them down. Also, *U.S.*, **ten′pins′.**

tenrec (tĕn′rĕk), *n.* any of several insectivorous mammals of Madagascar, which constitute the family *Tenrecidae*, esp. a common tailless species, *Tenrec ecaudatus*. Also, **tanrec.** [t. F, t. Malagasy: m. *tàndraka*]

Tenrec, *Tenrec ecaudatus* (Length 14 in.)

tense[1] (tĕns), *adj.*, **tenser, tensest,** *v.*, **tensed, tensing.** —*adj.* **1.** stretched tight, as a cord, fibre, etc.; drawn taut; rigid. **2.** in a state of mental or nervous strain, as a person. **3.** characterized by a strain upon the nerves or feelings: *a tense moment.* **4.** *Phonet.* pronounced with relatively tense muscles. —*v.t., v.i.* **5.** to make or become tense. [t. L: m. s. *tensus*, pp., stretched, taut] —**tense′ly,** *adv.* —**tense′ness,** *n.*

tense[2] (tĕns), *n. Gram.* **1.** a category of verb inflection found in some languages which specifies the time and length of occurrence of the action or state expressed by the verb. **2.** a set of such categories or constructions in a particular language. **3.** the meaning of, or typical of, such a category. **4.** such categories or constructions, or their meanings collectively. [ME *tens*, t. OF, g. L *tempus* time]

tensible (tĕn′sə bl), *adj.* capable of being stretched; tensile. —**ten′sibil′ity,** *n.* —**ten′sibly,** *adv.*

tensile (tĕn′sīl), *adj.* **1.** of or pertaining to tension: *tensile strain.* **2.** capable of being stretched or drawn out; ductile. [t. NL: m. s. *tensilis*, der. L *tendere* stretch] —**tensility** (tĕn sĭl′ĭ tĭ), *n.*

tensile stress, *Engineering.* **1.** the stress on a body or material under tension. **2.** Also, **tensile strength.** ultimate stress; tenacity.

tensimeter (tĕn sĭm′ĭ tə), *n.* an instrument for determining vapour pressure or tension. [f. TENSI(ON) + -METER[1]]

tensiometer (tĕn′sĭ ŏm′ĭ tə), *n.* an apparatus for measuring tensile stress, as in aeroplane members.

tension (tĕn′shən), *n.* **1.** the act of stretching or straining. **2.** the state of being stretched or strained. **3.** mental or emotional strain; intense suppressed anxiety, suspense, or excitement. **4.** a strained relationship between individuals, groups, countries, etc. **5.** *Physics.* pressure: *vapour tension.* **6.** *Mech.* **a.** a state in which a body is stretched or increased in size in one direction with a decrease in size in a certain ratio in a perpendicular direction. **b.** a force tending to elongate a body. **7.** *Elect.* **a.** the condition of a dielectric body when its opposite surfaces are oppositely electrified. **b.** electromotive force; potential. **8.** *Mach.* a device for stretching or pulling something. **9.** a device to hold the proper tension on the material being woven in a loom. [t. LL: s. *tensio* act of stretching] —**ten′sional,** *adj.* —**ten′sionless,** *adj.*

tensity (tĕn′sĭ tĭ), *n.* the state of being tense.

tensive (tĕn′sĭv), *adj.* stretching or straining. [f. TENSE + -IVE. Cf. F *tensif*]

tensor (tĕn′sə, -sô), *n.* **1.** *Anat.* a muscle that stretches or tightens some part of the body. **2.** *Maths.* a set of functions which, when changing from one set of coordinates to another, are transformed in a precisely defined manner. [t. NL: stretcher]

tent[1] (tĕnt), *n.* **1.** a portable shelter of skins, coarse cloth, or esp., canvas, supported by one or more poles and usually extended by ropes fastened to pegs in the ground. —*v.t.* **2.** to provide with or lodge in tents; cover as with a tent. —*v.i.* **3.** to live in a tent; encamp. [ME *tente*, t. OF, g. L *tenta*, der. *tentus*, pp., stretched] —**tent′less,** *adj.* —**tent′like′,** *adj.*

tent[2] (tĕnt), *Surg.* —*n.* **1.** a roll or pledget, usually of soft, absorbent material, as a lint or gauze, for dilating an orifice, keeping a wound open, etc. —*v.t.* **2.** to keep (a wound) open with a tent. [ME *tente* a probe, t. MF, der. *tenter*]

tentacle (tĕn′tə kl), *n.* **1.** *Zool.* any of various slender, flexible processes or appendages in animals, esp. invertebrates, which serve as organs of touch, prehension, etc.; a feeler. **2.** *Bot.* a sensitive filament or process, as one of the glandular hairs of the sundew. See illus. under **jellyfish.** [t. NL: m. s. *tentāculum*, f. L: *tentā(re)* feel, try + -*culum*, dim. suffix] —**ten′tacle-like′,** *adj.* —**tentacular** (tĕn tăk′yo͝o lə), *adj.*

tentacled (tĕn′tə kld), *adj.* having tentacles. Also, **tentaculate** (tĕn tăk′yo͝o lĭt).

tentage (tĕn′tĭj), *n.* tents collectively; equipment or supply of tents.

tentation (tĕn tā′shən), *n.* a method of making mechanical adjustments or the like by a succession of trials. [t. L: s. *tentātio*, late var. of *temptātio* attempt]

tentative (tĕn′tə tĭv), *adj.* **1.** of the nature of, or made or done as, a trial, experiment, or attempt; experimental. **2.** hesitant; cautious; diffident. [t. ML: m. s. *tentātīvus*, der. L *tentāre* (*temptāre*) try] —**ten′tatively,** *adv.* —**ten′tativeness,** *n.*

tent caterpillar, any of several caterpillars or moths (family *Lasiocampidae*), which spin tentlike, silken webs in which they live gregariously.

tenter[1] (tĕn′tə), *n.* **1.** (in the manufacture of cloth) a framework on which the cloth is stretched so that it may set or dry evenly. **2.** *Obs.* a tenterhook. —*v.t.* **3.** to stretch (cloth) on a tenter or tenters. —*v.i.* **4.** to be capable of being tentered. [ME *tentour*, f. s. L *tentus*, pp., stretched + -*our* -OR[2]]

tenter[2] (tĕn′tə), *n.* one who tends, or has the care of something, esp. a machine in a factory. [f. *tent* tend + -ER[1]]

tenterhook (tĕn′tə ho͝ok′), *n.* **1.** one of the hooks or bent nails which hold cloth stretched on a tenter. **2. on tenterhooks,** in a state of painful suspense or anxiety.

tenth (tĕnth), *adj.* **1.** next after the ninth. **2.** being one of ten equal parts. —*n.* **3.** a tenth part, esp. of one ($\frac{1}{10}$). **4.** the tenth member of a series. **5.** *Music.* **a.** a note distant from another note by an interval of an octave and a third. **b.** the interval between such notes. **c.** the harmonic combination of such notes. —**tenth′ly,** *adv.*

tent stitch, *Embroidery.* a series of diagonal stitches thought to resemble the shape of a tent.

tenuis (tĕn′yo͞o ĭs), *n., pl.* **tenues** (tĕn′yo͞o ēz′). *Gk Gram.* a voiceless stop consonant. [t. L: thin, fine, slender]

tenuity (tĕ nyo͞o′ĭ tĭ), *n.* **1.** the state of being tenuous. **2.** slenderness. **3.** thinness of consistency; rarefied condition.

tenuous (tĕn′yo͞o əs), *adj.* **1.** thin or slender in form. **2.** thin in consistency; rare or rarefied. **3.** of slight importance or significance; unsubstantial. **4.** flimsy; lacking a firm or sound basis; weak; vague. [f. s. L *tenuis* slender + -OUS] —**ten′uously,** *adv.* —**ten′uousness,** *n.*

tenure (tĕn′yo͞oə), *n.* **1.** the holding or possessing of anything: *the tenure of an office.* **2.** the holding of property, esp. real property, of a superior in return for services to be rendered. **3.** the period or terms of holding something. [ME, t. OF, der. *tenir*, g. L *tenēre* hold] —**tenurial** (tĕ nyo͞oə′rĭ əl), *adj.* —**tenu′rially,** *adv.*

tenuto (tĭ nyo͞o′tō; *It.* tĕ no͞o′tō), *adj., n., pl.* **-tos, -ti** (-tē). *Music. adj.* **1.** held or sustained to its full time value, as a note or chord; not staccato. —*n.* **2.** the mark to indicate this. [It.: held]

Tenzing (tĕn′zĭng), *n.* **Norkay** (nô′kā), born 1913?, Nepalese mountaineer: climbed Mt Everest 1953.

teocalli (tē′ō kăl′ĭ; *Sp.* tė ō kä′lyē), *n., pl.* **-lis.** a ceremonial structure of the Aztecs, consisting of a truncated terraced pyramid supporting a temple. [t. Nahuatl: f. *teo(tl)* a god + *calli* house]

teosinte (tē′ō sĭn′tĭ), *n.* a tall annual grass, *Euchlaena mexicana*, native in Mexico and Central America, closely related to maize, and occasionally cultivated as a fodder plant. [t. Sp., t. Nahuatl: m. *teocintli*, appar. f. *teo(tl)* god + *cintli* dry ear of maize]

tepee (tē′pē), *n.* a tent or wigwam of the Amerindians. Also, **teepee, tipi.** [t. Dakota Siouan: m. *tīpī*, f. *ti* to dwell + *pi* used for]

tepefy (tĕp′ĭ fī′), *v.t.*, **-fied, -fying.** to make or become tepid or lukewarm. [t. L: m. *tepefacere* make tepid] —**tepefaction** (tĕp′ĭ făk′shən), *n.*

tephrite (tĕf′rīt), *n. Geol.* a basaltic rock consisting essentially of pyroxene and plagioclase with nepheline or leucite. [f. s. Gk *tephrós* ash-coloured + -ITE[1]] —**tephritic** (tĕf rĭt′ĭk). *adj.*

tepid (tĕp′ĭd), *adj.* moderately warm; lukewarm. [ME, t. L: s. *tepidus*] —**tepid′ity, tep′idness,** *n.* —**tep′idly,** *adv.*

tepidarium (tĕp′ĭ dâr′ĭ əm), *n., pl.* **-daria** (-dâr′ĭ ə). *Roman Antiq.* a room having a lukewarm bath. [t. L]

Teplice (*Cz.* tĕ′plē tsĕ), *n.* a town in W Czechoslovakia. 51,000 (est. 1965).

tequila (tĭ kē′lə), *n.* a Mexican drink produced by distillation of a fermented mash of agave. [named after *Tequila*, district of Mexico]

ter., 1. terrace. 2. territory.

tera-, a prefix denoting one million million. [irreg. comb. form repr. Gk *téras* monster. See TERATO-]

teraphim (tĕ′rə fĭm), *n. pl., sing.* **teraph** (tĕ′rəf), **teraphim.** idols or images venerated by the ancient Hebrews and kindred peoples, apparently as household gods. [ME *t(h)eraphyn, -ym*, t. L (Vulgate), t. Gk (Septuagint), t. Heb.: m. *th'rāphīm*. Cf. Aram. *th'rāphīn*]

terato-, a word element meaning 'monster', as in *teratogenic*. Also, (before vowels), **terat-.** [comb. form repr. s. Gk *téras* monster]

teratogenic (tĕ′rə tə jĕn′ĭk), *adj. Pathol.* leading to the production of foetal abnormalities.

teratoid (tĕ′rə toid′), *adj. Biol.* resembling a monster.

teratology (tĕ′rə tŏl′ə jĭ), *n. Biol.* the science or study of monstrosities or abnormal formations in animals or plants. —**teratological** (tĕ′rə tə lŏj′ĭ kl), *adj.* —**ter′atol′ogist,** *n.*

terbia (tû′bĭ ə), *n. Chem.* the oxide of terbium, Tb_2O_3, an amorphous white powder.

terbium (tû′bĭ əm), *n. Chem.* a rare-earth, metallic element present in certain minerals, and yielding colourless salts. *Symbol:* Tb; *at. no.:* 65; *at. wt:* 158·924. [f. *(Yt)terb(y)*, name of Swedish town where found + -IUM. See YTTERBIUM] —**ter′bic,** *adj.*

terbium metals, *Chem.* See **rare-earth elements.**

Ter Borch (*Du.* tĕr bôrKH′), **Gerard** (*Du.* KHė′rŏrt), 1617–81, Dutch painter.

Terbrugghen (*Du.* tĕr brY′KHə), *n.* **Hendrick** (*Du.* hĕn′-drĭk), 1588–1629, Dutch painter.

terce (tûs), *n. Eccles.* tierce (def. 3).

Terceira (*Port.* tər sāy′rə), *n.* a Portuguese island in the N Atlantic: one of the Azores. 96,000 pop. (est. 1967); 153 sq. mi. *Cap.:* Angra do Heroismo.

tercel (tû′səl), *n.* a male hawk trained for falconry, esp. the male peregrine falcon. Also, **tiercel, tercelet** (tûs′lĭt). [ME, t. OF, der. *tierz* third, g. L *tertius*]

tercentenary (tû′sĕn tē′nə rĭ), *adj., n., pl.* **-ries.** —*adj.* **1.** of or pertaining to a 300th anniversary. —*n.* **2.** a 300th anniversary. **3.** its celebration. **4.** a period of 300 years. Also, **ter′centen′nial.** [f. L *ter* thrice + CENTENARY]

tercentennial (tû′sĕn tĕn′yəl), *adj.* **1.** consisting of or lasting 300 years. **2.** recurring every 300 years. —*n.* **3.** *U.S.* a tercentenary.

tercet (tû′sĭt), *n.* **1.** *Pros.* a group of three lines rhyming together, or connected by rhyme with the adjacent group or groups of three lines. **2.** *Music.* a triplet. [t. F, t. It.: m. *terzetto*, dim. of *terzo* third, g. L *tertius*]

terebene (tĕ′rĭ bēn′), *n. Chem.* a paint and varnish drier consisting of linseed oil, natural resin, and salts of lead and manganese, thinned with turpentine. Also, **terebine.**

terebic acid (tĕ rĕb′ĭk), *Chem.* an acid, $C_7H_{10}O_4$, formed by the action of nitric acid on oil of turpentine. [f. TEREB(INTH) + -IC]

terebinth (tĕ′rĭ bĭnth), *n.* a moderate-sized anacardiaceous tree, *Pistacia terebinthus*, of the Mediterranean regions, yielding turpentine. [t. L: s. *terebinthus*, t. Gk: m. *terébinthos*; r. ME *theribynte*, t. OF]

terebinthic (tĕ′rĭ bĭn′thĭk), *adj.* pertaining to or resembling turpentine.

terebinthine (tĕ′rĭ bĭn′thĭn), *adj.* **1.** of, pertaining to, consisting of, or resembling turpentine. **2.** of or pertaining to the terebinth.

teredo (tĕ rē′dō), *n., pl.* **-dos, -dines** (-dĭ nēz′). a shipworm (genus *Teredo*). [t. L, t. Gk: m. *terēdṓn* wood-boring worm]

Terence (tĕ′rəns), *n.* (*Publius Terentius Afer*), *c.* 190–*c.* 159 B.C., Roman dramatist.

Teresa (tə rē′ zə; *Sp.* tė rė′sȧ), *n.* See **Theresa.**

Tereshkova (*Russ.* tĭ rĭsh kô′və), *n.* **Valentina Vladimirovna** (*Russ.* və lĭn tē′nə vlȧ dē′mĭ rəv nə), born 1937, Soviet cosmonaut: first woman to fly in space.

Teresina (*Port.* tė rė zē′nȧ), *n.* a port in NE Brazil, on the Parnahiba river. 144,799 (1961).

terete (tĕ′rēt), *adj.* **1.** slender and smooth, with a circular transverse section. **2.** cylindrical or slightly tapering. [t. L: m. s. *teres* rounded]

Tereus (tĭə′rĭ əs), *n.* See **Philomela.**

tergal (tû′gl), *adj.* of or pertaining to the tergum. [f. s. L *tergum* back + -AL[1]]

tergite (tû′jīt), *n.* **1.** a dorsal sclerite of an arthropod. **2.** the dorsal sclerite of an abdominal segment of an insect.

tergiversate (tû′jĭ vû sāt′), *v.i.*, **-sated, -sating.** **1.** to change repeatedly one's attitude or opinions with respect to a cause, subject, etc. **2.** to turn renegade. [t. L: m. *tergiversātus*, pp., having turned the back] —**ter′giversa′tion,** *n.* —**ter′giversa′tor,** *n.*

tergum (tû′gəm), *n., pl.* **-ga** (-gə). *Zool.* the dorsal surface of a body segment of an arthropod. [t. L: the back]

term (tûm), *n.* **1.** any word or group of linguistic forms naming something, especially as used in some particular field of knowledge, as *atom* in physics, *quietism* in theology, or *adze* in carpentry. **2.** any word or group of linguistic forms considered as a member of a construction or utterance. **3.** the time or period through which something lasts. **4.** a period of time to which limits have been set: *elected for a term of four years.* **5.** each of certain stated periods of the year into which instruction is regularly organized for students or pupils in universities, colleges, and schools. **6.** an appointed or set time or date, as for the payment of rent, interest, wages, etc. **7.** (*pl.*) conditions with regard to payment, price, charge, rates, wages, etc.: *reasonable terms.* **8.** (*pl.*) conditions or stipulations limiting what is proposed to be granted or done: *the terms of a treaty.* **9.** (*pl.*) footing or standing: *on good terms with a person.* **10.** *Alg., Arith., etc.* each of the members of which an expression, a series of quantities, or the like, is composed, as one of two or more parts of an algebraic expression. **11.** *Logic.* **a.** the subject or predicate of a categorical proposition. **b.** the word or expression denoting the subject or predicate of a categorical preposition. **12.** *Archit., etc.* a boundary post with a statue or bust on it, esp. a bust of the ancient Roman god Terminus. **13.** *Law.* **a.** an estate or interest in land, etc., to be enjoyed for a fixed period: *a term of years.* **b.** the duration of an estate. **c.** each of the periods during which certain courts of law hold their sessions. **14.** the normal completion of the period of pregnancy. **15.** *Archaic.* end, conclusion, or termination. **16.** *Archaic.* a boundary or limit. **17.** (*pl.*) *Obs.* state, situation, or circumstance. **18. bring to terms,** to compel to agree to stated conditions; force into submission. **19. come to terms, a.** to reach agreement. **b.** to become accustomed or resigned. **20. contradiction in terms,** a statement which is self-contradictory. —*v.t.* **21.** to apply a particular term or name to; name; call; designate. [ME, t. OF: m. *terme*, g. L *terminus* boundary, limit, end]

term., 1. terminal. 2. termination.

termagant (tû′mə gənt), *n.* **1.** a violent, turbulent, or brawling woman. **2.** (*cap.*) *Archaic.* a mythical deity, understood in the Middle Ages to be worshipped by the Muslims, represented in some morality plays, etc., as a violent overbearing personage. —*adj.* **3.** violent; turbulent; brawling; shrewish. [ME *Termagaunt, Tervagant*, t. OF: m. *Tervagan* a supposed Muslim deity] —**ter′magancy,** *n.*

term day, a fixed or appointed day, as for the payment of money due; a quarter-day.

terminable (tû′mĭ nə bl, tûm′nə bl), *adj.* **1.** that may be terminated. **2.** (of an annuity) coming to an end after a certain term. —**ter′minabil′ity, ter′minableness,** *n.* —**ter′minably,** *adv.*

terminal (tû′mĭ nəl), *adj.* **1.** situated at or forming the end or extremity of something. **2.** occurring at or forming the end of a series, succession, or the like; closing; concluding. **3.** pertaining to or lasting for a term or definite period; occurring at fixed terms or in every term. **4.** pertaining to, situated at, or forming the terminus of a railway. **5.** *Bot.* growing at the end of a branch or stem, as a bud, inflorescence, etc. **6.** *Archit., etc.* designating a figure of the form of a term (def. 12). **7.** pertaining to or placed at a boundary, as a landmark. **8.** occurring at or causing the end of life: *terminal cancer.* —*n.* **9.** a terminal part or structure; end or extremity. **10.** a railway terminus. **11.** *Elect.* **a.** the mechanical device by means of which an electrical connection to an apparatus is established. **b.** the point of current entry to, or point of current departure from, any conducting component in an electric circuit. **12.** *Archit., etc.* **a.** a terminal figure. **b.** a carving or the like at the end of something, as a finial. [t. L: s. *terminālis* pertaining to an end or boundary] —**ter′minally,** *adv.*

terminal velocity, **1.** *Physics.* the maximum velocity attained by a body which falls through a resisting medium. **2.** *Aeron.* the maximum limiting velocity which an aircraft can attain as determined by its total drag. **3. a.** the velocity of a missile, rocket, shell, etc., on impact with its target. **b.** the maximum velocity attained by a missile, rocket, shell, etc., during the course of its flight.

terminate (tû′mĭ nāt′), *v.*, **-nated, -nating.** —*v.t.* **1.** bring to an end; put an end to. **2.** to occur at or form the conclusion of. **3.** to bound or limit spatially; form or be situated at the extremity of. —*v.i.* **4.** to end, conclude, or cease. **5.** (of a train, bus, etc.) to complete a scheduled journey at a certain place. **6.** to come to an end (often fol. by *at, in,* or *with*). **7.** to issue or result (usually fol. by *in*). [t. L: m. s. *terminātus*, pp., ended, limited, determined] —**terminative** (tû′mĭ nə tĭv), *adj.* —**ter′minatively,** *adv.*

termination (tû′mĭ nā′shən), *n.* **1.** the act of terminating. **2.** the fact of being terminated. **3.** the place at which or the part in which anything terminates; bound or limit. **4.** an end or extremity; close or conclusion. **5.** an issue or result. **6.** *Gram.* a suffix or ending. —**ter′mina′tional,** *adj.*

terminator (tû′mĭ nā′tə), *n.* **1.** one who or that which terminates. **2.** *Astron.* the dividing line between the illuminated and the unilluminated part of a heavenly body, esp. the moon.

terminism (tû′mĭ nĭz′əm), *n.* *Philos.* the doctrine, associated with Occam, that universals are solely terms. Cf. **nominalism.**

terminology (tû′mĭ nŏl′ə jĭ), *n.*, *pl.* **-gies.** **1.** the system of terms belonging to a science, art, or subject; nomenclature: *the terminology of botany.* **2.** the science of terms, as in particular sciences or arts. [t. G: m. *Terminologie*, f. *termino-* (comb. form repr. ML *terminus* term) + *-logie* -LOGY] —**terminological** (tû′mĭ nə lŏj′ĭ kl), *adj.* —**ter′minolog′ically,** *adv.* —**ter′minol′ogist,** *n.*

term insurance, life insurance for a stipulated term of years only, the heirs being paid the face value of the insurance upon death during the term, but nothing being paid upon survival at the completion of the term.

terminus (tû′mĭ nəs), *n.*, *pl.* **-ni** (-nī′), **-nuses.** **1.** the end or extremity of anything. **2.** either end of a railway line, bus route, etc. **3.** the station or town at the end of a railway line, bus route, etc. **4.** the point to which anything tends; goal or end. **5.** a boundary or limit. **6.** a boundary post or stone. **7.** (*cap.*) *Roman Myth.* the god who presided over boundaries and landmarks. **8.** a figure of this god, representing the upper part of the body and terminating below in a rectangular pillar, which serves as a pedestal. [t. L: boundary, limit, end]

terminus ad quem (ăd kwĕm′), *Latin.* the end to which; aim; finishing point.

terminus a quo (ä kwō′), *Latin.* the end from which; starting point; beginning.

termitarium (tû′mĭ tēə′rĭ əm), *n.*, *pl.* **-taria** (-tēə′rĭ ə), a termite colony's nest.

termite (tû′mīt), *n.* any of the pale-coloured, soft-bodied, mainly tropical, social insects constituting the order *Isoptera*, some of which are very destructive to buildings, furniture, household stores, etc.; white ant. [t. NL: m. s. *termes* termite (LL woodworm)]

Termite (Worker), *Termes flavipes* (¼ in. long)

termless (tûm′lĭs), *adj.* **1.** not limited; unconditional. **2.** boundless; endless.

termor (tû′mə), *n.* *Law.* one who has an estate for a term of years or for life.

terms of reference. See **reference** (def. 12).

tern¹ (tûn), *n.* any bird of the subfamily *Sterninae* (family *Laridae*), comprising numerous aquatic species which are allied to the gulls but usually with a more slender body and bill, smaller feet, a long and deeply forked tail, and a more graceful flight, esp. any of those constituting the genus *Sterna*, as the common sea-swallow of Europe and America, *S. hirundo*, a white bird with black crown and grey mantle. [t. Scand.; cf. Dan. *terne*]

Common tern, *Sterna hirundo* (15 in. long)

tern² (tûn), *n.* **1.** a set of three. **2.** three winning numbers drawn together in a lottery. **3.** a prize won by drawing these. [ME, t. F: m. *terne*, t. It.: m. *terno*, der. L *terni* three each]

ternary (tû′nə rĭ), *adj.*, *n.*, *pl.* **-ries.** —*adj.* **1.** consisting of or involving three; threehold; triple. **2.** third in order or rank. **3.** based on the number three. **4.** *Chem.* **a.** consisting of three different elements or radicals. **b.** (formerly) consisting of three atoms. **5.** *Maths.* having three variables. **6.** *Metall.* (of an alloy) having three constituents. —*n.* **7.** a group of three. [ME, t. LL: m. s. *ternārius* made up of three]

ternary fission, *Physics.* **1.** a rare form of nuclear fission in which a heavy nucleus breaks into three fragments of comparable mass. **2.** a more common form of fission in which one of the three fragments is much lighter than the others, as an alpha particle.

ternate (tû′nĭt, -nāt), *adj.* **1.** consisting of three; arranged in threes. **2.** *Bot.* **a.** consisting of three leaflets, as a compound leaf. **b.** having leaves arranged in whorls of three, as a plant. —**ter′nately,** *adv.*

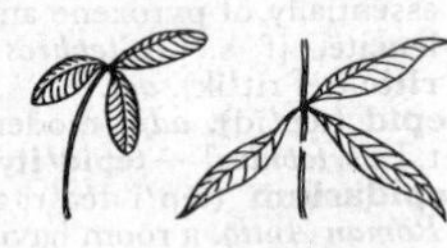

Ternate leaves

Ternate (tû nä′tĭ), *n.* an island in E Indonesia, W of Halmahera. 53 sq. mi.

terneplate (tûn′plāt′), *n.* an inferior tin plate, in which the tin is alloyed with a large proportion of lead. [f. *terne* (t. F: dull. See TARNISH) + PLATE¹]

Terni (*It.* tĕr′nē), *n.* a town in Italy, in S Umbria. 102,964 (1966).

ternion (tû′nĭ ən), *n.* a set or group of three; a triad. [t. L: s. *ternio*]

Ternopol (*Russ.* tĭr nô′pəly), *n.* a town in the SW Soviet Union in Europe: formerly in Poland. 52,000 (est. 1959). Also, **Tarnopol.**

terpene (tû′pēn), *n.* *Chem.* **1.** any of certain monocyclic hydrocarbons with the formula $C_{10}H_{16}$, occurring in essential or volatile oils. **2.** any of various compounds which contain isoprene structural units for their carbon skeletons and have the general formula $(C_5H_8)_n$. [t. G: m. *Terpen*, f. *Terp(entin)* TURPENTINE + *-en* -ENE].

terpinene (tû′pĭ nēn′), *n.* *Chem.* any of three isomeric liquid terpenes, $C_{10}H_{16}$, two of which occur naturally in various vegetable oils.

terpineol (tû pĭn′ĭ ŏl′), *n.* *Chem.* any of several unsaturated tertiary alcohols, $C_{10}H_{17}OH$, occurring naturally in essential oils or prepared synthetically, used in perfumery. [f. *terpine* (f. TERP(ENE) + -INE²) + -OL¹]

Terpsichore (tûp sĭk′ə rĭ), *n.* *Gk Myth.* the Muse of dancing and choral song.

terpsichorean (tûp′sĭ kə rĭən′), *adj.* **1.** pertaining to dancing. **2.** (*cap.*) of or pertaining to Terpsichore. —*n.* **3.** *Colloq.* a dancer.

terr., **1.** terrace. **2.** territory.

terra (tĕ′rə), *n.* earth; land. [t. L and It.: earth]

terra alba (tĕ′rə ăl′bə), any of various white, earthy or powdery substances as pipeclay, gypsum, kaolin, or magnesia. [t. L: white earth]

terrace (tĕ′rəs), *n.*, *v.*, **-raced, -racing.** —*n.* **1.** a raised level with a vertical or sloping front or sides faced with masonry, turf, or the like, esp. one of a series of levels rising one above another. **2.** a nearly level strip of land with a more or less abrupt descent along the margin of the sea, a lake, or a river. **3.** an open (usually paved) area connected with a house and serving as an outdoor living area. **4.** a row of houses running along the face or top of a slope, or a street with such a row or rows. —*v.t.* **5.** to form into or furnish with a terrace or terraces. [t. F, der. *terre* earth, g. L *terra*] —**ter′raceless,** *adj.*

terracotta (tĕ′rə kŏt′ə), *n.* **1.** a hard, usually unglazed earthenware of fine quality, used for architectural decorations, statuettes, vases, etc. **2.** something made of this, esp. a work of art. **3.** a brownish orange colour like that of much terracotta. —*adj.* **4.** made or having the colour of terracotta. [t. It.: baked earth, g. L *terra cocta*]

terra firma (tĕ′rə fû′mə), firm or solid earth; dry land, as opposed to water or air. [t. L: solid earth]

terrain (tĕ′rān), *n.* **1.** a tract of land, esp. as considered with reference to its natural features, military advantages, etc. **2.** *Geol.* terrane. [t. F, der. *terre* earth, g. L *terra*]

terra incognita (tĕ′rə ĭn kŏg′nĭ tə), an unknown or unexplored land. [L: unknown land]

terramara (tĕ′rə mä′rə), *n.*, *pl.* **-mare** (-mä′rĭ). a prehistoric settlement in N Italy, in the Po valley, whose remains are found in mounds. [t. It.: f. *terra* earth + *mara* var. of *marna* MARL¹]

terramycin (tĕ′rə mī′sĭn), *n.* **1.** an antibiotic similar to aureomycin. **2.** (*cap.*) a trademark for this.

terrane (tĕʹrān), *n.* *Geol.* a geological formation or series of formations. [see TERRAIN]

terrapin (tĕʹrə pĭn), *n.* **1.** any of various edible North American freshwater or tidewater turtles of the family *Emydidae*, esp. any of those constituting the genus *Malacylemmys* (**diamondback terrapins**) of the Atlantic and Gulf coasts of the U.S. **2.** any of various similar turtles. [t. Algonquian (of Virginia and Delaware), dim. of *torope, torupe* tortoise]

terraqueous (tĕ rāʹkwĭ əs), *adj.* consisting of land and water, as the earth. [f. s. L *terra* earth + AQUEOUS]

terrarium (tĕ rĕəʹrĭ əm), *n., pl.* **-rariums, -raria** (-rĕəʹrĭ ə). a vivarium for land animals (distinguished from *aquarium*). [t. NL, der. *terra* earth; modelled on AQUARIUM]

terra rossa (tĕʹrə rŏsʹə), a reddish clay soil characteristic of limestone regions which have a Mediterranean climate. [t. It.: red earth]

terrazzo (tĕ rătʹsō), *n.* a floor material of chippings of broken stone and cement, polished when in place. [t. It.: terrace, balcony, der. *terra* earth]

Terre Haute (tĕʹrə hōtʹ, tĕʹrĭ hŭtʹ), a town in the U.S., in W Indiana, on the Wabash. 72,500 (1960).

terrene (tĕʹrēn), *adj.* **1.** earthly; worldly. **2.** earthy. —*n.* **3.** the earth. **4.** a land or region. [ME, t. L: m. s. *terrēnus* pertaining to earth]

terreplein (tĕəʹplānʹ), *n.* *Fort.* the top platform or horizontal surface of a rampart, used to support cannon. [t. F: f. *terre* earth (g. L *terra*) + *plein* full (g. L *plēnus*)]

terrestrial (tĭ rĕsʹtrĭ əl), *adj.* **1.** pertaining to, consisting of, or representing the earth: *a terrestrial globe.* **2.** of or pertaining to the land as distinct from the water. **3.** *Bot.* **a.** growing on land; not aquatic. **b.** growing in the ground; not epiphytic or aerial. **4.** *Zool.* living on the ground; not aquatic, arboreal, or aerial. **5.** of or pertaining to the earth or this world; worldly; mundane. —*n.* **6.** an inhabitant of the earth, esp. a human being. [ME, f. L *terrestri(s)* pertaining to earth + -AL[1]] —**terresʹtrially,** *adv.* —**Syn. 5.** See **earthly.**

terrestrial magnetism, the magnetic field associated with the earth, due to which a freely suspended magnetized needle anywhere on the surface of the earth will set itself so that it points in the direction of the earth's magnetic North Pole.

terret (tĕʹrĭt), *n.* one of the round loops or rings on the saddle of a harness, through which the driving reins pass. [var. of ME *toret*, t. OF, dim. of *to(u)r* a round, circumference]

terre-verte (tĕəʹvĕətʹ), *n.* an olive-green pigment. [t. F: green earth]

terrible (tĕʹrə bl), *adj.* **1.** distressing; severe: *a terrible winter.* **2.** *Colloq.* extremely unpleasant or bad: *a terrible performance.* **3.** exciting or fitted to excite terror or great fear; dreadful; awful. [ME, t. L: m. s. *terribilis*] —**terʹribleness,** *n.* —**terʹribly,** *adv.* —**Syn. 1.** fearful, frightful, appalling, dire.

terricolous (tĕ rĭkʹə ləs), *adj.* *Bot., Zool.* living on or in the ground. [f. s. L *terricola* earth-dweller + -OUS]

terrier[1] (tĕʹrĭ ə), *n.* **1.** one of a variety of dogs, typically small, with a propensity to pursue prey, as the fox, badger, etc., into its burrow, occurring in many breeds including the fox-terrier, Irish terrier, Scottish terrier, Sealyham terrier, and Skye terrier. **2.** (*cap.*) *Colloq.* a soldier in the Territorial and Volunteer Reserve. [ME *terrere*, t. F: m. (*chien*) *terrier* a hunting dog to start badgers, etc., from their earth or burrow, der. *terre* earth, g. L *terra*]

terrier[2] (tĕʹrĭ ə), *n.* *Law.* a book or document in which are described the site, boundaries, acreage, etc., of lands privately owned by persons or corporations. [ME *terrere*, t. OF: m. *terreoir*, g. L *territōrium* territory]

terrific (tə rĭfʹĭk), *adj.* **1.** causing terror; terrifying. **2.** *Colloq.* extraordinarily great, intense, etc.: *terrific speed.* [t. L: s. *terrificus* frightening] —**terrifʹically,** *adv.*

terrify (tĕʹrĭ fīʹ), *v.t.,* **-fied, -fying.** to fill with terror; make greatly afraid. [t. L: m. s. *terrificāre*] —**terʹrifiʹer,** *n.* —**Syn.** See **frighten, afraid.**

terrigenous (tĕ rĭjʹĭ nəs), *adj.* **1.** produced by the earth. **2.** *Geol.* denoting or pertaining to sediments on the sea bottom derived directly from the neighbouring land, or to the rocks formed primarily by the consolidation of such sediments. [t. L: m. *terrigenus* earthborn]

terrine (tĕ rēnʹ), *n.* **1.** an earthenware cooking dish. **2.** a pâté of meat or game served in such a dish. **3.** a tureen. [t. F. See TUREEN]

territorial (tĕʹrĭ tôʹrĭ əl), *adj.* **1.** of or pertaining to territory or land. **2.** of, pertaining to, associated with, or restricted to a particular territory or district; local. **3.** pertaining or belonging to the territory of a state or ruler. **4.** (*cap.*) of or pertaining to a Territory of Australia, Canada, the U.S., or elsewhere. **5.** of or pertaining to a territorial army. —*n.* **6.** (*sometimes cap.*) a soldier in a territorial army. —**terʹritoʹrially,** *adv.*

territorial army, a voluntary force organized on a territorial basis to provide a reserve of trained, disciplined manpower for any emergency, as the British **Territorial and Volunteer Reserve.**

territorialism (tĕʹrĭ tôʹrĭ ə lĭzʹəm), *n.* **1.** the principle of the predominance of the landed classes. **2.** organization on a territorial basis. **3.** Also, **territorial system.** *Eccles.* the theory of Church policy according to which the supreme ecclesiastical authority is vested in the civil power. —**terʹritoʹrialist,** *n.*

territoriality (tĕʹrĭ tôʹrĭ ălʹĭ tĭ), *n.* **1.** territorial quality, condition, or status. **2.** the behaviour of an animal in claiming and defending its territory.

territorialize (tĕʹrĭ tôʹrĭ ə līzʹ), *v.t.,* **-lized, -lizing. 1.** to make a territory of. **2.** to extend by adding new territory. **3.** to organize or reorganize on a territorial basis. Also, **territorialise.** —**terʹritoʹrializaʹtion,** *n.*

territorial waters, that part of the sea adjacent to the coast of a country regarded under international law as within the territorial sovereignty of that country.

territory (tĕʹrĭ tə rĭ, -trĭ), *n., pl.* **-ries. 1.** any tract of land; region or district. **2.** the land and waters belonging to or under the jurisdiction of a state, sovereign, etc. **3.** any separate tract of land belonging to a state. **4.** (*often cap.*) a region administered by a government in which it is not fully represented. See **trust territory. 5.** *U.S.* formerly, a region or district not admitted to the Union as a state but having its own legislature, with a governor and other officers appointed by the President and confirmed by the Senate. **6.** the field of action, thought, etc.; domain or province of something. **7.** the region or district assigned to a representative, agent, or the like, for making sales, etc. **8.** the area which an animal or pair of animals claim as their own and defend against intruders of the same species. [ME, t. L: m. s. *territōrium* land round a town, district]

terror (tĕʹrə), *n.* **1.** intense, sharp, overpowering fear: *to be frantic with terror.* **2.** a feeling, instance or cause of intense fear: *to be a terror to evildoers.* **3.** (*cap.*) a period when a political group uses violence to maintain or achieve supremacy. See **Reign of Terror. 4.** (*cap.*) any terrorist group, regime, etc. **5.** *Colloq.* a person or thing that is a particular nuisance: *that boy is a little terror.* [t. L; r. ME *terrour*, t. F or L] —**terʹrorless,** *adj.*

—**Syn. 1.** TERROR, HORROR, PANIC, FRIGHT all imply extreme fear in the presence of danger or evil. TERROR implies an intense fear which is somewhat prolonged and may refer to imagined or future dangers: *frozen with terror at strange sounds in the night.* HORROR implies a sense of shock at a danger or evil which may be to others rather than to oneself: *to recoil in horror as the man threw himself into the fire.* PANIC and FRIGHT both imply a sudden shock of fear. FRIGHT is usually of short duration: *a spasm of fright.* PANIC is uncontrolled and unreasoning fear, often groundless, which may be prolonged: *the mob was in a panic when the horses stampeded.*

terrorism (tĕʹrə rĭzʹəm), *n.* **1.** the use of terrorizing methods. **2.** the state of fear and submission so produced. **3.** a method of resisting a government or of governing by deliberate acts of armed violence.

terrorist (tĕʹrə rĭst), *n.* **1.** one who uses or favours terrorizing methods of resisting a government or of governing. **2.** (formerly) a member of a political group in Russia aiming at the demoralization of the government by terror. **3.** an agent or partisan of the revolutionary tribunal during the Reign of Terror in France. —*adj.* **4.** Also, **terʹrorisʹtic.** denoting or pertaining to terrorists or their methods. [t. F: m. *terroriste*, der. L *terror* terror]

terrorize (tĕʹrə rīzʹ), *v.t.,* **-rized, -rizing. 1.** to fill or overcome with terror. **2.** to dominate or coerce by intimidation. Also, **terrorise.** —**terʹrorizaʹtion,** *n.* —**terʹrorizʹer,** *n.*

terror-stricken (tĕʹrə strĭkʹən), *adj.* smitten with terror; terrified. Also, **terror-struck** (tĕʹrə strŭkʹ).

terry (tĕʹrĭ), *n., pl.* **-ries,** *adj.* —*n.* **1.** the loop formed by the pile of a fabric when left uncut. **2.** Also, **terry cloth.** a pile fabric with loops on both sides, as in a Turkish towel. —*adj.* **3.** having the pile loops uncut: *terry velvet.* [? var. of TERRET]

Terry (tĕʹrĭ), *n.* **Dame Ellen (Alicia),** 1848–1928, English actress.

Tersanctus (tûʹsăngkʹtəs), *n.* *Eccles.* the Sanctus. [t. NL, lit. thrice holy]

terse (tûs), *adj.,* **terser, tersest.** neatly or effectively concise; brief and pithy, as language. [t. L: m. s. *tersus*, pp., polished] —**terseʹly,** *adv.* —**terseʹness,** *n.*

tertial (tûʹshəl), *Ornith.* —*adj.* **1.** pertaining to any of a set of flight feathers situated on the basal segment of a bird's wing. —*n.* **2.** a tertial feather. [f. s. L *tertius* third + -AL[1]]

tertian (tûʹshən), *adj.* **1.** (of a fever, ague, etc.) characterized by paroxysms which recur every other day. —*n.* 2. a tertian fever or ague. 3. (in certain Scottish universities) a third-year student. 4. a Jesuit during his tertianship. [ME *tercian*, t. L: m. s. (*febris*) *tertiāna* tertian (fever), der. *tertius* third]

tertianship (tûr′shən shĭp′), *n.* the third period in the training of a Jesuit when under strict discipline he prepares for full, lifelong membership of the Society.

tertiary (tûr′shə rĭ), *adj.*, *n.*, *pl.* **-ries.** —*adj.* 1. of the third order, rank, formation, etc.; third. 2. *Chem.* **a.** denoting or containing a carbon atom united to three other carbon atoms. **b.** formed by replacement of three atoms or radicals. 3. (*cap.*) *Geol.* pertaining to a geological period or a system of rocks which precedes the Quaternary and constitutes the earlier principal division of the Cainozoic era. 4. *Ornith.* tertial. 5. *Eccles.* denoting or pertaining to a branch (third order) of certain religious orders which consists of lay members living in community (**regular tertiaries**) or living in the world (**secular tertiaries**). —*n.* 6. (*cap.*) *Geol.* the period or system representing geological time from about 2 to 60 million years ago and comprising Palaeocene to Pliocene epochs or series. 7. *Ornith.* a tertial feather. 8. (*also cap.*) *Eccles.* a member of a tertiary branch of a religious order. [t. L: m. s. *tertiārius* of third part or rank]

tertiary colour, a colour produced by mixing two or more secondary colours, as brown or grey.

tertium quid (tûr′tyəm kwĭd′), something related in some way to two things, but distinct from both; something intermediate between two things. [t. L, trans. of Gk *trítos ti* some third thing]

tertius (tûr′shyəs), *adj.* (placed after the noun) (in some boys' schools) minimus.

Tertullian (tûr tŭl′ĭ ən), *n.* (*Quintus Septimius Florens Tertullianus*), A.D. *c.* 150–after 220, Christian theologian of N Africa.

tervalent (tûr′vā′lənt), *adj. Chem.* 1. trivalent. 2. possessing three different valencies, as cobalt with valencies 2, 3, and 4. [f. L *ter* thrice + VALENT]

Terylene (tĕ′rə lēn′), *n. Trademark.* a synthetic polyester fibre, used in the manufacture of clothing, etc., made from ethylene glycol and terephthalic acid.

terza rima (tĕə′tsə rē′mə), *Pros.* an Italian form of iambic verse consisting of eleven-syllable lines arranged in tercets, the middle line of each rhyming with the first and third lines of the following tercet. [It.: third rhyme]

tesla (tĕs′lə), *n. Physics.* the derived SI unit of magnetic flux density, defined as the density of one weber of magnetic flux per square metre. *Symbol:* T [named after Nikola *Tesla*, 1856–1943, U.S. electrical engineer]

tessellate (*v.* tĕs′ĭ lāt′; *adj.* tĕs′ĭ lĭt, -lāt′), *v.*, **-lated, -lating,** *adj.* —*v.t.* 1. to form of small squares or blocks, as floors, pavements, etc.; form or arrange in a chequered or mosaic pattern. —*adj.* 2. like a mosaic; tessellated. [t. LL: m. s. *tessellātus*, pp., formed in mosaic]

tessellation (tĕs′ĭ lā′shən), *n.* 1. the act or art of tessellating. 2. tessellated form or arrangement. 3. tessellated work.

tessera (tĕs′ə rə), *n.*, *pl.* **tesserae** (tĕs′ə rē′). 1. each of the small pieces used in mosaic work. 2. a small square of bone, wood, or the like, anciently used as a token, tally, ticket, due, etc. [t. L, t. d. Gk: lit., four] —**tes′seral,** *adj.*

Tessin (*Ger.* tĕ sēn′), *n.* German name of **Ticino.**

tessitura (tĕs′ĭ to͝oə′rə), *n.*, *pl.* **-turas, -ture** (-to͝oə′rĭ). *Music.* the range or compass of a voice or of a piece of music in relation to the normal range of a voice: *the song has a high tessitura.* [t. It.: lit., texture]

test[1] (tĕst), *n.* 1. that by which the presence, quality, or genuineness of anything is determined; a means of trial. 2. the trial of the quality of something: *to put to the test.* 3. a particular process or method of doing this. 4. *Educ.* a form of examination for evaluating the performance and capabilities of a student or class. 5. *Psychol.* a standardized procedure for eliciting responses upon which appraisal of the individual can be based: *an intelligence test.* 6. *Chem.* **a.** the process of detecting the presence of an ingredient in a compound or the like, or of determining the nature of a substance, commonly by the addition of a reagent. **b.** the reagent used. **c.** an indication or evidence of the presence of an ingredient, or of the nature of a substance, obtained by such means. 7. a cupel for assaying or refining metals. 8. *Sport.* a test match. —*v.t.* 9. to subject to a test of any kind; try. 10. *Chem.* to subject to a chemical test. 11. to assay or refine in a test or cupel. —*v.i.* 12. to conduct a test or series of tests. [ME, t. OF: cupel, g. L *testu(m)*, var. of *testa* tile, earthen vessel, pot] —**test′able,** *adj.* —**Syn.** 1. See **trial.**

test[2] (tĕst), *n.* 1. *Zool.* the hard covering of certain invertebrates, as molluscs, arthropods, tunicates, etc.; shell; lorica. 2. *Bot.* testa. [t. L: s. *testa* (see TEST[1])]

Test., Testament.

testa (tĕs′tə), *n.*, *pl.* **-tae** (-tē). *Bot.* the outer, usually hard, integument or coat of a seed. See diag. under **seed.** [t. L. See TEST[2]]

testaceous (tĕs tā′shəs), *adj. Bot.*, *Zool.* 1. having a hard shell. 2. of a brick red, brownish red, or brownish yellow colour. [t. L: m. *testāceus* shell-covered]

Test Act, *Hist.* a statute, passed 1673 and repealed 1828, requiring military officers and public officials to swear an oath of allegiance to the Crown and take the sacraments of the Church of England.

testacy (tĕs′tə sĭ), *n.* the state of being testate.

testament (tĕs′tə mənt), *n.* 1. *Law.* **a.** a formal declaration, usually in writing, of a person's wishes as to the disposition of his property after his death. **b.** a disposition to take effect upon death and relating to personal property. 2. a covenant, esp. between God and man. 3. (*cap.*) either of the two main divisions of the Bible: the Mosaic or old covenant or dispensation, or the Christian or new covenant or dispensation. 4. (*cap.*) the New Testament, as distinct from the Old Testament. 5. a copy of the New Testament. [ME, t. L: s. *testāmentum* will]

testamentary (tĕs′tə mĕn′tə rĭ), *adj.* 1. of, pertaining to, or of the nature of a testament or will. 2. given, bequeathed, done, or appointed by will. 3. set forth or contained in a will.

testate (tĕs′tāt, tĕs′tĭt), *adj.* having made and left a valid will. [late ME, t. L: m. s. *testātus*, pp.]

testation (tĕs tā′shən), *n.* 1. the disposal of property by will. 2. *Obs.* attestation; witnessing.

testator (tĕs tā′tə), *n.* 1. one who makes a will. 2. one who has died leaving a valid will. [t. L; r. ME *testatour*, t. AF]

testatrix (tĕs tā′trĭks), *n.*, *pl.* **-trices** (-trĭ sēz′). a female testator.

testatum (tĕs tā′təm), *n. Law.* the witnessing part of a deed or agreement.

test-ban (tĕst′băn′), *adj.* denoting or pertaining to a treaty or agreement between nations not to test nuclear weapons, or to test them only under limited conditions, as not in the atmosphere.

test bed, a framework and foundation on which an electrical machine or an engine is placed for the purpose of carrying out a test under load.

test case, a legal or other case which establishes a precedent for reference in similar cases.

tester[1] (tĕs′tə), *n.* one who or that which tests. [f. TEST[1], v. + -ER[1]]

tester[2] (tĕs′tə), *n.* a canopy or support, or both, as over a bed, altar, etc. [late ME. Cf. OF *testre* headboard of bed, *testiere* head covering, der. *teste* head, g. L *testa* pot]

tester[3] (tĕs′tə), *n.* 1. the teston of Henry VIII. 2. *Obs. Colloq.* a sixpence. [appar. alter. of TESTON]

testes (tĕs′tēz), *n.* pl. of **testis.**

testicle (tĕs′tĭ kl), *n. Anat.*, *Zool.* the male sex gland, either of two oval glands situated in the scrotal sac. [t. L: m. *testiculus*, dim. of *testis* TESTIS] —**testicular** (tĕs tĭk′yo͝o lə), *adj.*

testiculate (tĕs tĭk′yo͝o lĭt), *adj. Bot.* 1. shaped like a testicle. 2. having tubers shaped like testicles, as certain orchids.

testification (tĕs′tĭ fĭ kā′shən), *n.* the act of testifying or bearing witness.

testify (tĕs′tĭ fī′), *v.*, **-fied, -fying.** —*v.i.* 1. to bear witness; give or afford evidence. 2. to make solemn declaration. 3. *Law.* to give testimony under oath or solemn affirmation, usually in court. —*v.t.* 4. to bear witness to; affirm as fact or truth. 5. to give or afford evidence of in any manner. 6. to declare, profess, or acknowledge openly. 7. *Law.* to state or declare under oath or affirmation, usually in court. [ME, t. L: m. s. *testificārī* bear witness] —**tes′tifi′er,** *n.*

testimonial (tĕs′tĭ mō′nyəl), *n.* 1. a writing certifying to a person's character, conduct, or qualifications, or to a thing's value, excellence, etc.; a letter or written statement of recommendation. 2. something given or done as an expression of esteem, admiration, or gratitude. —*adj.* 3. pertaining to or serving as testimony.

testimonialize (tĕs′tĭ mō′nyə līz′), *v.t.*, **-lized, -lizing.** to present with a testimonial. Also, **testimonialise.**

testimony (tĕs′tĭ mə nĭ), *n.*, *pl.* **-nies.** 1. *Law.* the statement or declaration of a witness under oath or affirmation, usually in court. 2. evidence in support of a fact or statement; proof. 3. open declaration or profession, as of faith. 4. (*pl.*) the precepts of God. 5. *Bible.* the Decalogue as inscribed on the two tables of the law, or the ark in which the tables were kept. Ex. 25:16, 16:34. 6. *Archaic.* a declaration of disapproval; protest. [late ME, t. L: m. s. *testimōnium* evidence, attestation] —**Syn.** 1. See **evidence.**

testis (tĕs′tĭs), *n.*, *pl.* **-tes** (-tēz). testicle. [t. L]

test match, *Sport.* a match or one of a series of matches, esp. in cricket, between two nationally representative teams.

teston (tĕs′tən, tĕs to͞on′), *n.* **1.** an early silver coin in France, valued between 10 and 14½ sous. **2.** any of various silver coins formerly current, with a head or portrait on the obverse; in England, the shilling of Henry VIII, or Edward VI, reduced in value successively to tenpence, ninepence, and sixpence. Also, **testoon** (tĕs to͞on′). [t. F, t. It.: m. *testone*, aug. of *testa* head, g. L *testa* potsherd]

testosterone (tĕs tŏs′tə rōn′), *n. Biochem.* the hormone, $C_{19}H_{28}O_2$, secreted by the testes and obtained by extraction from animal testes and by synthesis. It stimulates the development of masculine characteristics. [f. *testo-* TESTIS + STER(OL) + -ONE]

test paper, 1. a set of questions to be answered under examination conditions, as one used in practice for an examination. **2.** *U.S.* a paper bearing answers given in an examination. **3.** *Chem.* paper impregnated with a reagent, as litmus, which changes colour when acted upon by certain substances.

test-pilot (tĕst′pī′lət), *n.* a pilot employed to test new aircraft by flying them in such a way that they are subjected to maximum strains.

test tube, *Chem.* a hollow cylinder of thin glass with one end closed, used in chemical tests.

test-tube baby (tĕst′tyo͞ob′), **1.** a child born as a result of artificial insemination. **2.** a child conceived artificially outside a mother's body under simulated conditions suitable for its survival.

testudinate (tĕs tyo͞o′dĭ nĭt, -nāt′), *adj.* formed like the carapace of a tortoise; arched; vaulted.

testudo (tĕs tyo͞o′dō), *n., pl.* **-dines** (-dĭ nēz′). **1.** *Fort.* (among the ancient Romans) a movable shelter with a strong and usually fireproof arched roof, used for protection of soldiers in siege operations. **2.** a shelter formed by soldiers overlapping their oblong shields above their heads. [ME, t. L: tortoise]

testy (tĕs′tĭ), *adj.,* **-tier, -tiest.** irritably impatient; touchy. [ME, t. AF: m. *testif* headstrong, der. OF *teste* head, g. L *testa* potsherd] —**tes′tily,** *adv.* —**tes′tiness,** *n.*

tetanic (tĭ tăn′ĭk), *adj.* **1.** *Pathol.* pertaining to, of the nature of, or characterized by tetanus. **2.** *Med.* denoting a remedy which acts on the nerves and through them on the muscles, and which, if taken in overdoses, causes tetanic spasms of the muscles and death. Also, **tetan′ical.**

tetanize (tĕt′ə nīz′), *v.t.,* **-nized, -nizing.** *Physiol.* to induce a condition of tetanus in (a muscle). Also, **tetanise.** —**tet′aniza′tion,** *n.*

tetanus (tĕt′ə nəs), *n.* **1.** *Pathol.* **a.** an infectious, often fatal disease, due to a specific micro-organism, the **tetanus bacillus,** which gains entrance to the body through wounds, characterized by more or less violent tonic spasms and rigidity of many or all the voluntary muscles, esp. those of the neck and lower jaw. Cf. **lockjaw. b.** the micro-organism, *Clostridium tetani,* which causes this disease. **2.** *Physiol.* tonic contractions of a skeletal muscle induced by rapid stimulation. [t. L, t. Gk: m. *tétanos* spasm (of muscles)] —**tet′anoid′,** *adj.*

tetany (tĕt′ə nĭ), *n. Pathol.* a state marked by severe intermittent tonic contractions and muscular pain, frequently due to a deficiency of calcium salts. [t. NL: m. s. *tetania.* See TETANUS]

tetartohedral (tĭ tä′tō hē′drəl), *adj.* (of a crystal) having one fourth the planes or faces required by the maximum symmetry of the system to which it belongs. [f. *tetarto-* (t. Gk, comb. form of *tétartos* fourth) + -HEDR(ON) + -AL[1]] —**tetar′tohe′drally,** *adv.* —**tetar′tohe′dralism,** *n.*

tetchy (tĕch′ĭ), *adj.,* **tetchier, tetchiest.** irritable; touchy. Also, **techy.** [orig. uncert.] —**tetch′ily,** *adv.* —**tetch′iness,** *n.*

tete-a-tete (tāt′ä tāt′), *adj.* **1.** of, between, or for two persons together, without others. —*n.* **2.** a private conversation or interview, usually between two people. **3.** a sofa shaped like an S so that two people are able to converse face to face. —*adv.* **4.** (of two persons) together in private: *to sit tete-a-tete.* Also, *French,* **tête-à-tête** (*Fr.* tĕ tȧ tĕt′). [t. F: head to head]

tete-beche (tĕt′bĕsh′), *adj. Philately.* (of an unsevered pair of stamps) reversed in relation to each other, either through error or intentionally. Also, *French,* **tête-bêche** (*Fr.* tĕt bĕsh′). [t. F: f. *tête* head + *bêche,* reduced from *bechenet* double-bed head]

tête-de-pont (*Fr.* tĕt də pôɴ′), *n., pl.* **têtes-de-pont** (*Fr.* tĕt də pôɴ′). *French.* bridgehead.

tether (tĕth′ə), *n.* **1.** a rope, chain, or the like, by which an animal is fastened, as to a stake, so that its range of movement is limited. **2.** the utmost length to which one can go in action; the utmost extent or limit of ability or resources. **3. at the end of one's tether,** having exhausted one's possibilities, patience, or resources. —*v.t.* **4.** to fasten or confine with or as with a tether. [ME *tethir,* appar. t. Scand.; cf. Icel. *tjōdhr*]

Tethys (tē′thĭs, tĕth′ĭs), *n. Gk Myth.* a Titaness and sea goddess, daughter of Uranus and consort of Oceanus.

tetra (tĕt′rə), *n.* any of several highly coloured tropical fish of the family *Characinidae,* often kept in home aquariums.

tetra-, a word element meaning 'four' as in *tetrabrach.* [t. Gk, comb. form of *téttares*]

tetrabasic (tĕt′rə bā′sĭk), *adj. Chem.* **1.** (of an acid) having four atoms of hydrogen replaceable by basic atoms or radicals. **2.** containing four basic atoms or radicals having a valency of one.

tetrabrach (tĕt′rə brăk′), *n. Class. Pros.* a metrical foot or word of four short syllables. [t. Gk: s. *tetrábrachys* having four short syllables]

tetrabranchiate (tĕt′rə brăng′kĭ ĭt, -āt′), *adj.* belonging or pertaining to the *Tetrabranchiata,* a subclass or order of cephalopods with four gills, including the pearly nautilus and numerous fossil forms. [t. NL: m. s. *tetrabranchiātum,* f. Gk *tetra-* TETRA- + s. Gk *bránchia* gills + *-ātum* -ATE[1]]

tetrachloroethylene (tĕt′rə klō′rō ĕth′ĭ lēn′), *n. Chem.* a colourless liquid, C_2Cl_4, used as a solvent, esp. in dry cleaning; perchlorethylene.

tetrachord (tĕt′rə kôd′), *n. Music.* a diatonic series of four notes, the first and last separated by a perfect fourth. [t. Gk: s. *tetráchordos* having four strings] —**tet′rachor′dal,** *adj.*

tetracid (tĕ trăs′ĭd), *n. Chem.* a base or an alcohol containing four hydroxyl (OH) groups.

tetrad (tĕt′răd), *n.* **1.** a group of four. **2.** the number four. **3.** *Chem.* a tetravalent or quadrivalent element, atom, or radical. [t. Gk: s. *tetrás* group of four]

tetradymite (tĕ trăd′ĭ mīt′), *n.* a mineral, bismuth telluride and sulphide, Bi_2Te_2S, occurring in soft grey to black foliated masses. [t. G: m. *Tetradymit,* f. s. Gk *tetrádymos* fourfold + *-it* -ITE[1]]

tetradynamous (tĕt′rə dī′nə məs, -dĭn′ə-), *adj. Bot.* having four long and two short stamens, as in many cruciferous flowers.

tetraethyl lead (tĕt′rə ĕth′ĭl), *Chem.* lead tetraethyl.

tetrafluoroethylene (tĕt′rə flo͞oə′rō ĕth′ĭ lēn′), *n. Chem.* a colourless gas, C_2F_4, which polymerizes into a thermoplastic material with good electrical-insulation properties.

tetragon (tĕt′rə gən), *n. Geom.* a plane figure having four angles; a quadrangle; a quadrilateral. [t. Gk: s. *tetrágōnon* quadrangle]

tetragonal (tĕ trăg′ə nəl), *adj.* **1.** pertaining to a tetragon. **2.** *Crystall.* denoting or pertaining to the tetragonal system.

tetragonal system, *Crystall.* a system of crystallization in which all three axes are at right angles to one another, and the two equal lateral axes differ in length from the vertical axis.

tetragram (tĕt′rə grăm′), *n.* **1.** a word of four letters. **2.** (*also cap.*) the Tetragrammaton. [t. Gk: m. s. *tetrágrammon*]

Tetragrammaton (tĕt′rə grăm′ə tən), *n.* the Hebrew word written JHVH (or JHWH, YHVH, YHWH), representing, without vowels, the 'ineffable name' of God, pronounced in Hebrew as 'Adonai' and commonly transliterated in English as 'Jehovah'. See **Yahweh.** [ME, t. Gk: the four-letter (word)]

tetrahedral (tĕt′rə hē′drəl), *adj.* **1.** pertaining to or having the form of a tetrahedron. **2.** having four lateral planes in addition to the top and bottom. —**tet′rahe′drally,** *adv.*

tetrahedrite (tĕt′rə hē′drīt), *n.* a steel-grey or blackish mineral with a brilliant metallic lustre, essentially copper and antimony sulphide (nearly Cu_3SbS_3), but often containing other elements, as silver, etc., occurring in tetrahedral crystals and massive, and forming an important ore of copper and sometimes of silver.

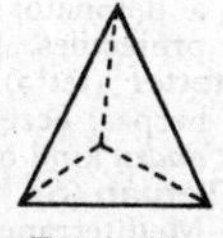
Tetrahedron

tetrahedron (tĕt′rə hē′drən), *n., pl.* **-drons, -dra** (-drə). *Geom.* a solid contained by four plane faces; a triangular pyramid. [t. LGk: m. *tetráedron,* neut. of *tetráedros* four-sided. See -HEDRON]

tetralogy (tĕ trăl′ə jĭ), *n., pl.* **-gies. 1.** a series of four related dramas, operas, etc. **2.** a group of four dramas, three tragic and one satiric, exhibited consecutively at the festival of Dionysus in ancient Athens. [t. Gk: m. s. *tetralogía*]

Tetramerous flower

tetramerous (tĕ trăm′ə rəs), *adj.* **1.** consisting of or divided into four parts. **2.** *Bot.* (of flowers) having four members in each whorl. [t. NL: m. *tetramerus*, t. Gk: m. *tetramerḗs* four-parted]

tetrameter (tĕ trăm′ĭ tə), *Pros.* —*adj.* **1.** having four measures. —*n.* **2.** a tetrameter line. In ancient poetry, it consisted of four dipodies (eight feet) in trochaic, iambic, or anapaestic metre. [t. L: m. s. *tetrametrus*, t. Gk: m. *tetrámetros*]

tetramorphism (tĕt′rə môr′fĭz′əm), *n. Crystall.* the property of some substances of crystallizing in four structurally distinct forms. —**tet′ramor′phic, tet′ramor′phous,** *adj.*

tetrandrous (tĕ trăn′drəs), *adj. Bot.* **1.** (of a flower) having four stamens. **2.** (of a plant) having flowers with four stamens.

tetrapetalous (tĕt′rə pĕt′ə ləs), *adj. Bot.* having four petals.

tetraplegia (tĕt′rə plē′jyə), *n. Pathol.* paralysis of all four limbs.

tetrapod (tĕt′rə pŏd′), *n.* any amphibian, reptile, bird, or mammal, the four classes of vertebrates, the members of which typically have four limbs.

tetrapody (tĕ trăp′ə dĭ), *n.* a group of four metrical feet. —**tetrapodic** (tĕt′rə pŏd′ĭk), *adj.*

tetrapterous (tĕ trăp′tə rəs), *adj.* **1.** *Zool.* having four wings or winglike appendages. **2.** *Bot.* having four winglike appendages. [t. Gk: m. *tetrápteros*]

Tetrapterous fruit
A, Silverbell tree, *Halesia carolina*; B, Transverse section

tetrarch (tē′trärk), *n.* **1.** any ruler of a fourth part, division, etc. **2.** a subordinate ruler generally. **3.** one of four joint rulers or chiefs. **4.** (in the ancient Roman Empire) the ruler of the fourth part of a country or province. [ME, t. LL: s. *tetrarcha*, var. of L *tetrarchēs*, t. Gk: ruler of one of four (parts)] —**tetrarchate** (tē′trä kāt′, -kĭt),

tetrarchy (tē′trä′kĭ), *n.*

tetrasporangium (tĕt′rə spô răn′ jĭ əm), *n., pl.* **-gia** (-jĭ ə). *Bot.* a sporangium containing four asexual spores (tetraspores).

tetraspore (tĕt′rə spô′), *n. Bot.* one of the four asexual spores produced within a tetrasporangium. —**tetrasporic** (tĕt′rə-spŏ′rĭk), **tetrasporous** (tĕt′rə spô′rəs, tĕ-trăs′pə rəs), *adj.*

tetrastich (tĕt′rə stĭk′), *n.* a poem, stanza, or set of four lines. —**tetrastichic** (tĕt′rə stĭk′ĭk), **tetrastichal** (tĕ-trăs′tĭ kl), *adj.*

tetrastichous (tĕ trăs′tĭ kəs), *adj. Bot.* **1.** arranged in a spike of four vertical rows, as flowers. **2.** having four such rows of flowers, as a spike. [t. Gk: m. *tetrástichos* having four rows]

tetrasyllable (tĕt′rə sĭl′ə bl), *n.* a word of four syllables. —**tetrasyllabic** (tĕt′rə sĭ lăb′ĭk), **tet′rasyllab′ical,** *adj.*

tetratomic (tĕt′rə tŏm′ĭk), *adj. Chem.* **1.** having four atoms in the molecule. **2.** having a valency of four. **3.** containing four replaceable atoms or groups.

tetravalent (tĕt′rə vā′lənt, tĕ trăv′ə lənt), *adj. Chem.* **1.** having a valency of four. **2.** quadrivalent.

Tetrazzini (*It.* tĕ trät tsē′nē), *n.* **Luisa** (*It.* lwē′zä), 1874–1940, Italian operatic soprano.

tetrode (tĕt′rōd), *n. Electronics.* a radio valve containing four electrodes, usually an anode, two grids, and a cathode.

tetrose (tĕt′rōs), *n. Chem.* a monosaccharide which contains four oxygen atoms in its molecule.

tetroxide (tĕ trŏk′sīd), *n. Chem.* an oxide which contains in its molecule four atoms of oxygen. Also, **tetroxid** (tĕ trŏk′sĭd).

tetryl (tĕt′rĭl), *n.* a military explosive, $C_7H_5N_5O_8$, used as a detonator and as a bursting charge in small-calibre projectiles. [f. TETR(A)- + -YL]

tetter (tĕt′ə), *n.* any of various cutaneous diseases, as herpes, eczema, impetigo, etc. [ME; OE *teter*, c. Skt *dadru* kind of skin disease]

Tetuán (*Sp.* tĕ twän′), *n.* a seaport in N Morocco, on the Mediterranean: former capital of the Spanish zone of Morocco. 100,000 (est. 1965).

Tetzel (*Ger.* tĕt′səl), *n.* **Johann** (*Ger.* yō′hän), 1465?–1519, German monk: seller of papal indulgences. Also, **Tezel.**

Teucer (tyōō′sə), *adj. Gk Legend.* **1.** the first king of Troy. **2.** a noted archer, son of Telamon.

Teucrian (tyōō′krĭ ən), *adj.* **1.** of or pertaining to the ancient Trojans, or to Teucer, their first king. —*n.* **2.** one of the ancient Trojans.

Teut., **1.** Teuton. **2.** Teutonic.

Teutoburger Wald (*Ger.* tŏy′tō bōōr gər vält), a chain of wooded hills in N West Germany, in Westphalia: German defeat of the Romans A.D. 9.

Teuton (tyōō′tən), *n.* **1.** a member of a Germanic people or tribe first mentioned in the 4th century B.C. and supposed to have dwelt in Jutland. **2.** a native of Germany or a person of German origin. —*adj.* **3.** Teutonic. [t. L: s. *Teutonēs, Teutonī* (pl.) tribal name]

Teutonic (tyōō tŏn′ĭk), *adj.* **1.** of or pertaining to the ancient Teutons. **2.** of or pertaining to the Teutons or Germans; German. **3.** denoting or pertaining to the northern European stock which includes the German, Dutch, Scandinavian, British, and related peoples. **4.** (of languages) Germanic. **5.** *Obs.* Nordic. —*n.* **6.** Germanic. —**Teuton′ically,** *adv.*

Teutonicism (tyōō tŏn′ĭ sĭz′əm), *n.* **1.** the character or spirit of the Teutons, esp. the Germans. **2.** a Teutonic characteristic. **3.** a Germanism.

Teutonic Order, a military and religious order founded (*c.*1190) in the Holy Land during the Third Crusade. At first devoted to charitable pursuits, it was later instrumental in the eastward expansion of medieval Germany against the Slavic and Baltic peoples. Also, **Teutonic Knights.**

Teutonism (tyōō′tə nĭz′əm), *n.* **1.** the culture of the Teutons. **2.** the study of Teutonic culture. —**Teu′tonist,** *n.*

Teutonize (tyōō′tə nīz′), *v.t., v.i.,* **-nized, -nizing.** to make or become Teutonic. Also, **Teutonise.** —**Teu′toniza′tion,** *n.*

Tevere (*It.* tĕ′vĕ rĕ), *n.* Italian name of the **Tiber.**

tew (tyōō), *Dial.* —*v.t.* **1.** to work up into proper condition; taw. —*v.i.* **2.** to work hard. —*n.* **3.** a state of worry, bustle, or excitement. [var. of TAW[2]]

Tewkesbury (tyōōks′bə rĭ, -brĭ), *n.* a town in W England, in Gloucestershire: final defeat of the Lancastrians in the Wars of the Roses, 1471. 5880 (1962).

TEWT (tyōōt), *n. Mil.* a training exercise that imitates war, in which commanders, staffs, and assistants perform war duties, but no troops are used. [*T*(*actical*) *E*(*xercise*) *W*(*ithout*) *T*(*roops*)]

Tex., **1.** Texan. **2.** Texas.

Texas (tĕk′səs), *n.* **1.** a state in the S United States. 9,579,677 pop. (1960); 267,339 sq. mi. *Cap.:* Austin. *Abbrev.:* Tex. **2.** (*l.c.*) a structure on the hurricane deck of an American river steamer, containing officers' cabins, etc., and having the pilot house in front or on top. —**Tex′an,** *adj., n.*

Texas fever, a North American tick fever which attacks some animals, esp. cattle.

Texas Rangers, the mounted police force of the State of Texas, originally a semi-official group of settlers organized to fight the Indians.

text (tĕkst), *n.* **1.** the main body of matter in a book or manuscript, as distinguished from notes, appendixes, etc. **2.** the original words of an author as distinct from a translation, paraphrase, commentary, or the like. **3.** the actual wording of anything written or printed. **4.** any of the various forms in which a writing exists. **5.** the wording adopted by an editor as representing the original words of an author. **6.** any theme or topic. **7.** the words of a song or the like. **8.** a textbook. **9.** a short passage of Scripture, esp. one chosen in proof of a doctrine, as the subject of a sermon, etc. **10.** *Eccles.* the letter of the Holy Scripture, or the Scriptures themselves. [ME, t. ML: m. *textus* wording (of the Gospel), L structure (of a discourse), orig. texture. See TEXTURE] —**text′less,** *adj.*

textbook (tĕkst′bŏŏk′), *n.* a book used by students as a standard work for a particular branch of study.

textile (tĕks′tīl), *n.* **1.** any material that is woven. **2.** a material suitable for weaving. —*adj.* **3.** woven or capable of being woven: *textile fabrics.* **4.** of or pertaining to weaving: *the textile industries.* [t. L: m. s. *textilis* woven]

textual (tĕks′tyōō əl), *adj.* **1.** of or pertaining to a text: *textual errors.* **2.** having the purpose of determining the true or best possible reading of a text: *textual criticism.* **3.** based on or conforming to the text, as of the Scriptures. [ME *textuel,* f. ML *textu(s)* TEXT + *-el* -AL[1]] —**tex′tually,** *adv.*

textualism (tĕks′tyōō ə lĭz′əm), *n.* strict adherence to the text, esp. of the Scriptures.

textualist (tĕks′tyōō ə lĭst), *n.* **1.** one who adheres closely to the text, esp. of the Scriptures. **2.** one who is well versed in the text of the Scriptures.

textuary (tĕks′tyōō ə rĭ), *adj., n., pl.* **-aries.** —*adj.* **1.** of or pertaining to the text; textual. —*n.* **2.** a textualist.

texture (tĕks′chə), *n., v.,* **-tured, -turing.** —*n.* **1.** the characteristic disposition of the interwoven or intertwined threads, strands, or the like, which make up a textile fabric. **2.** the characteristic disposition of the constituent parts of any body; general structure or constitution. **3.** the characteristic appearance or essential quality of something, esp. as conveyed to the touch. **4.** the structure of the surface of any work of art, or the simulation of the surface structure of the skin, garment, etc., of the object represented in paint, stone, or other medium. **5.** anything produced by weaving; woven fabric. —*v.t.* **6.** to give a specific or desired texture to, as clothes. [late ME, t. L: m. *textūra* weaving] —**tex′tural,** *adj.* —**tex′turally,** *adv.*

Tezel (*Ger.* tĕt′səl), *n.* Tetzel.

T.G.W.U., Transport and General Workers Union.

-th¹, a noun suffix referring to condition, quality, or action, added to words (*warmth*) and to stems related to words (*depth, length*). [OE *-thu, -tho, -th*, c. Icel. *-th*]

-th², the suffix of ordinal numerals (*fourth, tenth, twentieth*), the form *-th* being added in one or two cases to altered stems of the cardinal (*fifth, twelfth*). [OE *-tha, -the*; c. L *-tus*, Gk *-tos*]

-th³, *Archaic.* var. of **-eth¹**.

Th, *Chem.* thorium.

Th., Thursday.

Thabantshonyana (tä′bănt shŏn′yə nə), *n.* a mountain in Lesotho, the highest point in the Drakensberg range. 11,425 ft. Also, **Thabana Ntlenyana** (tä bä′nə ən tlā′nyə-nə).

Thackeray (thăk′ə rĭ), *n.* **William Makepeace** (māk′-pēs′), 1811–63, English novelist, born in India.

Thai (tī), *n.* **1.** a group of Sino-Tibetan languages spoken over a wide area of south-eastern Asia, including Siamese and Shan. **2.** the Siamese language. **3.** a native or inhabitant of Thailand. **4.** a Thai-speaking person. —*adj.* **5.** of, designating, or pertaining to the Thai languages or to the peoples that speak them. **6.** Siamese. Also, **Tai.**

Thailand (tī′lănd′), *n.* a kingdom in SE Asia. 30,591,000 pop. (est. 1965); 198,242 sq. mi. *Cap.:* Bangkok. Formerly, **Siam.**

Thaïs (thā′ĭs), *n.* Athenian courtesan, mistress of Alexander the Great and, after his death, of Ptolemy I.

thalamencephalon (thăl′ə mĕn sĕf′ə lŏn′), *n., pl.* **-la** (-lə). *Anat.* diencephalon. [NL. See THALAMUS, ENCEPHALON]

thalamus (thăl′ə məs), *n., pl.* **-mi** (-mī′). **1.** *Anat.* the middle part of the diencephalon through which sensory impulses pass to reach the cerebral cortex; optic thalamus. **2.** *Bot.* a receptacle or torus. **3.** the inner room or women's quarters of an ancient Greek house. [t. L, t. Gk: m. *thálamos* inner room] —**thalamic** (thə lăm′ĭk), *adj.*

thalassic (thə lăs′ĭk), *adj.* **1.** of or pertaining to the seas and oceans (sometimes distinguishing smaller bodies of water from *oceanic* bodies). **2.** growing, living, or found in the sea; marine. [f. s. Gk *thálassa* sea + -IC]

thalassography (thăl′ə sŏg′rə fĭ), *n.* oceanography, esp. the branch dealing with coastal waters. —**thal′assog′rapher,** *n.* —**thalassographic** (thăl′ə sə grăf′ĭk), *adj.* [f. s. Gk *thálassa* + -O- + -GRAPHY]

thale-cress (thāl′krĕs′), *n.* a small cruciferous herb, *Arabidopsis thaliana*, common in dry waste places of temperate regions. [f. *thale* (der. NL *Thāliāna*; named after Johann *Thal*, 1542–83, German physician) + CRESS]

thaler (tä′lə), *n., pl.* **-ler.** any of certain large silver coins of varying value formerly issued in Germany, esp. one of the value of 3 marks. Also, **taler.** [t. G: dollar]

Thales (thā′lēz), *n. c.* 640–*c.* 546 B.C., Greek philosopher born in Miletus.

Thalia (thə lī′ə), *n.* **1.** the Muse of comedy and idyllic poetry. **2.** *Gk Myth.* one of the three Graces. [t. Gk: m. *Tháleia*, lit., blooming]

thallic (thăl′ĭk), *adj.* *Chem.* of or containing thallium, esp. in the trivalent state.

thalidomide (thə lĭd′ə mīd′), *n.* *Med.* a crystalline solid, $C_{13}H_{10}N_2O_{41}$ formerly used as a sedative until it was discovered that it could affect the normal growth of the foetus if taken during pregnancy. [f. THAL(LIC) + (IM)IDO- + (*glutaril*)*mide* (f. GLUT(EN) + (TART)AR(IC) + -IMIDE)]

thallium (thăl′ĭ əm), *n.* *Chem.* a soft, malleable, rare, metallic element, used in alloys; its salts are also used in rat poisons. *Symbol:* Tl; *at. wt:* 204·37; *at. no.:* 81; *sp.gr.:* 11·85 at 20°C. [t. NL, f. s. Gk *thallós* green shoot + *-ium* -IUM]

thalloid (thăl′oid), *adj.* *Bot.* resembling or consisting of a thallus.

thallophyte (thăl′ə fīt′), *n.* *Bot.* any member of the *Thallophyta*, a phylum of plants (including the algae, fungi, and lichens) in which the plant body of larger species is typically a thallus. [t. NL: m. *thallophyta* (pl.). See THALLUS, -PHYTE] —**thallophytic** (thăl′ə fĭt′ĭk), *adj.*

thallous (thăl′əs), *adj.* *Chem.* containing monovalent thallium. Also, **thallious** (thăl′ĭ əs).

thallus (thăl′əs), *n., pl.* **thalli** (thăl′ī), **thalluses.** *Bot.* a simple vegetative plant body undifferentiated into true leaves, stem, and root: the plant body of typical thallophytes. [t. NL, t. Gk: m. *thallós* young shoot, twig]

thalofide cell (thăl′ə fīd′), a photoconductive cell which uses thallium oxysulphide as the light sensitive agent. [*thalofide* f. THAL(LIUM) + *o*(*xysul*)*fide* U.S. var. of OXYSULPHIDE]

thalweg (täl′vĕg), *n.* *Geol.* talweg.

Thames (tĕmz), *n.* **1.** the second longest river of Great Britain, rising in Gloucestershire and flowing to the North Sea; it forms the boundary of Oxfordshire and Buckinghamshire with Berkshire, and after flowing through London forms the boundary between Essex and Kent. 210 miles. **2.** the Waihou river of New Zealand.

Thames measurement, a system of determining the tonnage of a vessel, esp. a yacht, by using an equation based on the dimensions of the vessel.

Thames tonnage, the tonnage of a yacht as calculated by means of the **Thames measurement.**

Thammuz (tăm′o͞oz, -ŭz), *n.* Tammuz.

than (ŧħăn; *unstressed* ŧħən), *conj.* **1.** a particle used after comparative adjectives and adverbs and certain other words, such as *other, otherwise, else*, etc., to introduce the second member of a comparison: *he is taller than I am.* —*prep.* **2.** in comparison with: *he is taller than me.* [ME and OE; var. of ME and OE *thanne* than, then, c. G *denn.* See THEN]

Thana (tä′nə), *n.* a city in India, in W Maharashtra state. 101,107 (1961).

thanage (thā′nĭj), *n.* **1.** the tenure by which lands were held by a thane. **2.** the lands so held. **3.** the office, rank, or jurisdiction of a thane.

thanatophobia (thăn′ə tə fō′byə), *n.* morbid fear of death. —**than′atapho′bic,** *adj.*

thanatopsis (thăn′ə tŏp′sĭs), *n.* a view or contemplation of death. [f. Gk: s. *thánatos* death + *ópsis* sight, view]

Thanatos (thăn′ə tŏs′), *n.* *Gk Myth.* the personification of death. Cf. **Mors.**

thane (thān), *n.* **1.** *Early Eng. Hist.* a member of any of several classes of men ranking between earls and ordinary freemen, and holding lands of the king or lord by military service. **2.** *Scot. Hist.* a person, ranking with an earl's son, holding lands of the king; the chief of a clan, who became one of the king's barons. Also, **thegn.** [late ME, var. of ME *thain*, OE *thegn*, c. G *Degen* servant, warrior; akin to Gk *téknon* child]

Thanet (thăn′ĭt), *n.* **Isle of,** an island forming the NE tip of Kent, in SE England. ab. 40 sq. mi.

Thanjavur (tŭn′jə vo͞oə′), *n.* a city in SE India in Madras state. 111,099 (1961). Formerly, **Tanjore.**

thank (thăngk), *v.t.* **1.** to give thanks to; express gratitude to. **2. have oneself to thank,** to be oneself responsible or at fault. **3. have someone to thank for,** to rightly place blame or responsibility for (something) on someone. —*n.* **4.** (*usually pl.*) the expression of grateful feeling, or grateful acknowledgement of a benefit or favour, by words or otherwise: *to return a borrowed book with thanks.* **5.** (*pl.*) a common elliptical expression used in acknowledging a favour, service, courtesy, or the like. **6. thanks to, a.** thanks be given to. **b.** as a result or consequence of. [ME; OE *thanc* gratitude, orig. thoughtfulness, thought. See THINK¹] —**thank′er,** *n.*

thankee (thăng′kĭ), *interj.* *Dial.* thankyou.

thankful (thăngk′fəl), *adj.* feeling or expressing thanks. —**thank′fully,** *adv.* —**thank′fulness,** *n.*

thankless (thăngk′lĭs), *adj.* **1.** not such as to be rewarded with thanks; not appreciated. **2.** ungrateful. —**thank′lessly,** *adv.* —**thank′lessness,** *n.*

thank-offering (thăngk′ŏf′ə rĭng), *n.* an offering, as to some deity, to express gratitude for the turn of events or the like.

thanksgiver (thăngks′gĭv′ə), *n.* one who gives thanks.

thanksgiving (thăngks′gĭv′ĭng), *n.* **1.** the act of giving thanks; grateful acknowledgement of benefits or favours, esp. to God. **2.** an expression of thanks, esp. to God. **3.** a public celebration in acknowledgement of divine favour. **4.** *Chiefly U.S.* a day set apart for giving thanks to God. **5.** (*cap.*) *U.S.* Thanksgiving Day.

Thanksgiving Day, *U.S.* an annual festival in acknowledgement of divine favour, usually held on the fourth Thursday of November.

thankworthy (thăngk′wû′ŧħĭ), *adj.* deserving gratitude.

thankyou (thăngk′yo͞o), *interj.* **1.** (an expression of gratitude or thanks.) —*n.* **2.** the act of expressing thanks: *have you said your thankyous?* —*adj.* **3.** expressing thanks: *a thankyou letter.*

Thant (thănt, thŭnt), *n.* U (yo͞o, o͝o), born 1909, Burmese statesman: United Nations secretary-general since 1961.

Thapsus (thăp′səs), *n.* an ancient town on the N coast of Africa (in present-day Tunisia), ab. 100 mi. S of Carthage: decisive victory of Julius Caesar 46 B.C.

thar (tä), *n.* tahr.

Thar (tä), *n.* an extensive desert region on the border of West Pakistan and India, E of the river Indus. ab. 100,000 sq. mi. Also, **Great Indian Desert, Indian Desert.**

Thasos (thăs′ŏs), *n.* a Greek island in the N Aegean. 15,208 pop. (1951); ab. 170 sq. mi.

that (*conj.* t͟hət; *otherwise* t͟hăt), *pron. and adj.*, *pl.* **those;** *adv.*, *conj.* —*pron.* **1.** (a demonstrative pronoun used to indicate: **a.** a person, thing, idea, etc., as pointed out or present, before mentioned, about to be mentioned, supposed to be understood, or by way of emphasis. **b.** one of two or more persons, things, etc., already mentioned referring to the one more remote in place, time, or thought. **c.** one of two or more persons, things, etc., already mentioned, implying contradistinction (opposed to *this*).) **2.** (a relative pronoun used: **a.** as the subject or object of a relative clause, esp. one defining or restricting the antecedent (sometimes replaceable by *who*, *whom*, or *which*). **b.** as the object of a preposition, the preposition being at the end of the relative clause: *the man that I spoke of.* **c.** in various special or elliptical constructions: *fool that he is.*) **3. and all that,** together with all similar things (used dismissively). **4. at that,** additionally; besides: *it's an idea, and a good one at that.* **5. that is,** more precisely; in clarification or example. **6. that's that,** that is the end of the matter; the matter is closed or finished (used dismissively). **7. with that,** thereupon; immediately afterwards. —*adj.* **8.** (a demonstrative adjective used to indicate: **a.** a person, place, thing, idea, etc., as pointed out or present, before mentioned, supposed to be understood, or by way of emphasis. **b.** one of two or more persons, things, etc., already mentioned, referring to the one more remote in place, time, or thought. **c.** one of two or more persons, things, etc., already mentioned, implying contradistinction (opposed to *this*).) —*adv.* **9.** (an adverb used: **a.** with adjectives and adverbs of quality or extent to indicate precise degree or extent: *that much, that far.* **b.** *Chiefly Dial.* with other adjectives and adverbs to indicate extent or degree, or for emphasis: *poor lad, he was that weak!*) —*conj.* **10.** (a conjunction used: **a.** to introduce a clause as the subject or object of the principal verb or as the necessary complement to a statement made, or a clause expressing cause or reason, purpose or aim, result or consequence, etc.: *that he will come is certain.* **b.** elliptically, to introduce a sentence or clause expressing desire, surprise, or indignation.) [ME; OE *thæt* that, the, c. G *das(s)*, Gk *tó*]

—**Syn. 1.** THAT, WHICH, WHO are all relative pronouns in English. THAT as a relative pronoun originally referred to persons, animals, or things; it is now more frequently used of animals or things, though it can refer to all three: *the man that speaks evil of his friends; an animal that eats grass; a plant that likes the shade.* WHICH is used only of animals or things, except archaically of persons: *animals which bear burdens; plants which grow in the desert; Our Father which art in heaven.* WHO is used of persons and occasionally of the higher animals: *a man who works hard; a horse who runs successful races.* As the object of a preposition, only WHO (in the form WHOM) or WHICH can be used: *the people of whom I was speaking; the city to which I am going.* Only WHO and WHICH are found in non-restrictive clauses (those used parenthetically): *the cook, who was very nervous, sent us out of the kitchen; this house, which was just built, was burnt down last night.* Any of the three can be used in a clause which restricts or defines: *there is the house that is for sale.*

thatch (thăch), *n.* **1.** a material, as straw, rushes, leaves, or the like, used to cover roofs, haystacks, etc. **2.** a covering of such a material. **3.** *Colloq.* the hair covering the head. —*v.t.* **4.** to cover with or as with thatch. —*v.i.* **5.** to thatch houses, haystacks, etc. [ME *thacche*, var. of *thack*, OE *thæc* roof, thatch, c. G *Dach*, L *toga* covering; akin to Gk *tégos* roof] —**thatch′er,** *n.* —**thatch′less,** *adj.* —**thatch′y,** *adj.*

thatching (thăch′ĭng), *n.* **1.** the act or skill of covering with thatch. **2.** the material used for thatching; thatch (def. 1).

thaumatology (thô′mə tŏl′ə jĭ), *n.* the study or description of miracles. [f. *thaumato-* (t. Gk, comb. form of *thaûma* wonder) + -LOGY]

thaumatrope (thô′mə trōp′), *n.* a card with different pictures on opposite sides (as a horse on one side and a rider on the other), which, when twirled rapidly, causes the pictures to appear as if combined, thus illustrating the persistence of visual impressions. [f. Gk *thaûma* wonder + -TROPE]

thaumaturge (thô′mə tûj′), *n.* a worker of wonders or miracles. Also, **thau′matur′gist.**

thaumaturgic (thô′mə tû′jĭk), *adj.* **1.** pertaining to a thaumaturge or to thaumaturgy. **2.** having the powers of a thaumaturge. Also, **thau′matur′gical.**

thaumaturgy (thô′mə tû′jĭ), *n.* the working of wonders or miracles; magic. [t. Gk: m. s. *thaumatourgía* wonder-working, conjuring]

thaw (thô), *v.i.* **1.** to pass from a frozen to a liquid or semi-liquid state; melt. **2.** to be freed from the physical effect of frost or extreme cold (often fol. by *out*). **3.** (of the weather) to become warm enough to melt ice and snow: *it will probably thaw today.* **4.** to become less cold, formal, or reserved. **5.** to become less hostile, or aggressive: *relations between the Soviet Union and the U.S. have thawed.* —*v.t.* **6.** to cause to thaw. **7.** to make less cold, formal, reserved. —*n.* **8.** the act or process of thawing. **9.** a becoming less cold, formal, or reserved. **10.** a reduction in hostility or aggressiveness, esp. in international relations. **11.** a condition of the weather caused by the rise of the temperature above freezing point. [ME *thawe*, OE *thawian*, c. D *dooien*, Icel. *theyja*] —**thaw′er,** *n.* —**thaw′less,** *adj.* —**Syn. 1.** See **melt.**

Th.B., (L *Theologiae Baccalaureus*) Bachelor of Theology.

Th.D., (L *Theologiae Doctor*) Doctor of Theology.

the[1] (*stressed* t͟hē; *unstressed before a consonant* t͟hə; *unstressed before a vowel* t͟hĭ), *adj. or def. article.* a word used esp. before nouns: **1.** with a specifying or particularizing effect (opposed to *a* or *an*). **2.** to mark a noun as indicating something well known or unique: *the Alps, the earth.* **3.** with or as part of a title: *the Duke of Wellington, the Reverend John Smith.* **4.** to mark a noun as indicating the best-known, most approved, or most important of its kind: *the skiing centre of Europe.* **5.** to mark a noun as being used generically: *the dog is a quadruped.* **6.** in place of a possessive pronoun, to denote a part of the body or a personal belonging: *to hang the head and weep.* **7.** before adjectives used substantively and denoting an individual, a class or number of individuals, or an abstract notion: *to visit the sick.* **8.** distributively, to denote any one separately, where *a* or *an* is more commonly employed: *at five shillings the pound.* **9.** to specify one of a class or type: *Did you see the television last night?* **10.** to denote sufficiency or enough of something: *I don't have the money to buy a car.* **11.** *Scot.* to particularize in time, as replacing the standard English prefix *to-* in 'the day', 'the morrow', or in 'the now'. [ME and OE, uninflected var. of demonstrative pronoun. See THAT]

the[2] (t͟hə, t͟hĭ), *adv.* a word used to modify an adjective or adverb in the comparative degree: **1.** signifying 'in or by that', 'on that account', 'in or by so much', or 'in some or any degree': *he is taking more care of himself, and looks the better.* **2.** used correlatively, in one instance with relative force and in the other with demonstrative force, and signifying 'by how much . . . by so much' or 'in what degree . . . in that degree': *the more the merrier.* [ME and OE; orig. a case form of demon. pronoun. See THAT]

theaceous (thē ā′shəs), *adj.* belonging to the *Theaceae*, or tea family of plants. [f. s. NL *Theāceae* (der. NL *thea* TEA) + -OUS]

theandric (thē ăn′drĭk), *adj.* theanthropic. [t. MGk: m. s. *theandrikós.* See THEO-, ANDRO-, -IC]

theanthropic (thē′ăn thrŏp′ĭk), *adj.* of or pertaining to both God and man; both divine and human.

theanthropism (thē ăn′thrə pĭz′əm), *n.* **1.** the doctrine of the union of the divine and human natures, or of the manifestation of God as man in Christ. **2.** the attribution of human nature to the gods. [f. s. LGk *theánthrōpos* god-man + -ISM] —**thean′thropist,** *n.*

thearchy (thē′ä′kĭ), *n.*, *pl.* **-chies.** **1.** the rule or government of God or of a god. **2.** an order or system of deities. [t. Eccl. Gk: m. s. *thearchía.* See THEO-, -ARCHY] —**thear′chic,** *adj.*

theat., **1.** theatre. **2.** theatrical.

Theatine (thĭə′tīn), *n.* **1.** a member of a congregation of clerics founded in 1524. **2.** a member of a similar order for women, established in 1600.

theatre (thĭə′tə), *n.* **1.** a building expressly designed to house dramatic presentations, stage entertainments, or the like. **2.** any site used for dramatic presentations, etc., as one in the open air. **3.** Also, **film theatre.** a cinema. **4.** the audience at a performance in a theatre. **5.** dramatic performances as a branch of art; the drama. **6.** dramatic works collectively, as of a literature, a nation, a period, or an author. **7.** acting, writing, or the like with reference to its suitability for dramatic performance: *it's fine writing, but it's just not theatre.* **8.** a room or hall, fitted with tiers of seats rising like steps, as used for lectures, anatomical demonstrations, etc. **9.** a room in a hospital or elsewhere in which surgical operations are performed: *an operating theatre.* **10.** a place of action; field of operations: *theatre of war, theatre of operations.* **11.** a natural formation of land rising by steps or gradations. Also, *U.S.*, **theater.** [ME, t. L: m. s. *theātrum*, t. Gk: m. *théātron* seeing place, theatre]

theatregoer (thĭə′tə gō′ə), *n.* one who regularly attends the theatre.

theatre-in-the-round (thĭə′tə rĭn t͟hə round′), *n.* a theatre with seats arranged round a central stage.

theatrical (thĭ ăt′rĭ kl), *adj.* Also, **theat′ric.** **1.** of or pertaining to the theatre, or dramatic or scenic representations: *theatrical performances.* **2.** suggestive of the theatre or of acting; artificial, pompous, spectacular, or extravagantly histrionic: *a theatrical display of grief.* —*n.* **3.** (*pl.*)

dramatic performances, now esp. as given by amateurs. —**theat′ricalism,** *n.* —**theatricality** (thĭ ăt′rĭ kăl′ĭ tĭ), **theat′ricalness,** *n.* —**theat′rically,** *adv.*

theatricalize (thĭ ăt′rĭ kə līz′), *v.*, **-lized, -lizing.** —*v.t.* **1.** to represent, in dramatic form; dramatize. **2.** to express in a theatrical or extravagantly histrionic manner. —*v.i.* **3.** to behave in an extravagantly histrionic manner. Also, **theatricalise.**

Thebaid (thē′bā ĭd), *n.* **1.** the region around Egyptian or Grecian Thebes. **2.** an epic poem composed about A.D. 80–92 by Statius. [t. L, t. Gk: s. *Thēbaís*]

thebaine (thē′bə ēn′, thĭ bā′ēn, -ĭn), *n. Chem.* a white crystalline poisonous alkaloid, $C_{19}H_{21}NO_3$, present in opium in small quantities. [f. NL *thēba(ia)* thebaine (der. Gk *Thêbai* THEBES) + -INE²]

Thebes (thēbz), *n.* **1.** an ancient ruined city in Upper Egypt, on the Nile: a former capital of Egypt. **2.** a city of ancient Greece, in Boeotia: a rival of ancient Athens. —**Thebaic** (thē bā′ĭk), *adj.* —**Theban** (thē′bən), *adj.*, *n.*

theca (thē′kə), *n.*, *pl.* **-cae** (-sē). **1.** a case or receptacle. **2.** *Bot.* **a.** a sac, cell, or capsule. **b.** a spore case. **3.** *Anat.*, *Zool.* a case or sheath enclosing an organ, etc., as the horny covering of an insect pupa. [t. L, t. Gk: m. *thḗkē* case, cover] —**the′cal,** *adj.*

thecate (thē′kĭt, -kāt), *adj.* having, or contained in, a theca.

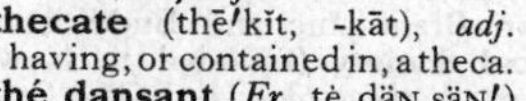

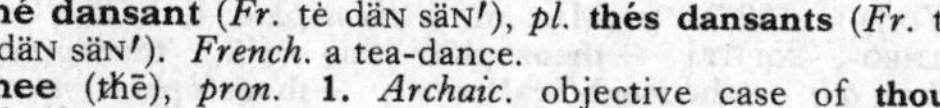

Thebes (def. 1) *c.* 1450 B.C.

thé dansant (*Fr.* tè däN säN′), *pl.* **thés dansants** (*Fr.* tè däN säN′). *French.* a tea-dance.

thee (t͟hē), *pron.* **1.** *Archaic.* objective case of **thou.** **2.** (formerly, chiefly among the Society of Friends) thou. [ME; OE *thē* (orig. dat., later dat. and acc.), c. LG *di*, G *dir*]

theelin (thē′lĭn), *n. Biochem.*, *Obsolesc.* oestrone. [irreg. f. Gk *thêl(ys)* female + -IN²]

theelol (thē′lōl), *n. Biochem.*, *Obsolesc.* oestriol.

theft (thĕft), *n.* **1.** the act of stealing; the wrongful taking and carrying away of the personal goods of another; larceny. **2.** an instance of this. **3.** *Obs.* something stolen. [ME; OE *thēoft*, earlier *thēofth*, f. *thēof* THIEF + -TH¹, c. Icel. *thýft*, obs. D *diefte*] —**theft′less,** *adj.*

thegn (thān), *n.* thane.

The Hague. See **Hague.**

theine (thē′ēn, -ĭn), *n.* caffeine found in tea. Also, **thein** (thē′ĭn). [f. s. NL *thea* TEA + -INE²]

their (t͟hâə), *adj.* **1.** the possessive form of *they* used before a noun. **2.** *Colloq.* (usually considered to be bad usage) a possessive adjective with singular force used in place of 'his' or 'her' when the sex of the antecedent is not determined: *Who has left their pen on my desk?* [ME, t. Scand.; cf. Icel. *their(r)a* of those. See THEY]

theirs (t͟hâəz), *pron.* **1.** a form of the possessive *their* used predicatively or without a noun following. **2.** *Colloq.* (usually considered to be bad usage) a possessive pronoun with singular force, used in place of 'his' or 'hers' when the sex of the antecedent is not determined: *Does anybody recognize this pen as theirs?*

theirselves (t͟hə sĕlvz′), *pron.*, *pl. Colloq.* (usually considered to be bad usage) themselves. [formed on analogy with MYSELF]

theism (thē′ĭz′əm), *n.* **1.** the belief in one God as the creator and ruler of the universe, without rejection of revelation (distinguished from *deism*). **2.** belief in the existence of a God or gods (opposed to *atheism*). [f. s. Gk *theós* god + -ISM] —**the′ist,** *n.*, *adj.* —**theistic** (thē ĭs′tĭk), **theis′tical,** *adj.* —**theis′tically,** *adv.*

Theiss (*Ger.* tīs), *n.* German name of **Tisza.**

thelitis (thĭ lī′tĭs), *n. Pathol.* inflammation of the nipple. [t. NL, f. Gk: s. *thēlḗ* nipple + *-ītis* -ITIS]

them (t͟hĕm; *unstressed* t͟həm), *pron.* **1.** the objective case of **they.** —*adj.* **2.** *Colloq.* (usually considered to be bad usage) those: *take them things out of here.* [ME *theym*, t. Scand.; cf. Icel. *theim* to those. See THEY]

thema (thē′mə), *n.*, *pl.* **themata** (thē′mə tə, thĕm′ə-). a theme (esp. def. 5).

thematic (thĭ măt′ĭk), *adj.* **1.** of or pertaining to a theme. **2.** *Gram.* **a.** of, pertaining to, or producing a theme or themes (def. 4). **b.** pertaining to the theme or stem. The thematic vowel is the vowel that ends the stem and precedes the inflectional ending of a word form, as *i* in Latin *audio* I hear. —**themat′ically,** *adv.*

theme (thēm), *n.* **1.** a subject of discourse, discussion, meditation, or composition; a topic. **2.** a short, informal essay, esp. a school composition. **3.** *Music.* **a.** a principal subject in a musical composition. **b.** a short subject from which variations are developed. **4.** *Gram.* the element common to all or most of the forms of an inflectional paradigm, often consisting in turn of a root with certain formative elements or modifications. Cf. **stem.** **5.** an administrative division of the Byzantine Roman Empire. [ME, t. L: m. *thema*, t. Gk] —**theme′less,** *adj.* —**Syn.** **1.** See **subject.**

theme song, **1.** a melody in an operetta, film or musical comedy, so emphasized by repetition as to dominate the presentation. **2.** a melody associated with a particular character or the like in such a production. **3.** a signature tune. Also, **theme tune.**

Themis (thē′mĭs, thĕm′ĭs), *n. Gk Myth.* a Greek goddess personifying justice.

Themistocles (thĭ mĭs′tə klēz′), *n.* 527?–460? B.C., Athenian statesman.

themselves (t͟həm sĕlvz′), *pron. pl.* **1.** a reflexive form of **them:** *they hurt themselves.* **2.** an emphatic form of **them** or **they** used: **a.** as object: *they used it for themselves.* **b.** in apposition to a subject or object: *they themselves did it.* **3.** their proper or normal selves; their usual state of mind (used after *be*, *become*, or *come to*): *they are themselves again.* **4.** Also, **themself.** *Colloq.* (usually considered to be bad usage) a reflexive pronoun with singular force, used in place of 'himself' or 'herself' when the sex of the antecedent is not determined: *someone is deceiving themselves.*

then (t͟hĕn), *adv.* **1.** at that time: *prices were lower then.* **2.** immediately or soon afterwards: *he stopped, and then began again.* **3.** next in order of time. **4.** at another time. **5.** next in order of place. **6.** in the next place; in addition; besides. **7.** in that case; in those circumstances. **8.** since that is so; therefore; consequently. **9. but then,** but at the same time; but on the other hand. —*adj.* **10.** being; being such; then existing: *the then prime minister.* —*n.* **11.** that time: *till then.* [ME, var. of ME *thenne*, OE *thænne*; orig. var. of THAN] —**Syn. 8.** See **therefore.**

thenar (thē′nə), *n. Anat.* **1.** the fleshy mass of the outer side of the palm of the hand. **2.** the fleshy prominence or ball of muscle at the base of the thumb. —*adj.* **3.** of or pertaining to the thenar. [t. NL, t. Gk: palm of hand or sole of foot]

thenardite (thĭ nä′dīt, tĭ-), *n.* a mineral, sodium sulphate, Na_2SO_4, occurring in white crystals and masses, esp. in dried lakes. [named after L. J. *Thénard*, 1777–1857, French chemist. See -ITE¹]

Thenard's blue (tā′näz, -nädz), a blue pigment consisting of a calcined mixture of cobalt oxide and alumina. [named after L. J. *Thénard.* See THENARDITE]

thence (t͟hĕns), *adv.* **1.** from that place. **2.** from that time; henceforth. **3.** from that source; for that reason; therefore. [ME *thennes*, f. *thenne* (OE *thanone* thence; c. D *dan*, G *dannen*) + *-s*, adv. gen. suffix]

thenceforth (t͟hĕns′fôth′), *adv.* from that time or place onwards. Also, **thenceforward** (t͟hĕns′fô′wəd), **thenceforwards.**

theo-, a word element meaning 'pertaining to the gods', 'divine'. Also, before vowels, **the-.** [t. Gk, comb. form of *theós* god]

Theobald (thĭə′bôld, tĭb′ld), *n.* **Lewis,** 1688–1744, English writer and Shakespearian editor.

theobromine (thē′ō brō′mēn, -mĭn), *n. Chem.* a powder, $C_7H_8N_4O_2$, in the form of microscopic crystals, having alkaline properties, obtained from the seeds and leaves of species of the genus *Theobroma*, and used as a nerve stimulant and a diuretic: the lower homologue of caffeine. [f. NL *theobrom(a)* genus of trees typified by cacao (t. Gk: lit., god-food) + -INE²]

theocentric (thĭə sĕn′trĭk), *adj.* having God as a focal point of concern.

theocracy (thĭ ŏk′rə sĭ), *n.*, *pl.* **-cies.** **1.** a form of government in which God or a deity is recognized as the supreme civil ruler, His laws being interpreted by the ecclesiastical authorities. **2.** a system of government by priests claiming a divine commission. **3.** a state or commonwealth under any such form or system of government. [t. Gk: m. s. *theokratía.* See THEO-, -CRACY]

theocrasy (thĭ ŏk′rə sĭ), *n.* **1.** a mixture of religious forms and deities worshipped. **2.** (in mysticism) the union of the soul and God. [t. Gk: m. s. *theokrāsía* mingling with god]

theocrat (thĭə′krăt), *n.* **1.** the ruler, or a member of a governing body, in a theocracy. **2.** one who favours theocracy. —**theocrat′ic, theocrat′ical,** *adj.* —**theocrat′ically,** *adv.*

Theocritus (thĭ ŏk′rĭ təs), *n.* fl. *c.* 270 B.C., Greek pastoral poet.

theodicy (thĭ ŏd′ĭ sĭ), *n.*, *pl.* **-cies.** a vindication of the divine attributes, particularly holiness and justice, in respect to the existence of physical and moral evil. [t. F: m. *théodicée*, title of work by Leibniz, f. Gk: *theó(s)* god + m. *dikē* justice] —**theodicean** (thĭ ŏd′ĭ sīən′), *adj.*, *n.*

theodolite (thĭ ŏd′ə līt′), *n.* *Survey.* an instrument for measuring horizontal or vertical angles. [coined word; orig. unknown] —**theodolitic** (thĭ ŏd′ə lĭt′ĭk), *adj.*

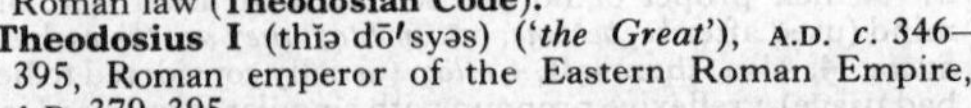

Theodolite
A, Telescope; B, Vertical scale; C, Horizontal scale

Theodora (thĭə dô′rə), *n.* A.D. 508–548, Byzantine empress: wife of Justinian I.

Theodoric (thĭ ŏd′ə rĭk), *n.* (‘*the Great*’) A.D. *c.* 454–526, king of the Ostrogoths, who conquered Italy in A.D. 493 and ruled it until his death.

Theodosian (thĭə dō′syən), *adj.* **1.** of or pertaining to Theodosius I, esp. with reference to his act making Christianity the established religion of the Eastern Roman Empire. **2.** of or pertaining to Theodosius II, esp. with reference to his codification of Roman law (**Theodosian Code**).

Theodosius I (thĭə dō′syəs) (‘*the Great*’), A.D. *c.* 346–395, Roman emperor of the Eastern Roman Empire, A.D. 379–395.

Theodosius II (thĭə dō′syəs), A.D. 401–450, Roman emperor of the Eastern Roman Empire, A.D. 408—450.

theogony (thĭ ŏg′ə nĭ), *n.*, *pl.* **-nies. 1.** the origin of the gods. **2.** an account of this; a genealogical account of the gods. [t. Gk: m. s. *theogonía*] —**theogonic** (thĭə gŏn′ĭk), *adj.* —**theog′onist,** *n.*

theol., **1.** theologian. **2.** theological. **3.** theology.

theologian (thĭə lō′jyən), *n.* one versed in theology, esp. Christian theology.

theological (thĭə lŏj′ĭ kl), *adj.* **1.** of, pertaining to, or connected with theology. **2.** based upon the nature and will of God as revealed to man. Also, **theologic.** —**theolog′ically,** *adv.*

theologize (thĭ ŏl′ə jīz′), *v.*, **-gized, -gizing.** —*v.i.* **1.** to theorize or speculate upon theological subjects. —*v.t.* **2.** to make theological; treat theologically. Also, **theologise.** —**theol′ogiza′tion,** *n.* —**theol′ogiz′er,** *n.*

theology (thĭ ŏl′ə jĭ), *n.*, *pl.* **-gies. 1.** the science which treats of God, His attributes, and His relations to the universe; the science or study of divine things or religious truth; divinity. **2.** a particular form, system, or branch of this science or study. [ME *theologie*, t. L: m. *theologia*, t. Gk]

theomachy (thĭ ŏm′ə kĭ), *n.*, *pl.* **-chies.** a battle with or among the gods. [t. Gk: m. s. *theomachía*]

theomania (thĭə mā′nyə), *n.* religious madness, esp. the belief that one is God. —**theomaniac** (thĭə mā′nĭ ăk′), *n.*

theomorphic (thĭə mô′fĭk), *adj.* having the form or likeness of God or a god. [f. s. Gk *theómorph(os)* of divine form + -IC] —**theomor′phism,** *n.*

theopathy (thĭ ŏp′ə thĭ), *n.* religious emotion excited by the contemplation of God. [t. Gk: m. s. *theopátheia* suffering of God] —**theopathetic** (thĭə′pə thĕt′ĭk), **theopathic** (thĭə păth′ĭk), *adj.*

theophany (thĭ ŏf′ə nĭ), *n.*, *pl.* **-nies.** a manifestation or appearance of God or a god to man. [t. LL: m. s. *theophania*, t. Gk] —**theophanic** (thĭə făn′ĭk), *adj.*

Theophrastus (thĭə frăs′təs), *n.* *c.* 372–287 B.C., Greek philosopher.

theophylline (thĭə fĭl′ēn, -ĭn), *n.* *Chem.* a white crystalline alkaloid, $C_7H_8N_4O_2$, derived from tea; an isomer of theobromine. [f. *theo-* (irreg. comb. form repr. NL *thea* TEA) + PHYLL(O)- + -INE[2]]

theor., theorem.

theorbo (thĭ ô′bō), *n.*, *pl.* **-bos.** an obsolete musical instrument of the lute class, having two necks, one above the other; archlute. [t. It.: m. *tiorba*] —**theor′bist,** *n.*

theorem (thĭə′rəm), *n.* **1.** *Maths.* a theoretical proposition; a statement embodying something to be proved. **2.** a rule or law, esp. one expressed by an equation or formula. **3.** *Logic.* a proposition which can be deduced from the premises or assumptions of a system. [t. LL: m. *theōrēma*, t. Gk: spectacle, theory, thesis (to be proved)] —**theorematic** (thĭə′rə măt′ĭk), *adj.*

theoretical (thĭə rĕt′ĭ kl), *adj.* **1.** of, pertaining to, or consisting in theory; not practical. **2.** existing only in theory; hypothetical. **3.** given to, forming, or dealing with theories; speculative. Also, **theoretic.** —**theoret′ically,** *adv.*

theoretical arithmetic, arithmetic (def. 2).

theoretician (thĭə′rə tĭsh′ən), *n.* one who deals with or is expert in the theoretical side of a subject.

theoretics (thĭə rĕt′ĭks), *n.* the theoretical or speculative part of a science or subject.

theorist (thĭə′rĭst), *n.* **1.** one who theorizes. **2.** one who deals mainly with the theory of a subject: *a theorist in medical research.*

theorize (thĭə′rīz), *v.i.*, **-rized, -rizing. 1.** to form a theory or theories. **2.** to speculate or conjecture. Also, **theorise.** —**theo′riza′tion,** *n.* —**theo′riz′er,** *n.*

theory (thĭə′rĭ), *n.*, *pl.* **-ries. 1.** a coherent group of general propositions used as principles of explanation for a class of phenomena: *Newton's theory of gravitation.* **2.** a proposed explanation whose status is still conjectural, in contrast to well-established propositions that are regarded as reporting matters of actual fact. **3.** *Maths.* a body of principles, theorems, or the like, belonging to one subject: *number theory.* **4.** that department of a science or art which deals with its principles or methods, as distinguished from the practice of it. **5.** a particular conception or view of something to be done or of the method of doing it; a system of rules or principles. **6.** conjecture or opinion. [t. LL: m. s. *theōria*, t. Gk: contemplation, theory]

—**Syn. 1.** THEORY, HYPOTHESIS are both often used colloquially to mean an untested idea or opinion. A THEORY properly is a more or less verified or established explanation accounting for known facts or phenomena: *the theory of relativity.* A HYPOTHESIS is a conjecture put forth as a possible explanation of certain phenomena or relations, which serves as a basis of argument or experimentation by which to reach the truth: *this idea is offered only as a hypothesis.* —**Ant. 1.** principle, axiom, law.

theos., **1.** theosophical. **2.** theosophy.

theosophy (thĭ ŏs′ə fĭ), *n.* **1.** any of various forms of philosophical or religious thought in which claim is made to a special insight into the divine nature or to a special divine revelation. **2.** the system of belief and doctrine, based largely on Brahmanic and Buddhistic ideas, of the **Theosophical Society** (founded in New York in 1875). [t. ML: m. s. *theosophia*, t. LGk. See THEO-, -SOPHY] —**theosophic** (thĭə sŏf′ĭk), **theosoph′ical,** *adj.* —**theosoph′ically,** *adv.* —**theos′ophist,** *n.*

Theotocópuli (thē′ō tō kŏp′ōō lĭ), *n.* **Domingo** (dō mĭng′gō). See **El Greco.**

theralite (thĕ′rə līt′), *n.* *Geol.* a coarse-grained basic igneous rock comprised of plagioclase, nepheline, augite, and often biotite, analcite, or olivine. [f. Gk *thēra* prey + -LITE]

therapeut., **1.** therapeutic. **2.** therapeutics. Also, **therap.**

therapeutic (thĕ′rə pyōō′tĭk), *adj.* pertaining to the treating or curing of disease; curative. Also, **ther′apeu′tical.** [t. NL: s. *therapeuticus*, t. Gk: m. *therapeutikós*, der. *therapeutes* one who treats medically] —**ther′apeu′tically,** *adv.*

therapeutics (thĕ′rə pyōō′tĭks), *n.* the branch of medicine concerned with the remedial treatment of disease. [pl. of *therapeutic*, n., t. NL: s. *therapeutica*, prop. fem. of *therapeuticus* THERAPEUTIC, adj. See -ICS]

therapist (thĕ′rə pĭst), *n.* a person trained to give therapy by any of various physical or psychological methods. Also, **therapeutist** (thĕ′rə pyōō′tĭst).

therapy (thĕ′rə pĭ), *n.*, *pl.* **-pies. 1.** the treatment of disease, as by some remedial or curative process. **2.** a curative power or quality. [t. NL: m. s. *therapia*, t. Gk: m. *therapeía* healing]

there (ŧħĕə), *adv.* **1.** in or at that place. **2.** at that point in an action, speech, etc. **3.** in that matter, particular, or respect. **4.** into or to that place; thither. **5.** (used less definitely and also unemphatically as by way of calling the attention to something: *there they go.* —*adj.* **6.** (used for emphasis with a demonstrative adjective, after the noun qualified): *that man there.* **7.** *Colloq.* (generally considered to be bad usage) used for emphasis between a demonstrative adjective and the noun qualified: *that there man.* **8. all there, a.** of sound mind. **b.** shrewd; quick-witted. —*pron.* **9.** that place: *he comes from there too.* **10.** used to introduce a sentence or clause in which the verb comes before its subject: *there is no hope.* **11.** used in interjectional phrases: *there's a good boy.* —*interj.* **12.** (an exclamation used to express satisfaction, encouragement, consolation, etc.): *there! it's done!* [ME; OE *thǣr*, c. D *daar*, G *da*]

there-, a word element meaning ‘that (place)’, ‘that (time)’, etc., used in combination with certain adverbs and prepositions. [special use of THERE, demonstrative adv.]

thereabouts (ŧħĕə′rə bouts′), *adv.* **1.** about or near that place or time. **2.** about that number, amount, etc. Also, **thereabout.**

thereafter (ŧħĕər′äf′tə), *adv.* **1.** after that in time or sequence; afterwards. **2.** *Obs.* accordingly.

thereagainst (ŧħĕə′rə gĕnst′), *adv.* *Archaic.* against, or in opposition to, that.

thereat (ŧħĕər′ăt′), *adv.* **1.** at that place, time, etc.; there. **2.** on that occasion; by reason of that.

thereby (ŧħĕə′bī′), *adv.* **1.** by that; by means of that.

2. in that connection or relation: *thereby hangs a tale.* 3. by or near that place. 4. *Scot.* about that number, quantity, or degree.

therefor (thĕə'fô'), *adv.* for that or this; for it.

therefore (thĕə'fô'), *adv.* in consequence of that; as a result; consequently. [ME *therefore,* f. *ther* THERE + *fore,* var. of *for* FOR]

—**Syn.** hence, whence. THEREFORE, WHEREFORE, ACCORDINGLY, CONSEQUENTLY, SO, THEN agree in introducing a statement resulting from, or caused by, what immediately precedes. THEREFORE ('for this or that reason') and WHEREFORE ('for which reason') imply exactness of reasoning; they are esp. used in logic, law, mathematics, etc., and in a formal style of speaking or writing. ACCORDINGLY ('in conformity with the preceding') and CONSEQUENTLY ('as a result, or sequence, or effect of the preceding') are less formal. SO ('because the preceding is true', or 'this being the case') and THEN ('since the preceding is true') are conversational in tone.

therefrom (thĕə'frŏm'), *adv.* from that place, thing, etc.

therein (thĕər'ĭn'), *adv.* 1. in that place or thing. 2. in that matter, circumstance, etc.

thereinafter (thĕə'rĭn äf'tə), *adv.* afterwards in that document, statement, etc.

thereinbefore (thĕə'rĭn bĭ fô'), *adv.* before in that document, statement, etc.

thereinto (thĕər'ĭn'to͞o), *adv.* into that place, thing, matter, etc.

theremin (thĕ'rĭ mĭn), *n.* an electronic musical instrument whose pitch and tone volume are controlled by the distance between the player's hands and two metal rods serving as aerials. [named after Léon *Thérémin,* born 1896, inventor in France]

thereof (thĕər'ŏv'), *adv.* 1. of that or it. 2. from or out of that as a source or origin.

thereon (thĕər'ŏn'), *adv.* 1. on or upon that or it. 2. immediately after that; thereupon.

thereout (thĕər'out'), *adv. Archaic.* out of that.

Theresa (tə rē'zə; *Sp.* tĕ rĕ'sä), *n.* **Saint** (*Theresa of Avila*), 1515–82, Spanish Carmelite nun, mystic, and writer. Also, **Teresa.**

thereto (thĕə'to͞o'), *adv.* 1. to that place, thing, matter, etc. 2. *Archaic.* in addition to that. Also, **thereunto** (thĕər'ŭn'to͞o).

theretofore (thĕə'to͞o fô'), *adv.* before that time.

thereunder (thĕər'ŭn'də), *adv.* 1. under or beneath that. 2. under the authority of, or in accordance with, that.

thereupon (thĕə'rə pŏn'), *adv.* 1. immediately following that. 2. in consequence of that. 3. upon that or it. 4. with reference to that.

therewith (thĕə'wĭth', -wĭth'), *adv.* 1. with that. 2. in addition to that. 3. following upon that; thereupon.

therewithal (thĕə'wĭth ôl', -wĭth-), *adv.* 1. together with that; in addition to that. 2. following upon that.

Therezina (*Port.* tĕ rĕ zē'nä), *n.* former name of **Teresina.**

theriac (thĭə'rĭ ăk'), *n.* an antidote to venomous bites, etc., esp. an electuary made with honey. —**theriacal** (thə rī'ə kl), *adj.*

therianthropic (thĭə'rĭ ăn thrŏp'ĭk), *adj.* 1. being partly animal and partly human in form. 2. of or pertaining to deities conceived or represented in such form. [f. s. Gk *thērion* wild beast + s. *ánthrōpos* man + -IC] —**therianthropism** (thĭə'rĭ ăn'thrə pĭz'əm), *n.*

theriomorphic (thĭə'rĭ ō mô'fĭk), *adj.* (of deities) conceived or represented as having the form of beasts. Also, **the'riomor'phous.** [f. s. Gk *thēriómorphos* having the shape of a wild beast + -IC]

therm (thûm), *n. Physics.* a unit of heat used as a basis for the selling of gas; equal to 100,000 British thermal units. [t. Gk: s. *thérmē* heat]

therm-, a word element representing **thermal.** Also, **thermo-.** [t. Gk, comb. form of *thermós* hot, *thérmē* heat]

thermae (thû'mē), *n.pl.* 1. hot springs; hot baths. 2. a public bathing establishment of the ancient Greeks or Romans. [t. L, t. Gk: m. *thérmai*]

thermaesthesia (thûm'ĕs thē'zyə), *n. Physiol.* ability to feel cold or heat; sensitiveness to heat. Also, *U.S.,* **thermesthesia.**

thermal (thû'məl), *adj.* 1. Also, **thermic.** of or pertaining to heat or temperature: *thermal capacity.* 2. of, pertaining to, or of the nature of thermae. —*n.* 3. *Aeron., Meteorol.* an ascending current of air caused by local heating, used by glider pilots to attain height. [f. s. Gk *thérmē* heat + -AL[1]] —**ther'mally,** *adv.*

thermal barrier, *Aeron.* an obstacle to flight above very high speeds owing to heating of the aircraft by air friction. Also, **heat barrier.**

thermal capacity, *Physics.* heat capacity.

thermal conductivity, *Physics.* the rate of heat transfer along a body by conduction, measured in calories flowing across a one-centimetre cube per second when the opposite faces have a temperature difference of 1° C. Also, **coefficient of thermal conductivity, specific thermal conductivity.**

thermal diffusion, *Physics.* a method of separating the constituents of fluid, as isotopes, due to diffusion along a temperature gradient within the fluid.

thermal efficiency, *Physics.* the ratio of the work done by a heat engine to the mechanical equivalent of the heat supplied by the fuel.

thermal equator, an imaginary line drawn round the earth for each month of the year, joining the point on each meridian where the highest average monthly temperature occurs.

thermalize (thû'mə līz'), *v.t.,* **-lized, -lizing.** *Physics.* to reduce the energy of neutrons, with a moderator, in order to produce thermal neutrons. Also, **thermalise.**

thermal neutrons, *Physics.* neutrons which have low speeds, their energy being of the same order as the thermal energy of the atoms or molecules of the substance through which they are passing.

thermal reactor, *Physics.* a nuclear reactor in which most of the fissions are caused by thermal neutrons.

thermal springs, natural hot-water springs.

thermanaesthesia (thûm'ăn'ēs thē'zyə), *n. Pathol.* loss of ability to feel cold or heat; loss of temperature sense. Also, *U.S.,* **thermanesthesia.**

Thermidor (thû'mĭ dô'; *Fr.* tĕr mē dŏr'), *n.* (in the calendar of the first French Republic) the eleventh month of the year, extending from July 19th to August 17th. [t. F, f. Gk: m. *thermē* heat + s. *dôron* gift]

thermion (thû'mĭ ən), *n. Physics.* any of a class of electrically charged particles such as ions or electrons emitted by incandescent materials.

thermionic (thû'mĭ ŏn'ĭk), *adj.* pertaining to thermionics or thermions: *thermionic emission.*

thermionic current, 1. a flow of thermions. 2. the electric current so produced.

thermionics (thû'mĭ ŏn'ĭks), *n.* the science of thermionic phenomena, esp. the design and study of thermionic valves.

thermionic valve, a radio valve which contains a heated cathode.

thermistor (thû mĭs'tə), *n. Electronics.* a semiconductor, the resistance of which decreases or increases rapidly with increase in temperature. [f. THERM- + (TRANS)ISTOR or THERM- + (RES)ISTOR]

thermit (thû'mĭt), *n.* 1. Also, **thermite** (thû'mīt). a mixture of finely divided metallic aluminium and one or more oxides, as of iron, producing when ignited an extremely high temperature as the result of the union of the aluminium with the oxygen of the oxide: used in welding, etc. 2. (*cap.*) a trademark for this substance. [t. G: f. *therm-* THERM- + *-it* -ITE[1]]

thermo-, var. of **therm-,** before consonants, as in *thermochemistry.*

thermobarograph (thû'mō bă'rə grăf', -gräf'), *n.* an apparatus combining a thermograph and a barograph.

thermobarometer (thû'mō bə rŏm'ĭ tə), *n.* 1. an apparatus in which the change in boiling point indicates the pressure. 2. a form of barometer so constructed that it may also be used as a thermometer.

thermochemistry (thû'mō kĕm'ĭs trĭ), *n.* the branch of chemistry that treats of the relations between chemical action and heat. —**ther'mochem'ical,** *adj.* —**ther'mochem'ist,** *n.*

thermocouple (thû'mō kŭp'l), *n.* two conductors of different metals joined at their ends and producing a thermoelectric current when there is a difference in temperature between the ends. Also, **thermoelectric couple.**

thermoduric (thû'mō dyo͝oə'rĭk), *adj.* resistant to relatively high temperatures.

thermodynam., thermodynamics.

thermodynamics (thû'mō dī năm'ĭks), *n.* the science concerned with the relations between heat and mechanical energy or work, and the conversion of one into the other. —**ther'modynam'ic, ther'modynam'ical,** *adj.* —**ther'modynam'ically,** *adv.*

thermoelectric (thû'mō ĭ lĕk'trĭk), *adj.* of or pertaining to thermoelectricity. Also, **thermoelectrical.** —**ther'moelec'trically,** *adv.*

thermoelectric couple, a thermocouple.

thermoelectric effect, *Physics.* the Seebeck effect.

thermoelectricity (thû'mō ĭ lĕk'trĭs'ĭ tĭ), *n.* electricity produced directly from heat, as that generated (in the form of a current) when the ends of two dissimilar metallic conductors are joined to form a closed circuit and one of the junctions is heated.

thermoelectric thermometer, a thermometer based on thermoelectricity containing a thermocouple with an indicator.

thermoelectromotive (thû′mō ĭ lĕk′trō mō′tĭv), *adj.* denoting or pertaining to electromotive force produced by heat, as with a thermoelectric couple.

thermogenesis (thû′mō jĕn′ĭ sĭs), *n.* the production of heat, esp. in an animal body by physiological processes. —**thermogenetic** (thû′mō jĭ nĕt′ĭk), *adj.*

thermograph (thû′mō grăf′, -gräf′), *n.* a self-registering thermometer.

thermography (thû mŏg′rə fĭ), *n.* any process of writing or printing involving the use of heat. —**thermog′rapher,** *n.* —**thermographic** (thû′mō grăf′ĭk), *adj.*

thermolabile (thû′mō lā′bĭl), *adj. Biochem.* subject to destruction or loss of characteristic properties through the action of moderate heat, as certain toxins and ferments (opposed to *thermostable*).

thermoluminescence (thû′mō lo͞o′mĭ nĕs′əns), *n. Physics.* phosphorescence produced by heat. —**ther′molu′minesc′ent,** *adj.*

thermolysis (thû mŏl′ĭ sĭs), *n.* **1.** *Physiol.* the dispersion of heat from the body. **2.** *Chem.* dissociation by heat. —**thermolytic** (thû′mō lĭt′ĭk), *adj.*

thermometer (thə mŏm′ĭ tə), *n.* an instrument for measuring temperature, as by means of the expansion and contraction of mercury or alcohol in a capillary tube and bulb. —**thermometric** (thû′mə mĕt′rĭk), **ther′momet′rical,** *adj.* —**ther′momet′rically,** *adv.*

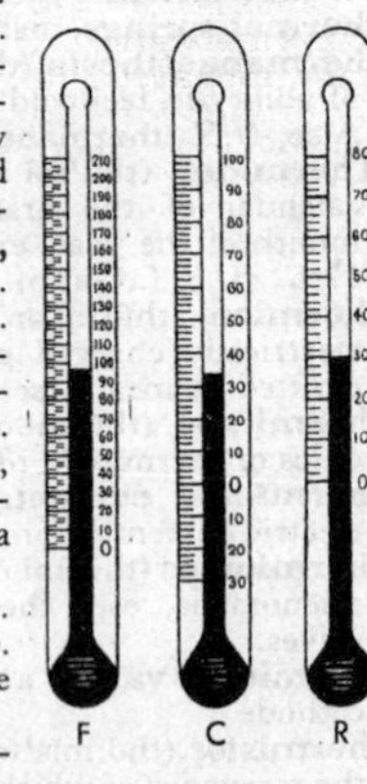
Thermometers
F, Fahrenheit;
C, Centigrade;
R, Reaumur

thermometry (thə mŏm′ĭ trĭ), *n.* **1.** the measurement of temperature. **2.** the science of the construction and use of thermometers.

thermomotive (thû′mō mō′tĭv), *adj.* **1.** pertaining to motion produced by heat. **2.** pertaining to a thermomotor.

thermomotor (thû′mō mō′tə), *n.* an engine operated by heat, esp. one driven by the expansive force of heated air.

thermonuclear (thû′mō nyo͞o′klĭ ə), *adj. Chem., Physics.* designating, or capable of producing, extremely high temperatures resulting from, caused by, or associated with nuclear fusion.

thermonuclear bomb, an atomic weapon which involves a fusion reaction, as a hydrogen bomb.

thermonuclear reaction, *Chem., Physics.* a nuclear fusion reaction that takes place between atomic nuclei which form part of a substance which has been heated to a temperature of several million degrees centigrade.

thermophil (thû′mō fĭl), *n.* something which requires or thrives best in comparatively hot conditions, as certain bacteria. Also, **thermophile** (thû′mō fīl′). —**ther′mophil′ic,** *adj.*

thermophone (thû′mō fōn′), *n.* a device for producing soundwaves in which an electrical conductor is heated and cooled according to the current passing through it; the soundwaves are produced by the expansion and contraction of the air around the conductor.

thermopile (thû′mō pīl′), *n. Physics.* a number of thermoelectric couples joined so as to produce a combined effect, used for generating currents or measuring small differences in temperature. [f. THERMO- + PILE[1]]

thermoplastic (thû′mō plăs′tĭk), *adj.* **1.** soft and pliable whenever heated, as some plastics, without any change of the inherent properties. —*n.* **2.** such a plastic.

Thermopylae (thû mŏp′ĭ lē′), *n.* a narrow pass in E Greece: heroic defence by the Spartans against the Persians 480 B.C.

Thermopylae, 480 B.C.

thermos (thû′mŏs), *n.* **1.** a double-walled container, usually made of silvered glass and having a vacuum in the interior cavity: used to keep substances that are hotter or colder than their surroundings at a constant temperature. **2.** (*cap.*) a trademark for this. [t. Gk: hot]

thermoscope (thû′mə skōp′), *n.* a device for indicating variations in temperature, usually without measuring their amount. —**thermoscopic** (thû′mə skŏp′ĭk), **ther′moscop′ical,** *adj.* —**ther′moscop′ically,** *adv.*

thermosetting (thû′mō sĕt′ĭng), *adj.* denoting or pertaining to a type of plastic which becomes hard and unmouldable when heated and, after setting, resistant to additional applications of heat, as the urea resins.

thermosiphon (thû′mō sī′fən), *n.* an arrangement of siphon tubes serving to induce circulation of water in a heating apparatus.

thermosphere (thû′mə sfĭə′), *n.* the region of the earth's atmosphere in which the temperature increases with altitude.

thermostable (thû′mō stā′bl), *adj. Biochem.* capable of being subjected to a moderate degree of heat without loss of characteristic properties, as certain toxins and ferments (opposed to *thermolabile*). —**thermostability** (thû′mō-stə bĭl′ĭ tĭ), *n.*

thermostat (thû′mə stăt′), *n.* a device, including a relay actuated by thermal conduction or convection, which functions to establish and maintain a desired temperature automatically, or signals a change in temperature for manual adjustment. —**ther′mostat′ic,** *adj.* —**ther′mostat′ically,** *adv.*

thermostatics (thû′mə stăt′ĭks), *n.* the science concerned with thermal equilibrium.

thermotaxis (thû′mō tăk′sĭs), *n.* **1.** *Biol.* the movement of an organism towards or away from a source of heat. **2.** *Physiol.* the regulation of the bodily temperature. —**ther′motax′ic,** *adj.*

thermotensile (thû′mō tĕn′sīl), *adj.* pertaining to tensile strength as affected by changes of temperature.

thermotherapy (thû′mō thĕ′rə pĭ), *n.* treatment of disease by means of heat, either moist or dry.

thermotropism (thû mŏt′rə pĭz′əm), *n. Biol.* the property in plants or other organisms of turning or bending (towards or away), as in growth, under the influence of heat. —**thermotropic** (thû′mə trŏp′ĭk), *adj.*

-thermy, a word element referring to heat. [comb. form repr. Gk *thérmē*]

theroid (thĭə′roid), *adj.* having animal propensities or characteristics. [t. Gk: m. s. *thēroeidḗs*]

Thersites (thû sī′tēz), *n. Gk Legend.* the most vindictive, impudent, and foul-mouthed of the Greeks before Troy.

thersitical (thû sĭt′ĭ kl), *adj.* scurrilous; foul-mouthed.

thesaurus (thĭ sô′rəs), *n., pl.* **-sauri** (-sô′rī). **1.** a storehouse or repository, as of words or knowledge; a dictionary, encyclopedia, or the like, esp. a dictionary of synonyms and antonyms. **2.** a treasury. [t. L, t. Gk: m. *thēsaurós* treasure, treasury]

these (thēz), *pron., adj.* pl. of **this.** [ME; r. OE *thās*]

Theseus (thē′syo͞os), *n. Gk Legend.* the chief hero of Attica, son of Aegeus, said to have organized a constitutional government and united the separate states at Athens. Among his many exploits he found his way through the Cretan labyrinth (aided by Ariadne, whom he loved but deserted), slew the Minotaur, fought the Amazons, was one of the Argonauts, and took part in the Calydonian hunt. —**Thesean** (thĭ sē′ən), *adj.*

thesis (thē′sĭs; *also for 4 and 5,* thĕs′ĭs), *n., pl.* **-ses** (-sēz). **1.** a proposition laid down or stated, esp. one to be discussed and proved or to be maintained against objections. **2.** a subject for a composition or essay. **3.** a dissertation, as one presented by a candidate for a diploma or degree, esp. a postgraduate degree. **4.** *Music.* (in conducting) the downward stroke in a measure (opposed to *arsis*). **5.** *Pros.* **a.** (orig.) the accented syllable of a foot in verse (opposed to *arsis*). **b.** (later) the stressed part of a metrical unit. [ME, t. Gk: setting down, something set down]

Thespian (thĕs′pĭ ən), *adj.* **1.** of Thespis. **2.** pertaining to tragedy or to the dramatic art in general; tragic; dramatic. —*n.* **3.** a tragedian; an actor or actress.

Thespis (thĕs′pĭs), *n.* fl. 6th cent. B.C., Greek poet.

Thess., Thessalonians. Also, **Thes.**

Thessalonian (thĕs′ə lō′nyən), *adj.* **1.** of or pertaining to Thessalonica (modern Salonika). —*n.* **2.** a native or inhabitant of Thessalonica. **3.** (*pl.*) either of the two books or epistles of the New Testament addressed by St Paul to the Thessalonian Christians.

Thessaloniki (thĕs′ə lə nī′kĭ), *n.* official name of **Salonika.** Also, **Thessalonike.** Ancient, **Thessalonica** (thĕs′ə lə nī′kə, -ə lŏn′ĭkə).

Thessaly (thĕs′ə lĭ), *n.* a region in E Greece: a former division of ancient Greece. 695,385 pop. (1961); 5208 sq. mi. —**Thessalian** (thĕ sā′lyən), *adj., n.*

Thessaly

theta (thē′tə), *n.* the eighth letter (Θ, θ) of the Greek alphabet.

thetic (thĕt′ĭk), *adj.* positive; dogmatic. Also, **thetical.** [t. Gk: m. s. *thetikós,* der. *thetós* placed] —**thet′ically,** *adv.*

Thetis (thē′tĭs), *n. Gk Myth.* the chief of the Nereids and mother by Peleus of Achilles.

theurgy (thē′û′jĭ), *n., pl.* **-gies.** **1.** a system of magic practised by the Egyptian Platonists and others professing to have communication with and aid from beneficent deities. **2.** the working of some divine or supernatural agency in human affairs; the effects brought about among men by such agency. [t. L: m. s. *theūrgia*, t. Gk: m. *theourgia* sorcery] —**theur′gic, theur′gical,** *adj.* —**theur′gically,** *adv.* —**the′urgist,** *n.*

thew (thyo͞o), *n.* **1.** (*usually pl.*) muscle or sinew. **2.** (*pl.*) physical strength. [ME; OE *thēaw* custom, usage, c. OHG *dau* discipline] —**thew′y,** *adj.*

thewless (thyo͞o′lĭs), *adj.* without vigour or energy.

they (t͟hā), *pron. pl., poss.* **theirs,** *obj.* **them. 1.** nominative plural of *he, she* and *it.* **2.** people in general: *they say he is rich.* **3.** *Colloq.* (generally regarded as bad usage) a person indefinitely (used in place of a singular pronoun where the sex of the antecedent is not determined): *If anybody moves they will get a bullet in their head.* [ME; t. Scand.; cf. Icel. *their* those, c. OE *thā*, pl. of *thæt* THAT]

they'd (t͟hād), the contraction of: **1.** they had. **2.** they would.

they'll (t͟hāl), the contraction of: **1.** they will. **2.** they shall.

they're (t͟hā′ə, t͟hēə), the contraction of: *they are.*

they've (t͟hāv), the contraction of: *they have.*

thi-, var. of **thio-,** as in *thiazine.*

thiamine (thī′ə mēn′, -mĭn), *n. Biochem.* a white crystalline solid forming part of the vitamin B complex, $C_{12}H_{17}$-ClN_4OS; a vitamin (B_1) required by the nervous system, absence of which causes beri-beri and other disorders; aneurin. Also, **thiamin.**

thiazine (thī′ə zēn′, -zīn′), *n. Chem.* any of a class of compounds containing a ring composed of one atom each of sulphur and nitrogen and four atoms of carbon. Also, **thiazin** (thī′ə zĭn). [f. THI- + AZ(O)- + -INE[2]]

thiazole (thī′ə zōl′), *n. Chem.* **1.** a colourless liquid, C_3H_3NS, with a pungent smell, serving as the parent substance of important dyestuffs. **2.** any of various derivatives of this substance. Also, **thiazol** (thī′ə zŏl′).

Thibet (tĭ bĕt′), *n. Obs.* Tibet. —**Thibet′an,** *adj., n.*

thick (thĭk), *adj.* **1.** having relatively great extent from one surface or side to its opposite; not thin: *a thick slice.* **2.** measuring as specified between opposite surfaces, or in depth, or in a direction perpendicular to that of the length and breadth: *a board one inch thick.* **3.** set close together; compact; dense: *a thick forest.* **4.** numerous, abundant, or plentiful. **5.** filled, covered, or abounding (fol. by *with*): *tables thick with dust.* **6.** having relatively great consistency; viscous: *a thick syrup.* **7.** (of darkness, etc.) dense, deep, or profound. **8.** husky, hoarse, muffled, or not clear in sound: *a thick voice.* **9.** (of an accent or dialect) very pronounced. **10.** containing much solid matter in suspension or solution. **11.** (of mist, smoke, etc.) having the component particles densely aggregated. **12.** (of the weather, etc.) foggy, misty, or hazy. **13.** sluggish; heavy-headed, as after dissipation. **14.** slow of mental apprehension; stupid; dull; slow-witted: *his mind is very thick.* **15.** *Colloq.* close in friendship; intimate. **16.** *Slang.* disagreeably excessive: *his demands are a bit thick.* —*adv.* **17.** in a thick manner. **18.** closely; near together: *flowers growing thick beside a wall.* **19. lay it on thick,** *Slang.* to be extravagant in flattery, praise, or the like. —*n.* **20.** that which is thick. **21.** the thickest, densest, or most crowded part; the place, time, stage, etc., of greatest activity or intensity: *in the thick of the fight.* **22.** *Slang.* a stupid, dull-witted person. **23. through thick and thin,** under all circumstances; unwaveringly. [ME; OE *thicce*, c. G *dick*] —**thick′ish,** *adj.* —**thick′ly,** *adv.*

thicken (thĭk′ən), *v.t., v.i.* **1.** to make or become thick or thicker. **2.** to make or grow more intense, profound, intricate, or complex. —**thick′ener,** *n.*

thickening (thĭk′ə nĭng), *n.* **1.** a making or becoming thick. **2.** a thickened part or area. **3.** something used to thicken; thickener.

thicket (thĭk′ĭt), *n.* a thick or dense growth of shrubs, bushes, or small trees; a thick coppice. [OE *thiccet*, f. *thicce* THICK + *-et*, n. suffix]

thickhead (thĭk′hĕd′), *n.* **1.** a stupid person; blockhead. **2.** any bird of the Australian family *Pachycephalidae.* —**thick′-head′ed,** *adj.* —**thick′-head′edness,** *n.*

thick-knee (thĭk′nē′), *n.* a wading bird of the family *Burhinidae*, as *Burhinus oedicnemus*, of Europe, Africa, and Asia; stone curlew.

thickleaf (thĭk′lēf′), *n., pl.* **-leaves.** any of the succulent herbs or shrubs constituting the genus *Crassula.*

thickness (thĭk′nĭs), *n.* **1.** the state or quality of being thick. **2.** the third dimension of a solid, as distinct from length and breadth. **3.** the thick part or body of something. **4.** a layer. —*v.t.* **5.** to cut or prepare to a required thickness.

thickset (thĭk′sĕt′), *adj.* **1.** set thickly or in close arrangement; dense: *a thickset hedge.* **2.** set, studded, or furnished thickly: *a sky thickset with stars.* **3.** of thick form or build; heavily or solidly built. —*n.* **4.** a thicket.

thick-skinned (thĭk′skĭnd′), *adj.* **1.** having a thick skin. **2.** not sensitive to criticism, reproach, rebuff, etc.

thick-skulled (thĭk′skŭld′), *adj.* **1.** having a thick skull. **2.** stupid; doltish.

thick-witted (thĭk′wĭt′ĭd), *adj.* stupid; dull.

thief (thēf), *n., pl.* **thieves.** one who steals, esp. secretly or without open force; one guilty of theft or larceny. [ME; OE *thēof*, c. G *Dieb*]

—**Syn.** THIEF, ROBBER refer to one who steals. A THIEF takes the goods or property of another by stealth without the latter's knowledge: *a horse thief; like a thief in the night.* A ROBBER trespasses upon the house, property, or person of another, and makes away with things of value, even at the cost of violence: *a robber held up two women in the street.*

Thiers (*Fr.* tyĕr), *n.* **Louis Adolphe** (*Fr.* lwē à dôlf′), 1797–1877, French statesman: president of France 1871–1873.

Thieu (tyo͞o), *n.* **Nguyen Van** (nyo͞o′ən văn), born 1923, Vietnamese statesman: president of South Vietnam since 1967.

thieve (thēv), *v.,* **thieved, thieving.** —*v.t.* **1.** to take by theft; steal. —*v.i.* **2.** to act as a thief; commit theft; steal. [OE *thēofian*, der. *thēof* THIEF]

thievery (thē′və rĭ), *n., pl.* **-eries. 1.** the act or practice of thieving; theft. **2.** something taken by theft.

thievish (thē′vĭsh), *adj.* **1.** given to thieving. **2.** of, pertaining to, or characteristic of a thief; stealthy. —**thiev′ishly,** *adv.* —**thiev′ishness,** *n.*

thig (thĭg), *v.t., v.i.,* **thigged, thigging.** *Scot.* to beg (alms, food, etc.); solicit (gifts). [ME, t. Scand.; cf. Icel. *thiggja* receive] —**thig′ger,** *n.*

thigh (thī), *n.* **1.** that part of the leg between the hip and the knee in man. **2.** a homologous or apparently corresponding part of the hind limb of other animals; the region of the femur. See illus. under **horse. 3.** (in birds) **a.** the true femoral region, buried in the general integument of the body. **b.** the segment below, containing the fibula and tibia. **4.** *Entomol.* femur. [ME; OE *thēoh*, c. D *dij*, MHG *diech*, Icel. *thjō*]

thighbone (thī′bōn′), *n.* femur.

thigmotaxis (thĭg′mə tăk′sĭs), *n. Biol.* the movement of an organism towards or away from any object which provides a mechanical stimulus; stereotaxis. [NL, f. Gk: m. *thígma* touch + *-taxis* -TAXIS] —**thigmotactic** (thĭg′mə tăk′tĭk), *adj.*

thigmotropism (thĭg mŏt′rə pĭz′əm), *n. Biol.* the property in plants or other organisms of turning or bending (towards or away), as in growth, under the influence of mechanical contact. [f. s. Gk *thígma* touch + -O- + -TROPISM] —**thigmotropic** (thĭg′mə trŏp′ĭk), *adj.*

thill (thĭl), *n.* either of the pair of shafts between which a single animal drawing a vehicle is placed. [ME *thylle.* Cf. OE *thille* plank, flooring]

thimble (thĭm′bl), *n.* **1.** a small cap, usually of metal, worn on the finger to push the needle in sewing. **2.** *Mech.* any of various devices or attachments likened to this. **3.** a short length of pipe encasing one of smaller diameter, as where a stovepipe passes through a wooden roof. **4.** *Naut.* a metal ring with a concave groove on the outside, used to line the outside of a ring of rope forming an eye. [ME *thym(b)yl*, OE *thȳmel*, der. *thūma* thumb] —**thim′ble-like′,** *adj.*

thimbleful (thĭm′bl fo͝ol′), *n., pl.* **-fuls.** as much as a thimble will hold; a small quantity.

thimblerig (thĭm′bl rĭg′), *n., v.,* **-rigged, -rigging.** —*n.* **1.** a swindling game in which the operator apparently covers a small ball or pea with one of three thimble-like cups, and then, moving the cups about, offers to bet that no-one can tell under which cup the ball or pea lies. —*v.t.* **2.** to cheat by or as by the thimblerig. —**thim′blerig′ger,** *n.*

thimbleweed (thĭm′bl wēd′), *n.* any of various plants with a thimble-shaped fruiting head, as the anemone, *Anemone virginiana*, and the rudbeckia, *Rudbeckia laciniata.*

Thimphu (tĭm′po͞o), *n.* the capital of Bhutan. Also, **Thimbu.** Cf. **Punakha.**

thin (thĭn), *adj.,* **thinner, thinnest,** *adv., v.,* **thinned, thinning.** —*adj.* **1.** having relatively little extent from one surface or side to its opposite; not thick: *thin ice.* **2.** of small cross-section in comparison with the length; slender: *a thin wire.* **3.** having little flesh; spare; lean. **4.** having the constituent or individual parts relatively few and not close together: *thin vegetation.* **5.** not dense; sparse; scanty. **6.** having relatively slight consistency, as a liquid; fluid; rare or rarefied, as air, etc. **7.** without solidity or substance; unsubstantial. **8.** easily seen through, transparent, or flimsy: *a thin excuse.* **9.** lacking fullness or volume, as sound; weak and shrill. **10.** faint, slight, poor, or feeble. **11.** lacking body, richness, or growth. **12.** lacking in chroma; of light tint. **13.** *Photog.* (of a developed negative) lacking in opaqueness and yielding prints without strong contrasts of light and shade. —*adv.* **14.** in a thin manner. —*v.t.* **15.** to make thin or thinner (often fol. by *down, out,* etc.). —*v.i.* **16.** to become thin or thinner; become reduced or diminished; go, pass, etc. (fol. by *down, off, away,* etc.). [ME and OE *thynne,* c. G *dünn*; akin to L *tenuis*] —**thin′ly,** *adv.* —**thin′ness,** *n.*

—**Syn. 3.** THIN, GAUNT, LEAN, SPARE, SLIM agree in referring to one having little flesh. THIN applies often to one in an unnaturally reduced state, as from sickness, overwork, lack of food, or the like: *a thin, dirty little waif.* GAUNT suggests the angularity of bones prominently displayed in a thin face and body: *to look ill and gaunt.* LEAN usually applies to a person or animal that is naturally thin: *looking lean but healthy after a camping holiday.* SPARE implies a muscular leanness with no diminution of vitality: *the mountaineer was spare in body.* SLIM usually applies to a person whose thinness is attractive and often cultivated: *her slim figure was greatly admired.*

thine (thīn), *pron., adj. Archaic.* the possessive form of *thou* used predicatively or without a noun following, or before a noun beginning with a vowel or *h.* Cf. **thy.** [ME; OE *thīn,* c. G *dein.* See THOU]

thin-face (thĭn′fās′), *adj. Print.* lean-face.

thing[1] (thĭng), *n.* **1.** a material object without life or consciousness; an inanimate object. **2.** some entity, object, or creature which is not or cannot be specifically designated or precisely described: *the stick had a brass thing on it.* **3.** that which is or may become an object of thought, whether material or ideal, animate or inanimate, actual, possible, or imaginary. **4.** a matter or affair: *things are going well now.* **5.** a fact or circumstance: *it is a curious thing.* **6.** an action, deed, or performance: *to do great things.* **7.** a particular or respect: *perfect in all things.* **8.** what is desired or required: *just the thing.* **9.** (*pl.*) clothes or apparel, esp. articles of dress added to ordinary clothing when going outdoors. **10.** (*pl.*) *Colloq.* implements, utensils, or other articles for service: *to help with the breakfast things.* **11.** (*pl.*) *Colloq.* personal possessions or belongings, often such as one carries along on a journey. **12.** *Law.* anything that may be the subject of a property right. **13.** that which is signified or represented, as distinguished from a word, symbol, or idea representing it. **14.** a living being or creature. **15.** *Colloq.* an unaccountable attitude or feeling about something, as of fear or aversion: *I have a thing about minced meat.* **16.** *Colloq.* a hallucination: *he's seeing things again.* **17. do the handsome thing by,** to treat generously. **18. know a thing or two,** *Colloq.* to be shrewd. **19. make a good thing out of,** to obtain an advantage from. **20. make a thing of,** *Colloq.* to turn into a major issue: *OK, so I made a mistake, but there's no need to make a thing of it.* **21. not to get a thing out of, a.** to fail to elicit something desired, as information, from. **b.** to fail to enjoy, appreciate, etc.: *I went to a performance of a play in Czech, but didn't get a thing out of it.* **22. old thing,** *Colloq.* (a familiar form of address.) **23. one of those things,** an event which was unavoidable or which is no longer remediable. **24. the thing, a.** that which is proper, correct, or fashionable. **b.** that which is important or necessary. **c.** the point or hub of a matter: *this is the thing.* [ME and OE, c. D and G *Ding* affair, matter, thing]

thing[2] (thĭng, tĭng), *n.* (in Scandinavian countries) a public meeting or assembly, esp. a legislative assembly or a court of law. [t. Icel.: assembly]

thing-in-itself (thĭng′ĭn ĭt sĕlf′), *n.* (in Kantian philosophy) reality as it is apart from experience; what remains to be postulated after space, time, and all the categories of the understanding are assigned to consciousness. See **noumenon.** [trans. of G *Ding an sich*]

thingumabob (thĭng′ə mə bŏb′), *n. Colloq.* (an indefinite name for a thing or person which a speaker cannot or does not designate more precisely.) Also, **thingumbob, thingumajig** (thĭng′mĭ jĭg′), **thingummy** (thĭng′ə mĭ).

think[1] (thĭngk), *v.,* **thought, thinking,** *n.* —*v.t.* **1.** to form or conceive in the mind; have in the mind as an idea, conception, or the like. **2.** to turn over in the mind; meditate; ponder: *he was thinking what it could mean.* **3.** to have the mind full of (a particular subject or the like). **4.** to form or have an idea or conception of (a thing, fact, circumstance, etc.). **5.** to bear in mind, recollect, or remember. **6.** to have in mind, intent, or purpose. **7.** to hold as an opinion; believe; suppose: *they thought that the earth was flat.* **8.** to consider (something) to be (as specified): *he thought the lecture was very interesting.* **9.** to anticipate or expect: *I did not think to find you here.* **10.** to bring by thinking.
—*v.i.* **11.** to use the mind, esp. the intellect, actively; cogitate or meditate. **12.** to form or have an idea or mental image (fol. by *of*). **13.** to reflect upon the matter in question: *think carefully before you begin.* **14.** to remember (usually fol. by *of*): *I can't think of his name.* **15.** to have consideration or regard (usually fol. by *of*): *to think of others first.* **16.** to make mental discovery; form or have a plan (usually fol. by *of*): *he thought of it first.* **17.** to have a belief or opinion as indicated. **18.** to have a high, low, or other opinion of a person or thing (fol. by *of*): *to think well of a person.* **19.** to have an anticipation or expectation (fol. by *of*). **20.** to have an opinion as indicated: *he thought fit to act alone.*
—*v.* **21.** Some special verb phrases are:
think aloud, to utter one's thoughts without considering all implications or putting them into a formal pattern.
think better of, to decide against an original intention.
think little of, to have a poor or low opinion of.
think nothing of, a. to have a very low opinion of. **b.** to disregard; take no account of.
think out, a. to finish or complete in thought. **b.** to understand or solve by process of thought. **c.** to devise or contrive by thinking.
think over, to consider carefully and at leisure.
think through, *U.S.* to think out.
think twice, to consider with great care (before taking action).
think up, to form as a concept; devise.
—*n.* **22.** *Colloq.* an act or process of thinking: *go away and have a good think.*
[ME; OE *thencan* (c. D and G *denken*), der. *thanc* thought. See THANK, n.] —**think′able,** *adj.* —**think′er,** *n.*

—**Syn. 4.** conceive, imagine, picture. **6.** intend, mean. **7.** THINK, DEEM, JUDGE, SUPPOSE mean to have an opinion. THINK is the general word for forming or having a thought, opinion, notion, or idea in the mind: *to think that a hat is becoming.* DEEM, used esp. in formal speech, implies having formed an opinion and holding to it as a standard for measuring, judging, etc.: *to deem it an honour to be invited to speak.* JUDGE suggests a careful balance of reason and evidence: *to judge from previous experience.* SUPPOSE suggests having an opinion not based on certainty, but which appears to be justified: *to suppose that a friend is honest.*

think[2] (thĭngk), *v.t.,* **thought, thinking.** *Archaic.* to seem or appear (usually impersonal, with indirect object; now only in *methinks* and *methought*). [ME; OE *thync(e)an,* c. G *dünken*]

thinking (thĭng′kĭng), *adj.* **1.** that thinks; reasoning. **2.** thoughtful; reflective. —*n.* **3.** thought; reflection.

thinking cap, a period or state of reflection or consideration: *they put on their thinking caps when confronted with the problem.*

thinner (thĭn′ə), *n.* **1.** one who or that which thins. **2.** a volatile liquid added to paints or varnishes to facilitate application and to aid penetration by lowering the viscosity.

thin-skinned (thĭn′skĭnd′), *adj.* **1.** having a thin skin. **2.** sensitive to criticism, reproach, rebuff, or the like; easily offended; touchy.

thio-, a word element used in chemical nomenclature to indicate the replacement of part or all the oxygen atoms in a compound by sulphur: often used to designate sulphur analogues of oxygen compounds. Also, **thi-.** [comb. form repr. Gk *theîon* sulphur]

thioaldehyde (thī′ō ăl′dĭ hīd′), *n. Chem.* any of a class of compounds formed by the action of hydrogen sulphide on aldehydes, and regarded as aldehydes with the oxygen replaced by sulphur.

thioamide (thī′ō ăm′īd, -ĭd), *n. Chem.* an amide group which contains a sulphur atom. See **polyamide.**

thiocarbamide (thī′ō kä′bə mīd′), *n. Chem.* thiourea.

thiocyanate (thī′ō sī′ə nāt′), *n. Chem.* a salt or ester of thiocyanic acid, characterized by the univalent SCN group, and used in hypertensions to relax and dilate smaller blood vessels.

thiocyanic acid (thī′ō sī ăn′ĭk), *Chem.* an unstable acid, HSCN, known chiefly in the form of its salts.

Thiokol (thī′ə kŏl′), *n. Trademark.* any of a group of rubber-like materials with the general formula $(RS_x)_n$, where R is a bivalent radical and *x* is a number usually between 2 and 4, used when oil and petrol resistance are required.

thionic (thī ŏn′ĭk), *adj. Chem.* of or pertaining to sulphur. [f. m. *Gk theîon* sulphur + -IC]

thionic acid, *Chem.* any of four acids of sulphur of the type $H_2S_xO_6$, where *x* is a number from 2 to 5.

thionine (thī′ō nēn′, -nīn′), *n. Chem.* **1.** a thiazine derivative occurring in dark crystalline plates, used as a violet dye, as in staining microscopic objects. **2.** any of various related dyes.

thiopentone sodium (thī′ō pĕn′tōn), sodium pentothal. Also, **thiopental sodium** (thī′ō pĕn′tl).

thiophen (thī′ō fĕn′), *n. Chem.* a colourless liquid, C_4H_4S, with physical properties resembling benzene, occurring in crude coal-tar benzene and prepared by high temperature interaction of butane and sulphur. Also, **thiophene** (thī′ō fēn′).

thiosinamine (thī′ō sĭn′ə mēn′, -sĭ năm′ĭn), *n. Chem.* a colourless crystalline compound, $C_4H_8N_2S$, with bitter taste and faint garlic-like smell: obtained by the action of ammonia on a sulphur compound, present in mustard oil.

thiosulphate (thī′ō sŭl′fāt), *n. Chem.* a salt of thiosulphuric acid. Also, *U.S.*, **thiosulfate.**

thiosulphuric acid (thī′ō sŭl fyŏŏə′rĭk), *Chem.* an acid, $H_2S_2O_3$, which may be regarded as sulphuric acid with one oxygen atom replaced by sulphur. Also, *U.S.*, **thiosulfuric acid.**

thiourea (thī′ō yŏŏə′rĭ ə), *n. Chem.* a colourless crystalline substance, $CS(NH_2)_2$, with a bitter taste, derived from urea by replacement of the oxygen with sulphur. Also, **thiocarbamide.**

third (thûd), *adj.* **1.** next after the second in order, place, time, rank, value, quality, etc. (the ordinal of three). **2.** one out of every three: *every third Monday.* **3.** *Music.* lowest of three parts for the same instrument or voice: *third cello.* **4.** uncommitted to either of two opposing extremes; following a middle course: *third force, Third World.* —*n.* **5.** one who or that which comes next after the second. **6.** a third part, esp. of one. **7.** the class of honours next below a second in a university degree examination. **8.** *Motor Vehicles.* third gear. **9.** (*usually pl.*) *Law.* **a.** the third part of the personal property of a deceased husband, which in certain circumstances goes absolutely to the widow. **b.** a widow's dower. **10.** *Music.* **a.** a note on the third degree from a given note (counted as the first). **b.** the interval between such notes. **c.** the harmonic combination of such notes. [ME *thirde*, OE (North.) *thirda*, var. of *thridda*, c. D *derde*, G *dritte*; akin to L *tertius*, Gk *trítos*] —**third′ly,** *adv.*

third class, a class of accommodation, as on a train, esp. formerly in Great Britain, cheaper and less luxurious than second or first class.

third-class (thûd′kläs′), *adj.* extremely shoddy and inferior.

third degree, 1. the use of bullying or torture by the police (or others) in some countries in examining a person in order to extort information or a confession. **2.** the degree of master mason in Freemasonry.

third estate, the commons. See **estate** (def. 6).

third gear, *Motor Vehicles.* the third forward gear ratio, usually the highest or next to highest.

third half, *Sport, Colloq.* a social gathering after a match.

third-hand (thûd′hănd′), *adj.* **1.** obtained after two previous possessors. **2.** old and shoddy. —*adv.* **3.** after having been owned by two previous persons.

Third International. See **international** (def. 7).

third man, 1. *Cricket.* **a.** a fielding position near the boundary on the off side behind the batsman's wicket. **b.** a fielder in this position. **2.** *Colloq.* the referee in a boxing or wrestling match.

third party, any person other than the principals to some transaction, proceeding, or agreement.

third-party (thûd′pä′tĭ), *adj.* denoting an insurance policy against liability caused by the insurer or his servants to the property or person of others.

third person, *Gram.* See **person** (def. 11).

third rail, a conductor in the form of a supplementary rail, laid beside or between the rails of the track of an electric railway to carry the current, which is collected by means of a sliding contact.

third-rate (thûd′rāt′), *adj.* **1.** of the third rate or class. **2.** distinctly inferior.

Third Reich. See **Reich** (def. 4).

Third Republic. See **Republic** (def. 4).

Third World, those countries collectively, esp. in Africa and Asia, which belong neither to the capitalist nor the communist spheres of influence.

thirl (thûl), *v.t., v.i. Dial.* **1.** to pierce. **2.** to thrill. [ME; OE *thyrlian*, der. *thyrel* hole. See NOSTRIL]

thirlage (thû′lĭj), *n. Scot. Law.* **1.** an obligation imposed on tenants of certain lands, requiring them to bring their grain to a particular mill. **2.** the price paid for such grinding. [var. of obs. *thrillage* bondage, der. THRALL]

thirst (thûst), *n.* **1.** an uneasy or painful sensation of dryness in the mouth and throat caused by need of drink. **2.** the physical condition resulting from this need. **3.** strong or eager desire; craving: *a thirst for knowledge.* —*v.i.* **4.** to feel thirst; be thirsty. **5.** to have a strong desire. [ME *thirsten* (v.), OE *thyrstan*, der. OE *thurst* (n.) c. D *dorst*, G *Durst*] —**thirst′er,** *n.* —**thirst′less,** *adj.*

thirsty (thûs′tĭ), *adj.*, **-tier, -tiest. 1.** having thirst; craving drink. **2.** needing moisture, as land; dry or arid. **3.** eagerly desirous; eager. **4.** *Colloq.* causing thirst. —**thirst′ily,** *adv.* —**thirst′iness,** *n.*

thirteen (thû′tēn′), *n.* **1.** a cardinal number, ten plus three. **2.** a symbol for this number, as 13 or XIII. —*adj.* **3.** amounting to thirteen in number. [ME *thrittene*, OE *thrēotēne*, c. G *dreizehn*. See THREE, -TEEN]

thirteenth (thû′tēnth′), *adj.* **1.** next after the twelfth. **2.** being one of thirteen equal parts. —*n.* **3.** a thirteenth part, esp. of one ($\frac{1}{13}$). **4.** the thirteenth member of a series.

thirtieth (thû′tĭ ĭth), *adj.* **1.** next after the twenty-ninth. **2.** being one of thirty equal parts. —*n.* **3.** a thirtieth part, esp. of one ($\frac{1}{30}$). **4.** the thirtieth member of a series.

thirty (thû′tĭ), *n., pl.* **-ties,** *adj.* —*n.* **1.** a cardinal number, ten times three. **2.** a symbol for this number, as 30 or XXX. **3.** (*pl.*) the numbers from 30 to 39 of a series, esp. with reference to the years of a person's age, or the years of a century, esp. the twentieth. —*adj.* **4.** amounting to thirty in number. [ME *thritty*, OE *thrītig*, f. *thrī* THREE + *-tig* -TY[1], c. G *dreissig*]

Thirty-nine Articles, the 39 points of doctrine subscribed to by ordinands of the Church of England, as prescribed by an act of Parliament of 1571.

thirty-second note (thû′tĭ sĕk′ənd), *U.S.* demisemiquaver.

thirty-twomo (thû′tĭ tōō′mō), *n., pl.* **-mos,** *adj. Bookbinding.* trigesimo-secundo.

Thirty Years War, a series of European wars (1618–48) primarily between Protestants and Catholics of the Holy Roman Empire.

this (ŧħĭs), *pron. and adj., pl.* **these;** *adv.* —*pron.* **1.** a demonstrative pronoun used to indicate: **a.** a person, thing, idea, etc., as pointed out, present, or near, as before mentioned or supposed to be understood, as about to be mentioned, or by way of emphasis. **b.** one of two or more persons, things, etc., already mentioned, referring to the one nearer in place, time, or thought. **c.** one of two or more persons, things, etc., already mentioned, implying contradistinction (opposed to *that*). **2. with this,** hereupon; immediately after this. —*adj.* **3.** a demonstrative adjective used to indicate: **a.** a person, place, thing, idea, etc., as pointed out, present, or near, before mentioned, supposed to be understood, or by way of emphasis. **b.** one of two or more persons, things, etc., already mentioned, referring to one nearer in place, time, or thought. **c.** one of two or more persons, things, etc., already mentioned, implying contradistinction (opposed to *that*). —*adv.* **4.** an adverb used with adjectives and adverbs of quantity or extent: *this much.* [ME and OE, c. G *dies*]

Thisbe (thĭz′bĭ), *n.* See **Pyramus and Thisbe.**

thistle (thĭs′əl), *n.* **1.** any of various prickly plants of the composite genus *Cirsium*, as *C. vulgare*, the **spear thistle. 2.** any prickly plant of related genera, as *Carduus*, *Carlina*, and *Onopordum.* **3.** any of various other prickly plants. [ME and OE *thistel*, c. D *distel*, G *Distel*] —**this′tle-like′,** *adj.* —**this′tly,** *adj.*

Thistle, *Cirsium vulgare*

Thistle (thĭs′əl), *n.* **Order of the,** a Scottish order of knighthood, founded in 1687.

thistledown (thĭs′əl doun′), *n.* the tufted feathery parachutes of thistle seeds.

thither (ŧħĭŧħ′ə), *adv.* **1.** Also, **thitherwards** (ŧħĭŧħ′ə wədz), **thitherward.** to or towards that place or point. —*adj.* **2.** on the side or in the direction away from the person speaking; farther; more remote. [ME; OE *thider*, earlier *thæder*, c. Icel. *thadhra* there; akin to THAT, THE]

thitherto (ŧħĭŧħ′ə tōō′, ŧħĭŧħ′ə tōō′), *adv. Rare.* up to that time; until then.

thixotropy (thĭk sŏt′rə pĭ), *n. Chem.* the property exhibited by certain gels of becoming liquid when stirred or shaken. [f. Gk *thíx(is)* a touch + -O- + -TROPY] —**thixotropic** (thĭk′sə trŏp′ĭk), *adj.*

tho (ŧħō), *conj., adv.* though. Also, **tho'.**

thole[1] (thōl), *n.* **1.** a pin inserted in a boat's gunwale or the like, to act as a fulcrum for the oar. **2.** either of two such pins between which the oar works. Also, **tholepin** (thōl′pĭn′). [ME *tholle*, OE *tholl*, c. LG *dolle*]

Thole pins

thole[2] (thōl), *v.t.*, **tholed, tholing.** *Dial.* to suffer; bear; endure. [ME; OE *tholian*, c. Icel. *thola*; akin to L *tolerāre*]

tholobate (thŏl′ə bāt′), *n. Archit.* the substructure supporting a dome or cupola. [f. Gk: m. *thólos* THOLUS + m. s. *-batēs* goer]

tholus (thō′ləs), *n., pl.* **tholi** (thō′lī). a circular building or part of one, as a dome, cupola, or lantern. Also, **tholos, thole.** [t. L, t. Gk: m. *thólos*]

Thomas (tŏm′əs; *Fr.* tô mȧ′ *for 3*), *n.* **1.** an apostle who demanded proof of Christ's resurrection. John 20:24–29. **2.** See **doubting Thomas. 3. Ambroise** (*Fr.* äN brwȧz′), 1811–96, French composer. **4. Dylan (Marlais)** (dĭl′ən mä′lā), 1914–53, Welsh poet writing in English. **5. (Philip) Edward** ('*Edward Eastaway*'), 1878–1917, English poet.

Thomas of Erceldoune (ûr′səl do͞on′) ('*Thomas the Rhymer*'), 1220?–1297?, Scottish poet.

Thomas of Woodstock (wo͝od′stŏk′), **Duke of Gloucester,** 1355–97, English prince (son of Edward III).

Thomism (tō′mĭz′əm), *n.* a system of philosophy and theology as taught by St Thomas Aquinas. —**Tho′mist,** *n., adj.*

Thompson (tŏmp′sən, tŏm′-), *n.* **1. Benjamin, Count Rumford,** 1753–1814, English physicist and administrator in Bavaria, born in America. **2. Francis,** 1859–1907, English poet.

Thompson submachine gun, a type of submachine gun. Also, **Tommy gun.** [named after J. T. *Thompson*, 1860–1940, U.S. army officer]

Thomson (tŏm′sən), *n.* **1. James,** 1700–1748, English poet, born in Scotland. **2. James** ('*B.V.*'), 1834–82, English poet; author of *The City of Dreadful Night.* **3. John Arthur,** 1861–1933, Scottish scientist and author. **4. Sir Joseph John,** 1856–1940, English physicist. **5. Sir William.** See **Kelvin. 6.** a river in E Australia flowing SW through Queensland, joining with the Barwon to form Copper Creek. ab. 240 mi.

Thomson effect, *Physics.* the production of a gradient of electrical potential along a conducting metal wire or strip which is subjected to a temperature gradient along its length. See **Kelvin scale.** [named after Sir William THOMSON]

Thonburi (tŏn′bo͞o rē′), *n.* a town in S Thailand, near Bangkok. 403,828 (1964).

thong (thŏng), *n.* **1.** a narrow strip of hide or leather, used as a fastening, as the lash of a whip, etc. **2.** a similar strip of some other material. [ME; OE *thwong*, akin to Icel. *thvengr*]

Thor (thô), *n. Scand. Myth.* the ancient Scandinavian god of thunder, represented as wielding a mighty hammer.

thoracic (thô răs′ĭk), *adj.* of or pertaining to the thorax. Also, **thoracal** (thô′rə kl).

thoracic duct, *Anat.* the main trunk of the lymphatic system, passing along the spinal column in the thoracic cavity, and conveying a large amount of lymph and chyle into the venous circulation.

thoracicolumbar (thô răs′ĭ kō lŭm′bə), *adj.* pertaining to the thoracic and lumbar areas of the body.

thoracoplasty (thô′rə kō plăs′tĭ), *n., pl.* **-ties.** *Surg.* the operation of removal of selected portions of the bony chest wall (ribs) to compress part of the underlying lung or an abnormal pleural space, usually in the treatment of tuberculosis. [f. *thoraco-* (t. Gk: m. *thōrako-*, comb. form of *thṓrāx* THORAX) + -PLASTY]

thorax (thô′răks), *n., pl.* **thoraces** (thô′rə sēz′, thô rā′sēz), **thoraxes. 1.** (in man and the higher vertebrates) the part of the trunk between the neck and the abdomen, containing the cavity (enclosed by the ribs, etc.) in which the heart, lungs, etc., are situated; the chest. **2.** a corresponding part in other animals. **3.** (in insects) the portion of the body between the head and the abdomen. See diag. under **insect.** [ME, t. L, t. Gk: breastplate, chest]

Thoreau (thô′rō, thô rō′), *n.* **Henry David,** 1817–62, U.S. naturalist and author.

Thorez (*Fr.* tŏ rĕz′), *n.* **Maurice** (*Fr.* mŏ rēs′), 1900–64, French politician: leader of the French Communist Party.

thoria (thô′rĭ ə), *n. Chem.* an oxide of thorium, ThO_2, a white powder, used in making gas mantles. [f. THORI(UM) + *-a*; modelled on MAGNESIA]

thorianite (thô′rĭ ə nīt′), *n.* a rare mineral, mainly thorium oxide, ThO_2, but containing also uranium, cerium, etc., occurring in small, black, cubic crystals, notable for its radioactivity: a minor source of thorium.

thoride (thô′rīd), *n. Physics.* any of several natural radioactive isotopes which occur in the radioactive series containing thorium.

thorite (thô′rīt), *n.* a radioactive mineral, thorium silicate, $ThSiO_4$, occurring as black or yellow crystals.

thorium (thô′rĭ əm), *n. Chem.* a radioactive metallic element present in monazite. Thorium oxide (thoria) with 1 per cent cerium oxide (ceria) constitutes Welsbach gas mantles. *Symbol:* Th; *at. wt:* 232·038; *at. no.:* 90; *sp. gr.:* 11·2. [t. NL: f. *Thor* THOR + *-ium* -IUM] —**thoric** (thô′rĭk), *adj.*

thorn (thôn), *n.* **1.** a sharp excrescence on a plant, esp. a sharp-pointed aborted branch; a spine; a prickle. **2.** any of various thorny shrubs or trees, esp. of the genus *Crataegus*, as *C. monogyna*, the common hawthorn, often planted for hedges. **3.** their wood. **4.** something that wounds, or causes discomfort or annoyance. **5.** the runic character þ for *th* (once used in the English alphabet; still used in Icelandic). **6. thorn in one's flesh** or **side,** a source of continual annoyance, discomfort, or the like. —*v.t.* **7.** to prick with a thorn; vex. [ME and OE, c. G *Dorn*, Icel. *thorn*] —**thorn′less,** *adj.* —**thorn′like′,** *adj.*

Thorn (*Ger.* tôrn), *n.* German name of **Torún.**

Thornaby-on-Tees (thô′nə bĭ ŏn tēz′), *n.* a town in England, in the North Riding of Yorkshire. 22,793 (1961).

thorn-apple (thôn′ăp′l), *n.* **1.** any of the poisonous solanaceous plants constituting the genus *Datura*, the species of which bear capsules covered with prickly spines, esp. the jimson weed, *D. stramonium.* **2.** a fruit of some species of thorn tree, genus *Crataegus*; haw.

thornback (thôn′băk′), *n.* a European skate, *Raia clavata*, with short spines on the back and tail.

thornbush (thôn′bo͝osh′), *n.* any thorny plant or bush.

Thorndike (thôn′dīk′), *n.* **Dame Sybil,** born 1882, English actress.

Thornhill (thôn′hĭl′), *n.* **Sir James,** 1675?–1734, English baroque painter.

thorny (thô′nĭ), *adj.,* **-nier, -niest. 1.** abounding in or characterized by thorns; spiny; prickly. **2.** thornlike. **3.** overgrown with thorns or brambles. **4.** painful; vexatious. **5.** full of points of dispute; difficult; *a thorny question.* —**thorn′iness,** *n.*

thoron (thô′rŏn), *n. Chem.* a radioactive isotope of radon, produced by the disintegration of thorium. *Symbol:* Tn; *at. wt:* 220; *at. no.:* 86. [der. *thoro-*, comb. form of THORIUM, modelled on NEON]

thorough (thŭ′rə), *adj.* **1.** carried out through the whole of something; fully executed; complete or perfect: *a thorough search.* **2.** being fully or completely (such): *a thorough fool.* **3.** thoroughgoing in action or procedure; leaving nothing undone. **4.** *Rare.* going, passing, or extending through. —*adv., prep.* **5.** *Archaic.* through. —*n.* **6.** (*cap.*) thoroughgoing action, procedure, or policy, as that of Strafford and Laud in the reign of Charles I of England. Also, *Colloq.*, **thoro** for 1–5. [ME; OE *thuruh*, var. of *thurh* THROUGH] —**thor′oughly,** *adv.* —**thor′oughness,** *n.*

thoroughbass (thŭ′rə bās′), *n. Music.* **1.** a bass part written out in full throughout an entire piece, and accompanied by figures which indicate the successive chords of the harmony. **2.** the science or method of indicating harmonies by such figures. **3.** harmonic composition in general.

thorough brace, *U.S.* either of two strong braces or bands of leather from the front to the back spring and supporting the body of a coach or other vehicle.

thoroughbred (thŭ′rə brĕd′), *adj.* **1.** of pure or unmixed breed, stock, or race, as a horse or other animal; bred from the purest and best blood. **2.** (*cap. or l.c.*) of or pertaining to the Thoroughbred breed of horses. **3.** (of human beings) having qualities characteristic of pure breeding; high-spirited; mettlesome; elegant or graceful. **4.** thoroughly educated or trained. —*n.* **5.** a thoroughbred animal. **6.** (*cap.*) a horse of the English breed of racehorses, developed by crossing domestic and Middle Eastern strains. **7.** a well-bred or thoroughly trained person.

thoroughfare (thŭ′rə fēə′), *n.* **1.** a road, street, or the like, open at both ends; esp. a main road. **2.** a passage or way through: *no thoroughfare.* **3.** a strait, river, or the like, affording passage.

thoroughgoing (thŭ′rə gō′ĭng), *adj.* **1.** doing things thoroughly. **2.** carried out to the full extent. **3.** complete; unqualified: *a thoroughgoing knave.*

thoroughpaced (thŭ′rə pāst′), *adj.* **1.** trained to go through all the possible paces, as a horse. **2.** thoroughgoing, complete, or perfect.

thoroughpin (thŭ′rə pĭn′), *n. Vet. Sci.* a morbid swelling just above the hock of a horse, usually appearing on both sides of the leg and sometimes causing lameness.

thorow-wax (thŭ′rə wăks′), *n.* the hare's-ear.

thorp (thôp), *n. Archaic except in Placenames.* a hamlet, village, or small town. Also, **thorpe.** [ME and OE, c. G *Dorf*, Icel. *thorp* village]

Thorpe (thôp), *n.* **Jeremy** (jĕ′rə mĭ), born 1929, British politician, leader of the Liberal Party since 1967.

Thorshavn (*Dan.* tôrs′hȧ wən), *n.* a town in and the capital of the Faeroes. 7,447 (1964).

Thorvaldsen (*Dan.* tŏr′vȧl sən), *n.* **Albert Bertal** (*Dan.* ȧl′bĕrt bĕr′təl), 1770–1844, Danish sculptor. Also, **Thorwaldsen** (*Dan.* tŏr′vȧl sən).

those (tħōz), *pron., adj.* pl. of **that.** [ME; OE *thās* these (change of meaning variously explained); r. *thō* (d., obs.)]

Thoth (thōth, tōt), *n.* an Egyptian divinity represented as a human form with the head of an ibis or baboon, whom the Greeks identified with Hermes: the scribe of the gods, the inventor of numbers and letters, and the god of learning, wisdom, and magic. [t. Gk, t. Egyptian: m. *Tehut*]

thou[1] (t͟hou), *pron., sing., nom.* **thou** *poss.* **thy** or **thine;** *obj.* **thee;** *pl., nom.* **you** or **ye;** *poss.* **your** or **yours;** *obj.* **you** or **ye;** *v.* —*pron.* **1.** the personal pronoun of the second person, in the singular number and nominative case, used to denote the person (or thing) spoken to: formerly in general use, often as indicating: **a.** equality, familiarity, or intimacy. **b.** superiority on the part of the speaker. **c.** contempt or scorn for the person addressed; but now little used (being regularly replaced by *you*, which is plural, and takes a plural verb) except provincially, archaically, in poetry or elevated prose, in addressing the Deity, and by the Friends or Quakers, who, however, usually say not *thou* but *thee*, putting with it a verb in the third person singular (*thee is*). —*v.t.* **2.** to address as 'thou'. —*v.i.* **3.** to use 'thou' in discourse. [ME; OE *thū*, c. G and MD *du*, L *tū*]

thou[2] (thou), *n. Slang.* a thousand (pounds, etc.).

though (t͟hō), *conj.* **1.** (introducing a subordinate clause, which is often marked by ellipsis) notwithstanding that; in spite of the fact that. **2.** even if; granting that. **3.** yet, still, or nevertheless (introducing an additional statement restricting or modifying a principal one): *I will go though I fear it will be useless.* **4.** if (usually in *as though*). —*adv.* **5.** for all that; however. Also, **tho, tho'.** [ME *thoh*, t. Scand.; cf. Icel. *thō*, c. OE *thēah* however]

thought[1] (thôt), *n.* **1.** the product of mental activity; that which one thinks. **2.** a single act or product of thinking; an idea or notion: *to collect one's thoughts.* **3.** the act or process of thinking; mental activity. **4.** the capacity or faculty of thinking. **5.** a consideration or reflection. **6.** meditation: *lost in thought.* **7.** intention, design, or purpose, esp. a half-formed or imperfect intention: *we had some thought of going.* **8.** anticipation or expectation: *I had no thought of seeing you here.* **9.** consideration, attention, care, or regard: *taking no thought for her appearance.* **10.** a judgement, opinion, or belief. **11.** the intellectual activity or the ideas, opinions, etc., characteristic of a particular place, class, or time: *Greek thought.* **12.** a very small amount; a trifle. **13. second thoughts,** reconsideration. [ME *thoght*, OE *thoht* (akin to THINK[1]). Cf. D *gedachte*] —**Syn. 2.** concept, conception, opinion, judgement, belief.

thought[2] (thôt), *v.* pt. and pp. of **think.**

thoughtful (thôt′fəl), *adj.* **1.** occupied with or given to thought; contemplative; meditative; reflective. **2.** characterized by or manifesting thought: *a thoughtful essay.* **3.** careful, heedful, or mindful: *to be thoughtful of one's safety.* **4.** showing consideration for others; considerate. —**thought′fully,** *adv.* —**thought′fulness,** *n.*

—**Syn. 4.** THOUGHTFUL, CONSIDERATE mean taking thought for the comfort and the good of others. THOUGHTFUL implies providing little attentions, offering services, or in some way looking out for the comfort or welfare of others: *it was thoughtful of you to send the flowers.* CONSIDERATE implies sparing others annoyance or discomfort, and being careful not to hurt their feelings: *not considerate, only polite.*

thoughtless (thôt′lĭs), *adj.* **1.** not taking thought; unthinking, careless, or heedless. **2.** characterized by or showing lack of thought. **3.** lacking in consideration for others; inconsiderate. **4.** devoid of or lacking capacity for thought. —**thought′lessly,** *adv.* —**thought′lessness,** *n.*

thought-reading (thôt′rē′dĭng), *n.* mind-reading. —**thought′-read′er,** *n.*

thought transference, telepathy.

thousand (thou′zənd), *n.* **1.** a cardinal number, ten times one hundred. **2.** a symbol for this number, as 1000 or M. **3.** a great number or amount. **4. one in a thousand,** exceedingly good; exceptional; outstanding. —*adj.* **5.** amounting to one thousand in number. [ME; OE *thūsend*, c. Dan. *tusind*]

Thousand and One Nights, The, The Arabian Nights' Entertainments.

thousandfold (thou′zən fōld′), *adj., adv.* a thousand times as great or as much.

Thousand Islands, a group of ab. 1500 islands in S Canada and the northern U.S., in the St Lawrence at the outlet of Lake Ontario: summer resorts.

thousandth (thou′zənth), *adj.* **1.** last in order of a series of a thousand. **2.** being one of a thousand equal parts. —*n.* **3.** a thousandth part, esp. of one (1/1000). **4.** the thousandth member of a series.

Thrace (thrās), *n.* **1.** an ancient region of varying extent in the E part of the Balkan Peninsula: later a Roman province; now in Bulgaria, Turkey, and Greece. **2.** a modern region corresponding to the S part of the Roman province: now divided between Greece (**Western Thrace**) and Turkey (**Eastern Thrace**).

Thrace (def. 2)

Thracian (thrā′shyən), *adj.* **1.** of or pertaining to Thrace or its inhabitants. —*n.* **2.** a native or inhabitant of Thrace. **3.** the language of ancient Thrace.

thraldom (thrôl′dəm), *n.* the state of being a thrall; bondage; slavery; servitude. Also, *U.S.*, **thralldom.**

thrall (thrôl), *n.* **1.** one who is in bondage; a bondman or slave. **2.** one who is in bondage to some power, influence, or the like. **3.** thraldom. —*v.t.* **4.** *Archaic.* to put or hold in thraldom; enslave. —*adj.* **5.** *Archaic.* in bondage; enslaved. [ME; OE *thrǣl*, t. Scand.; cf. Icel. *thrǣll*, c. OHG *dregil* servant]

thrash (thrăsh), *v.t.* **1.** to beat soundly by way of punishment; administer a beating to. **2.** to defeat thoroughly. **3.** *Naut.* to force (a ship) forward against the wind, etc. **4.** to thresh (wheat, grain, etc.). **5. thrash out,** to discuss (a matter) exhaustively; solve (a problem, etc.) by exhaustive discussion. —*v.i.* **6.** to beat, toss, or plunge wildly or violently about. **7.** *Naut.* to make way against the wind, tide, etc.; beat. **8.** to thresh. —*n.* **9.** the act of thrashing; a beating; a blow. **10.** *Swimming.* the upward and downward movement of the legs, as in the crawl. [var. of THRESH] —**Syn. 1.** See **beat.**

thrasher (thrăsh′ə), *n.* **1.** one who or that which thrashes. **2.** any of various long-tailed thrushlike birds, esp. of the genus *Toxostoma*, allied to the mockingbird, as the **brown thrasher. 3.** thresher (def. 3).

thrashing (thrăsh′ing), *n.* **1.** a flogging; beating. **2.** the act of one who or that which thrashes. **3.** a defeat.

thrasonical (thrə sŏn′ĭ kl), *adj.* boastful; vainglorious. [f. s. L *Thraso* a boastful soldier in Terence's play '*Eunuchus*' + -IC + -AL[1]] —**thrason′ically,** *adv.*

Thrasybulus (thrăs′ĭ byōō′ləs), *n.* died *c.* 389 B.C. Athenian patriot and general.

thread (thrĕd), *n.* **1.** a fine cord of flax, cotton, or other fibrous material spun out to considerable length; esp. such a cord composed of two or more filaments twisted together. **2.** twisted fibres of any kind used for sewing. **3.** one of the lengths of yarn forming the warp and woof of a woven fabric. **4.** a filament or fibre of glass or other ductile substance. **5.** something having the fineness or slenderness of a thread, as a thin continuous stream of liquid, a fine line of colour, or a thin seam of ore. **6.** the helical ridge of a screw. **7.** that which runs through the whole course of something, connecting successive parts, as the sequence of events in a narrative. **8.** something conceived as being spun or continuously drawn out, as the course of life supposed to be spun and cut by the Fates. **9. hang by a thread,** to be in a dangerous or precarious position.
—*v.t.* **10.** to pass the end of a thread through the eye of (a needle). **11.** to fix (beads, etc.) upon a thread that is passed through; string. **12.** to pass continuously through the whole course of (something); pervade. **13.** to make one's way through (a narrow passage, a forest, a crowd, etc.). **14.** to make (one's way, etc.) thus. **15.** to form a thread on or in (a bolt, hole, etc.).
—*v.i.* **16.** to thread one's way, as through a passage or between obstacles. **17.** to move in a threadlike course; wind or twine. **18.** *Cookery.* (of boiling syrup) to form a fine thread when dropped from a spoon.
[ME *threed*, OE *thrǣd*, c. G *Draht.* See THROW] —**thread′er,** *n.* —**thread′less,** *adj.* —**thread′like′,** *adj.*

threadbare (thrĕd′bĕə′), *adj.* **1.** having the nap worn off so as to lay bare the threads of the warp and woof, as a fabric, garment, etc. **2.** meagre, scanty, or poor. **3.** hackneyed or trite: *threadbare arguments.* **4.** wearing threadbare clothes; shabby: *a threadbare little old man.*

threadfin (thrĕd′fĭn′), *n.* any of the spiny-rayed fishes constituting the family *Polynemidae*, the lower part of whose pectoral fin is composed of numerous separate, slender, filamentous rays.

thread mark, a thin thread in paper currency used to prevent counterfeiting.

Threadneedle Street (thrĕd′nē′dl, thrĕd′nē′dl), a street in the City of London, noted for its banks, including the Bank of England.

threadworm (thrĕd′wûm′), *n.* any of various nematode worms, esp. a pinworm.

thready (thrĕd′ĭ), *adj.* **1.** consisting of or resembling a thread or threads; fibrous; filamentous. **2.** stringy or viscid, as a liquid. **3.** (of the pulse) thin and feeble. **4.** (of voice, etc.) lacking fullness; thin; weak. —**thread′iness,** *n.*

threat (thrĕt), *n.* **1.** a declaration of an intention or determination to inflict punishment, pain, or loss on someone in retaliation for, or conditionally upon, some action or course; menace. **2.** an indication of probable evil to come; something that gives indication of causing evil or harm. —*v.t., v.i.* **3.** *Archaic or Dial.* to threaten. [ME *threte,* OE *thrēat* throng, threat, distress. Cf. Icel. *thraut* labour, struggle] —**threat′less,** *adj.*

threaten (thrĕt′n), *v.t.* **1.** to utter a threat against; menace. **2.** to be a menace or source of danger to. **3.** to offer (a punishment, injury, etc.) by way of a threat. **4.** to give an ominous indication of: *the clouds threaten rain.* —*v.i.* **5.** to utter or use threats. **6.** to indicate impending evil or mischief. [ME *thretne,* OE *thrēatnian,* der. *thrēat* THREAT] —**threat′ener,** *n.* —**threat′eningly,** *adv.* —**Syn. 6.** See **imminent.**

three (thrē), *n.* **1.** a cardinal number, two plus one. **2.** a symbol for this number, as 3 or III. **3.** a set of this many persons or things. **4.** a playing card with three pips. —*adj.* **5.** amounting to three in number. [ME; OE *thrēo,* c. G *drei;* akin to Gk *treîs,* L *trēs*]

three-colour (thrē′kŭl′ə), *adj.* **1.** having or characterized by the use of three colours. **2.** denoting or pertaining to a photomechanical process for making reproductions of paintings, etc., usually carried out by making three plates or printing surfaces, each corresponding to a primary colour, by the halftone process, and taking superimposed impressions from these plates in three correspondingly coloured inks.

three-cornered (thrē′kô′nərd), *adj.* **1.** having three corners. **2.** pertaining to or involving three persons, parties, etc.

3-D (thrē′dē′), *adj.* **1.** three-dimensional: *3-D films.* —*n.* **2.** a three-dimensional form or appearance.

three-decker (thrē′dĕk′ə), *n.* **1.** any vessel, etc., having three decks, tiers, etc. **2.** (formerly) one of a class of sailing warships which carried guns on three decks. **3.** a sandwich made of three slices of bread and two layers of filling. **4.** anything having three layers, levels, tiers, etc.

three-dimensional (thrē′dĭ mĕn′shə nəl), *adj.* **1.** having or seeming to have, the dimension of depth. **2.** realistic; lifelike.

threefold (thrē′fōld′), *adj.* **1.** having three elements or parts. **2.** three times as great or as much; treble. —*adv.* **3.** in threefold manner or measure; trebly.

three-halfpence (thrē′hā′pəns), *n.* **1.** one penny and one halfpenny. **2.** an obsolete silver coin of this value.

three-halfpenny (thrē′hăp′nĭ), *adj.* **1.** of the amount or value of three-halfpence. —*n.* **2.** something purchased for three-halfpence.

Three Kings Islands, a group of islands off the NW tip of North Island, New Zealand, between the Tasman Sea and the Pacific Ocean. 3 sq. mi.

three-legged race (thrē′lĕg′ĭd, -lĕgd′), a race run by a number of contestants in pairs, each pair having their inside legs tied together.

three-master (thrē′mäs′tə), *n.* a sailing ship with three masts.

three-mile limit (thrē′mīl′), *Internat. Law.* the limit of the marine belt which is included within the jurisdiction of the state possessing the coast.

threepence (thrŏŏp′əns, thrĭp′əns, thrĕp′əns), *n.* **1.** three pennies. **2.** a threepenny bit. **3.** a former silver coin of Britain and certain other countries valued at three pennies.

threepenny (thrŏŏp′nĭ, thrĭp′nĭ, thrĕp′nĭ, -ə nĭ), *adj.* **1.** of the amount or value of threepence. —*n.* **2.** something purchased for threepence.

threepenny bit, (until 1971) a twelve-sided nickel-brass coin of Britain valued at threepence.

three-phase (thrē′fāz′), *adj.* *Elect.* **1.** denoting or pertaining to a circuit, system, or device which is energized by three electromotive forces which differ in phase by one third of a cycle, i.e., 120 degrees. **2.** having three phases.

three-piece (thrē′pēs′), *adj.* **1.** consisting of three matching pieces, as a women's coat, skirt, and blouse, or a man's jacket, trousers, and waistcoat. **2.** having three parts. —*n.* **3.** a three-piece outfit, suit, etc.

three-ply (thrē′plī′), *adj.* consisting of three thicknesses, layers, strands, or the like.

three-point landing (thrē′point′), *Aeron.* a smooth aircraft landing in which the two main wheels of the landing gear and the tail or nose wheel all touch the ground simultaneously.

three-point turn, the complete reversal of the direction of motion of a vehicle by swinging it round in the road to the opposite kerb, reversing on the opposite lock, and driving off forwards in the new direction.

three-quarter (thrē′kwô′tə), *adj.* **1.** consisting of or involving three quarters of a whole. **2.** *Rugby Football.* of or pertaining to a three-quarter. —*n.* **3.** *Rugby Football.* one of the four players in the three-quarter line.

three-quarter binding, *Bookbinding.* a binding in which the leather back extends farther towards the side covers than in half-binding.

three-ring circus (thrē′rĭng′), *U.S.* **1.** a circus with performances taking place simultaneously in three separate rings. **2.** something spectacular, tumultuous, or confusing.

Three Rivers, a town in Canada, in S Quebec, on the St Lawrence. 53,477 (1961). French, **Trois-Rivières.**

three R's, reading, (w)riting, and (a)rithmetic, regarded as the fundamentals of education.

threescore (thrē′skô′), *adj.* three times twenty; sixty.

threesome (thrē′səm), *adj.* **1.** consisting of three; threefold. **2.** performed or played by three persons. —*n.* **3.** three forming a group. **4.** something in which three persons participate. **5.** *Golf.* a match in which one player, playing his own ball, plays against two opponents with one ball, the two latter playing alternate strokes. [ME *thresum.* See THREE, -SOME[2]]

three-square (thrē′skwĕə′), *adj.* having an equilateral triangular cross-section, as certain files.

three-wheeler (thrē′wē′lə), *n.* a vehicle, esp. a motor car, having three wheels.

thremmatology (thrĕm′ə tŏl′ə jĭ), *n.* *Biol.* the science of breeding or propagating animals and plants under domestication. [f. Gk *thremmato-* (comb. form of *thrémma* nursling) + -LOGY]

threnode (thrē′nōd, thrĕn′ōd), *n.* threnody.

threnody (thrĕn′ə dĭ, thrē′nə dĭ), *n., pl.* **-dies.** a song of lamentation, esp. for the dead; a dirge or funeral song. [t. Gk: m. s. *thrēnōidia*] —**threnodial** (thrĭ nō′dyəl), **threnodic** (thrĭ nŏd′ĭk), *adj.* —**threnodist** (thrĕn′ə dĭst, thrē′nə dĭst), *n.*

threonine (thrē′ə nēn′, -nĭn), *n.* *Biochem.* an essential amino acid, $CH_3CHOHCH(NH_2)COOH$, obtained by the hydrolysis of proteins.

thresh (thrĕsh), *v.t.* **1.** to separate the grain or seeds from (a cereal plant, etc.) by some mechanical means, as by beating with a flail or by the action of a threshing machine. **2.** to beat as if with a flail. —*v.i.* **3.** to thresh wheat, grain, etc. **4.** to deliver blows as if with a flail. —*n.* **5.** the act of threshing. [ME *thresshe,* OE *threscan,* c. G *dreschen.* Cf. THRASH]

thresher (thrĕsh′ə), *n.* **1.** one who or that which threshes. **2.** one who separates grain or seeds from wheat, etc., by beating with a flail, using a threshing machine, etc. **3.** Also, **thrasher, thresher shark.** a large shark of the genus *Alopias,* esp. *A. vulpinus,* having a very long tail with which it threshes the water to drive together the small fish on which it feeds.

threshing machine, a machine for separating the grain and seeds from wheat, etc.

threshold (thrĕsh′ōld, thrĕsh′hōld), *n.* **1.** the sill of a doorway. **2.** the entrance to a house or building. **3.** any place or point of entering or beginning. **4.** *Psychol., Physiol.* the point at which a stimulus becomes perceptible or is of sufficient intensity to produce an effect; the limen. **5.** *Physics.* the lowest value of any signal, stimulus, or agency which will produce a specified effect, as a threshold frequency. [ME *threschold,* OE *threscold, -wold,* c. Icel. *threskjöldr;* appar. der. THRESH, v.]

threshold frequency, *Physics.* the lowest frequency of radiation which, when incident upon a photoelectric material, will produce a photoelectric effect.

threw (thrōō), *v.* pt. of **throw.**

thrice (thrīs), *adv.* **1.** three times, as in succession; on three occasions. **2.** in threefold quantity or degree. **3.** very; greatly; extremely. [ME *thries,* f. obs. *thrie* thrice (OE *thriga*) + *-s,* adv. gen. suffix]

thrift (thrĭft), *n.* **1.** economical management; economy; frugality. **2.** vigorous growth, as of a plant. **3.** the sea-pink. **4.** *Obs.* prosperity. [ME, der. THRIVE. Cf. Icel. *thrift* prosperity] —**thrift′less,** *adj.* —**thrift′lessly,** *adv.* —**thrift′lessness,** *n.*

thrifty (thrĭf′tĭ), *adj.,* **-tier, -tiest.** **1.** using or characterized by thrift or frugality; provident. **2.** *Rare.* thriving, prosperous, or successful. **3.** *Rare.* thriving physically; growing vigorously. —**thrift′ily,** *adv.* —**thrift′iness,** *n.* —**Syn. 1.** See **economical.**

thrill (thrĭl), *v.t.* **1.** to effect with a sudden wave of keen emotion, so as to produce a tremor or tingling sensation through the body. **2.** to cause to vibrate or quiver; utter or send forth tremulously, as a melody. —*v.i.* **3.** to affect one with a wave of emotion or excitement; produce a thrill. **4.** to be stirred by a thrill of emotion or excitement. **5.** to move tremulously; vibrate; quiver. —*n.* **6.** a tremor or tingling sensation passing through the body as the result of sudden keen emotion or excitement. **7.** thrilling property or quality, as of a story. **8.** a vibration or quivering. **9.** *Pathol.* an abnormal tremor or vibration, as in the respiratory system. [ME; metathetic var. of THIRL, v.]

thriller (thrĭl′ə), *n.* **1.** one who or that which thrills. **2.** a book, play, or film, dealing with crime, mystery, etc., in an exciting or sensational manner.

thrilling (thrĭl′ĭng), *adj.* **1.** producing deep emotion or excitement. **2.** vibrant. —**thrill′ingly,** *adv.* —**thrill′ingness,** *n.*

thrips (thrĭps), *n.* any of numerous small insects of the order *Thysanoptera*, characterized by long, narrow wings fringed with hairs, many species of which are destructive to plants. [t. L, t. Gk: woodworm]

thrive (thrīv), *v.i.*, **throve** or **thrived, thrived** or **thriven, thriving.** **1.** to prosper; be fortunate or successful; increase in property or wealth; grow richer or rich. **2.** to grow or develop vigorously; flourish. [ME, t. Scand.: cf. Icel. *thrífask*] —**thriv′er,** *n.* —**thriv′ingly,** *adv.* —**Syn. 2.** See **succeed.**

thro (thrōō), *prep., adv., adj.* through. Also, **thro′.**

throat (thrōt), *n.* **1.** the passage from the mouth to the stomach or to the lungs; the fauces, pharynx, and oesophagus; the larynx and trachea. **2.** some analogous or similar narrowed part or passage. **3.** the front of the neck below the chin and above the collarbones. **4.** *Naut.* nock (def. 4). **5. cut one's (own) throat,** to pursue a course of action which is injurious or ruinous to oneself. **6. jump down someone's throat,** to deliver a strong verbal attack on; berate; scold. **7. ram** or **thrust (something) down someone's throat,** to force something on someone's attention. **8. stick in one's throat, a.** to be difficult to express or utter. **b.** to be difficult to accept in one's mind. [ME and OE *throte.* Cf. THROTTLE] —**throat′less,** *adj.*

throatlatch (thrōt′lăch′), *n.* a strap which passes under a horse's throat and helps to hold a bridle or halter in place.

throaty (thrō′tĭ), *adj.*, **-tier, -tiest.** produced or modified in the throat, as sounds; hoarse; guttural. —**throat′ily,** *adv.* —**throat′iness,** *n.*

throb (thrŏb), *v.*, **throbbed, throbbing,** *n.* —*v.i.* **1.** to beat with increased force or rapidity, as the heart under the influence of emotion or excitement; palpitate. **2.** to feel or exhibit emotion. **3.** to pulsate; vibrate. —*n.* **4.** the act of throbbing. **5.** a violent beat or pulsation, as of the heart. **6.** any pulsation or vibration. [ME (in ppr. *throbbant*); orig. unknown] —**throb′ber,** *n.* —**throb′bingly,** *adv.* —**Syn. 3.** See **pulsate.**

throe (thrō), *n.* **1.** a violent spasm or pang; a paroxysm. **2.** a sharp attack of emotion. **3.** (*pl.*) the pains of childbirth. **4.** (*pl.*) the agony of death. **5.** (*pl.*) any violent convulsion or struggle. [ME *throwe*, var. of *thrawe*; akin to OE *thrēa*, *thrawu* threat, calamity]

thrombin (thrŏm′bĭn), *n.* *Biochem.* an enzyme catalysing the conversion of fibrinogen into fibrin in the clotting of blood. [f. THROMB(US) + -IN²]

thrombosis (thrŏm bō′sĭs), *n.* *Pathol.* intravascular coagulation of the blood in any part of the circulatory system, as in the heart, arteries, veins, or capillaries. [t. NL, t. Gk: curdling, clotting] —**thrombotic** (thrŏm bŏt′ĭk), *adj.*

thrombus (thrŏm′bəs), *n.*, *pl.* **-bi** (-bī). *Pathol.* a fibrinous clot which forms in and obstructs a blood vessel, or which forms in one of the heart's chambers. [t. NL, t. Gk: m. *thrómbos* lump, clot]

throne (thrōn), *n.*, *v.*, **throned, throning.** —*n.* **1.** the chair or seat occupied by a sovereign, bishop, or other exalted personage on ceremonial occasions, usually raised on a dais and covered with a canopy. **2.** the office or dignity of a sovereign. **3.** the occupant of a throne; a sovereign. **4.** sovereign power or authority. **5.** episcopal office or authority. **6.** (*pl.*) an order of angels. —*v.t., v.i.* **7.** to set or sit on or as on a throne. [ME, t. L: m. *thronus*, t. Gk: m. *thrónos* high seat; r. ME *trone*, t. OF] —**throne′less,** *adj.*

throng (thrŏng), *n.* **1.** a multitude of people crowded or assembled together; a crowd. **2.** a great number of things crowded or considered together. **3.** *Dial.* pressure, as of work. —*v.i.* **4.** to assemble, collect, or go in large numbers; crowd. —*v.t.* **5.** to crowd or press upon; jostle. **6.** to fill or occupy with or as with a crowd. **7.** to bring or drive together into a crowd. **8.** to fill by crowding or pressing into. [ME; OE *gethrang*; akin to D *drang*, G *Drang*] —**Syn. 1.** See **crowd.**

throstle (thrŏs′əl), *n.* **1.** the Old World songthrush, *Turdus philomelus.* **2.** a machine for spinning wool, cotton, etc., in which the twisting and winding are simultaneous and continuous. [ME and OE, c. D *drossel*, G *Drossel*, akin to L *turdus* thrush]

throttle (thrŏt′l), *n.*, *v.*, **-tled, -tling.** —*n.* **1.** a lever, pedal, or other device to control the amount of fuel being fed to an engine. **2.** a throttle valve. **3.** *Chiefly Dial.* the throat, gullet, or windpipe. [prob. dim. of ME *throte* THROAT] —*v.t.* **4.** to stop the breath of by compressing the throat; strangle. **5.** to choke or suffocate in any way. **6.** to compress by fastening something tightly about. **7.** to silence or check as if by choking. **8.** *Mach.* to obstruct the flow of (steam, etc.) by means of a throttle valve or otherwise; check the supply of steam, etc., to (an engine) in this way. [late ME *throtel*, freq. of earlier *throte*, v., strangle (der. *throte*, n., THROAT)] —**throt′tler,** *n.*

throttle lever, a lever, handle, etc., for manipulating a throttle valve.

throttle valve, the valve which regulates the flow of vapour received by the cylinders of an engine.

through (thrōō), *prep.* **1.** in at one end, side, or surface, and out at the other, of: *to pass through a tunnel.* **2.** past: *the car went through the traffic lights without stopping.* **3.** between or among the individual members or parts of: *to swing through the trees.* **4.** over the surface or within the limits of: *to travel through a country.* **5.** during the whole period of; throughout: *to work through the night.* **6.** having reached the end of: *to be through one's work.* **7.** having finished successfully: *to get through an examination.* **8.** by the means or instrumentality of: *it was through him they found out.* **9.** by reason of or in consequence of: *to run away through fear.* **10.** *U.S.* up to and including: *from Monday through Thursday.*
—*adv.* **11.** in at one end, side, or surface and out at the other: *to push a needle through.* **12.** all the way; along the whole distance: *this train goes through to Worthing.* **13.** throughout: *soaking wet through.* **14.** from the beginning to the end: *to read a letter through.* **15.** to the end: *to carry a matter through.* **16.** to a favourable or successful conclusion: *to pull through.* **17.** having completed an action, process, etc.: *he is not yet through.* **18. through and through, a.** through the whole extent or substance; from beginning to end. **b.** in all respects; thoroughly. **19. through with, a.** finished or done with. **b.** at an end of all relations or dealings with.
—*adj.* **20.** passing or extending from one end, side, or surface to the other. **21.** that extends, goes, or conveys through the whole of a long distance with little or no interruption, obstruction, or hindrance: *a through train.* Also, **thro, thro′, thru.**
[ME; metathetic var. of *thourgh*, OE *thurh*, c. G *durch*, akin to Goth. *thairh*] —**Syn. 8.** See **by.**

throughly (thrōō′lĭ), *adv.* *Archaic.* thoroughly.

throughout (thrōō out′), *prep.* **1.** in or to every part of; everywhere in. **2.** from the beginning to the end of. —*adv.* **3.** in every part. **4.** at every moment or point.

throughput (thrōō′pŏŏt′), *n.* **1.** the quantity or amount of raw material processed within a given time. **2.** *Computers.* the work done by a computer in a given time.

throughway (thrōō′wā′), *n.* thruway.

throve (thrōv), *v.* pt. of **thrive.**

throw (thrō), *v.*, **threw, thrown, throwing,** *n.* —*v.t.* **1.** to project or propel forcibly through the air by a sudden jerk or straightening of the arm; propel or cast in any way. **2.** to hurl or project (a missile), as a gun does. **3.** to project or cast (light, a shadow, etc.). **4.** to project (the voice). **5.** to make (a voice) appear to be coming from a place other than its source, as a ventriloquist does. **6.** to direct (words, a glance, etc.). **7.** to cause to go or come into some place, position, condition, etc., as if by throwing: *to throw a man into prison, to throw a bridge across a river, to throw troops into action.* **8.** to put hastily: *to throw a shawl over one's shoulders.* **9.** *Mach.* **a.** to move (a lever, etc.) in order to connect or disconnect parts of an apparatus or mechanism. **b.** to connect, engage, disconnect, or disengage by such a procedure. **10.** to shape on a potter's wheel. **11.** to bring to bear or exert (influence, authority, power, etc.). **12.** to deliver (a blow or punch). **13.** *Cards.* to play (a card). **14.** to cause to fall to the ground; bring to the ground, as an opponent in wrestling. **15.** *Chiefly U.S. Colloq.* to permit an opponent to win (a race, contest, or the like) deliberately, as for a bribe. **16.** to cast (dice). **17.** to make (a cast) at dice. **18.** (of a horse, etc.) to cause to fall off. **19.** (of domestic animals) to bring forth (young). **20.** *Colloq.* to astonish; disconcert; confuse. **21.** *Textiles.* to wind or twist silk, etc., into threads.
—*v.i.* **22.** to cast, fling, or hurl a missile, etc.
—*v.* **23.** Some special verb phrases are:
throw away, 1. to discard; dispose of. **2.** to squander; waste. **3.** to fail to use; miss (an opportunity, chance, etc.).
throw back, to revert to a type found in one's ancestors; show atavism.
throw in, 1. to add as an extra, esp. in a bargain. **2.** to interpose; interpolate; contribute (a remark, etc.).
throw off, 1. to free oneself from. **2.** to elude, escape

from (a pursuer, etc.). **3.** to discard or remove hastily. **4.** to recover from (a cold, etc.). **5.** to utter, write, compose, etc., with ease.

throw oneself at (someone), to attempt to excite the interest of in order to win the love of.

throw oneself into, to work enthusiastically at.

throw oneself on or **upon,** to entrust oneself to the mercy of; commit oneself completely to.

throw open, 1. to open wide. **2.** to permit general access to.

throw out, 1. to discard; cast away. **2.** to emit; give forth. **3.** to utter casually or indirectly (a remark, hint, etc.). **4.** to expel; eject; remove forcibly. **5.** to reject; refuse to accept. **6.** to cause to make a mistake.

throw over, to abandon; forsake; desert.

throw together, 1. to assemble in a hasty or haphazard manner. **2.** to bring together; cause to associate.

throw up, 1. to give up; abandon. **2.** to build hastily. **3.** to vomit.

—*n.* **24.** an act of throwing or casting; a cast or fling. **25.** the distance to which anything is or may be thrown: *a stone's throw.* **26.** a venture or chance: *it was his last throw.* **27.** *Mach.* **a.** the movement of a reciprocating part or the like from its central position to its extreme position in either direction, or the distance traversed (equivalent to one half the travel or stroke). **b.** the arm or the radius of a crank or the like; the eccentricity of an eccentric, or the radius of a crank to which an eccentric is equivalent, being equal to the distance between the centre of the disc and the centre of the shaft. **c.** the complete movement of a reciprocating part or the like in one direction, or the distance traversed (equivalent to the travel or stroke). **28.** *U.S.* a light blanket, as for use when reclining on a sofa; an afghan. **29.** a cast at dice. **30.** the number thrown. **31.** *Wrestling.* the act, instance, or method of throwing an opponent. **32.** *Geol., Mining.* the amount of vertical displacement produced by fault. [ME; OE *thrāwan* turn, twist, c. G *drehen* twist, twirl] —**throw′er,** *n.*

—**Syn. 1.** THROW, CAST, PITCH, TOSS imply projecting something through the air. THROW is the general word, often used with an adverb which indicates direction, destination, etc.: *throw a rope to him; the paper away.* CAST is a formal word for THROW, archaic except as used in certain idiomatic expressions (*cast a net; black looks; cast down*; the compound *broadcast,* etc.): *to cast off a boat.* PITCH implies throwing with some force and definite aim: *to pitch a ball.* To TOSS is to throw lightly as with an underhand or sideways motion, or to move irregularly up and down or backwards and forwards: *to toss a bone to a dog.*

throwaway (thrō′ə wā′), *n.* **1.** any advertisement, as a brochure or handbill, distributed in the streets, slipped under doors, etc. —*adj.* **2.** (of a remark, witticism, etc.) uttered in a deliberately casual manner with apparent disregard for effect.

throwback (thrō′băk′), *n.* **1.** an act of throwing back. **2.** a setback or check. **3.** reversion to an ancestral type or character. **4.** an example of this.

throw-in (thrō′ĭn′), *n.* *Soccer.* the act of throwing the ball into play after it has crossed one of the touchlines.

throwing stick, *Austral.* a wooden implement with which a spear or dart is thrown.

thrown (thrōn), *v.t.* pp. of **throw.**

thrown silk, raw silk that has been twisted into thread.

thru (thrōō), *prep., adv., adj.* through.

thrum[1] (thrŭm), *v.,* **thrummed, thrumming,** *n.* —*v.i.* **1.** to play on a stringed instrument, as a guitar, by plucking the strings, esp. in an idle, monotonous, or unskilful manner. **2.** to sound when thrummed on, as a guitar, etc. **3.** to drum or tap idly with the fingers. —*v.t.* **4.** to play (a stringed instrument, or a melody on it) by plucking the strings, esp. in an idle, monotonous, or unskilful manner. **5.** to drum or tap idly on. **6.** to recite or tell in a monotonous way. —*n.* **7.** the act or sound of thrumming; dull, monotonous sound. [imit.] —**thrum′mer,** *n.*

thrum[2] (thrŭm), *n., v.,* **thrummed, thrumming.** —*n.* **1.** one of the ends of the warp threads in a loom, left unwoven and remaining attached to a loom when the web is cut off. **2.** (*pl.*) the row or fringe of such threads. **3.** any short piece of waste thread or yarn; a tuft, tassel, or fringe of threads, as at the edge of a piece of cloth. **4.** (*pl. or sing.*) *Naut.* short bits of rope yarn used for mops, etc. —*v.t.* **5.** *Naut.* to insert short pieces of rope yarn through (canvas) and thus give it a rough surface, as in order that it may be wrapped about a part to prevent chafing. **6.** *Dial.* to furnish or cover with thrums, ends of thread, or tufts. [ME and OE, c. G *Trumm.* Cf. L *terminus* end]

thrumwort (thrŭm′wûrt′), *n.* an annual, aquatic herb, *Damasonium alisma,* of the family *Alismataceae,* of W and S Europe.

thruppence (thrŏŏp′əns), *n.* threepence.

thrush[1] thrŭsh), *n.* **1.** any of numerous passerine birds belonging to the family *Turdidae,* most of which are moderate in size, migratory, gifted as songsters, and not brightly coloured, as the European **song thrush** (*Turdus philomelus*). **2.** any of various superficially similar birds of other families, as the **water thrushes** of the genus *Seirus* (family *Compsothlypidae*). [ME *thrusche,* OE *thrȳsce,* akin to OHG *drōsca*] —**thrush′like′,** *adj.*

Thrush, *Turdus philomelus* (9 in. long)

thrush[2] (thrŭsh), *n.* **1.** *Pathol.* a disease, esp. in children, characterized by whitish spots and ulcers on the membranes of the mouth, fauces, etc., due to a parasitic fungus, *Saccharomyces albicans.* **2.** *Vet. Sci.* (in horses) a diseased condition of the frog of the foot. [cf. Dan. *troske,* d. Sw. *torsk* (def. 1)]

thrust (thrŭst), *v.,* **thrust, thrusting,** *n.* —*v.t.* **1.** to push forcibly; shove; put or drive with force: *he thrust a dagger into her back.* **2.** to put forcibly into some position, condition, etc.: *to thrust oneself into danger.* **3.** to stab or pierce, as with a sword. —*v.i.* **4.** to push against something. **5.** to push or force one's way, as against obstacles or through a crowd. **6.** to make a thrust, lunge, or stab at something. —*n.* **7.** the act of thrusting; a forcible push or drive; a lunge or stab. **8.** *Mach.* the linear force generated by an engine-driven propeller or by propulsive gases (as in jet propulsion). **9.** *Geol.* a compressive strain in the crust of the earth, which in its most characteristic development, produces reversed or thrust faults. **10.** *Mech., etc.* a pushing force or pressure exerted by a thing or a part against a contiguous one. **11.** *Archit.* the force exerted in a lateral direction by an arch, and tending to overturn the abutments. [ME *thruste(n),* t. Scand.; cf. Icel. *thrȳsta*] —**thrust′er,** *n.* —**Syn. 1.** See **push.**

thrust bearing, *Mach.* a bearing designed to take an axial load.

thruster (thrŭs′tə), *n.* **1.** one who or that which thrusts. **2.** *Fox-hunting.* one who rides well in front of the field or too close to hounds. **3.** *Astronautics.* a small rocket used to control the attitude of a spacecraft.

thruway (thrōō′wā′), *n.* *U.S.* an expressway. Also, **throughway.**

Thucydides (thyōō sĭd′ĭ dēz′), *n.* *c.* 460–*c.* 400 B.C., Greek historian.

thud (thŭd), *n., v.,* **thudded, thudding.** —*n.* **1.** a dull sound, as of a heavy blow or fall. **2.** a blow causing such a sound. —*v.i., v.t.* **3.** to beat or strike with a dull sound of heavy impact. [ME; OE *thyddan,* v.]

thug (thŭg), *n.* **1.** a brutal, vicious, or murderous ruffian, robber, or gangster. **2.** (*sometimes cap.*) one of a former body of professional robbers and murderers in India, who strangled their victims. [t. Hind.: m. *thag*] —**thuggery** (thŭg′ə rĭ), *n.* —**thug′gish,** *adj.*

thuggee (thŭ gē′), *n.* (*sometimes cap.*) the system or practices of the thugs in India. [t. Hind.: m. *thagī*]

thuja (thyōō′jə), *n.* any of the evergreen coniferous trees constituting the genus *Thuja,* esp. *T. occidentalis,* the common arborvitae, which yields an aromatic oil. [NL, t. Gk: m. *thyía* African tree]

Thule (thyōō′lĭ), *n.* **1.** the ancient Greek and Latin name for an island or region (variously identified as one of the Shetland Islands, Iceland, Norway, etc.) supposed to be the most northerly region of the world. **2.** ultima Thule. [t. L, t. Gk: m. *Thoúlē*; r. ME and OE *Tyle,* t. L: m. *Thȳlē,* t. Gk]

thulia (thyōō′lĭ ə), *n.* *Chem.* the oxide of thulium, Tm_2O_3. [t. NL, der. L *Thūlē* THULE]

thulium (thyōō′lĭ əm), *n.* *Chem.* a rare-earth metallic element found in the minerals euxenite, gadolinite, etc. *Symbol:* Tm; *at. wt:* 168·934; *at. no.:* 69. [t. NL, f. s. L *Thūlē* THULE + *-ium* -IUM]

thumb (thŭm), *n.* **1.** the short, thick inner digit of the human hand, next to the forefinger. **2.** the corresponding digit in other animals; the pollex. **3.** that part of a glove, etc., which covers the thumb. **4.** *Archit.* ovolo. **5. all thumbs,** clumsy; awkward. **6. thumbs up,** gesture or expression of triumph or approval. **7. under the thumb of,** under the power or influence of. —*v.t.* **8.** to soil or wear with the thumbs in handling, as the pages of a book. **9.** to run through (the pages of a book, etc.) quickly (often fol. by *through*). **10.** (of a hitchhiker) to solicit or obtain (a ride) by pointing the thumb in the direction in which one wishes to travel. **11. thumb one's nose,** to put one's thumb to one's nose and extend the fingers in a gesture of defiance or contempt. [ME; OE *thūma,* c. G *Daumen*] —**thumb′less,** *adj.* —**thumb′like′,** *adj.*

thumb index, a series of notches or indentations on the

outer edges of a book to indicate the various sections into which the book is divided.

thumbnail (thŭm′nāl′), *n.* **1.** the nail of the thumb. —*adj.* **2.** quite small; concise: *a thumbnail description.*

thumbscrew (thŭm′skrōō′), *n.* **1.** an ancient instrument of torture by which one or both thumbs were compressed. **2.** a screw whose head is so constructed that it may be turned easily with the thumb and a finger; used as a fastening device for window sashes.

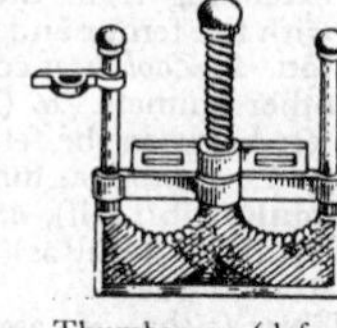
Thumbscrew (def. 1)

thumbtack (thŭm′tăk′), *n. U.S.* a drawing-pin.

thump (thŭmp), *n.* **1.** a blow with something thick and heavy, producing a dull sound; a heavy knock. **2.** the sound made by such a blow. —*v.t.* **3.** to strike or beat with something thick and heavy, so as to produce a dull sound; pound. **4.** (of an object) to strike against (something) heavily and noisily. **5.** *Colloq.* to thrash severely. —*v.i.* **6.** to strike or beat heavily, with a dull sound; pound. **7.** to walk with heavy-sounding steps. **8.** to beat violently, as the heart. [imit.] —**thump′er,** *n.*

thumping (thŭm′pĭng), *adj. Colloq.* very great; remarkably or unusually large; exceptional. —**thump′ingly,** *adv.*

Thun (*Ger.* tōōn), *n.* **1.** a town in central Switzerland, near Lake Thun. 34,500 (1966). **2. Lake.** German, **Thuner See.** a lake in central Switzerland, formed by a widening in the course of the river Aar. ab. 10 mi. long.

thunder (thŭn′də), *n.* **1.** the loud noise which accompanies a flash of lightning, due to violent disturbance of the air by a discharge of electricity. **2.** *Chiefly Poetic.* the destructive agent in a thunderstorm. **3.** any loud, resounding noise: *thunders of applause.* **4.** a threatening or startling utterance, denunciation, or the like. —*v.i.* **5.** to give forth thunder (often with impersonal *it* as subject): *it thundered last night.* **6.** to make a loud, resounding noise like thunder. **7.** to utter loud or vehement denunciations, threats, or the like. **8.** to speak in a very loud tone. **9.** to move or go with a loud noise. —*v.t.* **10.** to strike, drive, inflict, give forth, etc., with loud noise or violent action. [ME; OE *thunor*, c. G *Donner*, Icel. *Thōrr* Thor, akin to L *tonitrus* thunder] —**thun′derless,** *adj.*

thunderbird (thŭn′də bûd′), *n.* (in the folk belief of certain western American Indians) a huge bird capable of producing thunder, lightning, and rain.

thunderbolt (thŭn′də bōlt′), *n.* **1.** a flash of lightning with the accompanying thunder. **2.** an imaginary bolt or dart conceived as the material destructive agent cast to earth in a flash of lightning. **3.** any of various fossils, stones, or mineral concretions formerly supposed to have been cast to earth with the lightning. **4.** something very destructive, terrible, severe, sudden, or startling. **5.** one who acts with fury or with sudden and resistless force.

thunderclap (thŭn′də klăp′), *n.* a crash of thunder.

thundercloud (thŭn′də kloud′), *n.* an electrically charged cloud producing lightning and thunder.

thunderer (thŭn′də rə), *n.* **1.** one who thunders. **2.** (*cap.*) Jupiter; Zeus.

thundering (thŭn′də rĭng), *adj.* **1.** that thunders. **2.** producing a noise or effect like thunder. **3.** *Colloq.* extraordinary; very great. —**thun′deringly,** *adv.*

thunderous (thŭn′də rəs), *adj.* producing thunder or a loud noise like thunder. Also, **thun′dery.** —**thun′derously,** *adv.*

thunderpeal (thŭn′də pēl′), *n.* a crash of thunder.

thundershower (thŭn′də shou′ə), *n.* a shower accompanied by thunder and lightning, or a short heavy shower from a thundercloud.

thunder stick, a bullroarer.

thunderstone (thŭn′də stōn′), *n.* one of the fossils, stones, etc., popularly identified as thunderbolts.

thunderstorm (thŭn′də stôm′), *n.* a storm of thunder and lightning, and usually rain.

thunderstruck (thŭn′də strŭk′), *adj.* **1.** struck by a thunderbolt. **2.** overcome with consternation, confounded, or astounded: *he was thunderstruck by the news of his promotion.* Also, **thunderstricken** (thŭn′də strĭk′ən).

thundery (thŭn′də rĭ), *adj.* thunderous.

Thuner See (*Ger.* tōō′nər zė). See **Thun, Lake.**

Thur., Thursday.

Thurber (thû′bə), *n.* **James (Grover),** 1894–1961, U.S. artist and writer.

Thurgau (*Ger.* tōōr′gou), *n.* a canton in NE Switzerland. 166,420 pop. (1960); 388 sq. mi. *Cap.:* Frauenfeld.

thurible (thyōō′rĭ bl), *n.* a censer. [ME *turrible*, t. L: m. *t(h)ūribulum* censer, der. *t(h)ūs* incense]

thurifer (thyōō′rĭ fə), *n.* one who carries a thurible in religious ceremonies. [t. L: incense-bearing]

Thuringia (thyōō rĭn′jĭ ə), *n.* a former state in central Germany: formed originally from Thuringian duchies and principalities. German, **Thüringen** (*Ger.* tY′rĭng ən). —**Thurin′gian,** *adj., n.*

Thuringian Forest, a forested mountain region in central East Germany: holiday resort area. German, **Thüringer Wald** (*Ger.* tY′rĭng ər vält′).

Thurrock (thŭ′rək), *n.* an urban district in England, in Essex. 114,263 (1961).

Thurs., Thursday.

Thursday (thûz′dĭ), *n.* the fifth day of the week, following Wednesday. [ME, t. Scand.; cf. Icel. *Thorsdagr*, c. OE *Thunresdæg*, G *Donnerstag*, day of *Thunor* or Thor (trans. of LL *dies Jovis*)]

Thursday Island, an island in Torres Strait between NE Australia and New Guinea, forming part of Queensland: pearl-fishing centre. 2549 pop. (1966); 1¼ sq. mi.

Thurso (thû′sō), *n.* a seaport in Scotland, in Caithness. 8038 (1961).

thus (t͟hŭs), *adv.* **1.** in the way just indicated; in this way. **2.** in the following manner; in the manner now indicated. **3.** accordingly; consequently. **4.** to this extent or degree: *thus far.* [ME and OE, c. D *dus*]

thwack (thwăk), *v.t.* **1.** to strike or beat vigorously with something flat; whack. —*n.* **2.** a sharp blow with something flat; whack. [appar. imit.] —**thwack′er,** *n.*

thwart (thwôt), *v.t.* **1.** to oppose successfully; prevent from accomplishing a purpose; frustrate (a purpose, etc.); baffle. **2.** *Archaic.* to cross. **3.** *Archaic.* to extend across. —*n.* **4.** a seat across a boat, esp. one used by an oarsman. **5.** a transverse member spreading the gunwales of a canoe or the like. See diag. under **gunwale.** —*adj.* **6.** passing or lying crosswise or across; cross; transverse. **7.** *Archaic.* perverse; obstinate. **8.** adverse; unfavourable. —*prep., adv.* **9.** across; athwart. [ME *thwert*, adv., t. Scand.; cf. Icel. *thvert* across, neut. of *thverr* transverse, c. OE *thweorh* crooked, cross] —**thwart′er,** *n.*

—**Syn. 1.** THWART, FRUSTRATE, BAFFLE imply preventing someone, more or less completely, from accomplishing a purpose. THWART and FRUSTRATE apply to purposes, actions, plans, etc.; BAFFLE, to the psychological state of the person himself. THWART suggests stopping someone by opposing him, blocking him, or in some way running counter to his efforts. FRUSTRATE implies rendering all attempts or efforts useless or ineffectual, so that nothing ever comes of them. BAFFLE suggests causing defeat by confusing, puzzling, or perplexing, so that a situation seems too hard a problem to understand or solve.

thy (t͟hī), *pron., adj.* the possessive form corresponding to **thou** and **thee,** used before a noun. Cf. **thine.** [ME, var. of THINE]

Thyestes (thī ĕs′tēz), *n. Gk Legend.* son of Pelops and brother of Atreus. He seduced his brother's wife, in revenge for which Atreus slew Thyestes' sons and served them to their father at a banquet. —**Thyestean** (thī ĕs′tĭ ən, thī′ĕs tē′ən), **Thyes′tian,** *adj.*

thylacine (thī′lə sīn′), *n.* a carnivorous, wolf-like marsupial, *Thylacinus cynocephalus*, of Tasmania, tan-coloured, with black stripes across the back. [t. NL: m. s. *Thȳlacīnus*, f. s. Gk *thȳlakos* pouch + *-inus* -INE[1]]

thyme (tīm), *n.* any of the plants of the mint family constituting the genus *Thymus*, as *T. vulgaris*, a low sub-shrub with aromatic leaves used for seasoning, or a wild creeping species, *T. serpyllum* (**wild thyme**). [ME, t. L: m. *thymum*, t. Gk: m. *thýmon*]

Wild thyme, *Thymus serpyllum*

thymelaeaceous (thĭm′ĭ lĭ ā′shəs), *adj.* belonging to the *Thymelaeaceae*, a family of (chiefly) Old World trees, shrubs, and herbs including the mezereon, leatherwood, etc. [f. s. NL *Thymalaeāceae* (der. *Thymelaea* name of species, from Gk) + -OUS]

thymic[1] (tī′mĭk), *adj.* pertaining to or derived from thyme. [f. THYME + -IC]

thymic[2] (thī′mĭk), *adj.* of or pertaining to the thymus. [f. THYM(US) + -IC]

thymidine (thī′mĭ dēn′), *n. Biochem.* a compound of thymine and deoxyribose, present in all living cells, mainly in combined form, as in deoxyribonucleic acids.

thymidylic acid (thī′mĭ dĭl′ĭk), *Biochem.* the monophosphate of thymidine, present in all living cells, mainly in combined form, as in deoxyribonucleic acids.

thymine (thī′mēn), *n. Biochem.* a white crystalline pyrimidine base, $C_5H_6N_2O_2$, which occurs in DNA and is one of the four units upon which the genetic code is based.

thymol (thī′mŏl), *n. Chem.* a crystalline phenol, $C_{10}H_{13}OH$, present in an oil obtained from thyme, used as an antiseptic, etc. [f. THYM(E) + -OL[2]]

thymus (thī′məs), *n. Anat.* a glandular body or ductless gland of uncertain function found in vertebrate animals, in man lying in the thorax near the base of the neck and becoming vestigial in the adult. An animal thymus used as food is called *sweetbread.* Also, **thymus gland.** [NL, t. Gk: m. *thýmos*]

thyr-, a combining form of **thyroid,** as in *thyroxine.* Also, before consonants, **thyro-.**

thyratron (thīʹrə trŏnʹ), *n. Electronics.* a gas-filled valve used as a high-speed switch.

thyristor (thī rĭsʹtə), *n. Electronics.* a semiconductor controlled rectifier, often used as an electronic switch in control circuits.

thyroid (thīʹroid), *Anat.* **—*adj.* 1.** denoting or pertaining to the thyroid gland. **2.** denoting or pertaining to the principal cartilage of the larynx, forming the projection known in men as the Adam's apple. **—*n.* 3.** the thyroid gland. **4.** the thyroid cartilage. **5.** an artery, vein or the like, of the thyroid region. **6.** a preparation made from the thyroid glands of certain animals, used in treating hypothyroidism. [var. of *thyreoid,* t. Gk: m. *thyreoeidḗs* shield-shaped] —**thyʹroidless,** *adj.*

thyroidectomy (thīʹroi dĕkʹtə mĭ), *n., pl.* **-mies.** *Surg.* excision of the whole or a part of the thyroid gland.

thyroid gland, *Anat.* a bilobate ductless gland lying on either side of the windpipe or trachea and connected below the larynx by a thin isthmus of tissue. Its internal secretion is important in regulating the rate of metabolism and, consequently, body growth.

thyroiditis (thīʹroi dīʹtĭs), *n. Pathol.* inflammation of the thyroid gland. [NL. See THYROID, -ITIS]

thyrotoxicosis (thīʹrō tŏkʹsĭ kōʹsĭs), *n. Pathol.* a disease caused by an overactive thyroid gland.

thyroxine (thī rŏkʹsēn, -sĭn), *n. Biochem.* the hormone of the thyroid gland (often produced synthetically), $C_{15}H_{11}O_4NI_4$, used in treating hypothyroidism. Also, **thyroxin** (thī rŏkʹsĭn). [f. THYR- + *-oxin(e),* modelled on TOXIN(E)]

thyrsoid (thûrʹsoid), *adj. Bot.* having somewhat the form of a thyrsus. Also, **thyrsoiʹdal.** [t. Gk: m. s. *thyrsoeidḗs* thyrsus-like]

thyrsus (thûrʹsəs), *n., pl.* **-si** (-sī). **1.** Also, **thyrse** (thûs). *Bot.* a form of mixed inflorescence, as in the lilac, in which the primary ramification is centripetal or indeterminate, and the secondary and successive ramifications are centrifugal or determinate. **2.** *Gk Myth.* a staff tipped with a pine cone and sometimes twined with ivy and vine branches, borne by Dionysus (Bacchus) and his votaries. [t. L, t. Gk: m. *thýrsos* Bacchic staff, stem of plant]

thysanuran (thĭsʹə nyo͞oəʹrən), *adj.* **1.** belonging or pertaining to the *Thysanura,* an order of wingless insects with long, filamentous caudal appendages, to which the bristletails belong. **—*n.* 2.** a thysanuran insect. [f. s. NL *Thysanūra* (f. Gk: s. *thýsanos* tassel + m. *ourá* tail) + -AN] —**thysʹanuʹrous,** *adj.*

thyself (thī sĕlfʹ), *pron.* **1.** an emphatic appositive to **thou** or **thee. 2.** a substitute for reflexive **thee.**

ti[1] (tē), *n., pl.* **tis.** a tropical palmlike plant, *Cordyline australis.* [t. Polynesian]

ti[2] (tē), *n.* te[1].

Ti, *Chem.* titanium.

Tia Juana (*Sp.* tyȧ KHwäʹnȧ), Tijuana.

Tian Shan (tyănʹ shănʹ), Tien Shan.

tiapan (tīʹə pănʹ), *n.* a rare, highly venomous snake, *Oxyuranus scutellatus,* of Australia, that reaches a length of 12 feet and whose bite is almost certainly fatal.

tiara (tĭ äʹrə), *n.* **1.** a jewelled ornamental coronet worn by women. **2.** a diadem worn by the pope, surmounted by the mound (or orb) and cross of sovereignty, and surrounded with three crowns. **3.** the papal position or dignity. **4.** a headdress or turban worn by the ancient Persians and others. [t. L, t. Gk]

Tiber (tīʹbə), *n.* a river in central Italy, flowing through Rome into the Mediterranean. 244 mi. Italian, **Tevere.**

Tiberias (tī bĭəʹrĭ ăsʹ), *n.* **Sea of.** See **Galilee, Sea of.**

Tiberius (tī bĭəʹrĭ əs), *n.* (*Tiberius Claudius Nero Caesar*), 42 B.C. – A.D. 37, Roman emperor from A.D. 14 to 37.

Tibet (tĭ bĕtʹ), *n.* a country in S Asia, N of the Himalayas: a part of China since 1951; the highest country in the world. 1,321,500 pop. (est. 1965); ab. 469,400 sq. mi.; average elevation, ab. 16,000 ft. *Cap.:* Lhasa. Official name, **Tibetan Autonomous Region.** Also, *Obs.,* **Thibet.**

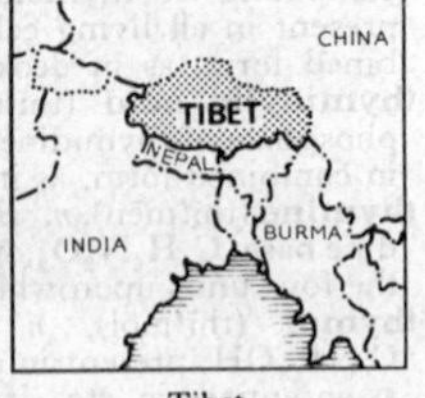

Tibet

Tibetan (tĭ bĕtʹn), *adj.* **1.** of or pertaining to Tibet, its inhabitants, or their language. **—*n.* 2.** a member of the native Mongolian race of Tibet. **3.** the language of Tibet, a Sino-Tibetan language, esp. its literary standard form. Also, *Obs.,* **Thibetan.**

Tibeto-Burman (tĭ bĕtʹō bûʹmən), *n.* a subfamily of Sino-Tibetan languages, including Tibetan and Burmese.

tibia (tĭbʹĭ ə), *n., pl.* **tibiae** (tĭbʹĭ ēʹ), **tibias. 1.** *Anat.* the shinbone; the inner of the two bones of the lower leg, extending from the knee to the ankle, and articulating with the femur and the astragalus. See diag. under **skeleton. 2.** *Zool.* **a.** a corresponding bone in the hind limb of other animals. **b.** (in insects) the fourth segment of the leg, between the femur and tarsus. See diag. under **coxa.** [t. L: shinbone, flute] —**tibʹial,** *adj.*

tibiale (tĭbʹĭ äʹlĭ), *n.* astragalus.

Tibullus (tĭ bŭlʹəs), *n.* **Albius** (ălʹbĭ əs), *c.* 54–*c.* 19 B.C., Roman poet.

Tibur (tīʹbə), *n.* ancient name of **Tivoli.**

tic (tĭk), *n. Pathol.* **1.** a sudden, painless, purposeless muscular contraction in the face or extremities, which can be reproduced by the victim of this habit and can be stopped at will. **2.** tic douloureux. [t. F, t. It.: m. *ticchis;* of Gmc origin]

tical (tĭ kälʹ, -kôlʹ, tēʹkl), *n., pl.* **-cals, -cal. 1.** a former Siamese unit of weight, equal to 231·5 grains, or about half an ounce. **2.** the monetary unit of Siam (Thailand) until 1928, now supplanted by the baht. **3.** a former Siamese silver coin. [t. Siamese, t. Pg., t. Hind.: m. *takā* weight]

tic douloureux (tĭkʹdo͞oʹlə rûʹ; *Fr.* tĕk do͞o lo͞o rœʹ), *Pathol.* trifacial or trigeminal neuralgia; paroxysmal darting pain and muscular twitching in the face which may be evoked by rubbing certain points of the face. [t. F: painful tic]

Ticino (*It.* tē chēʹnō), *n.* a canton in S Switzerland. 195,566 pop. (1960); 1086 sq. mi. *Cap.:* Bellinzona. German, **Tessin.**

tick[1] (tĭk), *n.* **1.** a slight, sharp recurring click or beat, as of a clock. **2.** *Colloq.* a moment or instant. **3.** a small mark, as a dash (often formed by two small strokes at an acute angle) serving to draw attention to something, to indicate that an item on a list, etc., has been noted or checked, or to indicate the correctness of something, as a piece of written work. **4. on the tick,** punctually. **—*v.i.* 5.** to emit or produce a tick, like that of a clock. **6.** to pass as with ticks of a clock: *the hours ticked by.* **—*v.t.* 7.** to sound or announce by a tick or ticks. **8.** to mark (an item, etc.) with a tick, as to indicate examination or correctness (often fol. by *off*). **—*v.* 9.** Some special verb phrases are:

tick off, to rebuke; scold.

tick over, 1. (of an internal-combustion engine) to run slowly with the gears disengaged. **2.** to be inactive, often in preparation for action.

what makes one tick, what motivates one's behaviour. [late ME *tek* little touch, akin to D *tik,* LG *tikk* a touch]

tick[2] (tĭk), *n.* **1.** any member of a group of large blood-sucking mitelike animals (*Acarina*) of the families *Ixodidae* and *Argasidae,* provided with a barbed proboscis which it buries in the skin of vertebrate animals. **2.** any of the dipterous insects of the family *Hippoboscidae,* often wingless, which are parasitic on certain animals, as sheep, camels, bats, pigeons. [ME *teke, tyke,* OE *ticia* (? mistake for *ticca*). Cf. LG *tieke,* G *Zecke*]

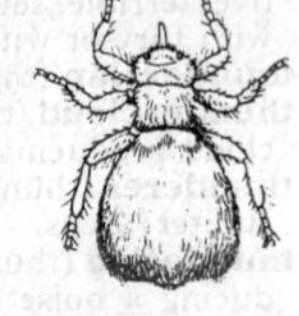
Tibet Sheep tick, *Melophagus ovinus* (Ab. ¼ in. long)

tick[3] (tĭk), *n.* **1.** the cloth case of a mattress, pillow, etc., containing hair, feathers, or the like. **2.** *Colloq.* ticking. [ME *tikke, teke, tyke* (c. D *tijk,* G *Zieche*). Cf. L *tēca, thēca,* t. Gk: m. *thḗkē* case]

tick[4] (tĭk), *n. Colloq.* **1.** a score or account. **2.** *Colloq.* credit or trust: *to buy on tick.* [short for TICKET]

tick-bird (tĭkʹbûdʹ), *n.* either of two African species of birds of the genus *Buphagus,* of the family *Sturnidae,* which have the habit of perching upon large mammals and feeding upon ticks.

ticker (tĭkʹə), *n.* **1.** one who or that which ticks. **2.** a tape machine. **3.** *Slang.* a watch. **4.** *Slang.* the heart.

ticker tape, the paper tape on which the tape machine prints its information.

ticket (tĭkʹĭt), *n.* **1.** a slip, usually of paper or cardboard, serving as evidence of the holder's title to some service, right, or the like: *a railway ticket, a theatre ticket.* **2.** a written or printed slip of paper, cardboard, etc., affixed to something to indicate its nature, price, or the like; a label or tag. **3.** *U.S.* a list of candidates nominated or put forward by a political party, faction, etc. **4.** *Slang.* a certificate. **5.** *Slang.* discharge from the armed forces: *to get one's ticket.* **6.** a preliminary recording of transactions prior to their entry in more permanent books of account. **7.** a summons issued for a traffic or parking offence. **8.** *Colloq.* the correct, right, or proper thing: *that's the ticket.* **9.** *Rare.*

a short note, notice, or memorandum. **10.** *Rare.* a placard. —*v.t.* **11.** to attach a ticket to; distinguish by means of a ticket; label. **12.** *U.S.* to furnish with a ticket. [t. F: m. *étiquette* ticket, label. See ETIQUETTE]

ticket collector, one who checks or collects passengers' tickets, as at a railway station.

ticket day, name-day.

ticket of leave, (formerly) permission given to a convict after serving part of his sentence to be at liberty with certain restrictions.

tickey (tĭk′ĭ), *n.* *S African Colloq.* **1.** (formerly) a threepenny piece. **2.** any small coin. **3.** something or somebody very small. [t. Malay: m. *tiga* three]

tickey box, *S African Colloq.* a coin-operated telephone callbox.

tick fever, any fever transmitted by ticks.

ticking (tĭk′ĭng), *n.* **1.** a strong cotton fabric, usually twilled, used esp. for ticks. **2.** a similar cloth in satin weave or Jacquard, used esp. for mattress covers. [f. TICK[3] + -ING[1]]

tickle (tĭk′l), *v.*, **-led, -ling,** *n.* —*v.t.* **1.** to touch or stroke lightly with the fingers, a feather, etc., so as to excite a tingling or itching sensation in; titillate. **2.** to poke in some sensitive part of the body so as to excite spasmodic laughter. **3.** to excite agreeably; gratify: *to tickle someone's vanity.* **4.** to excite amusement in. **5.** to get, move, etc., by or as by tickling. **6. tickled pink,** greatly pleased or amused. —*v.i.* **7.** to be affected with a tingling or itching sensation, as from light touches or strokes. **8.** to produce such a sensation. —*n.* **9.** the act of tickling. **10.** a tickling sensation. [ME *tikel(en)*; ? freq. of TICK[1] (in obs. sense) touch lightly]

tickler (tĭk′lə), *n.* **1.** one who or that which tickles. **2.** *U.S.* a memorandum book or the like kept to refresh the memory as to appointments, payments due, etc. **3.** *U.S. Accounting.* a single-entry account arranged according to the due dates of obligations. **4.** *Colloq.* a difficult or puzzling situation, problem, etc.

tickler coil, *Radio.* the coil by which the anode circuit of a radio valve is inductively coupled with the grid circuit in the process of regeneration.

ticklish (tĭk′lĭsh), *adj.* **1.** sensitive to tickling. **2.** requiring careful handling or action; risky; difficult: *a ticklish situation.* **3.** unstable or easily upset, as a boat; unsteady. —**tick′lishly,** *adv.* —**tick′lishness,** *n.*

tick-tack (tĭk′tăk′), *n.* a system of signalling used by bookmakers at race meetings. Also, **tic-tac.**

tick-tack man, an assistant to a bookmaker.

tick-tack-toe (tĭk′tăk′tō′), *n.* **1.** a children's game consisting of trying, with the eyes shut, to bring a pencil down upon one of a set of numbers, as on a slate, the number hit being scored. **2.** *U.S.* noughts-and-crosses. Also, **tick-tack-too** (tĭk′tăk′to͞o′), **tit-tat-toe.**

tick-tock (tĭk′tŏk′), *n.* an alternating ticking sound, as that made by a clock. Also, **tic-toc.** [imit. Cf. TICK[1]]

Ticonderoga (tī′kŏn də rō′gə), *n.* a town in the U.S., in NE New York State on Lake Champlain: French fort captured by the English 1759, and by the Americans 1775. 3568 (1960).

tidal (tī′dl), *adj.* **1.** of, pertaining to, or characterized by tides. **2.** dependent on the state of the tide as to time of departure: *a tidal steamer.*

tidal basin, **1.** a dock affected by tidal movement. **2.** a basin with gates which is filled with water at high tide; the water is released at low tide, scouring the adjacent harbour.

tidal current, the flow of seawater into and out of an estuary or through a strait at the ebb and flow of the tide.

tidal wave, **1.** a large destructive ocean wave produced by an earthquake or the like. **2.** either of the two great wavelike swellings of the ocean surface (due to the attraction of the moon and sun) which move round the earth on opposite sides and give rise to tide. **3.** any widespread or powerful movement, opinion, or the like: *a tidal wave of popular indignation.*

tidbit (tĭd′bĭt′), *n.* *U.S.* titbit. [f. d. *tyd* nice (akin to TIDE[1] (def. 8)) + BIT[2]]

tiddler (tĭd′lə), *n.* **1.** a very small fish, esp. a stickleback or minnow. **2.** *Colloq.* a small child, esp. one who is undersized.

tiddly (tĭd′lĭ), *n.* **1.** *Colloq.* slightly drunk; tipsy. **2.** *Naut.* smart; trim. Also, **tiddley.** [d. var. of OE *tīdlic* timely; sense development obscure]

tiddlywinks (tĭd′lĭ wĭngks′), *n.* a game, the object of which is to flick small discs into a cup placed some distance away. Also, **tiddleywinks.**

tide[1] (tīd), *n.*, *v.*, **tided, tiding.** —*n.* **1.** the periodic rise and fall of the waters of the ocean and its inlets, about every 12 hours and 26 minutes, due to the attraction of the moon and sun. **2.** the inflow, outflow, or current of water at any given place resulting from the tidal waves. **3.** the flood tide. **4.** a stream or current. **5.** anything that alternately rises and falls, increases and decreases, etc. **6.** a tendency, trend, current, etc., as of events, ideas, public opinion, etc. **7.** a season or period in the course of the year, day, etc. (now chiefly in compounds): *wintertide.* **8.** *Eccles.* a period of time which includes, and follows, an anniversary or festival, etc. **9.** *Archaic.* a suitable time or occasion. **10.** *Obs.* or *Dial.* an extent of time. —*v.i.* **11.** to flow as the tide; flow to and fro. **12.** to float or drift with the tide. —*v.t.* **13.** to carry, as the tide does. **14. tide over,** to get (a person, etc.) over a period of difficulty, distress, etc.; enable (a person, etc.) to cope. [ME; OE *tīd*, c. G *Zeit* time; akin to TIME] —**tide′less,** *adj.* —**tide′like′,** *adj.*

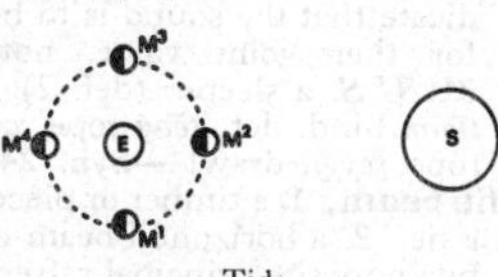

Tide
S, Sun; E, Earth
M1, M3, Moon at neap tide;
M2, M4, Moon at spring tide

tide[2] (tīd), *v.i.*, **tided, tiding.** *Archaic.* to happen or befall. [ME; OE *tīdan*, *getīdan* happen, der. *tīd* time]

tide-gate (tīd′gāt′), *n.* a gate which admits water at flood tide and closes when the tide is at ebb.

tide-gauge (tīd′gāj′), *n.* a gauge for measuring tide level.

tideland (tīd′lănd′), *n.* *U.S.* land in the intertidal zone.

tide-lock (tīd′lŏk′), *n.* a lock at the entrance to a tidal basin.

tidemark (tīd′mäk′), *n.* **1.** a mark left by the highest or lowest point of a tide. **2.** a mark made to indicate the highest or lowest point of a tide. **3.** any mark indicating the point which something has reached or below which it has fallen.

tide-race (tīd′rās′), *n.* a swift tidal current.

tide-rip (tīd′rĭp′), *n.* **1.** a disturbance in the sea caused by opposing currents or by a fast current passing over an uneven bottom. **2.** a tidal wave.

tidewaiter (tīd′wā′tə), *n.* (formerly) a customs officer who boarded ships to enforce the customs regulations.

tidewater (tīd′wô′tə), *n.* **1.** water affected by the ebb and flow of the tide. **2.** the water covering land which is dry at low tide. **3.** *U.S.* seacoast.

tideway (tīd′wā′), *n.* **1.** a channel in which a tidal current runs. **2.** a strong current running through such a channel.

tidings (tī′dĭngz), *n.pl.* (*sometimes construed as sing.*) news, information, or intelligence: *sad tidings.* [ME; OE *tīdung* (c. G *Zeitung* news), der. *tīdan* happen]

tidivate (tĭd′ĭ vāt′), *v.*, **-vated, -vating.** titivate.

tidy (tī′dĭ), *adj.*, **-dier, -diest,** *v.*, **-died, -dying,** *n.*, *pl.* **-dies.** —*adj.* **1.** neat; trim; orderly: *a tidy room.* **2.** *Colloq.* considerable: *a tidy sum.* —*v.t.*, *v.i.* **3.** to make tidy or neat (often fol. by *up*). —*n.* **4.** any of various articles for keeping things tidy, as a receptacle or box. **5.** *Chiefly U.S.* an ornamental covering for protecting the back of a chair, etc.; an antimacassar. [ME, der. *tīd* time, c. G *zeitig* timely] —**ti′dily,** *adv.* —**ti′diness,** *n.* —**Syn. 1.** See **neat[1].**

tie (tī), *v.*, **tied, tying,** *n.* —*v.t.* **1.** to bind or fasten with a cord, string, or the like, drawn together and knotted. **2.** to draw together the parts of with a knotted string or the like: *to tie a bundle.* **3.** to fasten by tightening and knotting the string or strings of: *to tie one's shoes.* **4.** to draw together into a knot, as a cord. **5.** to form by looping and interlacing, as a knot or bow. **6.** to fasten, join, or connect in any way. **7.** to bind or join closely or firmly. **8.** *Colloq.* to unite in marriage. **9.** to confine, restrict, or limit. **10.** to bind or oblige, as to do something. **11.** *Music.* to connect (notes) by a tie. **12. tie down, a.** to fasten down by tying. **b.** to hinder; confine; restrict; curtail. **13. tie up, a.** to fasten securely by tying. **b.** to bind or wrap up. **c.** to hinder. **d.** to bring to a stop or pause. **e.** to invest or place (money) in such a way as to make it unavailable for other purposes. **f.** to place (property) under such conditions or restrictions as to prevent sale or alienation. **g.** to occupy or engage completely. —*v.i.* **14.** to make a tie, bond, or connection. **15.** to make the same score; be equal in a contest. **16.** (of a ship) to moor. **17. tie up with,** to be closely connected or associated with. —*n.* **18.** that with which anything is tied. **19.** a cord, string, or the like, used for tying or fastening something. **20.** a narrow, decorative band, as of cotton or silk, worn round the neck, commonly under a collar, and tied in front. **21.** a low shoe fastened with a lace. **22.** a knot; an ornamental knot. **23.** anything that fastens, secures, or unites. **24.** a link, bond, or connection of kinship, affection, mutual interest, etc. **25.** something that restricts one's freedom of action. **26.** a state of equality in points, votes, etc., as among competitors: *the game ended in a tie.* **27.** a match or contest in which this occurs. **28.** anything, as a beam, rod, etc., connecting or holding together two or more things or parts. **29.** *Civ. Eng.* a member of a framework which is required to take only a tensile load. **30.** *Music.* a curved line connecting two notes on the same line or space to indicate that the sound is to be sustained for their joint value, not repeated. **31.** *U.S.* a sleeper (def. 2). [ME; OE *tīgan* bind, der. *tēag* rope, c. Icel. *taug* rope, *teygja* draw] **—Syn. 24.** See **bond.**

Ties (def. 30)

tie beam, 1. a timber or piece serving as a tie. **2.** a horizontal beam connecting the lower ends of two opposite principal rafters, forming the base of a roof truss. See diag. under **curb roof.**

Tieck (*Ger.* tēk), *n.* **Ludwig** (*Ger.* lo͞ot′vĭKH), 1773–1853, German author.

tied cottage, a cottage, usually owned by a farmer, and rented to one of his employees as long as he is in the farmer's employment.

tied house, a public house which is bound to obtain all its supplies of beer, etc., from one brewery (which usually owns the public house).

tie-in sale (tī′ĭn′), *U.S.* a sale in which the buyer is required to purchase, in addition, some undesired or undesirable item.

tie line, *Teleph.* a telephone line connecting two private branch exchanges or subscribers, which is not open to connection with the main telephone network, even though it may pass through a main exchange.

Tien Shan (tyĕn′ shăn′), a mountain system of central Asia, in Sinkiang, China and Kirghizia in the Soviet Union. Highest peak, Tengri Khan, ab. 23,950 ft. Also, **Tian Shan.**

Tientsin (tyĕn′tsĭn′), *n.* a port in China, the capital of Hopeh province, in the E part. 3,278,000 (1958).

tiepin (tī′pĭn′), *n.* an ornamental pin or clip for holding the halves of a tie together.

Tiepolo (*It.* tyĕ′pô lô), *n.* **1. Giovanni Battista** (*It.* jô vän′nē bät tēs′tä), 1696–1770, Venetian painter and decorator. **2.** his son, **Giovanni Domenico** (*It.* dô mĕ′nē kô), 1727–1804, Venetian painter.

tier[1] (tĭə), *n.* **1.** a row, range, or rank. **2.** one of a series of rows or ranks rising one behind or above another, as of seats in an amphitheatre, of boxes in a theatre, of guns in a man-of-war, or of oars in an ancient galley. **3.** a layer or level. *—v.t.* **4.** to arrange in tiers. *—v.i.* **5.** to rise in tiers. [t. F: m. *tire* sequence]

tier[2] (tī′ə), *n.* **1.** one who or that which ties. **2.** *U.S. Dial.* a child's apron or pinafore. [f. TIE + -ER[1]]

tierce (tĭəs; *also for* 5, tûs), *n.* **1.** an old measure of capacity equivalent to one third of a pipe, or 42 wine gallons. **2.** a cask or vessel holding this quantity. **3.** Also, **terce.** *Eccles.* the third of the seven canonical hours, or the service for it, orig. fixed for the third hour of the day (or 9 a.m.). **4.** *Fencing.* the third of eight defensive positions. **5.** *Cards.* (esp. in piquet) a sequence of three cards. **6.** *Obs.* a third or third part of the same suit. [ME *terce,* t. OF, g. L *tertius* third]

tiercel (tĭə′səl), *n.* tercel.

tie rod, a metal rod serving as a tie (def. 28).

Tierra del Fuego (tĭ ĕ′rə dĕl fo͞o ā′gō; *Sp.* tyĕr′rä dĕl fwĕ′gô), a group of islands at the S tip of South America, separated from the mainland by the Strait of Magellan, and belonging partly to Argentina (7900 pop. est. 1960; 8074 sq. mi.) and partly to Chile (4768 pop., 1952; 19,402 sq. mi.). See map under **Falkland Islands.**

tiers état (*Fr.* tyĕr zē tä′), *French.* the third estate.

tie-up (tī′ŭp′), *n.* **1.** an association, link, or connection. **2.** *U.S.* a stoppage of business, transportation, etc., on account of a strike, storm, accident, etc.

tiff[1] (tĭf), *n.* **1.** a slight or petty quarrel. **2.** a slight fit of ill humour. *—v.i.* **3.** to have a petty quarrel. **4.** to be in a tiff. [orig. uncert.]

tiff[2] (tĭf), *n. Obs.* alcoholic drink. [orig. uncert.]

tiffany (tĭf′ə nĭ) *n.* a gauze of silklike texture. [? t. MF: m. *tiphanie* Epiphany, t. LL: m. *theophania.* See THEOPHANY]

tiffin (tĭf′ĭn), *n. Anglo-Indian.* **1.** lunch. *—v.i.* **2.** to eat lunch. *—v.t.* **3.** to serve lunch to. [var. of *tiffing* drinking, der. TIFF[2]]

Tiflis (tĭf′lĭs; *Russ.* tĭf lēs′), *n.* a city in the SW Soviet Union in Europe and the capital of the Georgian Republic. 812,000 (est. 1965). Official name, **Tbilisi.** See map under **Georgia.**

tig (tĭg), *n.* tag[2].

tiger (tī′gə), *n.* **1.** a large, carnivorous feline, *Panthera tigris,* of Asia, tawny-coloured, striped with black, ranging in several races from India and the Malay Peninsula to Siberia. **2.** the puma, jaguar, thylacine, or other animal resembling the tiger. **3.** one who resembles a tiger in fierceness, courage, etc. **4.** *U.S.* an additional cheer (often the word *tiger*) at the end of a round of cheering. [ME *tigre,* OE *tīgras* (pl.), t. L: m. *tīgris, tigris,* t. Gk] **—ti′ger-like′,** *adj.*

Tiger, *Panthera tigris* (Total length ab. 10 ft, tail ab. 3 ft)

tiger beetle, any beetle of the family *Cicindelidae,* of active, predatory habits.

tiger cat, 1. a small spotted felid carnivore, *Felis tigrina,* of Central and South America. **2.** the margay, *Felis wiedi,* of South America. **3.** the golden cat, *Felis aurata,* of Africa.

tigereye (tī′gər ī′), *n.* tiger's-eye.

tigerfish (tī′gə fĭsh′), *n.* any of various striped fish, esp. those of the family *Theraponidae* of marine and brackish waters of Asia and the Pacific, or freshwater fish of the genus *Hydrocyon* (family *Cichlidae*).

tigerish (tī′gə rĭsh), *adj.* **1.** tiger-like. **2.** fiercely cruel; bloodthirsty; relentless. Also, **tigrish.** **—ti′gerishly,** *adv.* **—ti′gerishness,** *n.*

tiger lily, 1. a lily, *Lilium tigrinum,* with flowers of a dull orange colour spotted with black, and small bulbs or bulbils in the axils of the leaves. **2.** any lily, esp. *L. pardalinum,* of similar coloration.

tiger moth, any of a group of moths (family *Arctiidae*), many of which have conspicuously spotted or striped wings.

tiger's-eye (tī′gəz ī′), *n.* **1.** a golden brown chatoyant stone used for ornament, formed by the alteration of crocidolite, and consisting essentially of quartz coloured by iron oxide. **2.** a glaze on pottery, etc., giving the appearance of this stone. Also, **tigereye.**

tiger shark, a large voracious striped shark, *Galeocerdo cuvieri* (family *Carcharinidae*) of tropical oceans.

tiger snake, a highly venomous snake, *Notechis scutatus,* of Australia and Tasmania, considered the most dangerous of Australian snakes: grows to a length of six feet.

tight (tīt), *adj.* **1.** firmly or closely fixed in place; not easily moved; secure: *a tight knot.* **2.** drawn or stretched so as to be tense; taut. **3.** fitting closely, esp. too closely: *tight trousers.* **4.** difficult to deal with or manage: *to be in a tight corner.* **5.** of such close or compacted texture, or fitted together so closely, as to be impervious to water, air, steam, etc. **6.** strict; firm; rigid. **7.** closely packed; full. **8.** *Colloq.* close; nearly even: *a tight race.* **9.** *Colloq.* stingy; parsimonious. **10.** *Slang.* drunk; tipsy. **11.** *Com.* (of a commodity) difficult to obtain. **12.** *Finance.* (of credit) not easily obtained. **13.** *Dial.* competent or skilful. **14.** *Archaic or Dial.* tidy. **15.** *Archaic or Dial.* neatly or well built or made. *—adv.* **16.** in a tight manner; closely; firmly; securely; tensely. [ME, sandhi var. of *thight* dense, solid, c. Icel. *thēttr* tight, D and G *dicht* tight, close, dense] **—tight′ly,** *adv.* **—tight′ness,** *n.*

-tight, a suffix meaning 'impervious to', as in *watertight.*

tighten (tī′tn), *v.t., v.i.* to make or become tight or tighter. **—tight′ener,** *n.*

tight-fisted (tīt′fĭs′tĭd), *adj.* parsimonious.

tight-knit (tīt′nĭt′), *adj.* well organized; closely integrated.

tight-lipped (tīt′lĭpt′), *adj.* **1.** having the lips drawn tight. **2.** not saying much; taciturn.

tightrope (tīt′rōp′), *n.* a rope or wire stretched tight, on which acrobats perform feats of balancing.

tights (tīts), *n.pl.* a close-fitting garment covering the body from the waist downwards, and the legs.

tightwad (tīt′wŏd′), *n. U.S. Slang.* a close-fisted or stingy person. [f. TIGHT + WAD[1]]

Tiglath-pileser I (tĭg′lăth pĭ lē′zə, -pī-), died 1102? B.C., king of Assyria *c.* 1115–1102?

Tiglath-pileser III (tĭg′lăth pĭ lē′zə, -pī-), died 727 B.C., king of Assyria 745–727 B.C.

tigon (tī′gən), *n.* the offspring of a male tiger and a female lion. Cf. **liger.**

Tigré (tē′grā), *n.* a former kingdom in E Africa: now a province in Ethiopia. *Cap.:* Aduwa.

tigress (tī′grĭs), *n.* **1.** a female tiger. **2.** a fierce or cruel woman.

Tigris (tī′grĭs), *n.* a river flowing from SE Turkey SE through Iraq, joining the Euphrates to empty into the Persian Gulf through the Shatt-al-Arab. ab. 1150 mi. See map under **Babylon.**

tigrish (tī′grĭsh), *adj.* tigerish.

Tijuana (*Sp.* tē KHwä′nä), *n.* a border town in NW Mexico. 244,290 (est. 1965). Also, **Tia Juana.**

tike (tīk), *n.* tyke.

tiki (tē′kĭ), *n.* a carved image representing an ancestor worn as an amulet in some Polynesian cultures. [t. Maori]

til (tĭl, tēl), *n.* the plant sesame. [t. Hind.: sesame]

Tilburg (tĭl′bûg; *Du.* tĭl′bYrKH), *n.* a town in the S Netherlands in S central North Brabant province. 145,045 (1965).

tilbury (tĭl′bə rĭ, -brĭ), *n., pl.* **-ries.** a light two-wheeled carriage without a top. [named after the inventor]

Tilbury (tĭl′bə rĭ, -brĭ), *n.* a seaport in SE England, in Essex, on the Thames estuary. 18,387 (1961).

tilde (tĭl′də), *n.* a diacritical mark (˜) placed over a letter, as over the letter *n* in Spanish to indicate a palatal nasal sound, as in *señor.* [t. Sp., ult. t. ML: m. *titulus* TITLE]

tile (tīl), *n.*, *v.*, **tiled, tiling.** —*n.* **1.** a thin slab or shaped piece of baked clay, sometimes glazed and ornamented, used for covering roofs, lining walls, paving floors, draining land, in ornamental work, etc. **2.** any of various similar slabs or pieces, as of stone or metal. **3.** a pottery tube or pipe used for draining land. **4.** a hollow or cellular block used as a wall unit in masonry construction. **5.** *Colloq.* a stiff hat or a high top-hat. **6. on the tiles,** *Colloq.* having a wild, riotous, or debauched night's entertainment. —*v.t.* **7.** to cover with or as with tiles. [ME; OE *tigele,* c. G *Ziegel,* both t. L: m. *tēgula*] —**til′er,** *n.* —**tile′-like′,** *adj.*

tilefish (tīl′fĭsh′), *n.*, *pl.* **-fishes,** (*esp. collectively*) **-fish.** a large, brilliantly coloured food fish, *Lopholatilus chamaeleonticeps,* of the Atlantic Ocean.

tiliaceous (tĭl′ĭ ā′shəs), *adj.* belonging to the *Tiliaceae,* or linden family of plants. [t. LL: m. *tiliāceus,* der. L *tilia* lime tree]

tiling (tī′lĭng), *n.* **1.** the operation of covering with tiles. **2.** tiles collectively. **3.** a tiled surface.

till[1] (tĭl), *prep.* **1.** up to the time of; until: *to fight till death.* **2.** (with a negative) before: *he did not come till today.* **3.** near (a specified time): *till evening.* **4.** *Scot. and N Dial.* to; unto. —*conj.* **5.** to the time that or when; until. **6.** (with a negative) before. [ME; OE (Northern) *til,* t. Scand.; cf. Icel. *til* to]

till[2] (tĭl), *v.t.* **1.** to labour, as by ploughing, harrowing, etc., upon (land) for the raising of crops; cultivate. **2.** to plough. —*v.i.* **3.** to cultivate the soil. [ME *tille,* OE *tilian* strive, get, c. D *telen* breed, cultivate, G *zielen* aim (at)] —**till′able,** *adj.*

till[3] (tĭl), *n.* (in a shop, etc.) a container as a box, drawer, or the like, usually having separate compartments for coins and notes of different denominations, in which cash for daily transactions is temporarily kept. [late ME *tylle,* n. use of *tylle,* v., draw (now obs.), OE *tyllan*; akin to L *dolus* trick]

till[4] (tĭl), *n.* **1.** *Geol.* glacial drift consisting of an unassorted mixture of clay, sand, gravel, and boulders. **2.** a stiff clay. [orig. uncert.]

tillage (tĭl′ĭj), *n.* **1.** the operation, practice, or art of tilling land. **2.** tilled land.

tillandsia (tĭ lănd′zĭ ə), *n.* any of the tropical and subtropical American plants constituting the bromeliaceous genus *Tillandsia,* most of which are epiphytic on trees, as **Florida moss** (*T. usneoides*) which hangs from the branches of trees in long tufts. [t. NL; named after E. *Tillands,* 17th-cent. Swedish botanist]

tiller[1] (tĭl′ə), *n.* one who tills; a farmer. [f. TILL[2] + -ER[1]]

tiller[2] (tĭl′ə), *n.* *Naut.* a bar or lever fitted to the head of a rudder, to turn the rudder in steering. [ME *tiler,* t. OF: m. *telier* weaver's beam, der. *teile* cloth, g. L *tēla* web] —**till′erless,** *adj.*

tiller[3] (tĭl′ə), *n.* **1.** a shoot of a plant which springs from the root or bottom of the original stalk. **2.** a sapling. —*v.i.* **3.** (of a plant) to put forth new shoots from the root, or round the bottom of the original stalk. [OE *telgor* twig, shoot]

Till Eulenspiegel (tĭl′oi′lən spē′gl; *Ger.* tĭl′ŏʏ′lən shpē-gəl), a legendary German peasant figure of the 14th century, renowned for his practical jokes.

Tilley lamp (tĭl′ĭ), *Trademark.* a portable form of light which operates by burning vaporized paraffin in a special type of mantle, used on building sites, yachts, etc.

Tilly (*Ger.* tĭl′ē), *n.* **Count Johan Tserclaes von** (*Ger.* yō′hän tsĕr klĕs′ fŏn), 1559–1632, German general in the Thirty Years War.

Tilsit (*Ger.* tĭl′zĭt), *n.* former name of **Sovetsk**: peace treaty between France, Prussia, and Russia 1807.

tilt[1] (tĭlt), *v.t.* **1.** to cause to lean, incline, slope or slant. **2.** to rush at or charge, as in a joust. **3.** to hold poised for attack, as a lance. —*v.i.* **4.** to move into or assume a sloping position or direction. **5.** to strike, thrust, or charge with a lance or the like (fol. by *at*). **6.** to engage in a joust, tournament or similar contest. **7. tilt at windmills,** to fight imaginary enemies. —*n.* **8.** an act or instance of tilting. **9.** the state of being tilted; a sloping position. **10.** a slope. **11.** a joust or any other contest. **12.** a dispute. **13.** a thrust of a weapon, as at a tilt or joust. **14. full tilt,** with full force or speed. [ME *tylte,* der. OE *tealt* unsteady] —**tilt′er,** *n.*

tilt[2] (tĭlt), *n.* **1.** a cover of coarse cloth, canvas, etc., as for a wagon, boat, etc. **2.** an awning. —*v.t.* **3.** to furnish with a tilt. [ME, var. of *tild,* OE *teld,* c. G *Zelt* tent]

tilth (tĭlth), *n.* **1.** the act or operation of tilling; tillage. **2.** the state of being tilled. **3.** the physical condition of soil in relation to plant growth. **4.** tilled land. [ME and OE, der. OE *tilian* TILL[2]]

tilt hammer, a drop hammer used in forging, etc., consisting of a heavy head at one end of a pivoted lever.

tiltyard (tĭlt′yäd′), *n.* a courtyard or other area for tilting or jousting.

Tim., Timothy.

Timaru (tĭm′ə rōō′), *n.* a town in New Zealand, in E South Island. 26,400 (est. 1965).

timbal (tĭm′bl), *n.* **1.** a kettledrum. **2.** *Entomol.* a vibrating membrane in certain insects, as the cicada. Also, **tymbal.** [t. F: m. *timbale,* aphetic nasalized var. of *attabal,* t. Sp.: m. *atabal* Moorish drum, t. Ar.: m. *attabl*]

timbale (tăm băl′; *Fr.* tăN băl′), *n.* **1.** a preparation of minced meat, fish, or vegetables, cooked in a cup-shaped mould. **2.** a small mould of paste, baked and filled with some cooked food. [t. F: kettledrum. See TIMBAL]

timber (tĭm′bə), *n.* **1.** wood, esp. when suitable for building houses, ships, etc., or for use in carpentry, joinery, etc. **2.** the wood of growing trees suitable for structural uses. **3.** the trees themselves. **4.** *Chiefly U.S.* wooded land. **5.** a single beam or piece of wood forming, or capable of forming, part of a structure. **6.** *Naut.* (in a ship's frame) one of the curved pieces of wood which spring upwards and outwards from the keel; a rib. **7.** personal character or quality. —*v.t.* **8.** to furnish with timber. **9.** to support with timber. —*interj.* **10.** (a warning, as given by a lumberjack, that a tree is about to fall.) [ME and OE; orig. building, material for building, c. G *Zimmer* room, Icel. *timbr* timber; akin to L *domus* house, Gk *dómos*] —**tim′-berless,** *adj.*

timbered (tĭm′bəd), *adj.* **1.** made of or furnished with timber. **2.** covered with growing trees; wooded: *timbered acres.*

timber-framing (tĭm′bə frā′mĭng), *n.* a method of building construction in which the frame of timber forming the structure is filled in with plaster or bricks.

timberhead (tĭm′bə hĕd′), *n.* *Naut.* **1.** the top end of a timber, rising above the deck, and serving for belaying ropes, etc. **2.** a bollard resembling this in position and use.

timber hitch, *Naut.* a kind of hitch by which a rope is fastened to a spar.

timbering (tĭm′bə rĭng), *n.* **1.** building material of wood. **2.** timberwork.

timberland (tĭm′bə lănd′), *n.* *U.S.* land covered with timber-producing forests.

timber line, 1. the altitude above sea-level at which timber ceases to grow. **2.** the arctic or antarctic limit of tree growth.

timber wolf, the large brindled wolf, *Canis lupus lycaon,* of forested Canada and the northern United States. Also, **grey wolf.**

timberwork (tĭm′bə wûk′), *n.* work formed of timbers.

timber yard, a place where timber is stored.

timbre (tĭm′bə, tăm′bə; *Fr.* tăN′br), *n.* **1.** *Acoustics, Phonet.* that characteristic quality of a sound, independent of pitch and loudness, from which its source or manner of production can be inferred: the saxophone and the clarinet have different timbres, and so do the vowels of *bait* and *boat.* Timbre depends on the relative strengths of the components of different frequencies, which are determined by resonance. **2.** *Music.* the characteristic quality of sound produced by a particular instrument or voice; tone colour. [t. F: quality of sound, orig., kind of tambourine, g. L *tympanum,* t. Gk: m. *týmpanon* timbrel, kettledrum]

timbrel (tĭm′brəl), *n.* a tambourine or similar instrument. [dim. of ME *timbre.* See TIMBRE]

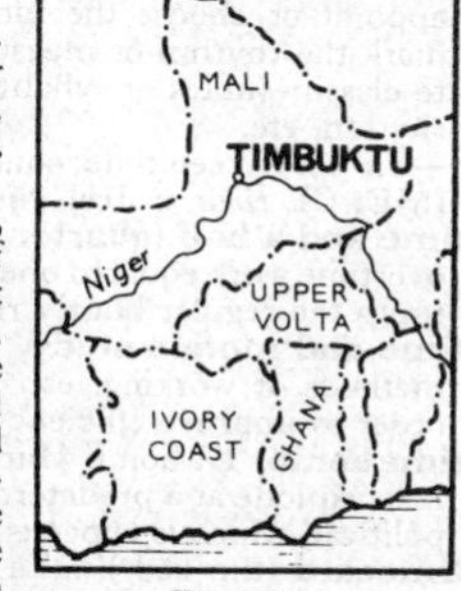

Timbuktu

Timbuktu (tĭm′bŭk tōō′), *n.* **1.** a town in central Mali, near the river Niger. 7,000 (est. 1963). French, **Tombouctou. 2.** any faraway place.

time (tīm), *n.*, *adj.*, *v.*, **timed, timing.** —*n.* **1.** the system of those relations which any event has to any other as past, present, or future; indefinite continuous duration regarded as that in which events succeed one another. **2.** duration regarded as belonging to the present life as distinct from the life to come, or from eternity. **3.** a system or method of measuring or reckoning the passage of time. **4.** a limited extent of time, as between two successive events: *a long time.* **5.** a particular period considered as distinct from other periods: *for the time being.* **6.** (*often pl.*) a period in the history of the world, or contemporary with the life or activities of a notable person: *ancient times.* **7.** (*often pl.*)

the period or era now (or then) present. **8.** (*often pl.*) a period considered with reference to its events or prevailing conditions, tendencies, ideas, etc.: *hard times.* **9.** a prescribed or allotted period, as of one's life, for payment of a debt, etc. **10.** the normal or expected moment of death. **11.** the natural termination of the period of gestation. **12.** a period with reference to personal experience of a specified kind: *to have a good time.* **13.** a period of work of an employee, or the pay for it. **14.** *Colloq.* a term of imprisonment: *to do time.* **15.** the period necessary for or occupied by something: *to ask for time to consider.* **16.** leisure or spare time: *to have no time.* **17.** a particular or definite point in time: *what time is it?* **18.** a particular part of a year, day, etc.: *Christmas time.* **19.** an appointed, fit, due, or proper time: *there is a time for everything.* **20.** the particular moment at which something takes place: *opening time.* **21.** an indefinite period in the future: *time will tell.* **22.** the period in which an action is completed, esp. a performance in a race: *the winner's time was just under four minutes.* **23.** the right occasion or opportunity: *to watch one's time.* **24.** each occasion of a recurring action or event: *to do a thing five times.* **25.** (*pl.*) used as a multiplicative word in phrasal combinations expressing how many instances of a quantity or factor are taken together: *four times five.* **26.** *Drama.* one of the three unities. See **unity** (def. 10). **27.** *Pros.* a unit or a group of units in the measurement of metre. **28.** *Music, etc.* **a.** tempo; relative rapidity of movement. **b.** the metrical duration of a note or rest. **c.** proper or characteristic tempo. **d.** the general movement of a particular kind of musical composition with reference to its rhythm, metrical structure, and tempo. **e.** the movement of a dance or the like to music so arranged: *waltz time.* **29.** *Mil.* the rate of marching, calculated on the number of paces taken per minute: *quick time.* **30. against time,** in an effort to finish something within a certain period. **31. ahead of one's time,** having ideas more advanced than those of the age in which one lives. **32. ahead of time,** before the time due; early. **33. at one time,** formerly. **34. at the same time,** nevertheless. **35. at times,** occasionally; at intervals. **36. behind the times,** old-fashioned. **37. for the time being,** temporarily. **38. from time to time,** occasionally, at intervals. **39. in good time, a.** punctually; at the right time. **b.** early; with time to spare. **40. in no time,** very quickly. **41. in time, a.** soon or early enough. **b.** eventually; after a lapse of time. **c.** following the correct rhythm or tempo. **42. keep time, a.** to function accurately, as a clock. **b.** to observe the tempo or rhythm. **c.** to perform movements in unison in the same rhythm. **43. kill time,** to occupy oneself in some manner so as to make the time pass quickly. **44. many a time,** often; frequently. **45. on time,** punctually. **46. pass the time of day,** to have a brief conversation. **47. take one's time,** to be slow or leisurely. **48. time after time,** often; repeatedly. **49. time and (time) again,** often; repeatedly; again and again. **50. time of one's life,** *Colloq.* a very enjoyable experience.
—*adj.* **51.** of, pertaining to, or showing the passage of time. **52.** (of an explosive device) containing a timing mechanism so that it will detonate at the desired moment: *a time bomb.* **53.** *Com.* payable a stated period of time after presentment. **54.** of or pertaining to purchases with payment postponed.
—*v.t.* **55.** to ascertain or record the time, duration, or rate of: *to time a race.* **56.** to fix the duration of. **57.** to fix or regulate the intervals between (actions, movements, etc.). **58.** to regulate as to time, as a train, a clock, etc. **59.** to appoint or choose the moment or occasion for. **60.** to mark the rhythm or measure of, as in music. **61.** *Music.* to classify (notes or syllables) according to metre, accent, rhythm, etc.
—*v.i.* **62.** to keep time; sound or move in unison.
[ME; OE *tima*, c. Icel. *tīmi*; akin to TIDE[1]]

time and a half (quarter, third, etc.), a rate of pay for overtime work equal to one and a half (quarter, third, etc.), times the regular hourly rate.

time and motion study, the systematic examination of methods of working, esp. in industrial organizations, in order to improve efficiency.

time bomb, 1. a bomb which contains a mechanism causing it to explode at a predetermined time. **2.** a situation, esp. political, which is expected to have a disastrous outcome.

timecard (tīm′käd′), *n.* a card for recording the time at which an employee arrives and departs.

time clock, a clock with an attachment by which a record may be made of the time of something, as of the arrival and departure of employees.

time deposit, *Banking.* a deposit that can be withdrawn by the depositor only after he has given advance notice or after a period of time agreed upon has elapsed.

time division multiplex, *Telecom.* a technique whereby two or more signals are formed into a single composite signal for transmitting over a link, and are recovered at the receiving end of the link.

time-expired (tīm′ik spī′əd), *adj.* (of a soldier, sailor, etc.) having completed a term of service.

time exposure, *Photog.* a long exposure in which the camera shutter is operated by hand, rather than by a built-in timing mechanism in the camera.

time-honoured (tīm′ŏn′əd), *adj.* revered or respected because of antiquity and long continuance: *a time-honoured custom.*

time immemorial, 1. Also, **time out of mind.** a time extending back beyond memory or record. **2.** *Law.* time beyond legal memory, fixed by English statute as prior to the beginning of the reign of Richard I (1189).

timekeeper (tīm′kē′pə), *n.* **1.** one who or that which keeps time. **2.** (in a sports contest, etc.) one who observes and records the time taken by competitors in a race, the duration of an event, etc. **3.** timepiece. **4.** a person employed to keep account of the hours of work done by others. **5.** one who beats time in music.

time-lag (tīm′lăg′), *n.* the period of time between the occurrence of two closely connected events.

time-lapse photography (tīm′lăps′), a form of cinema photography in which successive exposures are made after a lapse of time, in order to record a slow continuous process, as the opening of a flower.

timeless (tīm′lĭs), *adj.* **1.** eternal; unending. **2.** referring to no particular time. **—time′lessly,** *adv.* **—time′lessness,** *n.*

time limit, a period of time within which something must be done.

timely (tīm′lĭ), *adj.*, **-lier, -liest,** *adv.* **—***adj.* **1.** occurring at a suitable time; seasonable; opportune; well-timed: *a timely warning.* **2.** *Rare.* early. **—***adv.* **3.** seasonably; opportunely. **4.** *Archaic.* early or soon. **—time′liness,** *n.* **—Syn. 1.** See **opportune.**

timeous (tī′məs), *adj. Scot.* **1.** early. **2.** timely.

time out of mind, time immemorial (def. 1).

timepiece (tīm′pēs′), *n.* **1.** an apparatus for measuring and recording the progress of time; a chronometer. **2.** a clock or a watch.

timer (tī′mə), *n.* **1.** one who or that which times. **2.** one who measures or records time. **3.** a device for indicating or measuring time, as a stopwatch.

time-reflection symmetry (tīm′rĭ flĕk′shən), *Physics.* the concept that any physical situation should be reversible in time; on this principal the reflection in time of a given situation would correspond to what one would see by reflecting the situation in a space mirror, except that all particles would be replaced by their corresponding anti-particles.

timesaving (tīm′sā′vĭng), *adj.* reducing time required: *timesaving devices or methods.*

timeserver (tīm′sû′və), *n.* one who for selfish ends shapes his conduct to conform with the opinions of the time or of persons in power. **—time′serv′ing,** *adj., n.*

time-sharing (tīm′shēə′rĭng), *n. Computers.* the handling by a computer of several programs at the same time.

time sheet, a sheet or card recording the hours worked by an employee.

time signal, a signal, esp. one sent by radio, indicating a precise moment of time and used as a means of regulating clocks, etc.

time signature, *Music.* a sign, usually in the form of a fraction, indicating the rhythmical pattern of a piece or part of a piece of music, the numerator being the number of beats to the bar and the denominator the length of each beat as a fraction of a semibreve.

time switch, a switch operated by a clockwork or electric clock for activating a mechanism at a particular time.

timetable (tīm′tā′bl), *n.* **1.** a schedule showing the times at which railway trains, buses, aeroplanes, etc., arrive and depart. **2.** a schedule of times of classes, lectures, etc., in a school, university, etc. **3.** any plan listing the times at which certain things are due to take place.

timeworn (tīm′wôn′), *adj.* **1.** worn or impaired by time. **2.** showing the ravages or adverse effect of time.

time zone, one of the 24 regions or divisions of the globe approximately coinciding with meridians at successive hours from the observatory at Greenwich.

timid (tĭm′ĭd), *adj.* **1.** subject to fear; easily alarmed; timorous; shy. **2.** characterized by or indicating fear. [t. L: s. *timidus* frightened] **—timid′ity, tim′idness,** *n.* **—tim′idly,** *adv.* **—Syn. 1.** timorous, fearful, faint-hearted. See **cowardly.**

timing (tī′mĭng), *n.* **1.** *Theat.* **a.** a synchronizing of the various parts of a production for theatrical effect. **b.** the result or effect thus achieved. **c.** (in acting) the act of adjusting one's tempo of reading and movement for dramatic effect. **2.** *Sport.* the control of the speed of an action in order that it may reach its maximum at the proper moment. **3. a.** the mechanism which ensures that the valves in an internal-combustion engine open and close at the correct time. **b.** the process of adjusting this mechanism so that it operates correctly.

timing chain, the chain which operates the timing in an internal-combustion engine by driving the camshaft from the crankshaft.

Timişoara (*Rum.* tē mē shwä′rä), *n.* a town in W Rumania. 152,230 (est. 1964). Hungarian, **Temesvár.**

timocracy (tī mŏk′rə sī), *n., pl.* **-cies. 1.** a form of government in which love of honour is the dominant motive of the rulers. **2.** a form of government in which a certain amount of property is requisite as a qualification for office. [earlier *timocratie*, t. Gk: m. *tīmokratía*, der. *tīmé* price, (moral) worth] **—timocratic** (tī′mə krăt′ĭk), **ti′mocrat′ical,** *adj.*

Timor (tē′mô, tī′mô), *n.* **1.** an island in the Malay Archipelago: largest and easternmost of Lesser Sunda Islands; divided between Indonesia and Portugal. **2. Indonesian Timor** (formerly **Netherlands Timor),** the W part of this island. 310,000 pop. (est. 1966); 5765 sq. mi. **3. Portuguese Timor,** a Portuguese overseas territory comprising the E part of this island. 517,079 pop. (1961); 7330 sq. mi. *Cap.:* Dili.

timorous (tĭm′ə rəs), *adj.* **1.** full of fear; fearful. **2.** subject to fear; timid. **3.** characterized by or indicating fear. [late ME, t. ML: m. s. *timōrōsus* fearful, frightened] **—tim′orously,** *adv.* **—tim′orousness,** *n.*

Timor Sea, an arm of the Indian Ocean between Timor and NW Australia.

Timoshenko (tĭm′ə shĕng′kō; *Russ.* tĭ mä shĕn′kə), *n.* **Semeon Konstantinovich** (*Russ.* sĭ myôn′ kən stän tē′nə vĭch), 1895–1970, Soviet general.

timothy (tĭm′ə thĭ), *n.* a coarse grass, *Phleum pratense*, with cylindrical spikes, valuable as fodder. Also, **timothy grass.** [named after *Timothy* Hanson, American farmer who first cultivated it in the early 18th century]

Timothy (tĭm′ə thĭ), *n.* **1.** a disciple and companion of the apostle Paul, to whom Paul is supposed to have addressed the two New Testament epistles bearing his name. **2.** either of these epistles. [t. L: m. s. *Tīmotheus*, t. Gk: m. *Timótheos*, lit., God-honouring]

Timour (tē′mo͝oə), *n.* Tamerlane. Also, **Timur.**

timpani (tĭm′pə nī), *n.pl., sing.* **-no** (-nō′). kettledrums. [t. It., g. L *tympanum*, t. Gk: m. *týmpanon*] **—tim′panist,** *n.*

tin (tĭn), *n., adj., v.,* **tinned, tinning.** **—***n.* **1.** *Chem.* a low-melting, metallic element nearly approaching silver in colour and lustre, used in making alloys and in plating. *Symbol:* Sn (for *stannum*); *at. wt:* 118·69; *at. no.:* 50; *sp. gr.:* 7·31 at 20°C. **2.** tin plate. **3.** any shallow metal pan, esp. one used in baking. **4.** a hermetically sealed container for food, esp. one made of tin plate. **5.** any container made of tin plate. **6.** the contents of a tin. **7.** *Slang.* money. **—***adj.* **8.** made or consisting of tin or tin plate. **9.** mean; worthless; counterfeit. **10.** indicating the tenth event of a series, as a wedding anniversary. **—***v.t.* **11.** to cover or coat with a thin deposit of tin. **12.** to pack or preserve in tins, as foodstuffs. [ME and OE, c. G *Zinn*] **—tin′like′,** *adj.*

tinamou (tĭn′ə mo͞o′), *n.* any of a group of birds (family *Tinemidae*), of South and Central America, superficially resembling the gallinaceous birds but more primitive, and hunted as game. [t. F, t. Galibi: m. *tinamu*]

tincal (tĭng′kl), *n.* crude native borax (the oriental name). [t. Malay: m. *tingkal*]

tincan (tĭn′kăn′), *n.* a sealed or covered metal can for foodstuffs, esp. one made of tin plate.

tinct (tĭngkt), *v.t.* **1.** *Obs.* to tinge or tint, as with colour. **2.** *Obs.* to imbue. **—***adj.* **3.** *Poetic.* tinged; coloured; flavoured. **—***n.* **4.** *Obs.* tint; tinge; colouring. [t. L: s. *tinctus*, pp., coloured, tinged]

tinct., tincture.

tinctorial (tĭngk tô′rĭ əl), *adj.* pertaining to colouring or dyeing.

tincture (tĭngk′chə), *n., v.,* **-tured, -turing.** **—***n.* **1.** *Pharm.* a solution of a medicinal substance in alcohol (or sometimes in a mixture of alcohol and ammonia or ether), prepared by maceration, digestion, or percolation. **2.** a slight infusion, as of some element or quality. **3.** a trace; a smack or smattering. **4.** *Her.* any of the metals, colours, or furs used in coats of arms, etc. **5.** *Obs.* a dye or pigment. **—***v.t.* **6.** to impart a tincture or colour to; tinge. **7.** to imbue or impregnate with something. [ME, t. L: m. *tinctūra* dyeing, tingeing]

tinder (tĭn′də), *n.* **1.** a material or preparation formerly used for catching the spark from a flint and steel struck together for fire or light. **2.** any dry substance that readily takes fire from a spark. [ME; OE *tynder*, c. G *Zunder*] **—tin′der-like′,** *adj.*

tinderbox (tĭn′də bŏks′), *n.* **1.** a box for holding tinder, usually fitted with a flint and steel. **2.** one who or that which is highly excitable, inflammable, etc.

tin disease, *Metall.* tin plague.

tine (tīn), *n.* a sharp projecting point or prong, as of a fork or deer's antler. [ME *tyne*, var. of ME and OE *tind*, c. MHG *zint*]

tinea (tĭn′ĭ ə), *n. Pathol.* any of several skin diseases caused by fungi. [NL, in L gnawing worm]

tineid moth (tĭn′ĭ ĭd), any moth of the family *Tineidae*, as the clothes moth.

tinfoil (tĭn′foil′), *n.* **1.** tin, or an alloy of tin and lead, in the form of a thin sheet, formerly much used as a wrapping for drugs, confectionery, tobacco, etc. **2.** aluminium foil.

ting (tĭng), *v.t., v.i.* **1.** to cause to make, or to make, a high, clear, ringing sound. **—***n.* **2.** a tinging sound. [imit.]

ting-a-ling (tĭng′ə lĭng′), *n.* a tingling sound, esp. one made by a small bell.

tinge (tĭnj), *v.,* **tinged, tingeing** or **tinging,** *n.* **—***v.t.* **1.** to impart a trace or slight degree of some colour to; tint. **2.** to impart a slight taste or smell to. **—***n.* **3.** a slight degree of coloration. **4.** a slight admixture, as of some qualifying property or characteristic. [late ME, t. L: m. s. *tingere* dye, colour]

tingle (tĭng′gl), *v.,* **-gled, -gling,** *n.* **—***v.i.* **1.** to have a sensation of slight stings or prickly pains, from a sharp blow or from cold. **2.** to cause such a sensation. **—***n.* **3.** a tingling sensation. **4.** the tingling action of cold, etc. [ME; appar. var. of TINKLE] **—tin′gler,** *n.* **—tin′glingly,** *adv.*

tin god, 1. a pompous, self-satisfied, dictatorial person, esp. one of minor importance who exercises some authority over others. **2.** an unworthy person who is mistakenly made the object of veneration or worship.

tin hat, *Colloq.* a steel helmet worn by soldiers.

tinhorn (tĭn′hôn′), *U.S. Slang.* **—***n.* **1.** a pretentious or boastful person, esp. a gambler, who claims power, influence, resources, etc., which he does not possess. **—***adj.* **2.** insignificant; petty; cheap.

tinker (tĭng′kə), *n.* **1.** a mender of pots, kettles, pans, etc., usually an itinerant. **2.** an unskilful or clumsy worker; a bungler. **3.** one skilled in various minor kinds of mechanical work; a jack-of-all-trades. **4.** an act or instance of tinkering. **5.** *Irish and Scot.* a gipsy; vagrant. **6.** a small species of mackerel, *Pneumatophorus grex*, of the Atlantic coast of the U.S. **—***v.i.* **7.** to do the work of a tinker. **8.** to work unskilfully or clumsily at anything. **9.** to busy oneself with a thing without useful results. **—***v.t.* **10.** to mend as a tinker. **11.** to repair in an unskilful or makeshift way. [syncopated var. of earlier *tinekere* worker in tin]

tinkerbird (tĭng′kə bûd′), *n.* any small barbel of Africa and elsewhere, having a harsh call like intermittent tapping; anvilbird.

tinker's cuss, *Slang.* something worthless or trivial: *his opinion is not worth a tinker's cuss.* Also, **tinker's damn.**

tinkle (tĭng′kl), *v.,* **-kled, -kling,** *n.* **—***v.i.* **1.** to give forth or make a succession of short, light, ringing sounds. **—***v.t.* **2.** to cause to tinkle or jingle. **3.** to make known, call attention to, attract, or summon by tinkling. **—***n.* **4.** a tinkling sound. **5.** the act of tinkling. **6.** *Colloq.* a telephone call. [ME; freq. of obs. *tink*, v., make a metallic sound; imit.] **—tin′kling,** *n., adj.*

tinktinkie (tĭngk′tĭng′kĭ), *n. S African.* the Cape wren-warbler. [Afrikaans]

tin lizzie (tĭn′ lĭz′ĭ), *Slang.* any cheap, old, or decrepit motor vehicle.

tinman (tĭn′mən), *n., pl.* **-men.** tinsmith.

tinman's solder, a low-melting solder containing up to 65 per cent tin alloyed with lead, used for tinning.

tinned (tĭnd), *adj.* **1.** covered or coated with tin or solder. **2.** preserved or packed in a can, as foodstuffs.

tinner (tĭn′ə), *n.* tinsmith.

tinnitus (tĭ nī′təs), *n. Pathol.* a ringing or similar sensation of sound in the ears, due to disease of the auditory nerve, etc. [t. L: a ringing]

tinny[1] (tĭn′ĭ), *adj.,* **-nier, -niest. 1.** of or like tin. **2.** containing tin. **3.** characteristic of tin, as sounds; lacking resonance. **4.** not strong or durable. **5.** having the taste of tin. **—tin′nily,** *adv.* **—tin′niness,** *n.*

tinny[2] (tĭn′ĭ), *adj. Austral., N.Z. Colloq.* lucky.

tin-opener (tĭn′ōp′nə), *n.* a device for opening tins.

tin-pan alley (tĭn′păn′), **1.** the district of a city where most of the popular music is published. **2.** the realm of composers or publishers of popular music, or such persons as a group.

tin plague, *Metall.* an allotropic change which occurs to white tin, at low temperatures, causing it to change into the grey, powdery form. Also, **tin disease, tin pest.**

tin plate, thin sheet iron or sheet steel coated with tin.
tin-plate (tĭn′plāt′), *v.t.*, **-plated, -plating.** to plate (sheet iron or steel) with tin.
tin-pot (tĭn′pŏt′), *adj. Colloq.* inferior; petty; worthless.
tin pyrites, stannite.
tinsel (tĭn′səl), *n.*, *adj.*, *v.*, **-selled, -selling** or (*U.S.*) **-seled, -seling.** —*n.* **1.** an inexpensive glittering metallic substance, as copper, brass, etc., in thin sheets, used in pieces, strips, threads, etc., to produce a sparkling effect. **2.** a metallic yarn usually wrapped around a core yarn of silk, rayon, or cotton, for weaving brocade or lamé. **3.** anything showy or attractive with little or no real worth; showy pretence. **4.** *Obs.* a fabric of silk or wool interwoven with threads of gold, silver, or (later) copper. —*adj.* **5.** consisting of or containing tinsel. **6.** showy; gaudy; tawdry. —*v.t.* **7.** to adorn with tinsel. **8.** to adorn with anything glittering. **9.** to make showy or gaudy. [t. F: m. *étincelle* spark, flash, g. L *scintilla*] —**tin′sel-like′,** *adj.*
tinselly (tĭn′sə lĭ), *adj.* cheap; gaudy; tawdry.
tinsmith (tĭn′smĭth′), *n.* one who works in or with tin; a maker of tinware. Also, **tinman, tinner.**
tin soldier, 1. a miniature toy soldier usually made of lead. **2.** one who plays at being a soldier.
tinstone (tĭn′stōn′), *n.* cassiterite.
tint (tĭnt), *n.* **1.** a colour, or a variety of a colour; hue. **2.** a colour diluted with white; a colour of less than maximum chroma, purity, or saturation (as opposed to a *shade*, which is produced by adding black). **3.** a delicate or pale colour. **4.** *Engraving.* a uniform shading, as that produced by series of fine parallel lines. **5.** *Print.* a faintly or lightly coloured background upon which an illustration or the like is to be printed. **6.** any of various impermanent dyes for the hair. —*v.t.* **7.** to apply a tint or tints to; colour slightly or delicately; tinge. [var. of TINCT] —**tint′er,** *n.*
tintack (tĭn′tăk′), *n.* a short nail made of tin-plated iron.
Tintagel Head (tĭn tăj′əl), a cape in England, on the W coast of Cornwall: ruins of **Tintagel Castle,** the legendary birthplace of King Arthur.
tintinnabular (tĭn′tĭ năb′yŏŏ lə), *adj.* of or pertaining to bells or bellringing. Also, **tintinnabulary** (tĭn′tĭ năb′yŏŏ lə rĭ), **tin′tinnab′ulous.** [f. s. L *tintinnābulum* bell + -AR[1]]
tintinnabulation (tĭn′tĭ năb′yŏŏ lā′shən), *n.* the ringing or sound of bells.
tintometer (tĭn tŏm′ĭ tə), *n. Chem.* a colorimeter in which a colour is compared with a range of standard solutions or standard glass slides.
Tintoretto (tĭn′tə rĕt′ō; *It.* tēn tô rĕt′tô), *n.* **Il** (*It.* ēl) (*Jacopo Robusti*), 1518–94, Venetian painter.
tintype (tĭn′tīp′), *n.* a photograph (in the form of a positive) taken on a sensitized sheet of enamelled tin or iron; a ferrotype.
tinware (tĭn′wĕə′), *n.* articles made of tin plate.
tinwork (tĭn′wûk′), *n.* **1.** something made of tin. **2.** (*pl.*, *usually construed as sing.*) an establishment for the mining or manufacture of tin or for the making of tinware.
tiny (tī′nĭ), *adj.*, **-nier, -niest.** very small; minute; wee. [f. obs. *tine* very small (of unknown orig.) + -Y[1]]
-tion, a suffix used to form abstract nouns from verbs or stems not identical with verbs, whether as expressing action (*revolution, commendation*), or a state (*contrition, starvation*), or associated meanings (*relation, temptation*). Also, **-ation, -cion, -ion, -sion, -xion.** [t. L: s. *-tio* (f. *-t*, pp. stem ending, + *-io*, noun suffix); also repr. F *-tion*, G *-tion*, etc., from L]
tip[1] (tĭp), *n.*, *v.*, **tipped, tipping.** —*n.* **1.** a slender or pointed extremity, esp. of anything long or tapered: *the tips of the fingers.* **2.** the top, summit, or apex. **3.** a small piece or part, as of metal or leather, forming the extremity of something. —*v.t.* **4.** to furnish with a tip. **5.** to serve as or form the tip of. **6.** to mark or adorn the tip of. [ME *typ*, c. D and LG *tip*] —**tip′less,** *adj.*
tip[2] (tĭp), *v.*, **tipped, tipping,** *n.* —*v.t.* **1.** to cause to assume a slanting or sloping position; incline; tilt. **2.** to overthrow, overturn, or upset (often fol. by *over* or *up*). **3.** to take off or lift (the hat) in salutation. **4.** to dispose of (rubbish, etc.) by dumping. —*v.i.* **5.** to assume a slanting or sloping position; incline. **6.** to tilt up at one end and down at the other. **7.** to be overturned or upset. **8.** to tumble or topple (usually fol. by *over* or *up*). —*n.* **9.** the act of tipping. **10.** the state of being tipped. **11.** a rubbish dump, esp. one near a mine, on which unwanted material is dumped. [ME *tipe*; orig. uncert.]
tip[3] (tĭp), *n.*, *v.*, **tipped, tipping.** —*n.* **1.** a small present of money given to someone, as a waiter, porter, etc., for performing a service; a gratuity. **2.** a piece of private or secret information, as for use in betting, speculation, etc. **3.** a useful hint or idea. —*v.t.* **4.** to give a small present of money to. **5. tip off,** *Colloq.* **a.** to give private or secret information about; inform. **b.** to warn of impending trouble, danger, etc. —*v.i.* **6.** to give a gratuity. [orig. unknown]
tip[4] (tĭp), *n.*, *v.*, **tipped, tipping.** —*n.* **1.** a light, smart blow; a tap. —*v.t.* **2.** to strike or hit with a light, smart blow; tap. **3.** *Cricket, etc.* to strike (the ball) with a glancing blow. [? akin to TAP. Cf. G *tippen* tap]
tip-and-run (tĭp′ən rŭn′), *n.* a form of cricket in which the batsman must attempt to make a run each time he hits the ball.
tipcart (tĭp′kät′), *n.* a cart with a body that can be tipped or tilted to discharge the contents.
tipcat (tĭp′kăt′), *n.* **1.** a game in which a short piece of wood, tapering at both ends, is struck lightly at one end with a stick so as to make it spring up, and while in the air is struck again for the purpose of driving it as far as possible. **2.** the piece of wood used in this game. Also, **cat, pussy.**
tipi (tē′pĭ), *n.*, *pl.* **-pis.** tepee.
tip-off (tĭp′ŏf′), *n.* **1.** the act of tipping off. **2.** a hint or warning: *they got a tip-off about the raid.*
tipper (tĭp′ə), *n.* one who or that which tips.
Tipperary (tĭp′ə rĕə′rĭ), *n.* **1.** a county in the S Republic of Ireland, in Munster province. 123,882 pop. (1961); 1643 sq. mi. *Co. town:* Clonmel. **2.** a town in this county in the SW part. 4507 (1966).
tippet (tĭp′ĭt), *n.* **1.** a scarf, usually of fur or wool, for covering the neck, or the neck and shoulders, and usually having ends hanging down in front. **2.** *Eccles.* a band of silk or the like worn round the neck with the ends pendent in front. **3.** *Hist.* a long, narrow, pendent part of a hood, sleeve, etc. [ME: appar. der. TIP[1]]
Tippet (tĭp′ĭt), *n.* **Sir Michael (Kemp),** born 1905, English composer.
tipple[1] (tĭp′l), *v.*, **-pled, -pling,** *n.* —*v.t.* **1.** to drink (wine, spirits, etc.), esp. repeatedly, in small quantities. —*v.i.* **2.** to drink alcoholic drink, esp. habitually or to some excess. —*n.* **3.** intoxicating liquor. [orig. uncert.; appar. akin to TIP[2], TIPPLE[2]. Cf. Norw. *tipla* drink little and often] —**tip′pler,** *n.*
tipple[2] (tĭp′l), *n. U.S.* **1.** a device which tilts or overturns a goods wagon to dump its contents. **2.** a place where loaded wagons are emptied by tipping. [der. *tipple*, v., freq. of TIP[2]]
tipstaff (tĭp′stäf′), *n.*, *pl.* **-staves** (-stāvz′, -stävz′), **-staffs. 1.** an attendant or crier in a court of law. **2.** a staff tipped with metal, formerly carried as a badge of office, as by a constable. **3.** any official who carried such a staff.
tipster (tĭp′stə), *n. Colloq.* one who makes a business of furnishing tips, as for use in betting, speculation, etc.
tipsy (tĭp′sĭ), *adj.*, **-sier, -siest. 1.** slightly intoxicated. **2.** characterized by or due to intoxication: *a tipsy lurch.* **3.** tipping, unsteady, or tilted, as if from intoxication. [appar. der. TIP[2] in obs. sense of intoxicate] —**tip′sily,** *adv.* —**tip′siness,** *n.*
tipsy cake, a kind of trifle decorated with almonds and soaked in wine.
tiptoe (tĭp′tō′), *n.*, *v.*, **-toed, -toeing,** *adj.*, *adv.* —*n.* **1.** the tip or end of a toe. **2. on tiptoe, a.** on the tips of the toes collectively: *to walk on tiptoe.* **b.** eagerly expectant. **c.** cautious; stealthy. —*v.i.* **3.** to move or go on tiptoe, as with caution or stealth. —*adj.* **4.** characterized by standing or walking on tiptoe. **5.** straining upwards. **6.** eagerly expectant. **7.** cautious; stealthy. —*adv.* **8.** on tiptoe.
Tipton (tĭp′tən), *n.* a town in England, in Staffordshire. 38,100 (1961).
tiptop (tĭp′tŏp′), *n.* **1.** the extreme top or summit. **2.** *Colloq.* the highest point or degree, as of excellence. —*adj.* **3.** situated at the very top. **4.** *Colloq.* of the highest quality or excellence: *in tiptop condition.* [f. TIP[1] end + TOP highest point; or varied redupl. of TOP]
Tipu Sahib (tĭp′ōō sä′ĭb), *c.* 1750–99, sultan of Mysore 1782–99.
tirade (tī rād′), *n.* **1.** a prolonged outburst of denunciation. **2.** a long, vehement speech. **3.** a passage dealing with a single theme or idea, as in poetry. [t. F: draught, shot, t. It.: m. *tirata* volley, der. *tirare* draw]
tirailleur (*Fr.* tē rà yœr′), *n. French.* skirmisher; sharpshooter.
Tirana (tĭ rä′nə), *n.* the capital of Albania, in the central part. 152,500 (est. 1964). Albanian, **Tiranë** (*Alb.* tē rä′nə).
tire[1] (tī′ə), *v.*, **tired, tiring,** *n.* —*v.t.* **1.** to reduce or exhaust the strength of, as by exertion; make weary; fatigue (sometimes fol. by *out*). **2.** to exhaust the interest, patience, etc., of, as by long continuance or by dullness; make weary. —*v.i.* **3.** to have the strength reduced or exhausted, as by labour or exertion; become fatigued. **4.** to have one's appreciation, interest, patience, etc., exhausted; become or be weary (usually fol. by *of*). —*n.* **5.** *Dial.* fatigue. [ME *tyre*, OE *tȳrian*; of unknown orig.]
tire[2] (tī′ə), *n.*, *v.*, **tired, tiring.** *U.S.* tyre.
tire[3] (tī′ə), *v.*, **tired, tiring,** *n. Archaic.* —*v.t.* **1.** to attire

or array. **2.** to dress (the head or hair), esp. with a head-dress. —*n.* **3.** attire or dress. **4.** a headdress. [ME; aphetic var. of ATTIRE]

tired[1] (tī′əd), *adj.* **1.** exhausted, as by exertion; fatigued. **2.** weary; bored (usually fol. by *of*). **3.** *Colloq.* impatient or disgusted: *you make me tired!* **4.** trite; hackneyed; lacking originality. [f. TIRE[1] + -ED[2]] —**tired′ly,** *adv.* —**tired′ness,** *n.*

—**Syn. 1.** TIRED, EXHAUSTED, FATIGUED, WEARIED, WEARY suggest a condition in which a large part of one's energy and vitality has been consumed. One who is TIRED has used up a considerable part of his bodily or mental resources: *to feel tired at the end of the day.* One who is EXHAUSTED is completely drained of energy and vitality, usually because of arduous or long-sustained effort: *exhausted after a hard run.* One who is FATIGUED has consumed energy to a point where rest and sleep are demanded: *feeling rather pleasantly fatigued.* One who is WEARIED has been under protracted exertion or strain which has gradually worn out his strength: *wearied by a long vigil.* WEARY suggests a more permanent condition than WEARIED: *weary of struggling against misfortunes.*

tired[2] (tī′əd), *adj. U.S.* tyred.

Tiree (tī rē′), *n.* an island in Scotland, in the Inner Hebrides.

tireless (tī′ə lĭs), *adj.* untiring; indefatigable: *a tireless worker.* —**tire′lessly,** *adv.* —**tire′lessness,** *n.*

Tiresias (tī rē′sĭ ăs′), *n. Gk Legend.* a Theban seer blinded by Athena, whom he saw bathing. She relented, and gave him prophetic vision.

tiresome (tī′ə səm), *adj.* **1.** such as to tire one; wearisome. **2.** annoying or vexatious. —**tire′somely,** *adv.*

tirewoman (tī′ə wŏŏm′ən), *n., pl.* **-women.** *Archaic.* a lady's maid. [see TIRE[3]]

Tirich Mir (tē′rĭch mĭə′), a mountain in N West Pakistan: highest peak of the Hindu Kush range. 25,230 ft.

tiring room (tī′ə rĭng), *Archaic.* a dressing-room, esp. in a theatre. [aphetic var. of *attiring room*]

tiro (tī′ə rō′), *n., pl.* **-ros.** a beginner in learning anything; a novice. Also, *Chiefly U.S.,* **tyro.** [t. L: recruit]

Tirol (tĭ′rəl, tĭ rōl′; *Ger.* tē rōl′), *n.* Tyrol. —**Tirolese** (tĭ′rə lēz′), **Tirolean** (tĭ rō′lĭ ən), *adj., n.*

Tirpitz (*Ger.* tĭr′pĭts), *n.* **Alfred von** (*Ger.* äl′frĕt fŏn), 1849–1930, German admiral and statesman.

tirrivee (tĭ′rĭ vē′), *n. Scot.* a tantrum.

Tirso de Molina (*Sp.* tĕr′sō dĕ mō lē′nä) (*Gabriel Téllez*), 1571?–1648, Spanish dramatist.

Tiruchirapalli (tĭ′rŏŏ chĭ′rə pŭl′ĭ), *n.* a town in India, in central Madras. 249,862 (1961). Formerly, **Trichinopoly.**

'tis (tĭz), contraction of *it is.*

tisane (tĭ zăn′; *Fr.* tē zȧn′), *n.* **1.** a herbal tea. **2.** *Obs.* a ptisan. [t. F: barley water. See PTISAN]

Tishri (tĭsh′rĭ), *n.* (in the Jewish calendar) the first month of the year. [t. Heb.]

Tisiphone (tĭ sĭf′ə nĭ), *n. Gk Myth.* one of the Furies.

Tissot (*Fr.* tē sō′), *n.* **James Joseph Jacques** (*Fr.* zhȧm zhō zĕf zhȧk′), 1836–1902, French painter.

tissue (tĭs′yōō, tĭsh′ōō), *n., v.,* **-sued, -suing.** —*n.* **1.** *Biol.* **a.** the substance of which an organism or part is composed. **b.** an aggregate of cells and cell products forming a definite kind of structural material in an animal or plant: *muscular tissue.* **2.** a woven fabric, esp. one of light or gauzy texture, orig. woven with gold or silver. **3.** an interwoven or interconnected series or mass: *a tissue of falsehoods.* **4.** any of several kinds of soft gauzelike papers used for various purposes. **5.** a paper handkerchief. **6.** tissue paper. —*v.t. Rare.* **7.** to weave, esp. with threads of gold or silver. **8.** to clothe or adorn with tissue. [ME, t. OF: m. *tissu* rich kind of cloth, pp. of *tistre* weave, g. L *texere*]

tissue culture, 1. the science of cultivating animal tissue in a prepared medium. **2.** the process itself.

tissue paper, a very thin, almost transparent paper used for wrapping delicate articles, covering illustrations in books, copying letters, etc.

Tisza (*Hung.* tĕ′sŏ), *n.* a river in S central Europe flowing from the Carpathian Mountains through E Hungary and NE Yugoslavia into the Danube N of Belgrade. ab. 800 mi. German, **Theiss.**

tit[1] (tĭt), *n.* **1.** any of various birds of the family *Paridae,* as the **blue tit,** *Parus caeruleus.* **2.** any of various other small birds. **3.** *Archaic or Dial.* a girl or young woman. **4.** *Chiefly Dial.* a small or poor horse. [ME *tit-,* c. Icel. *tittr* titmouse, d. Norw. *titta* little girl]

tit[2] (tĭt), *n.* **1.** a teat. **2.** *Chiefly Taboo.* a female breast. [ME and OE, c. G *Zitze,* MD, LG *titte*]

Titan (tī′tn), *n.* **1.** *Gk Myth.* **a.** one of a family of primordial deities, the children of Uranus (heaven) and Gaea (earth), conceived as lawless beings of gigantic size and enormous strength, who overthrew Uranus, the ruler of the world, and raised Cronus, one of their number, to the throne, but were themselves overcome and cast into Tartarus by Zeus, the son of Cronus. **b.** the sun-god, Helios (Sol), son of the Titan Hyperion. **2.** (*usually l.c.*) a person or thing of enormous size, strength, etc. —*adj.* **3.** titanic. [t. Gk] —**Titaness** (tī′tn ĭs), *n.fem.*

titanate (tī′tə nāt′), *n. Chem.* a salt of titanic acid (def. 2).

Titanesque (tī′tə nĕsk′), *adj.* Titan-like; titanic.

titania (tī tā′nyə), *n. Chem.* titanium dioxide.

titanic[1] (tī tăn′ĭk), *adj.* **1.** of, pertaining to, or characteristic of the Titans. **2.** of enormous size, strength, etc.; gigantic. [f. TITAN + -IC]

titanic[2] (tī tăn′ĭk), *adj. Chem.* of or containing titanium, esp. in the tetravalent state. [f. TITAN(IUM) + -IC]

titanic acid, *Chem.* **1.** titanium dioxide. **2.** any of various acids derived from it.

titanic oxide, *Chem.* titanium dioxide.

titaniferous (tī′tə nĭf′ə rəs), *adj.* containing or yielding titanium. [f. TITANI(UM) + -FEROUS]

Titanism (tī′tə nĭz′əm), *n.* the characteristic Titan spirit or quality, esp. of revolt against tradition, convention, and established order.

titanite (tī′tə nīt′), *n.* sphene. [der. TITANIUM]

titanium (tī tā′nyəm), *n. Chem.* a metallic element occurring combined in various minerals, and isolated as a dark grey powder with a metallic lustre and an ironlike appearance. It is used in metallurgy to remove oxygen and nitrogen from steel and to toughen it. *Symbol:* Ti; *at. wt:* 47·90; *at. no.:* 22; *sp. gr.:* 4·5 at 20°C. [f. TITAN + -IUM]

titanium dioxide, *Chem.* a white insoluble powder, TiO_2, used as a white pigment and in ceramics. Also, **titanium oxide, titanic oxide, titanic acid, titania.**

Titanomachy (tī′tə nŏm′ə kĭ), *n. Gk Myth.* the revolt of the Titans.

titanosaurus (tī′tə nə sô′rəs), *n. Palaeontol.* a South American dinosaur (genus *Titanosaurus*) of the Cretaceous era. Also, **ti′tanosaur′.** [t. NL: f. *Titāno-* (t. Gk, comb. form of *Titán* Titan) + *-saurus* -SAURUS]

titanous (tī tăn′əs), *adj. Chem.* containing trivalent titanium.

titbit (tĭt′bĭt′), *n.* **1.** a delicate bit of food. **2.** a choice or pleasing bit of anything. Also, *U.S.,* **tidbit.** [var. of TIDBIT]

titer (tī′tə, tē′-), *n. U.S.* titre.

titfer (tĭt′fə), *n. Slang.* a hat. [reduction of rhyming slang TIT FOR TAT a hat]

tit for tat, blow for blow; an equivalent given in retaliation, repartee, etc. [? var. of earlier *tip for tap*]

tithable (tī′thə bl), *adj.* liable to be tithed; subject to the payment of tithes.

tithe (tīth), *n., v.,* **tithed, tithing.** —*n.* **1.** (*often pl.*) the tenth part of the annual produce of agriculture, etc., due or paid as a tax for the support of the priesthood, religious institutions, etc. **2.** any tax, levy, or the like, of one tenth. **3.** a tenth part, or any indefinitely small part, of anything. [ME *ti(ghe)the,* OE *teogotha* tenth] —*v.t.* **4.** to give or pay a tithe or tenth of (produce, earnings, etc.). **5.** to pay tithes on. **6.** to exact a tithe from (a person, etc.). **7.** to levy a tithe on (produce, goods, etc.). —*v.i.* **8.** *Obs.* to give or pay a tithe. [ME *tithen,* OE *te(o)g(o)thian,* v., der. *teogotha* tenth part] —**tithe′less,** *adj.* —**tith′er,** *n.*

tithing (tī′thĭng), *n.* **1.** a tithe. **2.** a giving or exacting of tithes. **3.** a company of householders, orig. ten in number, in the old English system of frankpledge. **4.** a rural division in England, orig. regarded as one tenth of a hundred, descended from this system. [ME: OE *tigething,* der. *teogotha* TITHE]

Tithonus (tĭ thō′nəs), *n. Gk Myth.* a son of Laomedon, beloved by Eos (Aurora). He asked and was granted immortality, but finding himself immortally old he asked Eos to take back her gift and was metamorphosed into a grasshopper.

titi[1] (tē′tē), *n., pl.* **-tis.** any of small reddish or greyish monkeys of the genus *Callicebus* of South America. [native name; orig. uncert.]

titi[2] (tē′tē), *n., pl.* **-tis.** any of the shrubs or small trees of the family *Cyrillaceae* of the southern U.S., esp. *Cliftonia monophylla* (**black titi**) and *Cyrilla racemiflora* (**white titi**), with glossy leaves and racemes of white flowers. [t. S Amer. Sp., t. Aymara]

Titian (tĭsh′ən), *n.* **1.** (*Tiziano Vecellio*), c. 1477–1576, Italian painter. **2.** (*l.c.*) a reddish or reddish brown colour made famous by this painter.

Lake Titicaca

Titicaca (*Sp.* tē tē kä′kä), *n.* **Lake,** a lake in the Andes between S Peru and W Bolivia: the largest in South America, and the highest large lake in the world. ab. 3500 sq. mi.; 12,508 ft high.

titillate (tĭt′ĭ lāt′), *v.t.*, **-lated, -lating.** **1.** to tickle; excite a tingling or itching sensation in, as by touching or stroking lightly. **2.** to excite agreeably: *to titillate the fancy.* [t. L: m. s. *titillātus* tickled] —**tit′illa′tion,** *n.* —**titillative** (tĭt′ĭ lā′tĭv), *adj.*

titivate (tĭt′ĭ vāt′), *v.*, **-vated, -vating.** *Colloq.* —*v.t.* **1.** to make smart or spruce. —*v.i.* **2.** to make oneself smart or spruce. Also, **tittivate, tidivate.** [earlier *tiddivate*, ? der. TIDY, modelled on CULTIVATE] —**tit′iva′tion,** *n.* —**tit′iva′tor,** *n.*

titlark (tĭt′läk′), *n.* any of the pipits, small larklike birds, esp. of the genus *Anthus*, as *A. spinoletta*, a migratory bird of northern parts of both the New and Old Worlds. [f. TIT¹ + LARK¹]

title (tī′tl), *n.*, *v.*, **-tled, -tling.** —*n.* **1.** the distinguishing name of a book, poem, picture, piece of music, or the like. **2.** a descriptive heading or caption, as of a chapter, section, or other part of a book. **3.** a titlepage. **4.** a descriptive or distinctive appellation, esp. one belonging to a person by right of rank, office, attainment, etc. **5.** *Sport.* the championship: *he lost the title.* **6.** established or recognized right to something. **7.** a ground for a claim. **8.** anything affording ground for a claim. **9.** *Law.* **a.** legal right to the possession of property, esp. real property. **b.** the ground or evidence of such right. **c.** the instrument constituting evidence of such right. **d.** a unity combining all the requisites to complete legal ownership. **e.** a division of a statute, lawbook, etc., esp. one larger than an article or section. **f.** (in pleading) the designation of one's basis for judicial relief; the cause of action sued upon, as contract, tort, etc. **10.** *Eccles.* **a.** a fixed sphere of work and source of income, required as a condition of ordination. **b.** any of certain Catholic churches in Rome, the nominal incumbents of which are cardinals. —*v.t.* **11.** to furnish with a title; designate by an appellation; entitle. [ME, t. OF, t. L: m. *titulus*; r. OE *titul*, t. L: s. *titulus*] —**Syn. 1, 4.** See **name.**

titled (tī′tld), *adj.* having title, esp. of nobility.

titledeed (tī′tl dēd′), *n.* a deed or document containing or constituting evidence of ownership.

titleholder (tī′tl hōl′də), *n.* **1.** one who holds a title. **2.** *Sport.* one who is the current holder of a championship.

titlepage (tī′tl pāj′), *n.* the page at the beginning of a volume which indicates the title, author's or editor's name, and publication information (usually the publisher, and the place and date of publication).

title role, (in a play, opera, etc.) the role or character from which the title is derived. Also, **title part.**

titmouse (tĭt′mous′), *n.*, *pl.* **-mice** (-mīs′). any of various small birds constituting the family *Paridae*, as *Parus atricapillus* of the New and Old Worlds. [ME *titmose*, f. TIT¹ + *mose* (OE *māse*) titmouse, by assoc. with MOUSE]

Tito (tē′tō), *n.* **Marshal** (*Josip Broz*), born 1891, president of Yugoslavia since 1953.

Titograd (*Serb.* tē′tô gråd), *n.* a town in Yugoslavia, in the S part. 30,657 (1961). Formerly, **Podgorica.**

Titoism (tē′tō ĭz′əm), *n.* the political theory and practice of Marshal Tito, esp. a type of national communist government independent of the Soviet Union. [f. TITO + -ISM] —**Ti′toist,** *adj.*, *n.*

titrate (tī′trāt), *v.t.*, *v.i.*, **-trated, -trating.** *Chem., etc.* to ascertain the quantity of a given constituent present in a solution by accurately measuring the volume of a liquid reagent of known strength necessary to convert the constituent into another form. [f. s. F *titrer* titrate + -ATE¹. See TITRE] —**titra′tion,** *n.*

titre (tī′tə, tē′-), *n.* *Chem.* **1.** the amount of a substance by volume or weight which exactly fulfils certain given requirements of titration. **2.** the strength of a standard solution used in titration. Also, *U.S.*, **titer.** [t. F: m. *titre* fineness, strength, t. L: m. *titulus* title]

tit-tat-toe (tĭt′tăt′tō′), *n.* tick-tack-toe.

titter (tĭt′ə), *v.i.* **1.** to laugh in a low, half-restrained way, as from nervousness or in ill-suppressed amusement. —*n.* **2.** a tittering laugh. [cf. d. Sw. *tittra* giggle] —**tit′terer,** *n.* —**tit′teringly,** *adv.*

tittie (tĭt′ĭ), *n.* *Scot.* titty¹.

tittivate (tĭt′ĭ vāt′), *v.t.*, *v.i.*, **-vated, -vating.** titivate.

tittle (tĭt′l), *n.* **1.** a dot or other small mark in writing or printing, used, e.g., as a diacritic. **2.** a very small part or quantity; a particle, jot, or whit. [ME *titel*, t. ML: m. s. *titulus* mark over letter or word. See TITLE]

tittle-tattle (tĭt′l tăt′l), *n.*, *v.*, **-tled, -tling.** gossip. [varied redupl. of TATTLE] —**tit′tle-tat′tler,** *n.*

tittup (tĭt′əp), *n.*, *v.*, **-tupped, -tupping.** —*n.* **1.** a prancing movement; a curvet. —*v.i.* **2.** to go with an up-and-down movement: prance; caper. [f. d. *tit* pull + UP]

titty¹ (tĭt′ĭ), *n.*, *pl.* **-ties.** *Scot.* sister. Also, **tittie.**

titty² (tĭt′ĭ), *n.* **1.** teat. **2.** *Taboo.* a female breast. [OE *tittig*]

titubation (tĭt′yo͞o bā′shən), *n.* *Pathol.* a disturbance of body equilibrium in standing or walking, resulting in an uncertain gait and trembling: the result of a disease of the cerebellum. [t. L: s. *titubātio* staggering, stammering]

titular (tĭt′yo͞o lə), *adj.* **1.** of, pertaining to, or of the nature of a title. **2.** having a title, esp. of rank. **3.** existing or being such in title only: *a titular prince.* **4.** from whom or which a title or name is taken. **5.** designating any of the Roman Catholic churches in Rome whose nominal incumbents are cardinals. —*n.* **6.** one who bears a title. **7.** one from whom or that from which a title or name is taken. **8.** the benefice or cure conferring its name or style upon a dignitary who may delegate the obligations of this office; sinecure. [f. s. L *titulus* TITLE + -AR¹] —**tit′ularly,** *adv.*

titulary (tĭt′yo͞o lə rĭ), *adj.*, *n.*, *pl.* **-laries.** titular.

Titus (tī′təs), *n.* **1.** a convert and companion of the apostle Paul, to whom Paul is supposed to have written the short New Testament epistle bearing Titus's name. **2.** this New Testament epistle. **3.** (*Flavius Sabinus Vespasianus*), A.D. 40?–81, Roman emperor A.D. 79–81.

Tiu (tē′o͞o), *n.* the Anglo-Saxon god of the sky and of war, the equivalent of Tyr in Scandinavian mythology. [var. of OE *Tiw* god of war. See TUESDAY]

Tiverton (tĭv′ə tən), *n.* a town in England, in Devonshire. 12,397 (1961).

Tivoli (tĭv′ə lĭ; *It.* tē′vô lē), *n.* a town in central Italy, E of Rome, in Latium: ruins of Roman villas. 21,517 (1962).

tizzy (tĭz′ĭ), *n.*, *pl.* **-zies.** *Slang.* **1.** dither. **2.** *Obsolesc.* a sixpence. [orig. uncert.]

Tjirebon (chĭ′rə bŏn′), *n.* a seaport in Indonesia, in N Java. 158,000 (est. 1961).

T-junction (tē′jŭngk′shən), *n.* a junction where a road meets another going across it at right angles, as in the letter T.

Tl, *Chem.* thallium.

T.L., total loss.

Tlemcen (*Fr.* tlĕm sĕn′), *n.* a town in NW Algeria. 83,000 (1960).

Tlingit (tlĭng′gĭt), *n.*, *pl.* **Tlingit** or **Tlingits. 1.** a group of Amerindian tribes of the coastal regions of S Alaska and N British Columbia. **2.** a member of this group. **3.** an Amerindian linguistic stock of SE Alaska and N British Columbia. Also, **Tlinkit** (tlĭng′kĭt). [t. d. Tlingit: m. *Lingit* people] .

Tm, *Chem.* thulium.

tmesis (tmē′sĭs, mē′sĭs), *n.* *Gram., Rhet.* the separation of words that constitute a compound or construction by the insertion of other elements, as *a great man and good* instead of *a great and good man.* [t. Gk: a cutting]

Tn, *Chem.* thoron.

tn, ton.

TNB, *Chem.* trinitrobenzene. Also, **T.N.B.**

TNT, *Chem.* trinitrotoluene. Also, **T.N.T.**

to (to͞o; *unstressed before vowels* to͝o; *unstressed before consonants* tə), *prep.* **1.** expressing motion or direction towards something: *from north to south.* **2.** indicating limit of movement or extension: *rotten to the core.* **3.** expressing contact or contiguity: *apply varnish to the surface.* **4.** expressing a point or limit in time: *to this day.* **5.** expressing time until and including: *Monday to Friday.* **6.** expressing aim, purpose, or intention: *going to the rescue.* **7.** expressing destination or appointed end: *sentenced to death.* **8.** indicating result or consequence: *to his dismay.* **9.** indicating state or condition: *he tore it to pieces.* **10.** indicating the object of inclination or desire: *they drank to his health.* **11.** expressing the object of a right or claim: *claimants to an estate.* **12.** expressing limit in degree or amount: *punctual to the minute, goods to the value of £100.* **13.** indicating addition or amount: *adding insult to injury; they danced to music.* **14.** expressing attachment or adherence: *the paper stuck to the wall; he held to his opinions.* **15.** expressing comparison or opposition: *the score was 9 to 5.* **16.** expressing agreement or accordance: *a position to one's liking.* **17.** expressing reference or relation: *what will he say to this?* **18.** expressing relative position: *one line parallel to another.* **19.** indicating proportion or ratio: *thirty miles to the gallon.* **20.** supplying the place or sense of the dative case in other languages, connecting transitive verbs with their indirect or distant objects, and adjectives, nouns, and intransitive or passive verbs with a following noun which limits their action or application. **21.** used as the ordinary sign or accompaniment of the infinitive (expressing orig. motion, direction, purpose, etc., as in the ordinary uses with a substantive object, but now appearing in many cases as a mere meaningless sign). —*adv.* **22.** towards a person, thing, or point implied or understood. **23.** to a contact point or closed position:

pull the shutters to. **24.** to a matter; to action or work: *we turned to with a will.* **25.** to consciousness; to one's senses: *after he came to.* **26. to and fro, a.** to and from some place or thing. **b.** in opposite or different directions alternately. [ME and OE *tō*, c. G *zu*]

t/o, turnover.

toad (tōd), *n.* **1.** the terrestrial species of tailless (i.e., frog-like) amphibians of the genus *Bufo* and allied genera. **2.** any of various tailless amphibians (order *Salientia*). **3.** any of various other animals, as certain lizards. See **horned toad. 4.** a person or thing as an object of disgust or aversion. [ME *tode*, OE *tādige*; orig. unknown] —**toad′like′,** *adj.*

toadeater (tōd′ē′tə), *n.* toady.

toadfish (tōd′fĭsh′), *n., pl.* **-fishes,** (*esp. collectively*) **-fish. 1.** any of the thick-headed, wide-mouthed fishes constituting the family *Batrachoididae*, as *Opsanus tau* of the Atlantic coast of the U.S. **2.** a puffer (def. 2).

toadflax (tōd′flăks′), *n.* **1.** a common European scrophulariaceous plant, *Linaria vulgaris*, having showy yellow-and-orange flowers, naturalized as a weed in many parts of the world; butter-and-eggs. **2.** any plant of the same genus.

Toad-flax, *Linaria vulgaris*

toad-in-the-hole (tōd′ĭn thə hōl′), *n.* meat, esp. sausages, baked in batter.

toad-rush (tōd′rŭsh′), *n.* a small annual rush, *Juncus bufonius*, common in wet muddy places throughout temperate regions.

toad spittle, cuckoo-spit (the secretion).

toadstone (tōd′stōn′), *n.* any of various stones or stonelike objects, formerly supposed to have been formed in the head or body of a toad, worn as jewels or amulets.

toadstool (tōd′stōōl′), *n.* **1.** any of various fleshy fungi having a stalk with an umbrella-like cap, esp. the agarics. **2.** a poisonous agaric, as distinguished from an edible one. **3.** any of various other fleshy fungi, as the puffballs, coral fungi, etc.

toady (tō′dĭ), *n., pl.* **toadies,** *v.,* **toadied, toadying.** —*n.* **1.** an obsequious sycophant; a fawning flatterer. —*v.t.* **2.** to be the toady to. —*v.i.* **3.** to be a toady. [TOAD + -Y[2]] —**toad′yish,** *adj.* —**toad′yism,** *n.*

to-and-fro (tōō′ən frō′), *adj.* back and forth.

toast[1] (tōst), *n.* **1.** bread in slices browned on both surfaces by heat. —*v.t.* **2.** to brown, as bread or cheese, by exposure to heat. **3.** to heat or warm thoroughly at a fire. —*v.i.* **4.** to become toasted. [ME *tost(en)*, t. OF: m. *toster*, der. L *torrēre* dry, parch]

toast[2] (tōst), *n.* **1.** a person whose health is proposed and drunk; an event, sentiment, or the like, to which one drinks. **2.** a call on another or others to drink to some person or thing. **3.** the act of thus drinking. **4.** words of congratulation, appreciation, loyalty, etc., spoken before drinking. **5.** a person who is very popular, celebrated, suddenly famous: *she was the toast of the town.* —*v.t.* **6.** to propose as a toast. **7.** to drink to the health of, or in honour of. —*v.i.* **8.** to propose or drink a toast. [fig. use of TOAST[1], n., with reference to a piece of toast being put into a beverage to flavour it]

toaster[1] (tōs′tə), *n.* **1.** one who toasts something. **2.** an instrument or apparatus for toasting bread, cheese, etc. [f. TOAST[1], v. + -ER[1]]

toaster[2] (tōs′tə), *n.* one who proposes, or joins in, a toast or health. [f. TOAST[2], v. + -ER[1]]

toasting fork, a fork with a long handle on which bread, or the like, can be toasted over a fire.

toastmaster (tōst′mäs′tə), *n.* **1.** one who presides at a dinner and introduces the after-dinner speakers. **2.** one who proposes or announces toasts.

toast-rack (tōst′răk′), *n.* a stand in which slices of toast are placed to stand upright, separated by partitions.

tobacco (tə băk′ō), *n., pl.* **-cos, -coes. 1.** any plant of the solanaceous genus *Nicotiana*, esp. one of those species, as *N. tabacum*, whose leaves are prepared for smoking or chewing or as snuff. **2.** the leaves so prepared. **3.** any of various similar plants of other genera. [t. Sp.: m. *tabaco*, t. Arawak (from Guarani): pipe for smoking, or roll of leaves smoked, or plant] —**tobac′coless,** *adj.*

tobacco heart, *Pathol.* a functional disorder of the heart, characterized by a rapid and often irregular pulse, due to excessive use of tobacco.

tobacconist (tə băk′ə nĭst), *n.* one who retails tobacco, cigarettes, and other items connected with smoking.

Tobago (tə bā′gō), *n.* an island off the NE coast of Venezuela: formerly a British colony in the Federation of the West Indies, now part of the independent state of Trinidad and Tobago. 33,333 pop. (1960); 116 sq. mi.

to-be (tə bē′), *adj.* future (esp. in combination): *mother-to-be.*

Tobit (tō′bĭt), *n.* a book of the Apocrypha.

toboggan (tə bŏg′ən), *n.* **1.** a light sledge with low runners, used in the sport of tobogganing. **2.** a long, narrow, flat-bottomed sledge made of a thin board curved upwards and backwards at the front end, used originally for transport over snow. —*v.i.* **3.** to use, or coast on, a toboggan. **4.** *U.S.* to fall rapidly, as prices, one's fortune, etc. [t. Canadian F: m. *tabagane*, etc., t. Abnaki: m. *udaba′gan* (what is) used for dragging, der. *uda′be* he drags; cf. *udabauask* sleigh] —**tobog′ganer, tobog′ganist,** *n.*

Tobol (*Russ.* tå bôl′), *n.* a river in the W Soviet Union in Asia, flowing NE to the river Irtish. ab. 800 mi.

Tobolsk (*Russ.* tå bôlysk′), *n.* a town in the W Soviet Union in Asia, on the river Irtish near the confluence of the Tobol. 47,000 (est. 1960).

Tobruk (tə brŏŏk′), *n.* a seaport in E Libya: the scene of much fighting, 1940–42. 5000 (est. 1965).

toby (tō′bĭ), *n., pl.* **-bies.** *Chiefly S African.* a puffer (fish); blaasop.

toby jug (tō′bĭ), **1.** Also, **toby.** a small jug or mug in the form of a stout old man wearing a three-cornered hat. **2.** *U.S. Slang.* a long, slender, cheap cigar. [short for *Tobias*]

Toby jug

Tocantins (*Port.* tö kəɴ tĕɴs′), *n.* a river in E Brazil, flowing N to the Pará river. ab. 1700 mi.

toccata (tə kä′tə; *It.* tök kä′tä), *n. Music.* a composition in the style of an improvisation, for the piano, organ, or other keyboard instrument, intended to exhibit the player's technique. [It. (pp. fem.) touched, der. *toccare* TOUCH]

Toc H (tŏk′āch′), a society formed to continue the spirit of comradeship of World War I, by promoting Christian fellowship by practical services. [obs. telegraphers' code for *T.H.*, initials of *Talbot House*, in Poperinge, Belgium, the first headquarters]

Tocharian (tŏ kä′rĭ ən), *n.* **1.** a member of a central Asiatic people of high culture, who disappeared about A.D. 1000. **2.** an Indo-European language or languages of central Asia, records of which date from A.D. 600.

tocher (tŏKH′ə, tŏk′ə), *Scot.* —*n.* **1.** a dowry. —*v.t.* **2.** to settle or provide with a dowry. [ME (Scot.) *toquhyr*, t. Ir. and OGael.: m. *tochar*, lit., assignment]

tocology (tō kŏl′ə jĭ), *n.* obstetrics. Also, **tokology.** [f. m. Gk *tóko(s)* child + -LOGY]

tocopherol (tō kŏf′ə rŏl′), *n. Biochem.* one of several alcohols which comprise the reproductive dietary factor known as vitamin E, occurring in wheat-germ oil, lettuce or spinach leaves, egg yolk, etc. The most active form is **alpha-tocopherol,** $C_{29}H_{50}O_2$. [f. m. Gk *tókos* child + s. Gk *phérein* + -OL[1]]

Tocqueville (tŏk′vĭl; *Fr.* tŏk vēl′), *n.* **Alexis Charles Henri Maurice Clérel de** (*Fr.* å lĕk sē shårl äɴ rē mō rēs klė rĕl′ də), 1805–59, French statesman and author.

tocsin (tŏk′sĭn), *n.* **1.** a signal, esp. of alarm, sounded on a bell or bells. **2.** a bell used to sound an alarm. [t. F, t. Pr.: m. *tocasenh*, f. *toca(r)* touch, strike + *senh* sign, bell (g. L *signum* sign, ML bell)]

tod[1] (tŏd), *n.* **1.** an English unit of weight, chiefly for wool, commonly equal to 28 lbs but varying locally. **2.** a load. **3.** a bushy mass, esp. of ivy. [ME *todde*. Cf. d. Swed. *todd* mass (of wool), E Fris. *todde* small load]

tod[2] (tŏd), *n. Scot. and N Dial.* **1.** a fox. **2.** a sly or crafty person. [ME, special use of TOD[1] (def. 3), with reference to the fox's bushy tail]

tod[3] (tŏd), *n. Slang.* **on one's tod,** alone. [rhyming slang on *Tod Sloan* (19th-cent. English jockey)]

today (tə dā′), *n.* **1.** this present day. **2.** this present time or age. —*adv.* **3.** on this present day. **4.** at the present time; in these days. [ME; OE *to dæg*. See TO, prep., DAY]

Todd (tŏd), *n.* **Baron Alexander Robertus** (rə bû′təs), born 1907, Scottish chemist.

toddle (tŏd′l), *v.,* **-dled, -dling,** *n.* —*v.i.* **1.** to go with short, unsteady steps, as a child or an old person. —*n.* **2.** the act of toddling. **3.** an unsteady gait. [b. TOTTER and WADDLE]

toddler (tŏd′lə), *n.* one who toddles, esp. a very young child.

toddy (tŏd′ĭ), *n., pl.* **-dies. 1.** a drink made of spirits and hot water, sweetened and sometimes spiced with cloves. **2.** the drawn sap, esp. when fermented, of various species of palm (**toddy palms**), used as a drink. [t. Hind.: m. *tārī*, der. *tār* palm tree]

Todmorden (tŏd′mô′dn, tŏd mô′dn), *n.* a town in England, in the West Riding of Yorkshire. 17,428 (1961).

to-do (tə dōō′), *n., pl.* **-dos.** *Colloq.* bustle; fuss. —**Syn.** See **ado.**

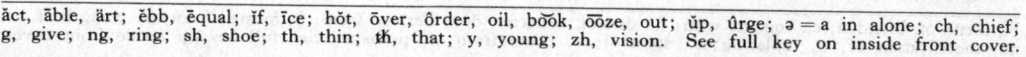

tody (tō′dĭ), *n., pl.* **-dies.** any of the small insectivorous West Indian birds constituting the family *Todidae*, related to the motmots and kingfishers, and having a brightly coloured green and red plumage. [t. F: m. *todier*, der. L *todus*, name of small bird]

toe (tō), *n.*, *v.*, **toed, toeing.** —*n.* **1.** (in man) one of the terminal members or digits of the foot. **2.** an analogous part in other animals. **3.** the forepart of the foot or hoof of a horse or the like. **4.** a part, as of a stocking or shoe, to cover the toes. **5.** a part resembling a toe in shape or position. **6.** the outer end of the hitting surface of a golf club or hockey stick. **7.** *Railways.* the end of a frog in front of the point and in the direction of travel. **8.** *Mach.* **a.** a journal or part placed vertically in a bearing, as the lower end of a vertical shaft. **b.** an arm or projecting part on which a cam or the like strikes. **9. on one's toes,** prepared to act; wide-awake. **10. tread on someone's toes,** to offend, esp. by ignoring (another's) area of responsibility. —*v.t.* **11.** to furnish with a toe or toes. **12.** to touch or reach with the toes. **13.** to kick with the toe. **14.** *Golf.* to strike (the ball) with the toe of the club. **15.** *U.S.* to place or move the toes in a manner specified: *to toe in* (in walking). **16.** *U.S.* to tap with the toe, as in dancing. [ME; OE *tā*, c. G *Zeh(e)*, Icel. *tā*] —**toe′less,** *adj.* —**toe′like′,** *adj.*

toecap (tō′kăp′), *n.* a cap to strengthen the toe of a shoe or boot.

toe-crack (tō′krăk′), *n.* a sand-crack on the front of a horse's hoof.

toed (tōd), *adj.* having a toe or toes: *five-toed.*

toe-dance (tō′däns′), *v.i.*, **-danced, -dancing.** *Ballet*, *Obs. except U.S.* to dance on points.

toehold (tō′hōld′), *n.* **1.** a small ledge or niche, just enough for the toe, in climbing. **2.** any means of support, entry, access, etc. **3.** *Wrestling.* a type of hold whereby the wrestler wrenches the foot of his opponent.

toe-in (tō′ĭn′), *n.* a slight forward convergence of the front wheels of a motor vehicle, used to improve steering stability.

toenail (tō′nāl′), *n.* the nail growing on each of the toes of the human foot.

toering (tŏŏə′rĭng), *n.* *S African.* a conical straw hat, as worn by Malays. [t. Afrikaans, ? t. Malay: m. *tudung*]

toe-shoe (tō′shōō′), *n.* *Obs. except U.S.* blocked shoe.

toff (tŏf), *n.* *Colloq.* a rich, upper-class, usually well-dressed person; a gentleman.

toffee (tŏf′ĭ), *n.* a sweet made of sugar or treacle boiled down, often with butter, nuts, etc. Also, **toffy;** *U.S.*, **taffy.** [earlier *taffy*, *tuffy*, of unknown orig.; ? assoc. with TOUGH]

toffee apple, an apple coated with toffee, held by a small stick.

toffee-nosed (tŏf′ĭ nōzd′), *adj.* *Slang.* snobbish; pretentious; upper-class.

toft (tŏft), *n.* **1.** *Dial.* a homestead or messuage. **2.** a piece of land on which a house, generally with outbuildings, is or has been situated, including the yard. [ME and OE, t. Scand.; cf. Icel. *toft* homestead]

tog (tŏg), *n.*, *v.*, **togged, togging.** *Colloq.* —*n.* **1.** a garment. **2.** (*usually pl.*) clothes. —*v.t.* **3.** to clothe; dress (often fol. by *out* or *up*). [appar. short for obs. cant term *togeman(s)* cloak, coat. Cf. D *tuig* trappings or L *toga* toga]

toga (tō′gə), *n.*, *pl.* **-gas.** **1.** the loose outer garment of the citizens of ancient Rome when appearing in public in time of peace. **2.** a robe of office, a professional gown, or some other distinctive garment. [t. L] —**togaed** (tō′gəd), *adj.*

togated (tō′gā tĭd), *adj.* **1.** peaceful. **2.** clad in a toga. [f. s. L *togātus* clad in toga + -ED²]

toga virilis (tō′gə vĭ rī′lĭs), *Latin.* the manly toga assumed by Roman youths at the age of fourteen.

tog-boy (tŏg′boi′), *n.* *S African.* a licensed native labourer in any of certain South African towns. [f. *tog* (m. Afrikaans *togt*, t. D: m. *tocht* journey, expedition) + BOY]

together (tə gĕth′ə), *adv.* **1.** into or in one gathering, company, mass, place, or body: *to call the people together.* **2.** into or in union, proximity, contact, or collision, as two or more things: *to sew things together.* **3.** into or in relationship, association, business, or friendly relations, etc., as two or more persons: *to bring strangers together.* **4.** taken or considered collectively or conjointly: *this one cost more than all the others together.* **5.** (of a single thing) into or in a condition of unity, compactness, or coherence: *to squeeze a thing together; the argument does not hang together well.* **6.** at the same time; simultaneously: *you cannot have both together.* **7.** without intermission or interruption; continuously; uninterruptedly: *for days together.* **8.** in cooperation; with united action; conjointly: *to undertake a task together.* **9.** with mutual action; mutually; reciprocally: *to confer together; to multiply two numbers together.* [ME *togethir*, OE *tōgædere*, f. TO, prep., + *gædere*, adv., together, c. D *tegader.* Cf. GATHER]

togetherness (tə gĕth′ə nĭs), *n.* a feeling or quality of being united with other people.

toggery (tŏg′ə rĭ), *n.* *Colloq.* garments; clothes; togs.

toggle (tŏg′l), *n.*, *v.*, **-gled, -gling.** —*n.* **1.** a transverse pin, bolt, or rod placed through an eye of a rope, link of a chain, or the like, for various purposes. **2.** a toggle joint, or a device furnished with one. **3.** a small wooden bar around which a loop is passed, to fasten the front of a garment as a duffel coat. —*v.t.* **4.** to furnish with a toggle or toggles. **5.** to secure or fasten with a toggle or toggles. [? akin to TACKLE]

toggle joint, *Mach.* a device consisting of two arms pivoted together at their inner ends and pivoted to other parts at their outer ends, utilized in printing presses, etc., for pressure at the outer ends when the arms are put into a straight line by force applied at the bend between them.

Toggle joint

toggle switch, *Elect.* a switch in which a projecting knob or arm, moving through a small arc, causes the contacts to open or close the circuit suddenly.

Togo (tō′gō), *n.* **Count Heilhachiro** (hā′hə chĭə′rō), 1847–1934, Japanese admiral.

Togo (tō′gō), *n.* **Republic of,** an independent country in W Africa; former French trusteeship of Togoland. 1,400,000 pop. (est. 1960); ab. 21,620 sq. mi. *Cap.*: Lomé.

Togoland (tō′gō lănd′), *n.* a former German protectorate in W Africa, on the Gulf of Guinea: the E part is now a republic (see **Togo**), the W part, formerly a British trusteeship, is now part of Ghana.

Togolese (tō′gō lēz′), *n.*, *pl.* **-lese,** *adj.* —*n.* **1.** a native of the Republic of Togo. —*adj.* **2.** of, pertaining to, or characteristic of the Republic of Togo or the Togolese.

toheroa (tō′ə rō′ə), *n.* **1.** a New Zealand shellfish (*Amphidesma ventricosum*). **2.** a soup made of this. [t. Maori]

to-hunga (tō′hŏŏng′ə), *n.* *N.Z.* a Maori priest or doctor. [t. Maori]

toil¹ (toil), *n.* **1.** hard and continuous work; exhausting labour or effort. **2.** a laborious task. **3.** *Archaic.* battle; strife; struggle. —*v.i.* **4.** to engage in severe and continuous work; labour arduously. **5.** to move or travel with difficulty, weariness, or pain. —*v.t.* **6.** to bring or effect by toil. [ME *toile(n)*, t. AF: m. *toiler* strive, dispute, wrangle, g. L *tudiculāre* stir] —**toil′er,** *n.* —**Syn. 1.** See **work.**

toil² (toil), *n.* **1.** (*usually pl.*) a net or nets set about a space into which game is driven or within which it is known to be. **2.** (*pl.*) power; clutches: *she was in the toils of her wicked uncle.* **3.** *Obs.* any snare or trap for wild beasts. [t. F: m. *toile*, g. L *tēla* web]

toile (twäl), *n.* **1.** a type of transparent linen. **2.** the made-up pattern in a cheap cloth of an exclusively designed gown before this is made in its intended material. [t. F. See TOIL²]

toilet (toi′lĭt), *n.* **1.** a lavatory. **2.** *U.S.* a bathroom. **3.** a dressing-room, esp. one with a bath. **4.** the act or process of dressing, including bathing, arranging the hair, etc. **5.** the articles used in dressing, etc., as mirror, brush, comb, etc. **6.** a dressing-table. **7.** the dress or costume of a person; any particular costume: *toilet of white silk.* **8.** *Surg.* the cleansing of the part or wound after an operation, esp. in the peritoneal cavity. Also, **toilette** (twä lĕt′; *Fr.* twȧ lĕt′) for 4, 7. [t. F: m. *toilette*, dim. of *toile* cloth. See TOIL²]

toilet paper, soft, thin paper for sanitary use after defecation.

toiletry (toi′lĭ trĭ), *n.*, *pl.* **-tries.** an article or substance used in dressing or making up.

toilet set, the articles used in dressing, etc., as mirror, brush, comb, etc.

toilet water, a scented liquid used as a light perfume; cologne.

toilful (toil′fəl), *adj.* characterized by or involving toil; laborious; toilsome. —**toil′fully,** *adv.*

toilsome (toil′səm), *adj.* characterized by or involving toil; laborious or fatiguing. —**toil′somely,** *adv.* —**toil′someness,** *n.*

toilworn (toil′wôn′), *adj.* **1.** worn by toil. **2.** showing the effects of toil.

Tojo (tō′jō), *n.* **Hideki** (hē′dĭ kĭ), 1885–1948, Japanese general.

tokay (tō′kā), *n.* a small lizard, *Gekko gecko* of the family *Gekkonidae*, of south-east Asia. [imit. of its cry]

Tokay (tō kā′), *n.* **1.** a rich, sweet, aromatic wine made near Tokay, Hungary. **2.** a variety of grape from which it is made. **3.** a similar wine made elsewhere.

token (tō′kən), *n.* **1.** something serving to represent or indicate some fact, event, feeling, etc.; sign: *to wear black as a token of mourning.* **2.** a characteristic mark or indication; symbol. **3.** a memento; a keepsake. **4.** something used to indicate authenticity, authority, etc. **5.** a stamped piece of metal issued as a limited medium of exchange, as for bus fares, at a nominal value much greater than its commodity value. **6.** anything of only nominal value similarly used, as paper currency. **7. by the same token,** in the same way; similarly. **8. in token of,** as a sign or evidence of. [ME; OE *tācen*, c. G *Zeichen*; akin to TEACH]

token payment, a small payment binding an agreement or acknowledging a debt.

tokology (tŏ kŏl′ə jĭ), *n.* tocology.

Tokushima (tō′ko͞o shē′mə), *n.* a seaport in SW Japan, on NE Shikoku island. 193,233 (1965).

Tokyo (tō′kyō), *n.* a seaport in and the capital of Japan, on **Tokyo Bay,** an inlet of the Pacific in SE Honshu island, one of the world's three largest cities: destructive earthquake and fire, 1923. 11,025,013 (1967). Also, **Tokio.** Formerly, **Yeddo** or **Yedo.** See map under **Hiroshima.**

tola (tō′lə), *n.* a unit of weight in India equal to 180 English grains, the weight of a silver rupee. [t. Hind.: a balance, weight]

tolan (tō′lăn), *n.* *Chem.* an unsaturated crystalline hydrocarbon, $C_6H_5C \equiv CC_6H_5$. Also, **tolane** (tō′lān). [f. TOL(U) + -AN(E)]

tolbooth (tŏl′bo͞oth′), *n.* **1.** a town hall or guildhall. **2.** *Chiefly Scot.* a town prison; a jail. Also, **tollbooth.** [ME *tolbothe.* See TOLL² + BOOTH]

Tolbuhin (*Bulg.* tôl bo͞o′KHĕn), *n.* a town in NE Bulgaria. 54,815 (1964). Formerly, **Dobrich.**

told (tōld), *v.* **1.** pt. and pp. of **tell. 2. all told,** in all.

tole (tōl), *n.* enamelled or lacquered metalware usually with gilt decoration, often used (esp. in the eighteenth century) for trays, lampshades, etc. Also, **tôle.** [t. F]

Toledo (tə lē′dō *for 3; for 1, 2 and 4,* tŏ lā′dō; *Sp.* tô lĕ′dô), *n.* **1. Francisco de** (*Sp.* frȧn thēs′kô dĕ), *c.* 1515–84?, Spanish administrator, viceroy of Peru 1569–81. **2.** a city in central Spain, on the river Tagus: the capital of Spain under the Romans. 39,871 (1965). **3.** a city in the U.S., in NW Ohio: a port on Lake Erie. 318,003 (1960). **4.** a sword or sword blade as one originally made at Toledo, Spain.

tolerable (tŏl′ə rə bl), *adj.* **1.** that may be tolerated; endurable. **2.** fairly good; not bad. **3.** *Colloq.* in fair health. [ME, t. L: m. s. *tolerābilis* bearable] —**tol′erableness,** *n.* —**tol′erably,** *adv.* —**Syn. 3.** so-so.

tolerance (tŏl′ə rəns), *n.* **1.** the disposition to be patient and fair towards those whose opinions or practices differ from one's own; freedom from bigotry. **2.** the disposition to be patient and fair to opinions which are not one's own. **3.** the ability to endure disagreeable circumstances. **4.** *Med.* the power of enduring or resisting the action of a drug, poison, etc. **5. a.** *Mach.* an allowable variation in the dimensions of a machined article or part. **b.** an allowable variation in some other characteristic of an article as weight, quality, etc. **6.** *Coining.* a permissible deviation in the fineness and weight of coin, owing to the difficulty of securing exact conformity to the standard.

—**Syn. 1.** TOLERANCE, TOLERATION agree in allowing the right of something which one does not approve. TOLERANCE suggests a liberal spirit towards the views and actions of others: *tolerance towards religious minorities.* TOLERATION implies the allowance or sufferance of conduct with which one is not in accord: *toleration of bribery.*

tolerance limits, *Statistics.* a pair of numbers obtained from a sample such that it can be stated with a given degree of probability that the numbers will include between them at least a specified percentage of values of a variable in the population.

tolerant (tŏl′ə rənt), *adj.* **1.** inclined or disposed to tolerate; showing tolerance; forbearing. **2.** favouring toleration. **3.** *Med.* able to endure or resist the action of a drug, poison, etc. —**tol′erantly,** *adv.*

tolerate (tŏl′ə rāt′), *v.t.*, **-rated, -rating. 1.** to allow to be, be practised, or be done without prohibition or hindrance; permit. **2.** to bear without repugnance; put up with. **3.** *Med.* to endure or resist the action of (a drug, poison, etc.). **4.** *Obs.* to endure or sustain, as pain or hardship. [t. L: m. s. *tolerātus* endured] —**tolerative** (tŏl′ə rə tĭv), *adj.* —**tol′era′tor,** *n.*

toleration (tŏl′ə rā′shən), *n.* **1.** the tolerating, esp. of what is not actually approved; forbearance. **2.** allowance, by a government, of the exercise of religions other than the one which is officially established or recognized; recognition of the right of private judgement in matters of faith and worship. —**tol′era′tionism,** *n.* —**tol′era′tionist,** *n.* —**Syn. 1.** See **tolerance.**

tolidine (tŏl′ĭ dēn′, -dĭn), *n.* *Chem.* any of three isomeric derivatives of toluene, $(NH_3.CH_3.C_6H_3)_2$, the orthoisomer of which is used in making dyes. [f. TOL(U) + -ID(E) + -INE²]

Tolima (*Sp.* tô lē′mȧ), *n.* a volcanic mountain in W Colombia, in the Andes. 18,438 ft.

Tolkien (tŏl′kēn), *n.* **John Ronald Reuel** (ro͞o′ĭl), born 1892, British medievalist, writer, and critic, born in South Africa.

toll¹ (tōl), *v.t.* **1.** to cause (a large bell) to sound with single strokes slowly and regularly repeated, as for summoning a congregation to church, or esp. for announcing a death. **2.** to sound (a knell, etc.) or strike (the hour), by such strokes. **3.** to announce (a death, etc.) by this means; ring a toll for (a dying or dead person). **4.** to summon or dismiss by tolling. **5.** *U.S.* to lure or decoy (game) by arousing curiosity. **6.** *Obs.* to attract, allure, or entice. —*v.i.* **7.** to sound with single strokes slowly and regularly repeated, as a bell. —*n.* **8.** the act of tolling a bell. **9.** a single stroke made in tolling a bell. **10.** the sound made. [ME; akin to OE *-tyllan* in *fortyllan* attract, allure]

toll² (tōl), *n.* **1.** Also, **tollage.** a payment exacted by the state, the local authorities, etc., for some right or privilege, as for passage along a road or over a bridge. **2.** formerly, the right to take such payment. **3.** a compensation for services, as for grinding corn or for transportation or transmission. **4.** *Dial.* grain retained by a miller in payment of his services. **5.** a payment made for a long-distance telephone call. **6.** a tax, duty, or tribute. **7.** exaction, cost, or the like, esp. in terms of death or loss: *the accident took a heavy toll of lives.* —*v.t.* **8.** to collect (something) as a toll. —*v.i.* **9.** to collect toll; levy toll. [ME and OE (c. G *Zoll*), var. of *toln*, t. LL: m. s. *tolōneum*, var. of L *telōnium*, t. Gk: m. *telṓnion* tollhouse]

tollbar (tōl′bä′), *n.* a barrier, esp. a gate, across a road or bridge, where toll is taken.

tollbooth (tŏl′bo͞oth′), *n.* tolbooth.

toll bridge, a bridge at which a toll is charged.

toll call, (formerly in Britain) a short-distance trunk call.

Toller (*Ger.* tŏl′ər), *n.* **Ernst** (*Ger.* ĕrnst), 1893–1939, German dramatist.

tollgate (tōl′gāt′), *n.* a gate where toll is taken.

tollhouse (tōl′hous′), *n.* a house at a tollgate, occupied by a tollkeeper.

tollie (tŏl′ĭ), *n.* *S African.* calf. [t. Zulu or Xhosa: m. *ithole* calf (after horns have begun to appear)]

tollkeeper (tōl′kē′pə), *n.* the collector at a tollgate.

Tolpuddle Martyrs, six farm labourers who were sentenced to seven years' transportation in 1834 for having formed a trade union in the village of Tolpuddle, Dorset.

Tolstoy (tŏl′stoi; *Russ.* tȧl stôy′), *n.* **Lev** (*Eng.* **Leo**) **Nikolaevich** (*Russ.* lyĕf nĭ kȧ lȧ′yĭ vĭch), 1828–1910, Russian novelist and social reformer. Also, **Tolstoi.**

Toltec (tŏl′tĕk), *n.* **1.** (*pl.*) an Indian people who flourished in central Mexico before the advent of the Aztecs, and who, according to tradition, laid the foundation of Aztec culture. —*adj.* **2.** Also, **Tol′tecan.** of or pertaining to the Toltecs.

tolu (tŏ lo͞o′), *n.* a fragrant yellowish brown balsam obtained from a South American tree, *Myroxylon balsamum,* used in medicine as a stomachic and expectorant, and in perfumery. [named after *Tolu* (now Santiago de Tolu) in Colombia, where balsam is obtained]

toluate (tŏl′yo͝o āt′), *n.* *Chem.* a salt or ester of toluic acid.

Toluca (*Sp.* tô lo͞o′kȧ), *n.* a town in S central Mexico. 156,033 (1960).

toluene (tŏl′yo͝o ēn′), *n.* *Chem.* a colourless liquid hydrocarbon, $C_6H_5CH_3$, obtained from tolu, coal tar, etc.: used as a solvent and in the manufacture of coal-tar substances, as TNT. [f. TOLU + -ENE]

toluic acid (tŏ lyo͞o′ĭk), *Chem.* any of three isomeric acids, $CH_3.C_6H_4.COOH$, which are derivatives of toluene.

toluide (tŏl′yo͝o ĭd′), *n.* *Chem.* an amide which contains a tolyl group united to the nitrogen. Also, **toluid** (tŏl′yo͝o ĭd).

toluidine (tŏ lyo͞o′ĭ dēn′), *n.* *Chem.* any of three isomeric amines, $CH_3C_6H_4NH_2$, derived from toluene, used in the dye and drug industries. Also, **toluidin** (tŏ lyo͞o′ĭ dĭn).

toluol (tŏl′yo͝o ŏl′), *n.* *Chem.* **1.** toluene. **2.** the commercial form of toluene. Also, **toluole** (tŏl′yo͝o ōl′). [f. TOLU + -OL²]

toluyl group (tŏl′yo͝o ĭl), *Chem.* a univalent radical, $CH_3.C_6H_4.CO$, present in toluic acids. Also, **toluyl radical.** [f. TOLU + -YL]

tolyl group (tŏl′ĭl), *Chem.* a univalent hydrocarbon radical, $CH_3C_6H_4$, from toluene. Also, **tolyl radical.** [f. TOL(U) + -YL]

tom (tŏm), *n.* **1.** the male of various animals (often used in composition, as in *tomcat*). **2.** tomcat. **3.** a name for a large bell. [short for *Thomas*]

tomahawk (tŏm′ə hôk′), *n.* **1.** a light axe used by the North American Indians as a weapon and tool, and serving as a token of war. **2.** any of various similar weapons or implements. **3.** (in Australia) a hatchet. —*v.t.* **4.** to strike, cut, or kill with or as with a tomahawk. [t. Algonquian (Virginia d.): m. *tommahick*, etc., war club, ceremonial object]

Tom and Jerry, *U.S.* a hot drink composed of rum and water (or milk) with beaten eggs, spiced and sweetened.

tomato (tə mä′tō), *n., pl.* **-toes. 1.** a widely cultivated solanaceous plant, *Lycopersicon lycopersicum*, bearing a slightly acid, pulpy fruit, commonly red, sometimes yellow, used as a vegetable. **2.** the fruit itself. **3.** any plant of the same genus. **4.** its fruit. [t. Sp.: m. *tomate*, t. Nahuatl: m. *tomatl*]

tomb (to͞om), *n.* **1.** an excavation in earth or rock for the reception of a dead body. **2.** a grave or mausoleum. **3.** any sepulchral structure. **4.** the state of death. **—*v.t.* 5.** to place in or as in a tomb; bury. [ME, t. OF: m. *tombe*, g. LL *tumba*, t. Gk: m. *týmbos*] **—tomb′less,** *adj.* **—tomb′-like′,** *adj.*

Tombalbaye (*Fr.* tôɴ bál bȧy′), *n.* **François** (*Fr.* fräɴ swȧ′), born 1918, president of Chad since 1960.

Tombigbee (tŏm bĭg′bĭ), *n.* a river in the U.S., flowing through NE Mississippi and SW Alabama, joining the Alabama river to form the Mobile river. ab. 450 mi.

tombola (tŏm bō′lə), *n.* a lottery in which competitors buy tickets which may entitle them to a prize. [t. It.: der. *tombolare* to tumble]

tombolo (tŏm′bə lō′), *n.* a spit of sand or shingle thrown up by the tides, linking an island or rock with the mainland. [t. It.]

Tombouctou (*Fr.* tôɴ bo͝ok to͞o′), *n.* French name of **Timbuktu.**

tomboy (tŏm′boi′), *n.* a boisterous, romping girl. **—tom′-boy′ish,** *adj.* **—tom′boy′ishness,** *n.*

tombstone (to͞om′stōn′), *n.* a stone, usually bearing an inscription, set to mark a tomb or grave.

tomcat (tŏm′kăt′), *n.* a male cat.

Tom Collins (kŏl′ĭnz), a long drink containing gin, lemon or lime juice, and soda-water, sweetened and served with ice.

Tom, Dick, and Harry, common people generally: *they invited every Tom, Dick, and Harry.*

tome (tōm), *n.* **1.** a volume forming a part of a larger work. **2.** any volume, esp. a ponderous one. [t. F, t. L: m. *tomus*, t. Gk: m. *tómos* volume, section of book]

-tome, a word element referring to cutting, used esp. in scientific terms, as *microtome, osteotome.* [comb. form repr. Gk *tomḗ* a cutting, section; *tómos* a cut, slice; *-tomos* cutting]

Tomé (*Sp.* tō mĕ′), *n.* **Narciso** (*Sp.* när thē′sō), fl. 1715–1742, Spanish sculptor.

tomentose (tə mĕn′tōs), *adj.* **1.** *Anat.* fleecy; flocculent. **2.** *Bot., Entomol.* closely covered with down or matted hair. [t. NL: m. s. *tōmentōsus*, der. L *tōmentum* TOMENTUM]

tomentum (tə mĕn′təm), *n., pl.* **-ta** (-tə). *Bot.* pubescence consisting of longish, soft, entangled hairs pressed close to the surface. [NL: special use of L *tōmentum* stuffing (of wool, hair, etc.) for cushions]

tomfool (tŏm′fo͞ol′), *n.* **1.** a grossly foolish person; a silly fool. **—*adj.* 2.** being, or characteristic of, a tomfool. **—*v.i.* 3.** to play the fool.

tomfoolery (tŏm′fo͞o′lə rĭ), *n., pl.* **-eries. 1.** foolish or silly behaviour. **2.** a silly act, matter, or thing.

Tomkinson Range (tŏm′kĭn sən), a mountain range in Australia, on the borders of Western Australia, Northern Territory, and South Australia. Highest point, Mt Aloysius, 3560 ft.

Tomlinson (tŏm′lĭn sən), *n.* **Henry Major,** 1873–1958, English journalist and novelist.

tommy (tŏm′ĭ), *n., pl.* **-mies.** short for **Tommy Atkins.** Also, **Tommy.**

Tommy Atkins (ăt′kĭnz), **1.** any private of the British Army. **2.** the rank and file collectively. [a familiar name for typical British soldier, arising out of the use of the name 'Thomas Atkins' in specimen forms given in official regulations from 1815]

tommy bar, a bar inserted into a capstan, box spanner, etc., to give leverage for turning.

Tommy gun, *Slang.* **1.** a Thompson submachine gun. **2.** any similar gun.

tommyrot (tŏm′ĭ rŏt′), *n.* *Slang.* nonsense.

tomography (tə mŏg′rə fĭ), *n.* *Med.* röntgenography of a selected plane in the body.

tomorrow (tə mŏ′rō), *n.* **1.** the day after this day: *tomorrow will be fair.* **2.** a day immediately following or succeeding another day. **3.** some future day or time. **—*adv.* 4.** on the morrow; on the day after this day: *come tomorrow.* Also, **to-morrow.** [ME *to morwe(n)*, OE *tō morgen(ne)* on the morrow, in the morning]

tompion (tŏm′pyən), *n.* tampion.

Tompion (tŏm′pyən), *n.* **Thomas,** 1639–1713, English clockmaker.

Tomsk (tŏmsk; *Russ.* tômsk), *n.* a town in the central Soviet Union in Asia, E of the river Ob. 302,000 (est. 1965).

Tom Thumb (thŭm), **1.** a diminutive hero of folk tales. **2.** a diminutive man; a dwarf. **3.** a midget, Charles Stratton (1838–83), exhibited in the circus of P. T. Barnum.

Tom Tiddler's Ground, 1. a children's game in which one player attempts to catch the others as they cross his 'territory'. **2.** the territory which he patrols. **3.** *Slang.* any place where money, etc., is easily acquired. **4.** *Slang.* a disputed territory. [def. 3 from the former cry of children playing this game, 'I'm on Tom Tiddler's ground, picking up gold and silver']

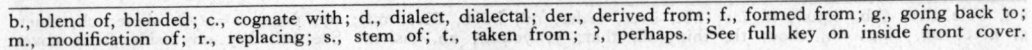

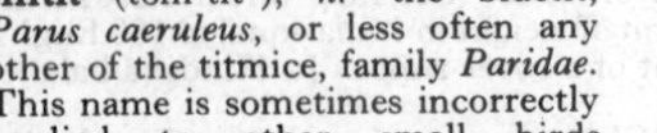

Tomtit, *Parus caeruleus* (Ab. 4½ in. long)

tomtit (tŏm′tĭt′), *n.* the bluetit, *Parus caeruleus*, or less often any other of the titmice, family *Paridae.* This name is sometimes incorrectly applied to other small birds. [f. TOM + TIT[1]]

tom-tom (tŏm′tŏm′), *n.* **1.** a native drum of indefinite pitch. **2.** a dully repetitious drumbeat or similar sound. Also, **tam-tam.** [t. Hind. or other East Ind. vernacular: m. *tam-tam.* Cf. Malay *tong-tong*; both imit.]

Tom-tom

-tomy, a noun termination meaning a 'cutting', esp. relating to a surgical operation, as in *appendectomy, lithotomy, phlebotomy*, or sometimes a division, as in *dichotomy.* [t. Gk: m. s. *-tomia*]

ton[1] (tŭn), *n.* **1.** a unit of weight equal to 2240 lbs (**long ton**) in Great Britain and 2000 lbs (**short ton**) in the U.S. **2.** Also, **tonne.** a unit of weight equal to 1000 kilos (**metric ton**). **3.** a unit of volume or weight for freight equal to either 40 cubic feet or 1000 kilos (**freight ton**). **4.** a unit of displacement of ships, equal to 35 cubic feet of salt water (**displacement ton**). **5.** a unit of internal capacity of ships, equal to 100 cubic feet. **6.** *Colloq.* a heavy weight: *that book weighs a ton.* **7.** (*pl.*) *Colloq.* very many; a good deal: *tons of things to see.* [ME; var. of TUN]

ton[2] (*Fr.* tôɴ), *n.* fashion; style. [F, g. L *tonus* TONE]

ton[3] (tŭn), *n.* *Slang.* a speed of a hundred miles an hour, esp. on a motorcycle.

-ton, noun suffix, as in *simpleton, singleton.* [var. of d. *tone* ONE. Cf. TOTHER]

tonal (tō′nəl), *adj.* **1.** *Music.* pertaining to tonality (opposed to *modal*). **2.** pertaining to tone. **—ton′ally,** *adv.*

tonalist (tō′nə lĭst), *n.* one who adheres to tonality in music, painting, etc.

tonality (tō năl′ĭ tĭ), *n., pl.* **-ties. 1.** *Music.* **a.** the sum of relations, melodic and harmonic, existing between the notes of a scale or musical system; key. **b.** particular scale or system of notes; a key. **2.** *Painting, etc.* the system of tones or tints, or the colour scheme, of a picture, etc.

to-name (to͞o′nām′), *n.* *Chiefly Scot.* a nickname, esp. one to distinguish a person from others of the same name. [ME; OE *tōnama*, f. *tō* TO + *nama* NAME]

Tonbridge (tŭn′brĭj′), *n.* a town in England, in Kent. 22,141 (1961).

tone (tōn), *n., v.,* **toned, toning. —*n.* 1.** any sound considered with reference to its quality, pitch, strength, source, etc.: *shrill tones.* **2.** quality or character of sound. **3.** vocal sound; the sound made by vibrating muscular bands in the larynx. **4.** a particular quality, way of sounding, modulation, or intonation of the voice as expressive of some meaning, feeling, spirit, etc.: *a tone of command.* **5.** an accent peculiar to a person, people, locality, etc., or a characteristic mode of sounding words in speech. **6.** stress of voice on a syllable of a word. **7.** *Phonet.* a musical pitch or melody which may serve to distinguish between words composed of the same sounds, as in Chinese. **8.** *Music.* **a.** an interval equivalent to two semitones; a whole tone. **b.** any of the nine plainsong melodies or tunes, to which the psalms are sung (called **Gregorian tones**). **c.** *Chiefly U.S.* note. **9.** a variety of colour; a tint; a shade. **10.** hue; that distinctive quality by which colours differ from one another in addition to their differences indicated by chroma, tint, shade; a slight modification of a given colour: *green with a yellowish tone, light tone, dull tone, etc.* **11.** *Art.* the prevailing effect of harmony of colour and values. **12.** *Physiol.* **a.** the state of tension or firmness proper to the organs or tissues of the body. **b.** that state of the body or of an organ in which all its animal functions are performed with healthy vigour. **c.** healthy sensitivity to stimulation. **13.** normal healthy condition of the mind. **14.** a particular state or temper of the mind; spirit, character, or tenor. **15.** prevailing character or style, as of manners or morals. **16.** style, distinction, or elegance.

—*v.t.* 17. to sound with a particular tone. **18.** to give the proper tone to (a musical instrument). **19.** to modify the tone or general colouring of. **20.** to give the desired tone to (a painting, etc.). **21.** *Photog.* to change the colour of (a print), usually by chemical means. 22. to render (as specified) in tone or colouring. 23. to modify the tone or character of. 24. to give physical or mental tone to. 25. **tone down, a.** *Painting.* to subdue; make (a colour) less intense in hue. **b.** to lower the tone, strength, intensity, etc., of; soften; moderate. 26. **tone up, a.** to give a higher or stronger tone to. **b.** to make stronger or more vigorous: *walking tones up the muscles.* —*v.i.* 27. to take on a particular tone; assume colour or tint. 28. to harmonize in tone or colour (fol. by *with* or *in with*). 29. **tone down,** to become softened or moderated. 30. **tone up,** to gain in tone or strength. [ME, t. ML: m. *tonus*, t. Gk: m. *tónos* tension, pitch, key] —**tone′less,** *adj.* —**tone′lessly,** *adv.* —**tone′-lessness,** *n.* —**ton′er,** *n.* —**Syn.** 1. See **sound**[1].

tone colour, *Music.* quality of tone; timbre.

tone deafness, the inability to distinguish differences in pitch in musical notes. —**tone′-deaf′,** *adj.*

tone poem, *Music.* an instrumental composition intended to suggest a train of poetic images or sentiments.

tong[1] (tŏng), *n.* 1. (*pl., sometimes construed as sing.*) any of various implements consisting of two arms hinged, pivoted, or otherwise fastened together, for seizing, holding, or lifting something. —*v.t.* 2. *U.S.* to seize, gather, hold, or handle with tongs, as logs or oysters. —*v.i.* 3. *U.S.* to use, or work with, tongs. [ME; OE *tang*, c. G *Zange*]

tong[2] (tŏng), *n.* 1. (in China) an association, society, or political party. 2. (in the U.S.) a Chinese society or association, usually considered by its members to be a private, closed society, but often believed by others to indulge in criminal practices. [t. Chinese: m. *t'ang* meeting place]

tonga (tŏng′gə), *n.* a light two-wheeled vehicle used in India. [t. Hind.: m. *tangā*]

Tonga (tŏng′ə), *n.* a Polynesian kingdom consisting of three groups of islands in the S Pacific, NE of New Zealand: a British protectorate. 67,495 pop. (est. 1962); ab. 250 sq. mi. *Cap.:* Nuku'alofa. Also, **Tonga Islands** or **Friendly Islands.**

Tongan (tŏng′ən), *n.* 1. a native of Tonga. 2. the language of the Tongans. —*adj.* 3. of or pertaining to Tonga, the Tongans, or their language.

Tongariro (tŏng′ə rĭə′rō), *n.* **Mount,** a volcanic peak in New Zealand, in central North Island. 6458 ft.

Tongking (tŏng′kĭng′), *n.* Tonkin.

tongue (tŭng), *n., v.,* **tongued, tonguing.** —*n.* 1. an organ in man and most vertebrates occupying the floor of the mouth and often protrusible and freely movable, being the principal organ of taste, and, in man, of articulate speech. See diag. under **mouth.** 2. *Zool.* an organ in the mouth of invertebrates, frequently of a rasping nature. 3. the tongue of an animal, as an ox, reindeer, or sheep, as used for food, often prepared by smoking or pickling. 4. the human tongue as the organ of speech. 5. the faculty or power of speech: *to find one's tongue, to lose one's tongue.* 6. speech or talk, esp. mere glib or empty talk. 7. manner or character of speech: *a flattering tongue.* 8. the language of a particular people, country, or locality: *the Hebrew tongue.* 9. a dialect. 10. a people as distinguished by its language (a biblical use): *I will gather all nations and tongues.* 11. the voice of a hound or other dog: *the dog gave tongue.* 12. something resembling or suggesting an animal's tongue in shape, position, or function. 13. a strip of leather under the lacing or fastening of a shoe. 14. a suspended piece inside a bell that produces a sound on striking against the side. 15. a vibrating reed or the like in a musical instrument. 16. the pole of a carriage or other vehicle, extending between the animals drawing it. 17. *Carp.* a projecting strip along the centre of the edge of a board, for fitting into a groove in another board. 18. a narrow strip of land extending into a body of water. 19. *Mach.* a long, narrow projection on a machine. 20. the pin of a buckle, brooch, etc. 21. **give tongue,** speak out, esp. loudly. 22. **hold one's tongue,** to be quiet. 23. **on the tip of one's tongue,** on the verge of being uttered. 24. **slip of the tongue,** an inadvertent remark. 25. **with one's tongue in one's cheek, tongue in cheek,** mockingly; insincerely. —*v.t.* 26. to articulate (the notes of a flute, cornet, etc.) by strokes of the tongue. 27. *Carp.* **a.** to cut a tongue on (a board). **b.** to join or fit together by a tongue-and-groove joint. 28. to touch with the tongue. 29. to reproach or scold. 30. to articulate or pronounce. 31. *Archaic.* to speak or utter. —*v.i.* 32. to tongue the notes of a flute, etc. 33. to talk or prate. 34. to project like a tongue or tongues. [ME and OE *tunge*, c. G *Zunge*; akin to L *lingua*] —**tongued** (tŭngd), *adj.* —**tongue′less,** *adj.*

tongue-and-groove joint (tŭng′ən grōōv′), *Carp.* a joint consisting of a tongue (def. 17) on the edge of one board and a matching groove on the edge of the next.

tongue graft, *Hort.* whip graft.

tongue-in-cheek (tŭng′ĭn chēk′), *adj.* mocking; insincere.

tongue-lash (tŭng′lăsh′), *v.i., v.t.* to scold or reprimand. —**tongue′lash′ing,** *n.*

tongueless frog, aglossa.

tongue-tie (tŭng′tī′), *n., v.,* **-tied, -tying.** —*n.* 1. impeded motion of the tongue caused esp. by shortness of the fraenum which binds down its underside. —*v.t.* 2. to make tongue-tied.

tongue-tied (tŭng′tīd′), *adj.* 1. unable to speak, as from shyness. 2. affected with tongue-tie.

tongue twister, 1. a contrived sentence which is difficult to say because of the constant repetition of a certain letter, or certain similar sounds: *the Leith police dismisseth us.* 2. any word or phrase that is difficult to say or pronounce without stumbling.

tonguing (tŭng′ĭng), *n.* *Music.* the manipulation of the tongue in playing a wind instrument to interrupt the note and produce a staccato effect.

tonic (tŏn′ĭk), *n.* 1. a medicine that invigorates or strengthens. 2. anything invigorating physically, mentally, or morally. 3. *Music.* the first degree of the scale; the keynote. —*adj.* 4. pertaining to, maintaining, increasing, or restoring the tone or healthy condition of the system or organs, as a medicine. 5. invigorating physically, mentally, or morally. 6. *Physiol., Pathol.* **a.** pertaining to tension, as of the muscles. **b.** marked by continued muscular tension: *a tonic spasm.* 7. characterized by distinctions of tone or accent: *a tonic language.* 8. pertaining to tone or accent in speech. 9. *Phonet.* **a.** accented, esp. with primary accent. **b.** *Obs.* voiced. 10. *Music.* **a.** pertaining to or founded on the keynote, or first note, of a musical scale: *a tonic chord.* **b.** *U.S.* of or pertaining to a note or notes. [t. Gk: m. s. *tonikós* pertaining to stretching or notes]

tonic accent, vocal accent, or syllabic stress, in pronunciation or speaking.

tonicity (tō nĭs′ĭ tĭ), *n.* 1. tonic quality or condition. 2. the state of bodily tone. 3. *Physiol.* the normal elastic tension of living muscles, arteries, etc., by which the tone of the system is maintained.

tonic sol-fa, a system of singing, in which tonality or key relationship is emphasized, the usual staff notation is discarded, and the notes are indicated by the initial letters of the syllables of the *sol-fa* system.

tonic water, effervescent water with quinine, often added to spirits.

tonight (tə nīt′), *n.* 1. this present or coming night; the night of this present day. 2. *Obs. except Dial.* last night. —*adv.* 3. on this present night; on the night of this present day. [ME; OE *tō niht.* See TO, prep., NIGHT]

tonite (tō′nīt), *n.* an explosive made of guncotton, a nitrate, and a nitro compound, used esp. for blasting. [f. s. L *tonāre* to thunder + -ITE[2]]

tonka bean (tŏng′kə), 1. the fragrant, black, almond-shaped seed of a tall leguminous tree, *Dipteryx* (or *Coumarouna*) *odorata*, of tropical South America, used in perfumes and snuff. 2. the tree itself. [t. Guiana Negro: m. *tanka* name of the bean + BEAN]

Tonkin (tŏn′kĭn′), *n.* 1. a former state in N French Indochina, now part of North Vietnam. 2. **Gulf of,** an arm of the South China Sea, W of Hainan. ab. 300 mi. long. Also, **Tongking** or **Tonking** (tŏn′kĭng′).

Tonle Sap (tŏn′lĭ săp′), a large lake in W Cambodia, draining into the Mekong river: great seasonal variation in area.

tonn., tonnage.

tonnage (tŭn′ĭj), *n.* 1. the carrying capacity of a vessel expressed in tons of 100 cubic feet. 2. ships collectively considered with reference to their carrying capacity or together with their cargoes. 3. a duty on ships or boats at so much per ton of cargo or freight, or according to the capacity in tons. Also, **tunnage.**

tonnage deck, *Naut.* the upper deck in all ships which have less than three decks, the second deck from below in other ships.

tonnage duty, a duty imposed on imported wines.

tonne (tŭn), *n.* See **ton**[1] (def. 2).

tonneau (tŏn′ō), *n., pl.* **tonneaus, tonneaux** (tŏn′ōz). 1. a rear body or compartment of a motor car with seats for passengers. 2. a flexible material covering a convertible motor car, often with a part which folds back around the driver to protect him from the weather. [t. F: cask, dim. of *tonne* TUN]

tonometer (tō nŏm′ĭ tə), *n.* 1. an instrument for measuring the frequencies of tones. 2. a tuning fork. 3. a graduated set of tuning forks, whose frequencies have been carefully determined. 4. any of various physiological instruments, as for measuring the tension within the eyeball, of for determining blood pressure. [f. Gk *tóno(s)* tension, tone + -METER[1]] —**tonometric** (tŏn′ə mĕt′rĭk), *adj.* —**tonom′etry,** *n.*

tonsil (tŏn′səl), *n. Anat.* either of two prominent oval masses of lymphoid tissue situated one on each side of the fauces. [t. L: m. s. *tonsillae*, pl.] —**ton′sillar,** *adj.*

tonsillectomy (tŏn′sĭ lĕk′tə mĭ), *n., pl.* **-mies.** *Surg.* the operation of excising or removing one or both tonsils. [f. s. L *tonsillae* tonsils + -ECTOMY]

tonsillitis (tŏn′sĭ lī′tĭs), *n. Pathol.* inflammation of a tonsil or the tonsils. [t. NL, f. s. L *tonsillae* + *-itis* -ITIS] —**tonsillitic** (tŏn′sĭ lĭt′ĭk), *adj.*

tonsorial (tŏn sô′rĭ əl), *adj.* (often in humorous use) of or pertaining to a barber or his work. [f. s. L *tonsōrius* pertaining to shaving + -AL[1]]

tonsure (tŏn′shə), *n., v.,* **-sured, -suring.** —*n.* **1.** the act of clipping the hair or shaving the head. **2.** the shaving of the head, or of some part of it, as a religious practice or rite, esp. in preparation for entering the priesthood or a monastic order. **3.** the part of a cleric's head left bare by shaving the hair. **4.** the state of being shorn. —*v.t.* **5.** to confer the ecclesiastical tonsure upon. **6.** to subject to tonsure. [ME, t. L: m. *tonsūra* shearing] —**ton′sured,** *adj.*

tontine (tŏn′tēn, tŏn tēn′), *n.* **1.** a scheme in which subscribers to a common fund share an annuity with the benefit of survivorship, the shares of the survivors being increased as the subscribers die, until the whole goes to the last survivor. **2.** the annuity shared. **3.** the share of each subscriber. **4.** the number who share. **5.** any of various forms of life assurance in which the chief benefits accrue to participants who are alive and whose policies are in force at the end of a specified period (**tontine period**). [t. F; named after Lorenzo *Tonti*, Neapolitan banker who started the scheme in France about 1653]

ton-up (tŭn′ŭp′), *adj. Slang.* **1.** capable of travelling at a speed of a hundred miles an hour or more. **2.** of or pertaining to a person who derives pleasure or prestige from excessive speed.

tonus (tō′nəs), *n. Physiol.* a normal state of slight continuous tension in muscle tissue which facilitates its response to stimulation. [NL: special use of L *tonus*, t. Gk: m. *tónos* tone]

too (too͞), *adv.* **1.** in addition; also; furthermore; moreover: *young, clever, and rich too.* **2.** to an excessive extent or degree; beyond what is desirable, fitting, or right: *too long.* **3.** more (as specified) than should be. **4.** extremely: *only too glad to help you.* [var. of TO, adv.]

took (to͝ok), *v.* pt. of **take.**

tool (too͞l), *n.* **1.** an instrument, esp. one held in the hand, for performing or facilitating mechanical operations, as a hammer, saw, file, etc. **2.** any instrument of manual operation. **3.** that part of a lathe, planer, drill, or similar machine, which performs the cutting or machining operation. **4.** the machine itself; a machine tool. **5.** anything used like a tool to do work or effect some result. **6.** a person used by another for his own ends; a cat's-paw. **7.** the design or ornament impressed upon a book cover. **8.** *Taboo.* the penis. —*v.t.* **9.** to work or shape with a tool. **10.** to work decoratively with a hand tool; to ornament with a bookbinders' tool, as on book covers. **11.** *Slang.* to drive (a coach, etc.). —*v.i.* **12.** to work with a tool or tools. **13.** *Slang.* to drive or ride in a vehicle. [ME; OE *tōl*, c. Icel. *tōl*, pl.] —**tool′er,** *n.*

—**Syn. 1.** TOOL, IMPLEMENT, INSTRUMENT, UTENSIL refer to contrivances for doing work. A TOOL is a contrivance held in and worked by the hand, for assisting the work of (especially) mechanics or labourers: *a carpenter's tools.* An IMPLEMENT is any tool or contrivance designed or used for a particular purpose: *agricultural implements.* An INSTRUMENT is anything used in doing a certain work or producing a certain result, esp. such as requires delicacy, accuracy, or precision: *surgical or musical instruments.* A UTENSIL is especially an article for domestic use: *kitchen utensils.* When used figuratively of human agency, TOOL is generally used in a contemptuous sense; INSTRUMENT, in a neutral or good sense: *a tool of unscrupulous men; an instrument of Providence.*

tooling (too͞′lĭng), *n.* the provision of tools, as in a factory.

tool-post (too͞l′pōst′), *n.* a vertical post, which is usually slotted and carries a clamping nut, for securing a lathe tool in its cutting position.

toolshed (too͞l′shĕd′), *n.* a shed in the garden of, or attached to, a house, in which tools are kept.

tool steel, any of various steels, containing up to about 1·5 per cent carbon and various alloying metals, which are suitable for use in tools for cutting metal.

toon (too͞n), *n.* **1.** a meliaceous tree, *Toona ciliata* (or *Cedrela toona*), of the East Indies and Australia, yielding a red wood resembling mahogany, but softer, and extensively used for furniture, carving, etc. **2.** the wood. [t. Hind.: m. *tūn*]

toot (too͞t), *v.i.* **1.** (of a horn) to give forth its characteristic sound. **2.** to make a sound resembling that of a horn or the like. **3.** to sound or blow a horn or other wind instrument. **4.** (of grouse) to give forth a characteristic cry or call. —*v.t.* **5.** to cause (a horn, etc.) to sound by blowing it. **6.** to sound (notes, etc.) on a horn or the like. —*n.* **7.** an act or sound of tooting. [late ME, cf. LG and G *tūten*, D *toeten* in same sense] —**toot′er,** *n.*

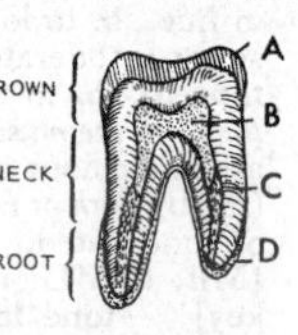

Tooth (human)
A, Enamel;
B, Pulp;
C, Dentine;
D, Cementum

tooth (too͞th), *n., pl.* **teeth** (tēth), *v.* —*n.* **1.** (in most vertebrates) one of the hard bodies or processes usually attached in a row to each jaw, serving for the prehension and mastication of food, as weapons of attack or defence, etc., and in mammals typically composed chiefly of dentine surrounding a sensitive pulp and covered on the crown with enamel. **2.** (in invertebrates) any of various similar or analogous processes occurring in the mouth or alimentary canal, or on a shell. **3.** any projection resembling or suggesting a tooth. **4.** one of the projections of a comb, rake, saw, etc. **5.** one of a series of projections (cogs) on the edge of a wheel, etc., which engage with corresponding parts of another wheel or body. **6.** *Bot.* one of the hard projections in the peristome of mosses. **7.** a sharp, distressing, or destructive attribute or agency. **8.** taste, relish, or liking. **9. a sweet tooth,** a liking for sweet things. **10. get one's teeth into,** to start to cope effectively with (a problem). **11. in the** (or **one's**) **teeth, a.** in direct opposition or conflict. **b.** to one's face; openly. **12. in the teeth of, a.** so as to face or confront; straight against. **b.** in defiance of; in spite of. **c.** in the face or presence of. **13. long in the tooth,** elderly. **14. to the teeth,** fully: *armed to the teeth.* —*v.t.* **15.** to furnish with teeth. **16.** to cut teeth upon. —*v.i.* **17.** to interlock, as cogwheels. [ME; OE *tōth*, c. G *Zahn*; akin to L *dens*, Gk *odoús*] —**toothed** (too͞tht), *adj.* —**tooth′less,** *adj.*

toothache (too͞th′āk′), *n.* a pain in a tooth or teeth or in the jawbone.

toothache tree, the eastern North American prickly ash, *Zanthoxylum americanum*, the bark of which is used as a remedy for toothache.

tooth and nail, fiercely; with all one's might: *we fought tooth and nail but lost.*

toothbrush (too͞th′brŭsh′), *n.* a small brush with a long handle, for cleaning the teeth.

toothcomb (too͞th′kōm′), *n.* a comb with very fine teeth, usually at each edge.

toothpaste (too͞th′pāst′), *n.* a dentifrice in the form of paste.

toothpick (too͞th′pĭk′), *n.* a small pointed piece of wood, etc., for removing food, etc., lodged between the teeth.

tooth-shell (too͞th′shĕl′), *n.* a member of the scaphopod mollusc genus *Dentalium*, common on northern British coasts.

toothsome (too͞th′səm), *adj.* pleasing to the taste; palatable: *a toothsome dish.* —**tooth′somely,** *adv.* —**tooth′someness,** *n.*

toothwort (too͞th′wût′), *n.* **1.** a European orobanchaceous plant, *Lathraea squamaria*, having a rootstock covered with toothlike scales. **2.** any plant of the cruciferous genus *Dentaria*, having toothlike projections upon the creeping rootstock.

toothy (too͞′thĭ), *adj.* having prominent teeth. —**too′thily,** *adv.* —**too′thiness,** *n.*

tootle[1] (too͞′tl), *v.,* **-tled, -tling,** *n.* —*v.i.* **1.** to toot gently or repeatedly on a flute or the like. —*n.* **2.** the sound itself. [freq. of TOOT]

tootle[2] (too͞′tl), *v.i. Slang.* **1.** to go or walk. **2.** to drive. **3. tootle off,** to depart.

too-too (too͞′too͞′), *adj. Colloq.* extremely or extravagantly.

tootsy (to͝ot′sĭ), *n., pl.* **-sies.** *Childish.* a foot. [f. d. *toot* foot (alteration of FOOT, or der. OE *tōtian* to protrude) + *-sy* hypocoristic suffix]

Toowoomba (to͝o wo͝om′bə), *n.* a town in NE Australia, in Queensland. 52,900 (est. 1964).

top[1] (tŏp), *n., adj., v.,* **topped, topping.** —*n.* **1.** the highest point or part of anything; the apex; the summit. **2.** the uppermost or upper part, surface, etc., of anything. **3.** the higher end of anything on a slope. **4.** a part considered as higher: *the top of a street.* **5.** the part of a plant above ground, as distinguished from the root. **6.** (*usually pl.*) one of the tender tips of the branches or shoots of plants. **7.** that part of anything which is first or foremost; the beginning. **8.** the highest or leading place, position, rank, etc.: *at the top of the class.* **9.** the highest point, pitch, or degree: *to talk at the top of one's voice.* **10.** one who or that which occupies the highest or leading position. **11.** *Poetic.* the most perfect example, type, etc.: *the top of all honours.* **12.** the best or choicest part: *the top of all*

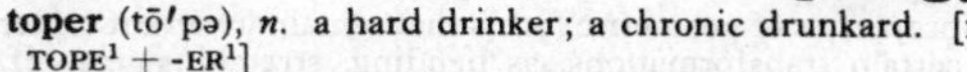

creation. **13.** a covering or lid, as of a box, motor car, carriage, etc. **14.** the head. **15.** the crown of the head. **16.** *Motor Vehicles.* a transmission gear providing the highest forward speed ratio, usually turning the drive shaft at the same rate as the engine crankshaft. **17.** *Naut.* a platform surrounding the head of a lower mast on a ship, and serving as a foothold, a means of extending the upper rigging, etc. **18.** *Chem.* that part of a mixture under distillation which volatilizes first. **19.** *Golf, etc.* **a.** a stroke above the centre of the ball, usually failing to give any height, distance, or accuracy. **b.** the forward spin given to the ball by such a stroke. **20.** See **big top. 21. blow one's top,** *Colloq.* to lose one's temper. **22. on top,** successful; victorious; dominant. **23. on top of, a.** upon. **b.** close upon; following upon. **24. over the top,** *Mil.* over the top of the parapet before a trench, as in issuing to charge against the enemy. **25. (the) tops,** *Colloq.* the very best: *that book really is the tops.*
—*adj.* **26.** pertaining to, situated at, or forming the top; highest; uppermost; upper: *the top shelf.* **27.** highest in degree; greatest: *to pay top prices.* **28.** foremost, chief, or principal: *to win top honours in a competition.* **29.** denoting or pertaining to the highest forward gear on a vehicle. **30. top dog,** the person in the highest or most important position.
—*v.t.* **31.** to furnish with a top; put a top on. **32.** to be at or constitute the top of. **33.** to reach the top of. **34.** to rise above: *the sun had topped the horizon.* **35.** to exceed in height, amount, number, etc. **36.** to surpass, excel, or outdo: *that tops everything!* **37.** to come up to or go beyond the requirements of (a part or character). **38.** to surmount with something specified. **39.** to complete by or as by putting the top on or constituting the top of. **40.** to remove the top of; crop; prune. **41.** to get or leap over the top of (a fence, etc.). **42.** *Chem.* to distil off only the most volatile part of a mixture. **43.** *Golf, etc.* **a.** to hit (the ball) above the centre. **b.** to make (a stroke, etc.) by hitting the ball in this way. **44.** to top-dress (land). **45. top up,** to fill by adding liquid to (a partly filled container).
—*v.i.* **46.** to rise aloft. **47.** *Golf, etc.* to hit the ball above the centre.
[ME and OE, c. D *top(p)*, G *Zopf* top, tuft of hair]

top[2] (tŏp), *n.* **1.** a child's toy, often inversely conical, with a point on which it is made to spin. **2. sleep like a top,** to sleep very soundly. [ME and OE, c. Flem. *top.* Cf. G *Topf*]

top-, var. of **topo-,** before vowels, as in *toponym.*

topaz (tō′păz), *n.* **1.** a mineral, a fluosilicate of aluminium, usually occurring in prismatic orthorhombic crystals of various colours, and used as a gem (**true topaz** or **precious topaz**). **2.** a yellow variety of sapphire (**oriental topaz**). **3.** a yellow variety of quartz (**false topaz** or **common topaz**). [t. L: s. *topazus*, t. Gk: m. *tópazos*; r. ME *topace*, t. OF]

topazolite (tō păz′ə līt′), *n.* a yellow or olive-green variety of andradite garnet found in Piedmont. [f. *topazo-* (comb. form repr. Gk *tópazos* TOPAZ) + -LITE]

top-boot (tŏp′bo͞ot′), *n.* a high boot, esp. one having the upper part of a different material from the rest.

topcoat (tŏp′kōt′), *n.* **1.** a lightweight overcoat. **2.** an outer coat; an overcoat.

top cross, *Genetics.* the progeny of the cross of a variety by one inbred line.

top drawer, the highest level, esp. of social class. —**top-drawer** (tŏp′drô′), *adj.*

top-dress (tŏp′drĕs′), *v.t.* to manure (land, etc.) on the surface.

top dressing, 1. a dressing of manure on the surface of land. **2.** the action of one who top-dresses. **3.** a top layer of gravel, crushed rock, etc., on a roadway. **4.** any superficial treatment or surface covering.

tope[1] (tōp), *v.,* **toped, toping.** —*v.i.* **1.** to consume alcoholic drink habitually and to excess. —*v.t.* **2.** to drink (alcohol) habitually and to excess. [var. of obs. *top* drink, appar. special use of *top* tip, tilt, topple; ? akin to TOP[2]]

tope[2] (tōp), *n.* **1.** a small shark, *Galeorhinus galeus*, found along the European coast. **2.** any of various related sharks of small to medium size. [orig. uncert., ? t. Cornish]

tope[3] (tōp), *n.* (in Buddhist countries) a dome-shaped monument, usually for religious relics. [t. Hind.: m. *tōp*]

Tope[3]

topee (tō′pē, tō′pĭ), *n.* (in India) a helmet of sola pith. Also, **topi.** [t. Hind.: hat]

Topeka (tə pē′kə), *n.* a town in the U.S., the capital of Kansas, in the NE part, on the Kansas river. 119,484 (1960).

toper (tō′pə), *n.* a hard drinker; a chronic drunkard. [f. TOPE[1] + -ER[1]]

top-flight (tŏp′flīt′), *adj.* first-rate; superior.

topgallant (tŏp′găl′ənt; *Naut.* tə găl′ənt), *Naut.* —*n.* **1.** the spars and rigging next above the topmast, in a square-rigged vessel. See illus. under **sail.** —*adj.* **2.** pertaining to the topgallant. [f. TOP[1] + GALLANT, adj.]

tophamper (tŏp′hăm′pə), *n.* *Naut.* **1.** the light upper sails and their gear and spars, sometimes used to refer to all spars and gear above the deck. **2.** any unnecessary weight, either aloft or about the upper decks.

top-hat (tŏp′hăt′), *n.* a man's tall silk hat.

top-heavy (tŏp′hĕv′ĭ), *adj.* **1.** having the top disproportionately heavy; liable to fall from too great weight above. **2.** *Finance.* **a.** having a financial structure overburdened with securities which have priority in the payment of dividends. **b.** overcapitalized. —**top′-heav′iness,** *n.*

Tophet (tō′fĕt), *n.* **1.** a place in the valley of Hinnom, near Jerusalem, where, contrary to the law, children were offered as sacrifices, esp. to Moloch, later used as a dumping ground for refuse. **2.** the place of punishment for the wicked after death; hell. **3.** some place, condition, etc., likened to hell. Also, **Topheth.** [ME, ult. t. Heb.]

top-hole (tŏp′hōl′), *adj.* *Slang.* first-rate.

tophus (tō′fəs), *n., pl.* **-phi** (-fī). *Pathol.* a calcareous concretion formed in the soft tissue about a joint, in the pinna of the ear, etc., esp. in gout; a gouty deposit. [t. L, var. of *tōfus* sandstone]

topi[1] (tō′pĭ), *n., pl.,* **-pis.** a medium-sized, short-horned East African antelope *Damaliscus korrigum.*

topi[2] (tō′pē, tō′pĭ), *n., pl.* **-pis.** topee.

topiary (tō′pyə rĭ), *adj., n., pl.* **-aries.** *Hort.* —*adj.* **1.** clipped or trimmed into (fantastic) shapes. **2.** of or pertaining to such trimming. —*n.* **3.** topiary work; the topiary art. **4.** a garden containing such work. [t. L: m. s. *topiārius*] —**topiarian** (tō′pĭ ĕə′rĭ ən), *adj.* —**to′-piarist,** *n.*

topic (tŏp′ĭk), *n.* **1.** a subject of conversation or discussion: *to provide a topic for discussion.* **2.** the subject or theme of a discourse or of one of its parts. **3.** *Rhet., Logic.* a general field of considerations from which arguments can be drawn. **4.** a general rule or maxim. [sing. of *topics*, t. L: anglicization of *topica*, pl., t. Gk: m. *tà topiká* name of work by Aristotle (lit., things pertaining to commonplaces)] —**Syn. 2.** See **subject.**

topical (tŏp′ĭ kl), *adj.* **1.** pertaining to or dealing with matters of current or local interest. **2.** pertaining to the subject of a discourse, composition, or the like. **3.** of a place; local. **4.** *Med.* pertaining or applied to a particular part of the body. —**top′ically,** *adv.*

topknot (tŏp′nŏt′), *n.* **1.** a tuft of hair growing on the top of the head. **2.** a knot of hair so worn in some styles of hairdressing. **3.** a knot or bow of ribbon worn on the top of the head. **4.** a tuft or crest of feathers on the head of a bird. **5.** any of the various flatfishes of the genus *Zeugopterus.*

topless (tŏp′lĭs), *adj.* **1.** without a top. **2.** having the breasts bare. **3.** allowing the breasts to be exposed, as a garment. —*n.* **4.** a topless garment, esp. a dress.

top-line (tŏp′līn′), *adj.* of the highest importance.

toplofty (tŏp′lŏf′tĭ), *adj.* *Colloq.* haughty; pompous; pretentious. —**top′loft′iness,** *n.*

topman (tŏp′mən), *n., pl.* **-men.** *Naut.* a man stationed for duty in a top (def. 17).

topmast (tŏp′mäst′; *Naut.* -məst), *n.* *Naut.* the second section of mast above the deck, being that just above the lower mast.

top minnow, any of several small surface-swimming cyprinodont fishes of the egg-laying family *Cyprinodontidae* and the live-bearing family *Poeciliidae.*

topmost (tŏp′mōst′), *adj.* highest; uppermost.

topnotch (tŏp′nŏch′), *adj.* *Colloq.* first-rate: *a topnotch job.*

topo-, a word element meaning 'place', as in *topography.* Also, **top-.** [t. Gk, comb. form of *tópos*]

topochemistry (tŏp′ō kĕm′ĭs trĭ), *n.* the study of chemical reactions which are confined to a specified part of a system.

topog., 1. topographical. **2.** topography.

topographer (tə pŏg′rə fə), *n.* **1.** a specialist in topography. **2.** one who describes the surface features of a place or region.

topography (tə pŏg′rə fĭ), *n., pl.* **-phies. 1.** the detailed description and analysis of the features of a relatively small area, district, or locality. **2.** the detailed description of particular localities, as cities, towns, estates, etc. **3.** the relief features or surface configuration of an area. [ME, t. LL: m. s. *topographia*, t. Gk] —**topographic** (tŏp′ə grăf′ĭk), **top′ograph′ical,** *adj.* —**top′ograph′ically,** *adv.*

topology (tə pŏl′ə jĭ), *n.* *Maths.* the study of those properties of geometric forms that remain invariant under certain transformations, as bending, stretching, etc. [f. TOPO- + -LOGY] —**topologic** (tŏp′ə lŏj′ĭk), **top′olog′ical,** *adj.* —**top′olog′ically,** *adv.*

toponym (tŏp′ə nĭm), *n.* **1.** a placename. **2.** a name derived from the name of a place. [f. TOP- + *-onym*, modelled on SYNONYM]

toponymy (tə pŏn′ĭ mĭ), *n., pl.* **-mies. 1.** the study of the placenames of a region. **2.** *Anat.* the nomenclature of the regions of the body. —**toponymic** (tŏp′ə nĭm′ĭk), **top′onym′ical,** *adj.*

topper (tŏp′ə), *n.* **1.** one who or that which tops. **2.** *Slang.* a top-hat. **3.** *Slang.* anything excellent.

topping (tŏp′ĭng), *n.* **1.** the act of one who or that which tops. **2.** a distinct part forming a top to something. **3.** something put on a thing at the top to complete it. **4.** (*pl.*) that which is removed in topping or cropping plants, as branches. —*adj.* **5.** very high in rank, degree, etc. **6.** *Colloq.* excellent. **7.** *Obs.* rising above something else; overtopping.

topping lift, *Naut.* a rope or wire used for lifting the end of a derrick or boom.

topple (tŏp′l), *v.,* **-pled, -pling.** —*v.t.* **1.** to fall forwards as having too heavy a top; pitch or tumble down. **2.** to lean over or jut, as if threatening to fall. —*v.t.* **3.** to cause to topple. [freq. of *top* topple. See TOPE¹]

topsail (tŏp′sāl′; *Naut.* -səl), *n. Naut.* **1.** a square sail (or either of two square sails) next above the lowest or chief square sail on a mast of a square-rigged vessel, or next above a chief fore-and-aft sail on topsail schooners, etc. See illus. under **sail. 2.** in a fore-and-aft rig, a square or triangular sail set above the gaff.

top-secret (tŏp′sē′krĭt), *adj. Chiefly Mil.* extremely secret.

topside (tŏp′sīd′), *n.* **1.** the upper side. **2.** (*usually pl.*) the upper part of a boat's or ship's side, above the main deck. **3.** a lean cut of beef, without bone, from the thigh of the animal.

topsoil (tŏp′soil′), *n.* **1.** the surface or upper part of the soil. —*v.t.* **2.** to cover (land) with topsoil.

topsy-turvy (tŏp′sĭ tû′vĭ), *adv., adj., n., pl.* **-vies.** —*adv.* **1.** with the top where the bottom should be; upside down. **2.** in or into a reversed condition or order. **3.** in or into a state of confusion or disorder. —*adj.* **4.** turned upside down; inverted; reversed. **5.** confused or disorderly. —*n.* **6.** inversion of the natural order. **7.** a state of confusion or disorder. [akin to TOP¹ and ME *terve* overturn (cf. OE *tearflian* roll)] —**top′sy-tur′vily,** *adv.* —**top′sy-tur′viness,** *n.*

topsy-turvydom (tŏp′sĭ tû′vĭ dəm), *n.* a state of affairs or a region in which everything is topsy-turvy.

toque (tōk), *n.* a hat with little or no brim and often with a soft or full crown, worn by women and (formerly) men. [t. F: a hat, bonnet, c. It. *tocca* cap, Sp. *toca* kerchief, Pg. *touca* coif]

Toque

tor (tô), *n.* a rocky eminence; a hill. [ME; OE *torr*, t. Celtic. Cf. Gael. *torr*, Welsh *twr* protuberance]

Torah (tô′rə), *n.* **1.** the teaching and judgements of the early Jewish priests. **2.** the Pentateuch. Also, **Tora.** [t. Heb.: instruction, law]

torbanite (tô′bə nīt′), *n.* a dark brown oil shale which is rich in carbonaceous matter (70–80 per cent). [named after *Torbane* Hill in Scotland. See -ITE¹]

torbernite (tô′bə nīt′), *n.* a mineral, hydrated copper uranium phosphate, $CuU_2P_2O_{12}.12H_2O$, occurring in square tabular crystals of a bright green colour, a minor ore of uranium; copper uranite. [named after *Torber* Bergmann, 1735–84, Swedish chemist. See -ITE¹]

torc (tôk), *n.* torque (def. 4).

torch (tôch), *n.* **1.** a small portable electric lamp powered by dry batteries. **2.** a light to be carried in the hand, consisting of some combustible substance, as resinous wood, or of twisted flax or the like soaked with tallow or other inflammable substance. **3.** something considered as a source of illumination, enlightenment, guidance, etc.: *the torch of learning.* **4.** any of various lamplike devices which produce a hot flame and are used for soldering, burning off paint, etc. **5. carry a torch for,** to suffer unrequited love for. [ME *torche*, t. OF] —**torch′less,** *adj.* —**torch′like′,** *adj.*

torchbearer (tôch′bĕə′rə), *n.* **1.** one who or that which carries a torch. **2.** one who brings knowledge or enlightenment, esp. in a new sphere of activity.

torchlight (tôch′līt′), *n.* the light of a torch or torches.

torchon lace (tô′shən; *Fr.* tŏr shôN′), **1.** bobbin-made linen or cotton lace with loosely twisted threads in simple, open patterns. **2.** a machine-made imitation of this, in linen or cotton. [*torchon*, t. F: dishcloth]

torch song, a moody, romantic song, popular in the 1930s, sung by a woman singer, esp. in a nightclub. —**torch-singer** (tôch′sing′ə), *n.*

torchwood (tôch′wŏŏd′), *n.* **1.** any of various resinous woods suitable for making torches, as the wood of the rutaceous tree, *Amyris balsamifera*, of Florida, the West Indies, etc. **2.** any of the trees yielding these woods.

Tordesillas (*Sp.* tôr dė sē′lyȧs), *n.* a town in NW Spain, SW of Valladolid: treaty defining the colonial spheres of Spain and Portugal 1494. 6500 (est. 1968).

tore¹ (tô), *v.* pt. of **tear**².

tore² (tô), *n.* torus. [t. F, t. L: m. *torus* TORUS]

toreador (tŏ′rĭ ə dô′), *n.* a Spanish bullfighter. [t. Sp., der. *torear* fight bulls, der. *toro* bull, g. L *taurus*]

torero (tŏ rĕə′rō), *n., pl.* **-ros** (-rōz). a bullfighter who fights on foot. [t. Sp.]

toreutic (tə rōō′tĭk), *adj.* of or pertaining to toreutics or to objects decorated by this work. [t. Gk: m. s. *toreutikós*, der. *toreúein* to emboss]

toreutics (tə rōō′tĭks), *n.* the art of decorating metal by embossing or engraving.

toric (tŏ′rĭk), *adj.* **1.** denoting or pertaining to a lens with a surface forming a portion of a torus, used for spectacles. **2.** *Geom.* of or pertaining to a torus. [f. TOR(US) + -IC]

torii (tô′rĭ ē′), *n., pl.* **torii.** a form of decorative gateway or portal in Japan, consisting of two upright wooden posts connected at the top by two horizontal crosspieces, and commonly found at the entrance to Shinto temples. [t. Jap.]

Torino (*It.* tȯ rē′nȯ), *n.* Italian name of **Turin.**

torment (*v.* tô mĕnt′; *n.* tô′mĕnt), *v.t.* **1.** to afflict with great bodily or mental suffering; pain: *to be tormented with violent headaches.* **2.** to worry or annoy excessively: *to torment one with questions.* **3.** to throw into commotion; stir up; disturb. —*n.* **4.** a state of great bodily or mental suffering; agony; misery. **5.** something that causes great bodily or mental pain or suffering. **6.** a source of pain, anguish, trouble, worry, or annoyance. **7.** *Archaic.* **a.** an instrument of torture, as the rack or the thumbscrew. **b.** the infliction of torture by means of such an instrument. **c.** the torture inflicted. [ME, t. OF: s. *tormenter*, der. *torment* torment, n., g. L *tormentum* something operated by twisting] —**torment′ingly,** *adv.*

—**Syn. 1.** TORMENT, RACK, TORTURE suggest causing great physical or mental pain, suffering, or harassment. To TORMENT is to harass as by incessant repetition of vexations or annoyances: *to be tormented with a toothache.* To RACK is to affect with such pain as that suffered by one stretched on a rack; to concentrate with painful effort: *to rack one's brains.* To TORTURE is to afflict with acute and more or less protracted suffering: *to torture a person by keeping him in suspense.*

tormentil (tô′mən tĭl), *n.* a low rosaceous herb, *Potentilla erecta*, of Europe and W Asia with small bright yellow flowers, and a strongly astringent root which is used in medicine and in tanning and dyeing. [ME *tormentille*, t. ML: m. *tormentilla*, dim. of *tormentum* TORMENT]

tormentor (tô mĕn′tə), *n.* **1.** one who or that which torments. **2.** *Theat.* a curtain or framed structure behind the proscenium at each side of the stage. Also, **tormenter.**

torn (tôn), *v.* pp. of **tear**².

tornado (tô nā′dō), *n., pl.* **-does, -dos. 1.** *Meteorol.* **a.** a violent whirlwind of small radius, advancing over the land, in which winds of destructive force circulate round a centre. It is characterized by strong ascending currents and is generally made visible by a funnel-shaped cloud. **b.** a violent squall or whirlwind of small extent, as those occurring during the summer months on the west coast of Africa. **2.** a violent outburst, as of emotion or activity. [t. Sp., der. *tornar* to turn, b. with *tronada* thunderstorm, der. *tronar* to thunder, g. L *tonāre*] —**tornadic** (tô năd′ĭk), *adj.* —**torna′do-like′,** *adj.*

toroid (tô′roid), *n. Geom.* **1.** a surface generated by the revolution of any closed plane curve or contour about an axis lying in its plane. **2.** the solid enclosed by such a surface. [f. TOR(US) + -OID]

toroidal (tô roi′dl), *adj. Geom.* denoting or pertaining to a torus.

Toronto (tə rŏn′tō), *n.* a city in SE Canada, on Lake Ontario: the capital of Ontario. 636,239; with suburbs, 1,717,875 (est. 1964).

torose (tô′rōs, tô rōs′), *adj.* **1.** *Bot.* cylindrical, with swellings or constrictions at intervals; knobbed. **2.** *Zool.* bulging. Also, **torous** (tô′rəs). [t. L: m. s. *torōsus* bulging. See TORUS]

torpedo (tô pē′dō), *n., pl.* **-does,** *v.,* **-doed, -doing.** —*n.* **1.** a self-propelled cigar-shaped missile containing explosives which is launched from a tube in a submarine, torpedo-boat, or the like, and explodes upon impact with the ship fired at. **2.** any of various submarine explosive devices for destroying hostile ships, as a mine. **3.** *U.S.* a cartridge of gunpowder, dynamite, or the like, exploded in an oilwell to start or increase the flow of oil, or elsewhere for other purposes. **4.** any of various other explosive devices. **5.** any of the fishes of the genus *Torpedo*, relatives of the rays and sharks, characterized by their ability to give electric shocks to aggressors. **—*v.t.*** **6.** to attack, hit, damage, or destroy with a torpedo or torpedoes. **7.** *U.S.* to explode a torpedo in (an oilwell) to start or increase the flow of oil. **—*v.i.*** **8.** to attack, damage, or sink a ship with torpedoes. [t. L: numbness, torpidity, torpedo-fish. Cf. TORPID]

torpedo-boat (tô pē′dō bōt′), *n.* a warship of small size and high speed used primarily for torpedo attacks.

torpedo-boat destroyer, a vessel somewhat larger than the ordinary torpedo-boat, designed for the destruction of enemy torpedo-boats, or as a more powerful form of torpedo-boat.

torpedo tube, a tube through which a self-propelled torpedo is launched, usually by the detonation of a charge of explosive.

torpid[1] (tô′pĭd), *adj.* **1.** inactive or sluggish, as a bodily organ. **2.** slow; dull; apathetic; lethargic. **3.** dormant, as a hibernating or aestivating animal. [t. L: s. *torpidus* numb] **—torpid′ity, tor′pidness,** *n.* **—tor′pidly,** *adv.* **—Syn. 3.** See **inactive.**

torpid[2] (tô′pĭd), *n.* *Rowing.* (at Oxford University) **1.** (*pl.*) a series of bumping races held in the Hilary term. **2.** an eight-oared clinker-built boat taking part in these. [special use of TORPID[1]]

torpor (tô′pə), *n.* **1.** a state of suspended physical powers and activities. **2.** sluggish inactivity or inertia. **3.** dormancy, as of a hibernating animal. **4.** lethargic dullness or indifference; apathy. [t. L: numbness]

torporific (tô′pə rĭf′ĭk), *adj.* causing torpor.

torquate (tô′kwĭt, -kwāt), *adj.* *Zool.* ringed about the neck, as with feathers or a colour; collared. [t. L: m. s. *torquātus*, pp., adorned with a necklace]

Torquay (tô kē′), *n.* a town in England, in Devonshire: seaside resort. 54,046 (1961).

torque (tôk), *n.* **1.** *Mech.* that which produces or tends to produce torsion or rotation; the moment of a system of forces which tends to cause rotation. **2.** *Mach.* the turning power of a shaft. **3.** the rotational effect on plane-polarized light passing through certain liquids or crystals. **4.** Also, **torc.** a collar, necklace, or similar ornament consisting of a twisted narrow band, usually of precious metal, worn esp. by the ancient Gauls and Britons. [t. L: m. *torques* twisted metal necklace]

torque converter. See **fluid drive.**

Torquemada (tô′kĭ mä′də; *Sp.* tòr kė mȧ′dȧ), *n.* **Tomás de** (*Sp.* tȯ mȧs′ dė), 1420–98, Spanish inquisitor general.

torquemeter (tôk′mē′tə), *n.* a device for measuring the torque of a rotating shaft enabling the power transmitted, or the power of an engine to which it is attached, to be calculated.

torques (tô′kwēz), *n.* *Zool.* a ringlike band or formation about the neck, as of feathers, hair, or integument of distinctive colour or appearance; a collar. [t. L: twisted neck chain or collar]

torr (tô), *n.* *Physics.* a unit of pressure, equal to 1 mm. of mercury, used in the field of high vacuum. [named after E. TORRICELLI]

Torrance (tŏ′rəns), *n.* a town in the U.S., in SW California, SW of Los Angeles. 100,991 (1960).

Torre Annunziata (*It.* tòr′rė ȧn no͞on tsyȧ′tȧ), a seaport in Italy, in Campania, on the Bay of Naples. 61,844 (1966).

Torre del Greco (*It.* tòr′rė dėl grĕ′kȯ), a seaport in Italy, in Campania, on the Bay of Naples. 87,391 (1966).

torrefy (tŏ′rĭ fī′), *v.t.*, **-fied, -fying. 1.** to dry or parch with heat, as drugs, etc. **2.** to roast, as metallic ores. Also, **torrify.** [t. L: m. s. *torrefacere* make dry or hot] **—torrefaction** (tŏ′rĭ făk′shən), *n.*

Torrens (tŏ′rənz), *n.* **Lake,** a salt lake in E South Australia. 2230 sq. mi. 25 ft below sea-level.

torrent (tŏ′rənt), *n.* **1.** a stream of water flowing with great rapidity and violence. **2.** a rushing, violent, or abundant and unceasing stream of anything: *a torrent of lava.* **3.** a violent downpour of rain. **4.** a violent, tumultuous, or overwhelming flow: *a torrent of abuse.* [t. L: s. *torrens* torrent, lit., boiling; r. ME *torrens*, t. L]

torrential (tŏ rĕn′shəl), *adj.* **1.** pertaining to or having the nature of a torrent. **2.** resembling a torrent in rapidity or violence. **3.** falling in torrents. **4.** produced by the action of a torrent. **5.** violent, vehement, or impassioned. **6.** overwhelming; extraordinarily copious. **—torren′tially,** *adv.*

Torreón (*Sp.* tòr rė ȯn′), *n.* a city in NE Mexico. 212,900 (est. 1965).

Torres Strait (tŏ′rĭs), a strait between NE Australia and S New Guinea. ab. 80 mi. wide.

Torricelli (*It.* tòr rē chĕl′lē), *n.* **Evangelista** (*It.* ė vȧn jė lĕ′stȧ), 1608–47, Italian physicist; discovered the principle of the barometer.

torrid (tŏ′rĭd), *adj.* **1.** subject to parching or burning heat, esp. of the sun, as regions, etc. **2.** oppressively hot, parching, or burning, as climate, weather, air, etc. **3.** ardent; passionate. [t. L: s. *torridus*] **—torrid′ity, tor′ridness,** *n.* **—tor′ridly,** *adv.*

Torrid Zone, the part of the earth's surface between the tropics of Cancer and Capricorn.

torrify (tŏ′rĭ fī′), *v.t.*, **-fied, -fying.** torrefy.

torsade (tô săd′), *n.* **1.** a twisted cord. **2.** any ornamental twist, as of velvet. [t. F: twisted fringe, der. *tordre*, g. LL *torcĕre*, r. L *torquēre* twist]

torsibility (tô′sə bĭl′ĭ tĭ), *n.* **1.** capability of being twisted. **2.** resistance to being twisted. **3.** capacity to return to original shape after being twisted.

torsion (tô′shən), *n.* **1.** the act of twisting. **2.** the resulting state. **3.** *Mech.* **a.** the twisting of a body by two equal and opposite torques. **b.** the internal torque so produced. [ME *torcion*, t. LL: m. *torsio*, der. *torquēre* twist] **—tor′sional,** *adj.* **—tor′sionally,** *adv.*

torsion balance, an instrument for measuring small forces (as electrical attraction or repulsion) by determining the amount of torsion or twisting they cause in a slender wire or filament.

torsk (tôsk), *n.* an edible marine fish, *Brosmius brosme*, of both coasts of the N Atlantic.

torso (tô′sō), *n., pl.* **-sos. 1.** the trunk of the human body. **2.** a sculptured form representing the trunk of a nude female or male figure. **3.** something mutilated or incomplete. Also, **torse.** [t. It.: trunk, stump, stalk, trunk of statue, g. L *thyrsus* THYRSUS]

tort (tôt), *n.* *Law.* a civil wrong (other than a breach of contract or trust) such as the law requires compensation for in damages. In typical cases it is a wilful or negligent injury to the person, property or reputation of a plaintiff. [ME, t. OF, t. LL: s. *tortum* wrong, injustice, L twisted]

torticollis (tô′tĭ kŏl′ĭs), *n.* *Pathol.* a condition in which the neck is twisted and the head inclined to one side, by spasmodic contraction of the muscles of the neck. [t. NL: crooked neck. See TORT, COLLAR]

tortile (tô′tīl), *adj.* twisted; coiled. [t. L: m. s. *tortilis* twisted, winding]

tortilla (*Sp.* tòr tē′lyȧ), *n.* (in Mexico, etc.) a thin, round, unleavened cake prepared from oatmeal, baked on a flat plate of iron, earthenware, or the like. [t. Sp., dim. of *torta* cake, g. LL *torta* (*pānis*) twisted (bread)]

tortious (tô′shəs), *adj.* *Law.* of the nature of or pertaining to a tort. [ME *torcious*, t. AF, der. ML *tortio* use of violence, in L torture] **—tor′tiously,** *adv.*

tortoise (tô′təs), *n.* **1.** any terrestrial or freshwater reptile of the order *Chelonia*, as *Testudo graeca*, commonly kept as a domestic pet. **2.** *U.S.* a turtle. **3.** a very slow person or thing. **4.** testudo (defs 1 and 2). [ME *tortuce*, t. ML: m. *tortuca*, der. L *tortus*, pp., twisted]

tortoiseshell (tô′tə shĕl′), *n.* **1.** the horny substance, with a mottled or clouded yellow-and-brown coloration, composing the plates or scales that cover the marine **tortoiseshell turtle,** *Eretmochelys*, formerly used for making combs and other articles, inlaying, etc. **2.** the shell of a tortoise. **3.** any synthetic substance made to appear like natural tortoiseshell. **4.** any of certain colourful butterflies (family *Nymphalidae*), as *Nymphalis polychloros*, with variegated undermarkings. **5.** Also, **tortoiseshell cat.** a domestic cat, usually female, with yellow-and-black colouring. **—*adj.*** **6.** mottled or variegated like tortoiseshell, esp. with yellow and black and sometimes other colours. **7.** made of tortoiseshell.

Tortola (tô′tə lə, tô tō′lə), *n.* the principal island in the British Virgin Islands, in the West Indies. 6262 (1964).

Tortuga (*Sp.* tòr to͞o′gȧ), *n.* an island off the N coast of, and belonging to, Haiti: formerly a pirate stronghold. ab. 25 mi. long. French, **La Tortue** (*Fr.* lȧ tòr tʏ′).

tortuosity (tô′tyo͞o ŏs′ĭ tĭ), *n., pl.* **-ties. 1.** the state of being tortuous; twisted form or course; crookedness. **2.** a twist, bend, or crook. **3.** a twisting or crooked part, passage, or thing.

tortuous (tô′tyo͞o əs), *adj.* **1.** full of twists, turns, or bends; twisting, winding, or crooked. **2.** not direct or straightforward as in a course of procedure, thought, speech, or writing. **3.** deceitfully indirect or morally crooked, as proceedings, methods, policy, etc. **4.** *Geom.* not in one plane, as a curve, such as a helix, which does not lie in a plane. [ME, t. L: m. s. *tortuōsus* full of turns or twists] **—tor′tuously,** *adv.* **—tor′tuousness,** *n.*

torture (tô′chə), *n., v.*, **-tured, -turing. —*n.*** **1.** the act of inflicting excruciating pain, esp. from sheer cruelty or in hatred, revenge, or the like. **2.** a method of inflicting such pain. **3.** (*often pl.*) the pain or suffering caused or undergone. **4.** extreme anguish of body or mind; agony. **5.** a cause of severe pain or anguish. *—v.t.* **6.** to subject to torture. **7.** to afflict with severe pain of body or mind. **8.** to twist, force, or bring into some unnatural position or form: *trees tortured by storms.* **9.** to wrest, distort, or pervert (language, etc.). [t. L: m. *tortūra* twisting, torment, torture] **—tor′turer,** *n.* **—tor′turous,** *adj.* **—Syn. 6.** See **torment.**

Toruń (*Pol.* tô′rōōyn), *n.* a town in N Poland, on the Vistula. 112,000 (1964). German, **Thorn.**

torus (tô′rəs), *n., pl.* **tori** (tô′rī). **1.** *Archit.* a large convex moulding, more or less semicircular in profile, commonly forming the lowest member of the base of a column, or that directly above the plinth (when present), and sometimes occurring as one of a pair separated by a scotia and fillets. See diag. under **column. 2.** *Geom.* **a.** a surface generated by the revolution of a conic (esp. a circle) about an axis lying in its plane. **b.** the solid enclosed by such a surface. **3.** *Bot.* the receptacle of a flower. **4.** *Anat., etc.* a rounded ridge; a protuberant part. [t. L: bulge, rounded moulding]

torus palatinus (tô′rəs păl′ə tī′nəs), *Anat.* a rounded ridge on the hard palate. [NL]

Tory (tô′rĭ), *n., pl.* **-ries. 1.** a member of a political party in Great Britain, in general favouring conservation of the existing order of things in State and Church, evolving into the Conservative Party in the early 19th century. Cf. **Whig** (def. 3). **2.** a member of the Conservative Party. **3.** an advocate of conservative principles; one opposed to reform or radicalism. **4.** *Amer. Hist.* one who remained loyal to the British Crown during the War of American Independence; a loyalist. **5.** (in the 17th century) one of a class of dispossessed Irish, nominally royalists, who became outlaws and were noted for their outrages and cruelties. *—adj.* **6.** of or belonging to or characteristic of the Tories. **7.** of or pertaining to the Conservative Party. **8.** being a Tory. **9.** conservative. Also, **tory** for 3, 9. [t. Irish: m. *tōraidhe* pursuer] **—To′ryism,** *n.*

Toscana (*It.* tôs kä′nä), *n.* Italian name of **Tuscany.**

Toscanini (tŏs′kə nē′nĭ; *It.* tôs kä nē′nē), *n.* **Arturo** (*It.* är tōō′rô), 1867–1957, Italian musician and conductor of operas and symphonies.

tosh (tŏsh), *n. Slang.* nonsense.

toss (tŏs), *v.,* **tossed** or (*Poetic*) **tost; tossing** *n. —v.t.* **1.** to throw, pitch, or fling, esp. to throw lightly or carelessly: *to toss a piece of paper into the wastepaper basket.* **2.** to throw or send (a ball, etc.) from one to another, as in play. **3.** to throw or pitch with irregular or careless motions; fling or jerk about: *a ship tossed by the waves, a tree tosses its branches in the wind.* **4.** to agitate, disturb, or disquiet. **5.** to throw, raise, or jerk upwards suddenly: *she tossed her head disdainfully.* **6.** to throw (a coin, etc.) into the air in order to decide something by the side turned up when it falls (often fol. by *up*). **7.** to drink or eat very quickly (fol. by *off*): *he tossed off a few drinks and then left.* **8.** (of an animal) to throw (someone or something) up into the air or to the ground. *—v.i.* **9.** to pitch, rock, sway, or move irregularly, as a ship on a rough sea, or a flag or plumes in the breeze. **10.** to fling or jerk oneself or move restlessly about, esp. on a bed or couch: *to toss in one's sleep.* **11.** to throw something. **12.** to throw a coin or other object into the air in order to decide something by the way it falls (often fol. by *up*). **13.** to go with a fling of the body: *to toss out of a room.* **14. toss off,** *Taboo.* **a.** (of a male) to ejaculate sperm; have an orgasm. **b.** to masturbate. *—n.* **15.** the act of tossing. **16.** a pitching about or up and down. **17.** a throw or pitch. **18.** a tossing of a coin or the like to decide something; a toss-up. **19.** a sudden fling or jerk of the body, esp. a quick upward or backward movement of the head. **20. argue the toss,** to go on arguing after a dispute has been settled. **21. take a toss,** to fall from a horse. [appar. t. Scand.; cf. d. Sw. *tossa* spread, strew] **—toss′er,** *n.* **—Syn. 1.** See **throw.**

tossed salad, a mixture of salad vegetables tossed in a dressing.

toss-up (tŏs′ŭp′), *n.* **1.** the tossing up of a coin or the like to decide something by the side on which it falls. **2.** *Colloq.* an even chance.

tost (tŏst), *v. Poetic.* pt. and pp. of **toss.**

tot[1] (tŏt), *n.* **1.** a small child. **2.** a small portion of drink. **3.** a small quantity of anything. [? short for *totterer* child learning to walk]

tot[2] (tŏt), *v.,* **totted, totting,** *n. Colloq. —v.t.* **1.** to add (often fol. by *up*). *—n.* **2.** a total. **3.** the act of adding. [t. L: so much, so many]

total (tō′tl), *adj., n., v.,* **-talled, -talling** or (*U.S.*) **-taled, -taling.** *—adj.* **1.** constituting or comprising the whole; entire; whole: *the total expenditure.* **2.** of or pertaining to the whole of something: *a total eclipse.* **3.** complete in extent or degree; absolute; unqualified; utter: *a total failure.* *—n.* **4.** the total amount; sum; aggregate: *to add the several items to find the total.* **5.** the whole; a whole or aggregate: *the costs reached a total of £200.* *—v.t.* **6.** to bring to a total; add up. **7.** to reach a total of; amount to. *—v.i.* **8.** to amount (often fol. by *to*). [ME, t. ML: s. *tōtālis,* der. L *tōtus* entire] **—Syn. 5.** See **whole.**

total abstainer, one who, for religious or other reasons, abstains from any form of alcoholic drink.

total depravity, *Theol.* the absolute unfitness of man, due to original sin, for the moral purposes of his being, until born again through the influence of the Spirit of God.

total eclipse, an eclipse in which the whole surface of the eclipsed body is obscured (opposed to *annular eclipse*).

total heat, *Physics.* enthalpy.

total internal reflection, *Optics.* the total reflection of a light ray which occurs when light from one medium strikes another of lower optical density, at an angle of incidence in excess of the critical angle.

totalitarian (tō′tăl ĭ tâə′rĭ ən), *adj.* **1.** of or pertaining to a centralized government in which those in control grant neither recognition nor tolerance to parties of differing opinion. *—n.* **2.** an adherent of totalitarian principles. **—to′talita′rianism,** *n.*

totality (tō tăl′ĭ tĭ), *n., pl.* **-ties. 1.** the state of being total; entirety. **2.** that which is total; the total; the total amount; a whole. **3.** *Astron.* total obscuration in an eclipse.

totalizator (tō′tə lī zā′tə), *n.* **1.** an apparatus for registering and indicating the total of operations, measurements, etc. **2.** a form of betting, as on horseraces, in which those who bet on the winners divide the bets or stakes, less a percentage for the management, taxes, etc. **3.** the apparatus that records the bets. Also, **totalisator.**

totalize (tō′tə līz′), *v.t.,* **-lized, -lizing.** to make total; combine into a total. Also, **totalise. —to′taliza′tion,** *n.*

totalizer (tō′tə lī′zə), *n.* **1.** totalizator. **2.** *Chiefly U.S.* an adding machine. Also, **totaliser.**

totally (tō′tə lĭ), *adv.* wholly; entirely; completely.

totara (tō′tə rə), *n.* the conifer, *Podocarpus totara,* found in New Zealand, the wood of which is widely used for building, furniture, etc. [t. Maori]

tote[1] (tōt), *v.,* **toted, toting,** *n. U.S. Colloq. and Dial.* *—v.t.* **1.** to carry, as on the back or in the arms, as a burden or load. **2.** to carry or have on the person: *to tote a gun.* **3.** to transport or convey, as in a vehicle or boat. *—n.* **4.** the act or course of toting. **5.** that which is toted. [orig. uncert.]

tote[2] (tōt), *n.* totalizator.

totem (tō′təm), *n. Anthropol.* **1.** an object or thing in nature, often an animal, assumed as the token or emblem of a clan, family, or related group. **2.** an object or natural phenomenon with which a primitive family or sib considers itself closely related, usually by blood. **3.** a representation of such an object serving as the distinctive mark of the clan or group. [t. Algonquian (Ojibwa): m. *ototeman* his brother-sister kin, der. *ote* parents, relations] **—totemic** (tō tĕm′ĭk), *adj.*

totemism (tō′tə mĭz′əm), *n.* **1.** the practice of having totems. **2.** the system of tribal division according to totems.

totemist (tō′tə mĭst), *n.* a member of a clan or the like distinguished by a totem. **—to′temis′tic,** *adj.*

totem pole, a pole or post carved and painted with totemic figures, erected by Indians of the north-west coast of North America, esp. in front of their houses. Also, **totem post.**

tother (tŭth′ə), *adj., pron. Dial.* the other. Also, **t'other.** [ME *the tother,* var. of *thet other* the other]

totidem verbis (tŏt′ĭ dĕm vû′bĭs), *Latin.* with just so many words; in these words.

totipalmate (tō′tĭ păl′mĭt, -māt), *adj. Zool.* having all toes fully webbed. [f. L *tōti-* (repr. *tōtus* whole) + PALMATE]

Totipalmate foot

totipalmation (tō′tĭ păl mā′shən), *n.* totipalmate condition or formation.

Totleben (*Russ.* tôt′lyĭ byĭn), *n.* **Franz Eduard Ivanovich, Count** (*Russ.* fränts ĕd värt′ ĭ vä′nə vĭch), 1818–84, Russian military engineer and general.

Tottenham (tŏt′nəm), *n.* a district of the N outer London borough of Haringey.

totter (tŏt′ə), *v.i.* **1.** to walk or go with faltering steps, as if from extreme weakness. **2.** to sway or rock on the base or ground, as if about to fall: *a tottering tower, a tottering government.* **3.** to shake or tremble: *a tottering load.* *—n.* **4.** the act of tottering; an unsteady movement or gait. **5.** *Slang.* a rag-and-bone man; a scavenger. [ME *totre,* t. Scand.; cf. d. Norw. *totra* quiver, shake] **—tot′terer,** *n.* **—tot′teringly,** *adv.* **—Syn. 1.** See **stagger.**

tottery (tŏt′ə rĭ), *adj.* tottering; shaky.

Tottori (tô′tə rĭ), *n.* a town in Japan, in W Honshu island. 108,860 (1965).

toucan (to͞o′kən), *n.* any of various fruit-eating birds (family *Ramphastidae*) of tropical America, with an enormous beak and usually a striking coloration. [ult. t. Tupi: m. *tucana*]

Toucan, *Ramphastos toco* (25 in. long)

Toucan (to͞o′kən), *n. Astron.* the southern constellation Tucana.

touch (tŭch), *v.t.* **1.** to put the hand, finger, etc., on or into contact with (something) to feel it. **2.** to come into contact with and perceive (something), as the hand or the like. **3.** to bring (the hand, finger, etc., or something held) into contact with something. **4.** to give a slight tap or pat to with the hand, finger, etc.; strike or hit gently or lightly. **5.** to hurt or injure. **6.** to come into or be in contact with. **7.** *Geom.* (of a line or surface) to be tangent to. **8.** to be adjacent to or border on. **9.** to come up to; reach; attain. **10.** to attain equality with; compare with (usually with a negative). **11.** to mark by strokes of the brush, pencil, or the like. **12.** to modify or improve by adding a stroke of paint, etc., here and there (often fol. by *up*). **13.** to mark or relieve slightly, as with colour: *a grey dress touched with blue.* **14.** to strike the strings, keys, etc., of (a musical instrument) so as to cause it to sound. **15.** to play or perform, as an air. **16.** to stop at (a place), as a ship. **17.** to treat or affect in some way by contact. **18.** to affect as if by contact; tinge; imbue. **19.** to affect with some feeling or emotion, esp. tenderness, pity, gratitude, etc.: *his heart was touched by their sufferings.* **20.** to handle, use, or have to do with (something) in any way: *he won't touch another drink.* **21.** to begin to eat; eat a little of: *he hardly touched his food.* **22.** to deal with or treat in speech or writing. **23.** to refer or allude to. **24.** to pertain or relate to: *a critic in all affairs touching the kitchen.* **25.** to be a matter of importance to; make a difference to. **26.** to stamp (tested metal) as being of standard purity, etc. **27.** *Slang.* to apply to for money, or succeed in getting money from. —*v.i.* **28.** to place the hand, finger, etc., on or in contact with something. **29.** to come into or be in contact. **30.** to make a stop or a short call at a place, as a ship or those on board (usually fol. by *at*). **31.** to speak or write briefly or casually (fol. by *on* or *upon*) in the course of a discourse, etc.: *he touched briefly on his own travels.* **32. touch down,** (of an aircraft) to land after a flight. —*n.* **33.** the act of touching. **34.** the state or fact of being touched. **35.** that sense by which anything material is perceived by means of the contact with it of some part of the body. **36.** the sensation or effect caused by touching something, regarded as a quality of the thing: *an object with a slimy touch.* **37.** a coming into or being in contact. **38.** a close relation of communication, agreement, sympathy, or the like: *to be in touch with public opinion.* **39.** a slight stroke or blow. **40.** a slight attack, as of illness or disease: *a touch of rheumatism.* **41.** a slight added action or effort in doing or completing any piece of work. **42.** manner of execution in artistic work. **43.** the act or manner of touching or fingering a musical instrument, esp. a keyboard instrument, so as to bring out the tone. **44.** the mode of action of the keys of an instrument. **45.** a partial series of changes on a peal of bells. **46.** a stroke or dash, as with a brush, pencil, or pen. **47.** a detail in any artistic work. **48.** a slight amount of some quality, attribute, etc.: *a touch of sarcasm in his voice.* **49.** a slight quantity or degree: *a touch of salt.* **50.** a distinguishing characteristic or trait: *the touch of the master.* **51.** quality or kind in general. **52.** the act of testing anything. **53.** something that serves as a test. **54.** *Slang.* the act of applying to a person for money, as a gift or loan. **55.** *Slang.* an obtaining of money thus. **56.** *Slang.* the money obtained. **57.** *Slang.* a person from whom such money can be obtained easily. **58.** an official mark or stamp put upon gold, silver, etc., after testing, to indicate standard fineness. **59.** a die, stamp, or the like for impressing such a mark. **60.** *Rugby Football, etc.* the portion of the land lying outside the field of play, including the touchlines in Rugby. **61.** *Fencing.* a hit with the point of the weapon which scores a point. [ME *touche(n)*, t. OF: m. *tochier*; orig. uncert.] —**touch′able,** *adj.* —**touch′er,** *n.*

touch and go, 1. something done quickly. **2.** a precarious or delicate state of affairs. **3.** a narrow escape.

touch-and-go (tŭch′ən gō′), *adj.* **1.** hasty, sketchy, or desultory. **2.** precarious, risky: *a highly touch-and-go situation.*

touchdown (tŭch′doun′), *n.* **1.** *Rugby Football.* the act of a player touching the ball down to the ground behind the opponent's goal line, so as to score a try. **2.** *American Football.* **a.** a similar act. **b.** the score made by this, counting 6 points. **3.** the landing of an aircraft.

touché (to͞o′shā), *interj.* **1.** *Fencing.* (an expression indicating a touch by the point of a weapon.) **2.** good point! (said in acknowledging a telling remark or rejoinder). [F: pp. of *toucher* to touch]

touched (tŭcht), *adj.* **1.** moved; stirred. **2.** slightly crazy; unbalanced: *touched in the head.*

touch-hole (tŭch′hōl′), *n.* (formerly) the vent in the breech of a firearm through which fire was communicated to the powder charge. See diag. under **flintlock.**

touching (tŭch′ĭng), *adj.* **1.** affecting; moving; pathetic. **2.** that touches. —*prep.* **3.** in reference or relation to; concerning; about. —**touch′ingly,** *adv.* —**touch′ingness,** *n.*

touch-in-goal (tŭch′ĭn gōl′), *n. Rugby Football.* the extension of the touchline between the dead-ball line and the goal line.

touch judge, *Rugby Football.* one of two officials, one on each side of the field of play, who decide whether the ball has gone into touch and which side last played it.

touchline (tŭch′līn′), *n. Rugby Football, etc.* any of the sidelines bordering the field of play.

touchmark (tŭch′mäk′), *n.* an official mark or stamp indicating a standard of purity, used in marking pewter articles.

touch-me-not (tŭch′mĭ nŏt′), *n.* **1.** a yellow-flowered balsaminaceous plant, *Impatiens noli-me-tangere,* whose ripe seed capsules burst open when touched. **2.** any of various other species of the same genus.

touchpaper (tŭch′pā′pə), *n.* paper saturated with a substance, as potassium nitrate, which makes it smoulder slowly; used as a fuse in fireworks and explosives.

touchstone (tŭch′stōn′), *n.* **1.** a black siliceous stone used to test the purity of gold and silver by the colour of the streak produced on it by rubbing it with either metal. **2.** a test or criterion for the qualities of a thing.

touch-type (tŭch′tīp′), *v.i.,* **-typed, -typing.** to type without looking at the keys of the typewriter.

touchwood (tŭch′wo͝od′), *n.* **1.** wood converted into an easily ignitable substance by the action of certain fungi, and used as tinder. **2.** amadou.

touchy (tŭch′ĭ), *adj.,* **touchier, touchiest.** **1.** apt to take offence on slight provocation; irritable. **2.** precarious, risky, or ticklish, as a subject. **3.** sensitive to touch. **4.** easily ignited, as tinder. [var. of TETCHY, by assoc. with TOUCH] —**touch′ily,** *adv.* —**touch′iness,** *n.*

tough (tŭf), *adj.* **1.** not easily broken or cut. **2.** not brittle or tender. **3.** difficult to masticate, as food. **4.** of viscous consistency, as liquid or semiliquid matter. **5.** capable of great endurance; sturdy; hardy. **6.** not easily influenced, as a person. **7.** hardened; incorrigible. **8.** difficult to perform, accomplish, or deal with; hard, trying, or troublesome. **9.** hard to bear or endure. **10.** vigorous; severe; violent: *a tough struggle.* **11.** rough, disorderly, or rowdyish. —*adv.* **12.** *Colloq.* aggressively; threateningly: *to act tough.* —*n.* **13.** a ruffian; a rowdy. [ME; OE *tōh.* Cf. D *taai,* G *zähe, zäh*] —**tough′ly,** *adv.* —**tough′ness,** *n.* —**Ant. 1.** fragile.

toughen (tŭf′ən), *v.i., v.t.* to make or become tough or tougher. —**tough′ener,** *n.*

Toul (*Fr.* to͞ol), *n.* a fortress town in NE France, on the Moselle: siege 1870. 15,031 (1962).

Toulon (*Fr.* to͞o lôɴ′), *n.* a seaport in SE France: naval base. 161,786 (1962).

Toulouse (*Fr.* to͞o lo͞oz′), *n.* a city in S France, on the river Garonne. 323,724 (1962).

Toulouse-Lautrec (*Fr.* to͞o lo͞oz lō trĕk′), *n.* **Henri Marie Raymond de** (*Fr.* äɴ rē mȧ rē rĕ môɴ′ də), 1864–1901, French painter and lithographer.

toupee (to͞o′pā), *n.* **1.** a wig or patch of false hair worn to cover a bald spot. **2.** (formerly) a curl or an artificial lock of hair on the top of the head, esp. as a crowning feature of a periwig. [t. F: m. *toupet,* der. OF *to(u)p* tuft of hair. See TOP[1]]

tour (to͞oə), *v.i.* **1.** to travel from place to place. **2.** to travel from place to place with a theatrical company. —*v.t.* **3.** to travel through (a place). **4.** (of a manager) to send or take (a theatrical company, its production, etc.) from place to place. —*n.* **5.** a travelling around from place to place. **6.** a long journey including the visiting of a number of places in sequence. **7.** a journey of a theatrical company from place to place to fulfil engagements: *to go on tour.* **8.** *Chiefly Mil.* a period of duty at one place. [ME, t. F, g. L *tornus,* t. Gk: m. *tórnos* tool for making a circle] —**Syn. 6.** See **excursion.**

touraco (to͞oə′rə kō′), *n., pl.* **-cos.** any of the large African birds constituting the family *Musophagidae* (genera

Turacus, Musophaga, etc.), notable for their brilliant plumage and helmet-like crest. [t. some W African language. Cf. Twi *aturukubu* turtle-dove]

Touraine (*Fr.* to͞o rĕn′), *n.* a former province in W France. *Cap.*: Tours.

Tourane (*Fr.* to͞o rȧn′), *n.* former name of **Da Nang.**

Tourcoing (*Fr.* to͞or kwăN′), *n.* town in N France, near the Belgian border. 89,258 (1962).

tour de force (*Fr.* to͞or də fôrs′), *French.* a feat requiring unusual strength, skill, or ingenuity.

Touré (to͞oə′rā; *Fr.* to͞o rĕ′), *n.* **Sékou** (sĕk′o͞o; *Fr.* sĕ ko͞o′), born 1922, president of the Republic of Guinea since 1958.

tourer (to͞oə′rə), *n.* **1.** one who or that which tours. **2.** an open motor car; sports car.

touring car, an open motor car designed for five or more passengers. Also, **tourer.**

tourism (to͞oə′rĭz′əm), *n.* **1.** the practice of touring, esp. for pleasure. **2.** the occupation of providing local services, as entertainment, lodging, food, etc., for tourists.

tourist (to͞oə′rĭst), *n.* one who tours, esp. for pleasure.

tourist class, a type of lower-priced fare accommodation for travel, as on a passenger ship or airliner.

Tourist Trophy, a series of international road races for motorcycles of different classes held annually over a mountainous course in the Isle of Man. *Abbrev.*: T.T.

tourmaline (to͞oə′mə lēn′), *n.* a mineral, essentially a complex silicate containing boron, aluminium, etc., occurring in various colours (black being common), the transparent varieties (red, pink, green, and blue) being used in jewellery. Also, **tourmalin** (to͞oə′mə lĭn), **turmaline.** [t. Sinhalese: m. *toramalli* cornelian]

Tournai (*Fr.* to͞or nĕ′), *n.* a town in W Belgium on the river Scheldt. 33,297 (est. 1965). Also, **Tournay.**

tournament (to͞oə′nə mənt, tô′-, tû′-), *n.* **1.** a meeting for contests in athletic or other sports. **2.** a trial of skill in some game, in which competitors play a series of contests: *a chess tournament.* **3.** *Hist.* **a.** a contest or martial sport in which two opposing parties of mounted and armoured combatants fought for a prize, with blunted weapons and in accordance with certain rules. **b.** a meeting at an appointed time and place for the performance of knightly exercises and sports. [ME *tornement*, t. OF: m. *torneiement*, der. *torneier* TOURNEY, v.]

tournedos (to͞oə′nə dō′; *Fr.* to͞or nə dō′), *n., pl.* **-dos.** *Cookery.* small slices taken from the middle of fillet of beef and sautéed or grilled. [t. F, f. *tourne(r)* turn + *dos* the back]

Tourneur (tû′nə), *n.* **Cyril** (sĭ′rĭl), 1575?–1626, English dramatist.

tourney (to͞oə′nĭ, tô′-), *n., pl.* **-neys,** *v.,* **-neyed, -neying.** *Archaic.* —*n.* **1.** a tournament (def. 3). —*v.i.* **2.** to contend or engage in a tournament. [def. 1, ME, t. OF: m. *tornei, tournay*, der. *torneier* tourney, v. def. 2, ME, t. OF: m. s. *tourneier*, der. *torn* turn, g. L *tornus* lathe] —**tour′neyer,** *n.*

tourniquet (to͞oə′nĭ kā′, tô′-), *n.* *Surg.* any device for arresting bleeding by forcibly compressing a blood vessel, as a pad pressed down by a screw, a bandage tightened by twisting, etc. [t. F, der. *tourner* turn]

tournure (to͞oə′nyo͞oə), *n.* *Obs.* **1.** manner or bearing; graceful carriage; elegance. **2.** form or contour, as of a person's figure. [t. F]

Tours (*Fr.* to͞or), *n.* a town in W France, the capital of Indre-et-Loire department, on the river Loire: Charles Martel defeated the Saracens near here A.D. 732. 92,944 (1962).

tousle (tou′zəl), *v.,* **-sled, -sling,** *n.* —*v.t.* **1.** to disorder or dishevel: *his hair was tousled.* **2.** to handle roughly. —*n.* *Rare.* **3.** a tousled mass of hair. **4.** a tousled condition; a disordered mass. [ME *tousel*; freq. of *touse* pull]

Toussaint L'Ouverture (*Fr.* to͞o săN lo͞o vĕr tyr′) (*Francis Dominique Toussaint*), 1743–1803, Negro military and political leader, one of the liberators of Haiti.

tout (tout), *v.i.* **1.** to solicit business, employment, votes, etc., importunately. **2.** *Racing.* to sell betting information, take bets, etc., esp. in public places. **3.** to spy on a racehorse, etc., to obtain information for betting purposes. —*v.t.* **4.** to solicit support for importunately. **5.** to describe or proclaim, esp. favourably: *to tout a politician as a friend of the people.* **6.** to sell information on (a racehorse, etc.). **7.** to spy on (a racehorse, etc.) in order to gain information for betting purposes. **8.** to watch; spy on. —*n.* **9.** one who solicits custom, employment, support, etc., importunately. **10.** one who spies on racehorses, etc., to gain information for betting purposes, or who gives tips on racehorses, etc., as a business. [ME *tute(n)*; akin to OE *tȳtan* peep out, become visible, shine (said of a star)]

tout à fait (*Fr.* to͞o tȧ fĕ′), *French.* entirely.

tout à vous (*Fr.* to͞o tȧ vo͞o′), *French.* yours sincerely.

tout de suite (*Fr.* to͞ot swēt′), *French.* at once.

tout ensemble (*Fr.* to͞o tăN săN′bl), *French.* **1.** all together. **2.** the assemblage of parts or details, as in a work of art, considered as forming a whole; the ensemble.

touter (tou′tə), *n.* *Colloq.* one who touts; a tout.

tout le monde (*Fr.* to͞ol mōNd′), *French.* all the world; everyone.

tovarich (tō vä′rĭch), *n.* *Russian.* comrade.

tow[1] (tō), *v.t.* **1.** to drag or pull (a boat, car, etc.) by means of a rope or chain. —*n.* **2.** the act of towing. **3.** the thing being towed. **4.** a rope, chain, etc., for towing. **5.** the state of being towed. **6. in tow, a.** in the condition of being towed. **b.** under guidance; in one's charge. **c.** in attendance; following or accompanying one around. **7. on** or **under tow,** in the condition of being towed. [ME *towe(n)*, OE *togian* pull by force, drag, c. MHG *zogen* draw, tug, drag. Cf. TUG]

tow[2] (tō), *n.* **1.** the fibre of flax, hemp, or jute prepared for spinning by scutching. **2.** the coarse and broken parts of flax or hemp separated from the finer parts in hackling. —*adj.* **3.** made of tow: *tow cloth.* **4.** resembling tow; pale yellow: *tow-coloured hair.* [ME; OE *tōw* (in *tōwlic* pertaining to thread, *tōwhūs* spinning house). Cf. Icel. *tō* wool]

towage (tō′ĭj), *n.* **1.** the act of towing. **2.** the state of being towed. **3.** a charge for towing.

toward (*adj.* tō′əd; *prep.* tə wôd′, tôd), *adj.* **1.** going on; in progress: *when there is work toward.* **2.** *Obs.* promising, hopeful, or apt, as a young person. **3.** *Obs.* that is to come; imminent or impending. —*prep.* **4.** towards. [ME, OE *tōweard*, f. *tō-* to + *-weard* -WARD]

towardly (tō′əd lĭ), *adj.* *Archaic.* **1.** promising; apt; tractable or docile. **2.** favourable or propitious; seasonable or suitable. —**to′wardliness, to′wardness,** *n.*

towards (tə wôdz′, tôdz), *prep.* **1.** in the direction of (with reference to either motion or position): *to walk towards the north.* **2.** with respect to; as regards: *one's attitude towards a proposition.* **3.** nearly as late as; shortly before: *towards two o'clock.* **4.** as a help or contribution to: *to give money towards a gift.* Also, **toward.** [TOWARD + -S[2]]

towboat (tō′bōt′), *n.* a tugboat.

towel (tou′əl), *n., v.,* **-elled, -elling** or (*U.S.*) **-eled, -eling.** —*n.* **1.** a cloth or the like for wiping and drying something wet, esp. one for the hands, face, or body after washing or bathing. **2. throw in the towel,** to give up; admit defeat. —*v.t.* **3.** to wipe or dry with a towel. [ME, t. OF: m. *toaille* cloth for washing or wiping, t. Gmc; cf. MHG *twähele* towel, OE *thwēal* washbasin]

towelling (tou′ə lĭng), *n.* **1.** any of various absorbent fabrics used for towels, and also for beachwear and the like. **2.** a rubbing with a towel. **3.** *Slang.* a thrashing. Also, *U.S.*, **toweling.**

tower (tou′ə), *n.* **1.** a building or structure high in proportion to its lateral dimensions, either isolated or forming part of any building. **2.** such a structure used as or intended for a stronghold, fortress, prison, etc. **3.** any of various tower-like structures, contrivances, or objects. **4.** a tall, movable structure used in ancient and medieval warfare in storming a fortified place. **5. tower of strength,** a source of mental and physical support, as a person; one who may be depended on. —*v.i.* **6.** to rise or extend far upwards like a tower; rise aloft. **7.** to surpass, as in ability, etc. (fol. by *over, above*, etc.). [ME *tour*, late OE *tūr*, t. OF; r. OE *torr*, t. L: m. *turris*] —**tow′ered,** *adj.* —**tow′erless,** *adj.* —**tow′er-like′,** *adj.*

tower block, a very tall building or part of a building, esp. one containing flats or offices.

Tower Bridge, a two-bascule lifting bridge in London, on the Thames, having two high towers, completed 1894.

tower crane, a crane mounted on a tall, lattice tower, used in the erection of multistorey buildings.

tower cress, a small cruciferous herb with pale yellow flowers, *Arabis turrita*, a native of central and S Europe.

Tower Hamlets, an E inner borough of London. 205,375 (1964).

towering (tou′ə rĭng), *adj.* **1.** that towers; very lofty or tall: *a towering oak.* **2.** very great. **3.** rising to an extreme degree of violence or intensity: *a towering rage.* —**tow′eringly,** *adv.* —**Syn. 1.** See **high.**

tower mustard, a biennial cruciferous herb, *Turritis glabra*, widespread in dry places in N temperate regions.

Tower of London, a historic fortress in London: originally a royal palace, later a prison, now a group of buildings containing an arsenal and museum.

towershell (tou′ə shĕl′), *n.* a gastropod mollusc of the genus *Turritella*, with a long, spiral shell.

towery (tou′ə rĭ), *adj.* **1.** having towers. **2.** lofty.

towhead (tō′hĕd′), *n.* **1.** a head of flaxen or light-coloured hair. **2.** a head of tousled hair. **3.** a person with such hair. —**tow′head′ed,** *adj.*

towline (tō′līn′), *n.* a line, hawser, or the like, by which anything is or may be towed.

town (toun), *n.* **1.** a distinct densely populated area of considerable size, having some degree of self-government. **2.** a group of buildings, larger than a village and administratively more independent, but smaller than a city. **3.** a city. **4.** a borough. **5.** urban life, opposed to rural: *I prefer the town to the country.* **6.** the particular town in question, as that in which one is. **7.** the nearest large town; in England, usually, London. **8.** the main shopping, business, or entertainment centre of a large town, contrasted with the suburbs. **9.** an urban community; the people of a town. **10.** the inhabitants of a university town (opposed to *gown*). **11.** *U.S.* any of various administrative divisions, usually urban, and smaller and less elaborately organized than a city; a township. **12. go to town, a.** to do something thoroughly. **b.** to do something enthusiastically; splash out. **c.** to overindulge or lose one's self-restraint. **d.** to celebrate. **e.** to be successful. **13. man about town,** a sophisticated, pleasure-seeking, and usually sociable man of high social status. **14. on the town, a.** seeking amusement in a town. **b.** supported by the municipal authorities or public charity. **15. talk of the town,** the subject of general gossip or rumour. [ME; OE *tūn*, c. D *tuin*, G *Zaun* hedge. Cf. Irish *dūn* fortified place] —**town′ish,** *adj.* —**town′less,** *adj.*

town clerk, an official who keeps the records, issues licences, and acts as secretary of a town. Also, **clerk of the council.**

town council, the governing body of a town.

town councillor, a member of a town council.

town crier, *Chiefly Hist.* a person employed by a town to make public proclamations.

townee (tou nē′), *n.* **1.** a townsman. **2.** (derogatory) an inhabitant of a university town. **3.** (derogatory) one who comes from a town and is ignorant of country ways.

town gas, gas made for domestic or industrial use.

town hall, a hall or building belonging to a town, used for the transaction of the town's business, etc., and often also as a place of public assembly.

town-hall clock (toun′hôl′), the moschatel.

town house, 1. a house or mansion in a town, as distinguished from a country residence. **2.** a modern house of two or three storeys, designed esp. for small sites in towns and suburbs.

town meeting, *U.S.* **1.** a general meeting of the inhabitants of a town. **2.** a meeting of the qualified voters of a town for the transaction of public business.

town-planning (toun′plăn′ĭng), *n.* the calculated control of urban physical conditions in the social interests of the community at large. —**town-planner** (toun′plăn′ə), *n.*

townsfolk (tounz′fōk′), *n.pl.* **1.** townspeople. **2.** people living or bred in towns or a town rather than the country.

Townshend (tounz′ĕnd′), *n.* **Charles, 2nd Viscount** ('*Turnip Townshend*'), 1674–1738, English statesman and agriculturist.

township (toun′shĭp), *n.* **1.** *Hist.* **a.** one of the local divisions or districts of a large parish, each containing a village or small town, usually with a church of its own. **b.** the manor, parish, etc., itself. **c.** its inhabitants. **2.** a small town. **3.** (in South Africa) an area set aside for Africans, as in an urban locality; a location. **4.** (in the U.S. and Canada) an administrative division of a county with varying corporate powers. **5.** (in U.S. surveys of public land) a region or district 6 miles square, containing 36 sections. [ME *tounshipe*, OE *tūnscipe*, f. *tūn* TOWN + *-scipe* -SHIP]

townsman (tounz′mən), *n., pl.* **-men. 1.** an inhabitant of a town. **2.** an inhabitant of one's own or the same town. —**towns′wom′an,** *n.fem.*

townspeople (tounz′pē′pl), *n.pl.* the inhabitants collectively of a town. Also, **townsfolk.**

Townsville (tounz′vĭl), *n.* a seaport in Australia, in NE Queensland. 55,200 (est. 1964).

towpath (tō′päth′), *n.* a path along the bank of a canal or river, for use in towing boats.

towrope (tō′rōp′), *n.* a rope, hawser, or the like, used in towing boats.

towy (tō′ĭ), *adj.* of the nature of or resembling tow².

Towy (tou′ĭ), *n.* the longest river in Wales, flowing from Cardiganshire SW to Carmarthen Bay. 68 mi.

tox-, var. of **toxo-,** before vowels, as in *toxaemia.*

toxaemia (tŏk sē′myə), *n.* *Pathol.* entry into, and persistence in, the bloodstream of bacterial toxins absorbed from a local lesion, by which stream these poisons are borne by the circulation to all parts of the body. Also, *Chiefly U.S.,* **toxemia.** [t. NL. See TOX-, -AEMIA]

toxaemic (tŏk sē′mĭk), *adj.* *Pathol.* **1.** pertaining to or of the nature of toxaemia. **2.** affected with toxaemia. Also, *Chiefly U.S.,* **toxemic.**

toxic (tŏk′sĭk), *adj.* **1.** of, pertaining to, affected with, or caused by a toxin or poison. **2.** poisonous. [t. ML: s. *toxicus*, der. L *toxicum* poison, t. Gk: m. *toxikón* (orig. short for *toxikòn* (*phármakon*), lit., (poison) pertaining to the bow, i.e. poison used on arrows)] —**tox′ically,** *adv.*

toxicant (tŏk′sĭ kənt), *adj.* **1.** poisonous; toxic. —*n.* **2.** a poison.

toxication (tŏk′sĭ kā′shən), *n.* poisoning.

toxicity (tŏk sĭs′ĭ tĭ), *n., pl.* **-ties.** toxic quality; poisonousness.

toxico-, a combining form of **toxic.** Cf. **toxo-.** [comb. form repr. Gk *toxikón* poison. See TOXIC]

toxicogenic (tŏk′sĭ kō jĕn′ĭk), *adj.* *Physiol., Pathol.* **1.** generating or producing toxic products or poisons. **2.** formed by poisonous matter.

toxicol., toxicology.

toxicology (tŏk′sĭ kŏl′ə jĭ), *n.* the science of poisons, their effects, antidotes, detection, etc. —**toxicological** (tŏk′sĭ kə lŏj′ĭ kl), *adj.* —**tox′icolog′ically,** *adv.* —**tox′icol′ogist,** *n.*

toxicosis (tŏk′sĭ kō′sĭs), *n., pl.* **-ses** (-sēz). *Pathol.* a morbid condition produced by the action of a poison. [t. NL. See TOXIC, -OSIS]

toxin (tŏk′sĭn), *n.* **1.** any of the specific poisonous products generated by pathogenic micro-organisms and constituting the causative agents in various diseases, as tetanus, diphtheria, etc. **2.** any of various organic poisons produced in living or dead organisms. **3.** their products, as a venom, etc. Also, **toxine** (tŏk′sĭn, -sēn). [f. TOX(IC) + -IN(E)²] —**Syn. 1.** See **poison.**

toxiphobia (tŏk′sĭ fō′byə), *n.* *Psychol.* a morbid fear of being poisoned. [f. *toxi-* (var. of TOXO-) + -PHOBIA]

toxo-, a combining form representing **toxin,** or short for **toxico-,** as in *toxoplasmosis.*

toxoid (tŏk′soid), *n.* a non-toxic toxin produced by treating a toxin with chemical agents or by physical means. [f. TOX(O)- + -OID]

toxophilite (tŏk sŏf′ĭ līt′), *n.* a devotee of archery; archer. [f. s. *Toxophilus* (coined Gk proper name: bow-lover) + -ITE¹] —**toxophilitic** (tŏk sŏf′ĭ lĭt′ĭk), *adj.* —**toxoph′ily,** *n.*

toxoplasmosis (tŏk′sō plăz mō′sĭs), *n.* *Vet. Sci., Pathol.* an infection caused by bodies believed to be protozoa which are known as *Toxoplasma gondii*, and occurring in dogs, cats, sheep, and man, the nervous system usually being the part involved.

toy (toi), *n.* **1.** an object, often a small imitation of some familiar thing, for children or others to play with, or otherwise derive amusement; a plaything. **2.** a thing or matter of little or no value or importance; a trifle. **3.** a small article of little real value, but prized for some reason; a knick-knack; a trinket. **4.** something diminutive. **5.** any of various breeds of dog bred or selected for their smallness; toy dog. **6.** *Obs.* amorous dallying. —*adj.* **7.** of or like a toy, esp. in size. **8.** made as a toy: *a toy train.* —*v.i.* **9.** to handle affectionately; play. **10.** to act idly, absent-mindedly, or without seriousness. **11.** to trifle; deal with as unimportant (usually fol. by *with*). [ME *toye* dalliance; orig. uncert.] —**toy′er,** *n.* —**toy′less,** *adj.* —**toy′like′,** *adj.*

Toyama (tô′yə mä′), *n.* a town in central Japan, in W Honshu island. 239,810 (1965).

toy dog, 1. toy (def. 5). **2.** any dog of unusually small size kept as a pet.

Toynbee (toin′bĭ), *n.* **1. Arnold,** 1852–83, English social reformer. **2.** his nephew, **Arnold Joseph,** born 1889, English historian.

Toyohashi (tô′yə hä′shĭ), *n.* a seaport in central Japan, on SW Honshu island. 238,672 (1965).

Toyonaka (tō yô′nə kə, tô′yə nä′kə), *n.* a town in Japan, in S Honshu island. 291,936 (1965).

Toyota (tô′yə tə), *n.* a town in Japan, in SW central Honshu island. 107,455 (1965).

toyshop (toi′shŏp′), *n.* a shop in which toys are sold.

tp, *U.S.* township.

tpi, 1. teeth per inch. **2.** turns per inch.

Tr, *Chem.* terbium.

tr., 1. transitive. **2.** translated. **3.** translator. **4.** transpose. **5.** treasurer. **6.** *Music.* trill. **7.** trustee.

trabeated (trā′bĭ ā′tĭd), *adj.* *Archit.* **1.** constructed with horizontal beams, as a flat, unvaulted ceiling, or with a lintel or entablature, as an unarched doorway. **2.** pertaining to such construction, as distinct from the vaulted or arched kind. Also, **trabeate** (trā′bĭ ĭt, -āt′). [der. *trabeat(ion)* beam structure, f. L *trabe(m)* beam (acc. of *trabs*) + -ATION] —**tra′bea′tion,** *n.*

trabecula (trə bĕk′yŏŏ lə), *n., pl.* **-lae** (-lē′). **1.** *Anat., Bot., etc.* a structural part resembling a small beam or crossbar. **2.** *Bot.* one of the projections from the cell wall which extend across the cell cavity of the ducts of certain plants, or the plate of cells across the cavity of the sporangium of a moss. [t. L, dim. of *trabs* beam] —**trabec′ular,** *adj.*

Trabzon (*Turk.* träb′zôn), *n.* official name of **Trebizond** (def. 2).

trace[1] (trās), *n., v.,* **traced, tracing.** —*n.* **1.** a mark, token, or evidence of the former presence, existence, or action of something; a vestige. **2.** a mark, indication, or evidence. **3.** a scarcely discernible quantity of something; a very small amount. **4.** *Psychol.* the residual effect of an experience in memory; an engram. **5.** a record traced by a self-registering instrument. **6.** a tracing, drawing, or sketch of a thing. **7.** *U.S.* the track made or left by the passage of a person, animal, or thing. **8.** (*esp. in pl.*) a single such mark. —*v.t.* **9.** to follow the footprints, track, or traces of. **10.** to follow or make out the course or line of: *to trace a river to its source.* **11.** to follow (footprints, traces, the history of something, the course or line of something, a drawn line, etc.). **12.** to follow the course, development, or history of: *to trace a political movement.* **13.** to find by investigation; find out; discover. **14.** to copy (a drawing, plan, etc.) by following the lines of the original on a superimposed transparent sheet. **15.** to draw (a line, outline, figure, etc.). **16.** to make a plan, diagram, or map of. **17.** to mark or ornament with lines, figures, etc. **18.** to make an impression or imprinting of (a design, pattern, etc.). **19.** to print in a curved, broken, or wavy-lined manner. **20.** to put down in writing.
—*v.i.* **21.** to trace one's or its history; go back in time. [ME, t. OF: m. *tracer* delineate, trace, pursue, der. L *tractus,* pp., drawn, trailed, or *tractus,* n., a dragging, trailing] —**trace′able,** *adj.* —**trace′abil′ity, trace′ableness,** *n.* —**trace′ably,** *adv.*

—**Syn. 1.** TRACE, VESTIGE agree in denoting marks or signs of something usually of the past. TRACE, the broader term, denotes any mark or slight indication of something past or present: *a trace of ammonia in water.* VESTIGE is more limited and refers to some slight, though actual, remains of something that no longer exists: *vestiges of one's former wealth.*

trace[2] (trās), *n.* **1.** each of the two straps, ropes, or chains by which a carriage, wagon, or the like is drawn by a harness horse or other draught animal. See illus. under **harness. 2.** *Mach.* a piece in a machine, as a bar, transferring the movement of one part to another part, being hinged to each. **3.** *Angling.* a short piece of gut or other strong material connecting the hook to a fishing line. **4. kick over the traces,** to reject discipline; to act in an independent manner. [ME *trays,* t. OF: m. *traiz,* pl. of *trait* strap for harness, act of drawing, g. L *tractus,* pp., drawn, or *tractus,* n., draught]

trace element, an element found in plants and animals in minute quantities and believed to be a critical factor in physiological processes.

tracer (trā′sə), *n.* **1.** one who or that which traces. **2.** any of various devices for tracing drawings, plans, etc. **3.** ammunition containing a chemical which by burning or smoking makes it visible, to show the path of the projectile and indicate the target to other firers. **4.** the composition contained in such ammunition. **5.** a radioactive substance used to study biological, chemical, and industrial processes by following its path on a photographic film, fluoroscope, or other detection device; radioactive tracer. **6.** one whose business is the tracing of missing property, parcels, etc. **7.** an enquiry form sent from point to point to trace a missing shipment, parcel, or the like.

tracer bullet, a bullet that leaves a trail of smoke or fire so that aim can be corrected.

traceried (trā′sə rīd), *adj.* ornamented with tracery.

tracery (trā′sə rī), *n., pl.* **-ries. 1.** ornamental work consisting of ramified ribs, bars, or the like, as in the upper part of a Gothic window, in panels, screens, etc. **2.** any delicate interlacing work of lines, threads, etc., as in carving, embroidery, etc.; network.

Window tracery

trache-, var. of **tracheo-** before vowels, as in *tracheid.*

trachea (trə kē′ə), *n., pl.* **tracheae** (trə kē′ē). **1.** (in air-breathing vertebrates) the tube extending from the larynx to the bronchi, serving as the principal passage for conveying air to and from the lungs; the windpipe. See diag. under **lung. 2.** (in insects and other arthropods) one of the air-conveying tubes of the respiratory system. **3.** *Bot.* a duct formed by a row of cells which have perforated end walls as in xylem vessels. [t. ML, var. of LL *trāchia,* t. Gk: m. *trācheîa,* short for *artēría trācheîa* rough artery (i.e. windpipe)]

tracheal (trə kē′əl), *adj.* **1.** *Anat. and Zool.* pertaining to or connected with the trachea or tracheae. **2.** *Bot.* of the nature of or composed of tracheae.

tracheid (trā′kī īd), *n. Bot.* an elongated, imperforate, dead xylem cell with a lignified wall. Also, **tracheide.**

tracheitis (trăk′ī ī′tĭs), *n. Pathol.* inflammation of the trachea. [t. NL. See TRACHE-, -ITIS]

tracheo-, a combining form representing **trachea,** as in *tracheoscopy.* Also, **trache-.**

tracheoscopy (trăk′ī ŏs′kə pī), *n. Med.* examination of the interior of the trachea, as with a laryngoscope. —**tracheoscopic** (trăk′ī ə skŏp′ĭk), *adj.* —**trach′eos′copist,** *n.*

tracheotomy (trăk′ī ŏt′ə mī), *n., pl.* **-mies.** *Surg.* the operation of cutting into the trachea. —**trach′eot′omist,** *n.*

trachoma (trə kō′mə), *n. Pathol.* a contagious inflammation of the conjunctiva of the eyelids, characterized by the formation of granulations or papillary growths. [t. NL, t. Gk: roughness] —**trachomatous** (trə kŏm′ə təs, -kō′mə-), *adj.*

trachyte (trā′kīt, trăk′īt), *n.* a volcanic rock, commonly of porphyritic texture, consisting essentially of alkali felspar and one or more subordinate minerals, as hornblende, mica, etc. [t. F, t. Gk: m. *trāchýtēs* roughness]

trachytic (trə kĭt′ĭk), *adj. Geol.* pertaining to the nearly parallel arrangement of felspar crystals in the groundmass of volcanic rocks.

tracing (trā′sĭng), *n.* **1.** a copy of a drawing, etc., made by tracing. **2.** the act of one who or that which traces. **3.** that which is produced by tracing. **4.** the record traced by a self-registering instrument.

tracing paper, a translucent paper used in tracing.

track[1] (trăk), *n.* **1.** a road, path, or trail. **2.** the structure of rails, sleepers, etc., on which a railway train or the like runs; a railway line. **3.** the mark, or series of marks, left by anything that has passed along. **4.** (*esp. pl.*) a footprint or other mark left by an animal, a person, or a vehicle. **5.** a rough roadway or path made or beaten by the feet of men or animals. **6.** a line of travel or motion: *the track of a bird.* **7.** an endless jointed metal band which is driven by the wheels of a track-laying vehicle to enable it to move, or pull loads, over rough ground. **8.** *Physics.* the path of an ionized particle which has been made visible in a cloud chamber or on a photographic emulsion. **9.** a course followed. **10.** a course of action or conduct; a method of proceeding: *to go on in the same track year after year.* **11.** a path or course made or laid out for some particular purpose. **12.** a course laid out for running or racing. **13.** *U.S.* **a.** the sports which are performed on a track, collectively; athletics. **b.** both track and field sports as a whole. **14.** *Motor Vehicles.* the measured distance at the ground line, between the centres of both front or rear tyres. **15.** *Aeron.* **a.** the distance between the port and starboard wheels of an undercarriage, or the distance between the centres of the port and starboard legs of multi-wheel landing gears. **b.** the projection of an aircraft's flight path on the surface of the earth. **16.** one of the distinct sections of a gramophone record containing a piece, or section of music, etc. **17.** one of the bands of recorded material made on the width of a magnetic tape. **18.** Some special noun phrases are:

in one's tracks, just where one is standing: *he was stopped in his tracks.*

in the tracks of, following; pursuing.

keep track of, to follow the course or progress of; keep sight or knowledge of.

lose track of, to fail to keep informed on or in view; fail to stay in touch with.

make tracks, *Colloq.* to leave or depart.

make tracks for, to head towards.

off the beaten track, secluded, unusual, or little known.

off the track, away from the subject in hand.

on the track of, pursuing; on the scent of.

the right or **wrong track,** *Colloq.* the right (or wrong) idea, plan, interpretation, etc.

(on) the wrong side of the tracks, *U.S.* (in) a low social position; (in) a low-class or poor neighbourhood.

—*v.t.* **19.** to follow up or pursue the track, traces, or footprints of. **20.** to hunt by following the tracks of. **21.** to follow the course of, as by radar. **22.** (fol. by *down*) to catch or find, after pursuit or searching. **23.** to follow (a track, course, etc.). **24.** *U.S.* **a.** to make a track of footprints upon (a floor, etc.). **b.** to make a track with (earth, snow, etc., carried on the feet) in walking. **25.** *U.S. Railways.* **a.** to furnish with a track or tracks, as for trains. **b.** to have (a certain distance) between wheels, runners, rails, etc. —*v.i.* **26.** to follow up a track or trail. **27. a.** to run in the same track, as the wheels of a vehicle. **b.** to be in alignment, as one gearwheel with another. **28.** *Films, Television, etc.* (of the camera) to move bodily in any direction while in operation. Cf. **pan, zoom. 29.** *U.S.* make one's way. —*adj.* **30.** *Athletics.* pertaining to those sports performed on a running track (contrasted with *field*).

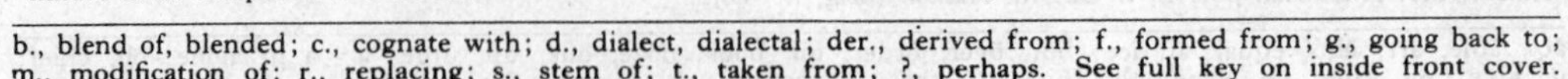

[late ME *trak*, t. F: m. *trac*, ? t. Gmc; cf. D *trekken* draw, pull] —**track′er,** *n.* —**track′less,** *adj.*

track[2] (trăk), *v.t.* to tow (a boat), esp. from a river bank.

trackage (trăk′ĭj), *n.* *U.S.* **1.** the tracks, collectively, of a railway. **2.** the provision of tracks. **3.** the right of one railway company to use the tracks of another. **4.** Also, **trackage charge.** the money paid for this right.

tracked (trăkt), *adj.* fitted with tracks, as a track-laying vehicle.

tracking station, a station used for following an object, esp. a satellite, moving through the atmosphere or space, usually by means of radio or radar.

track-laying vehicle (trăk′lā′ĭng), a vehicle, as a tank or tractor, the wheels on each side of which move on a track (see **track**[1] def. 7); a caterpillar.

trackless (trăk′lĭs), *adj.* **1.** without paths, roads, etc. **2.** untrodden. **3.** not running on rails, as a trolleybus. **4.** not leaving a track or trail. —**track′lessly,** *adv.* —**track′lessness,** *n.*

trackman (trăk′mən), *n.*, *pl.* **-men.** *U.S.* **1.** a man who assists in inspecting, installing, or maintaining railway tracks. **2.** a trackwalker.

track meet, *U.S.* an athletics meeting.

track rod, a rod which connects the two front wheels of a motor vehicle so that they can be steered together.

track shoe. See **spike**[1] (def. 6).

tracksuit (trăk′syōōt′), *n.* a warm, loose, two-piece overgarment worn by athletes in training, between events, etc.

trackwalker (trăk′wô′kə), *n.* *U.S.* a man employed to walk over and inspect a certain section of railway track at intervals.

tract[1] (trăkt), *n.* **1.** a stretch or extent of land, water, etc.; region. **2.** *Anat.* **a.** a definite region or area of the body, esp. a group, series, or system of related parts or organs: *the digestive tract.* **b.** a bundle of nerve fibres having a common origin and destination. **3.** a space or extent of time; a period. **4.** *Rom. Cath. Ch.* an anthem consisting of verses of Scripture, sung after the gradual in the mass from Septuagesima until the day before Easter and on certain other occasions, taking the place of the alleluias and the verse which ordinarily accompany the gradual. [late ME *tracte*, t. L: m. *tractus* drawing, stretch, extent, tract]

tract[2] (trăkt), *n.* a brief treatise or pamphlet suitable for general distribution, esp. one dealing with some topic of practical religion. [ME *tracte*; appar. short for L *tractātus* TRACTATE]

tractable (trăk′tə bl), *adj.* **1.** easily managed, or docile, as persons, their dispositions, etc. **2.** that may be easily handled or dealt with, as metals; malleable. [t. L: m. s. *tractābilis*] —**trac′tabil′ity, trac′tableness,** *n.* —**trac′tably,** *adv.* —**Ant. 1.** stubborn.

Tractarian (trăk tēə′rĭ ən), *n.* **1.** one of the promoters or adherents of Tractarianism. —*adj.* **2.** pertaining or belonging to the Tractarians.

Tractarianism (trăk tēə′rĭ ə nĭz′əm), *n.* a system of religious opinion and practice promulgated within the Church of England in a series of papers entitled *Tracts for the Times*, published at Oxford between 1833 and 1841. The movement began as a counter movement to the liberalizing tendency in ecclesiasticism and the rationalizing tendency in theology, and was in its inception an endeavour to bring the Church back to the principles of primitive and patristic Christianity. The last tract, No. 90, by Dr (afterwards Cardinal) Newman, evoked bitter criticism, and a part of the Tractarians (incl. Newman in 1845) entered the Roman Catholic Church.

tractate (trăk′tāt), *n.* a treatise; a tract. [late ME, t. L: m. s. *tractātus* handling, discussion, treatise]

tractile (trăk′tīl), *adj.* **1.** capable of being drawn. **2.** that may be drawn out in length; ductile. —**tractility** (trăktĭl′ĭ tĭ), *n.*

traction (trăk′shən), *n.* **1.** the act of drawing or pulling. **2.** the state of being drawn. **3.** the drawing of a body, vehicle, train, or the like along a surface, road, track, railway, waterway, etc. **4.** the adhesive friction of a body, as of a wheel on a rail. **5.** the pulling or drawing of a muscle, organ, or the like. **6.** the form or type of propulsion of a vehicle; motive power. **7.** *Obs.* attracting power or influence. [t. ML: s. *tractio* act of drawing, der. L trahere draw] —**trac′tional,** *adj.*

traction engine, a locomotive for drawing heavy loads along an ordinary road, over fields, etc., usually driven by steam.

tractive (trăk′tĭv), *adj.* serving to draw; drawing.

tractor (trăk′tə), *n.* **1.** a motor vehicle, usually fitted with deeply treaded tyres, used to draw loads and as a source of power for agricultural machinery, etc. **2.** a short motor vehicle used to draw a trailer, as in an articulated lorry. **3.** one who or that which draws or pulls. **4.** something used for drawing or pulling. **5.** Also, **tractor propeller.** a propeller mounted at the front of an aeroplane, thus exerting a pull. **6.** Also, **tractor aeroplane.** an aeroplane with a propeller so mounted. [f. obs. *tract*, v., draw (t. L: s. *tractus*, pp.) + -OR[2]]

trad (trăd), *n.* *Colloq.* **1.** traditional jazz. —*adj.* **2.** traditional; old-fashioned; conventional.

trade (trād), *n.*, *v.*, **traded, trading.** —*n.* **1.** the buying and selling, or exchanging, of commodities, either by wholesale or by retail, within a country or between countries: *domestic or foreign trade.* **2.** a purchase, sale, or exchange. **3.** a form of occupation pursued as a business or calling, as for a livelihood or profit. **4.** some line of skilled mechanical work: *the trade of a carpenter, plumber, or printer.* **5.** people engaged in a particular line of business: *a lecture of interest only to the trade.* **6.** traffic; amount of dealings: *a brisk trade in overcoats.* **7.** market: *the tourist trade.* **8.** commercial occupation (as against professional): *she could not marry him, for he was in trade.* **9.** (*pl.*) the trade winds. —*v.t.* **10.** to give in return; exchange; barter. **11.** to exchange: *to trade seats with a person.* **12. trade in,** to give in part exchange, as in a transaction. **13. trade on,** to exploit or take advantage of, esp. unfairly. —*v.i.* **14.** to carry on trade. **15.** to traffic (fol. by *in*): *to trade in wheat.* **16.** to make an exchange. —*adj.* **17.** of or pertaining to commerce, a particular trade or occupation, or trade as a whole. [ME, t. MLG: a track] —**trade′less,** *adj.*

—**Syn. 1.** TRADE, COMMERCE, TRAFFIC refer to the exchanging of commodities for other commodities or money. TRADE is the general word: *a brisk trade between the nations.* COMMERCE applies to trade on a large scale and over an extensive area: *international commerce.* TRAFFIC may refer to a particular kind of trade; but it usually suggests the travel, transportation and activity associated with or incident to trade: *the opium traffic; heavy traffic on the railways.* **3.** See **occupation. 11.** TRADE, BARGAIN, BARTER, SELL refer to exchange or transfer of ownership for some kind of material consideration. TRADE conveys the general idea, but often means to exchange articles of more or less even value: *to trade with Argentina.* BARGAIN suggests a somewhat extended period of coming to terms: *to bargain about the price of a horse.* BARTER applies esp. to exchanging goods, wares, labour, etc., with no transfer of money for the transaction: *to barter wheat for machinery.* SELL implies transferring ownership usually for a sum of money: *to sell a car.*

trade discount, a deduction from list prices made to members of the same or allied types of business, or by a wholesaler to a retailer.

trade gap, the difference between the value of a country's imports and of its exports when the former is a larger figure.

trade-in (trād′ĭn′), *n.* **1.** goods given in whole or, usually, part payment of a purchase. —*adj.* **2.** of or pertaining to such goods, or to such a method of payment.

trademark (trād′mäk′), *n.* the name, symbol, figure, letter, word, or mark adopted and used by a manufacturer or merchant in order to designate the goods he manufactures or sells, and to distinguish them from those manufactured or sold by others. Any mark entitled to registration under the provisions of a statute is a trademark.

trade name, **1.** the name or style under which a firm does business. **2.** a word or phrase used in trade whereby a business or enterprise or a particular class of goods is designated, but which is not technically a trademark, either because it is not susceptible of exclusive appropriation as a trademark or because it is not affixed to goods sold in the market. **3.** the name by which an article or substance is known to the trade.

trade price, the price at which goods are sold to members of the same trade, or to retail dealers by wholesalers.

trader (trā′də), *n.* **1.** one who trades; a merchant or businessman. **2.** a ship employed in trade.

trade reference, **1.** an individual or company in business to which one is referred for information concerning an applicant's credit standing. **2.** the reference itself.

trade route, a land or sea route habitually or commonly followed by caravans, trading ships, etc.

tradescantia (trā′dĕs kăn′shyə), *n.* any plant of the genus *Tradescantia* (family *Commelinaceae*); a spiderwort (def. 1). [NL; named after John *Tradescant*, gardener to Charles I]

trade school, a type of school for giving instruction in a trade or trades.

tradesman (trādz′mən), *n.*, *pl.* **-men. 1.** a man engaged in trade. **2.** a shopkeeper. **3.** a craftsman. **4.** one who calls on private houses to deliver goods. —**tradeswoman** (trādz′wŏŏm′ən), *n.fem.*

tradespeople (trādz′pē′pl), *n.pl.* **1.** people engaged in trade. **2.** shopkeepers collectively. Also, **tradesfolk** (trādz′fōk′).

Trades Union Congress, a voluntary organization of British trade unions enabling them to meet to consider matters of common concern, with authority to promote common action and also to discipline its members (affiliated unions). *Abbrev.*: T.U.C.

trade union, an organization of employees for mutual aid and protection, and for dealing collectively with employers. Also, **trades union.**

trade unionism, 1. the system, methods, or practice of trade or labour unions. **2.** trade unions collectively. **3.** advocacy of the general adoption of trade unions.

trade unionist, 1. a member of a trade union. **2.** one who favours trade unions.

trade wind, 1. one of the winds prevailing over the oceans from about 30° north latitude to about 30° south latitude, and blowing from north-east to south-west in the Northern Hemisphere, and from south-east to north-west in the Southern Hemisphere towards the equator. **2.** *Archaic.* a wind that blows in one regular course, or continually in the same direction.

trading certificate, a licence without which a public company may not start to trade.

trading estate, an industrial area consisting of factories built or financed by the government or local authority.

trading post, a general store for carrying on trade in an unsettled or thinly settled region.

trading stamp, a stamp with a certain value given as a premium by a seller to a customer, specified quantities of these stamps being exchangeable for various articles when presented to the issuers of the stamps.

tradition (trə dĭsh′ən), *n.* **1.** the handing down of statements, beliefs, legends, customs, etc., from generation to generation, esp. by word of mouth or by practice: *a story that has come down to us by popular tradition.* **2.** that which is so handed down: *the traditions of the Eskimos.* **3.** *Theol.* **a.** (among the Jews) an unwritten body of laws and doctrines, or any one of them, held to have been received from Moses and handed down orally from generation to generation. **b.** (among Christians) a body of teachings, or any one of them, held to have been delivered by Christ and His apostles but not committed to writing. **4.** *Law.* the act of handing over something to another, esp. in a formal legal manner; delivery; transfer. [ME, t. L: s. *trāditio* delivery, handing down]

traditional (trə dĭsh′ə nəl), *adj.* **1.** pertaining to tradition. **2.** handed down by tradition. **3.** in accordance with tradition. **4.** *Jazz.* **a.** of the style of music played in New Orleans *c.* 1900–20, characterized by extensive improvisation within a set instrumental framework. **b.** of a modern imitation of this style. Also, **traditionary** (trə-dĭsh′ə nə rĭ). **—tradi′tionally,** *adv.*

traditionalism (trə dĭsh′ə nə lĭz′əm), *n.* **1.** adherence to tradition as authority, esp. in matters of religion. **2.** a system of philosophy according to which all knowledge of religious truth is derived from divine revelation and received by traditional instruction. **—tradi′tionalist,** *n., adj.* **—tradi′tionalis′tic,** *adj.*

traditive (trăd′ĭ tĭv), *adj.* traditional. [f. TRADIT(ION) + -IVE]

traditor (trăd′ĭ tə), *n.* an early Christian who betrayed his fellows at the time of the Roman persecutions. [ME, t. L: traitor, betrayer]

traduce (trə dyōōs′), *v.t.*, **-duced, -ducing.** to speak evil or maliciously and falsely of; slander, calumniate, or malign: *to traduce someone's character.* [t. L: m. s. *trādūcere* transport, disgrace] **—traduc′er,** *n.* **—traduc′-ingly,** *adv.*

traducianism (trə dyōō′shə nĭz′əm), *n. Theol.* **1.** the doctrine that a man's soul is born of his parents with his body, and hence inherits their characteristics. **2.** the teaching that original sin is transmitted at birth from parent to child. **—tradu′cianist,** *n., adj.* **—tradu′-cianis′tic,** *adj.*

Trafalgar (trə făl′gə; *Sp.* trä fäl-gär′), *n.* **Cape,** a cape on the SW coast of Spain, W of Gibraltar: British naval victory under Nelson over the French and Spanish fleets 1805.

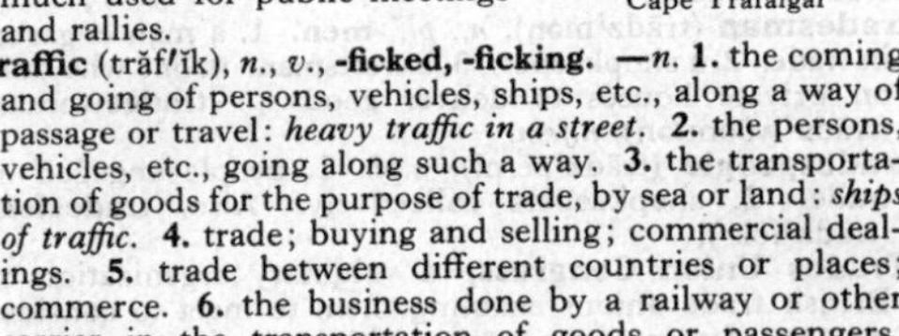

Cape Trafalgar

Trafalgar Square, a square in central London containing a columnar monument to Nelson; much used for public meetings and rallies.

traffic (trăf′ĭk), *n., v.*, **-ficked, -ficking.** *—n.* **1.** the coming and going of persons, vehicles, ships, etc., along a way of passage or travel: *heavy traffic in a street.* **2.** the persons, vehicles, etc., going along such a way. **3.** the transportation of goods for the purpose of trade, by sea or land: *ships of traffic.* **4.** trade; buying and selling; commercial dealings. **5.** trade between different countries or places; commerce. **6.** the business done by a railway or other carrier in the transportation of goods or passengers. **7.** the aggregate of goods, passengers, telephone or telegraph messages, etc., handled, esp. in a given period.

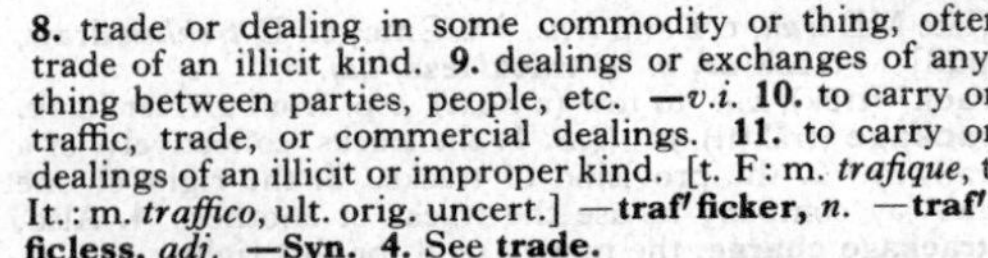

8. trade or dealing in some commodity or thing, often trade of an illicit kind. **9.** dealings or exchanges of anything between parties, people, etc. *—v.i.* **10.** to carry on traffic, trade, or commercial dealings. **11.** to carry on dealings of an illicit or improper kind. [t. F: m. *trafique*, t. It.: m. *traffico*, ult. orig. uncert.] **—traf′ficker,** *n.* **—traf′-ficless,** *adj.* **—Syn. 4.** See **trade.**

trafficator (trăf′ĭ kā′tə), *n. Motor Vehicles.* a flashing light or an illuminated arm which indicates a driver's intention to turn left or right.

traffic circle, *U.S.* a roundabout.

traffic light, (*usually pl.*) one of a set of coloured lights used to direct or control road traffic at crossings, junctions, etc.

tragacanth (trăg′ə kănth′), *n.* **1.** a mucilaginous substance derived from various low, spiny, Asiatic shrubs of the genus *Astragalus*, esp. *A. gummifer*, used to impart firmness to pills and lozenges, stiffen calicoes, etc. **2.** the plant itself. [t. L: s. *tragacantha* goat's thorn, t. Gk: m. *tragákantha*]

tragedian (trə jē′dyən), *n.* **1.** a writer of tragedy. **2.** an actor of tragedy.

tragedienne (trə jē′dĭ ĕn′), *n.* an actress of tragedy.

tragedy (trăj′ĭ dĭ), *n., pl.* **-dies. 1.** a dramatic composition of serious or sombre character, with an unhappy ending: *Shakespeare's tragedy of 'Hamlet'.* **2.** that branch of the drama which is concerned with this form of composition. **3.** the art and theory of writing and producing tragedies. **4.** any literary composition, as a novel, dealing with a sombre theme carried to a tragic conclusion. **5.** the tragic element of drama, of literature generally, or of life. **6.** a lamentable, dreadful, or fatal event or affair; a disaster or calamity. [ME *tragedie*, t. ML: m. *tragēdia*, L *tragoedia*, t. Gk: m. *tragōidia*, lit., goat song (reason for name variously explained)]

tragic (trăj′ĭk), *adj.* **1.** characteristic or suggestive of tragedy: *tragic solemnity.* **2.** mournful, melancholy, or pathetic in the extreme: *a tragic expression.* **3.** dreadful, calamitous, disastrous, or fatal: *a tragic death.* **4.** pertaining to or having the nature of tragedy: *the tragic drama.* **5.** acting in or composing tragedy. Also, **trag′ical.** [t. L: s. *tragicus*, t. Gk: m. *tragikós* of tragedy] **—trag′ically,** *adv.* **—trag′icalness,** *n.*

tragicomedy (trăj′ĭ kŏm′ĭ dĭ), *n., pl.* **-dies. 1.** a dramatic or other literary composition combining elements of both tragedy and comedy. **2.** an incident or series of incidents of mixed tragic and comic character. [t. LL: m. s. *tragicōmoedia*, r. L *tragico-cōmoedia*, f. *tragico-* TRAGIC + *cōmoedia* COMEDY] **—tragicomic** (trăj′ĭ kŏm′ĭk), **trag′icom′ical,** *adj.* **—trag′icom′ically,** *adv.*

tragion (trā′gĭ ən), *n., pl.* **tragia** (trā′gĭ ə). *Anat.* a point in the depth of the notch just over the tragus of the external ear.

tragopan (trăg′ə păn′), *n.* any of the Asiatic pheasants constituting the genus *Tragopan*, characterized by two fleshy erectile horns on the head, and wattles on the throat. [t. NL, special use of L *tragopān* fabulous Ethiopian bird, t. Gk]

tragus (trā′gəs), *n., pl.* **-gi** (-jī). *Anat.* a fleshy prominence at the front of the external opening of the ear. See diag. under **ear.** [t. LL, t. Gk: m. *trágos* hairy part of ear (lit., goat)] **—tra′gal,** *adj.*

Traherne (trə hûn′), *n.* **Thomas,** 1637?–74, English writer.

Traikov (*Bulg.* trảy′kŏf), *n.* **Georgi** (*Bulg.* gẻ ŏr′gē), born 1898, Bulgarian political leader: president since 1964.

trail (trāl), *v.t.* **1.** to drag or let drag along the ground or other surface; to draw or drag along behind. **2.** to bring or have floating after itself or oneself: *to trail clouds of dust.* **3.** to follow the track or trail of; track. **4.** to protract. **5.** to mark out, as a track. **6.** *U.S.* to beat down or make a path or way through (grass, etc.). **7.** *Colloq.* to follow along behind (another or others), as in a race. **8.** *Mil.* to carry (a rifle, etc.) in the right hand in a horizontal position, with the muzzle forwards and the butt near the ground. *—v.i.* **9.** to be drawn or dragged along the ground or some other surface, as when hanging from something moving: *her long gown trailed over the floor.* **10.** to hang down loosely from something. **11.** to stream or float from and after something moving, as dust, smoke, sparks, etc., do. **12.** to follow as if drawn along. **13.** to fish by trailing a line; to troll. **14.** to go slowly, lazily, or wearily along; straggle. **15.** to pass or extend in a straggling line. **16.** to move languidly. **17.** to pass by gradual change, as into silence; diminish (fol. by *off*): *her voice trailed off.* **18.** to fall behind the leaders, as a competitor in a race; be losing in a competition of any kind. **19.** to follow a track or scent, as of game. **20.** (of a plant) to extend itself in growth along the ground and over objects encountered, resting on these for support rather than taking root or clinging by tendrils, etc. —*n.* **21.** a path or track made across a wild region, over rough country, or the like, by the passage of men or animals: *to follow the trail.* **22.** the track, scent, or the like, left by an animal, person, or thing, esp. as followed by a hunter, hound, or other pursuer. **23.** something that is trailed or that trails behind, as the train of a skirt or robe. **24.** a stream of dust, smoke, light, people, vehicles, etc., behind something moving. **25.** *Astron.* **a.** a long bright tail seen in the sky in the wake of certain meteors. **b.** the trace left on a stationary photographic plate by a star during a long exposure. **26.** *Ordn.* that part of a guncarriage which rests on the ground when the piece is unlimbered. **27.** the act of trailing. [ME *traile(n)*, t. AF: m. *trailler* trail, OF tow (a boat), der. *traille* towrope, g. L *trāgula* dragnet, der. *trahere* draw, drag] —**trail′less,** *adj.* —**Syn. 21.** See **path.**

trailer (trā′lə), *n.* **1.** one who or that which trails. **2.** a vehicle drawn by another vehicle. **3.** *Films.* an advertisement for a forthcoming film, usually consisting of extracts from it. **4.** a trailing plant. **5.** *U.S.* a caravan.

trailing arbutus, arbutus (def. 2).

trailing edge, *Aeron.* the rear edge of a propeller blade or aerofoil.

trail rope, 1. a guide rope on a balloon. **2.** *Mil.* a prolonge.

train (trān), *n.* **1.** *Railways.* **a.** a set of carriages or wagons, whether self-propelled or connected to a locomotive. **b.** such a series without any motive power. **c.** a railway locomotive. **2.** a line or procession of persons, vehicles, etc., travelling together. **3.** *Mil.* an aggregation of vehicles, animals, and men accompanying an army to carry supplies, baggage, ammunition, etc. **4.** a series or row of objects or parts. **5.** *Mach.* a series of connected parts, as wheels and pinions, through which motion is transmitted. **6.** order, esp. proper order: *matters were in good train.* **7.** something that is drawn along; a trailing part. **8.** an elongated part of a skirt or dress trailing behind on the ground. **9.** a trail or stream of something from a moving object. **10.** a line or succession of persons or things following after. **11.** a body of followers or attendants; a retinue. **12.** a succession or series of proceedings, events, circumstances, etc. **13.** a succession of connected ideas; a course of reasoning: *to lose one's train of thought.* **14.** the aftermath; the events proceeding from an event. **15.** proper sequence; order: *putting matters in train.* **16.** *Astron.* a trail (def. 25a) or the tail of a comet. **17.** a line of combustible material, as gunpowder, for leading fire to an explosive charge. **18.** *Physics.* a succession of wave cycles, pulses, or the like, esp. one caused by a periodic disturbance of short duration. —*v.t.* **19.** to subject to discipline and instruction; educate; drill. **20.** to make proficient by instruction and practice, as in some art, profession, or work: *to train soldiers.* **21.** to make (a person, etc.) fit by proper exercise, diet, etc., as for some athletic feat or contest. **22.** to discipline and instruct (an animal) to perform specified action. **23.** to treat or manipulate so as to bring into some desired form, position, direction, etc. **24.** *Hort.* to bring (a plant, branch, etc.) into a particular shape or position, by bending, pruning, or the like. **25.** to bring to bear on some object or point, aim, or direct, as a firearm, a camera, a telescope, the glance, etc. —*v.i.* **26.** to give the discipline and instruction, drill, practice, etc., designed to impart proficiency or efficiency. **27.** to undergo discipline and instruction, drill, etc. **28.** to get oneself into condition by exercise, etc. **29.** to travel by train. [ME, t. OF: m. *tra(h)iner*, v., der. L *trahere* draw] —**train′able,** *adj.* —**train′er,** *n.* —**train′less,** *adj.*

trainband (trān′bănd′), *n. Hist.* one of the trained bands or forces of citizen soldiery organized in London and elsewhere in the 16th, 17th, and 18th centuries.

trainbearer (trān′bĕə′rə), *n.* one who holds up a train, as of a robe, cloak, or dress, in ceremonies, to prevent it from trailing on the ground.

trainee (trā nē′), *n.* **1.** one receiving training. —*adj.* **2.** receiving training: *a trainee designer.*

train ferry, a ferry designed to carry railway carriages and their passengers.

training (trā′nĭng), *n.* **1.** the development in oneself or another of certain skills, habits, and attitudes. **2.** the resulting condition. **3. in training, a.** undergoing such discipline. **b.** physically fit, as a result of training. **4. out of training,** physically unfit. —**Syn. 1.** See **education.**

training college, a college providing post-secondary education in specified skills, usually associated with a professional qualification or vocation, as teaching.

training school, 1. a school for giving training in some art, profession, or line of work. **2.** an institution for the reformation of juvenile delinquents.

training ship, a ship equipped for training boys in seamanship, as for naval service.

train oil, oil obtained by boiling, from the blubber of whales, or from seals, fishes, etc. [f. *train* (now obs.), earlier *trane* train oil (t. MLG or MD; appar. special use of MLG *trāne* tear, drop, c. G *Träne*) + OIL]

trainsick (trān′sĭk′), *adj.* made sick by the motion of riding in a train. —**train′sick′ness,** *n.*

trainspotter (trān′spŏt′ə), *n.* See **spotter** (def. 4).

traipse (trāps), *v.i.*, **traipsed, traipsing.** *Colloq.* **1.** to walk so as to be, or having become, tired; trudge. **2.** to walk (about) aimlessly; gad about. Also, **trapes.** [origin. uncert; ? akin to TRAMP]

trait (trā; trāt), *n.* **1.** a distinguishing feature or quality; characteristic: *bad traits of character.* **2.** *Rare.* a stroke or touch. [late ME, t. F: draught, g. L *tractus*]

traitor (trā′tə), *n.* **1.** one who betrays a person, a cause, or any trust. **2.** one who betrays his country by violating his allegiance; one guilty of treason. [ME, t. OF: m. *traitre*, g. L *trāditor* betrayer] —**traitress** (trā′trĭs), *n.fem.*

traitorous (trā′tə rəs, -trəs), *adj.* **1.** having the character of a traitor; treacherous; perfidious. **2.** characteristic of a traitor. **3.** having the nature of treason: *a traitorous action.* —**trai′torously,** *adv.* —**trai′torousness,** *n.*

Trajan (trā′jən), *n.* (*Marcus Ulpius Nerva Trajanus*), A.D. 53?–117, Roman emperor A.D. 98–117.

trajectory (trə jĕk′tə rĭ), *n.*, *pl.* **-ries. 1.** the curve described by a projectile in its flight. **2.** the path described by a body moving under the action of given forces. **3.** *Geom.* a curve or surface which cuts all the curves or surfaces of a given system at a constant angle. [t. ML: m. s. *trājectōrius*, adj., casting over]

Tralee (trə lē′), *n.* a seaport in SW Ireland: the county town of Kerry. 10,714 (1961).

tram[1] (trăm), *n.*, *v.*, **trammed, tramming.** —*n.* **1.** a passenger vehicle running on a tramway, having flanged wheels and usually powered by electricity taken by a current collector from an overhead conductor wire. **2.** a wheeled truck or car on which loads are transported in mines. **3.** the vehicle or cage of an overhead carrier. —*v.t.* **4.** to travel or convey by tram. —*v.i.* **5.** to travel by tram. [t. MLG or MD: m. *trame* beam, rung, etc.] —**tram′less,** *adj.*

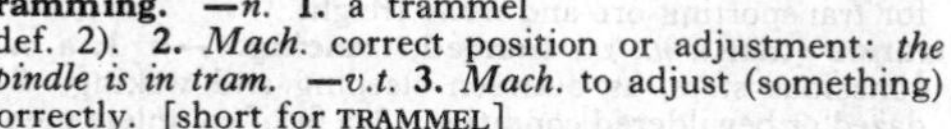

Tram[1]

tram[2] (trăm), *n.*, *v.*, **trammed, tramming.** —*n.* **1.** a trammel (def. 2). **2.** *Mach.* correct position or adjustment: *the spindle is in tram.* —*v.t.* **3.** *Mach.* to adjust (something) correctly. [short for TRAMMEL]

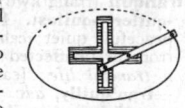

tram[3] (trăm), *n.* silk yarn of two or more strands or weft. [t. F: m. *trame*, t. L: m. *trāma* weft]

tramcar (trăm′kä′), *n.* **1.** a tram (def. 1). **2.** *Mining.* a car of various design for ore haulage on a mine railway system, esp. underground.

tramline (trăm′līn′), *n.* **1.** (*usually pl.*) the track on which trams run. **2.** one of the rails of such track. **3.** the route of a tram. **4.** (*pl.*) *Tennis, etc.* the outer marking lines of a tennis court, etc.

trammel (trăm′əl), *n.*, *v.*, **-melled, -melling** or (*U.S.*) **-meled, -meling.** —*n.* **1.** (*usually pl.*) anything that impedes or hinders free action; a restraint: *the trammels of custom.* **2.** an instrument for describing ellipses. **3.** a trammel net. **4.** a fowling net. **5.** a contrivance hung in a fireplace to support pots, kettles, etc., over the fire. **6.** a shackle, esp. one for teaching a horse to amble. —*v.t.* **7.** to involve or hold in trammels; hamper; restrain. **8.** to catch or entangle in or as in a net. [ME *tramail*, t. OF: net with three layers of meshes, g. LL *tremaculum*, f. L: *trē(s)* three + m. *macula* mesh] —**tram′meller,** *n.*

Trammel (def. 2)

trammel net, a three-layered net, the middle layer of which is fine-meshed, the others coarse-meshed, so that fish attempting to pass through the net will become entangled in one or more of the meshes.

tramontana (trăm′ŏn tä′nə), *n.* a cool, dry wind which blows down from the mountains in the Mediterranean region. [It.]

tramontane (trə mŏn′tān), *adj.* **1.** being or situated beyond the mountains, orig., beyond the Alps as viewed from Italy. **2.** pertaining to the other side of the mountains. **3.** foreign; barbarous. —*n.* **4.** one who lives beyond the mountains (orig. applied by the Italians to the peoples beyond the Alps, and by the latter to the Italians). **5.** a foreigner; a barbarian. [ME, t. It.: m. *tramontano*, g. L *transmontānus*, f. *trans* across + s. *mons* mountain + *-ānus* -AN]

tramp (trămp), *v.i.* **1.** to tread or walk with a firm, heavy, resounding step. **2.** to tread heavily or trample (fol. by *on* or *upon*): *to tramp on a person's toes.* **3.** to walk steadily; march; trudge. **4.** to go about as a vagabond or tramp. **5.** to make a voyage on a tramp (def. 19). **6.** *U.S.* to hike. —*v.t.* **7.** to tramp or walk heavily or steadily through or over. **8.** to traverse on foot: *tramp the streets.* **9.** to tread or trample underfoot. **10.** to travel over as a tramp. **11.** to run (a vessel) as a tramp (def. 19). —*n.* **12.** the act of tramping. **13.** a firm, heavy, resounding tread. **14.** the sound made. **15.** a long, steady walk; trudge. **16.** a walking excursion or expedition. **17.** a person who travels about on foot from place to place, esp. a vagabond living on occasional jobs or gifts of money or food. **18.** *Slang.* a promiscuous woman; a whore. **19.** a cargo boat which does not run regularly between fixed ports, but goes wherever shippers desire. [ME *trampe(n)*, c. LG *trampen* stamp] —**tramp′er,** *n.*

tram pinch. See **pinch** (def. 26).

trample (trăm′pl), *v.*, **-pled, -pling,** *n.* —*v.i.* **1.** to tread or step heavily and noisily; stamp. **2.** to tread heavily, roughly, or crushingly (fol. by *on, upon,* etc.), esp. repeatedly. **3.** to treat with contempt. **4.** to act in a harsh, domineering, or cruel way, as if treading roughly (fol. by *on, upon,* etc.): *to trample on an oppressed people.* —*v.t.* **5.** to tread heavily, roughly, or carelessly on or over; tread underfoot, etc. **6.** to treat with contempt. **7.** to domineer harshly over; crush: *to trample one's employees.* **8.** to put, force, reduce, etc., by trampling: *to trample out a fire.* —*n.* **9.** the act or sound of trampling. [ME, freq. of TRAMP, c. G *trampeln*] —**tram′pler,** *n.*

trampoline (trăm′pə lĭn, -lēn′), *n.* a sheet of canvas attached by resilient cords to a horizontal frame several feet above the floor: used by acrobats and gymnasts as a springboard in tumbling. [It.: springboard]

tramp steamer, a tramp (def. 19).

tramroad (trăm′rōd′), *n. Mining.* a tracked road within a mine for ore trucks.

tramway (trăm′wā′), *n.* **1.** usually, a system of grooved tracks laid in urban streets, forming routes for the conveyance of passengers in trams. **2.** such a system, together with the cars and other equipment. **3.** the company owning or operating it. **4.** an early type of railway, consisting of a crude track of wooden rails, or wooden rails capped with metal treads. **5.** *Mining.* **a.** a track (usually elevated) or roadway for mine haulage. **b.** an overhead cable system for transporting ore and mine freight.

trance (trăns), *n.*, *v.*, **tranced, trancing.** —*n.* **1.** a half-conscious state, as between sleeping and waking. **2.** a dazed or bewildered condition. **3.** a fit of complete mental absorption or deep musing. **4.** an unconscious, cataleptic, or hypnotic condition. **5.** *Spiritualism.* a temporary state in which a medium, with suspension of personal consciousness, is controlled by an intelligence from without and used as a means of communication, as from the dead. —*v.t.* **6.** to put in a trance. [ME, t. OF: m. *transe* passage, esp. from life to death, deadly suspense or fear, der. *transir* go across, pass over, t. L: m. *transīre*] —**trance′like′,** *adj.*

tranche (tränch), *n. Finance.* an additional block of stock, as bonds, etc., supplementary to an already existing issue. [t. F: slice]

tranquil (trăng′kwĭl), *adj.*, **-quiller, -quillest** or (*U.S.*) **-quiler, -quilest. 1.** free from commotion or tumult; peaceful; quiet; calm: *a tranquil country place.* **2.** free from or unaffected by disturbing emotions; unruffled: *a tranquil life.* [earlier *tranquill*, t. L: s. *tranquillus*] —**tran′quilly,** *adv.* —**tran′quilness,** *n.* —**Syn. 1.** See **peaceful.** —**Ant. 1.** agitated.

tranquillity (trăng kwĭl′ĭ tĭ), *n.* **1.** the state of being tranquil; calmness; peacefulness; quiet; serenity; composure. **2.** (*caps*) **Sea of,** a plain, *Mare Tranquillitatis*, in the first quadrant of the face of the moon: site of man's first landing on the moon, July 20th, 1969. Also, *U.S.*, **tranquility.**

tranquillize (trăng′kwĭ līz′), *v.t., v.i.*, **-lized, -lizing.** to make or become tranquil. Also, **tranquillise;** *U.S.*, **tranquilize.** —**tran′quilliza′tion,** *n.*

tranquillizer (trăng′kwĭ lī′zə), *n.* **1.** a drug that has a sedative or calming effect without inducing sleep. **2.** one who or that which tranquillizes. Also, **tranquilliser;** *U.S.*, **tranquilizer.**

trans-, 1. a prefix meaning 'across', 'beyond', freely applied in geographical terms (*transcontinental, trans-Siberian*), also found attached to stems not used as words, and in figurative meanings, e.g., *transpire, transport, transcend.* **2.** *Chem.* See **cis-trans isomerism.** [t. L, comb. form of *trans*, prep.]

trans., 1. transactions. **2.** transferred. **3.** transitive. **4.** translated. **5.** translation. **6.** translator. **7.** transparent. **8.** transpose.

transact (trăn zăkt′), *v.t.* **1.** to carry through (affairs, business, etc.) to a conclusion or settlement. **2.** to perform. —*v.i.* **3.** to carry through affairs or negotiations. [t. L: s. *transactus*, pp., carried out, driven through, accomplished] —**transac′tor,** *n.* —**Syn. 1.** See **perform.**

transaction (trăn zăk′shən), *n.* **1.** the act of transacting. **2.** the fact of being transacted. **3.** an instance or process of transacting something. **4.** that which is transacted; an affair; a piece of business. **5.** (*pl.*) **a.** records of the doings of a learned society or the like. **b.** reports of papers read, addresses delivered, discussions, etc., at the meetings. [late ME, t. L: s. *transactio* act of carrying out] —**transac′tional,** *adj.*

transalpine (trănz′ăl′pīn), *adj.* **1.** across or beyond the Alps, esp. as viewed from Italy. **2.** passing through or over the Alps. **3.** pertaining to people or places beyond the Alps. —*n.* **4.** a native or inhabitant of a country beyond the Alps.

transatlantic (trăn′zət lăn′tĭk), *adj.* **1.** passing or extending across the Atlantic: *a transatlantic liner.* **2.** beyond, or on the other side of, the Atlantic.

transcalent (trăns kā′lənt), *adj.* pervious to heat; permitting the passage of heat. [f. TRANS- + s. L *calens*, ppr., being hot] —**transcalency** (trăns kā′lən sĭ), *n.*

Transcaucasia (trăns′kô kā′zyə), *n.* a region in the SW Soviet Union in Asia, consisting of that part of Caucasia S of the Caucasus Mountains, formerly comprising (1927–36) the **Transcaucasian Socialist Soviet Republic,** which included the republics of Armenia, Azerbaijan, and Georgia. —**Transcaucasian** (trăns′kô kā′zyən), *adj., n.*

transceiver (trăn sē′və), *n.* a radio set capable of both transmitting and receiving.

transcend (trăn sĕnd′), *v.t.* **1.** to go or be above or beyond (a limit, something with limits, etc.); surpass or exceed. **2.** to go beyond in elevation, excellence, extent, degree, etc.; surpass, excel, or exceed. **3.** *Theol.* (of the Deity) to be above and independent of (the universe). —*v.i.* **4.** to be transcendent; excel. [ME, t. L: s. *transcendere* climb over or beyond]

transcendence (trăn sĕn′dəns), *n.* **1.** the state, quality, or fact of being transcendent. **2.** transcendent character. Also, **transcend′ency.**

transcendent (trăn sĕn′dənt), *adj.* **1.** transcending; going beyond ordinary limits; surpassing or extraordinary. **2.** superior or supreme. **3.** *Theol.* **a.** being beyond matter, and having a continuing existence therefore outside the created world. **b.** (of God) simultaneously concerned with the whole of the universe. **4.** *Philos.* **a.** Also, **transcendental.** (in scholastic philosophy) denoting that which is above the categories of Aristotle. **b.** (in Kantian philosophy) denoting that which is given neither as an *a priori* nor as an *a posteriori* element in experience, and so is beyond the Kantian categories of thought (contrasted with *transcendental*). —**transcend′ently,** *adv.* —**transcend′entness,** *n.*

transcendental (trăn′sĕn dĕn′tl), *adj.* **1.** transcendent, surpassing, or superior. **2.** transcending ordinary or common experience, thought, or belief; extraordinary; supernatural; abstract or metaphysical. **3.** idealistic, lofty, or extravagant. **4.** speculative; obscure. **5.** *Philos.* **a.** (in scholastic philosophy) transcendent (def. 4a). **b.** (in Kantian philosophy) denoting knowledge which is concerned less with the objects known than with the mode by which they are known, i.e., mainly with the presuppositions of knowledge (contrasted with *transcendent*). **c.** denoting certain theories that explain knowledge as partly determined by the process of knowing. **6.** *Maths.* not producible by the algebraic operations of addition, subtraction, multiplication, division, and the extraction of roots, each repeated only a finite number of times. —*n.* **7.** *Maths.* a transcendental number, such as π or e. **8.** (*pl.*) (in scholastic philosophy) categories which have universal application as being, one, true, good. —**tran′scenden′tally,** *adv.*

transcendentalism (trăn′sĕn dĕn′tə lĭz′əm), *n.* **1.** transcendental character, thought, or language. **2.** transcendental philosophy; any philosophy based upon the doctrine that the principles of reality are to be discovered by the study of the processes of thought, or emphasizing the intuitive and spiritual above the empirical (associated with Kant and subsequent German idealism, especially Schelling, and in America, with Emerson). **3.** that which is vague and elusive in philosophy. —**tran′scenden′talist,** *n., adj.*

transcontinental (trănz′kŏn′tĭ nĕn′tl), *adj.* **1.** passing or extending across a continent: *a transcontinental railway.* **2.** on the other side of a continent.

transcribe (trăn skrīb′), *v.t.*, **-scribed, -scribing. 1.** to make a copy of in writing: *to transcribe a document.* **2.** to reproduce in writing or print as from speech. **3.** to write out in other characters; transliterate: *to transcribe one's shorthand notes.* **4.** *Radio.* to make a recording of (a programme, announcement, etc.) for broadcasting. **5.** *Music.* to arrange (a composition) for a medium other than that for which it was originally written. [t. L: m. s. *transcrībere* copy off] —**transcrib′er,** *n.*

transcript (trăn′skrĭpt), *n.* **1.** something transcribed or made by transcribing; a written copy. **2.** a reproduction in writing or print. **3.** a form of something as rendered from one alphabet or language into another. **4.** *Law.* an official written copy of proceedings in a court. [ME, t. L: s. *transcriptum*, lit., thing copied, pp. (neut.) of *transcribere* TRANSCRIBE; r. ME *transcrit*, t. OF]

transcription (trăn skrĭp′shən), *n.* **1.** the act of transcribing. **2.** a transcript; a copy. **3.** *Music.* **a.** the arrangement of a composition for a medium other than that for which it was originally written. **b.** a composition so arranged. **4.** *U.S.* a gramophone record. See **transcribe** (def. 4). —**transcriptive** (trăn skrĭp′tĭv), *adj.*

transcrystalline fracture (trănz′krĭs′tə līn′), *Metall.* the fracture of a metal in which the line of failure passes through the crystals rather than round their boundaries. Cf. **intercrystalline fracture.**

transducer (trănz dyōō′sə), *n.* *Physics.* any device which receives energy from one medium or transmission system, and supplies related energy to another medium or transmission system. [var. of TRADUCER. See TRADUCE]

transect (trăn sĕkt′), *v.t.* to cut across; dissect transversely. —**transec′tion,** *n.*

transenna (trăn sĕn′ə), *n.* a lattice or openwork screen, generally of marble, enclosing a shrine in early Christian churches. [t. L: lit., latticework]

transept (trăn′sĕpt), *n.* *Archit.* **1.** the transverse portion (or, occasionally, portions) of a cruciform church. See diag. under **basilica. 2.** either of the two armlike divisions of this, one on each side of the crossing. [t. Anglo-L: s. *transēptum*, f. L: *trans* across + *sēptum* enclosure] —**transep′tal,** *adj.* —**transep′tally,** *adv.*

transeunt (trăn′sĭ ənt), *adj.* *Philos.* passing outwards; producing an effect outside itself (usually descriptive of activity, and then contrasted with *immanent*). [t. L: s. *transiens*, ppr., going across]

trans-Europe (trănz′yōōə′rəp), *adj.* crossing or extending across Europe: *the trans-Europe express.*

transf., transferred.

transfer (*v.* trăns fû′; *n.* trăns′fû), *v.*, **-ferred, -ferring,** *n.* —*v.t.* **1.** to convey or remove from one place, person, etc., to another. **2.** *Law.* to make over or convey: *to transfer a title to land.* **3.** to convey (a drawing, design, pattern, etc.) from one surface to another. —*v.i.* **4.** to transfer oneself. **5.** to be transferred. **6.** to change from one bus, train, or the like, to another, as on a transfer (def. 12). **7.** (of a professional football player) to change from one club to another. —*n.* **8.** the means or system of transferring. **9.** the act of transferring. **10.** the fact of being transferred. **11.** a point or place for transferring. **12.** a ticket, issued with or without extra charge, entitling a passenger to continue his journey on another bus, train, or the like; a transfer-ticket. **13.** a drawing, pattern, etc., which may be transferred to a surface, esp. by direct contact. **14.** (of a football player) the fact or act of transferring or being transferred. **15.** *Law.* a conveyance, by sale, gift, or otherwise, of real or personal property, to another. **16.** *Finance.* the act of having the ownership of a stock or registered bond transferred upon the books of the issuing company or its agent. **17.** *Finance.* a deed completed when stocks and shares change hands, which is registered with the company issuing the shares. [ME *transferre(n)*, t. L: m. *transferre* carry across] —**transfer′able,** *adj.* —**transfer′abil′ity,** *n.*

transferable vote, a vote which can be transferred to a second choice if the candidate first voted for should be out of the running.

transferase (trăns′fə rās′), *n.* *Biochem.* any enzyme that catalyses the transfer of a chemical group from one substrate to another.

transferee (trăns′fə rē′), *n.* **1.** one who is transferred or removed, as from one place to another. **2.** *Law.* one to whom a transfer is made, as of property.

transference (trăns′fə rəns, -frəns), *n.* **1.** the act or process of transferring. **2.** the fact of being transferred. **3.** *Psychol.* **a.** reproduction of emotions, originally experienced for the most part in childhood, towards a person other than the one towards whom they were initially experienced. **b.** displacement (def. 6).

transferential (trăns′fə rĕn′shəl), *adj.* pertaining to or involving transference.

transfer fee, a sum of money paid by one football club to another when a player is transferred between them.

transfer list, a list made by a football club of players to be transferred.

transferor (trăns fû′rə), *n.* *Law.* one who makes a transfer, as of property.

transfer-paper (trăns′fû pā′pə), *n.* *Print.* a specially prepared paper formerly used to transfer images from letterpress or engraved surfaces to lithographic surfaces. Images could also be drawn direct on to transfer-paper and transferred to lithographic surfaces.

transferrer (trăns fû′rə), *n.* one who or that which transfers.

transfer-ticket (trăns′fû tĭk′ĭt), *n.* a transfer (def. 12).

transfiguration (trăns′fĭg′yōō rā′shən), *n.* **1.** the act of transfiguring. **2.** the state of being transfigured. **3.** (*cap.*) the change in the appearance of Christ when glorified in the presence of three chosen disciples. Matt. 17:1–9. **4.** (*cap.*) the occasion when this happened. **5.** (*cap.*) the church festival commemorating this, observed on August 6th.

transfigure (trăns fĭg′ə), *v.t.*, **-ured, -uring. 1.** to change in outward form or appearance; transform, change, or alter. **2.** to change so as to glorify, exalt, or idealize. [ME, t. L: m. s. *transfigūrāre*] —**transfig′urement,** *n.*

transfix (trăns fĭks′), *v.t.* **1.** to pierce through, as with a pointed weapon, or as the weapon does. **2.** to fix fast with or on something sharp; thrust through. **3.** to make motionless with amazement, terror, etc. [t. L: s. *transfixus*, pp., pierced, transfixed] —**transfixion** (trăns fĭk′shən), *n.*

transform (trăns fôm′), *v.t.* **1.** to change in form; change to something of a different form; metamorphose. **2.** to change in appearance, condition, nature, or character, esp. completely or extensively. **3.** to change (one substance, element, or nuclide) into another. **4.** *Elect.* to change the voltage and current characteristics of (a circuit) by the use of a transformer. **5.** *Maths.* to change the form of (a figure, expression, etc.) without in general changing the value. **6.** *Physics.* to change (one form of energy) into another. —*v.i.* **7.** to change in form, appearance, or character; become transformed. [ME, t. L: s. *transformāre* change form] —**transform′able,** *adj.* —**transformative** (trăns-fô′mə tĭv), *adj.*

—**Syn. 1.** TRANSFORM, CONVERT mean to change one thing into another. TRANSFORM suggests changing from one form, appearance, structure, or type to another: *to transform oil into gas.* CONVERT suggests so changing the characteristics as to change the use or purpose: *to convert a barn into a house.*

transformation (trăns′fə mā′shən), *n.* **1.** the act of transforming. **2.** the state of being transformed. **3.** change in form, appearance, nature, or character. **4.** *Physics.* the change of one nuclide or element into another. **5.** *Theat.* Also, **transformation scene.** a seemingly miraculous change in the appearance of scenery or actors in view of the audience. **6.** *Gram., Logic.* one of a set of symbols or formulas substituted for the parts of a set or system, as the premises and conclusion of a statement, to show the functions of the parts and their relations to each other. **7.** *Obs.* a wig for a woman. —**trans′forma′tional,** *adj.*

transformational grammar, a system of analysis using transformations (def. 6) to show the relations between the constituent parts of a sentence, clause, etc.

transformer (trăns fô′mə), *n.* **1.** one who or that which transforms. **2.** *Elect.* an electric device, without continuously moving parts, which by electromagnetic induction transforms electric energy from one or more circuits to one or more circuits at the same frequency, usually with changed values of voltage and current; esp. one for transforming a comparatively small alternating current of higher voltage into a larger current of lower voltage (**step-down transformer**), or, conversely, a current of lower voltage into one of higher voltage (**step-up transformer**).

transformism (trăns fô′mĭz′əm), *n.* *Biol.* **1.** the doctrine of gradual transformation of one species into another by descent with modification through many generations. **2.** such transformation itself. **3.** any doctrine or instance of evolution. —**transform′ist,** *n.*

transfuse (trăns fyōōz′), *v.t.*, **-fused, -fusing. 1.** to pour from one container into another. **2.** to transfer or transmit as if by pouring; instil; impart. **3.** to diffuse through something; infuse. **4.** *Med.* **a.** to transfer (blood) from the veins or arteries of one person or animal into those of another. **b.** to inject, as a saline solution, into a blood vessel. [ME, t. L: m. s. *transfūsus*, pp., poured across] —**transfus′er,** *n.* —**transfus′ible,** *adj.* —**transfusive** (trăns fyōō′-sĭv), *adj.*

transfusion (trăns fyōō′zhən), *n.* **1.** the act or process of transfusing. **2.** *Med.* **a.** the transferring of blood taken from one person or animal to another, as in order to renew a depleted blood supply. **b.** the injecting of some other liquid into the veins. **3.** an act of imparting, injecting, transmitting, or the like: *a transfusion of new capital into a business.* [t. L: s. *transfūsio*]

transgress (trănz grĕs′), *v.t.* **1.** to pass over or go beyond (a limit, etc.): *to transgress the bounds of prudence.* **2.** to go beyond the limits imposed by (a law, command, etc.); violate; infringe; break. —*v.i.* **3.** to violate a law, command, etc.; offend or sin (fol. by *against*). [t. L: s. *transgressus*, pp., having stepped across] —**transgres′sive,** *adj.* —**transgres′sively,** *adv.* —**transgres′sor,** *n.*

transgression (trănz grĕsh′ən), *n.* the act of transgressing: violation of a law, command, etc.; sin.

tranship (trăn shĭp′), *v.t.*, *v.i.*, **-shipped, -shipping.** —*v.t.* **1.** to transfer from one ship or other conveyance to another. —*v.i.* **2.** to go or be taken from one ship or other conveyance to another. Also, **transship, trans-ship.** —**tranship′ment,** *n.*

transhumance (trăns hyōō′məns), *n.* the seasonal migration of livestock, and the people who tend them, between lowlands and adjacent mountains. [t. F, der. *transhumer*, t. Sp.: m. *trashumar* change ground. See TRANS-, HUMUS] —**transhum′ant,** *adj.*

transience (trăn′zĭ əns), *n.* transient state or quality. Also, **tran′siency.**

transient (trăn′zĭ ənt), *adj.* **1.** passing with time; not lasting or enduring; transitory. **2.** lasting only for a time; temporary: *transient authority.* **3.** remaining for only a short time, as a guest at a hotel. **4.** *Philos.* **a.** transeunt. **b.** (formerly) transcendent (def. 4b). —*n.* **5.** one who or that which is transient; a transient guest, boarder, or the like. [m. TRANSEUNT (with *-ie-* from L nom.)] —**tran′siently,** *adv.* —**tran′sientness,** *n.* —**Syn. 2.** See **temporary.** —**Ant. 2.** permanent.

transilient (trăn sĭl′ĭ ənt), *adj.* leaping or passing from one thing or state to another. [t. L: s. *transiliens*, ppr., leaping across] —**transil′ience,** *n.*

transilluminate (trăn′zĭ lyōō′mĭ nāt′), *v.t.*, **-nated, -nating.** **1.** to cause light to pass through. **2.** *Med.* to throw a strong light through (an organ or part) as a means of diagnosis. —**trans′illu′mina′tion,** *n.* —**trans′illu′mina′tor,** *n.*

transisthmian (trănz′ĭsth′mĭ ən), *adj.* passing or extending across an isthmus.

transistor (trăn zĭs′tə), *n.* **1.** *Electronics.* a miniature amplifying device, usually utilizing germanium, that performs nearly all the functions of, while having many advantages over, the electronic valve. **2.** *Colloq.* a transistorized radio. —*adj.* **3.** equipped with transistors, as a radio or gramophone. [f. TRANS(FER) + (RES)ISTOR]

transistorize (trăn zĭs′tə rīz′), *v.t.*, **-rized, -rizing.** *Electronics.* to equip with or convert to a circuit employing transistors. Also, **transistorise.**

transit (trăn′sĭt, -zĭt), *n.*, *v.*, **-sited, -siting.** —*n.* **1.** the act or fact of passing across or through; passage from one place to another. **2.** conveyance from one place to another, as of persons or goods: *the problem of rapid transit in cities.* **3.** a transition or change. **4.** *Astron.* **a.** the passage of a heavenly body across the meridian of a place or through the field of a telescope. **b.** the passage of an inferior planet (Mercury or Venus) across the disc of the sun, or of a satellite or its shadow across the face of its primary. **5.** *Survey, U.S.* a theodolite. **6. in transit,** passing through a place; staying for only a short time. —*v.t.* **7.** to pass across or through. **8.** *Survey.* to turn (the telescope of a theodolite) about its horizontal transverse axis so as to make it point in the opposite direction; reverse, invert, or plunge (the instrument). —*v.i.* **9.** to pass across or through a place or thing. [late ME, t. L: s. *transitus* act of crossing]

transition (trăn zĭsh′ən), *n.* **1.** passage from one position, state, stage, etc., to another. **2.** a passage or change of this kind. **3.** *Music.* **a.** a passing from one key to another; modulation. **b.** a brief or sudden modulation; a modulation used in passing. **c.** a passage serving as a connecting link between two more important passages. **4.** *Physics.* a change in the configuration of an atomic nucleus, either by changing to another nuclide with the emission of alpha or beta particles, or by changing its energy state with the emission of gamma rays. **5.** *Archit.* the period of change from one architectural style to another. [t. L: s. *transitio* act of going across] —**transi′tional, transitionary** (trăn zĭsh′ə nə rĭ), *adj.* —**transi′tionally,** *adv.*

transition element, *Chem.* any of several elements which occur in the middle of the long periods of the periodic table, have incomplete inner electron shells, variable valencies, and properties which generally resemble those of their horizontal neighbours in the periodic table.

transition temperature, **1.** *Chem.* the temperature at which one form of a polymorphous substance changes into another; the temperature at which both forms can coexist (**transition point**). **2.** *Physics.* the temperature at which a superconducting material becomes superconducting.

transitive (trăn′sĭ tĭv), *adj.* **1.** *Gram.* having the nature of a transitive verb. **2.** characterized by or involving transition; transitional; intermediate. **3.** passing over to or affecting something else; transeunt. —*n.* **4.** *Gram.* a transitive verb. [t. LL: m. s. *transitivus*] —**tran′sitively,** *adv.* —**tran′sitiveness,** *n.*

transitive verb, *Gram.* a verb that is regularly accompanied by a direct object.

transitory (trăn′sĭ tə rĭ, -trĭ), *adj.* **1.** passing away; not lasting, enduring, permanent or eternal. **2.** lasting for a short time; brief; transient. —**tran′sitorily,** *adv.* —**tran′sitoriness,** *n.* —**Syn. 2.** See **temporary.**

transit theodolite, *Survey.* a theodolite in which the telescope can be rotated completely around its horizontal axis.

Trans-Jordan (trănz′jô′dn), *n.* former name of **Jordan.**

Transkei (trăns′kī′), *n.* a native reserve in the Republic of South Africa, including the tribal areas of Tembuland, Pondoland, Griqualand East, and Transkei. 1,290,680 pop. (1960); 16,554 sq. mi.

transl., **1.** translated. **2.** translation.

translate (trăns lāt′, trănz-), *v.*, **-lated, -lating.** —*v.t.* **1.** to turn (something written or spoken) from one language into another: *to translate English into Spanish.* **2.** to change into another form; transform or convert. **3.** to bear, carry, or remove from one place, position, condition, etc., to another; transfer. **4.** to express in other terms; interpret; explain. **5.** *Mech.* to cause (a body) to move without rotation or angular displacement; subject to translation. **6.** *U.S. Teleg.* to retransmit or forward (a message), as by a relay. **7.** *Eccles.* **a.** to move (a bishop) from one see to another. **b.** to move (a see) from one place to another. **8.** to remove (the body of a saint) from one resting place to another, esp. a specially built shrine. **9.** to exalt in spiritual ecstasy or rapture. **10.** to convey or remove to heaven without death. —*v.i.* **11.** to practise translation. **12.** to admit of translation: *the book translates well.* [ME, t. L: m. s. *translātus*, pp., carried over] —**translat′able,** *adj.* —**translat′ableness,** *n.* —**translator** (trăns lā′tə, trănz-), *n.*

translation (trăns lā′shən, trănz-), *n.* **1.** the rendering of something into another language. **2.** a version in a different language: *a French translation of Hamlet.* **3.** conversion to a different form. **4.** the act of translating. **5.** the state of being translated; removal to another place, etc. **6.** *Mech.* motion in which all particles of a body move in straight-line paths. **7.** *U.S. Teleg.* the process of forwarding a message, as by a relay. —**transla′tional,** *adj.*

—**Syn. 2.** TRANSLATION, PARAPHRASE, VERSION refer to a rewording of something. A TRANSLATION is a rendering of the same ideas in a different language from the original: *a translation from Greek into English.* A PARAPHRASE is a free rendering of the sense of a passage in other words, usually in the same language: *a paraphrase of a poem.* A VERSION is a translation, esp. of the Bible, or else a rewriting for a particular purpose: *a new version of the theory.*

transliterate (trănz lĭt′ə rāt′), *v.t.*, **-rated, -rating.** to change (letters, words, etc.) into corresponding characters of another alphabet or language: *to transliterate the Greek X as ch.* [f. TRANS- + m. s. L *lĭterātus* lettered] —**trans′litera′tion,** *n.* —**translit′era′tor,** *n.*

translocate (trănz′lō kāt′), *v.t.*, **-cated, -cating.** to remove from one place to another; cause to change place; displace; dislocate. —**trans′loca′tion,** *n.*

translucent (trănz lōō′sənt), *adj.* **1.** transmitting light diffusely or imperfectly, as frosted glass. **2.** *Now Rare.* clear. [t. L: s. *translūcens*, ppr., shining through] —**translu′cence, translu′cency,** *n.* —**translu′cently,** *adv.* —**Syn. 1.** See **transparent.**

translucid (trănz lōō′sĭd), *adj.* translucent. —**trans′lucid′ity,** *n.*

translunary (trănz′lōō′nə rĭ), *adj.* **1.** situated beyond or above the moon; superlunary. **2.** celestial, rather than earthly. **3.** ideal; visionary.

transmarine (trănz′mə rēn′), *adj.* overseas.

transmeridional (trănz′mə rĭd′ĭ ə nəl), *adj.* crossing the meridians; running east and west.

transmigrant (trănz′mī′grənt, trănz′mĭ grənt), *n.* **1.** a person passing through a country or place on his way from his own country to a country in which he intends to settle. —*adj.* **2.** transmigrating. [t. L: s. *transmigrans*, ppr.]

transmigrate (trănz′mī grāt′), *v.*, **-grated, -grating.** —*v.i.* **1.** to remove or pass from one place to another. **2.** to migrate from one country to another in order to settle there. **3.** (of the soul) to be reborn with the same soul in another body, either immediately upon death or after a purgatorial or waiting period. —*v.t.* **4.** to cause to transmigrate, as a soul. [ME, t. L: m. s. *transmigrātus*, pp.] —**trans′migra′tor,** *n.* —**transmigratory** (trănz′mī grā′tə rĭ), *adj.*

transmigration (trănz′mī grā′shən), *n.* **1.** the act of transmigrating. **2.** the passage of a soul at death into another body; metempsychosis. [ME, t. LL: s. *transmigrātio*]

transmissible (trănz mĭs′ə bl), *adj.* capable of being transmitted. —**transmis′sibil′ity,** *n.*

transmission (trănz mĭsh′ən), *n.* **1.** the act of transmitting. **2.** the fact of being transmitted. **3.** that which is transmitted. **4.** *Mach.* **a.** the transmitting or transferring of motive force. **b.** a device for this purpose, esp. the mechanism or gearing for transmitting the power from the revolutions of the engine shaft in a motor vehicle to the driving wheels, at the varying rates of speed and direction of drive as selected in gear changes. **5.** *Radio.* the broadcasting of electromagnetic waves from the transmitting station to the receiving station. **6. a.** an instance of broadcasting a radio programme. **b.** such a programme. [t. L: s. *transmissio*] —**transmis′sive,** *adj.*

transmission factor, *Physics.* the ratio of the radiant flux transmitted by a body to the flux incident upon it; transmittance. Also, **transmittance.**

transmission line, *Elect.* the system of conductors (usually overhead) by which electromagnetic power is transmitted at high voltage from one place to another.

transmission loss, *Elect.* the power lost in a transmission line.

transmit (trănz mĭt′), *v.t.*, **-mitted, -mitting. 1.** to send over or along, as to a recipient or destination; forward, dispatch, or convey. **2.** to communicate, as information, news, etc. **3.** to pass on or hand down, as to heirs, successors, or posterity. **4.** to broadcast (a radio or television programme). **5.** *Physics.* **a.** to cause (light, heat, sound, etc.) to pass through a medium. **b.** to convey or pass along (an impulse, force, motion, etc.). **c.** to permit (light, heat, etc.) to pass through: *glass transmits light.* **6.** *Radio.* to emit (electromagnetic waves). [ME, t. L: m. s. *transmittere* send across] —**transmit′table, transmit′tible,** *adj.*
—**Syn. 1.** See **carry.**

transmittal (trănz mĭt′l), *n.* the act of transmitting (defs 1–3). Also, **transmit′tance.**

transmittance (trănz mĭt′ns), *n. Physics.* **1.** transmission factor. **2.** transmittal.

transmitter (trănz mĭt′ə), *n.* **1.** one who or that which transmits. **2.** Also, **transmitting set.** *Radio.* a device for sending electromagnetic waves; that part of the broadcasting apparatus which generates and modulates the radio frequency current and conveys it to the aerial. **3.** that part of a telephonic or telegraphic apparatus converting soundwaves or mechanical movements into corresponding electrical waves or impulses.

transmogrify (trănz mŏg′rĭ fī′), *v.t.*, **-fied, -fying.** to change as by magic; transform. [vulgar or humorous coinage] —**transmog′rifica′tion,** *n.*

transmontane (trănz mŏn′tān), *adj.* tramontane (def. 1).

transmundane (trănz′mŭn′dān), *adj.* beyond the (or this) world.

transmutation (trănz′myo͞o tā′shən), *n.* **1.** the act of transmuting. **2.** the fact or state of being transmuted. **3.** a change into another nature, substance, form, or condition. **4.** *Biol.* the transformation of one species into another. Cf. **transformism. 5.** *Physics.* the change of one element into another. **6.** *Alchemy.* the (attempted) conversion of base metals into metals of greater value, esp. into gold or silver. —**trans′muta′tional, transmutative** (trănz myo͞o′tə tĭv), *adj.*

transmute (trănz myo͞ot′), *v.t.*, **-muted, -muting.** to change from one nature, substance, or form into another; transform. [ME, t. L: m. *transmutāre*] —**transmut′able,** *adj.* —**transmut′abil′ity, transmut′ableness,** *n.* —**transmut′ably,** *adv.* —**transmut′er,** *n.*

transnormal (trănz′nô′məl), *adj.* beyond what is normal; supernormal.

transoceanic (trănz′ō′shĭ ăn′ĭk), *adj.* across, crossing, or beyond the ocean.

transom (trăn′səm), *n.* **1.** a crosspiece separating a door or the like from a window or fanlight above it. **2.** *Chiefly U.S.* a window above such a crosspiece; a fanlight. **3.** a crossbar, as of wood or stone, dividing a window horizontally. **4.** a window so divided. **5.** a lintel. **6.** any of several transverse beams or timbers fixed across the sternpost of a ship, to strengthen and give shape to the afterpart. [ME, t. L: m. *transtrum* (with loss of second *-tr-* by dissimilation)] —**tran′somed,** *adj.*

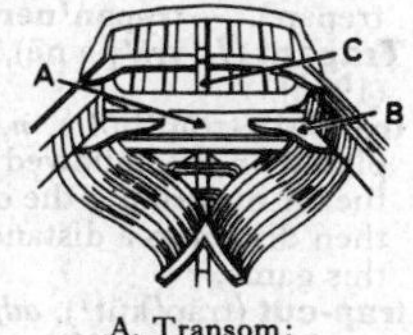

A, Transom; B, Transom knee; C, Sternpost

transonic (trăn sŏn′ĭk), *adj.* *Chiefly Aeron.* the speed at which the airflow relative to the body is subsonic in some places and supersonic in others, moving at 700–780 m.p.h. at sea-level.

transonic barrier. See **sound barrier.**

transpacific (trăns′pə sĭf′ĭk), *adj.* **1.** passing or extending across the Pacific. **2.** beyond or on the other side of, the Pacific.

transpadane (trăns′pə dān′, trăns pā′dān), *adj.* on the farther (or north) side of the river Po (from Rome). [t. L: m. s. *transpadānus*]

transparency (trăns pā′rən sĭ), *n.*, *pl.* **-cies. 1.** Also, **transpar′ence.** the property or quality of being transparent. **2.** something which is transparent; a picture, design, or the like on glass or some translucent substance, made visible by light shining through from behind. **3.** *Photog.* **a.** the fraction of the incident light transmitted by a specific photographic density. **b.** a transparent positive photographic image used for projection.

transparent (trăns pā′rənt), *adj.* **1.** having the property of transmitting rays of light through its substance so that bodies situated beyond or behind can be distinctly seen (opposed to *opaque*, and usually distinguished from *translucent*). **2.** admitting the passage of light through interstices. **3.** diaphanous. **4.** open, frank, or candid: *the man's transparent honesty.* **5.** easily seen through or understood: *transparent excuses.* **6.** manifest or obvious. **7.** *Obs.* shining through, as light. [ME, t. ML: s. *transpārens*, f. L: *trans* across + *pārens*, ppr., appearing] —**transpar′ently,** *adv.* —**transpar′entness,** *n.*
—**Syn. 1.** TRANSPARENT, TRANSLUCENT agree in describing material that light rays can pass through. That which is TRANSPARENT allows objects to be seen clearly through it: *clear water is transparent.* That which is TRANSLUCENT allows light to pass through, but diffusing it so that objects beyond are not distinctly seen: *ground glass is translucent.*

transpierce (trăns pĭəs′), *v.t.*, **-pierced, -piercing.** to pierce through; penetrate; pass through.

transpire (trăn spī′ə), *v.*, **-spired, -spiring.** —*v.i.* **1.** to occur, happen, or take place. **2.** to emit or give off waste matter, etc., through the surface, as of the body, of leaves, etc. **3.** to escape as through pores, as moisture, smell, etc. **4.** to escape from secrecy; leak out; become known. —*v.t.* **5.** to emit or give off (waste matter, watery vapour, a smell, etc.) through the surface, as of the body, of leaves, etc. [t. ML: m. s. *transpīrāre*, f. L *trans* across + *spīrāre* breathe] —**transpir′able,** *adj.* —**transpiration** (trăn′spə rā′shən), *n.* —**transpiratory** (trăn spī′ə rə tə rĭ, -trĭ), *adj.*

transplant (*v.* trăns plănt′, *n.* trăns′plănt′), *v.t.* **1.** to remove (a plant) from one place and plant it in another. **2.** *Surg.* to transfer, as an organ or a portion of tissue, from one part of the body to another or from one person or animal to another. **3.** to remove from one place to another. **4.** to bring (a colony, etc.) from one country to another for settlement. —*v.i.* **5.** to be capable of being transplanted. —*n.* **6.** a transplanting. **7.** something transplanted. **8.** a seedling which has been transplanted once or several times. [late ME, t. LL: s. *transplantāre*] —**transplant′able,** *adj.* —**trans′planta′tion,** *n.* —**transplant′er,** *n.*

transpolar (trănz′pō′lə), *adj.* across the (north or south) pole or polar region.

transponder (trăn spŏn′də), *n.* a transmitter controlled by a receiver so that it transmits information in response to interrogating signals.

transponible (trăns pō′nə bl), *adj.* capable of being transposed. [f. s. L *transpōnere* transpose + -IBLE] —**transpo′nibil′ity,** *n.*

transpontine (trănz′pŏn′tĭn), *adj.* **1.** across or beyond a bridge. **2.** on the southern side of the Thames. [f. TRANS- + s. L *pons* bridge + -INE[1]]

transport (*v.* trăns pôt′; *n.*, *adj.* trăns′pôt), *v.t.* **1.** to carry or convey from one place to another. **2.** to carry away by strong emotion. **3.** to carry into banishment, as a criminal to a penal colony. **4.** *Obs.* to kill. —*n.* **5.** the act or method of transporting or conveying; conveyance. **6.** a system of conveying passengers or freight: *public transport.* **7.** a means of transporting or conveying, as a ship employed for transporting soldiers or military stores, or convicts. **8.** a convict transported, or sentenced to be transported. **9.** an aeroplane carrying goods or passengers as part of a transport system. **10.** strong emotion; ecstatic joy, bliss, etc. —*adj.* **11.** relating to means, systems, or the personnel or equipment of transport: *transport workers.* [ME *transporte(n)*, t. L: m. *transportāre* carry across] —**transport′able,** *adj.* —**transport′abil′ity,** *n.* —**transport′er,** *n.*

transportation (trăns′pô tā′shən), *n.* **1.** the act of transporting. **2.** the state of being transported. **3.** *Chiefly U.S.* means of transport or conveyance. **4.** *U.S.* cost of transport or travel by public conveyance. **5.** *U.S.* tickets or permits for transport or travel. **6.** banishment, as of a criminal to a penal colony; deportation.

transport cafe (kăf), an inexpensive eating place on a main road, used principally by long-distance lorry drivers. Also, **transport café.**

transporter (trăns pô′tə), *n.* **1.** a lorry designed to carry large or bulky loads. **2.** a transporter bridge, crane, etc.

transporter bridge, a bridge having a tower on each bank connected by a span which supports a moving trolley from which a shore-level platform is suspended from cables. Used for carrying vehicles, passengers, etc., over waterways.

transporter crane, a crane having a high-level girder from which a grab or hoist is suspended; the structure can usually move on wheels and can run astride ships, trains, etc., to unload at any point.

transport number, *Chem.* in an electrolytic process, the fraction of the total current passed which is carried by one specified species of ion.

transpose (trăns pōz′), *v.t.*, **-posed, -posing.** **1.** to alter the relative position or order of (a thing in a series, or a series of things). **2.** to cause (two or more things) to change places; interchange. **3.** to alter the order of (letters in a word, or words in a sentence). **4.** *Alg.* to bring (a term) from one side of an equation to the other, with change of the plus or minus sign. **5.** *Music.* to reproduce in a different key, by raising or lowering in pitch. **6.** *Rare.* to transfer or transport. **7.** *Obs.* to transform; transmute. [ME *transpose(n)*, t. F: m. *transposer*, f. *trans-* across + *poser* place. See POSE¹] —**transpos′able,** *adj.* —**transpos′er,** *n.*

transposition (trăns′pə zĭsh′ən), *n.* **1.** the act of transposing, or the state of being transposed. **2.** a transposed form of something. Also, **transposal** (trăns pō′zəl). —**trans′posi′tional,** *adj.*

transship (trăns′shĭp′), *v.*, **-shipped, -shipping.** tranship. —**transship′ment,** *n.*

Trans-Siberian Railway (trăn′sī bĭə′rĭ ən), a railway constructed 1891–1916 by the Russian government, crossing Siberia and Manchuria from Kuibyshev to Vladivostok: over 4000 mi.

transubstantiate (trăn′səb stăn′shĭ āt′), *v.t.*, **-ated, -ating.** **1.** to change from one substance into another; transmute. **2.** *Theol.* to change (the substance of bread and wine) into the substance or body and blood of Christ, the species (def. 4a) alone remaining of bread and wine. [t. ML: m. s. *transubstantiātus*, pp.]

transubstantiation (trăn′səb stăn′shĭ ā′shən), *n.* **1.** the changing of one substance into another. **2.** *Theol.* the conversion, in the Eucharist, of the whole substance of the bread into the body, and of the whole substance of the wine into the blood, of Christ, only the appearance of bread and wine remaining, following the philosophical concept that any object whatever could be separately conceived as to its tangible form and its true nature (a doctrine of the Roman Catholic Church). —**tran′substan′tia′tionalist,** *n.*

transudation (trăn′syŏŏ dā′shən), *n.* **1.** the act or process of transuding. **2.** a substance which has transuded. Also, **transudate** (trăn′syŏŏ dāt′).

transude (trăn syōōd′), *v.i.*, **-suded, -suding.** to pass or ooze through pores or interstices, as a fluid. [t. NL: m. s. *transūdāre*, f. L: *trans* across + *sūdāre* sweat] —**transudatory** (trăn syōō′də tə rĭ, -trĭ), *adj.*

transumpt (trăn sŭmpt′, trăn′sŭmpt), *n.* a copy of a legal document. [t. L: s. *transumptus*, pp., transcribe]

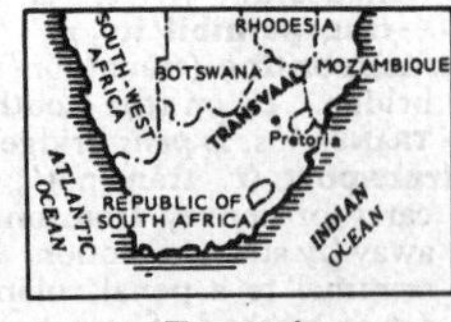

Transvaal

transuranic element (trănz′yŏŏ răn′ĭk), *Chem., Physics.* an element having a higher atomic number than uranium. Neptunium, plutonium, americium, curium, berkelium, californium, einsteinium, fermium, mendelevium, nobelium, and lawrencium (at. nos 93–103) are the ones known at present.

Transvaal (trănz′väl′), *n.* a NE province in the Republic of South Africa. 6,273,477 pop. (1960); 110,450 sq. mi. *Cap.*: Pretoria. Formerly, **South African Republic.** —**Trans′vaal′er,** *n.* —**Transvaal′ian,** *adj.*

transvalue (trănz văl′yōō), *v.t.*, **-ued, -uing.** to change the value of. —**trans′valua′tion,** *n.* —**transval′uer,** *n.*

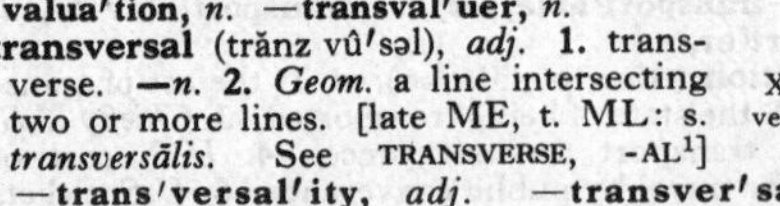

XY, Transversal (def. 2)

transversal (trănz vû′səl), *adj.* **1.** transverse. —*n.* **2.** *Geom.* a line intersecting two or more lines. [late ME, t. ML: s. *transversālis.* See TRANSVERSE, -AL¹] —**trans′versal′ity,** *adj.* —**transver′sally,** *adv.*

transverse (trănz vûs′), *adj.* **1.** lying or being across or in a crosswise direction; athwart. **2.** *Geom.* denoting that axis of a hyperbola which passes through the foci. **3.** (of a flute) held across the body, and having a mouth hole in the side of the tube, near its end, across which the player's breath is directed. —*n.* **4.** something which is transverse. **5.** *Geom.* a transverse axis. [t. L: m. s. *transversus*, pp., turned or directed across] —**transvers′ely,** *adv.*

transverse process, *Anat.* a process which projects from the sides of a vertebra.

transverse vibrations, *Acoustics.* periodic disturbances for which the particle oscillations of the medium are perpendicular to the direction of propagation.

transverse wave, *Physics.* a wave in which the displacement is perpendicular to the direction of propagation.

transvestism (trănz vĕs′tĭz′əm), *n.* **1.** the abnormal desire to wear clothing appropriate to the opposite sex. **2.** the act or state of so dressing. —**transvestite** (trănz vĕs′tīt), *n., adj.*

Transylvania (trăn′sĭl vā′nyə), *n.* a region and former province in W and central Rumania: formerly a part of Hungary. 24,027 sq. mi. —**Tran′sylva′nian,** *adj., n.*

Transylvanian Alps, a mountain range in S Rumania, forming a SW extension of the Carpathian system. Highest peak, Mt Negoiul, 8345 ft. See map under **Iron Gate.**

trap¹ (trăp), *n., v.*, **trapped, trapping.** —*n.* **1.** a contrivance used for taking game or other animals, as a mechanical device that springs shut suddenly, a pitfall, or a snare. **2.** any device, stratagem, or the like for catching one unawares. **3.** an ambush. **4.** any of various mechanical contrivances for preventing the passage of steam, water, etc. **5.** an arrangement in a pipe, as a double curve or a U-shaped section, in which liquid remains and forms a seal, for preventing the passage or escape of air or gases through the pipe from behind or below; stench trap; stink trap. **6.** (*pl.*) *Jazz, Obs. and U.S.* percussion instruments. **7.** a device for suddenly releasing or tossing into the air objects to be shot at, as pigeons or clay targets. **8.** the piece of wood, shaped somewhat like a shoe hollowed at the heel, and moving on a pivot, used in playing the game of trapball. **9.** trapball. **10.** a carriage, esp. a light two-wheeled one. **11.** a trapdoor. **12.** *Slang.* one's mouth. —*v.t.* **13.** to catch in a trap: *to trap foxes.* **14.** to take by stratagem; lead by artifice or wiles. **15.** to furnish or set with traps. **16.** to provide (a drain, etc.) with a trap. **17.** to stop and hold by a trap, as air in a pipe. —*v.i.* **18.** to set traps for game: *he was busy trapping.* **19.** to engage in catching animals in traps for their furs. [ME *trappe*, OE *træppe*, c. MD *trappe*. Cf. ML *trappa*] —**trap′like′,** *adj.*

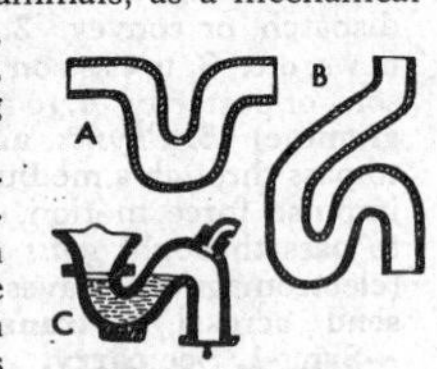

Traps (def. 5)
A, B, Common traps;
C, Ventilating trap

—**Syn. 1, 2.** TRAP, PITFALL, SNARE apply to literal or figurative contrivances for deceiving and catching animals or people. Literally, a TRAP is a mechanical contrivance for catching animals, the main feature usually being a spring: *a trap baited with cheese for mice.* Figuratively, TRAP suggests the scheme of one person to take another by surprise and gain an advantage from him: *a trap for the unwary.* A PITFALL is (usually) a concealed pit arranged for the capture of large animals or men who may fall into it; figuratively, it is any concealed danger, error, or source of disaster: *to catch elephants in a pitfall.* A SNARE is a device for entangling birds, rabbits, etc., with intent to capture; figuratively, it implies enticement and inveiglement: *a snare for small animals.*

trap² (trăp), *n., v.*, **trapped, trapping.** —*n.* **1.** (*pl.*) *Colloq.* personal belongings; luggage. **2.** *Obs.* a cloth or covering for a horse. —*v.t.* **3.** to furnish with trapping; caparison. [ME *trappe*; orig. uncert.]

trap³ (trăp), *n. Geol.* any of various fine-grained dark-coloured igneous rocks having a more or less columnar structure, esp. some form of basalt. [t. Sw.: m. *trapp*, var. of *trappa* stair (so named from their appearance)]

trapan (trə păn′), *n., v.t.*, **-panned, -panning.** *Archaic.* trepan². —**trapan′ner,** *n.*

Trapani (*It.* trä′pä nē), *n.* a seaport in NW Sicily. 79,248 (1966).

trapball (trăp′bôl′), *n.* **1.** an old game in which a ball placed on the hollowed end of a trap (def. 8) is thrown into the air by striking the other end of the trap with a bat and then driven to a distance with the bat. **2.** the ball used in this game.

trap-cut (trăp′kŭt′), *adj.* step-cut.

trapdoor (trăp′dô′), *n.* **1.** a door or the like, flush, or nearly so, with the surface of a floor, ceiling, roof, etc. **2.** the opening which it covers.

trapes (trāps), *v.i.*, **trapesed, trapesing.** *Colloq.* traipse.

trapeze (trə pēz′), *n.* **1.** an apparatus for gymnastics consisting of a short horizontal bar attached to the ends of two suspended ropes. **2.** (on a small sailing boat) a device resembling this by which one may lean almost completely outboard. **3.** *Geom.* trapezium. [t. F, t. L: m. *trapezium* small table, t. Gk: m. *trapézion*]

trapeziform (trə pē′zĭ fôrm′), *adj.* formed like a trapezium.

trapezium (trə pē′zyəm), *n., pl.* **-ziums, -zia** (-zyə). **1.** *Geom.* **a.** (as orig. used by Euclid) any rectilinear quadrilateral plane figure not a parallelogram. **b.** a quadrilateral plane figure in which only one pair of opposite sides are parallel. **2.** *Anat.* a bone of the carpus articulating with the metacarpal bone of the thumb. [t. NL. See TRAPEZE] —**trape′zial,** *adj.*

Trapezium (def. 1b)

trapezoid (trăp′ĭ zoid′), *n.* **1.** *Geom.* **a.** a quadrilateral plane figure of which no two sides are parallel. **b.** a trapezium (def. 1b). **2.** *Anat.* a bone of the carpus articulating with the metacarpal bone of the index finger. [t. NL: s. *trapezoidēs* table-like, t. LGk: m. *trapezoeidḗs*] —**trap′ezoid′, trap′ezoi′dal,** *adj.*

Trapezoid (def. 1a)

Trappe (*Fr.* tràp), *n.* **La** (*Fr.* là). See **La Trappe.**

trappean (trăp′ĭ ən, trə pē′ən), *adj. Obs.* consisting of, pertaining to, or having the nature of trap (rock).

trapper (trăp′ə), *n.* **1.** one who traps. **2.** one who makes a business of trapping wild animals for their furs.

trappings (trăp′ĭngz), *n.pl.* **1.** articles of equipment or dress, esp. of an ornamental character. **2.** conventional or characteristic articles of dress or adornment. **3.** that which necessarily accompanies or adorns: *the trappings of power.* **4.** a covering for a horse, esp. when ornamental in character. [ME. See TRAP[2], -ING[1]]

Trappist (trăp′ĭst), *n.* **1.** a member of a monastic body, a reformed branch of the Cistercian order, observing the extremely severe rule of austerity and silence established at the abbey of La Trappe, in Normandy, in 1664. —*adj.* **2.** of or pertaining to the Trappists. [t. F: m. *trappiste*]

traprock (trăp′rŏk′), *n. Geol.* trap[3].

traps (trăps), *n.pl.* See **trap**[1] (def. 6).

trapshooting (trăp′shōō′tĭng), *n.* the sport of shooting at live pigeons released from, or clay targets, etc., thrown into the air by, a trap (def. 7). Cf. **skeet.** —**trap′shoot′er,** *n.*

trash (trăsh), *n.* **1.** anything worthless or useless; rubbish. **2.** foolish notions, talk, or writing; nonsense. **3.** worthless or disreputable persons. **4.** broken or torn bits, as twigs, splinters, rags, or the like. **5.** that which is broken or lopped off from anything in preparing it for use. **6.** the refuse of sugar cane after the juice has been expressed. **7. white trash,** the poor white inhabitants of the southern U.S. —*v.t.* **8.** to free from trash or refuse, as outer leaves from growing sugar cane. **9.** to free from superfluous twigs or branches. [ME *trasche.* Cf. d. Norw. *trask,* Icel. *tros*] —**trash′er,** *n.*

trashy (trăsh′ĭ), *adj.,* **trashier, trashiest. 1.** of the nature of trash; rubbishy or worthless: *trashy novels.* **2.** *U.S.* encumbered with trash, as a field. —**trash′ily,** *adv.* —**trash′iness,** *n.*

Trasimeno (*It.* trä sē mĕ′nô), *n.* a lake in central Italy, in Umbria, W of Perugia: the Romans were disastrously defeated here by Hannibal 217 B.C. ab. 10 mi. long.

trass (trăs), *n.* a rock, common along the Rhine, composed chiefly of comminuted pumice or other volcanic material, used for making hydraulic cement. [t. D: m. *tras,* earlier *tarasse,* var. of *terras,* prob. t. F. See TERRACE]

trattoria (trăt′ə rĭə′; *It.* trät tô rē′ä), *n.* an Italian or Italian-style restaurant. [It.]

trauma (trô′mə), *n., pl.* **-mata** (-mə tə), **-mas. 1.** *Pathol.* **a.** a bodily injury produced by violence, or any thermal, chemical, etc., extrinsic agent. **b.** the condition produced by this; traumatism. **c.** the injurious agent or mechanism itself. **2.** *Psychol.* a startling experience which has a lasting effect on mental life; a shock. [t. Gk: wound]

traumatic (trô măt′ĭk), *adj.* **1.** pertaining to or produced by a trauma or wound. **2.** adapted to the cure of wounds. [t. LL: s. *traumaticus,* t. Gk: m. *traumatikós* pertaining to wound(s)]

traumatism (trô′mə tĭz′əm), *n. Pathol.* **1.** any morbid condition produced by a trauma. **2.** the trauma or wound itself.

traumatize (trô′mə tīz′), *v.t.,* **-tized, -tizing.** *Pathol.* to injure (tissues) by force, or by thermal, chemical, electrical, etc., agents. Also, **traumatise.**

travail (trăv′āl), *n.* **1.** physical or mental toil or exertion, esp. when painful. **2.** the labour and pain of childbirth. —*v.i.* **3.** to suffer the pangs of childbirth; be in labour. **4.** *Archaic.* to toil or exert oneself. [ME, t. OF: suffering, painful effort, trouble, der. *travailler* work (hard), ult. der. LL *trepālium* torture instrument, lit., object made of three stakes]

Travancore (trăv′əng kô′), *n.* a former state in S India; now included in Kerala.

trave (trāv), *n.* a device to inhibit a wild or untrained horse or one being shod. [ME *trave,* t. OF, g. L *trabs* beam]

travel (trăv′əl), *v.,* **-elled, -elling** or (*U.S.*) **-eled, -eling,** *n.* —*v.i.* **1.** to go from one place to another; make a journey: *to travel for pleasure.* **2.** to move or go from one place or point to another. **3.** to proceed or advance in any way. **4.** to go from place to place as a representative of a business firm. **5.** *Colloq.* to move with speed. **6.** to move in a fixed course, as a piece of mechanism. **7.** to pass, or be transmitted, as light, sound, etc. —*v.t.* **8.** to travel, journey, or pass through or over, as a country, district, road, etc. **9.** to journey (a specified distance). —*n.* **10.** the act of travelling; journeying, esp. in distant or foreign places. **11.** (*pl.*) journeys: *to start on one's travels.* **12.** (*pl.*) **a.** journeys as the subject of a written account or literary work. **b.** such an account or work. **13.** *Mach.* **a.** the complete movement of a moving part (esp. a reciprocating part) in one direction, or the distance traversed; stroke. **b.** length of stroke. **14.** movement or passage in general. [ME; var. of TRAVAIL]

travel agency, a business that arranges journeys and accommodation for travellers, as by procuring tickets, reservations, etc. Also, **travel bureau.**

travelled (trăv′əld), *adj.* **1.** having travelled, esp. to distant places; experienced in travel. **2.** frequented by travellers, as a road. **3.** *Geol.* moved to a distance from the original site, as a boulder. Also, *U.S.,* **traveled.**

traveller (trăv′lə), *n.* **1.** one who or that which travels. **2.** one who travels or has travelled in distant places or foreign lands. **3.** a travelling salesman; a commercial traveller. **4.** a piece of mechanism constructed to move in a fixed course. **5.** *Naut.* **a.** a wooden or metal ring or hoop fitted to move freely round a mast or spar. **b.** the rope, spar, or rod itself. **c.** a ring attached to the sheet of a fore-and-aft sail and sliding from side to side on a metal rod fastened to the deck. Also, *U.S.,* **traveler.**

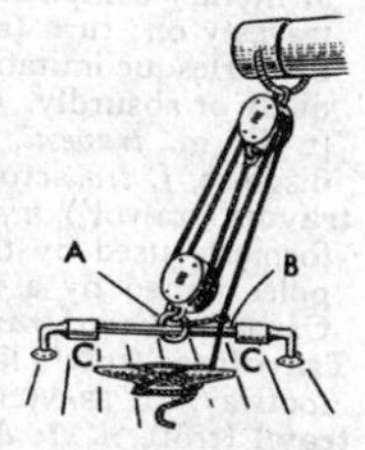

Traveller (def. 5)
A, Ring; B, Horse; C, Buffer

traveller's cheque, a cheque issued by a bank, express company, etc., to a traveller, which may be cashed only by endorsement in sight of the payee. Also, *U.S.,* **traveler's check.**

traveller's joy, the old-man's-beard, *Clematis vitalba.*

traveller's tree, a Madagascan tree, *Ravenala madagascariensis,* having two rows of large leaves the bases of which accumulate water.

travelling salesman, one who travels from place to place as the representative of a business firm, to solicit orders or sell goods; a representative; a traveller.

travelogue (trăv′ə lŏg′), *n.* **1.** a documentary film describing a country, travels, etc. **2.** a lecture describing travel, usually illustrated, as with photographs, slides, etc. [f. TRAVEL + *-logue,* modelled on DIALOGUE]

Travers (trăv′əz), *n.* **Mount.** See **Spenser Mountains.**

traverse (trăv′ûs), *v.,* **-ersed, -ersing,** *n., adj., adv.* —*v.t.* **1.** to pass across, over, or through. **2.** to go to and fro over or along, as a place. **3.** to extend across. **4.** to cause to move laterally. **5.** to pass in review; survey carefully. **6.** to go counter to; obstruct or thwart. **7.** *Law.* **a.** (in the law of pleading) to deny (an allegation of fact set forth in a previous pleading). **b.** to join issue upon. **c.** to deny formally, in pleading at law. **8.** to turn and point (a gun) in any direction. **9.** *Naut.* to brace (a yard) fore and aft.
—*v.i.* **10.** to pass or go across; cross; cross over. **11.** to turn horizontally, as a gun. **12.** *Mach.* to move crosswise or sideways. **13.** *Fencing.* to glide the blade towards the hilt of the contestant's foil while applying pressure to the blade. **14.** *Mountaineering.* to move horizontally or transversely.
—*n.* **15.** the act of traversing, or passing across, over, or through. **16.** something that crosses, obstructs, or thwarts; obstacle. **17.** a transversal or similar line. **18.** a place where one may traverse or cross; a crossing. **19.** *Archit.* a transverse gallery or loft of communication in a church or other large building. **20.** a member placed or extending across; a crosspiece or crossbar. **21.** a railing, lattice, or screen serving as a barrier. **22.** *Naut.* **a.** the

zigzag track of a vessel compelled by contrary winds or currents to sail on different courses. **b.** each of the runs in a single direction made in such sailing. **23.** *Fort.* **a.** a defensive barrier, parapet, or the like placed transversely. **b.** one thrown across the terreplein or the covered way of a fortification to protect it from enfilade fire. **24.** *Ordn.* the horizontal laying of a gun so as to make it point in any required direction. **25.** *Mach.* **a.** a crosswise or side movement or motion, as of a lathe carriage or tool. **b.** a part moving in this way. **26.** *Survey.* a movement across the country by a surveyor connected by continuous bearings and measurements. **27.** *Law.* a formal denial of some matter of fact alleged by the other side.
—*adj.* **28.** lying, extending, or passing across; cross; transverse.
—*adv.* **29.** *Obs.* across; crosswise; transversely.
[Defs 1–14, ME *traverse(n)*, t. F: m. *traverser* cross, thwart, der. *travers* TRAVERSE, n. or adj. Defs 15–29, ME; t. OF: m. *travers* lying athwart, g. LL *trāversus*, L *transversus*, pp.] —**trav′ersable,** *adj.* —**trav′erser,** *n.*

traversing bridge, a bridge that may be withdrawn horizontally to permit the passage of ships or the like.

travertine (trăv′ə tĭn), *n.* **1.** a form of limestone deposited by springs, etc., used in Italy for building purposes. **2.** a crusty deposit of calcium carbonate around a hot spring. Also, **travertin.** [t. It.: m. *travertino*, b. *tivertino*, g. L *Tīburtīnus* of Tibur (now Tivoli) and *tra-* across (g. L *trans*)]

travesty (trăv′ĭs tĭ), *n.*, *pl.* **-ties,** *v.*, **-tied, -tying. 1.** any grotesque or debased likeness or imitation: *a travesty of justice.* **2.** a literary composition characterized by burlesque or ludicrous treatment of a serious work or subject. **3.** literary composition of this kind. —*v.t.* **4.** to make a travesty on; turn (a serious work or subject) to ridicule by burlesque imitation or treatment. **5.** to imitate grotesquely or absurdly. **6.** to be a travesty of. See **burlesque.** [t. F: m. *travesti*, pp., disguised, t. It.: m. *travestire* disguise, f. *tra* across (g. L *trans*) + *vestire* dress (g. L)]

travois (trə voi′), *n.*, *pl.* **-vois** (-voiz′). a transport device, formerly used by the Plains Indians, consisting of two poles joined by a frame and drawn by an animal. [t. Canadian F: m. *travail* brake]

Travolator (trăv′ə lā′tə), *n.* *Trademark.* a type of moving footway. [f. TRAV(EL) + -O- + (ESCA)LATOR]

trawl (trôl), *n.* **1.** Also, **trawl net.** a strong fishing net dragged along the sea bottom in trawling. **2.** Also, *U.S.*, **trawl line.** a buoyed line used in sea fishing, having numerous short lines with baited hooks attached at intervals. —*v.i.* **3.** to fish with a net whose edge is dragged along the sea bottom to catch the fish living there. **4.** *U.S.* to fish with a trawl line. **5.** to troll. —*v.t.* **6.** to drag (a trawl net). **7.** to catch with a trawl net or a trawl line. **8.** to troll. [cf. MD *traghel* dragnet]

trawler (trô′lə), *n.* **1.** any of various types of vessels used in fishing with a trawl net. **2.** one who trawls.

tray (trā), *n.* **1.** any of various flat, shallow containers or receptacles of wood, metal, etc., with slightly raised edges used for carrying, holding, or exhibiting articles and for various other purposes. **2.** a removable receptacle of this shape in a cabinet, box, trunk, or the like, sometimes forming a drawer. **3.** a tray and what is in it. [ME; OE *trēg*, c. OSw. *trö* corn measure; akin to TREE]

treacherous (trĕch′ə rəs), *adj.* **1.** violating faith or betraying trust; disloyal; traitorous. **2.** deceptive, untrustworthy, or unreliable. **3.** unstable or insecure. **4.** likely or ready to betray. —**treach′erously,** *adv.* —**treach′erousness,** *n.*

treachery (trĕch′ə rĭ), *n.*, *pl.* **-eries. 1.** violation of faith; betrayal of trust; treason. **2.** an act of perfidy or faithlessness. **3.** readiness to betray. [ME *trecherie*, t. OF, der. *tricher* cheat; orig. uncert.] —**Syn. 1.** See **disloyalty.**

treacle (trē′kl), *n.* **1.** the dark, viscous, uncrystallized syrup obtained in refining sugar. Cf. **molasses. 2.** golden syrup. **3.** *Colloq.* cloying sentimentality as of music or behaviour. **4.** *Obs.* any of various medicinal compounds formerly in repute as antidotes for poisonous bites or for poisons. **5.** *Obs.* a sovereign remedy. [ME, t. OF: m. *triacle* antidote, g. L *thēriaca*, t. Gk: m. *thēriakḗ* (def. 4)] —**treacly** (trē′klĭ), *adj.* —**trea′cliness,** *n.*

treacle mustard, an annual cruciferous herb, *Erysimum cheiranthoides*, a common weed of cultivated land in N temperate regions.

tread (trĕd), *v.*, **trod** or (*Archaic*) **trode; trodden** or **trod; treading;** *n.* —*v.t.* **1.** to step or walk on, about, in, or along. **2.** to trample or crush underfoot. **3.** to put into some position or condition by trampling: *to tread grapes.* **4.** to domineer harshly over; crush. **5.** to execute by walking or dancing: *to tread a measure.* **6.** (of male birds) to copulate with. —*v.i.* **7.** to set down the foot or feet in walking; step; walk. **8.** to step, walk, or trample (fol. by *on* or *upon*). **9.** (of male birds) to copulate. **10. tread water,** *Swimming.* to move the arms and legs in such a way as to keep the body in an upright position with the head above water. —*n.* **11.** a treading, stepping, or walking, or the sound of this. **12.** manner of treading or walking. **13.** a single step as in walking. **14.** any of various things or parts on which a person or thing treads, stands, or moves. **15.** the sole of the foot or of a shoe that presses on the ground. **16.** the horizontal upper surface of a step in a stair, on which the foot is placed. **17.** the width of this from front to back. **18.** that part of a wheel, tyre, or runner which bears on the road, rail, etc. **19.** the part of a rail on which the wheels bear. [Defs 1–10, ME *trede(n)*, OE *tredan*, c. G *treten.* Defs 11–19, ME *trede, tredd*] —**tread′er,** *n.*

treadle (trĕd′l), *n.*, *v.*, **-dled, -dling.** —*n.* **1.** a lever or the like worked by the foot to impart motion to a machine. —*v.i.* **2.** to work a treadle. [ME and OE *tredel.* See TREAD, V.] —**tread′ler,** *n.*

treadmill (trĕd′mĭl′), *n.* **1.** an apparatus for producing rotary motion by the weight of men or animals, treading on a succession of moving steps that form a kind of continuous path, as around the periphery of a horizontal cylinder. **2.** a monotonous or wearisome round, as of work or life.

treas., 1. treasurer. **2.** treasury.

treason (trē′zən), *n.* **1.** violation by a subject of his allegiance to his sovereign or to the state; high treason. **2.** *Rare.* the betrayal of a trust or confidence; breach of faith; treachery. [ME, t. AF: m. *tre(y)soun*, g. L *trāditio* act of betraying]
—**Syn. 2.** See **disloyalty. 1.** TREASON, SEDITION mean disloyalty or treachery to one's country or its government. TREASON is any attempt to overthrow the government or well-being of a state to which one owes allegiance; the crime of giving aid or comfort to the enemies of one's government. SEDITION is any act, writing, speech, etc., directed unlawfully against state authority, the government, or constitution, or calculated to bring it into contempt or to incite others to hostility, ill will, or disaffection. —**Ant. 2.** loyalty.

treasonable (trē′zə nə bl), *adj.* **1.** of the nature of treason. **2.** involving treason; traitorous. —**trea′sonableness,** *n.* —**trea′sonably,** *adv.*

treasonous (trē′zə nəs), *adj.* treasonable. —**trea′sonously,** *adv.*

treasr, treasurer.

treasure (trĕzh′ə), *n.*, *v.*, **-ured, -uring.** —*n.* **1.** wealth or riches stored or accumulated, esp. in the form of precious metals or money. **2.** wealth, rich materials, or valuable things. **3.** any thing or person greatly valued or highly prized: *this book was his chief treasure.* —*v.t.* **4.** to put away for security or future use, as money; lay up in store. **5.** to retain carefully or keep in store, as in the mind. **6.** to regard as precious; prize; cherish. [ME *tresor*, t. OF, g. L *thēsaurus.* See THESAURUS] —**treas′ureless,** *adj.*

treasure-house (trĕzh′ə hous′), *n.* **1.** a repository or storehouse for valuables or money. **2.** a source of valuable things, as ideas.

treasurer (trĕzh′ə rə), *n.* **1.** one who is in charge of treasure or a treasury. **2.** one who has charge of the funds of a company, private society, or the like. **3.** an officer of a state, city, etc., entrusted with the receipt, care, and disbursement of public money. —**treas′urership′,** *n.*

treasure-trove (trĕzh′ə trōv′), *n.* **1.** *Law.* any money, bullion, or the like, of unknown ownership, found hidden in the earth or any other place. **2.** anything of similar nature which one finds. [t. AF: m. *tresor trové* treasure found]

treasury (trĕzh′ə rĭ), *n.*, *pl.* **-uries. 1.** a place where public revenues, or the funds of a company, etc., are deposited, kept, and disbursed. **2.** the funds or revenue of a state or a public or private company, etc. **3.** (*cap.*) the department of government which has control over the collection, management, and disbursement of the public revenue. **4.** a building, room, chest, or other place for the preservation of treasure or valuable objects. **5.** a repository or a collection of treasures of any kind; a thesaurus.

Treasury bench, the first row of seats on the Speaker's right in the House of Commons, occupied by members of the government.

Treasury bill, a bill, not carrying interest, issued under the authority of the Treasury, payable at not more than twelve months from its date, which is tendered for at a discount and forms part of the unfunded debt of the United Kingdom.

Treasury note, 1. a currency note issued by the Treasury between 1914 and 1928, for £1 and 10*s.*, being legal tender for the payment of any debt. **2.** *U.S.* a note or bill issued by the United States Treasury, receivable as legal tender for all debts except as otherwise expressly provided.

treat (trēt), *v.t.* **1.** to act or behave towards in some specified way: *to treat someone with respect.* **2.** to look upon, consider, or regard in a specified aspect, and deal with accordingly: *to treat a matter as unimportant.* **3.** to deal with (a disease, patient, etc.) in order to relieve or cure. **4.** to deal with in speech or writing; discuss. **5.** to deal with, develop, or represent artistically, esp. in some specified manner or style: *to treat a theme realistically.* **6.** to subject to some agent or action in order to bring about a particular result: *to treat a substance with an acid.* **7.** to entertain with food, drink, amusement, etc. **8.** to regale another at one's own expense. *—v.i.* **9.** to deal with a subject in speech or writing, or discourse. **10.** to give, or bear the expense of, a treat. **11.** to carry on negotiations with a view to a settlement, discuss terms of settlement, or negotiate. *—n.* **12.** an entertainment of food, drink, amusement, etc., given by way of compliment or as an expression of friendly regard. **13.** *Colloq.* anything that affords particular pleasure or enjoyment. **14.** the act of treating. **15.** one's turn to treat. **16. stand treat,** to bear the expense of an entertainment. [ME *trete(n)*, t. OF: m. *tretier*, *traitier*, g. L *tractāre* drag, handle, treat] **—treat′able,** *adj.* **—treat′er,** *n.*

treatise (trē′tĭz), *n.* **1.** a book or writing treating of some particular subject. **2.** one containing a formal or methodical exposition of the principles of the subject. [ME *treatis*, t. AF: m. *tretiz*, der. *traitier* TREAT]

treatment (trēt′mənt), *n.* **1.** the act or manner of treating. **2.** action or behaviour towards a person, etc. **3.** management in the application of medicines, surgery, etc. **4.** literary or artistic handling, esp. with reference to style. **5.** subjection to some agent or action.

treaty (trē′tĭ), *n., pl.* **-ties. 1.** a formal agreement between two or more states in reference to peace, alliance, commerce, or other international relations. **2.** the formal document embodying such an international agreement. **3.** any agreement or compact. **4.** *Rare.* negotiation with a view to settlement. **5.** *Obs.* entreaty. [ME *tretee*, t. AF: m. *treté*, pp., handled, treated. See TREAT] **—trea′tyless,** *adj.*

treaty port, (formerly) in the Far East, any of the ports opened by special treaty to foreign trade.

Trebbia (*It.* trĕb′byä), *n.* a river in N Italy, in Emilia province, flowing into the river Po near Piacenza: Hannibal decisively defeated the Romans near here 218 B.C. ab. 75 mi.

Trebizond (trĕb′ĭ zŏnd′), *n.* **1.** a medieval empire (1204–1461) in NE Asia Minor. **2.** Official name, **Trabzon.** a seaport in NE Turkey, on the Black Sea: an ancient Greek colony; capital of the medieval empire of Trebizond. 53,039 (1960).

treble (trĕb′l), *adj., n., v.,* **-bled, -bling.** *—adj.* **1.** threefold; triple. **2.** *Music.* **a.** of or pertaining to the highest part in harmonized music; soprano. **b.** of the highest pitch or range, as a voice part, voice, singer, or instrument. **c.** high in pitch; shrill. *—n.* **3.** *Music.* **a.** the treble or soprano part. **b.** a treble voice, singer, or instrument. **c.** a piano part for the right hand. **4.** a high or shrill voice or sound. **5.** the highest-pitched peal of a bell. *—v.t., v.i.* **6.** to make or become three times as much or as many; triple. [ME, t. OF, g. L *triplus* triple] **—trebly** (trĕb′lĭ), *adv.*

treble chance, a football pool where the chances of winning are related to the numbers of home and away wins as well as the number of draws forecast by the competitor.

treble clef, *Music.* a sign which indicates the G above middle C, placed on the second line of the stave, counting upwards. See illus. under **clef.**

Treblinka (trĕ blĭng′kə), *n.* a Nazi concentration camp in Poland, near Warsaw.

trebuchet (trĕb′yŏŏ shĕt′), *n.* a medieval military engine for hurling stones and making a breach. [ME, t. OF, der. *trebucher* overturn, fall, der. *tre(s)*, across, over (g. L *trans*) + *buc* trunk of body, t. Gmc; cf. OE *būc* belly]

trecento (*It.* trĕ chĕn′tô), *n.* the 14th century, with reference to Italy, and esp. to its art or literature. [It., short for *mille trecento* thirteen hundred]

Tredegar (trĭ dē′gə), *n.* a town in W Monmouthshire. 19,792 (1961).

tree (trē), *n., v.,* **treed, treeing.** *—n.* **1.** a perennial plant having a permanent, woody, self-supporting main stem or trunk, usually growing to a considerable height, and usually developing branches at some distance from the ground. **2.** any of various shrubs, bushes, and herbaceous plants, as the banana, resembling a tree in form or size. **3.** a family tree. **4.** something resembling a tree in shape, as a crosstree, etc. **5.** a pole, post, beam, bar, handle, or the like, as one forming part of some structure. **6.** a shoetree. **7.** a saddletree. **8.** a treelike group of crystals, as one forming in an electrolytic cell. **9.** *Maths.* a network with no loops. **10.** a gallows or gibbet. **11.** *Archaic or Poetic.* the cross on which Christ was crucified. *—v.t.* **12.** to drive into or up a tree, as a hunted animal, or a man pursued by an animal. **13.** *Colloq.* to put into a difficult position. **14.** to stretch or shape on a tree, as a shoe or boot. **15.** to furnish (a structure) with a tree. [ME: OE *trēo(w)*, c. Icel. *trē*, Goth. *triu*; akin to Gk *drȳs* tree, oak] **—tree′less,** *adj.* **—tree′lessness,** *n.* **—tree′like′,** *adj.*

Tree (trē), *n.* **Sir Herbert Beerbohm** (bĭə′bōm) (*Herbert Beerbohm*), 1853–1917, English actor and theatre manager.

tree creeper. See **creeper** (def. 4).

tree fern, any of various ferns, mostly tropical and chiefly of the family *Cyatheaceae*, which attain the size of trees, sending up a straight trunklike stem with foliage at the summit.

tree frog, any of the arboreal frogs of various families, characterized usually by toes with adhesive discs.

tree heath, a shrubby heath, *Erica arborea*, of Mediterranean regions; briar.

tree kangaroo, any kangaroo of the highly arboreal genus *Dendrolagus*, found in New Guinea and Queensland, Australia.

tree-mouse (trē′mous′), *n.* any of several arboreal rodents of Africa, belonging to the subfamily *Dendromyinae*.

treenail (trē′nāl′, trĕn′əl), *n.* a cylindrical pin of hard wood for fastening together timbers in ships, etc. Also, **trenail, trunnel.** [ME *trenayl*. See TREE, NAIL]

tree of heaven, ailanthus.

tree of knowledge of good and evil, *Bible.* a tree in the midst of the Garden of Eden, bearing the forbidden fruit, the eating of which destroyed the primal innocence of Adam and Eve. Gen. 2:9, etc.

tree of life, *Bible.* **1.** a tree in the midst of the Garden of Eden which yielded food giving everlasting life. Gen. 2:9; 3:22. **2.** a tree in the heavenly Jerusalem with leaves for the healing of the nations. Rev. 22:2. **3.** arbor vitae.

tree shrew, any mammal of the family *Tupaiadae*, of southern Asia and adjacent islands, squirrel-like in appearance and having a long snout.

tree sparrow, 1. a European weaverbird, *Passer montanus*, related to the house sparrow. **2.** a North American finch, *Spizella arborea*, common in winter in the northern U.S.

tree-surgeon (trē′sû′jən), *n.* one who practises tree-surgery.

tree-surgery (trē′sû′jə rĭ), *n.* the repair of damaged trees, as by the removal of diseased parts, filling of cavities, and prevention of further decay, and by strengthening branches with braces.

treetop (trē′tŏp′), *n.* the top part of a tree.

trefoil (trĕf′oil), *n.* **1.** any of the herbs constituting the leguminous genus *Trifolium*, usually having digitate leaves of three leaflets, and reddish, purple, yellow, or white flower heads, and including the common clovers. **2.** any of various similar plants, as the black medick. **3.** an ornamental figure or structure resembling a trifoliolate leaf. [ME *treyfoyle*, t. AF: m. *trifoil*, g. L *trifolium* triple leaf]

Trefoils (def. 3)

trehala (trĭ hä′lə), *n.* an edible, sugar-like secretion of the larvae of certain beetles of the genus *Larinus*, found in Asia Minor and neighbouring countries, forming a cocoon. [t. Turk.: m. *tiqālah*]

trehalose (trē′hə lōs′), *n.* *Chem.* a white crystalline disaccharide, $C_{12}H_{22}O_{11}$, found in yeast, certain fungi, etc., and used to identify certain bacteria. [f. TREHAL(A) + -OSE²]

treillage (trā′lĭj), *n.* latticework; a lattice or trellis. [t. F, der. *treille* arbour, trellis, g. L *trichila* arbour]

Treitschke (*Ger.* trīch′kə), *n.* **Heinrich von** (*Ger.* hīn′rĭKH fōn), 1834–96, German historian.

Trejos (*Sp.* trĕ KHôs′), *n.* **José Joaquín** (*Sp.* KHô sĕ′ KHwä kēn′), born 1917, president of Costa Rica since 1966.

trek (trĕk), *v.,* **trekked, trekking,** *n.* *—v.i.* **1.** to travel or migrate, esp. with difficulty. **2.** *S African.* to travel by ox wagon. *—v.t.* **3.** *S African.* (of a draught animal) to draw (a vehicle or load). *—n.* **4.** a journey, esp. a difficult one. **5.** *S African.* a migration or expedition, as by ox wagon. **6.** *S African.* a stage of a journey by ox wagon or otherwise, between one stopping place and the next. [t. D: m. s. *trekken* draw, travel] **—trek′ker,** *n.*

trellis (trĕl′ĭs), *n.* **1.** a frame or structure of latticework; a lattice. **2.** a framework of this kind used for the support of growing vines, etc. *—v.t.* **3.** to furnish with a trellis. **4.** to enclose in a trellis. **5.** to train or support on a trellis: *trellised vines.* **6.** to form into or like a trellis. [ME *trelis*, t. OF, orig. adj., g. LL *trilicius*, r. L *trilix* woven with three threads] **—trel′lis-like′,** *adj.*

Trellis

trelliswork (trĕl′ĭs wûk′), *n.* latticework.
trematode (trĕm′ə tōd′, trē′mə-), *n.* any of the *Trematoda,* a class or group of platyhelminths or flatworms, having one or more suckers, and living as ectoparasites or endoparasites on or in various animals; fluke. [t. NL: m. *Trēmatōda,* t. Gk: m. *trēmatṓdēs* having holes]
tremble (trĕm′bl), *v.,* **-bled, -bling,** *n.* —*v.i.* **1.** (of persons, the body, etc.) to shake involuntarily with quick, short movements, as from fear, excitement, weakness, cold, etc.; quake; quiver; shiver. **2.** to be agitated with fear, apprehension, or the like. **3.** (of things) to be affected with vibratory motion. **4.** to be tremulous, as light, sound, etc.: *his voice trembled as he spoke.* —*n.* **5.** an act of trembling. **6.** a state or fit of trembling. **7.** (*pl.*) any condition or disease characterized by continued trembling or shaking, as ague. **8.** (*pl.*) *Vet. Sci.* a toxic condition of cattle and sheep contracted by eating white snakeroot (*Eupatorium*), and marked by muscular tremors. [ME, t. F: m. *trembler,* g. LL *tremulāre,* ult. der. L *tremere*] —**trem′bler,** *n.* —**trem′blingly,** *adv.* —**Syn. 1.** See **shake.**
trembly (trĕm′blĭ), *adj.* trembling; tremulous.
tremendous (trĭ mĕn′dəs), *adj.* **1.** *Colloq.* extraordinarily great in size, amount, degree, etc. **2.** dreadful or awful, as in character or effect. **3.** *Colloq.* extraordinary; unusual; remarkable. [t. L: m. *tremendus* dreadful] —**tremen′dously,** *adv.* —**tremen′dousness,** *n.* —**Syn. 1.** See **huge.**
tremolant (trĕm′ə lənt), *n. Music.* tremulant. [t. G, t. It.: m. *tremolante* tremulant]
tremolite (trĕm′ə līt′), *n.* a white or greyish variety of amphibole, $Ca_2Mg_5Si_8O_{22}(OH)_2$, occurring usually in bladed crystals. [f. *Tremol(a)* valley in Switzerland + -ITE[1]]
tremolo (trĕm′ə lō′), *n., pl.* **-los.** *Music.* **1.** a tremulous or vibrating effect produced on certain instruments and in the human voice, as to express emotion. **2.** a tremulant. [t. It.: trembling, g. L *tremulus*]
tremor (trĕm′ə), *n.* **1.** involuntary shaking of the body or limbs, as from fear, weakness, etc.; a fit of trembling. **2.** any tremulous or vibratory movement; a vibration. **3.** a trembling or quivering effect, as of light, etc. **4.** a tremulous sound or note. [ME, t. L: trembling, terror] —**trem′orless,** *adj.*
tremulant (trĕm′yo͞o lənt), *adj.* **1.** trembling; tremulous. —*n.* **2.** Also, **tremolant, tremolo.** *Music.* a mechanical device on an organ for producing a tremolo effect.
tremulous (trĕm′yo͞o ləs), *adj.* **1.** (of persons, the body, etc.) characterized by trembling, as from fear, nervousness, weakness, excitement, etc. **2.** fearful; timorous. **3.** (of things) vibratory or quivering. **4.** (of writing, etc.) done with a trembling hand. [t. L: m. *tremulus*] —**trem′ulously,** *adv.* —**trem′ulousness,** *n.*
trenail (trē′nāl′, trĕn′əl), *n.* treenail.
trench (trĕnch), *n.* **1.** *Fort.* a long, narrow excavation in the ground, the earth from which is thrown up in front to serve as a shelter from the enemy's fire, etc. **2.** (*pl.*) a system of such excavations, with their embankments, etc. **3.** (*pl.*) the front line of battle in Europe in World War I. **4.** a deep furrow, ditch, or cut. —*v.t.* **5.** to surround or fortify with a trench or trenches; entrench. **6.** to cut a trench or trenches in. **7.** to set or place in a trench. **8.** to form (a furrow, ditch, etc.) by cutting into or through something. **9.** to make a cut in; divide by cutting. **10.** *Obs.* to cut. —*v.i.* **11.** to dig a trench or trenches. **12.** to encroach or infringe (fol. by *on* or *upon*). **13.** to come close or verge (fol. by *on* or *upon*). **14.** *Obs.* to enter or penetrate so as to affect intimately (fol. by *into* or *unto*). [ME *trenche,* t. OF: act of cutting, slice, der. *trenchier,* v., g. L *truncāre* cut off]
trenchant (trĕn′chənt), *adj.* **1.** incisive or keen, as language or a person; cutting: *trenchant wit.* **2.** thoroughgoing, vigorous, or effective: *a trenchant policy.* **3.** clearly or sharply defined, as an outline. **4.** *Chiefly Poetic.* sharp; keen-edged: *a trenchant blade.* [ME, t. OF, ppr. of *trenchier* cut] —**trench′ancy,** *n.* —**trench′antly,** *adv.*
Trenchard (trĕn′chäd), *n.* **Hugh Montague** (mŏn′tə gyo͞o′), **1st Viscount,** 1873–1956, Marshal of the Royal Air Force 1927–1956.
trench coat, a belted, military-style mackintosh.
trencher (trĕn′chə), *n.* **1.** one who trenches; one who makes trenches. **2.** *Archaic.* **a.** a rectangular or circular flat piece of wood on which meat, or other food, was formerly served or carved. **b.** such a piece of wood with that which it bears. **3.** *Archaic.* a supply of food. [ME, t. AF: m. *trenchour* a cutting place, trencher, der. *trenchier* cut. See TRENCH]
trencherman (trĕn′chə mən), *n., pl.* **-men. 1.** one who has a hearty appetite. **2.** a parasite or hanger on.
trench fever, *Pathol.* a recurrent fever, often suffered by soldiers in trenches in World War I, caused by a rickettsia transmitted by lice.
trench foot, *Pathol.* a disease of the feet due to exposure to cold and wet, common among soldiers serving in trenches.
trench mortar, a mortar, usually having a smooth bore, for firing projectiles short distances at high angles of elevation, used in trench warfare.
trench mouth, *Pathol.* Vincent's angina. [so called because of its prevalence among soldiers]
trench warfare, warfare in which the opposing sides occupy a system of trenches facing each other.
trend (trĕnd), *n.* **1.** the general course, drift, or tendency: *the trend of events.* **2.** the general direction which a road, river, coastline, or the like, tends to take. **3.** style; fashion. —*v.i.* **4.** to have a general tendency, as events, etc. **5.** to tend to take a particular direction; extend in some direction indicated. [ME *trende(n),* OE *trendan;* akin to OE *trinda* ball, D *trent* circumference, Sw. *trind* round. Cf. TRUNDLE] —**Syn. 1.** See **tendency.**
trendy (trĕn′dĭ), *adj. Colloq.* forming part of or influenced by fashionable trends; ultrafashionable.
Trengganu (trĕng gä′no͞o), *n.* a state in Malaysia, in the SE Malay Peninsula. 346,046 pop. (est. 1964); 5050 sq. mi. *Cap.:* Kuala Trengganu.
Trent (trĕnt), *n.* **1.** Italian, **Trento.** a town in Italy, in S Trentino-Alto Adige, on the river Adige. 84,833 (1966). **2. Council of,** the council of the Roman Catholic Church which met at Trent intermittently from 1545 to 1563, condemning the Reformation and defining Church doctrines. **3.** a river in central England, flowing NE from Staffordshire into the Humber. ab. 170 mi.
trente et quarante (*Fr.* träN tė kȧ räNt′), rouge et noir. [F: thirty and forty]
Trentino-Alto Adige (*It.* trĕn tē′nô äl′tô ä′dē jė) a region in NE Italy. 785,491 pop. (1961); 5256 sq. mi.
Trento (*It.* trĕn′tô), *n.* Italian name of **Trent** (def. 1).
Trenton (trĕn′tən), *n.* a town in the U.S., the capital of New Jersey, in the W part, on the Delaware river. 114,167 (1960).
trepan[1] (trĭ păn′), *n., v.,* **-panned, -panning.** —*n.* **1.** a boring tool for sinking shafts or the like. **2.** *Surg.* an obsolete form of the trephine resembling a carpenter's brace and bit. —*v.t.* **3.** *Mach.* **a.** to cut (circular discs) out of plate stock using a rotating cutter. **b.** to cut (a concentric groove) around a bored or drilled hole. **4.** to operate upon with a trepan; perforate by a trepan. [ME, t. ML: s. *trepanum* crown saw, t. Gk: m. *trýpanon* borer] —**trepanation** (trĕp′ə nā′shən), *n.*
trepan[2] (trĭ păn′), *n., v.,* **-panned, -panning.** *Archaic.* —*n.* **1.** one who ensnares or entraps others.**2.** a stratagem; a trap. —*v.t.* **3.** to ensnare or entrap. **4.** to entice. **5.** to cheat or swindle. Also, **trapan.** [orig. *trapan,* der. TRAP[1] and confused with TREPAN[1]] —**trepan′ner,** *n.*
trepang (trĭ păng′), *n.* any of various wormlike holothurians or sea-cucumbers, as *Holothuria edulis,* used as food in China. [t. Malay: m. *trīpang*]
trephine (trĭ fēn′), *n., v.,* **-phined, -phining.** —*n.* **1.** *Surg.* a small circular saw with a centre pin mounted on a strong hollow metal shaft to which is attached a transverse handle: used in surgery to remove circular discs of bone from the skull. —*v.t.* **2.** to operate upon with a trephine. [orig. *trafine,* explained by inventor as m. L *trēs fīnēs* three ends]
trepidation (trĕp′ĭ dā′shən), *n.* **1.** tremulous alarm or agitation; perturbation. **2.** vibratory movement; a vibration. **3.** *Pathol.* rapid, repeated, muscular flexion and extension of muscles of the extremities or lower jaw; clonus. [t. L: s. *trepidātio* act of hurrying, or of being alarmed]
treponema (trĕp′ə nē′mə), *n., pl.* **-mas, -mata** (-məz, -mə tə). any of several anaerobic spirochaetes of the genus *Treponema,* certain of which are pathogenic for man and warm-blooded mammals.
trespass (trĕs′pəs), *n.* **1.** *Law.* **a.** an unlawful act causing injury to the person, property, or rights of another, committed with force or violence, actual or implied. **b.** a wrongful entry upon the lands of another. **c.** the action to recover damages for such an injury. **2.** an encroachment or intrusion. **3.** an offence, sin, or wrong. —*v.i.* **4.** *Law.* to commit a trespass. **5.** to make an improper inroad on a person's presence, time, etc.; encroach or infringe (usually fol. by *on* or *upon*). **6.** to commit a transgression or offence; transgress; offend; sin. [ME *trespas(en),* t. OF: m. *trespasser,* v., f. *tres* across (g. L *trans*) + *passer* (g. L *passāre* PASS)] —**tres′passer,** *n.*

—**Syn. 5.** TRESPASS, ENCROACH, INFRINGE, INTRUDE imply overstepping boundaries and assuming possession of others' property or rights. To TRESPASS is to pass unlawfully within the boundaries of another's property: *hunters trespass on a farmer's fields.* To ENCROACH is to creep, as it were, gradually and often stealthily, upon territory, rights, or privileges, so that a footing is imperceptibly established: *the sea slowly encroached upon the land.* To INFRINGE is to break in upon or invade rights, customs, or the like, by violating or disregarding them: *to infringe a patent.* To INTRUDE is to thrust oneself into the presence of a person or into places or circumstances where one is not welcome: *to intrude into a private conversation.*

tress (trĕs), *n.* **1.** (*usually pl.*) any long lock or curl of hair, esp. of a woman, not plaited or braided. **2.** *Archaic.* a plait or braid of the hair of the head, esp. of a woman. [ME *tresse*, t. F: plait or braid of hair; orig. uncert.] —**tressed** (trĕst), *adj.*

-tress, a suffix forming some feminine agent-nouns, corresponding to masculine nouns in *-ter*, *-tor*, as *actor*, *actress*, etc. See **-ess.**

tressure (trĕsh′ə, trĕs′yo͝oə), *n. Her.* a diminutive of the orle, usually decorated with fleur-de-lis round the edges, and often doubled. [ME, t. OF: m. *tressur* braid of hair, der. *tresser* braid, plait. See TRESS]

trestle (trĕs′əl), *n.* **1.** a frame used as a support, consisting typically of a horizontal beam or bar fixed at each end to a pair of spreading legs. **2.** *Civ. Eng.* **a.** a supporting framework composed chiefly of vertical or inclined pieces with or without diagonal braces, etc., used for various purposes, as for carrying tracks across a gap. **b.** a bridge or the like of such structure. [ME, t. OF: m. *trestel* transom, beam, g. dim. of L *transtrum*]

trestle bridge, a bridge supported by trestles or trestlework.

trestle table, a table made of a board or boards laid upon trestles.

trestletree (trĕs′əl trē′), *n. Naut.* either of two horizontal fore-and-aft timbers or bars secured to a masthead, one on each side, to support the crosstrees.

trestlework (trĕs′əl wûk′), *n.* structural work consisting of a trestle or trestles.

tret (trĕt), *n. Com.* (formerly) an allowance for waste, after a deduction for tare. [ME, t. AF: m. *trait* TRAIT]

Trevelyan (trĭ vĕl′yən, -vĭl′-), *n.* **1. George Macaulay,** 1876–1962, English historian. **2.** his father, **Sir George Otto,** 1838–1928, English biographer, historian, and statesman.

Treves (trēvz), *n.* Trier. French, **Trèves** (*Fr.* trĕv).

Treviso (*It.* trė vē′zò), *n.* a town in Italy, in E Veneto. 84,443 (1966).

trews (tro͞oz), *n.pl.* close-fitting tartan trousers, worn esp. by certain Scottish Lowland regiments. [var. of *trouse* TROUSERS]

trey (trā), *n.* a playing card or a die having three pips. [ME, t. OF: m. *trei(s)*, g. L *trēs* three]

tri-, a word element meaning 'three', as in *triacid.* [t. L, comb. form of *trēs*, *tria* three; or t. Gk, comb. form of *treîs*, *tría* three and *trís* thrice]

triable (trī′ə bl), *adj.* **1.** that may be tried. **2.** subject or liable to judicial trial. [late ME, t. AF. See TRY, -ABLE] —**tri′ableness,** *n.*

triacid (trī ăs′ĭd), *adj. Chem.* **1.** capable of combining with three molecules of a monobasic acid: *a triacid base.* **2.** denoting acid salts containing three replaceable hydrogen atoms.

triad (trī′ăd), *n.* **1.** a group of three, esp. of three closely related or associated persons or things. **2.** *Chem.* an element, atom, or radical having a valency of three. **3.** *Music.* a chord of three notes, esp. one consisting of a given note with its major or minor third and its perfect, augmented, or diminished fifth. [t. L: s. *trias*, t. Gk: group of three. —**triad′ic,** *adj.*

tria juncta in uno (trē′ä yo͝ongk′tä ĭn o͞o′nō), *Latin.* three united in one (motto of the Order of the Bath).

trial (trī′əl, trīl), *n.* **1.** *Law.* **a.** the examination before a judicial tribunal of the facts put in issue in a cause (often including issues of law as well as of fact). **b.** the determination of a person's guilt or innocence by due process of law. **2.** the act of trying or testing, or putting to the proof. **3.** test; proof. **4.** an attempt or effort to do something. **5.** tentative or experimental action in order to ascertain results; an experiment. **6.** the state or position of a person or thing being tried or tested; probation. **7.** subjection to suffering or grievous experiences; affliction: *comfort in the hour of trial.* **8.** an affliction or trouble. **9.** a trying, distressing, or annoying thing or person. **10.** *Ceramics.* a piece of ceramic material used to try the heat of the kiln and the progress of the firing of its contents. **11. on trial, a.** undergoing a trial before a court of law. **b.** undergoing a test; on approval. —*adj.* **12.** pertaining to trial or a trial. **13.** done or used by way of trial, test, proof, or experiment. [t. AF, der. *trier* TRY]

—**Syn. 2.** TRIAL, EXPERIMENT, TEST imply an attempt to find out something or to find out about something. TRIAL is the general word for a trying of anything: *articles sent for ten days' free trial.* EXPERIMENT looks to the future, and is a trial conducted to prove or illustrate the truth or validity of something, or an attempt to discover something new: *an experiment in chemistry.* TEST is a stronger and more specific word, referring to a trial under approved and fixed conditions, or a final and decisive trial as a conclusion of past experiments: *a test of a new type of aeroplane.* **8.** See **affliction.**

trial and error, a process of experimentation to find the best way of achieving a desired result, in which various methods are tried and eliminated as unsuitable.

trial balance, *Bookkeeping.* a statement of all the open debit and credit items, made preliminary to balancing a double-entry ledger.

trial marriage, cohabitation of a man and woman in order to discover if they are suitable marriage partners.

trial run, **1.** a preliminary performance to test the efficiency of a motor vehicle, ship, etc. **2.** a preliminary testing period of anything.

triandrous (trī ăn′drəs), *adj. Bot.* **1.** (of a flower) having three stamens. **2.** (of a plant) having flowers with three stamens.

triangle (trī′ăng′gl), *n.* **1.** a geometrical plane figure formed by three (usually) straight lines which meet two by two in three points, thus forming three angles. **2.** *Chiefly U.S.* a set square. **3.** any three-cornered or three-sided figure, object, or piece: *a triangle of land.* **4.** *Music.* an instrument of percussion, made of a steel rod bent into the form of a triangle open at one of the corners, and sounded by being struck with a small, straight steel rod. **5.** a group of three; triad. **6.** (*cap.*) *Astron.* the constellation Triangulum. [ME, t. L: m. *triangulum*, lit. three-cornered object. See ANGLE[1]]

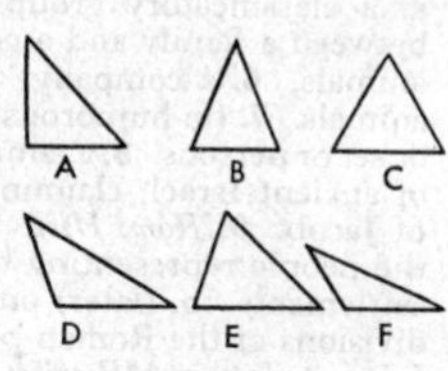

Triangles
A, Right-angled; B, Isosceles; C, Equilateral; D, Obtuse; E, Acute; F, Scalene

triangular (trī ăng′gyo͝o lə), *adj.* **1.** pertaining to or having the form of a triangle; three-cornered. **2.** having a triangle as base or cross-section: *a triangular prism.* **3.** comprising three parts or elements; triple. **4.** pertaining to or involving a group of three, as three persons, parties, or things. —**triangularity** (trī ăng′gyo͝o lă′rĭ tĭ), *n.* —**trian′gularly,** *adv.*

triangulate (*adj.* trī ăng′gyo͝o lĭt, -lāt′; *v.* trī ăng′gyo͝o lāt′), *adj.*, *v.*, **-lated, -lating.** —*adj.* **1.** triangular. **2.** composed of or marked with triangles. —*v.t.* **3.** to make triangular. **4.** to divide into triangles. **5.** *Survey.* **a.** to survey (a region, etc.) by establishing dividing points into triangles and measuring the angles of these triangles. **b.** to determine trigonometrically.

triangulation (trī ăng′gyo͝o lā′shən), *n. Survey.* **1.** the operation and immediate result of measuring, ordinarily with a theodolite, the angles of a network of triangles laid out on the earth's surface by marking their vertices. **2.** the triangles thus marked.

Triangulation
A, B, Points known; C, Point visible from both A and B, the position of which is plotted by measuring angles A and B

Triangulum (trī ăng′gyo͝o ləm), *n. Astron.* the Triangle, a northern constellation between Aries and Perseus.

triarchy (trī′ä′kĭ), *n.*, *pl.* **-chies.** **1.** government by three persons. **2.** a set of three joint rulers; a triumvirate. **3.** a country divided into three governments. **4.** a group of three countries or districts each under its own ruler. [t. Gk: m. s. *triarchia* triumvirate; See TRI-, -ARCHY]

Triassic (trī ăs′ĭk), *Geol.* —*adj.* **1.** pertaining to the geological period or system that constitutes the earliest principal division of the Mesozoic era. —*n.* **2.** the period or system characterized by widespread land deposits following Permian and preceding Jurassic. [f. LL *trias* the number three (t. Gk) + -IC; so called because deposits are divisible into three groups]

triatic stay (trī ăt′ĭk), *Naut.* a wire rope fitted horizontally between the tops of the masts in schooners. [orig. obscure]

triatomic (trī′ə tŏm′ĭk), *adj. Chem.* **1.** having three atoms in the molecule. **2.** containing three replaceable atoms or groups.

triaxial (trī ăk′sĭ əl), *adj.* having three axes.

triazine (trī′ə zēn′, -zĭn, trī ăz′ēn, -ĭn), *n. Chem.* **1.** any of a group of three compounds, $C_3H_3N_3$, containing three nitrogen and three carbon atoms arranged in a six-membered ring. **2.** any of a number of their derivatives. Also, **triazin** (trī′ə zĭn, trī ăz′ĭn). [f. TRI- + AZ(O)- + -INE[2]]

triazoic (trī′ə zō′ĭk), *adj.* hydrazoic.

triazole (trī′ə zōl′, trī ăz′ōl), *n. Chem.* any of a group of four compounds, $C_2H_3N_3$, containing three nitrogen and two carbon atoms arranged in a five-membered ring.

tribade (trĭb′əd), *n.* a woman who practises tribadism, esp. a female homosexual who assumes the male role. [t. L: m. s. *tribas* rubbing, t. Gk]

tribadism (trĭb′ə dĭz′əm), *n.* lesbianism.

tribal (trī′bl), *adj.* of, pertaining to, or characteristic of, a tribe or tribes: *tribal customs.* —**tri′bally,** *adv.*

tribalism (trī′bə lĭz′əm), *n.* **1.** the customs and belief of a tribe or tribes. **2.** loyalty to one's tribe, group, etc.

tribasic (trī bā′sĭk), *adj. Chem.* **1.** (of an acid) having three atoms of hydrogen replaceable by basic atoms or radicals. **2.** containing three basic atoms or radicals, each having a valency of one, as *tribasic sodium phosphate,* Na_3PO_4.

tribe (trīb), *n.* **1.** any aggregate of people united by ties of descent from a common ancestor, community of customs and traditions, adherence to the same leaders, etc. **2.** a local division of a primitive or aboriginal people. **3.** a division of some other people. **4.** a class, kind, or sort of animals, plants, articles, or other things. **5.** *Bot., Zool.* **a.** a classificatory group of animals or plants, ranking between a family and a genus. **b.** any group of plants or animals. **6.** a company, troop, or number of persons or animals. **7.** (in humorous or contemptuous use) **a.** a class or set or persons. **b.** a family. **8.** any of the twelve divisions of ancient Israel, claiming descent from the twelve sons of Jacob. **9.** *Rom. Hist.* **a.** any one of three divisions of the people representing the Latin, Sabine, and Etruscan settlements. **b.** (later) one of 30, afterwards 35, political divisions of the Roman people. **10.** *Gk Hist.* a phyle. [t. L: m. *tribus*; r. ME *tribu,* t. OF] —**tribe′less,** *adj.*

tribesman (trībz′mən), *n., pl.* **-men.** a man belonging to a tribe; a member of a tribe.

tribo-, a word element meaning 'friction', as in *triboelectricity.* [t. Gk, comb. form of *tribein* to rub]

triboelectricity (trī′bō ĭ lĕk′trĭs′ĭ tĭ), *n. Physics.* electricity generated by friction.

tribology (trī bŏl′ə jĭ), *n. Physics, Chem.* the study of the friction and wear between, and the lubrication of, interacting surfaces in relative motion.

triboluminescence (trī′bō lo͞o′mĭ nĕs′əns), *n. Physics.* the emission of light when certain crystals, as cane sugar, are crushed. —**tri′bolu′mines′cent,** *adj.*

tribrach (trī′brăk, trĭb′răk), *n. Pros.* a foot of three short syllables. [t. L: s. *tribachys,* t. Gk]

tribromoethanol (trī brō′mō ĕth′ə nōl′), *n. Chem.* a colourless crystalline compound, $CBr_3.CH_2OH$, used as an anaesthetic; avertin.

tribulation (trĭb′yo͝o lā′shən), *n.* **1.** grievous trouble; severe trial or experience. **2.** an instance of this, or an affliction, trouble, etc. [ME, t. L: s. *tribulātio,* der. L *tribulāre* afflict, der. *tribulum* threshing sledge]

tribunal (trī byo͞o′nəl), *n.* **1.** a court of justice. **2.** a place or seat of judgement. **3.** a raised platform for the seats of magistrates, orig. in a Roman basilica or hall of justice. [t. L: judgement seat, der. *tribūnus* tribune]

tribunate (trĭb′yo͝o nĭt), *n. Hist.* **1.** the office of tribune. **2.** a body of tribunes. [t. L: m. s. *tribūnātus*]

tribune[1] (trĭb′yo͞on), *n.* **1.** a person who upholds or defends popular rights. **2.** *Rom. Hist.* **a.** any of various administrative officers, esp. one of ten officers elected to protect the interests and rights of the plebeians from the patricians. **b.** a military officer, six of whom were assigned to a Roman legion. [ME, t. L: m. *tribūnus*] —**trib′uneship′,** *n.*

tribune[2] (trĭb′yo͞on), *n.* **1.** a raised platform, or dais; a rostrum or pulpit. **2.** a raised part, or gallery, with seats, as in a church. **3.** (in a Christian basilica) the bishop's throne in a corresponding recess, or apse. **4.** the apse itself. **5.** tribunal (def. 3). [t. It.: m. *tribuna* tribunal]

tributary (trĭb′yo͝o tə rĭ, -trĭ), *n., pl.* **-taries,** *adj.* —*n.* **1.** a stream contributing its flow to a larger stream or other body of water. **2.** one who pays tribute. —*adj.* **3.** (of a stream) flowing into a larger stream or other body of water. **4.** furnishing subsidiary aid; contributory; auxiliary. **5.** paying or required to pay tribute. **6.** paid as tribute. —**trib′utarily,** *adv.*

tribute (trĭb′yo͞ot), *n.* **1.** a personal offering, testimonial, compliment, or the like given as if due, or in acknowledgment of gratitude, esteem, or regard. **2.** a stated sum or other valuable consideration paid by one sovereign or state to another in acknowledgement of submission or as the price of peace, security, protection, or the like. **3.** a rent, tax, or the like, as that paid by a subject to a sovereign. **4.** anything paid as under exaction or by enforced contribution. **5.** the state of being liable or the obligation to make such payment. [ME *tribut,* t. L: s. *tribūtum*]

tricarboxylic acid cycle (trī′kä′bŏk sĭl′ĭk), *Biochem.* the citric acid cycle.

tricarpellary (trī′kä′pĭ lə rĭ), *adj. Bot.* having three carpels.

trice[1] (trīs), *n.* a very short time; a moment; an instant: *to come back in a trice.* [ME *tryse,* special use of TRICE[2] (*at a trice* at one tug)]

trice[2] (trīs), *v.t.,* **triced, tricing.** *Naut.* **1.** to pull or haul with a rope. **2.** to haul up and fasten with a rope (usually fol. by *up*). [ME, t. MD: m. s. *trīsen* hoist, appar. der. *trīse* pulley]

Tricel (trī′səl), *n. Trademark.* a man-made fibre, used in textile manufacturing.

tricentennial (trī′sĕn tĕn′yəl), *adj., n.* tercentenary.

triceps (trī′sĕps), *n. Anat.* a muscle having three heads, or points of origin, esp. the extensor muscle at the back of the upper arm. [t. L: three-headed]

triceratops (trī sĕ′rə tŏps′), *n.* any of the large, horned dinosaurs constituting the genus *Triceratops,* reptiles of great size with huge heads and heavily armoured necks.

trich-, var. of **tricho-,** before vowels, as in *trichite.*

trichiasis (trĭ kī′ə sĭs), *n. Pathol.* a state in which the eyelashes grow inwardly. [t. Gk, der. *trichiân* be hairy]

trichina (trĭ kī′nə), *n., pl.* **-nae** (-nē). the nematode worm, *Trichinella spiralis,* the adults of which live in the intestine and produce embryos which encyst in the muscle tissue, esp. in pigs, rats, and man. [t. NL, t. Gk, n. use of fem. of *tríchinos* of hair]

trichinize (trĭk′ĭ nīz′), *v.t.,* **-nized, -nizing.** to infect with trichinae. Also, **trichinise.** —**trich′iniza′tion,** *n.*

Trichinopoly (trĭch′ĭ nŏp′ə lĭ), *n.* former name of **Tiruchirapalli.**

trichinosis (trĭk′ĭ nō′sĭs), *n. Pathol.* a disease due to the presence of the trichina in the intestines and muscular tissues. [t. NL. See TRICHINA, -OSIS]

trichinous (trĭk′ĭ nəs), *adj.* **1.** pertaining to or of the nature of trichinosis. **2.** infected with trichinae.

trichite (trĭk′īt), *n. Geol.* any of various minute hairlike mineral bodies occurring in certain vitreous igneous rocks, esp. obsidian. [TRICH- + -ITE[1]] —**trichitic** (trĭ-kĭt′ĭk), *adj.*

trichlorethylene (trī′klô rĕth′ĭ lēn′), *n. Chem.* a colourless liquid, $CHCl.CCl_2$, used as a solvent, in dry-cleaning, and as an anaesthetic. Also, **trichloroethylene** (trī′-klô′rō ĕth′ĭ lēn′), **trilene.**

trichloride (trī′klô′rīd), *n. Chem.* a chloride having three atoms of chlorine, as ferric chloride, $FeCl_3$. Also, **trichlorid** (trī′klô′rĭd).

trichloronitromethane (trī′klô′rō nī′trō mē′thān), *n. Chem.* chloropicrin.

tricho-, a word element referring to hair, as in *trichocyst.* [t. Gk, comb. form of *thríx*]

trichocyst (trĭk′ə sĭst′), *n. Zool.* an organ of offence and defence embedded in the outer protoplasm of many infusorians, consisting of a small elongated sac containing a fine, hairlike filament capable of being ejected. —**trich′ocys′tic,** *adj.*

trichogyne (trĭk′ə jīn′, -jĭn), *n. Bot.* a hairlike prolongation of a carpogonium, serving as a receptive organ for the spermatium. [f. TRICHO- + Gk *gynḗ* woman]

trichoid (trĭk′oid), *adj.* hairlike.

trichology (trĭ kŏl′ə jĭ), *n.* the science of the hair and its diseases. —**trichol′ogist,** *n.*

trichome (trī′kōm, trĭk′ōm), *n. Bot.* an outgrowth from the epidermis of plants, as a hair. [t. Gk: m. *tríchōma* growth of hair] —**trichomic** (trĭ kŏm′ĭk), *adj.*

trichomonad (trĭk′ō mŏn′ăd), *n.* any flagellate protozoan of the genus *Trichomonas,* parasitic in man or animals.

trichosis (trĭ kō′sĭs), *n. Pathol.* any disease of the hair.

trichotomy (trī kŏt′ə mĭ), *n.* **1.** division into three parts. **2.** arrangement in three divisions. **3.** the three-part division of man into body, spirit, and soul. [f. *tricho-* (repr. Gk *trícha* triply) + -TOMY] —**trichotomic** (trĭk′ə tŏm′ĭk), **trichot′omous,** *adj.*

trichroic (trī krō′ĭk), *adj.* **1.** having or exhibiting three colours. **2.** pleochroic. —**trichro′ism,** *n.*

trichromatic (trī′krō măt′ĭk), *adj.* **1.** pertaining to the use or combination of three different colours, as in printing, or in photography in natural colours. **2.** pertaining to, characterized by, or involving three colours.

trichromatism (trī krō′mə tĭz′əm), *n.* **1.** trichromatic condition. **2.** the use or combination of three different colours.

trichromatopsia (trī′krō′mə tŏp′syə), *n. Ophthalm.* normal vision, in which the three fundamental colours, red, blue, and green, can be distinguished.

trick (trĭk), *n.* **1.** a crafty or fraudulent device, expedient, or proceeding; an artifice, stratagem, ruse, or wile. **2.** a deceptive or illusory appearance; mere semblance. **3.** a roguish or mischievous performance; prank: *to play a trick on someone.* **4.** a foolish, disgraceful, or mean performance or action. **5.** a clever device or expedient, dodge, or ingenious shift: *a rhetorical trick.* **6.** the art or knack of doing something. **7.** a clever or dexterous feat, as for exhibition or entertainment: *tricks in horsemanship.* **8.** a feat of jugglery, magic, or legerdemain. **9.** a particular habit or way of acting; characteristic quality, trait, or mannerism. **10.** *Cards.* the cards collectively which are played and won in one round. **11.** *U.S. Colloq.* a child or young girl. **12.** a spell or turn of duty. **13. do the trick,** to achieve the desired result. —*adj.* **14.** pertaining to or having the nature of tricks. **15.** made for tricks. —*v.t.* **16.** to deceive by trickery. **17.** to cheat or swindle (fol. by *out of*). **18.** to beguile by trickery (fol. by *into*). **19.** to dress, array, or deck (often fol. by *out* or *up*). —*v.i.* **20.** to practise trickery or deception; cheat. [ME *trik*, t. OF: m. *trique* deceit, der. *trichier* deceive; orig. uncert.] —**trick′er,** *n.* —**trick′less,** *adj.*

—**Syn. 1.** TRICK, DECEPTION, FRAUD, TRICKERY imply cheating or creating a false impression. A TRICK is usually an underhanded act designed to cheat someone. The word emphasizes the ingenuity, cleverness, or dexterity of the agent, and sometimes refers merely to a pleasurable deceiving of the senses: *to win by a trick.* DECEPTION is an intentional or unintentional act by means of which a false impression is created: *to practise the art of deception.* A FRAUD is an act or series of acts of subtle deceit or duplicity by which one tries to benefit himself at another's expense: *an advertiser convicted of fraud.* TRICKERY, the use of tricks and habitual deception, has esp. opprobrious connotations: *notorious for trickery in his business deals.* **16.** See **cheat.**

trickery (trĭk′ə rĭ), *n., pl.* **-eries. 1.** the use or practice of tricks; artifice. **2.** a trick. —**Syn. 1.** See **trick.**

trickish (trĭk′ĭsh), *adj.* tricky. —**trick′ishly,** *adv.* —**trick′ishness,** *n.*

trickle (trĭk′l), *v.,* **-led, -ling,** *n.* —*v.i.* **1.** to flow or fall by drops, or in a small, broken, or gentle stream: *tears trickled down her cheeks.* **2.** to come, go, pass, or proceed bit by bit, slowly, irregularly, etc.: *subscriptions are trickling in.* —*v.t.* **3.** to cause to trickle. —*n.* **4.** a trickling flow or stream. **5.** a small, slow, or irregular quantity of anything coming, going, or proceeding: *a trickle of visitors.* [sandhi var. of obs. *strickle*, freq. of STRIKE]

trickle charger, *Elect.* an apparatus which supplies a very small current to an accumulator.

trickster (trĭk′stə), *n.* **1.** a deceiver; a cheat. **2.** one who practises tricks.

tricksy (trĭk′sĭ), *adj.* **1.** tricky, crafty, or wily. **2.** mischievous, frolicsome, or playful. **3.** deceptive; uncertain. **4.** *Obs.* trim, spruce, or fine. —**trick′sily,** *adv.* —**trick′siness,** *n.*

tricktrack (trĭk′trăk′), *n.* a variety of backgammon. Also, **trictrac.**

tricky (trĭk′ĭ), *adj.,* **trickier, trickiest. 1.** given to or characterized by deceitful tricks; crafty; wily. **2.** skilled in clever tricks or dodges. **3.** deceptive, uncertain, or ticklish to deal with or handle. —**trick′ily,** *adv.* —**trick′iness,** *n.*

triclinic (trī klĭn′ĭk), *adj.* *Crystall.* denoting or pertaining to a system of crystallization in which the three axes are unequal and intersect at oblique angles. [f. TRI- + m. s. Gk *klínein* lean, slope + -IC]

triclinium (trī klĭn′ĭ əm), *n., pl.* **-clinia** (-klĭn′ĭ ə). *Rom. Hist.* **1.** a couch extending along three sides of a table, for reclining on at meals. **2.** a room containing such a couch, as a dining room. [t. L, t. Gk: m. *triklínion* three-couch dining room]

tricolour (trĭk′ə lə), *adj.* **1.** Also, **tricoloured** (trī′kŭl′əd). having three colours. —*n.* **2.** a tricolour flag or the like. **3.** the national flag of France, adopted during the Revolution, consisting of three equal vertical stripes of blue, white, and red. Also, *U.S.,* **tricolor.** [t. F: m. *tricolore,* t. LL: m. *tricolor*, adj., f. *tri-* TRI- + *-color* coloured]

tricorn (trī′kôn′), *adj.* **1.** having three horns, or hornlike projections, as a hat with the brim turned up on three sides. —*n.* **2.** a tricorn hat. Also, **tricorne.**

tricostate (trī′kŏs′tāt), *adj.* *Bot., Zool.* having three ribs, costae, or raised lines.

tricot (trĭk′ō; *Fr.* trē kó′), *n.* a warp-knit fabric, usually of rayon, with the right and wrong sides different. [t. F, der. *tricoter* knit, ult. of Gmc orig.]

tricresol (trī′krē′sŏl), *n.* *Chem.* a mixture of the three isomers of cresol.

trictrac (trĭk′trăk′), *n.* tricktrack.

tricuspid (trī kŭs′pĭd), *adj.* Also, **tricus′pidal. 1.** having three cusps or points, as a tooth. Cf. **bicuspid. 2.** *Anat.* denoting or pertaining to a valve of three segments, guarding the opening from the right auricle into the right ventricle of the heart. —*n.* **3.** *Anat.* a tricuspid valve. [t. L: s. *tricuspis* having three points]

tricuspidate (trī kŭs′pĭ dāt′), *adj.* *Anat.* having three cusps or flaps.

tricycle (trī′sĭ kl), *n.* **1.** a cycle with three wheels (usually one in front and one on each side behind) propelled by pedals or hand levers. **2.** three-wheeler. [t. F, f. *tri-* TRI- + *cycle* (see CYCLE)]

tricyclic (trī sī′klĭk, -sĭk′lĭk), *adj.* pertaining to or embodying three cycles.

trident (trī′dnt), *n.* **1.** a three-pronged instrument or weapon. **2.** *Rom. Hist.* a three-pronged spear used by the retiarius in gladiatorial combats. **3.** *Class. Myth.* the three-pronged spear forming a characteristic attribute of the sea-god Poseidon, or Neptune. **4.** a fish spear having three prongs. —*adj.* **5.** having three prongs or tines. [t. L: s. *tridens* having three teeth]

Neptune with trident

Tridentine (trī dĕn′tĭn), *adj.* pertaining to the Council of Trent, or conforming to its decrees and doctrines. [t. ML: m. s. *Tridentīnus*, der. *Tridentum* Trent]

tridimensional (trī′dĭ mĕn′shə nəl), *adj.* having three dimensions. —**tri′dimen′sional′ity,** *n.*

triecious (trī ē′shəs), *adj.* *Bot., U.S.* trioecious.

tried (trīd), *v.* **1.** pt. and pp. of **try.** —*adj.* **2.** tested; proved; having sustained the tests of experience.

triennial (trī ĕn′yəl), *adj.* **1.** lasting three years. **2.** occurring every three years. —*n.* **3.** a period of three years. **4.** a third anniversary. [f. s. L *triennium* period of three years + -AL[1]] —**trien′nially,** *adv.*

triennium (trī ĕn′yəm), *n., pl.* **-enniums, -ennia** (-ĕn′yə). a period of three years.

Trier (*Ger.* trēr), *n.* a town in West Germany, in SW Rhineland-Palatinate, on the river Moselle: extensive Roman ruins; cathedral. 105,000 (est. 1968). Also, **Treves.** French, **Trèves.**

trierarch (trī′ər äk′), *n.* *Gk Hist.* **1.** the commander of a trireme. **2.** (in Athens) a citizen who, singly, or jointly with other citizens, was required to fit out a trireme for the public service. [t. Gk: s. *triḗrarchos*]

trierarchy (trī′ər ä′kĭ), *n., pl.* **-chies.** *Gk Hist.* **1.** the office of a trierarch. **2.** trierarchs collectively. **3.** (in Athens) the duty of fitting out or furnishing triremes for the public service. [t. Gk: m. s. *triērarchía*]

Trieste (trī ĕst′; *It.* trē ĕs′tĕ), *n.* **1.** a seaport in Italy, in SE Friuli-Venezia Giulia, on the **Gulf of Trieste.** 280,692 (1966). **2. Free Territory of,** an area surrounding and including the town of Trieste, divided in 1954, the N part (86 sq. mi.; 302,200 pop.), incl. the town of Trieste, taken over by Italy; the S zone (199 sq. mi.; 73,500 pop.) by Yugoslavia.

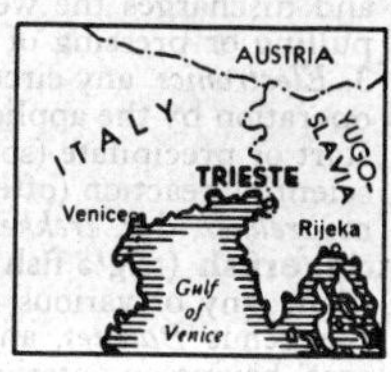

Trieste

triethylamine (trī ĕth′ĭ lə mēn′), *n.* *Chem.* a colourless liquid, $N(C_2H_5)_3$, used as a solvent.

trifacial (trī fā′shəl), *adj.* trigeminal.

trifid (trī′fĭd), *adj.* cleft into three parts or lobes. [t. L: s. *trifidus* split in three. See -FID]

trifle (trī′fəl), *n., v.,* **-fled, -fling.** —*n.* **1.** an article or thing of small value. **2.** a matter of slight importance; a trivial or insignificant affair or circumstance. **3.** a small, inconsiderable, or trifling sum of money. **4.** a small quantity or amount of anything; a little: *he's still a trifle angry.* **5.** a kind of pewter of medium hardness. **6.** (*pl.*) articles made of this. **7.** a dish typically consisting of sponge cake soaked in wine or liqueur, with jam, fruit, or the like topped with custard or whipped cream and (sometimes) almonds. —*v.i.* **8.** to deal lightly or without due seriousness or respect (usually fol. by *with*): *he was in no mood to be trifled with.* **9.** to amuse oneself or dally (usually fol. by *with*). **10.** to play or toy by handling or fingering (usually fol. by *with*): *he sat trifling with a pen.* **11.** to act or talk in an idle or frivolous way. **12.** to pass time idly or frivolously; waste time; idle. —*v.t.* **13.** to pass (time, etc.) idly or frivolously (usually fol. by *away*). [ME *treoflen*, t. OF: m. *trufler* make sport of, deceive; orig. uncert.] —**tri′fler,** *n.*

trifling (trī′flĭng), *adj.* **1.** of slight importance; trivial; insignificant: *a trifling matter.* **2.** of small value, cost, or amount: *a trifling sum.* **3.** frivolous, shallow, or light. **4.** *U.S. Dial.* mean; worthless. —**tri′flingly,** *adv.* —**tri′flingness,** *n.* —**Syn. 1.** See **petty.**

trifoliate (trī′fō′lĭ ĭt, -āt′), *adj.* **1.** having three leaves, leaf-like parts or lobes, or three foils. **2.** *Bot.* trifoliolate. Also, **tri′fo′liat′ed.** [f. TRI- + m. s. L *foliātus* leaved]

trifoliolate (trī′fō′lĭ ə lāt′), *adj.* *Bot.* **1.** having three leaflets, as a compound leaf. **2.** having leaves with three leaflets, as a plant.

trifolium (trī fō′lyəm), *n.* any plant of the leguminous genus *Trifolium*, as clover. [t. L: triple leaf]

triforium (trī fôʹ rī əm), *n.*, *pl.* **-foria** (-fôʹ rĭ ə). *Archit.* (in a church) the wall at the side of the nave, choir or transept, corresponding to the space between the vaulting or ceiling and the roof of an aisle, often having a blind arcade or an opening in a gallery. [t. AL; of unknown orig.]

Triforium

triform (trīʹfôm′), *adj.* **1.** formed of three parts, or in three divisions. **2.** existing or appearing in three different forms. **3.** combining three different forms. Also, **triʹformed′.** [t. L: s. *triformis*]

trifurcate (*v.* trīʹfû kāt′; *adj.* trīʹfû kĭt, -kāt′), *v.*, **-cated, -cating,** *adj.* —*v.t., v.i.* **1.** to divide into three forks or branches. —*adj.* **2.** Also, **triʹfurcat′ed.** divided into three forks or branches. [f. s. L *trifurcus* three forked + -ATE[1]] —**tri′furcaʹtion,** *n.*

trig[1] (trĭg), *adj.*, *v.*, **trigged, trigging.** —*adj.* **1.** neat, trim, smart, or spruce. **2.** in good physical condition; sound; well. —*v.t.* **3.** to make trig, trim, or smart (often fol. by *up* or *out*). [ME, t. Scand; cf. Icel. *tryggr* safe, c. Goth. *triggus* true, faithful. Cf. TRUE]

trig[2] (trĭg), *v.*, **trigged, trigging,** *n.* —*v.t.* **1.** to support or prop, as with a wedge. —*v.i.* **2.** to act as a check on the moving of wheels, vehicles, etc. —*n.* **3.** a wedge or block used to prevent a wheel, cask, or the like from rolling. [? t. Scand.; cf. Icel. *tryggja* make fast]

trig., **1.** trigonometric. **2.** trigonometry.

trigeminal (trī jĕmʹĭ nəl), *Anat.* —*adj.* **1.** denoting or pertaining to either of a pair of double-rooted cranial nerves, each dividing into three main branches to supply the face, etc. —*n.* **2.** a trigeminal nerve. [f. s. L *trigeminus* threefold + -AL[1]]

trigesimo-secundo (trī jĕs′ĭ mō sĭ kŭnʹdō), *n.*, *pl.* **-dos,** *adj. Bookbinding.* —*n.* **1.** a volume printed from sheets folded to form 32 leaves or 64 pages, approximately $4\frac{1}{2} \times 3$ inches. *Abbrev.:* 32 mo. or 32°. —*adj.* **2.** in trigesimo-secundo. Also, **thirty-twomo.** [t. It.: thirty-second]

trigger (trĭgʹə), *n.* **1.** (in firearms) a small projecting tongue which when pressed by the finger liberates the mechanism and discharges the weapon. **2.** a device, as a lever, the pulling or pressing of which releases a detent or spring. **3.** *Electronics.* any circuit which is used to set a system in operation by the application of a single pulse. —*v.t.* **4.** to start or precipitate (something), as a chain of events or a scientific reaction (often fol. by *off*). [earlier *tricker*, t. D: m. *trekker*, der. *trekken* pull] —**trigʹgerless,** *adj.*

triggerfish (trĭgʹə fĭsh′), *n.*, *pl.* **-fishes,** (*esp. collectively*) **-fish.** any of various compressed, deep-bodied fishes of the genus *Balistes*, and allied genera, chiefly of tropical seas, having an anterior dorsal fin with three stout spines.

trigger-happy (trĭgʹə hăp′ĭ), *adj. Colloq.* **1.** ready to fire a gun at the slightest provocation. **2.** reckless, irresponsible, or foolhardy, esp. in matters which could lead to war.

triglyceride (trī′glĭsʹə rīd′), *n. Biochem.* any ester of glycerol and fatty acids in which each glycerol molecule is combined with three fatty acid molecules.

triglyph (trīʹglĭf′), *n. Archit.* a structural member of a Doric frieze, separating two consecutive metopes, and consisting typically of a rectangular block with two vertical grooves or glyphs, and two chamfers or half grooves at the sides, together counting as a third glyph, and leaving three flat vertical bands on the face of the block. See illus. under **metope.** [t. L: s. *trīglyphus*, t. Gk: m. *tríglyphos* thrice-grooved] —**triglyphʹic,** *adj.*

trigo (trēʹgō), *n. Chiefly Southern U.S.* wheat; field of wheat. [t. Sp., g. L *trīticum* wheat]

trigon (trīʹgən), *n.* **1.** *Astrol.* the position or aspect of two planets distant 120° from each other. **2.** an ancient Greek harp or lyre triangular in shape. **3.** *Obs.* a triangle. [t. L: s. *trigōnum* triangle, t. Gk: m. *trígōnon*, prop. neut. adj., three-cornered]

trigon., **1.** trigonometric. **2.** trigonometry.

trigonal (trĭgʹə nəl), *adj.* **1.** triangular. **2.** *Crystall.* having threefold symmetry.

trigonometer (trĭg′ə nŏmʹĭ tə), *n.* an instrument for solving plane right-angled triangles by inspection. [back-formation from TRIGONOMETRY]

trigonometrical function, *Maths.* a function relating two sides of a right-angled triangle with one of the acute angles in the triangle, as tangent, sine, cosine, cotangent, secant, cosecant, or any function derived from any of these.

trigonometry (trĭg′ə nŏmʹĭ trĭ), *n.* the branch of mathematics that deals with the relations between the sides and angles of triangles (plane or spherical), and the calculations, etc., based on these. [t. NL: m. s. *trigōnometria*, f. Gk: *trígōno(n)* triangle + *-metria* -METRY] —**trigonometric** (trĭg′ə nə mĕtʹrĭk) **trig′onometʹrical,** *adj.* —**trig′onometʹrically,** *adv.*

trigonous (trĭgʹə nəs), *adj.* having three angles or corners; triangular, as stems, seeds, etc. [t. L: m. *trigōnus* triangular, t. Gk: m. *trígōnos*]

trigraph (trīʹgrăf, -gräf), *n.* a group of three letters representing a single speech sound, as *eau* in *beau.* —**trigraphic** (trī grăfʹĭk), *adj.*

trihedral (trī hēʹdrəl), *adj. Geom.* having, or formed by, three planes meeting in a point: *a trihedral angle.*

trihedron (trī hēʹdrən), *n.*, *pl.* **-drons, -dra** (-drə). *Geom.* the figure determined by three planes meeting in a point.

trihydric (trī′hīʹdrĭk), *adj. Chem.* containing three hydroxyl groups. Also, **trihydroxy.**

trijugate (trīʹjŏŏ gāt′, trī jŏŏʹgĭt, -gāt), *adj. Bot.* having three pairs of leaflets. Also, **trijugous** (trīʹjŏŏ gəs, trī jŏŏʹ-). [f. TRI- + m. s. L *jugātus* joined]

trike (trīk), *n. Colloq.* tricycle. [alter. of TRICYCLE]

trilateral (trī′lătʹə rəl), *adj.* having three sides. [f. s. L *trilaterus* three-sided + -AL[1]] —**tri′latʹerally,** *adv.*

trilby (trĭlʹbĭ), *n.*, *pl.* **-bies.** a man's soft felt hat with an indented crown. Also, **trilby hat.** [named after heroine of *Trilby*, novel by G. Du Maurier]

trilene (trīʹlēn), *n. Chem.* trichlorethylene.

trilinear (trīʹlĭnʹĭ ə), *adj.* pertaining to or involving three lines.

trilingual (trīʹlĭngʹgwəl), *adj.* using or involving three languages.

triliteral (trī′lĭtʹə rəl), *adj.* **1.** consisting of three letters, as a word. —*n.* **2.** a triliteral word or root.

triliteralism (trī′lĭtʹə rə lĭz′əm), *n. Gram.* the characteristic presence of triliteral roots in a language, as in the Semitic languages.

trill (trĭl), *v.t.* **1.** to sing with a vibratory effect of voice, esp. in the manner of a shake or trill. **2.** to play with like effect on an instrument. **3.** *Phonet.* to pronounce with rapid vibrations of an elastic organ of speech: *Spanish 'rr' is trilled with the tip of the tongue.* **4.** (of birds, etc.) to sing or give forth in a succession of rapidly alternating or changing sounds. —*v.i.* **5.** to resound vibrantly, or with a rapid succession of sounds, as the voice, song, laughter, etc. **6.** to utter, give forth, or make a sound or a succession of sounds more or less resembling such singing, as a bird, a frog, a grasshopper, a person laughing, etc. **7.** to execute a shake or trill with the voice or on a musical instrument. —*n.* **8.** the act or sound of trilling. **9.** *Music.* a trilled sound, or a rapid alternation of two consecutive notes, in singing or in instrumental music; a shake. **10.** a similar sound, or succession of sounds, uttered or made by a bird, an insect, a person laughing, etc. **11.** *Phonet.* **a.** a trilled articulation. **b.** a trilled consonant, as Spanish *rr.* [t. It.: m. *trillo*, n., quaver or warble in singing; of Gmc orig.]

Trill (def. 9)

trillion (trĭlʹyən), *n.* **1.** a cardinal number represented by one followed by 18 zeros (Britain and Germany) or 12 zeros (U.S. and France). —*adj.* **2.** amounting to one trillion in number. [t. F, f. *tri-* TRI- + *(m)illion* MILLION] —**trilʹlionth,** *n.*, *adj.*

trillium (trĭlʹyəm), *n.* any of the herbs constituting the liliaceous genus *Trillium*, characterized by a whorl of three leaves from the centre of which rises a solitary flower. [NL, appar. f. Sw. *trilling* triplet + L *-ium* -IUM]

trilobate (trī lōʹbāt, trīʹlə bāt′), *adj.* having three lobes.

Trilobate leaf

trilobite (trīʹlə bīt′), *n.* any of the *Trilobita*, a group of extinct arthropods, variously classed with the crustaceans or the arachnids or as intermediate between these, with a flattened oval body varying in length from an inch or less to two feet, their remains being found widely distributed in strata of the Palaeozoic era, and important as being among the earliest known fossils. [t. NL: m. *Trilobītēs*, f. *tri-* TRI- + s. Gk *lobós* lobe (of ear, etc.) + *-ītēs* -ITE[1]] —**trilobitic** (trī′lə bĭtʹĭk), *adj.*

trilocular (trī′lŏkʹyŏŏ lə), *adj.* having three loculi, chambers, or cells. [f. TRI- + s. L *loculus* small receptacle (dim. of *locus* place) + -AR[1]]

trilogy (trĭlʹə jĭ), *n.*, *pl.* **-gies.** **1.** a series or group of three related dramas, operas, novels, etc. **2.** a series of three complete and usually related tragedies performed in ancient Athens at the festival of Dionysus. **3.** a group of three related things. [t. Gk: m. s. *trilogía.* See TRI-, -LOGY]

trim (trĭm), *v.*, **trimmed, trimming,** *n.*, *adj.*, **trimmer, trimmest,** *adv.* —*v.t.* **1.** to reduce to a neat or orderly state by clipping, paring, pruning, etc.: *to trim a hedge.* **2.** to remove by clipping, paring, pruning, or the like:

(often fol. by *off*): *to trim off loose threads from a ragged edge.* **3.** to modify (opinions, etc.) according to expediency. **4.** *Carp.* to bring (a piece of timber, etc.) to the required smoothness or shape. **5.** *Aeron.* to level off (an aircraft in flight). **6.** *Naut.* **a.** to distribute the load of (a vessel) so that it sits well on the water. **b.** to stow or arrange, as cargo. **c.** to adjust (the sails or yards) with reference to the direction of the wind and the course of the ship. **7.** to decorate or deck with ornaments, etc.: *to trim a Christmas tree.* **8.** to upholster and line the interior of motor cars, etc. **9.** to rebuke or reprove. **10.** to beat or thrash. **11.** *U.S. Colloq.* to defeat. **12.** to prepare (a lamp, fire, etc.) for burning. **13.** *Obs.* to dress or array (often fol. by *up*). **14.** *Obs.* to equip. —*v.i.* **15.** *Naut.* **a.** to assume a particular position or trim in the water, as a vessel. **b.** to adjust the sails or yards with reference to the direction of the wind and the course of the ship. **16.** to pursue a neutral or cautious course or policy between parties. **17.** to accommodate oneself, or adjust one's principles, etc., to the prevailing climate of opinion. —*n.* **18.** proper condition or order: *to find everything out of trim.* **19.** condition or order of any kind. **20.** *Naut.* **a.** the set of a ship in the water, esp. the most advantageous one. **b.** the balance of a ship. **c.** the difference between the draught at the bow of a vessel and that at the stern. **d.** the condition of a ship with reference to her fitness for sailing. **e.** the adjustment of the sails, etc., with reference to the direction of the wind and the course of the ship. **f.** the condition of a submarine as regards buoyancy. **21.** dress, array, or equipment. **22.** material used for decoration; decorative trimming. **23.** *U.S.* window dressing. **24.** a trimming by cutting, clipping, or the like. **25.** a haircut which neatens the appearance of the hair without changing the style. **26.** that which is eliminated or cut off. **27.** *Aeron.* the attitude of an aeroplane with respect to the three axes at which balance occurs in forward flight with free controls. **28.** *Carp.* the visible woodwork of the interior of a building. **29. a.** the upholstery, knobs, handles, and other equipment inside a motor car. **b.** ornamentation on the exterior of a motor car, esp. in chromium or a contrasting colour. —*adj.* **30.** pleasingly neat or smart in appearance: *trim lawns.* **31.** in good condition or order. **32.** *Obs.* properly prepared or equipped. **33.** *Obs.* good, excellent, or fine. —*adv.* **34.** Also, **trim′ly,** in a trim manner. [OE *trymman, trymian* strengthen, prepare, der. *trum*, adj., firm, active] —**trim′ness,** *n.* —**Syn. 30.** See **neat**[1].

Trim (trĭm), *n.* a town in the Republic of Ireland, the county town of Neath. 1371 (1961).

trimer (trī′mə), *n.* *Chem.* a substance whose molecules consist of three molecules of a monomer.

trimerous (trĭm′ə rəs), *adj.* **1.** consisting of or divided into three parts. **2.** *Bot.* (of flowers) having three members in each whorl. **3.** *Entomol.* having three segments or parts. [t. NL: m. *trimerus*, t. Gk: m. *trimerés* made up of three parts]

trimester (trī mĕs′tə), *n.* a term or period of three months. [t. F: m. *trimestre*, t. L: m. s. *trimestris* of three months] —**trimes′tral, trimes′trial,** *adj.*

trimeter (trĭm′ĭ tə), *Pros.* —*n.* **1.** a verse of three measures or feet. —*adj.* **2.** consisting of three measures or feet. **3.** *Class. Pros.* composed of six feet or three dipodies. [t. L: m. s. *trimetrus* having three measures, t. Gk: m. *trímetros*]

trimetric (trī mĕt′rĭk), *adj.* **1.** pertaining to or consisting of a trimeter or trimeters. **2.** *Crystall.* orthorhombic. Also, **trimet′rical.**

trimetric projection, *Geom.* three-dimensional projection with three different linear scales at arbitrary angles.

trimmer (trĭm′ə), *n.* **1.** one who or that which trims. **2.** a tool or machine for trimming, clipping, paring, or pruning. **3.** a machine for trimming timber. **4.** *Bldg Trades.* a timber or beam into which one of the ends of a joist or rafter is fitted in the framing about an opening, a chimney, etc. **5.** an apparatus for stowing, arranging, or shifting cargo, coal, or the like. **6.** one who has no firm belief, policy, etc., esp. in politics. **7.** one who accommodates himself to one political party or other as expediency may dictate; an opportunist; time-server. **8.** one employed to upholster and otherwise finish the interior of a vehicle.

trimming (trĭm′ĭng), *n.* **1.** anything used or serving to trim or decorate: *the trimmings of a Christmas tree.* **2.** a decorative fitting or finish; a garnish. **3.** (*pl.*) *Colloq.* agreeable accompaniments or additions to plain or simple dishes or food. **4.** (*pl.*) pieces cut off in trimming, clipping, paring, or pruning. **5.** the act of one who or that which trims. **6.** a rebuking or reproving. **7.** a beating or thrashing. **8.** *U.S. Colloq.* a defeat: *our team took another trimming yesterday.*

trimolecular (trī′mə lĕk′yŏŏ lə), *adj.* *Chem.* relating to or having three molecules.

trimonthly (trī′mŭnth′lĭ), *adj.* taking place once each three months.

trimorph (trī′môf′), *n.* *Crystall.* **1.** a substance existing in three structurally distinct forms; a trimorphous substance. **2.** any one of the three forms.

trimorphism (trī mô′fĭz′-əm), *n.* **1.** *Zool.* the occurrence of three forms distinct in structure, coloration, etc., among animals of the same species. **2.** *Bot.* the occurrence of three different forms of flowers, leaves, etc., on the same plant or on distinct plants of the same species. **3.** *Crystall.* the property of some substances of crystallizing in three structurally distinct forms. **4.** the property or condition of occurring in three distinct forms. [f. s. Gk *trimorphos* having three forms + -ISM] —**trimor′phic, trimor′phous,** *adj.*

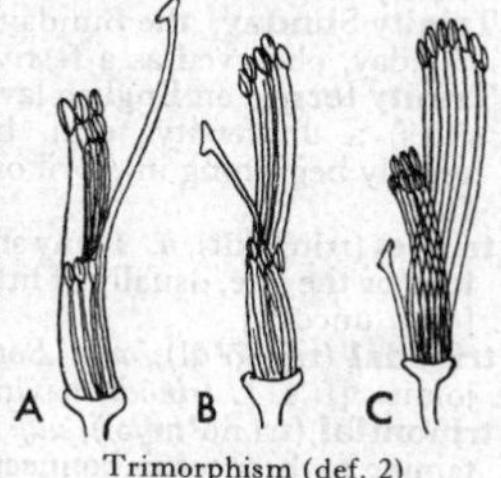

Trimorphism (def. 2)
A, Long style;
B, Intermediate style;
C, Short style

Trimurti (trĭ mŏŏə′tĭ), *n.* a Hindu trinity, consisting of Brahma the Creator, Vishnu the Preserver, and Siva the Destroyer, represented symbolically by one body with three heads. [t. Skt, f. *tri* three + *mūrti* shape]

Trinacrian (trī nā′krĭ ən, trĭ-, -năk′rĭ ən), *adj.* *Poetic or Lit.* Sicilian. [f. s. L *Trinacria* Sicily (t. Gk: m. *Trinakría*) + -AN]

trinal (trī′nəl), *adj.* threefold; triple; trine. [t. LL: s. *trīnālis*, f. L: s. *trīnus* threefold + *-ālis* -AL[1]]

trinary (trī′nə rĭ), *adj.* consisting of three parts, or proceeding by three; ternary.

Trincomalee (trĭng′kə mə lē′), *n.* a seaport in E Ceylon. 32,507 (1963).

trine (trīn), *adj.* **1.** threefold; triple. **2.** *Astrol.* denoting or pertaining to the trigon aspect of two planets distant from each other 120°, or the third part of the zodiac. —*n.* **3.** a set or group of three; a triad. **4.** (*cap.*) the Trinity. **5.** *Astrol.* the trine aspect of two planets. [ME, t. L: m. s. *trīnus* threefold]

Trinidad (trĭn′ĭ dăd′; *Sp.* trē-nē dȧd′), *n.* an island in the E West Indies, off the NE coast of Venezuela: part of Trinidad and Tobago. 792,624 pop. (1960); 1864 sq. mi.

Trinidad

Trinidad and Tobago, an independent state in the West Indies comprising the islands of Trinidad and Tobago: a member of the Commonwealth of Nations; formerly a British colony. 827,957 pop. (1960); 1980 sq. mi. *Cap.:* Port-of-Spain.

Trinitarian (trĭn′ĭ tēə′rĭ ən), *adj.* **1.** believing in the doctrine of the Trinity. **2.** pertaining to Trinitarians, or believers in the doctrine of the Trinity. **3.** belonging or pertaining to the religious order of Trinitarians. **4.** pertaining to the Trinity. **5.** (*l.c.*) forming a trinity; threefold; triple. —*n.* **6.** one who believes in the doctrine of the Trinity. **7.** a member of a religious order (**Order of the Holy Trinity**) founded in 1198 to redeem Christian captives of the Muslims.

Trinitarianism (trĭn′ĭ tēə′rĭ ə nĭz′əm), *n.* the belief in, or doctrine of, the Trinity.

trinitrine (trī nī′trĭn), *n.* *Med.* a nitroglycerine preparation used in the treatment of angina pectoris. Also, **trinitrin.**

trinitro-, *Chem.* a combining form meaning 'of three nitro groups', as in *trinitrobenzene.*

trinitrobenzene (trī′nī′trō bĕn′zēn, -bĕn zēn′), *n.* *Chem.* any of three highly explosive yellow crystalline compounds, $C_6H_3(NO_2)_3$, none of which is produced commercially. *Abbrev.:* TNB, T.N.B.

trinitrocresol (trī′nī′trō krē′sŏl), *n.* *Chem.* a yellow crystalline compound, $CH_3C_6H(OH)(NO_2)_3$, used in high explosives.

trinitrotoluene (trī′nī′trō tŏl′yŏŏ ēn′), *n.* *Chem.* a high explosive, $CH_3C_6H_2(NO_2)_3$, used in modern warfare, etc., exploded by detonators but unaffected by ordinary friction or shock. *Abbrev.:* TNT, T.N.T. Also, **trinitrotoluol** (trī′nī′trō tŏl′yŏŏ ŏl′).

Trinity (trĭn′ĭ tĭ), *n., pl.* **-ties. 1.** the union of three persons (Father, Son, and Holy Ghost) in one Godhead, or the threefold personality of the one Divine Being (**the Holy Trinity** or **Blessed Trinity**). **2.** Trinity Sunday. **3.** (*l.c.*)

a group of three; a triad. **4.** (*l.c.*) the state of being threefold or triple; threeness. **5.** Trinity term. [ME *trinite*, t. OF, t. L: m. *trīnitas* triad, trio, trinity]

Trinity House. See **Elder Brethren.**

Trinity Sunday, the Sunday next after Pentecost or Whit Sunday, observed as a festival in honour of the Trinity.

Trinity term, an English law sitting and (at some universities) a university term, between variable dates, but usually beginning in April or June and ending in June or July.

trinket (trĭng′kĭt), *n.* **1.** any small fancy article, bit of jewellery, or the like, usually of little value. **2.** anything trifling. [orig. uncert.]

trinodal (trī′nō′dl), *adj. Bot., etc.* having three nodes or joints. [f. s. L *trinōdis* having three knots + -AL[1]]

trinomial (trī nō′myəl), *adj.* **1.** *Alg.* consisting of or pertaining to three terms connected by the sign +, the sign −, or both of these. **2.** *Zool., Bot.* **a.** denoting a name comprising three terms, as of genus, species, and subspecies or variety. **b.** characterized by the use of such names. —*n.* **3.** *Alg.* a trinomial expression, as $a + b - c$. **4.** *Bot., Zool.* a trinomial name, as *Rosa gallica pumila.* [f. TRI- + (BI)NOMIAL] —**trino′mially,** *adv.*

trio (trē′ō), *n., pl.* **trios. 1.** a musical composition for three voices or instruments. **2.** a company of three singers or players. **3.** a subordinate division of a minuet, scherzo, march, etc., usually in a contrasted key and style (perhaps orig. written for three instruments or in three parts). **4.** any group of three persons or things. [t. It., der. *tre* three, modelled after *duo*]

triode (trī′ōd), *n. Electronics.* a radio valve containing three electrodes, usually an anode, a grid, and a cathode. [f. TRI- + -ODE[2]]

trioecious (trī ē′shəs), *adj. Bot.* having male, female, and hermaphrodite flowers on different plants. Also, *U.S.*, **triecious.** [f. s. NL *trioecia* (f. *tri-* TRI- + m. Gk *oikion* house) + -OUS] —**trioe′ciously,** *adv.*

triolet (trē′ō lĕt′), *n.* a short poem of fixed form, consisting of eight lines using two rhymes: ab aa abab. The first line is repeated as the fourth and seventh lines, and the second line is repeated as the eighth. [t. F; orig. uncert.]

trioxide (trī ŏk′sīd), *n. Chem.* an oxide containing three oxygen atoms, as As_2O_3. Also, **trioxid** (trī ŏk′sĭd).

trip (trĭp), *n., v.,* **tripped, tripping.** —*n.* **1.** a journey or voyage. **2.** a journey, voyage, or run made by a boat, train, or the like, between two points. **3.** a journey made for pleasure; excursion. **4.** *Colloq.* a period under the influence of a hallucinatory drug. **5.** a stumble. **6.** a sudden impeding or catching of a person's foot so as to throw him down, esp. in wrestling. **7.** a slip, mistake, or blunder. **8.** a wrong step in conduct. **9.** an act of stepping lightly; a light or nimble movement of the feet. **10.** *Mach.* **a.** a projecting part, catch, or the like for starting or checking some movement. **b.** a sudden starting or releasing.
—*v.i.* **11.** to stumble: *to trip over a child's toy.* **12.** to make a slip or mistake, as in a statement; make a wrong step in conduct. **13.** to step lightly or nimbly; skip; dance. **14.** to go with a light, quick tread. **15.** to tip or tilt. **16.** *Naut.* (of a boom) to roll under water in a seaway. **17.** *Horol.* to move over and beyond the pallet, as a tooth on an escapement wheel. **18.** *Rare.* to make a journey or excursion.
—*v.t.* **19.** to cause to stumble (often fol. by *up*): *the rug tripped him up.* **20.** cause to fail; hinder; overthrow. **21.** to cause to make a slip or error (often fol. by *up*): *to trip up a witness by artful questions.* **22.** to catch in a slip or error. **23.** to perform with a light or tripping step, as a dance. **24.** to dance upon (ground, etc.). **25.** to tip or tilt. **26.** *Naut.* **a.** to break out (an anchor) by turning it over or lifting it from the bottom by a line (**tripping line**) attached to its crown. **b.** to tip or turn (a yard) from a horizontal to a vertical position. **c.** to lift (an upper mast) before lowering. **27.** to operate, start, or set free (a mechanism, weight, etc.) by suddenly releasing a catch, clutch, or the like. **28.** *Mach.* to release or operate suddenly (a catch, clutch, etc.).
[ME *trippe*, t. OF: m. *tripper* strike with the feet, t. Gmc; cf. MD *trippen*]

—**Syn. 1.** TRIP, EXPEDITION, JOURNEY, PILGRIMAGE, VOYAGE are terms for a course of travel made to a particular place, usually for some specific purpose. TRIP is the general word, indicating going any distance and returning, by walking or any means of locomotion, for either business or pleasure, and in either a hurried or a leisurely manner: *a trip to the Continent; a holiday trip; a bus trip.* An EXPEDITION, made often by an organized company, is designed to accomplish a specific purpose: *an archaeological expedition.* JOURNEY indicates a trip of considerable length, usually by land, for business or pleasure or other reasons, and is now applied to travel which is more leisurely or more fatiguing than a trip; a return is not necessarily indicated: *the long journey to Siam.* A PILGRIMAGE is made as to a shrine, from motives of piety or veneration: *a pilgrimage to Lourdes.* A VOYAGE is travel by water or air, usually for a long distance and for business or pleasure; if by water, leisure is indicated: *a voyage round the world.*

tripalmitin (trī păl′mĭ tĭn), *n. Chem.* palmitin.

triparted (trī′pä′tĭd), *adj.* divided into three parts.

tripartite (trī′pä′tīt), *adj.* **1.** divided into or consisting of three parts. **2.** *Bot.* divided into three parts by incisions which extend nearly to the base, as a leaf. **3.** participated in by three parties, as a treaty. [ME, t. L: m. s. *tripartītus* divided into three parts] —**tri′par′titely,** *adv.*

Tripartite leaf

tripartition (trī′pä tĭsh′ən), *n.* division into three parts.

tripe (trīp), *n.* **1.** the first and second divisions of the stomach of a ruminant, esp. of the ox kind, prepared for use as food. **2.** *Slang.* anything poor or worthless, esp. written work; nonsense; rubbish. [ME, t. OF, ult. t. Ar.: m. *tarb* folds of peritoneum]

tripedal (trī′pĕd′l, trī′pēd′l), *adj.* having three feet. [t. L: s. *tripedālis*]

tripersonal (trī′pû′sə nəl), *adj.* consisting of or existing in three persons, as the Godhead.

tripetalous (trī pĕt′ə ləs), *adj. Bot.* having three petals.

triphammer (trĭp′hăm′ə), *n. Mach.* a heavy hammer raised and then let fall by means of some tripping device, as a cam. Also, **trip hammer.**

triphenylmethane (trī′fĕn′ĭl mē′thān, -fē′nīl-), *n. Chem.* a colourless, crystalline organic compound, $(C_6H_5)_3CH$, from which many dyes (the **triphenylmethane dyes**) are derived.

triphthong (trĭf′thŏng), *n.* **1.** a union of three vowel sounds pronounced in one syllable. **2.** a trigraph. [t. NL: s. *triphthongus*, t. MGk: m. *triphthongos* with three vowels] —**triphthong′al,** *adj.*

triphylite (trĭf′ĭ līt′), *n.* a mineral, a phosphate of lithium, iron, and manganese, usually occurring in masses of a bluish or greenish colour.

triphyllous (trī fĭl′əs), *adj. Bot.* having three leaves.

tripinnate (trī′pĭn′ĭt, -āt), *adj. Bot.* bipinnate, as a leaf, with the divisions also pinnate. Also, **tri′pin′nated.** —**tri′pin′nately,** *adv.*

triplane (trī′plān′), *n.* an aeroplane with three supporting wings, one above another.

triple (trĭp′l), *adj., n., v.,* **-pled, -pling.** —*adj.* **1.** threefold; consisting of three parts: *a triple knot.* **2.** of three kinds. **3.** three times as great. **4.** *Internat. Law.* tripartite. —*n.* **5.** an amount, number, etc., three times as great as another. **6.** something triple or threefold; a triad. —*v.t.* **7.** to make triple. —*v.i.* **8.** to become triple. [ME, t. L: m. *triplus*, t. Gk: m. *triploús* threefold] —**triply** (trĭp′lĭ), *adv.*

Triple Alliance, 1. the alliance (1882–1915) between Germany, Austria-Hungary, and Italy. **2.** a league (1717) of France, Great Britain, and the Netherlands against Spain. **3.** a league (1668) of England, Sweden, and the Netherlands against France.

triple bond, *Chem.* a chemical linkage between atoms in a molecule consisting of three covalent bonds, often represented in formulas by three lines, as in acetylene, $CH \equiv CH$.

triple crown, the tiara worn by the pope.

Triple Entente, 1. an informal understanding among Great Britain, France, and Russia based on (a) a Franco-Russian military alliance, 1894; (b) an Anglo-French entente, 1904; (c) an Anglo-Russian understanding, 1907: considered as a counterbalance to the Triple Alliance and terminating when the Bolsheviks came to power in Russia in 1917. **2.** the member nations of this entente.

triple-expansion (trĭp′l ĭk spăn′shən), *adj.* denoting or pertaining to a steam-engine in which the steam is expanded in three cylinders in succession, the exhaust steam from the first cylinder being the driving steam for the second, and so on.

triple jump, an Olympic field event, the object of which is to cover the greatest possible distance by taking in a continuous movement, a hop, a step, and a jump. Also, **hop, step, and jump.**

triple measure, *Music.* triple time.

triple-nerved (trĭp′l nûvd′), *adj. Bot.* denoting a leaf in which two prominent nerves emerge from the middle nerve a little above its base.

triple point, *Physics.* the unique temperature and pressure at which the gaseous, liquid, and solid phases of a substance are in equilibrium.

triplet (trĭp′lĭt), *n.* **1.** one of three children born at one birth. **2.** (*pl.*) three offspring born at one birth. **3.** any group or combination of three. **4.** *Pros.* three successive verses or lines, esp. when rhyming and of the same length; a stanza of three lines. **5.** *Music.* a group of three notes to be performed in the time of two ordinary notes of the same kind. **6.** an assembled imitation gem with three parts, the centre one giving the colour, the top and bottom supplying the wearing qualities. **7.** (*pl.*) (in some card games) three cards of the same denomination. **8.** *Chem.* a chemical bond consisting of three electrons shared between two atoms. [der. TRIPLE, modelled after DOUBLET. Cf. F *triplet*]

tripletail (trĭp′l tāl′), *n.* a large food fish, *Lobotes surinamensis*, of the warmer waters of the Atlantic Ocean and the Mediterranean Sea, with the lobes of its dorsal and anal fins extending backwards and with the caudal fin suggesting a three-lobed tail.

triple time, *Music.* time or rhythm characterized by three beats to the bar with an accent on the first beat. Also, **triple measure.**

triplex (trĭp′lĕks), *adj.* **1.** threefold; triple. —*n.* **2.** something triple. **3.** *Music.* triple time. [t. L: threefold]

Triplex (trĭp′lĕks), *n.* *Trademark.* a form of laminated safety glass.

triplicate (*v.* trĭp′lĭ kāt′; *adj.*, *n.* trĭp′lĭ kĭt), *v.*, **-cated, -cating,** *adj.*, *n.* —*v.t.* **1.** to make threefold; triple. **2.** to make or produce a third time or in a third instance. —*adj.* **3.** threefold; triple; tripartite. —*n.* **4.** one of three identical things. [t. L: m. s. *triplicātus*, pp., tripled] —**trip′lica′tion,** *n.*

triplicity (trĭ plĭs′ĭ tĭ), *n.*, *pl.* **-ties. 1.** the state of being triple; triple character. **2.** a group or combination of three; triad. **3.** *Astrol.* a set of three signs of the zodiac.

tripod (trī′pŏd), *n.* **1.** a stool, pedestal, or the like with three legs. **2.** a three-legged stand, as for a camera. [t. L: s. *tripūs*, t. Gk: m. *tripous* three-footed]

tripodal (trĭp′ə dl), *adj.* **1.** pertaining to or having the form of a tripod. **2.** having three feet or legs.

tripodic (trī pŏd′ĭk), *adj.* having or using three feet or legs.

tripody (trĭp′ə dĭ), *n.*, *pl.* **-dies.** *Pros.* a group or verse of three feet. [t. Gk: m. s. *tripodía*]

Tripoli (trĭp′ə lĭ; *It.* trē′pō lē), *n.* **1.** Also, **Tripolitania.** one of the former Barbary States of N Africa: later a province of Turkey; now a part of Libya. **2.** a seaport in and the capital of Libya, in the NW part. 212,577 (1964). **3.** a seaport in N Lebanon, on the Mediterranean. 114,443 (1961). **4.** (*l.c.*) any of several siliceous substances, as rottenstone and infusorial earth, used in polishing, etc. —**Tripolitan** (trĭ pŏl′ĭ tən), *adj.*, *n.*

Tripolitania (trĭp′ō lĭ tā′nyə; *It.* trē pō lē tá′nyȧ), *n.* Tripoli (def. 1).

tripos (trī′pŏs), *n.*, *pl.* **triposes.** (at Cambridge University) any of various final honours examinations for the B.A. degree. [t. L: pseudo-Hellenization of *tripūs* tripod]

tripper (trĭp′ə), *n.* **1.** one who or that which trips. **2.** *Mach.* **a.** a signal device; a trip. **b.** an apparatus causing a signal, or other operating mechanism, to be tripped or activated. **3.** *Colloq.* one who goes on a pleasure trip or excursion.

trippet (trĭp′ĭt), *n.* *Mach.* a projection, cam, or the like, for striking some other part at regular intervals.

tripping (trĭp′ĭng), *adj.* **1.** light and quick, as the step, pace, etc. **2.** proceeding with a light, easy movement or rhythm. —**trip′pingly,** *adv.*

tripping line. *Naut.* See **trip** (def. 26a).

tripple (trĭp′l), *n.*, *v.*, **-pled, -pling.** *Chiefly S African.* —*n.* **1.** a steady gait of horses, in which the animal moves both legs on each side together. —*v.i.* **2.** to move at a tripple. [t. Afrikaans: m. *trippel*, t. D: s. *trippelen*, v., TRIP (def. 14)]

tripterous (trĭp′tə rəs), *adj.* *Bot.* three-winged; having three wings or winglike expansions. [f. TRI- + s. Gk *pterón* wing + -OUS]

Triptolemus (trĭp tŏl′ĭ məs), *n.* *Gk Myth.* a favourite of Demeter: the inventor of the plough and patron of agriculture, and connected with the Eleusinian mysteries. Also, **Triptolemos.**

triptych (trĭp′tĭk), *n.* **1.** *Art.* a set of three panels or compartments side by side, bearing pictures, carvings, or the like. **2.** a hinged or folding three-leaved writing tablet. [t. Gk: m. s. *triptychos* of three plates]

Tripura (trĭp′o͝o rə), *n.* a union territory in NE India. 1,142,005 pop. (1961); 4116 sq. mi.

trip-wire (trĭp′wī′ə), *n.* a concealed wire designed to set off an alarm, explosive device, etc., when touched or pulled.

triquetral (trī kwē′trəl, -kwĕt′rəl), *adj.* **1.** triquetrous. —*n.* **2.** one of the eight bones of the carpus.

triquetrous (trī kwē′trəs, -kwĕt′rəs), *adj.* **1.** three-sided; triangular. **2.** having a triangular cross-section. Also, **triquetral.** [t. L: m. *triquetrus* three-cornered]

triradiate (trī rā′dĭ ĭt, -āt′), *adj.* having, or consisting of, three rays or raylike processes. Also, **trira′diat′ed.** —**trira′diately,** *adv.*

trireme (trī′rēm), *n.* *Class. Hist.* a galley with three rows or tiers of oars on each side, one above another, used chiefly as a warship. [t. L: m. s. *trirēmis*]

trisaccharide (trī săk′ə rīd′), *n.* *Chem.* a carbohydrate composed of three monosaccharide units, and hydrolysable to a monosaccharide or a mixture of monosaccharides.

trisect (trī sĕkt′), *v.t.* to divide into three parts, esp. into three equal parts. [f. TRI- + s. L *sectus*, pp., cut] —**trisection** (trī sĕk′shən), *n.* —**trisec′tor,** *n.*

trisepalous (trī sĕp′ə ləs), *adj.* *Bot.* having three sepals.

triseptate (trī sĕp′tāt), *adj.* *Bot.*, *Zool.* having three septa.

triserial (trī sĭə′rĭ əl), *adj.* **1.** arranged in three series or rows. **2.** *Bot.* having only three verticils.

triskelion (trĭs kĕl′ĭ ŏn′, -ən), *n.*, *pl.* **-kelia** (-kĕl′ĭ ə). a symbolic figure consisting of three legs, arms, or branches radiating from a common centre: the device of Sicily and the Isle of Man. Also, **triskele** (trĭs′kēl). [f. TRI- + s. Gk *skélos* leg + Gk *-ion* dim. suffix]

Triskelion

trismus (trĭz′məs), *n.* *Pathol.* lockjaw. [t. NL, t. Gk: m. *trismós* a grinding] —**tris′mic,** *adj.*

trisoctahedron (trĭs ŏk′tə hē′drən), *n.*, *pl.* **-drons, -dra** (-drə). a solid bounded by twenty-four equal faces, three corresponding to each face of an octahedron, called (esp. in *Crystall.*) **trigonal trisoctahedron** when the faces are triangles, and **tetragonal trisoctahedron** when the faces are quadrilaterals. [f. Gk *trís* thrice + OCTAHEDRON] —**trisoc′tahe′dral,** *adj.*

trispermous (trī spû′məs), *adj.* *Bot.* three-seeded. [f. TRI- + m. Gk *-spermos* having seed]

Tristan da Cunha (trĭs′tən də ko͞o′nə), a group of three volcanic islands in the S Atlantic, belonging to Great Britain. ab. 50 sq. mi.

tristearin (trī stĭə′rĭn), *n.* *Chem.* stearin (def. 1).

tristichous (trĭs′tĭ kəs), *adj.* **1.** arranged in three rows. **2.** *Bot.* arranged in or characterized by three vertical rows. [t. Gk: m. *trístichos* of three rows]

Tristram (trĭs′trəm), *n.* *Arthurian Legend.* one of the famous knights of the Round Table, whose love for Iseult, wife of King Mark, is the subject of many legends. Also, **Tristan** (trĭs′tən).

tristylous (trī stī′ləs), *adj.* *Bot.* having three styles. [f. TRI- + m. Gk *-stylos* columned]

trisulphide (trī sŭl′fīd), *n.* *Chem.* a sulphide containing three sulphur atoms.

trisyllable (trī′sĭl′ə bl), *n.* a word of three syllables, as *telephone.* —**trisyllabic** (trī′sĭ lăb′ĭk), **tri′syllab′ical,** *adj.* —**tri′syllab′ically,** *adv.*

tritanope (trī′tə nōp′, trĭt′-), *n.* *Ophthalm.* one who has tritanopia.

tritanopia (trī′tə nō′pyə, trĭt′-), *n.* *Ophthalm.* a form of defective colour vision in which hue discrimination is very poor in the green to blue region of the spectrum. [NL, f. Gk: s. *trítos* third + *an-* AN-[1] + *opia* -OPIA]

trite (trīt), *adj.*, **triter, tritest. 1.** hackneyed by constant use or repetition; commonplace: *a trite saying.* **2.** *Archaic.* rubbed or worn by use. [t. L: m. s. *trītus*, pp., rubbed, worn] —**trite′ly,** *adv.* —**trite′ness,** *n.* —**Syn. 1.** See **commonplace.** —**Ant. 1.** fresh.

tritheism (trī′thē ĭz′əm), *n.* *Theol.* belief in three Gods, esp. in the doctrine that the three persons of the Trinity (Father, Son, and Holy Ghost) are three distinct Gods, each an independent centre of self-consciousness and self-determination. —**tri′theist,** *n.*, *adj.* —**tri′theis′tic, tri′theis′tical,** *adj.*

tritium (trĭt′ĭ əm), *n.* *Chem.* a radioactive isotope of hydrogen containing two neutrons and a proton, with a mass number of 3.

Triton (trī′tn), *n.* **1.** *Class. Myth.* **a.** a sea-god, son of Poseidon and Amphitrite, represented as having the head and trunk of a man and the tail of a fish, and bearing a conch-shell trumpet. **b.** (later) one of a race of subordinate sea deities similarly represented, attendants on the greater sea-gods. **2.** (*l.c.*) any of various marine gastropods constituting the family *Tritonidae* (esp. of the genus *Triton*), having a large, spiral, often beautifully coloured shell. **3.** (*l.c.*) the shell of a triton. **4.** (*l.c.*) *Physics.* the nucleus of a tritium atom.

tritone (trī′tōn′), *n.* *Music.* an interval consisting of three whole tones. [t. ML: m. s. *tritonus*, t. Gk: m. *tritonos* having three tones]

triturable (trĭt′yo͞o rə bl), *adj.* that may be triturated.

triturate (trĭt′yo͞o rāt′), *v.*, **-rated, -rating,** *n.* —*v.t.* **1.** to reduce to fine particles or powder by rubbing, grinding, bruising, or the like; pulverize. —*n.* **2.** a triturated substance. **3.** a trituration. [t. LL: m. s. *trītūrātus*, pp., threshed] —**trit′ura′tor,** *n.*

trituration (trĭt′yo͞o rā′shən), *n.* **1.** the act of triturating. **2.** the state of being triturated. **3.** *Pharm.* **a.** a mixture of a medicinal substance with milk sugar, triturated to an impalpable powder. **b.** any triturated substance.

triumph (trī′əmf), *n.* **1.** the act or fact of being victorious, or triumphing; victory; conquest. **2.** a notable achievement; striking success. **3.** the exultation of victory; joy over success. **4.** *Rom. Hist.* the ceremonial entrance into ancient Rome of a victorious commander with his army, spoils, captives, etc., authorized by the senate in honour of an important military or naval achievement. **5.** *Obs.* a public pageant, spectacle, or the like. *—v.i.* **6.** to gain a victory; be victorious. **7.** to gain mastery; prevail. **8.** to achieve success. **9.** to exult over victory; rejoice over success. **10.** to be elated or glad; rejoice proudly; glory. **11.** to celebrate a triumph, as a victorious Roman commander. *—v.t.* **12.** *Obs.* to conquer; triumph over. [ME *triumphe*, OE *triumpha*, t. L: m. *triumphus*] **—tri′umpher,** *n.* **—Syn. 1.** See **victory.**

triumphal (trī ŭm′fəl), *adj.* **1.** of or pertaining to a triumph. **2.** celebrating or commemorating a triumph or victory.

triumphant (trī ŭm′fənt), *adj.* **1.** having achieved victory or success; victorious; successful. **2.** exulting over victory; rejoicing over success; exultant. **3.** *Rare.* triumphal. **4.** *Obs.* splendid; magnificent. [t. L: s. *triumphans*, ppr., triumphing] **—trium′phantly,** *adv.*

triumph card, *Cards.* one of the 22 cards in the tarot pack which bears a symbolic or mythological character, functioning as trumps in the old game of tarots, and now chiefly used in cartomancy, each card having a particular mystical significance ascribed to it.

triumvir (trī o͝om′və), *n., pl.* **-virs, -viri** (-vĭ rē′). **1.** *Rom. Hist.* one of three officers or magistrates sharing the same public function. **2.** one of three persons associated in any office. [t. L: s. *triumvirī*, pl., back-formation from *trium virōrum* of three men] **—trium′viral,** *adj.*

triumvirate (trī ŭm′vĭ rĭt), *n.* **1.** *Rom. Hist.* the office or magistracy of a triumvir. **2.** the government of three joint officers or magistrates. **3.** a coalition of three magistrates or rulers for joint administration. **4.** any association of three in office or authority. **5.** any group or set of three. [t. L: m. s. *triumvirātus*]

triune (trī′yo͞on), *adj.* **1.** three in one; constituting a trinity, as the Godhead. *—n.* **2.** (*cap.*) the Trinity. [f. TRI- + m. s. L *ūnus* one]

triunitarian (trī′yo͞o′nĭ tĕə′rĭ ən), *n.* Trinitarian.

triunity (trī′yo͞o′nĭ tĭ), *n., pl.* **-ties.** Trinity.

trivalent (trī vā′lənt, trĭv′ə lənt), *adj.* *Chem.* having a valency of three. **—triva′lence, triva′lency,** *n.*

trivalent carbon, *Chem.* a carbon atom which utilizes only three of its four valencies.

trivalve (trī′vălv′), *adj.* having three valves, as a shell.

Trivandrum (trĭ văn′drəm), *n.* a town in India: the capital of Kerala, in the S part: pilgrimages. 239,815 (1961).

trivet (trĭv′ĭt), *n.* **1.** a small metal plate with short legs put under a hot platter or dish at the table. **2.** a three-footed or three-legged stand or support, esp. one of iron placed over a fire to hold cooking vessels or the like. [ME *trevet*, OE *trefet*, appar. b. L *tripēs* and OE *thrifēte* three-footed (with VL *-e-* for L *-i-*)]

trivia (trĭv′ĭ ə), *n.pl.* inessential, unimportant, or inconsequential things; trifles; trivialities. [appar. back-formation from TRIVIAL]

trivial (trĭv′ĭ əl), *adj.* **1.** of little importance; trifling; insignificant. **2.** commonplace; ordinary. **3.** *Biol.* (of names of animals and plants) specific, as distinguished from *generic.* [ME, t. L: s. *triviālis* belonging to the crossroads, (hence) common] **—triv′ially,** *adv.* **—Syn. 1.** See **petty. —Ant. 1.** important.

trivialism (trĭv′ĭ ə lĭz′əm), *n.* **1.** trivial character. **2.** something trivial.

triviality (trĭv′ĭ ăl′ĭ tĭ), *n., pl.* **-ties. 1.** something trivial; a trivial matter, affair, remark, etc. **2.** Also, **triv′ialness.** trivial quality or character.

trivialize (trĭv′ĭ ə līz′), *v.t.,* **-lized, -lizing.** to make trivial or unimportant. Also, **trivialise.**

trivium (trĭv′ĭ əm), *n.* (during the Middle Ages) the lower division of the seven liberal arts, comprising grammar, rhetoric, and logic. Cf. **quadrivium.** [t. ML, special use of L *trivium* public place (lit. place where three roads meet)]

triweekly (trī′wēk′lĭ), *adv., adj., n., pl.* **-lies.** *—adv.* **1.** every three weeks. **2.** three times a week. *—adj.* **3.** occurring or appearing three times a week. **4.** occurring or appearing every three weeks. *—n.* **5.** a triweekly publication.

-trix, a suffix of feminine agent-nouns, as in *executrix.* Cf. **-or².** [t. L]

Troas (trō′ăs), *n.* a region in NW Asia Minor around ancient Troy. Also, **The Troad** (trō′ăd).

Trobriand Islands (trō′brĭ ănd′), a group of islands lying north of the eastern end of New Guinea: part of the Australian territory of Papua. 11,700 pop. (est. 1967); 170 sq. mi.

trocar (trō′kä), *n.* *Surg.* a sharp pointed instrument enclosed in a cannula, used for withdrawing fluid from a cavity, as the abdominal cavity, etc. [earlier *trocart*, t. F, var. of *trois-carts*, lit., three-faced]

trochaic (trō kā′ĭk), *Pros.* *—adj.* **1.** pertaining to the trochee. **2.** consisting of or employing a trochee or trochees. *—n.* **3.** a trochee. **4.** (*usually pl.*) a verse or poem consisting of trochees. [t. L: s. *trochaicus*, t. Gk: m. *trochaikós*]

trochal (trō′kl), *adj.* *Zool.* resembling a wheel. [f. s. Gk *trochós* wheel + -AL¹]

trochanter (trŏ kăn′tə), *n.* **1.** *Anat., Zool.* (in many vertebrates) a prominence or process on the upper part of the femur. See illus. under **coxa. 2.** *Zool.* (in insects and other arthropods) the lower segment of the leg. [t. F, t. Gk]

troche (trōsh), *n.* *Pharm.* a small tablet, esp. a circular one, made of some medicinal substance worked into a paste with sugar and mucilage or the like, and dried. [back-formation from obs. *trochisk* troche, t. L: m. s. *trochiscus*, t. Gk: m. *trochískos*]

trochee (trō′kē), *n.* *Pros.* a metrical foot of two syllables, a long followed by a short, or an accented followed by an unaccented. [t. L: m. s. *trochaeus*, t. Gk: m. *trochaîos* running]

trochilus (trŏk′ĭ ləs), *n., pl.* **-li** (-lī′). **1.** any of several small Old World warblers, as the willow warbler (*Phylloscopus trochilus*). **2.** the hummingbird. **3.** crocodile bird. [t. L, t. Gk: m. *trochílos*]

trochlea (trŏk′lĭ ə), *n., pl.* **-leae** (-lĭ ē′). *Anat.* a pulley-like structure or arrangement of parts affording a smooth surface upon which another part glides, as a tendon or bone. [t. L, t. Gk: m. *trochileía* pulley]

trochlear (trŏk′lĭ ə), *adj.* **1.** *Anat.* belonging to or connected with a trochlea. **2.** *Physiol., Anat.* pulley-like. **3.** *Bot.* circular and contracted in the middle so as to resemble a pulley. Also, **trochleariform** (trŏk′lĭ ă′rĭ fôm′).

trochlear nerve, *Anat.* the fourth cranial nerve in vertebrates.

trochoid (trō′koid), *n.* **1.** *Geom.* a curve traced by a point rigidly connected with, but not generally on the circumference of, a circle which rolls, without slipping, upon a curve, circle, or straight line. *—adj.* **2.** wheel-like; rotating like a wheel, as a joint. [t. Gk: m. *trochoeidēs* round like a wheel] **—trochoi′dal,** *adj.* **—trochoi′dally,** *adv.*

trochophore (trŏk′ə fô′), *n.* *Zool.* a ciliate free-swimming larva common to several invertebrate groups.

trod (trŏd), *v.* pt. and pp. of **tread.**

trodden (trŏd′n), *v.* pp. of **tread.**

trode (trōd), *v.* *Archaic.* pt. of **tread.**

troglodyte (trŏg′lə dīt′), *n.* **1.** a caveman or cavedweller. **2.** a person living in seclusion. **3.** one unacquainted with affairs of the world. [t. L: m. s. *trōglodyta*, t. Gk: m. *trōglodýtēs* one who creeps into holes] **—troglodytic** (trŏg′lə dĭt′ĭk), **trog′lodyt′ical,** *adj.*

trogon (trō′gŏn), *n.* any bird of the family *Trogonidae*, esp. of the genus *Trogon*, of tropical and subtropical regions, notable for brilliant plumage. See **quetzal** (def. 1). [t. NL, t. Gk: gnawing]

troika (troi′kə), *n.* **1.** a Russian vehicle drawn by a team of three horses abreast. **2.** a team of three horses driven abreast. **3.** any group of three persons acting together for a common purpose. [t. Russ.]

Troilus (troi′ləs, trō′ĭ ləs), *n.* *Class. and Medieval Legend.* the warrior son of King Priam of Troy, mentioned by Homer and Virgil, and greatly developed in medieval redactions of the Troy story as the lover of Cressida.

Trois-Rivières (*Fr.* trwȧ rē vyěr′), *n.* French name of **Three Rivers.**

Trojan (trō′jən), *adj.* **1.** of or pertaining to ancient Troy or its inhabitants. *—n.* **2.** a native or inhabitant of Troy. **3.** *Colloq.* one who shows pluck, determination, or energy: *to work like a Trojan.* [ME, t. L: s. *Trōjānus*]

Trojan group, *Astron.* a group of asteroids which have the same mean motion as the planet Jupiter: they are divided into two subgroups which oscillate between two points, equidistant from the sun and Jupiter, forming an equilateral triangle with the sun and Jupiter.

Trojan Horse, *Class. Legend.* **1.** the gigantic, hollow, wooden figure of a horse, filled with armed Greeks, and brought into Troy, thus ensuring the destruction of the city. **2.** one who or that which is designed to subvert or undermine from within.

Trojan War, *Class. Legend.* a ten-year war waged by the confederated Greeks, under the Greek king Agamemnon, against the Trojans to avenge the abduction of Helen, wife of the Greek king Menelaus, by Paris, son of the Trojan king Priam, and ending in the sack and burning of Troy.

troll¹ (trōl), *v.t.* **1.** to sing or utter in a full, rolling voice.

2. to sing in the manner of a round or catch. 3. to fish by trolling. 4. to move (the line or bait) in doing this. 5. to cause to turn round and round; roll. 6. *Obs.* to pass from one to another, as a bowl of drink at table. —*v.i.* 7. to sing with a full, rolling voice; give forth full, rolling tones. 8. to be uttered or sounded in such tones. 9. to fish with a moving line, as one worked up and down in fishing for pike with a rod, or one trailed behind a boat. 10. to roll; turn round and round. 11. *Slang.* to go; walk; saunter; stroll. 12. *Obs.* to move nimbly, as the tongue in speaking. —*n.* 13. a song whose parts are sung in succession; a round. 14. the act of trolling. 15. a lure used in trolling for fish. 16. the fishing line containing the lure and hook for use in trolling. [ME *trollen* roll, stroll, t. OF: m. *troller*, t. MHG: m. *trollen*] —**troll′er,** *n.*

troll[2] (trōl), *n.* (in Scandinavian folklore) one of a race of supernatural beings, sometimes conceived as giants and sometimes as dwarfs, inhabiting caves or subterranean dwellings. [t. Scand.; cf. Icel. *troll*]

trolley (trŏl′ĭ), *n., pl.* **-leys,** *v.* —*n.* 1. any of various kinds of low carts or vehicles. 2. a small table on castors for carrying dishes, serving food, etc. 3. a low truck running on rails, used on railways, in factories, mines, etc. 4. a pulley or truck travelling on an overhead track, or grooved metallic wheel or skid carried on the end of a sprung pole (**trolley pole**) by an electric tram or trolleybus and held in contact with an overhead conductor, usually a suspended wire (**trolley wire**), from which it collects the current for the propulsion of the vehicle. 5. a trolleybus. 6. *U.S.* a tram. —*v.t., v.i.* 7. to convey or go by trolley. [prob. der. TROLL[1]] —**trol′leyless,** *adj.*

trolleybus (trŏl′ĭ bŭs′), *n.* an electric bus, whose motor draws current from two overhead wires by means of twin trolley poles. Also, **trolley-bus, trolley bus.**

trolley car, *U.S.* a tram.

trollop (trŏl′əp), *n.* 1. an untidy or slovenly woman; a slattern. 2. an immoral woman; prostitute. [prob. der. TROLL[1], v.]

Trollope (trŏl′əp), *n.* **Anthony,** 1815–82, English novelist.

trombidiasis (trŏm′bĭ dī′ə sĭs), *n.* *Vet. Sci.* the condition of being infested with chiggers. [NL, f. s. L *trombidium* red mite + *-iāsis* -IASIS]

trombone (trŏm bōn′), *n.* a musical wind instrument consisting of a cylindrical metal tube expanding into a bell and bent twice in U shape, usually equipped with a slide. [t. It., der. *tromba* trumpet, t. OHG: m. *trumba*] —**trombonist** (trŏm bō′nĭst), *n.*

Trombone

trommel (trŏm′əl), *n.* *Metall.* a revolving cylindrical or conical sieve. [t. G: *Trommel* drum]

Tromp (*Du.* trômp), *n.* 1. **Cornelis** (*Du.* kôr nĕ′lĭs), 1629–1691, Dutch admiral. 2. his father, **Maarten Harpertszoon** (*Du.* mär′tən hŏr′pərt sôn), 1597–1653, Dutch admiral.

trompe (trŏmp), *n.* *Metall.* the apparatus by which the blast is produced in one type of forge. The principle is that water can be made to fall through a pipe in such a way that it will draw in through side openings a considerable amount of air which can be utilized as a constant current or blast. [t. F: lit., trump]

trompe l'oeil (trŏmp′lŭy′; *Fr.* trôNp lœy′), *Painting.* a type of painting intended to deceive the eye; illusionism. [F: trick the eye]

Tromsö (trŏm′sō; *Norw.* trōōm′sœ), *n.* a seaport in N Norway. 33,378 (1965).

trona (trō′nə), *n.* a mineral, greyish or yellowish hydrous sodium carbonate and bicarbonate, $Na_2CO_3 \cdot NaHCO_3 \cdot 2H_2O$, occurring in dried or partly evaporated lake basins. [t. Sw., appar. t. Ar.: m. *trōn*. Cf. NATRON]

Trondheim (trŏn′hām), *n.* a seaport on **Trondheim Fiord** (ab. 80 mi. long), in central Norway. 113,582 (1965). Formerly, **Nidaros** or **Trondhjem** (trŏn′yəm).

troop (trōōp), *n.* 1. an assemblage of persons or things; a company or band. 2. a great number or multitude. 3. *Mil.* a body of soldiers being a subdivision of a cavalry regiment. 4. (*pl.*) a body of soldiers, marines, etc. 5. a unit of 32 boy scouts, equal to four patrols. 6. a herd, flock, or swarm. 7. *Rare.* a band or troupe of actors. —*v.i.* 8. to gather in a company; flock together. 9. to go or come in great numbers. 10. to walk as if on a march. 11. to go, pass, or march in rank or order. 12. to associate or consort (fol. by *with*). —*v.t.* 13. to assemble in, form into, or unite with a troop or troops. 14. *Mil.* to carry (the flag or colours) in a ceremonial way before troops: *trooping the colour.* [t. F: m. *troupe*, g. LL *troppus* flock, from Gmc]

—**Syn.** 1. TROOP, TROUPE both mean a band, company, or group. TROOP has various meanings as indicated in the definitions above. With the spelling TROUPE the word has the specialized meaning of a company of actors, singers, or acrobats. See **company.**

troop-carrier (trōōp′kă′rĭ ə), *n.* a motorized vehicle, aircraft, or ship, used to transport troops.

trooper (trōō′pə), *n.* 1. a cavalry soldier. 2. a private soldier in a cavalry regiment. 3. this rank. 4. *U.S.* a state trooper. 5. a cavalry horse. 6. a troopship. 7. **swear like a trooper,** to swear vigorously. [der. TROOP. Cf. F *troupier*]

troopship (trōōp′shĭp′), *n.* a ship for the conveyance of military troops; a transport.

troostite[1] (trōōs′tīt), *n.* *Metall.* 1. the microstructure of hardened steel, consisting of ferrite and finely divided cementite, which is produced on tempering martensite below 450°C. 2. Also, **troostitic pearlite.** the constituent produced by the decomposition of austenite when cooled at a rate intermediate between that which will produce a martensitic or a sorbitic structure. [named after L. *Troost*, died 1911, French chemist] —**troostitic** (trōō stĭt′ĭk), *adj.*

troostite[2] (trōōs′tīt), *n.* a form of willemite in which some of the zinc is replaced by manganese. [named after G. *Troost*, 1776–1850, U.S. metallurgist]

tropaeolin (trō pē′ə lĭn), *n.* *Chem.* any of a number of orange or yellow azo dyes of complex composition.

tropaeolum (trō pē′ə ləm), *n., pl.* **-lums, -la** (-lə). any of the pungent herbs constituting the genus *Tropaeolum*, native in tropical America, species of which are well known in cultivation under the name of *nasturtium.* [NL, dim. of L *tropaeum* TROPHY]

-tropal, an adjective combining form identical in meaning with **-tropic.**

trope (trōp), *n.* 1. *Rhet.* **a.** a figure of speech. **b.** a word or phrase so used. 2. a phrase, sentence, or verse formerly interpolated in a liturgical text to amplify or embellish. [t. L: m. s. *tropus* figure in rhetoric, t. Gk: m. *trópos* turn]

-trope, a combining form referring to turning, as in *heliotrope.* [t. Gk: m. s. *-trópos*]

trophallaxis (trŏf′ə lăk′sĭs), *n., pl.* **-laxes** (-lăk′sēz). (among social insects) a method of feeding and communication by the mutual exchange of regurgitated food. [f. TROPH(O)- + Gk *állaxis* exchange] —**trophallactic** (trŏf′ə lăk′tĭk), *adj.*

trophic (trŏf′ĭk), *adj.* *Physiol.* of or pertaining to nutrition; concerned in nutritive processes. [t. Gk: m. s. *trophikós* pertaining to food] —**troph′ically,** *adv.*

trophied (trō′fĭd), *adj.* adorned with trophies.

tropho-, a word element referring to nourishment, as in *trophoplasm.* [t. Gk, comb. form of *trophḗ*]

trophoblast (trŏf′ə blăst′), *n.* *Embryol.* the extraembryonic part of a blastocyst, with mainly trophic or nutritive functions, or developing into foetal membranes with trophic functions.

trophoplasm (trŏf′ə plăz′əm), *n.* *Biol.* that kind of protoplasm which is regarded as forming the nutritive part of a cell.

trophy (trō′fĭ), *n., pl.* **-phies.** 1. anything taken in war, hunting, etc., esp. when preserved as a memento; a spoil or prize. 2. anything serving as a token or evidence of victory, valour, skill, etc. 3. a carved, painted, or other representation of objects associated with or symbolical of victory or achievement. 4. any memento or memorial. 5. a memorial erected by the ancient Greeks, Romans, and others in commemoration of a victory in war, consisting of arms or other spoils taken from the enemy and hung upon a tree, pillar, or the like. [t. F: m. *trophée*, t. L: m. *trop(h)aeum*, t. Gk: m. *trópaion*, der. *tropḗ* putting to flight, defeat] —**tro′phyless,** *adj.*

-trophy, a word element denoting nourishment, as in *hypertrophy.* [t. Gk: m. s. *-trophía* nutrition]

tropic (trŏp′ĭk), *n.* 1. *Geog.* **a.** either of two corresponding parallels of latitude on the terrestrial globe, one (**tropic of Cancer**) about 23½° north, and the other (**tropic of Capricorn**) about 23½° south of the equator, being the boundaries of the Torrid Zone. See diag. under **zone.** **b. the tropics,** the regions lying between and near these parallels of latitude; the Torrid Zone and neighbouring regions. 2. *Astron.* **a.** (now) either of two circles on the celestial sphere, parallel to the celestial equator, one (**tropic of Cancer**) about 23½° north of it, and the other (**tropic of Capricorn**) about 23½° south of it. **b.** (formerly) either of the two solstitial points, at which the sun reaches its greatest distance north and south of the celestial equator. —*adj.* 3. pertaining to the tropics; tropical. [ME, t. L: s. *tropicus*, t. Gk: m. *tropikós* pertaining to a turn]

-tropic, an adjective combining form corresponding to *-trope, -tropism*, as in *geotropic.*

tropical (trŏp′ĭ kl), *adj.* 1. pertaining to, characteristic of, occurring in, or inhabiting the tropics, especially the humid tropics: *tropical flowers.* 2. designed to be used in the tropics: *tropical clothing.* 3. of or pertaining to the astronomical tropics, or either one of them. 4. pertaining to, characterized by, or of the nature of a trope or tropes; metaphorical. —**trop′ically,** *adv.*

tropical black earth, regur.

tropical climate, a group of climate regions characterized by high temperatures throughout the year and pronounced wet and dry seasons.

tropical medicine, the branch of medicine which deals with diseases peculiar to the tropics.

tropical year, *Astron.* See **year** (def. 5).

tropic bird, any of several totipalmate seabirds of the family *Phaethontidae*, found chiefly in tropical regions, having white plumage with black markings and a pair of greatly elongated tail feathers.

tropine (trōʹpēn, -pĭn), *n. Chem.* a white crystalline, hygroscopic basic compound, $C_5H_{18}NO$, formed by the hydrolysis of atropine. Also, **tropin** (trōʹpĭn). [aphetic var. of ATROPINE]

tropism (trōʹpĭz ʹəm), *n. Biol.* the response, usually an orientation, of a plant or animal, as in growth, to the influences of external stimuli. [separate use of -TROPISM] —**tropistic** (trō pĭsʹtĭk), *adj.*

-tropism, a word element referring to tropism, as in *heliotropism.* [f. -TROP(E) + -ISM]

tropo-, a word element referring to turning or change. [t. Gk: comb. form of *trópos, tropḗ*]

tropology (trŏ pŏlʹə jĭ), *n., pl.* **-gies. 1.** the use of tropes or a trope in speech or writing. **2.** the use of a Scripture text so as to give it a moral interpretation or significance apart from its direct meaning. [t. LL: m. s. *tropologia*, t. Gk. See TROPE] —**tropologic** (trŏpʹə lŏjʹĭk), **tropʹologʹical,** *adj.* —**tropʹologʹically,** *adv.*

tropopause (trŏpʹə pôzʹ), *n. Meteorol.* the transition layer between the troposphere and the stratosphere.

tropophilous (trŏ pŏfʹĭ ləs), *adj. Ecol.* adapted to a climate with alternate growing and rest periods, as a plant. [f. TROPO- + m. Gk *-philos* loving]

tropophyte (trŏpʹə fītʹ), *n. Ecol.* a plant adapted to a climate alternately favourable or unfavourable to growth. —**tropophytic** (trŏpʹə fĭtʹĭk), *adj.*

troposphere (trŏpʹə sfĭəʹ), *n. Meteorol.* the inner layer of atmosphere, varying in height between about 6 miles and 12 miles, within which there is a steady fall of temperature with increasing altitude of about 2°C per 1000 ft, and within which nearly all cloud formations occur and weather conditions manifest themselves.

-tropous, a word element synonymous with **-tropal,** as in *heterotropous.* [t. Gk: m. *-tropos* pertaining to a turn]

Troppau (*Ger.* trŏpʹou), *n.* German name of **Opava.**

troppo (trŏpʹō; *It.* trŏpʹpō), *adv. Music.* too much: used esp. in directions. [t. It.; of Gmc orig. See TROOP]

-tropy, a word element synonymous with **-tropism.** [t. Gk: m. *tropḗ* turning] +]

Trossachs (trŏsʹəks), *n.* a valley in Scotland, in Perthshire, near Loch Katrine.

trot[1] (trŏt), *v.,* **trotted, trotting,** *n.* —*v.i.* **1.** (of a horse, etc.) to go at a gait between a walk and a run, in which the legs move in diagonal pairs, but not quite simultaneously, so that when the movement is slow one foot at least is always on the ground, and when fast all four feet are momentarily off the ground at once. **2.** to go at a quick, steady gait; move briskly, bustle, or hurry. —*v.t.* **3.** to cause to trot. **4.** to ride at a trot. **5.** to lead at a trot. **6.** to execute by trotting. **7. trot out,** *Colloq.* **a.** to bring forward for or as for inspection. **b.** to give voice to in a trite or boring way. —*n.* **8.** the gait of a horse, dog, etc., when trotting. **9.** the sound made. **10.** a jogging gait between a walk and a run. **11.** (in harness racing) a race for trotters. **12. on the trot, a.** in a state of continuous activity. **b.** one after another, in quick succession: *he won three races on the trot.* **13.** *U.S. Slang.* a crib, translation, or other illicit aid. **14.** *Rare.* a toddling child. **15.** (usually disparagingly) an old woman. [ME *trotten*, t. OF: m. *trotter*, t. MHG: m. *trotten* run, orig. tread]

trot[2] (trŏt), *n.* **1.** a trotline. **2.** a short line with hooks, attached to the trotline. [var. of *trat*; orig. obscure]

troth (trōth), *n. Archaic.* **1.** faithfulness, fidelity, or loyalty: *by my troth.* **2.** truth or verity: *in troth.* **3.** one's word or promise, esp. in engaging oneself to marry. [ME *trowthe, trouthe*, OE *trēowth.* See TRUTH]

trotline (trŏtʹlīnʹ), *n. Fishing.* a strong fishing line strung across a stream, or deep into a river, having individual hooks attached by smaller lines at intervals.

Trotsky (trŏtʹskĭ; *Russ.* trôtʹskĭy), *n.* **Leon** (*Russ.* lĭ ônʹ) (*Lev*, or *Leiba, Davidovich Bronstein*), 1879–1940, Russian revolutionary leader and writer: minister of war 1918–25; later exiled. Also, **Trotski.**

Trotskyism (trŏtʹskĭ ĭzʹəm), *n.* the political principles of Leon Trotsky, esp. the advocacy of worldwide proletarian revolution.

Trotskyite (trŏtʹskĭ ītʹ), *n.* **1.** a supporter of Trotsky or Trotskyism. —*adj.* **2.** of or pertaining to Trotsky or Trotskyism. Also, **Trotskyist** (trŏtʹskĭ ĭst).

trotter (trŏtʹə), *n.* **1.** an animal which trots; a horse bred and trained for harness racing. **2.** one who moves about briskly and constantly. **3.** the foot of an animal, esp. of a sheep or pig, used as food.

troubadour (trōōʹbə dōōəʹ), *n.* **1.** one of a class of lyric poets who flourished principally in southern France from the 11th century to the 13th century, and wrote in Provençal, chiefly on courtly love. **2.** a minstrel or ballad singer. [t. F, t. Pr.: m. *trobador*, der. *trobar*, ? g. LL *tropāre*, der. *tropus* song, orig. figure of speech. See TROPE]

trouble (trŭbʹl), *v.,* **-bled, -bling,** *n.* —*v.t.* **1.** to disturb in mind; distress; worry. **2.** to put to inconvenience, exertion, pains, or the like: *may I trouble you to shut the door?* **3.** to cause bodily pain or inconvenience to, as a disease or ailment does. **4.** to annoy, vex, or bother. **5.** to disturb or agitate, or stir up so as to make turbid, as water, etc. —*v.i.* **6.** to put oneself to inconvenience. **7.** to worry. —*n.* **8.** molestation, harassment, annoyance, or difficulty: *to make trouble for someone.* **9.** unfortunate position or circumstances; misfortunes. **10.** disturbance; disorder; unrest: *industrial trouble; political troubles.* **11.** physical derangement or disorder: *heart trouble.* **12.** disturbance of mind, distress, or worry. **13.** inconvenience endured, or exertion or pains taken, in some cause or in order to accomplish something. **14.** something that troubles; a cause or source of annoyance, difficulty, distress, or the like. **15.** a personal habit, characteristic, etc., which is disadvantageous or a source of anxiety or distress. **16. in trouble, a.** suffering or liable to suffer punishment, affliction, etc.; in difficulties. **b.** *Colloq.* pregnant while unmarried. [ME *troublen*, t. OF: m. *troubler*, g. LL *turbulāre*, r. L *turbidāre*, influenced by *turbulentus* turbulent] —**troubʹler,** *n.* —**Syn. 13.** See **care.**

troubled waters, a confused or disordered state of affairs; a state of unrest.

troublemaker (trŭbʹl māʹkə), *n.* one who causes trouble for others, esp. one who does so habitually and deliberately.

trouble-shooter (trŭbʹl shōōʹtə), *n.* an expert in discovering and eliminating the cause of trouble in the operation of something, in settling disputes, etc. —**trouble-shooting,** *n.*

troublesome (trŭbʹl səm), *adj.* **1.** causing trouble or annoyance; vexatious. **2.** laborious; difficult. **3.** *Archaic.* full of distress or affliction. —**trouʹblesomely,** *adv.* —**trouʹblesomeness,** *n.*

trouble spot, an area in which trouble or unrest exists or is liable to develop: *the Middle East is one of the world's trouble spots.*

troublous (trŭbʹləs), *adj. Archaic.* **1.** characterized by trouble; disturbed; unsettled. **2.** turbulent; restless. **3.** causing annoyance; troublesome.

trou-de-loup (trōōʹdə lōōʹ), *n., pl.* **trous-de-loup** (trōōʹdə lōōʹ). *Mil.* a conical or pyramidal pit with a pointed stake fixed vertically in the centre, rows of which are dug in front of a position to hinder an enemy's approach, formerly esp. used against cavalry. [F: wolf hole]

trough (trŏf), *n.* **1.** an open, boxlike receptacle, usually long and narrow, as for containing water or food for animals, or for any of various other purposes. **2.** any receptacle of similar shape. **3.** a channel or conduit for conveying water, as a gutter under the eaves of a building. **4.** any long depression or hollow, as between two ridges or waves. **5.** *Meteorol.* an elongated area of relatively low pressure. [ME; OE *trōh*, c. D, Icel. *trog*, G *Trog*] —**troughʹlikeʹ,** *adj.*

trounce (trouns), *v.t.,* **trounced, trouncing. 1.** to beat or thrash severely. **2.** to punish. **3.** *Colloq.* to defeat. [orig. uncert.]

troupe (trōōp), *n., v.,* **trouped, trouping.** —*n.* **1.** a troop, company, or band, esp. of actors, singers, or the like. —*v.i.* **2.** *U.S.* to travel as a member of a theatrical company; barnstorm. [t. F] —**Syn. 1.** See **troop.**

trouper (trōōʹpə), *n.* **1.** an actor in a theatrical company. **2.** a veteran actor. **3.** one who shows great devotion to duty, loyalty to a firm, colleagues, etc.

troupial (trōōʹpyəl), *n.* any of the birds of the American family *Icteridae*, including the American blackbirds, American orioles, etc., esp. one with brilliant plumage, as *I. icterus.* [t. F: m. *troupiale*, der. *troupe* TROOP]

trouser (trouʹzə), *adj.* of or pertaining to trousers: *trouser leg.*

trousered (trouʹzəd), *adj.* wearing trousers.

trousers (trouʹzəz), *n.pl.* a loose-fitting outer garment covering the lower part of the trunk and each leg separately, and usually extending to the ankles, worn esp. by men and boys. [extended form of *trouse*, t. Irish: m. *triubhas*] —**trouʹserless,** *adj.*

trousseau (trōōʹsō), *n., pl.* **-seaux, -seaus** (-sōz). a bride's outfit of clothes, linen, etc., which she brings with her at marriage. [t. F: lit., bundle, dim. of *trousse* truss]

trout (trout), *n., pl.* **trouts,** (*esp. collectively*) **trout. 1.** any fish of the genus *Salmo* other than the Atlantic salmon (*S. salar*), including the trout of Europe (*S. trutta*), and the American **rainbow trout** (*S. gairdnerii*) and **cutthroat trout** (*S. Clarkii*). **2.** any of various fishes of the salmon family of the genera *Salvelinus* and *Cristivomer*, also known as chars noted, by fishermen for their gameness and prized as food, and including several American species, as the **brook trout. 3.** any of several unrelated fishes, such as a bass (*Micropterus salmoides*), a drumfish of the genus *Cynoscion*, or a greenling of the genus *Hexagrammos*. **4.** *Colloq.* a woman of unattractive appearance: *an old trout.* [ME *troute*, OE *truht*, t. L: m. *tructa*, t. Gk: m. *trṓktēs* gnawer, a sea fish] —**trout′like′**, *adj.*

trouvaille (*Fr.* tro͞o väy′), *n. French.* a thing found by chance; unexpected good luck.

trouvère (*Fr.* tro͞o vĕr′), *n.* one of a class of poets who flourished in northern France during the 12th and 13th centuries and composed the chansons de geste and works on courtly love. Also, **trouveur** (*Fr.* tro͞o vœr′). [t. F, der. *trouver*. See TROUBADOUR]

Trouville-sur-Mer (*Fr.* tro͞o vēl sʏr mĕr′), *n.* a seaport in NW France, in Calvados department, on the English Channel: resort. 10,000 (est. 1965).

trover (trō′və), *n. Law.* a common-law action for the recovery of the value of personal property wrongfully converted by another to his own use (orig. brought against a finder of such goods). [t. OF: find, v., g. L *turbāre* disturb]

trow (trō), *v.i. Archaic.* to believe, think, or suppose. [ME *trowen*, OE *trūwian* believe, trust, c. G *trauen*]

Trowbridge (trō′brĭj′), *n.* a town in England, in Wiltshire. 15,833 (1961).

trowel (trou′əl), *n., v.,* **-elled, -elling** or (*esp. U.S.*) **-eled, -eling.** —*n.* **1.** any of various tools consisting of a plate of metal or other material, usually flat, fitted into a short handle, used for spreading, shaping, or smoothing plaster or the like. **2.** a similar tool with a curved, scooplike blade, used in gardening for taking up plants, etc. —*v.t.* **3.** to apply, shape, or smooth with or as with a trowel. [ME *truel*, t. OF: m. *truelle*, g. LL *truella*, r. L *trulla* small ladle] —**trow′eller**; *esp. U.S.,* **trow′eler**, *n.*

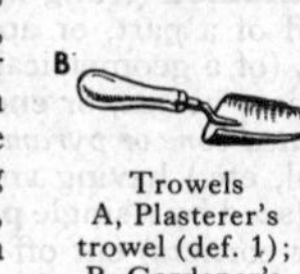

Trowels
A, Plasterer's trowel (def. 1); B, Gardener's trowel (def. 2)

troy (troi), *adj.* in or by troy weight. [named after TROYES]

Troy (troi), *n.* Latin, **Ilium.** Greek, **Ilion.** an ancient ruined city in NW Asia Minor: the seventh of nine settlements on the same site; besieged by the Greeks for ten years.

Troy

Troyat (*Fr.* trwȧ yȧ′), *n.* **Henri** (*Fr.* äɴ rē′), born 1911, French novelist.

Troyes (*Fr.* trwȧ), *n.* a town in NE France, the capital of Aube department, on the Seine. 67,406 (1962).

Troyon (*Fr.* trwȧ yôɴ′), *n.* **Constant** (*Fr.* kôɴ stäɴ′), 1813–65, French painter.

troy weight, a system of weights in use for precious metals and gems (formerly also for bread, etc.): 24 grains = 1 pennyweight; 20 pennyweights = 1 ounce; 12 ounces = 1 pound. The grain, ounce, and pound are the same as in apothecaries' weight, the grain alone being the same as in avoirdupois weight. In Great Britain only the ounce and its decimal subdivisions are now legally permitted in troy weight.

truant (tro͞o′ənt), *n.* **1.** a pupil who stays away from school without permission. **2.** one who shirks or neglects his duty. —*adj.* **3.** staying away from school without permission. **4.** pertaining to or characteristic of a truant. —*v.i.* **5.** to play truant. [ME, t. OF, prob. of Celtic orig.] —**tru′ancy**, *n.*

truce (tro͞os), *n.* **1.** a suspension of hostilities, as between armies, by agreement, for a specified period; an armistice. **2.** an agreement or treaty establishing this. **3.** respite or freedom, as from trouble, pain, etc. [ME, var. of *trewes*, pl. of *trewe*, OE *trēow* treaty, good faith. Cf. TRUE] —**truce′less**, *adj.*

Trucial States (tro͞o′shəl), a group of seven Arab sheikhdoms, Abu Dhabi, Dubai, Sharjah, Ajman, Umm al Qaiwain, Ras al Khaimah, Fujairah, on the S coast of the Persian Gulf, in treaty relations with Great Britain. 130,000 pop. (est. 1965); 32,278 sq. mi. Also, **Trucial Coast, Trucial Oman.**

truck[1] (trŭk), *n.* **1.** any of various vehicles for carrying goods, etc. **2.** a goods truck. **3.** *Chiefly U.S.* a lorry. **4.** any of various wheeled frames for moving heavy articles, as a barrow with two very low front wheels used to move heavy luggage, etc. **5.** a low rectangular frame on which heavy boxes, etc., are moved. **6.** a group of two or more pairs of wheels in a frame, for supporting a locomotive body, etc. **7.** a small wooden wheel, cylinder, or roller, as on certain old-style guncarriages. **8.** a circular or square piece of wood fixed on the head of a mast or the top of a flagstaff, and usually containing small holes for signal halyards. —*v.t.* **9.** to transport by a truck or trucks. **10.** to put on a truck. —*v.i.* **11.** to convey articles or goods on a truck. **12.** *Chiefly U.S.* to drive a truck. [back-formation from *truckle* wheel. See TRUCKLE[2]]

truck[2] (trŭk), *n.* **1.** dealings: *to have no truck with a person.* **2.** barter. **3.** a bargain or deal. **4.** the payment of wages in goods, etc., instead of money. **5.** miscellaneous articles; odds and ends. **6.** trash or rubbish. **7.** *U.S.* vegetables, etc., raised for the market. —*v.t.* **8.** to exchange; trade; barter; peddle. —*v.i.* **9.** to exchange commodities; barter; bargain or negotiate. **10.** to traffic; have dealings. [ME *truk(i)e*, t. OF: m. *troquer*; orig. uncert.]

truckage (trŭk′ĭj), *n.* **1.** conveyance by a truck or trucks. **2.** the charge for this.

truckdriver (trŭk′drī′və), *n. U.S.* a lorry driver.

trucker[1] (trŭk′ə), *n. U.S.* **1.** a lorry driver. **2.** one whose business is trucking goods. [f. TRUCK[1] + -ER[1]]

trucker[2] (trŭk′ə), *n. U.S.* one who grows vegetables, etc., for the market; market gardener. [f. TRUCK[2] + -ER[1]]

truck farm, *U.S.* a farm for growing vegetables for market; market garden. Also, **truck garden.**

trucking[1] (trŭk′ĭng), *n. U.S.* the act or business of conveying articles or goods on trucks. [f. TRUCK[1], v. + -ING[1]]

trucking[2] (trŭk′ĭng), *n.* **1.** commercial bartering. **2.** *U.S.* the growing of vegetables for the market. [f. TRUCK[2], v. + -ING[1]]

truckle[1] (trŭk′l), *v.i.,* **-led, -ling.** to submit or yield obsequiously or tamely (usually fol. by *to*). [special use of obs. *truckle*, v., sleep on truckle bed] —**truck′ler**, *n.* —**truck′lingly**, *adv.*

truckle[2] (trŭk′l), *n.* **1.** a pulley. **2.** a truckle bed. [late ME *trocle*, t. L: m. s. *trochlea*, t. Gk: m. *trochileia* pulley]

truckle bed, a low bed moving on castors, usually pushed under another bed when not in use.

truckman (trŭk′mən), *n., pl.* **-men.** *U.S.* **1.** a lorry driver. **2.** one who transports goods, etc. for a living.

truck system, the system of paying wages in kind.

truculent (trŭk′yo͝o lənt), *adj.* **1.** fierce; cruel; brutal; savage. **2.** scathing; harsh; vitriolic. **3.** aggressive; belligerent. [t. L: s. *truculentus*] —**truc′ulence, truc′ulency**, *n.* —**truc′ulently**, *adv.* —**Syn. 1.** See **fierce.**

Trudeau (tro͞o′dō), *n.* **Pierre Elliott** (pyĕər′ ĕl′yət), born 1921, Canadian statesman: prime minister since 1968.

trudge (trŭj), *v.,* **trudged, trudging,** *n.* —*v.i.* **1.** to walk. **2.** to walk laboriously or wearily. —*v.t.* **3.** to walk laboriously or wearily along or over: *he trudged the streets.* [orig. uncert.] —**trudg′er**, *n.* —**Syn. 2.** See **pace**[1].

trudgen (trŭj′ən), *n. Swimming.* a stroke in which a double overarm motion and a scissors kick are used. Also, **trudgen stroke.** [named after John *Trudgen*, 1852–1902, English swimmer]

true (tro͞o), *adj.,* **truer, truest,** *n., adv., v.,* **trued, truing.** —*adj.* **1.** being in accordance with the actual state of things; conforming to fact; not false: *a true story.* **2.** real or genuine: *true gold.* **3.** free from deceit; sincere: *a true interest in someone's welfare.* **4.** firm in allegiance; loyal; faithful; trusty. **5.** being or indicating the essential reality of something. **6.** agreeing with or conforming to a standard, pattern, rule, or the like: *a true copy.* **7.** exact, correct, or accurate: *a true balance.* **8.** of the right kind; such as it should be; proper: *to arrange things in their true order.* **9.** properly so called; rightly answering to a description: *true statesmanship.* **10.** legitimate or rightful: *the true heir.* **11.** reliable, unfailing, or sure: *a true sign.* **12.** exactly or accurately shaped, formed, fitted, or placed, as a surface, instrument, or part of a mechanism. **13.** *Biol.* belonging to a particular group; conforming to the norm; typical. **14.** *Stockbreeding.* purebred. **15.** *Navig.* (of a bearing) fixed in relation to the earth's axis rather than the magnetic poles: *true north.* **16.** *Archaic.* truthful. **17.** *Archaic.* honest; honourable; upright.
—*n.* **18.** exact or accurate formation, position, or adjustment: *to be out of true.* **19. the true,** that which is true.
—*adv.* **20.** in a true manner; truly or truthfully. **21.** exactly or accurately. **22.** in agreement with the ancestral type: *to breed true.* **23. to come true,** to happen in reality as desired, expected, dreamt, etc.: *if dreams came true.*
—*v.t.* **24.** to make true; shape, adjust, place, etc., exactly or accurately. [ME; OE *trēowe*, c. G *treu*] —**true′ness**, *n.* —**Syn. 1.** See **real**[1].

true blue, 1. a non-fading blue dye or pigment. 2. one who is true-blue. 3. the colour adopted by the 17th-century Covenanters in contradistinction to the royal red. 4. a staunch Conservative.

true-blue (trōō′blōō′), *adj.* 1. unchanging; unwavering; staunch; true. 2. staunchly conservative.

true-born (trōō′bôn′), *adj.* 1. of pure stock; legitimate; purebred. 2. having the qualities associated with pure breeding.

true-bred (trōō′brĕd′), *adj.* 1. thoroughbred; purebred. 2. showing good breeding.

true-hearted (trōō′hä′tĭd), *adj.* 1. faithful or loyal. 2. honest or sincere. —**true′-heart′edness,** *n.*

true level, an imaginary surface everywhere perpendicular to the plumbline, or line of gravity.

truelove (trōō′lŭv′), *n.* 1. a sweetheart; one truly loving or loved. 2. the herb Paris, *Paris quadrifolia*, having a whorl of four leaves suggesting a truelove knot.

truelove knot, a complicated ornamental knot, esp. one formed of intertwined loops, used as an emblem of true love or interwoven affections. Also, **true′-lov′er's knot′.**

truepenny (trōō′pĕn′ĭ), *n.* *Archaic.* a trusty person; an honest fellow.

true rib, *Anat.* any of the ribs which are attached to the sternum by costal cartilages (the first seven pairs in man).

true time, apparent solar time; the time as shown by a sundial.

Truffaut (*Fr.* trʏ fō′), *n.* **François** (*Fr.* fräɴ swȧ′), born 1932, French film director.

truffle (trŭf′əl), *n.* 1. any of various subterranean edible fungi of the ascomycetous genus *Tuber*. 2. any of various similar fungi of other genera. 3. a chocolate confection resembling this. [t. F: m. *truffe*, t. Pr.: m. *trufa*, or t. It.: m. *truffa*, g. LL *tūfera*, t. Osco-Umbrian: m. *tūfer*, c. L *tūber* esculent root] —**truf′fled,** *adj.*

trug (trŭg), *n.* a shallow, oblong, wooden basket for carrying fruit, vegetables, etc.

truism (trōō′ĭz′əm), *n.* a self-evident, obvious truth. —**truis′tic, truis′tical,** *adj.*

Trujillo (*Sp.* trōō ĸʜē′lyō), *n.* 1. **Rafael Leonidas** (*Sp.* rȧ fȧ ĕl′ lė ō nĕ′dȧs), 1891–1961, Dominican army officer and politician: president 1930–38, 1942–52. 2. a town in NW Peru. 99,808 (1961).

Truk Islands (trŭk), a group of the Caroline Islands, in the N Pacific: 25,820 pop. (1965); ab. 50 sq. mi.

trull (trŭl), *n.* *Archaic.* a prostitute; a strumpet. [t. G: m. *Trulle*, var. of *Trudel* loose woman]

truly (trōō′lĭ), *adv.* 1. in accordance with fact or truth; truthfully. 2. exactly; accurately; correctly. 3. rightly; duly; properly. 4. legitimately; rightfully. 5. genuinely; really. 6. indeed; verily. 7. *Archaic.* faithfully; loyally; constantly.

Truman (trōō′mən), *n.* **Harry S,** born 1884, 33rd president of the U.S., 1945–53.

Trumbull (trŭm′bl), *n.* 1. **John,** 1756–1843, U.S. painter. 2. his father, **Jonathan,** 1710–85, U.S. statesman.

trump[1] (trŭmp), *n.* 1. *Cards.* a. any playing card of a suit that for the time outranks the other suits, such a card being able to take any card of another suit. b. (*pl.*, *U.S. sometimes sing.*) the suit itself. 2. *Colloq.* a person of great excellence. —*v.t.* 3. *Cards.* to take with a trump. 4. to excel; surpass; be better than; beat. 5. **trump up,** to invent deceitfully or dishonestly, as an accusation; fabricate. —*v.i.* *Cards.* 6. to play a trump. 7. to take a trick with a trump. [unexplained var. of TRIUMPH] —**trump′less,** *adj.*

trump[2] (trŭmp), *Archaic or Poetic.* —*n.* 1. a trumpet. 2. its sound. 3. some similar sound. —*v.i.* 4. to blow a trumpet. 5. to make a trumpet-like sound. —*v.t.* 6. to proclaim, etc., by or as by a trumpet. [ME *trompe*, t. F: of Gmc orig.]

trump card, 1. *Cards.* trump[1] (def. 1a). 2. *Colloq.* a decisive factor; important advantage.

trumpery (trŭm′pə rĭ), *n.*, *pl.* **-ries,** *adj.* —*n.* 1. something showy but of little intrinsic value; worthless finery; useless stuff. 2. rubbish; nonsense. —*adj.* 3. showy but unsubstantial or useless; of little or no value; trifling; rubbishy. [t. F: m. *tromperie*, der. *tromper* deceive]

trumpet (trŭm′pĭt), *n.* 1. *Music.* a. any of a family of musical wind instruments with a penetrating, powerful tone, consisting of a tube, now usually metallic, and commonly once or twice curved round upon itself, having a cup-shaped mouthpiece at one end and a flaring bell at the other. b. an organ stop having a tone resembling that of a trumpet. c. a trumpeter. 2. a sound like that of a trumpet. 3. the loud cry of the elephant or some other animal. 4. an ear trumpet. 5. (*pl.*) any of several pitcher plants. —*v.i.* 6. to blow a trumpet. 7. to emit a sound like that of a trumpet, as an elephant. —*v.t.* 8. to sound on a trumpet. 9. to utter with a sound like that of a trumpet. 10. to proclaim loudly or widely. [ME, t. OF: m. *trompette*, dim. of *trompe*. See TRUMP[2]] —**trum′petless,** *adj.* —**trum′pet-like′,** *adj.*

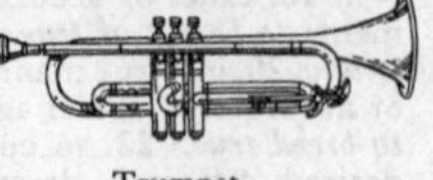
Trumpet

trumpeter (trŭm′pĭ tə), *n.* 1. one who sounds or plays a trumpet. 2. one who proclaims or announces something with a trumpet. 3. a soldier whose regular duty is to sound trumpet calls at stated hours. 4. one who proclaims or announces something loudly or widely. 5. any of the large South American birds constituting the family *Psophiidae*, esp. *Psophia crepitans* (**common trumpeter**), related to the rails. 6. Also, **trumpeter swan.** a large North American wild swan (*Cygnus buccinator*) having a sonorous cry. 7. one of a breed of domestic pigeons.

trumpet-fish (trŭm′pĭt fĭsh′), *n.* any of various long-snouted fish of the family *Aulostomidae*, esp. *Aulostomus maculatus*, of the S Atlantic Ocean.

trumpet flower, 1. any of various plants with pendent flowers shaped like a trumpet. 2. trumpet honeysuckle. 3. the flower of any of these plants.

trumpet honeysuckle, an American honeysuckle, *Lonicera sempervirens*, with large tubular flowers, deep red outside and yellow within.

trumpet-major (trŭm′pĭt mā′jə), *n.* the chief trumpeter of a band or regiment.

truncate (trŭng′kāt), *v.*, **-cated, -cating,** *adj.* —*v.t.* 1. to shorten by cutting off a part; cut short; mutilate. —*adj.* 2. truncated. 3. *Biol.* a. square or broad at the end, as if cut off transversely. b. lacking the apex, as certain spiral shells. [t. L: m. s. *truncātus*, pp., cut] —**trunca′tion,** *n.*

Truncate leaf

truncated (trŭng′kā tĭd), *adj.* 1. shortened by the cutting off of a part, or appearing as if so shortened; cut short. 2. (of a geometrical figure or solid) having the apex, vertex, or end cut off by a plane: *a truncated cone or pyramid.* 3. *Crystall.* a. (of a crystal, etc.) having angles or edges cut off or replaced by a single plane. b. (of one of the edges or corners) cut off or replaced by a modifying plane which makes equal angles with the adjacent similar planes. 4. *Biol.* truncate.

Truncated cone

truncheon (trŭn′chən), *n.* 1. a short club carried by a policeman. 2. a baton, or staff of office or authority. 3. *Archaic.* a club or cudgel. 4. *Archaic.* the shaft of a spear. —*v.t.* 5. to beat with a club. [ME *trunchon*, t. OF: m. *tronçon* piece cut off, ult. der. L *truncus* stump]

trundle (trŭn′dl), *v.*, **-dled, -dling,** *n.* —*v.t.* 1. to cause (a ball, hoop, etc.) to roll along; roll. 2. to cause to rotate; twirl; whirl. —*v.i.* 3. to roll along. 4. to move or run on a wheel or wheels. —*n.* 5. the act of trundling or rolling. 6. a small wheel, roller, or the like. 7. a small wheel adapted to support a heavy weight, as the wheel of a castor. 8. a lantern pinion. 9. each of the bars of a lantern pinion. 10. the impulse which causes something to roll. 11. *Now Rare.* a truck or carriage on low wheels. [OE *tryndel* wheel; cf. LG *tründeln* roll] —**trun′dler,** *n.*

trunk (trŭngk), *n.* 1. the main stem of a tree, as distinct from the branches and roots. 2. a box or chest for holding clothes and other articles, as for use on a journey. 3. the body of a human being or of an animal, excluding the head and limbs. 4. *Archit.* a. the shaft of a column. b. the dado or die of a pedestal. 5. the main line of a river, railway, or the like. 6. *Teleph.* a. (*pl.*) *U.S.* a trunk call exchange: *give me trunks.* b. *U.S.* a trunk line. 7. *Anat.* the main body of an artery, nerve, or the like, as distinct from its branches. 8. (*pl.*) a. shorts, either tight-fitting or loose, worn by swimmers, athletes, etc. b. short, tight-fitting breeches, as worn over tights in theatrical use. c. *Obs.* trunk hose. 9. the long, flexible, cylindrical nasal appendage of the elephant. 10. *Naut.* a. a large enclosed passage through the decks or bulkheads of a vessel, for coaling, ventilation, or the like. b. any of various watertight casings in a vessel, as the vertical one above the slot for a centre board in the bottom of a boat. 11. a shaft or chute. 12. *U.S.* boot[1] (def. 5). 13. *Obs.* any of various pipes or tubes, as a speaking tube, a blowpipe, or a telescope. —*adj.* 14. denoting or pertaining to the main line or artery, as of a railway, road, river, etc. [late ME *trunke*, t. L: m. s. *truncus*] —**trunk′less,** *adj.*

trunk call, *Teleph.* a telephone call made by a trunk line.

trunkfish (trŭngk′fĭsh′), *n.*, *pl.* **-fishes,** (*esp. collectively*) **-fish.** 1. any of the fishes of the genus *Mormyridae* of central and southern Africa, having extended mouth-parts forming a trunk. 2. any of the fishes of the genus *Ostracion.* 3. cowfish (def. 1).

trunk hose, full, baglike breeches covering the body from the waist to the middle of the thigh or lower, worn in the 16th and 17th centuries.

trunk line, *Teleph.* a telephone line or channel between two exchanges in different parts of a country or of the world, which is used to provide connections between subscribers making long-distance calls.

trunk piston, *Mach.* a piston with a long skirt to take the side thrust, as in an internal-combustion engine.

trunk road, a main road for long-distance travel.

trunnel (trŭn′əl), *n.* treenail.

trunnion (trŭn′yən), *n.* **1.** either of the two cylindrical projections on a cannon, one on each side, which support it on its carriage. **2.** any of various similar supports, gudgeons, or pivots. [t. F: m. *trognon* trunk, stump, ult. orig. uncert.]

Truro (trŏŏə′rō), *n.* a town in England, in Cornwall. 13,336 (1961).

truss (trŭs), *v.t.* **1.** to tie, bind, or fasten. **2.** to make fast with skewers or the like, as the wings of a fowl preparatory to cooking. **3.** *Bldg Trades, etc.* to furnish or support with a truss or trusses. **4.** to confine or enclose, as the body, by something fastened closely around.
—*n.* **5.** *Bldg Trades, etc.* **a.** a combination of members, as beams, bars, ties, or the like, so arranged, usually in a triangle or a collection of triangles, as to form a rigid framework, and used in bridges (**bridge truss**), roofs (**roof truss**), etc., to give support and rigidity to the whole or a part of the structure. **b.** any framework consisting of a number of members connected together and loaded principally at the joints so that the stresses in the members are essentially simple tensions or compressions. **6.** *Med.* an apparatus for maintaining a hernia in a reduced state. **7.** *Hort.* a compact terminal cluster or head of flowers growing upon one stalk. **8.** *Naut.* an iron fitting by which a lower yard is secured to the mast. **9.** a collection of things tied together or packed in a receptacle; a bundle; a pack. **10.** a bundle of hay or straw, now usually one containing about 56 lbs of old hay, 60 lbs of new hay, or 36 lbs. of straw.
[ME *trussen*, t. OF: m. *trusser*, ult. der. L *torca* bundle, r. *torques* necklace, something twisted] —**truss′er,** *n.*

truss bridge, *Civ. Eng.* a bridge in which the greatest strain is taken by trusses.

trussed beam (trŭst), *Bldg Trades, etc.* a beam that has been strengthened by the addition of tie rods and struts.

trussing (trŭs′ĭng), *n. Bldg Trades, etc.* **1.** the members which form a truss. **2.** a structure consisting of trusses. **3.** trusses collectively.

trust (trŭst), *n.* **1.** reliance on the integrity, justice, etc., of a person, or on some quality or attribute of a thing; confidence. **2.** confident expectation of something; hope. **3.** confidence in the ability or intention of a person to pay at some future time for goods, etc.; credit: *to sell goods on trust.* **4.** one on whom or that on which one relies. **5.** the state of being relied on, or the state of one to whom something is entrusted. **6.** the obligation or responsibility imposed on one in whom confidence or authority is placed: *a position of trust.* **7.** the condition of being confided to another's care or guard: *to leave something in trust with a person.* **8.** something committed or entrusted to one, as an office, duty, etc. **9.** *Law.* **a.** a fiduciary relationship in which one person (the trustee) holds the title to property (the **trust estate** or **trust property**) for the benefit of another (the beneficiary). **b.** a fund of securities, cash or other assets, held by trustees on behalf of a number of investors. **10.** *Com.* **a.** a combination of industrial or commercial companies having a central committee or board of trustees, controlling a majority or the whole of the stock of each of the constituent companies, thus making it possible to manage the concerns so as to economize expenses, regulate production, defeat competition, etc. **b.** a monopolistic organization or combination in restraint of trade whether in the form of a trust (def. 10a), contract, association or otherwise. **11.** *Rare.* reliability.
—*adj.* **12.** *Law.* of or pertaining to trusts or a trust.
—*v.i.* **13.** to have or place trust, reliance, or confidence (usually fol. by *in*). **14.** to have confidence; hope. **15. trust to,** to depend on; rely on.
—*v.t.* **16.** to have trust or confidence in; rely on. **17.** to believe. **18.** to expect confidently, hope (usually fol. by a clause or an infinitive). **19.** to commit or consign with trust or confidence. **20.** to permit to be in some place, position, etc., or to do something, without fear of consequences: *he will not trust it out of his sight.* **21.** to invest with a trust; entrust with something. **22.** to give credit to (a person) for goods, etc., supplied. [ME, t. Scand.; cf. Icel. *traust* trust, c. G *Trost* comfort] —**trust′er,** *n.*
—**Syn. 1.** TRUST, ASSURANCE, CONFIDENCE imply a feeling of security. TRUST implies instinctive unquestioning belief in and reliance upon something: *to have trust in the loyalty of friends.* CONFIDENCE implies conscious trust because of good reasons, definite evidence, or past experience: *to feel confidence in the outcome of events.* ASSURANCE implies absolute confidence and certainty: *to feel an assurance of victory.*

trust corporation, a corporation organized to exercise the functions of a trustee.

trust deed, *Law.* the legal document which appoints trustees and defines their power.

trustee (trŭs tē′), *n., v.* **-teed, -teeing.** *Law.* —*n.* **1.** a person, usually one of a body of persons, appointed to administer the affairs of a company, institution, etc. **2.** a person who holds the title to property for the benefit of another. **3.** (in New England) a garnishee. —*v.t.* **4.** to place in the hands of a trustee or trustees. **5.** (in New England) to garnish.

trustee process, *Law.* (in New England) garnishment.

trustee savings bank, a bank controlled by Act of Parliament in which trustees are appointed to ensure that savings are placed at interest for the sole benefit of depositors.

trusteeship (trŭs tē′shĭp′), *n.* **1.** the office or function of a trustee. **2.** the administrative control of a territory granted to a country by an organ (**Trusteeship Council**) of the United Nations. **3.** a trust territory.

trustful (trŭst′fəl), *adj.* full of trust; trusting; confiding. —**trust′fully,** *adv.* —**trust′fulness,** *n.*

trusting (trŭs′tĭng), *adj.* that trusts; confiding; trustful. —**trust′ingly,** *adv.* —**trust′ingness,** *n.*

trust instrument, *Law.* the document which sets out the trusts upon which the person entitled to the enjoyment of land holds the fee simple.

trust territory, a territory administered by a country on behalf of the Trusteeship Council of the United Nations.

trustworthy (trŭst′wû′thĭ), *adj.* worthy of trust or confidence; reliable. —**trust′wor′thily,** *adv.* —**trust′wor′thiness,** *n.* —**Syn.** See **reliable.**

trusty (trŭs′tĭ), *adj.*, **trustier, trustiest,** *n., pl.* **trusties.** —*adj.* **1.** that may be trusted or relied on; trustworthy; reliable. **2.** *Rare.* trustful. —*n.* **3.** one who or that which is trusted. **4.** a well-behaved and trustworthy convict to whom special privileges are granted. —**trust′ily,** *adv.* —**trust′iness,** *n.*

truth (trōōth), *n.* **1.** that which is true; the true or actual facts of a case: *to tell the truth.* **2.** conformity with fact or reality; verity: *the truth of a statement.* **3.** a verified or indisputable fact, proposition, principle, or the like: *mathematical truths.* **4.** the state or character of being true. **5.** genuineness, reality, or actual existence. **6.** agreement with a standard, rule, or the like. **7.** honesty, uprightness, or integrity. **8.** accuracy, as of position or adjustment. **9. in truth,** in fact; in reality; truly. **10.** *Archaic.* fidelity or constancy. [ME *treuthe*, OE *trēowth*, c. Icel. *tryggdh* faith] —**truth′less,** *adj.*

truthful (trōōth′fəl), *adj.* **1.** telling the truth, esp. habitually, as a person. **2.** conforming to truth, as a statement. **3.** corresponding with reality, as a representation. —**truth′fully,** *adv.* —**truth′fulness,** *n.*

try (trī), *v.*, **tried, trying,** *n., pl.* **tries.** —*v.t.* **1.** to attempt to do or accomplish: *it seems easy until you try it.* **2.** to test the effect or result of: *to try a new method.* **3.** to endeavour to ascertain by experiment: *to try one's luck.* **4.** to test the quality, value, fitness, accuracy, etc., of: *to try a new brand of soap powder.* **5.** to attempt to open (a door, window etc.) in order to find out whether it is locked. **6.** *Law.* to examine and determine judicially, as a cause; determine judicially the guilt or innocence of (a person). **7.** to put to a severe test; strain the endurance, patience, etc., of; subject to grievous experiences, affliction, or trouble. **8.** to melt (fat, etc.) to obtain the oil; render (usually fol. by *out*). **9.** *Rare.* to ascertain the truth or right of (a matter, etc.) by test (sometimes fol. by *out*). **10.** *Obs.* to show or prove by test or experience. **11.** *Obs.* to extract or refine by heat, as metal from ore; refine; purify (usually fol. by *out*). —*v.i.* **12.** to make an attempt or effort: *try harder next time.* —*v.* **13.** Some special verb phrases are:
try it on, *Colloq.* to attempt to hoodwink or test the patience of, esp. impudently.
try on, to put on (clothes, etc.) to see if they fit, look well, etc.
try out, 1. to test; experiment with. **2.** *U.S.* to compete (for a position, etc.).
—*n.* **14.** an attempt, endeavour, or effort: *to have a try at something.* **15.** *Rugby Football.* a score of three points earned by a touchdown. [ME *tryen*, t. OF: m. *trier* pick, cull] —**tri′er,** *n.*
—**Syn. 1.** TRY, ATTEMPT, ENDEAVOUR, STRIVE imply putting forth effort towards a specific end. TRY is the verb in most general use: *try to do your best.* ATTEMPT is more formal and often carries the idea of more effort: *he attempted to deceive me.* ENDEAVOUR suggests

resolve and continuous effort, esp. in the face of difficulties: *endeavour to effect a compromise.* STRIVE implies hard and earnest exertion to accomplish something difficult or laborious: *to strive mightily at a task.*

trying (trī′ĭng), *adj.* annoying; distressing; irritating; testing one's patience. **—try′ingly,** *adv.* **—try′ingness,** *n.*

trying plane, a very long plane used by carpenters to make the edges of boards straight. [var. of *truing plane.* See TRUE, v.]

tryma (trī′mə), *n., pl.* **-mata** (-mə tə). *Bot.* a drupaceous nut having a fibrous or fleshy epicarp which is ultimately dehiscent, as in the walnut and hickory. [t. NL, t. Gk: hole]

try-on (trī′ŏn′), *n. Colloq.* an attempt to hoodwink or test the patience of someone.

tryout (trī′out′), *n. Colloq.* a trial, practice, or test to ascertain fitness for some purpose.

trypaflavine (trĭp′ə flā′vĭn, -vēn), *n. Chem.* acriflavine.

trypanosome (trĭp′ə nə sōm′), *n.* any of the minute flagellate protozoans constituting the genus *Trypanosoma,* parasitic in the blood or tissues of man and other vertebrates, usually transmitted by insects, often causing serious diseases, as African sleeping sickness in man, and many diseases in domestic animals. [f. *trypano-* (comb. form of Gk *trýpanon* borer) + -SOME[3]] **—tryp′anoso′mic,** *adj.*

trypanosomiasis (trĭp′ə nə sə mī′ə sĭs), *n. Pathol.* any infection caused by a trypanosome.

tryparsamide (trĭ pär′sə mĭd), *n. Pharm.* a synthetic drug, $C_8H_{10}AsN_2O_4Na$, used for the cure of epilepsy.

trypsin (trĭp′sĭn), *n. Biochem.* **1.** a proteolytic enzyme of the pancreatic juice, capable of converting proteins into peptone. **2.** any of several proteolytic enzymes. [var. of *tripsin,* f. s. Gk *trîpsis* friction + -IN[2]] **—tryptic** (trĭp′tĭk), *adj.*

trypsinogen (trĭp sĭn′ə jĭn), *n. Biochem.* the inactive precursor of trypsin.

tryptophan (trĭp′tə făn′), *n. Biochem.* a colourless, solid, aromatic, essential amino acid, $C_{11}H_{12}N_2O_2$, occurring in proteins and found in the seed of some leguminous plants: necessary to animal life. It is released from proteins by tryptic digestion. Also, **tryptophane** (trĭp′tə fān′). [f. *trypto-* (comb. form repr. Gk *triptós* rubbed) + -PHAN(E)]

trysail (trī′sāl′; *Naut.* -səl), *n. Naut.* a small fore-and-aft sail set with or without a gaff, usually loose-footed, on the foremast or mainmast of a vessel, and used esp. in heavy weather.

try square, two straight edges fastened at right angles to each other, used for testing the squareness of work or for laying out right angles.

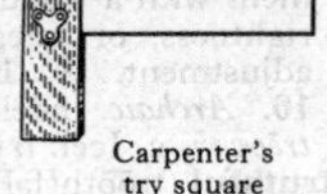
Carpenter's try square

tryst (trĭst, trīst), *n.* **1.** an appointment, esp. between lovers, to meet at a certain time and place; rendezvous. **2.** an appointed meeting. **3.** an appointed place of meeting. **—*v.t.*** **4.** *Chiefly Scot.* to make an engagement with (a person) for a meeting. **—*v.i.*** **5.** *Chiefly Scot.* to make an appointment or agreement. [ME *triste,* t. OF; orig. uncert.] **—tryst′er,** *n.*

trysting place, a place where a tryst is kept or is to be kept.

tsamma (tsä′mə), *n.* a common watermelon, *Citrullus vulgaris,* of southern Africa, a staple food of the Bushmen.

Tsana (tsä′nə), *n.* **Lake.** See **Tana, Lake.**

tsar (zä), *n.* **1.** an emperor or king. **2.** (*usually cap.*) the emperor of Russia. **3.** (*often cap.*) an autocratic ruler or leader. Also, **czar, tzar.** [t. Russ., ult. t. L: m. *Caesar*] **—tsardom** (zä′dəm), *n.*

tsarevitch (zä′rə vĭch), *n.* **1.** the son of a tsar. **2.** (later) the eldest son of a tsar. Also, **czarevitch, tzarevitch.**

tsarevna (zä rĕv′nə), *n.* a daughter of a tsar. Also, **czarevna, tzarevna.**

tsarina (zä rē′nə), *n.* the wife of a tsar; Russian empress. Also, **czarina, tzarina.** [f. TSAR + *-ina* (Latinization of G *-in,* fem. suffix, as in *Zarin* wife of tsar)]

tsarism (zä′rĭz′əm), *n.* dictatorship; autocratic government. Also, **czarism, tzarism.**

tsarist (zä′rĭst), *adj.* **1.** of, pertaining to, or characteristic of a tsar or the system of government under a tsar. **2.** dictatorial; autocratic; imperious. **—*n.*** **3.** an adherent or supporter of a tsar or tsarism. Also, **czarist, tzarist.**

tsaritsa (zä rĭt′sə), *n.* tsarina. Also, **czaritza, tsaritza, tzaritza.**

Tsaritsyn (*Russ.* tsä rĭt′sĭn), *n.* a former name of **Volgograd.**

Tsedenbal (*Russ.* tsĕd′ən băl), *n.* **Yumzhagiin** (*Russ.* yōōm′zhə gyĭn), Mongolian statesman: first secretary of the Mongolian People's Revolutionary Party since 1952.

Tselinograd (*Russ.* tsĭ lĭ nă grät′), *n.* a town in the SW Soviet Union in Asia. 159,000 (est. 1965).

tsetse fly (tsĕt′sĭ), any of the blood-sucking flies of the African genus *Glossina,* some of which transmit protozoan parasites (trypanosomes) which cause sleeping sickness and other serious diseases. Also, **tsetse, tzetze.** [native name]

Tsetse fly, *Glossina morsitans* (Ab. ½ in. long)

T-shirt (tē′shûrt′), *n.* a lightweight, close-fitting, collarless shirt, with short sleeves. Also, **tee-shirt.**

Tshombe (chŏm′bĭ), *n.* **Moise** (mō ēz′), 1919–69, Congolese politician: prime minister of the Democratic Republic of the Congo 1960–62.

Tsinan (tsē′năn′), *n.* a city in E China: the capital of Shantung province. 882,000 (est. 1958). See map under **Shantung.**

Tsinghai (tsĭng′hī′), *n.* Chinghai.

Tsingtao (tsĭng′tou′), *n.* a seaport in E China, in Shantung province. 1,144,000 (est. 1958).

Tsingling Shan (tsĭng′lĭng shăn′), a mountain range in central China. Highest peak, ab. 13,000 ft.

Tsiranana (*Fr.* tsē rȧ nȧ nȧ′), *n.* **Philibert** (*Fr.* fē lē bĕr′), born 1912, Malagasy statesman: president of the Malagasy Republic since 1960.

tsotsi (tsŏt′sĭ), *n. S African.* an African spiv, hoodlum, or gangster. [Johannesburg d.]

tsp., teaspoon.

T square, a T-shaped ruler used in mechanical drawing to make parallel lines, etc., the short crosspiece sliding along the edge of the drawing board as a guide.

Tsu (tsōō), *n.* a town in Japan, in S central Honshu island. 117,214 (1965).

tsunami (tsōō nä′mĭ), *n.* a large, often destructive sea wave caused by an underwater earthquake. [t. Jap.: tidal wave]

Tsushima (tsōō′shĭ mə), *n.* two adjacent Japanese islands between Korea and Kyushu island, Japan: the Japanese fleet decisively defeated the Russian fleet near here 1905. 66,000 pop. (est. 1963); 271 sq. mi.

tsutsugamushi fever (tsōō′tsōō gə mōō′shĭ), Japanese river fever.

Tswana (tswä′nə), *n.* **1.** any of various Bantu-speaking Negro peoples, centred esp. in Botswana. **2.** a member of such peoples. **3.** the Bantu language spoken by such peoples.

T.T., **1.** teetotal. **2.** teetotaller. **3.** Tourist Trophy. **4.** tuberculin tested.

Tu, *Chem. Obs.* thulium.

Tu., Tuesday.

Tuamotu Archipelago (tōōə mō′tōō), a group of French islands in the S Pacific. 6847 pop. (1962); 332 sq. mi. Also, **Low** or **Paumotu Archipelago.** See map under **Hawaiian Islands.**

Tuareg (twä′rĕg), *n.* **1.** a Berber or Hamitic-speaking member of the Muslim nomads of the Sahara. **2.** the language of the Tuaregs, a Berber dialect. [native name]

tuatara (tōō′ə tä′rə), *n.* a lizard-like reptile, *Sphaenodon punctatum,* found in a few islands off the coast of New Zealand, the only surviving member of the order *Rhynchocephalia.* [t. Maori]

tub (tŭb), *n., v.,* **tubbed, tubbing.** **—*n.*** **1.** a vessel or receptacle for bathing in; a bathtub. **2.** *Colloq.* a bath in a tub. **3.** a broad, round, open, wooden vessel, usually made of staves held together by hoops and fitted around a flat bottom. **4.** any of various vessels resembling or suggesting a tub. **5.** as much as a tub will hold. **6.** *Colloq.* a slow, clumsy ship or boat. **7.** *Rowing Colloq.* a heavy boat used for training novices. **8.** *Mining.* **a.** an ore wagon in a mine. **b.** a bucket, box, or the like, in which material is brought from or conveyed in a mine; a skip. **c.** installation of lining in an excavation (shaft) to prevent inflow of water or caving in. **—*v.t.*** **9.** to put or set in a tub. **10.** *Colloq.* to wash or bathe in a tub. **11.** *Rowing Colloq.* to coach (oarsmen) in a tub. **—*v.i.*** **12.** *Colloq.* to wash or bathe oneself in a tub. **13.** *U.S. Colloq.* to undergo washing, esp. without damage, as a fabric. [ME *tubbe,* c. LG *tubbe*; orig. unknown] **—tub′bable,** *adj.* **—tub′ber,** *n.* **—tub′like,** *adj.*

tuba (tyōō′bə), *n., pl.* **-bas, -bae** (-bē). **1.** a brass wind instrument of low pitch equipped with valves. **2.** an organ reed stop of large scale with notes of exceptional power. **3.** an ancient Roman trumpet. [t. L: trumpet; akin to TUBE]

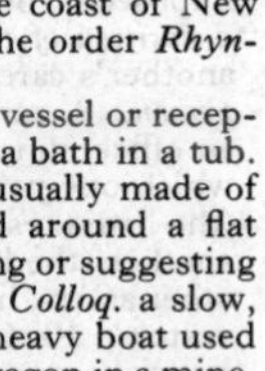

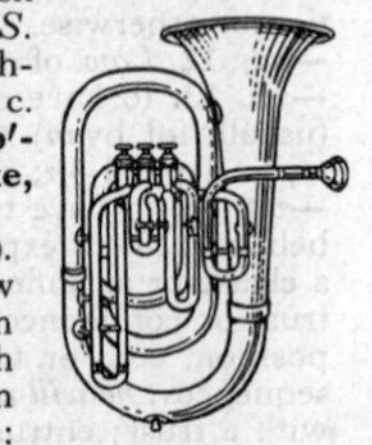
Tuba (def. 1)

tubal (tyōō′bl), *adj.* **1.** of or pertaining to a tube or tubes; tubular. **2.** *Anat.* pertaining to a tube, as the Fallopian tube.

Tubal-cain (tyōō′bl kān′), *n. Bible.* a maker of brass and iron articles. Gen. 4:22.

tubate (tyōō′bāt), *adj.* forming or having a tube or tubes.

tubby (tŭb′ĭ), *adj.*, **-bier, -biest. 1.** short and fat: *a tubby man.* **2.** having a dull sound; without resonance. —**tub′biness,** *n.*

tube (tyōōb), *n.*, *v.*, **tubed, tubing.** —*n.* **1.** a hollow usually cylindrical body of metal, glass, rubber, or other material, used for conveying or containing fluids, and for other purposes. **2.** a small, collapsible, metal cylinder closed at one end and having the open end provided with a cap, for holding paint, toothpaste, or other semiliquid substance to be squeezed out by pressure. **3.** *Anat.*, *Zool.* any hollow, cylindrical vessel or organ: *the bronchial tubes.* **4.** *Bot.* **a.** any hollow, elongated body or part. **b.** the united lower portion of a gamopetalous corolla or a gamosepalous calyx. **5.** the tubular tunnel in which an underground railway runs. **6.** the railway itself. **7.** valve (def. 7). **8.** *Archaic.* a telescope. —*v.t.* **9.** to furnish with a tube or tubes. **10.** to convey or enclose in a tube. **11.** to form in the shape of a tube; make like a tube. [t. L: m. s. *tubus* pipe] —**tube′less,** *adj.* —**tube′like′,** *adj.*

tubeless tyre, a pneumatic tyre which is so constructed that the outer cover makes an airtight seal with the wheel rims so that an inner tube is unnecessary.

tube of force, *Elect.*, *Magnetism.* a tubular space bounded by lines of force or induction.

tuber[1] (tyōō′bə), *n.* **1.** *Bot.* a fleshy, usually oblong or rounded thickening or outgrowth (as the potato) of a subterranean stem or shoot, bearing minute scalelike leaves with buds or eyes in their axils, from which new plants may arise. **2.** *Anat.*, *etc.* a rounded swelling or protuberance; a tuberosity; a tubercle. [t. L: bump, swelling]

tuber[2] (tyōō′bə), *n.* one who or that which tubes. [f. TUBE + -ER[1]]

tubercle (tyōō′bû′kl), *n.* **1.** a small rounded projection or excrescence, as on a bone, on the surface of the body in various animals, or on a plant. **2.** *Pathol.* **a.** a small, firm, rounded nodule or swelling. **b.** such a swelling as the characteristic lesion of tuberculosis. [t. L: m. s. *tūberculum* small swelling]

tubercle bacillus, the bacterium, *Myobacterium tuberculosis,* causing tuberculosis.

tubercular (tyōō bû′kyōō lə), *adj.* **1.** pertaining to tuberculosis; tuberculous. **2.** of, pertaining to, or having the nature of a tubercle or tubercles. **3.** characterized by tubercles. —*n.* **4.** a tuberculous person. —**tuber′cularly,** *adv.*

tubercularize (tyōō bû′kyōō lə rīz′), *v.t.*, *v.i.* **-rized, -rizing.** tuberculize. Also, **tubercularise.** —**tuber′culariza′tion,** *n.*

tuberculate (tyōō bû′kyōō lĭt), *adj.* **1.** tubercular. **2.** having tubercules. Also, **tuberculose.** [t. NL: m. s. *tūberculātus,* der. L *tūberculum* tubercle] —**tuber′cula′tion,** *n.*

tubercule (tyōō′bû kyōōl′), *n. Bot.* a nodule, esp. on the roots of certain legumes.

tuberculin (tyōō bû′kyōō lĭn), *n. Med.* a sterile liquid prepared from cultures of the tubercle bacillus, used in the diagnosis and treatment of tuberculosis.

tuberculize (tyōō bû′kyōō līz′), *v.*, **-lized, -lizing.** —*v.t.* **1.** to innoculate with tuberculin. **2.** to infect with a tubercle, or with tuberculosis. —*v.i.* **3.** to form tubercles or become tuberculous. Also, **tubercularize, tuberculinize, tuberculise.** —**tuber′culiza′tion,** *n.*

tuberculinize (tyōō bû′kyōō lĭ nīz′), *v.t.*, *v.i.*, **-nized, -nizing.** tuberculize. Also, **tuberculinise.** —**tuber′culiniza′tion,** *n.*

tuberculo-, a word element representing **tuberculous, tuberculosis,** or **tubercle bacillus.** [comb. form repr. L *tūberculum* tubercle]

tuberculoid (tyōō bû′kyōō loid′), *adj.* resembling a tubercle.

tuberculose (tyōō bû′kyōō lōs′), *adj.* tuberculate.

tuberculosis (tyōō bû′kyōō lō′sĭs), *n. Pathol.* **1.** an infectious disease affecting any of various tissues of the body, due to the tubercle bacillus, and characterized by the production of tubercles. **2.** this disease when affecting the lungs; pulmonary phthisis; consumption. [t. NL, der. L *tūberculum* TUBERCLE]

tuberculous (tyōō bû′kyōō ləs), *adj.* **1.** tubercular. **2.** affected with tuberculosis: *several tuberculous patients.*

tuberose[1] (tyōō′bə rōz′), *n.* a bulbous amaryllidaceous plant, *Polianthes tuberosa,* cultivated for its spike of fragrant, creamy white, lily-like flowers. [t. L: m. *tūberōsa,* fem. of *tūberōsus* tuberous, popularly confused with TUBE + ROSE]

tuberose[2] (tyōō′bə rōs′), *adj.* tuberous.

tuberosity (tyōō′bə rŏs′ĭ tĭ), *n.*, *pl.* **-ties.** a rough projection or protuberance of a bone as for the attachment of a muscle.

tuberous (tyōō′bə rəs), *adj.* **1.** covered with or characterized by rounded or wartlike prominences or tubers. **2.** of the nature of such a prominence. **3.** *Bot.* bearing tubers. **4.** having the nature of or resembling a tuber. [t. L: m. s. *tūberōsus*]

tuberous root, a true root so thickened as to resemble a tuber, but bearing no buds or eyes.

tube train, a train on an underground railway.

tube worm, *Zool.* any polychaete worm which constructs and inhabits a protective tube.

tubing (tyōō′bĭng), *n.* **1.** material in the form of a tube: *copper tubing.* **2.** tubes collectively. **3.** a piece of tube.

Tübingen (*Ger.* tʏ′bĭng ən), *n.* a town in West Germany, in central Baden-Württemberg. 53,900 (est. 1966).

Tubman (tŭb′mən), *n.* **William Vacanarat Shadrach** (wĭl′yəm văk′ə nə răt shăd′răk), born 1895, Liberian statesman: president since 1944.

tub-thumper (tŭb′thŭm′pə), *n.* a violent or declamatory orator, preacher, etc. —**tub′-thump′ing,** *adj.*, *n.*

tubular (tyōō′byōō lə), *adj.* **1.** of, or pertaining to a tube or tubes. **2.** characterized by or consisting of tubes. **3.** Also, **tubiform** (tyōō′bĭ fôm′). having the nature or form of a tube; tube-shaped. **4.** *Physiol.*, *Pathol.* denoting a respiratory sound resembling that produced by a current of air passing through a tube. [t. NL: s. *tubulāris,* der. L *tubulus* little tube] —**tubularity** (tyōō′byōō lă′rĭ tĭ), *n.*

tubulate (*adj.* tyōō′byōō lĭt, -lāt′; *v.* tyōō′byōō lāt′), *adj.*, *v.*, **-lated, -lating.** —*adj.* **1.** formed into or like a tube; tubular. —*v.t.* **2.** to form into a tube. **3.** to furnish with a tube. —**tu′bula′tion,** *n.* —**tu′bula′tor,** *n.*

tubule (tyōō′byōōl), *n.* a small tube; a minute tubular structure. [t. L: m. s. *tubulus* small pipe]

tubuliflorous (tyōō′byōō lĭ flô′rəs), *adj. Bot.* having the corolla tubular in all the perfect flowers of a head, as certain composite plants.

tubulous (tyōō′byōō ləs), *adj.* **1.** containing or composed of tubes. **2.** having the form of a tube; tubular. **3.** *Bot.* having tubular flowers. [t. NL: m. s. *tubulōsus*]

tubulure (tyōō′byōō lyōōə′), *n.* a short tubular opening, as in a glass jar or at the top of a retort. [t. F, der. L *tubulus* little pipe]

T.U.C., Trades Union Congress.

Tucana (tōō kä′nə), *n. Astron.* the southern constellation Toucan.

tuchun (tōō′chōōn′), *n.* (in Chinese history) the title of a military ruler of a province. [t. Chinese, lit., overseer of troops]

tuck[1] (tŭk), *v.t.* **1.** to thrust into some narrow space or close or concealed place: *tuck this in your pocket.* **2.** to thrust the edge or end of (a garment, covering, etc.) closely into place between retaining parts or things (usually fol. by *in, up,* etc.): *he tucked his napkin under his chin.* **3.** to cover snugly in or as in this manner: *to tuck one up in bed.* **4.** to draw up in folds or a folded arrangement: *to tuck one's legs under a chair.* **5.** *Needlework.* to sew tucks in. **6.** *Colloq.* to eat or drink (usually fol. by *in, away,* etc.). —*v.i.* **7.** to draw together; contract; pucker. **8.** *Needlework.* to make tucks. **9.** *Colloq.* to eat or drink heartily or greedily (usually fol. by *in, into, away,* etc.). —*n.* **10.** a tucked piece or part. **11.** *Needlework.* a fold, or one of a series of folds, made by doubling cloth upon itself, and stitching parallel with the edge of the fold. **12.** *Naut.* that part of a vessel where the after ends of the outside planking or plating unite at the sternpost. **13.** *Schoolboy Slang.* food, esp. sweet delicacies such as cakes, pastries, jam, etc. **14.** *Sport.* (in diving) a dive in which the knees are bent and pulled in close to the chest, the body being straightened again before hitting the water. [ME *t(o)uke(n)* stretch (cloth), torment, OE *tūcian* torment. Cf. MLG *tucken,* G *zucken* tug]

tuck[2] (tŭk), *n. Archaic.* a rapier with a stiff blade. [? sandhi var. of obs. *stock* sword. Cf. G *Stock,* F *estoc*]

tuck[3] (tŭk), *n. Chiefly Scot.* a stroke or tap, esp. on a drum; drumbeat.

Tuck (tŭk), *n.* **Friar,** the jolly priest of Robin Hood's band.

tuckahoe (tŭk′ə hō′), *n.* **1.** the edible underground sclerotium of the fungus *Poria cocos,* found on the roots of trees in the southern U.S. **2.** *U.S.* an inhabitant of Virginia, esp. the E part. [t. Algonquian (Virginia d.): m. *tockawhouge* it is globular]

tuckbox (tŭk′bŏks′), *n.* a box containing tuck (def. 13).

tucker[1] (tŭk′ə), *n.* **1.** one who or that which tucks. **2.** a piece of linen, muslin, or the like, worn by women about the neck and shoulders. **3.** a chemisette. **4.** *Austral.*, *N.Z. Colloq.* food. [f. TUCK[1] + -ER[1]]

tucker[2] (tŭk′ə), *v.t. U.S. Colloq.* to weary; tire; exhaust (often fol. by *out*).

tuckerbag (tŭk′ə băg′), *n. Austral.* any bag used for carrying food. Also, **tuckerbox** (tŭk′ə bŏks′).

tucket (tŭk′ĭt), *n.* a flourish or fanfare on a trumpet.

tuck-in (tŭk′ĭn′, tŭk′ĭn′), *n. Colloq.* a hearty meal.

tuckshop (tŭk′shŏp′), *n.* a shop, esp. one in a school, where cakes, pastries, etc., are sold.

Tucson (to͞o sŏn′, to͞o′sŏn), *n.* a town in the U.S., in S Arizona: health resort. 212,892 (1960).

Tucumán (*Sp.* to͞o ko͞o män′), *n.* a town in NW Argentina. 280,075 (1960).

-tude, a suffix forming abstract nouns (generally from Latin adjectives or participles) in words of Latin origin, as in *latitude, fortitude,* but sometimes used directly as an English formative element. [t. L: m. *-tūdo.* Cf. F *-tude*]

Tudor (tyo͞o′də), *adj.* **1.** of, pertaining to, or belonging to the English royal house of Tudor. **2.** of, pertaining to, or characteristic of the period of the reigns of the Tudor monarchs: *Tudor style of architecture.* **—***n.* **3.** a member of the royal family which ruled England from 1485 to 1603, and which was descended from **Sir Owen Tudor,** a Welshman who married the widow of Henry V.

Tues., Tuesday.

Tuesday (tyo͞oz′dĭ), *n.* the third day of the week, following Monday. [ME *Tewesday,* OE *Tiwesdæg* Tiw's day (trans. of L *Martis dies* day of Mars)]

tufa (tyo͞o′fə), *n. Geol.* a porous mass of mineral calcium carbonate deposited round a spring. [t. It.: m. *tufo,* g. L *tōfus* loose porous stone] **—tufaceous** (tyo͞o fā′shəs), *adj.*

tuff (tŭf), *n. Geol.* a rock of volcanic origin, comprising compacted or cemented volcanic ash and dust. Also, **volcanic tuff.** [t. F: m. *tuf,* t. It.: m. *tufo* TUFA] **—tuffaceous** (tŭ fā′shəs), *adj.*

tuffet (tŭf′ĭt), *n.* **1.** a hillock; mound. **2.** a footstool; hassock.

tuft (tŭft), *n.* **1.** a bunch of small, usually soft and flexible things, as feathers, hairs, etc., fixed at the base with the upper part loose. **2.** a small clump of bushes, trees, etc. **3.** a cluster of short-stalked flowers, leaves, etc., growing from a common point. **4.** any of the bunches of threads sewn through a mattress, quilt, etc., in order to strengthen the padding. **5.** a button through which a tuft is sewn. **6.** a gold tassel on the cap formerly worn at English universities by titled undergraduates. **7.** one who wore such a tassel. **—***v.t.* **8.** to furnish with a tuft or tufts. **9.** to arrange in a tuft or tufts. **10.** *Upholstery.* to draw together (a cushion, etc.) by passing a thread through at regular intervals, the depressions thus produced being usually ornamented with tufts or buttons. **—***v.i.* **11.** to form a tuft or tufts. [ME *toft;* orig. uncert.]

tufted (tŭf′tĭd), *adj.* **1.** furnished with a tuft or tufts. **2.** formed into a tuft or tufts.

tufthunter (tŭft′hŭn′tə), *n. Archaic.* **1.** one who seeks the acquaintance of titled persons. **2.** a toady; sycophant. [f. TUFT (defs 6, 7) + HUNTER] **—tuft′hunt′ing,** *adj.*

tufty (tŭf′tĭ), *adj.* **1.** abounding in tufts. **2.** covered or adorned with tufts. **3.** forming a tuft or tufts.

tug (tŭg), *v.,* **tugged, tugging,** *n.* **—***v.t.* **1.** to pull at with force or effort. **2.** to move by pulling forcibly; drag; haul. **3.** to tow (a vessel, etc.) by means of a tugboat. **—***v.i.* **4.** to pull with force or effort: *to tug at an oar.* **5.** to strive hard, labour, or toil. **—***n.* **6.** the act of tugging; a strong pull. **7.** a struggle; a strenuous contest. **8.** a tugboat. **9.** that by which something is tugged. **10. a.** a trace of a harness. **b.** any of various pulling or supporting parts of a harness. [ME *toggen,* appar. intensive var. of TOW[1]] **—tug′ger,** *n.* **—tug′less,** *adj.*

tugboat (tŭg′bōt′), *n.* a strongly built, heavily powered vessel for towing other vessels.

Tugela (to͞o gā′lə), *n.* a river in the Republic of South Africa, in Natal, flowing E to the Indian Ocean. ab. 300 mi.

tug of war, **1.** an athletic contest between two teams at opposite ends of a rope, each team trying to drag the other over a line. **2.** a severe or critical struggle.

tui (to͞o′ĭ), *n.* a green-black New Zealand honey-eater, *Prosthemadera novae-zealandiae,* having white tufts under the throat; parson-bird. [t. Maori]

Tuileries (twē′lə rĭ; *Fr.* twēl rē′), *n.* a former royal residence in Paris, begun by Catherine de' Medici, 1564: the seat of the convention in 1792; burned by supporters of the Commune, 1871.

tuition (tyo͞o ĭsh′ən), *n.* **1.** teaching or instruction, as of pupils. **2.** the charge or fee for instruction. **3.** *Archaic.* guardianship or custody. [late ME *tuicion,* t. L: m. s. *tuitio* guardianship] **—tui′tional, tuitionary** (tyo͞o ĭsh′ə nə rĭ), *adj.* **—tui′tionless,** *adj.*

Tula (*Russ.* to͞o′lə), *n.* a town in the central Soviet Union in Europe, S of Moscow. 366,000 (est. 1965).

tularaemia (to͞o′lə rē′myə), *n.* a disease of rabbits, squirrels, etc., caused by a bacterium, *Pasturella tularensis* (or *Bacterium tularense*), transmitted to man by insects or by the handling of infected animals, resembling the plague and taking the form in man of an irregular fever lasting several weeks. Also, *U.S.,* **tularemia.** [f. *Tulare,* county in California + -AEMIA]

Tuléar (*Fr.* tʏ lė är′), *n.* a seaport in SW Madagascar. 30,398 (1964).

tulip (tyo͞o′lĭp), *n.* **1.** any of the liliaceous plants constituting the genus *Tulipa,* cultivated in many varieties, and having large, showy, usually erect, cup-shaped or bell-shaped flowers of various colours. **2.** a flower or bulb of such a plant. [earlier *tulipa(n),* t. Turk.: m. *tülbend* TURBAN] **—tu′lip-like′,** *adj.*

tulip tree, a North American magnoliaceous tree, *Liriodendron tulipifera,* with tulip-like flowers and a wood that is used in cabinetwork, etc.

tulipwood (tyo͞o′lĭp wo͝od′), *n.* **1.** the wood of the tulip tree. **2.** any of various striped or variegated woods of other trees. **3.** any of these trees.

Tull (tŭl), *n.* **Jethro** (jĕth′rō), 1674–1741, English agriculturist who developed the seed drill.

Tullamore (tŭl′ə mô′), *n.* a town in the Republic of Ireland, the county town of Offaly. 6243 (1961).

tulle (tyo͞ol; *Fr.* tʏl), *n.* a thin silk or nylon net, used in millinery, dressmaking, etc. [t. F, named after TULLE]

Tulle (*Fr.* tʏl), *n.* a town in S central France, the capital of Corrèze department. 20,800 (est. 1965).

Tully (tŭl′ĭ), *n.* See **Cicero.**

Tulsa (tŭl′sə), *n.* a town in the U.S., in NE Oklahoma: centre of a rich oil-producing region. 261,685 (1960).

tumble (tŭm′bl), *v.,* **-bled, -bling,** *n.* **—***v.i.* **1.** to roll or fall over or down as by losing footing, support, or equilibrium: *to tumble down the stairs.* **2.** to fall rapidly, as stock market prices. **3.** to perform leaps, springs, somersaults, or other feats of bodily agility, as for exhibition or sport. **4.** to roll about by turning one way and another; pitch about; toss. **5.** to stumble or fall (usually fol. by *over*). **6.** to go, come, get, etc., in a precipitate or hasty way. **7.** *Colloq.* to become suddenly alive to some fact, circumstance, or the like (often fol. by *to*). **—***v.t.* **8.** to send falling or rolling; throw over or down. **9.** to move or toss about, or turn over, as in handling, searching, etc. **10.** to put in disorder by or as by tossing about. **11.** to throw, cast, put, send, etc., in a precipitate, hasty, or rough manner. **12.** to subject to the action of a tumbling box. **—***n.* **13.** an act of tumbling; a fall; a downfall. **14.** tumbled condition; disorder or confusion. **15.** a confused heap. [ME *tum(b)le* (freq. of *tumben,* OE *tumbian* dance), c. G *tummeln*]

tumbledown (tŭm′bl doun′), *adj.* dilapidated; ruinous.

tumbler (tŭm′blə), *n.* **1.** a drinking utensil with a flat bottom, without handle or stem, and usually of glass. **2.** one who or that which tumbles; one who performs leaps, somersaults, and other bodily feats. **3.** (in a lock) any locking or checking part which, when lifted or released by the action of a key or the like, allows the bolt to move. **4.** (in a gunlock) a lever-like piece which by the action of a spring forces the hammer forwards when released by the trigger. **5.** *Mach.* **a.** a part moving a gear into place in a selective transmission. **b.** a single cog or cam on a rotating shaft, transmitting motion to a part with which it engages. **6.** a tumbling box. **7.** a person who operates a tumbling box. **8.** one of a breed of dogs resembling small greyhounds, formerly used in hunting rabbits. **9.** one of a breed of domestic pigeons having the habit of turning over and over backwards in their flight. **10.** a toy, usually representing a fat, squatting figure, with a heavy or weighted and rounded base, so as to rock when touched. **11.** a machine in which damp clothes are slowly rotated and subjected to heat in order to dry them.

tumbler gear, *Mach.* a transmission having gears actuated by a tumbler.

tumbler switch, *Elect.* an electric switch having a quick action; used esp. in lighting circuits.

tumbleweed (tŭm′bl wēd′), *n.* any of various plants of North America (as an amaranth, *Amaranthus graecizans*) whose branching upper part becomes detached from the roots in autumn and is driven about by the wind.

tumbling box, an apparatus consisting of a box or cylindrical vessel pivoted at each end or at two corners, so that it can be made to revolve, used for polishing objects by allowing them to tumble about with an abrasive substance, for mixing materials, etc. Also, **tumbling barrel.**

tumbrel (tŭm′brəl), *n.* **1.** one of the carts used during the French Revolution to convey victims to the guillotine. **2.** a cart constructed so that the body tilts backwards to empty the load, esp. a dung cart. **3.** *Obs.* a two-wheeled covered cart accompanying artillery in order to carry tools, ammunition, etc. Also, **tumbril.** [ME *tumberell,* t. ML: s. *tumberellus,* ult. der. OLG *tumben* fall, c. OE *tumbian* dance. Cf. TUMBLE]

tumefacient (tyo͞o′mĭ fā′shyənt), *adj.* tumefying; swelling. [t. L: s. *tumefaciens,* ppr., tumefying]

tumefaction (tyōō′mĭ făk′shən), *n.* the act of making or becoming swollen or tumid. [t. L: m. s. *tumefacere*]
tumefy (tyōō′mĭ fī′), *v.t.*, *v.i.*, **-fied, -fying.** to make or become swollen or tumid. [t. L: m. s. *tumefacere*]
tumescent (tyōō mĕs′ənt), *adj.* swelling; slightly tumid. [t. L: s. *tumescens* beginning to swell] —**tumes′cence,** *n.*
tumid (tyōō′mĭd), *adj.* **1.** swollen, or affected with swelling, as a part of the body. **2.** pompous, turgid, or bombastic, as language, literary style, etc. [t. L: s. *tumidus* swollen] —**tumid′ity, tu′midness,** *n.* —**tu′midly,** *adv.*
tummy (tŭm′ĭ), *n.* *Colloq.* stomach.
tumour (tyōō′mə), *n.* **1.** a swollen part; a swelling or protuberance. **2.** *Pathol.* an abnormal or morbid swelling in any part of the body, esp. a more or less circumscribed morbid overgrowth of new tissue which is autonomous, differs more or less in structure from the part in which it grows, and serves no useful purpose. **3.** *Obs.* **a.** haughtiness; inflated pride. **b.** turgid or pompous language, style, etc. Also, *U.S.* **tumor.** [t. L: swollen state] —**tu′morous,** *adj.*
tump (tŭmp), *n.* *Dial.* **1.** a mound; hillock. **2.** a clump of trees or shrubs, esp. in a bog or fen.
tumular (tyōō′myōō lə), *adj.* of or like a tumulus or mound. [f. s. L *tumulus* mound + -AR[1]]
tumult (tyōō′mŭlt), *n.* **1.** the commotion or disturbance of a multitude, usually with noise; an uproar. **2.** a popular outbreak or uprising; commotion, disturbance, or violent disorder. **3.** agitation of mind; a mental or emotional disturbance. [ME, t. L: s. *tumultus*] —**Syn. 1.** See **ado.**
tumultuary (tyōō mŭl′tyōō ə rĭ), *adj.* **1.** tumultuous. **2.** confused; irregular.
tumultuous (tyōō mŭl′tyōō əs), *adj.* **1.** full of or marked by tumult or uproar. **2.** making a tumult; disorderly or noisy, as persons, etc. **3.** disturbed or agitated, as the mind, feelings, etc. [t. L: m. s. *tumultuōsus*] —**tumul′tuously,** *adv.* —**tumul′tuousness,** *n.* —**Ant. 3.** tranquil.
tumulus (tyōō′myōō ləs), *n., pl.* **-luses, -li** (-lī′). **1.** a mound or elevation of earth, etc., esp. of artificial origin and more or less antiquity. **2.** such a mound over a tomb; a barrow. [t. L: mound]
tun (tŭn), *n., v.,* **tunned, tunning.** —*n.* **1.** a large cask for holding liquids, etc., esp. wine, ale, or beer. **2.** a measure of capacity for wine, etc., usually equivalent to 252 wine gallons. —*v.t.* **3.** to put into or store in a tun or tuns. [ME and OE *tunne*, c. G *Tonne*]
tuna[1] (tyōō′nə), *n.* **1.** the tunny. **2.** any of various species and genera of large oceanic food and game fishes closely related to the tunny. Also, **tuna fish.** [t. Amer. Sp., var. of Sp. *atún* (t. Ar.: m. *tūn*) b. with d. *tun* tunny (g. L *thunnus*, t. Gk: m. *thýnnos*)]
tuna[2] (tyōō′nə), *n.* **1.** any of various prickly pears, esp. the erect, treelike species, *Opuntia tuna* and others, native in Mexico, bearing a sweet, edible fruit. **2.** the fruit. [t. Sp., t. Haitian]
tunable (tyōō′nə bl), *adj.* **1.** capable of being tuned. **2.** *Archaic.* in tune; harmonious; tuneful. Also, **tuneable.** —**tun′ableness,** *n.* —**tun′ably,** *adv.*
Tunbridge Wells (tŭn′brĭj′), a town in England, in Kent: mineral springs. 39,869 (1961).
tundra (tŭn′drə), *n.* one of the vast, nearly level, treeless plains of the arctic regions of Europe, Asia, and North America. [t. Russ.: marshy plain]
tune (tyōōn), *n., v.,* **tuned, tuning.** —*n.* **1.** a succession of musical sounds forming an air or melody, with or without the harmony accompanying it. **2.** a musical setting of a hymn or psalm, usually in four-part harmony. **3.** the state of being in the proper pitch: *to be in tune.* **4.** agreement in pitch; unison; harmony. **5.** due agreement, as of radio instruments or circuits with respect to frequency. **6.** accord; agreement. **7.** *Obs.* frame of mind; mood. **8.** *Obs.* a tone or sound. **9. call the tune,** to be in a position to give orders, dictate policy, etc.; command; control. **10. change one's tune, sing another (different) tune,** to change one's mind; reverse previously held views, attitudes, etc. **11. to the tune of,** to the amount of. —*v.t.* **12.** to adjust (a musical instrument) to a correct or given standard of pitch (often fol. by *up*). **13.** to bring into harmony. **14.** to adjust (an engine, machine or the like) for proper or improved running (often fol. by *up*). **15.** *Radio.* **a.** to adjust (a circuit, etc.) so as to bring it into resonance with another circuit, a given frequency, or the like. **b.** to adjust (a receiving apparatus) so as to make it in accord in frequency with a sending apparatus whose signals are to be received. **c.** to adjust a receiving apparatus so as to receive (the signals of a sending station). **16.** to put into a proper or a particular condition, mood, etc. **17.** *Rare.* to adapt (the voice, song, etc.) to a particular tone or to the expression of a particular feeling or the like; attune. **18.** *Archaic.* to utter, sound or express musically. **19.** *Archaic.* to play upon (a lyre, etc.). —*v.i.* **20.** to put a musical instrument, etc., in tune (often fol. by *up*). **21.** to give forth a musical sound. **22.** to sound or be in harmony. **23. tune in,** to adjust a radio so as to receive signals. **24. tune out,** to adjust a radio so as to avoid the signals of a sending station. [ME; unexplained var. of TONE]
tuneable (tyōō′nə bl), *adj.* tunable.
tuned circuit, *Radio.* a circuit consisting of an inductance and a capacitance which can be tuned to resonate at a given frequency by adjusting the values of the inductance or the capacitance; a resonant circuit.
tuneful (tyōōn′fəl), *adj.* **1.** full of melody; melodious: *tuneful compositions.* **2.** producing musical sounds or melody. —**tune′fully,** *adv.* —**tune′fulness,** *n.*
tuneless (tyōōn′lĭs), *adj.* **1.** unmelodious; unmusical. **2.** making or giving no music; silent: *in the corner stood a tuneless old piano.* —**tune′lessly,** *adv.*
tuner (tyōō′nə), *n.* **1.** one who or that which tunes. **2.** the part of a radio receiver which produces an output suitable for feeding into an amplifier.
tune-up (tyōōn′ŭp′), *n.* a check or adjustment of working order or condition, as an adjustment of the carburettor, ignition timing, etc., of a motor vehicle for maximum efficiency or power.
tung oil (tŭng), a drying oil, a valuable ingredient of varnishes, obtained from the seeds of a euphorbiaceous tree, *Aleurites fordii*; China wood-oil. [t. Chinese: m. *t'ung*]
tungstate (tŭng′stāt), *n.* a salt of any tungstic acid.
tungsten (tŭng′stən), *n.* *Chem.* a rare metallic element having a bright grey colour, a metallic lustre, and a high melting point (3410°C): found in wolframite, tungstite, and other minerals, and used to make high-speed steel cutting tools, for electric-lamp filaments, etc.; wolfram. *Symbol:* W (for *wolframium*); *at. wt:* 183·85; *at. no.:* 74; *sp. gr.:* 19·3. [t. Sw.: heavy stone] —**tungstenic** (tŭng-stĕn′ĭk), *adj.*
tungsten lamp, an incandescent electric lamp in which the filament is made of tungsten.
tungsten steel, a hard special steel containing tungsten.
tungsten trioxide, *Chem.* a yellow insoluble powder, WO_3, used in the manufacture of tungstates. Also, **tung′stic ac′id, tung′stic anhy′dride.**
tungstic (tŭng′stĭk), *adj.* *Chem.* of or containing tungsten, esp. in the pentavalent state or in the hexavalent state.
tungstic acid, *Chem.* **1.** a hydrate of tungsten trioxide, $H_2WO_4.H_2O$, used in the manufacture of tungsten-lamp filaments. **2.** any of a group of acids derived from tungsten by polymerization of tungsten trioxide. **3.** tungsten trioxide.
tungstite (tŭng′stīt), *n.* native tungsten trioxide, WO_3, a yellow or yellowish green mineral occurring usually in a pulverulent form.
Tungting (tōōng′tĭng′), *n.* a shallow lake in S China, in Hunan province. ab. 1500 sq. mi.
Tungus (tōōng′gōōs), *n., pl.* **-guses, -gus. 1.** a member of a Mongoloid people living in E Siberia. **2.** a language of Siberia and Manchuria of the Tungusic family.
Tungusic (tōōng gōōs′ĭk), *n.* **1.** a branch of the Altaic family of languages spoken in central and eastern Siberia and Manchuria. —*adj.* **2.** belonging to or pertaining to the Tunguses or to Tungusic. Also, **Tungusian** (tōōng-gōōs′ĭ ən).
Tunguska (*Russ.* tōōn gōōs′kə), *n.* any of three tributaries of the river Yenisei in the central Soviet Union in Asia: the **Lower Tunguska,** ab. 2000 mi.; the **Upper Tunguska** or the lower course of the Angara; and the **Stony Tunguska,** ab. 1000 mi.
tunic (tyōō′nĭk), *n.* **1.** a coat worn as part of a military or other uniform. **2.** a loose, sleeveless dress, esp. as worn by girls as part of a school uniform. **3.** a similar garment worn by women, as for gymnastics, dancing, etc. **4.** a garment like a shirt or gown, worn by both sexes among the ancient Greeks and Romans. **5.** *Eccles.* a tunicle. **6.** *Anat., Zool.* **a.** any covering or investing membrane or part, as of an organ. **b.** any loose membranous skin not formed from the epidermis. **7.** *Bot.* a natural integument. [OE *tunice*, t. L: m. *tunica*]
tunica (tyōō′nĭ kə), *n., pl.* **-cae** (-sē′). *Anat., Zool., Bot.* a tunic. [t. NL, special use of L *tunica* tunic]
tunicate (tyōō′nĭ kĭt, -kāt′), *n.* **1.** *Zool.* any marine chordate of the subphylum *Tunicata*, having a saclike body enclosed in a thick membrane (tunic) from which protrude two openings or siphons for the ingress and egress of water. —*adj.* Also, **tu′nicat′ed. 2.** (esp. of the *Tunicata*) having a tunic or covering. **3.** of or pertaining to the tunicates. **4.** *Bot.* having or consisting of a series of concentric layers, as a bulb. [t. L: m. s. *tunicātus*, pp., clothed with a tunic]
tunicle (tyōō′nĭ kl), *n.* *Eccles.* a vestment worn over the alb by subdeacons, as at the celebration of the mass, and by bishops. [ME, t. L: m. *tunicula*, dim. of *tunica* tunic]

tuning coil, *Electronics.* an inductive coil in a circuit which can be adjusted to tune the circuit.
tuning fork, a small steel instrument consisting of two prongs on a stem, designed to produce, when struck, a pure musical note of a definite constant pitch, and thus serving as a standard for tuning musical instruments, in acoustical investigation, etc.

Tuning fork

Tunis (tyo͞o′nĭs), *n.* **1.** the capital of Tunisia, in the NE part. 700,000 (est. 1961). See map under **Sardinia. 2.** one of the former Barbary States in N Africa, notorious for its pirates: modern Tunisia.
Tunisia (tyo͞o nĭz′ĭ ə, -nĭs′ĭ ə), *n.* a republic of N Africa on the Mediterranean; a French protectorate until 1956. 4,630,000 pop. (est. 1965); 48,330 sq. mi. *Cap.:* Tunis. See map under **Malta.** —**Tunis′ian,** *adj., n.*
Tunku (to͝ong′ko͞o), *n.* a Malayan title of respect before family names as an indication of nobility or rank. Also, **Tuanku.** [t. Malay: ruler] —**Tengku** (tĕng′ko͞o), **Tenku,** *n.fem.*
Tunku Abdul Rahman. See **Rahman, Tunku Abdul.**
tunnage (tŭn′ĭj), *n.* tonnage.
tunnel (tŭn′əl), *n., v.* **-nelled, -nelling** or (*U.S.*) **-neled, -neling. 1.** an underground passage. **2.** a passageway, as for trains, motor vehicles, etc., through or under an obstruction as a hill, mountain, river, town, harbour, etc. **3.** an approximately horizontal passageway or gallery in a mine. **4.** the burrow of an animal. **5.** *Dial.* a funnel. **6.** *Obs.* the flue of a chimney. —*v.t.* **7.** to make or form a tunnel through or under. **8.** to make or form as or like a tunnel: *to tunnel a passage under a river.* **9.** to perforate as with tunnels. —*v.i.* **10.** to make a tunnel or tunnels: *to tunnel through the Alps.* [late ME *tonel* funnel-shaped net. Cf. OF *tonel* cask, der. *tonne* TON[1]] —**tun′neller;** *esp. U.S.,* **tun′neler,** *n.*
tunnel diode, *Electronics.* a semiconductor which has a negative resistance over part of its operating range as a result of the tunnel effect.
tunnel effect, *Physics.* the passage of an electron through a narrow potential barrier in a semiconductor in spite of its energy level being too low to surmount the barrier according to classical mechanics. This is explained in terms of quantum mechanics on the assumption that most of the electron's energy can tunnel through the barrier.
tunny (tŭn′ĭ), *n., pl.* **-nies,** (*esp. collectively*) **-ny. 1.** any of a number of widely distributed, important, marine food fishes, genus *Thunnus,* of the mackerel family, esp. *T. thynnus,* occurring in the warmer parts of the Atlantic and Pacific oceans, sometimes reaching a weight of 750 lbs or more. **2.** any of various related scombroid fishes, as the albacore, *Germo alalunga* (the **long-finned tunny**). [t. F: m. *thon,* t. Pr.: m. *ton,* g. L *thunnus,* t. Gk: m. *thýnnos*]
tup (tŭp), *n., v.,* **tupped, tupping.** —*n.* **1.** a male sheep; ram. **2.** the head of a steam hammer or pile-driver. —*v.t.* **3.** (of a ram) to copulate with (a ewe).
tupelo (tyo͞o′pĭ lō′), *n., pl.* **-los. 1.** any of several trees of the cornaceous genus *Nyssa,* esp. a large tree, *N. aquatica,* of deep swamps and river bottoms of the southern U.S. **2.** the strong, tough wood of any of these trees, esp. in commercial use. [t. N Amer. Ind. (Creek): m. *ito opelwa* swamp tree]
Tupi (to͞o pē′), *n., pl.* **-pis. 1.** a member of a widespread group of tribes of South American Indians living along the lower Amazon and in the valleys of other Brazilian rivers. **2.** the language of this group. —**Tupi′an,** *adj.*
tuppence (tŭp′əns), *n.* twopence.
Tupungato (*Sp.* to͞o po͞on gä′tō), *n.* a mountain in the Andes, between Argentina and Chile. ab. 22,000 ft.
tuque (tyo͞ok), *n.* a kind of knitted cap worn in Canada. [t. Canadian F, var. of F *toque* cap]
tuquoque (tyo͞o′kwō′kwĭ), *Latin.* thou, too; you're another: a retort accusing of a similar crime an opponent who has brought charges against one.
Turanian (tyo͞o rā′nyən), *adj.* **1.** belonging or pertaining to a group of Asian peoples or languages comprising all or nearly all those which are neither Indo-European nor Semitic. **2.** *Obs.* Ural-Altaic. —*n.* **3.** a member of any of the races speaking a Turanian (esp. a Ural-Altaic) language. **4.** a member of any of the Ural-Altaic races. [f. Pers. *Turān,* name of district beyond the Oxus + -IAN]
turban (tû′bən), *n.* **1.** a form of headdress of Muslim origin worn by men chiefly in parts of N Africa, and SW and S Asia, consisting of a scarf of silk, linen, cotton, or the like, wound directly round the head or around a cap. **2.** any headdress resembling this. **3.** a small hat, either brimless or with a brim turned up close against the crown, worn by women. [earlier *turband,* t. Turk.: m. *tülbend,* t. Ar.: m. *dulband,* t. Pers., Hind.] —**tur′baned,** *adj.* —**tur′banless,** *adj.* —**tur′ban-like′,** *adj.*

Turban

turbary (tû′bə rĭ), *n., pl.* **-ries. 1.** land, or a piece of land, where turf or peat may be dug or cut. **2.** *Law.* the right to cut turf or peat on a common or another person's land. [ME *turbarye,* t. ML: m. *turbaria,* der. *turba* TURF]
turbellarian (tû′bĭ lĕə′rĭ ən), *adj.* **1.** belonging to the *Turbellaria,* a class of platyhelminths or flatworms, mostly aquatic, and characterized by cilia whose motions produce small currents or vortexes in water. —*n.* **2.** a turbellarian platyhelminth. [der. NL *Turbellāria,* f. s. L *turbella* little crowd + *-āria,* neut. pl. of *-ārius* -ARY[1]]
turbid (tû′bĭd), *adj.* **1.** (of liquids) opaque or muddy with particles of extraneous matter. **2.** not clear or transparent; thick, as smoke or clouds; dense. **3.** disturbed; confused; muddled. [t. L: s. *turbidus* disturbed] —**turbid′ity, tur′bidness,** *n.* —**tur′bidly,** *adv.*
turbidimeter (tû′bĭ dĭm′ĭ tə), *n.* a device for measuring the turbidity of water or other liquids.
turbinal (tû′bĭ nəl), *adj.* **1.** turbinate. —*n.* **2.** *Anat.* a turbinate bone. [f. s. L *turbo* top + -AL[1]]
turbinate (tû′bĭ nĭt, -nāt′), *adj.* Also, **tur′binat′ed. 1.** scroll-like; whorled; spiral. **2.** *Anat.* denoting or pertaining to certain scroll-like spongy bones of the nasal passages in the higher vertebrates. See diag. under **mouth. 3.** inversely conical. —*n.* **4.** a turbinate shell. **5.** *Anat.* a turbinate bone. [t. L: m. s. *turbinātus* shaped like a top]
turbine (tû′bĭn, -bīn), *n.* **1.** any of a class of hydraulic motors in which a vaned wheel or runner is made to revolve by the impingement of a free jet of fluid (**impulse turbine** or **action turbine**) or by the passage of fluid which completely fills the motor (**reaction** or **pressure turbine**). **2.** any of certain analogous motors using other fluids, as steam (**steam turbine**), products of combustion (**gas turbine**), or air (**air turbine**). [t. F, t. L: m. s. *turbo* anything that spins]
turbit (tû′bĭt), *n.* one of a breed of domestic pigeons with a stout, roundish body, a short head and beak, and a ruffled breast and neck. [appar. der. L *turbo* a top; so called because of its figure]
turbo-electric (tû′bō ĭ lĕk′trĭk), *adj.* having an electric motor powered by a turbine.
turbofan (tû′bō făn′), *n. Aeron.* a turbojet engine incorporating an oversize compressor acting as a ducted fan.
turbogenerator (tû′bō jĕn′ə rā′tə), *n.* an electric generator coupled to a steam turbine.
turbojet (tû′bō jĕt′), *n. Aeron.* **1.** Also, **jet engine.** a gas-turbine engine used for propelling an aircraft, in which the thrust is obtained solely from the reaction of a jet issuing from a propelling nozzle. **2.** an aeroplane driven by one or more of such engines.
turboprop (tû′bō prŏp′), *n. Aeron.* **1.** a gas-turbine engine coupled to a propeller, forming a propulsive unit of an aircraft. **2.** an aeroplane driven by one or more of such units. Also, **propjet.**
turbot (tû′bət), *n., pl.* **-bot, -bots. 1.** a European flatfish, *Psetta maxima,* with a diamond-shaped body. **2.** any of several other flatfishes. **3.** a triggerfish. [ME, t. MD (cf. OF *torbot*); orig. uncert.]
turbulence (tû′byo͞o ləns), *n.* **1.** a turbulent state. **2.** *Hydraulics.* the haphazard secondary motion due to eddies within a moving fluid. **3.** *Meteorol.* irregular motion of the atmosphere, as that indicated by gusts and lulls in the wind. Also, **tur′bulency.**
turbulent (tû′byo͞o lənt), *adj.* **1.** disposed or given to disturbances, disorder, or insubordination; violent; unruly. **2.** marked by or showing a spirit of disorder or insubordination: *a turbulent period.* **3.** disturbed; agitated; troubled; stormy. [t. L: s. *turbulentus* restless] —**tur′bulently,** *adv.*
turbulent flow, fluid flow in which the motion at any point varies rapidly in magnitude and direction.
Turco (tû′kō), *n., pl.* **-cos.** (formerly) an Algerian serving in the light infantry of the French army.
Turco-, a word element meaning 'Turkish'. [t. F, t. It.]
Turcoman (tû′kə mən), *n., pl.* **-mans.** Turkoman.
turd (tûd), *n. Taboo.* **1.** a piece of excrement. **2.** (used offensively) an unpleasant person. [ME; OE *tord*]
turdiform (tû′dĭ fôm′), *adj.* having the form of a thrush. [t. NL: s. *turdiformis,* f. s. L *turdus* thrush + -(*i*)*formis* -(I)FORM]
turdine (tû′dīn, dĭn), *adj.* belonging or pertaining to the thrushes, birds of the family *Turdidae.* [f. s. L *turdus* thrush + -INE[1]]
tureen (tə rēn′), *n.* a large deep dish with a cover, for holding soup, etc., at table. [earlier *terrine,* t. F: earthenware dish, ult. der. L *terra* earth]

Turenne (*Fr.* tʏ rěn′), *n.* **Henri de la Tour d'Auvergne de** (*Fr.* äɴ rē′ də là to͝or dō věrny′ də), 1611–75, French marshal.

turf (tûf), *n.*, *pl.* **turfs,** (*Archaic*) **turves** (tûvz); *v.* —*n.* **1.** the covering of grass, etc., with its matted roots, forming the surface of grassland. **2.** a piece cut or torn from the surface of grassland, with the grass, etc., growing on it; a sod. **3.** a block or piece of peat dug for fuel. **4.** peat as a substance for fuel. **5. the turf, a.** the grassy course or other track over which horseraces are run. **b.** the practice or institution of racing horses. **c.** the racing world. —*v.t.* **6.** to cover with turf or sod. **7. turf out,** *Colloq.* to throw out; eject. [ME and OE, c. G *Torf* peat; Latinized, *turba*] —**turf′less,** *adj.* —**turf′like′,** *adj.*

turf accountant, a bookmaker.

turfman (tûf′mən), *n.*, *pl.* **-men.** *U.S.* a man devoted to horseracing.

turfy (tû′fĭ), *adj.*, **turfier, turfiest. 1.** covered with or consisting of grassy turf. **2.** resembling turf; turf-like. **3.** abounding in, or of the nature of, turf or peat. **4.** pertaining to or characteristic of horseracing. —**turf′iness,** *n.*

Turgenev (tû gā′nyĕv; *Russ.* to͝or gyě′nyĭf), *n.* **Ivan Sergeevich** (*Russ.* ĭ vän′ sĭr gyě′yĭ vĭch), 1818–83, Russian novelist.

turgent (tû′jənt), *adj.* *Obs.* swelling; swollen; turgid. [t. L: s. *turgens*, ppr., swelling] —**tur′gently,** *adv.*

turgescent (tû jĕs′ənt), *adj.* becoming swollen; swelling. [t. L: s. *turgescens*, ppr.] —**turges′cence, turges′cency,** *n.*

turgid (tû′jĭd), *adj.* **1.** pompous or bombastic, as language, style, etc. **2.** swollen; distended; tumid. [t. L: s. *turgidus*] —**turgid′ity, tur′gidness,** *n.* —**tur′gidly,** *adv.*

turgite (tû′jīt), *n.* an iron ore, a hydrated ferric oxide, related to limonite but containing less water. [named after *Turginak* mine in Soviet Union. See -ITE[1]]

turgor (tû′gə), *n.* **1.** the state of being swelled or filled out. **2.** *Plant Physiol.* the normal distension or rigidity of plant cells, resulting from the pressure exerted from within against the cell walls by the cell contents. [t. L, der. *turgēre* swell]

Turgot (*Fr.* tʏr gō′), *n.* **Anne Robert Jacques** (*Fr.* àn rō běr zhàk′), 1727–81, French statesman, financier, and economist.

Turin (tyo͝o rĭn′), *n.* a city in NW Italy, in Piedmont, on the river Po: capital of the Kingdom of Italy 1860–65. 1,107,613 (1966). Italian, **Torino.**

Turk (tûk), *n.* **1.** a native or inhabitant of Turkey. **2.** (formerly) a native or inhabitant of the Ottoman Empire, esp. a Muslim. **3.** a member of any of the peoples speaking Turkic languages. **4.** a cruel, brutal, tyrannical, or unruly man. **5.** one of a breed of horses allied to the Arab. **6.** any Turkish horse. [ME, ult. t. Pers.]

Turk., **1.** Turkey. **2.** Turkish.

Turkestan (tû′kĭ stän′), *n.* a vast region in W and central Asia, E of the Caspian Sea, including the former **Eastern** or **Chinese Turkestan** (the S and central part of Sinkiang, China), **Russian Turkestan** (now the Kazak, Kirghiz, Tadzhik, Turkmen, and Uzbek republics of the Soviet Union), and a N strip of Afghanistan. Also, **Turkistan.**

turkey (tû′kĭ), *n.*, *pl.* **-keys,** (*esp. collectively for 1*) **-key. 1.** a large gallinaceous bird of the family *Meleagrididae*, esp. *Meleagris gallopava*, of America, which is domesticated in most parts of the world. **2.** the flesh of this bird, used as food. **3.** *U.S. Slang.* an unsuccessful theatrical production; flop. **4. talk turkey,** *Colloq.* to talk seriously; talk business.

Turkey (tû′kĭ), *n.* a republic in W Asia and SE Europe. 31,391,207 pop. (1965); 296,185 sq. mi. (286,928 sq. mi. in Asia; 9257 sq. mi. in Europe). *Cap.:* Ankara. See **Ottoman Empire.**

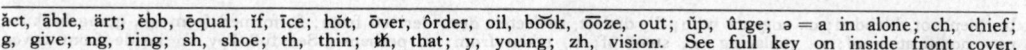

Turkey

turkey buzzard, a vulture, *Cathartes aura*, common in South and Central America and the southern U.S., having a bare reddish head and a dark plumage.

turkey cock, 1. the male of the turkey. **2.** a strutting, pompous, conceited person.

turkey oak, an oak tree with deeply cut, hairy leaves, *Quercus cerris*, a native of W and S Europe but often planted and naturalized elsewhere.

Turkey red, 1. a bright red produced in fabrics by madder or alizarin. **2.** cotton cloth of this colour.

turkey trot, a round dance popular during World War I, danced by couples, properly to ragtime, the step being a springy walk with little or no bending of the knees, and accompanied by a swinging motion of the body with shoulder movements up and down.

Turki (tû′kē), *n.* **1.** Turkic. —*adj.* **2.** pertaining or belonging to the peoples speaking Turkic. [t. Pers.]

Turkic (tû′kĭk), *n.* **1.** a branch of the Altaic family of languages that includes Turkish, Azerbaijani, Turkmen, Uzbeg, Kirghiz, and Yakut. —*adj.* **2.** of or pertaining to Turkic.

Turkish (tû′kĭsh), *adj.* **1.** pertaining or belonging to or derived from the Turks or Turkey. **2.** of or pertaining to the language of the Turks. —*n.* **3.** the language of Turkey; Ottoman Turkish. **4.** Turkic.

Turkish bath, a kind of bath introduced from the East, in which, after copious perspiration in a heated room, the body is washed, massaged, etc.

Turkish delight, a cubed, gelatine-stiffened confection covered with icing sugar.

Turkish Empire. See **Ottoman Empire.**

Turkish pound. See **lira** (def. 3).

Turkish towel, a thick cotton towel with a long nap usually composed of uncut loops.

Turkism (tû′kĭz′əm), *n.* the culture, beliefs, principles, etc., of the Turks.

Turkistan (tû′kĭ stän′), *n.* Turkestan.

Turkman (tûk′mən), *n.*, *pl.* **-men.** a native or inhabitant of Turkmenistan. —**Turkmenian** (tûk mē′nyən), *adj.*

Turkmen (tûk′mĕn), *n.* a Turkic language spoken mainly east of the Caspian Sea.

Turkmenistan (tûk′mĕn ĭ stän′; *Russ.* to͝ork mĭ nĭs tàn′), *n.* a constituent republic of the Soviet Union, bordering the Caspian Sea, Iran, and Afghanistan. 1,862,000 pop. (est. 1965); 187,100 sq. mi. *Cap.:* Ashkhabad. Also, **Turkomen** (tû′kə mĕn′). Official name, **Turkmen Soviet Socialist Republic.**

Turko-, var. of **Turco-.**

Turkoman (tû′kə mən), *n.*, *pl.* **-mans. 1.** a member of a Turkish people consisting of a group of tribes which inhabit the region about the Aral Sea and parts of Iran and Afghanistan. **2.** Turkmen. Also, **Turcoman.** [t. Pers.: m. *Turkumān* one resembling a Turk]

Turks and Caicos Islands (tûks′ən kī′kōs), two groups of islands in the SE part of the Bahamas: a British colony. 5716 pop. (1960); 166 sq. mi. *Cap.:* Grand Turk.

Turk's-cap lily (tûks′kăp′), either of two lilies, *Lilum martagon* and *L. superbum*, having nodding flowers with the perianth segments strongly revolute.

Turk's-head (tûks′hĕd′), *n.* *Naut.* a form of decorative knot made by weaving turns of small cord round a larger rope.

Turku (*Finn.* to͝or′ko͞o), *n.* a seaport in SW Finland. 138,299 (1965).

turmaline (tû′mə lēn′), *n.* tourmaline.

turmeric (tû′mə rĭk), *n.* **1.** the aromatic rhizome of *Curcuma longa*, an East Indian zingiberaceous plant. **2.** a powder prepared from it, used as a condiment (esp. in curry powder), a yellow dye, a medicine, etc. **3.** the plant itself. **4.** any of various similar substances or plants. [earlier *tarmaret*, t. ML: m. *terra merita*, lit., deserving earth]

turmeric paper, paper treated with turmeric: used to indicate the presence of alkalis, which turn it brown, or of boric acid, which turns it reddish brown.

turmoil (tû′moil), *n.* **1.** a state of commotion or disturbance; tumult; agitation; disquiet. **2.** *Obs.* harassing labour. [appar. f. TURN + MOIL] —**Syn. 1.** See **agitation.**

turn (tûn), *v.t.* **1.** cause to move round on an axis or about a centre; rotate: *to turn a wheel.* **2.** to cause to move round or partly round, as for the purpose of opening, closing, tightening, etc.: *to turn a key.* **3.** to reverse the position or posture of: *to turn a page.* **4.** to bring the underparts of (sod, soil, etc.) to the surface, as in ploughing. **5.** to change the position of, by or as by rotating; to move into a different position. **6.** to change or alter the course of; to divert; deflect. **7.** to change or alter the nature, character, or appearance of. **8.** to change or convert (fol. by *into* or *to*): *to turn water into ice.* **9.** to render or make by some change. **10.** to change the colour of (leaves, etc.). **11.** to cause to become sour, ferment, or the like: *warm weather turns milk.* **12.** to cause (the stomach) to reject food or anything swallowed. **13.** to change from one language or form of expression to another; translate. **14.** to put or apply to some use or purpose: *to turn a thing to good use.* **15.** to go or pass round or to the other side of: *to turn a street corner.* **16.** to get beyond or pass (a certain age, time, amount, etc.): *a man just turning forty.* **17.** to direct, aim or set going towards or away from a specified person or thing, or in a specified direction: *to turn towards the north.* **18.** to direct (the eyes, face, etc.) another way; avert. **19.** to shape (a piece of metal, etc.) into rounded form with a cutting instrument while rotating in a lathe. **20.** to bring into a rounded or curved form in any way. **21.** to shape artistically or gracefully, esp. in rounded form. **22.** to

form or express gracefully: *to turn a sentence.* **23.** to direct (thought, desire, etc.) towards or away from something. **24.** to cause to go; send; drive: *to turn a person from one's door.* **25.** to revolve in the mind (often fol. by *over*). **26.** to maintain a steady flow or circulation of (money or articles of commerce). **27.** to reverse (a garment, etc.) so that the inner side becomes the outer. **28.** to remake (a garment) by putting the inner side outwards. **29.** to curve, bend, or twist. **30.** to bend back or blunt (the edge of a knife, etc.). **31.** to execute, as a somersault, by rotating or revolving. **32.** to disturb the mental balance of, or make mad, distract; derange. **33.** to throw into disorder or confusion; upset: *the thief turned the room upside down.* **34.** *Obs.* to convert. **35.** *Obs.* to pervert.
—*v.i.* **36.** to move round on an axis or about a centre; rotate. **37.** to move partly round in this manner, as a door on a hinge. **38.** to direct the face or gaze towards or away from something, or in a particular direction. **39.** to direct or set one's course towards or away from something or in a particular direction. **40.** to direct one's thought, attention, desire, etc., towards or away from something. **41.** to hinge or depend (usually fol. by *on* or *upon*): *the question turns on this point.* **42.** to apply one's efforts, interest, etc., to something; devote oneself to something: *he turned to the study of music.* **43.** to change or reverse the course so as to go in a different or the opposite direction: *to turn to the right.* **44.** to change position so as to face in a different or the opposite direction. **45.** to change or reverse position or posture as by a rotary motion. **46.** to shift the body about as if on an axis: *to turn on one's side in sleeping.* **47.** to assume a curved form; bend. **48.** to be affected with nausea, as the stomach. **49.** to have a sensation as of whirling, or be affected with giddiness as the head. **50.** to adopt a different religion, manner of life, etc. **51.** to change one's position in order to resist or attack: *the worm will turn.* **52.** to change or alter, as in nature, character, or appearance. **53.** to become sour, fermented, or the like, as milk, etc. **54.** to become of a different colour, as leaves, etc. **55.** to be changed, transformed, or converted (fol. by *into* or *to*). **56.** to change so as to be; become: *to turn pale.* **57.** to put about or tack, as a ship.
—*v.* **58.** Some special verb phrases are:
turn against, 1. to make hostile towards; cause to be prejudiced against: *to turn a son against his father.* **2.** to take up an attitude of hostility or opposition: *to turn against a person.*
turn away, 1. to look or face in a different direction. **2.** to refuse to help; rebuff. **3.** to refuse admission to.
turn back, 1. to go back; return. **2.** to cause to go back or return. **3.** to fold.
turn down, 1. to fold. **2.** to lessen the intensity of; moderate. **3.** to refuse or reject (a person, request, etc.).
turn in, 1. *Colloq.* to go to bed. **2.** *Colloq.* to hand over to; deliver; surrender. **3.** to give back. **4.** *U.S.* to submit; hand in.
turn it up! *Slang.* stop it! shut up!
turn off, 1. to stop the flow of (water, gas, etc.) as by closing a valve, etc. **2.** to switch off (a radio, light, etc.). **3.** to branch off; diverge; change direction. **4.** *Obs.* to execute by hanging.
turn on, 1. to cause (water, gas, etc.) to flow as by opening a valve, etc. **2.** to switch on (a radio, light, etc.). **3.** Also, **turn upon.** to become suddenly hostile to; attack without warning. **4.** to show or display suddenly: *to turn on the charm.* **5.** *Slang.* to excite or interest (a person): *man, that jazz sure turns me on!*
turn out, 1. to extinguish or put out (a light, etc.). **2.** to produce as the result of labour; manufacture; make. **3.** to drive out; expel; send away; dismiss; discharge. **4.** to clear or empty (a cupboard, pocket, drawer, etc.) of contents. **5.** to equip; fit out. **6.** to result or issue. **7.** to come to be; become ultimately. **8.** to be found or known; prove. **9.** *Colloq.* to get out of bed. **10.** *Colloq.* to assemble, or cause to assemble; muster; parade; gather.
turn over, 1. to move or be moved from one side to another. **2.** to reverse the position of; invert. **3.** to meditate; ponder; reflect. **4.** to start (an engine). **5.** (of an engine) to start. **6.** hand over; transfer. **7.** *Com.* to purchase and then sell (goods or commodities). **8.** *Com.* to do business or sell goods to the amount of (a specified sum). **9.** *Com.* to invest or recover (capital) in some transaction or in the course of business.
turn to, 1. to apply to for help, advice, etc.; appeal to. **2.** to set oneself to a task; attend to.
turn up, 1. to fold, esp. so as to shorten, as a garment. **2.** to dig up; bring to the surface by digging; expose. **3.** to find; bring to light; uncover. **4.** to increase the intensity of. **5.** to happen; occur. **6.** to arrive; come. **7.** to come to light; be recovered. **8.** (of a person's nose, or the like) to point slightly upwards at the end. **9.** *Slang.* to make (a person) feel sick; nauseate.
—*n.* **59.** a movement of rotation, whether total or partial: *a slight turn of the handle.* **60.** the act of changing or reversing position or posture as by a rotary movement: *a turn of the dice.* **61.** the time for action or proceeding which comes in due rotation or order to each of a number of persons, etc.: *it's my turn to pay.* **62.** the act of changing or reversing the course: *to make a turn to the right.* **63.** a place or point at which such a change occurs. **64.** a place where a road, river, or the like turns. **65.** a single revolution, as of a wheel. **66.** the act of turning so as to face or go in a different direction. **67.** direction, drift, or trend: *the conversation took an interesting turn.* **68.** change or a change in nature, character, condition, circumstances, etc. **69.** the point or time of change. **70.** the time during which a workman or a set of workmen is at work in alternation with others. **71.** that which is done by each of a number of persons acting in rotation or succession. **72.** rounded or curved form in general. **73.** shape, form, or mould. **74.** a passing or twisting of one thing round another as of a rope round a mast. **75.** the condition or manner of being twisted. **76.** a single round, as of a wound or coiled rope. **77.** style, as of expression or language. **78.** a distinctive form or style imparted: *a happy turn of expression.* **79.** a short walk, ride, or the like which includes a going and a returning, esp. by different routes. **80.** natural inclination, bent, tendency, or aptitude. **81.** a spell or period of work; shift. **82.** a spell or bout of action. **83.** an attack of illness or the like. **84.** an act of service or disservice (with *good*, *bad*, *kind*, etc.). **85.** requirement, exigency, or need: *this will serve your turn.* **86.** *Colloq.* a nervous shock, as from fright or astonishment. **87.** *Stock Exchange.* the difference between the stockjobber's buying and selling price. **88.** *Music.* a melodic embellishment or grace, commonly consisting of a principal note with two auxiliary notes, one above and the other below it. **89.** an individual stage performance, esp. in a music hall, cabaret, etc. **90.** the performer in such an entertainment. **91.** a contest or round; a bout.
92. Some special noun phrases are:
at every turn, constantly; in every case.
by turns, one after another; alternately; in rotation.
in turn, in due order of succession.
on the turn, a. in the process of or about to turn or change. **b.** (of milk) on the point of turning sour.
out of turn, a. out of proper order. **b.** at the wrong time; at an unsuitable moment; indiscreetly; tactlessly.
take turns, to do in succession; alternate.
to a turn, to just the proper degree; perfectly.
turn and turn about, by turns; alternately.
[ME; OE *turnian*, t. L: m. *tornāre* turn (in a lathe)]
—**Syn. 36.** TURN, REVOLVE, ROTATE, SPIN indicate moving in a more or less rotary, circular fashion. TURN is the general and popular word for motion on an axis or round a centre, but it is used also of motion less than a complete circle: *a gate turns on its hinges.* REVOLVE refers esp. to movement in an orbit round a centre, but is sometimes exchangeable with ROTATE, which refers only to the motion of a body round its own centre or axis: *the moon revolves about the earth; the earth revolves (or rotates) on its axis.* To SPIN is to rotate very rapidly: *the blades of an electric fan spin.* **80.** TURN and CAST are colloquial in use and imply a bent, inclination, or habit. TURN means a tendency or inclination for something: *a turn for art.* CAST means an established habit of thought, a mould, a style: *a melancholy cast.*

turnabout (tûʹnə boutʹ), *n.* **1.** the act of turning in a different or opposite direction. **2.** *Chiefly U.S.* a change of opinion, loyalty, etc.
turnbuckle (tûnʹbŭkʹl), *n.* a link or sleeve with a swivel at one end and an internal screw thread at the other, or with an internal screw thread at each end, used as a means of uniting or coupling, and of tightening, two parts, as the ends of two rods.

Open turnbuckle

turncoat (tûnʹkōtʹ), *n.* one who changes his party or principles; a renegade. [f. TURN + COAT]
turncock (tûnʹkŏkʹ), *n.* stopcock.
turndown (tûnʹ dounʹ), *adj.* that is or may be turned down; folded or doubled down.
turned commas, *Print.* inverted commas.
turner (tûʹnə), *n.* **1.** one who or that which turns. **2.** one who fashions objects on a lathe. [ME, f. TURN + -ER[1]]
Turner (tûʹnə), *n.* **Joseph Mallord William** (mălʹəd), 1775–1851, English painter.
turnery (tûʹnə rĭ), *n.* **1.** the art or work of a turner; forming of objects on a lathe. **2.** articles fashioned on a lathe.
Turnhout (*Flem.* tʏrnʹhôwt), *n.* a town in Belgium, in N Antwerp province. 37,146 (est. 1964).
turn indicator, *Aeron.* an instrument that indicates the rate of turn of an aircraft about its vertical axis.

turning (tûr′nĭng), *n.* **1.** the act of one who or that which turns. **2.** a place where one road branches off from another. **3.** the forming of objects on a lathe. **4.** shaping or forming: *the turning of verses.*

turning point, 1. a point at which a decisive change takes place; a critical point; a crisis. **2.** *Survey.* a point on which a foresight and a backsight are taken in direct levelling. **3.** a point at which something turns, esp. the high or low point on a graph.

turnip (tûr′nĭp), *n.* **1.** the thick, fleshy edible root of the cruciferous plant *Brassica rapa,* the common **white turnip,** or of *Brassica napus,* the **Swedish turnip** or swede. **2.** the plant itself. **3.** the root of this plant used as a vegetable. [earlier *turnepe,* f. TURN (with reference to its neatly rounded shape) + ME *nepe* NEEP] —**tur′nip-like′,** *adj.*

turnkey (tûn′kē′), *n., pl.* **-keys.** one who has charge of the keys of a prison; a prison keeper.

turn-off (tûn′ŏf′), *n. Chiefly U.S.* a side road.

turnout (tûn′out′), *n.* **1.** the body of persons who come to an assemblage, muster, spectacle, or the like. **2.** the quantity produced; output. **3.** the act of turning out. **4.** the manner or style in which a person or thing is equipped, dressed, etc. **5.** an equipment or outfit. **6.** a short siding or passage which enables vehicles, etc., to pass one another.

turnover (tûn′ō′və), *n.* **1.** the act or result of turning over; upset. **2.** the aggregate of worker replacements in a given period in a given business or industry. **3.** the ratio of the labour turnover to the average number of employees in a given period. **4.** the number of times that capital is invested and reinvested in a line of merchandise during a specified period of time. **5.** the turning over of the capital or stock of goods involved in a particular transaction or course of business. **6.** the total amount of business done in a given time. **7.** the rate at which items are sold or stock used up and replaced. **8.** a small semicircular pie made by folding one half of the crust on to the other. —*adj.* **9.** turned over; that may be turned over. **10.** having a part that turns over.

turnpike (tûn′pīk′), *n.* **1.** *Hist.* a barrier set across a road to stop passage until toll is paid; a tollgate. **2.** *Hist.* a road on which a turnpike operated. **3.** *U.S.* a road for fast traffic, esp. one maintained by tolls.

turnplate (tûn′plāt′), *n.* a railway turntable.

turn-round (tûn′round′), *n.* **1.** the process of preparing a ship in port or a train, etc., at a terminus for the return journey. **2.** the time taken to do this.

turnspit (tûn′spĭt′), *n.* **1.** one who turns a spit. **2.** a dog of a breed with long body and short legs formerly used to work a treadmill which turned a spit.

turnstile (tûn′stīl′), *n.* a structure usually consisting of four arms at right angles to each other, revolving horizontally on top of a post, and set in a gateway or opening in a fence, to allow the passage of people one at a time after a fee has been paid; used to record or control the number of people passing through.

turnstone (tûn′stōn′), *n.* any of the small, migratory, limicoline shorebirds constituting the genus *Arenaria,* notable for their habit of turning over stones in search of food, esp. *A. interpres,* common in both Old and New Worlds.

turntable (tûn′tā′bl), *n.* **1.** the rotating disc on which the record in a gramophone rests. **2.** *Railways.* a rotating, track-bearing platform pivoted in the centre, used for turning round locomotives and other rolling stock.

turn-up (tûn′ŭp′), *n.* **1.** that which is turned up or which turns up. **2.** a turned-up fold at the bottom of a trouser leg. **3.** *Colloq.* a fight, row, or disturbance. **4.** *Colloq.* an unexpected or fortuitous occurrence, result, etc. —*adj.* **5.** that is or may be turned up.

turpentine (tûr′pən tīn′), *n., v.* **-tined, -tining.** —*n.* **1.** an oleoresin exuding from the terebinth, *Pistacia terebinthus.* **2.** any of various oleoresins derived from coniferous trees, esp. the longleaf pine, *Pinus palustris,* and yielding a volatile oil and a resin when distilled. **3.** oil of turpentine. **4.** any of various substitutes for these, esp. white spirit. —*v.t.* **5.** to treat with turpentine; apply turpentine to. **6.** to gather or take crude turpentine from (trees). [ME *ter(e)bentyn(e),* t. L: m. *terebinthina,* der. Gk *terébinthos*]

turpentine tree, the mopane, *Copaifera mopane,* an African leguminous tree of Zambezi forests, having dark, hard wood.

turpeth (tûr′pĭth), *n.* **1.** a drug obtained from the roots of a convolvulaceous plant, *Operculina turpethum,* of the East Indies, formerly used as a purgative. **2.** the plant itself. **3.** its root. [t. ML: s. *turpethum;* r. ME *turbit,* t. ML: m. *turbith(um),* t. Ar.: m. *turbid*]

Turpin (tûr′pĭn), *n.* **Dick,** 1706–39, English highwayman.

turpitude (tûr′pĭ tyo͞od′), *n.* **1.** shameful depravity. **2.** a depraved or shameful act. [t. L: m. *turpitūdo* baseness]

turps (tûps), *n. Colloq.* turpentine.

turquoise (tûr′kwäz, -kwoiz), *n.* **1.** a sky blue or greenish blue compact opaque mineral, essentially a hydrous phosphate of aluminium containing a little copper and iron, much used in jewellery. **2.** Also, **turquoise blue.** a greenish blue or bluish green. [t. F: Turkish (stone), der. *Turc* Turk; r. ME *turkeis,* t. OF]

Turrets (def. 2) 13th century

turret (tŭr′rĭt), *n.* **1.** a small tower, usually one forming part of a larger structure. **2.** a small tower at an angle of a building, frequently beginning some distance above the ground. **3.** Also, **tur′rethead′.** a pivoted attachment on a lathe, etc., for holding a number of tools, each of which can be presented to the work in rapid succession by a simple rotating movement. **4.** *Naval, Mil.* a low, tower-like, heavily armoured structure, usually revolving horizontally, within which guns are mounted. **5.** *Fort.* a tall structure, usually moved on wheels, formerly employed in breaching or scaling a fortified place, a wall, or the like. [ME *turet,* t. OF: m. *touret* dim. of *tour* TOWER] —**tur′retless,** *adj.*

turreted (tŭr′rĭ tĭd), *adj.* **1.** furnished with a turret or turrets. **2.** having a turret-like part or parts. **3.** *Zool.* having whorls in the form of a long or towering spiral, as certain shells.

Turreted shell

turret lathe, a lathe fitted with a turret (def. 3).

turri-, a word element meaning 'tower'. [t. L, comb. form of *turris*]

turrical (tŭr′rĭ kl), *adj.* pertaining to or resembling a turret or turrets.

turriculate (tŭ rĭk′yo͞o lĭt, -lāt′), *adj.* furnished with or resembling a turret or turrets. [f. s. L *turricula* little tower + -ATE[1]]

turtle[1] (tûr′tl), *n., v.,* **-tled, -tling.** —*n.* **1.** any of the *Chelonia,* an order or group of reptiles having the body enclosed in a shell consisting of a carapace and a plastron, from between which the head, tail, and four legs protrude. **2.** a marine species of turtle, as distinguished from freshwater and terrestrial tortoises. **3. turn turtle,** to capsize. —*v.i.* **4.** to catch turtles, esp. as a business. [t. Sp.: m. *tortuga* (g. LL *tortūca,* der. *tortus* twisted), influenced by TURTLE[2]]

turtle[2] (tûr′tl), *n. Archaic.* a turtledove. [ME and OE, var. of *turtur,* t. L]

turtleback (tûr′tl băk′), *n.* **1.** Also, **tur′tledeck′.** an arched protection erected over the deck of a steamer at the bow, and often at the stern also, to guard against damage from heavy seas. **2.** *Archaeol.* a crude stone implement having one or both faces slightly convex.

turtledove (tûr′tl dŭv′), *n.* a small, slender Old World dove, *Streptopelia turtur,* having a long, graduated tail which is conspicuous in flight.

turtleneck (tûr′tl nĕk′), *adj.* **1.** of or pertaining to a sweater, etc., having a high, close-fitting neck. —*n.* **2.** a turtleneck sweater.

turves (tûvz), *n. Archaic.* pl. of **turf.**

Tuscaloosa (tŭs′kə lo͞o′sə), *n.* a town in the U.S., in W Alabama. 63,370 (1960).

Tuscan (tŭs′kən), *adj.* **1.** of, pertaining to, or characteristic of Tuscany, its people, or their dialect. **2.** *Archit.* denoting or pertaining to a classical (Roman or Renaissance) order of architecture distinguished by a plain (not fluted) shaft, ring-shaped capital, and a frieze resembling the Doric. —*n.* **3.** the standard literary form of the Italian language. **4.** any Italian dialect of Tuscany. **5.** a native of Tuscany.

Tuscany (tŭs′kə nĭ), *n.* a region in W central Italy: formerly a grand duchy. 3,267,374 pop. (1961); 8879 sq. mi. *Cap.:* Florence. Italian, **Toscana.**

Tuscany

Tuscarora (tŭs′kə rô′rə), *n., pl.* **-ras,** (*esp. collectively*) **-ra. 1.** a member of a North American Indian people living originally in North Carolina, and later, after their admission to the Iroquois confederacy, in New York. **2.** an Iroquoian language spoken by the Tuscarora people.

Tusculum (tŭs′kyo͞o ləm), *n.* an ancient city of Latium, SE of Rome: Roman villas.

tush[1] (tŭsh), *interj.* **1.** (used as an exclamation expressing impatience, contempt, etc.). —*n.* **2.** an exclamation of 'tush'.

tush[2] (tŭsh), *n.* **1.** one of the four canine teeth of the horse. **2.** tusk. [ME; OE *tusc.* See TUSK]

tusk (tŭsk), *n.* **1.** (in certain animals) a tooth developed to great length, usually as one of a pair, as in the elephant, walrus, wild boar, etc., but singly in the narwhal. **2.** a long, pointed, or protruding tooth. **3.** a projecting part resembling the tusk of an animal. —*v.t., v.i.* **4.** to dig, tear, or gore with the tusks or tusk. [ME *tuske,* metathetic var. of ME and OE *tux,* metathetic var. of OE *tusc;* prob. akin to TOOTH] —**tusked** (tŭskt), *adj.* —**tusk′less,** *adj.* —**tusk′like′,** *adj.*

Tusks of walrus

tusker (tŭs′kə), *n.* an animal with tusks, as an elephant or a wild boar.

tussah (tŭs′ə), *n.* a coarse silk from India (called shantung in China) of a tan colour, obtained from the cocoon of various undomesticated Asiatic silkworms (*Antheraea mylitta,* etc.). [alter. of TUSSER]

tussal (tŭs′əl), *adj.* pertaining to tussis or a cough. [f. s. L *tussis* cough + -AL[1]]

Tussaud (*Fr.* tʏ sō′), *n.* **Marie** (*Fr.* mȧ rē′), 1760–1850, Swiss modeller in wax; founder of **Madame Tussaud's** (tə sôdz′) waxworks exhibition in London.

tusser (tŭs′ə), *n.* tussore. [t. Hind.: m. *tasar* shuttle]

tussis (tŭs′ĭs), *n. Pathol.* a cough. [t. L]

tussive (tŭs′ĭv), *adj. Pathol.* of or pertaining to a cough.

tussle (tŭs′əl), *v.,* **-sled, -sling,** *n.* —*v.i.* **1.** to struggle or fight roughly or vigorously; wrestle; scuffle. —*n.* **2.** a rough struggle as in fighting or wrestling; a scuffle. **3.** any vigorous conflict or contest. [var. of TOUSLE]

tussock (tŭs′ək), *n.* a tuft or clump of growing grass or the like. [appar. akin to MHG *zūsach* thicket, *zūse* lock (of hair), brushwood. See TOUSLE, -OCK]

tussock moth, any of various dull-coloured moths (family *Lymantriidae*), whose larvae are notorious pests of broad-leaved trees, as *Dasychira pudibunda,* the pale tussock moth of Europe.

tussocky (tŭs′ə kĭ), *adj.* **1.** abounding in tussocks. **2.** forming tussocks.

tussore (tŭs′ə), *n.* a fabric woven from tussah. Also, **tusser.** [alter. of TUSSER]

tut (tŭt; or *clicked* t), *interj., n., v.,* **tutted, tutting.** —*interj.* **1.** (used as an exclamation expressing impatience, contempt, etc.). —*n.* **2.** an exclamation of 'tut'. —*v.i.* **3.** to utter the exclamation 'tut'. Also, **tut′-tut′.**

Tutankhamen (tōō′tăng kä′mĕn), *n.* 14th century B.C., a king of Egypt of the 18th dynasty.

tutelage (tyōō′tĭ lĭj), *n.* **1.** the office or function of a guardian; guardianship. **2.** instruction. **3.** the state of being under a guardian or a tutor. [f. s. L *tūtēla* watching + -AGE]

tutelary (tyōō′tĭ lə rĭ), *adj.* **1.** having the position of guardian or protector of a person, place, or thing: *tutelary saint.* **2.** of or pertaining to a guardian or guardianship. —*n.* **3.** one having tutelary authority, as an angel, saint, or guardian. Also, **tutelar** (tyōō′tĭ lə). [t. L: m. s. *tūtēlārius* guardian]

Tuticorin (tōō′tĭ kô′rĭn), *n.* a town in India, in S Madras. 124,230 (1961).

tutor (tyōō′tə), *n.* **1.** one employed to instruct another in some branch or branches of learning, esp. a private instructor. **2.** a university teacher who supervises the studies of certain undergraduates assigned to him. **3.** (in some U.S. universities and colleges) a teacher of academic rank lower than instructor. **4.** a teacher without institutional connections who assists students in preparing for examinations. **5.** *Civil, Roman, and Scot. Law.* the guardian of a boy or girl below the age of puberty or majority. —*v.t.* **6.** to act as a tutor to; teach or instruct, esp. privately. **7.** to train, school, or discipline. **8.** to admonish or reprove. **9.** to have the guardianship or care of. —*v.i.* **10.** to act as a tutor or private instructor. **11.** to study under a tutor. [ME, t. L: protector] —**tu′torless,** *adj.* —**tu′torship′,** *n.*

tutorage (tyōō′tə rĭj), *n.* **1.** the office, authority, or care of a tutor; instruction. **2.** the charge for instruction by a tutor.

tutorial (tyōō tô′rĭ əl), *adj.* **1.** pertaining to or exercised by a tutor: *tutorial functions or authority.* —*n.* **2.** a period of instruction given by a university tutor to an individual student or a small group of students.

tutorial system, a system of education, esp. in some universities, in which instruction is given personally by tutors, who also act as general supervisors of a small group of students in their charge.

tutsan (tŭt′sən), *n.* a shrubby, hypericaceous perennial, *Hypericum androsaemum,* occurring in wet woods of Europe and W Asia.

Tutsi (tōōt′sĭ), *n., pl.* **-sis,** (*esp. collectively*) **-si.** Watutsi (def. 1).

tutti (tōōt′ĭ; *It.* tōōt′tē), *adj., n., pl.* **-tis.** *Music.* —*adj.* **1.** all; all the voices or instruments together (used as a direction). **2.** intended for or performed by all (or most of) the voices or instruments together, as a passage or movement in concerted music (opposed to *solo*). —*n.* **3.** a tutti passage or movement. **4.** the tonal product or effect of tutti performance. [It., pl. of *tutto* TUTTO]

tutti-frutti (tōō′tĭ frōō′tĭ), *n.* **1.** a preserve of chopped mixed fruits, often with brandy syrup. **2.** a variety of fruits (usually candied and minced), used in ice-cream, confections, etc. [t. It., lit., all fruits]

tutto (tōō′tō; *It.* tōōt′tō), *adj. Music.* all; entire; the whole (used as a direction in music). [It., t. OF: m. *tout*]

tut-tut (tŭt′tŭt′; *or clicked* t), *interj., n., v.i.,* **-tutted, -tutting.** tut.

tutty (tŭt′ĭ), *n.* an impure oxide of zinc obtained from the flues of smelting furnaces, or a similar substance occurring as a native mineral, used chiefly as a polishing powder. [ME *tutie,* t. ML: m. *tūtia,* t. Ar.: m. *tūtiyā* oxide of zinc, ? t. Pers.]

tutu (*Fr.* tʏ tʏ′), *n. French.* a short, full, ballet skirt, usually made of several layers of tarlatan or tulle.

Tutuila (tōō′tōō ē′lə), *n.* the largest of the islands of American Samoa: harbour at Pago Pago. 17,250 pop. (1950); 53 sq. mi.

tu-whit tu-whoo (tə wĭt′tə wōō′), (imitation of the cry of an owl).

tuxedo (tŭk sē′dō), *n., pl.* **-dos.** *U.S.* a dinner jacket. [short for *Tuxedo coat,* named after country club at *Tuxedo* Park, in New York State]

tuyère (twē′ĕə, twĭ′ə; *Fr.* tʏ yĕr′), *n. Metall.* an opening through which the blast of air enters a blast furnace, cupola forge, or the like, to facilitate combustion. Also, **twyere.** [t. F, der. *tuyau* pipe, of Gmc orig.]

TV, television.

TVA, Tennessee Valley Authority.

Tver (*Russ.* tvyĕry), *n.* former name of **Kalinin** (def. 2).

twa (twä), *n. Scot.* two.

Twaddell degree (twŏ dĕl′), a unit on a scale for measuring the specific gravity of liquids, equal to 200 (specific gravity −1). *Abbrev.:* °Tw. [named after W. *Twaddell,* died *c.* 1840, Scottish inventor]

twaddle (twŏd′l), *n., v.,* **-dled, -dling.** —*n.* **1.** trivial, feeble, silly or tedious talk or writing. —*v.i.* **2.** to talk in a trivial, feeble, silly or tedious manner; prate. —*v.t.* **3.** to utter as twaddle. [var. of *twattle,* b. TWIDDLE and TATTLE] —**twad′dler,** *n.*

twain (twān), *adj., n. Archaic.* two. [ME *twayn,* OE *twēgen,* c. G (obs.) *Zween*]

Twain (twān), *n.* **Mark** (*Samuel Langhorne Clemens*), 1835–1910, U.S. author and humorist.

twang (twăng), *v.i.* **1.** to give out a sharp, ringing sound, as the string of a musical instrument when plucked. **2.** to have a sharp, nasal tone, as the human voice. —*v.t.* **3.** to cause to make a sharp, ringing sound, as a string of a musical instrument. **4.** to produce (music) by plucking the strings of a musical instrument. **5.** to pluck the strings of (a musical instrument). **6.** to speak with a sharp, nasal tone. **7.** to pull or pluck the string of (a bow). **8.** to shoot (an arrow). —*n.* **9.** the sharp, ringing sound produced by plucking or suddenly releasing a tense string. **10.** a sound resembling this. **11.** the act of plucking or picking. **12.** a sharp, nasal tone, as of the human voice. [imit.] —**twang′y,** *adj.*

'twas (twŏz; *unstressed* twəz), contraction of *it was.*

twat (twŏt), *n. Taboo Slang.* **1.** the vagina. **2.** a woman considered as a sexual object. **3.** sexual intercourse. **4.** a despicable or unpleasant person. Also, **twot.** [orig. uncert.]

twayblade (twā′blād′), *n.* any of various orchidaceous plants, esp. of the genera *Listera, Ophrys,* or *Liparis,* characterized by two nearly opposite broad leaves. [f. *tway* (ME *twey,* OE *twēge* TWO) + BLADE]

tweak (twēk), *v.t.* **1.** to seize and pull with a sharp jerk and twist: *to tweak someone's ear.* —*n.* **2.** an act of tweaking; a sharp pull and twist. [OE *twician* (inferred from *twicere,* n.), var. of *twiccian* catch hold of, pluck, gather. See TWITCH] —**tweak′y,** *adj.*

twee (twē), *adj. Colloq.* affected; precious; excessively dainty; coy.

tweed (twēd), *n.* **1.** a coarse wool cloth in a variety of weaves and colours, either hand-spun and hand-woven in Scotland, or reproduced, often by machine, elsewhere. **2.** (*pl.*) garments made of this cloth. [appar. back-formation from Scot. *tweedling* twilling (now obs.), of unexplained orig.]

Tweed (twēd), *n.* **1. William Marcy** ('*Boss Tweed*'), 1823–78, U.S. politician: headed the **Tweed Ring,** a group of Tammany politicians who got control of the financial affairs of New York City about 1870 and misappropriated millions of dollars. **2.** a river flowing E from S Scotland along a part of the NE boundary of England into the North Sea. 97 mi.

Tweeddale (twēd′dāl′), *n.* Peeblesshire.

Tweedledum and Tweedledee (twē′dl dŭm′ən twē′-dl dē′), any two persons, things, etc., nominally different but practically the same. [humorous imit. coinage, appar. first applied as nicknames to Handel and Bononcini, with reference to their musical rivalry]

'tween (twēn), *prep. Poetic.* between.

tweeny (twē′nĭ), *n. Obs.* a maidservant who assists other servants. [f. TWEEN + -Y[2]]

tweet (twēt), *n.* **1.** the weak chirp of a young or small bird. *—v.i.* **2.** to utter a tweet or tweets. [imit.]

tweeter (twē′tə), *n.* a small loudspeaker designed for the reproduction of high-frequency sounds.

tweeter-woofer (twē′tə wōō′fə), *n.* a loudspeaker, usually coaxial, in which a tweeter is mounted in and in front of the cone of a woofer.

tweezers (twē′zəz), *n.pl.* small pincers or nippers for plucking out hairs, taking up small objects, etc. [pl. of *tweezer*, f. *tweeze* case, receptacle (see ETUI) + -ER[1]]

twelfth (twĕlfth), *adj.* **1.** next after the eleventh. **2.** being one of twelve equal parts. *—n.* **3.** a twelfth part, esp. of one ($\frac{1}{12}$). **4.** the twelfth one of a series.

Twelfth day, the twelfth day after Christmas, January 6th, on which the festival of the Epiphany is celebrated, formerly observed as the last day of the Christmas festivities.

Twelfth night, 1. the evening before Twelfth day, formerly observed with various festivities. **2.** the evening of Twelfth day itself.

Twelfthtide (twĕlfth′tīd′), *n.* the season of Twelfth night and Twelfth day.

twelve (twĕlv), *n.* **1.** a cardinal number, ten plus two. **2.** a symbol for this number, as 12 or XII. **3.** a set of this many persons or things. **4. the Twelve,** the twelve apostles chosen by Christ. *—adj.* **5.** amounting to twelve in number. [ME; OE *twelf*, c. G *zwölf*]

twelve-mile limit (twĕlv′mīl′), *Internat. Law.* the offshore boundary of a state, extending 12 miles out to sea. Cf. **three-mile limit.**

twelvemo (twĕlv′mō), *n., pl.* **-mos,** *adj.* duodecimo.

twelvemonth (twĕlv′mŭnth′), *n.* a year.

Twelve Tables, the, the tablets on which were engraved short statements of Roman law most important in the affairs of daily life, drawn up by the decemvirs in 451 and 450 B.C.

twelve-tone (twĕlv′tōn′), *adj. Music.* based on or incorporating the twelve-tone technique: *twelve-tone music.* Also, **twelve-note** (twĕlv′nōt′).

twelve-tone technique, *Music.* a modern system of note relationships in which the 12 notes of an octave are not subjugated to any one key, but are unified by a selected order of notes which form the basis of a given composition. Also, **twelve-note technique.**

twentieth (twĕn′tĭ ĭth), *adj.* **1.** next after the nineteenth. **2.** being one of twenty equal parts. *—n.* **3.** a twentieth part, esp. of one ($\frac{1}{20}$). **4.** the twentieth member of a series.

twenty (twĕn′tĭ), *n., pl.* **-ties,** *adj.* *—n.* **1.** a cardinal number, ten times two. **2.** a symbol for this number, as 20 or XX. **3.** a set of this many persons or things. **4.** (*pl.*) the numbers from 20 to 29 of a series, esp. with reference to the years of a person's age, or the years of a century, esp. the twentieth. *—adj.* **5.** amounting to twenty in number. [ME; OE *twēntig*, akin to G *zwanzig*]

twenty-fourmo (twĕn′tĭ fô′mō), *n., pl.* **-mos,** *adj. Bookbinding.* vigesimo-quarto.

twentymo (twĕn′tĭ mō′), *n., pl.* **-mos,** *adj. Bookbinding.* vigesimo.

twenty-one (twĕn′tĭ wŭn′), *n.* pontoon[2].

'twere (twû; *unstressed* twə), contraction of *it were.*

twerp (twûp), *n. Slang.* a contemptible or insignificant person. Also, **twirp.**

twi-, a word element meaning 'two', or 'twice', as in *twibill.* [ME and OE, c. G *zwei-*, L *bi-*. See TWO]

twibill (twī′bĭl′), *n.* **1.** a mattock with one arm like that of an adze and the other like that of an axe. **2.** *Archaic.* a double-bladed battle-axe. [ME and OE. See TWI-, BILL[3]]

twice (twīs), *adv.* **1.** two times, as in succession: *write twice a week.* **2.** on two occasions; in two instances. **3.** in twofold quantity or degree; doubly: *twice as much.* [ME *twies*, f. *twie* twice (OE *twiga*) + *-s*, adv. gen. suffix]

twice-laid (twīs′lād′), *adj.* **1.** made from strands of used rope. **2.** made from makeshift or used material.

twicer (twī′sə), *n. Austral. Slang.* a crook; double-crosser.

twice-told (twīs′tōld′), *adj.* told twice; told before.

Twickenham (twĭk′ə nəm), *n.* a district in the SW outer London borough of Richmond upon Thames. 100,822 (1961).

twiddle (twĭd′l), *v.,* **-dled, -dling,** *n.* *—v.t.* **1.** to turn round and round, esp. with the fingers. **2. twiddle one's thumbs** or **fingers, a.** to keep turning one's thumbs or fingers idly about each other. **b.** to do nothing; be idle. *—v.i.* **3.** to play with something idly, as by touching or handling. **4.** to turn round and round; twirl. *—n.* **5.** the act of twiddling; a twirl. [b. TWITCH and FIDDLE] **—twid′dler,** *n.*

twig[1] (twĭg), *n.* **1.** a slender shoot of a tree or other plant. **2.** a small offshoot from a branch or stem. **3.** a small dry, woody piece fallen from a branch: *a fire of twigs.* **4.** *Anat.* one of the minute branches of a blood vessel or nerve. [ME and OE *twigge*, akin to G *Zweig* branch] **—twig′less,** *adj.* **—twig′like′,** *adj.*

twig[2] (twĭg), *v.,* **twigged, twigging.** *Slang.* *—v.t.* **1.** to look at; observe. **2.** to catch sight of; perceive. **3.** to understand. *—v.i.* **4.** to understand. [orig. uncert.]

twiggy (twĭg′ĭ), *adj.* **1.** abounding in twigs. **2.** consisting of twigs. **3.** twiglike.

twilight (twī′līt′), *n.* **1.** the light from the sky when the sun is below the horizon, esp. in the evening. **2.** the time during which this light prevails. **3.** a condition or period preceding or succeeding full development, glory, etc. *—adj.* **4.** pertaining to or resembling twilight: *the twilight hour.* **5.** crepuscular, as a bat or moth. [ME, f. TWI- + LIGHT[1]; c. G *Zwielicht*] **—twi′light′less,** *adj.*

Twilight of the Gods, Ragnarok.

twilight sleep, *Obstet.* a state of semiconsciousness usually produced by hypodermic injections of scopolamine and morphine, in order to effect relatively painless childbirth. [trans. of G *Dämmerschlaf*]

twill (twĭl), *n.* **1.** a fabric woven with the weft threads so crossing the warp as to produce an effect of parallel diagonal lines, as in serge. **2.** the characteristic weave of such fabrics. *—v.t.* **3.** to weave in the manner of a twill. **4.** to weave in twill construction. [Scot. and North. E var. of *twilly*, ME *twyle*, OE *twili(c)*, half trans. half adoption of L *bilīc(em)* having double thread (acc. sing. of unrecorded *bilix*). See TWI-]

'twill (twĭl), contraction of *it will.*

twin (twĭn), *n., adj., v.,* **twinned, twinning.** *—n.* **1.** (*pl.*) two children or animals brought forth at a birth. **2.** one of two such children or animals. **3.** (*pl.*) two persons or things closely related or connected or closely resembling each other. **4.** either of two such persons or things. **5.** *Crystall.* a compound crystal, consisting of two or more parts or crystals definitely orientated each to the other. **6. Twins,** *Astron.* the zodiacal constellation or sign Gemini. *—adj.* **7.** being two, or one of two, children or animals born at the same birth: *twin sisters.* **8.** being two persons or things closely related or associated or much alike; forming a pair or couple. **9.** being one of two such persons or things; forming one of a couple or pair: *a twin peak.* **10.** consisting of two similar parts or elements joined or connected: *a twin vase.* **11.** *Bot., Zool.* occurring in pairs; didymous. **12.** *Crystall.* of the nature of a twin (def. 5). **13.** *Obs.* twofold or double. *—v.t.* **14.** to conceive or bring forth as twins. **15.** to pair or couple. **16.** to furnish a counterpart to. **17.** *Crystall.* to form into a twin. *—v.i.* **18.** to bring forth twins. **19.** to be twinborn. **20.** to be paired or coupled. [ME; OE *(ge)twinn*, c. Icel. *tvinnr* double]

twinborn (twĭn′bôn′), *adj.* born at the same birth.

twine (twīn), *n., v.,* **twined, twining.** *—n.* **1.** a strong thread or string composed of two or more strands twisted together. **2.** the act of twining. **3.** the state of being twined. **4.** a twined or twisted thing or part; a fold, convolution, or coil. **5.** a twist or turn. **6.** a knot or tangle. *—v.t.* **7.** to twist together; interwind; intertwine. **8.** to form by or as by twisting strands: *to twine a wreath.* **9.** to twist (one strand, thread, or thing) with another. **10.** to bring by or as by twisting or winding (fol. by *in, into,* etc.). **11.** to put or dispose by or as by winding (fol. by *about, around,* etc.). **12.** to encircle or wreathe with something wound about. **13.** to enfold. *—v.i.* **14.** to become twined or twisted together, as two things, or as one thing with another. **15.** to wind itself (fol. by *about, around,* etc.). **16.** to wind in a sinuous or meandering course. **17.** (of plants, stems, etc.) to grow in convolutions about a support. [ME; OE *twin*, c. D *twijn*] **—twin′er,** *n.*

Twining stems

twinflower (twĭn′flou′ə), *n.* a slender, creeping, evergreen caprifoliaceous plant, *Linnaea borealis*, of Europe, or the American variety or species, *L. americana*, with pink or purplish nodding flowers borne in pairs on threadlike peduncles.

twinge (twĭnj), *n., v.,* **twinged, twinging.** *—n.* **1.** a sudden, sharp pain (in body or mind): *a twinge of rheumatism, a twinge of remorse.* *—v.t.* **2.** to affect with sudden, sharp pain or pains (in body or mind). **3.** to give (a person, etc.)

a twinge or twinges. —*v.i.* **4.** to have or feel a twinge or twinges. **5.** to give a twinge. [ME *twenge(n)*, OE *twengan* pinch]

twink (twĭngk), *n.*, *v.i.* **1.** wink. **2.** twinkle. [ME *twinken*, c. G *zwinken* wink; akin to TWINKLE]

twinkle (twĭng′kl), *v.*, **-kled, -kling,** *n.* —*v.i.* **1.** to shine with quick, flickering, gleams of light, as stars, distant lights, etc. **2.** to sparkle in the light. **3.** (of the eyes) to be bright with amusement, pleasure, etc. **4.** to appear or move as if with little flashes of light. **5.** *Archaic.* to wink; blink. —*v.t.* **6.** to emit (light) in little gleams or flashes. **7.** *Archaic.* to blink (the eyes, etc.). —*n.* **8.** a twinkling with light. **9.** a twinkling brightness in the eyes. **10.** the time required for a wink; twinkling. **11.** a wink of the eye. [ME; OE *twinclian*] —**twin′kler,** *n.*

twinkling (twĭng′klĭng), *n.* **1.** the act of shining with little gleams of light. **2.** the time required for a wink; an instant. **3.** *Archaic.* winking; a wink.

twinned (twĭnd), *adj.* **1.** born as twins or as a twin. **2.** paired or coupled. **3.** united or combined. **4.** having the nature of a twin.

twinning (twĭn′ĭng), *n.* **1.** the bearing of twins. **2.** coupling; union. **3.** *Crystall.* the union of crystals to form a twin (def. 5).

twin-plate process (twĭn′plāt′), a process for making polished plate glass in which rolling, annealing, and grinding are carried out on a continuously produced ribbon of glass, both surfaces being ground simultaneously.

twin-screw (twĭn′skrōō′), *adj.* *Naut.* (of a vessel) having two screw propellers, which usually revolve in opposite directions.

twin-set (twĭn′sĕt′), *n.* a cardigan and matching sweater, worn by women.

twirl (twûl), *v.t.* **1.** to cause to rotate rapidly; spin; whirl; swing circularly. **2.** to twiddle: *to twirl one's thumbs.* **3.** to wind idly, as about something. —*v.i.* **4.** to rotate rapidly; whirl. **5.** to turn quickly so as to face or point another way. —*n.* **6.** a twirling or a being twirled; a spin; a whirl; a twist. **7.** something twirled; curl; convolution. [b. TWIST and WHIRL] —**twirl′er,** *n.*

twirp (twûp), *n.* twerp.

twist (twĭst), *v.t.* **1.** to combine, as two or more strands or threads, by winding together; intertwine. **2.** to combine or associate intimately. **3.** to form by or as by winding strands together. **4.** to entwine (one thing) with or in another; wind or twine (something) about a thing. **5.** to encircle (a thing) with something wound about. **6.** to alter in shape, as by turning the ends in opposite directions, so that parts previously in the same straight line and plane are situated in a spiral curve. **7.** to wring out of shape or place; contort or distort. **8.** to turn sharply and put out of place; sprain: *when she fell she twisted her ankle.* **9.** to wrest from the proper form or meaning; pervert. **10.** to form into a coil, knot, or the like by winding, rolling, etc.: *to twist the hair into a knot.* **11.** to bend tortuously. **12.** to cause to move with a rotary motion, as a ball pitched in a curve. **13.** to turn in another direction.
—*v.i.* **14.** to be or become intertwined. **15.** to wind or twine about something. **16.** to writhe or squirm. **17.** to take a spiral form or course; wind, curve, or bend. **18.** to turn or rotate, as on an axis; revolve, as about something. **19.** to turn so as to face in another direction. **20.** to change shape with a spiral or screwing movement of parts. **21.** to move with a progressive rotary motion, as a ball pitched in a curve. **22.** to dance the twist (def. 45).
—*n.* **23.** a curve, bend, or turn. **24.** a turning or rotating as on an axis; rotary motion; spin. **25.** anything formed by or as by twisting or twining parts together. **26.** the act or the manner of twisting strands together, as in thread, yarn, or rope. **27.** a wrench. **28.** a twisting awry. **29.** a wrestling or perverting, as of meaning. **30.** spiral disposition, arrangement, or form. **31.** spiral movement or course. **32.** an irregular bend; a crook or kink. **33.** a peculiar bent, bias, or the like, as in the mind or nature. **34.** the altering of the shape of anything by or as by turning the ends in opposite directions. **35.** the stress causing this alteration. **36.** the resulting state. **37.** a sudden, unexpected alteration to the course of events, as in a play. **38.** *Cricket, Baseball, etc.* **a.** a spin given to a ball in pitching, etc. **b.** a ball having such a spin. **39.** a twisting or torsional action, force, or stress. **40.** a kind of strong twisted silk thread, heavier than ordinary sewing silk, used for working buttonholes and for other purposes. **41.** a direction of twisting in weaving yarns, as S twist (left-hand twist), Z twist (right-hand twist). **42.** a loaf or roll of dough twisted and baked. **43.** a kind of tobacco manufactured in the form of a rope or thick cord. **44.** the degree of spiral formed by the grooves in a rifled firearm or cannon. **45.** a vigorous dance performed by couples and characterized by strongly rhythmic gyrations of the body and movements of the arms and legs in time to heavily accented music. [ME *twiste* divide, *twist* divided object, rope, OE *-twist*, c. D *twisten* quarrel. See TWI-] —**twist′abil′ity,** *n.* —**twist′able,** *adj.* —**twist′ingly,** *adv.* —**Syn. 33.** See **turn.**

twist drill, *Mech.* a drill with one or more deep spiral grooves in the body.

twister (twĭs′tə), *n.* **1.** one who or that which twists. **2.** a ball pitched or moving with a spinning motion. **3.** an untrustworthy, swindling person. **4.** *U.S.* a whirlwind or tornado.

twit[1] (twĭt), *v.*, **twitted, twitting,** *n.* —*v.t.* **1.** to taunt, gibe at, or banter by references to anything embarrassing. **2.** to reproach or upbraid. —*n.* **3.** the act of twitting. **4.** a derisive reproach; taunt; gibe. [aphetic var. of obs. *atwite*, ME *atwiten*, OE *ætwītan* taunt, f. *æt-* AT + *wītan* blame] —**twit′ter,** *n.*

twit[2] (twĭt), *n.* *Colloq.* a fool; twerp.

twitch (twĭch), *v.t.* **1.** to give a short, sudden pull or tug at; jerk. **2.** to pull or draw with a hasty jerk. **3.** to move (a part of the body) with a jerk. **4.** to pinch and pull sharply; nip. —*v.i.* **5.** to move or be moved in a quick, jerky way. **6.** to give a short, sudden pull or tug; tug (fol. by *at*). —*n.* **7.** a quick, jerky movement of the body, or of some part of it. **8.** a short, sudden pull or tug; a jerk. **9.** a twinge (of body or mind). **10.** a loop or noose, attached to a handle, for drawing tightly about the muzzle of a horse to bring it under control. [ME *twicchen*, akin to OE *twiccian* pluck] —**twitch′er,** *n.* —**twitch′ingly,** *adv.*

twitch-grass (twĭch′gräs′), *n.* couch-grass; quitch.

twite (twīt), *n.* a mountain linnet, *Carduelis flavirostris*, a common resident bird of the British Isles, similar to the linnet but distinguished by markings and the colour of the bill.

twitter (twĭt′ə), *v.i.* **1.** to utter a succession of small, tremulous sounds, as a bird. **2.** to titter; giggle. **3.** to tremble with excitement or the like; be in a flutter. —*v.t.* **4.** to express or utter by twittering. —*n.* **5.** the act of twittering. **6.** a twittering sound. **7.** a state of tremulous excitement. [ME *twiter*, akin to G *zwitschern*] —**twit′teringly,** *adv.*

twitterer (twĭt′ə rə), *n.* **1.** a bird that twitters. **2.** a person who twitters.

twittery (twĭt′ə rĭ), *adj.* **1.** given to or characterized by twittering. **2.** tremulous; shaky.

'twixt (twĭkst), *prep.* *Archaic.* betwixt.

two (tōō), *n.* **1.** a cardinal number, one plus one. **2.** a symbol for this number, as 2 or II. **3.** a set of this many persons or things. **4.** a playing card, die face, etc., with two pips. **5. in two,** in two pieces; apart: *to break in two.* **6. put two and two together,** to draw a conclusion from certain circumstances. —*adj.* **7.** amounting to two in number. [ME; OE *twā*, c. G *zwei.* Cf. L *duo*, Gk *dýo*]

two-by-four (tōō′bī fô′), *adj.* **1.** two units thick and four units wide, esp. in inches. **2.** *U.S. Slang.* unimportant; insignificant.

two-cycle engine (tōō′sī′kl), *U.S.* a two-stroke engine.

two-dimensional (tōō′dĭ mĕn′shə nəl), *adj.* having two dimensions, as height and width.

two-edged (tōō′ĕjd′), *adj.* **1.** having two edges, as a sword. **2.** cutting or effective both ways. **3.** having two possible meanings, results, etc., one favourable and one unfavourable.

two-faced (tōō′fāst′), *adj.* **1.** having two faces. **2.** deceitful, hypocritical. —**two-facedly** (tōō′fā′sĭd lĭ, -fāst′lĭ), *adv.* —**two′-fac′edness,** *n.*

two-fisted (tōō′fĭs′tĭd), *adj.* **1.** having two fists and able to use them. **2.** *U.S. Slang.* strong and vigorous.

twofold (tōō′fōld′), *adj.* **1.** having two elements or parts. **2.** twice as great or as much; double. —*adv.* **3.** in twofold measure; doubly.

two-four (tōō′fô′), *adj.* *Music.* characterized by two crotchets to the bar.

two-handed (tōō′hăn′dĭd), *adj.* **1.** having two hands. **2.** using both hands equally well; ambidextrous. **3.** involving or requiring both hands: *a two-handed sword.* **4.** requiring the hands of two persons to operate: *a two-handed saw.* **5.** engaged in by two persons: *a two-handed game.*

two-legged (tōō′lĕg′ĭd, -lĕgd′), *adj.* having two legs.

two-line brevier (tōō′līn′), a printing type (16 point) of a size between English and great primer.

two-master (tōō′mäs′tə), *n.* *Naut.* a vessel rigged with two masts.

two-party system (tōō′pä′tĭ), a system of government in which two major political parties, more or less equal in strength, contend for election to power.

twopence (tŭp′əns), *n.* **1.** a sum of money of the value of two pennies. **2.** a British copper coin of this value, issued in the reign of George III. **3.** a British silver coin of this value (since 1662 coined only as maundy money). **4.** a trifle. Also, **tuppence.**

twopenny (tŭp′ə nĭ), *adj.* **1.** of the amount or value of twopence. **2.** of very little value; trifling; worthless. Also, **tuppenny.**
twopenny-halfpenny (tŭp′ə nĭ hā′pə nĭ), *adj.* twopenny (def. 2).
two-phase (to͞o′fāz′), *adj. Elect.* diphase.
two-piece (to͞o′pēs′), *adj.* **1.** consisting of two pieces, usually matching, as an outfit of clothing. *—n.* **2.** a two-piece outfit.
two-ply (to͞o′plī′), *adj.* consisting of two thicknesses, layers, strands, or the like.
two-seater (to͞o′sē′tə), *n.* a motor vehicle, aeroplane, or the like, able to seat two people.
Two Sicilies, The. See **Sicilies, The Two.**
twosome (to͞o′səm), *adj.* **1.** consisting of two. **2.** performed or played by two persons. *—n.* **3.** two together or in company. **4.** a match, as in golf, between two persons. [f. TWO + -SOME[2]]
twostep (to͞o′stĕp′), *n., v.,* **-stepped, -stepping,** *—n.* **1.** a dance in duple time, characterized by sliding steps. **2.** a piece of music for, or in the rhythm of, this dance. *—v.i.* **3.** to perform this dance.
two-stroke (to͞o′strōk′), *adj.* **1.** denoting or pertaining to an internal-combustion engine cycle in which one piston stroke out of every two is a power stroke. **2.** powered by such an engine. *—n.* **3.** a two-stroke engine or vehicle.
twot (twŏt), *n. Taboo Slang.* twat.
two-time (to͞o′tīm′), *v.,* **-timed, -timing.** *Colloq. —v.t.* **1.** to deceive or doublecross. **2.** to deceive (someone) by having a similar relationship with another. *—v.i.* **3.** to deceive or doublecross someone. **4.** to deceive a friend or lover by having a similar relationship with another. **—two′-tim′er,** *n.*
two-tone (to͞o′tōn′), *adj.* having two tones, as of sound, colour, or the like: *a two-tone horn, a two-tone car.*
'twould (two͝od), contraction of *it would.*
two-up (to͞o′ŭp′), *n. Austral.* a gambling game similar to pitch-and-toss, in which coins are spun in the air.
two-way (to͞o′wā′), *adj.* **1.** letting persons or vehicles go either way. **2.** having two ways or passages. **3.** capable of having movement in two directions. **4.** *Maths.* having a double mode of variation.
two-way stretch, *Colloq.* a women's foundation garment of two-way elastic.
twp, township.
twyere (twē′ēə, twī′ə), *n. Metall.* tuyère.
-ty[1], a suffix of numerals denoting multiples of ten, as *twenty.* [OE *-tig,* c. G *-zig*]
-ty[2], a suffix of nouns denoting quality, state, etc., as *unity, enmity.* [ME *-te(e),* t. OF: m. *-te, -tet,* g. s. L *-tas*]
Ty, Territory.
Tyburn (tī′bûn′), *n.* a former place of public execution in London.
Tyche (tī′kĭ), *n. Gk Mythol.* the goddess of fortune, the counterpart of the Roman Fortuna.
tychism (tī′kĭz′əm), *n. Philos.* the philosophical theory of C. S. Peirce and others, that chance plays an active part in the universe and is not merely supposed to do so on account of our ignorance of particular facts. [f. TYCH(E) + -ISM]
tycoon (tī ko͞on′), *n.* **1.** a businessman having great wealth and power. **2.** a title used to describe the shogun of Japan to foreigners from 1603 to 1867. [t. Jap.: m. *taikun,* f. Chinese: *tai* great (d. var. of *ta*) + *kiun* prince]
Tydeus (tī′dyo͞os), *n. Gk Legend.* the brother of Meleager and one of the Seven against Thebes.
tyke (tīk), *n.* **1.** a cur. **2.** *Chiefly Scot.* a low contemptible fellow; a boor. **3.** a mischievous or troublesome child. **4.** any small child. Also, **tike.** [ME, t. Scand.; cf. Icel. *tīk* bitch]
Tyler (tī′lə), *n.* **1. John,** 1790–1862, 10th president of the United States, 1841–45. **2. Wat** (wŏt) (or **Walter**), died 1381, English rebel: leader of the Peasants' Revolt in 1381.
tylosis (tī lō′sĭs), *n. Bot.* balloon-like extensions of the walls of xylem vessels, found esp. in heartwood.
tymbal (tĭm′bl), *n.* timbal.
tympan (tĭm′pən), *n.* **1.** a sheet or plate of some thin material, in an apparatus. **2.** *Print.* a padlike device interposed between the platen or its equivalent and the sheet to be printed, in order to soften and equalize the pressure. **3.** *Archit.* a tympanum. [t. L: s. *tympanum,* t. Gk: m. *týmpanon* drum]
tympanic (tĭm păn′ĭk), *adj.* pertaining or belonging to a tympanum, esp. the tympanum of the ear.
tympanic bone, *Anat., Zool.* (in mammals) a bone of the skull, supporting the tympanic membrane and enclosing part of the tympanum or middle ear.
tympanic membrane, *Anat., Zool.* a membrane separating the tympanum or middle ear from the passage of the external ear; the eardrum. See diag. under **ear.**
tympanist (tĭm′pə nĭst), *n.* a person who plays the drums or other percussion instruments in an orchestra. Cf. **timpanist.**
tympanites (tĭm′pə nī′tēz), *n. Pathol.* distension of the abdomen caused by the presence of air or gas, as in the intestine. [t. NL, t. Gk: pertaining to a drum] **—tympanitic** (tĭm′pə nĭt′ĭk), *adj.*
tympanitis (tĭm′pə nī′tĭs), *n. Pathol.* inflammation of the lining membrane of the tympanum or middle ear. [f. TYMPAN(UM) + -ITIS]
tympanum (tĭm′pə nəm), *n., pl.* **-nums, -na** (-nə). **1.** *Anat., Zool.* the middle ear, comprising that part of the ear situated in a recess of the temporal bone. See diag. under **ear.** **2.** the tympanic membrane. **3.** *Archit.* **a.** the recessed, usually triangular space enclosed between the horizontal and sloping cornices of a pediment, often adorned with sculpture. **b.** a similar space between an arch and the horizontal head of a door or window below. **4.** *Elect., U.S.* the diaphragm of a telephone. **5.** a drum or similar instrument. **6.** the stretched membrane forming a drumhead. **7.** a scoop wheel for raising water. [t. L, t. Gk: m. *týmpanon* drum]

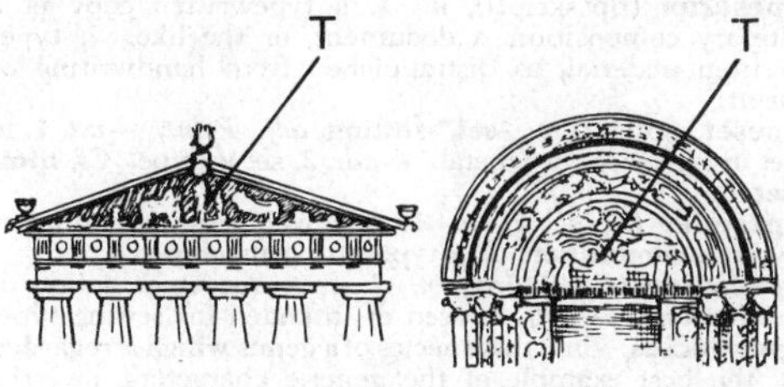

T, Tympanums (defs 3a and 3b)

Tyndale (tĭn′dl), *n.* **William,** *c.* 1492–1536, English religious reformer, translator of the Bible, and martyr.
Tyndall (tĭn′dl), *n.* **John,** 1820–93, English physicist.
Tyndall effect, *Physics.* the scattering of light by particles of matter which makes a beam of light visible by illuminating the particles of dust floating in the air. [named after John TYNDALL]
Tyndareus (tĭn dâ′rĭ əs), *n. Gk Myth.* the husband of Leda and father of Clytemnestra.
Tyne (tīn), *n.* a river in NE England, in Northumberland, flowing into the North Sea. ab. 80 mi.
Tynemouth (tīn′mouth′), *n.* a seaport in NE England at the mouth of the river Tyne. 70,112 (1961).
Tyneside (tīn′sīd′), *n.* a conurbation on the banks of the river Tyne extending from Tynemouth to Newcastle and including Newcastle, Gateshead, Wallsend, Jarrow, Tynemouth and South Shields. 850,000 (est. 1967).
Tynwald (tĭn′wəld, tīn′-), *n.* the parliament of the Isle of Man.
typ., **1.** typographer. **2.** typographic. **3.** typographical. **4.** typographically. **5.** typography.
typal (tī′pl), *adj.* pertaining to or forming a type.
type (tīp), *n., v.,* **typed, typing.** *—n.* **1.** a kind, class, or group as distinguished by a particular characteristic. **2.** a person or thing embodying the characteristic qualities of a kind, class, or group; a representative specimen. **3.** the general form, style, or character distinguishing a particular kind, class or group. **4.** *Biol.* **a.** the general form or plan of structure common to a group of animals, plants, etc. **b.** a genus or species which most nearly exemplifies the essential characteristics of a higher group and frequently gives the latter its name. **5.** *Agric.* **a.** the inherited features of an animal or breed favourable for any given purpose: *dairy type.* **b.** a strain, breed, or variety of animals, or a single animal, belonging to a specific kind. **6.** the pattern or model from which something is made. **7.** *Print.* **a.** a rectangular piece or block, now usually of metal, having on its upper surface a letter or character in relief. **b.** such pieces or blocks collectively. **c.** a similar piece in a typewriter or the like. **d.** such pieces collectively. **e.** a printed character or printed characters: *a headline in large type.* **8.** an image or figure produced by impressing or stamping, as the principal figure or device on either side of a coin or medal. **9.** a prefiguring symbol, as an Old Testament event prefiguring an event in the New Testament. *—v.t.* **10.** to

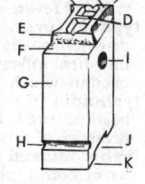

Type (def. 7a)
A, Stem;
B, Face;
C, Serif;
D, Hairline;
E, Beard or neck;
F, Shoulder;
G, Body;
H, Nick;
I, Pin mark;
J, Groove;
K, Foot

typewrite. **11.** to reproduce in type or in print. **12.** *Med.* to ascertain the type of (a blood sample). **13.** to be a type or symbol of. **14.** to represent by a symbol; symbolize. —*v.i.* **15.** to typewrite. [late ME, t. L: m. s. *typus*, t. Gk: m. *týpos* blow, impression]

-type, a word element representing **type,** as in *prototype*; especially used of photographic processes, as in *ferrotype.*

typecast (tīp′käst′), *v.*, **-cast, -casting,** *adj.* —*v.t.* **1.** to cast (an actor, etc.) continually in the same kind of role, esp. because of some physical characteristic. —*adj.* **2.** (of an actor) having acquired a particular image through frequent casting in similar roles.

typeface (tīp′fās′), *n. Print.* face (def. 17).

typefounder (tīp′foun′də), *n.* one engaged in the making of metallic types for printers.

type genus, *Biol.* that genus which is formally taken and held to be typical of the family or other higher group to which it belongs.

type-high (tīp′hī′), *adj. Print.* of the same height as type.

type metal, an alloy for making printing types, etc., consisting chiefly of lead and antimony, and sometimes small quantities of tin, copper, etc.

typescript (tīp′skrĭpt′), *n.* **1.** a typewritten copy of a literary composition, a document, or the like. **2.** typewritten material, as distinguished from handwriting or print.

typeset (tīp′sĕt′), *v.*, **-set, -setting,** *adj. Print.* —*v.t.* **1.** to set in type, esp. hot metal. —*adj.* **2.** set in type. Cf. **filmset.**

typesetter (tīp′sĕt′ə), *n.* **1.** one who sets or composes type; a compositor. **2.** a typesetting machine.

typesetting (tīp′sĕt′ĭng), *n.* **1.** the process or action of setting type. —*adj.* **2.** used or intended for setting type.

type species, *Biol.* that species of a genus which is regarded as the best example of the generic characters, i.e., the species from which a genus is named.

type specimen, *Biol.* an individual animal or plant from which the description of a species has been prepared.

typewrite (tīp′rīt′), *v.t., v.i.*, **-wrote, -written, -writing.** to write by means of a typewriter; type.

typewriter (tīp′rī′tə), *n.* **1.** a machine for writing mechanically in letters and characters. **2.** *Print.* a type style which gives the appearance of typewritten copy. **3.** (formerly) a typist.

typewriting (tīp′rī′tĭng), *n.* **1.** the act or art of using a typewriter. **2.** work done on a typewriter.

typhlitis (tĭf lī′tĭs), *n. Pathol.* inflammation of the caecum. [f. Gk *typhl(ón)* caecum + -ITIS] —**typhlitic** (tĭf lĭt′ĭk), *adj.*

typhlology (tĭf lŏl′ə jĭ), *n.* the sum of scientific knowledge concerning blindness.

typhlosole (tĭf′lə sōl′), *n. Zool.* an inwardly projecting fold of the intestine of some invertebrates such as the earthworm.

typho-, a word element representing **typhus** and **typhoid,** as in *typhogenic.*

Typhoeus (tī fē′əs), *n. Gk Myth.* a monster with a hundred serpents' heads, fiery eyes, and a terrifying voice. Zeus set him on fire with thunderbolts and flung him down into Tartarus under Mt Etna. Cf. **Typhon.**

typhogenic (tī′fō jĕn′ĭk), *adj. Pathol.* producing typhus or typhoid fever.

typhoid (tī′foid), *n.* typhoid fever. [f. TYPH(US) + -OID] —**typhoi′dal,** *adj.*

typhoid bacillus, a micro-organism found in the intestinal ulcers and elsewhere in the bodies of sufferers from typhoid fever.

typhoid fever, *Pathol.* an infectious, often fatal, febrile disease, usually of the summer months, characterized by intestinal inflammation and ulceration, due to the typhoid bacillus which is usually introduced with food or drink.

typhoidin (tī foi′dĭn), *n. Med.* a culture of dead typhoid bacillus used by cutaneous inoculation to detect the presence of a typhoid infection.

typhomalarial (tī′fō mə lĕə′rĭ əl), *adj.* having the character of both typhoid fever and malaria, as a fever.

Typhon (tī′fŏn), *n. Class. Myth.* **1.** a monster and a son of Typhoeus: later confused with Typhoeus. **2.** Greek name of **Set.**

typhoon (tī fo͞on′), *n.* **1.** a tropical cyclone or hurricane of the western Pacific area and the China seas. **2.** a violent storm or tempest of India. [t. Chinese: m. *tai fung* great wind; influenced by Gk *tȳphôn* violent wind] —**typhonic** (tī fŏn′ĭk), *adj.*

typhus (tī′fəs), *n. Pathol.* an acute infectious disease characterized by great prostration, severe nervous symptoms, and a peculiar eruption of reddish spots on the body, now regarded as due to a specific micro-organism transmitted by lice and fleas. Also, **typhus fever.** [t. NL, t. Gk: m. *tŷphos* vapour] —**ty′phous,** *adj.*

typical (tĭp′ĭ kl), *adj.* **1.** pertaining to, of the nature of, or serving as a type or emblem; symbolic. **2.** of the nature of or serving as a type or representative specimen. **3.** conforming to the type. **4.** *Biol.* exemplifying most nearly the essential characteristics of a higher group in natural history, and forming the type: *the typical genus of a family.* **5.** pertaining or belonging to a representative specimen; characteristic or distinctive. Also, **typ′ic.** —**typ′ically,** *adv.* —**typ′icalness,** *n.*

typify (tĭp′ĭ fī′), *v.t.*, **-fied, -fying. 1.** to serve as the typical specimen of; exemplify. **2.** to serve as a symbol or emblem of; symbolize; prefigure. **3.** to represent by a type or symbol. [f. s. L *typus* TYPE + -IFY] —**typification** (tĭp′ĭ fĭ kā′shən), *n.* —**typ′ifi′er,** *n.*

typist (tī′pĭst), *n.* **1.** one who operates a typewriter. **2.** one whose occupation is typewriting.

typog., 1. typographer. **2.** typography.

typographer (tī pŏg′rə fə), *n.* one skilled or engaged in typography.

typographical (tī′pə grăf′ĭ kl), *adj.* pertaining to typography: *typographical errors.* Also, **ty′pograph′ic.** —**ty′pograph′ically,** *adv.*

typography (tī pŏg′rə fĭ), *n.* **1.** the art or process of printing with types. **2.** the work of setting and arranging types and of printing from them. **3.** the general character or appearance of printed matter. [t. NL: m. s. *typographia*, f. Gk: *týpo(s)* type + *graphía* writing]

typology (tī pŏl′ə jĭ), *n.* **1.** the doctrine or study of types or symbols, esp. those of Scripture. **2.** symbolic significance or representation. —**typological** (tī′pə lŏj′ĭ kl), *adj.* —**typol′ogist,** *n.*

typothetae (tī pŏth′ĭ tē′, tī′pə thē′tē), *n.pl. U.S.* printers, esp. master printers (used in the names of associations). [f. Gk *týpo(s)* type + *-thetae*, Latinized pl. of Gk *thétēs* one who places]

Tyr (tyo͞oə, tīə), *n. Scand. Myth.* the god of war and victory, son of Odin. He is represented with one hand, the other having been bitten off by the wolf Fenrir. [Icel.]

tyramine (tī′rə mĭn, tī′-), *n. Chem.* a crystalline solid, $HO.C_6H_4(CH_2)_2NH_2$, formed by the action of bacteria on tyrosine, esp. in decaying animal products, as cheese.

tyrannical (tĭ răn′ĭ kl), *adj.* arbitrary or despotic; despotically cruel or harsh; severely oppressive. Also, **tyran′nic.** [f. s. L *tyrannicus* (t. Gk: m. *tyrannikós*) + -AL[1]] —**tyran′nically,** *adv.* —**tyran′nicalness,** *n.*

tyrannicide (tĭ răn′ĭ sīd′), *n.* **1.** one who kills a tyrant. **2.** the act of killing a tyrant. [t. L: m. s. *tyrannicīda* (def. 1), tyrannicīdium (def. 2). See -CIDE] —**tyran′nicid′al,** *adj.*

tyrannize (tĭ′rə nīz′), *v.*, **-nized, -nizing.** —*v.i.* **1.** to exercise power cruelly or oppressively. **2.** to reign as a tyrant. **3.** to rule despotically or cruelly. —*v.t.* **4.** to rule tyrannically. **5.** to act the tyrant to or over. Also, **tyrannise.** —**tyr′anniz′er,** *n.* —**tyr′anniz′ingly,** *adv.*

tyrannosaurus (tĭ răn′ə sô′rəs), *n.* a great carnivorous dinosaur, of the genus *Tyrannosaurus*, of the later Cretaceous period in North America, which walked erect on its powerful hind limbs. Also, **tyran′nosaur′.**

tyrannous (tĭ′rə nəs), *adj.* tyrannical. —**tyr′annously,** *adv.* —**tyr′annousness,** *n.*

tyranny (tĭ′rə nĭ), *n., pl.* **-nies. 1.** arbitrary or unrestrained exercise of power; despotic abuse of authority. **2.** the government or rule of a tyrant or absolute ruler. **3.** a state ruled by a tyrant or absolute ruler. **4.** oppressive or unjustly severe government on the part of any ruler. **5.** undue severity or harshness. **6.** a tyrannical act or proceeding. [ME *tirannie*, t. ML: m. *tyrannia*, der. *tyrannus* TYRANT]

tyrant (tī′ə rənt), *n.* **1.** a king or ruler who uses his power oppressively or unjustly. **2.** an absolute ruler, as in ancient Greece, owing his office to usurpation. **3.** any person who exercises power despotically. **4.** a tyrannical or compulsory influence. [ME *tirant*, t. OF, t. L: m. *tyrannus*, t. Gk: m. *týrannos*]

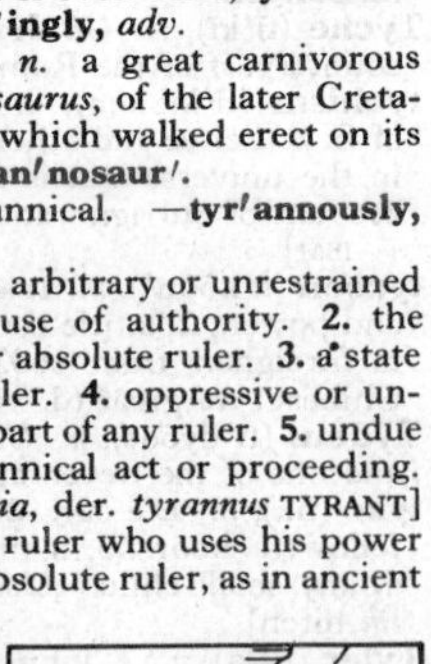

tyre (tī′ə), *n., v.*, **tyred, tyring.** —*n.* **1.** a band of metal or rubber, fitted round the rim of a wheel as a running surface: the inflated rubber **pneumatic tyre** provides good adhesion and resistance to shock. —*v.t.* **2.** to furnish with a tyre or tyres. Also, *U.S.*, **tire.** [late ME; special use of TIRE[3]]

Tyre, *c.* 1000 B.C.

Tyre (tī′ə), *n.* an ancient seaport of Phoenicia: one of the great cities of antiquity, famous for its navigators and traders.

Tyrian (tĭr′ĭ ən), *adj.* **1.** pertaining or belonging to ancient Tyre. **2.** of the colour of the dye called Tyrian purple. —*n.* **3.** a native of Tyre. [f. s. L *Tyrius* (t. Gk: m. *Týrios*) + AN]

Tyrian purple, a highly prized purple dye of classical antiquity, orig. obtained at great expense from a certain shellfish. It was later shown to be an indigo derivative and synthesized, and it has been displaced by other synthetic dyes. Cf. **murex.** Also, **Tyrian dye.**

tyro (tī′ə rō′), *n., pl.* **-ros.** *Chiefly U.S.* tiro.

Tyrol (tĭr′əl, tĭ rōl′; *Ger.* tē rōl′), *n.* **1.** an alpine region in W Austria and N Italy: a former Austrian crownland. **2.** a province in W Austria. 462,899 pop. (1961); 4883 sq. mi. *Cap.:* Innsbruck. Also, **Tirol.**

Tyrolese (tĭ′rə lēz′), *adj., n., pl.* **-ese.** —*adj.* **1.** of or pertaining to the Tyrol or its inhabitants. —*n.* **2.** a native of Tyrol. Also, **Tyrolean** (tĭ rō′lĭ ən, tĭ′rə lĭən′).

Tyrolienne (tĭ rō′lĭ ĕn′), *n.* **1.** a dance of the Tyrolese peasants. **2.** a song or melody, characteristically a yodel, suitable for such a dance. [t. F, fem. of *tyrolien* pertaining to Tyrol]

Tyrone (tĭ rōn′), *n.* a county in W Northern Ireland. 133,930 pop. (1961); 1218 sq. mi. *Co. town:* Omagh.

tyrosinase (tī′rō sĭ nās′, tĭ′rō-), *n. Biochem.* an oxidizing enzyme found in plant and animal tissues that catalyses the first stages of the conversion of tyrosine into melanin and other pigments.

tyrosine (tī′rə sēn′, -sĭn, tĭ′rə-), *n. Chem., Biochem.* an amino acid, $C_9H_{11}NO_3$, occurring in proteins. [f. Gk *tȳrós* cheese + -INE[2]]

Tyrrhenian Sea (tĭ rē′nyən), a part of the Mediterranean, partially enclosed by W Italy, Corsica, Sardinia, and Sicily. See map under **Salerno.**

Tyumen (*Russ.* tyŏŏ mėny′), *n.* a town in the W Soviet Union in Asia. 218,000 (est. 1967).

tzar (zä), *n.* tsar.

tzarevitch (zä′rə vĭch), *n.* tsarevitch.

tzarevna (zä rĕv′nə), *n.* tsarevna.

tzarina (zä rē′nə), *n.* tsarina.

tzarism (zä′rĭz′əm), *n.* tsarism.

tzarist (zä′rĭst), *n.* tsarist.

tzaritza (zä rĭt′sə), *n.* tsaritsa.

tzetze fly (tsĕt′sĭ), tsetse fly.

Tzigane (tsĭ gän′, sĭ-), *adj.* **1.** (*often l.c.*) pertaining to the Hungarian Gipsies. —*n.* **2.** a Hungarian Gipsy. Also, **Tzigany** (tsĭg′ä nĭ, sĭg′-). [t. Hung.]

U

U, u (yōō), *n., pl.* **U's** or **Us, u's** or **us.** a vowel, the 21st letter of the English alphabet.

U[1] (yōō), *adj.* **1.** denoting a cinema film which may be shown publicly to unaccompanied children as well as to adults. —*n.* **2.** such a film. Cf. **A, X.**

U[2] (yōō), *adj. Colloq.* appropriate to or characteristic of the upper class. Cf. **non-U.** [initial of UPPER (CLASS)]

U[3] (ōō, yōō), *n.* a Burmese title of respect for a man (used before the proper name). [t. Burm.: uncle]

U, *Chem.* uranium.

U., 1. uncle. **2.** union. **3.** united. **4.** university. **5.** upper.

u., 1. (G *und*) and. **2.** upper.

uakari (wə kä′rĭ), *n.* any of the short-tailed monkeys of the genus *Cacajao*, esp. *C. rubicundus* of the Amazon basin. [t. Tupi]

U.A.R., United Arab Republic. Also, **UAR.**

ubac (yōō′băk), *n. Mountaineering.* a mountain slope shaded from the sun. [t. d. F, g. L *opacus* dark]

Ubangi (yōō băng′gĭ), *n.* a river forming a part of the boundary between the Democratic Republic of the Congo and Republic of Congo flowing into the river Congo. ab. 700 mi. (with the Uele, ab. 1400 mi.). Also, **Mobangi, Mubangi;** *French,* **Oubangui.**

Ubangi-Shari (yōō băng′gĭ shä′rĭ), *n.* a former overseas territory of French Equatorial Africa: now independent within the French Community. See **Central African Republic.**

Ube (ōō′bā), *n.* a town in Japan, in S central Honshu island. 158,986 (1965).

Übermensch (*Ger.* Y′bər mĕnsh), *n.* See **superman** (esp. def. 2).

ubiety (yōō bī′ə tĭ), *n.* the state of being in a definite place; condition with respect to place; local relation. [t. NL: m. s. *ubietas*, der. L *ubi* where]

ubiquinone (yōō′bĭ kwĭn′ōn, -kwĭ nōn′), *n. Biochem.* any of a group of closely related quinone compounds found widely distributed in living tissues. [f. UBI(QUITOUS) + QUINONE]

ubiquitarian (yōō′bĭ kwĭ tĕə′rĭ ən, yōō bĭk′-), *n. Theol.* a member of the Lutheran communion who believes that Christ is fully present at all times and places, and therefore no more so within the Eucharistic elements than elsewhere.

ubiquitous (yōō bĭk′wĭ təs), *adj.* characterized by ubiquity; being everywhere at the same time; present everywhere; omnipresent. Also, *Rare,* **ubiquitary** (yōō bĭk′-wĭ tə rĭ). [f. UBIQUIT(Y) + -OUS] —**ubiq′uitously,** *adv.* —**ubiq′uitousness,** *n.* —**Syn.** See **omnipresent.**

ubiquity (yōō bĭk′wĭ tĭ), *n.* **1.** the state or capacity of being everywhere at the same time; omnipresence. **2.** (*cap.*) *Theol.* the omnipresent state of God or Christ. [t. NL: m. s. *ubiquitas*, der. L *ubique* everywhere]

ubi supra (ōō′bĭ sōō′prä), *Latin.* in the page or passage previously referred to. [L: where above]

U-boat (yōō′bōt′), *n.* a German submarine. [t. G: half adoption, half trans. of *U-boot*, short for *Unterseeboot* undersea boat]

U-bolt (yōō′bōlt′), *n.* a rod of iron bent into the form of the letter U, fitted at both ends with a screw thread which takes a nut.

u.c., 1. (It. *una corda*) *Music.* 'one string'; soft pedal. **2.** *Print.* upper case (capital letter or letters).

Ucayali (*Sp.* ōō kä yä′lē), *n.* a river flowing N through E Peru, joining the Marañón to form the Amazon. ab. 1000 mi.

Uccello (*It.* ōōt chĕl′lō), *n.* **Paolo** (*It.* pä′ō lō), 1396/7–1475, Italian painter.

Udaipur (ōō dī′pŏŏə), *n.* a town in India, in S Rajasthan. 111,139 (1961).

Udall (yōō′dl), *n.* **Nicholas,** 1505–56, English schoolmaster, translator, and dramatist. Also, **Uvedale.**

U.D.C., urban district council.

udder (ŭd′ə), *n.* a mamma or mammary gland, esp. when pendulous and with more than one teat, as in cows. [ME *uddre*, OE *ūder*, c. G *Euter*, akin to L *ūber*] —**ud′derless,** *adj.* —**ud′der-like′,** *adj.*

U.D.I., unilateral declaration of independence (specif. that declared by Rhodesia in 1965).

Udine (*It.* ōō′dē nė), *n.* a town in Italy, in Friuli-Venezia Giulia. 93,707 (1966).

udo (ōō′dō), *n.* a plant, *Aralia cordata*, cultivated esp. in Japan and China for its edible shoots. [t. Jap.]

udometer (yōō dŏm′ĭ tə), *n.* a rain gauge; a pluviometer. [t. F: m. *udomètre*, f. s. L *ūdus* wet, damp + *-o-* -O- + *-mètre* -METER[1]] —**udometric** (yōō′də mĕt′rĭk), *adj.* —**udom′etry,** *n.*

Uele (wä′lə), *n.* a river in central Africa, flowing from the NE Republic of Congo W to the river Ubangi. ab. 700 mi.

Ufa (*Russ.* ōō fä′), *n.* a city in the E Soviet Union in Europe: the capital of Bashkir Republic. 665,000 (est. 1965).

u.f.n., until further notice.

UFO (yōō′fō), *n.* unidentified flying object. Also, **U.F.O.**

Uganda (yōō găn′də), *n.* an independent state in E Africa between the NE Republic of Congo and Kenya: member of the Commonwealth of Nations. 6,845,000 pop. (est. 1961); 93,981 sq. mi. *Cap.:* Kampala. —**Ugan′dan,** *n., adj.*

Uganda

ugh (ŭKH, ōōh, ûh), *interj.* **1.** (an exclamation expressing disgust, aversion, horror, or the like.) **2.** (a representation of the sound of a cough or grunt.)

ugli fruit (ŭg′lĭ), a large, juicy fruit with a thick yellow skin, a cross between a tangerine, a grapefruit, and a Seville orange.

uglify (ŭg′lĭ fī′), *v.t.,* **-fied, -fying.** to make ugly. [f. UGLY + -FY] —**ug′lifica′tion,** *n.*

ugly (ŭg′lĭ), *adj.,* **-lier, -liest. 1.** repulsive or displeasing in appearance; offensive to the sense of beauty: *ugly furniture.* **2.** morally revolting: *ugly sin.* **3.** disagreeable;

unpleasant; objectionable: *ugly tricks.* **4.** of a troublesome nature; threatening disadvantage or danger: *ugly symptoms.* **5.** unpleasantly or dangerously rough: *ugly weather.* **6.** ill-natured; quarrelsome; vicious: *an ugly disposition.* [ME, t. Scand.; cf. Icel. *uggligr* fearful, dreadful] —**ugʹlily,** *adv.* —**ugʹliness,** *n.* —**Syn. 1.** ill-favoured, hard-featured, uncomely, unsightly. **2.** base, heinous, vile. **6.** surly, spiteful.

ugly duckling, an unattractive or unpromising child who becomes a beautiful or much admired adult. [name of a story by Hans Andersen]

Ugrian (o͞oʹgrĭ ən, yo͞oʹ-), *adj.* **1.** denoting or pertaining to a race or ethnological group including the Magyars and related peoples of western Siberia and the north-eastern Soviet Union in Europe. —*n.* **2.** a member of any of the Ugrian peoples. **3.** Ugric.

Ugric (o͞oʹgrĭk, yo͞oʹ-), *n.* **1.** the group of Finno-Ugric languages that consists of Hungarian and two languages spoken in western Siberia (Ostyak and Vogul). —*adj.* **2.** Ugrian.

Ugro-Finnic (o͞oʹgrō fĭnʹĭk, yo͞oʹgrō-), *n.* Finno-Ugric.

u.h.f., ultra high frequency.

uhlan (o͞oʹlän, yo͞oʹlən), *n.* **1.** one of a body of mounted soldiers first known in Europe in Poland, usually carrying lances. **2.** one of such a body in the former German army, classed as heavy cavalry. Also, **ulan.** [t. G, t. Pol.: m. *ulan*, t. Turk.: m. *oghlān* boy, lad]

Uhland (*Ger.* o͞oʹlänt), *n.* **Johann Ludwig** (*Ger.* yōʹhän lo͞otʹvĭKH), 1787–1862, German poet and writer.

Uigur (wēʹgo͝oə), *n.* **1.** a member of the Turkish race dominant in Mongolia and eastern Turkestan from the 8th to the 12th century A.D., now found mainly in Sinkiang. **2.** a Turkic language of north-western Mongolia. Also, **Uighur.** —**Uigurian** (wē go͝oəʹrĭ ən), **Uiguʹric,** *adj.*

uintaite (yo͞o ĭnʹtə ītʹ), *n.* gilsonite. Also, **uintahite.** [named after the *Uinta* Mountains in NE Utah, U.S.A. See -ITE[1]]

Uist (yo͞oʹĭst), *n.* two islands, **North Uist** and **South Uist,** of the Outer Hebrides in Inverness-shire, Scotland.

uitlander (ātʹlănʹdə, oitʹ-; *Du.* œytʹlŏn dər), *n. S African.* foreigner; anyone not an Afrikaner. [Afrikaans: outlander]

Ujiji (o͞o jēʹjĭ), *n.* a town in W Tanzania, on Lake Tanganyika: Stanley found Livingstone here 1871. ab. 12,000 (1957).

Ujjain (o͞o jānʹ), *n.* a town in India, in W Madhya Pradesh. 144,161 (1961).

Ujpest (*Hung.* o͞oyʹpĕsht), *n.* a town in N Hungary, on the Danube; part of Budapest. 68,530 (est. 1954).

U.K., United Kingdom.

ukase (yo͞o kāzʹ), *n.* **1.** (in Russia under the Tsars) an edict or order of the emperor, having the force of law. **2.** any absolute or arbitrary order, regulation, or proclamation. [t. Russ.: m. *ukaz*]

Ukr., Ukraine.

Ukraine (yo͞o krānʹ), *n.* a constituent republic of the Soviet Union, in the SW part: a rich agricultural region. 41,869,000 pop. (est. 1959); ab. 223,000 sq. mi. *Cap.:* Kiev. Official name, **Ukrainian Soviet Socialist Republic.**

Ukraine

Ukrainian (yo͞o krāʹnyən), *adj.* **1.** of or pertaining to the Ukraine. —*n.* **2.** a native or inhabitant of the Ukraine. **3.** a Slavic language closely related to Russian.

ukulele (yo͞oʹkə lāʹlĭ), *n.* a small musical instrument of the guitar kind with a long neck, much used in the Hawaiian Islands. Also, **ukelele.** [t. Hawaiian: lit., flea]

Ukulele

ulan (yo͞oʹlən), *n.* uhlan.

Ulan Bator (o͞oʹlän bäʹtô), a town in and the capital of the Mongolian People's Republic in E central Asia: former holy city of the Mongols. 250,000 (est. 1966). Also, **Ulan Bator Khoto** (kōʹtō). Formerly, **Urga.**

Ulan Ude (*Russ.* o͝o lănʹ o͝o dĕʹ), a city in the S Soviet Union in Asia, near Lake Baikal. 213,000 (est. 1965).

Ulbricht (*Ger.* o͝olʹbrĭKHt), *n.* **Walter** (*Ger.* välʹtər), born 1893, East German statesman: chairman of the East German Council of State and secretary of the Politburo of the Socialist Unity Party since 1960.

ulcer (ŭlʹsə), *n.* **1.** *Pathol.* a sore open either to the surface of the body or to a natural cavity, and accompanied by the disintegration of tissue and the formation of pus, etc. **2.** a corrupting influence or element. [ME, t. L: s. *ulcus*, akin to Gk *hélkos*]

ulcerate (ŭlʹsə rātʹ), *v.t., v.i.,* **-rated, -rating.** to effect or be affected with an ulcer; make or become ulcerous. [ME, t. L: m. s. *ulcerātus*, pp.] —**ulʹceraʹtion,** *n.*

ulcerative (ŭlʹsə răʹtĭv), *adj.* **1.** causing ulceration. **2.** of the nature of or characterized by ulceration.

ulcerous (ŭlʹsə rəs), *adj.* **1.** of the nature of an ulcer or ulcers; characterized by the formation of ulcers. **2.** affected with an ulcer or ulcers. **3.** corrupting; corruptive. —**ulʹcerously,** *adv.* —**ulʹcerousness,** *n.*

ule (o͞oʹlā), *n.* **1.** a latiferous Central American tree, *Castilla elastica.* **2.** the crude rubber obtained from this tree. [t. Mex. Sp., t. Nahuatl: m. *ulli*]

-ule, a diminutive suffix of nouns, as in *globule.* [t. L: m. *-ulus, -ula, -ulum*]

ulema (o͞oʹlĭ mə), *n.pl.* the doctors of Muslim religion and law, esp. in Turkey. [t. Ar.: learned (men)]

-ulent, an adjective suffix meaning 'abounding in', as in *fraudulent.* [t. L: s. *-ulentus* full of]

ulexite (yo͞oʹlĕk sītʹ), *n.* a mineral, hydrous borate of calcium and sodium which occurs in saline crusts in arid regions, esp. in Chile and Nevada, in the form of fine white acicular crystals. [named after G. L. *Ulex*, German chemist; see -ITE[1]]

Ulfilas (o͝olʹfĭ lăsʹ), *n.* A.D. *c.* 311–*c.* 382, Christian bishop among the Goths, and translator of the Bible into the Gothic language. Also, **Ulfila** (o͝olʹfĭ lə), **Wulfila.**

Ulhasnagar (o͞o läsʹnə gə), *n.* a new city in India, in Maharashtra. 107,760 (1961).

ullage (ŭlʹĭj), *n., v.i.,* **-laged, -laging.** —*n.* **1.** the amount by which the contents of a container, tank, ship, etc., fall short of filling it. **2.** the loss of wine or the like from its container by reason of leakage or evaporation. **3.** *Aeron.* the volume of a full tank in excess of the fuel. **4.** *Slang.* a worthless person or people; dregs. —*v.i.* **5.** to create an ullage. **6.** to measure an ullage. [late ME, t. AF: m. *ulliage* filling up (of a cask), der. *aouiller* fill up (a cask), ult. der. LL *oculus* bunghole, L eye]

ullage rocket, *Aeron.* a small rocket used to impart a forward thrust to a vehicle, to move the propellant to the rear of the tanks prior to firing the main engine.

Ullswater (ŭlzʹwôʹtə), *n.* a lake in England, on the border between Cumberland and Westmorland. 7½ mi. long.

Ulm (*Ger.* o͝olm), *n.* a town in West Germany, a river port in E Baden-Württemberg. 91,700 (est. 1966).

ulmaceous (ŭl māʹshəs), *adj.* belonging to the *Ulmaceae*, or elm family of dicotyledonous trees and shrubs, characterized by erect anthers, two stigmatic branches, flower buds produced on leafless yearly branches, and broad-winged samaras. [f. s. NL *Ulmāceae*, pl., genus name (der. L. *ulmus* elm) + -OUS]

ulna (ŭlʹnə), *n., pl.* **-nae** (-nē), **-nas. 1.** *Anat.* that one of the two bones of the forearm which is on the side opposite to the thumb. **2.** a corresponding bone in the forelimb of other vertebrates. [NL, special use of L *ulna* elbow, arm] —**ulʹnar,** *adj.*

-ulose, var. of **-ulous** in scientific terms, as in *granulose, ramulose.* [t. L: m. s. *-ulōsus.* See -ULE, -OSE[1]]

ulotrichous (yo͞o lŏtʹrĭ kəs), *adj.* having woolly hair. [f. Gk: m. *oûlo(s)* curly + m. *-trichos* -haired]

-ulous, a suffix forming adjectives meaning 'tending to', as in *credulous, populous.* [t. L: m. s. *-ulosus*, or m. *-ulus*]

Ulpian (ŭlʹpĭ ən), *n.* (*Domitius Ulpianus*), died A.D. 228?, Roman jurist.

Ulster (ŭlʹstə), *n.* **1.** an ancient province in Ireland, now comprising Northern Ireland and a part of the Republic of Ireland. 217,524 pop. (1961); 3123 sq. mi. **2.** Northern Ireland. **3.** (*l.c.*) a long, loose, heavy overcoat, orig. made of cloth from N Ireland.

Ulster (def. 1)

ult., 1. ultimate. **2.** ultimately. **3.** Also, **ulto.** ultimo.

ulterior (ŭl tĭəʹrĭ ə), *adj.* **1.** being beyond what is seen or avowed; intentionally kept concealed: *ulterior motives.* **2.** coming at a subsequent time or stage: *ulterior action.* **3.** being or situated beyond, or on the farther side: *ulterior regions.* [t. L: farther, compar. adj. akin to *ultrā*, adv., beyond] —**ulteʹriorly,** *adv.*

ultima (ŭlʹtĭ mə), *n.* the last syllable of a word. [t. L, fem. of *ultimus* farthest, last]

ultima ratio regum (o͝olʹtĭ mä räʹtĭ ō rĕgʹo͝om), *Latin.* the last (or final) argument of kings; resort to arms (motto engraved by Louis XIV on his cannon).

ultimate (ŭlʹtĭ mĭt), *adj.* **1.** forming the final aim or object: *his ultimate goal.* **2.** coming at the end, as of a course of action, a process, etc.; final; decisive: *ultimate lot in life.*

3. beyond which it is impossible to proceed, as by investigation or analysis; fundamental; elemental: *ultimate principles.* 4. impossible to exceed or override: *ultimate weapon.* 5. last, as in a series. —*n.* 6. the final point; final result. 7. a fundamental fact or principle. [t. LL: m. s. *ultimātus*, pp., ended, der. L *ultimus* last] —**ul′timately,** *adv.* —**ul′timateness,** *n.* —**Syn.** 2. See **last**[1].

ultimate load, *Aeron.* the maximum load which a structure is designed to withstand.

ultimate particle, elementary particle.

ultimate stress, *Engineering.* the load required to fracture a material, divided by the original area of cross-section at the point of fracture; tenacity; tensile strength; tensile stress. Also, **ultimate tensile stress** or **strength.**

ultima Thule (ŭl′tĭ mə thyo͞o′lĭ), 1. the uttermost degree obtainable. 2. the farthest limit or point possible. 3. the farthest north. Also, **Thule.** [L: farthest Thule (supposedly the northernmost point in the world)]

ultimatum (ŭl′tĭ mā′təm), *n., pl.* **-tums, -ta** (-tə). 1. the final terms of one of the parties in a diplomatic relationship, the rejection of which by the other party may involve a rupture of relations or lead to a declaration of war. 2. a final proposal or statement of conditions. [t. NL, prop. neut. of LL *ultimātus* ULTIMATE]

ultimo (ŭl′tĭ mō′), *adv.* in or of the month preceding the present: *on the 12th ultimo.* *Abbrev.:* ult., ulto. Cf. **proximo.** [t. L: short for *ultimō mense* in the last month]

ultimogeniture (ŭl′tĭ mō jĕn′ĭ chə), *n.* the principle of undivided inheritance or succession by the youngest son (distinguished from *primogeniture*). [f. *ultimo-* (comb. form repr. L *ultimus* last) + GENITURE]

ulto, ultimo.

ultra (ŭl′trə), *adj.* 1. going beyond what is usual or ordinary; excessive; extreme. —*n.* 2. one who goes to extremes, as of fashion, etc. [t. L: beyond, adv., prep.]

ultra-, a prefix meaning: 1. beyond (in space or time) as in *ultraplanetary.* 2. excessive; excessively, as in *ultraconventional.* [t. L, comb. form of *ultrā*, adv., prep., beyond] See the list following:

ultrabasic rock (ŭl′trə bā′sĭk), *Geol.* a rock which contains less silica than basic rock; rock containing less than 45 per cent of silica.

ultracentrifuge (ŭl′trə sĕn′trĭ fyo͞oj′), *n., v.t.,* **-fuged, -fuging.** *Chem.* —*n.* 1. a high-speed centrifuge capable of separating ultramicroscopic particles. —*v.t.* 2. to separate in an ultracentrifuge.

ultrafilter (ŭl′trə fĭl′tə), *Chem.* —*n.* 1. a filter for the separation of colloidal particles consisting of a semi-permeable membrane through which the filtrate passes under pressure or suction. —*v.t.* 2. to separate in an ultrafilter.

ultra high frequency, *Radio.* 1. any frequency between 300 and 3000 megahertz. 2. (of a device) designed to transmit or receive such a frequency. *Abbrev.:* u.h.f.

ultraism (ŭl′trə ĭz′əm), *n.* 1. extremism. 2. an extreme view or act. —**ul′traist,** *n., adj.* —**ul′trais′tic,** *adj.*

ultramarine (ŭl′trə mə rēn′), *adj.* 1. beyond the sea. 2. of an ultramarine colour; deep blue. —*n.* 3. a blue pigment consisting of powdered lapis lazuli. 4. a similar artificial blue pigment. 5. any of various other pigments. 6. a deep blue colour. [t. ML: m. s. *ultrāmarīnus.* See ULTRA-, MARINE]

ultramicrobalance (ŭl′trə mī′krō băl′əns), *n.* *Chem.* a balance capable of weighing very small quantities of a substance to an accuracy of one hundredth of a microgram.

ultramicrometer (ŭl′trə mī krŏm′ĭ tə), *n.* a micrometer calibrated to a very fine scale.

ultramicroscope (ŭl′trə mī′krə skōp′), *n.* an instrument for detecting, by means of diffractive effects, objects too small to be seen by the ordinary microscope. —**ultramicroscopic** (ŭl′trə mī′krə skŏp′ĭk), **ul′trami′croscop′ical,** *adj.*

ultramicroscopy (ŭl′trə mī krŏs′kə pĭ), *n.* the use of the ultramicroscope.

ultramontane (ŭl′trə mŏn′tān), *adj.* 1. beyond the mountains. 2. south of the Alps; Italian. 3. pertaining to or supporting the Roman Catholic belief that the pope is the spiritual head of the Church in all countries. 4. (formerly) north of the Alps; tramontane. —*n.* 5. one who lives beyond the mountains. 6. one living south of the Alps. 7. a member of the ultramontane party in the Roman Catholic Church. 8. (formerly) one living to the north of the Alps. [t. ML: m. s. *ultrāmontānus.* See ULTRA-, MONTANE] —**ultramontanism** (ŭl′trə mŏn′tĭ nĭz′əm), *n.*

ultramundane (ŭl′trə mŭn′dān), *adj.* 1. beyond the limits of the known universe. 2. *Obs.* beyond the present life. [t. LL: m. s. *ultrāmundānus.* See ULTRA-, MUNDANE]

ultrasonic (ŭl′trə sŏn′ĭk), *adj.* referring to periodic disturbances in a medium above the audible limit, i.e. above 20,000 hertz.

ultrasonic cleaning, a method of cleaning metallic parts by immersion in a fluid through which ultrasonic waves pass.

ultrasonics (ŭl′trə sŏn′ĭks), *n.pl.* (*construed as sing.*) the study of pressure waves which are of similar nature to soundwaves, but whose frequencies are above the audible limit; supersonics.

ultratropical (ŭl′trə trŏp′ĭ kl), *adj.* 1. outside the tropics. 2. warmer than the tropics.

ultraviolet (ŭl′trə vī′ə lĭt), *adj.* 1. beyond the violet, as the invisible rays of the spectrum lying outside the violet end of the visible spectrum. 2. pertaining to these rays. Cf. **infrared.**

ultraviolet microscope, *Physics.* a microscope in which the object to be viewed is illuminated by ultraviolet radiation: quartz lenses are used and the image is recorded photographically.

ultra vires (ŭl′trə vī′ə rēz′), *Latin.* going beyond the legal power or authority of an agent, company, tribunal, etc. [L: beyond the power]

ultravirus (ŭl′trə vī′ə rəs), *n.* an ultramicroscopic agent which passes through the finest bacterial filters.

ultroneous (ŭl trō′nĭ əs), *adj.* *Rare.* spontaneous; voluntary. [t. L: m. *ultrōneus*] —**ultro′neously,** *adv.* —**ultro′neousness,** *n.*

ulu (o͞o′lo͞o), *n.* a type of knife used by Eskimos.

ululant (yo͞o′lyo͞o lənt), *adj.* ululating; howling. [t. L: s. *ululans*, ppr.; imit.]

ululate (yo͞o′lyo͞o lāt′), *v.i.,* **-lated, -lating.** 1. to howl, as a dog or wolf. 2. to utter some similar sound; hoot; wail. 3. to lament loudly. [t. L: m. s. *ululātus*, pp.; imit.] —**u′lula′tion,** *n.*

-ulus, a diminutive suffix of nouns, as in *homunculus, calculus.*

Ulyanovsk (*Russ.* o͞o lyä′nəfsk), *n.* a city in the E Soviet Union in Europe: birthplace of Lenin. 265,000 pop. (est. 1965).

Ulysses (yo͞o′lĭ sēz′, yo͞o lĭs′ēz), *n.* Latin name for **Odysseus.** —**Ulyssean** (yo͞o lĭs′ĭ ən), *adj.*

um (m, əm), *interj.* 1. (an indication of hesitation or inarticulacy.) 2. (an expression of doubt, pensiveness, etc.) Cf. **humph.**

umbel (ŭm′bl), *n.* *Bot.* an inflorescence in which a number of flower stalks or pedicels, nearly equal in length, spread from a common centre: called a **simple umbel** when each pedicel is terminated by a single flower, and a **compound umbel** when each pedicel bears a secondary umbel. [t. L: m. s. *umbella* sunshade, parasol, dim. of *umbra* shadow]

Compound umbel

umbellate (ŭm′bĭ lĭt, -lāt′), *adj.* having or forming an umbel or umbels. Also, **umbellar** (ŭm bĕl′ə), **um′bellat′ed.** —**um′bellately,** *adv.*

umbelliferous (ŭm′bĭ lĭf′ə rəs), *adj.* 1. bearing an umbel or umbels. 2. belonging or pertaining to the *Umbelliferae*, a family of plants containing many important umbel-bearing herbs, as the parsley, carrot, etc. [f. NL *umbellifer* (see UMBEL, -(I)FER) + -OUS]

umbellule (ŭm bĕl′yo͞ol, ŭm′bĭ lyo͞ol′), *n.* one of the secondary umbels in a compound umbel. [t. NL: m. *umbellula*, dim. of *umbella* UMBEL] —**umbellulate** (ŭm-bĕl′yo͞o lĭt, -lāt′), *adj.*

umber (ŭm′bə), *n.* 1. an earth consisting chiefly of a hydrated oxide of iron and some oxide of manganese, used in its natural state (**raw umber**) as a brown pigment, or after heating (**burnt umber**) as a reddish brown pigment. 2. the colour of such a pigment; dark dusky brown or dark reddish brown. —*adj.* 3. of such a colour. —*v.t.* 4. to colour with or as with umber. [t. It.: m. (*terra di*) *ombra*, lit., (earth of) shade (see UMBRA); ? prop., Umbrian earth]

Umberto (o͞om bĕə′tō; *It.* o͞om bĕr′tō), *n.* (*Humbert I*), 1844–1909, king of Italy 1878–1909; assassinated.

umbilical (ŭm bĭl′ĭ kl, ŭm′bĭ lī′kl), *adj.* 1. of the umbilicus or umbilical cord. 2. formed or placed like a navel; central. —*n.* 3. an umbilical cord (esp. def. 2). [t. ML: s. *umbilīcālis*, der. L *umbilīcus* navel]

ul′tra-ambi′tious, *adj.*
ul′tracon′fident, *adj.*
ul′traconser′vatism, *n.*
ul′traconser′vative, *n., adj.*
ul′tracred′ulous, *adj.*
ul′tracrit′ical, *adj.*
ul′trafash′ionable, *adj.*
ul′tralib′eral, *adj., n.*
ul′traloy′al, *adj.*
ul′traloy′alist, *n.*
ul′tramod′ern, *adj., n.*
ul′tramod′est, *adj.*
ul′trana′tionalism, *n.*
ul′trana′tionalist, *n., adj.*
ul′trarad′ical, *adj., n.*
ul′trarap′id, *adj.*
ul′trara′tional, *adj.*
ul′trarefined′, *adj.*
ul′trarelig′ious, *adj.*
ul′traroy′alist, *adj.*

umbilical cord, 1. *Anat.* a cord or funicle connecting the embryo or foetus with the placenta of the mother, and transmitting nourishment from the mother. 2. Also, **umbilical connector, umbilical.** *Aerospace.* **a.** an electrical cable or fluid pipeline conveying supplies and signals from the ground to a rocket before the launch. **b.** an air or oxygen line connecting an astronaut to his spacecraft enabling him to walk in space.

umbilicate (ŭm bĭl′ĭ kĭt, -kāt′), *adj.* 1. having the form of an umbilicus or navel. 2. having an umbilicus. Also, **umbil′icat′ed.**

umbilication (ŭm bĭl′ĭ kā′shən), *n.* 1. a central navel-like depression. 2. umbilicate state or formation.

umbilicus (ŭm bĭl′ĭ kəs, ŭm′bĭ lī′kəs), *n., pl.* **-bilici** (-bĭl′ĭ sī′, -bĭ lī′sī). 1. *Anat.* the navel, or central depression in the surface of the abdomen indicating the point of attachment of the umbilical cord. 2. *Bot., Zool., etc.* a navel-like formation, as the hilum of a seed. 3. a central point or place. 4. a small, navel-like depression. [t. L; akin to Gk *omphalós* and NAVEL]

umbiliform (ŭm bĭl′ĭ fôm′), *adj.* having the form of an umbilicus or navel. [f. UMBILI(CUS) + -FORM]

umble pie (ŭm′bl), humble pie. [orig. spelling of HUMBLE PIE. See UMBLES]

umbles (ŭm′blz), *n.pl.* numbles. [var. of NUMBLES]

umbo (ŭm′bō), *n., pl.* **umbones** (ŭm bō′nēz), **umbos.** 1. the boss, knob, or projection at or near the centre of a shield. 2. any similar boss or protuberance. 3. the raised centre of the cup of some toadstools. 4. *Zool.* the beak of a bivalve shell; the protuberance of each valve above the hinge. [t. L] —**umbonic** (ŭm bŏn′ĭk), *adj.*

umbonate (ŭm′bə nĭt, -nāt′), *adj.* 1. bosslike. 2. having an umbo or boss. Also, **umbonal** (ŭm′bə nəl).

umbra (ŭm′brə), *n., pl.* **-brae** (-brē). 1. shade; shadow. 2. *Astron.* **a.** the complete or perfect shadow of an opaque body, as a planet, where the direct light from the source of illumination is wholly cut off. Cf. **penumbra. b.** the dark central portion of a sunspot. 3. ghost. [t. L] —**um′bral,** *adj.*

umbrage (ŭm′brĭj), *n.* 1. offence given or taken; resentful displeasure. 2. the foliage of trees, etc., affording shade. 3. *Obs.* shade or shadows, as that cast by trees, etc. 4. *Rare.* a shadowy appearance or semblance of something. [late ME, t. F: m. *ombrage*, g. L *umbrāticum*, neut. adj., of or in the shade; def. 1 through obs. meanings 'suspicion', 'disfavour']

umbrageous (ŭm brā′jəs), *adj.* 1. forming or affording shade; shady; shaded. 2. *Rare.* apt or disposed to take umbrage or offence, as a person. —**umbra′geously,** *adv.* —**umbra′geousness,** *n.*

umbrella (ŭm brĕl′ə), *n.* 1. a portable shade or screen for protection from sunlight, rain, etc., in its modern form consisting of a light circular canopy of silk, cotton, or other material on a folding frame of bars or strips of steel, cane, etc. 2. the saucer- or bowl-shaped gelatinous body of a medusa; the bell. 3. any general protection or cover. 4. *Mil.* a covering force of aircraft protecting ground troops. [t. It.: m. *ombrella*, der. *ombra* shade, g. L *umbra*] —**umbrel′la-less,** *adj.* —**umbrel′la-like′,** *adj.*

umbrella bird, 1. a South American bird, *Cephalopterus ornatus* (family *Cotingidae*) with an umbrella-like crest above the head. 2. another bird of this genus, *C. penduliger.*

umbrella pine. See **Japanese umbrella pine.**

umbrella stand, a rack or vertical container for walking sticks and closed umbrellas.

umbrella tree, 1. an American magnolia, *Magnolia tripetala*, a tree with large leaves in umbrella-like clusters. 2. any of various other trees suggesting an umbrella, as the tropical African moraceous tree, *Musanga smithii.*

Umbria (ŭm′brĭ ə; *It.* o͞om′bryä), *n.* 1. an ancient district in central and N Italy. 2. a region in central Italy. 788,546 pop. (1961); 3270 sq. mi. *Cap.:* Perugia.

Umbrian (ŭm′brĭ ən), *adj.* 1. of or pertaining to Umbria, its language, or its inhabitants. —*n.* 2. a native or inhabitant of Umbria. 3. an Italic language, which became extinct in ancient times.

umbriferous (ŭm brĭf′ə rəs), *adj.* casting or making shade. [f. L *umbrifer* shade-bearing + -OUS] —**umbrif′erously,** *adv.*

Umiak

umiak (o͞o′mĭ ăk′), *n.* an open Eskimo boat consisting of a wooden frame covered with skins and provided with several thwarts, for transport of goods and passengers. Also, **umiack, oomiak.** [t. Eskimo (Eastern d.): large skin boat, or woman's boat]

umlaut (o͝om′lout), *Gram.* —*n.* 1. (of vowels in Germanic languages) assimilation in which a vowel is influenced by a following vowel or semivowel. 2. a vowel which has resulted from such assimilation, esp. when written *ä, ö,* or *ü* in German. 3. two dots as a diacritic over a vowel to indicate a different vowel sound from that of the letter without the diacritic, esp. as so used in German. —*v.t.* 4. to modify by umlaut. 5. to write the umlaut over. [t. G, f. *um* about + *Laut* sound]

Umm al Qaiwain (o͞om′äl kī wān′). See **Trucial States.**

umph (əm, əmf), *interj.* humph.

umpirage (ŭm′pī′ə rĭj), *n.* 1. the office or authority of an umpire. 2. the decision of an umpire; arbitrament.

umpire (ŭm′pī′ə), *n., v.,* **-pired, -piring.** —*n.* 1. a person selected to rule on the plays in a game. 2. a person to whose decision a controversy between parties is referred; an arbiter or referee. —*v.t.* 3. to act as umpire in (a game). 4. to decide or settle (a controversy, etc.) as umpire; arbitrate. —*v.i.* 5. to act as umpire. [ME *oumpere*, r. *noumpere* (*a noumpere* taken as *an oumpere*), t. OF: m. *nonper* uneven, odd, f. *non* not (g. L *nōn*) + *per* (see PEER[1], n.)] —**um′pireship′,** *n.* —**Syn.** 1. referee, arbiter, arbitrator. 2. See **judge.**

umpteen (ŭmp tēn′), *adj.* of an indefinite, esp. a very large or immeasurable, number. —**umpteenth′,** *adj.*

Umtali (o͞om tä′lĭ), *n.* a town in E Rhodesia. 46,000 (est. 1964).

Umtamvuna (o͞om′təm vo͞o′nə), *n.* a river in the Republic of South Africa flowing SE along the border of Natal and Cape Province to the Indian Ocean. 50 mi.

umtiza (o͞om tē′zə), *n.* an evergreen tree, *Umtiza listeri*, of southern Africa, yielding hard and durable timber. [t. Xhosa: m. *umthiza*]

Umzimkulu (o͞om′zĭm ko͞o′lo͞o), *n.* a river in the Republic of South Africa flowing SE through S Natal to the Indian Ocean. 200 mi.

un-[1], a prefix meaning 'not', freely used as an English formative, giving a negative or opposite force, in adjectives (including participial adjectives) and their derivative adverbs and nouns, as in *unfair, unfairly, unfairness, unfelt, unseen, unfitting, unformed, unheard-of, unget-at-able*, and less freely in certain other nouns, as in *unease, unrest, unemployment.*

Note: Of the words in **un-**[1], only a selected number are separately entered below, since in most formations of this class, the meaning, spelling, and pronunciation may readily be determined by reference to the simple word from which each is formed. [ME and OE, c. D *on-*, G and Goth. *un-*, Icel. *ū-*, *ō-*; akin to L *in-*, Gk *an-*, *a-* (alpha privative)] —**Syn.** See **in-**[3].

un-[2], a prefix freely used in English to form verbs expressing a reversal of some action or state, or removal, deprivation, release, etc., as in *unbend, uncork, unfasten*, etc., or to intensify the force of a verb already having such a meaning, as in *unloose.* [ME and OE *un-*, *on-*, c. D *ont-*, G *ent-*, Goth. *and-*; akin to L *ante* before, Gk *anti* opposite to, against]

'un (ən), *pron. Dial.* one: *that's a big 'un.* Also, **un.**

U.N., United Nations.

U.N.A., United Nations Association.

unabbreviated (ŭn′ə brē′vĭ ā′tĭd), *adj.* not shortened; given in full.

unable (ŭn ā′bl), *adj.* not able (to do something); lacking ability or power (to do something); weak; impotent. —**Syn.** See **incapable.**

unabridged (ŭn′ə brĭjd′), *adj.* not abridged or shortened, as a book.

unaccented (ŭn′ăk sĕn′tĭd), *adj.* not accented; unstressed.

unacceptable (ŭn′ək sĕp′tə bl), *adj.* that cannot be accepted; unwelcome; unsuitable. —**un′accept′ableness,** *n.*

unaccommodated (ŭn′ə kŏm′ə dā′tĭd), *adj.* 1. not satisfied. 2. not accommodated; not adapted.

unaccompanied (ŭn′ə kŭm′pə nĭd), *adj.* 1. not accompanied. 2. *Music.* without an accompaniment.

unaccomplished (ŭn′ə kŏm′plĭsht), *adj.* 1. not accomplished; incomplete. 2. without accomplishments.

unaccountable (ŭn′ə koun′tə bl), *adj.* 1. not to be accounted for or explained. 2. not accountable or answerable. —**un′account′abil′ity, un′account′ableness,** *n.* —**un′account′ably,** *adv.* —**Syn.** 1. inexplicable, inscrutable, strange. 2. unanswerable, irresponsible.

unaccounted-for (ŭn′ə koun′tĭd fô′), *adj.* not explained, understood, or taken into account.

---

un′abashed′, *adj.* **un′abol′ished,** *adj.* **un′accep′tance,** *n.* **un′accus′able,** *adj.*
un′abat′ed, *adj.* **unab′rogat′ed,** *adj.* **un′accom′modat′ing,** *adj.* **un′accused′,** *adj.*

unaccustomed (ŭn′ə kŭs′təmd), *adj.* **1.** not habituated: *to be unaccustomed to hardships.* **2.** unusual; unfamiliar. —**un′accus′tomedness,** *n.*

unaddressed (ŭn′ə drĕst′), *adj.* not bearing an address, as a letter or the like.

unadmitted (ŭn′əd mĭt′ĭd), *adj.* **1.** not stated, said, or conceded. **2.** kept secret. **3.** refused admission, as to a society.

unadopted (ŭn′ə dŏp′tĭd), *adj.* **1.** not adopted. **2.** (of a road) not maintained by the local authority.

unadvised (ŭn′əd vīzd′), *adj.* **1.** not advised; without advice. **2.** indiscreet; rash. —**unadvisedly** (ŭn′əd vī′zĭd lĭ), *adv.* —**un′advis′edness,** *n.*

unaesthetic (ŭn′ēs thĕt′ĭk), *adj.* unattractive; offending the aesthetic sense. Also, *U.S.*, **unesthetic.** —**un′aesthet′ically,** *adv.*

unaffected[1] (ŭn′ə fĕk′tĭd), *adj.* free from affection; sincere; genuine. [f. UN-[1] + AFFECTED[2]] —**un′affect′edly,** *adv.* —**un′affect′edness,** *n.* —**Syn.** plain, natural, simple, naive.

unaffected[2] (ŭn′ə fĕk′tĭd), *adj.* not affected, acted upon, or influenced. [f. UN-[1] + AFFECTED[1]] —**Syn.** unmoved, untouched, unimpressed.

Unalaska (o͞o′nə lăs′kə), *n.* one of the Aleutian Islands, off the SW mainland of Alaska. ab. 75 mi. long.

unalienable (ŭn ā′lyə nə bl), *adj.* unable or not allowed to be taken away or withheld, as a right. —**una′lienably,** *adv.*

unalive (ŭn′ə līv′), *adj.* not awake to or conscious of (something) (fol. by *to*): *he was quite unalive to the possibilities.*

unalterable (ŭn ôl′tə rə bl), *adj.* not able to be changed. Also, **inal′terable.** —**unal′terably,** *adv.* —**unal′terableness,** *n.*

un-American (ŭn′ə mĕ′rĭ kən), *adj.* unfavourable to America; not characteristic of or proper to America; foreign or opposed to American character, usages, standards, etc. —**un′-Ame′ricanism,** *n.*

Unamuno (*Sp.* o͞o nä mo͞o′nō), *n.* **Miguel de** (*Sp.* mē gĕl′ dĕ), 1864–1936, Spanish philosopher, poet, novelist, and essayist.

unaneled (ŭn′ə nēld′), *adj.* *Archaic.* not having received extreme unction.

unanimity (yo͞o′nə nĭm′ĭ tĭ), *n.* complete accord or agreement.

unanimous (yo͞o năn′ĭ məs), *adj.* **1.** of one mind; in complete accord; agreed. **2.** characterized by or showing complete accord: *a unanimous vote.* [t. L: m. *ūnanimus*] —**unan′imously,** *adv.* —**unan′imousness,** *n.*

unanswerable (ŭn än′sə rə bl), *adj.* **1.** not able to be refuted or rebutted; conclusive: *an unanswerable accusation.* **2.** not having an answer, as a question. —**unan′swerableness,** *n.* —**unan′swerably,** *adv.*

unappealable (ŭn′ə pē′lə bl), *adj.* **1.** not appealable; that cannot be carried to a higher court by appeal, as a cause. **2.** not to be appealed from, as a judgement or a judge. —**un′appeal′ableness,** *n.*

unappreciative (ŭn′ə prē′shyə tĭv), *adj.* not appreciative; lacking in appreciation. Also, **inappreciative.** —**un′appre′ciatively,** *adv.* —**un′appre′ciativeness,** *n.*

unapproachable (ŭn′ə prō′chə bl), *adj.* **1.** not to be approached; inaccessible. **2.** remote; inaccessible to intimacy. **3.** unrivalled. —**un′approach′ableness,** *n.* —**un′approach′ably,** *adv.*

unappropriated (ŭn′ə prō′prĭ ā′tĭd), *adj.* **1.** not taken possession of. **2.** not assigned or allotted.

unapt (ŭn ăpt′), *adj.* **1.** unfitted; unsuited. **2.** not disposed, likely, or liable. **3.** not quick to learn; inapt. —**unapt′ly,** *adv.* —**unapt′ness,** *n.*

unargued (ŭn ä′gyo͞od), *adj.* **1.** not argued, justified, or explained. **2.** undisputed.

unarm (ŭn äm′), *v.t.* **1.** to disarm. **2.** *Archaic.* to divest or relieve of armour. —*v.i.* **3.** to lay down one's arms. **4.** *Archaic.* to take off one's armour. [ME *unarme.* See UN-[2], ARM[2]]

unarmed (ŭn ämd′), *adj.* **1.** without arms or armour. **2.** defenceless. **3.** not furnished with claws, prickles, scales, or other armature, as animals and plants. **4.** *Mil.* not having a detonator, as a bomb.

unashamed (ŭn′ə shāmd′), *adj.* **1.** not contrite; not restrained by moral scruples. **2.** unconcealed; unembarrassed: *unashamed gluttony.* —**unashamedly** (ŭn′ə shā′mĭd lĭ), *adv.*

unassuming (ŭn′ə syo͞o′mĭng), *adj.* unpretending; modest. —**un′assum′ingly,** *adv.* —**un′assum′ingness,** *n.*

unassured (ŭn′ə sho͝oəd′, -shôd′), *adj.* **1.** not certain; insecure. **2.** not confident. **3.** not having any life assurance.

unattached (ŭn′ə tăcht′), *adj.* **1.** not attached. **2.** not connected or associated with any particular body, group or the like; independent. **3.** not engaged or married.

unattached participle. See **misrelated participle.**

unattended (ŭn′ə tĕn′dĭd), *adj.* **1.** unaccompanied. **2.** alone. **3.** with no-one in charge. **4.** not taken care of. **5.** not heeded or paid attention to.

unau (yo͞o′nou), *n.* a two-toed sloth, *Choloepus didactylus.* [t. d. Tupi (Island of Maranhão)]

unauthentic (ŭn′ô thĕn′tĭk), *adj.* not authentic.

unavailing (ŭn′ə vā′lĭng), *adj.* ineffectual; useless. —**un′avail′ingly,** *adv.*

unavoidable (ŭn′ə voi′də bl), *adj.* **1.** not to be avoided. **2.** unable to be avoided; inevitable. —**un′avoid′ableness, un′avoid′abil′ity,** *n.* —**un′avoid′ably,** *adv.*

unaware (ŭn′ə wĕə′), *adj.* **1.** not aware; unconscious, as of something: *to be unaware of any change.* —*adv.* **2.** unawares. —**un′aware′ness,** *n.*

unawares (ŭn′ə wĕəz′), *adv.* **1.** while not aware or conscious of a thing oneself; unknowingly or inadvertently. **2.** while another is not aware; unexpectedly: *to come upon someone unawares.*

unbacked (ŭn băkt′), *adj.* **1.** without backing or support. **2.** not supported by bets. **3.** not endorsed. **4.** never having been mounted by a rider, as a horse.

unbalance (ŭn băl′əns), *v.*, **-anced, -ancing,** *n.* —*v.t.* **1.** to throw out of balance. **2.** to disorder or derange, as the mind. —*n.* **3.** unbalanced condition.

un′achiev′able, *adj.*
un′acknowl′edged, *adj.*
un′acquain′tance, *n.*
un′acquaint′ed, *adj.*
un′acquaint′edness, *n.*
unact′able, *adj.*
unact′ed, *adj.*
unac′tuat′ed, *adj.*
un′adapt′able, *adj.*
un′adapt′ed, *adj.*
un′adjust′ed, *adj.*
un′admired′, *adj.*
un′admir′ing, *adj.*
un′admon′ished, *adj.*
un′adorned′, *adj.*
un′adul′terat′ed, *adj.*
un′adven′turous, *adj.*
un′advis′able, *adj.*
un′advis′ableness, *n.*
un′afraid′, *adj.*
unaid′ed, *adj.*
unaired′, *adj.*
un′allot′ted, *adj.*
un′allow′able, *adj.*
un′alloyed′, *adj.*
unal′tered, *adj.*
un′ambig′uous, *adj.*
un′ambi′tious, *adj.*
un′ambi′tiously, *adv.*
un′amen′able, *adj.*
un′amend′able, *adj.*
un′amend′ed, *adj.*
una′miabil′ity, *n.*
una′miable, *adj.*
una′miableness, *n.*
un′amus′able, *adj.*
un′amused′, *adj.*
un′amus′ingly, *adv.*
unan′alys′able, *adj.*
unan′alysed′, *adj.*
un′analyt′ical, *adj.*
unan′chor, *v.t., v.i.*
unan′chored, *adj.*
unan′notat′ed, *adj.*
un′antic′ipat′ed, *adj.*
un′apol′oget′ic, *adj.*
un′apostol′ic, *adj.*
un′apostol′ically, *adv.*
un′appalled′, *adj.*
un′appeal′ing, *adj.*
un′appeas′able, *adj.*
un′appeased′, *adj.*
unap′petiz′ing, *adj.*
un′applaud′ed, *adj.*
un′applied′, *adj.*
un′appoint′ed, *adj.*
un′appre′ciat′ed, *adj.*
un′apprehend′ed, *adj.*
un′apprehen′sive, *adj.*
un′apprehen′siveness, *n.*
un′apprised′, *adj.*
un′approached′, *adj.*
un′approved′, *adj.*
un′approv′ingly, *adv.*
unar′guable, *adj.*
unar′moured, *adj.*
un′aroused′, *adj.*
un′arranged′, *adj.*
un′arrest′ed, *adj.*
unart′ful, *adj.*
unart′fully, *adv.*
un′artic′ulat′ed, *adj.*
un′artis′tic, *adj.*
un′ascend′able, *adj.*
un′ascend′ed, *adj.*
un′ascertain′able, *adj.*
un′ascertained′, *adj.*
unask′able, *adj.*
unasked′, *adj.*
un′aspir′ing, *adj.*
un′assail′able, *adj.*
un′assail′ably, *adv.*
un′assailed′, *adj.*
un′assayed′, *adj.*
un′assert′ed, *adj.*
un′assert′ive, *adj.*
un′assign′able, *adj.*
un′assigned′, *adj.*
un′assim′ilable, *adj.*
un′assim′ilat′ed, *adj.*
un′assist′ed, *adj.*
un′asso′ciat′ed, *adj.*
un′assuage′able, *adj.*
un′assuaged′, *adj.*
un′aston′ished, *adj.*
un′aton′able, *adj.*
un′atoned′, *adj.*
un′attain′abil′ity, *n.*
un′attain′able, *adj.*
un′attain′ableness, *n.*
un′attain′ably, *adv.*
un′attained′, *adj.*
un′attest′ed, *adj.*
un′attired′, *adj.*
un′attrac′tive, *adj.*
un′attrac′tively, *adv.*
un′attrac′tiveness, *n.*
unau′dited, *adj.*
un′augment′ed, *adj.*
un′authen′ticat′ed, *adj.*
un′authentic′ity, *n.*
un′author′itative, *adj.*
unau′thorized′, *adj.*
un′avail′able, *adj.*
un′avail′ableness, *n.*
un′avenged′, *adj.*
un′avert′able, *adj.*
un′avowed′, *adj.*
un′awak′ened, *adj.*
unawed′, *adj.*
unbag′, *v.t.*
unbail′able, *adj.*
unbait′ed, *adj.*
unbaked′, *adj.*

unbalanced (ŭn băl′ənst), *adj.* **1.** not balanced, or not properly balanced. **2.** lacking steadiness and soundness of judgement. **3.** mentally disordered or deranged. **4.** (of an account) not adjusted; not brought to an equality of debits and credits.

unballasted (ŭn băl′əs tĭd), *adj.* **1.** not ballasted. **2.** not properly steadied or regulated.

unbank (ŭn băngk′), *v.t.* to remove material from (a fire that has been banked).

unbar (ŭn bä′), *v.t., v.i.*, **-barred, -barring. 1.** to remove a bar or bars from. **2.** to open; unlock.

unbated (ŭn bā′tĭd), *adj.* unabated.

unbearable (ŭn bēə′rə bl), *adj.* not bearable; unendurable; intolerable. —**unbear′ableness,** *n.* —**unbear′ably,** *adv.*

unbeatable (ŭn bē′tə bl), *adj.* **1.** not able to be beaten or overtaken; unsurpassable. **2.** supremely good or excellent.

unbeaten (ŭn bē′tn), *adj.* **1.** not defeated. **2.** untrodden: *unbeaten paths.* **3.** not struck or pounded.

unbecoming (ŭn′bĭ kŭm′ĭng), *adj.* **1.** not becoming; not appropriate; unsuited. **2.** improper; unseemly. **3.** (of clothing, etc.) unattractively inappropriate. —**un′becom′ingly,** *adv.* —**un′becom′ingness,** *n.* —**Syn.** 2. See **improper.**

unbeknown (ŭn′bĭ nōn′), *adj. Colloq.* unknown; unperceived; without a person's knowledge (usually fol. by *to*, and often used adverbially): *unbeknown to her, he was married already.* Also, **unbeknownst** (ŭn′bĭ nōnst′).

unbelief (ŭn′bĭ lēf′), *n.* lack of belief; disbelief, esp. in divine revelation or in the truth of the gospel.

unbeliever (ŭn′bĭ lē′və), *n.* **1.** one who does not believe. **2.** one who does not accept any, or some particular, religious belief.

unbelieving (ŭn′bĭ lē′vĭng), *adj.* **1.** not believing; sceptical. **2.** not accepting any, or some particular, religious belief. —**un′believ′ingly,** *adv.* —**un′believ′ingness,** *n.*

unbelt (ŭn bĕlt′), *v.t.* **1.** to remove the belt from. **2.** to unbuckle or untie the belt of. **3.** to remove by undoing a supporting belt, as a sword.

unbend (ŭn bĕnd′), *v.*, **-bent** or **-bended, -bending.** —*v.t.* **1.** to release from the strain of effort or close application; relax by laying aside formality. **2.** to release from tension, as a bow. **3.** to straighten from a bent form or position. **4.** *Naut.* **a.** to loose or untie, as a sail, rope, etc. **b.** to unfasten from spars or stays, as sails. —*v.i.* **5.** to relax the strictness of formality or ceremony; act in an easy, genial manner. **6.** to become unbent.

unbending (ŭn bĕn′dĭng), *adj.* **1.** not bending; rigid; unyielding; inflexible. **2.** stern; rigorous; resolute. —*n.* **3.** a relaxing or easing. —**unbend′ingly,** *adv.* —**unbend′ingness,** *n.*

unbent (ŭn bĕnt′), *v.* **1.** pt. and pp. of **unbend.** —*adj.* **2.** not bent; unbowed. **3.** not forced to yield or submit.

unbeseeming (ŭn′bĭ sē′mĭng), *adj. Obs.* not beseeming; unbecoming. —**un′beseem′ingly,** *adv.* —**un′beseem′ingness,** *n.*

unbiased (ŭn bī′əst), *adj.* not biased; unprejudiced; impartial. Also, **unbiassed.** —**unbi′asedly,** *adv.* —**unbi′asedness,** *n.*

unbidden (ŭn bĭd′n), *adj.* **1.** not commanded; spontaneous. **2.** uninvited. Also, **unbid′.**

unbind (ŭn bīnd′), *v.t.*, **-bound, -binding. 1.** to release from bands or restraint, as a prisoner; free. **2.** to unfasten or loose, as a band or tie. [ME; OE *unbindan*, c. G *entbinden.* See UN-², BIND, v.]

unbitted (ŭn bĭt′ĭd), *adj.* **1.** not bitted or bridled. **2.** uncontrolled.

unblenched (ŭn blĕncht′), *adj. Obs.* undaunted.

unblessed (ŭn blĕst′), *adj.* **1.** excluded from a blessing. **2.** unhallowed; unholy. **3.** unhappy; wretched. Also, **unblest.** —**unblessedness** (ŭn blĕs′ĭd nĭs), *n.*

unblinking (ŭn blĭng′kĭng), *adj.* **1.** not blinking. **2.** without any show of response. **3.** fearless; undismayed. —**unblink′ingly,** *adv.*

unblock (ŭn blŏk′), *v.t.* to remove an obstruction or hindrance from.

unblushing (ŭn blŭsh′ĭng), *adj.* **1.** shameless. **2.** not blushing. —**unblush′ingly,** *adv.* —**unblush′ingness,** *n.*

unbodied (ŭn bŏd′ĭd), *adj. Poetic.* **1.** incorporeal. **2.** disembodied.

unbolt (ŭn bōlt′), *v.t.* **1.** to draw the bolt of (a door, etc.). **2.** to open, dismantle, release, or the like, by the removal of threaded bolts.

unbolted¹ (ŭn bōl′tĭd), *adj.* not fastened, as a door. [f. UN-¹ + BOLT¹ + -ED²]

unbolted² (ŭn bōl′tĭd), *adj.* not sifted, as grain. [f. UN-¹ + BOLT² + -ED²]

unboned (ŭn bōnd′), *adj.* **1.** boneless. **2.** not having the bones removed.

unbonnet (ŭn bŏn′ĭt), *v.i.* **1.** to uncover the head, as in respect. —*v.t.* **2.** to take off the bonnet from.

unbonneted (ŭn bŏn′ĭ tĭd), *adj.* bareheaded.

unborn (ŭn bôn′), *adj.* **1.** not yet born; yet to come; future: *ages unborn.* **2.** of a baby, still in the womb.

unbosom (ŭn bo͝oz′əm), *v.t.* **1.** to disclose (one's thoughts, feelings, etc.) esp. in confidence. **2. unbosom oneself,** to disclose (one's thoughts, etc., to another person). —*v.i.* **3.** to disclose one's thoughts, feelings, secrets, etc. [f. UN-² + BOSOM, v.] —**unbos′omer,** *n.*

unbottle (ŭn bŏt′l), *v.t.* to let out from or as from a bottle.

unbound (ŭn bound′), *v.* **1.** pt. and pp. of **unbind.** —*adj.* **2.** not bound, as a book.

unbounded (ŭn boun′dĭd), *adj.* **1.** unlimited; boundless. **2.** unrestrained; uncontrolled. —**unbound′edly,** *adv.* —**unbound′edness,** *n.*

unbowed (ŭn boud′), *adj.* **1.** not bowed or bent. **2.** not yielding or submitting.

unbrace (ŭn brās′), *v.t.*, **-braced, -bracing. 1.** to free from tension; relax. **2.** to weaken. **3.** *Obs.* to remove the braces of.

unbraid (ŭn brād′), *v.t.* to separate (anything braided, as hair) into its several strands.

unbranded (ŭn brăn′dĭd), *adj.* (of goods placed on sale) not bearing a manufacturer's label or trademark.

unbred (ŭn brĕd′), *adj. Obs.* **1.** ill-bred. **2.** not taught or trained.

unbreech (ŭn brēch′), *v.t.* **1.** to take off the trousers of (a person). **2.** *Obs. Mil.* to remove the breech from (a gun).

unbrick (ŭn brĭk′), *v.t.* **1.** to remove bricks from, as to set free. **2.** to reveal; free.

unbridle (ŭn brī′dl), *v.t.*, **-dled, -dling. 1.** to remove the bridle from (a horse, etc.). **2.** to free from restraint.

unbridled (ŭn brī′dld), *adj.* **1.** unrestrained or uncontrolled. **2.** not having a bridle on, as a horse.

un-British (ŭn brĭt′ĭsh), *adj.* not characteristic of Britain; opposed to British interests or standards.

unbroken (ŭn brō′kən), *adj.* **1.** whole; intact. **2.** not subdued or crushed, as one's spirit. **3.** uninterrupted; continuous. **4.** not tamed. **5.** undisturbed; unimpaired. **6.** (of a record) not improved on. **7.** (of a law) not infringed. Also, *Obs.*, **unbroke′.** —**unbro′kenly,** *adv.* —**unbro′kenness,** *n.*

unbuckle (ŭn bŭk′l), *v.t., v.i.*, **-led, -ling.** —*v.t.* **1.** to unfasten the buckle or buckles of; remove by unfastening the buckles of. —*v.i.* **2.** to unfasten buckles.

unbuild (ŭn bĭld′), *v.t.*, **-built, -building.** to demolish (something built); raze.

unbuilt (ŭn bĭlt′), *adj.* **1.** not yet built, as a structure. **2.** (fol. by *on* or *upon*) not yet built on, as land.

unburden (ŭn bû′dn), *v.t.* **1.** to free from a burden. **2.** to relieve (one's mind, conscience, etc., or oneself) by disclosure or confession of something. **3.** to cast off or get rid of, as a burden or something burdensome; disclose; reveal. Also, **unburthen.**

---

unbaled′, *adj.*
unban′dage, *v.t.*
un′baptized′, *adj.*
unbarbed′, *adj.*
unbar′bered, *adj.*
unbarred′, *adj.*
unbash′ful, *adj.*
unbathed′, *adj.*
unbeard′ed, *adj.*
unbeau′teous, *adj.*
unbeau′tified′, *adj.*
unbeau′tiful, *adj.*
unbed′, *v.t.*
unbed′ded, *adj.*
un′befit′ting, *adj.*
un′befriend′ed, *adj.*
un′beget′, *v.t.*
unbegged′, *adj.*
un′begin′ning, *adj.*
un′begot′ten, *adj.*
un′begun′, *adj.*
un′believ′able, *adj.*
un′believ′ably, *adv.*
un′believe′, *v.t., v.i.*
un′believed′, *adj.*
unbelt′ed, *adj.*
unben′eficed, *adj.*
un′benefi′cial, *adj.*
unben′efited, *adj.*
un′benev′olent, *adj.*
un′betrayed′, *adj.*
un′betrothed′, *adj.*
unbet′terable, *adj.*
unbet′tered, *adj.*
unbev′elled, *adj.*
un′bewil′dered, *adj.*
unbib′lical, *adj.*
unbid′dable, *adj.*
unbig′oted, *adj.*
unbleached′, *adj.*
unblem′ished, *adj.*
unblend′ed, *adj.*
unblind′ed, *adj.*
unblood′ed, *adj.*
unblood′ied, *adj.*
unblood′y, *adj.*
unblot′ted, *adj.*
unblown′, *adj.*
unblunt′ed, *adj.*
unboast′ful, *adj.*
unboiled′, *adj.*
unbooked′, *adj.*
unbook′ish, *adj.*
unboot′, *v.t., v.i.*
unbought′, *adj.*
unbranched′, *adj.*
unbreak′able, *adj.*
unbreath′able, *adj.*
unbreath′ing, *adj.*
unbrib′able, *adj.*
unbribed′, *adj.*
unbroth′erliness, *n.*
unbroth′erly, *adj.*
unbruised′, *adj.*
unbur′nished, *adj.*
unburnt′, *adj.*
unburst′, *adj.*
unbur′y, *v.t.*

---

unbusinesslike (ŭn bĭz′nĭs līk′), *adj.* not methodical or efficient; vague; unconcerned with the aims or principles of business.

unbutton (ŭn bŭt′n), *v.t.* **1.** to unfasten the button or buttons of (a garment, etc., or a person). **2.** to unfasten (a button). —*v.i.* **3.** to unfasten one's buttons. **4.** to relax one's formality.

unbuttoned (ŭn bŭt′nd), *adj.* **1.** having the buttons unfastened. **2.** not having a button or buttons. **3.** informal or relaxed.

uncage (ŭn kāj′), *v.t.*, **-caged, -caging.** to release from or as from a cage.

uncalculated (ŭn kăl′kyōō lā′tĭd), *adj.* **1.** not determined by calculation. **2.** not deliberate; unexpected.

uncalculating (ŭn kăl′kyōō lā′tĭng), *adj.* **1.** not calculating or scheming. **2.** not planning or trying to achieve a particular aim.

uncalled-for (ŭn kôld′fô′), *adj.* unnecessary and improper; unwarranted.

uncanny (ŭn kăn′ĭ), *adj.* **1.** such as to arouse superstitious uneasiness; unnaturally strange. **2.** preternaturally good: *uncanny judgement.* —**uncan′nily,** *adv.* —**uncan′niness,** *n.* —**Syn. 1.** See **weird.**

uncanonical (ŭn′kə nŏn′ĭ kl), *adj.* **1.** not in accordance with canons or rules. **2.** not belonging to the canon of Scripture. **3.** unsuitable for a clergyman. —**un′canon′ically,** *adv.*

uncap (ŭn kăp′), *v.*, **-capped, -capping.** —*v.t.* **1.** to remove the cap from (the head of a person). **2.** to remove a cap or cover from. —*v.i.* **3.** to remove the cap from the head, as in respect.

uncapable (ŭn kā′pə bl), *adj. Obs.* incapable.

uncareful (ŭn kĕə′fəl), *adj.* **1.** careless. **2.** inconsiderate. **3.** carefree. —**uncare′fully,** *adv.* —**uncare′fulness,** *n.*

uncase (ŭn kās′), *v.t.*, **-cased, -casing. 1.** to remove from its case; take the case or casing off. **2.** to strip or bare. **3.** to reveal; make known.

uncaused (ŭn kôzd′), *adj.* not resulting from a prior cause; self-existent.

uncensored (ŭn sĕn′səd), *adj.* **1.** not altered by a censor, as a publication or film. **2.** not criticized adversely, disapproved of, or reproved.

unceremonious (ŭn′sĕ rĭ mō′nyəs), *adj.* not ceremonious; informal; abrupt or rude. —**un′ceremo′niously,** *adv.* —**un′ceremo′niousness,** *n.*

uncert., uncertain.

uncertain (ŭn sû′tn), *adj.* **1.** not definitely or surely known; doubtful. **2.** not confident, assured, or decided. **3.** not fixed or determined. **4.** doubtful; vague; indistinct. **5.** not to be depended on. **6.** subject to change; variable; capricious. **7.** dependent on chance. **8.** unsteady or fitful, as light. —**uncer′tainly,** *adv.* —**uncer′tainness,** *n.*

—**Syn.** 1. UNCERTAIN, INSECURE, PRECARIOUS imply lacking in predictability. That which is UNCERTAIN is doubtful or problematical, it often involves danger through an inability to predict or to place confidence in the unknown: *the time of his arrival is uncertain.* That which is INSECURE is not firm, stable, reliable, or safe, and hence is likely to give way, fail, or be overcome: *an insecure foundation, footing, protection.* PRECARIOUS suggests great liability to failure, or exposure to imminent danger: *precarious means of existence.* —**Ant.** 1. definite, sure.

uncertainty (ŭn sû′tn tĭ), *n.*, *pl.* **-ties. 1.** an uncertain state or mood. **2.** unpredictability; indefiniteness. **3.** something uncertain.

uncertainty principle, *Physics.* the principle, first stated by W. Heisenberg, that it is not possible to determine simultaneously with complete accuracy both the position and momentum of a particle, as an electron. Accurate measurement of one leads to inevitable inaccuracy in the measurement of the other, so that the product of both uncertainties is never less than $\frac{h}{2\pi}$ where h is Planck's constant. Also, **Heisenberg's uncertainty principle, the indeterminacy principle.**

unchain (ŭn chān′), *v.t.* **1.** to free from chains. **2.** to set free; release.

unchancy (ŭn chăn′sĭ), *adj. Chiefly Scot.* **1.** unlucky. **2.** dangerous. [f. UN-[1] + CHANCY]

uncharge (ŭn chäj′), *v.t.*, **-charged, -charging.** *Obs.* to free from a load, charge, or burden; unload; relieve.

uncharitable (ŭn chă′rĭ tə bl), *adj.* **1.** unforgiving; harsh; censorious. **2.** miserly. —**unchar′itableness,** *n.* —**unchar′itably,** *adv.*

uncharted (ŭn chä′tĭd), *adj.* not mapped; unexplored; unknown, as a remote region.

unchartered (ŭn chä′təd), *adj.* **1.** without a charter. **2.** without regulation; lawless.

unchaste (ŭn chāst′), *adj.* **1.** not chaste or virtuous, as persons. **2.** marked by lewdness or sexual excess, as life, habits, etc. —**unchaste′ly,** *adv.* —**unchaste′ness, unchastity** (ŭn chăs′tĭ tĭ), *n.*

unchristian (ŭn krĭs′chən), *adj.* **1.** not Christian. **2.** unworthy of Christians; uncharitable; improper. —**unchris′tianly,** *adv.*

unchurch (ŭn chûch′), *v.t.* **1.** to expel (individuals) from a church; excommunicate. **2.** to divest of the status and nature of a church. **3.** to deprive of the authority over, or possession of the building of, or jurisdiction within, a church. **4.** to exclude (an entire group, body, or sect) from membership of the church. [f. UN-[2] + CHURCH]

uncial (ŭn′sĭ əl), *adj.* **1.** designating, written in, or pertaining to ancient majuscule letters distinguished from capital majuscules by relatively great roundness, inclination, and inequality in height. **2.** pertaining to an inch or an ounce. **3.** pertaining to the duodecimal system. —*n.* **4.** an uncial letter. **5.** uncial writing. **6.** a manuscript in uncials. [t. L: s. *unciālis* pertaining to an inch] —**un′cially,** *adv.*

Uncials (Latin) 8th century

unciform (ŭn′sĭ fôm′), *adj.* **1.** hook-shaped. —*n.* **2.** *Anat.* a bone of the carpus with a hooklike process projecting from the palmar surface. [t. NL: s. *unciformis,* f. *unci-* (comb. form repr. L *uncus* hook) + *-formis* -FORM]

uncinariasis (ŭn′sĭ nə rī′ə sĭs), *n.* hookworm disease. [t. NL: f. *Uncinār(ia)* genus of hookworms (der. L *uncīnus* hook) + *-iāsis* -IASIS]

uncinate (ŭn′sĭ nĭt, -nāt′), *adj. Biol.* hooked; bent at the end like a hook. Also, **uncinal** (ŭn′sĭ nəl), **un′cinat′ed.** [t. L: m. s. *uncinātus*]

Uncinate prickles

uncinus (ŭn sī′nəs), *n.*, *pl.* **uncini** (ŭn sī′nī). *Zool.* any small hooked structure such as one of the marginal teeth of the radula of a gastropod mollusc. [L: hooked]

uncircumcised (ŭn sû′kəm sīzd′), *adj.* **1.** not circumcised. **2.** not Jewish; gentile. **3.** not spiritually purified; irreligious; heathen.

uncircumcision (ŭn′sû kəm sĭzh′ən), *n.* **1.** condition of being uncircumcised. **2.** *Rare.* gentiles collectively.

uncivil (ŭn sĭv′əl), *adj.* **1.** without good manners; rude; impolite; discourteous. **2.** uncivilized. —**uncivility** (ŭn′sĭ vĭl′ĭ tĭ), **unciv′ilness,** *n.* —**unciv′illy,** *adv.*

uncivilized (ŭn sĭv′ĭ līzd′), *adj.* barbarous; unenlightened. Also, **uncivilised.**

unclad (ŭn klăd′), *v.* **1.** pt. and pp. of **unclothe.** —*adj.* **2.** not clad; unclothed.

unclasp (ŭn kläsp′), *v.t.* **1.** to undo the clasp or clasps of; unfasten. **2.** to release from the grasp, as something held. —*v.i.* **3.** to become unclasped, as the hands, etc. **4.** to release or relax the grasp.

---

unbut′tered, *adj.*
uncal′cined, *adj.*
uncalled′, *adj.*
uncan′did, *adj.*
uncan′didly, *adv.*
uncan′dour, *n.*
uncan′onized′, *adj.*
uncan′vassed, *adj.*
un′capsiz′able, *adj.*
uncap′tained, *adj.*
uncap′tured, *adj.*
uncared′-for′, *adj.*
uncar′ing, *adj.*
uncar′peted, *adj.*
uncart′, *v.t.*
uncarved′, *adj.*
uncashed′, *adj.*
un′castrat′ed, *adj.*
uncat′alogued′, *adj.*
uncat′echized′, *adj.*
uncath′olic, *adj.*
uncaught′, *adj.*
unceas′ing, *adj.*
unceas′ingly, *adv.*
uncel′ebrat′ed, *adj.*
un′censor′ious, *adj.*
un′certif′icat′ed, *adj.*
uncer′tified′, *adj.*
unchal′lengeable, *adj.*
unchal′lengeably, *adv.*
unchange′able, *adj.*
unchange′ably, *adv.*
unchanged′, *adj.*
unchang′ing, *adj.*
unchang′ingly, *adv.*
unchap′eroned′, *adj.*
un′char′acteris′tic, *adj.*
un′char′acteris′tically, *adv.*
uncharm′ing, *adj.*
uncharred′, *adj.*
uncha′stened, *adj.*
un′chastised′, *adj.*
uncheck′able, *adj.*
unchecked′, *adj.*
uncheered′, *adj.*
uncheer′ful, *adj.*
uncheer′fully, *adv.*
uncheer′fulness, *n.*
uncheer′ing, *adj.*
unchild′ish, *adj.*
unchilled′, *adj.*
unchipped′, *adj.*
unchis′elled, *adj.*
unchiv′alrous, *adj.*
unchiv′alrously, *adv.*
uncho′sen, *adj.*
unchris′tened, *adj.*
unchron′icled, *adj.*
un′chronolog′ical, *adj.*
uncir′cumscribed′, *adj.*
uncir′cumspect′, *adj.*
uncit′ed, *adj.*
unclaimed′, *adj.*
unclamp′, *v.t.*
unclar′ified′, *adj.*
unclassed′, *adj.*
unclas′sical, *adj.*

unclassified (ŭn klăs′ĭ fīd′), *adj.* **1.** not arranged in some order or according to some classification. **2.** (of information) not secret. **3.** (of football results) not arranged in divisions. **4.** (of roads) not having a classification number; maintained by a local authority.

uncle (ŭng′kl), *n.* **1.** a brother of one's father or mother. **2.** an aunt's husband. **3.** *Slang.* a pawnbroker. **4.** a familiar title applied to any elderly man. **5. talk like a Dutch uncle,** talk severely (to someone). [ME, t. AF, g. L *avunculus* mother's brother] —**un′cle-less′,** *adj.*

unclean (ŭn klēn′), *adj.* **1.** morally or spiritually impure. **2.** ceremonially or ritually defiled. **3.** (of food) unfit to be eaten; forbidden. **4.** physically defiled or defiling; foul; dirty.

uncleanly[1] (ŭn klēn′lĭ), *adv.* in an unclean manner. [f. UNCLEAN + -LY]

uncleanly[2] (ŭn klĕn′lĭ), *adj.* not cleanly; unclean. [f. UN-[1] + CLEANLY] —**unclean′liness,** *n.*

unclench (ŭn klĕnch′), *v.t., v.i.* to open or become opened from a clenched state.

Uncle Sam (săm), a personification of the government or people of the United States. [extension of the initials *U.S.*]

Uncle Tom, *U.S.* (usually in contemptuous use) a Negro who is openly servile to whites. [after the principal character in Harriet Beecher Stowe's '*Uncle Tom's Cabin*']

uncloak (ŭn klōk′), *v.t.* **1.** to remove the cloak from. **2.** to reveal; expose. —*v.i.* **3.** to take off the cloak, or the outer garments generally.

unclog (ŭn klŏg′), *v.t.,* **-clogged, -clogging.** to free from being clogged or from anything that clogs.

unclose (ŭn klōz′), *v.t., v.i.,* **-closed, -closing.** to bring or come out of a closed state; open.

unclothe (ŭn klōth′), *v.t.,* **-clothed** or **-clad, -clothing. 1.** to strip of clothes. **2.** to strip of anything; divest; uncover.

unclubbable (ŭn klŭb′ə bl), *adj.* (of a person) unsuitable or unwilling to be fitted into a club and its rules. —**un′clubbabil′ity,** *n.*

unco (ŭng′kō), *adj., adv., n., pl.* **-cos.** *Scot. and N Dial.* —*adj.* **1.** remarkable; extraordinary. **2.** unknown; strange. **3.** uncanny. —*adv.* **4.** remarkably; extremely. —*n.* **5.** something extraordinary. **6.** (*pl.*) news. **7.** *Obs.* a stranger. [var. of UNCOUTH]

uncoil (ŭn koil′), *v.t.* **1.** to unwind. —*v.i.* **2.** to unwind itself.

uncome-at-able (ŭn′kŭm ăt′ə bl), *adj.* inaccessible; unattainable.

uncomfortable (ŭn kŭmf′tə bl), *adj.* **1.** causing discomfort; disquieting. **2.** in a state of discomfort; uneasy; ill-at-ease. —**uncom′fortableness,** *n.* —**uncom′fortably,** *adv.*

uncommercial (ŭn′kə mû′shəl), *adj.* **1.** not engaged in commerce or trade. **2.** not in accordance with commercial principles or practices. **3.** not likely to be commercially successful. **4.** not profit-seeking.

uncommitted (ŭn′kə mĭt′ĭd), *adj.* **1.** not committed, esp. not bound by pledge or assurance, as to a course or party. **2.** not having a particular point of view; not partisan.

uncommon (ŭn kŏm′ən), *adj.* **1.** not common; unusual or rare. **2.** unusual in amount or degree; above the ordinary. **3.** exceptional. —*adv.* **4.** very; remarkably. —**uncom′monness,** *n.* —**Syn. 1.** scarce, infrequent.

uncommonly (ŭn kŏm′ən lĭ), *adv.* **1.** in an uncommon or unusual degree; remarkably. **2.** rarely; infrequently.

uncommunicative (ŭn′kə myōō′nĭ kə tĭv), *adj.* not disposed to impart information, opinions, etc.; reserved; taciturn. —**un′commu′nicatively,** *adv.* —**un′commu′nicativeness,** *n.*

uncompromising (ŭn kŏm′prə mī′zĭng), *adj.* not admitting of compromise; unyielding; inflexible. —**uncom′promis′ingly,** *adv.*

unconcern (ŭn′kən sûn′), *n.* lack of concern; freedom from solicitude or anxiety; indifference. —**Syn.** See **indifference.**

unconcerned (ŭn′kən sûnd′), *adj.* **1.** not concerned; disinterested; free from solicitude or anxiety; uninterested. **2.** not involved (with) or taking part (in). —**unconcernedly** (ŭn′kən sû′nĭd lĭ), *adv.* —**un′concern′edness,** *n.*

unconditional (ŭn′kən dĭsh′ə nəl), *adj.* not limited by conditions; absolute: *an unconditional promise.* —**un′condi′tional′ity, un′condi′tionalness,** *n.* —**un′condi′tionally,** *adv.*

unconditioned (ŭn′kən dĭsh′ənd), *adj.* **1.** not subject to conditions; absolute. **2.** *Psychol.* unlearned; natural; innate. Cf. **conditioned reflex** or **response.**

unconfessed (ŭn′kən fĕst′), *adj.* **1.** not admitted, confessed, or avowed. **2.** not having received confession from a priest.

unconformable (ŭn′kən fô′mə bl), *adj.* **1.** not conformable; not conforming. **2.** *Geol.* denoting discontinuity of any type in stratigraphic sequence. —**un′conform′abil′ity,** *n.* —**un′conform′ably,** *adv.*

unconformity (ŭn′kən fô′mĭ tĭ), *n., pl.* **-ties. 1.** lack of conformity; incongruity; inconsistency. **2.** *Geol.* **a.** a discontinuity in rock sequence denoting interruption of sedimentation, commonly accompanied by erosion of rocks below the break. **b.** the fault plane separating such strata.

unconnected (ŭn′kə nĕk′tĭd), *adj.* **1.** not connected; separate; distinct (sometimes fol. by *with*). **2.** not internally coherent, as a piece of writing; disunited; broken up. —**un′connect′edly,** *adv.* —**un′connect′edness,** *n.*

unconscionable (ŭn kŏn′shə nə bl), *adj.* **1.** unreasonably excessive. **2.** not in accordance with what is just or reasonable: *unconscionable behaviour.* **3.** not guided by conscience; unscrupulous. —**uncon′scionableness,** *n.* —**uncon′scionably,** *adv.*

unconscious (ŭn kŏn′chəs), *adj.* **1.** not conscious; unaware. **2.** temporarily devoid of consciousness. **3.** not endowed with knowledge of one's own existence, etc. **4.** occurring below the level of conscious thought. **5.** unintentional: *an unconscious slight.* **6.** *Psychol.* pertaining to mental processes which the individual cannot bring into consciousness. —*n.* **7. the unconscious,** *Psychol.* an organization of the mind containing all psychic material not available in the immediate field of awareness. —**uncon′sciously,** *adv.* —**uncon′sciousness,** *n.*

unconsidered (ŭn′kən sĭd′əd), *adj.* **1.** not considered or thought worthy of consideration; not paid attention to; unimportant. **2.** not resulting from or accompanied by consideration, esp. prior consideration; careless or unthinking.

unconstitutional (ŭn′kŏn stĭ tyōō′shə nəl), *adj.* not constitutional; unauthorized by, contrary to, or inconsistent

unclas′sifi′able, *adj.*
uncleaned′, *adj.*
uncleansed′, *adj.*
unclear′, *adj.*
uncleared′, *adj.*
unclear′ly, *adv.*
unclear′ness, *n.*
uncler′ical, *adj.*
unclimb′able, *adj.*
unclimbed′, *adj.*
unclipped′, *adj.*
unclois′ter, *v.t.*
unclois′tered, *adj.*
uncloud′ed, *adj.*
uncloud′y, *adj.*
unclutch′, *v.t.*
un′coag′ulat′ed, *adj.*
uncoat′ed, *adj.*
uncock′, *v.t.*
uncocked′, *adj.*
uncof′fined, *adj.*
un′collat′ed, *adj.*
un′collect′ed, *adj.*
uncol′oured, *adj.*
uncome′liness, *n.*
uncome′ly, *adj.*
un′command′ed, *adj.*
un′commend′able, *adj.*
un′commend′ably, *adv.*
un′commis′sioned, *adj.*
un′commu′nicable, *adj.*
un′commu′nicably, *adv.*
un′commu′nicat′ed, *adj.*
un′commu′nicat′ing, *adj.*
un′commut′ed, *adj.*
un′compact′ed, *adj.*
un′compan′ionable, *adj.*
un′compas′sionate, *adj.*
un′compelled′, *adj.*
uncom′pensat′ed, *adj.*
un′compet′itive, *adj.*
un′complain′ing, *adj.*
un′complain′ingly, *adv.*
un′compli′ant, *adj.*
uncom′plicat′ed, *adj.*
un′complimen′tary, *adj.*
un′compound′ed, *adj.*
un′comprehend′ed, *adj.*
un′comprehend′ing, *adj.*
un′comprehen′sive, *adj.*
un′compressed′, *adj.*
un′concealed′, *adj.*
un′conceiv′able, *adj.*
un′conceiv′ably, *adv.*
un′conceived′, *adj.*
un′concil′iat′ing, *adj.*
un′conclud′ed, *adj.*
un′condemned′, *adj.*
un′condensed′, *adj.*
un′condu′cive, *adj.*
uncon′fident, *adj.*
un′confid′ing, *adj.*
un′confin′able, *adj.*
un′confined′, *adj.*
un′confirmed′, *adj.*
un′confused′, *adj.*
un′confus′edly, *adv.*
un′confut′able, *adj.*
un′confut′ed, *adj.*
un′congealed′, *adj.*
un′conge′nial, *adj.*
un′conge′nial′ity, *n.*
un′conjec′turable, *adj.*
un′conjec′tured, *adj.*
uncon′querable, *adj.*
uncon′querably, *adv.*
uncon′quered, *adj.*
un′conscien′tious, *adj.*
un′conscien′tiously, *adv.*
un′conscien′tiousness, *n.*
uncon′secrat′ed, *adj.*
un′consent′ing, *adj.*
un′consol′idat′ed, *adj.*
un′constrained′, *adj.*
un′constrain′edly, *adv.*
un′constraint′, *n.*
un′construc′tive, *adj.*
un′consult′ed, *adj.*
un′consumed′, *adj.*
uncon′summat′ed, *adj.*
un′contam′inat′ed, *adj.*
uncon′templat′ed, *adj.*
un′conten′tious, *adj.*
un′contest′able, *adj.*
un′contest′ed, *adj.*
un′contract′ed, *adj.*
un′contradict′able, *adj.*
un′contradict′ably, *adv.*
un′contradict′ed, *adj.*
un′control′labil′ity, *n.*
un′control′lable, *adj.*
un′control′lably, *adv.*
un′controlled′, *adj.*
un′controver′sial, *adj.*
uncon′trovert′ed, *adj.*
un′controvert′ible, *adj.*
un′controvert′ibly, *adv.*

with the constitution, as of a country. —**un′constitu′tional′ity,** *n.* —**un′constitu′tionally,** *adv.*

unconventional (ŭn′kən vĕn′shə nəl), *adj.* not conventional; not bound by or conforming to convention, rule, or precedent; free from conventionality. —**un′conven′tionally,** *adv.*

unconventionality (ŭn′kən vĕn′shə năl′ĭ tĭ), *n.*, *pl.* **-ties.** **1.** disregard for or freedom from rules and precedents; originality. **2.** something unconventional, as an act.

uncork (ŭn kôk′), *v.t.* to draw the cork from.

uncounted (ŭn koun′tĭd), *adj.* **1.** not counted. **2.** innumerable.

uncouple (ŭn kŭp′l), *v.t.*, **-pled, -pling.** to undo from being coupled; disconnect.

uncourteous (ŭn kû′tyəs), *adj.* discourteous. —**uncour′teously,** *adv.* —**uncour′teousness,** *n.*

uncourtly (ŭn kôt′lĭ), *adj.* not courtly; rude. —**uncourt′liness,** *n.*

uncouth (ŭn ko͞oth′), *adj.* **1.** awkward, clumsy, or unmannerly, as persons, behaviour, actions, etc. **2.** strange and ungraceful in appearance or form. **3.** unusual or strange. [ME; OE *uncūth* (f. *un-* UN-[1] + *cūth*, pp., known), c. D *onkond*] —**uncouth′ly,** *adv.* —**uncouth′ness,** *n.*

uncovenanted (ŭn kŭv′ĭ nən tĭd), *adj.* **1.** not agreed to or promised by covenant. **2.** not having joined in a covenant.

uncover (ŭn kŭv′ə), *v.t.* **1.** to lay bare; disclose; reveal. **2.** to remove the cover or covering from. **3.** to remove (the hat, or other head covering). —*v.i.* **4.** to remove a cover or covering. **5.** to take off one's hat or other head covering, as in respect.

uncovered (ŭn kŭv′əd), *adj.* **1.** having no cover or covering. **2.** having the head bare. **3.** not protected by security, as a debt.

uncritical (ŭn krĭt′ĭ kl), *adj.* **1.** disinclined to make critical analysis: *an uncritical reader.* **2.** without discrimination or critical perception. **3.** not in accordance with the rules of just criticism: *an uncritical estimate.* —**uncrit′ically,** *adv.*

uncross (ŭn krŏs′), *v.t.* to remove from a crossed position: *to uncross one's legs.*

uncrossed (ŭn krŏst′), *adj.* **1.** (of a cheque) not crossed; negotiable. **2.** not thwarted.

uncrown (ŭn kroun′), *v.t.* **1.** to deprive or divest of a crown. **2.** to reduce from dignity or pre-eminence.

uncrowned (ŭn kround′), *adj.* **1.** not crowned; not having yet assumed the crown. **2.** having royal status or power without royal rank. **3. uncrowned king,** one who is regarded as ruler of his own particular circle: *he was the uncrowned king of the dockers.*

uncrushable (ŭn krŭsh′ə bl), *adj.* **1.** that cannot or cannot easily be crushed. **2.** (of textiles) not retaining the creases when crumpled.

unction (ŭngk′shən), *n.* **1.** the act of anointing, esp. for medical purposes or as a religious rite. **2.** *Relig.* **a.** the act of ceremonial anointing with oil, esp. within the seventh sacrament to strengthen the mortally sick, or at the consecration of a monarch before his coronation, or of an altar or a new church. **b.** the consecrating grace of God bestowed freely on the faithful. **3.** something soothing or comforting. **4.** a soothing, sympathetic, and persuasive quality in discourse, esp. on religious subjects. **5.** a professional, conventional, or affected earnestness or fervour in utterance. [ME, t. L: s. *unctio*] —**unc′tionless,** *adj.*

unctuous (ŭngk′tyo͞o əs), *adj.* **1.** of the nature of or characteristic of an unguent or ointment; oily; greasy. **2.** characterized by religious unction or fervour, esp. of an affected kind; excessively smooth, suave, or bland. **3.** having an oily or soapy feel, as certain minerals. [ME, t. ML: m. s. *unctuōsus*, der. L *unctum* ointment] —**unctuosity** (ŭngk′tyo͞o ŏs′ĭ tĭ), **unc′tuousness,** *n.* —**unc′tuously,** *adv.*

uncurl (ŭn kûl′), *v.t.*, *v.i.* to straighten out, as something curled.

uncustomed (ŭn kŭs′təmd), *adj.* on which customs duty has not been paid.

uncut (ŭn kŭt′), *adj.* **1.** not shortened, condensed, or abridged, as a work of literature, by censorship, etc. **2.** (of a book) not having its pages trimmed at the edges after printing. **3.** (of gems, velvet, etc.) not shaped by cutting. **4.** not cut.

undamped (ŭn dămpt′), *adj.* **1.** undiminished, as energy, spirits, etc. **2.** *Physics.* (of a vibrating string or other oscillation) having no extrinsic restriction on amplitude.

undaunted (ŭn dôn′tĭd), *adj.* not discouraged; fearless; undismayed. —**undaunt′edly,** *adv.* —**undaunt′edness,** *n.*

undé (ŭn′dā), *adj.* *Her.* wavy. Also, **undée.** [t. OF, f. *unde* wave (g. L *unda*) + *-e(e)*, adj. suffix (see -ATE[1])]

undecagon (ŭn dĕk′ə gən), *n.* a polygon having eleven angles and eleven sides. [f. L *undec(im)* eleven + (DEC)-AGON]

undeceive (ŭn′dĭ sēv′), *v.t.*, **-ceived, -ceiving.** to free from deception, fallacy, or mistake. —**un′deceiv′able,** *adj.* —**un′deceiv′er,** *n.*

undecided (ŭn′dĭ sī′dĭd), *adj.* **1.** not decided or determined. **2.** not having one's mind made up; irresolute. —**un′decid′edly,** *adv.* —**un′decid′edness,** *n.*

undecimal (ŭn dĕs′ĭ məl), *adj.* based upon the number eleven.

undecked (ŭn dĕkt′), *adj.* **1.** without a deck, as a ship. **2.** not adorned or embellished.

undecorticated (ŭn′dĭ kô′tĭ kā′tĭd), *adj.* not having had the shell, husk, or back removed.

undefended (ŭn′dĭ fĕn′dĭd), *adj.* **1.** without defences or protection; not defended. **2.** (of a legal action) not defended by counsel; having no defence put forward.

undefined (ŭn′dĭ fīnd′), *adj.* **1.** not definitely limited; indefinite. **2.** not described by definition or explanation; not explained.

undemonstrative (ŭn′dĭ mŏn′strə tĭv), *adj.* reserved; not inclined to demonstrations of enthusiasm, affection, etc. —**un′demon′stratively,** *adv.* —**un′demon′strativeness,** *n.*

undeniable (ŭn′dĭ nī′ə bl), *adj.* **1.** not to be refuted; indisputable. **2.** that cannot be refused. **3.** unquestionably good; unexceptionable. —**un′deni′ableness,** *n.* —**un′deni′ably,** *adv.*

under (ŭn′də), *prep.* **1.** beneath and covered by: *under a table or a tree.* **2.** below the surface of: *under the sea.* **3.** at a point or position lower than or farther down than: *to stand under a window.* **4.** in the position or state of bearing, supporting, sustaining, undergoing, etc.: *to sink under a load; a matter under consideration.* **5.** subject to: *under the influence of drink.* **6.** bearing as a crop: *land under barley.* **7.** beneath (a head, heading, or the like), as in classification. **8.** as designated, indicated, or represented by: *under a new name.* **9.** below in degree, amount, price, etc.; less than: *under age.* **10.** below in rank, dignity, or the like. **11.** subject to the rule, direction, guidance, etc., of: *under supervision; to study under a professor.* **12.** during the reign or

---

un′convers′ant, *adj.*
un′convert′ed, *adj.*
un′convert′ible, *adj.*
un′convict′ed, *adj.*
un′convinced′, *adj.*
un′convinc′edly, *adv.*
un′convinc′ing, *adj.*
uncooked′, *adj.*
uncooled′, *adj.*
un′coop′erative, *adj.*
un′coor′dinat′ed, *adj.*
uncop′ied, *adj.*
un′coquet′tish, *adj.*
uncor′dial, *adj.*
uncor′dially, *adv.*
un′correct′ed, *adj.*
un′corrob′orat′ed, *adj.*
un′corrupt′ed, *adj.*
un′corrupt′edly, *adv.*
uncost′ly, *adj.*
uncoun′selled, *adj.*
uncount′able, *adj.*
uncoun′teract′ed, *adj.*
uncourt′ed, *adj.*
uncov′etous, *adj.*
uncracked′, *adj.*
uncramped′, *adj.*
un′creat′abil′ity, *n.*
un′creat′able, *adj.*
un′creat′ed, *adj.*
un′creat′ive, *adj.*
un′creat′iveness, *n.*
uncred′itable, *adj.*
uncred′ited, *adj.*
uncrip′pled, *adj.*
uncrit′icized′, *adj.*
uncrit′iciz′ing, *adj.*
uncrit′iciz′ingly, *adv.*
uncropped′, *adj.*
uncrowd′ed, *adj.*
uncrushed′, *adj.*
uncrys′talliz′able, *adj.*
uncrys′tallized′, *adj.*
uncul′tivable, *adj.*
uncul′tivat′ed, *adj.*
uncul′tured, *adj.*
uncurbed′, *adj.*
uncured′, *adj.*
un′curtailed′, *adj.*
uncur′tain, *v.t.*
uncur′tained, *adj.*
uncus′tomary, *adj.*
undam′aged, *adj.*
undarned′, *adj.*
undashed′, *adj.*
undat′ed, *adj.*
undaz′zled, *adj.*
undead′ened, *adj.*
undealt′, *adj.*
un′debased′, *adj.*
un′debat′able, *adj.*
un′debat′ed, *adj.*
un′debauched′, *adj.*
un′decid′able, *adj.*
un′deci′pherable, *adj.*
un′deci′pherabil′ity, *n.*
un′declared′, *adj.*
un′decomposed′, *adj.*
undec′orat′ed, *adj.*
un′defaced′, *adj.*
un′defeat′ed, *adj.*
un′defiled′, *adj.*
un′defin′able, *adj.*
un′defin′ably, *adv.*
un′deformed′, *adj.*
un′defrayed′, *adj.*
un′degen′erate, *adj.*
un′delayed′, *adj.*
undel′egat′ed, *adj.*
un′delib′erate, *adj.*
un′delib′erat′ed, *adj.*
un′deliv′erable, *adj.*
un′deliv′ered, *adj.*
un′delud′ed, *adj.*
un′demand′ed, *adj.*
un′demand′ing, *adj.*
un′democrat′ic, *adj.*
un′democrat′ically, *adv.*
un′demon′strable, *adj.*
undem′onstrat′ed, *adj.*
un′denied′, *adj.*
un′denom′ina′tional, *adj.*
un′depend′able, *adj.*
un′depend′ably, *adv.*
un′depre′ciat′ed, *adj.*
un′depressed′, *adj.*

---

rule of. **13.** subject to the influence, conditioning force, etc., of: *under these circumstances, born under Taurus.* **14.** with the favour or aid of: *under protection.* **15.** authorized, warranted, or attested by: *under one's hand or seal.* **16.** in accordance with: *under the provisions of the law.* **17.** in the state or process of: *under repair.* —*adv.* **18.** under or beneath something. **19.** beneath the surface. **20.** in a lower place. **21.** in a lower degree, amount, etc. **22.** in a subordinate position or condition. **23.** in or into subjection or submission. **24.** in or into cover or submersion: *to send a boat under.* **25. down under,** Australia and New Zealand. —*adj.* **26.** beneath. **27.** lower in position. **28.** lower in degree, amount, etc. **29.** lower in rank or condition. **30.** facing downwards: *the under fringe of a curtain.* [ME and OE; c. D *onder*, G *unter*, Icel. *undir*, akin to L *infrā* below] —**Syn. 2.** See **below.**

under-, a prefixal attributive use of *under*, as to indicate place or situation below or beneath, as in *underbrush, undertow;* lower in grade or dignity, as in *undersheriff, understudy;* of lesser degree, extent, or amount, as in *undersized;* or insufficiency, as in *underfeed.*

underact (ŭn′dər ăkt′), *v.t., v.i.* to act (a part, as in a play) with a lack of dramatic quality; act in an excessively restrained style.

underage (ŭn′də rĭj), *n.* shortage; amount of deficiency, as below a set level.

underarm (ŭn′dər äm′), *adj.* **1.** under the arm: *an underarm seam.* **2.** *Cricket, Tennis, etc.* executed with the hand below the shoulder as in bowling, service, etc. —*adv.* **3.** *Cricket, Tennis, etc.* with an underarm action.

underarmed (ŭn′dər ämd′), *adj.* not having sufficient weapons.

underbelly (ŭn′də bĕl′ĭ), *n.* **1.** the lower part of the belly. **2.** an insufficiently protected area or aspect.

underbid (ŭn′də bĭd′), *v.t.*, **-bid, -bidding. 1.** to make a lower bid than (another), as in seeking a contract to be awarded to the lowest bidder. **2.** to make a lower bid than. —**un′derbid′der,** *n.*

underbody (ŭn′də bŏd′ĭ), *n.* the lower part of the body, as of an animal, vehicle, etc.

underbred (ŭn′də brĕd′), *adj.* **1.** of inferior breeding or manners; vulgar. **2.** not of pure breed, as a horse.

underbrush (ŭn′də brŭsh′), *n.* shrubs, small trees, etc., growing under large trees in a wood or forest.

underbuy (ŭn′də bī′), *v.t.*, **-bought, -buying. 1.** to buy more cheaply than (another). **2.** to buy at less than the actual value.

undercapitalize (ŭn′də kăp′ĭ tə līz′), *v.t., v.i.*, **-lized, -lizing.** to provide insufficient capital for (a business venture). Also, **undercapitalise.**

undercarriage (ŭn′də kă′rĭj), *n.* **1.** the supporting framework beneath the body of a carriage, etc. **2.** the portions of an aeroplane beneath the body, serving as a support when on the ground or water or when taking off and alighting. Also, *Chiefly U.S.*, **landing gear.**

undercharge (*v.* ŭn′də chäj′; *n.* ŭn′də chäj′), *v.*, **-charged, -charging,** *n.* —*v.t.* **1.** to charge (a person, etc.) less than the proper or fair price. **2.** to charge (so much) less than a fair price. **3.** to put an insufficient charge or load into. —*n.* **4.** a charge or price less than is proper or fair. **5.** an insufficient charge or load.

underclassman (ŭn′də kläs′mən), *n.*, *pl.* **-men.** *U.S.* a freshman or sophomore.

underclay (ŭn′də klā′), *n.* *Geol.* a bed of clay underlying a coal seam, representing the soil in which the plants grew.

underclothes (ŭn′də klōthz′), *n.pl.* clothes worn under outer clothes, esp. those worn next to the skin. Also, **un′dercloth′ing.**

undercoat (ŭn′də kōt′), *n.* **1.** a coat or coats of paint applied to a surface after priming and filling, or after preparation of a previously painted surface, before the application of the finishing coat. **2.** the paint used for this. **3.** a coat worn beneath another. —*v.t.* **4.** to apply an undercoat to.

undercoating (ŭn′də kō′tĭng), *n.* **1.** undercoat. **2.** *U.S.* underseal.

undercover (ŭn′də kŭv′ə), *adj.* working or done out of public sight; secret: *an undercover agent.*

undercroft (ŭn′də krŏft′), *n.* **1.** the crypt of a church. **2.** a vault or chamber under the ground. [f. UNDER- + obs. *croft* vault (ult. t. L: m. *crypta* CRYPT)]

undercurrent (ŭn′də kŭ′rənt), *n.* **1.** a current below the upper currents or below the surface. **2.** an underlying or concealed condition or tendency.

undercut (*v.* ŭn′də kŭt′; *n., adj.* ŭn′də kŭt′), *v.*, **-cut, -cutting,** *n., adj.* —*v.t.* **1.** to cut under or beneath. **2.** to cut away material from so as to leave a portion overhanging, as in carving or sculpture. **3.** to sell or work at a lower price than. **4.** *Sport.* to hit (the ball) so as to cause a backspin. —*v.i.* **5.** to undercut material, a competitor, a ball, etc. —*n.* **6.** a cut, or a cutting away, underneath. **7.** *U.S.* a notch cut in a tree to determine the direction in which the tree is to fall and to prevent splitting. **8.** *Sport.* a slice or cut made with an underhand motion. **9.** the tenderloin or fillet of beef or underside of sirloin. —*adj.* **10.** cut away underneath.

underdevelop (ŭn′də dĭ vĕl′əp), *v.t.* to develop short of the required amount: *to underdevelop film.*

underdeveloped (ŭn′də dĭ vĕl′əpt), *adj.* **1.** (of a country) in the primitive stages of industrial and economic development, and lacking the surplus capital to advance. **2.** (of film) developed less than normal, producing a lack of contrast. **3.** less fully developed than average. —**un′der-devel′opment,** *n.*

underdo (ŭn′də do͞o′), *v.i., v.t.*, **-did, -done, -doing.** —*v.t.* **1.** to do insufficiently or imperfectly. **2.** to cook lightly or insufficiently. —*v.i.* **3.** *Obs.* to do less than is necessary.

underdog (ŭn′də dŏg′), *n.* **1.** a victim of oppression. **2.** the loser or expected loser in a competitive situation, fight, etc.

underdone (ŭn′də dŭn′), *adj.* (of food, esp. meat) cooked lightly or less than completely; (of meat) cooked so that it is still pink; rare; seignant.

underdrainage (ŭn′də drā′nĭj), *n.* drainage of agricultural lands and removal of excess water and alkali by drains buried beneath the surface.

underdraw (ŭn′də drô′), *v.t.* **1.** to depict inadequately. **2.** *Bldg Trades.* to cover (a ceiling) by fixing the plasterwork to the underside of the joists. —*v.i.* **3.** to construct an underdrawn ceiling.

underdress (*n.* ŭn′də drĕs′; *v.* ŭn′də drĕs′), *n.* **1.** a dress worn under another. —*v.i.* **2.** to dress too plainly; wear an outfit which is not smart or elaborate enough for the occasion.

underestimate (*v.* ŭn′dər ĕs′tĭ māt′; *n.* ŭn′dər ĕs′tĭ mĭt), *v.*, **-mated, -mating,** *n.* —*v.t.* **1.** to estimate at too low a value, rate, or the like. —*n.* **2.** an estimate that is too low. —**un′deres′tima′tion,** *n.*

underexpose (ŭn′də rĭk spōz′), *v.t.*, **-exposed, -exposing.** to expose to light too little, as in photography.

underexposure (ŭn′də rĭk spō′zhə), *n.* **1.** inadequate exposure to light rays. **2.** a photographic negative or print which has been underexposed. **3.** insufficient exposure to anything, as publicity.

underfeed (ŭn′də fēd′), *v.t.*, **-fed, -feeding. 1.** to feed insufficiently. **2.** to feed with fuel from beneath.

underfeed stoker, an automatic stoker which feeds fuel into a furnace from below the fire.

underfelt (ŭn′də fĕlt′), *n.* a thick felt laid under a carpet to make it more resilient.

underfoot (ŭn′də fo͝ot′), *adv.* **1.** under the foot or feet; on the ground; underneath or below. **2.** in a state of subjection. —*adj.* **3.** lying under the foot or feet. **4.** abject; downtrodden.

underfur (ŭn′də fû′), *n.* the fur, or fine, soft, thick, hairy coat, under the longer and coarser outer hair in certain animals, as seals, otters, and beavers.

undergarment (ŭn′də gä′mənt), *n.* a garment worn under another garment, esp. next to the skin.

underglaze (ŭn′də glāz′), *adj.* *Ceramics.* applied before the glaze is put on, as decoration or colours in porcelain painting.

undergo (ŭn′də gō′), *v.t.*, **-went, -gone, -going. 1.** to be subjected to; experience; pass through. **2.** to endure; sustain; suffer. —**Syn. 2.** See **experience.**

undergrad (ŭn′də grăd′), *n.* *Colloq.* an undergraduate.

undergraduate (ŭn′də grăd′yo͞o ĭt), *n.* **1.** a student in a university or college who has not taken his first degree. —*adj.* **2.** having the standing of an undergraduate. **3.** pertaining to, characteristic of, or consisting of undergraduates. —**un′dergrad′uateship′,** *n.*

undergraduette (ŭn′də grăd′yo͞o ĕt′), *n.* *Colloq.* a female undergraduate.

underground (*adv.* ŭn′də ground′; *adj., n.* ŭn′də-ground′), *adv.* **1.** beneath the surface of the ground. **2.** in concealment or secrecy; not openly. —*adj.* **3.** existing,

un′deractiv′ity, *n.*
un′der-a′gent, *n.*
un′derbridge′, *n.*
un′derbuild′, *v.t.*
un′der-build′er, *n.*
un′derbush′, *n.*
un′der-but′ler, *n.*
un′derclad′, *adj.*
un′der-clerk′, *n.*
un′dercliff′, *n.*
un′derclothe′, *v.t.*
un′derclothed′, *adj.*
un′dercook′, *v.t.*
un′derdeck′, *n.*
un′derdrain′, *v.t.*
un′derdrain′, *n.*
un′derdressed′, *adj.*
un′derdrift′, *n.*
un′deremploy′ment, *n.*
un′derfed′, *adj.*
un′derfloor′, *adj.*
un′derframe′, *n.*
un′dergar′dener, *n.*

situated, operating, or taking place beneath the surface of the ground. **4.** used, or for use, underground. **5.** hidden or secret; not open. **6.** not public; not generally known about. —*n.* **7.** the place or region beneath the surface of the ground; the underworld. **8.** a railway running mainly through tunnels laid beneath the roadway or in deeply laid tubes. **9.** a secret organization fighting the established government or occupation forces, esp. one in the fascist-overrun nations of Europe before and during World War II.

underground railroad, *U.S. Hist.* (before the abolition of slavery) an arrangement among opponents of slavery for helping fugitive slaves to escape into Canada or some other place of safety.

undergrowth (ŭn′də grōth′), *n.* **1.** shrubs or small trees growing beneath or among large trees. **2.** condition of being undergrown or undersized.

underhand (ŭn′də hănd′), *adj.* **1.** not open and aboveboard; secret and crafty or dishonourable. **2.** done or delivered underhand. —*adv.* **3.** with the hand below the shoulder, as in pitching or bowling a ball. **4.** *Tennis.* with the racket held below the wrist. **5.** secretly; stealthily; slyly.

underhanded (ŭn′də hăn′dĭd), *adj.* **1.** underhand. **2.** short-handed. —**un′derhand′edly,** *adv.* —**un′derhand′edness,** *n.*

underhung (ŭn′də hŭng′), *adj.* **1.** *Anat.* **a.** (of the lower jaw) projecting beyond the upper jaw. **b.** having the lower jaw so projecting. **2.** resting on a track beneath, instead of being overhung, as a sliding door.

underinsure (ŭn′də rĭn shŏŏə′, -shô′), *v.t.,* **-sured, -suring. 1.** to insure (possessions) for less than their full value. **2.** to insure (oneself) for less than the full value of one's possessions. —**un′derinsu′rance,** *n.*

underived (ŭn′dĭ rīvd′), *adj.* not derived; fundamental, as an axiom.

underjaw (ŭn′də jô′), *n.* the lower jaw.

underlaid (ŭn′də lād′), *adj.* **1.** put beneath. **2.** having an underlay. —*v.* **3.** pt. and pp. of **underlay.**

underlap (ŭn′də lăp′), *v.t.,* **-lapped, -lapping.** to extend partly under.

underlay (*v.* ŭn′də lā′; *n.* ŭn′də lā′), *v.,* **-laid, -laying,** *n.* —*v.t.* **1.** to lay (one thing) under or beneath another. **2.** to provide with something laid underneath; raise or support with something laid underneath. **3.** *Print.* to add (packing material) beneath a printing block in order to give added impression or to bring up to type height. **4.** to extend beneath. —*n.* **5.** something underlaid. **6.** felt, paper, rubber, or the like, laid under a floor-covering to increase its insulation, resilience, etc. **7.** *Printing.* a piece or pieces of paper put under types, etc., to bring them to the proper height for printing.

underlet (ŭn′də lĕt′), *v.t.,* **-let, -letting. 1.** to let below the true value. **2.** to sublet. —**un′derlet′ter,** *n.*

underlie (ŭn′də lī′), *v.t.,* **-lay, -lain, -lying. 1.** to lie under or beneath; be situated under. **2.** to be at the basis of; form the foundation of. **3.** *Finance.* to support another right or security. [ME *underly*, OE *underlicgan* (see UNDER-, LIE[2])]

underline (ŭn′də līn′), *v.t.,* **-lined, -lining. 1.** to mark with a line or lines underneath; underscore. **2.** to emphasize or stress the importance of.

underling (ŭn′də lĭng), *n.* a subordinate (esp. in disparagement). [ME and OE; f. UNDER, adv. + -LING[1]]

underlying (ŭn′də lī′ĭng), *adj.* **1.** lying under or beneath (something). **2.** fundamental; existing beneath the apparent aspect of. —*v.* **3.** pt. and pp. of **underlie.**

undermanned (ŭn′də mănd′), *adj.* lacking a sufficient number of troops, workers, etc.; short-handed.

undermanning (ŭn′də măn′ĭng), *n.* the fact of being undermanned.

undermine (ŭn′də mīn′), *v.t.,* **-mined, -mining. 1.** to form a mine or passage under, as in military operations; make an excavation under. **2.** to render unstable by digging into or wearing away the foundations. **3.** to affect injuriously or weaken by secret or underhand means. **4.** to weaken insidiously; destroy gradually. —**un′dermin′er,** *n.*

undermost (ŭn′də mōst′), *adj., adv.* lowest.

underneath (ŭn′də nēth′), *prep.* **1.** under; beneath. —*adv.* **2.** beneath; below. —*adj.* **3.** lower. —*n.* **4.** the under or lowest part or aspect. [ME *undernethe*, OE *underneothan*. See UNDER, BENEATH]

undernourish (ŭn′də nŭ′rĭsh), *v.t.* to provide with less nourishment than is necessary to maintain normal health. —**un′dernour′ished,** *adj.* —**un′dernour′ishment,** *n.*

underofficer (*v.* ŭn′dər ŏf′ĭ sə; *n.* ŭn′dər ŏf′ĭ sə), *v.t.* to furnish inadequately with officers. —*n.* **2.** *Mil.* an officer of cadets.

underogatory (ŭn′dĭ rŏg′ə tə rĭ, -trĭ), *adj.* not derogatory.

underpants (ŭn′də pănts′), *n.pl.* an undergarment, usually for men, in the form of more or less close-fitting short or long trousers, made of light cotton or the like; pants; drawers.

underpart (ŭn′də pät′), *n.* the lower part or face.

underpass (ŭn′də päs′), *n.* a passage running underneath, esp. a passage for vehicles or pedestrians, or both, crossing under a railway, road, etc.

underpay (ŭn′də pā′), *v.t.,* **-paid, -paying.** to pay insufficiently. —**un′derpay′-ment,** *n.*

underpin (ŭn′də pĭn′), *v.t.,* **-pinned, -pinning. 1.** to pin or support underneath; place something under for support or foundation. **2.** to support with masonry, stones, etc., as a building. **3.** to support; prop.

underpinning (ŭn′də pĭn′ĭng), *n.* *Archit.* supports or latticework placed under a completed wall.

underplay (ŭn′də plā′), *v.t.* **1.** to act (a part) sketchily. **2.** to act subtly and restrainedly. **3.** to perform or deal with in a subtle or restrained manner. —*v.i.* **4.** to leave out of one's acting all subtlety and enriching detail. **5.** to achieve an effect in acting with a minimum of emphasis. **6.** *Cards.* to play a low card while retaining a higher.

underplot (ŭn′də plŏt′), *n.* **1.** a subplot. **2.** a secret scheme; trick.

underprice (ŭn′də prīs′), *v.t.,* **-priced, -pricing.** to price (something offered for sale) below its value or normal price.

underprivileged (ŭn′də prĭv′ĭ lĭjd), *adj.* denied the enjoyment of the normal privileges or rights of a society because of poverty and low social status.

underproduction (ŭn′də prə dŭk′shən), *n.* production that is less than normal, or than the demand.

underproof (ŭn′də proof′), *adj.* containing a smaller proportion of alcohol than proof spirit does.

underprop (ŭn′də prŏp′), *v.t.,* **-propped, -propping.** to prop underneath; support; uphold.

underquote (ŭn′də kwōt′), *v.t.,* **-quoted, -quoting. 1.** to quote at a price below another price or the market price. **2.** to quote lower prices than (another).

underrate (ŭn′də rāt′), *v.t.,* **-rated, -rating.** to rate or value too low; underestimate.

underrun (ŭn′də rŭn′), *v.,* **-ran, -run, -running,** *n.* —*v.t.* **1.** to run, pass, or go under. —*n.* **2.** an undercurrent.

underscore (*v.* ŭn′də skô′; *n.* ŭn′də skô′), *v.,* **-scored, -scoring,** *n.* —*v.t.* **1.** to mark with a line or lines underneath; underline. —*n.* **2.** a line drawn beneath something written or printed, as for emphasis.

undersea (ŭn′də sē′), *adj.* **1.** submarine. **2.** for use below the surface of the sea. —*adv.* **3.** underseas.

underseal (ŭn′də sēl′), *n.* **1.** a preparation of tar, bitumen, or the like used to protect the underside of a motor vehicle from corrosion, rust, etc. —*v.t.* **2.** to coat with a protective layer of underseal.

underseas (ŭn′də sēz′), *adv.* beneath the surface of the sea.

undersecretary (ŭn′də sĕk′rə trĭ), *n., pl.* **-taries.** a secretary subordinate to a principal secretary. —**un′dersec′retaryship′,** *n.*

undersell (ŭn′də sĕl′), *v.t.,* **-sold, -selling. 1.** to advertise or publicize with restraint. **2.** to sell things at a lower price than (a competitor). **3.** to sell for less than the actual value. —**un′dersell′er,** *n.*

undersense (ŭn′də sĕns′), *n.* an inner or subconscious awareness.

underservant (ŭn′də sû′vənt), *n.* an inferior or subordinate servant.

underset (ŭn′də sĕt′), *n., v.,* **-set, -setting.** —*n.* **1.** an ocean undercurrent. **2.** *Mining.* a lower vein of ore. —*v.t.* **3.** to support from below.

undersexed (ŭn′də sĕkst′), *adj.* having unusually little interest in sex or sexual activity; lacking sexual drive.

undersheriff (ŭn′də shĕ′rĭf), *n.* a sheriff's deputy, esp. a deputy on whom the sheriff's duties devolve when the sheriff is incapacitated or when the office is vacant.

undershirt (ŭn′də shût′), *n.* *U.S.* a vest or singlet.

undershoot (ŭn′də shoot′), *v.,* **-shot, -shooting.** —*v.i.*

---

un′dergrown′, *adj.*
un′derhang′ing, *adj.*
un′derhorsed′, *adj.*
un′derkeep′er, *n.*
un′derlease′, *n., v.t., v.i.*
un′derlessee′, *n.*
un′derlid′, *n.*
un′derlip′, *n.*
un′derman′ager, *n.*
un′dermast′ed, *adj.*
un′dermas′ter, *n.*
un′dermen′tioned, *adj.*
un′dernamed′, *adj.*
un′dernote′, *n.*
un′dernot′ed, *adj.*
un′derpeo′pled, *adj.*
un′derpraise′, *v.t., v.i.*
un′derprize′, *v.t.*
un′derqual′ified′, *adj.*
un′der-rep′resent′ed, *adj.*
un′der-roast′, *v.t.*
un′der-robe′, *n.*
un′derroof′, *n.*
un′dershaft′ed, *adj.*

---

1. *Aeron.* to land an aircraft before it reaches the correct landing strip as a result of insufficient speed or height. 2. to shoot or launch a projectile so that it falls short of the target. —*v.t.* 3. *Aeron.* to land short of (a landing strip, etc.). 4. to shoot or launch a projectile so that it falls short of (a target).

undershorts (ŭn′də shôts′), *n.pl. Chiefly U.S.* short underpants.

undershot (ŭn′də shŏt′), *adj.* 1. underhung; driven by water passing beneath, as a kind of vertical waterwheel. 2. having the upper jaw shorter than the lower jaw, as a dog; usually considered to be a malformation.

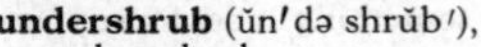

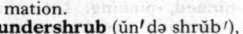

Undershot waterwheel

undershrub (ŭn′də shrŭb′), *n.* a low shrub.

underside (ŭn′də sīd′), *n.* the under or lower side.

undersign (ŭn′də sīn′), *v.t.* to sign one's name under, or at the end of (a letter or document); to affix one's signature to.

undersigned (ŭn′də sīnd′), *adj.* 1. having signed, as a person, at the end of a letter or document. 2. signed, as a name. —*n.* 3. **the undersigned,** the person or persons undersigning a letter or document.

undersized (ŭn′də sīzd′), *adj.* below the usual size. Also, **un′dersize′.**

underskirt (ŭn′də skût′), *n.* a skirt worn under an outer skirt or under an overskirt or drapery.

undersleeve (ŭn′də slēv′), *n.* 1. a sleeve worn under an outer sleeve. 2. an ornamental inner sleeve extending below the outer sleeve.

underslung (ŭn′də slŭng′), *adj.* 1. attached to the axles from below, as the chassis frame of a car. 2. having a low centre of gravity. 3. supported from above.

undersoil (ŭn′də soil′), *n.* subsoil.

undersparred (ŭn′də späd′), *adj. Naut.* having insufficient masts, yards, gaffs, etc., to carry enough sail.

understaffed (ŭn′də stäft′), *adj.* having too few employees; inadequately staffed.

understand (ŭn′də stănd′), *v.*, **-stood, -standing.** —*v.t.* 1. to perceive the meaning of; grasp the idea of; comprehend. 2. to be thoroughly familiar with; apprehend clearly the character or nature of. 3. to comprehend by knowing the meaning of the words employed, as a language. 4. to interpret, or assign a meaning to; take to mean. 5. to grasp the significance, implications, or importance of. 6. to regard or take as a fact, or as settled. 7. to get knowledge of; learn or hear. 8. to accept as a fact; believe. 9. to conceive the meaning of in a particular way: *you are to understand the phrase literally.* 10. to supply mentally, as a word necessary to complete sense. —*v.i.* 11. to perceive what is meant. 12. to have the use of the intellectual faculties. 13. to have information or knowledge about something: *to understand about a matter.* 14. to accept sympathetically: *if you go away, I shall understand.* 15. to be informed; believe. [ME; OE *understondan*, c. D *onderstaan*, G *unterstehen*] —**Syn.** 1. See **know.**

understandable (ŭn′də stăn′də bl), *adj.* that may be understood. —**un′derstand′ableness,** *n.* —**un′derstand′ably,** *adv.*

understanding (ŭn′də stăn′dĭng), *n.* 1. the act of one who understands; comprehension; personal interpretation. 2. intelligence; wit. 3. superior intelligence; superior power of recognizing the truth: *men of understanding.* 4. a mutual comprehension of each other's meaning, thoughts, etc. 5. a state of (good or friendly) relations between persons. 6. a mutual agreement of a private or unannounced kind. 7. *Philos.* discursive knowledge based on premises and observations. 8. **on the understanding that,** on condition that. —*adj.* 9. that understands; possessing or showing intelligence or understanding. 10. sympathetically discerning; tolerant. —**un′derstand′ingly,** *adv.*

understate (ŭn′də stāt′), *v.t.*, **-stated, -stating.** to state or represent less strongly than is desirable or necessary; state with too little emphasis. —**un′derstate′ment,** *n.*

understeer (*v.* ŭn′də stĭə′; *n.* ŭn′də stĭə′, ŭn′də stĭə′), *v.i.* 1. (of a motor vehicle) to tend to turn in a wider circle than indicated by the geometry of the wheels. —*n.* 2. such a tendency.

understock (ŭn′də stŏk′), *v.t.* to supply insufficiently with stock.

understood (ŭn′də stŏŏd′), *v.* 1. pt. and pp. of **understand.** —*adj.* 2. agreed upon by all concerned. 3. implied; assumed.

understrapper (ŭn′də străp′ə), *n.* an underling.

understratum (ŭn′də strä′təm), *n., pl.* **-strata** (-strä′tə), **-stratums.** a substratum.

understudy (ŭn′də stŭd′ĭ), *n., v.*, **-studied, -studying.** —*n.* 1. an actor or actress who stands by to replace a performer when the latter is unable to appear. —*v.t.* 2. to act as an understudy to (an actor or actress). 3. to be the understudy for (a particular role). —*v.i.* 4. to be an understudy.

undersurface (ŭn′də sû′fĭs), *n.* the surface of the lower part of something; the surface that faces downwards.

undertake (ŭn′də tāk′), *v.*, **-took, -taken, -taking.** —*v.t.* 1. to take on oneself (some task, performance, etc.); take in hand; essay; attempt. 2. to take on oneself by formal promise or agreement; lay oneself under obligation to perform or execute. 3. to warrant or guarantee (fol. by a clause). 4. to take in charge; assume the duty of attending to (a person). 5. *Obs.* to engage with, as in a duel. —*v.i.* 6. *Archaic.* to take on oneself any task of responsibility. 7. *Archaic.* to engage oneself by promise (*for*); give a guarantee, or become surety (*for*).

undertaker (ŭn′də tā′kə *for 1*; ŭn′də tā′kə *for 2*), *n.* 1. one who undertakes something. 2. one whose business it is to prepare the dead for burial and to take charge of funerals; funeral director; mortician.

undertaking (ŭn′də tā′kĭng *for 1–3*; ŭn′də tā′kĭng *for 4*), *n.* 1. the act of one who undertakes any task or responsibility. 2. a task, enterprise, etc., undertaken. 3. a promise; pledge; guarantee. 4. the business of an undertaker or funeral director.

undertenant (ŭn′də tĕn′ənt), *n.* a subtenant. —**un′derten′ancy,** *n.*

under-the-counter (ŭn′də thə koun′tə), *adj.* 1. pertaining to goods kept hidden for sale in some improper way, as on the black market. —*adv.* 2. sold illegally, as black-market goods. Also (esp. in predicative use), **under the counter.**

underthings (ŭn′də thĭngz′), *n.pl.* underclothes.

undertint (ŭn′də tĭnt′), *n.* 1. a subdued tint. 2. a partly or wholly concealed tint under another.

undertone (ŭn′də tōn′), *n.* 1. a low or subdued tone, as of utterance. 2. an underlying quality, element, or tendency. 3. a subdued colour; a colour modified by an underlying colour.

undertook (ŭn′də tŏŏk′), *v.* pt. of **undertake.**

undertow (ŭn′də tō′), *n.* 1. the backward flow or draught of the water, below the surface, from waves breaking on a beach. 2. any strong current below the surface of a body of water, moving in a direction different from that of the surface current.

undertrick (ŭn′də trĭk′), *n. Bridge.* a trick lacking from the number needed to make a contract. Cf. **overtrick.**

undertrump (ŭn′də trŭmp′), *v.t. Cards.* 1. to trump with a lower trump than has already been played. 2. to play a lower trump than.

undervalue (ŭn′də văl′yōō), *v.t.*, **-ued, -uing.** 1. to value below the real worth; put too low a value on. 2. to diminish in value; make of less value. 3. to esteem too low; esteem lightly; hold in mean estimation. —**un′derval′ua′tion,** *n.* —**un′derval′uer,** *n.*

undervest (ŭn′də vĕst′), *n.* a vest.

underwater (ŭn′də wô′tə), *adj.* 1. being or occurring under water. 2. designed to be used under water. 3. situated below the waterline of a ship.

underwear (ŭn′də wĕə′), *n.* underclothes.

underweight (*n.* ŭn′də wāt′; *adj.* ŭn′də wāt′), *n.* 1. deficiency in weight. —*adj.* 2. lacking usual or required weight.

underwent (ŭn′də wĕnt′), *v.* pt. of **undergo.**

underwing (ŭn′də wĭng′), *n.* a hind wing of an insect.

underwood (ŭn′də wŏŏd′), *n.* 1. shrubs or small trees growing under larger trees; underbrush. 2. a growth of underbrush.

underworld (ŭn′də wûld′), *n.* 1. the lower, degraded, or criminal part of human society. 2. the lower or nether world; Hades. 3. the place or region below the surface of the earth. 4. the opposite side of the earth; the antipodes. 5. *Archaic.* the world below the skies; the earth.

underwrite (ŭn′də rīt′, ŭn′də rīt′), *v.*, **-wrote, -written, -writing.** —*v.t.* 1. to write (something) under a thing, esp. under other written matter. 2. to sign one's name to (a document, etc.). 3. to subscribe to, agree with, or support (a statement, etc.), as by signature. 4. *Obs.* to agree to give or pay (a certain sum of money) by signing one's name. 5. to agree to meet the expense of; undertake to finance. 6. to guarantee the sale of (shares or bonds to be offered to

un′dertaxed′, *adj.* | un′derten′ancy, *n.* | un′der-u′tilize′, *v.t.*, -lized, -lizing. | un′der-u′tiliza′tion, *n.*
un′der-teach′er, *n.* | un′der-treas′urer, *n.* | | un′der-waist′coat′, *n.*

the public for subscription). **7.** *Insurance.* **a.** to write one's name at the end of (a policy of insurance), thereby becoming liable in case of certain losses specified therein. **b.** to insure. **c.** to assume liability to the extent of (a certain sum) by way of insurance. —*v.i.* **8.** to underwrite something. **9.** to carry on the business of an underwriter. [ME; OE *underwrītan* (trans. of L *subscrībere*)]

underwriter (ŭn′də rī′tə), *n.* **1.** one who underwrites policies of insurance, or carries on insurance as a business. **2.** one who underwrites shares or bonds.

underwritten (ŭn′də rĭt′n, ŭn′də rĭt′n), *v.* pp. of **underwrite.**

underwrote (ŭn′də rōt′, ŭn′də rōt′), *v.* pt. of **underwrite.**

undesigning (ŭn′dĭ zī′nĭng), *adj.* without underhand or selfish designs.

undesirable (ŭn′dĭ zī′ə rə bl), *adj.* **1.** objectionable; detrimental. **2.** not desirable. —*n.* **3.** an undesirable person or thing. —**un′desir′ableness,** *n.* —**un′desir′ably,** *adv.*

undetermined (ŭn′dĭ tû′mĭnd), *adj.* **1.** not definitely settled or decided; uncertain. **2.** not fixed, limited, or restricted, as in meaning, extent, etc.; indefinite. **3.** undecided, irresolute, or uncertain, as a person.

undeveloped (ŭn′dĭ vĕl′əpt), *adj.* **1.** not developed; not fully grown or matured. **2.** (of land) not built on; not made to yield a profit. —**Syn. 1.** See **imperfect.**

undid (ŭn dĭd′), *v.* pt. of **undo.**

undies (ŭn′dĭz), *n.pl. Colloq.* women's underclothes.

undigested (ŭn′dĭ jĕs′tĭd), *adj.* **1.** (of food) not digested; unassimilated. **2.** (of information, ideas, discourse, etc.) not ordered or arranged in intelligible fashion.

undine (ŭn′dīn), *n.* one of a class of mythological female water-sprites. According to Paracelsus, when an undine married a mortal and bore a child, she received a soul. Also, **ondine.** [t. NL (Paracelsus): m. *Undina*, der. L *unda* wave] —**Syn.** See **sylph.**

undirected (ŭn′dĭ rĕk′tĭd), *adj.* **1.** not directed; not guided. **2.** bearing no address, as a letter.

undischarged (ŭn′dĭs chäjd′), *adj.* **1.** not cleared, as debts. **2.** not performed, as obligations or duties. **3.** not set free or released, as a bankrupt, soldier, etc. **4.** *Archaic.* not fired, as a gun. **5.** not unloaded, as a ship's cargo.

undisciplined (ŭn dĭs′ĭ plĭnd), *adj.* **1.** lacking in discipline; unruly; disorderly. **2.** not having been subjected to training or discipline.

undistinguished (ŭn′dĭs tĭng′gwĭsht), *adj.* **1.** lacking distinctive features. **2.** not outstanding; mediocre.

undivided (ŭn′dĭ vī′dĭd), *adj.* **1.** not divided, or separated into parts. **2.** not partial; whole; not diluted: *they gave him their undivided loyalty.* —**un′divid′edly,** *adv.* —**un′divid′edness,** *n.*

undo (ŭn do͞o′), *v.t.,* **-did, -done, -doing. 1.** to unfasten and open (something closed, locked, barred, etc.). **2.** to untie or loose (strings, etc.). **3.** to open (a parcel, a sealed letter, etc.). **4.** to reverse the doing of; cause to be as if never done. **5.** to do away with; efface. **6.** to bring to ruin or disaster; destroy. **7.** *Obs.* to explain; interpret. [ME; OE *undōn*, c. D *ontdoen*; f. UN-[2] + DO[1]] —**undo′er,** *n.*

undoing (ŭn do͞o′ĭng), *n.* **1.** the reversing of what has been done; annulling. **2.** a bringing to destruction, ruin, or disaster. **3.** a cause of destruction or ruin. **4.** the act or fact of unfastening or opening.

undone[1] (ŭn dŭn′), *adj.* **1.** not done; not accomplished or completed, or finished. **2.** unfastened. **3.** *Archaic.* neglected or omitted. [f. UN-[1] + DONE]

undone[2] (ŭn dŭn′), *v.* **1.** pp. of **undo.** —*adj.* **2.** reversed. **3.** brought to destruction or ruin. [see UNDO]

undouble (ŭn dŭb′l), *v.t., v.i.,* **-bled, -bling.** to unfold; straighten out, as a fist.

undoubted (ŭn dou′tĭd), *adj.* not called in question; accepted as beyond doubt; undisputed. —**undoubt′edly,** *adv.*

undramatic (ŭn′drə măt′ĭk), *adj.* **1.** lacking drama or excitement; dull. **2.** not suitable for the theatre.

undrape (ŭn drāp′), *v.t.,* **-draped, -draping.** to strip of drapery; bare.

undraw (ŭn drô′), *v.,* **-drew, -drawn, -drawing.** *Rare.* —*v.t.* **1.** to draw back or away. —*v.i.* **2.** to be drawn back or withdrawn.

undress (*adj.* ŭn′drĕs′; *otherwise* ŭn drĕs′), *v.t.* **1.** to take off the clothes of; disrobe. **2.** to strip of whatever adorns. **3.** to remove the dressing from (a wound, etc.). —*v.i.* **4.** to take off one's clothes. —*n.* **5.** the state of having little or no clothes on. **6.** ordinary or informal dress. **7.** *Mil.* a uniform for ordinary occasions (as opposed to *full dress* or *battledress*). —*adj.* **8.** of or pertaining to ordinary dress. **9.** informal as to dress.

undressed (ŭn drĕst′), *adj.* **1.** not dressed; not specially prepared. **2.** without clothes on. **3. a.** (of leather) having a napped finish on the flesh side. **b.** (of textiles, masonry, etc.) not prepared in some way.

Undset (*Nor.* o͞on′sĕt), *n.* **Sigrid** (*Nor.* sē′grē), 1882–1949, Norwegian novelist.

und so weiter (*Ger.* o͝ont zō vī′tər), *German.* and so forth.

undue (ŭn dyo͞o′), *adj.* **1.** unwarranted; excessive; too great: *undue haste.* **2.** not proper, fitting, or right; unjustified: *to exert undue influence.* **3.** not yet owing or payable.

undulant (ŭn′dyo͝o lənt), *adj.* undulating; waving; wavy. [t. L: s. *undulans*, ppr.]

undulant fever, an irregular, relapsing fever, with swelling of joints, spleen, and rheumatic pains, caused by *Brucella melitensis* ingested in raw milk of diseased cows and goats; Malta fever; Mediterranean fever; brucellosis.

undulate (*v.* ŭn′dyo͝o lāt′; *adj.* ŭn′dyo͝o lĭt, -lāt′), *v.,* **-lated, -lating,** *adj.* —*v.i.* **1.** to have a wavy motion; rise and fall or move up and down in waves. **2.** to have a wavy form or surface; bend with successive curves in alternate directions. —*v.t.* **3.** to cause to move in waves. **4.** to give a wavy form to. —*adj.* **5.** Also, **un′dulat′ed.** wavy; bending with successive curves in alternate directions; having a waved form, surface, margin, etc. [t. L: m. s. *undulātus* wavy, der. *unda* wave]

undulation (ŭn′dyo͝o lā′shən), *n.* **1.** the act of undulating; a waving motion. **2.** wavy form or outline. **3.** one of a series of wavelike bends, curves, or elevations. **4.** *Physics.* the motion of waves; a wave; a vibration.

undulatory (ŭn′dyo͝o lə tə rĭ, -trĭ), *adj.* **1.** moving in undulations. **2.** having the form or appearance of waves. Also, **undulative** (ŭn′dyo͝o lə tĭv).

unduly (ŭn dyo͞o′lĭ), *adv.* **1.** excessively. **2.** inappropriately; improperly; unjustifiably.

undying (ŭn dī′ĭng), *adj.* deathless; immortal; unending. —**undy′ingly,** *adv.*

unearned (ŭn ûnd′), *adj.* **1.** not earned by one's own labour or effort, as income derived from stocks and shares. **2.** not deserved.

unearned increment, the increase in the value of land, etc., due to natural causes, as growth of population, rather than to any labour or expenditure by the owner.

---

un'described′, *adj.*
un'descrip′tive, *adj.*
un'deserve′, *v.t.*
un'deserved′, *adj.*
un'deserv′edly, *adv.*
un'deserv′ing, *adj.*
un'designed′, *adj.*
un'design′edly, *adv.*
un'desired′, *adj.*
un'desir′ing, *adj.*
un'desir′ous, *adj.*
un'despair′ing, *adj.*
un'despair′ingly, *adv.*
un'detect′ed, *adj.*
unde′viat'ing, *adj.*
undev′iat'ingly, *adv.*
un'devout′, *adj.*
undex′terous, *adj.*
undex′terously, *adv.*
undi′agnosed', *adj.*
un'dictat′ed, *adj.*
un'differen′tiat'ed, *adj.*
undig′nified', *adj.*
undig′nify', *v.t.*
undil′igent, *adj.*
un'dilut′ed, *adj.*
un'dimin′ished, *adj.*
undimmed′, *adj.*
un'diplomat′ic, *adj.*
undipped′, *adj.*
un'discerned′, *adj.*
un'discern′ing, *adj.*
undis′ciplinable, *adj.*
undis′cipline, *n.*
un'disclosed′, *adj.*
un'discour′ageable, *adj.*
un'discour′aged, *adj.*
un'discov′erable, *adj.*
un'discov′ered, *adj.*
un'discrim′inat'ing, *adj.*
un'discrim′inat'ingly, *adv.*
un'discussed′, *adj.*
un'disfig′ured, *adj.*
un'disguis′able, *adj.*
un'disguis′ably, *adv.*
un'disguised′, *adj.*
un'disguis′edly, *adv.*
un'disheart′ened, *adj.*
un'dismayed′, *adj.*
un'dispersed′, *adj.*
un'disposed′, *adj.*
un'disput′ed, *adj.*
un'disput′edly, *adv.*
un'dissem′bled, *adj.*
un'dissem′bling, *adj.*
undis′sipat'ed, *adj.*
un'dissolved′, *adj.*
un'distinc′tive, *adj.*
un'distin′guishable, *adj.*
un'distin′guishably, *adv.*
un'distort′ed, *adj.*
un'distract′ed, *adj.*
un'distract′edly, *adv.*
un'distrib′uted, *adj.*
un'disturbed′, *adj.*
un'disturb′edly, *adv.*
un'diver′sified', *adj.*
un'divert′ed, *adj.*
un'divert′ing, *adj.*
un'divulged′, *adj.*
undock′, *v.t.*
undoc′tored, *adj.*
undoc′ument'ed, *adj.*
un'dogmat′ic, *adj.*
un'domes′ticat'ed, *adj.*
undoubt′able, *adj.*
undoubt′ing, *adj.*
undoubt′ingly, *adv.*
undrain′able, *adj.*
undrained′, *adj.*
undreamed′, *adj.*
undreamed′-of', *adj.*
undream′ing, *adj.*
undreamt′, *adj.*
undried′, *adj.*
undrink′able, *adj.*
undrowned′, *adj.*
undrunk′, *adj.*
undug′, *adj.*
undulled′, *adj.*
undu′tiful, *adj.*
undu′tifully, *adv.*
undu′tifulness, *n.*
undyed′, *adj.*

---

unearth (ŭn ûth′), *v.t.* **1.** to dig or get out of the earth; dig up. **2.** to uncover or bring to light by digging, searching, or discovery.

unearthly (ŭn ûth′lĭ), *adj.* **1.** not of this earth or world. **2.** supernatural; ghostly; unnaturally strange; weird: *an unearthly scream.* **3.** *Colloq.* unreasonable; absurd: *to get up at an unearthly hour.* **—unearth′liness,** *n.* **—Syn. 2.** See **weird.**

uneasy (ŭn ē′zĭ), *adj.*, **-easier, -easiest. 1.** not easy in body or mind; uncomfortable; restless; disturbed; perturbed. **2.** not easy in manner; constrained. **3.** *Obs.* not conducive to ease; causing bodily discomfort. **—uneas′ily,** *adv.* **—uneas′iness,** *n.*

uneconomic (ŭn′ē kə nŏm′ĭk), *adj.* not productive of economic benefit.

uneconomical (ŭn′ē kə nŏm′ĭ kəl), *adj.* wasteful, as a method, activity, etc.; unprofitable. **—un′econom′ically,** *adv.*

uneducated (ŭn ĕd′yŏŏ kā′tĭd), *adj.* **1.** not educated. **2.** not showing signs of education: *an uneducated handwriting.* **—Syn. 1.** See **ignorant.**

unembarrassed (ŭn′ĭm bă′rəst), *adj.* **1.** not embarrassed; not ashamed, constrained, or self-conscious; at ease. **2.** not hampered or obstructed. **—un′embar′rassedly,** *adv.*

unemotional (ŭn′ĭ mō′shə nəl), *adj.* **1.** (of a person) not subject to strong emotions or reactions; imperturbable; unenthusiastic. **2.** lacking in or unmodified by strong emotion. **—un′emo′tionally,** *adv.*

unemployable (ŭn′ĭm ploi′ə bəl), *adj.* **1.** unable to keep a job; not fit to be employed; unusable. **—***n.* **2.** a person or thing that is unfit to be employed or used. **—un′employ′abil′ity,** *n.*

unemployed (ŭn′ĭm ploid′), *adj.* **1.** out of work, esp. temporarily and involuntarily; without work or employment. **2.** not employed; not in use; not kept busy or at work. **3.** not in productive or profitable use. **—***n.* (*sing. construed as pl.*) **4.** those who are not employed. **5.** those who are out of work, esp. temporarily and involuntarily.

unemployment (ŭn′ĭm ploi′mənt), *n.* **1.** lack of employment; unemployed condition. **2.** the number of people out of work: *unemployment is down this year.* **3.** the excess of unemployed over available jobs.

unenlightened (ŭn′ĭn lī′tnd), *adj.* **1.** not informed or instructed. **2.** characterized by unreason, prejudice, illiberality, ignorance, superstition, or the like.

unenterprising (ŭn ĕn′tə prī′zĭng), *adj.* lacking in adventurousness or initiative. **—unen′terpris′ingly,** *adv.*

unenviable (ŭn ĕn′vĭ ə bəl), *adj.* disagreeable: *an unenviable predicament.* **—unen′viably,** *adv.*

unequal (ŭn ē′kwəl), *adj.* **1.** not equal; not of the same quantity, value, rank, ability, merit, etc.: *unequal size.* **2.** not adequate, as in amount, power, ability, etc. (fol. by *to*): *strength unequal to the task.* **3.** not evenly proportioned or balanced; not having the parts alike or symmetrical: *an unequal leaf.* **4.** not even or regular, as motion, extent, duration, etc. **5.** in which the parties are unevenly matched: *an unequal contest.* **6.** uneven or variable in character, quality, etc. **—***n.* **7.** (*pl.*) people or things not equal to one another. **—une′qually,** *adv.* **—une′qualness,** *n.*

unequalled (ŭn ē′kwəld), *adj.* not equalled; unparalleled; matchless. Also, *U.S.*, **unequaled.**

unequivocal (ŭn′ĭ kwĭv′ə kəl), *adj.* not equivocal; not ambiguous; clear; plain: *an unequivocal reply.* **—un′equiv′ocally,** *adv.* **—un′equiv′ocalness,** *n.*

unerring (ŭn û′rĭng), *adj.* **1.** not erring; not going astray or missing the mark; without error or mistake. **2.** unfailingly right, exact, or sure. **—unerr′ingly,** *adv.* **—unerr′ingness,** *n.*

UNESCO (yŏŏ nĕs′kō), *n.* the United Nations Educational, Scientific, and Cultural Organization. Also, **U.N.E.S.C.O.**

unessential (ŭn′ĭ sĕn′shəl), *adj.* **1.** not of prime importance; not indispensable; inessential. **2.** having no essence or being. **—***n.* **3.** an inessential thing; a nonessential. **—un′essen′tially,** *adv.*

unesthetic (ŭn′ĕs thĕt′ĭk), *adj.* *U.S.* unaesthetic.

unethical (ŭn ĕth′ĭ kəl), *adj.* contrary to moral precept; immoral. **2.** in contravention of some code of professional conduct. **—uneth′ically,** *adv.*

uneven (ŭn ē′vən), *adj.* **1.** not level or flat; rough; rugged. **2.** irregular; varying; not uniform. **3.** not equally balanced; not equal: *an uneven contest.* **4.** (of a number) odd; not divisible into two equal integers: *3, 5, and 7 are uneven numbers.* [ME; OE *unefen*, c. G *uneben*. See UN-[1], EVEN[1]] **—une′venly,** *adv.* **—une′venness,** *n.*

uneventful (ŭn′ĭ vĕnt′fəl), *adj.* not eventful; lacking in important or striking occurrences: *an uneventful day at the office.* **—un′event′fully,** *adv.* **—un′event′fulness,** *n.*

unexacting (ŭn′ĭg zăk′tĭng), *adj.* **1.** not exacting; undemanding. **2.** easily satisfied; uncritical.

unexampled (ŭn′ĭg zăm′pəld), *adj.* unlike anything previously known; without parallel; unprecedented: *unexampled kindness, unexampled lawlessness.*

unexceptionable (ŭn′ĭk sĕp′shə nə bəl), *adj.* not open or liable to any exception or objection; beyond criticism. **—un′excep′tionableness,** *n.* **—un′excep′tionably,** *adv.*

unexceptional (ŭn′ĭk sĕp′shə nəl), *adj.* **1.** not exceptional; not unusual or extraordinary. **2.** admitting of no exception. **3.** unexceptionable. **—un′excep′tionally,** *adv.*

unexpected (ŭn′ĭk spĕk′tĭd), *adj.* unforeseen; surprising. **—un′expect′edly,** *adv.* **—un′expect′edness,** *n.* **—Syn.** See **sudden.**

unexperienced (ŭn′ĭk spĭə′rĭ ənst), *adj.* **1.** not furnished with or taught by experience; inexperienced. **2.** not known by experience, as facts; not having been experienced, as sensations.

unexpired (ŭn′ĭk spī′əd), *adj.* not having expired, as a period of time, lease, etc.; remaining.

unexplainable (ŭn′ĭk splā′nə bəl), *adj.* (of events) such that no explanation can be found; mysterious; inexplicable.

unexposed (ŭn′ĭk spōzd′), *adj.* *Photog.* (of film) not having been exposed to the light; unused.

unexpressed (ŭn′ĭk sprĕst′), *adj.* **1.** not expressed, stated, or communicated. **2.** not stated explicitly; tacit.

unexpressive (ŭn′ĭk sprĕs′ĭv), *adj.* **1.** inexpressive. **2.** *Obs.* inexpressible. **—un′expres′sively,** *adv.* **—un′expres′siveness,** *n.*

unfading (ŭn fā′dĭng), *adj.* **1.** not diminishing: *unfading enthusiasm.* **2.** not fading, as colour. **—unfad′ingly,** *adv.* **—unfad′ingness,** *n.*

unfailing (ŭn fā′lĭng), *adj.* **1.** not failing or giving way; totally dependable: *unfailing good humour.* **2.** never giving out; unceasing; continuous: *an unfailing supply.* **3.** certain; infallible: *an unfailing test.* **—unfail′ingly,** *adv.* **—unfail′ingness,** *n.*

unfair (ŭn fĕə′), *adj.* **1.** not fair; biased or partial; not just or equitable; unjust. **2.** marked by deceptive dishonest practices. [ME; OE *unfæger*, c. Icel. *úfagr*. See UN-[1], FAIR[1]] **—unfair′ly,** *adv.* **—unfair′ness,** *n.*

unfaithful (ŭn fāth′fəl), *adj.* **1.** false to duty or promises; disloyal; perfidious; faithless. **2.** not upright; dishonest. **3.** not faithfully accurate or exact, as a copy or description.

---

unease′, *n.*
uneat′able, *adj.*
uneat′en, *adj.*
un′eclipsed′, *adj.*
uned′ified′, *adj.*
uned′ify′ing, *adj.*
uned′ited, *adj.*
un′effaced′, *adj.*
un′elab′orat′ed, *adj.*
un′elapsed′, *adj.*
un′elat′ed, *adj.*
un′elect′ed, *adj.*
un′eman′cipat′ed, *adj.*
un′embel′lished, *adj.*
un′embit′tered, *adj.*
un′embod′ied, *adj.*
un′embraced′, *adj.*
un′emphat′ic, *adj.*
un′emphat′ically, *adv.*
un′enclosed′, *adj.*
un′encour′aged, *adj.*
un′encum′bered, *adj.*
un′endear′ing, *adj.*
unend′ing, *adj.*
unend′ingly, *adv.*
unend′ingness, *n.*
un′endorsed′, *adj.*
un′endowed′, *adj.*
un′endur′able, *adj.*
un′endur′ably, *adv.*
un′endur′ing, *adj.*
un′enforce′able, *adj.*
un′enfran′chised, *adj.*
un′engaged′, *adj.*
un′engag′ing, *adj.*
un′enjoy′able, *adj.*
un′enlist′ed, *adj.*
un′enliv′ened, *adj.*
un′enquir′ing, *adj.*
un′enriched′, *adj.*
un′enrolled′, *adj.*
un′entailed′, *adj.*
unen′tered, *adj.*
un′enthu′siast′ic, *adj.*
un′enti′tled, *adj.*
unen′vied, *adj.*
unen′vious, *adj.*
uneq′uable, *adj.*
une′qualized′, *adj.*
uneq′uitable, *adj.*
un′erad′icat′ed, *adj.*
un′escap′able, *adj.*
un′escort′ed, *adj.*
un′estab′lished, *adj.*
un′evangel′ical, *adj.*
un′evap′orat′ed, *adj.*
un′evolved′, *adj.*
un′exag′gerat′ed, *adj.*
un′exam′ined, *adj.*
un′excelled′, *adj.*
un′excit′able, *adj.*
un′excit′ed, *adj.*
un′excit′ing, *adj.*
un′exclu′sive, *adj.*
un′exclu′sively, *adv.*
un′exclu′siveness, *n.*
unex′ecut′ed, *adj.*
un′exem′plified′, *adj.*
unex′ercised′, *adj.*
un′exhaust′ed, *adj.*
unex′orcized′, *adj.*
un′expand′ed, *adj.*
un′expan′sive, *adj.*
un′expend′ed, *adj.*
un′explain′able, *adj.*
un′explain′ably, *adv.*
un′explained′, *adj.*
un′exploit′ed, *adj.*
un′explored′, *adj.*
unex′purgat′ed, *adj.*
un′extend′ed, *adj.*
un′exten′uat′ed, *adj.*
un′extin′guished, *adj.*
unfad′ed, *adj.*
unfal′len, *adj.*
unfal′sified′, *adj.*
unfal′tering, *adj.*
unfal′teringly, *adv.*

---

4. adulterous. 5. *Obs.* unbelieving; infidel. —**unfaith′fully,** *adv.* —**unfaith′fulness,** *n.*

unfamiliar (ŭn′fə mĭl′yə), *adj.* **1.** not familiar; not acquainted or conversant: *be unfamiliar with a subject.* **2.** not well known; unaccustomed; unusual; strange: *a subject unfamiliar to me.* —**unfamiliarity** (ŭn′fə mĭl′ĭ ăr′rĭ tĭ), *n.* —**un′famil′iarly,** *adv.*

unfashionable (ŭn făsh′nə bl), *adj.* **1.** not in accordance with the prevailing fashion or taste. **2.** not in demand, as styles, objects, etc. **3.** (of people) not following the current fashion. **4.** (of people) not concerned with or interested in fashion; continuously out of fashion. —**un′fashionabil′ity, unfash′ionableness,** *n.* —**unfash′ionably,** *adv.*

unfasten (ŭn fä′sən), *v.t.* **1.** to loose from, or as from, fastenings. **2.** to undo or open (a fastening). —*v.i.* **3.** to become unfastened.

unfathered (ŭn fä′thəd), *adj.* **1.** of unknown paternity; bastard. **2.** having no father; deprived of a father; fatherless. **3.** not ascribable to a particular author or responsible person; unauthenticated.

unfathomable (ŭn făth′ə mə bl), *adj.* **1.** not fathomable; incapable of being fathomed. **2.** impenetrable by the mind; inscrutable; incomprehensible. —**unfath′omableness,** *n.* —**unfath′omably,** *adv.*

unfavourable (ŭn fā′və rə bl, -vrə bl), *adj.* not favourable; not propitious; disadvantageous; adverse. Also, *U.S.,* **unfavorable.** —**unfa′vourableness,** *n.* —**unfa′vourably,** *adv.*

unfeatured (ŭn fē′chəd), *adj.* **1.** not featured; not given special prominence. **2.** *Obs.* featureless.

unfeeling (ŭn fē′lĭng), *adj.* **1.** not feeling; devoid of feeling; insensible or insensate. **2.** unsympathetic; callous; hard-hearted. —**unfeel′ingly,** *adv.* —**unfeel′ingness,** *n.* —**Syn. 2.** See **hard.**

unfeigned (ŭn fānd′), *adj.* not feigned; sincere. —**unfeignedly** (ŭn fā′nĭd lĭ), *adv.* —**unfeign′edness,** *n.*

unfeminine (ŭn fĕm′ĭ nĭn), *adj.* **1.** (of dress, behaviour, etc.) unsuitable for a woman. **2.** exhibiting such characteristics. —**unfem′inineness,** *n.*

unfetter (ŭn fĕt′ə), *v.t.* **1.** to free from fetters. **2.** to free from restraint of any kind.

unfettered (ŭn fĕt′əd), *adj.* unrestrained; not hindered or restricted.

unfilled aperture, *Astron.* a method of constructing a radio telescope in which two aerials are combined into one radio interferometer, giving the effect of two large apertures, although only two perpendicular arms of the aerial system need be constructed.

unfinished (ŭn fĭn′ĭsht), *adj.* **1.** not finished; incomplete. **2.** lacking some special finish. **3.** not sheared, as cloth.

unfired (ŭn fī′əd), *adj.* **1.** not having been fired, as a gun. **2.** (of pottery, etc.) not baked in a kiln. **3.** not roused or excited.

unfit (ŭn fĭt′), *adj., v.,* **-fitted, -fitting.** —*adj.* **1.** not fit; not adapted or suited; unsuitable; not deserving or good enough. **2.** unqualified or incompetent. **3.** not physically fit or in due condition. —*v.t.* **4.** to render unfit or unsuitable; disqualify. —**unfit′ly,** *adv.* —**unfit′ness,** *n.*

unfix (ŭn fĭks′), *v.t.* **1.** to render no longer fixed; unfasten; detach; loosen. **2.** to unsettle.

unflagging (ŭn flăg′ĭng), *adj.* not slackening or weakening, as from fatigue; untiring. —**unflag′gingly,** *adv.*

unflappable (ŭn flăp′ə bl), *adj.* imperturbable; not easily upset. —**unflap′pably,** *adv.* —**unflap′pableness,** *n.*

unfledged (ŭn flĕjd′), *adj.* **1.** not fledged; without feathers sufficiently developed for flight, as a young bird. **2.** immature; undeveloped; callow.

unfleshly (ŭn flĕsh′lĭ), *adj.* not fleshly; not carnal or corporeal; spiritual.

unflinching (ŭn flĭn′chĭng), *adj.* not flinching; unshrinking: *he faced dangers with unflinching courage.* —**unflinch′ingly,** *adv.*

unfold (ŭn fōld′), *v.t.* **1.** to bring out of a folded state; spread or open out: *unfold your arms.* **2.** to develop. **3.** to spread out or lay open to view. **4.** to reveal or display. **5.** to reveal or disclose in words; set forth; explain. —*v.i.* **6.** to become unfolded; open out. **7.** to become plain, as by expansion; develop; be revealed: *his story unfolded slowly.* [ME; OE *unfealdan,* c. G *entfalten.* See UN-[2], FOLD[1]] —**unfold′er,** *n.* —**unfold′ment,** *n.*

unforced (ŭn fôst′), *adj.* not compelled; produced without difficulty; spontaneous; natural. —**unforcedly** (ŭn-fô′sĭd lĭ), *adv.* —**unforc′edness,** *n.*

unforeseen (ŭn′fô sēn′), *adj.* not predicted; unexpected.

unforgettable (ŭn′fə gĕt′ə bl), *adj.* not forgettable; never to be forgotten; remarkable: *scenes of unforgettable beauty.* —**un′forget′tably,** *adv.*

unformed (ŭn fômd′), *adj.* **1.** not formed; not definitely shaped; shapeless or formless. **2.** undeveloped; crude. **3.** not trained or educated, as the mind. **4.** not made or created.

unfortunate (ŭn fô′chə nĭt), *adj.* **1.** not lucky; tending to suffer mishaps. **2.** regrettable; disastrous; constituting a misfortune. **3.** unpropitious; likely to have undesirable results: *an unfortunate decision.* **4.** unsuitable; inept: *an unfortunate choice of words.* **5.** deserving of sympathy; sad. —*n.* **6.** an unfortunate person. **7.** *Obs.* a prostitute. —**unfor′tunately,** *adv.* —**unfor′tunateness,** *n.*

unfounded (ŭn foun′dĭd), *adj.* without foundation; baseless: *unfounded suspicions.* —**unfound′edly,** *adv.* —**unfound′edness,** *n.*

unfreeze (ŭn frēz′), *v.,* **-froze, -frozen, -freezing.** —*v.t.* **1.** to thaw out; cause to thaw. **2.** to relax restrictions on (prices, incomes, credit, etc.). **3.** to lift controls from the manufacture of or dealing in (a commodity or the like). —*v.i.* **4.** to thaw.

unfrequented (ŭn′frĭ kwĕn′tĭd), *adj.* not frequented, as places; little resorted to or visited; solitary.

unfriended (ŭn frĕn′dĭd), *adj.* without friends; friendless. —**unfriend′edness,** *n.*

unfriendly (ŭn frĕnd′lĭ), *adj.* **1.** not friendly; hostile; inimical; unkindly. **2.** unfavourable, as a climate. —*adv.* **3.** *Rare.* in an unfriendly manner. —**unfriend′liness,** *n.*

unfrock (ŭn frŏk′), *v.t.* to deprive of priestly status.

unfruitful (ŭn froot′fəl), *adj.* not fruitful; unproductive; barren; fruitless. —**unfruit′fully,** *adv.* —**unfruit′fulness,** *n.*

unfurl (ŭn fûl′), *v.t.* **1.** to spread or shake out from a furled state, as a sail or a flag; unfold. —*v.i.* **2.** to become unfurled.

unfurnished (ŭn fû′nĭsht), *adj.* **1.** (of rented living accommodation) not furnished by the landlord; rented without furniture. **2.** not equipped or provided (often fol. by *with*).

ungainly (ŭn gān′lĭ), *adj.* **1.** not gainly; not graceful or shapely; awkward; clumsy; uncouth. —*adv.* **2.** in an awkward manner. [ME *ungaynly,* adv. See UN-[1], GAINLY, adj.] —**ungain′liness,** *n.*

Ungaretti (*It.* ōōn gä rĕt′tē), *n.* **Giuseppe** (*It.* jōō zĕp′pĕ), 1888–1970, Italian poet.

---

unfamed′, *adj.*
un′famil′iarized′, *adj.*
unfan′cied, *adj.*
unfan′ciful, *adj.*
unfanned′, *adj.*
unfash′ioned, *adj.*
un′fastid′ious, *adj.*
unfath′omed, *adj.*
un′fatigued′, *adj.*
un′fati′guing, *adj.*
unfa′voured, *adj.*
unfeared′, *adj.*
unfear′ful, *adj.*
unfear′fully, *adv.*
un′feasibil′ity, *n.*
unfea′sible, *adj.*
unfeath′ered, *adj.*
unfeign′ing, *adj.*
unfelled′, *adj.*
un′feminin′ity, *n.*
unfenced′, *adj.*
unfer′tile, *adj.*
un′ferment′ed, *adj.*
unfer′tilized′, *adj.*
unfig′ured, *adj.*
unfiled′, *adj.*
unfil′ially, *adv.*
unfil′lable, *adj.*
unfilled′, *adj.*
unfil′leted, *adj.*
unfilmed′, *adj.*
unfil′terable, *adj.*
unfil′tered, *adj.*
unfind′able, *adj.*
unfin′ishable, *adj.*
unfirm′, *adj.*
unfirm′ly, *adv.*
unfished′, *adj.*
unfit′ted, *adj.*
unfit′ting, *adj.*
unfit′tingly, *adv.*
unfix′ity, *n.*
unflanked′, *adj.*
unflat′tened, *adj.*
unflat′tered, *adj.*
unflat′tering, *adj.*
unflat′teringly, *adv.*
unflawed′, *adj.*
unflick′ering, *adj.*
unfloored′, *adj.*
unfluc′tuat′ing, *adj.*
unflur′ried, *adj.*
unflushed′, *adj.*
unflut′ed, *adj.*
un′forbid′den, *adj.*
unford′able, *adj.*
un′foresee′able, *adj.*
un′foresee′ably, *adv.*
unfor′feitable, *adj.*
unforge′able, *adj.*
unforged′, *adj.*
un′forgiv′able, *adj.*
un′forgiv′ably, *adv.*
un′forgiv′en, *adj.*
un′forgiv′ing, *adj.*
un′forgiv′ingly, *adv.*
un′forgot′ten, *adj.*
unfor′mulat′ed, *adj.*
unfor′tified′, *adj.*
unfos′silized′, *adj.*
unfought′, *adj.*
unframed′, *adj.*
unfran′chised, *adj.*
unfranked′, *adj.*
unfre′quently, *adv.*
unfret′ted, *adj.*
unfright′ened, *adj.*
unfrost′ed, *adj.*
unfrown′ing, *adj.*
unfro′zen, *adj.*
unfu′elled, *adj.*
un′fulfilled′, *adj.*
unfund′ed, *adj.*
unfun′ny, *adj.*
unfurn′ish, *v.t.*
unfurred′, *adj.*
unfur′rowed, *adj.*
unfused′, *adj.*
unfus′sy, *adj.*
ungagged′, *adj.*
ungain′ful, *adj.*
ungal′lant, *adj.*
ungal′lantly, *adv.*
ungal′lantry, *n.*
ungar′nered, *adj.*
ungar′nished, *adj.*
ungar′risoned, *adj.*
ungar′tered, *adj.*
ungath′ered, *adj.*
ungauged′, *adj.*

Ungava (ŭng gā′və, -gä′və), *n.* former name of a region in NE Canada comprising the larger part of the peninsula of Labrador: incorporated into Quebec province 1912.
ungenerous (ŭn jĕn′ə rəs), *adj.* not generous; ignoble; illiberal; mean. —**ungen′erously,** *adv.* —**ungen′erousness, un′generos′ity,** *n.*
ungentle (ŭn jĕn′tl), *adj.* **1.** rough or harsh, as people or their speech or actions. **2.** *Archaic or Rare.* not possessing the attributes of good birth and breeding. —**ungent′ly,** *adv.* —**ungen′tleness,** *n.*
unget-at-able (ŭn′gĕt ăt′ə bl), *adj.* inaccessible. Also, **ungetatable.** —**un′get-at′-ably,** *adv.*
ungird (ŭn gûrd′), *v.t. Archaic.* **1.** to unfasten or take off the girdle or belt of. **2.** to loosen, or take off, by unfastening a girdle. [UN-² + GIRD¹. Cf. G *entgürten*]
ungirt (ŭn gûrt′), *adj. Archaic.* **1.** having a girdle loosened or removed. **2.** not taut or tightened for use; loose.
unglue (ŭn gloo′), *v.t.*, **-glued, -gluing.** **1.** to separate or open (something fastened with, or as with, glue). **2.** to separate; dissolve.
ungodly (ŭn gŏd′lĭ), *adj.* **1.** not godly; not conforming to God's laws; irreligious; impious; sinful. **2.** wicked. **3.** *Colloq.* dreadful; outrageous. —*n.* **4. the ungodly,** wicked people. —**ungod′lily,** *adv.* —**ungod′liness,** *n.*
ungotten (ŭn gŏt′n), *adj.* **1.** not obtained or gained. **2.** *Obs.* not begotten.
ungovernable (ŭn gŭv′ə nə bl), *adj.* that cannot be governed, ruled, or restrained; uncontrollable. —**ungov′ernableness,** *n.* —**ungov′ernably,** *adv.*
ungraceful (ŭn grās′fəl), *adj.* not graceful; lacking grace or elegance; clumsy; awkward. —**ungrace′fully,** *adv.* —**ungrace′fulness,** *n.*
ungracious (ŭn grā′shəs), *adj.* **1.** not gracious; lacking in gracious courtesy or affability. **2.** unacceptable; unwelcome. **3.** *Obs.* ungraceful; unpleasing. —**ungra′ciously,** *adv.* —**ungra′ciousness,** *n.*
ungrammatical (ŭn′grə măt′ĭ kl), *adj.* **1.** not conforming to the rules of grammar; grammatically clumsy or wrong. **2.** not in accordance with a particular method or set of rules. **3.** not according to native usage, as the language of a foreigner. —**un′grammat′ically,** *adv.*
ungrateful (ŭn grāt′fəl), *adj.* **1.** not grateful; not feeling or displaying gratitude; giving no return or recompense. **2.** unpleasant; disagreeable. **3.** (of land) responding badly to cultivation. **4.** thankless; not repaying one's efforts. —**ungrate′fully,** *adv.* —**ungrate′fulness,** *n.*
ungrounded (ŭn groun′dĭd), *adj.* baseless; without grounds or justification. —**unground′edly,** *adv.* —**unground′edness,** *n.*
ungrudging (ŭn grŭj′ĭng), *adj.* not grudging; willing; hearty; liberal. —**ungrudg′ingly,** *adv.*
ungual (ŭng′gwəl), *adj.* of or pertaining to, bearing, or shaped like a nail, claw, or hoof. [f. s. L *unguis* nail, claw + -AL¹]
unguarded (ŭn gä′dĭd), *adj.* **1.** not guarded; unprotected; undefended. **2.** incautious; imprudent; characterized by carelessness or indiscretion: *a confession made in an unguarded moment.* **3.** open; guileless; candid. **4.** *Chess, Cards, etc.* open to attack by an opponent. **5.** having no guard, screen, or the like. —**unguard′edly,** *adv.* —**unguard′edness,** *n.*
unguent (ŭng′gwənt), *n.* any soft preparation or salve, usually of butter-like consistency, applied to sores, etc.; an ointment. [ME, t. L: s. *unguentum*] —**unguentary** (ŭng′gwən tə rĭ, -trĭ), *adj.*
unguessed (ŭn gĕst′), *adj.* **1.** not known or solved by guessing. **2.** unexpected (often fol. by *at*).
unguiculate (ŭng gwĭk′yoo lĭt, -lāt′), *adj.* Also, **unguic′ulat′ed.** **1.** bearing or resembling a nail or claw. **2.** *Zool.* having nails or claws, as distinguished from hoofs. **3.** *Bot.* having a clawlike base, as certain petals. See illus. under **corolla.** —*n.* **4.** an unguiculate animal. [t. NL: m. s. *unguiculātus*, der. L *unguiculus* fingernail, dim. of *unguis* claw]
unguinous (ŭng′gwĭ nəs), *adj.* consisting of or resembling fat or oil; oily. [t. L: m. s. *unguinōsus* oily]
unguis (ŭng′gwĭs), *n., pl.* **-gues** (-gwēz). **1.** a nail, claw, or hoof. **2.** *Bot.* the clawlike base of certain petals. [t. L]
ungula (ŭng′gyoo lə), *n., pl.* **-lae** (-lē′). **1.** *Geom.* a part cut off from a cylinder, cone, or the like, by a plane oblique to the base. **2.** *Zool.* a hoof. [t. L]

Ungula (def. 1)

ungular (ŭng′gyoo lə), *adj.* pertaining to or of the nature of an ungula; ungual.
ungulate (ŭng′gyoo lĭt, -lāt′), *adj.* **1.** having hoofs. **2.** belonging or pertaining to the *Ungulata*, a group sometimes set up, though without phylogenetic justification, in order to classify all hoofed mammals together in one category. **3.** hoof-like. —*n.* **4.** a hoofed mammal. [t. L: m. s. *ungulātus* having claws]
unguligrade (ŭng′gyoo lĭ grād′), *adj. Zool.* walking on hoofs. [f. *unguli-* (comb. form repr. UNGULA) + -GRADE]
unhair (ŭn hĕə′), *v.t.* **1.** *Tanning.* to free from hair. —*v.i.* **2.** to become free of hair.
unhallow (ŭn hăl′ō), *v.t. Obs. Rare.* to desecrate; profane.
unhallowed (ŭn hăl′ōd), *adj.* **1.** not hallowed or consecrated. **2.** profane; impious or wicked.
unhand (ŭn hănd′), *v.t. Archaic.* to take the hand or hands from; release from a grasp; let go.
unhandsome (ŭn hăn′səm), *adj.* **1.** lacking good looks; plain or ugly. **2.** ungracious; discourteous; unseemly; mean. **3.** ungenerous; illiberal. —**unhand′somely,** *adv.* —**unhand′someness,** *n.*
unhandy (ŭn hăn′dĭ), *adj.* **1.** not handy; not easy to handle or manage, as things. **2.** not skilful in using the hands, as persons. —**unhand′ily,** *adv.* —**unhand′iness,** *n.*
unhanged (ŭn hăngd′), *adj.* not yet executed by hanging.
unhappy (ŭn hăp′ĭ), *adj.*, **-ier, -iest.** **1.** sad, miserable, or wretched. **2.** unfortunate; unlucky. **3.** unfavourable; inauspicious. **4.** infelicitous: *an unhappy remark.* **5.** *Obs.* of wretched character; objectionable. —**unhap′pily,** *adv.* —**unhap′piness,** *n.* —**Syn.** **1.** sorrowful, downcast, cheerless, disconsolate. **4.** inappropriate, inapt.
unharness (ŭn hä′nĭs), *v.t.* **1.** to strip of harness; free (a horse, etc.) from harness or gear. **2.** to divest of armour.
unharnessed (ŭn hä′nĭst), *adj.* **1.** (of a horse, etc.) divested of harness. **2.** not under control for industrial exploitation, as a river.
unhasp (ŭn häsp′), *v.t.* to loose the hasp of.
unhat (ŭn hăt′), *v.*, **-hatted, -hatting.** *Rare.* —*v.t.* **1.** to remove the hat from. —*v.i.* **2.** to take off one's hat, as in respect.
unhealthy (ŭn hĕl′thĭ), *adj.*, **-healthier, -healthiest.** **1.** not healthy; not possessing health; not in a healthy or sound condition. **2.** characteristic of or resulting from bad health. **3.** hurtful to health; unwholesome. **4.** morally harmful; noxious. **5.** morbid: *an unhealthy interest in death.* **6.** *Slang.* dangerous. —**unheal′thily,** *adv.* —**unheal′thiness,** *n.* —**Syn.** **1.** sickly, delicate, frail, weak, ill, diseased. **3.** unhealthful, unsanitary, unhygienic, unsalubrious.
unheard (ŭn hûd′), *adj.* **1.** not heard; not perceived by the ear. **2.** not given a hearing or audience. **3.** not heard of; unknown.
unheard-of (ŭn hûd′ŏv′), *adj.* **1.** that was never heard of; unknown. **2.** such as was never known before; unprecedented.
unheeding (ŭn hē′dĭng), *adj.* not attentive or watchful; unobservant (sometimes fol. by *of*). —**unheed′ingly,** *adv.*
unhelm (ŭn hĕlm′), *v.t. Archaic.* to deprive of the helm or helmet.
unhinge (ŭn hĭnj′), *v.t.*, **-hinged, -hinging.** **1.** to take (a door, etc.) off the hinges. **2.** to unbalance (the mind, etc.). **3.** to remove the hinges from. **4.** to detach or separate from something. **5.** to deprive of fixity or stability; throw into confusion or disorder. **6.** to upset or discompose (a person). **7.** to unsettle (opinions, etc.).
unhistorical (ŭn′hĭs tŏr′ĭ kl), *adj.* **1.** not in accordance with historical principles or the accepted methods of historians. **2.** not in history; not having occurred. —**un′histor′ically,** *adv.*
unhitch (ŭn hĭch′), *v.t.* to free from being hitched or fastened; unfasten.

ungear′, *v.t.*
ungeld′ed, *adj.*
ungelt′, *adj.*
ungen′eraliz′able, *adj.*
ungen′eralized′, *adj.*
unge′nial, *adj.*
un′genial′ity, *n.*
unge′nially, *adv.*
ungen′tlemanly, *adj.*
ungen′tlemanliness, *n.*
ungift′ed, *adj.*
ungild′, *v.t.*
ungild′ed, *adj.*
ungilt′, *adj.*
ungirth′, *v.t.*
ungirthed′, *adj.*
ungiv′en, *adj.*
unglam′orous, *adj.*
unglazed′, *adj.*
unglor′ified′, *adj.*
unglove′, *v.t.*
ungod′like′, *adj.*
ungov′erned, *adj.*
ungraced′, *adj.*
ungrad′ed, *adj.*
ungrad′uat′ed, *adj.*
ungraft′ed, *adj.*
ungrant′ed, *adj.*
ungrasp′able, *adj.*
ungrasp′ably, *adv.*
ungrasped′, *adj.*
ungrat′ified′, *adj.*
ungrat′ify′ing, *adj.*
ungreased′, *adj.*
ungroomed′, *adj.*
unground′, *adj.*
ungrudged′, *adj.*
unguid′able, *adj.*
unguid′ed, *adj.*
ungum′, *v.t.*
ungummed′, *adj.*
unhack′neyed, *adj.*
unhalt′ing, *adj.*
unham′pered, *adj.*
unhan′dicapped′, *adj.*
unhan′dled, *adj.*
unhang′, *v.t.*
unhar′dened, *adj.*

unholy (ŭn hō′lĭ), *adj.*, **-lier, -liest.** **1.** not holy; not sacred or hallowed. **2.** impious; sinful; wicked. **3.** *Colloq.* dreadful; outrageous. [ME; OE *unhālig*, c. D *onheilig*, Icel. *ūheilagr*. See UN-[1], HOLY] —**unho′lily,** *adv.* —**unho′liness,** *n.*

unhood (ŭn ho͝od′), *v.t.* to divest of a hood, esp. that of a hawk.

unhook (ŭn ho͝ok′), *v.t.* **1.** to loose from a hook. **2.** to open or undo by loosening a hook or hooks. —*v.i.* **3.** to become unhooked.

unhoped-for (ŭn hōpt′fô′), *adj.* not hoped or looked for; unexpected.

unhorse (ŭn hôs′), *v.t.*, **-horsed, -horsing.** **1.** to throw from a horse, as in battle. **2.** to cause to fall from the saddle. **3.** to dislodge; overthrow.

unhouse (ŭn houz′), *v.t.*, **-housed, -housing.** to drive from a house or habitation; deprive of shelter.

unhung (ŭn hŭng′), *adj.* (of a picture) not yet publicly exhibited.

unhusk (ŭn hŭsk′), *v.t.* to free from, or as from, a husk.

uni-, a word element meaning 'one', 'single', as in *unisexual.* [t. L, comb. form of *ūnus* one]

Uniat (yo͞o′nĭ ăt′), *n.* a member of any of various communities of Greek and other Eastern Christians which acknowledge the supremacy of the pope and are in communion with the Church of Rome, but retain their own liturgy, rites, discipline, etc. Also, **Uniate** (yo͞o′nĭ ĭt, -āt′). [t. Russ.]

uniaxial (yo͞o′nĭ ăk′sĭ əl), *adj.* **1.** having one axis. **2.** *Crystall.* (of a crystal) having one direction in which no double refraction occurs. **3.** *Bot.* (of a plant) having a primary stem which does not branch. **4.** (of certain red seaweeds) having a structure in which the main axis is derived from a single filament of cells.

unicameral (yo͞o′nĭ kăm′ə rəl), *adj.* having, characterized by, or consisting of a single chamber, as a legislative assembly. —**u′nicam′eralism,** *n.* —**u′nicam′eralist,** *n.*

UNICEF (yo͞o′nĭ sĕf′), *n.* an organization created by the United Nations in 1946 to assist child health, nutrition, and welfare programmes. [*U*(*nited*) *N*(*ations*) *I*(*nternational*) *C*(*hildren's*) *E*(*mergency*) *F*(*und*)]

unicellular (yo͞o′nĭ sĕl′yo͞o lə), *adj.* pertaining to or consisting of a single cell.

unicellular animals, the protozoans.

unicity (yo͞o nĭs′ĭ tĭ), *n.* **1.** oneness; the fact of being single. **2.** the fact or state of being unique.

unicolour (yo͞o′nĭ kŭl′ə), *adj.* *Zool.* having only one colour.

unicorn (yo͞o′nĭ kôn′), *n.* **1.** a mythological animal with a single long horn, said to elude every captor save a virgin, and seldom caught. **2.** a conventional and heraldic representation of this animal, in the form of a horse with a lion's tail and with a long, straight, and spirally twisted horn. **3.** (in the Authorized Version of the Bible, Deut. 33:17, and elsewhere) a two-horned animal now usually identified with the rhinoceros or the aurochs. **4.** (formerly) a carriage drawn by three horses, two abreast behind one leader. **5.** the team of horses. **6.** the narwhal. **7.** *Obs.* the rhinoceros. —*adj.* **8.** having one horn. [ME, t. L: s. *ūnicornis* having one horn]

Unicorn

unicostate (yo͞o′nĭ kŏs′tāt), *adj.* **1.** having only one costa, rib, or ridge. **2.** *Bot.* (of a leaf) having only one primary or prominent rib, the midrib.

unicum (yo͞o′nĭ kəm), *n.* *Rare.* a unique example or thing.

unicycle (yo͞o′nĭ sī′kl), *n.* a vehicle with only one wheel, esp. a pedal-driven one used by acrobats.

unideal (ŭn′ī dĭəl′), *adj.* **1.** not having ideals, as a person. **2.** not marked by idealism. **3.** not ideal; not perfect. —**un′ideal′ism,** *n.*

unidirectional (yo͞o′nĭ dĭ rĕk′shə nəl), *adj.* having, or moving in, only one direction.

unifiable (yo͞o′nĭ fī′ə bl), *adj.* that may be unified.

unific (yo͞o nĭf′ĭk), *adj.* making one; forming unity; unifying.

unification (yo͞o′nĭ fĭ kā′shən), *n.* **1.** the act or process of unifying. **2.** the state of being unified.

unified field theory, *Physics.* any theory which is capable of describing the electromagnetic field and the gravitational field in one set of equations; no such satisfactory theory yet exists.

unifilar (yo͞o′nĭ fī′lə), *adj.* having or involving only one thread, wire, or the like.

uniflorous (yo͞o′nĭ flô′rəs), *adj.* *Bot.* having or bearing one flower only.

unifoliate (yo͞o′nĭ fō′lĭ ĭt, -āt′), *adj.* **1.** one-leafed. **2.** unifoliolate.

unifoliolate (yo͞o′nĭ fō′lĭ ə lāt′), *adj.* *Bot.* **1.** compound in structure yet having only one leaflet, as the leaf of the orange. **2.** bearing such leaves, as a plant.

Unifoliate leaf

uniform (yo͞o′nĭ fôm′), *adj.* **1.** having one form; having always the same form or character; unvarying. **2.** without diversity in appearance, colour, etc.; not discontinuous; unbroken. **3.** regular; even: *a uniform pace.* **4.** consistent in action, opinion, etc., as a person, or as action, etc.; being the same in all places or in all parts of a country: *a uniform divorce law.* **5.** agreeing with one another in form, character, appearance, etc.; alike; of the same form, character, etc., with another or others. —*n.* **6.** a distinctive dress of uniform style, materials, and colour worn by and identifying all the members of a group or organization, esp. a military body, school, etc. **7.** a distinctive dress characteristic of a particular social group or type of person. **8.** a single suit of such dress. —*v.t.* **9.** to clothe or furnish with or as with a uniform. **10.** to make uniform. [t. L: s. *ūniformis*] —**u′niform′ly,** *adv.* —**u′niform′ness,** *n.* —**Syn. 1.** invariable, unchanging. **3.** See **even.**

uniformalize (yo͞o′nĭ fô′mə līz′), *v.t.*, **-lized, -lizing.** *Rare.* to bring into uniformity. Also, **uniformalise.**

uniformed (yo͞o′nĭ fômd′), *adj.* wearing a uniform.

uniformitarian (yo͞o′nĭ fô′mĭ tëə′rĭ ən), *adj.* **1.** pertaining to uniformity or a doctrine of uniformity, esp. in geological theory. **2.** *Geol.* pertaining to the thesis that early geological processes are not different from those observed now. —*n.* **3.** one who adheres to a doctrine of uniformity. —**u′niform′itar′ianism,** *n.*

uniformity (yo͞o′nĭ fô′mĭ tĭ), *n.*, *pl.* **-ties.** **1.** the state or character of being uniform; sameness of form or character throughout; absence of variation or diversity. **2.** conformity among several things to each other or to a standard. **3.** regularity or evenness; consistency or agreement of structure or composition. **4.** wearisome sameness; monotony. **5.** conformity of opinions, attitudes, or the like, esp. in religion. **6.** something uniform; an extent or expanse of a uniform character.

uniform system, *Photog.* a system for marking the stops on a camera lens in which each stop corresponds to doubling or halving the exposure. On this scale unity is equal to an aperture of f4 on the f number scale. *Abbrev.*: u.s.

unify (yo͞o′nĭ fī′), *v.t.*, **-fied, -fying.** to form into one; make a unit of; reduce to unity. [t. ML: m. *ūnificāre*, f. L: *ūni-* UNI- + *-ficāre* -FY] —**u′nifi′er,** *n.*

unigeniture (yo͞o′nĭ jĕn′ĭ chə), *n.* (of Christ) the state or fact of being the only begotten.

Unigenitus (yo͞o′nĭ jĕn′ĭ təs), *n.* a papal bull of 1713 which condemned the teachings of the Jansenists in every particular, and by which they were suppressed.

unijugate (yo͞o′nĭ jo͞o′gĭt, -gāt), *adj.* *Bot.* (of a pinnate leaf) having a single pair of leaflets. [f. s. L *ūnijugus* having one yoke + -ATE[1]]

Unijugate leaf

unilabiate (yo͞o′nĭ lăb′ĭ ĭt, -āt′), *adj.* *Bot.* one-lipped, as a corolla.

unilateral (yo͞o′nĭ lăt′ə rəl), *adj.* **1.** pertaining to, occurring on, or affecting one side only. **2.** leaning or tending to one side. **3.** affecting one side, party, or person only. **4.** undertaken or performed by one side only: *unilateral disarmament.* **5.** concerned with or

---

unharmed′, *adj.*
un′harmo′nious, *adj.*
un′harmo′niously, *adv.*
unhar′mony, *n.*
unhar′vested, *adj.*
unhatched′, *adj.*
unhaz′ardous, *adj.*
unheal′able, *adj.*
unhealed′, *adj.*
unhear′ing, *adj.*
unheat′ed, *adj.*
unhedged′, *adj.*
unheed′ed, *adj.*
unheed′ful, *adj.*
unhel′meted, *adj.*
unhelped′, *adj.*
unhelp′ful, *adj.*
unhelp′fulness, *n.*
unhemmed′, *adj.*
unher′alded, *adj.*
un′hero′ic, *adj.*
un′hero′ically, *adv.*
unhes′itat′ing, *adj.*
unhes′itat′ingly, *adv.*
unhewn′, *adj.*
unhid′den, *adj.*
unhin′dered, *adj.*
unhome′like′, *adj.*
unhome′liness, *n.*
unhome′ly, *adj.*
unhon′oured, *adj.*
unhope′ful, *adj.*
unhope′fully, *adv.*
unhop′ing, *adj.*
un′hospit′able, *adj.*
unhulled′, *adj.*
unhu′man, *adj.*
unhu′manize′, *v.t.*
unhunt′ed, *adj.*
unhur′ried, *adj.*
unhur′riedly, *adv.*
unhur′rying, *adj.*
unhurt′, *adj.*
unhus′banded, *adj.*
un′ide′alis′tic, *adj.*
un′iden′tified, *adj.*
un′idiomat′ic, *adj.*
un′ignit′ed, *adj.*

---

considering but one side of a matter or question; one-sided. 6. *Law.* (of contracts and obligations) binding one party only; more generally, affecting one party only. 7. *Bot.* having all the parts disposed on one side of an axis, as an inflorescence. 8. *Sociol.* indicating line of descent through parents of one sex only. 9. *Phonet.* produced on one side of the tongue, as *unilateral l.* —**u′nilat′eral′ity,** *n.* —**u′nilat′erally,** *adv.*

unilingual (yōō′nĭ lĭng′gwəl), *adj.* knowing, using, concerning, or in only one language.

unilluminating (ŭn′ĭ lyōō′mĭ nā′tĭng), *adj.* 1. failing to clarify or inform. 2. failing to shed light.

unilobed (yōō′nĭ lōbd′), *adj.* having, or consisting of, a single lobe.

unilocular (yōō′nĭ lŏk′yŏŏ lə), *adj. Bot., Zool.* having, or consisting of, but one loculus, chamber, or cell.

unimaginable (ŭn′ĭ măj′ĭ nə bl), *adj.* 1. impossible to conceive or comprehend. 2. remarkable, tremendous, or extraordinary. —**un′imag′inableness,** *n.* —**un′imag′inably,** *adv.*

unimpassioned (ŭn′ĭm păsh′ənd), *adj.* free of strong emotion; unmoved; uninfluenced by emotion.

unimpeachable (ŭn′ĭm pē′chə bl), *adj.* 1. that cannot be doubted; beyond question. 2. irreproachable; blameless. —**un′impeach′abil′ity,** *n.* —**un′impeach′ably,** *adv.*

unimportant (ŭn′ĭm pô′tnt), *adj.* lacking importance; insignificant. —**un′impor′tance,** *n.*

unimposing (ŭn′ĭm pō′zĭng), *adj.* not imposing or impressive.

unimproved (ŭn′ĭm prōōvd′), *adj.* 1. not made better, more useful, more efficient, etc. 2. (of land) **a.** not built upon or developed. **b.** not cultivated; left in the wild state. 3. not bred for better quality or productiveness, as crops, domestic animals, etc. 4. not better, as health.

unincorporated company, a company formed for business purposes without sanction of a special charter or an act of Parliament.

uninformed (ŭn′ĭn fômd′), *adj.* 1. lacking knowledge in some or any respect; uneducated. 2. lacking knowledge or information (as to some matter).

uninhibited (ŭn′ĭn hĭb′ĭ tĭd), *adj.* 1. not restrained by social conventions; informal; free. 2. not impeded or restricted by inhibitions.

uninspired (ŭn′ĭn spī′əd), *adj.* dull; lacking inspiration or spiritedness; unimaginative.

uninspiring (ŭn′ĭn spī′ə rĭng), *adj.* not stimulating or exciting; dreary.

unintelligent (ŭn′ĭn tĕl′ĭ jənt), *adj.* 1. deficient in intelligence; dull or stupid. 2. marked by lack of intelligence. 3. not endowed with intelligence: *plants are an unintelligent form of life.* —**un′intel′ligence,** *n.* —**un′intel′ligently,** *adv.*

unintelligible (ŭn′ĭn tĕl′ĭ jə bl), *adj.* not intelligible; not capable of being understood. —**un′intel′ligibil′ity, un′intel′ligibleness,** *n.* —**un′intel′ligibly,** *adv.*

unintentional (ŭn′ĭn tĕn′shə nəl), *adj.* not intentional; not acting with intention; not done purposely, or not designed. —**un′inten′tional′ity,** *n.* —**un′inten′tionally,** *adv.*

uninterested (ŭn ĭn′trĭs tĭd), *adj.* 1. having or showing no feeling of interest; indifferent. 2. not personally concerned in something. 3. *Colloq.* disinterested. —**unin′terestedly,** *adv.* —**unin′terestedness,** *n.* —**Syn.** 1. See **disinterested.**

uninterrupted (ŭn′ĭn tə rŭp′tĭd), *adj.* 1. unbroken; continuous. 2. unified; having no divisions between the parts. —*adv.* 3. without interruption. —**un′interrupt′edly,** *adv.* —**un′interrupt′edness,** *n.*

uninucleate (yōō′nĭ nyōō′klĭ ĭt), *adj. Biol.* (of a cell) containing only one nucleus.

union (yōō′nyən), *n.* 1. the act of uniting two or more things into one. 2. the state of being so united; conjunction; combination. 3. something formed by uniting two or more things; a combination. 4. a number of persons, societies, states, or the like, joined together or associated for some common purpose. 5. the uniting of persons, parties, etc., in general agreement. 6. a uniting of states or nations into one political body, as that of the American colonies at the time of the War of American Independence, that of England and Scotland in 1707, or that of Great Britain and Ireland in 1801. 7. **the Union, a.** the United States of America. **b.** (from 1603) the uniting of the English and Scottish crowns; (from 1707) the uniting of their parliaments. **c.** (from 1801) the uniting of the parliaments of Great Britain and Ireland. **d.** (from 1920) the uniting of the countries of Great Britain and Northern Ireland. 8. a device emblematic of union, used in a flag or ensign, sometimes occupying the upper corner next to the staff, or sometimes occupying the entire field. 9. a uniting or being united in marriage, or some similar relationship. 10. a trade union. 11. *Hist.* a number of parishes united for the administration of the poor laws, etc. 12. a union house. 13. any of various contrivances for connecting parts of machinery, etc., esp. a fitting composed of three parts used to connect the ends of two pipes, neither of which can be turned. 14. a fabric made of two kinds of yarn, of which one is usually cotton. 15. (*cap.*) a club or debating society for the members of certain universities. [late ME, t. L: s. *ūnio*]

—**Syn.** 2. UNION, UNITY agree in referring to a oneness, either created by putting together, or by being undivided. A UNION is a state of being united, a combination, as the result of joining two or more things into one: *to promote the union between two families, the Union of England and Scotland.* UNITY is the state or inherent quality of being one, single, individual, and indivisible (often as consequence of union): *to find unity in diversity, to give unity to a work of art.* 4. See **alliance.** —**Ant.** 2. division.

union card, a card identifying one as a member of a trade union.

Union Flag, the Union Jack.

union house, *Hist.* a workhouse erected and maintained by a poor law union.

unionism (yōō′nyə nĭz′əm), *n.* 1. the principle of union, esp. trade unionism. 2. advocacy of this. 3. *Chiefly Hist.* loyalty to or advocacy of the union between Great Britain and Ireland. 4. (*cap.*) *U.S.* loyalty to the federal union of the United States of America, esp. at the time of the Civil War.

unionist (yōō′nyə nĭst), *n.* 1. one who promotes or advocates union. 2. a trade unionist. 3. *Politics.* **a.** (*cap.*) a member of the party upholding the legislative union of Great Britain and Ireland or (since 1920) Northern Ireland. **b.** (formerly) an opponent of home rule in Ireland. 4. (*cap.*) an adherent of the federal union of the United States of America, esp. during the Civil War. —*adj.* 5. of or pertaining to unionism, esp. trade unionism, or union, esp. that between Great Britain and Ireland. —**u′nionis′tic,** *adj.*

Unionist Party, a political party of Northern Ireland, upholding the principle of the Union (def. 7d); traditionally allied to the Conservative Party.

unionize (yōō′nyə nīz′), *v.*, **-nized, -nizing.** —*v.t.* 1. to organize into a trade union; bring into or incorporate in a trade union. 2. to subject to the rules of a trade union. 3. to enforce recognition of trade unions (on an industry, business, etc.). Also, **unionise.** —**u′nioniza′tion,** *n.*

un-ionized (ŭn ī′ə nīzd′), *adj. Chem.* not ionized. Also, **un-ionised.**

Union Jack, 1. Also, **Union Flag.** the national flag of the United Kingdom, symbolizing the union of its component countries. 2. its design, used as a national symbol and

un′illu′minat′ed, *adj.*
unil′lustrat′ed, *adj.*
un′imag′inative, *adj.*
un′imag′inatively, *adv.*
un′imag′inativeness, *n.*
un′imag′ined, *adj.*
un′imbued′, *adj.*
un′impaired′, *adj.*
un′impeached′, *adj.*
un′imped′ed, *adj.*
un′imped′edly, *adv.*
un′impressed′, *adj.*
un′impres′sible, *adj.*
un′impres′sionable, *adj.*
un′impres′sive, *adj.*
un′impris′oned, *adj.*
un′improv′able, *adj.*
un′improv′ing, *adj.*
un′impugn′able, *adj.*
un′impul′sive, *adj.*
un′inclined′, *adj.*
un′increas′able, *adj.*
un′increased′, *adj.*
un′indebt′ed, *adj.*
un′indent′ed, *adj.*
unin′dexed, *adj.*
unin′dicat′ed, *adj.*
un′indulged′, *adj.*
un′indus′trious, *adj.*
un′infect′ed, *adj.*
un′inflamed′, *adj.*
un′inflam′mable, *adj.*
un′inflam′mabil′ity, *n.*
un′inflat′ed, *adj.*
un′inflect′ed, *adj.*
unin′fluenced, *adj.*
un′influen′tial, *adj.*
un′inform′ative, *adj.*
un′inform′ing, *adj.*
un′inhab′itable, *adj.*
un′inhab′itableness, *n.*
un′inhab′itably, *adv.*
un′inhab′ited, *adj.*
un′inher′itable, *adj.*
un′ini′tiat′ed, *adj., n.*
unin′jured, *adj.*
un′inquir′ing, *adj.*
un′inquis′itive, *adj.*
un′inscribed′, *adj.*
un′instruct′ed, *adj.*
un′instruc′tive, *adj.*
unin′sulat′ed, *adj.*
un′insur′able, *adj.*
un′insur′ably, *adv.*
un′insured′, *adj.*
unin′tegrat′ed, *adj.*
un′intellec′tual, *adj.*
un′intend′ed, *adj.*
unin′teresting, *adj.*
unin′terestingly, *adv.*
unin′terestingness, *n.*
un′inter′pretable, *adj.*
un′interred′, *adj.*
un′intim′idat′ed, *adj.*
un′intox′icat′ing, *adj.*
un′introduced′, *adj.*
un′inured′, *adj.*
un′invad′ed, *adj.*
un′invent′ed, *adj.*
un′inven′tive, *adj.*
un′inven′tively, *adv.*
un′inven′tiveness, *n.*
un′invest′ed, *adj.*
un′inves′tigable, *adj.*
un′inves′tigat′ed, *adj.*
un′invit′ed, *adj.*

for decoration. **3.** *Naut.* this flag, flown as the jack of a ship.

Union of South Africa, former name of the Republic of South Africa. See **South Africa.**

Union of Soviet Socialist Republics, official name of the **Soviet Union.** *Abbrev.:* U.S.S.R.

union suit, *U.S.* combinations (def. 9).

uniparous (yo͞o nĭp′ə rəs), *adj.* **1.** producing only one at a birth. **2.** *Bot.* (of a cyme) producing only one axis at each branching. [t. NL: m. *ūniparus.* See UNI-, -PAROUS]

unipartite (yo͞o′nĭ pä′tīt), *adj.* not divided; consisting of or concerning a single part.

uniped (yo͞o′nĭ pĕd′), *adj.* **1.** having a single foot; one-footed; one-legged. —*n.* **2.** a person, animal, or thing having only one foot or leg.

unipersonal (yo͞o′nĭ pû′sə nəl), *adj.* **1.** consisting of or existing as but one person. **2.** *Gram.* used in only one person, esp. the third person singular, as certain verbs.

unipetalous (yo͞o′nĭ pĕt′ə ləs), *adj. Bot.* having only one petal.

uniplanar (yo͞o′nĭ plā′nə), *adj.* lying or taking place in one plane: *uniplanar motion.*

unipolar (yo͞o′nĭ pō′lə), *adj.* **1.** *Physics.* having or pertaining to one pole only. **2.** *Anat.* denoting a nerve cell in spinal and cranial ganglia in which the incoming and outgoing processes fuse outside the cell body. —**unipolarity** (yo͞o′nĭ pō lă′rĭ tĭ), *n.*

unique (yo͞o nēk′), *adj.* **1.** of which there is only one; sole. **2.** having no like or equal; standing alone in comparison with others; unequalled. **3.** remarkable, rare or unusual: *a unique experience.* [t. F, t. L: m. *ūnicus*; r. earlier *unic,* t. L: s. *ūnicus*] —**unique′ly,** *adv.* —**unique′ness,** *n.* —**Syn. 1.** See **only.**

uniseptate (yo͞o′nĭ sĕp′tāt), *adj.* having only one septum or partition, as a silicula.

uniseriate (yo͞o′nĭ sē′rĭ ĭt), *adj. Bot.* having, or consisting of, a single row or layer of cells. —**u′niser′iately,** *adv.*

unisexual (yo͞o′nĭ sĕk′syo͝o əl), *adj.* **1.** of or pertaining to one sex only. **2.** having only male or female organs in one individual, as an animal or a flower. —**u′nisex′ual′ity,** *n.* —**u′nisex′ually,** *adv.*

unison (yo͞o′nĭ sən, -zən), *n.* **1.** coincidence in pitch of two or more notes, voices, etc. **2.** the theoretical interval between any note and a note of exactly the same pitch; a prime. **3.** a sounding together at the same pitch or in octaves, as of different voices or instruments performing the same part. **4.** a sounding together in octaves, esp. of male and female voices or of higher and lower instruments of the same class. **5.** accord or agreement. **6. in unison,** in agreement, concordant; in perfect accord; simultaneously. [t. LL: s. *ūnisonus* having one sound, f. L *ūni-* UNI- + *-sonus* sounding]

unisonous (yo͞o nĭs′ə nəs), *adj.* according in sound or pitch; being in unison. Also, **unis′onal, unisonant** (yo͞o-nĭs′ə nənt). [t. LL: m. *ūnisonus*]

unissued (ŭn ĭsh′o͞od), *adj.* not issued, as esp. shares, stock, or the like.

unit (yo͞o′nĭt), *n.* **1.** a single thing or person; any group of things or persons regarded as an individual. **2.** one of the individuals or groups making up a whole, or into which a whole may be analysed. **3.** any magnitude regarded as an independent whole; a single, undivided entity. **4.** any specified amount of a quantity, as of length, volume, force, momentum, time, by comparison with which any other quantity of the same kind is measured or estimated. **5.** *Maths.* the lowest positive integer; one. **6.** *Educ.* the quantity of educational instruction, determined usually by a number of hours of classroom and, sometimes, laboratory work. **7.** *Mil.* **a.** an organized body of soldiers of any size, which is a subdivision of a larger body. **b.** a vessel, vehicle, or large piece of equipment, as a tank, battleship, etc. **8.** *Mech.* any piece of equipment which has a specific function: *a power unit.* **9.** *Immunol., Pharm.* **a.** the measured amount of a substance necessary to cause a certain effect; a clinical unit used when a substance cannot readily be isolated in pure form and its activity determined directly. **b.** the amount necessary to cause a specific effect upon a specific animal or upon animal tissues. —*adj.* **10.** of, pertaining to, equivalent to, containing, or forming a unit or units. [appar. back-formation from UNITY]

Unit., Unitarian.

unitarian (yo͞o′nĭ tēə′rĭ ən), *n.* **1.** one who maintains that God is one being, rejecting the doctrine of the Trinity, and emphasizing freedom in religious belief, tolerance of difference in religious opinion, character as the fundamental principle in religion, and the use of all religious history and experience interpreted by reason as a guide to conduct. Cf. **Monarchian. 2.** (*cap.*) a member of a Christian denomination founded upon the doctrine that God is one being, and giving each congregation complete control over its affairs. **3.** an advocate of some theory of unity or centralization, as in government. **4.** a member of a non-Christian religion holding monotheistic views, esp. a Muslim. —*adj.* **5.** (*cap.*) pertaining to the Unitarians or their doctrines; accepting Unitarianism; belonging to the Unitarians. **6.** pertaining to a unit or unity; unitary. **7.** advocating or directed towards national or administrative unity or centralization. —**u′nitar′ianism,** *n.*

unitary (yo͞o′nĭ tə rĭ, -trĭ), *adj.* **1.** of or pertaining to a unit or units. **2.** pertaining to, characterized by, or based on unity. **3.** of the nature of a unit; having the individual character of a unit. **4.** serving as a unit, as of measurement or estimation.

unit character, *Biol.* a characteristic, usually dependent on a single gene, transmitted according to Mendel's laws.

unit cost, the cost of a specified unit of a product or service.

unite[1] (yo͞o nīt′), *v.,* **united, uniting.** —*v.t.* **1.** to join so as to form one connected whole; join, combine, or incorporate in one; cause to be one. **2.** to cause to hold together or adhere. **3.** to join in marriage. **4.** to associate (persons, etc.) by some bond or tie; join in action, interest, opinion, feeling, etc. **5.** to have or exhibit in union or combination. —*v.i.* **6.** to join together so as to form one connected whole; become one; combine. **7.** to join in marriage. **8.** to enter into alliance or association; join in action; act in concert or agreement; become one in opinion or feeling. [ME, t. L: m. *ūnitus,* pp., joined together, made one] —**unit′er,** *n.* —**Syn. 1.** connect, conjoin, join, couple, link, yoke. See **join. 2.** blend, fuse, weld. —**Ant. 1.** divide. **2.** separate.

unite[2] (yo͞o′nīt, yo͞o nīt′), *n.* (during the reigns of James I and Charles I) a gold coin worth 20 shillings, and later 22 shillings. [der. UNITE[1]; named with reference to the union of England and Scotland]

united (yo͞o nī′tĭd), *adj.* **1.** joined or brought together; combined. **2.** of or produced by two or more persons, etc., in combination. **3.** in agreement. **4.** in association for a common purpose. **5.** formed by the union of two or more things, bodies, etc. —**unit′edly,** *adv.* —**unit′edness,** *n.*

United Arab Republic, **1.** a former republic in NE Africa, created by the union of Egypt and Syria in 1958, and dissolved by Syria's withdrawal in 1961. **2.** the official name of **Egypt.** *Abbrev.:* U.A.R., UAR.

United Arab States, the federation (in 1958) of the United Arab Republic and the kingdom of Yemen; dissolved in 1961.

United Brethren, an American Protestant denomination which arose early in the 19th century and sought to unite members of various confessions; the Moravian Church.

United Kingdom, Great Britain and Northern Ireland: formerly (1801–1922) it comprised Great Britain and Ireland. 51,402,623 pop. (1961). 93,377 sq. mi. *Cap.:* London. *Abbrev.:* U.K. Official name, **United Kingdom of Great Britain and Northern Ireland.**

United Nations, **1.** an international association of 113 states formed in 1945 to promote international peace and cooperation. **2.** the nations that signed the joint declaration in Washington, D.C., January 2nd 1942, pledging to employ full resources against the Axis powers, not to make a separate peace, etc.

United Nations Children's Fund. See **UNICEF.**

United Nations Educational, Scientific, and Cultural Organization. See **UNESCO.**

United Press International, a private agency for the gathering and distributing of news. Formerly, **United Press.** *Abbrev.:* U.P., U.P.I.

United Provinces, **1.** the former name of **Uttar Pradesh.** Official name was, **United Provinces of Agra and Oudh. 2.** *Hist.* the seven northern provinces of the Netherlands which seceded from Spain in 1581 under the Union of Utrecht to form the basis of modern Holland.

United States, a republic in North America, consisting of 50 states and the District of Columbia. 179,323,175 pop. (1960); continental United States, 3,608,787 sq. mi.; United States and possessions, 3,680,114 sq. mi. *Cap.:* Washington, D.C. *Abbrev.:* U.S. Also, **United States of America** (*abbrev.:* U.S.A.), **America, the States.**

unit factor, *Biol.* a gene; a substance which functions as the hereditary unit for a single character.

unitive (yo͞o′nĭ tĭv), *adv.* serving or tending to unite. —**u′nitively,** *adv.* [t. LL: m. s. *ūnītīvus,* der. L *ūnītus,* pp., made one]

---

un′invit′ing, *adj.* **un′involved′,** *adj.* **uni′roned,** *adj.* **unir′rigat′ed,** *adj.*

unit organ, *Music.* an organ in which, to save space, stops of different pitch but the same tone quality are derived from a single rank of pipes.

unit pole, *Physics.* a magnetic pole which when placed one centimetre from an identical pole experiences a repulsive force of one dyne.

unit process, *Chem. Engineering.* any of several operations which are common to many chemical industries and which form part of a sequence of operations, as filtration, distillation, evaporation, etc. The plant employed is usually standardized, requiring only minor modifications for specific industries.

unit rule, *U.S.* (in Democratic national conventions) a rule whereby some states vote as a unit, not recognizing minority votes within the delegation.

unit trust, **1.** a trust whose management purchases shares from a number of companies. The portfolio of such shares is divided into equal units for sale to the public, whose interests are served by an independent trustee company. **2.** the units issued for sale by such a trust.

unity (yōō′nĭ tĭ), *n., pl.* **-ties. 1.** the state or fact of being one; oneness. **2.** one single thing; something complete in itself, or regarded as such. **3.** the oneness of a complex or organic whole or of an interconnected series; a whole or totality as combining all its parts into one. **4.** the fact or state of being united or combined into one, as of the parts of a whole. **5.** freedom from diversity or variety. **6.** unvaried or uniform character, as of a plan. **7.** oneness of mind, feeling, etc., as among a number of persons; concord, harmony, or agreement. **8.** *Maths.* the number one; a quantity regarded as one. **9.** (in literature and art) a relation of all the parts or elements of a work constituting a harmonious whole and producing a single general effect. **10.** one of the three principles of dramatic structure, esp. in neoclassical drama: **unity of time** (action taking place during twenty-four hours); **unity of place** (no extensive shifts in setting); **unity of action** (a single plot). [ME *unite,* t. L: m. *ūnitas*] **—Syn. 1.** See **union. 7.** unison, concert. **—Ant. 1.** diversity.

Unity of Brethren. See **Moravian** (def. 4).

Univ., 1. Universalist. **2.** University.

univ., 1. universal. **2.** universally. **3.** university.

univalent (yōō′nĭ vā′lənt, yōō nĭv′ə lənt), *adj.* **1.** *Chem.* monovalent. **2.** *Biol.* one only; applied to a chromosome which does not possess, or does not join, its homologous chromosome in synapsis. [f. UNI- + -VALENT] **—u′niva′lency,** *n.*

univalve (yōō′nĭ vălv′), *adj.* Also, **u′nivalved′, univalvular** (yōō′nĭ văl′vyōō lə). **1.** having one valve. **2.** (of a shell) composed of a single valve or piece. **—*n.* 3.** a univalve mollusc or its shell.

universal (yōō′nĭ vû′səl), *adj.* **1.** extending over, including, proceeding from, all or the whole (of something specified or implicit); without exception. **2.** applicable to many individuals or single cases; general. **3.** affecting, concerning, or involving all: *universal military training.* **4.** used or understood by all: *a universal language.* **5.** existing or prevailing in all parts; everywhere: *universal calm of southern seas.* **6.** versed in or embracing many or all subjects, fields, etc.: *universal scholarship.* **7.** given or extended to all: *universal revelation.* **8.** of or pertaining to the universe, all nature, or all existing things: *universal cause.* **9.** *Logic.* pertaining to a proposition that concerns all members of a class: *all men are wealthy* is a universal proposition. Cf. **particular** (def. 9); **singular** (def. 6). **10.** *Mach., etc.* adapted or adaptable for all or various uses, angles, sizes, etc. **11.** (of a joint or the like) allowing free movement in all directions within certain limits. **12.** *Archaic.* comprising all; whole; entire. **—*n.* 13.** that which may be applied throughout the universe to many things, usually thought of as an entity which can be in many places at the same time (distinguished from *particular*). **14.** a trait or characteristic, as distinguished from a particular individual or event, which can be possessed in common by many distinct things, e.g. *mortality.* **15.** *Logic.* a universal proposition. **16.** *Philos.* **a.** a general term or concept, or the generic nature which such a term signifies; a Platonic idea or Aristotelian form. **b.** a metaphysical entity which is repeatable and remains unchanged in character in a series of changes or changing relations. Cf. **particular** (def. 12). **17.** *Mach.* a universal joint, esp. one at the end of the propeller shaft in a motor vehicle. [ME, t. L: s. *ūniversālis*] **—u′niver′salness,** *n.* **—Syn. 1.** See **general. —Ant. 9.** particular.

universal class, *Logic.* that class which includes all other classes, and has for its members the individuals who are members of any of these subordinate classes.

Universal Copyright Convention, an international agreement to protect literary and artistic copyright, signed at Geneva in 1952 and effective from 1955.

universal coupling, universal joint.

universal donor, *Med.* a blood donor whose blood is of a group that may be transfused to persons of other groups.

universalism (yōō′nĭ vû′sə lĭz′əm), *n.* **1.** universal character; universality. **2.** the fact of having a great variety of knowledge, interests, or activities. **3.** (*cap.*) the doctrine or belief of Universalists.

universalist (yōō′nĭ vû′sə lĭst), *n.* **1.** one characterized by universalism, as in knowledge, interests, or activities. **2.** (*cap.*) one who believes in the doctrine that all men will finally be saved, or brought back to holiness and God; a member of a Christian denomination which holds this doctrine as its distinctive belief.

universalistic (yōō′nĭ vû′sə lĭs′tĭk), *adj.* **1.** of, pertaining to, or affecting, the whole of something, esp. mankind; inclined to be universal. **2.** of or pertaining to universalism.

universality (yōō′nĭ vû săl′ĭ tĭ), *n., pl.* **-ties. 1.** the character or state of being universal; existence or prevalence everywhere. **2.** relation, extension, or applicability to all. **3.** very great versatility or range of knowledge, interests, etc.

universalize (yōō′nĭ vû′sə līz′), *v.t.,* **-lized, -lizing.** to make universal. Also, **universalise. —u′niver′saliza′tion,** *n.*

universal joint, *Mach.* a joint allowing free movement in all directions within certain limits. Also, **universal coupling.**

Universal joint

universal language, a language understood or intended to be understood everywhere.

universally (yōō′nĭ vû′sə lĭ), *adv.* in a universal manner; in every instance, part, or place, without exception.

universal motor, *Elect.* a series-wound electrical motor which can be operated on either direct or alternating current.

Universal Postal Union, an international organization founded in 1875 to further international efficiency and collaboration in the postal services.

universal suffrage, the principle that the right to vote for one's government, etc., should be extended to everyone.

universal time, a system of time measurement based on Greenwich Mean Time, but counted from 0 hr, which is equivalent to midnight Greenwich Mean Time. *Abbrev.:* U.T.

universe (yōō′nĭ vûs′), *n.* **1.** all of space, and all the matter and energy which it contains; the cosmos. **2.** the whole world; mankind generally: *the whole universe knows it.* **3.** a world or sphere in which something exists or prevails. **4.** a galaxy. **5.** *Logic.* the collection of all the objects to which any discourse refers. [t. L: m. s. *ūniversum*]

universe of discourse, *Logic.* the aggregate of objects, ideas, or facts assumed or implied in discourse.

university (yōō′nĭ vû′sĭ tĭ), *n., pl.* **-ties. 1.** an institution of higher learning with power to grant degrees. **2.** its members, as teachers, undergraduates, graduate members, etc. **3.** its buildings. **4.** its governing body. **5.** a sports team or crew representing it in competition. **6.** anything considered as a source of learning: *the great university of life.* [ME, t. ML: m. s. *ūniversitas* (*magistrōrum et scholārium*) guild (of teachers and students)]

university extension course, a course prepared by a university and pursued in evening classes. Cf. **extension course.**

univocal (yōō′nĭ vō′kl), *adj.* having only one possible meaning; unambiguous; unmistakeable.

unjoint (ŭn joint′), *v.t.* to take apart the joints of; disjoint.

unjust (ŭn jŭst′), *adj.* **1.** not just; not acting justly or fairly, as persons. **2.** not in accordance with justice or fairness, as actions. **3.** *Archaic.* unfaithful or dishonest. **—unjust′ly,** *adv.* **—unjust′ness,** *n.* **—Syn. 1.** inequitable, partial, unfair. **2.** undeserved, unmerited, unjustifiable.

unkempt (ŭn kĕmpt′), *adj.* **1.** not combed, as the hair. **2.** having the hair not combed or cared for. **3.** in an uncared-for, neglected, or untidy state; rough. **4.** crude, coarse, or unpolished, as persons. [var. of *unkembed,* f. UN-² + *kembed,* pp. of obs. *kemb* (ME *kembe,* OE *cemban*) comb] **—unkempt′ness,** *n.*

unkenned (ŭn kĕnd′; *Scot.* -kĕnt′), *adj. Obs. or Dial.* unknown.

unjad′ed, *adj.*
unjaun′diced, *adj.*
unjeal′ous, *adj.*
unjoy′ful, *adj.*
unjudged′, *adj.*
unjudg′ing, *adj.*
un′judi′cial, *adj.*
unjus′tifi′able, *adj.*

unkennel (ŭn kĕn′əl), *v.t.*, **-nelled, -nelling** or (*esp. U.S.*) **-neled, -neling.** **1.** to drive or release from or as from, a kennel; dislodge. **2.** to dislodge a fox from its hole. **3.** to bring to light.

unkind (ŭn kīnd′), *adj.* **1.** not kind; harsh; cruel; unmerciful; unfeeling and distressing. **2.** *Archaic or Dial.* of the weather, soil, etc., harsh; unwelcoming; not mild. —**unkind′ly,** *adv.* —**unkind′ness,** *n.*

unkindly (ŭn kīnd′lĭ), *adj.* **1.** not kindly; ill-natured; unkind. **2.** inclement or bleak, as weather, climate, etc.; unfavourable for crops, as soil. —**unkind′liness,** *n.*

unknightly (ŭn nīt′lĭ), *adj.* **1.** unworthy of a knight. **2.** not like a knight. —*adv.* **3.** in a manner unworthy of a knight. —**unknight′liness,** *n.*

unknit (ŭn nĭt′), *v.t.*, **-knitted** or **-knit, -knitting.** **1.** to untie or unfasten (a knot, etc.); unravel (something knitted). **2.** to dissolve, destroy, unloose, weaken, etc. [ME *unknytte(n)*, OE *uncnyttan*. See UN-², KNIT, v.]

unknowable (ŭn nō′ə bl), *adj.* **1.** not knowable; incapable of being known; transcending human knowledge. —*n.* **2.** something unknowable. **3. the Unknowable.** *Philos.* the (postulated) reality lying behind all phenomena but not cognizable by any of the processes by which the mind cognizes phenomenal objects. —**unknow′abil′ity,** *n.* —**unknow′ableness,** *n.* —**unknow′ably,** *adv.*

unknowing (ŭn nō′ĭng), *adj.* **1.** lacking knowledge; ignorant. **2.** without knowledge (of something). —**unknow′ingly,** *adv.* —**unknow′ingness,** *n.*

unknown (ŭn nōn′), *adj.* **1.** not known; not within the range of one's knowledge, cognizance, or acquaintance; unfamiliar; strange. **2.** not ascertained, discovered, explored, or identified. —*n.* **3.** one who or that which is unknown; an unknown person. **4.** *Maths.* an unknown quantity or a symbol representing this.

Unknown Warrior, (in various countries) an unidentified soldier killed in a war, esp. World War I, and entombed as a memorial to all similar victims of the war. Also, **Unknown Soldier.**

unlace (ŭn lās′), *v.t.*, **-laced, -lacing.** **1.** to undo the lacing of (a garment, etc.). **2.** to loosen or remove the garments, etc., of by undoing lacing.

unlade (ŭn lād′), *v.t.*, **-laded, -lading.** **1.** to take the lading, load, or cargo from; unload. **2.** to discharge (the load or cargo). —*v.i.* **3.** to discharge the load or cargo.

unladen (ŭn lā′dn), *adj.* not carrying any load, as a goods-carrying vehicle, etc.

unlaid (ŭn lād′), *adj.* **1.** (of a table) not set for a meal. **2.** (of a ghost) not yet exorcized. **3.** (of paper) not laid; not having the lined texture of laid paper. **4.** untwisted, as a rope.

unlash (ŭn lăsh′), *v.t.* to loosen or unfasten, as something lashed or tied fast.

unlatch (ŭn lăch′), *v.t.* **1.** to unfasten or open (a door, etc.) by lifting the latch. —*v.i.* **2.** to become unlatched; open through the lifting of a latch.

unlawful (ŭn lô′fəl), *adj.* **1.** not lawful; contrary to law; illegal; not sanctioned by law. **2.** contrary to moral rule; immoral; irreligious. **3.** born out of wedlock; illegitimate. —**unlaw′fully,** *adv.* —**unlaw′fulness,** *n.*

unlawful assembly, *Law.* a meeting of three or more persons with intent to commit a crime or breach of the peace.

unlay (ŭn lā′), *v.t.*, **-laid, -laying.** to untwist, as a rope into separate strands.

unleaded (ŭn lĕd′ĭd), *adj.* **1.** not furnished with lead. **2.** *Print.* not separated or spaced with leads, as lines of type or printed matter.

unlearn (ŭn lûn′), *v.t.* **1.** to put aside from knowledge or memory (something learned); discard or lose knowledge of; forget. —*v.i.* **2.** to put aside knowledge.

unlearned (ŭn lû′nĭd *for 1, 4*; ŭn lûnt′ *for 2, 3*), *adj.* **1.** not learned; not scholarly or erudite; uneducated; ignorant. **2.** not acquired by learning; never learned. **3.** known without being learned. **4.** of or pertaining to unlearned persons. Also, (*for 2 and 3*), **unlearnt.** —**unlearn′edly,** *adv.*

unleash (ŭn lēsh′), *v.t.* **1.** to let loose or give vent to (rage, violence, or the like). **2.** to release from or as from a leash; set free to pursue or run at will; let loose.

unleavened (ŭn lĕv′ənd), *adj.* **1.** (of bread, etc.) not made to rise by the addition of leaven, as yeast or bicarbonate of soda. **2.** unmodified by the addition of some influence.

unless (ən lĕs′), *conj.* **1.** except on condition that; except if it be, or were, that; except when; if . . . not: *I shan't come unless you really want me to.* —*prep.* **2.** *Obs.* except; but. [ME *onlesse*, f. ON, prep. + *lesse* LESS, orig. meaning on a lower condition (than)]

unlettered (ŭn lĕt′əd), *adj.* not educated; illiterate; without knowledge of books. —**Syn.** See **ignorant.**

unlicensed (ŭn lī′sənst), *adj.* **1.** having no licence. **2.** done or undertaken without licence; unauthorized.

unlike (ŭn līk′), *adj.* **1.** not like; different or dissimilar; having no resemblance. —*prep.* **2.** otherwise than like; different from. **3.** uncharacteristic of: *it is unlike you to be so cheerful.* —*n.* **4.** (*esp. pl.*) that which is unlike (another). —**unlike′ness,** *n.* —**Syn. 1.** diverse, variant, heterogeneous.

unlikelihood (ŭn līk′lĭ hŏŏd′), *n.* the state of being unlikely; improbability.

unlikely (ŭn līk′lĭ), *adj.* **1.** not likely to happen or be; improbable; probably not going (to do, be, etc.). **2.** not likely to be true; doubtful. **3.** holding out little prospect of success; unpromising. **4.** *Archaic or Dial.* unprepossessing. —*adv.* **5.** improbably. —**unlike′liness,** *n.*

unlimber (ŭn lĭm′bə), *v.t.* **1.** to detach (a gun) from its limber or prime mover. —*n.* **2.** the act of changing a gun from travelling to firing position.

unlimited (ŭn lĭm′ĭ tĭd), *adj.* **1.** not limited; unrestricted. **2.** boundless; limitless. —**unlim′itedly,** *adv.* —**unlim′itedness,** *n.*

unlimited company, *Finance.* a company whose members are each liable for its debts to the full extent of their property.

unlined¹ (ŭn līnd′), *adj.* not marked or incised with lines.

unlined² (ŭn līnd′), *adj.* not furnished with a lining, as a garment.

unlink (ŭn lĭngk′), *v.t.* **1.** to separate the links of (a chain, etc.). **2.** to detach from being linked; to separate or detach by, or as by, undoing a connecting link. —*v.i.* **3.** to become unlinked.

unlisted (ŭn lĭs′tĭd), *adj.* **1.** not listed; not entered in a list. **2.** (of stock exchange securities) not entered in the official list of those admitted for dealings. **3.** *Chiefly U.S.* (of a telephone number) ex-directory.

unlive (ŭn lĭv′), *v.t.*, **-lived, -living.** **1.** to undo or annul (past life, etc.). **2.** to live down.

unload (ŭn lōd′), *v.t.* **1.** to take the load from; remove the burden, cargo, or freight from. **2.** to relieve of anything burdensome. **3.** to withdraw the charge from (a firearm). **4.** to remove or discharge (a load, etc.). **5.** to relieve oneself of (something burdensome). **6.** to get rid or dispose of (stock, etc.) by sale. —*v.i.* **7.** to unload something; remove or discharge a load. —**unload′er,** *n.*

unlock (ŭn lŏk′), *v.t.* **1.** to undo the lock of, esp. with a key. **2.** to open or release by, or as by, undoing a lock. **3.** to open (anything firmly closed or joined): *to unlock the jaws.* **4.** to lay open; disclose. —*v.i.* **5.** to become unlocked.

unlockable (ŭn lŏk′ə bl), *adj.* **1.** that cannot be locked. **2.** that can be unlocked.

unlooked-for (ŭn lŏŏkt′fô′), *adj.* not looked for; unexpected; unforeseen.

unloose (ŭn lōōs′), *v.t.*, **-loosed, -loosing.** **1.** to set or let loose; release from bonds, fastenings, etc.; set free from restraint. **2.** to loose or undo (a bond, fastening, knot, etc.). **3.** to loosen or relax (the grasp, hold, fingers, etc.).

unloosen (ŭn lōō′sən), *v.t.* to unloose; loosen.

unlovely (ŭn lŭv′lĭ), *adj.* **1.** not lovely; without beauty or charm of appearance; unpleasing to the eye. **2.** unattractive, repellent, or disagreeable in character; unpleasant; objectionable.—**unlove′liness,** *n.*

unlucky (ŭn lŭk′ĭ), *adj.* not lucky; not having good luck; unfortunate or ill-fated; not attended with good luck. —**unluck′ily,** *adv.* —**unluck′iness,** *n.*

unmade (ŭn mād′), *adj.* **1.** not yet made. **2.** not having a maker; not having been made; uncreated.

unmake (ŭn māk′), *v.t.*, **-made, -making.** **1.** to cause to be as if never made; reduce to the original matter,

unjus′tifi′ably, *adv.*
unjus′tified′, *adj.*
unkin′dled, *adj.*
unla′belled, *adj.*
un′labor′ious, *adj.*
unla′boured, *adj.*
unla′dylike′, *adj.*
un′lament′ed, *adj.*
unlaunched′, *adj.*
unleased′, *adj.*
unled′, *adj.*
unles′sened, *adj.*
unlet′, *adj.*
unlet′table, *adj.*
unlib′erat′ed, *adj.*
unlicked′, *adj.*
unlid′ded, *adj.*
unliq′uidat′ed, *adj.*
unlis′tened-to′, *adj.*
unlis′tening, *adj.*
unlit′, *adj.*
unlit′erary, *adj.*
unlooped′, *adj.*
unlopped′, *adj.*
unlos′able, *adj.*
unlost′, *adj.*
unlov′able, *adj.*
unloved′, *adj.*
unlov′ing, *adj.*
unlov′ingly, *adv.*
unlov′ingness, *n.*
unmai′denly, *adj.*
un′maintain′able, *adj.*
un′mal′leabil′ity, *n.*
unmal′leable, *adj.*
unmalt′ed, *adj.*

elements, or state. **2.** to take to pieces; destroy; ruin or undo. **3.** to depose from office or authority. —**un-mak′er,** *n.*

unman (ŭn măn′), *v.t.*, **-manned, -manning. 1.** to deprive of the character or qualities of a man or human being. **2.** to deprive of virility; emasculate. **3.** to deprive of manly courage or fortitude; break down the manly spirit of. **4.** to deprive of men: *to unman a ship.*

unmanageable (ŭn măn′ĭ jə bl), *adj.* **1.** impossible to govern or control, as a horse, child, etc.; refractory. **2.** incapable of being satisfactorily dealt with or handled, as affairs, objects, etc.; unwieldy. —**unman′ageably,** *adv.*

unmanly (ŭn măn′lĭ), *adj.* **1.** not manly; not like or befitting a man; womanish or childish. **2.** ignoble; weak; cowardly. —**unman′liness,** *n.*

unmanned (ŭn mănd′), *adj.* **1.** without a crew, controlled automatically: *an unmanned ship.* **2.** desolate; having no population. **3.** castrated. **4.** (of a falcon) not trained for hunting.

unmannered (ŭn măn′əd), *adj.* **1.** without manners; unmannerly. **2.** not affected or insincere.

unmannerly (ŭn măn′ə lĭ), *adj.* **1.** not mannerly; ill-bred; rude; churlish. —*adv.* **2.** *Obs.* with ill manners. —**unman′nerliness,** *n.*

unmarked (ŭn mäkt′), *adj.* **1.** not marked; bearing no marking, stain, etc. **2.** not bearing the marks of blows, punches, etc.; unbruised. **3** not distinguished; not characterized (by some quality). **4.** *Archaic.* unnoticed.

unmarketable (ŭn mä′kĭ tə bl), *adj.* incapable of being sold or unsuitable for sale; not finding or likely to find a buyer. —**un′mar′ketabil′ity,** *n.* —**unmar′ketably,** *adv.*

unmask (ŭn mäsk′), *v.t.* **1.** to strip of a mask or disguise. **2.** to lay open (anything concealed); expose in the true character. **3.** *Mil.* to reveal the presence of (guns, etc.) by firing. —*v.t.* **4.** to put off a mask or disguise. —**un-mask′er,** *n.*

unmatched (ŭn mächt′), *adj.* not matched, rivalled, or equalled.

unmeaning (ŭn mē′nĭng), *adj.* **1.** not meaning anything; without meaning or significance, as words or actions; meaningless. **2.** expressionless, vacant, or unintelligent, as the face, etc. —**unmean′ingly,** *adv.* —**unmean′-ingness,** *n.*

unmeant (ŭn mĕnt′), *adj.* not intended or deliberate; accidental.

unmeasured (ŭn mĕzh′əd), *adj.* **1.** of undetermined or indefinitely great extent or amount; unlimited; measureless. **2.** unrestrained; intemperate. —**unmeas′urable,** *adj.* —**unmeas′urably,** *adv.*

unmechanical (ŭn′mĭ kăn′ĭ kl), *adj.* **1.** not pertaining to or working by means of a mechanism. **2.** (of a person) having little or no mechanical aptitude or inclination. —**un′mechan′ically,** *adv.*

unmeet (ŭn mēt′), *adj.* *Obs.* not meet; unfitting; unbecoming; unseemly. [ME *unmete,* OE *unmǣte.* See UN-[1], MEET[2]] —**unmeet′ly,** *adv.* —**unmeet′ness,** *n.*

unmentionable (ŭn mĕn′shə nə bl), *adj.* not mentionable; unworthy or unfit to be mentioned. —**unmen′-tionableness,** *n.* —**unmen′tionably,** *adv.*

unmentionables (ŭn mĕn′shə nə blz), *n.pl.* *Obs.* (humorous) trousers, breeches, or undergarments.

unmerciful (ŭn mû′sĭ fəl), *adj.* **1.** not merciful; merciless; pitiless; relentless; unsparing. **2.** unsparingly great; unconscionable. —**unmer′cifully,** *adv.* —**unmer′ciful-ness,** *n.*

unmindful (ŭn mīnd′fəl), *adj.* not mindful; regardless; heedless; careless. —**unmind′fully,** *adv.* —**unmind′-fulness,** *n.*

unmistakeable (ŭn′mĭs tā′kə bl), *adj.* not mistakeable; admitting of no mistake; clear; plain; evident. Also, **unmistakable.** —**un′mistake′ableness,** *n.* —**un′mis-take′ably,** *adv.*

unmitigated (ŭn mĭt′ĭ gā′tĭd), *adj.* **1.** not mitigated; not softened or lessened. **2.** unqualified or absolute; utter. —**unmit′igat′edly,** *adv.*

unmixed (ŭn mĭkst′), *adj.* not mixed; unmingled; pure; unalloyed. Also, **unmixt.** —**unmixedly** (ŭn mĭkst′lĭ, -mĭk′sĭd lĭ), *adv.*

unmoor (ŭn mo͞o͞ə′), *v.t.* **1.** to loose (a ship, etc.) from moorings or anchorage. —*v.i.* **2.** (of a ship, etc.) to become unmoored.

unmoral (ŭn mŏ′rəl), *adj.* non-moral; having no moral aspect, neither moral nor immoral. Cf. **amoral.** —**un-morality** (ŭn′mə răl′ĭ tĭ), *n.* —**unmor′ally,** *adv.*

unmounted (ŭn moun′tĭd), *adj.* **1.** (of a picture) not having a mount. **2.** not having or riding a horse: *un-mounted soldiers.* **3.** not mounted on something, as a stand.

unmoved (ŭn mo͞ovd′), *adj.* unaffected; calm; unemotional. —**unmovedly** (ŭn mo͞o′vĭd lĭ), *adv.*

unmoving (ŭn mo͞o′vĭng), *adj.* **1.** not moving; motionless. **2.** *Rare.* arousing no feeling.

unmuffle (ŭn mŭf′əl), *v.*, **-fled, -fling.** —*v.t.* **1.** to strip of or free from that which muffles. —*v.i.* **2.** to throw off that which muffles.

unmurmuring (ŭn mû′mə rĭng), *adj.* without complaint, grumbling, or demur; willing. —**unmur′muringly,** *adv.*

unmusical (ŭn myo͞o′zĭ kl), *adj.* **1.** not musical; not melodious or harmonious. **2.** harsh or discordant in sound. **3.** not fond of or skilled in music. —**unmu′-sically,** *adv.* —**unmu′sicalness,** *n.*

unmuzzle (ŭn mŭz′əl), *v.t.*, **-zled, -zling. 1.** to free from restraint, as upon speech or expression. **2.** to remove a muzzle from (a dog, etc.).

unnail (ŭn nāl′), *v.t.* to take out the nails from.

unnamed (ŭn nāmd′), *adj.* **1.** having no name; nameless. **2.** not specified or mentioned by name.

unnatural (ŭn năch′rəl), *adj.* **1.** not natural; not proper to the natural constitution or character. **2.** having or showing a lack of natural or proper instincts, feelings, etc. **3.** contrary to the nature of things. **4.** at variance with the ordinary course of nature; unusual, strange, or abnormal. **5.** contrary to accepted or expected modes of behaviour. **6.** artificial or affected; forced or strained. **7.** more than usually cruel or evil. —**unnat′urally,** *adv.* —**unnat′uralness,** *n.*

unnavigable (ŭn năv′ĭ gə bl), *adj.* not able to be navigated, as because there is insufficient depth of water, lack of room for a vessel to manoeuvre, ice, etc.

unnecessary (ŭn nĕs′ĭ sə rĭ, -ĭs rĭ), *adj.* not necessary; superfluous; needless. —**unnec′essarily,** *adv.* —**unnec′-essariness,** *n.*

unnerve (ŭn nûv′), *v.t.*, **-nerved, -nerving.** to deprive of nerve, strength, or physical or mental firmness; break down the self-control of; upset.

unnumbered (ŭn nŭm′bəd), *adj.* **1.** not numbered; uncounted. **2.** countless; innumerable. **3.** not marked with or bearing a number or numbers.

UNO (yo͞o′nō), *n.* United Nations Organization.

unobjectionable (ŭn′əb jĕk′shə nə bl), *adj.* that cannot be objected to; acceptable. —**un′objec′tionableness,** *n.* —**un′objec′tionably,** *adv.*

unobtrusive (ŭn′əb tro͞o′sĭv), *adj.* not obvious; discreet. —**un′obtru′sively,** *adv.* —**un′obtru′siveness,** *n.*

unoccupied (ŭn ŏk′yo͞o pīd′), *adj.* **1.** not occupied; not possessed or held; vacant. **2.** not employed; idle. **3.** not controlled by a foreign army.

unofficial (ŭn′ə fĭsh′əl), *adj.* **1.** not official; informal. **2.** (of news) not confirmed by official sources. **3.** *Sport.* (of a time or speed, or a record) not confirmed by official timekeepers. —**un′offi′cially,** *adv.*

unman′acle, *v.t.*
unman′acled, *adj.*
unman′fully, *adv.*
un′manufac′turable, *adj.*
un′manured′, *adj.*
unmapped′, *adj.*
unmarred′, *adj.*
unmar′riageable, *adj.*
unmar′ried, *adj.*
unmar′tyred, *adj.*
unmatch′able, *adj.*
unmat′ed, *adj.*
un′mathemat′ical, *adj.*
unme′diat′ed, *adj.*
unmed′ical, *adj.*
unmed′itative, *adj.*
unmel′lowed, *adj.*
unmelt′ed, *adj.*
unmelt′ing, *adj.*
unmem′orable, *adj.*
unmen′tioned, *adj.*
unmer′cenary, *adj.*
unmer′chantable, *adj.*
unmer′ited, *adj.*
unmer′itedly, *adv.*
un′merito′rious, *adj.*
un′method′ical, *adj.*
un′method′ically, *adv.*
unmil′itary, *adj.*
unmilked′, *adj.*
unmilled′, *adj.*
unmind′ed, *adj.*
unmined′, *adj.*
unmin′gled, *adj.*
un′ministe′rial, *adj.*
unmint′ed, *adj.*
unmissed′, *adj.*
unmod′ern, *adj.*
unmod′ernize′, *v.t., v.i.*
unmod′ernized′, *adj.*
unmod′ifi′able, *adj.*
unmod′ulat′ed, *adj.*
un′molest′ed, *adj.*
un′molest′edly, *adv.*
un′molest′ing, *adj.*
unmor′tared, *adj.*
unmort′gaged, *adj.*
unmor′tified′, *adj.*
unmoth′erly, *adj.*
unmould′ed, *adj.*
unmount′, *v.t., v.i.*
unmourned′, *adj.*
unmov′able, *adj.*
unmov′ably, *adv.*
unmown′, *adj.*
unmus′cular, *adj.*
unmu′tilat′ed, *adj.*
unname′able, *adj.*
unnat′uralized′, *adj.*
unneed′ed, *adj.*
unneed′ful, *adj.*
unneed′fully, *adv.*
un′nego′tiable, *adj.*
unneigh′bourly, *adj.*
unnot′ed, *adj.*
unno′ticeable, *adj.*
unno′ticed, *adj.*
unnour′ishing, *adj.*
un′oblit′erat′ed, *adj.*
un′obscured′, *adj.*
un′observ′able, *adj.*
un′observ′ant, *adj.*
un′observed′, *adj., adv.*
un′obstruct′ed, *adj.*
un′obtain′able, *adj.*
un′offend′ing, *adj.*

unorganized (ŭn ô′gə nīzd′), *adj.* **1.** not organized; without organic structure. **2.** not formed into an organized or systematized whole. **3.** not having membership in a trade union. Also, **unorganised.**

unpack (ŭn păk′), *v.t.* **1.** to undo or take out (something packed). **2.** to remove the contents packed in (a suitcase, trunk, etc.). **3.** to remove a pack or load from (a horse, etc.); unload (a vehicle, etc.). —*v.i.* **4.** to unpack articles, goods, etc. —**unpack′er,** *n.* —**unpack′ing,** *n.*

unpaged (ŭn pājd′), *adj.* (of a publication) having unnumbered pages.

unpalatable (ŭn păl′ə tə bl), *adj.* **1.** disagreeable; distasteful. **2.** not agreeable to the palate; ill-tasting. —**un′pal′atabil′ity, unpal′atableness,** *n.* —**unpal′atably,** *adv.*

unparalleled (ŭn pă′rə lĕld′), *adj.* not paralleled; having no parallel; unequalled; unmatched.

unparliamentary (ŭn′pä lə mĕn′tə rĭ, -trĭ), *adj.* **1.** not parliamentary; not in accordance with parliamentary practice. **2.** (of language) foul or abusive. —**un′parliamen′tarily,** *adv.* —**un′parliamen′tariness,** *n.*

unpeg (ŭn pĕg′), *v.t.*, **-pegged, -pegging.** **1.** to remove the peg or pegs from. **2.** to open, unfasten, or unfix by removing a peg or pegs. **3.** to permit (wages, prices, etc.) to be increased.

unpen (ŭn pĕn′), *v.t.*, **-penned, -penning.** to release from, or as from, a pen.

unpeople (ŭn pē′pl), *v.t.*, **-pled, -pling.** **1.** to deprive of people; depopulate. **2.** to deprive or divest (of something).

unpick (ŭn pĭk′), *v.t.* to undo the stitches of (something sewn, etc.).

unpin (ŭn pĭn′), *v.t.*, **-pinned, -pinning.** **1.** to remove the pin or pins from. **2.** to unfasten by removing a pin or pins; release from being pinned or pinned down.

unplaced (ŭn plāst′), *adj.* **1.** not assigned to, or put in, a particular place. **2.** *Horseracing.* not among the first three (or sometimes four) runners.

unplait (ŭn plăt′), *v.t.* to bring out of a plaited state; unbraid, as hair.

unpleasant (ŭn plĕz′ənt), *adj.* not pleasant; unpleasing; disagreeable. —**unpleas′antly,** *adv.*

unpleasantness (ŭn plĕz′ənt nĭs), *n.* **1.** the quality or state of being unpleasant. **2.** something unpleasant; an unpleasant state of affairs. **3.** a disagreement or quarrel.

unplug (ŭn plŭg′), *v.t.*, **-plugged, -plugging.** **1.** to disconnect (electrical apparatus) by pulling the plug from it or from a power socket. **2.** to remove the plug from, as to open.

unplumbed (ŭn plŭmd′), *adj.* **1.** not plumbed; unfathomed; of unknown depth. **2.** not investigated in depth.

unpocket (ŭn pŏk′ĭt), *v.t.* to take out of or as if out of one's pocket, disburse.

unpolished (ŭn pŏl′ĭsht), *adj.* **1.** not smoothed by polishing. **2.** rough or inelegant in style, language, etc. **3.** not cultured or refined. **4.** (of rice) unmilled, retaining the husk.

unpolitic (ŭn pŏl′ĭ tĭk), *adj. Obs. Rare.* impolitic.

unpolled (ŭn pōld′), *adj.* **1.** not polled. **2.** not voting or not cast at the polls. **3.** not consulted by opinion poll.

unpopular (ŭn pŏp′yo͝o lə), *adj.* not popular; not liked by the public or by persons generally. —**unpopularity** (ŭn′pŏp yo͝o lă′rĭ tĭ), *n.* —**unpop′ularly,** *adv.*

unpractical (ŭn prăk′tĭ kl), *adj.* not practical; impractical; lacking practical usefulness or wisdom. —**un′practical′ity, unprac′ticalness,** *n.* —**unprac′tically,** *adv.*

unpractised (ŭn prăk′tĭst), *adj.* **1.** not practised; not done habitually or as a practice. **2.** not trained or skilled; inexpert.

unprecedented (ŭn prĕs′ĭ dən tĭd), *adj.* having no precedent or preceding instance; never known before; unexampled. —**unprec′edentedly,** *adv.*

unprejudiced (ŭn prĕj′o͝o dĭst), *adj.* **1.** not prejudiced; unbiased; impartial. **2.** *Obs.* not impaired. —**Syn. 1.** See **fair**[1].

unpremeditated (ŭn′prĭ mĕd′ĭ tā′tĭd), *adj.* (of actions, etc.) not planned or decided upon in advance. —**un′premed′itat′edly,** *adv.*

unpresentable (ŭn′prĭ zĕn′tə bl), *adj.* not fit to be seen.

unpretending (ŭn′prĭ tĕn′dĭng), *adj.* not pretending; unassuming; modest. —**un′pretend′ingly,** *adv.*

unpretentious (ŭn′prĭ tĕn′shəs), *adj.* not pretentious; modest; without ostentation. —**un′preten′tiously,** *adv.* —**un′preten′tiousness,** *n.*

unpriced (ŭn prīst′), *adj.* **1.** not priced; having no price set or indicated. **2.** *Poetic.* beyond price; priceless.

unprincipled (ŭn prĭn′sĭ pld), *adj.* **1.** lacking sound moral principles, as a person. **2.** showing want of principle, as conduct, etc. **3.** not instructed in the principles of something (fol. by *in*). —**unprin′cipledness,** *n.* —**Syn. 1.** See **unscrupulous.**

unprintable (ŭn prĭn′tə bl), *adj.* **1.** unfit to be printed, as offending against taste, morals, the laws of libel, or the like. **2.** not able to be printed.

unproductive (ŭn′prə dŭk′tĭv), *adj.* **1.** not fruitful; producing nothing. **2.** not producing or providing (fol. by *of*). —**un′produc′tively,** *adv.* —**un′produc′tiveness,** *n.*

unprofessional (ŭn′prə fĕsh′ə nəl), *adj.* **1.** contrary to professional ethics; unbecoming in members of a profession. **2.** not professional; not pertaining to or connected with a profession. **3.** not belonging to a profession. **4.** not of professional quality; amateur. —**un′profes′sionally,** *adv.*

unprofitable (ŭn prŏf′ĭ tə bl), *adj.* **1.** not showing a profit, as a business enterprise. **2.** not beneficial; disadvantageous. —**unprof′itably,** *adv.*

unpromising (ŭn prŏm′ĭ sĭng), *adj.* not showing signs of future excellence or improvement. —**unprom′isingly,** *adv.*

---

unoiled′, *adj.*
uno′pened, *adj.*
un′opposed′, *adj.*
un′oppressed′, *adj.*
un′oppres′sive, *adj.*
un′ordained′, *adj.*
unor′dered, *adj.*
unor′derly, *adj.*
unor′ganiz′able, *adj.*
un′orig′inal, *adj.*
un′orig′inal′ity, *n.*
un′orig′inat′ed, *adj.*
unor′nament′ed, *adj.*
unor′thodox, *adj.*
unor′thodox′y, *n.*
un′ostenta′tious, *adj.*
un′ostenta′tiously, *adv.*
unowned′, *adj.*
unpac′ified′, *adj.*
unpaid′, *adj.*
unpain′ful, *adj.*
unpaint′able, *adj.*
unpaint′ed, *adj.*
unpaired′, *adj.*
unpal′liat′ed, *adj.*
unpam′pered, *adj.*
unpan′elled, *adj.*
unpa′pered, *adj.*
unpar′allel′, *adj.*
unpar′alysed′, *adj.*
unpar′donable, *adj.*
unpar′donably, *adv.*
unpar′doned, *adj.*
unpar′doning, *adj.*
un′partic′ipat′ing, *adj.*
unpas′sable, *adj.*
unpassed′, *adj.*
unpas′sionate, *adj.*
unpas′sionately, *adv.*
unpat′ented, *adj.*
unpathed′, *adj.*
un′patriot′ic, *adj.*
un′patriot′ically, *adv.*
unpat′ronized′, *adj.*
unpat′terned, *adj.*
unpaus′ing, *adj.*
unpaved′, *adj.*
unpawned′, *adj.*
unpay′able, *adj.*
unpay′ing, *adj.*
unpeace′able, *adj.*
un′pedan′tic, *adj.*
unpeeled′, *adj.*
unpen′etrat′ed, *adj.*
unpen′sioned, *adj.*
unpep′pered, *adj.*
un′perceiv′able, *adj.*
un′perceived′, *adj.*
un′percep′tive, *adj.*
un′perfect′ed, *adj.*
unper′forat′ed, *adj.*
un′performed′, *adj.*
unper′fumed, *adj.*
unper′ishable, *adj.*
un′persuad′able, *adj.*
un′persuad′ed, *adj.*
un′persuas′ive, *adj.*
un′persuas′ively, *adv.*
un′perturbed′, *adj.*
un′perturb′edly, *adv.*
un′pervert′ed, *adj.*
un′philosoph′ical, *adj.*
un′philosoph′ically, *adv.*
unpicked′, *adj.*
unpierced′, *adj.*
unpi′loted, *adj.*
unpit′iable, *adj.*
unpit′ied, *adj.*
unpit′ying, *adj.*
unpit′yingly, *adv.*
unplanned′, *adj.*
unplant′ed, *adj.*
unplas′tered, *adj.*
unplay′able, *adj.*
unplayed′, *adj.*
unpleas′able, *adj.*
unpleased′, *adj.*
unpleas′ingly, *adv.*
unpli′able, *adj.*
unpli′ancy, *n.*
unpli′ant, *adj.*
unploughed′, *adj.*
unplucked′, *adj.*
unplun′dered, *adj.*
un′poet′ic, *adj.*
un′poet′ically, *adv.*
unpoint′ed, *adj.*
unpoised′, *adj.*
unpo′larized′, *adj.*
un′policed′, *adj.*
unpol′ishable, *adj.*
un′pollut′ed, *adj.*
unpop′ulous, *adj.*
un′portray′able, *adj.*
un′possessed′, *adj.*
un′postpon′able, *adj.*
unpraised′, *adj.*
unpraise′wor′thy, *adj.*
un′predict′able, *adj.*
un′preoc′cupied′, *adj.*
un′prepared′, *adj.*
un′prepar′edly, *adv.*
un′prepossess′sing, *adj.*
un′prevail′ing, *adj.*
un′prevent′able, *adj.*
un′prevent′ably, *adv.*
unpriest′ly, *adj., adv.*
unpriv′ileged, *adj.*
unprized′, *adj.*
un′proclaimed′, *adj.*
un′procur′able, *adj.*
un′progres′sive, *adj.*
un′progres′sively, *adv.*
un′prolif′ic, *adj.*
unprompt′ed, *adj.*
un′pronounce′able, *adj.*
un′propi′tious, *adj.*
un′propi′tiously, *adv.*
unpros′perous, *adj.*
unpros′perously, *adv.*
un′protect′ed, *adj.*
un′protect′edness, *n.*
un′protest′ing, *adj.*
unprov′able, *adj.*
unproved′, *adj.*
unprov′en, *adj.*

---

unprovided (ŭn′prə vī′dĭd), *adj.* **1.** not furnished or supplied with something. **2.** lacking something, esp. the necessities of life (fol. by *for*).

unpublished work (ŭn pŭb′lĭsht), *Copyright Law.* a literary work which, at the time of registration, has not been reproduced for sale or been publicly distributed.

unqualified (ŭn kwŏl′ĭ fīd′), *adj.* **1.** not qualified; not fitted; not having the requisite qualifications. **2.** not modified, limited, or restricted in any way: *unqualified praise.* **3.** absolute; out-and-out. —**unqual′ified′ly,** *adv.* —**unqual′ified′ness,** *n.* —**Syn. 3.** See **absolute.**

unquestionable (ŭn kwĕs′chə nə bl), *adj.* **1.** not questionable; not open to question; beyond dispute or doubt; indisputable; indubitable. **2.** beyond criticism; unexceptionable. —**un′ques′tionabil′ity, unques′tionableness,** *n.* —**unques′tionably,** *adv.*

unquestioned (ŭn kwĕs′chənd), *adj.* **1.** not enquired into. **2.** not called in question; undisputed. **3.** not questioned; not interrogated.

unquiet (ŭn kwī′ət), *adj.* **1.** not quiet; restless; turbulent; tumultuous. **2.** uneasy; perturbed. **3.** agitated or in commotion; not silent or still. —**unqui′etly,** *adv.* —**unqui′etness,** *n.*

unquote (ŭn kwōt′), *v.i.*, **-quoted, -quoting.** to close a quotation.

unravel (ŭn răv′əl), *v.*, **-elled, -elling** or (*esp. U.S.*) **-eled, -eling.** —*v.t.* **1.** to free from a ravelled or tangled state; disentangle; disengage the threads or fibres of (a woven or knitted fabric, a rope, etc.). **2.** to take apart (a piece of knitting). **3.** to free from complication or difficulty; make plain or clear; solve. —*v.i.* **4.** to become unravelled. —**unrav′eller,** *n.* —**unrav′elment,** *n.*

unread (ŭn rĕd′), *adj.* **1.** not read or perused, as a book. **2.** not having gained knowledge by reading. **3.** not having read (some subject or matter) (fol. by *in*).

unreadable (ŭn rē′də bl), *adj.* **1.** not readable; illegible; undecipherable. **2.** not interesting to read; tedious. —**unread′abil′ity, unread′ableness,** *n.* —**unread′ably,** *adv.*

unready (ŭn rĕd′ĭ), *adj.* **1.** not ready; not made ready, as for action or use. **2.** not in a state of readiness or preparation, as a person. **3.** not prompt or quick. **4.** *Obs. or Dial.* not dressed, or not fully dressed. —**unread′ily,** *adv.* —**unread′iness,** *n.*

unreal (ŭn rĭəl′), *adj.* not real; not substantial; imaginary; artificial; unpractical or visionary. —**unreal′ly,** *adv.* —**Syn.** sham, spurious, fictitious, illusive, theoretical, impractical.

unrealistic (ŭn′rĭə lĭs′tĭk), *adj.* **1.** not closely or accurately resembling an object or situation depicted. **2.** not practical, hard-headed or clear-sighted.

unreality (ŭn′rĭ ăl′ĭ tĭ), *n.*, *pl.* **-ties. 1.** lack of reality; quality of being unreal. **2.** something unreal or without reality.

unreason (ŭn rē′zən), *n.* **1.** lack of reason; inability or unwillingness to think or act rationally, reasonably, or sensibly. **2.** that which is devoid of or contrary to reason.

unreasonable (ŭn rēz′nə bl), *adj.* **1.** not reasonable; not endowed with reason. **2.** not guided by reason or good sense. **3.** not agreeable to or willing to listen to reason. **4.** not based on or in accordance with reason or sound judgement. **5.** exceeding the bounds of reason; immoderate; exorbitant. —**unrea′sonableness,** *n.* —**unrea′sonably,** *adv.* —**Syn. 1, 2.** irrational, senseless, foolish, silly. **5.** excessive.

unreasoned (ŭn rē′zənd), *adj.* worked out or arrived at by some method other than reasoning; irrational.

unreasoning (ŭn rē′zə nĭng), *adj.* **1.** not employing reason; illogical; unthinking. **2.** irrational, as emotions: *an unreasoning fear.* —**unrea′soningly,** *adv.*

unrecognized (ŭn rĕk′əg nīzd′), *adj.* **1.** not accorded adequate credit or appreciation. **2.** not recognized. Also, **unrecognised.**

unredeemed (ŭn′rĭ dēmd′), *adj.* **1.** unmitigated, unrelieved, or unmodified, as by some good feature. **2.** not recovered from pawn or by ransom.

unreel (ŭn rēl′), *v.t., v.i.* to unwind from a reel. —**unreel′able,** *adj.*

unreeve (ŭn rēv′), *v.*, **-rove** or **-reeved, -reeving.** —*v.t.* **1.** *Naut.* to withdraw (a rope, etc.) from a block, thimble, etc. —*v.i.* **2.** to unreeve a rope. **3.** (of a rope, etc.) to become unreeved.

unrefined (ŭn′rĭ fīnd′), *adj.* **1.** not refined; not purified, as substances. **2.** coarse or vulgar; lacking nice feeling, taste, etc. —**Syn. 1.** unpurified, crude, coarse. **2.** unpolished, uncultured, ill-bred, rude, boorish, vulgar, gross.

unreflected (ŭn′rĭ flĕk′tĭd), *adj.* **1.** not returned by reflection, as by a polished surface. **2.** not considered or thought out (fol. by *on*).

unreflecting (ŭn′rĭ flĕk′tĭng), *adj.* not given to the exercise of reflection, meditation, or thought; thoughtless.

unreformed (ŭn′rĭ fômd′), *adj.* **1.** not changed for the better, as persons, their character, etc. **2.** not reformed, as institutions, esp. the Church. **3.** not affected by the Reformation.

unregenerate (ŭn′rĭ jĕn′ə rĭt), *adj.* **1.** unreformed; wicked or sinful; unconverted. **2.** not regenerate; not born again spiritually. **3.** remaining at enmity with God. Also, **unregenerated** (ŭn′rĭ jĕn′ə rā′tĭd). —**unregeneracy** (ŭn′rĭ jĕn′ə rə sĭ), *n.* —**un′regen′erately,** *adv.*

unrelated (ŭn′rĭ lā′tĭd), *adj.* **1.** not connected by blood or marriage; not kin. **2.** having no relationship; unconnected. **3.** untold, as a story.

unrelenting (ŭn′rĭ lĕn′tĭng), *adj.* **1.** not relenting; not yielding to feelings of kindness or compassion. **2.** not slackening in severity or determination. **3.** maintaining speed or rate of advance. —**un′relent′ingly,** *adv.* —**un′relent′ingness,** *n.*

unreliable (ŭn′rĭ lī′ə bl), *adj.* not reliable; not to be relied or depended on. —**un′reli′abil′ity, un′reli′ableness,** *n.* —**un′reli′ably,** *adv.*

unrelieved (ŭn′rĭ lēvd′), *adj.* **1.** not varied, moderated, or made less monotonous. **2.** not provided with relief or aid. —**unrelievedly** (ŭn′rĭ lē′vĭd lĭ), *adv.*

unreligious (ŭn′rĭ lĭj′əs), *adj.* **1.** irreligious. **2.** having no connection with or relation to religion; neither religious nor irreligious.

unremarkable (ŭn′rĭ mä′kə bl), *adj.* ordinary; unexciting; not worthy of note. —**un′remark′ably,** *adv.*

unremarked (ŭn′rĭ mäkt′), *adj.* not noticed.

unremitting (ŭn′rĭ mĭt′ĭng), *adj.* not remitting or slackening; not abating for a time; incessant. —**un′remit′tingly,** *adv.* —**un′remit′tingness,** *n.*

unrepeatable (ŭn′rĭ pē′tə bl), *adj.* **1.** too vulgar, abusive or otherwise unpleasant to be repeated. **2.** unable to be repeated: *an unrepeatable offer of goods on sale.* —**un-**

un′provoc′ative, *adj.*
un′provoked′, *adj.*
unpruned′, *adj.*
unpub′lishable, *adj.*
unpub′lished, *adj.*
unpunc′tual, *adj.*
un′punctual′ity, *n.*
unpunc′tuat′ed, *adj.*
unpunc′turable, *adj.*
unpun′ishable, *adj.*
unpun′ishably, *adv.*
unpun′ished, *adj.*
unpur′chaseable, *adj.*
unpur′chased, *adj.*
unpurged′, *adj.*
unpur′ified′, *adj.*
un′pursued′, *adj.*
unquail′ing, *adj.*
unquail′ingly, *adv.*
unqual′ifi′able, *adj.*
unquan′tified′, *adj.*
unquar′ried, *adj.*
unqueen′ly, *adj.*
unquench′able, *adj.*
unquench′ably, *adv.*
unquenched′, *adj.*
unques′tioning, *adj.*
unquick′ened, *adj.*
un′quotabil′ity, *n.*
unquot′able, *adj.*
unraised′, *adj.*
unraked′, *adj.*
unran′sacked, *adj.*
unran′somed, *adj.*
unrate′able, *adj.*
unrat′ed, *adj.*
unrat′ified′, *adj.*
unra′tioned, *adj.*
unrav′ished, *adj.*
unra′zored, *adj.*
unreach′able, *adj.*
unre′alism, *n.*
unre′aliz′able, *adj.*
unre′alized′, *adj.*
unreaped′, *adj.*
unre′bated, *adj.*
un′rebuked′, *adj.*
un′rebut′ted, *adj.*
un′recall′able, *adj.*
un′recalled′, *adj.*
un′recep′tive, *adj.*
un′recep′tively, *adv.*
un′receptiv′ity, *n.*
un′recip′rocat′ed, *adj.*
unreck′onable, *adj.*
un′reclaimed′, *adj.*
un′recogni′tion, *n.*
unrec′ogniz′able, *adj.*
unrec′ogniz′ably, *adv.*
unrec′ogniz′ing, *adj.*
un′recommend′able, *adj.*
unrec′ompensed′, *adj.*
unrec′onciled′, *adj.*
un′reconstruct′ed, *adj.*
un′record′ed, *adj.*
unrec′tified′, *adj.*
un′redeem′able, *adj.*
un′redressed′, *adj.*
un′reduced′, *adj.*
un′reduc′ible, *adj.*
un′reflec′tive, *adj.*
un′reform′able, *adj.*
un′refract′ed, *adj.*
un′refreshed′, *adj.*
un′refresh′ing, *adj.*
un′refresh′ingly, *adv.*
un′refus′able, *adj.*
un′refut′ed, *adj.*
un′regard′ed, *adj.*
un′regard′ing, *adj.*
unreg′istered, *adj.*
un′regret′ted, *adj.*
unreg′ulat′ed, *adj.*
un′rehearsed′, *adj.*
unreined′, *adj.*
un′relaxed′, *adj.*
un′relax′ing, *adj.*
unrel′ished, *adj.*
un′remem′bered, *adj.*
un′remem′bering, *adj.*
un′remit′tent, *adj.*
un′remit′tently, *adv.*
un′remorse′ful, *adj.*
un′removed′, *adj.*
un′remu′nerative, *adj.*
un′remu′nerativeness, *n.*
unren′derable, *adj.*
un′renew′able, *adj.*
un′repaid′, *adj.*
un′repair′, *n.*
un′repair′able, *adj.*
un′repay′able, *adj.*
un′repelled′, *adj.*
un′repen′tance, *n.*

repeatability (ŭn′rĭ pē′tə bĭl′ĭ tĭ), *n.* —**un′repeat′ably,** *adv.*
unrequited (ŭn′rĭ kwī′tĭd), *adj.* (used esp. of affection) not returned or reciprocated. —**un′requit′edly,** *adv.* —**un′requit′edness,** *n.*
unreserve (ŭn′rĭ zûv′), *n.* absence of reserve; frankness.
unreserved (ŭn′rĭ zûvd′), *adj.* **1.** not reserved; without reservation; full; entire. **2.** free from reserve; frank; open. **3.** not set aside or ordered in advance; not booked. —**unreservedly** (ŭn′rĭ zû′vĭd lĭ), *adv.* —**un′reserv′edness,** *n.*
unresolved (ŭn′rĭ zŏlvd′), *adj.* **1.** (of questions, problems, etc.) not decided or solved. **2.** (of persons) uncertain how to act, or in an opinion. —**unresolvedly** (ŭn′rĭ zŏl′vĭd lĭ), *adv.* —**un′resolv′edness,** *n.*
unrest (ŭn rĕst′), *n.* **1.** lack of rest; restless or uneasy state; inquietude. **2.** strong, almost rebellious, dissatisfaction and agitation.
unresting (ŭn rĕs′tĭng), *adj.* not stopping or pausing, tireless, seeking or taking no rest. —**unrest′ingly,** *adv.*
unrestraint (ŭn′rĭ strānt′), *n.* absence of or freedom from restraint.
unrewarded (ŭn′rĭ wô′dĭd), *adj.* **1.** (of persons) without appropriate recompense. **2.** (of good or bad actions) not recompensed.
unriddle (ŭn rĭd′l), *v.t.*, **-dled, -dling.** to solve (a riddle, etc.). —**unrid′dler,** *n.*
unrig (ŭn rĭg′), *v.t.*, **-rigged, -rigging. 1.** to strip of rigging, as a ship. **2.** *Obs. and Dial.* to undress.
unrighteous (ŭn rī′chəs), *adj.* **1.** not righteous; not upright or virtuous; wicked. **2.** not in accordance with right; unjust. —*n.* **3. the unrighteous,** wicked and unjust people collectively. [ME *unrightwyse,* OE *unrihtwis*] —**unright′eously,** *adv.* —**unright′eousness,** *n.*
unrip (ŭn rĭp′), *v.t.*, **-ripped, -ripping.** *Rare.* to undo by ripping; cut or tear open; rip.
unripe (ŭn rīp′), *adj.* **1.** not ripe; immature; not fully developed. **2.** *Obs.* too early; premature. Also, **unripened.** —**unripe′ness,** *n.*
unrivalled (ŭn rī′vəld), *adj.* having no rival or competitor; having no equal; peerless. Also, *U.S.*, **unrivaled.**
unrobe (ŭn rōb′), *v.t., v.i.*, **-robed, -robing.** to disrobe.
unroll (ŭn rōl′), *v.t.* **1.** to open or spread out (something rolled, coiled, or folded). **2.** to extend or spread out. **3.** to lay open; display; reveal. —*v.i.* **4.** to become unrolled. **5.** to become visible or apparent.
unroof (ŭn ro͞of′), *v.t.* to take the roof off.
unroot (ŭn ro͞ot′), *v.t.* to uproot.
unround (ŭn round′), *v.t. Phonet.* to pronounce without rounding the lips: the vowel of *bit* is normally unrounded, the vowel of *put* is often unrounded. —**unround′ed,** *adj.*
unrove (ŭn rōv′), *Naut.* —*v.* **1.** pt. and pp. of **unreeve.** —*adj.* **2.** withdrawn from a block, thimble, etc.
UNRRA (ŭn′rə), *n.* United Nations Relief and Rehabilitation Administration.
unruffled (ŭn rŭf′əld), *adj.* **1.** (of a person) calm; undisturbed. **2.** not physically ruffled or disturbed; not choppy, as the sea.
unruly (ŭn ro͞o′lĭ), *adj.* not submissive or conforming to rule; ungovernable; turbulent; refractory; lawless. —**unru′liness,** *n.*
unsaddle (ŭn săd′l), *v.*, **-dled, -dling.** —*v.t.* **1.** to take the saddle from. **2.** to cause to fall or dismount from a saddle; unhorse. —*v.i.* **3.** to take the saddle from a horse.
unsafe (ŭn sāf′), *adj.* **1.** not safe or secure, as a person. **2.** not safe to be in, as a place. **3.** not to be trusted; unreliable. —**unsafe′ly,** *adv.* —**unsafe′ness,** *n.*
unsafety (ŭn sāf′tĭ), *n.* the state of being unsafe; exposure to danger or risk; insecurity.
unsaid (ŭn sĕd′), *v.* **1.** pt. and pp. of **unsay.** —*adj.* **2.** not uttered.
unsatisfactory (ŭn′săt ĭs făk′tə rĭ, -trĭ), *adj.* not satisfactory; not satisfying specified desires or requirements; inadequate. —**un′satisfac′torily,** *adv.* —**un′satisfac′toriness,** *n.*
unsaturated (ŭn săch′ə rā′tĭd), *adj.* **1.** not saturated; having the power to dissolve still more of a substance. **2.** *Chem.* capable of taking on an element, etc., by direct chemical combination without the liberation of other elements or compounds, esp. as a result of the presence of a double or triple bond between carbon atoms.
unsavoury (ŭn sā′və rĭ), *adj.* **1.** unpleasant in taste or smell. **2.** socially or morally unpleasant or offensive. Also, *esp. U.S.*, **unsavory.** —**unsa′vourily,** *adv.* —**unsa′vouriness,** *n.*
unsay (ŭn sā′), *v.t.*, **-said, -saying.** to retract (something said).
unscathed (ŭn skāthd′), *adj.* not scathed; unharmed; uninjured physically or spiritually.
unscholarly (ŭn skŏl′ə lĭ), *adj.* not in accordance with principles or standards of scholarship; not learned; inappropriate to a scholar. —**unschol′arliness,** *n.*
unschooled (ŭn sko͞old′), *adj.* **1.** uneducated; having received no schooling. **2.** not disciplined. **3.** not acquired by training; natural.
unscientific (ŭn′sī ən tĭf′ĭk), *adj.* **1.** not scientific; not in accordance with the requirements of science. **2.** not conforming to the principles or methods of science. —**un′scientif′ically,** *adv.*
unscramble (ŭn skrăm′bl), *v.t.*, **-bled, -bling. 1.** *Colloq.* to bring out of a scrambled condition; reduce to order. **2.** to restore (a scrambled telephone message, or the like) to intelligibility. —**unscram′bler,** *n.*
unscratched (ŭn skrăcht′), *adj.* **1.** not having been scratched. **2.** having received no injury; totally unharmed.
unscreened (ŭn skrēnd′), *adj.* **1.** not protected by a screen or screening. **2.** not sifted or separated through or as through a screen. **3.** not yet shown in a cinema. **4.** not investigated for security purposes.
unscrew (ŭn skro͞o′), *v.t.* **1.** to draw the screw or screws from; unfasten by withdrawing screws. **2.** to remove (the lid of a screw-top jar, etc.) by turning. **3.** to loosen or withdraw (a screw, screwlike plug, etc.). —*v.i.* **4.** to permit of being unscrewed. **5.** to become unscrewed.
unscripted (ŭn skrĭp′tĭd), *adj.* (of a radio or television programme, theatrical performance, etc.) performed without a prepared script.
unscrupulous (ŭn skro͞o′pyo͝o ləs), *adj.* not scrupulous; unrestrained by scruples; conscienceless; unprincipled. —**unscru′pulously,** *adv.* —**unscru′pulousness,** *n.*
—**Syn.** UNSCRUPULOUS, UNPRINCIPLED refer to lack of moral standards or conscience to guide one's conduct. The UNSCRUPULOUS man is without scruples of conscience, and disregards, or has contempt for, laws of right or justice with which he is perfectly well acquainted, and which should restrain him in his actions: *unscrupulous methods of making money, in taking advantage of the unfortunate.* The UNPRINCIPLED man is without moral principles or ethical standards in his conduct or actions: *an unprincipled rogue, unprincipled conduct.*
unseal (ŭn sēl′), *v.t.* **1.** to break or remove the seal of. **2.** to open, as something sealed or firmly closed: *nothing will unseal my lips on that topic.*
unsealed (ŭn sēld′), *adj.* **1.** not closed with or bearing a seal. **2.** not closed, as a letter.
unseam (ŭn sēm′), *v.t.* to open the seam or seams of.
unsearchable (ŭn sû′chə bl), *adj.* not searchable; not to be searched into or understood by searching; inscrutable; unfathomable. —**unsearch′ableness,** *n.* —**unsearch′ably,** *adv.*

un′repen′tant, *adj.*
un′repen′tantly, *adv.*
un′repent′ed, *adj.*
un′repent′ing, *adj.*
un′replace′able, *adj.*
un′report′able, *adj.*
un′report′ed, *adj.*
un′represen′tative, *adj.*
un′represent′ed, *adj.*
un′repressed′, *adj.*
un′reproach′ful, *adj.*
un′reproduc′ible, *adj.*
un′reproved′, *adj.*
un′resent′ed, *adj.*
un′resent′ful, *adj.*
un′resent′fully, *adv.*
un′resent′fulness, *n.*
un′resent′ing, *adj.*
un′resist′ing, *adj.*
un′resist′ingly, *adv.*
un′resolv′able, *adj.*
un′respect′able, *adj.*
un′respect′ed, *adj.*
un′respon′sive, *adj.*
un′respon′sively, *adv.*
un′respon′siveness, *n.*
unrest′ful, *adj.*
un′restored′, *adj.*
un′restrain′able, *adj.*
un′restrained′, *adj.*
un′restrain′edly, *adv.*
un′restrict′ed, *adj.*
un′restrict′edly, *adv.*
un′reten′tive, *adj.*
un′retract′ed, *adj.*
un′return′able, *adj.*
un′return′ing, *adj.*
un′reveal′able, *adj.*
un′reveal′ing, *adj.*
un′revenged′, *adj.*
unrev′erent, *adj.*
un′reversed′, *adj.*
un′reviewed′, *adj.*
un′revised′, *adj.*
un′revoked′, *adj.*
un′reward′ing, *adj.*
un′rhetor′ical, *adj.*
unrid′den, *adj.*
unride′able, *adj.*
unri′fled, *adj.*
unris′en, *adj.*
unriv′et, *v.t.*
un′roman′tic, *adj.*
un′roman′tically, *adv.*
un′roman′ticized′, *adj.*
unrope′, *v.t.*
unrouged′, *adj.*
unroused′, *adj.*
unroy′al, *adj.*
unroy′ally, *adv.*
unrubbed′, *adj.*
unrum′pled, *adj.*
unsaint′liness, *n.*
unsaint′ly, *adj.*
unsal′aried, *adj.*
unsale′able, *adj.*
unsalt′ed, *adj.*
unsanc′tified′, *adj.*
unsanc′tioned, *adj.*
unsan′itary, *adj.*
unsat′isfi′able, *adj.*
unsat′isfied′, *adj.*
unsat′isfy′ing, *adj.*
unsay′able, *adj.*
unscale′able, *adj.*
unscaled′, *adj.*
unscarred′, *adj.*
unscored′, *adj.*
unscru′tinized′, *adj.*
unsearched′, *adj.*

unseasonable (ŭn sē′zə nə bl, -sēz′nə-), *adj.* **1.** inappropriate to the time of year or the hour. **2.** untimely; ill-timed; inopportune. **—unsea′sonableness,** *n.* **—unsea′sonably,** *adv.*

unseasoned (ŭn sē′zənd), *adj.* **1.** (of things) not seasoned; not matured, dried, etc., by due seasoning. **2.** (of persons) not inured to a climate, work, etc.; inexperienced. **3.** (of food) not flavoured with seasoning.

unseat (ŭn sēt′), *v.t.* **1.** to throw from a saddle, as a rider. **2.** to depose from an official seat or from office. **3.** to displace from a seat.

unsecured (ŭn′sĭ kyo͝ord′), *adj.* **1.** not made secure or fastened. **2.** not insured against loss, as by a mortgage, bond, pledge, etc.

unseemly (ŭn sēm′lĭ), *adj.* **1.** not seemly; unfitting; unbecoming; improper; indecorous. **2.** *Obs.* unattractive. *—adv.* **3.** in an unseemly manner. **—unseem′liness,** *n.* **—Syn. 1.** See **improper.**

unseen (ŭn sēn′), *adj.* **1.** not seen; unperceived; unobserved; invisible. **2.** (of passages of writing or music) not previously seen. **—***n.* **3.** an unprepared passage for translation, as in an examination.

unsegregated (ŭn sĕg′rĭ gā′tĭd), *adj.* not subject to racial segregation.

unselfish (ŭn sĕl′fĭsh), *adj.* not selfish; disinterested; altruistic. **—unself′ishly,** *adv.* **—unself′ishness,** *n.*

unserviceable (ŭn sûr′vĭ sə bl), *adj.* **1.** not useful, as for its proper purpose. **2.** incapable of being put to use, as through wear or damage. **—un′ser′viceabil′ity,** *n.*

unset (ŭn sĕt′), *adj.* **1.** not solidified or become firm. **2.** (of gems) unmounted.

unsettle (ŭn sĕt′l), *v.*, **-tled, -tling.** *—v.t.* **1.** to bring out of a settled state; cause to be no longer firmly fixed or established; render unstable; disturb; disorder. **2.** to shake or weaken (beliefs, feelings, etc.); derange (the mind, etc.). *—v.i.* **3.** to become unfixed or disordered.

unsettled (ŭn sĕt′ld), *adj.* **1.** not settled; not fixed in a place or abode. **2.** not populated, as a region. **3.** not fixed or stable, as conditions; without established order, as times. **4.** liable to change, as weather. **5.** wavering or uncertain, as the mind, opinions, etc., or the person. **6.** undetermined, as a point at issue. **7.** not adjusted, closed, or disposed of finally, as an account or an estate. **—unset′tledness, unset′tlement,** *n.*

—Syn. 3, 4. UNSETTLED, UNSTABLE, UNSTEADY imply a lack of fixity, firmness, and dependability. That which is UNSETTLED is not fixed or determined: *unsettled weather, unsettled claims.* That which is UNSTABLE is wavering, changeable; easily moved, shaken, or overthrown: *unstable equilibrium, an unstable decision.* That which is UNSTEADY is infirm or shaky in position or movement: *unsteady on one's feet, unsteady of purpose.* **—Ant. 3.** stable.

unsew (ŭn sō′), *v.t.*, **-sewed, -sewed** or **-sewn, -sewing.** to undo (the sewing of something).

unsex (ŭn sĕks′), *v.t.* **1.** to deprive (a person, esp. a woman) of the qualities appropriate to his or her sex. **2.** to castrate.

unshackle (ŭn shăk′l), *v.t.* **1.** to free from restraint. **2.** to free from shackles; unfetter.

unshadow (ŭn shăd′ō), *v.t.* to free from shadow; disclose.

unshadowed (ŭn shăd′ōd), *adj.* not shadowed; not darkened or obscured; free from gloom.

unshakeable (ŭn shā′kə bl), *adj.* (of opinions, beliefs, positions, etc.) tenaciously held; not open to dissuasion. Also, **unshakable. —unshake′ably,** *adv.*

unshapen (ŭn shā′pən), *adj.* not shaped or definitely formed; shapeless; formless; indefinite.

unsheathe (ŭn shēth′), *v.t.*, **-sheathed, -sheathing. 1.** to draw from a sheath, as a sword, knife, or the like. **2.** to bring or put forth from a covering, threateningly or otherwise.

unshell (ŭn shĕl′), *v.t.* to take out of the shell; remove or release, as from a shell.

unship (ŭn shĭp′), *v.t.*, **-shipped, -shipping. 1.** to put or take off from a ship, as persons or goods. **2.** to remove from the proper place for use, as a mast, oar, tiller, etc.

unshoulder (ŭn shōl′də), *v.t.* to remove (a load) from the shoulder.

unshrinking (ŭn shrĭng′kĭng), *adj.* not shrinking or drawing back; firm; unyielding. **—unshrink′ingly,** *adv.* **—unshrink′ingness,** *n.*

unshriven (ŭn shrĭv′ən), *adj.* *Rom. Cath. Ch.* not having received the last sacrament; not having received the sacramental grace of penance by confession before a priest.

unshroud (ŭn shroud′), *v.t.* to remove the shroud from; divest of something that shrouds; uncover; unveil.

unsight (ŭn sīt′), *adj.* *Obs.* without inspection or examination (used in the phrase *unsight, unseen*): *to buy a thing unsight, unseen* (that is, without seeing it).

unsighted (ŭn sī′tĭd), *adj.* **1.** (of a gun) not provided with sights. **2.** (of a shot) fired without proper aiming. **3.** not yet in view.

unsightly (ŭn sīt′lĭ), *adj.* not pleasing to the sight; forming an unpleasing sight. **—unsight′liness,** *n.*

unskilful (ŭn skĭl′fəl), *adj.* not skilful; inexpert; awkward; bungling. Also, *U.S.*, **unskillful. —unskil′fully,** *adv.* **—unskil′fulness,** *n.*

unskilled (ŭn skĭld′), *adj.* **1.** of or pertaining to workers lacking specialized training or ability. **2.** not skilled (in some activity). **3.** not requiring or exhibiting skill.

unslaked lime (ŭn slākt′). See **lime** (def. 1).

unsling (ŭn slĭng′), *v.t.*, **-slung, -slinging. 1.** to remove (something) from a position in which it is slung. **2.** *Naut.* to take off the slings of; release from slings.

unsnap (ŭn snăp′), *v.t.*, **-snapped, -snapping.** to release by opening a snap or catch.

unsnarl (ŭn snäl′), *v.t.* to bring out of a snarled condition; disentangle.

unsociable (ŭn sō′shə bl), *adj.* not sociable; having, showing, or marked by a disinclination to friendly social relations. **—un′sociabil′ity, unso′ciableness,** *n.* **—unso′ciably,** *adv.*

unsolder (ŭn sŏl′də), *v.t.* **1.** to separate (something soldered). **2.** to disunite; dissolve.

unsolicited (ŭn′sə lĭs′ĭ tĭd), *adj.* **1.** not asked for: *unsolicited contributions.* **2.** (of persons) not approached or solicited (for some purpose).

unsonsy (ŭn sŏn′sĭ), *adj.* *Scot., Irish, and N Dial.* bringing or boding ill luck. [f. UN-[1] + SONSY]

unsophisticated (ŭn′sə fĭs′tĭ kā′tĭd), *adj.* **1.** not sophisticated; simple; artless. **2.** not complicated, as a mechanism; unsubtle. **3.** unadulterated; pure; genuine. **—un′sophis′ticat′edly,** *adv.* **—un′sophis′ticat′edness, un′sophis′tica′tion,** *n.*

unsound (ŭn sound′), *adj.* **1.** not sound; diseased, as the body or mind. **2.** decayed, as timber or fruit; impaired or defective, as goods. **3.** not solid or firm, as foundations. **4.** not well-founded or valid; fallacious. **5.** easily broken; light: *unsound slumber.* **6.** not financially strong; unreliable. **—unsound′ly,** *adv.* **—unsound′ness,** *n.*

---

unsea′wor′thiness, *n.*
unsea′wor′thy, *adj.*
unsec′onded, *adj.*
un′second′ed, *adj.*
un′sectar′ian, *adj.*
un′sectar′ianism, *n.*
unsec′ular, *adj.*
unsec′ularize′, *v.t.*
un′seduced′, *adj.*
unsee′able, *adj.*
unsee′ing, *adj.*
un′segment′ed, *adj.*
unseized′, *adj.*
un′selec′tive, *adj.*
un′selfcon′scious, *adj.*
un′selfcon′sciously, *adv.*
un′selfcon′sciousness, *n.*
un′sensa′tional, *adj.*
unsen′sitized′, *adj.*
unsen′sual, *adj.*
unsen′sualize′, *v.t.*
unsen′tenced, *adj.*
un′sentimen′tal, *adj.*
unsep′arat′ed, *adj.*
unserved′, *adj.*
unsex′ual, *adj.*
unshad′ed, *adj.*
unsha′ken, *adj.*
unshaped′, *adj.*
unshape′liness, *n.*
unshape′ly, *adv.*
unshared′, *adj.*
unshaved′, *adj.*
unsha′ven, *adj.*
unshed′, *adj.*
unshel′tered, *adj.*
unshield′ed, *adj.*
unshift′ing, *adj.*
unshock′able, *adj.*
unshod′, *adj.*
unshorn′, *adj.*
unshor′tened, *adj.*
unshrink′able, *adj.*
unshuf′fled, *adj.*
unshut′ter, *v.t.*
unshut′tered, *adj.*
unsift′ed, *adj.*
unsigned′, *adj.*
unsigned′-for′, *adj.*
unsig′nify′ing, *adj.*
unsi′lenced, *adj.*
unsil′vered, *adj.*
unsinged′, *adj.*
un′sinkabil′ity, *n.*
unsink′able, *adj.*
unsis′terliness, *n.*
unsis′terly, *adj.*
unskimmed′, *adj.*
unskinned′, *adj.*
unslack′ened, *adj.*
unslack′ening, *adj.*
unsleep′ing, *adj.*
unsleep′ingly, *adv.*
unslept′-in′, *adj.*
unsmart′, *adj.*
unsmil′ing, *adj.*
unsmil′ingly, *adv.*
unsmil′ingness, *n.*
unsmoked′, *adj.*
unsmooth′, *v.t.*
unsmoothed′, *adj.*
unsmoth′erable, *adj.*
unsmoth′ered, *adj.*
unsnub′bable, *adj.*
unsnuffed′, *adj.*
unso′cial, *adj.*
un′social′ity, *n.*
unsoft′ened, *adj.*
unsoft′ening, *adj.*
unsoiled′, *adj.*
unsold′, *adj.*
unsol′dierlike′, *adj.*
unsol′dierly, *adv.*
unsol′emn, *adj.*
un′solic′itous, *adj.*
unsol′id, *adj.*
un′solid′ity, *n.*
unsol′idly, *adv.*
unsolv′able, *adj.*
unsolved′, *adj.*
unsort′ed, *adj.*
unsought′, *adj.*
unsound′able, *adj.*
unsoured′, *adj.*
unsov′ereign, *adj.*
unsown′, *adj.*

unsounded[1] (ŭn soun′dĭd), *adj.* not sounded, uttered, or caused to make a noise.

unsounded[2] (ŭn soun′dĭd), *adj.* not sounded or fathomed.

unsparing (ŭn spĕə′rĭng), *adj.* **1.** not sparing; liberal or profuse. **2.** unmerciful. —**unspar′ingly,** *adv.* —**unspar′ingness,** *n.*

unspeak (ŭn spēk′), *v.t.*, **-spoke, -spoken, -speaking.** to retract (something spoken); unsay.

unspeakable (ŭn spē′kə bl), *adj.* **1.** inexpressibly bad or objectionable. **2.** impossible to express in words; unutterable; inexpressible. **3.** not speakable; that may not be spoken. —**unspeak′ably,** *adv.*

unsphere (ŭn sfĭə′), *v.t.*, **-sphered, -sphering.** *Obs. or Poet.* to remove from its or one's sphere.

unspoilt (ŭn spoilt′), *adj.* not impaired; not having deteriorated, as the character of a person or place. Also, **unspoiled** (ŭn spoilt′).

unspoken (ŭn spō′kən), *adj.* **1.** not spoken; not expressed aloud. **2.** understood without needing to be uttered.

unspotted (ŭn spŏt′ĭd), *adj.* **1.** not having spots or marks. **2.** (esp. of a reputation) having no moral blemish.

unsprung (ŭn sprŭng′), *adj.* not equipped with a spring or springing, as upholstery, vehicles, etc.

unstable (ŭn stā′bl), *adj.* **1.** not stable; not firm or firmly fixed; unsteady. **2.** liable to fall, change, or cease. **3.** unsteadfast; inconstant; wavering. **4.** lacking emotional stability. **5.** *Chem.* denoting compounds which readily decompose or change into other compounds. —**unsta′bleness,** *n.* —**unsta′bly,** *adv.* —**Syn. 2, 3.** See **unsettled.**

unstable equilibrium, a state of equilibrium in a body such that any slight displacement will cause the body to move away from its position of equilibrium.

unstable oscillation, a mechanical or electrical oscillation which tends to increase in amplitude with time, esp. in an aircraft structural member, or an electrical circuit.

unsteady (ŭn stĕd′ĭ), *adj.* **1.** not steady; not firmly fixed; not secure or stable. **2.** fluctuating or wavering; unsteadfast. **3.** irregular or uneven. —*v.t.* **4.** to make unsteady. —**unstead′ily,** *adv.* —**unstead′iness,** *n.* —**Syn. 1, 2.** See **unsettled.**

unstep (ŭn stĕp′), *v.t.*, **-stepped, -stepping.** to remove (a mast, etc.) from its step.

unstick (ŭn stĭk′), *v.t.*, **-stuck, -sticking. 1.** to free, as one thing stuck to another. **2. come unstuck,** *Colloq.* to fail; suffer defeat or disaster, often as a result of questionable practice or being too clever.

unstop (ŭn stŏp′), *v.t.*, **-stopped, -stopping. 1.** to remove the stopper from. **2.** to free from any obstruction; open. **3.** to draw out the stops of (an organ).

unstoppable (ŭn stŏp′ə bl), *adj.* **1.** that cannot be stopped, prevented, or halted; inexorable. **2.** that cannot be stopped up or obstructed. —**unstop′pably,** *adv.*

unstopped (ŭn stŏpt′), *adj.* **1.** *Pros.* denoting a line of verse the sense of which continues into the following line. **2.** not stopped up or prevented.

unstrained (ŭn strānd′), *adj.* **1.** not under strain or tension. **2.** not separated or cleared by straining.

unstrap (ŭn străp′), *v.t.*, **-strapped, -strapping.** to take off or slacken the strap of.

unstratified (ŭn străt′ĭ fīd′), *adj.* not stratified; not arranged in strata or layers: *unstratified rocks* (such as the igneous rocks granite, porphyry, etc.).

unstressed (ŭn strĕst′), *adj.* **1.** not under stress or strain. **2.** not stressed or accented.

unstring (ŭn strĭng′), *v.t.*, **-strung, -stringing. 1.** to deprive of a string or strings. **2.** to take from a string. **3.** to loosen the strings of. **4.** to relax the tension of. **5.** to relax unduly, or weaken (the nerves). **6.** to weaken the nerves of.

unstriped (ŭn strīpt′), *adj.* not striped; non-striated, as muscular tissue.

unstrung (ŭn strŭng′), *v.* **1.** pt. and pp. of **unstring.** —*adj.* **2.** having the string or strings loosened or removed, as a bow or harp. **3.** having the nerves weakened or in bad condition, as a person.

unstudied (ŭn stŭd′ĭd), *adj.* **1.** not premeditated or laboured; natural; unaffected. **2.** not having studied; unversed.

unsubstantial (ŭn′səb stăn′shəl), *adj.* **1.** not substantial; not solid, firm, or strong; flimsy; slight; unreal; insubstantial. **2.** not substantiated; having no foundation in fact. **3.** immaterial; having no substance. —**un′substan′tial′ity,** *n.* —**un′substan′tially,** *adv.*

unsuccess (ŭn′sək sĕs′), *n.* lack of success; failure.

unsuccessful (ŭn′sək sĕs′fəl), *adj.* not successful; without success; unfortunate. —**un′success′fully,** *adv.* —**un′success′fulness,** *n.*

unsuitable (ŭn syo͞o′tə bl), *adj.* not suitable; inappropriate; unfitting; unbecoming. —**un′suitabil′ity, unsuit′ableness,** *n.* —**unsuit′ably,** *adv.*

unsuited (ŭn syo͞o′tĭd), *adj.* **1.** not suited or fit; inappropriate: *unsuited to the purpose to which it is put.* **2.** badly matched; incompatible.

unsullied (ŭn sŭl′ĭd), *adj.* **1.** not tarnished or soiled. **2.** blameless.

unsung (ŭn sŭng′), *adj.* **1.** not sung; not uttered or rendered by singing. **2.** not celebrated in, or as if in, song.

unsure (ŭn sho͝oə′, -shô′), *adj.* **1.** not certain; not confident. **2.** not to be relied on: *an unsure method.* **3.** precarious; dependent on chance.

unsuspected (ŭn′sə spĕk′tĭd), *adj.* **1.** clear of or not under suspicion. **2.** not imagined to exist. —**un′suspect′edly,** *adv.* —**un′suspect′edness,** *n.*

unswathe (ŭn swāth′), *v.t.*, **-swathed, -swathing.** to free from that which swathes; take wrappings from.

unswayed (ŭn swād′), *adj.* not influenced or affected.

unswear (ŭn swĕə′), *v.t.*, **-swore, -sworn, -swearing.** to retract (something sworn, or sworn to); recant by a subsequent oath; abjure.

unswerving (ŭn swû′vĭng), *adj.* steady; constant; not turning aside: *unswerving loyalty.* —**unswerv′ingly,** *adv.*

unsympathetic (ŭn′sĭm pə thĕt′ĭk), *adj.* **1.** not offering sympathy; lacking understanding; hostile. **2.** not inspiring sympathy; unpleasing. —**un′sympathet′ically,** *adv.*

untack (ŭn tăk′), *v.t.* to remove the tacking from (a piece of sewing).

untangle (ŭn tăng′gl), *v.t.*, **-gled, -gling. 1.** to bring out of a tangled state; disentangle; unsnarl. **2.** to straighten out or clear up (anything confused or perplexing).

untapped (ŭn tăpt′), *adj.* **1.** not drawn on, as resources, potentialities, etc.: *an untapped fund of money, of enthusiasm.* **2.** not tapped.

untaught (ŭn tôt′), *v.* **1.** pt. and pp. of **unteach.** —*adj.*

---

unspe′cialized′, *adj.*
un′specif′ic, *adj.*
unspec′ified′, *adj.*
unspec′tacled, *adj.*
un′spectac′ular, *adj.*
unspec′ulative, *adj.*
unspel′lable, *adj.*
unspent′, *adj.*
unspir′itualize′, *v.t.*
unsplin′terable, *adj.*
unsport′ing, *adj.*
unsports′manlike′, *adj.*
unsprayed′, *adj.*
unspun′, *adj.*
unspurred′, *adj.*
unsquared′, *adj.*
unstack′, *v.t.*
unstain′able, *adj.*
unstained′, *adj.*
unstamped′, *adj.*
unstarched′, *adj.*
unstart′ed, *adj.*
unstart′led, *adj.*
unstart′ling, *adj.*
unstat′ed, *adj.*
unstates′manlike′, *adj.*
unstead′fast, *adj.*
unstead′fastly, *adv.*
unstead′fastness, *n.*
unsteered′, *adj.*
unstif′fen, *adj.*
unstif′fened, *adj.*
unsti′fled, *adj.*
unstilled′, *adj.*
unstim′ulat′ed, *adj.*
unstim′ulat′ing, *adj.*
unstint′ed, *adj.*
unstint′ing, *adj.*
unstint′ingly, *adv.*
unstir′ring, *adj.*
unstitch′, *v.t.*
unstocked′, *adj.*
unstock′inged, *adj.*
unstop′per, *v.t.*
unstop′pered, *adj.*
un′straightfor′ward, *adj.*
unstreaked′, *adj.*
unstrength′ened, *adj.*
unstrick′en, *adj.*
unstripped′, *adj.*
unstruck′, *adj.*
unstuck′, *adj.*
unsty′lish, *adj.*
un′subdu′able, *adj.*
un′subdued′, *adj.*
unsub′ject, *adj.*
un′subject′ed, *adj.*
un′submerged′, *adj.*
unsub′sidized′, *adj.*
un′substan′tiat′ed, *adj.*
unsub′tle, *adj.*
unsub′tlety, *n.*
unsug′ared, *adj.*
unsuit′, *v.t.*
unsum′moned, *adj.*
unsun′ny, *adj.*
un′supersti′tious, *adj.*
un′supplied′, *adj.*
un′support′ed, *adj.*
un′suppressed′, *adj.*
un′surmised′, *adj.*
un′surmount′able, *adj.*
un′surpas′sable, *adj.*
un′surpas′sably, *adv.*
un′surpassed′, *adj.*
un′surprised′, *adj.*
un′surveyed′, *adj.*
un′suspect′ing, *adj.*
un′suspect′ingly, *adv.*
un′suspi′cious, *adj.*
un′suspi′ciously, *adv.*
un′sustain′able, *adj.*
un′sustained′, *adj.*
un′sustain′ing, *adj.*
unswal′lowed, *adj.*
unsweet′, *adj.*
unswept′, *adj.*
unsworn′, *adj.*
un′symbol′ic, *adj.*
un′symmet′rical, *adj.*
un′symmet′rically, *adv.*
un′systemat′ic, *adj.*
un′systemat′ically, *adv.*
unsys′tematized′, *adj.*
untact′ful, *adj.*
untact′fully, *adv.*
untaint′ed, *adj.*
unta′ken, *adj.*
untame′able, *adj.*
untame′ably, *adv.*
untamed′, *adj.*
untanned′, *adj.*
untar′nished, *adj.*
untarred′, *adj.*
untast′ed, *adj.*
untaste′ful, *adj.*
untaste′fully, *adv.*

2. natural or inborn; not acquired by teaching. 3. not instructed or educated; ignorant; naive.

untaxed (ŭn tăkst′), *adj.* 1. not subjected to taxation. 2. not under a burden or strain.

unteach (ŭn tēch′), *v.t.*, **-taught, -teaching.** 1. to cause to be forgotten or disbelieved, as by contrary teaching. 2. to cause to forget or disbelieve something previously taught.

unteachable (ŭn tē′chə bl), *adj.* 1. (of a subject) unable to be taught or imparted. 2. (of a person) incapable of being instructed; having no capacity or will to learn. —**unteach′ably,** *adv.* —**un′teachabil′ity, unteach′ableness,** *n.*

untenable (ŭn tĕn′ə bl), *adj.* 1. incapable of being held against attack. 2. incapable of being maintained against argument, as an opinion, scheme, etc. 3. not fit to be occupied. —**un′tenabil′ity,** *adv.* —**unten′ably,** *n.*

Unter den Linden (ŏŏn′tə dĕn lĭn′dən), a street in East Berlin, formerly noted for its cafes, shops, etc. [G: under the lime trees]

Untermeyer (ŭn′tə mī′ə), *n.* **Louis,** born 1885, U.S. poet, critic, and anthologist.

Unterwalden (*Ger.* ŏŏn′tər väl dən), *n.* a canton in central Switzerland. 45,273 pop. (1960); 296 sq. mi.

unthankful (ŭn thăngk′fəl), *adj.* 1. not thankful; ungrateful. 2. not repaid with thanks; thankless. —**unthank′fully,** *adv.* —**unthank′fulness,** *n.*

unthatch (ŭn thăch′), *v.t.* to throw off the thatch from.

unthink (ŭn thĭngk′), *v.t.*, **-thought, -thinking.** 1. to dispel from the mind or thoughts. 2. to reverse or retract by thinking, as in changing one's mind.

unthinkable (ŭn thĭng′kə bl), *adj.* 1. inconceivable; unimaginable. 2. not to be considered; utterly out of the question. —**unthink′ably,** *adv.*

unthinking (ŭn thĭng′kĭng), *adj.* 1. not thinking; thoughtless; heedless. 2. indicating lack of thought or reflection. 3. not given to reflection; uncritical. 4. not possessing the faculty of thought. —**unthink′ingly,** *adv.* —**unthink′ingness,** *n.*

unthread (ŭn thrĕd′), *v.t.* 1. to draw out or take out the thread from. 2. to thread one's way out of. 3. to disentangle; restore from a confused condition.

untidy (ŭn tī′dĭ), *adj.*, *v.t.*, **-tidied, -tidying.** —*adj.* 1. not tidy or neat; slovenly; disordered. —*v.t.* 2. to make untidy; disorder. —**unti′dily,** *adv.* —**unti′diness,** *n.*

untie (ŭn tī′), *v.*, **-tied, -tying.** —*v.t.* 1. to loosen or unfasten (anything tied); let or set loose by undoing a knot. 2. to undo the string or cords of. 3. to undo, as a cord or a knot; unknot. 4. to free from or as from bonds or restraint. 5. to resolve, as perplexities. —*v.i.* 6. to become untied.

until (ən tĭl′), *conj.* 1. up to the time that or when; till. 2. (with negatives) before: *he did not come until the meeting was half over.* —*prep.* 3. onward to, or till (a specified time); up to the time of (some occurrence). 4. (with negatives) before: *he did not go until night.* 5. *Scot. and N Dial.* to; unto. [ME *untill*, f. *un-* (t. Scand.; cf. Icel. *unz* up to, as far as) + TILL]

untimely (ŭn tīm′lĭ), *adj.* Also, *Scot.*, **untimeous** (ŭn tī′məs). 1. not timely; not occurring at a suitable time or season; ill-timed or inopportune. 2. premature; not fully mature or ripe. —*adv.* 3. unseasonably. —**untime′liness,** *n.*

untinged (ŭn tĭnjd′), *adj.* 1. not modified or affected: *untinged by sentiment.* 2. not coloured, as by paint, light, etc.

untitled (ŭn tī′tld), *adj.* 1. not titled; without a title, as of nobility. 2. *Archaic.* having no right or claim.

unto (ŭn′tōō *finally,* ŭn′tŏŏ *before vowels,* ŭn′tə *before consonants*), *prep. Archaic.* 1. to (in its various uses, except as the accompaniment of the infinitive). 2. until; till. [ME; f. *un-* (see UNTIL) + TO]

untold (ŭn tōld′), *adj.* 1. not told; not related; not revealed. 2. more than can be numbered or enumerated; uncounted. 3. too much to be measured; incalculable.

untouchability (ŭn′tŭch ə bĭl′ĭ tĭ), *n.* the defiling character ascribed to low-caste Indians or non-Hindus by high-caste Hindus or Brahmans.

untouchable (ŭn tŭch′ə bl), *adj.*, *n.* 1. that may not be touched; of a nature such that it cannot be touched; not palpable; intangible. 2. too distant to be touched. 3. vile or loathsome to the touch. 4. unable to be equalled. —*n.* 5. a member of the lower classes in India, whose touch is believed to defile a high-caste Hindu.

untouched (ŭn tŭcht′), *adj.* 1. not touched or handled. 2. not harmed or damaged in the least. 3. not used at all, esp. entirely uneaten or undrunk. 4. not affected, modified or influenced; innocent. 5. not discussed or mentioned (sometimes fol. by *upon* or *on*). 6. not moved or affected in mind; undisturbed; calm.

untoward (ŭn′tə wôd′, ŭn tō′əd), *adj.* 1. unfavourable or unfortunate. 2. unseemly. 3. *Archaic.* unruly, stubborn, or perverse. [f. UN-[1] + TOWARD] —**un′toward′ly,** *adv.* —**un′toward′ness,** *n.*

untrammelled (ŭn trăm′əld), *adj.* unrestricted; unhampered. Also, *U.S.*, **untrammeled.**

untravelled (ŭn trăv′əld), *adj.* 1. not having travelled, esp. to distant places; not having gained experience by travel. 2. not travelled through or over; not frequented by travellers. Also, *U.S.*, **untraveled.**

untread (ŭn trĕd′), *v.t.*, **-trod, -trodden** or **-trod, -treading.** to go back through in the same steps; retrace.

untried (ŭn trīd′), *adj.* 1. not tried; not tested or put to the proof; not attempted. 2. not yet tried at law.

untrue (ŭn trōō′), *adj.* 1. not true, as to a person or a cause, to fact, or to a standard. 2. unfaithful; false. 3. incorrect or inaccurate. —**untrue′ness,** *n.* —**untru′ly,** *adv.*

untruss (ŭn trŭs′), *v.t. Obs.* to loose from or as from a fastening; unfasten or untie; undress.

untruth (ŭn trōōth′, ŭn′trōōth′), *n.* 1. the state or character of being untrue. 2. want of veracity; divergence from truth. 3. something untrue; a falsehood or lie. 4. *Obs.* unfaithfulness or disloyalty. —**Syn.** 3. See **falsehood.**

untruthful (ŭn trōōth′fəl), *adj.* not truthful; wanting in veracity; diverging from or contrary to the truth; not corresponding with fact or reality. —**untruth′fully,** *adv.* —**untruth′fulness,** *n.*

untuck (ŭn tŭk′), *v.t.* to release from or bring out of a tucked condition.

unturned (ŭn tûnd′), *adj.* 1. not having been turned or turned over. 2. **leave no stone unturned,** to make an exhaustive search.

untutored (ŭn tyōō′təd), *adj.* not tutored; untaught; uninstructed.

untwine (ŭn twīn′), *v.t.*, *v.i.*, **-twined, -twining.** to bring or come out of a twined condition.

untwist (ŭn twĭst′), *v.t.*, *v.i.* to bring or come out of a twisted condition.

U Nu. See **Nu, U.**

unused (ŭn yōōzd′ *for 1 and 2*; ŭn yōōst′ *for 3*), *adj.* 1. not used; not put to use. 2. never having been used. 3. not accustomed.

unusual (ŭn yōō′zhŏŏ əl), *adj.* not usual, common, or ordinary; uncommon in amount or degree; of an exceptional kind. —**unu′sually,** *adv.* —**unu′sualness,** *n.*

unutterable (ŭn ŭt′ə rə bl, -ŭt′rə bl), *adj.* 1. not communicable by utterance; incapable of being expressed. 2. inexpressibly great or remarkable; unspeakable. 3. incapable of being uttered; unpronounceable. —**unut′terably,** *adv.*

unvalued (ŭn văl′yōōd), *adj.* 1. not regarded as of value. 2. not assessed in a formal valuation. 3. *Obs.* invaluable. 4. *Obs.* valueless.

unvarnished (ŭn vä′nĭsht), *adj.* 1. (of statements, etc.)

---

untax′able, *adj.*
untear′able, *adj.*
untech′nical, *adj.*
untel′lable, *adj.*
untem′pered, *adj.*
untempt′ed, *adj.*
untempt′ing, *adj.*
unten′antable, *adj.*
unten′anted, *adj.*
untend′ed, *adj.*
unten′der, *adj.*
unter′minat′ed, *adj.*
unter′rified′, *adj.*
untest′ed, *adj.*
unteth′er, *v.t.*
unteth′ered, *adj.*
unthanked′, *adj.*
unthatched′, *adj.*
un′theolog′ical, *adj.*
unthick′ened, *adj.*
unthought′-of′, *adj.*
un′thought-out′, *adj.*
unthreat′ened, *adj.*
unthrif′ty, *adj.*
untiled′, *adj.*
until′lable, *adj.*
untilled′, *adj.*
untinc′tured, *adj.*
untinned′, *adj.*
untint′ed, *adj.*
untipped′, *adj.*
untir′able, *adj.*
untir′ing, *adj.*
untir′ingly, *adv.*
untoned′, *adj.*
un′torment′ed, *adj.*
untorn′, *adj.*
untrace′able, *adj.*
untrace′ably, *adv.*
untraced′, *adj.*
untrain′able, *adj.*
untrained′, *adj.*
un′transformed′, *adj.*
un′translat′abil′ity, *n.*
un′translat′able, *adj.*
un′translat′ably, *adv.*
untreat′able, *adj.*
untreat′ed, *adj.*
untrimmed′, *adj.*
untrod′den, *adj.*
untroub′led, *adj.*
untroub′lesome, *adj.*
untrust′ing, *adj.*
untrust′wor′thiness, *n.*
untune′ful, *adj.*
untune′fully, *adv.*
untune′fulness, *n.*
unty′ing, *adj.*
untyp′ical, *adj.*
unu′niformed′, *adj.*
unus′able, *adj.*
unut′tered, *adj.*
unvan′quishable, *adj.*
unvan′quished, *adj.*
unvar′ied, *adj.*
unvar′iegat′ed, *adj.*
unvar′ying, *adj.*
unvar′yingly, *adv.*

not embellished; plain. 2. not covered with varnish.
unveil (ŭn vāl′), *v.t.* 1. to remove a veil from; disclose to view. 2. to disclose, as if by removing a veil; reveal. —*v.i.* 3. to remove a veil; reveal oneself; become unveiled.
unveiling (ŭn vā′lĭng), *n.* 1. the act of showing a monument or the like for the first time, as in a ceremonial removal of a covering. 2. the presentation of something for the first time.
unvoice (ŭn vois′), *v.t.*, **-voiced, -voicing.** *Phonet.* to pronounce a voiced sound in such a way that vocal cord vibrations are heard during part of its duration only: before a pause, the end of a voiced fricative is *unvoiced* in English, as in *if you please*, when the final *z* sound ends like *s*.
unvoiced (ŭn voist′), *adj.* 1. not uttered, spoken, or sounded. 2. See **voiceless.**
unwarrantable (ŭn wŏ′rən tə bl), *adj.* 1. unable to be justified, confirmed, or proved, as an assertion or argument. 2. unable to be justified, or vindicated, as an action. —**unwar′rantableness,** *n.* —**unwar′rantably,** *adv.*
unwarranted (ŭn wŏ′rən tĭd), *adj.* 1. not justified, confirmed, or supported: *an unwarranted supposition.* 2. not authorized, as actions. —**unwar′rantedly,** *adv.*
unwary (ŭn wĕə′rĭ), *adj.* not wary; not cautious; unguarded. —**unwar′ily,** *adv.* —**unwar′iness,** *n.*
unwashed (ŭn wŏsht′), *adj.* 1. (of things) not cleaned by washing. 2. (of people) not clean; not habitually or usually kept clean by washing. —*n.* 3. **the great unwashed,** *Colloq.* (contemptuous) the masses; the rabble.
unwatched (ŭn wŏcht′), *adj.*—*Naut.* denoting or pertaining to a construction, as a beacon, which is worked automatically and not normally manned.
unwearied (ŭn wĭə′rĭd), *adj.* 1. not wearied; not fatigued. 2. indefatigable. 3. (of qualities, actions, etc.) unremitting. —**unwea′riedly,** *adv.* —**unwea′riedness,** *n.*
unweave (ŭn wēv′), *v.t.*, **-wove, -woven, -weaving.** *Archaic and Poetic.* to undo, take apart, or separate (something woven); ravel.
unweighed (ŭn wād′), *adj.* 1. not weighed; not tested as to weight. 2. not pondered upon or considered.
unwelcome (ŭn wĕl′kəm), *adj.* 1. not welcome, as a person. 2. not acceptable; unpleasing. —**unwel′comely,** *adv.* —**unwel′comeness,** *n.*
unwell (ŭn wĕl′), *adj.* not well; ailing; somewhat ill.
unwept (ŭn wĕpt′), *adj.* 1. not wept, or wept for; unmourned. 2. *Rare.* not wept or shed, as tears.
unwholesome (ŭn hōl′səm), *adj.* 1. not wholesome; unhealthful; deleterious to health or well-being, physically or morally. 2. not sound in health; unhealthy, esp. in appearance; suggestive of disease. —**unwhole′somely,** *adv.* —**unwhole′someness,** *n.*
unwieldy (ŭn wēl′dĭ), *adj.* 1. not wieldy; wielded with difficulty; not readily handled or managed in use or action, as from size, shape, or weight. 2. ungainly; awkward. —**unwield′ily,** *adv.* —**unwield′iness,** *n.*
unwill (ŭn wĭl′), *v.t.* 1. to will or determine upon (the reversal of something). 2. to deprive of will. 3. to revoke or reverse (one's will or purpose).
unwilled (ŭn wĭld′), *adj.* not willed; involuntary.
unwilling (ŭn wĭl′ĭng), *adj.* 1. not willing; loath; reluctant. 2. performed or given reluctantly: *the unwilling admiration of the scornful.* —**unwill′ingly,** *adv.* —**unwill′ingness,** *n.*
unwind (ŭn wīnd′), *v.*, **-wound, -winding.** —*v.t.* 1. to undo (something wound); loose or separate, as what is wound. 2. to remove the windings from around (something). 3. to disentangle. —*v.i.* 4. to become unwound. 5. to relax or calm down.
unwinking (ŭn wĭng′kĭng), *adj.* not winking; having a fixed stare; watchful; unsleeping. —**unwink′ingly,** *adv.*
unwisdom (ŭn wĭz′dəm), *n.* 1. lack of wisdom. 2. unwise action; folly.
unwise (ŭn wīz′), *adj.* not wise; foolish; imprudent; injudicious. —**unwise′ly,** *adv.* —**unwise′ness,** *n.*
unwish (ŭn wĭsh′), *v.t.* 1. to retract (a wish). 2. to wish for (something) not to be; desire the cessation of.
unwished (ŭn wĭsht′), *adj.* not wished; undesired; unwelcome.
unwitnessed (ŭn wĭt′nĭst), *adj.* 1. unseen; unobserved. 2. not attested by a witness, as a signature on a document.
unwitting (ŭn wĭt′ĭng), *adj.* 1. not witting or knowing; ignorant; unaware; unconscious. 2. performed unintentionally or unknowingly; unpremeditated. —**unwit′tingly,** *adv.* —**unwit′tingness,** *n.*
unwonted (ŭn wōn′tĭd), *adj.* *Archaic.* 1. not customary, habitual, or usual. 2. unused or unaccustomed (to something). —**unwont′edly,** *adv.* —**unwont′edness,** *n.*
unworkable (ŭn wû′kə bl), *adj.* 1. incapable of being put into operation, as a system, or into practice, as a theory. 2. unable to be worked on, or worked. —**un′workabil′ity,** *n.*
unworldly (ŭn wûld′lĭ), *adj.* 1. not worldly; not seeking material advantage or gain; spiritually minded. 2. naive; unsophisticated. 3. not terrestrial; unearthly. —**unworld′liness,** *n.*
unworn (ŭn wôn′), *adj.* 1. not damaged or deteriorating, etc., as from use. 2. (of clothing) never worn; not hitherto worn.
unworthy (ŭn wû′thĭ), *adj.* 1. not worthy; lacking worth or excellence. 2. not commendable or creditable. 3. not of adequate merit or character. 4. of a kind not worthy (with *of*, expressed or understood). 5. beneath the dignity (*of*). 6. undeserving. 7. not deserved or justified. —**unwor′thily,** *adv.* —**unwor′thiness,** *n.*
unwound (ŭn wound′), *v.* 1. pt. and pp. of **unwind.** —*adj.* 2. not wound, or wound up.
unwrap (ŭn răp′), *v.*, **-wrapped, -wrapping.** —*v.t.* 1. to bring out of a wrapped condition; unfold or open, as something wrapped. —*v.i.* 2. to become unwrapped.
unwrinkle (ŭn rĭng′kl), *v.t.*, **-kled, -kling.** to smooth the wrinkles from.
unwritten (ŭn rĭt′n), *adj.* 1. not written; not reduced to or recorded in writing. 2. not actually formulated or expressed; customary. 3. containing no writing; blank. [ME and OE *unwriten*; f. UN-[1] + *writen*, pp. of WRITE]
unwritten law, 1. law which rests for its authority on custom, judicial decision, etc., as distinguished from law originating in written command, statute, or decree. 2. the supposed principle of the right of the individual to avenge wrongs against personal or family honour, esp. in cases involving relations between the sexes (sometimes urged in justification of persons guilty of criminal acts of vengeance).
unyoke (ŭn yōk′), *v.*, **-yoked, -yoking.** —*v.t.* 1. to free from or as from a yoke. 2. to part or disjoin, as by removing a yoke. —*v.i.* 3. to remove a yoke. 4. to cease work.
unzip (ŭn zĭp′), *v.t.*, *v.i.*, **-zipped, -zipping.** —*v.t.* 1. to open the zip of (a garment). —*v.i.* 2. to become unzipped.
up (ŭp), *adv.*, *prep.*, *adj.*, *n.*, *v.*, **upped, upping,** *interj.* —*adv.* 1. to, towards, or in a more elevated position: *to climb up to the top of a ladder.* 2. into the air: *to throw up a ball.* 3. out of the ground: *to dig up potatoes.* 4. to or in an erect position: *to stand up.* 5. out of bed: *to get up.* 6. above the horizon: *the moon came up.* 7. to or at any point that is considered higher, as the north, a capital city, or the like. 8. to or at a source, origin, centre, or the like: *to follow a stream up to its source.* 9. to or at a higher point or degree in a scale, as of rank, size, value, pitch, etc. 10. to or at a point of equal advance, extent, etc.: *to catch up in a race.* 11. ahead; into a leading or more advanced position: *to move up into the lead.* 12. well advanced or versed, as in a subject: *to keep up in nuclear physics.* 13. in or into activity, operation, etc.: *to set up vibrations.* 14. in or into a state of agitation or excitement: *worked up.* 15. into existence, view, prominence, or consideration: *a problem has cropped up, the lost papers have turned up, his case comes up in court on Thursday.* 16. to a state of maturity: *to bring up a child.* 17. into or in a place of safekeeping, storage, retirement, etc.: *to lay up riches.* 18. to a state of completion; to an end:

unven′tilat′ed, *adj.*
un′vera′cious, *adj.*
unver′ifi′able, *adj.*
unver′ified′, *adj.*
unversed′, *adj.*
unvi′olat′ed, *adj.*
unvir′tuous, *adj.*
unvir′tuously, *adv.*
unvis′ited, *adj.*
unvit′iat′ed, *adj.*
unvit′rifi′able, *adj.*
unvo′cal, *adj.*
unvul′canized′, *adj.*
unwan′dering, *adj.*
unwant′ed, *adj.*
unwar′like′, *adj.*
unwarmed′, *adj.*
unwarped′, *adj.*
unwatch′ful, *adj.*
unwatch′fully, *adv.*
unwatch′fulness, *n.*
unwa′tered, *adj.*
unwa′vering, *adj.*
unwa′veringly, *adv.*
unweaned′, *adj.*
unwear′able, *adj.*
unwear′ying, *adj.*
unwear′yingly, *adv.*
unweath′ered, *adj.*
unwebbed′, *adj.*
unwed′, *adj.*
unwed′ded, *adj.*
unweed′ed, *adj.*
unweight′ed, *adj.*
unwel′comed, *adj.*
unwel′coming, *adj.*
unwigged′, *adj.*
unwind′ing, *adj.*, *n.*
unwiped′, *adj.*
unwire′, *v.t.*
un′withdrawn′, *adj.*
unwith′erable, *adj.*
unwith′ered, *adj.*
unwith′ering, *adj.*
unwom′anliness, *n.*
unwom′anly, *adj.*, *adv.*
unwood′ed, *adj.*
unwork′manlike′, *adj.*
unwor′ried, *adj.*
unwound′able, *adj.*
unwound′ed, *adj.*
unwo′ven, *adj.*
unwrin′kled, *adj.*
unwrought′, *adj.*
unwrung′, *adj.*
unyield′ing, *adj.*
unyield′ingly, *adv.*
unyield′ingness, *n.*
unyoked′, *adj.*
unzoned′, *adj.*

to finish something up. **19.** in or into a state of union, contraction, etc.: *to add up a column of figures, to fold up a blanket.* **20.** to the required or final point: *to pay up one's debts, to burn up rubbish.* **21.** to a standstill: *to rein up, seize up.* **22.** *U.S.* equally; each; apiece; all: *the score was seven points up.* **23.** *Naut.* towards or facing into the wind. **24. up with,** towards a higher or more favourable position. —*prep.* **25.** to, towards, or at a higher place on or in: *up the stairs, up a tree.* **26.** to, towards, near, or at a higher station, condition, or rank in. **27.** to, towards, or at a farther or higher point of: *up the street.* **28.** towards the source, origin, etc., of: *up the stream.* **29.** towards or in the interior of (a region, etc.): *the explorers went up-country.* **30.** in a course or direction contrary to that of: *to sail up wind.* **31.** *Dial. or Colloq.* towards or at: *up London, up the Junction.*

—*adj.* **32.** upwards; going or directed upwards. **33.** travelling towards a terminus or centre: *an up train.* **34.** in an upright position or pointing upwards: *the signal is up.* **35.** standing and speaking: *the prime minister was up for three hours.* **36.** out of bed: *I have been up since six o'clock.* **37.** risen above the horizon: *the sun is up.* **38.** at a high point or full: *the tide is up.* **39.** in the air; above the ground: *the aeroplane is six thousand feet up.* **40.** on horseback; in the saddle. **41.** well informed or advanced, as in a subject: *to be up in mathematics.* **42.** in activity or operation: *the wind is up, the lights are up.* **43.** under consideration; on offer: *a candidate up for election.* **44.** appearing before a court or the like on some charge: *he is up for speeding again.* **45.** in the process of going on or happening, esp. something amiss: *they wondered what was up.* **46.** in a state of agitation or excitement: *his anger was up.* **47.** impassable to wheeled traffic, as a road under repair. **48.** in a leading or advanced position: *to be up in social standing.* **49.** winning or having won money at gambling or the like: *he was £30 up after an hour in the casino.* **50.** *Games.* winning or ahead of an opponent by a specified number of points, holes, etc. **51. all up,** at an end; at the point of defeat or failure. **52. up against,** *Colloq.* faced with: *they are up against enormous problems.* **53. up against it,** *Colloq.* in difficulties; in severe straits. **54. up and about,** active; out of bed, esp. after recovering from an illness. **55. up to, a.** engaged in; doing: *what are you up to?* **b.** incumbent upon, as a duty: *it is up to him to make the next move.* **c.** as many as and no more: *I will take up to eight pupils.* **d.** as far as and no farther: *he is up to his knees in water.* **e.** *Colloq.* capable of: *he is not up to the job.*

—*n.* **56.** an upward movement; an ascent. **57.** a rise of fortune, mood, etc.: *to have one's ups and downs.* **58. on the up and up,** *Colloq.* **a.** honest, frank, or credible. **b.** tending upwards; improving; having increasing success.

—*v.t. Colloq.* **59.** to put or take up. **60.** to make larger; step up: *to up output.* **61.** to raise; go better than (a preceding wager). **62.** *Naut.* to turn (the helm) to windward, thus turning the ship's head away from the wind.

—*v.i.* **63.** *Colloq.* to get or start up (usually fol. by *and*). **64. up to windward,** *Naut.* to bring a ship into the wind.

—*interj.* **65.** (a command to rise or stand up.)

[ME and OE, c. LG *up*, and akin to G *auf*]

up-, a prefixal, attributive use of **up,** in its various meanings, as in *upland, upshot, upheaval.* [ME and OE]

U.P., **1.** United Press. **2.** United Provinces.

up-and-coming (ŭp′ən kŭm′ing), *adj.* becoming successful, well-known, fashionable, etc.; promising. Also (esp. in predicative use), **up and coming.**

up-and-down (ŭp′ən doun′), *adj.* taking place, performed, or formed alternately or both upwards and downwards. Also (esp. in predicative use), **up and down.**

Upanishad (o͞o pŭn′ĭ shəd), *n.* the chief theological documents of ancient Hinduism, expounding more elaborately the mystical knowledge contained in the earlier Vedas, esp. the pantheistic doctrine that, in all things, but pre-eminently in each human soul, there may be seen manifested the supreme, impersonal Brahma or Atman, the World Soul. —**Upanishadic** (o͞o pŭn′ĭ-shŭd′ĭk), *adj.*

upas (yo͞o′pəs), *n.* **1.** the poisonous milky sap of *Antiaria toxicaria,* a large moraceous tree of Java, used for arrow poison. **2.** Also, **upas tree.** the tree. **3.** a destructive or deadly power or influence. [t. Malay: poison]

upbear (ŭp′bēə′), *v.t.*, **-bore, -borne, -bearing.** *Rare.* to bear up; raise aloft; support; sustain. —**up′bear′er,** *n.*

up-beat (ŭp′bēt′), *n.* **1.** *Music.* **a.** the last beat of a bar, esp. when the piece of music or section or phrase starts with a note on that beat. **b.** the introductory beat of a conductor when bringing in the orchestra. —*adj.* **2.** *Colloq.* optimistic; cheerful.

up-bow (ŭp′bō′), *n.* (in bowing on a stringed instrument) a stroke towards the nut of the bow: indicated in scores by the symbol V (opposed to *down-bow*).

upbraid (ŭp brād′), *v.t.* **1.** to reproach for some fault or offence; reprove severely; chide. **2.** to censure or find fault with (things). —*v.i.* **3.** to utter reproaches. [ME; OE *upbregdan.* See UP-, BRAID, V.] —**upbraid′er,** *n.*

upbraiding (ŭp brā′dĭng), *n.* **1.** the act or language of one who upbraids. —*adj.* **2.** reproachful; chiding. —**upbraid′ingly,** *adv.*

upbringing (ŭp′brĭng′ĭng), *n.* the bringing up or rearing of a person from childhood; care and training devoted to the young while growing up.

upbuild (ŭp bĭld′), *v.t.*, **-built, -building.** **1.** to build up; establish. **2.** to develop or improve. —**upbuild′er,** *n.*

upburst (ŭp′bûst′), *n.* a burst upwards.

upcast (ŭp′käst′), *n.* **1.** the act or an act of casting upwards. **2.** the state of being cast upwards. **3.** something that is cast up. **4.** a shaft or passage up which air passes, as from a mine (opposed to *downcast*); uptake. —*adj.* **5.** *Geol., Mining.* the upthrow of a fault. **6.** cast up; directed upwards.

up-country (ŭp′kŭn′trĭ), *adj.* **1.** being or living remote from the coast or border; interior: *an up-country village.* **2.** (used derogatorily) unsophisticated. —*n.* **3.** the interior of the country. —*adv.* **4.** towards or in the interior of a country.

update (ŭp′dāt′), *v.t.*, **-dated, -dating.** to bring up to date.

Updike (ŭp′dīk′), *n.* **John,** born 1932, U.S. author.

up-end (ŭp′ĕnd′), *v.t.* **1.** to set on end, as a barrel. **2.** to upset or alter drastically. —*v.i.* **3.** to stand on end.

upgrade (*n.* ŭp′grād′; *v., adj., adv.* ŭp′grād′), *v.*, **-graded, -grading,** *n., adj., adv.* —*v.t.* **1.** to assign (a person, job, or the like) to a higher status, usually with a larger salary. —*n. U.S.* **2.** an uphill slope. **3. on the upgrade,** improving; up-and-coming. —*adj., adv. U.S.* **4.** uphill.

upgrowth (ŭp′grōth′), *n.* **1.** the process or fact of growing up; development. **2.** something that grows up.

upheaval (ŭp hē′vəl), *n.* **1.** the act of upheaving. **2.** the state of being upheaved. **3.** a thorough, violent, or revolutionary change or disturbance, esp. in a society. **4.** *Geol.* an upward warping of a part of the earth's crust, forcing certain areas into a relatively higher position than before.

upheave (ŭp hēv′), *v.*, **-heaved** or **-hove, -heaving.** —*v.t.* **1.** to heave or lift up; raise up or aloft. **2.** to disturb or change violently or radically. —*v.i.* **3.** to be lifted up; rise as if thrust up.

upheld (ŭp hĕld′), *v.* pt. and pp. of **uphold.**

uphill (ŭp′hĭl′), *adv.* **1.** up, or as if up, the slope of a hill; upwards. —*adj.* **2.** going or tending upwards on or as on a hill. **3.** at a high place or point. **4.** laboriously fatiguing or difficult. —*n.* **5.** an ascent or rise.

uphold (ŭp hōld′), *v.t.*, **-held, -holding.** **1.** to support, sustain, or preserve unimpaired: *to uphold the old order.* **2.** to keep up, or keep from sinking; support. **3.** to support or maintain, as by advocacy or agreement: *to uphold the decision of a lower court.* —**uphold′er,** *n.* —**Syn. 3.** See **support.**

upholster (ŭp hōl′stə), *v.t.* **1.** to provide (stools, armchairs, sofas, etc.) with coverings, cushions, stuffing, springs, etc. **2.** to cover or cushion in the manner of upholstery. —*v.i.* **3.** to do upholstery work. [back-formation from UPHOLSTERER]

upholsterer (ŭp hōl′stə rə, -strə), *n.* one whose business it is to make, finish, or repair the coverings and stuffing of chairs, couches, cushions, etc. [f. earlier *upholster* (f. UPHOLD, V. + -STER) + -ER [1]]

upholstery (ŭp hōl′stə rĭ, -strĭ), *n., pl.* **-ries.** **1.** the cushions, furniture coverings and other material used to stuff and cover furniture and cushions. **2.** the interior padding and lining for the seats, etc., of a car. **3.** the business of an upholsterer.

uphroe (yo͞o′frō), *n. Naut.* euphroe.

U.P.I., United Press International.

upkeep (ŭp′kēp′), *n.* **1.** the process of keeping up or maintaining; the maintenance, or keeping in operation, due condition, and repair, of an establishment, a machine, etc. **2.** the cost of this, including operating expenses, cost of renewal or repair, etc.

upland (ŭp′lənd), *n.* **1.** an area of high ground; a stretch of hilly or mountainous country. **2.** the higher ground of a region or district; an elevated region. —*adj.* **3.** of or pertaining to uplands or elevated regions.

uplift (*v.* ŭp′lĭft′; *n.* ŭp′lĭft′), *v.t.* **1.** to lift up; raise; elevate. **2.** to raise socially or morally. **3.** to exalt emotionally or spiritually. —*n.* **4.** the act of lifting up or raising; elevation. **5.** the process or work of improving socially or morally. **6.** emotional or spiritual exaltation. **7.** *Geol.* an upheaval. —**up′lift′er,** *n.* —**up′lift′ment,** *n.*

uplifted (ŭp′lĭf′tĭd), *adj.* **1.** raised up; exalted. **2.** intellectually or spiritually elevated.

upmost (ŭp′mōst′), *adj.* uppermost.

Upolu (o͞o pō′lo͞o), *n.* an island in Western Samoa, in the

S Pacific: the home of Robert Louis Stevenson for the last five years of his life. 82,479 pop. (1961); 430 sq. mi.

upon (ə pŏn′), *prep.* **1.** up and on; upwards so as to get or be on: *to climb upon a table.* **2.** in an elevated position on. **3.** on, in any of various senses (used as an equivalent of *on* with no added idea of ascent or elevation, and preferred in certain cases only for euphonic or metrical reasons). [ME. See UP, adv., ON, prep.]

upper (ŭp′ə), *adj.* **1.** higher (than something implied) or highest, as in place, or position, or in a scale: *the upper slopes of a mountain, upper register of a voice.* **2.** occupying or consisting of high or rising ground, or farther into the interior. **3.** forming the higher of a pair of corresponding things or sets. **4.** (of a surface) facing upwards. **5.** superior, as in rank, dignity, or station. **6.** higher or highest in respect of wealth, rank, office, birth, influence, etc.: *the upper classes or orders.* **7.** (*cap.*) *Geol.* denoting a later division of a period, system, or the like: *the Upper Devonian.* —*n.* **8.** anything which is higher (than another, as of a pair) or highest. **9.** the part of a shoe or boot above the sole, comprising the vamp and quarters. **10. be on one's uppers,** *Colloq.* to be reduced to poverty or want.

upper atmosphere, that part of the earth's atmosphere which can be reached by rocket or satellite, but not by balloon; the atmosphere from about 30 kilometres upwards.

Upper Austria, a province in N Austria. 1,131,623 pop. (est. 1961); 4631 sq. mi. *Cap.:* Linz. German, **Oberösterreich.**

Upper Canada, a former British province (1791–1840) in Canada: now forms the S part of Ontario province.

upper case, *Print.* the upper half of a pair of cases, which contains the capital letters of the alphabet.

upper-case (ŭp′ə kās′), *adj., v.,* **-cased, -casing.** —*adj.* **1.** (of a letter) capital (as opposed to *small*). **2.** *Print.* pertaining to or belonging in the upper case. See **case**[2] (def. 8). —*v.t.* **3.** to print or write with an upper-case letter or letters.

upper circle, one of the sections of seats in the auditorium of a theatre, concert hall, or the like, between the dress circle and the gallery.

upper class, *pl.* **classes.** the class of people socially and conventionally regarded as being higher or highest in the social hierarchy and commonly identified by wealth or aristocratic birth.

upper-class (ŭp′ə kläs′), *adj.* belonging, pertaining to, or typical of the upper class.

upperclassman (ŭp′ə kläs′mən), *n., pl.* **-men.** *U.S.* a member of either the junior or senior class in a high school or college.

upper crust, *Colloq.* the aristocracy; the higher orders of society.

uppercut (ŭp′ə kŭt′), *n., v.,* **-cut, -cutting.** —*n.* **1.** a swinging blow directed upwards, as to an adversary's chin. —*v.t., v.i.* **2.** to strike with an uppercut.

upper deck, the highest continuous deck above the main deck.

Upper Egypt. See **Egypt.**

upper hand, the dominating or controlling position; the advantage.

Upper House, (*often l.c.*) **1.** one of two branches of a legislature, generally smaller and less representative than the lower branch. **2.** (in Great Britain) the House of Lords.

Upper Karoo, *Geol.* **1.** pertaining to the lower Mesozoic period or system in southern Africa roughly equivalent to the Triassic and Lower Jurassic. **2.** a period or system following the Lower Karoo and preceding the Cretaceous in southern Africa. Also, **Upper Karroo.**

uppermost (ŭp′ə mōst′), *adj.* **1.** highest in place, order; rank, power, etc. **2.** topmost; predominant; foremost. —*adv.* **3.** in the highest or topmost place. **4.** in the foremost place in respect of rank or precedence.

Upper Silesia, a highly industrialized region divided between Germany and Poland after World War I, and included in Poland since World War II.

Upper Tunguska (*Russ.* to͞on go͞os′kə). See **Angara.**

Upper Volta, a republic in W Africa, formerly part of French West Africa. 4,716,000 pop. (est. 1964); 106,011 sq. mi. *Cap.:* Ougadougou. Also, **Voltaic Republic.** See map under **Timbuktu.**

upper works, *Naut.* the structures on the main or freeboard deck, or in any deck above.

uppish (ŭp′ĭsh), *adj. Colloq.* affecting superiority; presumptuous; self-assertive. Also, **uppity** (ŭp′ĭ tĭ). [f. UP, adv. + -ISH[1]] —**up′pishly,** *adv.* —**up′pishness,** *n.*

Uppsala (ŭp′sä′lə; *Swed.* o͝op′sä lä), *n.* a town in SE Sweden. 84,272 (1964). Also, **Upsala.**

upraise (ŭp′rāz′), *v.t.,* **-raised, -raising.** to raise or elevate; direct upwards; exalt.

uprear (ŭp′rĭə′), *v.t.* to rear up; raise.

upright (ŭp′rīt′), *adj.* **1.** erect or vertical, as in position or posture. **2.** raised or directed vertically or upward; not inclined or leaning over. **3.** adhering to rectitude; righteous, honest, or just. **4.** in accord with moral rectitude. —*n.* **5.** the state of being upright or vertical. **6.** something standing erect or vertical, as a piece of timber. **7.** an upright piano. **8.** one of the vertical members of a framework, as a goalpost. —*adv.* **9.** in an upright position or direction; vertically. [ME; OE *uppriht*, c. G *aufrecht*] —**up′right′ly,** *adv.* —**up′right′ness,** *n.*

—**Syn. 1.** plumb. UPRIGHT, ERECT, VERTICAL, PERPENDICULAR imply that something is in the posture of being straight upwards, not leaning. That which is UPRIGHT is in a position corresponding to that of a man standing up: *a tree which has fallen is no longer upright, an upright piano.* ERECT emphasizes the straightness of position or posture: *proud and erect, a flagpole stands erect.* VERTICAL esp. suggests upward direction along the shortest line from the earth to a level above it: *the vertical edge of a door, ornamented by vertical lines.* PERPENDICULAR, a term frequently interchangeable with VERTICAL, is esp. used in mathematics: *the perpendicular side of a right triangle, to erect a perpendicular line from the base of a figure.* —**Ant. 1.** leaning, bent, horizontal.

upright piano. See **piano** (def. 3).

uprise (*v.* ŭp′rīz′; *n.* ŭp′rīz′), *v.,* **-rose, -risen, -rising,** *n. Archaic.* —*v.i.* **1.** to rise; get up, as from a lying or sitting posture. **2.** to come into view. **3.** to come into being or action. **4.** to move upwards; mount up; ascend. **5.** to come above the horizon. **6.** to slope upwards. **7.** to become erect. —*n.* **8.** the act of rising.

uprising (ŭp′rī′zĭng, ŭp′rī′zĭng), *n.* **1.** an insurrection or revolt. **2.** the act of rising. **3.** an ascent or acclivity.

uproar (ŭp′rô′), *n.* **1.** violent and noisy disturbance, as of a multitude; tumultuous or confused noise or din. **2.** an instance of this. [t. D: m. *oproer* tumult; sense affected by ROAR] —**Syn. 1.** See **disorder.**

uproarious (ŭp rô′rĭ əs), *adj.* **1.** characterized by or in a state of uproar; tumultuous. **2.** making or given to making an uproar, or disorderly and noisy, as an assembly, persons, etc. **3.** confused and loud, as sounds, utterances, etc. **4.** expressed by or producing uproar. **5.** extremely funny. —**uproar′iously,** *adv.* —**uproar′iousness,** *n.*

uproot (ŭp′ro͞ot′), *v.t.* **1.** to root up; tear up by or as if by the roots. **2.** to eradicate; remove utterly. **3.** to remove (people) from their native environment; displace. —**up′root′er,** *n.*

uprose (ŭp′rōz′), *v.* pt. of **uprise.**

uprouse (ŭp rouz′), *v.t.,* **-roused, -rousing.** to arouse.

uprush (ŭp′rŭsh′), *n.* a sudden or violent upward flow, movement, etc.

upsadaisy (ŭp′sə dā′zĭ), *interj.* (used to encourage or reassure a child when being lifted, climbing, or standing up.) [fanciful redup. of UP] Also, **upsidaisy, upsydaisy.**

Upsala (ŭp′sä′lə; *Swed.* o͝op′sä lä), *n.* Uppsala.

upset (*v., adj.* ŭp sĕt′; *n.* ŭp′sĕt′), *v.,* **-set, -setting,** *n., adj.* —*v.t.* **1.** to overturn; knock or tip over; capsize. **2.** to spill by knocking over; tip out. **3.** to throw into disorder; disarrange; overthrow or undo. **4.** to disturb (someone) mentally or emotionally; distress. **5.** to disorder physically or make ill, esp. in the digestive system. **6.** to nullify or invalidate: *to upset someone's plans.* **7.** to defeat a competitor or opponent. **8.** *Mach.* to shorten and thicken by hammering on the end, as a heated piece of iron. —*v.i.* **9.** to become overturned or knocked over. —*n.* **10.** a physical upsetting or being upset; overthrow. **11.** the act or fact of disordering or deranging (ideas, plans, patterns, etc.). **12.** a physical disorder; a slight illness, esp. gastric. **13.** an emotional disturbance. **14.** a quarrel. **15.** a defeat, esp. unexpected. **16.** *Mach.* **a.** a tool for upsetting. **b.** something upset, as a bar end. —*adj.* **17.** emotionally disturbed; distressed; affected by emotional disturbance. **18.** affected by slight illness, as the gastric system. **19.** overturned or capsized.

—**Syn. 1.** UPSET, CAPSIZE, OVERTURN imply a change from an upright or other stable position to a prostrate one. UPSET is a familiar word, applied to simple, everyday actions: *to upset a table, a glass of water.* CAPSIZE is applied especially to the upsetting of a boat or vessel: *to capsize a canoe.* OVERTURN usually suggests violence in upsetting something supposedly stable: *the earthquake overturned houses.* All three are used figuratively, also: *to upset the stock market, to capsize a plan, to overturn a government.*

upset price, *U.S.* reserve price.

upsetting (ŭp sĕt′ĭng), *adj.* causing or tending to cause distress.

upshot (ŭp′shŏt′), *n.* **1.** the final issue, the conclusion, or the result. **2.** the conclusion (of an argument). [f. UP- (in sense of termination) + SHOT[1]]

upside (ŭp′sīd′), *n.* the upper side or part.

upside down, 1. with the upper part undermost. **2.** in complete disorder; topsy-turvy. [alter. of ME *up so down*]

upsides (ŭp′sīdz′), *adv. Colloq.* **1.** alongside; on a level with (fol. by *of* or *with*). **2.** revenged or even by retaliation or rivalry (fol. by *with*).

upsilon (yōōp sī′lən), *n.* the twentieth letter (Υ, υ = English U, u, or Y, y) of the Greek alphabet. [t. Gk: m. *ŷ psilón* simple or slender *u* or *y*]

upspring (ŭp′sprĭng′), *v.i.*, **-sprang** or **-sprung, -sprung, -springing.** to spring up; come into being.

upstage (ŭp′stāj′), *adv., adj., v.t.*, **-staged, -staging.** —*adv.* **1.** on or to the back of the stage, which was at one time higher in elevation than the front. —*adj.* **2.** of or pertaining to the back of the stage. **3.** haughtily aloof; haughty; supercilious. —*v.t.* **4.** *Theat.* to manoeuvre (an actor) into a less favourable position for holding the audience's attention, as by moving him upstage. **5.** to steal attention (from another) by some manoeuvre.

upstairs (ŭp′stĕəz′), *adv.* **1.** up the stairs; to or on an upper floor. **2.** *Colloq.* into the air. **3.** to or in a higher rank or office. **4. kick upstairs,** to promote (someone) esp. to a position of diminished power, in order to get him out of the way. —*adj.* **5.** on or pertaining to an upper floor. —*n.* **6.** an upper storey or storeys; that part of a building above the ground floor.

upstanding (ŭp stăn′dĭng), *adj.* **1.** standing erect; erect and tall, esp. of persons or animals; erect, well grown and vigorous in body or form. **2.** straightforward, open, or independent; upright; honourable.

upstart (*n., adj.* ŭp′stät′; *v.* ŭp stät′), *n.* **1.** one who has risen suddenly from a humble position to wealth or power, or to assumed consequence; a parvenu. **2.** one who is pretentious and objectionable through being thus exalted. —*adj.* **3.** (of persons, families, etc.) newly or suddenly risen to importance; without pedigree. **4.** lately come into existence or notice. **5.** characteristic of an upstart. —*v.i.* **6.** *Archaic.* to start up. —*v.t.* **7.** *Archaic.* to cause to start up.

upstate (ŭp′stāt′), *U.S.* —*n.* **1.** the part of a state farther north or away from the coast, esp. the more northerly part of New York State. —*adj.* **2.** of or coming from the parts of a state farther north or away from the coast. —*adv.* **3.** to or towards such parts of a state. —**up′stat′er,** *n.*

upstream (ŭp′strēm′), *adv.* **1.** towards or in the higher part of a stream; against the current. —*adj.* **2.** situated farther up the stream. **3.** moving or facing upstream.

upstroke (ŭp′strōk′), *n.* an upward stroke, esp. of a pen or pencil, or of a piston in a vertical cylinder.

upsurge (*v.* ŭp sûj′; *n.* ŭp′sûj′), *v.*, **-surged, -surging,** *n.* —*v.i.* **1.** to surge up. —*n.* **2.** a surging upwards.

upsweep (*v.* ŭp′swēp′; *n.* ŭp′swēp′), *v.*, **-swept, -sweeping,** *n.* —*v.t., v.i.* **1.** to sweep upwards. —*n.* **2.** a sweeping upwards. **3.** a steep slope.

upswell (ŭp′swĕl′), *v.t., v.i.*, **-swelled, -swelled** or **-swollen, -swelling.** *Rare.* to swell up.

upswing (*n.* ŭp′swĭng′; *v.* ŭp′swĭng′), *n., v.*, **-swung, -swinging.** —*n.* **1.** an upward swing or swinging movement, as of a pendulum. **2.** marked advance or increase. —*v.i.* **3.** to make an upward swing.

upsydaisy (ŭp′sĭ dā′zĭ), *interj.* upsadaisy.

uptake (ŭp′tāk′), *n.* **1.** the action of understanding or comprehension; mental grasp. **2.** the act of taking up. **3.** a pipe or passage leading upwards from below, as for conducting smoke, a current of air, or the like. **4. quick (slow) on the uptake,** quick (slow) to grasp new or complicated ideas, or to learn.

upthrow (ŭp′thrō′), *n.* **1.** an upheaval. **2.** *Geol., Mining.* that side of a fault where a mass of rock is higher than its continuation on the other side of the fault plane. Also, **upthrow side.**

upthrust (ŭp′thrŭst′), *n.* **1.** a thrust in an upward direction. **2.** *Geol.* an upheaval or uplift.

uptight (ŭp′tīt′), *adj. Slang.* **1.** tense, nervous, or irritable. **2.** angry. **3.** conforming to established conventions, esp. despised conventions. **4.** destitute.

uptilt (ŭp′tĭlt′), *v.t.* to tilt up.

up-to-date (ŭp′tə dāt′), *adj.* **1.** extending to the present time; including the latest facts: *an up-to-date record.* **2.** in accordance with the latest or newest standards, ideas, or style; modern. **3.** (of persons, etc.) keeping up with the times, as in information, ideas, methods, style, etc. Also (esp. in predicative use), **up to date.** —**up′-to-date′ness,** *n.*

up-to-the-minute (ŭp′tə thə mĭn′ĭt), *adj.* **1.** most recent or current; extending to the immediate present, as a news report. **2.** entirely modern. Also (esp. in predicative use), **up to the minute.**

uptown (ŭp′toun′), *U.S.* —*adv.* **1.** to, towards, or in any of various parts of a town or city, esp. one considered to be higher, or away from the centre. —*adj.* **2.** moving towards, situated in, or pertaining to such a part. —*n.* **3.** such a part.

upturn (*v.* ŭp′tûn′; *n.* ŭp′tûn′), *v.t.* **1.** to turn up or over. **2.** to direct upwards. —*v.i.* **3.** to turn upwards. —*n.* **4.** an upward turn, or a changing and rising movement, as in prices, business, etc.

upturned (ŭp′tûnd′), *adj.* **1.** turned or directed upwards. **2.** turned over; upside down. **3.** having a turned-up end.

upward (ŭp′wəd), *adj.* **1.** directed, tending, or moving towards a higher point or level; ascending. —*adv.* **2.** upwards. [ME, OE *upweard*, c. D *opwaart*; f. UP- + -WARD] —**up′wardly,** *adv.*

upwards (ŭp′wədz), *adv.* **1.** towards a higher place or position; in a vertical direction. **2.** towards a higher level, degree, or standard, as of thought, feeling, distinction, rank, age, amount, etc. **3.** towards the source, as of a stream; towards the interior, as of a country; towards the centre, most important part, etc. **4.** so as to be uppermost; in or facing the highest position. **5.** to or into later life. Also, **upward.**

upwards of, **1.** more than; above. **2.** approximately. Also, **upward of.**

upwind (ŭp′wĭnd′), *adv.* **1.** against the wind; contrary to the course of the wind. **2.** towards or in the direction from which the wind is blowing: *he was standing upwind of us and could be heard clearly.* —*adj.* **3.** tending, facing, or moving towards the direction from which the wind is blowing.

Ur (û), *n.* an ancient Sumerian city and district in S Babylonia, on the Euphrates, now in SE Iraq.

uracil (yōōə′rə sĭl), *n. Biochem.* a pyrimidine base, $C_4H_4N_2O_2$, present in all living cells, mainly in combined form, as in ribonucleic acids. [f. UR(O)-[1] + AC(ETIC) + -IL]

uraemia (yōōə rē′myə), *n. Pathol.* the morbid condition resulting from the retention of urinary constituents. Also, *U.S.*, **uremia.** [t. NL. See URO-[1], -AEMIA]

uraemic (yōōə rē′mĭk), *adj.* **1.** pertaining to uraemia. **2.** afflicted with uraemia. Also, *U.S.*, **uremic.**

uraeus (yōōə rē′əs), *n., pl.* **uraei, -ses.** the sacred asp (a cobra, *Naja haje*) as represented upon the headdress of divinities and royal personages of ancient Egypt, usually directly over the forehead, as an emblem of supreme power. [NL, t. Gk: m. *ouraîos*, repr. Egyptian name of cobra]

Ural (yōōə′rəl), *n.* **1.** Usually, **Urals** or **Ural Mountains.** a mountain system in the Soviet Union, extending N and S from the Arctic Ocean to near the Caspian Sea, forming a natural boundary between Europe and Asia. Highest peak, Mt Telpos, 5540 ft. **2.** a river flowing from the Urals into the Caspian Sea. ab. 1400 mi. **3.** a former administrative division comprising a region in the Urals. —*adj.* **4.** of or pertaining to these mountains or this river.

Ural-Altaic (yōōə′rəl ăl tā′ĭk), *adj.* **1.** of or pertaining to the Urals, on the border between the Soviet Union in Europe and Siberia, and the Altai Mountains, in southern Siberia and north-western Mongolia, or the country or peoples around them. **2.** pertaining to the peoples using Ural-Altaic (def. 3). —*n.* **3.** a supposed, but unproved, linguistic phylum combining the Uralian, Turkic, Tungusic, and Mongolian families of languages.

Uralian (yōōə rā′lyən), *n.* **1.** a linguistic stock or family comprising the Finno-Ugric and Samoyed languages. —*adj.* **2.** of or pertaining to the Urals or the district around them, or the people living there.

Uralic (yōōə răl′ĭk), *n.* Finno-Ugric.

Uralsk (*Russ.* ōō rályskʹ), *n.* a town in the W Soviet Union in Asia. 117,000 (est. 1965).

Urania (yōōə rā′nyə), *n.* **1.** *Gk Myth.* the Muse of astronomy. **2.** a name of Aphrodite. [t. L, t. Gk: m. *Ourania* heavenly one]

Uranian (yōōə rā′nyən), *adj.* pertaining to the planet Uranus.

Uranian (yōōə rā′nyən), *adj.* **1.** of or pertaining to the heavens; celestial. **2.** (as an epithet of Venus) heavenly; spiritual. **3.** pertaining to astronomy. **4.** pertaining to the muse Urania.

uranic[1] (yōōə răn′ĭk), *adj. Chem.* **1.** of or containing uranium, esp. in the tetravalent state. **2.** containing uranium in a valency state higher than the corresponding uranous compound. [f. URAN(IUM) + -IC]

uranic[2] (yōōə răn′ĭk), *adj.* of or pertaining to the heavens; celestial; astronomical. [f. s. Gk *ouranós* heaven + -IC]

uranide (yōōə′rə nīd′), *n. Chem.* any of the sequence of natural radioactive elements which includes uranium.

uraninite (yōōə răn′ĭ nīt′), *n.* a mineral, probably originally uranium dioxide (UO_2), but altered by radioactive decay, and usually containing uranium trioxide, lead, radium, and helium, occurring in several varieties including the impure form known as pitchblende: the most important ore of uranium. [f. URAN(IUM) + -IN[2] + -ITE[1]]

uranite (yōōə′rə nīt′), *n.* either of two minerals, autunite (lime uranite) or torbernite (copper uranite). [t. G: m. *Uranit.* See URANIUM, -ITE[1]] —**uranitic** (yōōə′rə nĭt′ĭk), *adj.*

uranium (yōōə rā′nyəm), *n. Chem.* a white, lustrous,

radioactive, metallic element, having compounds which are used in photography and in colouring glass. The natural element consists of 99·28 per cent of the isotope U-238 and 0·71 per cent of the isotope U-235. The latter is capable of sustaining a nuclear chain reaction and is the basis of the atomic bomb and nuclear reactors. *Symbol:* U; *at. wt:* 238·03; *at. no.:* 92; *sp. gr.:* 18·7. [NL; see URAN(US), -IUM]

urano-, a word element meaning 'heaven', as in *uranography*. [t. Gk, comb. form of *ouranós*]

uranography (yŏŏə′rə nŏg′rə fĭ), *n.* the branch of astronomy concerned with the description and mapping of the heavens, and esp. of the fixed stars. [t. Gk: m. s. *ouranographía.* See URANO-, -GRAPHY] —**u′ranog′rapher, u′ranog′raphist,** *n.* —**uranographic** (yŏŏə′rə nō grăf′ĭk), **u′ranograph′ical,** *adj.*

uranology (yŏŏə′rə nŏl′ə jĭ), *n. Astron. Obs.* astronomy or a treatise on astronomy. —**u′ranol′oger,** *n.* —**uranological** (yŏŏə′rə nə lŏj′ĭ kl), *adj.*

uranometry (yŏŏə′rə nŏm′ĭ trĭ), *n. Astron. Obs.* **1.** a treatise on the magnitudes and positions of celestial bodies, esp. the fixed stars. **2.** the measurement of the relative positions of celestial bodies.

uranous (yŏŏə′rə nəs), *adj. Chem.* containing trivalent uranium.

Uranus (yŏŏə′rə nəs), *n.* **1.** *Astron.* the seventh major planet in order from the sun. Its period of revolution is 84·02 years, its mean distance from the sun about 1783 million miles, and its diameter 29,270 miles. It has 5 satellites. **2.** *Gk Myth.* the personification of Heaven, and ruler of the world, son and husband of Gaea (Earth) and father of the Titans, the Cyclopes, etc., who confined his children in Tartarus and was dethroned by his son Cronus, youngest of the Titans, at the instigation of Gaea. [t. L, t. Gk: m. *Ouranós* (def. 2)]

uranyl (yŏŏə′rə nĭl), *n. Chem.* the divalent radical UO_2-, which forms salts with acids. [f. URAN(IUM) + -YL] —**u′ranyl′ic,** *adj.*

urao (ōō rä′ō), *n.* natural crystalline sodium sesquicarbonate, $NaCO_3 \cdot NaHCO_3 \cdot 2H_2O$.

urate (yŏŏə′răt), *n. Chem.* a salt of uric acid. [f. UR(O)-[1] + -ATE[2]]

urban (û′bən), *adj.* **1.** of, pertaining to, or comprising a city or town. **2.** living in a city or cities. **3.** occurring or situated in a city or town. **4.** characteristic of or accustomed to cities; citified. [t. L: s. *urbānus*]

Urban (û′bən), *n.* the name of eight popes.

Urban II (*Odo* or *Otho*), *c.* 1042–99, French ecclesiastic; pope 1088–99.

urban district, a minor administrative division in England and Wales, with local self-government by an urban district council but lacking the charter of a borough.

urbane (û bān′), *adj.* **1.** having the refinement and manners considered to be characteristic of city-dwellers; civilized; sophisticated. **2.** smoothly polite; suave or bland. **3.** exhibiting elegance, refinement, or courtesy, as in expression. [t. L: m. s. *urbānus*] —**urbane′ly,** *adv.* —**urbane′ness,** *n.*

urbanity (û băn′ĭ tĭ), *n., pl.* **-ties. 1.** the quality of being urbane; refined or elegant courtesy or politeness; suavity. **2.** (*pl.*) civilities; courtesies. [t. L: m. *urbānitas*]

urbanize (û′bə nīz′), *v.t.,* **-nized, -nizing.** to render urban, as in character. Also, **urbanise.** —**ur′baniza′tion,** *n.*

urban renewal, the rehabilitation of urban areas, by replacement, repair, or innovation, in accordance with comprehensive plans.

urbi et orbi (û′bĭ ĕt ô′bĭ), *Latin.* to the city (Rome) and the world. Papal bulls are so addressed.

urceolate (û′sĭ ə lĭt, -lāt′), *adj.* shaped like a pitcher; swelling out like the body of a pitcher and contracted at the orifice, as a corolla. [t. NL: m. s. *urceolātus*, der. L *urceolus*, dim. of *urceus* pitcher]

urchin (û′chĭn), *n.* **1.** a small boy or youngster, esp. one who is mischievous and impudent, or ragged and shabbily dressed. **2.** a sea-urchin. **3.** *Archaic.* a kind of elf or mischievous sprite. **4.** *Archaic or Dial.* a hedgehog. —*adj.* **5.** of the nature of or resembling an urchin. [ME *urchone*, t. d. OF: m. *hirechon*, ult. der. L *ēricius* hedgehog]

Urdu (ŏŏə′dōō), *n.* one of the official languages of Pakistan, a dialect used by Muslims derived from Hindustani but using Arabic characters and drawing on Persian and Arabic vocabulary. [t. Hind.: camp (speech), t. Turki: m. *ordu* camp. See HORDE]

-ure, a suffix of abstract nouns indicating action, result, and instrument, as in *legislature, pressure.* [repr. F *-ure* and L *-ūra*]

urea (yŏŏə′rĭ ə), *n. Chem.* a colourless crystalline substance, $CO(NH_2)_2$, occurring in wine, used in fertilizers and in making plastics and adhesives; the principal nitrogenous excretory product of mammals, amphibians, elasmobranch fishes, and some reptiles; carbamide. [NL, f. m. Gk *oúrē(sis)* urination + *-a*, noun ending] —**ureal** (yŏŏə′rĭ əl), *adj.*

urea resins, a group of resins formed by the interaction of urea and formaldehyde. Also, **urea-formaldehyde resins.**

urease (yŏŏə′rĭ ās′), *n. Biochem.* an enzyme found in many plants, bacteria, fungi, etc., which catalyses the conversion of urea into ammonia and carbon dioxide. [f. URE(A) + -ASE]

uredium (yŏŏə rē′dĭ əm), *n. Bot.* the fructification of the rust-fungi-bearing uredospores. Also, **uredinium** (yŏŏə′rĭ dĭn′ĭ əm), **uredosorus** (yŏŏə rē′də sô′rəs).

uredo (yŏŏə rē′dō), *n., pl.* **uredos** or **uredines** (yŏŏə rē′dĭ nēz′). a skin irritation; hives; urticaria. [t. L: rust fungus, itch]

uredospore (yŏŏə rē′də spô′), *n. Bot.* the spore of the rust fungi which appears between the aeciospore and the teliospore, commonly the summer spore.

uredostage (yŏŏə rē′də stāj′), *n. Bot.* the phase in the life cycle of a rust fungus when the uredospores are formed. Also, **uredial stage** (yŏŏə rē′dĭ əl).

ureide (yŏŏə′rĭ īd′), *n. Chem.* any of several derivations of urea containing an acyl group.

uremia (yŏŏə rē′myə), *n. U.S.* uraemia.

uremic (yŏŏə rē′mĭk), *adj. U.S.* uraemic.

-uret, a suffix having the same force as **-ide,** as in *arseniuret.* [t. NL: s. *-urētum*]

ureter (yŏŏə rē′tə), *n. Anat.* a muscular duct or tube conveying the urine from a kidney to the bladder or cloaca. See diag. under **kidney.** [t. L, t. Gk] —**ure′teral, ureteric** (yŏŏə′rĭ tĕ′rĭk), *adj.*

urethane (yŏŏə′rĭ thān′, yŏŏə rē′thān), *n. Chem.* **1.** any derivative of carbamic acid with the type formula, NH_2COOR. **2.** a colourless, crystalline compound, the ethyl ester of carbamic acid, $NH_2COOC_2H_5$, used in the synthesis of organic compounds, esp. in the manufacture of **urethane resins,** and as a mild hypnotic drug. Also, **urethan** (yŏŏə′rĭ thăn′). [f. UR(EA) + ETHANE]

urethr-, var. of **urethro-** before vowels, as in *urethritis.*

urethra (yŏŏə rē′thrə), *n., pl.* **-thrae** (-thrē), **-thras.** *Anat.* the membranous tube which extends from the bladder to the exterior. In the male it conveys semen as well as urine. [t. LL, t. Gk] —**ure′thral,** *adj.*

urethritis (yŏŏə′rĭ thrī′tĭs), *n. Pathol.* inflammation of the urethra. —**urethritic** (yŏŏə′rĭ thrĭt′ĭk), *adj.*

urethro-, a word element representing **urethra,** as in *urethroscope.* Also, **urethr-.**

urethroscope (yŏŏə rē′thrə skōp′), *n. Med.* an apparatus for observing the urethra.

urethroscopy (yŏŏə′rĭ thrŏs′kə pĭ), *n. Med.* observation of the urethra by a urethroscope.

Urey (yŏŏə′rĭ), *n.* **Harold Clayton,** born 1893, U.S. chemist; discovered heavy hydrogen.

Urfa (*Turk.* ōōr′fä), *n.* a town in SE Turkey, E of the river Euphrates. 72,870 (1965). See **Edessa.**

Urga (û′gə), *n.* former name of **Ulan Bator.**

urge (ûj), *v.,* **urged, urging,** *n.* —*v.t.* **1.** to endeavour to induce or persuade, as by entreaties or earnest recommendations; entreat or exhort earnestly: *urge a person to take more care.* **2.** to press by persuasion or recommendation, as for acceptance, performance, or use; recommend or advocate earnestly: *urge a plan of action.* **3.** to press (something) upon the attention: *urge a claim.* **4.** to insist on, allege, or assert with earnestness: *urge the need of haste.* **5.** to push or force along; impel with force or vigour: *urge the cause along.* **6.** to drive with incitement to speed or effort: *urge dogs on with shouts.* **7.** to press, push, or hasten (the course, activities, etc.): *urge one's flight.* **8.** to impel, constrain, or move to some action: *urged by necessity.* —*v.i.* **9.** to make entreaties or earnest recommendations. **10.** to exert a driving or impelling force; to give an impulse to haste or action: *hunger urges.* **11.** to press, push, or hasten on (often fol. by *on, onwards, along,* etc.). —*n.* **12.** the fact of urging or being urged; impelling action, influence, or force; impulse. **13.** an involuntary, natural, or instinctive impulse. [t. L: m. s. *urgēre* press, drive] —**urg′er,** *n.*

urgency (û′jən sĭ), *n., pl.* **-cies. 1.** urgent character; imperativeness; pressing importance. **2.** insistence; importunateness.

urgent (û′jənt), *adj.* **1.** pressing; compelling or requiring immediate action or attention; imperative. **2.** insistent or earnest in solicitation; importunate, as a person. **3.** expressed with insistence, as requests or appeals. [t. L: s. *urgens*, ppr.] —**ur′gently,** *adv.*

urger (û′jə), *n. Austral. Slang.* a racecourse tipster.

-urgy, a word element meaning 'a technology', as in *metallurgy.* [t. Gk: m. s. *-ourgia*, der. *érgon* work]

Uri (*Ger.* o͞o′rē), *n.* a canton in central Switzerland. 32,021 pop. (1961); 415 sq. mi. *Cap.*: Altdorf.
-uria, a word element meaning 'urine'. [NL, t. Gk: m. *-ouria*, der. *oûron* urine]
Uriah (yo͝oə rī′ə), *n.* a Hittite officer, husband of Bathsheba. David contrived his death in battle. II Sam. 11. [t. Heb.: m. *Urīyāh*]
urial (o͝oə′rĭ əl), *n.* a wild sheep of the Himalayas and southern Asia, *Ovis orientalis.* [t. Punjabi: m. *hoorēal*]
uric (yo͝oə′rĭk), *adj.* pertaining to or obtained from urine. [f. UR(O)-[1] + -IC]
uric acid, *Biochem.* a colourless, scaly compound, $C_5H_4N_4O_3$, found in the joints in gout: the principal nitrogenous excretory product of birds and most reptiles.
uridine (yo͝oə′rĭ dīn′), *n. Biochem.* a compound of uracil and ribose, present in all living cells, mainly in combined form, as in ribonucleic acids.
uridylic acid (yo͝oə′rĭ dĭl′ĭk), *Biochem.* the monophosphate of uridine, present in all living cells, mainly in combined form, as in ribonucleic acids.
Uriel (yo͝oə′rĭ əl), *n.* one of the archangels in Jewish angelology. [t. Heb.: m. *Urī'el*]
Urim and Thummim (yo͝oə′rĭm ən thŭm′ĭm), *Bible.* objects (or parts of one object) worn upon the breastplate of the high priests of Israel. These or other objects bearing the same name were used ceremonially in cases of doubt to ascertain the will of God. (Exodus 28:30.)
urinal (yo͝oə′rĭ nəl, yo͝oə rī′nəl), *n.* **1.** a fixture, room, or building for discharging urine in. **2.** a glass or metallic receptacle for urine. [ME, t. L]
urinalysis (yo͝oə′rĭ năl′ĭ sĭs), *n., pl.* **-ses** (-sēz′). urine analysis. [f. URIN(E) + (AN)ALYSIS]
urinary (yo͝oə′rĭ nə rĭ), *adj., n., pl.* **-naries.** —*adj.* **1.** of or pertaining to urine. **2.** pertaining to the organs secreting and discharging urine. —*n.* **3.** *Archaic.* a reservoir for the reception of urine, etc., for manure. **4.** a urinal.
urinary calculus, *Pathol.* a calcareous concretion in the urinary tract.
urinate (yo͝oə′rĭ nāt′), *v.i.,* **-nated, -nating.** to pass or discharge urine. —**u′rina′tion,** *n.* —**urinative** (yo͝oə′rĭ nə tĭv), *adj.*
urine (yo͝oə′rĭn), *n.* the secretion of the kidneys (in mammals, a fluid), which in most mammals is conducted to the bladder by the ureter, and from there to the exterior by the urethra. [ME, t. L: m. *ūrīna*, akin to Gk *oûron*]
urine analysis, analysis of urine chemically or microscopically.
uriniferous (yo͝oə′rĭ nĭf′ə rəs), *adj.* conveying urine.
urinogenital (yo͝oə′rĭ nō jĕn′ĭ tl), *adj.* urogenital.
urinous (yo͝oə′rĭ nəs), *adj.* pertaining to, resembling, or containing urine. Also, **urinose** (yo͝oə′rĭ nōs′).
Urmia (û′myə), *n.* **1.** former name of **Rizaiyeh. 2. Lake,** a salt lake in NW Iran. ab. 2000 sq. mi. (large seasonal variation).
urn (ûn), *n.* **1.** a kind of vase, of various forms, esp. one with a foot or pedestal. **2.** such a vase for holding the ashes of the dead after cremation. **3.** (esp. among the ancient Greeks) an electoral vase or other receptacle for votes. **4.** *Bot.* the spore-bearing part of the capsule of a moss, between lid and seta. **5.** a vessel or apparatus with a tap, used for making tea, coffee, etc., in quantity. [ME *urne*, t. L: m. *urna*] —**urn′like′,** *adj.*
uro-[1], a word element referring to urine and the urinary tract, as in *urochrome.* [t. Gk, comb. form of *oûron* urine]
uro-[2], a word element meaning 'tail', as in *urochord.* [comb. form repr. Gk *ourá*]
urochord (yo͝oə′rō kôd′), *n. Zool.* the notochord of an ascidian or tunicate, found mostly in the larva, or more conspicuous in the larva than in the adult, and confined chiefly to the caudal region. [f. URO-[2] + CHORD[1]] —**u′rochor′dal,** *adj.*
urodele (yo͝oə′rō dēl′), *adj. Zool.* belonging or pertaining to the suborder of the *Amphibia*, including the newts and salamanders, which retain tails throughout adult life.
urogenital (yo͝oə′rō jĕn′ĭ tl), *adj.* genito-urinary. [f. URO-[1] + GENITAL]
urogenous (yo͝oə rŏj′ĭ nəs), *adj. Physiol.* **1.** secreting or producing urine. **2.** contained in urine.
urolith (yo͝oə′rə lĭth), *n. Pathol.* a urinary calculus. [f. URO-[1] + -LITH] —**u′rolith′ic,** *adj.*
urology (yo͝oə rŏl′ə jĭ), *n.* the scientific study of the urine and the genito-urinary tract, with special reference to the diagnostic significance of changes in its anatomy and physiology. [f. URO-[1] + -LOGY] —**urologic** (yo͝oə′rə-lŏj′ĭk), **u′rolog′ical,** *adj.* —**urol′ogist,** *n.*
uropod (yo͝oə′rə pŏd′), *n.* an abdominal limb of an arthropod, esp. one of those on either side of the telson, as in a lobster. [f. URO-[2] + -POD]
uropygial (yo͝oə′rə pĭj′ĭ əl), *adj. Ornith.* of or pertaining to the uropygium. [f. UROPYGI(UM) + -AL[1]]
uropygial gland, *Ornith.* a gland opening on the uropygium at the root of the tail in most birds, and secreting an oily fluid used by the bird in preening its feathers.
uropygium (yo͝oə′rə pĭj′ĭ əm), *n. Ornith.* the projecting terminal portion of a bird's body, from which the tail feathers spring. [t. ML, t. Gk: m. *ouropýgion*]
uroscopy (yo͝oə rŏs′kə pĭ), *n. Med.* inspection of the urine as a means of diagnosis, etc. [f. URO-[1] + -SCOPY] —**uroscopic** (yo͝oə′rə skŏp′ĭk), *adj.* —**uros′copist,** *n.*
urostyle (yo͝oə′rō stīl′), *n. Zool.* a bone formed by the fusion of all or part of the caudal vertebrae in some fish and such amphibians as frogs and toads.
Urquhart (û′kət), *n.* **Sir Thomas,** 1611–60, Scottish author and translator.
Ursa Major (û′sə mā′jə), *gen.* **Ursae Majoris** (û′sē mə-jô′rĭs). *Astron.* the Great Bear. [L: greater bear]
Ursa Minor (û′sə mī′nə), *gen.* **Ursae Minoris** (û′sē mĭ nô′rĭs). *Astron.* the Little Bear. [L: lesser bear]
ursiform (û′sĭ fôm′), *adj.* having the form of a bear; bearlike. [f. *ursi-* (comb. form of L *ursus* bear) + -FORM]
ursine (û′sīn), *adj.* **1.** of or pertaining to a bear or bears. **2.** bearlike. [t. L: m. s. *ursīnus*]
ursine dasyure, Tasmanian devil.
Ursprache (*Ger.* o͞or′shprä KHə), *n. German.* a hypothetically reconstructed parent language, as primitive Germanic (reconstructed by comparative linguistics) from which the Germanic languages have developed. [G: f. *ur-* primitive, original + *Sprache* language]
Ursula (û′syo͝o lə), *n.* **Saint,** a legendary British Christian princess supposed to have been put to death, with 11,000 attendant virgins, by the Huns at Cologne.
Ursuline (û′syo͝o lĭn′), *n.* **1.** one of a religious order of Roman Catholic women founded by St Angela Merici at Brescia, Italy, in 1537, and devoted to the teaching of girls. —*adj.* **2.** of or pertaining to the Ursulines. [f. URSUL(A) + -INE[1]]
urticaceous (û′tĭ kā′shəs), *adj.* belonging to *Urticaceae*, or nettle family of plants. [f. s. NL *Urtīcāceae*, pl. (der. L *urtīca* nettle) genus of nettles + -OUS]
urticant (û′tĭ kənt), *adj.* adapted for, or producing, stinging.
urticaria (û′tĭ kēə′rĭ ə), *n. Pathol.* a skin disease characterized by transient eruptions of itching weals caused chiefly by gastric derangement; nettlerash; hives. [NL, der. L *urtīca* nettle] —**ur′ticar′ial, ur′ticar′ious,** *adj.*
urticate (û′tĭ kāt′), *v.,* **-cated, -cating.** —*v.t.* **1.** to cause a stinging sensation in or on (a body, etc.) with, as with, or like nettles. **2.** to whip; flagellate; flog with nettles. **3.** *Obs.* to whip (a benumbed or paralytic limb) with nettles in order to restore sensation. —*v.i.* **4.** to sting as or like a nettle. **5.** *Obs.* to use urtication in treating paralysis, etc. [t. ML: m. s. *urticātus*, pp., der. L *urtīca* nettle]
urtication (û′tĭ kā′shən), *n.* the action or result of urticating or stinging.
Uru., Uruguay.
Uruguay (yo͝oə′rə gwī′; *Sp.* o͞o ro͞o gwäy′), *n.* **1.** a republic in SE South America. 2,590,158 pop. (1963); 72,172 sq. mi. *Cap.*: Montevideo. **2.** a river flowing from S Brazil along the E boundary of Argentina into the River Plate. 981 mi. —**Uruguayan** (yo͝oə′rə gwī′ən), *adj., n.*
Urumchi (o͞o ro͞om′chĭ), *n.* a city in NW China: the capital of Sinkiang province. 320,000 (est. 1958). Also, **Urumtsi** (o͞o ro͞om′chĭ).
Urundi (o͞o ro͞on′dĭ), *n.* See **Ruanda-Urundi.**
urus (yo͝oə′rəs), *n.* the aurochs. [t. L; of Gmc orig.]
urushiol (o͞o′ro͞o shĭ ŏl′, o͞o ro͞o′shĭ ŏl′), *n.* a toxic, liquid, catechol derivative, the active irritant principle in several species of the plant genus *Rhus*, as poison ivy. [f. Jap. *urushi* lacquer + -OL[2]]
us (ŭs), *pron.* objective case of **we.** [ME and OE, c. G and Goth. *uns*]
U.S., United States.
U/S, 1. unserviceable. **2.** useless. Also, **U.S.**
u.s., 1. ubi supra. **2.** uniform system. **3.** unserviceable. **4.** useless. **5.** ut supra.
U.S.A., United States of America.
usable (yo͞o′zə bl), *adj.* useable. —**us′abil′ity, us′ableness,** *n.*
U.S.A.F., United States Air Force.
usage (yo͞o′sĭj, yo͞o′zĭj), *n.* **1.** customary way of doing; a custom or practice: *the usages of the last fifty years.* **2.** customary manner of using a language or any of its forms, esp. standard practice in a given language: *English usage.* **3.** a particular instance of this: *a usage borrowed from the French.* **4.** the body of rules or customs followed by a particular set of people. **5.** usual conduct or behaviour. **6.** way of using or treating, or treatment: *hard or rough usage.* **7.** habitual or customary use; long-continued practice: *immemorial usage.* **8.** the act or fact of using or employing; use. [ME, t. OF, der. *us* use, g. L *ūsus*]

usance (yo͞o′zəns), *n.* **1.** *Com.* the length of time, exclusive of days of grace, allowed by custom or usage for the payment of foreign bills of exchange (it varies between different places). **2.** *Econ.* the income of benefits of every kind derived from the ownership of wealth. **3.** *Archaic.* use. **4.** *Archaic.* interest, as on a loan. **5.** *Obs.* custom. **6.** *Obs.* usury. [ME, t. OF, der. *user* USE, v.]

Usbeg (ŭs′bĕg, ŭz′bĕg), *n.* Uzbek.

use (*v.* yo͞oz, *def. 11* also yo͞os; *n.* yo͞os), *v.*, **used, using,** *n.* —*v.t.* **1.** to employ for some purpose; put into service; turn to account: *use a knife to cut, use a new method.* **2.** to avail oneself of; apply to one's own purposes: *use the front room for a conference.* **3.** to expend or consume in use: *his car uses a lot of oil.* **4.** to act or behave towards, or treat (a person) in some manner. **5.** to exploit (a person) for one's own ends. **6.** to utter (words) or speak (a language). **7.** to operate or put into effect. **8.** *Archaic.* to practise habitually or customarily; make a practice of. **9.** to habituate or accustom. See **used²**. **10. use up, a.** to consume completely. **b.** to exhaust; tire out. —*v.i.* **11.** to be accustomed, wont, or customarily found (with an infinitive expressed or understood, and, except in archaic use, now only in the past): *he used to go every day.* **12.** *Archaic or Dial.* to resort, stay, or dwell customarily. —*n.* **13.** the act of employing or using, or putting into service: *the use of tools.* **14.** the state of being employed or used: *this book is in use.* **15.** an instance or way of employing or using something: *each successive use of the tool.* **16.** a way of being employed or used; a purpose for which something is used: *the instrument has different uses.* **17.** the power, right, or privilege of employing or using something: *to lose the use of the right eye.* **18.** service or advantage in or for being employed or used; utility or usefulness: *of no practical use.* **19.** help; profit; resulting good: *what's the use of doing that?* **20.** occasion or need, as for something to be employed or used: *have you any use for another calendar?* **21.** continued, habitual, or customary employment or practice; custom; practice: *follow the prevailing use of such occasions.* **22.** way of using or treating; treatment. **23.** consumption, as of food or tobacco. **24.** *Law.* **a.** the enjoyment of property, as by the employment, occupation, or exercise of it. **b.** the benefit or profit of property (lands and tenements) in the possession of another who simply holds them for the beneficiary. **c.** the equitable ownership of land the legal title to which is in another; a passive trust. **25.** *Eccles.* the distinctive form of ritual or of any liturgical observance used in a particular church, diocese, community, etc. **26.** *Obs.* interest; usury. **27.** Some special noun phrases are:

bring into use, to introduce so as to become customary or generally employed.

come into use, to become customary or generally employed.

have no use for, 1. to have no occasion or need for. **2.** to have no liking or tolerance for.

in use, 1. occupied; currently employed to some purpose. **2.** in general employment.

make use of, to employ; put to use; use for one's own purposes or advantages.

of no use, or (elliptically) **no use,** of no service, advantage, or help; useless: *it's no use crying.*

of use, useful.

out of use, not in current or general employment.

put to use, to employ.

[ME, t. OF: m. *user*, der. L *ūsus*, pp.]

—**Syn. 1.** USE, UTILIZE mean to make something serve one's purpose. USE is the general word: *to use a telephone, to use a saw and other tools, to use one's eyes, to use coal, eggs in cooking.* (What is USED often has depreciated or been diminished, sometimes completely consumed: *a used car, all the butter has been used up.*) As applied to persons, USE implies some selfish or sinister purpose: *to use another to advance oneself.* UTILIZE implies practical or profitable use, turning to account as for a particular end, etc.: *to utilize all one's resources, the most modern systems.* In some cases it has replaced USE as the general word.

useable (yo͞o′zə bl), *adj.* **1.** that is available for use. **2.** that is in condition to be used. Also, **usable.** —**use′abil′ity, use′ableness,** *n.*

used¹ (yo͞ozd), *adj.* **1.** that has been made use of, esp. as showing signs of wear. **2.** second-hand. **3. used up,** completely consumed or exhausted. [pp. of USE]

used² (yo͞ost), *adj.* accustomed; habituated; inured (fol. by *to*). [special use of USE, v. See def. 11]

useful (yo͞os′fəl), *adj.* **1.** being of use or service; serving some purpose; serviceable, advantageous, helpful, or of good effect. **2.** of practical use, as for doing work; producing material results; supplying common needs: *the useful arts.* **3.** *Colloq.* competent; able. —**use′fully,** *adv.* —**use′fulness,** *n.*

useless (yo͞os′lĭs), *adj.* **1.** of no use; not serving the purpose or any purpose; unavailing or futile. **2.** without useful qualities; of no practical good. —**use′lessly,** *adv.* —**use′lessness,** *n.*

—**Syn. 1.** inutile, fruitless, profitless, valueless, worthless. USELESS, FUTILE, INEFFECTUAL, VAIN refer to that which is unavailing. That is USELESS which is unavailing because of the circumstances of the case or some inherent defect: *it is useless to cry over spilt milk.* FUTILE suggests wasted effort and complete failure to attain a desired end: *all attempts were futile.* That is INEFFECTUAL which weakly applies energy in an ill-advised way and does not produce a desired effect: *an ineffectual effort.* That which is VAIN is fruitless or hopeless even after all possible effort: *it is vain to keep on hoping.* **2.** unserviceable, unusable. —**Ant. 1.** effective.

user (yo͞o′zə), *n.* **1.** one who or that which uses. **2.** *Law.* **a.** the right to the enjoyment of property. **b.** the exercise of a right to the enjoyment of property.

Ushant (ŭsh′ənt), *n.* an island off the NW coast of France: naval battles, 1778, 1794. 1940 pop. (1962); 4½ mi. long. French, **Ouessant.**

U-shaped (yo͞o′shāpt′), *adj.* being in the form of a U.

Ushas (o͞o′shəs), *n.* Dawn, a Vedic deity, daughter of Sky, and sister of Night. [t. Skt: m. *Usas*]

usher (ŭsh′ə), *n.* **1.** one who escorts persons to seats in a church, theatre, etc. **2.** an attendant who keeps order in a law court. **3.** (formerly) a subordinate teacher or assistant in a school. **4.** (formerly) an officer whose business it is to introduce strangers or walk before persons of rank. **5.** *Archaic.* one who goes before; a precursor. **6.** *Obs.* an officer or servant having charge of an entrance door; a doorkeeper. —*v.t.* **7.** to act as an usher to; conduct or show (fol. by *in, into, out,* etc.). **8.** to attend or bring at the coming or beginning. [ME, t. AF: m. *usser*, g. LL *ustiārius* doorkeeper, r. L *ostiārius*] —**ush′erless,** *adj.*

usherette (ŭsh′ə rĕt′), *n.* a female attendant, esp. one who shows people to their seats in a cinema or theatre.

Usk (ŭsk), *n.* a river in SE Wales and SW England, flowing into the Severn estuary. 57 mi.

Üsküdar (*Turk.* ʏs′kʏ där), *n.* Turkish name of **Scutari** (def. 1).

U.S.N., United States Navy.

Usnach (o͝osh′nəᴋʜ, -nə), *n.* See **Deirdre.**

Uspallata Pass (*Sp.* o͞os pä lyä′tä), a mountain pass in the Andes, linking Mendoza, Argentina, and Santiago, Chile: 'Christ of the Andes' statue nearby. ab. 12,800 ft high.

usquebaugh (ŭs′kwĭ bô′), *n.* (in Scotland and Ireland) whisky. [t. Irish and Scot. Gaelic: m. *uisge beatha* water of life]

U.S.S., 1. United States Ship. **2.** United States Steamer. **3.** United States Steamship.

U.S.S.R., Union of Soviet Socialist Republics.

Ussuri (*Russ.* o͝os so͞o rē′), *n.* a river forming a part of the boundary between E Manchuria and the SE Soviet Union in Asia, flowing N to the river Amur. 365 mi.

ustilagineous (ŭs′tĭ lə jĭn′ĭ əs), *adj.* of or pertaining to the smut fungi belonging to the family *Ustilaginaceae.* [f. s. LL *ūstilāgo* smut fungus (der. L *ūrere* to burn) + -EOUS]

Ústí nad Labem (*Cz.* o͞os′tyē näd lä′bĕm), a town in NW Czechoslovakia. 70,000 (1965).

Ust-Kamenogorsk (*Russ.* o͞ostу′kə mĭ nä gôrsk′), *n.* a town in the W Soviet Union in Asia. 202,000 (est. 1965).

ustulate (ŭs′tyo͝o lĭt, -lāt′), *adj.* coloured or blackened as if scorched. [t. L: m.s. *ūstulātus*, pp., burnt]

ustulation (ŭs′tyo͝o lā′shən), *n.* **1.** the act of scorching or burning. **2.** *Pharm.* the roasting or drying of moist substances so as to prepare them for pulverizing.

usu., 1. usual. **2.** usually.

usual (yo͞o′zho͝o əl), *adj.* **1.** habitual or customary: *his usual skill.* **2.** such as is commonly met with or observed in experience; ordinary: *the usual January weather.* **3.** in common use; common: *say the usual things.* **4. as usual,** as is (or was) usual; in the customary or ordinary manner: *he will come as usual.* —*n.* **5.** that which is usual or habitual. [ME, t. L: s. *ūsuālis*] —**u′sually,** *adv.* —**u′sualness,** *n.*

—**Syn. 1.** USUAL, CUSTOMARY, HABITUAL refer to a settled and constant practice. USUAL indicates that which is to be expected by reason of previous experience, which shows it to occur more often than not: *there were the usual crowds at the races.* That which is CUSTOMARY is in accordance with prevailing usage or individual practice: *it is customary to finish up with a bonfire.* That which is HABITUAL has become settled or constant as the result of habit on the part of the individual: *the harassed manager wore a habitual frown.* **2.** general, prevailing, prevalent, everyday. —**Ant. 1.** unexpected, extraordinary.

usucapion (yo͞o′zyo͝o kā′pyən), *n.* *Law.* the acquisition of a thing through long continuance of its use; title by prescription. Also, **usucaption** (yo͞o′zyo͝o kăp′shən). [t. L: s. *ūsūcapio*]

usufruct (yo͞o′syo͝o frŭkt′), *n.* *Rom. and Civ. Law.* the right of enjoying all the advantages to be derived from the use of something which belongs to another, so far as compatible with the substance of the thing not being destroyed or injured. [t. LL: s. *ūsūfructus*, L *ūsusfructus*, for *ūsus et fructus* use and fruit]

usufructuary (yo͞o′syo͞o frŭk′tyo͞o ə rĭ), *adj.*, *n.*, *pl.* **-aries.** —*adj.* **1.** of, pertaining to, or of the nature of a usufruct. —*n.* **2.** a person who has a usufruct property. [t. LL: m. s. *ūsūfructuārius*, der. *ūsūfructus* USUFRUCT]

Usumbura (o͝o′zəm bo͞o′rə), *n.* the capital of Burundi, in the SW part, on Lake Tanganyika. See map under **Rwanda.**

usurer (yo͞o′zhə rə, yo͞ozh′rə), *n.* **1.** one who lends money at an exorbitant rate of interest. **2.** *Obs.* one who lends money at interest. [ME, t. AF, der. *usure* USURY]

usurious (yo͞o′zyo͞o′rĭ əs), *adj.* **1.** practising usury; taking exorbitant interest for the use of money. **2.** pertaining to or of the nature of usury: *usurious interest.* —**usu′riously,** *adv.* —**usu′riousness,** *n.*

usurp (yo͞o zûp′), *v.t.* **1.** to seize and hold (an office or position, power, etc.) by force or without right. **2.** to appropriate or make use of (rights, property, etc.) not one's own. —*v.i.* **3.** to commit forcible or illegal seizure of an office, power, etc.; encroach. [ME *usurpe*, t. L: m. *ūsūrpāre*] —**usurp′er,** *n.* —**usurp′ingly,** *adv.*

usurpation (yo͞o′zû pā′shən), *n.* **1.** the act of usurping; the seizing and holding of the place, power, or the like, of another without right. **2.** the wrongful seizure and occupation of a throne.

usury (yo͞o′zho͞o rĭ), *n.*, *pl.* **-ries.** **1.** an exorbitant amount or rate of interest, esp. in excess of the legal rate. **2.** the lending, or practice of lending money at an exorbitant rate of interest. **3.** *Archaic.* the fact or practice of lending money at interest. **4.** *Obs.* interest paid for the use of money. [ME *usurie*, t. ML: m. *ūsūria* interest]

usw, (G *und so weiter*) and so forth. Also, **u.s.w.**

ut (ŭt, o͞ot), *n. Music.* the syllable once generally used for the first note or keynote of a scale and sometimes for the note C: now commonly superseded by *do.* See **sol-fa.** [t. L. See GAMUT]

Ut., Utah.

U.T., universal time. Also, **u.t.**

Utah (yo͞o′tô, yo͞o′tä), *n.* a state in the W United States. 890,627 pop. (1960); 84,916 sq. mi. *Cap.:* Salt Lake City. *Abbrev.:* Ut. —**U′tahan,** *adj.*, *n.*

ut dict., (L *ut dictum*) as directed.

Ute (yo͞ot, yo͞o′tĭ), *n.*, *pl.* **Utes,** (*collectively*) **Ute.** **1.** a member of an important tribe of the Shoshonean stock of North American Indians, now on reservations in Utah and Colorado. **2.** their language, of Uto-Aztecan stock.

utensil (yo͞o tĕn′səl), *n.* **1.** any of the instruments or vessels commonly used in a kitchen, dairy, etc. **2.** any instrument, vessel, or implement. [ME *utensyl(e)*, t. ML: m. *ūtensile*, prop. neut. of L *ūtensilis* useful] —**Syn. 2.** See **tool.**

uterine (yo͞o′tə rīn′), *adj.* **1.** of or pertaining to the uterus or womb. **2.** related through having the same mother. [ME, t. LL: m. s. *uterinus*, der. L *uterus* uterus]

utero-, a word element representing **uterus.**

uterus (yo͞o′tə rəs), *n.*, *pl.* **uteri** (yo͞o′tə rī′). *Anat.*, *Zool.* that portion of the oviduct in which the fertilized ovum implants itself and develops or rests during prenatal development; the womb of mammals. See **oviduct.** [t. L]

Utgard (o͞ot′gäd, o͞ot′-), *n.* Jotunheim.

U Thant. See **Thant.**

Uther (yo͞o′thə), *n. Arthurian Legend.* king of Britain and father of Arthur. Also, **Uther Pendragon.**

Utica (yo͞o′tĭ kə), *n.* **1.** a town in the U.S., in central New York State, on the Mohawk river. 100,410 (1960). **2.** an ancient city on the N coast of Africa, NW of Carthage.

utile (yo͞o′tĭl, -tīl), *adj. Obs.* useful. [t. L: m. s. *ūtilis*]

utilitarian (yo͞o′tĭ lĭ tēə′rĭ ən), *adj.* **1.** pertaining to or consisting in utility; concerning practical or material things. **2.** having regard to utility or usefulness rather than beauty, ornamentality, etc. **3.** of, pertaining to, or adhering to the doctrine of utilitarianism. —*n.* **4.** an adherent of utilitarianism. **5.** one who is only concerned with practical matters, or who assumes a practical attitude.

utilitarianism (yo͞o′tĭ lĭ tēə′rĭ ə nĭz′əm), *n.* **1.** the ethical doctrine that virtue is based on utility, and that conduct should be directed towards promoting the greatest happiness of the greatest number of persons. **2.** utilitarian spirit.

utility (yo͞o tĭl′ĭ tĭ), *n.*, *pl.* **-ties.** **1.** the state or character of being useful. **2.** something useful; a useful thing. **3.** a public service, as a bus or railway service, gas or electricity supply, or the like. Cf. **public utility.** **4.** *Econ.* the capacity of an object for satisfying a human want. **5.** well-being or happiness; that which is conducive to the happiness and well-being of the greatest number: the principle and purpose of utilitarianism. **6.** *U.S.* (*pl.*) stocks or shares of public utilities. —*adj.* **7.** provided, designed, bred, or made for usefulness or profitability rather than beauty. [ME *utilite*, t. L: m. s. *ūtilitas*]

utility man, *U.S.* **1.** a worker expected to serve in any capacity when called on. **2.** an actor of miscellaneous small parts.

utilize (yo͞o′tĭ līz′), *v.t.*, **-lized, -lizing.** to put to use; turn to profitable account: *to utilize water power for driving machinery.* Also, **utilise.** —**u′tiliz′able,** *adj.* —**u′tiliza′tion,** *n.* —**u′tiliz′er,** *n.* —**Syn.** See **use.**

ut infra (o͞ot ĭn′frä), *Latin.* as below.

uti possidetis (yo͞o′tī pŏs′ĭ dē′tĭs), *Internat. Law.* the principle which vests in either of the belligerents at the end of a war all territory actually occupied and controlled by them. [L: lit., as you possess]

utmost (ŭt′mōst′), *adj.* **1.** of the greatest or highest degree, quantity, or the like; greatest: *of the utmost importance.* **2.** being at the farthest point or extremity; farthest: *the utmost boundary of the East.* —*n.* Also, **uttermost.** **3.** the greatest degree or amount: *the utmost that can be said.* **4.** the highest, greatest, or best of one's power: *do your utmost.* **5.** the extreme limit or extent. [ME *utmest*, OE *ūtemest*, f. *ūte* OUT + *-mest* -MOST]

Uto-Aztecan (yo͞o′tō ăz′tĕk′ən), *n.* an American Indian linguistic stock, widespread from Idaho to the Isthmus of Tehuantepec, and from the Rocky Mountains to the Pacific; this stock includes Hopi, Ute, Shoshone, Comanche, Nahuatl (Aztec), Piman, and other languages.

utoo (yo͞o′to͞o), *n. N.Z.* payment; satisfaction. [t. Maori]

Utopia (yo͞o tō′pyə), *n.* **1.** an imaginary island described in Sir Thomas More's *Utopia* (1516) as enjoying the utmost perfection in law, politics, etc. **2.** (*often l.c.*) a place or state of ideal perfection. **3.** (*often l.c.*) any visionary system of political or social perfection. [NL, f. Gk: m. *ou* not + *-topia*, der. *tópos* place]

Utopian (yo͞o tō′pyən), *adj.* **1.** of, pertaining to, or resembling a Utopia. **2.** (*often l.c.*) founded upon or involving imaginary or ideal perfection. **3.** given to dreams or schemes of such perfection. —*n.* **4.** an inhabitant of Utopia. **5.** (*often l.c.*) an ardent but unpractical political or social reformer; a visionary; an idealist.

utopianism (yo͞o tō′pyə nĭz′əm), *n.* the views or habit of mind of a utopian; impracticable schemes of political or social reform.

Utrecht (yo͞o′trĕkt; *Du.* Y′trĕKHT), *n.* **1.** a city in the Netherlands, the capital of Utrecht province: treaties ending the War of the Spanish Succession were signed here, 1714. 267,001 (1965). **2.** a province in the central Netherlands. 673,601 pop. (est. 1959); 526 sq. mi.

Utrecht

utricle (yo͞o′trĭ kl), *n.* **1.** a small sac or baglike body, as an air-filled cavity in a seaweed. **2.** *Bot.* a membranous sheath surrounding the fruit in sedges of the cyperaceous genus *Carex.* **3.** *Anat.* the larger of two sacs in the membranous labyrinth of the internal ear and concerned with equilibrium. Cf. **saccule.** [t. L: m. s. *ūtriculus*, dim. of *ūter* bag]

utricular (yo͞o trĭk′yo͞o lə), *adj.* **1.** pertaining to or of the nature of a utricle; baglike. **2.** having a utricle or utricles.

utriculate (yo͞o trĭk′yo͞o lĭt, -lāt′), *adj.* having a utricle; utricular; baglike.

utriculitis (yo͞o trĭk′yo͞o lī′tĭs), *n. Pathol.* inflammation of the utricle bone of the middle ear. [f. s. L *ūtriculus* UTRICLE + -ITIS]

Utrillo (yo͞o trĭl′ō; *Fr.* Y trē yó′), *n.* **Maurice** (*Fr.* mō rēs′), 1883–1955, French painter.

Uttar Pradesh (o͞ot′ə prä′dĕsh), a state in N India, formerly United Provinces. 73,746,401 pop. (1961); 113,409 sq. mi. *Cap.:* Lucknow.

utter[1] (ŭt′ə), *v.t.* **1.** to give audible expression to (words, etc.); speak or pronounce: *the words were uttered in my hearing.* **2.** to give expression to (a subject, etc.): *unable to utter her opinions.* **3.** to give forth (cries, sounds, etc.) with or as with the voice: *utter a sigh.* **4.** to express or make known in any manner. **5.** to express by written or printed words. **6.** to make publicly known; publish: *utter a libel.* **7.** to put into circulation, as coins, notes, etc., and esp. counterfeit money, forged cheques, etc. **8.** *Dial. Rare.* to expel; emit. **9.** *Obs.* to publish, as a book. **10.** *Obs.* to sell. —*v.i.* **11.** to use the faculty of speech. [ME *outre* (freq. of OUT, v.), c. G *äussern* declare] —**ut′terable,** *adj.* —**ut′terableness,** *n.*

utter[2] (ŭt′ə), *adj.* **1.** complete; total; absolute: *her utter abandonment to grief.* **2.** unconditional; unqualified: *an utter denial.* [ME; OE *ūtera* (compar. of *ūt* OUT), c. G *äusser*] —**Syn. 1.** See **absolute.**

utterance[1] (ŭt′ə rəns, ŭt′rəns), *n.* **1.** the act of uttering;

vocal expression. 2. manner of speaking; power of speaking. 3. something uttered, as a word or words uttered, a cry, animal's call, or the like. 4. a putting into circulation. [ME; f. UTTER[1], + -ANCE]

utterance[2] (ŭt′ə rəns, ŭt′rəns), *n. Obs.* the utmost extremity; death. [ME, t. OF: m. *oultrance*, der. *oultrer* pass beyond, der. L *ultrā* beyond]

utter barrister, a barrister who is not a Queen's Counsel.

utterer (ŭt′ə rə), *n.* one who utters; one who puts into circulation, publishes, or expresses audibly.

uttering (ŭt′ə rĭng), *n. Crim. Law.* the crime of knowingly tendering or showing a forged instrument or counterfeit coin to another with intent to defraud.

utterless (ŭt′ə lĭs), *adj.* unutterable.

utterly (ŭt′ə lĭ), *adv.* in an utter manner; completely; absolutely.

uttermost (ŭt′ə mōst′), *adj.* **1.** utmost; furthest; extreme. **2.** of the greatest degree, etc.: *uttermost distress.* —*n.* **3.** the extreme limit or extent; the utmost. [ME; f. UTTER[2] + -MOST]

U-turn (yōō′tûn′), *n.* a reversal of direction, as by a motor vehicle, performed in a single U-shaped movement so as to end up facing in the opposite direction on the other side of the road.

uvarovite (ōō vä′rə fīt′), *n.* an emerald green variety of garnet containing chromium, to which its colour is due. [named after Count S. S. *Uvarov*, 1785–1855, president of St Petersburg Academy. See -ITE[1]]

uvea (yōō′vyə), *n. Anat.* the middle tunic of the eye (iris, choroid, and ciliary body, taken collectively). [t. ML, der. L *ūva* grape] —**u′veal, u′veous,** *adj.*

Uvedale (yōō′dl, yōōv′dāl′), *n.* **Nicholas.** See **Udall.**

uveitis (yōō′vĭ ī′tĭs), *n. Pathol.* inflammation of the uvea. [NL, f. s. ML *ūvea* UVEA + *-ītis* -ITIS] —**uveitic** (yōō′vĭ ĭt′ĭk), *adj.*

uvula (yōō′vyōō lə), *n., pl.* **-las, -lae** (-lē′). *Anat.* the small, fleshy, conical body projecting downwards from the middle of the soft palate. See diag. under **mouth.** [ME, t. ML, dim. of L *ūva* grape]

uvular (yōō′vyōō lə), *adj.* **1.** of or pertaining to the uvula. **2.** *Phonet.* pronounced with the back of the tongue held close to or touching the uvula: *Parisian French uses the uvular 'r'.* —*n.* **3.** *Phonet.* a uvular sound. —**u′vularly,** *adv.*

uvulitis (yōō′vyōō lī′tĭs), *n. Pathol.* inflammation of the uvula. [NL, f. s. ML *ūvula* UVULA + *-ītis* -ITIS]

ux., (L *uxor*) wife.

Uxbridge (ŭks′brĭj′), *n.* a town in the W outer London borough of Hillingdon.

Uxmal (*Sp.* ōōz mäl′), *n.* an ancient ruined city in SE Mexico: a centre of later Mayan civilization.

uxorial (ŭk sô′rĭ əl), *adj.* of or pertaining to a wife; typical of or befitting a wife.

uxoricide (ŭk sô′rĭ sīd′), *n.* **1.** one who kills his wife. **2.** the act of killing one's wife. [f. L *uxori-* wife + -CIDE] —**uxo′rici′dal,** *adj.*

uxorious (ŭk sô′rĭ əs), *adj.* excessively or foolishly fond of one's wife; doting on a wife. [t. L: m. *uxōrius*] —**uxo′riously,** *adv.* —**uxo′riousness,** *n.*

Uzbek (ŭz′bĕk), *n.* **1.** a member of a Turkish people of mixed origin and high culture, resident in W central Asia, where they form an influential class, largely urban. **2.** a Turkic language spoken in Turkestan. —*adj.* **3.** of or pertaining to this people or their language. Also, **Usbeg, Uzbeg** (ŭz′bĕg).

Uzbekistan (ŭz′bĕ kĭ stän′), *n.* a constituent republic of the Soviet Union in Asia, in the S part, N of Afghanistan. 9,492,000 pop. (est. 1963); 158,500 sq. mi. *Cap.:* Tashkent. Official name, **Uzbek Soviet Socialist Republic** (ŭz′bĕk; *Russ.* ōōz byĕk′).

V, v, (vē), *n., pl.* **V's** or **Vs, v's** or **vs.** **1.** a consonant, the 22nd letter of the English alphabet. **2.** (*sometimes l.c.*) the Roman numeral for five. Cf. **Roman Numerals.** **3.** something shaped like the letter V. **4.** the symbol of victory, esp. in World War II.

V, 1. *Chem.* vanadium. **2.** *Maths.* vector. **3.** velocity. **4.** *Elect.* volt.

v, 1. velocity. **2.** *Elect.* volt.

V., 1. Venerable. **2.** Viscount.

v., 1. valve. **2.** *Bot.* variety (of). **3.** vector. **4.** verb. **5.** verse. **6.** version. **7.** versus. **8.** vice-. **9.** vide. **10.** violin. **11.** vocative. **12.** voice. **13.** volt. **14.** voltage. **15.** volume. **16.** von.

V-1, a flying bomb developed by the Germans in World War II and launched against England. Also, **V-one.** [t. G: part trans. of *Vergeltungswaffe* retaliation weapon]

V-2, a long-range rocket developed by the Germans in World War II and used as a missile against England. Also, **V-two.**

Va, 1. Virginia. **2.** *Music.* viola.

V.A., 1. Vicar Apostolic. **2.** Vice-Admiral. **3.** (Order of) Victoria and Albert.

v.a., verb active.

Vaal (väl), *n.* a river in the Republic of South Africa flowing SW from Transvaal, then forming the border of Transvaal and Orange Free State, and joining the Orange river in Cape Province. ab. 750 mi.

vac (văk), *n. Colloq.* vacation.

vac., vacant.

vacancy (vā′kən sĭ), *n., pl.* **-cies.** **1.** the state of being vacant; emptiness; unoccupied state. **2.** something vacant; vacant space. **3.** a gap or opening. **4.** an unoccupied office or position: *to fill vacancies by election.* **5.** lack of thought or intelligence; vacuity. **6.** *Crystall.* an irregularity in a lattice caused by a site normally occupied by an atom or ion being vacant. **7.** *Rare.* absence of occupation; idleness or inactivity. **8.** *Obs.* unoccupied or leisure time.

vacant (vā′kənt), *adj.* **1.** having no contents; empty; void. **2.** devoid or destitute (*of*). **3.** having no occupant: *vacant chairs.* **4.** untenanted, as a house, etc. **5.** not in use, as a room. **6.** free from work, business, etc., as time. **7.** characterized by or proceeding from absence of occupation: *a vacant life.* **8.** unoccupied with thought or reflection, as the mind. **9.** characterized by, showing, or proceeding from lack of thought or intelligence. **10.** not occupied by an incumbent, official, or the like, as a benefice, office, etc. **11.** *Law.* **a.** idle or unutilized; open to any claimant, as land. **b.** without an incumbent; abandoned: *a vacant estate* (one having no heir or claimant). [ME, t. L: s. *vacans*, ppr.] —**va′cantly,** *adv.* —**Syn. 1.** See **empty. 9.** blank, vacuous, inane.

vacate (və kāt′), *v.,* **-cated, -cating.** —*v.t.* **1.** to make vacant; cause to be empty or unoccupied. **2.** to give up the occupancy of. **3.** to give up or relinquish (an office, position, etc.). **4.** to render inoperative; deprive of validity; annul: *to vacate a legal judgement.* —*v.i.* **5.** to withdraw from occupancy or possession; leave; quit. [t. L: m. s. *vacātus*, pp., freed, emptied]

vacation (və kā′shən), *n.* **1.** a part of the year when law courts, universities, etc., are suspended or closed. **2.** *Chiefly U.S.* a holiday. **3.** the act of vacating. —*v.i.* **4.** *U.S.* to take or have a vacation or holiday. [ME, t. L: s. *vacātio*] —**vaca′tionless,** *adj.*

vacationist (və kā′shə nĭst), *n. U.S.* one who is taking a vacation or holiday. Also, **vaca′tioner.**

vaccinal (văk′sĭ nəl), *adj. Med.* of, pertaining to, or due to vaccine or vaccination.

vaccinate (văk′sĭ nāt′), *v.,* **-nated, -nating.** *Med.* —*v.t.* **1.** to inoculate with the vaccine of cowpox, so as to render the subject immune to smallpox. **2.** to inoculate with the modified virus of any of various other diseases, as a preventive measure. —*v.i.* **3.** to perform or practise vaccination. [der. VACCINE, adj.]

vaccination (văk′sĭ nā′shən), *n. Med.* the act or practice of vaccinating; inoculation with vaccine.

vaccinationist (văk′sĭ nā′shə nĭst), *n. Med.* an advocate of vaccination.

vaccinator (văk′sĭ nā′tə), *n. Med.* **1.** one who vaccinates. **2.** an instrument used in vaccination.

vaccine (văk′sēn), *n.* **1.** the virus of cowpox, obtained from the vesicles of an affected cow or person, and used in vaccination. **2.** the modified virus of any of various other diseases, used for preventive inoculation. —*adj.* **3.** pertaining to vaccinia or to vaccination. **4.** of, pertaining to, or derived from cows. [t. L: m. s. *vaccinus* pertaining to cows]

vaccine point, *Med.* a thin, pointed, vaccine-coated piece of bone or the like, for use in vaccinating.

vaccinia (văk sĭn′ĭ ə), *n. Pathol.* cowpox. [NL, der. L *vaccinus* VACCINE (def. 4)]

vacciniaceous (văk sĭn′ĭ ā′shəs), *adj.* belonging to the *Vacciniaceae*, a family of plants usually included in the *Ericaceae*, containing the blueberry, whortleberry, huckleberry, cranberry, etc. [f. s. NL *Vacciniāceae*, pl., genus of plants (der. L *vaccinium* blueberry) + -ous]

vaccinization (văk′sĭ nī zā′shən), *n. Med.* a vaccination produced by a series of virus inoculations. Also, **vaccinisation.**

vacherin (*Fr.* vȧsh răN′), *n. Cookery.* a sweet made with meringue on a pastry base and filled with ice-cream, cream and sometimes fruit. [t. F]

vacillate (văs′ĭ lāt′), *v.i.*, **-lated, -lating. 1.** to sway unsteadily; waver; stagger. **2.** to fluctuate. **3.** to waver in mind or opinion; be irresolute or hesitant. [t. L: m. s. *vacillātus*, pp.] **—Syn. 1.** See **waver.**

vacillating (văs′ĭ lā′tĭng), *adj.* **1.** that vacillates; wavering. **2.** characterized by vacillation. Also, **vacillatory** (văs′ĭ lā′tə rĭ, -trĭ). **—vac′illat′ingly,** *adv.*

vacillation (văs′ĭ lā′shən), *n.* **1.** the act of vacillating; wavering in mind or opinion; irresolution. **2.** an instance of this. **3.** unsteady movement.

vacua (văk′yo͞o ə), *n.* a pl. of **vacuum.**

vacuity (vă kyo͞o′ĭ tĭ), *n.*, *pl.* **-ties. 1.** the state of being vacuous or empty; absence of contents; emptiness. **2.** an empty space; a vacuum. **3.** absence or lack of something specified. **4.** vacancy of mind, thought, etc.; mental inactivity. **5.** absence of ideas or intelligence; inanity. **6.** something inane or senselessly stupid. [t. L: m. *vacuitas*]

vacuolate (văk′yo͞o ə lĭt, -lāt′), *adj.* provided with or containing a vacuole or vacuoles. Also, **vac′uolat′ed.**

vacuolation (văk′yo͞o ə lā′shən), *n.* **1.** the formation of vacuoles. **2.** the state of being vacuolate. **3.** a system of vacuoles.

vacuole (văk′yo͞o ōl′), *n.* **1.** a cavity within a cell, often containing a watery liquid or secretion. See diag. under **cell. 2.** a minute cavity or vesicle in organic tissue. [t. NL: m. s. *vacuolum*, dim. of *vacuum* VACUUM]

vacuous (văk′yo͞o əs), *adj.* **1.** empty; without contents. **2.** empty of ideas or intelligence; stupidly vacant. **3.** showing mental vacancy: *a vacuous look.* **4.** purposeless; idle. [t. L: m. *vacuus*] **—vac′uously,** *adv.* **—vac′uousness,** *n.*

vacuum (văk′yo͞o əm), *n.*, *pl.* **vacuums, vacua** (văk′yo͞o ə), *adj.*, *v.* **—***n.* **1.** a space entirely void of matter (**perfect** or **complete vacuum**). **2.** an enclosed space from which air (or other gas) has been removed, as by an air pump (**partial vacuum**). **3.** the state or degree of exhaustion in such an enclosed space. **4.** empty space. **—***adj.* **5.** pertaining to, employing, or producing a vacuum. **6.** (of a hollow container) partly exhausted of gas. **7.** pertaining to apparatuses or processes which utilize gas pressures below atmospheric pressure. **—***v.t.* **8.** to clean with a vacuum cleaner or treat with any vacuum device. [t. L, prop. neut. of *vacuus* empty]

vacuum brake, a type of brake used on railway trains, motor vehicles, etc., operated by a vacuum system.

vacuum cleaner, an apparatus for cleaning carpets, floors, etc., by suction.

vacuum crystallization, *Chem.* the process of crystallization carried out under a reduced pressure at a temperature below the temperature required at normal pressures.

vacuum distillation, *Chem.* the process of distillation carried out under a reduced pressure, thus depressing the boiling point of the substance to be distilled and enabling the process to be carried out at a reduced temperature.

vacuum filtration, *Chem.* the process of filtration carried out under a reduced pressure, in order to increase the rate of filtration by sucking the filtrate through the filter.

vacuum flask, a flask or bottle protected by a vacuum jacket which prevents the escape of heat from hot contents or the entrance of heat to cold contents; Dewar flask; thermos. Also, **vacuum bottle.**

vacuum gauge, a device for measuring pressures below atmospheric pressure in the receiver of an air pump, in steam condensers, and the like.

vacuum pump, a pump or device by which a partial vacuum can be produced.

vacuum tube, *Electronics.* **1.** valve (def. 7). **2.** a sealed glass tube containing a partial vacuum or a highly rarefied gas, in which may be observed the effects of a discharge of electricity passed through the tube between electrodes leading into it.

vade mecum (vä′dĭ mā′ko͝om), *Latin.* **1.** anything a person carries about as being of service. **2.** a book for ready reference; a manual or handbook. [L: go with me]

Vaduz (*Ger.* fä do͝ots′), *n.* a town in and the capital of Liechtenstein. 3826 (1964).

vae victis (vē′ vĭk′tĭs), *Latin.* woe to the vanquished.

vagabond (văg′ə bŏnd′), *adj.* **1.** wandering from place to place without settled habitation; nomadic. **2.** leading an irregular or disreputable life. **3.** good-for-nothing; worthless. **4.** of or pertaining to a vagabond or vagrant: *vagabond habits.* **5.** moving about without certain direction. **—***n.* **6.** one who is without a fixed abode and wanders from place to place. **7.** an idle wanderer without visible means of support; a tramp or vagrant. **8.** an idle, worthless fellow; a scamp; a rascal. [ME, t. L: m. s. *vagābundus* strolling about] **—Syn. 7.** See **vagrant.**

vagabondage (văg′ə bŏn′dĭj), *n.* **1.** the state or habits of a vagabond; idle wandering. **2.** the class of vagabonds. Also, **vag′abondism.**

vagarious (və gĕə′rĭ əs), *adj.* **1.** characterized by vagaries; erratic. **2.** wandering; roving; roaming.

vagary (vā′gə rĭ, və gĕə′rĭ), *n.*, *pl.* **-ries. 1.** an extravagant idea or notion. **2.** a wild, capricious, or fantastic action; a freak. [appar. t. L: m. *vagārī* wander]

vagina (və jī′nə), *n.*, *pl.* **-nas, -nae** (-nē). **1.** *Anat.* **a.** the passage leading from the uterus to the vulva in a female mammal. Cf. **oviduct. b.** a sheathlike part or organ. **2.** *Bot.* the sheath formed by the basal part of certain leaves where they embrace the stem. [t. L: sheath]

A, Vaginate culm; B, Vaginate leaf

vaginal (və jī′nəl), *adj.* **1.** *Anat., etc.* pertaining to the vagina of a female mammal. **2.** pertaining to or resembling a sheath.

vaginate (văj′ĭ nĭt, -nāt′), *adj.* furnished with a vagina or sheath; sheathed.

vaginitis (văj′ĭ nī′tĭs), *n. Pathol.* inflammation of the vagina; colpitis. [NL. See VAGINA, -ITIS]

vagrancy (vā′grən sĭ), *n.*, *pl.* **-cies. 1.** the state or condition of being a vagrant. **2.** the conduct of a vagrant. **3.** mental wandering; digression in thought.

vagrant (vā′grənt), *n.* **1.** one who wanders from place to place and has no settled home or work; vagabond; tramp. **2.** *Law.* an idle or disorderly person, as a tramp, beggar, unlicensed pedlar, prostitute, etc., whose habits of life are inconsistent with the good order of society, and who is liable to arrest and imprisonment. **—***adj.* **3.** wandering or roaming from place to place; nomadic. **4.** living in vagabondage; wandering idly without a settled home or work. **5.** of, pertaining to, or characteristic of a vagrant: *a vagrant life.* **6.** (of plants) straggling in growth. **7.** (of things) not fixed or settled; moving hither and thither. [late ME *vag(a)raunt* wandering (person), der. freq. of ME *vague*, v., wander, t. L: m. s. *vagārī*] **—va′grantly,** *adv.* **—va′grantness,** *n.*

—Syn. 2. VAGRANT, VAGABOND describe an idle, disreputable person who lacks a fixed abode. VAGRANT suggests the idea of a tramp, a person with no settled abode or livelihood, an idle and disorderly person: *picked up by police as a vagrant.* VAGABOND especially emphasizes the idea of worthless living, often by trickery, thieving, or other disreputable means: *actors were once classed with rogues and vagabonds.*

vagrom (vā′grəm), *adj. Archaic.* vagrant.

vague (vāg), *adj.*, **vaguer, vaguest. 1.** not definite in statement or meaning; not explicit or precise: *vague promises.* **2.** of an indefinite or indistinct character, as ideas, feelings, etc. **3.** indistinct to the sight or other sense, or perceptible or recognizable only in an indefinite way: *vague forms seen through mist*; *vague murmurs.* **4.** not definitely fixed, determined, or known; uncertain. **5.** (of persons, etc.) indefinite in statement; not clear in thought or understanding. **6.** (of the eyes, expression, etc.) showing absence of clear perception or understanding. [t. L: m. *vagus* wandering] **—vague′ly,** *adv.* **—vague′ness,** *n.*

vagus nerve (vā′gəs), *Anat.* either of two cranial nerves extending through the neck into the thorax and the upper part of the abdomen; a pneumogastric nerve. [*vagus* t. L: wandering]

vail (vāl), *v.t. Archaic.* **1.** to cause or allow to descend or sink; lower. **2.** to take off or doff (a hat, etc.), as in respect or submission. [ME *vale*, aphetic var. of obs. *avale*, t. OF: m. *avaler* descend, der. phrase *à val* down, g. L *ad vallem* to the valley]

vain (vān), *adj.* **1.** without real value or importance; hollow, idle or worthless. **2.** futile; useless; ineffectual. **3.** having an excessive pride in one's own appearance, qualities, gifts, achievements, etc.; conceited. **4.** proceeding from or showing personal vanity: *vain boasts.* **5.** *Archaic.* senseless or foolish. **6. in vain, a.** without effect or avail; to no purpose. **b.** improperly; blasphemously: *to take God's name in vain.* [ME, t. OF, g. L *vānus* empty, idle] **—vain′ly,** *adv.* **—vain′ness,** *n.* **—Syn. 1.** unimportant; trivial. **2.** See **useless. 3.** egotistical, complacent, vainglorious, proud, arrogant, overweening. **—Ant. 2.** effective. **3.** modest.

vainglorious (vān glô′rĭ əs), *adj.* **1.** filled with or given to vainglory. **2.** characterized by, showing, or proceeding from vainglory. **—vainglo′riously,** *adv.* **—vainglo′riousness,** *n.*

vainglory (vān glô′rĭ), *n.* **1.** inordinate elation or pride in one's achievements, abilities, etc. **2.** vain pomp or show. [ME; trans. of ML *vāna glōria*]
vair (vĕə), *n.* a kind of fur much used for lining and trimming garments during the 13th and 14th centuries, and generally assumed to have been the skin of a variety of squirrel with a grey back and white belly. Cf. **miniver.** [ME, t. OF, g. L *varius* particoloured]
vaivode (vā′vōd, vī′-), *n.* voivode.
Valais (văl′ā; *Fr.* vȧ lĕ′), *n.* a canton in SW Switzerland. 177,783 pop. (1960); 2021 sq. mi. *Cap.:* Sion. German, **Wallis.**
valance (văl′əns), *n.* **1.** a short curtain or piece of dependent drapery, as at the edge of a canopy, from the frame of a bed to the floor, etc. **2.** a pelmet. [late ME; ? der. OF *avaler* descend. See VAIL] **—val′anced,** *adj.*
Valdai Hills (*Russ.* vȧl dȧy′), a region of hills and plateaus in the W Soviet Union at the source of the river Volga. Highest point, ab. 1150 ft. See map under **Volgograd.**
Valdemar I (văl′dĭ mä′). See **Waldemar I.**
Val-de-Marne (*Fr.* vȧl də mȧrn′), *n.* a department in N France, SE of Paris. 1,100,000 pop. (est. 1962); 94 sq. mi. *Cap.:* Créteil.
Valdivia (*Sp.* bȧl dē′byȧ), *n.* a seaport in S Chile. 57,262 (est. 1959).
Val-d'Oise (*Fr.* vȧl dwȧz′), *n.* a department in N France, N of Paris. 640,000 (est. 1965); 482 sq. mi. *Cap.:* Pontoise.
vale[1] (vāl), *n.* *Chiefly Poetic.* a valley. [ME, t. OF: m. *val*, g. L *vallis*]
vale[2] (vā′lĭ), *interj.*, *n.* *Latin.* goodbye; farewell.
valediction (văl′ĭ dĭk′shən), *n.* **1.** a bidding farewell; a leave-taking. **2.** an utterance, speech, etc., made at the time of or by way of leave-taking. [f. s. L *valedictus*, pp., bidden goodbye + -ION]
valedictorian (văl′ĭ dĭk tô′rĭ ən), *n.* *U.S.* (in colleges and schools) the student (usually the one who ranks highest academically) who pronounces the valedictory oration at the commencement exercises.
valedictory (văl′ĭ dĭk′tə rĭ), *adj.*, *n.*, *pl.* **-ries.** **—***adj.* **1.** bidding farewell; farewell. **2.** of or pertaining to an occasion of leave-taking. **—***n.* **3.** a valedictory address or oration. **4.** *U.S.* (in colleges and schools) the oration delivered by the valedictorian.
Valence (*Fr.* vȧ läɴs′), *n.* a town in SE France, the capital of Drôme department. 52,532 (1962).
Valencia (və lĕn′shĭ ə; *Sp.* bȧ lĕn′thyȧ), *n.* **1.** a region in E Spain: formerly a Moorish kingdom. 1,429,708 pop. (1960); 9085 sq. mi. **2.** a seaport in E Spain. 583,151 (1965). **3.** a town in N Venezuela. 163,601 (1961).
Valenciennes (văl′ən sĭ ĕn′; *Fr.* vȧ läɴ syĕn′), *n.* **1.** a town in N France, in Nord department. 46,650 (1967). **2.** a fine bobbin-made lace of which the pattern and the net ground are made together, of the same threads. **3.** a machine-made imitation of it. Also, **Valenciennes lace** for 2, 3.
valency (vā′lən sĭ), *n.*, *pl.* **-cies.** *Chem.* **1.** the quality which determines the number of atoms or radicals with which any single atom or radical will unite chemically. **2.** the relative combining capacity of an atom or radical compared with the standard hydrogen atom: *a valency of one* (the capacity to unite with one atom of hydrogen or its equivalent). Also, *Chiefly U.S.*, **valence.** [t. L: m. s. *valentia* strength]
valency band, *Physics.* the range of energies in a semiconductor corresponding to states which can be occupied by the valency electrons which bind the crystal together. Also, *Chiefly U.S.*, **valence band.**
valency bond, *Chem.* a true chemical bond between atoms in a molecule formed by the interaction of valency electrons. Also, *Chiefly U.S.*, **valence bond.**
valency electron, *Chem.* an electron from the outer shell of an atom which can take part in the formation of valency bonds. Also, *Chiefly U.S.*, **valence electron.**
Valens (vā′lĕnz), *n.* **Flavius** (flā′vyəs), A.D. *c.* 328–378, emperor of the Eastern Roman Empire A.D. 364–378.
-valent, a word element meaning having worth or value, used esp. in scientific terminology to refer to valency, as in *quadrivalent*. [t. L: s. *valens*]
valentine (văl′ən tīn′), *n.* **1.** an amatory or sentimental (sometimes satirical or comic) card or the like, or some token or gift, sent by one person to another on St Valentine's Day. **2.** a sweetheart chosen on St Valentine's Day.
Valentine (văl′ən tīn′), *n.* **Saint,** died A.D. *c.* 270, Christian martyr at Rome.
Valentinian (văl′ən tĭn′ĭ ən), *n.* name of three Roman emperors: **Valentinian I** (A.D. 321?–375), **Valentinian II** (A.D. *c.* 371–392), and **Valentinian III** (A.D. 419?–455). Also, **Valentinianus** (văl′ən tĭn′ĭ ā′nəs).
valentinite (văl′ən tĭ nīt′), *n.* a mineral, trioxide of antimony, Sb_2O_3, occurring as white orthorhombic crystals, usually as a result of the decomposition of other antimony ores. [named after Basil *Valentine*, 15th-century German alchemist]
Valentino (văl′ən tē′nō), *n.* **Rudolph** (ro͞o′dŏlf) (*Rodolpho d'Antonguolla*), 1895–1926, U.S. film actor, born in Italy.
Valera (və lĕə′rə, -lĭə′rə), *n.* **Eamon De** (ā′mən). See **De Valera.**
Valera y Alcalá Galiano (*Sp.* bȧ lĕ′rȧ ē ȧl kȧ lȧ′ gȧ lyȧ′nō), **Juan** (*Sp.* KHwȧn), 1824–1905, Spanish novelist, critic, and statesman.
valerian (və lĭə′rĭ ən), *n.* **1.** any of the perennial herbs constituting the genus *Valeriana*, as *V. officinalis*, a plant with white or pink flowers and a medicinal root. **2.** a drug consisting of or made from the root, used as a nerve sedative and antispasmodic. [ME, t. ML: s. *valeriāna*, fem., der. *Valerius*, personal name]
Valerian (və lĭə′rĭ ən), *n.* (*Publius Licinius Valerianus*), died after A.D. 260, Roman emperor A.D. 253–260.
valerianaceous (və lĭə′rĭ ə nā′shəs), *adj.* belonging to the *Valerianaceae*, a family of plants containing valerian, spikenard, etc. [f. s. NL *Valeriānāceae* (see VALERIAN) + -OUS]
valeric (və lĕ′rĭk, -lĭə′rĭk), *adj.* pertaining to or derived from valerian. Also, **valerianic** (və lĭə′rĭ ăn′ĭk). [f. VALER(IAN) + -IC]
valeric acid, *Chem.* any of several isomeric organic acids, C_4H_9COOH, the common one being a liquid of pungent smell obtained from valerian roots.
Valéry (*Fr.* vȧ lĕ rē′), *n.* **Paul** (*Fr.* pŏl), 1871–1945, French poet and philosopher.
valet (văl′ĭt, văl′ā; *Fr.* vȧ lĕ′), *n.*, *v.*, **-leted, -leting.** **—***n.* **1.** a manservant who is his employer's personal attendant, caring for his clothing, etc.; manservant. **2.** one who performs similar services for patrons of a hotel, etc. **3.** any of various contrivances, as a rack or stand, for holding coats, hats, etc. **—***v.t.*, *v.i.* **4.** to attend or act as valet. [t. F, var. of MF *vaslet*. See VARLET, VASSAL] **—val′etless,** *adj.*
valeta (və lē′tə), *n.* veleta.
valet de chambre (*Fr.* vȧ lĕ də shäɴ′br), *pl.* **valets de chambre** (*Fr.* vȧ lĕ də shäɴ′br). *French.* valet (def. 1).
valetudinarian (văl′ĭ tyo͞o′dĭ nĕə′rĭ ən), *n.* **1.** an invalid. **2.** one who is constantly or excessively concerned about the state of his health. **—***adj.* **3.** in poor health; sickly; invalid. **4.** constantly or excessively concerned about the state of one's health. **5.** characterized by or pertaining to invalidism: *valetudinarian habits.* [f. s. L *valētūdinārius* in poor health + -AN]
valetudinarianism (văl′ĭ tyo͞o′dĭ nĕə′rĭ ə nĭz′əm), *n.* valetudinarian condition or habits.
valetudinary (văl′ĭ tyo͞o′dĭ nə rĭ), *n.*, *pl.* **-ries,** *adj.* valetudinarian.
valgus (văl′gəs), *Pathol.* **—***n.* **1.** an abnormal position of part of the bone structure of the human body. **—***adj.* **2.** of or in such a position. [t. L: bow-legged]
Valhalla (văl hăl′ə), *n.* *Scand. Myth.* the hall of immortality into which the souls of heroes slain in battle are received. Also, **Valhall** (văl hăl′), **Walhalla.** [t. NL, t. Icel.: m. *valhöll* hall of the slain]
valiance (văl′yəns), *n.* the quality of being valiant; valour; bravery; courage. Also, **valiancy.** [var. of late ME *vailance*, t. AF, var. of OF *vaillance*, der. *vaillant* VALIANT]
valiant (văl′yənt), *adj.* **1.** brave, courageous, or stout-hearted, as persons. **2.** marked by or showing bravery or valour, as deeds, attempts, etc. [ME, t. OF: m. *vaillant*, der. *valeir* be strong, g. L *valēre*] **—val′iantly,** *adv.* **—val′iantness,** *n.*
valid (văl′ĭd), *adj.* **1.** sound, just, or well-founded: *a valid reason, a valid objection.* **2.** having force, weight, or cogency; authoritative. **3.** legally sound, effective, or binding; having legal force; sustainable in law. **4.** *Logic.* denoting arguments in which the premises imply the conclusion (opposed to *invalid*). **5.** *Archaic.* robust or well. [t. L: s. *validus* strong] **—val′idly,** *adv.* **—val′idness,** *n.*
validate (văl′ĭ dāt′), *v.t.*, **-dated, -dating.** **1.** to make valid; confirm; corroborate; substantiate. **2.** to give legal force to; legalize. **—val′ida′tion,** *n.*
validity (və lĭd′ĭ tĭ), *n.*, *pl.* **-ties.** **1.** the state or quality of being valid. **2.** legal soundness or force.
valine (vā′lēn, văl′ēn), *n.* *Biochem.* a white, crystalline amino acid $(CH_3)_2CH.CH(NH_2)COOH$, obtained by the hydrolysis of many proteins.
valise (və lēz′), *n.* a traveller's case for holding clothes, toilet articles, etc., esp. a small one for carrying by hand; a travelling bag. [t. F, t. It.: m. *valigia*; orig. uncert.]
Valkyrie (văl kĭə′rĭ), *n.* *Scand. Myth.* one of the handmaids of Odin who ride through the air to battle and choose the heroes who are to be slain and taken to Valhalla.

Also, **Valkyr** (vălʹkĭə), **Walkyrie.** [t. Icel.: m. *valkyrja* chooser of the slain] —**Valkyrʹian,** *adj.*

Valladolid (*Sp.* bä lyä dô lĕdʹ), *n.* a town in N Spain: Columbus died here 1506. 172,239 (1965).

vallation (və lāʹshən), *n. Fort.* **1.** a rampart or entrenchment. **2.** the process or technique of constructing ramparts. [t. LL: s. *vallātio*, der. L *vallum* rampart]

vallecula (və lĕkʹyo͝o lə), *n.*, *pl.* **-lae** (-lēʹ). *Anat.*, *Bot.* a furrow or depression. [t. LL, dim. of L *valles* valley] —**vallecʹular,** *adj.*

valleculate (və lĕkʹyo͝o lātʹ), *adj.* having a vallecula or valleculae.

Valle d'Aosta (*It.* välʹlĕ dä ôsʹtä), a region in NW Italy, on the Swiss border. 99,754 pop. (1961); 1260 sq. mi.

Valle Inclán (*Sp.* bäʹlyĕ ēn klänʹ), **Ramón del** (*Sp.* rä mônʹ dĕl), 1870–1936, Spanish novelist and poet.

Vallejo (və lāʹō), *n.* a town in the U.S., in W California, on San Pablo Bay, NE of San Francisco. 60,877 (1960).

Valletta (və lĕtʹə), *n.* a seaport in and the capital of Malta, on the NE coast. 17,725 (est. 1963).

valley (vălʹĭ), *n.*, *pl.* **-leys. 1.** an elongated depression, usually with an outlet, between uplands, hills, or mountains, esp. one following the course of a stream. **2.** an extensive, more or less flat, and relatively low region drained by a great river system. **3.** any hollow or structure likened to a valley. **4.** *Archit.* a depression or angle formed by the meeting of two inclined sides of a roof. **5.** the lower phase of a horizontal wave motion. [ME *valey*, t. OF: m. *valee*, der. *val*, g. L *vallis*] —**valʹley-likeʹ,** *adj.*

Valley of Ten Thousand Smokes, a volcanic area in SW Alaska, in the Katmai National Park.

Vallombrosa (*It.* väl lôm brôʹsä), *n.* a resort in central Italy, near Florence: famous abbey.

vallum (vălʹəm), *n.* a defensive wall of earth or stone, as those erected by the Romans in N England and Scotland. [t. L]

Valois (*Fr.* vä lwäʹ), *n.* **1.** a member of a ruling family of France which reigned from 1328 to 1589. **2.** a duchy of the Ile de France in the Middle Ages.

Valona (və lōʹnə; *It.* vä lôʹnä), *n.* a seaport in SW Albania, on **Valona Bay,** an inlet of the Adriatic. 45,350 (est. 1964). Also, **Avlona.** Albanian, **Vlónë.**

valonia (və lōʹnĭ ə), *n.* acorn cups of the **valonia oak,** *Quercus aegilops*, used in tanning, dyeing, and making ink. [t. It.: m. *vallonia*, t. mod. Gk: m. *balánia* acorns]

valor (vălʹə), *n. U.S.* valour.

valorize (vălʹə rīzʹ), *v.t.*, **-rized, -rizing.** *Chiefly U.S.* **1.** to assign a value to. **2.** (of a government) to fix the value or price of (a commercial commodity) and provide for maintaining it against a decline (as to a price below the cost of production), by purchase of the commodity at the fixed price or by other means (esp. with reference to the action of Brazil in fixing the price of coffee). Also, **valorise.** [f. obs. *valor* worth (see VALOUR) + -IZE] —**valʹorizaʹtion,** *n.*

valorous (vălʹə rəs), *adj.* **1.** having or displaying valour; valiant or brave, as persons. **2.** characterized by valour, as actions, etc. [late ME, t. ML: m. s. *valorōsus*] —**valʹorously,** *adv.* —**valʹorousness,** *n.*

valour (vălʹə), *n.* boldness or firmness in braving danger; bravery or heroic courage, esp. in battle. Also, *U.S.*, **valor.** [ME, t. OF, t. LL: m. *valor* (der. L *valēre* be strong, be worth)]

Valparaiso (vălʹpə rīʹzō), *n.* a seaport in central Chile. 259,241 (est. 1960). Spanish, **Valparaíso** (*Sp.* bäl pä rä ēʹsô).

valse (*Fr.* väls), *n. French.* waltz.

valuable (vălʹyo͝o ə bl), *adj.* **1.** of monetary worth. **2.** representing a large market value: *valuable paintings.* **3.** of considerable use, service, or importance: *valuable information, valuable aid.* **4.** capable of having the value estimated. —*n.* **5.** (*usually pl.*) a valuable article, as of personal property or of merchandise, esp. one of comparatively small size. —**valʹuableness,** *n.* —**valʹuably,** *adv.*

—**Syn. 2.** costly, expensive, rare. VALUABLE, PRECIOUS refer to that which has pecuniary or other value. VALUABLE applies to whatever has value, but esp. to what has considerable value either in money or because of its usefulness, rarity, etc: *a valuable watch.* That which is PRECIOUS has a very high intrinsic value, or is very dear for its own sake, associations, or the like: *a precious jewel, friendship.* —**Ant. 1.** worthless.

valuation (vălʹyo͝o āʹshən), *n.* **1.** an estimating or fixing of the value of a thing. **2.** a value estimated or fixed; estimated worth. —**valʹuaʹtional,** *adj.*

valuator (vălʹyo͝o āʹtə), *n.* an appraiser.

value (vălʹyo͝o), *n.*, *v.*, **-ued, -uing.** —*n.* **1.** that property of a thing because of which it is esteemed, desirable, or useful, or the degree of this property possessed; worth, merit, or importance: *the value of education.* **2.** material or monetary worth, as in traffic or sale: *even the waste has value.* **3.** the worth of a thing as measured by the amount of other things for which it can be exchanged, or as estimated in terms of a medium of exchange. **4.** equivalent worth or equivalent return: *for value received.* **5.** estimated or assigned worth; valuation. **6.** force, import, or significance: *the value of a word or phrase.* **7.** *Maths.* the magnitude of any quantity, measurement, or function. **8.** (*pl.*) *Sociol.* the things of social life (ideals, customs, institutions, etc.) towards which the people of the group have an affective regard. These values may be positive, as cleanliness, freedom, education, etc., or negative, as cruelty, crime, or blasphemy. **9.** *Ethics.* any object or quality desirable as a means or as an end in itself. **10.** *Painting.* degree of lightness or darkness in a colour. **11.** *Music.* the relative length or duration of a note. **12.** *Phonet.* **a.** quality. **b.** the phonetic equivalent of a letter: *one value of the letter 'a' is the vowel sound in 'hat', 'sang', etc.* —*v.t.* **13.** to estimate the value of; rate at a certain value or price; appraise. **14.** to consider with respect to worth, excellence, usefulness, or importance. **15.** to regard or esteem highly.
[ME, t. OF, pp. of *valeir* be worth, g. L *valēre*]

—**Syn. 1.** VALUE, WORTH imply intrinsic excellence or desirability. VALUE is that quality of anything which renders it desirable or useful: *the value of sunlight or good books.* WORTH implies esp. spiritual qualities of mind and character, or moral excellence: *few knew his true worth.* **15.** See **appreciate.**

valued (vălʹyo͞od), *adj.* **1.** highly regarded or esteemed. **2.** estimated or appraised. **3.** having the value specified.

valued policy, *Insurance.* a form of insurance policy in which the value of the object insured is specified. Cf. **open policy.**

valueless (vălʹyo͞o lĭs), *adj.* without value; worthless. —**valʹuelessness,** *n.*

valuer (vălʹyo͞o ə), *n.* **1.** one who estimates or assesses values. **2.** one who values highly.

valuta (və lo͞oʹtə), *n. Banking.* the value of a currency in terms of another currency. [t. It.: value]

valvate (vălʹvāt), *adj.* **1.** furnished with or opening by a valve or valves. **2.** serving as or resembling a valve. **3.** *Bot.* **a.** opening by valves, as certain capsules and anthers. **b.** meeting without overlapping, as the parts of certain buds. **c.** composed of or characterized by such parts. [t. L: m. s. *valvātus* having folding doors]

valve (vălv), *n.*, *v.*, **valved, valving.** —*n.* **1.** any device for closing or modifying the passage through a pipe, outlet, inlet, or the like, in order to control the flow of liquids, gases, etc. **2.** a hinged lid or other movable part in such a device, which closes or modifies the passage. **3.** *Anat.* a membranous fold or other structure which controls the flow of a fluid, as one which permits blood to flow in one direction only. **4.** (in musical wind instruments of the trumpet class) a device for changing the length of the air column to alter the pitch of a note. **5.** *Zool.* **a.** one of the two or more separable pieces composing certain shells. **b.** either half of the silicified shell of a diatom. **6.** *Bot.* **a.** one of the segments into which a capsule dehisces. See diag. under **septicidal. b.** a flap or lidlike part of certain anthers. **7.** *Electronics.* an electrical device consisting of two or more electrodes in an evacuated or gas-filled cylinder of glass or metal, which can be used for controlling a flow of electricity. **8.** *Archaic.* one of the halves or leaves of a double or folding door. —*v.t.* **9.** to provide with a means of control of fluid flow, as gas from a balloon, by inserting a valve. [ME, t. L: m. *valva* leaf of a door (pl. folding doors)] —**valveʹless,** *adj.* —**valveʹlikeʹ,** *adj.*

Globe valve
A, Wheel; B, Spindle; C, Stuffing nut; D, Disc; E, Valve seat; F, Pipe end

valve base, *Electronics.* **1.** the part of a radio valve envelope from which the connecting pins to the various electrodes project, enabling the valve to be fitted into a valve socket and thus connected to the rest of the circuit. **2.** the specific configuration of these connecting pins.

valve gear, the mechanism for opening and closing the valves in an internal-combustion engine.

valve house, a house or structure at the gate of a dam, reservoir, etc., with apparatus for regulating the flow of water; gatehouse.

valvelet (vălvʹlĭt), *n.* a small valve; a valvule.

valve socket, *Electronics.* a plastic or ceramic connector, attached to the chassis of an electronic device, into which the pins of the valve base connect, enabling the valve to be connected to the rest of the circuit. Also, **valve-holder.**

valve spring, a helical spring used to close a poppet valve, esp. in an internal-combustion engine.

valvotomy (văl vŏt′ə mĭ), *n., pl.* **-mies.** valvulotomy.

valvular (văl′vyo͝o lə), *adj.* **1.** having the form of a valve. **2.** furnished with or operating by a valve or valves. **3.** of a valve or valves, esp. of the heart.

valvule (văl′vyo͞ol), *n.* a small valve or valvelike part. [t. L: m. *valvula*, dim. of *valva*. See VALVE]

valvulitis (văl′vyo͝o lī′tĭs), *n. Pathol.* inflammation of the cardiac-valve leaflets, caused by an acute infectious process, usually rheumatic fever or syphilis. [f. s. NL *valvula* valvule + -ITIS]

valvulotomy (văl′vyo͝o lŏt′ə mĭ), *n., pl.* **-mies.** *Surg.* the opening, slitting, or fracturing of a heart valve along natural lines of cleavage. Also, **valvotomy.** [NL, f. VALVUL(E) + -O- + -TOMY]

vambrace (văm′brās′), *n.* a piece of armour for the forearm or the whole arm. [ME, t. AF: m. (*a*) *vantbras*, f. *avant-* fore- + *bras* arm. Cf. BRACE]

vamoose (və mo͞os′), *v.*, **-moosed, -moosing.** *U.S. Slang.* —*v.i.* **1.** to make off; decamp; depart quickly. —*v.t.* **2.** to decamp from; quit hurriedly. Also, **vamose** (və mōs′). [t. Sp.: m. *vamos* let us go]

vamp[1] (vămp), *n.* **1.** the front part of the upper of a shoe or boot. **2.** anything patched up or pieced together. **3.** *Music.* an accompaniment, usually improvised, consisting of a succession of simple chords. —*v.t.* **4.** to furnish with a vamp, esp. to repair with a new vamp, as a shoe or boot. **5.** to patch up or repair; renovate (often fol. by *up*). **6.** to give an appearance of newness to. **7.** *Music.* to improvise (an accompaniment or the like). —*v.i.* **8.** *Music.* to improvise an accompaniment, tune, etc. [ME *vampe*, t. OF: alter. of *avanpie* forepart of the foot, f. *avant* before (g. L *ab ante* from in front) + *pie* foot, g. s. L *pēs*] —**vamp′er,** *n.*

vamp[2] (vămp), *Slang.* —*n.* **1.** a woman who uses her charms to seduce and exploit men. —*v.i.* **2.** to act as a vamp. —*v.t.* **3.** to use one's feminine charms or arts upon (a man). [short for VAMPIRE] —**vamp′er,** *n.*

vampire (văm′pī′ə), *n.* **1.** a preternatural being, in the common belief a reanimated corpse of a person improperly buried, supposed to suck blood of sleeping persons at night. **2.** one who preys ruthlessly on others; an extortionist. **3.** Also, **vampire bat. a.** any of various South and Central American bats including *Desmodus rotundus*, *Diphylla ecaudata* and *Diaemus youngi*, the **true vampires,** which feed on the blood of animals including man. **b.** any large South American bat of the genera *Phyllostomus* and *Vampyrus*, erroneously reputed to suck blood. **c.** any of the false vampires of Asia and Australia. See **false vampire. 4.** *Theat.* a trapdoor on a stage. [t. F, t. G: m. *Vampir*, ? ult. t. Turk.: m. *uber* witch] —**vampiric** (văm pĭ′rĭk), **vampirish** (văm′pī′ə rĭsh), *adj.*

vampirism (văm′pī ə rĭz′əm), *n.* **1.** the belief in the existence of preternatural vampires. **2.** acts or practices of vampires. **3.** the unscrupulous exploitation of others.

vamplate (văm′plāt′), *n.* a metal plate mounted on a lance serving as a guard for the hand. [ME *vaunplate*, t. AF: f. *avant-* fore- + *plate* PLATE[1]]

van[1] (văn), *n.* **1.** (formerly) the foremost division or the front part of an army, a fleet, or any body of individuals advancing, or in order for advancing. **2.** the forefront in any movement, course of progress, or the like. **3.** those who are in the forefront of a movement or the like. [short for VANGUARD]

van[2] (văn), *n.* **1.** a covered vehicle, usually large in size, for moving furniture, goods, etc. **2.** a closed railway wagon. [short for CARAVAN]

van[3] (văn; *Du.* vŏn), *prep.* (*often cap.*) from; of (used in Dutch in personal names, originally to indicate place of origin). [t. D]

van[4] (văn), *n. Poetic.* a wing. [var. of FAN[1]]

van[5] (văn), *n. Tennis.* advantage.

Van (*Turk.* văn), *n.* **1. Lake,** a salt lake in E Turkey. ab. 1450 sq. mi. **2.** a town on this lake. 42,881 (1960).

vanad-, a word element indicating the presence of vanadium, as in *vanadate.*

vanadate (văn′ə dāt′), *n. Chem.* a salt of a vanadic acid. Also, **vanadiate** (və nā′dĭ āt′).

vanadic (və năd′ĭk, -nā′dĭk), *adj. Chem.* of or containing vanadium, esp. in the trivalent or pentavalent state.

vanadic acid, any of certain acids containing vanadium, esp. one with the formula H_3VO_4.

vanadinite (və năd′ĭ nīt′), *n.* a mineral, lead chlorovanadate, $Pb_5(VO_4)_3Cl$, occurring in yellow, brown, or greenish crystals: an ore of lead and vanadium.

vanadium (və nā′dyəm), *n. Chem.* a rare element occurring in certain minerals, and obtained as a light grey powder with a silvery lustre: used as an ingredient of steel to toughen it and increase shock resistance. *Symbol:* V; *at. wt:* 50·942; *at. no.:* 23; *sp. gr.:* 5·96. [f. Icel. *Vanad(is)* epithet of goddess FREYA + -IUM; so called because discovered in Sweden]

vanadium steel, a special steel containing approximately 0·10–0·20 per cent vanadium to increase elasticity, etc.

vanadous (văn′ə dəs), *adj. Chem.* containing divalent or trivalent vanadium. Also, **vanadious** (və nā′dyəs).

Van Allen (văn ăl′ən), **James Alfred,** born 1914, U.S. physicist.

Van Allen belt, *Physics.* either of two belts of charged particles trapped within the earth's magnetic field; the inner belt lies above 1500 to 3500 mi. above the earth's surface and the outer belt between 8000 and 12,000 mi. above the earth. [named after J. A. VAN ALLEN]

Vanbrugh (văn′brə), *n.* **John,** 1664–1726, English dramatist and architect.

Van Buren (văn byo͞oə′rən), **Martin,** 1782–1862, 8th president of the U.S., 1837–41.

Vancouver Island

Vancouver (văn ko͞o′və), *n.* **1.** a large island in SW Canada, off the SW coast of British Columbia. 333,951 pop. (1966); 12,408 sq. mi. **2.** a seaport in SW British Columbia, on Georgia Strait opposite SE Vancouver Island. 384,522 (1961). **3. Mount,** a mountain in Canada, in SW Yukon, near the Alaskan border. 15,700 ft.

Vandal (văn′dl), *n.* **1.** a member of a Germanic people which in the 5th century A.D. ravaged Gaul and Spain, settled in Africa, and in 455 sacked Rome. **2.** (*l.c.*) one who wilfully or ignorantly destroys or damages anything, as property or works of art. —*adj.* **3.** of or pertaining to the Vandals. **4.** (*often l.c.*) imbued with or characterized by vandalism. [t. LL: s. *Vandalus*, Latinization of native tribal name] —**Vandalic** (văn dăl′ĭk), *adj.*

vandalism (văn′də lĭz′əm), *n.* **1.** wanton or malicious destruction or damage of property. **2.** wilful or ignorant destruction of artistic or literary treasures. **3.** conduct or spirit characteristic of the Vandals.

vandalize (văn′də līz′), *v.t.*, **-lized, -lizing.** to destroy or damage by vandalism. Also, **vandalise.**

Van de Graaff generator (văn′də grăf′), *Physics.* an electrostatic generator in which a high potential is developed in a metal conductor by accumulating the charge from a high-speed belt; often used as a particle accelerator. [named after R. J. *Van de Graaff*, born 1901, U.S. physicist]

Vanderbilt (văn′də bĭlt), *n.* **Cornelius,** 1794–1877, U.S. capitalist.

Van der Hum (văn′də hŭm′), a South African liqueur made from naartjies and aromatic herbs.

Van der Waals' equation (văn′də wălz′; *Du.* vŏn dər wáls′), *Chem.* a modification of the gas laws taking into account Van der Waals' forces and the finite size of the atoms or molecules. [named after J. D. *Van der Waals*, 1837–1923, Dutch physicist]

Van der Waals' forces, *Chem.* weak attractive forces between atoms or molecules arising as a result of electrons in neighbouring atoms or molecules moving in sympathy with each other. [see VAN DER WAALS' EQUATION]

Van Diemen's Land (văn dē′mənz), former name of **Tasmania.**

Van Dyck (văn dīk′), **Sir Anthony,** 1599–1641, Flemish painter living in England. Also, **Vandyke.**

Vandyke (văn′dīk), *n., v.*, **-dyked, -dyking.** —*n.* **1.** (*sometimes l.c.*) a Vandyke beard. **2.** (*sometimes l.c.*) a Vandyke collar. —*v.t.* **3.** to cut or shape (material) with deep points.

Vandyke beard, a short, pointed beard.

Vandyke brown, any of several dark brown pigments consisting of iron oxide admixed with lampblack or similar materials.

Vandyke collar, a wide collar with deeply pointed edge.

vane (vān), *n.* **1.** a flat piece of metal, or some other device fixed upon a spire or other elevated object in such a way as to move with the wind and indicate its direction; a weathercock. **2.** a similar piece, or sail, in the wheel of a windmill, to be moved by the air. **3.** any plate, blade, or the like, attached to an axis, and moved by or in air or a liquid: *a vane of a screw propeller.* **4.** *Ornith.* the web of a feather. **5.** *Navig., Survey.* a sight on a quadrant or other surveying instrument. [ME; OE *fana* flag, c. G *Fahne*] —**vaned,** *adj.* —**vane′less,** *adj.*

Vane (vān), *n.* **Sir Henry** (*Sir Harry Vane*), 1613–62, English statesman and author.

Vänern (*Sw.* vĕ′nərn), *n.* a lake in SW Sweden. ab. 2150 sq. mi. Also, **Väner** (*Sw.* vĕ′nər), **Vener.**

Van Eyck (văn īk′). See **Eyck.**

vang (văng), *n. Naut.* a rope extending from the peak of a gaff to the ship's rail, or to a mast, and used to steady the gaff. [t. D: catch]

Van Gogh (văn gŏKH′; *Du.* vŏn KHÔKH′), **Vincent** (*Du.* vĭn sĕnt′), 1853–90, Dutch painter.

vanguard (văn′gäd′), *n.* **1.** the foremost division or the front part of an army; the van. **2.** the leading position in any field. **3.** the leaders of any intellectual or political movement. [late ME *vandgard*, t. OF: aphetic m. *avan(t)-garde*, f. *avant* before + *garde* guard]

Vanier (văn′ĭ ā′; *Fr.* vȧ nyĕ′), *n.* **Georges Philias** (jôj′ fĭl′ĭ əs; *Fr.* zhôrzh fē lē ȧs′), 1888–1967, Canadian statesman and diplomat, governor-general 1959–67.

vanilla (və nĭl′ə), *n.* **1.** any of the tropical climbing orchids constituting the genus *Vanilla*, esp. *V. planifolia*, whose podlike fruit (**vanilla bean**) yields an extract used in flavouring food, in perfumery, etc. **2.** the fruit or bean. **3.** the extract. [t. NL, t. Sp.: m. *vainilla* little pod, der. *vaina* sheath, g. L *vāgina*]

A B

Vanilla, *Vanilla planifolia*
A, Flowering branch; B, Fruit

vanillic (və nĭl′ĭk), *adj.* pertaining to, derived from, or resembling vanilla or vanillin.

vanillin (văn′ĭ lĭn, və nĭl′ĭn), *n.* a white crystalline compound, $C_8H_8O_3$, the active principle of vanilla, now prepared artificially and used as a flavouring agent and a substitute for vanilla. Also, **vanilline** (văn′ĭ lĭn, -lēn′, və nĭl′ĭn, -ēn).

Vanir (vä′nĭə), *n.pl. Scand. Myth.* a race of gods originally at war with the Aesir, but later received into Asgard. Frey and Freya belonged to the Vanir. [t. Icel.]

vanish (văn′ĭsh), *v.i.* **1.** to disappear from sight, or become invisible, esp. quickly. **2.** to disappear by ceasing to exist; come to an end; cease. **3.** *Maths.* (of a number or quantity) to become zero. **—***n.* **4.** *Phonet.* the last part of a vowel sound when it differs noticeably in quality from the main sound. [ME *vanisshen*, t. OF: aphetic m. *evaniss-*, s. *evanir*. See EVANESCE] **—van′isher,** *n.* **—Syn. 1.** See **disappear.**

vanishing cream, a white foundation cream which becomes colourless on application.

vanishing point, 1. a point of disappearance. **2.** (in perspective) that point towards which receding parallel lines appear to converge.

vanity (văn′ĭ tĭ), *n., pl.* **-ties. 1.** the quality of being personally vain; excessive pride in one's own appearance, qualities, gifts, achievements, etc. **2.** an instance or display of this quality or feeling. **3.** something about which one is vain. **4.** vain or worthless character; want of real value; hollowness or worthlessness. **5.** something vain or worthless. [ME *vanite*, t. OF, t. L: m. s. *vānitas* emptiness] **—Syn. 1.** conceit, self-esteem, egotism. See **pride. 4.** emptiness, unreality, sham, folly.

vanity case, a small case or bag for holding cosmetics, toilet articles, etc., carried by a woman. Also, **vanity box, vanity bag.**

Vanity Fair, 1. (*often l.c.*) any place or group, as the world, a great city, fashionable society, etc., regarded as given over to vain pleasure or empty show. **2.** (in Bunyan's *Pilgrim's Progress*) a fair which goes on perpetually in the town of Vanity. It symbolizes worldly ostentation and frivolity.

Van Loon (văn lōn′), **Hendrik Willem** (hĕn′drĭk vĭl′əm), 1882–1944, U.S. author, born in the Netherlands.

Vannes (*Fr.* vȧn), *n.* a town in NW France, the capital of Morbihan department. 40,700 (est. 1967).

vanquish (văng′kwĭsh), *v.t.* **1.** to conquer or defeat in battle or conflict; reduce to subjection by superior force. **2.** to defeat in any contest. **3.** to overcome or overpower. [ME *vencusche*, t. OF: m. *vencus*, pp. of *veintre*, g. L *vincere*] **—van′quishable,** *adj.* **—van′quisher,** *n.*

Vansittart (văn sĭt′ət), *n.* **Robert Gilbert, 1st Baron,** 1881–1957, British statesman and diplomat.

vantage (vän′tĭj), *n.* **1.** position or condition affording superiority, as for action. **2.** opportunity likely to give superiority. **3.** *Tennis.* advantage. [ME, aphetic m. *avantage* ADVANTAGE]

vantage ground, a position which gives one an advantage, as for action or defence; favourable position.

vantage point, a position or place affording an advantageous or clear view or perspective.

Van't Hoff's law (văn tŏfs′), *Chem.* the law which states that the osmotic pressure of a dilute solution is equal to the pressure which the solute would exert in the gaseous state, if it occupied a volume equal to the volume of the solution, at the same temperature. [named after J. H. *Van't Hoff*, 1852–1911, Dutch chemist]

Vanua Levu (vä nōō′ə lĕv′ōō), an island in the S Pacific, one of the Fiji Islands. ab. 40,000 pop. (est. 1967); 2137 sq. mi.

vanward (văn′wəd), *adj.* towards or in the van or front (opposed to *rearward*).

Vanzetti (văn zĕt′ĭ; *It.* vȧn dzĕt′tē), *n.* **Bartolomeo** (*It.* bȧr tȯ lȯ mĕ′ȯ), 1888–1927, Italian political radical, in the U.S. See **Sacco, Nikola.**

vapid (văp′ĭd), *adj.* **1.** having lost life, sharpness, or flavour; insipid; flat. **2.** without animation or spirit; dull, uninteresting or tedious, as talk, writings, persons, etc. [t. L: s. *vapidus*] **—vapid′ity, vap′idness,** *n.* **—vap′idly,** *adv.* **—Ant. 1.** pungent. **2.** stimulating.

vapor (vā′pə), *n., v.t., v.i. U.S.* vapour. **—va′porabil′ity,** *n.* **—va′porable,** *adj.* **—va′porer,** *n.* **—va′porless,** *adj.* **—va′por-like′,** *adj.*

vaporescence (vā′pə rĕs′əns), *n.* a changing into vapour. [d. VAPO(U)R + -ESCENCE] **—va′pores′cent,** *adj.*

vaporific (vā′pə rĭf′ĭk), *adj.* **1.** producing vapour, or connected with the production of vapour; tending towards vapour. **2.** pertaining to or of the nature of vapour. [t. NL: s. *vaporificus*]

vaporimeter (vā′pə rĭm′ĭ tə), *n.* an instrument for measuring vapour pressure or volume.

vaporing (vā′pə rĭng), *adj., n. U.S.* vapouring. **—va′poringly,** *adv.*

vaporish (vā′pə rĭsh), *adj. U.S.* vapourish. **—va′porishness,** *n.*

vaporization (vā′pə rī zā′shən), *n.* **1.** the process by which a liquid is converted into a vapour. **2.** the rapid change of water into steam, esp. in a boiler. **3.** *Med.* a vapour therapy. Also, **vaporisation.**

vaporize (vā′pə rīz′), *v.,* **-rized, -rizing. —***v.t.* **1.** to cause to pass into the gaseous state. **—***v.i.* **2.** to become converted into vapour. Also, **vaporise. —va′poriz′able,** *adj.*

vaporizer (vā′pə rī′zə), *n.* **1.** one who or that which vaporizes. **2.** a form of atomizer. Also, **vaporiser.**

vaporous (vā′pə rəs), *adj.* **1.** full of or abounding in vapour; foggy or misty. **2.** dimmed or obscured with vapour. **3.** of the form of vapour; unsubstantial. **4.** given to fanciful or foolish ideas or discourse. **—va′porously,** *adv.* **—va′porousness, vaporosity** (vā′pə rŏs′ĭ tĭ), *n.*

vapory (vā′pə rĭ), *adj. U.S.* vapoury.

vapour (vā′pə), *n.* **1.** a visible exhalation, as fog, mist, condensed steam, smoke, etc. **2.** a substance in the gaseous state (sometimes restricted to substances in the gaseous state when below their critical points); a gas. **3.** matter converted into vapour for technical or medicinal uses, etc. **4.** a combination of vaporized matter and air. **5.** gaseous particles of drugs that can be inhaled as a therapeutic agent. **6.** an invisible exhalation, as of moisture, noxious gases, etc. **7.** *Archaic.* something unsubstantial or transitory. **8.** (*pl.*) *Archaic.* hypochondria, low spirits. **9.** (*pl.*) *Obs.* injurious exhalations formerly supposed to be produced within the body, esp. the stomach. **—***v.t.* **10.** to cause to rise or pass off in, or as in, vapour. **11.** *Archaic.* to affect with vapours. **—***v.i.* **12.** to rise or pass off in the form of vapour. **13.** to emit vapour or exhalations. **14.** to talk or act grandiloquently or boastfully; bluster. Also, *U.S.*, **vapor.** [ME, t. AF, t. L: m. *vapor* steam] **—va′pourabil′ity,** *n.* **—va′pourable,** *adj.* **—va′pourer,** *n.* **—va′pourless,** *adj.* **—va′pour-like′,** *adj.*

vapour concentration, *Meteorol.* humidity (def. 2c).

vapour density, *Physics.* **1.** the mass which a unit volume of a vapour would possess if it could exist as an ideal gas at 0°C at a pressure of 760 mm. of mercury. **2.** the ratio of the mass of a given volume of a gas to the mass of an equal volume of hydrogen under the same conditions of temperature and pressure.

vapouring (vā′pə rĭng), *adj.* **1.** that vapours. **2.** foolishly boastful. **—***n.* **3.** the act of bragging or blustering; windy talk. Also, *U.S.*, **vaporing. —va′pouringly,** *adv.*

vapourish (vā′pə rĭsh), *adj.* **1.** of the nature of vapour. **2.** abounding in vapour. **3.** *Archaic.* inclined to or affected by the vapours or low spirits; depressed. Also, *U.S.*, **vaporish. —va′pourishness,** *n.*

vapour pressure, *Physics.* **1.** the pressure exerted by the molecules of a liquid which escape from the surface of that liquid as a vapour. **2.** the maximum pressure that this vapour can exert, at a given temperature, in a system consisting of a liquid (or solid) in equilibrium with its vapour; saturated vapour pressure.

Vapours (vā′pəz), *n.* **Sea of,** a plain, *Mare Vaporum*, in the first quadrant of the face of the moon.

vapour trail, a trail of condensed vapour left by high-flying aeroplanes, rockets, etc.

vapoury (vā′pə rĭ), *adj.* **1.** vaporous. **2.** vapourish. Also, *U.S.*, **vapory.**

vaquero (vă kĕə′rō), *n., pl.* **-ros** (-rōz). *South-western U.S.* a herdsman or cowboy. [t. Sp., der. *vaca* cow, g. L *vacca*]
Var (*Fr.* vȧr), *n.* a department in SE France. 469,557 pop. (1962); 2333 sq. mi. *Cap.*: Draguignan.
var., **1.** variant. **2.** variation. **3.** variety. **4.** various.
vara (vä′rə), *n.* **1.** a unit of length in Spanish- and Portuguese-speaking countries, varying from about 32 in. to about 43 in. **2.** the square vara, used as a unit of area. [t. Sp., Pg.: rod, pole, g. L *vāra* forked pole]
varactor (vĕə′răk′tə), *n. Electronics.* a semiconductor device with variable capacitance.
Varanasi (vă′rə nə sĭ), *n.* a city in India, in SE Uttar Pradesh, on the Ganges: holy city of Hinduism. 471,258 (1961). Also, **Benares.**
Varangian (və răn′jĭ ən), *n.* **1.** one of the Northmen who under Rurik established a dynasty in Russia in the 9th century. **2.** a member of the bodyguard (**Varangian guard**) of the Byzantine emperors. —*adj.* **3.** of or pertaining to the Varangians. [der. ML *Varangus*, ult. t. Scand.; cf. Icel. *Væringi*]
Vardar (*Serb.* vȧr′dȧr), *n.* a river flowing from SE Yugoslavia through N Greece to the Gulf of Salonika. 200 mi.
varec (vă′rĕk), *n.* the ash of kelp. [t. F, ult. t. Gmc: cf. ME, MD, MLG *wrak* WRACK]
Varese (*It.* vȧ rĕ′sĕ), *n.* a town in Italy, in N Lombardy. 76,245 (1966).
Vargas (*Port.* vȧr′gȧs), *n.* **Getulio Dornelles** (*Port.* zhĕ tōō′lyōō dōōr nĕ′lĕs), 1883–1954, Brazilian statesman.
variable (vĕə′rĭ ə bl), *adj.* **1.** apt or liable to vary or change; changeable. **2.** capable of being varied or changed; alterable. **3.** inconsistent or fickle, as a person. **4.** *Biol.* deviating from the usual type, as a species or a specific character. **5.** *Elect.* (of a circuit component) being so constructed that the characteristic value of the component may be continuously varied. **6.** *Astron.* (of a star) changing in brightness. **7.** *Meteorol.* (of wind) tending to change in direction. —*n.* **8.** something variable. **9.** *Maths.* a symbol, or the quantity or function which it signifies, which may represent any one of a given set of values. **10.** *Astron.* a star whose light varies in intensity. **11.** *Meteorol.* a shifting wind, esp. as opposed to a trade wind. **12.** (*pl.*) a region where such winds occur. —**var′iabil′ity, var′iableness,** *n.* —**var′iably,** *adv.* —**Ant. 1.** constant.
variable geometry, *Aeron.* the principle upon which swing-wing aircraft are designed.
variable time fuse, proximity fuse.
Variable Zone, Temperate Zone.
varia lectio (vä′rĭ ä lĕk′tĭ ō′), *pl.* **variae lectiones** (vä′rĭ ē lĕk′tĭ ō′nēz). *Latin.* a variant reading.
variance (vĕə′rĭ əns), *n.* **1.** the state or fact of varying; divergence or discrepancy. **2.** an instance of this; difference. **3.** *Statistics.* the square of the standard deviation. **4.** *Law.* **a.** a difference or discrepancy, as between two statements or documents in law which should agree. **b.** a departure from the cause of action originally stated in the complaint. **5.** a disagreement, dispute, or quarrel. **6. at variance, a.** in a state of difference, discrepancy, or disagreement, as things. **b.** in a state of controversy or of dissension, as persons. [ME, t. OF]
variant (vĕə′rĭ ənt), *adj.* **1.** exhibiting diversity; varying; tending to change or alter. **2.** being an altered or different form of something: *a variant spelling of a word.* —*n.* **3.** a variant form. **4.** a different form or spelling of the same word: *'lanthorn' is an old variant of 'lantern'.* **5.** a different reading of a passage. **6.** *Statistics.* variate. [ME, t. L: s. *varians*, ppr., varying]
variate (vĕə′rĭ ĭt), *n. Statistics.* the numerical value of an attribute belonging to a statistical item. Also, **variant.**
variation (vĕə′rĭ ā′shən), *n.* **1.** the act or process of varying; change in condition, character, degree, etc. **2.** an instance of this. **3.** amount or rate of change. **4.** a different form of something; a variant. **5.** *Music.* **a.** the transformation of a melody or theme with changes or elaborations in harmony, rhythm, and melody. **b.** a varied form of a melody or theme, esp. one of a series of such forms developing the capacities of the subject. **6.** *Astron.* **a.** any deviation from the mean orbit of a heavenly body, esp. of a planetary or satellite orbit. **b.** an inequality in the moon's motion having a period of half a synodic month. **7.** declination (def. 2). **8.** *Biol.* **a.** a deviation in the structure or character of an organism from that of others of the same species or group, or that of the parents. **b.** an organism exhibiting such deviation; variety. **9.** *Ballet.* a solo dance. [ME *variacio(u)n*, t. L: m. s. *variātio*] —**var′ia′tional,** *adj.*
varic-, var. of **varico-** before vowels.
varicella (vă′rĭ sĕl′ə), *n. Pathol.* chickenpox. [t. NL: f. *vari(ola)* VARIOLA + *-cella*, dim. suffix]
varicellate (vă′rĭ sĕl′ĭt, -āt), *adj.* having small varices, as certain shells. [f. s. NL *varicella* (alter. of L *varicula*, dim. of *varix* varicose vein) + -ATE[1]]
varicelloid (vă′rĭ sĕl′oid), *adj.* resembling varicella.
varices (vă′rĭ sēz′), *n.* pl. of **varix.**
varico-, a word element meaning 'varicose veins', as in *varicocele.* Also, before vowels, **varic-.** [comb. form repr. L *varix* VARIX]
varicocele (vă′rĭ kō sēl′), *n. Pathol.* a varicose condition of the spermatic veins of the scrotum.
varicoloured (vĕə′rĭ kŭl′əd), *adj.* **1.** having various colours; variegated in colour; motley. **2.** varied; assorted. Also, *U.S.,* **varicolored.**
varicose (vă′rĭ kōs′), *adj.* **1.** abnormally or unusually enlarged, swollen, or dilated. **2.** pertaining to or affected with varices or varicose veins, which often affect the superficial portions of the lower limbs. [t. L: m. s. *varicōsus.* See VARIX]
varicosis (vă′rĭ kō′sĭs), *n. Pathol.* **1.** the formation of varices. **2.** varicosity. [f. VARIC(O)- + -OSIS]
varicosity (vă′rĭ kŏs′ĭ tĭ), *n., pl.* **-ties.** *Pathol.* **1.** the state or condition of being varicose. **2.** varix.
varied (vĕə′rĭd), *adj.* **1.** made various, diversified; characterized by variety: *a varied assortment.* **2.** changed or altered: *a varied form of a word.* **3.** variegated, as in colour, as an animal. —**var′iedly,** *adv.* —**var′iedness,** *n.*
variegate (vĕə′rĭ gāt′), *v.t.,* **-gated, -gating. 1.** to make varied in appearance; mark with different colours, tints, etc. **2.** to give variety to; diversify. [t. LL: m. s. *variegātus*, pp. (def. 1)]
variegated (vĕə′rĭ gā′tĭd), *adj.* **1.** varied in appearance or colour; marked with patches or spots of different colours. **2.** varied; diversified; diverse.
variegation (vĕə′rĭ gā′shən), *n.* **1.** the act of variegating. **2.** the state or condition of being variegated; varied coloration.
varietal (və rī′ə tl), *adj.* **1.** of, pertaining to, or characteristic of a variety. **2.** constituting a variety. —**vari′etally,** *adv.*
variety (və rī′ə tĭ), *n., pl.* **-ties,** *adj.* —*n.* **1.** the state or character of being various or varied; diversity, or absence of uniformity or monotony. **2.** difference or discrepancy. **3.** a number of things of different kinds. **4.** a kind or sort. **5.** a different form, condition, or phase of something. **6.** a category within a species, based on some hereditary difference not considered great enough to distinguish species. **7.** a group or type of animals or plants produced by artificial selection. **8.** *Theat.* entertainment of mixed character, consisting of a number of individual performances or acts, as of singing, dancing, comic turns, acrobatics, etc. —*adj.* **9.** *Theat.* of, pertaining to, or characteristic of a variety. [t. L: m. s. *varietas*] —**Syn. 1.** diversity, multiplicity. **3.** assortment, collection, group. **5.** kind, sort, class, species.
variform (vĕə′rĭ fôm′), *adj.* varied in form; having various forms. [f. s. L *varius* various + -FORM]
variola (və rī′ə lə), *n. Pathol.* smallpox. [t. ML, der. L *varius* various, spotted]
variolar (və rī′ə lə), *adj.* variolous.
variolate (vĕə′rĭ ə lāt′), *v.t.,* **-lated, -lating.** to inoculate with virus of variola. —**var′iola′tion,** *n.*
variole (vĕə′rĭ ōl′), *n.* **1.** a shallow pit or depression like the mark left by a smallpox pustule; a foveola. **2.** *Geol.* any of the spherules of variolite.
variolite (vĕə′rĭ ə līt′), *n. Geol.* any of certain fine-grained, basic igneous rocks containing light-coloured spherules, which, esp. on weathered surfaces, give them a pock-marked appearance. [f. VARIOL(A) + -ITE[1]]
variolitic (vĕə′rĭ ə lĭt′ĭk), *adj.* **1.** *Geol.* of or resembling variolite, esp. in texture. **2.** spotted; speckled.
varioloid (vĕə′rĭ ə loid′), *adj.* **1.** resembling variola or smallpox. **2.** of or pertaining to a mild case of smallpox. —*n.* **3.** a mild smallpox, esp. as occurring in persons who have been vaccinated or have previously had smallpox.
variolous (və rī′ə ləs), *adj.* **1.** pertaining to variola or smallpox. **2.** affected with smallpox. **3.** having pits like those left by smallpox. Also, **variolar.**
variometer (vĕə′rĭ ŏm′ĭ tə), *n.* **1.** *Elect.* an instrument for comparing the intensity of magnetic forces, esp. the magnetic force of the earth, at different points. **2.** *Elect.* an instrument for varying inductance, consisting of a fixed coil and a movable coil connected in series (used as a tuning device). **3.** *Aeron.* an instrument for measuring the rate of climb or descent of an aircraft. [f. *vario-* (comb. form repr. L *varius* various) + -METER[1]]
variorum (vĕə′rĭ ô′rəm), *adj.* **1.** (of an edition, etc.) characterized by various versions of the text or commentaries by various editors: *a variorum edition of Shakespeare.* —*n.* **2.** a variorum edition, text, etc. [short for L *ēditio cum notīs variōrum* edition with notes of various persons]
various (vĕə′rĭ əs), *adj.* **1.** differing one from another, or of different kinds, as two or more things. **2.** divers, several,

or many: *in various parts of the world.* **3.** exhibiting or marked by variety or diversity. **4.** differing in different parts, or presenting differing aspects. [t. L: m. *varius*] —**var′iously,** *adv.* —**var′iousness,** *n.*

—**Syn. 1.** VARIOUS, DIFFERENT, DISTINCT, DIVERSE refer to things which are sufficiently unlike to be perceivably of more than one kind. VARIOUS implies that there are several kinds of the same general thing: *various types of seaweed.* DIFFERENT is applied either to a single thing differing in identity or character from another, or to two or more things differing thus from one another: *two different stories concerning an event.* DISTINCT implies want of connection between things, which, however, may possibly be alike or similar: *two distinct accounts which coincide.* DIVERSE commonly implies a number or assortment of things or parts differing one from another: *three completely diverse proposals for preventing inflation.* —**Ant. 1.** identical, same, similar, uniform.

variscite (vă′rĭ sīt′), *n.* a mineral, aluminium phosphate, $Al(PO_4).2H_2O$, which occurs as nodular masses principally in the U.S., in Utah. [t. G: m. *Variscit*, named after *Variscia* Latinized name of district in Saxony]

varix (vĕə′rĭks), *n.*, *pl.* **varices** (vă′rĭ sēz′). **1.** *Pathol.* a permanent abnormal dilation and lengthening of a vein, usually accompanied by some tortuosity; a varicose vein. **2.** *Zool.* a mark or scar on the surface of a shell at a former position of the lip of the aperture. [ME, t. L: dilated vein]

varlet (vä′lĭt), *n.* *Archaic.* **1.** an attendant. **2.** a page attached to a knight. **3.** a low fellow or a rascal. [ME, t. OF, var. of *va(s)let* VALET. See VASSAL]

varletry (vä′lĭ trĭ), *n.* *Archaic.* **1.** varlets collectively. **2.** the mob or rabble.

varmint (vä′mĭnt), *n.* *Dial.* **1.** vermin. **2.** an objectionable or undesirable animal. **3.** an objectionable or undesirable person. Also, **var′ment.**

Varna (*Bulg.* vȧr′nȧ), *n.* a seaport in NE Bulgaria, on the Black Sea. 175,352 (1964). Formerly (1949–57), **Stalin.**

varnish (vä′nĭsh), *n.* **1.** a preparation which consists of resinous matter (as copal, lac, etc.) dissolved in an oil (**oil varnish**) or in alcohol (**spirit varnish**) or other volatile liquid, and which, when applied to the surface of wood, metal, etc., dries and leaves a hard, more or less glossy, usually transparent coating. **2.** the sap of certain trees, used for the same purpose (**natural varnish**). **3.** any of various other preparations similarly used, as one having indiarubber, pyroxylin, or asphalt for the chief constituent. **4.** a coating or surface of varnish. **5.** something resembling a coating of varnish; a gloss. **6.** a merely external show, or a veneer. —*v.t.* **7.** to lay varnish on. **8.** to invest with a glossy appearance. **9.** to give an improved appearance to; embellish; adorn. **10.** to cover with a specious or deceptive appearance. [ME *vernisshe(n)*, t. OF: m. *vernisser*, der. *vernis* varnish, n., t. ML: m. *vernicium* sandarac, sweet-smelling resin, t. MGk: m. *bernĭkē*, Gk *Berenĭkē*, a city in Cyrenaica] —**var′nisher,** *n.*

varnish tree, any of various trees yielding sap or other substances used for varnish, as *Rhus verniciflua* of Japan. See **lacquer.**

Varro (vă′rō), *n.* **Marcus Terentius** (mä′kəs tə rĕn′tyəs), *c.* 116–27? B.C., Roman scholar and author.

varsity (vä′sĭ tĭ), *n.*, *pl.* **-ties.** *Colloq.* university. [var. of (UNI)VERSITY]

Varuna (vă′rōō nə, vŭ′-), *n.* (in the Hindu Rig-Veda) the god of the sky or heaven, all-encompassing and all-seeing. [t. Skt: deity]

varus (vĕə′rəs), *n.* *Pathol.* abnormal angulation of a bone or joint, with the angle pointing away from mid-line. [t. L: bandy-legged]

varve (väv), *n.* *Geol.* the layer of sediment deposited during a year in a melt-water lake, consisting of a lower layer of sand deposited in spring and an upper layer of silt deposited in the summer. [t. Sw: m. *varv*, lit., full circle]

vary (vĕə′rĭ), *v.*, **-ried, -rying.** —*v.t.* **1.** to change or alter, as in form, appearance, character, substance, degree, etc. **2.** to cause to be different, one from another. **3.** to diversify (something); relieve from uniformity or monotony. **4.** *Music.* to alter (a melody or theme) by modification or embellishments, without changing its identity. —*v.i.* **5.** to be different, or show diversity. **6.** to undergo change in form, appearance, character, substance, degree, etc. **7.** *Maths.* to be subject to change. **8.** to change in succession, follow alternately, or alternate. **9.** to diverge; deviate (usually fol. by *from*). **10.** *Biol.* to exhibit variation. [ME, t. L: m. s. *variāre*, der. *varius* various] —**var′ier,** *n.* —**var′yingly,** *adv.*

vas (văs), *n.*, *pl.* **vasa** (vā′sə). *Anat., Zool., Bot.* a vessel or duct. [t. L: vessel]

Vasari (*It.* vȧ zȧ′rē), *n.* **Giorgio** (*It.* jôr′jô), 1511–74, Italian painter, architect, and art historian.

vascular (văs′kyŏŏ lə), *adj.* *Zool., Bot.* pertaining to, composed of, or provided with vessels or ducts which convey fluids, as blood, lymph, or sap. Also, **vasculose** (văs′kyŏŏ lōs′), **vasculous** (văs′kyŏŏ ləs). [t. NL: s. *vāsculāris*, der. L *vāsculum* little vessel] —**vascularity** (văs′kyŏŏ lă′rĭ tĭ), *n.* —**vas′cularly,** *adv.*

vascular bundle, bundle (def. 4).

vascular cambium, *Bot.* a cambium which gives rise to secondary vascular tissues, usually a large quantity of xylem and a small amount of phloem.

vascular tissue, *Bot.* plant tissue consisting of ducts or vessels which, in highly developed plants, form the system by which sap is conveyed through the plant.

vasculum (văs′kyŏŏ ləm), *n.*, *pl.* **-la** (-lə), **-lums.** a kind of case or box used by botanists for carrying specimens as they are collected. [t. L, dim. of *vās* vessel]

vas deferens (văs′dĕf′ə rĕnz′), *pl.* **vasa deferentia** (vā′-sə dĕf′ə rĕn′shĭ ə). the deferent duct of the testicle which transports the sperm from the epididymus to the penis. [L: vessel carrying down]

vase (väz), *n.* a hollow vessel, generally higher than it is wide, made of glass, earthenware, porcelain, etc., now chiefly used as a flower container or for decoration. [t. F, t. L: m. *vās* vessel] —**vase′like′,** *adj.*

vasectomy (vă sĕk′tə mĭ), *n.*, *pl.* **-mies.** *Surg.* excision of the vas deferens, or of a portion of it.

Vaseline (văs′ĭ lēn′), *n.* *Trademark.* a translucent, yellow or whitish, semisolid petroleum product (a form of petrolatum), used as a remedial ointment and internal remedy, and in various medicinal and other preparations. [f. *vas* (t. G: m. *Wasser* water) + *-el-* (t. Gk: m. *élaion* oil) + -INE[2]]

vaso-, a word element meaning 'vessel', as in *vasoconstrictor.* [comb. form repr. L *vās* vessel]

vasoconstriction (vā′zō kən strĭk′shən), *n.* *Physiol.* constriction of the blood vessels, as by the action of a nerve.

vasoconstrictor (vā′zō kən strĭk′tə), *Physiol.* —*adj.* **1.** serving to constrict blood vessels. —*n.* **2.** a nerve or drug that causes vasoconstriction.

vasodilatation (vā′zō dī′lā tā′shən), *n.* *Physiol.* dilatation of the blood vessels, as by the action of a nerve.

vasodilator (vā′zō dī lā′tə), *Physiol.* —*adj.* **1.** serving to dilate or relax blood vessels. —*n.* **2.** a nerve or drug that causes vasodilatation.

vasoinhibitor (vā′zō ĭn hĭb′ĭ tə), *n.* an agent or drug that inhibits the action of the vasomotor nerves. —**vasoinhibitory** (vā′zō ĭn hĭb′ĭ tə rĭ, -trĭ), *adj.*

vasomotor (vā′zō mō′tə), *adj.* *Physiol.* serving to regulate the diameter of blood vessels, as certain nerves.

vassal (văs′əl), *n.* **1.** (in the feudal system) a person holding lands by the obligation to render military service or its equivalent to his superior. **2.** a feudatory tenant. **3.** a person holding some similar relation to a superior; a subject, follower, or retainer. **4.** *Archaic.* a servant or slave. —*adj.* **5.** pertaining to or characteristic of a vassal. **6.** being a vassal or in vassalage. [ME, t. OF, g. LL *vassallus*, der. *vassus* servant; of Celtic orig.] —**vas′salless,** *adj.*

vassalage (văs′ə lĭj), *n.* **1.** the state of being a vassal; the status of a vassal. **2.** homage or service due from a vassal. **3.** a territory held by a vassal. **4.** *Hist.* a body of vassals. **5.** dependence, subjection, or servitude.

Vassar (văs′ə), *n.* a private college for women in the U.S., in Poughkeepsie, New York State: founded in 1861.

vast (väst), *adj.* **1.** of very great extent or area; very extensive, or immense. **2.** of very great size or proportions; huge; enormous. **3.** very great in number, quantity, or amount, etc.: *a vast army, a vast sum.* **4.** very great in degree, intensity, etc.: *in vast haste, vast importance.* —*n.* **5.** *Chiefly Poetic.* a vast expanse or space. [t. L: s. *vastus*] —**vast′ly,** *adv.* —**vast′ness,** *n.*

Västerås (*Sw.* vĕs tər ôs′), *n.* a town in E Sweden. 85,007 (1964).

vastitude (väs′tĭ tyōōd′), *n.* **1.** vastness or immensity. **2.** a vast expanse or space.

vasty (väs′tĭ), *adj.* *Poetic.* vast; immense.

vat (văt), *n.*, *v.*, **vatted, vatting.** —*n.* **1.** a large container for liquids. —*v.t.* **2.** to put into or treat in a vat. [ME; OE *fæt*, c. G *Fass* keg]

Vat., Vatican.

vat dye, *Chem.* any of a group of insoluble dyes which are applied to fabrics by first reducing them to alkali-soluble leuco bases. After dyeing, the insoluble dye is regenerated in the fibres of the material by oxidization.

vatic (văt′ĭk), *adj.* of, pertaining to, or characteristic of a prophet. Also, **vat′ical.** [appar. back-formation from VATICINAL]

Vatican (văt′ĭ kən), *n.* **1.** the palace of the popes in Rome and their chief residence since 1377: includes a library, art museum, archives, administrative offices, etc. **2.** the papal power or government, as distinguished from the Quirinal (representing the Italian government). [t. L: s. *Vāticānus (mons)* Vatican (hill)]

Vatican City, an independent state within the city of Rome, on the right bank of the Tiber: established in 1929, it is ruled by the pope and includes St Peter's church and the Vatican. ab. 1000 pop.; 109 acres. Italian, **Città del Vaticano** (*It.* chĕt tȧd′dĕl vȧ tē kȧ′nȯ).

vaticinal (və tĭs′ĭ nəl), *adj.* of, pertaining to, or characterized by prophecy; prophetic. [f. s. L *vāticinus* prophetic + -AL[1]]

vaticinate (və tĭs′ĭ nāt′), *v.t., v.i.,* **-nated, -nating.** to prophesy. [t. L: m. s. *vāticinātus*, pp.] —**vatic′ina′tor,** *n.*

vaticination (văt′ĭ sĭ nā′shən), *n.* **1.** the act of prophesying. **2.** a prophecy.

Vätter (*Sw.* vĕ′tər), *n.* a lake in S Sweden. ab. 80 mi. long; 733 sq. mi. Also, **Vättern** (*Sw.* vĕ′tərn), **Vetter.**

Vauban (*Fr.* vȯ bäɴ′), *n.* **Sébastien le Prestre de** (*Fr.* sĕbȧs tyăɴ lə prĕ′trə də), 1633–1707, French military engineer and marshal.

Vaucluse (*Fr.* vȯ klʏz′), *n.* a department in SE France. 303,536 pop. (1962); 1381 sq. mi. *Cap.:* Avignon.

Vaud (*Fr.* vȯ), *n.* a canton in W Switzerland. 429,512 pop. (1960); 1239 sq. mi. *Cap.:* Lausanne. German, **Waadt.**

vaudeville (vō′də vĭl, vô′-), *n.* **1.** *U.S.* variety entertainment. **2.** a theatrical piece of light or amusing character, interspersed with songs and dances. [t. F, alter. of *chanson du Vau de Vire* song of the Valley of Vire (in Normandy)]

Vaudois (*Fr.* vȯ dwȧ′), *n., pl.* **-dois. 1.** a native or inhabitant of Vaud. **2.** the dialect spoken there.

Vaudois (*Fr.* vȯ dwȧ′), *n.pl.* the Waldenses.

Vaughan (vôn), *n.* **Henry,** 1622–95, English poet and mystic, born in Wales.

Vaughan Williams (vôn′wĭl′yəmz), **Ralph,** 1872–1958, English composer.

vault[1] (vôlt), *n.* **1.** an arched structure, commonly made of stones, concrete, or bricks, forming a ceiling or roof over a hall, room, sewer, or other wholly or partially enclosed construction. **2.** an arched space, chamber, or passage, esp. one underground. **3.** an underground chamber, as a cellar or a division of a cellar. **4.** a burial chamber. **5.** a strongroom for storing and safeguarding valuables. **6.** *Anat.* an arched roof of a cavity. **7.** something resembling an arched roof: *the vault of heaven.* —*v.t.* **8.** to construct or cover with a vault. **9.** to make in the form of a vault; arch. [ME *vaute*, t. OF: m. *voute*, g. Rom. *volta*, der. *vol(vi)tus*, r. L *volūtus*, pp., turned, rolled] —**vault′like′,** *adj.*

Vaults
A, Barrel; B, Groin

vault[2] (vôlt), *v.i.* **1.** to leap or spring, as to or from a position or over something. **2.** to leap with the aid of the hands supported on something, sometimes on a pole: *to vault over a fence or a bar.* —*v.t.* **3.** to leap or spring over: *to vault a fence.* —*n.* **4.** the act of vaulting. [t. OF: m. *volter*, t. It.: m. *voltare*, g. frequentative of L *volvere* roll] —**vault′er,** *n.* —**Syn. 1.** See **jump.**

vaulted (vôl′tĭd), *adj.* **1.** constructed or covered with a vault, as a building, chamber, etc. **2.** provided with a vault or vaults, as below the ground.

vaulting[1] (vôl′tĭng), *n.* **1.** the act or process of constructing vaults. **2.** the structure forming a vault or vaults. **3.** a vault, vaulted ceiling, or the like, or such structures collectively. [f. VAULT[1] + -ING[1]]

vaulting[2] (vôl′tĭng), *adj.* **1.** that vaults. **2.** used in vaulting: *a vaulting pole.* **3.** exaggerated: *vaulting conceit.* [f. VAULT[2] + -ING[2]]

vault light, pavement light.

vaunt (vônt), *v.t.* **1.** to speak vaingloriously or boastfully of. —*v.i.* **2.** *Archaic or Literary.* to talk vaingloriously or boastfully; boast; brag. —*n.* **3.** vainglorious or boastful utterance. [ME *vaunt(en)*, t. MF: m. *vanter*, g. LL *vānitāre*, der. L *vānus* vain] —**vaunt′er,** *n.* —**vaunt′ingly,** *adv.*

vaunt-courier (vônt′kŏŏə′rĭ ə), *n. Archaic.* one who goes in advance, as a herald. [t. OF: m. *avaunt-courrier* forerunner]

vaunty (vôn′tĭ), *adj. Scot.* boastful; vainly ostentatious.

vavasor (văv′ə sō′), *n.* (in the feudal system) a vassal, or feudal tenant, next in rank to a baron. Also, **vavasour** (văv′ə sŏŏə′). [ME, t. OF, g. ML *vassus vassōrum* vassal of vassals]

vb, verb.

VC, Vietcong.

V.C., **1.** Vice-Chairman. **2.** Vice-Chancellor. **3.** Vice-Consul. **4.** Victoria Cross.

V.D., venereal disease.

v.d., various dates.

Veadar (vē′ə dä′, vā′-), *n.* (in the Jewish calendar) an intercalary month of 29 days inserted, when required, after Adar. [t. Heb.: and (yet another) Adar]

veal (vēl), *n.* **1.** a calf, esp. as intended or used for food. **2.** the flesh of the calf as used for food. [ME *veel*, t. OF, g. L *vitellus* little calf]

Veblen (vĕb′lən), *n.* **Thorstein** (thô′stīn), 1857–1929, U.S. economist.

Vectis (vĕk′tĭs), *n.* the Latin name of the **Isle of Wight.**

vector (vĕk′tə), *n.* **1.** *Maths.* a quantity which possesses both magnitude and direction. Two such quantities acting on a point may be represented by the two sides of a parallelogram, so that their resultant is represented in magnitude and direction by the diagonal of the parallelogram. **2.** *Biol.* an insect or other organism transmitting germs or other agents of disease. [t. L: carrier] —**vectorial** (vĕk tô′rĭ əl), *adj.*

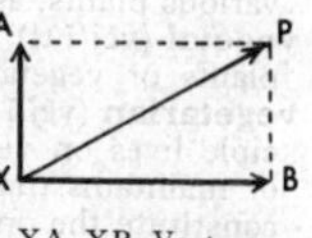

XA, XB, Vectors; XP, Resultant

vector field, a region, each point of which is characterized by a definite value of some vector quantity; a field of force.

Ved., Vedic.

Veda (vā′də), *n.* (*sometimes pl.*) the entire sacred scriptures of Hinduism, esp. as comprising the four Books of Wisdom which have the word 'Veda' in their titles: **Rig-Veda** or The Veda of Psalms or Verses, the **Yajur-Veda** or The Veda of Sacred Formulas, **Sama-Veda** or The Veda Chants, and the **Atharva-Veda** or The Veda of Charms. [t. Skt: lit., knowledge] —**Vedaic** (vĭ dā′ĭk), *adj.* —**Vedaism** (vā′də ĭz′əm), *n.*

Vedanta (vĭ dän′tə, -dăn′-), *n.* the chief philosophy among the Hindus, a system of idealistic monism, chiefly as expounded by the philosopher S(h)ankara about 800 A.D., with some varieties occurring later. It is concerned with the end of the Vedas, both chronologically and teleologically. [t. Skt, f. *Veda* VEDA + *anta* end] —**Vedan′tic,** *adj.* —**Vedan′tism,** *n.* —**Vedan′tist,** *n.*

V-E Day, the day of victory in Europe for the Allies in World War II (May 8th, 1945). [V(ictory in) E(urope)]

Vedda (vĕd′ə), *n.* a Ceylonese aborigine. Also, **Veddah.** [t. Sinhalese: hunter]

vedette (vĭ dĕt′), *n.* **1.** Also, **vedette boat.** a small naval launch used for scouting. **2.** a mounted sentry in advance of the outposts of an army. Also, **vidette.** [t. F, t. It.: m. *vedetta*, der. *vedere* see, g. L *vidēre*]

Vedic (vā′dĭk), *adj.* **1.** of or pertaining to the Veda or Vedas. —*n.* **2.** the language of the Veda, closely related to classical Sanskrit.

vee (vē), *n.* **1.** *U.S. Slang.* a five-dollar note. —*adj.* **2.** in the shape of a V.

veer[1] (vĭə), *v.i.* **1.** to turn or shift to another direction; change from one direction or course to another. **2.** to change; alter; be variable or changeable; pass from one state to another. **3.** (of the wind) **a.** to change direction by moving clockwise round the points of the compass. See **back**[1] (def. 22). **b.** *Naut.* to shift more aft in relation to the vessel's course (opp. to *haul*). —*n.* **4.** a change of direction. [t. F: m. *virer*, g. LL *gīrāre* turn (der. *gȳrus* a turn, t. Gk: m. *gŷros*) b. with *vertere* turn] —**veer′ingly,** *adv.*

veer[2] (vĭə), *v.t. Naut.* to slacken or let out: *to veer chain.* [late ME *vere*, t. MD: m. s. *vieren* let out]

Vega (vē′gə), *n. Astron.* a brilliant white star of the first magnitude, in the constellation Lyra. [t. Sp. or t. ML, t. Ar.: m. *wāqi* the falling (vulture)]

Vega (*Sp.* bĕ′gȧ), *n.* **Lope de.** See **de Vega.**

vegetable (vĕj′tə bl), *n.* **1.** any herbaceous plant, annual, biennial, or perennial, whose fruits, seeds, roots, tubers, bulbs, stems, leaves, or flower parts are used as food, mainly with the entree, as tomato, bean, beet, potato, asparagus, cabbage, etc. **2.** the edible part of such plants, as the fruit of the tomato or the tuber of the potato. **3.** any member of the vegetable kingdom; a plant. **4.** *Colloq.* a dull or uninspiring person. **5.** *Colloq.* a person who, due to physical injury or mental deficiency, is entirely dependent on the agencies of others for subsistence. —*adj.* **6.** of, consisting of, or made from edible vegetables: *a vegetable diet, a vegetable dinner.* **7.** of, pertaining to or characteristic of plants: *vegetable life or processes.* **8.** derived from plants or some part of plants: *vegetable fibre, vegetable oils.* **9.** consisting of or containing the substance or remains of plants: *vegetable matter.* **10.** of the nature of a plant; consisting of or comprising plants: *a vegetable organism, the vegetable kingdom.* [ME, t. LL: m. *vegetābilis* vivifying]

vegetable butter, any of various fixed vegetable fats which usually melt at or below body temperature.

vegetable garden, kitchen garden.

vegetable ivory. See **ivory** (def. 8).

vegetable kingdom, the plants of the world collectively (distinguished from *animal kingdom*).

vegetable marrow. See **marrow** (def. 5).

vegetable oil, any of a group of soils which are obtained from plants or their seeds or fruits, usually consisting of esters of fatty acids and glycerol.

vegetable silk, a fine, glossy fibre, similar to silk cotton, from the seeds of a Brazilian tree, *Chorisia speciosa.*

vegetable tallow, any of several tallow-like substances of vegetable origin, used in making candles, soap, etc., and as lubricants.

vegetable wax, a wax or waxlike substance obtained from various plants, as the wax-palm.

vegetal (vĕj′ĭ tl), *adj.* **1.** pertaining to or of the nature of plants or vegetables; vegetable. **2.** vegetative (def. 3).

vegetarian (vĕj′ĭ tĕə′rĭ ən), *n.* **1.** one who on moral principle lives on vegetable food (refusing meat, fish, etc.), or maintains that vegetables and farinaceous substances constitute the only proper food for man. —*adj.* **2.** of or pertaining to the practice or principle of living solely or chiefly on vegetable food. **3.** devoted to or advocating this practice. **4.** consisting solely of vegetables.

vegetarianism (vĕj′ĭ tĕə′rĭ ə nĭz′əm), *n.* the beliefs and practices of a vegetarian.

vegetate (vĕj′ĭ tāt′), *v.i.*, **-tated, -tating. 1.** to grow in the manner of plants; increase as if by vegetable growth. **2.** to live like vegetables, in an inactive, passive, or unthinking way. **3.** *Pathol.* to grow, or increase by growth, as an excrescence. [t. L: m. s. *vegetātus*, pp., enlivened]

vegetation (vĕj′ĭ tā′shən), *n.* **1.** plants collectively; the plant life of a particular region considered as a whole. **2.** the act or process of vegetating. **3.** *Pathol.* a morbid growth or excrescence. —**veg′eta′tional,** *adj.*

vegetative (vĕj′ĭ tə tĭv), *adj.* **1.** growing or developing as or like plants; vegetating. **2.** of, pertaining to, or connected with vegetation or vegetable growth. **3.** denoting the parts of a plant not specialized for reproduction. **4.** (of reproduction) asexual. **5.** denoting or pertaining to those bodily functions which, being performed unconsciously or involuntarily, are likened to the processes of vegetable growth. **6.** having the power to produce or support growth in plants: *vegetative mould.* Also, **vegetive** (vĕj′ĭ tĭv). —**veg′etatively,** *adv.* —**veg′etativeness,** *n.*

vehemence (vē′ĭ məns), *n.* **1.** the quality of being vehement; violent ardour; fervour; fire. **2.** impetuosity; violence; fury. Also, **ve′hemency.**

vehement (vē′ĭ mənt), *adj.* **1.** eager, impetuous, or impassioned. **2.** characterized by anger, bitterness, or rancour: *vehement opposition.* **3.** passionate, as feeling; strongly emotional: *vehement desire, vehement dislike.* **4.** (of actions) marked by great energy, exertion, or unusual force. [late ME, t. L: s. *vehemens*] —**ve′hemently,** *adv.*

vehicle (vē′ĭ kl), *n.* **1.** any receptacle, or means of transport, in which something is carried or conveyed, or travels. **2.** a carriage or conveyance moving on wheels or runners. **3.** *Astronautics.* a rocket excluding the payload or spacecraft. **4.** a means of conveyance, transmission, or communication: *air is the vehicle of sound.* **5.** a medium by which ideas or effects are communicated: *language is a vehicle for the conveyance of thought.* **6.** *Pharm.* a substance, usually fluid, possessing little or no medicinal action, used as a medium for active remedies. **7.** *Painting.* the liquid portion of a paint, in which the pigment is dispersed. [t. L: m. s. *vehiculum* conveyance]

vehicular (vĭ hĭk′yŏŏ lə), *adj.* **1.** of, pertaining to, or associated with vehicles. **2.** serving as a vehicle. **3.** carried or transported by means of a vehicle or vehicles.

Vehmgericht (*Ger.* fēm gə rĭKHT′), *n.*, *pl.* **-richte** (*Ger.* -rĭKH′ tə). *German.* any of a class of irregular tribunals in medieval Germany, esp. in Westphalia, often meeting in secret, and exercising broad powers, including the power of life and death in case of serious crimes. [t. MHG: *Vehm* (var. of *veime* guild court; c. G *Feme*) + *Gericht* court]

Veii (vē′yī), *n.* an ancient Etruscan city in central Italy, near Rome: often at war with ancient Rome.

veil (vāl), *n.* **1.** a piece of material, usually light and more or less transparent, worn, esp. by women, over the head or face, as to conceal the face or to protect it from the sun or wind. **2.** a piece of material worn so as to fall over the head and shoulders on each side of the face, forming a part of the headdress of a nun. **3.** the life accepted or the vows made by a woman, when she makes either her novice's vows and takes the white veil, or her irrevocable vows and takes the black veil of a nun. **4.** something that covers, screens, or conceals: *a veil of smoke or mist.* **5.** a mask, disguise, or pretence. **6.** *Bot., Anat., Zool.* a velum. **7.** *Dial.* a caul. **8. take the veil,** to become a nun. —*v.t.* **9.** to cover or conceal with or as with a veil. **10.** to hide the real nature of; mask; disguise. [ME, t. AF, g. L *vēlum* sail, covering] —**veiled,** *adj.* —**veil′less,** *adj.* —**veil′-like′,** *adj.*

veiled (vāld), *adj.* **1.** covered with or wearing a veil. **2.** concealed or covered, with or as with a veil. **3.** not openly expressed or declared; disguised. **4.** lacking distinctness or clarity; muffled.

veiling (vā′lĭng), *n.* **1.** a veil. **2.** a thin net used in making veils.

vein (vān), *n.* **1.** one of the system of branching vessels or tubes conveying blood from various parts of the body to the heart. **2.** (loosely) any blood vessel. **3.** one of the tubular, riblike thickenings that ramify in an insect's wing. **4.** one of the strands or bundles of vascular tissue forming the principal framework of a leaf. **5.** any body or stratum of ore, coal, etc., clearly separated or defined. **6.** a body or mass of igneous rock, deposited mineral, or the like, occupying a crevice or fissure in rock; a lode. **7.** a small natural channel or watercourse under the surface of the earth. **8.** the water running through it. **9.** a streak or marking, as of a different shade or colour, running through marble, wood, etc. **10.** mood; temper; disposition. **11.** a strain or quality traceable in character or conduct, writing, etc.: *a vein of stubbornness, to write in a poetic vein.* —*v.t.* **12.** to furnish with veins. **13.** to mark with lines or streaks suggesting veins. **14.** to extend over or through (something) in the manner of veins. [ME *veine*, t. OF, g. L *vēna*] —**veined,** *adj.* —**vein′less,** *adj.* —**vein′like′,** *adj.*

veining (vā′nĭng), *n.* **1.** the act or process of forming veins or veinlike markings. **2.** a pattern of veins or veinlike markings.

veinlet (vān′lĭt), *n.* a small vein.

veinstone (vān′stōn′), *n.* gangue.

veinule (vā′nyo͞ol), *n.* a venule (def. 2). [t. F, t. L: m. *vēnula* little vein]

veiny (vā′nĭ), *adj.*, **-nier, -niest.** full of veins; veined.

vel., vellum.

vela (vē′lə), *n.* pl. of **velum.**

velamen (vĕ lā′mĕn), *n.*, *pl.* **-lamina** (-lăm′ĭ nə). **1.** *Anat.* a membranous covering; a velum. **2.** *Bot.* the thick, spongy integument or epidermis covering the aerial roots of epiphytic orchids. [t. L: covering]

velar (vē′lə), *adj.* **1.** of or pertaining to a velum or veil, esp. that of the palate. **2.** *Phonet.* with the back of the tongue held close to or touching the soft palate. —*n.* **3.** a velar sound. [t. L: s. *vēlāris*, der. *vēlum* curtain]

velarium (vĭ lĕə′rĭ əm), *n.*, *pl.* **-laria** (-lĕə′rĭ ə). *Rom. Antiq.* an awning drawn over a theatre or amphitheatre as a protection from rain or the sun. [t. L]

velarize (vē′lə rīz′), *v.t.*, **-rized, -rizing.** *Phonet.* to pronounce with velar articulation. Also, **velarise.** —**ve′lariza′tion,** *n.*

velate (vē′lĭt, -lāt), *adj.*, *v.*, **-lated, -lating.** —*adj.* **1.** *Bot., Zool.* having a velum. —*v.t.* **2.** *Phonet.* to velarize. [t. L: m. s. *vēlātus* veiled]

velation (vĭ lā′shən), *n.* *Phonet.* pronunciation with velar articulation. [t. LL: s. *vēlātio*]

Velázquez (*Sp.* bė lȧth′kėth), *n.* **Diego Rodríguez de Silva y** (*Sp.* dyė′gȯ rȯ drē′gėth dė sēl′bȧ ē), 1599–1660, Spanish painter. Also, **Velásquez** (vĭ lăs′kwĭz).

Velbert (*Ger.* fĕl′bərt), *n.* a town in West Germany, in central North Rhine-Westphalia. 55,900 (est. 1966).

veld (vĕlt), *n.* the open country, bearing grass, bushes, or shrubs, or thinly forested, characteristic of parts of southern Africa. Also, **veldt.** [t. Afrikaans, t. D: FIELD]

Velde (*Fr.* vĕld), *n.* **Henri van de** (*Fr.* äN rē′ väN də), 1863–1957, Belgian designer and architect.

veldschoen (vĕlt′sko͞on, fĕlt′-), *n. sing. and pl.* any strong, watertight shoe, esp. one having the uppers and the sole moulded as one piece. [var. of VELSKOEN by assoc. with VELD]

veleta (və lē′tə), *n.* a ballroom dance in waltz time. Also, **valeta.** [t. Sp.: weathercock]

veliger (vĕl′ĭ jə), *n.* the free-swimming, larval stage in the development of a mollusc. [t. NL. See VELUM, -I-, -GEROUS]

velites (vē′lĭ tēz′), *n.pl.* light-armed ancient Roman soldiers. [t. L]

velleity (vĕ lē′ĭ tĭ), *n.*, *pl.* **-ties. 1.** volition in its weakest form. **2.** a mere wish, unaccompanied by an effort to obtain it. [t. ML: m. s. *velleitas*, der. L *velle* wish]

vellicate (vĕl′ĭ kāt′), *v.t.*, **-cated, -cating.** to pluck; nip; pinch. [t. L: m. s. *vellicātus*, pp., der. *vellere*] —**vel′lica′tion,** *n.* —**vellicative** (vĕl′ĭ kə tĭv), *adj.*

Vellore (vĕl′ô), *n.* a town in India, in NE Madras. 113,742 (1961).

vellum (vĕl′əm), *n.* **1.** a sheet of calfskin prepared as parchment for writing or bookbinding. **2.** a manuscript or the like on such parchment. **3.** a texture of paper or cloth resembling that of such parchment. —*adj.* **4.** made of or resembling vellum. **5.** bound in vellum. [ME *velym*, t. OF: m. *velin*, der. *veel* VEAL]

veloce (vĭ lō′chĭ; *It.* vė lȯ′chė), *adj.* *Music.* played at a quick tempo. [It., quick, g. s. L *vēlox*]

velocipede (vĭ lŏs′ĭ pēd′), *n.* **1.** a bicycle-like vehicle, usually with two or three wheels, propelled by the rider. **2.** an early kind of bicycle or tricycle. [t. F: m. *vélocipède*, f. L: *vēlōci-* swift + m. s. *pēs* foot]

velocity (vĭ lŏs′ĭ tĭ), *n.*, *pl.* **-ties. 1.** rapidity of motion or operation; swiftness; quickness. **2.** *Physics.* rate of motion, esp. when the direction of motion is also specified.

[t. L: m. s. *vēlōcitas* swiftness] **—Syn. 1.** See **speed.**

velocity modulation, *Electronics.* the process of altering the velocity of a beam of electrons in proportion to the strength of a control signal.

velocity of light, *Physics.* a universal constant defining the rate of propagation of any electromagnetic radiation in vacuo, equal to $2{\cdot}9979 \times 10^{10}$ cm. per sec. or 186,281 miles per second. *Symbol:* c.

velocity ratio, *Physics.* (of a machine) the ratio of the distance through which the point of application of the applied force moves, to the distance through which the point of application of the load moves in the same time.

velours (və lo͝oəʹ; *Fr.* və lo͞orʹ), *n. sing. and pl.* **1.** a French term for velvet. **2.** any of various fabrics with a fine, raised finish. Also, **velour.** [t. F: velvet, earlier *velous,* t. Pr.: m. *velos,* ult. der. L *villus* hair]

velouté (və lo͞oʹtā; *Fr.* və lo͞o tėʹ), *n. French.* a smooth white sauce made with chicken or veal stock. Also, **velouté sauce.** [F, der. *velours* velvet]

Velsen (*Du.* vĕlʹsə), *n.* a town in the Netherlands, in SE North Holland. 67,806 (1965).

velskoen (vĕlʹsko͞on, fĕlʹ-), *n., pl.* **-skoene** (-sko͞oʹnə). **1.** *S African.* a type of comfortable, sturdy, rawhide boot, usually ankle-length. **2.** veldschoen. [Afrikaans: skin shoe]

velum (vēʹləm), *n., pl.* **-la** (-lə). **1.** *Biol.* any of various veil-like or curtain-like membranous partitions. **2.** *Anat.* the soft palate. [t. L: sail, covering]

velure (və lo͝oəʹ), *n., v.,* **-lured, -luring.** **—n. 1.** velvet or a substance resembling it. **2.** a hatters' pad of velvet, plush, or the like, for smoothing or dressing silk hats. **—*v.t.* 3.** to smooth or dress (a hat) with a velure. [var. of *velour* VELOURS]

velutinous (və lo͞oʹtĭ nəs), *adj.* having a soft, velvety surface, as certain plants. [t. NL: m. *velūtinus,* der. ML *velutum* velvet]

velvet (vĕlʹvĭt), *n.* **1.** a fabric of silk, silk and cotton, cotton, etc., with a thick, soft pile formed of loops of the warp thread either cut at the outer end (as in ordinary velvet) or left uncut (as in uncut or terry velvet). **2.** something likened to the fabric velvet in softness, etc. **3.** the soft, deciduous covering of a growing antler. **4.** *Colloq.* a very agreeable or desirable position or situation. **5.** *Slang.* money gained through gambling or speculation. **6.** *Slang.* clear gain or profit. **—*adj.* 7.** Also, **velʹveted.** made of velvet or covered with velvet. **8.** resembling velvet; velvety; smooth and soft. [ME, t. ML: s. *velvetum,* ult. der. L *villus* shaggy hair] **—velʹvet-likeʹ,** *adj.*

velvet carpet, a carpet or rug of pile weave resembling Wilton.

velveteen (vĕlʹvĭ tēnʹ), *n.* **1.** a cotton pile fabric with short pile. **2.** (*pl.*) trousers or knickerbockers made of velveteen. **—*adj.* 3.** Also, **velʹveteenedʹ.** made of velveteen. [der. VELVET]

velvet glove, a superficially pleasant manner concealing ruthless determination.

velvety (vĕlʹvĭ tĭ), *adj.* **1.** like or suggestive of velvet; smooth and soft. **2.** (of wines, spirits, etc.) having no harshness; smooth. **3.** gentle and smooth in contact. **—velʹvetiness,** *n.*

Ven., 1. Venerable. **2.** Venice.

vena (vēʹnə), *n., pl.* **-nae** (-nē). *Anat.* a vein. [L]

vena cava (vēʹnə kāʹvə), *pl.* **venae cavae** (vēʹnē kāʹvē). *Anat.* either of two large veins discharging into the right auricle of the heart. See diag. under **heart.** [L: hollow vein]

venal (vēʹnəl), *adj.* **1.** ready to sell one's services or influence unscrupulously; accessible to bribery; corruptly mercenary. **2.** purchasable like mere merchandise, as things not properly bought and sold. **3.** characterized by venality: *a venal period, a venal agreement.* [t. L: s. *vēnālis* for sale] **—veʹnally,** *adv.* **—Syn. 1.** See **corrupt.**

venality (vē nălʹĭ tĭ), *n., pl.* **-ties.** the quality of being venal; prostitution of talents or principles for money or reward.

venatic (vē nătʹĭk), *adj.* of or pertaining to hunting. Also, **venatʹical.** [t. L: s. *vēnāticus*] **—venatʹically,** *adv.*

venation (vē nāʹshən), *n.* **1.** the arrangement of veins, as in a leaf or an insect's wing. **2.** these veins collectively. [t. NL: s. *vēnātio,* der. L *vēna* vein] **—venaʹtional,** *adj.*

Venations of leaves
A, Pinnate; B, Palmate; C, Parallel

vend (vĕnd), *v.t.* **1.** to dispose of by sale; peddle. **2.** to give utterance to (an opinion, etc.). **—*v.i.* 3.** to vend something. **4.** to be disposed of by sale. [t. L: s. *vendere* sell]

vendace (vĕnʹdāsʹ), *n.* either of two species of whitefish of the genus *Corogenus, C. vandesius* or *C. gracilior.* [t. OF: m. *vendese,* ? t. Celt: m. **vindasia,* der. **vindos* white (cf. OIr. *find* white), influenced by DACE]

vendee (vĕn dēʹ), *n. Chiefly Law.* the person to whom a thing is vended or sold.

Vendée (*Fr.* väɴ dėʹ), *n.* a department in W France, on the Atlantic: royalist revolt 1793–95. 408,928 pop. (1962); 2690 sq. mi. *Cap.:* La Roche-sur-Yon.

Vendémiaire (*Fr.* väɴ dė myĕrʹ), *n. French.* (in the calendar of the first French republic) the first month of the year, extending from September 22nd to October 21st. [F, der. L *vindēmia* grape-gathering]

vender (vĕnʹdə), *n.* vendor.

vendetta (vĕn dĕtʹə), *n.* **1.** a private feud in which the relatives of a murdered person seek to obtain vengeance by killing the murderer or a member of his family, esp. as existing in Corsica and parts of Italy; blood feud. **2.** any prolonged or persistent quarrel, rivalry, etc. [t. It., g. L *vindicta* vengeance] **—vendetʹtist,** *n.*

vendible (vĕnʹdə bl), *adj.* **1.** capable of being vended or sold; saleable. **—*n.* 2.** a vendible article. **—vendʹibilʹity, vendʹibleness,** *n.* **—vendʹibly,** *adv.*

vending machine, a coin-operated machine for selling goods.

vendition (vĕn dĭshʹən), *n.* the act of vending; sale.

Vendôme (*Fr.* väɴ dōmʹ), *n.* **Louis Joseph de** (*Fr.* lwē zhō zĕfʹ də), 1654–1712, French general and marshal.

vendor (vĕnʹdô), *n. Chiefly Law.* one who vends or disposes of a thing by sale. Also, **vender.** [f. VEND + -OR[2]]

vendue (vĕnʹdyo͞o), *n.* a public auction. [t. D: m. *vendu,* t. OF: m. *vendue* sale, der. *vendre* sell]

veneer (vĭ nĭəʹ), *n.* **1.** a thin layer of wood or other material used for facing or overlaying wood. **2.** one of the several layers of plywood. **3.** a superficially pleasing appearance or show: *a veneer of good manners.* **—*v.t.* 4.** to overlay or face (wood) with thin sheets of some material, as a fine wood, ivory, tortoiseshell, etc. **5.** to cover (an object) with a thin layer of costly material to give an appearance of superior quality. **6.** to cement (layers of wood veneer) to form plywood. **7.** to give a superficially pleasing appearance to. [t. G: m. *furniren,* t. F: m. *fournir.* See FURNISH] **—veneerʹer,** *n.*

veneering (vĭ nĭəʹrĭng), *n.* **1.** the process, work, or craft of applying veneers. **2.** material applied as a veneer. **3.** the surface thus formed. **4.** a merely superficial show or outward display: *a veneering of civilization.*

venenose (vĕnʹĭ nōsʹ), *adj. Rare.* poisonous.

Vener (*Sw.* vĕʹnər), *n.* Vänern.

venerable (vĕnʹə rə bl, vĕnʹrə bl), *adj.* **1.** worthy of veneration or reverence, as on account of high character or office. **2.** commanding respect by reason of age and dignity of appearance. **3.** (of places, buildings, etc.) hallowed by religious, historic, or other lofty associations. **4.** impressive or interesting from age, antique appearance, etc. **5.** ancient: *a venerable error.* [ME, t. L: m. *venerābilis*] **—venʹerabilʹity, venʹerableness,** *n.* **—venʹerably,** *adv.*

venerate (vĕnʹə rātʹ), *v.t.,* **-rated, -rating.** to regard with reverence, or revere. [t. L: m. s. *venerātus,* pp., having reverenced] **—venʹeraʹtor,** *n.*

veneration (vĕnʹə rāʹshən), *n.* **1.** the act of venerating. **2.** the state of being venerated. **3.** the feeling of one who venerates; reverence: *filled with veneration for the traditions of one's country.* **4.** the outward expression of reverent feeling. **—Syn. 3.** See **respect.**

venereal (vĭ nĭəʹrĭ əl), *adj.* **1.** arising from or connected with sexual intercourse with an infected person: *venereal disease.* **2.** pertaining to diseases so arising. **3.** infected with or suffering from veneral disease. **4.** adapted to the cure of such disease: *a venereal remedy.* **5.** of or pertaining to sexual desire or intercourse. [ME; f. s. L *venereus* pertaining to Venus + -AL[1]]

venereal disease, any of those diseases which are transmitted by sexual intercourse with an infected person, esp. syphilis and gonorrhoea.

venerer (vĕnʹə rə), *n. Archaic.* a huntsman.

venery[1] (vĕnʹə rĭ), *n. Archaic.* the gratification of sexual desire. [f. s. L *Venus* goddess of love + -Y[3]]

venery[2] (vĕnʹə rĭ), *n. Archaic.* the practice or sport of hunting; the chase. [ME *venerye,* t. OF: m. *venerie,* der. *vener* hunt, g. L *vēnārī*]

venesection (vĕnʹĭ sĕkʹshən), *n. Med.* phlebotomy. [f. ML *vēnē* (gen. sing. of *vēna* vein) + s. L *sectio* a cutting]

Venetia (vĭ nēʹshə), *n.* **1.** an ancient Roman province in N Italy between the river Po and the Alps. **2.** Veneto.

Venetian (vĭ nēʹshən), *adj.* **1.** of or pertaining to Venice or its inhabitants. **—*n.* 2.** a native or inhabitant of Venice. **3.** (*l.c.*) *Colloq.* a venetian blind. **4.** (*l.c., pl.*) a tape or braid for holding the slats of venetian blinds in place. **5.** (*l.c.*) a cotton or wool cloth of superior quality, used for linings.

venetian blind, a blind, as for a window, having overlapping horizontal slats that may be opened or closed, esp. one in which the slats may be raised and drawn together above the window by pulling a cord.

Venetian glass, ornamental glassware made at or near Venice.

Venetian red, 1. a red pigment, orig. prepared from a natural oxide of iron, but now usually made by calcining a mixture of lime and iron sulphate. 2. a dark shade of orangy red.

Venetian white, a mixture of white lead and barium sulphate in equal parts, used as a pigment.

Veneto (*It.* vĕ′nĕ tô), *n.* a region in NE Italy. 3,833,837 pop. (1961); 7095 sq. mi. Also, **Venetia, Venezia.**

Venez., Venezuela.

Venezia (*It.* vĕ nĕt′tsyä), *n.* **1.** Italian name of **Venice. 2.** Veneto.

Venezia Giulia (*It.* jōō′lyä), a former region in NE Italy, at the N end of the Adriatic. The larger part, including the area surrounding the Free Territory of Trieste, was ceded to Yugoslavia 1947: the area remaining in Italy now forms part of Friuli-Venezia Giulia.

Venezia Giulia

Venezia Tridentina (*It.* trĕ dĕn tē′nä), a former department in N Italy, including the Trentino region, now part of Trentino-Alto Adige.

Venezuela (vĕn′ĭ zwā′lə; *Sp.* bĕ nĕ thwĕ′lä), *n.* a republic in N South America. 8,880,000 pop. (est. 1965); 352,143 sq. mi. *Cap.:* Caracas. See map under **Caribbean.** —**Ven′ezue′lan,** *adj., n.*

venge (vĕnj), *v.t.,* **venged, venging.** *Archaic.* to avenge. [ME, t. OF: m. *venger,* g. L *vindicāre*]

vengeance (vĕn′jəns), *n.* **1.** the avenging of wrong, injury, or the like, or retributive punishment. **2.** infliction of injury or suffering in requital for wrong done or other cause of bitter resentment. **3. with a vengeance, a.** with force or violence. **b.** extremely. **c.** to a surprising or unusual degree. [ME, t. OF, der. *venger* VENGE] —**Syn. 1.** See **revenge.**

vengeful (vĕnj′fəl), *adj.* **1.** desiring or seeking vengeance, as persons; vindictive. **2.** characterized by or showing a vindictive spirit: *a vengeful sort of person.* **3.** taking or executing vengeance. —**venge′fully,** *adv.* —**venge′fulness,** *n.*

venial (vē′nyəl), *adj.* **1.** that may be forgiven or pardoned; not seriously wrong, as a sin (opposed to *mortal*). **2.** excusable, as an error or slip. [ME, t. L: s. *veniālis,* der. *venia* pardon] —**veniality** (vē′nĭ ăl′ĭ tĭ), **ve′nialness,** *n.* —**ve′nially,** *adv.*

venial sin, 1. *Rom. Cath. Ch.* a voluntary transgression of God's law, which without destroying charity or union with God retards man in attaining final union with Him.

Venice (vĕn′ĭs), *n.* **1.** a seaport in NE Italy, built on numerous small islands in the **Lagoon of Venice,** an inlet of the Adriatic. 365,371 (1966). **2. Gulf of,** the N part of the Adriatic Sea. Italian, **Venezia.**

venipuncture (vĕn′ĭpŭngk′chə), *n. Med.* the puncture of a vein for surgical or therapeutic purposes. [f. *veni-* (comb. form repr. L *vēna* vein) + PUNCTURE]

venire facias (vĭ nī′ə rĭ fā′shĭ ăs′), *Obs. Law.* a writ or precept directed to the sheriff, requiring him to summon qualified citizens to act as jurors in the trial of cases. Also, **veni′re.** [L: lit., cause to come]

venireman (vĭ nī′ə rĭ mən), *n., pl.* **-men.** *Obs. Law.* a man summoned under a venire facias.

venison (vĕn′zən, vĕn′ĭ zən), *n.* the flesh of a deer or similar animal. [ME, t. OF: m. *veneson,* g. s. L *vēnātio* hunting]

Venite (vĭ nī′tĭ), *n.* **1.** the 95th Psalm (94th in the Vulgate and Douay), used as a canticle at matins or morning prayers. **2.** a musical setting of this psalm. [L: come ye; so called from first word of L version]

veni, vidi, vici (vā′nī, vē′dī, vē′kī), *Latin.* I came, I saw, I conquered (words used by Julius Caesar in reporting one of his victories).

Venizelos (vĕn′ĭ zā′lŏs), *n.* **Eleutherios** (ĕ′lyōō thĕ′rĭ ŏs′), 1864–1936, prime minister of Greece 1910–15, 1917–20, 1928–33.

Venlo (*Du.* vĕn′lō), *n.* a town in the Netherlands, in E Limburg. 59,313 (1965).

venom (vĕn′əm), *n.* **1.** the poisonous fluid which some animals, as certain snakes, spiders, etc., secrete, and introduce into the bodies of their victims by biting, stinging, etc. **2.** something resembling or suggesting poison in its effect; spite or malice. **3.** *Rare.* poison in general. —*v.t.* **4.** *Archaic.* to infect with venom; make venomous; envenom. [ME *venim,* t. OF, var. of *venin,* g. L *venēnum* poison] —**ven′omer,** *n.* —**ven′omless,** *adj.* —**Syn. 1.** See **poison.**

venomous (vĕn′ə məs), *adj.* **1.** (of an animal) having a gland or glands for secreting venom; inflicting a poisoned bite, sting, or wound. **2.** full of venom; poisonous. **3.** spiteful or malignant: *a venomous disposition, a venomous attack.* —**ven′omously,** *adv.* —**ven′omousness,** *n.*

venose (vē′nōs), *adj.* **1.** having many or prominent veins. **2.** venous. [t. L: m. s. *vēnōsus*]

venosity (vĭ nŏs′ĭ tĭ), *n. Physiol.* venous or venose state, quality, or characteristic.

venous (vē′nəs), *adj.* **1.** of, pertaining to, or of the nature of a vein or veins. **2.** pertaining to the blood of the veins which has given up oxygen and become charged with carbon dioxide, and, in the higher animals, is dark red in colour. [t. L: m. s. *vēnōsus*] —**ve′nously,** *adv.* —**ve′nousness,** *n.*

vent[1] (vĕnt), *n.* **1.** an opening or aperture serving as an outlet for air, smoke, fumes, etc. **2.** the small opening at the breech of a gun by which fire is communicated to the charge. **3.** *Zool.* the anal or excretory opening of animals, esp. of those below mammals, as birds and reptiles. **4.** a means of escaping or passing out; an outlet, as from confinement. [appar. coalescence of VENT[2] and VENT[3]] —**vent′less,** *adj.*

vent[2] (vĕnt), *n.* **1.** expression or utterance: *to give vent to emotions, to complaints.* **2.** *Obs.* the act or fact of venting; emission or discharge; issue. —*v.t.* **3.** to give free course or expression to (an emotion, passion, etc.): *glad of any excuse to vent her pique.* **4.** to give utterance to; publish or spread abroad. **5.** to relieve by giving vent to something. **6.** to let out or discharge (liquid, smoke, etc.). **7.** to furnish with a vent or vents. [t. F: aphetic m. *évent* a breaking forth, *évenier* break forth, der. *vent* (g. L *ventus*) wind] —**vent′er,** *n.*

vent[3] (vĕnt), *n.* the slit in the back or sides of a coat. [ME, var. of *fente,* t. OF: slit]

ventage (vĕn′tĭj), *n.* a small hole or vent, as one of the finger holes of a flute.

ventail (vĕn′tāl), *n.* the pivoted middle element of a face defence of a close helmet. [ME, t. OF: m. *ventaille,* der. *vent* wind]

venter (vĕn′tə), *n.* **1.** *Anat., Zool.* the abdomen or belly. **2.** a belly-like cavity or concavity. **3.** a belly-like protuberance. **4.** *Law.* the womb, or a wife or mother, as a source of offspring. [t. L: belly, womb]

ventiduct (vĕn′tĭ dŭkt′), *n.* a duct, pipe or passage for wind or air, as for ventilating an apartment or room. [f. *venti-* (comb. form repr. L *ventus* wind) + DUCT]

ventilate (vĕn′tĭ lāt′), *v.t.,* **-lated, -lating. 1.** to provide (a room, mine, etc.) with fresh air in place of air which is vitiated. **2.** to introduce fresh air: *the lungs ventilate the blood.* **3.** (of air, wind, etc.) to circulate through, blow on, etc., so as to freshen. **4.** to expose (substances, etc.) to the action of air or wind. **5.** to submit (a question, etc.) to free examination and discussion. **6.** to give utterance or expression to (an opinion, etc.). **7.** to furnish with a vent or opening, as for the escape of air or gas. [t. L: m. s. *ventilātus,* pp., fanned]

ventilation (vĕn′tĭ lā′shən), *n.* **1.** the act of ventilating. **2.** the state of being ventilated. **3.** any means of or device for ventilating.

ventilative (vĕn′tĭ lā′tĭv), *adj.* **1.** promoting or producing ventilation. **2.** of or pertaining to ventilation.

ventilator (vĕn′tĭ lā′tə), *n.* **1.** one who or that which ventilates. **2.** any contrivance for replacing foul or stagnant air by fresh air.

Ventôse (*Fr.* väɴ tōz′), *n. French.* (in the calendar of the first French republic) the sixth month of the year, from February 19th to March 20th. [F, t. L: m. *ventōsus* windy]

ventral (vĕn′trəl), *adj.* **1.** of or pertaining to the venter or belly; abdominal. **2.** situated on the abdominal side of the body. **3.** of, pertaining to, or situated on the anterior or lower side or surface, as of an organ or part. **4.** *Bot.* of or designating the lower or inner surface, as of a petal, etc. —*n.* **5.** a ventral fin. [t. L: s. *ventrālis*] —**ven′trally,** *adv.*

V, Ventral fin

ventral fin, (in fishes) either of a pair of fins on the lower surface of the body, and corresponding to the hind limbs of higher vertebrates.

ventricle (vĕn′trĭ kl), *n.* **1.** any of various hollow organs or parts in an animal body. **2.** one of the two main cavities of the heart which receive the blood from the auricles and propel it into the arteries. See diag. under **heart. 3.** one of a series of connecting cavities of the brain. [ME, t. L: m. *ventriculus*, dim. of *venter* belly]

ventricose (vĕn′trĭ kōs′), *adj.* **1.** swelling out, esp. on one side or unequally; protuberant. **2.** having a large abdomen. [t. NL: m. s. *ventricōsus*, der. L *venter* belly] —**ventricosity** (vĕn′trĭ kŏs′ĭ tĭ), *n.*

ventricular (vĕn trĭk′yŏŏ lə), *adj.* **1.** of, pertaining to, or of the nature of a ventricle. **2.** swelling out; distended.

ventriculus (vĕn trĭk′yŏŏ ləs), *n.* **1.** the stomach of an insect, the part of the food tract where digestion and absorption take place. **2.** the muscular portion of a bird's stomach. [t. L, dim. of *venter* belly]

ventriloquial (vĕn′trĭ lō′kwĭ əl), *adj.* of, pertaining to, or using ventriloquism. Also, **ventriloqual** (vĕn trĭl′ə kwəl). —**ven′trilo′quially,** *adv.*

ventriloquism (vĕn trĭl′ə kwĭz′əm), *n.* the art or practice of speaking or of uttering sounds with little or no lip movement, in such a manner that the voice appears to come not from the speaker but from some other source, as a dummy. Also, **ventril′oquy.** [f. s. LL *ventriloquus* one who apparently speaks from the belly + -ISM]

ventriloquist (vĕn trĭl′ə kwĭst), *n.* one who performs or is expert in ventriloquism. —**ventril′oquis′tic,** *adj.*

ventriloquize (vĕn trĭl′ə kwīz′), *v.i.*, *v.t.*, **-quized, -quizing.** to speak or produce sounds in the manner of a ventriloquist. Also, **ventriloquise.**

Ventris (vĕn′trĭs), *n*, **Michael George Francis,** 1922–56, English philologist.

venture (vĕn′chə), *n.*, *v.*, **-tured, -turing.** —*n.* **1.** a hazardous or daring undertaking; any undertaking or proceeding involving uncertainty as to the outcome. **2.** a business enterprise or proceeding in which loss is risked in the hope of profit; a commercial or other speculation. **3.** that on which risk is taken in a business enterprise or speculation, as a ship, cargo, merchandise, etc. **4.** *Archaic.* hazard or risk. **5. at a venture,** according to chance; at random. —*v.t.* **6.** to expose to hazard; risk. **7.** to take the risk of; brave the dangers of. **8.** to dare; presume; be so bold as; go so far as. **9.** *Archaic.* to take the risk of sending. —*v.i.* **10.** to make a venture; risk oneself. **11.** to take a risk; dare or presume (often fol. by *on* or *upon* or an infinitive): *to venture on an ambitious project.* [ME, aphetic var. of *aventure*, earlier form of ADVENTURE] —**ven′turer,** *n.* —**Syn. 11.** See **dare.**

venturesome (vĕn′chə səm), *adj.* **1.** having or showing a disposition to venture or take risks, often rashly; daring. **2.** attended with risk; hazardous. —**ven′turesomely,** *adv.* —**ven′turesomeness,** *n.*

Venturi meter (vĕn tyŏŏə′rĭ; *It.* vĕn tōō′rē), *Physics.* a device for measuring the rate of flow of fluids, consisting of a narrow tube, in the centre of which is a constriction, means being provided for measuring the drop in pressure across this constriction. The drop in pressure is directly related to the rate of fluid flow. [named after G. B. *Venturi*, 1746–1822, Italian physicist]

venturous (vĕn′chə rəs), *adj.* **1.** disposed to venture; bold; daring; adventurous. **2.** hazardous; risky. —**ven′turously,** *adv.* —**ven′turousness,** *n.* —**Ant. 1.** timid.

venue (vĕn′yōō), *n.* **1.** *Law.* **a.** the place of a crime or cause of action. **b.** the county or place where the jury is gathered and the cause tried. **c.** the designation, in the pleading, of the jurisdiction where trial will be held. **d.** the statement naming the place and person before whom an affidavit was sworn. **2.** the scene of any action or event. [ME, t. OF: coming]

venule (vĕn′yōōl), *n.* **1.** a small vein. **2.** one of the branches of the veins in an insect's wing. Also, **veinule.** [t. L: m. *vēnula*, dim. of *vēna* vein] —**venular** (vĕn′yŏŏ lə), *adj.*

venulose (vĕn′yŏŏ lōs′), *adj.* having veinlets. Also, **venulous** (vĕn′yŏŏ ləs).

Venus (vē′nəs), *n.* **1.** an ancient Italian goddess of gardens and spring, identified by the Romans with Aphrodite as the goddess of love and beauty. **2.** a beautiful woman. **3.** *Astron.* the most brilliant planet, having an orbit next inside the earth's and second from the sun. Its period of revolution is 224·701 days, its mean distance from the sun 67,240,000 miles, and its diameter 7640 miles. It has no satellites. **4.** *Chem. Obs.* copper. **5. mount of Venus,** the elevation at the base of the thumb.

Venusberg (vē′nəs bûg′; *Ger.* vĕ′nŏŏs bĕrk), *n.* a mountain in central Germany, in the caverns of which, according to medieval legend, Venus held her pagan court.

Venus de Milo (də mī′lō), a Greek statue of antiquity portraying Venus in marble, found in 1820 on Melos and now in the Louvre, Paris. Also, **Venus of Melos.**

Venusian (vĭ nyōō′zĭ ən), *adj.* **1.** of or pertaining to the planet Venus. —*n.* **2.** a supposed inhabitant of Venus.

Venus's flower basket, a deep-sea sponge of the genus *Euplectella*, having an intricate skeleton of siliceous spicules.

Venus's flytrap, a plant, *Dionæa muscipula*, native to North and South Carolina, whose leaves have two lobes which close like a trap when certain delicate hairs on them are irritated, as by a fly.

Venus's flytrap, *Dionæa muscipula*

Venus's girdle, a pelagic ctenophore of the Mediterranean, *Cestus veneris*, with a flattened, ribbon-like shape.

Venus's hair, a delicate maidenhair fern, *Adiantum capillus-veneris.*

Venus's looking glass, a small, campanulaceous, annual herb, *Legousia hybrida*, occurring on cultivated land in Europe and W Asia.

ver., 1. verse; verses. **2.** version.

veracious (vĕ rā′shəs), *adj.* **1.** speaking truly; truthful or habitually observant of truth: *a veracious witness.* **2.** characterized by truthfulness; true: *a veracious statement or account.* [f. VERACI(TY) + -OUS] —**vera′ciously,** *adv.* —**vera′ciousness,** *n.*

veracity (vĕ răs′ĭ tĭ), *n.*, *pl.* **-ties. 1.** truthfulness in speaking or statement; habitual observance of truth. **2.** conformity to truth or fact, as of statements. **3.** correctness or accuracy, as of the senses, a scientific instrument, etc. **4.** something veracious; a truthful statement; a truth. [t. ML: m. s. *vērācitas*, ult. der. L *vērus* true]

Veracruz (vĕ′rə krōōz′; *Sp.* bĕ rä krōōth′), *n.* a seaport in E Mexico: the chief port of Mexico. 173,347 (est. 1965). Formerly, **Vera Cruz.**

veranda (və răn′də), *n.* an open portico or gallery, usually roofed and sometimes partly enclosed, attached to the exterior of a house or other building; a piazza, porch, or gallery. Also, **verandah.** [orig. from India, in several native languages, appar. m. Pg. and OSp. *varanda* railing, der. L *vāra* rod] —**veran′daless,** *adj.*

veratric acid (vĭ răt′rĭk), *Chem.* a white crystalline acid, $(CH_3O)_2C_6H_3COOH$, obtained by the decomposition of veratrine and in other ways. [*veratric*, f. s. L *vērātrum* hellebore + -IC]

veratridine (vĭ răt′rĭ dēn′), *n. Chem.* a soluble amorphous alkaloid, $C_{36}H_{51}NO_{11}$, occurring with veratrine in the seeds of the sabadilla. Also, **veratridin** (vĭ răt′rĭ dĭn).

veratrine (vĕ′rə trēn′), *n. Chem.* a slightly soluble, crystalline alkaloid, $C_{32}H_{49}NO_9$, obtained from the seeds of the sabadilla, formerly used in medicine, chiefly in the local treatment of rheumatism, neuralgia, etc., and causing prolonged contraction of voluntary muscle. Also, **veratria** (və rā′trĭ ə, -răt′rĭ ə), **veratrin** (vĕ′rə trĭn), **veratrina** (vĕ′rə trī′nə).

verb (vûb), *n. Gram.* **1.** one of the major form classes, or parts of speech, comprising words which express the occurrence of an action, existence of a state, and the like, and such other words as show similar grammatical behaviour, as English *discover*, *remember*, *write*, *be.* **2.** any such word. **3.** any word or construction of similar function or meaning. [ME, t. L: s. *verbum* word, verb] —**verb′less,** *adj.*

verbal (vû′bl), *adj.* **1.** of or pertaining to words: *verbal symbols.* **2.** consisting of or in the form of words: *a verbal picture of a scene.* **3.** expressed in spoken words; oral rather than written: *verbal tradition, a verbal message.* **4.** pertaining to or concerned with words only, rather than ideas, facts, or realities: *a purely verbal distinction.* **5.** corresponding word for word; verbatim: *a verbal copy or quotation.* **6.** *Gram.* **a.** of, pertaining to, or derived from a verb. **b.** used in a sentence as or like a verb, as participles and infinitives. —*n.* **7.** *Gram.* a word, particularly a noun or adjective, derived from a verb. [late ME, t. L: s. *verbālis*, der. *verbum* word] —**ver′bally,** *adv.* —**Syn. 3.** See **oral.**

verbalism (vû′bə lĭz′əm), *n.* **1.** a verbal expression; a word or phrase. **2.** a formal phrase or sentence, with little or no meaning. **3.** predominance of mere words, as over ideas or realities.

verbalist (vû′bə lĭst), *n.* **1.** one skilled in words. **2.** one who deals with words merely, rather than ideas or realities.

verbalize (vû′bə līz′), *v.*, **-lized, -lizing.** —*v.t.* **1.** to express in words. **2.** *Gram.* to convert into a verb: *to verbalize 'butter' into 'to butter'.* —*v.i.* **3.** to use many words; be verbose. **4.** to express in words. Also, **verbalise.** —**ver′baliza′tion,** *n.* —**ver′baliz′er,** *n.*

verbal noun, *Gram.* a noun derived from a verb, esp. in a language where nouns are derived by the same or similar means from all or nearly all verbs, as (in English) by adding *-ing.*

verbatim (vû bā′tĭm), *adv.* **1.** word for word, or in exactly the same words. —*adj.* **2.** corresponding word for word to an original. [t. ML, der. L *verbum* word]

verbatim et litteratim (vû bā′tĭm ĕt lĭt′ə rā′tĭm), *Latin.* word for word and letter for letter; in the same words.

verbena (vû bē′nə), *n.* any plant of the genus *Verbena*, comprising species characterized by elongated or flattened spikes of sessile flowers, some of which are much cultivated as garden plants. [t. L: foliage]
verbenaceous (vû′bĭ nā′shəs), *adj.* belonging to the *Verbenaceae*, or verbena family of plants, which includes also the lantana, teak, etc.
verbiage (vû′bĭ ĭj), *n.* abundance of useless words, as in writing or speech; wordiness. [t. F, der. *verbier* gabble, ult. der. L *verbum* word. See -AGE]
verbid (vû′bĭd), *n.* *Gram.* a non-finite verb form; an infinitive or participle.
verbose (vû bōs′), *adj.* expressed in, characterized by the use of, or using many or too many words; wordy. [t. L: m. s. *verbōsus* full of words] —**verbose′ly,** *adv.* —**verbose′ness,** *n.* —**Ant.** laconic.
verbosity (vû bŏs′ĭ tĭ), *n.* the quality of being verbose; wordiness; superfluity of words. —**Ant.** reticence.
verbum sapienti satis (vû′bəm săp′ĭ ĕn′tĭ săt′ĭs), *Latin.* a word to the wise is sufficient. Also, **verb. sap., verb. sat., verbum sap.**
Vercelli (*It.* vėr chĕl′lē), *n.* a town in Italy, in E Piedmont. 55,085 (1966).
Vercingetorix (vû′sĭn jĕt′ə rĭks), *n.* died 45? B.C., Gallic chieftain conquered by Caesar.
verdant (vû′dnt), *adj.* **1.** green with vegetation; covered with growing plants or grass: *a verdant valley.* **2.** of a green colour. **3.** inexperienced; unsophisticated. [f. VERD(URE) + -ANT] —**ver′dancy,** *n.* —**ver′dantly,** *adv.*
verd antique (vûd′ ăn tēk′), **1.** a green, mottled or impure serpentine, used for decorative purposes. **2.** any of various similar greenish stones. [t. OF: antique green]
Verde (vûd), *n.* **Cape,** a cape in Senegal, near Dakar: the westernmost point of Africa.
verderer (vû′də rə), *n.* *Hist.* a judicial officer in the royal forests having charge esp. of the vert, or trees and undergrowth. Also, **verderor.** [t. AF, ult. g. LL *viridārius* forester, der. *viridis* green]
Verdi (vĕə′dĭ; *It.* vėr′dē), *n.* **Giuseppe** (*It.* jōō zĕp′pė), 1813–1901, Italian composer.
verdict (vû′dĭkt), *n.* **1.** *Law.* the finding or answer of a jury given to the court concerning a matter submitted to their judgement. **2.** a judgement or decision: *the verdict of the public.* [b. ML *vērēdictum* verdict (lit., truly said) and ME *verdit* (t. OF: lit., true saying)]
verdigris (vû′dĭ grĭs), *n.* a green or bluish patina formed on copper, brass, or bronze surfaces exposed to the atmosphere for long periods of time, consisting principally of basic copper sulphate. [ME *verdegres(e),* t. AF, m. *vert de Grece,* lit., green of Greece]
verditer (vû′dĭ tə), *n.* **1.** either of two pigments, consisting usually of carbonate of copper prepared by grinding either azurite (**blue verditer**) or malachite (**green verditer**). **2.** *Obs.* verdigris. [t. F: m. *vert de terre,* lit., green of earth]
Verdun (vĕə′dŭn; *Fr.* vĕr dœɴ′), *n.* **1.** a fortress town in NE France, on the river Meuse: a German offensive was stopped here in 1916 in the bloodiest fighting of World War I. 25,250 (1967). **2.** a town in Canada, in S Quebec. 78,317 (1961).
verdure (vû′jə), *n.* **1.** greenness, esp. of fresh, flourishing vegetation. **2.** green vegetation, esp. grass or herbage. **3.** freshness in general; flourishing condition. [ME, t. OF, f. *verd* green (g. L *viridis*) + *-ure* -URE] —**ver′dureless,** *adj.*
verdurous (vû′jə rəs), *adj.* **1.** rich in verdure or fresh greenness, as vegetation. **2.** covered with verdure or green vegetation, as places. **3.** consisting of verdure. **4.** pertaining to or characteristic of verdure. —**ver′durousness,** *n.*
verecund (vĕ′rĭ kŭnd′), *adj.* *Rare.* bashful; modest. [t. L: s. *verēcundus*]
Vereeniging (və rē′nĭ gĭng), *n.* a town in the Republic of South Africa, in S Transvaal: treaty ending Boer War signed here 1902. 78,835 (1960).
Vereshchagin (*Russ.* vĭ rĭ shchä′gĭn), *n.* **Vasili Vasilievich** (*Russ.* vä sĕ′lĭy vä sĕ′lyĭ vĭch), 1842–1904, Russian painter, esp. of military subjects.
verge[1] (vûj), *n., v.,* **verged, verging.** —*n.* **1.** the edge, rim, or margin of something. **2.** the limit or point beyond which something begins or occurs: *to be on the verge of tears.* **3.** a limiting belt, strip, or border of something. **4.** a narrow strip of turf bordering the edge of a road, pathway, etc. **5.** space within boundaries; room or scope. **6.** an area or district subject to a particular jurisdiction. **7.** *Hist.* an area in England, including the royal court, subject to the jurisdiction of the lord high steward. **8.** the edge of the tiling projecting over the gable of a roof. **9.** *Archit.* the shaft of a column; a small ornamental shaft. **10.** a rod, wand, or staff, esp. one carried as an emblem of authority or ensign of office of a bishop, dean, and the like. **11.** *Horol.* a lever with lips or projections, in a clock, which intermittently lock the escape wheel and transmit impulses from the escape wheel to the pendulum. **12.** *Obs.* a stick or wand held in the hand by a person swearing fealty to the lord on being admitted as a tenant. —*v.i.* **13.** to be on the verge or border, or touch at the border. **14.** to come close to, approach, or border on some state or condition (usually fol. by *on* or *upon*). [ME, t. F, g. L *virga* rod]
verge[2] (vûj), *v.i.,* **verged, verging.** to incline or tend; slope (usually fol. by *to* or *towards*). [t. L: m. s. *vergere* turn, incline]
verger (vû′jə), *n.* **1.** an official who takes care of the interior of a church and acts as attendant. **2.** an official who carries the verge or other symbol of office before a bishop, dean, or other dignitary. [late ME, t. F (obs.), der. *verge* rod. See VERGE[1]]
Vergil (vû′jĭl), *n.* Virgil. —**Vergil′ian,** *adj.*
Verhaeren (*Fr.* vĕ rà rĕn′), *n.* **Emile** (*Fr.* ė mēl′), 1855–1916, Belgian poet.
veridical (vĭ rĭd′ĭ kl), *adj.* truth-telling; truthful; veracious. Also, **verid′ic.** [f. s. L *vēridicus* truth-telling + -AL[1]] —**verid′ical′ity,** *n.* —**verid′ically,** *adv.*
veriest (vĕ′rĭ ĭst), *adj.* utmost; thoroughgoing: *the veriest stupidity.*
verification (vĕ′rĭ fĭ kā′shən), *n.* **1.** the act of verifying. **2.** the state of being verified. **3.** formal assertion of the truth of something. **4.** *Obs. Law.* a short confirmatory affidavit at the end of a pleading or petition. —**ver′ifica′tive,** *adj.*
verifier (vĕ′rĭ fĭ′ə), *n.* **1.** one who or that which verifies. **2.** *Computers.* a machine which checks that punched cards have been punched correctly.
verify (vĕ′rĭ fĭ′), *v.t.,* **-fied, -fying.** **1.** to prove (something) to be true, as by evidence or testimony; confirm or substantiate. **2.** to ascertain the truth or correctness of, esp. by examination or comparison: *to verify dates, spelling, or a quotation.* **3.** to state to be true, esp., in legal use, formally or upon oath. [ME *verifie,* t. OF: m. *verifier,* t. LL: m. *vērificāre,* der. L *vērus* true] —**ver′ifi′able,** *adj.*
verily (vĕ′rĭ lĭ), *adv.* *Archaic.* in very truth; truly; really; indeed. [ME; f. VERY + -LY]
verisimilar (vĕ′rĭ sĭm′ĭ lə), *adj.* having the appearance of truth; likely or probable. [m. L *vērisimilis* to agree with SIMILAR] —**ver′isim′ilarly,** *adv.*
verisimilitude (vĕ′rĭ sĭ mĭl′ĭ tyōōd′), *n.* **1.** appearance or semblance of truth; probability. **2.** something having merely the appearance of truth. [t. L: m. *vērī similitūdo* likeness of truth]
verism (vĭə′rĭz′əm), *n.* the theory that rigid representation of truth and reality is essential to art and literature and therefore the ugly and vulgar must be included. [f. s. L *vērus* true + -ISM] —**ver′ist,** *n., adj.* —**veris′tic,** *adj.*
veritable (vĕ′rĭ tə bl), *adj.* **1.** being truly such; genuine or real: *a veritable triumph.* **2.** *Rare.* true, as statements, etc. [late ME, t. AF, der. *verite,* t. L: m. s. *vēritas* truth] —**ver′itableness,** *n.* —**ver′itably,** *adv.*
verity (vĕ′rĭ tĭ), *n., pl.* **-ties.** **1.** quality of being true, or in accordance with fact or reality. **2.** a truth, or true statement, principle, belief, idea, or the like. [ME *verite,* t. L: m. s. *vēritas*]
verjuice (vû′jōōs′), *n.* **1.** an acid liquor made from the sour juice of crab apples, unripe grapes, etc., formerly much used for culinary and other purposes. **2.** sourness, as of temper or expression. —*adj.* Also, **ver′juiced′.** **3.** of or pertaining to verjuice. **4.** sour in temper, expression, etc. [ME *verjous,* t. OF: m. *vertjus,* f. *vert* green + *jus* juice]
Verlaine (*Fr.* vĕr lĕn′), *n.* **Paul** (*Fr.* pōl), 1844–96, French symbolist poet.
Vermeer (vĕə mĭə′; *Du.* vər mėr′), *n.* **Jan** (*Du.* yŏn) (*Jan van der Meer of Delft*), 1632–75, Dutch painter.
vermeil (vû′māl), *n.* **1.** vermilion red. **2.** metal, as silver or bronze, coated with gilt. —*adj.* **3.** of the colour vermilion. [ME *vermaile,* t. OF: m. *vermail* bright red, g. L *vermiculus* little worm, applied to cochineal]
vermi-, a word element meaning 'worm', as in *vermiform.* [t. L, comb. form of *vermis*]
vermicelli (vû′mĭ sĕl′ĭ, -chĕl′ĭ), *n.* a kind of pasta of Italian origin in the form of long, slender, solid threads (thinner than spaghetti), to be cooked for food. Cf. **macaroni** (def. 1). [t. It., pl. of *vermicello* little worm, der. *verme* worm, g. L *vermis*]
vermicide (vû′mĭ sīd′), *n* any agent that kills worms, esp. a drug used to kill parasitic intestinal worms. —**ver′micid′al,** *adj.*
vermicular (vû mĭk′yōō lə), *adj.* **1.** consisting of or

characterized by sinuous or wavy outlines or markings, resembling the tracks of worms. **2.** of, pertaining to, or characteristic of a worm or worms. [t. ML: s. *vermiculāris*, der. L *vermiculus* little worm] —**vermic′ularly,** *adv.*

vermiculate (*v.* vû mĭk′yŏŏ lāt′; *adj.* vû mĭk′yŏŏ lĭt, -lāt′), *v.*, **-lated, -lating,** *adj.* —*v.t.* **1.** to work or ornament with winding or wavy outlines or markings, resembling the tracks of worms. —*adj.* **2.** worm-eaten, or appearing as if worm-eaten; vermiculated. **3.** vermicular. **4.** (of thought processes) subtly sinuous. [t. L: m. s. *vermiculātus*, pp., worm-eaten] —**vermic′ula′tion,** *n.*

vermicule (vû′mĭ kyōōl′), *n.* any small worm.

vermiculite (vû mĭk′yŏŏ lĭt′), *n.* any of various micaceous minerals, usually formed by alteration of the common micas, occurring in yellow to brown foliated masses with inelastic laminae. They exfoliate and expand after heating and in the exfoliated form are used extensively as insulating material. [f. s. L *vermiculus* little worm + -ITE[1]]

vermiform (vû′mĭ fôm′), *adj.* like a worm in form; long and slender. [t. ML: s. *vermiformis*. See VERMI, -FORM]

vermiform appendix, *Anat.* a narrow, blind tube protruding from the caecum: in man, situated in the lower right-hand part of the abdomen and having no known useful function, its diameter being about that of a pencil and its length 3 to 4 inches. See diag. under **intestine.**

vermiform process, *Anat.* **1.** the median lobe or division of the cerebellum. **2.** the vermiform appendix.

vermifuge (vû′mĭ fyōōj′), *adj.* **1.** serving to expel worms or other animal parasites from the intestines, as a medicine. —*n.* **2.** a vermifuge medicine or agent.

vermilion (və mĭl′yən), *n.* **1.** brilliant scarlet red. **2.** a bright red pigment consisting of mercuric sulphide; cinnabar. —*adj.* **3.** of the colour of vermilion. —*v.t.* **4.** to colour with or as with vermilion. [ME *vermilioun*, t. OF: m. *vermillon* bright red, der. *vermeil* VERMEIL]

vermin (vû′mĭn), *n.pl. or sing.* **1.** noxious, troublesome, or objectionable animals collectively, esp. troublesome or disgusting insects or other minute animals, more particularly creeping ones parasitic on living animals or plants. **2.** *Obs.* a single animal of this kind. **3.** obnoxious persons collectively. **4.** a single person of this kind. [ME *vermyne*, t. OF: m. *vermin*, der. *verm* worm, g. L *vermis*]

vermination (vû′mĭ nā′shən), *n.* **1.** the breeding of vermin. **2.** the fact of being infested with vermin, esp. parasitic vermin.

verminous (vû′mĭ nəs), *adj.* **1.** of the nature of or resembling vermin. **2.** pertaining to or caused by vermin. **3.** infested with vermin, esp. parasitic vermin. —**ver′minously,** *adv.* —**ver′minousness,** *n.*

vermis (vû′mĭs), *n., pl.* **-mes** (-mēz). *Anat.* the median lobe of the cerebellum.

Vermont (vû mŏnt′), *n.* a state of the NE United States: a part of New England. 389,881 pop. (1960); 9609 sq. mi. *Cap.:* Montpelier. *Abbrev.:* Vt.

Vermonter (vû mŏn′tə), *n.* a native or inhabitant of Vermont.

vermouth (vû′məth; *Fr.* vĕr mōōt′), *n.* an aromatized white wine in which herbs, roots, barks, bitters, and other flavourings have been steeped. [t. F: m. *vermout*, t. G: m. *Wermuth* wormwood]

vernacular (və năk′yŏŏ lə), *adj.* **1.** native or originating in the place of its occurrence or use, as language or words (often as opposed to *literary* or *learned* language). **2.** expressed or written in the native language of a place, as literary works. **3.** using such a language, as a speaker or a writer. **4.** pertaining to such a language. **5.** denoting or pertaining to the common name for a plant or animal. **6.** native or peculiar to popular taste, as a style of architecture. **7.** *Obs.* endemic, as a disease. —*n.* **8.** the native speech or language of a place. **9.** the language or phraseology peculiar to a class or profession. **10.** a vernacular word or expression. **11.** the common name for a plant or animal rather than the scientific term which gives genus and species. [f. s. L *vernāculus* native + -AR[1]] —**vernac′ularly,** *adv.* —**Syn. 8.** See **language.**

vernacularism (və năk′yŏŏ lə rĭz′əm), *n.* **1.** a vernacular word or expression. **2.** the use of the vernacular.

vernacularize (və năk′yŏŏ lə rīz′), *v.t.*, **-rized, -rizing.** to translate into the native speech of a people. Also, **vernacularise.** —**vernac′ularist,** *n.* —**vernac′ulariza′tion,** *n.*

vernal (vû′nəl), *adj.* **1.** of or pertaining to spring. **2.** appearing or occurring in spring. **3.** appropriate to or resembling spring. **4.** belonging or pertaining to youth. [t. L: s. *vernālis*] —**ver′nally,** *adv.*

vernal equinox. See **equinox.** Also, **vernal point.**

vernalize (vû′nə līz′), *v.t.*, **-lized, -lizing.** to shorten the growth period before blossoming and fruit or seed bearing of (a plant), as by chilling its seed or bulb. Also, **vernalise.** —**ver′naliza′tion,** *n.*

vernation (vû nā′shən), *n. Bot.* the disposition of the foliage leaves within the bud. [t. L: s. *vernātio* shedding of the skin of snakes, ult. der. *ver* spring]

Verne (vĕən, vûn; *Fr.* vern), *n.* **Jules** (jōōlz; *Fr.* zhYl), 1828–1905, French novelist.

Verner (vû′nə; *Dan.* vĕr′nər), *n.* **Karl Adolph** (*Dan.* kärl ä′dŏlf), 1846–96, Danish linguist.

Verner's law, (in the history of Indo-European languages) the statement by Verner of some hitherto unexplained features in the system formulated by Grimm's law, showing the continuance into later languages of the effects of the primitive Indo-European word accent. —**Vernerian** (vû nĕə′rĭ ən), *adj.*

vernicle (vû′nĭ kl), *n.* veronica (defs 2–4).

vernier (vû′nyə), *n.* **1.** Also, **vernier scale.** a small, movable, graduated scale running parallel with the fixed graduated scale of a sextant, theodolite, barometer, or other graduated instrument, and used for measuring a fractional part of one of the divisions of the fixed scale. **2.** *Mach.* an auxiliary device for giving a piece of apparatus a higher adjustment accuracy. —*adj.* **3.** equipped with a vernier: *a vernier barometer.* **4.** *Aerospace.* denoting or pertaining to a low-thrust rocket engine used to achieve fine adjustments of the velocity or attitude of a spacecraft. [t. F; named after Pierre *Vernier*, 1580–1637, French mathematician]

Vernoleninsk (*Russ.* vĭr nə lyĭ nĕnsk′), *n.* former name of **Nikolaev.**

Vernon (vû′nən), *n.* **Edward** ('*Old Grog*'), 1684–1757, English admiral.

Verona (və rō′nə; *It.* vĕ rô′nä), *n.* a city in N Italy, on the river Adige. 247,948 (1966).

Veronal (vĕ′rə nəl), *n. Trademark*, barbitone. [t. G, said to have been named after VERONA]

Veronese (vĕ′rə nēz′), *adj., n., pl.* **-ese.** —*adj.* **1.** of or pertaining to Verona or its inhabitants. —*n.* **2.** a native or inhabitant of Verona.

Veronese (vĕ′rə nā′zĭ; *It.* vĕ rô nĕ′sĕ), *n.* **Paolo** (*It.* pä′ô lô) (*Paolo Cagliari*), 1528–88, Venetian painter.

veronica (və rŏn′ĭ kə), *n.* **1.** any plant of the scrophulariaceous genus *Veronica*, as the speedwell. **2.** the representation of the face of Christ which, according to a legend, was miraculously impressed on a cloth which St Veronica offered to Him to wipe His brow as He carried His cross to Calvary. **3.** the cloth itself. Cf. **sudarium. 4.** any similar picture of Christ's face, as on a garment. Also (defs 2–4), **vernicle.** [t. ML, appar. named after St *Veronica*]

Verrazano (*It.* vĕr rä tsä′nô), *n.* **Giovanni da** (*It.* jô vän′nē dä), *c.* 1480–1527?, Italian navigator who explored along the coast of North America for France. Also, **Verrazzano** or **Verrazani** (*It.* vĕr rä tsä′nē).

Verrocchio (*It.* vĕr rôk′kyô), *n.* **Andrea del** (*It.* än drĕ′ä dĕl), 1435–88, Italian goldsmith, sculptor, and painter.

verruca (vĕ rōō′kə), *n., pl.* **-cae** (-sē). **1.** *Med.* a wart. **2.** *Zool.* a small, flattish, wartlike prominence. [t. L]

verrucose (vĕ′rōō kōs), *adj.* studded with wartlike excrescences or elevations. Also, **verrucous** (vĕ′rŏŏ kəs, vĕ rōō′kəs). —**verrucosity** (vĕ′rŏŏ kŏs′ĭ tĭ), *n.*

vers., *Trig.* versed sine.

Versailles (vĕə sī′; *Fr.* vĕr säy′), *n.* a town in N France, ab. 12 miles SW of Paris, capital of Yvelines department: palace of Louis XIV; treaty of peace between the Allies and Germany 1919. 95,149 (1962).

versant (vû′sənt), *n.* **1.** a slope of a mountain or mountain chain. **2.** the general slope of a country or region. [t. F, ppr. of *verser* turn, g. L *versāre*, der. *vertere*]

versatile (vû′sə tīl′), *adj.* **1.** capable of or adapted for turning with ease from one to another of various tasks, subjects, etc.; many-sided in abilities. **2.** *Bot.* attached at or near the middle so as to swing freely, as an anther. **3.** *Zool.* turning either forwards or backwards: *a versatile toe.* **4.** variable or changeable, esp. in feeling, purpose, policy, etc. [t. L: m. s. *versātilis* turning about] —**ver′satile′ly,** *adv.* —**versatility** (vû′sə tĭl′ĭ tĭ), **ver′satile′ness,** *n.*

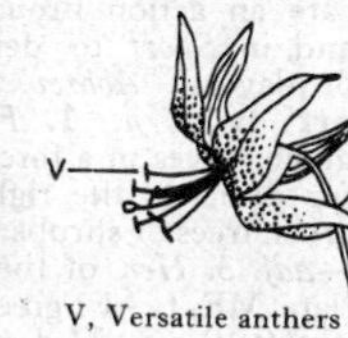

V, Versatile anthers

vers de société (*Fr.* vĕr də sō syĕ tĕ′), *French.* humorous light verse dealing with fashions and foibles of the time.

verse (vûs), *n.* **1.** (not in technical use) a stanza or other subdivision of a metrical composition: *the first verse of a hymn.* **2.** a succession of metrical feet written or printed or orally composed as one line; one of the lines of a poem. **3.** a particular type of metrical line: *a hexameter verse.* **4.** a poem, or piece of poetry. **5.** metrical composition; poetry, esp. as involving metrical form. **6.** a particular type of metrical composition: *iambic verse, elegiac verse.*

7. the metrical compositions of an author, period, or the like, considered collectively: *Elizabethan verse.* **8.** *Obs.* a line of prose, esp. a sentence, or part of a sentence, written as one line; a stich. **9.** a short division of a chapter in the Bible, usually one sentence, or part of a long sentence. *—adj.* **10.** written in poetry: *a verse drama.* [ME and OE *vers,* t. L: s. *versus* line, row]

—**Syn. 1.** VERSE, STANZA, STROPHE, STAVE are terms for a metrical grouping in poetic composition. VERSE is often mistakenly used for STANZA, but is properly only a single metrical line. A STANZA is a succession of lines (verses) commonly bound together by a rhyme scheme, and usually forming one of a series of similar groups which constitute a poem: *the four-line stanza is the one most frequently used in English.* STROPHE (originally the section of a Greek choral ode sung while the chorus was moving from right to left) is in English poetry practically equivalent to 'section'; a STROPHE may be unrhymed or without strict form, but may be a stanza: *strophes are divisions of odes.* STAVE is a word (now seldom used) which meant a stanza set to music or intended to be sung: *a stave of a hymn, of a drinking song.* **5.** See **poetry.**

versed (vûst), *adj.* experienced; practised; skilled (fol. by *in*): *well versed in a subject.* [half adoption, half trans. of L *versātus*, pp., busied, engaged]

versed sine, *Trig.* one minus the cosine (of a given angle or arc). *Abbrev.:* vers.

verset (vû′sĕt), *n.* **1.** a short verse or scrap of metrical writing. **2.** *Music.* a short organ prelude or interlude. **3.** *Archaic.* a versicle.

versicle (vû′sĭ kl), *n.* **1.** a little verse. **2.** *Eccles.* one of a series of short sentences, or parts of sentences, usually from the Psalms, said or sung by the officiant, as distinguished from the response of the choir or congregation. Cf. **response** (def. 4a). [ME, t. L: m. s. *versiculus* little verse]

versicolour (vû′sĭ kŭl′ə), *adj.* **1.** changeable in colour. **2.** of various colours; particoloured. Also, **ver′sicol′oured;** *U.S.,* **versicolor.** [t. L: m. *versicolor*]

versicular (vû sĭk′yŏŏ lə), *adj.* of or consisting of versicles or verses. [f. s. L *versiculus* little verse + -AR[1]]

versification (vû′sĭ fĭ kā′shən), *n.* **1.** the act of versifying. **2.** form or style of verse; metrical structure. **3.** a metrical version of something. **4.** the rules or customs of verse-making.

versify (vû′sĭ fī′), *v.,* **-fied, -fying.** *—v.t.* **1.** to relate or describe in verse; treat as the subject of verse. **2.** to turn into verse or metrical form. *—v.i.* **3.** to compose verses. [ME *versifie,* t. L: m. *versificāre* put into verse] —**ver′sifi′er,** *n.*

version (vû′shən), *n.* **1.** a particular account of some matter, as from one person or source, as contrasted with some other account or accounts. **2.** a translation. **3.** a particular form or variant of anything. **4.** (*often cap.*) a translation of the Bible or a part of it: *the King James Version.* **5.** *Med.* the act of turning a child in the uterus so as to bring it into a more favourable position for delivery. **6.** *Pathol.* an abnormal direction of the axis of the uterus. [t. L: s. *versio* turning] —**ver′sional,** *adj.* —**Syn. 2.** See **translation.**

vers libre (vĕə′lē′brə; *Fr.* vĕr lē′br), *French.* free verse. —**vers librist** (vĕə′lē′brĭst).

verso (vû′sō), *n., pl.* **-sos. 1.** *Print.* Also, **reverso.** a left-hand page of a book or manuscript. **2.** the reverse, back, or other side of some object, as a coin or medal. [t. L: short for *versō foliō*, lit., on the turned leaf]

verst (vĕəst, vûst), *n.* a Russian measure of distance, equivalent to 3500 feet (about 2/3 of a mile). [t. Russ.: s. *versta*]

versus (vû′səs), *prep.* against (used esp. in *Law* to indicate an action brought by one party against another, and in *Sport* to denote a contest between two teams or players). *Abbrev.:* v. *or* vs. [t. L]

vert[1] (vût), *n.* **1.** *Forest Law.* **a.** vegetation bearing green leaves in a forest and capable of serving as a cover for deer. **b.** the right to cut such green trees or shrubs. **2.** *Her.* green. *—adj.* **3.** *Her.* of the colour green. [late ME, t. AF: green]

vert[2] (vût), *v.t. Med.* to turn (a foetus) by application of pressure on the abdomen. [t. L: s. *vertere*]

vert., vertical.

vertebra (vû′tĭ brə), *n., pl.* **-brae** (-brē′), **-bras.** *Anat., Zool.* any of the bones or segments composing the spinal column: in man and the higher animals consisting typically of a more or less cylindrical body (centrum) and an arch (neural arch) with various processes, forming a foramen through which the spinal cord passes. [t. L]

Vertebra
A, Spine; B, Facet of rib; C, Pedicel; D, Body; E, Lamina; F, Transverse process; G, Articular process; H, Spinal canal

vertebral (vû′tĭ brəl), *adj.* **1.** of or pertaining to a vertebra or the vertebrae; spinal. **2.** of the nature of a vertebra. **3.** composed of vertebrae. **4.** having vertebrae. —**ver′tebrally,** *adv.*

vertebral column, the spinal column.

vertebrate (vû′tĭ brāt′, -brĭt), *n.* **1.** a vertebrate animal. *—adj.* **2.** having vertebrae; having a backbone or spinal column. **3.** belonging or pertaining to the *Vertebrata*, a subphylum of the phylum *Chordata*, all members of which have backbones. [t. L: m. s. *vertebrātus* jointed]

vertebrated (vû′tĭ brā′tĭd), *adj.* **1.** having vertebrae; vertebrate. **2.** consisting of vertebrae.

vertebration (vû′tĭ brā′shən), *n.* vertebrate formation.

vertex (vû′tĕks), *n., pl.* **-texes, -tices** (-tĭ sēz′). **1.** the highest point of something; the apex; the top; the summit. **2.** *Anat., Zool.* the crown or top of the head. **3.** *Astron., etc.* a point in the celestial sphere towards which or from which the common motion of a group of stars is directed. **4.** *Maths.* the point farthest from the base. **5.** *Geom.* **a.** a point in a plane figure common to two or more sides. **b.** a point in a solid common to three or more sides. **c.** the point of intersection of the tangents extended from each end of a circular curve. [t. L: whirl, crown of the head, summit]

vertical (vû′tĭ kl), *adj.* **1.** being in a position or direction perpendicular to the plane of the horizon; upright; plumb. **2.** of, pertaining to, or situated at the vertex. **3.** *Bot.* **a.** (of a leaf) having the blade in a perpendicular plane, so that neither of the surfaces can be called upper or under. **b.** in the same direction as the axis; lengthways. **4.** of or pertaining to the consolidation of businesses or industries that are closely related in the manufacture or sale of a certain commodity. *—n.* **5.** a vertical line, plane, or the like. **6.** vertical or upright position. **7.** (in a truss) a vertical member. [t. LL: s. *verticālis*, der. *vertex* VERTEX] —**ver′tical′ity, ver′ticalness,** *n.* —**ver′tically,** *adv.* —**Syn. 1.** See **upright.** —**Ant. 1.** horizontal.

vertical angle, 1. *Geom.* **a.** either of the two opposite angles formed by two intersecting lines or planes; vertically opposite angle. **b.** the angle at the vertex of a triangle or polygon. **2.** *Astron.* an angle measured on a vertical circle.

vertical circle, 1. *Astron.* a great circle on the celestial sphere which passes through the zenith and cuts the horizon at right angles. **2.** *Survey.* the graduated circular plate of a theodolite used for measuring vertical angles.

vertices (vû′tĭ sēz′), *n.* a pl. of **vertex.**

verticil (vû′tĭ sĭl), *n. Bot., Zool.* a whorl or circle, as of leaves, hairs, etc., arranged round a point on an axis. [t. L: m. s. *verticillus*, dim. of *vertex* whorl (of a spindle)]

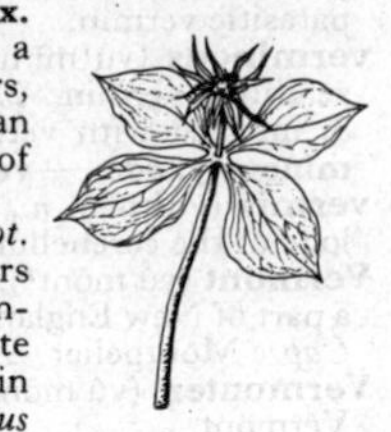
Verticil

verticillaster (vû′tĭ sĭ lăs′tə), *n. Bot.* an inflorescence in which the flowers are arranged in a seeming whorl, consisting in fact of a pair of opposite axillary, usually sessile, cymes, as in many mints. [t. NL: f. s. L *verticillus* whorl + *-aster* -ASTER[2]]

verticillate (vû tĭs′ĭ lĭt, -lāt′, vû′tĭ sĭl′āt), *adj.* **1.** disposed in or forming verticils or whorls, as flowers, etc. **2.** (of plants) having flowers, etc., so arranged or disposed. Also, **vertic′illat′ed.** —**vertic′illately,** *adv.* —**vertic′illa′tion,** *n.*

vertiginous (vû tĭj′ĭ nəs), *adj.* **1.** whirling or rotary. **2.** affected with vertigo. **3.** liable to cause vertigo. **4.** apt to change quickly; unstable. [t. L: m. s. *vertīginōsus* suffering from giddiness] —**vertig′inously,** *adv.* —**vertig′inousness,** *n.*

vertigo (vû′tĭ gō′), *n., pl.* **vertigos, vertigines** (vû tĭj′ĭ nēz′). *Pathol.* a disordered condition in which an individual, or whatever is around him, seems to be whirling about; dizziness. [t. L: lit., whirling round]

vertu (vû too′), *n.* virtu.

Vertumnus (vû tŭm′nəs), *n.* the Roman divinity of gardens and orchards, worshipped as the god of the changing seasons. Also, **Vortumnus.** [t. L, der. *vertere* turn, change]

Verulamium (vĕ′roo lā′myəm), *n.* ancient name of **St Albans.**

vervain (vû′vān), *n.* any plant of the genus *Verbena* (see **verbena**), esp. one of the species with small spicate flowers, as *V. officinalis,* a common European species. [ME *verveine,* t. OF, g. L *verbēna* green bough]

verve (vûv), *n.* **1.** enthusiasm or energy, as in literary or artistic work; spirit, liveliness, or vigour: *her novel lacks verve.* **2.** *Rare.* talent. [t. F: enthusiasm, fancy; orig. uncert.]

vervet (vû′vĭt), *n.* an African monkey, *Cercopithecus æthiops pygerythrus,* allied to the green monkey and the grivet, but distinguished by a rusty patch at the root of the tail. [f. F, b. *ver(t)* green and *(gri)vet* grivet]

Verwoerd (fēə vo͝oət′), *n.* **Hendrik Frensch** (hĕn′-drĭk frĕnch′), 1901–66, South African politician, born in the Netherlands: prime minister 1958–66.

very (vĕr′ĭ), *adv., adj.,* **-rier, -riest.** *—adv.* **1.** in a high degree, extremely, or exceedingly. **2.** (used as an intensive emphasizing superlatives or stressing identity or oppositeness): *the very best thing to be done, in the very same place.* *—adj.* **3.** precise or identical: *the very thing you should not have done.* **4.** even (what is specified): *they grew to dread his very name.* **5.** mere: *the very thought is distressing.* **6.** sheer: *to weep for very joy.* **7.** actual: *caught in the very act.* **8.** (with emphatic or intensive force) being such in the true or full sense of the term: *the very heart of the matter.* **9.** true, genuine, or real: *the very God.* **10.** *Archaic.* rightful or legitimate. [ME, t. OF: m. *verai,* der. L *vērus* true]

very high frequency, *Radio.* any frequency between 30 and 300 megacycles per second. *Abbrev.:* v.h.f.

Very light (vīə′rĭ), a small coloured flare which is fired from a special pistol (**Very pistol**) for the purposes of illumination or signalling. [named after E. W. *Very,* 1847–1907, American inventor]

very low frequency, *Radio.* any frequency below 30 kilocycles per second. *Abbrev.:* v.l.f.

Very Rev., Very Reverend (a title of ecclesiastical deans).

vesica (vĕs′ĭ kə), *n., pl.* **-cae** (-sē′). **1.** a bladder; a sac. **2.** the urinary bladder, *Vesica urinaria,* or gall bladder, *V. fellea.* [L: bladder, blister]

vesical (vĕs′ĭ kl), *adj.* **1.** of or pertaining to a vesica or bladder, esp. the urinary bladder. **2.** having the shape of a vesica, esp. elliptical.

vesicant (vĕs′ĭ kənt), *adj.* **1.** vesicating; producing a blister or blisters, as a medicinal substance. *—n.* **2.** a vesicant agent or substance. **3.** *Chem. War.* a chemical agent that causes burns and destruction of tissue both internally and externally. [t. NL: s. *vēsicans* blistering]

vesicate (vĕs′ĭ kāt′), *v.t.,* **-cated, -cating.** to raise vesicles or blisters on; blister. **—ves′ica′tion,** *n.*

vesicatory (vĕs′ĭ kā′tə rĭ), *adj., n., pl.* **-ries.** vesicant.

vesicle (vĕs′ĭ kl), *n.* **1.** a little sac or cyst. **2.** *Anat., Zool.* a small bladder-like cavity, esp. one filled with fluid. **3.** *Pathol.* a circumscribed elevation of the epidermis containing serous fluid. **4.** *Bot.* a small bladder, or bladder-like air cavity, esp. one present in plants which float on water. **5.** *Geol.* a small, usually spherical cavity in a rock or mineral, due to gas or vapour. [t. L: m. s. *vēsicula,* dim. of *vēsica* bladder, blister]

vesicular (vĕ sĭk′yo͝o lə), *adj.* **1.** of or pertaining to vesicles. **2.** having the form of a vesicle. **3.** characterized by or consisting of vesicles. **—vesic′ularly,** *adv.*

vesicular exanthema, a specific infectious disease of swine, closely resembling foot-and-mouth disease.

vesiculate (*adj.* vĕ sĭk′yo͝o lĭt, -lāt′; *v.* vĕ sĭk′yo͝o lāt′), *adj., v.,* **-lated, -lating.** *—adj.* **1.** characterized by or covered with vesicles. **2.** of the nature of a vesicle. *—v.t., v.i.* **3.** to make or become vesiculate or vesicular. **—vesic′-ula′tion,** *n.*

Vespasian (vĕs pā′zhyən), *n.* (*Titus Flavius Sabinus Vespasianus*), A.D. 9–79, Roman emperor A.D. 70–79.

vesper (vĕs′pə), *n.* **1.** evening. **2.** (*cap.*) the evening star, esp. Venus; Hesperus. **3.** an evening prayer, service, song, etc. **4.** a vesper bell; a bell rung at evening. **5.** (*pl.*) vespers. *—adj.* **6.** of, pertaining to, appearing in, or proper to the evening. **7.** of or pertaining to vespers. [ME, t. L]

vesperal (vĕs′pə rəl), *n.* *Eccles.* **1.** that part of the antiphonary which contains the chants for vespers. **2.** a cloth used between offices to cover the altar cloth.

vespers (vĕs′pəz), *n.pl.* (*sometimes cap.*) **1.** a religious service held in the late afternoon or the evening. **2.** the sixth of the seven canonical hours, or the service for it, occurring in the late afternoon or evening. **3.** *Rom. Cath. Ch.* a part of the office to be said in the evening by those in major orders, frequently made a public ceremony in the afternoons or evenings of Sundays and holy days. **4.** Evensong. [t. ML: m. *vesperae,* pl., vespers, special use of L *vespera* evening]

vespertilionine (vĕs′pə tĭl′ĭ ə nīn′, -nĭn), *adj.* of or pertaining to the bats of the subfamily *Vespertilioninae,* common in temperate regions and including many well-known species. [f. s. L *vespertilio* bat + -INE[1]] **—vespertilionid** (vĕs′pə tĭl′ĭ ə nĭd), *n., adj.*

vespertine (vĕs′pə tīn′), *adj.* **1.** of, pertaining to, or occurring in the evening. **2.** *Bot.* opening or expanding in the evening, as certain flowers. **3.** *Zool.* appearing or flying in the early evening; crepuscular. Also, **vespertinal** (vĕs′pə tī′nəl). [t. L: m. s. *vespertīnus* of the evening]

vespiary (vĕs′pĭ ə rĭ), *n., pl.* **-ries.** a wasp's nest. [f. s. L *vespa* wasp + *-iary* as in APIARY]

vespid (vĕs′pĭd), *n.* **1.** any member of the *Vespidae,* a widely distributed family of social wasps, including the hornets, which live in communities composed of males (drones), females (queens), and workers. *—adj.* **2.** belonging or pertaining to the *Vespidae.* [t. NL: s. *Vespidae,* der. L *vespa* wasp]

vespine (vĕs′pīn), *adj.* **1.** of or pertaining to wasps. **2.** wasp-like.

Vespucci (*It.* vĕs po͞ot′chē), *n.* **Amerigo** (*It.* ä mē rē′gô) (*Americus Vespucius*), 1451–1512, Italian merchant, adventurer, and explorer after whom America was named.

vessel (vĕs′əl), *n.* **1.** a craft for travelling on water, now esp. one larger than an ordinary rowing boat; a ship or boat. **2.** a hollow or concave article, as a cup, bowl, pot, pitcher, vase, bottle, etc., for holding liquid or other contents. **3.** *Anat., Zool.* a tube or duct, as an artery, vein, or the like, containing or conveying blood or some other body fluid. **4.** *Bot.* a duct formed of connected cells which have lost their intervening partitions, containing or conveying sap, etc. **5.** a person regarded as a receptacle or container (chiefly in or after biblical expressions). [ME, t. OF, g. L *vascellum* small vase. See VASE]

vest (vĕst), *n.* **1.** a short undergarment with or without sleeves, usually worn next to the skin under a shirt. **2.** *Now Chiefly U.S.* a waistcoat. **3.** *U.S.* a similar garment, or a part or trimming simulating the front of such a garment, worn by women. **4.** a long garment resembling a cassock, worn by men in the times of Charles II. **5.** *Archaic.* dress, apparel, or vesture. **6.** *Archaic.* an outer garment, robe, or gown. **7.** *Rare.* an ecclesiastical vestment. [t. It.: m. *veste,* g. L *vestis* garment] *—v.t.* **8.** to clothe, dress, or robe. **9.** to dress in ecclesiastical vestments. **10.** to cover or drape (an altar). **11.** to place or settle (something, esp. property, rights, powers, etc.) in the possession or control of a person or persons (usually fol. by *in*): *to vest an estate or a title in a person.* **12.** to invest or endow (a person, etc.) with something, esp. with powers, functions, etc. *—v.i.* **13.** to put on vestments. **14.** to become vested in a person or persons, as a right. **15.** to pass into possession; to devolve upon a person as possessor. [ME, t. OF: m. *vestir,* g. L *vestīre* clothe] **—vest′less,** *adj.* **—vest′like′,** *adj.*

Vesta (vĕs′tə), *n.* **1.** *Rom. Myth.* the goddess of the hearth and hearth fire, worshipped in a temple containing an altar on which a sacred fire was kept burning under the care of the vestal virgins. **2.** (*l.c.*) a short match with a wood or wax stem which can be struck on any rough surface.

vestal (vĕs′tl), *adj.* **1.** of, pertaining to, or consecrated to Vesta. **2.** pertaining to, characteristic of, or resembling a vestal virgin; virgin; chaste. *—n.* **3.** a vestal virgin. **4.** a virgin; a chaste unmarried woman. **5.** a nun.

vestal virgin, (among the ancient Romans) one of four, later six, virgins consecrated to Vesta and to the service of watching the sacred fire kept burning perpetually on her altar.

vested (vĕs′tĭd), *adj.* **1.** settled or secured in the possession of a person or persons, as a complete or fixed right, an interest sometimes possessory, sometimes future, which has substance because of its relative certainty. **2.** clothed or robed, esp. in ecclesiastical vestments: *a vested choir.*

vested interests, 1. personal interests or rights in a system, institution, or the like, usually protected by law or custom. **2.** the persons, groups, etc., who have acquired rights or powers by which they are able to further or maintain their position of dominance in some sphere of a country's activities, as business or finance.

vestee (vĕs tē′), *n.* *U.S.* a decorative front piece worn under a woman's jacket or blouse and visible between its open edges; dicky (def. 1). [f. VEST, n. + *-ee,* dim. suffix]

vestiary (vĕs′tĭ ə rĭ), *adj.* of or pertaining to garments or dress. [t. L: m. s. *vestiārius*]

vestibular (vĕs tĭb′yo͝o lə), *adj.* of, pertaining to, or resembling a vestibule.

vestibule (vĕs′tĭ byo͞ol′), *n., v.,* **-buled, -buling.** *—n.* **1.** a passage, hall, or antechamber between the outer door and the interior parts of a house or building. **2.** *Anat., Zool.* any of various cavities or hollows regarded as forming an approach or entrance to another cavity or space: *the vestibule of the ear.* See diag. under **ear. 3.** an enclosed space at the end of a railway carriage, affording entrance to the carriage from outside and from the next carriage. *—v.t.* **4.** to provide with a vestibule or vestibules, as a railway carriage. [t. L: m. s. *vestibulum*]

vestibule school, *U.S.* a department of an industrial establishment in which new employees are trained for the work they are to perform.

vestige (vĕs′tĭj), *n.* **1.** a mark, trace, or visible evidence of something which is no longer present or in existence. **2.** a surviving evidence or memorial of some condition, practice, etc. **3.** a very slight trace or amount of something. **4.** *Biol.* a degenerate or imperfectly developed organ or structure having little or no utility, but which in an earlier stage of the individual or in preceding organisms performed a useful function. **5.** *Archaic.* a footprint or track. [t. F, t. L: m. *vestigium* footprint] **—Syn. 1.** See **trace**[1].

vestigial (vĕs tĭj′ĭ əl), *adj.* pertaining to or of the nature of a vestige. —**vestig′ially,** *adv.*

vestigium (vĕs tĭj′ĭ əm), *n., pl.* **-tigia** (-tĭj′ĭ ə). *Anat.* a vestige; a vestigial structure of any kind.

vesting (vĕs′tĭng), *n. Now Chiefly U.S.* any of various medium or heavy cloths used for making waistcoats, etc.

vestment (vĕst′mənt), *n.* **1.** a garment, esp. an outer garment, robe, or gown. **2.** an official or ceremonial robe. **3.** *Eccles.* **a.** one of the garments worn by the clergy and their assistants, choristers, etc., during divine service and on other occasions. **b.** one of the garments worn by the celebrant, deacon, and subdeacon during the celebration of the Eucharist. **4.** something that covers like a garment. [ME *vestement*, t. OF, der. *vestir* clothe, on model of L *vestīmentum* clothing] —**vestmental** (vĕst mĕn′tl), *adj.*

vest-pocket (vĕst′pŏk′ĭt), *adj. Now Chiefly U.S.* miniature, as something designed for a waistcoat pocket.

vestry (vĕs′trĭ), *n., pl.* **-tries. 1.** a room in or a building attached to a church, in which the vestments, and sometimes also the sacred vessels, etc., are kept; a sacristy. **2.** (in some churches) a room in or a building attached to a church, used as a chapel, for prayer meetings, for the Sunday school, etc. **3.** (in parishes of the Church of England) **a.** a meeting of all the parishioners, or of a committee of parishioners, held in the vestry for the dispatch of the official business of the parish. **b.** the body of parishioners so meeting; parish council. **4.** (in the Protestant Episcopal Church in the U.S.) a committee, chosen by the members of a congregation, who, in conjunction with the churchwardens, manage the temporal affairs of a church. [ME, f. VEST, v. + -RY]

vestry book, a parish register.

vestryman (vĕs′trĭ mən), *n., pl.* **-men.** a member of a church vestry.

vesture (vĕs′chə), *n., v.,* **-tured, -turing.** —*n.* **1.** *Law.* **a.** everything growing on and covering the land, with the exception of trees. **b.** any such product, as grass or wheat. **2.** *Archaic.* clothing; garments. **3.** *Archaic.* something that covers like a garment; a covering. —*v.t.* **4.** *Archaic.* to clothe, as with vesture. [ME, t. OF, der. *vestir* clothe, influenced by ML *vestītūra* clothing] —**ves′tural,** *adj.*

Vesuvian (vĭ so͞o′vyən), *adj.* **1.** of, pertaining to, or resembling Mount Vesuvius; volcanic. —*n.* (*l.c.*) **2.** a kind of slow-burning match formerly used for lighting cigars, etc.; a fusee. **3.** vesuvianite.

vesuvianite (vĭ so͞o′vyə nīt′), *n.* a mineral, a hydrous silicate of calcium and aluminium chiefly, commonly in prismatic crystals and usually of a brown to green colour; idocrase.

Vesuvius (vĭ so͞o′vyəs), *n.* **Mount,** an active volcano in SW Italy, near Naples: many severe eruptions; the ancient cities of Pompeii and Herculaneum were buried by an eruption A.D. 79. ab. 4000 ft. See map under **Salerno.**

vet[1] (vĕt), *n., v.,* **vetted, vetting.** *Colloq.* —*n.* **1.** a veterinary surgeon. —*v.t.* **2.** to examine or treat as a veterinary surgeon does. **3.** to examine or treat (a person) medically. **4.** to examine (a product, proposal, or the like) with a view to acceptance, rejection, or correction. —*v.i.* **5.** to work as a veterinary surgeon. [short for VETERINARY]

vet[2] (vĕt), *n. U.S. Colloq.* a veteran.

Vet (vĕt), *n.* a river in the Republic of South Africa, flowing NW through Orange Free State to the Vaal. 130 mi.

vetch (vĕch), *n.* **1.** any of various leguminous plants, mostly climbing herbs, of the genus *Vicia*, as *V. sativa*, the common vetch, cultivated for forage and soil improvement. **2.** any of various allied plants, as *Lathyrus sativus*, of Europe, cultivated for its edible seeds and as a forage plant. **3.** the beanlike seed or fruit of any such plant. [ME *veche*, t. d. OF, g. L *vicia*] —**vetch′like′,** *adj.*

vetchling (vĕch′lĭng), *n.* any of the plants constituting the leguminous genus *Lathyrus*, as *L. pratensis*, common in meadows.

veter., veterinary.

veteran (vĕt′ə rən, vĕt′rən), *n.* **1.** one who has seen long service in any occupation or office. **2.** a soldier who has seen active service: *a veteran of the desert war.* **3.** *U.S.* anyone who has had any experience in some field, esp. a soldier. —*adj.* **4.** experienced through long service or practice; having served for a long period; grown old in service. **5.** of, pertaining to, or characteristic of veterans. **6.** denoting or pertaining to a motor vehicle built before 1904. **7.** (of soldiers) having had service or experience in warfare: *veteran troops.* [t. L: s. *veterānus*, der. *vetus* old]

veterinarian (vĕt′ə rĭ nĕə′rĭ ən, vĕt′rĭ-), *n. U.S.* a veterinary surgeon.

veterinary (vĕt′ə rĭ nə rĭ, vĕt′rĭn rĭ), *n., pl.* **-ries,** *adj.* —*n.* **1.** a veterinary surgeon. —*adj.* **2.** of the medical and surgical treatment of animals, esp. domesticated ones. [t. L: m. s. *veterīnārius*, der. *veterīnus* pertaining to cattle]

Veteran's Day, *U.S.* Armistice Day.

veterinary medicine, that branch of medicine that concerns itself with the study, prevention, and treatment of animal diseases.

veterinary surgeon, one who practises veterinary medicine or surgery.

vetiver (vĕt′ĭ və), *n.* **1.** the long, fibrous, aromatic roots of an Indian grass, *Vetiveria zizanoides*, used for making hangings and screens, and yielding **vetiver oil,** used in perfumery. **2.** the grass itself. [t. Tamil: m. *vettivēru*]

veto (vē′tō), *n., pl.* **-toes,** *v.,* **-toed, -toing.** —*n.* **1.** the power or right of preventing action by a prohibition. **2.** a prohibition directed against some proposed or intended act. **3.** the right of any one of the five members of the United Nations Security Council to prevent the Council acting on any except procedural matters. **4.** *U.S.* the power or right vested in one branch of government to cancel or postpone the decisions of another, esp. the right of the president or the governor of a state to reject bills passed by the legislature. **5.** the exercise of such a right. **6.** *U.S.* a document or message by which the right of veto is exercised, on which the reasons for exercising the right are officially stated. —*v.t.* **7.** to prevent (a proposal, legislative bill, etc.) being put into action by exercising the right of veto. **8.** to refuse to consent to. [t. L: I forbid] —**ve′toer,** *n.* —**ve′toless,** *adj.*

vet. sci., veterinary science.

Vetter (*Sw.* vĕ′tər), *n.* Vätter.

vex (vĕks), *v.t.* **1.** to irritate; annoy; provoke; make angry: *enough to vex a saint.* **2.** to torment; plague; worry: *want of money vexes many.* **3.** to agitate, discuss, or debate (a subject, etc.) with vigour: *a vexed question.* **4.** *Archaic.* to disturb by motion; stir up; toss about. **5.** *Archaic.* to trouble or afflict physically. [ME *vexe(n)*, t. L: m. *vexāre* agitate] —**vex′er,** *n.* —**vex′ingly,** *adv.*

vexation (vĕk sā′shən), *n.* **1.** the act of vexing. **2.** the state of being vexed. **3.** something that vexes.

vexatious (vĕk sā′shəs), *adj.* **1.** causing vexation; vexing; annoying. **2.** *Law.* (of legal actions) instituted without sufficient grounds, and serving only to cause annoyance. —**vexa′tiously,** *adv.* —**vexa′tiousness,** *n.*

vexed (vĕkst), *adj.* **1.** disturbed; troubled; annoyed. **2.** much discussed or disputed. **3.** tossed about, as waves. —**vexedly** (vĕk′sĭd lĭ), *adv.* —**vex′edness,** *n.*

vexillary (vĕk′sĭ lə rĭ), *n., pl.* **-ries,** *adj.* —*n.* **1.** one of a class of ancient Roman veteran soldiers, who served under a special standard. —*adj.* **2.** Also, **vexillar** (vĕk sĭl′ə). of or pertaining to a vexillum. [t. L: m. s. *vexillārius*]

vexillate (vĕk′sĭ lĭt, -lāt′), *adj.* having a vexillum or vexilla.

vexillum (vĕk sĭl′əm), *n., pl.* **vexilla** (vĕk sĭl′ə). **1.** a military standard or flag carried by ancient Roman troops. **2.** a body of men serving under such a standard. **3.** Also, **vexil** (vĕk′sĭl). *Bot.* the large upper petal of a papilionaceous flower. See illus. under **papilionaceous. 4.** *Ornith.* the web or vane of a feather. [t. L: standard]

VF, 1. video frequency. **2.** voice frequency.

V.F.R., *Aeron.* Visual Flight Rules.

V.G., Vicar-General.

v.g., 1. (L *verbi gratia*) for example. **2.** very good.

v.h.f., *Radio.* very high frequency.

Vi, *Chem. Obs.* virginium.

V.I., 1. Vancouver Island. **2.** Virgin Islands.

v.i., 1. verb intransitive. **2.** vide infra.

via (vī′ə), *prep.* **1.** by way of; by a route that passes through: *go to Italy via Paris.* **2.** by means of: *to reach a conclusion via three logical steps.* [t. L, abl. of *via* way]

viable (vī′ə bl), *adj.* **1.** capable of living. **2.** practicable; workable. **3.** *Physiol.* **a.** physically fitted to live. **b.** (of a foetus) having reached such a stage of development as to permit continued existence, under normal conditions, outside the womb. **4.** *Bot.* able to live and grow. [t. F, der. *vie* life, g. L *vīta*] —**vi′abil′ity,** *n.*

via dolorosa (vē′ə dŏl′ə rō′sə), **1.** Christ's way to Golgotha. **2.** any distressing, difficult, or sorrowful course.

Viaduct (def. 1)

viaduct (vī′ə dŭkt′), *n.* **1.** a bridge consisting of a series of narrow masonry arches with high supporting piers, for carrying a road, railway, etc., over a valley, ravine, or the like. **2.** a similar bridge of steel girders. [f. L *via* way + *-duct* as in AQUEDUCT]

vial (vī′əl, vīl), *n.* **1.** (*pl. or sing.*) a store or accumulation of wrath, indignation, etc. (Rev. 15:17; 16:1–17). **2.** phial (def. 1). [ME *viole*, var. of *fiole* PHIAL]

via media (vī′ə mē′dĭ ə), *Latin.* a middle way; a mean between two extremes.

viand (vī′ənd), *n.* **1.** an article of food. **2.** (*pl.*) articles or dishes of food, now usually of a choice or delicate kind. [ME *vyaunde*, t. OF: m. *viande*, g. L *vīvenda* things to be lived on]

Viareggio (*It.* vyȧ rĕd′jō), *n.* a seaport in NW Italy: resort. 52,837 (1966).

viaticum (vī ăt′ĭ kəm), *n.*, *pl.* **-ca** (-kə), **-cums.** **1.** *Eccles.* the Eucharist or communion as given to a person dying or in danger of death. **2.** (among the ancient Romans) a provision or allowance for travelling, orig. of transport and supplies, later of money, made to officials on public missions. **3.** money or necessities for any journey. [t. L]

viator (vī ā′tô), *n.*, *pl.* **viatores** (vī′ə tô′rēz). a traveller; a wayfaring person. [t. L]

vibes (vībz), *n.pl. Colloq.* vibraphone. **—vi′bist,** *n.*

Viborg (*Sw.* vē′bŏry), *n.* Swedish name of **Vyborg.**

vibraculum (vī brăk′yōō ləm), *n.*, *pl.* **-la** (-lə). one of the long, tapering, whiplike, movable appendages possessed by certain polyzoans. [NL, der. L *vibrāre* shake] **—vibrac′ular,** *adj.*

Vibracula

vibraharp (vī′brə häp′), *n. U.S.* a vibraphone.

vibrant (vī′brənt), *adj.* **1.** moving to and fro rapidly; vibrating. **2.** vibrating so as to produce sound, as a string. **3.** (of sounds) characterized by perceptible vibration, or resonant. **4.** pulsating with energy. **5.** full of vigour; energetic; powerful; forceful. **6.** exciting; producing a thrill. **7.** *Phonet.* voiced. **—***n.* **8.** *Phonet.* a voiced sound. [t. L: s. *vibrans*, ppr.] **—vi′brancy,** *n.* **—vi′brantly,** *adv.*

vibraphone (vī′brə fōn′), *n.* a xylophone-like musical instrument with electronically operated resonators controlled by a pedal. Also, *U.S.*, **vibraharp.** [f. L *vibrā*(*re*) shake, vibrate + -PHONE] **—vibraphonist** (vī′brə fō′nĭst), *n.*

vibrate (vī brāt′), *v.*, **-brated, -brating.** **—***v.i.* **1.** to move to and fro, as a pendulum; oscillate. **2.** to move to and fro or up and down quickly and repeatedly; quiver; tremble. **3.** (of sounds) to produce or have a quivering or vibratory effect; resound. **4.** to thrill, as in emotional response. **5.** to move between extremes; fluctuate; vacillate. **—***v.t.* **6.** to cause to move to and fro, swing, or oscillate. **7.** to cause to move to and fro or up and down quickly and repeatedly; cause to quiver or tremble. **8.** to give forth or emit (sound, etc.) by or as by vibratory motion. [t. L: m. s. *vibrātus*, pp., shaken] **—Syn. 2.** See **shake.**

vibratile (vī′brə tīl′), *adj.* **1.** capable of vibrating or of being vibrated. **2.** having a vibratory motion. **3.** pertaining to or of the nature of vibration. **—vibratility** (vī′brə tĭl′ĭ tĭ), *n.*

vibration (vī brā′shən), *n.* **1.** the act of vibrating; oscillation. **2.** the state of vibrating; tremulous effect. **3.** *Physics.* **a.** the oscillating, reciprocating, or other periodic motion of a rigid or elastic body forced from a position or state of equilibrium. **b.** the analogous motion of the particles of a mass of air, etc., whose state of equilibrium has been disturbed, as in transmitting sound, etc. **c.** the vibratory motion of a string or other sonorous body, producing musical sound. **4.** a single vibrating motion; an oscillation; a quiver or tremor. **—vibra′tional,** *adj.* **—vibra′tionless,** *adj.*

vibrative (vī brā′tĭv), *adj.* vibratory.

vibrato (vĭ brä′tō), *n.*, *pl.* **-tos.** *Music.* a pulsating effect, produced in singing by the rapid reiteration of emphasis on a note, and on bowed instruments by a rapid change of pitch corresponding to the vocal tremolo. [It., pp. of *vibrare* vibrate, t. L]

vibrator (vī brā′tə), *n.* **1.** one who or that which vibrates. **2.** any of various instruments or devices causing a vibratory motion or action. **3.** an appliance with a rubber or other tip of variable shape, made to oscillate very rapidly, used in vibratory massage. **4.** *Elect.* **a.** a device containing a vibrating member for converting a direct current into an oscillating current. **b.** a device for producing electrical oscillations.

vibratory (vī′brə tə rĭ, -trĭ), *adj.* **1.** producing vibration. **2.** vibrating, or admitting of vibration. **3.** of the nature of or inherent in vibration. **4.** pertaining to vibration. Also, **vibrative.**

vibrio (vĭb′rĭ ō′), *n.*, *pl.* **-rios.** *Bacteriol.* any bacterium of the genus *Vibrio*, made up of comma-shaped organisms, the most important of which is *V. comma*, the causative agent of Asiatic cholera. [NL, der. L *vibrāre* shake] **—vibrioid** (vĭb′rĭ oid′), *adj.*

vibrionic (vĭb′rĭ ŏn′ĭk), *adj.* of, pertaining to, or caused by an infection by any bacterium of the genus *Vibrio.*

vibrissa (vī brĭs′ə), *n.*, *pl.* **-brissae** (-brĭs′ē). **1.** one of the stiff, bristly hairs growing about the mouth of certain animals, as a cat's whisker. **2.** one of the long, slender, bristle-like feathers growing along the side of the mouth in many birds. [t. L: hair in the nostrils]

viburnum (vī bû′nəm), *n.* **1.** any of the shrubs or small trees constituting the caprifoliaceous genus *Viburnum*, species of which, as the cranberry bush, *V. opulus*, or snowball, are cultivated for ornament. **2.** the dried bark of various species of *Viburnum*, used in medicine. [t. L: the wayfaring tree]

vicar (vĭk′ə), *n.* **1.** *C. of E.* a clergyman acting as priest of a parish. **2.** *Rom. Cath. Ch.* **a.** an ecclesiastic representing the pope or a bishop. **b.** the pope as the representative on earth of God or Christ. **3.** one acting in place of another. **4.** a person authorized to perform the functions of another; a deputy. [ME *vicare*, t. AF, t. L: m. s. *vicārius* substitute] **—vic′arship′,** *n.*

vicarage (vĭk′ə rĭj), *n.* **1.** the residence of a vicar. **2.** the benefice of a vicar. **3.** the office or duties of a vicar.

vicar apostolic, *Rom. Cath. Ch.* **1.** a missionary or titular bishop stationed either in a country where no episcopal see has yet been established, or in one where the succession of bishops has been interrupted. **2.** (formerly) an archbishop, bishop, or other ecclesiastic to whom the pope delegated a portion of his jurisdiction.

vicarate (vĭk′ə rĭt), *n.* vicariate.

vicar choral, *C. of E.* a cleric or layman who sings in a cathedral choir.

vicar forane (fō rān′), *Rom. Cath. Ch.* an ecclesiastical dignitary appointed by the bishop to exercise a limited jurisdiction in a particular town or district of his diocese; a rural dean. [f. VICAR + s. L *forāneus* living outside; see FOREIGN]

vicar-general (vĭk′ə jĕn′rəl), *n.*, *pl.* **vicars-general.** **1.** *Rom. Cath. Ch.* a priest appointed by a bishop to assist him in the administration of a diocese. **2.** *C. of E.* an ecclesiastical officer, usually a layman, who assists a bishop or an archbishop in the discharge of his judicial or administrative duties. **3.** a deputy with extensive power or jurisdiction (a title given to Thomas Cromwell).

vicarial (vī kēə′rĭ əl), *adj.* **1.** of or pertaining to a vicar or vicars. **2.** acting as or holding the office of a vicar. **3.** delegated or vicarious, as powers.

vicariate (vī kēə′rĭ ĭt), *n.* **1.** the office or authority of a vicar. **2.** a district under a vicar. Also, **vicarate.**

vicarious (vī kēə′rĭ əs), *adj.* **1.** performed, exercised, received, or suffered in place of another: *vicarious pleasure.* **2.** taking the place of another person or thing; acting or serving as a substitute. **3.** pertaining to or involving the substitution of one for another. **4.** *Physiol.* pertaining to or denoting the performance by one organ of part of the functions normally performed by another. [t. L: m. *vicārius* substituted] **—vicar′iously,** *adv.* **—vicar′iousness,** *n.*

vicarly (vĭk′ə lĭ), *adj.* pertaining to, resembling, or suggesting a vicar.

Vicar of (Jesus) Christ, *Rom. Cath. Ch.* the pope, with reference to his claim to stand in the place of Jesus Christ and possess His authority in the Church.

vice[1] (vīs), *n.* **1.** an immoral or evil habit or practice; a grave moral fault. **2.** immoral conduct or life; indulgence in impure or degrading practices. **3.** a particular form of depravity. **4.** a fault, defect, or imperfection: *a vice of literary style.* **5.** a physical defect or infirmity: *a constitutional vice.* **6.** a bad habit, as in a horse. **7.** (*cap.*) a character in the English morality plays, a personification of general vice or of a particular vice, serving as the buffoon. [ME, t. OF, g. L *vitium* fault] **—Syn. 1.** See **fault.**

vice[2] (vīs), *n.*, *v.*, **viced, vicing.** **—***n.* **1.** any of various devices, usually having two jaws which may be brought together or separated by means of a screw, lever, or the like, used to hold an object firmly while work is being done upon it. **—***v.t.* **2.** to hold, press, or squeeze with or as with a vice. Also, *U.S.*, **vise.** [ME *vyse*, t. OF: m. *vis* screw, g. L *vītis* vine] **—vice′like′,** *adj.*

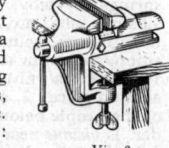

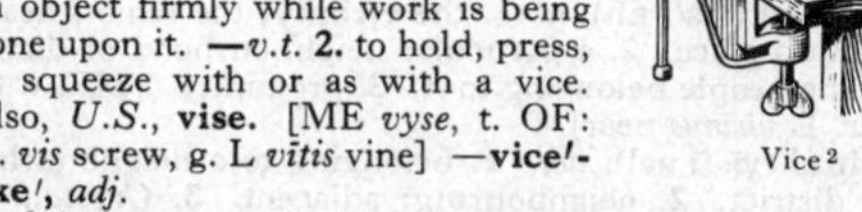

Vice[2]

vice[3] (vī′sĭ), *prep.* instead of; in the place of. [t. L, abl. of *vicis* turn]

vice-, a prefix denoting a substitute, deputy, or subordinate: *vice-chairman, viceroy, viceregent.* [See VICE]

vice-admiral (vīs′ ăd′mə rəl), *n.* a naval officer next in rank below an admiral. **—vice′-ad′miralty,** *n.*

vice-chairman (vīs′ chēə′mən), *n., pl.* **-men** (-mən). a member of a board, committee, or the like, immediately below the chairman in rank, and taking the place of the chairman in his absence. **—vice′-chair′manship′,** *n.*

vice-chancellor (vīs′ chăn′sə lə), *n.* **1.** the executive head of a university, usually a member of the teaching staff. **2.** a substitute, deputy, or subordinate chancellor. **3.** a chancery judge acting as assistant to the chancellor. **—vice′-chan′cellorship′,** *n.*

vice-consul (vīs′ kŏn′səl), *n.* a consular officer of a grade below that of consul. **—vice′-con′sular,** *adj.* **—vice′-con′sulate,** *n.* **—vice′-con′sulship′,** *n.*

vicegeral (vīs′jĕ′rəl), *adj.* of a vicegerent or his position.

vicegerency (vīs′jĕ′rən sĭ), *n., pl.* **-cies.** **1.** the position, government, or office of a vicegerent. **2.** the territory or district under a vicegerent.

vicegerent (vīs′jĕ′rənt), *n.* **1.** an officer deputed by a ruler or supreme head to exercise the powers of the ruler or head. **2.** any deputy. *—adj.* **3.** exercising delegated powers. **4.** characterized by delegation of powers. [t. ML: s. *vicegerens*, ppr., place-holding, substituting]

viceless (vīs′lĭs), *adj.* free from vices or vice.

vicenary (vĭs′ĭ nə rĭ), *adj.* pertaining to or consisting of twenty. [t. L: m. s. *vicēnārius*]

vicennial (vī sĕn′yəl), *adj.* **1.** of or for twenty years. **2.** occurring every twenty years. [f. s. L *vicennium* period of twenty years + -AL[1]]

Vicente (*Port.* vē sĕn′tə), *n.* **Gil** (*Port.* zhēl), *c.* 1470–1536, Portuguese dramatist.

Vicenza (*It.* vē chĕn′tsä), *n.* a city in NE Italy, in Veneto. 107,091 (1966).

Vice-Pres., Vice-President.

vice-president (vīs′prĕz′ĭ dənt), *n.* an officer next in rank to a president and taking his place under certain conditions (as the **Vice-President of the United States,** who is elected at the same time as the President, and succeeds to the presidential office on the resignation, removal, death, or disability of the President). **—vice′-pres′idency,** *n.* **—vice-presidential** (vīs′ prĕz′ĭ dĕn′shəl), *adj.*

viceregal (vīs′rē′gl), *adj.* of or pertaining to a viceroy. **—vice′re′gally,** *adv.*

vice-regent (vīs′rē′jənt), *n.* **1.** a deputy regent; one who acts in the place of a ruler, governor, or sovereign. *—adj.* **2.** of, pertaining to, or occupying the position of a vice-regent. **—vice′-re′gency,** *n.*

vicereine (vīs′ rān′), *n.* a viceroy's wife. [t. F: equiv. to *vice-* VICE- + *reine* queen]

viceroy (vīs′roi), *n.* **1.** one appointed to rule a country or province as the deputy of the sovereign: *the viceroy of India.* **2.** anyone to whom rank or authority has been delegated. [t. F, f. *vice-* VICE- + *roi* king] **—vice′roy-ship′,** *n.*

viceroyalty (vīs′roi′əl tĭ), *n., pl.* **-ties.** **1.** the dignity, office, or period of office of a viceroy. **2.** a country or province ruled by a viceroy.

vice versa (vī′sĭ vû′sə), conversely; the order being changed (from that of a preceding statement): *A distrusts B, and vice versa.* [t. L]

Vichy (vē′shĭ; *Fr.* vē shē′), *n.* a town in central France: the capital of unoccupied France 1940–44; hot springs. 32,200 (1967).

Vichy, 1940–44

Vichyite (vē′shĭ īt′), *n.* **1.** a member or adherent of the French government at Vichy 1940–44. *—adj.* **2.** of or pertaining to this government.

vichyssoise (*Fr.* vē shē swäz′), *n. French.* a creamy potato and leek soup, usually served cold.

vichy water (vē′shĭ), **1.** a natural mineral water from springs at Vichy, containing sodium bicarbonate, other alkaline salts, etc., used in the treatment of digestive disturbances, gout, etc. **2.** some water of similar composition, natural or artificial. Also, **Vichy, vichy.**

vicinage (vĭs′ĭ nĭj), *n.* **1.** the vicinity; the region near or about a place. **2.** a particular neighbourhood or district, or the people belonging to it. **3.** proximity. [ME, t. OF, der. L *vīcīnus* near]

vicinal (vĭs′ĭ nəl), *adj.* **1.** belonging to a neighbourhood or district. **2.** neighbouring; adjacent. **3.** *Crystall.* denoting planes whose position varies very little from planes of much simpler indices which they replace. **4.** *Chem.* denoting a compound in which adjacent carbon atoms have been substituted. [t. L: s. *vīcīnālis* neighbouring]

vicinity (vĭ sĭn′ĭ tĭ), *n., pl.* **-ties.** **1.** the region near or about a place; the neighbourhood or vicinage. **2.** the state or fact of being near in place; proximity; propinquity. [t. L: m. s. *vīcīnitas*]

vicious (vĭsh′əs), *adj.* **1.** addicted to or characterized by vice or immorality; depraved; profligate. **2.** given or disposed to evil; bad. **3.** reprehensible, blameworthy, or wrong, as an action, practice, etc. **4.** spiteful or malignant: *a vicious attack.* **5.** *Colloq.* unpleasantly severe: *a vicious headache.* **6.** characterized or marred by faults or defects; faulty; defective: *vicious reasoning.* **7.** (of a horse, etc.) having bad habits or an ugly disposition. **8.** *Obs.* morbid, foul, or noxious. [ME, t. L: m. s. *vitiōsus* faulty] **—vi′ciously,** *adv.* **—vi′ciousness,** *n.*

vicious circle, 1. a situation in which solution of one problem creates further problems and increased difficulties. **2.** *Logic.* **a.** (in demonstration) the use of one proposition to establish a second, when the second proposition is in turn used to establish the first. **b.** (in definition) the use of one term in defining a second, the second in turn being used to define the first. **3.** *Pathol.* a series of unhealthy changes in which the first change produces the second which in turn affects the first.

vicissitude (vĭ sĭs′ĭ tyōōd′), *n.* **1.** a change or variation, or something different, occurring in the course of something. **2.** interchange or alteration, as of states or things. **3.** (*pl.*) changes, variations, successive or alternating phases or conditions, etc., in the course of anything. **4.** regular change or succession of one state or thing to another. **5.** change, mutation, or mutability. [t. L: m. *vicissitūdo* change] **—vicissitudinary** (vĭ sĭs′ĭ tyōō′dĭ nə rĭ), **vicis′situ′dinous,** *adj.*

Vickers (vĭk′əz), *n.* **Jon,** born 1926, Canadian tenor.

Vicky (vĭk′ĭ), *n.* (*Victor Weisz*), 1913–66, British cartoonist, born in Germany of Hungarian parents.

vicomte (*Fr.* vē kôNt′), *n. French.* viscount. **—vicomtesse** (*Fr.* vē kôN tĕs′), *n.fem.*

vicontiel (vī kŏn′tĭ əl), *adj. Early Eng. Law.* pertaining to the sheriff or viscount. [t. AF, der. *viconte* sheriff]

victim (vĭk′tĭm), *n.* **1.** a sufferer from any destructive, injurious, or adverse action or agency: *victims of disease or oppression.* **2.** a dupe, as of a swindler. **3.** a person or animal sacrificed, or regarded as sacrificed: *war victims.* **4.** a living creature sacrificed in religious rites. [t. L: s. *victima* beast for sacrifice]

victimize (vĭk′tĭ mīz′), *v.t.,* **-mized, -mizing.** **1.** to make a victim of. **2.** to discipline or punish selectively, esp. as a result of an industrial dispute: *four men were victimized by management after the strike.* **3.** to punish unfairly. **4.** to dupe, swindle, or cheat: *to victimize poor widows.* **5.** to slay as or like a sacrificial victim. Also, **victimise.** **—vic′timiza′tion,** *n.* **—vic′timiz′er,** *n.* **—Syn. 4.** See **cheat.**

victor (vĭk′tə), *n.* **1.** one who has vanquished or defeated an adversary; a conqueror. **2.** a winner in any struggle or contest. [ME, t. L]

Victor Emmanuel I (ĭ măn′yōō əl) (*Vittorio Emanuele*), 1759–1824, king of Sardinia 1802–21.

Victor Emmanuel II, 1820–78, king of Sardinia 1849–78, and first king of Italy 1861–78.

Victor Emmanuel III, 1869–1947, king of Italy 1900–46.

Victoria (vĭk tô′rĭ ə), *n.* **1.** 1819–1901, queen of Great Britain and Ireland 1837–1901, and empress of India 1876–1901. **2.** *Rom. Myth.* the goddess of victory, identified with the Greek Nike. **3.** a state in SE Australia. 3,130,960 pop. (1964); 87,884 sq. mi. *Cap.:* Melbourne. **4.** Also, **Hong Kong.** a seaport in and the capital of Hong Kong colony, on the SE coast of China. 1,005,041 (1964). **5.** a seaport in SW Canada, on Vancouver Island: the capital of British Columbia. 54,741 (1961); with suburbs, 154,152 (1961). See map under **Vancouver.** **6.** a seaport in and the capital of the Seychelles. 10,500 (1964). **7.** a river in N Australia flowing NW through Northern Territory to Joseph Bonaparte Gulf. ab. 440 mi. **8. Lake.** Also, **Victoria Nyanza.** a lake in E Africa: the second largest freshwater lake in the world; principal headwaters of the Nile. 26,828 sq. mi. **9. Mount,** a mountain of the Owen Stanley Range, in SE New Guinea. 13,030 ft. **10.** (*l.c.*) a low, light, four-wheeled carriage with a folding hood, a seat for two passengers, and a perch in front for the driver. **11.** Also, **victoria plum.** a large, sweet, pinkish red variety

Lake Victoria

Victoria (def. 10)

of plum. **12.** a waterlily, *Victoria regia* (or *amazonica*), a native of still waters from Paraguay to Venezuela, with leaves 6 feet, and flowers 12 to 18 inches across.

Victoria Cross, a British decoration in the shape of a bronze Maltese cross awarded to members of the armed services for acts of conspicuous bravery in the presence of the enemy, founded by Queen Victoria in 1856.

Victoria Falls, **1.** falls of the river Zambezi in southern Africa between Zambia and Rhodesia, near Livingstone. ab. 400 ft high; over a mile wide. **2.** Iguassú Falls.

Victoria Land, a region in Antarctica, bordering on the Ross Sea; largely in Ross Dependency.

Victorian (vĭk tôʹrĭ ən), *adj.* **1.** of or pertaining to Queen Victoria or her reign or period: *the Victorian age.* **2.** having the characteristics usually attributed to the Victorians, as bigotry and prudishness. **3.** of or pertaining to the state of Victoria in Australia. —*n.* **4.** a person living in the Victorian period. **5.** a person having the characteristics usually attributed to the Victorians; a prude. **6.** a native or inhabitant of the state of Victoria in Australia.

Victoriana (vĭk tôʹrĭ äʹnə), *n.* ornaments, bric-a-brac, etc., of the Victorian period.

Victorianism (vĭk tôʹrĭ ə nĭzʹəm), *n.* **1.** the distinctive character, thought, tendencies, etc., of the Victorian period. **2.** a Victorian characteristic.

Victoria Nyanza (nyănʹzə). See **Victoria** (def. 8).

victoria sandwich, a type of sponge cake made with equal quantities of fat and sugar.

victorine (vĭkʹtə rēnʹ), *n.* a fur tippet with long ends.

victorious (vĭk tôʹrĭ əs), *adj.* **1.** having achieved a victory. **2.** characterized by or pertaining to victory. **3.** conquering; triumphant. —**victoʹriously,** *adv.* —**victoʹriousness,** *n.*

victory (vĭkʹtə rĭ), *n., pl.* **-ries. 1.** the ultimate and decisive superiority in a battle or any contest. **2.** a success or triumph won over the enemy in battle or war, or an engagement ending in such a triumph: *naval victories.* **3.** any success or successful performance achieved over an adversary or opponent, opposition, difficulties, etc. **4.** (*cap.*) the Roman goddess Victoria, or Greek Nike. [ME *victorie*, t. L: m. *victōria*] —**vicʹtoryless,** *adj.*

—**Syn. 1.** VICTORY, CONQUEST, TRIUMPH refer to a successful outcome of a struggle. VICTORY suggests the decisive defeat of an opponent in a contest of any kind: *victory in battle, a football victory.* CONQUEST implies the taking over of control by the victor, and the obedience of the conquered: *a war of conquest, the conquest of Peru.* TRIUMPH implies a particularly outstanding victory: *the triumph of a righteous cause, of justice.* —**Ant. 1.** defeat.

victress (vĭkʹtrĭs), *n.* a female victor.

victual (vĭtʹl), *n., v.,* **-ualled, -ualling** or (*U.S.*) **-ualed, -ualing.** —*n.* **1.** (*pl.*) *Chiefly Dial or Colloq.* articles of food prepared for use. **2.** *Archaic. or Dial.* food or provisions, usually for human beings. —*v.t.* **3.** to supply or store with victuals. —*v.i.* **4.** to take or obtain victuals. **5.** *Archaic.* to eat or feed. [ME *vitaile*, t. OF, g. LL *victuālia* provisions] —**victʹualless,** *adj.*

victualler (vĭtʹə lə, vĭtʹlə), *n.* **1.** one who furnishes victuals or provisions; a sutler. **2.** a supply ship. **3.** a licensed victualler. Also, *U.S.*, **victualer.**

vicuña (vĭ kyo͞oʹnə), *n.* **1.** a wild South American ruminant, *Lama vicugna*, of the Andes, related to the guanaco but smaller, and having a soft, delicate wool. **2.** a fabric made of this wool, or of some substitute, usually twilled and finished with a soft nap. **3.** a garment of this fabric. [t. Sp., t. Quechua: m. *vicunna*]

Vicuña, *Lama vicugna* (2½ ft or more high at the shoulder)

vid., vide.

Vidar (vēʹdä), *n.* *Scand. Myth.* a taciturn god of great strength, son of Odin and the giantess Grid.

vide (vīʹdĭ), *v.* *Latin.* see (used esp. in making reference to parts of a text).

vide ante (vīʹdĭ ănʹtĭ), *Latin.* see before.

vide infra (vīʹdĭ ĭnʹfrä), *Latin.* see below.

videlicet (vĭ dēʹlĭ sĕtʹ), *adv.* namely; that is to say (used to introduce examples, details, lists, etc.). *Abbrev.*: viz. [t. L, for *vidēre licet* it is permitted to see]

video (vĭdʹĭ ōʹ), *adj.* **1.** *Television.* pertaining to or employed in the transmission or reception of a televised image. —*n.* **2.** *U.S. Colloq.* television. [t. L: I see]

video frequency, the frequency of the signal which conveys the image and synchronizing pulses in a television broadcasting system. *Abbrev.*: VF.

video-tape (vĭdʹĭ ō tāpʹ), *n., v.,* **-taped, -taping.** —*n.* **1.** magnetic tape upon which a video-frequency signal is recorded; used for storing a television programme or film. —*v.t.* **2.** to record on video-tape.

vide post (vīʹdĭ pōstʹ), *Latin.* see after or afterwards; refer to later material.

vide supra (vīʹdĭ so͞oʹprä), *Latin.* see above.

vidette (vĭ dĕtʹ), *n.* vedette.

vide ut supra (vīʹdĭ o͝ot so͞oʹprä), *Latin.* see as above; refer as directed previously.

vidual (vĭdʹyo͞o əl), *adj.* of or pertaining to a widow or the state of widowhood. [t. L: s. *viduālis*]

viduity (vĭ dyo͞oʹĭ tĭ), *n.* the state of being a widow; widowhood. [ME (Scot.) *viduite*, t. OF, t. L: m. s. *viduitas*]

vie (vī), *v.,* **vied, vying.** —*v.i.* **1.** to strive in competition or rivalry with another; to contend for superiority. —*v.t.* **2.** *Archaic.* to put forward or offer in competition or rivalry. **3.** *Obs.* to stake in card playing. [t. F: aphetic m. *envier* challenge, t. L: m. *invitāre* invite]

vielle (vĭ ĕlʹ), *n.* a hurdy-gurdy (def. 2). [t. F]

Vienna (vĭ ĕnʹə), *n.* **1.** the capital of Austria, in the NE part: a port on the Danube. 1,627,566 (1961). German, **Wien.** See **Congress of Vienna. 2.** Also, **Vienna loaf.** (*sometimes l.c.*) a cigar-shaped loaf of white bread about 12 inches long. **3.** a smoked sausage, eaten boiled, usually made of beef or pork.

Vienna Circle, a group of philosophers, many of them also mathematicians or scientists, active in Vienna from about 1930, who developed logical positivism.

Vienna International. See **international** (def. 8).

Vienna white, a paint consisting of pure white lead.

Vienne (*Fr.* vyĕn), *n.* **1.** a town in SE France, on the river Rhône, S of Lyons: Roman ruins. 28,163 (1962). **2.** a department in W central France. 331,619 pop. (1962); 2711 sq. mi. *Cap.*: Poitiers.

Viennese (vĭə nēzʹ), *adj., n., pl.* **-nese.** —*adj.* **1.** of Vienna. —*n.* **2.** a native or inhabitant of Vienna.

Vientiane (vyĕnʹtĭ änʹ), *n.* a town in NW Laos, on the Mekong river: administrative capital. 100,000 (est. 1962).

vi et armis (vīʹ ĕt äʹmĭs), *Latin.* by force of arms (lit., by force and arms).

Vietcong (vyĕtʹkŏngʹ), *n.* **1.** a communist-led organization and guerrilla army in South Vietnam, supported by North Vietnam, fighting the Americans and South Vietnamese and seeking to overthrow the existing government. **2.** a member of this force. —*adj.* **3.** of or pertaining to this organization.

Vietminh (vyĕtʹmĭnʹ), *n.* **1.** a revolutionary nationalist organization in Vietnam which fought first the Japanese, then the French 1941–54. —*adj.* **2.** of or pertaining to this organization.

Vietnam (vyĕtʹnămʹ), *n.* a country in SE Asia, comprising the former states of Annam, Tonkin, and Cochin-China; formerly part of French Indochina; divided in 1954 at 17°N. See **North Vietnam** and **South Vietnam.**

Vietnam

Vietnamese (vyĕtʹnə mēzʹ), *adj., n., pl.* **-ese.** —*adj.* **1.** of or pertaining to Vietnam or its inhabitants. —*n.* **2.** a native or inhabitant of Vietnam. **3.** Formerly, **Annamese, Annamite.** the official language of Vietnam. **4.** the Annamese linguistic family.

Viëtor (*Ger.* fēʹĕ tŏr), *n.* **Wilhelm** (*Ger.* vĭlʹhĕlm), 1850–1918, German philologist and phonetician.

view (vyo͞o), *n.* **1.** a seeing or beholding; an examination by the eye. **2.** sight or vision: *exposed to view.* **3.** range of sight or vision: *objects in view.* **4.** a sight or prospect of some landscape, scene, etc. **5.** a picture of a scene. **6.** the aspect, or a particular aspect, of something. **7.** mental contemplation or examination; a mental survey. **8.** contemplation or consideration of a matter with reference to action: *a project in view.* **9.** aim, intention, or purpose. **10.** prospect or expectation: *with no view of success.* **11.** a general account or description of a subject. **12.** a particular way of regarding something. **13.** a conception, notion, or idea of a thing; an opinion or theory. **14.** a survey or inspection. **15. a dim view,** an unfavourable opinion. **16. in view, a.** within range of vision. **b.** under consideration. **c.** near to realization. **17. in view of, a.** in sight of. **b.** in prospect or anticipation of. **c.** in consideration of. **d.** on account of. **18. on view,** in a place for public inspection; on exhibition. **19. with a view to, a.** with an aim or intention directed to. **b.** with an expectation or hope of. **c.** in consideration of. **d.** with regard to. —*v.t.* **20.** to see or behold. **21.** to watch (a television programme). **22.** to look at, survey, or inspect. **23.** to contemplate mentally; consider. **24.** to regard in a particular light or as specified. **25.** *Hunting.* to sight (a hunted animal).

—*v.i.* **26.** to inspect a prospective purchase or the like. **27.** to watch television or a television programme. [ME *vewe*, t. AF, var. of *veue*, pp. of *veoir* see, g. L *vidēre*] —**Syn. 4.** VIEW, PROSPECT, SCENE, VISTA refer to a landscape or perspective. VIEW is a general word, referring to whatever lies open to sight: *a fine view of the surrounding country.* PROSPECT suggests a sweeping and often distant view, as from a place of vantage: *a beautiful prospect to the south.* SCENE suggests an organic unity in the details such as is to be found in a picture: *a woodland scene.* VISTA suggests a long narrow view, as along an avenue between rows of trees: *a pleasant vista.* **13.** See **opinion.**

viewable (vyōō′ə bl), *adj.* **1.** able to be viewed; visible. **2.** ready to be inspected: *the house is viewable now.*

viewer (vyōō′ə), *n.* **1.** one who or that which views. **2.** one who watches television or a television programme. **3.** a device for viewing photographic transparencies. **4.** an official inspector, as of a colliery.

viewfinder (vyōō′fīn′də), *n. Photog.* an attachment to a camera enabling the photographer to determine what will be included in his picture.

view halloo, the shout uttered by a huntsman on seeing a fox break cover. Also, **view halloa.**

viewless (vyōō′lĭs), *adj.* **1.** that cannot be viewed or seen; invisible. **2.** without views or opinions. **3.** not having a pleasant view, or having no view at all. —**view′lessly,** *adv.*

viewpoint (vyōō′point′), *n.* **1.** a place affording a view of something. **2.** a point of view; an attitude of mind: *the viewpoint of an artist.*

viewy (vyōō′ĭ), *adj. Colloq.* **1.** theorizing; visionary. **2.** opinionated. —**view′iness,** *n.*

Vigée-Lebrun (*Fr.* vē zhė lə brœɴ′), *n.* **Madame.** See **Lebrun, Marie Anne Elisabeth Vigée.**

vigesimal (vĭ jĕs′ĭ məl), *adj.* **1.** pertaining to or based upon twenty. **2.** twentieth. **3.** proceeding by twenties. [f. s. L *vīgēsimus* twentieth + -AL[1]]

vigesimo (vĭ jĕs′ĭ mō′), *n., pl.* **-mos,** *adj. Bookbinding.* —*n.* **1.** a volume printed from sheets folded to form 20 leaves or 40 pages, approximately 3 × 5 inches. *Abbrev.*: 20mo or 20°. —*adj.* **2.** in vigesimo. Also, **twentymo.** [t. L, abl. sing. of *vīgēsimus* twentieth]

vigesimo-quarto (vĭ jĕs′ĭ mō kwô′tō), *n., pl.* **-tos,** *adj. Bookbinding.* —*n.* **1.** a volume printed from sheets folded to form 24 leaves or 48 pages, approximately $3\frac{5}{8} \times 5\frac{1}{8}$ inches. *Abbrev.*: 24mo or 24°. —*adj.* **2.** in vigesimo-quarto. Also, **twenty-fourmo.** [t. L, abl. sing. of *vīgēsimus-quartus* twenty-fourth]

Vigevano (*It.* vē jĕ′vä nō), *n.* a town in Italy, in Lombardy. 64,029 (1966).

vigia (vĭ jĭə′), *n. Naut.* **1.** a mark on a navigational chart indicating a hazard or supposed hazard the precise location and nature of which is uncertain. **2.** an unidentified object sighted in the water and regarded as a possible hazard to navigation. [t. Sp.: lookout, reef; akin to VIGILANT]

vigil (vĭj′ĭl), *n.* **1.** a keeping awake for any purpose during the normal hours of sleep. **2.** a watch kept by night or at other times; a course or period of watchful attention. **3.** a period of wakefulness from inability to sleep. **4.** *Eccles.* **a.** a devotional watching, or keeping awake, during the customary hours of sleep. **b.** (*often pl.*) a nocturnal devotional exercise or service, esp. on the eve before a church festival. **c.** the eve, or day and night, before a church festival, esp. an eve which is a fast. [ME *vigile*, t. AF, g. L *vigilia* watch]

vigilance (vĭj′ĭ ləns), *n.* **1.** the quality or fact of being vigilant; watchfulness. **2.** *Pathol.* insomnia.

vigilance committee, *U.S.* **1.** an unauthorized committee of citizens organized for the maintenance of order and the summary punishment of crime in the absence of regular or efficient courts. **2.** *Hist.* (in the South) an organization of citizens using non-legal means to control or intimidate Negroes and abolitionists, and, during the Civil War, to suppress loyalty to the Union.

vigilance man, a vigilante.

vigilant (vĭj′ĭ lənt), *adj.* **1.** keenly attentive to detect danger; wary: *a vigilant sentry.* **2.** ever awake and alert; sleeplessly watchful. [late ME, t. L: s. *vigilans* watching] —**vig′ilantly,** *adv.* —**vig′ilantness,** *n.* —**Syn. 1.** See **alert.** —**Ant. 1.** careless.

vigilante (vĭj′ĭ lăn′tĭ), *n. U.S.* a member of a vigilance committee. [t. Sp.: vigilant]

vigilantism (vĭj′ĭ lăn′tĭz′əm), *n. U.S.* the qualities attributed to vigilantes, esp. militantism and extreme suspiciousness.

vigneron (*Fr.* vē nyə rôɴ′), *n. French.* a wine-grower.

vignette (vĭ nyĕt′), *n., v.,* **-gnetted, -gnetting.** —*n.* **1.** a decorative design or small illustration used on the title-page of a book, or at the beginning or end of a chapter. **2.** an engraving, drawing, photograph, or the like, shading off gradually at the edges; a design without a borderline. **3.** decorative work representing meandering branches, leaves, or tendrils, as in architecture or in manuscripts. **4.** any small, pleasing picture or view. **5.** a small, graceful literary sketch. —*v.t.* **6.** to finish (a picture, photograph, etc.) in the manner of a vignette. [t. F, dim. of *vigne* vine] —**vignet′tist,** *n.*

vignetter (vĭ nyĕt′ə), *n. Photog.* a device for shading off the edges of a print into a plain margin.

Vignola (*It.* vēn nyŏ′lä), *n.* **Giacomo da** (*It.* jä′kō mō dä) (*Giacomo Barocchio*), 1507–73, Italian architect.

Vigny (*Fr.* vē nyē′), *n.* **Alfred Victor de** (*Fr.* äl frĕd vēk tōr′ də), 1797–1863, French poet, novelist, and dramatist.

Vigo (vē′gō; *Sp.* bē′gō), *n.* a seaport in NW Spain, on the **Bay of Vigo,** an inlet of the Atlantic (19 mi. long): naval battle 1702. 165,671 (1965).

vigoroso (vĭg′ə rō′sō; *It.* vē gō rō′sō), *adj. Music.* vigorous or spirited in manner. [t. It.]

vigorous (vĭg′ə rəs), *adj.* **1.** full of or characterized by vigour. **2.** strong and active; robust. **3.** energetic or forcible. **4.** powerful in action or effect. **5.** growing well, as a plant. [ME, t. ML: m. s. *vigorōsus*] —**vig′orously,** *adv.* —**vig′orousness,** *n.* —**Syn. 2.** See **active.** —**Ant. 2.** lethargic.

vigour (vĭg′ə), *n.* **1.** active strength or force, as of body or mind. **2.** healthy physical or mental energy or power. **3.** energy; energetic activity. **4.** force of healthy growth in any living matter or organism, as a plant. **5.** active or effective force. Also, *U.S.,* **vigor.** [ME, t. OF, t. L: m. *vigor*]

vihara (vĭ hä′rə), *n.* a Buddhist or Jain temple or monastery. [t. Skt]

Viipuri (*Finn.* vē′pōō rē), *n.* former name of **Vyborg.**

Vijayawada (vē′jĭ ə wä′də), *n.* a town in Andhra Pradesh, India. 230,397 (1961). Also, **Bezwada.**

Viking (vī′kĭng), *n.* (*sometimes l.c.*) a Scandinavian rover or sea-robber of the type that infested the seas about northern and western Europe during the 8th, 9th, and 10th centuries, making raids upon the coasts. [t. Icel.: s. *víkingr* free-booter, pirate, c. OE *wīcing*]

vil., village.

vilayet (vĭ lä′yĕt), *n.* a province, or main administrative division of Turkey. Also, **eyalet.** [t. Turk., t. Ar.: m. *welāyet* district]

vile (vīl), *adj.,* **viler, vilest. 1.** wretchedly bad: *vile weather.* **2.** highly offensive, obnoxious, or objectionable. **3.** repulsive or disgusting, as to the senses or feelings; despicably or revoltingly bad. **4.** morally base, depraved, or despicable, as persons or the mind, character, actions, etc.: *vile thoughts.* **5.** foul, as language. **6.** poor or wretched, as in quality or state. **7.** of mean or low condition, as a person. **8.** mean or menial, as tasks, etc. **9.** low, degraded, or ignominious, as a condition, etc.: *vile servitude.* **10.** of little value or account; paltry. [ME, t. AF, g. L *vīlis* cheap, base] —**Syn. 3.** See **mean².** **4.** iniquitous, vicious, villainous. —**vile′ly,** *adv.* —**vile′ness,** *n.*

vilify (vĭl′ĭ fī′), *v.t.,* **-fied, -fying. 1.** to speak evil of; defame; traduce. **2.** *Obs.* to make vile. [ME, t. LL: m. s. *vīlificāre*] —**vil′ifica′tion,** *n.* —**vil′ifi′er,** *n.* —**Syn. 1.** depreciate, disparage, slander, calumniate, malign. —**Ant. 1.** praise.

vilipend (vĭl′ĭ pĕnd′), *v.t.* **1.** to regard or treat as of little value or account. **2.** to vilify. [late ME, t. L: s. *vīlipendere,* f. *vīli(s)* vile + *pendere* consider] —**vil′-ipend′er,** *n.*

villa (vĭl′ə), *n.* **1.** a detached or semidetached dwelling house, usually suburban, esp. one built before 1914. **2.** a mansion in the suburbs or at a resort. **3.** a country residence, usually of some size and pretensions; a country seat. **4.** an ancient Roman rural dwelling associated with agriculture, usually one built round a courtyard. [t. L or It.: country house] —**vil′la-like′,** *adj.*

Villa (*Sp.* bē′lyä), *n.* **Francisco** (*Sp.* frän thēs′kō) (*Doroteo Arango, 'Pancho Villa'*), 1877–1923, Mexican general and revolutionary.

villadom (vĭl′ə.dəm), *n. U.S.* **1.** villas collectively. **2.** the narrow and dull section of society regarded as villa occupants; suburban society. [f. VILLA + -DOM]

village (vĭl′ĭj), *n.* **1.** a small assemblage of houses in a country district, larger than a hamlet and smaller than a town. **2.** the inhabitants collectively. **3.** an assemblage of animal dwellings or the like, resembling a village. **4.** *U.S.* a small municipality. —*adj.* **5.** of, belonging to, or characteristic of a village; rustic. [ME, t. OF, der. *ville,* g. L *villa* villa] —**vil′lageless,** *adj.*

village community, an early form of organization, in which the land belonged to the village, the arable land being allotted by it to the members or households of the community, by more or less permanent arrangements, the waste or common land remaining undivided.

villager (vĭl′ĭ jə), *n.* **1.** an inhabitant of a village. **2.** a rustic.

villain (vĭl′ən), *n.* **1.** a wicked person; scoundrel. **2.** a character in a play, novel, or the like, who constitutes an important evil agency in the plot. **3.** *Colloq.* a criminal. **4.** a villein. [ME, t. OF, g. L *villānus* farm servant] —**villainess** (vĭl′ə nĭs), *n. fem.*

villainage (vĭl′ə nĭj), *n.* villeinage. Also, **villanage.**

villainous (vĭl′ə nəs), *adj.* **1.** having the character of a villain. **2.** pertaining to or befitting a villain. **3.** base; wicked; vile. **4.** very bad or unpleasant: *villainous weather.* —**vil′lainously,** *adv.* —**vil′lainousness,** *n.*

villainy (vĭl′ə nĭ), *n., pl.* **-nies. 1.** the action or conduct of a villain or scoundrel. **2.** a villainous act or deed. **3.** *Obs.* villeinage.

Villa-Lobos (*Port.* vē′lyȧ lō′bōōs), *n.* **Heitor** (*Port.* əy tôr′), 1881–1959, Brazilian composer.

villanella (vĭl′ə nĕl′ə; *It.* vĕl lȧ nĕl′lȧ), *n., pl.* **-nelle** (-nĕl′ĭ; *It.* -nĕl′lĕ), **-nellas.** an Italian rustic part-song without accompaniment. [t. It.: rustic, dim. of *villano* peasant, der. *villa* villa]

villanelle (vĭl′ə nĕl′), *n. Pros.* a short poem of fixed form, written in tercets (usually five) with a final quatrain, all based on two rhymes. [t. F, t. It. See VILLANELLA]

Villanovan (vĭl′ə nō′vən), *adj.* **1.** denoting or pertaining to an early Iron Age culture in N Italy, characterized by lake dwellings and the primitive use of iron and extensive use of bronze. —*n.* **2.** this culture. **3.** a member of the people which founded this culture. [named after *Villanova,* town in NE Italy near Bologna, where the first such remains were found in 1853]

Villard de Honnecourt (*Fr.* vē lȧr də ŏn kōōr′), fl. *c.* 1225–35, French architect.

Villars (*Fr.* vē lȧr′), *n.* **Claude Louis Hector de** (*Fr.* klōd lwē ĕk tōr′ də), 1653–1734, marshal of France.

villatic (vĭ lăt′ĭk), *adj.* of or pertaining to a farm; rural. [t. L: s. *villāticus,* der. *villa* villa]

villein (vĭl′ĭn), *n.* a member of a class of half-free persons under the feudal system who were serfs with respect to their lord but had the rights and privileges of freemen with respect to others. Also, **villain.** [var. of VILLAIN]

villeinage (vĭl′ĭ nĭj), *n.* **1.** the tenure by which a villein held land and tenements from his lord. **2.** the condition or status of a villein. Also, **villainage, villanage, villenage.** [ME, t. OF. See VILLAIN, -AGE]

Villeneuve (*Fr.* vēl nœv′), *n.* **Pierre Charles Jean Baptiste Silvestre de** (*Fr.* pyĕr shȧrl zhäɴ bȧ tēst sēl vĕs′trə də), 1763–1806, French admiral.

Villeurbanne (*Fr.* vē yœr bȧn′), *n.* a town in E France, near Lyons. 107,630 (1962).

villi (vĭl′ī), *n.* pl. of **villus.**

Villiers (vĭl′əz, vĭl′yəz), *n.* **George.** See **Buckingham** (defs 1, 2).

villiform (vĭl′ĭ fôm′), *adj.* **1.** having the form of a villus. **2.** so shaped and closely set as to resemble the pile of velvet, as the teeth of certain fishes. [t. NL: s. *villiformis.* See VILLUS, -FORM]

Villon (*Fr.* vē yôɴ′), *n.* **François** (*Fr.* fräɴ swȧ′), 1431–after 1463, French poet.

villosity (vĭ lŏs′ĭ tĭ), *n., pl.* **-ties. 1.** a villous surface or coating. **2.** a number of villi together. **3.** a villus.

villous (vĭl′əs), *adj.* **1.** covered with or of the nature of villi. **2.** abounding in villiform processes. **3.** *Bot.* pubescent with long and soft hairs which are not interwoven. Also, **villose** (vĭl′ōs). [t. L: m. s. *villōsus* hairy] —**vil′lously,** *adv.*

villus (vĭl′əs), *n., pl.* **villi. 1.** *Anat.* one of the minute, wormlike, vascular processes on certain animal membranes, esp. on the mucous membrane of the small intestine, where they serve in absorbing nutriment. **2.** *Bot.* one of the long, soft, straight hairs covering the fruit, flowers, and other parts of certain plants. [t. L: tuft of hair, shaggy hair]

Vilna (vĭl′nə; *Russ.* vēl′nə), *n.* a city in the W Soviet Union: capital of the Lithuanian Republic; formerly in Poland. 298,000 (est. 1965). Polish, **Wilno.** Lithuanian, **Vilnius** (vĭl′nĭ ōōs).

vim (vĭm), *n. Slang.* force; energy; vigour in action. [t. L, acc. of *vis*]

vimen (vī′mĕn), *n., pl.* **vimina** (vĭm′ĭ nə). *Bot.* a long, flexible shoot of a plant. [t. L: twig] —**viminal** (vĭm′ĭ nəl), *adj.*

Viminal (vĭm′ĭ nəl), *n.* the north-easternmost of the Seven Hills of ancient Rome, north of the Esquiline.

vimineous (vĭ mĭn′ĭ əs), *adj. Bot.* **1.** of, like, or producing long, flexible shoots. **2.** of or made of twigs. [t. L: m. *vimineus* made of twigs]

v. imp., verb impersonal.

Vimy (*Fr.* vē mē′), *n.* a town in N France, N of Arras: battle of Vimy Ridge 1917. 3050 (1965).

vina (vē′nə), *n.* an Indian musical instrument with numerous strings stretched over a long, sticklike fingerboard with movable frets, to which up to three gourds are attached to increase resonance. [t. Skt]

vinaceous (vī nā′shəs), *adj.* **1.** relating to, or resembling, wine or grapes. **2.** wine-coloured. [t. L: m. *vīnāceus*]

Viña del Mar (*Sp.* bē′nyȧ dĕl mȧr′), a city and seaside resort in central Chile. 126,460 (1960).

vinaigrette (vĭn′ā grĕt′), *n.* **1.** Also, **vinegarette.** a small ornamental bottle or box for holding aromatic vinegar, smelling salts, or the like. —*adj.* **2.** served with a vinaigrette sauce. [t. F, f. *vinaigre* VINEGAR + *-ette* -ETTE]

vinaigrette sauce, a cold, tart sauce of oil, vinegar, seasonings, and herbs.

vinasse (vĭ năs′), *n. Distilling.* the residuum in a still after distillation, esp. the residual liquid obtained after the distillation of beetroot molasses which is used as a source of potassium carbonate. Cf. **slop**[1] (def. 12). [t. F, t. Pr.: m. *vinassa,* g. L *vīnācea* grapeskin]

Vincennes (*Fr.* văɴ sĕn′), *n.* a town in N France near Paris: castle; park. 50,499 (1962).

Vincent de Paul (vĭn′sənt də pôl′; *Fr.* văɴ säɴ də pŏl′), **Saint,** 1576–1660, French Roman Catholic priest and reformer.

Vincentian (vĭn sĕn′shyən), *n.* **1.** a member of the **Congregation of the Mission,** founded in France in 1625 as a charitable association by Saint Vincent de Paul. —*adj.* **2.** of or pertaining to Saint Vincent de Paul or the association founded by him.

Vincent's angina, *Pathol.* a disease characterized by ulceration of the mucosa of the tonsils, pharynx, and mouth, and the development of a membrane, caused by a bacillus and a spirillum; trench mouth. Also, **Vincent's infection.** [named after J. H. *Vincent,* 1862–1950, French physician]

Vinci (vĭn′chĭ; *It.* vēn′chē), *n.* See **Leonardo.**

vincible (vĭn′sĭ bl), *adj.* capable of being conquered or overcome. [t. L: m. s. *vincibilis*] —**vin′cibil′ity, vin′cibleness,** *n.*

vincit omnia veritas (vĭng′kĭt ŏm′nĭ ä vĕ′rĭ tăs′), *Latin.* truth conquers all things.

vinculum (vĭng′ kyōō ləm), *n., pl.* **-la** (-lə). **1.** a bond of union; a tie. **2.** *Maths.* a stroke or brace drawn over a quantity consisting of several members or terms, as $\overline{a+b}$, in order to connect them and show that they are to be considered together. [t. L: fetter]

Vindhya Hills (vĭn′dyə), a mountain range in central India, N of the river Narbada.

Vindhya Pradesh (prä′dĕsh), *n.* a former state in central India: now part of Madhya Pradesh.

vindicable (vĭn′dĭ kə bl), *adj.* that may be vindicated. —**vin′dicabil′ity,** *n.*

vindicate (vĭn′dĭ kāt′), *v.t.,* **-cated, -cating. 1.** to clear, as from a charge, imputation, suspicion, or the like. **2.** to afford justification for: *subsequent events vindicated his policy.* **3.** to uphold or justify by argument or evidence. **4.** to assert, maintain, or defend (a right, cause, etc.) against opposition. **5.** to lay claim to, for oneself or another. **6.** *Rom. and Civ. Law.* to regain possession, under claim of title of property through legal procedure or to assert one's right to its possession. **7.** *Obs.* to deliver from something. **8.** *Obs.* to avenge, revenge, or punish. [t. L: m. s. *vindicātus,* pp., set free, punished] —**vin′dica′tor,** *n.*

vindication (vĭn′dĭ kā′shən), *n.* **1.** the act of vindicating. **2.** the state of being vindicated. **3.** defence or justification. **4.** something that vindicates: *the success of his plan was the real vindication.*

vindicatory (vĭn′dĭ kā′tə rĭ), *adj.* **1.** serving to vindicate. **2.** justificatory. **3.** punitive; retributive. Also, **vindicative** (vĭn′dĭ kə tĭv).

vindictive (vĭn dĭk′tĭv), *adj.* **1.** disposed or inclined to revenge; revengeful: *a vindictive person.* **2.** proceeding from or showing a revengeful spirit. **3. vindictive damages,** *Law.* damages over and above the actual amount suffered, given punitively. [f. s. L *vindicta* vengeance + -IVE] —**vindic′tively,** *adv.* —**vindic′tiveness,** *n.* —**Syn. 1.** See **spiteful.**

vine (vīn), *n.* **1.** a long, slender stem that trails or creeps on the ground or climbs by winding itself about a support or holding fast with tendrils or claspers. **2.** a plant bearing such a stem. **3.** any of the climbing plants constituting the genus *Vitis,* having a woody stem and bearing grapes, esp. *V. vinifera,* the common European species; a grapevine. [ME, t. OF, g. L *vīnea*] —**vine′less,** *adj.* —**vine′like′,** *adj.*

vinedresser (vīn′drĕs′ə), *n.* one who dresses, trims, or cultivates vines, esp. grapevines.

vinegar (vĭn′ĭ gə), *n.* **1.** a sour liquid consisting of dilute and impure acetic acid, obtained by acetous fermentation from wine, cider, beer, ale, or the like, and used as a condiment, preservative, etc. 2. *Pharm.* a solution of a medicinal substance in dilute acetic acid, or vinegar. 3. sour or crabbed speech, temper, or countenance. —*v.t.* 4. to apply vinegar to. [ME *vinegre*, t. OF, f. *vin* wine + *egre* sour] —**vin′egar-like′**, *adj.*

vinegar eel, a minute nematode worm, *Anguillula aceti*, found in vinegar, etc. Also, **vinegar worm.**

vinegarette (vĭn′ĭ gə rĕt′), *n.* vinaigrette.

vinegar fly, any fly of the genus *Drosophila*, esp. *D. melanogaster*; fruit-fly.

vinegarish (vĭn′ĭ gə rĭsh), *adj.* slightly sour; resembling vinegar.

vinegar-plant (vĭn′ĭ gə plänt′), *n. Bot.* a bacterium, *Acetobacter xylinum*, causing acetic fermentation.

vinegarroon (vĭn′ĭ gə ro͞on′), *n.* a large whip scorpion, *Thelyphonus giganteus*, of the southern U.S., etc., which emits a vinegar-like smell when alarmed. [t. Sp.: m. *vinagrón*, der. *vinagre* vinegar]

vinegary (vĭn′ĭ gə rĭ), *adj.* 1. of the nature of or resembling vinegar; sour. 2. ill-natured, as a person.

Vineland (vīn′lənd), *n.* Vinland.

vine-mildew (vīn′mĭl′dyo͞o), *n.* a serious fungal disease of grapevines caused by *Uncinula necator*.

vinery (vī′nə rĭ), *n., pl.* **-eries.** 1. a vineyard. 2. *U.S.* vines collectively.

vineyard (vĭn′yəd), *n.* 1. a plantation of grapevines, for producing grapes for wine-making, etc. 2. a sphere of activity, esp. on a high spiritual plane. [ME; f. VINE + YARD[2]] —**vine′yardist,** *n.*

vingt-et-un (*Fr.* văN tĕ œN′), *n. Cards.* pontoon. [F]

vinic (vī′nĭk, vĭn′ĭk), *adj.* of, pertaining to, found in, or extracted from wine. [f. s. L *vīnum* wine + -IC]

viniculture (vĭn′ĭ kŭl′chə), *n.* 1. the cultivation of the vine. 2. the study or science of wine-making. [f. *vini-* (comb. form of L *vīnum* wine) + CULTURE] —**vin′icul′tural,** *adj.* —**vin′icul′turist,** *n.*

viniferous (vī nĭf′ə rəs), *adj.* producing wine.

vinificator (vĭn′ĭ fĭ kā′tə), *n.* a condenser for alcohol vapours escaping from fermenting wine. [f. *vini-* (comb. form of L *vīnum* wine) + L *-ficātor* maker]

Vinland (vĭn′lənd), *n.* a region on the E coast of North America, variously identified, visited by Norsemen in about A.D. 1000. Also, **Vineland.**

Vinnitsa (*Russ.* vē′nĭt sə), *n.* a city in the central Ukraine, in the SW Soviet Union in Europe, on the river Bug. 144,000 (est. 1964).

vinometer (vĭ nŏm′ ĭ tə, vī-), *n.* a hydrometer for measuring the percentage of alcohol in wine. [f. *vino-* (comb. form repr. L *vīnum* wine) + -METER[1]]

vin ordinaire (*Fr.* văN ôr dē nĕr′), *French.* a cheap wine generally for popular consumption. [F: common wine]

vinous (vī′nəs), *adj.* 1. having the nature of or resembling wine. 2. pertaining to or characteristic of wine. 3. produced by, indicative of, or given to indulgence in wine. 4. wine-coloured; wine-red. [t. L: m. s. *vīnōsus*] —**vinosity** (vī nŏs′ĭ tĭ), *n.*

vintage (vĭn′tĭj), *n., adj., v.,* **-taged, -taging.** —*n.* 1. the wine from a particular harvest or crop. 2. the annual produce of the grape harvest, esp. with reference to the wine obtained: *a luxuriant vintage.* 3. an exceptionally fine wine from the crop of a good year, designated and sold as the produce of that year. 4. wine, esp. good wine. 5. the act of gathering ripe grapes. 6. the season of gathering grapes, or of wine-making. 7. wine-making. 8. *Colloq.* the crop or output of anything: *a hat of last year's vintage.* —*adj.* 9. of or pertaining to wine or wine-making. 10. (of wines) designated and sold as the produce of a specified year. 11. of high quality; exceptionally fine: *the actor gave a vintage performance last night.* 12. denoting or pertaining to a motor vehicle built between 1918 and 1930, or a racing car more than ten years old. 13. old-fashioned; out of date. —*v.t.* 14. to gather (grapes) for wine-making. 15. to make (wine, esp. vintage wine) from grapes gathered. [late ME, t. AF, b. *vinter* VINTNER and *vendage*, OF *vendange* (g. L *vindēmia* grape gathering)]

vintager (vĭn′tĭ jə), *n.* one who gathers harvest grapes.

vintner (vĭnt′nə), *n.* a dealer in wine; a wine merchant. [late ME *vyntenere*, alter. of ME *viniter*, t. AF. Cf. ML *vinetārius* wine-seller]

vinum (vī′nəm), *n. Pharm.* a solution of a medicinal substance in wine. [special use of L *vīnum* wine]

viny (vī′nĭ), *adj.,* **-nier, -niest.** 1. pertaining to, of the nature of, or resembling vines. 2. abounding in or producing vines.

vinyl (vī′nĭl), *n.* 1. *Chem.* the univalent radical CH_2:CH, derived from ethylene, compounds of which undergo polymerization to form high-molecular-weight plastics and resins. 2. vinylite. [f. s. L *vīnum* wine + -YL]

vinyl acetate, *Chem.* a colourless, easily polymerized fluid, $CH_3COOCH = CH_2$, used in the plastics industry.

vinyl chloride, *Chem.* an inflammable gas, CH_2CHCl, widely used in the plastics industry.

vinylidene (vī nĭl′ĭ dēn′), *n. Chem.* the bivalent radical CH_2:C:, derived from ethylene, polymerized compounds of which are used in plastics and resins. [f. VINYL + -ID[3] + -ENE]

vinylidene chloride, *Chem.* a colourless liquid, CH_2—CCl_2, which is widely used in the plastics industry to form a copolymer, esp. with vinyl chloride.

vinylite (vī′nĭ līt′), *n.* 1. a synthetic, thermoplastic substance used in the manufacture of moulded plastic ware, esp. gramophone records. 2. (*cap.*) a trademark for this substance. Also, **vinyl.**

vinyl polymers, a group of compounds derived from vinyl compounds such as vinyl acetate, styrene, etc., by polymerization.

viol (vī′əl), *n.* a bowed musical instrument, differing from the violin in having deeper ribs, sloping shoulders, a greater number of strings (usually 6) and frets: common in the 16th and 17th centuries in various sizes from the **treble viol** to the **bass viol.** [earlier *viole*, t. F; r. late ME *vyell*, t. F: m. *vielle*; ? both g. ML *vitula, vidula*]

viola[1] (vĭ ō′lə), *n.* 1. a four-stringed musical instrument of the violin family, slightly larger than the violin; a tenor or alto violin. 2. a labial organ stop of 8-foot or 4-foot pitch, giving notes of a penetrating stringlike quality. [t. It. See VIOL]

viola[2] (vī′ə lə, vī ō′lə), *n.* 1. any of a genus of plants, *Viola*, including the violet and the pansy, bearing irregular flowers on axillary peduncles. 2. a pansy, *V. cornuta*, cultivated as a garden plant. [t. L: violet]

violable (vī′ə lə bl), *adj.* that may be violated. [t. L: m. s. *violābilis*] —**vi′olabil′ity, vi′olableness,** *n.* —**vi′olably,** *adv.*

violaceous (vī′ə lā′shəs), *adj.* 1. belonging to the *Violaceae*, or violet family of plants. 2. of a violet colour; bluish purple. [t. L: m. *violāceus* violet-coloured]

viola da braccio (vĭ ō′lə də brăch′ĭ ō′), an old musical instrument of the viol family, held against the shoulder like a violin: superseded by the modern viola. [It.: lit., viol for the arm]

viola da gamba (vĭ ō′lə də găm′bə), 1. an old musical instrument of the viol family, held on or between the knees: superseded by the modern cello; bass viol. 2. an organ stop of 8-foot pitch giving a stringlike tone. [It.: lit., viol for the leg]

Viola da gamba

viola d'amore (vĭ ō′lə dă môʹrĭ), a viol with numerous sympathetic strings (in addition to several gut strings), producing a characteristic silvery tone. [It.: lit., viol of love]

violate (vī′ə lāt′), *v.,* **-lated, -lating,** *adj.* —*v.t.* 1. to break, infringe, or transgress (a law, rule, agreement, promise, instructions, etc.). 2. to break in upon or disturb rudely: *to violate privacy, peace, or a peaceful spot.* 3. to break through or pass by force or without right: *to violate a frontier.* 4. to do violence to. 5. to deal with or treat in a violent or irreverent way; desecrate or profane: *to violate a temple or an altar.* 6. to rape (esp. a woman). —*adj.* 7. *Archaic.* defiled; violated. [late ME, t. L: m. s. *violātus*, pp.] —**vi′ola′tor,** *n.*

violation (vī′ə lā′shən), *n.* 1. the act of violating. 2. the state of being violated. 3. a breach, infringement, or transgression, as of a law, promise, etc. 4. desecration. 5. ravishment or rape. 6. *Obs.* the act of treating with violence. [ME, t. L: s. *violātio*]

violative (vī′ə lə tĭv), *adj. Chiefly U.S.* pertaining to or involving violation.

violence (vī′ə ləns), *n.* 1. rough force in action: *the violence of the wind.* 2. rough or injurious action or treatment: *to die of violence.* 3. any unjust or unwarranted exertion of force or power, as against rights, laws, etc.; injury; wrong; outrage. 4. a violent act or proceeding. 5. rough or immoderate vehemence, as of feeling or language; fury; intensity; severity. 6. a distortion of meaning or fact. [ME, t. OF, t. L: m. *violentia* vehemence]

violent (vī′ə lənt), *adj.* 1. acting with or characterized by uncontrolled, strong, rough force: *a violent blow, explosion, tempest, etc.* 2. acting with, characterized by, or due to injurious or destructive force: *violent measures, a violent death.* 3. intense in force, effect, etc.; severe; extreme: *violent heat, pain, contrast, etc.* 4. roughly or immoderately vehement, ardent, or passionate: *violent feeling.* 5. furious in impetuosity, energy, etc.: *violent haste.* [ME, t. L: s. *violentus*] —**vi′olently,** *adv.*

violescent (vī′ə lĕs′ənt), *adj.* tending to a violet colour. [f. s. L *viola* violet + -ESCENT]

violet (vī′ə lĭt), *n.* **1.** any plant of the genus *Viola*, comprising chiefly low, stemless or leafy-stemmed herbs with purple, blue, yellow, white, or variegated flowers, as *V. cucullata*, a species common in wet woods, *V. odorata* (**English violet** or **sweet violet**), a fragrant species much cultivated, and *V. tricolor*, the pansy, whose flowers often bear petals differing in colouring. **2.** any such plant except the pansy and the viola. **3.** any of the various similar plants of other genera. **4.** a bluish purple colour. *—adj.* **5.** of the colour called violet; bluish purple. [ME, t. OF: m. *violete*, der. L *viola*] **—vi′olet-like′,** *adj.*

violet ray, light of the shortest visible wavelength.

violet wood, kingwood.

violin (vī′ə lĭn′), *n.* **1.** the treble of the family of modern bowed instruments, which is held nearly horizontal by the player's arm, with the lower part supported against the collarbone or shoulder; a fiddle. **2.** a violinist. [t. It.: m. *violino*, dim. of *viola* viol] **—vi′olin′less,** *adj.*

Violin

violinist (vī′ə lĭn′ĭst), *n.* a player on the violin.

violin-maker (vī′ə lĭn′ mā′kə), *n.* one who designs and builds violins and instruments of the violin family.

violist (vī′ə lĭst), *n.* a player on the viol.

Viollet-le-Duc (*Fr.* vyô lĕl dʏk′), *n.* **Eugène Emmanuel** (*Fr.* œ zhĕn ė må nwĕl′), 1814–79, French architect.

violoncellist (vī′ə lən chĕl′ĭst), *n.* a cellist.

violoncello (vī′ə lən chĕl′ō), *n., pl.* **-los, -li** (-lē). a cello. [t. It., dim. of *violone* bass viol]

violone (vī′ə lōn′), *n.* **1.** the double-bass viol, or contrabass. **2.** a sixteen-foot organ pedal stop, resembling the cello. [t. It., aug. of *viola* viol]

V.I.P., *Colloq.* very important person.

viper (vī′pə), *n.* **1.** any of the Old World venomous snakes of the genus *Vipera*, esp. *V. berus*, a small European species; the adder. **2.** any snake of the highly venomous family *Viperidae*, confined to the Old World and including the common vipers, the puff adder, and various other types, all characterized by erectile venom-conducting fangs. **3.** any of various venomous or supposedly venomous snakes of allied or other genera, as the **horned viper,** *Cerastes cornutus*, a venomous species of Egypt, Palestine, etc., with a horny process above each eye. **4.** a venomous, malignant, or spiteful person. **5.** a false or treacherous person. [t. L: s. *vīpera*, for *vivipera*, f. *vivi-* (comb. form of *vivus*) + *-pera* bringing forth (vipers were formerly thought to be viviparous)] **—vi′per-like′,** *adj.*

viperine (vī′pə rīn′), *adj.* of or like a viper.

viperish (vī′pə rĭsh), *adj.* viper-like; viperous.

viperous (vī′pə rəs), *adj.* **1.** of the nature of a viper or vipers; viper-like. **2.** pertaining to vipers. **3.** characteristic of vipers. **4.** venomous or malignant. **—vi′perously,** *adv.*

viper's bugloss, a bristly, boraginaceous Old World weed, *Echium vulgare*, with showy blue flowers. Also, *U.S.*, **blueweed.**

virago (vĭ rä′gō), *n., pl.* **-goes, -gos. 1.** a turbulent, violent, or ill-tempered, scolding woman; a shrew. **2.** a woman of masculine strength or spirit. [ME and OE, t. L: manlike woman] **—viraginous** (vĭ răj′ĭ nəs), *adj.* **—vira′go-like′,** *adj.*

viral (vī′ə rəl), *adj.* pertaining to or caused by a virus.

Virchow (*Ger.* fĭr′KHō), *n.* **Rudolf** (*Ger.* rōō′dôlf), 1821–1902, German pathologist, anthropologist, and political leader.

virelay (vĭr′ĭ lā′), *n.* **1.** an old French form of short poem, with short lines running on two rhymes, and having two opening lines recurring at intervals. **2.** any of various similar or other forms of poem, as one consisting of stanzas made up of longer and shorter lines, the lines of each kind rhyming together in each stanza, with the rhyme of the shorter lines of one stanza forming the rhyme of the longer lines of the next stanza. Also, *French*, **virelai** (*Fr.* vēr lĕ′). [ME, t. OF, f. *virel(i)* dance + *lai* song]

vireo (vĭr′ĭ ō′), *n., pl.* **-reos.** any of several small, American, insectivorous birds constituting the family *Vireonidae*, having the plumage olive green or grey above, and white or yellow below; a greenlet. [t. L: some small bird, ? the greenfinch]

vires (vī′ə rēz′), *n. Latin.* pl. of **vis.**

virescence (vĭ rĕs′əns), *n. Bot.* the state of becoming green, though usually not entirely so, due to the abnormal presence of chlorophyll.

virescent (vĭ rĕs′ənt), *adj.* **1.** turning green. **2.** tending to a green colour; slightly greenish. [t. L: s. *virescens*, ppr.]

virga (vû′gə), *n. Meteorol.* rain or snow that is dissipated in falling and does not reach the ground, commonly appearing in trails descending from a cloud layer. [t. L: twig, streak]

virgate[1] (vû′gĭt, -gāt), *adj.* shaped like a rod or wand; long, slender, and straight. [t. L: m. s. *virgātus*]

virgate[2] (vû′gĭt, -gāt), *n.* an early English measure of land of varying extent, generally regarded as having been equivalent to a quarter of a hide, or about thirty acres. [t. ML: m. s. *virgāta*, short for *virgāta terrae* (trans. of OE *geard landes*, lit., yard of land)]

Virgil (vû′jĭl), *n.* (*Publius Vergilius Maro*), 70–19 B.C., Roman poet. Also, **Vergil.** [t. ML: m. s. *Virgilius*, misspelling of L *Vergilius*] **—Virgil′ian,** *adj.*

virgin (vû′jĭn), *n.* **1.** a woman, esp. a young woman, who has had no sexual intercourse. **2.** a girl, young woman, or unmarried woman. **3.** *Eccles.* (usually of saints) an unmarried religious woman. **4. the Virgin,** Mary, the mother of Christ (often called **the Blessed Virgin**). **5.** (*cap.*) any representation of the Virgin, esp. a statue or statuette. **6.** any female animal that has not copulated. **7.** a youth or man who has not had sexual intercourse. **8.** an unfertilized insect. **9.** (*cap.*) the zodiacal constellation or sign Virgo. *—adj.* **10.** being a virgin: *Virgin Mother.* **11.** consisting of virgins. **12.** pertaining to, characteristic of, or befitting a virgin. **13.** resembling or suggesting a virgin; pure; unsullied; undefiled: *virgin snow.* **14.** without admixture, alloy, or modification: *virgin gold.* **15.** untouched, untried, or unused: *virgin soil.* **16.** *Zool.* unfertilized. **17.** *Metall.* made directly from ore or from first smelting. **18.** denoting the oil obtained as from olives, etc., by the first pressing without the application of heat. **19.** *Physics.* (of a neutron) not having experienced a collision of any kind. [ME *virgine*, t. OF, t. L: m. s. *virgo* maiden]

virginal[1] (vû′jĭ nəl), *adj.* **1.** of, pertaining to, characteristic of, or befitting a virgin. **2.** continuing in a state of virginity. **3.** pure or unsullied; untouched; fresh. **4.** *Zool.* unfertilized. [t. L: s. *virginālis* maidenly] **—vir′ginally,** *adv.*

virginal[2] (vû′jĭ nəl), *n.* Also, **virginals, pair of virginals. 1.** a small harpsichord of rectangular shape, with the strings stretched parallel to the keyboard, the earlier types placed on a table: common in the 16th and 17th centuries. **2.** (loosely) any harpsichord. [appar. special use of VIRGINAL[1]] **—vir′ginalist,** *n.*

virgin birth, 1. *Theol.* the doctrine or dogma that the birth of Christ did not, by the miraculous agency of God, impair or prejudice the virginity of Mary. Cf. **Immaculate Conception. 2.** *Zool.* parthenogenesis; a birth resulting from a female who has not copulated.

Virginia (və jĭn′yə), *n.* **1.** a state in the E United States, on the Atlantic coast. 3,966,949 pop. (1960); 40,815 sq. mi. *Cap.:* Richmond. *Abbrev.:* Va. **2.** tobacco grown in Virginia. **—Virgin′ian,** *adj., n.*

Virginia creeper, a vitaceous climbing plant, *Parthenocissus quinquefolia*, of North America and elsewhere, having palmate leaves, usually with five leaflets, and bluish black berries; woodbine.

Virginia deer, 1. the common white-tailed deer, *Odocoileus virginianus*, of eastern North America. **2.** any related variety of white-tailed deer.

Virginia fence, *U.S.* a snake fence. Also, **Virginia rail fence.**

Virginia stock, a commonly cultivated cruciferous annual, *Malcolmia maritima*, a native of the Mediterranean region.

virginibus puerisque (vû gĭn′ĭ bəs pōōə rĭs′kwĭ), *Latin.* for girls and boys.

Virgin Islands, 1. a group of islands in the West Indies E of Puerto Rico, forming the E extremity of the Greater Antilles. **2.** Official name, **Virgin Islands of the United States** (formerly, **Danish West Indies**). a group of these islands forming an unincorporated territory of the United States, including St Thomas, St John, and St Croix: purchased from Denmark 1917. 32,099 pop. (1960); 133 sq. mi. *Cap.:* Charlotte Amalie. **3.** Official name, **British Virgin Islands.** the remaining thirty-six of these islands, an administrative territory formerly part of the British colony of the Leeward Islands. 7338 pop. (1961); 67 sq. mi. *Cap.:* Road Town. *Abbrev.:* V.I.

virginity (vû jĭn′ĭ tĭ), *n.* **1.** the condition of being a virgin; virginal chastity; maidenhood. **2.** the condition of being unsullied or unused.

virginium (və jĭn′ĭ əm), *n. Chem.* former name of **francium.** [t. NL; named after the state *Virginia*]

Virgin Mary, Mary, the mother of Jesus.

Virgin Queen, the, Queen Elizabeth I of England.

virgin's-bower (vû′jĭnz bou′ə), *n.* any of several climbing varieties of clematis with small white flowers in large panicles, as *Clematis virginiana*, of the U.S.

Virgo (vû′gō), *n., gen.* **Virginis** (vû′jĭ nĭs). **1.** an equatorial constellation south of Ursa Major, containing the bright star Spica; the Virgin. **2.** the sixth sign of the zodiac. See diag. under **zodiac.** [t. L: maiden]

virgo intacta (vû′gō ĭn tăk′tə), *Law.* a virgin with hymen unbroken. [L: untouched virgin]

virgulate (vû′gyŏŏ lĭt, -lāt′), *adj.* rod-shaped; virgate.

virgule (vû′gyōōl), *n. Print.* **1.** a short oblique stroke (/) between two words designating that the interpretation may be made in either sense. Example: *and/or.* **2.** such a stroke used as a mark of division. [t. L: m. *virgula* little rod]

viridescent (vĭ′rĭ dĕs′ənt), *adj.* slightly green or greenish. [t. LL: s. *viridescens* becoming green] **—vir′ides′cence,** *n.*

viridian (vĭ rĭd′ĭ ən), *n.* a bluish green pigment of great permanency, consisting of a hydrated oxide of chromium. [f. L *viridi(s)* green + -AN]

viridity (vĭ rĭd′ĭ tĭ), *n.* **1.** greenness; verdancy; verdure. **2.** inexperience or simplicity. [late ME, t. L: m. s. *viriditas* greenness]

virile (vĭ′rĭl), *adj.* **1.** of, pertaining to, or characteristic of a man, as opposed to a woman or a child; masculine or manly; natural to or befitting a man. **2.** having or exhibiting in a marked degree masculine strength, vigour, or forcefulness. **3.** characterized by a vigorous masculine spirit: *a virile literary style.* **4.** pertaining to or capable of procreation. [t. L: m. s. *virilis*, der. *vir* man] **—Syn. 2.** See **male.**

virilism (vĭ′rĭ lĭz′əm), *n.* hermaphroditism in which a female has certain minor sexual characteristics resembling those of a male, as a deep voice, etc.

virility (vĭ rĭl′ĭ tĭ), *n., pl.* **-ties. 1.** the state or quality of being virile; manhood; masculine or manly character, vigour, or spirit. **2.** the power of procreation.

virology (vĭ′ə rŏl′ə jĭ), *n.* the study of viruses and the diseases caused by them. [f. *viro-* (comb. form of VIRUS) + -LOGY] **—virological** (vĭ′ə rə lŏj′ĭ kl), *adj.* **—vi′rolog′ically,** *adv.* **—vi′rol′ogist,** *n.*

virtu (vû tōō′), *n.* **1.** excellence or merit in objects of art, curios, and the like. **2.** *(construed as pl.)* such objects or articles collectively. **3.** a taste for or knowledge of such objects or articles. Also, **vertu.** [t. It., t. L: m. *virtūs* VIRTUE]

virtual (vû′chŏŏ əl), *adj.* **1.** being such in power, force, or effect, although not actually or expressly such: *the regent is a virtual king.* **2.** *Optics.* **a.** denoting an image formed by the apparent convergence of rays geometrically (but not actually) prolonged, as the image in a mirror (opposed to *real*). **b.** denoting a focus of a corresponding nature. **3.** *Archaic.* having virtue or inherent power to produce effects. [ME *vertual*, t. ML: m. s. *virtuālis*] **—vir′tual′ity,** *n.* **—vir′tually,** *adv.*

virtual state, *Physics.* **1.** (in quantum mechanics) the state of a particle when it is representing a force between interacting bodies, as a **virtual photon,** representing an electromagnetic force. **2.** the state of an atomic nucleus which appears as an intermediate state when the transition between two other states of that nucleus is computed.

virtual work, *Mech.* the work done by a set of forces acting on a body, when the body is imagined to undergo a small displacement; the principle is used to calculate the equilibrium position of a body, or system of bodies, under the action of a given set of forces.

virtue (vû′tyōō, vû′chōō), *n.* **1.** moral excellence or goodness. **2.** conformity of life and conduct to moral laws; uprightness; rectitude. **3.** a particular moral excellence: *the cardinal virtues* (justice, prudence, temperance, and fortitude); *the theological virtues* (faith, hope, and charity). **4.** an excellence, merit, or good quality: *brevity is often a virtue.* **5.** chastity, esp. in women. **6.** effective force: *there is no virtue in such measures.* **7.** a power or property of producing a particular effect. **8.** inherent power to produce effects; potency or efficacy: *a medicine of sovereign virtue.* **9.** *(pl.)* an order of angels. See **angel** (def. 1). **10.** *Obs.* manly excellence, spirit, or valour. **11. by** or **in virtue of,** by reason of: *to act by virtue of authority conferred.* [ME *virtu*, t. L: m. *virtus* manliness (der. *vir* man); r. ME *vertu*, t. OF] **—Syn. 1.** See **goodness. —Ant. 1.** vice.

virtuose (vû′tyŏŏ ō′zĭ), *adj.* exhibiting the qualities of a virtuoso. Also, **virtuosic** (vû′tyŏŏ ō′zĭk).

virtuosity (vû′tyŏŏ ŏs′ĭ tĭ), *n., pl.* **-ties. 1.** the character or skill of a virtuoso. **2.** a fondness for or interest in virtu.

virtuoso (vû′tyŏŏ ō′zō), *n., pl.* **-sos, -si** (-zē), *adj.* **—n. 1.** one who has special knowledge or skill in any field, as in music. **2.** one who excels in musical technique or execution. **3.** one who has a cultivated appreciation of artistic excellence; a connoisseur of works or objects of art; a student or collector of objects of art, curios, antiquities, etc. **4.** *Obs.* one who has special interest or knowledge in art and science. **—adj. 5.** characteristic of a virtuoso; virtuose. [t. It.: learned, skilful]

virtuous (vû′chŏŏ əs), *adj.* **1.** morally excellent or good; conforming or conformed to moral laws; upright; righteous; moral. **2.** *Archaic.* having effective virtue; potent; efficacious. [ME, t. LL: m. s. *virtuōsus*; r. ME *vertuous*, t. OF, der *vertu* VIRTUE] **—vir′tuously,** *adv.* **—vir′tuousness,** *n.* **—Ant. 1.** vicious.

virulence (vĭ′rŏŏ ləns), *n.* **1.** the quality of being virulent; actively poisonous or malignant quality. **2.** venomous hostility. **3.** intense acrimony. Also, **vir′ulency.**

virulent (vĭ′rŏŏ lənt), *adj.* **1.** actively poisonous, malignant, or deadly: *a virulent poison, a virulent form of a disease.* **2.** *Med.* highly infective; malignant or deadly. **3.** *Bacteriol.* of the nature of an organism causing specific or general clinical symptoms. **4.** violently or venomously hostile. **5.** intensely bitter, spiteful, or acrimonious. [ME, t. L: s. *virulentus* poisonous. See VIRUS] **—vir′ulently,** *adv.*

virus (vĭ′ə rəs), *n.* **1.** an infective agent; in a restricted sense, an infective agent smaller than a common micro-organism, and requiring living cells for multiplication. Cf. **filterable** (def. 2). **2.** any disease caused by a virus. **3.** the venom of a poisonous animal. **4.** a moral or intellectual poison; a corrupting influence. [t. L: slimy liquid, poison] **—vi′rus-like′,** *adj.* **—Syn. 1.** See **poison.**

vis (vĭs), *n., pl.* **vires** (vĭ′ə rēz′). *Latin.* force.

Vis., 1. Viscount. **2.** Viscountess.

visa (vē′zə), *n., v.,* **-saed, -saing. —n. 1.** an endorsement made by an authorized representative of a country upon the passport of a citizen of another country, testifying that the passport has been examined and found in order, and permitting passage to the country making the endorsement. **—v.t. 2.** to put a visa on; examine and endorse, as a passport. Also, **visé.** [t. L, short for *carta vīsa* paper (has been) seen]

visage (vĭz′ĭj), *n.* **1.** the face, esp. of a human being, and commonly with reference to shape, features, expression, etc.; the countenance. **2.** aspect; appearance. [ME, t. AF and OF, der. *vis* face (g. L *vīsus*). See -AGE] **—vis′aged,** *adj.* **—Syn. 1.** See **face.**

Visakhapatnam (vē shä′kə pət nəm), *n.* a seaport in Andhra Pradesh, E India. 182,000 (1961).

visard (vĭz′əd), *n.* vizard.

vis-a-vis (vē′ zä vē′), *adv., adj., prep., n., pl.* **-vis. —adv. 1.** face to face. **—adj. 2.** face to face; opposite. **—prep. 3.** face to face with; opposite. **4.** regarding; with relation to: *discussions with the treasurer vis-a-vis the finances of a proposal.* **—n. 5.** one face to face with or situated opposite to another. **6.** a person corresponding in status or function to another; opposite number. **7.** *Furniture.* tete-a-tete (def. 3). **8.** (formerly) a carriage in which the occupants sit face to face. Also, *French,* **vis-à-vis** (*Fr.* vē zȧ vē′). [t. F: face to face]

Visayan (vĭ sä′yən), *n.* **1.** one of a Malay people, the most numerous native race of the Philippine Islands. **2.** the language of this people. Also, **Bisayan.**

Visayan Islands, an island group in the central Philippine Islands, including Panay, Negros, Cebú, Bohol, Leyte, Samar, Masbate, and smaller islands. Spanish, **Bisayas.**

Visby (*Sw.* vēs′bʏ), *n.* a seaport on and the capital of the Swedish island of Gotland, in the Baltic: an important member of the Hanseatic League. 53,662 (1964). German, **Wisby.** See map under **Hanseatic League.**

Visc., 1. Viscount. **2.** Viscountess.

viscacha (vĭs kăch′ə), *n.* **1.** a burrowing rodent, *Lagostomus maximus*, about the size of a domestic cat, inhabiting the pampas of Paraguay and Argentina, related to the chinchilla. **2.** a rodent of a related genus, *Lagidium*, of the Andes (**alpine** or **mountain viscacha**), about the size of a grey squirrel, having long rabbit-like ears and a squirrel-like tail. Also, **vizcacha.** [t. Sp., t. Quechua]

viscera (vĭs′ə rə), *n.pl., sing.* **viscus. 1.** the soft interior organs in the cavities of the body, including the brain, lungs, heart, stomach, intestines, etc., esp. such of these as are confined to the abdomen. **2.** (in popular use) the intestines or bowels. [t. L]

visceral (vĭs′ə rəl), *adj.* **1.** of the viscera. **2.** affecting the viscera. **3.** having the character of viscera.

viscid (vĭs′ĭd), *adj.* **1.** sticky, adhesive, or glutinous; of a glutinous consistency; viscous. **2.** *Bot.* covered by a sticky substance, as a leaf. [t. LL: s. *viscidus*, der. L *viscum* birdlime] **—viscid′ity, vis′cidness,** *n.* **—vis′cidly,** *adv.*

viscoid (vĭs′koid), *adj.* somewhat viscous. Also, **viscoi′dal.** [f. VISC(OUS) + -OID]

viscometer (vĭs kŏm′ĭ tə), *n. Chem.* any instrument used to measure the viscosity of a liquid. Also, **viscosimeter. —viscometrical** (vĭs′kə mĕt′rĭ kl), *adj.* **—viscom′etry,** *n.*

Visconti (*It.* vēs kōn′tē), *n.* an Italian family that ruled Milan and Lombardy from 1277 to 1447.

viscose (vĭs′kōs), *Chem.* —*n.* **1.** a viscous solution prepared by treating cellulose with caustic soda and carbon bisulphide: used in manufacturing regenerated cellulose fibres, sheets, or tubes, as rayon or cellophane. —*adj.* **2.** relating to or made from viscose. [t. L: m. s. *viscōsus.* See VISCOUS]

viscosimeter (vĭs′kō sĭm′ĭ tə), *n.* viscometer.

viscosity (vĭs kŏs′ĭtĭ), *n., pl.* **-ties. 1.** the state or quality of being viscous. **2.** *Physics.* a property of a fluid in resisting change in the shape or arrangement of its elements during flow, and the degree to which this property exists in a particular fluid.

viscount (vī′kount), *n.* **1.** a nobleman next below an earl or count and next above a baron. **2.** the son or younger brother of an earl or a count. **3.** (formerly) a deputy of a count or earl. **4.** *Hist.* a sheriff. [ME, t. AF: m. *viscounte,* f. *vis* VICE- + *counte* COUNT[2]]

viscountcy (vī′kount sĭ), *n., pl.* **-cies.** the rank or dignity of a viscount. Also, **vis′countship′.**

viscountess (vī′koun tĭs), *n.* **1.** the wife or widow of a viscount. **2.** a woman holding in her own right a rank equivalent to that of a viscount.

viscounty (vī′koun tĭ), *n., pl.* **-ties. 1.** viscountcy. **2.** *Hist.* the jurisdiction of a viscount, or the territory under his authority.

viscous (vĭs′kəs), *adj.* **1.** sticky, adhesive, or glutinous; of a glutinous character or consistency; thick. **2.** having the property of viscosity. [ME *viscouse,* t. L: m. *viscōsus,* der. *viscum* birdlime] —**vis′cously,** *adv.* —**vis′cousness,** *n.*

Visct, Viscount.

viscus (vĭs′kəs), *n.* sing. of **viscera.**

vise (vīs), *n., v.,* **vised, vising.** *U.S.* vice[2].

visé (vē′zā), *n., v.t.,* **-séed, -séing.** visa. [t. F. See VISA]

Vishnu (vĭsh′nōō), *n.* **1.** 'the Pervader', one of a half-dozen solar deities in the Rig-Veda, daily traversing the sky in three strides, morning, noon, and night. **2.** (in popular Hinduism) a deity believed to have descended from heaven to earth in several incarnations, or avatars, varying in number from nine to twenty-two, but always including animals. His most important human incarnation is the Krishna of the Bhagavad-gita. **3.** (in later Hinduism) 'the Preserver', the second member of an important trinity, together with Brahma the Creator and Shiva the Destroyer. [t. Skt]

visibility (vĭz′ĭ bĭl′ĭ tĭ), *n., pl.* **-ties. 1.** the state or fact of being visible; capability of being seen. **2.** the relative capability of being seen under given conditions of distance, light, atmosphere, etc.: *low or high visibility.* **3.** *Meteorol.* the greatest distance at which an object of specified characteristics can be seen and identified; visual range. **4.** *Photog.* the ratio of the luminous flux, in lumens, to the corresponding energy flux in watts. **5.** something visible; a visible thing.

visibility meter, *Meteorol.* a meter for measuring and giving a standardized scale value to visibility through the atmosphere.

visible (vĭz′ə bl), *adj.* **1.** capable of being seen; perceptible by the eye; open to sight or view. **2.** *Physics.* (of electromagnetic radiation) having a wavelength between 3800 and 7600 angstrom units. **3.** perceptible by the mind. **4.** apparent; manifest; obvious. **5.** represented visually; prepared or converted for visual presentation: *visible sound* (an oscillograph of a soundwave). [ME, t. L: m. s. *vīsibilis*] —**vis′ibleness,** *n.* —**vis′ibly,** *adv.*

visible horizon. See **horizon** (def. 1).

visible speech, *Phonet.* a system of notation in which each symbol shape is designed to indicate diagrammatically the articulatory position of the sound it stands for and in which phonetically related sounds are represented by related symbol shapes.

Visigoth (vĭz′ĭ gŏth′), *n.* a member of the westerly division of the Goths, which formed a monarchy about A.D. 418, maintaining it in southern France until A.D. 507 and in Spain until A.D. 711. [t. LL: s. *Visigothī* (pl.), Latinization of Gmc tribal name] —**Vis′igoth′ic,** *adj.*

visile (vĭz′ĭl), *n. Psychol.* one in whose mind visual images are especially distinct.

vision (vĭzh′ən), *n.* **1.** the act of seeing with the eye; the power, faculty, or sense of sight. **2.** the act or power of perceiving what is not actually present to the eye, whether by some supernatural endowment or by natural intellectual acuteness: *to lack vision in dealing with great problems.* **3.** something seen or presented to the mind otherwise than by natural, ordinary sight in the normal waking state. **4.** a mental view or image, whether of supernatural origin or merely imaginative, of what is not actually present in place or time: *visions of the past or the future.* **5.** a vivid imaginative conception or anticipation: *visions of wealth or glory.* **6.** something seen; an object of sight. **7.** a sight seen in a dream, ecstasy, trance, or the like. **8.** a sight such as might be seen in a vision, dream, etc.: *a vision of loveliness.* **9.** a scene, person, etc., of extraordinary beauty. —*v.t.* **10.** to show, or to see, in or as in a vision. [ME, t. L: s. *vīsio* sight] —**vi′sionless,** *adj.*

visional (vĭzh′ə nəl), *adj.* **1.** of or pertaining to visions. **2.** belonging to or seen in a vision. —**vi′sionally,** *adv.*

visionary (vĭzh′ə nə rĭ), *adj., n., pl.* **-ries.** —*adj.* **1.** given to or characterized by radical, often unpractical ideas, views, or schemes: *a visionary enthusiast.* **2.** given to or concerned with seeing visions. **3.** belonging to or seen in a vision. **4.** unreal or imaginary: *visionary evils.* **5.** purely ideal or speculative; unpractical. **6.** proper only to a vision. —*n.* **7.** one who sees visions. **8.** one who is given to novel ideas or schemes which are not immediately practicable; an unpractical theorist or enthusiast: *although a visionary, he was an excellent economist.* —**vi′sionariness,** *n.*

visit (vĭz′ĭt), *v.t.* **1.** to go to see (a person, place, etc.) in the way of friendship, ceremony, duty, business, curiosity, or the like. **2.** to call upon (a person, family, etc.) for social or other purposes. **3.** to make a stay or sojourn with, as a guest. **4.** (in general) to come or go to. **5.** to go to for the purpose of official inspection or examination; inspect or examine. **6.** to come to in order to comfort or aid. **7.** to come upon or assail: *the plague visited London in 1665.* **8.** to afflict with suffering, trouble, etc. **9.** *Obs.* to inflict punishment for. —*v.i.* **10.** to make a visit or visits. **11.** *U.S.* to talk casually; chat. **12.** *Obs.* to inflict punishment. —*n.* **13.** an act of visiting. **14.** a going to see a person, place, etc. **15.** a call paid to a person, family, etc. **16.** a stay or sojourn as a guest. **17.** a going to a place to make an official inspection or examination. **18.** the visiting of a vessel, as at sea, by an officer of a hostile state, to ascertain its nationality, the nature of its cargo (whether contraband), etc.: *the right of visit and search.* [ME, t. L: s. *vīsitāre* go to see]

visitable (vĭz′ĭ tə bl), *adj.* **1.** capable of or suitable for being visited. **2.** liable or subject to official visitation.

visitant (vĭz′ĭ tənt), *n.* **1.** a visitor; a guest; a temporary resident. **2.** a supernatural visitor; an apparition; a ghost. **3.** one who visits a place of interest, a shrine, etc., for sightseeing, on a pilgrimage, or the like. **4.** a migratory bird, or other animal, at a temporary feeding place, etc., or on its nesting-ground (**summer visitant**) or wintering ground (**winter visitant**). —*adj.* **5.** visiting; paying a visit. —**Syn. 1.** See **visitor.**

visitation (vĭz′ĭ tā′shən), *n.* **1.** the act of visiting; a visit. **2.** visiting or a visit for the purpose of making an official inspection or examination. **3.** (*cap. or l.c.*) the visit of the Virgin Mary to her cousin Elizabeth. (See Luke 1:39–56.) **4.** (*cap.*) a church festival, held on July 2nd, in commemoration of this visit. **5.** a visiting with comfort or aid, or with affliction or punishment, as by God. **6.** a special dispensation from heaven, whether of favour or of affliction. **7.** any experience or event, esp. an unpleasant one, regarded as occurring by divine dispensation. **8.** an affliction or punishment from God. —**vis′ita′tional,** *adj.*

visitatorial (vĭz′ĭ tə tô′rĭ əl), *adj.* **1.** pertaining to an official visitor or to official visitation. **2.** having the power of visitation.

visiting card, 1. a small card bearing one's name, used on various social or business occasions. **2.** *Colloq.* any article or thing, esp. a recognizable one, which serves to announce its owner.

visiting professor, a university professor invited to teach at a university not his own for a short period, usually an academic year.

visitor (vĭz′ĭ tə), *n.* one who visits, or makes a visit, as for friendly, business, official, or other purposes. —**visitress** (vĭz′ĭ trĭs), *n. fem.*

—**Syn.** VISITOR, CALLER, GUEST, VISITANT are terms for one who comes to spend time with or stay with others, or in a place. A VISITOR often stays some time, for social pleasure, for business, sightseeing, etc.: *we have a visitor for the weekend.* A CALLER comes for a brief (usually) formal visit: *the caller merely left her card.* A GUEST is anyone receiving hospitality, and the word has been extended to include anyone who pays for meals and lodging: *a welcome guest, a paying guest.* VISITANT applies to a migratory bird or to a supernatural being: *a warbler as a visitant.*

visitorial (vĭz′ĭ tô′rĭ əl), *adj.* of or pertaining to a visitor; visitatorial.

visitors' book, a book kept at a private home, a place of interest, a hotel, etc., in which visitors sign their names and sometimes write comments about their visit.

vis major (vĭs′mā′jə), *Law.* force majeure. [L: lit., greater force]

visor (vī′zə), *n.* **1.** the movable front parts of a helmet, covering the face, esp. the uppermost part which protects the eyes. **2.** any disguise or means of concealment. **3.** *Chiefly U.S.* the projecting forepiece of a cap, for protecting the eyes. **4.** a small shield attached to the inside roof of a car, which may be swung down to protect the driver's eyes from glare or sunlight. —*v.t.* **5.** to protect or mask with a visor; shield. Also, **vizor.** [ME *viser*, t. AF, der. *vis* face] —**vi′sored,** *adj.* —**vi′sor-less,** *adj.*

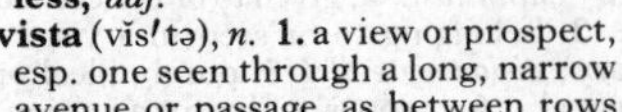
Spanish helmet with V, Visor 16th century

vista (vĭs′tə), *n.* **1.** a view or prospect, esp. one seen through a long, narrow avenue or passage, as between rows of trees, houses, or the like. **2.** such an avenue or passage. **3.** a mental view of a far-reaching kind: *vistas of thought.* **4.** a mental view extending over a long time or a stretch of remembered, imagined, or anticipated experiences, etc.: *dim vistas of the past or the future.* [t. It.: sight, view; fem. of *visto*, pp. of *vedere* see, g. L *vidēre*] —**vistaed** (vĭs′təd), *adj.* —**vis′taless,** *adj.* —**Syn. 1.** See **view.**

Vistula (vĭs′tyŏŏ lə), *n.* a river in Poland, flowing from the Carpathian Mountains past Warsaw into the Baltic near Danzig. ab. 650 mi. Polish, **Wisla.** German, **Weichsel.** See map under **Polish Corridor.**

visual (vĭz′yŏŏ əl), *adj.* **1.** of or pertaining to sight. **2.** *Optics.* optical. **3.** perceptible by the sight; visible. **4.** perceptible by the mind; of the nature of a mental vision. —*n.* **5.** (in advertising) the preliminary sketch of a layout showing the arrangement of copy. [ME, t. LL: s. *visuālis* belonging to sight]

visual aid, *Educ.* a device, technique, or the like, which uses the student's sense of sight in carrying on or assisting the learning process: *television and photographs are good visual aids.*

visual flight rules, *Aeron.* the aviational code of regulations for visual flying which specifies minimum horizontal visibility, etc.

visualize (vĭz′yŏŏ ə līz′), *v.*, **-lized, -lizing.** —*v.i.* **1.** to call up or form mental images or pictures. —*v.t.* **2.** to make visual or visible. **3.** to form a mental image of. **4.** to make perceptible to the mind or to the imagination. Also, **visualise.** —**vis′ualiza′tion,** *n.* —**vis′ualiz′er,** *n.*

visually (vĭz′yŏŏ ə lĭ), *adv.* in a visual manner or respect; by sight.

visual purple, the substance in the rod cells of the retina of the eye which is photosensitive to dim light; rhodopsin.

visual range, *Meteorol.* visibility (def. 3).

vitaceous (vī tā′shəs), *adj.* belonging to the *Vitaceae*, or grape family of plants, many of which are climbers, as the ampelopsis, Japanese ivy, Virginia creeper, etc. [f. s. NL *Vītāceae* the grape genus (der. L *vītis* vine) + -OUS]

Vita glass (vī′tə), *Trademark.* a type of glass which allows ultraviolet radiation to be transmitted.

vital (vī′tl), *adj.* **1.** of or pertaining to life: *vital functions or processes.* **2.** having life, or living. **3.** having remarkable energy, enthusiasm, vivacity: *he has a very vital personality.* **4.** being the seat or source of life: *the vital parts or organs.* **5.** necessary to life. **6.** necessary to the existence, continuance, or well-being of something; indispensable; essential: *a vital necessity.* **7.** affecting the existence, well-being, truth, etc., of something: *a vital error.* **8.** of critical importance: *vital problems.* **9.** imparting life or vigour; vitalizing, or invigorating. **10.** affecting life; destructive to life: *a vital wound.* —*n.* **11.** (*pl.*) those bodily organs which are essential to life, as the brain, heart, lungs, and stomach. **12.** (*pl.*) the essential parts of anything. [ME, t. L: s. *vītālis*] —**vi′tally,** *adv.* —**vi′talness,** *n.*

vital force, the animating force in animals and plants. Also, **vital principle.**

vitalism (vī′tə lĭz′əm), *n.* **1.** the doctrine that phenomena are only partly controlled by mechanical forces and that they are in some measure self-determining (opposed to *mechanism*). **2.** *Biol.* the doctrine that ascribes the functions of a living organism to a vital principle distinct from chemical and other forces. —**vi′talist,** *n., adj.* —**vi′talis′tic,** *adj.*

vitality (vī tăl′ĭ tĭ), *n., pl.* **-ties. 1.** exuberant physical vigour; energy; enthusiastic vivacity: *of terrific vitality.* **2.** vital force. **3.** the principle of life. **4.** power to live, or physical strength as a condition of life. **5.** power of continued existence, as of an institution, a book, etc. **6.** something having vital force.

vitalize (vī′tə līz′), *v.t.*, **-lized, -lizing. 1.** to make vital or living, or give life to. **2.** to give vitality or vigour to; animate. Also, **vitalise.** —**vi′taliza′tion,** *n.* —**vi′taliz′er,** *n.*

vital statistics, 1. statistics concerning human life or the conditions affecting human life and the maintenance of population. **2.** *Colloq.* the measurements of a woman's figure, as at the bust, waist, and hips.

vitamin (vĭt′ə mĭn, vī′tə mĭn), *n. Biochem.* any of a group of food factors essential in small quantities to maintain life but not themselves supplying energy. The absence of any one of them results in a characteristic deficiency disease. They were named in 1912 by Casimir Funk. Also, **vitamine** (vĭt′ə mĭn, vī′tə-). [f. L *vīt(a)* life + AMIN(E)] —**vit′amin′ic,** *adj.*

vitamin A, *Biochem.* a yellow, fat-soluble, solid terpene alcohol, obtained from carotene and found in green and yellow vegetables, egg yolk, etc.; essential to growth, the protection of epithelial tissue, and the prevention of night blindness.

vitamin A_2, *Biochem.* a vitamin similar to vitamin A, derived from liver oils of freshwater fish.

vitamin B_1, *Biochem.* thiamine.

vitamin B_2, *Biochem.* riboflavine.

vitamin B_6, *Biochem.* pyridoxine together with the closely related compounds pyridoxal and pyridoxamine.

vitamin B complex, *Biochem.* an important group of water-soluble vitamins containing vitamin B_1, vitamin B_2, etc.

vitamin C, *Biochem.* ascorbic acid.

vitamin D, *Biochem.* any of the several fat-soluble antirachitic vitamins D_1, D_2, D_3, found in milk and fish-liver oils, esp. cod and halibut, or obtained by irradiating provitamin D with ultraviolet light.

vitamin D_1, *Biochem.* a mixture of lumisterol and calciferol, obtained by ultraviolet irradiation of ergosterol.

vitamin D_2, *Biochem.* calciferol.

vitamin D_3, *Biochem.* the naturally occurring D-vitamin, found in fish-liver oils, differing from vitamin D_2 by slight structural differences in the molecule.

vitamin E, *Biochem.* a pale yellow viscous fluid, found in wheat-germ oil, which promotes fertility in mammals and prevents human abortions. See **tocopherol.**

vitamin G, *Biochem.* vitamin B_2; riboflavine.

vitamin H, *Biochem.* biotin; sometimes included in the vitamin B complex.

vitaminize (vĭt′ə mĭ nīz′, vī′tə-), *v.t.*, **-nized, -nizing.** to add vitamins to (a food). Also, **vitaminise.**

vitamin K_1, *Biochem.* a vitamin found in leafy vegetables, rice, bran, pig's liver, etc., and obtained from alfalfa oil or putrefied sardine meat, which promotes blood clotting by increasing the prothrombin content of the blood.

vitamin K_2, *Biochem.* a compound similar in activity to vitamin K_1.

vitamin P, *Biochem.* a water-soluble vitamin, present in citrus fruits, rose hips, and paprika, which maintains the resistance of cell and capillary walls to permeation and change of pressure; citrin.

Vitebsk (*Russ.* vĕ′tĭpsk), *n.* a city in the W Soviet Union, on the river Dvina. 174,000 (est. 1963).

vitellin (vĭ tĕl′ĭn), *n. Biochem.* a phosphoprotein in the yolk of eggs. [f. VITELL(US) + -IN[2]]

vitelline (vĭ tĕl′ĭn, -īn), *adj.* **1.** pertaining to the egg yolk. **2.** having a yellow colour.

vitelline membrane, the membrane surrounding the egg yolk.

vitellus (vĭ tĕl′əs), *n.* the yolk of an egg. [t. L]

Viterbo (*It.* vē tĕr′bô), *n.* a town in central Italy, in Lazio. 51,502 (1966).

vitiable (vĭsh′ĭ ə bl), *adj.* subject to being vitiated.

vitiate (vĭsh′ĭ āt′), *v.t.*, **-ated, -ating. 1.** to impair the quality of; make faulty; mar. **2.** to contaminate; corrupt; spoil. **3.** to make legally defective or invalid; invalidate. [t. L: m. s. *vitiātus*, pp., spoiled] —**vi′tia′tion,** *n.* —**vi′tia′tor,** *n.*

vitiated (vĭsh′ĭ ā′tĭd), *adj.* spoiled; corrupted; rendered invalid.

viticulture (vĭt′ĭ kŭl′chə), *n.* **1.** the culture or cultivation of the grapevine; grape-growing. **2.** the study or science of grapes and their culture. [f. *viti-* (t. L, comb. form of *vītis* vine) + CULTURE] —**vit′icul′tural,** *adj.* —**vit′icul′turer, vit′icul′turist,** *n.*

Viti Levu (vē′tĭ lĕv′ōō), the largest of the Fiji Islands, in the S Pacific. ab. 185,000 pop. (est. 1966); 4010 sq. mi. *Cap.:* Suva.

vitiligo (vĭt′ĭ lī′gō), *n. Pathol.* a disease in which smooth white patches are formed on various parts of the body, owing to loss of the natural pigment. [t. L: tetter]

Vitoria (*Sp.* bē tô′ryä), *n.* a town in N Spain: decisive defeat of the French forces in Spain 1813. 92,885 (1965).

vitreosil (vĭt′rĭ ə sĭl), *n. Trademark.* a vitreous silica used for laboratory apparatus which has to withstand large and sudden temperature changes.

vitreous (vĭt′rĭ əs), *adj.* **1.** of the nature of glass; resembling glass, as in transparency, brittleness, hardness, etc.; glassy: *vitreous china.* **2.** of or pertaining to glass. **3.** obtained from glass. [t. L: m. *vitreus,* der. *vitrum* glass] —**vit′reously,** *adv.* —**vit′reousness, vitreosity** (vĭt′rĭ ŏs′ĭ tĭ), *n.*

vitreous electricity, positive electricity; electricity produced on glass by rubbing with silk.

vitreous enamel, a coloured glassy coating, stoved on to metal articles, as baths, signs, etc., giving resistance to heat, corrosion, etc.

vitreous humour, *Anat.* the transparent gelatinous substance filling the eyeball behind the crystalline lens. See diag. under **eye.**

vitreous silica, silica glass.

vitrescent (vĭ três′ənt), *adj.* **1.** turning into glass. **2.** tending to become glass. **3.** capable of being formed into glass. [f. s. L *vitrum* glass + -ESCENT] —**vitres′cence,** *n.*

vitri-, a word element meaning 'glass', as in *vitriform.* [comb. form repr. L *vitrum*]

vitric (vĭt′rĭk), *adj.* **1.** of or pertaining to glass. **2.** of the nature of glass; glasslike. [f. s. L *vitrum* glass + -IC]

vitrification (vĭt′rĭ fĭ kā′shən), *n.* **1.** the act or process of vitrifying. **2.** the state of being vitrified. **3.** something vitrified. Also, **vitrifaction** (vĭt′rĭ făk′shən).

vitriform (vĭt′rĭ fôm′), *adj.* having the form or appearance of glass.

vitrify (vĭt′rĭ fī′), *v.t., v.i.,* **-fied, -fying. 1.** to convert or be converted into glass. **2.** to make or become vitreous. —**vit′rifi′able,** *adj.* —**vit′rifi′abil′ity,** *n.*

vitriol (vĭt′rĭ əl), *n., v.,* **-olled, -olling** or (*U.S.*) **-oled, -oling.** —*n.* **1.** *Chem.* any of certain metallic sulphates of glassy appearance, as of copper (blue vitriol), or iron (green vitriol), or zinc (white vitriol), etc. **2.** sulphuric acid. **3.** something highly caustic, or severe in its effects, as criticism. —*v.t.* **4.** to injure or burn with vitriol or sulphuric acid; vitriolize. [ME, t. ML: s. *vitriolum,* der. L *vitrum* glass]

vitriolic (vĭt′rĭ ŏl′ĭk), *adj.* **1.** of, resembling, or pertaining to vitriol. **2.** obtained from vitriol; resembling vitriol. **3.** severely caustic or scathing: *vitriolic criticism.*

vitriolize (vĭt′rĭ ə līz′), *v.t.,* **-lized, -lizing. 1.** to treat with or change into vitriol. **2.** to injure or burn with vitriol or sulphuric acid, as by throwing it in one's face. Also, **vitriolise.** —**vit′rioliza′tion,** *n.*

Vitrolite (vĭt′rə līt′), *n. Trademark.* an opaque type of glass with a fire-finished surface.

Vitruvius Pollio (vĭ troo′vyəs pŏl′ĭ ō′), **Marcus** (mä′kəs), lived in the first century B.C., Roman architect, engineer, and author. —**Vitru′vian,** *adj.*

vitta (vĭt′ə), *n., pl.* **vittae** (vĭt′ē). **1.** *Bot.* a tube or receptacle for oil, found in the fruits of most umbelliferous plants. **2.** *Zool., Bot.* a streak or stripe, as of colour. [t. L: ribbon, fillet]

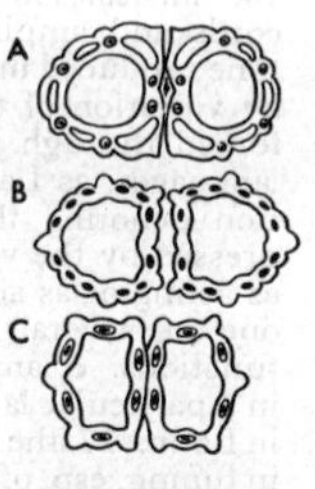

A

B

C

Vitta (def. 1) The black spots indicate the vittae in the transverse section of the fruits of A, spotted cowbane, B, celery, and C, parsley

vittate (vĭt′āt), *adj.* **1.** provided with or having a vitta or vittae. **2.** striped longitudinally.

Vittorini (*It.* vēt tō rē′nē), *n.* **Elio** (*It.* ĕ′lyō), 1908–66, Italian novelist.

vituline (vĭt′yŏŏ līn′, -lĭn), *adj.* of, pertaining to, or resembling a calf or veal. [t. L: m. s. *vitulīnus*]

vituperate (vĭ tyōō′pə rāt′), *v.,* **-rated, -rating.** —*v.t.* **1.** to find fault with abusively. **2.** to address abusive language to; revile; objurgate. —*v.i.* **3.** to use abusive language. [t. L: m. s. *vituperātus,* pp.] —**vitu′pera′tor,** *n.*

vituperation (vĭ tyōō′pə rā′shən), *n.* **1.** the act of vituperating. **2.** verbal abuse. —**Ant. 1.** praise.

vituperative (vĭ tyōō′pə rə tĭv, -prə tĭv), *adj.* characterized by or of the nature of vituperation; abusive. —**vitu′peratively,** *adv.*

viva[1] (vē′və), *interj.* **1.** *Italian.* (used in phrases of acclamation) long live (the person or idea named)! —*n.* **2.** a shout of 'viva!' [t. It.: lit., may he live, subj. of *vivere* live]

viva[2] (vī′və), *n. Colloq.* viva voce (def. 2).

vivace (vĭ vä′chĭ; *It.* vē vä′chĕ), *adj. Music.* vivacious; lively. [It., g. L *vivax*]

vivacious (vĭ vā′shəs), *adj.* **1.** lively, animated, or sprightly: *a vivacious manner or style, vivacious conversation.* **2.** *Archaic.* long-lived, or tenacious of life. [f. VIVACI(TY) + -OUS] —**viva′ciously,** *adv.* —**viva′ciousness,** *n.* —**Ant. 1.** languid.

vivacity (vĭ văs′ĭ tĭ), *n., pl.* **-ties. 1.** the quality of being vivacious. **2.** liveliness; animation; sprightliness. **3.** a vivacious act or speech; a lively sally. [late ME, t. L: m. s. *vīvācitas*]

Vivaldi (vĭ văl′dĭ; *It.* vē väl′dē), *n.* **Antonio** (*It.* än tô′nyō), 1680?–1741, Italian composer and violinist.

vivandière (*Fr.* vē väɴ dyĕr′), *n.* (formerly) a woman accompanying a French or other European regiment to sell provisions and spirits to the soldiers. [t. F, fem. of *vivandier* sutler, der. ML *vīvenda* victuals]

vivarium (vī vĕə′rĭ əm), *n., pl.* **-riums, -ria** (-rĭ ə). a place where animals are kept alive in conditions simulating their natural state. Cf. **terrarium** and **aquarium.** [t. L: enclosure for live game]

viva voce (vī′və vō′sĭ), **1.** by word of mouth; orally. **2.** an oral examination. [t. ML: lit., with the living voice] —**vi′va-vo′ce,** *adj.*

vive (vēv), *interj. French.* (used in phrases of acclamation) long live (the person or idea named)!

vive le roi (*Fr.* vēv lə rwä′), *French.* long live the king!

viverrine (vĭ vĕ′rĭn), *adj.* **1.** of or pertaining to the *Viverridae,* a family of small carnivorous mammals including the civets, genets, palm civets, etc. —*n.* **2.** a viverrine animal. [t. NL: m. s. *viverrīnus,* der. L *viverra* ferret]

Vivian (vĭv′ĭ ən), *n. Arthurian Legend.* an enchantress, the mistress of Merlin: known as 'the Lady of the Lake.' Also, **Viv′ien.**

vivianite (vĭv′ĭ ə nīt′), *n.* a rare, blue, crystalline mineral phosphate of iron, $Fe_3(PO_4)_2.8H_2O$. [named after J. G. *Vivian,* 19th-century English mineralogist]

vivid (vĭv′ĭd), *adj.* **1.** strikingly bright, as colour, light, objects, etc.: *a vivid green.* **2.** strikingly alive; full of life: *a vivid personality.* **3.** lively or intense, as feelings, etc. **4.** vigorous, as activities, etc. **5.** lively, or presenting the appearance, freshness, spirit, etc., of life, as a picture. **6.** clearly perceptible to the eye or mind. **7.** strong and distinct, as an impression or recollection. **8.** forming distinct and striking mental images, as the imagination. **9.** lively in operation. [t. L: s. *vividus* animated] —**viv′idly,** *adv.* —**viv′idness,** *n.* —**Syn. 1.** bright, brilliant, intense. **2.** animated, spirited, lively. **5.** See **picturesque.**

vivify (vĭv′ĭ fī′), *v.t.,* **-fied, -fying. 1.** to give life to; quicken. **2.** to enliven; render lively or animated; brighten. [t. L: m. s. *vīvificāre*] —**viv′ifica′tion,** *n.* —**viv′ifi′er,** *n.*

vivipara (vĭ vĭp′ə rə), *n.pl.* viviparous animals.

viviparous (vĭ vĭp′ə rəs), *adj.* **1.** *Zool.* bringing forth living young (rather than eggs), as most mammals and some reptiles and fishes. **2.** *Bot.* producing seeds that germinate on the plant. [t. L: m. *vīviparus* bringing forth living young] —**viviparity** (vĭv′ĭ păr′ĭ tĭ), **vivip′arousness,** *n.* —**vivip′arously,** *adv.*

vivisect (vĭv′ĭ sĕkt′, vĭv′ĭ sĕkt′), *v.t.* **1.** to dissect the living body of. —*v.i.* **2.** to practise vivisection. [f. *vīvi-* (t. L, comb. form of *vīvus* alive) + -SECT] —**viv′isec′tor,** *n.*

vivisection (vĭv′ĭ sĕk′shən), *n.* **1.** the action of cutting into or dissecting a living body. **2.** the practice of subjecting living animals to cutting operations, esp. in order to advance physiological and pathological knowledge. —**viv′isec′tional,** *adj.*

vivisectionist (vĭv′ĭ sĕk′shə nĭst), *n.* **1.** one who practises vivisection. **2.** one who favours or defends the practice of vivisection.

vixen (vĭk′sən), *n.* **1.** a female fox. **2.** an ill-tempered or quarrelsome woman; a spitfire. [southern d. var. of ME *fixen* she-fox, f. OE *fyxe* she-fox + *-en,* obs. fem. suffix] —**vix′enish, vix′enly,** *adj.* —**vix′enishly,** *adv.* —**vix′enishness,** *n.*

Viyella (vĭ ĕl′ə), *n. Trademark.* a soft fabric made of cotton and wool, used esp. for blouses, shirts, and children's clothing.

viz., videlicet.

vizard (vĭz′əd), *n.* **1.** a mask. **2.** *Obs.* a visor. Also, **visard.** [alter. of VISOR] —**viz′arded,** *adj.*

vizcacha (vĭs kăch′ə), *n.* viscacha.

vizier (vĭ zĭə′), *n.* **1.** a high official in various Muslim countries. **2.** a minister of state. Also, **vizir.** [t. Turk.: m. *vezīr,* t. Ar.: m. *wazīr* bearer of burdens] —**vizierate** (vĭ zĭə′rĭt, -rāt), **vizier′ship,** *n.* —**vizier′ial,** *adj.*

vizor (vī′zə), *n., v.t.* visor. —**vi′zored,** *adj.* —**vi′zorless,** *adj.*

V-J Day, August 15th, 1945 (in the U.S. September 2nd, 1945), the day of victory over Japan for the Allies in World War II. [V(ictory over) J(apan)]

VL, Vulgar Latin.

vl., violin.

v.l., varia lectio.

Vlaardingen (*Du.* vlär′dĭng ə), *n.* a town in the W Netherlands, at the mouth of the Rhine. 72,905 (1965).

Vladikavkaz (*Russ.* vlə dĭ kăf kăs′), *n.* former name of **Ordzhonikidze.**

Vladimir (vlăd′ĭ mĭə′; *Russ.* vlä dē′mĭr), *n.* **1. Saint.**

Also, **Wladimir,** A.D. *c.* 956–1015, grand prince of Russia A.D. 980–1015: first Christian Russian ruler of Russia. **2.** a city in the central Soviet Union, in Europe. 196,000 (est. 1965).

Vladivostok (vlăd′ĭ vŏs′-tŏk; *Russ.* vlə dĭ vȧs tôk′), *n.* a seaport in the SE Soviet Union in Asia, on the Sea of Japan: eastern terminus of the Trans-Siberian Railway. 367,000 (est. 1965).

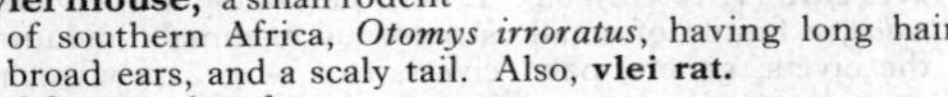

Vladivostok

Vlaminck (*Fr.* vlȧ mănk′), *n.* **Maurice de** (*Fr.* mō-rēs′ də), 1876–1958, French painter.

vlei (vlī), *n. S African.* a watery hollow. [t. Afrikaans]

vlei mouse, a small rodent of southern Africa, *Otomys irroratus,* having long hair, broad ears, and a scaly tail. Also, **vlei rat.**

v.l.f., very low frequency.

Vlissingen (*Du.* vlĭs′ĭng ə), *n.* Dutch name of **Flushing.**

Vlónë (*Alb.* vlô′nə), *n.* Albanian name of **Valona.**

Vltava (*Cz.* vəl′tȧ vȧ), *n.* a river flowing from the Bohemian Forest N through W Czechoslovakia to the Elbe. ab. 270 mi. German, **Moldau.**

V.M.D., (L *Veterinariae Medicinae Doctor*) Doctor of Veterinary Medicine.

V neck, a neckline shaped in front like a V.

V.O., (Royal) Victorian Order.

vo, verso.

voc., vocative.

vocab., vocabulary.

vocable (vō′kə bl), *n.* **1.** a word; a term. **2.** a word considered merely as composed of certain sounds or letters, without regard to meaning. *—adj.* **3.** that may be spoken. [t. L: m. s. *vocābulum* name, term]

vocabulary (və kăb′yŏŏ lə rĭ), *n., pl.* **-ries. 1.** the stock of words used by a people, or by a particular class or person. **2.** a list or collection of the words of a language, book, author, branch of science, or the like, usually in alphabetical order and defined; a wordbook, glossary, dictionary, or lexicon. **3.** the words of a language. [t. ML: m. s. *vocābulārius,* der. L *vocābulum* vocable]

vocal (vō′kl), *adj.* **1.** of or pertaining to the voice; uttered with the voice; oral: *the vocal organs.* **2.** rendered by or intended for singing, as music. **3.** having a voice: *a vocal being.* **4.** giving forth sound with or as with a voice. **5.** inclined to express oneself in speech; stridently insistent. **6.** *Phonet.* **a.** vocalic (def. 1). **b.** voiced. *—n.* **7.** a vocal sound. **8.** a piece of music, usually pop, performed by a singer. Cf. **instrumental.** [ME, t. L: s. *vōcālis,* der. *vox* voice] **—vocality** (vō kăl′ĭ tĭ), **vo′calness,** *n.* **—vo′cally,** *adv.*

vocal cords, *Anat.* folds of mucous membrane projecting into the cavity of the larynx, the edges of which can be drawn tense and made to vibrate by the passage of air from the lungs, thus producing vocal sound.

vocalic (vō kăl′ĭk), *adj.* **1.** of or pertaining to a vowel or vowels; vowel-like. **2.** containing many vowels.

vocalism (vō′kə lĭz′əm), *n.* **1.** *Phonet.* **a.** the system of vowels of a particular language. **b.** the nature of one or more given vowels. **2.** the use of the voice, as in speech or song. **3.** the act, principles, or art of singing.

vocalist (vō′kə lĭst), *n.* a singer.

vocalize (vō′kə līz′), *v.,* **-lized, -lizing.** *—v.t.* **1.** to make vocal; form into voice; utter or articulate; sing. **2.** to endow with voice or utterance. **3.** *Phonet.* **a.** to use as a vowel, as the *l* of *bottle.* **b.** to change into a vowel. **c.** to voice. **4.** (of Hebrew, Arabic, and similar systems of writing) to furnish with vowels or vowel points. *—v.i.* **5.** to use the voice, as in speech or song. **6.** to sing on a vowel or vowel sounds. Also, **vocalise. —vo′caliza′tion,** *n.* **—vo′caliz′er,** *n.*

vocat., vocative.

vocation (vō kā′shən), *n.* **1.** a particular occupation, business, or profession; a trade or calling. **2.** a calling or summons, as to a particular activity or career. **3.** a divine call to God's service or to the Christian life. **4.** a function or station to which one is called by God. [late ME *vocacion,* t. L: m. s. *vocātio* calling]

vocational (vō kā′shə nəl), *adj.* of or pertaining to a vocation or occupation: *vocational schools* (schools that train people for various trades or occupations), *vocational guidance* (the process of helping pupils and students choose their future careers). **—voca′tionally,** *adv.*

vocative (vŏk′ə tĭv), *adj.* **1.** *Gram.* **a.** (in some inflected languages) designating a case that indicates the person or thing addressed. **b.** similar to such a case form in function or meaning. **2.** pertaining to or used in calling. *—n.* **3.** *Gram.* **a.** the vocative case. **b.** any other formation of vocative meaning. **c.** a word therein, as Latin *Paule,* 'Paul' (nominative *Paulus*). [late ME, t. L: m. s. *vocātīvus,* der. *vocāre* call] **—voc′atively,** *adv.*

voces (vō′sēz), *n.* pl. of **vox.**

vociferance (vō sĭf′ə rəns), *n.* vociferant utterance; vociferation.

vociferant (vō sĭf′ə rənt), *adj.* **1.** vociferating. *—n.* **2.** one who vociferates.

vociferate (vō sĭf′ə rāt′), *v.i., v.t.,* **-rated, -rating.** to cry out loudly or noisily; shout; bawl. [t. LL: m. s. *vōciferātus,* pp.] **—vocif′era′tor,** *n.*

vociferation (vō sĭf′ə rā′shən), *n.* noisy outcry; a clamour.

vociferous (vō sĭf′ə rəs), *adj.* **1.** crying out noisily; clamorous. **2.** of the nature of vociferation; uttered with clamour. [f. VOCIFER(ATE) + -OUS] **—vocif′erously,** *adv.* **—vocif′erousness,** *n.*

vodka (vŏd′kə), *n.* an alcoholic drink, originally Russian, distilled orig. from wheat, but now from corn, other cereals, and potatoes. [t. Russ., dim. of *voda* water]

Vogelweide (*Ger.* fô′gəl vī də), *n.* See **Walther von der Vogelweide.**

vogue (vōg), *n.* **1.** the fashion, as at a particular time: *a style in vogue fifty years ago.* **2.** popular currency, acceptance, or favour: *the book had a great vogue in its day.* [t. F, der. *voguer* row, t. It.: m. *vogare,* ? g. L *vocāre* call (through use in sailors' shanties)] **—Syn. 1.** See **fashion.**

Vogul (vō′gl), *n.* a Finno-Ugric language of the Ugric group, spoken east of the Ural Mountains.

voice (vois), *n., v.,* **voiced, voicing.** *—n.* **1.** the sound or sounds uttered through the mouth of living creatures, esp. of human beings in speaking, shouting, singing, etc. **2.** the sounds naturally uttered by a single person in speech or vocal utterance, often as characteristic of the utterer. **3.** such sounds considered with reference to their character or quality: *a manly voice, a sweet voice.* **4.** the condition of the voice for speaking or singing, esp. effective condition: *she was in poor voice.* **5.** the ability to sing well: *she has a wonderful voice.* **6.** any sound likened to vocal utterance: *the voice of the wind.* **7.** anything likened to speech as conveying impressions to the mind: *the voice of nature.* **8.** the faculty of uttering sounds through the mouth, esp. articulate sounds; utterance; speech. **9.** expression in spoken or written words, or by other means: *to give voice to one's disapproval by a letter.* **10.** expressed opinion or choice: *his voice was for compromise.* **11.** the right to express an opinion or choice; vote; suffrage: *have no voice in a matter.* **12.** expressed wish or injunction: *obedient to the voice of God.* **13.** the person or other agency by which something is expressed or revealed. **14.** musical sound created by the vibration of the vocal cords and amplified by oral and other throat cavities; tone produced in singing. **15.** *Phonet.* the sound produced by vibration of the vocal cords, as air from the lungs is forced through between them. **16.** *Gram.* **a.** (in some languages, as Latin) a group of categories of verb inflection denoting the relationship between the action expressed by the verb and the subject of the sentence (e.g., as acting or as acted upon). **b.** (in some other languages) one of several contrasting constructions with similar functions. **c.** any one of such categories or constructions in a particular language, e.g., the *active* and *passive* voices in Latin. **17.** the finer regulation, as of intensity and colour, in tuning, esp. of a piano or organ. **18.** a singer. **19.** a voice part. **20.** *Obs.* rumour. **21.** *Obs.* reputation. **22. with one voice,** in chorus; unanimously.

—v.t. **23.** to give voice, utterance, or expression to (an emotion, opinion, etc.); express; declare; proclaim: *to voice one's discontent.* **24.** *Music.* **a.** to regulate the tone of, as the pipes of an organ. **b.** to write the voice parts for (music). **25.** *Phonet.* to utter with vibration of the vocal cords.

[ME, t. AF, g. L *vox*] **—voic′er,** *n.*

voice box, the larynx.

voiced (voist), *adj.* **1.** having a voice of a specified kind: *low-voiced.* **2.** expressed vocally. **3.** *Phonet.* having voice (def. 15).

voice frequency, *Electronics.* a frequency within the range suitable for the transmission of speech; a frequency in the range 200 to 3500 cycles per second. *Abbrev.*: VF.

voiceful (vois′fəl), *adj.* having a voice, esp. a loud voice; sounding; sonorous.

voiceless (vois′lĭs), *adj.* **1.** having no voice; mute; dumb. **2.** uttering no speech or words; silent. **3.** having an unmusical voice. **4.** unspoken or unuttered. **5.** *Phonet.* uttered without tonal vibration of the vocal cords: *p, f,* and *s* are *voiceless*; surd; unvoiced. **6.** having no voice or vote. **—voice′lessly,** *adv.* **—voice′lessness,** *n.* **—Syn. 1.** See **dumb.**

voice part, *Music.* the melody or succession of notes for one of the voices or instruments in a harmonic or concerted composition.

void (void), *adj.* **1.** *Law.* without legal force or effect; not legally binding or enforceable. **2.** useless; ineffectual; vain. **3.** completely empty; devoid; destitute (fol. by *of*). **4.** without contents. **5.** without an incumbent, as an office. —*n.* **6.** an empty space: *the void of heaven.* **7.** a place without the usual or desired occupant: *his death left a void among us.* **8.** a gap or opening, as in a wall. **9.** emptiness; vacancy. —*v.t.* **10.** to make void or of no effect; invalidate; nullify. **11.** to empty or discharge (contents); evacuate (excrement, etc.). **12.** *Archaic.* to make empty or vacant. **13.** *Archaic.* to clear or rid (fol. by *of*). **14.** *Archaic.* to leave, as a place. [ME, t. OF: m. *voide,* g. LL *vocitus,* ult. der. *vocuus,* r. L *vacuus* empty] —**void′er,** *n.* —**void′ness,** *n.*

voidable (voi′də bl), *adj.* **1.** capable of being voided. **2.** *Law.* capable of being made or adjudged void. —**void′ableness,** *n.*

voidance (voi′dns), *n.* **1.** the act of voiding. **2.** annulment, as of a contract. **3.** ejection from a benefice. **4.** vacancy, as of a benefice.

voided (voi′dĭd), *adj. Her.* cut out (with a narrow rim left) so as to show the field.

voile (voil; *Fr.* vwȧl), *n.* a semitransparent dress fabric of wool, silk, rayon, or cotton, with an open weave. [t. F: veil. See VEIL]

voir dire (*Fr.* vwȧr dēr′), *Law.* **1.** an oath administered to a proposed witness or juror by which he is sworn to speak the truth in an examination to ascertain his competence. **2.** the examination itself, i.e., the preliminary examination of a prospective witness or juror touching his competence. [t. AF, f. *voir* true, truly + *dire* say]

voivode (voi′vōd), *n.* (in various Slav countries) **1.** a military commander. **2.** the administrative head of a town, province, etc. Also, **vaivode.** [t. Serbo-Croat: m. *vojevoda*]

voix céleste (vwä′sĕ lĕst′), an organ stop having two pipes for each note tuned to very slightly different pitches and producing a wavering, gentle sound. [F: heavenly voice]

vol., 1. volcano. **2.** volume. **3.** volunteer.

Volans (vō′lănz), *n.* the constellation Flying Fish.

volant (vō′lənt), *adj.* **1.** flying; having the power of flight. **2.** *Poetic.* moving lightly; nimble. **3.** *Her.* represented as flying. [t. L: s. *volans,* ppr. of *volāre* fly]

Bird volant

volante (vŏ lăn′tĭ), *adv., adj.* moving quickly and lightly. [It.: flying]

Volapük (vŏl′ə pŏŏk′), *n.* one of the earliest of the artificially constructed international auxiliary languages, invented about 1879. Also, **Volapuk** (vŏl′ə pŏŏk′). [f. *vol* (repr. E *world*) + *pük* (repr. E *speak, speech*)] —**Vol′apük′ist,** *n.*

volar (vō′lə), *adj.* of or pertaining to the palm of the hand or the sole of the foot. [f. s. L *vola* hollow of the hand or foot + -AR[1]]

volatile (vŏl′ə tīl′), *adj.* **1.** evaporating rapidly; passing off readily in the form of vapour: *a volatile oil.* **2.** light and changeable of mind; frivolous; flighty. **3.** fleeting; transient. **4.** *Archaic.* able or accustomed to fly, as winged creatures. [ME *volatil,* t. L: s. *volātilis* flying] —**volatility** (vŏl′ə tĭl′ĭ tĭ), **vol′atile′ness,** *n.*

volatile oil, a distilled oil, esp. an essential oil distilled from plant tissue. Such oils are distinguished from glyceride oils by their volatility and failure to saponify.

volatile salt, sal volatile.

volatilize (vŏ lăt′ĭ līz′), *v.,* **-lized, -lizing.** —*v.i.* **1.** to become volatile; pass off as vapour. —*v.t.* **2.** to make volatile; cause to pass off in the form of vapour. Also, **volatilise.** —**volat′iliz′able,** *adj.* —**volat′iliza′tion,** *n.* —**volat′iliz′er,** *n.*

vol-au-vent (*Fr.* vŏl ō väN′), *n.* a pastry case, often filled with meat in a sauce, or with fruit, or the like. [F: flight on the wind]

volcanic (vŏl kăn′ĭk), *adj.* **1.** of or pertaining to a volcano or volcanoes: *a volcanic eruption.* **2.** discharged from or produced by volcanoes: *volcanic mud.* **3.** characterized by the presence of volcanoes. **4.** suggestive of a volcano, or its eruptive violence, etc. **5.** *Geol.* denoting a class of igneous rocks which have solidified on the earth's surface. **6.** mud volcano. —**volcan′ically,** *adv.* —**volcanicity** (vŏl′kə nĭs′ĭ tĭ), *n.*

volcanic glass, a natural glass produced when molten lava cools very rapidly; obsidian.

volcanic tuff. See **tuff.**

volcanism (vŏl′kə nĭz′əm), *n.* the phenomena connected with volcanoes and volcanic activity.

volcano (vŏl kā′nō), *n., pl.* **-noes, -nos. 1.** an opening in the earth's crust through which molten rock (lava), steam, ashes, etc., are expelled from within, either continuously or at irregular intervals, gradually forming a conical heap (or in time a mountain), commonly with a cup-shaped hollow (crater) about the opening. **2.** a mountain or hill having such an opening and formed wholly or partly of its own lava. [t. It., g. L *Volcānus* Vulcan, god of fire]

Volcano Islands, three small Japanese islands in the W Pacific, ab. 750 mi. S of Tokyo. See **Iwo Jima.**

volcanology (vŏl′kə nŏl′ə jĭ), *n.* vulcanology. —**volcanological** (vŏl′kə nə lŏj′ĭ kl), *adj.* —**vol′canol′ogist,** *n.*

vole (vōl), *n.* any of the rodents of the genus *Microtus* and allied genera, resembling and belonging to the same family as the common rats and mice, and usually of heavy build and having short limbs and tail. [short for *volemouse* field mouse; *vole,* t. Scand.; cf. Norw. *voll* field, c. OE *weald* forested area]

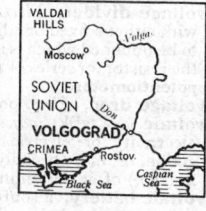

Vole, *Microtus agrestis* (Total length 6 in., tail $1\frac{1}{2}$ in.)

Volga (vŏl′gə; *Russ.* vôl′gə), *n.* a river flowing from the Valdai Hills in the W Soviet Union E and then S to the Caspian Sea: the longest river in Europe. 2325 mi.

Volgograd (vŏl′gə grăd′; *Russ.* vəl gȧ grȧt′), *n.* a city in the SE Soviet Union in Europe, on the Volga: siege and battles in World War II, September 1942 to February 1943. 700,000 (est. 1965). Formerly, (until 1925) **Tsaritsyn,** (1925–61) **Stalingrad.**

Volgograd

volitant (vŏl′ĭ tənt), *adj.* **1.** flying; having the power of flight; volant. **2.** active; moving. [t. L: s. *volitans,* ppr., flying to and fro]

volitation (vŏl′ĭ tā′shən), *n.* the act or power of flying; flight. [t. ML: s. *volitātio,* der. *volitāre,* freq. of *volāre* fly] —**vol′ita′tional,** *adj.*

volition (və lĭsh′ən), *n.* **1.** the act of willing; exercise of choice to determine action. **2.** a determination by the will. **3.** the power of willing; will. [t. ML: s. *volitio,* der. L *volo* I wish] —**voli′tional, volitionary** (və lĭsh′ə nə rĭ), *adj.* —**voli′tionally,** *adv.* —**Syn. 1.** See **will[2].**

volitive (vŏl′ĭ tĭv), *adj.* **1.** characterized by or pertaining to volition. **2.** *Gram.* expressing a wish or permission: *a volitive construction.* [f. VOLIT(ION) + -IVE]

Volkslied (*Ger.* fōlks′lēt), *n., pl.* **-lieder** (*Ger.* -lē dər). *German.* a folksong.

volley (vŏl′ĭ), *n., pl.* **-leys,** *v.,* **-leyed, -leying.** —*n.* **1.** the flight of a number of missiles together. **2.** the discharge of a number of missiles or firearms simultaneously. **3.** a burst or outpouring of many things at once or in quick succession. **4.** *Tennis, etc.* **a.** a flight of a ball in play before striking the ground. **b.** a return of the ball before it touches the ground. **c.** a succession of such returns. **5.** *Cricket.* a ball so bowled that it reaches the batsman before it touches the ground; full toss. **6.** *Mining.* the explosion of several blasts in the rock at one time. —*v.t.* **7.** to discharge in or as in a volley. **8.** *Tennis, etc.* to return (the ball) before it strikes the ground. **9.** *Cricket.* to bowl (a ball) in such a manner that it is pitched near the top of the wicket. —*v.i.* **10.** to fly or be discharged together, as missiles. **11.** to move or proceed with great rapidity, as in a volley. **12.** to fire a volley or sound together, as firearms. **13.** to emit or produce loud sounds simultaneously or continuously. [t. F: m. *volée* flight, der. *voler* fly, g. L *volāre*] —**vol′leyer,** *n.*

volleyball (vŏl′ĭ bôl′), *n.* **1.** a game, played outdoors or in a gymnasium, the object of which is to prevent a large ball from touching the ground by striking it from side to side over a high net with the hands. **2.** the ball used in this game.

Vologda (*Russ.* vô′ləg də), *n.* a city in the N Soviet Union in Europe. 152,000 (est. 1963).

volost (vō′lŏst), *n.* **1.** (formerly) a small administrative peasant division in Russia. **2.** a rural soviet. [t. Russ.]

volplane (vŏl′plān′), *v.i.,* **-planed, -planing.** to glide towards the earth in an aeroplane, with no engine power or with the engine shut off. [t. F: m. *vol plané* glided flight]

vols, volumes.

Volsci (vŏl′skē), *n.pl.* an ancient people of southern Latium, subdued by Rome late in the 4th century B.C.

Volscian (vŏl′skĭ ən), *adj.* **1.** of or pertaining to the Volsci or to their language. —*n.* **2.** one of the Volsci.

Volsteadism (vŏl′stĕ dĭz′əm), *n. U.S.* **1.** the policy of prohibiting the sale of liquor to be used as or for a beverage. **2.** the enforcement of this policy. [named after Congressman A. J. *Volstead*, 1860–1946, author of such a prohibition bill passed in 1919 and repealed in 1933]

Volsung (vŏl′so͝ong), *n.* (in Icelandic legend) **1.** a descendant of Odin, the grandfather of Sigurd. **2.** any of his family.

Volsunga saga (vŏl′so͝ong gə sä′gə), an Icelandic saga about the Nibelungs and the Volsungs, centring on the adventures of Sigurd. [t. Icel.: m. *Völsungasaga*]

volt[1] (vōlt), *n. Elect.* the derived SI unit of electric potential or electromotive force, defined as the difference of potential between two points of a conducting wire carrying a constant current of one ampere, when the power dissipated between these points is one watt; approximately 10^8 c.g.s. electromagnetic units. *Symbol.:* V. [named after Alessandro VOLTA]

volt[2] (vŏlt), *n.* volte.

volta (vŏl′tə; *It.* vŏl′tȧ), *n., pl.* **-te** (*It.* -tĕ). *Music.* turn; time (used in phrases): *una volta* (once); *due volte* (twice); *prima volta* (first time); *etc.* [It.: turn]

Volta (*It.* vŏl′tȧ *for 1*; vŏl′tə *for 2*), *n.* **1. Count Alessandro** (*It.* ȧ lĕs sȧn′drŏ), 1745–1827, Italian physicist. **2.** a river in W Africa, in Ghana, flowing into the Bight of Benin. ab. 200 mi. long (with its main upper branch, the **Black Volta,** ab. 790 mi. long).

volta-, combining form of **voltaic,** as in *voltameter*.

voltage (vŏl′tĭj), *n. Elect.* electromotive force reckoned or expressed in volts.

voltage divider, *Elect.* a resistor (or series of resistors) with either a fixed or adjustable tapping allowing a voltage to be obtained which is a fraction of the total voltage across the resistor (or series of resistors). Also, **potential divider, potentiometer.**

voltage drop, *Elect.* potential difference.

voltaic (vŏl tā′ĭk), *adj.* **1.** denoting or pertaining to the electricity or electric currents produced by chemical action, or, more broadly, to any electric current; galvanic. **2.** (*cap.*) of or pertaining to Alessandro Volta.

voltaic battery, a source of electric current consisting of one or more voltaic cells; an electric battery.

voltaic cell. See **cell** (def. 7).

voltaic couple, (in a voltaic cell) the substances (commonly two metallic plates) in the dilute acid or other electrolyte, giving rise to the electric current.

voltaic electricity, electric current; moving electric charges.

voltaic pile, *Elect.* an early form of voltaic battery consisting of a number of voltaic cells joined in series, each one containing a sheet of copper and a sheet of zinc separated by a piece of cloth moistened with dilute sulphuric acid. [named after A. VOLTA]

Voltaic Republic. See **Upper Volta.**

Voltaire (vŏl′tēə; *Fr.* vŏl tĕr′), *n.* **François Marie Arouet de** (*Fr.* fräN swȧ mȧ rē ȧ rwĕ′ də), 1694–1778, French philosopher, historian, dramatist, and essayist. **—Voltairean** (vŏl tēə′rĭ ən), **Voltairian,** *adj.*

voltaism (vŏl′tə ĭz′əm), *n.* the branch of electrical science that deals with the production of electricity or electric currents by chemical action.

voltameter (vŏl tăm′ĭ tə), *n.* a device for measuring the quantity of electricity passing through a conductor by the amount of electrolytic decomposition it produces, or for measuring the strength of a current by the amount of such decomposition in a given time. **—voltametric** (vŏl′tə mĕt′rĭk), *adj.*

voltammeter (vōlt′ăm′mē′tə), *n.* an instrument which can be used for measuring either volts or amperes.

volt-ampere (vōlt′ăm′pĕə), *n.* an electrical unit equal to the product of one volt and one ampere, which with direct current circuits is equivalent to one watt.

volte (vŏlt), *n.* **1.** *Fencing.* a sudden movement or leap to avoid a thrust. **2.** *Manège.* **a.** a circular or turning movement of a horse. **b.** a gait in which a horse going sideways turns around a centre, with the head turned outward. Also, **volt.** [t. F: m. *volte*, t. It.: m. *volta* turn, ult. der. L *volvere* turn]

volte-face (vŏlt′fäs′; *Fr.* vŏl tə fȧs′), *n.* **1.** a turning so as to face in the opposite direction. **2.** a reversal of opinion or policy. [F, t. It.: m. *volta faccia* turn the face, f. *volta* (der. *voltare* turn) + *faccia* face (g. L *facies*)]

volti (vŏl′tĭ; *It.* vŏl′tē), *imp. v. Music.* turn; turn over (a direction to turn the page). [It.]

voltmeter (vōlt′mē′tə), *n. Elect.* an instrument for measuring the voltage between two points.

Volturno (*It.* vŏl to͞or′nŏ), *n.* a river flowing from the Apennines in central Italy into the Tyrrhenian Sea. ab. 110 mi. See map under **Salerno.**

voluble (vŏl′yo͞o bl), *adj.* characterized by a ready and continuous flow of words, as a speaker or his tongue or speech; glibly fluent: *a voluble talker.* [t. L: m. s. *volūbilis*, der. *volvere* roll, turn] **—vol′ubil′ity, vol′ubleness,** *n.* **—vol′ubly,** *adv.* **—Syn.** See **fluent.**

volume (vŏl′yo͞om), *n.* **1.** a collection of written or printed sheets bound together and constituting a book. **2.** a book forming one of a related set or series. **3.** *Hist.* a roll of papyrus, parchment, or the like, or of manuscript. **4.** the size, measure, or amount of anything in three dimensions; the space occupied by a body or substance in cubic units. **5.** a mass or quantity, esp. a large quantity, of anything: *a volume of sound, to pour out volumes of abuse.* **6.** amount: *the volume of travel on a railway for a given period.* **7.** loudness or softness. **8.** fullness or quantity of tone or sound. [ME *volym*, t. OF: m. *volum*, t. L: m. *volūmen* roll (of papyrus or parchment); def. 4, etc., developed from meaning 'dimensions of a book'] **—Syn. 4.** See **size**[1].

volume control, a manually operated potentiometer for controlling the output of an electronic circuit, esp. of the sound of a radio, television, or gramophone.

volumed (vŏl′yo͞omd), *adj.* **1.** consisting of a volume or volumes (usually with a qualifying adverb): *a many-volumed work.* **2.** in volumes of rolling or rounded masses, as smoke.

volume resistivity, the electrical resistance between opposite faces of a unit cube of insulating material.

volumeter (vŏ lyo͞o′mĭ tə), *n.* any of various instruments or devices for measuring volume, as of gases, liquids, or solids.

volumetric (vŏl′yo͞o mĕt′rĭk), *adj. Chem., Physics.* denoting, pertaining to, or depending upon measurement by volume. Also, **vol′umet′rical. —vol′umet′rically,** *adv.* **—volumetry** (vŏ lyo͞o′mĭ trĭ), *n.*

volumetric analysis, 1. chemical analysis by volume, esp. by titration. **2.** determination of the volume of gases or changes in their volume during combination.

voluminous (və lyo͞o′mĭ nəs), *adj.* **1.** forming, filling, or writing a large volume or book, or many volumes: *a voluminous author.* **2.** sufficient to fill a volume or volumes: *a voluminous correspondence.* **3.** of great volume, size, or extent; in great volumes: *a voluminous flow of lava.* **4.** of ample size, extent, or fullness, as garments, draperies, etc. **5.** *Obs.* having many coils, convolutions, or windings. [t. LL: m. s. *volūminōsus* full of folds. See VOLUME] **—volu′minously,** *adv.* **—volu′minousness, voluminosity** (və lyo͞o′mĭ nŏs′ĭ tĭ), *n.*

voluntarism (vŏl′ən tə rĭz′əm), *n. Philos.* any theory regarding the will rather than the intellect as the fundamental agency or principle. **—vol′untarist,** *n., adj.* **—vol′untaris′tic,** *adj.*

voluntary (vŏl′ən tə rĭ, -trĭ), *adj., n., pl.* **-taries. —***adj.* **1.** done, made, brought about, undertaken, etc., of one's own accord or by free choice: *a voluntary contribution.* **2.** acting of one's own will or choice: *a voluntary substitute.* **3.** pertaining to or depending on voluntary action or contribution. **4.** *Law.* **a.** acting or done without compulsion or obligation. **b.** done by intention, and not by accident: *voluntary manslaughter.* **c.** made without valuable consideration: *a voluntary conveyance or settlement.* **5.** *Physiol.* subject to or controlled by the will: *voluntary muscles.* **6.** having the power of willing or choosing: *a voluntary agent.* **7.** proceeding from a natural impulse; spontaneous: *voluntary faith.* **—***n.* **8.** something done voluntarily. **9.** a piece of music, frequently spontaneous and improvised, performed as a prelude to a larger work, esp. a piece of organ music performed before, during, or after an office of the church. [ME, t. L: m. s. *voluntārius*] **—vol′untarily,** *adv.* **—vol′untariness,** *n.*
—Syn. 1. See **deliberate. 7.** VOLUNTARY, SPONTANEOUS agree in applying to something which is a natural outgrowth or natural expression arising from circumstances and conditions. VOLUNTARY implies having given previous consideration, or having exercised judgement: *a voluntary confession, a voluntary movement, the offer was a voluntary one.* That which is SPONTANEOUS arises as if by itself from the nature of the circumstances or condition: *spontaneous applause, combustion, expression of admiration.* **—Ant. 7.** forced.

voluntaryism (vŏl′ən tə rĭ ĭz′əm, -trĭ-), *n.* the principle or system of supporting churches, schools, etc., by voluntary contributions or aid, independently of the state. **—vol′untaryist,** *n.*

voluntary school, a school built by voluntary bodies (chiefly religious), but maintained by local education authorities. Formerly, **non-provided school.**

volunteer (vŏl′ən tĭə′), *n.* **1.** one who enters into any service of his own free will, or who offers himself for any service or undertaking. **2.** *Mil., etc.* one who enters one of the armed services voluntarily (rather than through conscription), specif. for special or temporary service (rather than as a member of the regular or permanent army). **3.** *Law.* **a.** a person whose actions are not founded on any legal obligation to so act. **b.** one to whom a conveyance is made or promise given without valuable consideration. **4.** *Obs. Agric.* a volunteer plant. *—adj.* **5.** entering voluntarily into any service; being a volunteer; consisting of volunteers. **6.** *Agric.* springing up spontaneously, or without being planted. *—v.i.* **7.** to offer oneself for some service or undertaking. **8.** to enter service or enlist as a volunteer. *—v.t.* **9.** to offer (one's services, etc., or oneself) for some duty or purpose. **10.** to offer to undertake or undergo: *volunteer a dangerous duty.* **11.** to offer to give, or to give, bestow, show, etc., voluntarily: *volunteer advice* (without being asked). **12.** to offer in speech; communicate, tell, or say voluntarily: *to volunteer an explanation.* [t. F: m. *volontaire*, t. L: m. *voluntārius* VOLUNTARY]

voluptuary (və lŭp′tyo͞o ə rĭ), *n., pl.* **-aries,** *adj.* *—n.* **1.** one given up to luxurious or sensuous pleasures. *—adj.* **2.** pertaining to or characterized by luxurious or sensuous pleasures: *voluptuary habits.* [t. L: m. s. *voluptuārius*, var. of *voluptārius*, der. *voluptas* pleasure]

voluptuous (və lŭp′tyo͞o əs), *adj.* **1.** full of, characterized by, or ministering to pleasure or luxurious or sensuous enjoyment: *a voluptuous life.* **2.** derived from luxurious or full gratification of the senses: *voluptuous pleasure.* **3.** directed towards luxurious or sensuous enjoyment: *voluptuous desires.* **4.** given or inclined to luxurious enjoyment of the pleasures of the senses: *a voluptuous woman.* **5.** suggestive of an inclination to sensuous pleasure: *a voluptuous mouth.* **6.** sensuously pleasing or delightful: *voluptuous beauty.* [ME, t. L: m. *voluptuōsus*, der. *voluptas* pleasure] **—volup′tuously,** *adv.* **—volup′tuousness, voluptuosity** (və lŭp′tyo͞o ŏs′ĭ tĭ), *n.* **—Syn. 1.** See **sensual.**

volute (və lyo͞ot′), *n.* **1.** a spiral or twisted formation or object. **2.** *Archit.* a spiral scroll-like ornament, esp. one forming the distinctive feature of the Ionic capital or a more or less important part of the Corinthian and Composite capitals. **3.** *Zool.* **a.** a turn or whorl of a spiral shell. **b.** any of the *Volutidae*, a family of tropical marine gastropods, many species of which have shells prized for their beauty. *—adj.* **4.** in the form of a volute; rolled up. **5.** *Mach.* **a.** spirally shaped or having a part so shaped. **b.** moving in a circular way, esp. if combined with a lateral motion. [t. L: m. s. *volūta* scroll] **—volu′tion,** *n.*

Volute on an Ionic capital

volva (vŏl′və), *n. Bot.* a cuplike membranous sheath at the base of the stalk in some toadstools and mushrooms. [t. L: covering]

volvulus (vŏl′vyo͞o ləs), *n. Pathol.* a torsion or twisting of the intestine causing intestinal obstruction. [t. NL, der. L *volvere* turn]

vomer (vō′mə), *n. Anat.* a bone of the skull in most vertebrates, in man being shaped like a ploughshare, and forming a large part of the nasal septum, or partition between the right and left nasal cavities. [t. L: ploughshare] **—vomerine** (vō′mə rīn′, -rĭn), *adj.*

vomica (vŏm′ĭ kə), *n., pl.* **-cae** (-sē′). *Pathol.* **1.** a cavity, usually in the lungs, containing pus. **2.** the pus content of such a cavity. [t. L: ulcer]

vomit (vŏm′ĭt), *v.i.* **1.** to eject the contents of the stomach by the mouth; spew; be sick. **2.** to be ejected or come out with force or violence. *—v.t.* **3.** to throw up or eject from the stomach through the mouth; spew. **4.** to cast out or eject as if in vomiting; to send out with force or copiously. **5.** to cause (a person) to vomit. *—n.* **6.** the act of vomiting. **7.** matter ejected in vomiting. [late ME *vomyte*, t. L: m. *vomitāre*] **—vom′iter,** *n.* **—vom′itive,** *adj.*

vomito negro (vŏm′ĭ tō nē′grō), *Pathol.* the black vomit of yellow fever. [Sp., t. L: m. s. *vomitus*]

vomitory (vŏm′ĭ tə rĭ, -trĭ), *adj., n., pl.* **-ries.** *—adj.* **1.** inducing vomiting; emetic. **2.** pertaining to vomiting. *—n.* **3.** an emetic. **4.** an opening through which something is ejected or discharged.

vomiturition (vŏm′ĭ tyo͞o rĭsh′ən), *n. Pathol.* **1.** ineffectual efforts to vomit. **2.** the vomiting of a little matter. **3.** *Obs.* vomiting with little effort.

von (vŏn; *Ger.* fŏn), *prep. German.* from; of (much used in German personal names, orig. before names of places or estates, and later before family names as an indication of nobility or rank).

von Braun (*Ger.* fŏn broun′). See **Braun, Wernher von.**

V-one (vē′wŭn′), *n.* V-1.

Von Neumann (vŏn nyo͞o′mən; *Ger.* fŏn noĭ′män), **John,** 1903–57, U.S. mathematician, born in Hungary.

von Siemens (*Ger.* fŏn zē′məns). See **Siemens, Werner von.**

voodoo (vo͞o′do͞o), *n., pl.* **-doos,** *adj., v.,* **-dooed, -dooing.** *—n.* **1.** a class of mysterious rites or practices, of the nature of sorcery, witchcraft, or conjuration, prevalent among the Negroes of the West Indies and the southern U.S., and probably of African origin. **2.** one who practises such rites. **3.** a fetish or other object of voodoo worship. *—adj.* **4.** pertaining to, associated with, or practising voodoo or voodooism. *—v.t.* **5.** to affect by or as by voodoo sorcery or conjuration. [t. Haitian Creole: m. *vodu*, t. some African language. See HOODOO]

voodooism (vo͞o′do͞o ĭz′əm), *n.* the voodoo rites or practices; voodoo sorcery; the voodoo superstition. **—voo′dooist,** *n.* **—voo′doois′tic,** *adj.*

Voortrekker (fôr′trĕk′ə), *n.* (in southern Africa) **1.** any of the settlers of Dutch descent who moved up-country in the Great Trek of 1838 in an effort to evade the British administration. **2.** a member of an Afrikaner youth movement.

voracious (və rā′shəs), *adj.* **1.** devouring or craving food in large quantities: *a voracious appetite.* **2.** greedy in eating; ravenous. **3.** eager and indefatigable: *she is a voracious reader.* [f. *voraci(ty)* (t. L: m. s. *vorācitas* greediness) + -OUS] **—vora′ciously,** *adv.* **—voracity** (vŏrăs′ĭ tĭ), **vora′ciousness,** *n.* **—Syn. 1.** See **ravenous.**

Vorarlberg (*Ger.* fôr′ärl bĕrk), *n.* a province in W Austria. 226,323 pop. (1961); 1004 sq. mi. *Cap.:* Bregenz.

Vorlage (*Ger.* fôr′lä gə), *n. German.* (in skiing) a position in which the skier leans forward but keeps his heels in contact with the skis. [G: forward position]

Voronezh (*Russ.* vä rô′nĭsh), *n.* a city in the central Soviet Union in Europe, near the river Don. 576,000 (est. 1965).

Voronoff (*Russ.* vô′rə nəf), *n.* **Serge** (*Russ.* sĕrzh), 1866–1951, Russian physician.

Voroshilov (*Russ.* və rä shĭ′ləf), *n.* **Kliment Efremovich** (*Russ.* klĕ′mĭnt yĭ fryĕ′mə vĭch), 1881–1969, Soviet general: president of the Soviet Union 1953–60.

Voroshilovgrad (*Russ.* və rə shĭ lăf grät′), *n.* former name of **Lugansk** 1935–57.

Voroshilovsk (*Russ.* və rä shē′ləfsk), *n.* former name of **Stavropol.**

-vorous, a word element meaning 'eating', as in *carnivorous, herbivorous, omnivorous.* [t. L: m. *-vorus* devouring]

vortex (vô′tĕks), *n., pl.* **-texes, -tices** (-tĭ sēz′). **1.** a whirling movement or mass of water, as a whirlpool. **2.** a whirling movement or mass of air, as a whirlwind. **3.** a whirling mass of fire, flame, etc. **4.** a state of affairs likened to a whirlpool for violent activity, irresistible force, etc. **5.** something looked upon as drawing into its powerful whirl or current everything that is near it. **6.** (in old theories, as in the Cartesian philosophy) a rapid rotatory movement of cosmic matter about a centre, regarded as accounting for the origin or phenomena of bodies or systems of bodies in space. [t. L, var. of *vertex* VERTEX]

vortical (vô′tĭ kl), *adj.* **1.** of or pertaining to a vortex. **2.** resembling a vortex. **3.** moving in a vortex. **—vor′tically,** *adv.*

vorticella (vô′tĭ sĕl′ə), *n., pl.* **-cellae** (-sĕl′ē). a transparent, bell-shaped animalcule on a fine elastic stem.

vortices (vô′tĭ sēz′), *n.* a pl. of **vortex.**

vorticism (vô′tĭ sĭz′əm), *n.* (*sometimes cap.*) an English modern art movement initiated in 1914 and inspired by cubism and futurism. **—vor′ticist,** *n.*

vorticose (vô′tĭ kōs′), *adj.* vortical; whirling. [t. L: m. s. *vorticōsus*, der. *vortex* VORTEX]

vortiginous (vô tĭj′ĭ nəs), *adj.* whirling; vortical. [var. of VERTIGINOUS]

Vortumnus (vô tŭm′nəs), *n.* Vertumnus.

Vosges (vōzh; *Fr.* vôzh), *n.* **1.** a range of low mountains in NE France. Highest peak, 4668 ft. **2.** a department in NE France. 380,676 pop. (1962); 2303 sq. mi. *Cap.:* Épinal.

votable (vō′tə bl), *adj.* subject to a vote. Also, **voteable.**

votary (vō′tə rĭ), *n., pl.* **-ries,** *adj.* *—n.* Also, **vo′tarist. 1.** one who is bound by a vow, esp. one bound by vows to a religious life; a monk or a nun. **2.** a devotee of some form of religious worship; a devoted worshipper, as of God, a saint, etc. **3.** one devoted to some pursuit, study, etc. **4.** a devoted follower or admirer. *—adj. Obs.* **5.** consecrated by a vow. **6.** votive. [f. s. L *vōtum* vow + -ARY[1]] **—votaress** (vō′tə rĭs), **votress** (vō′trĭs), *n. fem.*

vote (vōt), *n., v.,* **voted, voting.** *—n.* **1.** a formal expression of will, wish, or choice in some matter, whether of a single individual, as one of a number interested in common, or of a body of individuals, signified by voice, by ballot, etc. **2.** the means by which such expression is made, as a ballot, ticket, etc. **3.** the right to such expression; suffrage. **4.** the decision reached by voting, as by a majority of ballots cast. **5.** a number of votes (or expressions of will) collectively: *the Labour vote, a light vote was polled.* **6.** an expression of feeling, as approval, or the like: *they gave him a vote of confidence.* **7.** an award, grant, or the like, voted: *a vote of £100,000 for a new building.* **8.** *Obs.* a vow. **9.** *Obs.* an ardent wish or prayer. —*v.i.* **10.** to express or signify choice in a matter undergoing decision, as by a voice, ballot, or otherwise; give or cast a vote or votes: *for whom will you vote at the election?* —*v.t.* **11.** to enact, establish, or determine by vote; bring or put (*in, out, down,* etc.) by vote; grant by vote: *to vote an appropriation for a new school.* **12.** to support by one's vote: *to vote Liberal.* **13.** to advocate by or as by one's vote: *to vote that the report be accepted.* **14.** to declare by general consent: *they voted the trip a success.* [late ME, t. L: m. s. *vōtum* vow, wish]

voteable (vō′tə bl), *adj.* votable.

voter (vō′tə), *n.* **1.** one who votes. **2.** one who has a right to vote; an elector.

voting machine, *U.S.* a mechanical substitute for the ballot-paper which automatically registers and counts votes.

voting paper, a ballot-paper.

votive (vō′tĭv), *adj.* **1.** offered, given, dedicated, etc., in accordance with a vow: *a votive offering.* **2.** performed, undertaken, etc., in consequence of a vow. **3.** of the nature of or expressive of a wish or desire. **4.** *Rom. Cath. Ch.* optional; not prescribed: *a votive mass* (a mass which does not correspond with the office of the day, but is said at the choice of the priest). [t. L: m. s. *vōtīvus* pertaining to a vow] —**vo′tively,** *adv.* —**vo′tiveness,** *n.*

Votyak (vō′tĭ ăk′), *n.* a Finno-Ugric language of the Permian group.

vouch (vouch), *v.i.* **1.** to answer (*for*) as being true, certain, reliable, justly asserted, etc. **2.** to give warrant or attestation; give one's own assurance, as surety or sponsor (fol. by *for*): *I can vouch for him.* —*v.t.* **3.** to warrant; attest; confirm. **4.** to sustain or uphold by some practical proof or demonstration, or as such proof does. **5.** to affirm or declare as with warrant; vouch for. **6.** to adduce or quote in support, as extracts from a book or author; cite in warrant or justification, as authority, instances, facts, etc. **7.** to support or authenticate with evidence. **8.** *Law.* (formerly) to call or summon (a person) into court to make good a warranty of title. **9.** *Obs.* to call or take to witness, as a person. —*n. Obs.* **10.** a vouching. **11.** a supporting warrant or attestation. [ME *vouche,* t. AF: m. *voucher,* akin to L *vocāre* call]

voucher (vou′chə), *n.* **1.** one who or that which vouches, as for something. **2.** a document, receipt, stamp, or the like, which proves the truth of a claimed expenditure. **3.** a ticket used as a substitute for cash, as a gift voucher, luncheon voucher, etc. **4.** (in early English law) **a.** one called into court to warrant another's title. **b.** the act of vouching another person to make good a warranty.

vouchsafe (vouch sāf′), *v.,* **-safed, -safing.** —*v.t.* **1.** to grant or give, by favour, graciousness, or condescension: *to vouchsafe a reply.* **2.** to allow or permit, by favour or graciousness. —*v.i.* **3.** to condescend; deign; have the graciousness (to do something). [ME *vouche sauf,* lit., guarantee as safe. See VOUCH] —**vouchsafe′ment,** *n.*

vouge (vo͞ozh), *n.* a long-handled weapon with a kind of axe blade prolonged to a point at the top, used by foot soldiers in the 14th century and later.

voussoir (*Fr.* vo͞o swȧr′), *n. Archit.* any of the pieces, in the shape of a truncated wedge, which form an arch or vault. See diag. under **arch.** [ME, t. F, ult. der. L *volvere* turn]

vow (vou), *n.* **1.** a solemn promise, pledge, or personal engagement: *marriage vows, a vow of secrecy.* **2.** a solemn or earnest declaration. **3.** a solemn, religiously binding promise made to God or to any deity or saint, as to perform some act, make some offering or gift, or enter some service or condition. **4.** a promise, limited in duration and in subject, made at the novitiate by one seeking to become a member of a religious community (**simple vow**). **5.** a promise, binding for life, and usually undertaking absolute chastity, total poverty, and unquestioning obedience, made at the profession of a religious when the habit is taken (**solemn vow**). **6. take vows,** to enter a religious order or house. —*v.t.* **7.** to make a vow of; promise by a vow, as to God or a saint: *to vow a crusade or a pilgrimage.* **8.** to pledge oneself to do, make, give, observe, etc.; make a solemn threat or resolution of: *I vowed revenge.* **9.** to declare solemnly or earnestly; assert emphatically, or asseverate (often with a clause as object): *she vowed she would go to law.* **10.** to make (a vow). **11.** to dedicate or devote by a vow: *to vow oneself to the service of God.* —*v.i.* **12.** to make a solemn or earnest declaration; bind oneself by a vow. [ME *vou,* t. AF, g. L *vōtum*] —**vow′er,** *n.* —**vow′less,** *adj.*

vowel (vou′əl), *n.* **1.** *Phonet.* a voiced speech sound during the articulation of which air from the lungs is free to pass out through the middle of the mouth without causing undue friction. **2.** *Gram.* a letter which usually represents a vowel, as in English, *a, e, i, o,* and *u,* and sometimes *y.* —*adj.* **3.** pertaining to a vowel. [ME, t. OF: m. *vouel,* g. L *vōcālis* (*littera*) vocal (letter)] —**vow′elless,** *adj.*

vowelize (vou′ə līz′), *v.t.,* **-lized, -lizing.** to provide (a Hebrew, Arabic, etc., text) with vowel points. Also, **vowelise.** —**vow′eliza′tion,** *n.*

vowel point, (in Hebrew and Arabic writing and systems derived from them) any of certain marks placed above or below consonant letters to indicate vowels.

vox (vŏks), *n., pl.* **voces** (vō′sēz). voice; sound. [L]

vox angelica (ăn jĕl′ĭ kə), *Music.* an organ stop producing delicate tones, and having two pipes for each digital, one of which is tuned slightly sharp, so that by their dissonance a wavy effect is produced. Also, **vox caelestis** (sĭ lĕs′tĭs). [L: angelic voice]

vox barbara (bä′bə rə), *Latin.* a word or term not conforming to classical standards or accepted usage (applied esp. to Neo-Latin terms in botany, zoology, etc., formed from elements that are neither Latin nor Greek).

vox humana (hyo͞o mä′nə), *Music.* an organ stop designed to produce tones resembling those of the human voice. [L: human voice]

vox pop., vox populi.

vox populi (pŏp′yo͝o lī′), *Latin.* the voice or opinion of the people.

vox populi, vox Dei (dā′ē), the voice of the people (is) the voice of God. Alcuin, *Epistles, c.* 800.

voyage (voi′ĭj), *n., v.,* **-aged, -aging.** —*n.* **1.** a passage, or course of travel, by sea or water, esp. to a distant place. **2.** a flight through air or space, as a journey in an aeroplane. **3.** (formerly) a journey or passage from one place to another by land. **4.** (*often pl.*) a voyage as the subject of a written account, or the account itself. **5.** *Obs.* an enterprise or undertaking. —*v.i.* **6.** to make or take a voyage; travel by sea or water. —*v.t.* **7.** to traverse by a voyage. [t. F; r. ME *viage,* t. OF, g. L *viāticum* provision for a journey] —**voy′ager,** *n.* —**Syn. 1.** See **trip.**

voyageur (*Fr.* vwȧ yȧ zhœr′), *n., pl.* **-geurs** (*Fr.* -zhœr′). *French.* a French Canadian or half-breed who is an expert woodsman and boatman, esp. one hired as a guide by a fur company whose stations are in remote and unsettled regions. [F, der. *voyager* travel]

voyeur (vwī û′; *Fr.* vwȧ yœr′), *n.* one who attains sexual gratification by looking at sexual objects or situations. [t. F, der. *voir* see]

voyeurism (vwī′û rĭz′əm), *n.* a deviation in which sexual gratification is obtained by looking at sexual objects or situations; the condition of a voyeur.

Voysey (voi′zĭ), *n.* **Charles Francis Annesley,** 1857–1941, English architect.

V.P., Also, **V. Pres.** Vice-President.

v.p., verb passive.

V.R., **1.** Vice-Regent. **2.** (L *Victoria Regina*) Queen Victoria. **3.** Volunteer Reserve.

v.r., verb reflexive.

vraisemblance (vrā′sŏm blŏns′; *Fr.* vrĕ säɴ bläɴs′), *n. French.* appearance of truth; verisimilitude. [F, f. *vrai* true + *semblance* appearance]

V. Rev., Very Reverend.

Vries (*Du.* vrēs), *n.* See **De Vries.**

vrouw (vrou; *Afrik., Du.* frou), *n. Afrikaans, Dutch.* **1.** a woman; a wife; a lady. **2.** Mrs. Cf. **Frau.**

vs., **1.** verse. **2.** versus.

V.S., Veterinary Surgeon.

v.s., vide supra.

V-shaped (vē′shāpt′), *adj.* in the shape of the letter V.

V-sign (vē′sīn′), *n.* **1.** a symbol of victory indicated by raising the index and middle fingers, palm outwards. **2.** a similar gesture indicating contempt, palm inwards.

V.S.O., a scheme whereby young volunteers are sent overseas, esp. to developing countries, to teach, use various skills, etc. [*V*(*oluntary*) *S*(*ervice*) *O*(*verseas*)]

Vt, Vermont.

v.t., verb transitive.

Vte, Vicomte.

Vtesse, Vicomtesse.

VTO, *Aeron.* vertical take-off.

VTOL (vē′tŏl), *n. Aeron.* an aircraft capable of taking off and landing vertically. [*V*(*ertical*) *T*(*ake*) *O*(*ff and*) *L*(*anding*)]

V-two (vē′to͞o′), *n.* V-2.

Vuelta Abajo (*Sp.* bwĕl′tȧ ȧ bȧ′ᴋʜō), a region in W Cuba: famous for its tobacco.

vug (vŭg), *n. Mining.* a small cavity in a rock or lode, often lined with crystals. Also, **vugg, vugh.** [t. Cornish: m. *vooga* cave] —**vug′gy,** *adj.*

Vuillard (*Fr.* vwē yȧr′), *n.* **Edouard** (*Fr.* ė dwȧr′), 1868–1940, French intimist painter and decorator.

Vul., Vulgate.

Vulcan (vŭl′kən), *n.* **1.** the Roman god of fire and metalworking. Cf. **Hephaestus. 2.** an imaginary planet with a smaller orbit than that of Mercury, which was believed to exist in the 19th century but whose existence has now been disproved.

Vulcanian (vŭl kā′nyən), *adj.* **1.** of or associated with Vulcan. **2.** (*l.c.*) volcanic. **3.** (*l.c.*) of metalworking.

vulcanism (vŭl′kə nĭz′əm), *n. Geol.* the phenomena connected with the genesis and movement of molten rock material within and at the surface of the earth (including those phenomena connected with plutonic rocks as well as volcanism). Also, **vulcanicity** (vŭl′kə nĭs′ĭ tĭ).

vulcanite (vŭl′kə nīt′), *n.* a hard rubber, readily cut and polished,. used for making combs, buttons, etc., and for electrical insulation, and obtained by vulcanizing indiarubber with a large amount of sulphur; ebonite.

vulcanize (vŭl′kə nīz′), *v.t.*, **-nized, -nizing. 1.** to treat (indiarubber) with sulphur or some compound of sulphur, and subject to a moderate heat (110°–140°C), in order to render it non-plastic and give greater elasticity, durability, etc., or, when a large amount of sulphur and a more extensive heat treatment are employed, in order to make it very hard, as in the case of vulcanite. **2.** to treat (indiarubber) similarly with sulphur or sulphur compounds but without heat, in which case the effects are only superficial. **3.** to subject (substances other than indiarubber) to some analogous process, as to harden. Also, **vulcanise.** —**vul′caniz′able,** *adj.* —**vul′caniza′tion,** *n.* —**vul′caniz′er,** *n.*

vulcanized fibre, a fibre obtained by treating paper pulp with zinc chloride solution: used as a low-voltage electrical insulator.

vulcanology (vŭl′kə nŏl′ə jĭ), *n.* the scientific study of volcanoes and volcanic phenomena. Also, **volcanology.** —**vulcanological** (vŭl′kə nə lŏj′ĭ kl), *adj.* —**vul′canol′ogist,** *n.*

Vulg., Vulgate.

vulg., 1. vulgar. 2. vulgarly.

vulgar (vŭl′gə), *adj.* **1.** marked by ignorance of or want of good breeding or taste, as manners, actions, language, dress, display, etc.: *her appearance and manners were very vulgar.* **2.** crude; coarse; unrefined. **3.** obscene; indecent: *a vulgar joke.* **4.** ostentatious; unsubtle; lacking in good taste, as works: *a vulgar piece of architecture.* **5.** belonging to or constituting the common people of society: *the vulgar herd.* **6.** of, pertaining to, or current among the multitude or general mass of the people: *vulgar errors or superstitions.* **7.** spoken by or being in the language spoken by the people generally; vernacular: *a vulgar translation of the Greek text of the New Testament.* **8.** common or ordinary: *a vulgar fraction.* —*n.* **9.** *Archaic.* the common people. **10.** *Obs.* the vernacular. [ME, t. L: s. *vulgāris* pertaining to the common people] —**vul′garly,** *adv.* —**vul′garness,** *n.* —**Syn. 1.** unrefined, inelegant, low, coarse, ribald. See **common. 2.** crude; boorish.

vulgar fraction, common fraction.

vulgarian (vŭl gĕə′rĭ ən), *n.* a vulgar person, esp. one whose vulgarity is the more conspicuous for his wealth, prominence, or pretensions to good breeding.

vulgarism (vŭl′gə rĭz′əm), *n.* **1.** vulgar character or action; vulgarity. **2.** a vulgar expression; a word or phrase used only in common colloquial, and esp. in coarse, speech.

vulgarity (vŭl găr′ĭ tĭ), *n., pl.* **-ties. 1.** the state or quality of being vulgar; commonness; plebeian character; want of good breeding, manners, or taste; coarseness. **2.** something vulgar; a vulgar act or speech; a vulgar expression; vulgarism.

vulgarize (vŭl′gə rīz′), *v.t.*, **-rized, -rizing. 1.** to make vulgar, common or commonplace; to lower; debase: *to vulgarize manners or taste.* **2.** to put into general use; make known to the general public. Also, **vulgarise.** —**vul′gariza′tion,** *n.* —**vul′gariz′er,** *n.*

Vulgar Latin, popular Latin, as opposed to literary or standard Latin; esp. those forms of popular Latin speech from which sprang the Romance languages of later times.

Vulgate (vŭl′gāt, -gĭt), *n.* **1.** the Latin version of the Scriptures, accepted as the authorized version of the Roman Catholic Church. It was prepared mainly by Jerome near the end of the 4th century. **2.** (*l.c.*) any vulgate text or version. —*adj.* **3.** of or pertaining to the Vulgate. **4.** (*l.c.*) common, or in common use. [t. L: m. s. *vulgātā*, short for *vulgāta ēditio* popular edition]

vulnerable (vŭl′nə rə bl, -nrə bl), *adj.* **1.** susceptible to being wounded; liable to physical hurt. **2.** not protected against emotional hurt; highly sensitive. **3.** not immune to moral attacks, as of criticism or calumny, or against temptations, influences, etc. **4.** (of a place, fortress, etc.) open to attack or assault; weak in respect of defence. **5.** *Contract Bridge.* exposed to greater than usual penalties (applied to the partners who have won one game towards a rubber). [t. LL: m. s. *vulnerābilis* wounding] —**vul′nerabil′ity, vul′nerableness,** *n.* —**vul′nerably,** *adv.*

vulnerary (vŭl′nə rə rĭ), *adj., n., pl.* **-ries.** —*adj.* **1.** used or useful for healing wounds, as plants or remedies. —*n.* **2.** a remedy for wounds.

Vulpecula (vŭl pĕk′yŏŏ lə), *n. Astron.* the Little Fox, a northern constellation lying between Cygnus and Aquila. [t. L, dim. of *vulpes* fox] .

vulpecular (vŭl pĕk′yŏŏ lə), *adj.* pertaining to or of the nature of a young fox or any fox; vulpine.

vulpine (vŭl′pīn), *adj.* pertaining to, like, or characteristic of a fox. [t. L: m. s. *vulpīnus*]

vulpinite (vŭl′pĭ nīt′), *n.* a mineral form of anhydrite which occurs at Vulpino in Italy; used for ornamental purposes.

vulture (vŭl′chə), *n.* **1.** any of various large, carrion-eating birds related to the eagles, kites, hawks, falcons, etc. but having less powerful toes and straighter claws and usually a naked head, esp. the species of the Old World family *Vulturidae*, as the **Egyptian vulture** (*Neophron percnopterus*), and those of the New World family *Cathartidae*, as the **turkey vulture** (*Cathartes aura*). **2.** a person or thing that preys ravenously and ruthlessly. [ME *vultur*, t. L] —**vul′ture-like′,** *adj.*

Vulture, *Gyps indicus* (3 ft long)

vulturine (vŭl′chə rīn′), *adj.* **1.** pertaining to or characteristic of vultures. **2.** resembling a vulture. Also, **vulturous** (vŭl′chə rəs). [t. L: m. s. *vulturīnus*]

vulva (vŭl′və), *n., pl.* **-vae** (-vē), **-vas.** *Anat.* the external female genitalia, specif. the two pairs of labia and the cleft between them. [t. L: wrapper] —**vul′val, vul′var,** *adj.* —**vulviform** (vŭl′vĭ fôm′), *adj.*

vv., 1. verses. 2. violins.

v.v., vice versa.

vv. ll., variae lectiones.

Vyatka (*Russ.* vyät′kə), *n.* former name of **Kirov.**

Vyborg (*Russ.* vĭ′bərk), *n.* a seaport in the NW Soviet Union, on the Gulf of Finland: formerly in Finland. 50,000 (est. 1960). Formerly, **Viipuri.** Swedish, **Viborg.**

Vyernyi (*Russ.* vyĕr′nyĭ), *n.* former name of **Alma-Ata.**

vying (vī′ĭng), *adj.* that vies; competing: *women vying with one another for attention.* —**vy′ingly,** *adv.*

Vyrnwy (*Welsh* vĭr′nŏŏy), *n.* **Lake,** the largest lake in Wales, in Montgomeryshire; a man-made reservoir. 3½ sq. mi.

Vyshinsky (*Russ.* vĭ shĭn′skĭy), *n.* **Andrei Yanuarievich** (*Russ.* än dryĕy′ yän wär′yĭ vĭch), 1883–1954, Soviet politician and lawyer.

W

W, w (dŭb′l yŏŏ′), *n., pl.* **W's** or **Ws, w's** or **ws. 1.** the 23rd letter of the English alphabet. **2.** the twenty-third in order or of a series.

W, 1. *Elect.* watt; watts. 2. west. 3. western. 4. *Chem.* **a.** wolfram. **b.** wolframium.

W., 1. Wales. 2. warden. 3. Wednesday. 4. Welsh. 5. west. 6. western.

w., 1. *Elect.* watt; watts. 2. week; weeks. 3. weight. 4. west. 5. western. 6. wide. 7. width. 8. wife. 9. with.

W.A., 1. West Africa. 2. Western Australia.

Waadt (*Ger.* vat), *n.* German name of **Vaud.**

WAAF (wăf), *n.* **1.** Women's Auxiliary Air Force. **2.** a member of the Women's Auxiliary Air Force.

Waal (*Ger.* väl; *Du.* wäl), *n.* See **Rhine.**

Wabash (wô′băsh), *n.* a river in the U.S., flowing from W Ohio through Indiana and S along part of the boundary between Indiana and Illinois into the Ohio river. 475 mi.

wabble (wŏb′l), *v.i., v.t.*, **-bled, -bling,** *n.* wobble. —**wab′bler,** *n.* —**wab′bling,** *adj.* —**wab′blingly,** *adv.* —**wab′bly,** *adj., adv.*

WAC (wăk), *n. U.S.* **1.** Women's Army Corps. **2.** a member of the Women's Army Corps.

Wace (wās; *Fr.* vȧs), *n.* **Robert** (rŏb′ət; *Fr.* rō bĕr′), fl. 1170, Anglo-Norman poet.

wack (wăk), *n.* **1.** *U.S. Slang.* an erratic, irrational, or unconventional person. **2.** *Dial.* (a familiar term of address).

wacke (wăk′ə), *n.* a soft rock of fine texture, derived from disintegrated basaltic rocks. [t. G: kind of stone]

wacky (wăk′ĭ), *adj.*, **wackier, wackiest.** *U.S. Slang.* erratic, irrational, or unconventional; crazy. Also, **whacky.**

Waco (wā′kō), *n.* a town in the U.S., in central Texas, on the Brazos river. 97,808 (1960).

wad[1] (wŏd), *n.*, *v.*, **wadded, wadding.** —*n.* **1.** a small mass or lump of anything soft. **2.** a small mass of cotton, wool, or other fibrous or soft material, used for stuffing, padding, packing, etc. **3.** a ball or mass of something squeezed together: *a wad of folded paper.* **4.** a roll or bundle, esp. of banknotes. **5.** *U.S. Slang.* a large quantity of something, esp. money. **6.** a plug of cloth, tow, paper, or the like, used to hold the powder or shot, or both, in place in a gun or cartridge. **7.** *Dial.* a bundle, esp. a small one, of hay, straw, etc. —*v.t.* **8.** to form into a wad. **9.** *U.S.* to roll tightly (often fol. by *up*): *wadding his cap into his pocket.* **10.** to hold in place by a wad, as powder or shot. **11.** to put a wad into (a gun, etc.). **12.** to fill out with or as with wadding; stuff; pad. [orig. uncert.; akin to Sw. *wadd,* G *Watte* wadding] —**wad′der,** *n.*

wad[2] (wŏd), *n.* a soft, earthy, black to dark brown mass of manganese oxide minerals. [orig. uncert.]

wad[3] (wäd, wəd), *v. Scot.* would.

Wadai (wŏ dī′), *n.* a former independent sultanate of the Sudan in N central Africa: now the E part of the Republic of Chad.

wadding (wŏd′ĭng), *n.* **1.** any fibrous or soft material for stuffing, padding, packing, etc., esp. carded cotton in specially prepared sheets. **2.** material for wads for guns, etc. **3.** a wad or lump.

waddle (wŏd′l), *v.*, **-dled, -dling,** *n.* —*v.i.* **1.** to walk with short steps and swaying or rocking from side to side, as a duck. **2.** to move with a similar movement. —*n.* **3.** the act of waddling; a waddling gait. [freq. of WADE] —**wad′dler,** *n.* —**wad′dlingly,** *adv.*

waddy (wŏd′ĭ), *n.*, *pl.* **-dies,** *v.*, **-died, -dying.** *Austral.* —*n.* **1.** a heavy wooden war club of the Australian aborigines. —*v.t.* **2.** to beat or strike with a waddy.

wade (wād), *v.*, **waded, wading,** *n.* —*v.i.* **1.** to walk through any substance, as water, snow, sand, etc., that impedes free motion: *wading in mud, wading through high grass.* **2.** to make one's way with labour or difficulty: *to wade through a dull book.* **3.** *Obs.* to go or proceed. **4. wade in** or **into,** *Colloq.* **a.** to begin energetically. **b.** to attack strongly. —*v.t.* **5.** to pass through or cross by wading; ford: *to wade a stream.* —*n.* **6.** the act of wading. [ME; OE *wadan* go, c. G *waten,* L *vādāre*]

wader (wā′də), *n.* **1.** one who or that which wades. **2.** any of various long-legged birds, as cranes, herons, storks, sandpipers, plovers, etc., that wade in water in search of food. **3.** (*pl.*) high waterproof boots used for wading.

wadi (wŏd′ĭ), *n.*, *pl.* **-ies.** (in Arabia, Syria, northern Africa, etc.) **1.** the channel of a watercourse which is dry except during periods of rainfall. **2.** the stream or watercourse itself.. [t. Ar.]

Wadi Halfa (wŏd′ĭ häl′fə), a town in N Sudan, on the Nile. 52,454 (1967).

wading bird, wader (def. 2).

Wad Medani (wŏd′mē dä′nĭ), a town in E Sudan. 57,000 (est. 1964).

wadset (wŏd′sĕt′), *n.*, *v.t.*, **-setted, -setting.** *Scot. Law.* mortgage. [ME *wedset,* OE *tō wedde settan* set for pledge]

wady (wŏd′ĭ), *n.*, *pl.* **-ies.** wadi.

wae (wā), *n. Scot. and N Dial.* woe.

waesucks (wā′sŭks), *interj. Scot.* alas! [Scot., f. *wae* WOE + *sucks,* var. of SAKE(s)]

waf (wăf, wäf), *adj. Scot.* waff².

WAF (wăf), *U.S.* **1.** Women in the Air Force. —*n.* **2.** a member of Women in the Air Force.

Wafd (wŏft), *n.* the nationalist party in Egypt. [t. Ar.: deputation] —**Wafd′ist,** *n.*, *adj.*

wafer (wā′fə), *n.* **1.** a thin, crisp cake or biscuit, variously made, and often sweetened and flavoured, usually eaten with ice-cream. **2.** a thin disc of unleavened bread, used in the Eucharist, as in the Roman Catholic Church. **3.** any of various other thin, flat cakes, sheets, or the like. **4.** a thin disc of dried paste, gelatine, adhesive paper, or the like, used for sealing letters, attaching paper, etc. **5.** *Med.* a thin, circular sheet of dry paste or the like, or a pair of such sheets, used upon moistening to wrap about or enclose a powder to be swallowed. —*v.t.* **6.** to seal, close, or attach by means of a wafer or wafers: *to wafer a letter.* [ME *wafre,* t. OF: m. *waufre,* t. MLG: m. *wafel* honeycomb. Cf. WAFFLE] —**wa′fer-like′, wa′fery,** *adj.*

wafer-thin (wā′fə thĭn′), *adj.* very thin.

waff[1] (wăf, wäf), *n. Scot. and N Dial.* **1.** a puff or blast of air, wind, etc. **2.** a brief view; glimpse. [var. of WAVE]

waff[2] (wăf, wäf), *adj. Scot.* worthless. Also, **waf.**

waffle[1] (wŏf′əl), *n.* a batter cake with a grid of deep indentations formed by baking it in a metal appliance having two hinged parts (**waffle iron**). [t. D: m. *wafel.* Cf. WAFER]

waffle[2] (wŏf′əl), *v.*, **-fled, -fling.** *Colloq.* —*v.i.* **1.** to speak or write vaguely, pointlessly, and at considerable length. **2.** to talk or write nonsense. —*n.* **3.** useless verbiage. **4.** nonsense; twaddle. Also, **woffle.** [freq. of d. *waff* to yelp]

waft[1] (wäft), *v.t.* **1.** to bear or carry through the air or over water: *the gentle breeze wafted the sound of voices.* **2.** to bear or convey lightly as if in flight: *he wafted her away.* **3.** *Obs.* to signal to, summon, or direct by waving. —*v.i.* **4.** to float or be carried, esp. through the air. —*n.* **5.** a sound, smell, etc., carried through the air: *a waft of bells.* **6.** a wafting movement; current or gust: *a waft of wind.* **7.** the act of wafting. **8.** *Naut.* waif (def. 4). [backformation from obs. *wafter,* late ME *waughter* armed escort vessel, t. D or LG: m. *wachter* guard; in some senses confused with WAFF¹ wave] —**waft′er,** *n.*

waft[2] (wăft, wäft), *n. Scot.* weft.

waftage (wäf′tĭj), *n. Archaic.* **1.** the act of wafting. **2.** the state of being wafted.

wafture (wäf′chə), *n.* **1.** the act of wafting. **2.** something wafted: *waftures of incense.*

wag (wăg), *v.*, **wagged, wagging,** *n.* —*v.t.* **1.** to move from side to side, forwards and backwards, or up and down, esp. rapidly and repeatedly: *a dog wagged his tail.* **2.** to move (the tongue) in talking. **3.** to shake (a finger) at someone, esp. in reproval, reproach, or admonition. —*v.i.* **4.** to be moved from side to side or one way and the other, esp. rapidly and repeatedly, as the head or the tail. **5.** (of the tongue) to move busily, esp. in idle or indiscreet talk. **6.** to get along; travel; proceed: *how the world wags.* **7.** to totter or sway. **8.** *Slang.* to play truant. —*n.* **9.** the act of wagging. **10.** a humorous person; joker. [ME *wagge,* t. Scand.; cf. Icel. *vaga* to rock]

wage (wāj), *n.*, *v.*, **waged, waging.** —*n.* **1.** (*often pl.*) that which is paid for work or services, as by the day or week; hire; pay. **2.** (*pl.*) *Econ.* the share of the products of industry received by labour for its work, as distinct from the share going to capital. **3.** (*usually pl., sometimes construed as sing.*) recompense or return: *the wages of sin is death.* **4.** *Obs.* a pledge or security. —*v.t.* **5.** to carry on (a battle, war, conflict, etc.): *to wage war against a nation.* **6.** *Obs. or Dial.* to hire. **7.** *Obs.* **a.** to stake or wager. **b.** to pledge. —*v.i.* **8.** *Obs.* to contend; battle. [ME, t. OF: m. *wagier,* der. *wage* pledge. See GAGE¹] —**wage′less,** *adj.* —**Syn. 1.** remuneration, emolument, earnings.

wage-earner (wāj′û′nə), *n.* one who works for wages (sometimes distinguished from a salaried employee).

wage freeze, freeze (def. 29).

wager (wā′jə), *n.* **1.** something staked or hazarded on an uncertain event; a bet. **2.** the act of betting. **3.** the subject of a bet. **4.** *Early Eng. Law.* a pledge to make good one's cause: *wager of law.* —*v.t.* **5.** to hazard (something) on the issue of a contest or any uncertain event or matter; stake; bet. **6.** *Hist.* to pledge oneself to (battle) for the decision of a case. —*v.i.* **7.** to make or offer a wager; bet. [ME, t. AF: m. *wageure.* See WAGE] —**wa′gerer,** *n.* —**Syn. 1.** stake, hazard, risk, venture.

wageworker (wāj′wû′kə), *n. U.S.* a member of the labouring class; a worker for wages; wage-earner.

Wagga Wagga (wŏg′ə wŏg′ə), a town in Australia, in SE New South Wales. 23,300 (est. 1964).

waggery (wăg′ə rĭ), *n.*, *pl.* **-geries. 1.** the action, spirit, or language of a wag. **2.** a waggish act; a jest.

waggish (wăg′ĭsh), *adj.* **1.** like a wag; roguish in merriment and good humour; jocular. **2.** characteristic of or befitting a wag: *waggish humour..* —**wag′gishly,** *adv.* —**wag′gishness,** *n.* —**Syn. 1.** See **humorous.**

waggle (wăg′l), *v.*, **-gled, -gling,** *n.* —*v.t.*, *v.i.* **1.** to wag with short, quick movements. —*n.* **2.** a waggling motion. [freq. of WAG. Cf. G *wackeln* stagger] —**wag′glingly,** *adv.*

waggly (wăg′lĭ), *adj.* waggling; unsteady.

waggon (wăg′ən), *n.* wagon. —**wag′gonage,** *n.* —**wag′goner,** *n.* —**wag′gonette′,** *n.*

waggon-headed (wăg′ən hĕd′ĭd), *adj.* wagon-headed.

Wagner (väg′nə; *Ger.* vȧg′nər), *n.* **1. Otto** (ŏt′ō; *Ger.* ō′tō), 1841–1918, Austrian architect. **2. Richard** (rĭch′əd; *Ger.* rĭKH′ärt), 1813–83, German composer.

Wagnerian (väg nĭə′rĭ ən), *adj.* **1.** of, pertaining to, or like Richard Wagner or his works. —*n.* **2.** Also, **Wagnerite** (väg′nə rīt′). a follower or admirer of the music or theories of Richard Wagner.

Wagnerism (väg′nə rĭz′əm), *n.* **1.** Richard Wagner's theory of method as exemplified in his music dramas, which, departing from the conventional methods of earlier (esp. Italian) opera, shows constant attention to dramatic and emotional effect, and the abundant use of the leitmotiv. **2.** the study, imitation, or influence of the music of Richard Wagner. —**Wag′nerist,** *n.*

Wagner tuba, 1. either of two modified French horns, designed by Richard Wagner, of tenor and bass range. **2.** a double-bass tuba.

wagon (wăg′ən), *n.* **1.** any of various kinds of four-wheeled vehicles, esp. one designed for the transport of heavy loads, delivery, etc. **2.** a railway truck. **3.** (*cap.*) *Astron.* Charles's Wain, or the Plough. **4.** *U.S.* a police van for transporting prisoners. **5.** *Obs.* a chariot. **6. on the wagon,** *Slang.* abstaining from alcoholic drink. —*v.t.* **7.** to transport or convey by wagon. Also, **waggon.** [t. D: m. *wagen,* c. OE *wægn* WAIN] —**wag′onless,** *adj.* —**Syn. 1.** cart, van, wain, truck, dray, lorry.

wagonage (wăg′ə nĭj), *n. Archaic.* **1.** transport or conveyance by wagon. **2.** money paid for this. **3.** a collection of wagons; wagons collectively. Also, **waggonage.**

wagoner (wăg′ə nə), *n.* **1.** one who drives a wagon. **2.** (*cap.*) *Astron.* the northern constellation Auriga. **3.** *Obs.* a charioteer. Also, **waggoner.**

wagonette (wăg′ə nĕt′), *n.* a four-wheeled pleasure vehicle, with or without a top, having a crosswise seat in front and two lengthwise seats facing each other at the back. Also, **waggonette.**

wagon-headed (wăg′ən hĕd′ĭd), *adj. Archit.* of the form of a round arch or a semicylinder, like the cover of a wagon when stretched over the bows, as a ceiling, roof, etc. Also, **waggon-headed.**

wagon-lit (*Fr.* vá gôɴ lē′), *n., pl.* **wagon-lits** (*Fr.* vá gôɴ-lē′). (in French and other Continental use) a railway sleeping-car. [F: f. *wagon* railway coach, WAGON + *lit* bed]

wagonload (wăg′ən lōd′), *n.* the load carried by a wagon.

wagon soldier, *U.S. Mil. Slang.* a field artillery soldier.

wagon train, a train of wagons and horses, esp. one carrying military supplies.

Wagram (*Ger.* väg′räm), *n.* a village in NE Austria: Napoleon defeated the Austrians here, 1809.

wagtail (wăg′tāl′), *n.* any of numerous small, chiefly Old World birds of the family *Motacillidae,* having a slender body with a long, narrow tail which is habitually wagged up and down.

Wahabi (wə hä′bĭ), *n., pl.* **-bis.** *Islam.* one of the followers of Abd al-Wahhab (1691?–1787?), a Muslim reformer who opposed all practices which are not sanctioned by the Koran. They are today the most conservative Muslim group and are found mainly in Saudi Arabia. Also, **Wahabee, Wahhabi, Wahabite** (wə hä′bīt). [t. Ar.] —**Waha′biism, Waha′bism,** *n.*

wahine (wä hē′nĭ), *n.* **1.** *N.Z.* a Maori girl or woman. **2.** *U.S., N.Z., Austral., etc.* an attractive girl, esp. one who frequents beaches. [t. Maori]

wahoo[1] (wä ho͞o′, wä′ho͞o), *n., pl.* **-hoos. 1.** a shrub or small tree, *Euonymus atropurpureus,* native to North America, with pendulous capsules which in dehiscing reveal the bright scarlet arils of the seeds; burning bush. **2.** any of various other American shrubs or small trees, as an elm, *Ulmus alata,* or a linden, *Tilia heterophylla.* [t. Dakota (Siouan): m. *wanku* arrowwood; or t. Creek (Muskhogean): m. *uhawha* cork or winged elm]

wahoo[2] (wä ho͞o′, wä′ho͞o), *n., pl.* **-hoos.** a large, swift game fish, *Acanthocybium solandri,* of the high seas. [t. Amer. Ind.]

Waiapu (wī ä′po͞o), *n.* a river in New Zealand, in E North Island, flowing NE to the Pacific Ocean. 75 mi.

Waiau (wī′ou), *n.* **1.** a river in New Zealand, in S South Island, flowing S to Foveaux Strait. 135 mi. **2.** Waiau-uha.

Waiau-uha (wī′ou o͝oə′), *n.* a river in New Zealand, in N South Island, flowing S then E to the Pacific Ocean. 105 mi. Also, **Waiau.**

waif (wāf), *n.* **1.** a person without home or friends, esp. a child. **2.** a stray thing or articles. **3.** something found, of which the owner is not known, as an animal. **4.** Also, **waft.** *Naut.* a signalling, or a signal given, by a flag rolled and stopped or fastened. **5.** *Law, Obs.* stolen property thrown away by a thief in flight, which was formerly forfeited to the king or lord of the manor. [ME, t. AF, prob. t. Scand.; cf. Icel. *veif* oscillation]

Waihou (wī′hō), *n.* a river in New Zealand, in N North Island, flowing N to the Pacific Ocean. 95 mi. Also, **Thames.**

Waikato (wī kăt′ō, -kä′tō), *n.* the longest river in New Zealand, in W North Island, flowing NW then W to the Tasman Sea. 270 mi.

Waikiki (wī′kĭ kē′, wī′kĭ kē′), *n.* a pleasure resort in the Hawaiian Islands, in SE Oahu, formerly part of Honolulu.

wail (wāl), *v.i.* **1.** to utter a prolonged, inarticulate, mournful cry, usually high-pitched or clear-sounding, as in grief or suffering: *the child wailed when he fell over.* **2.** to sound mournfully, as music, the wind, etc. **3.** to lament or mourn bitterly. —*v.t.* **4.** to wail over; bewail; lament: *to wail the dead.* **5.** to cry or say in lamentation. —*n.* **6.** the act of wailing. **7.** a wailing cry, as of grief, pain, etc. **8.** any similar mournful sound: *the wail of an old tune.* [ME *weile,* t. Scand.; cf. Icel. *vǣla* wail, der. *vǣ,* var. of *vei* woe] —**wail′er,** *n.* —**wail′ingly,** *adv.*

wailful (wāl′fəl), *adj.* mournful; plaintive. —**wail′-fully,** *adv.*

Wailing Wall, a wall in Jerusalem where Jews assemble on certain occasions for prayers and lamentation. It is reputedly the remains of part of the temple built by Herod. Also, **Wailing Wall of the Jews.**

wailsome (wāl′səm), *adj.* wailing.

Waimakariri (wī′măk′ə rĭə′rĭ), *n.* a river in New Zealand, in E central South Island, flowing E to the Pacific Ocean. 100 mi.

wain (wān), *n.* **1. the Wain,** Charles's Wain; the Plough. **2.** *Chiefly Poetic.* a wagon or cart. [ME; OE *wægn,* c. D *wagen,* G *Wagen.* Cf. OE *wegan* carry]

wainscot (wān′skət), *n., v.,* **-scoted, -scoting** or **-scotted, -scotting.** —*n.* **1.** oak or other wood, usually in panels, serving to line the walls of a room, etc. **2.** a dado, or a facing of any material on interior walls, etc. **3.** the lower portion of a wall surfaced in a different manner or material from the upper portion. **4.** (orig.) a superior quality of oak imported into England for fine panelled work and the like. —*v.t.* **5.** to line (a room, walls, etc.) with wainscot or wood: *a room wainscoted in oak.* [ME *waynscot,* half trans., half adoption of MLG *wagenschot,* f. *wagen* WAIN + *schot,* of doubtful meaning]

wainscoting (wān′skə tĭng), *n.* **1.** panelling or woodwork with which walls, etc., are wainscoted. **2.** wainscots collectively. Also, **wainscotting.**

wainwright (wān′rīt′), *n.* a wagon-maker.

Wairau (wī′rou), *n.* a river in New Zealand, in N South Island, flowing NE to Cook Strait. 105 mi.

Wairoa (wī rō′ə), *n.* **1.** a river in New Zealand, in NW North Island, flowing SE then W to the Tasman Sea. 115 mi. **2.** a river in New Zealand, in E North Island, flowing SE to Hawke Bay on the Pacific Ocean. 85 mi.

waist (wāst), *n.* **1.** the part of the human body between the ribs and the hips. **2.** the part of a garment covering the waist. **3.** *U.S.* a woman's blouse. **4.** *U.S.* a bodice. **5.** that part of an object, esp. a central or middle part, which bears some analogy to the human waist: *the waist of a violin.* **6.** *Naut.* the central part of a ship; that part of the deck between the forecastle and the quarterdeck. **7.** the narrow part or petiole of the abdomen of certain insects, as the wasp. [ME *wast,* c. Icel. *vöxtr,* OHG *wahst* growth. See WAX[2], v., grow] —**waist′less,** *adj.*

waistband (wāst′bănd′), *n.* a band encircling the waist, esp. as a part of a skirt, trousers, etc.

waistcloth (wāst′klŏth′), *n.* a loincloth.

waistcoat (wās′kōt′), *n.* **1.** a close-fitting, sleeveless garment for men which reaches to the waist and buttons down the front, and is designed to be worn under a jacket. **2.** a similar garment sometimes worn by women. **3.** a body garment for men, formerly worn under the doublet. —**waist′coat′ed,** *adj.*

waist-deep (wāst′dēp′), *adj.* waist-high.

waisted (wās′tĭd), *adj.* shaped like or so as to form a waist.

waist-high (wāst′hī′), *adj.* reaching as high as the waist. Also, **waist-deep.**

waistline (wāst′līn′), *n.* **1.** a line around the body at the smallest part of the waist. **2.** that part of a woman's dress, coat, etc., which lies at or close to the waist.

wait (wāt), *v.i.* **1.** to stay or rest in expectation; remain in a state of quiescence or inaction, as until something expected happens (often fol. by *for, till,* or *until*): *waiting for him to go.* **2.** (of things) to be in readiness: *a letter waiting for you.* **3.** to remain neglected for a time: *a matter that can wait.* **4.** to postpone or delay something or to be postponed or delayed. **5. wait on** or **upon, a.** to perform the duties of an attendant or servant for. **b.** to supply the wants of (a person) at table. **c.** to call upon or visit (a person, esp. a superior): *to wait on the emperor in his palace.* **d.** to attend as an accompaniment or consequence. **6. to wait up,** to delay going to bed to await someone's arrival. —*v.t.* **7.** to continue stationary or inactive in expectation of; await: *to wait one's turn in a queue.* **8.** (of things) to be in readiness for; be reserved for: *glory waits thee.* **9.** *Colloq.* to defer or postpone in expectation of the arrival of someone: *to wait dinner for the guests.* **10.** *Obs.* to attend upon or escort, esp. as a sign of honour. **11. wait table,** to wait at table; serve. —*n.* **12.** the act of waiting or awaiting; delay; halt. **13.** a period or interval of waiting. **14.** *Theat.* the time between two acts or the like. **15.** (*usually pl.*) one of a band of singers and musicians who go about the streets by night at Christmas singing and playing carols, etc. **16.** *Obs.* one of a body of musicians in the employ of a city or town. **17.** *Obs.* a watchman. **18. lie in wait,** to wait in ambush. [ME *waite(n)*, t. OF: m. *waitier*, t. OHG: m. *wahtēn* watch; akin to WATCH]

—**Syn. 1.** await, linger, remain, abide. WAIT, TARRY imply pausing to linger and thereby putting off further activity until later. WAIT usually implies staying for a limited time and for a definite purpose, that is, for something expected: *to wait for a train.* TARRY is a somewhat archaic word for WAIT but it suggests lingering, perhaps aimlessly delaying, or pausing (briefly) in a journey: *to tarry on the way home, to tarry overnight at an inn.* **12.** waiting, tarrying, lingering, pause, stop.

wait-a-bit (wāt′ə bĭt′), *n.* any of various plants bearing thorns or prickly appendages, as a procumbent herb, *Harpagophytum procumbens*, of southern Africa, or the greenbrier. [trans. of Afrikaans *wacht-een-beetje*]

Waitaki (wī tăk′ī), *n.* a river in New Zealand, in SE South Island, flowing SE to the Pacific Ocean. 135 mi.

Waitara (wī′tə rə), *n.* a river in New Zealand, in W North Island, flowing SW then NW to the Tasman Sea. 85 mi.

waiter (wā′tə), *n.* **1.** a man who waits at table, as in a restaurant, hotel, etc. **2.** a tray on which dishes, etc., are carried; salver. **3.** one who waits or awaits. **4.** *Obs.* an attendant. —**wait′erless,** *adj.*

waiting (wā′tĭng), *n.* **1.** a period of waiting. **2. in waiting,** in attendance, as upon a king, queen, prince, etc. —*adj.* **3.** that serves or attends: *a waiting man, waiting maid.*

waiting game, the postponement of action on a particular matter for the time being in order to have an opportunity for more effective action later on.

waiting list, a list of persons waiting for something to become available, as applicants for housing accommodation, etc.

waiting room, a room for the use of persons waiting, as in a railway station or a doctor's surgery.

waitress (wā′trĭs), *n.* a woman who waits at table, as in a restaurant, hotel, etc. —**wait′ressless,** *adj.*

waive (wāv), *v.t.*, **waived, waiving. 1.** to forbear to insist on; relinquish; forgo: *to waive one's rank, to waive honours.* **2.** *Law.* to relinquish (a known right, etc.) intentionally. **3.** to put aside for the time; defer. **4.** to put aside or dismiss from consideration or discussion: *waiving my attempts to explain.* [ME *weyven*, t. AF: m. *weyver* abandon. See WAIF]

waiver (wā′və), *n. Law.* **1.** an intentional relinquishment of some right, interest, or the like. **2.** an express or written statement of such relinquishment. [t. AF: m. *weyver*. See WAIVE]

Wajda (*Pol.* vȧy′dȧ), *n.* **Andrzej** (*Pol.* ȧnd′zhĕy), born 1926, Polish film director.

Wakashan (wä kăsh′ən, wô′kə shăn′), *n.* an Amerindian linguistic stock including languages spoken in British Columbia and Washington, esp. Nootka and Kwakiutl.

Wakatipu (wä′kä tē′po͞o), *n.* **Lake,** a lake in New Zealand, in S South Island. 113 sq. mi.

Wakayama (wăk′ə yä′mə), *n.* a seaport in Japan, on S Honshu island. 328,657 (1965).

wake¹ (wāk), *v.*, **woke, woken, waking** or (*Chiefly U.S.*) **waked, waken, waking,** *n.* —*v.i.* **1.** to become roused from sleep; awake (often fol. by *up*). **2.** to be or continue awake. **3.** to remain awake for some purpose, duty, etc. **4.** to become roused from a quiescent or inactive state. **5.** to become alive, as to something perceived; become aware of. **6.** *Dial.* to hold a wake over a corpse. **7.** *Archaic or Dial.* to keep watch or vigil. —*v.t.* **8.** to rouse from sleep; awake (often fol. by *up*). **9.** to rouse from quiescence, inactivity, lethargy, unconsciousness, etc. (often fol. by *up*). **10.** *Dial.* to hold a wake over (a corpse). **11.** *Archaic or Dial.* to keep watch or vigil over. —*n.* **12.** a watching, or a watch kept, esp. for some solemn or ceremonial purpose. **13.** a watch, esp. at night, by the body of a dead person before burial, often accompanied by drinking and feasting. **14.** an annual festival held formerly, or now locally in England in commemoration of the dedication of a parish church. **15.** the state of being awake: *between sleep and wake.* [ME *wake(n)*, OE *wacian*, c. D *waken*, G *wachen*, Icel. *vaka* wake, watch; ME *woke*, OE *wōc* (past tense)] —**wak′er,** *n.* —**Syn. 8.** waken, arouse.

wake² (wāk), *n.* **1.** the track left by a ship or other object moving in the water. **2.** the path or course of anything that has passed or preceded. **3. in the wake of, a.** following behind. **b.** following as a result or consequence of. [t. Scand.; cf. Icel. *vök* hole in the ice]

Wakefield (wāk′fēld′), *n.* a city in England, in the West Riding of Yorkshire: battle, 1460. 61,268 (1961).

wakeful (wāk′fəl), *adj.* **1.** indisposed or unable to sleep, as a person. **2.** characterized by absence of sleep: *a wakeful night.* **3.** watchful or vigilant: *a wakeful foe.* —**wake′fully,** *adv.* —**wake′fulness,** *n.* —**Syn. 1.** sleepless, insomnious, restless.

Wake Island, an island in the N Pacific, belonging to the U.S.: air-base. 3 sq. mi. See map under **Hawaiian Islands.**

waken (wā′kən), *v.t.* **1.** to rouse from sleep; awake. **2.** to rouse from inactivity; stir up or excite; arouse. —*v.i.* **3.** to wake, or become awake; awaken. [ME; OE *wæcnan*, c. Icel. *vakna.* See WAKE¹] —**wa′kener,** *n.*

wakerife (wāk′rīf′), *adj. Scot. and N Dial.* wakeful. —**wake′rife′ness,** *n.*

wake-robin (wāk′rŏb′ĭn), *n.* **1.** the cuckoopint. **2.** any or various other arums or araceous plants. **3.** any of various plants of the U.S. of the liliaceous genus *Trillium*, as *T. erectum*, a species with ill-scented purple, pink, or white flowers.

wake-up (wāk′ŭp′), *n. U.S. Dial.* flicker².

Wal., 1. Walachian. **2.** Walloon.

Walachia (wŏ lā′kyə), *n.* a former principality in SE Europe: it united with Moldavia to form Rumania, 1861. 29,569 sq. mi. *Cap.*: Bucharest. Also, **Wallachia.** —**Wala′chian,** *adj., n.*

Walachia

Walbrzych (*Pol.* vȧw′bzhĭKH), *n.* a town in SW Poland. 123,000 (est. 1964). German, **Waldenburg.**

Walcheren (väl′kə rən; *Du.* wŏl′KHə rə), *n.* an island in SW Netherlands, forming part of Zeeland province. 77,839 pop. (est. 1956); 82 sq. mi.

Waldemar I (väl′dĭ mä′) (*'the Great'*), 1131–82, king of Denmark 1157–82. Also, **Valdemar I.**

Waldenburg (*Ger.* vȧl′dən bo͝ork), *n.* German name of **Walbrzych.**

Waldenses (wŏl dĕn′sēz), *n.pl.* a Christian sect which arose after 1170 in southern France under the leadership of Pierre Waldo, a merchant of Lyons, and in the 16th century joined the Reformation movement. [t. ML, pl. of *Waldensis*, der. *Waldo*] —**Waldensian** (wŏl dĕn′sĭ ən), *adj., n.*

waldgrave (wôld′grāv), *n.* (in the old German Empire) an officer having jurisdiction over a royal forest. [t. G: m. *Waldgraf*, f. *Wald* forest + *Graf* count]

Waldstein (*Ger.* vält′shtīn), *n.* See **Wallenstein.**

wale¹ (wāl), *n., v.*, **waled, waling.** —*n.* **1.** a streak, stripe, or ridge produced on the skin by the stroke of a rod or whip; a welt. **2.** a ridge or raised line formed in the weave of cloth. **3.** the texture of a fabric; the kind of weave. **4.** a ledger, esp. one used to support the poling boards in a trench. **5.** *Naut.* **a.** any of certain strakes of thick outside planking on the sides of a wooden ship. **b.** the gunwale. —*v.t.* **6.** to mark with wales. **7.** to weave with wales. [ME; OE *walu* weal, ridge, prob. akin to Icel. *völr*, Goth *walus* rod, wand]

wale² (wāl), *n., v.*, **waled, waling.** *Scot. and N Dial.* —*n.* **1.** the choicest or best specimen, part, etc. —*v.t.* **2.** to choose; select; pick out. [ME *wal(e)*, t. Scand.; cf. Icel. *val* choice, c. G *Wahl*]

Waler (wā′lə), *n.* (in the 19th century) a horse bred in Australia, esp. in New South Wales, and exported to India.

Wales (wālz), *n.* a division of the United Kingdom: a principality forming the SW part of Great Britain. 2,640,632 pop. (1961); 8016 sq. mi.

Wales

Walhalla (văl hăl′ə), *n. Scand. Myth.* Valhalla.

waling (wā′lĭng), *n.* a set or row of wales (def. 4).

walk (wôk), *v.i.* **1.** to go or travel on foot at a moderate pace; to proceed by steps, or by advancing the feet in turn, at a moderate pace (in bipedal locomotion, so that there is always one foot on the ground, and in quadrupedal locomotion, so that there are always two or more feet on the ground). **2.** to go about or travel on foot for exercise or pleasure. **3.** to go about on the earth, or appear to living persons, as a ghost. **4.** (of things) to move in a manner suggestive of walking, as through repeated vibrations or the effect of alternate expansion and contraction. **5.** to conduct oneself in a particular manner, or pursue a particular course of life: *to walk humbly with thy God.* **6.** *Obs.* to be in motion or action.
—*v.t.* **7.** to proceed through, over, or upon by walking:

walking London streets by night. **8.** to cause to walk; lead, drive, or ride at a walk, as an animal: *walking their horses towards us.* **9.** to force or help to walk, as a person. **10.** to conduct or accompany on a walk: *he walked them about the park.* **11.** to move (an object, as a box or a trunk) in a manner suggestive of walking, as by a rocking motion. **12.** to examine, measure, etc., by traversing on foot: *to walk a track.*
—*v.* **13.** Some special verb phrases are:
walk away with, to win easily.
walk off, to get rid of by walking: *to walk off a headache.*
walk off with, **1.** to remove without permission; steal. **2.** to win, as in a competition. **3.** to outdo one's competitors; win easily.
walk out, **1.** to go on strike. **2.** to leave in protest; leave angrily.
walk out on, to abandon; forsake; desert.
walk out with, to court, woo, or be courted or wooed by.
walk over, **1.** *Horseracing.* (of an unopposed contestant) to go over (the course) at walking pace and thus be judged the winner. **2.** to win easily.
walk the streets, **1.** to wander about the streets. **2.** to be a prostitute, esp. one who solicits on the streets.
walk up, **1.** to ascend; go upstairs. **2.** to approach; draw near.
—*n.* **14.** the act or course of walking, or going on foot. **15.** a spell of walking for exercise or pleasure: *to take a walk.* **16.** a distance walked or to be walked, often in terms of the time required: *ten minutes' walk from the station.* **17.** the gait or pace of a person or animal that walks. **18.** manner of walking: *impossible to mistake her walk.* **19.** a department or branch of activity, or a particular line of work: *they found every walk of life closed against them.* **20.** *Athletics.* a walking race. **21.** a way for pedestrians at the side of a street or road; a path or pavement. **22.** a place prepared or set apart for walking. **23.** a path in a garden or the like. **24.** a passage between rows of trees. **25.** an enclosure in which poultry may run about freely. **26.** a sheepwalk. **27.** a ropewalk. **28.** a plantation of coffee or other trees, as in the West Indies. **29.** *Obs.* **a.** the route or round of a tradesman, hawker, or the like. **b.** the district traversed. **30.** *Obs.* a division of a forest under the charge of a forester or keeper. **31.** *Obs.* a haunt or resort. **32.** *Obs.* manner of behaviour; conduct.
[ME; OE *wealcan* roll, toss, *gewealcan* go, c. D and G *walken* to full (cloth), Icel. *vālka* toss] —**walk′able,** *adj.* —**walk′er,** *n.*
—**Syn.** **1.** step, stride, stroll, saunter, ambulate, perambulate, promenade, pace, march, tramp, hike, tread. **15.** stroll, promenade, march, tramp, hike, constitutional.

walkabout (wô′kə bout′), *n.* *Austral.* wandering; roaming. [t. Aboriginal pidgin English]

walkaway (wô′kə wā′), *n.* an easy victory or conquest.

walkie-talkie (wô′kĭ tô′kĭ), *n.* *Radio.* a combined transmitter and receiver light enough to be carried by one man: developed originally for military use in World War II and subsequently widely used by police, medical services, etc.

walking (wô′kĭng), *adj.* **1.** that walks; able to walk. **2.** used for or in walking: *walking shoes.* **3.** characterized by or consisting of walking: *a walking holiday.* **4.** of or pertaining to an implement, machine, etc., drawn by an animal and operated by a person on foot: *a walking plough.* —*n.* **5.** the act of one who or that which walks: *walking was the best exercise for him.* **6.** manner or style of walking. **7.** the state of that on which one walks: *dry walking in the garden.*

walking bass, *Jazz.* an accompanying bass part played with one note to a beat, usually at medium tempo.

walking delegate, (formerly) an official appointed by a trade union to go from place to place in the interests of the union.

walking fern, a fern of the family *Polypodiaceae, Camptosorus rhizophyllus,* with simple fronds tapering into a prolongation which often takes root at the apex.

walking papers, *Colloq.* dismissal.

walking stick, a stick used in walking; a cane.

walk of life, occupation, profession, or social position.

walk-on (wôk′ŏn′), *n.* *Theat.* a small part in a play, esp. one in which the actor does not speak at all. Also, **walking part.**

walkout (wôk′out′), *n.* **1.** a strike by workers. **2.** the act of leaving or boycotting a conference, meeting, etc., esp. as an act of protest.

walkover (wôk′ō′və), *n.* *Colloq.* **1.** *Racing.* a going over the course at a walk or otherwise by a contestant who is the only starter. **2.** an unopposed or easy victory.

walk-up (wôk′ŭp′), *U.S. Colloq.* —*n.* **1.** a flat or a block of flats without a lift. —*adj.* **2.** having no lift.

Walkyrie (văl kĭə′rĭ), *n.* Valkyrie.

wall (wôl), *n.* **1.** an upright work or structure of stone, brick, or similar material, serving for enclosure, division, support, protection, etc., as one of the upright enclosing sides of a building or a room, or a solid fence of masonry. **2.** (*usually pl.*) a rampart raised for defensive purposes. **3.** anything which resembles or suggests a wall: *a wall of prejudice.* **4.** a wall-like enclosing part, thing, mass, etc.: *a wall of fire; a wall of troops.* **5.** an embankment to prevent flooding. **6.** the external layer of structural material surrounding an object, as an organ of the body or a plant or animal cell. **7.** *Mountaineering.* a vertical or nearly vertical stretch of unbroken rock. **8.** **go to the wall,** **a.** to give way or suffer defeat in a conflict or competition. **b.** to fail in business, or become bankrupt. **9.** **up the wall,** *Colloq.* in or into a state of exasperation, confusion, etc. **10.** **with one's back to the wall,** in a very difficult predicament —*adj.* **11.** of or pertaining to a wall. **12.** growing against or on a wall. **13.** situated or placed in or on a wall. —*v.t.* **14.** to enclose, shut off, divide, protect, etc., with or as with a wall (often fol. by *in* or *off*). **15.** to fill up (a doorway, etc.) with a wall. **16.** to shut up within walls; entomb; immure (usually fol. by *up*). [ME and OE, t. L: m. s. *vallum*] —**walled,** *adj.* —**wall′-less,** *adj.* —**wall′-like′,** *adj.* —**Syn.** **2.** battlement, breastwork, bulwark.

walla (wŏl′ə), *n.* wallah.

wallaby (wŏl′ə bĭ), *n., pl.* **-bies,** (*esp. collectively*) **-by.** any of various small and medium-sized kangaroos of the genera *Macropus, Thylogale, Petrogale,* etc., some of which are no larger than rabbits. [t. native Australian]

Wallaby, *Wallabia agilis* (Total length 5 ft, tail ab. 2 ft)

Wallace (wŏl′ĭs), *n.* **1.** **Alfred Russel,** 1823–1913, English naturalist, explorer, and author. **2.** **Edgar,** 1875–1932, English novelist. **3.** **Henry Agard,** 1888–1965, U.S. statesman: vice-president of the U.S. 1941–45. **4.** **Lewis** (or **Lew**), 1827–1905, U.S. general and novelist. **5.** **Sir William,** *c.* 1272–1305, Scottish military leader and patriot.

Wallachia (wŏ lā′kyə), *n.* Walachia. —**Walla′chian,** *adj., n.*

wallah (wŏl′ə), *n.* *Colloq.* a person employed at or concerned with a particular thing (used esp. in combination with another word): *laundry wallah; cleaning wallah.* Also, **walla.** [t. Hind.: m. *-wālā*]

wallaroo (wŏl′ə rōō′), *n., pl.* **-roos,** (*esp. collectively*) **-roo.** any of several large kangaroos, of the genus *Osphranter,* of the grassy plains of Australia.

Wallasey (wŏl′ə sĭ), *n.* a town in England, in Cheshire. 103,213 (1961).

wall bars, a gymnasium apparatus consisting of rows of vertical wooden bars attached to a wall and used for various exercises.

wallboard (wôl′bôd′), *n.* an artificial sheet material for use in making or covering walls, ceilings, etc., as a substitute for wooden boards or plaster.

wall creeper, a small grey and crimson Old World bird, *Tichodroma muraria,* which makes its home among precipitous rocks.

walled plain, *Astron.* one of a number of large ring mountains or craters on the surface of the moon, whose diameters vary between about 30 and 200 miles.

Wallenstein (wŏl′ən stīn′; *Ger.* văl′ən shtīn), *n.* **Albrecht Wenzel Eusebius von** (*Ger.* ăl′brĕKHt vĕn′tsəl ôY zĕ′bĭ ōōs fŏn) (*Duke of Friedland*), 1583–1634, Austrian general born in Bohemia. Also, **Waldstein.**

Waller (wŏl′ə), *n.* **1.** **Edmund,** 1607–87, English poet. **2.** **Thomas** ('*Fats*'), 1904–43, U.S. jazz musician.

wallet (wŏl′ĭt), *n.* **1.** a small, booklike folding case for carrying papers, paper money, etc., in the pocket. **2.** a bag for holding food, clothing, toilet articles, or the like, as for use on a journey. [ME *walet*; orig. uncert.]

walleye (wôl′ī′), *n.* **1.** any of various North American fishes with large staring eyes, esp. the **walleyed pike,** a pike-perch, *Stizostedion vitreum.* **2.** an eye such as is seen in a walleyed person or animal.

walleyed (wôl′īd′), *adj.* **1.** having eyes in which there is an abnormal amount of the white showing, because of divergent strabismus. **2.** having an eye or the eyes presenting little or no colour, as the result of a light-coloured or white iris or of white opacity of the cornea. **3.** having large, staring eyes, as some fishes. [ME *wawileghed,* t. Scand.; cf. Icel. *vagl-eygr,* f. *vagl* film over eye + *-eygr* -eyed]

wallflower (wôl′flou′ə), *n.* **1.** a European perennial, *Cheiranthus cheiri,* growing wild on old walls, cliffs, etc., and also cultivated in gardens, with sweet-scented flowers, commonly yellow or orange but in cultivation varying from pale yellow to brown, red, or purple. **2.** any plant of the brassicaceous genera *Cheiranthus* and *Erysimum*. **3.** *Colloq.* a person, esp. a woman, who looks on at a dance, esp. from failure to obtain a partner.

wall game, a kind of football, played against a wall, as at Eton College.

Wallington (wŏl′ĭng tən), *n.* a district in the SW outer London borough of Sutton.

Wallis (*Ger.* vȧ′lĭs), *n.* German name of **Valais.**

wall lettuce, a perennial composite herb of walls and dry rocks, *Mycelis muralis*, widespread in Europe and W Asia.

Walloon (wŏ lo͞on′), *n.* **1.** one of a people inhabiting chiefly the southern and south-eastern parts of Belgium and adjacent regions in France. **2.** the French dialect of Belgium, esp. of the south-east. —*adj.* **3.** of or pertaining to the Walloons or their language. [t. F: m. Wallon, g. ML *Wallo*, t. Gmc.; cf. OHG *walh* foreigner]

wallop (wŏl′əp), *v.t. Colloq.* **1.** to beat soundly; thrash. **2.** to strike with a vigorous blow. **3.** to defeat thoroughly, as in a game. —*v.i.* **4.** *Dial.* to move heavily and clumsily about. —*n.* **5.** *Colloq.* a vigorous blow. **6.** *Colloq.* (in boxing, etc.) an ability to deliver such blows. **7.** *Colloq.* a forceful impression or impact. **8.** *Slang.* beer. **9.** *Dial.* a heavy, clumsy movement; a lurch. [ME *walop*, t. OF, akin to F *galoper* gallop]

walloper (wŏl′ə pə), *n.* **1.** *Colloq.* one who or that which wallops. **2.** *Dial.* something strikingly large or huge.

walloping (wŏl′ə pĭng), *Colloq.* —*n.* **1.** a sound beating or thrashing. **2.** a thorough defeat. —*adj.* **3.** of large size; whopping.

wallow (wŏl′ō), *v.i.* **1.** to roll the body about, or lie, in water, snow, mud, dust, or the like, as for refreshment: *pigs wallowing in the mud.* **2.** to live self-indulgently or luxuriously: *to wallow in wealth; to wallow in sensuality.* **3.** to flounder about clumsily or with difficulty: *the gunboat wallowing in the water.* **4.** to surge up, as smoke, heat, etc. —*n.* **5.** the act of wallowing. **6.** a place to which animals, as buffaloes, resort to wallow. **7.** the indentation produced by their wallowing. [ME *walwe*, OE *wealwian* roll, akin to Goth. *walwjan*, L *volvere* roll] —**wal′lower,** *n.* —**Syn.** **1.** welter, flounder.

wallpaper (wôl′pā′pə), *n.* **1.** paper, commonly with printed decorative patterns in colour, for pasting on and covering the walls or ceilings of rooms, etc. —*v.t.* **2.** to put wallpaper on; furnish with wallpaper.

wall pellitory, a small, bushy, Old World urticaceous plant, *Parietaria officinalis*, growing on walls, and said to be a diuretic and refrigerant.

wall pepper, a small, perennial, crassulaceous herb, *Sedum acre*, having fleshy leaves with a hot peppery taste, occurring in dry places in Europe and W Asia.

wall plate, **1.** *Bldg Trades.* a plate or timber placed horizontally in or on a wall, under the ends of girders, joists, or other timbers, in order to distribute pressure. **2.** *Mach.* a vertical metal plate secured against a wall or the like, as to attach a bracket.

wall rock, *Mining.* the rock forming the walls of a vein.

wall rocket, a European cruciferous plant, *Diplotaxis tenuifolia*, growing along old walls, etc.

wall rue, a small delicate fern, *Asplenium rutamuraria*, growing on walls and cliffs.

Wallsend (wôlz′ĕnd′), *n.* a town in England, in Northumberland: on the site of the eastern end of Hadrian's Wall. 49,822 (1961).

Wall Street, **1.** a street in New York City, in S Manhattan: the chief financial centre of the U.S. **2.** the money market or the financiers of the U.S.

wall-to-wall (wôl′tə wôl′), *adj.* covering the entire floor space of a room, as a carpet.

wally (wā′lĭ), *adj., n., pl.* **-lies.** *Scot.* —*adj.* **1.** fine; handsome. **2.** ample; strong; big. —*n.* **3.** a toy; gewgaw. [? akin to WALE[2]]

wallydrag (wā′lĭ drăg′, wŏl′ĭ-), *n. Scot.* a feeble, ill-grown creature. Also, **wallydraigle** (wā′lĭ drā′gl, wŏl′ĭ-).

walnut (wôl′nŭt′, -nət), *n.* **1.** the edible nut of trees of the genus *Juglans*, of the North Temperate zone. **2.** a tree bearing this nut, as *J. regia* (**common walnut**), or *J. nigra* (**black walnut**), which yields both a valuable timber and a distinctively flavoured nut. **3.** the wood of such a tree. **4.** any of various fruits or trees resembling the walnut. **5.** a shade of brown, as that of the heartwood of the black walnut tree. [ME *walnotte*, OE *walhhnutu*, lit., foreign nut]

Walpole (wôl′pōl′), *n.* **1.** **Horace** (*4th Earl of Orford*), 1717–97, English author. **2.** **Sir Hugh Seymour,** 1884–1941, English novelist, born in New Zealand. **3.** **Sir Robert** (*1st Earl of Orford*), 1676–1745, British statesman: prime minister 1721–42.

Walpurgis Night (văl po͝oə′gĭs), the evening preceding May 1st, the feast day of **St Walpurgis** (an English missionary and abbess in Germany, who died about A.D. 780), on which, according to German popular superstition, witches ride to some appointed rendezvous, esp. the Brocken, the highest of the Harz Mountains. Also, *German*, **Walpurgisnacht** (*Ger.* vȧl po͝or′gĭs nȧKHt).

walrus (wôl′rəs, wŏl′-), *n., pl.* **-ruses,** (*esp. collectively*) **-rus.** either of two large marine mammals of the genus *Odobenus*, of arctic seas, related to the seals, and having flippers, a pair of large tusks, and a thick, tough skin. [t. D: lit., whalehorse. Cf. G *Walross*, Dan. *hvalros*; also OE *horshwæl* horse-whale]

Atlantic walrus, *Odobenus rosmarus* (Up to 11 ft long)

walrus moustache, a thick moustache hanging down loosely at both ends.

Walsall (wôl′sôl), *n.* a town in England, in Staffordshire. 118,498 (1961).

Walser (*Ger.* vȧl′zər), *n.* **Martin** (*Ger.* mȧr′tēn), born 1924, German novelist and dramatist.

Walsingham (wôl′sĭng əm), *n.* **Sir Francis,** 1530?–1590, English statesman: secretary of state 1573–90.

Walter (*Ger.* vȧl′tər), *n.* **Bruno** (*Ger.* bro͞o′nō) (*Bruno Schlesinger*), 1876–1962, German conductor in the U.S.

Waltham Forest (wôl′thəm), a NE outer London borough. 248,500 (est. 1965).

Walthamstow (wôl′thəm stō′), *n.* a district in the NE outer London borough of Waltham Forest.

Walther von der Vogelweide (*Ger.* vȧl′tər fōn dėr fō′gəl vī də), *c.* 1170–*c.* 1230, German poet.

Walton (wôl′tən), *n.* **1.** **Izaak** (ī′zək), 1593–1683, English writer and famous fisherman. **2.** **Sir William Turner,** born 1902, English composer.

waltz (wôls), *n.* **1.** a ballroom dance in moderately fast triple time, in which the dancers move in a series of circles, taking one step to each beat. **2.** a slower dance, also in triple time. **3.** a piece of music for, or in the rhythm of, this dance. —*adj.* **4.** of, pertaining to, or characteristic of the waltz, as music, rhythm, or dance. —*v.i.* **5.** to dance or move in the movement or step of a waltz. **6.** *Colloq.* to take away with great ease: *he waltzed off with the first prize.* **7.** *Slang.* to move nimbly or quickly. —*v.t.* **8.** to cause to waltz; accompany in a waltz. [t. G: m. *walzer*, der. *walzen* roll, dance a waltz] —**waltz′er,** *n.* —**waltz′like′,** *adj.*

Walvis Bay (wôl′vĭs), **1.** a bay on the coast of South-West Africa. **2.** a seaport on this bay. **3.** an exclave of the Republic of South Africa around this bay, administered by South-West Africa. 15,594 pop. (1961); 374 sq. mi. Also, **Walfish Bay** (wôl′fĭsh′).

wamble (wŏm′əl), *v.,* **wambled, wambling,** *n. Chiefly Dial.* —*v.i.* **1.** to move with an uncertain motion. **2.** to twist; roll the body. —*n.* **3.** an unsteady or rolling movement or gait. [ME *wamle*. Cf. Norw. *vamla* stagger] —**wam′blingly,** *adv.* —**wam′bly,** *adj.*

wame (wām), *n. Scot. and N Dial.* belly. [var. of WOMB]

wampish (wăm′pĭsh), *v.i. Scot.* to toss about.

wampum (wŏm′pəm), *n.* **1.** cylindrical beads made from shells, pierced and strung, used by North American Indians as money and for ornament: properly denoting a white variety but applied also to a black or dark purple variety commonly considered more valuable than the white; peag. **2.** *U.S. Slang.* money. [short for *wompanpeag*, t. Algonquian (New England area): m. *wanpanpiak* string of shell beads, der. *wap* white + *anpi* string of shell beads + *-ak*, animate pl. suffix]

wampumpeag (wŏm′pəm pēg′), *n.* wampum (def. 1). [See WAMPUM]

wamus (wô′məs, wŏm′əs), *n. U.S.* **1.** a type of cardigan. **2.** Also, **wammus** (wŏm′əs), **wampus** (wŏm′pəs). a durable, coarse, outer jacket. [t. D: m. *wammes*, earlier *wambuis*, t. OF: m. *wambois* leather doublet, der. OHG *wamba* belly. See WOMB]

wan (wŏn), *adj.,* **wanner, wannest,** *v.,* **wanned, wanning.** —*adj.* **1.** of an unnatural or sickly pallor; pallid: *his wan face flushed.* **2.** pale in colour or hue: *cowslips wan.* **3.** showing or suggesting ill health, worn condition, unhappiness, etc.: *a wan look, a wan smile.* **4.** *Archaic.* dark or gloomy. —*v.i., v.t.* **5.** *Poetic.* to become or make wan. [ME; OE *wann* dark, gloomy] —**wan′ly,** *adv.* —**wan′ness,** *n.* —**Syn.** **1.** See **pale**[1].

Wanaka (wŏn′ə kə), *n.* **Lake,** a lake in New Zealand, in SW South Island. 74 sq. mi.

Wanchüan (wăn′cho͝o än′), *n.* a city in N China, in Hopei province. 480,000 (est. 1958).

wand (wŏnd), *n.* **1.** a slender stick or rod, esp. one used by a conjurer, or supposedly by a magician or fairy to work magic. **2.** a rod or staff borne as an ensign of office or authority. **3.** a slender shoot, stem, or branch of a shrub or tree: *lissom as a hazel wand.* **4.** *U.S. Archery.* a slat 6 feet by 2 inches placed at a distance of 100 yards for men and 60 yards for women, and used as a mark. [ME, t. Scand.; cf. Icel. *vöndr*, c. Goth. *wandus*] —**wand′like′**, *adj.*

wander (wŏn′də), *v.i.* **1.** to ramble without any certain course or object in view; roam, rove, or stray: *to wander over the earth.* **2.** to go aimlessly or casually: *wandering into the adjoining room.* **3.** to pass or extend in an irregular course or direction: *off to the south wandered the purple hills.* **4.** to move, pass, or turn idly, as the hand, the pen, the eyes, etc. **5.** (of the mind, thoughts, desires, etc.) to take one direction or another without intention or control. **6.** to stray from a path, place, companions, etc. **7.** to deviate in conduct, belief, etc.; err; go astray: *let me not wander from thy commandments.* **8.** to think or speak confusedly or incoherently. —*v.t.* **9.** *Poetic.* to wander over or through. [ME *wandre(n)*, OE *wandrian*, c. MD *wanderen*, G *wandern*] —**wan′derer,** *n.* —**wan′deringly,** *adv.* —**Syn. 1.** range, stroll, meander, saunter.

wandering albatross, a large albatross, *Diomedea exulans*, of southern waters, having the plumage mostly white with dark markings on the upper parts.

Wandering Jew, 1. a legendary character condemned to roam without rest because he struck or mocked Christ on the day of Crucifixion. **2.** Also, **wandering Jew, Wandering jew.** any of various trailing or creeping plants, as *Zebrina pendula* or *Tradescantia fluminensis.*

Wanderjahr (*Ger.* vän′dər yär), *n., pl.* **-jahre** (*Ger.* -yä rə). *German.* **1.** a year or period of wandering or travelling away from one's work. **2.** (formerly) a year in which an apprentice travelled and improved his skills and knowledge before settling down to work.

wanderlust (wŏn′də lŭst′; *Ger.* vän′dər lo͝ost), *n.* an instinctive impulse to rove or travel about. [t. G]

wanderoo (wŏn′də ro͞o′), *n.* **1.** any of several langurs, of Ceylon. **2.** a macaque, *Macacus silenus*, of southern India. [t. Sinhalese: m. *wanderu* monkey]

wandle (wŏn′dl), *adj. Scot.* supple.

wandoo (wŏn′do͞o), *n.* the white gum of Western Australia, *Eucalyptus redunca.* [t. native Australian]

Wandsworth (wŏnz′wəth), *n.* a SW inner London borough. 335,000 (est. 1965).

wane (wān), *v.*, **waned, waning,** *n.* —*v.i.* **1.** (of the moon) to decrease periodically in the extent of its illuminated portion after the full moon (opposed to *wax*). **2.** to decline in power, importance, prosperity, etc. **3.** to decrease in strength, intensity, etc.: *daylight waned, and night came on.* **4.** to draw to a close. —*n.* **5.** gradual decline in strength, intensity, power, etc. **6.** the drawing to a close of life, a time, etc.: *the wane of life.* **7.** the waning of the moon. **8.** a period of waning. **9.** a bevelled edge of a plank or board as sawn from an unsquared log, due to the curvature of the log. **10. on the wane,** decreasing; diminishing. [ME; OE *wanian* lessen, c. MD and MHG *wanen*]

Wanganui (wŏng′ə no͞o′ĭ), *n.* **1.** a town in New Zealand, in W North Island. 36,000 (est. 1965). **2.** a river in New Zealand, in SW North Island, flowing S to the Tasman Sea. 180 mi.

wangle (wăng′gl), *v.*, **-gled, -gling,** *n. Colloq.* —*v.t.* **1.** to bring about, accomplish, or obtain by contrivance, scheming, or often, indirect or insidious methods. **2.** to fake; falsify; manipulate. —*v.i.* **3.** to use contrivance, scheming, or indirect methods to accomplish some end. **4.** to manipulate or continue something for dishonest purposes. —*n.* **5.** an act or instance of wangling. [b. WAG and DANGLE] —**wan′gler,** *n.*

Wanhsien (wăn′shyĕn′), *n.* a town in central China, on the Yangtze. 110,000 (est. 1950).

waning moon. See **moon** (def. 2f).

wanion (wŏn′yən), *n. Archaic.* curse; vengeance (used esp. in *with a wanion*). [ME *waniand*, ppr. of *wanien* WANE]

wank (wăngk), *Taboo Slang.* —*v.i.* **1.** to masturbate. —*n.* **2.** an act or instance of masturbation. —**wank′er,** *n.*

Wankel engine (*Ger.* văng′kəl), an internal-combustion engine with one or more combustion chambers, each shaped like an ellipse with its longer sides slightly indented and within each of which a triangular-shaped piston rotates eccentrically and in so doing encloses varying volumes between its sides and the chamber walls which provide the same cycle as a reciprocating engine. [named after Dr Felix *Wankel*, born 1902, German engineer]

Wanne-Eickel (*Ger.* vä′nə ī′kəl), *n.* a town in West Germany, in W North Rhine-Westphalia. 108,669 (est. 1964).

wannish (wŏn′ĭsh), *adj.* somewhat wan.

Wanstead (wŏn′stĭd), *n.* a district in the NE outer London borough of Redbridge.

want (wŏnt), *v.t.* **1.** to feel a need or a desire for; wish for: *to want one's dinner; always wanting something new.* **2.** to wish or desire (often fol. by infinitive): *I want to see you, he wants to be notified.* **3.** to be without or be deficient in: *to want judgement or knowledge.* **4.** to fall short by (a specified amount): *the sum collected wants but a few pounds of the desired amount.* **5.** to require or need: *the car wants cleaning.* —*v.i.* **6.** to wish; like; feel inclined to (often fol. by *to*): *they can go out if they want.* **7.** to be deficient by the absence of some part or thing, or fall short (sometimes fol. by *for*): *he did not want for abilities.* **8.** to have need (usually fol. by *for*): *if you want for anything, let him know.* **9.** to be in a state of destitution or poverty. **10.** to be lacking or absent, as a part or thing necessary to completeness. —*n.* **11.** something wanted or needed; a necessity. **12.** a need or requirement: *the wants of mankind.* **13.** absence or deficiency of something desirable or requisite; lack: *plants dying for want of rain.* **14.** the state of being without something desired or needed; need: *to be in want of an assistant.* **15.** the state of being without the necessities of life; destitution; poverty. **16.** a sense of lack or need of something: *to feel a vague want.* [ME *wante*, t. Scand.; cf. Icel. *vanta* lack] —**want′er,** *n.* —**want′less,** *adj.* —**Syn. 1.** See **wish. 3.** lack, need. **11.** desideratum. **13.** dearth, scarcity, scarceness, inadequacy, insufficiency, scantiness, paucity. **15.** privation. See **poverty.**

want ad, *Chiefly U.S.* small ad.

wantage (wŏn′tĭj), *n. U.S.* that which is wanting or lacking; an amount lacking.

wanted (wŏn′tĭd), *adj.* (of a suspected criminal, etc.) sought by the police.

wanting (wŏn′tĭng), *adj.* **1.** lacking or absent: *an apparatus with some of the parts wanting.* **2.** deficient in some part, thing, or respect: *to be wanting in courtesy.* —*prep.* **3.** lacking; without. **4.** less; minus: *a century, wanting three years.*

wanton (wŏn′tən), *adj.* **1.** done, shown, used, etc., maliciously or unjustifiably: *a wanton attack, injury, or affront; wanton cruelty.* **2.** deliberate and uncalled for: *Why ruin your career in this wanton way?* **3.** reckless or disregardful of right, justice, humanity, etc., as persons: *a wanton disturber of men's religious convictions.* **4.** lawless or unbridled with respect to sexual behaviour; loose, lascivious, or lewd. **5.** extravagantly luxurious or self-indulgent, as a person, way of life, etc. **6.** *Now Poetic.* sportive or frolicsome, as children, young animals, etc. **7.** *Chiefly Poetic.* having free play: *wanton breezes, a wanton brook.* **8.** *Poetic.* luxuriant, as vegetation. —*n.* **9.** a wanton or lascivious person, esp. a woman. —*v.i.* **10.** to act, grow, etc., in a wanton manner. —*v.t.* **11.** to squander (away), as in pleasure. [ME *wantowen*, lit., undisciplined, f. *wan-* not + OE *togen* disciplined] —**wan′tonly,** *adv.* —**wan′tonness,** *n.* —**Syn. 1.** reckless, malicious. **3.** unruly, wild. **4.** dissolute, licentious, immoral.

wap (wŏp), *v.t., v.i.*, **wapped, wapping,** *n. U.S. and Dial.* whop.

wapentake (wŏp′ən tāk′, wăp′-), *n.* (formerly in N England and the Midlands) a subdivision of a shire or county corresponding to a hundred. [ME; OE *wǣpen(ge)tæc*, t. Scand.; cf. Icel. *vāpnatak*, lit. taking of weapons, i.e. show of weapons at public voting]

wapiti (wŏp′ĭ tĭ), *n., pl.* **-tis,** (*esp. collectively*) **-ti.** a North American species of deer, *Cervus canadensis*, with long, slender antlers: usually called *elk.* [t. Shawnee (Algonquian): white rump]

wappenshaw (wăp′ən shô′, wŏp′ən-), *n.* a muster or review of persons under arms, formerly held at certain times in certain districts of Scotland, to satisfy the military chiefs that their men were properly armed. [short for *wappenshawing* (Scot.) weapon-showing]

wapperjaw (wŏp′ə jô′), *n. U.S. Colloq.* a projecting underjaw. —**wap′per-jawed′,** *adj.*

war[1] (wô), *n., v.*, **warred, warring,** *adj.* —*n.* **1.** a conflict carried on by force of arms, as between nations or states, or between parties within a state; warfare (by land, by sea, or in the air). **2.** a contest carried on by force of arms, as in a series of battles or campaigns. **3.** active hostility or contention; conflict; contest: *a war of words.* **4.** armed fighting, as a department of activity, a profession, or an art: *war is our business.* **5.** *Obs., Poetic.* a battle; engagement. **6. at war,** in a state of hostility or active military operations. —*v.i.* **7.** to make or carry on war; fight. **8.** to carry on active hostility or contention: *to war with evil.* **9.** to be in a state of strong opposition: *warring principles.*

—*adj.* **10.** of, belonging to, used in, or due to war. [ME *werre*, t. OF, t. OHG: m. *werra* strife] —**war′less,** *adj.*

war[2] (wä), *adv., adj. Scot.* worse.

Warangal (vä′rəng gl), *n.* a city in India, in N Andhra Pradesh. 156,106 (1961).

waratah (wŏ′rə tä′), *n.* a red-flowering Australian plant of the genus *Telopea.* [t. native Australian]

Warbeck (wô′bĕk), *n.* **Perkin,** 1474–99, Walloon impostor, pretender to the English throne.

War between the States, the American Civil War: used esp. in the former Confederate states.

warble[1] (wô′bl), *v.,* **-bled, -bling,** *n.* —*v.i.* **1.** to sing with trills, quavers, or melodic embellishments. **2.** *U.S.* to yodel. —*v.t.* **3.** to sing with trills, quavers, or melodious turns; carol. **4.** to express or celebrate in song. —*n.* **5.** a warbled song. **6.** the act of warbling. [ME *werblen*, t. OF: m. *werbler* quaver, t. Gmc; cf. OHG *werbel* something that revolves]

warble[2] (wô′bl), *n.* **1.** a small, hard tumour on a horse's back, produced by the galling of the saddle. **2.** a lump in the skin of an animal's back, containing the larva of a warble fly. [orig. uncert. Cf. obs. Sw. *varbulde* boil] —**war′bled,** *adj.*

warble fly, any of various flies of the family *Hypodermatidae*, whose larvae produce warbles.

warbler (wô′blə), *n.* **1.** one who or that which warbles. **2.** any of the small, chiefly Old World songbirds constituting the family *Sylviidae*, including the reedwarbler, blackcap, etc. **3.** Also, **wood warbler.** any of numerous small, insectivorous, New World birds of the family *Parulidae*, many of which are brightly coloured. **4.** *Elect.* any device, as a rotating capacitor, for rapidly varying the carrier frequency in a radiotelephone system to ensure secrecy.

Warburton (wô′bə tən), *n.* a river in Australia flowing SW through NE South Australia into Lake Eyre. 275 mi.

war cloud, something that threatens war.

war correspondent, a journalist employed by a newspaper, etc., to send home first-hand reports from a battle area.

war crime, a crime, such as genocide, maltreatment of prisoners, etc., committed during wartime.

war cry, 1. a cry or a word or phrase, shouted in charging or in rallying to attack; a battle cry. **2.** a party cry or slogan in any contest.

ward (wôd), *n.* **1.** a division or district of a city or town, as for administrative or representative purposes. **2.** one of the districts into which certain English and Scottish counties are divided. **3.** a division of a hospital or the like, as for a particular class of patients: *a convalescent ward.* **4.** each of the separate divisions of a prison. **5.** *Fort.* an open space within walls, or between lines of walls, of a castle or fortified place: *the castle's lower ward.* **6.** *Law.* **a.** a person, esp. a minor, who has been legally placed under the care of a guardian or a court. **b.** the state of being under the care or control of a legal guardian. **c.** guardianship over a minor or some other person legally incapable of managing his own affairs. **7.** the state of being under restraining guard or in custody. **8.** one who is under the protection or control of another. **9.** a movement or posture of defence, as in fencing. **10.** a curved ridge of metal inside a lock, forming an obstacle to the passage of a key which does not have a corresponding notch. **11.** the notch or slot in the bit of a key, into which such a ridge fits. **12.** the act of keeping guard or protective watch: *watch and ward.* —*v.t.* **13.** to avert, repel, or turn aside, as danger, an attack, assailant, etc. (usually fol. by *off*): *to ward off a blow.* **14.** to place in a ward, as of a hospital. **15.** *Archaic.* to guard. [ME; OE *weardian*, c. MD *waerden*, G *warten.* See GUARD, v.] —**ward′less,** *adj.*

Ward (wôd), *n.* **1. Artemus** (*Charles Farrar Browne*), 1834–67, U.S. humorist. **2. Mrs Humphry** (*Mary Augusta Arnold*), 1851–1920, English novelist, born in Tasmania.

-ward, an adjectival and adverbial suffix indicating direction, as in *onward, seaward, backward.* [ME; OE *-weard* towards]

war dance, (among primitive people) a dance preliminary to a warlike excursion or in celebration of a victory.

warded (wô′dĭd), *adj.* having notches, slots, or wards, as in locks and keys.

warden[1] (wô′dn), *n.* **1.** one charged with the care or custody of something; a keeper. **2.** any of various public officials charged with superintendence, as over a port, etc. **3.** *Chiefly U.S.* the chief administrative officer in charge of a prison. **4.** (formerly) the principal official in a region, town, etc. **5.** the head of certain colleges, schools, hospitals, youth hostels, etc. **6.** a member of the governing body of a guild. **7.** *U.S.* (in Connecticut) the chief executive officer of a borough. **8.** a churchwarden. **9.** an air-raid warden. **10.** a traffic warden. **11.** *Now Rare.* a gatekeeper. [ME *wardein*, t. OF. See GUARDIAN] —**ward′enship′,** *n.* —**Syn. 1.** warder, guardian, guard, custodian.

warden[2] (wô′dn), *n.* one of a group of cooking pears distinguished for crisp, firm flesh. [orig. uncert.]

wardenry (wô′dn rĭ), *n., pl.* **-ries.** the office, jurisdiction, or district of a warden.

warder[1] (wô′də), *n.* **1.** an official having charge of prisoners in a jail; prison officer. **2.** one who wards or guards something. [ME, der. WARD, v.] —**ward′ership′,** *n.*

warder[2] (wô′də), *n.* a truncheon or staff of office or authority, used in giving signals. [late ME; orig. uncert.]

ward-heeler (wôd′hē′lə), *n. U.S.* a minor official who canvasses voters and performs other minor duties for a political party.

wardress (wôd′rĭs), *n.* a female warder.

wardrobe (wôd′rōb′), *n.* **1.** a stock of clothes or costumes, as of a person or of a theatrical company. **2.** a piece of furniture for holding clothes, now usually a tall, upright, movable cupboard fitted with hooks, shelves, etc. **3.** a room or place for keeping clothes or costumes in. **4.** the department of a royal or other great household charged with the care of wearing apparel. [ME *warderobe*, t. OF. See WARD, ROBE]

wardroom (wôd′ro͝om′, -ro͞om′), *n.* (in a warship) **1.** the mess room for all officers not lower in rank than lieutenant and not including the commanding officer or flag officers. **2.** these officers collectively.

-wards, an adverbial suffix indicating direction, as in *onwards, seawards, backwards.* Also, *Now Chiefly U.S.*, **-ward.** [ME *-wardes*; OE *-weardes*, adv. genitive of *-weard* -WARD; cf. D *-waarts*, OHG *-wartes*]

wardship (wôd′shĭp), *n.* **1.** guardianship; custody. **2.** *Law.* the guardianship over a minor or ward.

ware[1] (wēə), *n.* **1.** (*usually pl.*) articles of merchandise or manufacture, or goods: *a pedlar selling his wares.* **2.** a particular kind or class of articles of merchandise or manufacture (now chiefly in composition): *tinware, silverware.* **3.** pottery, or a particular kind of pottery: *Delft ware.* [ME; OE *waru*, c. G *Ware*]

ware[2] (wēə), *adj., v.,* **wared, waring.** *Archaic.* —*adj.* **1.** watchful, wary, or cautious. **2.** aware or conscious. —*v.t.* **3.** to beware of (usually used in the imperative). [ME; OE *wær*, c. Icel. *varr*, Goth. *wars*]

ware[3] (wēə), *v.t.,* **wared, waring.** *Scot. and N Dial.* to spend (money, time, care, etc.). [ME, t. Scand.; cf. Icel. *verja* spend, invest (also wrap), c. OE *werian* WEAR[1]]

warehouse (*n.* wēə′hous′; *v.* wēə′houz′, -hous′), *n., v.,* **-housed, -housing.** —*n.* **1.** a storehouse for wares or goods. **2.** the building in which a wholesale dealer keeps his stock of merchandise. —*v.t.* **3.** to deposit or store in a warehouse. **4.** to place in a government or bonded warehouse, to be kept until duties are paid.

warehouseman (wēə′hous′mən), *n., pl.* **-men. 1.** one who is employed in or has charge of a warehouse. **2.** a wholesale merchant who has a warehouse for the storing of merchandise.

Warerite (wēə′rīt), *n. Trademark.* a decorative laminated plastic sheeting, used for facing walls, furniture, etc.

warfare (wô′fēə′), *n.* **1.** the act of waging war. **2.** armed conflict. **3.** military operations.

war game, *Mil.* See TEWT.

warhead (wô′hĕd′), *n.* the forward section of a self-propelled missile, bomb, torpedo, etc., containing explosives.

warhorse (wô′hôs′), *n.* **1.** a horse used in war; a charger. **2.** a veteran soldier or politician, esp. an aggressive one.

warily (wēə′rĭ lĭ), *adv.* in a wary manner.

wariness (wēə′rĭ nĭs), *n.* the state or quality of being wary.

warison (wă′rĭ sən), *n.* (erroneously) a note sounded as a signal for assault. [ME, t. OF: protection. Cf. GARRISON]

wark (wäk), *n., v.i. Dial.* pain; ache. [var. of WORK]

Warks., Warwickshire.

warlike (wô′līk′), *adj.* **1.** fit, qualified, or ready for war; martial: *warlike fleet, warlike tribes.* **2.** threatening or betokening war: *a warlike tone.* **3.** of or pertaining to war: *a warlike expedition, warlike deeds.* —**war′like′ness,** *n.* —**Syn. 2.** bellicose, belligerent, hostile.

warlock (wô′lŏk′), *n.* **1.** one who practises magic arts by the aid of the devil; a sorcerer or wizard. **2.** a fortune-teller, conjurer, or the like. [ME *warloghe*, OE *wǣrloga* oath-breaker, devil]

war lord, 1. a military commander or commander-in-chief, esp. of a warlike country. **2.** a military leader, esp. one who has seized power in part of a country: *the Chinese war lords.*

warm (wôm), *adj.* **1.** having or communicating a moderate degree of heat, as perceptible to the senses. **2.** of or at a moderately high temperature; characterized by comparatively high temperature: *a warm climate.* **3.** having a sensation of bodily heat: *to be warm from fast walking.*

4. keeping or maintaining warmth: *warm clothes.* 5. (of colour, effects of colour, etc.) suggestive of warmth; inclining towards red or orange, as yellow (rather than towards green or blue). 6. characterized by or showing lively feelings, passions, emotions, sympathies, etc.: *a warm heart, warm interest.* 7. strongly attached, or intimate: *warm friends.* 8. cordial or hearty: *a warm welcome.* 9. heated, irritated, or angry: *to become warm when contradicted.* 10. animated, lively, brisk, or vigorous: *a warm debate.* 11. strong or fresh: *a warm scent.* 12. *Colloq.* relatively close to something sought, as in a game. 13. *Colloq.* uncomfortable or unpleasant.
—*v.t.* 14. to make warm; heat (often fol. by *up*): *to warm one's feet; warm up a room.* 15. to heat, as cooked food for reuse. 16. to excite ardour, enthusiasm, or animation in. 17. to inspire with kindly feeling; affect with lively pleasure. —*v.i.* 18. to become warm (often fol. by *up*). 19. to become ardent, enthusiastic, animated, etc. (often fol. by *up* or *to*). 20. to grow kindly, friendly, or sympathetically disposed (often fol. by *to* or *towards*): *my heart warms towards him.* 21. **warm up,** to prepare for a game, sporting event, etc., by exercising beforehand.
—*n.* 22. *Colloq.* a warming or heating: *sit at the fire and have a warm.*
[ME; OE *wearm*, c. D, G *warm*] —**warm′er,** *n.* —**warm′ish,** *adj.* —**warm′ly,** *adv.* —**warm′ness,** *n.* —**Syn.** 1. lukewarm, tepid, heated. 6. hearty, enthusiastic, zealous, fervent, fervid.

warm-blooded (wôm′blŭd′ĭd), *adj.* 1. denoting or pertaining to animals, as mammals and birds, whose blood ranges in temperature from about 98° to 112°F, and remains relatively constant, irrespective of the temperature of the surrounding medium. 2. ardent, impetuous, or passionate: *young and warm-blooded valour.*

warm front, *Meteorol.* 1. the contact surface between two air masses where the warmer mass is advancing against and over the cooler mass. 2. the line of intersection of this surface with the surface of the earth.

warm-hearted (wôm′hä′tĭd), *adj.* having or showing sympathy, cordiality, etc. —**warm′-heart′edly,** *adv.* —**warm′-heart′edness,** *n.*

warming pan, a long-handled, covered, flat vessel, as of brass, for holding hot coals or the like, formerly in common use for warming beds before they were to be occupied.

warmonger (wô′mŭng′gə), *n.* one who advocates war or seeks to bring it about.

warmongering (wô′mŭng′gə rĭng), *n.* the principles and practices of a warmonger.

warm sector, *Meteorol.* a body of warm air found in a recently formed active depression, bounded by the cold and warm fronts.

warmth (wômth), *n.* 1. the state of being warm; moderate or gentle heat. 2. the sensation of moderate heat. 3. liveliness of feelings, emotions, or sympathies; ardour or fervour; cordiality; enthusiasm or zeal. 4. slight irritation: *his denial betrayed some warmth.*

warm-up (wôm′ŭp′), *n.* the act or instance of warming up.

warn (wôn), *v.t.* 1. to give notice or intimation to (a person, etc.) of danger, impending evil, possible harm, or anything unfavourable: *to warn a person of a plot against him; warned that he was in danger.* 2. to urge or advise to be on one's guard; caution: *to warn a foolhardy person.* 3. to admonish or exhort as to action or conduct: *to warn a person to be on time.* 4. to notify, apprise, or inform: *to warn a person of an intended visit.* 5. to give notice to (a person, etc.) to go, stay, or keep (away, off, etc.): *to warn trespassers off private grounds.* 6. to give authoritative or formal notice to, order, or summon. —*v.i.* 7. to give a warning: *to warn of impending disaster.* [ME; OE *warnian*, c. G *warnen*. Cf. WARE[2]] —**warn′er,** *n.*
—**Syn.** 1. WARN, CAUTION, ADMONISH imply attempting to prevent another from running into danger or getting into unpleasant or undesirable circumstances. To WARN is to speak plainly and usually in strong terms: *to warn him about danger and possible penalties.* To CAUTION is to advise about necessary precautions, legal rights, etc., to put one on his guard about or against some circumstance or condition: *caution him against trying to go, the police caution a suspect,* thus emphasizing avoidance of penalties. ADMONISH suggests giving earnest, authoritative advice, exhortation, with only tacit references to danger or penalty: *to admonish one for neglecting duties.*

warning (wô′nĭng), *n.* 1. the act of warning, giving notice, or cautioning. 2. something serving to warn, give notice, or caution. —*adj.* 3. that warns. —**warn′ingly,** *adv.* —**Syn.** 2. caution, admonition, advice.

war nose, a device in the front end of a projectile, as a torpedo, for detonating the explosive charge.

War of American Independence, the war between Great Britain and its American colonies, 1775–83, by which the colonies won their independence. Also, *U.S.*, **American Revolution.**

War of 1812, a war (1812–15) between Great Britain and the United States.

war of nerves, a conflict in which the aim is to intimidate or demoralize the enemy by using psychological methods such as threats, propaganda, etc.

War of the Austrian Succession, a war (1740–48) in which Austria, England, and Holland opposed Prussia, France, and Spain over the right of succession of Maria Theresa of Austria.

War of the Spanish Succession, a war (1701–14) fought by Austria, England, the Netherlands, and Prussia, against France and Spain, arising out of disputes about the succession to the throne in Spain after the death of Charles II of Spain.

warp (wôp), *v.t.* 1. to bend or twist out of shape, esp. from a straight or flat form, as timbers, flooring, etc. 2. to bend or turn from the natural or true direction or course. 3. to distort from the truth, fact, true meaning, etc.; bias or pervert: *prejudice warps the mind; warped in his political principles.* 4. *Aeron.* to bend (a wing, plane or aerofoil) at the end or ends, to promote equilibrium or to secure lateral control. 5. *Naut.* to move (a ship, etc.) into some desired place or position by hauling on a rope or warp which has been fastened to something fixed, as a buoy, anchor, or the like. 6. *Agric.* to treat (land) by inundation with water that deposits alluvial matter. —*v.i.* 7. to become bent or twisted out of shape, esp. out of a straight or flat form: *the wood has warped in drying.* 8. to turn or change from the natural or proper course, state, etc. 9. *Geol.* (of the earth's crust) to undergo a slow bending process. 10. *Naut.* a. to warp a ship or the like along. b. to move by being warped, as a ship. [ME *werpe*, OE *weorpan* throw, c. D *werpen*, G *werfen*]
—*n.* 11. a bend or twist in something, as in wood that has dried unevenly. 12. a mental twist or bias. 13. yarns placed lengthwise in the loom, across the weft or woof, and interlaced. See diag. under **weave.** 14. *Naut.* a rope for warping or hauling a ship or the like along or into a position. 15. alluvial matter deposited by water, esp. water let in to inundate low land so as to enrich it. [ME *warpe*, OE *wearp*, c. G *Warf*] —**warp′er,** *n.* —**Syn.** 1. turn, contort, distort.

war paint, 1. paint applied to the face and body by savages upon going to war. 2. *Colloq.* make-up; cosmetics. 3. *Colloq.* full dress; finery.

warpath (wô′päth′), *n.* 1. the path or course taken by American Indians on a warlike expedition. 2. **on the warpath, a.** engaging in, seeking, or preparing for war. **b.** in state of wrath; angry; indignant.

warped (wôpt), *adj.* twisted; distorted; perverted.

warp knitted, (of textiles) knitted on a warp loom to a close pattern and often in a locknit.

warpland (wôp′lănd′), *n.* *Geol.* an area of land subject to the deposition of alluvial sediment in flooding.

warplane (wô′plān′), *n.* *U.S.* an aeroplane for warfare.

warrant (wŏ′rənt), *n.* 1. authorization, sanction, or justification. 2. that which serves to give reliable or formal assurance of something; a guarantee. 3. something having the force of a guarantee or positive assurance of a thing. 4. a writing or document certifying or authorizing something, as a certificate, receipt, licence, or commission. 5. *Law.* an instrument, issued by a magistrate, authorizing an officer to make an arrest, seize property, make a search, or carry a judgement into execution. 6. (in the army and navy) the certificate of authority or appointment issued to an officer below the rank of a commissioned officer. 7. a warehouse receipt. 8. a written authorization for the payment or receipt of money: *a treasury warrant; dividend warrant.*
—*v.t.* 9. to give authority to; authorize. 10. to afford warrant or sanction for, or justify: *the circumstances warrant such measures.* 11. to give one's word for; vouch for (often used with a clause in mere emphatic assertion): *I'll warrant he did!* 12. to give a formal assurance, or a guarantee or promise, to or for; guarantee: *to warrant payment; to warrant safe delivery.* 13. to guarantee the quantity, quality, and other representations made to a purchaser of goods. 14. to guarantee or secure title to (the purchaser of goods); assure indemnification against loss to. 15. *Law.* to guarantee title of an estate or other granted property (to a grantee).
[ME *warant*, t. OF, var. of *guarant* defender, t. Gmc; cf. MHG *warend* warranty] —**war′rantable,** *adj.* —**war′rantably,** *adv.* —**war′rantless,** *adj.*
—**Syn.** 12. WARRANT, GUARANTEE are etymologically the same and frequently interchangeable to indicate pledging that something is safe or genuine. To WARRANT is to give such a pledge: *to warrant the soundness of a horse, warranted silverware.* To GUARANTEE is to make something sure or certain by binding oneself to replace it or refund its price if it is not as represented: *to guarantee a watch.*

warrantee (wŏ′rən tē′), *n. Law.* one to whom a warranty is made.
warranter (wŏ′rən tə), *n.* one who warrants.
warrant officer, a member of the armed forces holding, by warrant, an intermediate rank between that of commissioned and non-commissioned officers.
warrantor (wŏ′rən tô′), *n. Law.* one who warrants, or makes a warranty.
warranty (wŏ′rən tĭ), *n., pl.* **-ties. 1.** the act of warranting; warrant; assurance. **2.** *Law.* **a.** an engagement, express or implied, in assurance of some particular in connection with a contract, as of sale: *an express warranty of the quality of goods.* **b.** a covenant in a deed to land by which the party conveying assures the grantee that he will enjoy the premises free from interference by any person claiming under a superior title. A **warranty deed** is a deed containing such a covenant, as distinguished from a *quitclaim deed,* which conveys without any assurances only such title as the grantor may have. **c.** (in the law of insurance) a statement or promise, made by the party insured, and included as an essential part of the contract, falsity or nonfulfilment of which renders the policy void. **d.** a judicial document, as a warrant or writ. [ME *warantie,* t. OF. Cf. GUARANTEE, WARRANT]
Warrego (wŏ′rĭ gō′), *n.* a river in E Australia flowing S through Queensland, then New South Wales to the river Darling. ab. 495 mi.
warren (wŏ′rən), *n.* **1.** a place where rabbits breed or abound. **2.** a building, district, etc., containing many poor people living in overcrowded conditions. [ME, t. AF: m. *warenne* game park; akin to GUARD, WARD]
Warren (wŏ′rən), *n.* **1. Earl,** born 1891, chief justice of the U.S. Supreme Court 1953–69. **2. Robert Penn,** born 1905, U.S. novelist and poet.
warrener (wŏ′rə nə), *n.* the keeper of a warren (def. 1).
warrigal (wŏ′rĭ gl), *Austral.* **—***n.* **1.** the dingo. **—***adj.* **2.** wild; untamed. [t. native Australian]
Warrington (wŏ′rĭng tən), *n.* a town in England, in Lancashire. 75,964 (1961).
warrior (wŏ′rĭ ə), *n.* a man engaged or experienced in warfare; soldier. [ME *werreour,* t. ONF: m. *werreieor.* See WAR[1]] **—war′rior-like′,** *adj.*
Warsaw (wô′sô), *n.* the capital of Poland, in the E central part, on the river Vistula. 1,241,000 (est. 1964). Polish, **Warszawa** (*Pol.* vȧr shȧ′vȧ). See map under **Prussia.**
Warsaw Pact, a military alliance established in 1955 between Albania, Bulgaria, Czechoslovakia, East Germany, Hungary, Poland, Rumania, and the Soviet Union. Also, **Warsaw Treaty Organization.**
warship (wô′shĭp′), *n.* a ship built or armed for use in war.
warsle (wä′səl), *v.i., v.t.,* **-sled, -sling,** *n. Scot.* wrestle. Also, **warstle.**
Wars of the Roses, the civil struggle between the royal house of Lancaster, whose emblem was a red rose, and the royal house of York, whose emblem was a white rose, beginning in 1455 and ending in the accession of Henry VII and the union of the two houses in 1485.
wart (wôt), *n.* **1.** a small, usually hard, abnormal elevation on the skin, caused by a filterable virus. **2.** a small protuberance. [ME; OE *wearte,* c. G *Warze*] **—wart′-like′,** *adj.*
Warta (*Pol.* vȧr′tȧ), *n.* a river in Poland, flowing NW and W into the Oder. 445 mi. German, **Warthe** (*Ger.* vȧr′tə).
Wartburg (*Ger.* vȧrt′bo͝ork), *n.* a castle in East Germany, in Thuringia, near Eisenach: Luther translated the New Testament here 1521–22.
wartcress (wôt′krĕs′), *n.* swinecress.
wart-hog (wôt′hŏg′), *n.* an African wild swine, *Phacochoerus aethiopicus,* having large tusks, and warty excrescences on the face.

Wart-hog, *Phacochoerus aethiopicus,* (2½ ft high at the shoulder, total length ab. 5½ ft)

wartime (wô′tīm′), *n.* **1.** a time or season of war. **—***adj.* **2.** of, pertaining to, or occurring during war: *wartime conferences.*
warty (wô′tĭ), *adj.,* **wartier, wartiest. 1.** having warts; covered with or as with warts. **2.** like a wart.
war-weary (wô′wĭə′rĭ), *adj.* completely exhausted by war, esp. after a long conflict.
Warwick (wŏ′rĭk), *n.* **1. Richard Neville, Earl of** ('*the Kingmaker*'), 1428–71, English soldier and statesman. **2.** a town in England, the county town of Warwickshire. 16,051 (1961). **3.** Warwickshire.
Warwickshire (wŏ′rĭk shĭə′, -shə), *n.* a county in central England. 2,023,289 pop. (1961); 983 sq. mi. *Co. town:* Warwick. Also, **Warwick.** *Abbrev.:* Warks.
wary (wĕə′rĭ), *adj.,* **warier, wariest. 1.** watchful, or on one's guard, esp. habitually; on the alert; cautious; careful. **2.** characterized by caution. [f. WARE[2], adj. + -Y[1]] **—war′ily,** *adv.* **—war′iness,** *n.* **—Syn. 1.** alert, vigilant, circumspect. See **careful.**
was (wŏz; *unstressed* wəz), *v.* first and third pers. sing., pt. indicative of **be.** [ME; OE *wæs,* c. G *war*]
wash (wŏsh), *v.t.* **1.** to apply water or some other liquid to for the purpose of cleansing; cleanse by dipping, rubbing, or scrubbing in water, etc. **2.** to remove (dirt, stains, paint, or any matter) by or as by the action of water, or as water does (fol. by *out, off,* etc.). **3.** to free from spiritual defilement, or from sin, guilt, etc. **4.** to wet with water or other liquid, or as water does. **5.** to flow over or against: *a shore or cliff washed by waves.* **6.** to carry or bring with water or any liquid, or as the water or liquid does (often fol. by *up, down,* or *along*). **7.** to wear, as water does, by flowing over or against a surface (often fol. by *out* or *away*). **8.** to form (a channel, etc.), as flowing water does. **9.** *Mining, etc.* **a.** to subject (earth, etc.) to the action of water in order to separate valuable material. **b.** to separate (valuable material, as gold) thus. **10.** to purify (a gas or gaseous mixture) by passage through or over a liquid. **11.** to cover with a watery or thin coat of colour. **12.** to overlay with a thin coat or deposit of metal: *to wash brass with gold.* **13. wash down, a.** to clean completely by washing. **b.** to swallow (food) with the aid of liquid. **14. wash out, a.** to remove or get rid of by washing. **b.** to cancel or abandon (an arrangement, sporting event, etc.). **15. wash up,** to wash (dishes, saucepans, etc.) after a meal. **—***v.i.* **16.** to wash oneself: *time to wash for supper.* **17.** to wash clothes. **18.** to cleanse anything with or in water or the like. **19.** to undergo washing, esp. without injury. **20.** *Colloq.* to stand being put to the proof; bear investigation. **21.** to be carried or driven (along, ashore, etc.) by water. **22.** to flow or beat with a lapping sound, as waves on a shore. **23.** to move along in or as in waves, or with a rushing movement, as water. **24.** to be eroded, as by a stream, rainfall, etc.: *a hillside that washes frequently.* **25.** to be worn by the action of water, as a hill (often fol. by *away*). **26. wash out,** *Rowing.* to allow the blade to rise wholly or partly out of the water before a stroke is properly finished.
—*n.* **27.** the act of washing with water or other liquid. **28.** a quantity of clothes, etc., washed, or to be washed, at one time. **29.** a liquid with which something is washed, wetted, coloured, overspread, etc. **30.** the flow, sweep, dash, or breaking of water. **31.** the sound made by this: *listening to the wash of the Atlantic.* **32.** water moving along in waves or with a rushing movement. **33.** the rough or broken water left behind a moving ship, etc. **34.** *Aeron.* the disturbance in the air left behind by a moving aeroplane or any of its parts. **35.** any of various liquids for toilet purposes: *a hair wash.* **36.** a medicinal lotion. **37.** earth, etc., from which gold or the like can be extracted by washing. **38.** the wearing away of the shore by breaking waves. **39.** a tract of land washed by the action of the sea or a river. **40.** a fen, marsh, or a bog. **41.** a small stream or shallow pool. **42.** a shallow arm of the sea or a shallow part of a river. **43.** a depression or channel formed by flowing water. **44.** alluvial matter transferred and deposited by flowing water. **45.** *Western U.S.* the dry bed of an intermittent stream; dry wash. **46.** a broad, thin layer of colour applied by a continuous movement of the brush, as in watercolour painting. **47.** a thin coat of metal applied in liquid form. **48.** waste liquid matter, refuse food, etc., from the kitchen, as for pigs. **49.** washy or weak drink or liquid food. **50.** the fermented wort from which the spirit is extracted in distilling. **51. come out in the wash,** to be revealed eventually; become known.
[ME; OE *wascan,* c. D *wasschen,* G *waschen,* Icel. *vaska*] **—Syn. 1.** clean, lave, rinse, launder, scrub, mop, swab.
Wash (wŏsh), *n.* **The,** a shallow bay of the North Sea, on the E coast of England. ab. 22 mi. long; ab. 15 mi. wide.
Wash., Washington.
washable (wŏsh′ə bl), *adj.* capable of being washed, esp. without injury: *a washable fabric.*
washbasin (wŏsh′bā′sən), *n.* a large basin or bowl for washing face and hands, etc. Also, **washbowl** (wŏsh′bōl′).
washboard (wŏsh′bôd′), *n.* **1.** a board or frame with a corrugated metallic or other surface, on which clothes are scrubbed in the process of washing. **2.** such a board or frame used as a rhythm instrument in certain types of folk music. **3.** *U.S.* a skirting board. **4.** *Naut.* **a.** a thin broad plank fastened to and projecting above the gunwale or side of a boat to keep out the spray and sea. **b.** a similar board on the sill of a port.
washcloth (wŏsh′klŏth′), *n.* **1.** a small cloth for washing the face or body; face flannel. **2.** a cloth used for washing dishes, etc.
washday (wŏsh′dā′), *n.* the day set apart in a household for washing clothes. Also, **washing day.**

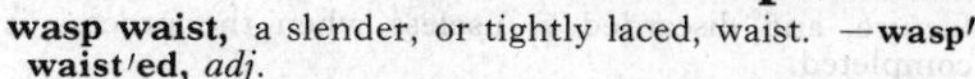

washed-out (wŏsht′out′), *adj.* **1.** faded, esp. during washing. **2.** *Colloq.* **a.** utterly fatigued; exhausted. **b.** tired-looking; pale; wan.

washed-up (wŏsht′ŭp′), *adj. Colloq.* having failed completely; finished; ruined.

washer (wŏsh′ə), *n.* **1.** one who or that which washes. **2.** a machine or apparatus for washing something. **3.** a flat ring or perforated piece of leather, rubber, metal, etc., used to give tightness to a joint, to prevent leakage, and to distribute pressure (as under the head of a bolt, under a nut, etc.).

washerman (wŏsh′ə mən), *n., pl.* **-men.** a man who washes clothes, etc., for hire.

washerwoman (wŏsh′ə wo͝om′ən), *n., pl.* **-women.** a woman who washes clothes, etc., for hire.

washhouse (wŏsh′hous′), *n.* a house or building, as an outhouse, where clothes are washed.

washing (wŏsh′ĭng), *n.* **1.** the act of one who or that which washes; ablution. **2.** clothes, etc., washed or to be washed, esp. those washed at one time. **3.** (*sing. or pl.*) liquid that has been used to wash something. **4.** matter removed in washing something. **5.** material, as gold dust, obtained by washing earth, etc. **6.** a placer or other superficial deposit so washed. **7.** a thin coating or covering applied in liquid form.

washing day, washday.

washing machine, an apparatus for washing clothing, etc.

washing powder, a powdered preparation, usually a detergent, used for washing clothes.

washing soda, crystalline sodium carbonate, or sal soda, used as a cleansing agent.

Washington (wŏsh′ĭng tən), *n.* **1. Booker T(aliaferro)** (bo͝ok′ə tŏl′ə və), 1856–1915, U.S. educational reformer and author. **2. George,** 1732–99, American general and 1st president of the U.S., 1789–97. **3.** the capital of the United States, on the Potomac between Maryland and Virginia: coextensive with the District of Columbia. 763,956 (1960). **4.** a state in the NW United States, on the Pacific coast. 2,853,214 pop. (1960); 68,192 sq. mi. *Cap.:* Olympia. *Abbrev.:* Wash. **5. Mount,** a peak of the White Mountains, in N New Hampshire: the highest peak in the NE United States. 6293 ft. **6. Lake,** a lake in W Washington, near Seattle. 20 mi. long. **7.** a town in England, in Durham. 18,808 (1961).

Washingtonian (wŏsh′ĭng tō′nyən), *adj.* **1.** of Washington (the city or the state). —*n.* **2.** a native or inhabitant of Washington (the city or the state).

Washington palm, either of the fan palms of the U.S., *Washingtonia filifera* and *W. gracilis* (*robusta*), native in southern California and adjoining regions.

Washita (wŏsh′ĭ tô′), *n.* Ouachita.

wash-leather (wŏsh′lĕth′ə), *n.* a soft leather, usually sheepskin, prepared in imitation of chamois leather, used for gloves, etc., and polishing surfaces as glass.

wash-out (wŏsh′out′), *n.* **1.** a washing out of earth, etc., by water, as from an embankment or a roadway by heavy rain or a freshet. **2.** the hole or break produced. **3.** *Colloq.* a failure or fiasco. **4.** *Med.* lavage of the bowels or bladder.

washrag (wŏsh′răg′), *n.* washcloth.

washroom (wŏsh′ro͞om′, -ro͝om′), *n.* a room having washbasins and other toilet facilities.

washstand (wŏsh′stănd′), *n.* **1.** a piece of furniture for holding a basin, a ewer, etc., for use in washing one's hands and face. **2.** a stationary fixture having taps with running water, for the same purpose.

washtub (wŏsh′tŭb′), *n.* a tub for use in washing something, esp. clothes, etc.

washwoman (wŏsh′wo͝om′ən), *n., pl.* **-women.** washerwoman.

washy (wŏsh′ĭ), *adj.*, **washier, washiest. 1.** overdiluted; weak: *washy coffee.* **2.** weak, thin, or poor, as if from excessive dilution: *washy colouring.* —**wash′iness,** *n.*

wasn't (wŏz′nt), contraction of *was not.*

wasp (wŏsp), *n.* **1.** any of numerous hymenopterous, stinging insects, included for the most part in two superfamilies, *Sphecoidea* and *Vespoidea.* Their habits vary from a solitary life to colonial organization. **2.** a waspish person. [ME *waspe,* OE *wæsp,* akin to D *wesp,* G *Wespe,* L *vespa*] —**wasp′like′,** **wasp′y,** *adj.*

Wasp, *Eumenes fraternus* (½ in. long)

WASP (wŏsp), *n.* (in the U.S.) a white Anglo-Saxon Protestant, esp. considered as a dominant or privileged group in American society.

waspish (wŏs′pĭsh), *adj.* **1.** like or suggesting a wasp. **2.** quick to resent a trifling affront or injury; snappish. **3.** showing irascibility or petulance: *waspish writing.* **4.** having a slender waist, like a wasp. —**wasp′ishly,** *adv.* —**wasp′ishness,** *n.*

wasp waist, a slender, or tightly laced, waist. —**wasp′-waist′ed,** *adj.*

wassail (wŏs′āl), *n.* **1.** *Hist.* a salutation wishing health to a person, used when presenting a cup of drink or when drinking to the person. **2.** a festivity or revel with drinking of healths. **3.** alcoholic drink for toasting on festive occasions, esp. spiced ale, as on Christmas Eve and Twelfth-night. **4.** *Obs.* a song sung in wassailing. —*v.i.* **5.** to drink healths; revel with drinking. —*v.t.* **6.** to drink to the health or success of. [early ME *wes hail,* t. Scand.; cf. early Icel. *ves heill,* c. OE *wes hāl* be hale or whole] —**was′sailer,** *n.*

Wassermann (*Ger.* väs′ər män), *n.* **1. August von** (*Ger.* ou′go͞ost fōn), 1866–1925, German physician and bacteriologist. **2. Jakob** (*Ger.* yä′kŏp), 1873–1934, German novelist.

Wassermann reaction (wăs′ə mən; *Ger.* väs′ər män), a diagnostic test for syphilis using the fixation of a complement by the serum of a syphilitic individual. Also, **Wassermann test.** [named after A. von WASSERMANN]

wast (wŏst; *unstressed* wəst), *v. Archaic.* a 2nd pers. sing. pt. indic. of **be.**

wastage (wās′tĭj), *n.* loss by use, wear, decay, wastefulness, etc.

waste (wāst), *v.*, **wasted, wasting,** *n., adj.* —*v.t.* **1.** to consume, spend, or employ uselessly or without adequate return; use to no avail; squander: *to waste money, time, effort, or words.* **2.** to fail or neglect to use, or let go to waste: *to waste an opportunity.* **3.** to destroy or consume gradually, or wear away. **4.** to wear down or reduce in bodily substance, health, or strength; emaciate; enfeeble: *to be wasted by disease or hunger.* **5.** to destroy, devastate, or ruin: *a country wasted with fire and sword.*

—*v.i.* **6.** to be consumed or spent uselessly or without being fully utilized. **7.** to become gradually consumed, used up, or worn away: *a candle wastes in burning.* **8.** to become physically wasted, lose flesh or strength, or become emaciated or enfeebled (often fol. by *away*). **9.** to diminish gradually, or dwindle, as wealth, power, etc. (often fol. by *away*). **10.** to pass gradually, as time.

—*n.* **11.** useless consumption or expenditure, or use without adequate return: *waste of material, money, or time.* **12.** neglect, instead of use: *waste of opportunity.* **13.** gradual destruction, impairment, or decay: *the waste and repair of bodily tissue.* **14.** devastation or ruin, as from war, fire, etc. **15.** a region or place laid waste or in ruins. **16.** anything unused, unproductive, or not properly utilized. **17.** an uncultivated tract of land. **18.** a tract of wild land, desolate country, or desert. **19.** *Law.* positive damage to, or neglect of land by a tenant. **20.** an empty, desolate, or dreary tract or extent: *a waste of snow.* **21.** anything left over or superfluous, as excess material, byproducts, etc., not of use for the work in hand. **22.** remnants from the working of cotton, etc., used for wiping machinery, absorbing oil, etc. **23.** *Phys. Geog.* material derived by mechanical and chemical disintegration of rock, as the detritus transported by streams, etc. **24. go to waste,** to be wasted; fail to be used. **25. lay waste,** to destroy; devastate; ruin.

—*adj.* **26.** not used or in use: *waste energy.* **27.** (of land, regions, etc.) uninhabited and wild, desolate and barren, or desert. **28.** (of regions, towns, etc.) in a state of desolation and ruin, as from devastation or decay. **29.** left over or superfluous: *to utilize waste products of manufacture.* **30.** having served a purpose and no longer of use. **31.** rejected as useless or worthless, or refuse: *waste products.* **32.** *Physiol.* pertaining to material unused by or unusable to the organism. **33.** intended to receive, hold, or carry away refuse or surplus material, etc.

[ME, t. AF: m. *wast,* g. b. L *vastus* desert and OHG *wuosti* desert] —**Syn. 1.** misspend, dissipate, fritter away. **13.** diminution, decline, emaciation, consumption. **18.** See **desert**[1]. **21.** refuse, rubbish, trash.

wastebasket (wāst′bäs′kĭt), *n.* wastepaper basket.

wasteful (wāst′fəl), *adj.* **1.** given to or characterized by useless consumption or expenditure: *wasteful methods of living* **2.** squandering, or grossly extravagant. **3.** devastating or destructive: *wasteful war.* —**waste′fully,** *adv.* —**waste′fulness,** *n.*

wasteness (wāst′nĭs), *n.* the state of being waste or desolate.

wastepaper (wāst′pā′pə), *n.* paper thrown away or otherwise disposed of as useless.

wastepaper basket, a basket for wastepaper, or papers, scraps of paper, etc., to be disposed of as refuse. Also, **wastebasket.**

wastepipe (wāst′pīp′), *n.* **1.** a pipe for conveying away water, etc. **2.** *Plumbing.* a pipe carrying liquid wastes from all fixtures except water closets. Cf. **soil pipe.**

waste product, material produced in a process, as manufacture, and discarded as useless when the process is completed.

waster (wās′tə), *n.* **1.** one who or that which wastes. **2.** a spendthrift. **3.** an idler or good-for-nothing. **4.** something rejected as waste, esp. an inferior or badly made article. **5.** one who destroys or lays waste.

wasting (wās′tĭng), *adj.* **1.** gradually reducing the fullness and strength of the body: *a wasting disease.* **2.** laying waste; devastating; despoiling.

wastrel (wās′trəl), *n.* **1.** a wasteful person; spendthrift. **2.** an idler, or good-for-nothing. [f. WAST(E) + -REL]

watch (wŏch), *v.i.* **1.** to be on the lookout, look attentively, or be closely observant, as to see what comes, is done, happens, etc.: *to watch while an experiment is performed.* **2.** to look or wait attentively and expectantly (usually fol. by *for*): *to watch for a signal, an opportunity.* **3.** to be careful or cautious. **4.** to keep awake, esp. for a purpose; keep a vigilant watch as for protection or safekeeping. **5.** to keep vigil, as for devotional purposes. **6.** to keep guard. **7. watch out,** to be on one's guard; be alert or cautious. **8. watch over,** to guard; protect.
—*v.t.* **9.** to keep under attentive view or observation, as in order to see or learn something; view attentively or with interest: *to watch a game of cricket.* **10.** to contemplate or regard mentally: *to watch his progress.* **11.** to look or wait attentively and expectantly for: *to watch one's chance or opportunity.* **12.** to guard for protection or safekeeping.
—*n.* **13.** close, constant observation for the purpose of seeking or discovering something. **14.** a lookout, as for something expected: *to be on the watch.* **15.** vigilant guard, as for protection, restraint, etc. **16.** a keeping awake for some special purpose: *a watch beside a sickbed.* **17.** a period of time for watching or keeping guard. **18.** something that measures and indicates the progress of time. **19.** a small, portable timepiece. **20.** *Naut.* **a.** a period of time (usually four hours) during which one part of a ship's crew is on duty, taking turns with another part. **b.** a certain part (usually half) of the officers and crew of a vessel who together attend to working it for an allotted period of time. **21.** one of the periods into which the night was divided by the ancients: *the fourth watch of the night.* **22.** a watchman, or a body of watchmen.
[ME *wacche*, OE *wæcca* (North.), var. of *wacian* WAKE[1]]
—**watch′er,** *n.*
—**Syn. 1.** WATCH, LOOK, SEE imply being aware of things around one by perceiving them through the eyes. TO WATCH is to be a spectator, to look on or observe, or to fix the attention upon during passage of time: *to watch while a procession passes.* TO LOOK is to direct the gaze with the intention of seeing, to use the eyesight with attention: *to look for violets in the spring, to look at articles displayed for sale.* TO SEE is to perceive with the eyes, to obtain a visual impression, with or without fixing the attention: *animals able to see in the dark.*

watchcase (wŏch′kās′), *n.* the case or outer covering for the works of a watch.

watch-chain (wŏch′chān′), *n.* a chain for securing a pocket watch to the clothing.

watch committee, a committee of a local government body which exercises supervision over local police services, etc.

watchdog (wŏch′dŏg′), *n.* **1.** a dog kept to guard property. **2.** a watchful guardian.

watch-fire (wŏch′fī′ə), *n.* a fire maintained during the night as a signal and for a watching party.

watchful (wŏch′fəl), *adj.* **1.** vigilant or alert; closely observant. **2.** characterized by vigilance or alertness. **3.** *Archaic.* wakeful or sleepless. —**watch′fully,** *adv.* —**watch′fulness,** *n.* —**Syn. 1.** attentive, heedful, careful, circumspect. See **alert.**

watch-glass (wŏch′gläs′), *n.* a transparent cover for the face of a watch.

watch-guard (wŏch′gäd′), *n.* a chain, cord, or ribbon for securing a watch when worn on the person.

watchmaker (wŏch′mā′kə), *n.* one whose occupation it is to make and repair watches. —**watch′mak′ing,** *n.*

watchman (wŏch′mən), *n., pl.* **-men. 1.** one who keeps guard over a building at night, to protect it from fire or thieves. **2.** (formerly) one who guarded or patrolled the streets at night.

watch-night (wŏch′nīt′), *n.* **1.** a religious service or meeting held on the last night of the year and lasting till midnight. **2.** the night on which the service is held.

watchout (wŏch′out′), *n.* the act of looking out for something; lookout.

watchstrap (wŏch′străp′), *n.* a strap for attaching a watch to the wrist.

watchtower (wŏch′tou′ə), *n.* a tower on which a sentry keeps watch.

watchword (wŏch′wûd′), *n.* **1.** a word or short phrase to be communicated, on challenge, to a sentinel or guard; a password; a countersign. **2.** a word or phrase expressive of a principle or rule of action. **3.** a rallying cry of a party, etc.; a slogan.

Watenstedt-Salzgitter (*Ger.* vä′tən shtĕt zälts gĭt′ər), *n.* See **Salzgitter.**

water (wô′tə), *n.* **1.** the liquid which in a more or less impure state constitutes rain, oceans, lakes, rivers, etc., and which in a pure state is a transparent, odourless, tasteless liquid, a compound of hydrogen and oxygen, H_2O, freezing at 32°F or 0°C, and boiling at 212°F or 100°C. It contains 11·188 per cent hydrogen and 88·812 per cent oxygen, by weight. **2.** a special form or variety of this liquid, as rain. **3.** (*often pl.*) the liquid obtained from a mineral spring. **4.** the water of a river, etc., with reference to its relative height, esp. as dependent on tide: *high or low water.* **5.** that which enters a vessel through leaks: *the ship is taking water.* **6.** the surface of water: *above, below,* or *on the water.* **7.** (*pl.*) flowing water, or water moving in waves. **8.** (*pl.*) a body of water as a sea or seas bordering a particular country or situated in a particular region. **9.** a liquid solution or preparation: *toilet water.* **10.** any of various solutions of volatile or gaseous substances in water: *ammonia water.* **11.** any liquid or aqueous organic secretion, exudation, humour, or the like, as tears, perspiration, urine, the amniotic fluids, etc. **12.** a wavy, lustrous pattern or marking, as on silk fabrics, metal surfaces, etc. **13.** the degree of transparency and brilliancy of a diamond or other precious stone. **14. above water,** out of embarrassment or trouble, esp. of a financial nature. **15. by water,** by ship or boat. **16. in deep water,** in trouble; in a difficult situation. **17. like water,** abundantly; freely: *to spend money like water.* **18. of the first water,** of the finest quality or rank: *a literary critic of the first water.* **19. throw cold water on,** to discourage.
—*v.t.* **20.** to sprinkle, moisten, or drench with water: *to water a road or street.* **21.** to supply (animals) with water for drinking. **22.** to furnish with a supply of water, as a ship. **23.** to furnish water to (a region, etc.), as by streams; supply (land, etc.) with water, as by irrigation. **24.** to dilute or adulterate with water (often fol. by *down*): *to water soup.* **25.** *Finance.* to issue (shares of stock) without receiving a corresponding amount of cash or property. **26.** to produce a wavy lustrous pattern, marking, or finish on (fabrics, metals, etc.).
—*v.i.* **27.** to discharge, fill with, or secrete water or liquid, as the eyes, or as the mouth at the sight or thought of tempting food. **28.** to drink water, as an animal. **29.** to take in a supply of water, as a ship.
—*adj.* **30.** of or pertaining to water in any way. **31.** holding water: *a water bucket.* **32.** worked or powered by, or treating, water: *a water mill.* **33.** used in or on water: *a water vehicle.* **34.** prepared with water for hardening, dilution, etc.: *water mortar.* **35.** situated or occurring on, in, or by water: *water music, water frontage.* **36.** residing by or in, or ruling over, water: *water people, water deity.*
[ME; OE *wæter*, c. D *water*, G *Wasser*; akin to Icel. *vatn*, Goth. *wato*] —**wa′terer,** *n.* —**wa′terless,** *adj.* —**wa′terlike′,** *adj.*

waterage (wô′tə rĭj), *n.* **1.** delivery of goods over water routes. **2.** the cost of this.

water-back (wô′tə băk′), *n.* a reservoir, set of pipes, or the like, at the back of a stove or fireplace, providing a supply of hot water.

Water-bearer (wô′tə bĕə′rə), *n.* Aquarius.

water-beetle (wô′tə bē′tl), *n.* any of the aquatic beetles of the family *Dytiscidae* (diving beetles) or *Hydrophilidae.*

Waterberg-Matsap (wô′tə bûg măt′săp), *Geol.* —*adj.* **1.** pertaining to the earliest Palaeozoic period or system of rocks in southern Africa. —*n.* **2.** a period or system following the Pre-Cambrian periods or systems in southern Africa.

water-betony (wô′tə bĕt′ə nĭ), *n.* a perennial scrophulariaceous herb, *Scrophularia aquatica*, common in wet places in Europe.

waterbird (wô′tə bûd′), *n.* an aquatic bird, or bird that frequents the water; a swimming or wading bird.

water-biscuit (wô′tə bĭs′kĭt), *n.* a thin, crisp biscuit prepared from flour and water.

water-blister (wô′tə blĭs′tə), *n.* a blister which contains a clear, serous fluid, as distinguished from a blood blister, in which the fluid is sanguineous.

water-boatman (wô′tə bōt′mən), *n., pl.* **-men. 1.** a hemipterous insect of the family *Corixidae*, members of which swim in fresh water, using their long legs. **2.** pond-skater.

waterborne (wô′tə bôn′), *adj.* **1.** supported by the water; carried by the water. **2.** conveyed by ship or boat. **3.** transmitted by water, as a disease.

water-bottle (wô′tə bŏt′l), *n.* a flask or vessel of leather, glass, etc., for holding drinking water, esp. as used by soldiers, travellers, etc.

waterbrain (wô′tə brān′), *n.* gid, in sheep.

waterbrash (wôʹtə brăsh′), *n. Pathol.* heartburn.

waterbuck (wôʹtə bŭk′), *n.*, *pl.* **-bucks,** (*esp. collectively*) **-buck.** any of various African antelopes of the genus *Kobus*, frequenting marshes and reedy places, esp. *K. ellipsiprymnus*, a large species of southern and central Africa. [t. D: m. *waterbok*]

Common waterbuck, *Kobus ellipsiprymnus* (4 to 4½ ft high at the shoulder, total length 6 ft)

water-buffalo (wôʹtə bŭfʹələ̄′), *n.* the common flat-horned buffalo, *Bubalus bubalus*, of the Old World tropics. Also, **water-ox.**

Waterbury (wôʹtə bə rĭ, -brĭ), *n.* a town in the U.S., in W. Connecticut. 107,130 (1960).

water-butt (wôʹtə bŭt′), *n.* an open-ended barrel or container for collecting and storing rain-water.

water-carrier (wôʹtə kăʹrĭ ə), *n.* **1.** a man who or an animal which carries water. **2.** a container for carrying water.

water-cart (wôʹtə kät′), *n.* a vehicle that carries water, esp. one which waters the roads.

water-chestnut (wôʹtə chĕsʹnŭt), *n.* **1.** any of the aquatic plants constituting the genus *Trapa*, bearing an edible, nutlike fruit, esp. *T. natans* of the Old World. **2.** the fruit. Also, **water-caltrop** (wôʹtə kălʹtrəp).

water-chickweed (wôʹtə chĭkʹ-wēd), *n.* a slender caryophyllaceous perennial herb, *Myosoton aquaticum*, common in wet places in Europe and temperate Asia.

Water-buffalo, *Bubalus bubalus* (5 to 6 ft high at the shoulder)

water cider, ciderkin.

water-clock (wôʹtə klŏk′), *n.* a device, as a clepsydra, for measuring time by the flow of water.

water-closet, **1.** a receptacle in which human excrement is flushed down a drain by water from a cistern. **2.** a lavatory (def. 1). *Abbrev.*: w.c.

watercolour (wôʹtə kŭlʹə), *Painting.* **—*n.*** **1.** a pigment for which water rather than oil is used as a vehicle. **2.** the art or method of painting with such pigments. **3.** a painting or design executed by this method. **—*adj.*** **4.** of or pertaining to watercolour or a watercolour painting. Also, *U.S.*, **watercolor.** **—waʹtercolʹourist,** *n.*

water-cool (wôʹtə ko͞ol′), *v.t.* to cool by means of water, esp. by water circulating in pipes or a jacket. **—waʹter-cooled′,** *adj.*

water-cooler (wôʹtə ko͞oʹlə), *n.* a vessel for holding drinking water which is cooled and drawn off for use by a tap.

watercourse (wôʹtə kôs′), *n.* **1.** a stream of water, as a river or brook. **2.** the bed of such a stream. **3.** a natural channel conveying water. **4.** a channel or canal made for the conveyance of water.

watercraft (wôʹtə kräft′), *n.* **1.** skill in boating and water sports. **2.** any boat or ship. **3.** boats and ships collectively.

water-crake (wôʹtə krāk′), *n.* **1.** the spotted crake. **2.** the Old World water-ouzel (*Cinclus aquaticus*).

watercress (wôʹtə krĕs′), *n.* **1.** a perennial cress, *Rorippa nasturtium-aquaticum*, usually growing in clear, running water, and bearing pungent leaves. **2.** the leaves, used for salads, soups, and as a garnish.

water cure, **1.** hydropathy or hydrotherapy. **2.** *Colloq.* torture by means of forcing water in great quantities into the victim's stomach.

water-diviner (wôʹtə dĭ vīʹnə), *n.* one who uses a divining rod to discover water in the ground. Also, **waterfinder.**

water-dog (wôʹtə dŏg′), *n.* **1.** a dog accustomed to or delighting in the water, or trained to go into the water to retrieve game. **2.** *Colloq.* a person who is at home on or in the water.

water-dropwort (wôʹtə drŏpʹwût), *n.* any of several perennial umbelliferous herbs of the genus *Oenanthe*, as *O. fistulosa*, a plant of wet places in Europe and SW Asia.

watered-down (wôʹtəd doun′), *adj.* made weaker, less effective, by or as by the addition of water.

water equivalent, *Physics.* heat capacity.

waterfall (wôʹtə fôl′), *n.* a steep fall or flow of water from a height; a cascade.

waterfinder (wôʹtə fīnʹdə), *n.* a water-diviner.

water-flea (wôʹtə flē′), *n.* daphnia.

Waterford (wôʹtə fəd), *n.* **1.** a county in the Republic of Ireland, in SE Munster. 71,439 pop. (1961); 710 sq. mi. **2.** its county town, in the E part: a seaport. 28,216 (1961).

waterfowl (wôʹtə foul′), *n.* **1.** a waterbird, esp. a swimming bird. **2.** such birds collectively, esp. swimming game birds.

waterfront (wôʹtə frŭnt′), *n.* **1.** land abutting on a body of water. **2.** a part of a city or town so abutting.

water-gap (wôʹtə găp′), *n.* a transverse gap in a mountain ridge, cut by and giving passage to a stream.

water-gas (wôʹtə găs′), *n.* a poisonous gas used for lighting, etc., made by passing steam over incandescent coal or other carbon fuel, and consisting of a mixture of various gases, chiefly carbon monoxide and hydrogen.

water-gate (wôʹtə gāt′), *n.* **1.** a floodgate. **2.** a gateway giving access to a body of water.

water-gauge (wôʹtə gāj′), *n.* any device for indicating the height of water in a reservoir, tank, boiler, or other vessel.

Boiler water-gauge
A, Water-level; B, Upper cock; C, Lower cock

waterglass (wôʹtə gläs′), *n.* **1.** a glass or goblet for drinking. **2.** a vessel of glass to hold water. **3.** a glass tube used to indicate water-level, as in a boiler. **4.** a device for observing objects beneath the surface of the water, consisting essentially of an open tube or box with a glass bottom. **5.** sodium silicate.

water-gum (wôʹtə gŭm′), *n.* **1.** (in the U.S.) a tupelo, *Nyassa sylvatica*, v. *biflora*, of the southern states. **2.** (in Australia) any of several myrtaceous trees growing near water.

water-hammer (wôʹtə hămʹə), *n.* the concussion which results when a moving volume of water in a pipe is suddenly arrested.

water-hemlock (wôʹtə hĕmʹlŏk), *n.* any of the poisonous plants constituting the umbelliferous genus *Cicuta*, as *C. virosa* of Europe, and *C. maculata* of North America, growing in swamps and marshy places.

waterhen (wôʹtə hĕn′), *n.* the moorhen or gallinule, *Gallinula chloropus*, of Europe, Asia, North Africa, and Australia.

water-hole (wôʹtə hōl′), *n.* a natural hole or hollow in which water collects, as a spring in a desert, a cavity in the dried-up course of a river, etc.

water-ice (wôʹtər īs′), *n.* **1.** ice formed by direct freezing of fresh or salt water, and not by compacting of snow. **2.** a frozen confection made with fruit juice and sugar syrup.

water-inch (wôʹtər ĭnch′), *n. Hydraulics.* the quantity of water (very nearly 500 cubic feet) discharged in 24 hours through a circular opening of 1 inch diameter leading from a reservoir in which the water is constantly only high enough to cover the orifice. Also, **miner's inch.**

wateriness (wôʹtə rĭ nĭs), *n.* a watery state.

watering (wôʹtə rĭng), *n.* **1.** the act of one who or that which waters. **2.** a watered appearance on silk, etc. **—*adj.*** **3.** that waters. **4.** pertaining to medicinal springs or a sea-bathing resort.

watering-can (wôʹtə rĭng kăn′), *n.* a vessel, esp. with a spout having a perforated nozzle, for watering or sprinkling plants, etc.

watering-place (wôʹtə rĭng plās′), *n.* **1.** a health resort with mineral springs; spa. **2.** a seaside resort. **3.** a place where drinking water may be obtained.

waterish (wôʹtə rĭsh), *adj.* watery.

water-jacket (wôʹtə jăkʹĭt), *n.* a casing or compartment containing water, placed about something to keep it cool or otherwise regulate its temperature, as round the cylinder or cylinders of an internal-combustion engine.

water-jump (wôʹtə jŭmp′), *n.* any small body of water which a horse must jump over, as in a steeplechase.

water-level (wôʹtə lĕvʹəl), *n.* **1.** the surface level of any body of water. **2.** *Naut.* waterline.

waterlily (wôʹtə lĭlʹĭ), *n.* **1.** any of the aquatic plants constituting the genus *Nymphaea* (*Castalia*) family *Nymphaeceae*, the species of which have large, disclike, floating leaves and showy, fragrant flowers, esp. *N. alba* of Europe or *N. odorata* of America. **2.** any plant of the genus *Nuphar* of the same family (**yellow waterlily** or **yellow pond-lily**). **3.** a nymphaeaceous plant. **4.** the flower of any such plant.

Waterlily, *Nymphaea alba*

waterline (wôʹtə līn′), *n.* **1.** *Naut.* **a.** that part of the outside of the hull of a ship that is just at the water-level. **b.** any of several lines marked on the hull of a ship, showing the depth to which it sinks when unloaded and when partially or fully loaded. **2.** water-level. **3.** the line in which water at its surface borders upon a floating body.

waterlog (wô′tə lŏg′), *v.t.*, **-logged, -logging. 1.** to cause (a ship, etc.) to become unmanageable as a result of flooding. **2.** to soak or saturate with water.

waterlogged (wô′tə lŏgd′), *adj.* **1.** so filled with water, by leakage or overflow, as to be heavy or unmanageable, as a ship, etc. **2.** excessively saturated with water: *waterlogged ground.*

Waterloo (wô′tə lo͞o′; *for 1 also Flem.* wä′tər lō), *n.* **1.** a village in central Belgium, S of Brussels: Napoleon decisively defeated here June 18th, 1815. **2.** a decisive or crushing defeat.

Waterloo

water main, a main or principal pipe or conduit in a system for conveying water.

waterman (wô′tə mən), *n.*, *pl.* **-men. 1.** a man who manages, or works on, a boat; boatman. **2.** one skilled in rowing or boating.

watermanship (wô′tə mən shĭp′), *n.* **1.** the function of a waterman. **2.** skill in rowing, etc.

watermark (wô′tə mäk′), *n.* **1.** a mark indicating the height to which water rises or has risen, as in a river, etc. **2.** a figure or design impressed in the fabric in the manufacture of paper and visible when the paper is held to the light. —*v.t.* **3.** to mark (paper) with a watermark. **4.** to impress (a design, etc.) as a watermark.

water-meadow (wô′tə mĕd′ō), *n.* a meadow kept fertile by flooding from a stream.

watermelon (wô′tə mĕl′ən), *n.* **1.** the large, roundish or elongated fruit of a trailing cucurbitaceous vine, *Citrullus vulgaris,* having a hard, green rind and a (usually) pink or red pulp which abounds in a sweetish, watery juice. **2.** the plant or vine.

water-meter (wô′tə mē′tə), *n.* a device for measuring and registering the quantity of water that passes through a pipe, etc.

water-milfoil (wô′tə mĭl′foil), *n.* any of various aquatic plants, chiefly of the genus *Myriophyllum,* the submersed leaves of which are very finely divided.

watermill (wô′tə mĭl′), *n.* a mill with machinery driven by water.

water-mint (wô′tə mĭnt′), *n.* a perennial labiate herb, *Mentha aquatica* of wet places in Europe, SW Asia, northern and southern Africa.

water-moccasin (wô′tə mŏk′ə sĭn), *n.* a venomous snake, *Ancistrodon piscivorus,* of the rattlesnake family, inhabiting swamps of the southern U.S.

water-motor (wô′tə mō′tə), *n.* any form of prime mover, or motor, that is operated by the kinetic energy, pressure, or weight of water, esp. a small turbine or waterwheel fitted to a pipe supplying water.

water-nymph (wô′tə nĭmf′), *n.* **1.** a nymph of the water, as a naiad, a nereid, or an oceanid. **2.** a waterlily. **3.** any of the aquatic plants constituting the genus *Naias.*

water-oak (wô′tər ōk′), *n.* **1.** an oak, *Quercus nigra,* of the southern U.S., growing chiefly along streams and swamps. **2.** any of several other American oaks.

water of constitution, *Chem.* that portion of the water of hydration which is retained more tenaciously than the rest, as the molecule of water in $CuSo_4 . 5H_2O$ which remains after the four molecules have been driven off at 100°C.

water of crystallization, *Chem.* water of hydration: formerly thought necessary to crystallization, but now usually regarded as affecting crystallization only as it forms new molecular combinations.

water of hydration, *Chem.* that portion of a hydrate which is represented as, or can be driven off as, water: now usually regarded as being in true molecular combination with the other atoms of the compound, and not existing in the compound as water.

water-ouzel (wô′tər o͞o′zəl), *n.* any of several plump, thick-plumaged, aquatic birds of the family *Cinclidae,* allied to the thrushes, esp. *Cinclus cinclus* of Europe, and *C. mexicanus* of western North America, having the habit of jerking the body or 'dipping' as they perch, walk, etc.; a dipper.

water-ox (wô′tər ŏks′), *n.* water-buffalo.

water-paint (wô′tə pānt′), *n.* any paint in which the volatile portion is mainly water, esp. an emulsion paint in which the binder is, or becomes, insoluble in water.

water-parsnip (wô′tə päs′nĭp), *n.* a large, perennial, umbelliferous herb, *Sium latifolium,* occurring in wet places in Europe.

water-parting (wô′tə pä′tĭng), *n.* a watershed or divide.

water-pepper (wô′tə pĕp′ə), *n.* any of various plants of the polygonaceous genus *Polygonum,* growing in wet places, esp. *P. hydropiper.*

water-pimpernel (wô′tə pĭm′pə nĕl), *n.* **1.** the brookweed. **2.** the pimpernel, *Anagallis arvensis.*

water-pipit (wô′tə pĭp′ĭt), *n.* pipit.

water-pistol (wô′tə pĭs′tl), *n.* a toy gun that squirts a jet of water or other liquid.

water-plantain (wô′tə plăn′tĭn), *n.* any of the aquatic herbs of the genus *Alisma,* esp. *A. plantago-aquatica,* a species growing in shallow water and having leaves suggesting those of the common plantain.

water-polo (wô′tə pō′lō), *n.* a water game played by two teams, each having seven swimmers, in which the object is to carry or pass the ball over the opponent's goal line.

water-power (wô′tə pou′ə), *n.* **1.** the power of water used, or capable of being used, to drive machinery, etc. **2.** a fall or descent in a stream, capable of being so used. **3.** a water right possessed by a mill.

waterpox (wô′tə pŏks′), *n. Pathol.* chickenpox.

waterproof (wô′tə pro͞of′), *adj.* **1.** impervious to water. **2.** rendered impervious to water by some special process, as coating or treating with rubber or the like. —*n.* **3.** any of several coated or rubberized fabrics which will hold water. **4.** an outer garment of waterproof material. —*v.t.* **5.** to make waterproof.

waterproofing (wô′tə pro͞o′fĭng), *n.* **1.** the material used to make something waterproof. **2.** the act or process of making something waterproof.

water-purslane (wô′tə pûs′lĭn), *n.* any of various marsh plants somewhat resembling purslane, as a lythraceous plant, *Peplis portula,* of Europe.

water-rail (wô′tə rāl′), *n.* a brown and grey bird, *Rallus aquaticus,* of the coot family, about 12 inches long, inhabiting marshes and rivers of Europe and Asia.

water-rat (wô′tə răt′), *n.* **1.** any of several different rodents of aquatic habits, as the water-vole, *Arvicola amphibius.* **2.** the American muskrat, *Fiber zibethicus.* **3.** (in Australia and New Guinea) any of the aquatic rats of the subfamily *Hydromyinae,* esp. of the genus *Hydromys.* **4.** *U.S. Slang.* a vagrant or thief who frequents a waterfront.

water-repellent (wô′tə rĭ pĕl′ənt), *adj.* having a finish which is resistant to water.

water right, the right to make use of the water from a particular stream, lake, or canal.

water-sapphire (wô′tə săf′ī ə), *n.* a transparent variety of cordierite, found in Ceylon, Madagascar, and elsewhere, sometimes used as a gem. [trans. of F *saphir d'eau*]

waterscape (wô′tə skāp′), *n.* a picture or view of the sea or other body of water. [f. WATER + *-scape,* modelled on LANDSCAPE]

water-scorpion (wô′tə skô′pyən), *n.* any of the aquatic hemipterous insects constituting the family *Nepidae* (genera *Nepa, Ranatra,* etc.), having a tail-like process through which respiration is effected.

watershed (wô′tə shĕd′), *n.* **1.** the ridge or crest line dividing two drainage areas; a water-parting; divide. **2.** *U.S.* the region or area drained by a river, etc.; a drainage area. [f. WATER + SHED[2]]

water-shield (wô′tə shēld′), *n.* any of the aquatic plants of the nymphaeaceous genera *Brasenia* and *Cabomba,* with peltate floating leaves.

water-shrew (wô′tə shro͞o′), *n.* either of two small aquatic shrews of the genus *Neomys,* inhabiting Europe and parts of Asia.

water-sick (wô′tə sĭk′), *adj. Agric.* excessively watered, esp. by irrigation, so that tilling and planting cannot be done.

waterside (wô′tə sīd′), *n.* **1.** the margin, bank, or shore of the sea, a river, a lake, etc. —*adj.* **2.** of, relating to, or situated at the waterside: *waterside insects.* **3.** working by the waterside: *waterside police.*

water-ski (wô′tə skē′), *n., v.,* **-ski'd** or **-skied, -skiing.** —*n.* **1.** a type of ski used for gliding over water. —*v.i.* **2.** to glide over water on water-skis by grasping a rope towed by a speedboat.

water-snake (wô′tə snāk′), *n.* **1.** any of the harmless colubrine snakes of the genus *Natrix,* found in or near fresh water. **2.** any of various other snakes living in or frequenting water.

water-soak (wô′tə sōk′), *v.t.* to soak with water.

water-softener (wô′tə sŏf′nə), *n.* any substance or device for destroying the hardness of water, usually by causing the precipitation, or removal from solution, of the metals whose salts cause the hardness.

water-soldier (wô′tə sōl′jə), *n.* a floating aquatic herb, *Stratiotes aloides* (family *Hydrocharitaceae*), with rosettes of fleshy, serrated leaves, occurring in ponds in Europe and NW Asia.

water-soluble (wô′tə sŏl′yo͞o bl), *adj.* able to dissolve in water: *water-soluble vitamins B and C.*

water-spaniel (wô′tə spăn′yəl), *n.* a curly-haired spaniel of either of two varieties, taking to water and readily trained for hunting.

Irish water-spaniel (Ab. 2 ft high at the shoulder)

water-speedwell (wô′tə spēd′-wĕl), *n.* a speedwell, *Veronica anagallis-aquatica*, found esp. in marshes.
water-spider (wô′tə spī′də), *n.* an aquatic spider, *Argyroneta aquatica*, of Europe and N Asia which lives under water in an air bubble trapped by a web.
waterspout (wô′tə spout′), *n.* **1.** a pipe running down the side of a house to take away water from the gutter of the roof. **2.** a spout, nozzle, or orifice from which water is discharged. **3.** *Meteorol.* **a.** a tornado-like storm or whirlwind over the ocean or other body of water, which takes the form of a progressive gyrating mass of air laden with mist and spray, presenting the appearance of a solid column of water reaching upwards to the clouds. **b.** a sudden and violent downpour of rain; cloudburst.
water-sprite (wô′tə sprīt′), *n.* a sprite or spirit inhabiting the water.
water-starwort (wô′tə stä′wût), *n.* any plant of the genus *Callitriche*, of aquatic herbs.
water-strider (wô′tə strī′də), *n.* any of the hemipterous insects constituting the family *Gerridae*, having long, slender legs, and darting about on the surface of water; pond-skater.
water-table (wô′tə tā′bl), *n.* **1.** the depth below which the ground is saturated with water. **2.** *Archit.* a projecting string-course or similar member placed to throw off or divert water.
watertight (wô′tə tīt′), *adj.* **1.** impervious to water. **2.** without fault; irrefutable; flawless: *a watertight argument or alibi.* —**wa′tertight′ness,** *n.*
water-tower (wô′tə tou′ə), *n.* **1.** a vertical pipe or tower into which water is pumped to obtain a required head; a standpipe. **2.** a fire-extinguishing apparatus throwing a stream of water on the upper parts of a tall burning building.
water-tube boiler (wô′tə tyo͞ob′ boi′lə), a boiler in which the water passes through tubes in the combustion zone.
water-tunnel (wô′tə tŭn′əl), *n.* *Aeron.* a device similar to a wind-tunnel, except that water is the circulating fluid instead of air, used for aerodynamic tests at slow stream velocities.
water-vapour (wô′tə vā′pə), *n.* gaseous water, esp. when diffused and below the boiling point: distinguished from steam.
water-violet (wô′tə vī′ə lĭt), *n.* a floating, aquatic, perennial, primulaceous herb, *Hottonia palustris*, with projecting pale mauve flowers, occurring in ponds in Europe.
water-vole (wô′tə vōl′), *n.* a large dark brown vole, *Arvicola amphibius*, of western Europe, which infests river banks in Britain.
water-wagon (wô′tə wăg′ən), *n.* water-cart.
water-wagtail (wô′tə wăg′tāl), *n.* a long-tailed, grey and white bird, *Motacilla alba*, of Europe, including Britain.
water-wave (wô′tə wāv′), *n.*, *v.*, **-waved, -waving.** —*n.* **1.** a wave on the surface of a body of water. **2.** a wave set into lotioned hair with combs and then allowed to dry by the application of heat from a drier. —*v.t.* **3.** to set (hair) in a water-wave.
waterway (wô′tə wā′), *n.* **1.** a river, canal, or other body of water as a route or way of travel or transport. **2.** a channel for vessels, esp. a fairway in a harbour, etc. **3.** *Naut.* a drainage gutter on the deck of a ship which carries water to the scuppers.
waterweed (wô′tə wēd′), *n.* any aquatic plant without special use or beauty.
waterwheel (wô′tə wēl′), *n.* **1.** a wheel turned by water and used to perform mechanical work; a water turbine. **2.** a wheel with buckets for raising water, as a noria.
water whorl-grass (wûl′gräs′), a perennial grass, *Catabrosa aquatica*, of wet places in Europe and W Asia.
water-wings (wô′tə wĭngz′), *n.* a device shaped like a pair of wings and inflated with air, usually worn under the arms to keep the body afloat while learning to swim.
water-witch (wô′tə wĭch′), *n.* *U.S.* a water-diviner. —**wa′ter-witch′ing,** *n.*
waterworks (wô′tə wûks′), *n.pl.* **1.** (*often construed as sing.*) an aggregate of apparatus and structures by which water is collected, preserved, and distributed for domestic and other purposes, as for a town. **2.** *Colloq.* tears, or the source of tears. **3.** *Colloq.* the bladder or its functioning.
waterworn (wô′tə wôn′), *adj.* worn by the action of water; smoothed by water in motion.
watery (wô′tə rĭ), *adj.* **1.** pertaining to or connected with water: *watery Neptune.* **2.** full of or abounding in water, as soil, a region, etc. **3.** containing much or too much water. **4.** soft or soggy as a result of too much water or overcooking: *watery cabbage.* **5.** tearful. **6.** of the nature of water: *watery vapour.* **7.** resembling water in appearance or colour: *a watery blue.* **8.** resembling water in consistency: *a watery fluid.* **9.** weak, thin, washy, vapid, or poor: *watery writing.* **10.** consisting of water: *a watery grave.* **11.** discharging, filled with, or secreting a water-like morbid discharge.
Watford (wŏt′fəd), *n.* a town in England, in Hertfordshire, near London. 75,662 (1961).
Watlings Island (wŏt′lĭngz), San Salvador (def. 1).
Watson-Watt (wŏt′sən wŏt′), *n.* **Sir Robert Alexander,** born 1892, Scottish physicist.
watt (wŏt), *n.* *Physics.* the derived SI unit of power, defined as one joule per second; the power of a current of one ampere flowing across a potential difference of one volt. *Symbol:* W [named after James WATT]
Watt (wŏt), *n.* **James,** 1736–1819, Scottish engineer and inventor.
wattage (wŏt′ĭj), *n.* **1.** *Elect.* power, in watts. **2.** the watts required to operate an electrical device.
Watteau (wŏt′ō; *Fr.* vȧ tō′), *n.* **Jean Antoine** (*Fr.* zhäɴ-äɴ twȧn′), 1684–1721, French painter.
watt-hour (wŏt′ou′ə), *n.* *Elect.* the product of average power in watts and the time in hours during which such power is maintained: the commonly used unit of electrical energy.
wattle (wŏt′l), *n.*, *v.*, **-tled, -tling,** *adj.* —*n.* **1.** (*pl. or sing.*) rods or stakes interwoven with twigs or branches of trees, used for making fences, walls, roofs, etc. **2.** (*pl.*) the poles forming the framework of a thatched roof. **3.** any of various Australian acacias, esp. the shrub *Acacia aneura*, with spikes of small flowers. **4.** the huilbos of southern Africa, *Peltophorum africanum.* **5.** *Dial.* a twig, wand, stick, or rod. **6.** *Dial.* a hurdle. **7.** a fleshy lobe or appendage hanging down from the throat or chin of certain birds, etc., as the domestic fowl, the turkey, etc. —*v.t.* **8.** to bind, wall, fence, or otherwise fit with wattles. **9.** to roof or frame with wattles or in similar fashion. **10.** to form into a basketwork; interweave; interlace. **11.** to form by interweaving twigs or branches: *to wattle a fence.* —*adj.* **12.** built or roofed with wattles. [ME *wattel*, OE *watul* covering, var. of *wætla* bandage] —**wat′-tled,** *adj.*
wattle and daub, wattles plastered with mud or clay and used as a building material.
wattlebird (wŏt′l bûd′), *n.* an Australian honey-eater, *Anthochaera paradoxa*, having a pendulous wattle on each side of the throat.
wattless (wŏt′lĭs), *adj.* *Elect.* without watts or power: *a wattless alternating current* (one differing in phase by 90 degrees from the associated e.m.f.); *a wattless electromotive force* (one differing in phase by 90 degrees from the current).
wattmeter (wŏt′mē′tə), *n.* *Elect.* an instrument for measuring electric power in watts.
Watts (wŏts), *n.* **George Frederick,** 1817–1904, English painter and sculptor.
watt-second (wŏt′ sĕk′ənd), *n.* *Elect.* joule.
Watutsi (wə to͝ot′sĭ), *n.*, *pl.* **-sis** (*esp. collectively*) **-si.** **1.** Also, **Tutsi.** a member of a tall, slender people of Burundi and Rwanda. **2.** (*usually l.c.*) a dance resembling the frug. —*v.i.* **3.** to dance the watutsi. Also, **Watusi** (wə to͞o′zĭ).
waucht (*Scot.* wŏKHt; *Eng. Dial.* wäft), *n.*, *v.t.*, *v.i.* waught.
Waugh (wô), *n.* **Evelyn Arthur St John** (sĭn′jən), 1903–1966, English novelist.
waught (*Scot.* wŏKHt; *Eng. Dial.* wäft), *Scot. and N Dial.* —*n.* **1.** a copious draught. —*v.t.*, *v.i.* **2.** to drink fully. Also, **waucht.**
waul (wôl), *v.i.* to cry as a cat or a newborn baby; squall. Also, **wawl.**
wave (wāv), *n.*, *v.*, **waved, waving.** —*n.* **1.** a disturbance of the surface of a liquid body, as the sea or a lake, in the form of a ridge or swell. **2.** any surging or progressing movement or part resembling a wave of the sea: *a wave of the pulse.* **3.** a swell, surge, or rush, as of feeling, excitement, prosperity, etc.: *a wave of anger swept over him.* **4.** a widespread movement, feeling, opinion, tendency, etc.: *a wave of anti-Americanism.* **5.** one of a succession of movements of people migrating into a region, country, etc. **6.** a line of soldiers advancing or attacking. **7.** a movement of migrating birds, animals, etc. **8.** an outward curve, or one of a series of such curves, in a surface or line; an undulation. **9.** *Physics.* a progressive vibrational disturbance propagated through a medium, as air, without corresponding progress or advance of the parts

or particles themselves, as in the transmission of sound or electromagnetic energy. **10.** the act of waving, as a flag or the hand. **11.** a sign made with a wave of the hand, a flag, etc. **12.** a period or spell of exceptionally hot or cold weather. **13.** *Archaic.* water; a body of water; the sea. —*v.i.* **14.** to move loosely to and fro or up and down; flutter. **15.** to curve alternately in opposite directions; have an undulating form. **16.** to bend or sway up and down or to and fro, as branches or plants in the wind. **17.** to be moved, esp. alternately in opposite directions: *the lady's handkerchief waved in token of encouragement.* **18.** to give a signal by waving something: *she waved to me as I left.* —*v.t.* **19.** to cause to move loosely to and fro or up and down. **20.** to cause to bend or sway up and down or to and fro. **21.** to give an undulating form to; cause to curve up and down or in and out. **22.** to give a wavy appearance or pattern to, as silk. **23.** to impart a wave to (the hair). **24.** to move, esp. alternately in opposite directions: *to wave the hand.* **25.** to signal to by waving a flag or the like; direct by a waving movement: *to wave a train to a halt.* **26.** to signify or express by a waving movement: *to wave a last goodbye.*
[ME; OE *wafian,* akin to Icel. *vāfa* swing] —**wav′er,** *n.* —**wave′less,** *adj.* —**wave′like′,** *adj.*
—**Syn. 1.** WAVE, RIPPLE, BREAKER, SURF refer to a ridge or swell on the surface of water. WAVE is the general word: *waves in a high wind.* A RIPPLE is the smallest kind of wave, such as is caused by a stone thrown into a pool: *ripples in a brook.* A BREAKER is a wave breaking, or about to break, upon the shore or upon rocks: *the roar of breakers.* SURF is the collective name for breakers: *heavy surf makes bathing dangerous.* **14.** undulate, fluctuate, flutter, float, sway, rock.

waveband (wāv′bănd′), *n. Radio.* a range of wavelengths or frequencies in which the waves have similar propagation characteristics.

wave-equation (wāv′ĭ kwā′zhən), *n. Physics.* any equation, based on quantum theory, in which a wave motion is described in terms of a wave-function, or the solution to which is a wave-function.

wave-form (wāv′fôm′), *n. Physics.* the trace or shape of a wave; the shape of the graph obtained by plotting the instantaneous values of a function, which varies periodically, against time.

wave-front (wāv′frŭnt′), *n. Physics.* an imaginary surface that is the locus of all adjacent points at which the phase of vibration is the same.

wave-function (wāv′fŭngk′shən), *n. Physics.* **1.** a function used in wave-mechanics to define the three-dimensional stationary wave system which represents the orbital electrons around an atomic nucleus. **2.** a solution of a wave-equation in wave-mechanics.

waveguide (wāv′gīd′), *n. Electronics.* a piece of hollow, conducting tubing, usually rectangular or circular in cross-section, used as a conductor or directional transmitter for microwaves which are propagated through its interior.

wavelength (wāv′lĕngth′), *n.* **1.** *Physics.* the distance, measured in the direction of propagation of a wave, between two successive points that are characterized by the same phase of vibration. **2.** *Radio.* the wavelength (def. 1) of the carrier wave of a particular radio transmitter or station. **3.** a mode of thinking or understanding: *the teacher was obviously not on the same wavelength as his pupils.*

wavelet (wāv′lĭt), *n.* a small wave; ripple.

Wavell (wā′vəl), *n.* **Archibald Percival, 1st Earl,** 1883–1950, British field marshal: viceroy of India 1943–47.

wavellite (wā′və līt′), *n.* a white to yellowish green or brown mineral, a hydrous aluminium fluophosphate. [named after W. *Wavell,* died 1829, English physician, its discoverer]

wave-mechanics (wāv′mĭ kăn′ĭks), *n. Physics.* a development of quantum mechanics in which elementary particles are considered to be associated with periodic waves, the frequency and amplitude of which are determined by rules deriving from analogy with light propagation, hypothesis from known quantum conditions, and conditions of continuity.

wavemeter (wāv′mē′tə), *n. Radio.* an instrument for measuring wavelengths or frequencies.

wave-number (wāv′nŭm′bə), *n. Physics.* the number of waves per unit length; the reciprocal of wavelength.

waver (wā′və), *v.i.* **1.** to sway to and fro; flutter: *leaves wavering in the breeze.* **2.** to flicker or quiver, as light, etc.: *wavering tongues of flame.* **3.** to become unsteady or begin to fail or give way: *his mind is wavering.* **4.** to shake or tremble, as the hands, etc.: *his voice wavered.* **5.** to feel or show doubt or indecision, or vacillate: *he wavered in his determination.* **6.** (of things) to fluctuate or vary. **7.** to totter. [ME, freq. of OE *wafian* WAVE; c. d. G *wabern* move about. Icel. *vafra* toddle] —**wa′verer,** *n.* —**wa′veringly,** *adv.*
—**Syn. 5.** WAVER, FLUCTUATE, VACILLATE refer to an alternation or hesitation between one direction and another. WAVER means to hesitate between choices: *to waver as to what course to pursue.* FLUCTUATE suggests irregular change from one side to the other or up and down: *the prices of shares fluctuate when there is bad news followed by good.* VACILLATE is to make up one's mind and change it again suddenly; to be undecided as to what to do: *we must not vacillate but must set a day.*

WAVES (wāvz), *n. U.S.* (*construed as sing. or pl.*) Women's Reserve, U.S. Naval Reserve. [from the initial letters of *W*(*omen's*) *A*(*ppointed*) *V*(*olunteer*) *E*(*mergency*) *S*(*ervice*)]

wave-train (wāv′trān′), *n. Physics.* a group or series of successive waves sent out along the same path or course by a vibrating body, a radio aerial, or the like.

wavy (wā′vĭ), *adj.,* **-vier, -viest. 1.** curving alternately, in opposite directions in movement or form: *a wavy course, wavy hair.* **2.** abounding in or characterized by waves: *the wavy sea.* **3.** resembling or suggesting waves. **4.** *Bot.* **a.** bending with successive curves in opposite directions, as a margin. **b.** having such a margin, as a leaf. **5.** vibrating or tremulous; unsteady; wavering. —**wav′ily,** *adv.* —**wav′iness,** *n.*

wawl (wôl), *v.i.* waul.

wax[1] (wăks), *n.* **1.** any of a group of amorphous solid materials consisting of esters of monohydric alcohols and the higher homologues of fatty acids, as beeswax, an ester of palmitic acid, $C_{30}H_{61}OCOC_{15}H_{31}$. **2.** any of various other similar substances, as spermaceti, the secretions of certain insects (wax insects), and the secretions (vegetable wax) of certain plants. **3.** any of a group of solid, non-greasy, insoluble substances which have a low melting or softening point, esp. mixtures of the higher hydrocarbons, as paraffin wax. **4.** *Physiol.* cerumen. **5.** a resinous substance used by shoemakers for rubbing their thread. **6.** sealing wax. **7.** something suggesting wax as being readily moulded, worked upon, handled, managed, etc.: *helpless wax in their hands.* —*v.t.* **8.** to rub, smear, stiffen, polish, etc., with wax; treat with wax: *waxed moustaches, a waxed floor.* —*adj.* **9.** made of or resembling wax. [ME; OE *weax,* c. D *was,* G *Wachs,* Icel. *vax*] —**wax′er,** *n.* —**wax′like′,** *adj.*

wax[2] (wăks), *v.i.,* **waxed; waxed** or (*Poetic*) **waxen; waxing. 1.** to increase in extent, quantity, intensity, power, etc.: *discord waxed daily.* **2.** (of the moon) to increase in the extent of its illuminated portion before the full moon (opposed to *wane.*) **3.** to grow or become (as stated). [ME; OE *weaxan,* c. G *wachsen*]

wax[3] (wăks), *n. Colloq.* a fit of anger. [orig. uncert.; ? from phrase *to wax angry* (see WAX[2], def. 3)]

wax-bean (wăks′bēn′), *n. U.S.* any variety of snap-bean with a yellowish colour and waxy appearance.

waxberry (wăks′bə rĭ, -brĭ), *n., pl.* **-ries. 1.** the wax-myrtle, or the bayberry. **2.** the snowberry.

waxbill (wăks′bĭl′), *n.* any of various weaverbirds, esp. of the genus *Estrilda,* having white, pink, or red bills of waxlike appearance, and including many well-known cagebirds, as an African species, *Estrilda astrild,* the amadavat, and the Java sparrow.

waxen (wăk′sən), *adj.* **1.** made of or covered with wax. **2.** resembling or suggesting wax: *his face had an unhealthy waxen appearance.* **3.** weak or impressionable, as a person or his characteristics. —*v.* **4.** *Poetic.* pp. of **wax**[2].

wax-eye (wăks′ī′), *n.* the blightbird.

waxing moon. See **moon** (def. 2e).

wax-insect (wăks′ĭn′sĕkt), *n.* any of various homopterous insects which secrete a wax or waxlike substance, as a Chinese scale insect, *Ericerus pela.*

wax-moth (wăks′mŏth′), *n.* bee-moth.

wax-myrtle (wăks′mû′tl), *n.* a shrub or tree of the genus *Myrica,* as *M. cerifera,* which bears small berries coated with wax (sometimes used in making candles, etc.), or *M. pensylvanica.* Cf. **bayberry.**

wax-palm (wăks′päm′), *n.* **1.** a tall pinnate-leaved palm, *Ceroxylon andicola,* of the Andes, whose stem and leaves yield a resinous wax. **2.** Also, **carnauba.** a palmate-leaved palm, *Copernicia cerifera,* of Brazil, whose young leaves are coated with a hard wax.

wax-paper (wăks′pā′pə), *n.* paper made moistureproof by coating with paraffin wax.

waxplant (wăks′plänt′), *n.* any of the climbing or trailing plants of the asclepiadaceous genus *Hoya,* natives of tropical Asia and Australia, having glossy leaves and umbels of pink, white, or yellowish waxy flowers.

waxwing (wăks′wĭng′), *n.* any bird of the passerine family *Bombycillidae,* having a showy crest and small red appendages at the tips of the secondary wing feathers and sometimes the tail feathers, as *Bombycilla garrula* of the northern hemisphere.

waxwork (wăks′wûk′), *n.* **1.** figures, ornaments, etc., made of wax, or one such figure. **2.** (*pl. construed as sing.*) an exhibition of wax figures, ornaments, etc.

waxy[1] (wăk′sĭ), *adj.*, **-ier, -iest.** **1.** resembling wax, as in substance or appearance. **2.** abounding in, covered with, or made of wax. **3.** *Pathol.* pertaining to or suffering from a degeneration caused by deposits of a waxlike insoluble material in an organ. **4.** pliable, yielding, or impressionable. **—wax′iness,** *n.*

waxy[2] (wăk′sĭ), *adj.*, **-ier, -iest.** angry. [f. WAX[3] + -Y[1]]

way (wā), *n.* **1.** manner, mode, or fashion: *a new way of looking at a matter; to reply in a polite way.* **2.** characteristic or habitual manner: *that is only his way.* **3.** a course, plan, or means for attaining an end: *to find a way to reduce friction.* **4.** respect or particular: *a plan defective in several ways.* **5.** direction: *look this way.* **6.** passage or progress on a course: *to make one's way on foot, to lead the way.* **7.** distance: *a long way off.* **8.** a path or course leading from one place to another. **9.** an old Roman road: *Icknield Way.* **10.** a minor street in a town. **11.** a road, route, passage, or channel (usually used in combination): *a highway, waterway, doorway.* **12.** *Law.* a right of way. **13.** any line of passage or travel used or available: *blaze a way through dense woods.* **14.** space for passing or advancing: *he cleared a way through the throng of people.* **15.** (*often pl.*) a habit or custom: *I don't like his ways at all.* **16.** the course of mode or action which one prefers or upon which one is resolved: *to have one's own way, the local Don Juan was reputed to have had his way with numerous young women.* **17.** *Colloq.* condition, as to health, prosperity, etc.: *to be in a bad way.* **18.** range of experience or notice: *the best device that ever came my way.* **19.** course of life, action, or experience: *the way of transgressors is hard.* **20.** *Colloq.* calling or business. **21.** (*pl.*) (in shipbuilding) the timbers on which a ship is launched. **22.** *Mach.* a longitudinal strip, as in a planer, guiding a moving part along a surface. **23.** *Naut.* movement or passage through the water. **24.** Some special noun phrases are:

by the way, incidentally; in the course of one's remarks: *by the way, have you received that letter yet?*

by way of, 1. by the route of; via; through. **2.** as a method or means of: *to number articles by way of distinguishing them.* **3.** having a reputation for; ostensibly (being, doing, etc.): *he is by way of being an authority on the subject.*

come one's way, to come to one; happen to one.

each way, (of a bet) laid for a win or a place. Also, **both ways.**

give way, 1. to withdraw; retreat. **2.** to yield; break down; collapse.

give way to, 1. to yield to. **2.** to lose control of (one's emotions, etc.).

go out of one's way, to make a special effort; inconvenience oneself.

have a way with, to have a skill in dealing with: *she has a way with children.*

have a way with one, to have a charming or persuasive manner.

have it both ways, to gain or succeed by each of two contrary means, situations, etc.

in a way, to a certain extent; after a fashion: *in a way he's a pleasant person.*

in the way, forming an obstruction or hindrance.

lead the way, 1. to proceed in advance of others. **2.** to take the initiative; show by example.

make one's way, 1. to proceed. **2.** to achieve advancement, recognition, or success: *to make one's way in the world.*

make way, 1. to allow to pass. **2.** to give up or retire in favour of: *the manager resigned to make way for a younger man.*

out of the way, 1. so as not to obstruct or hinder. **2.** disposed of; dealt with. **3.** murdered: *to put a person out of the way.* **4.** out of the frequented way; off the beaten track. **5.** unusual; extraordinary.

pay one's or **its way,** to remain solvent or financially self-supporting.

under way, 1. in motion or moving along, as a ship that has weighed anchor. **2.** in progress, as an enterprise. [ME; OE *weg*, c. D *weg*, G *Weg*, Icel. *vegr*, Goth. *wigs*] **—Syn. 3.** See **method. 7.** space, interval.

waybill (wā′bĭl′), *n.* **1.** a list of goods sent by a common carrier, as a railway, with directions. **2.** (on a bus, etc.) a list showing the number of passengers carried or tickets sold.

wayfarer (wā′fĕə′rə), *n.* a traveller, esp. on foot.

wayfaring (wā′fĕə′rĭng), *adj.*, *n.* travelling, esp. on foot.

wayfaring tree, a deciduous, caprifoliaceous shrub, *Viburnum lantana*, having hairy leaves and black fruits, occurring on calcareous soils in Europe and W Asia.

waygoing (wā′gō′ĭng), *Scot. and N Dial.* —*adj.* **1.** going away; departing: *a waygoing tenant.* **2.** of or pertaining to one who goes away. —*n.* **3.** the act of leaving; departure.

waylaid (wā′lād′), *v.* pt. and pp. of **waylay.**

Wayland the Smith (wā′lənd), (in English and Scandinavian folklore) a demigod who became a smith of great skill. Also, **Wayland.**

waylay (wā′lā′), *v.t.*, **-laid, -laying. 1.** to fall upon or assail from ambush, as in order to rob, seize, or slay. **2.** to await and accost unexpectedly. [f. WAY + LAY[1]. Cf. MLG *wegelagen*] **—way′lay′er,** *n.*

wayleave (wā′lēv′), *n.* right of way.

way-out (wā′out′), *adj. Colloq.* **1.** advanced in technique, style, etc. **2.** unusual; odd; eccentric.

-ways, a suffix of manner creating adverbs, as in *sideways, lengthways.* See **-wise.** [orig. gen. of WAY]

ways and means, 1. legislation, methods, and means of raising revenue for the use of the government. **2.** methods of accomplishing something.

wayside (wā′sīd′), *n.* **1.** the side of the way; the border or edge of the road or highway. —*adj.* **2.** being, situated, or found at or along the wayside: *a wayside inn.*

way station, *U.S.* a station intermediate between principal stations, as on a railway.

way train, *U.S.* a local train.

wayward (wā′wəd), *adj.* **1.** turned or turning away from what is right or proper; perverse: *a wayward son.* **2.** swayed or prompted by caprice, or capricious: *a wayward fancy or impulse.* **3.** turning or changing irregularly; irregular: *a wayward stream or breeze.* [ME; aphetic var. of *awayward*] **—way′wardly,** *adv.* **—way′wardness,** *n.* **—Syn. 1.** contrary, headstrong, stubborn, obstinate, disobedient, unruly, refractory, intractable. See **wilful.**

wayworn (wā′wôn′), *adj.* worn or wearied by travel.

Waziristan (wə zĭə′rĭ stän′), *n.* a mountainous district in Pakistan, in NW West Pakistan province.

W/B, waybill. Also, **W.B.**

Wb, *Elect.* weber.

w.b., 1. warehouse book. **2.** waybill. **3.** westbound.

W.C., West Central (postal district, London).

w.c., 1. water closet. **2.** without charge.

W.C.T.U., Women's Christian Temperance Union.

wd, 1. ward. **2.** word.

W.D., War Department.

we (wē; *unstressed* wĭ), *pron., pl.; poss.* **our** or **ours;** *obj.* **us. 1.** nominative pl. of **I. 2.** (used by a speaker or writer to denote people in general, including himself): *we usually take our holidays in August.* **3.** (used by a sovereign when alluding to himself or herself in formal speech): *we are not amused.* **4.** (used by an editor or other writer to avoid any appearance of egotism from the use of *I*): *we deplore the present economic situation.* **5.** (used as a term of encouragement or cajolery where the 2nd person sing. is meant): *we really should work a little harder.* [ME and OE, c. D *wij*, G *wir*, Icel. *vēr*, Goth. *weis*]

W.E.A., Workers' Educational Association.

weak (wēk), *adj.* **1.** liable to yield, break, or collapse under pressure or strain; fragile; frail; not strong: *a weak fortress, a weak spot in armour.* **2.** deficient in bodily strength or healthy vigour, as from age, sickness, etc.; feeble; infirm: *a weak old man; weak eyes.* **3.** deficient in political strength, governing power, or authority: *a weak nation or ruler.* **4.** lacking in force, potency, or efficacy; impotent, ineffectual, or inadequate: *weak prayers.* **5.** lacking in rhetorical force or effectiveness: *a weak style.* **6.** lacking in logical or legal force or soundness: *a weak argument.* **7.** deficient in mental power, intelligence, or judgement: *a weak mind.* **8.** deficient in moral strength or firmness, resolution, or force of character: *prove weak under temptation, weak compliance.* **9.** deficient in amount, volume, loudness, intensity, etc.; faint; slight: *weak vibrations, a weak current of electricity.* **10.** deficient, wanting, or poor in something specified: *a hand weak in trumps, weak in spelling.* **11.** deficient in the essential or desirable properties or ingredients: *weak tea, a weak infusion.* **12.** inconclusive; anticlimactic or logically unsatisfactory, as the ending of a book, play, or the like. **13.** unstressed, as a syllable, word, etc. **14.** (of Germanic verbs) inflected with suffixes, without inherited change of the root vowel, as English *work, worked* or *keep, kept* (in which the vowel change is not inherited). **15.** (of Germanic nouns and adjectives) inflected with endings originally appropriate to stems terminating in *-n. Alte* in German *der alte Mann* 'the old man' is a weak adjective. **16.** pertaining to a flour or wheat which has a low gluten content. **17.** *Photog.* thin; not dense. **18.** *Com.* characterized by falling prices. [ME *weik*, t. Scand.; cf. Icel. *veikr*, c. OE *wāc*, G *weich*] **—weak′ish,** *adj.*

—Syn. 2. WEAK, DECREPIT, FEEBLE, WEAKLY imply a lack of strength or of good health. WEAK means not physically strong, because of extreme youth, old age, illness, etc.: *weak after an attack of fever.* DECREPIT means old and broken in health to a marked degree: *decrepit and barely able to walk.* FEEBLE denotes much the same as WEAK, but connotes being pitiable or inferior: *feeble and almost senile.* WEAKLY suggests a longstanding sickly condition, a state of chronic bad health: *a weakly child may become a strong man.* **6.** unsound, ineffective, inadequate, illogical, inconclusive, unsustained, unsatisfactory, lame. **8.** vacillating, wavering, unstable, irresolute, weak-kneed. **—Ant. 2.** strong, robust.

weaken (wē′kən), *v.t., v.i.* to become or make weak or weaker. **—weak′ener,** *n.* **—Syn.** enfeeble, debilitate, enervate, undermine, sap, exhaust, deplete, lessen, diminish, lower, reduce, impair, minimize, invalidate.

weak ending, *Pros.* a verse ending in which the metrical stress falls on a word or syllable which would not be stressed in natural utterance, as a preposition whose object is carried over to the next line.

weaker sex, women.

weak-kneed (wēk′nēd′), *adj.* yielding readily to opposition, intimidation, etc.

weakling (wēk′lĭng), *n.* **1.** a weak or feeble creature (physically or morally). **—***adj.* **2.** weak; not strong.

weakly (wēk′lĭ), *adj.*, **-lier, -liest,** *adv.* **—***adj.* **1.** weak or feeble in constitution; not robust; sickly. **—***adv.* **2.** in a weak manner. **—weak′liness,** *n.* **—Syn. 1.** See **weak.**

weak-minded (wēk′mīn′dĭd), *adj.* **1.** having or showing a want of firmness of mind. **2.** having or showing a weak or feeble mind. **—weak′-mind′edness,** *n.*

weakness (wēk′nĭs), *n.* **1.** the state or quality of being weak; feebleness. **2.** a weak point, as in a person's character; slight fault or defect. **3.** a self-indulgent inclination or liking, as for a person, object, etc. **—Syn. 2.** See **fault.**

weak nuclear interaction, *Physics.* an interaction of the type responsible for the decay of all particles except protons, electrons, neutrons, and photons.

weak sister, *U.S. Colloq.* one who does not do his fair share of work; a person or element in a group that is weak and ineffective.

weak-willed (wēk′wĭld′), *adj.* **1.** lacking strength of will; easily swayed, persuaded, etc. **2.** vacillating.

weal[1] (wēl), *n.* **1.** *Archaic.* well-being, prosperity, or happiness: *in weal or woe; zealous only for the public weal.* **2.** *Obs.* wealth or riches. [ME *wele,* OE *wela.* See WELL[1]]

weal[2] (wēl), *n.* **1.** a small burning or itching swelling on the skin, as from a mosquito bite or from urticaria. **2.** a wale or welt. [var. of WALE[1]]

weald (wēld), *n.* *Archaic.* open or wooded country. [ME *weeld,* OE *weald* forest, var. of *wald* WOLD[1]]

Weald (wēld), *n.* **The,** a former wooded district of SE England, in the counties of Kent, Surrey, and Sussex: now primarily an agricultural region.

wealth (wĕlth), *n.* **1.** a great store of valuable possessions, property, or riches: *the wealth of a city.* **2.** a rich abundance or profusion of anything: *a wealth of imagery.* **3.** *Econ.* **a.** all things having a value in money, in exchange, or in use. **b.** anything having utility and capable of being appropriated or exchanged. **4.** rich or valuable contents or produce: *the wealth of the soil.* **5.** the state of being rich; affluence: *persons of wealth and standing.* **6.** *Obs. or Archaic.* well-being or prosperity. [ME *welth,* f. *wel* WELL[1] + -TH[1]] **—Syn. 3a.** possessions, assets, goods, property. **5.** opulence, fortune.

wealthy (wĕl′thĭ), *adj.*, **-thier, -thiest. 1.** possessed of wealth; rich: *a wealthy person or nation.* **2.** characterized by, pertaining to, or suggestive of wealth: *a wealthy appearance.* **3.** rich in character, quality, or amount; abundant or ample. **—wealth′ily,** *adv.* **—wealth′iness,** *n.* **—Syn. 1.** affluent, opulent, prosperous, well-to-do, moneyed. See **rich.**

wean[1] (wēn), *v.t.* **1.** to accustom (a child or animal) to food other than its mother's milk. **2.** to withdraw from any object or form of habit or enjoyment (usually fol. by *from*). [ME *wene,* OE *wenian,* c. D *wennen* accustom, G *gewöhnen,* Icel. *venja*] **—wean′er,** *n.*

wean[2] (wēn), *n. Scot.* a child. [contraction of *wee ane* little one]

weanling (wēn′lĭng), *n.* **1.** a child or animal newly weaned. **—***adj.* **2.** newly weaned.

weapon (wĕp′ən), *n.* **1.** any instrument for use in attack or defence in combat, fighting, or war, as a sword, rifle, cannon, etc. **2.** anything serving as an instrument for making or repelling an attack: *the deadly weapon of meekness.* **3.** *Zool.* any part or organ serving for attack or defence, as claws, horns, teeth, stings, etc. [ME *wepen,* OE *wǣpen,* c. G *Waffe*] **—weap′oned,** *adj.* **—weap′onless,** *adj.*

weaponry (wĕp′ən rĭ), *n.* weapons collectively.

wear[1] (wēə), *v.*, **wore, worn, wearing,** *n.* **—***v.t.* **1.** to carry or have on the body or about the person as a covering, equipment, ornament, or the like: *wear a coat, a watch, wear a disguise.* **2.** to have or use on the person habitually: *to wear a beard.* **3.** to bear or have in the aspect or appearance: *to wear a smile, or an air of triumph.* **4.** to impair (garments, etc.) by wear: *gloves worn at the fingertips.* **5.** to impair, deteriorate, or consume gradually by use or any continued process: *a well-worn volume.* **6.** to waste or diminish gradually by rubbing, scraping, washing, etc.: *rocks worn by the waves.* **7.** to make (a hole, channel, way, etc.) by such action. **8.** to bring, reduce, make, take, etc. (as specified), by wear or any gradual change: *to wear clothes to rags or a person to a shadow.* **9.** to weary or exhaust: *worn with toil or care.* **10.** to pass (time, etc.) gradually or tediously (commonly fol. by *away* or *out*). **11.** *Colloq.* to accept, tolerate, or be convinced by: *he told me a lie but I wouldn't wear it.* **12. wear out, a.** to wear or use until no longer fit for use: *to wear out clothes or tools.* **b.** to use up. **c.** to exhaust by continued use, strain, or any gradual process: *to wear out patience.* **—***v.i.* **13.** to undergo gradual impairment, diminution, reduction, etc., from wear, use, attrition, or other causes (often fol. by *away, down, out,* or *off*). **14.** to hold out or last under wear, use, or any continued strain: *materials or colours that will wear, or wear well.* **15.** to become; grow gradually: *my patience is wearing thin.* **16.** to pass, as time, etc., esp. slowly or tediously (often fol. by *away* or *on*). **—***n.* **17.** the act of wearing; use, as of a garment: *I have had very good wear from this dress.* **18.** the state of being worn, as on the person. **19.** clothing, garments, or other articles for wearing. **20.** style of dress, adornment, etc., esp. for a particular time, activity, etc.: *evening wear; beach wear.* **21.** gradual impairment, wasting, diminution, etc., as from use: *the carpet shows wear.* [ME *were,* OE *werian,* c. Icel. *verja,* Goth. *wasjan* clothe] **—wear′er,** *n.*

wear[2] (wēə), *v.*, **wore, wearing,** *n. Naut.* **—***v.t.* **1.** to bring (a vessel) on another tack by turning her head away from the wind until the wind is on her stern, and then bringing her head up towards the wind on the other side. **—***n.* **2.** a tactical manoeuvre by which a sailing vessel is changed from one tack to another. [orig. uncert.]

wearability (wēə′rə bĭl′ĭ tĭ), *n.* the ability to withstand the wear and stress of normal use.

wearable (wēə′rə bl), *adj.* **1.** that may be worn. **—***n.* **2.** (*chiefly pl.*) that which may be worn, esp. clothing.

wear and tear, diminution, decay, damage, or injury sustained by ordinary use.

weariful (wĭə′rĭ fəl), *adj.* **1.** wearisome; tedious. **2.** full of weariness. **—wea′rifully,** *adv.* **—wea′rifulness,** *n.*

weariless (wĭə′rĭ lĭs), *adj.* unwearying; tireless.

wearing (wēə′rĭng), *adj.* **1.** relating to or made for wear. **2.** gradually impairing or wasting. **3.** wearying or exhausting. **—wear′ingly,** *adv.*

wearing apparel, dress in general; garments.

wearisome (wĭə′rĭ səm), *adj.* **1.** causing weariness; fatiguing: *a difficult and wearisome march.* **2.** tiresome or tedious: *a wearisome person, day, or book.* **—wea′risomely,** *adv.* **—wea′risomeness,** *n.* **—Syn. 2.** irksome, monotonous, humdrum, dull, prosy. See **tedious.**

weary (wĭə′rĭ), *adj.*, **-rier, -riest,** *v.*, **-ried, -rying. —***adj.* **1.** exhausted physically or mentally by labour, exertion, strain, etc.; fatigued; tired: *weary eyes, feet, or brain.* **2.** characterized by or causing fatigue: *a weary journey.* **3.** impatient or dissatisfied at excess or overlong continuance (often fol. by *of*): *weary of excuses.* **4.** characterized by or causing such impatience or dissatisfaction; tedious; irksome: *a weary wait.* **—***v.t., v.i.* **5.** to make or become weary; fatigue or tire. **6.** to make or grow impatient or dissatisfied at having too much of something (often fol. by *of*). [ME *wery,* OE *wērig*] **—wea′rily,** *adv.* **—wea′riness,** *n.* **—Syn. 1.** wearied, spent. See **tired**[1].

weasand (wē′zənd), *n. Archaic.* **1.** the windpipe or trachea. **2.** the gullet. **3.** the throat. [ME *wesand,* OE *wǣsend,* var. of *wāsend* gullet]

weasel (wē′zəl), *n.* **1.** any of certain small carnivores of the genus *Mustela* (family *Mustelidae*), esp. *M. nivalis,* common in Europe and much of northern Asia, having a long, slender body, and feeding largely on small rodents. **2.** any of various similar animals of the *Mustelidae.* **3.** a cunning, sneaking fellow. **4.** a tracked vehicle used in snow; a kind of tractor. **—***v.i.* **5.** *Chiefly U.S.* to go back on one's word; evade, as an obligation (often fol. by *out*). [ME *wesel,* OE *weosul,* c. G *Wiesel*] **—wea′selly,** *adj.*

weasel's-snout (wē′zəlz snout′), *n.* the calf's-snout.

weasel words, *U.S.* intentionally ambiguous statements.

weather (wĕth′ə), *n.* **1.** the state of the atmosphere with respect to wind, temperature, cloudiness, moisture, pressure, etc. **2.** windy or stormy weather. **3. keep one's weather eye open,** *Colloq.* to be on one's guard; keep a sharp lookout. **4. make heavy weather of,** to have a lot of difficulty coping with (something). **5. under the weather,** *Colloq.* **a.** indisposed; ill; ailing. **b.** drunk. *—v.t.* **6.** to expose to the weather; to dry, season, or otherwise affect by exposure to the air or atmosphere. **7.** to discolour, disintegrate, or affect injuriously, as by atmospheric agencies. **8.** to bear up against and come safely through (a storm, danger, trouble, etc.). **9.** *Naut.* (of a ship, mariner, etc.) to pass or sail to the windward of: *to weather a cape.* **10.** *Archit.* to cause to slope, so as to shed water. *—v.i.* **11.** to undergo change, as discoloration or disintegration, as the result of exposure to atmospheric conditions. **12.** to endure or resist exposure to the weather. **13.** to go or come safely through a storm, danger, trouble, etc. (fol. by *through*). *—adj.* **14.** of or pertaining to the side or part, as of a ship, that is exposed to the wind: *the weather bow.* [ME and OE *weder*, c. D *weder*, G *Wetter*, Icel. *vedhr*]

weather-beaten (wĕŧħ′ə bē′tn), *adj.* **1.** bearing evidences of exposure to the weather. **2.** seasoned or hardened by exposure to weather: *a weather-beaten face.*

weatherboard (wĕŧħ′ə bôd′), *n.* **1.** one of a series of thin boards, usually thicker along one edge than the other, nailed on an outside wall or a roof in overlapping fashion to form a protective covering which will shed water. **2.** *Naut.* the side of a vessel towards the wind. *—v.t.* **3.** to cover or furnish with weatherboards.

weatherboarding (wĕŧħ′ə bô′dĭng), *n.* **1.** a covering or facing of weatherboards or the like. **2.** weatherboards collectively.

weatherbound (wĕŧħ′ə bound′), *adj.* delayed by bad weather.

Weather Bureau, a branch of the U.S. Department of Commerce, performing the functions of the Meteorological Office in Britain.

weathercock (wĕŧħ′ə kŏk′), *n.* **1.** a weathervane in the shape of a cock. **2.** any weathervane. **3.** a fickle or inconstant person or thing. *—v.i.* **4.** (of an aeroplane or missile) to tend to turn into the relative wind.

weathered (wĕŧħ′əd), *adj.* **1.** seasoned or otherwise affected by exposure to the weather or elements. **2.** (of wood) discoloured or stained by the action of air, rain, etc., or by artificial means. **3.** (of rocks) worn, disintegrated, or changed in colour or composition, by the action of the elements. **4.** *Archit.* made sloping or inclined, as a window-sill, to prevent the lodgement of water.

weather forecast, a description of the prevailing weather conditions and a forecast of those of the immediate future, based on meteorological observation.

weather-gauge (wĕŧħ′ə gāj′), *n.* **1.** the (advantageous) position of a ship when it is to windward of another ship. **2.** the position of advantage; the upper hand.

weatherglass (wĕŧħ′ə gläs′), *n.* any of various instruments, as a barometer or a hygroscope, designed to indicate the state of the atmosphere.

weatherly (wĕŧħ′ə lĭ), *adj.* *Naut.* (of a boat) making very little leeway when close-hauled. **—weath′erliness,** *n.*

weatherman (wĕŧħ′ə măn′), *n., pl.* **-men.** *Colloq.* **1.** one who foretells weather. **2.** one who is employed in a meteorological office.

weather map, a map or chart showing meteorological conditions over a wide area at a particular time, compiled from simultaneous observations at different places.

weatherproof (wĕŧħ′ə prōōf′), *adj.* **1.** proof against the weather; able to withstand exposure to all kinds of weather. *—v.t.* **2.** to make proof against the weather.

weathership (wĕŧħ′ə shĭp′), *n.* a ship that goes to sea specifically to make meteorological observations.

weatherside (wĕŧħ′ə sīd′), *n.* *Naut.* the windward side.

weather station, an installation equipped and used for the making of meteorological observations.

weather strip, a narrow strip, as of rubber, metal, wood, etc., covering the joint between a door, window sash, or the like, and the jamb, casing, etc., to exclude wind, rain, etc.

weather-strip (wĕŧħ′ə strĭp′), *v.t.,* **-stripped, -stripping.** to fit with weather strips.

weather-stripping (wĕŧħ′ə strĭp′ĭng), *n.* **1.** a weather strip. **2.** weather strips collectively.

weathervane (wĕŧħ′ə vān′), *n.* a vane for indicating the direction of the wind; a weathercock.

weatherwise (wĕŧħ′ə wīz′), *adj.* **1.** skilful in predicting weather. **2.** skilful in predicting reactions, opinions, etc.

weatherworn (wĕŧħ′ə wôn′), *adj.* weatherbeaten.

weave (wēv), *v.,* **wove** or (*esp. for defs 5 and 9*) **weaved; woven** or **wove; weaving;** *n.* *—v.t.* **1.** to interlace (threads, yarns, strips, fibrous material, etc.) so as to form a fabric or texture. **2.** to form by interlacing threads, yarns, strands, or strips of some material: *to weave a basket, to weave cloth.* **3.** to form by combining various elements or details into a connected whole: *to weave a tale or a plot.* **4.** to introduce as an element or detail into a connected whole: *to weave a melody into a musical composition.* **5.** to follow in a winding course; to move from side to side: *to weave one's way through traffic.* *—v.i.* **6.** to weave cloth, etc. **7.** to become woven or interwoven. **8.** to move from side to side. **9.** to wind in and out of or through: *she weaved through the crowd.* **10. get weaving,** *Colloq.* to make a start, esp. hurriedly, enthusiastically, etc. *—n.* **11.** a manner of interlacing yarns: *plain, twill, or satin weave.* [ME *weve*, OE *wefan*, c. G *weben*] **—Syn. 3.** contrive, fabricate, construct.

Weave
A, Warp; B, Weft

weaver (wē′və), *n.* **1.** one who weaves. **2.** one whose occupation is weaving. **3.** a weaverbird.

weaverbird (wē′ və bûd′), *n.* any of numerous (chiefly African and Asiatic) passerine birds of the family *Ploceidae,* related to the finches and building elaborately woven nests.

Weaverbird,
Ploceus cucullatus
(Ab. 7 in. long)

weaver's knot, sheet bend. Also, **weaver's hitch.**

web (wĕb), *n., v.,* **webbed, webbing.** *—n.* **1.** something formed as by weaving or interweaving. **2.** a thin silken fabric spun by spiders, and also by the larvae of some insects, as the tent caterpillars, etc.; cobweb. **3.** a woven fabric, esp. a whole piece of cloth in the course of being woven or after it comes from the loom. **4.** anything resembling this, as seeming to be interlaced, tightly woven, or closely linked. **5.** a tangled intricate state of circumstances, events, etc.: *the web of intrigue.* **6.** *Zool.* **a.** a membrane which connects the digits of an animal. **b.** that which connects the toes of aquatic birds and aquatic mammals. **7.** *Ornith.* **a.** the series of barbs on each side of the shaft of a feather. **b.** the series on both sides, collectively. **8.** the vertical member in a rolled or fabricated beam. **9.** *Mach.* the radius portion of a crank, connecting the axle and the crankpin. **10.** cell (def. 10). **11.** a large reel of paper, esp. as used in certain types of printing. *—v.t.* **12.** to cover with or as with a web; envelop. [ME and OE, c. D and LG *webbe*, Icel. *vefr*; akin to WEAVE] **—web′less,** *adj.* **—web′like′,** *adj.*

Webb (wĕb), *n.* **1. Beatrice Potter,** 1858–1943, English writer on economic and social problems. **2.** her husband, **Sidney James** (*Lord Passfield*), 1859–1947, English economist and sociologist. **3. John,** 1611–72, English architect.

webbed (wĕbd), *adj.* **1.** having the digits connected by a web, as the foot of a duck or a beaver. **2.** (of the digits) connected thus. **3.** formed like or with a web.

webbing (wĕb′ĭng), *n.* **1.** woven material of hemp, cotton, or jute, in bands of various widths, for use where strength is required. **2.** such woven bands nailed on furniture under springs or upholstery, for support. **3.** *Zool.* the membrane forming a web or webs.

webby (wĕb′ĭ), *adj.* **1.** pertaining to, of the nature of, or resembling a web. **2.** webbed.

weber (vā′bə, wē′bə), *n.* *Elect.* the derived SI unit of magnetic flux, defined as the flux which, linking a circuit of one turn, produces in it an electromotive force of one volt as it is reduced to zero at a uniform rate in one second; equal to 10^8 maxwells. *Symbol:* Wb [named after Wilhelm WEBER]

Weber (vā′bə; *Ger.* vĕ′bər), *n.* **1. Baron Karl Maria von** (*Ger.* kärl mä rē′ä fŏn), 1786–1826, German composer. **2. Ernst Heinrich** (*Ger.* ĕrnst hīn′rĭкн), 1795–1878, German physiologist. **3.** his brother, **Wilhelm Eduard** (*Ger.* vĭl′hĕlm ĕ′dōō ärt), 1804–91, German physicist. **4. Max** (*Ger.* mäks), 1864–1920, German sociologist and economist.

Webern (vā′bən; *Ger.* vĕ′bərn), *n.* **Anton von** (*Ger.* än′tōn fŏn), 1883–1945, Austrian composer.

webfoot (wĕb′fŏŏt′), *n., pl.* **-feet.** a foot with the toes joined by a web. **—web′-foot′ed,** *adj.*

web-offset (wĕb′ŏf′sĕt′), *n.* **1.** the offset lithographic printing process adapted for printing a continuous reel in one or several colours on both sides of the paper. *—adv., adj.* **2.** (printed) by this process.

webster (wĕb′stə), *n. Obs. or Dial.* a weaver.
Webster (wĕb′stə), *n.* **1. Daniel,** 1782–1852, U.S. statesman and orator. **2. John,** 1580?–1625?, English dramatist. **3. Noah,** 1758–1843, U.S. lexicographer.
web-toed (wĕb′tōd′), *adj.* web-footed.
wed (wĕd), *v.*, **wedded** or **wed, wedding.** —*v.t.* **1.** to bind oneself to (a person) in marriage; take for husband or wife. **2.** to unite (a couple) or join (one person to another) in marriage or wedlock; marry. **3.** to bind by close or lasting ties; attach firmly: *to be wedded to a theory.* —*v.i.* **4.** to contract marriage; marry. **5.** to become united as if in wedlock. [ME; OE *weddian* pledge, c. G *wetten* bet, Icel. *vedhja* pledge]
we'd (wēd; *unstressed* wĭd), contraction of *we had, we should,* or *we would.*
Wed., Wednesday.
wedded (wĕd′ĭd), *adj.* **1.** united in matrimony; married. **2.** joined. **3.** joined by devotion: *he was wedded to the cause.*
Weddell Sea (wĕd′l), a wide arm of the S Atlantic, in Antarctica.
wedding (wĕd′ĭng), *n.* **1.** the act or ceremony of marrying; marriage; nuptials. **2.** a celebration of an anniversary of a marriage, as a silver wedding, celebrated on the 25th anniversary of a marriage. [ME; OE *weddung.* See WED] —**Syn. 1.** See **marriage.**
wedding breakfast, a meal taken after a wedding ceremony in celebration of the event.
wedding cake, a cake, traditionally made in tiers and coated with icing, cut by a bride and bridegroom and eaten at a wedding reception.
wedding dress, a dress, usually white and floor-length, often having a train, worn by a bride at her wedding.
wedding ring, 1. a ring, usually of gold, silver, or platinum, placed on the finger of the bride during a wedding ceremony, and worn afterwards. **2.** a similar ring sometimes worn by married men.
Wedekind (*Ger.* vā′də kĭnt), *n.* **Frank** (*Ger.* frängk), 1864–1918, German poet and dramatist.
wedge (wĕj), *n., v.,* **wedged, wedging.** —*n.* **1.** a device (one of the so-called simple machines) consisting of a piece of hard material with two principle faces meeting in a sharply acute angle. **2.** a piece of anything of like shape: *a wedge of pie or cheese.* **3.** *Meteorol.* a region of relatively high pressure, extending from an anticyclone, with isobars in the shape of a wedge. **4.** a wedge-shaped cuneiform character or stroke. **5.** something that serves to part, divide, etc.: *a disrupting wedge divided the loyalties of party members.* **6.** *Mil.* (formerly) a tactical formation generally in the form of a V with the point towards the enemy. **7. thin end of the wedge,** something small or insignificant which is likely to lead to something large and important. —*v.t.* **8.** to cleave or split with or as with a wedge. **9.** to pack or fix tightly by driving in a wedge or wedges. **10.** to thrust, drive, or fix (in, between, etc.) like a wedge: *to wedge oneself through a narrow opening.* **11.** to knead (clay) so as to gain a uniform consistency. —*v.i.* **12.** to force a way (in, etc.) like a wedge. [ME; OE *wecg,* c. d. G *Weck*] —**wedge′like′, wedg′y,** *adj.*

Wedge

wedge heel, a solid wedge-shaped piece on a woman's shoe, widest at the back of the sole, tapering to nothing at the front.
Wedgwood (wĕj′wo͝od′), *n.* **1. Josiah,** 1730–95, English potter. **2.** a type of artistic pottery with tinted (usually blue) ground and white decoration in relief in designs based on Greek and Roman models. —*adj.* **3.** pertaining to or made or originated by Josiah Wedgwood.
Wedgwood blue, a light shade of greyish blue, characteristic of that used on Wedgwood pottery.
wedlock (wĕd′lŏk), *n.* the state of marriage; matrimony. [ME *wedlok,* OE *wedlāc,* f. *wed* pledge + *-lāc,* suffix making neut. nouns]
Wednesbury (wĕnz′bə rĭ, -brĭ), *n.* a town in England, in Staffordshire. 34,511 (1961).
Wednesday (wĕnz′dĭ), *n.* the fourth day of the week, following Tuesday. [ME *Wednesdai,* OE *Wōdnes dæg* Woden's day, c. D *Woensdag,* Dan. *Onsdag*; trans. of L *Mercurii diēs*]
wee (wē), *adj.,* **weer, weest,** *n.* —*adj.* **1.** little; very small. —*n.* **2.** *Scot.* a short space of time. [ME *we,* var. of *wei* (small) quantity, OE *wēg* weight, amount]
weed[1] (wēd), *n.* **1.** a plant growing wild, esp. in cultivated ground to the exclusion or injury of the desired crop. **2.** any useless, troublesome, or noxious plant, esp. one that grows profusely. **3.** *Colloq.* a cigar or cigarette. **4.** *Colloq.* a marijuana cigarette. **5.** a thin or weakly person esp. one regarded as stupid or infantile. **6.** a sorry animal, esp. a horse unfit for racing or breeding purposes. **7. the weed,** *Colloq.* **a.** tobacco. **b.** marijuana. —*v.t.* **8.** to free from weeds or troublesome plants: *to weed a garden.* **9.** to root out or remove (a weed) (often fol. by *out*). **10.** to remove as being undesirable or superfluous (often fol. by *out*): *to weed out undesirable members.* **11.** to rid of what is undesirable or superfluous. —*v.i.* **12.** to remove weeds or the like. [ME *wede,* OE *wēod*] —**weed′er,** *n.* —**weed′less,** *adj.* —**weed′like′,** *adj.*
weed[2] (wēd), *n.* **1.** (*pl.*) mourning garments: *widow's weeds.* **2.** a mourning band of black crepe or cloth, as on a man's hat or coat sleeve. **3.** *Archaic or Dial.* a garment or clothing or dress: *clad in rustic weeds.* [ME *wede,* OE *wǣd,* var. of *wǣd* garment, c. Icel. *vādh* cloth]
weedkiller (wēd′kĭl′ə), *n.* a substance or preparation used for killing weeds.
weedy (wē′dĭ), *adj.,* **-dier, -diest. 1.** abounding in weeds. **2.** consisting of or pertaining to weeds. **3.** of a poor, straggling growth, as a plant. **4.** thin and weakly, as a person or animal. —**weed′iness,** *n.*
week (wēk), *n.* **1.** a period of seven successive days, commonly understood as beginning (unless otherwise specified or implied) with Sunday, followed by Monday, Tuesday, Wednesday, Thursday, Friday, and Saturday. **2.** the working days or working portion of the seven-day period: *a working week of 40 hours.* **3.** seven days after a specified day: *I shall come Tuesday week.* **4. week in, week out,** continuously; incessantly. [ME *weke,* OE *wice,* c. D *week,* akin to G *Woche*]
weekday (wēk′dā′), *n.* **1.** any day of the week except Sunday and sometimes Saturday. —*adj.* **2.** of or on a weekday: *weekday occupations.*
weekend (*n.* wēk′ĕnd′; *adj., v.* wēk′ĕnd′), *n.* **1.** the end of the working week, esp. the period from Friday night or Saturday to Monday, as a time for recreation, visiting, etc. —*adj.* **2.** of, for, or on a weekend. —*v.i.* **3.** to pass the weekend, as at a place. —**week′en′der,** *n.*
weekly (wēk′lĭ), *adj., adv., n., pl.* **-lies.** —*adj.* **1.** pertaining to a week, or to each week. **2.** done, happening, appearing, etc., once a week, or every week. **3.** continuing or staying for a week: *a weekly boarder.* —*adv.* **4.** once a week. **5.** by the week. —*n.* **6.** a periodical appearing once a week.
Weelkes (wēlks), *n.* **Thomas,** 1575?–1623, English composer of madrigals.
ween (wēn), *v.i., v.t. Archaic.* to think or suppose. [ME *wene,* OE *wēnan* expect, c. G *wähnen* imagine]
weeny (wē′nĭ), *adj. Colloq.* very small; tiny.
weep[1] (wēp), *v.,* **wept, weeping,** *n.* —*v.i.* **1.** to manifest grief or anguish, orig. by outcry, now by tears; shed tears, as from sorrow, unhappiness, or any overpowering emotion; cry: *to weep for joy or rage.* **2.** to let fall drops of water or liquid; drip. **3.** to exude water or liquid, as soil, rock, a plant stem, a sore, etc. —*v.t.* **4.** to weep for; mourn with tears or other expression of sorrow: *he wept his dead brother.* **5.** to shed (tears, etc.). **6.** to let fall or give forth in drops: *trees weeping odorous gums.* **7.** to pass, bring, put, etc., with the shedding of tears (fol. by *away, out,* etc.): *to weep one's eyes out.* —*n.* **8.** *Colloq.* weeping, or a fit of weeping. **9.** exudation of water or liquid. [ME *wepe,* OE *wēpan* wail, c. Goth. *wōpjan* call] —**Syn. 1.** sob, bewail, lament.
weep[2] (wēp), *n.* the lapwing, *Vanellus vanellus,* of Europe, so called from its cries.
weeper (wē′pə), *n.* **1.** one who weeps. **2.** a hired mourner at a funeral. **3.** something worn as a symbol of mourning.
weepie (wē′pĭ), *n. Colloq.* a sentimental film or play. [WEEP[1] + -IE]
weeping (wē′pĭng), *adj.* **1.** that weeps. **2.** expressing sorrow by shedding tears. **3.** (of trees, etc.) having slender, drooping branches.
weeping willow, a commonly cultivated willow with long pendulous branches; probably a native of China.
weepy (wē′pĭ), *adj.* **1.** tearful; likely to burst into tears for the slightest reason. **2.** exuding moisture or the like.
weever (wē′və), *n.* **1.** either of two small marine fishes of the genus *Trachinus, T. vipera* (**lesser weever**), common in British waters, and the rarer *T. draco* (**greater weever**), notable for their poison glands at the base of certain spinous fins. **2.** any fish of the same family (*Trachinidae*). [? OE *wifer* dart (c. Icel. *vifr* sword); modern meaning by association with obs. *wyver* WYVERN]
weevil (wē′vĭl), *n.* **1.** any of the numerous beetles of the family *Curculionidae,* many of which are economically important, being destructive to nuts, grain, fruit, the stems of leaves, the pitch of trees, etc.; a snout-beetle. **2.** any of the beetles of the family *Lariidae,* known as **seed-weevils** or **bean-weevils.** [ME *wevel,* OE *wifel*; akin to WAVE or WEAVE]
weevilly (wē′vĭ lĭ), *adj.* infested with weevils. Also, **weevilled** (wē′vĭld); *Chiefly U.S.,* **weevily, weeviled.**
wee-wee (wē′wē′), *Childish.* —*n.* **1.** urine. —*v.i.* **2.** to urinate.

weft (wĕft), *n.* **1.** woof or filling yarns which interlace with warp running from selvage to selvage. See diag. under **weave. 2.** a woven piece. [ME and OE. See WEAVE]

Wehrmacht (vĕə′mäkt; *Ger.* vĕr′mäKHt), *n.* the armed forces of Germany (1935–45), prior to and during World War II. [G: defence force]

Weichsel (*Ger.* vīk′səl), *n.* German name of the **Vistula.**

weigela (wī gē′lə, -jē′-, wī′gĭ lə), *n.* any of various shrubby, caprifoliaceous plants of the genus *Weigela*, native in E Asia, including species or varieties familiar in cultivation, with funnel-shaped white, pink, or crimson flowers. [t. NL, after C.E. *Weigel*, 1748–1831, German physician]

weigh[1] (wā), *v.t.* **1.** to ascertain the weight of by means of a balance, scale, or other mechanical device: *to weigh gold, gases, persons, etc.* **2.** to hold up or balance, as in the hand, in order to estimate the weight. **3.** to measure (a certain quantity of something) according to weight (usually fol. by *out*): *to weigh out 5 lbs of sugar.* **4.** to bear (down) by weight, heaviness, oppression, etc.: *weighed down with care, a bough weighed down by fruit.* **5.** to balance in the mind; consider carefully in order to reach an opinion, decision, or choice (sometimes fol. by *up*): *to weigh facts or a proposal; to weigh up the pros and cons.* **6.** to raise or lift (now chiefly in the phrase *to weigh anchor*). **7.** *Obs.* to regard or esteem. **8. weigh one's words,** to consider and choose one's words carefully in speaking or writing. *—v.i.* **9.** to have weight or heaviness: *to weigh little or less, to weigh a ton.* **10.** to have importance, moment, or consequence: *wealth weighs little in this case.* **11.** to bear down as a weight or burden: *such responsibility weighed upon him.* **12. weigh in, a.** (of a boxer or wrestler) to be weighed before a fight. **b.** (of a jockey) to be weighed after a race. [ME *weghe*, OE *wegan* carry, weigh, c. D *wegen*, G *wägen*, Icel. *vega*] **—weigh′able,** *adj.* **—weigh′er,** *n.* **—Syn. 5.** See **study.**

weigh[2] (wā), *n. Naut.* **under weigh,** in motion, as a ship that has weighed anchor. [special use of WEIGH[1]]

weighbridge (wā′brĭj′), *n.* a road-level weighing machine for vehicles; used esp. to determine the weight of their loads.

weigh-in (wā′ĭn′), *n.* the checking of a contestant's weight, as before a boxing or wrestling match, or a jockey's weight after a horserace.

weight (wāt), *n.* **1.** amount of heaviness; amount a thing weighs. **2.** the force which gravitation exerts upon a material body. It varies with altitude and latitude. It is often taken as a measure of the mass, which does not vary, and is equal to the mass times the acceleration due to gravity. **3.** a system of units for expressing weight or mass: *avoirdupois weight.* **4.** a unit of weight or mass. **5.** a body of determinate mass, as of metal, for using on a balance or scale in measuring the weight or mass of (or weighing) objects, substances, etc. **6.** one of a series of standard divisions within which boxers or wrestlers fight, according to how much they weigh. **7.** a quantity of a substance determined by weighing: *a half-ounce weight of gold dust.* **8.** any heavy mass or object, esp. an object used because of its heaviness: *the weights of a clock.* **9.** pressure or oppressive force, as of something burdensome: *the weight of cares, sorrows.* **10.** a heavy load or burden: *that is such a weight I can't lift it.* **11.** a burden, as of care or responsibility: *to remove a weight from my mind.* **12.** importance, moment, consequence, or effective influence: *an opinion of great weight, men of weight.* **13.** stress (def. 7). **14.** a measure of the relative importance of an item in a statistical population. **15.** (of clothing) the relative thickness as determined by the weather. **16.** *Print.* the degree of blackness of a typeface; the extent to which a bold typeface is heavier than its roman equivalent. **17. by weight,** according to weight measurement. *—v.t.* **18.** to add weight to; load with additional weight. **19.** to load (fabrics, threads, etc.) with mineral or other matter to increase the weight or bulk. **20.** to burden with or as with weight: *to be weighted with years.* **21.** *Statistics.* to give a (statistical) weight to. **22. carry weight,** to have influence or importance. **23. pull one's weight,** to do one's fair share of work. **24. throw one's weight around** or **about, a.** to behave in an aggressive or selfish fashion. **b.** to use one's influence, personality, etc., to gain one's own ends without regard for others. [ME; OE *wiht*, c. D *wicht*, G *Wucht*. See WEIGH[1]]

weight density, the weight per unit volume.

weighting (wā′tĭng), *n.* an increased amount, as of salary or the like, to balance the higher cost of living in a particular area.

weightlessness (wāt′lĭs nĭs), *n.* the state of being without apparent weight as experienced in free fall, due to the absence of any apparent gravitational pull. Also, **zero gravity.**

weight-lifting (wāt′lĭf′tĭng), *n.* the sport of lifting barbells of specified weights, in competition or for exercise. **—weight′-lift′er,** *n.*

weighty (wā′tĭ), *adj.*, **-tier, -tiest. 1.** having considerable weight; heavy; ponderous. **2.** burdensome or onerous: *the weighty cares of sovereignty.* **3.** important or momentous: *weighty negotiations.* **4.** influential: *a weighty financier.* **—weight′ily,** *adv.* **—weight′iness,** *n.* **—Syn. 3.** See **heavy.**

Weihaiwei (wā′hī wā′), *n.* a seaport and district in NE China, in Shantung province: leased to Great Britain 1898–1930. 175,000 pop. (est. 1950); 285 sq. mi.

Weil (*Fr.* vĕy), *n.* **Simone** (*Fr.* sə mōn′), 1903–43, French philosopher.

Weill (*Ger.* vīl), *n.* **Kurt** (*Ger.* ko͝ort), 1900–50, German composer, in the U.S. after 1935.

Weimar (vī′mä; *Ger.* vī′mär), *n.* a city in SW East Germany. 66,675 (est. 1955).

Weimaraner (vī′mə rä′nə), *n.* one of a breed of hunting dogs, originating in Germany, about 2 ft high, having a smooth grey coat and docked tail.

Weimar Republic, the German Republic from 1919 to 1933: founded at Weimar.

Weingartner (vīn′gät′nə; *Ger.* vīn′gärt nər), *n.* **Paul Felix von** (*Ger.* poul fē′lĭks fōn), 1863–1942, Austrian conductor and composer.

weir (wĭə), *n.* **1.** a dam in a river or stream to stop and raise the water, as for conducting it to a mill, for purposes of irrigation, etc. **2.** an obstruction placed across a stream thereby causing the water to pass through a particular opening or notch, thus measuring the quantity flowing. **3.** a fence, as of brush, narrow boards, or a net, set in a stream, channel, etc., for catching fish. [ME and OE *wer*, c. G *Wehr*]

weird (wĭəd), *adj.* **1.** involving or suggesting the supernatural; unearthly or uncanny: *a weird scene, light, or sound.* **2.** *Colloq.* startlingly or extraordinarily singular, odd, or queer: *a weird get-up.* **3.** concerned with fate or destiny.
—n. **4.** *Archaic or Scot.* fate or destiny. **5.** (*cap.*) *Obs. or Archaic.* fate personified, or one of the Fates. [ME *werd*, n., OE *wyrd* fate; akin to WORTH[2], v.] **—weird′ly,** *adv.* **—weird′ness,** *n.*

—Syn. 1. WEIRD, EERIE, UNEARTHLY, UNCANNY refer to that which is mysterious and apparently outside natural law. That is WEIRD which is suggestive of the fateful intervention of supernatural influences in human affairs: *the weird adventures of a group lost in the jungle.* That is EERIE which, by suggesting the ghostly, makes one's flesh creep: *an eerie moaning from a deserted house.* That is UNEARTHLY which seems by its nature to belong to another world: *an unearthly light which preceded the storm.* That is UNCANNY which is mysterious because of its apparent defiance of the laws established by experience: *an uncanny ability to recall numbers.*

weirdie (wĭə′dĭ), *n. Colloq.* one who behaves in a strange, abnormal, or eccentric way. Also, **weirdy.** [f. WEIRD + -IE]

weird sisters, 1. the Fates. **2.** the Norns.

Weismann (*Ger.* vīs′män), *n.* **August** (*Ger.* ou′go͝ost), 1834–1914, German biologist.

Weismannism (vīs′mə nĭz′əm), *n.* the theories and teachings of the German biologist August Weismann, esp. his theory respecting the continuity of the germ plasm and its isolation from the body plasm, with the accompanying doctrine that acquired characters in the latter are not and cannot be inherited.

Weisshorn (vīs′hôn′; *Ger.* vīs′hŏrn), *n.* a mountain in the Alps in S Switzerland, in Valais canton. 14,804 ft.

Weizmann (vīts′mən; *Ger.* vīts′män), *n.* **Chaim** (kī′ĭm), 1874–1952, Israeli chemist and Zionist leader, born in Russia: first president of Israel, 1948–52.

weka (wā′kə, wē′kə), *n.* any of several large, flightless, New Zealand rails constituting the genus *Gallirallus.* [t. Maori]

welch (wĕlsh), *v.t., v.i. Slang.* welsh. **—welch′er,** *n.*

Welch (wĕlsh), *adj., n.* Welsh.

Welchman (wĕlsh′mən), *n., pl.* **-men.** Welshman.

welcome (wĕl′kəm), *interj., n., v.,* **-comed, -coming,** *adj.* *—interj.* **1.** (a word of kindly greeting as to one whose coming gives pleasure): *welcome, friends!* *—n.* **2.** a kindly greeting or reception, as of one whose coming gives pleasure: *to give one a warm welcome.* *—v.t.* **3.** to greet the coming of (a person, etc.) with pleasure or kindly courtesy. **4.** to receive or regard as welcome: *to welcome a change.* **5.** to receive or greet the arrival (of a person) with displeasure, or the like: *they welcomed the leader with silence.* *—adj.* **6.** gladly received, as one whose coming gives pleasure: *a welcome visitor.* **7.** agreeable, as something coming, occurring, or experienced: *a welcome letter, a welcome rest.* **8.** given full right by the cordial consent of others: *welcome to anything he can find.* **9.** free to enjoy courtesies, etc., without being under obligation (used in conventional response to thanks): *you are quite welcome.* [ME; OE *wilcuma,* f. *wil-* pleasure + *cuma* guest] **—wel′comeless,** *adj.* **—wel′comely,** *adv.* **—wel′comeness,** *n.* **—wel′comer,** *n.*

welcome-home-husband-however-drunk-you-be (wĕl′kəm hōm′hŭz′bənd hou ĕv′ə drŭngk′yo͞o bē′), *n.* a houseleek.

weld[1] (wĕld), *v.t.* **1.** to unite or fuse (pieces of metal, etc.) by hammering, compression, or the like, esp. after rendering soft or pasty by heat, and sometimes with the addition of fusible material like or unlike the pieces to be united. **2.** to bring into complete union. *—v.i.* **3.** to undergo welding; be capable of being welded. *—n.* **4.** a welded junction or joint. **5.** the act of welding. [var. of WELL², v.] **—weld′able,** *adj.* **—weld′er,** *n.*

weld[2] (wĕld), *n.* **1.** a mignonette, *Reseda luteola,* a native of southern Europe, yielding a yellow dye. **2.** the dye. Also, **wold, woald.** [ME *welde,* c. MLG *walde*]

Welensky (wə lĕn′skĭ), *n.* **Sir Roy,** born 1907, Rhodesian politician: prime minister of the Federation of Rhodesia and Nyasaland 1956–63.

welfare (wĕl′fêə′), *n.* **1.** the state of faring well; well-being: *one's welfare, the physical or moral welfare of society.* **2.** welfare work. **3. the welfare,** any social security agency or such agencies collectively. [ME; see WELL¹, FARE] **—Syn. 1.** prosperity, success, happiness, weal.

welfare state, a state (def. 8) in which the welfare of the people in such matters as social security, health and education, housing, and working conditions is the responsibility of the government.

welfare work, work devoted to the welfare of persons in a community, esp. the aged, sick, poor, etc.

welkin (wĕl′kĭn), *n. Archaic.* the sky; the vault of heaven. [ME *welken(e),* OE *wolcen* cloud, c. G *Wolke*]

Welkom (wĕl′kəm, vĕl′-), *n.* a town in the Republic of South Africa, in the Orange Free State. 97,614 (1960).

well[1] (wĕl), *adv., adj., compar.* **better,** *super.* **best,** *interj.* *—adv.* **1.** in a satisfactory, favourable, or advantageous manner; fortunately or happily: *affairs are going well, to be well supplied, well situated.* **2.** in a good or proper manner: *he behaved very well.* **3.** commendably, meritoriously, or excellently: *to act, write, or reason well, a good work well done.* **4.** with propriety, justice, or reason: *I could not well refuse.* **5.** in satisfactory or good measure; adequately or sufficiently: *think well before you act.* **6.** thoroughly or soundly: *shake well before using; beat well.* **7.** easily; clearly: *I can see it very well.* **8.** to a considerable extent or degree: *a sum well over the amount fixed, dilute the acid well.* **9.** personally; to a great degree of intimacy: *to know a person well.* **10.** Some special adverbial phrases are:
as well, in addition: *she is bringing a friend as well.*
as well as, in addition to; no less than: *he was handsome as well as rich.*
just as well, preferable; more favourable; advisable: *it would be just as well if you went.*
very well, 1. with certainty; undeniably: *you know very well you are late.* **2.** (a phrase used to indicate consent, often with reluctance): *very well, you may go out, but not for long.* **3.** (used ironically and with discontent) satisfactory; pleasing: *it's all very well for you, you don't have to worry about money.*
—adj. **11.** in good health, or sound in body and mind: *I am well; a well man.* **12.** satisfactory or good: *all is well with us.* **13.** proper or fitting. **14.** in a satisfactory position; well-off: *I am very well as I am.* *—interj.* **15.** (used to express surprise, agreement): *well, who would have thought it?* **16.** (used as a preliminary to further speech): *well, as I was saying.* [ME and OE *wel(l),* c. D *wel,* G *wohl,* Icel. *vel,* Goth. *waila*] **—Syn. 11.** healthy, hale, sound, hearty.

well[2] (wĕl), *n.* **1.** a hole drilled into the earth, generally by boring, for the production of water, petroleum, natural gas, brine, or sulphur. **2.** a spring or natural source of water. **3.** a fountain, fountainhead, or source: *Chaucer, well of English undefiled.* **4.** a vessel, receptacle, or reservoir for a liquid: *an inkwell.* **5.** any sunken or deep enclosed space, as a shaft for air or light, or for stairs, a lift, or the like, extending vertically through the floors of a building. **6.** a compartment or enclosure around a ship's pumps to render them easy of access and protect them from being injured by the cargo. [ME and OE, c. G *Welle* wave] *—v.i.* **7.** to rise, spring, or gush, as water, from the earth or some source (often fol. by *up, out,* or *forth*): *tears well up in the eyes.* *—v.t.* **8.** to send welling up or forth: *a fountain welling its pure water.* [ME *welle,* OE *wellan* (c. D *wellen,* Icel. *vella*), var. of *wiellan,* causative of *weallan* boil]

we'll (wēl; *unstressed* wĭl), contraction of *we will* or *we shall.*

well-advised (wĕl′əd vīzd′), *adj.* prudent; acting with care and wisdom. Also (esp. in predicative positions), **well advised.**

Welland Canal (wĕl′ənd), a ship canal in S Canada, in Ontario, connecting lakes Erie and Ontario: 8 locks raise or lower ships 325 ft. 25 mi. long; 25 ft deep.

well-appointed (wĕl′ə poin′tĭd), *adj.* comfortably and adequately equipped, decorated, furnished, etc., as a hotel, house, or the like. Also (esp. in predicative positions), **well appointed.**

wellaway (wĕl′ə wā′), *interj. Archaic.* (an exclamation of sorrow.) Also, **welladay** (wĕl′ə dā′). [ME *welawei,* r. ME and OE *weilāwei* (*wei* t. Scand.; cf. Icel. *vei* woe), r. OE *wā lā wā* woe! la! woe!]

well-balanced (wĕl′băl′ənst), *adj.* **1.** rightly balanced, adjusted, or regulated. **2.** sensible; sane. Also (esp. in predicative positions), **well balanced.**

well-behaved (wĕl′bĭ hāvd′), *adj.* characterized by good behaviour or conduct. Also (esp. in predicative positions), **well behaved.**

well-being (wĕl′bē′ĭng), *n.* good or satisfactory condition of existence; welfare.

well-beloved (wĕl′bĭ lŭvd′), *adj.* dearly loved; very dear. Also (esp. in predicative positions), **well beloved.**

well-born (wĕl′bôn′), *adj.* of good birth or family. Also (esp. in predicative positions), **well born.**

well-bred (wĕl′brĕd′), *adj.* **1.** well brought up, as persons. **2.** showing good breeding, as behaviour, manners, etc. **3.** of good breed, as a domestic animal. Also (esp. in predicative positions), **well bred.**

well-built (wĕl′bĭlt′), *adj.* **1.** that has been built soundly: *a well-built house.* **2.** (of a person) strongly built; broad. Also (esp. in predicative positions), **well built.**

well-chosen (wĕl′chō′zən), *adj.* chosen with care, consideration, and aptness: *her speech centred round a few well-chosen topics.* Also (esp. in predicative positions), **well chosen.**

well-connected (wĕl′kə nĕk′tĭd), *adj.* **1.** having important, powerful, or influential relatives. **2.** having useful connections with influential people. Also (esp. in predicative positions), **well connected.**

well deck, *Naut.* a deck on a ship lying between two raised decks and forming a well below their level.

well-disposed (wĕl′dĭs pōzd′), *adj.* **1.** rightly or properly disposed; well-meaning. **2.** favourably or kindly disposed: *well-disposed hearts.* Also (esp. in predicative positions), **well disposed.**

welldoer (wĕl′do͞o′ə), *n.* **1.** one who does well or acts rightly. **2.** a doer of good deeds.

welldoing (wĕl′do͞o′ĭng), *n.* good conduct or action.

well-dressed (wĕl′drĕst′), *adj.* wearing clothes that are smart, fit well, and are suitable for the occasion. Also (esp. in predicative positions), **well dressed.**

well-earned (wĕl′ûnd′), *adj.* well deserved, as after much effort, hard work, etc.: *a well-earned rest.* Also (esp. in predicative positions), **well earned.**

well-educated (wĕl′ĕd′yo͞o kā′tĭd), *adj.* **1.** having had a good education. **2.** apparently cultured and refined. Also (esp. in predicative positions), **well educated.**

Welles (wĕlz), *n.* **(George) Orson,** born 1915, U.S. actor, producer, and film director.

Wellesley (wĕlz′lĭ), *n.* **1. Arthur.** See **Wellington, 1st Duke of. 2.** his brother, **Richard Colley, Marquis,** 1760–1842, British statesman and administrator: governor-general of India, 1797–1805. **3. Islands,** a group of islands at the head of the Gulf of Carpentaria, in N Australia. **4. College,** a women's university in the U.S., in Massachusetts, founded in 1870.

well-established (wĕl′ĭs tăb′lĭsht), *adj.* **1.** having a reliable reputation, often of some years' standing, and an apparently stable and successful future: *a well-established bank.* **2.** firmly set and unlikely to change: *a well-established fashion.* Also (esp. in predicative positions), **well established.**

well-favoured (wĕl′fā′vəd), *adj.* of pleasing appearance; good-looking. Also (esp. in predicative positions), **well favoured.**

well-fed (wĕl′fĕd′), *adj.* **1.** having a plentiful, balanced diet. **2.** fat; plump. Also (esp. in predicative positions), **well fed.**

---

well′-act′ed, *adj.*
well′-aimed′, *adj.*
well′-ar′gued, *adj.*
well′-armed′, *adj.*
well′-arranged′, *adj.*
well′-bound′, *adj.*
well′-condi′tioned, *adj.*
well′-conduct′ed, *adj.*
well′-consid′ered, *adj.*
well′-cov′ered, *adj.*
well′-cut′, *adj.*
well′-defend′ed, *adj.*
well′-defined′, *adj.*
well′-deserved′, *adj.*
well′-devel′oped, *adj.*
well′-direct′ed, *adj.*
well′-disguised′, *adj.*
well′-drawn′, *adj.*
well′-dried′, *adj.*
well′-drilled′, *adj.*
well′-endowed′, *adj.*
well′-equipped′, *adj.*
well′-fash′ioned, *adj.*
well′-feath′ered, *adj.*

well-found (wĕl′found′), *adj.* well furnished with supplies, necessaries, etc. Also (esp. in predicative positions), **well found.**

well-founded (wĕl′foun′dĭd), *adj.* rightly or justly founded, as on good grounds: *well-founded suspicions.* Also (esp. in predicative positions), **well founded.**

well-groomed (wĕl′grōōmd′), *adj.* **1.** having a fresh, clean, tidy appearance; neatly dressed. **2.** tended, cleaned, curried, etc., with great care, as a horse. Also (esp. in predicative positions), **well groomed.**

well-grounded (wĕl′groun′dĭd), *adj.* **1.** based on good grounds or reasons: well-founded. **2.** well or thoroughly instructed in the first principles of a subject. Also (esp. in predicative positions), **well grounded.**

wellhead (wĕl′hĕd′), *n.* a fountainhead; source.

well-heeled (wĕl′hēld′), *adj. Colloq.* wealthy; prosperous. Also (esp. in predicative positions), **well heeled.**

well-hung (wĕl′hŭng′), *adj.* **1.** of meat or game, hung for a sufficient length of time. **2.** arranged so as to hang well, as a gate. Also (esp. in predicative positions), **well hung.**

well-informed (wĕl′ĭn fômd′), *adj.* **1.** having reliable or full information on a subject. **2.** having information on a variety of subjects: *a well-informed man.* Also (esp. in predicative positions), **well informed.**

Wellington (wĕl′ĭng tən), *n.* **1. Arthur Wellesley, 1st Duke of,** 1769–1852, British general and statesman, prime minister 1828–30. **2.** a seaport in and the capital of New Zealand, in the S part of North Island. 126,700 (est. 1965). See map under **New Zealand.**

wellington boot, 1. Also, **wellington.** a waterproof boot made of rubber, stretching up to the knee. **2.** originally, a leather boot with the front stretching up to above the knee. [named after the Duke of WELLINGTON]

well-knit (wĕl′nĭt′), *adj.* firmly and compactly built.

well-known (wĕl′nōn′), *adj.* **1.** clearly or fully known. **2.** familiarly known, or familiar: *his well-known face.* **3.** generally or widely known: *the well-known sculptor.* Also (esp. in predicative positions), **well known.**

well-lined (wĕl′līnd′), *adj.* (of a purse, pocket, etc.) full of money. Also (esp. in predicative positions), **well lined.**

well-mannered (wĕl′măn′əd), *adj.* polite; courteous. Also (esp. in predicative positions), **well mannered.**

well-meaning (wĕl′mē′nĭng), *adj.* **1.** meaning or intending well: *a well-meaning but tactless person.* **2.** proceeding from good intentions. Also (esp. in predicative positions), **well meaning.**

well-meant (wĕl′mĕnt′), *adj.* well-meaning (def. 2). Also (esp. in predicative positions), **well meant.**

wellnigh (wĕl′nī′), *adv.* very nearly; almost. **—Syn.** See **almost.**

well-off (wĕl′ôf′), *adj.* **1.** in a satisfactory, favourable, or good position or condition. **2.** in good or easy circumstances as to money or means; moderately rich. Also (esp. in predicative positions), **well off.**

well-oiled (wĕl′oild′), *adj. Slang.* drunk. Also (esp. in predicative positions), **well oiled.**

well-ordered (wĕl′ô′dəd), *adj.* properly or efficiently regulated or arranged. Also (esp. in predicative positions), **well ordered.**

wellpoint (wĕl′point′), *n. Civ. Eng.* one of a series of pipes with perforated tips, driven into the ground around an excavation site in order to pump the ground-water level below that of the excavation.

well-preserved (wĕl′prĭ zûvd′), *adj.* **1.** having been kept in good condition. **2.** preserving a young or youthful appearance. Also (esp. in predicative positions), **well preserved.**

well-proportioned (wĕl′prə pô′shənd), *adj.* **1.** having pleasing proportions, esp. as regards size and shape. **2.** (of a person) having a good figure. Also (esp. in predicative positions), **well proportioned.**

well-read (wĕl′rĕd′), *adj.* **1.** having read much: *well-read in science.* **2.** having an extensive and intelligent knowledge of books or literature. Also (esp. in predicative positions), **well read.**

well-rounded (wĕl′roun′dĭd), *adj.* **1.** having an agreeable rounded shape. **2.** full and varied, as a person's life. **3.** sonorous and well constructed, as a phrase or sentence. Also (esp. in predicative positions), **well rounded.**

Wells (wĕlz), *n.* **1. H(erbert) G(eorge),** 1866–1946, English novelist and writer on social and political problems. **2.** a town in SW England, in Somersetshire: cathedral. 6960 (est. 1962).

well-spoken (wĕl′spō′kən), *adj.* **1.** having a cultured, refined accent. **2.** speaking well, fittingly, or pleasingly. **3.** polite in speech. **4.** spoken well, appropriately, etc. Also (esp. in predicative positions), **well spoken.**

wellspring (wĕl′sprĭng′), *n.* **1.** a fountainhead. **2.** a source of anything.

well sweep, sweep (def. 27).

well-thought-of (wĕl′thôt′ŏv′), *adj.* having a good reputation; held in estimation. Also (esp. in predicative positions), **well thought of.**

well-timed (wĕl′tīmd′), *adj.* fittingly timed; opportune; timely: *a well-timed attack.* Also (esp. in predicative positions), **well timed.**

well-to-do (wĕl′tə dōō′), *adj.* **1.** having a sufficiency of means for comfortable living, well off, or prosperous. **2.** characterized by or showing a comfortable sufficiency of means, or prosperity: *well-to-do circumstances.*

well-tried (wĕl′trīd′), *adj.* **1.** thoroughly tried or tested. **2.** (of a person) refined and proper in one's manner of speech and its content. Also (esp. in predicative positions), **well tried.**

well-turned (wĕl′tûnd′), *adj.* **1.** having a pleasing shape: *a well-turned ankle.* **2.** aptly and pleasingly expressed: *a well-turned compliment.* Also (esp. in predicative positions), **well turned.**

well-wisher (wĕl′wĭsh′ə), *n.* one who wishes well to a person, a cause, etc. **—well′-wish′ing,** *adj., n.*

well-worn (wĕl′wôn′), *adj.* **1.** much worn or affected by use: *well-worn garments or carpets, a well-worn volume.* **2.** trite, hackneyed, or stale: *a well-worn saying or theme.* **3.** *Archaic.* fittingly or becomingly worn or borne: *well-worn reserve.* Also (esp. in predicative positions), **well worn.**

Wels (*Ger.* vĕls), *n.* a town in N central Austria. 41,060 (1961).

Welsbach burner (wĕlz′băk; *Ger.* vĕlz′bäKH), a gas burner, consisting essentially of a Bunsen burner, about the flame of which is placed an incombustible mantle (**Welsbach mantle**) composed of thoria and some ceria, which becomes brilliantly incandescent. [named after Karl Auer von *Welsbach*, 1858–1929, Austrian chemist who devised it]

welsh (wĕlsh), *v.t., v.i. Slang.* to cheat by evading payment, esp. of a gambling debt (sometimes fol. by *on*). Also, **welch.** [orig. obscure] **—welsh′er,** *n.*

Welsh (wĕlsh), *adj.* **1.** of or pertaining to Wales, its people, or their language. **—***n.* **2.** the people of Wales. **3.** the Celtic language of Wales. Also, **Welch.** [ME *Welische*, OE *Welisc*, der. *Walh* Briton, foreigner]

Welsh corgi (kô′gĭ). See **corgi.**

Welsh dresser, a sideboard having drawers or compartments below and open shallow shelves above.

Welshman (wĕlsh′mən), *n., pl.* **-men.** a native or inhabitant of Wales. Also, **Welchman.**

Welsh pony, one of a breed of very small, stocky ponies, originally from Wales.

Welsh poppy, a papaveraceous perennial herb with yellow flowers, *Meconopsis cambrica*, occurring in shady places in W Europe.

Welsh rarebit, melted cheese, sometimes mixed with ale or beer, milk, etc., eaten on toast. Also, **Welsh rabbit.** [var. of *Welsh rabbit*, prob. of jocular origin]

---

well′-filled′, *adj.*
well′-fin′ished, *adj.*
well′-fit′ting, *adj.*
well′-formed′, *adj.*
well′-for′tified′, *adj.*
well′-fought′, *adj.*
well′-fur′nished, *adj.*
well′-gov′erned, *adj.*
well′-grown′, *adj.*
well′-horsed′, *adj.*
well′-instruct′ed, *adj.*
well′-intend′ed, *adj.*
well′-inten′tional, *adj.*
well′-judged′, *adj.*
well′-kept′, *adj.*
well′-liked′, *adj.*
well′-look′ing, *adj.*
well′-made′, *adj.*
well′-man′aged, *adj.*
well′-marked′, *adj.*
well′-matched′, *adj.*
well′-mount′ed, *adj.*
well′-named′, *adj.*
well′-or′ganized′, *adj.*
well′-paid′, *adj.*
well′-paint′ed, *adj.*
well′-placed′, *adj.*
well′-planned′, *adj.*
well′-plant′ed, *adj.*
well′-pol′ished, *adj.*
well′-print′ed, *adj.*
well′-rea′soned, *adj.*
well′-reg′ulat′ed, *adj.*
well′-remem′bered, *adj.*
well′-respect′ed, *adj.*
well′-rigged′, *adj.*
well′-sea′soned, *adj.*
well′-served′, *adj.*
well′-set′, *adj.*
well′-set′-up′, *adj.*
well′-sharp′ened, *adj.*
well′-shod′, *adj.*
well′-spent′, *adj.*
well′-stacked′, *adj.*
well′-stocked′, *adj.*
well′-tai′lored, *adj.*
well′-tanned′, *adj.*
well′-taught′, *adj.*
well′-tem′pered, *adj.*
well′-thumbed′, *adj.*
well′-tim′bered, *adj.*
well′-told′, *adj.*
well′-trained′, *adj.*
well′-trav′elled, *adj.*
well′-trimmed′, *adj.*
well′-trod′den, *adj.*
well′-tuned′, *adj.*
well′-ven′tilat′ed, *adj.*
well′-warmed′, *adj.*
well′-wa′tered, *adj.*
well′-wood′ed, *adj.*
well′-word′ed, *adj.*
well′-worked′-out′, *adj.*
well′-writ′ten, *adj.*

Welsh springer spaniel, one of the two breeds of springer spaniel, slightly smaller than the English springer spaniel, and having a distinctive red-and-white coat.

Welsh terrier, a black-and-tan terrier of a breed developed in Wales as a hunting dog.

welt (wĕlt), *n.* **1.** a ridge or wale on the surface of the body, as from the stroke of a stick or whip. **2.** a stroke of this kind. **3.** a strip of leather set in between the edges of the inner sole and upper and the outer sole of a shoe. **4.** a strengthening or ornamental finish along a seam, the edge of a garment, etc. **5.** a type of seam in which one edge is cut close to the stitching line and covered by the other edge which is stitched over it. *—v.t.* **6.** to beat soundly, as with a stick or whip. **7.** to furnish with a welt or welts. [ME *welte, walt*; cf. OE *wæltan, weltan* roll]

Weltanschauung (*Ger.* vĕltʹänʹshou o͝ong), *n. German.* the philosophy of an individual or a group (esp. a race) with an interpretation of world history or civilization.

Weltansicht (*Ger.* vĕltʹän zĭKHt), *n. German.* a world view; an attitude towards, or interpretation of, reality.

welter (wĕlʹtə), *v.i.* **1.** *Archaic.* to roll, toss, or heave, as waves, the sea, etc. **2.** *Archaic.* to lie bathed or be drenched in something, esp. blood. **3.** *Obs.* to roll or tumble about, or wallow, as animals. *—n.* **4.** a rolling or tumbling about: *in the welter of the sea.* **5.** commotion, turmoil, or chaos: *the welter of our mutable world.* [ME, freq. of obs. *welt* roll, OE *weltan.* Cf. MD *welteren,* LG *weltern* roll]

welterweight (wĕlʹtə wātʹ), *n.* a boxer or wrestler with a maximum weight of 10 st. 7 lbs for professionals, 10 st. 8 lbs for amateurs, intermediate in weight between a middleweight and lightweight. [f. *welter* heavyweight rider or boxer (lit. beater, der. WELT, v.) + WEIGHT]

Weltpolitik (*Ger.* vĕltʹpō lĭ tēkʹ), *n. German.* the policy of a nation with respect to the world. [G: world politics]

Weltschmerz (*Ger.* vĕltʹshmĕrts), *n. German.* sorrow felt and accepted as the necessary portion of the world; sentimental pessimism. [G: world-pain]

welwitschia (wĕl wĭchʹĭ ə), *n.* a plant, *Welwitschia mirabilis,* of desert regions of southern Africa, having an extremely long taproot, and a life of several centuries. [named after Friedrich Martin Josef *Welwitsch,* 1807–1872, Portuguese botanist born in Austria]

Welwyn (wĕlʹĭn), *n.* a town in England, in Hertfordshire: one of the first garden cities, founded in 1920. 35,179 (1961). Also, **Welwyn Garden City** (wĕlʹĭn gäʹdn sĭtʹĭ).

Wembley (wĕmʹblĭ), *n.* a district in the NW outer London borough of Brent: football stadium.

Wemyss (wēmz), *n.* a parish in E Scotland, in Fife, on the Firth of Forth: castle. 28,465 (1951).

wen[1] (wĕn), *n.* **1.** *Pathol.* a benign encysted tumour of the skin, esp. on the scalp, containing sebaceous matter; a sebaceous cyst. **2.** *Colloq.* a very large, overcrowded town, esp. London. [ME and OE *wenn,* c. D *wen*]

wen[2] (wĕn), *n.* wynn.

Wenceslaus (wĕnʹsĭs ləs), *n.* **1.** 1361–1419, emperor of the Holy Roman Empire 1378–1400, and king of Bohemia as Wenceslaus IV 1378–1419. **2. Saint** (*Good King Wenceslaus*), *c.* 907–929, prince of Bohemia. Also, **Wenceslas.** German, **Wenzel.**

wench (wĕnch), *n.* **1.** a girl, or young woman. **2.** a rustic or working girl. **3.** *Archaic or Dial.* a prostitute or promiscuous woman. *—v.i.* **4.** to consort with promiscuous women or prostitutes. [ME, var. of *wenchel,* OE *wencel* child. Cf. OE *wancol* weak] **—wenchʹer,** *n.*

Wenchow (wĕnʹchouʹ), *n.* former name of **Yungkia.**

wend (wĕnd), *v.,* **wended** or (*Archaic*) **went; wending.** *—v.t.* **1.** to direct or pursue (one's way, etc.): *he wended his way to the riverside.* *—v.i.* **2.** *Archaic.* to proceed or go. [ME; OE *wendan,* c. D and G *wenden*]

Wend (wĕnd), *n.* a member of a Slavic people in Saxony and adjoining parts of Prussia; Sorb. [t. G: m. *Wende*]

Wendish (wĕnʹdĭsh), *adj.* **1.** of or pertaining to the Wends or their language; Sorbian. *—n.* **2.** Sorbian (def. 2). Also, **Wendʹic.**

Wendy house, a playhouse for children, built in the corner of a room or out of doors as a miniature house. [named after the house built for *Wendy,* character in '*Peter Pan*', a play by J. M. Barrie produced in 1904]

Wenlock (wĕnʹlŏkʹ), *n.* a town in England, in Shropshire. 14,935 (1961).

wenny (wĕnʹĭ), *adj.* **1.** like a wen. **2.** having a wen.

Wensleydale (wĕnsʹlĭ dālʹ), *n.* **1.** a white cheese, having a subtle flavour and a flaky texture. **2.** a breed of long-haired woolly sheep.

went (wĕnt), *v.* **1.** pt. of **go. 2.** archaic pt. and pp. of **wend.**

wentletrap (wĕnʹtl trăpʹ), *n.* any of the handsome, usually white, spiral-shelled marine gastropods constituting the genus *Scalaria* or the family *Scalariidae.* [t. D: m. *wenteltrap* winding stair, spiral shell]

Wentworth (wĕntʹwûthʹ), *n.* **Thomas.** See **Strafford, 1st Earl of.**

Wenzel (*Ger.* vĕnʹtsəl), *n.* German name of **Wenceslaus.**

wept (wĕpt), *v.* pt. and pp. of **weep**[1].

were (wû; *unstressed* wə), *v.* pt. ind. pl. and subj. sing. and pl. of **be.** [ME; OE *wǣron, wǣre(n),* c. G *waren.* See WAS]

we're (wĭə), contraction of *we are.*

weren't (wûnt), contraction of *were not.*

werewolf (wĭəʹwo͝olfʹ), *n., pl.* **-wolves** (-wo͝olvzʹ). (in old superstition) a human being turned preternaturally into a wolf, or capable of assuming the form of a wolf, while retaining human intelligence. Also, **werwolf.** [ME *werwolf,* OE *wer(e)wulf,* f. *wer* man (c. L *vir*) + WOLF]

Werfel (*Ger.* vĕrʹfəl), *n.* **Franz** (*Ger.* fränts), 1890–1945, German novelist, dramatist, and poet, born in Prague.

wergild (wûʹgĭldʹ, wēəʹ-), *n. Early Eng. Law.* a fine for manslaughter and other crimes against the person, by paying which to the relatives of the deceased, or to the injured person, the offender freed himself from every further obligation or punishment. Also, **weregild** (wĭəʹ-gĭldʹ, wēəʹ-). [ME (Scot.) *weregylt,* OE *wer(e)gild,* f. *wer* man + *gild* compensation (see YIELD)]

Werner (*Ger.* vĕrʹnər), *n.* **Alfred** (*Ger.* älʹfrĕt), 1866–1919, Swiss chemist.

wernerite (wûʹnə rītʹ), *n.* scapolite.

wert (wût; *unstressed* wət), *v. Archaic.* 2nd pers. sing. pt. indic. and subj. of **be.**

Weser (vāʹzə; *Ger.* vėʹzər), *n.* a river flowing through northern West Germany into the North Sea. ab. 300 mi.

Wesermünde (*Ger.* vė zər mʏnʹdə), *n.* former name of **Bremerhaven.**

Wesker (wĕsʹkə), *n.* **Arnold,** born 1932, English dramatist.

Wesley (wĕzʹlĭ, wĕsʹlĭ), *n.* **1. Charles,** 1707–88, English Methodist preacher and hymn-writer. **2.** his brother, **John,** 1703–91, English preacher, founder of Methodism.

Wesleyan (wĕzʹlĭ ən), *adj.* **1.** of or pertaining to John Wesley, founder of Methodism. **2.** pertaining to Methodism. *—n.* **3.** a follower of John Wesley. **4.** a member of the denomination founded by him; a Methodist. **—Wesʹleyanism,** *n.*

Wessex (wĕsʹĭks), *n.* **1.** an Anglo-Saxon kingdom, later an earldom, in S England. *Cap.:* Winchester. See map under **Mercia. 2.** (in recent times) a region principally in Dorsetshire, described in Hardy's novels.

Wessex saddleback, a breed of pig, black with a white saddle over its shoulder, reared for pork and bacon.

west (wĕst), *n.* **1.** a cardinal point of the compass, (90° to the right of north) corresponding to the point where the sun is seen to set. **2.** the direction in which this point lies. **3.** (*l.c. or cap.*) a quarter or territory situated in this direction. **4. the West, a.** the western part of the world as distinct from the East or Orient; the Occident. **b.** the countries of Western Europe and the Americas not under Communist government. **c.** the whole western or Pacific part of the United States. **5.** *Ancient and Medieval Hist.* the Western Empire. *—adj.* **6.** directed or proceeding towards the west. **7.** coming from the west: *a west wind.* **8.** lying towards or situated in the west: *the west side.* **9.** *Eccles.* designating, lying towards, or in that part of a church opposite to and farthest from the altar. *—adv.* **10.** in the direction of the sunset; towards or in the west. **11.** from the west (as of wind). **12. go west,** *Colloq.* **a.** to die. **b.** to disappear; be lost. **c.** to go to America. [ME and OE, c. D *west,* G *West,* Icel. *vestr*]

West (wĕst), *n.* **1. Benjamin,** 1738–1820, American painter in England. **2. Mae,** born 1892, U.S. film actress. **3. Dame Rebecca** (*Cicily Fairfield*), born 1892, English novelist and critic.

West Bengal, a state in E India; formerly part of the province of Bengal. 34,926,279 pop. (1961); 33,805 sq. mi. *Cap.:* Calcutta. See **Bengal.**

West Berlin, a city and Land associated with but isolated from West Germany, forming the western part of Berlin (the former **western sector**). 2,190,000 (est. 1966). See **Berlin.**

westbound (wĕstʹboundʹ), *adj.* travelling towards the west.

West Bromwich (brŏmʹĭj, -ĭch), a town and county borough in England, in Staffordshire, near Birmingham. 96,041 (1961).

west by north, *Navig., Survey.* 11° 15′ (one point) north of west; 281° 15′ from due north. *Abbrev.:* W by N.

west by south, *Navig., Survey.* 11° 15′ (one point) south of west; 258°45′ from due north. *Abbrev.:* W by S.

West Country, 1. the SW counties of England (Somerset, Devon, etc.). **2.** a district of England in Somerset and Gloucestershire around Bath and Bristol.

West End, a district of central London noted for its shops, theatres, etc.

wester (wěs′tə), *v.i.* to move or tend westwards.

westering (wěs′tə rĭng), *adj.* moving towards the west.

westerly (wěs′tə lĭ), *adj., adv., n., pl.* **-lies.** —*adj.* **1.** moving, directed, or situated towards the west. **2.** coming from the west: *a westerly gale.* —*adv.* **3.** towards the west. **4.** from the west. —*n.* **5.** a westerly wind.

Westermarck (wěs′tə mäk′; *Fin.* věs′tər màrk), *n.* **Edward Alexander,** 1862–1939, Finnish sociologist in England.

western (wěs′tən), *adj.* **1.** lying towards or situated in the west. **2.** directed or proceeding towards the west. **3.** coming from the west, as a wind. **4.** (*usually cap.*) of or pertaining to the west: *the Western Church.* **5.** (*cap.*) Occidental. —*n.* **6.** *Colloq.* a story or film about the American West. [ME and OE *westerne*]

Western Australia, a state in W Australia. 789,917 pop. (1964); 975,920 sq. mi. *Cap.:* Perth.

Western Church, 1. the Roman Catholic Church, sometimes with the Anglican Church, or, more broadly, the Christian Churches of western Europe and those churches elsewhere which are connected with or have sprung from them. **2.** the Christian Church in the countries once comprised in the Western Empire and in countries evangelized from these countries, or that part of the Christian Church which acknowledged the popes after the split between Greek and Latin Christianity.

Western Empire, the western portion of the Roman Empire A.D. 395–476.

westerner (wěs′tə nə), *n.* (*often cap.*) a native or inhabitant of a western area, esp. of the western U.S.

Western Ghats. See **Ghats.**

Western Hemisphere, 1. a hemisphere of the earth cut along a meridian so chosen as to include all of North and South America, but no part of any other continent. **2.** that half of the earth traversed in passing westwards from the prime meridian to 180° longitude.

western hemlock, a coniferous tree, *Tsuga heterophylla,* a native of N America but frequently planted for forestry elsewhere.

Western Islands, Hebrides. Also, **Western Isles.**

westernism (wěs′tə nĭz′əm), *n.* a word, idiom, or practice peculiar to western people, esp. those of the western U.S.

Westernize (wěs′tə nīz′), *v.t.*, **-nized, -nizing.** to make Western in ideas, character, ways, etc. Also, **Westernise.** —**Wes′terniza′tion,** *n.*

westernmost (wěs′tən mōst′), *adj.* farthest west.

Western red cedar, red cedar.

Western Samoa, an independent state comprising the islands of Savai'i, Upolu, and several smaller islands: formerly under the trusteeship of New Zealand. 114,427 pop. (1961); 1133 sq. mi. *Cap.:* Apia.

Westfalen (*Ger.* věst fä′lən), *n.* German name of **Westphalia.**

West Germany, a country in central Europe, formed after World War II as the British, French, and U.S. zones of occupation. 57,864,500 pop. (est. 1963); 94,905 sq. mi. *Cap.:* Bonn. Official name, **Federal Republic of Germany.**

West Ham, a district in the E outer London borough of Newham.

West Hartlepool (hät′lĭ pōōl′), a seaport in England, in Durham. 77,035 (1961).

West Indies, 1. an archipelago in the N Atlantic between North and South America, enclosing the Caribbean Sea and the Gulf of Mexico: divided into the Greater Antilles, the Lesser Antilles, and the Bahamas. **2. Federation of the,** a former federation (1958–62) of British islands in the Caribbean, comprising Barbados, Jamaica, Trinidad and Tobago, and the Windward and Leeward Island colonies. 3,138,458 pop. (1961); 7931 sq. mi. —**West Indian.**

West Indies

westing (wěs′tĭng), *n.* **1.** westward movement or deviation. **2.** the distance due west made on any course tending westwards.

Westinghouse (wěs′tĭng hous′), *n.* **George,** 1846–1914, U.S. inventor, esp. of a type of air-brake.

West Irian (ĭ′rĭ ən), the W part of the island of New Guinea: formerly the Dutch territory of Netherlands New Guinea; since 1963 a province of Indonesia. 750,000 pop. (est. 1961); ab. 159,000 sq. mi. Also, **West New Guinea.** Formerly, **Dutch New Guinea.**

West Lothian (lō′thyən), a county in S Scotland. 92,764 pop. (1961); 120 sq. mi. *Co. town:* Linlithgow. Formerly, **Linlithgow.**

Westm., Westminster.

Westmeath (wěst′mēth′), *n.* a county in the central Republic of Ireland, in Leinster. 52,861 pop. (1961); 680 sq. mi. *Co. town:* Mullingar.

Westminster (wěst′mĭn′stə), *n.* **1.** a central borough (officially a city) in London: Westminster Abbey; Houses of Parliament; Buckingham Palace. 270,140 (est. 1962). **2.** a public school for boys founded in 1339. **3. Statute of.** See **Statute of Westminster.**

Westminster Abbey, a collegiate church in London founded in 1065 by King Edward the Confessor; the place of coronation of every English king and queen, of most royal marriages, and of many national ceremonies.

Westminster Assembly, a convocation, mostly of divines, which met at Westminster from 1643 to 1649, whose decisions on matters of faith and discipline have become the standard of orthodoxy in most English-speaking Presbyterian churches.

Westmld, Westmorland.

Westmorland (wěst′mə lənd, wěs′mə-), *n.* a county in NW England, partially in the Lake District. 67,222 pop. (1961); 789 sq. mi. *Co. town:* Appleby.

west-north-west (wěst′nôth′wěst′), *Navig., Survey.* —*n.* **1.** the point of the compass midway between west and north-west; 290°30′ from north. —*adj.* **2.** lying or situated in this direction. —*adv.* **3.** to, in or from this direction. *Abbrev.:* WNW. Also, *esp. Naut.*, **west-nor'-west** (wěst′nô wěst′).

Weston cell (wěs′tən), *Elect.* a type of primary cell used as a standard of electromotive force, consisting of mercury and cadmium electrodes in a saturated solution of cadmium sulphate; produces 1·0183 volts at 20°C. Also, **cadmium cell.**

Weston-super-Mare (wěs′tən sōō′pə mēə′), *n.* a seaside resort in England, in Somerset. 43,938 (1961).

West Pakistan, a province of Pakistan, NW of India and N of the Arabian Sea. 42,880,378 pop. (1961); 310,236 sq. mi. *Cap.:* Lahore.

Westphalia (wěst fā′lyə), *n.* a former province in NW Germany: treaty (1648) ending the Thirty Years War. Now part of North Rhine-Westphalia. German, **Westfalen.** —**Westpha′lian,** *adj., n.*

West Point, a military reservation in SE New York State, on the Hudson: site of the U.S. Military Academy.

West Prussia, a former province of Prussia, now in Poland. German, **Westpreussen** (*Ger.* věst′proy sən).

West Punjab, a former state in N West Pakistan.

West Riding (rī′dĭng), an administrative division in Yorkshire. 3,644,582 pop. (1961); 2790 sq. mi. *Chief town:* York.

west-south-west (wěst′south′wěst′), *Navig., Survey.* —*n.* **1.** the point of the compass midway between west and south-west; 247°30′ from north. —*adj.* **2.** lying or situated in this direction. —*adv.* **3.** to, in, or from this direction. *Abbrev.:* WSW. Also, *esp. Naut.*, **west-sou'-west** (wěst′sou wěst′).

West Suffolk, an administrative division of Suffolk. 128,918 pop. (1961); 611 sq. mi. *Chief town:* Bury St Edmunds.

West Sussex, an administrative division of Sussex. 411,224 pop. (1961); 628 sq. mi. *Chief town:* Chichester.

West Virginia, a state in the E United States. 1,860,421 pop. (1960); 24,181 sq. mi. *Cap.:* Charleston. *Abbrev.:* W.Va. —**West Virginian.**

westward (wěst′wəd), *adj.* **1.** moving, bearing, facing, or situated towards the west. —*adv.* **2.** westwards. —*n.* **3.** the westward part, direction, or point.

westwardly (wěst′wəd lĭ), *adj.* **1.** having a westward direction or situation. **2.** coming from the west, as a wind. —*adv.* **3.** towards the west. **4.** from the west.

westwards (wěst′wədz), *adv.* towards the west; west. Also, **westward.**

wet (wět), *adj.*, **wetter, wettest,** *n., v.*, **wet** or **wetted, wetting.** —*adj.* **1.** covered or soaked, wholly or in part, with water or some other liquid: *wet hands, a wet sponge.* **2.** moist, damp, or not dry: *wet ink or paint.* **3.** characterized by the presence or use of water or other liquid: *the wet of chemical analysis.* **4.** rainy; having a rainy climate. **5.** characterized by or favouring allowance of the manufacture and sale of alcoholic beverages. **6.** *Colloq.* weak; feeble; spiritless. **7. wet behind the ears,** *Colloq.* naive, lacking maturity, experience, or the like. —*n.* **8.** that which makes wet, as water or other liquid; moisture. **9.** a wet state, condition, or place. **10.** rain. **11.** *U.S.* one who favours allowance of the manufacture and sale of alcoholic beverages. —*v.t.* **12.** to make wet. **13.** to make wet, as by urinating: *the child wet the bed.* **14. wet one's whistle,** *Colloq.* to take a drink. —*v.i.* **15.** to become wet. [ME *wett*, prop. pp. of *wete*, OE *wǣtan* to wet; r. ME *weet*, OE *wǣt*, c. Icel. *vātr*] —**wet′ly,** *adv.* —**wet′ness,** *n.* —**wet′ter,** *n.* —**wet′tish,** *adj.*

—Syn. 1. dampened, drenched. 4. humid, misty, drizzling. 12. WET, DRENCH, SATURATE, SOAK imply moistening something thoroughly. To WET is to moisten in any manner with water or other liquid: *to wet or dampen a cloth.* DRENCH suggests wetting completely as by a downpour: *a heavy rain drenched the fields.* SATURATE implies wetting to the limit of absorption: *to saturate a sponge.* To SOAK is to keep covered or partially covered by a liquid for a time: *to soak beans.*

wet and dry, fine emery paper used either with a lubricant to reduce clogging or in a dry state, for producing a good finish on metal or the like.

wet-and-dry bulb hygrometer (wĕt′n drī′), *Physics.* a psychrometer.

wetback (wĕt′băk′), *n.* a Mexican labourer who enters the U.S. illegally, as by wading across the Rio Grande.

wet blanket, a person or thing that dampens ardour or has a discouraging or depressing effect.

wet-blanket (wĕt′blăng′kĭt), *v.t.* to dampen the ardour of.

wet cell, *Elect.* a cell whose electrolyte is in liquid form and free to flow.

wet dock, a basin into which vessels enter and in which the water is kept at one level by dock gates, irrespective of outside tides.

wet dream, a sexually exciting dream, resulting in an emission while or just after being asleep.

wether (wĕth′ə), *n.* a castrated ram. [ME and OE, c. G *Widder*; akin to L *vitulus* calf]

wet nurse, a woman hired to suckle another's infant.

wet-nurse (wĕt′nûs′), *v.t.*, **-nursed, -nursing.** 1. to act as wet nurse to. 2. *Colloq.* to cosset or pamper.

wet pack, *Med.* a type of bath in which wet sheets are applied to the patient.

wet rot, a state of decay in timber caused by alternate wetting and drying.

wet steam, a mixture of steam and water resulting from the cooling of dry saturated steam.

Wetterhorn (vĕt′ə hôn′; *Ger.* vĕt′ər hŏrn), *n.* a mountain in S Switzerland, in the Bernese Alps. 12,149 ft.

Wettich (*Ger.* vĕt′ĭKH), *n.* **Adrien** (*Ger.* á′drī ĕn). See **Grock.**

wetting agent, *Chem.* any substance added to a liquid to increase its penetrating, spreading, or wetting properties.

we've (wēv; *unstressed* wĭv), contraction of *we have.*

Wexford (wĕks′fəd), *n.* 1. a county in SE Ireland, in Leinster province. 83,308 pop. (1961); 908 sq. mi. 2. its county town: a seaport. 11,328 (1961).

wey (wā), *n.* a former unit of weight for dry goods, varying according to the commodity and often according to the county or region. [ME, OE *wǣg* weight, c. G *Wage*, Icel. *vāg*]

Weyden (*Flem.* wĕy′də), *n.* **Rogier van der** (*Flem.* rō KHēr′ vŏn dər), 1399?–1464, Flemish painter. Also, *French,* **Roger de la Pasture.**

Weygand (*Fr.* vĕ găN′), *n.* **Maxime** (*Fr.* mák sēm′), 1867–1965, French general.

Weymouth (wā′məth), *n.* a seaside resort in England, in Dorsetshire. 41,045 (1961).

wf, *Print.* wrong fount. Also, **w.f.**

W.F.T.U., World Federation of Trade Unions.

W.Ger., West Germanic.

wh., watt-hour.

whack (wăk), *v.t.* 1. *Colloq.* to strike with a smart, resounding blow or blows. 2. to exhaust completely: *I am whacked from all that work.* —*v.i.* 3. *Colloq.* to strike a smart, resounding blow or blows. —*n.* 4. *Colloq.* a smart, resounding blow: *a whack with his hand.* 5. *Slang.* a trial or attempt: *to take a whack at a job.* 6. *Slang.* a portion or share. [? imit.; ? var. of THWACK] —**whack′er,** *n.*

whacking (wăk′ĭng), *adj.* *Colloq.* large.

whacko (wăk′ō′), *interj.* (an expression denoting pleasure, delight, etc.)

whacky (wăk′ĭ), *adj.*, **-ier, -iest,** wacky.

Bowhead whale, *Balaena mysticetus* (50 to 65 ft long)

whale¹ (wāl), *n.*, *pl.* **whales,** (*esp. collectively*) **whale,** *v.*, **whaled, whaling.** —*n.* 1. *Zool.* any of the larger marine mammals of the order *Cetacea,* which includes the large sperm and whalebone whales, and the smaller dolphins and porpoises. All have fishlike bodies, modified foreflippers, and a horizontally flattened tail. 2. *Slang.* something extraordinarily big, great, or fine of its kind: *a whale of a lot, a whale of a scholar.* —*v.i.* 3. to carry on the work of taking whales. [ME; OE *hwæl,* c. MHG *wal,* Icel. *hvalr*]

whale² (wāl), *v.t.*, **whaled, whaling.** *U.S. Colloq.* to whip, thrash, or beat soundly. [orig. uncert.; ? var. of WALE¹]

whaleback (wāl′băk′), *n.* a vessel having a rounded deck which meets the sides in a continuous curve, sometimes with upper works, much used on the Great Lakes.

whaleboat (wāl′bōt′), *n.* a type of very handy boat designed for quick turning and use in rough sea; formerly used in whaling, now mainly for sea rescue.

whalebone (wāl′bōn′), *n.* 1. an elastic horny substance growing in place of teeth in the upper jaw of certain whales, and forming a series of thin, parallel plates on each side of the palate; baleen. 2. a thin strip of this material, used for stiffening corsets.

whaleman (wāl′mən), *n.*, *pl.* **-men.** a man engaged in whaling.

whaler (wā′lə), *n.* a person or vessel engaged in whaling.

Whales (wālz), *n.* **Bay of,** an inlet of the Ross Sea, in Antarctica: Little America is situated here.

whaling (wā′lĭng), *n.* the work or industry of taking whales; whale fishing.

wham (wăm), *n.*, *v.*, **whammed, whamming,** *adv.* —*n.* 1. a forceful stroke or blow. 2. the sound of this. —*v.i.*, *v.t.* 3. to hit forcefully, esp. with a single loud noise. —*adv.* 4. with force, suddenness, and often a loud noise.

whang (wăng), *Scot. and Dial.* —*n.* 1. a resounding blow, or bang. —*v.t.* 2. to strike with such a blow, or bang. [partly imit., partly var. of *thwang* THONG]

Whangaehu (wŏng′ə ā′hōō), *n.* a river in S North Island, New Zealand, flowing S to the Tasman Sea. 100 mi.

Whangarei (wăng′ä rā′), *n.* a town in N North Island, New Zealand. 20,800 (est. 1965).

whangee (wăng ē′), *n.* 1. one of the species of the bamboo genus *Phyllostachys,* native to China. 2. a cane made from the stem of one of these. [t. Chinese: alter. of *huang* hard bamboo]

whap (wŏp), *v.t.*, *v.i.*, **whapped, whapping,** *n.* *U.S. and Dial.* whop.

whare (wŏ′rĭ), *n.* *N.Z.* 1. a Maori hut. 2. any makeshift home, as temporary shearers' quarters. [t. Maori]

wharf (wôf), *n.*, *pl.* **wharves** (wôvz, wôfs), **wharfs,** *v.* —*n.* 1. a structure built on the shore of, or projecting out into, a harbour, stream, etc., so that vessels may be moored alongside to load or unload or to lie at rest; a quay; a pier. 2. *Obs.* a bank or shore. —*v.t.* 3. to provide with a wharf or wharves. 4. to place or store on a wharf. [ME; OE *hwearf* dam, akin to G *Werft* wharf] —**wharf′less,** *adj.*

wharfage (wô′fĭj), *n.* 1. the use of a wharf. 2. storage of goods at a wharf. 3. the charge or payment for the use of a wharf. 4. wharves collectively.

wharfinger (wô′fĭn jə), *n.* one who owns, or has charge of, a wharf. [f. WHARFAGE + -ER¹, with n-infix as in *passenger,* etc.]

Wharton (wô′tn), *n.* **Edith** (*Mrs Edith Newbold Jones Wharton*), 1862–1937, U.S. novelist.

wharve (wôv), *n.* *Spinning.* a wheel or round piece of wood on a spindle, serving as a flywheel or as a pulley. [ME *wherve,* OE *hweorfa*]

wharves (wôvz), *n.* 1. pl. of **wharf.** 2. pl. of **wharve.**

what (wŏt), *pron.* (*sing. and pl.*), *adv.*, *conj.* —*interrog. pron.* 1. (asking for the specifying of some thing (not person)): *what is your name? what did he do?* 2. (enquiring as to the nature, character, class, origin, etc., of a thing or person): *what is that animal?* 3. (enquiring as to the worth, usefulness, force, or importance of something): *what is wealth without health?* 4. (asking, often elliptically, for repetition or explanation of some word or words used, as by a previous speaker): *you need five what? you claim to be what?* 5. how much?: *what did it cost?* 6. *Colloq.* (used with a general or vague interrogative force, esp. at the end of a sentence): *a sort of anarchical fellow, what?* 7. (used adjectively, before a noun (whether thing or person)): *what news? what men?* 8. (often used interjectionally to express surprise, disbelief, indignation, etc.) 9. (often used with intensive force in exclamatory phrases, preceding an indefinite article, if one is used): *what luck! what an idea!* 10. **and what not** (Also, **and what have you**), and anything whatever; and anything else that there may be; et cetera. 11. **so what?** (an exclamation of contempt, dismissal, or the like). 12. **what for?** for what reason or purpose. 13. **what of it?** what does it matter? (an exclamation of dismissal, etc.). —*rel. pron.* 14. (as a compound relative) that which: *this is what he says, I will send what was promised.* 15. the kind of thing or person that, or such: *the book is just what it professes to be, the old man is not what he was.* 16. anything that, or whatever: *say what you please, come what may.* 17. (in parenthetic clauses) something that: *but he went, and, what is more surprising, gained a hearing.* 18. (as a simple relative) that, which, or who: now regarded as non-standard English. 19. (used adjectively) that or any . . . which; such . . . as: *take what time and what assistants you need.* 20. **know what it is to,** to have experience of. 21. **what for,** *Colloq.* severe treatment, punishment, or violence: *he hit me, so I gave him what for.* 22. **what it takes,** the necessary ability, personality,

or the like: *he may look stupid, but he's got what it takes to hold the job down.* **23. what's what,** the true position. —*adv.* **24.** to what extent or degree, or how much?: *what does it matter?* **25.** (in certain expressions) in what or some manner or measure, or partly: *what with storms and sickness his return was delayed.* **26.** *Obs.* in what respect or how?: *what are men better than sheep?* **27.** *Obs.* for what reason or purpose or why?
—*conj.* **28.** *Dial or Colloq.* to the extent that, as much as, or so far as: *he helps me what he can.* **29. but what,** *Colloq.* but that, but who; who or that . . . not.
[ME; OE *hwæt,* c. D *wat,* G *was,* Icel. *hvat,* Goth. *hwa*]
what-d'ye-call-it (wŏt′dyə kôl′ĭt), *n.* (a name used in place of one temporarily forgotten): *please pass me the what-d'ye-call it.*
whatever (wŏt ĕv′ə), *pron.* **1.** *indef. rel. pron.* **a.** anything that: *do whatever you like.* **b.** any amount or measure (of something) that: *whatever of time or energy may be mine.* **c.** no matter what: *do it, whatever happens.* **2.** *interrog. Colloq.* what ever? what? (used emphatically): *whatever do you mean?* —*adj.* **3.** any . . . that: *whatever merit the work has.* **4.** no matter what: *whatever rebuffs he might receive.* **5.** being what or who it may be: *for whatever reason he is unwilling, any person whatever.* Also, *Poetic,* **whate'er** (wŏt ĕə′).
whatnot (wŏt′nŏt′), *n.* **1.** a stand with shelves for bric-a-brac, books, etc. **2.** *Colloq.* anything; no matter what; what you please: *a chronicler of whatnots.* **3.** an insignificant or unspecified article. **4.** (a name for a person, used esp. in contempt): *the examiner was such a whatnot.*
what's (wŏts), contraction of *what is.*
what's-his-name (wŏt′sĭz nām′), *n.* (a name of a person substituted for one temporarily forgotten): *I met what's-his-name in the library.*
whatsoever (wŏt′sō ĕv′ə), *pron., adj.* intensive form of **whatever:** *whatsoever it be, in any place whatsoever.* Also, *Poetic,* **whatsoe'er** (wŏt′sō ĕə′).
whaup (wôp), *n. Chiefly Dial.* the large common curlew, *Numenius arquata,* of Europe. [cf. OE *hwilpe* plover]
wheal (wēl), *n.* weal. [ME *whele,* akin to obs. *wheal* v., OE *hwelian* suppurate]
wheat (wēt), *n.* **1.** the grain of a widely distributed cereal grass, genus *Triticum,* esp. *T. aestivum* (*T. sativum*), used extensively in the form of flour for white bread, cakes, pastry, etc. **2.** the plant, which bears the edible grain in dense spikes that sometimes have awns **(bearded wheat)** and sometimes do not **(beardless wheat** or **bald wheat).** [ME *whete,* OE *hwǣte,* c. D *weit,* G *Weizen*] —**wheat′less,** *adj.*
wheatear (wēt′ĭə′), *n.* a small oscine passerine bird, *Oenanthe oenanthe,* found principally in the Old World, notable for its boldly marked tail.
wheaten (wē′tn), *adj.* **1.** made of the grain or flour of wheat: *wheaten bread.* **2.** of or pertaining to wheat.
Wheatstone (wēt′stən), *n.* **Sir Charles,** 1802–75, English physicist and inventor.
Wheatstone bridge, *Elect.* an instrument designed for measuring the electrical resistance of a circuit or a circuit component. Also, **Wheatstone's bridge.** [named after Sir Charles WHEATSTONE]
wheatworm (wēt′wûm′), *n.* a small nematode worm, *Anguina tritici,* causing disease in wheat.
wheedle (wē′dl), *v.,* **-dled, -dling.** —*v.t.* **1.** to endeavour to influence (a person) by smooth, flattering, or beguiling words. **2.** to get by artful persuasions: *wheedling my money from me.* —*v.i.* **3.** to use beguiling or artful persuasions. [orig. obscure. Cf. OE *wǣdlian* beg] —**whee′dler,** *n.* —**whee′dlingly,** *adv.*
wheel (wēl), *n.* **1.** a circular frame or solid disc arranged to turn on an axis, as in vehicles, machinery, etc. **2.** any instrument, machine, apparatus, etc., shaped like this, or having such a frame or disc as an essential feature: *a potter's wheel.* **3.** a circular frame with or without projecting handles and an axle connecting with the rudder, for steering a ship. **4.** an old instrument of torture in the form of a circular frame on which the victim was stretched while his limbs were broken with an iron bar. **5.** anything resembling or suggesting a wheel (in first sense) in shape, movement, etc., as a decoration, or the trochal disc of a rotifer. **6.** a circular firework which revolves while burning. **7.** a rotating instrument which Fortune is represented as turning in order to bring about changes or reverses in human affairs. **8.** *Poetry.* a set of rhyming lines, usually four, forming the conclusion of a stanza of Middle English alliterative poetry. Cf. **bob.** See **bob and wheel. 9.** (*pl.*) moving, propelling, or animating agencies: *the wheels of trade or of thought.* **10.** a wheeling or circular movement: *merrily whirled the wheels of the dizzying dances.* **11.** *Mil.* a change of direction. **12.** (formerly) a movement of troops, ships, etc., drawn up in line, as if turning on a pivot. **13.** *Chiefly U.S. Colloq.* a person of considerable importance or influence: *a big wheel.* **14. at the wheel, a.** at the steering wheel of a motor car, ship, etc. **b.** in command or control. **15. wheels within wheels,** a complicated situation in which many different factors are involved. **16. put one's shoulder to the wheel,** to exert oneself greatly, as in a combined effort to achieve some end.
—*v.t.* **17.** to cause to turn, rotate, or revolve, as on an axis. **18.** to perform in a circular or curving direction. **19.** to move, roll, or convey on wheels, castors, etc.: *the maid wheels in the trolley.* **20.** to provide (a vehicle, etc.) with a wheel or wheels.
—*v.i.* **21.** to turn on or as on an axis or about a centre; rotate, revolve. **22.** *Mil.* to change direction while marching: *to wheel left.* **23.** to move in a circular or curving course: *pigeons wheeling above.* **24.** to turn or change in procedure or opinion (often fol. by *about* or *round*). **25.** to roll along on, or as on, wheels; to travel along smoothly. [ME; OE *hwēol, hweogol,* c. D *wiel,* Icel. *hjōl*] —**wheeled** (wēld), *adj.* —**wheel′less,** *adj.*
wheel and axle, a device (one of the so-called simple machines) consisting, in its typical form, of a cylindrical drum to which a wheel concentric with the drum is firmly fastened. Ropes are so applied that as one unwinds from the wheel the other is wound on to the drum.
wheel animalcule, a rotifer.
wheelbarrow (wēl′bă′rō), *n.* **1.** a frame or box for conveying a load, usually supported at one end by a wheel and at the other by two vertical legs above which are two horizontal shafts used in lifting the legs from the ground when the vehicle is pushed or pulled. **2.** a similar vehicle with more than one wheel. **3. wheelbarrow race,** a race in which the contestants walk on their hands, their legs being supported by a person at the rear. —*v.t.* **4.** to move or convey in a wheelbarrow.
wheelbase (wēl′bās′), *n.* the distance between the front and rear axles of a vehicle.
wheelchair (wēl′chēə′), *n.* a chair mounted on large wheels, and used by invalids.
wheeler (wē′lə), *n.* **1.** one who or that which wheels. **2.** something provided with a wheel or wheels: *a side-wheeler, a stern-wheeler.* **3.** a wheel-horse (def. 1).
wheel-horse (wēl′hôs′), *n.* **1.** a horse harnessed between others and next to the front wheels of a vehicle. **2.** a person who bears a principal burden of work.
wheelhouse (wēl′hous′), *n.* pilot house.
wheel-lock (wēl′lŏk′), *n.* an old type of gunlock in which sparks are produced by the friction of a small steel wheel against a piece of iron pyrites.
wheelman (wēl′mən), *n., pl.* **-men.** *U.S.* a helmsman. Also, **wheelsman.**
wheel of life, zoetrope.
wheel ore, bournonite.
wheelwork (wēl′wûk′), *n. Mach.* a train of gears.
wheelwright (wēl′rīt′), *n.* one whose trade it is to make or repair wheels, wheeled carriages, etc.
wheen (wēn), *n. Scot. and N Dial.* a few. [ME *quheyn,* OE *hwēne* instrumental case of *hwōn* few, a few]
wheeze (wēz), *v.,* **wheezed, wheezing,** *n.* —*v.i.* **1.** to breathe with difficulty and with a whistling sound: *wheezing with asthma.* —*v.t.* **2.** to utter such a sound. —*n.* **3.** a wheezing breath or sound. **4.** a theatrical gag. **5.** *Colloq.* a trite saying, story, etc. **6.** *Colloq.* a trick, dodge, or idea, esp. a cunning or artful one. [ME *whese,* prob. t. Scand.; cf. Icel. *hvæsa* hiss] —**wheez′er,** *n.* —**wheez′ingly,** *adv.*
wheezy (wē′zĭ), *adj.,* **-zier, -ziest.** affected with or characterized by wheezing. —**wheez′ily,** *adv.* —**wheez′iness,** *n.*
whelk[1] (wĕlk) *n.* any of various large spiral-shelled marine gastropods of the family *Buccinidae,* esp. *Buccinum undatum,* used for food in Europe. [ME *welke,* OE *weoloc;* orig. uncert.]

Whelk, *Buccinum undatum* (3 in. long)

whelk[2] (wĕlk), *n.* a pimple or pustule. [ME *whelke,* OE *hwylca.* See WHEAL]
whelm (wĕlm), *v.t.* **1.** to submerge; engulf. **2.** to overcome utterly, or overwhelm: *sorrow whelmed him.* [ME, appar. b. obs. *whelve* (OE *gehwelfan* bend over) and *helm* (OE *helmian* cover)]
whelp (wĕlp), *n.* **1.** the young of the dog, or of the wolf, bear, lion, tiger, seal, etc. **2.** (in contemptuous use) a youth. **3.** *Mach.* **a.** any of a series of longitudinal projections or ridges of iron or the like on the barrel of a capstan, windlass, etc. **b.** one of the teeth of a sprocket wheel. —*v.t., v.i.* **4.** (of a bitch, lioness, etc.) to bring forth (young). [ME; OE *hwelp,* c. G *Welf*]
when (wĕn), *adv.* **1.** at that time: *when are you coming?* **2. say when,** to tell one when to stop, esp. in pouring a

drink. —*conj.* **3.** at what time: *to know when to be silent.* **4.** at the time that: *when we were young, when the noise stopped.* **5.** at any time, or whenever: *he is impatient when he is kept waiting.* **6.** upon or after which; and then. **7.** while on the contrary, or whereas: *you cover up the wound when you should clean it first.* —*pron.* **8.** what time: *since when have you known this?* **9.** which time: *they left on Monday, since when we have heard nothing.* —*n.* **10.** the time of anything: *the when and the where of an act.* [ME *when(ne)*, OE *hwenne*, c. G *wann* when, *wenn* if, Goth. *hwan* when, how; akin to WHO, WHAT]

whenas (wĕn ăz′), *conj. Archaic.* when; whereas.

whence (wĕns), *adv. Archaic.* **1.** from what place?: *whence comest thou?* **2.** from what source, origin or cause?: *whence hath he wisdom?* —*conj.* **3.** from what place, source, cause, etc.: *he told whence he came.* [ME *whennes*, f. *whenne* (OE *hwanone* whence) + *-s*, adv. gen. suffix]

whencesoever (wĕns′sō ĕv′ə), *adv., conj. Archaic.* from whatsoever place, source, or cause.

whenever (wĕn ĕv′ə), *conj.* **1.** at whatever time; at any time when: *come whenever you like.* —*adv.* **2.** *Colloq.* when ever? when? (used emphatically): *whenever did he say that?* Also, *Poetic,* **whene'er** (wĕn ĕə′).

whensoever (wĕn′sō ĕv′ə), *adv., conj. Archaic.* at whatsoever time.

where (wĕə), *adv.* **1.** in or at what place?: *where is he?, where do you live?* **2.** in what position or circumstances?: *where do you stand on this question? without money where are you?* **3.** in what particular, respect, way, etc.?: *where does this affect us?* **4.** to what place, point, or end, or whither?: *where are you going?* **5.** from what source, or whence: *where did you get such a notion?* —*conj.* **6.** in or at what place, part, point, etc.: *find where he is, or where the trouble is.* **7.** in or at the place, part, point, etc., in or at which: *the book is where you left it.* **8.** in a position, case, etc., in which: *where ignorance is bliss, 'tis folly to be wise.* **9.** in any place, position, case, etc., in which, or wherever: *use the lotion where pain is felt.* **10.** to what or whatever place, or to the or any place to which: *go where you will, I will go where you go.* **11.** in or at which place; and there: *they came to the town, where they lodged for the night.* —*pron.* **12.** what place: *from where, where from?* **13.** the place in which: *this is where we live.* —*n.* **14.** *U.S. Colloq.* a place: *the wheres and hows of job hunting.* [ME *wher*, OE *hwǣr*, c. D *waar*; akin to Icel. *hvar*, Goth. *hwar*]

where-, a word element meaning 'what' or 'which'. [special use of WHERE]

-where, suffixal use of 'where', as in *somewhere.* Also, *U.S. Dial.,* **-wheres.**

whereabouts (*interrogatively* (wĕə′rə bouts′; *otherwise* wĕə′rə bouts′), *adv.* **1.** Also, *Rare,* **where′about′.** about where? where? —*conj.* **2.** near or in what place: *seeing whereabouts in the world we were.* —*n.pl.* **3.** (sometimes construed as sing.) the place where a person or thing is; the locality of a person or thing: *no clue as to his whereabouts.*

whereas (wĕər ăz′), *conj., n., pl.* **whereases.** —*conj.* **1.** while on the contrary: *one came, whereas the others didn't.* **2.** it being the case that, or considering that (esp. used in formal preambles). —*n.* **3.** a statement having 'whereas' as the first word: *to read the whereases in the will.*

whereat (wĕər ăt′), *adv., conj.* at what or at which.

whereby (wĕə bī′), *adv., conj.* **1.** by what or by which. **2.** *Obs.* by what? how?

where'er (wĕər ĕə′), *conj., adv. Poetic.* wherever.

wherefore (wĕə′fô′), *adv.* **1.** for what? why? —*conj.* **2.** for what or which cause or reason. —*n.* **3.** the cause or reason. [ME; f. WHERE + *fore* because of, FOR] —**Syn. 1.** See **therefore.**

wherefrom (wĕə frŏm′), *adv., conj. Archaic.* from which; whence.

wherein (wĕər ĭn′), *adv., conj.* in what or in which.

whereinto (wĕər ĭn′to͞o), *adv., conj.* into what or into which.

whereof (wĕər ŏv′), *adv., conj.* of what, which or whom.

whereon (wĕər ŏn′), *adv., conj.* on what or on which.

-wheres, *U.S. Dial.* var. of **-where.**

wheresoever (wĕə′sō ĕv′ə), *adv., conj.* in or to whatsoever place; wherever. Also, *Poetic,* **wheresoe'er** (wĕə′sō ĕə′).

wherethrough (wĕə thro͞o′), *adv., conj. Archaic.* through which.

whereto (wĕə to͞o′), *adv., conj.* to what or to which. Also, *Archaic,* **whereunto** (wĕər ŭn′to͞o).

whereupon (wĕə′rə pŏn′), *adv.* **1.** *Archaic.* upon what? whereon? —*conj.* **2.** at or after which. **3.** upon what or upon which.

wherever (wĕər ĕv′ə), *conj.* **1.** in, at, or to whatever place. **2.** in any case or condition: *wherever it is heard of.* —*adv.* **3.** *Colloq.* where ever? where? (used emphatically): *wherever did you find that?* Also, *Poetic,* **where'er.**

wherewith (wĕə wĭth′, -wĭth′), *adv., conj.* **1.** with what? **2.** with what or which. **3.** (by ellipsis) that with which: *I shall have wherewith to answer him.* —*n.* **4.** wherewithal.

wherewithal (*n.* wĕə′wĭth ôl′; *adv., conj.* wĕə′wĭth ôl′), *n.* **1.** that wherewith to do something; means or supplies for the purpose or need, esp. money: *the wherewithal to pay my rent.* —*adv., conj.* **2.** *Archaic.* wherewith.

wherry (wĕ′rĭ), *n., pl.* **-ries,** *v.,* **-ried, -rying.** —*n.* **1.** any of certain larger boats (fishing vessels, barges, etc.) used locally in Great Britain. **2.** a kind of light rowing boat used chiefly in England for carrying passengers and goods on rivers. **3.** *U.S.* a skiff. —*v.t., v.i.* **4.** to use, or transport in, a wherry. [late ME; orig. uncert.] —**wher′ryman,** *n.*

whet (wĕt), *v.,* **whetted, whetting,** *n.* —*v.t.* **1.** to sharpen (a knife, tool, etc.) by grinding or friction. **2.** to make keen or eager: *to whet the appetite or the curiosity.* **3. whet one's whistle.** wet one's whistle. —*n.* **4.** the act of whetting. **5.** something that whets; an appetizer. [ME *whette*, OE *hwettan*, c. G *wetzen*] —**whet′ter,** *n.*

whether (wĕth′ə), *conj.* **1.** a word introducing, in dependent clauses or the like, the first of two or more alternatives, and sometimes repeated before the second or later alternative (used in correlation with *or*): *it matters little whether we go or stay; whether we go or whether we stay, the result is the same.* **2.** used to introduce a single alternative (the other being implied or understood), and hence some clause or element not involving alternatives: *see whether he has come (or not), I doubt whether we can do any better.* **3. whether or no,** under whatever circumstances: *he threatens to go, whether or no.* —*pron. Archaic.* **4.** which (of two)? **5.** a word introducing a question presenting alternatives (usually with the correlative *or*). [ME; OE *hwether, hwæther*, c. Icel. *hvadharr*, Goth. *hwathar*]

whetstone (wĕt′stōn′), *n.* **1.** a stone for sharpening cutlery or tools by friction. **2.** anything that sharpens: *a whetstone for dull wits.*

whew, *interj.* **1.** (a whistling exclamation or sound expressing astonishment, dismay, etc.) —*n.* **2.** an utterance of 'whew'.

whey (wā), *n.* milk serum, separating as a watery liquid from the curd after coagulation, as in cheese-making. [ME *wheye*, OE *hwæg*, c. D and LG *wei*] —**whey′ish, whey′like′,** *adj.*

wheyey (wā′ĭ), *adj.* of, like, or containing whey.

wheyface (wā′fās′), *n.* a face or a person that is pallid, as from fear. —**whey′faced′,** *adj.*

whf, wharf.

which (wĭch), *interrog. pron.* **1.** what one (of a certain number mentioned or implied)?: *which of these, or which, do you want?* —*rel. pron.* **2.** as a simple relative with antecedent (a thing, body of persons, formerly a person) expressed: **a.** in clauses conveying an additional idea: *I read the book, which was short; five sons, of which he was the eldest.* **b.** used in clauses defining or restricting the antecedent, regularly after that (*that which must be will be*), or after a preposition (*the horse on which I rode*), or otherwise in place of the restrictive that (*the book which I gave you*). **c.** used adjectivally: *be careful which way you turn.* **3.** (as a compound relative representing both antecedent and consequent (either thing or person), what particular one, or the or any one that: *choose which you like; any one of these men, be it which it may.* **4.** (in parenthetic clauses) a thing that: *and, which is worse, all you have done is wrong.* —*adj.* **5.** what one of (a certain number mentioned or implied): *which book do you want?* **6.** no matter what; any that: *go which way you please, you'll end up here.* **7.** being previously mentioned: *it stormed all day, during which time the ship broke up.* [ME; OE *hwilc*, c. D *welk*, G *welch*, Goth. *hwileiks*, lit., of what form, like whom or what. See WHO, WHAT, LIKE[1]] —**Syn. 2.** See **that.**

whichever (wĭch ĕv′ə), *pron.* **1.** any one (of those in question) that: *take whichever you like.* **2.** no matter which: *whichever you choose, the others will be offended.* **3.** (used adjectivally) no matter which: *whichever day, whichever person.*

whichsoever (wĭch′sō ĕv′ə), *pron.* intensive form of **whichever.**

whicker (wĭk′ə), *v.i.* **1.** to snigger; titter. **2.** (of a horse) to neigh or whinny. [der. OE **hwican* (in *hwicung* squeaking) + -ER[6], akin to G *wiehern* neigh]

whid[1] (wĭd), *Scot.* —*n.* **1.** a word. **2.** a lie or falsehood. —*v.i.* **3.** to tell lies; exaggerate.

whid[2] (wĭd), *v.i.,* **whidded, whidding.** *Scot.* to move briskly and quietly.

whidah (wĭd′ə), *n.* whydah. Also, **whidah-bird** (wĭd′ə bûd′).

whiff (wĭf), *n.* **1.** a slight blast or puff of wind or air: *a whiff of fresh air.* **2.** a puff or waft of scent or smell: *a whiff of honeysuckle.* **3.** a puff of vapour, smoke, etc. **4.** a single inhalation or exhalation of air, tobacco smoke, or the like.

5. a slight outburst: *a little whiff of temper.* **6.** a light clinker boat with outriggers, for one sculler. *—v.i.* **7.** to blow or come in whiffs or puffs, as wind, smoke, etc. **8.** to inhale or exhale whiffs, as in smoking tobacco. **9.** to have an unpleasant smell. *—v.t.* **10.** to blow or drive with a whiff or puff, as the wind. **11.** to inhale or exhale (air, tobacco smoke, etc.) in whiffs. **12.** to smoke (a pipe, cigar, etc.). [? b. WHIP and PUFF] —**whiff′er,** *n.*

whiffet (wĭf′ĭt), *n. U.S.* **1.** a small dog. **2.** *Colloq.* an insignificant person; whippersnapper. [f. WHIFF + -ET, modelled on *whippet*]

whiffle (wĭf′əl), *v.,* **-fled, -fling.** *—v.i.* **1.** to blow in light or shifting gusts or puffs, as the wind; veer irregularly (about). **2.** to shift about; vacillate. *—v.t.* **3.** to blow with light, shifting gusts. [freq. of WHIFF, v.] —**whif′fler,** *n.*

whiffletree (wĭf′əl trē′, -trĭ), *n.* whippletree.

whig (wĭg), *v.i.,* **whigged, whigging.** *Scot.* to move at an easy, steady pace; jog along.

Whig (wĭg), *n.* **1.** in 17th-century Scotland, an adherent of the Presbyterian cause. **2.** one opposed to the succession of the Duke of York from 1679, on the grounds of his Catholicism. **3.** a member of one of the two major political parties in England in the 18th and early 19th centuries, associated at first with the Hanoverians, then with attempts to limit royal authority and increase parliamentary power, supporting Nonconformists as opposed to the established church, generally favouring various reforms, and finally evolving into the Liberal Party. Cf. **Tory** (def. 1). **4.** one of the more conservative members of the Liberal Party. **5.** *Amer. Hist.* **a.** a member of the group supporting the American War of Independence. **b.** a member of a political party (*c.* 1834–55) which was formed in opposition to the Democratic Party, and favoured a loose construction of the Constitution and a high protective tariff. *—adj.* **6.** being a Whig. **7.** of, pertaining to, or characteristic of the Whigs. [prob. short for *whiggamore*, one of a body of rebels who marched on Edinburgh, 1648]

Whiggery (wĭg′ə rĭ), *n., pl.* **-geries.** the principles or practices of Whigs.

Whiggish (wĭg′ĭsh), *adj.* **1.** of, pertaining to, or characteristic of Whigs. **2.** inclined to Whiggism. —**Whig′gishly,** *adv.* —**Whig′gishness,** *n.*

Whiggism (wĭg′ĭz′əm), *n.* the principles of Whigs.

while (wīl), *n., conj., v.,* **whiled, whiling.** *—n.* **1.** a space of time: *a long while, a while ago.* **2. once in a while,** occasionally. **3. the while,** during this time. **4. worth one's while,** worth time, pains, or expense. **5.** *Archaic or Dial.* a particular time or occasion. *—conj.* **6.** Also, **whilst.** during or in the time that. **7.** throughout the time that, or as long as. **8.** at the same time that (implying opposition or contrast): *while he appreciated the honour, he could not accept the position.* **9.** *Dial.* until. *—v.t.* **10.** to cause (time) to pass, esp. in some easy or pleasant manner (usually fol. by *away*). [ME; OE *hwīl*, c. D *wijl*, G *Weile*, Goth. *hweila*]

whiles (wīlz), *adv.* **1.** *Archaic or Dial.* at times. **2.** *Obs.* in the meantime. *—conj.* **3.** *Archaic or Dial.* while.

whilom (wī′ləm), *Archaic. —adv.* **1.** at one time; formerly. *—adj.* **2.** former. [ME; OE *hwīlum* at times, dat. pl. of *hwīl* WHILE, n.]

whilst (wīlst), *conj.* while. [earlier *whilest*, f. WHILES + inorganic *-t*, as in AMONGST]

whim (wĭm), *n.* **1.** an odd or fanciful notion; a freakish or capricious fancy or desire. **2.** capricious humour: *to be swayed by whim.* **3.** *Mining.* a vertical drum on which a hoisting rope winds, usually operated by a horse or horses. [prob. t. Scand.; cf. Icel. *hvim* unsteady look. In some senses short for *whim-wham*, itself der. *whim*, modelled on *trim-tram* gewgaw] —**Syn. 1.** whimsy, humour, caprice, vagary, quirk, notion, crotchet, chimera.

Whim (def. 3)

whimbrel (wĭm′brəl), *n.* a small European curlew, *Numenius phaeopus.*

whimper (wĭm′pə), *v.i.* **1.** to cry with low, plaintive, broken sounds, as a child, a grown person, a dog, etc. *—v.t.* **2.** to utter in a whimper. *—n.* **3.** a whimpering cry or sound. [freq. of *whimp* (now d.) whine, orig. uncert.; cf. Icel. *hvimpinn* shy (said of horse)] —**whim′perer,** *n.* —**whim′peringly,** *adv.*

whimsey (wĭm′zĭ), *n., pl.* **-seys.** whimsy.

whimsical (wĭm′zĭ kl), *adj.* **1.** given to whimsies or odd notions. **2.** of the nature of or proceeding from a whimsy, as thoughts, actions, etc. **3.** of an odd, quaint, or comical kind. —**whim′sically,** *adv.* —**whim′sicalness,** *n.* —**Syn. 1.** capricious, changeable, freakish, fanciful.

whimsicality (wĭm′zĭ kăl′ĭ tĭ), *n., pl.* **-ties. 1.** whimsical character. **2.** a whimsical notion, speech, or act.

whimsy (wĭm′zĭ), *n., pl.* **-sies. 1.** an odd or fanciful notion. **2.** anything odd or fanciful; a product of playful fancy, as a literary trifle. Also, **whimsey.**

whim-wham (wĭm′wăm′), *n.* any odd or fanciful object or thing; a gimcrack.

whin[1] (wĭn), *n.* gorse, furze. [late ME *whynne*, appar. t. Scand.; cf. Icel. *hvingras* bent grass]

whin[2] (wĭn), *n.* **1.** whinstone. **2.** any of various other dark-coloured rocks such as dolerite and basalt trap. [orig. uncert.]

whinchat (wĭn′chăt′), *n.* a small Old World oscine passerine bird, *Saxicola rubetra*, having buff-coloured breast and white at the base of the tail, and closely related to the stonechat. [f. WHIN[1] + CHAT warbler]

whine (wīn), *v.,* **whined, whining,** *n. —v.i.* **1.** to utter a low, complaining cry or sound, as from uneasiness, discontent, peevishness, etc. **2.** to complain in a feeble, plaintive way. *—v.t.* **3.** to utter with a whine. *—n.* **4.** a whining utterance, sound, or tone. **5.** a feeble, peevish complaint. [ME; OE *hwīnan*, c. Icel. *hvīna* whiz] —**whin′er,** *n.* —**whin′ingly,** *adv.* —**whin′y,** *adj.* —**Syn. 2.** See **complain.**

whinge (wĭnj), *v.i. Austral., N.Z. Dial.* to complain, whine. [WH(INE) + (CR)INGE]

whinny (wĭn′ĭ), *v.,* **-nied, -nying,** *n., pl.* **-nies.** *—v.i.* **1.** (of a horse) to utter its characteristic cry; neigh. *—v.t.* **2.** to express by whinnying. *—n.* **3.** a neigh. [alter. of WHINE in (now obs.) sense 'whinny']

whinstone (wĭn′stōn′), *n.* any of the dark-coloured fine-grained rocks such as dolerite and basalt trap.

whip (wĭp), *v.,* **whipped** or **whipt, whipping,** *n. —v.t.* **1.** to strike with quick, repeated strokes of something slender and flexible; lash. **2.** to beat with a whip or the like, esp. by way of punishment or chastisement; flog; thrash. **3.** to lash or castigate with words. **4.** to drive (*on, out, in*, etc.) by strokes or lashes. **5.** to spin (a top) by whipping. **6.** to bring (*in, into line, together*, etc.) as a party whip. **7.** *Chiefly U.S. Colloq.* to beat, outdo, or defeat, as in a contest. **8.** *Naut.* to hoist or purchase by means of a whip. **9.** to move quickly and suddenly; pull, jerk, snatch, seize, put, etc., with a sudden movement (fol. by *away, out, up, into*, etc.). **10.** to fish (a stream, etc.) with a rod and line. **11.** to overlay or cover (cord, etc.) with cord, thread, or the like wound about it. **12.** to wind (cord, twine, thread, etc.) about something. **13.** to gather, or form into pleats by overcasting the turned edge with small stitches and then drawing up the thread. **14.** to beat (eggs, cream, etc.) to a froth with a whisk, fork, or other implement in order to incorporate air and produce expansion. **15. whip up, a.** to create quickly: *I whipped up a meal when I heard he was coming.* **b.** to arouse to fury, intense excitement, etc.: *his speech soon whipped up the crowd. —v.i.* **16.** to move or go quickly and suddenly (*away, off, out, in*, etc.); dart; whisk. **17.** to beat or lash about, as a pennant in the wind. **18.** to fish with a rod and line. **19. whip in,** *Hunting.* to prevent from wandering, as hounds. **20. whip round,** to make a collection of money.

—n. **21.** an instrument to strike with, as in driving animals or in punishing, typically consisting of a lash or other flexible part with a more rigid handle. **22.** a whipping or lashing stroke or motion. **23.** a windmill vane. **24.** one who handles a whip; a driver of horses, a coach, etc. **25.** one who has charge of the hounds in hunting. **26.** *Parl. Proc.* **a.** a party manager in a legislative body, who secures attendance for voting, and directs other members. **b.** a written call made on members of a party to be in attendance for voting, etc. **27.** a contrivance for hoisting, consisting essentially of a rope and pulley. **28.** a wooden percussion instrument imitating the crack of a whip. **29.** a dish made of cream or eggwhites whipped to a froth with flavouring, etc., often with fruit pulp or the like: *prune whip.*

[ME *whippe*, earlier *(h)wippen*, c. D *wippen* wing, oscillate] —**whip′like′,** *adj.* —**whip′per,** *n.* —**Syn. 2.** scourge, lash, flagellate, beat, switch, punish, chastise. **7.** overcome, conquer. **21.** switch, rattan.

whipcord (wĭp′kôd′), *n.* **1.** a worsted fabric with a diagonally ribbed surface. **2.** a kind of strong, hard-twisted cord, sometimes used for the lashes of whips.

whip graft, a graft prepared by cutting both the scion and the stock in a sloping direction and inserting a tongue in the scion into a slit in the stock. See illus. under **graft.** Also, **whip grafting, whip graftage.**

whip hand, 1. the hand that holds the whip, in driving. **2.** the position of control, or the advantage.

whiplash (wĭp′lăsh′), *n.* the lash of a whip.

whipper-in (wĭp′ər ĭn′), *n., pl.* **whippers-in.** one who whips in hounds.

whippersnapper (wĭp′ə snăp′ə), *n.* a petty or insignificant person, often young, who affects importance.

whippet (wĭp′ĭt), *n.* a dog of an English breed, probably a cross between the greyhound and the terrier, used especially in rabbit coursing and racing. [n. use of obs. v., to frisk, orig. the phrase *whip it* move briskly]

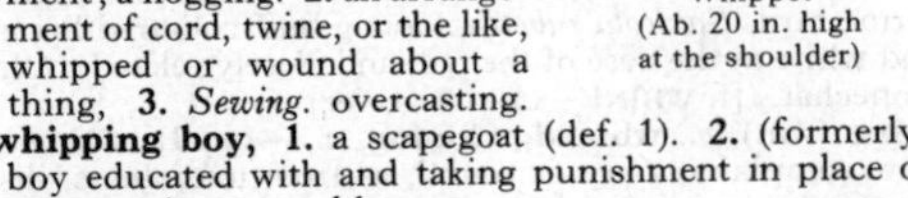

Whippet (Ab. 20 in. high at the shoulder)

whipping (wĭp′ĭng), *n.* **1.** a beating administered with a whip or the like, as for punishment; a flogging. **2.** an arrangement of cord, twine, or the like, whipped or wound about a thing. **3.** *Sewing.* overcasting.

whipping boy, 1. a scapegoat (def. 1). **2.** (formerly) a boy educated with and taking punishment in place of a young prince or nobleman.

whipping post, (formerly) a post to which persons were fastened to undergo whipping as a legal penalty.

whipping top, a top² (def. 1) spun by striking with a whip.

whippletree (wĭp′l trē′, -trĭ), *n.* a crossbar, pivoted at the middle, to which the braces of the harness are fastened in a cart, carriage, plough, etc.; swingletree. Also, **whiffletree.** [? der. WHIP]

whippoorwill (wĭp′po͝oə wĭl′), *n.* a nocturnal North American goatsucker (bird), *Caprimulgus vociferus*, having a variegated plumage of grey, black, white, and tawny. [imit., from its cry]

whip-round (wĭp′round′), *n.* *Colloq.* an impromptu collection of money.

whipsaw (wĭp′sô′), *n.* **1.** any flexible saw, as a bandsaw. —*v.t.* **2.** to cut with a whipsaw. **3.** *U.S.* to win two bets from (a person) at one turn or play, as in faro. **4.** *U.S.* to defeat or worst in two ways at once.

whip scorpion, any of various arachnids of the order *Uropygi*, resembling the true scorpions, but having (in the typical members) an abdomen ending in a slender whiplike part.

whipsnake (wĭp′snāk′), *n.* any of various slender snakes in which the scaling of the tail resembles a braided whip.

whipstall (wĭp′stôl′), *n.* *Aeron.* **1.** a stall during a vertical climb in which there is often a momentary slide of the aircraft tail first, the nose then pitching violently forward and down in a whiplike movement. —*v.t.* **2.** to cause (an aircraft) to perform a whipstall. —*v.i.* to perform a whipstall.

whipstitch (wĭp′stĭch′), *v.t.* **1.** to sew with stitches passing over an edge, in joining, finishing, or gathering. —*n.* **2.** one such stitch. **3.** *U.S. Colloq.* an instant.

whipstock (wĭp′stŏk′), *n.* the handle of a whip.

whipworm (wĭp′wûm′), *n.* any of certain parasitic nematode worms of the genus *Trichuris*, having a long, slender anterior end, giving a whiplike shape.

whir (wû), *v.i., v.t., n.* whirr.

whirl (wûl), *v.i.* **1.** to turn round, spin, or rotate rapidly. **2.** to turn about or aside quickly. **3.** to move, travel, or be carried rapidly along on wheels or otherwise. **4.** to have the sensation of turning round rapidly. —*v.t.* **5.** to cause to turn round, spin, or rotate rapidly. **6.** to send, drive, or carry in a circular or curving course. **7.** to drive, send, or carry along with great or dizzying rapidity. **8.** *Obs.* to hurl. —*n.* **9.** the act of whirling; rapid rotation or gyration. **10.** a whirling movement; a quick turn or swing. **11.** a short drive, run, walk, or the like, or a spin. **12.** something that whirls; a whirling current or mass. **13.** a rapid round of events, affairs, etc. **14.** a state marked by a dizzying succession or mingling of feelings, thoughts, etc. [ME *whirle*, t. Scand.; cf. Icel. *hvirfla*] —**whirl′er,** *n.* —**Syn. 1.** gyrate, pirouette. **5.** revolve, twirl.

whirlabout (wûl′l ə bout′), *n.* **1.** a whirling about. **2.** a whirligig. —*adj.* **3.** whirling about.

whirligig (wûl′lĭ gĭg′), *n.* **1.** something that whirls, revolves, or goes round; a revolving agency or course. **2.** a continuous round or succession. **3.** a giddy or flighty person. **4.** a merry-go-round. **5.** a toy for whirling or spinning, as a top. [der. WHIRL. See GIG¹]

whirligig beetle, any of the aquatic beetles of the family *Gyrinidae*, commonly seen circling rapidly about in large numbers on the surface of the water.

whirlpool (wûl′po͞ol′), *n.* a whirling eddy or current, as in a river or the sea, produced by irregularity in the channel or stream banks, by the meeting of opposing currents, by the interaction of winds and tides, etc.; a vortex of water.

whirlwind (wûl′wĭnd′), *n.* **1.** a mass of air rotating rapidly round and towards a more or less vertical axis, and having at the same time a progressive motion over the surface of the land or sea. **2.** anything resembling a whirlwind, as in violent activity. **3.** any circling rush or violent onward course. [ME, t. Scand.; cf. Icel. *hvirfilvindr*. See WHIRL, WIND¹]

whirlybird (wûl′lĭ bûd′), *n.* *U.S. Slang.* a helicopter.

whirr (wû), *v.,* **whirred, whirring,** *n.* —*v.i., v.t.* **1.** to go, fly, dart, revolve, or otherwise move quickly with a vibratory or buzzing sound. —*n.* **2.** the act or sound of whirring: *the whirr of wings.* Also, **whir.** [ME, t. Scand.; cf. Dan. *hvirre*; akin to WHIRL]

whish (wĭsh), *v.i.* **1.** to make, or move with, a whiz or swish. —*n.* **2.** a whishing sound.

whisht (wĭst), *interj., adj.* *Obs. or Dial.* whist¹.

whisk¹ (wĭsk), *v.t.* **1.** to sweep (dust, crumbs, etc.) or a surface with a brush, or the like. **2.** to move with a rapid, sweeping stroke. **3.** to draw, snatch, carry, etc., lightly and rapidly. —*v.i.* **4.** to sweep, pass, or go lightly and rapidly. —*n.* **5.** the act of whisking. **6.** a rapid, sweeping stroke; light, rapid movement. [late ME, t. Scand.; cf. Dan. *viske* wipe]

whisk² (wĭsk), *v.t.* **1.** to whip (eggs, cream, etc.) to a froth with a whisk or beating implement. —*n.* **2.** a small bunch of grass, straw, hair, or the like, esp. for use in brushing. **3.** an implement, in one form a bunch of loops of wire held together in a handle, for beating or whipping eggs, cream, etc. [ME *wisk*, t. Scand.; cf. Icel. *visk* wisp, c. G *Wisch* wisp of straw]

whisker (wĭs′kə), *n.* **1.** (*usually pl.*) the hair growing on the sides of a man's face, esp. when worn long and with the chin clean-shaven. **2.** (*pl.*) the beard generally. **3.** a single hair of the beard. **4.** (formerly) the moustache. **5.** one of the long, stiff, bristly hairs growing about the mouth of certain animals, as the cat, rat, etc.; a vibrissa. **6.** Also, **whisker boom.** *Naut.* either of two bars of wood or iron projecting laterally one from each side of the bowsprit, to give more spread to the guys which support the jib boom. **7.** *Obs.* one who or that which whisks. [ME; der. WHISK². Cf. LG *wisker* duster] —**whisk′ered, whisk′ery,** *adj.* —**whisk′erless,** *adj.*

whisky (wĭs′kĭ), *n., pl.* **-kies.** —*n.* **1.** a distilled spirit made from grain, as barley, rye, oats, etc. **2.** a drink of whisky. —*adj.* **3.** made of, relating to, or resembling, whisky. Also, *U.S. and Irish,* **whiskey.** [short for *whiskybae*, t. Gaelic: m. *uisgebeatha* water of life]

whisper (wĭs′pə), *v.i.* **1.** to speak with soft, low sounds, using the breath, lips, etc., without vibration of the vocal cords. **2.** to talk softly and privately (often with implication of gossip, slander, or plotting). **3.** (of trees, water, breezes, etc.) to make a soft, rustling sound. —*v.t.* **4.** to utter with soft, low sounds, using the breath, lips, etc. **5.** to say or tell in a whisper; to tell privately. **6.** to utter as a rumour, gossip, etc. **7.** to speak to or tell (a person) in a whisper, or privately. —*n.* **8.** the mode of utterance, or the voice, of one who whispers: *to speak in a whisper.* **9.** a sound, word, remark, or the like, uttered by whispering; something said or repeated privately: *low whispers.* **10.** a soft, rustling sound, as of leaves moving in the wind. [ME *whysper*, OE *hwisprian*, c. G *wispern*] —**whis′perer,** *n.*

whispering (wĭs′pə rĭng), *n.* **1.** whispered talk or conversation; a whisper or whispers. —*adj.* **2.** that whispers; making a sound like a whisper. —**whis′peringly,** *adv.*

whispering gallery, a gallery or dome in which sounds, however soft, are reflected and can be heard at a considerable distance.

whist¹ (wĭst), *interj.* **1.** hush! silence! be still! —*adj.* **2.** *Archaic or Dial.* hushed; silent; still. Also, **whisht.** [cf. SHUSH, etc.]

whist² (wĭst), *n.* a card game played by four players, two against two, with 52 cards. [earlier *whisk*, ? special use of WHISK¹, altered by confusion with WHIST¹]

whist-drive (wĭst′drīv′, wĭs′-), *n.* a series of games of whist played by a number of sets of partners at different tables, winning pairs moving to the next table at the end of each game.

whistle (wĭs′əl), *v.,* **-tled, -tling,** *n.* —*v.i.* **1.** to make a kind of clear musical sound, or a series of such sounds, by the forcible expulsion of the breath through a small orifice formed by contracting the lips, or through the teeth, together with the aid of the tongue. **2.** to make such a sound or series of sounds otherwise, as by blowing on a particular device. **3.** to produce a more or less similar sound by an instrument operated by steam or the like, or as such an instrument does. **4.** to emit somewhat similar sounds from the mouth, as birds. **5.** to move, go, pass, etc., with a whizzing sound, as a bullet. —*v.t.* **6.** to produce or utter by whistling. **7.** to call, direct, or signal by or as by whistling. **8.** to send with a whistling or whizzing sound. **9. whistle for,** to ask or wish for (something) in vain. —*n.* **10.** an instrument for producing whistling sounds, as by the breath, steam, etc., as a small wooden or tin tube or a small pipe. **11.** a fipple flute. **12.** a sound produced by or as by whistling: *a long-drawn whistle of astonishment.*

13. *Slang.* the mouth and throat: *to wet one's whistle.* [ME; OE *hwistlian*]

whistler (wĭs′lə), *n.* **1.** one who or that which whistles. **2.** something that sounds like a whistle. **3.** an atmospheric whistle which is sometimes picked up on radio receivers, caused by electromagnetic radiations emanating from lightning flashes being reflected back to earth by the ionosphere. **4.** any of various birds whose wings whistle in flight, esp. the goldeneye and European widgeon. **5.** a horse affected with whistling.

Whistler (wĭs′lə), *n.* **James Abbott McNeill,** 1834–1903, U.S. painter and etcher, living in England and France after 1855. —**Whistlerian** (wĭs lĭə′rĭ ən), *adj.*

whistlestop (wĭs′əl stŏp′), *v.*, **-stopped, -stopping,** *n.*, *adj.* —*v.i.* **1.** *Chiefly U.S.* to travel about the country, esp. by train, in campaigning for political office, stopping at small communities to reach voters in small groups. —*n.* **2.** *U.S.* a small unimportant community, esp. one on a railway line. **3.** *U.S.* a brief appearance, speech, or the like, in a small community, as during a political campaign. —*adj.* **4.** denoting or pertaining to whistlestopping or a whistlestop: *a whistlestop tour*; *whistlestop speeches.*

whistling (wĭs′lĭng), *n.* **1.** the act of one who or that which whistles. **2.** the sound produced. **3.** *Vet. Sci.* a form of roaring characterized by a peculiarly shrill sound. [ME; OE *hwistlung*, der. *hwistlian* WHISTLE, v.]

whistling swan, a large North American swan, *Cygnus columbianus.* The adult is pure white with black bill and feet, and a small yellow spot on the bill in front of the eye.

whit (wĭt), *n.* a particle; bit; jot (used esp. in negative phrases): *not a whit better.* [unexplained alter. of WIGHT[1]]

Whit (wĭt), *n.* Whitsuntide.

Whitby (wĭt′bĭ), *n.* a seaport in NE England, in Yorkshire: ruins of an abbey; church council A.D. 664. 11,662 (1961).

white (wīt), *adj.*, **whiter, whitest,** *n.*, *v.*, **whited, whiting.** —*adj.* **1.** of the colour of pure snow, reflecting all or nearly all the rays of sunlight (see def. 26). **2.** light or comparatively light in colour. **3.** lacking colour; transparent. **4.** having a light skin; marked by comparatively slight pigmentation of the skin. **5.** denoting or pertaining to the Caucasian race. **6.** dominated by or exclusively for only members of the white race. **7.** pallid or pale, as from fear or other strong emotion, or pain or illness. **8.** silvery, grey, or hoary: *white hair.* **9.** *Archaic.* blond or fair. **10.** snowy: *a white Christmas.* **11.** royalist, reactionary, or politically extremely conservative (opposed to *red*). **12.** blank, as an unoccupied space in printed matter. **13.** (of silverware) not burnished. **14.** *Armour.* composed of polished steel plates without fabric covering or the like. **15.** wearing white clothing: *a white friar.* **16.** *Electronics.* (of a signal) containing components of all frequencies at random: *a white noise.* **17.** benevolent, beneficent, or good: *white magic.* **18.** auspicious or fortunate. **19.** free from spot or stain. **20.** pure or innocent. **21.** *Colloq.* honourable; trustworthy. **22.** (of wines) light-coloured or yellowish (opposed to *red*). **23.** (of coffee) with milk or cream. **24.** (of bread) made with white flour having a high gluten content. **25. bleed white,** to deprive or be deprived of resources.
—*n.* **26.** an achromatic visual sensation of relatively high luminosity. A white surface reflects light of all hues completely and diffusely. Most so-called whites are very light greys: fresh snow, for example, reflects about 80 per cent of the incident light, but to be strictly white, snow would have to reflect 100 per cent of the incident light. It is the ultimate limit of a series of progressively lightening tints of any colour, as black is the ultimate limit of a series of darkening shades of any colour. **27.** the quality or state of being white. **28.** lightness of skin pigment. **29.** (*sometimes cap.*) a member of the white or Caucasian race. **30.** something white, or a white part of something. **31.** a pellucid viscous fluid which surrounds the yolk of an egg; albumen. **32.** the white part of the eyeball. **33.** (*pl.*) *Pathol.* leucorrhoea. **34.** white wine. **35.** a type or breed which is white in colour. **36.** any of several white-winged butterflies of the family *Pieridae*, as the cabbage white. **37.** (*cap.*) a pig of a white-haired breed. **38.** white fabric. **39.** (*pl.*) household goods as sheets, tablecloths, and sometimes underclothes, esp. goods made of cotton or linen and usually but not necessarily coloured white. **40.** a blank space in printing. **41.** *Archery.* **a.** the outermost ring of the butt. **b.** an arrow that hits this portion of the butt. **c.** the central part of the butt (target) formerly painted white, but now painted gold or yellow. **d.** *Archaic.* a target painted white. **42.** *Chess, Draughts.* the men or pieces which are light-coloured. **43.** a member of a royalist or reactionary party. **44. in the white,** (of furniture or wood) unvarnished or unpainted.
—*v.t.* **45.** *Print.* to make white by leaving blank spaces (often fol. by *out*). **46.** *Obs.* to make white; whiten.
—*v.* **47. white out,** to lose or lack clear visibility in daylight, due to snow, fog, or the like. [ME; OE *hwit*, c. G *weiss*, Icel. *hvítr*, Goth. *hweits*]

White (wīt), *n.* **1. Gilbert,** 1720–93, English clergyman and writer on natural history. **2. Patrick (Victor Martindale),** born 1912, Australian novelist.

white admiral, a butterfly, *Limenitis camilla*, with brown wings with prominent white markings: inhabiting Europe and much of Asia.

white alkali, *Agric.* a whitish layer of mineral salts, esp. sodium sulphate, sodium chloride, and magnesium sulphate, often found on top of soils under low rainfall.

white ant, a termite.

white-ant (wīt′ănt′), *v.t.* *Austral. Slang.* to undermine politically; sabotage.

white arsenic, arsenic trioxide. See **arsenic** (def. 2).

whitebait (wīt′bāt′), *n.*, *pl.* **-bait.** any small delicate fish cooked whole without being cleaned, esp. the young of herring and sprat.

white beam, a variable, deciduous, rosaceous tree, *Sorbus aria*, the leaves of which are densely hairy underneath, occurring on calcareous soil in W and S Europe.

white bear, the polar bear.

whitebeard (wīt′bĭəd′), *n.* a man having a white or grey beard; an old man.

white birch, **1.** the European birch, *Betula pendula*, having a hard wood of many uses. **2.** paper birch.

white book, *U.S.* white paper.

Whiteboy (wīt′boi′), *n.* *Hist.* a member of a secret association of Irish peasants, formed in about 1761 for the purposes of redressing grievances against landlords, protesting against tithes, etc., by acts of terrorism and arson. They wore white shirts for recognition on night raids.

white bryony, a European bryony, *Bryonia dioica.*

whitecap (wīt′kăp′), *n.* **1.** a wave with a broken white crest. **2.** (*cap.*) *U.S.* a member of a self-constituted committee in a community as one of the Ku Klux Klan, who attempts by terrorism, lynchings, etc., to control the community and keep out outsiders.

white cast iron, *Metall.* cast iron in which the carbon is present predominantly as iron carbide.

white cedar, **1.** a coniferous tree, *Chamaecyparis thyoides*, of the swamps of the eastern U.S. **2.** its wood, from which wooden utensils and building articles are often made. **3.** the arbor vitae, *Thuja occidentalis.*

Whitechapel (wīt′chăp′l), *n.* **1.** a district of the E inner London borough of Tower Hamlets. **2.** *Whist, etc.* a lead of a one-card suit with a view to subsequent trump. **3.** *Billiards.* the intentional pocketing of an opponent's ball.

white clover, a clover, *Trifolium repens*, with white flowers, common in pastures and meadows.

white coal, *Obs.* water, as of a stream, used for power.

white-collar (wīt′kŏl′ə), *adj.* belonging or pertaining to non-manual workers, as those in professional and clerical work who are expected to wear conventional dress at work.

white currant, a variety of the redcurrant, *Ribes sativum*, having white berries.

whitedamp (wīt′dămp′), *n.* carbon monoxide.

white dragon, a species of salamander, *Batrachuperus karlschmidti*, worshipped by Chinese monks in a temple on Mount Omei.

whited sepulchre, a specious hypocrite. Matt. 23:27.

white dwarf, *Astron.* one of a class of highly dense stars of low luminosity, as the companion of Sirius. Having consumed most of their available hydrogen they are near to the end of their active lives.

white elephant, **1.** an abnormally whitish or pale elephant, found usually in Siam; an albino elephant. **2.** an annoyingly useless possession. **3.** a possession of great value but entailing even greater expense.

white ensign, the flag borne by ships of the Royal Navy and the Royal Yacht Squadron, consisting of a red cross on a white field, with a Union Jack in canton.

white-eye (wīt′ī′), *n.* any of the numerous small, chiefly tropical, singing birds of the Old World and some Pacific islands, constituting the family *Zosteropidae*, most species of which have a ring of white feathers round the eye.

white-faced (wīt′fāst′), *adj.* **1.** having a white or pale face. **2.** marked with white on the front of the head, as a horse. **3.** having a white front or surface.

white feather, a symbol of cowardice: orig. from a white feather in a gamecock's tail taken as a sign of inferior breeding and hence of poor fighting qualities.

Whitefield (wĭt′fēld′), *n.* **George,** 1714–70, English Methodist preacher.

whitefish (wīt′fĭsh′), *n.*, *pl.* **-fishes,** (*esp. collectively*) **-fish.** **1.** any fish of the family *Coregonidae*, similar to the trout but with smaller mouths and larger scales, esp. *Coregonus clupeaformis*, the common whitefish, a highly valued and important food fish of the Great Lakes. **2.** an edible sea fish of any kind except herring, any of the salmon species or any species of migratory trout, including all shellfish.

white flag, an all-white flag, used as a symbol of surrender, etc.

white flax, the gold-of-pleasure, *Camelina sativa.*

White Friar, a Carmelite friar so called from the white cloak worn.

Whitefriars (wīt′frī′əz), *n.* a district (a sanctuary until 1697) in central London: named after a Carmelite monastery in Fleet Street, founded in 1241.

white frost, frost (def. 3).

white gold, any of several gold alloys possessing a white colour due to the presence of nickel or platinum. Commercial alloys contain gold, nickel, copper, and zinc.

white gum, any of various Australian eucalyptuses with a whitish bark.

white-haired (wīt′hĕəd′), *adj.* **1.** having grey hair, esp. as a mark of old age. **2.** *U.S. Colloq.* favourite; blue-eyed: *a white-haired boy.*

Whitehall (wīt′hôl′), *n.* **1.** Also, **Whitehall Palace.** a former palace in central London, originally built in the reign of Henry III: execution of Charles I, 1649. **2.** a major London thoroughfare between Trafalgar Square and the Houses of Parliament, flanked by government offices. **3.** the British government or its policies.

white-handed (wīt′hăn′dĭd), *adj.* **1.** having white hands. **2.** innocent; guiltless.

Whitehaven (wīt′hā′vən), *n.* a seaport in England, in Cumberland. 27,566 (1961).

Whitehead (wīt′hĕd′), *n.* **Alfred North,** 1861–1947, English mathematician and philosopher.

white-headed (wīt′hĕd′ĭd), *adj.* **1.** having white hair. **2.** having fair or flaxen hair. **3.** (of an animal) having the head wholly or partly white. **4.** *U.S. Colloq.* white-haired.

whiteheart (wīt′hät′), *n.* a kind of cherry bearing a large, sweet, soft-fleshed fruit.

white heat, **1.** a stage of intense activity, excitement, feeling, etc.: *to work at a white heat.* **2.** an intense heat at which a substance glows with white light.

white hope, one who is expected to bring glory, etc., to a country, team, or other group which he represents.

white horehound, a perennial labiate herb, *Marrubium vulgare,* widespread in waste places of Europe and W Asia.

white horse, **1.** a figure of a horse made on a hillside by removing the turf from the underlying chalk, usually of prehistoric origin, as one in Berkshire at Uffington. **2.** a white-topped wave; a whitecap.

Whitehorse (wīt′hôs′), *n.* a town in NW Canada; the capital of Yukon territory. 5031 (1961).

white-hot (wīt′hŏt′), *adj.* **1.** very hot. **2.** showing white heat.

White House, the, **1.** the official residence ('Executive Mansion') of the President of the United States, at Washington, D.C.: a large two-storey freestone building painted white. **2.** *Colloq.* the U.S. president's office; the executive branch of the Federal government.

white lead, **1.** basic lead carbonate, $2PbCO_3.Pb(OH)_2$, a white, heavy powder used as a pigment, in putty, and in medicinal ointments for burns. **2.** the putty made from this substance in oil.

white lead ore, cerussite.

white leather, whitleather.

white leg, *Pathol.* milk leg.

white lie, a lie uttered from polite, amiable, or pardonable motives; a harmless fib.

white light, *Physics.* light which contains all the wavelengths of the visible spectrum at approximately the same intensity, as light from an incandescent white-hot solid.

white line, **1.** any blank or white part or margin. **2.** *Print.* a line of space. **3.** a line of white paint or the like, either continuous or interrupted, laid along the centre of a road to separate traffic lanes. **4.** a white layer in a horse's hoof.

white-livered (wīt′lĭv′əd), *adj.* **1.** pale or unhealthy. **2.** cowardly.

whitely (wīt′lĭ), *adv.* with a white hue or colour.

white magic, magic used for benevolent or good purposes.

white man, **1.** a member of the white race. **2.** *Colloq.* an honest, straightforward, or reliable person.

white man's burden, the supposed duty of the white race to care for and educate peoples of other races in the colonies. [coined by Rudyard Kipling]

white matter, *Anat.* nervous tissue, esp. of the brain and spinal cord, containing fibres only, and nearly white in colour.

white meat, any light-coloured meat, as veal, the breast of chicken, etc. (distinguished from *red meat*).

white metal, **1. a.** any of various light-coloured alloys containing a high proportion of tin, as Babbitt metal, Britannia metal, etc.; used for bearings, light castings, and domestic articles. **b.** any of various similar alloys containing a high proportion of lead instead of tin. **2.** the intermediate metal in the conversion of copper matter.

White Mountains, a mountain range in N New Hampshire: a part of the Appalachian system. Highest peak, Mt Washington, 6293 ft.

whiten (wī′tn), *v.t., v.i.* to make or become white. —**whit′ener,** *n.*

—**Syn.** WHITEN, BLANCH, BLEACH mean to make or become white. To WHITEN implies giving a white colour or appearance by putting a substance of some kind on the outside: *to whiten shoes.* To BLANCH implies taking away original colour throughout: *to blanch celery by keeping it in the dark.* To BLEACH implies making white by placing in (sun) light or by using chemicals: *to bleach linen, hair.* —**Ant.** blacken.

whiteness (wīt′nĭs), *n.* **1.** the quality or state of being white. **2.** paleness. **3.** purity. **4.** a white substance.

white nickel, chloanthite.

white night, a sleepless night.

White Nile. See **Nile** (def. 3).

whitening (wīt′nĭng), *n.* **1.** the act or process of making or turning white. **2.** a preparation for making something white; whiting.

white oak, **1.** an oak, *Quercus alba,* of eastern North America, having a light grey to white bark and a hard, durable wood. **2.** the wood of this or any of several other related oaks.

white paper, **1.** paper bleached white. **2.** an official report of a government on a specific subject.

white pepper, a condiment prepared from the husked dried berries of the pepper plant, used either whole or ground. See **pepper.**

white pine, **1.** a pine, *Pinus strobus,* of eastern North America, yielding a light-coloured, soft, light wood of great commercial importance. **2.** the wood itself. **3.** the New Zealand tree kahikatea. **4.** any of various other similar species of pine.

white plague, tuberculosis, esp. pulmonary tuberculosis.

white poplar, **1.** an Old World poplar, *Populus alba,* having the underside of the leaves covered with a dense silvery white down. **2.** the soft, straight-grained wood of the tulip tree.

white potato. See **potato** (def. 1).

white race, the Caucasian race.

white rat, an albino variety of the common rat, *Rattus norvegicus,* used in biological experiments.

white rhinoceros, a two-horned rhinoceros, *Rhinoceros simus,* of Africa, characterized by wide square lips. [*white* t. Afrikaans: m. *wyd* WIDE (so called on account of its broad lips), influenced by WHITE]

white rose. *Hist.* See **rose** (def. 9b).

White Russia, **1.** Official name, **White Russian Soviet Socialist Republic.** Also, **Byelorussian Soviet Socialist Republic.** a constituent republic of the Soviet Union, in the W part. 8,100,000 (est. 1959); 86,100 sq. mi. *Cap.:* Minsk. **2.** a region in the W part of tsarist Russia, inhabited by the White Russians.

White Russian, a member of a division of the Russian people dwelling in White Russia and adjoining parts.

white sale, a sale of linen and cotton goods at bargain prices.

white sapphire, a white variety of corundum, used as a gem.

white sauce, a sauce made of butter, flour, seasoning, and milk or sometimes chicken or veal stock.

White Sea, an arm of the Arctic Ocean, in the NW Soviet Union. ab. 36,000 sq. mi.

white slave, **1.** a white woman who is sold or forced to serve as a prostitute, esp. outside her native land. **2.** a person held as a slave or in some condition resembling slavery.

white-slaver (wīt′slā′və), *n.* a person engaged in the traffic in white slaves.

white slavery, the condition of or the traffic in white slaves.

white-slaving (wīt′slā′vĭng), *n.* traffic in white slaves.

whitesmith (wīt′smĭth′), *n.* a tinsmith.

white spirit, a mixture of petroleum hydrocarbons in the boiling range 150°–200°C, used as a solvent for paints and varnishes as a substitute for turpentine.

white spruce. See **spruce** (def. 1).

white squall, *Naut.* a whirlwind or violent disturbance of small radius, which is not accompanied by the usual clouds, but is indicated merely by the whitecaps and turbulent water beneath it.

white supremacist, a believer in white supremacy.

white supremacy, the belief or theory that white men have a natural or god-given supremacy over people of other races.

white-tailed deer, (wīt′tāld′), a common deer of North America, *Odocoileus virginianus,* and related species,

whose tail is white on the underside. Also, **white′tail′.**
whitethorn (wīt′thôn′), *n.* the common hawthorn.
whitethroat (wīt′thrōt′), *n.* **1.** a small Old World songbird, *Sylvia communis*, reddish brown above, with white throat, and distinguishable from its closest allies by the white marks on its outer tail feathers. **2.** any of several other Old World birds of the same genus.
white tie, 1. a white bow tie for men, worn with the most formal style of evening dress. **2.** the most formal style of evening dress for men, of which the characteristic garments are a white bow tie and a tail coat (distinguished from *black tie*).
white trash, (used derogatorily) **1.** poor white people collectively, esp. in the southern U.S. **2.** one such person.
white turnip. See **turnip** (def. 1).
white vitriol, zinc sulphate heptahydrate, $ZnSO_4.7H_2O$, a white crystalline compound, used as an antiseptic, mordant, preservative, etc.
whitewall (wīt′wôl′), *n.* **1.** a vehicle tyre having a white sidewall. *—adj.* **2.** of or pertaining to such a tyre.
whitewash (wīt′wŏsh′), *n.* **1.** a composition, as of lime and water or of whiting, size, and water, used for whitening walls, woodwork, etc. **2.** anything used to cover up defects, gloss over faults or errors, or give a specious semblance of respectability, honesty, etc. **3.** *U.S. Colloq.* (in various games) a defeat in which the loser fails to score. *—v.t.* **4.** to whiten with whitewash. **5.** to cover up or gloss over the defects, faults, errors, etc., of by some means. **6.** *U.S. Colloq.* (in various games) to subject to a whitewash. **—white′wash′er,** *n.*
white water, any stretch of water in which the surface is broken, as in rapids or breakers, due to movement over a shallow bottom.
white wax, any of various waxes, as paraffin wax or beeswax, that are naturally white or artificially whitened.
white whale, the beluga, *Delphinapterus leucas.*
whitewing (wīt′wĭng′), *n. U.S.* a roadsweeper who wears a white uniform, as in New York City.
whitewood (wīt′wo͝od′), *n.* **1.** any of numerous trees, as the tulip tree or the linden, having a white or light-coloured wood. **2.** the wood. **3.** the cottonwood of the genus *Populus.*
whitey (wī′tĭ), *n. Slang.* (used contemptuously) a white man.
whither (wĭth′ə), *Archaic; now replaced by* **where.** *—adv.* **1.** to what place? **2.** to what point, end, course, etc., or to what? *—conj.* **3.** to what, whatever, or which place, point, end, etc. [ME and OE *hwider*, alter. of *hwæder* (c. Goth. *hwadrē*) on model of *hider* HITHER]
whithersoever (wĭth′ə sō ĕv′ə), *adv. Archaic.* to whatsoever place.
whitherward (wĭth′ə wəd), *adv. Archaic.* towards what place; in what direction. Also, **whitherwards.**
whiting[1] (wī′tĭng), *n.* **1.** any of several European species of the cod family, esp. *Merlangus merlangus.* **2.** the American Atlantic hake (*Merluccius bilinearis*). **3.** a slender Atlantic shore fish of the genus *Menticirrhus*, of the croaker family (*Sciaenidae*). [late ME *whytynge*, ? alter. of OE *hwitling* kind of fish. Cf. D *wijting*]
whiting[2] (wī′tĭng), *n.* pure white chalk (calcium carbonate) which has been ground and washed, used in making putty, whitewash, etc., and for cleaning silver, etc. [f. WHITE + -ING[1]]
whitish (wī′tĭsh), *adj.* somewhat white; tending to white. **—whit′ishness,** *n.*
whitleather (wĭt′lĕth′ə), *n.* leather dressed with alum, salt, or other chemicals; white leather.
Whitley Bay (wĭt′lĭ), a seaside resort in England, in Northumberland. 36,517 (1961).
whitlow (wĭt′lō), *n. Pathol.* an inflammation of the deeper tissues of a finger or toe, esp. of the terminal phalanx, usually terminating in suppuration. [ME *whitflawe, whitflowe*, f. WHITE + FLAW[1]]
whitlow grass, any of several small herbaceous plants of the cruciferous genera *Draba* and *Erophila*, as *E. verna*, a common plant of walls and rocks in temperate regions. [so called because once believed to cure whitlows]
Whitman (wĭt′mən), *n.* **Walt(er),** 1819–92, U.S. poet.
Whit Monday (wĭt), the Monday following Whit Sunday.
Whitney (wĭt′nĭ), *n.* **1. Eli,** 1765–1825, American inventor (of the cotton gin). **2. William Dwight,** 1827–94, U.S. philologist and lexicographer. **3. Mount,** a mountain in the U.S., in E California, in the Sierra Nevada Mountains: the second highest peak in the United States. 14,495 ft.
Whitstable (wĭt′stə bl), *n.* a seaport in England, in Kent, on the Thames estuary. 19,534 (1961).
Whitsun (wĭt′sən), *adj.* **1.** of or pertaining to Whit Sunday or Whitsuntide. *—n.* **2.** Whitsuntide.
Whit Sunday (wĭt), the seventh Sunday after Easter, celebrated as a festival in commemoration of the descent of the Holy Spirit on the day of Pentecost. [ME *whytsonenday*, OE *Hwīta Sunnandæg*, lit., white Sunday, from the white (baptismal) robes worn on that day]
Whitsuntide (wĭt′sən tīd′), *n.* the week beginning with Whit Sunday, esp. the first three days of this week.
Whittington (wĭt′ĭng tən), *n.* **Dick,** died 1423, lord mayor of London 1398, 1406–07, and 1419–20, about whom many legends survive.
whittle (wĭt′l), *v.*, **-tled, -tling,** *n.* *—v.t.* **1.** to cut, trim, or shape (a stick, piece of wood, etc.) by taking off bits with a knife. **2.** to cut off (a bit or bits). **3.** to cut by way of reducing amount (esp. fol. by *down*): *to whittle down expenses.* *—v.i.* **4.** to cut bits or chips from wood or the like with a knife, as in shaping something or as a mere aimless diversion. *—n.* **5.** *Scot. and N Dial.* a knife. [alter. of *thwittle*, ME *thwitel* knife, der. OE *thwītan* whittle] **—whit′tler,** *n.*
Whittle (wĭt′l), **Sir Frank,** born 1907, English aircraft designer; developed the jet engine.
whittling (wĭt′lĭng), *n.* **1.** the act of one who whittles. **2.** (*usually pl.*) a bit or chip whittled off.
whity (wī′tĭ), *adj.* whitish.
whiz (wĭz), *v.*, **whizzed, whizzing,** *n.* *—v.i.* **1.** to make a humming or hissing sound, as an object passing rapidly through the air. **2.** to move or rush with such a sound. *—v.t.* **3.** to cause to whiz. **4.** to treat with a whizzer. *—n.* **5.** the sound of a whizzing object. **6.** a swift movement producing such a sound. Also, **whizz.** [imit.]
whiz-bang (wĭz′băng′), *n.* **1.** *Mil.* a small shell which travels through the air at or near the speed of sound, so that it explodes at the same times as or shortly before the sound of its flight is heard. **2.** a firework making such a sound. **3.** the sound itself. *—v.i.* **4.** to make such a sound. Also, **whizz-bang.**
whizzer (wĭz′ə), *n.* **1.** something that whizzes. **2.** a centrifugal machine for drying sugar, grain, clothes, etc.
who (ho͞o), *pron.*; *possessive* **whose;** *objective* **whom.** *—interrog. pron.* **1.** what person?: *who told you so? whose book is this? of whom are you speaking?* **2.** (of a person) what as to character, origin, position, importance, etc.: *who is the man in uniform?* *—rel. pron.* **3.** (as a compound relative:) **a.** the or any person that; any person, be it who it may. **b.** *Archaic.* one that (after *as*). **4.** (as a simple relative, with antecedent (a person, or sometimes an animal or a personified thing) expressed): **a.** in clauses conveying an additional idea: *we saw men who were at work.* **b.** used in clauses defining or restricting the antecedent: *one on whose word we rely, the man to whom it was told.* **5. who's who,** the people who carry influence or importance. [ME; OE *hwā*, c. D *wie*, G *wer*, Goth. *hwas*] **—Syn. 4.** See **that.**
W.H.O., World Health Organization.
whoa (wō), *interj.* stop! (used esp. to horses).
who'd (ho͞od), contraction of *who would.*
whodunit (ho͞o′dŭn′ĭt), *n. Slang.* a novel dealing with a murder or murders and the detection of the criminal.
whoever (ho͞o ĕv′ə), *pron.*; *possessive* **whosever;** *objective* **whomever.** *—indef. rel. pron.* **1.** whatever person, or anyone that: *whoever wants it may have it.* **2.** no matter who. *—interrog. pron.* **3.** *Colloq.* who ever? who? (used emphatically): *whoever is that?* Also, *Poetic,* **whoe'er** (ho͞o ĕə′).
whole (hōl), *adj.* **1.** comprising the full quantity, amount, extent, number, etc., without diminution or exception; entire, full, or total. **2.** containing all the elements properly belonging; complete: *a whole set.* **3.** undivided, or in one piece: *to swallow a thing whole.* **4.** *Maths.* integral, or not fractional: *a whole number.* **5.** uninjured, undamaged, or unbroken; sound; intact: *to get off with a whole skin.* **6.** *Archaic.* sound; healthy. **7.** fully developed and balanced, in all aspects of one's nature: *educated to be a whole man.* **8.** being fully or entirely such: *whole brother.* **9. out of whole cloth,** *U.S. Colloq.* without foundation in fact: *a story made out of whole cloth.* *—n.* **10.** the whole assemblage of parts or elements belonging to a thing; the entire quantity, account, extent, or number. **11.** a thing complete in itself, or comprising all its parts or elements. **12.** an assemblage of parts associated or viewed together as one thing; a unitary system. **13. as a whole,** all things included or considered. **14. on** or **upon the whole, a.** on consideration of the whole matter, or in view of all the circumstances. **b.** as a whole or in general, without regard to exceptions. [ME *hole*, OE *hāl*, c. D *heel*, G *heil*, Icel. *heill*; spelling *wh-* (15th cent.) from d. pronunciation. Cf. HALE[1], HEAL] **—whole′ness,** *n.*
—Syn. 10. WHOLE, TOTAL mean the entire or complete sum or amount. The WHOLE is all there is; every part, member, aspect; the complete sum, amount, quantity of anything, not divided; the entirety: *the whole of one's property, family.* TOTAL also means whole, complete amount, or number, but conveys the idea of something added together or added up: *the total of his gains amounted to millions.* **—Ant. 10.** part.

whole brother, full brother.
whole gale, *Meteorol.* a wind of Beaufort scale force 10, i.e. one about 55–63 miles per hour.
wholehearted (hōl′hä′tĭd), *adj.* hearty; cordial; earnest; sincere. —**whole′heart′edly,** *adv.* —**whole′heart′edness,** *n.*
whole hog, *Slang.* **1.** entireness; completeness. **2. go the whole hog,** to involve oneself to the fullest extent; do something thoroughly or completely. —**whole′-hog′-ger,** *n.*
whole-length (hōl′lĕngth′), *adj.* full-length.
whole-life insurance (hōl′līf′), a life insurance contract where the capital sum is only payable on the death of the insured.
wholemeal (hōl′mēl′), *adj.* prepared with the complete wheat kernel, as flour or the bread baked with it; whole-wheat.
whole milk, milk containing all its constituents as received from the cow, or other milk-giving animal.
whole note, *U.S.* semibreve.
whole number, an integer, as 0, 1, 2, 3, 4, 5, etc.
wholesale (hōl′sāl′), *n., adj., adv., v.,* **-saled, -saling.** —*n.* **1.** the sale of commodities in large quantities, as to retailers or jobbers rather than to consumers directly (distinguished from *retail*). **2. by wholesale, a.** in large quantities, as in the sale of commodities. **b.** on a large scale and without discrimination: *slaughter by wholesale.* —*adj.* **3.** of, pertaining to, or engaged in sale by wholesale. **4.** extensive and indiscriminate: *wholesale discharge of workers.* —*adv.* **5.** in a wholesale way. **6.** on wholesale terms. —*v.t., v.i.* **7.** to sell by wholesale. —**whole′sal′er,** *n.*
whole-seas over (hōl′sēz ō′və), completely under the influence of alcohol.
whole sister, full sister.
wholesome (hōl′səm), *adj.* **1.** conducive to moral or general well-being; salutary; beneficial: *wholesome advice.* **2.** conducive to bodily health; healthful; salubrious: *wholesome food, air, or exercise.* **3.** suggestive of health (physical or moral), esp. in appearance. **4.** healthy or sound. [ME *holsum,* f. *hol* WHOLE + *-sum* -SOME¹] —**whole′somely,** *adv.* —**whole′someness,** *n.* —**Syn. 2.** nourishing, nutritious. **3.** See **healthy.**
whole-souled (hōl′sōld′), *adj. Obs.* whole-hearted; hearty.
whole tone, *Music.* an interval of two semitones, as A-B or B-C; a major second. Also, *U.S.,* **whole step.**
whole-tone scale (hōl′tōn′), a scale progressing exclusively by whole tones; a scale of six whole tones.
whole-wheat (hōl′wēt′), *adj. U.S.* wholemeal.
who'll (ho͞ol), contraction of *who will* or *who shall.*
wholly (hōl′lĭ), *adv.* **1.** entirely; totally; altogether; quite. **2.** to the whole amount, extent, etc. **3.** so as to comprise or involve all.
whom (ho͞om), *pron.* objective case of **who.** [ME; OE *hwām,* dat. of *hwā* WHO]
whomever (ho͞om ĕv′ə), *pron.* objective case of **whoever.**
whomsoever (ho͞om′sō ĕv′ə), *pron.* objective case of **whosoever.**
whoop (ho͞op), *n.* **1.** a loud cry or shout, as one uttered by children or warriors. **2.** the whooping sound characteristic of whooping cough. **3. not worth a whoop,** *Colloq.* not worth a thing; utterly valueless. —*v.i.* **4.** to utter a loud cry or shout (orig. the syllable whoop, or hoop), as a call, or in enthusiasm, excitement, frenzy, etc. **5.** to cry as an owl, crane, or certain other birds. **6.** to make the characteristic sound accompanying the deep indrawing of breath after a series of coughs in whooping cough. —*v.t.* **7.** to utter with or as with a whoop or whoops. **8.** to whoop to or at. **9.** to call, urge, pursue, or drive with whoops: *to whoop dogs on.* **10. whoop it** (or **things**) **up,** *Slang.* to raise an outcry or disturbance. —*interj.* **11.** (a cry to show excitement, encouragement, enthusiasm, etc.) [ME *whope,* OE *hwōpan* threaten, c. Goth. *hwōpan* boast]
whoopee (wo͝op′ĭ *for 1 and 2;* wo͝o pē′ *for 3*), *Colloq.* —*n.* **1.** uproarious festivity. **2. make whoopee,** to engage in uproarious merry-making. —*interj.* **3.** (a shout of 'whoopee'.) [extended var. of WHOOP]
whooper (ho͞o′pə), *n.* **1.** one who or that which whoops. **2.** Also, **whooper swan.** a common Old World swan, *Cygnus cygnus,* notable for its whooping cry.
whooping cough (ho͞o′pĭng), an infectious disease of the respiratory mucous membrane, esp. of children, characterized by a series of short, convulsive coughs followed by a deep inspiration accompanied by a whooping sound; pertussis.
whoops (wo͝ops), *interj.* (an exclamation of surprise, etc.)
whoosh (wo͝osh), *n.* **1.** a loud rushing noise, as of water or air. —*v.i.* **2.** to move with a loud rushing noise.
whop (wŏp), *v.,* **whopped, whopping,** *n. Colloq.* —*v.t.* **1.** to throw with force, pitch, or dash. **2.** to strike forcibly. **3.** to defeat soundly, as in a contest. **4.** to strike out or move suddenly. —*v.i.* **5.** to plump suddenly down; flop. —*n.* **6.** a forcible blow or impact. **7.** the sound made by it. **8.** a bump; a heavy fall. Also, *U.S. and Dial.,* **whap, wap.** [orig. uncert.]
whopper (wŏp′ə), *n. Colloq.* **1.** something uncommonly large of its kind. **2.** a big lie. **3.** one who or that which whops. [f. WHOP + -ER¹]
whopping (wŏp′ĭng), *adj. Colloq.* very large of its kind; huge.
whore (hô), *n., v.,* **whored, whoring.** —*n.* **1.** a prostitute. —*v.i.* **2.** to act as a whore. **3.** to consort with whores. —*v.t.* **4.** to make a whore of; debauch. [ME and OE *hōre,* c. G *Hure;* akin to L *cārus* dear]
who're (ho͞o′ə), contraction of *who are.*
whoredom (hô′dəm), *n.* **1.** prostitution. **2.** (in biblical use) idolatry.
whorehouse (hô′hous′), *n., pl.* **-houses** (-hou′zĭz). a brothel; house of prostitution.
whoremonger (hô′mŭng′gə), *n.* one who consorts with whores. Also, **whoremaster** (hô′mäs′tə).
whoreson (hô′sən), *Obs.* —*n.* **1.** the son of a whore; a bastard. **2.** (in contemptuous or abusive use) a person. —*adj.* **3.** being a bastard. **4.** mean; wretched; contemptible. [f. WHORE + SON]
whorish (hô′rĭsh), *adj.* being or having the character of a whore; lewd; unchaste. —**whor′ishly,** *adv.* —**whor′ishness,** *n.*
whorl (wûl), *n.* **1.** a circular arrangement of like parts, as leaves, flowers, etc., round a point on an axis; a verticil. **2.** one of the turns or volutions of a spiral shell. **3.** one of the principal ridge-shapes of a fingerprint, forming at least one complete circle (distinguished from *loop* and *arch*). **4.** *Anat.* one of the turns in the cochlea of the ear. **5.** anything shaped like a coil. [ME *whorvil,* f. *whorve* (OE *hweorfa* whorl) + *-l,* suffix]

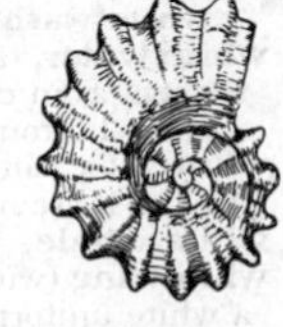
Whorls of ammonite

whorled (wûld), *adj.* **1.** having a whorl or whorls. **2.** disposed in the form of a whorl, as leaves.
whortleberry (wû′tl bĕ′rĭ), *n., pl.* **-ries. 1.** the edible, black berry of the ericaceous shrub, *Vaccinium myrtillus,* of Europe and Siberia. **2.** the shrub itself. [d. var. of *hurtleberry,* f. *hurtle* (der. *hurt,* OE *horta* whortleberry) + BERRY]
who's (ho͞oz), contraction of *who is* or *who has.*
whose (ho͞oz), *pron.* **1.** possessive case of the relative and interrogative pronoun **who**: *the man whose book I borrowed; whose is this book?* **2.** possessive case of the relative pronoun **which** (historically, of **what**): *a pen whose point is broken.* [ME *whos,* OE *hwæs,* gen. of *hwā* who]
whosesoever (ho͞oz′sō ĕv′ə), *pron.* possessive case of **whosoever.**
whosever (ho͞oz ĕv′ə), *pron.* possessive case of **whoever.**
whoso (ho͞o′sō), *pron.* whosoever; whoever.
whosoever (ho͞o′sō ĕv′ə), *pron., possessive* **whosesoever;** *objective* **whomsoever.** whoever; whatever person.
who've (ho͞ov), contraction of *who have.*
whr, watt-hour.
why (wī), *adv., conj., n., pl.* **whys,** *interj.* —*adv.* **1.** for what? for what cause, reason, or purpose? —*conj.* **2.** for what cause or reason. **3.** for which, or on account of which (after *reason,* etc., to introduce a relative clause): *the reason why he refused.* **4.** the reason for which: *that is why I raised this question again.* —*n.* **5.** the cause or reason. —*interj.* **6.** (an expression of surprise, hesitation, etc., or sometimes a mere expletive): *Why, it is all gone!* [ME; OE *hwī, hwȳ,* instrumental case of *hwæt* WHAT]
Whyalla (wī ăl′ə), *n.* a town in South Australia, on the Spencer Gulf. 18,000 (est. 1965).
whydah (wĭd′ə), *n.* **1.** any of the small African birds which constitute the subfamily *Viduinae,* comprising species of weaverbirds the males of which have elongated drooping tail feathers. **2.** any of the birds of the genera *Coliuspasser, Drepanoplectes,* and *Diatropura.* Also, **whidah, whidah-bird, widowbird.** [alter. of WIDOW BIRD to agree with name of town in Dahomey, western Africa, one of its haunts]
Whymper (wĭm′pə), *n.* **Edward,** 1840–1911, English mountaineer.
W.I., 1. West Indian. **2.** West Indies. **3.** Women's Institute.
Wichita (wĭch′ĭ tô′), *n.* a city in the U.S., in S Kansas on the Arkansas river. 254,698 (1960).
Wichita Falls, a city in the U.S., in N Texas. 101,724 (1960).
wick¹ (wĭk), *n.* **1.** a bundle or loose twist or braid of soft threads, or a woven strip or tube, as of cotton, which in a candle, lamp, oilstove, or the like serves to draw up the

melted tallow or wax or the oil or other inflammable liquid to be burned at its top end. 2. *Slang.* **to get on one's wick,** to irritate. [ME *wicke, weke,* OE *wice, wēoc(e),* c. MD *wiecke,* OHG *wiohha*] —**wick′less,** *adj.*

wick[2] (wĭk), *n. Curling.* a narrow opening in the field, bounded by other players' stones. [n. use of v., to drive a stone through an opening]

Wick (wĭk), *n.* a seaport in Scotland, the county town of Caithness. 7,397 (1961).

wicked (wĭk′ĭd), *adj.* **1.** evil or morally bad in principle or practice; iniquitous; sinful. **2.** mischievous or playfully malicious. **3.** *Colloq.* distressingly severe, as cold, pain, wounds, etc. **4.** *Colloq.* ill-natured, savage, or vicious: *a wicked horse.* **5.** *Colloq.* extremely trying, unpleasant, or troublesome. [ME, f. *wick(e)* wicked (now d.) + -ED[2]. Cf. OE *wicca* wizard] —**wick′edly,** *adv.* —**Syn. 1.** unrighteous, ungodly, godless, impious, profane; unprincipled; immoral, profligate, corrupt, depraved; heinous; infamous, vicious, vile. See **bad**[1].

wickedness (wĭk′ĭd nĭs), *n.* **1.** the quality or state of being wicked. **2.** wicked conduct or practices. **3.** a wicked act or thing.

wicker (wĭk′ə), *n.* **1.** a slender, pliant twig; an osier; a withe. **2.** wickerwork. **3.** *Obs.* something made of wickerwork, as a basket. —*adj.* **4.** consisting or made of wicker: *a wicker basket.* **5.** covered with wicker. [ME, t. Scand.; cf. d. Sw. *vikker* willow]

wickerwork (wĭk′ə wûk′), *n.* **1.** work consisting of plaited or woven twigs or osiers; articles made of wicker. —*adj.* **2.** wicker.

wicket (wĭk′ĭt), *n.* **1.** a small door or gate, esp. one beside, or forming part of, a larger one. **2.** a window or opening, often closed by a grating or the like, as in a door, or forming a place of communication in a ticket office or the like. **3.** a turnstile. **4.** a small gate by which a canal lock is emptied. **5.** a gate by which a flow of water is regulated, as to a waterwheel. **6.** *Cricket.* **a.** either of the two frameworks, each consisting of three stumps with two bails in grooves across their tops, at which the bowler aims the ball. **b.** the area between the wickets, esp. with reference to the state of the ground. **c.** one end of the pitch, esp. the area between the stumps and the popping crease. **d.** one batsman's turn at the wicket. **e.** the period during which two men bat together. **f.** the achievement of a batsman's dismissal by the fielding side. **7. a sticky wicket,** *Colloq.* a difficult or disadvantageous situation or set of circumstances. [ME, t. AF, ult. der. Scand.; cf. Icel. *vikja* move]

wicket-keeper (wĭk′ĭt kē′pə), *n. Cricket.* the player on the fielding side who stands immediately behind the wicket to stop balls that pass it.

wicking (wĭk′ĭng), *n.* material for wicks.

wickiup (wĭk′ĭ ŭp′), *n. U.S.* **1.** (in Nevada, Arizona, etc.) an American Indian hut made of brushwood or covered with mats. **2.** *Dial.* any rude hut. Also, **wikiup.** [prob. t. Algonquian (Sac-Fox-Kickapoo): m. *wikiyapi* lodge, dwelling]

Wickliffe (wĭk′lĭf), *n.* **John.** See **Wyclif.** Also, **Wiclif.**

Wicklow (wĭk′lō), *n.* **1.** a county in the E Republic of Ireland, in Leinster. 58,473 pop. (1961); 782 sq. mi. **2.** its county town. 3125 (1961). **3.** (*pl.*) Also, **Wicklow Mountains.** a low mountain range in this county. Highest point, 3039 ft.

wicopy (wĭk′ə pĭ), *n., pl.* **-pies.** *U.S.* **1.** the leatherwood, *Dirca palustris.* **2.** any of various willow herbs, as *Chamaenerion angustifolium.* **3.** basswood. [t. d. Algonquian: m. *wik′pi, wighebi,* etc., inner bark]

widdershins (wĭd′ə shĭnz′), *adv. Dial. and Archaic.* withershins.

wide (wīd), *adj.,* **wider, widest,** *adv., n.* —*adj.* **1.** having considerable or great extent from side to side; broad; not narrow. **2.** having a certain or specified extent from side to side: *3 feet wide.* **3.** of great horizontal extent; extensive; vast; spacious. **4.** of great range or scope; embracing a great number or variety of subjects, cases, etc.: *wide reading, experience, etc.* **5.** open to the full or a great extent; expanded; distended: *to stare with wide eyes, or a wide mouth.* **6.** full, ample, or roomy, as clothing. **7.** apart or remote from a specified point or object: *a guess wide of the truth.* **8.** too far or too much to one side: *a wide ball in cricket.* **9.** *Phonet.* pronounced with relatively lax muscles. **10.** *Slang.* astute; shrewd. —*adv.* **11.** to a great, or relatively great, extent from side to side. **12.** over an extensive space or region, or far abroad: *scattered far and wide.* **13.** to the full extent of opening: *to open the eyes or the mouth wide.* **14.** to the utmost, or fully: *to be wide awake.* **15.** away from or to one side of a point, mark, purpose, or the like; aside; astray: *the shot went wide.* —*n.* **16.** *Cricket.* a bowled ball that passes outside the batsman's reach, and counts as a run for the side batting. [ME; OE *wīd,* c. D *wijd,* G *weit*] —**wide′ness,** *n.* —**wid′ish,** *adj.* —**Syn. 1.** WIDE, BROAD refer to dimensions. They are often interchangeable, but WIDE especially applies to things of which the length is much greater than the width: *a wide road, piece of ribbon.* BROAD is more emphatic, and applies to things of considerable or great width, esp. to surfaces extending laterally: *a broad valley.* **4.** extensive, ample, comprehensive. —**Ant. 1.** narrow.

wide-angle (wīd′ăng′gl), *adj. Photog.* denoting or pertaining to a camera lens with a wide angle of view (up to 100°) and a short focal length.

wide-awake (wī′də wāk′), *adj.* **1.** fully awake; with the eyes wide open. **2.** alert, keen, or knowing. —*n.* **3.** Also, **wide-awake hat.** a soft, wide-brimmed felt hat.

wide-band (wīd′bănd′), *adj. Electronics.* denoting or pertaining to equipment which can respond to a wide range of frequencies.

wide-eyed (wīd′īd′), *adj.* having the eyes habitually or temporarily wide open, as from innocence, amazement, wakefulness, or the like.

widely (wīd′lĭ), *adv.* **1.** to a wide extent. **2.** over a wide space or area: *a widely distributed plant.* **3.** throughout a large number of persons: *a man who is widely known.* **4.** in many or various subjects, cases, etc.: *to be widely read.* **5.** greatly, very much, or very: *two widely different accounts of an affair.*

widen (wī′dn), *v.t., v.i.* to make or become wide or wider; expand. —**wid′ener,** *n.*

wide-open (wīd′ō′pən), *adj.* **1.** opened to the full extent. **2.** open to attack or dispute: *a wide-open statement.* **3.** *U.S.* denoting the loose or irregular enforcement or the non-enforcement of laws concerning the consumption of alcoholic drinks, vice, gambling, etc.

wide-screen (wīd′skrēn′), *adj.* denoting films projected on to a screen having greater width than height, intended to give the audience a greater sense of actuality. The width is generally 2½ times the height.

widespread (wīd′sprĕd′), *adj.* **1.** spread over or occupying a wide space. **2.** distributed over a wide region, or occurring in many places or among many persons or individuals. Also, **wide′spread′ing.**

widgeon (wĭj′ən), *n.* **1.** any of several freshwater ducks between the mallard and teal in size, esp. the **European widgeon** (*Anas penelope*). **2.** *Obs.* a fool. Also, **wigeon.** [orig. obscure]

Widnes (wĭd′nĭs), *n.* a town in England, in S Lancashire. 52,186 (1961).

widow (wĭd′ō), *n.* **1.** a woman who has lost her husband by death and has not married again. **2.** (used in combination) a woman whose husband is often absent, devoting his attention to some sport or other activity: *a golf widow.* **3.** *Cards.* an additional hand or part of a hand, as one dealt to the table. **4.** *Print.* a short line at the end of a paragraph, esp. one which makes less than half the full width. —*v.t.* **5.** to make (one) a widow (chiefly in pp.). **6.** to deprive of anything valued, or bereave. **7.** *Obs.* **a.** to endow with a widow's right. **b.** to survive as the widow of. [ME; OE *widuwe,* c. G *Witwe*; akin to L *vidua* widow (fem. of *viduus* deprived of)]

widowbird (wĭd′ō bûd′), *n.* whydah.

widower (wĭd′ō ə), *n.* a man who has lost his wife by death and has not married again.

widowhood (wĭd′ō ho͝od′), *n.* the state or period of being a widow (or, sometimes, a widower).

widow's cruse, a source of supply that never fails: in allusion to the pot of oil of the widow of Zarephath which, at the word of Elijah, yielded an unfailing supply until the coming of rain on the earth (I Kings 17:10–16. Cf. II Kings 4:1–7).

widow's mite, a small gift of money given in good spirit by one who can ill afford it.

widow's peak, a point formed by the hair growing down in the middle of the forehead.

width (wĭdth), *n.* **1.** extent from side to side; breadth; wideness. **2.** a piece of the full wideness, as of cloth.

widthwise (wĭdth′wīz′), *adv.* in the direction of the width. Also, **widthways** (wĭdth′wāz′).

Widukind (vē′do͞o kĭnt), *n.* Wittekind.

Wieland (*Ger.* vē′lănt), **Christoph Martin** (*Ger.* krĭs′tŏf mär′tēn), 1733–1813, German poet, novelist, and critic.

wield (wēld), *v.t.* **1.** to exercise (power, authority, influence, etc.), as in ruling or dominating. **2.** to manage (a weapon, instrument, etc.) in use; handle or employ in action. **3.** *Archaic.* to guide or direct. [ME *welde(n),* OE *wieldan* control, der. *wealdan* rule, govern, c. G *walten*] —**wield′able,** *adj.* —**wield′er,** *n.*

wieldy (wēl′dĭ), *adj.,* **wieldier, wieldiest.** readily wielded or managed, as in use or action.

Wien (*Ger.* vēn), *n.* German name of **Vienna.**

wiener (wē′nə), *n. U.S.* a frankfurter. Also, **wienerwurst** (wē′nə wûst′). [t. G, short for *wiener Wurst* Viennese sausage]

Wiener schnitzel (vē′nə shnĭt′səl), *German.* a breaded veal cutlet or escalope, variously seasoned or garnished. [t. G: Viennese cutlet]

Wiesbaden (*Ger.* vēs′bä dən), *n.* a city in West Germany, in SW Hesse: health resort; mineral springs. 261,100 (est. 1966).

wife (wīf), *n., pl.* **wives** (wīvz), **1.** a woman joined in marriage to a man as husband. **2.** a woman (*archaic* or *dial.*, except in compounds): *housewife, midwife.* [ME: OE *wīf* woman, wife, c. D *wijf*, G *Weib*, Icel. *vīf*] —**wife′dom,** *n.* —**wife′less,** *adj.* —**wife′lessness,** *n.*

wifehood (wīf′hŏŏd), *n.* **1.** the position or relation of a wife. **2.** wifely character.

wifely (wīf′lĭ), *adj.*, **-lier, -liest.** of, like, or befitting a wife. Also, **wifelike** (wīf′līk′). —**wife′liness,** *n.*

wig (wĭg), *n., v.,* **wigged, wigging.** —*n.* **1.** an artificial covering of hair for the head, worn to conceal baldness, for disguise, theatricals, etc., or formerly as an ordinary head covering. **2.** real or synthetic hair worn by women over their own hair, attached to a base or entwined with it, to create a new hairstyle, for a change of hair colour, etc. —*v.t.* **3.** to furnish with a wig or wigs. **4.** *Colloq.* to reprimand or reprove severely. —*v.i.* **5.** *Colloq.* to scold. [short for PERIWIG] —**wigged,** *adj.* —**wig′less,** *adj.* —**wig′like′,** *adj.*

Wig., Wigtownshire.

wigan (wĭg′ən), *n.* a stiff, canvas-like fabric used for stiffening parts of garments. [named after WIGAN, where first made]

Wigan (wĭg′ən), *n.* a town in W England, in Lancashire: coal-mining. 78,690 (1961).

wigeon (wĭj′ən), *n.* widgeon.

wiggery (wĭg′ə rĭ), *n., pl.* **-geries.** **1.** wigs or a wig; false hair. **2.** the wearing of wigs.

wigging (wĭg′ĭng), *n. Colloq.* a scolding or reproof.

wiggle (wĭg′l), *v.,* **-gled, -gling,** *n.* —*v.i.* **1.** to move or go with short, quick, irregular movements from side to side; wriggle. —*v.t.* **2.** to cause to wiggle; move quickly and irregularly from side to side. —*n.* **3.** a wiggling movement or course. **4.** a wiggly line. [ME *wigle(n)*, freq. of *wig* (now d.) wag. Cf. Norw. *vigla* totter, freq. of *vigga* rock oneself, and D and LG *wiggelen*]

wiggler (wĭg′lə), *n.* one who or that which wiggles.

wiggly (wĭg′lĭ), *adj.* **1.** undulating; wavy: *a wiggly line.* **2.** wriggly.

wight[1] (wīt), *n. Archaic.* **1.** a human being or person. **2.** a supernatural being. **3.** a living being or creature. [ME; OE *wiht*, c. G *Wicht*]

wight[2] (wīt), *adj. Archaic.* **1.** strong and brave, or valiant. **2.** active; nimble or swift. [ME, t. Scand.; cf. Icel. *vīgt*, neut. of *vīgr* able to fight]

Wight (wīt), *n.* **Isle of,** an island off the S coast of England, forming an administrative division of Hampshire. 95,753 pop. (1961); 147 sq. mi. *Chief town:* Newport.

wigmaker (wĭg′mā′kə), *n.* one who makes wigs.

Wigner (wĭg′nə), *n.* **Eugene Paul,** born 1902, U.S. physicist, born in Hungary.

Wigner effect, *Physics.* an effect produced on certain crystalline substances by irradiation, as the change of dimensions which occurs when graphite is bombarded by neutrons. [named after E. P. WIGNER]

Wigner nuclide, *Physics.* one of a pair of nuclides both of which have odd mass numbers and in which the atomic numbers and neutron numbers differ by one, as $^{3}_{1}$H and $^{3}_{2}$He. [named after E. P. WIGNER]

Wigtown (wĭg′tən), *n.* **1.** a burgh in Scotland, the county town of Wigtownshire. 1201 (1961). **2.** Wigtownshire.

Wigtownshire (wĭg′tən shĭə′, -shə), *n.* a county in SW Scotland. 29,107 pop. (1961); 487 sq. mi. *Co. town:* Wigtown. *Abbrev.:* Wig. Also, **Wigtown.**

wigwag (wĭg′wăg′), *v.,* **-wagged, -wagging,** *n.* —*v.t., v.i.* **1.** to move to and fro. **2.** *Naval, etc.* to signal by movements of two flags or the like waved according to a code. —*n. Naval, etc.* **3.** wigwagging, or signalling by movements of flags or the like. **4.** a message so signalled. —*adj.* **5.** *Naval, etc.* signalled in this manner. [contraction of phrase *wig and wag.* See WIGGLE, WAG] —**wig′wag′ger,** *n.*

wigwam (wĭg′wăm′), *n.* **1.** an American Indian hut or lodge, usually of rounded or oval shape, formed of poles overlaid with bark, mats, or skins. **2.** *U.S. Slang.* a structure, esp. of large size, used for political conventions, etc. **3. the Wigwam,** Tammany Hall. [t. Abnaki (Algonquian): dwelling]

wikiup (wĭk′ĭ ŭp′), *n. U.S.* wickiup.

Wilberforce (wĭl′bə fôs′), *n.* **William,** 1759–1833, British statesman, philanthropist, and religious writer.

wilco (wĭl′kō′), *interj.* message received and will be complied with (used in signalling and telecommunications). [shortened form of *will comply*]

Wilcox (wĭl′kŏks), *n.* **Ella Wheeler,** 1850–1919, U.S. poet.

wild (wīld), *adj.* **1.** living in a state of nature, as animals that have not been tamed or domesticated. **2.** growing or produced without cultivation or the care of man, as plants, flowers, fruit, honey, etc. **3.** uncultivated, uninhabited, or waste, as land. **4.** uncivilized or barbarous, as tribes or savages. **5.** of unrestrained violence, fury, intensity, etc.; violent; furious: *wild fighting, wild storms.* **6.** characterized by or indicating violent excitement, as actions, the appearance, etc. **7.** frantic; distracted, crazy, or mad: *to drive someone wild.* **8.** violently excited: *wild with rage, fear, or pain.* **9.** undisciplined, unruly, lawless, or turbulent: *wild boys, a wild crew.* **10.** unrestrained, untrammelled, or unbridled: *wild gaiety, wild orgies.* **11.** disregardful of moral restraints as to pleasurable indulgence. **12.** unrestrained by reason or prudence: *wild schemes.* **13.** extravagant or fantastic: *wild fancies.* **14.** disorderly or dishevelled: *wild locks.* **15.** wide of the mark: *a wild throw.* **16.** *Colloq.* intensely eager or enthusiastic. **17.** *Cards.* (of a card) having its value decided by the wishes of the players or the player who holds it. —*adv.* **18.** in a wild manner; wildly. **19. run wild, a.** to grow without cultivation or check. **b.** to behave in an unrestrained or uncontrolled manner: *he allows his children to run wild.* —*n.* **20.** (*often pl.*) an uncultivated, uninhabited, or desolate region or tract; a waste; a wilderness; a desert. [ME and OE *wilde*, c. D and G *wild*] —**wild′ly,** *adv.* —**wild′ness,** *n.* —**Syn. 1.** undomesticated, untamed, feral, ferine, savage. **5.** boisterous, stormy, tempestuous. **6.** enthusiastic, eager. **9.** self-willed, ungoverned, unrestrained, riotous, wayward. **12.** reckless, rash, extravagant, impracticable. **13.** weird, grotesque, bizarre. —**Ant. 1.** tame.

wild basil, a perennial labiate herb, *Clinopodium vulgare,* common on calcareous soils in N temperate regions.

wild boar, a wild Old World swine, *Sus scrofa,* the supposed original of most domestic pigs.

Wild boar, *Sus scrofa* (4 ft long, ab. 3 ft high at the shoulder)

wild brier, **1.** dogrose. **2.** sweetbrier, *Rosa eglanteria.* **3.** any other brier growing wild.

wild carrot, a biennial umbelliferous herb with white flowers and hooked fruits, *Daucus carota,* widespread in temperate regions, esp. near the coast: the original of the cultivated carrot.

wildcat (wīld′kăt′), *n., adj., v.,* **-catted, -catting.** —*n.* **1.** a forest-dwelling European feline, *Felis sylvestris,* somewhat larger than, but very much like, the domestic cat, to which it is closely related and with which it interbreeds freely. **2.** a similar North African species, *Felis libyca,* probably the main source of the domesticated cat. **3.** any of several North American felines of the genus *Lynx,* esp. *L. rufus* and *L. canadensis,* the former widely distributed, the latter largely restricted to Canada. **4.** any of several other of the smaller felines, as the serval, ocelot, etc. **5.** a quick-tempered or savage person. **6.** *U.S.* a reckless or unsound enterprise, business, etc. **7.** an exploratory well drilled in an effort to discover deposits of oil or gas; a prospect well. —*adj.* **8.** characterized by or proceeding from reckless or unsafe business methods: *wildcat companies or shares.* **9.** of or pertaining to an illicit enterprise or product. —*v.i., v.t.* **10.** to search for oil, ore, or the like, as an independent prospector. —**wild′cat′ting,** *n., adj.*

wildcat strike, a strike which has not been called or sanctioned by officials of a trade union; unofficial strike.

wildcatter (wīld′kăt′ə), *n. U.S. Colloq.* one who prospects for oil or ores; a prospector.

wild cherry, the gean, *Prunus avium.*

Wilde (wīld), *n.* **Oscar (Fingal O'Flahertie Wills)** (fĭng′gl ō flĕə′tĭ), 1854–1900, Irish dramatist, poet, novelist, essayist, and critic.

wildebeest (wĭl′dĭ bēst′), *n., pl.* **-beests.** gnu. [t. Afrikaans: lit., wild beast]

wilder (wĭl′də), *Archaic.* —*v.t.* **1.** to cause to lose one's way. **2.** to bewilder. —*v.i.* **3.** to lose one's way. **4.** to be bewildered. —**wil′derment,** *n.*

Wilder (wīl′də), *n.* **Thornton (Niven),** born 1897, U.S. novelist and playwright.

wilderness (wĭl′də nĭs), *n.* **1.** a wild region, as of forest or desert; a waste; a tract of land inhabited only by wild animals. **2.** any desolate tracts, as of water. **3.** a part of a garden set apart for plants growing with unchecked luxuriance. **4.** a bewildering mass or collection. **5. in the wilderness,** *Colloq.* **a.** in a state or place of isolation; away from the centre of things. **b.** out of political office. [ME, f. *wilder(n)* wild (OE *wilddēoren* of wild beasts) + -NESS] —**Syn. 1.** See **desert**[1].

wild-eyed (wīld′īd′), *adj.* glaring in an angry or wild manner.
wildfire (wīld′fī′ə), *n.* **1.** a highly inflammable composition, as Greek fire, difficult to extinguish when ignited, formerly used in warfare. **2.** something that runs or spreads with extraordinary rapidity: *the news spread like wildfire.* **3.** sheet lightning, unaccompanied by thunder. **4.** the will-o'-the-wisp or ignis fatuus. **5.** *Obs. Pathol.* erysipelas or some similar disease. **6.** *Obs. Vet. Sci.* an inflammatory disease of the skin of sheep; scabies.
wild flower, 1. the flower of an uncultivated plant. **2.** such a plant. Also, **wild′flow′er.**
wildfowl (wīld′foul′), *n.* **1.** a game bird, esp. a wild duck or wild goose. **2.** game birds collectively. **—wild′fowl′er,** *n.* **—wild′fowl′ing,** *n., adj.*
wild goose, 1. any undomesticated goose, esp. the European greylag and the Canada goose. **2.** *Colloq.* a foolish person.
wild-goose chase, 1. a wild or absurd chase, as after something non-existent or unobtainable. **2.** any senseless pursuit of an object or end.
wild grape, the grapevine in its wild state, several species of the genus *Coccoloba*, esp. *C. uvifera.*
Wild Hunt, *Germanic Legend.* a host of phantoms hunting, accompanied by the cries of huntsmen and baying of dogs.
Wild Huntsman, *Germanic Legend.* the leader of the Wild Hunt, often associated with Odin.
wild indigo, any of the American leguminous plants constituting the genus *Baptisia*, esp. *B. tinctoria*, a species with yellow flowers.
wilding (wīl′dĭng), *n.* **1.** a wild apple tree or apple. **2.** its fruit. **3.** any plant that grows wild. **4.** an escape (plant). **5.** a wild animal. **—***adj.* **6.** *Archaic.* not cultivated or domesticated; wild.
wildish (wīl′dĭsh), *adj.* somewhat wild.
wild leek, a liliaceous, bulbous plant, *Allium ampeloprasum*, a native of the Mediterranean region.
wild lettuce, any of various uncultivated species of lettuce (genus *Lactuca*), growing as weeds in fields and waste places, esp. an English species (*L. scariola*) or a North American species (*L. canadensis*).
wildlife (wīld′līf′), *n.* wild animals, esp. those hunted.
wildling (wīld′lĭng), *n.* a wild plant, flower, or animal.
wild madder, madder (defs 1, 2).
wild mustard, the charlock.
wild oat, 1. any uncultivated species of *Avena*, esp. *A. fatua*, a common grass or weed resembling the cultivated oat. **2.** (*pl.*) dissolute life in one's youth. **3. sow one's wild oats,** to live a dissolute life, esp. to be promiscuous.
wild pansy, the common pansy, *Viola tricolor*, in a wild state, varying between inconspicuous field weeds and showy varieties.
wild parsley, any of numerous umbelliferous plants resembling the parsley in shape and structure.
wild parsnip, an umbelliferous weed, *Pastinaca sativa*, having an inedible acrid root, common in fields and waste places: the original of the cultivated parsnip.
wild plum, bullace.
wild rose, any native species of rose, usually having a single flower with the corolla consisting of one circle of roundish spreading petals.
wild rubber, caoutchouc from trees growing wild.
wild rye, any of the grasses of the genus *Elymus*, somewhat resembling rye.
wild silk, any silk having a rough texture, as tussah.
wild spinach, any of various plants of the genus *Chenopodium*, sometimes used in place of spinach.
wild thyme, a thyme, *Thymus serpyllum.*
Wild West, the western frontier region of the U.S., before the establishment of stable government, esp. as a setting or background for cowboy films and stories or the like.
wildwood (wīld′wo͝od′), *n. Archaic.* a wood growing in the wild or natural state; a forest.
wile (wīl), *n., v.,* **wiled, wiling.** **—***n.* **1.** a trick, artifice, or stratagem. **2.** (*often pl.*) an artful or beguiling procedure. **3.** deceitful cunning; trickery. **—***v.t.* **4.** to beguile, entice, or lure (*away, from, into,* etc.). **5. wile away,** while away. [ME *wil(e)*, prob. t. Scand.; cf. Icel. *vēl* craft, fraud, *vēla* defraud]
wilful (wĭl′fəl), *adj.* **1.** willed, voluntary, or intentional: *wilful murder.* **2.** self-willed or headstrong; perversely obstinate or intractable. Also, *U.S.,* **willful.** [ME; OE *wilful-* willing (in *wilful-līce* willingly). See WILL², -FUL] **—wil′fully,** *adv.* **—wil′fulness,** *n.*

—Syn. 2. WILFUL, HEADSTRONG, PERVERSE, WAYWARD refer to one who stubbornly insists upon doing as he pleases. WILFUL suggests a stubborn persistence in doing what one wishes, esp. in opposition to those whose wishes or commands ought to be respected or obeyed: *a wilful child who disregarded his parents' advice.* One who is HEADSTRONG is often foolishly, and sometimes violently, self-willed: *reckless and headstrong youths.* The PERVERSE person is unreasonably or obstinately intractable or contrary, often with the express intention of being disagreeable: *perverse out of sheer spite.* WAYWARD in this sense has the connotation of rash wrongheadedness which gets one into trouble: *a reform school for wayward girls.* **—Ant. 2.** obedient.

Wilhelm I (vĭl′hĕlm), William I (def. 3).
Wilhelm II, William II (def. 2).
Wilhelmina I (wĭl′ə mē′nə; *Du.* wĭl hĕl mē′nȧ) (*Wilhelmina Helena Pauline Maria of Orange-Nassau*), 1880–1962, Queen of the Netherlands from 1890 until her abdication in 1948.
Wilhelmshaven (*Ger.* vĭl hĕlms hȧ′fən), *n.* a seaport in West Germany, in NW Lower Saxony. 101,400 (est. 1966).
Wilhelmstrasse (*Ger.* vĭl′hĕlm shtrȧ sə), *n.* **1.** a street in the centre of Berlin, in which many government and foreign office buildings were situated before 1945. **2.** (before 1945) the foreign office or policies of the German government.
Wilkes (wĭlks), *n.* **1. Charles,** 1798–1877, U.S. rear admiral and explorer. **2. John,** 1727–97, English politician, journalist, and writer.
Wilkes-Barre (wĭlks′bă′rĭ), *n.* a town in the U.S., in E Pennsylvania, on the Susquehanna river. 63,551 (1960).
Wilkes Land, a coastal area of Antarctica, south of Australia.
Wilkins (wĭl′kĭnz), *n.* **Sir George Hubert,** 1888–1958, Australian antarctic explorer and aviator.
will¹ (wĭl), *v.; pres. sing.* 1 **will**; 2 **will** or (*Archaic*) **wilt;** 3 **will;** *pl.* **will;** *pt.* 1 **would**; 2 **would** or (*Archaic*) **wouldst;** 3 **would;** *pl.* **would;** *pp.* (*Obs.*) **would;** imperative and infinitive lacking. **—***aux. v.* **1.** am (is, are, etc.) about or going to (in future constructions, denoting in the first person promise or determination, in the second and third persons mere futurity). **2.** am (is, are, etc.) disposed or willing to. **3.** am expected or required to. **4.** may be expected or supposed to: *you will not have forgotten him, this will be right.* **5.** am (is, are, etc.) determined or sure to (used emphatically): *you would do it, people will talk.* **6.** am (is, are, etc.) accustomed to, or do usually or often: *he would write for hours at a time.* **—***v.t., v.i.* **7.** to wish; desire; like: *as you will, would it were true.* [ME; OE *wyllan*, c. D *willen*, Icel. *vilja*, Goth. *wiljan*; akin to G *wollen*, L *velle* wish] **—Syn. 1.** See **shall.**
will² (wĭl), *n., v.,* **willed, willing.** **—***n.* **1.** the faculty of conscious and esp. of deliberate action: *the freedom of the will.* **2.** the power of choosing one's own actions: *to have a strong or a weak will.* **3.** the act of using this power. **4.** the process of willing, or volition. **5.** wish or desire: *to submit against one's will.* **6.** purpose or determination, often hearty determination: *to have the will to succeed.* **7.** the wish or purpose as carried out, or to be carried out: *to work one's will.* **8.** disposition (good or ill) towards another. **9.** *Law.* **a.** a legal declaration of a person's wishes as to the disposition of his (real) property, etc., after his death, usually in writing, and either signed by the testator and attested by witnesses or, in Scotland, holographic. **b.** the document containing such a declaration. **10. at will,** at one's discretion or pleasure: *to wander at will.* **11. a will of one's own,** a strong power of asserting oneself. **12. with a will,** willingly; readily; eagerly. **13. work one's will,** to do as one chooses. **—***v.t.* **14.** to give by will or testament; to bequeath or devise. **15.** to influence by exerting willpower. **16.** to wish or desire. **17.** to decide by act of will. **18.** to purpose, determine on, or elect, by act of will. **—***v.i.* **19.** to exercise the will. **20.** to determine, decide, or ordain, as by act of will. [ME and OE (also ME *wille*, OE *willa*); c. D *wil*, G *Wille*, Icel. *vili*, Goth. *wilja*] **—will′er,** *n.*

—Syn. 6. WILL, VOLITION refer to conscious choice as to action or thought. WILL denotes fixed and persistent intent or purpose: *where there's a will there's a way.* VOLITION is the power of forming an intention or the incentive for using the will; *to exercise one's volition in making a decision.*

willable (wĭl′ə bl), *adj.* capable of being willed, or fixed by will.
Willard (wĭl′əd, wĭl′äd), *n.* **1. Emma,** 1787–1870, U.S. educational reformer. **2. Frances Elizabeth,** 1839–98, U.S. teacher, writer, and temperance advocator.
willed (wĭld), *adj.* having a will of the kind specified (used in combination): *strong-willed.*
willemite (wĭl′ə mīt′), *n.* a mineral, a zinc silicate, Zn_2SiO_4, sometimes containing manganese, occurring in prismatic crystals or granular masses, usually greenish, sometimes white, brown, or red: a minor ore of zinc. [t. D: m. *Willemit*, named after King *Willem* I of the Netherlands]
Willemstad (*Du.* wĭl′əm stŏt), *n.* a seaport on the island of Curaçao in the West Indies: the capital of Netherlands Antilles. 43,457 (est. 1956).

Willesden (wĭlz′dən), *n.* a district in the NW outer London borough of Brent.

Willesden paper, *Bldg Trades.* a strong waterproof paper used as roof-lining, air-ducting in mines, and the like.

willet (wĭl′ĭt), *n.* a large North American semipalmate shorebird, *Catoptrophorus semipalmatus,* with striking black-and-white wing pattern. [short for *pill-will-willet,* imit. of cry of bird]

willful (wĭl′fo͝ol), *adj. U.S.* wilful. —**will′fully,** *adv.* —**will′fulness,** *n.*

William I (wĭl′yəm). **1.** (*William the Conqueror*), Duke of Normandy, 1027–87; king of England 1066–87, first king of Norman line. **2.** (*Prince of Orange and Count of Nassau*; '*William the Silent*'), 1533–84, Dutch statesman and soldier, born in Germany, leader of the revolt of the Netherlands against Spain. **3.** Also, **Wilhelm I.** 1797–1888, king of Prussia 1861–88, and German emperor 1871–88 (brother of Frederick William IV).

William II, 1. (*William Rufus, William the Red*), 1056?–1100, king of England 1087–1100 (son of William I). **2.** Also, **Wilhelm II.** 1859–1941, German emperor from 1888 until he abdicated in 1918.

William III (*Prince of Orange*), 1650–1702, king of Great Britain and Ireland 1689–1702 (successor and nephew of James II, and husband of Mary II). Also, **William of Orange.**

William IV, 1765–1837, king of Great Britain and Ireland 1830–37 (brother of George IV).

William of Malmesbury (mämz′bə rĭ, -brĭ), *c.* 1090–*c.* 1143, English historian.

Williams (wĭl′yəmz), *n.* **1. Emlyn,** born 1905, Welsh actor and dramatist. **2. Eric,** born 1911, prime minister of Trinidad and Tobago since 1961. **3. Ralph Vaughan,** see **Vaughan Williams. 4. Tennessee** (*Thomas Lanier Williams*), born 1914, U.S. dramatist. **5. William Carlos** (kä′lōs), 1883–1963, U.S. author and physician.

Williamsburg (wĭl′yəmz bûg′), *n.* a city in the U.S., in SE Virginia, its colonial capital: now restored to its former condition. 6832 (1960).

William Tell. See **Tell.**

willies (wĭl′ĭz), *n.pl. Slang.* a state of nervous fear, irritation, or dislike: *that boring old man gives me the willies.*

willing (wĭl′ĭng), *adj.* **1.** disposed or consenting (without being particularly desirous): *willing to take what one can get.* **2.** cheerfully consenting or ready: *a willing worker.* **3.** done, given, borne, used, etc., with cheerful readiness. —**will′ingly,** *adv.* —**will′ingness,** *n.* —**Syn. 1.** inclined, minded.

will-o'-the-wisp (wĭl′ə thə wĭsp′), *n.* **1.** ignis fatuus. **2.** anything that deludes or misleads by luring on.

willow (wĭl′ō), *n.* **1.** any of the trees or shrubs constituting the genus *Salix,* many species of which have tough, pliable twigs or branches which are used for wickerwork, etc. **2.** the wood of the willow. **3.** *Colloq.* something made of this, as a cricket bat. **4.** a machine consisting essentially of a cylinder armed with spikes revolving within a spiked casing, for opening and cleaning cotton or other fibre. —*v.t.* **5.** to treat (cotton, etc.) with a willow. [ME *wilwe,* var. of *wilghe,* OE *welig,* c. D *wilg,* LG *wilge*] —**wil′low-like′,** *adj.*

willower (wĭl′ō ə), *n.* **1.** a person or a thing that willows. **2.** willow (def. 4).

willowherb (wĭl′ō hûb′), *n.* **1.** an onagraceous plant, *Chamaenerion angustifolium,* with narrow willow-like leaves and racemes of purple flowers. **2.** any plant of the related genus *Epilobium.*

willowish (wĭl′ō ĭsh), *adj.* willowy.

willow pattern, a pattern used on china, employing the design of the willow tree, and originated in approximately 1780 by Thomas Turner in England.

willow warbler, a small brown bird of the family *Sylviidae*; *Phylloscopus trochilus,* of Europe and N Asia.

willow-ware (wĭl′ō wēə′), *n.* china using willow pattern.

willowy (wĭl′ō ĭ), *adj.* **1.** pliant; lithe. **2.** gracefully slender and supple. **3.** abounding with willows.

willpower (wĭl′pou′ə), *n.* **1.** control over one's impulses and actions. **2.** strength of will: *he has great willpower.*

willy-nilly (wĭl′ĭ nĭl′ĭ), *adv.* **1.** willingly or unwillingly. —*adj.* **2.** shilly-shallying; vacillating. [from phrase *will I* (*he, ye*), *nill I* (*he, ye*); *nill* be unwilling]

willy-willy (wĭl′ĭ wĭl′ĭ), *n. Austral.* a cyclonic storm whirlwind. [t. native Australian]

Wilmington (wĭl′mĭng tən), *n.* a seaport in the U.S., in N Delaware. 95,827 (1960).

Wilmslow (wĭlmz′lō), *n.* a town in England, in Cheshire. 21,393 (1961).

Wilno (vĭl′nə; *Pol.* vēl′nŏ), *n.* Polish name of **Vilna.**

Wilryck (*Flem.* wĭl′rĕyk), *n.* a town in N Belgium, in Antwerp province. 40,565 (est. 1964).

Wilson (wĭl′sən), *n.* **1. Angus (Frank Johnstone),** born 1913, English novelist and essayist. **2. Charles Thomson Rees** (tŏm′sən rēs′), 1869–1959, Scottish physicist. **3. Edmund,** born 1895, U.S. critic and essayist. **4. (James) Harold,** born 1916, British statesman: prime minister 1964–70. **5. John** ('*Christopher North*'), 1785–1854, Scottish poet and essayist. **6. Richard,** *c.* 1713–82, Welsh landscape painter. **7. (Thomas) Woodrow** (wo͝od′rō), 1856–1924, 28th president of the U.S., 1913–21. **8. Mount,** a mountain in the U.S., in SW California, near Pasadena: observatory. 5710 ft. —**Wilsonian** (wĭl sō′nyən), *adj.*

Wilson cloud chamber, *Physics.* See **cloud chamber.** Also, **Wilson chamber.** [named after C. T. R. WILSON]

Wilson Dam, a power dam on the Tennessee river, in NW Alabama: a part of the Tennessee Valley Authority. ab. 4600 ft long; 137 ft high.

Wilson's petrel, a small petrel or Mother Carey's chicken, *Oceanites oceanicus,* black with white rump, of antarctic and tropical oceans, and occasionally found farther north.

Wilson's Promontory, a headland on the S coast of Victoria: the most southerly point of mainland Australia.

wilt[1] (wĭlt), *v.i.* **1.** to become limp and drooping, as a fading flower; wither. **2.** to lose strength, vigour, assurance, etc. —*v.t.* **3.** to cause to wilt. —*n. Chiefly U.S.* **4.** the act of wilting. **5.** a spell of depression, lassitude, or dizziness. [d. var. of *wilk* wither, itself var. of *welk,* ME *welken.* Cf. D and G *welken* wither]

wilt[2] (wĭlt), *Archaic.* second pers. sing. pres. ind. of **will**[1].

wilt[3] (wĭlt), *n.* **1.** *Bot.* any of various plant diseases in which the leaves droop, become flaccid and then dry, usually because water cannot pass through the plant. **2.** a highly infectious disease in certain caterpillars, which causes their bodies to liquefy. Also, **wilt disease.** [special use of WILT[1]]

Wilten (*Ger.* vĭl′tən), *n.* a town in West Germany, in central North Rhine-Westphalia. 98,500 (est. 1966).

Wilton carpet (wĭl′tən), a kind of carpet, woven on a Jacquard loom like Brussels carpet, but having the loops cut to form a velvet pile. Also, **Wilton.** [named after *Wilton,* a town in Wiltshire]

Wilts., Wiltshire.

Wiltshire (wĭlt′shĭə, -shə), *n.* **1.** a county in S England, 422,753 pop. (1961); 1345 sq. mi. *Co. town:* Salisbury. *Abbrev.:* Wilts. **2.** one of an English breed of pure white sheep with long spiral horns.

wily (wī′lĭ), *adj.,* **-lier, -liest.** full of, marked by, or proceeding from wiles; crafty; cunning. [ME, f. WIL(E) + -Y[1]] —**wi′lily,** *adv.* —**wi′liness,** *n.* —**Syn.** artful, sly, designing, intriguing, tricky, foxy.

wimble (wĭm′bl), *n., v.,* **-bled, -bling.** —*n.* **1.** a device in mining, etc., for extracting the rubbish from a bored hole. **2.** a brace for drilling marble, etc. **3.** any of various other instruments for boring, etc. —*v.t.* **4.** to bore or perforate with or as with a wimble. [ME, t. AF. Cf. GIMLET]

Wimbledon (wĭm′bl dən), *n.* a district of the SW outer London borough of Merton: international tennis tournaments.

wimple (wĭm′pl), *n., v.,* **-pled, -pling.** —*n.* **1.** a woman's headcloth drawn in folds about the chin, formerly worn out of doors, and still in use by nuns. **2.** *Chiefly Scot.* a fold, wrinkle, or ripple. **3.** *Chiefly Scot.* a bend, wind, or turn. —*v.t.* **4.** to cover or muffle with or as with a wimple. **5.** to cause to ripple or undulate, as water. **6.** *Archaic.* to lay in folds, as a veil. —*v.i.* **7.** to ripple, as water. **8.** *Archaic.* to lie in folds, as a veil. [ME; var. of ME and OE *wimpel,* c. D and LG *wimpel*]

Wimple

Wimpy (wĭm′pĭ), *n. Trademark.* a kind of hamburger.

Wimshurst machine (wĭmz′hûst), *Physics.* a laboratory apparatus for generating and storing at high potential the static electricity produced by the friction between two coaxial, counter-revolving, insulating discs; a static machine. [named after J. *Wimshurst,* died 1903, English scientist]

win[1] (wĭn), *v.,* **won, winning,** *n.* —*v.i.* **1.** to succeed by striving or effort (sometimes fol. colloquially by *out*). **2.** to gain the victory. **3.** to be placed first in a race or the like. **4.** to get (*in, out, through, to,* etc., *free, loose,* etc.). —*v.t.* **5.** to get by effort, as through labour, competition, or conquest. **6.** to gain (a prize, fame, etc.). **7.** to be successful in (a game, battle, etc.). **8.** to make (one's way), as by effort, ability, etc. **9.** to attain or reach (a point, goal, etc.): *to win the shore in a storm.* **10.** to gain (favour, love, consent, etc.) as by qualities or influence. **11.** to gain the favour, regard, or adherence of. **12.** to bring (*over*) to favour, consent, etc.; persuade. **13.** to persuade to love or marriage, or gain in marriage. **14.** *Mining.* **a.** to obtain (ore, coal, etc.). **b.** to prepare (a vein, bed, mine, etc.) for working, by means of shafts, etc. *—n.* **15.** an act of winning; a success; a victory. **16.** the act or fact of finishing first, esp. in a horserace. [ME *winne(n)*, OE *winnan* work, fight, bear, c. G *gewinnen*] **—Syn. 5.** obtain, secure, acquire, earn, achieve, attain, reach. See **gain**[1].

win[2] (wĭn), *v.t.*, **won** or **winned, winning.** *Scot. and N Dial.* to dry (hay, seed, turf, or the like) by exposure to air or heat. [special use of WIN[1] (obs. sense, to harvest), influenced by WINNOW]

wince (wĭns), *v.*, **winced, wincing,** *n.* *—v.i.* **1.** to shrink, as in pain or from a blow; start; flinch. *—n.* **2.** a wincing or shrinking movement; a slight start. [ME *wynse.* Cf. OF *guenchir* turn aside] **—winc′er,** *n.*

wincey (wĭn′sĭ), *n.* a plain or twilled cloth, usually with a linen or cotton warp and woollen filling. Also, **winsey.** [orig. Scot. d.: der. LINSEY-WOOLSEY]

winceyette (wĭn′sĭ ĕt′), *n.* a plain lightweight cotton cloth raised slightly on both sides. [f. WINCEY + -ETTE]

winch (wĭnch), *n.* **1.** the crank or handle of a revolving machine. **2.** a windlass turned by a crank, for hoisting, etc. **3.** any one of a number of contrivances to crank objects by. *—v.t.* **4.** to hoist or haul by means of a winch. [ME *wynch*, OE *wince*] **—winch′er,** *n.*

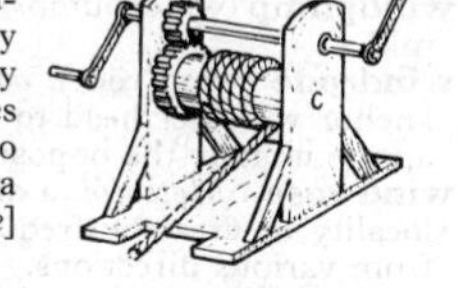

Winch

Winchester (wĭn′chĭs tə), *n.* **1.** a city in England, in Hampshire: cathedral; public school, founded 1388; capital of the early kingdom of Wessex. 28,770 (1961). **2.** a narrow-necked, cylindrical bottle used for transporting chemical and pharmaceutical liquids, which contains between 80 and 90 fluid ounces. **3.** Winchester rifle.

Winchester measures, a system of dry and liquid measures the originals of which were kept at Winchester; now obsolete in the U.K. although some still form the basis of American measures, as **Winchester bushel.** See **bushel**[1] (def. 1).

Winchester rifle, a type of magazine rifle, first made about 1866. [named after Oliver F. *Winchester*, 1810–80, U.S. manufacturer]

Winckelmann (*Ger.* vĭng′kəl mȧn), *n.* **Johann Joachim** (*Ger.* yō′hȧn yō′ȧ KHĭm), 1717–68, German archaeologist and historian of ancient art.

wind[1] (wĭnd), *n.* **1.** air in natural motion, as along the earth's surface. **2.** a gale; storm; hurricane. **3.** any stream of air, as that produced by a bellows, a fan, etc. **4.** air impregnated with the scent of an animal or animals. **5.** a hint or intimation: *get wind of the scandal.* **6.** any tendency or likely course: *the wind of public opinion, wind of change.* **7.** breath or breathing; power of breathing freely, as during continued exertion. **8.** empty talk; mere words. **9.** vanity; conceitedness. **10.** gas generated in the stomach and bowels. **11.** *Colloq.* the solar plexus, where a blow may cause shortness of breath. **12.** See **second wind.** **13.** *Music.* **a.** a wind instrument or wind instruments collectively. **b.** (*often pl.*) the players on such instruments collectively. **14.** *Naut.* the point or direction from which the wind blows. **15.** a point of the compass, esp. a cardinal point: *the four winds of heaven.* **16.** Some special noun phrases are:

before the wind, carried along by the wind; (of a ship) running with the wind astern.

between wind and water, 1. *Naut.* denoting the part of a ship, esp. the deck of a heavily laden ship, which the waves wash over. **2.** in a vulnerable or precarious position.

cast, fling, or **throw to the wind** or **winds,** to throw off or discard recklessly or in an abandoned manner: *throw all caution to the winds.*

close to the wind, 1. *Naut.* sailing as near as possible to the direction from which the wind is blowing. **2.** taking a calculated risk. **3.** transgressing or nearly transgressing conventions of taste, propriety, or the like.

get the wind up, *Colloq.* to take fright.

how the wind blows or **lies,** what the tendency or likelihood is. Also, **which way the wind blows** or **lies.**

in the teeth of the wind, 1. *Naut.* sailing directly against the wind. **2.** against opposition.

in the wind, 1. likely to happen; imminent. **2.** circulating as a rumour.

put the wind up, *Colloq.* to frighten.

raise the wind, *Colloq.* to obtain the necessary finances.

take the wind out of one's sails, to frustrate, disconcert, or deprive of an advantage.

—v.t. **17.** to expose to wind or air. **18.** to follow by the scent. **19.** to make short of wind or breath, as by vigorous exercise. **20.** to deprive momentarily of breath, as by a blow. **21.** to let recover breath, as by resting after exertion. [ME and OE, c. D *wind* and G *Wind*, Icel. *vindr*, Goth. *winds*, L *ventus*]

—Syn. 1. WIND, AIR, BLAST, BREEZE, GUST refer to a quantity of air set in motion naturally. WIND applies to any such air in motion, blowing with whatever degree of gentleness or violence. AIR, usually poetic, applies to a very gentle motion of the air. A BREEZE is usually a cool, light wind. BLAST and GUST apply to quick, forceful winds of short duration: BLAST implies a violent rush of air, often a cold one, whereas a GUST is little more than a flurry.

wind[2] (wīnd), *v.*, **wound, winding,** *n.* *—v.i.* **1.** to change direction; bend; turn; take a frequently bending course; meander. **2.** to have a circular or spiral course or direction. **3.** to coil or twine about something. **4.** to be twisted or warped, as a board. **5.** to proceed circuitously or indirectly. **6.** to undergo winding, or winding up. **7. wind up,** *Colloq.* **a.** to conclude action, speech, etc. **b.** to end: *wind up in the poorhouse.* *—v.t.* **8.** to encircle or wreathe, as with something twined, wrapped, or placed about. **9.** to roll or coil (thread, etc.) into a ball or on a spool or the like (often fol. by *up*). **10.** to remove or take off by unwinding (fol. by *off*). **11.** to twine, fold, wrap, or place about something. **12.** to adjust (a mechanism, etc.) for operation by some turning or coiling process (often fol. by *up*): *to wind a clock.* **13.** to haul or hoist by means of a winch, windlass, or the like (often fol. by *up*). **14.** to make (one's or its way) in a winding or frequently bending course. **15.** to make (the way) by indirect or insidious procedure. **16. wind up, a.** to bring to a state of great tension; key up; excite. **b.** to conclude (action, affairs, etc.). *—n.* **17.** a winding; a bend or turn. **18.** a twist producing an uneven surface. [ME; OE *windan*, c. D and G *winden*, Icel. *vinda*, Goth. *-windan*]

wind[3] (wīnd), *v.t.*, **winded** or **wound, winding. 1.** to blow (a horn, a blast, etc.). **2.** to sound by blowing. **3.** to signal or direct by blasts of the horn or the like. [special use of WIND[1]]

windable (wīn′də bl), *adj.* that can be wound.

windage (wĭn′dĭj), *n.* **1.** the influence of the wind in deflecting a missile. **2.** the amount of such deflection. **3.** the amount of movement of a gunsight necessary to compensate for this deflection. **4.** a difference between the diameter of a projectile and that of the gun bore, for the escape of gas and the preventing of friction. **5.** the friction between any rotating part of a machine and the air within the casing which encloses it. **6.** *Naut.* that portion of a vessel's surface upon which the wind acts.

windbag (wĭnd′băg′), *n.* **1.** *Slang.* an empty, voluble, pretentious talker. **2.** the bag of a bagpipe.

wind band, a military band.

windblown (wĭnd′blōn′), *adj.* **1.** blown by the wind. **2.** (of trees) growing in a certain shape because of strong prevailing winds. **3.** (of hair) windswept.

windborne (wĭnd′bôn′), *adj.* carried by the wind, as pollen or seed.

windbound (wĭnd′bound′), *adj.* (of a sailing ship) prevented from sailing by a contrary or high wind.

windbreak (wĭnd′brāk′), *n.* a growth of trees, a structure of boards, or the like, serving as a shelter from the wind.

windbreaker (wĭnd′brā′kə), *n.* *U.S.* a windcheater.

wind-broken (wĭnd′brō′kən), *adj.* (of horses, etc.) having the breathing impaired; affected with heaves.

windburn (wĭnd′bûn′), *n.* inflammation of the face, hands, etc., caused by excessive exposure to the wind.

windcheater (wĭnd′chē′tə), *n.* any close-fitting garment for the upper part of the body designed to give protection against the wind, as an anorak.

windchest (wĭnd′chĕst′), *n.* a box or reservoir that supplies air under pressure to the pipes or reeds of an organ.

wind cone, a windsock.

winded (wĭn′dĭd), *adj.* **1.** having wind or breath: *short-winded.* **2.** out of breath. **3.** momentarily unable to breathe, as after a blow in the solar plexus. **—wind′edness,** *n.*

winder (wīn′də), *n.* **1.** one who or that which winds (bends, turns, etc.) or is wound. **2.** a single one of a winding flight of steps. **3.** a plant that coils or twines itself about something. **4.** an instrument or a machine for winding thread, etc. **5.** a small knob on a watch for winding it up. **6.** *Mining.* a winding engine for raising cages in a mineshaft.

Windermere (wĭn′də mĭə′), *n.* **Lake,** a lake in NW England in Westmorland and Lancashire: the largest lake in England. 10½ mi. long; 5⅔ sq. mi.

windfall (wĭnd′fôl′), *n.* **1.** something blown down by the wind, as fruit. **2.** an unexpected piece of good fortune.

windflower (wĭnd′flou′ə), *n.* any plant of the genus *Anemone.* [trans. of Gk *anemṓnē* ANEMONE]

windgall (wĭnd′gôl′), *n.* *Vet. Sci.* a puffy distension of the synovial bursa at the fetlock joint. **—wind′galled′,** *adj.*

wind-gap (wĭnd′găp′), *n.* a gap in a mountain ridge where a stream once flowed; usually higher than a water-gap.

wind gauge, 1. *Meteorol.* anemometer. 2. an appliance attached to a gun to enable allowance to be made for the force of the wind on the projectile when sighting. 3. a gauge for measuring the pressure of the wind in an organ.
wind harp, aeolian harp.
Windhoek (*Afrik.* vĭnt′hŏŏk), *n.* the capital of South-West Africa, in the central part. 48,000 (est. 1965).
windhover (wĭnd′hŏv′ə), *n.* the European kestrel, *Falco tinnunculus.* [f. WIND[1], n. + HOVER]
winding (wīn′dĭng), *n.* 1. the act of one who or that which winds. 2. a bend, turn, or flexure. 3. a coiling, folding, or wrapping, as of one thing about another. 4. something that is wound or coiled, or a single round of it. 5. *Elect.* a. a symmetrically laid, electrically conducting current path in any device. b. the manner of such coiling: *a series winding.* —*adj.* 6. bending or turning; sinuous. 7. spiral, as stairs. —**wind′ingly,** *adv.*
winding sheet, 1. a sheet in which a corpse is wrapped for burial. 2. a mass of tallow or wax that has run down and hardened on the side of a candle.
winding strip, *Carp.* one of a pair of parallel battens which are looked through to examine a piece of wood for twist.
wind instrument (wĭnd), a musical instrument sounded by the player's breath or any current of air.
windjammer (wĭnd′jăm′ə), *n.* 1. any vessel propelled wholly by sails. 2. a member of its crew. 3. a windcheater.
windlass (wĭnd′ləs), *n.* 1. a device for raising weights, etc., usually consisting of a horizontal cylinder or barrel turned by a crank, lever, or the like, upon which a cable or the like winds, the outer end of the cable being attached directly or indirectly to the weight to be raised or the thing to be hauled or pulled. —*v.t.* 2. to raise, haul, or move by means of a windlass. [ME *windelas,* f. *windel* to wind (freq. of WIND[2]) + *-as* pole (t. Scand.; cf. Icel. *āss*)]

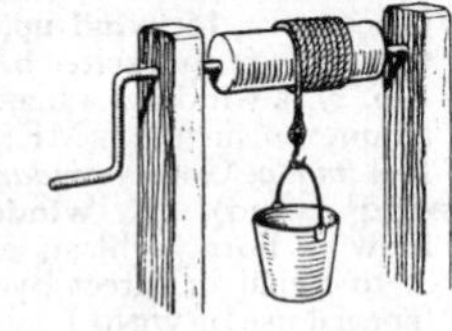
Windlass (hand-operated)

windless (wĭnd′lĭs), *adj.* 1. free from wind; calm. 2. out of breath.
windlestraw (wĭn′dl strô′), *n. Scot. and N Dial.* 1. a dry stalk of various grasses. 2. anything weak or slender.
wind-machine (wĭnd′mə shēn′), *n. Theat.* a device for producing a sound resembling a howling gale, usually consisting of a ribbed drum revolved against a silk or canvas sheet.
windmill (wĭnd′mĭl′, wĭn′-), *n.* 1. a mill or machine, as for grinding or pumping, operated by the wind, usually by the wind acting on a set of arms, vanes, sails, or slats attached to a horizontal axis so as to form a vertical revolving wheel. 2. the wheel itself. 3. *Aeron.* a small air turbine with blades, like those of an aeroplane propeller, exposed on a moving aircraft and driven by the air, used to operate fuel pumps, radio apparatus, etc. 4. an imaginary opponent, wrong, etc. (in allusion to Cervantes' *Don Quixote*): *to fight windmills.* —*v.i.* 5. *Aeron. Colloq.* (of an aeroplane propeller or turbojet) to rotate freely under the influence of a passing airstream.
window (wĭn′dō), *n.* 1. an opening in the wall or roof of a building, the cabin of a boat, etc., for the admission of air or light, or both, commonly fitted with a frame in which are set movable sashes containing panes of glass. 2. such an opening with the frame, sashes, and panes of glass, or any other device, by which it is closed. 3. the frame, sashes, and panes of glass, or the like, intended to fit such an opening. 4. a windowpane. 5. anything likened to a window in appearance or function, as a transparent section in an envelope, displaying the address. 6. any area, interval, or range of frequencies whose existence permits a particular event or phenomenon to be observed or accomplished, as the launching of a spacecraft aimed at a particular target. 7. strips of metal foil which when dropped from an aircraft give confusing reflections on enemy radar screens. —*v.t.* 8. to furnish with a window or windows. [ME, t. Scand.; cf. Icel. *vindauga,* f. *vind(r)* WIND[1] + *auga* eye] —**win′dowless,** *adj.*
window box, 1. a box for growing plants, placed at or in a window. 2. one of the vertical hollows at the sides of the frame of a window, for the weights counterbalancing a sliding sash.
window-dresser (wĭn′dō drĕs′ə), *n.* a person employed to dress the windows of a shop, or arrange in them attractive displays of goods for sale.
window-dressing (wĭn′dō drĕs′ĭng), *n.* 1. the act or fact of preparing a display in a shopwindow. 2. the presentation of the most favourable aspect of something, esp. when unpleasant facts are concealed.
windowpane (wĭn′dō pān′), *n.* a plate of glass used in a window.
window sash, the frame holding the pane or panes of a window.
window seat, a seat built beneath the sill of a recessed or other window.
window shade, *Chiefly U.S.* a blind or awning for a window.
window-shop (wĭn′dō shŏp′), *v.i.,* **-shopped, -shopping.** to look at articles in shopwindows instead of actually buying. —**win′dow-shop′per,** *n.* —**win′dow-shop′ping,** *adj., n.*
windowsill (wĭn′dō sĭl′), *n.* the sill under a window.
window tax, a graduated tax on houses with more than six windows, imposed in Great Britain 1697–1851.
windpipe (wĭnd′pīp′), *n.* the trachea of an air-breathing vertebrate.
wind-pollinated (wĭnd′pŏl′ĭ nā′tĭd), *adj. Bot.* pollinated by airborne pollen. —**wind′-pol′lina′tion,** *n.*
windproof (wĭnd′prōōf′), *adj.* resisting penetration by the wind.
windpump (wĭnd′pŭmp′), *n.* a pump operated by a windmill.
windrode (wĭnd′rōd′), *adj. Naut.* (of a vessel) riding at anchor with her head to the wind, and the tide running approximately the opposite way.
wind rose, *Meteorol.* a diagram which shows for a given locality or area the frequency and strength of the wind from various directions.
windrow (wĭnd′rō′, wĭn′-), *n.* 1. a row or line of hay raked together to dry before being made into cocks or heaps. 2. any similar row, as of sheaves of grain or stacks of peat, made for the purpose of drying. 3. a row of dry leaves, dust, etc., swept together by the wind. —*v.t.* 4. to arrange in a windrow or windrows. [f. WIND[1] + ROW[1]] —**wind′row′er,** *n.*
windsail (wĭnd′sāl′), *n. Naut.* a canvas funnel facing into the wind used to ventilate a ship's hold.
wind scale, a numerical scale, like the Beaufort scale, for designating relative wind intensities.
windscreen (wĭnd′skrēn′), *n.* the sheet of glass which forms the front window of a motor vehicle. Also, *Chiefly U.S.,* **windshield.**
windscreen-wiper (wĭnd′skrēn wī′pə), *n.* a mechanically operated, rubber-bladed wiper for keeping the windscreen of a motor vehicle clear of rain, snow, etc.
wind shake, 1. a flaw in wood supposed to be caused by the action of strong winds upon the trunk of the tree. 2. such flaws collectively.
wind-shaken (wĭnd′shā′kən), *adj.* 1. affected by wind-shake. 2. shaken by the wind.
windshear (wĭnd′shĭə′), *n. Meteorol.* a change of wind velocity with distance along an axis at right angles to the wind direction.
windshield (wĭnd′shēld′), *n. Chiefly U.S.* windscreen.
windsock (wĭnd′sŏk′), *n.* a wind-direction indicator, installed at airports and elsewhere, consisting of an elongated truncated cone of textile material, flown from a mast. Also, **airsock, wind cone, wind sleeve.**
Windsor (wĭn′zə), *n.* 1. the royal house of England since 1917. It comprises the Kings George V, Edward VIII, George VI, and Queen Elizabeth II. 2. **Duke of.** See **Edward VIII.** 3. a town in England, in Berkshire, on the Thames: the site of **Windsor Castle,** a residence of English sovereigns since William the Conqueror. 27,165 (1961). 4. a city in SE Canada, in Ontario, opposite Detroit, Michigan. 113,459 (1964).
Windsor chair, a wooden chair of many varieties, having a spindle back and legs slanting outwards: common in eighteenth-century England.
Windsor knot, a wide, triangular knot in a tie produced by extra turns when tying.
Windsor soap, a kind of perfumed toilet soap, usually coloured brown.
Windsor tie, a wide, soft, silk tie in a loose bow.
windstorm (wĭnd′stôm′), *n.* a storm with heavy wind, but little or no precipitation.
windsucker (wĭnd′sŭk′ə), *n.* a horse afflicted with cribbing.
wind-sucking (wĭnd′sŭk′ĭng), *adj.* cribbing (def. 1).
windswept (wĭnd′swĕpt′), *adj.* 1. open or exposed to the wind. 2. (of hair) blown about by the wind, or styled to give such an effect.
windtight (wĭnd′tīt′), *adj.* so tight as to prevent passage of wind or air.
wind-tunnel (wĭnd′tŭn′əl), *n.* a tunnel-like device through which a controlled airstream can be drawn at various speeds, in order to subject scale models of aircraft, parts of aircraft, or complete aircraft, to aerodynamic tests.
wind-up (wĭnd′ŭp′), *n. Chiefly U.S.* 1. the conclusion of

any action, etc.; the end or close. **2.** a final act or part.

windvane (wĭnd′vān′), *n.* a device using a pivoted arm with a vertical vane to indicate the direction of the wind.

windward (wĭnd′wəd), *adv.* **1.** towards the wind; towards the point from which the wind blows. *—adj.* **2.** pertaining to, situated in, or moving towards the quarter from which the wind blows (opposed to *leeward*). *—n.* **3.** the point or quarter from which the wind blows. **4.** the side towards the wind. **5. get to the windward of,** to get the advantage of.

Windward Islands, 1. an island group in the West Indies, comprising the S part of the Lesser Antilles. **2.** four former British colonies in this island group, Dominica, Grenada, St Lucia, and St Vincent and their dependencies. 314,295 pop. (1960); 821 sq. mi.

Windward Passage, a strait in the West Indies between Cuba and Hispaniola. ab. 50 mi. wide.

windy (wĭn′dĭ), *adj.*, **windier, windiest. 1.** accompanied or characterized by wind: *windy weather.* **2.** exposed to or swept by the wind: *a windy hill.* **3.** consisting of or resembling wind: *the windy tempest of my heart.* **4.** towards the wind, or windward. **5.** unsubstantial or empty. **6.** of the nature of, characterized by, or given to prolonged, empty talk; voluble. **7.** characterized by or causing flatulence. **8.** *Colloq.* frightened; nervous. **9.** *Colloq.* boastful. [ME; OE *windig*, f. *wind* WIND[1] + *-ig* -Y[1]] **—wind′ily,** *adv.* **—wind′iness,** *n.*

wine (wīn), *n.*, *v.*, **wined, wining.** *—n.* **1.** the fermented juice of the grape, in many varieties (red, white, sweet, dry, still, sparkling, etc.), used as a beverage and in cookery, religious rites, etc. **2.** a particular variety of such fermented grape juice: *port and sherry wines.* **3.** the juice, fermented or unfermented, of various other fruits or plants, used as a beverage, etc.: *gooseberry wine, currant wine.* **4.** a dark reddish colour, as of red wines. **5.** *U.S. Pharm.* vinum. **6.** something that invigorates, cheers, or intoxicates like wine. **7.** intoxication due to the drinking of wine. **8.** a party for wine-drinking. *—adj.* **9.** wine-coloured; dark purplish red. *—v.t.* **10.** to entertain with wine. **11.** to supply with wine. *—v.i.* **12.** to drink wine. [ME; OE *wīn*, c. D *wijn*, G *Wein*, Icel. *vīn*, Goth. *wein*, all g. to a prehistoric Gmc word t. L: m. *vīnum*] **—wine′less,** *adj.*

winebibber (wīn′bĭb′ə), *n.* one who drinks much wine; a drunkard. **—wine′bib′bing,** *n.*, *adj.*

wine biscuit, a semisweet biscuit originally intended to be eaten with wine.

wine cellar, 1. a cellar for the storage of wine. **2.** the wine stored there; a store or stock of wines.

wine-cooler (wīn′ko͞o′lə), *n.* a bucket with ice for cooling wine in bottles to be served at table.

wine gallon, a former gallon of 231 cu. in., equal to the present U.S. standard gallon.

wineglass (wīn′gläs′), *n.* a small drinking glass for wine.

wineglassful (wīn′gläs fo͝ol′), *n.*, *pl.* **-fuls.** the capacity of a wineglass, commonly considered as equal to 2 fluid ounces or 4 tablespoons.

wine-grower (wīn′grō′ə), *n.* one who owns or works in a vineyard or wine-making business.

wine-growing (wīn′grō′ĭng), *n.* the act or business of a wine-grower.

wine-making (wīn′mā′kĭng), *n.* the process of preparing wine from grapes or other fruit.

wine measure, a former English system of measures for wine, etc., in which the gallon (wine gallon) was equal to 231 cu. in., and hence smaller than the gallon for beer, etc.

wine palm, any of various palms yielding toddy (def. 2).

winepress (wīn′prĕs′), *n.* a machine in which the juice is pressed from grapes for wine.

winery (wī′nə rĭ), *n.*, *pl.* **-eries.** *U.S.* an establishment for making wine.

wineshop (wīn′shŏp′), *n.* a shop where wine is sold.

wineskin (wīn′skĭn′), *n.* **1.** a vessel made of the nearly complete skin of a goat, or the like, used, esp. in the East, for holding wine. **2.** *Colloq.* one who drinks great or excessive quantities of wine.

wine-taster (wīn′tās′tə), *n.* one whose occupation is to sample wines to examine their quality.

wine-tasting (wīn′tās′tĭng), *n.* **1.** the occupation of a wine-taster. **2.** a social or other gathering to sample various wines.

winey (wī′nĭ), *adj.*, **winier, winest.** winy.

wing (wĭng), *n.* **1.** either of the two anterior extremities, or appendages of the scapular arch or shoulder girdle, of most birds and of bats, which constitute the forelimbs and correspond to the human arms, but are adapted for flight. **2.** either of two corresponding but rudimentary or functionless parts in certain other birds, as ostriches and penguins. **3.** any of certain other winglike structures of other animals, as the patagium of a flying squirrel. **4.** (in insects) one of the thin, flat, movable, lateral extensions from the back of the mesothorax and the metathorax by means of which the insects fly. See diag. under **coleopteron. 5.** a similar structure with which gods, angels, demons, etc., are conceived to be provided for the purpose of flying. **6.** *U.S. Colloq.* an arm of a human being. **7.** a means or instrument of flight, travel, or progress. **8.** the act or manner of flying. **9.** flight; departure: *to take wing.* **10.** something resembling or likened to a wing, as a vane or sail of a windmill. **11.** *Aeron.* **a.** that portion of a main supporting surface confined to one side of an aeroplane. **b.** any complete winglike structure; plane. **12.** the mudguard of a motor vehicle. **13.** *Archit.* a part of a building projecting on one side of, or subordinate to, a central or main part. **14.** *Furniture.* an extension on the side of the back of an armchair above the arms. **15.** *Mil.*, *Naval.* either of the two side portions of an army or fleet (usually called right wing and left wing, and distinguished from the centre); flank unit. **16. a.** (in fighter command of the RAF and certain other airforces) a number of squadrons, usually three, four, or five, operating together as a tactical unit. **b.** (in the U.S. Air Force) an administrative and tactical unit consisting of two or more groups, a headquarters, and certain supporting and service units. **17.** (*pl.*) the insignia or emblem worn by a qualified pilot. **18.** *Fort.* either of the longer sides of a crownwork, uniting it to the main work. **19.** *Football, Hockey, etc.* **a.** either of the two areas of the pitch near the touchline and ahead of the halfway line, known as the left and right wings respectively, with reference to the direction of the opposing goal. **b.** a player in either of these positions. **20.** *Theat.* **a.** the platform or space on the right or left of the stage proper. **b.** one of the long, narrow side pieces of scenery. **21.** *Anat.* an ala: *the wings of the sphenoid.* **22.** *Bot.* **a.** any leaf-like expansion, as of a samara. **b.** one of the two side petals of a papilionaceous flower. See illus. under **papilionaceous. 23.** either of the parts of a double door, etc. **24.** the feather of an arrow. **25.** a group within a political party: *right wing, left wing.* **26.** *Naut.* **a.** the side part of a ship's hold. **b.** a side piece of an awning. **27. clip one's wings,** to restrict the independence or freedom of action of. **28. in the wings,** unobtrusively ready to take action when required; in reserve. **29. on the wing, a.** in flight; flying. **b.** in motion; travelling; active. **c.** *Football, Hockey, etc.* playing in the position on the left or right extreme of the forward line. **30. take wing, a.** to fly off. **b.** to leave hastily. **31. under one's wing,** in or into one's care or protection. *—v.t.* **32.** to equip with wings. **33.** to enable to fly, move rapidly, etc.; lend speed or celerity to. **34.** to supply with a winglike part, a side structure, etc. **35.** to transport on or as on wings. **36.** to perform or accomplish by wings. **37.** to traverse in flight. **38.** to wound or disable (a bird, etc.) in the wing. **39.** to wound (a person) in an arm or other non-vital part. **40.** to bring down (an aeroplane, etc.) by a shot. **41.** to brush or clean with a wing. **42.** *Theat. Colloq.* to perform (a part, etc.) relying on prompters in the wings. *—v.i.* **43.** to travel on or as on wings; fly; soar. [ME *wenge*, pl., t. Scand.; cf. Icel. *vængir*, pl.] **—wing′like′,** *adj.*

wing-and-wing (wĭng′ən wĭng′), *n.* *Naut.* with a sail extended on each side by a boom, as a schooner sailing with the foresail out on one side and the mainsail out on the other.

Wingate (wĭng′gĭt), *n.* **Orde Charles** (ôd), 1903–44, British general: organizer and commander of the Chindits.

wing-case (wĭng′kās′), *n.* elytron. Also, **wing-cover** (wĭng′kŭv′ə).

wing chair, a large upholstered chair, with winglike parts projecting from the back above the arms.

wing collar, a stand-up collar with the corners turned down above the tie, formerly worn with formal dress.

wing-commander (wĭng′kə män′də), *n.* **1.** a commissioned officer in the Royal Air Force ranking above a squadron leader and below group captain. **2.** an officer of equivalent rank in any of various other airforces.

wing-coverts (wĭng′kŭv′əts), *n.* *Ornith.* the feathers which cover the bases of the quill feathers of the wing in birds, divided into greater, middle, lesser, and primary coverts.

wing dam, *U.S.* spur (def. 10).

winged (wĭngd *or, esp. Poetic.*, wĭng′ĭd), *adj.* **1.** having wings. **2.** having a winglike part or parts: *a winged bone, a winged seed.* **3.** moving or passing on or as if on wings: *winged words.* **4.** rapid or swift. **5.** elevated or lofty: *winged sentiments.* **6.** disabled in the wing, as a bird. **7.** wounded in an arm or other non-vital part. **8.** *Archaic.* abounding with wings or winged creatures.

Winged Horse, *Astron.* the constellation Pegasus.

Winged Victory, a marble statue (*c.* 200 B.C.) of the Greek goddess Nike, found at Samothrace and now in the Louvre.

winger (wĭng′ə), *n. Football, Hockey, etc.* a player on the left or right wing.

wing-footed (wĭng′fo͝ot′ĭd), *adj. Archaic.* having winged feet; rapid; swift.

wing-forward (wĭng′fô′wəd), *n.* **1.** *Soccer, etc.* either of the two players at the ends of the forward line. **2.** *Rugby Union.* either of the two outside players on the outside of the back row of the scrum.

wing-half (wĭng′häf′), *n. Soccer, etc.* a left half or right half.

winging out, *Naut.* stowing cargo at the extreme sides of a ship's hold.

wingless (wĭng′lĭs), *adj.* **1.** having no wings. **2.** having only rudimentary wings, as an apteryx. —**wing′less-ness,** *n.*

winglet (wĭng′lĭt), *n.* **1.** a little wing. **2.** *Zool.* alula.

wing-loading (wĭng′lō′dĭng), *n. Aeron.* See **loading** (def. 4).

wing nut, a nut which incorporates two flat projecting wings enabling it to be turned by thumb and forefinger. Also, **butterfly nut.**

wing-sheath (wĭng′shēth′), *n.* a wing-case; elytron.

wingspan (wĭng′spăn′), *n.* the distance between the wingtips of an aeroplane, bird, or insect. Also, **wingspread.**

wingspread (wĭng′sprĕd′), *n.* wingspan.

wing-three-quarter (wĭng′thrē kwô′tə), *n. Rugby Football.* either of the two outside players in the three-quarter line; left wing or right wing.

wingtip (wĭng′tĭp′), *n.* the extreme outer edge of the wing of an aeroplane, bird, or insect.

wingy (wĭng′ĭ), *adj.* **1.** having wings. **2.** rapid; swift. **3.** *Slang.* tall; lofty.

wink[1] (wĭngk), *v.i.* **1.** to close and open the eyes quickly. **2.** (of the eyes) to close and open thus; blink. **3.** to close and open one eye quickly as a hint or signal or with some sly meaning (often fol. by *at*). **4.** to be purposely blind to a thing, as if to avoid the necessity of taking action (usually fol. by *at*): *to wink at petty offences.* **5.** to shine with little flashes of light, or twinkle. —*v.t.* **6.** to close and open (the eyes or an eye) quickly; execute or give (a wink). **7.** to drive or force (away, back, etc.) by winking: *to wink back one's tears.* **8.** to signal or convey by a wink. —*n.* **9.** the act of winking. **10.** a winking movement, esp. of one eye as in giving a hint or signal. **11.** a hint or signal given by winking. **12.** the time required for winking once; an instant or twinkling. **13.** a little flash of light; a twinkle. **14.** *Colloq.* a bit: *I didn't sleep a wink.* **15. forty winks,** *Colloq.* a short sleep or nap. **16. tip (someone) the wink,** *Colloq.* to give information or a vital hint to (someone). [ME; OE *wincian,* c. G *winken*]

—**Syn. 1.** WINK, BLINK refer to rapid motions of the eyelid. To WINK is to close and open either one or both eyelids with a rapid motion. To BLINK suggests a sleepy, dazed, or dazzled condition in which it is difficult to focus the eyes or see clearly: *a dazzling light makes one blink.*

wink[2] (wĭngk), *n.* one of the discs used in tiddleywinks.

Winkelried (*Ger.* vĭng′kəl rēt), *n.* See **Arnold von Winkelried.**

winker (wĭng′kə), *n.* **1.** one who or that which winks. **2.** a blinker for a horse. **3.** the nictitating membrane of a bird's eye. **4.** *Colloq.* a trafficator on a vehicle. **5.** *Colloq.* an eyelash or an eye.

winkle (wĭng′kl), *n., v.,* **-kled, -kling.** —*n.* **1.** any of various marine gastropods; a periwinkle. —*v.t.* **2.** *Colloq.* to prise or extract (something) out of, as a winkle from its shell with a pin (fol. by *out*). [short for PERIWINKLE[1]]

winkle-picker (wĭng′kl pĭk′ə), *n. Colloq.* a shoe having a sharp-pointed toe.

Winnebago (wĭn′ĭ bā′gō), *n.* **1.** a member of a North American Indian tribe speaking a Siouan language, living in NE Wisconsin and NE Nebraska. **2.** this tribe.

Winnepesaukee (wĭn′ĭ pĭ sô′kĭ), *n.* **Lake,** a lake in the U.S., in central New Hampshire: summer resort. 25 mi. long.

winner (wĭn′ə), *n.* **1.** one who or that which wins. **2.** *Colloq.* something successful or highly valued: *this song is a real winner.*

winning (wĭn′ĭng), *n.* **1.** the act of one who or that which wins. **2.** (*usually pl.*) that which is won. **3.** *Mining.* **a.** an opening of any kind by which coal is being, or has been, won. **b.** a bed of coal ready for mining. —*adj.* **4.** that wins; successful or victorious, as in a contest. **5.** taking, engaging, or charming, as a person or the manner, qualities, ways, etc. —**win′ningly,** *adv.* —**win′ningness,** *n.*
—**Syn. 5.** captivating, attractive, winsome.

winning gallery, *Real Tennis.* the opening that is farthest from the spectators' gallery (so named because any ball struck into it is called a winning ball).

winning opening, *Real Tennis.* the dedans, winning gallery, or the grille (so named because it is a winning stroke to hit a ball into any of them).

winning post, a post on a racecourse, forming the goal or finishing point of a race.

Winnipeg (wĭn′ĭ pĕg′), *n.* **1.** a city in S Canada, on the Red River: the capital of Manitoba. 256,613 (1964). **2. Lake,** a lake in S Canada, in Manitoba. ab. 260 mi. long; ab. 9000 sq. mi.

Winnipegosis (wĭn′ĭ pĭ gō′sĭs), *n.* **Lake,** a lake in S Canada, in W Manitoba, W of Lake Winnipeg, ab. 2000 sq. mi.

winnow (wĭn′ō), *v.t.* **1.** to free (grain, etc.) from chaff, refuse particles, etc., by means of wind or driven air; fan. **2.** to blow upon, as the wind does upon grain in this process. **3.** to drive or blow (chaff, etc.) away by fanning. **4.** to subject to some process of separating or distinguishing; analyse critically; sift: *to winnow a mass of statements.* **5.** to separate or distinguish: *to winnow truth from falsehood.* **6.** to pursue (a course) with flapping wings in flying. **7.** *Archaic.* to fan or stir (the air) as with the wings in flying. —*v.i.* **8.** to free grain from chaff by wind or driven air. **9.** to fly with flapping wings; flutter. —*n.* **10.** a device or contrivance for winnowing grain, etc. **11.** the act of winnowing. [ME *win(d)we,* OE *windwian* (der. WIND[1], n.). Cf. L *ventilāre*] —**win′nower,** *n.*

winnowing machine, a machine for cleaning grain by the action of riddles and sieves and an air blast. Also, *U.S.,* **fanning mill.**

winsey (wĭn′sĭ), *n.* wincey.

winsome (wĭn′səm), *adj.* winning, engaging, or charming: *a winsome smile.* [ME *winsom,* OE *wynsum,* f. *wyn* joy + *-sum* -SOME[1]] —**win′somely,** *adv.* —**win′someness,** *n.*

Winston-Salem (wĭn′stən sā′ləm), *n.* a city in the U.S., in North Carolina. 111,135 (1960).

winter (wĭn′tə), *n.* **1.** the last and the coldest season of the year. **2.** a period of cold weather associated with this season. **3.** a whole year as represented by this season: *a man of sixty winters.* **4.** a period like winter, as the last or final period of life, a period of decline, decay, inertia, dreariness, or adversity. —*adj.* **5.** of, pertaining to, or characteristic of winter. **6.** suitable for wear or use in winter. **7.** (of fruit and vegetables) of a kind that may be kept for use during the winter. **8.** *Agric.* designating varieties of grain, esp. wheat, oats, and barley, which are sown before winter to be harvested the following spring or summer. —*v.i.* **9.** to spend or pass the winter: *planning to winter in Italy.* —*v.t.* **10.** to keep, feed, or manage during the winter, as plants or cattle. [ME and OE, c. D *winter* and G *Winter,* Icel. *vetr,* Goth. *wintrus*] —**win′terer,** *n.* —**win′terless,** *adj.* —**win′ter-like′, win′terish,** *adj.*

winter aconite, a small ranunculaceous herb, *Eranthis hyemalis,* a native of the Old World, often cultivated for its bright yellow flowers, which appear very early in the spring.

winterbourne (wĭn′tə bôn′), *n.* a channel filled only at a time of excessive rainfall.

winter cherry, a solanaceous herb, *Physalis alkekengi,* widespread from SE Europe to Japan, often cultivated for the persistent, inflated, bright red calyx which contains a red, edible berry.

winter cress, a small cruciferous herb, *Barbarea vulgaris,* formerly grown for salad.

winterfeed (wĭn′tə fēd′), *v.t.,* **-fed, -feeding.** to feed in the winter, as cattle.

wintergarden (wĭn′tə gä′dn), *n.* **1.** an ornamental garden of evergreen plants, etc. **2.** a conservatory in which flowers are cultivated to bloom in the winter.

wintergreen (wĭn′tə grēn′), *n.* **1.** a small, creeping evergreen ericaceous shrub, *Gaultheria procumbens,* common in eastern North America, with white bell-shaped flowers, a bright red berry-like fruit, and aromatic leaves which yield a volatile oil. **2.** this oil (**oil of wintergreen**). **3.** the flavour of oil of wintergreen or something flavoured with it. **4.** any of various other plants of the same genus. **5.** any of various small evergreen herbs of the genera *Pyrola* and *Chimaphila.*

winter heliotrope, a rhizomatous composite herb with pale mauve, scented capitula, *Petasites fragrans,* a native of the Mediterranean region but frequently cultivated and sometimes naturalized elsewhere.

winterize (wĭn′tə rīz′), *v.t.,* **-rized, -rizing.** *U.S., Canada, etc.* to prepare (a motor vehicle, house, etc.) for cold weather by (in motor vehicles) adding antifreeze and changing weight of oil, (in houses) adding insulation, heating units, etc.

winterkill (wĭn′tə kĭl′), *v.t., v.i. U.S.* to kill by or die from exposure to the cold of winter, as wheat. —**win′terkil′ling,** *adj., n.*

winter lamb, a well-fed lamb born in the autumn or early winter and sold before May 20th.

winter quarters, 1. the quarters of an army during winter. **2.** a winter residence.

winter solstice, *Astron.* See **solstice** (def. 1).
winter sports, sports which take place on snow and ice, esp. skiing, skating, and bobsleighing.
wintersweet (wĭn′tə swēt′), *n.* a winter-flowering shrub with scented flowers, *Chimonanthus praecox*, native of China and Japan.
Winterthur (*Ger.* vĭn′tər to͞or), *n.* a town in N Switzerland, in Zurich canton. 87,900 (1964).
wintertime (wĭn′tə tīm′), *n.* the season of winter. Also, *Archaic*, **wintertide** (wĭn′tə tīd′).
wintry (wĭn′trĭ), *adj.*, **-trier, -triest.** **1.** of or characteristic of winter. **2.** having the season, storminess, or cold of winter. **3.** suggestive of winter, as in lack of warmth or cheer. Also, **wintery** (wĭn′tə rĭ, -trĭ), **winterly** (wĭn′tə lĭ). —**win′trily,** *adv.* —**win′triness,** *n.*
winy (wī′nĭ), *adj.*, **winier, winiest.** **1.** of, like, or characteristic of wine. **2.** affected by or intoxicated with wine. Also, **winey.**
winze (wĭnz), *n. Mining.* a small underground shaft, esp. one sunk from one level to another, as for ventilation, etc. [earlier *winds*, appar. der. WIND[1], n.]
wipe (wīp), *v.*, **wiped, wiping,** *n.* —*v.t.* **1.** to rub lightly with or on a cloth, towel, paper, the hand, etc., in order to clean or dry. **2.** to remove by rubbing with or on something (usually fol. by *away, off, out*, etc.). **3.** to remove as if by rubbing: *wipe the smile off your face.* **4.** to destroy or eradicate, as from existence or memory. **5.** to rub or draw (something) over a surface, as in cleaning or drying. **6.** *Plumbing.* **a.** to apply (solder in a semifluid state) by spreading with leather or cloth over the part to be soldered. **b.** to form (a joint) in this manner. **7. wipe out,** to destroy completely. **8. wipe the floor with,** *Slang.* to defeat utterly; overcome completely. —*n.* **9.** the action of wiping. **10.** a rub, as of one thing over another. **11.** *Films.* a technique in film editing by which the projected image of a scene appears to be pushed or wiped off the screen by the image that follows. **12.** *Obs. or Dial.* a sweeping stroke or blow. **13.** *Obs. Colloq.* a gibe. **14.** *Obs. Slang.* a handkerchief. [ME; OE *wīpian*, c. OHG *wīfan* wind round, Goth. *weipan* crown; akin to VIBRATE]
wiper (wī′pə), *n.* **1.** one who or that which wipes. **2.** that with which anything is wiped, as a towel or a handkerchief. **3.** *Elect.* that portion of the moving member of a selector, or other similar device, which makes contact with the terminals of a bank; a type of brush (def. 8a). **4.** *Mach.* a projecting piece, as on a rotating axis, acting on another part, as a stamper, esp. to raise it so that it may fall by its own weight. **5.** a windscreen-wiper.
wire (wī′ə), *n.*, *adj.*, *v.*, **wired, wiring.** —*n.* **1.** a piece of slender, flexible metal, ranging from a thickness that can be bent by the hand only with some difficulty down to a fine thread, and usually circular in section. **2.** such pieces as a material. **3.** a length of such material used as a conductor of electricity, usually insulated in a flex. **4.** a crosswire or crosshair. **5.** a barbed-wire fence. **6.** a long wire or cable used in a telegraph, telephone, or cable system. **7.** *Colloq.* a telegram. **8.** *Colloq.* the telegraphic system: *to send a message by wire.* **9.** (*pl.*) a system of wires by which puppets are moved. **10.** a metallic string of a musical instrument. **11.** *Ornith.* one of the extremely long, slender, wirelike filaments or shafts of the plumage of various birds. **12.** a metal device used to snare rabbits, etc. **13. pull wires,** *Chiefly U.S.* to exert hidden influence; pull strings. —*adj.* **14.** made of wire; consisting of or constructed with wires. **15.** wirelike. —*v.t.* **16.** to furnish with a wire or wires. **17.** to install an electric system of wiring, as for lighting, etc. **18.** to fasten or bind with wire. **19.** to put on a wire, as beads. **20.** *Colloq.* to send by telegraph, as a message. **21.** *Colloq.* to send a telegraphic message to. **22.** to snare by means of a wire or wires. **23.** *Croquet.* to arrange (a ball) in such a manner that it will rest behind an arch and thus prevent a shot which would be successful. —*v.i.* **24.** *Colloq.* to send a telegraphic message; telegraph. [ME and OE *wīr*, c. LG *wīr*, Icel. *vīrr*] —**wire′like′,** *adj.*
wirecloth (wī′ə klŏth′), *n.* **1.** a material of wires of moderate fineness, used for strainers, or in the manufacture of paper, etc. —*adj.* **2.** made of this material.
wire-cutter (wī′ə kŭt′ə), *n.* a tool designed to cut wire.
wiredancer (wī′ə dän′sə), *n.* one who dances or performs other feats upon a high wire. —**wire′danc′ing,** *n.*
wired glass, glass having wire netting embedded within it to increase its strength.
wiredraw (wī′ə drô′), *v.t.*, **-drew, -drawn, -drawing.** **1.** to draw (metal) out into wire, esp. by pulling forcibly through a series of holes gradually decreasing in diameter. **2.** to draw out to great length, in quantity or time; stretch out to excess. **3.** to strain unwarrantably, as in meaning. —**wire′draw′er,** *n.* —**wire′draw′ing,** *n.*
wire entanglement, *Fort.* heavy barbed-wire erected to impede the advance of the enemy.
wire-gauge (wī′ə gāj′), *n.* a gauge calibrated for standard wire diameters.
wire gauze, a gauzelike texture woven of very fine wires.
wire-haired (wī′ə hĕəd′), *adj.* having coarse, stiff, wirelike hair.
wire-haired terrier, a fox-terrier having a wiry coat. Also, *Chiefly U.S.*, **wirehair.**
wireless (wī′ə lĭs), *adj.* **1.** having no wire. **2.** denoting or pertaining to any of various devices which are operated with or set in action by electromagnetic waves. **3.** radio. —*n.* **4.** radio. **5.** wireless telegraphy or telephony. **6.** a wireless telegraph or telephone, or the like. —*v.t.*, *v.i.* **7.** to telegraph or telephone by wireless.

Wire-gauge

wireless link, radio link.
wireless receiver, radio receiver.
wireless relay, radio relay.
wireless set, a radio receiver, or a radio receiver and transmitter.
wireless signal, radio signal.
wireless station, radio station.
wireless telegraphy, radiotelegraphy.
wireless telephone, radiotelephone.
wireless telephony, radiotelephony.
wireless transmitter, radio transmitter.
wireman (wī′ə mən), *n.*, *pl.* **-men.** one who installs and maintains electric wiring.
wire netting, a texture or area of wire woven in the form of a net.
wirephoto (wī′ə fō′tō), *n.* **1.** a method of sending photographs by telegraphy. **2.** a photograph sent by this method.
wire-pulling (wī′ə po͝ol′ĭng), *n. Chiefly U.S.* string-pulling. —**wire′-pul′ler,** *n.*
wirer (wī′ə rə), *n.* **1.** one who wires. **2.** one who uses wire to snare game.
wire recorder, a device to record sound on a steel wire by magnetizing the wire as it passes an electromagnet, the sound being reproduced by the motion of the wire past a receiver.
wire rope, a rope made of strands of wire.
wire-tapper (wī′ə tăp′ə), *n.* **1.** one who illicitly taps telegraph or telephone wires to learn the nature of messages passing over them. **2.** *U.S. Colloq.* a swindler who professes to secure by this or some similar means advance information for betting or the like. —**wire′-tap′ping,** *n.*, *adj.*
wirewalker (wī′ə wô′kə), *n. Chiefly U.S.* tightrope-walker.
wire wheel, *Motor Vehicles.* a wheel having wire spokes, as used on high-speed sports cars.
wire wool, steel wool.
wirework (wī′ə wûk′), *n.* **1.** work consisting of wire. **2.** fabrics or articles made of wire.
wireworks (wī′ə wûks′), *n.pl. or sing.* an establishment where wire is made, or is put to some industrial use. —**wire′work′er,** *n.*
wireworm (wī′ə wûm′), *n.* **1.** any of the slender, hard-bodied larvae of click beetles, which in many species live underground and feed on the roots of plants. **2.** any of various small myriapods. **3.** a stomach worm.
wire-wound (wī′ə wound′), *adj. Elect.* wound with wire, as a resistor or armature.
wirewove (wī′ə wōv′), *adj.* **1.** made of woven wire. **2.** denoting fine glazed paper used esp. for letter paper.
wiring (wī′ə rĭng), *n.* **1.** the act of one who wires. **2.** *Elect.* the aggregate of wires, in a lighting system, switchboard, radio, etc. —*adj.* **3.** that installs, or is used in, wiring.
wirra (wĭ′rə), *interj. Irish.* (an exclamation of sorrow or lament.) [in full, *O wirra*, half trans., half adoption of Irish *a Muire* O Mary]
wiry (wī′ə rĭ), *adj.*, **wirier, wiriest.** **1.** made of wire. **2.** in the form of wire. **3.** resembling wire, as in form, stiffness, etc.: *wiry grass.* **4.** lean and sinewy. **5.** produced by or resembling the sound of a vibrating wire: *wiry tones.* —**wir′ily,** *adv.* —**wir′iness,** *n.*
wis (wĭs), *v.t.*, *v.i. Archaic.* to know. [abstracted from *iwis* certainly (OE *gewiss*), misread as *I wis* I know]
Wis., Wisconsin. Also, **Wisc.**
Wisbech (wĭz′bēch), *n.* a town in England, in N Cambridgeshire. 17,528 (1961).
Wisby (wĭz′bĭ; *Ger.* vĭz′bē), *n.* German name of **Visby.**
Wisconsin (wĭs kŏn′sĭn), *n.* **1.** a state in the N central United States: a part of the Midwest. 3,951,777 pop. (1960); 56,154 sq. mi. *Cap.:* Madison. *Abbrev.:* Wis. or Wisc. **2.** a river in the U.S., flowing from N Wisconsin SW to the Mississippi. ab. 430 mi.
Wisd., Wisdom of Solomon (Apocrypha).

wisdom (wĭz′dəm), *n.* **1.** the quality or state of being wise; knowledge of what is true or right coupled with just judgement as to action; sagacity, prudence, or common sense. **2.** scholarly knowledge, or learning: *the wisdom of the schools.* **3.** wise sayings or teachings. **4.** a wise act or saying. [ME and OE, c. Icel. *vīsdōmr.* See WISE[1], -DOM] —**wis′domless,** *adj.* —**Syn. 2.** discretion, judgement. See **information. 2.** learning, sapience, erudition.

Wisdom of Jesus, Son of Sirach (sī′ə′ răk), Ecclesiasticus.

Wisdom of Solomon, a book of the Apocrypha, on wisdom and its relation to righteousness.

wisdom tooth, the third molar tooth; the last tooth in each quadrant of the jaw; the last tooth to erupt (usually between the ages of 17–25).

wise[1] (wīz), *adj.*, **wiser, wisest. 1.** having the power of discerning and judging properly as to what is true or right. **2.** characterized by or showing such power; shrewd, judicious, or prudent. **3.** possessed of or characterized by scholarly knowledge or learning; learned; erudite: *wise in the law.* **4.** having knowledge or information as to facts, circumstances, etc.: *we are wiser for his explanations.* **5.** *Colloq.* in the know (about something implied); alerted; cognizant (often fol. by *to*): *they tried to keep it secret, but he was wise; I'm wise to your tricks.* **6. get wise,** *Colloq.* **a.** to face facts or realities. **b.** to learn something. **7. none the wiser,** still in ignorance. **8. put wise, a.** to explain something (to someone, esp. a naive person). **b.** to warn. —*v.i.* **9. wise up,** *Colloq.* **a.** to become aware, informed, or alerted; face the realities. **b.** to make (someone) aware, informed or alerted. [ME and OE *wīs,* c. D *wijs,* G *weise*] —**wise′ly,** *adv.* —**Ant. 2.** foolish.

wise[2] (wīz), *n. Archaic.* **1.** way of proceeding; manner; fashion. **2.** respect; degree (now usually in composition or in certain phrases): *in any wise* (in any way, respect, or degree). [ME and OE; c. D *wijze,* G *Weise* manner, tune]

-wise, a suffixal use of **wise**[2] in adverbs denoting: **1.** attitude or direction: *lengthwise, clockwise.* **2.** with reference to; in respect of: *moneywise.* **3.** *U.S.* var. of **-ways:** *sidewise.*

wiseacre (wīz′ā′kə), *n.* **1.** (esp. in ironical or humorous use) one who possesses or affects to possess great wisdom. **2.** a know-all. [t. MD: m. *wijsseggher* soothsayer]

wisecrack (wīz′krăk′), *Slang.* —*n.* **1.** a smart, pungent, or facetious remark. —*v.i.* **2.** to make wisecracks. —*v.t.* **3.** to say as a wisecrack. —**wise′crack′er,** *n.*

wise guy, *Chiefly U.S. Slang.* a cocksure or impertinent person of either sex.

Wiseman (wīz′mən), *n.* **Nicholas Patrick Stephen,** 1802–65, English cardinal and writer.

wish (wĭsh), *v.t.* **1.** to want; desire; long for (often with an infinitive or a clause as object): *I wish to see him, I wish that he would come.* **2.** to desire (a person or thing) to be (as specified): *to wish oneself elsewhere.* **3.** to entertain wishes of something favourable or otherwise, for: *to wish one well or ill.* **4.** to bid, as in greeting or leave-taking: *to wish one a good morning.* **5.** to command, request, or entreat: *I wish him to come.* **6.** to force or impose (fol. by *on*): *to wish a hard job on someone.* —*v.i.* **7.** to have a desire, longing, or yearning. **8.** to express a desire (for something), as in a magic ritual: *blow out the candles and wish.* **9. wish on** or **upon,** to perform such a ritual, using something as a talisman or charm: *to wish upon a forked hazel twig.* —*n.* **10.** a distinct mental inclination towards the doing, obtaining, attaining, etc., of something; a desire, felt or expressed: *disregard the wishes of others.* **11.** an expression of a wish, often one of a kindly or courteous nature: *send one's best wishes.* **12.** that which is wished: *get one's wish.* **13.** an act of ritual wishing: *to make a wish.* [ME *wisshe,* OE *wȳscan,* c. G *wünschen,* Icel. *œskja*] —**wish′er,** *n.* —**wish′less,** *adj.*

—**Syn. 1.** WISH, DESIRE, WANT indicate a longing for something. To WISH is to feel an impulse towards attainment or possession of something; the strength of the feeling may be of greater or less intensity: *I wish I could go home.* DESIRE, a more formal word, suggests a strong wish: *they desire a new regime.* WANT suggests a feeling of lack or need which imperatively demands fulfilment: *people all over the world want peace.*

wishbone (wĭsh′bōn′), *n.* the forked bone (a united pair of clavicles) in front of the breastbone in most birds; the furcula.

wishful (wĭsh′fəl), *adj.* **1.** having or showing a wish; desirous; longing. **2. wishful thinking,** a belief that a thing will happen or is so, based on one's hopes rather than on reality.

wish fulfilment, *Psychol.* the satisfaction of conscious or unconscious desires, esp. through realistic or symbolic gratification in dreams.

wishy-washy (wĭsh′ĭ wŏsh′ĭ), *adj.* **1.** washy or watery, as a liquid; thin and weak. **2.** lacking in substantial qualities; without strength or force; weak, feeble, or poor. [reduplication of WASHY]

Wisla (*Pol.* vē′swȧ), *n.* Polish name of the **Vistula.**

Wismar (*Ger.* vĭs′mȧr), *n.* a seaport in northern East Germany, on the Baltic. 57,277 (1963).

wisp (wĭsp), *n.* **1.** a handful or small bundle of straw, hay, or the like. **2.** any small or thin tuft, lock, mass, etc.: *wisps of hair.* **3.** anything small or thin, as a shred, bundle, or slip of something, sometimes used as a brush or whisk. **4.** a small or slight person. **5.** a flock (of birds, esp. snipe). —*v.t.* **6.** to rub (a horse) down with a wisp of straw. **7.** *Rare.* to twist into a wisp. [ME *wisp, wips;* akin to WIPE] —**wisp′-like′,** *adj.*

wispy (wĭs′pĭ), *adj.*, **wispier, wispiest.** being a wisp or in wisps; wisplike; thin, weak-looking, or pale: *a wispy plant.* Also, **wisp′ish.**

wist (wĭst), *v.* pt. and pp. of **wit**[2].

wisteria (wĭs tĭə′rĭ ə), *n.* any of the climbing shrubs, with handsome pendent racemes of purple flowers, which constitute the leguminous genus *Wisteria,* as *W. chinensis* (**Chinese wisteria**), much used to cover verandas and walls. Also, **wistaria** (wĭs tēə′rĭ ə). [after Caspar *Wistar,* 1761–1818, American anatomist]

wistful (wĭst′fəl), *adj.* **1.** pensive or melancholy. **2.** showing longing tinged with melancholy; regretful; sad. [f. obs. *wist* attentive (back-formation from *wistly* attentively, var. of *whistly;* see WHIST[1]) + -FUL] —**wist′fully,** *adv.* —**wist′fulness,** *n.*

wit[1] (wĭt), *n.* **1.** keen perception and cleverly apt expression of connections between ideas which may arouse pleasure and especially amusement. **2.** speech or writing showing such perception and expression. **3.** a person endowed with or noted for such wit. **4.** understanding, intelligence, or sagacity: *wit enough to come in out of the rain.* **5.** (*pl.*) mental abilities, or powers of intelligent observation, keen perception, ingenious contrivance, etc.: *to have one's wits about one.* **6.** (*pl.*) mental faculties, or senses: *to lose or regain one's wits.* **7.** *Archaic.* mental capacity; reason; intellect. **8.** *Archaic.* a clever or learned person. **9. at one's wits'** (or **wit's**) **end,** at the end of one's powers of knowing, thinking, etc.; utterly at a loss or perplexed. **10. five wits,** the five senses, or the perceptions generally. **11. live by one's wits,** to gain a livelihood by resourcefulness and quick-wittedness rather than by hard work. **12. out of one's wits,** in or into a state of great fear or incoherence: *to frighten someone out of his wits.* [ME and OE, c. G *Witz,* Icel. *vit*] —**Syn. 1.** drollery, facetiousness, repartee. See **humour. 4.** wisdom.

wit[2] (wĭt), *v.t., v.i., pres.* 1 **wot,** 2 **wost,** 3 **wot,** *pl.* **wit;** *pt.* and *pp.* **wist;** *pres. p.* **witting.** —*v.t., v.i. Archaic.* **1.** to know. **2. God wit,** *Archaic.* God knows (used to emphasize a statement). **3. to wit,** that is to say; namely. [ME; OE *witan,* c. D *weten,* G *wissen*]

witan (wĭt′ən), *n.pl. Early Eng. Hist.* **1.** the members of the national council or witenagemot. **2.** (*construed as sing.*) the witenagemot. [OE, pl. of *wita* man of knowledge, councillor]

witch[1] (wĭch), *n.* **1.** a person, now esp. a woman, who professes or is supposed to practise magic, esp. black magic or the black art; a sorceress. **2.** an ugly or malignant old woman; a hag. **3.** a fascinatingly attractive woman. —*v.t.* **4.** to affect by or as by witchcraft; bewitch; charm. **5.** to change by or as by witchcraft (fol. by *into, to,* etc.). **6.** to fascinate. [ME *wiche,* OE *wicce,* der. *wiccian* practise sorcery] —**witch′like′,** *adj.*

witch[2] (wĭch), *n.* a flatfish of the N Atlantic, *Pleuronectes cynoglossus,* resembling the lemon sole.

witchcraft (wĭch′kräft′), *n.* **1.** the art or practices of a witch; sorcery; magic. **2.** magical influence; witchery. —**Syn. 1.** See **magic.**

witchdoctor (wĭch′dŏk′tə), *n.* (in various primitive societies) **1.** a person possessing or supposed to possess magical powers of healing or of harming; medicine-man. **2.** a person thought to have the power of detecting witches.

witch-elm (wĭch′ĕlm′), *n.* wych-elm.

witchery (wĭch′ə rĭ), *n., pl.* **-eries. 1.** the use or practice of witchcraft; magic. **2.** magical influence; fascination; charm: *the witchery of her beauty.*

witches'-broom (wĭch′ĭz brōōm′), *n.* a dense mass of small thin branches frequently emerging from a swelling on a tree branch, as on cherry (caused by the fungus *Taphrina*) and on conifers (caused by various mistletoes). Also, **witches'-besom** (wĭch′ĭz bē′zəm).

witchetty (wĭch′ə tĭ), *n.* a large wood-boring grub of Australia, *Xyleutes leucomochla,* regarded by Aborigines as a delicacy. [t. native Australian]

witch-hazel (wĭch′hā′zəl), *n.* **1.** a shrub, *Hamamelis virginiana,* of eastern North America, whose bark and leaves afford medicinal preparations used for inflammation, bruises, etc. **2.** a liquid medicinal preparation used externally for inflammation and bruises. Also, **wych-hazel.**

witch-hunt (wĭch′hŭnt′), *n.* **1.** *Chiefly Hist.* the searching out of people to be accused of, and executed for witchcraft. **2.** an intensive effort to discover and expose disloyalty, subversion, dishonesty, or the like, usually based on slight, doubtful, or irrelevant evidence. —**witch′-hunt′er,** *n.* —**witch′-hunt′ing,** *n., adj.*

witching (wĭch′ĭng), *n.* **1.** the use of witchcraft. **2.** fascination. —*adj.* **3.** characterized by or suitable for sorcery, etc. **4.** enchanting. **5. witching hour,** (usually) midnight. —**witch′ingly,** *adv.*

wite (wīt), *n.* **1.** *Obs.* a punishment or fine. **2.** *Scot.* blame; reproach. [ME; OE: punishment]

witenagemot (wĭt′ĭ nə gĭ mōt′), *n.* *Early Eng. Hist.* the assembly of the witan; the national council attended by the king, aldermen, bishops, and nobles. [OE: councillors' assembly. See WITAN, MOOT]

with (wĭth, wĭth), *prep.* **1.** accompanied by or accompanying: *I will go with you.* **2.** in some particular relation to (esp. implying interaction, company, association, conjunction, or connection): *to deal, talk, sit, side, or rank with; to mix, compare, or agree with.* **3.** visiting; at the house of or in the company of: *he is with the doctor at the moment; she is with her cousin in the country.* **4.** (expressing similarity or agreement): *in harmony with.* **5.** (expressing equality or identity): *to be level with someone.* **6.** on the side of; in favour of; of the same opinion as: *are you with us or against us?* **7.** comprehending of: *are you with me?* **8.** of the same opinion as: *I'm with you on that subject.* **9.** in the same direction as: *with the stream, to cut timber with the grain.* **10.** in the same way as: *let us, with Solomon, be judicious.* **11.** characterized by or having: *a man with long arms.* **12.** carrying (a child or young), as a pregnant female. **13.** (of means or instrument) by the use of: *to line a coat with silk, to cut with a knife.* **14.** (of manner) using or showing: *to work with diligence.* **15.** in correspondence or proportion to: *their power increased with their number.* **16.** on the occasion or occurrence of; at the same time as, or immediately after, and because of: *to rise with the dawn, he swayed with every step he took.* **17.** in consequence of (the passage of time): *to alter with the years.* **18.** in regard to: *to be pleased with a thing.* **19.** in the estimation or view of: *if that's all right with you.* **20.** in the practice or experience of, or according to: *it's always the way with him.* **21.** (expressing power or influence over): *to prevail with someone.* **22.** (expressing subjection to power or influence): *to sway with the wind.* **23.** (of cause) owing to: *racked with pain.* **24.** in the region, sphere, or view of: *it is day with us while it is night with the Chinese.* **25.** (of separation, etc.) from: *to part with a thing.* **26.** against, as in opposition or competition: *to fight or vie with.* **27.** in the hands, care, keeping or service of: *leave it with me.* [ME and OE, c. Icel. *vidh*] —**Syn. 13.** See **by.**

with-, limited prefixal use of *with*, separative or opposing, as in *withdraw, withstand.* [ME and OE. See WITH]

-with, a suffix indicating conjunction: *herewith, therewith.*

withal (wĭ thôl′), *Archaic.* —*adv.* **1.** with it all; also; as well; besides. **2.** nevertheless. **3.** therewith. —*prep.* **4.** with (used after its object). [f. WITH + AL(L)]

withdraw (wĭth drô′), *v.*, **-drew, -drawn, -drawing.** —*v.t.* **1.** to draw back or away; take back; remove. **2.** to retract or recall: *to withdraw a charge.* —*v.i.* **3.** to retire; retreat; go apart or away. **4.** to retract a statement or expression. **5.** *Parl. Proc.* to remove an amendment, motion, etc., from consideration. —**withdraw′er,** *n.* —**Syn. 3.** See **depart.**

withdrawal (wĭth drô′əl), *n.* the act of withdrawing. Also, **withdraw′ment.**

withdrawal symptom, any distressing or painful symptom experienced by an addict due to the withdrawal of the drug (or other substance, as alcohol) of his addiction.

withdrawing room, *Obs.* a sitting room; a drawing room.

withdrawn (wĭth drôn′), *v.* **1.** pp. of **withdraw.** —*adj.* **2.** shy, retiring, or modest. **3.** secluded, as a place.

withdrew (wĭth dro͞o′), *v.* pt. of **withdraw.**

withe (wĭth), *n., v.*, **withed, withing.** —*n.* **1.** a willow twig or osier. **2.** any tough, flexible twig or stem suitable for binding things together. **3.** an elastic handle for a tool, to lessen shock in using. **4.** a thin brick partition dividing the flues in a chimney. —*v.t.* **5.** to bind with withes. [ME and OE *withthe*, c. LG *wedde*]

wither (wĭth′ə), *v.i.* **1.** to shrivel; fade; decay. **2.** to deteriorate or lose freshness (also fol. by *away*). —*v.t.* **3.** to make flaccid, shrunken, or dry, as from loss of moisture; cause to lose freshness, bloom, vigour, etc. **4.** to affect harmfully; blight: *reputations withered by scandal.* **5.** to abash, as by a scathing glance. [ME; ? var. of WEATHER, v.]

—**Syn. 1.** wrinkle, shrink, dry, decline, languish. WITHER, SHRIVEL imply a shrinking, wilting, and wrinkling. WITHER (of plants and flowers) is to dry up, shrink, wilt, fade, whether as a natural process or as the result of exposure to excessive heat or drought: *plants withered in the hot sun.* SHRIVEL, used of thin, flat objects and substances, such as leaves, the skin, etc., means to curl, roll up, become wrinkled: *the leaves shrivel in cold weather, paper shrivels in fire.* —**Ant. 1.** expand.

withered (wĭth′əd), *adj.* faded, dry, or wizened.

withering (wĭth′ə rĭng), *adj.* **1.** scathing, contemptuous, or crushing, as a remark, look, etc. **2.** causing to become withered. —**with′eringly,** *adv.*

witherite (wĭth′ə rīt′), *n.* a white to greyish mineral, barium carbonate ($BaCO_3$), occurring in crystals and masses: a minor ore of barium. [named after W. *Withering*, 1741–99, English physician]

withers (wĭth′əz), *n.pl.* the highest part of a horse's or other animal's back, behind the neck. See illus. under **horse.** [orig. uncert.]

withershins (wĭth′ə shĭnz′), *adv. Dial. and Archaic.* in a direction contrary to the apparent course of the sun; anticlockwise. Also, **widdershins.** [t. MLG: m. *weddersins* in an opposite direction]

withhold (wĭth hōld′), *v.*, **-held, -holding.** —*v.t.* **1.** to hold back; restrain or check. **2.** to refrain from giving or granting: *to withhold payment.* —*v.i.* **3.** *Obs.* to hold back; refrain. [ME *withholde(n)*. See WITH-, HOLD[1], v.] —**withhold′er,** *n.* —**Syn. 2.** See **keep.**

withholding tax, that part of one's tax liability withheld by the employer and paid directly to the government.

within (wĭ thĭn′), *adv.* **1.** in or into the interior or inner part, or inside. **2.** in or into a house, building, etc., or indoors. **3.** in or into an inner or farther room. **4.** on, or as regards, the inside, or internally. **5.** in the mind, heart, or soul; inwardly. —*prep.* **6.** in or into the interior of or the parts or space enclosed by: *within a city or its walls.* **7.** inside of; in. **8.** in the compass or limits of; not beyond: *within view, to live within one's income.* **9.** at or some point not beyond, as in length or distance; not farther than: *within a radius of a mile.* **10.** at or to some amount or degree not exceeding: *within two degrees of freezing.* **11.** in the course or period of, as in time: *within one's lifetime or memory.* **12.** inside of the limits fixed or required by; not transgressing: *within the law, within reason.* **13.** in the field, sphere, or scope of: *within the family, within one's power.* —*n.* **14.** the inside of a building, enclosed space, etc. [ME; OE *withinnan*]

withindoors (wĭ thĭn′dôz′), *adv. Obs.* indoors.

without (wĭ thout′), *prep.* **1.** not with; with no; with absence, omission, or avoidance of; lacking (as opposed to *with*). **2.** free from; excluding. **3.** *Archaic or Rare.* at, on, or to the outside of; outside of: *both within and without the house or the city.* **4.** beyond the compass, limits, range, or scope of (now used chiefly in opposition to *within*): *whether within or without the law.* —*adv.* **5.** in or into space without, or outside. **6.** outside a house, building, etc. **7.** without, or lacking, something implied or understood: *we must take this or go without.* **8.** as regards the outside, or externally. **9.** as regards external acts, or outwardly. **10.** *Dial.* unless. —*adj.* **11.** lacking means, possessions, etc.; destitute: *to be without.* [ME; OE *withūtan*]

withoutdoors (wĭ thout′dôz′), *adv. Obs.* out of doors.

withstand (wĭth stănd′), *v.*, **-stood, -standing.** —*v.t.* **1.** to stand or hold out against; resist or oppose, esp. successfully. —*v.i.* **2.** to stand in opposition. —**withstand′er,** *n.* [ME *withstande*, OE *withstandan*, c. Icel. *vidhstanda.* See WITH-, STAND] —**Syn. 1.** See **oppose.**

withy (wĭth′ĭ), *n., pl.* **withies,** *adj.* —*n.* **1.** a willow, esp. an osier. **2.** a flexible twig, or withe. **3.** a band or halter made of a willow twig, or the like. —*adj.* **3.** *Rare.* withe-like, as in slenderness, flexibility, etc. [ME *withie*, OE *withig.* See WITHE]

withywind (wĭth′ĭ wīnd′), *n.* *Dial.* the bindweed, or similar climbing plant.

witless (wĭt′lĭs), *adj.* lacking wits or intelligence; stupid; foolish. —**wit′lessly,** *adv.* —**wit′lessness,** *n.*

witling (wĭt′lĭng), *n.* a petty or would-be wit.

witness (wĭt′nĭs), *v.t.* **1.** to see or know by personal presence and perception. **2.** to be present at (an occurrence) as a formal witness or otherwise. **3.** to bear witness to; testify to; give or afford evidence of. **4.** to attest by one's signature. **5.** to be the scene of. —*v.i.* **6.** to bear witness; testify; give or afford evidence (also fol. by *to*). —*n.* **7.** one who, being present, personally sees or perceives a thing; a beholder, spectator, or eyewitness. **8.** a person or thing that affords evidence. **9.** one who gives testimony, as in a court of law. **10.** one who signs a document in attestation of the genuineness of its execution. **11.** testimony or evidence: *to bear witness to the truth of a statement.* [ME and OE *witnes.* See WIT[1], n., -NESS] —**wit′nesser,** *n.* —**Syn. 2.** See **observe.**

witness box, the place occupied by one giving evidence in a court. Also, *U.S.*, **witness stand.**

witness mark, a mark or stake set to identify a property corner or a survey point.

Witte (*Russ.* vĭt′tə), *n.* **Sergei Yulievich** (*Russ.* sĭr gyĕy′ yo͞o′lyĭ vĭch), 1849–1915, Russian statesman.

witted (wĭt′ĭd), *adj.* having wit or wits (only used in combination): *quick-witted, slow-witted.*

Wittekind (vĭt′ə kĭnt), *n.* died A.D. *c.* 807, Saxon warrior against Charlemagne. Also, **Widukind.**

Wittenberg (vĭt′n bûg′; *Ger.* vĭt′ən bĕrk), *n.* a town in central East Germany, on the Elbe: Luther taught in the university here; beginnings of the Reformation 1517. 46,544 (1963).

Wittgenstein (*Ger.* vĭt′gən shtīn), *n.* **Ludwig (Josef Johann)** (*Ger.* lo͞ot′vĭ KH yō′zĕf yō′hȧn), 1889–1951, British philosopher born in Austria.

witticism (wĭt′ĭ sĭz′əm), *n.* a witty remark; a joke. [der. WITTY; modelled on CRITICISM]

witting (wĭt′ĭng), *adj. Archaic.* knowing; aware; conscious.

wittingly (wĭt′ĭng lĭ), *adv.* knowingly; deliberately.

wittol (wĭt′l), *n. Obs.* a man who knows and tolerates his wife's infidelity. [ME *wetewold,* f. *wete* WIT[2], v. + *-wold,* modelled on *cokewold* CUCKOLD]

witty (wĭt′ĭ), *adj.,* **-tier, -tiest. 1.** possessing wit in speech or writing; amusingly clever in perception and expression. **2.** characterized by wit: *a witty remark.* **3.** *Obs. or Dial.* wise; intelligent. [ME; OE *wittig,* f. *witt* WIT[1] + *-ig* -Y[1]] —**wit′tily,** *adv.* —**wit′tiness,** *n.* —**Syn. 1.** facetious, droll, clever, original, sparkling, brilliant. See **humorous.**

Witwatersrand (wĭt wô′təz rănd′), *n.* a rocky ridge in the Republic of South Africa, in the Transvaal, near Johannesburg: goldfields. Also, **The Rand.**

wive (wīv), *v.,* **wived, wiving.** *Rare.* —*v.i.* **1.** to take a wife; marry. —*v.t.* **2.** to take as wife; marry. **3.** to marry off. **4.** to provide with a wife. [ME; OE *wīfian.* See WIFE]

wivern (wī′vən), *n. Her.* wyvern.

wives (wīvz), *n.* pl. of **wife.**

wizard (wĭz′əd), *n.* **1.** one who professes to practise magic; a magician or sorcerer. **2.** a person of exceptional or prodigious accomplishment (esp. in a specified field). **3.** *Archaic.* a sage; wise man. —*adj.* **4.** of or pertaining to a wizard. **5.** *Colloq.* superb; marvellous. [ME *wysard,* f. *wys* WISE[1] + -ARD] —**wiz′ard-like′,** *adj.* —**Syn. 1.** enchanter, necromancer.

wizardly (wĭz′əd lĭ), *adj.* **1.** of, like, or befitting a wizard. **2.** *Colloq.* extremely well.

wizardry (wĭz′ə drĭ), *n.* the art or practices of a wizard; sorcery; magic.

wizen (wĭz′ən), *Dial.* —*v.i., v.t.* **1.** to wither; shrivel; dry up. —*adj.* **2.** wizened. [ME *wisen,* OE *wisnian,* c. Icel. *visna* wither]

wizened (wĭz′ənd), *adj.* dried-up; withered; shrivelled.

wk, *pl.* **wks. 1.** week. **2.** work.

wkly, weekly.

w.l., wavelength.

Wladimir (vlăd′ĭ mĭə′; *Russ.* vlȧ dē′mĭr), *n.* See **Vladimir.**

Wm, William.

wmk, watermark.

WNW, west-north-west. Also, **W.N.W.**

wo (wō), *n., interj.* **1.** whoa. **2.** woe.

W.O., 1. walkover. **2.** War Office. **3.** warrant officer. **4.** wireless operator.

w/o, 1. walkover; walked over. **2.** write off; written off.

woad (wōd), *n.* **1.** a European cruciferous plant, *Isatis tinctoria,* formerly much cultivated for a blue dye extracted from its leaves. **2.** the dye. [ME *wode,* OE *wād,* c. G *Waid*]

woaded (wō′dĭd), *adj.* dyed or coloured blue with woad.

woald (wōld), *n.* weld[2].

wobble (wŏb′l), *v.,* **-bled, -bling,** *n.* —*v.i.* **1.** to incline to one side and to the other alternately, as a wheel, top, or other rotating body, when not properly balanced. **2.** to move unsteadily from side to side. **3.** to show unsteadiness; tremble; quaver: *his voice wobbled.* **4.** to vacillate; waver. —*v.t.* **5.** to cause to wobble. —*n.* **6.** *Colloq.* the act or fact of wobbling; a wobbling motion. Also, **wabble.** [t. LG: m. *wabbeln,* c. Icel. *vafla* toddle] —**wob′bler,** *n.*

wobbling (wŏb′lĭng), *adj.* that wobbles, or causes to wobble. Also, **wabbling.** —**wob′blingly,** *adv.*

wobbly (wŏb′lĭ), *adj.* Also, **wabbly.** shaky; unsteady. —**wob′bliness,** *n.*

Wobbly (wŏb′lĭ), *n., pl.* **-blies.** *U.S. Slang.* a member of the Industrial Workers of the World (trade union).

Wodehouse (wo͝od′hous′), *n.* **P(elham) G(renville)** (pĕl′əm), born 1881, English humorous novelist living in the U.S.

Woden (wō′dn), *n.* the chief Anglo-Saxon god, identical with the Scandinavian Odin. Also, **Wodan, Wotan.** [ME and OE, akin to WOOD[2]]

woe (wō), *n.* **1.** grievous distress, affliction, or trouble. **2.** an affliction. —*interj.* **3.** (an exclamation of grief, distress, or lamentation). Also, **wo.** [ME *wo,* OE *wā,* interj., c. D *wee,* G *Weh,* L *vae*] —**Syn. 1.** See **sorrow.**

woebegone (wō′bĭ gŏn′), *adj.* **1.** beset with woe; mournful or miserable; affected by woe, esp. in appearance. **2.** showing or indicating woe: *he had a perpetul woebegone look on his face.* Also, **wobegone.**

woeful (wō′fəl), *adj.* **1.** full of woe; wretched; unhappy. **2.** affected with, characterized by, or indicating woe: *her poetry is a conglomeration of woeful ditties.* **3.** of wretched quality; sorry; poor. Also, **woful.** —**woe′fully,** *adv.* —**woe′fulness,** *n.*

Woffington (wŏf′ĭng tən), *n.* **Margaret** (*Peg*), 1714–60, Irish actress in England.

woffle (wŏf′əl), *v.i.* waffle[2].

wog (wŏg), *n. Slang.* (derogatory) **1.** a native, esp. a dark-skinned one, of the Middle East or North Africa, esp. an Arab or Egyptian. **2.** any foreigner, esp. a dark-skinned one. [orig. disputed]

woke (wōk), *v.* a pt. of **wake.**

woken (wō′kən), *v.* pp. of **wake.**

Woking (wō′kĭng), *n.* a town in England, in N Surrey. 67,519 (1961).

wold[1] (wōld), *n.* an open, elevated tract of country: esp. applied (*in pl.*) to districts in parts of England (as Yorkshire and Lincolnshire) resembling the downs of the southern counties. [ME; OE *wald* forest, c. G *Wald.* Cf. Icel. *völlr* plain]

wold[2] (wōld), *n.* weld[2].

wolf (wo͝olf), *n., pl.* **wolves** (wo͝olvz), *v.* —*n.* **1.** a large, wild carnivore, *Canis lupus,* of Europe, Asia, and North America, belonging to the dog family, a swift-footed, cunning, rapacious animal, destructive to game, sheep, etc. **2.** the fur of such an animal. **3.** some wolf-like animal not of the dog family, as the thylacine (Tasmanian wolf). **4.** *Entomol.* the larva of any of various small insects infesting granaries. **5.** any of various rapacious fishes, as the pike. **6.** a cruelly rapacious person. **7.** *Colloq.* a man who is boldly flirtatious or amorous towards many women. **8.** *Music.* **a.** the harsh discord heard in certain chords of keyboard instruments, esp. the organ, when tuned to some system of unequal temperament. **b.** a chord or interval in which such a discord appears. **c.** (in bowed instruments) a discordant or false vibration in a string due to a defect in structure or adjustment of the instrument. **9. cry wolf,** to give false alarms habitually. **10. keep the wolf from the door,** to ward off or keep away poverty or hunger. **11. lone wolf,** a person or animal who prefers to be and act alone. **12. wolf in sheep's clothing,** one who hides hostile or malicious intentions behind a harmless appearance. —*v.t.* **13.** *Colloq.* to eat ravenously. —*v.i.* **14.** to hunt for wolves. [ME; OE *wulf,* c. D *wolf,* G *Wolf,* Icel. *ulfr*] —**wolf′-like′,** *adj.*

Wolf (*Ger.* vôlf), *n.* **1. Friedrich August** (*Ger.* frē′drĭKH ou′go͞ost), 1759–1824, German classical scholar. **2. Hugo** (*Ger.* ho͞o′gō), 1860–1903, Austrian composer, chiefly of Lieder.

wolf cub, 1. a young wolf. **2.** a cub (def. 4).

wolf-dog (wo͝olf′dŏg′), *n. Chiefly U.S.* **1.** any of various dogs of different breeds used for hunting wolves. See **wolfhound. 2.** a cross between a wolf and a domestic dog. **3.** an Eskimo dog.

Wolfe (wo͝olf), *n.* **1. James,** 1727–59, English general, killed at the Battle of Quebec. **2. Thomas (Clayton),** 1900–38, U.S. novelist.

wolf-eel (wo͝olf′ēl′), *n.* a large eel-like fish, *Anarrhichthys ocellatus,* of the Pacific coast of North America, like the wolf-fish but with the tail drawn out to a point.

wolfer (wo͝ol′fə), *n.* wolver.

Wolff (*Ger.* vôlf), *n.* **1.** Also, **Wolf. Christian von** (*Ger.* krĭs′tē ȧn fōn), 1679–1754, German philosopher and mathematician. **2. Kaspar Friedrich** (*Ger.* kȧs′pȧr frē′drĭKH), 1733–94, German anatomist and physiologist. —**Wolffian** (vôl′fĭ ən), *adj.*

Wolf-Ferrari (*It.* vôlf′fĕr rȧ′rē), *n.* **Ermanno** (*It.* ĕr mȧn′-nō), 1876–1948, Italian composer.

Wolffian body, *Embryol.* mesonephros.

wolf-fish (wo͝olf′fĭsh′), *n.* **1.** a large fish of the genus *Anarhichas,* as *A. lupus* of the northern Atlantic, allied to the blenny, and noted for its ferocious aspect and habits. **2.** lancet fish.

wolfhound (wo͝olf′hound′), *n.* a dog of various breeds formerly much used in hunting wolves, as the borzoi.

wolfish (wo͝ol′fĭsh), *adj.* **1.** resembling a wolf, as in form or characteristics. **2.** characteristic of or befitting a wolf. —**wolf′ishly,** *adv.* —**wolf′ishness,** *n.*

wolf note, wolf (def. 8c).

wolfram (wo͝ol′frəm), *n.* **1.** tungsten. **2.** wolframite. [t. G; ? orig. proper name]

wolframite (wo͝ol′frə mīt′, vôl′-), *n.* a mineral, iron manganese tungstate, (Fe, Mn)WO_3, occurring in heavy, greyish to brownish black tabular or bladed crystals (*sp. gr.*: 7·0–7·5): an important ore of tungsten. Also, **wolfram.** [t. G: m. *Wolframit*, f. *Wolfram* + *-it* -ITE¹]

wolframium (wo͝ol frā′myəm), *n. Chem.* tungsten.

Wolfram von Eschenbach (*Ger.* vŏl′främ fōn ĕsh′-ən bäKH), died 1220?, German epic poet.

wolf's-bane (wo͝olfs′bān′), *n.* a plant of the genus *Aconitum*, esp. a yellow-flowered species, *A. lycoctonum.* See **aconite** (def. 1). Also, **wolfsbane.**

Wolfsburg (*Ger.* vōlfs′bo͝ork), *n.* a town in NE West Germany. 84,600 (est. 1966).

wolf-spider (wo͝olf′spī′də), *n.* any spider of the family *Lycosidae*, members of which do not spin webs, but pursue their prey.

wolf-whistle (wo͝olf′wĭs′əl), *n.*, *v.*, **-led, -ling.** —*n.* **1.** a whistle in appreciation of an attractive woman, typically sliding up to a high note and then sliding down to a low one. —*v.t.* **2.** to make such a whistle at (someone). —*v.i.* **3.** to whistle in this manner.

Wolgemut (*Ger.* vôl′gə mo͞ot), *n.* **Michael** (*Ger.* mĭKH′ĭl), 1434–1519, German painter and designer.

wollastonite (wo͝ol′əs tə nīt′), *n.* a mineral, calcium silicate, $CaSiO_3$, occurring usually in fibrous white masses. [named after W. H. *Wollaston*, 1766–1828, English chemist]

Wollaston prism (wo͝ol′ə stən), *Optics.* a quartz prism for obtaining plane-polarized light, which is suitable for use with ultraviolet radiation. [See WOLLASTONITE]

Wollongong (wo͝ol′ən gŏng′), *n.* a seaport in Australia, in E New South Wales. 146,000 (est. 1965).

Wolof (wŏl′ŏf), *n.* **1.** a language spoken in W Africa around Dakar related to Fulani (def. 3). **2.** the people, or one of its members, who live in this region and speak this language.

Wolseley (wo͝olz′lĭ), *n.* **Garnet Joseph, 1st Viscount,** 1833–1913, British field marshal.

Wolsey (wo͝ol′zĭ), *n.* **Thomas,** 1475?–1530, English cardinal and statesman.

wolver (wo͝ol′və), *n.* one who hunts for wolves. Also, **wolfer.**

Wolverhampton (wo͝ol′və hămp′tən), *n.* a town in England, in S Staffordshire. 150,385 (1961).

wolverine (wo͝ol′və rēn′), *n.* the glutton, *Gulo gulo*, of America. Also, **wolverene.** [earlier *wolvering*, f. *wolver* wolf-like creature + -ING¹]

Wolverine, *Gulo gulo* (3 to 3½ ft long)

wolves (wo͝olvz), *n.* pl. of **wolf.**

woman (wo͝om′ən), *n.*, *pl.* **women** (wĭm′ĭn), *v.*, *adj.* —*n.* **1.** the female human being (distinguished from *man*). **2.** an adult female person (distinguished from *girl*). **3.** a mistress or paramour. **4.** a female servant, esp. one who does domestic chores, as cleaning, cooking, etc. **5.** (formerly) a female personal maid. **6.** feminine nature, characteristics, or feelings. **7.** *Dial. and U.S.* a wife. **8. kept woman,** a girl or woman maintained as a mistress by one man. **9. old woman,** a man who is pedantic or tends to fuss, gossip, etc. **10. scarlet woman,** a prostitute. —*v.t.* **11.** to call (one) 'woman', esp. rudely or condescendingly. **12.** *Obs.* to cause to act or be like a woman; make effeminate. —*adj.* **13.** female: *a woman doctor.* **14.** of, characteristic of, or belonging to women: *woman talk.* [ME; OE *wīfman*, f. *wīf* female + *man* human being] —**wom′anless,** *adj.*

—**Syn. 2.** WOMAN, FEMALE, LADY apply to the adult of the human race correlative with man. WOMAN is the general term: *a woman nearing middle age.* FEMALE refers esp. to sex. It was formerly used interchangeably with WOMAN, but now sometimes has a contemptuous implication: *a strong-minded female.* LADY formerly implied superior family or social position, but is now used conventionally and politely for any woman: *say hello to the lady;* also courteously for one engaged in menial tasks: *a charlady.*

womanhood (wo͝om′ən ho͝od′), *n.* **1.** the state of being a woman. **2.** womanly character or qualities. **3.** the state of being a grown woman (as opposed to a *girl*). **4.** women collectively.

womanish (wo͝om′ə nĭsh), *adj.* **1.** weakly feminine; effeminate. **2.** womanlike or feminine. —**wom′anishly,** *adv.* —**wom′anishness,** *n.*

womanize (wo͝om′ə nīz′), *v.i.*, **-nized, -nizing.** to have numerous casual affairs; philander. Also, **womanise.** —**wom′aniz′er,** *n.*

womankind (wo͝om′ən kīnd′), *n.* women, as distinguished from men; the female sex.

womanlike (wo͝om′ən līk′), *adj.* **1.** like a woman; womanly. —*adv.* **2.** in a manner characteristic of or befitting a woman.

womanly (wo͝om′ən lĭ), *adj.* **1.** like or befitting a woman; feminine; not masculine or girlish. —*adv.* **2.** *Obs.* in the manner of, or befitting, a woman. —**wom′anliness,** *n.*

woman of the world, a sophisticated woman, versed in the ways and usages of the world and society.

womb (wo͞om), *n.* **1.** the uterus of the human female and some of the higher mammalian quadrupeds. **2.** a hollow space. **3.** a place of origin, conception, etc. **4.** *Obs.* the belly. [ME and OE, c. D *wam*, G *Wamme*, Goth. *wamba* belly]

wombat (wŏm′bət), *n.* any of three species of burrowing marsupials of Australia, constituting the family *Vombatidae*, somewhat resembling ground hogs. [native Australian name]

Common wombat, *Vombatus hirsutus* (3 ft long)

Wombwell (wo͞om′wĕl), *n.* a town in England, in the West Riding of Yorkshire. 18,701 (1961).

women (wĭm′ĭn), *n.* pl. of **woman.**

womenfolk (wĭm′ĭn fōk′), *n.pl.* **1.** women in general; all women. **2.** a particular group of women, esp. those of one's family. Also, **womenfolks.**

Women's Institute, an association of women in rural areas, formed for social, cultural, and recreational purposes. *Abbrev.*: W.I.

Women's Land Army, an organization, operating during both world wars, of women working in agriculture to make up the shortage of manpower.

Women's Voluntary Service, a women's organization founded in World War II for work in civil defence, welfare, and other work. *Abbrev.*: W.V.S.

womera (wo͞om′ə rə), *n.* woomera.

won¹ (wŭn), *v.* pt. and pp. of **win.**

won² (wŭn, wo͞on, wōn), *v.i.*, **wonned, wonning.** *Archaic.* to dwell, abide, or stay. [ME *wone*, OE *wunian*, c. G *wohnen*]

won³ (wŏn), *n.* **1.** the monetary unit of South Korea, equivalent to about £0·0016 sterling. **2.** a note of this value.

wonder (wŭn′də), *v.i.* **1.** to think or speculate curiously: *to wonder about a thing.* **2.** to be affected with wonder; marvel (often fol. by *at*). **3.** to doubt (that something will or will not happen): *I wonder if she will come after all; I wonder if she'll really come.* —*v.t.* **4.** to speculate curiously or be curious about; be curious to know (fol. by a clause): *to wonder what happened.* **5.** to feel wonder at (now only fol. by a clause as object): *I wonder that you went.* —*n.* **6.** something strange and surprising; a cause of surprise, astonishment, or admiration: *it is a wonder he declined such an offer.* **7.** the emotion excited by what is strange and surprising; a feeling of surprised or puzzled interest, sometimes tinged with admiration. **8.** a miracle, or miraculous deed or event. **9.** See **Seven Wonders of the World. 10. nine days' wonder,** a subject of general surprise and interest for a short time. **11. no wonder,** (it is) not at all surprising (that). **12. small wonder,** (it is) hardly surprising (that). [ME; OE *wundor*, c. D *wonder*, G *Wunder*] —**won′derer,** *n.* —**Syn. 7.** surprise, astonishment, amazement, bewilderment, awe.

wonderful (wŭn′də fəl), *adj.* **1.** excellent; delightful; extremely good or fine. **2.** of a kind to excite wonder; marvellous; extraordinary; remarkable. [OE *wundorfull.* See WONDER, -FUL] —**won′derfully,** *adv.* —**won′derfulness,** *n.* —**Syn.** wondrous, miraculous, prodigious, astonishing, amazing, phenomenal, curious, strange.

wondering (wŭn′də rĭng), *adj.* **1.** expressing admiration or amazement; marvelling. —*n.* **2.** the act or process of expressing amazement or curiosity. —**won′deringly,** *adv.*

wonderland (wŭn′də lănd′), *n.* **1.** an imaginary land or place of wonders or marvels. **2.** a wonderful country or region: *a wonderland of snow, a winter wonderland.*

wonderment (wŭn′də mənt), *n.* **1.** wondering or wonder, **2.** a cause or occasion of wonder.

wonderstruck (wŭn′də strŭk′), *adj.* struck or affected with wonder. Also, **wonder-stricken** (wŭn′də strĭk′ən).

wonderwork (wŭn′də wûk′), *n.* **1.** a wonderful work; a marvel; a miracle. [ME *wonderworc*, OE *wundor weorc.* See WONDER, WORK]

wonder-worker (wŭn′də wû′kə), *n.* a worker or performer of wonders or marvels. —**won′der-work′ing,** *adj.*

wondrous (wŭn′drəs), *Archaic.* —*adj.* **1.** wonderful; marvellous. —*adv.* **2.** in a wonderful or surprising degree; remarkably. [metathetic var. of ME *wonders* (gen. of WONDER) wonderful; sp. conformed to -OUS] —**won′drously,** *adv.* —**won′drousness,** *n.*

wonga-wonga (wŏng′ə wŏng′ə), *n. Austral.* a large pigeon, *Leucosarcia picata.* [t. native Australian]

wonky (wŏng′kĭ), *adj. Slang.* **1.** shaky; unsound. **2.** askew; awry. **3.** unwell; upset. [var. of d. *wanky*, itself alter. of *wankle*, ME *wankel*, OE *wancol* shaky, unsteady]

Wönsan (wŏn′sän′), *n.* a seaport in E North Korea. 112,952 (1949). Japanese, **Gensan.**

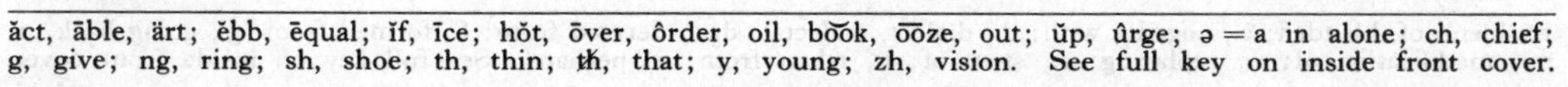

wont (wōnt), *adj.*, *n.*, *v.*, **wont, wont** or **wonted, wonting.** *Archaic.* —*adj.* **1.** accustomed; used (commonly followed by an infinitive). —*n.* **2.** custom; habit; practice. —*v.t.* **3.** to accustom (a person), as to a thing. **4.** to render (a thing) customary or usual (commonly in the passive). —*v.i.* **5.** to be wont or accustomed. [ME *woned*, OE *ge-wunod*, pp. of *gewunian* be accustomed]

won't (wōnt), contraction of *will not.*

wonted (wōnʹtĭd), *adj. Archaic.* **1.** accustomed; habituated; used. **2.** rendered customary; habitual or usual: *the old man was in his wonted place.* —**wontʹedly,** *adv.* —**wontʹedness,** *n.*

woo (wōō), *v.t.* **1.** to seek the favour, affection, or love of, esp. with a view to marriage. **2.** to seek to win: *to woo fame.* **3.** to invite (consequences, good or bad) by one's own action: *to woo one's own destruction.* **4.** to seek to persuade (a person, etc.), as to do something; solicit; importune. —*v.i.* **5.** to pay court to a woman. [ME *wowe*, OE *wōgian*] —**wooʹer,** *n.* —**wooʹingly,** *adv.*

wood[1] (wŏŏd), *n.* **1.** the hard, fibrous substance composing most of the stem and branches of a tree or shrub, and lying beneath the bark; the xylem. **2.** the trunks or main stems of trees as suitable for architectural and other purposes; timber or lumber. **3.** firewood. **4.** the cask, barrel, or keg in which wine, beer, or spirits are stored, as distinguished from the bottle: *aged in the wood.* **5.** *Print.* a woodblock (def. 1). **6.** *Music.* **a.** a wooden wind instrument. **b.** such instruments collectively in a band or orchestra; woodwind. **7.** (*often pl.*) a large and thick collection of growing trees, usually less extensive than a forest. **8.** *Golf.* a club with a wooden head. **9.** *Tennis, etc.* the frame part of a racket, usually made of wood. **10.** *Bowls.* bowl[2] (def. 2). **11. out of the wood,** disengaged or escaped from a series of difficulties or dangers. **12. can't see the wood for the trees,** to be unable to distinguish the essential or cardinal points of a problem, situation, or the like from the mass of detail. —*adj.* **13.** made of wood; wooden. **14.** used to store or carry wood. **15.** used to cut, carve, or otherwise shape wood. **16.** dwelling or growing in woods: *a wood owl.* —*v.t.* **17.** to cover or plant with trees. **18.** to supply with wood; get supplies of wood for. —*v.i.* **19.** to take in or get supplies of wood. [ME; OE *wudu*, earlier *widu*, c. Icel. *vidhr*, OHG *witu*, OIrish *fid*] —**woodʹless,** *adj.* —**Syn. 7.** See **forest.**

wood[2] (wŏŏd), *adj. Obs. except Dial.* mad or wild, as with rage or excitement. [ME; OE *wōd*, c. Icel. *ōdhr*; akin to G *Wut* rage, OE *wōth* song, L *vātes* seer]

Wood (wŏŏd), *n.* **1. Grant,** 1892–1942, U.S. painter. **2. Sir Henry (Joseph),** 1869–1944, English musician and conductor. **3. Mrs Henry,** 1814–87, English novelist and editor.

wood alcohol, 1. the product of the destructive distillation of wood, consisting principally of methyl alcohol. **2.** methyl alcohol.

wood anemone, any of certain species of anemone, esp. *Anemone nemorosa* of the Old World.

Wood anemone, *Anemone nemorosa*

wood ant, a large ant, *Formica ruta*, of woodlands of Europe.

wood avens, herb bennet (def. 1).

woodbin (wŏŏdʹbĭnʹ), *n.* a box for wood fuel. Also, **woodʹboxʹ.**

woodbine (wŏŏdʹbīnʹ), *n.* **1.** the common European honeysuckle, *Lonicera periclymenum.* **2.** any of various other honeysuckles, as *L. caprifolium* (**American woodbine**). **3.** *U.S.* the Virginia creeper, *Parthenocissus quinquefolia.* [ME *wodebinde*, OE *wudubind*, f. *wudu* WOOD[1] + *-bind* binding]

woodblock (wŏŏdʹblŏkʹ), *n.* **1.** *Print.* **a.** a block of wood engraved in relief, for printing from; a woodcut. **b.** a print or impression from such a block. **2.** a wooden block or sett, as used for flooring, roadmaking, etc. **3.** *Music.* a hollow block used in the percussion section of an orchestra. —*adj.* **4.** printed with or made from a woodblock or blocks.

wood-borer (wŏŏdʹbôʹrə), *n.* any animal that bores wood, as some marine molluscs, some crustaceans, and certain insect larvae.

woodcarving (wŏŏdʹkäʹvĭng), *n.* **1.** the art, craft, or activity of carving wood into useful or ornamental forms. **2.** a carved wooden object, esp. as a work of art. **3.** such objects collectively.

woodchat (wŏŏdʹchătʹ), *n.* **1.** Also, **woodchat shrike.** a shrike or butcher-bird, *Lanius senator*, of Europe and North Africa, having black forehead and chestnut crown, nape, and upper mantle. **2.** any of various Asiatic thrushes, esp. of the genus *Larvivora.*

woodchuck (wŏŏdʹchŭkʹ), *n.* a common North American marmot, *Marmota monax*, of stout, heavy form, that burrows in the ground and hibernates in the winter; the ground hog. [alter. of Algonquian (Cree or Chippewa) *otchek*, *otchig*, *odjik* fisher, weasel]

Woodchuck, *Marmota monax* (Total length ab. 2 ft, tail 6 in.)

wood coal, lignite.

woodcock (wŏŏdʹkŏkʹ), *n.*, *pl.* **-cocks,** (*esp. collectively*) **-cock. 1.** an Old World snipelike game bird, *Scolopax rusticula*, with long bill, short legs and large eyes placed far back in the head. **2.** *Obs.* a simpleton. [ME *wodecok*, OE *wuducoc.* See WOOD[1], n., COCK[1], n.]

Woodcock, *Scolopax rusticula* (14 in. long)

woodcraft (wŏŏdʹkräftʹ), *n.* *Chiefly U.S.* **1.** skill in anything which pertains to the woods or forest, esp. in making one's way through the woods, or in hunting, trapping, etc. **2.** forestry. **3.** the art of making or carving wooden objects. —**woodʹcraftsʹman,** *n.*

woodcut (wŏŏdʹkŭtʹ), *n.* **1.** a carved or engraved block of wood for printing from. **2.** a print or impression from such a block.

woodcutter (wŏŏdʹkŭtʹə), *n.* **1.** one who cuts wood, fells trees, etc. **2.** an engraver in wood, or maker of woodcuts. —**woodʹcutʹting,** *n.*

wooded (wŏŏdʹĭd), *adj.* **1.** covered with or abounding in woods or trees. **2.** having wood (of a specified kind): *a hard-wooded tree.*

wooden (wŏŏdʹn), *adj.* **1.** consisting or made of wood. **2.** stiff, ungainly, or awkward. **3.** without spirit or animation: *a wooden stare.* **4.** dull or stupid: *wooden wits.* **5.** (of a sound) as if issuing from a hollow wooden object when struck. **6.** indicating the fifth event of a series, as a wedding anniversary. —**woodʹenly,** *adv.* —**woodʹenness,** *n.*

wood-engraving (wŏŏdʹĭn grāʹvĭng), *n.* **1.** the art or process of engraving designs in relief with a burin on the end grain of wood, for printing. **2.** a block of wood so engraved. **3.** a print or impression from it. —**woodʹ-engraʹver.**

woodenhead (wŏŏdʹn hĕdʹ), *n. Colloq.* a blockhead; a dull or stupid person.

wooden-headed (wŏŏdʹn hĕdʹĭd), *adj. Colloq.* thick-headed; dull; stupid. —**woodʹen-headʹedness,** *n.*

wooden horse. See **Trojan Horse.**

wooden leg, an artificial leg, esp. (formerly) one made of wood.

woodenware (wŏŏdʹn wĕəʹ), *n.* vessels, utensils, etc., made of wood.

wood flour, waste wood reduced to a flourlike consistency, used as a filler, as a constituent of many synthetic materials, etc.

Woodford (wŏŏdʹfəd), *n.* a district of the NE outer London borough of Redbridge.

Wood Green, a district of the N outer London borough of Haringey.

woodgrouse (wŏŏdʹgrousʹ), *n.* capercailzie.

woodhouse (wŏŏdʹhousʹ), *n.* a house or shed in which wood is stored.

wood hyacinth, the bluebell.

wood ibis, a large naked-headed wading bird, *Mycteria americana*, of the family *Threskiornithidae*, of the wooded swamps of the southern U.S. and regions southwards.

woodland (wŏŏdʹlənd), *n.* **1.** land covered with woods or trees. —*adj.* **2.** of, pertaining to, or inhabiting the woods; sylvan.

woodlander (wŏŏdʹlən də), *n.* an inhabitant of the woods.

woodlark (wŏŏdʹläkʹ), *n.* a small European songbird, *Lullula arborea*, less famous than the skylark but equally gifted as an aerial songster.

wood lot, a tract, esp. on a farm, set aside for trees.

woodlouse (wŏŏdʹlousʹ), *n.*, *pl.* **-lice** (-līsʹ). *Zool.* any of certain small terrestrial isopod crustaceans of the genera *Oniscus*, *Armadillo*, etc., having a flattened elliptical body sometimes capable of being rolled up into a ball.

woodman (wŏŏdʹmən), *n.*, *pl.* **-men. 1.** one who tends trees or fells them for timber. **2.** *Hist.* an officer having charge of the king's woods. **3.** *Obs.* a hunter of forest game.

wood millet, a tall perennial grass, *Milium effusum*, occurring in shady woods in N temperate regions.

wood naphtha, wood alcohol.

woodnote (wŏŏdʹnōtʹ), *n.* a wild or natural musical note, as that of a forest bird.

wood nymph, a nymph of the woods, or a dryad.

woodpecker (wŏŏdʹpĕkʹə), *n.* any of numerous scansorial birds constituting the family *Picidae*, having a hard, chisel-like bill for boring into wood after insects, stiff tail feathers to assist in climbing, and usually a more or less boldly patterned plumage.

woodpigeon (wŏŏd′pĭj′ĭn), *n.* a large wild pigeon, *Columba palumbus*, of Europe; the ringdove.

woodpile (wŏŏd′pīl′), *n.* a pile or stack of wood, esp. wood for fuel.

wood pitch. See **wood tar.**

wood pulp, wood reduced to pulp through mechanical and chemical treatment and used in the manufacture of paper.

wood rat, a pack rat.

Woodroffe (wŏŏd′rŏf, -rŭf, -rəf), *n.* **Mount,** a peak in central Australia, the highest point in South Australia. 4970 ft.

woodruff (wŏŏd′rŭf′), *n.* a low, aromatic rubiaceous herb, *Asperula odorata*, of the Old World, having small, sweet-scented, white flowers. [ME *woderove*, OE *wudu-rōfe*, f. *wudu* WOOD[1] + *rōfe* (c. MLG *rōve* carrot)]

woodrush (wŏŏd′rŭsh′), *n.* any plant of the juncaceous genus *Luzula*, as the **hairy woodrush,** *L. pilosa*, widespread in N temperate regions.

wood sage, a perennial labiate herb with pale yellow flowers, *Teucrium scorodonia*, occurring in woods and heaths of W Europe.

woodscrew (wŏŏd′skrōō′), *n.* a metal screw used in carpentry.

woodshed (wŏŏd′shĕd′), *n.* a shed, esp. one for firewood.

woodsia (wŏŏd′zĭ ə), *n.* any fern of the genus *Woodsia*, comprising small and medium-sized species in temperate and cold regions. [named after Joseph *Woods*, 1776–1864, English botanist]

woodsman (wŏŏdz′mən), *n.*, *pl.* **-men. 1.** one accustomed to life in the woods and skilled in the arts of the woods, as hunting, trapping, etc. **2.** one who works in the woods, esp. a lumberjack.

Wood's metal, an alloy consisting of 50 per cent bismuth, 25 per cent lead and 12·5 per cent each of tin and cadmium, which melts at 71°C.

wood sorrel, a perennial oxalidaceous herb, *Oxalis acetosella*, with a slender creeping rhizome, trifoliate leaves and solitary white or pink flowers, widespread in shady places of temperate Europe and Asia.

Wood sorrel, *Oxalis acetosella*

wood spirit, 1. methyl alcohol. **2.** a supernatural being supposed to inhabit woods.

wood swallow, any insectivorous bird of the family *Artamidae*, of Australia.

woodsy (wŏŏd′zĭ), *adj.* *U.S.* of, like, suggestive of, or associated with the woods: *a woodsy fragrance.*

wood tar, a dark viscid product obtained from wood by distillation or burning slowly without flame, used in its natural state to preserve timber, etc., or subjected to further distillation, when it yields creosote, oils, and a final residuum called **wood pitch.**

wood-turning (wŏŏd′tû′nĭng), *n.* **1.** the forming of wood articles upon a lathe. *—adj.* **2.** used for or pertaining to wood-turning. **—wood′-turn′er,** *n.*

wood vinegar, 1. an impure acetic acid obtained by the distillation of wood. **2.** pyroligneous acid.

woodwind (wŏŏd′wĭnd′), *n.* **1.** (*sing., sometimes construed as pl.*) the group of wind instruments which comprises the flutes, clarinets, oboes, and bassoons. **2.** this group considered as a section of an orchestra. **3.** an instrument of this group. *—adj.* **4.** of or pertaining to wind instruments of this group.

woodwool (wŏŏd′wŏŏl′), *n.* fine wood shavings used as a packing material for fragile or delicate objects and as a filler for plaster.

woodwork (wŏŏd′wûk′), *n.* **1.** objects or parts made of wood. **2.** the interior wooden fittings of a house or the like. **3.** the art or craft of working in wood; carpentry.

woodworker (wŏŏd′wû′kə), *n.* a worker in wood, as a carpenter, joiner, or cabinetmaker.

woodworking (wŏŏd′wû′kĭng), *n.* **1.** the act or craft of one who works in wood. *—adj.* **2.** pertaining to or used for shaping wood: *woodworking tools.*

woodworm (wŏŏd′wûm′), *n.* a worm or larva that is bred in or bores in wood, esp. the larva of the beetle *Anobium striatum*, which attacks domestic woodwork.

woody (wŏŏd′ĭ), *adj.*, **woodier, woodiest. 1.** abounding with woods; wooded. **2.** belonging or pertaining to the woods; sylvan. **3.** situated in a wood. **4.** consisting of or containing wood; ligneous. **5.** resembling wood, as in hardness, texture, etc. **—wood′iness,** *n.*

woody nightshade, the bittersweet.

woof[1] (wōōf), *n.* **1.** yarns which travel from selvage to selvage in a loom, interlacing with the warp; weft; filling. **2.** texture; fabric. [ME *oof*, OE *ōwef*. See WEB, WEAVE]

woof[2] (wŏŏf), *n.* **1.** the sound of a dog barking, esp. deeply and loudly. **2.** a sound in imitation of this; a deep, resonant sound. *—v.i.* **3.** to make any such sound. [imit.]

woofer (wōō′fə), *n.* a loudspeaker designed for the reproduction of low-frequency sounds.

wool (wŏŏl), *n.* **1.** the fine, soft, curly hair, characterized by minute, overlapping surface scales, to which its felting property is mainly due, that forms the fleece of sheep and certain other animals, that of sheep constituting one of the most important materials of clothing. **2.** a fibre produced from sheep's fleece or the like, that may be spun into yarn, or made into felt, upholstery materials, etc. **3.** any of various types of yarn spun from this, as worsted, tweed, etc. **4.** fabric made from sheep's wool. **5.** woollen yarn used for knitting, crocheting, ornamental needlework, etc. **6.** any of various substances used commercially as substitutes for the wool of sheep, etc. **7.** a kind of wool-like yarn or material made from cellulose by a process similar to that used in manufacturing rayon or artificial silk. **8.** any of certain vegetable fibres, such as cotton, flax, etc., so used, esp. after preparation by special process (**vegetable wool**). **9.** any finely fibrous or filamentous matter suggestive of the wool of sheep: *glass wool.* **10.** *Colloq.* the human hair, esp. when short, thick, and curly. **11. dyed in the wool,** inveterate. **12. keep** (or **lose**) **one's wool,** to keep (or lose) one's temper; not become (or become) angry. **13. pull the wool over one's eyes,** to deceive or delude one. [ME *wole*, OE *wull*, c. D *wol*, G *Wolle*, Icel. *ull*, Goth. *wulla*]

wool-classing (wŏŏl′klä′sĭng), *n.* *Austral., N.Z.* the trade or occupation of grading wool. **—wool′-clas′ser,** *n.*

Woolf (wŏŏlf), *n.* **1. Leonard,** 1881–1969, English publisher, editor, and political writer. **2.** his wife, **Virginia,** 1882–1941, English novelist and critic.

wool fat, lanolin.

woolfell (wŏŏl′fĕl′), *n.* *Obs.* the skin of a wool-bearing animal with the fleece still on it. [f. WOOL + FELL[4]]

wool-gathering (wŏŏl′găth′ə rĭng), *n.* **1.** indulgence in desultory fancies or a fit of abstraction. **2.** gathering of the tufts of wool as caught on bushes, etc., by passing sheep. *—adj.* **3.** inattentive; abstracted. **—wool′-gath′erer,** *n.*

wool-grower (wŏŏl′grō′ə), *n.* one who raises sheep or other wool-bearing animals for the production of wool. **—wool′-grow′ing,** *n.*

Woollcott (wŏŏl′kət), *n.* **Alexander,** 1887–1943, U.S. author and journalist.

woollen (wŏŏl′ən), *n.* **1.** a fabric made from wool, esp. a soft loose one. **2.** (*pl.*) knitted woollen clothing, esp. jerseys. *—adj.* **3.** made or consisting of wool. **4.** of or pertaining to wool, or products made of wool, or their manufacture. Also, *U.S.*, **woolen.**

Woolley (wŏŏl′ĭ), *n.* **Sir (Charles) Leonard,** 1880–1960, English archaeologist and explorer.

woolly (wŏŏl′ĭ), *adj.*, **-lier, -liest,** *n.*, *pl.* **-lies.** *—adj.* **1.** consisting of wool. **2.** resembling wool. **3.** clothed or covered with wool or something resembling it. **4.** not clear or firm, as thinking, expression, depiction, etc.; blurred, confused, or indistinct. **5.** *Bot.* covered with a pubescence of soft hairs resembling wool. **6.** *U.S. Colloq.* like the rough atmosphere of the early West: *the wild and woolly West.* *—n.* **7.** *Colloq.* an article of clothing made of wool. **8.** *Western U.S., Austral.* a sheep. **—wool′lily,** *adv.* **—wool′liness,** *n.*

woolly bear, the caterpillar of any of various moths, as tiger moths, covered with a dense coat of woolly hairs.

woolly betony, the lamb's-ear.

woolmark (wŏŏl′mäk′), *n.* **1.** a mark on sheep for their identification. **2.** (*cap.*) *Trademark.* the trademark of the Wool Marketing Board.

woolpack (wŏŏl′păk′), *n.* **1.** the bale in which wool was formerly done up, as for transporting. **2.** *Meteorol.* a cumulus cloud of fleecy appearance.

woolsack (wŏŏl′săk′), *n.* **1.** (in England) the seat of the Lord Chancellor in the House of Lords, made of a large, square, cloth-covered bag of wool. **2.** the office of the Lord Chancellor. **3. sit on the woolsack,** to occupy the office of Lord Chancellor. **4.** a sack or bag of wool.

wool-shears (wŏŏl′shĭəz′), *n.* large shears specially designed for shearing sheep.

woolshed (wŏŏl′shĕd′), *n.* *Austral., N.Z.* a large shed for shearing and baling of wool.

wool-sorters' disease (wŏŏl′sô′təz), pulmonary anthrax in man caused by inhaling the spores of *Bacillus anthracis.*

wool staple, *Chiefly Hist.* a wool market.

wool-stapler (wo͝ol′stā′plə), *n.* a dealer in wool, esp. one who sorts it according to the staple or fibre, before selling it to the manufacturer. —**wool′-sta′pling,** *adj.*

Woolwich (wo͝ol′ĭj), *n.* a district on the Thames, now chiefly in the E inner London borough of Greenwich: site of royal military academy and former royal arsenal.

Woolworth (wo͝ol′wəth), *n.* **F(rank) W(infield)**, 1852–1919, U.S. merchant, founder of international chain-stores.

woomera (wo͞om′ə rə), *n. Austral.* a type of throwing stick with a notch at one end for holding a dart or spear, thus giving increased leverage in throwing: used by Australian Aborigines. Also, **womera.** [t. native Australian]

Woomera (wo͞om′ə rə), *n.* a town in central South Australia: rocket-launching and missile-testing site. 6735 (1966).

Woop Woop (wo͝op′ wo͝op′), *Austral., N.Z.* any remote and backward settlement.

Woosung (wo͞o′so͝ong′), *n.* a seaport in E China, at the mouth of the Yangtze: a suburb of Shanghai.

Wootton (wo͝ot′n), *n.* **Barbara Frances, Baroness,** born 1897, English social scientist.

woozy (wo͞o′zĭ), *adj. Slang.* **1.** muddled, or stupidly confused. **2.** out of sorts physically, as with dizziness, nausea, or the like. **3.** slightly or rather drunk. [? der. *wooze*, var. of OOZE[2]] —**wooz′ily,** *adv.* —**wooz′iness,** *n.*

wop (wŏp), *Slang.* (usually derogatory). —*n.* **1.** an Italian or any foreigner thought to be of Italianate appearance. —*adj.* **2.** of or pertaining to any Latin country, its culture, or inhabitants. [? t. It. (Neapolitan d.): m. *guapo* dandy]

Worcester (wo͝os′tə), *n.* **1.** a city in England, the county town of Worcestershire, on the river Severn: cathedral; Cromwell's defeat of the Scots 1651. 65,923 (1961). **2.** a town in the U.S., in central Massachusetts. 186,587 (1960). **3.** Worcestershire. **4.** Also, **Royal Worcester, Worcester china, Worcester porcelain.** a soft-paste porcelain containing little or no clay, made in Worcester, England, since 1751.

Worcester Pearmain (pĕə′mān′), a firm, sweet variety of apple, with greenish yellow and crimson skin.

Worcester sauce, a sharp sauce made with soya, vinegar, spices, etc., orig. from Worcester, England. Also, **Worcestershire sauce.**

Worcestershire (wo͝os′tə shĭə′, -shə), *n.* a county in W central England. 568,642 pop. (1961); 699 sq. mi. *Co. town:* Worcester. Also, **Worcester.**

Worcs., Worcestershire.

word (wûd), *n.* **1.** a sound or a combination of sounds, or its written or printed representation, used in any language as the sign of a concept. **2.** *Gram.* an element which can stand alone as an utterance, not divisible into two or more parts similarly characterized; thus *boy* and *boyish*, but not *-ish* or *boy scout*, the former being less than a word, the latter more. **3.** a speech element which signifies; a term used to describe or refer: *'blue' is not an accurate word for the sea.* **4.** (*often pl.*) speech or talk: *to have a word with someone.* **5.** an utterance or expression, usually brief: *a word of praise, or of warning.* **6.** (*pl.*) the text or lyrics of a song as distinguished from the music. **7.** (*pl.*) contentious or angry speech; a quarrel. **8.** warrant, assurance, or promise: *to give or keep one's word.* **9.** intelligence or tidings: *to get word of an occurrence.* **10.** a verbal signal, as a password, watchword, or countersign. **11.** an authoritative utterance, or command: *his word was law.* **12.** a rumour; hint. **13.** (*cap.*) *Theol.* **a.** the Scriptures, or Bible (often **the Word of God**). **b.** the Logos; the concept of the second person of the Trinity (often, **the Word made Flesh**). **14.** *Computers.* a unit of information, usually consisting of a number or of a group of alphanumeric characters, in the memory of a computer. **15.** *Obs.* a proverb; motto. **16.** some special noun phrases are:

as good as one's word, dependable; reliable; true to one's promises or stated intentions.

eat one's words, *Colloq.* to retract something said or written.

have a word with, to speak briefly to.

in a word, 1. in short; briefly. **2.** by way of summing up.

in so many words, explicitly; unequivocally; without prevarication.

my word! (an expression of surprise, mild annoyance, etc.)

of few words, taciturn or laconic; disinclined to talk.

of many words, loquacious.

of one's word, reliable; dependable: *he is a man of his word.*

play on words, a verbal construction making use of the peculiarities of words, esp. ambiguities of spelling or pronunciation, as a pun.

put in a (good) word for, to recommend (someone); mention in a favourable way.

suit the action to the word, to do what one has said one would do.

take one at one's word, to act on the assumption that someone means what he says literally.

take the words out of one's mouth, to say exactly what another was about to say.

the last word, 1. the closing remark, as of an argument. **2.** the very latest, most modern, or most fashionable; the best, or most sophisticated: *this machine is the last word in automation; the last word in chic.*

word for word, 1. (of a repetition, report, etc.) using exactly the same words as the original; verbatim. **2.** translated by means of exact verbal equivalents rather than by general sense.

word of honour, a promise.

word perfect, knowing (a lesson, part in a play, formula, etc.) completely and correctly; by rote: *study this until you are word perfect.*

—*v.t.* **17.** to express in words, or phrase; select words to express: *he words his speeches carefully to avoid causing offence.* [ME and OE, c. D *woord*, G *Wort*, Icel. *ordh*, Goth. *waurd*] —**Syn. 9.** news, report.

wordage (wû′dĭj), *n.* **1.** words collectively. **2.** quantity of words.

word-blind (wûd′blīnd′), *adj.* suffering from alexia.

word-blindness (wûd′blīnd′nĭs), *n.* alexia.

wordbook (wûd′bo͝ok′), *n.* **1.** a book of words, usually with explanations, etc.; a dictionary. **2.** the libretto of an opera.

wordbreak (wûd′brāk′), *n. Print.* the point of division in a word which runs over from one line to the next. The exact placing of the division is usually determined in England according to the etymological structure of the word; in the U.S. the stress pattern is a major determinant.

worded (wû′dĭd), *adj.* expressed by words selected in a specified way: *a carefully worded report.*

wording (wû′dĭng), *n.* **1.** the act or manner of expressing in words; phrasing. **2.** the form of words in which a thing is expressed. —**Syn.** See **diction.**

wordless (wûd′lĭs), *adj.* **1.** speechless, silent, or mute. **2.** not put into words; unexpressed.

word order, *Gram.* the arrangement in a sequence of the words of a sentence or smaller construction, usually to show meaning, as *Jack ate the beef* compared with *the beef Jack ate.*

word-painting (wûd′pān′tĭng), *n.* the art or practice of verbal description.

word picture, a verbal description, esp. a vivid one.

word play, verbal witticisms, quips, puns, etc.

word-square (wûd′skwĕə′), *n.* a set of words such that when arranged one beneath another in the form of a square they read alike horizontally and vertically.

s a t e d
a t o n e
t o a s t
e n s u e
d e t e r

Word-square

Wordsworth (wûdz′wəth), *n.* **William,** 1770–1850, English poet. —**Wordsworthian** (wûdz wû′thyən), *adj., n.*

wordy (wû′dĭ), *adj.,* **wordier, wordiest. 1.** characterized by or given to the use of many, or too many, words; verbose. —**word′ily,** *adv.* —**word′iness,** *n.*

wore (wô), *v.* pt. of **wear.**

work (wûk), *n., adj., v.,* **worked** or **wrought, working.** —*n.* **1.** exertion directed to produce or accomplish something; labour; toil. **2.** that on which exertion or labour is expended; something to be made or done; a task or undertaking. **3.** productive or operative activity. **4.** manner of working or quality of workmanship. **5.** *Physics.* **a.** *Mech.* the product of the force acting upon a body and the distance through which the point of application of force moves. Cf. **erg; kilogram-metre. b.** the transference of energy from one body or system to another. **6.** employment; a job, esp. that by which one earns a living. **7.** materials, things, etc., on which one is working, or is to work. **8.** the result of exertion, labour, or activity; a deed or performance. **9.** a product of exertion, labour, or activity: *a work of art, literary or musical works.* **10.** an engineering structure, as a building, bridge, dock, or the like. **11.** (*usually pl.*) a building, wall, trench, or the like, constructed or made as a means of fortification. **12.** (*pl. often construed as sing.*) a place or establishment for carrying on some form of labour or industry: *iron works.* **13.** (*pl.*) the working parts of a mechanical contrivance. **14.** the piece being cut, formed, ground, or otherwise processed in a machine tool, grinder, punching machine, etc. **15.** (*pl.*) *Theol.* acts performed in obedience to the law of God, or righteous deeds. **16.** some special noun phrases are:

at work, 1. at one's place of work. **2.** engaged in working: *danger, men at work.* **3.** operating; functioning: *strange forces have been at work in the neighbourhood.*

have one's work cut out, to be pressed; have a difficult task.

make short work of, to dispose or deal with quickly.

out of work, unemployed.

set to work, to start; begin.
the works, **1.** everything there is; the whole lot. **2.** *Slang.* a violent assault.
—adj. **17.** of, for, or concerning work: *work clothes.* [ME *worke,* n., OE *worc* (r. ME *werk,* OE *weorc*), c. D *werk,* G *Werk,* Icel. *verk,* Gk *érgon*]
—v.i. **18.** to do work, or labour; exert oneself (contrasted with *play*). **19.** to be employed, as for one's livelihood: *he works in a laundry.* **20.** to be in operation, as a machine. **21.** to act or operate effectively: *the pump will not work, the plan works.* **22.** to get (*round, loose,* etc.), as if by continuous effort. **23.** to move (*into, round, through,* etc.) gradually, carefully, or with effort: *to work carefully through a subject.* **24.** to have an effect or influence, as on a person or on the mind or feelings. **25.** to move in agitation, as the features under strong feeling. **26.** to make way with effort or difficulty: *a ship works to windward.* **27.** *Naut.* to give slightly at the joints, as a vessel under strain at sea. **28.** *Mach.* to move improperly, as from defective fitting of parts or from wear. **29.** to undergo treatment by labour in a given way: *this dough works slowly.* **30.** to ferment, as a liquid.
—v.t. **31.** to use or manage (an apparatus, contrivance, etc.) in operation. **32.** to bring, put, get, render, etc., by work, effort, or action (fol. by *in, off, out,* or other completive words): *to work off a debt, to work up a case.* **33.** to get, or cause (something or someone) to go or be (*in, into, up,* etc.) gradually, carefully, or with difficulty: *to work a broom up the chimney.* **34.** to bring about (any result) by or as by work or effort: *to work a change.* **35.** to effect, accomplish, cause, or do. **36.** to expend work on; manipulate or treat by labour: *to work butter.* **37.** to put into effective operation. **38.** to operate (a mine, farm, etc.) for productive purposes. **39.** to carry on operations in (a district or region). **40.** to make, fashion, or execute by work. **41.** to achieve, win, or pay for by work or effort: *to work one's way through college.* **42.** to arrange or contrive: *it'll be difficult but I think I can work you a day off.* **43.** to keep (a person, a horse, etc.) at work. **44.** to move, stir, or excite in feeling, etc. (often fol. by *up*): *he worked himself into a frenzy.* **45.** to make or decorate by needlework or embroidery. **46.** to cause (a liquid, etc.) to ferment.
—v. **47.** Some special verb phrases are:
work at, to attempt to achieve or master (something) with application and energy: *skating isn't easy; you've got to work at it.*
work in, **1.** to introduce, insert, or cause to penetrate, esp. gradually: *work in the butter and sugar; he managed to work in the question of money.* **2.** to find room for or fit in, as into a programme.
work into, **1.** to make (one's) way gradually into; penetrate slowly. **2.** to introduce or cause to mingle gradually, with care, etc. **3.** to get (something) into (somewhere) slowly, or with difficulty: *he worked his feet into his boots.*
work off, **1.** to get rid of by working. **2.** to discharge (a debt) by one's labour.
work one's passage, to pay for one's fare on a sea trip, or the like, by working as a member of the crew.
work out, **1.** to effect or achieve by labour: *to work out one's own salvation.* **2.** to discharge (a debt, etc.) by one's labour. **3.** to solve (a problem) by a reasoning process. **4.** to find (the answer to a problem) by reasoning. **5.** to calculate (the best way of doing something, etc.): *to work out a plan of campaign.* **6.** to amount to a total or calculated figure: *it works out at £1 a foot.* **7.** to cause to finish up, turn out, or culminate (satisfactorily, unless otherwise specified): *to work out one's difficulties.* **8.** to turn out; prove (effective or suitable, unless otherwise specified). **9.** to develop; elaborate: *he doesn't always work out his plots.* **10.** to exhaust (a mine, or the like). **11.** to expiate by or as by one's effort or labour. **12.** to undergo training or practice, esp. intensively, as an athlete.
work to rule, to operate or take part in a work-to-rule.
work up, **1.** to excite or arouse (as feelings in oneself or others): *to work up an appetite.* **2.** to expand or elaborate (something). **3.** to move or cause to move gradually upwards. **4.** to rise gradually, as in intensity: *to work up to a climax.* **5.** to get gradually to something considered as higher, more important, etc.: *I was working up to that topic.*
[ME *worke* (v. use of *worke,* n.), r. ME *wyrche,* OE *wyrcean,* c. G *wirken,* Icel. *verkja,* Goth. *waurkjan*] **—work′less,** *adj.*
—Syn. 1. WORK, DRUDGERY, LABOUR, TOIL refer to exertion of body or mind in performing or accomplishing something. WORK is the general word, and may apply to exertion which is either easy or hard: *heavy work, part-time work, outdoor work.* DRUDGERY suggests continuous, dreary, and dispiriting work, esp. of a menial or servile kind: *the drudgery of household tasks.* LABOUR particularly denotes hard manual work: *labour on a farm, in a steel mill.* TOIL suggests wearying or exhausting labour: *toil which breaks down the worker's health.* **2.** enterprise, project, job. **8.** product, achievement, feat. **31.** operate, manipulate, manage, handle. **34.** perform, execute, produce. **40.** form, shape. **—Ant. 1.** play, rest.

workable (wûr′kə bl), *adj.* **1.** practicable or feasible. **2.** capable of or suitable for being worked. **—work′abil′ity, work′ableness,** *n.*
workaday (wûr′kə dā′), *adj.* **1.** of or befitting working days; working; practical; everyday. **2.** commonplace; humdrum.
workbag (wûk′băg′), *n.* a bag for holding implements and materials for work, esp. needlework.
workbasket (wûk′bäs′kĭt), *n.* a small basket for holding equipment for needlework or the like.
workbench (wûk′bĕnch′), *n.* a bench or table at which someone works.
workbook (wûk′bo͝ok′), *n.* **1.** a manual of operating instructions. **2.** a book designed to guide the work of a student by inclusion of some instructional material, and usually providing questions, etc. **3.** a book in which a record is kept of work completed or planned.
workbox (wûk′bŏks′), *n.* a box to hold instruments and materials for work, esp. needlework.
workday (wûk′dā′), *n.* **1.** working day. *—adj.* **2.** workaday.
worked (wûkt), *adj.* that has undergone working; wrought; ornamented; embroidered: *a prettily worked handbag.*
—Syn. WORKED, WROUGHT both apply to something on which effort has been applied. WORKED implies expended effort of almost any kind: *a worked silver mine.* WROUGHT implies fashioning, moulding, or making, esp. by hand: *wrought-iron railings.*
worker (wûr′kə), *n.* **1.** one who or that which works: *he's a good steady worker.* **2.** one employed in manual or industrial labour. **3.** an employee, esp. as contrasted with a capitalist or a manager. **4.** one who works in a specified occupation: *office workers, research workers.* **5.** (in the Soviet Union) a citizen, excluding the peasants and members of the army or navy. **6.** *Entomol.* the sterile or infertile female of bees, wasps, ants, or termites, which does the work of the colony. **—work′erless,** *adj.*
Workers' Educational Association, a non-political, non-sectarian federation of educational and workers' organizations, founded 1903, providing inexpensive adult education esp. in the social sciences.
workfellow (wûk′fĕl′ō), *n.* one who works in the same place or at the same job as another.
workfolk (wûk′fōk′), *n.pl.* workpeople. Also, *U.S. Colloq.,* **workfolks.**
work function, *Physics.* the energy required to free an electron from the surface of a metal.
work-hardening (wûk′häd′nĭng), *n.* strain-hardening.
workhorse (wûk′hôs′), *n.* a horse used for draught or riding purposes, rather than recreation or sport.
workhouse (wûk′hous′), *n.* **1.** *Hist.* a publicly supported institution for the maintenance of able-bodied paupers who performed unpaid work. **2.** *U.S.* a house of correction.
working (wû′kĭng), *n.* **1.** the act of a person or thing that works. **2.** operation; action. **3.** the process of skilful working of something into a shape. **4.** the act of manufacturing or building a thing. **5.** the act of solving a problem. **6.** (*usually pl.*) a part of a mine, quarry, or the like, in which work is being or has been carried on. **7.** (*pl.*) the intermediate stages of a calculation, esp. in mathematics. **8.** the process of fermenting, as of yeasts. **9.** a slow advance involving exertion. **10.** disturbed or twisting motions.
—adj. **11.** that performs work or labour, esp. of a manual, mechanical or industrial kind. **12.** that performs the work of a business or the like, as against providing the capital or administration. **13.** that is functional or operative, as a machine. **14.** that is sufficient to permit work of a particular kind to proceed: *a working majority, working knowledge.* **15.** of a theory, arrangement, etc., providing a basis to work on (esp. for the time being, to prevent work from being delayed, etc.). **16.** pertaining to, connected with, or used in operating or working. **17.** that moves with jerks or twists, as the face when chewing or under emotional stress.
working capital, **1.** the amount of capital needed to carry on a business. **2.** *Accounting.* current assets minus current liabilities. **3.** *Finance.* liquid as distinguished from fixed capital assets.
working class, *pl.* **classes.** the class of people composed chiefly of manual workers and labourers; the proletariat.
working-class (wû′kĭng kläs′), *adj.* belonging or pertaining to, or characteristic of the working class; proletarian.
working day, **1.** the amount of time that a worker must work for an agreed daily wage. **2.** a day ordinarily given to working (opposed to *holiday*). **3.** the daily period of hours for working.

working-day (wûrʹkĭng dāʹ), *adj.* workaday; everyday.
working drawing, a drawing, as of the whole or part of a structure or machine, made to scale and in such detail with regard to dimensions, etc., as to form a guide for the workmen in the construction of the object.
working edge, an edge of a piece of wood trued square with the working face to assist in truing the other surfaces square; face edge.
working face, that face of a piece of wood or the like which is first trued and then used as a basis for truing the other surfaces; face side.
working load, the maximum load in normal conditions.
workingman (wûrʹkĭng mănʹ), *n., pl.* **-men.** a man of the working class; a man (skilled or unskilled) who earns his living at some manual or industrial work.
working memory, *Computers.* a high-speed memory unit used to hold intermediate results during a calculation.
working model, a model, as of a machine, having a moving mechanism which reproduces that of the original.
working order, the state of something, as a mechanism, when it is functioning properly.
working papers, legal papers giving information often required for employment.
working party, 1. a group, committee, etc., appointed to study a problem in detail, solve a difficulty, conduct an investigation, etc. **2.** *Mil.* a group of soldiers, etc., who are detailed to carry out a special task.
working substance, *Mech.* the substance, as a working fluid, which operates a prime mover.
Workington (wûrʹkĭng tən), *n.* a seaport in England, in W Cumberland. 29,552 (1961).
workman (wûkʹmən), *n., pl.* **-men. 1.** a man employed or skilled in some form of manual, mechanical, or industrial work. **2.** a male worker. **—workʹmanless,** *adj.*
workmanlike (wûkʹmən līkʹ), *adj.* **1.** like or befitting a good workman; skilful; well executed. **2.** efficient, smart, or businesslike. **—***adv.* **3.** in a manner characteristic of a good workman. Also, **workʹmanly.**
workmanship (wûkʹmən shĭpʹ), *n.* **1.** the art or skill of a workman; skill in working or execution. **2.** quality or mode of execution, as of a thing made. **3.** the product or result of the labour and skill of a workman; work executed.
workmen's compensation insurance, insurance required by law from employers for the protection of employees while engaged in the employer's business. The amount of the claim is stipulated by law (**workmen's compensation act**).
work of art, 1. a piece of creative work in the arts, esp. a painting or a piece of sculpture. **2.** anything executed extremely well or in particularly good taste.
work-out (wûkʹoutʹ), *n.* **1.** a trial at running, boxing, a game, or the like, usually preliminary to and in preparation for a contest, exhibition, etc. **2.** any performance for practice or training, or as a trial or test. **3.** physical exercise.
workpeople (wûkʹpēʹpl), *n.pl.* people employed at work or labour, esp. manual or industrial workers.
workroom (wûkʹro͞omʹ, -ro͝omʹ), *n.* a room in which work is carried on.
works committee, 1. an elected body of employee representatives which deals with management regarding grievances, working conditions, wages, etc., and which is consulted by management in regard to labour matters. **2.** a joint council or committee representing employer and employees which discusses working conditions, wages, etc., within a factory or office. Also, **works council.**
workshop (wûkʹshŏpʹ), *n.* **1.** a room or building in which work, esp. mechanical work, is carried on (considered as smaller than a factory). **2.** a group meeting to exchange ideas and study techniques, skills, etc.: *theatre workshop.*
workshy (wûkʹshīʹ), *adj.* disliking and tending to avoid work or effort of any kind; lazy.
Worksop (wûkʹsŏp), *n.* a town in England, in N Nottinghamshire. 34,311 (1961).
work-table (wûkʹtāʹbl), *n.* a table for working at; often with drawers or receptacles for materials, etc., as for sewing.
work-to-rule (wûkʹtə ro͞olʹ), *n.* **1.** a deliberate curtailment of output by workers, by slavish observation of rules, as an industrial sanction. **2.** a go-slow.
world (wûld), *n.* **1.** the earth or globe. **2.** a particular division of the earth: *the New World.* **3.** the earth, with its inhabitants, affairs, etc., during a particular period: *the ancient world.* **4.** a particular section of the world's inhabitants: *the Third World.* **5.** mankind; humanity. **6.** the public generally: *the whole world knows it.* **7.** the class of persons devoted to the affairs, interests, or pursuits of this life: *the world worships success.* **8.** society; secular, social, or fashionable life, with its ways and interests: *to withdraw from the world.* **9.** a particular class of mankind, with common interests, aims, etc.: *the fashionable world.* **10.** any sphere, realm, or domain, with all that pertains to it: *woman's world, the world of dreams, the insect world.* **11.** the totality of a person's immediate environment or context; one's physical and spiritual surroundings: *the little world of Don Camillo.* **12.** the entire system of created things; the universe; the macrocosm. **13.** any complex whole conceived as resembling the universe (cf. **microcosm**). **14.** one's life, conceived of as complete and separate from the rest of society; one's private mental universe. **15.** one of the three general groupings of physical nature, as the **animal world, mineral world, vegetable world. 16.** any period, state, or sphere of existence: *this world, the world to come.* **17.** a very great quantity or extent: *to do a world of good.* **18.** any indefinitely great expanse or amount. **19.** *Colloq.* all that is important, agreeable, or necessary to one's happiness: *you're the world to me.* **20.** any heavenly body: *the starry worlds.* **21.** Some special noun phrases are:
a world of one's own, a state of being out of touch with other people.
bring into the world, 1. to bear (a child), as a mother. **2.** to deliver (a child), as a midwife.
come into the world, to be born.
dead to the world, *Colloq.* **1.** unaware of one's surroundings. **2.** totally drunk. **3.** utterly tired; exhausted.
for all the world, 1. for any consideration, no matter how great: *he wouldn't come for all the world.* **2.** in every respect, or precisely: *he looks for all the world like a drug addict.*
for the world or **for worlds,** on any account.
in the world, 1. in the universe, or on earth anywhere. **2.** at all; ever: *nothing in the world will make me change my mind, where in the world did you get that hat?*
on top of the world, elated; delighted; exultant.
out of this world, excellent; supremely or sublimely good.
set the world on fire, to be a great success.
think the world of, to esteem very highly.
world without end, through all eternity; for ever.
[ME and OE, var. of OE *weorold,* c. D *wereld,* G *Welt,* Icel. *veröld,* all g. Gmc **wer-ald,* lit., man-age]
—Syn. 1. See **earth.**
World Bank, an international bank set up by the U.N. in 1944 to assist the development of poor countries, esp. by loans. Official name, **International Bank for Reconstruction and Development.**
world-beater (wûldʹbēʹtə), *n.* a surpassingly good thing, person, etc. **—worldʹ-beatʹing,** *adj., n.*
World Council of Churches, the ecumenical organization established jointly by the Anglican and most Protestant Churches to work for the eventual reunification of Christendom.
World Court, an international tribunal, sitting at The Hague, provided for in the Covenant of the League of Nations, and established in September, 1921, by action of the assembly of that body, and empowered to render decisions or advisory opinions in disputes threatening future war. Official name, **International Court of Justice.**
World Health Organization, an agency of the U.N., formed in 1948, to improve the health of all countries and control disease by the collection of information, training, and guidance of all kinds. *Abbrev.:* W.H.O.
worldling (wûldʹlĭng), *n.* one devoted to the interests and pleasures of this world; a worldly person.
worldly (wûldʹlĭ), *adj.,* **-lier, -liest,** *adv.* **—***adj.* **1.** earthly or mundane (as opposed to *heavenly, spiritual,* etc.). **2.** devoted to, directed towards, or connected with the affairs, interests, or pleasures of this world. **3.** secular (as opposed to *ecclesiastic, religious,* etc.). **4.** *Obs.* of or pertaining to this world. **—***adv.* **5.** in a worldly manner. **—worldʹliness,** *n.* **—Syn. 1.** See **earthly.**
worldly-minded (wûldʹlĭ mīnʹdĭd), *adj.* having or showing a worldly mind, or devotion to the affairs and interests of this world. **—worldʹly-mindʹedly,** *adv.* **—worldʹly-mindʹedness,** *n.*
worldly-wise (wûldʹlĭ wīzʹ), *adj.* wise as to the affairs of this world.
world power, a nation so powerful that it is capable of influencing or changing the course of world events.
World Series, *Baseball.* a group of games played each autumn between the winning teams of the two major leagues to determine the professional champions of the U.S. Also, **World's Series.**
world-shaking (wûldʹshāʹkĭng), *adj.* remarkable; of great importance or significance.
world war, a war involving a large number of countries, esp. the most powerful ones, and waged in many parts of the world.
World War I, the war, conducted mainly in Europe and the Middle East, between the Triple Entente (Great Britain, France, and Russia, aided by the U.S., Belgium, Japan, and others) and the Central Powers (Germany

and Austria-Hungary, aided by Turkey and Bulgaria) from July 28th, 1914, until the Central Powers' surrender on November 11th, 1918. Also, **First World War, Great War.**

World War II, the war, conducted mainly in Europe and the Far East, between the Allies (Great Britain and France and later the Soviet Union and the U.S.) and the Axis (Germany, Italy, and Japan), from September 3rd, 1939, until the surrender of Germany on May 8th, 1945, and of Japan on August 14th, 1945. Also, **Second World War.**

world-weary (wûld′wĭə′rĭ), *adj.* weary of the world or of existence and its pleasures; blasé.

worldwide (wûld′wīd′), *adj.* extending or spread throughout the world.

worm (wûm), *n.* **1.** *Zool.* any of the long, slender, soft-bodied bilateral invertebrates including the flatworms, roundworms, acanthocephalans, nemerteans, and annelids. **2.** (in popular language) any of numerous small creeping animals with more or less slender, elongated bodies, and without limbs or with very short ones, including individuals of widely differing kinds, as earthworms, tapeworms, insect larvae, adult forms of some insects, etc. **3.** woodworm, or its presence, as indicated by wormholes, etc. **4.** something resembling or suggesting a worm in appearance, movement, etc. **5.** the spiral pipe in a still, in which the vapour is condensed. **6.** a screw or screw thread. **7.** an endless screw (shaft on which one or more helical grooves are cut), or a device in which this is the principal feature. **8.** the endless screw which engages with a worm wheel or worm gear. **9.** a grovelling, abject, or contemptible person. **10.** a downtrodden or miserable person. **11.** something that penetrates, injures, or consumes slowly or insidiously, like a gnawing worm. **12.** (*pl.*) *Pathol.* any disease or disorder arising from the presence of parasitic worms in the intestines or other tissues. **13.** the lytta of a dog, etc.
—*v.i.* **14.** to move or act like a worm; creep, crawl, or advance slowly or stealthily. **15.** to get by insidious procedure (fol. by *into*, etc.).
—*v.t.* **16.** to make, cause, bring, etc., along by creeping or crawling, or by stealthy or devious advances. **17.** to get by persistent, insidious efforts (esp. fol. by *out* or *from*): *to worm a secret out of a person.* **18.** to free from worms. **19.** *Naut.* to wind yarn or the like spirally round (a rope) so as to fill the spaces between the strands and render the surface smooth.
[ME; OE *wyrm* worm, serpent, c. D *worm*, G *Wurm*, Icel. *ormr*, akin to L *vermis*] **—worm′er,** *n.* **—worm′less,** *adj.* **—worm′like′,** *adj.*

wormcast (wûm′käst′), *n.* an irregular coil of compacted soil or sand voided on the surface by some annelid worms, as earthworms and lugworms.

worm-eaten (wûm′ē′tn), *adj.* **1.** eaten into or gnawed by worms. **2.** impaired by time, decayed, or antiquated.

worm fence, snake fence.

worm gear, *Mach.* **1.** a worm wheel. **2.** such a worm wheel together with the endless screw forming a device by which the rotary motion of one shaft can be transmitted to another shaft at right angles to it.

wormhole (wûm′hōl′), *n.* a hole made by a burrowing or gnawing worm, as in timber, nuts, etc.

Worms (wûmz; *Ger.* vōrms), *n.* **1.** a town in SW West Germany, in Rhineland-Palatinate, on the Rhine. 63,700 (est. 1966). **2. Diet of,** an assemblage held here (1521), at which Luther was condemned as a heretic.

wormseed (wûm′sēd′), *n.* **1.** the dried, unexpanded flower heads of santonica, *Artemisia cina* (**Levant wormseed**), or the fruit of certain goosefoots, esp. *Chenopodium anthelminticum* (**American wormseed**), used as an anthelmintic drug. **2.** any of these plants. **3.** any plant with anthelmintic properties.

worm wheel, *Mach.* a toothed wheel which engages with a revolving worm, or endless screw, in order to receive or impart motion. Cf. **worm gear.**

W, Worm wheel

wormwood (wûm′wŏŏd′), *n.* **1.** any plant of the composite genus *Artemisia*, as *A. cina* (*santonica*), *A. moxa* (*moxa*), etc. **2.** a bitter, aromatic herb, *Artemisia absinthium*, a native of the Old World, formerly much used as a vermifuge and a tonic, but now chiefly in making absinth. **3.** something bitter, grevious, or extremely unpleasant; bitterness. [f. WORM + WOOD[1]; r. ME *wermode*, OE *wermōd*, c. G *Wermut*. See VERMOUTH]

wormy (wû′mĭ), *adj.*, **wormier, wormiest. 1.** containing a worm or worms; infested with worms. **2.** worm-eaten. **3.** wormlike; grovelling; low. **—worm′iness,** *n.*

worn (wôn), *v.* **1.** pp. of **wear. —*adj.* 2.** impaired by wear or use: *worn clothing.* **3.** wearied or exhausted. **—worn′ness,** *n.*

worn-out (wôn′out′), *adj.* **1.** worn or used until no longer fit for use. **2.** exhausted by use, strain, etc.

worried (wŭ′rĭd), *adj.* **1.** affected by worry; anxious; troubled; distressed. **2.** indicating or expressing worry.

worriment (wŭ′rĭ mənt), *n. Colloq.* **1.** trouble; harassing annoyance. **2.** worry, anxiety.

worrisome (wŭ′rĭ səm), *adj.* **1.** worrying, annoying, or disturbing; causing worry. **2.** inclined to worry. **—wor′risomely,** *adv.*

worry (wŭ′rĭ), *v.*, **-ried, -rying,** *n.*, *pl.* **-ries.** —*v.i.* **1.** to feel uneasy or anxious; fret; torment oneself with or suffer from disturbing thoughts. **2. worry along** or **through,** to progress by constant effort, in spite of difficulties. —*v.t.* **3.** to cause to feel uneasy or anxious; trouble; torment with annoyances, cares, anxieties, etc.; plague, pester, or bother. **4.** to seize (orig. by the throat) with the teeth and shake or mangle, as one animal does another. **5.** to harass by repeated biting, snapping, etc. **6.** to cause to move, etc., by persistent efforts, in spite of difficulties. —*n.* **7.** worried condition or feeling; uneasiness or anxiety. **8.** a cause of uneasiness or anxiety, or a trouble. **9.** the act of worrying. [ME *wory*, var. of *wery*, *wiry*, OE *wyrgan* strangle, c. G *würgen*] **—wor′rier,** *n.*

—Syn. 3. WORRY, ANNOY, HARASS all mean to disturb or interfere with someone's comfort or peace of mind. To WORRY is to cause anxiety, apprehension, or care: *to worry one's parents.* To ANNOY is to vex or irritate by continued repetition of interferences: *to annoy the neighbours.* HARASS implies long-continued worry and annoyance: *cares of office harass a president.* **7.** apprehension, solicitude. See **concern.**

worse (wûs), *adj.*, *used as compar.* of **bad. 1.** bad or ill in a greater or higher degree; inferior in excellence, quality, or character. **2.** more unfavourable or injurious. **3.** in less good condition; in poorer health. **4. none the worse for, a.** not harmed by. **b.** *Colloq.* positively benefited by. **5. the worse for wear, a.** showing signs of considerable wear; shabby or worn out. **b.** *Colloq.* drunk. —*n.* **6.** that which is worse. **7. for the worse,** so as to deteriorate: *a change for the worse.* **8. go from bad to worse,** to deteriorate. —*adv.* **9.** in a more disagreeable, evil, wicked, severe, or disadvantageous manner. **10.** with more severity, intensity, etc.; in a greater degree. **11.** in a less effective manner. **12. worse off,** in worse circumstances; poorer; less fortunate or well placed. [ME; OE *wyrsa*, c. Icel. *verri*, Goth. *wairsiza*] **—worse′ness,** *n.*

worsen (wû′sən), *v.t.*, *v.i.* to make or become worse.

worser (wû′sə), *adj.*, *adv. Dial. and Non-standard.* worse.

worship (wû′shĭp), *n.*, *v.*, **-shipped, -shipping** or (*U.S.*) **-shiped, -shiping.** —*n.* **1.** reverent honour and homage paid to God, a god, or a sacred personage, or to any object regarded as sacred. **2.** formal or ceremonious rendering of such honour and homage. **3.** adoring reverence or regard: *hero worship.* **4.** (with *your*, *his*, etc.) a title of honour used in addressing or mentioning certain magistrates and others of rank or station. **5.** *Archaic.* honourable character or standing: *men of worship.* —*v.t.* **6.** to render religious reverence and homage to. **7.** to feel an adoring reverence or regard for (any person or thing). —*v.i.* **8.** to render religious reverence and homage, as to a deity. **9.** to attend services of divine worship. **10.** to feel an adoring reverence or regard. [ME; OE *worthscip*, northern var. of *weorthscipe*, f. *weorth* WORTH[1] + *-scipe* -SHIP] **—wor′shipable,** *adj.* **—wor′shipper;** *U.S.*, **wor′shiper,** *n.* **—Syn. 1.** See **reverence. 3.** honour, homage, adoration, idolizing, idolatry. **7.** honour, venerate, revere, glorify, idolize.

worshipful (wû′shĭp fəl), *adj.* **1.** given to the worship of something. **2.** (an honorific title for persons or bodies of distinguished rank, as civil dignitaries, the London city companies, etc.). **—wor′shipfully,** *adv.* **—wor′shipfulness,** *n.*

worst (wûst), *adj.*, *used as superl of* **bad. 1.** bad or ill in the greatest or highest degree. **2.** most faulty, unsatisfactory, or objectionable. **3.** most unfavourable or injurious. **4.** in the poorest condition. **5.** most unpleasant or disagreeable. **6.** most unsuccessful, ineffective, or unskilful. —*n.* **7.** that which or one who is worst or the worst part. **8. come off worst** or **get the worst (of),** to be defeated (in a contest). **9. if (the) worst comes to (the) worst,** if the very worst happens. **10. one's worst,** the utmost, esp. the utmost harm, that a person is capable of: *to do one's worst to someone.* —*adv.* **11.** in the most evil, wicked, or disadvantageous manner. **12.** with the most severity, intensity, etc.; in the greatest degree. **13.** in the least satisfactory, complete or effective manner: *the worst-dressed girl in the room.* —*v.t.* **14.** to give (one) the worst of a contest or struggle; defeat; beat. [ME; OE *wurresta*, northern var. of *wyr(re)sta*, *wer(re)sta*, c. Icel. *verstr*]

worsted[1] (wŏŏs′tĭd), *n.* **1.** firmly twisted yarn or thread spun from combed long-staple wool, used for weaving, etc. **2.** wool cloth woven from such yarns, having a hard, smooth surface, and no nap. —*adj.* **3.** consisting or made of worsted. [named after ME *Worsted,* parish in Norfolk, England (now Worstead)]

worsted[2] (wŭs′tĭd), *v.* pp. of **worst.**

wort[1] (wût), *n.* the unfermented or fermenting infusion of malt which after fermentation becomes beer or mash. [ME; OE *wyrt,* c. G *Würze* spice. See WORT[2]]

wort[2] (wût), *n.* a plant; herb; vegetable (now used chiefly in combination, as in *liverwort, figwort, colewort,* etc.). [ME; OE *wyrt* root, plant, c. G *Wurz;* akin to ROOT[1]]

worth[1] (wûth), *adj.* **1.** good or important enough to justify (what is specified): *advice worth taking, a place worth visiting.* **2.** having a value of, or equal in value to, as in money. **3.** having property to the value or amount of. —*n.* **4.** excellence of character or quality as commanding esteem: *men of worth.* **5.** usefulness or importance, as to the world, to a person, or for a purpose. **6.** value, as in money. **7.** a quantity of something, of a specified value. **8.** wealth; the value of one's property. **9. for all one's worth,** with all one's might; to one's utmost. **10. for what it is worth,** in spite of possible doubts about the accuracy or veracity of what is said: *I tell you this for what it is worth.* [ME and OE; c. G *wert*] **—Syn. 4.** See **value. 5.** See **merit.**

worth[2] (wûth), *v.i. Archaic.* to happen or betide: *woe worth the day.* [ME; OE *weorthan,* c. G *werden*]

Worthing (wû′thĭng), *n.* a town in England, in West Sussex: seaside resort. 80,329 (1961).

worthless (wûth′lĭs), *adj.* without worth; of no use, importance, or value; good-for-nothing; useless; valueless. —**worth′lessly,** *adv.* —**worth′lessness,** *n.*

worthwhile (wûth′wīl′), *adj.* such as to repay one's time, attention, interest, work, trouble, etc.: *a worthwhile book.*

worthy (wû′thĭ), *adj.,* **-thier, -thiest,** *n., pl.* **-thies.** —*adj.* **1.** of adequate merit or character. **2.** of commendable excellence or merit; deserving (often fol. by *of,* an infinitive, or occasionally a clause). —*n.* **3.** a person of eminent worth or merit or of social importance. **4.** a person (often humorously). —**wor′thily,** *adv.* —**wor′thiness,** *n.* **—Syn. 2.** meritorious, estimable, excellent, exemplary.

wortle (wû′tl), *n., v.,* **wortled, wortling.** —*n.* **1.** a perforated plate through which metal is drawn to produce wire or tubing. —*v.t., v.i.* **2.** to produce (wire or tubing) by this means.

wot (wŏt), *Archaic.* first and third pers. sing. pres. of **wit**[2]. [ME *woot,* OE *wāt,* c. G *weiss*]

Wotan (*Ger.* vō′tän), *n. Germanic Myth.* the chief of the gods, corresponding to the Anglo-Saxon Woden, and the Scandinavian Odin. [t. G]

Wotton (wŏt′n, wo͝ot′n), *n.* **Henry,** 1568–1639, English poet and diplomat.

would (wo͝od; *unstressed* wəd), *v.* pt. of **will**[1] used: **1.** specially in expressing a wish: *I would it were true.* **2.** often in place of *will,* to make a statement or question less direct or blunt: *that would scarcely be fair, would you be so kind?* [ME and OE *wolde.* See WILL[1]]

would-be (wo͝od′bē′), *adj.* **1.** wishing or pretending to be: *a would-be wit.* **2.** intended to be: *a would-be kindness.*

wouldn't (wo͝od′nt), contraction of *would not.*

wouldst (wo͝odst), *v. Archaic and Poetic.* second pers. sing. pt. of **will**[1].

Woulfe's bottle (wo͝olfs), *Chem.* a flat-bottomed glass bottle with two or three necks, used for washing or dissolving gases. [first described in 1784 by Peter *Woulfe,* 1727–1803, English chemist]

wound[1] (wo͞ond), *n.* **1.** an injury to an organism, usually one involving division of tissue or rupture of the integument or mucous membrane, due to external violence or some mechanical agency rather than disease. **2.** a similar injury to the tissue of a plant. **3.** an injury or hurt to feelings, sensibilities, reputation, etc. —*v.t.* **4.** to inflict a wound upon; injure; hurt. —*v.i.* **5.** to inflict a wound or wounds. [ME; OE *wund,* c. G *Wunde*] —**wound′able,** *adj.* —**wound′er,** *n.* —**wound′less,** *adj.* **—Syn. 1.** hurt, cut, stab, laceration, lesion. See **injury.**

wound[2] (wound), *v.* pt. and pp. of **wind**[2] and **wind**[3].

wounded (wo͞on′dĭd), *adj.* **1.** injured; suffering bodily harm. **2.** damaged, marred, or impaired. —*n.* **3.** wounded people collectively.

woundwort (wo͞ond′wût′), *n.* any of several labiate herbs of the genus *Stachys,* as *S. sylvatica,* the **hedge woundwort** of W and S Europe.

wove (wōv), *v.* pt. and occasional pp. of **weave.**

woven (wō′vən), *v.* pp. of **weave.**

wove paper, paper having no pattern impressed into its surface by the dandy-roller, as opposed to *laid paper,* which has such patterns.

wow (wou), *n.* **1.** *Slang.* something that proves an extraordinary success. **2.** a slow variation in pitch fidelity resulting from fluctuations in the speed of a recording. —*interj.* **3.** *Colloq.* (an exclamation of surprise, wonder, pleasure, dismay, etc.)

wowser (wou′zə), *n. Austral.* an excessively puritanical person.

WPA, Works Projects Administration.

wpm, words per minute. Also, **w.p.m.**

W.R., West Riding (of Yorkshire).

WRAC, Women's Royal Army Corps.

wrack (răk), *n.* **1.** any brown seaweed of the genus *Fucus,* as *F. serratus,* the **serrated wrack,** and *F. vesciculosus,* the **bladderwrack. 2.** any seaweed or marine vegetation cast ashore. **3.** wreck or wreckage. **4.** ruin or destruction; disaster; rack[2]. [ME *wrak* wreck, t. MD or MLG]

WRAF, Women's Royal Air Force.

wraith (rāth), *n.* **1.** an apparition of a living person, or one supposed to be living, reputed to portend or indicate his death. **2.** a visible spirit. **3.** an insubstantial copy or replica of something. **4.** something pale, thin, and insubstantial, as a plume of vapour, smoke, or the like. [orig. uncert.] —**wraith′like′,** *adj.*

wrangle (răng′gl), *v.,* **-gled, -gling,** *n.* —*v.i.* **1.** to argue or dispute, esp. in a noisy or angry manner. **2.** to engage in argument, debate, or disputation. —*v.t.* **3.** to influence, persuade, or otherwise affect by arguing. **4.** *Western U.S.* to tend (horses). —*n.* **5.** a noisy or angry dispute; altercation. [appar. t. LG: m. *wrangeln,* freq. of *wrangen* struggle, make uproar. Cf. WRING]

wrangler (răng′glə), *n.* **1.** one who wrangles or disputes. **2.** (formerly, at Cambridge University) one of those who attained first-class honours in mathematics. **3.** *Western U.S.* one who tends or wrangles horses.

wrap (răp), *v.,* **wrapped** or **wrapt, wrapping,** *n.* —*v.t.* **1.** to enclose, envelop, or muffle in something wound or folded about (often fol. by *up*). **2.** to enclose and make fast (an article, bundle, etc.) within a covering of paper or the like (often fol. by *up*). **3.** to wind, fold, or bind (something) about as a covering. **4.** to protect with coverings, outer garments, etc. (usually fol. by *up*). **5.** to surround, envelop, shroud, or enfold. **6.** to fold or roll up. **7. wrapped up in, a.** engrossed or absorbed by. **b.** *Colloq.* involved or implicated in: *a businessman wrapped up in a series of illegal transactions.* **8. wrap up,** *Colloq.* to conclude or settle: *to wrap up a financial transaction.* —*v.i.* **9.** to wrap oneself (*up*). **10.** to become wrapped, as about something; fold. **11. wrap up,** *Slang.* to be silent; stop talking; shut up. —*n.* **12.** something to be wrapped about the person, esp. in addition to the usual indoor clothing, as a shawl, scarf, or mantle. **13.** (*pl.*) outdoor garments, or coverings, furs, etc. [b. obs. *wry,* v., cover and LAP[2]]

wrapper (răp′ə), *n.* **1.** that in which something is wrapped; a covering or cover. **2.** a long, loose outer garment. **3.** a book jacket. **4.** one who or that which wraps. **5.** the tobacco leaf used for covering a cigar.

wrapping (răp′ĭng), *n.* (*usually pl.*) that in which something is wrapped.

wrapround (răp′round′), *adj.* **1.** curved so as to follow the contours of what it covers, as a windscreen, sunglasses, etc. **2.** that wraps around or overlaps, as a skirt. —*n.* **3.** something that is wrapped round. **4.** *Print.* a sheet of colour plates or the like which is printed separately and wrapped round a signature in binding. Also, **wraparound** (răp′ə round′).

wrapt (răpt), *v. Obs.* a pt. and pp. of **wrap.**

wrasse (răs), *n.* any of various marine fishes of the family *Labridae,* esp. of the genus *Labrus,* having thick, fleshy lips, powerful teeth, and usually a brilliant colour, certain species being valued as food fishes. [t. Cornish: m. *wrach,* var. of *gwrach*]

wrath (rŏth), *n.* **1.** strong, stern, or fierce anger; deeply resentful indignation; ire. **2.** vengeance or punishment, as the consequence of anger. —*adj.* **3.** *Archaic.* wroth; angry. [ME; OE *wrǣththo,* der. *wrāth* WROTH. See -TH[1]] —**wrath′less,** *adj.*

Wrath (rŏth, rôth), *n.* **Cape,** a promontory in Scotland, in NW Sutherland.

wrathful (rŏth′fəl), *adj.* **1.** full of wrath, very angry, or ireful. **2.** characterized by or showing wrath: *wrathful words.* —**wrath′fully,** *adv.* —**wrath′fulness,** *n.* **—Syn. 1.** angry, irate, furious, raging, incensed, resentful, indignant.

wrathy (rŏth′ĭ), *adj. Colloq.* wrathful; angry. —**wrath′ily,** *adv.* —**wrath′iness,** *n.*

wreak (rēk), *v.t.* **1.** to inflict or execute (vengeance, etc.). **2.** to carry out the promptings of (one's rage, ill humour, will, desire, etc.), as on a victim or object. [ME *wreke(n),* OE *wrecan,* c. G *rächen*] —**wreak′er,** *n.*

wreath (rēth), *n., pl.* **wreaths** (rēthz). **1.** something twisted or bent into a circular form; a circular band of flowers, foliage, or any ornamental work, for adorning the head or for any decorative purpose; a garland or chaplet. **2.** a garland of flowers, laurel leaves, etc., worn on the head as a mark of honour. **3.** such a circular band of flowers, foliage, etc., left at a grave, tomb, or memorial as a mark of respect or affection for the dead. **4.** any ringlike, curving, or curling mass or formation. **5.** any object having a helical path, as a rising curve in the handrail of a staircase. **6.** a defect in glass having a circular shape. [ME *wrethe*, OE *wrǣth*; akin to WRITHE] **—wreath′less,** *adj.* **—wreath′like′,** *adj.*

wreathe (rēth), *v.*, **wreathed; wreathed** or (*Archaic*) **wreathen; wreathing.** **—*v.t.*** **1.** to encircle or adorn with or as with a wreath or wreaths. **2.** to form as a wreath, by twisting, twining, or otherwise. **3.** to surround in curving or curling masses or form. **4.** to envelop: *a face wreathed in smiles.* **—*v.i.*** **5.** to take the form of a wreath or wreaths. **6.** to move in curving or curling masses, as smoke.

wreck (rĕk), *n.* **1.** the ruin or destruction of a vessel in the course of navigation; shipwreck. **2.** a vessel in a state of ruin from disaster at sea, on rocks, etc. **3.** any building, structure, or thing reduced to a state of ruin. **4.** the ruin or destruction of anything: *the wreck of one's hopes.* **5.** that which is cast ashore by the sea, as the remains of a ruined vessel or of its cargo; shipwrecked property, or wreckage, cast ashore or (less strictly) floating on the sea. In Great Britain such property belongs legally to the crown. **6.** a broken-down or debilitated person; someone in poor physical or mental health. **—*v.t.*** **7.** to cause the wreck of (a vessel), as in navigation; shipwreck. **8.** to involve in a wreck. **9.** to cause the ruin or destruction of; spoil. **—*v.i.*** **10.** to suffer wreck. [ME *wrek*, t. Scand.; cf. Icel. *rek*; akin to WREAK, WRACK] **—Syn.** **9.** See **spoil.**

wreckage (rĕk′ĭj), *n.* **1.** remains or fragments of something that has been wrecked. **2.** the act of wrecking. **3.** the state of being wrecked.

wrecker (rĕk′ə), *n.* **1.** one who or that which wrecks. **2.** one whose business it is to tear down buildings as in clearing sites for other uses; a demolition worker. **3.** one who causes shipwrecks, as by false lights on shore, to secure wreckage, or who makes a business of plundering wrecks. **4.** *Chiefly U.S.* a salvager. **5.** *U.S.* a person, train, or the like, employed in removing wreckage, etc., as from railway lines.

wreckful (rĕk′fəl), *adj.* *Archaic.* causing wreckage.

wrecking (rĕk′ĭng), *adj.* *U.S.* designed or intended for the salvaging or clearing up of wrecked trains, boats, etc.: *wrecking train, wrecking company.*

wren (rĕn), *n.* **1.** any of numerous small, active, oscinine passerine birds constituting the family *Troglodytidae*, esp. *Troglodytes troglodytes*, known as the wren in England and as the **winter wren** in America; and the common **house wren** (*T. aedon*) of North America. **2.** any of various similar birds of other families, as the **golden-crested wren** (*Regulus regulus*). [ME *wrenne*, OE *wrenna*. Cf. Icel. *rindill*]

Wren (rĕn), *n.* **Sir Christopher,** 1632–1723, English architect.

Wren (rĕn), *n.* *Colloq.* a member of the WRNS.

wrench (rĕnch), *v.t.* **1.** to twist suddenly and forcibly; pull, jerk, or force by a violent twist. **2.** to overstrain or injure (the ankle, etc.) by a sudden, violent twist. **3.** to affect distressingly as if by a wrench. **4.** to wrest, as from the right use or meaning: *to wrench facts or statements.* **—*v.i.*** **5.** to twist, turn, or move suddenly aside. **6.** to give a wrench or twist at something. **—*n.*** **7.** a wrenching movement; a sudden, violent twist. **8.** a painful, straining twist, as of the ankle or wrist. **9.** a sharp, distressing strain, as to the feelings, esp. on parting or separation. **10.** a wrestling, as of meaning; a forced interpretation. **11.** an adjustable spanner. **12.** a spanner. [ME *wrenche(n)*, OE *wrencan* twist, turn, c. G *renken*]

Wrench (def. 11)

wrest (rĕst), *v.t.* **1.** to twist or turn; pull, jerk, or force by a violent twist. **2.** to take away by force. **3.** to get by effort: *to wrest a living from the soil.* **4.** to twist or turn from the proper course, application, use, meaning, or the like. **—*n.*** **5.** a wresting; a twist or wrench. **6.** a key or small wrench for tuning stringed musical instruments, as the harp or piano, by turning the pins to which the strings are fastened. [ME *wreste(n)*, OE *wrǣstan*, c. Icel. *reista*; akin to WRIST] **—wrest′er,** *n.* **—Syn.** **3.** See **extract.**

wrestle (rĕs′əl), *v.*, **-tled, -tling,** *n.* **—*v.i.*** **1.** to engage in wrestling. **2.** to contend, as in a struggle for mastery; grapple. **3.** to deal (with a subject) as a difficult task or duty. **—*v.t.*** **4.** to contend with in wrestling. **5.** to force by or as if by wrestling. **6.** *Western U.S.* to throw (an animal) for the purpose of branding. **—*n.*** **7.** an act of or a bout at wrestling. **8.** a struggle. [ME, freq. of WREST] **—wrestler** (rĕs′lə), *n.*

wrestling (rĕs′lĭng), *n.* **1.** an exercise or sport, subject to special rules, in which two persons struggle hand to hand, each striving to throw or force the other to the ground. **2.** the act of one who wrestles.

wretch (rĕch), *n.* **1.** a deplorably unfortunate or unhappy person. **2.** a person of despicable or base character. [ME *wretche*, OE *wrecca* exile, adventurer, c. G *Recke* warrior, hero, Icel. *rekkr* man]

wretched (rĕch′ĭd), *adj.* **1.** very unfortunate in condition or circumstances; miserable; pitiable. **2.** characterized by or attended with misery. **3.** despicable, contemptible, or mean. **4.** poor, sorry, or pitiful; worthless: *a wretched blunderer, wretched little daubs.* **—wretch′edly,** *adv.* **—wretch′edness,** *n.*

—Syn. **1.** dejected, distressed, afflicted, woeful, woebegone, forlorn, unhappy. **2.** WRETCHED, MISERABLE, SORRY refer to that which is unhappy, afflicted, or distressed. WRETCHED refers to a condition of extreme affliction or distress, esp. as outwardly apparent: *wretched hovels.* MISERABLE refers more to the inward feeling of unhappiness or distress: *a miserable life.* SORRY applies to distressed, often poverty-stricken outward circumstances; but it has connotations of unworthiness, incongruousness, or the like, so that the beholder feels more contempt than pity: *in a sorry plight.* **3.** base, vile, worthless, bad. **—Ant.** **1.** comfortable, happy, admirable.

Wrexham (rĕk′səm), *n.* a town in Wales, in Denbighshire. 35,438 (1961).

wrick (rĭk), *v.t., v.i., n.* wrench or strain; rick. [ME *wrike(n)* jerk; ? akin to WRENCH, WRINKLE]

wrier (rī′ə), *adj.* compar. of **wry.**

wriest (rī′ĭst), *adj.* superl. of **wry.**

wriggle (rĭg′l), *v.*, **-gled, -gling,** *n.* **—*v.i.*** **1.** to twist to and fro, writhe, or squirm. **2.** to move along by twisting and turning the body, as a worm or snake. **3.** to make one's way by shifts or expedients: *to wriggle out of a difficulty.* **4.** to insinuate oneself into a position of advantage; wheedle. **—*v.t.*** **5.** to cause to wriggle. **6.** to bring, get, make, etc., by wriggling. **—*n.*** **7.** an act of wriggling; a wriggling movement. **8.** a sinuous formation or course. [t. MLG: m. *wriggeln*, c. D *wriggelen*] **—wrig′gler,** *n.* **—wrig′gly,** *adj.*

wright (rīt), *n.* a workman, esp. a constructive workman (now chiefly in *wheelwright, playwright*, etc.). [ME; OE *wryhta*, metathetic var. of *wyrhta* worker. See WORK]

Wright (rīt), *n.* **1. Frank Lloyd,** 1869–1959, U.S. architect. **2. Joseph,** 1855–1930, English linguist and lexicographer. **3. Orville,** 1871–1948, and his brother, **Wilbur,** 1867–1912, U.S. aeronautical inventors: made first powered aeroplane flight, 1903.

wring (rĭng), *v.*, **wrung** or (*Rare*) **wringed; wringing;** *n.* **—*v.t.*** **1.** to twist forcibly, as something flexible. **2.** to twist and compress, or compress without twisting, in order to force out moisture (often fol. by *out*): *to wring one's clothes out.* **3.** to extract or expel by twisting or compression (usually fol. by *out* or *from*). **4.** to affect painfully by or as if by some contorting or compressing action; pain, distress, or torment. **5.** to clasp (another's hand) fervently. **6.** to clasp (one's hands) together, as in grief, etc. **7.** to force (*off*, etc.) by twisting. **8.** to extract or extort as if by twisting. **9. wringing wet,** soaking wet; fit to be wrung out. **—*v.i.*** **10.** to perform the action of wringing something. **11.** to writhe, as in anguish. **—*n.*** **12.** a wringing; forcible twist or squeeze. [ME; OE *wringan*, c. G *ringen*]

wringer (rĭng′ə), *n.* **1.** one who or that which wrings. **2.** an apparatus or machine which wrings water or the like out of anything wet; a mangle.

wrinkle[1] (rĭng′kl), *n.*, *v.*, **-kled, -kling.** **—*n.*** **1.** a ridge or furrow on a surface, due to contraction, folding, rumpling, or the like; corrugation; slight fold; crease. **—*v.t.*** **2.** to form a wrinkle or wrinkles in; corrugate; crease. **—*v.i.*** **3.** to become contracted into wrinkles; become wrinkled. [late ME *wrynkle*; back-formation from *wrinkled*, OE *gewrinclod* serrate] **—wrin′kleless,** *adj.* **—wrin′kly,** *adj.*

wrinkle[2] (rĭng′kl), *n.* *Colloq.* an ingenious, indirect or artful procedure or method; a novel or clever trick or device. [der. ME *wrink*, OE *wrenc* trick]

wrist (rĭst), *n.* **1.** the part of the arm between the forearm and the hand; technically, the carpus. **2.** the joint between the radius and the carpus (**wrist joint**). **3.** that part of an article of clothing which fits round the wrist. **4.** *Mach.* a wristpin. [ME and OE, c. G *Rist* back of hand, Icel. *rist* instep; akin to WRITHE]

wristband (rĭst′bănd′), *n.* the band or part of a sleeve, as of a shirt, which covers the wrist.

wrist drop, *Pathol.* paralysis of the extensor muscles of the hand causing it to droop, due to injuries or some poisons, as lead or arsenic.

wristlet (rĭst′lĭt), *n.* **1.** a band worn round the wrist, esp. to protect it from cold. **2.** a bracelet.

wristlock (rĭst′lŏk′), *n.* *Wrestling.* a hold by which the opponent is made defenceless by a wrenching grasp on the wrist.

wristpin (rĭst′pĭn′), *n. Mach.* a stud or pin projecting from the side of a crank, wheel, or the like, and attaching it to a connecting rod leading to some other part of the mechanism.

A, Wristpin; B, Wheel; C, Connecting rod

wrist shot, *Golf.* a short chopping stroke pivoting from the wrists with the arms held almost still.

wristwatch (rĭst′wŏch′), *n.* a watch attached to a strap or band worn about the wrist.

wristwork (rĭst′wûk′), *n.* skilful use of the flexibility of the wrist, as in sport.

wristy (rĭs′tĭ), *adj.* using very flexible wrist movements, as in cricket or similar sports.

writ[1] (rĭt), *n.* **1.** *Law.* **a.** a formal order under seal, issued in the name of a sovereign, government, court, or other competent authority, enjoining the officer or other person to whom it is issued or addressed, to do or refrain from some specified act. **b.** (in early English law) any formal document in letter form, under seal, and in the king's name. **2.** *Archaic.* something written: *Holy Writ* (the Bible). [ME and OE, c. Icel. *rit* writing. See WRITE]

writ[2] (rĭt), *v.* **1.** *Archaic.* pt. and pp. of **write. 2. writ large,** substantially the same, if on a large or larger scale.

write (rīt), *v.*, **wrote** or (*Archaic*) **writ; written** or (*Archaic*) **writ; writing.** —*v.t.* **1.** to trace or form (characters, letters, words, etc.) on the surface of some material, as with a pen, pencil, or other instrument or means; inscribe. **2.** to express or communicate in writing; give a written account of. **3.** to fill in the blank spaces of (a form, etc.) with writing: *to write a cheque.* **4.** to execute or produce by setting down words, etc.: *to write two copies of a letter.* **5.** to compose and produce in words or characters duly set down: *to write a letter to a friend.* **6.** to produce as author or composer. **7.** to trace significant characters on, or mark or cover with writing. **8.** to impress the marks or indications of: *honesty is written in his face.* **9.** *U.S.* to write a letter to (someone). **10.** *Computers.* to store (information) on a medium, esp. magnetic tape. —*v.i.* **11.** to trace or form characters, words, etc., with a pen, pencil, or other instrument or means, or as a pen or the like does. **12.** (of a writing implement) to produce characters, words, etc., in a specified manner: *this pen writes well.* **13.** to be a writer, journalist, or author for one's living. **14.** to express ideas in writing. **15.** to write a letter or letters, or communicate by letter. —*v.* **16.** Some special verb phrases are:

write down, 1. to set down in writing. **2.** to write in deprecation of; injure as by writing against. **3.** to write in consciously simple terms for a supposedly ignorant readership. **4.** *Com.* to reduce the book value of.

write for, to request or apply for by letter.

write in, 1. to write a letter to a newspaper, business firm, or the like. **2.** *U.S. Politics.* (in a ballot) to add the name of a candidate not listed in the printed ballot.

write off, 1. to cancel, as an entry in an account, as by an offsetting entry. **2.** to treat as an irreparable or non-recoverable loss. **3.** to consider as dead.

write out, 1. to put into writing. **2.** to write in full form. **3.** to exhaust the capacity or resources of by excessive writing: *an author who has written himself out.*

write up, 1. to write out in full or in detail. **2.** to bring up to date or to the latest fact or transaction in writing. **3.** to present to public notice in a written description or account. **4.** to commend to the public by a favourable written description or account. **5.** *Accounting.* to make an excessive valuation of (an asset).

[ME; OE *wrītan*, c. G *reissen* tear, draw, akin to Icel. *rīta* write]

write-in (rīt′ĭn′), *U.S. Colloq.* —*adj.* **1.** filled in by hand, instead of being printed (esp. referring to a vote cast for a name, etc., not on the ballot but added by the individual voter). —*n.* **2.** a vote or a candidate that is written in.

write-off (rīt′ŏf′), *n.* **1.** *Accounting.* something written off from the books. **2.** *Slang.* something irreparably damaged, as an aircraft, car, etc.

writer (rī′tə), *n.* **1.** one who expresses ideas in writing. **2.** one engaged in literary work. **3.** one whose occupation is writing, as a journalist or author. **4.** a composer of music. **5.** one who paints or draws lettering; signwriter. **6.** *Obs. or U.S.* a manual for teaching how to write: *a letterwriter.* **7.** *Scot.* a lawyer or solicitor. **8. the writer,** he who is writing this (referring to oneself in a piece of writing).

writer's cramp, *Pathol.* muscular incapacity of the thumb and fore finger affecting those who constantly write.

write-up (rīt′ŭp′), *n.* **1.** a written description or account, as in a newspaper or magazine. **2.** *Finance, U.S.* an illegally excessive statement of corporate assets.

writhe (rīth), *v.*, **writhed; writhed** or (*Obs. except Poetic*) **writhen; writhing;** *n.* —*v.i.* **1.** to twist the body about, or squirm, as in pain, violent effort, etc. **2.** to shrink mentally, as in acute discomfort, embarrassment, etc. —*v.t.* **3.** to twist or bend out of shape or position; distort; contort. **4.** to twist (oneself, the body, etc.) about, as in pain. —*n.* **5.** a writhing movement; a twisting of the body, as in pain. [ME; OE *wrīthan* twist, wind, c. Icel. *rīdha* knit, twist] —**writh′er,** *n.* —**writh′ingly,** *adv.*

writhen (rĭth′ən), *adj. Obs.* twisted.

writing (rī′tĭng), *n.* **1.** the act of one who or that which writes. **2.** the state of being written; written form: *to commit one's thoughts to writing.* **3.** that which is written; characters or matter written with a pen or the like. **4.** such characters or matter with respect to style, kind, quality, etc. **5.** handwriting. **6.** an inscription. **7.** a letter. **8.** any written or printed paper, document, or the like. **9.** literary matter or work, esp. with respect to style, kind, quality, etc. **10.** a literary composition or production. **11. writing on the wall,** an event presaging disaster, etc.

writing case, a portable case containing writing materials.

writing desk, 1. a piece of furniture with a surface for writing upon, usually with drawers and pigeonholes to hold writing materials, etc. **2.** a portable case for holding writing materials and affording, when opened, a surface for writing upon.

writing paper, paper for writing letters on.

writing table, a table fitted or used for writing on.

writ of assistance, *Amer. Hist.* a writ issued by a superior colonial court authorizing officers of the crown to summon aid and enter and search any premises.

writ of execution, a writ granted to enforce a judgement.

writ of prohibition, *Law.* (formerly) a command by a higher court that a lower court shall not exercise jurisdiction in a particular case: now replaced by a prerogative order.

writ or right, *Law.* **1.** (formerly) one of two writs issued by a manorial court in a dispute between feudal tenants as to ownership or extent of a freehold. **2.** *U.S.* a similar writ, now supplanted by ejectment actions.

written (rĭt′n), *v.* pp. of **write.**

WRNS, Women's Royal Naval Service.

Wroclaw (*Pol.* vrŏts′wáf), *n.* Polish name of **Breslau.**

wrong (rŏng), *adj.* **1.** not in accordance with what is morally right or good. **2.** deviating from truth or fact; erroneous. **3.** not correct in action, judgement, opinion, method, etc., as a person; in error. **4.** not in accordance with a code, convention or set of rules; not proper: *the wrong way to talk to one's betters.* **5.** not in accordance with needs or expectations: *to take the wrong road; the wrong way to hold a golf club.* **6.** out of order, awry, or amiss: *something is wrong with the machine.* **7.** not suitable or appropriate: *to say the wrong thing.* **8.** (of a fabric, etc.) pertaining to or constituting the side that is less finished, which forms the inner side of a garment, etc. **9. get on the wrong side of,** to incur the hostility of. **10. in wrong with,** *U.S.* in disfavour with. **11. wrong in the head,** *Colloq.* crazy; mad. —*n.* **12.** that which is wrong, or not in accordance with morality, goodness, justice, truth, or the like; evil. **13.** an unjust act; injury. **14.** *Law.* an invasion of right, to the damage of another person. **15. in the wrong, a.** responsible for some error or accident; guilty; to blame. **b.** mistaken; in error. —*adv.* **16.** in a wrong manner; not rightly; awry or amiss. —*v.t.* **17.** to do wrong to; treat unfairly or unjustly; injure or harm. **18.** to impute evil to unjustly. **19.** to seduce. [ME; OE *wrang*, t. Scand.; cf. Icel. *rangr* awry, c. D *wrang* acid, tart; akin to WRING]

—**Syn. 1.** bad, evil, wicked, sinful, immoral, iniquitous, reprehensible, unjust, crooked. **2.** inaccurate, incorrect, false, untrue, mistaken. **7.** improper, unsuitable. **12.** misdoing, wickedness, sin, vice. **17.** maltreat, abuse, oppress, cheat, defraud, dishonour.

wrongdoer (rŏng′dōō′ə), *n.* one who does wrong.

wrongdoing (rŏng′dōō′ĭng), *n.* blameworthy action; evil behaviour.

wrong fount, *Printing.* the incorrect fount, or size and style, for its place. *Abbrev.*: wf *or* w.f.

wrongful (rŏng′fəl), *adj.* **1.** full of or characterized by wrong. **2.** having no legal right; unlawful. —**wrong′fully,** *adv.* —**wrong′fulness,** *n.*

wrong-headed (rŏng′hĕd′ĭd), *adj.* wrong in judgement or opinion; misguided and stubborn; perverse. —**wrong′head′edly,** *adv.* —**wrong′-head′edness,** *n.*

Wronski (*Pol.* vrŏyN′skē), *n.* **Josef** (*Pol.* yōō′zĕf), 1778–1853, Polish philosopher, mathematician, and scientist.

wrote (rōt), *v.* pt. of **write.**

wroth (rōth, rŏth), *adj.* angry; wrathful (used predicatively). Also, *Archaic,* **wrath.** [ME; OE *wrāth*, c. D *wreed* cruel, Icel. *reidhr* angry. See WRITHE]

wrought (rôt), *v.* **1.** *Archaic.* a pt. and pp. of **work.** —*adj.* **2.** fashioned or formed; resulting from or having been subjected to working or manufacturing. **3.** produced or shaped by beating with a hammer, etc., as iron or silver articles. **4.** ornamented or elaborated. **5.** not rough or crude.

wrought iron, a comparatively pure form of iron (as that produced by puddling pig-iron) which contains practically no carbon, and which is easily forged, welded, etc., and does not harden when suddenly cooled.

wrought-iron (rôt′ī′ən), *adj.* made of, or used in the working or manufacture of, wrought iron.

wrought-iron casting, **1.** casting with mitis. **2.** a casting made from mitis.

wrought-up (rôt′ŭp′), *adj.* excited; perturbed.

wrung (rŭng), *v.* pt. and pp. of **wring.**

wry (rī), *adj.* **wryer, wryest** or **wrier, wriest. 1.** produced by the distortion of the facial features, usually to indicate dislike, dissatisfaction, or displeasure. **2.** ironically or bitterly amusing. **3.** abnormally bent or turned to one side; twisted or crooked: *a wry nose.* **4.** devious in course or purpose; misdirected. **5.** distorted or perverted, as in meaning. **6.** wrong, unsuitable, or ill-natured, as thoughts, words, etc. [adj. use of v., ME *wrye(n)*; OE *wrigian* go forward, swerve] **—wry′ly,** *adv.* **—wry′ness,** *n.*

wrybill (rī′bĭl′), *n.* a shorebird, *Anarhynchus frontalis,* of New Zealand, related to the plovers, and having its bill twisted to the right.

wryneck (rī′nĕk′), *n.* **1.** either of two species of small Old World scansorial birds constituting the family *Jynginae,* allied to the woodpeckers, and notable for their peculiar manner of twisting the neck and head. **2.** *Colloq.* **a.** torticollis. **b.** a person having torticollis.

wry-necked (rī′nĕkt′), *adj.* afflicted with wryneck (def. 2).

WSW, west-south-west. Also, **W.S.W.**

wt, weight.

W.T., **1.** wireless telegraphy. **2.** wireless telephony. **3.** wireless transmitter. Also, **W/T.**

Wuhan (wo͞o′hăn′), *n.* the three cities of Hankow, Hanyang, and Wuchang in E China at the junction of the rivers Han and Yangtze, forming one extensive metropolitan area: the capital of Hupeh province. 2,226,000 (est. 1958).

Wuhsien (wo͞o′shyĕn′), *n.* a city in E China, in Kiangsu province. 651,000 (est. 1958). Formerly, **Soochow.**

wulfenite (wo͝ol′fə nīt′), *n.* a mineral consisting of lead molybdate, occurring usually in tabular crystals, and varying in colour from greyish to bright yellow or red. [named after F. X. von *Wulfen,* 1728–1805, Austrian mineralogist]

Wulfila (wo͝ol′fĭ lə), *n.* See **Ulfilas.**

Wundt (*Ger.* vo͝ont), *n.* **Wilhelm Max** (*Ger.* vĭl′hĕlm mäks), 1832–1920, German physiologist and psychologist.

Wuppertal (*Ger.* vo͝op′ər täl), *n.* a city in W West Germany, in the Ruhr: formed (1929) by the union of Barmen, Elberfeld, and smaller communities. 422,900 (est. 1966).

wurley (wû′lē), *n. Austral.* an Aborigine's hut. [t. native Australian]

Wurlitzer (wû′lĭt sə), *n. Trademark.* a type of unit organ incorporating many special effects, formerly much used in cinemas, etc.

wurst (wûst, vo͝oəst; *Ger.* vo͝orst), *n.* sausage, esp. of a Continental type. [t. G: lit., mixture; akin to WORSE]

Württemberg (vû′təm bûg′; *Ger.* vʏr′təm bĕrk), *n.* a former state in SW West Germany; now a part of Baden-Württemberg.

wurtzite (wût′sīt), *n.* a mineral sulphide of zinc which crystallizes in the hexagonal system. [named after Charles *Wurtz,* 1817–1884, French chemist]

Würzburg (vûts′bûg′; *Ger.* vʏrts′bo͝ork), *n.* a town in West Germany, in NW Bavaria, on the river Main. 122,200 (est. 1966).

Wusih (wo͞o′sē′, -shē′), *n.* a city in eastern China, in Kiangsu province. 616,000 (est. 1958). Also, **Wuhsi.**

W.Va., West Virginia.

W.V.S., Women's Voluntary Service.

Wy., Wyoming.

Wyandot (wī′ən dŏt′), *n.* **1.** an Indian of the former Huron tribe or confederacy. A few survivors of mixed blood now live in Oklahoma, but the Huron language is extinct. **2.** an Iroquoian language.

Wyandotte (wī′ən dŏt′), *n.* **1.** one of an American breed of medium-sized domestic fowls, valuable for eggs and for the table. **2.** Wyandot.

Wyatt (wī′ət), *n.* **1. James,** 1747–1813, English architect. **2. Sir Thomas,** 1503?–42, English poet.

wych-elm (wĭch′ĕlm′), *n.* an elm, *Ulmus glabra,* of northern and western Europe. Also, **witch-elm.** [f. *wych* (ME *wyche,* OE *wice* wych-elm) + ELM]

Wycherley (wĭch′ə lĭ), *n.* **William,** *c.* 1640–1716, English dramatist.

wych-hazel (wĭch′hā′zəl), *n.* witch-hazel.

Wyclif (wĭk′lĭf), *n.* **John,** 1320?–1384, English religious reformer, and theologian. Also, **Wycliffe, Wickliffe, Wiclif.**

Wyclifite (wĭk′lĭ fīt′), *adj.* **1.** of or pertaining to Wyclif or the Wyclifites. **—***n.* **2.** a follower of John Wyclif; a Lollard. Also, **Wycliffite.**

wydah (wĭd′ə), *n.* whidah.

wye (wī), *n., pl.* **wyes. 1.** the letter Y, or something having a similar shape. **2.** *Elect.* a form of three-phase circuit arrangement in which 3 line conductors are connected to terminals of 3 circuit elements, as represented by the 3 arms of a Y, the centre connection becoming the so-called 'neutral'.

Wye (wī), *n.* a river flowing from central Wales through SW England into the Severn estuary. ab. 130 mi.

wye level, *Survey.* an instrument consisting of a spirit level mounted under and parallel to a telescope which can be rotated in its supports (Y's) for adjustment. Also, **Y level.**

Wykeham (wĭk′əm), *n.* **William of,** 1324–1404, English churchman and statesman.

wykehamist (wĭk′ə mĭst), *n.* **1.** a pupil or former pupil of Winchester School. **—***adj.* **2.** pertaining to the school or its pupils. [named after the school's founder, William of WYKEHAM]

Wyld (wīld), *n.* **Henry Cecil Kennedy,** 1870–1945, English lexicographer and linguist.

wynd (wīnd), *n. Scot.* an alleyway or narrow street. [ME (N dial.) *wynde,* OE *gewind*]

wynn (wĭn), *n.* the name of the rune for *w.* Also, **wen.** [OE: joy]

Wyo., Wyoming.

Wyoming (wī ō′mĭng), *n.* a state in the NW United States. 330,066 pop. (1960); 97,914 sq. mi. *Cap.:* Cheyenne. *Abbrev.:* Wyo. or Wy. **—Wyomingite** (wī ō′mĭng īt′), *n.*

Wyszynski (*Pol.* vĭ shĭɴ′skē), *n.* **Stefan** (*Pol.* stĕ′fän), born 1901, Polish Roman Catholic cardinal.

wyvern (wī′vən), *n. Her.* a two-legged, winged dragon having the hinder part of a serpent with a barbed tail. Also, **wivern.** [f. obs. *wiver* viper (t. OF) + *-n,* of obscure orig. and sense]

Wyvern

X, x (ĕks), *n., pl.* **X's** or **Xs, x's** or **xs. 1.** the 24th letter of the English alphabet. **2.** *Maths., etc.* a symbol for an unknown quantity or a variable. **3.** a term often used to designate a person, thing, agency, factor, or the like, whose true name is unknown or withheld. **4.** the Roman numeral for 10. See **Roman numerals. 5.** *U.S.* a ten-dollar bill.

X (ĕks), *Cinema.* **—***adj.* **1.** denoting a film which may not be shown publicly to children under 16, or a certificate issued to such a film. **—***n.* **2.** such a film.

X, **1.** Christ. **2.** Christian. [form of Greek letter *chi,* first letter of *Christós* Christ]

x, **1.** abscissa. **2.** *Com.* ex[1]; without or not including.

xalostockite (zăl′ə stŏk′īt), *n.* a pale pink form of grossularite which occurs in white marble at Xalostoc, Mexico.

xanth-, var. of **xantho-,** before vowels, as in *xanthine.*

xanthate (zăn′thāt), *n. Chem.* a salt or ester of xanthic acid. [f. XANTH- + -ATE[2]]

xanthein (zăn′thĭ ĭn), *n.* that part of the yellow colouring matter in yellow flowers soluble in water. Cf. **xanthin** (def. 1). [t. F: m. *xanthéine,* f. *xanth-* yellow + *-éine,* to distinguish it from *xanthine* XANTHIN]

xanthene (zăn′thēn), *n. Chem.* a colourless crystalline solid, $C_6H_4OC_6H_4CH_2$, which forms the basis for a group of dyestuffs.

xanthic (zăn′thĭk), *adj.* **1.** *Chiefly Bot.* yellow. **2.** *Chem.* of or derived from xanthine or xanthic acid.

xanthic acid, *Chem.* an unstable organic acid with the type formula ROCSSH, the methyl and ethyl esters of which are colourless, oily liquids with a penetrating smell.

Its copper salts are bright yellow. [t. F: m. *xanthique*. See XANTHO-, -IC]

xanthin (zăn′thĭn), *n.* **1.** that part of the yellow colouring matter in yellow flowers which is insoluble. **2.** a yellow colouring matter in madder. [t. F: m. *xanthine*, or t. G. See XANTH-, -IN[2]]

xanthine (zăn′thēn, -thĭn), *n. Chem.* a crystalline nitrogenous compound, $C_5H_4N_4O_2$, related to uric acid, found in urine, blood, and certain animal and vegetable tissues. [t. F. See XANTHO-, -INE[2]]

Xanthippe (zăn thĭp′ĭ), *n.* **1.** the wife of Socrates, proverbial as a scold. **2.** a scolding or ill-tempered wife; a shrewish woman. Also, **Xantippe** (zăn tĭp′ĭ).

xanthium (zăn′thĭ əm), *n.* any plant of the genus *Xanthium*, as the cocklebur, which bears hooked prickles often troublesome to animals.

xantho-, a word element meaning 'yellow', as in *xanthochroid*. Also, **xanth-.** [t. Gk, comb. form of *xanthós*]

xanthochroid (zăn′thō kroid′), *Ethnol.* —*adj.* **1.** belonging or pertaining to the light-complexioned or light-haired white peoples. —*n.* **2.** one having xanthochroid characteristics. [der. *xanthochroi* yellow-pale ones, f. Gk: *xanth-* XANTH- + *ōchroi* (pl. of *ōchrós* pale)]

xanthophyll (zăn′thō fĭl), *n. Biochem.* a yellow vegetable pigment, $C_{40}H_{56}O_2$, occurring in grain or leaves; oxygenated derivatives of carotene hydrocarbons. Also, *U.S.*, **xanthophyl.** [t. F: m. *xanthophylle*, f. *xantho-* XANTHO- + m. s. Gk *phýllon* leaf] —**xanthophyllous** (zăn′thō fĭl′əs), *adj.*

xanthoproteic acid (zăn′thō prō tē′ĭk), *Chem.* a yellow substance of unknown structure formed by the action of nitric acid on proteins. [f. XANTHO- + PROTE(IN) + -IC]

xanthosiderite (zăn′thō sĭd′ə rīt′), *n.* a mineral, hydrated iron oxide, $Fe_2O_3.2H_2O$, which occurs in yellow needles usually in association with other iron oxides.

xanthous (zăn′thəs), *adj.* **1.** yellow. **2.** denoting or pertaining to the peoples with a yellow complexion (the Mongolians). [t. Gk: m. *xanthós* yellow]

Xanthus (zăn′thəs), *n.* an ancient city of Lycia, in SW Asia Minor, near the mouth of the river Xanthus: valuable archaeological remains have been found in the ruins. —**Xanthian** (zăn′thĭ ən), *adj.*

Xavier (zā′vĭ ə, zăv′ĭ ə), *n.* **St Francis** (*Francisco Javier*, '*the Apostle of the Indies*'), 1506–52, Spanish Jesuit missionary, esp. in India and Japan. Also, **Zavier.**

X chromosome, *Biol.* the sex chromosome having major control in sex determination, often paired with an unlike or Y chromosome. In humans and most mammals the XX condition controls femaleness and XY maleness; in poultry and some insects the reverse is true, the female being the heterozygous sex. See **sex chromosome.**

x-div., *Com.* ex dividend.

Xe, *Chem.* xenon.

xebec (zē′bĕk), *n.* a small three-masted vessel of the Mediterranean, formerly much used by corsairs, and now employed to some extent in commerce. Also, **zebec, zebeck.** [alter. of *chebec*, t. F, influenced by Sp. *xabeque*, now *jabeque*, t. It.: m. *sciabecco*, ult. t. Ar.: m. *sabbāk*]

Xebec.

xenia (zē′nĭ ə), *n. Bot.* the immediate influence or effect on the seed or fruit by the pollen other than on the embryo. [t. NL, t. Gk, der. *xénos* guest]

xeno-, a word element meaning 'alien', 'strange', 'foreign', as in **xenogenesis.** Also (before a vowel), **xen-.** [t. Gk, comb. form of *xénos*, n., stranger, guest and *xénos*, adj., foreign, alien]

Xenocrates (zĕ nŏk′rə tēz′), *n.* 396–314 B.C., Greek philosopher. —**Xenocratic** (zĕn′ə krăt′ĭk), *adj.*

xenocryst (zĕn′ə krĭst′), *n. Geol.* a crystal which becomes included in a magma as it rises and is not formed by the magma itself. [f. XENO- + CRYST(AL)]

xenodiagnosis (zĕn′ə dī′ăg nō′sĭs), *n. Med.* a method of diagnosing certain diseases having insects, ticks, etc., as vectors, by feeding uninfected vectors on the patient and later examining them for infection.

xenodochium (zĕn′ə dŏk′ĭ əm, zĕn′ə də kī′əm), *n., pl.* **-dochia** (-dŏk′ĭ ə, -də kī′ə). **1.** an ancient Roman or Greek inn. **2.** a guesthouse in a monastery. [t. NL, f. Gk *xéno-* XENO- + *docheîon* holder]

xenogamy (zĕ nŏg′ə mĭ), *n. Bot.* cross-fertilization (distinguished from *self-fertilization*).

xenogenesis (zĕn′ə jĕn′ĭ sĭs), *n. Biol.* **1.** heterogenesis. **2.** the supposed generation of offspring completely and permanently different from the parent. Also, **xenogeny** (zĕ nŏj′ĭ nĭ). —**xenogenetic** (zĕn′ō jĭ nĕt′ĭk), **xen′ogen′ic,** *adj.*

xenoglossia (zĕn′ə glŏs′yə), *n.* the supposed ability of a person, as a psychic medium, to speak a language which he has not previously learned. [f. Gk *xéno-* XENO- + *glōss(a)* language + *-ia* -IA]

xenolith (zĕn′ə lĭth), *n. Geol.* a rock fragment foreign to the igneous rock in which it is embedded.

xenomorphic (zĕn′ə mô′fĭk), *adj. Geol.* denoting or pertaining to a mineral constituent of a rock, which does not have its characteristic crystalline form, but one forced upon it by other constituents of the rock. —**xen′omor′phically,** *adv.*

xenon (zĕn′ŏn), *n. Chem.* a heavy, colourless, chemically inactive, monatomic gaseous element present in the atmosphere, one volume in 170,000,000 volumes of air. *Symbol:* Xe; *at. wt:* 131·3; *at. no.:* 54. [t. Gk, neut. of *xénos* strange]

Xenophanes (zĕ nŏf′ə nēz′), *n. c.* 570–*c.* 480 B.C., Greek philosopher and poet.

xenophobe (zĕn′ə fōb′), *n.* one who fears or hates foreigners or things foreign.

xenophobia (zĕn′ə fō′byə), *n.* fear or hatred of foreigners. —**xen′opho′bic,** *adj.*

Xenophon (zĕn′ə fən), *n. c.* 434–*c.* 355 B.C., Greek historian and writer.

xenopus (zĕn′ə pəs), *n.* any frog of the African clawed genus *Xenopus*, used in pregnancy testing.

xenotime (zĕn′ə tīm′), *n. Chem.* a mineral, yttrium phosphate, YPO_4, often containing cerium, erbium, and thorium, of which it is a source.

Xeres (*Sp.* KHĕ′rĕth), *n.* former name of **Jerez.**

xero-, a word element meaning 'dry', as in *xeroderma*. Also, before a vowel, **xer-.** [comb. form repr. Gk *xērós*]

xeroderma (zĭə′rō dû′mə), *n. Pathol.* a disease in which the skin becomes dry and hard, and usually scaly. Also, **xerodermia** (zĭə′rō dû′mĭ ə).

xerography (zĭə rŏg′rə fĭ), *n.* a method of photographic copying in which an electrostatic image is formed on a surface coated with selenium when it is exposed to an optical image. A dark resinous powder is dusted on to this surface after exposure so that the particles adhere to the charged regions; the image so formed is transferred to a sheet of charged paper and fixed by heating. [f. Gk: *xērō(s)* dry + m. s. *graphē* writing. See -GRAPHY] —**xerograph** (zĭə′rə grăf′, -gräf′), *n.* —**xerographic** (zĭə′rə grăf′ĭk), *adj.*

xerophilous (zĭə rŏf′ĭ ləs), *adj.* **1.** *Bot.* growing in or adapted to dry, esp. dry and hot, regions. **2.** *Zool.* living in dry situations. —**xeroph′ily,** *n.*

xerophthalmia (zĭə′rŏf thăl′mĭ ə), *n. Pathol.* abnormal dryness of the eyeball, usually due to long-continued conjunctivitis.

xerophyte (zĭə′rə fīt′), *n.* a plant adapted for growth under dry conditions. —**xerophytic** (zĭə′rə fĭt′ĭk), *adj.*

Xerox (zĭə′rŏks), *Trademark.* —*n.* **1.** a xerographic process. **2.** a copy obtained by this process. —*v.t., v.i.* **3.** to obtain copies (of) by this process.

Xerxes I (zûk′sēz), *c.* 519–465 B.C., king of Persia 486?–465 B.C., son of Darius I and Atossa.

Xhosa (kô′sə), *n.* **1.** a Bantu language of Cape Province in the Republic of South Africa, related to Zulu. **2.** a member of the people speaking this language.

xi (sī), *n.* the fourteenth letter (Ξ, ξ, = English X, x) of the Greek alphabet.

Ximenes (zĭm′ĭ nēz′; *Sp.* KHē mĕ′nĕth), *n.* See **Jiménez de Cisneros.** Also, **Ximenez.**

Xingú (*Port.* shēng gōō′), *n.* a river flowing N through central Brazil into the Amazon. ab. 1300 mi.

x-int., *Com.* ex interest. Also, **X-i.**

-xion, var. of **-tion,** as in inflexion, flexion.

xiphisternum (zĭf′ĭ stû′nəm), *n., pl.* **-na** (-nə). *Anat., Zool.* the hindmost (or, in man, the lowermost) segment or division of the sternum. [f. *xiphi-* (comb. form repr. Gk *xiphos* sword) + STERNUM] —**xiph′ister′nal,** *adj.*

xiphoid (zĭf′oid), *Anat., Zool.* —*adj.* **1.** sword-shaped; ensiform. —*n.* **2.** the xiphisternum. [t. NL: s. *xiphoīdēs*, t. Gk: m. *xiphoeidḗs* swordlike]

xiphosuran (zĭf′ə syŏŏ′rən), *adj.* **1.** of or pertaining to the horseshoe crabs (order *Xiphosura*). —*n.* **2.** a member of the order *Xiphosura*; a horseshoe crab. [f. NL *Xiphosūra* (irreg. f. Gk: *xiphos* sword + *ourá* tail) + -AN]

Xmas (ĕks′məs), *n. Colloq.* Christmas.

Xn, Christian. Also, **Xtian.**

x-new, *Com.* ex the right to new shares.

Xnty, Christianity. Also, **Xty.**

xoanon (zō′ə nən), *n., pl.* **-na** (-nə). *Gk Antiq.* a primitive statue, originally wooden, later overlaid with ivory or gold.

XP (kī′rō′), *n.* the Christian monogram made from the first two letters of the Greek word for Christ. [t. Gk, repr. *chi* and *rho*]

x-pr., *Com.* ex privileges.
X-radiation (ĕks′rā′dĭ ā′shən), *n. Physics.* X-ray.
X-ray (ĕks′rā′), *n.* **1.** *Physics.* (*often pl.*) electromagnetic radiation of shorter wavelength than light (5×10^{-7} to 6×10^{-10} cm.) which are able to penetrate solids, ionize gases, and expose photographic plates; Röntgen ray. **2.** an examination of the interior of a person or an opaque substance by means of an apparatus using X-rays. *—v.t.* **3.** to examine by means of X-rays. **4.** to make an X-ray radiograph of. See **röntgenize. 5.** to treat with X-rays. [t. G: trans. of *X-Strahlen*, so called because their nature was not known]
X-ray crystallography, *Physics.* the study of a crystalline substance by observing the diffraction patterns which occur when a beam of X-rays is passed through it.
X-ray photograph, a radiograph made with X-rays.
X-ray therapy, *Med.* treatment of a disease, such as cancer, using controlled quantities of X-rays.
X-ray tube, *Physics.* an evacuated tube for the production of X-rays in which a heavy metal target is bombarded with a high-velocity stream of electrons.
x-rts, *Com.* ex rights. Also, **x-r.**
Xt, Christ.
Xtian, Christian.
X-unit (ĕks′yōō′nĭt), *n. Physics.* a unit of length equal to 10^{-11} cm. used to express the wavelengths of X- and gamma-radiation. *Abbrev.:* X.U.
xyl-, var. of **xylo-,** before vowels, as in *xylem.*
xylan (zī′lăn), *n. Chem.* the pentosan occurring in woody tissue which hydrolyses to xylose, used as the source of furfural. [f. XYL- + -AN]
xylem (zī′lĕm), *n. Bot.* that part of a vascular bundle which consists of tracheids and immediately associated cells, forming the woody portion; woody tissue. See **phloem.** [f. XYL- + *-em* (t. Gk: m. *-ēma* noun suffix)]
xylene (zī′lēn), *n. Chem.* any of three isomeric hydrocarbons, $C_6H_4(CH_3)_2$, of the benzene series, occurring as oily, colourless liquids obtained chiefly from coal tar, and used in making dyes, etc. Also, **xylol.**
xylenol (zī′lĭ nōl′), *n. Chem.* any of six isomeric phenols derived from xylene, $C_6H_3(CH_3)_2.OH$, used in the manufacture of plastics and derivatives of which are used in antiseptics.
xylenol resin, *Chem.* a synthetic resin produced by the condensation of a xylenol with an aldehyde.
xylic acid (zī′lĭk), *Chem.* any of six isomeric acids derived from xylene, $C_6H_3(CH_3)_2.COOH$.
xylidine (zī′lĭ dēn′, -dĭn′, zĭl′ĭ-), *n. Chem.* **1.** any of six isomeric compounds, $C_6H_3(CH_3)_2.NH_2$, derived from xylene and resembling aniline, used in dye manufacture. **2.** an oily liquid consisting of a mixture of certain of these compounds, used commercially in making dyes. Also, **xylidin** (zī′lĭ dĭn, zĭl′ĭ-). [f. XYL(ENE) or XYL(IC) + -ID[3] + -INE[2]]
xylo-, a word element meaning 'wood', as in *xylograph.* Also, **xyl-.** [t. Gk, comb. form of *xýlon*]
xylocarp (zī′lə kärp′), *n.* any fruit having a hard woody pericarp.
xylograph (zī′lə grăf′, -gräf′), *n.* an engraving on wood. **—xylographer** (zī lŏg′rə fə), *n.*
xylography (zī lŏg′rə fĭ), *n.* the art of engraving on wood, or of printing from such engravings. [t. F: m. *xylographie.* See XYLO-, GRAPHY] **—xylographic** (zī′lə grăf′ĭk), **xy′lograph′ical,** *adj.*
xyloid (zī′loid), *adj.* resembling wood; ligneous. [t. Gk: m. s. *xyloeidḗs*, f. *xylo-* XYLO- + *-eidēs* -oid]
xylol (zī′lōl), *n.* xylene.
Xylonite (zī′lə nīt′), *n. Trademark.* a thermoplastic material of the cellulose nitrate type.
xylophage (zī′lə fāj′), *n. Obs.* a wood-eating insect.
xylophagous (zī lŏf′ə gəs), *adj.* **1.** eating wood, as the larvae of certain insects. **2.** perforating or destroying timber, as certain molluscs and crustaceans.
xylophone (zī′lə fōn′), *n.* a musical instrument consisting of a graduated series of wooden bars, usually sounded by striking with small wooden hammers. **—xylophonic** (zī′lə fŏn′ĭk), *adj.*, **—xylophonist** (zī lŏf′ə-nĭst), *n.*

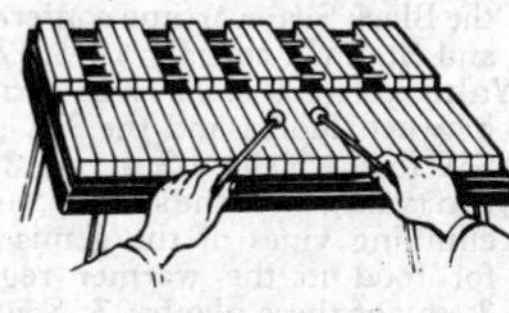
Xylophone

xylose (zī′lōs), *n. Chem.* a colourless crystalline aldopentose, $C_5H_{10}O_5$ derived from xylan, straw, corncobs, etc., by treating with heated dilute sulphuric acid, and dehydrating to furfural if stronger acid is used.
xylotomous (zī lŏt′ə məs), *adj.* boring into or cutting wood, as certain insects.
xylotomy (zī lŏt′ə mĭ), *n.* the art of cutting sections of wood, as with a microtome, for microscopic examination. **—xylot′omist,** *n.*
xylyl (zī′lĭl), *adj. Chem.* denoting any of the univalent radicals, $C_6H_4.CH_3.CH_2$-, derived from xylene.
xyst (zĭst), *n.* **1.** *Gk Antiq.* a covered portico used by athletes for their exercises. **2.** an open colonnade or tree-lined walk. [t. Gk: s. *xystós*]
xyster (zĭs′tə), *n.* a surgical instrument for scraping bones. [t. Gk: scraping tool]

Y

Y, y (wī), *n., pl.* **Y's** or **Ys, y's** or **ys. 1.** the 25th letter of the English alphabet. **2.** something resembling the letter Y in shape.
y-, *Obs.* an inflective prefix used in past participles, as in *y-clept* 'named'.
-y[1], a suffix of adjectives meaning 'characterized by or inclined to' the substance or action of the word or stem to which the suffix is attached, as in *juicy, dreamy, chilly.* Also, **-ey[1].** [OE *-ig.* Cf. G *-ig*]
-y[2], a diminutive suffix, often affectionate, common in names, as in *Billy, pussy.* Also, **-ey[2], -ie.** [ME; often through Scot. influence]
-y[3], a suffix forming action nouns from verbs, as in *enquiry*, also found in other abstract nouns, as *carpentry, infamy.* [repr. L *-ia, -ium*, Gk *-ia, -eia, -ion*, F *-ie*, G *-ie*]
Y, *Chem.* yttrium.
y, *Maths.* **1.** an ordinate. (See **abscissa**) **2.** an unknown quantity.
Y., *U.S.* Young Men's Christian Association.
y., 1. yard; yards. **2.** year; years.
yabber (yăb′ə), *n. Austral.* jabber. [t. native d. Australian: m. *yabba* language]
yabby (yăb′ĭ), *n. Austral.* any of several small crayfish, mostly freshwater. [t. native Australian]
Yablonoi Mountains (*Russ.* yə blä nôy′), a mountain range in the SE Soviet Union in Asia, E of Lake Baikal. Also, **Yablonovoi** (*Russ.* yə blə nä vôy′).
yacht (yŏt), *n.* **1.** a vessel used for private cruising, racing, or other like non-commercial purposes. *—v.i.* **2.** to sail, voyage, or race in a yacht. [earlier *yaught*, t. early mod. D: m. *jaght*, short for *jaghtschip* ship for chasing. Cf. G *Jacht, Jagd* hunting]
yachting (yŏt′ĭng), *n.* the practice or sport of sailing or voyaging in a yacht.
yachtsman (yŏts′mən), *n., pl.* **-men.** one who owns or sails a yacht. **—yachts′manship′, yacht′manship′,** *n.* **—yachts′wom′an,** *n. fem.*
yackety-yak (yăk′ə tĭ yăk′), *n., v.,* **-yakked, -yakking.** *Slang.* *—n.* **1.** empty conversation. *—v.i.* **2.** to talk or chatter, esp. pointlessly and continuously. [imit.]
yager (yā′gə), *n.* jaeger.
yah (yä), *interj.* (an exclamation of impatience or derision.)
Yahata (yä′hə tä′), *n.* Yawata.
Yahoo (yə hōō′), *n.* **1.** (in Swift's *Gulliver's Travels*) one of a race of brutes having the form of man and all his degrading passions, who are subject to the Houyhnhnms. **2.** (*l.c.*) a rough, coarse, or uncouth person. [name coined by Swift]
Yahweh (yä′wā), *n.* a name of God in the Hebrew text of the Old Testament, commonly transliterated Jehovah. See **Tetragrammaton.** Also, **Yahve, Yahveh** (yä′vā), **Jahveh, Jahve.**
Yahwism (yä′wĭz′əm), *n.* **1.** the religion of the ancient Hebrews, as based on the worship of Yahweh as the national deity. **2.** the use of Yahweh as the name of God. Also, **Yahvism** (yä′vĭz′əm).
Yahwist (yä′wĭst), *n.* the writer (or writers) of one of the major sources of the Hexateuch, in which God is characteristically spoken of as Yahweh (or erroneously, Jehovah) instead of Elohim. See **Elohist.** Also, **Yahvist** (yä′vĭst).
Yahwistic (yä wĭs′tĭk), *adj.* **1.** of or pertaining to the Yahwist. **2.** characterized by the use of Yahweh (Jehovah) instead of Elohim. Also, **Yahvistic** (vä vĭs′tĭk).
Yajur-Veda (yŭj′ŏŏə vā′də), *n.* See **Veda.**

yak (yăk), *n.* **1.** the long-haired wild ox, *Poephagus grunniens,* of the Tibetan highlands. **2.** a domesticated variety of the same species. [t. Tibetan: m. *gyag*]

Yak, *Poephagus grunniens* (5 ft high at the shoulder)

yakka (yăk′ə), *Austral. Colloq.* —*n.* **1.** work. —*v.i.* **2.** to work.

Yakut (yă ko͝ot′), *n.* a Turkic language of NE Siberia.

Yakutsk (yă ko͝otsk′; *Russ.* yĭ-ko͝otsk′), *n.* a city in the NE Soviet Union in Asia, on the river Lena. 92,000 (est. 1966).

Yale (yāl), *n.* **1. Elihu** (ĕl′ĭ hyo͞o′), 1648–1721, English colonial official, born in America: principal benefactor of Yale College, now Yale University. **2.** the university in New Haven, Connecticut, founded in 1701.

yale lock (yāl), **1.** a type of cylinder lock. **2.** (*cap.*) a trademark for this. [named after Linus *Yale,* 1821–68, U.S. locksmith]

y'all (yôl), *pron. Southern U.S.* you'all.

Yalta (yăl′tə), *n.* a seaport in the SW Soviet Union, on the Black Sea: wartime conference of Roosevelt, Churchill, and Stalin, February 1945. 47,100 (1959).

Yalu (yä′lo͞o), *n.* a river forming part of the boundary between Korea and the NE provinces of China, flowing SW to the Yellow Sea. ab. 300 mi.

yam (yăm), *n.* **1.** the starchy, tuberous root of any of various climbing vines of the genus *Dioscorea,* much cultivated for food in the warmer regions of both hemispheres. **2.** any of these plants. **3.** *Southern U.S.* the sweet potato. **4.** *Scot.* the common white potato. [t. Sp.: m. *(i)ñame*; ult. of African orig.; cf. Senegalese *nyami* eat]

Yamagata (yăm′ə gä′tə), *n.* **Prince Aritomo** (ă′rĭ tō′mō), 1838–1922, Japanese field marshal and statesman.

Yamashita (yăm′ə shē′tə), *n.* **Tomoyuki** (tō′mō yo͞o′kĭ), 1885–1946, Japanese general.

Yambol (*Bulg.* yàm′bòl), *n.* a town in E central Bulgaria. 56,998 (1964).

yamen (yä′mĕn), *n.* (in China, under the imperial system prior to 1912) the residence or office (often combined) of any official. [var. of *yamun,* t. Chinese, f. *ya* office + *mun* gate]

yammer (yăm′ə), *Colloq. or Dial.* —*v.i.* **1.** to whine or complain. **2.** to make an outcry or clamour; talk loudly and persistently. —*v.t.* **3.** to utter or say in complaint. —*n.* **4.** the act of yammering. [ME *yamur,* var. of *yomer,* OE *geōmrian* complain, akin to G *Jammer* lamentation] —**yam′merer,** *n.*

Yang (yăng), *n.* one of the two fundamental principles of the universe in Chinese philosophy, regarded as masculine, active, and assertive. Cf. **Yin.**

Yangkü (yăng′ko͞o′), *n.* Taiyüan.

Yangtze (yăngk′sĭ), *n.* a river flowing from the Tibetan plateau generally E through central China to the East China Sea. ab. 3200 mi. Also, **Yangtze-Kiang** (yăngk′-sĭ-kyăng′).

Yangtze

Yanina (yä′nĭ nə), *n.* Serbian name of **Ioannina.** Also, **Yannina.**

yank (yăngk), *Colloq.* —*v.t., v.i.* **1.** to pull or move with a sudden jerking motion; tug sharply. —*n.* **2.** a jerk or tug. [orig. uncert.]

Yank (yăngk), *n., adj. Slang.* Yankee.

Yankee (yăng′kĭ), *n.* **1.** a native or inhabitant of New England. **2.** a native or inhabitant of a northern state of the U.S. **3.** a native or inhabitant of the U.S. **4.** a Federal soldier in the American Civil War. —*adj.* **5.** of, pertaining to, or characteristic of the Yankees. [? back-formation from D *Jan Kees* John Cheese, nickname (mistaken for plural)]

Yankeedom (yăng′kĭ dəm), *n.* **1.** the region inhabited by the Yankees. **2.** Yankees collectively.

Yankee Doodle (do͞o′dl), an English song taken over by the American troops during the War of Independence.

Yankeeism (yăng′kĭ ĭz′əm), *n.* **1.** Yankee character or characteristics. **2.** a Yankee peculiarity, as of speech.

Yankeeland (yăng′kĭ lănd′), *n. Colloq.* **1.** the United States. **2.** *Chiefly Southern U.S.* the northern states of the U.S. **3.** *Chiefly Northern U.S.* New England.

Yaoundé (*Fr.* yà o͞on dĕ′), *n.* the capital of Cameroun in the SW part. 90,340 (est. 1962). Also, **Yaunde.**

yap (yăp), *v.,* **yapped, yapping,** *n.* —*v.i.* **1.** to yelp; bark snappishly. **2.** *Slang.* to talk snappishly, noisily, or foolishly. —*v.t.* **3.** to utter by yapping. —*n.* **4.** a yelp; a snappish bark. **5.** *Slang.* snappish, noisy, or foolish talk. **6.** *Slang.* the mouth. [imit.]

Yap (yäp, yăp), *n.* one of the Caroline Islands, in the W Pacific: U.S. telegraph station. 6021 pop. including adjacent islands (est. 1963); 83 sq. mi.

yapok (yə pŏk′), *n.* a small South and Central American aquatic opossum, *Chironectes minimus,* with webbed hind feet and variegated fur. [named after *Oyapok,* river in Brazil and French Guiana]

yapp (yăp), *n.* **1.** a style of bookbinding in limp leather or the like with projecting flaps overlapping the edges of the pages, used esp. on Bibles. —*adj.* **2.** of or pertaining to this style of binding.

Yapurá (*Port.* zhä po͞o rä′), *n.* Japurá.

Yaqui (*Sp.* yä′kē), *n., pl.* **-quis,** (*esp. collectively*) **-qui** for 1. **1.** a member of a Piman Indian people, in Sonora, Mexico. **2.** the language of the Yaqui Indians. **3.** a river in NW Mexico, flowing into the Gulf of California.

Yarborough (yä′bə rə, -brə), *n. Whist, Bridge.* a hand of cards, none of which is higher than a nine. [named after the 2nd Earl of *Yarborough,* died 1897]

yard[1] (yäd), *n.* **1.** a common unit of linear measure in English-speaking countries, equal to 3 ft or 36 in., defined as 0·9144 metres. **2.** *Naut.* a long cylindrical spar with a taper towards each end, slung crosswise to a mast and suspending a square sail, lateen sail, etc. [ME *yerd(e),* OE *gerd* (Anglian), c. D *gard,* G *Gerte* rod]

yard[2] (yäd), *n.* **1.** a piece of enclosed ground adjoining or surrounding a house or other building, or surrounded by it. **2.** a piece of enclosed ground for use as a garden, for animals, or for some other purpose. **3.** an enclosure within which any work or business is carried on: *a brickyard, a shipyard.* **4.** *Railways.* **a.** a goods yard. **b.** a marshalling yard. **5.** *U.S.* the winter pasture or browsing ground of moose and deer. **6. the Yard,** Scotland Yard. —*v.t.* **7.** to put into or enclose in a yard. [ME *yerd,* OE *geard* enclosure, c. D *gaard* garden, Icel. *gardhr* yard, Goth. *gards* house]

yardage[1] (yä′dĭj), *n.* measurement, or the amount measured, in yards. [f. YARD[1] + -AGE]

yardage[2] (yä′dĭj), *n.* **1.** the use of a yard or enclosure, as in lading or unlading cattle, etc., at a railway station. **2.** the charge for such use. [f. YARD[2] + -AGE]

yardang (yä′dăng), *n.* a sharp rib of rock up to 20 ft high, formed in a desert by the action of sand-laden winds on rocks of varying hardness. [t. Turki: ablative of *yar* cliff]

yardarm (yäd′äm′), *n. Naut.* either end of a yard of a square sail.

yard grass, a coarse annual grass, *Eleusine indica,* of the Old World, common in backyards and fields.

yardmaster (yäd′mäs′tə), *n.* a man employed to superintend a railway yard.

yardstick (yäd′stĭk′), *n.* **1.** a stick a yard long, commonly marked with subdivisions, used to measure with. **2.** any standard of measurement.

yare (yêə), *adj.,* **yarer, yarest.** *Archaic or Dial.* **1.** ready or prepared. **2.** prompt; brisk or quick. **3.** easily handled or manageable. [ME; OE *gearu, gearo,* c. D *gaar,* G *gar* done, dressed (as meat)] —**yare′ly,** *adv.*

Yarkand (yä′kănd′), *n.* a city in NW China, in Sinkiang province. 80,000 (est. 1953).

Yarmouth (yä′məth), *n.* See **Great Yarmouth.**

yarn (yän), *n.* **1.** thread made by twisting fibres, as nylon, cotton or wool, and used for knitting and weaving. **2.** the thread, in the form of a loosely twisted aggregate of fibres, as of hemp, of which rope is made (**rope yarn**). **3.** *Colloq.* a story or tale of adventure, esp. a long one about incredible events. —*v.i.* **4.** *Colloq.* to spin a yarn; tell stories. [ME; OE *gearn,* c. G *Garn*; akin to Icel. *görn* gut]

yarn-dyed (yän′dīd′), *adj.* (of fabrics) woven from yarns previously dyed.

Yaroslavl (*Russ.* yĭ rä slàvly′), *n.* a city in the central Soviet Union in Europe, on the Volga. 478,000 (est. 1965).

yarrow (yă′rō), *n.* **1.** an asteraceous plant, *Achillea millefolium,* of Europe and America, with finely divided leaves and whitish flowers, sometimes used in medicine as a tonic and astringent; milfoil. **2.** any of various other plants of the genus *Achillea.* Cf. **sneezewort.** [ME *yarowe, yarwe,* OE *gearwe,* c. G *Garbe*]

Yarrow (yă′rō), *n.* a river in SE Scotland, flowing through Selkirk into the Tweed. 14 mi.

yashmak (yăsh′măk), *n.* the veil worn by Muslim women in public. Also, **yashmac.** [t. Ar.]

yataghan (yăt′ə gən), *n.* a Turkish sabre with a curved blade, having an eared pommel and lacking a guard. Also, **ataghan, yatagan.** [t. Turk.]

ya-ta-ta (yä′tə tä′), *n. U.S. Slang.* empty conversation. [imit.]

yauld (yôd, yäd, yäld), *adj. Scot.* supple; active.

Yaundé (*Fr.* yà o͞on dĕ′), *n.* Yaoundé.

yaup (yôp), *v.i.*, *n.* yawp. —**yaup′er,** *n.*

yaupon (yô′pən), *n.* a shrub or small tree, *Ilex vomitoria,* a species of holly, of the southern U.S., with leaves which are sometimes used as a substitute for tea.

yaw (yô), *v.i.* **1.** to deviate temporarily from the straight course, as a ship. **2.** (of an aircraft, rocket, etc.) to have a motion about its vertical axis. —*v.t.* **3.** to cause to yaw. —*n.* **4.** a movement of deviation from the direct course, as of a vessel. **5.** a motion of an aircraft, etc., about its vertical axis. [orig. uncert.]

Yawata (yä′wə tä′), *n.* a town in SW Japan, on N Kyushu island. 210,051 (1951). Also, **Yahata.**

yawl[1] (yôl), *n.* **1.** a fore-and-aft-rigged vessel with a large mainmast forward and a much smaller mast set far aft, usually abaft the rudderpost. **2.** *Obs.* a jolly-boat. Cf. **ketch.** [t. D: m. *jol* kind of boat; orig. unknown]

Yawl (def. 1)

yawl[2] (yôl), *n.*, *v.i.* *Colloq. or Dial.* yowl; howl. [akin to YOWL]

yawn (yôn), *v.i.* **1.** to open the mouth involuntarily with a prolonged, deep intake of breath, as from drowsiness or weariness. **2.** to open wide like a mouth. **3.** to extend or stretch wide, as an open (and usually deep) space. —*v.t.* **4.** to say with a yawn. **5.** *Archaic.* to open wide, or lay open, as if by yawning. —*n.* **6.** the act of yawning. **7.** an opening, open space, or chasm. [ME *yane, yone,* OE *geonian,* akin to OE *gānian, gīnan,* G *gähnen*] —**yawn′er,** *n.* —**yawn′ingly,** *adv.*

yawp (yôp), *Colloq. or Dial.* —*v.i.* **1.** to utter a loud, harsh cry or sound; bawl. **2.** to talk noisily and foolishly. —*n.* **3.** a yawping cry. **4.** any harsh or raucous sound. **5.** a noisy, foolish utterance. Also, **yaup.** [imit.] —**yawp′er,** *n.*

yaws (yôz), *n.pl.* *Pathol.* a contagious disease resembling syphilis, caused by the spirochaete, *Treponema pertenue,* prevalent in certain tropical regions and characterized by an eruption of raspberry-like excrescences. Also, **frambœsia.**

Yb, *Chem.* ytterbium.

Y.B., yearbook.

Y chromosome, *Biol.* the mate of the X chromosome in one sex of species having differentiated sex chromosomes.

y-clad (ĭ klăd′), *v.* *Archaic.* pp. of **clothe.**

y-clept (ĭ klĕpt′), *v.*, *pp.* *Archaic.* called; named; styled. Also, **y-cleped.** [ME; OE *geclypod,* pp. See CLEPE]

yd, yard; yards.

yds, yards.

ye[1] (yē; *unstressed* yĭ), *pron.* *Archaic or Dial.* **1.** (nominative or objective plural of **thou**) you. **2.** (nominative singular) you. [ME; OE *gē,* c. D *gij,* G *ihr,* Icel. *ēr,* Goth. *jus*]

ye[2] (t͟hē; *spelling pron.* yē), *def. art.* an archaic spelling of **the**[1]. [var. of THE[1] due to misreading of ME symbol þ (see THORN, def. 5)]

yea (yā), *adv.* **1.** yes (used in affirmation or assent). **2.** *Archaic.* indeed or truly (used to introduce a sentence or clause). **3.** *Archaic.* not only so, but also (used in adding something which intensifies and amplifies). —*n.* **4.** an affirmation; an affirmative reply or vote. **5.** one who votes in the affirmative. [ME *ye, ya,* OE *gēa,* c. D, G, Icel., and Goth. *ja*]

yeah (yĕə), *adv.*, *n.* *Colloq.* yes.

yean (yēn), *v.t.*, *v.i.* (of a sheep or goat) to bring forth (young). [ME *yene,* OE *geēanian* bring forth (young)]

yeanling (yēn′lĭng), *n.* **1.** the young of a sheep or a goat; a lamb or a kid. —*adj.* **2.** just born; infant.

year (yĭə), *n.* **1.** a period of 365 or 366 days, divided into 12 calendar months, now reckoned as beginning January 1st and ending December 31st (**calendar year**). **2.** a period of approximately the same length in other calendars. **3.** a space of 12 calendar months reckoned from any point: *he left on May 15th to be gone a year.* **4.** a period consisting of 12 lunar months (**lunar year**). **5.** (in scientific use) the time interval between one vernal equinox and the next, or the period of one complete apparent circuit of the ecliptic by the sun, being equal to about 365 days, 5 hours, 48 minutes, 46 seconds (**tropical year, solar year, astronomical year**). **6.** the true period of the earth's revolution round the sun; the time it takes for the apparent travelling of the sun from a given star back to it again, being about 20 minutes longer than the tropical year, which is affected by the precession of the equinoxes (**sidereal year**). **7.** the time in which any planet completes a revolution round the sun. **8.** a full round of the seasons. **9.** a period out of every 12 months, devoted to a certain pursuit, activity, or the like: *the academic year.* **10.** (*pl.*) age, esp. of a person. **11.** (*pl.*) old age: *a man of years.* **12.** (*pl.*) time, esp. a long time. **13. a year and a day,** a period specified as the limit of time in various legal matters, as in determining a right or a liability, to allow for a full year by any way of counting. **14. year in, year out,** occurring regularly year after year; continuously. [ME *yeer,* OE *gēar,* c. D *jaar,* G *Jahr,* Icel. *ār,* Goth. *jēr*]

yearbook (yĭə′bo͝ok′), *n.* a book published annually, containing information, statistics, etc., about the year.

yearling (yĭə′lĭng), *n.* **1.** an animal one year old or in the second year of its age. **2.** *Horseracing.* a horse one year old, dating from January 1st of the year of foaling. —*adj.* **3.** a year old. **4.** of a year's duration. [f. YEAR + -LING[1]. Cf. G *Jährling*]

yearlong (yĭə′lŏng′), *adj.* lasting for a year.

yearly (yĭə′lĭ), *adj.*, *adv.*, *n.*, *pl.* **-lies.** —*adj.* **1.** pertaining to a year, or to each year. **2.** done, made, happening, appearing, coming, etc., once a year, or every year. **3.** continuing for a year. **4.** lasting only a year. —*adv.* **5.** once a year; annually. —*n.* **6.** a publication appearing once a year.

yearn (yûn), *v.i.* **1.** to have an earnest or strong desire; long. **2.** to be moved or attracted tenderly. [ME *yerne,* OE *giernan,* c. Icel. *girna*]

yearning (yû′nĭng), *n.* **1.** deep longing, esp. when tinged with tenderness or sadness. **2.** an instance of it. —**yearn′ingly,** *adv.* —**Syn. 1.** See **desire.**

year of grace, the year as reckoned from the birth of Christ; A.D.

yeast (yēst), *n.* **1.** a yellowish, somewhat viscid, semifluid substance consisting of the aggregated cells of certain minute fungi, which appears in saccharine liquids (fruit juices, malt worts, etc.), rising to the top as a froth (**top yeast** or **surface yeast**) or falling to the bottom as a sediment (**bottom yeast** or **sediment yeast**), employed to induce fermentation in the manufacture of alcoholic drink, esp. beer, and as a leaven to render bread, etc., light and spongy, and also used in medicine. **2.** a commercial substance made of living yeast cells and some meal-like material, used in raising dough for bread, etc. **3.** a yeast plant. **4.** spume or foam. **5.** ferment or agitation. —*v.i.* **6.** to ferment. **7.** to be covered with froth. [ME *yeest,* OE *gist,* c. G *Gischt*] —**yeast′less,** *adj.* —**yeast′-like′,** *adj.*

yeast cake, living yeast cells compressed with a little starch into a small cake. In **dried yeast cake,** yeasts are inactive; in a **compressed yeast cake** they are active and the product is perishable.

yeast plant, any of the minute, unicellular ascomycetous fungi constituting the genus *Saccharomyces,* and related genera.

yeasty (yēs′tĭ), *adj.*, **yeastier, yeastiest. 1.** of, containing, or resembling yeast. **2.** frothy or foamy. **3.** trifling or frivolous. —**yeast′ily,** *adv.* —**yeast′iness,** *n.*

Yeats (yāts), *n.* **William Butler,** 1865–1939, Irish poet, dramatist, and essayist.

Yeddo (yĕd′ō, yĕd′dō′), *n.* former name of **Tokyo.** Also, **Yedo.**

yegg (yĕg), *n.* *U.S. Slang.* **1.** a burglar, esp. a petty one. **2.** a thug. Also, **yeggman.** [orig. obscure; ? var. of *yekk* beggar, a term once popular in California Chinatowns]

yeggman (yĕg′mən), *n.*, *pl.* **-men.** yegg.

Yeisk (*Russ.* yĕysk), *n.* Eisk.

yeld (yĕld), *adj.* *Scot.* (of a cow, etc.) **1.** barren. **2.** not giving milk. [ME; OE *gelde,* c. G *Gelt.* Cf. GELD]

yelk (yĕlk), *n.* *Archaic or Dial.* yolk.

yell (yĕl), *v.i.* **1.** to cry out with a strong, loud, clear sound. **2.** to scream with pain, fright, etc. —*v.t.* **3.** to utter or tell by yelling. —*n.* **4.** a cry uttered by yelling. **5.** *U.S.* a cry or shout of fixed sounds or words, as one adopted by a school or college. [ME *yelle,* OE *gellan, giellan,* c. G *gellen* resound] —**yell′er,** *n.*

Yell (yĕl), *n.* the second largest of the Shetland Islands, Scotland. 1150 pop. (est. 1965); 81 sq. mi.

yellow (yĕl′ō), *adj.* **1.** of a bright colour like that of butter, lemons, etc.; between green and orange in the spectrum. **2.** having the yellowish skin characteristic of the Mongoloid peoples. **3.** denoting or pertaining to the Mongoloid race. **4.** *U.S. Colloq.* (often disparaging) having the yellowish skin characteristic of mulattos or dark-skinned quadroons. **5.** of sallow complexion. **6.** *Colloq.* cowardly; mean or contemptible. **7.** *Colloq.* (of newspapers, etc.) sensational, esp. morbidly or offensively sensational. —*n.* **8.** a hue between green and orange in the spectrum. **9.** the yolk of an egg. **10.** a yellow pigment or dye. —*v.t.*, *v.i.* **11.** to make or become yellow. [ME *yelou,* OE *geolu,* c. G *gelb,* L *helvus*] —**yel′lowish,** *adj.* —**yel′lowness,** *n.*

yellow archangel, a perennial labiate herb with yellow flowers, *Galeobdelon luteum,* occurring in woods throughout Europe.

yellow avens, herb bennet.

yellow-bellied (yĕl′ō bĕl′ĭd), *adj.* *Slang.* cowardly.

yellow-belly (yĕl′ō bĕl′ĭ), *n. Slang.* a coward.

yellowbill (yĕl′ō bĭl′), *n.* geelbek (def. 1).

yellowbird (yĕl′ō bûd′), *n.* **1.** any of various yellow or golden birds, as the golden oriole of Europe. **2.** any of several American goldfinches.

yellow bird's-nest, a non-green, saprophytic herb, *Monotropa hypopitys,* occurring in beech and fine woods of temperate regions.

yellow cress, any of several cruciferous herbs of the genus *Rorippa,* as *R. islandica,* the **marsh yellow cress,** of wet places throughout temperate regions.

yellow fever, *Pathol.* a dangerous, often fatal, infectious febrile disease of warm climates, due to a filterable virus transmitted by a mosquito, *Aëdes* (or *Stegomyia*) *calopus,* and characterized by jaundice, vomiting, haemorrhages, etc. Temporary immunization is possible.

yellow-fin tuna (yĕl′ō fĭn′), an important Pacific food fish, *Neothunnus macropterus.*

yellow flag, a rhizomatous, iridaceous perennial with yellow flowers, *Iris pseudacorus,* occurring in swampy places in Europe and W Asia.

yellow-green (yĕl′ō grēn′), *n.* **1.** a colour about midway between green and yellow in the spectrum. —*adj.* **2.** of the colour yellow-green.

yellowhammer (yĕl′ō hăm′ə), *n.* **1.** the common yellow bunting, *Emberiza citrinella,* of Europe, the male of which is marked with bright yellow. **2.** *U.S. Dial.* the flicker, *Colaptes auratus.* [earlier *yelambre,* f. OE *geolu* YELLOW + *omer* kind of bird (? bunting); *-h-* ? from obs. *yellow-ham,* repr. OE *geolu* YELLOW + *hama* covering (i.e. yellow-feathered bird)]

yellow jack, 1. the (yellow) flag of quarantine. **2.** yellow fever. **3.** any carangoid fish, esp. a Caribbean food fish, *Caranx bartholomaei.*

yellow jacket, any of several social wasps of the family *Vespidae,* having the body marked with bright yellow.

yellow jasmine. See **jasmine.** Also, **yellow jessamine.**

yellow metal, 1. a yellow alloy consisting of approximately three parts of copper and two of zinc. **2.** gold.

yellow peril, 1. the alleged danger of a predominance of the yellow race, with its enormous numbers, over the white race and Western civilization generally. **2.** the yellow race, regarded as presenting such a danger.

yellow pine, 1. any common American pine with a notably strong yellowish wood, usually with needles in clusters of three. **2.** the wood of any such tree.

yellow poplar, the tulip tree, *Liriodendron tulipifera.*

yellow quartz, citrine (def. 3).

yellow rattle, any of several annual, scrophulariaceous herbs of the genus *Rhinanthus,* as *R. minor,* which occurs in grassland of Europe and W Asia.

Yellow River, Hwang Ho.

yellows (yĕl′ōz), *n.* **1.** *Bot.* one of various plant diseases such as **peach yellows, cabbage yellows,** and **aster yellows,** whose most prominent symptom is a loss of green pigment in the leaves. **2.** jaundice, esp. in animals. **3.** *Obs.* jealousy.

Yellow Sea, an arm of the Pacific N of the East China Sea, between China and Korea.

yellow sorrel, any of several oxalidaceous herbs of the genus *Oxalis,* as *O. corniculata,* the procumbent yellow sorrel, a worldwide garden weed.

yellow spot, *Anat.* a small, circular, yellowish area on the retina, opposite the pupil. See diag. under **eye.**

Yellowstone (yĕl′ō stōn′), *n.* a river in the U.S., flowing from NW Wyoming through **Yellowstone Lake** (20 mi. long; ab. 140 sq. mi.) in Yellowstone National Park, and NE through Montana into the Missouri river in W North Dakota: two falls; deep canyon. 671 mi.

Yellowstone National Park, a park in the U.S., in NW Wyoming and adjacent parts of Montana and Idaho: geysers, hot springs, falls, canyon. 3458 sq. mi.

yellow streak, a cowardly trait in a person's character.

yellowtail (yĕl′ō tāl′), *n., pl.* **-tails,** (*esp. collectively*) **-tail.** any of several fishes with a yellow caudal fin, as *Ocyurus chrysurus,* a small snapper of the Caribbean, or the edible *Seriola lalandii* of southern African coasts.

yellow waterlily, a European waterlily, *Wuphar lutea,* with deep yellow, globular flowers and green bottle-shaped fruits.

yellowweed (yĕl′ō wēd′), *n.* **1.** the European ragwort, *Senecio jacobaea.* **2.** *U.S. Dial.* any of certain coarse species of goldenrod.

yellowwood (yĕl′ō wo͝od′), *n.* **1.** the hard, yellow wood of *Cladrastis lutea,* a fabaceous tree found locally in the southern U.S., which bears showy white flowers and yields a yellow dye. **2.** the tree. **3.** any of various other yellow woods, as that of *Podocarpus falcatus,* a large, long-lived tree of southern Africa. **4.** any of the trees yielding these woods.

yellowwort (yĕl′ō wût′), *n.* a small gentianaceous annual herb with yellow flowers, *Blackstonia perfoliata,* occurring on chalk grassland in Europe and SW Asia.

yellowy (yĕl′ō ĭ), *adj.* somewhat yellow.

yelp (yĕlp), *v.i.* **1.** to give a quick, sharp, shrill cry, as dogs, foxes, etc. **2.** to call or cry out sharply. —*v.t.* **3.** to utter or express by, or as by, yelps. —*n.* **4.** a quick, sharp bark or cry. [ME *yelpe,* OE *gelpan* boast; akin to LG *galpen* croak] —**yelp′er,** *n.*

Yemen (yĕm′ən), *n.* **1.** a republic in SW Arabia; formerly a member of United Arab States. 5,000,000 pop. (est. 1965); ab. 75,000 sq. mi. *Cap.:* San'a. **2.** See **South Yemen.**

yen[1] (yĕn), *n., pl.* **yen. 1.** the monetary unit of Japan, equivalent to about £0·0012 sterling. **2.** a coin of this value. [t. Jap., t. Chinese: m. *yüan* a round thing, a dollar]

yen[2] (yĕn), *n., v.,* **yenned, yenning.** *Colloq.* —*n.* **1.** desire; longing. —*v.i.* **2.** to desire. [? alter. of YEARN]

Yenan (yĕ′năn′), *n.* a city in N China, in Shensi province: the capital of Communist China prior to the capture of the city by Nationalist forces, 1947.

Yenisei (yĕn′ĭ sā′ĭ; *Russ.* yĭ nĭ syĕy′), *n.* a river flowing from the S Soviet Union in Asia, N to the Arctic Ocean. ab. 2800 mi.

yeoman (yō′mən), *n., pl.* **-men. 1.** a countryman, esp. one of some social standing, who cultivates his own land. **2.** a petty officer in the Royal Navy (in the U.S. Navy, having chiefly clerical duties). **3.** *Archaic or Hist.* a servant, attendant, or subordinate official in a royal or other great household. **4.** *Archaic or Hist.* a subordinate or assistant, as of a sheriff or other official or in a craft or trade. **5.** *Archaic or Hist.* one of a class of lesser freeholders (below the gentry) who cultivated their own land, early admitted in England to political rights. —*adj.* **6.** of, pertaining to, or characteristic of a yeoman. [ME *yeman, yoman,* f. *ye, yo* (of uncert. orig.) + MAN]

yeomanly (yō′mən lĭ), *adj.* **1.** of the condition or rank of a yeoman. **2.** pertaining to or befitting a yeoman. —*adv.* **3.** like or as befits a yeoman.

yeoman of the guard, 1. a member of the bodyguard of the English sovereign, instituted in 1485, which now consists of 100 men (with their officers), having purely ceremonial duties. **2. Yeomen of the Guard,** this company.

yeomanry (yō′mən rĭ), *n.* **1.** a volunteer cavalry force in Britain, orig. composed largely of yeomen, which became part of the Territorial Army. **2.** yeomen collectively.

yeoman service, good, useful, or substantial service. Also, **yeoman's service.**

Yeovil (yō′vĭl), *n.* a town in England, in Somerset. 24,598 (1961).

Yerba Buena (yĕə′bə bwā′nə, yû′bə-), an island in San Francisco Bay between Oakland and San Francisco, California: a 500-ft two-storey tunnel across this island connects the two spans of the San Francisco–Oakland bridge.

Yerevan (*Russ.* yĭ rĭ vȧn′), *n.* the capital of Armenia, in the S Soviet Union in Europe. Also, **Erevan.** 633,000 (est. 1965).

Yerwa-Maiduguri (yĕə′wə mī do͞o′go͝o rĭ, -mā-), *n.* a town in NE Northern Nigeria. 57,000 (est. 1963).

yes (yĕs), *adv., n., pl.* **yeses.** —*adv.* **1.** (used to express affirmation or assent or to mark the addition of something emphasizing and amplifying a previous statement.) —*n.* **2.** an affirmative reply. [ME; OE *gēse;* appar. f. *gēa* yes + *sī* be it]

yes-man (yĕs′măn′), *n. Colloq.* one who always agrees with his superiors; an obedient or sycophantic follower.

yester (yĕs′tə), *adj. Archaic.* being that preceding the present: *yester sun.*

yester-, 1. being, or belonging to, the day next before the present: *yesterevening, yesternight, yestermorning.* **2.** being that preceding the present: *yesterweek.* [back-formation from YESTERDAY]

yesterday (yĕs′tə dĭ), *adv.* **1.** on the day preceding this day. **2.** a short time ago. —*n.* **3.** the day preceding this day. **4.** time in the immediate past. —*adj.* **5.** belonging or pertaining to the day before or to a time in the immediate past. [ME; OE *geostrandæg,* f. *geostran* (c. G *gestern* yesterday) + *dæg* day]

yestern (yĕs′tən), *adj. Archaic.* yester.

yesteryear (yĕs′tə yĭə′), *adv., n. Chiefly Poetic.* last year.

yestreen (yĕs trēn′), *n., adv. Scot. and Poetic.* contraction of **yesterevening.**

yet (yĕt), *adv.* **1.** at the present time: *don't go yet.* **2.** up to a particular time, or thus far: *he had not yet come.* **3.** in the time still remaining, or before all is done: *there is yet time.* **4.** at this or that time, as previously: *he is here yet.* **5.** in addition, or again: *yet once more.* **6.** moreover: *he won't do it for you nor yet for me.* **7.** even or still (with comparatives): *a yet milder tone.* **8.** though the case be such;

nevertheless: *strange and yet true.* **9. as yet,** up to the present time. **—*conj.*** **10.** and yet, but yet, nevertheless: *it is good, yet it could be improved.* [ME; OE *gīet(a)*, c. MHG *ieze* yet, now (whence G *jetzt*)] **—Syn.** See **but**[1].

yeti (yĕt′ĭ), *n.* the abominable snowman. [t. Tibetan]

Yevtushenko (*Russ.* yĭf to͝o shĕn′kə), *n.* **Yevgeny Aleksandrovich** (*Russ.* yĭv gyĕ′nĭy ə lĭk sän′drə vĭch), born 1933, Soviet poet.

yew (yo͞o), *n.* **1.** an evergreen coniferous tree, of the genus *Taxus*, of moderate height, native of the Old World, western North America, and Japan, having a thick, dark foliage and a fine-grained elastic wood. **2.** the wood of such a tree. **3.** a bow for shooting, made of this wood. [ME *ew*, OE *īw*, *ēow*, c. G *Eibe*, Icel. *ȳr*]

Yezd (yĕzd), *n.* a town in central Iran. 74,170 (est. 1964).

Yezo (yĕz′ō), *n.* former name of **Hokkaido.**

Ygerne (ē gĕən′), *n.* *Arthurian Legend.* Igraine.

Yggdrasil (ĭg′drăs′ĭl), *n.* *Scand. Myth.* the ash tree which binds earth, heaven, and hell. Also, **Igdrasil.**

Y.H.A., Youth Hostels Association.

YHVH. See **Tetragrammaton.** Also, **YHWH.**

Yid (yĭd), *n.* *Offensive.* a Jew.

Yiddish (yĭd′ĭsh), *n.* **1.** a language consisting of a group of closely similar High German dialects, with vocabulary admixture from Hebrew and Slavic, written in Hebrew letters, spoken mainly by Jews in countries E of Germany and by Jewish emigrants from these regions, and now the official language of Birobidzhan, an autonomous Jewish region in the SE Soviet Union in Asia. **—*adj.*** **2.** Jewish. [t. G: m. *jüdisch* Jewish]

yiddisher (yĭd′ĭ shə), *n.* **1.** a Jew. **—*adj.*** **2.** of or pertaining to a Jew; Jewish.

yield (yēld), *v.t.* **1.** to give forth or produce by a natural process or in return for cultivation. **2.** to produce or furnish as payment, profit, or interest. **3.** to give up, as to superior power or authority. **4.** to give up or surrender (oneself) (often fol. by *up*). **5.** to give up or over, relinquish, or resign. **—*v.i.*** **6.** to give a return, as for labour expended; produce or bear. **7.** to surrender or submit, as to superior power. **8.** to give way to influence, entreaty, argument, or the like. **9.** to give place or precedence (fol. by *to*). **10.** to give way to force, pressure, etc., so as to move, bend, collapse, or the like. **—*n.*** **11.** the action of yielding or producing. **12.** that which is yielded. **13.** the quantity or amount yielded. **14.** *Chem.* the ratio of the product actually formed in a chemical process to that theoretically possible, usually expressed as a percentage. [ME *yelde(n)*, OE *g(i)eldan* pay, c. G *gelten* be worth, apply to] **—yield′er,** *n.*
—Syn. 1. furnish, supply, render. **3.** YIELD, SUBMIT, SURRENDER mean to give way or give up to someone or something. To YIELD is to concede under some degree of pressure, if not absolute compulsion, but not to cease opposition: *to yield ground to an enemy.* To SUBMIT is to give up more completely to authority, superior force, etc., and to cease opposition: *to submit to control.* To SURRENDER is to yield complete possession of, relinquish, and cease claim to: *to surrender a fortress, one's freedom, rights.* **12.** produce, harvest, fruit. See **crop. —Ant. 3.** resist.

yielding (yēl′dĭng), *adj.* submissive or compliant. **—yield′ingly,** *adv.* **—yield′ingness,** *n.*

yield point, *Metall.* the stress at which an elongation of the test piece in a tensile test first occurs without increase of load. Also, **yield stress.**

yill (yĭl), *n.* *Scot.* ale.

yin (yĭn), *adj., n., pron.* *Scot.* one.

Yin (yĭn), *n.* one of the two fundamental principles of the universe in Chinese philosophy, regarded as feminine, passive, and yielding. Cf. **Yang.**

Yinchuan (yĭn′chwän′), *n.* a town in NW China. 91,000 (est. 1958).

yip (yĭp), *v.i.*, **yipped, yipping,** *n.* *Chiefly U.S.* yap, as a small dog. [imit.]

yippee (yĭ pē′, yĭp′pē′), *interj.* (an exclamation used to express joy, pleasure, or the like.)

yird (yûd), *n., v.i.* *Scot.* earth.

-yl, a word element used in names of chemical radicals, as in *ethyl.* [comb. form repr. Gk *hýlē* wood, matter]

ylang-ylang (ē′läng ē′läng), *n.* **1.** an aromatic tree, *Canangium odoratum* (or *Cananga odorata*), of the Philippines, Java, etc., bearing fragrant drooping flowers which yield a volatile oil used in perfumery. **2.** the oil or perfume. Also, **ilang-ilang.** [t. Tagalog]

ylem (ī′ləm), *n.* a proposed name for the hypothetical substance out of which all atomic nuclei may have been formed: it would consist chiefly of neutrons and have a density of about 10^{13} grams per cc. [NL, ML basic substance, var. of L *hȳlem*, acc. of *hȳlē*, t. Gk: matter, wood]

Y level, wye level.

Y.M.C.A., Young Men's Christian Association.

Ymir (ē′mĭə), *n.* *Scand. Myth.* a giant, the first created being, progenitor of the race.

yobbo (yŏb′ō), *n.* *Slang.* a loutish, aggressive, or surly youth. Also, **yob** (yŏb).

yodel (yō′dl), *v.*, **-delled, -delling** or (*U.S.*) **-deled, -deling,** *n.* **—*v.t., v.i.*** **1.** to sing with frequent changes from the natural voice to falsetto and back again, in the manner of the Swiss and Tyrolean mountaineers. **—*n.*** **2.** a song, refrain, etc., so sung. Also, **yodle.** [t. G: m. s. *jodeln*] **—yo′deller,** *n.*

yodle (yō′dl), *v.t., v.i.*, **-dled, -dling,** *n.* yodel. **—yo′dler,** *n.*

Yoga (yō′gə), *n.* (*also l.c.*) (in Hindu religious philosophy) the union of the human soul with the Universal Spirit; ascetic practice aiming to effect such union through the withdrawal of the senses from all external objects, often for this purpose employing unfamiliar movements or postures. [t. Hind., t. Skt: lit., union; akin to YOKE]

yogh (yōKH), *n.* the name of the Middle English letter (ȝ), used to represent a voiced or voiceless fricative made against the roof of the mouth; the voiced fricative eventually became *y* or *x* according to whether it was palatal or velar; the voiceless fricative finally came to be written *gh* and this is kept in current spelling, though the old fricative has been lost (as in *light*) or has become an *f* (as in *tough*).

yoghurt (yŏg′ət), *n.* a prepared food of custard-like consistency, sometimes sweetened or flavoured, made from milk that has been curdled by the action of enzymes or other cultures. Also, **yoghourt, yogurt.** Cf. **kumiss.** [t. Turk.]

yogi (yō′gĭ), *n., pl.* **-gis** (-gĭz). one who practises yoga.

yo-heave-ho (yō′hēv′hō′), *interj.* (a chant formerly shouted by sailors when hauling together.)

yo-ho (yō′hō′), *interj., v.*, **-hoed, -hoing. —*interj.*** **1.** (used as a call or shout to attract attention, accompany effort, etc.) **—*v.i.*** **2.** to shout 'yo-ho!'

yoicks (yoiks), *interj.* (a cry used to urge on the hounds in fox-hunting.) [cf. HOICKS]

yoke (yōk), *n., v.*, **yoked, yoking. —*n.*** **1.** a contrivance for joining a pair of draught animals, esp. oxen, usually consisting of a crosspiece with two bow-shaped pieces (oxbow) beneath, one at each end, each bow enclosing the head of an animal. **2.** a pair of draught animals fastened together by a yoke (*pl.* after a numeral, **yokes** or **yoke**): *five yoke of oxen.* **3.** something resembling a yoke or a bow of a yoke in form or use. **4.** a frame fitting the neck and shoulders of a person, for carrying a pair of buckets or the like, one at each end. **5.** *Mach.* a vicelike piece gripping two parts firmly together. **6.** a crosshead attached to the upper piston of an opposed piston engine with rods to transmit power to the crankshaft. **7.** a crossbar on the head of a boat's rudder. **8.** a shaped piece in a garment, fitted about or below the neck, shoulders, or about the hips, from which the rest of the garment hangs. **9.** an emblem or token of subjection, servitude, slavery, etc., as one under which prisoners of war were compelled to pass by the ancient Romans and others. **10.** something that couples or binds together, or a bond or tie. **11.** *Dial.* the time during which a ploughman and his team work at one stretch; a period of ploughing. **12.** *Dial.* a part of the working day. **—*v.t.*** **13.** to put a yoke on; join or couple by means of a yoke. **14.** to attach (a draught animal) to a plough or vehicle; harness a draught animal to (a plough or vehicle). **15.** to join, couple, link, or unite. **16.** *Obs.* to bring into subjection or servitude. **—*v.i.*** **17.** to be or become joined, linked, or united. [ME *yok*, OE *geoc*, c. D *juk*, G *Joch*, Icel. *ok*, L *jugum*] **—yoke′less,** *adj.* **—Syn. 2.** See **pair.**

yokefellow (yōk′fĕl′ō), *n.* **1.** an intimate associate; a partner. **2.** a spouse. Also, **yokemate** (yōk′māt′).

yokel (yō′kl), *n.* a countryman or rustic; a country bumpkin. [orig. uncert.]

Yokohama (yō′kə hä′mə), *n.* a seaport in central Japan, in SE Honshu island, on Tokyo Bay: destructive earthquake, 1923. 1,619,000 (est. 1964). See map under **Hiroshima.**

Yokosuka (yō′kə so͞o′kə), *n.* a seaport in central Japan, in SE Honshu island, on Tokyo Bay: naval base. 310,000 (est. 1964).

Yokuts (yō′kŭts), *n., pl.* **-kuts. 1.** a member of a North American Indian group of small tribes speaking related dialects and occupying the southern half of the Great Valley of California and the adjoining eastern foothill regions. Nearly all the Valley Yokuts are extinct; some foothill groups remain. **2.** a Penutian family of languages spoken by the Yokuts.

yolk (yōk), *n.* **1.** the yellow and principal substance of an egg, as distinguished from the white. **2.** *Biol.* that part of the contents of the egg of an animal which enters directly into the formation of the embryo (**formative yolk,** or archiblast), together with any material which nourishes the embryo during its formation (**nutritive yolk,** deutoplasm, or parablast): distinguished from a mass of albumen (the white of the egg) which may surround it, and from the membrane or shell enclosing the whole. **3.** the essential part; the inner core. **4.** a natural grease exuded from the skin of sheep. [ME *yolke, yelke,* OE *geolca,* der. *geolu* yellow] **—yolk′less,** *adj.* **—yolk′y,** *adj.*

Yom Kippur (yŏm′kĭp′ə), the Day of Atonement, an annual Jewish fast day observed on the tenth day of the month Tishri. See Lev. 16:29–34. [t. Heb: Day of Atonement]

yon (yŏn), *Archaic or Dial.* —*adj., adv.* **1.** yonder. —*pron.* **2.** that or those yonder. [ME; OE *geon,* akin to G *jener* that]

yond (yŏnd), *adv., adj. Archaic or Dial.* yonder. [ME; OE *geond,* c. D *ginds.* Cf. YON, YONDER]

yonder (yŏn′də), *adj.* **1.** being the more distant, or farther. **2.** being in that place or over there, or being that or those over there. —*adv.* **3.** at, in, or to that place (specified or more or less distant); over there. [ME; cf. Goth. *jaindre* there]

yoni (yō′nĭ), *n. Hinduism.* the external female genitalia, considered as the symbol of Sakti. [t. Skt]

Yonkers (yŏng′kəz), *n.* a city in the U.S., in SE New York State, on the Hudson, near New York City. 190,634 (1960).

Yonne (*Fr.* yŏn), *n.* a department in NE central France. 269,826 pop. (1962); 2892 sq. mi. *Cap.:* Auxerre.

yore (yô), *adv., adj. Archaic.* of old; years ago; long ago: now only in the phrase **of yore:** *the knights-errant of yore.* [ME; OE *geāra,* appar. der. *gēar* YEAR]

York (yôk), *n.* **1.** an English royal house, 1461–85. It comprised three kings: Edward IV, Edward V, and Richard III. **2. Edmund of Langley, 1st Duke of,** 1341–1402, son of Edward III of England. **3.** Yorkshire. **4.** Ancient, **Eboracum.** a city in NE England, the county town of Yorkshire; the capital of Roman Britain: cathedral, university. 104,392 (1961). **5. Cape,** a cape at the NE extremity of Australia, at the end of the **Cape York Peninsula** in Queensland.

Yorke Peninsula (yôk), a promontory on the coast of South Australia between Spencer Gulf and Gulf St Vincent; at its tip is **Cape Spencer.** ab. 120 mi. long and 35 mi. wide.

yorker (yô′kə), *n. Cricket.* a ball so bowled that it pitches directly under the bat. [? der. YORKSHIRE]

Yorkist (yô′kĭst), *n.* **1.** an adherent or member of the house of York, esp. in the Wars of the Roses. —*adj.* **2.** belonging or pertaining to the royal house of York. **3.** of or pertaining to the Yorkists.

Yorks., Yorkshire.

Yorkshire (yôk′shĭə, -shə), *n.* a county in N England, divided for administrative purposes into the East Riding, West Riding, and North Riding. 4,725,976 pop. (1961); 6089 sq. mi. *Co. town:* York. *Abbrev.:* **Yorks.**

Yorkshire fog, a tufted perennial grass, *Holcus lanatus,* widespread in Europe and temperate Asia.

Yorkshire pudding, a baked pudding made from batter and served with gravy before or with roast beef.

Yorkshire terrier, a small short-legged terrier with silky hair, golden tan on the head, and bluish or silver on the body.

Yorkshire terrier (8 in. high at the shoulder)

Yorktown (yôk′toun′), *n.* a town in the U.S., in SE Virginia: surrender of Cornwallis to Washington, 1781.

Yoruba (yō′rŏŏ bə), *n., pl.* **-bas,** (*esp. collectively*) **-ba** for 1. **1.** a member of a numerous West African coastal Negro people and linguistic stock. **2.** the language of the Yoruba. **—Yo′ruban,** *adj.*

Yorubaland (yŏ′rŏŏ bə lănd′), *n.* a former kingdom in W Africa, in the E part of the Slave Coast: now a region in SW Nigeria.

Yosemite (yō sĕm′ĭ tĭ), *n.* a deep valley in the U.S., in E California, in the Sierra Nevada Mountains: a part of Yosemite National Park. ab. 7 mi. long.

Yosemite Falls, a series of falls in Yosemite National Park. Upper Fall, 1436 ft high; Middle Fall, 626 ft high; Lower Fall, 320 ft high. Total height (including rapids), 2526 ft.

Yosemite National Park, a national park in E California: waterfalls, sequoia trees, etc. 1162 sq. mi.

Yoshihito (yō′shĭ hē′tō), *n.* 1879–1926, emperor of Japan, 1912–26 (son of Emperor Mutsuhito).

you (yōō), *pron., poss.* **your** or **yours,** *obj.* **you,** *n., pl.* **yous.** —*pron.* **1.** the ordinary pronoun of the second person, orig. the objective (plural) of *ye,* but now used regularly as either objective or nominative, and with either plural or singular meaning, but always, when used as subject, taking a plural verb. **2.** one; anyone; people in general. —*n.* **3.** something resembling or closely identified with the person addressed: *that dress simply isn't you.* [ME; OE *ēow,* c. D *u*]

you'all (yōō ôl′), *pron. Chiefly Southern U.S.* you (used in addressing two or more persons): *you'all can come to dinner tomorrow.*

you'd (yōōd), contraction of *you had* or *you would.*

you'll (yōōl), contraction of *you will* or *you shall.*

young (yŭng), *adj.* **1.** being in the first or early stage of life, or growth; youthful; not old. **2.** having the appearance, freshness, vigour, or other qualities of youth. **3.** of or pertaining to youth: *in one's young days.* **4.** inexperienced. **5.** not far advanced in years in comparison with another or others. **6.** junior (applied to the younger of two persons of the same name). **7.** being in an early stage generally, as of existence, progress, operation, etc.; new; early. **8.** representing or advocating recent or progressive tendencies, policies, or the like. —*n.* **9.** young offspring. **10.** young people collectively. **11. with young,** pregnant. [ME *yong,* OE *geong,* c. G *jung*] **—young′ish,** *adj.*

—Syn. 1. YOUNG, YOUTHFUL both refer to lack of years and to inexperience. YOUNG is the general word for that which is undeveloped, immature, and in process of growth: *a young colt, child, shoots of wheat.* YOUTHFUL has connotations suggesting the favourable characteristics of youth, such as vigour, enthusiasm, and hopefulness: *youthful sports, energy.* **—Ant. 1.** mature, old.

Young (yŭng), *n.* **1. Brigham,** 1801–77, U.S. Mormon leader. **2. Edward,** 1683–1765, English poet.

youngberry (yŭng′bə rĭ, -brĭ), *n., pl.* **-ries.** *Hort.* the large, dark purple, sweet fruit of a trailing blackberry in the south-western U.S., a cross between several blackberries. [named after B. M. *Young,* U.S. fruitgrower, who developed it]

young blood, youthful people, ideas, practices, etc.

young-eyed (yŭng′īd′), *adj.* **1.** clear-eyed; bright-eyed. **2.** having a youthful outlook; enthusiastic; fresh.

Younghusband (yŭng′hŭz′bənd), *n.* **Sir Francis,** 1863–1942, English explorer.

Young Italy, a secret society in Italy, founded by Mazzini in 1831 to replace the Carbonari.

youngling (yŭng′lĭng), —*n.* **1.** a young person. **2.** anything young, as a plant, etc. **3.** a novice; a beginner. —*adj.* **4.** young; youthful. [ME *yongling,* OE *geongling,* c. G *Jüngling.* See YOUNG, -LING[1]]

Young Pretender, Charles Edward Stuart, grandson of James II of England, and son of James, the Old Pretender, whose landing in Scotland precipitated the rebellion of 1745. Also, **Young Chevalier.**

Young's modulus (yŭngz), *Physics.* the modulus of elasticity of a material in tension or compression, equal to the ratio of the stress applied to a wire or rod of the material to the longitudinal strain produced. [named after Thomas *Young,* 1773–1829, English physicist]

youngster (yŭng′stə), *n.* **1.** a child. **2.** a young person. **3.** a young horse or other animal. **4.** (in the Royal Navy) a midshipman of less than four years' standing. **5.** (in the U.S. Naval Academy) a midshipman in his second year.

Youngstown (yŭngz′toun′), *n.* a town in the U.S., in NE Ohio. 166,689 (1960).

Young Turk, 1. a member of a Turkish reformist and nationalist party founded in the latter half of the 19th century, which was the dominant political party in Turkey from 1908–18. **2.** any person in a political party who agitates for radical reforms.

younker (yŭng′kə), *n.* **1.** *Archaic.* a youngster. **2.** *Obs.* a young gentleman or knight. [t. MD: m. *jonchere* (f. *jonc* young + *here* master), c. G *Junker*]

your (yô, yōōə), *pron.* **1.** the possessive form of *you, ye,* used before a noun. **2.** (used to indicate all members of a particular group): *your suburban housewife; your typical old-age pensioner.* Cf. **yours.** [ME; OE *ēower* (gen. of *gē* YE), c. G *euer*]

you're (yōōə, yô), contraction of *you are.*

yours (yôz, yōōəz), *pron.* form of *your* used predicatively or without a noun following.

yourself (yô sĕlf′, yōōə-), *pron., pl.* **-selves. 1.** a reflexive form of *you*: *you've cut yourself.* **2.** an emphatic form of *you* or *ye* used **a.** as object: *you took it for yourself.* **b.** in apposition to a subject or object: *you yourself did it.* **3.** your proper or normal self: *you'll soon be yourself again.*

yours truly, 1. a conventional phrase used at the end of a letter. **2.** *Colloq.* I, myself, or me.

youth (yōōth), *n., pl.* **youths** (yōōthz), (*collectively*) **youth. 1.** the condition of being young, or youngness. **2.** the appearance, freshness, vigour, spirit, etc., characteristic of one that is young. **3.** the time of being young; early life. **4.** the period of life from puberty to the attainment of full growth; adolescence. **5.** the first or early period of anything. **6.** young persons collectively. **7.** a young person,

esp. a young man. [ME *youthe*, OE *geoguth*, c. G *Jugend*] —**youth′less,** *adj.*
youthful (yo͞oth′fəl), *adj.* **1.** characterized by youth; young. **2.** of, pertaining to, or befitting youth. **3.** having the appearance, freshness, vigour, etc., of youth. **4.** early in time. **5.** *Phys. Geog.* (of topographical features) having advanced in reduction of the land surface by erosion, etc., to a slight extent only. —**youth′fully,** *adv.* —**youth′fulness,** *n.* —**Syn. 3.** See **young.**
youth hostel, a simple lodging place for young travellers.
you've (yo͞ov), contraction of *you have*.
yow (you), *interj.*, *n.* (a shout of pain, dismay, etc.)
yowl (youl), *v.i.* **1.** to utter a long distressful or dismal cry, as an animal or a person; howl. —*n.* **2.** a yowling cry; a howl. [ME *yowle*, earlier *yuhele*, appar. der. OE *gēoh*- in *gēohthu* care, sorrow]
yoyo (yō′yō′), *n.*, *pl.* **-yos.** a toy, consisting of a round, flat-sided block of wood, plastic, etc., with a groove round the edge, in which a string is wound. The yoyo is spun out and reeled in by the string, one end of which remains attached to the finger.
yperite (ē′pə rīt′), *n.* mustard gas. [named after YPRES]
Ypres (*Fr.* ē′pr), *n.* a town in Belgium, in S West Flanders: the scene of many battles, 1914–18. 18,461 (1966). Flemish, **Ieper.**
Ypsilanti (ĭp′sĭ lăn′tĭ), *n.* **1. Prince Alexander,** 1792–1828, Greek patriot and revolutionary leader. **2.** his brother, **Demetrios** (dĭ mē′trĭ ŏs′), 1793–1832, Greek patriot and revolutionary leader. Also, **Ypsilantis, Ypselantes** (ĭp′sĭ lăn′tĭs).
Yquem (*Fr.* ē kĕm′), *n.* Château d'Yquem.
yr, **1.** year. **2.** your.
yrs, **1.** years. **2.** yours.
Yser (*Fr.* ē zĕr′), *n.* a river flowing from N France through NW Belgium into the North Sea: battles, 1914–18. 55 mi.
Yseult (ĭ so͞olt′), *n.* *Arthurian Legend.* Iseult.
Yt, *Chem.* yttrium.
Y.T., Yukon Territory.
ytterbia (ĭ tû′byə), *n.* *Chem.* ytterbium oxide, Yb_2O_3, which is white and forms colourless salts. [t. NL, g. *Ytterb(y)* in Sweden, where found + -IA. Cf. ERBIUM, TERBIUM, TERBIA, YTTRIA]
ytterbite (ĭ tû′bīt), *n.* gadolinite.
ytterbium (ĭ tû′byəm), *n.* *Chem.* a rare metallic element found in the mineral gadolinite, and forming compounds resembling those of yttrium. *Symbol:* Yb; *at. wt:* 173·04; *at. no.:* 70. [t. NL; f. YTTERB(ITE) + -IUM] —**ytter′bic,** *adj.*
yttria (ĭt′rĭ ə), *n.* *Chem.* a white insoluble oxide of yttrium, Y_2O_3, used in making incandescent mantles. [NL, der. *Ytter(by)* in Sweden]
yttriferous (ĭ trĭf′ə rəs), *adj.* yielding or containing yttrium.
yttrium (ĭt′rĭ əm), *n.* *Chem.* a rare trivalent metallic element, found in gadolinite and other materials. *Symbol:* Y or Yt; *at. wt:* 88·905; *at. no.:* 39; *sp. gr.:* 5·5. See **rare-earth elements.** [t. NL: f. YTTR(IA) + -IUM] —**yt′tric,** *adj.*
yttrocerite (ĭt′rə sĭə′rīt), *n.* a blue mineral, calcium fluoride, which contains metals of the yttrium and cerium groups.
yttrotantalite (ĭt′rə tăn′tə līt′), *n.* a dark brown mineral tantalite of yttrium, which also contains iron, cerium, and niobates.
yuan (yo͞o ăn′), *n.* **1.** the unit of currency of the People's Republic of China, equivalent to about £0·17 sterling; jenminpi. **2.** a banknote of this value. **3.** a copper coin of Nationalist China, equivalent to about £0·01 sterling. **4.** (*usually cap.*) (formerly in China) a department of government, or a council.
Yüan Shih-kai (yo͞o än′ shē′kī′), 1859–1916, president of China, 1912–16.
Yucatán (yo͞o′kə tăn′; *Sp.* yo͞o kä tän′), *n.* a peninsula comprising parts of SE Mexico, N Guatemala, and British Honduras. See map under **Tehuantepec.**
yucca (yŭk′ə), *n.* any liliaceous plant of the genus *Yucca*, of the warmer regions of America, having pointed usually rigid leaves, and whitish flowers in terminal central racemes. [t. NL, t. Sp.: m. *yuca*, t. Arawak]
Yüen (yo͞o ĕn′), *n.* a river in S China flowing NE to Tungting. ab. 500 mi. Also, **Yüan.**
Yuga (yo͞o′gə), *n.* (in Hindu use) **1.** an age of time. **2.** one of four ages distinguished in a period of the world's existence, the first being a golden age, with deterioration in those following. [t. Skt: age, orig. yoke]
Yugo., Yugoslavia.
Yugoslav (yo͞o′gō släv′), *n.* **1.** a native or inhabitant of Yugoslavia. **2.** a southern Slav; a member of the southern group of Slavic peoples. —*adj.* **3.** of or pertaining to the Yugoslavs. Also, **Jugoslav, Jugo-Slav.** 
Yugoslavia (yo͞o′gō slä′vyə), *n.* a republic in S Europe: formed in 1918 from the kingdoms of Serbia and Montenegro and part of Austria-Hungary. 18,549,291 pop. (1961); 98,725 sq. mi. *Cap.:* Belgrade. Also, **Jugoslavia.** —**Yu′gosla′vian,** *adj.*, *n.* —**Yu′gosla′vic,** *adj.*

AUSTRIA
HUNGARY
RUMANIA
Belgrade
YUGOSLAVIA
ADRIATIC SEA
ALBANIA

Yugoslavia

Yukon (yo͞o′kŏn), *n.* **1.** a river flowing from NW Canada generally W through central Alaska to the Bering Sea. ab. 2300 mi. **2.** a territory in NW Canada. 14,628 pop. (1961); 207,076 sq. mi. *Cap.:* Whitehorse.
yule (yo͞ol), *n.* Christmas, or the Christmas season. [ME *yole*, OE *geōl(a)* Christmastide, c. Icel. *jōl*]
yule log, a large log of wood which traditionally formed the foundation of the fire at Christmas. Also, **yule block, yule clog.**
yuletide (yo͞ol′tīd′), *n.* the Christmas season.

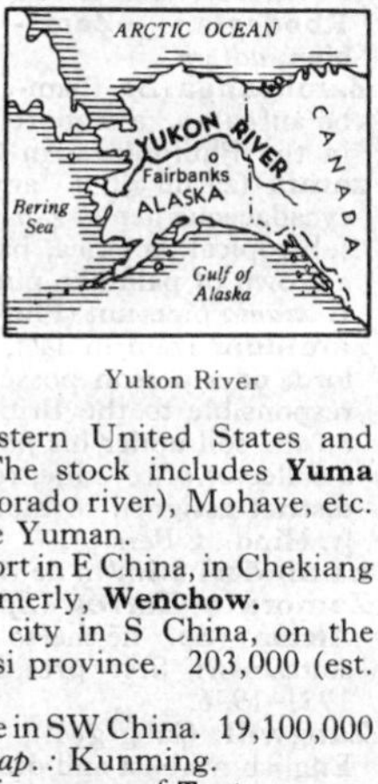

ARCTIC OCEAN
YUKON RIVER
CANADA
Fairbanks
ALASKA
Bering Sea
Gulf of Alaska

Yukon River

Yuman (yo͞o′mən), *n.* **1.** a North American Indian linguistic stock of the south-western United States and northern Lower California. The stock includes **Yuma** (a specific tribe of the lower Colorado river), Mohave, etc. —*adj.* **2.** of or pertaining to the Yuman.
Yungkia (yo͝ong′kyä′), *n.* a seaport in E China, in Chekiang province. 157,000 (1960). Formerly, **Wenchow.**
Yungning (yo͝ong′nĭng′), *n.* a city in S China, on the river Si: the capital of Kwangsi province. 203,000 (est. 1950).
Yünnan (yo͞o′năn′), *n.* a province in SW China. 19,100,000 pop. (1957); 162,342 sq. mi. *Cap.:* Kunming.
Yurev (*Russ.* yo͞or′yĭf), *n.* Russian name of **Tartu.**
Yuzovka (*Russ.* yo͞o′zəf kə), *n.* former name (until 1918) of **Donetsk.** See **Stalino.**
Yvelines (*Fr.* ēv lēn′), *n.* a department in N France. 800,000 pop. (est. 1965); 876 sq. mi. *Cap.:* Versailles.
Y.W.C.A., Young Women's Christian Association.
ywis (ĭ wĭs′), *adv.* *Obs.* iwis.

Z

Z, z (zĕd), *n.*, *pl.* **Z's** or **Zs, z's** or **zs.** a consonant, the 26th letter of the English alphabet. See **izzard, zed** (def. 1).
Z, **1.** *Chem.* atomic number. **2.** *Astron.* zenith distance. **3.** Also, **z.** zone.
z, **1.** an unknown quantity. **2.** zone.
Zaandam (*Du.* zän dŏm′), *n.* a town in the W Netherlands, in North Holland, on the river **Zaan.** 53,557 (1965).
zabaglione (zăb′ə lyō′nĭ; *It.* zä bäl lyô′nĕ), *n.* a cream mousse of Italian origin composed of egg yolks, sugar, and wine, usually Marsala. French, **sabayon.**
Zabrze (*Pol.* zäb′zhĕ), *n.* a city in SW Poland: formerly in Germany. 200,000 (est. 1964). German, **Hindenburg.**
Zacharias (zăk′ə rī′əs), *n.* *Bible.* the father of John the Baptist (Luke 1:5). Also, **Zachariah** (zăk′ə rī′ə), **Zachary** (zăk′ə rĭ).
zack (zăk), *n.* *Austral. Slang.* sixpence.
Zacynthos (zä′kĭn thŏs′), *n.* Greek name of **Zante** (def. 1).
Zadar (*Serb.* zä′där), *n.* a seaport in W Yugoslavia, on the Dalmatian coast: formerly, with surrounding territory, it constituted an exclave of Italy. 22,000 (est. 1959). Formerly, **Zara.**
Zadkine (*Russ.* tsät′kĭn), *n.* **Ossip** (*Russ.* ô′sĭp), 1890–1967, Russian sculptor, in France.

zaffre (zăf′ə), *n.* an artificial mixture containing cobalt oxide and usually silica, used to produce a blue colour in glass and other ceramic products (related to *smalt*). Also, **zaffer.** [t. F: m. *zafre*, ult. t. Ar.: m. *sufr* yellow copper, influenced by *za'farān* saffron. Cf. SAPPHIRE]

Zagazig (zăg′ə zĭg), *n.* a town in N Egypt, in the Nile delta. 124,000 (1960).

Zagreb (zä′grĕb), *n.* a city in NW Yugoslavia: the capital of Croatia. 457,499 (1961). German, **Agram.**

Zahir Shah (zĭ′ĭə shä′), **Mohammed,** born 1914, king of Afghanistan since 1933.

Zahlé (zä lā′), *n.* a town in central Lebanon. 33,000 (est. 1963).

zaibatsu (zī′băt so͞o′), *n.pl. or sing. Japanese.* the great industrial families of Japan.

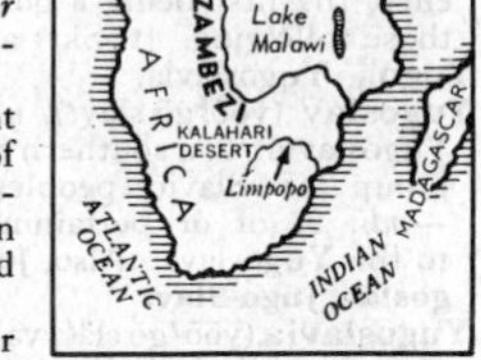

Zambezi

Zama (zä′mə), *n.* an ancient town in N Africa, SW of Carthage: the Romans defeated Hannibal near here in the final battle of the second Punic War, 202 B.C.

Zambezi (zăm bē′zĭ), *n.* a river in southern Africa, rising in Zambia, flowing through E Angola, Rhodesia, and Mozambique into the Indian Ocean: Victoria Falls. ab. 650 mi. long. Also, **Zambesi.**

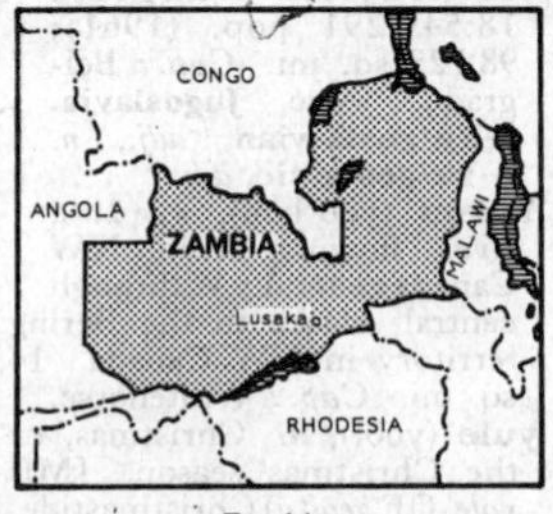

Zambia

Zambia (zăm′byə), *n.* an independent state in central Africa, formerly a British protectorate and part of the Federation of Rhodesia and Nyasaland; member of the Commonwealth of Nations. 3,732,700 pop. (est. 1964); 290,323 sq. mi. *Cap.:* Lusaka. Formerly, **Northern Rhodesia.** —**Zam′bian,** *adj.*, *n.*

Zamboanga (*Sp.* thäm bȯ än′gä), *n.* a seaport in the Philippines, in SW Mindanao. 131,489 (1960).

zamia (zā′mĭ ə), *n.* any of the plants constituting the cycadaceous genus *Zamia*, chiefly natives of tropical and subtropical America, having a short, tuberous stem and a crown of palmlike pinnate leaves. [NL, misreading of L *azānia* pine-nut (Pliny)]

zamindar (zăm′ĭn där′), *n. Indian Hist.* **1.** a native landlord, or a person possessing some property in the soil, responsible to the British government for the land tax on the soil under his jurisdiction. **2.** (under Mogul rule) a collector of revenue, required to pay a fixed sum on the district assigned to him. Also, **zemindar** (zĕm′ĭn där′). [t. Hind., t. Pers.]

zamindari (zăm′ĭn də rĭ), *n.* zemindari.

Zamora y Torres (*Sp.* thä mō′rä ē tōr′rĕs), **Niceto Alcalá** (*Sp.* nē thĕ′tō äl kä lä′), 1877–1949, Spanish statesman: first president of the Spanish Republic, 1931–1936.

Zangwill (zăng′gwĭl), *n.* **Israel** (ĭz′rāl), 1864–1926, English novelist and dramatist.

Zante (zăn′tĭ), *n.* **1.** Greek, **Zacynthos.** one of the Ionian Islands, off the W coast of Greece. 35,451 pop. (1961); 157 sq. mi. **2.** the capital of this island: a seaport. 9506 (1961).

zanthoxylum (zăn thŏk′sĭ ləm), *n.* the barks of various shrubs or trees of the genus *Zanthoxylum*, esp. *Z. americanum* and *Z. clavaherculis*, used in medicine.

Zanuck (zăn′ək), *n.* **Darryl F(rancis)** (dă′rəl), born 1902, U.S. film producer.

zany (zā′nĭ), *adj.*, **-nier, -niest,** *n.*, *pl.* **-nies.** —*adj.* **1.** extremely comical; clownish. **2.** slightly crazy; fantastic or ludicrous. —*n.* **3.** an apish buffoon; clown. **4.** a silly person; simpleton. [t. F: m. *zani*, t. d. It. (Venetian): m. *zanni* clown, lit., Johnny, c. It. *Giovanni* John] —**za′nyism,** *n.*

Zanzibar

Zanzibar (zăn′zĭ bä′), *n.* **1.** an island off the E coast of Africa, off Tanzania, formerly, together with Pemba and adjacent smaller islands, a British protectorate which became an independent state, now part of Tanzania. 165,253 pop. (1958); 640 sq. mi. **2.** a seaport on W Zanzibar. 57,923 (1958).

Zapata (*Sp.* thä pä′tä), *n.* **Emiliano** (*Sp.* ĕ mē lyä′nō), 1877?–1919, Mexican political leader: revolutionary 1911–16.

zapateado (*Sp.* thä pä tĕ ä′dō), *n.* a vigorous Spanish dance for a solo performer, accompanied by much tapping of the heels.

Zaporozhe (*Russ.* zə pä rô′zhyĭ), *n.* a city in the SW Soviet Union, in Europe, on the river Dnieper. 550,000 (est. 1965). Formerly, **Aleksandrovsk.**

Zara (zä′rə; *It.* dzä′rä), *n.* former name of **Zadar.**

Zaragoza (*Sp.* thä rä gō′thä), *n.* Spanish name of **Saragossa.**

Zarathustra (ză′rə tho͞os′trə), *n.* Zoroaster. —**Zarathustrian** (ză′rə tho͞os′trĭ ən), *adj.*, *n.*

zaratite (ză′rə tīt′), *n.* a green mineral, hydrated nickel carbonate, often occurring with chromite and magnetite. [t. Sp.: m. *zaratita*, der. surname *Zarate.* See -ITE[1]]

zareba (zə rē′bə), *n.* (in the Sudan and adjoining regions) a protective enclosure, as of thorn bushes. Also, **zareeba.** [t. Ar.]

zarf (zäf), *n.* a cuplike holder, usually of ornamental metal, for a coffee cup without a handle, as used in the Levant. [t. Ar.: vessel]

Z

Z, Zarf

Zaria (zä′rĭ ə), *n.* a town in N central Nigeria. 54,000 (est. 1963).

Zarqa (zä′kə), *n.* a town in Jordan, NE of Amman. 130,000 (est. 1965).

zarzuela (zä zwā′lə; *Sp.* thär thwĕ′lä), *n.* a traditional type of Spanish entertainment, usually satirical, in the form of an operetta.

Zavier (zā′vĭ ə, zăv′ĭ-), *n.* See **Xavier,** St Francis.

Zea (zē′ə), *n.* Kea.

zeal (zēl), *n.* ardour for a person, cause, or object; eager desire or endeavour; enthusiastic diligence. [ME *zele*, t. L: m. *zēlus*, t. Gk: m. *zêlos*, der. *zéein* boil]

Zealand (zē′lənd), *n.* the largest island of Denmark: Copenhagen is situated here. 1,855,102 pop. (est. 1954) 2709 sq. mi. Also, **Seeland.** Danish, **Sjælland.**

zealot (zĕl′ət), *n.* **1.** one who displays zeal. **2.** one carried away by excess of zeal. **3.** *Colloq.* a religious fanatic. **4.** (*cap.*) (in the 1st century A.D) a member of a society vowed to liberate the Jewish people from Roman domination, who attempted to do so by force. [t. LL: m. s. *zēlōtēs*, t. Gk, der. *zêlos* zeal]

zealotry (zĕl′ə trĭ), *n.* undue or excessive zeal; fanaticism.

zealous (zĕl′əs), *adj.* full of, characterized by, or due to zeal; ardently active, devoted, or diligent. —**zeal′ously,** *adv.* —**zeal′ousness,** *n.*

zebec (zē′bĕk), *n.* xebec. Also, **zebeck.**

Zebedee (zĕb′ĭ dē′), *n.* father of the apostles James and John (Matt. 4:21).

zebra (zē′brə, zĕb′rə), *n.* a wild, horselike animal, fully and regularly striped with dark bands on a light ground, or with alternating dark and light bands, occurring in three species, each with its own characteristic pattern of markings: the **mountain zebra,** *Equus zebra*, of southern Africa; the **common zebra,** *E. burchelli*, of southern, central, and eastern Africa; and **Grevy's zebra,** *E. grevyi*, of north-eastern Africa. [t. Congolese] —**zebrine** (zē′brīn, zĕb′rīn), *adj.*

Zebra, *Equus burchelli* (4 ft high at the shoulder)

zebra crossing, a pedestrian crossing marked with broad black and white stripes.

zebra-fish (zē′brə fĭsh′, zĕb′rə-), *n.* a popular egg-laying aquarium fish, *Brachydanio rerio*, with zebra-like stripes.

zebrawood (zē′brə wo͝od′), *n.* **1.** the striped hardwood of a tropical American tree, *Connarus guianensis*, used for cabinetwork, etc. **2.** the tree itself. **3.** any of various similar woods or trees.

zebu (zē′bo͞o), *n.* a bovine animal, *Bos indicus*, varying greatly in size and colour in different breeds, but having a characteristic large hump (sometimes double) over the shoulders and a very large dewlap: widely domesticated in India, China, eastern Africa, etc. [t. F; orig. uncert.]

Zebu, *Bos indicus* (6 ft high at the shoulder)

zecchino (zĕ kē′nō), *n.*, *pl.* **-ni** (-nē). sequin (def. 2). Also, **zechin** (zĕk′ĭn).

Zech., Zechariah.

Zechariah (zĕk′ə rī′ə), *n.* **1.** a Hebrew prophet of the sixth century (fl. 520 B.C.). **2.** a book of the Old Testament bearing his name.

b., blend of, blended; c., cognate with; d., dialect, dialectal; der., derived from; f., formed from; g., going back to; m., modification of; r., replacing; s., stem of; t., taken from; ?, perhaps. See full key on inside front cover.

zed (zĕd), *n.* **1.** a name for the letter Z. **2.** a Z-shaped bar. [ME, t. F: m. *zède*, t. L: m. *zēta*, t. Gk]

zedoary (zĕd′ō ə rĭ), *n.* an East Indian drug consisting of the rhizome of either of two species of curcuma, *Curcuma zedoaria* or *C. aromatica*, used as a stimulant. [late ME, t. ML: m. s. *zedoārium*, t. Ar.: m. *zedwār*]

zee (zē), *n. Chiefly U.S.* a name for the letter Z.

Zeebrugge (zē′brŏŏg′ə; *Du.* zė′brY KHə), *n.* a seaport in NW Belgium, connected with Bruges by a ship canal: German submarine base in World War I.

Zeeland (zē′lənd; *Du.* zė′lŏnt), *n.* a province in the SW Netherlands, consisting almost entirely of islands. 290,178 pop. (1964); 1041 sq. mi. *Cap.:* Middelburg.

Zeeman effect (zē′mən), *Spectroscopy.* the splitting of spectral lines into components when the light source is operated in a magnetic field. [named after P. *Zeeman*, 1865–1943, Dutch physicist]

Zeffirelli (zĕf′ə rĕl′ĭ; *It.* zĕf fē rĕl′lē), *n.* **Franco** (*It.* frȧn′kō), born 1923, Italian film and theatrical producer and designer.

zein (zē′ĭn), *n. Biochem.* a protein found in maize, yielding on hydrolysis mainly glutamic acid and bucine. [f. NL *zē(a)* maize (in L, spelt) + -IN²]

Zeist (*Du.* zĕyst), *n.* a town in the Netherlands, in Utrecht province. 55,034 (1965).

Zeitgeist (*Ger.* tsīt′gīst), *n. German.* the spirit of the time; general drift of thought or feeling characteristic of a particular period of time. [G: time-spirit]

zemindari (zĕm′ĭn də rĭ), *n.* one of the principal systems of land tenure in India, in which land is held by one or more persons in large estates and there may be intermediaries between the tenant and the government. See **mahalwari, ryotwari.** Also, **zamindari.** [t. Hind.]

Zemstrom (zĕm′strəm), *n.* (in the Soviet Union) an elective assembly of a local district or of a province, having the supervision and regulation of affairs within its territory.

zemstvo (zĕm′stvō; *Russ.* zyĕm′stfə), *n., pl.* **-stvos** (-stvōz). *Russian Hist.* one of the district councils founded by Alexander II in 1864, to replace the abolished authority of the nobles, containing the core of the liberal movement from 1905–17.

Zen (zĕn), *n.* a Buddhist sect, popular in Japan (where it was introduced from China in the 12th century), advocating self-contemplation as the key to the understanding of the universe. [Jap., t. Chinese: m. *ch'an*, t. Pali: m. *jhāna*, Skt *dhyāna* religious meditation]

zenana (zĕ nä′nə), *n.* (in India and Persia) **1.** that part of the house in which the women and girls of a family are secluded. **2.** its occupants collectively. [t. Hind., t. Pers.: m. *zanāna*, der. *zan* woman]

Zend (zĕnd), *n.* **1.** the translation and exposition, in a later form of Persian (Pahlavi), of the Zoroastrian Avesta. **2.** *Rare.* Avestan. **—Zendic** (zĕn′dĭk), *adj.*

Zend-Avesta (zĕnd′ə vĕs′tə), *n.* the Avesta, including the traditional exposition, the Zend. [t. Parsee: alter. of *Avesta-va-Zend* AVESTA with commentary]

Zener diode (zē′nə), *Electronics.* a diode which has a stable Zener voltage which is used for a reference. [named after Clarence Melvin *Zener*, born 1905, U.S. physicist]

Zener voltage, *Electronics.* the voltage at which the insulating properties of a semiconductor break down.

zenith (zĕn′ĭth), *n.* **1.** the point of the celestial sphere vertically above any place or observer, and diametrically opposite to the nadir. **2.** highest point or state; culmination. [ME *senyth*, t. ML: m. *cenit*, ult. t. Ar.: m. *semt ar-rās*, lit., way over the head] **—zen′ithal,** *adj.*

zenithal projection, *Cartog.* azimuthal projection.

zenith tube, *Astron.* a telescope mounted to point only at the zenith, used at observatories for taking time from the stars.

Zeno of Citium (zē′nō əv sĭt′ĭ əm), *c.* 336–*c.* 264 B.C., Greek philosopher and founder of the Stoic school.

Zeno of Elea, fl. *c.* 475 B.C., Greek philosopher.

Zenobia (zĭ nō′byə), *n.* **Septimia** (sĕp tĭm′ĭ ə), died after A.D. 272, queen of Palmyra in Syria A.D. 267–272.

zeolite (zē′ə līt′), *n.* **1.** any of a group of hydrated silicates of aluminium with alkali metals, commonly occurring as secondary minerals in cavities in igneous rocks. **2.** any similar artificial substance used in water softening by the ion-exchange method. [f. *zeo-* (comb. form repr. Gk *zeein* boil) + -LITE] **—zeolitic** (zē′ə lĭt′ĭk), *adj.*

Zephaniah (zĕf′ə nī′ə), *n.* **1.** a Hebrew prophet of the seventh century B.C. **2.** a book of the Old Testament bearing his name.

zephyr (zĕf′ə), *n.* **1.** a soft, mild breeze. **2.** (*cap.*) *Poetic.* the west wind personified. **3.** any of various things of fine, light quality, as a fabric, yarn, etc. [t. L: s. *zephyrus*, t. Gk: m. *zéphyros*]

zephyr cloth, a light type of material used for women's clothing.

Zephyrus (zĕf′ə rəs), *n.* the west wind personified.

zephyr yarn, a soft worsted yarn used in embroidery and knitting. Also, **zephyr worsted.**

zeppelin (zĕp′ə lĭn; *Ger.* tsĕp′ə lēn), *n.* a large dirigible consisting of a long, cylindrical, covered framework containing compartments or cells filled with gas, and of various structures for holding the engines, passengers, etc. [named after F. von ZEPPELIN]

Zeppelin (*Ger.* tsĕp′ə lēn), *n.* **Ferdinand von** (*Ger.* fĕr′dĭ nȧnt fōn), **Count,** 1838–1917, German general and airship builder.

Zermatt (zûr′măt; *Ger.* tsĕr mȧt′), *n.* a village in S Switzerland, near the Matterhorn: winter sports resort. 5315 ft high.

zero (zĭə′rō), *n., pl.,* **-ros, -roes,** *v.,* **-roed, -roing.** *—n.* **1.** the figure or symbol 0, which stands for the absence of quantity in the Arabic notation for numbers; a cipher. **2.** the origin of any kind of measurement; line or point from which all divisions of a scale (as a thermometer) are measured in either a positive or a negative direction. **3.** naught or nothing. **4.** the lowest point or degree. **5.** *Gram.* a hypothetical affix or other alteration of an underlying form to derive a complex word, not present in the phonemic shape of the word but functioning in the same way as other affixes or alterations in the language; e.g., the plural of *deer* is formed by adding a zero ending (that is, by adding nothing). **6.** *Ordn.* a sight setting for both elevation and windage for any given range. *—v.t.* **7.** *Chiefly U.S.* to adjust (any instrument or apparatus) to a zero point or to an arbitrary reading from which all other readings are to be measured. **8. zero in,** to adjust the sight settings of (a rifle) by calibrated firing on a standard range with no wind blowing. [t. It., t. Ar.: m. *ṣifr* CIPHER]

zero gravity, weightlessness.

zero hour, 1. *Mil.* the time set for the beginning of an attack. **2.** *Colloq.* the time at which any contemplated move is to begin.

zero point energy, *Physics.* the energy possessed by the atoms or molecules of a substance at the absolute zero of temperature.

zest (zĕst), *n.* **1.** anything added to impart flavour or cause relish. **2.** an agreeable or piquant flavour imparted. **3.** piquancy, interest, or charm. **4.** keen relish, hearty enjoyment, or gusto. **5.** the thin outer skin of citrus fruits. *—v.t.* **6.** to give zest, relish, or piquancy to. [t. F: m. *zeste* orange or lemon peel (used for flavouring); orig. unknown] **—zest′less,** *adj.* **—zest′y,** *adj.*

zestful (zĕst′fəl), *adj.* **1.** full of zest. **2.** characterized by keen relish or hearty enjoyment. **—zest′fully,** *adv.* **—zest′fulness,** *n.*

zeta (zē′tə), *n.* the sixth letter (Z, ζ, = English Z, z) of the Greek alphabet.

ZETA (zē′tə), *n. Physics.* a torus-shaped apparatus for studying controlled thermonuclear reactions. [*Z(ero) E(nergy) T(hermonuclear) A(pparatus)*]

Zethus (zē′thəs), *n. Gk Legend.* See **Amphion.**

Zetland (zĕt′lənd), *n.* Shetland Islands.

zeuge (zyōō′gə, zōō′gə), *n., pl.* **zeugen** (zyōō′gən, zōō′gən). a tabular mass of rock, 5–150 ft high, standing up from a stratum of softer rock, formed in a desert by the action of sand-laden winds. [t. G: lit., witness]

zeugma (zyōōg′mə), *n. Gram., Rhet.* a figure in which a verb is associated with two subjects or objects, or an adjective with two nouns, although appropriate to only one of the two, as in 'to wage war and peace'. [t. NL, t. Gk: yoking] **—zeugmatic** (zyōōg măt′ĭk), *adj.*

Zeus (zyōōs), *n.* **1.** the chief god of the ancient Greeks, ruler of the heavens, identified by the Romans with Jupiter. **2.** his statue, by Phidias at Olympia, one of the Seven Wonders of the World.

Zeuxis (zyōōk′sĭs), *n.* fl. *c.* 430–*c.* 400 B.C., Greek painter.

Zhamsarangin (zhăm′sä răng gĭn), *n.* **Sambu** (săm′bōō), born 1895, head of state of the Mongolian People's Republic since 1954.

Zhdanov (*Russ.* zhdȧ′nəf), *n.* a seaport in the SW Soviet Union, in Europe, on the Sea of Azov. 361,000 (est. 1965).

Zhitomir (*Russ.* zhĭ tȧ mĭr′), *n.* a city in the SW Soviet Union, in Europe, in the Ukraine. 120,000 (est. 1963).

Zhivkov (*Bulg.* zhĕf′kŏf), *n.* **Todor** (*Bulg.* tōd′ŏr), born 1911, Bulgarian political leader: prime minister since 1962.

Zhukov (*Russ.* zhōō′kəf), *n.* **Georgi Konstantinovich** (*Russ.* gĭ ôr′gĭy kən stȧn tē′nə vĭch), born 1896, Soviet marshal.

zibeline (zĭb′ə līn′, -lĭn), *adj.* **1.** of or pertaining to the sable. *—n.* **2.** the fur of the sable. **3.** a thick woollen cloth with a flattened hairy nap. Also, **zibelline.** [t. F, t. It.: m. *zibellino*, t. ML: m. *sabellīnus*, der. *sabellum* sable, t. Slav.: m. *sobol.* Cf. SABLE]

zibet (zĭb′ĭt), *n.* a civet, *Viverra zibetha*, of India, the Malay Peninsula, etc. [t. ML: m. s. *zibethum.* See CIVET]

Ziegfeld (zēg′fĕld′), *n.* **Florenz** (flō′rənz), 1867–1932, U.S. theatrical producer.

Ziegler catalysts (zē′glə; *Ger.* tsē′glər), *Chem.* catalysts which promote the polymerization of ethylene and propylene at normal temperatures and pressures, as titanium trichloride. [named after Carl *Ziegler*, born 1897, German chemist]

Ziel (zēl), *n.* **Mount,** a peak in central Australia, the highest point in Northern Territory. 4955 ft.

ziggurat (zĭg′o͝o răt′), *n.* (among the ancient Babylonians and Assyrians) a temple (of Sumerian origin) in the form of a pyramidal tower consisting of a number of storeys, and having about the outside a broad ascent winding round the structure and presenting the appearance of a series of terraces. Also, **zikkurat, zikurat** (zĭk′o͝o răt′). [t. Assyrian: m. *ziggurratu* pinnacle]

zigzag (zĭg′zăg′), *n., adj., adv., v.,* **-zagged, -zagging.** —*n.* **1.** a line, course, or progression characterized by sharp turns first to one side and then to the other. **2.** one of a series of such turns, as in a line or path. **3.** anything in the form of a zigzag. —*adj.* **4.** proceeding or formed in a zigzag. —*adv.* **5.** with frequent sharp turns from side to side. —*v.t.* **6.** to make zigzag, as in form or course; move in a zigzag direction. —*v.i.* **7.** to proceed in a zigzag line or course. [t. F, t. G: m. *Zickzack*, reduplication of *Zacke* point, tooth]

Zigzag lines

Zilpah (zĭl′pə), *n. Bible.* mother of Gad and Asher by Jacob. Gen. 30:10–13.

Zimbabwe (zĭm bä′bwĭ), *n.* the site of ruins in NE Rhodesia discovered in 1868, consisting of **Great Zimbabwe,** and, 8 miles away, a smaller group, **Little Zimbabwe,** probably of Bantu origin, dating possibly from about the 14th or 15th century.

Zimbalist (zĭm′bə lĭst), *n.* **Efrem** (ĕf′rəm), born 1889, U.S. violinist, born in Russia.

Zimmermann (*Ger.* tsĭm′ər män), *n.* **Dominikus** (*Ger.* dō mē′nĭ ko͞os), 1685–1766, German architect.

zinc (zĭngk), *n., v.,* **zincked, zincking** or **zinced** (zĭngkt), **zincing** (zĭng′kĭng). —*n.* **1.** *Chem.* a bluish white metallic element occurring combined as the sulphide, oxide, carbonate, silicate, etc., resembling magnesium in its chemical relations, and used in making galvanized iron, alloys such as brass and die-casting metal, etc., as an element in voltaic cells, and, when rolled out into sheets, as a protective covering for roofs, etc. *Symbol:* Zn; *at. wt:* 65·37; *at. no.* 30; *sp. gr.:* 7·14 at 20°C. **2.** a piece of this metal used as an element in a voltaic cell. —*v.t.* **3.** to coat or cover with zinc. [t. G: m. *Zink*, orig. uncert.] —**zincic** (zĭng′kĭk), **zinck′y,** *adj.*

zincate (zĭng′kāt), *n. Chem.* a salt derived from H_2ZnO_2, the acid form of amphoteric zinc hydroxide.

zinc blende, sphalerite.

zinc chloride, *Chem.* a white crystalline soluble solid, $ZnCl_2$, used as a wood preservative, disinfectant, and for various industrial purposes.

zinc chromate. See **zinc yellow.**

zinc chrome, zinc yellow.

zinc dust, finely divided zinc used as a pigment in protective paints for iron and steel.

zinciferous (zĭng kĭf′ə rəs), *adj.* yielding or containing zinc.

zincify (zĭng′kĭ fī′), *v.t.,* **-fied, -fying.** to cover or impregnate with zinc.—**zin′cifica′tion,** *n.*

zincite (zĭng′kīt), *n.* native zinc oxide, ZnO, a brittle deep red to orange-yellow mineral, usually massive or granular, and an important ore of zinc.

zinckenite (zĭng′kə nīt′), *n.* zinkenite.

zincograph (zĭng′kō grăf′, -gräf′), *n.* **1.** a zinc plate produced by zincography. **2.** a print from such a plate.

zincography (zĭng kŏg′rə fĭ), *n.* the art or process of producing a printing surface on a zinc plate, esp. of producing one in relief by etching away unprotected parts with acid. —**zincog′rapher,** *n.* —**zincographic** (zĭng′kō grăf′ĭk), **zin′cograph′ical,** *adj.*

zinc ointment, *Pharm.* a skin ointment composed of paraffin, white petroleum, and 20 per cent of zinc oxide.

zincous (zĭng′kəs), *adj.* pertaining to zinc.

zinc oxide, *Chem.* a compound of zinc and oxygen, ZnO, having a mild antiseptic and astringent action, used for the treatment of certain skin diseases, and as a pigment.

zinc-spinel (zĭngk′spĭn′əl), *n.* gahnite.

zinc white, a white pigment consisting of zinc oxide, used in paints.

zinc yellow, a yellow pigment consisting of **zinc chromate,** $ZnCrO_4$, used in paints. Also, **zinc chrome.**

zing (zĭng), *n.* **1.** a sharp singing sound. **2.** *Colloq.* vitality; enthusiasm: *she has lots of zing.* —*interj.* **3.** (used to imitate a sharp singing sound.) —**zing′y,** *adj.*

zingara (zĭng′gə rə; *It.* tsēn′gä rä), *n., pl.* **-re** (*It.* -rĕ). *Italian.* a female gipsy.

zingaro (zĭng′gə rō′; *It.* tsēn′gä rō), *n., pl.* **-ri** (-rĭ; *It.* -rē). *Italian.* a gipsy.

zingiberaceous (zĭn′jĭ bə rā′shəs), *adj.* belonging to the *Zingiberaceae*, or ginger family of plants. Also, **zinziberaceous** (zĭn′zĭ bə rā′shəs). [f. s. NL *zingiberāceae* (see GINGER) + -OUS]

zinkenite (zĭng′kə nīt′), *n.* a steel grey mineral with metallic lustre, lead antimony sulphide ($PbSb_2S_4$). Also, **zinckenite.** [t. G: m. *Zinkenit*, named after J. K. L. *Zincken*, 1790–1862, German mining director]

zinkosite (zĭng′kə sīt′), *n.* a mineral, anhydrous zinc sulphate, which occurs in Spain.

zinnia (zĭn′yə), *n.* any of the annual composite plants of the genus *Zinnia*, especially the colourful, cultivated varieties of *Z. elegans*, a native of Mexico. [t. NL, named after J. G. *Zinn*, 1727–59, German botanist]

zinnwaldite (zĭn′wəl dīt′, tsĭn′vəl-), *n.* a brown mineral mica, containing iron, which occurs in association with cassiterite ores. [named after *Zinnwald*, town in S East Germany, where it was first found]

Zinoviev (*Russ.* zĭ nôv′yĭf), *n.* **Grigori Evseevich** (*Russ.* grĭ gô′rĭy yĭv syĕ′yĭ vĭch), 1883–1936, Soviet politician.

Zinovievsk (*Russ.* zĭ nôv′yĭfsk), *n.* former name of **Kirovograd.**

Zion (zī′ən), *n.* **1.** a hill or mount of Jerusalem, the site of the Temple. **2.** the Israelites. **3.** the Jewish people. **4.** Israel as the national home of the Jews. **5.** the theocracy, or Church of God. **6.** heaven as the final gathering place of true believers. Also, **Sion.** [ME and OE *Sion*, t. LL (Vulgate), t. Gk (Septuagint), t. Heb.: m. *tsīyōn*]

Zionism (zī′ə nĭz′əm), *n.* a worldwide movement founded with the purpose of establishing a national home for the Jews in Palestine, which now provides support to the state of Israel. —**Zi′onist,** *n., adj.* —**Zi′onis′tic,** *adj.*

zip (zĭp), *n., v.,* **zipped, zipping. 1.** Also, **zip-fastener.** a fastener consisting of an interlocking device set along two edges to unite (or separate) them when an attached piece sliding between them is pulled, and used in place of buttons, hooks, or the like, on clothing, bags, etc. **2.** *Colloq.* a sudden, brief hissing sound, as of a bullet. **3.** energy or vim. —*v.i.* **4.** to make or move with a zip. **5.** to proceed with energy. —*v.t.* **6.** to fasten with a zip. [imit.]

Zipangu (zĭ păng′go͞o), *n.* Marco Polo's name for Japan.

zip code, *U.S.* a system to speed the delivery of post, whereby a code number consisting of five digits (the first three indicating the state and place of delivery, the last two the post office or postal zone) is written after the address.

zip-fastener (zĭp′fäs′nə), *n.* a zip (def. 1).

zipper (zĭp′ə), *n.* a zip (def. 1).

zippy (zĭp′ĭ), *adj.,* **-pier, -piest.** *Colloq.* lively; bright.

zircon (zû′kŏn), *n.* a common mineral, zirconium silicate, $ZrSiO_4$, occurring in square prismatic crystals or grains of various colours, usually opaque: used as a refractory when opaque and as a gem when transparent. [earlier *cicon*, var. of JARGON², ? t. Pers.: m. *zargūn* gold-coloured]

zirconate (zû′kə nāt′), *n.* a salt of the acid form of zirconium hydroxide.

zirconia (zû kō′nyə), *n. Chem.* an oxide of zirconium, ZrO_2, notable for its infusibility, used as a pigment, abrasive and refractory. [NL. See ZIRCON]

zirconium (zû kō′nyəm), *n. Chem.* a metallic element found combined in zircon, etc., resembling titanium chemically, used in steel metallurgy, as a scavenger, as a refractory, and to create opacity in vitreous enamel. *Symbol:* Zr; *at. wt:* 91·22; *at. no.:* 40; *sp. gr.:* 6·4 at 20°C. [NL. See ZIRCON] —**zirconic** (zû kŏn′ĭk), *adj.*

zirconyl (zû′kə nĭl), *adj. Chem.* containing the radical ZrO.

Ziska (zĭs′kə), *n.* **Jan** (yăn), *c.* 1370–1424, Bohemian general, and leader of the followers of John Huss.

zither (zĭth′ə), *n.* a musical folk instrument consisting of a flat soundbox with numerous strings stretched over it, which is placed on a horizontal surface and played with a plectrum and the fingertips. [t. G, t. L: m. *cithara.* See CITHARA] —**zith′erist,** *n.*

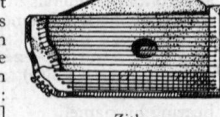

Zither

zithern (zĭth′ən), *n.* **1.** a cittern. **2.** a zither.

zittern (zĭt′ən), *n.* cittern.

zizith (tsĭt′sĭs, tsē′tsēt), *n.pl.* the fringes or tassels of entwined blue and white threads at the four corners of the tallith. See **tallith.** [t. Heb.]

zizz (zĭz), *n. Colloq.* a nap or doze.

Zlatoust (*Russ.* zlə tä ōōst′), *n.* a city in the W Soviet Union, in Asia. 175,000 (est. 1965).

zloty (zlŏt′ĭ; *Pol.* zwŏt′ĭ), *n.*, *pl.* **-tys,** (*collectively*) **-ty. 1.** the monetary unit of Poland, equivalent to £0·1042 sterling. **2.** a coin of this value. *Abbrev.:* Zl. [t. Pol.: lit., golden]

Zn, *Chem.* zinc.

-zoa, plural combining form naming zoological groups as in *Protozoa.* [NL, pl. See ZOON]

Zoan (zō′ăn), *n.* Biblical name of **Tanis.**

zod., zodiac.

zodiac (zō′dĭ ăk′), *n.* **1.** an imaginary belt of the heavens, extending about 8° on each side of the ecliptic, within which are the apparent paths of the sun, moon, and principal planets. It contains twelve constellations and hence twelve divisions (called *signs*), each division, however, because of the precession of the equinoxes, now containing the constellation west of the one from which it took its name. **2.** a circular or elliptical diagram representing this belt, and usually containing pictures of the animals, etc., which are associated with the constellations and signs. **3.** *Rare.* a circuit or round. [ME, t. L: s. *zōdiacus*, t. Gk: m. *zōidiakós* (*kýklos*) circle of the signs, der. *zôion* animal] —**zodiacal** (zō dī′ə kl), *adj.*

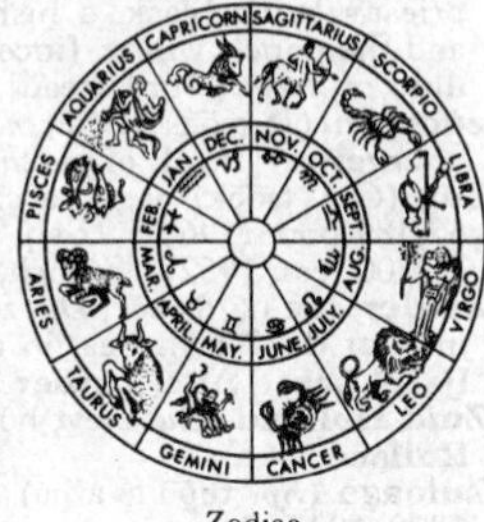

Zodiac

zodiacal light, a luminous tract in the sky, seen in the west after sunset or in the east before sunrise and supposed to be the light reflected from a cloud of meteoric matter revolving round the sun. A faint extension of this light along the ecliptic is called the **zodiacal band.**

zoetrope (zō′ĭ trōp′), *n.* an optical device consisting of a drum with a sequence of pictures on the inside and slits through which the viewer looks. When the drum is spun an illusion of a single moving picture is obtained. Also, **wheel of life.**

zoisite (zoi′sīt), *n.* a mineral, aluminium silicate of calcium, which crystallizes in the orthorhombic system. [named after the discoverer, Baron *Zois* von Edelstein, 1747–1819, Slovenian mineralogist]

Zola (zō′lə; *Fr.* zŏ lȧ′), *n.* **Emile** (*Fr.* ĕ mēl′), 1840–1902, French novelist.

Zollner's lines (zŏl′nəz), parallel lines, intersected by short oblique lines, which appear to converge or diverge. [named after J. K. F. *Zöllner*, 1834–82, German physicist]

Zollverein (*Ger.* tsŏl′fər īn), *n.* **1.** a union which by 1844 included practically all German states, for the maintenance of a uniform tariff on imports from other countries, and of free trading among themselves. **2.** any similar union or arrangement between a number of states; a customs union.

Zomba (zŏm′bə), *n.* a town in and the capital of Malawi. 12,000 (est. 1963). See map under **Malawi.**

zombi (zŏm′bĭ), *n.*, *pl.* **-bis. 1.** the python god among certain West Africans. **2.** the snake god worshipped in the voodoo ceremonies in the West Indies and certain parts of the southern United States. **3.** a supernatural force which brings a corpse to physical life. **4.** a dead body brought to life in this way. **5.** a person thought to resemble the walking dead. **6.** (used derogatorily) a person having no independent judgement, intelligence, etc. Also, **zombie.** [t. West Afr.] —**zom′biism,** *n.*

zonal (zō′nəl), *adj.* **1.** pertaining to a zone or zones. **2.** of the nature of a zone. Also, **zonary** (zō′nə rĭ). —**zon′ally,** *adv.*

zonal soil, one of a group of mature soils in the formation of which climate and vegetation have played a dominant part.

zonate (zō′nāt), *adj.* **1.** marked with a zone or zones, as of colour, texture, or the like. **2.** arranged in a zone or zones. Also, **zon′ated.**

zonation (zō nā′shən), *n.* **1.** zonate state or condition. **2.** arrangement or distribution in zones.

zone (zōn), *n.*, *v.*, **zoned, zoning.** —*n.* **1.** any continuous tract or area, usually circular, which differs in some respect, or is distinguished for some purpose, from adjoining tracts or areas, or within which certain distinguishing circumstances exist or are established. **2.** *Geog.* any of five divisions of the earth's surface, bounded by lines parallel to the equator, and named according to the prevailing temperature (as, the Torrid Zone, extending from the tropic of Cancer to the tropic of Capricorn; the North Temperate Zone, extending from the tropic of Cancer to the Arctic Circle; the South Temperate Zone, extending from the tropic of Capricorn to the Antarctic Circle; the North Frigid Zone, extending from the Arctic Circle to the North Pole; the South Frigid Zone, extending from the Antarctic Circle to the South Pole). **3.** *Phytogeog.*, *Zoogeog.* an area characterized by a particular set of organisms, which are determined by a particular set of environmental conditions, as an altitudinal belt on a mountain such as the alpine zone. **4.** *Geol.* a geological horizon. **5.** *Geom.* a part of the surface of a sphere included between two parallel planes. **6.** a ringlike or surrounding area, or one of a series of such areas, about a particular place, to all points within which a uniform charge is made for transport or some similar service. **7.** *U.S.* the total number of available railway terminals within a given circumference round a given shipping centre. **8.** an area or district under special restrictions or where certain conditions or circumstances prevail: *a military zone; parking-meter zone.* **9.** *Chiefly Poetic.* a girdle, belt, or cincture. —*v.t.* **10.** to encircle with or surround like a zone, girdle, or belt. **11.** to mark with zones or bands. **12.** to divide into zones, tracts or areas, as according to existing characteristics, or as distinguished for some purpose. [t. L: m. *zōna*, t. Gk: m. *zṓnē* girdle] —**Syn. 1.** See **belt.**

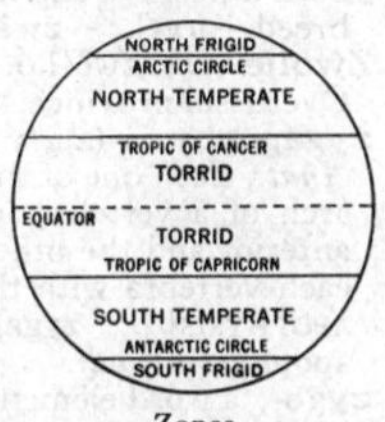

Zones

zone-melting (zōn′mĕl′tĭng), *n.* a process of purifying solids whereby a small portion is heated for a short time by moving it through a heated zone or by moving the zone along the solid. The process is employed to obtain very pure metals for use in transistors.

Zonguldak (*Turk.* zôn′gōōl däk), *n.* a seaport in NW Turkey. 54,010 (1960).

zonule (zō′nyōōl), *n.* a little zone, belt, or band. [t. NL: m. *zōnula*, dim. of L *zōna* girdle]

zoo (zōō), *n.* a park or other large enclosure in which live animals are kept for public exhibition; a zoological garden.

zoo-, a word element meaning 'living being', as in *zoochemistry.* [t. Gk: m. *zōio-*, comb. form of *zôion* animal]

zoochemistry (zō′ə kĕm′ĭs trĭ), *n. Biochem.* the chemistry of the constituents of the animal body; animal chemistry. —**zoochemical** (zō′ə kĕm′ĭ kl), *adj.*

zoogamy (zō ŏg′ə mĭ), *n. Zool.* reproduction by means of gametes; sexual reproduction. —**zoog′amous,** *adj.*

zoogeog., zoogeography.

zoogeography (zō′ə jĭ ŏg′rə fĭ), *n.* **1.** the science of the geographical distribution of animals. **2.** the study of the causes, effects, and other relations involved in such distributions. —**zo′ogeog′rapher,** *n.* —**zoogeographic** (zō′ə jĭə grăf′ĭk), **zo′ogeograph′ical,** *adj.* —**zo′ogeograph′ically,** *adv.*

zoogloea (zō′ə glē′ə), *n. Bacteriol.* a jelly-like mass or aggregate of bacteria formed when the cell walls swell through absorption of water and become contiguous. [f. ZOO- + *gloea* (Latinization of Gk *gloia* glue)] —**zo′ogloe′al,** *adj.*

zoography (zō ŏg′rə fĭ), *n.* that branch of zoology which deals with the description of animals. —**zoographic** (zō′ə grăf′ĭk), **zo′ograph′ical,** *adj.* —**zo′ograph′ically,** *adv.*

zooid (zō′oid), *n.* **1.** *Biol.* any organic body or cell which is capable of spontaneous movement and of an existence more or less apart from or independent of the parent organism. **2.** *Zool.* **a.** any animal organism or individual capable of separate existence, and produced by fission, gemination or some method other than direct sexual reproduction. **b.** one of the individuals, as certain free-swimming medusas, which intervene in the alternation of generations between the products of proper sexual reproduction. **c.** any one of the recognizably distinct individuals or elements of a compound or colonial animal, whether detached or detachable or not. —*adj.* **3.** Also, **zooi′dal.** resembling or of the nature of an animal. [f. ZO(O)- + -OID]

zool., **1.** zoological. **2.** zoologist. **3.** zoology.

zoolatry (zō ŏl′ə trĭ), *n.* **1.** worship of animals. **2.** excessive attention to a domestic pet. —**zool′atrous,** *adj.*

zoological (zō′ə lŏj′ĭ kl), *adj.* **1.** of or pertaining to zoology. **2.** relating to or concerned with animals. Also, **zo′olog′ic.** —**zo′olog′ically,** *adv.*

zoological garden, (*often pl.*) a zoo.

zoologist (zō ŏl′ə jĭst), *n.* one versed in zoology.

zoology (zō ŏl′ə jĭ), *n.*, *pl.* **-gies. 1.** the science that treats of animals or the animal kingdom. **2.** a treatise on this subject. **3.** the animals existing in a particular region. [t. NGk: m. s. *zōiología.* See ZOO-, -LOGY]

zoom (zo͞om), *v.i.* **1.** to make a continuous humming sound. **2.** to move with this sound: *he zooms along in his new car.* **3.** (of prices) to rise rapidly. **4.** *Aeron.* to gain height in an aircraft, in a sudden climb, using the kinetic energy of the aircraft. **5.** *Films, Television, etc.* to use a zoom lens so as to make an object appear to approach (often fol. by *in*) or recede from the viewer. *—v.t.* **6.** to cause (an aeroplane) to zoom. **7.** to fly over (an obstacle) by zooming. *—n.* **8.** the act of zooming. [imit.]

zoometry (zō ŏm′ĭ trĭ), *n.* measurement of the proportionate lengths or sizes of the parts of animals. —**zoometric** (zō′ə mĕt′rĭk), *adj.*

zoom lens, (in a camera or projector) a lens system which can be adjusted so as to give continuously varying magnification of an image without loss of focus.

zoomorphic (zō′ə mô′fĭk), *adj.* **1.** ascribing animal form or attributes to beings or things not animal; representing a deity in the form of an animal. **2.** characterized by or involving such ascription or representation. **3.** representing or using animal forms.

zoomorphism (zō′ə mô′fĭz′əm), *n.* **1.** zoomorphic representation, as in ornament. **2.** zoomorphic conception, as of a deity.

zoon (zō′ŏn), *n., pl.* **zoa** (zō′ə), **zoons.** *Zool.* any of the individuals of a compound organism. [NL, t. Gk: m. *zôion* animal]

-zoon, a combining form of **zoon.**

zoonosis (zō′ə nō′sĭs), *n., pl.* **-noses** (-nō′sēz). any disease which is communicable to man from another animal species.

zoophilous (zō ŏf′ĭ ləs), *adj.* **1.** *Bot.* adapted to pollination by the agency of animals. **2.** loving animals. **3.** (of insects) feeding on animals.

zoophobia (zō′ə fō′byə), *n.* morbid fear of animals.

zoophyte (zō′ə fīt′), *n.* any of various animals resembling a plant, as a coral, a sea-anemone, etc. [t. NL: m. *zōophyton,* t. Gk. See ZOO-, -PHYTE] —**zoophytic** (zō′ə fĭt′ĭk), —**zo′ophyt′ical,** *adj.*

zooplankton (zō′ə plăngk′tən), *n. Zool.* animal plankton.

zooplasty (zō′ə plăs′tĭ), *n. Surg.* the transplanting of living tissue from a lower animal to the human body. —**zo′oplas′tic,** *adj.*

zoosperm (zō′ə spûm′), *n. Bot. Obs.* a zoospore. —**zoospermatic** (zō′ə spû măt′ĭk), *adj.*

zoosporangium (zō′ə spô răn′jĭ əm), *n., pl.* **-gia** (-jĭ ə). *Bot.* a sporangium or spore case in which zoospores are produced. —**zo′osporan′gial,** *adj.*

zoospore (zō′ə spô′), *n.* **1.** *Bot.* an asexual spore, produced by certain algae and some fungi, capable of moving about by means of flagella. **2.** *Zool.* any of the minute motile flagelliform or amoeboid bodies which issue from the sporocyst of certain protozoans. —**zoosporic** (zō′ə-spô′rĭk), **zoosporous** (zō ŏs′pə rəs, zō′ə spô′rəs), *adj.*

zootomy (zō ŏt′ə mĭ), *n.* the dissection or the anatomy of animals. [t. NL: m. s. *zōotomia.* See ZOO-, -TOMY] —**zootomic** (zō′ə tŏm′ĭk), **zo′otom′ical,** *adj.* —**zo′otom′ically,** *adv.* —**zoot′omist,** *n.*

zootoxin (zō′ə tŏk′sĭn), *n.* any poison excreted by an animal, as snake venom. —**zo′otox′ic,** *adj.*

zoot suit (zo͞ot), *Slang.* **1.** *U.S.* a flashy suit consisting of baggy trousers with tight bottoms and an oversized jacket. **2.** any flashy suit.

zori (zô′rĭ), *n.* a low, flat Japanese sandal having thongs passing between the two inner toes. [t. Jap.]

zoril (zŏ′rĭl), *n.* a weasel-like animal of southern Africa, *Ictonyx striatus,* resembling a skunk, and capable of emitting a fetid odour. Also, **zorilla** (zŏ rĭl′ə). [t. F: m. *zorille,* t. Sp.: m. *zorrilla,* dim. of *zorra* fox]

Zorn (*Sw.* sŏrn), *n.* **Anders Leonhard** (*Sw.* ăn′dərs lĕ′ō nărd), 1860–1920, Swedish painter, etcher, and sculptor.

Zoroaster (zŏ′rō ăs′tə), *n.* fl. *c.* 600? B.C. Persian religious teacher. Also, **Zarathustra.**

Zoroastrian (zŏ′rō ăs′trĭ ən), *adj.* **1.** pertaining to Zoroaster, or to the ancient Persian religion founded by him. *—n.* **2.** one of the followers of Zoroaster, now represented by the Gabars and the Parsees.

Zoroastrianism (zŏ′rō ăs′trĭ ə nĭz′əm), *n.* the strongly ethical code founded upon the teaching of Zoroaster, which teaches a continuous struggle between Good, Ormazd, against Evil, Angra Mainyu. Also, **Zo′roas′trism.**

Zorrilla y Moral (*Sp.* thŏr rē′lyä ē mō răl′), **José** (*Sp.* KHō sĕ′), 1817–93, Spanish poet and dramatist.

zoster (zŏs′tə), *n.* **1.** *Pathol.* herpes zoster. **2.** *Gk Antiq.* a belt or girdle. [t. L, t. Gk: girdle]

Zouave (zo͞o äv′, zwäv), *n.* **1.** (*also l.c.*) one of a body of infantry in the French army, composed orig. of Algerians, distinguished for their dash and hardiness, and wearing a picturesque oriental uniform. **2.** a member of any body of soldiers wearing a similar dress. [t. F, from the name of the Algerian tribe from which recruits were mostly drawn]

zounds (zoundz), *interj. Archaic.* (a minced oath, often used as a mere emphatic exclamation, as of surprise, indignation, or anger.) [short for *by God's wounds*]

Zr, *Chem.* zirconium.

Zrenjanin (*Serb.* zrĕn′yä nĕn), *n.* a town in NE Yugoslavia. 55,578 (1961).

Zsigmondy (*Ger.* shĭg′mŏn dē), *n.* **Richard** (*Ger.* rĭKH′ärt), 1865–1929, German chemist, born in Austria.

Zuccari (*It.* tso͝ok′kä rē), *n.* **Federigo** (*It.* fĕ dĕ rē′gō), 1543?–1609, and his brother **Taddeo** (*It.* täd dĕ′ō), 1529–66, Italian painters. Also, **Zuccaro** (*It.* tso͝ok′kä rō), **Zucchero** (*It.* tso͝ok′kĕ rō).

zucchetto (tso͞o kĕt′ō, so͞o-, zo͞o-), *n., pl.* **-tos.** a small, round skullcap worn by Roman Catholic ecclesiastics, a priest's being black, a bishop's violet, a cardinal's red, and the pope's white. [incorrect var. of It. *zucchetta* cap, dim. of *zucca* gourd, head]

zucchini (*It.* tso͞ok kē′nē), *n., pl.* **-ni, -nis.** Italian name for **courgette.** [It, pl. of *zucchino*]

Zug (*Ger.* tso͞ok), *n.* **1.** a canton in central Switzerland. 52,489 pop. (1960); 92 sq. mi. **2.** a town in this canton. 15,700 (est. 1952). French, **Zoug** (*Fr.* zo͞og).

Zuider Zee (zī′də zē′; *Du.* zœy dər zė′), a former shallow inlet of the North Sea, in the central Netherlands; now **IJssel Lake.** Also, **Zuyder Zee.**

Zuid Holland (*Du.* zœyt hô′lŏnt), Dutch name of **South Holland.**

Zuloaga (*Sp.* tho͞o lō ä′gä), *n.* **Ignacio** (*Sp.* ēg nä′thyō), 1870–1945, Spanish painter.

Zulu (zo͞o′lo͞o), *n., pl.* **-lus, -lu,** *adj.* *—n.* **1.** a Bantu people of south-eastern Africa, occupying the coastal region between Natal and Lourenço Marques. **2.** a member of the Zulu nation. **3.** their language. *—adj.* **4.** of or pertaining to the Zulus or their language.

Zululand (zo͞o′lo͞o lănd′), *n.* a territory in the Republic of South Africa, in NE Natal province.

Zuñi (zo͞o′nyē, so͞o′-), *n., pl.* **-ñis.** **1.** (*pl.*) a tribe of North American Indians, of a linguistic stock related to Penutian, inhabiting the largest of the Indian pueblos, in western New Mexico. **2.** a member of this tribe. **3.** the language of this tribe. [t. Sp., t. Keresan: m. *Súnyitsa*] —**Zunian** (zo͞o′nyĭ ən, so͞o′-), *adj., n.*

Zurbarán (*Sp.* tho͞or bä rän′), *n.* **Francisco de** (*Sp.* frän thēs′kō dĕ), 1598–1668, Spanish painter.

Zurich (zyo͝o′rĭk), *n.* **1.** a canton in N Switzerland. 952,304 pop. (1960): 668 sq. mi. **2.** the capital of this canton, on **Lake Zurich** (25 mi. long; 34 sq. mi.). 438,800 (1964). German, **Zürich** (*Ger.* tsY′rĭKH).

Zuyder Zee (zī′də zē′; *Du.* zœy dər zė′). Zuider Zee.

Zwartberg (zwät′bûg′, zwôt′-; *Afrik.* zwŏrt′bĕrKH), *n.* **1.** Also, **Groote Swartberg.** a range of mountains in the Republic of South Africa, in Cape Province; part of the Karoo region. 5000–7000 ft. *—adj.* **2.** of or pertaining to earth movements which occurred in southern Africa in the Upper Karoo and which formed the Cape mountain ranges. Also, **Swartberg.**

Zweig (*Ger.* tsvīk), *n.* **1. Arnold** (*Ger.* är′nŏlt), 1887–1968, German novelist, essayist, and dramatist. **2. Stefan** (*Ger.* shtĕ′fän), 1881–1942, Austrian dramatist, critic, biographer, and novelist.

Zwickau (*Ger.* tsvĭk′ou), *n.* a city in East Germany, in Saxony. 128,505 (1964).

zwieback (zwī′băk, zwē′-; *Ger.* tsvē′bäk), *n.* a kind of bread cut into slices and dried in the oven. [t. G: twice-baked. Cf. BISCUIT]

Zwingli (*Ger.* tsvĭng′lē), *n.* **Ulrich** (*Ger.* o͝ol′rĭKH) or **Huldreich** (*Ger.* ho͝ol′drīKH), 1484–1531, Swiss Protestant reformer.

Zwinglian (zwĭng′glĭ ən, tsvĭng′lĭ-), *adj.* **1.** of or pertaining to Ulrich Zwingli or his doctrines, which were largely in agreement with those of Luther and offered a distinctive, spiritualist interpretation of the Lord's Supper. *—n.* **2.** a follower of Zwingli. —**Zwing′lianism,** *n.* —**Zwing′lianist,** *n., adj.*

zwitterion (tsvĭt′ər ī′ən), *n. Phys. Chem.* an ion carrying both a positive and a negative charge. [f. G *Zwitter* half-breed + ION] —**zwitterionic** (tsvĭt′ə rĭ ŏn′ĭk), *adj.*

Zwolle (*Du.* zwô′lə), *n.* a town in the E Netherlands, in Overijssel province. 58,492 (1965).

zygapophysis (zĭg′ə pŏf′ĭ sĭs, zī′gə-), *n., pl.* **-ses** (-sēz′). *Anat., Zool.* one of the articular processes upon the neural arch of a vertebra, usually occurring in two pairs, one anterior and the other posterior, and serving to interlock each vertebra with the one above and below. [f. ZYG- + APOPHYSIS] —**zygapophyseal** (zĭg′ăp ə fĭz′ĭ əl), **zyg′apophys′ial,** *adj.*

zygo-, a word element meaning 'yoke', especially referring to shape, as in *zygodactyl.* Also, before vowels, **zyg-.** [t. Gk, comb. form of *zygón*]

zygodactyl (zī′gō dăk′tĭl, zĭg′ō-), *adj.* **1.** Also, **zygodactylous.** (of a bird or bird's foot) having the toes disposed in pairs, one pair before and one pair behind on each foot. —*n.* **2.** a zygodactyl bird. —**zy′godac′tylism,** *n.*

Zygodactyl foot

zygoma (zī gō′mə, zĭ-), *n., pl.* **-mata** (-mə tə). *Anat.* **1.** the bony arch below the orbit of the skull, which is formed by the maxillary, jugal, and temporal bones. **2.** Also, **zygomatic process.** a process of the temporal bone forming part of this arch. **3.** the jugal bone. [t. NL t. Gk, der. *zygón* yoke] —**zygomatic** (zī′gō măt′ĭk, zĭg′ō-), *adj.*

zygomatic bone, *Anat.* the malar bone.

zygomorphic (zī′gō mô′fĭk, zĭg′ō-), *adj. Bot.* (of flowers, etc.) divisible into similar or symmetrical halves by one plane only. Cf. **actinomorphic.** Also, **zy′gomor′phous.** —**zy′gomor′phism, zy′gomor′phy,** *n.*

zygophyllaceous (zī′gō fĭ lā′shəs, zĭg′ō-), *adj.* belonging to the *Zygophyllaceae,* or bean caper family of plants. See **bean caper, guaiacum.** [f. s. NL *zygophyllāceae* (der. *Zygophyllum;* see ZYGO-, PHYLLO-) + -OUS]

zygophyte (zī′gō fīt′, zĭg′ō-), *n. Bot.* a plant which is reproduced by means of zygospores.

zygopteran (zī gŏp′tə rən), *Zool.* —*adj.* **1.** of or pertaining to the suborder *Zygoptera,* containing the smaller dragonflies. —*n.* **2.** a member of the *Zygoptera.*

zygosis (zī gō′sĭs, zĭ-), *n. Biol.* the coming together of two apparently identical cells as a prelude to the fusion of two similar gametes; conjugation.

zygospore (zī′gō spô′, zĭg′ō-), *n. Bot.* a cell formed by fusion of two similar gametes, as in certain algae and fungi.

zygote (zī′gōt, zĭg′ōt), *n. Biol.* **1.** the cell produced by the union of two gametes. **2.** the individual developing from such a cell. [t. Gk: m. s. *zygōtós* yoked] —**zygotic** (zī-gŏt′ĭk, zĭ-), *adj.*

zygotene (zī′gə tēn′), *n. Biol.* a phase of meiotic cell division in which the chromosomes come together in pairs.

zymase (zī′mās), *n. Biochem.* an extract obtained from yeast that is capable of fermenting sugar to alcohol and carbon dioxide. It was originally thought to contain a single enzyme, but it is now known that more than a dozen enzymes are involved in the fermentation process. [t. F, der. Gk *zýmē* leaven; modelled on DIASTASE]

zyme (zīm), *n. Obs.* the specific principle regarded as the cause of a zymotic disease. Cf. **zymosis.** [t. Gk: leaven]

zymo-, a word element meaning 'leaven', as in *zymogen.* Also, before vowels, **zym-.** [comb. form repr. Gk *zýmē*]

zymogen (zī′mō jĕn′), *n.* **1.** *Biochem.* any of various inactive precursors which can be converted into an enzyme; enzymogen. **2.** *Biol.* any of various bacterial organisms which produce enzymes. Also, **zymogene** (zī′mō jēn′). [t. G. See ZYMO-, -GEN]

zymogenesis (zī′mō jĕn′ĭ sĭs), *n. Biochem.* the conversion of a zymogen into an enzyme; enzymogenesis.

zymogenic (zī′mō jĕn′ĭk), *adj. Biochem., Biol.* of or pertaining to a zymogen or zymogene.

zymogenic organism, any micro-organism producing an enzyme which causes fermentation.

zymology (zī mŏl′ə jĭ), *n.* enzymology. —**zymologic** (zī′mō lŏj′ĭk), *adj.* —**zymol′ogist,** *n.*

zymolysis (zī mŏl′ĭ sĭs), *n. Biochem.* **1.** the digestive and fermentative action of enzymes. **2.** fermentation or other lytic actions produced by an enzyme; enzymolysis. —**zymolytic** (zī′mō lĭt′ĭk), *adj.*

zymometer (zī mŏm′ĭ tə), *n.* an instrument for ascertaining the degree of fermentation.

zymosis (zī mō′sĭs), *n., pl.* **-ses** (-sēz). **1.** an infectious or contagious disease. **2.** *Obs.* a process analogous to fermentation, by which certain infectious and contagious diseases were supposed to be produced. [t. NL, t. Gk: fermentation]

zymotic (zī mŏt′ĭk), *adj.* **1.** pertaining to, or caused by or as if by fermentation. Cf. **zymosis. 2.** pertaining to a zymotic disease. [t. Gk: m. s. *zymōtikós* causing fermentation]

zymotic disease, *Obs.* an infectious disease, as smallpox, typhoid fever, etc., which was regarded as due to the presence in the body of a morbific principle acting in a manner analogous to fermentation.

zymurgy (zī′mû′jĭ), *n.* that branch of chemistry which deals with fermentation, as in winemaking, brewing, distilling, the preparation of yeast, etc. [f. ZYM(O)- + -URGY]

Zyrian (zĭ′rĭ ən), *n.* a Finno-Ugric language of the Permian group, with written documents from the 13th century.

zzz, (used, esp. by cartoonists, to represent sleep or the sound of snoring.)

Signs and Symbols

Astronomy

1. Astronomical Bodies

☉ **a.** the sun. **b.** Sunday.
⊖ centre of sun.
upper limb of sun.
lower limb of sun.
☿ **a.** Mercury. **b.** Wednesday.
♀ **a.** Venus. **b.** Friday.
⊕, ♁, ⊖ the earth.
☾, ☽ **a.** the moon. **b.** Monday.
● new moon.
☽, ☽, ◐, ☽ the moon, first quarter.
○ full moon.
☾, ☾, ◑, ☾ the moon, last quarter.
☾ upper limb of moon.
☾ lower limb of moon.
♂ **a.** Mars. **b.** Tuesday.
①, ②, ③, etc. asteroids. Each of the known asteroids is designated by a number within a circle, as ① for Ceres, ② for Pallas, etc.
♃ **a.** Jupiter. **b.** Thursday.
♄ **a.** Saturn. **b.** Saturday.
⛢, ♅ Uranus.
♆ Neptune.
P Pluto.
☄ comet.
✳, ∗ star.
α, β, etc. the first, second, etc., brightest star in a specified constellation (fol. by the Latin name of the constellation in the genitive).

2. Signs of Position

☌ in conjunction; having the same longitude or right ascension. Thus, ☌♀☉ signifies the conjunction of Venus and the sun.
⚹ sextile; 60° apart in longitude or right ascension.
□ quadrature; 90° apart in longitude or right ascension.
△ trine; 120° apart in longitude or right ascension.
☍ in opposition; 180° apart in longitude or right ascension. Thus, ☍♂☉ signifies the opposition of Mars and the sun.
☊ ascending node. See **node.**
☋ descending node. See **node.**
♈ vernal equinox.
♎ autumnal equinox.
α, RA, AR right ascension.
β celestial latitude.
δ, Decl. declination.
θ sidereal time.
λ celestial (or geographical) longitude.

3. Signs of the Zodiac

A. SPRING SIGNS

♈ Aries, the Ram.
♉ Taurus, the Bull.
♊, Π Gemini, the Twins.

B. SUMMER SIGNS

♋, ♋ Cancer, the Crab.
♌ Leo, the Lion.
♍ Virgo, the Virgin.

C. AUTUMN SIGNS

♎ Libra, the Balance.
♏ Scorpio, the Scorpion.
♐ Sagittarius, the Archer.

D. WINTER SIGNS

♑ ♑ Capricorn, the Goat.
♒ Aquarius, the Water Bearer.
♓ Pisces, the Fishes.

Biology

♂ a male organism, organ, cell, etc.
♀ a female organism, organ, cell, etc.
⚥ an organism having both male and female organs—hermaphrodite.
□ an individual organism, esp. a male.
○ an individual organism, esp. a female.
× (of a hybrid organism) crossed with.
P parent or parental generation; the first generation in a specified line of descent.
F filial generation; any generation following a parental generation.
F_1, F_2, F_3, etc. the first, second, third, etc., filial generations.
\+ **1.** denoting the presence of a specified trait or characteristic. **2.** used to indicate computable mating strains of heterothallic fungi which show no morphological differences.
– **1.** denoting the absence of a specified trait or characteristic. **2.** used to indicate computable mating strains of heterothallic fungi which show no morphological differences.
n haploid number of chromosomes.
2n, 3n, 4n, etc. diploid, triploid, tetraploid, etc., chromosomes, i.e. having 2, 3, 4, etc., haploid sets.
☉ annual plant.
☉☉ biennial plant.
♃ a perennial herb or plant.
△ an evergreen.
⚹ Northern Hemisphere.
⚹ Southern Hemisphere.
|∗ Old World.
∗| New World.

Books

f° folio.
4 to, 4° quarto.
8 vo, 8° octavo.
12 mo, 12° duodecimo.
16 mo, 16° sextodecimo.
18 mo, 18° octodecimo.

NOTE: The fold symbols and names above designate the most common types of book manufacture. Each indicates the number of leaves into which a single sheet is folded, and thus the number of pages to a sheet and (usually) the approximate size of the book itself. For full definitions, see the entries under the words. Other, less commonly used, symbols and names (not defined in the text) are:

24 mo, 24° twenty-fourmo: consisting of twenty-four leaves, or forty-eight to a sheet.
32 mo, 32° thirty-twomo: consisting of thirty-two leaves, or sixty-four pages, to a sheet.
48 mo, 48° forty-eightmo: consisting of forty-eight leaves, or ninety-six pages, to a sheet.

Chemistry

1. Elements

Each of the chemical elements is represented by a letter or combination of letters, consisting of the initial or an abbreviation of the English or Latin name of the element.

Symbol	Name	Atomic Number
Ac	Actinium	89
Ag	Silver (L *argentum*)	47
Al	Aluminium	13
Am	Americium	95
Ar	Argon	18
As	Arsenic	33
At	Astatine	85
Au	Gold (L *aurum*)	79
B	Boron	5
Ba	Barium	56
Be	Beryllium	4
Bi	Bismuth	83
Bk	Berkelium	97
Br	Bromine	35
C	Carbon	6
Ca	Calcium	20
Cd	Cadmium	48
Ce	Cerium	58
Cf	Californium	98
Cl	Chlorine	17
Cm	Curium	96
Co	Cobalt	27
Cr	Chromium	24
Cs	Caesium	55
Cu	Copper (L *cuprum*)	29
Dy	Dysprosium	66
Er	Erbium	68
Es	Einsteinium	99
Eu	Europium	63
F	Fluorine	9
Fe	Iron (L *ferrum*)	26
Fm	Fermium	100
Fr	Francium	87
Ga	Gallium	31
Gd	Gadolinium	64
Ge	Germanium	32
H	Hydrogen	1
He	Helium	2
Hf	Hafnium	72
Hg	Mercury (L *hydrargyrum*)	80
Ho	Holmium	67
I	Iodine	53
In	Indium	49
Ir	Iridium	77
K	Potassium (L *kalium*)	19
Kr	Krypton	36
La	Lanthanum	57
Li	Lithium	3
Lu	Lutetium	71
Lw	Lawrencium	103
Md	Mendelevium	101
Mg	Magnesium	12
Mn	Manganese	25
Mo	Molybdenum	42
N	Nitrogen	7
Na	Sodium (L *natrium*)	11
Nb	Niobium	41
Nd	Neodymium	60
Ne	Neon	10
Ni	Nickel	28
No	Nobelium	102
Np	Neptunium	93
O	Oxygen	8
Os	Osmium	76
P	Phosphorus	15
Pa	Protactinium	91
Pb	Lead (L *plumbum*)	82
Pd	Palladium	46
Pm	Promethium	61
Po	Polonium	84
Pr	Praseodymium	59
Pt	Platinum	78
Pu	Plutonium	94
Ra	Radium	88
Rb	Rubidium	37
Re	Rhenium	75
Rh	Rhodium	45
Rn	Radon	86
Ru	Ruthenium	44
S	Sulphur	16
Sb	Antimony (L *stibium*)	51
Sc	Scandium	21
Se	Selenium	34
Si	Silicon	14
Sm	Samarium	62
Sn	Tin (L *stannum*)	50
Sr	Strontium	38
Ta	Tantalum	73
Tb	Terbium	65
Tc	Technetium	43
Te	Tellurium	52
Th	Thorium	90
Ti	Titanium	22
Tl	Thallium	81
Tm	Thulium	69
U	Uranium	92
V	Vanadium	23
W	Tungsten (G *Wolfram*)	74
Xe	Xenon	54
Y	Yttrium	39
Yb	Ytterbium	70
Zn	Zinc	30
Zr	Zirconium	40

2. Compounds

Compounds are represented by combinations of the symbols of their constituent elements, with an inferior numeral to the right of each symbol indicating the number of atoms of the element entering into the compound (number 1 is, however, omitted). Thus, in some simple cases, NaCl (sodium chloride, or common salt) is a compound containing one atom of sodium and one of chlorine, H_2O (water) contains two atoms of hydrogen and one of oxygen, H_2O_2 (hydrogen peroxide, or common peroxide) contains two atoms apiece of hydrogen and oxygen. A molecule may also consist entirely of atoms of a single element, as O_3 (ozone), which consists of three atoms of oxygen.

Other symbols used in the formulas of molecules and compounds are:

a. denoting radicals, as in CH_3·-COOH. **b.** denoting water of crystallization (or hydration) as in $Na_2CO_3 \cdot 10H_2O$ (washing soda).

( ) denoting a radical within a compound, as $(C_2H_5)_2O$ (ether).

3. Valency and Electric Charge

–, =, ≡, etc. **a.** denoting a negative charge of one, two, three, etc., as $(OH)^-$, $(SO_4)^=$. **b.** denoting a single, double, triple, etc., bond, as H–O–H.

1, 2, 3, etc. (before a symbol or formula) denoting a multiplication of the symbol or formula. Thus 3H = three atoms of hydrogen; $6H_2O$ = six molecules of water, etc.

1-, 2-, 3-, etc. (in names of compounds) denoting one of several possible positions of substituted atoms or groups.

$^{-1}$, $^{-2}$, $^{-3}$, etc. Same as –, =, ≡, etc. (def. **a**); as $(OH)^{-1}$; $(SO_4)^{-2}$.

$^+$, $^{++}$, $^{+++}$, etc. denoting a positive charge of one, two, three, etc., as K^+, Ca^{++}.

$^{+1}$, $^{+2}$, $^{+3}$, etc. Same as $^+$, $^{++}$, $^{+++}$, etc., as K^{+1}, Ca^{+2}

α, β, etc. (in names of compounds) denoting one of several possible positions of substituted atoms or groups.

+ denoting dextrorotation, as +120°.

– denoting laevorotation, as –120°.

′, ″, ‴, etc. **a.** denoting a valency of one, two, three, etc. **b.** denoting a charge, esp. a negative charge, of one, two, three, etc.

·, :, ⁝, etc. denoting a single, double, triple, etc., bond.

4. Chemical Reactions

+ added to; together with.

= form; are equal to; as H + H + O = H_2O.

→, ← denoting a reaction in the direction specified.

⇄ denoting a reversible reaction, i.e. a reaction which proceeds simultaneously in both directions.

↓ (after a symbol or formula) denoting the precipitation of a specified substance.

↑ (after a symbol or formula) denoting the appearance of a specified substance as a gas.

≡, ≃ (in a quantitative equation) denoting the quantities of specified substances which will enter completely into a reaction, without leaving excess material.

Language

ˆ circumflex accent; as in *s'il vous plaît*.

¸ (with c) cedilla; as in *Alençon*.

´ acute accent; as in *passé*.

` grave accent; as in *à la mode*.

˜ tilde; as in *São Paulo*.

¨ **1.** dieresis; as in *Laocoön*. **2.** umlaut; as in *Aufklärung*.

¯ macron.

˘ breve.

’ smooth breathing.

‘ rough breathing.

* denoting a hypothetical or reconstructed form: used esp. in etymologies.

Mathematics

1. Arithmetic and Algebra

+ **a.** plus. **b.** positive. **c.** denoting approximate accuracy, with some figures omitted at the end; as in $\pi = 3{\cdot}141592+$.

– **a.** minus. **b.** negative. **c.** denoting approximate accuracy, with some figures omitted at the end. Cf. + (def. **c**).

±, ∓, ±, ∓ **a.** plus or minus: $4 \pm 2 = 6$ or 2. **b.** positive or negative: $\pm a = +a$ or $-a$. **c.** denoting the probable error associated with a figure derived by experiment and observation, approximate calculation, etc.

×, · times; multiplied by: $3 \times 3 = 9$; $3 \cdot 3 = 9$.

NOTE: multiplication may also be indicated by writing the algebraic symbols for multiplicand(s) and multiplier(s) consecutively; as in: xy; $a(a+b) = a^2 + ab$.

÷, /, –, divided by; denoting the ratio of; as in $8 \div 2 = 8/2 = \frac{8}{2} = 8:2 = 4$.

= equals; is equal to.

≡ is identical with.

≠ ≠ is not equal to.

~, ∽ **a.** is equivalent to. **b.** is similar to.

> is greater than.

< is less than.

≧ ≥ is equal to or greater than.

≦ ≤ is equal to or less than.

^{1}, ^{2}, ^{3}, etc. (at the right of a symbol, figure, etc.) exponents, indicating the raising of a power to the first, second, third, etc., power: $(ab)^2 = a^2b^2$; $4^3 = 64$.

√ √ the radical sign, indicating the square root of, as in: $\sqrt{81} = 9$.

∛, ∜, ⁵√, etc. the radical sign used with indices, indicating the third, fourth, etc., root of; as in: $\sqrt[3]{125} = 5$.

$^{\frac{1}{2}}$, $^{\frac{1}{3}}$, $^{\frac{1}{4}}$, etc. fractional exponents, used to indicate roots, and equal to √, ∛, ∜, etc.; as $9^{\frac{1}{2}} = \sqrt{9} = 3$; $a^{\frac{3}{8}} = (a^{\frac{1}{8}})^3 = (a^3)^{\frac{1}{8}} = \sqrt[8]{a^3}$.

$^{-1}$, $^{-2}$, $^{-3}$, etc. negative exponents, used to indicate the reciprocal of the same quantity with a positive exponent; as in: $9^{-2} = \frac{1}{9^2} = \frac{1}{81}$; $a^{-\frac{1}{2}} = \frac{1}{\sqrt{a}}$.

( ) parentheses; as in: 2(a + b).

[ ] brackets; as in: 4 + [3(a – b)].

{ } braces; as in:

$5+\{6[2-(a+2)+4]\}$.

‾‾ vinculum; as in: $\overline{a+b}$.

NOTE: Parentheses, brackets, braces, and vinculum are usually applied to quantities consisting of more than one member or term, to connect them and show that they are to be considered together.

∝ varies directly as; is directly proportional to: x ∝ y.

!, ∟ factorial of: 4! = ⌊4 = 1×2×3×4 = 24.

f, F, *ϕ*, etc. function of; as in: *f*(x) = a function of x.

NOTE: In addition to *ϕ*, other symbols (esp. letters from the Greek alphabet) may be used to indicate functions, as *ψ*, *γ*, etc.

′, ″, ‴, etc. prime, double prime, triple prime, etc., used to indicate: **a.** first, second, third, etc., derivatives of a function, as in: f′(x); f″(x); etc. **b.** constants, as distinguished from the variable denoted by a letter alone. **c.** different variables using the same letters, as in y, y′, y″, etc.

σ standard deviation.

r correlation coefficient.

e, ∈. Same as **e** (def. 1), p. 503.

∞ infinity.

2. Geometry

∠, *pl.* ∠s angle; as in: ∠ACB.

⊥ **a.** a perpendicular (*pl.* ⊥s). **b.** is perpendicular to; as in: AB ⊥ CD.

|| **a.** a parallel (*pl.* ||s). **b.** is parallel to; as in: AB || CD.

△, *pl.* ⊿s triangle, as in: △ ABC.

▱ parallelogram, as in: ▱ ABCD.

□ square, as in: □ ABCD.

○, *pl.* Ⓢ circle.

π the Greek letter pi, representing the ratio (3·141592+) of the circumference of a circle to its diameter.

⌒ arc.

° degree(s), esp. of arc or (in physics, etc.) of temperature; as in: 60°.

′ minute(s); as in: 60° 20′.

″ second(s); as in: 60° 20′ 5″.

≅, ≡ is congruent to.

∴ therefore; hence.

∵ since; because.

3. Calculus

$\frac{d}{d}$ derivative; as in: $\frac{dy}{dx}$ = the derivative of y with respect to x.

△, *δ* an increment; as △ y or *δ* y = an increment of y.

d differential, as *d*y = differential y.

$\sum_{1}^{n}$ sum of *n* terms.

Σ sum of an infinite number of terms.

$\prod_{1}^{n}$ product of *n* terms.

Π product of an infinite number of terms.

lim, limit. An example of the use of this abbreviation is: $\lim_{y\to b}$ (x) = a; i.e. the limit of x as y approaches b is a.

∫ integral. An example of the use of this symbol is: ∫*f*(*x*)*dx*; i.e. the integral of *f*(x) with respect to x.

$\int_a^b$ definite integral, giving limits. Thus, $\int_a^b f(x)dx$ is the definite integral of *f*(x) between limits a and b.

Medicine and Pharmacy *

A̅A̅, A̅, a̅a̅ of each (used after two or more substances to indicate that equal quantities of each are to be used).

a.c. before food (L *ante cibum*).

b.d. twice a day (L *bis die*).

d.d. daily (L *de die*).

ex. aq. in water (L *ex aqua*).

G. (in the British Pharmacopoeia) gram (when stating doses).

γ microgram.

γγ micro-microgram.

h.d. at bedtime (L *hora decubitus*).

h.s. at bedtime (L *hora somni*).

♏ minim.

m. **1.** morning (L *mane*). **2.** mix (L *misce*).

m.d. (use) as directed (L *more dicto*).

m. et v. morning and evening (L *mane et vespere*).

n. at night (L *nocte*).

n. et m. night and morning (L *nocte et mane*).

qq.h. every hour (L *quaque hora*).

℞ take (L *recipe*): presumably based on ♃, the sign of Jupiter, and used to propitiate the god in writing a prescription.

s. let him take, or to be taken (L *sumat* or *sumendus*).

S. or Sig. write or label (L *signa*): indicating directions to be written on a package or label for the use of the patient.

Ss., ss. one half (L *semis*).

t.d.d. thrice a day (L *ter de die*).

t.d.s. to be taken thrice a day (L *ter die sumendum*).

t.i.d. thrice a day (L *ter in die*).

v. in the evening (L *vespere*).

+ **1.** acid reaction. **2.** positive reaction (to a clinical or diagnostic test). **3.** excess of.

− **1.** alkaline reaction. **2.** negative reaction (to a clinical or diagnostic test). **3.** deficiency of.

* For *Apothecaries' Measure, Apothecaries' Weight*, see p. 105.

Miscellaneous

@ at: material @ £1 per yard.

&, &, & the ampersand meaning *and*. Cf. **ampersand** (p. 84).

&c. et cetera; and others; and so forth; and so on. Cf. **et cetera** (p. 548).

© copyright; copyrighted.

′ foot; feet; as in: 6′ = six feet.

″ inch(es); as in: 6′ 2″ = six feet, two inches.

× **1.** by: used in stating dimensions, as in: a vat that is 2′×4′×1′; a 2″×4″ board. **2.** a sign (the cross) made in place of a signature by a person who cannot write; as in:

his
John × Jones
mark.

% per cent.

♠ *Cards.* spade.

♥ *Cards.* heart.

♦ *Cards.* diamond.

♣ *Cards.* club.

† died: used esp. in genealogical tables.

Money

$, $ **1.** (in the United States, Canada, Australia, Hong Kong, Liberia, Malaysia, etc.) dollar(s); as in $1; $10. **2.** (in certain countries, as Chile, Mexico, etc.) peso(s). **3.** (in Portugal) escudo(s). **4.** (in Brazil) cruzeiro; as in Cr. $5.

Eth. $, NT $, Ethiopian dollar(s); New Taiwan dollar(s).

¢ (in the United States, Canada, etc.) cent(s); as in 1¢; 50¢.

£ (in the United Kingdom, etc.) pound(s); as in £10.

/, *s.* (in the United Kingdom, etc.) shilling(s); as in 10/–; 10*s.*

d. (in the United Kingdom, etc.) penny (pence); as in 10*d.*

p. (in the United Kingdom decimal system, etc.) new pence; as in 10*p.*

£L, £T, £E, etc. (in Libya, Turkey, Egypt, etc.) pound(s).

₱ (in the Philippines) peso(s).

R, R, *pl.* Rs. (in India, Pakistan, etc.) rupee(s); as in R1, Rs10.

R (in the Republic of South Africa) rand; as in R20.

¥, Y (in Japan) yen; as in ¥50, Y50.

The International System of Units (SI)

1. Basic SI Units

BASIC PHYSICAL QUANTITY	SI UNIT	SYMBOL
length	metre	m
mass	kilogram	kg
time	second	s
electric current	ampere	A
thermodynamic temperature	kelvin	K
amount of substance	mole	mol
luminous intensity	candela	cd

2. Some Derived SI Units with Special Names

PHYSICAL QUANTITY	SI UNIT	SYMBOL
frequency	hertz	Hz
energy	joule	J
force	newton	N
power	watt	W
electric charge	coulomb	C
potential difference	volt	V
resistance	ohm	Ω
capacitance	farad	F
magnetic flux	weber	Wb
inductance	henry	H
magnetic flux density	tesla	T
luminous flux	lumen	lm
illumination	lux	lx

3. Prefixes for SI Units

FRACTION	PREFIX	SYMBOL	MULTIPLE	PREFIX	SYMBOL
10^{-1}	deci	d	10	deka	da
10^{-2}	centi	c	10^2	hecto	h
10^{-3}	milli	m	10^3	kilo	k
10^{-6}	micro	μ	10^6	mega	M
10^{-9}	nano	n	10^9	giga	G
10^{-12}	pico	p	10^{12}	tera	T
10^{-15}	femto	f			
10^{-18}	atto	a			

Religion

† the cross, a symbol or emblem for Christianity or its tenets, for a crucifix, etc. For various modifications, see illus. under **cross.**

✠, + **1.** *Rom. Cath. Ch.* a modification of the cross used by the pope and by archbishops and bishops before their names. **2.** (in certain service and prayer books) an indication inserted at those points in the service at which the sign of the cross is to be made. See **cross** (def. 6).

℟ response (def. 4a): used in

prayer books, esp. of the Roman Catholic Church.

✳ *Rom. Cath. Ch.* an indication used in service books to separate the verses of a psalm into two parts, showing where the response begins.

℣, V', V an indication used in service books to show the point at which a versicle (def. 2) begins.

P, P, Ᵽ a monogram for the first two letters (XP) of the Greek form of the name of Christ, inscribed on a labarum (def. 2).

Proofreaders' Marks

Instruction	Textual mark	Marginal mark
Insert in text the matter indicated in margin	⋏	*New matter* / *followed by*
Delete	Strike through characters to be deleted	₰
Delete and close up	Strike through characters to be deleted and use linking marks	₰ (with linking marks)
Leave as printed	.... under characters to remain	*stet*
Change to italic	— under characters to be altered	*ital*
Change to even small capitals	═ under characters to be altered	*s.c.*
Change to capital letters	≡ under characters to be altered	*caps*
Use capital letters for initial letters and small capitals for rest of words	≡ under initial letters and ═ under the rest of the words	*c. & s.c.*
Change to bold type	∿ under characters to be altered	*bold*
Change to lower case	Encircle characters to be altered	*l.c.*
Change to roman type	Encircle characters to be altered	*rom*
Underline word or words	— under words affected	*underline*
Substitute or insert character(s) under which this mark is placed, in 'superior' position	/ through character or ⋏ where required	*7 under character* (e.g. ⁷ₓ)
Substitute or insert character(s) over which this mark is placed, in 'inferior' position	/ through character or ⋏ where required	⌃ *over character* (e.g. ⌃ₓ)
Change damaged character(s)	Encircle character(s) to be altered	*x*
Close up—delete space between characters	⊂ linking characters	⊂⊃
Insert space	⋏	#
Transpose	⊔⊓ between characters or words,	*trs*
Move matter to right	⊏ at left side of group to be moved	⊏
Move matter to to left	⊐ at right side of group to be moved	⊐
Raise lines	⊤ over lines to be moved ⊥ under lines to be moved	*raise*
Lower lines	⊓ over lines to be moved ⊥ under lines to be moved	*lower*
Correct the vertical alignment	‖	‖
Straighten lines	═ through lines to be straightened	═
Begin a new paragraph	⊏ before first word of new paragraph	*n.p.*
No fresh paragraph here	⁀ between paragraphs	*run on*
Insert en (half-em) rule	⋏	*en*
Insert one-em rule	⋏	*em*

Extracted from BS 1219: 1958

Weights and Measures

Linear Measure

12 inches	= 1 foot
3 feet	= 1 yard
5½ yards	= 1 rod, pole, or perch
4 rods	= 1 chain
10 chains	= 1 furlong
8 furlongs (5280 feet)	= 1 statute mile

Mariners' Measure

6 feet	= 1 fathom
1000 fathoms (approx.)	= 1 nautical mile
3 nautical miles	= 1 league

Square Measure

144 square inches	= 1 square foot
9 square feet	= 1 square yard
30¼ square yards	= 1 square rod, pole, or perch
160 square rods	= 1 acre
640 acres	= 1 square mile

Cubic Measure

1728 cubic inches	= 1 cubic foot
27 cubic feet	= 1 cubic yard

Surveyors' Measure

7·92 inches	= 1 link
100 links	= 1 chain
80 chains	= 1 mile

Liquid Measure

60 minims	= 1 fluid drachm
8 fluid drachms	= 1 fluid ounce
5 fluid ounces	= 1 gill
4 gills	= 1 pint
2 pints	= 1 quart
4 quarts	= 1 gallon
31½ gallons	= 1 barrel
2 barrels	= 1 hogshead

Dry Measure

2 pints	= 1 quart
8 quarts	= 1 peck
4 pecks	= 1 bushel

Wood Measure

16 cubic feet	= 1 cord foot
8 cord feet	= 1 cord

Time Measure

60 seconds	= 1 minute
60 minutes	= 1 hour
24 hours	= 1 day
7 days	= 1 week
4 weeks (28 to 31 days)	= 1 month
12 months (365 or 366 days)	= 1 year
100 years	= 1 century

Angular and Circular Measure

60 seconds	= 1 minute
60 minutes	= 1 degree
90 degrees	= 1 right angle
180 degrees	= 1 straight angle
360 degrees	= 1 circle

Troy Weight

24 grains	= 1 pennyweight
20 pennyweights	= 1 ounce
12 ounces	= 1 pound

Avoirdupois Weight

$27\frac{11}{32}$ grains	= 1 dram
16 drams	= 1 ounce
16 ounces	= 1 pound
14 pounds	= 1 stone
2 stones	= 1 quarter
4 quarters	= 1 hundredweight
20 hundredweights	= 1 long ton (2240 pounds)
2000 pounds	= 1 short ton

Apothecaries' Weight

20 grains	= 1 scruple
3 scruples	= 1 drachm
8 drachms	= 1 ounce
12 ounces	= 1 pound

The Metric System *

Linear Measure

10 millimetres	= 1 centimetre
10 centimetres	= 1 decimetre
10 decimetres	= 1 metre
10 metres	= 1 decametre
10 decametres	= 1 hectometre
10 hectometres	= 1 kilometre

Square Measure

100 sq. millimetres	= 1 sq. centimetre
100 sq. centimetres	= 1 sq. decimetre
100 sq. decimetres	= 1 sq. metre
100 sq. metres	= 1 sq. decametre
100 sq. decametres	= 1 sq. hectometre
100 sq. hectometres	= 1 sq. kilometre

Cubic Measure

1000 cu. millimetres	= 1 cu. centimetre
1000 cu. centimetres	= 1 cu. decimetre
1000 cu. decimetres	= 1 cu. metre

Liquid Measure

10 millilitres	= 1 centilitre
10 centilitres	= 1 decilitre
10 decilitres	= 1 litre
10 litres	= 1 decalitre
10 decalitres	= 1 hectolitre
10 hectolitres	= 1 kilolitre

Weights

10 milligrams	= 1 centigram
10 centigrams	= 1 decigram
10 decigrams	= 1 gram
10 grams	= 1 decagram
10 decagrams	= 1 hectogram
10 hectograms	= 1 kilogram
100 kilograms	= 1 quintal
10 quintals	= 1 tonne

* See the entries *metric system* and *metre*[1] in the main body of this dictionary.

Conversion Factors

Imperial and Metric Units

Length

	cm	m	in.	ft	yd
1 centimetre	1	0·01	0·393701	0·0328084	0·0109361
1 metre	100	1	39·3701	3·28084	1·09361
1 inch	2·54	0·0254	1	0·0833333	0·0277778
1 foot	30·48	0·3048	12	1	0·333333
1 yard	91·44	0·9144	36	3	1

	km	mile	na. mile
1 kilometre	1	0·621371	0·539957
1 mile	1·60934	1	0·868976
1 nautical mile	1·852	1·15078	1

1 light year = $5{\cdot}87848 \times 10^{12}$ miles = $9{\cdot}4605 \times 10^{15}$ metres
1 Astronomical Unit = $1{\cdot}495 \times 10^{11}$ metres
1 Parsec = 3·26 light years = $3{\cdot}084 \times 10^{16}$ metres

Area

	cm^2	m^2	$in.^2$	ft^2
1 square centimetre	1	10^{-4}	0·155	$1{\cdot}07639 \times 10^{-3}$
1 square metre	10,000	1	1550	10·7639
1 square inch	6·4516	$6{\cdot}4516 \times 10^{-4}$	1	$6{\cdot}94444 \times 10^{-3}$
1 square foot	929·03	$9{\cdot}2903 \times 10^{-2}$	144	1

	yd^2	acre	km^2	$mile^2$
1 square yard	1	$2{\cdot}06612 \times 10^{-4}$	$8{\cdot}36127 \times 10^{-7}$	$3{\cdot}22831 \times 10^{-7}$
1 acre	4840	1	$4{\cdot}04686 \times 10^{-3}$	$1{\cdot}5625 \times 10^{-3}$
1 square kilometre	$1{\cdot}19599 \times 10^{6}$	247·105	1	0·386019
1 square mile	$3{\cdot}0976 \times 10^{6}$	640	2·58999	1

1 are = 100 square metres   1 hectare = 2·471 acres

Volume

	cm^3	$in.^3$	l.	ft^3	gal. (UK)
1 cubic centimetre	1	0·0610236	$9{\cdot}99972 \times 10^{-4}$	$3{\cdot}53146 \times 10^{-5}$	$2{\cdot}19969 \times 10^{-4}$
1 cubic inch	16·3871	1	0·0163866	$5{\cdot}78704 \times 10^{-4}$	$3{\cdot}60464 \times 10^{-3}$
1 litre	1000·028	61·0253	1	$3{\cdot}53159 \times 10^{-2}$	0·219975
1 cubic foot	28316·8	1728	28·3160	1	6·2282
1 gallon (UK)	4546·09	277·42	4·54596	0·160544	1

1 gallon (US) = 0·83268 gallons (UK) = 3·78533 litres
1 cubic yard = 0·764555 cubic metres

Speed

	mile/hr	ft/sec.	km/hr	m/sec.
1 mile per hour	1	1·46667	1·609344	0·447040
1 foot per second	0·681817	1	1·09728	0·3048
1 kilometre per hour	0·621371	0·911346	1	0·277778
1 metre per second	2·23694	3·28084	3·6	1

Mass

	lb.	kg.	cwt	tonne	ton
1 pound	1	0·453592	$8{\cdot}92857 \times 10^{-3}$	$4{\cdot}53593 \times 10^{-4}$	$4{\cdot}46429 \times 10^{-4}$
1 kilogram	2·20462	1	0·196841	0·001	$9{\cdot}84207 \times 10^{-4}$
1 hundredweight	112	50·8023	1	0·0508023	0·05
1 metric ton	2204·62	1000	19·6841	1	0·984207
1 long ton	2240	1016·05	20	1·01605	1

1 slug = 14·5939 kg. = 32·174 lbs

Force

	lb.	kg. f.	pdl	dyn.	N
1 pound force	1	0·453592	32·174	444,822	4·44822
1 kilogram force	2·20462	1	70·9316	980,665	9·80665
1 poundal	0·031081	$1{\cdot}40981 \times 10^{-2}$	1	13,825·5	0·138255
1 dyne	$2{\cdot}24809 \times 10^{-6}$	$1{\cdot}01972 \times 10^{-6}$	$7{\cdot}23300 \times 10^{-5}$	1	10^{-5}
1 newton	0·224809	0·101972	7·23300	10^5	1

Pressure

	$lb/in.^2$	kg/cm^2	atmos.	$dyne/cm^2$
1 pound per sq. inch	1	0·0703068	0·068046	$6{\cdot}89476 \times 10^4$
1 kilogram per sq. centimetre	14·2234	1	0·967841	$980{\cdot}665 \times 10^3$
1 atmosphere	14·6959	1·03323	1	$1{\cdot}01325 \times 10^6$
1 dyne per sq. centimetre	$1{\cdot}45038 \times 10^{-5}$	$1{\cdot}01972 \times 10^{-6}$	$9{\cdot}86923 \times 10^{-7}$	1

1 newton per sq. metre = 10 dynes per sq. centimetre
1 atmosphere = 760 mm Hg = 29·92 in.Hg = 33·90 ft H_2O all at 0°C
1 bar = 10^6 dynes per sq. centimetre = 0·986927 atmosphere
1 torr = $\frac{1}{760}$ atmospheres = 133·322 newtons per sq. metre

Work and Energy

	cal	J	Btu	kw-h
1 calorie (IT)	1	4·1868	$3{\cdot}96831 \times 10^{-3}$	$1{\cdot}163 \times 10^{-6}$
1 joule	0·238846	1	$9{\cdot}47813 \times 10^{-4}$	$2{\cdot}77778 \times 10^{-7}$
1 British thermal unit	251·997	1055·06	1	$2{\cdot}93071 \times 10^{-4}$
1 kilowatt hour	$8{\cdot}59845 \times 10^5$	$3{\cdot}6 \times 10^6$	3412·14	1

1 joule = 1 newton metre = 1 watt-second = 10^7 ergs = 0·737561 ft lbs
1 electron volt = $1{\cdot}602 \times 10^{-19}$ joules

Conversion of Currency from New Pence to £sd

$\frac{1}{2}$p = 1·2d
1p = 2·4d
2p = 4·8d
5p = 1s
10p = 2s
50p = 10s
100p = £1

Conversion of Temperatures from Fahrenheit to Centigrade

Subtract 32° and multiply by $\frac{5}{9}$, e.g. 68°F = 20°C

Conversion of Temperatures from Centigrade to Fahrenheit

Multiply by $\frac{9}{5}$ and add 32°, e.g. 10°C = 50°F.

Indo-European Languages

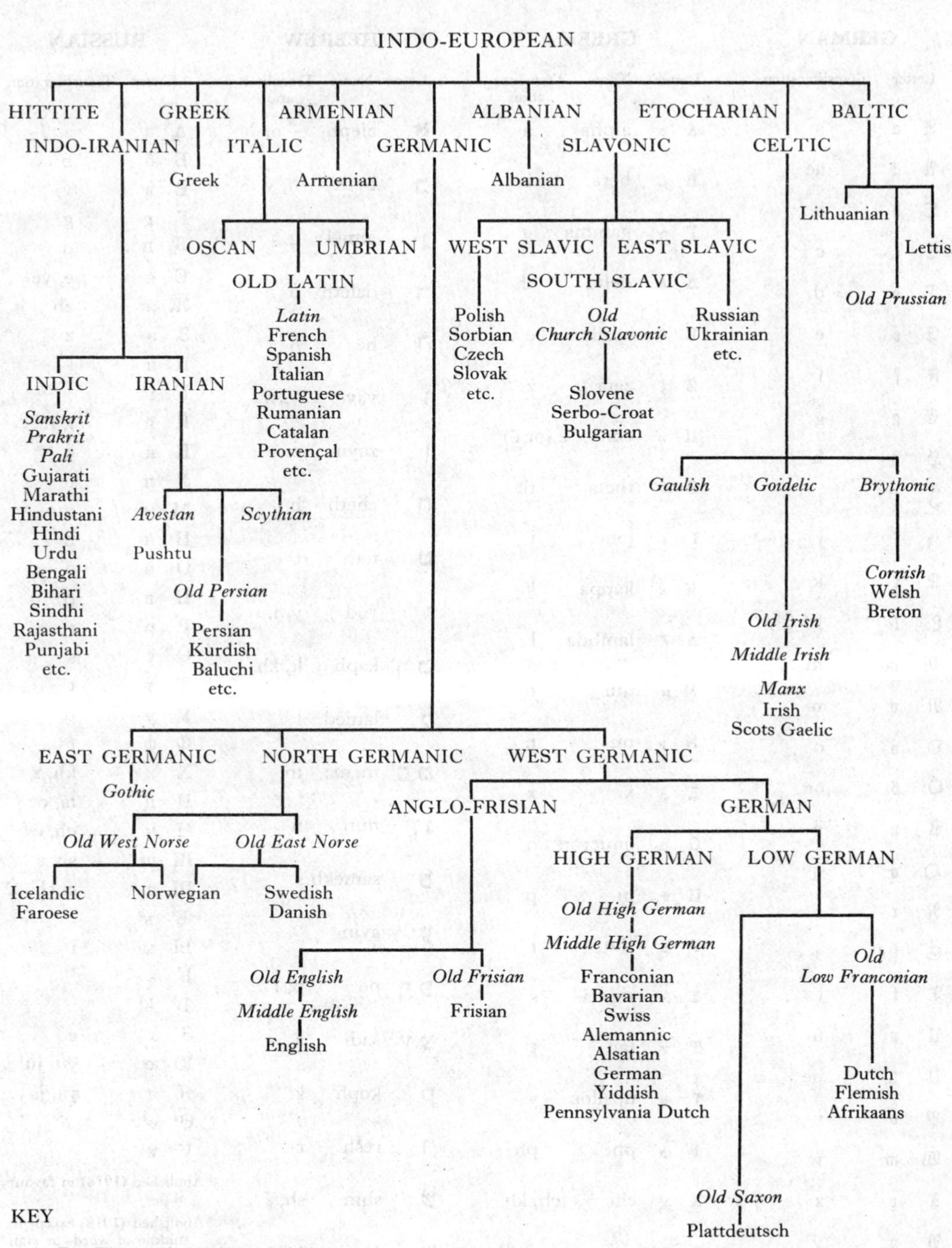

KEY

1. Families are shown in capital letters.
2. Dead languages are shown in italics.
3. Living languages are shown in capital and small letters.

Foreign Alphabets

GERMAN

Letter		Transliteration
A	a	a
Ä	ä	ae
B	b	b
C	c	c
D	d	d
E	e	e
F	f	f
G	g	g
H	h	h
I	i	i
J	j	j
K	k	k
L	l	l
M	m	m
N	n	n
O	o	o
Ö	ö	oe
P	p	p
Q	q	q
R	r	r
S	ſ s[1]	s
T	t	t
U	u	u
Ü	ü	ue
V	v	v
W	w	w
X	x	x
Y	y	y
Z	z	z

[1] At end of syllable.

GREEK

Letter		Name	Transliteration
Α	α	alpha	a
Β	β	beta	b
Γ	γ	gamma	g
Δ	δ	delta	d
Ε	ε	epsilon	e
Ζ	ζ	zeta	z
Η	η	eta	e (or ē)
Θ	θ	theta	th
Ι	ι	iota	i
Κ	κ	kappa	k
Λ	λ	lambda	l
Μ	μ	mu	m
Ν	ν	nu	n
Ξ	ξ	xi	x
Ο	ο	omicron	o
Π	π	pi	p
Ρ	ρ	rho	r
Σ	σ, ς[1]	sigma	s
Τ	τ	tau	t
Υ	υ	upsilon	y
Φ	φ	phi	ph
Χ	χ	chi	ch, kh
Ψ	ψ	psi	ps
Ω	ω	omega	o (or ō)

[1] At end of word.

HEBREW

Letter	Name	Transliteration
א	aleph	– or ʼ
ב	beth	b, v
ג	gimel	g
ד	daleth	d
ה	he	h
ו	vav	v, w
ז	zayin	z
ח	cheth	ḥ
ט	teth	ṭ
י	yod	y, j, i
כ ך[1]	kaph	k, kh
ל	lamed	l
מ ם[1]	mem	m
נ ן[1]	nun	n
ס	samekh	s
ע	ayin	ʻ
פ ף[1]	pe	p, f
צ ץ[1]	sadi	ṣ
ק	koph	ḳ
ר	resh	r
שׁ	shin	sh, š
שׂ	śin	ś
ת	tav	t

[1] At end of word.

RUSSIAN

Letter		Transliteration
А	а	a
Б	б	b
В	в	v
Г	г	g
Д	д	d
Е	е	e, ye
Ж	ж	zh
З	з	z
И	и	i
І[1]	і[1]	
Й	й	ĭ, i
К	к	k
Л	л	l
М	м	m
Н	н	n
О	о	o
П	п	p
Р	р	r
С	с	s
Т	т	t
У	у	u
Ф	ф	f
Х	х	kh, x
Ц	ц	ts, c
Ч	ч	ch, č
Ш	ш	sh, š
Щ	щ	shch, šč
Ъ[2]	ъ[2]	
Ы	ы	i
Ь	ь	ʼ
Ѣ[3]	ѣ[3]	
Э	э	e
Ю	ю	yu, ju
Я	я	ya, ja
Ѳ[4]	ѳ[4]	
Ѵ[1]	ѵ[1]	

[1] Abolished (1918) in favour of и.

[2] Abolished (1918) except in middle of words as sign of division (where it often is replaced by ').

[3] Abolished (1918) in favour of e.

[4] Abolished (1918) in favour of ф.

Ancient Alphabets

PHOENICIAN | EARLY GREEK | LATIN (Early Monumental) | EARLY ETRUSCAN | RUNIC (Anglo Saxon) | MODERN ROMAN CAPITALS

A
B
C
D
E
F
G
H
I
J
K
L
M
N
O
P
Q
R
S
T
U
V
W
X
Y
Z

Phonetic Value

þ
a
i
ng
ae
ea
io

(1) = ʾ
(2) = g
(3) = k
(4) = h
(5) = w
(6) = z
(7) = ṭ
(8) = th
(9) = y
(10) = s
(11) = ʿ
(12) = ṣ
(13) = š
(14) = kh

Guide to Punctuation

I. **Full stop** or **period** (.)

1. The full stop is used to indicate the end of any sentence other than an exclamation or question. Sentences which for politeness or other reasons are worded as exclamations or questions may also end in a full stop:

That is a good idea.

Would you pass me that book please.

A declarative sentence which contains an indirect question ends in a full stop, not a question mark:

He wanted to know when I would arrive.

2. The full stop is also used after an abbreviated word:

Abbrev. (abbreviation) mi. (mile, miles)
cf. (Latin *confer* compare)

Many British publishers and printers distinguish between abbreviations and contractions, and do not place a full stop after a contraction. A contraction is any shortened form of a word in which the last letter of the full word is shown:

Mr ([originally] master) Dr (doctor)

Abbreviations do not take a full stop if they are regarded as symbols:

N (north) m (metre) H (hydrogen)

II. **Question mark** or **mark of interrogation** (?)

1. The question mark is used to end an interrogative sentence, phrase, or word standing alone:

What do you mean? Under there?

It is not used after an interrogative subordinate clause:

I asked what you meant.

2. The question mark is also used to indicate uncertainty about stated facts:

The emperor Aurelian, A.D. 212?–275

In such cases the question mark may be placed in parentheses and/or before the uncertain information.

III **Exclamation mark** (!)

1. The exclamation mark is used to end an emphatic utterance of surprise, admiration, disgust, or other strong feeling. The utterance need not necessarily be a finite sentence:

Good heavens! That's a beautiful boat!

2. The exclamation mark may also be used to lend emphasis to a command (imperative sentence). It is not necessary to place an exclamation mark after every imperative sentence:

Come here this instant! he cried.

Please give me that book.

IV. **Comma** (,)

The comma is the most frequent mark of punctuation. Its basic function is to separate or set off within a sentence. We may consider this function under three headings.

1. Uses of the comma to separate off introductory matter.

a. The comma is used to separate introductory words of address, hesitation, transition, interjection, or the like from the main sentence:

John, what are you doing?

Ah, here's the train.

In some cases where the introductory or transitional word is very closely linked with the phrase, clause, or sentence which follows, the comma may be omitted:

Nevertheless I dislike it, I tell you.

In such cases the whole phrase, clause, or sentence may be regarded as forming part of a transition or introduction.

b. It is also used to separate off a word or phrase which has been placed first for emphasis or for some other reason:

Scientifically, what he said had no basis in fact.

Hopeful about the outcome of the negotiations, he asked for a summit conference.

c. It may be used as a convenience to the reader to show where one phrase or clause ends and the next begins:

If, after hearing the delegate speak, this assembly remains unconvinced, you may count on me, as your representative, to press for militant action.

There is, however, no need to use a comma after a short introductory phrase or clause:

If he does not come soon we'll go.

2. Use of the comma in lists, sets, and groups.

a. The comma is used to separate three or more items in a series:

In this class the children are taught English, Mathematics, History, Art, and Scripture.

The comma before the final conjunction (*and*, *or*) is regularly omitted by some writers. This practice is not recommended, however, since useful distinctions of sense may be achieved by omitting this comma only when the sense requires.

The raw materials of the writer are a keen eye, a fertile imagination, and pen and paper.

But:

In the stationery shop I bought office files, paper clips, a pen, and paper.

b. Groups of adjectives preceding the noun they modify are separated by commas only if they form a series of separate ideas:

Yellow, white, purple, and pink flowers

But:

Graceful red-brick Georgian houses

In the latter example the adjective 'serene' may be said to modify not only the noun 'man' but also the phrase 'old man'. Mixtures of both types of groups of adjectives may occur:

Yellow, white, purple, and pink little flowers.

A rule of thumb is that if the word 'and' could be meaningfully placed between two adjectives, then a comma is appropriate.

c. A comma may be used to divide two independent main clauses linked by a coordinating conjunction:

A large number of people are concerned about pollution, but very few are prepared to take active steps to combat it.

The comma in such cases is optional, and should be used only as an aid to sense or clarity.

3. Restrictive and non-restrictive.

a. One of the most important functions of the comma is to set off a non-restrictive phrase or clause. Its absence from a restrictive phrase or clause is equally significant. A restrictive phrase or clause is one whose meaning restricts or forms an essential part of the rest of the sentence and which should therefore not be divided from the rest of the sentence by commas. The relative clause in:

My daughter who is six has blonde hair

is restrictive in that it implies that I have other

daughters who are not six, and this sentence is restricted to the one who is. On the other hand:

My daughter, who is six, has blonde hair

does not restrict, but merely gives further information about my daughter.

In non-restrictive clauses and phrases commas should be placed before and after the clause or phrase:

Augustus and Tiberius, who were capable administrators, ruled the Roman Empire in the time of Christ.

But:

Emperors who were capable administrators became increasingly rare in the later history of Rome.

b. Words and phrases in apposition, which are by definition non-restrictive, should be preceded and followed by commas:

Oxford, the city of dreaming spires, is England's oldest university town.

c. Words, phrases, and clauses introduced parenthetically into a sentence may be set off by commas:

That is, however, not completely accurate.

d. See also section XIII 1 (a) on quotes.

V. **Semicolon (;)**

1. The semicolon is a mark of punctuation midway in function between the full stop and the comma. Its function, like theirs, is to separate. It is used to separate main clauses not joined by a conjunction:

Hitler expected to defeat Russia within six months; in this expectation he was disappointed.

2. It is also used to separate main clauses linked by a conjunctive adverb such as *nevertheless, therefore, moreover* and conjunctive adverbial phrases such as *all the same*.

The plan has not worked; all the same, it was worth trying.

3. A semicolon is also used to separate items in a series when there are already series within the items:

This book contains information about distribution and habitat; form, dimensions, and colouring; life-cycle; and economic significance.

In such cases the use of the semicolon avoids ambiguity.

4. Some writers prefer a semicolon to introduce examples or specification:

The most nerve-racking time in a space flight is before it actually happens; i.e., the moment before liftoff.

However, in such cases a dash is the punctuation recommended by us.

VI. **Colon (:)**

The main function of the colon is to introduce.

1. It is used to introduce a series or list of items or examples:

In England five types of tree are more common than any other: oak, ash, birch, elm, and beech.

The colon is used where there is a grammatical hiatus, and should not be placed before a list of items forming the direct or indirect object of a verb, the complement of the verb to be, or some other integral part of a sentence structure:

The five most common types of tree in England are the oak, ash, birch, elm, and beech.

2. The colon is commonly used after some introductory form of words such as the phrase 'as follows', whether before speech, a list of items, a formal statement or the like:

His precise words were as follows: 'I wish to place on record my dissent.'

The following men are to parade at 0930 hours: Blenkinsop, Jones, Levy, Williamson.

Some writers use a capital letter after a colon if what follows is a complete sentence. We recommend, however, that a lower-case letter be preferred after a colon except in direct quotations.

3. A colon is also used in dialogue, in verbatim court reports, plays, etc., following the name of the speaker:

Macduff: Your royal father's murder'd.
Malcolm: O, by whom?

VII. **Parentheses** or **round brackets ()**

1. Parentheses are used to enclose matter which does not form part of the flow of thought in the sentence or paragraph in which it occurs:

Hugo Wolf wrote his *Italian Song Book* in the year 1891. (The text is not in Italian, but is a German translation of some Italian poems.) This is considered by many musicians to be the culmination of the art of *Lieder*.

The comma, as I have said (see above), is easily misused.

Note that other punctuation may accompany parentheses. If the mark of punctuation applies only to the matter inside the parentheses then it comes before the close parenthesis. If it applies to the text outside the part in parentheses it is placed after the close parenthesis.

2. Series of numbers or letters enumerating parts of a list or series are placed within parentheses:

The aims of a good teacher are (1) to help his pupils to grow into integrated adults, (2) to give them an understanding of the subject he is teaching, (3) to extend human understanding of his own subject.

3. Parentheses are also used to enclose explanatory matter within the sentence which does not form part of the sentence itself:

When he arrived at Ashford (Middlesex), he decided to stay the night.

4. Parentheses are placed round an *-s* plural marker to avoid a cumbrous circumlocution, showing that a noun may or may not be plural, depending on context.

A teacher must aim to impart an understanding of the subject(s) he is teaching.

VIII. **Brackets** or **square brackets ()** or **[ ]**

Square brackets are used to indicate a deliberate interpolation in a text. The interpolation may be one of the following:

1. Correction or comment on a text that is for some reason reproduced verbatim:

Mussolini was killed in 1944 [1945—ed.].

2. Indication that the matter within the brackets is substituted for other words in the original version:

And [God] was made flesh.

3. The addition of some explanatory words:

This failing [making misleading statements in public] destroyed his political career.

4. The addition of some comment within the text of a verbatim transcript:

The Witness: Your Honour, I don't know what the word 'obscene' means. [Laughter in Court.]

5. Square brackets are used as 'brackets within brackets', as a substitute for parentheses:

$3x(24y-[2x+3]) = 119.$

Their behaviour, which discredits tigers, crocodiles and worms (some people [in Adlestrop and the Scrubs] would put it more strongly), surprised him.

IX. **Dash or em rule (—)**

The dash is used mainly to indicate interruption.

1. It is used, especially in writing direct speech, to show that a sentence remains unfinished:

'Now George, I don't want you to—'

'I shall do what I please,' he cut in.

2. It is used to indicate an interruption in the grammatical flow of a sentence, or an abrupt change of idea, subject, etc.

'Last Tuesday I was at the — but I don't think I ought to tell you about that.'

3. It is used to indicate hesitation or indistinctness in speech:

'I—er—um—well, frankly, I can't help you.'

Ellipsis may also be used to indicate hesitation. See section XI below.

4. It is used to show that a sentence is interrupted by some parenthetical observation. Enclosing such an observation in dashes lends rather more emphasis to it than using commas or parentheses.

The late Senator Kennedy—the second product of the great Kennedy political machine—was a victim of his own image.

5. A dash may be used to replace a word or part of a word which is taboo:

'What the — are you doing?'

6. Another use of the dash is to join two ends or points of a route, date, or the like:

The Cologne–Hanover–Berlin autobahn

I shall be taking the car Dover–Boulogne.

In such cases a dash is always appropriate; a hyphen may be confusing. In such cases and in giving dates and other numerals the convention in printing is to use a slightly shorter dash (en rule):

1797–1805. 15–27 May.

X. **Hyphen (-)**

The principal function of the hyphen is to join two words or parts of words together. In British English it is often used excessively and inconsistently. The current trend is to avoid using the hyphen except where there is a real justification for it. The functions of the hyphen are considered here under three headings: joining for syntactical reasons, joining for morphological reasons, and use of the hyphen as a separator.

1. Use of the hyphen to join two words or word elements for syntactical reasons.

The hyphen is used to join two or more words in order to make them function syntactically as a single word.

a. Attributive phrases take a hyphen where the second (or main) element is a noun. The same phrases used predicatively or independently do not take a hyphen. Thus:

An English-language dictionary

A machine-tool minder

But:

A dictionary of the English language

A man who minds a machine tool

The purpose of the hyphen in the first pair of examples is to make clear that what is meant is not a 'language dictionary published in English', or a 'tool-minder that is a machine'. In other words, the phrases 'English-language' and 'machine-tool' have precisely the same syntactic function as an attributive adjective.

b. Phrases consisting of noun plus modifier take a hyphen whatever their position in the sentence:

A computer-readable tape

A human-eye-readable print-out

The reason for using a hyphen in such positions is to make clear that the noun is subordinate to the modifier—a reversal of the usual pattern of English.

c. Adverbs should never be hyphenated with adjectives:

Beautifully made shoes

d. However, there is an exception. The adverbs 'ill' and 'well' (also 'better', 'best', 'worse', 'worst') are commonly hyphenated with adjectives, but only in attributive positions:

A well-known person is coming to see you.

A worse-shaped handle I have never known.

But:

He is very well known.

This handle is worse shaped than the others.

'Well' and 'ill' are not hyphenated to nouns which they may modify:

Ill feeling arose between them.

e. Some other compounds take hyphens if placed before the noun they modify (i.e., in attributive positions):

A hand-to-mouth existence

But:

They lived hand to mouth.

f. The common names of certain plants are composed of phrases which in another context would have a quite different meaning. Such names are hyphenated:

Welcome-home-husband-however-drunk-you-be is another name for the houseleek.

The Aaron's-beard is supposed to resemble the beard of a Jewish rabbi.

2. Use of the hyphen to join two or more words or word elements for morphological reasons.

a. Certain compound nouns are customarily hyphenated, although other compounds of the same grammatical type are customarily written or printed as one word (set solid). Thus:

has-been march-past

But:

newsreel eyelid

blackbird firedamp

b. Agentive and gerundive compounds are normally hyphenated:

marble-worker stone-quarrying

but:

engineering worker, etc.

are not, for they are not agent compounds; nor are:

watchmaker bookbinder

on the grounds of common usage. The more common the compound, the more likely it is to be set solid. Compounds consisting of single-syllabled elements are more likely to be hyphenated than those made up of polysyllabic words.

c. Nouns and adjectives formed from prepositional verbs take a hyphen:

To go ahead Give the go-ahead

A go-ahead young man

There are a number of exceptions, in which the noun or adjective compound is set solid in common usage—usually because the word is a very common one:

breakthrough changeover etc.

d. The following prefixes are customarily hyphenated to the word with which they are compounded:

ex-: ex-directory, ex-serviceman, ex-wife
non-: non-restrictive, non-swimmer
self-: self-assurance, self-discipline

The following prefixes are customarily set solid with the main word element, unless the latter begins with a capital letter, in which case a hyphen is used:

anti: anti-Corn Laws, anticorrosive
co: cooperate, copilot
counter: counteract, counterproposal
neo: neo-Catholic, neoclassicism
pan: pan-American, panplegia

As a general rule, suffixes are set solid with the rest of the word. Some adjectives which follow the noun are regarded by some writers as suffixes and hyphenated to the main noun—e.g. 'president-elect', 'secretary-designate'. However, we prefer two words in such cases.

e. In some compounds which might otherwise be set solid, a hyphen is introduced for phonetic reasons. In:

damp-proof counter-revolutionary

it is there to indicate that the doubled consonant is pronounced. In:

anti-alcoholic re-election, etc.

it is there to indicate that the two vowels are pronounced as two, and not as a diphthong.

3. Use of the hyphen as a separator.

a. In spelling out a compound number between 21 and 99, a hyphen is used:

Twenty-one; one hundred and ninety-two

b. In spelling out a fraction, a hyphen is sometimes used between the numerator and the denominator, unless either is a compound number.

Two-thirds; eight-seventeenths

The hyphen should never be used if either numerator or denominator is a compound number:

one thirty-second; forty-four fiftieths

c. The hyphen is used to divide part of a long word which falls at the end of a line from its continuation on the next line. The rules for the division of words are many and various. In British English division takes account of the etymological structure and the pronunciation of a word. Words consisting of one syllable only such as 'stroked' should not be divided.

XI. **Leaders** or **Ellipsis** (. . . or . . . .)

Leaders are used to indicate an omission in some quoted matter.

1. If the omission occurs at the beginning or in the middle of a sentence, the leaders consist of three full points with a space before and after them:

Shaw wrote, '. . . this is a brilliant . . . book.'

2. If the omission occurs at the end of a sentence, the usual practice is that a fourth leader is used if the sentence is complete, in which case there is no space before the first leader:

Down with all traitors. . . .

When the ellipsis is not part of quoted matter it should be placed outside the quotes:

'Down with all traitors.' . . .

XII. **Apostrophe** (')

The apostrophe is used to indicate the omission of letters or figures, and to distinguish in writing the possessive case of nouns.

1. It is used to indicate the omission of a vowel and certain other letters where two words have been run together to form a single word:

he'll John'll come

Frequently the apostrophe distinguishes between two quite different pronunciations and senses of the same group of letters as *he'll* and *hell* or *I'll* and *ill*. The distinction in writing between *it's* (a contraction of *it is*) and *its* (possessive case of *it*) should be carefully observed.

2. Certain conventions are observed in the placing of the apostrophe in contractions derived from the negative adverb *not*:

can't couldn't ain't etc.

3. In certain contractions an apostrophe may be used to show where letters are omitted. This is done especially where the contracted form might be unclear or confused with another word, or where it is particularly desired to draw attention to the fact that the form given is a contraction:

e'er e'en m'f'g chemists

4. An apostrophe is also used to indicate the omission of numerals, especially of the century in a date:

the gay '90s back in '43

5. a. The addition of an apostrophe and an *s* is the regular way of forming the possessive of singular nouns, and certain indefinite pronouns:

a gentleman's gentleman anyone's guess

b. In the case of singular nouns which end in *-s*, the possessive *s* may be omitted if it creates an unpleasant sound or visual effect.

For goodness' sake Thucydides' *History*

But:

Keats's poetry St James's Square

c. Plural nouns ending in *-s* form their possessive by the addition of an apostrophe alone:

the horses' hoofs politicians' arguments

A few plural nouns, those which form their plural in some way other than the addition of *-s*, form their possessive plural by adding an apostrophe and an *s*:

the men's room geese's wings

d. In indicating joint possession by more than one person or other proper noun, an apostrophe and *s* is added to the last name:

Paul and Anne's house

e. However, if the several individuals are all in individual possession of the named object, an apostrophe and *s* are added to all nouns:

Paul's and Anne's clothes

6. An apostrophe is sometimes used before a plural *s* in forming plurals of figures and abbreviations, especially where there is possibility of confusion with other words:

8's and 9's a's, e's, i's, o's, and u's

However, as long as there is no possibility of confusion, no apostrophe should be shown:

the 1940s M.P.s pros and cons

XIII. **Quotes**, **Quotation Marks**, or **Inverted Commas** ('' or "")

The primary use of quotes is to set off spoken words from the rest of the text. The modern practice is to prefer single quotes ('') to double (""), and this is the practice recommended here. This section will consider not only the use of quotes but also the conventions of all punctuation surrounding quoted matter.

1. In reporting speech, quotes are placed before and after the paragraph, sentence, phrase, or word quoted. If the quoted matter consists of more than one paragraph, a raised turned comma (') is placed at the beginning of each new para-

graph, but a raised unturned comma (') is placed only at the end of the whole quotation.

a. A comma is placed at the end of quoted matter before the raised comma if what follows is a verb or expression of speech such as 'I said', 'he explained', 'they asked' and the word following the quotation begins with a lower-case letter, unless it is a proper noun:

'I've got indigestion,' said John.

b. However, if the last sentence in the quoted matter is a question or an exclamation, a question mark or exclamation mark is the point used, although the following word still begins with a lower-case letter:

'What are you doing?' he demanded.

c. If the verb of saying precedes quoted matter, it is followed by a comma, but the first word of the quoted matter begins with a capital:

He exclaimed, 'That is a very good idea.'

d. If the verb of saying falls in the middle of a sentence in the quoted matter, there is a comma before the final raised comma, and another one before the raised turned comma, and both are followed by a lower-case letter:

'That,' said John, 'is a very good idea.'

If the punctuation following the quoted matter is applicable to the whole of the sentence and not just the quoted part, the punctuation is placed after the final raised comma:

What do you mean by 'I don't like it'?

In all other cases the punctuation is placed before the final raised comma:

'I believe . . .'

e. To give a quotation within a quotation, double quotes are used:

He asked, 'What do you mean by "no"?'

2. Quotes are also used to surround short passages quoted from a text, especially in the middle of a sentence:

The words of Dowland's madrigal 'Weep you no more, sad fountains' are thought to have been written by the composer himself.

Longer quotes are generally preceded by a colon and set off in a new, indented paragraph.

3. Titles of essays, articles, chapters, etc., within a publication are usually placed within quotes, the name of the publication being italicized in print or underlined in type. Quotes may also be used to mark names of works of art, pieces of music, radio and television programmes, and other works, especially if they are referred to as part of a larger collection:

Joseph L. Henderson's essay 'Ancient Myths and Modern Man' in *Man and His Symbols*, edited by C. G. Jung.

An article entitled 'Stress in Society' in *New Society*.

4. Quotes may be used to denote the names of aeroplanes, vehicles, etc.

The 'Diddler' was London's first trolleybus.

Lindbergh flew the Atlantic in the 'Spirit of St Louis'.

5. Quotes may be placed round a letter, word, or phrase to which the writer wishes to draw special attention. This may be because the word itself is the subject of special discussion, or because the word is used in an unusual, new, or special sense or is a newly coined word or expression, or because the word is used ironically or is a slang, colloquial, dialectal, or other non-standard expression.

By 'oosphere' they mean an unfertilized egg.

The countdown is interrupted as soon as a 'glitch' is discovered.

XIV. Capital Letters

1. A capital letter is used for the first letter of the first word of any sentence. See also the section on quotes (XIII 1 (c) and (d)) above:

That is quite right.

Now is the winter of our discontent . . .

2. All proper nouns and adjectives begin with a capital letter.

Charles — the French

Charles the Bold — French people

3. Names of particular regions, as opposed to points of the compass, are capitalized:

the Industrial North — the Far East

But:

The sun rises in the east and sets in the west.

4. In names of geographical features, words such as 'river', 'islands', 'street', etc., are capitalized if they form an integral part of the name:

the Yellow River *but:* the river Thames

County Durham *but:* the county of Essex

5. Except in some modern poetry, where the poet may specifically direct otherwise, each line of a piece of verse begins with a capital letter:

In pious times, ere priestcraft did begin,
Before polygamy was made a sin,
When man on many multiplied his kind
Ere one to one was cursedly confined. . . .

6. In titles of works of literature, art, music, etc., some writers capitalize all words except articles, prepositions, and conjunctions. Others capitalize only the first word, nouns and adjectives, and this is the practice recommended here:

All's well that ends well — *The Magic Flute*

7. In expressions of time, the abbreviations A.D., B.C. are usually capitalized in handwriting or typing, and in printing set in small capitals. B.C. follows the year, but A.D. normally precedes it:

436 B.C. — A.D. 1914

XV. Italics

Italics are useful for highlighting certain words in a text. In manuscript or typewriting, italics are indicated by underlining.

1. Names of publications, titles or works of literature, art, music, etc., are usually set in italics.

Orwell's *Animal Farm* — the London *Times*

2. Certain names, as names of ships or vehicles, may be placed in italics or surrounded by inverted commas:

the *Ark Royal* — the *Flying Scotsman*

3. Italics are used to show that a word is emphasized, or particularly stressed:

'Can't you see? I *want* to come,' she said.

4. In quoting the words of another writer or speaker, attention may be drawn to a particular word or phrase by italicizing it. In such cases it is customary to place the words '[my italics]' in square brackets after the quoted matter:

Some of our words will be harsh, fierce, destructive words, aimed in defiance *and contempt* at men and policies we detest [my italics].

5. Italics may be used to indicate that a letter, word, or phrase is itself the subject of discussion. However, we recommend inverted commas for this purpose.

6. Foreign words and phrases are placed in italics:

A significant period in European thought and literature was the *Aufklärung* in Germany.

Etymology Key

abl.	ablative	**inf.**	infinitive
acc.	accusative	**irreg.**	irregularly
alter.	alteration	**lit.**	literally
appar.	apparently	**m.**	modification of
assoc.	association	**nom.**	nominative
aug.	augmentative	**orig.**	origin, original, originally
b.	blend of, blended	**pop.**	popular
c.	cognate with	**prob.**	probably
comb. form	combining form	**prop.**	properly
d.	dialect, dialectal	**r.**	replacing
dat.	dative	**redupl.**	reduplication
der.	derived from	**repr.**	representing
deriv.	derivative	**s.**	stem of
dim.	diminutive	**syll.**	syllable
f.	formed from	**t.**	taken from
fig.	figurative, figuratively	**trans.**	translation
freq.	frequentative	**ult.**	ultimately
g.	going back to	**uncert.**	uncertain
gen.	genitive	**var.**	variant
ger.	gerund, gerundive	**voc.**	vocative
imit.	imitative	**?**	perhaps
impv.	imperative	*****	hypothetical form

Languages

AF	Anglo-French	**M**	1. Middle 2. Medieval
Amer. Ind.	American Indian	**ME**	Middle English (1100–1500)
Ar.	Arabic	**Mex.**	Mexican
Aram.	Aramaic	**MF**	Middle French (1400–1600)
D	Dutch	**MGk**	Medieval Greek (700–1500)
Dan.	Danish	**ML**	Medieval Latin (700–1500)
E	English	**NL**	Neo-Latin (after 1500)
Egypt.	Egyptian	**Norw.**	Norwegian
F	French	**O**	Old
Fris.	Frisian	**OE**	Old English (before 1100)
G	German	**OF**	Old French (before 1400)
Gk	Greek	**OS**	Old Saxon
Gmc	Germanic	**Pers.**	Persian
Goth.	Gothic	**Pg.**	Portuguese
Heb.	Hebrew	**Pol.**	Polish
HG	High German	**Pr.**	Provençal
Hind.	Hindustani	**Rom.**	Romance, Romanic
Hung.	Hungarian	**Russ.**	Russian
Icel.	Icelandic	**Scand.**	Scandinavian
IE	Indo-European	**Scot.**	Scottish
It.	Italian	**Skt**	Sanskrit
Jap.	Japanese	**Sp.**	Spanish
L	Latin	**Sw.**	Swedish
LG	Low German	**Turk.**	Turkish
LGk	Late Greek (300–700)	**VL**	Vulgar Latin
LHeb.	Late Hebrew	**WGmc**	West Germanic
LL	Late Latin (300–700)		